The CAMBRIDGE WORLD HISTORY *of* FOOD

EDITORS

Kenneth F. Kiple
Kriemhild Coneè Ornelas

VOLUME TWO

CAMBRIDGE
UNIVERSITY PRESS

PUBLISHED BY THE PRESS SYNDICATE OF THE UNIVERSITY OF CAMBRIDGE
The Pitt Building, Trumpington Street, Cambridge, United Kingdom

CAMBRIDGE UNIVERSITY PRESS
The Edinburgh Building, Cambridge CB2 2RU, UK
40 West 20th Street, New York, NY 10011-4211, USA
10 Stamford Road, Oakleigh, VIC 3166, Australia
Ruiz de Alarcón 13, 28014 Madrid, Spain
Dock House, The Waterfront, Cape Town 8001, South Africa

http://www.cambridge.org

First published 2000
Reprinted 2000, 2001

Printed in the United States of America

Typeface Garamond Book 9.5/10.25 pt.   *System* QuarkXPress®   [GH]

The following illustrations in Part II are from the LuEsther T. Mertz Library, The New York Botanical Garden, Bronx, New York: Corn, Sorghum.

The following illustrations in Parts II and III are from the General Research Division, The New York Public Library, Astor, Lenox and Tilden Foundations: Banana plant, White potato, Prickly sago palm, Taro, Early onion, Lentil, Cabbage, Brussels sprouts, Cucumber, Watermelon, Field mushroom, Long white squash, Tomato, Chestnut, Peanut, Sesame, Soybean, Coriander, Peking duck, Geese, Goat, Cacao, Kola.

The following illustrations in Parts II and III are from the Rare Book and Manuscript Library, Columbia University: Oat, Olive, Sugar, Reindeer, Cattle, Turkey, Coffee.

A catalog record for this book is available from the British Library.

Library of Congress Cataloging in Publication Data

The Cambridge world history of food / editors, Kenneth F. Kiple, Kriemhild Coneè Ornelas.
        p. cm.
    Includes bibliographical references and index.
    ISBN 0-521-40214-X (v. 1) – ISBN 0-521-40215-8 (v. 2) – ISBN 0-521-40216-6 (slipcase set)
    1. Food–History. I. Kiple, Kenneth F., 1939– II. Ornelas, Kriemhild Coneè.

TX353.C255 2000
641.3'09–dc21   00-057181

ISBN   0 521 40214 X (Volume 1)
ISBN   0 521 40215 8 (Volume 2)
ISBN   0 521 40216 6 (Set)

CONTENTS

VOLUME ONE

Part II   Staple Foods: Domesticated Plants and Animals

VOLUME TWO

PART V

Food and Drink around the World

Part V comprises a history of food and drink around the world, from the beginnings of agriculture in the Near East to recent excitement generated by the "Mediterranean diet." It is divided chronologically as well as geographically, which invariably creates anomalies and overlap that invite explanation. Illustrative is the treatment together of South Asia and the Middle East in view of the culinary impact of Islam on both regions. Or again, because of an abundance of available authorities on food and drink in the various European countries (and their many regions), that section could easily have mushroomed to the point of giving lie to a title that promised "world history." Thus, we have dealt with Greece, Italy, and the Iberian countries under the rubrics of "The Mediterranean" and "Southern Europe."

For the Americas, we have two Caribbean entries, which might seem somewhat disproportionate. But it should be noted that the chapter that provides a pre-Columbian historical background for the Caribbean region does so for South America and lowland Central America as well, whereas the chapter treating the period since 1492 reveals the mélange of cultures and cuisines of the region, in which those of Africa blended with others of Europe and Asia, even though the dishes often centered on plants originally cultivated by the region's indigenous peoples.

In Part V, alarm about the danger of the demise of national and regional cuisines is sometimes expressed – triggered, at least in part, by fast-food chains, born in the United States but now reproducing wildly across the globe from Mexico City to Moscow, Bridgetown to Brussels, and Phnom Penh to Paris. It is interesting to note how the standardized nature of fast foods contrasts so starkly with the usage of foods in an earlier period of globalization, which took place during the centuries following the Columbian voyages. Then, burgeoning nationalism ensured that although various cultures adopted most of the same foods, they prepared them differently, just as regional cuisines arose in similar fashion to proclaim a distinctiveness from the metropolis.

Yet, even though nationalism has faded in the West, the ongoing globalization of everything from economics to politics seems once again, in the case of foods, to be provoking a like reaction, doubtless because the homogenization process appears paradoxically to spur a need for cultural autonomy. Thus, although fast food has its place in a world in a hurry, it is almost certainly not the harbinger of planetary food uniformity it stands accused of being. Indeed, it is probably best to conceive of food globalization as a process of expanding the availability of more and more foods, reaching the point at which the ingredients of the national dishes of the world are increasingly available to anyone anywhere. Another comforting indication that national cuisines are not on the verge of extinction is the vital and rapidly expanding field of culinary history, discussed in the last chapter of Part V.

V.A

The Beginnings of Agriculture:
The Ancient Near East and North Africa

The Sumerians may have said it best: "Food: That's the thing! Drink: That's the thing!" (Gordon 1959: 142). From bread and beer to wine and cheese, the people of the ancient Near East and North Africa developed a rich cuisine based on a set of crops and livestock domesticated in Southwest Asia, and a sophisticated technology of food preparation and preservation. This chapter traces the history of diet and foods of hunter-gatherers who lived at the end of the Stone Age in the Near East and North Africa, the impact of the development and spread of agriculture, and the social context of food and drink in early Mesopotamian and Egyptian civilization.

Geographical Background

Patterns of subsistence in any society reflect geography and cultural development. The civilizations of the ancient Near East and North Africa developed in a complex environmental mosaic that encompassed coasts and inland plateaus, high mountains and lands below sea level, barren deserts, fertile plains, and dense woodlands. The boundaries of the environmental zones have shifted over the years because the region has known both dry periods and moister phases.

People, too, have wrought changes on the land as they assisted the movement of plants and animals from their original homelands. Over the millennia, humans have turned deserts into gardens with irrigation, and have transformed naturally productive lands into deserts by overgrazing and fuel cutting. Specifying the environmental picture at any particular place and time is not an easy task.

Elevation has also had a profound influence on vegetation and climate in the Near East and, ultimately, the productive capacity of the land. Levantine mountains form the western border of the Fertile Crescent, and the Taurus-Zagros chain lies to the north and east, from Mediterranean Anatolia to southwestern Iran. The winter months bring the snow and rain that support forests and grasslands. The three main vegetational zones are forests in the mountains and hill zones surrounding the Fertile Crescent, steppe at slightly lower elevations, and desert in the lowlands.

The natural forest and steppe forest formations are dominated by oaks. Conifers of various types occur throughout. Pistachio is common in both the Mediterranean forests and the southern Zagros (Zohary 1973). This band of hilly country borders undulating grasslands and shrubby steppe to the south. Lying south of the steppe are the hot deserts of Arabia. The Tigris and Euphrates river systems originate in the mountains in the north, run through Mesopotamia, and drain into the Persian Gulf, providing a distinct riparian habitat, as well as an important source of water for irrigation. During the last 15,000 years, the margins of these environmental zones have shifted back and forth with drier and moister climatic phases (Zeist and Bottema 1991).

North Africa has a less hospitable environment than the Near East. The Sahara desert spans the continent; on its southern margins are the dry Sahel grasslands, and along its northern periphery are more semiarid lands. The immense Sahara has a varied terrain with scattered oases, depressions, high ground, rugged hills along the Red Sea coast, and mountains in the central region. Higher mountains lie to the northwest in the Maghreb. Along the North African coast, light winter rains sustain a narrow band of green. The Nile Valley is the lushest region in North Africa because of the river water derived from Equatorial Africa, but the desert lies just beyond the river valley.

The Near East

Foragers

Fourteen thousand years ago, human populations throughout this region were mobile hunter-gatherers who relied on wild plants and animals for sustenance (Table V.A.1). Little is known of the full range of foods eaten by these people. There is scant evidence of the plant foods consumed even though nuts, starchy seeds, and tubers were probably important contributors to the diet (Colledge 1991). But the skeletal remains of forest and steppe animals attest to a variety of game that was eaten, including several types of deer and gazelle, wild cattle, pigs, sheep, goats, and onagers (Hesse 1995).

Table V.A.1. *Chronology of the Near East and Egypt*

Near East		Egypt	
Calibrated date B.C.	Uncalibrated date B.C.		Calibrated date B.C.
Literate civilizations of Mesopotamia		**Pharaonic state**	
3,100 –	2,600	-	3,100
Early states		Predynastic	
3,500 –	2,800	Later villages & towns	
Later villages &	3,000	-	3,750
proto-urban societies		Early predynastic villages	
	3,700	-	4,500
		Semisedentary farmers/foragers	
	6,300	-	5,200
Pottery Neolithic			
6,900 –	6,000	-	
Aceramic Neolithic		**Mobile foragers**	
10,200 –	8,300	-	
Sendentary and semisedentary foragers			
12,000 –	10,000	-	
Mobile foragers			

Source: Adapted from Evin (1995) for the Near East and Hassan (1985) for Egypt. Calibrated dates interpreted from Stuiver et al. (1986, fig. 7) and uncalibrated dates based on Libby half-life (5,568 years).

Note on Chronology: Scientists have developed ways to calibrate radiocarbon dates so that they more accurately reflect calendar years. Most of the reports and papers cited here, however, use uncalibrated radiocarbon dates for periods before the early states. In order to be consistent, we have decided to use calibrated and historical dates throughout (cf. Evin 1995). We hope this does not cause confusion for readers who investigate some of our source material.

By 12,000 B.C., seeds and nuts had become an important part of the diet (Flannery 1973). At this time, foraging populations in the more favorable areas became less mobile and began to stay in settlements for extended periods. People living in the steppe and steppe forest began to concentrate on a few main species of animals and plants. The faunal evidence is fairly straightforward; at sites from the Levant to the Syrian steppe, gazelle appears to have been the primary source of animal protein (Garrard 1984). At Abu Hureyra, for example, gazelle constitutes about 80 percent of the animal bone (Legge 1975). Depending on local availability, the meat diet in other areas also seemed to focus on only one or two wild ungulates, like sheep, goat, pig, and onager (Hesse 1995).

As the climate changed during this period, the habitat of wild grasses expanded. Analysis of isotopes in human bone from archaeological sites suggests that people were now eating more plant foods. The most extensive collection of archaeological plant remains comes from the site of Abu Hureyra. Though Gordon C. Hillman, Susan M. Colledge, and David R. Harris (1989) suggest that the Abu Hureyrans consumed a wide array of plants, some of the plant remains they have turned up as evidence may have derived from animal dung burned as fuel, and so may not fairly represent human food choices (Miller 1996). Slightly later samples from nearby Mureybit (Zeist and Bakker-

Heeres 1984) have a few concentrations of seeds that are more likely to be human food remains, especially those of wild einkorn.

Accompanying the shift to a settled lifestyle were advances in food technology that probably contributed to a more stable food supply and population growth. In addition to cooking, which probably had been practiced for about a million years, archaeological evidence points to improvements in grinding and storage technology. Without grinding and cooking, the digestibility of wild cereals and pulses would have been low, but with such techniques, even pulses that are toxic when fresh could be nutritious, and, consequently, the amount of food available from a given tract of land would have been increased. Moreover, storing food in pits reduced both intra- and interannual variation in food availability.

These technological changes encouraged an increase in sedentism as well as in population during the early village period. Food, a welcome addition to most social interactions, probably also became important for greasing the wheels of human relations. Feasting, practiced on a grand scale in later periods, was doubtless begun for a variety of reasons, ranging from the cementing of alliances to the attracting of labor. Such activities would have encouraged sedentary foragers to accumulate surplus beyond bare subsistence needs (Bender 1978).

Farmers

Sometime after 12,000 B.C., sedentary hunter–gatherer communities in the Levant, followed slightly later by inhabitants of Anatolia and parts of the Zagros Mountains, embarked on a path that led to the domestication of plants and animals and, ultimately, food production. This shift in subsistence that archaeologists refer to as the "Neolithic Revolution" was the most profound change in human history and one that still has a far-reaching impact on the planet.

Current consensus is that plant domestication in the Near East began in the Jordan Valley around 9500 B.C. (Zeist 1988), and animal husbandry started about the same time or a little later in the Zagros Mountains and, possibly, North Africa (Hole 1984; Rosenberg et al. 1995). By the middle of the ninth millennium B.C., domesticated plants could also be found in Anatolia and the Zagros. Even with advances in agriculture, however, wild plant gathering and hunting continued to play an important role in the economy. In fact, it is probable that the ancestors of the first domesticated plants in the Near East – emmer, einkorn, and barley – had been important food plants for local foraging populations.

Domesticated plants entered the archaeological record at different times and places. For example, emmer wheat originated in the Jordan Valley, but bitter vetch is probably Anatolian. The earliest farming villages did not use pottery or domestic animals and, like their forebears, stored grain in pits. As early as the ninth and eighth millennia B.C., the ability to store surplus food enabled small, undifferentiated settlements of farmers to develop into larger communities of more complex social and economic organization. Changes are evidenced by public architecture (shrines), differences in wealth as reflected in the goods accompanying burials, specialized occupations for a few, and elaborate mortuary cults (see Voigt 1990). Some of the communities were also vastly larger than the earliest villages and may have housed a thousand or more inhabitants.

Nomadic foragers who followed herds of goat and sheep in the mountains of Iran began managing wild herds about 12,000 years ago, and pigs may have been domesticated at about that time as well (Rosenberg et al. 1995). Cattle were domesticated in Anatolia about 7000 B.C. By determining the age and sex of the animals slaughtered, faunal analysts can infer herd management strategies. For example, if the bone assemblage includes both adult males and females, it is unlikely that milk production was the goal; whether hunted or herded, the primary product supplied by the animals of the early herders was meat.

By 6700 B.C., a fully agricultural economy that relied almost entirely on farming and herding was established over much of the Near East. The staple crops grown over a broad area were cereals (emmer, einkorn, durum wheat, bread wheat, and two- and six-row barley) and pulses (lentil, bitter vetch, and chickpea). It is likely that these crops were eaten, even toxic ones (like bitter vetch) because they are sometimes found in concentrations in roasting pits. Whereas cereals satisfied much of the caloric needs of the early villagers, the addition of domesticated pulses and livestock helped satisfy protein needs. A variety of wild plants, including such nuts as pistachio, almond, and acorn, continued to enhance the diet as well (see, for example, Mason 1995).

Farming spread to the hot, dry lowlands of Mesopotamia where techniques for water management developed. Late in the sixth millennium B.C., the Near Eastern complex of crops and livestock also spread to the Nile Valley, where still other irrigation techniques emerged to take advantage of the Nile floods. Farming villages proliferated as the new subsistence systems proved to be highly productive and capable of supporting a burgeoning population. After the initial phase of domestication, such fruits as grape, olive, fig, and date were domesticated. Their dietary and economic potential, however, was not fully realized until relatively late.

The Near Eastern agro-pastoral subsistence system proved very productive, initially supporting ever-increasing populations. Although one might think the domesticated pulses would be the perfect dietary complement to the cereals, the inclusion of domestic animals in a mixed economy had several advantages lacking in a purely plant-based system. First, animals provided ready access to dietary fat; aside from wild nut trees (especially pistachio and almond), oil plants (olive, flax, and sesame) do not appear to have been utilized at this early date. Second, land marginal for agriculture could have been used productively for pasture. Third, animals convert inedible pasture plants into tasty meat, which would have increased the food supply. Finally, domestic animals may have been traded with other groups to "set up reciprocal obligations and maximize sharing during lean years" (Flannery 1969: 87).

In the short run, the new farming methods seem to have been successful in evening out seasonal and year-to-year fluctuations in the food supply. On a theoretical level, the combined effect of plant and animal husbandry should have been a more stable food supply for growing populations (Raish 1992; Redding 1993). Yet the land could not continue to support expanding populations without some change in management (Köhler-Rollefson 1988). In fact, the first half of the sixth millennium B.C. saw a fairly widespread abandonment of settlements and the reestablishment of smaller communities on other sites, and faunal assemblages from Iran to Syria show a renewed emphasis on hunted animals (Buitenhuis 1990, Zeder 1994). Overgrazing and inadequate fallowing may have exacerbated a long-term impact of fuel cutting by village farmers, with inevitable results.

It was the development of new techniques of chemically transforming food that allowed the theoretical advantages of the agro-pastoral system to be realized. Pottery, widespread by 6000 B.C., permitted new forms of storage and cooking possibilities (though stone boiling in animal skins would have been possible even in prepottery days) (Moore 1995). Fermentation allowed farmers to transform grain and fruits into psychotropic substances; though alcohol is itself not digested, the fermentation process makes many nutrients more available.

Fermented grapes could also have yielded vinegar, a pickling agent. In the Near East, the earliest evidence for fermentation comes from Iran – wine residues at Hajji Firuz, around 5500 B.C., and beer (and wine) residues at Godin Tepe, around 3500 B.C. (Michel, McGovern, and Badler 1993; McGovern et al. 1996); it did not take long for people to appreciate the added value of fermentation. Beer became a convenient and pleasant way to consume grain's carbohydrates and vitamins. It is probably no accident that olives, which must be cured before eating, were domesticated in this era, and olive oil would have been a welcome addition to the diet.

Early Near Eastern farmers did not just experiment with plants. Although we do not know when adults in these populations lost at least some of their inability to absorb lactose (Simoons 1979), at some point they probably began to consume milk from their herds. Cheese, ghee, yoghurt, and other cultured milk products were most likely innovations of the later village societies. Based on the age of slaughter, the zooarchaeologist Simon Davis (1984) suggests that dairy products were not emphasized until relatively late, around 4500 to 4000 B.C. in western Iran. In the Levant, ceramic vessels considered to be churns date to this time (Kaplan 1954). And in the earliest archaic texts from Mesopotamia (before 3000 B.C.), mention of an elaborate array of storable dairy products that were produced in institutional quantities suggest strongly that these items had long been part of the culinary repertoire (Nissen, Damerow, and Englund 1993).

Finally, the period of the later villages seems to have been the time when people began to use salt as a food preservative, although the mineral may have been used for animal hide preparation as early as the seventh millennium B.C. Archaeological evidence for the production and procurement of salt at this time is not available (Potts 1984), but it is difficult to imagine that the large quantities of fish placed as offerings in the fifth millennium B.C. temple at Eridu were fresh! Certainly by the third millennium, drying and salting were well-known techniques of food preservation (see Reiner 1980). In summary, it seems that the major food-transforming technologies developed and spread between about 5500 and 3500 B.C.

By about 3500 B.C., orchard crops began to make a noticeable contribution to the diet. Grape and olive in the Mediterranean region and date in Mesopotamia, so important to the earliest civilizations, had been domesticated. Such fruits as fig, pomegranate, and apple came under cultivation, too. By this time domesticated livestock had almost completely replaced their wild relatives and other hunted animals. The ability to preserve large quantities of varied foods permitted surplus accumulation that, in turn, provided an impetus toward the developments we associate with civilization: urbanization, a high degree of economic specialization, and social inequality (Sherratt 1981; Redding 1993).

The First States

Productive surplus-generating agriculture may not have caused the changes set in motion, but it certainly permitted them to occur. Towns began to appear across Mesopotamia and the northern plains, which individually, as well as collectively, had all the trappings of a society more complex than any previously seen in the Near East. Among them were monuments and temples, full-time craft specialists, social stratification, and large populations.

Specialized nomadic pastoralists who began to share the landscape with settled agricultural populations joined in feeding the growing urban populations, and by 3500 B.C. the trend toward larger and more complex communities culminated in the emergence of the literate civilizations of Mesopotamia and, around 3100 B.C., in the appearance of a state in Egypt. Such social and cultural changes accompanying the rise of complex societies also had profound implications for foodways.

In earlier times, differences in consumption patterns had resulted from seasonal and local resource availability. But these early civilizations were now composed of people divided by wealth, class, occupation, and ethnicity, and their diets varied accordingly. Social status, in other words, had become an additional factor in determining who ate what.

Moreover, the basic Near Eastern crop complex was joined by a few new plants, as indicated by the archaeological record of the third and second millennia B.C. (see Miller 1991). For example, a grave offering included dried apples at Ur (Ellison et al. 1978), and coriander, fruits, and garlic cloves have been uncovered at Tell ed-Der (Zeist 1984). Plants originally domesticated beyond the borders of the Near East also began to appear, including millets, sesame, and rice (Zohary and Hopf 1993). Wild plants continued to add variety to the diet, as evidenced by occasional finds in food-related contexts: a jar of caper buds and fruits at Sweyhat (Zeist and Bakker-Heeres 1985), *Prosopis* seeds at Nimrud (Helbaek 1966), and *Chenopodium* at Shahr-i Sokhta (Costantini n.d.).

Deposits in cesspits provide direct evidence of diet, but they are not commonly found. A mineralized cess deposit from the third millennium B.C. city of Malyan, however, produced dozens of grape seeds and incompletely digested seeds of wheat and barley (Miller 1984). Most plant remains found are charred, however, so they do not directly represent food remains. Rather, they reflect fuel use, trash disposal, and cooking accidents. Archaeobotanical analysis is, therefore, not the primary means of understanding class or ethnic distinctions in human food consumption, but the situation is different for faunal remains.

As in earlier times, the major food animals were sheep, goat, cattle, and pig. Such domesticates as donkey, horse, and camel became more common, but they do not appear to have been eaten to any great extent. A variety of wild animals, such as gazelle, small game, birds, turtles, and fish, are frequent but minor contributors to faunal assemblages (Hesse 1995).

Several studies of the pattern of animal bone disposal on urban sites demonstrate the strategies employed to ensure a steady access to animal products, as well as social differences among the inhabitants. On most Near Eastern sites, the bulk of the bone is from sheep or goat, yet a fluctuating percentage of pig bone consistently appears. Pigs do well in forest and thickets, and can only survive harsh summers with shade and water. Generally then, pork-consuming regions are ecologically suited to the pig (Hesse 1995: 215).

The distribution of pigs in the later periods probably reflects the economics of pig production; they are a fine animal for town dwellers because they reproduce quickly and eat garbage. Thus, in Mesopotamia, the town residents of al-Hiba ate more pork than their rural counterparts in the community of Sakheri Sughir (Mudar 1982: 33). The difficulty in managing large numbers of pigs was another variable in pork consumption. At Lahav, in Israel, their numbers increased when the site was occupied by relatively isolated independent households. But when the settlement was integrated into a regional economy and, presumably, pig raising was more strictly regulated, production declined (Zeder 1995a). Faunal studies have not yet detected specific evidence for the Jewish prohibition on pork consumption because it is difficult to segregate ecological and economic from symbolic values reflected in archaeological bone remains (Hesse 1995: 215).

The dietary impact of wealth is exhibited at al-Hiba, a site where residents of the temple precinct had greater access to domestic animals, and residents of the lower town ate relatively more wild animals, along with pork (Mudar 1982). At Leilan, too, the lower town residences of poorer people had relatively large quantities of pig bones (Zeder 1995b). At Malyan, differential distribution of species and of meat-bearing elements across the site suggests that some residents had more direct access to the herds of sheep and goat than others, and some higher-status households appear to have had greater access to choicer cuts than did lower-status ones (Zeder 1991: 199).

Our sources of evidence for food multiply after the advent of complex society. Visual representations of food and texts concerning its production, distribution, preparation, and consumption fill out a picture constructed with more ubiquitous archaeological remains like seeds and bones. Writing, glyptic, and monumental art are associated with the upper strata of society and comprise evidence that begins to overshadow the archaeological plant remains among the literate societies. Animal bones, however, continue to be the primary source of information about meat consumption.

Among the earliest written signs in Mesopotamia is the one for beer, a necked jar (Green and Nissen 1987: 229). Even after the pictograph was transformed into a more abstract cuneiform sign, the image of two people sitting opposite each other and drinking (beer) with reed straws out of a necked vessel became one of the major elements in banquet scenes on seals (Selz 1983). Bread baking, beer brewing, and other food procurement and preparation scenes give some idea of the vast establishment that was necessary to support the major palace and temple institutions (Strommenger n.d.).

Plants of any sort are rarely depicted in the art of the ancient Near East, as either landscape elements or food. In contrast, images of animals are relatively common. There is no reason to suppose, however, that they are literal symbols of food sources, even when the subject is a food animal. Stylized animal representations in clay figurines are a normal part of assemblages from the aceramic Neolithic on. Although they frequently show important food species (bovids, caprids, and dogs), the animal taxa do not occur in proportion to bone refuse. The famous installations and wall paintings of Çatal Hüyük (eighth to seventh millennium B.C.) depict cattle, but they also depict vultures (Mellaart 1967). The pottery of some late farming cultures includes stylized birds and caprids, but again, there is no direct correlation with the faunal remains.

Depictions of animals in the art of the early civilization of Mesopotamia include many different life forms: scorpions, fish, turtles, birds, and wild and domestic mammals, along with imaginary creatures (Strommenger n.d.). Files of animals on cylinder seals and wall art seem to show sheep, goat, and cattle heading toward byres and are probably depictions of offerings to temple or palace. Haunches of meat and other comestibles are also elements in offering scenes. Portrayals of capture, such as men fishing with nets, sometimes suggest food procurement, but at other times, sport, as with the Assyrian royal lion hunts. A victory stela, showing human captives caught in a net, illustrates a new use for an old technology (Strommenger n.d.: 67), further demonstrating that pictorial evidence cannot be taken at face value. Moreover, scenes directly reflecting diet or dining only refer to a small segment of society. Their symbolic message is more significant than their documentary value.

Mesopotamians began keeping records on clay toward the end of the fourth millennium B.C. In the third millennium, the Sumerians developed writing for a variety of additional purposes. Hundreds of plant and animal names, many of which were used as foods and medicines, occur in ancient Sumerian and Akkadian texts from Mesopotamia (see, for example, Powell 1984; Stol 1985, 1987; Waetzoldt 1985, 1987; Postgate 1987). Economic and literary texts from Mesopotamia point to the importance of wheat, barley (and beer), date (and date wine), cattle, goat, sheep, dairy products, fish, and some fowl. Onion, garlic, and leek were the most important condiments. Different types of food preparation, such as roasting, brewing, and baking, are mentioned, as are names for many types of beer, cheese, and the like (Civil 1964; Ellison 1984; Bottéro 1985).

With textual evidence, it becomes easier to assess geographical, cultural, and social dietary variations. For example, although the staple plant foods of the Near East continued over a wide area, they had overlapping distributions. Cultural preference within the irrigation civilizations of southern Mesopotamia favored barley and beer, as well as date and date wine, whereas wheat and grape wine prevailed in the hilly regions and were joined by olive oil around the Mediterranean (see Powell 1995). Many regional differences are a function of ecology – grapes are more suited to a Mediterranean regime, and dates cannot be grown in the cooler climes. But these "natural" explanations for food preferences do not exclude cultural differences in attitudes toward various kinds of food. Wine, for example, came to have a religious significance in the Mediterranean civilizations that carries through to this day.

Distribution of food in the urban societies of lower Mesopotamia reflected social distinctions. It would seem that in the stratified societies of the ancient Near East, meat was a less important part of the diet for those of the lower classes. Economic texts from some of the major third millennium institutions show that careful track was kept of food provided to workers. Barley comprised the bulk of the rations for people working for the state or temple, although oil, malt products, meat, and other animal products were also distributed. Amounts varied according to the age and sex of the recipients, but scholars still disagree about whether daily ration for a worker constituted his or her whole diet or just a part of it (Gelb 1965; Ellison 1981).

Palace and temple archives also give a glimpse of herd management and production, but they deal exclusively with the large institutional herds of cattle, sheep, and goats. It has long been recognized that such archives tell only part of the story. Illustrative is sheep milk. Textual evidence suggests that only cattle and goats were milk producers, and sheep were grown for their wool and meat (Stol 1993). Yet sheep milk is high in fat and protein and would hardly have been wasted. Perhaps shepherds were allowed to milk the herds directly, or, as is ethnographically attested, sheep milk was mixed with cow's milk, but not recorded separately. Similarly, although quantities of fish were frequently deposited in temple and palace storehouses, no mention is made of fish preservation; because large quantities of fresh fish spoil rapidly, it seems likely that fish preservation and processing (for oil) was carried out by the private sector (Potts 1984).

Textual evidence of food preparation is slender. Perhaps best known is a hymn to the Mesopotamian beer goddess, which describes how *bappir*, an aromatic-flavored dough, is mixed with barley malt and fermented with herbs and other flavorings to make beer (Civil 1964). Three culinary texts from the second millennium B.C. (Bottéro 1985, 1995) contain recipes of sorts, although they are by no means step-by-step cooking instructions. Jean Bottéro, the Assyriologist who has studied them, considers them to be a codification of court cuisine that sets down general guidelines. Although the texts do not contain materials representative of the entire range of foods eaten by the upper stratum of society, let alone ordinary people, a few things are worth noting. The recipes include words for a variety of birds. They also contain words for meats and a method of cooking that included repeated washing of meat at different stages of food preparation. The number of plant types mentioned is relatively low, and those that have been identified appear to have been cultivated (with the possible exception of the potherbs). Finally, Mesopotamian cuisine was based on the use of sauces, which, as Bottéro points out, permitted the blending of subtle flavors unavailable with less elaborate forms of food preparation.

In earliest times, subsistence depended on wild resources available locally. The advent of agriculture brought together plants and animals from different regions and led to the creation of the Near Eastern agricultural complex of wheat and barley, pulses, sheep, goat, cattle, and pig. People of the Near East came to depend on domesticates, but wild plants and animals always constituted at least a minor portion of the diet. Advances in food preparation and storage technologies transformed agriculture into a highly productive and reasonably stable food procurement system, and effective food preservation techniques, in turn, permitted dense populations in towns and cities. Allowing for differences rooted in geography and culture, the diet and cuisine of Egyptian civilization developed along a similar path.

Egypt and North Africa

Beginning some 11,000 to 12,000 years ago, North Africa experienced a moist phase that lasted until historic times, although it was broken by several brief arid spells. During this period, summer rains produced seasonal lakes and dry grasslands, and the boundary of the Sahel shifted hundreds of kilometers north of its present location (Grove 1993). Hunter-gatherers who had been living on the margins of the Sahara began moving out onto what had been desert to subsist on wild plants, such fauna as gazelle and hare, and, in some cases, even fish (Muzzolini 1993).

By the seventh millennium B.C., these groups were growing larger and becoming more settled, as in the Near East. At Nabta Playa in southwestern Egypt, there were seasonal settlements that included storage pits, wells, and oval huts arranged in rows. Archaeological remains of plant foods indicate that the inhabitants gathered wild grasses, especially sorghum *(Sorghum)* and millet *(Pennisetum),* as well as Christ's-thorn fruits *(Zizyphus spina-christi)* and other wild fruits and seeds.

They cooked the plant foods in vessels, possibly made of hide, set in the sand of the hut floors (Wasylikowa et al. 1993). They may have also used the grinding stones that have been found in abundance at these sites to process grain. By the sixth millennium B.C., the Nabta Playa folk herded domestic cattle, sheep, and goats. The cattle were probably kept mainly for milk and blood, rather than meat (Wendorf and Schild 1984, 1994). Some scholars believe they were herded as early as 8000 B.C., but others reject this very early date (Gautier 1987; Muzzolini 1993; Wendorf and Schild 1994).

Livestock raising was gradually adopted by various groups of hunter-gathers in the Sahara and surrounding regions. Eventually pastoralism, combined with the gathering of wild plants, became a common pattern across North Africa, persisting in some areas until Roman conquerors introduced farming (Muzzolini 1993). In fact, in some regions of the desert, pastoralism and plant gathering are still practiced, although by 3,000 to 4,000 years ago, much of the Sahara had become far too arid to support any life (Grove 1993). It is believed that the African cereals, such as millet and sorghum, were domesticated in the Sahel, but little archaeological evidence of these plants has been collected (Harlan 1992). In contrast, the Egyptian Nile Valley has yielded a rich archaeological record of food and diet.

Nile Valley Hunter-Gatherers

Just off the Nile Valley in Wadi Kubbaniya, investigation of a series of 18,000-year-old camps has revealed one of the most detailed records of a hunting and gathering diet in the Old World (Wendorf and Schild 1989). Root foods from wetland plants, such as tubers, rhizomes, corms of sedges, rushes, and cattails, were dietary staples. The most important of these was purple nutgrass *(Cyperus rotundus)* (Hillman, Madeyska, and Hather 1989), which grows abundantly in wet ground and can be easily harvested with a digging stick. Young tubers are simply prepared by rubbing off the outer skin and roasting. Although older nutgrass tubers become woody and bitter with toxic alkaloids, grinding and washing renders them palatable. All of the archaeological specimens were found charred, suggesting roasting as the method for preparing young tubers. Aging tubers were probably prepared with the grinding stones found scattered across the Kubbaniyan sites (Hillman et al. 1989). Root foods were abundant through the fall and winter but became woody and eventually inedible by summer. Seeds of wetland plants helped fill the gap, but during the summer, the Nile's annual inundation restricted plant foods to wild dates and dom (or doom) palm fruits (Hillman et al. 1989).

The flood also brought catfish, the main source of animal protein for the Kubbaniyans. Catfish would have been exceptionally easy to catch at the onset of the inundation, when they spawned (Gautier and van Neer 1989). As the Nile waters moved across the floodplain, catfish would move to shallow water, where they congregated in dense masses and where they were doubtless readily taken with baskets, nets, spears, clubs, and even by hand. At the Kubbaniyan campsites, catfish were prepared for storage by drying or smoking after their heads had been removed. The vast quantities of catfish bones that littered the campsites suggest that they may have been eaten for some months after having been caught. Fish were supplemented with migratory waterfowl and small quantities of gazelle, hartebeest, and aurochs (Gautier and van Neer 1989).

The Nilotic adaptation, focused on root foods and catfish, appears to have persisted up until the beginnings of agriculture in Egypt, though the scant record of diet throughout these millennia does not provide incontrovertible evidence for either stability or change (Wetterstrom 1993). There are clues, however. Fishing gear and catfish bones are common at late hunter-gatherer sites. Fishing may have become even more important in the diet as fishing techniques apparently improved. Three fish of the deep Nile channel (Nile perch, *Bagrid,* and *Synodontes*) became common at sites after about 9,000 to 10,000 years ago (Neer 1989). The bones of aurochs, hartebeest, and gazelle indicate that they were the most abundant mammals. Occasional finds of other animals, such as hippopotamus or wild sheep, suggest rare catches.

Evidence of plant use for this period in the Nile Valley has not been collected systematically except at one site – a camp in the Fayum. Here, seeds of wetland plants were recovered, but no root foods were found, probably because preservation was poor (Wetterstrom 1993). The only other clue to the use of root foods is the fact that many sites during this period were located in ideal situations for collecting wetland tubers – next to embayments where the marshlike conditions necessary for wetland plants would have prevailed.

The Early Farmers of Egypt

The earliest traces of domestic plants and animals in Egypt are dated to roughly 5000 B.C. at a series of campsites in the Fayum Depression and in the oldest level of Merimde, a site on the western edge of the delta (Wetterstrom 1993). The Fayum data suggest that local forager groups adopted a few domestic crops and livestock but continued subsisting on wild plants and animals (Caton-Thompson and Gardiner 1934). Merimde, slightly younger than the early Fayum sites, may have been farther along in this transition. Although the settlement was probably only used seasonally, livestock bones found there are far more abundant than those of wild fauna (Driesch and Boessneck 1985). At this point, however, crops may not have supplied the bulk of the plant foods, as the facilities necessary for storing harvests were very limited (Wetterstrom 1993).

It is not clear when ancient Egyptians finally crossed the threshold from foraging to farming, shifting the balance in their diet from wild products to crops and livestock, but this appears to have occurred within a few centuries after domesticates were taken into the economy. Before 4400 B.C., Merimde had become a substantial village with abundant settlement debris and capacious storage facilities, while similar sites began to appear elsewhere, first in the north and later in the south. By 4000 to 3800 B.C., full-time farmers lived in permanent villages in the south as well as the north (Wetterstrom 1993).

The Near Eastern crop complex was the source of Egypt's first domesticates, and it formed the core of the agricultural economy through later periods (emmer wheat, six-row barley, lentils, peas, and flax, along with sheep, goats, cattle, and pigs). All of these, except perhaps cattle, probably came to Egypt from the Levant by way of the Sinai. As noted, cattle could have been independently domesticated in North Africa. The Near Eastern crops, all adapted to the Mediterranean climate, were planted in the fall after the annual flood had receded. As in the Near East, domesticated crops and livestock probably evened out the large seasonal fluctuations in the diet. Stored food may also have reduced the impact of year-to-year variations in Nile floods.

After Egyptians had become dependent on farming, they doubtless continued to supplement their diet with wild foods (Wetterstrom 1993). Fish were an important resource in many communities year-round, as were migratory waterfowl in the winter months. Larger animals, like gazelle, hippopotamus, and crocodile, occasionally show up among archaeological remains. But hunting was probably a rare adventure by this time. Where bone remains have been collected, wild fauna are extremely uncommon, as is hunting gear.

The archaeological evidence for wild plant foods is also unfortunately very limited. A small number of types have been recovered from archaeological sites, including the fruits of Christ's-thorn *(Zizyphus spina-christi)*, sycamore fig *(Ficus sycamorus)*, dom palm *(Hyphaene thebiaca)*, and balanites *(Balanites aegyptiaca)*, which has an edible oil in its seed. The small nutlike tubers of nutgrass *(Cyperus esculentus)* have been recovered from a variety of contexts: burials, inside a pot at a settlement, and from the stomach of a body mummified by the desert sands. This sedge, related to the *Cyperus* eaten at Wadi Kubbaniya, has been cultivated for its tubers since pharaonic times (Täckholm and Drar 1950). Seeds of grasses, sedges, vetches, and other wild plants have also been found at pre-Dynastic sites, although it is not clear if these were all used as foods. A variety of wild plants that do not preserve very well, if at all, were probably also gathered, including leafy vegetables and the stalk and rhizome of papyrus that we know were eaten in later periods (Täckholm and Drar 1950).

How prehistoric Egyptians prepared these foods and combined them into meals is very difficult to determine. Without the texts or representations of foods, so abundant in later periods, pre-Dynastic foodways must be inferred from a meager archaeological record. Cuts of meat – ribs, blades, legs – found in pre-Dynastic burial pots (Brunton 1928, 1937) hint at simple cooking techniques: boiling in pots or roasting over a fire. Headless remains of fish found in pots at settlements (Brunton 1928) suggest that fish were boiled after beheading. Fish may have also been smoked for storage as in earlier times, but there is no clear evidence of this.

Perhaps the easiest way to use cereals is in porridge, and this dish was probably on the early Egyptian farmer's menu. Bread is another simple way to turn grain into food. There is abundant documentation of bread in the Pharaonic Period, but for prehistoric periods, the evidence is limited to coarse loaves found in graves and settlement sites. At one site, a charred piece of bread was made of flour described as "more crushed than ground grain" (Debono 1948: 568). Though the pre-Dynastic breads seem crude, some may have been leavened with yeast, as they are porous (Brunton 1928). This would not necessarily have required any sophisticated understanding of baking techniques; a simple sourdough can easily be produced if flour and water are left to sit and collect wild yeast from the air. Fermentation could also have been readily discovered when grain and water or fruit juices were allowed to sit for a while. Egyptians certainly realized early the potential of fermentation, as attested to by traces of beer dregs found in the bottoms of vessels (Lucas and Harris 1962; Helck 1975a). Beginning around 3500 to 3400 B.C., formal brewery installations appeared at a number of sites (Geller 1989), associated with increasing economic specialization in Egypt.

Like Mesopotamia before it, Egypt, after the mid–fourth millennium B.C., was transformed from a society of simple autonomous villages into an organized, hierarchical state. In southern Egypt, burials showed marked differences in wealth and status among different groups, as well as individuals (Trigger 1983, Bard 1994). Large centers with temple and palace complexes and industrial and residential areas began to appear in southern Egypt. By around 3100 B.C., a centralized state had emerged with domain over the whole Nile Valley from the delta south to the First Cataract near Aswan (Bard 1994).

Pharaonic Egypt

The Pharaonic Period in Egypt, which spanned nearly 3,000 years, was an extraordinarily stable, conservative era (Map V.A.1.). From the beginning, a strong centralized government ruled Egypt as a single polity. The reign of the pharaohs was disrupted only three times when the power of that government broke down as a result of civil war or foreign invasion. Following these three so-called "intermediate" periods between the Old, Middle, and New Kingdoms and the Late Period, the central government was reestablished (Table V.A.2).

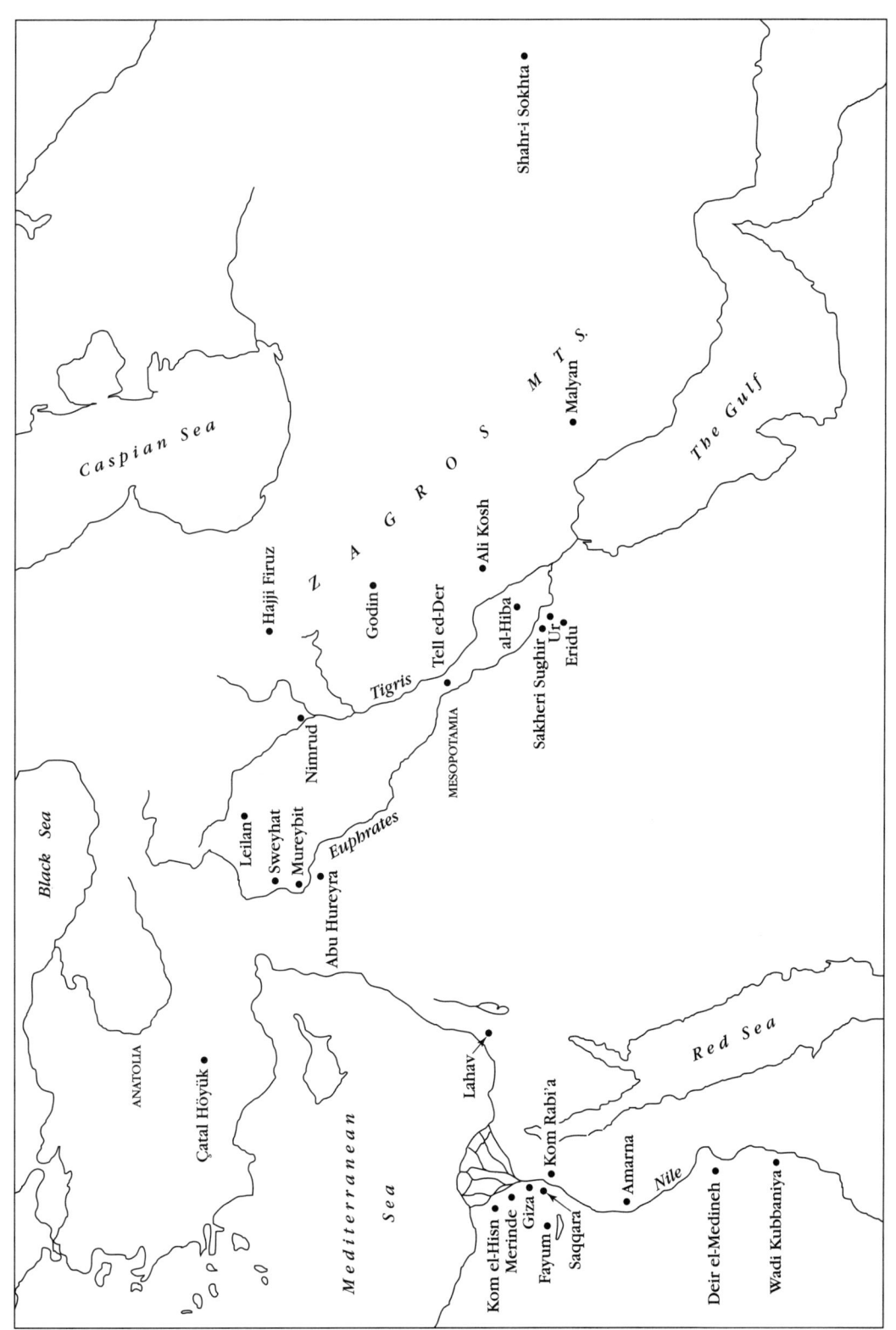

Map V.A.1. The world of Pharaonic Egypt.

Table V.A.2. *Pharaonic Egypt*

Period	Dynasties	Dates
Early Dynastic	1–2	c. 3100–2686 B.C.
Old Kingdom	3–6	c. 2686–2181 B.C.
First Intermediate	7–10	c. 2181–2040 B.C.
Middle Kingdom	11–12	c. 2133–1786 B.C.
Second Intermediate	13–17	c. 1786–1567 B.C.
New Kingdom	18–20	c. 1567–1085 B.C.
Third Intermediate	21–25	c. 1085–664 B.C.
Late Dynastic	26–31	c. 664–332 B.C.

Source: Bienkowski and Tooley (1995), p. 16.

Like early Mesopotamian civilization, pharaonic Egypt had a complex economic and social organization. People were divided by wealth, class, and occupation. Whereas the pharaoh, a divine king, presided at the top of the hierarchy, most of the people belonged to the lowest classes, working in myriad trades and as farmers and laborers (O'Connor 1983). In theory, the pharaoh owned all of Egypt; in practice, much of the land was held by the crown, but there were also large private estates. Crown-land harvests and taxes in kind from private lands supported the state bureaucracy, the military, and the conscripted laborers. Some land was also held as trusts, which supplied food to mortuary cults and temples (O'Connor 1983; Trigger 1983).

Pharaonic foods and diet are documented by a wealth of sources. These include artistic depictions in tombs, food offerings and offering lists in tombs and temples, tomb models, texts, and archaeological remains (Helck 1975b). Artistic depictions of everyday life, including food preparation, are common in Old and Middle Kingdom tombs, but less common in those of the New Kingdom. They are a rich source of information but can be difficult to interpret, as Egyptians tended to use a highly standardized iconography (Weeks 1979; Samuel 1989, 1993a, 1993b, 1994). Tomb models, most frequent in Middle Kingdom contexts, pose some of the same problems. Offerings and offering lists present a selective set of foods, the significance of which may elude present-day observers (Weeks 1979). Texts dealing with economic matters are abundant for the New Kingdom but less common for earlier periods. In addition, many words in the texts, including names of foods, are not yet understood (Janssen 1975).

Popular tales from the Middle and New Kingdoms offer clues to diet, but they are limited in scope. Archaeological data provide actual evidence of foods, allowing proper taxonomic identification in many cases, and may be useful in refining insights gained from textual sources and representations in tombs. Unfortunately, for the Pharaonic Period most archaeological material comes from tomb and temple contexts, with very little recovered from settlements. Other kinds of archaeological evidence, such as ovens, bakeries, and hearths, indicate something of

food processing and preparation, but the precise ways in which they were used is not always apparent. Recently, archaeologists have tried to test insights and theories gained from tomb depictions and other evidence by experimenting with baking, milling, and brewing techniques (Samuel 1989, 1993a, 1993b, 1994; Lehner 1994, 1997).

What emerges from the assorted lines of evidence is that all members of Egyptian society shared the same basic foods, with the upper strata having access to larger quantities and greater variety. At the core of the ancient Egyptian diet were bread and beer, consumed as staples by pharaoh and peasant alike throughout pharaonic history. Indeed, bread and beer were the basic wages, along with oils, grain, and clothing, paid to workmen on public and private projects (Eyre 1987). They were also the foods mentioned most often in popular tales, such as in the Middle Kingdom "Tale of the Eloquent Peasant" (Darby, Ghalioungui, and Grivetti 1977). As the hero set out on a trip, he commanded his wife, "[Y]ou shall make for me the six measures of barley into bread and beer for every day on which [I shall be traveling]" (Simpson 1973: 31).

Bread and beer were also fit for a king, however. An economic text from the Thirteenth Dynasty recorded a daily delivery of 1,630 loaves and 130 jugs of beer to the king's court (Scharff 1922). Bread and beer were also delivered to the temples every day and were viewed as essentials for the afterlife. The elite placed offerings of bread and beer in their tombs and enumerated them on offering lists. For example, Pharaoh Tutankhamen's tomb was stocked with bread (Hepper 1990).

Bread was produced in modest village kitchens (Janssen 1975) and in the large "commissaries" of elite households, the court, temples, and civic projects (Helck 1975b; Samuel 1993a, 1993b). Whereas the village breads that have been recovered are simple round loaves baked in an oven (Darby et al. 1977), professional bakers used a variety of techniques. Ceramic molds, which first appeared in late pre-Dynastic times, were commonly employed in the Old and Middle Kingdoms to bake offering breads and probably also rations for workmen (Jacquet-Gordon 1981; Lehner 1994). These coarse, thick-walled molds, shaped like flowerpots, were used as a kind of portable oven for baking in open pits (Lehner 1994). By the time of the New Kingdom, molded breads appear to have been made for special purposes and were baked in ovens in long, narrow, cylindrical molds (Samuel 1989, 1993b).

In addition to the mold-made loaves, a wide assortment of other breads and cakes were prepared for the temple and for the elite, employing a variety of techniques, temperatures, and grains (Drenkhahn 1975; Wild 1975; Samuel 1994). This was especially true during the New Kingdom, when loaf shapes proliferated; tomb art depicts spirals, cows, human figures, and other fanciful forms (Wreszinski 1926). Forty different kinds of breads and cakes were known at this time, compared to about a dozen in the Old Kingdom (Wild 1975). Emmer flour appears to have been the main ingredient in Egyptian bread, but other ingredients were also used (Grüss 1932; Täckholm, Täckholm, and Drar 1941), such as barley flour, ground nutgrass *(Cyperus esculentus)* tubers (Wilson 1988b), and sprouted wheat, which gave bread a slightly sweet flavor (Samuel 1994). Bakers sometimes added honey, dates, figs, and other fruits (Wilson 1988a; Samuel 1993a). For example, bread found in Tutankhamen's tomb was flavored with Christ's-thorn fruits (Hepper 1990).

Like bread, beer was brewed in modest households and in commissaries. Little is known of home-brewed beer, but breweries are frequently depicted in tomb scenes and models (Montet 1925). Archaeological traces of them have been found at a number of sites, as have vats and jars with beer residues (Lutz 1922; Lucas and Harris 1962; Helck 1975a; Geller 1992a, 1992b). The brewing process carried on at these ancient breweries, however, has not been well understood (Nims 1958; Geller 1992a; Samuel 1993a). The depictions are often ambiguous and the texts accompanying them subject to various interpretations because of difficulties in translating the language.

Delwen Samuel (1996) sidestepped these problems by turning to the direct evidence of brewing – ancient beer dregs and brewing by-products from the New Kingdom. Using scanning electron microscopy, she examined the microscopic structure of the starch granules in the residues and determined the processes they were subject to while being transformed into beer. It appears that Egyptians prepared grains intended for brewing in several different ways. After the grain was malted, or sprouted, some of the moist malt was heated while the rest was dried gently. The latter would have provided active enzymes for breaking down starch granules into simple sugars, which would support the yeast or lactic acid that is essential for producing alcohol. The roasted malted grains would have imparted a pleasant flavor and yielded a gelatinized starch that would be particularly susceptible to enzymatic attack. In addition, unsprouted, cooked grains may also have been used to make some beers. A large variety of named beers may have been produced by using different kilning and cooking techniques to prepare malted or unsprouted grains prior to brewing (Samuel 1996).

Both emmer and barley were used for beer in institutional breweries (Samuel 1996). In modest households, though, barley seems to have been the choice for brewing; as suggested in the "Tale of the Eloquent Peasant" and the evidence at Deir el-Medineh, a New Kingdom artisans' village, beer was brewed from barley rations (Lucas and Harris 1962; Janssen 1975). Bread, which has long been regarded as an essential ingredient of Egyptian brewing (Faltings 1991), played no role in these beers, according to the evidence that Samuel examined. As for flavorings in ancient Egyptian beer, there is little substantial evidence (Samuel 1996), although dates have often been propounded as a basic ingredient (Faltings 1991). As for Old Kingdom brewing techniques, Samuel's findings for the New Kingdom may well apply. No comparable studies have been conducted on beer dregs of the former period, and the archaeological evidence poses the ambiguities noted.

While bread and beer were basic subsistence to ancient Egyptians, vegetables and fruits were apparently regarded as above the level of basic needs. They were sometimes distributed as wages but were also depicted in market scenes, indicating that they could have been acquired through barter (Eyre 1994). The lower classes probably saw only the most common fruits and vegetables. The high labor costs of watering fruits and vegetables would have put many of them out of the reach of the poor (Eyre 1994). For the elite, on the other hand, "a variety and abundance of fresh produce was the mark of a luxury diet, emphasized by the elaboration of the fruits and vegetables recorded as offerings on the walls of tombs and temples" (Eyre 1994: 73).

Common vegetables in ancient Egypt included lettuce, leeks, onions, garlic, cucumbers, and radishes (Helck 1975b). Other names are listed in texts, but they have not yet been translated (Janssen 1975). How vegetables were prepared is not clear; they are shown as fresh produce in temple and tomb depictions. For lower classes, vegetables probably served mainly as condiments, as suggested by a New Kingdom tomb scene in which a workmen eats a lunch of bread, cucumber, and onion (Wilson 1988a).

The lower classes may have also supplemented their diet with wild plants. A host of weedy plants found in the fields and gardens, such as amaranth, chenopod, knotweed, sheep's sorrel, and wild grasses, could have been used as potherbs and grains. Their seeds have been found in settlement sites, such as Kom el-Hisn, an Old Kingdom community in the delta (Moens and Wetterstrom 1988), and Kom Rabi'a, a Middle and New Kingdom artisans' village at Memphis (Murray 1993), but it is not known for certain that these were actually consumed; many probably arrived at settlements as contaminants of cereal harvests. Still, many of these herbs have edible greens and/or seeds, which, ethnographic accounts indicate, have been used by others as foods (Fernald and Kinsey 1958; Nicolaisen 1963; Goodman and Hobbs 1988; Harlan 1989; Facciola 1990).

A number of fruits were known in ancient Egypt. Starting in the Old Kingdom with a short list – sycamore fig, dom palm, balanites, date, Christ's-thorn, and grape – the assortment grew as new types were introduced. Early additions were the true fig *(Ficus carica)*, melon *(Cucumis melo)*, persea, and a small watermelon *(Citrullus lunatus)* cultivated for its seeds (Germer 1985). Later, cordia *(Cordia myxa)*, pomegranate, and olive were adopted. During the

New Kingdom, exotic tropical fruits, such as grewia *(Grewia tenex),* were imported, as were pinenuts and almonds (Hepper 1990).

For peasants, the most important fruits were probably those that grew in Egypt with little or no care, such as Christ's-thorn, sycamore fig, and dom palm, as they would have been relatively cheap. Pomegranate, grape, and olive, on the other hand, all require tending and watering and were probably the prerogative of the elite. In tomb paintings and reliefs, fruits were usually displayed in large, overflowing baskets, perhaps to be consumed fresh, but fruits were also enjoyed dried, or cooked, and used as ingredients in other dishes. At Saqqara, a funerary meal laid out in a Second Dynasty tomb belonging to an elderly woman included plain Christ's-thorn berries placed on a plate and figs (probably *Ficus sycamorus*) prepared as a stew (Emery 1962). Fruits, particularly grapes, were also used to prepare wines imbibed by the elite (Janssen 1975). Wine production, which required substantial labor and skill, took place primarily in the delta and oases. But wine was also imported from Palestine, starting, perhaps, as early as pre-Dynastic times (Stager 1992). Often listed as an offering, wine was frequently depicted in New Kingdom funerary banquet scenes and was included in the funerary meal at Saqqara just discussed (Emery 1962).

Animal products were highly valued in the ancient Egyptian diet and together constituted the third most frequently mentioned food item in popular tales, after bread and beer (Darby et al. 1977). But they were not considered basic for subsistence, as indicated by the fact that meat was not given as rations. Market scenes in tombs show peasants buying pieces of meat through barter (Harpur 1987). For the well-to-do, meat figures prominently in tomb scenes, offering lists, and actual food offerings in tombs. The Saqqara funerary meal included four plates of meat out of a total of twelve dishes (Emery 1962).

Cattle were the most highly valued livestock in ancient Egypt, serving as draft animals and sacrificial beasts, as well as a source of food. Associated with the bovine deity Hathor (a mother goddess), they were considered sacred. Costly to raise, cattle were the premier choice for sacrifice at temples and tombs. Countless tomb paintings and reliefs show scenes of cattle husbandry, sacrificial processions, and the sacrifice of young, well-fed oxen. Beef consumption was almost certainly a prerogative of the elite, and the priests who butchered the cattle may have eaten the largest share (Darby et al. 1977). At the pyramid complex of Giza, for example, cattle bones from animals under two years of age predominate among the faunal remains (Redding 1992). The "middle classes," however, were not entirely excluded from enjoying beef. At Deir el-Medineh, cattle were delivered for feast days and periodically at other times for butchering, providing an occasional, but not rare, treat for the king's artisans (Janssen 1975).

For the lowest classes, beef was probably an extremely rare luxury. At Kom el-Hisn, for example, there is almost no bovine bone among the abundant faunal remains, although cattle were raised there (Moens and Wetterstrom 1988; Wenke 1990; Redding 1992). Kom el-Hisn peasants consumed only the occasional elderly or very young animal that died of natural causes, although they raised cattle destined for sacrifice at major ceremonial centers, such as the pyramid complex at Giza (Redding 1992).

Small livestock (sheep, goat, and pig) were more important sources of protein for lower classes. Bones of sheep and goats are common at settlement sites (Redding 1992). At Kom el-Hisn, peasants may have maintained their own small flocks while raising sacrificial cattle (Redding 1992). Pig remains are even more abundant at Kom el-Hisn and other settlement sites, such as the workmen's village at Amarna (Hecker 1982). Richard W. Redding (1991) proposes that peasants in rural areas raised small numbers of pigs for their own consumption, particularly in marginal regions where grain agriculture was not important.

Small livestock apparently played a minor role in the diet of the well-to-do. Large herds of sheep and goat were kept primarily for wool, hair, and milk. They were seldom depicted as sacrificial animals or placed in tombs as offerings. On the other hand, the Saqqara funerary repast did include a pair of kidneys from a small domestic animal (Emery 1962), and texts indicate that goats were occasionally sacrificed for certain festivals (Darby et al. 1977).

Relatively little is known about how meat was prepared, but food offerings placed in tombs during the Old Kingdom provide clues. Ribs and legs of beef found in the Saqqara funerary meal were most likely boiled or roasted. A dish that could not be identified (perhaps a stew) included ribs of beef among its ingredients (Emery 1962). A kitchen scene from a Fifth Dynasty tomb shows a cook cutting chunks of ox meat into pieces that were placed in a large cauldron. The hieroglyphic label underneath reads "cooking meat" (Hayes 1953: 97). Texts and a few tomb scenes indicate that beef was roasted as well (Darby et al. 1977).

While domestic livestock played an important role in ancient Egyptian life, the major sources of animal protein for rich and poor appear to have been fish and wild fowl. Both were abundant, and because little investment was required to produce them, they were probably inexpensive, compared with domestic animals. Texts from Deir el-Medineh indicate that they were very cheap at the time (Nineteenth Dynasty), with fish nearly as cheap as bread and beer (Janssen 1975). Fish are often shown in market scenes being purchased by barter (Eyre 1987). At Deir el-Medineh, fish were apparently a major source of protein, because they were distributed as rations (Janssen 1975). At Kom Rabi'a, abundant fish bones suggest that fish were an important source of food there as well (Ghaleb 1993).

As virtually the entire population lived close to the Nile waters, nearly everyone would have had some access to fish, at least during the flood season.

Poor Egyptians would, likewise, have had access to waterfowl during the winter migration. Fish and fowl were also common foods of the elite, who included them in tomb offerings and, particularly during the Old Kingdom, depicted fishing and fowling on their tomb walls (Montet 1925; Harpur 1987). Tomb scenes of food preparation indicate that fish were usually sun dried, pickled, or salted, whereas fowl was commonly roasted on a spit (Montet 1925). Wild fowl were also kept and fattened for consumption. The funerary meal from the Saqqara tomb included a cooked fish, cleaned, dressed, and beheaded, as well as a pigeon "stew" (Emery 1962).

Wild mammals were another potential source of meat, but hunting, already on the decline during the pre-Dynastic Period, had become an insignificant source of food by Old Kingdom times. At settlement sites, bones of wild mammals are rare; at Kom el-Hisn, for example, gazelle and hartebeest accounted for only 3 percent of the total faunal remains (Wenke 1990).

The traditional "poor man's meat" – pulses – were probably eaten by most of the people of ancient Egypt, although there is scant documentation. Pulses do not appear as tomb offerings or art, nor are they mentioned with any frequency in texts. But there are scattered archaeological finds, hinting at their importance. Lentils, for example, occur frequently in Tutankhamen's tomb as a contaminant of baskets of food offerings, suggesting that they were a common crop in ancient Egypt (Vartavan 1990, 1993). At Giza, lentils were found in trash left by workmen (Wetterstrom unpublished data). In Zoser's Third Dynasty tomb at Saqqara, lentils occurred in straw fill (Lauer, Täckholm, and Åberg 1950). They are also common in Middle and New Kingdom deposits at Kom Rabi'a (Murray 1993).

Records of other pulses in Egypt are few (scattered reports of lupine and fava beans [see, for example, Germer 1988]). Peas occasionally appear in archaeological contexts, such as Kom el-Hisn (Moens and Wetterstrom 1988). Chickpeas were apparently introduced in New Kingdom times; a few occurred in Tutankhamen's tomb as contaminants (Vartavan 1990, 1993). They are mentioned in texts from the Eighteenth Dynasty on but do not occur as offerings.

Dietary oil was considered an essential food, as indicated by the fact that it was among the rations allotted. Flaxseeds, castor beans, moringa nuts (*Moringa aptera*), olives, and, in later periods, sesame and safflower were all sources of oil (Germer 1985). Sesame seeds occur as offerings in Tutankhamen's tomb (Vartavan 1990), but they were not restricted to the elite; at Deir el-Medineh, artisans were given rations of sesame oil (Janssen 1975). In contrast, olive oil, most of which was imported from Palestine beginning in pre-Dynastic times (Stager 1992), was food for the elite.

The first cultivated spice found in Egypt is fenugreek, dated to 3000 B.C. (Renfrew 1973). From the New Kingdom on, and perhaps earlier, a wider range of seasonings was available in Egypt. In Tutankhamen's tomb, black cumin (*Nigella sativa*) and coriander occurred frequently as contaminants among baskets of foods, suggesting that they were grown widely and, therefore, were popular condiments (Vartavan 1990). Dill and cumin were also known in New Kingdom Egypt (Germer 1985). How these seasonings were used is not known, as recipe texts from ancient Egypt have yet to be found.

Honey and fruits were the only sweeteners known in ancient Egypt. In the Old Kingdom, honey, a scarce and costly resource, was under Pharaoh's control. Still expensive by the Middle Kingdom, honey was a frequent offering in private tombs and was employed extensively in temple rituals (Kueny 1950). It is unlikely that lower classes ever saw honey, relying instead on fruits and fruit juices as sweeteners. Sweetened breads and flavored beers, however, were probably a rare treat among the poorest classes.

During the 3,000 years of pharaonic history, it appears that the diet changed slowly, showing great conservatism and stability, like other aspects of Egyptian culture. The most visible changes relate to the introduction of new crops, new technologies, and new imports. Although the core of the agricultural system remained unchanged, with emmer wheat and barley the dominant crops, improvements in water management made it possible to grow fruits and vegetables in orchards and plantations (Eyre 1994) and, probably, to raise many of the new introductions, such as olives. While bread and beer retained their place as staples, baking and brewing technologies became more sophisticated.

Changes in the diet and the rewards of new technologies were probably not universally experienced. Initially, the diets of rich and poor were likely not vastly different. The elite would have had access to greater quantities of food, particularly meat, and sole access to a few costly goods, such as wine and olive oil. The elite may also have eschewed some low-status foods, such as pulses. But by New Kingdom times, and perhaps earlier, the gulf between rich and poor diets may have expanded into a chasm. The upper classes, undoubtedly, had greater access, and in some cases exclusive access, to new crops and imports, such as pine nuts, almonds, and pomegranates. In addition, tomb art and textual evidence suggest an elaboration of cooking techniques among the well-to-do during the New Kingdom.

Conclusion

In this chapter we have traced the history of food and diet over a heterogeneous territory and through a long time period that extended from the end of the Stone Age to the first civilizations. This era saw what are arguably the most significant changes ever to occur in the human diet, establishing the food patterns that still sustain people today.

With the adoption of farming and herding, peoples in the Near East and Egypt abandoned their diverse hunting-gathering diet and came to rely on the Near Eastern complex of domesticated plants and animals. After the shift to agriculture, both areas followed similar cultural trajectories, which involved the development of larger and more complex communities and, eventually, the emergence of civilizations. In both regions, improvements in food production and food storage technologies led to surplus accumulation and permitted the growth of large, dense populations and urban centers.

With the advent of complex society, people no longer had equal access to all types of food. An elite class ultimately controlled the production and distribution of much of the food supply. Some foods even became their sole prerogative, particularly exotic imports and those requiring extensive labor to produce. Most of the population, however, subsisted mainly on grain and grain products as earned wages in kind. In both Egypt and the Near East, the diet was based on plants, primarily cereal products like bread and beer, supplemented with vegetables, fish, and meat. For the lower classes, meat was probably a rare commodity except for the pigs that households could raise without interference from state authorities. Yet, although Egypt and the Near East followed similar social trajectories and shared the same core diet, they developed their own distinctive cuisines. Today much of the world shares that same core diet based on the Near Eastern domesticates, and variations on it are still developing.

Naomi F. Miller
Wilma Wetterstrom

Bibliography

Bard, Kathryn. 1994. The Egyptian Predynastic: A review of the evidence. *Journal of Field Archaeology* 21: 265-88.
Bender, Barbara. 1978. Gatherer-hunter to farmer: A social perspective. *World Archaeology* 10: 204-22.
Bienkowski, Piotr, and Angela M. J. Tooley. 1995. *Gifts of the Nile.* London.
Borowski, Oded. 1987. *Agriculture in Iron Age Israel.* Winona Lake, Ind.
Bottéro, Jean. 1985. The cuisine of ancient Mesopotamia. *Biblical Archaeologist* 48: 36-47.
  1995. *Textes culinaires Mésopotamiens.* Winona Lake, Ind.
Brunton, Guy. 1928. The Badarian civilization, Part. I. In *The Badarian civilization and Predynastic remains near Badari,* ed. Guy Brunton and Gertrude Caton-Thompson, 1-68. London.
  1937. *Mostagedda and the Tasian culture.* London.
Buitenhuis, Hijlke. 1990. Archaeozoological aspects of late Holocene economy and environment in the Near East. In *Man's role in the shaping of the eastern Mediter-*

ranean landscape, ed. S. Bottema, J. Entje-Neiborg, and W. van Zeist, 195-205. Rotterdam.
Caton-Thompson, Gertrude, and E. W. Gardiner. 1934. *The desert Fayum.* London.
Civil, M. 1964. A hymn to the beer goddess and a drinking song. In *Studies presented to A. Leo Oppenheim,* ed. Anon., 67-89. Chicago.
Colledge, Susan M. 1991. Investigations of plant remains preserved on epipalaeolithic sites in the Near East. In *The Natufian culture in the Levant,* ed. O. Bar-Yosef and F. R. Valla, 391-8. Ann Arbor, Mich.
Costantini, Lorenzo. N.d. Le piante. In *La città bruciata del deserto salato,* ed. Guiseppe Tucci, 159-228. Venice.
Darby, William J., Paul Ghalioungui, and Louis Grivetti. 1977. *Food: The gift of Osiris.* 2 vols. London and New York.
Davis, Simon J. M. 1984. The advent of milk and wool production in western Iran: Some speculations. In *Animals and archaeology: Early herders and their flocks,* ed. J. Clutton-Brock and C. Grigson, 265-78. Oxford.
Debono, Fernand. 1948. Helouan-el Omari: Fouilles du Service des Antiquités, 1943-1945. *Chronique d'Égypte* 21: 561-83.
Drenkhahn, Rosemarie. 1975. Brot. *Lexikon der Ägyptologie* 1: 871.
Driesch, Angela von den, and Joachim Boessneck. 1985. *Die Tierknochenfunde aus der neolithischen Siedlung von Merimde-Benisalame am westlichen Nildelta.* Deutsches Archäologisches Institut, Abteilung Kairo. Munich.
Ellison, Rosemary. 1981. Diet in Mesopotamia: The evidence of the barley ration texts c. 3000-1400 B.C. *Iraq* 43: 35-45.
  1984. Methods of food preparation in Mesopotamia (c. 3000-600 B.C.). *Journal of the Economic History of the Orient* 27: 89-98.
Ellison, R., J. Renfrew, D. Brothwell, and N. Seeley. 1978. Some food offerings from Ur, excavated by Sir Leonard A. Woolley, and previously unpublished. *Journal of Archaeological Science* 5: 167-77.
Emery, W. B. A. 1962. *A funerary repast in an Egyptian tomb of the Archaic Period.* Leiden, the Netherlands.
Evin, J. 1995. Possibilité et necessité de la calibration des datations C-14 de l'archéologie du proche-orient. *Paléorient* 21: 5-16.
Eyre, Christopher J. 1987. Work and the organization of work in the Old Kingdom. In *Labor in the ancient Near East,* ed. Marvin A. Powell, 5-47. New Haven, Conn.
  1994. The water regime for orchards and plantations in pharaonic Egypt. *Journal of Egyptian Archaeology* 80: 57-80.
Facciola, Stephen. 1990. *Cornucopia: A sourcebook of edible plants.* Vista, Calif.
Faltings, Dina. 1991. Die Bierbrauerei in AR. *Zeitschrift für Ägyptische Sprache und Altertumskunde* 118: 104-16.
Fernald, Merrit L., and Alfred C. Kinsey. 1958. *Edible wild plants of eastern North America.* Revised by Reed C. Rollin. New York.
Flannery, Kent V. 1969. Origins and ecological effects of early domestication in Iran and the Near East. In *The domestication and exploitation of plants and animals,* ed. P. J. Ucko and G. W. Dimbleby, 73-100. Chicago.
  1973. The origins of agriculture. *Annual Review of Anthropology* 2: 271-310.
Garrard, Andrew N. 1984. The selection of south-west Asian animal domesticates. In *Animals and archaeology 3. Early herders and their flocks,* ed. J. Clutton-Brock and C. Grigson, 117-39. Oxford.
Gautier, Achille. 1987. Prehistoric men and cattle in North Africa: A dearth of data and a surfeit of models. In *Pre-*

history of arid North Africa: Essays in honor of Fred Wendorf, ed. Angela E. Close, 163-87. Dallas, Tex.

Gautier, Achille, and Wim van Neer. 1989. Animal remains from the Late Paleolithic sequence at Wadi Kubbaniya. In *The Prehistory of Wadi Kubbaniya,* Vol. 2, *Palaeoeconomy, Environment and Stratigraphy,* ed. Angela E. Close, comp. Fred Wendorf and Romouald Schild, 119-58. Dallas, Tex.

Gelb, I. J. 1965. The ancient Mesopotamian ration system. *Journal of Near Eastern Studies* 24: 230-43.

Geller, Jeremy. 1989. Recent excavations at Hierakonpolis and their relevance to Predynastic production and settlement. *Cahier de recherches de l'Institut de Papyrologie et d'Égyptologie de Lille* 11: 41-52.

1992a. Bread and beer in fourth-millennium Egypt. *Food and Foodways* 5: 1-13.

1992b. From prehistory to history: Beer in Egypt. In *The followers of Horus: Studies dedicated to Michael Allen Hoffman.* Egyptian Studies Association Publication No. 2, ed. Renee Friedman and Barbara Allen, 19-26. Oxford.

Germer, Renate. 1985. *Flora des pharaonischen Ägypten.* Deutsches Archäologisches Institut, Abteilung Kairo, Sonderschrift 14. Munich.

1988. *Katalog der altägyptischen Pflanzenreste der Berliner Museen.* Wiesbaden.

Ghaleb, Barbara. 1993. Aspects of current archaeozoological research at the ancient Egyptian capital of Memphis. In *Biological anthropology and the study of ancient Egypt,* ed. V. Vivian Davies and Roxie Walker, 186-90. London.

Goodman, Steven M., and Joseph J. Hobbs. 1988. The ethnobotany of the Egyptian Eastern Desert: A comparison of common plant usage between two culturally distinct Bedoui groups. *Journal of Ethnopharmacology* 23: 73-89.

Gordon, Edmund I. 1959. *Sumerian proverbs.* Philadelphia, Pa.

Green, M. W., and H. J. Nissen. 1987. *Zeichenliste der archäischen Texte aus Uruk.* Berlin.

Grove, A. T. 1993. Africa's climate in the Holocene. In *The archaeology of Africa: Food, metal and towns,* ed. Thurstan Shaw, Paul Sinclair, Bassey Andah, and Alex Okpoko, 32-42. London.

Grüss, Johannes von. 1932. Untersuchung von Broten aus der ägyptischen Sammlung der staatlichen Museen zu Berlin. *Zeitschrift für Ägyptische Sprache und Altertumskunde* 68: 79-80.

Harlan, Jack. 1989. Wild-grass seed harvesting in the Sahara and the Sub-Sahara of Africa. In *Foraging and farming: The evolution of plant exploitation,* ed. D. R. Harris and G. C. Hillman, 79-98. London.

1992. *Crops and man.* Madison, Wis.

Harpur, Yvonne. 1987. *Decoration in Egyptian tombs of the Old Kingdom: Studies in orientation and scene content.* London.

Hassan, Fekri. 1985. A radiocarbon chronology of Neolithic and Predynastic sites in Upper Egypt and the Delta. *African Archaeological Review* 3: 95-116.

Hayes, William C. 1953. *The scepter of Egypt, Part. I: From earliest times to the end of the Middle Kingdom.* New York.

Hecker, Howard M. 1982. A zooarchaeological inquiry into pork consumption in Egypt from prehistoric to New Kingdom times. *Journal of the American Research Center in Egypt.* 19: 59-71.

Helbaek, Hans. 1966. The plant remains from Nimrud. In *Nimrud and its remains,* Vol. 2, ed. M. E. L. Mallowan, 613-20. 3 vols. London.

Helck, Wolfgang. 1975a. Bier. *Lexikon der Ägyptologie* 1: 789-92.

1975b. Ernährung. *Lexikon der Ägyptologie* 1: 1267-71.

Hepper, F. Nigel. 1990. *Pharaoh's flowers: The botanical treasures of Tutankhamun.* London.

Hesse, Brian. 1995. Animal husbandry and human diet in the ancient Near East. In *Civilizations of the ancient Near East,* ed. J. Sasson, 203-22. New York.

Hillman, Gordon C., Susan M. Colledge, and David R. Harris. 1989. Plant food economy during the epipaleolithic period at Tell Abu Hureyra, Syria: Dietary diversity, seasonality, and modes of exploitation. In *Foraging and farming, the evolution of plant exploitation,* ed. D. R. Harris and G. C. Hillman, 240-68. London.

Hillman, Gordon C., Eva Madeyska, and Jonathan G. Hather. 1989. Wild plant foods and diet at Late Paleolithic Wadi Kubbaniya: The evidence from charred remains. In *The prehistory of Wadi Kubbaniya, Vol. 2, Palaeoeconomy, environment and stratigraphy,* ed. Angela E. Close, comp. Fred Wendorf and Romuald Schild, 159-242. Dallas, Tex.

Hoffner, Harry A. Jr. 1974. *Alimenta Hethaeorum; food production in Hittite Asia Minor.* New Haven, Conn.

Hole, F. 1984. A reassessment of the Neolithic revolution. *Paléorient* 19: 49-60.

Jacquet-Gordon, Helen. 1981. A tentative typology of Egyptian bread moulds. In *Studien zur altägyptischen Keramik,* ed. Dorothea Arnold, 11-24. Mainz.

Janssen, J. J. 1975. *Commodity prices from the Ramessid period: An economic study of the village of the necropolis workmen at Thebes.* Leiden, the Netherlands.

Kaplan, J. 1954. Two Chalcolithic vessels from Palestine. *Palestine Exploration Quarterly* 86: 97-100.

Köhler-Rollefson, I. 1988. The aftermath of the Levantine Neolithic revolution in the light of ecological and ethnographic evidence. *Paléorient* 14: 87-93.

Kueny, G. 1950. Scènes apicoles dans l'ancienne Égypte. *Journal of Near Eastern Studies* 9: 84-93.

Lauer, J. P., V. Laurent Täckholm, and E. Åberg. 1950. Les plantes découvertes dans les souterraines de l'enceinte du roi Zoser. *Bulletin de l'Institut d'Égypte* 32: 121-52.

Legge, Anthony J. 1975. Appendix B. The fauna of Tell Abu Hureyra: Preliminary analysis. *Proceedings of the Prehistoric Society* 41: 74-7.

Lehner, Mark. 1994. Giza. In *The Oriental Institute 1993-1994 Annual Report,* ed. William M. Sumner, 26-30. Chicago.

1997. Replicating an ancient bakery. *Archaeology* 30: 36.

Lucas, A., and H. J. Harris. 1962. *Ancient Egyptian materials and industries.* Third edition. London.

Lutz, H. F. 1922. *Viticulture and brewing in the ancient orient.* Leipzig.

Mason, Sarah. 1995. Acornutopia? Determining the role of acorns in past human subsistence. In *Food in antiquity,* ed. J. Wilkins, D. Harvey, and D. Mobson, 12-24. Exeter, England.

McGovern, Patrick E., Donald L. Glusker, Lawrence J. Exner, and Mary M. Voigt. 1996. Neolithic resinated wine. *Nature* 381: 480-1.

Mellaart, James. 1967. *Çatal Hüyük: A Neolithic town in Anatolia.* New York.

Michel, Rudolph H., Patrick E. McGovern, and Virginia R. Badler. 1993. The first wine and beer: Chemical detection of ancient fermented beverages. *Analytical Chemistry* 65: 408A-13A.

Miller, Naomi F. 1984. The use of dung as fuel: An ethnographic example and an archaeological application. *Paléorient* 10: 71-9.

1991. The Near East. In *Progress in Old World palaeoeth-nobotany,* ed. W. van Zeist, K. E. Behre, and K. Wasy-likowa, 133-60. Rotterdam.

1996. Seed-eaters of the ancient Near East: Human or her-bivore? *Current Anthropology* 37: 521-8.

Moens, Marie-Francine, and Wilma Wetterstrom. 1988. The agricultural economy of an Old Kingdom town in Egypt's West Delta: Insights from the plant remains. *Journal of Near Eastern Studies* 47: 159-73.

Montet, Pierre. 1925. *Scènes de la vie privée dans les tombeaux égyptiens de l'ancien empire.* Strasbourg.

Moore, Andrew M. T. 1995. The inception of potting in west-ern Asia and its impact on economy and society. In *The emergence of pottery,* ed. W. K. Bennett and J. W. Hoopes, 39-53. Washington, D.C.

Mudar, Karen. 1982. Early Dynastic III animal utilization in Lagash: A report on the fauna of Tell al-Hiba. *Journal of Near Eastern Studies* 41: 23-34.

Murray, Mary Anne. 1993. Recent archaeobotanical research at the site of Memphis. In *Biological anthropology and the study of ancient Egypt,* ed. V. Vivian Davies and Roxie Walker, 165-8. London.

Muzzolini, A. 1993. The emergence of a food-producing econ-omy in the Sahara. In *The archaeology of Africa: Food, metal and towns,* ed. Thurstan Shaw, Paul Sinclair, Bassey Andah, and Alex Okpoko, 227-39. London.

Neer, Wim van. 1989. Fishing along the prehistoric Nile. In *Late prehistory of the Nile Basin and the Sahara,* ed. L. Krzyzaniak and M. Kobusiewicz, 49-56. Poznan, Poland.

Nicolaisen, Johannes. 1963. *Ecology and culture of the pas-toral Tuareg.* Nationalmuseets Skrifter Ethnografisk Raekke IX. Copenhagen.

Nims, Charles F. 1958. The bread and beer problem in the Moscow mathematical papyrus. *Journal of Egyptian Archaeology* 44: 56-65.

Nissen, Hans J., Peter Damerow, and Robert K. Englund. 1993. *Archaic bookkeeping,* trans. Paul Larsen. Chicago.

O'Connor, David. 1983. New Kingdom and Third Intermedi-ate Period, 1552-664 B. C. In *Ancient Egypt: A social history,* ed. B. G. Trigger, B. J. Kemp, D. O'Connor, and A. B. Lloyd, 183-271. Cambridge.

Postgate, J. N. 1987. Notes on fruit in the cuneiform sources. *Bulletin on Sumerian Agriculture* 3: 115-44.

Potts, Daniel. 1984. On salt and salt gathering in ancient Mesopotamia. *Journal of the Economic and Social History of the Orient* 27: 225-71.

Powell, Marvin A. 1984. Sumerian cereal crops. *Bulletin on Sumerian Agriculture* 1: 48-72.

1995. Wine and the vine in ancient Mesopotamia: The cuneiform evidence. In *The origins and ancient his-tory of wine,* ed. P. E. McGovern, S. J. Fleming, and S. H. Katz, 97-122. New York.

Raish, Carol. 1992. *Domestic animals and stability in pre-state farming societies.* Oxford.

Redding, Richard W. 1991. The role of the pig in the subsis-tence system of ancient Egypt: A parable on the poten-tial of faunal data. In *Animal use and culture change,* ed. P. J. Crabtree and K. Ryan, 20-30. MASCA Research Papers in Science and Archaeology 8, Supplement: 20-30. Philadelphia, Pa.

1992. Egyptian Old Kingdom patterns of animal use and the value of faunal data in modeling socioeconomic systems. *Paléorient* 18: 99-107.

1993. Subsistence security as a selective pressure favoring increasing cultural complexity. *Bulletin on Sumerian Agriculture* 7: 77-98.

Reiner, Erica, ed. 1980. *The Assyrian dictionary of the Oriental Institute of the University of Chicago,* Vol. 2. Chicago.

Renfrew, Jane. 1973. *Palaeoethnobotany.* New York.

Rosenberg, Michael, R. Mark Nesbitt, Richard W. Redding, and Thomas F. Strasser. 1995. Hallan Çemi Tepesi: Some preliminary observations concerning early Neolithic subsistence behaviors in eastern Anatolia. *Anatolica* 21: 1-12.

Samuel, Delwen. 1989. Their staff of life: Initial investigations of ancient Egyptian bread baking. *Amarna Reports* 5: 253-90.

1993a. Ancient Egyptian bread and beer: An interdiscipli-nary approach. In *Biological anthropology and the study of ancient Egypt,* ed. V. Vivian Davies and Roxie Walker, 156-64. London.

1993b. Ancient Egyptian cereal processing: Beyond the artistic record. *Cambridge Archaeological Journal* 3: 276-83.

1994. A new look at bread and beer. *Egyptian Archaeol-ogy: Bulletin of the Egypt Exploration Society* 4: 9-11.

1996. Archaeology of ancient Egyptian beer. *Journal of the American Society of Brewing Chemists* 54: 3-12.

Scharff, Alexander. 1922. Ein Rechnungsbuch des königlichen Hofes aus der 13. Dynastie (Papyrus Boulaq #18). *Zeitschrift für Ägyptische Sprache und Ältertums-kunde* 57: 53-8.

Selz, Gudrun. 1983. *Die Bankettszene, Entwicklung eines "überzeitlichen" Bildmotivs in Mesopotamien.* Wies-baden.

Sherratt, Andrew. 1981. Plough and pastoralism: Aspects of the secondary products revolution. In *Pattern of the past,* ed. I. Hodder, G. Isaac, and N. Hammond, 261-305. Cambridge.

Simoons, Frederick J. 1979. Dairying, milk use, and lactose malabsorption in Eurasia: A problem in culture history. *Anthropos* 74: 61-80.

Simpson, William Kelly. 1973. *The literature of ancient Egypt.* New Haven, Conn.

Stager, Lawrence. 1992. The periodization of Palestine from Neolithic through Early Bronze times. In *Chronologies in Old World archaeology.* Third edition, ed. Robert W. Ehrich, 22-41. Chicago.

Stol, Marten. 1985. Beans, peas, lentils and vetches in Akka-dian texts. *Bulletin on Sumerian Agriculture* 2: 127-39.

1987. Garlic, onion, leek. *Bulletin on Sumerian Agricul-ture* 3: 57-80.

1993. Milk, butter, and cheese. *Bulletin on Sumerian Agriculture* 7: 99-113.

Strommenger, Eva. N.d. *5000 years of the art of Mesopota-mia.* New York.

Stuiver, M., B. Kromer, B. Becker, and C. W. Ferguson. 1986. Radiocarbon age calibration back to 13,300 years B.P. and the 14C age matching of the German oak and U.S. bristlecone pine chronologies. *Radiocarbon* 28: 969-79.

Täckholm, Vivi, and Mohammed Drar. 1950. *Flora of Egypt,* Vol. 2. Bulletin of the Faculty of Science 23. Cairo.

Täckholm, Vivi, Gunnar Täckholm, and Mohammed Drar. 1941. *Flora of Egypt,* Vol. 1. Bulletin of the Faculty of Science 17. Cairo.

Trigger, Bruce. 1983. The rise of Egyptian civilization. In *Ancient Egypt: A social history,* ed. B. G. Trigger, B. J. Kemp, D. O'Connor, and A. B. Lloyd, 1-70. Cambridge.

Vartavan, C. de. 1990. Contaminated plant-foods from the tomb of Tutankhamun: A new interpretative system. *Journal of Archaeological Science.* 17: 473-94.

1993. Analyse plurisystématique pour l'interprétation des restes végétaux de la tombe de Toutankhmon. *Annales de la Fondation Fyssen* 8: 9–22.

Voigt, Mary M. 1990. Reconstructing neolithic societies and economies in the Middle East: An essay. *Archaeomaterials* 4: 1–14.

Waetzoldt, H. 1985. Ölpflanzen und Pflanzenöle im 3. Jahrtausend. *Bulletin on Sumerian Agriculture* 2: 77–96.

1987. Knoblauch und Zwiebeln nach den Texten des 3 JT. *Bulletin on Sumerian Agriculture* 3: 23–56.

Wasylikova, K., J. R. Harlan, J. Evans, et al. 1993. Examination of botanical remains from early neolithic houses at Nabta Playa, Western Egypt, with special reference to sorghum grains. In *The archaeology of Africa: Food, metal and towns,* ed. Thurstan Shaw, Paul Sinclair, Bassey Andah, and Alex Okpoko, 154–64. London.

Weeks, Kent R. 1979. Egypt and the comparative study of early civilizations. In *Egyptology and the social sciences,* ed. Kent R. Weeks, 59–81. Cairo.

Wendorf, Fred, and Romuald Schild. 1984. Conclusions. In *Cattle-keepers of the eastern Sahara: The Neolithic of Bir Kiseiba.* ed. Angela E. Close, comp. Fred Wendorf and Romuald Schild, 404–28. Dallas, Tex.

1989. Summary and synthesis. In *The prehistory of Wadi Kubbaniya, Vol. 3, Late Paleolithic archaeology,* ed. Angela E. Close, comp. Fred Wendorf and Romouald Schild, 768–824. Dallas, Tex.

1994. Are the early Holocene cattle in the eastern Sahara domestic or wild? *Evolutionary Anthropology* 3: 118–27.

Wenke, Robert. 1986. Old Kingdom community organization in the west Egyptian Delta. *Norwegian Archaeological Review* 19: 15–33.

1990. Excavations at Kom el-Hisn: The 1988 season. *Newsletter of the American Research Center in Egypt* 149: 1–6.

Wetterstrom, Wilma. 1993. Foraging and farming in Egypt: The transition from hunting and gathering to horticulture in the Nile Valley. In *The archaeology of Africa: Food, metal and towns,* ed. Thurstan Shaw, Paul Sinclair, Bassey Andah, and Alex Okpoko, 165–226. London.

Wild, Henri. 1966. Brasserie et panification au tombeau de Ti. *Bulletin de l'Institut Français d'Archéologie Orientale* 64: 95–120.

1975. Backen. *Lexikon der Ägyptologie* 1: 594–8. Wiesbaden.

Wilson, Hilary. 1988a. *Egyptian food and drink.* Aylesbury, England.

1988b. A recipe for offering loaves? *Journal of Egyptian Archaeology* 74: 214–17.

Wreszinski, Walter von. 1926. Bäckerei. *Zeitschrift für Ägyptische Sprache und Altertumskunde* 61: 1–15.

Zeder, Melinda A. 1991. *Feeding cities.* Washington, D.C.

1994. After the revolution: Post-Neolithic subsistence strategies in northern Mesopotamia. *American Anthropologist* 96: 97–126.

1995a. The role of pigs in Near Eastern subsistence from the vantage point of the southern Levant. In *Retrieving the past: Essays on archaeological research and methodology in honor of Gus van Beek,* ed. J. D. Seger, 297–312. Winona Lake, Ind.

1995b. The archaeobiology of the Khabur Basin. *Bulletin of the Canadian Society for Mesopotamian Studies* 29: 21–32.

Zeist, W. van. 1984. Palaeobotanical investigations of Tell ed-Der. In *Tell ed-Der IV,* ed. L. de Meyer, 119–43. Leuven, Belgium.

1988. Some aspects of early neolithic plant husbandry in the Near East. *Anatolica* 15: 49–67.

Zeist, W. van, and J. A. H. Bakker-Heeres. 1984. Archaeobotanical Studies in the Levant 3. Late paleolithic Mureybit. *Palaeohistoria* 26: 171–99.

1985. Archaeobotanical Studies in the Levant 4. Bronze Age sites on the north Syrian Euphrates. *Palaeohistoria* 27: 247–316.

Zeist, W. van and S. Bottema. 1991. Late Quaternary vegetation of the Near East. In *Beiheft zum Tübinger Atlas des vorderen Orients,* Reihe A nr. 18. Wiesbaden.

Zohary, Daniel, and Maria Hopf. 1993. *Domestication of plants in the Old World.* Second edition. Oxford.

Zohary, Michael. 1973. *Geobotanical foundations of the Middle East.* 2 vols. Stuttgart.

V.B

The History and Culture
of Food and Drink in Asia

V.B.1 ॐ The Middle East and South Asia

Although the regions we call the Middle East and South Asia constitute a very wide area, their collective culture has been shaped by a shared history from the conquest of Alexander the Great to the Islamic empires. The precepts of Islam have been adopted in most of the countries in the area under scrutiny, if not always by the majority, as in India. There are, therefore, many similarities in their cultures and especially in their preparation of foods. Each country, region, and town has its own cooking traditions, but it is easy to spy the similarities behind the differences.

This region of the world is socially traditional; therefore, women stay at home most of the time and are in charge of the kitchen. Food is often prepared in the company of other women in Muslim houses, which makes it a time for socializing. Professional cooks (always male) are employed for special occasions in wealthier homes.

The cooking is done mostly on a stove. The process is very long and slow, resulting in a very tender meat or vegetable, literally ready to disintegrate. The people of the Middle East and South Asia have no liking for red meat (even pieces of meat or kebabs for roasting are cooked previously or at least marinated).

Food is almost never cooked in water alone. Rather, it is first fried, then simmered or boiled, and finally enriched with fat. There is also a wide consumption of street food, fried or grilled. Savory pastries, such as *borek, samossa,* and *brik,* are popular.

Meat is an important item of the diet for those (except for the vegetarians) who can afford it, and it is used as often as possible, even as part of a stuffing or in a broth. Lamb is the favorite meat, although the less expensive chicken dominates in poorer houses. Because of the Islamic influence, pork is avoided, except by minorities, such as the Goanese Christians, for example.

The cookery is also characterized by the use of many pulses, clarified butter (*samn* or *ghee,* mainly from buffalo's milk), and fresh yoghurt (as a drink and a cooking liquid). Unlike in the Far East, milk, milk products, and milk sweets are important here, and all the people of the region rely on a basic cereal, mostly rice or wheat. Food is very colorful as well as flavorful because of the use of such spices as saffron and turmeric. Spices are used extensively, even if only in small quantities. There is a spice street in every bazaar in the Middle East and South Asia. All the countries of the region are on the same spice route, which begins in Asia, with the Middle East a conduit for spices on the way to Africa and Europe.

Scents are also typical of this exotic cookery: Rose, amber, musk, camphor, santal, orange blossom, jasmine, and orchid are used in many a sherbet and dish. People share a fondness for sour things: Lemon or lime, vinegar, tamarind, sumac, pomegranate juice, and sour cherries add zest to meat dishes.

Spices are also used for their assumed medicinal properties, and the composition and preparation of foods is often explained in terms of health needs created by climatic conditions. In fact, another similarity between the cultures of South Asia and the Middle East is a belief in medico-magic properties of food. This, in turn, encourages secrecy in cooking, and the preparation of aphrodisiacs and other potions at times tends to blur the tasks of cook and alchemist.

The History and Culture of Food in the Middle East

The Middle East encompasses a large area stretching from the Arabian Peninsula to Afghanistan and includes the border states of the eastern Mediterranean. It is divided into many countries: Turkey, Syria, Lebanon, Jordan, Israel, Egypt, Saudi Arabia, Iraq, and Iran. The people of the Middle East are of several racial types and have embraced different religions. Geographic and climatic conditions are extremely diverse in the region. Nonetheless, the Middle East can be described as a single cultural entity. Islam has played a unifying role in the area through the building of vast "Islamic" empires that rule over most of these people and the conversion of a vast majority of the population.

There is, therefore, a Middle Eastern civilization with a collection of several culinary traditions, each of which will be given due attention (although the food of the minorities of the region, Coptic, for example, or the cosmopolitan cuisine of Israel will be ignored for the sake of coherence). Overriding similarities in tastes and manners, however, will also be pointed out.

Before the Arrival of Islam

Long before dwellers in Europe could imagine the possibilities of fire, the civilizations of the Middle East had invented agriculture, cattle breeding, and numerous ways of preparing and enjoying foods.

Pre-Islamic Arabia. The diet of pre-Islamic Arabia was the typical diet of a pastoral people in a desert region. It was simple and monotonous, with the most important roles played by dairy foods. According to ancient poems and the *Koran,* milk, milk products, and dates were the main items of the diet. Camel milk was most frequently used, but goat and sheep milk were also available. The milk could be diluted with water and was used in the preparation of a sort of cheese and of clarified butter *(samn)* for cooking.

The oases provided the nomads with dates, which were sometimes the only food available. Dates supplied energy, were easy to carry, and, over time, acquired a symbolic value. They were served at festivals, and the Prophet Mohammed later stressed their importance by making them one of his favorite foods, especially for the breaking of fasts.

Meat was seldom eaten, except for festive occasions, when sheep were frequently consumed and especially appreciated for their fatty tails. Camels, sometimes slaughtered and their coagulated blood shaped into sausages to be cooked, were another source of animal protein. Beef, pork, or fowl were quite unknown. Hare, bustard, large lizards, and grasshoppers could become food in harsh environments.

Cereals were scarce. The Prophet ate cakes of coarse barley with a little vinegar, oil, and perhaps a few dates. Dried barley was also made into a meal that was easily cooked into a gruel with the addition of water and fat. Another type of gruel *(harira)* was prepared from flour cooked in milk. A richer gruel could be made with bran and meat.

A number of vegetables were also available throughout the settled communities of the desert. Cucumbers, vegetable marrows, beets, chicory, and olives were common, as well as leeks, onions, and garlic. Lemons, pomegranates, and grapes or raisins were the main fruits, although figs and apples are mentioned in some texts. By combining all these products, the Arabs could prepare a few elaborate dishes. *Tharid* was one: bread pieces soaked in a meat and vegetable broth. *Hayes* was another. Made of milk, butter, and dates, it is said to

have been another favorite of the Prophet. These dishes and the more common broths were quite bland. The nomads preferred to sell the spices they had rather than use them themselves. Imported wine was a luxury, but the Arabs were familiar with fermented drinks, prepared from dates, barley, honey, or raisins.

Pharaonic Egypt. Thanks to numerous archeological remains, it is possible to imagine how the kings and people of ancient Egypt would dine. Cattle and sheep were slaughtered in the palace and then might be roasted whole or grilled in pieces. Lamb chops were a delicacy, and fowl was also served, as were different types of bread and pastries. The food was seasoned with cream and, perhaps, imported olives from Greece. Lentils and fish constituted a simpler diet, and beverages consisted of beer, milk, and wine. Beer was prepared from the fermentation of barley, wheat, and dates. The country was so rich in wheat that during its Roman period (30 B.C. to A.D. 395) it became the empire's granary.

Ancient Mesopotamia. It was in ancient Mesopotamia that agriculture and cattle breeding were invented, and we can infer much about the diet of these early inventors from that of the people living in the region today. The staple food for this population of agriculturists was bread made of barley rather than wheat. Barley was often eaten in the form of gruel as well.

The banks of the Mediterranean are famous for their olives and grapes. The whole of the region that was once ancient Mesopotamia is very fertile: Cucumbers, turnips, onions, leeks, fennels, herbs, lentils, and chickpeas are among the vegetables grown. Many types of fruit can also be found, most importantly, dates, figs, and pomegranates. Fish is sometimes served, but meat is scarce. In the past, a sheep or goat was occasionally slaughtered for sacrifice or in honor of a guest. But as a rule, beef and pork, along with fowls and pigeons, were rarely eaten. Apart from pulses, most of the protein came from eggs, milk, and milk products, which included curd and cheese. Honey was and is a common treat. Olive and sesame oils are abundant. The common beverages were water, milk, or beer. The rich, however, enjoyed palm or grape wine.

Cooking was done on a stove. For the poor this consisted (and still consists) of a simple cavity, dug in the ground of a house or courtyard, and coated with clay in which embers were piled. These hearths are sometimes built in raised fashion along a wall, and some are ovens entirely of clay.

The arrangement of ovens designed for the baking of the bread is quite complex. They are built in the shape of beehives, with a side opening to introduce the embers. The bread cakes are placed against the hot walls inside and cook very quickly. These ovens are located in a courtyard or in empty ground between houses, where the meal is usually prepared by grinding grain with hand millstones made out of a long, flat stone and a pestle, or by pounding meal in three-legged stone mortars.

General Features of Food in the Middle East

The Imprint of Islam

In pre-Islamic Arabia, there were few prohibitions on food, although certain holy families did not eat meat, and each tribe had customs that might prohibit the eating of a certain part of an animal. Wine was drunk quite often and sometimes ritually. But, even before the time of the Prophet, certain Arabs had been influenced by Judaism and Christianity. Thus, they abstained from eating animals not ritually slaughtered or those sacrificed to idols and, perhaps, refrained from drinking alcohol. The Prophet, however, established what was lawful (*halal*) and unlawful (*haram*) to eat. Prohibitions in some instances included blood, the flesh of an animal that had died, or that of an animal not properly slaughtered. In addition, pork was proscribed, along with a few marginal animals that were snakelike in appearance or wild.

Mohammed insisted that the restrictions for his people were not as excessive as they were for Jews. He also stressed that food should be regarded as a divine blessing and, therefore, thoroughly appreciated. The Koran at first praised the virtue of wine but soon showed reservations about it and, finally, forbade it. In addition to these rules, Islam decreed a periodic general fast during the month of Ramadan.

Middle Eastern Table Manners

Food is traditionally eaten with three fingers of the right hand, from dishes or trays that can be shared by four to eight people. The thumb, index and middle fingers are used to pick up the food. It is polite to take the piece of food nearest to you in the serving dish. Pieces of meat or vegetables are usually taken with the help of a piece of bread, and fingers are licked after the meal.

The "table" is laid in a simple manner: Cloth is spread on the floor, or a large tray is placed on a low stool to form a table. Today, people sit cross-legged around these arrangements, although Pierre Belon, a sixteenth-century observer, noted that Arabs rested on their heels while eating and Turks sat on the floor. Dishes for those dining are displayed in front of them, usually all at the same time. If there is dessert, it is brought after the meal, and coffee follows in many Middle Eastern countries. Hands are washed with the help of a basin and a flask and dried on towels before and after meals.

The meals are inaugurated in Islam with an invocation of God. Islam dislikes the mixing of the sexes, and so in traditional homes, women and men usually eat apart. Everyone stops eating at the same time, and it is polite to nibble until your neighbors are finished. The choicest parts are offered to special guests. A host can also honor a guest by offering him a good morsel from his hand. There is a strong sense of hospitality, and the expected, or unexpected, guest will always be offered something to drink and eat.

Basic Ingredients and Cooking Techniques

Much of the Middle East is desert, with only about 10 percent of the land useful for cultivation. As a consequence, the common diet can be quite monotonous. Chickpeas and lentils have been part of Middle Eastern cuisine for thousands of years, along with a number of vegetables and fruits. The aubergine (eggplant), for example, is omnipresent on Middle Eastern tables. The Turks claim they know more than 40 ways of preparing this vegetable. It can be smoked, roasted, fried, or mashed for a "poor man's caviar." According to a Middle Eastern saying, to dream of three aubergines is a sign of happiness.

Because of the shortage of pasture land, sheep, goats, and chickens are the main animals raised. Pork is not eaten by Muslims and, generally, beef is not much appreciated. Animals are slaughtered by Muslim ritual; the throat is slit quickly, cutting through the trachea and the esophagus. Thus, the animal does not suffer. At the moment of cutting, the name of God is invoked. Ideally, the animal will have its left side facing Mecca at the moment of death.

Barley has become increasingly neglected in favor of wheat and rice. Wheat is used as flour in many leavened and unleavened breads. So too is *burghul* or cracked wheat, a preparation in which the whole grains are partially cooked, then dried and cracked. Three sizes of burghul are available, medium and large grains found in pilafs and stuffings, and a fine variety that is preferred for salads and *kibbeh*. Medium and large grains must be soaked before use.

Rice arrived in the Middle East later than wheat and is used mainly by urban populations, whereas wheat is the staple food of the countryside. Many types of rice are available, with the best and longest grains coming from Iran. It is prepared differently in every region, although rice is soaked everywhere. In Syria, it is boiled for 2 minutes in the same water it was soaked in, then simmered for 20 minutes until the water is absorbed. Melted butter is poured on it and the rice left to stand for a few minutes before eating. In Lebanon, water and butter are boiled together. In Egypt, the rice is fried in fat, then simmered. Iranians claim to have the best method of cooking rice: They parboil for 6 to 8 minutes, then steam with butter in a sealed dish. The rice is fluffy and flavorful, with a golden crust at the bottom of the pan.

Milk is widely used, especially in the form of thin or thick yoghurt. It is also churned into clarified butter (*samn*). Other cooking oils are derived from olives, cottonseeds, nuts, corn and sesame seeds. Olive oil is often associated with fish and salad dishes. A very sought-after delicacy is the rendered fat of sheep tails.

Because the region has long been involved in spice trading, some spices, mostly of Indian origin, are part of the diet. These include turmeric, cumin, coriander, and cinnamon. If they can be afforded, nuts are widely used in cooking (walnuts in Iran and pine nuts in Lebanon, for example). A few exotic items in a Middle Eastern pantry are *sumac,* a red spice with a sour lemony flavor that is the powder of dried, round berries and gives color and taste to many dishes (in Iran it is sprinkled on rice or kebabs); *tahina,* which is sesame seed paste; and *mahlab,* the powder of black cherry stones. Rose and orange blossom water, mastic, and powdered orchid root are also used, but more rarely.

Traditional cooking is done on a stove or *fatayel,* with bread usually baked by a professional. Moreover, in the past, the baker's oven also served as a public oven. Families sent their pans or dishes to be placed in the oven for very slow cooking. Today domestic ovens play this role most of the time. Middle Eastern cooking is a painstaking and slow process, made possible on an everyday basis because most women of the Middle East spend the day at home. For this reason, these women are able to carry on cooking traditions and people remain very much attached to the dishes of the past.

There is a considerable pride of craftsmanship that goes into Middle Eastern cookery. Miniature foods (like miniature paintings) are favorites, stuffings can be incredibly elaborate, and mock dishes are sometimes invented to puzzle the guests. Pastries are elaborate and reflect craftsmanship, as do the numerous finger foods, such as small pizzas, stuffed grape leaves, fried meat balls with delicate moist fillings, and confections that are jewel-like.

Coffee was first popular in Yemen and Saudi Arabia, then spread throughout the region. There is no ceremony, no bargaining, nor any counseling session without coffee. Cups are small and made of different materials, which vary from country to country. The sugar is usually boiled together with the coffee in water (although Egyptians like their coffee unsweetened). When the water boils, sugar and coffee are thrown into the pot. The beverage is stirred, simmered briefly, then poured, still frothy, into cups. In Lebanon, coffee is often flavored with orange blossom water.

Other Middle Eastern favorites are pickled vegetables or fruit (raw or lightly cooked and soaked in a salt-and-vinegar marinade) and fruit syrups (sherbet) of many kinds: orange, rose water, quince, apricot, and tamarind (in Egypt). A meat and wheat soup is usually served, especially for celebrations. Meat is often minced or hand pounded before cooking. If not, it is cubed, or at least cooked so as to be easily torn to pieces, because it is eaten with the fingers. A typical salad dressing in the Middle East is a simple mixture of olive oil and lemon juice, seasoned with salt, pepper, garlic, and herbs.

The dietary similarities of Middle Eastern countries reflect the long unification and acculturation process under Arab, "Islamic," and Ottoman domination. Under the Abbassids, for example (ninth to twelfth century), during the Golden Age of Islam, there was one single empire from Afghanistan to Spain and the North of Arabia. The size of the empire allowed many foods to spread throughout the Middle East. From India, rice went to Syria, Iraq, and Iran, and eventually, it became known and cultivated all the way to Spain. The use of sugar was common among wealthy people, along with spices from Asia, coffee from Arabia, olive oil from Syria, cheese from Crete, saffron from Tuscany, and even wine from the south of France. Dried and salted fish, honey, and hazelnuts also reached the Middle East from Russia and the Slavic countries.

To keep the products from deteriorating in transit, different techniques were used. Melons from Transoxiana were packed in ice inside lead boxes before they were sent to Baghdad. Nuts and desert truffles were dried. The crystallizing of fruit in honey or sugar, an old process developed in ancient Rome, was also employed, and milk was often preserved in the form of cheese.

Cooks also traveled; those from Egypt and Bolu, in Turkey, were the most famous and in the most demand. In addition, recipes spread, making Iranian and, later on, Turkish dishes fashionable. The culinary arts were considerably elevated early on under the Caliph Hârûn-al-Rashîd (786–801). The gastronomy of the time is depicted in poetry, as well as in medical treatises on food hygiene. The caliphs of Baghdad were renowned for their lavish and sophisticated tables. The rulers liked to converse about food and encouraged people to write about it and experiment with it. Manuals on good manners stressed that the well-bred man of the time could not ignore the culinary arts.

Palace food was characterized by its expense (plenty of meat, spices, sugar, rice), complexity (elaborate combinations of flavors, as well as stuffings), beauty (rich colors), and mock dishes. Palace doctors offered advice in the choice and preparation of food, as dietetics was important for the elite.

Many dishes of that period are still prepared today with ingredients available to the common people. Some of these are vinegar preserves, roasted meat, and cooked livers, which could be bought in the streets, eaten in the shops, or taken home. Such dishes considerably influenced medieval European and Indian cookery; for example, *paella,* which evolved from *pulao,* and pilaf and meat patties that started out as *samosa* or *sambusak.*

Despite the rich and relatively coherent cultural area created by the Muslim conquest, three main types of Middle Eastern cookery can subsequently be distinguished. One is that of Iran, another that of the Fertile Crescent, and the last that of Turkey. Each of these will be examined in turn.

Iranian Cookery

General Features

Iran is a vast land of varied climatic conditions. The coast of the Caspian Sea is known for its heavy rainfall and a verdant vegetation. But such a climate precludes the growing of long-grain rice and citrus fruits, such as oranges, tangerines, lemons, and limes. The region along the Persian Gulf is one of extreme heat, suitable for palm trees and the production of dates. Wheat is grown everywhere except on the Caspian coast, and the whole of the country produces tea, olives, peaches, apricots, pomegranates, pistachios, and walnuts. The famous red and white Damask roses, cultivated in Iran, yield an excellent rose water. The melons and grapes of Iran are also renowned. Although alcohol is prohibited in the Islamic religion, Iran was known in the past for good wines, especially those from Shiraz.

Sheep and goats are raised in large areas of Iran, with the main breed of sheep having fat tails and lean meat (fat is concentrated in the tail). These animals also provide milk from which large quantities of yoghurt are made.

Iranian dishes have changed little over the centuries, and many of them are somewhat unique in the Middle East because sweet and savory ingredients are often cooked together. A lamb stew with spinach and prunes is one example and duck in a sour cherry or pomegranate sauce is another.

Another feature of Iranian dishes is the wide use of fresh herbs, such as parsley, dill, coriander, mint, and cress, and a bowl of fresh herbs can play the role of a salad. Herbs mixed with rice flavor the green *sabzi pollo.* Iranian dishes are very subtly and lightly spiced. Saffron and cinnamon are among the most commonly used spices, dill and coriander seeds among the herbs most frequently employed.

Rice is an Iranian specialty, with many different kinds available, ranging from the longest and most flavorful to the quite ordinary. Rice is used in various ways: as *chilau* (white) or as *pollos* (with different meats and vegetables), and as a dessert (a *shol-e-zard* or saffron rice pudding served, among other occasions, for the annual observance of the martyrdom of Imam Hassan).

There is an Iranian legend explaining the high value of rice. When the Prophet Mohammed was accidentally conveyed into paradise, he sweated with terror at the idea of facing the throne of the Almighty. Six drops of his precious sweat came to earth from paradise. The second of these became a grain of rice.

As noted, Iranians have a unique method of preparing rice. This method is designed to leave the grains separate and tasty, making the rice fluffy and very flavorful. After soaking, parboiling, and draining, the rice is poured into a dish smeared with melted butter. The lid is then sealed tightly with a cloth and a paste of flour and water. The last stage is to steam it on low heat for about half an hour, after which the rice is removed and fluffed. The golden crust on the bottom of the pan, or *tah-dig,* is crumbled on top or served separately.

In addition to *pollo,* other typical Iranian preparations are *koresht* (stews of meat or fowl to be served with rice, such as chicken in walnut-lemon sauce or lamb in pomegranate sauce); *khorak* (eggplant casserole); and kebabs (pieces of roasted meat or game).

Iran is also famous for its soups, which include meat broth with chickpeas, typical rice and spinach soup, and hot yoghurt soup. Spinach originated in Iran and is used in many dishes. In a *kookoo,* or Iranian omelette, for example, the eggs are beaten and sometimes enhanced with a little baking soda so that the result is a very thick souffle, quite unlike an ordinary omelette. This versatile preparation comes in many variations, as does yoghurt, which when combined with fruit, herbs, and nuts is a common side dish, called *borani.* Their *dolmehs,* or stuffed vegetables, the Iranians borrowed from Turkey. Bread, in the past, served as a plate to hold food but today is employed in the Western way, on the side.

Historical Background

The early Persian empire (500 B.C.) was influenced by the Macedonians, Greeks, Romans, and Parthians. At the time of the Achaemenids, the king and the 1,500 individuals who generally dined with him had a great assortment of animal flesh from which to choose, including camels and ostriches. The satraps, or governors, also had to feed many guests. The satrap in Jerusalem, Nehemiah, often fed up to 150 notables at each meal. Food was prepared by a number of specialists, including chefs, bakers, pastry makers, drink mixers, and wine attendants. Tablecloths spread on the floor were of costly fabrics, and gold and silver vessels were in use among the nobility. Indeed, the Persians had such a passion for gold cups that Darius III once lost three or four tons of them, made of gold and encrusted with gems, to an enemy.

Like Nebuchadnezzar and the Assyrian kings before him, the Persian monarch enjoyed the special Helbon wine, from the vineyards on the slopes above Damascus, as well as wheat from Assos, salt from the oases of Ammon, oil from Karmanice, and water from the Nile and Danube.

With Alexander the Great (330 B.C.), links were established between India and Persia, that created common features in their cooking traditions. Under the Sassanids (third to seventh century), Persians seem to have become masters in the art of fine living. A Pahlavi text notes that the study of gastronomy was part of the education of a well-bred boy at the time of the Khusraus (end of sixth and early seventh century). Many of the words used in Middle Eastern cooking are of Persian origin and were popularized during this period. The cookery book of the Roman Apicius gives two recipes "in the Parthian manner." Both include *asafoetida,* a resin, appreciated as a condiment in spite of its unpleasant smell, which used to be important in Persian cooking. One of these recipes is a chicken dish; another uses kid or lamb, flavored with ground pepper, rue, onion, and stoned damson plums. Clearly, Iranian taste for sweet and sour combinations was already apparent at this early date.

During the reign of Khusrau II (early seventh century), a very lavish and sumptuous cookery was invented to satisfy the appetites of the monarch who had conquered Antioch, Damascus, Jerusalem, and Alexandria. It consisted of hot (grilled on a spit or fried) and cold meats, stuffed grape leaves, and marinated chicken. Other foods included mutton in pomegranate juice and rice pudding rich with honey, butter, and eggs. Young kid was popular, as was beef cooked with spinach and vinegar. Meat was marinated in spiced yoghurt, as it is today. Jams of quince, almond pastries, and dates stuffed with almonds and walnuts were served for dessert. *Rishta,* a kind of pasta similar to tagliatelle, was also known in ancient Persia.

In his twelfth-century writings, Marco Polo was impressed with the region and its wealth of foodstuffs: pomegranates, peaches, quince, and big fat sheep. But he noted that whereas the people of the countryside ate meat and wheat bread, those of Ormuz dined on dates, salted fish, and onions. Some 600 years later, John Bell, a visitor to Ispahan, took part in a big dinner:

> The entertainment consisted mostly of different kinds of rice boiled with butter, fowls, mutton, boiled and roasted lamb. The whole was served in large gold or china dishes and placed in the baskets, which stood on a long cloth spread above the carpets. The dishes were interspaced with saucers filled with aromatic herbs, sugar, and vinegar. [In addition to] the common bread, [there were] some very large thin cakes, which were used instead of napkins to wipe our fingers. They were made of wheat flour. (Bell 1965)

Sherbet was served cooled with ice, the latter from water frozen in the winter, then kept in cellars.

Food in the Arab Countries

General Features

In contrast to the Iranians, the Arabs have subsisted on a fairly rustic diet. Its origin is in the simple food of the Bedouins, which has not evolved much. The wealthy prefer rice; bread is the staple food of the common people. Bread of millet is made in the Aden protectorate; elsewhere, it is more generally of wheat, with sour or sweet fresh dough. It can be baked or fried on a griddle. Porridge and wheat gruel are still popular, as they were in ancient Arabia.

Fresh dates are a staple food in the poorest houses and are common everywhere. Individuals who consume *meshwi,* or meat grilled or roasted on a spit, betray tribal origins. Those who cannot afford lamb eat chicken or eggs often baked in an *eggah* or thick omelette. This is a versatile preparation that can be flavored with all kinds of vegetables, herbs, or meat. It is very close to the Spanish *tortilla* or the Iranian *kookoo.* Arab dishes of bread broken in pieces and soaked in stock, with various toppings, are reminiscent of *tharid,* the Prophet's favorite.

In coastal areas, fresh and dried fish are pounded and cooked with clarified butter and onions, or broken into pieces for easy consumption. Milk products are somewhat rare, with sour milk a common drink among the wealthy but not the common people. The mixture of milk, butter, and dates that Mohammed enjoyed is still prepared today. Spices and condiments, such as salt, pepper, chillies, tamarind, coriander, cloves, and cinnamon, are sometimes used.

A *mansaf,* or normal dinner, in a Bedouin family is simple, but served in a festive manner. Women cook huge wheat "pancakes" *(shrak)* on an iron plate. Several of these are piled on top of each other on a tray, then covered with rice and lamb, with butter poured over the top. A more elaborate meal for special occasions is a whole roasted lamb stuffed with rice, onions, nuts, and spices, and surrounded with mounds of rice, with hard-boiled eggs as a decoration. This meal is considered magnificent if the lamb is stuffed with a chicken, which, in turn, is stuffed with eggs and rice.

Meat balls *(kofte)* are another typical way of serving meat in Arab countries. They can be stewed in a soup, simmered in their own juice, or fried, and rice and spinach can be added to stretch the meat if it is scarce.

A meal is usually followed by one to three cups of boiling hot coffee. In the Aden protectorate, a kind of coffee prepared from the husks of the bean is a popular drink. It is not sweetened but flavored with ginger. A raisin tea made with boiled raisins and cinnamon is a specialty in Saudi Arabia.

Historical Background

Some travelers have left vivid written images of the foods and table manners of seventeenth-century Arabia. Among other things, their writings show how food was served. A large skin or woolen cloth was spread on the floor and dishes were placed on top. On great occasions, more than 10 dishes were offered and served six or seven times. In the middle of the table was placed the spectacular whole lamb or sheep with its trimmings. Arabs of rank ate at a small table 1 foot high with a large plate of tinned copper on it. Their food was served in copper dishes, tinned within and without. Instead of napkins, they used long linen cloths placed on their knees.

Western observers stressed the fraternity around these "tables." Sir Thomas Roe noted that Arabs make no great differences among table guests – the king and common soldiers, masters, and slaves, sat together and took food from dish (Roe 1926). Such fraternity is a value in Islam and still a tradition in Arabia. Travelers remarked, however, that women ate apart.

They also stressed the simplicity of the meals. Arabs had only a few cooking utensils of copper and big wooden bowls to use as large dishes or for kneading bread dough. They were reported to be fond of fresh bread and said to have baked it in a number of ways. Three examples of baking techniques are the use of an earthen pot in which a fire of charcoal was kindled (the bread was cooked on the sides of the pot), the placing of the dough on a heated plate of iron, and baking directly on charcoal.

In the desert, however, even the "more eminent schiechs *[sic]*," wrote Carsten Niebuhr, "eat of nothing but pilau or boiled rice. It is served up in a very large wooden plate" (Pinkerton 1811). A little mutton was consumed on occasion, but pastries were rare.

Most Arabs in poorer circumstances dined on bread and onions, sometimes with a little sour milk, salt, cheese, or oil. "But the most plenty and useful of all their fruits are their dates, which support and sustain many millions of people," wrote Roe (1926). Travelers, such as Roe, were also impressed by the use of coffee: "As soon as everyone is seated a servant brings a pot of coffee. It is very hot and poured in tiny cups. They are filled two, even three times, then a pipe of tobacco is presented" (Roe 1926).

Even though Islamic regulations were strictly observed and prayers said before and after meals, some inquisitive foreigners remarked that Muslims sometimes drank alcohol privately at night. Notwithstanding these "mistakes," the travelers gave the picture of a very traditional and modest food consumed by the Arabs, the same food that the Prophet himself had eaten.

Food in Egypt

General Features
Dishes served in Egypt constitute another type of old and simple tradition that goes back to pharaonic times, like the *melokhia* soup, a broth with the leaves of *corchorus olitorius,* (Tussa jute) which imparts a glutinous texture. Also old is the *batarekh,* or salted dried roe of the gray mullet, served sliced with bread. Pulses play an important role in the diet. Lentil soup is common, and the national dish is *ful medames,* brown Egyptian beans boiled and seasoned with olive oil, lemon juice, and parsley. To eat *ful medames* according to custom, one must first eat some of the beans whole, then mash some in the juice, and finally crush the rest with a hard-boiled egg placed on top of the dish. Cooked white broad beans, shaped into patties *(falafel),* spiced, and fried, are another favorite of the Egyptians, especially when eaten in a pita, or hollow flat bread.

Egypt is not a country where people consume animal protein in large amounts, but *hamud,* a chicken soup with lemon, is very popular. It is traditionally served with rice, cooked in the Egyptian way, fried then boiled. A kind of *kibbeh* (pounded meat and cereal) is prepared in Egypt, with ground rice instead of cracked wheat as in the Fertile Crescent. Fish kebabs are also quite common, and pigeons are frequently consumed. Couscous, a North African dish of a sort of semolina prepared with meat and vegetables, is served in Egypt as a dessert, topped with butter and fried raisins.

Nonetheless, the diet of the *fellahs,* or peasants, is mostly vegetarian. They usually have three meals a day, *futour* at sunrise, *ghada* taken while working in the fields, and a hot meal in the evening called *acha.* All of these meals consist mainly of raw or stewed vegetables.

Historical Background
In a fifteenth century Egyptian market, all kinds of foodstuffs could be purchased. Among them were wheat, barley, rice, beans, peas, chickpeas, carrots, cucumbers, lemons, watermelons, beef, mutton, chicken, goose, camel flesh, sugar, olive oil, sesame oil, clarified butter, and white cheese.

Pierre Belon du Mans, visiting in the sixteenth century, noted that Egyptians knew how to preserve foodstuffs. Lamb, for example, was cubed and boiled, cut in very small pieces, and boiled again in fat with cooked onions. Then the preparation was salted, spiced, and stored in barrels for up to two weeks. The French traveler also mentioned other preservation techniques, such as olives in brine, dried sea bream, salted gray mullet roe, and dried cheese (Belon 1557). These are not particularly sophisticated techniques, but they do show that Egyptians were able to make good and prolonged use of the products of their land.

Food in the Fertile Crescent
Syria, Jordan, and Lebanon have similar culinary traditions because all three were influenced by early Greek and Roman civilizations. In addition, Lebanon has recently been the recipient of a strong French influence, which is said to have enhanced the quality of its cookery.

This region is marked by the use of *burghul,* or cracked wheat, which is often consumed in the form of the traditional *tabouleh,* an herb salad with burghul and lemon juice. Burghul also plays an important role in another specialty of the area, *kibbeh,* which is said to have been mentioned in ancient Assyrian and Sumerian writings. Certainly, archeological evidence indicates that all the utensils and products necessary for this dish were on hand in the region long before Islam put its imprint upon it.

Kibbeh is made by pounding lamb with burghul, onions, and a little cinnamon; it is a mixture that can be eaten raw *(kibbeh naye)*, grilled, or fried. Stuffed kibbeh is a variation that has become an art in Syria. A kibbeh shell is shaped around the finger of the cook as evenly and thinly as possible. It is then filled with meat, nuts, and herbs and sealed. Once fried, it becomes crisp with a moist inside. Kibbeh is one of the many possible items one can choose as a typical snack *(mezze)*, along with a variety of olives, nuts, small pizzas, and pies. In Syria, a favorite is *muhamara*, a mixture of chopped nuts with hot pepper sauce. In Lebanon, another favorite is *mankoush*, a spicy herb flat bread. Lebanese people can spend hours nibbling these sorts of snacks while enjoying a drink of *arak*, an anise-flavored liquor. Local specialties include rice with almond sauce (Damascus), brown lentils and rice (Lebanon), bean salad (Lebanon), and lamb with yoghurt (Jordan). *Fattoush*, or bread salad, with a dressing of olive oil, onions, and lemon juice is common throughout the region.

Turkish Food

General Features

In Turkish food, one encounters the same differences between country food and the palace cookery that we have seen in other countries and regions once parts of the Ottoman empire. A classic Turkish meal starts with hot or cold yoghurt soup. In some villages the soup is made on baking day in a pit oven. A Turkish menu also offers *mezzes* (appetizers), such as sausage, vegetables in oil, cheese, *pastirma* (dried pressed meat cured with garlic and spices), or *borek* (flaky pastries with different fillings). A classic Turkish menu will feature soup, a meat dish, a borek, a vegetable dish, and a dessert.

Meat is a very important item in Turkish cookery. It comes in dozens of varieties of kebabs. Mutton and lamb are favorites, especially minced or pounded. Meat is even used in fruit dishes and puddings; examples include stewed apricots or quinces with lamb and a pudding of chicken breast. For big parties, a whole kid is roasted on a spit. Minced meat is the filling for the numerous *dolmasi*, or stuffed vegetables, such as peppers, tomatoes, vegetable marrow, and grape leaves.

Eggs are an important item of food, and many Turks raise chickens in their backyard. There are more than 130 varieties of fish available in the Bosporus Straits, with mackerel the most popular. A kind of unleavened flat bread made at home is the Turk's staple food. The baker offers many varieties of white bread, the most famous of which is the ring-shaped *simit*.

Turkey is well known for its pilafs, or rice dishes, made from long-grain rice, pounded ripe wheat *(dogme)*, toasted unripe wheat *(firik)*, and bulgur, or couscous. They are enriched with meat, dried fruit, vegetables, spices, and yoghurt.

Yoghurt is used in two forms in Turkey, one semi-liquid and the other firm. The latter is often eaten with jam or used for cooking, while the former, as a yoghurt drink *(ayran)*, is often served with meals.

A very special Turkish drink is *salep*, which is made with the infusion of a powder from the root of the salep orchid in milk and served hot. Coffee has been prepared and served in coffeehouses in Turkey since the fifteenth century. It is offered black and strong, usually with confections. Turks are very proud of their sweets, and a confectionery in Istanbul can feature more than 100 sorts of halvah (sweetmeats), such as plain and rose *lokum* and almond and pistachio marzipan.

In the past, vendors made and sold all kinds of foods on the streets. Today, these individuals are not so numerous, but sesame-sprinkled *simits* are still sold everywhere, the water or juice seller is still seen, and the streets of Istanbul still often smell of grilled fresh mackerel or roasted lamb.

Regional differences are important in Turkish food. The Aegean region is renowned for its fish and seafood. The Mediterranean region is rich in vegetables, with aubergines, peppers, tomatoes, and garlic featured in many stews. People of the Black Sea region enjoy cabbage soup and anchovies in many dishes, including a pilaf. Anatolia is the home of the best Turkish roast meat. Bursa is the town that gave birth to the world-famous *doner kebab*, meat roasted on a vertical revolving spit.

Historical Background

The nomadic period (before the eleventh century). In the Turkish city of Konya, people ate bulgur and lentils and knew how to use the pit oven, or tandor, 7,000 to 8,000 years ago. Turks in central Asia probably drank soups of *tarhana* (dried curd and cereals) and, when still nomads, they relied on mutton and horse meat, unleavened bread, milk, and milk products. *Manti* (a kind of ravioli) and *corek* (ring-shaped buns) were probably also known.

The Seljuk sultans and principalities period (1038-1299). During these centuries, the nomads were drawn from their steppes into the armies of the caliphate. They began to settle down, ruled a number of local dynasties, and as they did so, acquired more refined manners and tastes. Dishes of the period reveal that cooking was becoming an art. In an eleventh-century dictionary, for example, there is mention of a layered pastry, of noodle soup, grape syrup, and a corn-flour halvah.

Mowlavi Jalâl-al-Dîn Rumi, founder of the order of Whirling Dervishes, was a philosopher who, nonetheless, showed great interest in the subject of food. Thus, it is possible to infer from his writings the types of comestibles consumed in the thirteenth century. A few examples include saffron rice, homemade noodles with meat, *kadayif* (layered nut filled pastry), all kinds of halvah, wine, and fruit syrups. Within the order, strict rules were established concerning the organization of the kitchen and tables manners. Among other things, such rules show that social distinctions were made among those involved in food preparation, from sherbet makers to coffee masters to waiters, dishwashers, and cooks.

The Ottoman period (1299–1923). One group of nomads, the Osmanlis, or Ottomans, came to control the Islamic empire. Their rulers were cosmopolitan, having previously been slaves (or descendants of slaves) in all parts of the known world as far north as Russia and western Europe. These new rulers first took Persia as a model for their court life, then developed their own, including the culinary arts, borrowing from all over their empire.

The first Turkish cooks employed in the palace came from Bolu, the region where the sultans did their hunting. The men of Bolu were accustomed to leaving their land to learn this craft at the palace. Food was so important to the sultans that the insignia of their renowned janissary force was a pot and a spoon, symbols of their higher standard of living. The titles of janissary officers were drawn from the camp kitchen, such as "first maker of soup" and "first cook." The sacred object of the regiment was the stew pot around which the soldiers gathered to eat and take counsel.

When Sultan Mehmet II, the Conqueror, captured Constantinople (1453), he laid down the rules for food preparation, to be followed at the court for a long time to come. The palace kitchen was divided into four main areas: the king's kitchen; the sovereign's kitchen (responsible for food for his mother, the princes, and privileged members of the harem); the harem kitchen; and a kitchen for the palace household. That there was a movement toward culinary specialization seems clear in that the kitchen staff included bakers, confection and pastry makers, a yoghurt maker, and a pickle maker.

Ottaviano Bon (1653) has provided us with a good account of the kitchen in the seraglio in the seventeenth century, which shows how complex the organization had become. Food was prepared by the *Ajo-moglans* (Christian renegades) and 200 cooks and scullions who began their work before daybreak.

The sultan would eat three or four times a day, commonly dining at 10 in the morning and 6 in the evening, with snacks in between. He ate cross-legged, with an expensive towel upon his knees and another hanging on his left arm. Three or four kinds of white bread and two wooden spoons were placed before him (one for soup, one for dessert) upon a piece of Bulgar leather. The sultan's ordinary diet consisted of roasted pigeons, geese, lamb, hens, chickens, mutton and sometimes wild fowl. He would eat fish only when he was at the seaside. Preserves and syrups were always on the "table," though pies were "after their fashion, made of flesh" (Bon 1653). Sherbet followed the meal, since the ruler had adopted Islam and could not take wine.

When he finished, the leftover food was given to high officers. Lesser officers ate from a different kitchen where the food was of lesser quality. Odah youths (young Christians or Turks raised to become officers of the sultan) were fed on two loaves of bread a day, boiled mutton, and a thin pudding of rice with butter and honey. Queens had the same food as the sultan but consumed more sweets and fruit, reflective of their sweet and delicate nature. They drank their sherbet mixed with snow in the summer.

The hierarchy in the palace may be seen in many ways. Four kinds of bread were baked, the best for the sultan (with flour from Bursa), middle-quality loaves for ordinary officers, and a black and coarse bread for the servants; sailors received only sea biscuits.

Reaching the sultan's kitchen were luxury items from all over the empire. Alexandria sent rice, lentils, spices, pickled meats, and sugar, as well as prunes and dates. The latter were used in the dressing of roasted or boiled meats. Although few spices were used in Turkish cooking, an incredible amount of sugar was invested in pies, sherbets, and confections. Even common people offered each other sweets.

In addition, Valachia, Transylvania, and Moldavia sent honey to be used in broth, sherbets, and meat stews. Olive oil arrived from Greece and butter from the Black Sea region.

Bon noted that Turks used the flesh of calves in the same way that Christians used pork in puddings, pies, and sausages. They also dried the meat to make *basturma.* The serai kitchen was lavish in its use of meat, with 200 sheep, 100 kids, 10 calves, 50 geese, 200 hens, 100 chickens, and 200 pigeons slaughtered daily.

This aristocratic tradition of opulent dining that Bon depicted in the seventeenth century would continue into twentieth-century Turkey. Every meal of wealthy families would feature seven courses: fish, egg or *borek,* meat or fowl, cold vegetables in oil, hot vegetables with butter, pilaf, and pastry or pudding. Such meals were certainly not the democratic and rustic affairs of the Arabs.

The History and Culture of Food in the Indian Subcontinent

The Indian subcontinent is a huge triangle extending from the Himalayas to Cape Comorin and from the Baluchistan deserts to the rice fields of Bengal. It is divided into the countries of India, Bangladesh, Pakistan, Sri Lanka, and the Himalayan states. A diversity of physical environment in this area explains the diversity of the various agrarian civilizations and, in turn, the diversity of cookery traditions. The obvious contrast between the wheat eaters of the North and the rice eaters of the South is but one of numerous possible means of classification. Opposition is also found in the vegetarian ideal of Hinduism and the Muslims' fondness for meat. But it is interesting to note that the art of cooking unites, rather than divides, the people of the peninsula. This is an art that has evolved into a very rich and complex affair called "Indian cookery."

Indian Cookery: A Kaleidoscope

Three Cereals

As noted, we can divide the subcontinent into agricultural zones in which either wheat, rice, or millets are predominant. Although cereals are supplemented by various plants and pulses, they nonetheless constitute the staple food in each zone.

Rice is eaten everywhere in the Indian world, but it is the staple food only of the South and of Bengal, where it is boiled and served with a *dahl* (made from one of the many pulses of the peninsula), or perhaps with different curries and fresh yoghurt. When rice is ground and parboiled with split peas *(urad dahl),* it becomes a batter that the cooks of Tamil Nadu leave to ferment and to steam in molds to make the spongy *idlis.* The same batter can be shaped into small doughnuts and fried, or spread on the griddle to make a crispy pancake called *dosa.* All these preparations are served with chutney, a spicy vegetable curry, or a souplike *sambar.*

Millets like *jowar* (sorghum), *bajra,* or *ragi* are cultivated on the poorest soils and are found mainly in the Dekkan, Western Ghats, Gujerat, and Rajputana. They have been the staple food of the peasants, although "richer" cereals are increasingly becoming more preferred.

Wheat is mainly cultivated in the northern provinces. Most of the time it is used as bleached and unbleached flour. When mixed with water and salt (and for richer loaves, with milk, butter, or oil), it is the basis for the numerous Indian breads.

Roti or *chapati,* a thin whole-wheat griddle bread, is the daily accompaniment of *dahl.* With butter in the dough or on the pan, it becomes a golden *paratha.* Deep fried, it turns into a puffy *puri.* But thanks to the Muslim influence, northern India and Pakistan also know oven bread in its various forms. The most commonly found are the unleavened oblong *nan* or the round and soft *shirmal,* which is smeared with saffron milk. Lucknow and Hyderabad are also famous for their sourdough square breads or *kulchas.* All these oven breads are made of white flour and traditionally baked on the sides of the tandoor, the central Asian clay oven.

Such bread goes well, and is best associated, with the nonvegetarian cookery of the North, which includes kebabs and rich stews *(kormas)* of lamb or chicken.

North and South

Like the differing architecture of their temples and linguistic features, the North and South of the subcontinent have separate staple foods, and there are many differences between their cookeries.

With the curries, for example, the *masalas* (spice mixtures) that give each dish its character are not the same. In the North, the spices are dried, ground, and then dry-roasted or fried before being added to a dish. The dishes themselves are often nonvegetarian, due to a stronger Muslim influence, and tend to be dry so that food can be scooped up with bread. In the South, fresh spices are pounded with a liquid into a paste. The dishes these pastes flavor are mostly vegetarian, and rather liquid, to moisten the plain rice that generally is an important part of the meal.

Northern cooks will, therefore, have many dry spices on hand, such as cardamom, ginger, turmeric, black pepper, chillies, coriander, cumin, and, sometimes, dried vegetables or fruits that could not endure in the humid climate of the South. They use *ghee* (clarified butter) to cook the meat and oil (mustard oil, if possible) for the vegetables. Among the many pulses employed is the chickpea, which is a favorite in the North. Green tea in Kashmir and black tea, elsewhere, is boiled with water and sugar, spiced with ginger and cardamom, and whitened with rich buffalo milk.

By contrast, southerners use few dried spices and no dried vegetables. Rather, the latter are bought fresh on a day-to-day basis. Fruit and vegetables are preserved, however, in oil and chillies *(achar)* and in vinegar (pickles). In addition to jars of these relishes, a good kitchen will have different varieties of rice, some for everyday use, others for festivals and desserts, and still others for the servants. Rice flour will be present, as well as many types of pulses. In the vegetarian South, pulses are a major source of protein. Ghee is seldom used, but sesame and coconut oils are common.

The South, in tropical Asia, is also a land of coconuts and many other exotic products, such as mangoes, limes, bananas, "drumsticks," *moringa oleifera,* and jackfruit, all of which are often part of the diet. Coffee, introduced by the Arabs, is preferred to tea in the South, where it is prepared with milk and sugar. Now it is also found everywhere in its instant form.

Cooking utensils differ from north to south, although the *chula* (square hearth), the *tawa* (griddle), and the *karkhai* (deep frying pan) are common to the entire peninsula. In the North, the dry spices are ground on a grindstone *(chakki),* and in the South, the fresh ingredients are pounded with a mortar and pestle. The coconut grater is also typical of the South. Food is served on individual metal trays *(thali)* in the North, but on a clean banana leaf in the South. Finally, although all people of the subcontinent eat with their right hand, northerners tend to use the tips of the fingers, whereas southerners will dip their whole hand into the food.

More Regional Variations

The diversity of the culture of food and drink in the Indian world is much more complex, however, than simply differences between north and south. There are many interesting variations within the vast regions.

For example, the valley of Kashmir in the northernmost part of India has a somewhat cold climate, which is perfect for growing fruits, walnuts, and cumin, and for breeding sheep. Thus, as one might expect, the cookery is more closely related to that of central Asia. The tea there is made in a samovar and is a green tea, as in Tibet. The bread is closer to that made in Afghanistan than to Indian *chapatis* and is generally baked in clay ovens by professionals.

In Rajasthan, culture has dictated other food habits. Historically, their men have been warriors and, thus, have long been accustomed to outdoor cooking. For this reason, many of their dishes include marinated and grilled meats (including game), often prepared by males.

In contrast to this rugged fare, a Maharashtran meal starts with a sweet, eaten with a *puri* or *chapati.* Maharashtra is rich in seafood and coconuts, and both are often blended together. Every morning the ladies of many houses begin their day by grinding coconut and spices on a grinding stone. The milk of the coconut is also present in practically every dish, even in *pulao* (flavored rice, the Indian rendition of the Turkish pilaf).

Bengali food is reputed to be quite plain, but the sweets of the region (*sandesh, rasmalai, gulab jamen,* and all-milk sweets soaked in syrup) are famous. The waters of the Bay of Bengal yield hundreds of varieties of fish and shellfish. In fact, the "vegetarian" Brahmans of the region, who theoretically should avoid seafood, eat it nonetheless, calling it "vegetables of the sea."

The Portuguese, in their quest for empire, settled in Goa as well as in other places. Thus, personal names, architecture, and festivals, along with the foods of the region, reveal this influence. Indeed, Goanese food is Portuguese food, save for the lavish inclusion of red chillies and coconut milk. The use of onions and tomatoes in many soups is very Portuguese, and the Goanese consumption of pork is unique in India. Vinegar gives many dishes a typical sour-hot taste. Sweets include a lot of egg yolks and almonds. Thus, dishes such as *caldine, bife, souraca,* and *assada* are all reminders of the colonial past.

Malabar Muslim cookery constitutes another example of a blending of local and foreign traditions in India. Kerala Muslims are supposed to have descended from intermarriage between local Kerala women and Arab traders who settled there. Malabar food has a great deal in common with food elsewhere in Kerala in that it testifies to an extensive employment of coconuts, coconut oil, and rice. But the Arab influence is evident in dishes such as *alisa* (a wheat and meat porridge), or stuffed chicken. Another dish (*byriani*) shows the linkage with the Muslims of northern India, although it contains coconut and prawns. A Muslim love for bread is reflected in the Moplah specialty called *pathiri,* which is a rice *chapati.*

Cultural Background

The four major religions of India are Hinduism, Buddhism, Jainism, and Islam. The Islamic influence, which arrived in the eighth century, placed great emphasis on the enjoyment of food because it was considered a reward from God to the believer. Yet food is not a petty matter in the view of other dominant religions either. "All doings come from food" is an Indian saying. For the traditional Hindu, cooking and eating are not just matters of survival but moral investments and rituals as well. The *Mahabharata,* one of the sacred books, refers to the necessity of ensuring purity in food and drink as one of the ten essential disciplines of life; and even in the big cities, a majority of Indians still live according to such age-old customs.

Vegetarianism is a precept of the three Indian religions although, of course, the people of India were not always vegetarian. The first humans who appeared near the basin of the river Indus around 15,000 B.C. ate meat along with rice, molasses, spices, and betel leaves. It was not before the Vedic era (1500–800 B.C.) that an aversion toward meat consumption appeared in ancient texts. At this time, milk acquired a symbolic value and the cow was described as a "gift." Little by little, animals were replaced by clay or flour figurines for sacrifices, and instead of consuming the cows that constituted much of their wealth, the people of India began revering them.

It was the new religions of Buddha and Mahavira Jina (sixth century B.C.), however, which provided the decisive impulse to the vegetarian doctrine. Both prescribed nonviolence *(ahimsa)* and the abstinence from meat. This ideal is still subscribed to by the orthodox Hindus, whereas Jains go so far as not to touch foods that resemble meat, such as tomatoes, beet roots, and so forth.

However, there has always been an ambivalence in the Hindu attitude toward meat consumption. If Brahmans avoided it, it was recommended to the *Kshatriyas* (kings and warriors) and was not forbidden to the castes of merchants, agriculturists, and servants. All this suggests that the Hindu concepts on food were elaborated for a whole society, in which everyone had duties and a diet suited to those duties. Those who lived close to the world and its violence were urged to eat meat to gain energy. By contrast, the Hindu priests and Brahmans embraced vegetarianism; indeed, those who prayed were enjoined to avoid everything exciting to the senses, even onions.

Each individual can follow many diets. Hindus believe that a perfect life is lived in the four stages of student, householder, hermit, and ascetic. A man, therefore, might be vegetarian while single, then be nonvegetarian, and finish his life in abstinence and fasts.

The cow is still held sacred, its products considered excellent for health, as well as religious purposes. Pure *ghee* (clarified butter) is highly esteemed, and many Indians still feed the newborn baby with a spoonful of ghee after the Brahman ritual. They also give ghee to sick individuals and, although very expensive, it is still considered the best cooking medium.

While vegetarian doctrine was being elaborated, concepts of pure and impure foods were being developed as well. A ritual is organized around the meal to ensure its purity, which includes bathing and the wearing of clean clothes for both the cook and those who dine. The kitchen must be as clean as a temple and separated by a little wall from the rest of the house, far from the refuse area and near the prayer room. It is often swept and washed, and, traditionally, the floors are covered with cow dung, a sacred substance and one regarded as an antiseptic.

Purity also shapes the whole Hindu society as a hierarchical structure with the Brahmans at the top. An exchange of food is traditionally prohibited among the segments or castes of this society, especially from the lowest (most impure) to the highest (Brahmins). Even in the same family, it is considered "unclean" to touch food that has been touched by someone else, which is why the food is served directly from the cooking vessels onto the *thalis* (leaves). This also explains why there is no tradition of dining out in India. The quest for purity is too strong.

These age-old principles are still professed by most Hindus, but orthodoxy is sometimes sacrificed for the sake of health (diets low in fat, sugar, and spices), diversity (new recipes), status (for example, the Western habit of going to restaurants), and convenience (ready-made food).

As we have noted, Islam also strongly imposed itself on the cookery of the subcontinent for religious, as well as for purely gastronomic, reasons. Although a late cultural and religious arrival, Islam came to India via many channels. Arab traders, Afghan and Turk soldiers, along with Iranian administrators, all settled down there and made converts to their religion, as well as to portions of their culture.

If Hinduism has given a high spiritual content to the meal, it has paid little attention to the art of cooking. Boiled cereals and griddle bread, stewed vegetables, and pulses had been the usual diet since the beginning of Indian civilization. Islam gave to Indian cookery its masterpiece dishes from the Middle East. These include *pilau* (from Iranian pollo and Turkish pilaf), *samossa* (Turkish *sambussak*), *shir kurma* (dates and milk), kebabs, sherbet, stuffed vegetables, oven bread, and confections (halvah). Such dishes became so well acclimated in India that vegetarian versions of them were elaborated. It is this cross-cultural art that is now acclaimed all around the world.

Delphine Roger

Bibliography

Bell, J. 1965. *A journey from St. Petersburg to Pekin,* ed. J. L. Stevenson. Edinburgh.
Belon, P. 1557. *Portraits d'oyseaux, animaux, serpens, herbes, arbres, hommes et femmes, d'Arabie & Égypte.* Paris.
Bon, O. 1653. *A description of the grand signor's seraglio or Turkish emperours court,* trans. Robert Withers, ed. John Greaves. London.
Daumas, F. 1965. *La civilisation de l'Égypte pharaonique.* Paris.
Deshayes, J. 1969. *Les civilisations de l'Orient ancien.* Paris.
Foster, W., ed. 1968. *Early travels in India.* London.
Halici, N. 1989. *Turkish cookbook.* London.
Miquel, A. 1968. *L'islam et sa civilisation.* Paris.
Pinkerton, J. 1811. *A general collection of the best and most interesting voyages and travels in all parts of the world.* London.
Polo, M. 1926. *The book of Marco Polo, the Venetian, concerning the kingdoms and marvels of the East,* trans. and ed. Henry Yule. New York.
Popper, W. 1957. *Egypt and Syria under the Circassian sultans.* Berkeley, Calif.
Purchas, S. 1619. *Purchas his pilgrim. Microcosmus; or, The historie of man. . . .* London.
Ramazani, N. 1982. *Persian cooking.* Charlottesville, Va.
Ridgwell, J. 1990. *Middle Eastern cooking.* London
Roden, C. 1985. *A new book of Middle Eastern food.* London.
Roe, T. 1926. *The embassy of Sir Thomas Roe to India, 1615-19,* ed. William Foster. London.
Rumi, Jaelal-Din R-um-ii Poet and Mystic, 1207-73. *Selections from his writings,* trans. Reynold A. Nicholson. Oxford 1995.
Sauneron, S., ed. 1970. *Voyage en Égypte de Pierre Belon du Mans.* Cairo.

V.B.2 ❧ Southeast Asia

Southeast Asia, geographically and culturally diverse, stretches from Burma (Myanmar), through Thailand and the Indochinese and Malay peninsulas, to islanded Indonesia. Some would include the Philippines and Indonesian New Guinea as parts of Southeast Asia, but this study adds only the Philippines. European scholars called the region "Farther India" for its location "beyond the Ganges" (Coedes 1968). It is separated from China by the Himalayas and their eastern extension. Each country in the region has other mountain chains, channeling rivers to the South China, Java, Celebes, and other Indonesian seas, and to the Indian Ocean. Lowland plains south of the highest ranges of the mainland are home to most of the populations of Burma, Thailand, Malaysia, Cambodia (Kampuchea), Laos, and Vietnam. The region is also insular: Indonesia has over 13,000 islands, spreading some 5,400 kilometers (3,300 miles). Most people live on or near oceans or river deltas.

Southeast Asia is in the tropical belt along the equator, with little temperature variation – about 15.5 to 24 degrees Celsius (60 to 75 degrees Fahrenheit) in winter to 29 to 32 degrees Celsius (85 to 90 degrees Fahrenheit) in the dry summer months (Hanks 1972).

This is monsoon Asia, and annual rainfall amounts to several hundred millimeters (over 100 inches). North Pacific winds bring rain from the northeast down the South China Sea from October until March, and there is a southwesterly monsoon in summer from May to September (Jin-Bee 1963). Rain is not constant, but brief showers or thunderstorms are always imminent. Temperatures and precipitation are noticeably lower in higher parts of the region. Europeans early recognized the comfort of the foothills and built hill-station retreats where their accustomed temperate plants – fruits, flowers, trees, and vegetables – all flourished.

The mountains, rivers, plains, seas, climate, and laterite, "red-earth" soil have combined to influence what foods are grown or have been available for the choosing since human beings first dwelt there. But despite northern mountain barriers and north–south mountain chains that hinder passage within and beyond the region and keep hill-tribe people (with their different agricultures and religions) apart from lowland dwellers, outside influences have managed to modify behavior and material objects, including what there is to eat. In other words, historically, political, economic, and social factors have frequently resulted in new technologies, products, foodstuffs, and behaviors.

European exploitation of Southeast Asia began with the Portuguese during the Western Age of Exploration in the sixteenth century. But Indians had ventured there much earlier, perhaps in prehistoric times (Jin-Bee 1963; Burling 1965), and had founded kingdoms and introduced Buddhism (Coedes 1968). China has also had a long history and influential relationship with Southeast Asia. Northern Vietnam was part of the Chinese empire for a thousand years until the tenth century A.D. (Burling 1965). Malacca, commanding the waterway through which ships passed from the west to China or the Spice Islands, came under Chinese control in the fifteenth century as a hub of trade. But by the fourteenth century, Islam had been introduced to Southeast Asia by Gujarat Indians, Arabian merchants, or both.

Later colonizers included the Portuguese, Dutch, British, Germans, French, and, in the Philippines, Spaniards and North Americans. All of these cultures influenced foods and the implements for producing and eating them, as indicated among other things by Romanized names for both foods and implements in the languages of the region. It is interesting to note, however, that the World War II occupation of much of the area by Japan had little effect on food practices.

And finally, increased air travel, tourism, commercial marketing, television, advertising, and imported foodstuffs have certainly made the diets of indigenous people more complex, although not necessarily more nutritionally or culturally worthy (Wilson 1994).

Obviously, then, from the foregoing, much of the history of food and drink in Southeast Asia is the history of introductions, some of which can only be guessed at. Written records of the movements of peoples and their political and religious struggles were first made by early Chinese regimes (Coedes 1968). Pre-Aryanized, preliterate kingdoms (Cambodia and Burma) are known to have had complex material cultures, irrigated rice, domesticated cattle and plants, ancient belief systems, temples, and art objects, and also to have bestowed important roles on women. Archaeological records are intermittent, with imprecise dating (Burling 1965; Coedes 1968), so the written Chinese records provide most of our knowledge of early history. But other clues come from linguistic changes, plant distributions, local lore and myth, and, for recent centuries, reports of administrators, travelers, and ethnographers.

Despite the region's diversity, a basic eating pattern common throughout Southeast Asia is a heavy reliance on white rice, consumed with smaller quantities of an accompanying side dish, most often fish, prepared with a sauce from grated coconut meat and a variety of spices, many of which originated in the region (Wilson 1975).

Staples

Rice

Rice *(Oryza sativa)* belongs to the family of grasses, Gramineae. The cultivated species is chiefly *O. sativa*, which, some authorities believe, originated from wild rices native to southeastern Asia (Burkill 1966). *Oryza sativa* is polymorphic, responding with changes in structure to altered environmental growth conditions. This trait earlier led to reports of many different genuses and species until plant genetic studies showed which species were fertile when crossed and which were sterile. Botanists reduced the number of distinct species to 25, but hundreds or thousands of varieties (also termed races) of *O. sativa* exist, having different growing seasons, or responding with inflorescence to less sunlight or drier soils (Burkill 1966; Hanks 1972).

Rice will grow on dry uplands, which may have been the site of its first cultivation in late Mesolithic or early Neolithic times (Coedes 1968; Hanks 1972). The early cultivators could also have accidentally created new species by tying awns of different varieties together to prevent lodging. However, present species and races could also have developed in nature because they grow under similar conditions in the same places and readily interbreed. Quite likely, the process goes on at present when different races are planted for specific characteristics, as suggested by Douglas E. Yen (cited in Crawford 1992).

Rice is a plant of warm, damp areas and, hence, is climate-dependent. It grows satisfactorily in the tropical and subtropical belt from Asia through Africa to warm, moist parts of North and South America. Recognition of its reliability must have been gradual, and the initial understanding of its potential for dependable growth again and again in the same locale (initiated by inserting seeds in the ground) was probably fortuitous suggested when ungathered seeds germinated in a rain-fed field. A liking for the taste of this intermittent crop probably led to efforts to husband its growth, though when and how rice cultivation dawned as a regular agricultural pursuit can only be guessed at (Hanks 1972).

Based on archaeological finds (shards and tools) made in this century (Coedes 1968), together with recent techniques of carbon dating and ethnobotanical research, it has been estimated that the "first" crops of rice appeared some 10,000 to 15,000 years before the present. But "primitive" rice culture continues in some remote areas today, and its ecological and economic consequences that have been recorded also provide insights into early rice cultivation (Conklin 1957).

Rice requires moisture, warmth, and soil with organic matter. The soils of Southeast Asia, like those of much of the tropics, are lateritic, from iron compounds above underlying clay that oxidize upon exposure to air. For plants to grow, a top layer of organic matter, humus, is needed. This may be deposited naturally as fallen detritus in forests or as silt brought by rivers to the deltas. Many of Asia's rice bowls are located between inland forests and coastal mangrove swamps that hold these deposits.

But "dry" rice, which preceded irrigated rice, is still grown in Southeast Asia's upland forest areas, as well as in small dooryard plots (Wilson 1970). Most dryland rice involves shifting cultivation, for the plant removes much of the soil's nutrients, and considerable fallow time must be allowed before a new crop can be nourished (Hanks 1972).

Early growers had to be keenly aware of and attuned to the rhythms of the seasons and plants before regularizing their planting activities. These began by cutting forest growth well ahead of the onset of the rainy season, then drying and burning it. The latter tended to destroy competing plants, and the ash provided phosphates and potassium otherwise lacking in the soil. Still before the rains, seeds were planted through the ash. Such soil could produce crops for two years; after this, the agriculturists would either select another nearby area to plant or move on. Overpopulation and continued land use could lead to erosion and incursion of hardy weeds, and with prolonged soil use, trees would not be able to regenerate to restore the forest.

The other principal method of rice culture is wet-rice cultivation, with its use of shallow water to kill off competing plants. In all countries where rice constitutes the "bulk of consumption" (Wilson 1985), each step in rice raising, from selecting grains for the next year's crop to harvest, storage, and husking for cooking, is accompanied by rituals of worship. People from Burma to the Philippines have long felt that this paramount food is the homesite of a potent god and have made it central to civil and religious rites.

Indeed, beliefs regarding the efficacy and supernatural or curative properties of rice antedate the introduction of organized religions to the region (Geertz 1960; Rosemary Firth 1966; Wilson 1970).

Varieties in which the endosperm starch is partially replaced by soluble starch and dextrin produce glutinous, "sticky" rice that is sweeter, but less easily digested, than ordinary rice (Burkill 1966). Dyed yellow with turmeric (formerly saffron, which is the color of royalty in Southeast Asia), glutinous rice is served for ceremonial occasions as part of the meal or made into sweetmeats exchanged at religious holidays (Geertz 1960; Rosemary Firth 1966; Wilson 1985). One of the most popular of these "cakes" is Malay-Indonesian *ketupat,* usually made of steamed glutinous rice (white, red, or black) mixed with coconut cream and recooked in a woven or folded leaf (Wilson 1985). In Sumatra this mixture is called *lemang* and may be served with fruits or with festival meats such as *sate* or *rendang.* The rice sometimes is made into a fermented liquidlike toddy.

Despite the widespread visibility of wet-rice paddy fields, they are a relatively recent phenomenon. Wet rice was not extensively cultivated in Indonesia, the Philippines, Thailand, or Burma until the latter part of the nineteenth century. Its cultivation coincided with the opening of the Suez Canal and a greatly expanded trade to the area, at a time when colonial powers were encouraging increased food production for growing populations (J. N. Anderson, personal communication).

A continuous need for water and its control has increased sensitivity to seasonal fluctuations in the rains and has also encouraged an elaborate technology to harness and store it – all accompanied by rituals similar to those used for the rice that grows in the water. Where hillside erosion prevented regular upland cropping, terracing was introduced and is still used. Terraces require substantial investments of time and energy because effective structures can be realized only gradually. Notable examples of terracing are to be found in Java and Bali. It has been suggested that the terraces of the northern Philippines were constructed for earlier propagation of taro and other root crops, which may have preceded rice planting (Pollock 1992).

Dry-rice growers practice various means to delay fallowing and maintain soil fertility, including intercropping, a common technique among shifting cultivators. Indonesians, for example, have recently introduced peanuts *(Arachis hypogaea)* in some areas. Moreover, at the International Rice Research Institute in the Philippines, and elsewhere, high-yielding, fast-growing, more highly nutritious strains of rice have been bred to meet increasing demand.

This "Green Revolution" was technically successful, but preexisting races cultivated by small growers were often preferred for taste or for aroma, and when hand-hulled by pounding in a mortar, they retained much of the germ removed by machine hulling. The new strains that replaced them, however, required greater input in terms of time, technology, fertilizers, and water control, and have, therefore, proven too expensive for many small cultivators. Because of these developments, some compromises have ensued, and gene banks for rice now recognize the value of older varieties.

Root Crops

In addition to rice, or as a substitute, Southeast Asians have eaten a variety of other starchy staples (chiefly root vegetables) that are indigenous as well as introduced. Notable among them are yams of the *Dioscorea* species, chiefly *Dioscorea alata,* the greater yam, and *Dioscorea esculenta,* the lesser yam, both of which are ancient plants thought to have been domesticated several thousand years ago in Southeast Asia (Burkill 1966; Pollock 1992). *Dioscorea alata,* is a cultigen unknown in the wild, whereas *D. esculenta,* still has wild varieties. Robert Dentan (1968) notes that the Semai (Malaysian aborigines) tend wild yam patches, which may give us a glimpse of how agriculture began. The plants have climbing vines and starchy tubers that can be stored in the ground. Now chiefly famine foods, these roots, propagated by cuttings, contain alkaloids and other toxins not yet identified, among them acrid substances used by indigenous peoples as fish poisons (Heiser 1990). Consequently, those who rely upon wild yams are careful to boil or roast them before eating.

Another root that may have preceded rice as a staple is *Colocasia esculenta,* together with other members of this family, *Alocasia macrorrhiza, Cyrtosperma chamissonis,* and *Xanthosoma sagittifolium,* that are collectively known as taro. Except for *Xanthosoma,* which is American in origin, taros are Asian or Pacific plants. *Alocasia* and *Colocasia* have been cultivated "from remote times" throughout Southeast Asia (Burkill 1966). *Colocasia,* unknown as a wild plant (Herklots 1972), probably originated in northern India. Its common names are *dasheen, eddo, cocoyam,* or *keladi* (Malay). Taros have not been relied on as a starch food in much of Southeast Asia for many years. They contain crystals of calcium oxalate that must be leached out before the corms are cooked. Occasionally, however, the stems and leaves are boiled or fried in coconut oil.

Two other starchy roots, introduced to Southeast Asia, are the white potato *(Solanum tuberosum)* and manioc (cassava, yuca) *(Manihot utilissima),* both of South American origin. The potato was probably brought by the Spaniards to the Philippines in the sixteenth century and by the Dutch to Java in the following century (Burkill 1966). A taste for it has been slow to develop, but the same cannot be said of manioc. Of the family that includes figs *(Ficus)* and other latex-producing species, manioc was widespread in tropical America (Jones 1959). It was noted by voyagers who followed Christopher Columbus and was taken early to Africa; it reached Asia much later, however, and although the date of its arrival in Southeast Asia is not certain (Burkill 1966), it may have been as late as the eighteenth century.

According to Robert Hefner (1990), in the nineteenth century the Dutch colonial government introduced manioc to Java, where rural people resisted its cultivation until a serious food crisis was experienced in the 1880s. Although a comparative latecomer, manioc is now ubiquitous throughout the region. The roots may be left in the ground for long periods, and because manioc produces more food per unit of land than any other crop, it is increasingly relied upon as a famine food. Yet manioc is nutritionally inferior to most other foods, and it drains soils of nutrients without contributing any. Moreover, most races contain hydrogen cyanide (prussic acid), and South American techniques for removing this poison by boiling or roasting did not accompany manioc to Africa and the East. In Java (Burkill 1966), Malaysia, and other parts of the region, sun-dried strips of manioc are sold and consumed as snacks. In both countries, parboiled tubers are fermented several days with locally produced yeast to make an inexpensive *tapai* (Burkill 1966; Wilson 1986). In addition, the young leaves are sometimes used as a vegetable.

Grain Staples

Another New World staple, maize *(Zea mays),* caught on considerably more swiftly in Southeast Asia than did manioc and the potato. Lucien Hanks (1972) quotes the European traveler Nicholas Gervaise, who wrote, in 1688, that the grain had first been sown just 12 to 15 years earlier in Siam, yet it already covered the upland plains. Maize was also relied upon as a staple by upland dwellers in precolonial Java (Hefner 1990) – before Dutch rule in the nineteenth century. Although the Semai adopted it (together with manioc) as a staple food (Dentan 1968), it has tended to be a substitute grain in the region, and despite introduction of newer varieties, it is used primarily as feed for animals or as a snack, roasted or boiled, for humans.

Some staple grains of importance elsewhere also grow in Southeast Asia. Foxtail, or Italian millet *(Setaria italica),* and some other races have been food sources for tribal peoples (Burkill 1966). Wheat *(Triticum vulgare)* flour is of some importance in bread, biscuits, crackers, and cookies. Wheat was introduced following European settlement and used to make, among other things, noodles, which came to Southeast Asia from China (Chang 1977). Noodles are made and eaten in all the countries of the region, often as snack foods (Wilson 1986). Bread is of some importance in Vietnam and is increasingly common in other parts of the region. Bakeries in major urban centers produce bread and rolls that are sold in shops and markets and by itinerant salespeople. Such baked goods are usually consumed as morning snacks but are considered inferior to rice in relieving hunger.

Palm Staples

The sago palms (*Metroxylon sagu* or *Metroxylon rumphii*) yield a starch from the inner parts of the trunk after they are grated and soaked. This starch is a fallback food, consumed when rice supplies are short in the region. The trees are cut at maturity, about 9 to 15 years after planting, when the starch is at its peak (Burkill 1966). Sago flour is also used in making snack foods.

Another palm, the lontar (*Borassus flabellifer,* also known as the palmyra), grows from India eastward to the Celebes and yields sugar and toddy (wine) in the juices of its trunk. The time required for the lontar to reach maturity is similar to that of the sago (Burkill 1966). The tip of the tree is cut, and the juice collects in a vessel. It may be tapped for several months with daily cuts. J. J. Fox (1977) studied an Indonesian group on the island of Roti, Lesser Sundas, who subsist largely on this juice. Vinegar is made from overfermented lontar toddy (Burkill 1966), and the leaves have long been used in Indonesia for writing; books of leaves fastened together are known as *lontar.*

Staple Qualities

Southeast Asians believe that foods have inherent qualities that affect the body. Such beliefs stem from the humoral systems of Ayurvedic (Indian), Chinese, and Islamic medicine, all of which have influenced these populations over the last millennium (Hart, Rajadhon, and Coughlin 1965; Hart 1969; Lindenbaum 1977; Laderman 1983). Although with ethnic and individual differences, objects, physiological states (including disease), weather, and behaviors are categorized as having degrees of "hot," "cold," and "neutral." Most staple foods are defined as "neutral" among these populations. Manioc, however, is "hot," and eating it is thought to make the body hot, a situation also brought about by consuming animal protein, salt, and some anomalous fruits and seeds. The definition of manioc as "hot" may indicate recognition of the toxic chemical in the raw tuber.

Fish, Meat, and Fowl

Fish

There is little disagreement among experts (Raymond Firth 1966; Hanks 1972) that the dietary staples of Southeast Asians during the historical era have been primarily rice and fish. But the archaeological record is less clear regarding the presence of fish in diets of prehistoric hunter-gatherers, in large part because archaeological research in the area is far from complete. Finds in northern Vietnam of middens of mollusk shells in Hoabhinian-era levels (Burling 1965) indicate an early reliance on foods from the sea, and E. N. Anderson (1988) writes of rich sources of fish and game for central and southern China in Neolithic times. For later periods, Ying-Shi Yu (1977) has noted

the finding of several species of fish in the tomb of a Han aristocrat who died in the first century before the present era in Hunan Province (southern China).

The bony fishes antedate mammals by several hundred million years. When the continents reached their present-day positions, land masses blocked fish migration through the tropical seas, but species found in Southeast Asia range throughout these latitudes as far as Africa or Australia. Relatively few comprehensive listings have been compiled, yet Raymond Firth (1966) cites C. N. Maxwell, who described 250 species of marine food fishes for Malaya, and J. S. Scott (1959) lists 294, including the skate, shark, and ray family, and the dolphin, *Coryphaena hippurus,* as sea fishes of Malaya. Though many are edible, the list of favored marine fish is shorter. Raymond Firth (1966) notes that over 20 types were landed at a Malay village in amounts greater than 1,000 tons. Most were of the mackerel family, *Scombroidii,* including herring (*Clupea* spp.) and small horse mackerel (*Scomberomerus* spp.) (Scott 1959). Of deepwater fish feeding near the surface Firth notes dorab or wolf herring (*Chirocentrus dorab),* shad (*Clupea kanagurta),* sprat or whitebait (*Stolephorus* spp.), and anchovies (*Anchoviella* and *Thrissocles* spp.). Bottom feeders taken in quantity during Firth's research included jewfish (among which are numbered croaker, *Umbrina dussumierii, Corvina* spp., *Otolithes ruber,* and several types of *Johnius*), sea bream (*Synagris* spp.), sea perch *(Lates calcarifer),* snapper (*Lutianus* spp.), gray mullet (*Mugil* spp.), and flatfish (including sole, flounder, *Pseudorhombus,* and *Synaptura* spp.) (Scott 1959; Raymond Firth 1966). This list is echoed by Thomas Fraser (1960), Carol Laderman (1983), and Christine S. Wilson (1983).

Other fish common to the region and mentioned by Raymond Firth include pomfret (*Stromateus* spp., generally prized in Southeast Asia), catfish (*Chilinus* spp., not a popular food), sardines (*Sardinella* spp.), bluefish (*Pomatomus salatrix),* grouper (*Epinephelus* spp.), pike (*Sphyraena* spp.), and scad *(Caranx leptolepis).* Fish have been caught with indigenous methods developed over time, chiefly by nets from shore or small boats, or by handline. Before the existence of motorized transport, these activities were local and subsistent, but commercial trade of sea products seems to have begun with Chinese embassies early in the first millennium (Fraser 1960).

Additional sea animals eaten by Southeast Asians include squid or cuttlefish (*Loligo* and *Sepia* spp.) (Burkill 1966), crabs (*Charybdis* spp.), prawns and crayfish (*Penaeus, Penaeopsis, Parapenaeopsis* spp. and *Peneus semisulcatus;* the spiny lobsters *Panulirus*), and the lobsterlike *Squilla.* Shrimp (*Acetes erythraeus*) (Burkill 1966) and other crustaceans caught in tidal nets are the source of a fermented paste eaten as a side relish with rice meals (Wilson 1970).

A fish of continuing commercial value, used in dishes such as cooked vegetables, is the small whitebait or anchovy *(Stolephorus* spp.). The green sea turtle *(Chelonia mydas)* (Burkill 1966) provides meat occasionally and widely prized eggs seasonally. Mollusks – cockles *(Cardium),* clams, mussels *(Mytilus* spp.), and oysters *(Ostrea edulis* and *Ostrea rivularis)* – are collected along shorelines, often by women and children (Burkill 1966).

Sharks and rays, the Elasmobranchs, are widely found in tropical seas. The gelatinous skeletons are prized by the Chinese, and members of the Carcharidae and Dasybatidae families provide income to fishermen who sell the valued fins (Burkill 1966). The dogfish *(Scoliodon sorrakowah C.),* and other members of this class, are usually eaten by poorer people (Scott 1959; Burkill 1966). Salting (curing in brine) and drying fish have long been practiced. Before ice machines and mechanical refrigeration, these preservation methods permitted the sale of surplus fish at a distance and storage for monsoon months when fishing was unsafe.

Animal Meats

Meat – the flesh of mammals – is chiefly reserved for feasts and special occasions (Geertz 1960; Kirsch 1973; Volkman 1985). Often the flesh is that of the water buffalo *(Bubalus bubalis)* (Burkill 1966), that ancient ricefield plough-laborer. A native of Asia, the water buffalo is said to have been domesticated in many locales, but at present the best evidence points to southern China some time around 5000 B.C. (Hoffpauir, this work). Buffalo milk is higher in fat than that of most cattle, about 7 percent (Heiser 1990), but is little used in Southeast Asia because the populations exhibit high incidences of primary adult lactose intolerance (Simoons 1970).

Other *Bos* species have been domesticated in the region, such as the *seladang (Bos gaurus)* of Malaysia, the *mithan (Bos frontalis)* of Indochina, and the *banteng (Bos sondaicus)* of Java. Some cattle *(Bos taurus),* the species common in the West, are found in the region – mainly in Java and the Philippines (Burkill 1966). *Zebu,* Indian cattle, though well adapted to the climate are relatively rare.

Another ruminant of the bovine family, the goat *(Capra hircus),* is widespread throughout the region, where it has substituted for more expensive meat species despite its strong flavor. Its Malay name, *kambing,* is well known throughout the region and is applied locally to sheep – *kambing biri-biri* – as well. Rural people neutralize goats' destructive grazing with fences or by staking. Archaeological remains of domesticated sheep have been dated from 9000 B.C.; goat domestication probably was almost that early (Heiser 1990). K. C. Chang (1977) indicates that goats were introduced to China from western Asia in prehistoric times.

The pig *(Sus scrofa)* is said to have been domesticated in the Near East (Anderson 1988; Heiser 1990) around 7000 to 5000 B.C., when villages developed, although Frederick Simoons (1994) suggests that pigs were first domesticated in Southeast Asia. When Islam came to Southeast Asia, its prohibition against eating pork stopped pig raising among many peoples, although others who were not converted continued the practice. Wild pigs are native to Asia as they are to Europe, and it has been suggested that in rural Asian Muslim countries, the animals may be called something other than "pigs" by the natives and, thus, may be hunted and eaten.

Although many wild mammals and birds are protected by legislation (Medway 1969), some are still hunted for meat, particularly by aboriginal peoples. Well liked by all inhabitants of Southeast Asia is another local ruminant, the deer *(Cervus unicolor)* (Medway 1969), along with the mouse deer or chevrotain *(Tragulus javanicus* and *Tragulus napu).* The flesh of this smallest of hoofed mammals is said to be excellent and is salted, dried, and smoked (jerked) throughout Malaysia. Other wild animals that have acted as occasional food sources include the large fruit-eating flying fox or fruit bat *(Pteropus edulis* or *Pteropus vampyrus)* (Burkill 1966; Medway 1969). In addition, jungle tribes may hunt birds, monkeys, and other small animal species for food.

Poultry or Fowl

Chickens *(Gallus gallus)* are generally the most important domestic fowl in Southeast Asia and may have been domesticated there. The archaeological record is not clear, and experts differ as to whether this Asian jungle bird was first domesticated in India or Southeast Asia (Heiser 1990). Yet there is general agreement with I. H. Burkill (1966) that the chicken was early selected for gaming as well as divination, in which both entrails and thigh bones were and still are used (Heiser 1990). Chickens are kept for meat and eggs in rural areas, with the meat often prepared for feasts (Geertz 1960), along with other animal meats. Clifford Geertz and other anthropologists (e.g., Fraser 1960) have noted the frequency of *kenduri* or *slametan,* special feasts of a familial or community nature, with curried chicken dishes to accompany the glutinous rice. Chicken is generally liked and is sometimes a meal-saver during monsoon months when fresh fish is not obtainable.

Fowl eggs have also been valued for use in divination. Simoons (1994), for example, has commented on their use in this capacity by hill-tribe peoples from Assam eastward, while also noting their avoidance (along with fowl meat) because of beliefs associating them with fertility. Others (Rosemary Firth 1966; Strange 1981) have noted the symbolic use of eggs as fertility symbols that are given to female guests at weddings and as spirit offerings to launch a boat or enter a new house.

Simoons (1994) notes a particular preference in this region for brooded eggs, with the embryo well developed – these are especially relished in the

Philippines. He hypothesizes that the practice may have originated, before domestication, in the gathering of wild fowl eggs, which, if they contained half-hatched chicks as recognizable forms of life, were judged as not dangerous to eat. Other poultry kept by Southeast Asians include ducks (the *Anas* species, related to the mallard), which were domesticated independently in both Europe and China (Burkill 1966). In Indonesia, ducks are part of an ecological system that includes rice fields and irrigation ditches containing fish. The ducks subsist on the rice (after threshing) as well as on the fish, while providing eggs and meat for their caretakers. Geese (*Anser anser*, the European domestic species, or an Indian hybrid, *Anser cygnoides*) (Burkill 1966) sometimes play similar roles in rural Southeast Asia. The goose probably reached the region via India.

Nonstaple Plant Foods

Vegetables

Although Western visitors to Southeast Asia have noted native plants sometimes used as food (for example, Burbidge 1989; Wallace 1989), and have commented on "curries" for main meals without always specifying their components (Lewis 1991), nutritionists and anthropologists have been those most concerned with the importance of vegetable foods in Southeast Asian diets. Rosemary Firth (1966), for example, has noted that for Malay fishing people, vegetables are a marginal need. The sandy soil near the sea is not conducive to vegetable propagation, and the people who might have time for such an effort, and who play significant roles in rice raising, have no tradition of gardening. Before the advent of motorized transport, the attitude toward vegetables seemed to be that they made a nice addition to a meal but were not essential to it (Wilson 1988).

Traditionally, the growers of vegetables for market in Southeast Asia have been the Chinese. But others living in rural areas long ago learned of wild plants growing on empty lands and in the forests, including wild ferns, and well into this century, older women made gathering trips to bring these wild plants back for consumption (Wilson 1970). Burkill (1966) lists a number of edible ferns, such as *Diplazium esculentum* and *Stenochlaena palustris*, although most of the species cited are used for making woven objects or for medicinal purposes.

During colonial times, Europeans introduced a number of Western vegetables to the hill stations at higher altitudes. The carrot – *Daucus carota sativus* – is an example: It was carried from Persia to India and then China in the thirteenth century (Herklots 1972). (The Dutch introduced quick-maturing cultivars in Indonesia during the nineteenth century, but roots such as carrots do best at higher elevations.)

Laderman (1983) lists three dozen vegetables that she identified as collected or purchased in an East

Coast Malay village. Among those eaten occasionally that are grown locally are many types of spinach, gucil (*Antidesma ghaesembilla*), sweet shoot (*Sauropus androgynus*), and bamboo shoots (*Bambusa* spp.) (Burkill 1966). Several species of amaranths (*Amaranthus gangeticus*) (Herklots 1972) are ancient potherbs here, native to the region and eaten like spinach. Another local spinach abundant in the region is *kangkung* (*Ipomoea reptans*) (Burkill 1966; Herklots 1972). It grows on or near water, has a peppery taste like watercress, and is also called swamp cabbage.

The Western view that Southeast Asians have little interest in eating vegetables probably results from the climatically difficult enterprise of raising temperate species. Those that are grown are often natives of China or India, such as *Brassica chinensis*, Chinese cabbage, and *Brassica juncea* (Burkill 1966). Among the leguminous plants that are found is the long bean (*Vigna sinensis*), which became a cultigen during ancient times in Asia or Africa and has pods that may measure 1 meter in length (Burkill 1966). Another legume, *Psophocarpus tetragonolobus*, the winged or four-angled bean, was noted in the seventeenth century in the Moluccas as introduced from elsewhere. On the basis of its Malay name, *kachang botor* (*botor* means lobe in Arabic), Burkill (1966) infers that it was brought by Arabs from the African side of the Indian Ocean. The pods and beans are eaten raw or cooked, as is the root. This plant has received international attention in recent decades thanks to its high protein content, along with some derogatory comments because of preparation difficulties (National Academy of Sciences 1975; Henry, Donachie, and Rivers 1985; Sri Kantha and Erdman 1986).

Another legume is the yam bean (*Pachyrhizus erosus*). A native of tropical America, this bean was brought by the Spaniards to the Philippines in the sixteenth century. From there it quickly spread as far as Indochina and Thailand and soon grew wild (Burkill 1966; Herklots 1972). Both young pods and the starchy root are eaten.

Several other leguminous seed pods that originated in Africa or Asia have added protein and variety to Southeast Asian diets. Examples are the gram beans: red (*Cajanus indicus*), the Indian *dhal* (sometimes known as the pigeon pea), green or mung (*Phaseolus aureus*), and black, also known as mung or *dhal* (*Phaseolus mungo* L.) (Burkill 1966; Herklots 1972). Sprouts as well as vegetable cheese have been prepared from both *dhal* beans.

The other bean-cheese source for the region is the soybean, *Glycine max*, which has been cultivated by the Chinese for at least 4,500 years (Herklots 1972). In addition to sprouts and oil, the beans have been fermented to produce *tempe* or tofu and soy sauce, a fermented product soaked in brine and exposed to the sun (Burkill 1966).

The South American groundnut or peanut (*Arachis*

hypogaea) may have reached Asia early by western as well as eastern routes (Burkill 1966). A variety of races have developed over the last two centuries, some of which have been selected for oil content. Peanut oil production has been a Southeast Asian industry for over a century, with the oil (chemically similar to olive oil) sold in the region. Nuts, ground into paste, cooked with onions, peppers, and other spices, are served with curries, roasted meat, and in fresh fruit and vegetable salads in several Southeast Asian countries.

Two leguminous trees of the *Parkia* and *Pithecolobium* genera provide seeds that are eaten with meals as a relish and also used as diuretics (Burkill 1966). *Parkia biglobosa* is also found in Africa, where the seeds are eaten after roasting, but the preferred species in Southeast Asia is *Parkia speciosa,* the *petai. Pithecolobium* species are found in Asia and America. *Pithecolobium jiringa,* the *jering,* is the seed of choice for both medicinal and food purposes. It may be boiled or roasted. Both seeds smell and taste like garlic, and the odor lingers on the eater's breath.

One vegetable seemingly native to the region is eggplant (also called *brinjal* and *aubergine,* or *terong* in Malay). *Solanum melongena,* related to the potato and tomato, reached India, Africa, and Europe via Spain (Burkill 1966). Charles Heiser (1990) and G. A. C. Herklots (1972) believe it originated in India, reaching Spain and Africa via the Arabs and Persians. The latter authority notes its mention in a Chinese work on agriculture of the fifth century. The plant produces large, egg-shaped fruits, ranging in color from white through golden to green and blackish purple.

Another vegetable – this one has been cultivated in the region for at least two millennia and may, indeed, have originated there – is the climbing snake gourd *(Trichosanthes anguina* or *Trichosanthes cucumerina)* (Burkill 1966; Herklots 1972). The Chinese obtained it from the south, presumably Malaysia, suggesting that it was cultivated there at least from the early Christian era. Another native gourd is the wax gourd *(Benincasa cerifera)* (Burkill 1966; Herklots 1972). Bitter melon or cucumber (*Momordica charantia* L.), a long, green, warty-looking gourd (Herklots 1972) with seeds inside bright red arils, has long been an ingredient in curries (Burkill 1966). It is probably African in origin. The bottle gourd *(Lagenaria leucantha)* may also have originated in Africa; known to the Egyptians, it reached China sometime during the past 2,000 years (Burkill 1966). Other gourds of ancient origin, such as the *Luffah* species, have also served as vegetables (Herklots 1972).

The Chinese or Japanese radish *(Raphanus sativus),* a cultigen of eastern Asia with a long white root, has origins similar to the European radish (Burkill 1966; Herklots 1972). Okra, or "lady's fingers" *(Hibiscus esculentus),* a vegetable assumed to be of African origin (Burkill 1966), is sometimes named a bean in local languages; the Malay term *bendi* is from Hindi (Burkill 1966; Herklots 1972).

The tomato *(Lycopersicum esculentum)* (Burkill 1966) was brought from America to Europe and thence to Asia more than 300 years ago. Eaten raw or cooked, it is also the source of bottled sauces called in many lands *kichap* – the name usually given in Malay to soy sauce. (A Malay calls catsup *sos tematu.*)

Edible toadstools or mushrooms *(Volvariella volvacea)* are grown and eaten in some countries of Southeast Asia (Burkill 1966). With the advent of refrigeration and tinned foods in the twentieth century, a variety of Western vegetable foods became available to people in money economies, particularly in urban locales.

Fruits

Southeast Asia has a wealth of native fruits, as well as some introduced from other regions. Best known is the banana *(Musa* species). Heiser (1990) believes that *Musa acuminata,* the wild banana of Malaysia, was the progenitor of all other banana species. In fact, Heiser feels that Southeast Asia was the original home of all bananas, although Betty Allen (1967) suggests that the place of origin may have been India.

Cultivated bananas may be small or large, red- as well as yellow-skinned, and sweet or tart. Plantains have always been eaten cooked; some other races, cultivated for centuries, are dipped in batter and fried. Flowers from banana plants of a Philippine race are served as a vegetable. For millennia the leaves have been used as wrappings for food and as temporary rain cover.

Citrus fruits are also of Asian origin, although grapefruit may be an exception (Burkill 1966; Heiser 1990). Species have been cultivated in subtropical climes from before the time of Alexander the Great. *Citrus microcarpa* (Burkill 1966) is a small, round, green ball of a fruit (sometimes called the music lime) long used in cooking and making drinks, as is *Citrus aurantifolia* (much like the West Indian lime). *Citrus nobilis* (Burkill 1966) is the Mandarin orange or sweet lime, not to be confused with *Citrus sinensis,* the sweet or Chinese orange familiar to Western palates, though both may have originated in China. The rind of the Mandarin orange, green to orange in color, peels easily like that of a tangerine, and the segments are readily removed. Native to Southeast Asia is *Citrus maxima* or *Citrus grandis* (Burkill 1966; Allen 1967), the sweet pomelo, as large as a grapefruit. It reached Europe in the twelfth century (Eiseman and Eiseman 1988) and is now sold in U.S. markets. It is highly valued in Southeast Asia, where it is associated with the Chinese New Year.

Garcinia is a genus of trees of the rubber family in the Old World tropics (Burkill 1966). A number of species have edible fruits, and several yield dyes, ink, or watercolor paint. *Garcinia mangostana,* the mangosteen, is a favorite throughout Southeast Asia and has been known elsewhere since the voyages of exploration; it is also famous for having earned the admiration of Queen Victoria. The small, round fruit has a ¼-inch (0.635 centimeter), dark red to purple rind, and five or more white, fleshy segments of edible matter with a delicate, slightly tart flavor. F. W. Burbidge (1989) was enthusiastic about the mangosteen when he wrote in 1880, as was Alfred Wallace (1989: 148), who commented in his mid-1850s report on the Malay Archipelago that "those celebrated fruits, the mangosteen and . . . durion . . . will hardly grow" elsewhere. *Garcinia atroviridis,* a bright yellow-orange, acid-astringent, fluted fruit about 3 to 4 inches (8 to 9 centimeters) in diameter, and eaten as a relish (Burkill 1966), is native to Malaysia and Burma and common in Thailand (Allen 1967).

Several members of the Sapindaceae family have a tart-sweet pulp, with the best known, *rambutan (Nephelium lappaceum),* named for the hairlike cilia extending from its red or yellow rind. Native to the region, it is widely cultivated, but wild forest specimens are also found (Burkill 1966). Also native is *Nephelium malaiense* ("cat's eyes"), which is small with a buff skin (Allen 1967). The litchi (lychee) from southern China *(Litchi chinensis)* is cultivated as well (Burkill 1966).

Other fruits with refreshing pulp include the langsat *(Lansium domesticum)* – an indigenous fruit that is now cultivated. It was noted by the Chinese in Java in the fifteenth century (Burkill 1966). *Salak (Zalacca edulis)* is a similar fruit from a palm that grows throughout Southeast Asia. Its thin, brown skin looks like that of a lizard (Burkill 1966; Eiseman and Eiseman 1988).

Two members of the rubber and castor oil family produce pleasant fruits. One, *Cicca acida* (Burkill 1966; Allen 1967), known in English and Malay as *chermai,* the Malay or Otaheite gooseberry, is a very tart tree fruit. Although it has been cultivated for centuries, its place of origin is not known. The other fruit, *rambai (Baccaurea motleyana),* is a Southeast Asian native and has long been cultivated there (Allen 1967).

Perhaps the most famed Southeast Asian fruit is durian *(Durio zibethinus)* (Burkill 1966), which grows on trees too tall to climb (70 to 80 meters or more). Ovoid or round, variable in size, each fruit may weigh several kilograms. The thick, green rind has sharp spines that cushion its fall. Inside are four or five arils of soft pulp surrounding seeds. Durian smells and tastes like onion, garlic, or cheese. The fruit is edible for only a few days after dehiscing, after which it undergoes rapid chemical change (Wilson 1970). Most Southeast Asians and some Europeans relish this seasonal fruit, and the seeds are roasted and eaten as well. Durian conserves, sweet or salty, have been made by local people, and in recent decades durian ice cream has been developed.

The mango *(Mangifera indica)* is the most famous member of its family, which originated in India (Burkill 1966). Other species grow throughout Southeast Asia. It has been known for more than 4,000 years (Allen

1967) and was one of the earliest tree fruits to be cultivated (Eiseman and Eiseman 1988). Fruits may be 17 centimeters (7 inches) long, and about 7 centimeters (3 inches) in diameter. When ripe, the flesh is yellow to reddish, sweet, aromatic, and much prized. *Mangifera odorata,* called *kuini* in Malay, is also sweet when ripe, with a resinous smell. The horse mango, *Mangifera foetida,* is inedible until ripe. Both *M. odorata* and *M. foetida* are fibrous and are sometimes eaten to help remove intestinal parasites.

A New World member of this family, *Anacardium occidentale* – the cashew – was brought by the Portuguese in the sixteenth century to become one of the first American trees cultivated in Southeast Asia (Burkill 1966; Allen 1967). The tart fruit, a greenish pedicel the size of an apple, which is rich in ascorbic acid, and its appended nut are both well liked. The nut must be boiled or roasted to remove an irritant chemical, cardol. In rural areas, monkeys and fruit bats vie with human consumers for the fruit, which otherwise serves as a cooked relish with a rice meal.

Two members of the Urticaceae family, *Artocarpus integra* and *Artocarpus champeden* (jackfruit and chempedak), are native to Asia, the jackfruit coming from India (Burkill 1966). Both have large fruits as long as 30 centimeters (1 foot), with mottled green, bumpy rinds and yellowish, creamy flesh surrounding seeds that are boiled before eating. The fruits are used to make sweetmeats. Historically very popular, they were known to Pliny. *Artocarpus communis* (breadfruit), a member of this family, is less common and not much consumed.

Two small trees native to Malaysia produce acid fruits that are cooked and used as tart, refreshing relishes, *Averrhoa bilimbi* and *Averrhoa carambola* (Burkill 1966). The latter, brought to the West by early explorers, is known in Western countries as starfruit because of its shape when cut horizontally. In Asia, both are called *belimbing.* Four tropical American fruits, *Annona muricata* (soursop, or "Dutch durian"), *Annona reticulata* (custard apple or bullock's heart), *Annona cherimola* (cherimoya), and *Annona squamosa* (sweetsop), were brought very early to Southeast Asia (Burkill 1966).

Eugenia, found throughout the tropics, has more than two dozen species in south India and Southeast Asia that have grown wild and been cultivated for centuries for their valued fruits. One, *Eugenia aromatica,* produces cloves. Others have pearlike, rosy or pink-tinted fruits, about 5 to 7 or more centimeters long (2 to 3 inches), that are called *jambu* in Malay, and "apples" by English speakers: *Eugenia aquea* (or *Eugenia jambos*) are water or rose apples, *Eugenia malaccensis* is the Malay apple, and *Eugenia javanica* is the Java apple (Burkill 1966). Also of this Myrtaceae family is the guava, *Psidium guajava,* an American native brought by the Spanish across both the Atlantic and Pacific at an early date (Burkill 1966). The thin, green skin becomes yellow and soft at maturity;

the pulp is white, greenish, or rose, with many small seeds. They are good eaten raw and make excellent juice drinks.

Other well-liked, early introductions from the Americas are papaya *(Carica papaya)*, pineapple *(Ananas comosus)*, and passion fruit *(Passiflora laurifolia)*. Papaya reached Southeast Asia via the West Indies before the sixteenth century (Burkill 1966; Allen 1967). A large herb, it is fast-growing, producing fruit in six months. Ever-bearing, the papaya is a useful dooryard plant, rich in nutrients, green-skinned until ripe, with yellow to red flesh, and 15 to 35 centimeters (6 to 14 inches) in length.

Pineapple was cultivated in America from remote times, and the Europeans brought it around the world to all parts of Asia before the seventeenth century (Burkill 1966). A pineapple plantation industry was developed during the nineteenth century in Malaysia, Indonesia, and the Philippines, when canning was introduced (Allen 1967). Passion fruit, a climbing herb of tropical America, was also introduced to India and other Asian countries in the nineteenth century (Burkill 1966).

Fruits of purple *Passiflora edulis* and yellow *Passiflora laurifolia* are sweet in smell and taste and suitable for both eating or juice. *Passiflora quadrangularis,* the grenadilla, is popular in Indonesia. Unripe it serves as a vegetable and is also preserved in sugar. Not a fruit but a similar snack is sugarcane *(Saccharum officinarum)*, a grass eaten by chewing the cane, or drunk as pressed juice (Burkill 1966). It was domesticated in New Guinea or Indonesia during remote times (Heiser 1990). Burkill (1966) has documented its spread through Asia, and Sidney Mintz (1985) has provided its later history. Early Indian references to the crystallized form of sugar date from several hundred years B.C., and Alexander the Great noted it during his voyages (Burkill 1966). The watermelon *(Citrullus vulgaris),* an African plant known to the Egyptians (Burkill 1966), reached China via India in the tenth century and is grown in some Southeast Asian countries. The fruits resemble North American varieties in color and character.

Fruits native to the region but less well known because they are seldom marketed are cultivated in dooryards for local consumption. Among these are *Sandoricum indicum* (the *sentul)* (Burkill 1966) and *Erioglossum rubiginosum (mertajam),* a tree with small red to black astringent fruits, called *kerian* by Malays. The *kundungan (Bouea macrophylla)* is a small tree related to the cashew that is cultivated in villages (Burkill 1966). It is native to Malaysia and much of Indonesia, with a sour-to-sweet taste. Further north, it is called *setar* for the capital of Kedah, Alor Star (Allen 1967).

Kemuntung, or rose myrtle, a shrub of the Myrtaceae family *(Rhodomyrtus tomentosa),* produces small, wild fruits prized by children. Still other fruits have been available since refrigerated shipping began;

pears, grapes, and oranges are enjoyed by rural people who can afford market prices. Some grow in hill stations or at high altitudes. A few wild species of *Prunus,* relatives of the peach *(Prunus persica),* as well as species of *Pyrus,* related to the pear *(Pyrus communis)* and the apple *(Pyrus malus),* are grown, but most are of European origin (Burkill 1966).

Spices and Seasonings

Southeast Asia encompasses the Spice Islands, whose lure motivated the fifteenth- and sixteenth-century European voyages of discovery. Most sought after were pepper *(Piper nigrum),* cloves *(Eugenia aromatica),* and nutmeg *(Myristica fragrans)* (Reid 1993). Although clove and nutmeg trees are Southeast Asian natives and have been cultivated for centuries, their early history is dim (Burkill 1966). Clove was known to the Chinese by 300 B.C.; it was in Egypt by the first century A.D. and reached the Mediterranean by the fourth century. Arabs brought nutmeg to Europe in the sixth century. Nutmeg, which is also the source of mace, is made into a sweet by boiling to remove tannin before adding sugar (Burkill 1966). Before the twentieth century, it was candied for sale in Europe.

Piper is a genus of many species that grow in moist, warm parts of the world (Burkill 1966). *Piper nigrum,* with both black and white berries, was apparently first cultivated in India; its name in countries to which it subsequently spread are cognates of the Sanskrit *pippah.* By the sixteenth century, it became an export plantation crop in Dutch-controlled Sumatra and in other countries (Andaya 1993). Supplanting the Portuguese, the Dutch assured their profit by allowing cultivation only in areas they controlled by treaty with local rulers. All these spices remain important cuisine condiments and, thus, important commercial crops (Steinberg 1970).

Cinnamon *(Cinnamomum zeylanicum),* the bark of a tree of eastern and southeastern Asia, is another aromatic spice of ancient origin (Burkill 1966). The genus was once common in Europe and was known to the Egyptians, Hebrews, and Aryans. *Cinnamomum cassia,* a Chinese tree known over the last two millennia, provides cassia, an alternate form of cinnamon in Southeast Asia. *Cinnamomum zeylanicum* grows wild at high elevations in western India and Sri Lanka (Ceylon) and still produces the best cinnamon (Burkill 1966). Both cassia and cinnamon are known in Malay as *kayu manis* ("sweet wood") and are used medicinally as well as for seasoning.

Ginger *(Zingiber* species) is an herb native to tropical Asia and the Pacific (Burkill 1966), where several species and races grow wild. *Zingiber officinale* was cultivated in India and China before the Christian era (Yu 1977). The fresh rhizomes are used medicinally and as flavoring and are also dried and candied. Another family member, galangal *(Zingiber galanga)*

(Burkill 1966), is also native to tropical Asia and India and has been extensively used in Malaysia and Java. Its history and use compare to that of ginger.

Turmeric *(Curcuma domestica),* from the same family, is a Southeast Asian native as well and was used as a condiment (a substitute for saffron) and dye long before the Aryans reached India (Burkill 1966). Its color was the same as the royal color of India and the Indianized states of Southeast Asia, and turmeric was used in weddings and to tint ceremonial rice (Rosemary Firth 1966). Cardamom *(Amomum kepulaga)* (Burkill 1966), still one more herb of the ginger family, grows wild in Java and is cultivated as a breath sweetener and for use in curries.

Other important seasonings in general use have reached Southeast Asia from the outside world. Chief among these are members of the lily family (*Allium* species, such as onions, garlic, shallots, leeks, and chives) and chilli peppers (*Capsicum* species, which are natives of the Americas). Alliums are northern plants, mainly from the Mideast, where they have been grown since ancient times (Burkill 1966). But garlic *(Allium sativum)* and others were also cultivated long ago in India, spreading east from there. Bulbs of the *Allium* species (for example, shallot – *Allium ascalonicum*) are grown for market in hilly parts of Indonesia and the Philippines; most, however, are imported from India. All are ingredients in curries and used as seasonings, and most have also been employed medicinally for generations (Skeat 1967; Gimlette and Thomson 1971). Shallots are eaten raw individually or in salads along with other vegetables and are pickled in brine. Garlic is more prominent in areas closer to China. *Allium cepa,* the white or red onion, may be shredded and deep-fried as a condiment for other foods, as may shallots.

Columbus brought *Capsicum* (the chilli pepper) to Europe, whereupon writers of the time commented on its introduction (Burkill 1966). But less than 50 years later it was termed the "pepper of Calicut," a misnomer that ignored its New World origin. Chilli peppers have long been cultivated in Central and South America, and their European names reflect Spanish versions of the Mexican term *aji* as well as the desire of Dutch black pepper traders to save their own product from confusion by means of another Spanish translation, "*chilli.*" Early on, naturalists distinguished over a dozen races, but the main species remain *Capsicum frutescens,* the sweeter, less pungent type represented by bell peppers, and *Capsicum annuum,* the very hot, small perennial known as bird pepper, which is the source of tabasco.

A number of races of both grow in Southeast Asia. *Capsicum baccatum* var. *baccatum,* the source of cayenne (Herklots 1972), has been used medicinally and for arrow poisons in Asia as it was in South America (Burkill 1966). Certainly the chillies are much appreciated in Southeast Asia. Burkill has noted that

Malays prefer *Capsicum* to "black" pepper in cookery, and Westerners have long commented on the fiery nature of Thai cuisine (Steinberg 1970). The active principle in peppers is capsaicin, an alkaloid known to irritate skin and mucous membranes (Burkill 1966). It is also said to be addicting (Pangborn 1975), which may explain its lengthy history of use in Southeast Asia as well as in America (Rozin and Schiller 1980). Chillies have long been dried for market sale throughout Southeast Asia.

Tamarind, a leguminous tree with pulp-filled pods, was known to Greeks in the fourth century B.C. Although it probably originated in Africa or India, it was early cultivated in Southeast Asia (Burkill 1966). The pulp of *Tamarindus indica,* which is sweet to tart, looks in its marketable form like dates, which prompted Arabs and Persians to call it *tamar,* the Indian date (Burkill 1966). It is used as a relish and in cooking, and the flowers are sometimes eaten as well. In Java, the pulp is salted and made into balls that are steamed for preservation. Tamarind has also been used for medicinal purposes, to fix dyes, and to clean metal.

A grass native to the region, *Cymbopogon citratus* – lemon or citronella grass – has been cultivated as a food flavoring, a liquor spice, and a tea (Burkill 1966). In Java it is part of a spicy sherbet drink, and in Malay it plays a role in medicine and magic. The Portuguese took it to Madras in the seventeenth century, and it subsequently spread to all the tropics (Skeat 1967).

Three herbs of the temperate Old World or Levant, caraway, coriander, and cumin *(Carum carvi, Coriandrum sativum, Cuminum cyminum),* have been seasonings in Southeast Asia since their introduction at about the beginning of the Christian era. Because they have a past prior to written records (Burkill 1966), they are sometimes thought of as interchangeable, and anise *(Pimpinella anisum),* another family member, has been associated with them because of its odor and flavor. Anise was known to the Egyptians and, within the past thousand years, was carried by Arabs or Persians to China and India. In Malay, anise, caraway, and cumin are all called *jintan* (Winstedt 1966). Fresh coriander leaves (cilantro, or Chinese parsley) are used to flavor soups, meat, and fish dishes; the Thais, in particular, have a passion for them uncooked in many dishes.

Basil *(Ocimum basilicum* and *Ocimum canum),* an herb of the warmer parts of the world, has religious or symbolic roles as well as seasoning and medicinal ones in Southeast Asia (Burkill 1966). The Hindus, to whom it is sacred, may have introduced *Ocimum* species to Southeast Asia during "Indianization" (Coedes 1968). Mint *(Mentha arvensis* and other species), a similarly fragrant herb, is cultivated at higher elevations and used for flavoring and for medicines (Burkill 1966).

Salt has been a substance of physical as well as economic need (to produce dried seafoods) in Southeast Asia and, therefore, has been an item of commerce as well (Kathirithamby-Wells 1993). The salt trade probably antedates written records. Seacoast areas have long been local sources, and sea salt from solar evaporation has been produced in Thailand, Indonesia, and Vietnam for export as well as domestic use (ICNND 1960, 1962; Raymond Firth 1966); in addition, Thailand has salt deposits in the northeast (ICNND 1962).

Unfortunately, the local salt is not iodized, and iodine-deficiency diseases are a health problem in several of these countries (ICNND 1962) despite reliance on seafood, which is a good source of the mineral. The incidence of goiter on Bali, for example, may result from the Balinese preference for pork instead of seafood.

Although honey was undoubtedly the earliest sweetener, the boiling of the inflorescence of the nipa palm *(Nipa fruticans)* to make sugar has been an enduring cottage industry (Burkill 1966; Winstedt 1966). Refined white cane sugar has been much prized for hot drinks, but although refining was done in Java and other locales from early colonial times (Burkill 1966), it has proved too expensive for rural people, even in recent decades (Rosemary Firth 1966). Perhaps unfortunately, however, it has become a dietary essential (Wilson 1970, 1988).

Vinegar has been made from both palm and cane sugar, as well as from rice and fruit pulp (Burkill 1966). It occurs naturally if palm or fruit syrup is allowed to ferment more than 40 days. It is used in food preparation, and much of it has been imported from China in recent decades.

Soy sauce and the fish soy of Vietnam, *nuoc mam,* have already been briefly discussed. *Nam pla* or *pla-ra* (ICNND 1962) is the Thai version. Malay coastal villagers make *budu* by salting small fish, such as anchovies, in vats until the mixture ferments (Wilson 1986). A Philippine version is called *patis* (Steinberg 1970). A similar product, *gnapi,* is made in Burma by allowing fish to decay in the open (Lewis 1991). Shrimp paste is similarly made in most of these countries. The Malay version is *belacan,* the Indonesian *terasi,* and the Philippine *bagung.* These products are relishes or side dishes, often enlivened with fresh raw chillies; all are excellent sources of calcium and protein (Wilson 1986) and, with the chillies, of vitamin C.

Although not a condiment or a seasoning, yeast for household cooking is locally made (Wilson 1986). Burkill (1966) reports that the Javanese use their word for yeast, *tapai* (of Arabic origin), to include the Malaysian preparation *ragi* (from the Hindu) (Winstedt 1970). To rice flour and several spices, *Aspergillus* fungi as well as *Saccharomyces* spores are added, some adventitiously. This combination results in the fermented glutinous rice cakes, *tapai* (Wilson 1986), and also toddy.

Cooking Fats and Oils

Until the past few decades, the cooking mediums in Southeast Asia have been water, oils, sauces, and coconut milk. To save fuel, most cooking was done over wood fires, as quickly as possible, and long, slow roasting was done over coals. The premium oil has been coconut *(Cocos nucifera)*. The nut of this palm is the seed of the fruit, and its grated ripe flesh, squeezed in water, also provides coconut milk *(santan* in Malay), the base for the curries of the region. This "most useful of trees" (Heiser 1990) requires warmth and moisture to grow well, and seacoasts provide the best climate. Southeast Asia produces 90 percent of the world's coconuts.

When the coconut was domesticated is not known (Heiser 1990). Its importance to Southeast Asians can be seen in the Malay names given it at every stage of development (Burkill 1966). It is planted by human effort at house sites, and when the trunk has formed, it will fruit in 4 or 5 years, yielding about 50 fruits a year for decades. The nut reaches full size before the meat forms and is fully ripe in one year. People generally pick coconuts, but the Malays and Thais also train the macaque, or "pig-tailed," monkey *(Macacus nemestrina)* to climb the trees and gather ripe fruits when they are ready to fall (Wilson 1970).

The water inside can be drunk for refreshment before the fruit ripens, but it is astringent. The endosperm of a 10-month fruit is eaten with a spoon as a delicacy, whereas the meat of the ripe endosperm is grated for consumption. It is also sun- or heat-dried to make copra, which is pressed for oil as both a cottage and commercial industry. The oil, milk, and meat of coconuts were used in cooking long before the arrival of Europeans. In addition, the husk provides coir for rope, and the shell is both employed as a utensil and made into charcoal. Different parts of the coconut at different development stages are used in pregnancy, in childbirth, and in magical rites (Burkill 1966). The immature inflorescence of the tree is bound in anticipation of later tapping for toddy production.

The oil palm *(Elaeis guineensis)* (Burkill 1966) was brought to Southeast Asia from West Africa as a plantation crop in the nineteenth century by colonial powers, and new plantations have continued to be planted. Most production goes into oil for commercial export to make soap and margarine as well as cooking oil. Palm oil is chemically similar to coconut oil. Other vegetable oils, such as that of the soybean, are imported from China and India.

Beverages

The most important beverages for early humans in Southeast Asia, as elsewhere, were water from rain, streams, ponds, and lakes, and liquids that could be obtained from fresh fruits (Robson 1978). All other drinkables are introductions, although tea *(Camellia sinensis)* is grown in the region. Anderson (1988) indicates that tea probably originated somewhere in the Burma–India border country and was taken to China by Buddhist monks, to become a passion there before the middle of the first millennium A.D. Burkill (1966), however, relying on earlier writers, suggests that tea did not reach western Asia before the thirteenth century. The Dutch and British independently established a sea trade in green tea, and in the eighteenth and nineteenth centuries, the plant was introduced to India and to various locales in Southeast Asia. Basic tea flavors come from postharvest processing of the leaves. Green tea is dried and rolled; black tea is fermented before drying (Burkill 1966).

Coffee originated around the Red Sea (Heiser 1990), where it still grows wild (Burkill 1966). As its Latin name, *Coffea arabica,* suggests, the Arabs were the first to use it as a drink (in the thirteenth century), but whether this was done before or after the technique of roasting (to enhance the flavor and aroma) was developed is unclear. Coffee beans (like some tea leaves) are fermented before roasting. Use of the beverage spread, with the drink reaching Europe in the seventeenth century. The first planting of coffee outside Arabia was in Java in 1696, under Dutch direction. In the next century, the plant radiated to all parts of the world's tropics and had become an industry in Java by the 1800s. Early in that century, Dutch administrators enforced greater cultivation of the shrub, particularly at higher elevations in Java, and entire forest ecosystems were replaced in the process (Hefner 1990).

Smaller plantations in other countries of the region were begun at about this time. A number of species have been cultivated in Southeast Asia, with some, including *C. arabica,* susceptible to the fungus *Hemileia vastatrix,* which spread from Ceylon in the mid–nineteenth century (Burkill 1966). The fungus drove some planters to Malaya, and one resistant species, *Coffea liberica,* was introduced at that time. Coffee (like tea) has generally been drunk hot, often with sugar and sweetened condensed milk.

Adoption of both tea and coffee no doubt owes much to their stimulating effects (Heiser 1990), but how this became recognized is not known, for processing is needed to make their action noticeable. The alkaloids causing the effects are caffeine and similar compounds. Cocoa, another beverage containing a related substance, theobromine, is much less used in Southeast Asia, although the tree, *Theobroma cacao,* was introduced in several locales by planters as a replacement for coffee destroyed by the fungus. Originating in the New World, cacao trees were in the Philippines by the seventeenth century and in Malacca during the following century. Thus, Spaniards, Portuguese, and Dutch all took part in its dissemination. The cocoa bean is fermented and roasted (like coffee) to produce the powdered material from which the drink is made.

Commercial bottled or tinned beverages are recent introductions. Rosemary Firth (1966) has commented that soft drinks and sweetened condensed milk were considered luxuries in Kelantan, Malaya, in 1963, and prior to World War II were largely unknown. By the late 1960s, however, colas and other carbonated beverages had reached remote villages and, by the mid-1980s, advertisements for well-known brands were common. Local or regional industries produced bottled soy milk for adult consumption. By then, bovine milk processed to remain fresh without refrigeration, and packaged in cardboard containers, had reached village shops, as had similarly processed and packaged fruit drinks. Instant coffee and juice powders, for reconstitution with water, also became available.

Alcoholic Beverages

Muslims are forbidden alcohol-containing beverages, but non-Islamic Southeast Asians have produced local beers and wines as well as toddy. Early dwellers probably sampled sap and other fermentable products and learned how to encourage the process (Burkill 1966). Toddy, the most common of old Southeast Asian drinks, is made from palm sap. Fermented glutinous rice *(tapai)* produces wine during processing that is 3 percent alcohol (ICNND 1964). Spirits had become familiar in Southeast Asia before the end of the sixteenth century, when the Chinese began distilling alcohol in Java (Burkill 1966).

Nonnutritive Ingestants and Inhalants

Oral activity may take place for behavioral or physiological reasons not related to nutrition (Oswald, Merrington, and Lewis 1970). Southeast Asians' most common nonnourishing oral activities involve the substances betel nut and tobacco, which are often chewed together (Burkill 1966; Reid 1985).

Areca nut *(Areca catechu)* is the seed of a native Malaysian palm (called the betel palm) that spread to India and East Africa between A.D. 1000 and 1400. Betel is also the name of the leaf of the pepper *(Piper betel),* also Malaysian, in which the quid is wrapped (Burkill 1966). The nuts are sun- or heat-dried, split, and cut into pieces for the chew. The active principles are alkaloids affecting the nervous system, as does nicotine (Burkill 1966). The quid usually includes lime (calcium carbonate from seashells) that helps to release the stimulants. When these substances came into use in Southeast Asia is unclear, but their oral use was known in southern China by the fourth century A.D. (Anderson 1988). Ash of the nut has been used as tooth powder, and the nut itself is used medicinally, magically, and ceremonially (Wilson 1970).

Christine S. Wilson

Bibliography

Allen, Betty M. 1967. *Malayan fruits. An introduction to the cultivated species.* Singapore.

Andaya, Barbara W. 1993. Cash cropping and upstream-downstream tensions. In *Southeast Asia in the early modern era,* ed. Anthony Reid, 91-122. Ithaca, N.Y.

Anderson, E. N. 1988. *The food of China.* New Haven, Conn.

Burbidge, F. W. [1880] 1989. *The gardens of the sun.* Singapore.

Burkill, I. H. 1966. *A dictionary of the economic products of the Malay Peninsula,* Vols. 1-2. Kuala Lumpur, Malaysia.

Burling, Robbins. 1965. *Hill farms and paddy fields.* Englewood Cliffs, N.J.

Chang, K. C. 1977. *Food in Chinese culture.* New Haven, Conn.

Coedes, G. 1968. *The Indianized states of Southeast Asia.* Honolulu.

Conklin, Harold C. 1957. Hanunoo agriculture, a report on an integral system of shifting cultivation in the Philippines. *FAO Forestry Development Paper No. 12.* Rome.

Crawford, Gary W. 1992. Prehistoric plant domestication in East Asia. In *The origins of agriculture,* ed. C. W. Cowan and P. J. Watson. Washington, D.C.

Dentan, Robert K. 1968. *The Semai.* New York.

Eiseman, Fred, and Margaret Eiseman. 1988. *Fruits of Bali.* Berkeley, Calif.

Firth, Raymond. 1966. *Malay fishermen.* London.

Firth, Rosemary. 1966. *Housekeeping among Malay peasants.* London.

Fox, J. J. 1977. *Harvest of the palm: Ecological change in eastern Indonesia.* Cambridge, Mass.

Fraser, Thomas M. 1960. *Rusembilan: A Malay fishing village in southern Thailand.* Ithaca, N.Y.

Geertz, Clifford. 1960. *The religion of Java.* New York.

Gimlette, John D. 1971. *Malay poisons and charm cures.* Kuala Lumpur, Malaysia.

Gimlette, John D., and H. W. Thomson. 1971. *A dictionary of Malayan medicine.* Kuala Lumpur, Malaysia.

Hanks, Lucien M. 1972. *Rice and man.* Chicago.

Hart, Donn V. 1969. *Bisayan Filipino and Malayan humoral pathologies.* Southeast Asia Program Data Paper No. 76. Ithaca, N.Y.

Hart, Donn V., Phya Anuman Rajadhon, and Richard J. Coughlin. 1965. *Southeast Asian birth customs.* New Haven, Conn.

Hefner, Robert W. 1990. *The political economy of mountain Java.* Berkeley, Calif.

Heiser, Charles B. 1990. *Seed to civilization: The story of food.* New edition. Cambridge, Mass.

Henry, C. J. K., P. A. Donachie, and J. P. W. Rivers. 1985. The winged bean. Will the wonder crop be another flop? *Ecology of Food and Nutrition* 16: 331-8.

Herklots, G. A. C. 1972. *Vegetables in South-East Asia.* London.

Hobhouse, Henry. 1987. *Seeds of change.* New York.

ICNND (Interdepartmental Committee on Nutrition for National Defense). 1960. *Republic of Vietnam nutrition survey.* Washington, D.C.

1962. *The kingdom of Thailand nutrition survey.* Washington, D.C.

1964. *Federation of Malaya nutrition survey.* Washington, D.C.

Jin-Bee, Ooi. 1963. *Land, people and economy in Malaya.* London.

Jones, W. O. 1959. *Manioc in Africa.* Stanford, Calif.

Kathirithamby-Wells, Jeyamalar. 1993. Restraints on the development of merchant capitalism in Southeast Asia before c. 1800. In *Southeast Asia in the early modern era,* ed. Anthony Reid, 123-48. Ithaca, N.Y.

Kirsch, A. Thomas. 1973. *Feasting and social oscillation.* Southeast Asia Program Data Paper No. 92. Ithaca, N.Y.

Laderman, Carol. 1983. *Wives and midwives.* Berkeley, Calif.

Lewis, Norman. 1991. *Golden earth. Travels in Burma.* London.

Lindenbaum, Shirley. 1977. The "last course": Nutrition and anthropology in Asia. In *Nutrition and anthropology in action,* ed. T. K. Fitzgerald, 141-55. Assen, the Netherlands.

Medway, Lord. 1969. *The wild animals of Malaya and offshore islands including Singapore.* London.

Mintz, Sidney W. 1985. *Sweetness and power.* New York.

National Academy of Sciences. 1975. *The winged bean.* Report. Washington, D.C.

Oswald, I., J. Merrington, and H. Lewis. 1970. Cyclical "on demand" oral intake by adults. *Nature* 225: 959-60.

Pangborn, Rosemarie M. 1975. Cross-cultural aspects of flavor preference. *Food Technology* 26: 34-6.

Pollock, Nancy J. 1992. *These roots remain.* Honolulu.

Reid, Anthony. 1985. From betel-chewing to tobacco-smoking in Indonesia. *Journal of Asian Studies* 44: 529-47.

1993. Introduction: A time and a place. In *Southeast Asia in the early modern era,* ed. Anthony Reid, 1-9. Ithaca, N.Y.

Robson, John R. K. 1978. Fruit in the diet of prehistoric man and of the hunter-gatherer. *Journal of Human Nutrition* 32: 19-6.

Rozin, Paul, and D. Schiller. 1980. The nature and acquisition of a preference for chili pepper by humans. *Motivation and Emotion* 4: 77-101.

Scott, J. S. 1959. *An introduction to the sea fishes of Malaya.* Kuala Lumpur, Malaysia.

Simoons, Frederick J. 1970. The traditional limits of milking and milk use in southern Asia. *Anthropos* 65: 547-93.

1994. *Eat not this flesh.* Second edition. Madison, Wisc.

Skeat, Walter. 1961. *Fables and folk tales from an eastern forest.* Singapore.

1967. *Malay magic.* New York.

Sri Kantha, Sachi, and John W. Erdman. 1986. Letter to the editor, Is winged bean a flop? *Ecology of Food and Nutrition* 18: 339-41.

Steinberg, Rafael. 1970. *Pacific and Southeast Asian cooking.* New York.

Strange, Heather. 1981. *Rural Malay women in tradition and transition.* New York.

Volkman, Toby Alice. 1985. *Feasts of honor.* Illinois Studies in Anthropology No. 16. Chicago.

Wallace, Alfred R. 1989. *The Malay archipelago.* Singapore.

Wilson, Christine S. 1970. Food beliefs and practices of Malay fishermen. Ph.D. thesis, University of California, Berkeley.

1975. Rice, fish and coconuts – the bases of Southeast Asian flavors. *Food Technology* 29: 42-4.

1983. Malay fishers of protein and other nutrients. Unpublished paper presented at the Eleventh International Congress of Anthropological and Ethnological Sciences, Vancouver, B.C.

    1985. Staples and calories in Southeast Asia. In *Food energy in tropical ecosystems,* ed. Dorothy J. Cattle and Karl H. Schwerin, 65-81. New York.

    1986. Social and nutritional context of "ethnic foods": Malay examples. In *Shared wealth and symbol: Food, culture, and society in Oceania and Southeast Asia,* ed. Lenore Manderson, 259-72. Cambridge.

    1988. Commerciogenic food habit changes in a modernizing society. Unpublished paper presented at the Second Annual Meeting, Association for the Study of Food and Society, Washington, D.C.

    1994. Traditional diets; their value and preservation. *Ecology of Food and Nutrition* 32: 89-90.

Winstedt, Richard O. 1966. *An unabridged English-Malay dictionary.* Kuala Lumpur, Malaysia.

    1970. *An unabridged Malay-English dictionary.* Kuala Lumpur, Malaysia.

Yu, Ying-Shih. 1977. Han. In *Food in Chinese culture,* ed. K. C. Chang, 53-83. New Haven, Conn.

V.B.3   China

Legend has it that when Emperor Tang, the founder of the Shang dynasty (sixteenth to eleventh centuries B.C.), appointed his prime minister, he chose Yi Yin, a cook widely renowned for his great professional ability. Indeed, in the Chinese classics (the oldest of which date from the eighth and seventh centuries B.C.) the art of proper seasoning and the mastery of cooking techniques are customary metaphors for good government (Chang 1977: 51; Knechtges 1986). Moreover, in certain contexts the expression *tiaogeng,* literally "seasoning the soup," must be translated as "to be minister of state"!

That government should be likened to the cooking process is not really surprising, considering that the foremost task of the emperor was to feed his subjects.[1] Seeing the sovereign, the intermediary between heaven and earth, in the role of provider of food is in keeping with a mythical vision of primeval times. According to legend, the first humans, clad in animal skins, lived in caves or straw huts and fed on raw animals, indiscriminately devouring meat, fur, and feathers in the same mouthful. Shennong, the Divine Farmer, one of the mythical Three August Sovereigns and founders of civilization, taught men to cultivate the five cereals and acquainted them with the blessings of agriculture (Zheng 1989: 39) after Suiren had taught them to make fire for cooking their foods. In mythology, cooking is associated with the process of civilization that put an end to the disorder of the earliest ages and led to a distinction between savagery and civilized human behavior.

Throughout Chinese history, the cooking of foodstuffs and the cultivation and consumption of cereals

were considered the first signs of the passage from barbarity to culture. Thus the Chinese of the Han ethnic group set themselves apart from surrounding nationalities who, they said, had no knowledge of agriculture or did not know about the cooking of food (Legge 1885: 223; Couvreur 1950, 1: 295; Chang 1977).

Cooking and food, then, were assigned a major role in ancient China. This is very clear in the *Zhou Ritual,* a compendium describing the idealized administration of the Zhou dynasty (1066-771 B.C.). Written in the fifth century B.C., this compendium indicates that half of the personnel of the imperial palace were occupied in the preparation of food, meaning that more than 2,000 persons were involved in handling the food of the sovereign and his family (Knechtges 1986: 49).

In the third century B.C., the authors of the *Lüshi chunqiu,* a compendium of the cosmological and philosophical knowledge of the time, credited cook and prime minister Yi Yin with inventing a theory of cuisine and gastronomy that became a major point of reference for posterity. The culinary principles of Emperor Tang's minister (in fact a set of rules of good government) were to remain the implicit standard adopted by all the subsequent authors of culinary works. Yi Yin classifies all foodstuffs according to their origin, categorizes flavors, indicates the best sources of supply and the best products, and stresses the importance of the mastery of cooking techniques and the harmony of flavors. He points out that raw foods, whether they belong to the vegetable, animal, or aquatic kingdom, have a naturally disagreeable odor, which can be corrected or intensified by the combination of the five flavors and the mastery of the three elements, water, fire, and wood. These techniques make it possible to create, at will, balanced sweetness, sourness with acidity, saltiness without an excess of brine, sharp flavor that does not burn, and delicate but not insipid tastes (Chen Qiyou 1984; Knechtges 1986).

To this day, cuisine in China is implicitly defined as the art of using cooking and seasoning to transform ingredients steeped in savagery - as their unique smells indicate - into edible dishes fit for human beings living in society. Dishes cooked in this manner are not only edible but healthful. In ancient China, all foodstuffs were considered both nutriment and medicine. In principle, the dietary regime was supposed to provide all that was needed to maintain the body's vital energy. It was - and still is - believed that the first step in treating an illness must be a change of diet and that medications should be brought to bear only if diet proves ineffectual. Foodstuffs were, therefore, classified by their "nature" (hot, cold, temperate, cool) and their flavor (salty, sour, sweet, bitter, acrid) as part of a humoral medicine founded on matching, contrasting, or combining these qualities with those of the illness to be treated. Although there is some controversy as to where ideas of hot and cold foods originated (with Greece and India leading candidates along with China), it is a credit to the great originality of the Chinese that they invented what one might call a "medicinal gastronomy," which, still in vogue, endeavors to heal by using the pharmacopoeia without sacrificing the aesthetics or the tastes of high-class cuisine.

The Importance of Cereals

Although emperors and the princes enjoyed the privilege of savoring the very finest dishes, they, like everybody else, could not get along without cooked cereals. For in ancient as in modern China, cereals have been assigned the function of nourishing and sustaining life, which has given birth to the model of the Chinese meal, whose antiquity is suggested by the classic texts. When Confucius asserted, for instance, that a little coarse rice washed down with water was enough to make him happy, he meant to indicate that he was humble and modest, but he also was making the point that no one can survive without these two ingredients. In normal times, Confucius liked to eat his rice accompanied by fine dishes and complemented by wine. But he made it clear that the quantity of meat should never exceed that of rice. Underlying this recommendation is the norm that makes cereal the centerpiece of the meal (Legge 1893).

Cereal, or more precisely starch, remains the basic ingredient of the daily meal in China, and despite an increased meat consumption of late in urban areas, a very large majority of the population continues to derive almost 90 percent of its proteins from vegetable foods.

An ordinary meal consists of a starch cooked in water or steamed and a choice of several dishes prepared with meat, fish, eggs, vegetables, and products derived from soybeans. Such a pattern is not peculiar to China. This kind of meal was also the norm in preindustrial Europe and still exists in many countries where foods such as couscous, corn tortillas, polenta, and bread are considered the staff of life. The dishes or sauces that accompany them are more a matter of seasoning and gastronomic pleasure than of dietary bulk.

In China, not all staples have the same status. Two of them, rice and wheat, are the most highly valued, with millet and maize less appreciated. Tuberous plants, such as taros, yams, and white and sweet potatoes, are generally disliked and considered poor substitutes for the prestigious cereals.[2]

From an agricultural point of view, wheat, various millets, and maize are the typical cereals of the north,[3] whereas rice is characteristic of the regions south of the Yangtze River and of western China. But that more wheat buns are eaten in Beijing than in certain poor country places of Guangdong Province is not simply a matter of climate and geography. When in the past the prince and his entourage enjoyed ravioli made of fine wheat flour, the peasant, the soldier in the field, and the hermit made do with gruel, in keeping with their social status (Sabban 1990). Access to "fancy" cereals still depends on a family's economic situation. Sometimes the inequalities are stark. Whereas prosperity and city living attenuate the differences by offering wide food choices to the inhabitants of Beijing, Shanghai, or Canton (Guangzhout), who thus do not experience the constraints of local supply, poorer people and peasants living far from urban centers have access only to the cheapest local products.

It is, therefore, only on festive occasions that ordinary people treat themselves to a good banquet, during which they almost dismiss the tyranny of the daily cereal. On such occasions cooked dishes become the center of the meal, and when rice or steamed buns are served at the end, the guests will casually take only a mouthful or two. For once, they have filled up on dishes that ordinarily only complement the meal. Such short-lived disdain for a foodstuff that is venerated in day-to-day life is a way of expressing one's pleasure and satisfaction.

The Historical Roots of the Different Chinese Cuisines

In an area larger than that of Europe, the territory of China stretches some 5,000 kilometers from the Siberian border in the north to the tropics in the south and a similar distance from the Pamir Mountains in the west to the shores of the Yellow Sea in the east. This climatic and geographical diversity makes for a variety of Chinese cuisines. However, the division of China into gastronomic regions is relatively recent and does not obscure the ancient contrast between North and South China, which is as pertinent as ever.

As already suggested, the production of different cereals as basic staples has made North China and South China two distinct entities with identifiable political, cultural, and economic roots. Throughout Chinese history the location of the capital has moved back and forth between the north and the south, and with it the court and the decision-making bodies. Such shifts also meant that each new capital became the center of innovation in fashions and taste, and on such occasions the other part of the Chinese world was made to adopt the values and views of the capital.

This struggle for preeminence has always been mirrored in the cuisine and food habits of the Chinese. A political exile, for instance, might evoke a specific food to signify his homesickness and indignation about the injustice he is suffering. Or, again, one who has betrayed an unfamiliarity with foods peculiar to the "other" China gives a reason for others to stigmatize his or her ignorance, or naivete, or haughtiness.

The strong allusive value of some foodstuffs that assumed the rank of regional emblems thus made deep or nuanced comparisons unnecessary.[4]

As we have seen, wheat was to the north what rice was to the south. Most characteristically northern, however, were the breads, cakes, and wheat-based noodles, all subsumed under the generic term *bing* until the end of the Tang (A.D. 618–907) (Sabban 1990). These foodstuffs were highly appreciated by the aristocracy and identified those who ate them as "northerners," as did mutton and milk products.

The cuisine of the south, by contrast, was characterized by rice and also by pork, vegetables, and fish. Indeed, as shown by archaeological findings from ancient times and supported by more recent texts, fish have long occupied an important dietary role for the Chinese, who very early developed techniques of pisciculture. But even more important than pond-raised aquatic animals were the freshwater fish and shellfish present in the rice paddies of the lower Yangtze River. In this area, covered with rivers, lakes, and streams, large carp grew naturally along with an abundance of vegetables.

If before the Song (A.D. 960–1279), the northerners with their noodles, butter, and milk tended to elevate their own preferences as the standard of taste, the southerners were occasionally able to defend their indigenous products. King Wu of Jin who reigned from A.D. 266 to 290, for instance, unfavorably compared *lao* – a kind of yoghurt made from the milk of sheep and highly prized for its excellence in the north at the time – with a soup made of young aquatic plants growing in the southern lakes (Xu Zhen'e 1984).

Between the end of the Tang and the beginning of the Song, the center of gravity of Chinese civilization shifted from the north to the south. Subsequently, the Song period marked the rise of a new urban society and of a nationwide economy based on a network of transportation and distribution (Shiba 1970). Kaifeng and Hangzhou, the respective capitals of the northern and southern Song dynasties, were the scenes of an unprecedented mixing of populations, for it was here that inhabitants of north and south, as well as people from Sichuan, met and mingled. In this encounter, each group became conscious of its own food habits. Once they were recognized as distinct, the culinary styles of the north, the south, and Sichuan could be combined and finally become the cuisine of the capital.

In a parallel development, the discourse on cooking and food habits assumed new dimensions. The food of the emperor and his entourage had always been commented upon, and it was understood that the governing class and the well-to-do ate choice dishes (and sometimes too much of them), whereas the rest of the population, in keeping with its rank, consumed coarse cereals and vegetables. Before the Song period, testimonies to these contrasting habits were rare and widely scattered. Only the recipes of

the agricultural treatise *Qimin yaoshu,* written in the fourth century by a northern notable, provided a glimpse of the tastes of the contemporary elites (Shi Shenghan 1982).

In the Song period, the discourse on food practices began to take a larger view. Although the opposition between north and south remained at its core, some attention was now paid to other, more remote and even foreign regions, and, at times, value judgments yielded to quasi-ethnological descriptions. In this way, the customs and cuisines of foreign peoples came to be considered as legitimate as those of the Chinese. Thus, the culinary part of a household encyclopedia of the early fifteenth century contains a list of Muslim recipes and another of Jürchet (also Juchen or Jurchen) recipes (Qiu Pangtong 1986).[5] It is true that beginning in the late thirteenth century, the Mongol domination added impetus to the greater openness that had emerged in the Song period. A diet book containing many recipes, visibly influenced by foreign customs practiced in central Asia and India, was written in Chinese by the court dietician and presented to Emperor Tuq Temür in 1330 (Sabban 1986a).

In the sixteenth century, the literati Wang Shixing commented on the proverb "[t]hose who dwell on the mountain live off the mountain, those who haunt the seashore live off the sea" by noting that

> the inhabitants of the southern seashore eat fish and shrimp, whose odor makes the people of the north sick, while the men of the northern frontiers consume milk and yoghurt that southerners find nauseating. North of the Yellow River, people eat onions, garlic, and chives, which do them much good, whereas south of the Yangzi people are chary of spicy foods. (Wang Shixing 1981: 3)

Then he tolerantly and wisely concluded: "These are ways peculiar to different regions, and any attempt to make them uniform by force would be useless."

Beginning with the Qing or Manchu dynasty (A.D. 1644–1912), regional differences of cuisine were no longer perceived as the traceable consequences of geographic and climatic diversity but rather as veritable styles defined by a series of criteria involving the nature of the ingredients, seasonings, and types of preparation. The schema founded on three culinary styles, and supplemented by the cuisine of Sichuan dating from the Song period, gave rise to the notion of a China divided into four major gastronomical regions. But as the country's frontiers expanded as a result of the Manchu domination, what was called the "North" stretched even farther north, reaching as far as Shandong, Beijing, and Tianjin; the "South" came to include Zhejiang and Jiangsu, as well as Anhui, with the region of Canton becoming the country's "Deep South." The West still meant Sichuan but also came to include Guizhou, Yunnan, Hunan, and Hubei.

This division is still recognized today, although the limits of these four regions are often drawn very loosely. For example, the cuisine of Canton is seen as including that of Fujian Province and Taiwan, which may not be altogether justified.[6] Nonetheless, once travelers from Beijing have crossed the Yangtze River, they are in the south, and everything is different for the palate.

A regional cuisine is defined by certain dishes, by the frequent use of certain modes of cooking, by the use of specific ingredients, and especially by its condiments and spices – in short, by the tastes that set the one Chinese cuisine apart from all the others.

North of the Yellow River, garlic and onions have always been in favor, as Wang Shixing said long ago. Peking duck, with its fat and crunchy skin, must absolutely be eaten with a garnish of raw scallions and sweet sauce, *tianmianjiang*. The aroma of mutton blends with that of garlic, and the taste of balsamic vinegar cleanses these strong flavors with its tempered acidity.

Sichuan has the strongest condiments and spices, and the sharpest among them, chilli pepper and fagara, or Sichuan pepper *(Xanthoxylum Piperitum)*, are highly prized. Together with sesame oil or puree and fermented broad bean paste *(doubanjiang)*, they are used to flavor dishes and produce harmonies of flavors bearing such evocative names as "strange flavor" *(guai wei)*, "family flavor" *(jiachang wei)*, or "hot-fragrant" flavor *(xiangla wei).*[7]

The inhabitants of the low-lying plains of the Yangtze, a land of fish and rice, produce the most tender vegetables and raise the biggest carp and the fattest crabs. They slowly simmer dishes of light and subtle flavor enlivened by the presence of refreshing ginger and the fillip of Shaoxing wine. This is the only region of China where gentle flavors and sweet-and-sour tastes are truly appreciated and beautifully cooked.

The complexity and richness of Cantonese cuisine cannot be reduced to a few dominant flavors, for the art of the Cantonese cook is characterized by mastery in blending different flavors or, alternatively, permitting each one of them to stand out on its own. Seafood, however, is one of the main features of this cuisine. Its preparation emphasizes freshness by, for instance, simply steaming a fish au naturel. Oyster sauce is used to season poached poultry, fish, and briefly blanched green vegetables. But Canton is also famous for its roasted whole suckling pigs and its lacquered meats hung up as an appetizing curtain in the windows of restaurants.

China's culinary diversity can also be seen in the streets, where itinerant vendors sell small specialties *(xiaochi)* to hungry passersby at all hours of the day. Soups, fritters, skewers, fried, cooked, or steamed ravioli, cakes, crepes, tea, fruit juice – the choices seem infinite, though they depend, of course, on the season and the region. In the streets of Beijing, skewers of caramelized haws are offered in winter, whereas ruby-red slices of watermelon appear on the hottest days of summer.

To this mosaic of practices, habits, and tastes, one must add the cuisines of some 50 ethnic minorities. Among these are those of Turkish origin living in the autonomous region of Xinjiang and the Hui families, who in every other way are indistinguishable from the Han Chinese disseminated throughout the territory. These Islamic communities have developed a "Chinese" cuisine from which pork and all its derivatives are absent but are replaced with mutton and beef, which are consumed after Islamic ritual slaughtering.

Nor must one forget *su* cooking, which goes back very far and was already highly regarded under the Song. Based on the exclusion of all animal foods, this cuisine was adopted by the Buddhists and others who wished to eat a meatless or light diet. In their gastronomic version, *su* dishes bear the names of normal meat-containing dishes, and the cook's art consists of using vegetable ingredients to reproduce the taste, consistency, and shape of the meat normally included in these dishes.

Such diversity might make it appear as if there were no Chinese cuisine but several Chinese cuisines, and it is true that there is no haute cuisine without regional roots or affiliation with a genre (be it *su*, Islamic, or even traditional court cooking) that imparts its rhythm, its style, and its specific flavors to a gourmet meal. Nonetheless, everyday cooking is the same from one end of China to the other in its principles and its results. Throughout the territory, people use the same flavoring agents, namely soy sauce, ginger, scallions, and chilli peppers, supplemented, to be sure, by local condiments. Moreover, certain originally regional dishes, among them "Mother Ma's soy curds," "vinegar carp of the Western Lake," and "sweet-sour pork," have become so widely known that they are on the menu of ordinary restaurants in all parts of the country.

The Principles of Cooking Technique

The Chinese word for "to cook" is *pengtiao*, composed of two morphemes signifying, respectively, "to cook" and "to season." In China, cooking foods and combining their flavors are thus two equally important operations.

Certain condiments, as well as mastery of the techniques of chopping and cooking – which, in turn, are related to the use of specialized tools such as the wok and chopsticks – are indispensable in the practice of Chinese cooking. In other words, there is a close connection between the manners of the eater and the work of the cook. Small pieces and foods that can be broken up without using a knife are better suited to the use of chopsticks than any other food. But it would be naive to attribute the functioning of the Chinese culinary system merely to the way food is served and eaten, for Chinese cooking developed out of the interaction of all its constituent parts.

A clear distinction must be made, however, between day-to-day cooking designed to feed a family as economically as possible and professional cooking by specialists highly trained in every technique. The endeavors of the latter have nothing to do with necessity and are exclusively concerned with providing satisfaction and pleasure to the senses.

Home Cooking

Characteristic of cooking in the home is the chopping of ingredients into uniform small pieces, followed by their rapid cooking, usually sautéing in a semispherical iron skillet or wok.[8] The cooking is done with little fat but with a gamut of seasonings dominated by soy sauce, fresh ginger, scallions, sesame oil, Chinese vinegar, fagara, and chilli peppers. Such preparation of food makes for a remarkable economy of equipment. In addition to a rice cooker,[9] all that is needed to prepare any dish is a chopping board – a simple tree "slice" 5 to 10 centimeters in thickness – a cleaver, the wok, and a cooking spatula.

In the city most people cook on a gas ring; in the countryside they have a brick stove with several holes in the top so that the wok can be placed directly over the flame. Since fuel is scarce and expensive, it is always used sparingly, which has given rise to the widespread practice of quick stir-frying over high heat. Sometimes the cook will make use of the heat generated by cooking the rice to steam one of the dishes of the meal above the rice on the rice cooker. Several different dishes are cooked in the same wok, one right after the other, but this is done so rapidly that they have little time to cool. And even if they do cool, the rice, always served piping hot, will provide a balance.

Professional Cooking

Becoming a professional cook demands long years of apprenticeship under the watchful eye of a great chef, and before the aspiring kitchen boy can himself become a chef, he must pass through all the work stations. If he chooses the specialty of meat and vegetable cooking, he will go to the "red work bench" *(hongan),* where he will learn all about chopping and carving, composing, cooking techniques, and seasoning. If he prefers the white vest of the "pastry cook" he will go to the "white work bench" *(baian)* to learn the meticulous art of preparing little dishes made from flours and cereals, including the proper cooking times for pasta products.

A great chef does not, of course, have to be concerned with economy, for he is called upon to use ingredients to their best advantage and to bring out their quintessential flavor by treating them according to the rules of the subtle and difficult techniques he has mastered. He will, thus, use the hump or the heels of a camel without worrying about the rest of the animal when asked to create two of the great dishes of the haute cuisine of North China. Nor is there any economy in the use of fat, a great deal of which is used for deep frying, a practice generally absent from family cooking. Ovens, which are unknown in private homes, are part of the equipment of professional kitchens, particularly in restaurants located in such culinary regions as Beijing or Canton, where roast meat is a specialty.

Even though the same basic principles inform both the great gastronomy and the home cooking of China, professional practice gives cooking a scope and a complexity that cannot possibly be achieved at home. And so one usually turns to a restaurant if one wants to taste the grand specialties prepared with rare, costly, and such delicate ingredients as shark fins, bird's nests, sea cucumbers, abalones, shark's skin, and mountain mushrooms.

A Rich Repertory of Products and Condiments

Because most Chinese enjoy such a wide variety of foods, it is often asserted that there are no food taboos in China. In fact, the Chinese make the claim themselves,[10] even though they recognize that China's Muslims avoid pork and devout Buddhists reject all flesh as well as garlic and onions. Doubtless, such a claim stems, in part, from the popular understanding that a number of unexpected animal species such as the cat, the dog, the snake, and even the anteater end up as a ragout under the chopsticks of Cantonese food lovers, and from the knowledge that Chinese cooks do not, in principle, shun any edible product as long as they are able to prepare it according to the rules of the art. Indeed, haute cuisine calls for "the precious fruits of sea and mountain," essentially animal by-products whose consumption is limited because they are so rare and costly. If their strangeness strikes the imagination, they are not the only gustatory exotica that speak to the originality and the history of China's culinary repertory.

Such consumption of animal foods has a long history in China despite the frequent assertion that the country was traditionally a kind of "vegetal kingdom." Neither hunting nor pastoral activities were proscribed in ancient China and both classical written sources and archaeological findings testify to the importance of cattle breeding in ancient and medieval China. The first millennium of the Christian era probably paralleled the "golden age" of domestication in China in which the utilization of draft animals and the production of meat products gave rise to increasing leisure (and increasing warfare). It has only been in more recent times that activities leading to meat production and to specialized breeding of animals for hunting have become progressively marginalized (Cartier 1993; Elisseeff 1993).

China also stands out for the exceptional richness of vegetal species grown and eaten there – many times more than the fruits and vegetables known in the West. Moreover, these plants are used in an intensive manner, and roots, stems, leaves, shoots, seeds, and sometimes flowers are all exploited for their respective qualities.

The original stock of plants in China was later supplemented by large numbers of new plants, which were very quickly assimilated. As early as the first century B.C. the Chinese acclimatized plants imported from central Asia (which had mostly reached there from the Near East, India, and Africa) such as cucumbers, coriander, peas, sesame, onions, grapes, and pomegranates. Under the Tang (618–907), spinach was acquired from Persia. This was a time when there was great interest in the exotic, and in North China, fresh fruits that grew in faraway southern countries were highly prized. Thus we know that citrus fruit and litchi were carried from Lingnan (today in the Canton region) by special courier for Empress Yang Guifei.

Finally, in the mid–sixteenth century under the Ming, the "American plants" appeared in the coastal areas of Fujian and Guangdong, with the Portuguese and their ships instrumental in bringing maize, sweet potatoes, and peanuts to China. The tomato did not become known until the following century, and the chilli pepper had to await the eighteenth century. These new arrivals became highly popular in China, and scholars subsequently went so far as to attribute the country's population growth in the eighteenth century to the availability of maize and the sweet potato (Ho Ping-ti 1955). The chilli pepper wrought a deep change in the fundamental taste of the cuisines of Sichuan, Hunan, and Yunnan, which are known today for their highly spiced character.

To these expanding natural resources must be added a large number of "processed" foods made from meat, fish, vegetables, and fruit and subsequently used in the culinary process as basic ingredients or condiments. These processed foods have their own history, for their production is predicated on the availability of the appropriate technologies. The oldest texts (of the fourth and fifth centuries B.C.) mention the names of forcemeats, *coulis,* and seasoning sauces, as well as vinegars, pickled and fermented vegetables, and "smoked and salted meats," all of which shows beyond a doubt that aside from day-to-day cooking there was already a whole food "industry" founded on foresight and the stockpiling or conservation of foodstuffs.

The oldest example of this kind of organization is provided by the description of the ideal functioning of the imperial household of the Zhou in the *Zhou Ritual.* The household administration naturally included brigades of pigtailed officials in charge of preparing the daily meals, along with pork butchers *(laren),* the wine steward *(jiuzheng),* and the employees of the manufactory of spiced preserves *(yanren)* and of vinegar *(xiren)* (Biot 1851; Lin Yin 1985).

For the period before the sixth century of the current era we have no idea what these functions involved or, rather, what items were produced under the supervision of these officials. A weighty agricultural treatise of this period devotes a fourth of its space to food preparation. This section contains as many cooking recipes in the narrow sense as it does recipes pertaining to brewing, pickling, malting, and preserving. All of these recipes testify to great expertise and to the widespread use of preserved foods (Shih Sheng-han 1962). The most remarkable, and probably the oldest, of these recipes are those for making seasoning sauces by fermenting grains and legumes and the more than 20 recipes for different vinegars, which are also obtained by subjecting cooked cereals to acetic fermentation. In addition, this text contains a large number of recipes for pickled vegetables, "smoked and salted meats," and, of course, alcoholic beverages, the role and importance of which in Chinese culture we shall examine next.

Contrary to what one might expect, however, this treatise does not even allude to certain products that are today considered the very emblems of Chinese cooking. An example is soy sauce, which is so universally used in our day. Then it was probably perceived as nothing more than the residual liquid of a spicy paste until the Song period, when it became clearly identified with its own name. Similarly, the clotting of soy milk for a curd called *doufu* (tofu) seems to have been unknown in the written sources until the tenth century, when the first reference to this subject can be found (Hong Guangzhu 1987: 8).[11]

Conversely, some foods that have almost disappeared today seem to have enjoyed a certain vogue in the past. *Lao,* for example, which is a kind of fermented milk, and butter were luxury foods highly prized by the upper classes of society, at least until the end of the Song (Sabban 1986b). The reputation of these products (and the taste for them) lasted until the Qing period, although they were probably difficult to obtain outside of court circles, which had access to cows and ewes as well as to a "dairy" that produced for the emperor and his entourage. Perhaps the popularity of the Beijng yoghurt today and the recent fashion of "dairy cafés" offering traditional sweets made of milkcurd are vestiges of these ancient and prestigious treats.

This entire food "industry" was predicated on a remarkable knowledge of the phenomenon of fermentation, which is still used in the production of popular ready-to-use condiments such as soy sauce *(jiangyou),* salted black beans *(douchi),* sweet-salty sauce *(tianmianjiang),* and fermented broad bean paste *(doubanjiang).*

In addition to these condiments produced by fermentation, the Chinese developed original techniques for turning plant materials into edible substances much sought after for their consistency, their malleability, and their taste. In this category one finds a considerable variety of noodles made with cereal or leguminous plant flours. *Mianjin,* or "gluten," is a kind of firm but elastic dough obtained by rinsing a sponge of wheat flour. Also used are all the secondary products of soy milk, such as fresh or dried curd and its skin and gelatin. The textures of these particular substances have stimulated the imaginations of many cooks; thus, they not only have played a vital role in the development of *su* cooking diffused by Buddhist temples but also have made their mark on home cooking and on the cuisine of great restaurants. In this area the Chinese developed a technical prowess that may well be unmatched by other societies (Sabban 1993).

A Culture of Alcoholic Beverages

China is known as the land of tea, but in fact alcohol has been drunk there longer than the brew of the plant that has conquered the world. Yet tea has come to overshadow the other Chinese beverages called *jiu.* Difficult to translate into Western languages, this word *jiu* designates today all alcoholic liquids, from the lightest beer to the strongest distilled alcohol, with wines made from grapes and rice and sweet liqueurs in the middle.[12]

Before the advent of distillation, which is generally assumed to have occurred around the fourteenth or fifteenth century, *jiu* meant all alcoholic beverages obtained through the fermentation of cereals. But these were not beers whose fermentation was induced by malt, such as are found in several other ancient societies, but rather beverages with alcohol contents of between 10 and 15 percent obtained through a "combined fermentation" that called for the preliminary production of an ad hoc ferment that subsequently started the fermenting process in a mash of cooked cereals (Needham 1980; Sabban 1988). Each of these two processes involved fairly lengthy preparation and maturation. The cereal, the water, and the ferment *(qu)* were so indissolubly associated that the Chinese sometimes compared the *jiu* that had resulted from their transmutation to a body in which the cereal occupied the place of the flesh and muscle, the ferment that of the skeleton, and the water, like blood, irrigated all the veins.

This original technique, which subsequently spread to Japan, Korea, and all of Southeast Asia, has existed in China for a very long time. The first texts that have come down to us allude to the precise fermenting time of the *qu* needed for making *jiu* (Hong Guangzhu 1984). The "invention" of this precious liquid is attributed to Du Kang, a legendary figure venerated as the "immortal of *jiu*" who is the object of a cult in several villages of North China. He is supposed to have lived at the end of the Shang dynasty (1324–1066 B.C.). We do know from the texts and from an abundance of magnificent utensils found in archaeological sites that the Shang aristocrats loved to

drink, and there is evidence that some of their predecessors had also succumbed to this passion. In fact, the production of alcoholic beverages in China seems to go all the way back to the end of the Neolithic and perhaps even further. The site of Dawenkou in Shandong (4000 B.C.) has yielded a great variety of earthen vessels used for preserving, storing, and consuming alcoholic beverages.

There is no question that since the presumed time of their appearance alcoholic beverages have enjoyed considerable popularity in China. The sixth-century agricultural treatise *Qimin yaoshu* gives more than 30 recipes, each one for a specific beverage identified by its mode of production, its ingredients, and its flavor, color, strength, and so forth (Shi Shenghan 1982). We also learn from the texts that these beverages played an important role at all levels of society. Their production was controlled by the institution of state monopolies in the course of the first dynasties, and there were times when their consumption was forbidden. Every ritual involved alcoholic beverages as offerings to the gods or the ancestors. But alcohol was regularly used for more mundane purposes, and families were consequently ruined and promising careers cut short. In a word, it is clear that alcoholic beverages were present at every moment of people's lives. In the sixteenth century 70 kinds of *jiu* were counted (Du Shiran et al. 1982), and to this profusion should be added the exotic "grape wines" imported from central Asia, which became very fashionable in court circles under the Han and the Tang.

Alcoholic beverages maintain their importance in the present. No banquet, for example, would be complete without them. Indeed, the ceremony of marriage is referred to by the expression *he xijiu* or "drinking the wine of happiness," and each of the guests is invited to raise a glass in honor of the bride. The latter, as she was already enjoined to do in the ritual books of the third and fourth centuries B.C., must exchange a goblet with the groom. To testify to their mutual commitment, betrothed couples no longer drink out of the two halves of the same gourd but now cross their arms and give to each other the goblet they hold in their hands.

In eastern Zhejiang, a region where the production of a renowned rice wine is a tradition, people would bury several earthenware jars of good wine at the birth of a child and not open them until the day of his or her marriage. A family celebration without alcoholic beverages is unthinkable, and even on the occasion of a funeral it is customary to offer a drink to friends who have come to salute the deceased for the last time. Seasonal and religious festivities as well have always included generous libations, and until the advent of the republic in 1912 the winter solstice was celebrated with libations to heaven performed by the emperor and his ministers, whereas families made offerings of alcohol to their ancestors.

Alcoholic beverages are also items of gastronomy

consumed for no particular reason at a drinking party or to accompany a meal. Drinking with friends is a social activity mentioned in the oldest literature. In grave no. 1 of the Mawangdui site dating from the Eastern Han period (about 168 B.C.), where the spouse of the Marquis of Dai is buried, the arrangement of the objects contained in the northernmost funerary chamber is thought to represent the deceased seated at a lacquered table laden with meat dishes and goblets containing two kinds of wine. There is little doubt that this scene depicts either a drinking party or the first part of a banquet devoted, as usual, to the drinking of alcoholic beverages (Pirazzoli-t'-Serstevens 1991).

Although drinking parties sometimes had a political function, for instance when the seating arrangements concretely showed patterns of social hierarchy (Yü Ying-shih 1979), they were mainly moments of joy and exaltation. Almost all the poets have devoted some of their writings to the celebration of wine and the inspiring inebriation it brings. Poets of the Tang and Song period felt that wine was as necessary as paper, brush, and ink, and there was no lack of hardened drinkers among the rhymesters. It is even said that once when the great Li Bai (701–62) was in his cups, he thought that he could catch the moon when he saw its quivering reflection in the river and so perished by drowning. Perhaps it was a befitting end for a poet who, certain of his modern confreres do not hesitate to say, was permanently steeped in alcohol.

Drinking in China is a form of entertainment and a way to shed inhibitions. Sometimes it also gives rise to games and contests that make the losers drink more and more. At popular banquets the game of *morra* marks the time for drinking amid peals of laughter and screams of excitement. The famous eighteenth-century novel *The Dream in the Red Pavilion* furnishes a fine example of the jousts associated with wine drinking in literary circles: Any participant who did not succeed in improvising a song or poem with prearranged constraints within a limited time was made to drain his cup on the spot.

Although getting drunk is the admitted aim of these drinking bouts, drinking without eating is unthinkable. In order to "make the wine go down" *(xiajiu)*, one must sip it while nibbling at some tidbits or little dishes that not only fill the stomach but also sharpen one's thirst, although they should never distract the drinker from the appreciation of the wine.

The social standing of the drinker determines how fancy these indispensable accompaniments can be. A small bowl of fennel-toasted beans is all there was for poor Kong Yiji, the hero of a novel of Lu Xun, who occasionally treated himself to a nice bowl of warm wine at the corner tavern (Yang and Yang 1972). By contrast, goose braised in marc, pork of five flavors, fish with crayfish eggs, and the finest specialties of Suzhou carefully selected to go with the drinks were enjoyed by Zhu Ziye, the gourmet of the recent novel by Lu Wenfu (Lu Wenfu 1983). A contemporary of poor Kong Yiji, Zhu Ziye was vastly more wealthy.

The prewar taverns no longer exist, and the wine of Shaoxing is now rarely served warm, but people never fail to drink at a banquet or any other celebration. The choice of beverages has become wider: There are now clear alcohols made of rice or sorghum like the famous *maotai* and wines made of glutinous rice, the best of which is probably the yellow wine of Shaoxing. In addition, there is osmanthus-flavored liqueur, grape wines, which are now produced in China, and also port wine and even cognac.

Beer has been regularly consumed ever since it was introduced by the Europeans early in this century. "Qingdao," the best known and most renowned brand, is manufactured at Qingdao in Shandong, a town and region taken over in 1897 by the Germans, who established a brewery there in 1903 (Wang Shangdian 1987). Today, beer is the first alcoholic beverage people will buy if they are looking for a little treat.

The Art of Making Tea

Appearing much later than alcoholic beverages, tea began to acquire considerable importance in the Tang period, when its use became widespread. At first it was perceived as a serious competitor of wine, which it implicitly is to this day. Certain "weak natures" who could not tolerate alcohol very well actually replaced wine with tea when they attended official drinking parties. A *Discourse on Tea and Wine* (Wang Zhongmin 1984) from the late Tang period pits Tea against Wine in a debate that allows each of them to argue and preach in favor of his own brotherhood. Wine calls himself more precious than his opponent and better able to combat death, whereas Tea accuses Wine of causing the ruin of families and prides himself on being a virtuous drink of beautiful color that clears away confusion. But in the end Wine and Tea make peace when Water reminds them that without her neither of them amounts to much and that they should get along, since tea often helps to dissipate the vapors of drunkenness. And it is true that infusions of tea were first used for medicinal purposes (Sealy 1958; Chen Chuan 1984). Tea, however, very quickly became much more than a mere remedy.

Part of its enormous success can be attributed to its commercial value both within and without the borders of China, in nearby regions, and throughout the world. Of the three stimulating beverages – coffee (from Ethiopia and Yemen), tea (from China), and cocoa (from the New World) – that the Europeans "discovered" in the late Renaissance, tea was the most widely disseminated and is still the most commonly consumed today. China gave us this custom of drinking tea, which also took root in Japan, Korea, and northern India. It should be noted that all of the tea consumed in western Europe was initially imported from China until the

British broke this monopoly by launching their highly successful tea plantations in Ceylon and India toward the end of the nineteenth century.

Sichuan was the cradle of the decoction of a bitter plant thought to be tea, which was probably first used toward the end of the Western Han period (206–23). The names employed at the time are still somewhat doubtful, but the plant was clearly *Camellia sinensis.* At that time tea was not infused but prepared in decoction, perhaps seasoned with salt, onions, ginger, or citrus peels, and its leaves were sometimes simmered in cooked dishes. Clearly this was a far cry from what we call "tea" today. Two factors are thought to have facilitated the spread of tea throughout China to its northernmost frontiers, beginning with the Sui (581–618) and the Tang (618–907). One is that tea soon came to be an item of tribute and, thus, became known and appreciated in court circles. The other has to do with the vigorous growth of Buddhism between the beginning of the Christian era and the Tang period. It is reported that tea was a great help to Buddhist monks, whose religion prohibited the drinking of "intoxicating" beverages like wine and whose practice of meditation demanded fasting and staying awake for many hours at a time. Tea plantations therefore followed the founding of Buddhist temples in the mountains.

Most would agree, however, that it was Lu Yu, author of the famous *Classic of Tea* (Carpenter 1974; Lu Yu 1990), who in the middle of the eighth century provided the Chinese culture of tea with its veritable birth certificate. The Tang period, moreover, marks the beginning of the "tea policy" adopted by the Chinese government. More or less successful, depending on the period, this policy, which lasted until the Qing period, regulated the monopoly, the tribute, and the taxation of tea and monitored an official trade in which tea was exchanged for "barbarian" horses on the country's northern and northeastern frontiers. Doubtless the vast scope of tea consumption and the potential profits of its cultivation played a decisive role in the elaboration of this policy. Lu Yu himself probably only codified and formally described the practices and the techniques peculiar to his time and to the literati. His work in three chapters was devoted to the origins, the cultivation, the processing, and the drinking of tea. It had enormous influence on the rise of the culture of tea, which developed not only in China but in Japan as well.

Lu Yu's work gave rise to an endless number of treatises that either followed in the same vein or provided more elaborate information. It is important to note that in China – unlike Japan, where tea was associated with a Zen discipline – the art of tea was always in the realm of practical "know-how," somewhat ritualized but only done so to encourage a more thorough enjoyment of life. Lu Yu explains the comparative merits of different beverages in perfectly straightforward terms: "To quench one's thirst, one should drink water; to dissipate sadness and anger,

one should drink wine; to drive away listlessness and sleepiness, one should drink tea" (Fu Shuqin and Ouyang Xun 1983: 37). But despite such straightforwardness, he insists that the processing, preparation, and drinking of tea must be done according to the rules, and he heaps scorn on those who, believing that they are drinking tea, settle for "stuff that has washed out of the rain spout" (Fu Shuqin and Ouyang Xun 1983: 37).

It goes without saying that although Lu Yu was sometimes worshiped as the "God of Tea," planters, processors, and lovers of the divine brew have gone beyond the master's instructions. As processing techniques evolved, they led to modifications in the preparation of tea and changes in the consumers' tastes. As early as the Tang period, "steam wilting" was discovered, a technique that made it possible to free the brew of its "green taste." Then, under the Song, planters began to wash the leaves before wilting them, and loose-leaf tea replaced the kind that had hitherto been pressed into "cakes" that had to be crumbled before being used in decoctions. In the early Ming period the growing taste for loose-leaf tea spelled the victory of infusions over decoctions. The leaves of *C. sinensis* were now mixed with fragrant flower petals whose scent is imparted to the infusion. Today the best known of these infusions is jasmine tea.

In the Tang period, several local teas had already acquired a great reputation, and by the Song period 41 kinds of tea were considered worthy of serving as tributes. Today there are three major types of Chinese teas: green tea, oolong tea, and black tea. Green tea, which is the kind most frequently consumed in China and Japan, is not made to undergo fermentation, whereas oolong tea, most popular in the southern provinces, is semifermented. Black teas, mainly produced for export, are called "fermented."

Drinking and serving tea today are such commonplace activities that they do not elicit any commentary. Wherever they might be, people can expect to find a thermos of boiling hot water, covered mugs, and tea leaves ready to be steeped. In any waiting or reception area, the visitor is offered tea. Tea is never drunk with the meal.[13] But when invited to share a meal, visitors are always received with a cup of tea. And this little offering is repeated to mark the end of the meal. On all such occasions this gesture must be made, whether or not the tea is actually drunk.

Every Chinese worker – blue or white collar – and every traveler carries a glass receptacle whose lid is tightly closed over some hot water in which a small handful of tea is steeping. In the course of the day more water is added and the liquid becomes paler and paler. This type of consumption, which in Taiwan is facilitated by automatic dispensers, is suited to the normal use of tea conceived as a mildly stimulating internal lubricant that will aid the digestion. The tea used throughout the day is usually of rather poor quality and in principle affordable for everyone. In lean times, the habit continues even without tea and people drink hot water, calling it "tea."

Along with such routine tea drinking in all parts of the country, the southern provinces have developed a veritable culture of tea. Every town or village has its "tea house," which can be quite modest, where people go to relax, to talk to their friends, and to share and comment on the latest news. These "tea parlors" have a long history in China. Indeed, those of the capitals of the northern and southern Song have become legendary thanks to the authors of the *Descriptions of the Capital* (Gernet 1962), who vaunted their lively and refined character.

In Canton and its region, however, and in Hong Kong, too, tea drinking is a more serious matter, as is everything that involves food. In Canton, the gastronomic capital of China, there are vast numbers of establishments that from morning until midafternoon offer tea lovers the opportunity to order a large pot of their favorite tea along with, if they choose, an incredible variety of "little dishes" – ravioli, fritters, dumplings, tartlets, pâtés, noodles, and so forth – all of them especially designed to accompany tea without overpowering its taste.

Françoise Sabban
(translated by Elborg Forster)

Notes

1. This assertion is according to the hallowed expression taken from the *History of the Han* (compiled in the first century of our era): *Wangzhe yi min wei tian, er min yi shi wei tian,* "The most important thing(s) in the world for the prince are his subjects, for whom nothing is more important than food."
2. In the food trade, a distinction is made between "fine cereals," *xiliang,* that is to say, rice and wheat, and "coarse cereals," *culiang,* meaning all the others. Counted among the latter are the tuberous vegetables, which are the mainstay of the diet in the poorest regions and in times of shortage.
3. To this list should be added sorghum, which can also be consumed as the mainstay of the diet when nothing else is available but which is generally used for the production of alcoholic beverages.
4. Until the Tang (618–907), North China, the cradle of Chinese civilization, imposed its values on the rest of the territory and hot and humid South China remained a neglected part of the huge empire, to cite Jacques Gernet (1962). But as a result of the continuous onslaught of nomadic barbarians from central Asia, who made increasing inroads on the great northern plain, the Yangtze Basin assumed ever greater importance. Under the Song, when South China had become conscious of its strength, it developed a refined urban civilization, which in turn gave birth to a genuine national cuisine based on the recognition of three major regional cuisines.
5. The Jürchet were a Tungusic tribe of the present Heilongjian Province in northeastern China who adopted the dynastic name of Jin in 1115. They were neighbors of the northern Song, with whom they concluded an alliance to attack the Liao empire. But they eventually turned on the

Song, whom they finally annexed when they conquered their capital of Kaifeng in 1126.
6. The present literature on Chinese cuisine contains a great many typologies of regional cuisines, but all of them are based on the historical division into four major zones. Certain specialists assign different culinary schools to eight geographic regions. In reality, each province lays claim to its own cuisine and every provincial publishing house has published works devoted to the cooking of its own provincial cuisine.
7. Here are two of the most typical flavor combinations of Sichuan: One is *yuxiang wei,* literally "fish flavor," which does not contain a single fish-based ingredient but consists of a mixture of chilli pepper, fermented broad bean paste, soy sauce, scallions, and so forth. The other is *mala wei,* literally "numbing hot flavor," which, consisting essentially of chilli pepper and fagara, or Sichuan pepper, is said to produce in the mouth a blended sensation of numbness, relaxation, and heat.
8. "Wok" is the Cantonese pronunciation of the word for this utensil, pronounced *huo* in standard Chinese. In North China this type of skillet is given another word, pronounced *guo.*
9. Today, this is often an automatic electric cooker.
10. This assertion holds except with respect to certain combinations of foods whose consumption during the same meal is not recommended for reasons of health. Works on diet, but also peasant calendars, contain lists of pernicious, that is, poisonous, "combinations" of foodstuffs, although not without indicating the corresponding antidotes. Their presence in calendars makes it seem likely that in addition to medical reasons, considerations of a magic and religious nature are also involved here.
11. See also the arguments of Chen Wenhau (1991), who advances the hypothesis that tofu was a much earlier invention dating back to the end of the Eastern Han period (25–220).
12. Although fully aware of the inadequacy of this choice, I shall here translate *jiu* as "wine" or "alcoholic beverage," as a matter of convenience. But it does seem better than the word "beer," which today designates a product that has nothing to do with the Chinese *jiu,* since it has always involved the use of malt. This is not the case for various Chinese *jiu,* which are produced by "combined fermentation" with ferments from cereal mashes. (In this connection see the essay by Ankei Takao 1986.) The few available recipes from the sixth century actually indicate that malt, though well known in China, was by that time used only to make "cereal sugars" or "maltoses."
13. One must be clear about what is called a "meal." An implicit classification defines the standard meal by its composition, namely, a staple cereal accompanied by its cooked dishes and often a light soup, and by the time at which it is eaten, essentially at noon and in the evening. If, in Guangdong, tea sometimes appears as part of a "snack" that might be considered a meal – for the "Cantonese breakfast" can be eaten any time between the morning and early afternoon – such a snack is really a matter of drinking tea and eating some accompanying dishes, even though it might take the place of a meal by virtue of the quantity of food and even the time when it is eaten.

Bibliography

Anderson, Eugene N. 1988. *The food of China.* New Haven, Conn., and London.
Ankei Takao. 1986. Discovery of SAKE in central Africa: Mold

fermented liquor of the Songola. *Journal d'Agriculture et de Botanique Appliquée* 33: 30.

Biot, Edouard, trans. 1851. *Rites des Tcheou,* Vol. 1. Paris.

Bray, Francesca. 1984. Part II: Agriculture. In *Science and civilisation in China,* ed. Joseph Needham. Vol. 6, *Biology and Biological Technology.* Cambridge and London.

Buck, John Lossing. 1956. *Land utilization in China.* . . . Facsimile reprint of vol. 1 of the original 1937 edition. New York.

Carpenter, Francis Ross, trans. 1974. *The classic of tea.* Boston, Mass., and Toronto.

Cartier, Michel. 1993. La marginalisation des animaux en Chine. *Anthropozoologica* 18: 7–16.

Chang K. C. 1977. Ancient China. In *Food in Chinese culture,* ed. K. C. Chang, 23–52. New Haven, Conn., and London.

Chen Chuan. 1984. *Chaye tongshi.* Beijing.

Chen Qiyou, ed. 1984. *Lüshi chunqiu jiaoshi,* Vol. 14. Shanghai.

Chen Wenhua. 1991. Doufu qiyuan yu heshi. *Nongye kaogu* 1: 245–8.

Couvreur, Séraphin, trans. 1950. *Mémoires sur les bienséances et les cérémonies. Li Ki* (Liji), 2 vols. Paris.

Du Shiran et al. 1982. *Zhongguo kejishu shigao,* Vol. 1. Beijing.

Elisseeff, Danielle. 1993. Des animaux sous une chape de plomb. *Anthropozoologica* 18: 17–28.

Epstein, Helmut. 1969. *Domestic animals of China.* Edinburgh.

Fu Shuqin and Ouyang Xun, eds. 1983. *Lu Yu chajing shizhu.* Hubei.

Gernet, Jacques. 1962. *Daily life in China in the eve of the Mongol invasion, 1250–1276,* trans. H. M. Wright. New York.

Ho Ping-ti. 1955. The introduction of American food plants into China. *American Anthropologist* 57: 191–201.

Hong Guangzhu. 1984. *Zhongguo shipin keji shi gao.* Beijing.
  1987. *Zhongguo doufu.* Beijing.

Knechtges, David R. 1986. A literary feast: Food in early Chinese literature. *Journal of the American Oriental Society* 106: 49–63.

Knightley, David N., ed. 1983. *The origins of Chinese civilization.* Berkeley, Calif.

Laufer, Berthold. 1919. Sino-Iranica: Chinese contributions to the history of civilization in ancient Iran. *Field Museum of Natural History, Anthropological Series* 15: 185–630.

Legge, James, trans. 1885. The Lî Kî. In *The sacred books of China,* Part 3, Oxford (The royal regulations, Sect. III/14).
  1893. Confucian analects. In *The Chinese classics,* Vol. 1. Oxford.

Lin Yin. 1985. *Zhouli jinzhu.* Beijing.

Lu Wenfu. 1983. *The gourmet,* trans. Yu Fanqin. Beijing.

Lu Yu. 1990. *Il canone del tè,* trans. Marco Ceresa. Milan.

Needham, Joseph. 1980. *Science and civilisation in China,* Vol. 5. Cambridge.

Pirazzoli-t'-Serstevens, Michèle. 1991. The art of dining in the Han period: Food vessels from tomb no. 1 at Mawangdui. *Food and Foodways* 3 and 4: 209–19.

Qiu Pangtong, ed. 1986. *Jujia biyong shilei quanji.* Beijing.

Sabban, Françoise. 1986a. Court cuisine in fourteenth-century imperial China: Some culinary aspects of Hu Sihui's *Yinshan Zhengyao. Food and Foodways* 2: 161–96.
  1986b. Un savoir-faire oublié: Le travail du lait en Chine ancienne. *Zinbun [Memoirs of the Research Institute for Humanistic Studies].* Kyoto, 21: 31–65.
  1988. Insights into the problem of preservation by fermentation in 6th-century China. In *Food Conservation. Ethnological Studies,* ed. A. Riddervold and A. Ropeid, 45–55. London.
  1990. De la main à la pâte: Réflexion sur l'origine des pâtes alimentaires et les transformations du blé en Chine ancienne (3e siècle av. J.-C.–6e siècle ap. J.-C.). *L'Homme* 31: 102–37.
  1993. La viande en Chine. Imaginaire et usages culinaires. *Anthropozoologica* 18: 79–90.

Sealy, Robert. 1958. *A revision of the genus Camellia.* London.

Shiba Yoshinobu. 1970. *Commerce and society in Sung China,* trans. Mark Elvin. Ann Arbor, Mich.

Shih Sheng-han. 1962. *A preliminary survey of the book "Ch'i Min Yao Shu," an agricultural encyclopaedia of the sixth century.* Beijing.

Shi Shenghan. 1982. *Qimin yaoshu jiaoshi.* Beijing.

Simoons, Frederick J. 1991. *Food in China: A cultural and historical inquiry.* Boca Raton, Fla.

Wang Shangdian, ed. 1987. *Zhongguo shipin gongye fazhan jianshi.* Taiyuan.

Wang Shixing. [1597] 1981. *Guangzhiyi.* Beijing.

Wang Zhongmin, ed. 1984. Chajiu lun. In *Dunhuang bianwenji.* Beijing.

Xu Zhen'e, ed. 1984. *Shishuo xinyu jiaojian,* Vol. 1. Beijing.

Yang Hsien Yi and Gladys Yang, trans. 1972. Kung I-chi. In *Selected stories of Lu Hsun.* Third edition. Beijing.

Yü Ying-shih. 1979. Han. In *Food in Chinese culture,* ed. K. C. Chang, 53–83. New Haven, Conn., and London.

Zheng, Chantal. 1989. *Mythes et croyances du monde chinois primitif.* Paris.

V.B.4 ☙ Japan

Rice and Staple Food

Rice has long been the main staple of the traditional Japanese diet. It is not only consumed daily as a staple food but also used to brew sake, a traditional alcoholic drink. Japanese cuisine has developed the art of providing side dishes to complement consumption of the staple food. Table manners were also established in the quest for more refined ways of eating rice and drinking sake at formal ceremonial feasts. The history of the Japanese diet, which is inseparable from rice, started therefore with the introduction of rice cultivation.

Subsistence during the Neolithic period in Japan (known as the Jōmon era, beginning about 12,000 years ago) was provided by hunting and gathering. Agriculture did not reach the Japanese archipelago until the very end of the Neolithic period. Collecting nuts (especially acorns and chestnuts) and hunting game were common activities, and a large variety of marine resources was intensively exploited throughout the period. The Jōmon era, however, ended with a shift from hunting and gathering to sedentary agriculture.

The Yangtze delta in China is considered to be the original source for the practice of rice cultivation in Japan. Continuous waves of migrants bearing knowledge of the technique reached Japan from the continent around 2,400 years ago via two major routes. One was through the Korean peninsula and the other was a direct sea route from China. Rice production techniques were accompanied by the use of metal tools, which provided high productivity and a stable supply. Population increased rapidly, and localized communities appeared in the following Yayoi era (1,700 to 2,400 years ago). Paddy-field rice cultivation was then under way except in the northern Ainu-dominated region of Hokkaido and in the southern Okinawa islands, an island chain between Kyūmshū (the southernmost main island of Japan) and Taiwan.

From the beginning of cultivation, only short-grain rice was known in Japan. Although long-grain rice was common in Southeast Asia and India, its absence from Japan caused the Japanese to develop prejudices about rice that persist until today. For them, rice means exclusively the short-grain variety; the long-grain type is regarded as inferior and unpalatable.

Traditionally, a meal consists of boiled plain rice, called *gohan* or *meshi,* and seasoned side dishes, called *okazu.* Cooked rice has always been the staple of a meal, so much so that the words *gohan* and *meshi* are used colloquially as synonyms for the word "meal." Side dishes complement rice consumption with their seasoned flavors, and as a rule, the sophistication and variety of such dishes has betokened the affluence of those who served them.

Peasants living in mountain areas with low rice productivity, along with poor people in general, formerly mixed millet with rice. The sweet potato, introduced in the eighteenth century, also became popular as a staple in the south of Japan, where it supplemented a low yield of rice. However, even the poor cooked pure boiled rice and pounded rice cake from pure glutinous rice for important meals. Pounded rice cakes *(mochi),* prepared by pounding steamed glutinous rice with a mortar and pestle, have been indispensable food items for Japanese ceremonial feasts. People thought that the essence – the sacred power of rice – was made purer by pounding, and *mochi* was believed to contain the "spirit of rice." Naturally this was and is the most celebrated form of rice and therefore the most appropriate food for feasts. Thus, New Year's day, the principal annual feast in Japan, sees *mochi* always consumed as a ceremonial food.

In a census record of 1873, nutritional information for the Hida Region (Gife Prefecture, Central Honsyū) shows that rice was the most important food, notwithstanding the general unsuitability of the area for the crop's cultivation (Koyama et al. 1981: 548–51). The same data reveal a typical daily intake of nutriments for premodern Japanese people. The recorded population of this mountainous region was about 90,000, and these people are thought to have maintained the highest dependency in Japan on millet as a rice substitute. The average daily energy intake per capita was 1,850 kilocalories (kcal) (in 1980 it was 2,600 kcal), of which 55 percent was supplied by rice, which also supplied 39 percent of the protein.

Both rice and millet, when served as a staple, have always been either boiled or steamed. Milling, however, was not developed generally, and processed powder was used only for cakes or snacks and not for bread. Later, noodle products made from the powder became popular. The oldest form of the noodles, *sakubei,* produced by adding rice powder to flour, was introduced from China in the eighth century.

Noodles made from flour as a light lunch or snack became popular during the fourteenth and fifteenth centuries, and consumption increased considerably after the seventeenth century, when a processing technique for buckwheat noodles *(soba)* was developed in Edo, now Tokyo. Since then, *soba* has become popular mainly in eastern Japan, where Tokyo is located, whereas *udon* noodles (made from flour) have always been popular in western Japan (Ishige 1991a).

Meat and Fish

A unique feature of Japanese dietary history has been the country's various taboos on meat eating. The first recorded decree prohibiting the eating of cattle, horses, dogs, monkeys, and chickens was issued by Emperor Temmu in A.D. 675. Similar decrees, based on the Buddhist prohibition of killing, were issued repeatedly by emperors during the eighth and ninth centuries. The number of regulated meats increased to the point that all mammals were included except whales, which, given their marine habitat, were categorized as fish.

The taboo against the consumption of animal flesh developed further when the Japanese aboriginal religion, Shintō, adopted a philosophy similar to that of the Buddhists. This did not mean, however, that meat eating was totally banned in Japan. Professional hunters in mountain regions ate game (especially deer and wild boar), and it was not uncommon for hunted bird meat to be consumed. However, a lack of animal breeding for meat kept its consumption very low. Indeed, it was only during the fifteenth century and its aftermath that the tradition of eating both the meat and eggs of domestic fowl was revived. Fowls, until then, had been regarded in Shintō as God's sacred messengers and were reared to announce the dawn rather than as a mere food resource.

Milk and other dairy products failed to become popular in Japan, China, and Korea. In fact, the only Japanese dairy product known to history was *so,* produced between the eighth and fourteenth centuries. Milk was boiled down to yield this semisolid product. But even this food, consumed at the court and among the noble class, disappeared as a result of the demise of the aristocracy. Cattle were raised only for drawing carts or plowing fields. To utilize them for meat or even for milk was, until relatively recently, a long-forgotten practice.

Lack of meat and dairy products in the Japanese diet produced an aversion to oily tastes, so that even vegetable oil was not commonly used for cooking. Tempura, fish or vegetables fried in a vegetable oil, is one of the best-known Japanese dishes today, but it became popular only after the mid-eighteenth century.

The lack of meat products also minimized spice utilization. Pepper and cloves were known from the eighth century and were imported either via China or directly from Southeast Asia, and garlic was also grown on a small scale. But these spices were used mainly to make medicines and cosmetics.

In the coastal seas of Japan, warm and cold currents mix to provide bountiful fishing grounds. This favorable natural environment and the traditional exclusion of fish from the meat taboo meant an extensive exploitation of marine resources. The Japanese developed a special liking for fish, and most people enjoyed a variety, although consumption was still largely forbidden for Buddhist monks.

Fish dishes, with a higher status as well as a more attractive taste than vegetable dishes, were formerly considered indispensable at feasts. However, before the introduction of modern delivery systems, the difficulty of preserving and transporting fresh marine fish minimized consumption in inland areas where freshwater fish were commonly eaten instead.

The basic concept of fish preparation in Japan is suggested by the following proverb: "Eat it raw first of all, then grill it, and boil it as the last resort." To amplify, it is felt that the taste and texture of fish is best appreciated when it is very fresh and eaten raw. If the fish is a little less than fresh then its best taste will be produced by sprinkling it with salt and grilling it. If the fish is not fresh, then it is better boiled with seasonings, such as soy sauce *(shoyu)* or soybean paste (miso).

The consumption of fish raw has been traditional since ancient times. *Namasu,* or the eating of thinly sliced raw fish dipped in a sauce with a vinegar base, is a typical example. However, the better-known sashimi has been popular only since the seventeenth century – its popularity increasing as the general consumption of soy sauce increased. Delicately sliced raw fish of the utmost freshness and quality is eaten after being dipped in soy sauce flavored with a small amount of grated wasabi *(Wasabia japonica),* which is similar to horseradish.

As a rule, the philosophy of cooking aims at the creation of new tastes that do not exist naturally – such creation is a result of imposing artificial processes on food materials. But Japanese cooking methods are antithetical to this philosophy. The ideal of Japanese cooking is to retain the natural tastes of food with the minimum of artificial processes. Thus sashimi, for example, can be viewed as a representative product of the Japanese cooking philosophy.

Nigiri-sushi, prepared by putting a slice of raw fish onto a bite-size portion of hand-rolled, vinegar-flavored rice, has recently become internationally popular. But sushi originated as a means of preserving fish by fermenting it in boiled rice. Fish that are salted and placed in rice are preserved by lactic acid fermentation, which prevents proliferation of the bacteria that bring about putrefaction. A souring of flavor occurs during the process, and the fish is eaten only after the sticky decomposed rice has been cleaned off.

This older type of sushi is still produced in the areas surrounding Lake Biwa in western Japan, and similar types are also known in Korea, southwestern China, and Southeast Asia. In fact, the technique first originated in a preservation process developed for freshwater fish caught in the Mekong River and is thought to have diffused to Japan along with the rice cultivation.

A unique fifteenth-century development shortened the fermentation period of sushi to one or two weeks and made both the fish and the rice edible. As a result, sushi became a popular snack food, combining fish with the traditional staple food, rice. Sushi without fermentation appeared during the Edo period (1600–1867), and sushi was finally united with sashimi at the end of the eighteenth century, when the hand-rolled type, *nigiri-sushi,* was devised. Various styles of hand-rolled sushi were developed, such as *norimaki,* in which vinegar-flavored rice and seasoned boiled vegetables are rolled in paper-thin layers. In addition, sushi restaurants became popular during this era. They offered ready-made rice prepared with vinegar and other seasonings and rolled with different toppings according to the taste of the guests. In this manner, sushi has changed from its original character as a preserved food to that of a fast food (Ishige and Ruddle 1990: 21–94).

Vegetable Food

In daily meals, vegetables have generally constituted the main ingredients of side dishes and soups accompanying rice. Among these vegetables are a variety of sea plants that have been utilized since ancient times and remain a unique feature of Japanese cooking even today. Sea plants are usually dried and soaked in water before cooking. Sea tangle has been the most important of all. It is commonly used to prepare broth, and owing to its rich content of glutamic acid, it enhances the original taste of the foodstuffs with which it is boiled.

Traditionally, salted vegetables have been an indispensable part of the daily diet of even the poorest classes of people. Some several hundred varieties of salted vegetables are known in Japan; however, the method of pickling common in the West, using vinegar, has not developed there.

Of all beans, the soybean is the most significant. It is a good source of vegetable protein, and its importance in the Japanese diet is surpassed only by that of rice. Varieties of soya in a processed state, such as tofu and *nattō,* have played an extremely prominent dietary role over the ages. Tofu, or soybean curd, which diffused from China and is first mentioned in Japan in an eleventh-century document, has been one of the most widespread of the processed foods. A cookbook providing 100 different recipes for tofu cooking was published in 1782 and became so popular that a second volume, containing another 138 recipes, was issued the following year. Many of these recipes were devised by Buddhist monks, who abstained from eating meat for doctrinal reasons and relied heavily on tofu as a source of protein.

Bacillus subtilis bacteria, which grow on rice straw, are cultivated on boiled soybeans to produce *nattō. Nattō* has a unique sticky consistency and is usually seasoned with soy sauce and mustard before eating; minced *nattō* is used as an ingredient of soybean-paste soup. *Nattō* contains abundant protein and vitamin B_2 and has been popular as a breakfast food because it is easily digestible.

Vegetarian diets, or *shōjin-ryōri,* rely on a variety of foods processed from soybeans. These include tofu, *abura-age* (fried tofu), *kōri-dōfu* (freeze-dried tofu), and *yuba* (paper-thin processed tofu), as well as mushrooms, sea plants, sesame, walnuts, and, of course, vegetables. *Fu,* which is produced by condensing wheat gluten, has also been a popular foodstuff. *Shōjin-ryōri* has generally been served during periods of mourning, for Buddhist rituals, and on the anniversary of the death of close kin.

From a dietetic point of view, the Japanese vegetarian diet is both well balanced and quite rational. It supplies protein from tofu and similar products, fat from sesame, walnuts, and vegetable oil, vitamins from vegetables, and minerals from sea plants. Such a diet not only is nutritious but also offers many palatable recipes, which have been refined by such techniques as employing a broth made from dried sea tangle and mushrooms as a base for cooking. Vegetable oils, which are extensively used, were especially developed by those Zen Buddhist monks who had maintained contacts with China.

Seasonings and Flavorings

Because of an absence of rock salt in Japan, salt made from seawater has been prevalent since the Neolithic era. But a salty residue fermented from soybeans has traditionally been used as a basic and versatile seasoning in Japan (as well as in China and Korea). Miso (soybean paste) and *shōyu* (soy sauce), the two major products of this residue, have been used to season boiled dishes and as ingredients in the preparation of various sauces.

Of the *kōji* fungi that are employed as starters for soybean fermentation, *Aspergillus oryzae,* which grows on rice grains, is the most common. The fermented products of soybeans were first recorded in

a law book called the *Taihō-ritsuryō,* compiled in A.D. 702. But it is known that by that time a type of miso was already being produced, using a technique thought to have been introduced from Korea. The indigenous Japanese processing method, which employs artificially cultivated starters like *kōji* and combines soybeans with rice and barley, was devised later. It differs from the Korean method, which relies on natural bacteria in the air to ferment pure soybeans, to which salt is added.

The traditional Japanese method of processing miso is to mash boiled or steamed beans while the *kōji* fungus is cultured on boiled or steamed rice or barley. All these ingredients are then mixed together with salt and placed in a container. After a maturation period of more than a year, the mixture changes into miso, a pastelike substance. The liquid that oozes out in the maturation container is sometimes used as a type of soy sauce. Other types of miso are also made; these all vary by region in processing techniques.

Similarly, the general method of processing *shōyu* (soy sauce) is to culture *kōji* fungus on pounded, preparched wheat grains and then to mix this with boiled beans and a large amount of salt water in a maturation container. The mixture is stirred occasionally, and fermentation is completed within three or four months. During the maturation period following fermentation, the contents intensify in color and flavor, owing to chemical reactions among the ingredients. After one year of maturation, the liquid obtained by squeezing the contents is pasteurized and becomes *shōyu.* As with miso, *shōyu* also has many regional varieties.

The use of the liquid by-product of miso processing as a seasoning has been known for a long time, but commercial production of *shōyu* dates only from the sixteenth century. Propagation of recipes from major cities where *shōyu* was employed extensively during the Edo period gave *shōyu* national status as a seasoning, and more than 70 percent of present-day Japanese recipes employ it in some way. In contrast to *shōyu,* miso has decreased in importance as a seasoning for both boiled dishes and sauces, and its daily use has generally been restricted to soup.

Rice is employed to make the traditional Japanese vinegar. In addition, a type of sake with a strong sweet taste, called *mirin* (which is processed in a slightly different way from the usual brew), serves as a cooking wine.

Another unique feature of Japanese food culture is the extensive development of dried foods for the preparation of soup stock (broth), or *dashi.* Dried sea tangle *(konbu),* dried bonito *(katsuo-bushi),* and dried brown mushrooms *(shiitake)* are some examples. They are not only used for *dashi* but also often added to boiling vegetables.

Katsuo-bushi, or dried bonito, is produced by boiling the fish, after which it is heat-dried and cooled. This process is repeated more than 10 times until the water content of the fish is reduced to less than 20 percent and the surface is covered by "tar." The covering of "tar" and fat is scraped off and the remaining meat is placed in a wooden box and left for two weeks to propagate an artificially planted fungus of the genus *Aspergillus*. After two weeks the surface is cleaned, and the fungus-planting process is repeated four more times.

At completion, a majority of the remaining contents are protein and flavor essence. Water content is reduced to 15 percent of the original, and the final product, *katsuo-bushi,* appears dry and hard like a block of wood. The fungus-planting process, which yields a better flavor and helps extract the water, was invented in the seventeenth century, although the rest of the process has been known since ancient times.

When used, small amounts of very thin flakes of *katsuo-bushi* are shaved from the block with a specially designed plane, then placed in boiling water to extract their flavor. When the water is strained it becomes a pure soup stock, and the flakes are usually discarded except in rare cases when they are combined with soy sauce to prepare a salty side dish. *Konbu* and *shiitake* are similarly boiled to prepare soup stocks yielding their particular flavors.

Dried foods for making *dashi* were developed essentially to add subtle and enhancing flavors to traditional dishes that consisted mainly of vegetables with little intrinsic taste. But the traditional interest in such products led Japanese scientists to conduct chemical analyses of their flavors. The analyses found that inosinic acid from *katsuo-bushi,* monosodium glutamate from *konbu,* and guanylic acid from *shiitake* were the sources of their natural tasty flavors. This research was the forerunner of Japan's modern natural and artificial flavor research industry.

Table Manners and Tableware

As is the case in China and Korea, Japanese food is usually served in sizes suitable for picking up by chopsticks, the use of which is thought to have been introduced from China in the seventh century. That the Japanese ate with the fingers prior to the introduction of chopsticks was recorded by a Chinese mission in the early third century. Spoons, however, although common in China and Korea, did not catch on in Japan, perhaps because the habit of sipping soup from handheld wooden bowls made the use of spoons superfluous. Japan's abundant forest resources meant that wooden tableware was more readily available than ceramic ware, and a wooden bowl can be more comfortably held than a ceramic or metal one.

Traditionally, only lacquered wooden ware was used for formal feasts. Chinaware remained unpopular until the seventeenth century, when mass production became possible as a result of new manufacturing techniques learned from Korea. The more widespread use of china caused a functional division between wooden and chinaware to evolve for daily use. Chinaware was used for rice and side dishes, whereas boiling hot soup was served in wooden lacquered bowls.

As a rule, every individual has his or her own chopsticks and a set of tableware. An extra set of chopsticks is used to serve food from a communal food vessel to each individual vessel. If extra chopsticks are not provided with the communal food vessel, then individuals reverse their own chopsticks and use them to transfer food to their own vessels. This practice, however, reflects more a psychological cleanliness derived from Shintoism (in order to prevent one's spoiled spirit from passing to others through shared foods) than it does practical sanitary concerns.

No chairs were used in Japan before the general adoption of dining tables in the latter half of the twentieth century. Diners sat either on tatami (straw mats) or on the wooden floor. Vessels containing food were served on a small, low, portable table called a *zen.* Usually, each dish was set on a *zen* in the kitchen and then brought to and placed in front of the diner. Several *zen* tables were used for each person at a formal feast, as the numerous separate dishes could not all be placed on just one. The number of small tables at a feast consequently became a standard for evaluating the event as well as the host. One unique feature of a Japanese meal is that all the dishes are served simultaneously. The only exceptions are meals served as part of a tea ceremony, in which dishes arrive in an orderly manner one after the other.

As a diner's personal table is very low, vessels containing food are handheld and lifted close to the mouth, to which the food is delivered with chopsticks. When sipping soup it is not considered bad manners to make a slurping sound. Modern Japanese table manners, for the most part, originated at the formal feasts of the samurai warrior class during the sixteenth and seventeenth centuries. From these feasts evolved the rituals and complicated manners for using tableware and chopsticks that are still commonly practiced today.

A big change, however, has occurred in the traditional table setting during the twentieth century. During the first half of the century, a larger portable table called *cyabu-dai,* on which there is space enough to place all the diners' dishes, gradually replaced the traditional personal table. Family members sat on tatami mats and surrounded the dining table for their daily meals. But the biggest change has been the increasing use of Western-style tables and chairs in ordinary households during the last few decades. This has drastically westernized Japanese dining settings: About 70 percent of all households now use a table and chairs for meals (Ishige 1991b).

Tea and Liquor

The first record of tea in Japan mentions an offering of prepared tea to the Emperor Saga, in A.D. 815, by a Buddhist monk who had studied in China. This particular tea was prepared by pounding a roasted block of compacted tea leaves into powder and then boiling it in water. The emperor became fond of it and ordered the planting of tea trees. Tea drinking quickly became fashionable among the aristocracy but, for some unknown reason, lost popularity in the tenth century. The taste and flavor may have been too strong for the Japanese palate at that time.

In the thirteenth century, tea drinking again became a popular custom as a result of the reintroduction of the tree, on the one hand, and on the other a new method of tea preparation, brought from China by a Buddhist monk called Yōsai. Yōsai's book, which recommended tea as healthful, caused a strong revival of interest in tea drinking among aristocrats and monks, and the popularity of tea has continued undiminished until the present. After its reintroduction, steamed tea sprouts were dried and then ground to produce powder, which was mixed with boiling water in a tea bowl, a method basically the same as that which continues today as the tea ceremony.

The tea ceremony, or *cha-dou*, was established in the sixteenth century by Rikyu, who refined the custom to an aesthetic form based on Zen philosophy. It was an attempt to create an aesthetic whole, unifying architecture, gardening, fine arts, crafts, religion, philosophy, literature, food preparation, and presentation. The meal that accompanies the ceremony, called *kaiseki-ryōri*, has come to be regarded as the most refined form of cuisine and is still served in the best Japanese restaurants today.

The drinking of powdered tea, however, did not achieve general popularity owing to the intricate preparation and drinking etiquette required. Even today it is limited to the tea ceremony or other special occasions. The popular green tea is a leaf-type tea, or *sen-cha*, which is prepared by pouring boiling water on dried tea leaves in a teapot. Neither milk nor sugar are added. Drinking of this type of tea started in China during the Ming dynasty, and in the seventeenth century was introduced to Japan, where it became a custom widespread throughout the population and, thus, was incorporated into the Japanese way of life. People who had drunk only hot water prior to the introduction of tea now finished meals with it, had tea breaks, and served tea to welcome guests. That this tradition has survived is evident in the free tea service still offered in virtually every Japanese restaurant.

Only in recent times have alcoholic drinks such as wine or beer (produced by the saccharification of cereal germination) existed in Japan. The oldest-known such beverage, mentioned in eighth-century literature, utilized the starch saccharification potential of saliva. Raw or boiled rice was chewed and expectorated into a container where it mixed with saliva. This primitive technique survived until the beginning of the twentieth century in Okinawa. By tradition, virgins prepared this type of liquor for special religious ceremonies. Another practice – that of applying *kōji* fungus to rice as an initiator of fermentation (introduced from China) – has also been in general use since ancient times.

Rice wine or sake, which was homemade by farmers, is a result of the alcoholic fermentation of a simple mixture of steamed rice, *kōji*, and water. Professional brewers would prepare sake by adding low-alcohol sake to newly mixed steamed rice and *kōji* without previous filtering. This process causes saccharification and alcoholic fermentation at the same time and increases the alcoholic strength of the mixture. In contemporary commercial production, such a process is repeated three times to increase the amount of alcohol to nearly 20 percent. The mixture is then placed in a cloth bag and squeezed with a press. The pasteurization of the clear liquid from the press is the last part of the process.

The latter technique was first mentioned in A.D. 1568, in the *Tamonin-nikki*, the diary of a Buddhist monk, indicating its practice in Japan some 300 years before Louis Pasteur. In China, the first country in East Asia to develop the technique, the earliest record of the process dates from A.D. 1117 (Yoshida 1991).

Today, sake is normally served by warming it to nearly 50 degrees centigrade in a china bottle immersed in boiling water, after which it is poured into a small ceramic cup. This popular procedure began in the seventeenth century, although at that time hot sake was regarded as appropriate only in autumn and winter.

Shōchū, a traditional distilled liquor first mentioned in a sixteenth-century record, uses rice, sake lees, or sweet potatoes as a base material. A similar distillate from Okinawa, *awamori*, employs rice exclusively. In this case, the production technique is thought to have been diffused from Thailand in the fifteenth century, but the true forerunner of Japanese *shōchū* has yet to be firmly identified. One theory regards Okinawa and its *awamori* as the origin, whereas another insists that China was the source. We do know that *shōchū* was produced mainly in southern Kyūshū and Okinawa, where the hot climate made the brewing of good-quality sake difficult, and the liquor has been consistently consumed there since the Edo period. In other regions, *shōchū* has been regarded as a drink for the lower classes, who wanted a stronger (and cheaper) beverage than the more expensive sake.

Establishing Traditional Food Culture

As already mentioned, since the introduction of rice cultivation, various foods and their processing or cooking techniques have reached Japan from both China and Korea. In addition, European foods, brought by Portuguese traders and missionaries, started to flow into Japan between the late fifteenth and the early seventeenth centuries. But European styles of cooking, which mainly used meat, were not accepted by the mostly Buddhist Japanese, who were banned from eating meat by religious decree. Nonetheless, Western desserts and sweet snacks were welcomed, and some of the techniques of preparing these were adopted locally and still survive today. A typical example is a sponge cake called *kasutera* that derived from the Portuguese *bolo de Castelo,* a cake from the Castelo region of Portugal (Etchū 1982: 78–9).

Fearing that the propagation of Christianity by Western missionaries was merely a pretext to disguise Western attempts to colonize Japan, the Tokugawa Shogunate banned Christianity and closed the country to outsiders in 1639. The resulting near-total isolation from the rest of the world, lasting until 1854, brought domestic peace during the Edo period (named for the Shogunate's city). Domestic social stability, combined with isolation, tended to lend an unchanging quality to Japanese culture, including the culture of food. Indeed, most traditional dishes served in homes and restaurants today had their origins in the Edo period.

During the Edo period, Japanese food culture was developed and refined among wealthy urban middle-class merchants and artisans. This was a situation much different from that of many other countries, the food cultures of which, including styles of cooking, preparation techniques, table settings, and manners, were first developed and refined in the social life of the court and aristocracy before they diffused to the general society. But the Imperial Court in Kyoto had only a symbolic status at that time, with little political, economic, or social influence. The warrior class that supported the shogunate administration adopted the ritualized court cuisine of former times, which placed great emphasis on an intricate etiquette of food consumption, rather than on the food itself. The ruling class that regulated its members through ascetic morals had little interest in developing better or different flavors and tastes in their cuisine, whereas the majority of the peasants lived in poverty and were scarcely able to sustain themselves on the meanest of foods.

Wealthy merchants controlled (at least economically) Edo society, and Japanese haute cuisine restaurants came into being about the middle of the eighteenth century to cater to them. These restaurants were mostly located in the three major cities of Edo, Osaka, and Kyoto, and were similar to those established in Paris for the French bourgeoisie. With their superb interior decorations and ornamental gardens, such restaurants made every effort to serve refined, palatable dishes that were utterly different from those offered at the formal banquets of the court and the warrior class. The new and innovative recipes and food preparation techniques gradually spread to influence eating habits nationwide and ultimately became the core of today's traditional Japanese cuisine.

The emphasis on aesthetic food presentation in contemporary Japanese cuisine also originated in these restaurants with presentation devices of *kaiseki-ryōri.* The Japanese philosophy of food presentation seeks to reflect the Japanese view of nature in the elimination of anything artificial from the plate. Thus, symmetrical presentation, for example, is the antithesis of this philosophy, which would rather have imbalance and a blank space on a plate. This approach provides an elegant appearance, whereas to cover a whole plate with various foods is considered vulgar, even though it gives an affluent impression at first glance. Conceptually similar to an empty space in an India ink oriental painting, this deliberately proportioned space becomes an integral part of the art of food presentation. The representation of a season of the year in the display of a dish (by utilizing specific materials such as bonito fish in May or the taro potato in August – both lunar months) is also an important dimension of this philosophy.

Along with the haute cuisine restaurants, inexpensive eating houses and pubs for craftsmen and store employees also appeared in big cities. Not only did various noodles, along with sushi and tempura, become popular snacks in these eating houses, but other specialty restaurants and stalls serving only specific items proliferated. One *soba* shop and two sushi shops to a block was a common sight in the center of Edo, even in the eighteenth century, and according to the 1804 census, 6,165 eating houses existed in the city. This meant that there was one eating house for every 170 persons in the population, not counting peddlers' stalls and eating houses in the red-light district, which were excluded from the census. Another record (which again excluded peddlers' stalls) shows that in 1860, representatives of 3,763 *soba* shops from all over Edo held a meeting to discuss raising prices to meet the increased cost of ingredients.

Restaurant guidebooks for urban gourmets and visitors from the country became popular from the late eighteenth century, corresponding to the rapid increase of dining-out facilities in big cities. Indeed, there were urban bourgeoisie who enjoyed restaurant hunting in Japanese cities with help from guidebooks nearly a century before the publication of the *Michelin Guide* in France (Ishige 1990). Cookbook publication was also brisk, with about 130 originals and several hundred later editions of the originals known to have been printed.

Modernization of Foods

The Meiji Restoration, which put an end to the Tokugawa Shogunate in 1868, gave expression to the need for rapid social modernization. The government-led industrial revolution introduced Western technology and culture and developed a capitalistic economy with the ultimate goal of enriching and strengthening the Japanese nation in the world. A change of eating habits, which occurred in accordance with social improvements, can be seen in government encouragement of meat eating and milk drinking so as to make the physique of Japanese people comparable to that of Western people.

The change began with a public report in 1872, which mentioned that Emperor Meiji enjoyed beef dishes. Following this declaration, it became a custom of the court to entertain international guests with formal dinner parties at which French cuisine was served, and the traditional taboo against meat eating disappeared rather quickly. The first popular meat dish was boiled, thinly sliced meat served with tofu and leeks. It was seasoned with soy sauce and sugar and later became known as sukiyaki. Yet Western cuisine in general was reserved for special occasions and was prepared exclusively by professional chefs; thus, although the number of Western restaurants in big cities increased, Western cuisine was not commonly adopted in Japanese homes for a long time to come.

Milk drinking, although introduced by resident Westerners and repeatedly praised as nutritious by the government, met nonetheless with stubborn resistance from a general public unwilling to accept it as part of the normal diet. Indeed, until the mid-twentieth century, milk was regarded as either a medicine or a special health drink for the sick or persons of weak constitution. Except for canned condensed milk, welcomed by nursing mothers as a supplement to breast milk, few people adopted the custom of consuming dairy products (such as butter and cheese) before the general introduction of bread as a breakfast food in the 1960s. Yet even in the present, the limited consumption of dairy products in the home is another of the features that set Japanese eating habits apart from those of other developed countries.

It is interesting to note that although Western cuisine became progressively more popular after the Meiji Restoration, Chinese cuisine was largely ignored, even though it shared with Japanese cuisine a common food element (rice) and eating method (chopsticks) and had long influenced Japanese food culture. Western cuisine was regarded as a symbol of modernization, whereas the late nineteenth century Japanese victory in the Sino-Japanese War over Korea strengthened contempt for the Chinese people and their culture. Such factors delayed the Japanese patronage of Chinese restaurants until the 1920s, though there were many such restaurants in Japan, catering to Chinese merchants and students. The Japanese maintained a similar prejudice against Korean cuisine, arrogantly disregarding the culture of a people whom they had annexed. But also at the time, the spicy flavor of Korean food created by the use of garlic and pepper was contrary to the traditional plain taste of Japanese food. Korean barbecues and pickles have, however, subsequently become common in Japanese homes.

The production of beer and wine began in the early Meiji era. Beer, despite its bitter and unfamiliar taste, soon became popular, while sake drinking also continued. The government tried to promote a wine industry for export, but the project was destroyed by phylloxera, which raged through European vineyards at that time and reached Japan in 1884 via imported vine stock. After the devastation, only artificially sweetened wine, consumed as a nourishment for the sick or by people of weak constitution, was produced – and this on a small scale. However, quite recently a resumption of domestic table wine production has occurred in Japan to meet a demand that has increased since the 1970s. This development has paralleled Japanese economic growth and with it a growth of interest in European and Californian wines. But although wine was unpopular until recently, by the 1920s beer, whiskey, coffee, and black tea were regularly drunk at an increasing number of bars, beerhouses, cafés, and teahouses in the big cities.

The modernization of Japanese food culture after the Meiji Restoration was interrupted by the rise of militarism and World War II. Following the Manchurian incident of 1931, 15 years of war and large-scale mobilizations, along with trade sanctions by Western nations, caused food imports to decline severely and slowed domestic agricultural production as well. Consequently, major food items, including meat and dairy products, were rationed under government control. Even fish was in short supply as war destroyed the fishing industry, and a return to the traditional meal of rice with vegetable side dishes was strongly encouraged by the government.

As the war progressed, even the minimum food ration could not be distributed regularly, and malnutrition became a serious problem. People were forced to supplement their rations by growing sweet potatoes (as a rice substitute) and other vegetables in home gardens; even after the defeat in 1945, it took 10 years for the nation to regain its prewar level of agricultural output. However, as a result of the rapid growth of the Japanese economy since the 1960s, diets previously concentrated on carbohydrates and poor in fat and animal protein have greatly improved. As foreign foods and styles of cooking have been embraced for cooking in the home, with their original tastes altered to conform with Japanese preferences, a large-scale fusion of foreign and traditional cuisines has taken place.

Thus, annual per capita rice consumption, which reached a maximum of 171 kilograms (kg) in 1962, has since declined and has remained at around 70 kg since the late 1980s. The consumption of sweet potatoes and barley as rice substitutes has declined drastically, and only a few people still eat them regularly. Such traditional carbohydrate foods have been largely supplanted by bread, which school-lunch programs made popular. These programs served bread made from American flour to schoolchildren. The flour had been received as food aid during the postwar food shortage.

Today, about 30 percent of the adult population

eats bread for breakfast, but very few people eat bread at lunch or dinner. In contrast with the laborious preparation needed for rice, timesaving bread is suitable for the breakfast needs of a developing urban society in which many people commute and so have less time for meals.

Although there has been a rapid increase in the consumption of previously rare foods, such as meat, eggs, dairy products, and fats, the consumption of traditional foods, like fish and vegetables, has also increased. People in Japan no longer maintain the attitude that meals are merely a source of energy for labor and that a staple food is the most efficient source of such energy. Now people enjoy the meal itself through the various tastes of side dishes, and a greater emphasis on side dishes than on staple foods has kept pace with increases in the national income.

A large variety of foreign foods and cuisines are now part of the household menu. But they have become popular only as it was determined that their flavors complement rice, soy sauce, green tea, and so on. Moreover, their tastes and preparation have often been adapted to moderate flavors, and their size or form has been arranged for use with chopsticks. In other words, such modifications should be viewed as part of an expansion of Japanese eating habits and cuisine, rather than a headlong adoption of foreign dietary patterns.

The Japanese intake of the chief nutrients reached an almost ideal level by the end of the 1970s, except for a little too much salt and a lack of calcium. The general physique has improved accordingly and the average life span has become the longest in the world. This ideal situation, however, may not continue long, as the generation now being raised in this affluent society on a high-protein diet may later pay a stiff price in geriatric diseases as a result of overnutrition – a problem that is becoming acute in other developed nations.

Naomichi Ishige

Bibliography

Etchū, Tetsuya. 1982. *Nagasaki no seiyō ryōri-yōshoku no yoake.* Tokyo.
Ishige, Naomichi. 1990. Développement des restaurants Japonais pendant la périod Edo (1603-1867). In *Les restaurants dans le monde et à trâvers les ages,* ed. A. H. de Lamps and Jean-Robert Pitte. Paris.
  1991a. *Bunka menruigaku kotohajime.* Tokyo.
  1991b. Shokutaku bunkaron. In *Bulletin of the National Museum of Ethnology,* Special Issue No. 16: 3-51.
Ishige, Naomichi, and Kenneth Ruddle. 1990. *Gyoshō to narezushi no kenkyū.* Tokyo.
Koyama, Shūzō, et al. 1981. Hidagofudoki ni yoru shokuryōshigen no keiryōteki kenkyū. In *Bulletin of the National Museum of Ethnology* 6 (3): 363-596.
Yoshida, Hajime. 1991. *Nihon no shoku to sake - chūsei matsu no hakkōgijutsu wo chūsin ni.* Kyoto.

V.B.5 ❧ Korea

Historical Background

If the history of a dietary culture is, in many ways, the history of a people, then the evolution of Korea's dietary traditions clearly reflects that nation's turbulent history. Geography and environment play a decisive role in determining the foundation of a nation's dietary culture, whereas complex political, economic, and social conditions and interactions with other cultures contribute to further development.

Traditional dietary strategies must balance the need for sufficient calories and specific nutrients with the need to avoid or minimize diseases associated with foods that are contaminated, spoiled, or otherwise unhealthy. An account of traditional diets should, therefore, deal with food- and waterborne diseases as well as with typical foods and cooking methods. Once dietary habits and food preferences have been established, they become a central part of the culture and are highly resistant to change.

It is not uncommon, however, to find that in the course of exchanges between cultures, foreign foods have become so thoroughly adapted to local conditions that their origins are quite forgotten. In a rapidly changing and interdependent world, it is important to understand the historical background of traditional diets and the impact of modernization in order to maintain and develop dietary strategies that balance cherished traditions with new circumstances. An understanding of the traditional foods of Korea, therefore, requires a brief overview of Korean geography and history.

Korea occupies the mountainous peninsula south of Manchuria; the Yellow Sea separates Korea from mainland China to the west. Japan is only 206 kilometers (km) away across the southern Korea Straits. Because of its strategic location, Korea has a history that has been intimately linked to developments in China, Japan, and other Asian countries. The total size of the peninsula is about that of the state of New York. It was artificially divided along the 38th parallel as the result of World War II and the Korean War, with the area of the northern zone about 122,370 square kilometers (sq km) and that of the Republic of Korea about 98,173 sq km. The peninsula is approximately 1,000 km in total north-south length and 216 km wide at its narrowest point, with a rugged coastline about 17,269 km long. Korea has long been a cultural bridge and a mediator between China and Japan and often the target of their territorial ambitions and aggression. Devastated and exhausted by centuries of conflict, the "Hermit Kingdom" during the sixteenth century embarked on a policy of isolationism that kept Korea virtually unknown to the West until the last decades of the nineteenth century.

Only vague outlines of Korea's early history have been reconstructed. Old Choson – the first of the periods of Korean history – is traditionally, but unreliably, dated from 2333 to 562 B.C. Ancient sources recall a period of settled village life in which the people cultivated the five grains, domesticated the six animal species, and harvested foods from the sea.

The Three Kingdoms period encompassed the era of Koguryo (37 B.C. to A.D. 688), Paekche (18 B.C. to A.D. 660), and Silla (57 B.C. to A.D. 935). Since the fourth century A.D., Buddhism has provided a sense of spiritual unity for the peninsula, despite conflicts among the Three Kingdoms.

The period from A.D. 618 to 935 is known as the time of Unified Silla. The Koryo dynasty lasted from 918 to 1392 and was followed by the establishment of Modern Choson under the rule of the Yi dynasty (1392–1910), whose bureaucratic and administrative structures were based on Confucian principles. During the Three Kingdoms period, the adaptation of the Chinese writing system to the Korean language stimulated state-supported compilation of national histories, but none of these annals survive. Extracts from the annals compiled during the Koryo era are the oldest extant Korean historical texts.

Korean Foodways

Staples

As might be predicted from what we know of Korea's long history and the struggles of its people to maintain their independence and their unique culture, Korean dietary patterns, traditions, and customs can be described as deeply rooted and not easily changed. Some modern Korean nutritionists not very modestly proclaim that traditional Korean foods constitute the perfect diet, outstanding in nutrition, taste, appearance, and variety. In sum, Korean cuisine is said to provide a nutritious, well-balanced answer to the weight and cholesterol problems that plague the developed world. Moreover, presenting traditional foods in the proper manner is said to promote a sense of peace and well-being that enhances the stability of the family and the nation.

The Korean diet is about 70 percent carbohydrate, 13 percent fat, and 14 to 17 percent protein. The European diet, in contrast, is usually about 40 percent carbohydrate, 30 to 40 percent fat, 15 to 20 percent protein, and 10 to 15 percent sugar. Scientific studies of traditional Korean foods, however, find both good and bad aspects. On the positive side, by combining and mixing a variety of materials, Korean cooks have been able to balance the nutritional qualities of available foods. On the other hand, traditional foods and seasonings provide a very high salt intake. Rice is regarded as the staple food, and other foods are described as subsidiary. Of course, although rice may satisfy hunger, it is not a complete food, and essential elements must be added to the diet to avoid malnutrition. Korea's famous fermented vegetable preparations, known as kim-chee, almost invariably accompany each meal.

The traditional arts of cooking and presentation are said to be fundamental aspects of Korean culture; the proper preparation of food is considered a noble art as well as a science. Although it is difficult to precisely analyze and describe the special "Korean taste," preserving special dietary traditions and transmitting them to future generations is highly valued. Beyond nostalgia, Korean nutritionists are also concerned with the scientific analysis of the many components of the Korean diet and methods of preparation.

Historically, Korean food components and methods of preparation have been adapted to the four distinct seasons of the year and the different regions. Seasonal and regional adaptations bring out the best tastes in available foods and provide the balance needed to supply the body's nutritional requirements. Food etiquette is inextricably linked to food preparation and presentation, which is expressed in terms of rules for the placement of food on the table and rules for facing the table. Although the original Korean low food table, around which diners sit on the floor, has been largely displaced by Western-type tables and chairs, the etiquette of food presentation has not been forgotten.

Generally, the traditional Korean diet features three meals a day in which the foods are divided into two parts: the main dish or staple food – almost invariably boiled rice – and subsidiary foods or side dishes, such as soup, bean curd, cooked meat or fish, cooked vegetables, and fermented vegetables. Proper meal planning dictates diversity in methods of preparation and ingredients. The simplest meal has three side dishes, whereas more elaborate meals are characterized by an increasing number of side dishes. An ordinary everyday meal might consist of a serving of rice and soup for each person and a series of shared side dishes. The table setting shows a clear distinction between the main and the subsidiary dishes. For rituals and festivals, the table setting becomes more elaborate and includes a variety of appetizers, soups, noodles, vegetables, rice cakes, pastries, and beverages.

The evolution of Korea's traditional grain-based diet required the development of farming techniques as well as tools for hulling and pulverizing the grains. The evolution of the house, the kitchen, and the utensils for cooking, serving, and eating food was also part of this process. Cereals, such as millet and sorghum *(kaoliang),* were cultivated in Korea from about 2000 B.C. Excavations at ancient sites have yielded stone farming tools and the remains of different kinds of millet. Millet is probably the only grain native to the whole peninsula, but rice has long been the most important component of the Korean diet, with short-grain rice ultimately the favorite staple.

Rice was introduced from China, perhaps as early as 2000 B.C., although, according to some accounts, a

Chinese nobleman brought rice to Korea in 1122 B.C. Though small in area, the Korean peninsula has an extremely varied climate, so other cereals predominated in regions not suited to rice farming. In southern areas, rice was the mainstay, whereas millet was the staple grain in the north. Barley was introduced to Korea earlier than wheat, but the exact date is unknown. Barley was grown mainly in the southeastern region, where it was consumed as a staple in combination with rice. Wheat was not cultivated until about the first or second century A.D. It was probably introduced into Korea from China around the first century, but it has never been considered a staple. Even in the 1930s, the area devoted to wheat farming was only about half that occupied by barley.

During the Three Kingdoms era, Koguryo, Paekche, and Silla all engaged in land-reform policies, expanded irrigation systems, and actively encouraged the propagation of improved iron farming implements. Rice became the staple food of Paekche, whereas the people of Silla still depended on barley, and millet remained as important as rice in Koguryo. During the Unified Silla period, further developments in land use and farming techniques led to significant increases in rice production. But other important crops, in addition to barley, millet, and sorghum, were soybeans, red beans, mung beans, and buckwheat. Policies that increased farming productivity and land use were of primary importance to the government of Koryo. Rice reserves were maintained for emergency use, and the price of grain was regulated in order to increase rice production.

The soybean, a legume, is the most widely eaten plant in the world and is used in many forms, especially in China, Korea, and Japan. With only slight exaggeration, the ancients called the soybean a treasure-house of life, well suited to sustain, restore, and enrich the soil and the human body. The nutritious quality and versatility of the soybean make it an important part of the diet in areas like Korea, where adults do not drink milk and dairy products are not used. Soybeans can be eaten fresh, dried, ground, fermented, sprouted, or processed into bean curd and various pastes and sauces. Both soybeans and mung beans yield bean sprouts, a good source of vitamin C.

The soybean is also an excellent source of oil, although sesame oil is a favorite component in Korean cooking, and both toasted sesame seeds and sesame oil are important flavoring agents. Many different kinds of vegetables, fruits, and nuts have been part of the Korean diet since ancient times, among them radishes, turnips, lotus roots, taro, leeks, lettuce, green onions, garlic, cucumbers, eggplants, pears, peaches, chestnuts, pine nuts, and hazelnuts. In addition, there are wild plants, such as bamboo shoots, ferns, mushrooms, ginseng, and the broad bellflower obtained from the mountains and fields. During the Koryo era, radishes and pears were especially grown for the preparation of kim-chees that were said to be superior in taste to the fermented vegetables of the Three Kingdoms period. Vegetable leaves were also used as wrapping for little packages of rice or meat.

Agricultural techniques developed further during the Choson era, and practical farming manuals, stressing methods appropriate to Korea, were written during this period. The Yi dynasty actively encouraged an expansion of the trade in exotic foreign drugs and foods that had begun during the Koryo era. For example, the great king Sejong (reigned 1418–50) supported attempts to grow orange and grapefruit trees in several provinces in order to determine whether these fruit trees could be established in Korea. These and other experiments made it possible for Korean farmers to cultivate various foreign plants and trees.

New Foods

Somewhat later, important foods from the Americas, including chilli peppers, pumpkins, sweet potatoes, white potatoes, maize, and tomatoes, were introduced. The sweet potato reached Korea from Japan in 1763 with an official returning from a diplomatic mission. Originally regarded as a famine-prevention food, it eventually became a popular part of the diet. The white potato was introduced by way of China about 1840. It proved well suited to cultivation in the northern regions.

Chilli peppers and tobacco were brought to Korea about the time of the devastating war with Japan known as the Hideyoshi Invasion (1592–8). But today it is impossible to imagine Korean food without chilli peppers, which constitute the main seasoning in most Korean dishes, especially in kim-chee and hot soybean paste.

One of the early names for the plant was "Japanese mustard," because the Japanese had acquired knowledge of the chilli pepper, and probably its seeds as well, from Portuguese Catholic priests. King Sonjo (reigned 1567–1608) made numerous requests to Japan and even to China in attempts to obtain the seeds. Unwilling to lose their monopoly, however, the Japanese claimed that the pepper plant could grow only in foreign tropical areas, and that even if seeds could be obtained, they would not necessarily grow in Korea. They also claimed that the foreigners who sold peppers always boiled the seeds so that they would be useless in attempts to grow new plants. The Korean king countered that various other plants and animals that had been brought to Korea from foreign lands had flourished, and after the difficulties in obtaining the seeds had finally been overcome, the pepper plant was easily adapted to Korea.

Some authorities thought that chilli peppers contained a powerful poison, but the new food quickly became widely used as a seasoning and even was sold in winehouses, where drinkers added it to liquor for a sensation of hotness. Presumably, given the eager acceptance of chilli peppers, Korean cuisine had not been bland before their arrival. And, in fact, Koreans had previously used a hot spice from China, which was probably similar to the Sichuan peppercorn. The ancients thought that pepper was valuable in the cure of fever, whereas modern admirers of the chilli pepper claim that its active agent strengthens the stomach, offers protection against dysentery, and prevents the oxidation of fats.

Cooking and Eating

Bowl-shaped earthenware pots were used for cooking in Korea from the beginning of the farming period. But steaming was thought to improve the quality of the food, and earthenware steamers for cooking grains have been found in Bronze Age shell mounds that date from 1000 to 300 B.C. Koguryo wall paintings in third-century tombs depict food cooked in an earthenware steamer. The kinds of food cooked in the steamer apparently included five-grain rice (a mixture of rice, millet, soybeans, red beans, and barley or sorghum), steamed rice cakes, and glutinous rice cakes. Sauteed rice cakes or sorghum pancakes were also consumed. Cast-iron kettles for rice cooking did not become common until the later part of the Three Kingdoms era, and the traditional chinaware and brassware used for serving foods developed during the Choson period. One interesting example is a special large dish with nine compartments that was used to hold an assortment of side dishes placed in the individual compartments. Wealthy people used this dish for outdoor meals and picnics.

Ideas about the ideal configuration of the house reflect the importance of the kitchen and the proper handling of rice. According to custom and classical texts, the house with the most auspicious configuration was one that faced south and had a mountain behind it. The mountain protected the house from the northeasterly winter winds and the sun could shine into the front of the house. The kitchen would be located to the west so that when the rice was scooped out of the pot, the flat wooden spoon faced the inside of the house. If the kitchen faced east, the spoon would face the outside; this was thought likely to bring bad fortune.

A unique aspect of Korean table manners is that Koreans, unlike the other peoples of East Asia, use spoons for soup and rice and came to believe, unlike the Chinese, that it was rude to bring bowls up to their mouths. In the northern parts of the Korean peninsula, where staple foods included millet and barley, it was found that the grains of these cereals (especially when mixed with nonglutinous rice) were not easily managed with chopsticks. Thus, bronze spoons as well as chopsticks have been found in fifth- and sixth-century royal tombs.

Bronze spoons from the Unified Silla Kingdom (618–935) differed in shape from spoons found in China in that they were bent, thin, and long, and were apparently used together with chopsticks in sets (the shape of Korean chopsticks is also different from those of the Chinese and Japanese). Silver spoons were used at court and by the ruling class. In addition to being elegant, silver was supposed to detect poison in food.

The short-grain sticky rice favored in Korea can readily be picked up with chopsticks, but the use of the spoon is essential in dealing with the ubiquitous soups, stews, and porridgelike preparations found at almost every meal. Another important utensil is the *chori,* a bamboo strainer used to separate rice from sand and stones. Because the *chori* sifts good from bad it has been used as a symbol of good fortune.

It was during the Choson period that Confucianism came to exert a profound impact on political and moral standards, family structure, rituals, and ceremonies. Under the influence of Confucian ideals, the rules concerning food for the extended family and for ceremonial occasions became increasingly strict and rigid. Some concept of the most elaborate cuisine of this time period can be obtained through studies of the foods prepared in the palaces of the kings of Choson. Although the rituals and regulations governing royal cuisine were not common knowledge, some aspects of the art of royal cuisine influenced the dietary culture of the ruling class and diffused beyond the palace walls.

By the end of the Choson period, the art of royal cooking was on the verge of disappearing, and in 1970, when only one former palace chef still remained alive, royal cuisine was designated a major cultural property. Chef Han Hi-san, who had served King Kojong, King Sunjong, and Queen Yun, was awarded the title of Human Cultural Property of Royal Cuisine in 1971. After Han died, Professor Hwang Hye-song, who had studied with Chef Han, inherited the title. Hwang published many books on Korean cooking, established a research institute for royal cuisine, and held exhibitions to bring royal cuisine to the attention of the general public.

Traditions

A grain-based diet need not be bland or totally monotonous, even when boiled rice remains the single most important component. Thus, cereals were also made into gruel, noodles, and dumplings. Well-cooked porridge-like dishes, especially those made of millet, are still considered particularly nourishing and appropriate to the needs of the sick. Another simple, nourishing ancient food product called *misu karu* was made by washing, drying, roasting, and pounding cereal grains into a fine powder that could be mixed with water and used as an instant food. The roasted flour of assorted grains was useful for travelers, students, and others who needed a simple, ready-to-eat food.

Noodles and dumplings are such an ancient and popular part of the traditional Korean diet that, like China, Italy, Japan, Germany, and France, Korea also claims to have invented pasta (Korea has not, however, asserted this claim as passionately as Italy).

Dumplings and noodles have been made from rice and barley and prepared by boiling, steaming, or frying. They were usually served as main dishes for lunch or on special occasions. Noodles were considered especially appropriate for birthdays because they are a symbol of long life. Various kinds of noodles were made of wheat, buckwheat, rice, soya, or mung beans. Steamed wheat-flour buns were first brought from China and also became very popular for festive occasions.

Many different kinds of rice cakes and pancakes have been associated with holidays and festivals ever since the Koryo period. Steamed rice cakes were made with regular or glutinous rice and flavored with chestnuts, honey, jujubes, sorghum, and mugwort. Rice cakes, flavored with mugwort leaves or flowers, are a specialty of the southern provinces, and many therapeutic virtues have been attributed to mugwort *(Artemisia vulgaris),* which is also known as *moxa.* *Moxa* is supposed to increase the user's level of energy and ward off disease. Mugwort is dried and used in making *moxa* for cauterization *(moxibustion)* and other medicines. Rice cakes made with mugwort paste are traditionally served at the *Tano* festival.

Mugwort figures prominently in the foundation myth of Old Choson. According to ancient sources, the King of Heaven, leader of the gods of wind, rain, and clouds, ruler of grains of all kinds, who presided over life, disease, punishment, and goodness and evil, established his Holy City at the summit of Mount Taebaeksan. The god was approached by a bear and a tiger who beseeched him to make them human. The god gave them each a stick of *moxa* and 20 cloves of garlic and told them to eat them and avoid the sun for 100 days. The tiger failed to follow these instructions, but the bear did and became a woman. The god married her and she had a son called Tan-gun, the founder of Old Choson. Thus, both *moxa* and garlic were regarded as powerful drugs and foods in early times.

Among the most treasured traditional Korean foods are those associated with holidays, ceremonies, and seasons. Traditionally, Korean women prepared special dishes for folk holidays according to the lunar calendar. During the Choson period, with the rise of Confucianism, great attention was paid to rituals attached to holidays, including the preparation of foods thought to supply nutrition appropriate to each season. Such foods were a part of the ceremonies that expressed the hope of good harvests and harmony within the family and the village. Special holiday foods are often described as particularly nourishing and are said to encourage harmony between man and nature. Among these are rice cake soup, dumpling soup, cakes made of glutinous rice, rice cakes steamed on a layer of pine needles, five-grain rice, rice gruel prepared with red beans, sweet rice beverages, and seasoned dried vegetables. Cooking methods and ingredients have varied with regional customs, products, and increasing modernization.

The custom of making a red bean porridge with small dumplings of glutinous rice to mark the winter solstice has been practiced since the Koryo era, and sharing this dish with neighbors has also been part of the tradition. Eating certain foods on holidays was said to prevent different kinds of misfortune: For example, consuming red bean porridge on the day of the winter solstice was supposed to ensure good health, prevent colds, and drive away ghosts.

Five-grain rice and nine kinds of vegetables are typical holiday fare for the first full moon of the lunar year; rice cake soup was eaten on New Year's Day; crescent-shaped rice cakes were prepared for the second lunar month; azalea flower pancakes for the third lunar month; and grilled wheat cakes for the sixth lunar month. In the heat of mid-July, holiday foods that included chicken broth with ginseng, red dates and glutinous rice, and croaker stews were thought to revive the appetite and ward off illness. Foods appropriate to the August harvest moon festival have included taro soup, wine, rice cakes, and new fruits such as pears and persimmons.

Food and flower customs expressed the theme of seeking harmony with nature and incorporating its beauty in delicacies. A document from the Choson period describes an especially fragrant delicacy made by boiling together apricot petals, melted snow, and white-rice porridge. It was customary to go on "flower outings" several times a year, and while admiring the beauty of the flowers, participants would eat foods that incorporated them, such as chrysanthemum pancakes, chrysanthemum wines, chestnut balls, and citron tea.

Different kinds of rice cakes still retain symbolic value. For the ceremonial feast on a child's 100th day of life, steamed rice cakes represent purity and cleanliness; glutinous rice cakes, coated with mashed red beans, represent endurance; rice cakes steamed on a layer of pine needles represent generosity; and stuffed rice cakes represent intelligence. Collectively, the ceremonial foods represent longevity, purity, and divinity. At the feast held for a child's first birthday, there are, in addition to rice cakes, cakes made with cinnamon bark, steamed rice balls rolled in colored powders, and even a steamed, layered, rainbow rice cake that represents the parents' hope that the child will enjoy a wide range of accomplishments.

Seafood

Because Korea is surrounded by the sea on three sides and has many large rivers, its supply of seafood has been plentiful and varied. The remains of abalone, clams, oysters, snails, mackerel, pike, shark, and sea urchins have been found in ancient shell mounds. Different kinds of seaweed were also harvested, dried, and prepared in various ways. For example, seaweed can be made into paper-thin sheets, called *laver,* which are usually seasoned with hot sauce and wrapped around small portions of rice, vegetables, and meat. Seaweed soup is still considered essential for women recovering from the birth of a baby. At the ceremonial feast held when the baby is 100 days old, the mother again eats seaweed soup.

By the Three Kingdoms period, shipbuilding skills had been highly developed, so that many kinds of seafoods could be harvested. The challenge of storing highly perishable aquatic animals led to the development of methods for preserving them by fermentation. Fresh shrimp, fish, and other seafoods were salted and allowed to ferment. Pickled fish were often added to winter kim-chee.

During the Choson period, fishing techniques were further developed, fisheries became significant enterprises, and the production of herring, anchovies, pollack, codfish, and croakers increased rapidly. So, too, did the production of seaweed, and particular kinds were cultivated and processed on offshore islands.

All these products of the sea were dried, salted, or fermented and sold throughout the peninsula. Some were regarded in China as valuable medicines and desirable exotics. Chinese physicians were very interested, for example, in the properties of a certain mollusk that was eaten by the people of Silla; the medical men thought that a soup made from this mollusk and seaweed would cure "knotted-up breath."

Meat

Although geographic conditions in Korea were not suitable for livestock farming, cows, pigs, and hens were raised on a small scale, and, thus, some meat also entered the diet. Wild game could be found in the mountains, and the Koguryo people were known as skillful hunters of pheasants, roe deer, and wild boar. The people of Silla kept semiwild livestock on nearby islands. Cattle, hens, pigs, horses, and oxen were raised by the people of Paekche.

During the early Koryo period, when the influence of Buddhism was especially strong, kings and commoners alike generally refrained from eating meat, but pickled fish and shellfish were often served as side dishes. By the middle of the Koryo period, cattle were being raised on Cheju Island, and those whose religion and finances permitted it ate beef, pork, lamb, chicken, pheasant, and swan meat. Wealthy people might have their meats cooked whole, but cooking thinly sliced pieces of meat became popular during this time. Among the favorite meat dishes of the Koryo period were roasted ribs and bone and tripe soup. Significant changes in dietary customs developed during the Choson era, including increased (and perhaps guilt-free) consumption of beef, pork, chicken, and pheasant.

Fermented Food and Drink

Korea's famous pickled cabbage, kim-chee, has probably been an important side dish since agriculture began, but the first appearance of the word "kim-chee" occurred in the collected poems of Lee Kyu-bo (1168–1241), an eminent Koryo poet. Fermented vegetables were essential parts of the diet during the long, harsh Korean winter, when fresh vegetables were not available. Kim-chee is said to retain all the nutrition of almost any fresh vegetable.

Making kim-chee for the winter was a major annual event for each household. Traditionally, relatives and neighbors took turns helping each other, sharing the ingredients and the freshly made kim-chee. Originally, kim-chee contained only simple vegetables, but eventually a large number of regional and seasonal variations evolved, including those flavored with fermented seafoods, such as shrimp, anchovies, cuttlefish, crabs, and oysters. When hot chilli peppers were introduced in the middle of the Yi dynasty, the method of making this traditional food underwent substantial changes and improvements.

Although kim-chee is eaten as an essential side dish throughout the year, different ingredients and methods of preparation are associated with the changing seasons and different regions. Almost all varieties include Chinese cabbage, radishes, red pepper, and garlic. Salted shrimp provides the special flavor characteristic of the kim-chee preferred by residents of Seoul; salted anchovy is used in southern regions, and various kinds of fish are favored in northern regions, but the art of making kim-chee can be applied to an almost endless variety of basic ingredients, spices, and flavorings. Even the stems of the sweet potato vine can be turned into kim-chee.

Today, except for rice, kim-chee is the most important and popular food in the Korean diet. Another interesting fermented food, however, is made from a mixture of chopped fish, rice, radishes, and malt. This preparation is said to ward off indigestion, especially during festivals when overindulgence is likely to occur. Similar health-promoting benefits have been ascribed to kim-chee. There is no doubt that it is a good source of vitamins, including ascorbic acid, which protects against scurvy. Kim-chee is also said to regulate body fluids and intestinal fermentation, prevent constipation, and stimulate the appetite. Certainly, fermented foods add taste, texture, and important nutrients to the bland main dish of rice and other grains. They are said to provide the five different tastes: sweet, salty, hot, sour, and bitter.

In addition, wine and soy sauce are important products of fermentation. The production of alcoholic beverages from fermented grains probably developed during the early stages of farming. Similarly, soy sauce and hot soybean pastes, made by processing soybeans, have long been used as seasonings and condiments that contribute to the characteristic flavor of Korean foods. Techniques for making wine and soy sauces became highly advanced in the Three Kingdoms period, but the art of making soybean paste was revolutionized by the addition of the hot chilli pepper. Soy sauce and hot soybean pastes are still indispensable seasoning agents in Korean cooking. Koreans consider Japanese soybean sauces excessively sweet in comparison to their own, which they characterize as salty, light, simple, and refreshing. Each household traditionally prepared soy sauce and soybean pastes in the spring or autumn and stored them in large earthenware jars on special terraces. Recent health claims have been made for soy sauces: It is suggested that they not only prevent the oxidation of dietary fats but also contain anticancer factors.

Various kinds of rice wine were made during the Koryo period, including several that served for medicinal purposes. Other wines derived from sources as diverse as roots, barks, irises, chrysanthemums, and bamboo leaves. Many of these were made at home – an important task for the housewife. Farmers and laborers traditionally drank rice wine from a gourd before and after meals and with their midmorning snack to wet the throat and clear away the kim-chee aftertaste.

Exactly when techniques for the distillation of hard liquor were imported into Koryo is unknown. However, records of the time of King Kongmin, who reigned from 1351 to 1374, suggest that hard liquor was already being used and misused. During the twentieth-century Japanese occupation (1910–45), Japanese wines, grape wines, and Western liquors gradually became popular. After liberation from Japan in 1945, Western liquor and beer became widely available, and cocktails and mixed drinks were commonly served at social functions, especially in the cities.

Hot Beverages

In Korea, hot beverages have been collectively referred to as *ch'a*, or tea. Green tea, made of dried tea leaves steeped in hot water, was introduced to Korea in the eighth century by a Buddhist monk from China. Ancient Chinese texts associated tea with Taoist philosophy and referred to tea as the elixir of immortality. Tea plants and the seeds of tea bushes arrived from China in the ninth century. At first, tea drinking was associated primarily with Buddhist temples, the court, and the aristocracy. Drinking the beverage was said to soothe the mind and refresh the spirit while cleansing and improving the body. But it soon became popular among the common people as well, and offerings of tea and tea-drinking ceremonies were part of all national rites. Buddhist temples operated large tea plantations and sponsored tea-brewing competitions.

With the establishment of the Yi dynasty, the custom of tea drinking declined among members of the upper class, who were now professing Confucianism. The Choson government denounced Buddhism and levied high taxes on tea plantations. Alcoholic beverages, such as rice wine, generally took the place of tea in official ceremonies. But despite government repression, tea drinking remained popular, and people cultivated small tea gardens near their homes. Buddhist monks and nuns also continued to drink tea, which was always included in offerings to the Buddha, and men of letters associated tea drinking with artistic endeavors and the contemplation of nature.

The opinions of tea-loving scholars, monks, and poets profoundly influenced Korean culture, especially those of the Buddhist monk and scholar Ch'o Ui (1786–1866), who is credited with reviving interest in the rituals and traditions of tea drinking. In his *Eulogy to Oriental Tea* (1837), Ch'o asserted, among other things, that Korean tea was superior to Chinese tea in taste, fragrance, and medicinal virtues.

In addition to green tea, other such drinks, made from barley, corn, rice, sesame seeds, ginseng, ginger, cinnamon bark, citron, quince, dates, pears, strawberries, cherries, watermelon, and peaches, are also popular. Even the pollen of pine tree flowers can be mixed with honey and made into a sweet tea. Sweet beverages based on honey or fruits are often accompanied by rice or barley cakes. Indeed, many pastries were developed as accompaniments for tea, including fried honey cookies, fried cookies made from glutinous rice, small cakes made with green tea, and candied fruits.

Another important traditional beverage is the scorched-rice tea served with everyday family meals. It is made by pouring water over the rice that sticks to the bottom of the pot in which the rice was cooked. Boiling this rice with water creates a fragrant drink, and rice that is not consumed with the meal can also be mixed with this tea. Making such a beverage also has the virtue of making it easier to clean the spoon, rice bowl, and rice kettle.

Since the 1940s, coffee has become very popular in Korea, but King Kojong, who reigned from 1864 to 1906, appears to have been the first Korean king with the coffee-drinking habit. He was introduced to coffee by the Russian consul general in Seoul. In 1898 Kojong's enemies tried to murder him along with the crown prince by putting poison in their morning coffee. Fortunately, Kojong noticed a peculiar odor and did not drink his coffee. The prince was not so observant, but he vomited the tainted brew before it could do him significant harm.

Famine and Food-Related Disease

Famine

Ancient sources refer to famines and epidemics, floods, severe droughts, and grasshoppers that consumed all the grain. Early agricultural societies were very vulnerable to crop failures and famines. The importance of agriculture in the early Three Kingdoms period is reflected in references to Paekche kings punished for crop failures by removal from the throne, or even by death.

Other sources mention the Koryo relief system and the efforts made by these kings to deal with famines and epidemics. Warehouses were established in various provinces and opened as needed to ward off mass starvation. Government officials were charged with aiding and feeding the poor, and they provided a set measure of millet per day per person. During the Choson period, food reserves were maintained for use during natural disasters and for famine relief. To prepare for famine years, farmers were ordered to gather various edible roots, flowers, fruits, and leaves. Texts written in the sixteenth century describe hundreds of different kinds of foods that could be stored for famine relief. In order to disseminate such information to the general population, books on famine relief were written in the Korean alphabet, the script for the people, rather than in scholarly Chinese characters. Other texts provided discussions of the relationship between diet and health.

Food-Related Disease

Thirteenth-century texts dealing with traditional Korean medicine describe food poisoning that was variously attributed to the consumption of domestic animals, fish, crabs, mushrooms, alcohol, medicines, and miscellaneous chemicals. Given the age-old problem of contaminated food and water, it is not surprising that dysentery was historically one of Korea's more common diseases, to which even members of the royal family fell victim.

Despite the many virtues ascribed to kim-chee, including those of preventing everything from scurvy to dysentery, the symptoms of some vitamin deficiency diseases seem to have been described in early Korean medical texts. One recurrent condition suggests the possibility of beriberi. The symptoms described included swelling of the lower limbs, followed by swelling of the heart and stomach, difficulty in urination, weakness in the feet, and dizziness. However, early accounts are vague, and the symptoms of beriberi are not easily differentiated from those of other diseases.

According to Koryo sources, the Chinese apparently believed that beriberi could be cured by wearing shoes made from the skin of a remarkable fish found in Korea. The skin of this fish was said to be similar to that of the cow. Beriberi was probably rare in Korea, when compared to other parts of Asia, because few Koreans subsisted on a thiamine-deficient polished white rice diet. But the disease was noted among Japanese living in Korean cities because the Japanese were more likely to consume polished rice. During World War II, polished rice became more common in Korea, and beriberi was sometimes observed even in villages. Scurvy and pellagra seem to have been rare, but anemia was not uncommon, and symptoms that suggest rickets, including a condition referred to as "turtle chest," appear in the pediatric sections of ancient medical texts. Classic descriptions of "gentle wind" disease probably refer to osteomalacia, a form of adult rickets. In modern Korea, osteo-

malacia, a gradual deformation of improperly calcified bones, is fairly common among older women.

Parasitic infections are widespread in Asia, and presumably always have been, but ancient texts are too ambiguous to provide specific diagnostic clues as to the agents involved or the specific sources of infection, although various herbal remedies were prescribed to remove parasites. Gastritis seems to have been the major disease in the category of digestive disorders, but symptoms are also described that suggest gastric ulcers, intestinal disorders, and parasitic infestations.

Paragonimiasis (or pulmonary distomiasis) is caused by infection with members of the genus *Paragonimus,* and references to a disorder characterized by rusty-brown mucus are suggestive of this disease, which could have been acquired by eating contaminated raw crabmeat or other seafoods. The developing parasites lodge in the lungs and cause an intense inflammatory reaction that results in the production of the rusty-brown sputum.

Other parasites were still widespread in the early twentieth century. Infestation with flukes was generally caused by eating raw fish and crustaceans contaminated with the lung fluke *(Paragonimus westermani),* the liver fluke *(Clonorchis sinensis),* or the intestinal fluke *(Metagonimus yokogawai).* Until recent times, contaminated food and water were also a constant source of intestinal diseases such as bacillary and amebic dysentery. The custom of drinking tea or water boiled in the rice kettle provided some protection, as did the use of kim-chee instead of fresh vegetables. Noting that Korean patients recovered from dysentery more easily than Japanese patients, early-twentieth-century medical missionaries advised the latter to eat kim-chee.

Nutritional Status Today

The history of disease in twentieth-century Korea illustrates the remarkable impact of improved sanitary conditions, public-health measures, land reform, and economic development. Despite the devastation caused by World War II and the Korean War, and the repatriation of millions of Koreans from Manchuria, China, and Japan, many epidemic and endemic diseases have been virtually eliminated.

Since land reform policies were put in place in 1948, South Korean agricultural policy has encouraged the development of small, intensively worked farms. This policy was vindicated by the achievement of self-sufficiency in rice production and an increased food output that has kept pace with population growth. South Korea, Japan, and Taiwan have among the world's highest per-acre rice yields. Because much of the peninsula is mountainous and unsuitable for farming, agricultural development policy has focused on maximizing yields by means of high-yield crop varieties. Today, genetic engineering is seen as a principal means of increasing crop yields.

In addition, in the 1960s, South Korea embarked on a vigorous and highly successful program of economic development, and since 1962 the Korean economy has grown at one of the fastest rates in the world. In a remarkably short period of time, South Korea's traditionally agrarian society has undergone a major structural transformation, and the country has become one of the key industrialized nations of the Pacific Rim.

Since the late 1940s, numerous studies of the nutritional status of the South Korean people have addressed the question of shortages in the quantity and quality of the food supply. Most of these investigations reached the same general conclusions, despite some relatively minor regional differences. Overall, the traditional South Korean diet is high in carbohydrates and low in protein and fats. Studies of the state of nutrition in Korea undertaken in 1946 found that over 90 percent of foods consumed came from plant sources.

When similar studies were conducted in the 1960s, the proportion of grains consumed had been somewhat reduced. Rice, however, remained the main food, which may reflect a reaction to years of food rationing and shortages during the Japanese occupation. But rice shortages from 1960 to 1975 led the government to establish rice conservation measures, such as the increased production of wheat, the importation of American surplus foods, and attempts to create two "rice-free days" each week, during which, as a patriotic duty, wheat products would be eaten instead of rice. Bread was used in school lunches, restaurants were ordered to use wheat-flour foods, and a nationwide mass communication campaign was launched to encourage the consumption of wheat products. Although resistance to these attempts to change dietary habits was quite strong, at least students and some white-collar workers seem to have adopted the custom of eating bread for breakfast. Nevertheless, Korea remains primarily a rice-eating culture.

Although self-sufficiency in rice production was attained in the 1980s, imports of wheat products and maize were still essential. In fact, increased demand for wheat flour, used in bread and instant noodles, reflects a significant change in South Korean dietary patterns. Beef imports have also increased, whereas the production of traditional cattle has decreased. Fish and other seafoods have become increasingly important sources of protein.

In general, the intake of animal protein has significantly increased since the 1970s, and the growth in the amount of protein consumed was accompanied by a threefold jump in fat intake between 1962 and 1982. Consumption of beef and pork increased about two times; chicken consumption increased almost five times, and the use of milk and other dairy products also increased about five times. Although the intake of some minerals, particularly calcium, increased significantly, that of iron did not, and many Korean women have exhibited symptoms of iron-deficiency anemia. Investigations of infant and child nutrition in different regions during the 1970s led nutritionists to urge mothers to increase the use of eggs, fish, and vegetables as supplemental foods. One problem with the typical Korean diet is a very high intake of salt and hot chilli peppers; these factors appear to be linked to high blood pressure and a high incidence of gastroenteritis and stomach cancer. Researchers report that the use of great amounts of salt becomes habitual for South Koreans prior to reaching 6 years of age.

It is interesting to note that studies of nutritional status and dietary patterns conducted in the 1960s indicated that at that point, despite changes associated with rapid industrialization, many people had maintained traditional food habits. Indeed, the Korean dietary pattern seems to have been remarkably stable from the early beginnings of Korean history to the end of the Yi dynasty and beyond. Researchers have found little evidence of changes in the basic ingredients and cooking methods used by Korean families other than an increase, in urban areas, in the consumption of dairy products such as butter and cheese.

Between 1970 and 1990, however, the combination – already mentioned – of urbanization, modernization, industrialization, socioeconomic development, and the influence of Western culture wrought significant changes in the typical South Korean diet. In addition, factors such as the 1988 Seoul Olympic Games, the expansion of the fast-food industry, and the influence of mass media have helped accelerate such changes. South Korean nutritionists predict that in coming years, the pattern of food consumption in South Korea will involve a continuing decrease in the amount of grains used and an increase in the consumption of foods of animal origin. Consequently, they urge the development of a national health and nutrition policy that will focus on the prevention of the kinds of diseases associated with these new dietary patterns. Since the 1970s, the pattern of major diseases and causes of death in South Korea has become that of the Western world, whereby cardiovascular diseases, circulatory problems, and stroke are the most important killers. Those who value Korea's unique historical culture warn against losing the harmony and balance encapsulated in the traditional dietary culture and etiquette of the table.

Lois N. Magner

Work on this chapter was supported in part by NIH Grant R01 LM 04175 from the National Library of Medicine.

Bibliography

Handelman, Howard, ed. 1981. *The politics of agrarian change in Asia and Latin America*. Bloomington, Ind.

Han Woo-keun. 1970. *The history of Korea,* trans. Lee Kyung-shik, ed. Grafton K. Mintz. Seoul.

Im Dong-kwon. 1994. Village rites. A rich communal heritage. *Koreana: Korean Art and Culture* (Special Issue) 8: 6–11. (Special issue entitled *Village rites and festivals: Celebrating the spirits, feasting the gods.*)

Kim Tu-jong. 1966. *A history of Korean medicine* (in Korean). Seoul.

Korean Nutrition Society. 1989. *Korean nutrition resource data.* Seoul.

Lee, Florence C., and Helen C. Lee. 1988. *Kimchi: A natural health food.* Elizabeth, N.J.

Lee Ki-baik. 1984. *A new history of Korea,* trans. Edward W. Wagner. Cambridge, Mass.

Lee, K. Y. 1985. Korean food life 100 years (1880–1980). (One hundred years of Korean food habits, main dishes and side dishes): Evaluation and trends in dietary status (in Korean). *Yonsei Nonchong* (Korea) 21: 297–318.

Magner, Lois N. 1993. Diseases of antiquity in Korea. In *The Cambridge world history of human disease,* ed. Kenneth F. Kiple, 389–92. Cambridge and New York.

Marks, Copeland, with Manjo Kim. 1993. *The Korean kitchen: Classic recipes from the Land of the Morning Calm.* San Francisco.

Medical News Company, ed. 1984. *Centennial of modern medicine in Korea (1884–1983)* (in Korean). Seoul.

Miki, Sakae. 1962. *History of Korean medicine and of disease in Korea* (in Japanese). Japan.

Mo, Sumi. 1991. Present-day dietary patterns of Korea, influenced by social, economic and technological forces, and cultural processes. *Journal of the Asian Regional Association for Home Economics* (Supplement) 1: 87–95.

Ravenholt, Albert. 1981. Rural mobilization for modernization in South Korea. In *The politics of agrarian change in Asia and Latin America,* ed. Howard Handelman, 48–62. Bloomington, Ind.

Sohn, Kyunghee. 1991. A review of traditional Korean food. *Journal of the Asian Regional Association for Home Economics* (Supplement) 1: 81–6.

Yu Geh-won. 1976. *Season and food table* (in Korean). 4 vols. Seoul.

Yun Seo-Seok. 1993. History of Korean dietary culture. *Koreana: Korean Art and Culture* (Special Issue) 7: 7–11. (Special issue entitled *Traditional food: A taste of Korean life.*)

V.C

The History and Culture
of Food and Drink in Europe

V.C.1 ❧ The Mediterranean (Diets and Disease Prevention)

The basic elements of healthful diets are well established (USDHHS 1988; National Research Council 1989; USDA/USDHHS 1995). They provide adequate amounts of energy and essential nutrients, reduce risks for diet-related chronic diseases, and derive from foods that are available, affordable, safe, and palatable. A very large body of research accumulated since the mid-1950s clearly indicates that healthful diets are based primarily on fruits, vegetables, and grains, with smaller quantities of meat and dairy foods than are typically included in current diets in the United States and other Western countries (James 1988; USDHHS 1988; National Research Council 1989).

Throughout the course of history, societies have developed a great variety of ways to combine the foods that are available to them (as a result of geography, climate, trade, and cultural preferences) into characteristic dietary patterns. In some areas, typical diets have developed patterns so complex, varied, and interesting in taste that they have come to be identified as particular cuisines. Some of these, most notably those of Asia and the Mediterranean, seem to bless the populations that consume them with substantially lower levels of coronary heart disease, certain cancers, diabetes mellitus, and other chronic diseases than those suffered by other peoples. Consequently, such apparent relationships between cuisines and health have created much interest in traditional dietary patterns.

Illustrative is the current interest in Mediterranean diets that has been stimulated by the unusually low levels of chronic diseases and the longer life expectancies enjoyed by adults residing in certain regions bordering the Mediterranean Sea (WHO 1994). Such good health cannot be understood within the context of those factors usually associated with disease prevention in industrialized countries, such as educational levels, financial status, and health-care expenditures. Indeed, the percentages of those who are poor in

Mediterranean regions are often quite high relative to those of more developed economies (World Bank 1993). To explain this paradox, researchers have focused on other lifestyle characteristics associated with good health, and especially on the various constituents of the typical Mediterranean diet.

Data from the early 1960s best illustrate the intriguing nature of the paradox. At that time, the overall life expectancy of Greeks at age 45 exceeded that of people in any other nation reporting health statistics to the World Health Organization (WHO/FAO 1993). Subsequently, the ranking of life expectancy in Greece has declined somewhat, at least partly because of undesirable changes in dietary practices that have occurred (Kafatos et al. 1991). But even with such changes, in 1991 life expectancy at age 45 in Greece was an additional 32.5 years, second in rank only to the 33.3 years yet available to Japanese people. By comparison, in the same year, life expectancy at age 45 for adults in the United States, United Kingdom, and Canada was respectively 30.8, 30.9, and 32.1 years (WHO 1994).

Even these brief observations raise interesting historical questions. For example: What, precisely, is a "Mediterranean" diet? When and under what circumstances did it develop? What are the health effects of specific dietary patterns? In what ways do diets change, and what are the health implications of such changes? Should – and could – a Mediterranean-style diet be adopted elsewhere, and if such a diet were to be adopted in, for example, the United States, what would be the impact on agriculture, the food economy, and health patterns? Because such questions address fundamental issues of food and nutrition research and policy, the Mediterranean diet constitutes an especially useful model for studying healthful dietary patterns (Nestle 1994).

Historical Antecedents

Diets of the Ancient Mediterranean
In the absence of written records, knowledge of ancient diets must be inferred from other kinds of evidence. Fortunately, evidence related to Mediterranean

diets is extraordinarily abundant, including a vast and extensively documented archaeological record of food debris and a large quantity of food-related art, pottery, tools, and inscribed tablets excavated from prehistoric, Neolithic, Bronze Age, and later sites throughout the region (Fidanza 1979). The evidence also includes information derived from scholarly analyses of the writings of Homer and other classical authors. (The many and varied sources of information about the diets of ancient Egyptians, for example, are summarized in Table V.C.1.1.)

Inferences based on such sources must, however, be tempered by consideration of the difficulties inherent in evaluation: poor preservation of materials, incomplete fragments, errors of oversight, biased opinions, false information, and problems of translation, classification, dating, and interpretation (Darby, Ghalioungui, and Grivetti 1977). Nonetheless, scholars have used these sources over the years to firmly establish the availability in ancient times of an astonishing variety of plant and animal foods, breads, spices, sweets, and beers and wines (Seymour 1907; Vickery 1936; Vermeule 1964).

Discovery of the presence of various foods in a region suggests – but does not prove – that people ate those foods on a routine basis. Reports of actual dietary intake in ancient times are scanty and are especially lacking for the diets of the general population. When classical authors described foods at all, they wrote almost exclusively about those consumed by warriors or noblemen. Such accounts do not seem entirely credible; the writings of Homer, for example, leave the impression that Hellenic heroes consumed nothing but meat, bread, and wine (Seymour 1907). Homeric texts mention vegetables and fruits only rarely, perhaps because such foods were considered

Table V.C.1.1. *Sources of information about diets in ancient Egypt*

Archaeology (preserved remains of animals and plants)
    Stomach and intestines of human mummies
    Tombs (sealed and opened)
    Mud bricks

Art (depictions of foods, food preparation, domestic animals)
    Temple and tomb paintings and reliefs
    Statues, models, dioramas

Literature
    Papyrus, tomb, or temple texts
        Daily food allowances
        Lists of food offerings
        Foods in medical prescriptions
        Cosmology and mythology texts
    Greek, Roman, and Arabic texts
    Religious texts
    Descriptive accounts by travelers, historians, naturalists

Source: Adapted from Darby, Ghalioungui, and Grivetti (1977), 1:23.

inadequate to the dignity of gods and of heroes (Yonge 1909), and olive oil is mentioned only in the context of its use as an unguent (Seymour 1907).

Perhaps as a result of such research, scholars have concluded that the typical diet of the common people in ancient times must have been rather sparse, based mainly on plant foods and bread, with meat and seafood only occasional supplements. In fact, such a diet was characteristic of the Mediterranean region even in the early twentieth century (Seymour 1907; Vickery 1936). However, a second- to third-century A.D. review of the food writings of classical poets and authors has provided a vivid contrast. It described foods and drinks in great detail, classifying them by flavor and aroma, means of preparation, and contribution to meals and banquets, suggesting that people of all classes ate and enjoyed a vast array of foods and ingredients (Yonge 1909).

Modern scholars have related dietary practices to the health of ancient Mediterranean populations through inferences from examinations of prehistoric skeletal remains, analyses of sepulchral inscriptions, and other kinds of evidence, as indicated by the listings in Table V.C.1.1. Some of this evidence provides insights into dental lesions, anemia, and other diseases, and taken together, it all suggests that the average life span in ancient Greece and Rome was probably on the order of 20 to 30 years (Wells 1975). The evidence also indicates, however, that this brief life expectancy had much more to do with infection and civil conflict than with malnutrition and starvation (Darby et al. 1977).

Modern History: The Rockefeller Study

The first systematic attempt to investigate dietary intake in the Mediterranean region took place shortly after the end of World War II. In 1948, the government of Greece, concerned about the need to improve the economic, social, and health status of its citizens, invited the Rockefeller Foundation to conduct an epidemiological study on the island of Crete. The aim was to identify factors that would best contribute to raising the standard of living of the Greek population, and Leland Allbaugh, an epidemiologist, was appointed to oversee the study. Allbaugh and his colleagues designed and conducted an extraordinarily comprehensive survey of the demographic, economic, social, medical, and dietary characteristics of the members of 1 out of each 150 households on the island, a sample chosen through a carefully designed randomization process. The foundation published the results of these investigations as a monograph in the early 1950s (Allbaugh 1953).

The report of the survey was remarkable in several important respects. It was, for example, extraordinarily thorough. It included a 75-page appendix that contained descriptions and critical evaluations of statistical methods and a 50-page compendium of the questionnaires used to obtain information. The survey's numerous dietary components included a review of agricultural data on the Greek food supply; the administration to 128 households of several distinct questionnaires examining cooking practices, daily menus, food expenditures, household food production, and food handling and consumption practices; and three dietary-intake surveys: one of pregnant women and nursing mothers, another of children and adolescents aged 7 to 19 years, and yet another of children aged 1 to 6, with the information in the latter obtained from the parents. These multiple surveys, however, constituted only the most peripheral components of the overall dietary probe.

The core of the survey's dietary sections consisted of 7-day weighed food inventories collected from the 128 households, 7-day dietary-intake records obtained from more than 500 individuals in those households, and food-frequency questionnaires administered to 765 households. These extensive dietary investigations were conducted in the early fall by volunteer nurses from the Greek Red Cross who, after 5 full days of training, went to live in the survey communities for periods of 7 to 10 days and made daily visits to the sample households. The work of these nurses was closely supervised and their data cross-checked in several ways. Given the extent, complexity, and comprehensiveness of these investigations, it is difficult to imagine that anything like a survey of this magnitude could be initiated – or funded – today.

Table V.C.1.2 compares selected data on Cretan dietary practices obtained through the various dietary survey methods. The methods yielded substantial agreement about the daily amount of energy consumed by the population – an average of 2,500 kilocalories per day – and the amounts of meat and dairy foods consumed on an average day. Agricultural food "balance" data, which represented the amounts of food available throughout the entire country of Greece on a per capita daily basis, indicated a higher intake of cereals and sugar and a lower intake of potatoes, pulses, nuts, oils, and fats than did data derived from the Crete surveys. However, as is discussed later in this chapter, these differences can be attributed to sources of random and systematic error inherent in methods of dietary-intake measurement. Data on alcohol consumption best illustrate the nature of such errors. Allbaugh was able to explain the discrepancy between the small amount reported in the dietary-intake records and the much larger amount indicated by food balance or household inventory data as a result of systematic underreporting. This was confirmed by his own observations as well as by "an expressed feeling by the respondents that the visiting Americans might be expected to frown upon heavy wine consumption where food was short" (Allbaugh 1953: 106).

A comparison of the food sources of energy in the diets of people in Crete, Greece, and the United States, as reported in the Rockefeller study, may be found in

Table V.C.1.2. *Dietary intake in Crete in 1948 as estimated by three methods*

	Greece	Crete	
	Food balance 1948–9	7-day diet record	Household inventory[a]
Energy, MJ (kcal)/d	10.2 (2,443)	10.7 (2,547)	10.7 (2,554)
Foods, kg/person/y			
Cereals	158.2	127.7	128.2
Potatoes	30.9	59.1	38.6
Sugar, honey	9.1	5.5	5.5
Pulses, nuts	15.0	20.0	23.2
Vegetables, fruits, olives	120.5	175.9	132.3
Meat, fish, eggs	23.2	28.6	27.7
Milk, cheese	35.0	25.5	34.5
Oils, fats	15.0	30.9	30.9
Wine, beer, spirits	37.7	10.0	38.6

Source: Adapted from Allbaugh (1953), p. 107.

[a]Adjusted for information obtained from food-frequency questionnaires.

Table V.C.1.3. It displays data derived from dietary-intake surveys for Crete and reports data taken from food-supply surveys for Greece and the United States, even though these types of data are not truly comparable. The results indicate that plant foods – cereals, pulses, nuts, potatoes, vegetables, and fruits – comprised 61 percent of total calories reported as consumed by people in Crete, whereas plant foods comprised 74 percent of the energy available in the Greek food supply (although not necessarily consumed in the Greek diet) and 37 percent of the energy in the U.S. food supply (again, available but not necessarily consumed).

Table V.C.1.3. *Percentage of total energy contributed by major food groups in the diet of Crete as compared to their availability in the food supplies of Greece and the United States in 1948–9*

	Crete (7-day record)	Greece (food balance)	U.S. (food balance)
Total energy, MJ (kcal)/d	10.7 (2,547)	10.4 (2,477)	13.1 (3,129)
	Energy (%)		
Food group			
Cereals	39	61	25
Pulses, nuts, potatoes	11	8	6
Vegetables, fruits	11	5	6
Meat, fish, eggs	4	3	19
Dairy products	3	4	14
Table oils, fats	29	15	15
Sugar, honey	2	4	15
Wine, beer, spirits	1	–[a]	–[a]

Source: Adapted from Allbaugh (1953), p. 132.

[a]Data not available.

Similarly, foods of animal origin - meat, fish, eggs, and dairy products - comprised only 7 percent of energy in the Cretan diet, in contrast to 19 percent of the energy in the Greek food supply and 29 percent of the energy in the U.S. food supply, but table oils and fats were reported to contribute 29 percent of the energy in the Cretan diet, whereas they constituted only 15 percent of that in the Greek and U.S. food supplies. In Crete, however, 78 percent of the table fats derived from olives and olive oil. The total amount of fat from all sources in the Cretan diet, including that "hidden" in animal foods, was reported as 107 grams per day, or an estimated 38 percent of total energy, a percentage similar to that in the U.S. food supply in the late 1940s (USDA 1968) and considerably higher than that recommended today as a means to reduce chronic disease risk factors (Cannon 1992; USDA 1992; USDA/USDHHS 1995).

The data in Tables V.C.1.2 and V.C.1.3 constitute the basis for the conclusion of the Rockefeller report that "olives, cereal grains, pulses, wild greens and herbs, and fruits, together with limited quantities of goat meat and milk, game, and fish have remained the basic Cretan foods for forty centuries . . . no meal was complete without bread . . . Olives and olive oil contributed heavily to the energy intake . . . food seemed literally to be 'swimming' in oil" (Allbaugh 1953: 100). The Rockefeller survey data also indicated that wine was frequently consumed at all meals - midmorning, noon, and evening.

Whether olive oil made such a contribution to the diet for 40 centuries, however, is doubtful. At least one analysis of tree cultivation in southern Italy suggests that olive oil must have been a scarce commodity until at least the sixteenth century and that its principal use in medieval times was in religious rituals (Grieco 1993).

Thus, in attempting to correlate his current observations of dietary intake with the nutritional and general health of the population, Allbaugh noted certain limitations of his study. Few data were available on the nutrient and energy composition of Cretan foods, and virtually no information was available on the clinical and biochemical status of the Cretan population. Nevertheless, the study reported few serious nutritional problems in Crete; those that existed "were limited to a relatively small number of households, living under conditions of very low income and little home production of food" (Allbaugh 1953: 124). Diets generally were nutritionally adequate as measured against the U.S. Recommended Dietary Allowances of that time (National Research Council 1948). The investigators concluded that the diets and food consumption levels observed for most individuals "were surprisingly good. On the whole, their food pattern and food habits were extremely well adapted to their natural and economic resources as well as their needs" (Allbaugh 1953: 31).

This favorable conclusion, however, was one not necessarily shared by the study subjects. Allbaugh reported that only one out of six of the interviewed families judged the typical diet to be satisfactory. He quoted one family as complaining: "We are hungry most of the time" (Allbaugh 1953: 105). When asked what they would most like to eat to improve their diets, survey respondents listed meat, rice, fish, pasta, butter, and cheese, in order of priority. A large majority of respondents (72 percent) listed meat as the favorite food. On the basis of such views, Allbaugh concluded that the diet of Crete could best be improved by providing more foods of animal origin - meat, fish, cheese, eggs - on a daily basis.

Ancel Keys and the Seven Countries Study

Despite the great wealth of information provided by the Rockefeller report, interest in the health implications of Mediterranean diets is more often thought to have begun with the work of Ancel Keys, an epidemiologist from the University of Minnesota. In 1952, impressed by the low rates of heart disease that he had observed on vacations in the Mediterranean (Keys 1995), Keys initiated a series of investigations of dietary and other coronary risk factors with colleagues in seven countries. Keys and his wife, Margaret, have reported the genesis of these investigations in vivid detail:

> Snowflakes were beginning to fly as we left Strasbourg on the fourth of February. All the way to Switzerland we drove in a snowstorm . . . On the Italian side the air was mild, flowers were gay, birds were singing, and we basked at an outdoor table drinking our first espresso coffee at Domodossola. We felt warm all over. (Keys and Keys 1975: 2)

The two were particularly impressed by the difference between the diet they were eating in Italy and the typical diet consumed by people in the United States. As they described it, the Italian diet included:

> [H]omemade minestrone . . . pasta in endless variety . . . served with tomato sauce and a sprinkle of cheese, only occasionally enriched with some bits of meat, or served with a little local sea food . . . a hearty dish of beans and short lengths of macaroni . . . lots of bread never more than a few hours from the oven and never served with any kind of spread; great quantities of fresh vegetables; a modest portion of meat or fish perhaps twice a week; wine of the type we used to call "Dago red". . . always fresh fruit for dessert. Years later, when called on to devise diets for the possible prevention of coronary heart disease we looked back and concluded it would be hard to do better than imitate the diet of the common folk of Naples in the early 1950s. (Keys and Keys 1975: 4)

Keys and his colleagues published the results of their Neapolitan investigations, which found Italian diets to be remarkably low in fat – 20 percent of energy, or just half the proportion observed in the diets of comparable American groups (Keys et al. 1954). By that time (and long before such ideas became commonplace), Keys had associated the typical American diet, rich in meat and dairy fats, with higher levels of blood cholesterol and, therefore, with increased risk of coronary heart disease.

In 1959, the the principal lines of evidence for these associations were reviewed in a cookbook designed to help the general public reduce risks for coronary heart disease (Keys and Keys 1959). In a foreword to this volume, the eminent cardiologist Paul Dudley White, who had made several expeditions with the authors "to study the health and the ways of life of native populations" in southern Italy and Crete, extolled both the health benefits and the taste of the lowfat foods – and the wine – that they had routinely consumed during their Mediterranean travels.

In this cookbook, perhaps the first of the "healthy heart" genre, the authors summarized their "best advice" for lifestyle practices to reduce coronary risk (Keys and Keys 1959: 40). Table V.C.1.4 lists their precepts in comparison to the 1995 U.S. dietary guidelines for health promotion and disease prevention (USDA/USDHHS 1995). As is evident, the guidelines closely follow the 1959 advice that Ancel and Margaret Keys derived from their observations of diet and coronary risk in southern Italy and Crete. This comparison demonstrates that the Mediterranean diet of the 1950s can be considered to constitute the original prototype for development of current dietary guidance policy in the United States.

Beginning in the early 1950s, and for more than 20 years thereafter, Keys and his colleagues identified dietary and other risk factors for coronary heart disease through a large-scale study of nearly 13,000 middle-aged men from 7 countries distributed among 16 cohorts (Keys 1970; Keys et al. 1980). The overall results of the Seven Countries Study provided strong epidemiological evidence for the effects of fat and various fatty acids on serum cholesterol levels and on coronary heart disease risk (Kromhout, Menotti, and Blackburn 1994).

Dietary-intake data for foods and food components other than fat, however, were published in English for the first time only in 1989 (Kromhout et al. 1989). That report compared the 16 cohorts in the 7 countries with respect to their intake of bread, cereals, various vegetables, fruit, meat, fish, eggs, dairy foods, table fats, pastries, and alcoholic beverages. These data confirmed that Mediterranean diets in the early 1960s were based primarily on foods from plant sources, but that some versions were higher in fat – mainly olive oil – than might be expected in a population with such good health. The Seven Countries' data, as confirmed by subsequent investigations (Cresta et al. 1969; Kafatos et al. 1991; Trichopoulou et al. 1992), constituted the principal research basis for the pro-

Table V.C.1.4. *Ancel and Margaret Keys' 1959 dietary advice for prevention of coronary heart disease compared to the 1995 U.S. dietary guidelines*

The Keyses' "best advice"	1995 dietary guidelines
	Eat a variety of foods.
Do not get fat; if you are fat, reduce. Get plenty of exercise and outdoor recreation.	Balance the food you eat with physical activity – maintain or improve your weight.
Restrict saturated fats, the fats in beef, pork, lamb, sausages, margarine, solid shortenings, fats in dairy products. Prefer vegetable oils to solid fats, but keep total fats under 30 percent of your diet energy.	Choose a diet low in fat, saturated fat, and cholesterol.
Favor fresh vegetables, fruits, and nonfat milk products.	Choose a diet with plenty of grain products, vegetables, and fruits.
Avoid heavy use of salt and refined sugar.	Choose a diet moderate in salt and sodium. Choose a diet moderate in sugars.
Be sensible about cigarettes, alcohol, excitement, business strain.	If you drink alcoholic beverages, do so in moderation.

Sources: Adapted from Keys and Keys (1959) and USDA/USDHHS (1995).

portions of foods from plant and animal sources proposed recently as a Mediterranean diet pyramid (Willett et al. 1995) or a Greek column (Simopoulos 1995).

The EURATOM Study

One additional large-scale study, from a rather unexpected source, yielded comparative information about dietary intake in the Mediterranean and other regions of Europe. From 1963 to 1965, the European Atomic Energy Commission (EURATOM) examined household food consumption among 3,725 families in 11 regions of 6 European countries in an effort to identify the foods among those most commonly consumed that were likely to be sources of radioactive contaminants. Investigators conducted dietary interviews for 7 consecutive days in each of the selected households and weighed all foods present in the households on those days. After applying several correction factors, the researchers converted the data on household food consumption to daily average amounts of food consumed per person. These data were published in 1969 (Cresta et al. 1969).

Of the regions selected by EURATOM for the study, nine were in the north of Europe and two in the south. One of the northern regions was in Italy (Friuli).

Because both of the southern regions also were in Italy (Campania and Basilicata), the data could be used to compare the typical dietary intake of the Italian north – which was quite similar to dietary patterns throughout the rest of northern Europe – with that of the Mediterranean regions. A detailed comparative analysis of these data is now available (Ferro-Luzzi and Branca 1995).

The EURATOM study revealed distinct differences in dietary-intake patterns between the northern and southern Italian regions. Diets in the Mediterranean areas were characterized by a much greater intake of cereals, vegetables, fruit, and fish, but a much smaller intake of potatoes, meat and dairy foods, eggs, and sweets. Although no consistent differences were observed in overall consumption of table fats, the foods contributing to total fat intake were quite different. Consumption of butter and margarine was much higher in the north, whereas in the south, the principal fat was olive oil, and margarine was not consumed at all. Taken together, the results of the EURATOM study provide further evidence that the Mediterranean diet of the mid-1960s was based predominantly on plant foods and included olive oil as the principal fat.

Recent Observations

In the years following these investigations, the Keys' description of the role of diet in coronary risk has become more widely accepted (James 1988; USDHHS 1988; National Research Council 1989). Along with this acceptance has come increasing recognition that the traditional dietary patterns of many cultures meet current dietary guidelines and that the cuisines of these cultures – especially those of Mediterranean and Asian countries – could serve as models for dietary improvement (Nestle 1994). In recent years, reports of investigations of the scientific basis and health implications of Mediterranean diets have been published in at least five edited collections of papers (Helsing and Trichopoulou 1989; Spiller 1991; Giacosa and Hill 1993; Serra-Majem and Helsing 1993; Nestle 1995). Public interest in Mediterranean diets has been stimulated by numerous articles in the popular press (Kummer 1993; Hamlin 1994), and their palatability has been celebrated in cookbooks emphasizing the dual themes of good taste and good health (Shulman 1989; Goldstein 1994; Jenkins 1994; Wolfert 1994).

Historical and Research Issues

As noted previously, studies of Mediterranean dietary patterns raise research issues that are also applicable to a more general understanding of the role of diet in health.

Definition of the Mediterranean Diet

The peoples of the 16 or more countries that border the Mediterranean Sea vary greatly in culture, ethnicity, religion, economic and political status, and other factors that might influence dietary intake, and their food supplies vary widely in the quantity used of every item that has been examined. Thus, the identification of common dietary elements within the region has proved a challenging task to researchers (Ferro-Luzzi and Sette 1989; Giacco and Riccardi 1991; Varela and Moreiras 1991; Giacosa et al. 1993).

Because the studies of Ancel Keys found the typical dietary pattern of the Greek island of Crete in the 1950s and 1960s to be associated with especially good health, this pattern has come to be viewed as the model, and because olive oil was a principal source of fat in the Cretan diet, the model has been extended to include diets consumed in olive-producing Mediterranean regions. In this manner, the generic term "Mediterranean diet" has come to be used, in practice, as referring to dietary patterns similar to those of Crete in the early 1960s and other regions in the Mediterranean where olive oil is the principal source of dietary fat (Willett et al. 1995).

Dietary Epistemology: Research Methods

Knowledge of the content of Mediterranean diets in the early 1960s – or at present – necessarily depends upon the reliability of methods used to determine the typical food intake of the population. National diet surveys, such as those that are conducted regularly in the United States, have not been generally available in Mediterranean countries. The Rockefeller study of Crete was a notable exception, remarkable by any standard of epidemiological investigation (see Table V.C.1.2) in its use of multiple methods, lengthy personal interviews, and critical analysis of results to attempt to define dietary intake (Allbaugh 1953). The Seven Countries Study also used multiple methods. For most of the 16 cohorts, Keys and his colleagues obtained 7-day diet records from small subsamples of each group and corroborated these records by analyzing the energy and nutrient composition of weighed, duplicate meals. For a few cohorts, investigators collected dietary data from 24-hour recalls as verified through food-frequency questionnaires (Keys 1970). Finally, the EURATOM study attempted to corroborate daily reports of household food intake by weighing all foods present in the house on each of the seven consecutive interview days (Cresta et al. 1969).

These investigations were designed to overcome fundamental flaws in each of the methods commonly used to evaluate the dietary intake of individuals and populations; all provide opportunities for random and systematic errors in reporting food intake, estimating serving sizes, and determining nutrient content (Mertz 1992; Buzzard and Willett 1994; Young and Nestle 1995). Such problems are compounded in studies that attempt to compare dietary-intake data from one country to another, or within one country over time. If the methods for determination of dietary intake differ, their results are not strictly comparable – a situation similar to comparing apples to oranges (see Tables V.C.1.2 and V.C.1.3).

For purposes of international comparison, investigators must often rely on food-balance data – agricultural data on specific commodities present in the food supply from one year to the next. As already noted, these data are distinctly different from those that describe dietary intake. They reflect the amounts of specific foods produced in a country during a given year, with imports of foods added and food exports subtracted, expressed on a per capita basis through dividing by the population total on a defined day of the year.

Such data are also known by other names: food supply, food availability, food disappearance, and food consumption. Among these terms, "consumption" is a misnomer, because food-balance data are only an indirect estimate of dietary intake. A food that is produced but then wasted, fed to animals, or used for industrial purposes is not consumed; for many foods, therefore, food-balance data overestimate dietary intake. In the case of foods produced at home, however, food-balance data underestimate consumption. The average annual per capita availability of a food commodity only rarely – and accidentally – is an accurate measure of actual consumption by an individual man, woman, or child. These limitations may explain observed discrepancies in study results, and they emphasize the need for caution in interpreting comparative data such as those presented in Tables V.C.1.2 and V.C.1.3.

Despite such limitations, food-balance data are often the best – or only – data available to estimate time trends in dietary practices, and they are used frequently in comparative descriptions of Mediterranean diets (Ferro-Luzzi and Sette 1989; Helsing 1995). Three agencies of the United Nations (UN) produce such data. The Organization of Economic Cooperation and Development (OECD) has published data for the supply and use in 23 countries of specific food items, such as pork, cheese, or olive oil, from 1979 to 1988 (OECD 1991).

The Food and Agriculture Organization (FAO) publishes individual food-balance sheets for 145 countries that include data for per capita supply of major food groups (e.g., meat, legumes, alcohol); its most recent edition provides data in 3-year averages from 1961–3 through 1986–8 (FAO 1991). The World Health Organization (WHO) Regional Office for Europe has established a comprehensive computerized database that incorporates FAO food-balance data as well as the WHO annual health statistics since 1961 for each of the countries that supply such data to the UN (WHO/FAO 1993). This program makes it possible to generate an immediate display of the relationship between the availability of any food and the disease rates in any country of interest (Ferro-Luzzi and Sette 1989; Helsing 1995).

Health Impact

By the definition used here, the Mediterranean diet can be considered a near-vegetarian diet. As such, it would be expected to produce the well-established health benefits of vegetarian diets and to solve any deficiencies of energy or micronutrients (especially vitamin B_{12}) that are occasionally associated with such diets (Johnston 1994). Vegetarian or near-vegetarian diets are especially plentiful in key nutrients, particularly antioxidant vitamins, fiber, and a variety of phenolic compounds that have been identified as protective against cancer and other chronic diseases (Dwyer 1994; Kushi, Lenart, and Willett 1995a, 1995b). Researchers, however, have yet to establish the relative contribution of any single nutrient or food component, the foods that contain such factors, or physical activity and lifestyle patterns – alone or in combination – to the favorable health indices observed in the Mediterranean region.

In this context, the role of olive oil is of particular interest. The Greek diet, for example, contains a higher proportion of fat than is usually recommended. Yet much of this fat is olive oil, and the diet is associated with very good health. Diets rich in olive oil are associated with exceptionally low rates of coronary heart disease, even when blood cholesterol levels are high (Verschuren et al. 1995). The traditional Greek diet is also associated with an exceptionally low risk for breast cancer (Trichopoulou et al. 1995).

Changing Dietary Patterns

If it is indeed true that Mediterranean diets of the 1960s protected adult populations against premature death, it would seem highly desirable to preserve the protective elements of those diets. Evidence from dietary-intake surveys and from food-balance data indicates, however, that dietary patterns throughout the region are changing rapidly, and generally in an undesirable direction. For example, one dietary-intake study of an urban population on Crete (obtained by 24-hour diet recalls corroborated by food models, photographs, and clinical and biochemical measurements) reported an increase in the intake of meat, fish, and cheese but a decrease in the intake of bread, fruit, potatoes, and olive oil (Kafatos et al. 1991) from levels reported by Keys and his colleagues in the early 1960s (Kromhout, Keys, Aravanis, et al. 1989). Similar changes have been observed in Italy (Ferro-Luzzi and Branca 1995). Food-balance data also document large increases in the availability of meat, dairy foods (FAO 1991), and animal fats (Serra-Majem and Helsing 1993) throughout the region since the early 1960s. Given this situation, the traditional Mediterranean diet may well become a historical artifact.

Increasing evidence suggests that the recent changes in Mediterranean dietary patterns have been accompanied by increases in chronic disease risk factors among the populations. These risk factors include a decline in levels of physical activity, along with higher levels of serum cholesterol (Kafatos et al. 1991), hypertension, and obesity (Spiller 1991). Associated with these changes in risk factors are reports of rising rates of coronary heart disease, diabetes (Spiller 1991), and several types of diet-related cancers (LaVecchia et al. 1993) in several Mediterranean countries. These trends confirm well-established relationships between diet and chronic disease risk (James 1988; USDHHS 1988; National Research Council 1989) and suggest the need to reverse current practices through widespread efforts at preserving and promoting traditional diets within the region (Nestle 1994).

Preservation and Adaptation

Overall dietary patterns in a country are the result of an ongoing interaction between culturally determined food traditions and the assimilation of new foods through economic improvement, foreign contact, or international food marketing. Education also has a role in influencing personal food preferences and dietary change (Heimendinger and Van Duyn 1995). Until recently, Mediterranean dietary patterns were quite resistant to change. Allbaugh and Keys both remarked on the similarity of the foods commonly eaten in Italy and Crete to those produced and consumed in those areas in the ancient past. Despite suggestions that traditional dietary patterns are beginning to be abandoned (Alberti-Fidanza et al. 1994), such foods are still routinely consumed by at least some older population groups (Trichopoulou, Katsouyanni, and Cnardellis 1993).

Issues related to the assimilation of Mediterranean dietary patterns within other countries are best illustrated by the adaptation of southern Italian foods to American tastes (Levenstein and Conlin 1990). Italian immigrants of the late nineteenth and early twentieth centuries retained many of their food traditions despite North American–held views of their diets as insufficiently nutritious, indigestible, unsanitary, and inadequate in amounts of milk and meat. Such views, however, began to change during the economic restrictions of World War I, when Italian pastas became popular as inexpensive, well-balanced alternatives to meat, and since the 1920s, Italian food products have been widely marketed in the United States (Levenstein 1985). But today many Italian-style foods have been "Americanized" to the point that they are far higher in energy, fat, cholesterol, and sodium than the traditional foods from which they were derived (Hurley and Liebman 1994).

Policy Implications

Policies designed to encourage consumption of traditional diets within their country of origin, or to promote the adaptation of traditional models to new locations, will have to address many well-defined cultural, economic, and institutional barriers (Nestle 1994). They will also need to recognize that diet is only one of a great many behavioral factors that influence health and that other determinants may command higher national priorities for action (Jamison

and Mosley 1991). Moreover, the transfer of traditional Mediterranean dietary patterns to a country such as the United States would be likely to affect agriculture, the food industry, the overall economy, and the environment in highly complex ways, some of which may be beneficial, but others undesirable (Gussow 1994, 1995; O'Brien 1995).

The role of the Mediterranean diet in U.S. dietary guidance policy is of particular interest. As is demonstrated in Table V.C.1.4, the Mediterranean observations of Keys' led directly to the formulation of dietary guidelines for the prevention of coronary heart disease. In turn, such guidelines eventually encompassed more general advice for health promotion and disease prevention in American statements of dietary guidance policy, as expressed in the Dietary Guidelines for Americans (USDA/USDHHS 1995). Because animal foods are principal sources of fat, saturated fat, and cholesterol in American diets (Gerrior and Zizza 1994), dietary guidelines necessarily should promote predominantly plant-based diets similar to those traditionally consumed in the Mediterranean region or in Asia. That this may not be evident from standard American food guides (USDA 1992) is, at least in part, a result of political pressures from producers of meat and dairy foods to ensure that their products retain a dominant position in the American food supply and diet (Nestle 1993). Such pressures may well have resulted in dietary recommendations that are ambiguous and confusing to the public (Nestle 1995a).

Research Directions

Traditional Mediterranean diets appear to have been based mainly on plant foods, to contain foods from animal sources in very small amounts, to use olive oil as the principal dietary fat, to feature alcohol in moderation, and to balance energy intake with energy expenditure. Substantial research – in quantity and quality – supports the very great health benefits of just such dietary and activity patterns (Willett 1994; Kushi et al. 1995a, 1995b).

Mediterranean diets are consistent with current food guide recommendations for public-health promotion and disease prevention, as well as with recommendations for nutritionally adequate vegetarian diets (Haddad 1994). Because they also are appreciated for their gastronomic qualities, they are well worth further study as a cultural model for dietary improvement. Several areas of historical and applied research related to Mediterranean diets seem especially worthy of additional investigation; these are listed in Table V.C.1.5. While awaiting the results of such studies, immediate efforts should be instituted to preserve the ancient – and healthful – dietary traditions within the Mediterranean region and to encourage greater consumption of plant foods among industrialized populations as a means to improve health.

Table V.C.1.5. *Suggestions for further historical and applied research on the health impact of Mediterranean diets*

Historical research needs

Identification of methods to determine the typical dietary intake of individuals and populations in Mediterranean countries in the past, present, and future.

Identification of methods to determine time trends in Mediterranean dietary patterns.

Determination of the impact of dietary changes on nutritional status and health risks in Mediterranean countries in the past and present.

Identification of cultural, behavioral, economic, and environmental determinants of dietary change in Mediterranean countries in the past and present.

Determination of the impact of dietary changes on the agriculture, food industry, economy, and environment of Mediterranean countries in the past and present.

Determination of the impact of adoption of Mediterranean foods or dietary patterns on the agriculture, food industry, economy, and environment of countries outside the Mediterranean region in the past and present.

Applied research needs

Identification of the roles of specific plant foods characteristic of Mediterranean diets – fruits, vegetables, legumes, cereals, nuts, oils, wine – in health promotion and disease prevention.

Identification of the roles of specific plant-food nutrients – vitamins, minerals, monounsaturated fatty acids, linolenic acid, fiber, alcohol, phytochemicals – in the low rates of chronic diseases observed in Mediterranean countries.

Determination of the proportions of plant and animal foods in Mediterranean diets optimal for reducing disease risk.

Determination of the proportion of energy from fat and specific fatty acids in Mediterranean diets associated with the lowest risk of disease.

Development of dietary recommendations and food guides that best reflect current scientific knowledge of the health benefits of Mediterranean diets.

Identification of effective methods to educate the public in Mediterranean countries about traditional dietary practices that best promote health.

Marion Nestle

This chapter was adapted from the author's "Mediterranean Diets: Historical and Research Overview," which appeared in the *American Journal of Clinical Nutrition* 61 (Supplement), June 1995, pp. 1313s–20s.

Bibliography

Alberti-Fidanza, A., C. A. Paolacci, M. P. Chiuchiù, et al. 1994. Dietary studies on two rural Italian population groups of the Seven Countries Study. 1. Food and nutrient intake at the thirty-first year follow-up in 1991. *European Journal of Clinical Nutrition* 48: 85–91.

Allbaugh, L. G. 1953. *Crete: A case study of an undeveloped area.* Princeton, N.J.

Buzzard, I. M., and W. C. Willett, eds. 1994. First international conference on dietary assessment methods: Assessing diets to improve world health. *American Journal of Clinical Nutrition* 59 (Supplement): 143s–306s.

Cannon, G. 1992. *Food and health: The experts agree.* London.

Cresta, M., S. Ledermann, A. Garnier, et al. 1969. *Étude des consommations alimentaires des population de onze régions de la Communauté Européenne en vue de la détermination des niveaux de contamination radioactive.* Rapport établi au Centre d'Étude Nucléaire de Fontenay-aux-Roses, France EUR 4218 f. Bruselles.

Darby, W. J., P. Ghalioungui, and L. Grivetti. 1977. *Food: The gift of Osiris.* 3 vols. London.

Dwyer, J. T. 1994. Vegetarian eating patterns: Science, values, and food choices – where do we go from here? In Second International Congress on Vegetarian Nutrition: Proceedings of a symposium held in Arlington, Virginia, June 28–July 1, 1992, ed. P. K. Johnston. *American Journal of Clinical Nutrition* 59 (Supplement): 1255s–62s.

Ferro-Luzzi, A., and F. Branca. 1995. The Mediterranean diet, Italian style: Prototype of a healthy diet. *American Journal of Clinical Nutrition* 61 (Supplement): 1338s–45s.

Ferro-Luzzi, A., and S. Sette. 1989. The Mediterranean diet: An attempt to define its present and past composition. *European Journal of Clinical Nutrition* 43: 13–30.

Fidanza, F. 1979. Diets and dietary recommendations in ancient Greece and Rome and the school of Salerno. *Progress in Food and Nutrition Science* 3: 79–99.

FAO (Food and Agriculture Organization of the United Nations). 1991. *Food balance sheets, 1984–1986 average.* Rome.

Gerrior, S. A., and C. Zizza. 1994. *Nutrition content of the U.S. food supply, 1909–1990.* U.S. Department of Agriculture Home Economic Research Report No. 52. Hyattsville, Md.

Giacco, R., and G. Riccardi. 1991. Comparison of current eating habits in various Mediterranean countries. In *The Mediterranean diets in health and disease,* ed. G. A. Spiller, 3–9. New York.

Giacosa, A., and M. J. Hill, eds. 1993. *The Mediterranean diet and cancer prevention: Proceedings of a workshop organized by the European Cancer Prevention Organization and the Italian League Against Cancer, Cosenza, Italy, June 28-30, 1991.* Andover, England.

Giacosa, A., F. Merlo, P. Visconti, et al. 1993. Mediterranean diet: An attempt at a clear definition. In *The Mediterranean diet and cancer prevention: Proceedings of a workshop organized by the European Cancer Prevention Organization and the Italian League Against Cancer, Cosenza, Italy, June 28-30, 1991,* ed. A. Giacosa and M. J. Hill, 1–14. Andover, England.

Gifford, K. D., G. Drescher, and N. H. Jenkins, eds. 1993. *Diets of the Mediterranean: A summary report of the 1993 International Conference on the Diets of the Mediterranean, Cambridge, Massachusetts, January 20-23, 1993.* Boston, Mass.

Goldstein, J. 1994. *Mediterranean the beautiful: Authentic recipes from the Mediterranean lands.* New York.

Grieco, A. J. 1993. Olive tree cultivation and the alimentary use of olive oil in late medieval Italy (ca. 1300-1500). In *Oil and wine production in the Mediterranean area,* ed. M.-C. Amouretti and J.-P. Brun. *Bulletin de Correspondance Hellenique* (Supplement 26). Paris.

Gussow, J. D. 1994. Ecology and vegetarian considerations: Does environmental responsibility demand the elimination of livestock? In Second International Congress on Vegetarian Nutrition: Proceedings of a symposium held in Arlington, Virginia, June 28–July 1, 1992. *American Journal of Clinical Nutrition* 59 (Supplement): 1110s–16s.

1995. Mediterranean diets: Are they environmentally responsible? *American Journal of Clinical Nutrition* 61 (Supplement): 1383s–9s.

Haddad, E. H. 1994. Development of a vegetarian food guide. In Second International Congress on Vegetarian Nutrition: Proceedings of a symposium held in Arlington, Virginia, June 28–July 1, 1992. *American Journal of Clinical Nutrition* 59 (Supplement): 1248s–54s.

Hamlin, S. 1994. Mediterranean madness. *The Washington Post,* June 8, pp. E1, E10.

Heimendinger, J., and M. A. S. Van Duyn. 1995. Dietary behavior change: The challenge of recasting the role of fruits and vegetables in the American diet. *American Journal of Clinical Nutrition* 61 (Supplement): 1397s–1401s.

Helsing, E. 1995. Traditional diets and disease patterns of the Mediterranean circa 1960. *American Journal of Clinical Nutrition* 61 (Supplement): 1329s–37s.

Helsing, E., and A. Trichopoulou, eds. 1989. The Mediterranean diet and food culture – a symposium. *European Journal of Clinical Nutrition* 43: 1–92.

Hurley, J., and B. Liebman. 1994. When in Rome. . . . *Nutrition Action Healthletter* 21: 1, 5–7.

James, W. P. T. 1988. *Healthy nutrition: Preventing nutrition-related diseases in Europe.* Copenhagen.

Jamison, D. T., and W. H. Mosley. 1991. Disease control priorities in developing countries: Health policy responses to epidemiological change. *American Journal of Public Health* 81: 15–22.

Jenkins, N. H. 1994. *The Mediterranean diet cookbook: A delicious alternative for lifelong health.* New York.

Johnston, P. K., ed. 1994. Second International Congress on Vegetarian Nutrition: Proceedings of a symposium held in Arlington, Virginia, June 28–July 1, 1992. *American Journal of Clinical Nutrition* 59 (Supplement): 1099s–1262s.

Kafatos, A., I. Kouroumalis, I. Vlachonikolis, et al. 1991. Coronary-heart-disease risk-factor status of the Cretan urban population in the 1980s. *American Journal of Clinical Nutrition* 54: 591–8.

Keys, A. 1995. The Mediterranean diet and public health: Reflections. *American Journal of Clinical Nutrition* 61 (Supplement): 1321s–24s.

ed. 1970. Coronary heart disease in seven countries. *Circulation* 41 (Supplement): 9–13 and 1186–95.

Keys, A., C. Aravanis, H. Blackburn, et al. 1980. *Seven countries: A multivariate analysis of death and coronary heart disease.* Cambridge, Mass.

Keys, A., F. Fidanza, V. Scardi, et al. 1954. Studies on serum cholesterol and other characteristics on clinically healthy men in Naples. *Archives of Internal Medicine* 93: 328–35.

Keys, A., and M. Keys. 1959. *Eat well and stay well.* New York.

1975. *How to eat well and stay well the Mediterranean way.* New York.

Kromhout, D., A. Keys, C. Aravanis, et al. 1989. Food consumption patterns in the 1960s in the seven countries. *American Journal of Clinical Nutrition* 49: 809–94.

Kromhout, D., A. Menotti, and H. Blackburn, eds. 1994. *The Seven Countries Study: A scientific adventure in cardiovascular disease epidemiology.* Utrecht, the Netherlands.

Kummer, C. 1993. The Mediterranean diet. *Self* (July): 75–9, 129.

Kushi, L. E., E. B. Lenart, and W. C. Willett. 1995a. Health implications of Mediterranean diets in the light of contemporary knowledge. 1. Plant foods and dairy products. *American Journal of Clinical Nutrition* 61 (Supplement): 1407s–15s.

1995b. Health implications of Mediterranean diets in the light of contemporary knowledge. 2. Meat, wine, fats, and oil. *American Journal of Clinical Nutrition* 61 (Supplement): 1416s–27s.

LaVecchia, C., F. Lucchini, E. Negri, et al. 1993. Patterns and trends in mortality from selected cancers in Mediterranean countries. In *The Mediterranean diet and cancer prevention: Proceedings of a workshop organized by the European Cancer Prevention Organization and the Italian League Against Cancer, Cosenza, Italy, June 28–30, 1991,* ed. A. Giacosa and M. J. Hill, 81–103. Andover, England.

Levenstein, H. 1985. The American response to Italian food, 1880-1930. *Food and Foodways* 1: 1–24.

Levenstein, H. A., and J. R. Conlin. 1990. The food habits of Italian immigrants to America: An examination of the persistence of a food culture and the rise of "fast food" in America. In *Dominant symbols in popular culture,* ed. R. B. Browne, M. W. Fishwick, and K. O. Browne, 231–46. Bowling Green, Ohio.

Mertz, W. 1992. Food intake measurements: Is there a "gold standard"? *Journal of the American Dietetic Association* 92: 1463–5.

National Research Council. 1948. *Recommended dietary allowances.* Revised edition. Washington, D.C.

1989. *Diet and health: Implications for reducing chronic disease risk.* Washington, D.C.

Nestle, M. 1993. Food lobbies, the food pyramid, and U.S. nutrition policy. *International Journal of Health Services* 23: 483–96.

Traditional models of healthy eating: Alternatives to "techno-food." *Journal of Nutrition Education* 26: 241–5.

1995a. Dietary guidance for the 21st century: New approaches. *Journal of Nutrition Education* 27: 272–5.

Nestle, M. 1995b. Mediterranean diets: Historical and research overview. *American Journal of Clinical Nutrition* 61 (Supplement): 1313s–20s.

1995. Mediterranean diets: Science and policy implications. *American Journal of Clinical Nutrition* 61 (Supplement): 1313s–1427s.

O'Brien, P. 1995. Dietary shifts and implications for U.S. agriculture. *American Journal of Clinical Nutrition* 61 (Supplement): 1390s–96s.

OECD (Organization of Economic Cooperation and Development). 1991. *Food consumption statistics, 1979-88.* Paris.

Serra-Majem, L., and E. Helsing, eds. 1993. Changing patterns of fat in Mediterranean countries. *European Journal of Clinical Nutrition* 47 (Supplement).

Seymour, T. D. 1907. *Life in the Homeric age.* New York.

Shulman, M. R. 1989. *Mediterranean light: Delicious recipes from the world's healthiest cuisines.* New York.

Simopoulos, A. P. 1995. The Mediterranean food guide: Greek column rather than an Egyptian pyramid. *Nutrition Today* 30: 54–61.

Spiller, G. A., ed. 1991. *The Mediterranean diets in health and disease.* New York.

Trichopoulou, A., K. Katsouyanni, and C. Cnardellis. 1993. The traditional Greek diet. *European Journal of Clinical Nutrition* 47 (Supplement 1): 76s–81s.

Trichopoulou, A., K. Katsouyanni, S. Stuver, et al. 1995. Consumption of olive oil and specific food groups in relation to breast cancer risk in Greece. *Journal of the National Cancer Institute* 87: 110-16.

Trichopoulou, A., N. Toupadaki, A. Tzonou, et al. 1992. The macronutrient composition of the Greek diet: Estimates derived from six case-control studies. *European Journal of Clinical Nutrition* 47: 549-58.

USDA (U.S. Department of Agriculture). 1968. *Food consumption, prices, and expenditures.* Agriculture Economic Report No. 138. Washington, D.C.

    1992. *The food guide pyramid.* Home and Garden Bulletin No. 252. Hyattsville, Md.

USDA/USDHHS (U.S. Department of Agriculture and U.S. Department of Agriculture and Human Services). 1995. *Nutrition and your health: Dietary guidelines for Americans.* Fourth edition. Washington, D.C.

USDHHS (U.S. Department of Health and Human Services). 1988. *The surgeon general's report on nutrition and health.* Washington, D.C.

Varela, G., and O. Moreiras. 1991. Mediterranean diet. *Cardiovascular Risk Factors* 1: 313-21.

Vermeule, E. 1964. *Greece in the Bronze age.* Chicago.

Verschuren, M., D. R. Jacobs, Bennie P. M. Bloemberg, et al. 1995. Serum total cholesterol and long-term coronary heart disease mortality in different cultures: Twenty-five-year follow-up of the Seven Countries Study. *Journal of the American Medical Association* 274: 131-6.

Vickery, K. F. 1936. Food in early Greece. *Illinois Studies in Social Sciences* 20: 1-97.

Wells, C. 1975. Prehistoric and historical changes in nutritional diseases and associated conditions. *Progress in Food and Nutrition Science* 1: 729-79.

Willett, W. C. 1994. Diet and health. What should we eat? *Science* 264: 532-7.

Willett, W. C., F. Sacks, A. Trichopoulou, et al. 1995. Mediterranean diet pyramid: A cultural model for healthy eating. *American Journal of Clinical Nutrition* 61 (Supplement): 1402s-6s.

Wolfert, P. 1994. *The cooking of the Eastern Mediterranean: 215 healthy, vibrant, and inspired recipes.* New York.

World Bank. 1993. *World development report: Investment in health.* Washington, D.C.

WHO (World Health Organization of the United Nations). 1994. *World health statistics annual, 1993.* Geneva.

WHO/FAO (World Health Organization and Food and Agriculture Organization). 1993. *Food and health indicators in Europe: Nutrition and health, 1961-1990.* Computer program. Copenhagen.

Yonge, C. D., trans. 1909. *The Deipnosophists or banquet of the learned of Athenaeus.* 3 vols. London.

Young, L., and M. Nestle. 1995. Portion sizes in dietary assessment: Issues and policy implications. *Nutrition Reviews* 53: 149-58.

V.C.2   Southern Europe

The basic ingredients that have historically comprised the southern European diet are well known and have recently received much attention for their health-promoting benefits: These are bread, wine, olive oil, and a wide variety of fruits and vegetables supple-mented by fish, dairy products, and a relatively small amount of animal flesh.

Less known, however, are the historical forces that shaped how southern Europeans think about food. Essentially, three rival systems have influenced the culture of food in southern Europe since late antiquity, and in various combinations these systems have informed eating patterns at all levels of society.

The most pervasive of these food systems might be called "Christian," although its roots are not necessarily found in the teachings of Jesus and his disciples. It encompasses monastic asceticism as well as the calendar of fasts and feasts that have historically regulated food consumption. In all its manifestations, the ideal goal of Christian foodways has been spiritual purity through the control of bodily urges, though this can easily be lost sight of when rules are bent and holidays become occasions for excess.

The second major system is medical in origin and has gained and lost popularity in the past two millennia depending on the state of nutritional science, though it continues to influence common beliefs to this day. The object of this system of "humoral physiology," of course, is the maintenance or recovery of health by means of dietary regimen.

Lastly, the "courtly" or gastronomic food culture has also profoundly influenced southern Europe, radiating from urban centers of power such as Rome, Naples, Venice, and the courts of Aragon, Castile, and Provence. Its goal is ostensibly pleasure, but this is usually mixed with motives of conscious ostentation in order to impress guests.

Whereas religious, medical, and gastronomic considerations shape the foodways of most cultures, it is their unique and often surprising combinations that make those of southern Europe especially fascinating. The gourmand monk, the duke surrounded by swarms of physicians, the parvenu townsman indulging his taste for spices - all reveal glimpses into the dynamics of society and the ways that individuals express themselves through food preferences, which in southern Europe are to a great extent informed by one or more of these fundamental systems.

Christianity

Although "Quadragesima," or Lent, was instituted in remembrance of Christ's 40-day fast in the desert, there is little in the biblical account of Christ and his followers that would warrant either regular fasting or placing restrictions on which foods can be consumed. In fact, the Gospels consciously reject the dietary legalism of the Old Testament and assert that all foods are clean: "Not that which goeth into the mouth defileth a man" (Matt. 15: 11). Furthermore, Christ celebrated numerous feasts - the marriage at Cana, supper at Emmaus, the "Last Supper."

Fasting, or a denial of bodily urges to achieve spiritual purity, seems to be more directly rooted in

Greek and Eastern ideas about the dualism of body and soul. If the body is merely a temporary corruptible prison for the eternal soul, then suppressing its sinful demands will cleanse the spirit in anticipation of its release from bodily constraint. Rejecting the appetites for food, sex, and sleep becomes a path to righteousness.

St. Anthony (c. 250-350) was the most popular of the early ascetics, and the example of his austerities in the Egyptian desert would inspire many future Christians. The church fathers also adopted a favorable stance toward fasting and abstinence. St. Augustine (354-430) recommended abstinence from meat and drink in an epistle to his sister's nunnery, and both St. Ambrose (340?-397) and St. Jerome (340?-420) were influential in advocating an abstemious diet for monastics in Italy.

It was St. Benedict of Nursia (c. 480-547) who would be most influential in framing a rule that would form the foundation for European monasticism. However, before we examine this specific institution, the more general topic of public fasts demands attention.

In the fourth and fifth centuries, the Christian church gradually defined the fast as an abstention from meat and animal products such as milk and eggs and a limitation of meals to one a day. The 40 days between Ash Wednesday and Easter, as well as the 30 days of Advent preceding Christmas, were set aside as the most important fasts. Wednesdays and Fridays, and sometimes a third day of the week, were also designated as fast days, as were the evenings preceding holidays. Although originally proscribed, fish increasingly became the ideal food for these periods.

In principle, fasts were intended to be public expressions of self-denial in atonement for sins. Minor mortifications would presumably quell the passions and turn the mind to spiritual exercise in preparation for major holy celebrations. Depending on their budgets, people could, in practice, consume rare and expensive fish, dried fruits, and spiced confections, so Lent did not necessarily involve a sacrifice of luxury. Rather in wealthy households it could become the occasion for the ingenious invention of meatless dishes incorporating almond milk to replace cream. But for the majority of people a normally meager diet would now be limited to bread, legumes, and the often reviled stockfish.

The cyclical seasons of want were bracketed by festivals of plenty, and numerous saint's days and local celebrations punctuated the medieval calendar. The festival of St. Iago in Spain and that of St. Joseph in Italy are two examples. Many of these feasts originated in pagan agricultural rites that were absorbed into the early church and transformed into holy days. Each town across southern Europe would also celebrate the feast of its own patron saint with specially prepared foods.

The most universal feast was held on the day before Ash Wednesday, Martedi Grasso or Mardi Gras, when all meat and eggs had to be consumed before Lent. This day of meat eating or "Carnevale" often became the occasion for gross indulgence. Drunkenness, flesh eating, violence, and sexual license were all associated with this binge preceding the rigors of abstinence.

By the late Middle Ages, mock battles would be held between personifications of Carnival and Lent, and the natural order of society would be subverted in mock trials, mock weddings, and even mock prayers. Indeed, the world was said to be turned upside down in this brief catharsis of revelry (Burke 1978). Gluttony was still considered among the seven deadly sins, though this rule, too, was momentarily suspended.

The most important "feast" in the Christian calendar, however, was of a more sacred nature. The sacrament of the Eucharist, in which bread or a thin wafer consecrated by a priest is placed in the mouth of each communicant, offers a form of spiritual nourishment. After the Fourth Lateran Council in 1215, the official doctrine of transubstantiation held that the substance of the bread is transformed into the actual body of Christ while its "accidents" or shape still appear to be bread. Through this miracle, and the act of eating the bread, one receives merit, which aids in salvation. Drinking wine is also central to the sacrament, although it was customarily reserved only for priests. The wine becomes the blood of Christ in the same way that the bread becomes the body. Thus, the everyday acts of eating and drinking were transformed into one of the central mysteries of the Christian church.

Also central to the culture of food as influenced by Christianity was the development of monasticism. In his "Rule" for monks at Monte Cassino in the sixth century, St. Benedict laid down specific regulations for food consumption that spread across Europe. Two cooked dishes were to be offered at either the noontime (prandium) or late afternoon (cena) meal and a third dish of fresh fruit or vegetables when available. Each monk was to be given a pound of bread daily as well as a "hemina" of wine, which was roughly two glasses (St. Benedict 1981: chap. 40, n. 40.3).

St. Benedict noted that wine was hardly a proper drink for monks, but few could be convinced of that in his day. Benedict also carefully fit meals into the daily schedule of prayers, though over the years his original provisions were supplemented by snacks such as the "collation," eaten while hearing readings from St. Cassian's Collations. There might also have been extra portions of food, the "pittance" provided by pious benefactors, though this may not have amounted to much, considering what this word has come to mean.

Most important, in addition to the regular cycles of fasting, monks were expected to abstain entirely from meat, except perhaps on rare occasions, as when dining in private with the abbot or when ill. These rules were often observed only in the breach, especially as monasteries grew more wealthy and lax in the tenth and eleventh centuries. Cheese was eventually allowed, following the logic that it is no more flesh than olive oil is wood (Moulin 1978: 87). Other prohibitions were also avoided: St. Benedict cannot have been referring to fowl when demanding that monks abstain from the meat of quadrupeds (St. Benedict 1981: chap. 39).

Rather than models of austerity, many monasteries became gastronomic enclaves, and there is, no doubt, some truth to the complaints of St. Peter Damian and Dante Alighieri about portly Benedictines (Dante 1939: 130). In addition to preserving and spreading viticulture throughout Europe, the monks originated many renowned cheeses, pastries, and confections. From their medicinal gardens they also concocted many celebrated cordials, chartreuse, and vermouth – not to mention champagne (Dom Perignon in the seventeenth century).

It was precisely in reaction to this gastronomic luxury and laxity that many new and more rigorous orders were founded in successive waves of religious revival. In contrast to lavish Cluniac monasteries, Cistercian simplicity began to flourish in the late twelfth century, influenced by St. Bernard of Clairvaux. Later came new austere mendicant orders such as the Franciscans, and following the advent of bubonic plague, a number of intensely penitential and flagellant orders flourished, such as the Gesuati. At any rate, the ascetic attitude toward food remained active in spite of the luxury of wealthier orders.

Many holy men and women so successfully mortified their flesh through abstinence that we can only conclude they deliberately starved themselves to death. This was precisely the goal of some Cathars in the South of France, who believed (heretically) that the world was created by the devil and that everything in it, the body as well as food, was evil. For the Cathars, starvation was a way to attain spiritual perfection. The Carthusians, an entirely different vegetarian order, had to go out of their way to assert the goodness of food to avoid being suspected of the Cathar heresy.

Self-starvation itself, however, was not necessarily considered heretical or demoniacal. St. Catherine of Siena, it has been suggested, suffered from a form of anorexia and subsequently became a model consciously imitated for centuries (Bell 1985). For many young women, conquering the self and hunger may have been the only outlet for expressing their pious urges in an entirely male-dominated society, the ideal of holiness being achieved only with the destruction of appetites and often the body itself.

Following the Counter Reformation, asceticism was gradually supplanted by activism as the ideal fruit of devotion. The Lenten fast, however, remained in force up until Vatican II, and to this day many Catholics continue the practice as an integral part of their food heritage.

Humoral Physiology

Physicians promulgated another theoretical food system, humoral physiology, which had a profound impact on the culture of food in southern Europe. As a legacy of Greek science, nutritional theory survived in more or less threadbare form through the early Middle Ages. Among the Moors of Spain it did undergo a rich development, but its first major revival in the Latin West was within the walls of the earliest universities, most notably at Salerno, Montpellier, Bologna, and, later, at Padua and Valladolid.

Translating Galen and Hippocrates via Arabic sources and commentaries, Gerard of Cremona (1140–1187) and Arnald of Villanova (1235–1312) provided Europe with its first guides to nutrition. The popular *Regimen Sanitatis* (c. 1160) of Salerno was the most widely known of the early diet books, and works continued to be written through the Middle Ages by individuals such as Magninus of Milan and Ugo Benzo.

During the Renaissance, dozens of new works were printed throughout southern Europe, the most popular by Marsilio Ficino, Platina, and Girolamo Savonarola. A second major revival followed in the sixteenth century, as complete and accurate translations of ancient Greek texts became available. Despite extensive scientific research in the seventeenth and eighteenth centuries, the old humoral system was fully abandoned only in the nineteenth century, and it still survives in the popular consciousness, most notably in Latin America.

Humoral physiology is based on the idea that four major fluids dominate the human body: blood, phlegm, choler, and black bile (or melancholy). Each "humor" is composed of two basic elements: Heat and moisture are the elements that make up blood; cold and moisture constitute phlegm; heat and dryness combine to form choler; and cold and dryness make up melancholy. When the body is in a state of health, the four humors were said to be balanced, or in the correct proportion of 16 parts to 4 parts to 1 part to 1/4 part. An imbalance of humors was seen as the origin of sickness and disease. Each individual, however, was also said to have his or her own natural "complexion" or constitution in which one humor dominated, and this distinctive makeup determined the nature of bodily functions, character, and intelligence.

That this system was well known is confirmed by frequent references to it in southern European art and literature from the High Middle Ages onward. But the system was not merely a philosophical abstraction or literary conceit. People did try to judge the state of their bodies' vital signs and tried to correct imbalances through regulation of the "nonnaturals" or external influences, such as sleep, exercise, air quality, sexual activity, and – most important for this discussion – diet.

Essential to this system was the belief that each food also had its own complexion or dominant humor and would thus interact with the humoral balance of the individual who consumed it. Several signs revealed the qualities of a food: color, aroma, and, most notably, taste. Sweetness was evidence of heat and moisture. Spicy, salty, and bitter foods were all considered hot and dry in varying degrees; we still describe foods like chilli peppers as "hot." Cold and dry foods tasted sour, styptic, or tannic (hence a "dry" wine). Lastly, insipid and watery foods were composed of cold and moist elements. Foods in each of these categories also promoted their own specific humor in the body when eaten. Cool and moist cucumbers supposedly converted into phlegm; hot and dry cinnamon became choler; and sugar made good blood.

As a rule, healthy individuals were advised to consume foods similar to their own natural complexions. When "distempered" or ill, one should consume the opposite foods to correct the imbalance. Medicines were prescribed following the same logic. A "cold" or phlegmatic imbalance might be corrected with hot and dry spices, or a more potent medicine if more serious. Tobacco was first taken for such conditions. When a person was overheated, a cold acidic drink was viewed as a good corrective.

By the mid-sixteenth century, physicians most frequently recommended nourishment opposite to the natural complexion, but such advice merely assumed that the patient was usually somewhat distempered, and the recommendation did not constitute a change in theory (Flandrin 1982, 1987: 295-6).

The complexion of each food also determined how it would best combine with other foods. An excessively cold and moist food, such as melon, was best corrected with salt or prosciutto. Fatty phlegmatic meats were more digestible with hot and dry spices. A food whose substance was difficult to "concoct" in the stomach, such as crass and gluey fish, would be improved by a cutting lemon juice or vinegar.

Indeed, humoral physiology is at the very heart of many culinary traditions that persist in southern Europe to this day. Salads are a perfect example. Cold and moist lettuce is combined with hot and dry herbs, both of whose humoral natures are counteracted by hot and dry salt and cold and dry vinegar, given further balance by hot and moist oil. Consider quail with grapes, strawberries with balsamic vinegar, or pork with mustard. All these combinations have their origin in humoral dietary theory.

According to dietary theorists, however, deciding exactly what to eat was a far more complicated affair than simply balancing flavors. Each meal also required consideration of the season, because the body was thought to respond to atmospheric conditions and air quality. The age and gender of the diner was also essential; young people were thought to have hotter systems, as were all males. This is why wine was considered harmful for boys but excellent for the aged *(Vinum lac senum est)*. The amount of physical exercise people performed also helped determine the most healthful diet for them. According to the theory, laborers had hotter stomachs and could digest tougher, denser, and darker foods such as beans, sausages, coarse whole grain breads, and porridge, but the leisured required more subtle and rarefied foods such as chicken, eggs, white bread, light wines, and refined sweets. Clearly, social prejudice was built right into the system.

The amount of sexual activity also had to be taken into account, for this heated and dried the body, using up nutrients as blood was supposedly converted into semen. Hot foods could overheat the sexually active or actually incite lust. Conversely, a less nutritious diet was seen as an aid to celibacy; less blood, and ultimately less semen, would be produced. Cold foods, such as lettuce, became effective anaphrodisiacs recommended for priests and others with a need for them.

Mood was also directly related to diet. A diet of cold and dry foods, such as beef, could lead to depression, as could crass, indigestible foods, which clogged the body and permitted humors to accidentally corrupt. Laziness could be triggered by a debilitating "phlegmatic" humor, just as overly hot foods could provoke wrath. Equally, the emotional state of the individual determined which foods were corrective. Melancholic people, for example, were cheered up with aromatics, borage, hot (and moist) wines, and sweets.

Many popular dietary recommendations, however, appear to have derived from a source other than standard humoral physiology. Frequently, physicians mentioned that the character traits of a particular animal would produce similar traits in the person who ate it. Thus, the flesh of rabbits would make one timid, and it was often described as a melancholic food. But highly strung birds could make one nervous and edgy, even causing insomnia. The same elements that materially caused these characteristics in the animal were transferred into the consumer. In similar fashion, a light and subtle wine was thought to produce, in a process not unlike distillation, light "spirits" that flowed easily through the brain and instilled subtlety of thought. This process of direct transference was also applied to specific animal parts: Testicles promoted virility, brains gave rise to wit, blood (or milk, which was believed to be produced from blood in the mammary glands) fortified the weak and blood-deficient.

Direct transference began to be criticized in the mid-sixteenth century and was eventually banished from nutritional theory along with the doctrine of signatures, which posited that foods good for specific ailments would bear the marks of their potency in their outward form. That is, brain-shaped walnuts were good for the intellect; red wine was an analogue for blood. But by the mid-seventeenth century the entire system of humoral physiology had been called into question, particularly after systematic research had been conducted into the process of digestion. An entirely new system to replace humoral theory appeared in the nineteenth century with Justus von Liebig and the discovery of the role of proteins, carbohydrates, and fats, and in the twentieth century with the discovery of vitamins.

The Courtly Aesthetic

The third major influence on the foodways of southern Europe derives from the social connotations of particular foods and methods of preparation. Historically, it was usually the court that set culinary trends, which then spread to lower ranks of society. But this was not simply a process of invention and imitation. Specific items could be devalued or revived, depending on which social class they were currently associated with.

In southern Europe it is particularly the proliferation of social strata and the specialization of the economy that have generated a wealth of food prejudices (Goody 1982). In a relatively unstratified society, where the majority of the population is involved in food production and eats essentially the same diet, few foods will be associated with particular classes. This was most likely the case in the early Middle Ages. But in many parts of southern Europe, particularly in trading and manufacturing centers, where there always have been both noble and impoverished classes, food prejudices become central, and this has been increasingly true from the High Middle Ages to the present.

Specific foods also rise and fall in popularity. For example, in the Middle Ages and early Renaissance, saffron was a symbol of wealth and privilege because it was expensive and because it lent a dazzling effect to foods. The way to impress a guest was to present a saffron-daubed dish, sparkling like gold. Indeed, saffron became a symbol for gold, and to eat it represented a literal incorporation of wealth. However, enthusiasm for saffron abated during the sixteenth century, when for the first time it was cultivated on a large scale (Toussaint-Samat 1992: 522). As a consequence, it became far more affordable, less potent as a symbol of wealth, and at court it went out of fashion. Sugar had much the same history, beginning when it was first processed in Portuguese and Spanish colonies (Mintz 1985).

Economic factors can also influence the association of a particular food with a certain class. For example, in the sixteenth century, as populations grew and the living standard of the majority dropped, the price of meat rose considerably faster than that of grains. Thus, a greater proportion of expendable income had to be spent on the former, a process described as "depecoration." Poorer people were forced to purchase less fresh meat, and what meat products they could afford would necessarily be long-

lasting or preservable. Examples include sausages and smoked meats, as well as herring and salted codfish. As these items became identifiable as peasant food, they were increasingly reviled at court – and, it is interesting to note, condemned by dieticians.

Other foods readily identified with the peasantry – beans and onions and porridges of barley and millet (and later maize, as in polenta) – were stigmatized as southern European society was increasingly stratified. Particular foods became more obvious symbols of class. To consume something beyond one's budget was an act of social climbing, just as eating "common" foods showed a lack of taste and breeding.

Oddly enough, though, peasant foods came back into fashion, particularly during periods of nostalgia for simplicity and earthiness, as in the Romantic movement or in recent decades. The most interesting and subtly malleable food prejudices always have and still do center around bread. Because it has been the staple of the West, bread preferences are almost always an encapsulation of social climate. In fact, at times, the whiteness and texture of bread have been arranged hierarchically and have matched precisely the structure of society.

Illustrative is fifteenth-century Ferrara, where an essentially two-tiered society was reflected in the distinction between fine white bread and all other types (Camporesi 1989). Seventeenth-century works depict each social level with its own proper type of bread, but in other periods, brown, whole wheat, and multigrained breads have gained popularity. When ethnic awareness is valued, rustic, homemade loaves reappear.

If we specifically examine courtly food fashions, a number of interesting patterns emerge. The oldest and most obvious symbols of nobility were large game animals, such as roast boar or venison, presented whole to a large hall of retainers. Such viands would be carved and apportioned according to rank, and naturally the most honored (and favored) guests would be seated closest to the lord (Visser 1991). This type of meal perfectly matched the feudal warrior society in which prowess on the hunt was valued as much as it was in battle.

Gradually, however, this rustic sort of meal was replaced on noble tables with meals of magnificence and sophistication. Perhaps originating in the Burgundian court, dishes including peacocks (resewn into their feathers), swans, baked porpoises, and sturgeons became fashionable and quickly spread to Italy and the rest of southern Europe. Exotic spices and sugar, liberally strewn over each dish, also became requisite symbols of wealth; even pearls, amber, and gold might be incorporated into elaborately prepared confections. Disguised foods and hybrid creations, such as half-pig and half-chicken, also became popular. These new foods signified aesthetically new symbols of power and new values of wealth, as well as new far-flung connections.

An entire literary genre flourished that described the proper way to throw a banquet, and by the time of the Renaissance, precise rules for carving and using newly introduced cutlery were elaborated (Rosselli 1516; Romoli 1560). This new "civilized" behavior at the table reflected a pacification of society as governments claimed a monopoly on violence (Elias 1982). A profusion of tastes and textures became the hallmark of sophistication. Cristophoro di Messisbugo described a Ferrarese banquet for 54 guests held during Lent in 1529. It included over a dozen courses that consisted of 15 to 54 individual servings of 140 separate foods and required over 2,500 plates. It is interesting to note that each course also contained savories, sweets, soups, and salads in no discernible order (Messisbugo 1549).

When lower social classes (such as wealthy merchants) began to imitate such ostentatious meals, however, once again courtly fashion shifted – this time toward simplicity and refinement. New American products made their appearance. Chocolate drinking spread quickly from Spain as the ideal drink for indolent aristocrats (Schivelbusch 1992). Italian chefs were lured to northern courts, and the French entirely transformed haute cuisine in the seventeenth century by increasingly abandoning spices and the juxtaposition of flavor and texture. The new culinary aesthetic became one of simple ingredients, delicacy of preparation, and careful ordering of courses (Revel 1982; Mennell 1985: 71). French classicism in art, absolutism in government, and courtly cuisine thereafter dominated in southern Europe, though regional variations did not disappear. The tomato, for example, caught on in the south much more than elsewhere in Europe.

The influence of the courtly aesthetic declined in nineteenth-century Europe in the wake of popular revolutions, and the democratization of governments ushered in a similarly leveling tendency in taste. A "bourgeois" cuisine introduced a greater simplicity that was, in part, a reaction against aristocratic refinement, and there eventually arose a new awareness and appreciation of folk recipes and traditional foodways, especially with the growth of nationalism.

In the modern era in southern Europe an even greater splintering of society into various groups has resulted in further proliferation of eating styles and a greater need of individuals to be associated with a distinctive group on the basis of taste. Today, vegetarianism, fast food, health food, ethnic food, and nouvelle cuisine all vie for adherents with their own distinctive ideologies and approaches. The modern era in southern Europe can also be sharply contrasted with preceding centuries because of the advance of food technologies in areas such as scientific methods of farming, canning, refrigeration, and factory processing. Food industries are now entirely geared toward a consumer society and are firmly linked to global markets. Not only have subsistence crises and hunger become things of the past for most in the developed world, but they have been replaced with the problem of overeating.

To conclude, three ideologies of food – Christian, dietetic, and courtly – reveal some of the ways southern Europeans have thought about food and indicate the kinds of considerations that entered into their food choices. But little, thus far, has been mentioned of what they actually had to choose from, and thus, in closing, a very brief catalog of the most common ingredients and their particular social or medical associations is offered.

Wheat has always been southern Europe's dominant grain, used primarily in leavened breads. Until recently, the whitest and most finely bolted flour was considered the most prestigious as well as the most healthful; flours containing bran were thought to be crass and fit only for laborers. Various pastries and cookies were praised by physicians for their restorative power and were certainly indulged in at court as well as within monasteries throughout the Middle Ages. Only in the early modern period were they judged to be unhealthy enticements, precisely at the time when sugar and spices became available to ordinary people.

Pasta made its appearance in the late Middle Ages, and from the start was condemned by physicians as difficult to digest. Although pasta was usually associated with common kitchens, courts did not entirely reject it, as is evidenced by Bartolomeo Scappi's references to macaroni (Scappi 1570). Extruded pasta, usually made with semolina flour, has come in dozens of sizes and shapes since the late nineteenth century.

Barley has also been popular since ancient times and was most frequently used in porridges and polenta, as were millets, although these were replaced entirely by maize, introduced in the sixteenth century. Rice had been an expensive luxury, usually served with milk and sweetened. It was first cultivated widely in the fifteenth century in Lombardy, and later in Spain, after which a stout variety (arborio) became the basis of risotto and paella.

Legumes, particularly fava beans, peas, and chickpeas, have flourished since Roman times. None were considered suitable for delicate constitutions, and since the late Renaissance were increasingly stigmatized as peasant food. Nonetheless, beans were perhaps the quintessential Lenten fare for those with modest budgets, and new varieties of beans introduced from the Americas have also been popular.

As for vegetables, few were considered especially nutritious, but watery cucumbers, zucchini, and squashes, although frowned upon by physicians, were nonetheless cultivated and enjoyed at all levels of society. The vegetables particularly associated with southern Europe have been salad greens: lettuce, sorrel, endive, purslane, orache, radicchio, dandelion, spinach, and beet and turnip greens. In addition, all varieties of the Brassica family were consumed: cabbages, broccoli, cauliflower, and kale, as well as such others as artichokes, cardoons, asparagus, and fennel. Eggplants were probably introduced by the Arabs, but they were considered very dangerous, along with other members of the Solanaceae. Tomatoes have been a staple of southern European cuisine for only the past few centuries; along with capsicum peppers, they were widely used after their introduction from the New World in the sixteenth century.

Onions and garlic, traditionally, have been indispensable flavorings, though the latter, in the past as now, has strong peasant associations. Truffles, particularly the white variety from Piedmont and the black from Perigord, have always been highly prized luxuries. But as with mushrooms, physicians usually considered them dangerous "excrements of the earth."

The most distinctively southern European herbs are parsley, oregano, rosemary, thyme, sage, fennel, aniseed (the fruit of the anise plant), and mint – all praised as hot and dry "correctives." Also widely used are bay laurel, myrtle, juniper, lovage, lemon balm, saffron, wormwood, borage, rue, savory, lavender, and, finally, basil, which had a mixed reception among physicians. Spices most frequently imported into Venice, Genoa, Marseilles, and, later, Lisbon and Seville include pepper, cinnamon and cassia, cloves, nutmeg and mace, grains of paradise (malagueta pepper), coriander and cumin, ginger, and galanga – although these have all waxed and waned in popularity on aristocratic tables.

Olives and olive oil have been traditional staple commodities, along with grapes, citrus fruits (since late antiquity), figs, and imported dates. Peaches and melons were wildly popular in early modern courts but were strongly denounced by dietary theorists as excessively cold, moist, and corruptible. Cherries, plums, strawberries, pomegranates, quinces, apples, and pears have also been popular – especially in art – as symbols for the Nativity. Among nuts, almonds, pistachios, pine nuts, walnuts, and hazelnuts take first place, and chestnuts, too, have been important, particularly in the Cévennes Mountains and around Rome. Chestnuts, however, were often described as peasant food.

Cheese from Piacenza seems to have been the first cheese to be universally praised in southern Europe. It was superseded, however, by *parmigiano-reggiano* and *pecorino romano. Mozarella di bufala* and *ricotta* are also renowned. The south of France boasts many incomparable cheeses as well, and Spain and Portugal both produce especially good cheeses made from the milk of goats and ewes.

Fowl, both domestic and wild, were credited by physicians with being the most tempered of foods and were lauded at court. They included chickens, pheasants, pigeons and partridges, and later guinea fowl and turkeys, as well as numerous tiny birds or "ucelli" (larks, thrushes, and sparrows). Ducks and

geese were quite often associated with Jews, who salted and cured them. Eggs were esteemed as the ideal food for convalescents and as symbols of Christ's resurrection.

With the coming of Lent, fish appeared on most tables, although for the poor it was usually dried cod. Sardines and anchovies, squid and octopus, crustaceans, and shellfish were all consumed, along with a wide variety of fresh fish from the Atlantic, the Mediterranean, the Adriatic, and from lakes and rivers. Among these were tuna, mackerel, mullet, bass, trout, perch, pike, carp, sole, and turbot – to name but a few. At court, mammoth sturgeons, newly born eels, turtles, snails, and even tender young frogs (eaten whole) were all fashionable at one time or another.

Among the meats consumed, veal and kid were considered the most healthful and the easiest to digest. Beef was to be reserved for robust laborers, as were innumerable varieties of pork sausage, blood sausage, organ meats, and other "salume" – though prosciutto was served on wealthy tables as well as poor. Lamb and rabbits generated a good deal of medical controversy, as did those game meats most readily associated with rural nobility.

Lastly, to do justice to the topic of wine would be impossible in this chapter. But in short, it is indispensable to Christianity, has been viewed as essential to a healthful diet in both past and very recent nutritional theories, and remains a principal object of gastronomic snobbery. Perhaps coffee has been its only serious rival in recent times.

Kenneth Albala

Bibliography

Bell, Rudolph M. 1985. *Holy anorexia.* Chicago and London.

Benedict of Nursia, St. 1981. *The rule of St. Benedict,* ed. Timothy Fry. Collegeville, Minn.

Burke, Peter. 1978. *Popular culture in early modern Europe.* New York.

Camporesi, Piero. 1989. *Bread of dreams* (Il pane salvaggio), trans. David Gentilcore. Cambridge.

Dante Alighieri. 1939. *Paradiso,* trans. John Sinclair. New York.

Elias, Norbert. 1982. *The history of manners,* trans. Edmund Jephcott. New York.

Flandrin, Jean-Louis. 1982. Médecine et habitudes alimentaire anciennes. In *Pratique et discours alimentaires à la Renaissance,* ed. Jean Claude Margolin and Robert Sauzet, 85–97. Paris.

  1987. Distinction through taste. In *A history of private life,* Vol. 3, ed. Phillipe Aries and George Duby, 295–6. Cambridge, Mass.

Goody, Jack. 1982. *Cooking, cuisine and class.* Cambridge.

Henisch, Bridget Ann. 1976. *Fast and feast: Food in medieval society.* University Park, Pa., and London.

Mennell, Stephen. 1985. *All manners of food.* Oxford.

Messisbugo, Christophoro di. 1549. *Banchetti.* Ferrara, Italy.

Mintz, Sidney W. 1985. *Sweetness and power: The place of sugar in modern history.* Harmondsworth, England.

Moulin, Leo. 1978. *La Vie Quotidienne des Religieux au Moyen Age.* Paris.

Revel, Jean-Francois. 1982. *Culture and cuisine* (Un festin en paroles), trans. Helen R. Lane. New York.

Romoli, Domenico. 1560. *La singolar dottrina.* Venice.

Rosselli, Giovanni. 1516. *Opera nuova chiamata epulario.* Venice.

Scappi, Bartolomeo. 1570. *Opera.* Rome.

Schivelbusch, Wolfgang. 1992. *Tastes of paradise* (Das Paradies, Geschmack und die Vernunft), trans. David Jacobson. New York.

Toussaint-Samat, Maguelonne. 1992. *History of food* (Histoire naturelle et morale de la nourriture), trans. Anthea Bell. Oxford.

Visser, Margaret. 1991. *The rituals of dinner.* New York.

V.C.3 ❧ France

The Dominance of the French *Grande Cuisine*

Many in Western societies as well as upper-class members of non-Western societies consider French cookery to be the world's most refined method of food preparation. This reputation has mainly to do with the *grande cuisine,* a style of cooking offered by high-class restaurants and generally regarded as the national cuisine of France. The *grande cuisine* attained its status because it emphasizes the pleasure of eating rather than its purely nutritional aspects. Whereas all cuisines embody notions of eating for pleasure, it was only in France, specifically in Paris at the beginning of the nineteenth century, that a cuisine that focused on the pleasure of eating became socially institutionalized. Moreover, it was the bourgeois class of the period that used this emphasis on eating for pleasure for their cultural development. Previously, the aristocracy had determined the styles and fashions of the times, including the haute cuisine, but this privilege was temporarily lost with the French Revolution.

The middle class also used the *grande cuisine* to demonstrate a cultural superiority over other social groups with growing economic power and, thus, the potential to rise on the social ladder. At the same time, restaurants – new and special places created for the *grande cuisine* – came into being. Spatially institutionalized, the *grande cuisine* was transformed into a matter of public concern and considerable debate (Aron 1973).

The institutionalization of a cuisine that emphasized the pleasure of eating had many effects, not the least of which was that in France, more than in other European societies, eating and drinking well came to symbolize the "good life" (Zeldin 1973-7). As such, the *grande cuisine* became culturally important for all French classes, not only for the middle class that had created it, with the result that cooking and discussions about food and the qualities of wines came

to be of paramount moment. Indeed, this self-conscious stylization of eating and drinking by all classes of France led to the description of the French by other Europeans as pleasure-oriented, and the characterization of the French style of living as *savoir vivre.*

Within French society, the manner of eating became an important indication of an entire lifestyle because eating habits represented a part of culture in which social differences and dissimilarities were expressed more intensely and more subtly than in any other area. Pierre Bourdieu's study, *La Distinction,* impressively showed this phenomenon in relation to French society (1979).

Another effect of the institutionalization of the *grande cuisine* went beyond French society: The *grande cuisine* became the model and the basis for an internationally renowned cuisine and one that is culturally and socially more highly valued than other regional and national cuisines. Prices reflect this valuation most clearly. French restaurants not only are associated with gourmet food but are also the most expensive restaurants in practically any country. This internationalization of the *grande cuisine* has led to the adoption and variation, in other nations, of French recipes, French food decoration, and French ideas of service, such as the order that dinner courses should follow. The international dominance of the *grande cuisine* can be most clearly seen by the fact that the menu, the cooking language, the organization of the kitchen, and the training of the cooks are all to a large extent based on French models.

Outside of France, the *grande cuisine* holds the reputation of being a national cuisine, with people forgetting perhaps that there also exist a number of different French regional cuisines. These are bound to each other not so much by common cooking traditions as by a complicated cultural rating scheme that determines the cultural superiority or inferiority of cuisines of similar regional and social origin. This cultural judgment is also applied to those who cook and eat these regional dishes, which means that foods can be used to establish symbolic boundaries and to produce social inequality (cf. Gusfield 1992).

We can illustrate this social process with the *grande cuisine* and the regional cuisines. The former originated in an urban, aristocratic, and bourgeois environment; the latter represent rural and lower-middle-class cooking. They are not variations, one on the other, but opposites, each with different "cultural capital" (Bourdieu 1979). The *grande cuisine* is considered to be well developed, refined, and luxurious; rural cooking is described as simple, plain, and modest (Bonnain-Moerdyk 1972). Not only do these descriptions standardize the styles of cooking, they also express the meaning and function of eating and drinking in those social classes that have a special cuisine. The cultural meanings that can be derived from the *grande cuisine* suggest that members of the bourgeois and aristocratic classes are elevated beyond the mere physical need of nourishment, whereas characterizations of the styles of cooking of the lower, middle, and rural classes emphasize the physical aspect of eating. It is said that these classes do not possess the "cultural capital" necessary to go beyond the physical need to eat and drink. Thus, different cuisines are used for cultural and social differentiation and establish (as well as reflect) social inequality.

The History of the French Cuisine

One might think that there are no better resources than recipe collections and cookbooks to reconstruct what in former centuries was considered delicious cooking. Such sources, however, are inherently biased because only the wealthy classes could read and write, and there are no written reports about the cooking customs of the majority of the population. Moreover, it is doubtful that we can deduce from those recipe collections and cookbooks we do have what foodstuffs were even eaten by the upper classes. Most of the time recipes were not written by cooks because the majority of them could not read and, consequently, could not always have strictly followed recipes. Most cookbooks, then, presumably served more to idealize the aristocratic style of eating than to give cooking instructions, and we can only hope to learn from them something about the cooking notions of a certain class of literate people at a particular time.

In general, cookbooks and recipe collections are examined historically for two reasons (Barlösius 1992). One of them is to discover tendencies in the regionalization of cookery. In France this is apparent only from the nineteenth century onward because it was then that "the upper classes began to take interest in regional folklore," and of course, this included an interest in regional cookery as well (Flandrin and Hyman 1986: 4). A second reason is to reconstruct long-term changes in cooking customs in order to discern processes of cultivation and civilization (see, for example, the works of Jean-Louis Flandrin [1983, 1984, 1986]).

The Fourteenth to the Eighteenth Century
The earliest known French recipe collection is the "Ménagier de Paris" from the fourteenth century. The oldest known French cookbook is the *Viandier de Taillevant,* published by Pierre Gaudol between 1514 and 1534. In both, we can find only a few clues to the regional origins of the recipes and other instructions (Stouff 1982; Bonnet 1983; Laurioux 1986), and in fact, it can be shown that some recipes were taken from previously published collections. Some were entirely plagiarized, others only partly changed.

Another resource, very famous and popular in Europe at that time, was the cookbook *De Honesta Voluptate* (c. 1475) by Platina (Bartolomeo Sacchi). Taken together these cookbooks give the impression that there was no regional or rural differentiation in cooking in Europe during the Middle Ages. "Cookbooks, regardless of who their readers might have been, diffused culinary models inspired more by aristocratic practices than by those of the common people, and were more cosmopolitan than regional" (Flandrin and Hyman 1986: 4). The European aristocracy had, then, a common culture in eating and drinking that was not restricted by state borders. The later development and proclamation of national cuisines is closely connected to the process of state formation, which was reinforced by the assertion of independent cultures in support of national identities (Barlösius in press).

Common European cooking traditions endured until the seventeenth century, when national cuisines began to develop. It was only when French cookery became culturally stylized and was used to mark social differences that it also became a model for the courtly and aristocratic cuisines of Europe. This conscious cultural creation of cookery and table manners shows itself most clearly in the fact that before the seventeenth century, cookbooks and recipe collections were rarely published. Then, suddenly, in the seventeenth and eighteenth centuries, many cookbooks appeared. The first of this series was *Cuisinier François* by François Pierre de la Varenne, published again and again from 1651 until 1738. Other very influential cookbooks were the 1656 *Le Cuisinier* by Pierre de Lune, the 1674 *L'Art de Bien Traiter* by L. S. R., François Massialot's *Le Cuisinier Royal et Bourgeois* (published 1691–1750), and Menon's *Nouveau Traité de la Cuisine* (1739).

In these books, changes in cooking were described with terms like *ancien* and *moderne,* which were also used to indicate changes in other arts (Barlösius 1988). The cookery of the Middle Ages was criticized as being rude, even ridiculous (whereas the new cookery was considered to be refined and cultivated). Culinary tastes had obviously changed. The cooks of the seventeenth century, especially, complained about the medieval customs of cooking food too long and overseasoning it. One result was that Asian spices, like saffron, ginger, cinnamon, passion fruit seeds, and mace, were hardly used in the new cuisine, although native herbs, such as chervil, tarragon, basil, thyme, bay leaves, and chives, became popular (Flandrin 1986).

The new culinary taste was also apparent in meat choices. During the Middle Ages, the menu of the aristocracy consisted mainly of dishes with chicken and venison (Revel 1979). Beef and pork were scarcely ever eaten, although beef was an ingredient in broths and soups. Other meats that were consumed seem exotic even today, as for example, swans, storks, cranes, peacocks, herons, and large sea mammals.

During the first decades of the seventeenth century, recipes for big birds and sea mammals like whales, dolphins, and seals disappeared from the cookbooks. It was not just that such meats were believed to have no gastronomical value; they were no longer considered edible, and attempts to prepare them marked one as uncultivated, to say the least. In fact, all animals were scratched from the menu that were not especially raised or chased for food. Also out of fashion was the medieval penchant for realistic presentation, in which, for example, cooked birds might be redecorated with their feathers before being served. At this point, then, beef dishes and some pork dishes came into fashion, but only those that used the most valuable and exquisite meat parts, such as fillets, loins, legs, and hams (cf. Flandrin 1986).

Such changes give the impression that cooking was natural and bland in the seventeenth and eighteenth centuries, but this is the case only when measured against medieval cookery. In comparison with today's food preparation, however, the courtly eighteenth-century aristocratic cuisine was heavy, excessive, and complicated. Original flavors were altered, even overwhelmed, with excessive seasoning and the mixing of different kinds of foods. The aristocratic love of splendor demanded as many dishes as possible on the table, and flavor and taste were subordinated to food decoration. Until the nineteenth century, it was common to serve food *à la française,* which signified that many different kinds of dishes were offered at the same time. There were no strict rules concerning the number of dishes, but often, depending on the number of guests, there might be as many different dishes per course as there were guests, and there was a minimum of three courses. Thus, this could mean that a meal with 25 persons in attendance required 25 different dishes per course, meaning that 75 dishes were served altogether (Malortié 1881). It is true that the guests had a much greater choice than today, but inevitably many of the dishes were cold by the time they were finally served and people had the opportunity to eat them.

Table manners also changed with culinary tastes to become standardized and strictly regulated. During the Middle Ages, everybody shared the same plate and cutlery. But in the seventeenth and eighteenth centuries, each person had his or her own plate, glass, cutlery, and napkin. People were embarrassed to eat from the same plate as others or to use the same knife or glass, and with the new regulations, the distance between guests became wider (Elias 1981). Table manners were constantly cultivated and regulated down to the tiniest details. Some of the rules even changed to their opposites. In the sixteenth and seventeenth centuries, for example, it was proper to cut one's bread with a knife, but in the eighteenth century, this was considered bad form. Instead, one broke bread with the hands.

Thus, medieval notions (albeit aristocratic ones) of how to organize eating, drinking, meals, and cooking were culturally devalued, and new (but also aristocratic) ones were put in their place. Most likely much

of the reason for this change was that the aristocrats were interested in creating greater social distance between themselves and the growing masses, and contributing to this desire was an increased emphasis on cultural characteristics, such as refined culinary taste and distinguished table manners. Certainly it is the case that social differentiation processes were at work at the dinner table as well as in other areas of everyday life. Thus, the aristocracy developed a lifestyle in which culinary and other cultural attitudes became an important means of establishing as well as reflecting social distances and defining social units. This new development was the haute cuisine.

The Emergence of the Grande Cuisine in the Nineteenth Century

In the seventeenth and eighteenth centuries, like music, painting, and literature, the haute cuisine served to express courtly aristocratic lifestyles. Only cooking and eating that demonstrated wealth, luxury, and pomp could accomplish this goal and distinguish the aristocracy in no uncertain terms from the rising middle class.

Haute cuisine was institutionalized in the *salle à manger* (dining room) of the aristocracy. Alexandre Dumas once complained that in the salons, commoners like Montesquieu (Charles Louis de Secondat), Voltaire (François-Marie Arouet), and Denis Diderot discussed important social issues in a serious and enlightened fashion, but sophisticated cookery was available only to the aristocrats (Dumas 1873: 30). Middle-class notions about cookery were excluded from the *salle à manger.* It is noteworthy that in the second half of the eighteenth century, haute cuisine was one of the last cultural areas in which the aristocratic taste still dominated (Barlösius 1988).

The aristocratic host (amphitryon) was called, after the verse by Molière [Jean-Baptiste Pocquelin]), *le véritable Amphitryon est l'Amphitryon où on mange.* He invited his guests, selected the menu, and made sure that the *salle à manger* looked splendid. At the beginning of the nineteenth century, Alexandre L. B. Grimod de la Reynière, in his book *Manuel des Amphitryon,* described standards of behavior for aristocratic hosts (Grimod 1808). Indispensable characteristics were wealth, good taste, an innate sensitivity, the desire to eat well, generosity, gracefulness, vividness, and a predilection for order. That money alone was not enough to run an excellent household could be observed again and again among the nouveaux riches (the "new rich") of the French Revolution (Grimod 1808).

The cooks who provided the haute cuisine were craftsmen who had an excellent knowledge of their craft. No aesthetic creativity was needed, however, and because of social position, they could not pursue their artistic inclinations, which were frequently directed toward the simplification of food presentation and spicing as well as a refined design of taste and flavor.

The aristocracy demanded a visible stylization that was in contrast to the cook's focus on the taste of the food rather than its appearance. The *salle à manger* as well as the amphitryon (host) were symbols of the ancien régime, so that the bourgeois *grande cuisine* was, to a great extent, developed in the restaurants. In fact, as already noted, it was at the time of the French Revolution that restaurants were established in Paris in great number (Andrieu 1955; Guy 1971; Mennell 1985). Before 1789, there were fewer than 50 restaurants in Paris; by 1820, the number had climbed to 3,000 (Zeldin 1973–77: Vol. 1, 739). It was in these restaurants that a bourgeois eating culture was established and the *salle à manger* disparaged, although its example was followed in standards of service, tableware, crystal, and cutlery.

The founding of the restaurants was the most important step in the process of changing aristocratic haute cuisine to bourgeois *grande cuisine*. Everybody who had enough money could eat in restaurants, where cookery was no longer the privilege solely of the aristocrats (Aron 1973; Barlösius and Manz 1988), and a cuisine that placed emphasis on the pleasure of eating was no longer influenced by aristocratic taste. In short, restaurants and their cooks succeeded in making cooking an aesthetic, taste-oriented art, which did not focus on a certain class (Barlösius and Manz 1988).

Indeed, the cooks helped to institutionalize the *grande cuisine* (Barlösius 1988). Many who had previously worked for the aristocracy now became cooks in the restaurants. They were responsible for menu planning, food design, and the financial aspects of meal production and began a process of professionalizing themselves as they assumed total responsibility for the design of the cuisine. Not only did they regard their cookery as an art, they defined themselves as artists whose task it was to make cooking equal to already established arts such as music and painting. Like other arts, that of cooking constantly changed because the cooks were competitive and strove for social recognition. But in calling themselves artists, they overlooked the fact that many of them were not working independently, and thus, it is not surprising that their working conditions and wages were often below those of other skilled workers.

Another factor in the institutionalization of the *grande cuisine* was the gourmand. Gourmands, who were supposed to be well informed in food matters and to have well-developed tastes, began to educate the public with an outpouring of gastronomic literature. Important works were Grimod de la Reynière's *Almanach des Gourmands* and Anthèlme Brillat-Savarin's *La Physiologie du Goût* (Grimod 1803–12; Brillat-Savarin 1833).

In fact, the gourmand took the place of the traditional aristocratic amphitryon, who did not fit into the sophisticated bourgeois culture of eating. Whereas an amphitryon was considered to be a gourmand because of his social position, social background was not important for a gourmand, who represented the bourgeois idea of a connoisseur. The following characteristics necessary to a gourmand were listed: a sensitive and well-developed sense of flavor, a distinctive aesthetic taste, and the ability to put the pleasure of eating into words. Finally, the gourmand was supposed to know in theory what the cook knew and did in practice, because only with that knowledge would the gourmand be able to make a sound judgment about food and drink (Brillat-Savarin 1833).

From the gourmand, professional gastronomic critics evolved. They ranked the restaurants according to a rating scheme and also published gastronomic guides. One of the first institutions of gastronomic criticism was the Société des Mercredis, founded in 1781 or 1782 by Grimod de la Reynière and some 17 gourmand friends, with Grimod as its chairman until 1810. This jury examined the quality of restaurants, with the members meeting once a week to jointly determine their expert opinions. Grimod was the first to have the idea of forming a jury whose only task was to taste and rate food. Inevitably, his jury was also the first to be accused of partiality in its judgments and, thus, of jeopardizing those restaurants that got low marks. With only a few exceptions, the jury's judgments were published from 1803 until 1812 in the *Almanach des Gourmands* (Guy 1971; Revel 1979).

The Société des Mercredis and the *Almanach des Gourmands* were forerunners of all those institutions of gastronomic criticism that followed, such as the various restaurant guides. Early in the twentieth century, the most influential gastronomic critic was Curnonsky (pseudonym Maurice-Edmond Sailland), who in 1928 founded the *Académie de Gastronome* on the model of the *Académie Française* (Curnonsky and Rouff 1921–8). In France, the best-known restaurant guides are those by Michelin and Kléber-Colombes.

Journals can also be indirect instruments of gastronomic criticism. For example, they give obligatory descriptions of the kinds of food to eat and how to enjoy eating them, and superficially, one cannot detect any traditional regulations and standardizations in these publications, such as, for example, rules of behavior. But such publications, nevertheless, belong to a genre in which questions of taste and table manners are dealt with, even if in subtle ways and not in the form of regulations. As in the past, today's media that focus on gastronomic criticism and the development of taste constitute a means of potentially producing social distance, as well as other distinctions, and setting a certain standard of cooking and taste.

The Change of the Grande Cuisine

At the beginning of the nineteenth century, the bourgeois *grande cuisine* was still detached from the traditions of the aristocratic haute cuisine, although not completely so, as is shown by recipes and food decoration. During this phase, the *grande cuisine* was influenced by Antonin Carême, said to be its founder, and by Antoine Beauvilliers, one of the first of the restaurant cooks (Beauvilliers 1814–16; Carême 1821, 1843–8). In his three-volume work *L'Art Culinaire de la Cuisine Française au Dix-neuvième Siècle,* first published in 1830, Carême described this cuisine extensively and depicted it in very detailed and exact drawings. He claimed the Italian architect Andrea Palladio (1508–80) as his model and adapted classical architectural forms to food presentation. No wonder the *grande cuisine* of this period, with its preference for regulated forms and symmetrical arrangement, can be called *cuisine classique.*

Carême concentrated on the visual aspect of cookery and not so much on food flavor. He also held to the *service à la française,* viewing as much less elegant the *service à la russe,* which was becoming more and more popular in restaurants. The latter corresponds mainly to today's style of service: The food is put on plates in the kitchen and served immediately to guests instead of being arranged aesthetically on the table beforehand.

Two cookbooks published later in the nineteenth century became very famous: These were Felix Urbain Dubois and Émile Bernard's *La Cuisine Classique* and Jules Gouffé's *Le Livre de la Cuisine.* In these volumes the tension between artful food decoration and the development of flavor and taste was discussed, but no unanimous decision was arrived at (Gouffé 1867; Dubois and Bernard 1874). Dubois and Bernard did not favor the *service à la russe* because, for them, cookery had to appeal to all of the senses. They did, however, simplify food decoration.

The contradiction between style and flavor became a point of dispute among Parisian chefs in the 1880s: Should food presentation be simplified in order to enhance the pleasure of eating? And if so, did that mean that cooks had to give up their claim to be artists? This debate, carried on in the cooks' clubs and journals, was a reaction to the criticisms that cookery was in crisis and had become decadent because it had neither adapted to alterations in taste nor paid attention to social changes in the clientele of the restaurants. The discussion was led by cook Prosper Montagné, who slowly succeeded in establishing that cookery had to focus primarily on food flavor and taste (Montagné and Salles 1900). At this juncture, the *cuisine classique* was developing into a cuisine that was aimed at an integration into new social realities – a *cuisine moderne.*

The cooks of the *cuisine moderne* reacted to alterations in taste as well as to social changes. Among these was the fact that people increasingly had limited time when eating in a restaurant. Another had to do with a change in the mixture of restaurant customers by the late nineteenth and early twentieth centuries. Auguste Escoffier, the most famous cook of that period, recommended that his colleagues study the tastes and habits of their guests and adapt their cookery to them, with special attention to those tastes that had changed over the years (Escoffier 1921). The cooks went into action. They simplified their recipes, shortened cooking times, left out superfluous decoration, and tried to speed up service in order to satisfy their new kinds of customers. Their artistry now focused fully on the composition of the food's flavor and taste (Barlösius 1988).

Yet the *cuisine moderne* was itself soon due for modification. Formerly it was thought that there existed universally valid rules for cooking; these determined which foods went well together and how they were to be prepared and decorated. In other words, people believed that recipes were independent of the cook. Cookery was regarded as an art, but not as an individual art whereby each cook had his own particular style that distinguished him from all others. In the 1930s, however, the obligatory cooking rules of the *cuisine moderne* were relaxed. Now cooks were asked to improvise when cooking. Traditional notions of matching foods were not taught anymore. Cooking came to be treated as an experiment, and this cookery was called *cuisine de liberté,* or the nouvelle cuisine.

Fernand Point, its most famous practitioner, placed emphasis on the arrangement of side dishes while simplifying existing recipes and developing new ones (Point 1969). The *cuisine de liberté* stressed the food's own taste and aimed at the perfection of cookery so as to create the best-quality dishes. In order to achieve this effect, new cooking methods were developed to retain the natural flavors, tastes, and colors of food. Although Point had not yet thought in terms of the nutritional and physiological aspects of his cookery, the nouvelle cuisine did integrate modern knowledge about nutrition that appealed to a new health consciousness.

The *grande cuisine* had scarcely been concerned with the health aspects of food, but now cooks attempted to link the pleasures of eating with foods that were healthful. It became very important to cook foods that were light and easily digestible. Moreover, the cooks of the nouvelle cuisine distanced themselves from industrialized food production. They disapproved of canned and prefabricated foods on the grounds of poor quality and demanded a return to small-farm food production.

The nouvelle cuisine also accepted regional cooking traditions to an unprecedented extent, and with this development, the dominance of Parisian cuisine, which had existed since the emergence of haute cuisine, was diminished. Nonetheless, in restaurants the nouvelle cuisine was expensive, and relatively few were able to afford it. For its part, the *grande cuisine* had begun to influence private cooking. Through television shows and mass-produced cookbooks, chefs were able to introduce their cookery to large segments of the population. Whereas original haute cuisine cookbooks had been written only for aristocratic and bourgeois households, and those in the first phase of the *grande cuisine* had addressed cooks in restaurants, now many cookbooks focused on family and household cooking. Thus, on one hand, the cooks opened up new sources of revenue with their books and shows, and on the other hand, the public became more interested in the art of cooking.

French Regional Cuisines

The term "regional cuisines" refers to the cookery and foodways of specific geographic areas whose borders frequently correspond with ethnic boundaries. The emergence of regional cuisines is often explained in climatic, biological, and geographic terms, and certainly these naturally caused differences help explain the more or less distinct division between northern and southern French cookery. The cuisines of southern France are marked by Mediterranean culture and more resemble Italian and Spanish regional cuisines than those of northern France. The latter are similar to cuisines found in Belgium and in the region of Baden, in Germany. The natural differences between the Mediterranean and northern French cuisines are certainly demonstrated by their use of fats. Southern cookery is based on cooking oils, such as nut and olive oils, whereas northern cookery uses butter and lard. There is also a difference in beverage preference, with those in southern France preferring wine and those in northern France beer or cider (Hémardinquer 1961; Mandrou 1961).

Such differences are not sufficient, however, to explain the emergence of small regional differences in cookery (Flandrin 1983). The concept of regional cookery presupposes that common ways of preparing food are cultural specialties that are further developed to become objects of cultural identity. Through these processes, demarcation from other cuisines occurs because of different methods of food preparation. Cooking, then, is a sociocultural phenomenon, and different recipes and foodways are the products of this phenomenon. And when certain recipes become cultural characteristics, the cuisines are distinguishable and can be regarded as independent cultural products. Therefore, cuisines can establish cultural differences as well as common grounds.

These social contexts explain why cooking traditions, which frequently differ from region to region, are stylized as regional cuisines only if the region as a whole is perceived as a cultural, ethnic, or political unity. Most of the time, the process of regionalization has been a reaction against the centralizing tendencies of the state. Thus, the first explicitly regional cookbooks published in France, appearing during the course of the nineteenth century, can be looked upon as evidence of a conscious cultural upgrading of typically regional ways of cooking (Capatti 1989). But they can also be seen as constituting a reaction against the increasing cultural dominance of the *grande cuisine,* which emanated, of course, from Paris.

Rural traditions, however, were not included in such regional cookbooks. They described urban bourgeois cookery only because the increasing centralizing tendency of Paris meant that the urban bourgeoisie in the rest of the country were not only spatially but also socially and culturally pushed into a peripheral border position. In short, the formation of independent regional cultural identities, even if only in terms of eating and drinking, can be interpreted as cultural self-assertion in the face of the emergence of a "national" cuisine.

The conscious development of regional cuisines led to popular dishes, beverages, and often cheeses that are frequently pointed to as typical and characteristic of particular regions. Wines, dishes featuring sausages with sauerkraut, the now-famous quiche, and Muenster cheese, for example, are culinary features of the Alsace-Lorraine region. Typical of the cuisine of Normandy are seafood, cider, and Calvados and the cheeses Camembert, Brie, and Pont l'Évêque. The cuisine of Provence is based on garlic, tomatoes, and olive oil. Bouillabaisse is often noted as one of its typical dishes; it consists of fish and crustaceans from the Mediterranean. The most famous dishes of the cuisine of Brittany are thin, sweet, or salty pancakes called crepes and galettes. Some areas are more famous for their wines than their cookery, especially Bordeaux, Bourgogne, Touraine, and Champagne. But in these regions, even though the wines are deemed more important than food, they nonetheless symbolize true eating enjoyment (Fischer 1983).

Although certain dishes and beverages have been pointed to as characteristic of specific regional cuisines, it is not always safe to conclude that they are consumed very heavily in their region, and in fact, statistics bear this out. One reason is that many typically regional dishes are traditionally prepared for festive occasions but not for everyday consumption. Another is that these dishes may be quantitatively a small part of the diet when compared to basic foods like bread. The main reason, however, is that regional cuisines tend to reflect the national cuisine in the sense that they assign to some foods a special historical status that is not deserved. To take Provence as an example, it can be demonstrated that foods that are supposed to be native and indispensable to its cuisine do not necessarily originate in that region. Tomatoes, beans, potatoes, and artichokes are the basic elements of the cuisine of Provence. But none of these foods originated there; rather, they reached southern France only following the fifteenth century (cf. Stouff 1982; Flandrin and Hyman 1986).

French Cuisine – Today and the Future

In recent years, it has become apparent that for many in the West, French cookery is no longer seen as the culinary standard, or even as the most refined cuisine. Other cuisines, such as those of Italy or Japan, are regarded as on an equal level, even though, both nationally and internationally, the French government and lobbies for the country's gastronomic arts attempt to forestall this loss of predominance by means of advertising, awards, "taste-training" events, and even great state dinners.

Why is the French style of cuisine (which was, after all, something of a standard for more than 300 years) losing its dominant position now? Two important reasons, among many, are directly connected with each other. One is that the European aristocracy and the established middle classes, for whom France served for so long as the culturally guiding nation, in language and cuisine as well as in civilization generally, no longer hold a culture-forming position, and the new cultural elites have oriented themselves to other lifestyles. The second reason reflects the shifting of political, economic, and cultural positions of power within the global society. Although French cuisine, in particular, maintained a European dominance in the past, the increasing acceptance and popularity of, say, Japanese cuisine illustrates something of the cultural competition internationally at the turn of the twenty-first century. In other words, both within Europe and in other parts of the world, French culture and, therefore, French cuisine have become devalued in terms of prestige.

The future will show if another cuisine will replace that of France in a position of prominence. It is more likely, however, that several different national styles of cookery will achieve acceptance as equally delightful and ideal. One thing is already certain: The French cuisine (and French wines as well) are no longer matchless in quality.

Eva Barlösius

Bibliography

Andrieu, Pierre. 1955. *Histoire du restaurant.* Paris.
Aron, Jean-Paul. 1973. *Le mangeur du 19ième siècle.* Paris.
Barlösius, Eva. 1988. Eßgenuß als eigenlogisches soziales Gestaltungsprinzip. Zur Soziologie des Essens und Trinkens, dargestellt am Beispiel der grande cuisine Frankreichs. Ph.D. thesis, Universität Hannover.
1992. The history of diet as a part of the *vie matérielle* in France. In *European food history,* ed. H. J. Teuteberg, 90–108. Leicester, England.
In press. Cucina. In *Enciclopedia del corpo.* Rome.
Barlösius, Eva, and Wolfgang Manz. 1988. Der Wandel der Kochkunst als genußorientierte Speisengestaltung. Webers Theorie der Ausdifferenzierung und Rationalisierung als Grundlage einer Ernährungssoziologie. *Kölner Zeitschrift für Soziologie und Sozialforschung* 4: 728–46.
Beauvilliers, Antoine. 1814-16. *L'art du cuisinier.* Paris.
Bonnain-Moerdyk, Rolande. 1972. Sur la cuisine traditionelle comme culte culinaire du passé. *Revue de la Société d'Ethnologie Française* 3-4: 287–94.
Bonnet, Jean-Claude. 1983. Les manuels de cuisine. *18ième Siècle* 15: 53–64.

Bourdieu, Pierre. 1979. *La distinction. Critique sociale du jugement.* Paris.
Brillat-Savarin, Anthèlme. 1833. *La physiologie du goût.* Paris.
Capatti, Alberto. 1989. *Le goût du nouveau. Origines de la modernité alimentaire.* Paris.
Carême, Antonin. 1821. *Projets d'architecture dédiés à Alexandre Ier.* Paris.
1843-8. *L'art culinaire de la cuisine française au dix-neuvième siècle. Traité alimentaire et practique.* Paris.
Curnonsky [Maurice-Edmond Sailland] and Marcel Rouff. 1921-8. *La France gastronomique. Guide des merveilleuses culinaires et des bonnes auberges françaises.* Paris.
Dubois, Felix Urbain, and Émile Bernand. 1874. *La cuisine classique.* Paris.
Dumas, Alexandre. 1873. *Le grand dictionnaire de la cuisine.* Paris.
Elias, Norbert. 1981. *Über den Prozeß der Zivilisation.* 2 vols. Frankfurt.
Escoffier, Auguste. 1921. *Guide culinaire.* Paris.
Fischer, M. F. K., trans. 1983. *Die Küche in Frankreichs Provinzen.* Stuttgart.
Flandrin, Jean-Louis. 1983. Le goût et la nécessité: Sur l'usage des graisses dans les cuisines d'Europe occidentale (XIVe–XVIIIe siècle). *Annales* E.S.C. 369–401.
1984. Internationalisme, nationalisme, et régionalisme dans la cuisine du 14e et 15e siècles: Le témoignage des livres de cuisine. In *Manger et boire au Moyen Age.* 2 vols. 75–91.
1986. La distinction par le goût. In *Histoire de la vie privée,* Vol. 3, ed. Philippe Ariès and Georges Duby, 266–309. Paris.
Flandrin, Jean-Louis, and Philip Hyman. 1986. Regional tastes and cuisines: Problems, documents and discourses on food in southern France in the sixteenth and seventeenth centuries. *Food and Foodways* 2: 1–31.
Gouffé, Jules. 1867. *Le livre de la cuisine.* Paris.
Grimod de la Reynière, Alexandre L. B. 1803-12. *Almanach des gourmands.* Paris.
1808. *Manuel des amphitryon.* Paris.
Gusfield, Joseph R. 1992. Nature's body and the metaphors of food. In *Cultivating differences. Symbolic boundaries and the making of inequality,* ed. Michèle Lamont and Marcel Fournier, 75–104. Chicago.
Guy, Christian. 1971. *La vie quotidienne de la société gourmande en France au XIXe siècle.* Paris.
Hémardinquer, Jean-Jacques. 1961. Essai de cartes de graisses en France. *Annales* E.S.C. 747–9.
Laurioux, Bruno. 1986. Les premiers livres de cuisine. *Histoire* 3: 51–7.
Malortie, Karl Ernst von. 1881. *Das Menü.* Second edition. Hannover.
Mandrou, Robert. 1961. Les consommations des villes françaises (viandes et boissons) au milieu du XIXième siècle. *Annales* E.S.C. 740–4.
Mennell, Stephen. 1985. *All manners of food: Eating and taste in England and France from the Middle Ages to the present.* Oxford.
Montagné, Prosper, and Prosper Salles. 1900. *La grande cuisine illustrée.* Paris.
Point, Fernand. 1969. *Ma gastronomie.* Paris.
Revel, Jean-Francois. 1979. *Un festin en paroles.* Paris.
Stouff, L. 1982. Y avait-il à la fin du moyen-age une alimentation et une cuisine provençale originale? *Manger et boire au moyen age,* Vol. 2. Paris.
Zeldin, Theodore. 1973-77. *France, 1848-1945.* 2 vols. Oxford.

V.C.4 ❧ The British Isles

Prehistory (6000 B.C. to 54 B.C.)

Until very recently, all settled communities have eaten the foods that their geographic contexts offered. Once Britain was cut off from the mainland of the Continent (by 6500 B.C.) and fishing was feasible in the clement weather of the summer, fish became as integral a part of the local diet as meat was in the winter. Yet the bulk of the diet (about 85 percent) was made up of plant foods, as it always had been. Humankind has relied on wild foods for 99.8 percent of its time on the planet. There are over 3,000 species of plants that can be eaten for food, but only 150 of these have ever been cultivated, and today the peoples of the world sustain themselves on just 20 main crops. We underestimate the harvest from the wild that humankind gathered and the detailed knowledge, passed on from generation to generation, about which plants were toxic, which were healing, and which were sharp, bitter, sweet, and sour; such knowledge must have been encyclopedic.

The women and children gathered roots, leaves, fungi, berries, nuts, and seeds. Early in the spring the new shoots of sea kale, sea holly, hogweed, bracken, "Good King Henry," and asparagus could be picked. Then there were bulbs to be dug up that had stored their energy during the winter. These included the bulbs of lilies and of the *Alliums* (including wild garlic), the rhizomes of "Solomon's Seal," and the tubers of water plants that were dried and then ground to make a flour. Baby pinecones and the buds of trees were also springtime foods, not to mention the cambium, the inner live skin beneath the outside bark of the tree, which in the spring was full of sweet sap and yielded syrup. The new leaves of wild cabbage, sea spinach, chard, and sea purslane could be picked, as could fat hen, orache, nettle, purslane, mallow, and much else. Other edible leaves were those of yellow rocket, ivy-leaved toadflax, lamb's lettuce, wood sorrel, dandelion, red clover, wild marjoram, and salad burnet (Colin Renfrew, in Black 1993). The flavoring herbs, like wild mustard, coriander, poppies, corn mint, juniper, and tansy, would have been gathered with pleasure. Wild birds' eggs were also eaten in the spring, with a small hole made in an egg's shell and the egg sucked out raw. The bigger eggs, however, would have been cooked in their shells in the warm embers of a fire.

In the autumn, there were fruits to be gathered, like crabapples that were sliced and dried for the winter, along with berries (sloes, elderberries, strawberries, and blackberries), mushrooms, large tree fungi (like *Fistulina hepatica*), and nuts. Hazelnuts, walnuts, sweet chestnuts, pine nuts, beechnuts, acorns, and different kinds of seeds were also stored. In addition, lichens and algae (both very nutritious) were gathered and dried, and cakes were made out of them.

Fishing communities grew up at the mouths of estuaries and along coasts where there were sheltered coves and inlets that could harbor boats and fishing equipment. Dragnets of nettle fiber were held between boats, woven basketlike traps caught crabs and lobsters, and fresh fish (trout, salmon, and pike) were speared with tridents of sharpened bone lashed to a stick. Fish were wind-dried and smoked over peat or wood fires.

Seabirds, killed with clay pellets flung by slings or with arrows having blunt wooden heads, were another source of food (Wilson 1973). Unplucked birds were covered with a thick layer of smeared clay and cooked in the embers of a fire. Large seabirds – oily and strong in flavor – could also have been smoked over a fire and stored for the winter. Smaller game birds in the forest were more difficult to catch, though traps made of nets might have been used. In the late Upper Paleolithic site at Kent's Cavern, Torquay, the bones of grouse, ptarmigan, greylag goose, and whooper swan were found (Renfrew, in Black 1993).

In the winter, red deer, roe deer, elk, wild oxen, and wild boar were hunted, whereas smaller game like wildcats, foxes, otters, beavers, and hares were frequently caught in traps. Nooses, hung from trees, served as one form of trap. Hounding animals into gullies was another method of capture. Deer-antler mattocks were wielded to hack meat off the carcass, whereas flint knives were employed for skinning. Nothing was wasted: The gut and stomach were used as casing for the soft offal, cut up small and mixed with fat and herbs, then slowly roasted.

The first domestic animals were brought to Britain around 3500 B.C. by the islands' first farmers, Neolithic immigrants from the coasts of western and northwestern Europe. Following their introduction, herds of sheep, goats, cattle, and pigs grazed in forest clearings. Unwanted male cattle were poleaxed, and many of the bones were split to extract the marrow. That a large number of calves were killed suggests that there would also have been a generous supply of milk with which to make butter and cheese.

The Celts, who began to settle in Britain from the eighth century B.C., added hens, ducks, and geese to the list of Britain's domesticated animals. They refused to eat the wild horses and instead tamed them for riding and for drawing wagons and chariots. The Celts were the first to recognize that the soil of Britain is more fertile than that of continental Europe, and they cleared forests to plant cereals and to allow pasture to grow for grazing. They preserved meat, fish, and butter in salt and exported British beef to the Continent. The Celts also tilled the soil so successfully that they exported grain to many parts of Europe. In Britain, they built underground grain storage silos.

The Celts processed wheat by setting ears alight,

then extinguishing the fire when the husks were burnt. The wheat was then winnowed and baked, and saddle querns were used to grind it into flour. These industrious farmers also began beekeeping, with conical hives made from wickerwork daubed with mud or dung. They employed shallow earthenware pots as drinking vessels, whereas deeper pots were made for cooking pottages (mixtures of meat, grains, leaves, roots, and herbs) slowly over a fire.

Honey and water, left together in a pot, will ferment, and this drink - mead - was often flavored with wild herbs and fruits. Some cow, ewe, and goat milk might have been drunk fresh, but most of it would have been made into cheese and only the whey drunk. The Celts made an unhopped beer from barley and wheat, first allowing the grain to germinate, then stopping this process with heat and allowing it to ferment. Finally, they also imported wine and, later, began to grow vines themselves.

The Roman Period (54 B.C. to A.D. 407)

The Romans raised vines in southern England and grew peaches, apricots, figs, and almonds in sheltered gardens. Beef and mutton were consumed in large quantities by Roman soldiers, as was pork where it was plentiful in the south and east of England.

The Romans introduced animal farming by enclosing large tracts of land, where they kept red, roe, and fallow deer, and wild boar, as well as bears captured in Wales and Scotland. Moreover, their villas had *leporaria* for keeping hares and rabbits in estate gardens, along with pheasants, peacocks, guinea fowl, partridges, and wild pigeons - the latter kept in columbaria (dovecotes). The Romans' pigs were confined in sties in order to fatten them. Snails were confined upon islands, so that they could not escape, and were fattened on milk, wine must, and spelt; when they became so fat that they could not get back into their shells, they were fried in oil. The Romans tamed barnacle geese and mallards and, of course, also raised chickens and capons (castrated male chicks), which (like other food animals) they kept in confinement and fattened.

They considered all kinds of shellfish to be great delicacies, and many of the oyster beds that still exist today were started by the Romans. They also brought into Britain many new spices, as well as the traditions of Greek and Roman cuisine that were as refined and sophisticated as a civilization could demand. Columella (Lucius Junius Moderatus), the Roman poet and agronomist, mentioned the use of lamb or kid rennet for making cheese. Previously, plant rennet - wild thistle, nettle, or lady's bedstraw - may have been used, perhaps discovered by accident when stirring warm milk with a stem or twig of one of these plants.

The Romans also introduced the cultivation of oat and rye, though barley was the predominant crop.

They brought their bread ovens and even the *cilabus* (a portable oven) to Britain and used eggs in cooking, a practice unknown to the Celts. Eggs and milk were heated together to make a custard; eggs were fried in oil and eaten with a sauce poured over them; eggs were mixed with pounded meat or fish to make rissoles, sausages, and stuffings. With Roman rule came imported pepper, ginger, cinnamon, cassia, and other spices from the East, and white mustard cultivation was introduced. The grains of the white mustard were pounded and mixed with white vinegar to preserve vegetables. For table use, the mustard was mixed with almonds, honey, and oil.

The Romans were obsessed with two flavorings. One was the powdered root of *silphium*, which no longer exists but is thought to have been a little like asafetida. The other was *liquamen*, a sauce made from rotting small fish, which was a cross between anchovy essence and the clear fish sauce of the Orient. There were *liquamen* factories all over the Roman Empire. Honey was also a favorite flavoring, and several writers devoted pages to the craft of beekeeping in their farming manuals. In addition, cheese was much used in cooking, quite often with fish.

The Romans introduced lentils into Britain and, for the first time, cultivated globe artichokes, asparagus, shallots, and endive. They also popularized wild plants like "Good King Henry," corn salad, nettles, and pennycress. In addition, they brought new herbs to Britain, among them borage, chervil, dill, fennel, lovage, sage, and thyme.

There is an assumption that Roman banquets were an excuse for gluttony and vulgarity, even though many of their writers reveal both fine taste and moderation in their selection of foods. Notorious gluttons like the emperor Vitellius Aulus might eat four huge meals a day, but many others, like Pliny the Younger (Gaius Plinius Caecilius Secundas), would partake only of meals that were simple and informal. Pliny (1748) condemned a dinner of oysters, sow's innards, and sea urchins while listing his own notion of an evening meal: lettuce, snails, eggs, barley cake, and snow-chilled wine with honey. A dinner described by Martial (Marcus Valerius Martialis) (1993) was rather more elaborate, though he called it modest, and it was served in a single course: a kid with meatballs, chicken, ham, beans, lettuce, and leek, flavored with mint and rocket. Such a sense of a modest, well-balanced meal, with plenty of fresh green vegetables and fruits, would not be found in Britain for another 2,000 years.

The Romans encouraged wine making. They had wines flavored with salt water, resinated wines flavored with myrtle or juniper, and medicated wines mixed with herbs and taken for various ailments. Sweet wines were made by adding honey, rose petals, or citron leaves; spiced wine was made by adding wormwood. By contrast, the Britons continued to drink unhopped beer.

The Early Medieval Period (407 to 1066)

After the Romans departed, sheep, pigs, and goats were the main livestock kept, and cattle were raised as plough and draft beasts. Sheep supplied wool and milk; pigs were economical, as they ate waste and foraged in the woodlands. The rabbits escaped from the *leporaria* and died out in the wild, as did the guinea fowl and the peacocks. But hens and geese were still kept by some for their eggs and flesh, although wild birds were the only kinds available to the majority of people. Fowlers hunted birds with nets, snares, birdlime, traps, and hawks, and falconry became the sport of kings.

Germanic tribesmen added ale to the alcoholic beverages of Britain. Ale is a drink made from fermented barley or wheat, and alehouses sprang up in every village and hamlet. The beer of Britain tended to be sweeter and darker, whereas ale could be both light and mild. Mead, however, remained the drink of the elite.

After the rites of the Catholic church had taken hold in Britain (by the sixth century A.D.), fast days numbered half of the year and, later on, even more than half. This encouraged fishing, which had declined under the Germanic settlers, who were mainly farmers. But now fishermen had larger boats and longer lines and could venture farther out to sea. Drift nets grew larger, so that shoals of herrings might be caught, and the herring industry on the east coast of Britain had become important to the economy by the time of the Norman conquest in 1066. Stranded whales belonged to the Crown, but except for the tongue (thought to be a delicacy), they were generally granted to the tenant who owned that piece of shoreline. Whale meat was salted and preserved for Lenten food.

The use of olive oil disappeared with the Romans to be replaced with butter (much of it made from ewes' milk), which found its way into all cooking. The majority of the population lived, as they always had, on daily pottage, which was a stew of cereal grains with green leaves and herbs (generally orache, cabbage, or wild beet) flavored with thyme, rosemary, and onion. The starches in the cereal thickened the stew, but a richer meal was made by adding fat from a carcass or animal bones. Plants with seeds that have a high oil content were particularly treasured, and linseed was eaten extensively in rural communities from prehistory until very recently.

The seasons dramatically influenced what people could eat. Winter was a time of scarcity. From November to April there was no pasture, and the little hay that could be cut had to be saved for the draft animals, the warhorses, and the breeding stock. Thus, most of the animals were slaughtered before the winter began. The slaughter of hogs began in September, whereas cows were killed for the Feast of St. Martin (November 11). On this day all the offal was cooked and eaten, for it could not be preserved (like the carcass meat) by salting, drying, or smoking. Chitterlings, tripe, black puddings, pasties of liver, and dishes of kidneys were all eaten during this feast that was called Yule. Later, the offal was also pickled in spiced ale for a short time to make "'umble pie" for Christmas.

Beginning in the sixth century, the Slavs introduced a new type of plow in Europe, which made it possible to bring new expanses of land under cultivation. It needed six to eight oxen to pull it, but it cut deeply into the soil and turned the furrow over at the same time. One result was that a three-field system of crop rotation came into being; one field was planted with wheat or rye, the second with peas, lentils, or beans, and the third was left fallow. The countryside fed the towns, where people also kept hens, cows, and pigs. The latter are excellent scavengers. They frequented the dark, narrow alleys where the refuse from the houses was discharged; without pigs, the people of medieval towns would have been practically buried under their own sewage and rubbish, especially after those towns began to grow in population. Certainly, epidemics like the plague would have decimated towns and their peoples long before they did.

The Medieval Period (1066 to 1485)

In the thirteenth century, herrings were gutted, salted, then smoked. The industry grew, and a century later, the fish were also salted and packed into barrels. Smoked and pickled herring became a major source of protein for the poor throughout the winter.

Fish played a large role in medieval banquets as well. They were baked in pies, made into shapes or jellies, and large creatures like the porpoise were cooked whole and carved as if they were big roasts. But because of the great number of fast days, the nobles ate three courses of meat – beef or mutton, fowl, and game – on those days when meat was permitted.

The invading Normans brought with them new varieties of apples and pears and other fruits such as peaches, cherries, gooseberries, plums, medlars, and quinces. Returning Crusaders introduced citrus fruits and pomegranates to Britain from the Middle East, though these remained rare and expensive. Dried fruits were imported from the Mediterranean and were considered medicinally better for the body than fresh fruits.

The medieval garden was well stocked with a great variety of herbs and salad plants that appeared in herbals with instructions on what ailments they would cure. Salads were eaten with oil, vinegar, and salt. The earliest salad recipe, from around 1390, called for such plants as parsley, sage, onions, leek, borage, fennel, cress, rosemary, rue, and purslane to be mixed together. Over a hundred herbs are listed as necessary to the garden in a fifteenth-century list.

The Crusaders also brought back with them a great range of spices, along with many ideas about the dishes that they were used in. Meat and fish dishes were flavored with such things as ginger, cinnamon, nutmeg, cloves, and grains of paradise. Indeed, in the thirteenth century, ginger, cinnamon, cloves, galingale, mace, nutmeg, cubebs, coriander, and cumin were listed as occupants of at least one English cupboard. The old Roman trade routes, which began in southern China, the Moluccas, Malaya, and India, and extended to the ports of the eastern Mediterranean, were flourishing again. The Crusaders had discovered sugarcane growing on the plains of Tripoli, and by the end of the eleventh century, sugar had begun creeping into British recipes. Even then, sugar came in the same hard, pyramid-shaped loaves (which had to be scraped or hacked at) that were still around at the beginning of the nineteenth century.

Cider making was introduced to Britain from Normandy in the middle of the twelfth century and, at first, was confined to Kent and Sussex in the southeast. But it soon spread to East Anglia and Yorkshire. If cider was made from pears, it was called "perry." Whey and buttermilk were drunk by peasants. Sweet wines, which became immensely popular, were imported from southern Europe and the eastern Mediterranean, another result of the Crusades. Wines from Crete, southern Italy, Tuscany, Spain, and Provence were also highly valued. Madeira malmsey was exported by the Portuguese after 1421, following the planting of malvasia grapes from Crete.

Wheat was cultivated for the fine white bread of the nobility, whereas barley was grown for brewing. Oats (that withstood both cold and rain) were raised in northern Britain to be used in pottages, porridges, and thick soups. Rye was grown to make bread for the majority, who lived off their daily pottages, supplemented by curd cheese, eggs, and whey. Poaching was a capital offense, as the forests belonged to the king. Nonetheless, much netting of game birds and trapping of deer and boar continued because, for the people, starvation was never far away. If the weather destroyed a harvest, then famine was likely that winter. Beginning around 1315, at the start of the Little Ice Age (caused by an advance of polar and alpine glaciers that lasted until 1700), Britain suffered years of famine that brought on revolts and rebellion (Tuchman 1978).

Cheese was made from the milk of goats, ewes, and cows, sometimes mixed together, at other times separated to make particular cheeses. Milk was seldom drunk fresh; the nobility thought it was unhealthy as it curdled in the stomach. Besides, the popularity of butter, cheese, whey, curds, cream, and buttermilk was such that fresh milk was thought too valuable to be used simply for drinking. In the summer, strawberries and cream constituted a rural banquet. Drinks called possets were fashioned with milk curdled by ale. Often flavored with fruits and honey, possets could also be drained and made into a dessert to be cut into slices.

Fast days provoked much ingenuity (among the rich) in replacing forbidden foods with alternative concoctions. Almond milk, an expensive substitute for cows' milk, was curdled, pressed, drained, and transformed into cream cheese. Eggs were modeled from fish roe, and ham and bacon were made from salmon masquerading as lean meat, with pike as the fat (Wheaton 1985). St. Thomas Aquinas, at one point, stipulated that chickens were aquatic in origin; therefore, because they counted as fish, they could be eaten on fast days. At rich monasteries, rabbits were bred for their embryos, as these did not count as meat either.

Those who could afford it ate from "trenchers," which were thick slices of coarse rye and wheat bread with a little of the center scooped out. "After the meal, these were collected and given to the poor. During a meal, the nobility used several trenchers, made from a better class of bread. Much of the meat consumed by the rich came from hunting, and so a great variety of fresh game could be eaten throughout the winter. In addition to wild boar and deer, there were also birds, ranging from herons, swans, and peacocks to curlews, partridges, pigeons, quail, snipe, and woodcocks.

Medieval feasts could be as elaborate as those of Roman times. Illustrative is the banquet of three courses given upon the coronation of Henry IV in 1399. The first course had 10 different dishes: slices of meat, cooked in a spiced sweet-and-sour sauce; a puree of rice and mulberries, sweetened with honey and flavored with wine and spices; a boar's head; baby swans; a capon; pheasants; herons; and a pie made from cream, eggs, dates, prunes, and sugar. Then the "subtlety," a highly decorated dish of pastry, jelly, almond paste, and sugar, was brought in to indicate the end of the first course.

A second course, of nine dishes, comprised venison, calf's-foot jelly, stuffed suckling pigs, peacocks, cranes, rabbits, pies, chickens, and fritters. Another subtlety was followed by the third course of 16 dishes, which included a lot of small game birds as well as jellied eggs and custard tarts. What is interesting about medieval menus is the similarity of the courses. There was no sense of a first course being an appetizer to whet the palate or of the last course being something to refresh or pacify the diner. Those ideas were lost with the Romans, and it was many centuries before they returned. Meanwhile, simple gluttony and gorging prevailed.

Pie makers were familiar figures in medieval England. The pie was a development of the Roman idea of using a flour and water paste to seal the cooked juices of a piece of meat. But because in England butter and lard were mixed in with the flour, it was possible to make a free-standing paste container that could be packed full of a mixture of meat, game, fish, and vegetables. In 1378, a special ordinance of Richard II regulated the prices cooks and pie bakers in London could charge for their roasted and baked meats (Wilson 1973).

Except for the peasants, who still gathered much wild food, people did not eat many vegetables, which were believed to be sources of disease, especially when raw. *The Book of Keruynge* (1508), for example, warned its readers to "beware of green sallettes." But onions, leeks, garlic, and cabbage were thought not to be harmful so long as they were cooked thoroughly. This was usually the case after stewing for long hours with meat or carcass bones to make soup.

Craftsmen and workers in the towns enjoyed a better diet than peasants in the countryside. An act passed in 1363 ordered that servants of noblemen, as well as artisans and tradesmen, were to have meat or fish once a day, as well as milk and cheese. Breakfast was bread and ale, with possibly some pickled herrings or cheese. A midday meal bought at a tavern or cookshop could be roast meat, stew or soup, bread, cheese, and ale. Supper was bread and cheese again, perhaps with cold meats, and ale or wine. The law's concern with the welfare of servants was a direct result of the Black Death, which had severely pruned the population, making the survivors substantially more valuable.

In the few decades that came before the onset of the plague, however, a rise in population outpaced agricultural production, which meant overpopulation, undernutrition, and a people more vulnerable to disease. Agricultural methods and tools had not advanced for 800 years; the clearing of productive land had been pushed to its limits, and poor soils could not be made more productive nor crop yields raised. When the plague appeared, in 1348, people starved by the thousands, and the peasantry bore the brunt. The chronicler Henry Knighton, canon of Leicester Abbey, reported 5,000 dead in one field alone, "their bodies so corrupted by the plague that neither beast nor bird would touch them" (Tuchman 1978: 103). Fields went uncultivated, seeds were unsown, dikes crumbled, and salt water soured the land. "So few servants and labourers were left," wrote Knighton, "that no one knew where to turn for help."

The plague killed 40 percent of Europe's population by 1380 and halved it by the end of the century. Yet as with servants, the catastrophic event improved the lives of those peasants who survived. Landowners reduced rents and sometimes even forgave them altogether. The acreage sowed in grain 30 years after the onset of the plague was only half what it had been before the calamity. But the plague did mean that some peasants became tenant farmers, and the size of their holdings continued to grow in ensuing centuries.

Tudor, Elizabethan, and Stuart England (1485 to 1688)

Many of the foods and dishes eaten during the Middle Ages remained popular into the sixteenth and seventeenth centuries. Although new and exotic American foodstuffs could be obtained, many of these took centuries to become part of the diet. An exception was the turkey, which had found its place upon English tables by the 1540s. However, potatoes, tomatoes, peppers, and haricot beans took 200 years or more before they were ever eaten, except as rare, exotic ingredients on the tables of the wealthy.

As Iberian sugar production on islands off Africa and in the Americas increased, the national consumption of sugar rose. Queen Elizabeth was inordinately fond of sweetmeats, and the wealthy all suffered from tooth decay. Sugar was used to make the most intricate shapes and sculptures for banquets. Birds, beasts, and fruits were contrived from spun sugar, placed in baskets of marzipan, and sometimes made even more lifelike by painting and gilding.

Hunting – still the most popular pastime of the nobility – also provided occasions for ornate al fresco breakfast banquets. The gentry ate dinner at 11:00 in the morning and supper between 5:00 and 6:00 in the evening. Meals were now served on plates, and trenchers were unknown, although they lived on in the practice of serving cubes of bread beneath boiled or stewed meats. Potteries producing tin-glazed earthenware were established in Norwich and London at the end of the sixteenth century by Andries and Jacob Jansen from Antwerp (Peter Brears, in Black 1993), and glass became fashionable for drinking vessels, although silver and gold cups remained popular with the nobility.

An act of Parliament in 1548 made Saturday a fish day so as to encourage both shipbuilding and fishing. The English fishing fleet on the east coast was in constant competition with the Dutch, who fished openly in England's coastal waters and sold their catch in English ports. Salted fish was never very popular in Britain, and more effort was made to bring in fresh fish for sale. Shellfish remained the most popular seafoods; lobsters, crabs, shrimps, and prawns were boiled and eaten cold, and sometimes lobsters were boiled, then wrapped in brine-soaked rags and kept for a few months buried in sand. Oysters were eaten both fresh and pickled in vinegar. Anchovies from the Mediterranean became increasingly popular; pickled in brine, they served as appetizers before meals and were added to meat and fish dishes for flavor. Fish pies were a common dish in Lenten fare. These were filled with a mixture of herrings, salmon, eels, and sturgeon and made with butter, egg yolks, spices, and dried fruits. There were various recipes for an Elizabethan fish-day salad that usually included herbs and periwinkles, along with white endive and alexander buds, with whelks to garnish the whole.

Local cheeses became widely known through the popularity of cheese fairs that were visited by merchants, factors, and peddlers, who bought cheeses for resale elsewhere. The best were selected for the rich. Highly thought of were Banbury and Cheshire cheeses, in which, it was said, neither the rennet nor the salt could be tasted. Cheeses were also imported from abroad; Parmesan was the most popular, although Dutch cheeses were also appreciated.

In the seventeenth century, a much greater range of salad plants were grown in the walled gardens of the great estates. John Evelyn (1620–1706), in his *Acetaria, a Discourse on Sallets,* enthused over the health-giving properties of the "Herby-Diet." Yet vegetables were still frowned upon by the majority of people, with the lack of fresh vegetables in the diet evidenced by the prominence of scurvy. Gideon Harvey, physician to Charles II, spoke of it in 1675 as the "Disease of London" (Spencer 1993: 214).

Distillation of plant juices became a public activity following the dissolution of the monasteries, as monks found new vocations as apothecaries and distillers, and English soldiers, returning from the Dutch wars, spread the popularity of strong liquors. Nonetheless, beer and ale remained the most popular beverages.

Early Modern England: The Agricultural Revolution (1688–1750)

Farming technology had progressed little between the sixth and eighteenth centuries. Because there was no winter pasture, the animals were still killed at the beginning of winter. But new ways of feeding cattle began to change this situation. It was discovered that cattle could be fattened very nicely on turnips, and a manual, *The Practical Farmer* by William Ellis (1732), advised giving cattle rapeseed cakes and turnips for winter provision, as was done in Holland. There, it had been discovered that cattle would thrive on the residue left after the oil (used for lighting) had been pressed from crushed rapeseed. Later, other vegetables, such as swedes, mangelwurzels, clover, and cabbages, were also used for winter cattle feeding.

At the same time, more efficient farm tools were being invented. Jethro Tull devised the first horse-drawn hoe and field drill, which wasted less seed and allowed more grain to be harvested. Farm tools were now made of cast iron and could be mass produced; the Rotherham plow was invented, and the first threshing machine appeared before 1800. Other machines were designed that could prepare animal feed, chop turnips, and cut chaff. Because animals could at last be maintained throughout the winter, those with the most valuable traits could be retained and used to breed in the spring. Robert Blackwell (1725–95), a Derbyshire breeder, introduced the longhorn, a cow that gave a high milk yield, and John Ellman (1755–1832) introduced a new breed of sheep, the Southdown, that fattened in half the time of other breeds. The growing size of animals not only increased yields of carcass meat and milk but also ensured finer-quality fleece from sheep and more hide from cows.

At the end of the seventeenth century came the creation of the Norfolk four-course system, whereby wheat was grown in the first year, turnips in the second, then barley with clover and ryegrass undersown in the third. In the fourth year the clover and ryegrass were either cut or used for grazing.

With this new farming technology came a need for larger fields, unimpeded by hedges. Gradually, the common land, where farmworkers traditionally had kept a cow, a pig, and a few hens, and where they gathered wood for cooking fires, was removed from public use by a series of Enclosures Acts. In the reign of George III (1760–1820) alone, 3 million acres of common land were added to private farming estates, hindering the ability of thousands of farmworkers to feed their families. Many emigrated to America, whereas others went into the factories in the new and burgeoning industrial cities.

The effect of the Enclosures Acts was far-reaching. Rural life was radically altered and partially destroyed, and whole villages were abandoned. Within a generation, cooking skills and traditional recipes were lost forever, as the creative interrelationship between soil and table (the source of all good cuisine) had been severed.

From then on, the diet of the workers rapidly declined, although in the north of England the potato had, at last, been accepted. In the south, wheat, the source of fashionable white bread, had taken over the land. A farm laborer with a wife and four children averaged £46 in annual earnings, but the cost of the same family's food amounted to £52 a year. Each week, such a family typically consumed 8 loaves of bread, 2 pounds of cheese, 2 pounds of butter, 2 ounces of tea, a half-pound of boiled bacon, and 2 pints of milk. By contrast, dinner for a late-eighteenth-century middle-class family of six has been depicted as consisting of three boiled chickens, a haunch of venison, a ham, a flour-and-suet pudding, and beans, followed by gooseberries and apricots (Drummond and Wilbraham 1959). Jonas Hanway, the reformer, said of the poor in Stevenage in 1767: "The food of the poor is good bread, cheese, pease and turnips in winter with a little pork or other meat, when they can afford it; but from the high price of meat, it has not lately been within their reach. As to milk, they have hardly sufficient for their use" (Drummond and Wilbraham 1959: 208).

The eighteenth century, however, was one in which vast amounts of meat were eaten by those who could afford it. Sydney Smith, canon of St. Paul's Cathedral, calculated that during his 77 years, he had consumed 44 wagonloads of meat and drink, which had starved to death fully 100 persons. In Smith's letters, and in Parson James Woodforde's diaries, accounts of meals are laden with meats: game, fowl, cold tongue and hams, roasted sweetbreads, giblet soup, pigeons, veal, and marrow sauces. Obesity was caricatured by artists like William Hogarth and Thomas Rowlandson, and huge weights, up to 40 stone (about 560 pounds), were attained by some people. Among meat eaters, meat consumption averaged about 147 pounds per person annually, about the per capita amount eaten today in the United States.

Throughout the century, market gardens had been started around growing cities and towns. London had gardens at Lewisham, Blackheath, Wanstead, and Ilford. A vegetable market at Liverpool arose because an influx of French Canadians wanted cheap vegetables for their soups. Most vegetables, however, were of poor quality and little variety (cabbages, carrots, spinach, sprouts, and turnips), although special vegetables were still grown in the walled gardens of great estates. Unfortunately, eighteenth-century practices of hygiene were not very advanced, and many of the barges that brought fruit and vegetables to the city of London took away the contents of the city's cesspits on their return journey.

Not only did overeating typify the times, so did an excess of fats used in cooking. Hannah Glasse (1971: 5) commented in her cookery book: "I have heard of a cook that used six pounds of butter to fry twelve eggs, when everybody knows (that understands cooking) that half a pound is full enough." Fashionable food centered around huge pies made from turkey and swan, or mixtures of game with veal, sweetbreads, mushrooms, and potatoes. Dr. Samuel Johnson's favorite dinner was "a leg of pork boiled till it dropped from the bone, a veal pie with plums and sugar and the outside cut of a salt buttock of beef" (Pullar 1970: 170).

Beer and ale remained the most popular drinks in Britain until the beginning of the eighteenth century, when home-brewed distilled spirits took over. Dutch *genever,* or gin, had begun to appear in England as early as Stuart times, and ginlike liquors, flavored with juniper berries, were made from beer dregs, lees of wine or cider, and soaked dried fruits. With the addition of extra yeast, large quantities of spirit could be distilled from any of these mixtures. Molasses fermented with barm (the yeasty froth on fermenting malt liquors) made a crude rum, and "grains of paradise" made the spirits hot and fiery in the mouth. British brandy was a spirit drawn from newly fermented barley malt.

Dutch-cultivated coffee beans spread from East Indian colonies to the West Indies and then to England. Coffeehouses became fashionable places to meet and gossip, and coffee was taken up by the nobility. It grew in popularity until the Georgian era, when tea began to compete with it. Drinking chocolate was perhaps not quite as popular, as the manner of making it was a chore. Cocoa beans were exported to England, where they were dried, peeled, and powdered. Next, sugar, cinnamon, vanilla, nutmeg, and ambergris were added, and then the mixture was rolled, made into cakes, and cast into molds. It was these cakes that had to be scraped and grated for use in drinks and puddings.

The foods eaten by the majority (the working and lower-middle classes) were all either grown locally or preserved by pickling and smoking. Jane Austen's father – a modest country clergyman – farmed a smallholding where he kept cows, pigs, and sheep and grew wheat for making bread. His wife kept fowl and looked after the vegetables, herb garden, and orchard. She taught her daughters how to supervise the making of butter, cheese, preserves, pickles, and homemade wines, as well as how to brew beer and cure bacon and hams (Black 1993). But such a life and its lessons were lost as the century grew older, the towns larger, and the world smaller.

Later Modern England: The Industrial Revolution (1700 to 1900)

As more and more factories were built for the mass production of goods, so towns and cities grew to serve the factories. The population of London quadrupled in the nineteenth century. In 1800, Manchester had 75,000 inhabitants; some 50 years later, there were 400,000. Social reformers were astonished that although riches grew and a new bourgeoisie of affluence appeared, the most abject poverty afflicted the majority of workers. Potatoes, bread, and tea constituted the main diet of the poor; about once a week there was some milk and sugar and, perhaps once a year, a piece of bacon. Almost half of the children born in towns died before they were 5 years old, whereas those who survived were severely undernourished, low in stature, physically weak, and frequently grew up deformed by rickets.

Nearly all food was adulterated with illegal additions to make it stretch further. Alum was added to bleach flour for white bread; various drugs and flavorings, even sulfuric acid, were put into hops. The leaves of ash, sloe, and elder were mixed into tea. Copper was used to color pickles green, red lead colored the rind of Gloucester cheese, and coffee contained roasted corn and red ocher.

The growing, well-off middle class in the towns and cities did not possess large estates, as the old landed gentry still did, which meant that the middle classes owned no source of natural foods. Thus, the nineteenth century produced the modern grocer, and railroads made it possible for milk and produce from the country to be delivered to the center of any great metropolis. Steam trawlers replaced sailing boats, and the railways also carried fresh fish, well-chilled in ice, to inland areas. Cod became commonplace, and the first fish-and-chips shops opened. The invention of bottling and canning methods of food preservation put many cheaper items onto grocers' shelves, where bottled sauces, along with canned foods – vegetables, meats, fish, and fruits – were now essential provisions. Aberdeen, although 515 miles away, became the abattoir of London because of the ability to send carcasses overnight by rail. The world had become one huge food market. After 1880, Australian beef could be sent by sea in refrigerated ships. Tea from India was no longer expensive, nor was wheat from America; hence, not only was a greater range of cheaper food now available, but much of it was packaged beguilingly, with certain brand names becoming household words.

The middle-class Victorian housewife had most of her fresh foods delivered. The baker, muffin man, and milkman made their rounds daily. The fishmonger brought cod, hake, salmon, skate, eels, herring, and shellfish; the greengrocer called with a wide range of seasonal vegetables delivered to him early from the market gardens. If a housewife left her basement kitchen to shop, it was only to buy from the butcher and the poulterer. Veal was the cheapest meat; calf's-feet jelly and a pig's-head brawn would both be appreciated by the family. Capons and pheasants were thought of as party dishes, and small game birds were kept to be served as savories (Black 1993).

A German chemist, Justus von Liebig, helped increase food production with his advocacy of artificial fertilizers at the same time that his research in nutrition attempted to classify foods scientifically. His main discovery in this endeavor was that of the food chain – the interdependence of plants and animals – and his research into plant nutrients led to his identification of protein, which resulted, during the next century, in fundamental changes in the ways that food was thought of, grown, and eaten.

The diet of the poor, however, did not improve; their wages were still low and malnutrition was widespread. In 1847, the Vegetarian Society was founded in the midst of industrial Britain. It was very much a social reforming movement, dedicated to temperance and the improvement of the working classes. Vegetarianism also flourished for a time among members of the affluent middle classes, who saw themselves as social reformers. They were shocked at the inadequacy of the diets of working people. Bread and jam (with the jam made from colored, sweetened fruit or vegetable pulp) was all that some children ate throughout the day. This scandal was at last drawn to the government's attention when cannon fodder was needed; in the enlistment for the Boer War (1899–1902), it was discovered that 37 percent of the volunteers were so unfit for service that they had to be invalided out.

The Twentieth Century

British society and its food did not change until after the end of World War I (1914–18). The postwar period was one of intense trading and competition in the world market. For the first time, people could eat tropical fruits (imported from the East) in winter; shipments of chilled apples and pears came all the way from New Zealand. Canada, Australia, and the Argentine grew wheat and exported it to Britain, and

in addition to fruits, butter and lamb from New Zealand competed with Danish butter, eggs, and bacon. But the British farmer, too, had to compete with these cheaper imports.

More foods were now packaged under brand names that soon became familiar, and consumers grew to expect an improved quality of service from retailers and food producers. Many of the household cooking chores had already been eliminated, as much of the food – custard, blancmange, jellies, gravy, and porridge – now came out of packages. Breakfast revolved around corn flakes or other cereal products, and the range of canned foods included not only soups but salmon, corned beef, vegetables, fruits like pineapple, and even game birds and condensed milk. Many of the favorite dishes for special occasions might come from a variety of containers, which was a boon for many, as servants were rapidly becoming nonexistent, except in extremely wealthy households. Food retailing in Britain in the 1930s absorbed nearly one-third of the national income.

What consumers failed to realize was that many additives entered these new foods. Food manufacturers added preservatives and improvers – anticaking agents to stop flour, milk, salt, and sugar from forming lumps; emulsifying agents, to blend substances that tended to separate; sequestrants, to keep fats from going rancid – none of which were disclosed on the labels.

Evidence of vitamins and how they contribute to health was published in 1911, and the subject, from then on, was never far from the public eye. It was gradually realized that afflictions like pellagra, rickets, scurvy, and beriberi, once believed to be contagious, were actually the result of deficiencies in vital elements of the diet. Of course, some of the new knowledge required generations to take hold. For example, the idea that brown flour, which contained all the bran and minerals, was more healthful than white flour was first mooted in the last quarter of the nineteenth century but required a full hundred years to be accepted.

In 1914, as in the Boer War, it was once more noted that volunteers for the armed services were grossly undernourished, and at last, the government took action by stressing the importance of the health of munitions workers and the importance of adequate nutrition to the workforce as a whole. By the end of World War I, a thousand industrial canteens were supplying a million meals a day, and workers in British industry, now for the first time had hot, well-cooked meals at reasonable prices (Burnett 1966).

By the time of World War II (1939–45), the government was far better prepared than before to ration food while increasing its production. A Food (Defence Plans) Department had been set up in 1936, but in 1939 Britain was only 30 percent self-sufficient in food compared with 86 percent for Germany. Rationing, however, was begun immediately because all the details had been worked out and the ration books printed. The science of nutrition was now so advanced that the nation's diet could be planned informatively and wisely. Food technology, it was also seen, could play a vital part in economizing on shipping space by dehydrating vegetables, drying eggs and bananas, importing boneless meat, and compressing carcasses. A good example is "Spam" – the bane of the wartime kitchen. A Food Advice Division was set up to give nutrition information to the public through radio and newspapers.

Britain rationed meat, bacon, cheese, fats, sugar, and preserves on a per person basis. Bread was brown, and vitamins A and D were added to margarine. Additional proteins, vitamins, and minerals were given to small children and to pregnant or nursing mothers. Communal feeding grew in importance; firms employing more than 250 people were required to provide a canteen service, and school canteens began to ensure that all children had at least one well-balanced meal a day. British restaurants in the blitzed areas provided hot, cheap, nutritious meals to the general public and grew to number 2,000 in 1943.

Millions of people "dug for victory." Flower beds and lawns gave way to vegetable gardens. A great amount of potatoes was eaten, and the consumption of green vegetables and fresh fruit also increased. Throughout the war, there was a decline in infant mortality, and the general health of children improved. On average, they were taller and heavier, and for the first time in British history, the poorest third of the population was eating an adequate and balanced diet. In fact, the British diet has never been more healthful, before or since the war, however much the people complained. They were then consuming a great deal more fiber, much less sugar and refined flours, little meat, and more fresh fruit and vegetables. The war encouraged people to go into the woods and hedgerows to harvest wild foods, to make jams out of sloes and rose hips, and to gather fungi, wild herbs, and greens for flavoring.

Rationing continued until 1953, and for a time there was even less food available than during the war. Women had tasted independence during the war years, and they were not always prepared to return to full-time domesticity. There was a move for women to go out to work, and to encourage this, there was a growth in domestic technology. From the mid-1950s onward, certain trends are noticeable. Less food was bought for home consumption, meals were smaller and lighter, and there was a growing demand for "convenience foods." This was a new concept: processed foods that are labor-saving because they can be prepared and brought to the table in only a few minutes. In this category, the greatest rise in consumption has been in quick-frozen foods (Burnett 1966), followed by precooked chilled dishes and microwave meals.

Such a change in diet would not have been possible had it not been for a postwar revolution in farming methods throughout the world, occurring on a scale far greater than that of the previous agricultural revolution in the eighteenth century. Intensive factory farming was an idea explored because of the rigors of wartime rationing and the fear that there would not be enough protein for a growing world population. Various factors coming together in the 1950s allowed for new methods. First, there was research in cellular growth and DNA, so that natural hormones could be extracted from livestock, then used to stimulate desired characteristics. Second, the ability was enhanced for chemical companies to research and produce a varied range of drugs, including antibiotics, that allowed farmers to keep greater numbers of animals than ever envisioned before. And third, new building technology could provide cheap housing units for animals, with concrete stalls and automatic feeders and timers that made controlled feeding, watering, and lighting feasible. One result was that fewer and fewer stockmen were needed on the farm to watch over and care for the animals.

Also in the 1950s, agriculture began to spawn a vast number of different but interdependent industries engaged in the development of new equipment, fertilizers, and seeds, as well as new techniques and products for the storage, processing, and preservation of foods. As a consequence, heavily mechanized farms with computer technology made farmers more and more dependent on a host of suppliers. A farmer might often be unable to make a choice on the way he reared his livestock because of the rules laid down by a particular supplier. Large companies, such as those of the pharmaceutical industry, were financing farming with millions of pounds of capital, which meant that the farmer was controlled from a remote city office. Agriculture had become a highly sophisticated energy-intensive system for transforming one series of industrial products into another series of industrial products that just happened to be edible (George 1986).

Selective breeding of livestock also became a new skill, and improvements in the control of selective breeding are certain to continue in the future. But this development also means that we lose genetic diversity (21 British cattle breeds have become extinct since the beginning of the twentieth century). When one bull can sire over a quarter of a million offspring, it allows for enormous inbreeding, which can reveal hitherto unsuspected defects (Johnson 1991). One of the drawbacks for the consumer with these new methods of rearing livestock is that a lack of exercise, combined with a rich protein diet, produces a carcass high in saturated fats. There is also a wide belief that food produced in such a way has less flavor than when natural rearing and feeding is employed. Fully 63 percent of housewives in Britain in the 1980s felt that food had less flavor than it did 20 years earlier (Johnson 1991).

This sense that basic English foods have become

blander (Johnson 1991) may partly explain the great popularity of ethnic foods and restaurants. Since the 1950s, Chinese, Indian, Cypriot, Thai, and Mexican restaurants have grown up throughout the towns and cities of Britain. No doubt, the willingness to try new foods was encouraged by postwar travel, although packaged holidays in the popular cheaper resorts of Europe now cater to the most conservative of British tastes with fish and chips, roast beef, and Yorkshire pudding. Popular food is also controlled by American companies that produce hamburgers, fried chicken, and the like. This is poor food nutritionally, with a high amount of saturated fat; nonetheless, it symbolizes the American way of life, and by consuming fast food, the eater becomes a part of that way of life. Indeed, this demonstrates how atavistic food consumption still is and how little it has changed from the days of prehistory, when to eat the meat of an ox meant that one was hoping to attain the strength of oxen.

In reaction to factory farming, to the widespread exploitation of animals, and to the high amount of saturated fat in the British diet, the vegetarian movement has grown in the last 40 years. In 1945, there were 100,000 vegetarians in Britain; by the 1990s there were 3 million, the number having doubled during the 1980s. Moreover, 40 percent of British people have reduced their consumption of red meat or entirely eliminated it from their diets (Spencer 1993).

Because of the worldwide market, there is now a far greater range of food available to more people than ever before in history. Yet the diet of the majority tends to be high in refined carbohydrates, sugars, and salt and relies on convenience foods, which lack the fiber and essential vitamins and minerals provided by fresh vegetables and fruits. Food has become blander and more stereotyped over the last 30 years, and the divide between rich and poor has not gotten any smaller. In fact, with a doubling of the population predicted within the next 40 years, it can only grow wider.

Colin Spencer

Bibliography

Ayrton, Elizabeth. 1974. *The cookery of England.* Harmondsworth, England.
Black, Maggie. 1993. *A taste of history.* London.
Burnett, John. 1966. *Plenty and want.* London.
Drummond, J. C., and Anne Wilbraham. 1959, new edition 1991. *The Englishman's food.* London.
George, Susan. 1986. *How the other half dies.* London.
Glasse, Hannah. [1796] 1971. *The art of cookery made plain and easy.* Hamden, Conn.
Johnson, Andrew. 1991. *Factory farming.* Oxford U.K., and Cambridge, Mass.
Martial. 1993. *Epigrams,* ed. and trans. D. R. Shackleton. 3 vols. Cambridge, Mass.
Pliny the Younger. 1748. *Correspondence,* trans. William Melmoth. 2 vols. Dublin.
Pullar, Phillipa. 1970. *Consuming passions: A history of English food and appetite.* London.
Spencer, Colin. 1993. *The heretic's feast: A history of vegetarianism.* London.
Tannahill, Reay. 1973. *Food in history.* New York.
Tuchman, Barbara W. 1978. *A distant mirror: The calamitous 14th century.* New York.
Wheaton, Barbara Ketcham. 1983. *Savouring the past.* London.
Wilson, C. Anne. 1973. *Food and drink in Britain.* Harmondsworth, England.

V.C.5 Northern Europe – Germany and Surrounding Regions

The majority of foods found in modern northern Europe – which includes the lands around the North Sea and the Baltic Sea and those of northern Alpine region – are not indigenous to the area. It is here, however, that one of the most stable of humankind's agricultural systems was established, and one that has proved capable of providing densely populated areas with a high standard of living. Such an agricultural bounty has helped northern Europe to become one of the most prosperous areas of the world.

The Paleolithic Period

The northern European environment underwent drastic change several times during the Pleistocene. Glaciers coming from Scandinavia and the Alps covered a large part of the landscape with glacigenic sediment several times during the Ice Age. Forests retreated from northern Europe and were replaced by a type of vegetation that can be regarded as a mixture of those of tundra and steppe. In this environment, forest-adapted herbivores were replaced by large grazing species such as caribou *(Rangifer tarandus),* wild horse *(Equus* sp.), and mammoth *(Mammonteus primigenius).* These species, associated in small or bigger herds, migrated from the north to the south and vice versa in a yearly cycle. In summer they fled north from the multitude of biting insects (to Jutland, for example), and in winter they were attracted by the somewhat higher temperatures in areas of the south, such as that just north of the Alps.

Reindeer herds proved to be a very good source of food for Paleolithic reindeer hunters, whose widespread presence in northern Europe is well established by excavations. The hunters migrated with the herds from the south to the north and back again. Prehistoric humans located their temporary dwelling places so as to achieve a maximum vantage point – usually so they could hunt downhill using their lances and bows or a kind of harpoon made of stone and bone material (Bandi 1968: 107–12; Kuhn-Schnyder 1968: 43–68; Rust 1972: 19–20, 65–9).

Although the archaeological evidence for hunting is very clear, hunters doubtless also gathered wild plants. The latter, however, is very difficult to demonstrate, as it is rarely possible to find plant material, such as fruits and seeds, preserved in the layers of Paleolithic camp excavations.

During the late glacial period, trees from the south colonized northern Europe so thoroughly that the landscape was nearly totally forested. Unfortunately, we know little about human nutrition following the return of forested conditions to northern Europe. Reindeer and other steppe-tundra fauna became locally extinct in the newly forested regions.

The Mesolithic Period

There is clearer evidence for human nutrition at the beginning of the postglacial period (the interglacial hiatus in which we live), approximately 11,000 years ago. Following the retreat of the Würmian glaciers, forests again established themselves in most parts of northern Europe to the extent that these landscapes became unsuitable for reindeer and other large herd herbivores. The reindeer herds retreated to those parts where tundra was established: northern Scandinavia, northern Finland, and northern Russia. It is only in these regions that a "Paleolithic way of life" has remained possible up to the present day, because the relationship between reindeer herds and hunters has remained as in millennia before. In the unforested region of the extreme north it is also still possible to practice Paleolithic hunting methods, as exemplified by the Laplanders and Inuit.

In most landscapes of northern Europe, however, hunting methods and nutrition changed, reflecting the changing environment. The forests were invaded by smaller and less frequent solitary woodland fauna, such as red deer *(Cervus elaphus)*, boar *(Sus scrofa)*, and badger *(Meles)*. These species are difficult to hunt in dense forests, and they do not provide a large meat yield. Changes in the vegetational environment were reflected in the hunter's tool kit. Long-range projectile weapons, for example, cannot be used in a wooded landscape. Smaller hunting tools constructed from "microliths" (typical archaeological remnants of the Mesolithic period) were better suited to the vegetation and woodland prey (Wyss 1968–71, 3: 123–44).

Life during the Mesolithic was perhaps harder than during the Paleolithic. It was more difficult to hunt an animal in a wooded landscape, and thus meat was certainly not available all the time. Possibly the plant component of the diet became more important during the Mesolithic. For example, at the very few Mesolithic dwelling places that have been examined by environmental archaeologists, there is evidence of the use of hazelnuts *(Corylus avellana)* (Vaughan 1987: 233–8).

During the Mesolithic, hazelnut bushes spread rapidly to many parts of Europe, as evidenced by pollen diagrams. This is in contrast to the vegetation development of the earlier interglacials. Hazelnuts are heavy, with low dispersal rates, so that it is very unlikely that the plant diffused unaided to all parts of northern Europe at the same time. Instead, it has often been assumed that hazelnuts were culturally dispersed by Mesolithic peoples (Firbas 1949: 149; Smith 1970: 81–96). Indeed, the distribution of these nuts is recorded by pollen analysis in the Mesolithic layer of Hohen Viecheln at the border of Lake Schwerin in northern Germany (Schmitz 1961: 29).

Most likely the expansion of hazelnut distribution was due to the nuts' chance spread during the preparation of "hazelnut meals" by migratory Mesolithic people. Most of the other wild fruits available in the present-day northern European woodlands are not archaeologically recorded for the Mesolithic, nor for the Neolithic period, which has been much more intensively examined by environmental archaeologists. Thus, it is unlikely that strawberries, wild apples, and pears, for example, contributed to human nutrition during the Mesolithic (Küster 1986: 437).

The Neolithic Period

The transition from the Mesolithic to the Neolithic has often been regarded as a revolution by northern European archaeologists (Childe 1956: 66–104). But the Mesolithic–Neolithic transition, with its change from a hunter–gatherer community to a sedentary food-producing farming community, was not a revolution in other parts of the world such as the Near East. In these areas a gradual evolution can be traced from the one stage to the other. In contrast, the transition from hunting and gathering to farming in northern Europe seems to have indeed been a revolutionary process, in which none of the nutritional mainstays of the Mesolithic was incorporated into the Neolithic food-production system.

Rather, all wild elements of the new farming system had been previously cultivated or domesticated elsewhere, mainly in the Near East. Both domesticated animals and cultivated crops were introduced into northern Europe, primarily from the Near East, and were, therefore, exotic elements at the beginning of the Neolithic. Near East domesticates, such as cattle *(Bos primigenius f. taurus)*, goats *(Capra aegagrus f. hircus)*, sheep *(Ovis ammon f. aries)*, and pigs *(Sus scrofa f. domestica)* were introduced into many parts of northern Europe during the Neolithic.

Although most had been introduced in the Balkans, only some of the ancient Near Eastern crops became important in Neolithic northern Europe. It is very likely, however, that each component of a well-balanced vegetarian regime (starch from cereal crops, proteins from pulses, and fat from oil plants) was available to all Neolithic settlements in the region.

In most parts of northern Europe, einkorn *(Triticum monococcum)* and emmer *(Triticum dicoccon)* were the predominant cereals during the Neolithic. Both traveled upstream on the Danube River and downstream on the Rhine River from the Balkans to northern Europe. The same expansion route can be traced for peas *(Pisum sativum)* and lentils *(Lens culinaris),* the major pulses of the Neolithic, although at that time lentils had a more extensive distribution. Today, lentil production is restricted by climatic conditions in many parts of northern Europe. Linseed *(Linum usitatissimum)* was the major oil (and also fiber) crop (Knörzer 1991: 190-3; Küster 1991: 180-2). Only in the extreme west - in southwestern Germany, along the Rhine, in the Netherlands, and in some parts of Scandinavia - were different crops apparently grown. Wheat *(Triticum aestivum* and/or *Triticum durum)* and naked barley *(Hordeum vulgare)* cultivation is evidenced in southwestern Germany and Switzerland (Jacomet and Schlichtherle 1984: 153-76; Küster 1991: 180-2), in the Netherlands, and in southwestern Scandinavia. These plants had their origins in the Near East but likely expanded via the Mediterranean and western Europe (Bakels 1982: 11-3). The only crop not of Near Eastern origin found in the Neolithic of northern Europe, the opium poppy *(Papaver somniferum),* most likely arrived from the western Mediterranean. Inside northern Europe, regional differences in agriculture and nutrition are traceable from the early Neolithic onward, making clear the borders between "economic provinces." For example, barley was important from the very beginning in southwestern Germany and the Netherlands but not in Bavaria and the Rhineland. Yet barley did become important later on in areas where it had not been grown during the early Neolithic.

Through agriculture, the northern European landscape was totally changed by humans. The clearing of the earlier wooded landscape caused environmental changes that are not completely understood today. Hunting, fishing, and the gathering of plants were activities still practiced by the early farmers, but the bulk of human nutrition was certainly derived from agricultural products.

Yet the variety of nutriments available in the Neolithic was severely limited. Because there were very few crops, no herbs and spices, and no cultivated fruits, all meals must have tasted very nearly the same, day in and day out, save on those rare occasions when a meat dish was available.

Toward the end of the Neolithic, some Mediterranean flavorings were introduced in northern Europe, but only in those parts that had cultural and economic contacts with Mediterranean areas. Among the imports were parsley *(Petroselinum crispum),* celery *(Apium graveolens* var. *juice),* and dill *(Anethum graveolens),* which reached some areas of southwestern Germany and northern Switzerland to enliven drab fare (Küster 1985; Jacomet 1988). Other spices were employed in the preservation and storage of meats. This importation of Mediterranean spices is the earliest indication we have of some sophistication in food preparation, as well as a gardening culture, in the southern parts of northern Europe. Following the end of the Neolithic, herbs and spices disappear from the record, and there are no remains of such plants in northern Europe in Bronze Age and even Iron Age settlements.

The Bronze Age and Iron Age

After the Neolithic Revolution, the development of northern European agriculture was influenced more by evolutionary than revolutionary processes. Although the people still did not personally participate in the process of domesticating animals and plants, they did continue to import new cultigens and domesticates. The basic diet, however, does not seem to have undergone any dramatic shifts.

Through trial and error, Bronze Age and Iron Age farmers discovered those crops that were best adapted to the environmental conditions of northern Europe. As they did so, einkorn, which provides only a small yield, became less common, whereas emmer, barley, and (from the early Bronze Age onward) spelt *(Triticum spelta)* were increasingly cultivated. Spelt, however, was common only in some regions: at the northern border of the Alps, in Jutland, and in southern Sweden, where it possibly was grown as a winter crop.

As a rule, only two different crops were grown in a settlement, which left such agricultural communities susceptible to crises when one or the other cereal had poor yields. Indeed, it seems likely that at times famine may have been the result of the ecological instability that a farming community relying on the cultivation of just two different crop species can create. And, of course, the crops were not just for human consumption; they also helped to feed the livestock.

During the Bronze Age, the horse *(Equus przewalskii f. caballus)* was domesticated. This probably took place in eastern Europe, but horses were subsequently introduced into northern Europe, where they not only were used for riding, transport, and agriculture but also became an important component of the human diet (Wyss 1971). Unlike other livestock, horses cannot subsist solely on leaf hay; they require special supplemental feed. Thus, it is striking that the introduction of domesticated horses coincided with the expansion of the millets *(Panicum miliaceum* and *Setaria italica)* and the horsebean *(Vicia faba)* into northern Europe. But whereas the impetus for the adoption of these plants may have been the feeding of horses, during the late Bronze and Iron Ages millets and beans doubtless also contributed to human nutrition.

Over time, agricultural methods became more sophisticated, with better ploughs (as metals were increasingly available), bigger fields, the use of better-adapted plants, and concomitant greater yields. But the basic elements of human nutrition remained more or less the same. Cereal crops, pulses, and oil plants still provided the bulk of the daily fare, and milk was plentiful. But meat was eaten only on special occasions, as reflected in hoary rules concerning the consumption of meat that have persisted until today.

Since animals were not hunted every day and only seasonally slaughtered, meat, as a scarce item, became regarded as an important component of banquets. In fact, from ancient times onward a good reason for inviting numerous guests to a banquet was so that the bulk of any meat served was consumed before it became rancid. Because slaughtering was commonly done in autumn, banquets were (and often still are) given in late autumn and around the time of Christmas. By contrast, meat was normally not consumed during the winter and spring months, when people maintained only as many cattle as were necessary for breeding. This period corresponds to the fasting season (Lent) of the Catholic church between Shrove Tuesday and Easter. Lamb was and remains a traditional dish at an Easter banquet, for this was the time of year when an abundance of newborn sheep could be culled from the flock.

The Roman Age

Around the time of the birth of Christ, parts of northern Europe situated southwest of the Rhine and south of the Danube became colonies of the Roman Empire. Within this area, foodstuffs took on an increasingly important role in Roman commerce, with the Rhine serving as an important trading route. Wheat, rice *(Oryza sativa),* and exotic spices were transported downstream to Roman garrisons and to towns in northwestern Germany and the Netherlands. However, colonies not situated near the Rhine, although involved in the trade of spices and wine, did not trade in bulky items such as grain. Thus, in these regions, the Romans had to force the subdued peoples to deliver crops to the towns and settlements where their soldiers and civilians lived.

There were great efforts during Roman times to increase crop yields, which can be seen in the construction of the villa system. Sophisticated agricultural methods were practiced. But ultimately, difficulties in transporting enough food to the Roman soldiers in those parts of the Imperium not accessible by river routes may be one of the reasons for the decline of the Roman Empire in the Danube provinces. By contrast, the area between Cologne and the Netherlands was one of the economically most powerful parts of the Imperium even in the late Roman age.

Outside of the Roman Empire, some improvement of agricultural methods also took place. Rye *(Secale cereale)* and oats *(Avena sativa)* were grown as additional crops, certainly enlarging and stabilizing of the food supply and possibly enabling the local farmers to export crops to Roman towns. Yet despite the influence of Roman commerce and the presence of trade routes in the area, the peasant diet, at least, seems to have been similar to that of prehistoric times.

The inhabitants of towns and garrisons, by contrast, enjoyed considerably more variety in viands. Those who had the ability bought many different spices at market, and cultivated fruits became available. In fact, the oldest fruit-tree groves and vineyards in northern Europe date from the Roman Age. The basic requirement for these was the stability that Roman rule brought to settlements. Prehistoric settlements had lasted for only a few decades at the most – not long enough for the fruits of groves and vines to appear in any abundance.

The Middle Ages

Many of the Roman trade routes were still used after the Romans departed. For example, the trade route along the Rhine remained important, and its commerce was extended by Viking merchants to the coasts, to northwestern Germany, and to the islands and peninsulas around the North Sea: England, Ireland, Iceland, Norway, and Jutland. Artifacts that represent importations into Viking settlements, such as wine and wine vessels in Haithabu (Behre 1983), serve to document the existence and extensiveness of these routes.

The Hanse merchants added the areas around the Baltic Sea to their economic empire, bringing exotic food to the towns along the Baltic coast. Indeed, at times there was more imported food inside the towns than local products. As an example, during a period of grain shortage in Lubeck, marzipan, a bread that is baked not of ordinary flour but of almond "flour" and sugar, is said to have been invented (Küster 1987).

The food trade in northern Europe experienced yet another shift when the exchange began of meat (or livestock) and crops between the agricultural and grassland areas. In the Netherlands, oxen were taken from Frisia westward to the big towns, whereas crops were transported from the dry, sandy areas to the fen landscapes where cattle farms came into existence (Bieleman 1989). The trade of oxen, in turn, led to the development of "oxen routes" inside northern Europe. In the late Middle Ages, as food transport and trade became more important, these activities were no longer confined to waterways but were also carried out over such overland routes.

All parts of northern Europe that were distant from the trade routes had remained rural, and the diets of their residents continued to be restricted to the few elements of food (cereals, pulses, oil plants) that had been exploited since prehistoric times. Only the species of plants had changed. Rye, oats, and, in some areas, wheat had become more important, whereas emmer was only rarely cultivated.

Urban growth meant a continuing demand for as much food as possible, which led to intensive agricultural production. Nearly all woods were cleared, and a sophisticated rotation system – winter crop, summer crop, and fallow – came into existence. The settlements became stable and were usually arranged around a church. As during Roman times, such stability (in towns, monasteries, and castles) promoted the cultivation of fruit trees and vines, the produce of which was available in the markets. Yet the demands of rapidly growing urban populations frequently led to shortages in basic foodstuffs like flour, which in turn led to conflict and even civil war between city peoples and peasants. The *Bauernkrieg* ("Peasants' War") of 1525 was perhaps the most famous of these conflicts, signaling the end of the Middle Ages and its accompanying social system in northern Europe.

Modern Times

During the following centuries, it became even more difficult for rural farmers to supply enough food for urban populations that continued to swell (Abel 1978). There was one crisis after another, which brought periods of famine in northern Europe and periods of migration to North America. But at the same time, American food plants were taking root in Europe.

In the period of mercantilism, just prior to the Age of Industrialization, factories were founded in many parts of northern Europe. People began working for wages, and thus many more became dependent on the food market, which had difficulty meeting demand, especially in years with low crop yields. In response, northern European landowners forced peasants to cultivate the American potato *(Solanum tuberosum)*, which delivered a high yield of food per unit of land cultivated.

In principle, such cultivation made it possible for ordinary workers to buy sufficient food in the form of potatoes to sustain themselves. But the expanded food supply caused rapid population growth and a concomitant growth of towns. Indeed, the industrialization of northern Europe would not have been possible without the introduction of the potato (Küster 1992a).

It was not, however, until the nineteenth and twentieth centuries that the peasants' diet began to include imported food items, such as spices, long enjoyed by town dwellers. This change was precipitated by an extensive construction of railways that linked the countryside with the cities. With the new foodstuffs came grocers to the villages. They were called "Kolonialwarenhändler" in the German language, which means "colonial produce merchants." Yet only exotic food imports were sold in the grocery shops, whereas the most important constituents of the diet were provided by the farmers themselves.

During the nineteenth and twentieth centuries, the construction of railways has also led to further spatial concentration of cattle raising and crop production.

With the invention of mineral fertilizers that were transported by rail, crop production was abandoned in mountainous areas but intensified in the plains. In addition, the great increase in yield on fertilized fields led to the abandonment of remote acres where spruce forests could be planted.

Another agrarian and nutritional revolution was caused by the beginning of extensive maize *(Zea mays)* cultivation during the past few decades. Maize silage provides enough food for large cattle and chicken producers, causing meat and eggs to become relatively cheap to northern European consumers. Since World War II there has been a marked shift toward increased meat consumption. The protein-rich diet causes health problems, and dietitians recommend eating more grains and vegetables and less meat and eggs. In northern Europe today, food shortages are not a problem, and the price of food plays less of a role in determining an individual's nutrition than it did in the past. It is interesting that despite the great variety of foods available on the shelves in the supermarket, dietitians are recommending a return to the dietary staples of prehistoric times (Haenel 1986).

Nonetheless, a huge variety of foods is now produced in northern Europe, and other foods produced outside of that region can be purchased by almost everyone. Some of the crops produced, such as wheat, barley, oats, and rye, have been grown and consumed for millennia. Others, such as potatoes and maize from the Americas, are relatively new but very important. Also important are certain foods brought in from abroad. Rice, which is imported in large quantities from South Asia, is one of these. Coffee and tea are others. The northern Europeans have long been fond of hot beverages, and today Dutch and Saxonian coffees are famous the world over.

In a remarkable turnaround compared with the past, today more crops and meat are produced in northern Europe than can be consumed by the people of the region, and such abundance has created great political and economic problems. Oversupply of such items as pork, butter, wine, and apples has prompted the common market of the European Union to insist on less production, and farmers have been forced to destroy a portion of their harvests and cut back on the amount of meat produced. Because areas where long-established crops can be cultivated have become increasingly restricted, farmers are turning to alternative crops such as spelt, flax, and sunflowers. Many products from these new crops arc available in health-food stores as well as supermarkets, as northern Europeans, like people in other developed countries, are giving more thought to improving their nutrition.

Another important nutritional development in the region began in the 1950s, when labor shortages there opened the way for southern European workers to move north. With them came their national cuisines and specialty restaurants; Italian and Greek foods are very popular in northern Europe today. Pizza restaurants can be found even in small villages, and frozen pizza is one of the most common fast-food dishes in the home.

In addition to the influence of southern Europeans, there has been a substantial culinary contribution made by the people of now-independent overseas colonies to their former mother countries. Just as Indian food and restaurants are common in England, and North African cookery is widespread in France, there are many Indonesian restaurants in the Netherlands.

As the northern European countries have become more prosperous, they have also attracted the peoples (and thus the foods) of most of the rest of the world. Chinese restaurants, for example, are ubiquitous, and spring rolls and other Chinese dishes are available in all the supermarkets.

Indeed, because of prosperity on the one hand and all of these culinary choices on the other, cooking at home has come to an end in many households. It is easy and inexpensive to purchase already prepared dishes from the supermarket in cans, or frozen, or dried. Moreover, it has become very common to eat in what might be termed "neighborhood" restaurants where one encounters friends and can relax. Fast-food restaurants from America have been introduced but are still not all that popular because they are too hurried.

Clearly, then, the history of food and drink in northern Europe has entered into a unique chapter. There is an abundant variety of both native and exotic foods available, and famine is unknown. More and more customers are demanding higher-quality foodstuffs, and it has become fashionable, for example, to use the very best olive oils and spiced vinegars in the preparation of salads. Factories that turn out convenience foods, such as mashed potato powder and instant soups and sauces, are supplemented by a market network that supplies frozen and fresh fruits, vegetables, meats, and fish, all of which combine to supply a high – perhaps too high – level of nutrition for the northern European.

This situation stands in stark contrast to nutritional levels in the poorer regions of the world. For economic and political as well as logistical reasons, it is a complicated matter to ship foods from northern European countries to the underdeveloped nations. But some, especially the Scandinavians, have done much to help improve the standard of living, including the level of nutrition, of developing-world peoples. Moreover, there are regular airlifts from northern Europe to famine-ravaged regions of the world, although, of course, balanced diets are hardly provided in such bulk shipments.

In conclusion, it is worth stressing that the sheer amount of nutrients available to northern Europeans today also stands in stark contrast to their own long past of undernutrition and even famine. One hopes that one day soon, like the northern Europeans, the people in today's developing countries will be confronting the problem of overnutrition.

Hansjörg Küster

Bibliography

Abel, W. 1978. *Agrarkrisen und Agrarkonjunktur.* Third edition. Hamburg and Berlin.

Bakels, C. C. 1982. Der Mohn, die Linearbandkeramik und das westliche Mittelmeergebiet. *Archäologisches Korrespondenzblatt* 12: 11-13.

Bandi, H.-G. 1968. Das Jungpaläolithikum. In *Archäologie der Schweiz,* ed. Schweizerische Gesellschaft für Archäologie, Vol. 1, 107-22. Basel.

Behre, K.-E. 1983. *Ernährung und Umwelt der wikingerzeitlichen Siedlung Haithabu. Die Ergebnisse der Untersuchungen der Pflanzenreste.* Neumünster, Germany.

Bieleman, J. 1989. Die Verschiedenartigkeit der Landwirtschaftssysteme in den Sandgebieten der Niederlande in der frühen Neuzeit. *Siedlungsforschung* 7: 119-30.

Childe, V. G. 1956. *Man makes himself.* Third edition. London.

Firbas, F. 1949. *Waldgeschichte Mitteleuropas,* Vol. 1. Jena, Germany.

Haenel, H. 1986. Ernährung in der Steinzeit – Ernährung heute. *Wissenschaft und Fortschritt* 36: 287-90.

Jacomet, S. 1988. *Planzen mediterraner Herkunft in neolithischen Seeufersiedlungen der Schweiz.* In *Der prähistorische Mensch und seine Umwelt,* ed. H. Küster. *Forschungen und Berichte zur Vor- und Frühgeschichte in Baden-Württemberg* 31: 205-12. Stuttgart, Germany.

Jacomet, S., and H. Schlichtherle. 1984. Der kleine Pfahlbauweizen Oswald Heers. Neue Untersuchungen zur Morphologie neolithischer Nacktweizen-Ähren. In *Plants and ancient man,* ed. W. van Zeist and W. A. Casparie, 153-76. Rotterdam.

Knörzer, K.-H. 1970. *Römerzeitliche Pflanzenfunde aus Neuss.* Berlin.

  1981. *Römerzeitliche Pflanzenfunde aus Xanten.* Cologne, Germany.

  1991. Deutschland nördlich der Donau. In *Progress in Old World palaeoethnobotany,* ed. W. van Zeist, K. Wasylikowa, and K.-E. Behre, 189-206. Rotterdam.

Kuhn-Schnyder, E. 1968. Die Geschichte der Tierwelt des Pleistozäns und Alt-Holozäns. In *Archäologie der Schweiz,* ed. Schweizerische Gesellschaft für Archäologie, Vol. 1, 43-68. Basel.

Küster, H. 1985. Neolithische Pflanzenreste aus Hochdorf, Gemeinde Eberdingen (Kreis Ludwigsburg). In *Forschungen und Berichte zur Vor- und Frühgeschichte in Baden-Württemberg* 19: 13-83. Stuttgart, Germany.

  1986. Sammelfrüchte des Neolithikums. *Abhandlungen aus dem Westfälischen Museum für Naturkunde* 48 (2/3): 433-40.

  1987. *Wo der Pfeffer wächst. Ein Lexikon zur Kulturgeschichte der Gewürze.* Munich.

  1991. Mitteleuropa südlich der Donau, einschliesslich Alpenraum. In *Progress in Old World palaeoethno-*

botany, ed. W. van Zeist, K. Wasylikowa, and K.-E. Behre, 179-87. Rotterdam.

1992a. Neue Pflanzen für die Alte Welt. Kartoffel und Mais als Kärrner der Industriellen Revolution. *Kultur und Technik* 16: 30-5.

1992b. Römerzeitliche Pflanzenreste. In *Ein Geschirr-depot des 3. Jahrhunderts. Grabungen im Lagerdorf des Kastells Langenhain,* ed. H.-G. Simon and H.-J. Köhler, 184-8. Bonn, Germany.

Rust, A. 1972. *Vor 20000 Jahren. Rentierjäger der Eiszeit.* Third edition. Neumünster, Germany.

Schmitz, H. 1961. Pollenanalytische Untersuchungen in Hohen Viecheln am Schweriner See. In *Hohen Viecheln. Ein mittelsteinzeitlicher Wohnplatz in Mecklenburg,* ed. E. Schuldt, 14-38. Berlin.

Smith, A. G. 1970. The influence of Mesolithic and Neolithic man on British vegetation: A discussion. In *Studies in the vegetational history of the British Isles,* ed. D. Walker and R. G. West, 81-96. London.

Vaughan, D. 1987. The plant macrofossils. In *Prehistoric and Romano-British sites at Westward Ho!, Devon. Archaeological and palaeoenvironmental surveys 1983 and 1984. Studies in palaeoeconomy and environment in South West England,* ed. N. D. Balaam et al., 233-8. Oxford.

Wyss, R. 1968-1971. Technik, Wirtschaft und Handel. In *Archäologie der Schweiz,* ed. Schweizerische Gesellschaft für Archäologie, 3 vols. 3: 123-44. Basel.

V.C.6 ❧ The Low Countries

The term "Low Countries" is used here to mean the Netherlands. Belgium, known in the past as the southern Netherlands, has been independent since the 1830s. Situated between France to the south and the Netherlands to the north, Belgium has had a different history and has developed different cultural characteristics since the seventeenth century. Thus, in this chapter, Belgian culinary culture is employed for comparative purposes only.

A general overview of the history and culinary culture of the Netherlands should, perhaps, start with the observation that the Dutch have never succeeded in being proud of their cuisine. This seems to be a reflection of a lack of national pride that sometimes borders on indifference. If asked, most would probably not be able to identify important, genuinely national, dishes. Moreover, if such a dish were named, it might well be *rijsttafel,* which is not Dutch in origin but Indonesian and is a product of the Dutch East Indian colonies. Such a lack of concern with indigenous culinary culture forms a more or less sharp contrast to the attitudes of the inhabitants of neighboring Western European countries like Belgium, France, and, to some degree, Germany.

Over the centuries, foreign visitors have repeatedly expressed amazement at the Dutch lack of exaltation of the table. But since the late Middle Ages, daily food has always been prepared according to the general rule that it must be simple, nourishing, and cheap. Only after World War II did this undemanding attitude begin to change.

Contrasts and Similarities:
The Late Middle Ages (1300 to 1500)

Little evidence is available about food and drink in the late medieval Low Countries. Cookery books in this era were exclusively aimed at the secular and ecclesiastical upper classes. The recipes, nevertheless, give some indication of the extremely wide range of possible dishes at the tables of the elite. The first Dutch-language cookbook, printed in Brussels by Thomas van der Noot in 1510 and titled *Een notabel boecxken van cokeryen* ("A notable book of cookery"), offers medieval recipes for festivities such as weddings and banquets that deal with the preparation of sauces, jellies, fish, meat, fowl and game, pies, tarts and other pastries, eggs, dairy products, various sugars, wine, and, finally, candied quinces and ginger.

The recipes come from various sources, many of them French, which underlines the observations of Stephen Mennell (1985) about the essential similarity of the tables of the medieval rich everywhere in western Europe, with the elite following culinary standards that were mostly Italian and French. It was especially at such festivals that princes, nobles, and church dignitaries ate and drank lavishly. The festive banquets of the Burgundian dukes, at that time rulers in northern France and the southern Netherlands (Flanders), initiated a luxurious and flamboyant civilization that served as a model all over Europe, as did the ceremonies of their peripatetic courts.

Prodigious consumption at the courts, particularly of meat (from pigs, calves, sheep, various fowl, and game) and wine, contributed to the maintenance of the high social position of the nobility. So, too, did the lavish use of precious spices and sugar in the preparation of a large number of dishes to be presented all at once. A refined taste, however, still had to be acquired, and social standards in eating, appetite, and table manners evolved only over the course of a lengthy civilizing process (Elias 1994). In the Middle Ages, quantity prevailed over quality, in no small part because of the irregularity of the food supply. It was a time when harvests failed, diseases killed domestic animals, and life was made even more insecure by pestilence and war (Mennell 1985: 20-39).

Religious restrictions on the consumption of meat and dairy produce also exerted a profound influence on cooking and eating. Prescribed days of abstinence were not confined to the period of Lent but (in addition to special days of fasting) were in force twice each week, which made for a total of about 150 days of food proscriptions every year. These religious rules of abstinence and fasting raised impediments to, and at the same time opened possibilities for, the culinary creativity of the cooks at the courts as well as those in ordinary kitchens. Fish – a preferred Lenten food – was abundantly available from the sea as well as from the many rivers and lakes in the Low Countries. Thus, meals at the court of the Bishop of Utrecht in the fourteenth century included about 20 different fish dishes, such as haddock, plaice, whiting, eel, herring (in various preparations), sturgeon, pike, perch, and carp. But Lenten abstinence may also have hindered the use of certain cooking methods – such as frying in northern Europe, where butter was the principal edible fat – and in such areas hampered the development of culinary variety in general. By contrast, in southern Europe, where olive oil – not proscribed during Lent – was the major fat, the days of abstinence may have encouraged the inventiveness of cooks, especially in the competition for prestige at noble and royal courts (Jobse-van Putten 1995).

Thus, sharp contrasts existed between festive and daily eating, between feasting and fasting, and between years of plenty and those of scarcity. Other contrasts and variations were related to the rhythm of the seasons, to the church calendar, to the regional agricultural produce, and, above all, to the social strata. To this might be added the contrast between fresh and preserved foods. Except for the short periods during harvest and slaughter, no possibility existed of eating one's fill of fresh vegetables and meat. Rather, because of the rapid deterioration of foodstuffs, they were generally consumed as salted and dried products.

The ecological and geographic conditions typical of a northwestern European delta, with its rivers, lakes, sea inlets, and clay soils, applied especially to the western and northern parts of the Netherlands – Holland, Zeeland, and Friesland – that were to assume a dominant position in the Dutch Republic. The eastern and southern parts of the territory were higher and more sandy, with vegetation different from the lower regions. Such a division between the northwest and the southeast was for centuries an important factor in the economic and agricultural structure, influencing the products available for consumption. The cultivation of grains, for instance, was a matter largely defined by climate and soil.

In fourteenth-century Europe, famines and epidemics, most notably the Black Death, caused a considerable reduction of the population that in turn led to a transformation in the production and distribution of food. The grazing of cattle increased relative to the growing of crops, and for a time, meat was available in larger quantities, even for the poor. Later on, however, the cultivation of grains increased in the Low Countries as elsewhere in Europe, transforming them into staple foods.

A moderate maritime climate in the Low Countries allowed the growing of several types of cereals, including barley, oats, and rye. At least initially, wheat could be cultivated only in the southwest, and rye became the prominent grain in the Netherlands, even

though wheat was the more appreciated of the two (Jobse-van Putten 1995: 83). Unfortunately, the quantity of grain produced was not sufficient for the population and had to be supplemented by imports from eastern Europe. In the thirteenth and fourteenth centuries, this took place within the flourishing trade network of the Hanse – towns of the Hanseatic League – through which substantial parts of northern Europe were commercially interrelated, forming a line from the Baltic Sea and the river Danube in the east to Bruges (Flanders) and London in the west. In the fifteenth century, the position of the Hanse deteriorated, and the grain trade shifted to Amsterdam, which became the most important grain center, not only for the Low Countries but for Europe as a whole.

From the fourteenth century onward (although in Flanders much earlier), economic differentiation began to take place. The importance of money and trade increased; means of transport were improved; and cities came into being. Consequently, some farmers began to produce for the market. Butter and cheese, for example, were made in the low-lying grasslands of Holland and Friesland (where animal husbandry was important) and later became very famous delicacies. Despite such surplus production, however, subsistence agriculture remained the dominant economic pattern, especially on the small and isolated mixed farms in the eastern and southern parts of the Low Countries (Burema 1953: 29).

This type of economy substantially influenced attitudes toward preserving, cooking, and eating home-produced foods, an influence that endured, in part at least, until the second half of the twentieth century (Jobse-van Putten 1995: 379–84). Meals everywhere in the Low Countries were prepared in roughly similar fashion, although local and regional differences in agricultural products and technical conditions of cookery caused variations from place to place in the composition and taste of dishes and drinks. Grain was cooked as porridge (often the poorer qualities), baked as pancakes or bread, and brewed for beer. Porridge could be made in a pot over an open fire, but bread required an oven and, thus, tended to be found in the households of those in more fortunate circumstances. Beer was the common drink, as water was of poor quality and milk was mainly used for making butter and cheese. Vegetables and fruits – thought to be unhealthy – were not much appreciated. Nonetheless, tubers, beetroots, turnips, and peas were often daily foods by necessity. Green leafy vegetables were little known and eaten only among the upper strata. The number of meals per day depended on social position. The elite preferred two meals, but those performing physical labor often ate three or more times daily. In rural areas, frequent hot meals were common.

The ordinary medieval hot meal among country people and townsfolk consisted of a half-liquid pottage, which was a mush made of water, milk, or beer, root vegetables, and pulses (various types of peas) or grain, sometimes enriched with a piece of meat or lard. This dish, prepared over an open fire, like porridge, underwent changes as different ingredients became available throughout the seasons. If an oven was available, bread went with each of the day's hot and cold meals.

In the consumption of pottage, the Low Countries were not very different from other western European countries during the Middle Ages. The records of two hospitals in the cities of Leiden and Utrecht between 1367 and 1500 indicate that pottages were an important dish in both institutions. Meat and fish (salted herring was a preferred Lenten food) were served with bread once or twice a day, and smaller meals consisted of bread, butter, cheese, eggs, and milk, buttermilk, or beer (Jobse-van Putten 1995: 145-50). Every part of an animal (head, brain, eyes, and entrails) was utilized in meat dishes, and the frequency with which such dishes were served by the two hospitals in question is an indication of both the relative prosperity of the cities and the abundance of meat in this period.

Is it possible to discern some traits of an emerging national cuisine in the Low Countries during the late Middle Ages? And is there any indication of a continuity with later developments in Dutch foodways? The little available evidence suggests a negative answer to both questions. The similarities in foodways with other western European countries seem to have been substantially greater than the differences. National states were later inventions, and local and regional networks were dominant in determining the production, distribution, and preparation of foods. The contrasts between common and festive fare, and between meal preparation among the elite, on one hand, and the masses, on the other, were everywhere alike.

There were, of course, some contrasts. One was the Dutch dependency on butter and meat fat for cooking instead of olive oil. That Dutch butter and cheese were famous products at an early stage, and continued to be so for centuries, was another. A final difference was the Dutch expertise in horticulture, which had gained a widespread reputation.

Gardening was initially practiced in the monasteries, but castles and country houses also began to develop cabbage patches and orchards for pears and apples. In addition, commercial gardens were cultivated near cities. Like butter and cheese, horticultural produce was later promoted for export. Foreigners came to regard it as "typically Dutch," and it also achieved fame. Catherine of Aragon, for example, had salad vegetables brought to the English court from Holland by a special courier (Burema 1953: 16).

Rise and Fall of the Dutch Republic (1500 to 1800)

As already noted, strangers visiting the Netherlands over the centuries have often noted a simplicity in cuisine and lack of refinement in the eating and drinking habits of its citizens. The latter were frequently portrayed as people with little discrimination but fond of large quantities of food, which they swallowed quickly. By the late Middle Ages, the Dutch were also well known for their exorbitant drinking habits (Burema 1953: 53). Seventeenth-century paintings by Rembrandt and others show overloaded tables and bacchanalian parties of guilds and fraternities. Yet other paintings show families praying before a simple meal of nothing but bread and cheese. Although some of the latter may carry moral and religious messages, the same simplicity is also mentioned in foreigners' descriptions (Schama 1987: 159-75). Together, these images give an impression of both the exception and the rule in Dutch eating and drinking in the sixteenth and seventeenth centuries. Feasting was characterized by excessive indulgence, reminiscent of the late medieval Burgundian court. Yet daily meals were frugal and consisted, more often than not, of only one or two courses, even among the well-to-do and the aristocracy. As both types of meals lack refinement, how does one interpret the combination of excess and simplicity that has become a distinguishing mark of Dutch culinary culture?

Popular wisdom has it that Dutch culinary mediocrity was caused by Calvinism, which frowned on mundane pleasures. Indeed, the economic and social influence of religion, especially of Calvinism, has been a much-discussed topic among historians and sociologists, who have pondered, among other things, the extent to which it was a force in the sociogenesis of the Dutch Republic and in subsequent public and private spheres of life. Culinary attitudes and preferences, of course, belong to both spheres and are part of the lifestyles and mentalities of the social groups in power. Thus, to understand the culinary culture of the Netherlands, a look at the process of state formation and related economic development is indispensable.

Certainly, the shift of the commercial and industrial center of gravity in Europe from the south to the northwest was an important marker in the beginning of the modern age, and the Low Countries were at the heart of this process. But the forces that led to the flourishing economic position of the Republic of the Seven United Provinces from 1588 to 1795 had already been set in motion by the end of the fifteenth century. At that time, the Low Countries were under the rule of the Habsburg monarchs, who were able, through fortuitous marriages, to enlarge their domains to include Austrian, Burgundian, and Spanish territories.

Situated as they were around the estuaries of the rivers Scheldt, Maas, and Rhine, the inhabitants of the Low Countries knew how to take advantage of the new economic opportunities this expansion provided. The development of new technologies to master floodwaters, the reclamation of land, and the construction of an early infrastructure of navigable canals and windmills were an important Dutch contribution to modern European economic growth. In addition, there were well-known Dutch advances in shipping and commerce, and development also occurred in other important fields such as agriculture, fisheries (especially herring), and industry (principally textiles and timber). It is important to note that all of this economic upsurge had already taken place before the Reformation, with its various brands of Protestantism (especially Calvinism), could have had any influence (De Vries and Van der Woude 1995: 23–67, 205–13).

Moreover, even the Calvinist influence was often moderated by a liberal and humanistic Christian faith in the tradition of Desiderius Erasmus. Consequently, Calvinism never succeeded in achieving a religious monopoly; indeed, many citizens clung to the old Roman Catholic church. This is not to say, however, that Calvinism was not an important force in Dutch history. It helped sustain the country during its revolt against the Spanish Habsburgs, and the great merchants who emerged as the Dutch Republic came into existence were supporters of the Reformation. These men found their rising influence in the affairs of the state legitimized by the new Protestant faith, and they, along with the patricians, did impress a cultural style on the public and private spheres of daily life that was typical of the urban bourgeois from Holland and Zeeland.

This meant that the exceptionally broad, but differentiated, middle classes in the cities were at the heart of the republican society (Huizinga 1984: 39–59; Van Deursen 1992) – a situation that was fundamentally different from other European countries such as England and France. In England, both the royal court and the rural gentry left their mark on cultural life, whereas in France, new cultural models, in foodways as in other areas, were pioneered at the urban court where the king and nobility resided (Mennell 1985: 102–34). But in the Netherlands, during the sixteenth and seventeenth centuries, the dominance of bourgeois influence, legitimized by the characteristic Christian lay religiosity of either the orthodox Calvinist or the liberal humanist, resulted in a frugal and simple culinary style.

This simplicity was not the case on festive occasions, however, despite the complaints of some Calvinist ministers about the collapse of tables under the weight of too many dishes, and despite the decrees issued by Doctor Nicolaas Tulp (the mayor of Amsterdam around 1660) against excessive expenditures for eating and drinking at weddings, christenings, and funerals. Indeed, such festivals were occasions when considerations of social status and competition overcame the ever-present virtue of thriftiness (Van Otterloo 1986: 39–43).

From 1500 to 1800, as in the late Middle Ages, the main foods remained grain, tubers, meat, lard, fish, cheese, and butter. The central importance of the grain market in Amsterdam meant an increasing abundance of wheat, and wheat bread became the most popular farinaceous food among the urban well-to-do, as well as among the patricians in their country houses. In addition, spices, for those who could afford them, were increasingly available from 1602 onward because of the trading efforts of the Dutch East India Company.

The diets of artisans and farmers centered mainly on a daily porridge, sometimes interchanged with or complemented by pancakes and rye bread. Bread might be accompanied by butter or cheese, but not both. The two together were viewed as a needless luxury, even as "devil's work." If possible, bread was eaten at breakfast with fish, porridge, or another hot dish, and perhaps at a third or even fourth meal in the early evening with a pottage. Many varieties of bread were used, depending on social position and the type, rhythm, and place of work.

In distinguished circles, the salad, an invention diffused from the south, often accompanied the early evening meal or was used as an entrée at the beginning of a hot meal. Initially, beer was the beverage of choice at meals, but later on it was largely replaced by milk, buttermilk, or whey, although the poor generally drank water. After 1680, coffee began to be used; in the eighteenth century, it became a popular drink, and there were many coffeehouses in the cities and towns. Tea – called "women's tobacco" – also came into use and long remained a high-status beverage, partly because of the costly tea set required by social custom. Tea was drunk by the wives of patricians and bourgeois regents and diffused very slowly among the lower social strata during the eighteenth and nineteenth centuries (Jobse-van Putten 1995: 151–226).

For many, the day's two hot meals generally consisted of one to three courses: a starter, a main course, and possibly a dessert. The starter might have been a salad or a *sop* (pottage) from groats or bread soaked in milk or broth. Other possibilities were a dish of pulses with butter and onions, braised root vegetables, or cabbage. Dessert was usually buttermilk porridge in rural areas; among the urban merchants, however, pastry (for example, "shoemaker's tart," made from apples, bread, and eggs) and fruits were common. The main course was a dish of fish or meat, served, if possible, with green herbs, prunes, or currants. In wealthy households, this course might be followed by oysters or lobster with sweet sauces (Burema 1953: 96).

The relative simplicity of the bourgeois kitchen was reflected in the unique cookbook of Dutch origin *De verstandige Kock of Sorghvuldige Huyshoudster* ("The Prudent Cook or Careful Housekeeper"), published in Amsterdam in 1667. This frequently reprinted book was intended for wealthy merchants who owned country houses and had access to produce from their own gardens (gardening was a relatively new pursuit of the urban elite). The book opens with instructions for building a kitchen range that permitted the simultaneous preparation of separate dishes. Next, the book deals with the preparation of salads (both cooked and raw); vegetables (braised in sauces thickened with bread crumbs); meat, game, and fowl; salted fish, fish from the sea, and freshwater fish (the three separate chapters on fish indicate the importance of this food); and cakes, tarts, and pastry. The traditional Dutch pottage of meat and vegetables is present in the cookbook as a "Spanish hodgepodge," and a few recipes are given for a festive mixed-meat dish, *olipodrigo,* that was widely known in Europe (Van't Veer: 1966: 69–93).

In the eighteenth century, there was a growing French cultural influence among the elite, and a modest refinement can be discerned in cookery, table manners, table coverings, and tableware. The fork increasingly became an obligatory instrument after the 1750s, and pewter and silver, as decorative materials, were now preferred over copper or iron. For the upper classes, ambivalence about luxury at the table now belonged to the past. But at the same time, the gulf between rich and poor increased considerably, and the potato would soon become crucial to the survival of the latter.

That gulf was also manifested in poems and plays that ridiculed bourgeois virtues, such as, for example, the preference of aristocrats and their bourgeois imitators for game and white bread (*Heerenbroot* or "lord's bread") instead of rye bread and cheese (Schama 1987: 172; Zahn 1989: 48–52, 272). Indeed, a widespread contempt for the upper classes and their ostentation helped bring about a society without a steep social hierarchy or an influential central court. This situation, however, as suggested by Jack Goody (1982: 97–134) and Stephen Mennell (1985: 103–34), may have discouraged the rise of a uniquely Dutch haute cuisine.

Modernization and Industrialization: The Modern World (1800 to 1960)

In 1795, the Low Countries became a part of Napoleonic France. The administration by regents and merchants came to an end, and Amsterdam's trade monopoly shifted to England. These developments increased the general impoverishment of many in the population that had already begun with economic deterioration during the late eighteenth century. Following the period of French control, the Low Countries became a kingdom ruled by the princes of Orange. William I (1813–40), the "king-merchant," tried to restore the old Dutch commercial position and to give the country new economic life by the founding of trading companies, the construction of roads and canals, the reclamation of land, and other modernizing measures. But his efforts were more or less unsuccessful. Moreover, during his reign, there was the 1830 separation of Flanders and the Walloon provinces in the south from the rest of the nation; these united to become the country of Belgium.

The 1840s are well known in western European history as a decade of turbulence and revolution, caused in part by recurring shortages of food. This was certainly the case in the Netherlands, where the decade represents a low point in Dutch history. A dearth of grain put even bread and porridge out of reach of both the masses in the cities and many in the countryside. Meat and lard virtually disappeared from the diet, and countless people ate potatoes, carrots, and turnips, or perhaps only potatoes, morning, noon, and evening.

Indeed, from the end of the eighteenth century onward, potatoes increasingly became a staple food for the nation and a substitute for unaffordable bread. In 1847 and 1848 this near-exclusive dependence on potatoes had disastrous consequences, as the potato blight during these years triggered crop failures and famine. Food shortages were joined by epidemics – as was often the case in the preindustrial period – to produce high death rates, primarily in the strongly urbanized province of North Holland. Fortunately, many of the urban poor were helped by local administrations or by charitable institutions. Soup kitchens and eatinghouses provided portions of cheap or free food, and the thin soup (invented by Count Benjamin Rumford and composed of bone-jelly, beans, potatoes, and sometimes turnips or carrots) that became famous all over Europe was also popular in the Netherlands.

Slight improvements in the food supply were made intermittently during the decades that followed, but in the 1880s, a deep agricultural crisis, caused by a sudden profusion of overseas grain, again brought widespread shortages and misery, this time mainly in the countryside, as local grain prices tumbled. After 1890, however, substantial economic growth took place in the Netherlands, and industrialization, improved transportation, and an ensuing rise in income brought an expansion of the distribution and affordability of foodstuffs.

In the twentieth century, two World Wars and the economic crisis of the 1930s again caused shortages, but after the 1950s, food scarcity and hunger became things of the past, and a new age of plenty was under way. Paralleling these developments was the modernization of Dutch foodways that took place between 1880 and 1960. This modernization involved the diffusion of food and drink innovations, new dishes, and new sequences of meals that passed, in general, from the upper to the lower classes, from town to country, and from the western market-oriented regions to the eastern and southern provinces, hitherto geared to subsistence agriculture. At the start of this period, contrasts were sharp, but by the end, similarities were the norm, brought about by increasing education, democratization, and uniformity (Van Otterloo 1990: 127–84; Jobse-van Putten 1995: 499–506).

These were long-term processes that involved, among other things, what might be called the replacement of foods of necessity with foods of luxury, as qualitatively better and more expensive foods gradually became more accessible to more people. In other words, potatoes, pulses, root vegetables, and grains such as buckwheat and rye were little by little replaced by wheat, meat, butter, cheese, other dairy produce, and sugar. The change began with the replacement of rye (cheaper but nutritious) with wheat, most preferred but more expensive. The next phase, after World War II, saw a decline in the consumption of wheat (bread) but steep increases in the per capita intake of meat, cheese, and sugar. The position of potatoes as a staple food, strong during the entire nineteenth century, began to deteriorate after 1900, and after 1920, potato consumption declined at an accelerated pace (Van Otterloo 1990: 45–8).

Industrialization also had revolutionizing effects on food and meals in the production of foodstuffs and in the organization of work and the family. The shifting of food production to the factory was made possible by rapidly increasing scientific knowledge in relation to the mechanization and "chemicalization" of food. Industrially processed ingredients, like corn flour, *fécule* (custard powder), "Oxo" (bouilion cubes), margarine, canned vegetables, meat, and fish, had become available at the end of the nineteenth century and were readily so during the interwar years. The food industry promoted its products through advertisements and educational campaigns, sometimes enlisting cookery teachers, even doctors, to inspire public trust in the new time- and energy-saving processed foods.

As elsewhere, the level of education in the Low Countries increased considerably after 1900. Women benefited from cooking classes and schools of home economics that taught the principles of hygiene and nutrition and, not incidentally, how to prepare tasty and healthy meals. (Although similar institutions were known elsewhere in western Europe, cookery books used in Dutch schools were distinguished by meticulous calculations of the prices of ingredients.) After 1930, radio and women's magazines helped to diffuse such knowledge, and in this way, the culinary cultures of Europe, especially that of France, trickled down to the middle and lower classes in the cities and, finally, to the country people in the eastern and southern provinces of the Netherlands. Also crucial to such a democratization of taste was the metamorphosis of the kitchen range, along with an increasing ease of securing water, gas, and electricity.

The modern industrial organization of work and the family also brought about several important changes in the dishes of Dutch people and in their meal system as a whole. The number, type, and composition of meals one consumed had for centuries reflected social, regional, and rural–urban differences. But now there was a movement toward uniformity (Jobse-van Putten 1995: 275–498). The number of meals in a day became three – generally a cold breakfast, a cold lunch, and a hot dinner at about 6:00 in the evening. Coffee and tea, popular among the urban middle classes since the end of the eighteenth century, now diffused (coffee in particular) to the whole Dutch populace and were drunk throughout the day, both with and between meals; these drinks replaced to a great extent other beverages like beer, milk, and buttermilk. Tea, at first a prestigious middle-class beverage drunk in the afternoon with a biscuit or a sweet, began somewhat later than coffee to accompany breakfast or lunch.

At breakfast, potatoes, porridge, and pancakes gave way to just bread and tea or coffee. A cold lunch around noon was an invention of the industrial age, suited to the new rhythm of work. Initially, hot potato meals were taken to the factory, but these were soon replaced with packets of bread brought from home. Much later, canteens supplied foods for employees, as they did elsewhere in Europe. Dinner in the Netherlands evolved into a three-course hot meal, ideally with a starter, preferably (vegetable) soup based on a meat stock, a French custom that between 1900 and 1940 was gradually adopted in the Low Countries (where pork or chicken was used as a stock instead of beef). The main course (again ideally) consisted of potatoes and gravy, cooked vegetables with a sauce, and a meat dish. Following this was a sweet dessert of (partly industrially processed) pudding, custard, or fresh or preserved fruits.

At first, this highly prestigious bourgeois meal was consumed exclusively on Sundays and festive occasions in the countryside, but it was later adopted in the cities as well. Thus, the centuries-old regional diversity of meals, comprising pancakes, porridges, stews, and thick soups based on pulses, grain, rice, and turnips, largely disappeared.

We might pause to ask and answer the question of whether any aspect of culinary culture in the Netherlands during this period was typically Dutch and thus unique in Europe. This was certainly not the case with breakfast, which seems to have followed the common Continental evolutionary path. At most, it was different only because of particular bread fillings, like chocolate sprinkles. The singular addiction of the Dutch to coffee and tea breaks at work is perhaps a national sin, not elsewhere indulged to the same extent.

Lunch took on a very simple form; it was mainly served cold and without frills. Except for an occasional salad, it continued the Dutch tradition of simplicity and frugality. This was also generally true of dinner, which had a simple and straightforward character, in which quantity (but also nutritiousness) continued to be preferred above quality and refinement. Another illustration of simplicity and frugality was the late development of habitually eating out in the Netherlands. In Belgium, restaurants had become popular as early as 1840, but restaurants in the Netherlands were only hesitantly visited beginning in about the 1890s, and eating out did not become a socially acceptable habit until the 1960s and later (Scholliers 1993: 71).

Globalization and Civilization: The Low Countries since the 1960s

World War II shook the Netherlands much more violently than World War I, and the populace experienced the distress of occupation and a scarcity of goods, even the pangs of hunger. Following the war, reconstruction of the economy and the country's infrastructure were priorities for the government and goals that required the utmost efforts of the entire population. Consumption was therefore postponed, and frugality continued.

The eating and drinking habits in the Netherlands were also patterned on the prewar model. No fundamental developments occurred except for a limited upsurge of interest in Indonesian food. This arose because of the tens of thousands of soldiers and people of mixed Dutch-Indonesian descent who flooded into the Netherlands during the years following the independence of this former Dutch colony.

Dutch postwar industriousness ultimately resulted in economic prosperity, and with it came a climate of widespread opposition to old ways and established authority. This was, of course, not unique to the Netherlands. In other Western countries, such as the United States, France, and Germany, similar developments took place, particularly at universities, where forces of change were aimed at questions of power and dependency in relationships between authorities and citizens, younger and older generations, and men and women. Institutional practices in the spheres of government, education, work, family life, and leisure were fundamentally altered by a cultural revolution in which the young formed the vanguard.

Frugality and hard work yielded to the drive for enjoyment, and pleasures such as popular music, sports, and travel became paramount. Consumption in the private sphere arose as a respected goal; certain brands of clothes became status symbols; homes were equipped with new furniture, televisions, washing machines, refrigerators, and other appliances. With Saturday as well as Sunday decreed days of leisure, weekends underwent a complete metamorphosis in family activities that encouraged the more convenient preparation of foods. As incomes rose and leisure hours increased, sociability became more important. Visits and parties were – as always – accompanied by food and drink, and traveling abroad led to exposure to the foodways of other cultures. Mediterranean countries such as France, Spain, Italy, and the former Yugoslavia became preferred holiday destinations for wide segments of the population.

At the same time, migrant workers came from areas of southern Europe to take jobs in the Netherlands. In the 1970s and 1980s, many foreigners, along with nonwhite citizens of the Caribbean, especially Suriname, were attracted by the high levels of welfare and social security, all of which transformed the Netherlands into a multicultural and, in some respects, a multiethnic society.

Other important transformations took place in the private sphere. These had to do with changing relationships among family members, now that people increasingly worked outside of the home. A growing divorce rate, an earlier independence of the young, and a rise in the number of old people combined to stimulate a substantial growth in the number of one- and two-person households. Such new and distinct conditions of life in the Netherlands led, among other things, to a fundamental alteration of the Dutch attitude toward food, which started among the middle classes but reached into innovative groups in the lower strata.

As elsewhere in the West, eating became less associated with a physical need to fill the stomach and more with a fashion of dining well, even elegantly, and the status that this conveyed. A flood of cookbooks, glossy cookery magazines, even serious treatises on culinary culture, swept into the bookshops and newsstands; cooking classes and culinary demonstrations on television became popular, and the media increasingly devoted columns and programs to the pleasures of the table.

Exotic herbs, spices, and other ingredients became available, and the figure of the gourmet was no longer one likely to be scorned or ridiculed. This does not mean that a genuine high culinary culture developed in the Netherlands, as it did in Belgium (Scholliers 1993), but it was the case that a "civilizing" of eating and taste spread throughout the various social strata. Eating out in restaurants and inviting nonfamilial guests for dinner at home – practices that formerly had never been common – gradually became the norm, and the per capita use of alcoholic beverages and soft drinks rose to heights never seen before. Between 1965 and 1990, the consumption of beer multiplied by two and a half times, wine by four, and soft drinks by slightly more than two and a half (CBS 1994).

The new and discriminating Dutch taste was not characterized by uniformity. Rather, there were various (and sometimes contradictory) trends, as international foodstuffs were increasingly distributed across the globe. A demand for exotic food was first apparent in the success of Chinese and Indonesian restaurants, which appealed to the Dutch because the food was cheap and large quantities were provided. Asian food was followed by Mediterranean cuisine from the various countries visited by vacationing Dutch, and from this point, culinary inquisitiveness spread to include foods from more distant parts of the world, like Mexico and Japan.

Indeed, the Dutch developed a world cuisine of their own, although the exotic dishes that comprised it were often not relished in their original forms and strong flavors but were shaped and moderated to meet the Dutch preference for bland tastes. Another international eating trend was adopted in the form of fast food from the United States, which had, in many respects, replaced France as a postwar cultural model for the Netherlands.

Like others in the West, the Dutch have embraced the tendency to make cooking in the home as easy as possible, which has meant a greater use of convenience food in preparing meals, and the use of snack foods has become marked. Many working housewives and mothers (whose numbers have increased substantially) now regularly escape their previously important duty of cooking for the family, and in fact, the rhythms of work and leisure of individual household members no longer coincide, which has changed the pattern of meals. Nowadays, the hot family meal in the evening might be the only one shared; yet even then, individual members of the household frequently have other commitments that oblige them to use the microwave to heat their share of the meal at a later time.

The consumption of snacks (described as grazing) in between, instead of, or in combination with regular meals has increased considerably. In addition, many restaurants, ranging from very exclusive to very simple, have come into existence to meet the new needs of the different strata of the population. Between 1965 and 1990, the number of restaurants multiplied five times (CBS 1994). Typically, these establishments borrow from cuisines the world over: snack bars and take-out restaurants feature American hamburgers, Indonesian *nasi,* Belgian *patates frites,* and Italian pizza.

As elsewhere, such changes in eating habits have brought anxiety about extremely processed food and concomitant concerns about obesity, food allergies, eating disorders, and food additives and contaminants. Vegetarianism and other movements supporting specific dietary principles have grown in popularity and in acceptance. In short, various trends and countertrends emphasizing the enjoyment, but also the dangers, inherent in food developed in contradiction with one another. This is, indeed, a remarkable change in a country that has never been characterized by a pronounced culinary culture! Both developments may be interpreted as aspects of the globalization of eating and drinking in the Netherlands (Elias 1994).

Summary

In this chapter, it has been suggested that the development of Dutch eating habits over the centuries has been influenced by a complex set of interrelated economic, political, and sociocultural forces. Processes of state formation and nation building, civilization, and democratization have marked the culinary culture of the Low Countries since the Middle Ages.

Until the last few decades, the Dutch maintained a preference for cheap, simple, and nourishing food, even though their cooks had obtained ideas and inspiration from foreigners, particularly the French, since the Middle Ages. That a high culinary culture was never created in the Netherlands differs greatly from the experience of Belgium, where, in the last 150 years, one has developed that is much appreciated abroad as well as at home.

The lack, however, of a haute cuisine in the Netherlands does not mean that the Dutch retained their seventeenth-century habits of binge eating and drinking at festivals. Rather, the French influence on daily life among the elite increased substantially in the eighteenth century, with Dutch patricians losing their bourgeois mentality and coming to resemble aristocrats in the usual sense. This change increasingly shaped their preferences and manners according to French (courtly) ways, particularly in dress and in the choice of dishes and recipes. The growing "civilizing of appetite" (Mennell 1985: 20–40) impeded immoderate "guzzling" among broader strata of the urban middle classes and encouraged them at the same time to permit themselves the luxury of refinement in eating, tableware, and table manners. Later rounds of democratization and civilization took place during the nineteenth and twentieth centuries and ultimately reached farmers and other country people and urban workers.

In the aftermath of World War II, new culinary models from America, the Mediterranean, and the (postcolonial) Far East became available. Subsequently, a decrease in the consumption of bread and potatoes, backbones of the earlier Dutch meal, bore witness to fundamental changes at the Dutch table. The movement from potatoes to pasta has meant a fading both of the traditional composition of meals and of national boundaries. To eat in a typically Dutch way seems to mean "going global" in the Netherlands at the turn of the twenty-first century.

Anneke H. van Otterloo

Many thanks to Dr. Jozien Jobse-van Putten and to Prof. Dr. Stephen Mennell for their fruitful comments on an earlier version of this chapter.

Bibliography

Burema, L. 1953. *De voeding in Nederland van de Middeleeuwen tot de twintigste eeuw* (Food in the Netherlands from the Middle Ages to the twentieth century). Assen, the Netherlands.

CBS (Centraal Bureau voor de Statistiek) (Central Bureau of Statistics). 1994. *Vijfennegentig jaren statistiek in tijdreeksen, 1899–1994.* The Hague.

De Vries, Jan, and Ad van der Woude. 1995. *Nederland 1500–1815. De eerste ronde van moderne economische groei* (The Netherlands 1500–1815: The first round of modern economic growth). Amsterdam.

Elias, Norbert. [1939] 1994. *The civilizing process.* Oxford.

Goody, Jack. 1982. *Cooking, cuisine and class. A study in comparative sociology.* Cambridge.

Huizinga, Johan. [1941] 1984. *Nederlands beschaving in dezeventiende eeuw. Een schets* (Dutch civilization in the seventeenth century: A sketch). Groningen, the Netherlands.

Jobse-van Putten, Jozien. 1995. *Eenvoudig maar voedzaam. Cultuurgeschiedenis van de dagelijkse maaltijd in Nederland* (Simple, but nutritious: A cultural history of the daily meal in the Netherlands). Nijmegen, the Netherlands.

Mennell, Stephen. 1985. *All manners of food. Eating and taste in England and France from the Middle Ages to the present.* Oxford.

1988. Voorspel: Eten in de Lage Landen. In his *Smaken verschillen. Eetcultuur in Engeland en Frankrijk van de Middeleeuwen tot nu,* 15–29. Amsterdam.

Mennell, Stephen, Anne Murcott, and Anneke H. van Otterloo. 1992. *The sociology of food: Eating, diet and culture.* London and Delhi.

Romein, Jan, and Annie Romein. 1979. *De Lage Landen bij de zee. Een geschiedenis van het Nederlandse volk* (The Low Countries: A history of the Dutch nation). Utrecht.

Schama, Simon. 1987. *Overvloed en onbehagen* (The embarrassment of riches). Amsterdam and London.

Scholliers, Peter. 1993. *Arm en rijk aan tafel. Tweehonderd jaar eetcultuur in België* (Rich and poor at table: Two hundred years of culinary culture in Belgium). Berchem and Brussels, Belgium.

Van Deursen, A. Th. [1978] 1992. *Mensen van klein vermogen: Het 'kopergeld' van de Gouden Eeuw* (People of little riches: The small coins of the Golden Age). Amsterdam.

Van Otterloo, Anneke H. 1986. Over de culinaire culturen in Noord en Zuid. Enkele opmerkingen bij de sociogenese van nationale stijl en regionale variaties (About culinary cultures in the north and south). *Groniek* 95: 36–55.

1990. *Eten en eetlust in Nederland (1840–1990). Een historisch-sociologische studie* (Eating and appetite in The Netherlands (1840–1990): A historical and sociological study). Amsterdam.

Van 't Veer, Annie. 1966. *Oud-Hollands kookboek* (Old Dutch cookbook). Utrecht and Antwerp.

Zahn, Ernest. 1989. *Regenten, rebellen en reformatoren. Een visie op Nederland en de Nederlanders* (Regents, rebels and reformers: A view on the Netherlands and the Dutch). Amsterdam.

V.C.7 ✎ Russia

Dietary patterns in Russia display marked continuities over most of the past millennium or so. Staple foodstuffs have remained remarkably constant, and despite the introduction of new foods and beverages in later centuries and the gradual eclipse of a few items, the diets of the vast majority of the population underwent little qualitative change until well into the nineteenth century. Russia, relatively isolated from the West until the reigns of Peter I and Catherine in the eighteenth century, was as conservative in its cuisine as it was in politics and society, and the sharp gap between rich and poor was reflected in what they ate and drank.

Russia is defined for the purposes of this study as the lands inhabited by the modern eastern Slavic peoples, the Belorussians in the west, the Ukrainians in the south, and the Russians in the north and center of "European Russia." Brief mention is made of the Baltic, Transcaucasian, Siberian, and central Asian peoples, primarily as their foods influenced the diets of their Slavic rulers in the Russian Empire and the Soviet Union. Imperial Russia also controlled Finland and much of Poland during the nineteenth century, but these areas are not considered here.

Peoples ancestral to the modern eastern Slavs apparently began spreading out from their homeland in the territory near the modern borders of Poland, Belarus, and Ukraine around the seventh century. They moved into the forests of central and northern Russia at the expense of scattered Finnic peoples, most of whom were eventually absorbed or displaced. Expansion into the grasslands of the Ukraine and beyond was much slower because the steppes were dominated by pastoral peoples of Turkic and Mongol stock. The medieval Kievan state was able to hold the horsemen at bay for a while, but by the twelfth century the Slavs began to retreat northward under nomad pressure. Not until the sixteenth century was the new Muscovite state strong enough to begin the reconquest of the Ukraine and extend Russian power down the Volga. Traditional Russian cuisine developed in the forest zone but was profoundly influenced by expansion into the grasslands and along trade routes.

Early Russian Diets

Archaeological evidence indicates that the early Slavic inhabitants of the forest, like their Finnic neighbors, were farmers who used slash-and-burn techniques to make clearings for their villages and farms. Their primary grain was rye; oats, buckwheat, and barley played secondary roles, and wheat was always uncommon in the north. Grain was consumed primarily as bread, including the famous Russian black rye bread, but gruels (kasha) and porridges were common as well. Noodles were borrowed from the Tatars in the thirteenth or fourteenth century. Grain was also converted into beverages ranging from the virtually nonalcoholic *kvas* to light beer *(braga)* and beer.

A variety of fruits and vegetables were also grown. Turnips, hardy enough to thrive in the harsh northern climate, were an important root crop; carrots, beets, and radishes were also significant. Garlic and onions were common seasonings. Cabbages and cucumbers were important in diets, both fresh or preserved by pickling or in salt. Such preparations provided the main supply of vegetables during the long winter and were essential as antiscorbutics. Cabbage soup *(shchi)* was and remains a dietary staple. There was at least limited cultivation of apple and cherry orchards from very early times.

The long winters created severe forage problems that precluded large-scale stock raising, but limited numbers of cows, horses, pigs, chickens, and ducks were kept. Possession of livestock was a measure of family wealth. Slaughtering was usually done in the fall. Milk, meat, and eggs were scarce and expensive and generally appeared in meals on feast days and festivals. Hard cheeses were not important, but cottage cheese was fairly common.

The forests also supplied many foods. Game animals provided welcome meat, especially in areas with sparse populations. Ducks, geese, and other birds were widely hunted and traded. Fish, fresh from local streams and ponds, or traded in salted or dried form, were the major source of animal protein. Wild nuts and berries provided seasonal variety, and mushroom gathering was and remains a popular activity. The forest was also a habitat for bees, whose hives were raided for wax and honey. The latter was a prized sweetener and was often fermented into mead. Bee-keeping eventually became a lucrative sideline for some farmers.

Salt, crucial for preserving fish, meat, and vegetables, was mined in rock form in a few places and was later obtained from the sea in the Crimea and salt lakes near Astrakhan at the mouth of the Volga. The major sources of salt, however, were well north of Moscow. Boiling seawater to crystalline salt was being done on the White Sea by the twelfth century, and salt production developed into an important industry in this remote region. By the fourteenth century wells were being drilled to tap underground brine pools at many sites between Moscow and the White Sea. Salt was an essential commodity and its production and trade were lucrative and heavily taxed enterprises.

In the tundra zone of the far north, from the Lapps (Saami) of the Kola Peninsula to the Chuckchi in extreme northeastern Siberia, Russian fur traders and pioneers encountered peoples who survived by hunting land and sea mammals, fishing, and herding reindeer. Further south, in the Siberian taiga forest, aboriginal peoples like the Yakuts supplemented hunting and fishing with stock raising. Russians venturing into such environments had, of course, to adapt to local conditions, but they traded with their countrymen for grain and introduced bread and other grain products, including fermented and distilled beverages, to their northern neighbors.

Daily diets were strongly influenced by religious requirements and the seasons. Conversion to Christianity, traditionally dated to 988, had a profound impact on food consumption patterns. The Orthodox calendar included a large number of feast and fast days which, to the amazement of some foreign observers, were widely observed. Church fasts included Lent, the 40 days before Christmas, and the Saints Peter and Paul fast. This fast, which ended on June 28 and could last from one to six weeks, depending on when Easter fell, came at a time when stored food was running low and caloric demands for agricultural work were very high.

Meat was forbidden during all fasts; fish and all foods of animal origin were forbidden during Lent. Wealthy Russians, however, frequently enjoyed elaborate fish dishes and fine wines during fast periods. Feast days, including Christmas, Easter, weddings, harvest celebrations, and, sometimes, funerals, were the major occasions for eating meat, pastries, and other rarities and for hearty drinking bouts. Binge drinking, and to some extent, binge eating, were regular features of Russian life, reflecting both the agricultural cycle and religious observances.

Peasants ate best in the fall, when the new harvest was gathered and animals were slaughtered. Mushrooms were hunted all over Russia and the Ukraine. They were both a prized food and an excuse for convivial excursions. The autumn was a common time for weddings and associated feasts. Fresh fruits and vegetables were available during the warmer months, but stored grain, pickled cabbage, and salted cucumbers were the winter staples. Food supplies often ran low in the spring; diminished stores and religious fasts meant lean meals during plowing and planting time in the late spring.

The conquest of the entire Volga River to its mouth on the Caspian Sea, completed by 1569, placed Russia in an advantageous position to trade for spices, notably pepper, saffron, and cinnamon. Melons and fruits from central Asia became more accessible, and the empire gained new sources of salt. The Volga and its tributaries provided a rich variety of fish, including sturgeon and its caviar and the sterlets, a variety of small sturgeon that delighted both Russian and visiting foreign gourmands. Fish were sold dried or salted and even transported live in special boats for the tables of the Tsar and other notables. Frozen fish were widely distributed during the winter. *Pirogi* (sing. *pirog*), pastries filled with meat, fish, or other delicacies, and *pel'meni,* small Siberian dumplings, probably entered the Russian diet during the sixteenth century. They may have been borrowed from Finnic or Tatar peoples of the Volga valley.

Russia slowly and erratically expanded into the Ukraine and southern Russia during the sixteenth, seventeenth, and eighteenth centuries. The conquest of these rich black-earth grasslands provided the basis for extensive wheat cultivation and a growing export of grain. Ukrainians and Russian colonists were able to raise more fruit and vegetables in these milder climes and to keep more livestock. Meat, though not milk, played a larger role in diets. Beets were a popular crop, and beet soup (*borshch*) held the place of cabbage soup (*shchi*) in the Ukrainian cuisine. Beets were also made into *kvas,* which was not only a beverage but a common stock for Ukrainian soups and stews. Large quantities of watermelons and eggplants were grown in some districts for local consumption and for trade.

The Eighteenth Century

The eighteenth century was a period of change in Russian diets, particularly among the elite, as many new foodstuffs were introduced. Peter the Great's opening to the West, symbolized by his construction of a new capital on the recently conquered shores of the Baltic, and complemented by the modernizing policies of Catherine at the end of the century, exposed the growing Russian Empire to an array of new foods and drinks from Europe, Asia, and the Americas. European, especially French, chefs appeared in many noble homes, and gourmet cooking spread among courtiers and other members of the elite. The first Russian cookbook appeared in 1779; it was followed by many translations of German and French cookbooks, sometimes adapted to local ingredients and tastes.

A few Russians learned to eat salads, an innovation dismissed by others as the equivalent of eating grass. The Dutch had introduced asparagus in the 1600s; at the end of the century a French visitor was treated to "dates from Egypt" by a clergyman in the far north. Tea, coffee, sugar, and the tomato were introduced among the upper classes. Elegant finger foods for hors d'oeuvres *(zakuski)* provided refreshment at receptions.

Wine had always been imported in small quantities by the church for communion and had occasionally graced the tables of the elite, but in the eighteenth century wines from Europe, and later from Armenia, Georgia, and parts of the southern Ukraine, gained popularity in gentry homes. Distilled spirits, first introduced from the Baltic and Poland in the 1500s, began to displace mead and beer, even in some poor households. Tea, known as a curiosity from the seventeenth century, was brewed in ornate samovars in the homes of the rich and in new urban cafés during the 1700s, and tea drinking began to percolate down the social scale. Tea was often served with cane sugar from the West Indies. Sugar, a major import by the late 1700s, gradually replaced honey as a sweetener, first in the homes of the wealthy, and then, like tea and vodka, it spread to more humble abodes.

Two other New World cultigens reached Russia during the eighteenth century. The potato, as in Ireland and Hungary (and like cassava in western Africa), was introduced to prevent famines. Catherine issued an edict recommending its cultivation after a dearth in food production in 1765, but this directive garnered little response except in the Baltic provinces dominated by German nobles, who took more interest in the tuber and made sure that their Baltic peasants did, too. For decades, however, the potato was scorned by the Slavic peasantry, remaining only a curiosity on the tables of sophisticates. Maize, introduced into eastern Europe in the eighteenth century and a staple crop in Hungary, Serbia, and Romania by the nineteenth century, remained insignificant in Russia, except in Bessarabia (Moldova) in the far southwest.

The tradition of keeping foreign dignitaries busy with lengthy banquets, featuring numerous rich dishes served in a seemingly endless sequence and even more numerous alcoholic toasts, reached a high stage of development during this period. Such ostentatious hospitality, already given mixed notice by sixteenth-century English and Dutch visitors, has continued until the present. The foreigners were well treated, kept in a haze during their visit, and distracted from seeing or hearing things that their hosts preferred they not know about.

The Nineteenth Century

Dietary innovations began to reach the peasantry, the vast majority of the population, only in the nineteenth century. The gradual spread of sugar beets and tomatoes in the Ukraine and southern Russia, and potatoes, especially in northern and central regions, did make something of a difference in the nutritional regimen. Still, dietary surveys and travelers' reports indicate strong continuity in the consumption patterns of most Russians. Tastes in beverages underwent more significant change as tea and vodka became widely used at all levels of society.

Bread, generally the familiar dark rye loaf, remained the staff of life. Wheat bread became a little more common, especially in the Black Earth areas of the Ukraine and in the Volga provinces, but most wheat was produced for export. A working man commonly ate 3 to 5 pounds of bread daily. Kasha was also a frequent dish. On feast days, and sometimes more often in prosperous households, dough was used to make *pirogi* filled with meat, cottage cheese, cabbage, or berries; or *blini,* thin yeast-leavened pancakes rolled up and filled with sweets or smothered in butter and sour cream; or *knyshi,* pastry puffs filled with cream.

Cabbage and cucumbers were the most important vegetables, but serf and free-peasant gardens generated a variety of produce. Onions and garlic continued to be popular seasonings, and peas, melons, berries, turnips, and other garden produce were appreciated during the summer. Oils from hemp, flax, and sunflower seeds (another American introduction) were used in cooking. Mushrooms, nuts, and berries were collected in the forest and could be salted or dried for the winter. Apiaries, providing honey, were common, and many peasants kept pigs, sheep, and/or poultry. The diet was monotonous and often lacked protein, especially for the poor. A rural doctor in the 1860s blamed the bad health of peasants in Pskov Province largely on their diet, which was mostly rye bread and cabbage. However, a study of villages in Tambov Province suggested that serfs in the early nineteenth century had better diets than contemporary French or Belgian peasants. In particular, these rural Russians enjoyed more meat.

The most important addition to the diets of most nineteenth-century Russians was the potato. Except in the Baltic and Polish provinces, potato cultivation was negligible until the 1830s. The peasants saw no need for them, especially since land and labor would have to be diverted from rye, and some even opposed potatoes on religious grounds. But government interest in and encouragement of potato cultivation grew after famines in the 1830s to the extent that heavy-handed official pressure produced several potato riots. By 1843, however, a German traveler, Baron von Haxthausen, noted that potatoes were being introduced into parts of Yaroslavl Province. Some peasants were interested in the tubers, others were coerced into planting them, and potato cultivation spread slowly. Nobles sometimes used them to feed livestock. In general, the potato spread into Belorussia and the northwestern provinces during the 1840s and 1850s, and thence into most of northern and central Russia and the Ukraine. By 1900 it had become a staple in most areas, often eaten in soup.

Meat and dairy products remained too expensive for most peasants, but the growing towns provided a market for cattle and milk. Milk and butter were most extensively consumed in the Baltics and in the north; peasants in the south and in the Ukraine generally had more meat. Even in areas of the south and southeast with large cattle herds, few peasants ate beef. Cattle were destined for urban markets. Peasants were more likely to eat pork, mutton, or poultry, the frequency of such meals being directly correlated with household wealth. Fish remained an important food during the numerous fasts, especially for those living near rivers and lakes or wealthy enough to purchase dried or salted fish.

Diets of the gentry were obviously richer and more diversified than those of the peasantry, but they varied greatly according to wealth and individual preference. City dwellers, including the merchant and artisan groups, had access to more imported foods and items from distant parts of the empire than all but the most opulent country residents. Many nobles spent the summers on their estates, where fresh foods were readily available, and wintered in the city. Even the petty rural landowner tended to take afternoon tea with pastries, biscuits, cheeses, caviar, jellies, jams, and other snacks, and have a heavy evening meal.

Hospitality was generous on country estates, and guests could expect to be well fed. Picnics were popular on pleasant days. In the evening, diners enjoyed *zakuski,* followed by a soup course with *pirogi,* a fish or poultry course often served cold, and a meat course with potatoes and vegetables. Salads remained unusual. Beef was especially popular with those who could afford it. Appropriate wines and champagnes might be served with each course. A meal would be capped by sweets and cognac or a dessert wine. Wealthy nobles sometimes maintained fishponds and built hothouses to provide fruits and vegetables off-season and icehouses to preserve them. Rich and even middle-class Russians employed skilled cooks, sometimes specially trained serfs, in their kitchens. A French- or Paristrained chef was a mark of distinction. Conspicuous food consumption, the use of luxury foods and beverages from abroad, and elaborate meals for guests were marks of high status and gentility.

Servants in great houses ate less grandly, though they did have access to leftovers and could sometimes appropriate items meant for the master's table. Still, if the recommendations of the leading nineteenth-century cookbook are any indication, household servants ate better than the peasants. For breakfast they might have had potatoes with fried eggs or porridge; dinner menus included *shchi* with buckwheat kasha, or *borshch* with dumplings, or barley soup and roast beef with mashed potatoes, or vegetable soup with a meat and barley kasha. On feast days servants were to have meat or poultry and assorted *pirogi.*

Alcoholic Beverages

Patterns of beverage consumption showed some dramatic changes in the nineteenth century. *Kvas,* a barely alcoholic product of bread or grain fermentation over a few days, was the basic daily drink and an important part of the diet. It was widely made and consumed in the home and dispensed by peddlers in towns and markets. *Kvas* could be produced from barley, oats, rye, and wheat, or, in the Ukraine, from beets, and was sometimes flavored with berries or fruit. It was most popular in central Russia and Siberia. There were numerous regional varieties.

Light beer *(braga)* and beer were popular, especially in the Baltics, Belorussia, and the Ukraine, but were less widely consumed in Russia and Siberia. Much was home-brewed, but taverns selling commercial beers appeared in the villages and towns. The state levied heavy taxes on commercial beer. Mead continued to decline and became a rarity by midcentury. Tea drinking, accompanied by sugar, spread slowly but became widespread in the villages by the 1880s.

The drink that became most popular, most destructive, most controversial, and most profitable for the government was vodka. According to legend, Vladimir of Kiev, the ruler who chose Orthodox Christianity as the new religion in 988, rejected Islam because strong drink was "the joy of the Rus." Small-scale distilleries began operating in the late sixteenth century in the Baltic region and along the trade routes between Moscow and the White Sea port of Archangelsk, but vodka, "little water," did not begin to make inroads in the general population until the second half of the eighteenth century.

Distillation of grain was a monopoly of the state and privileged nobles and was heavily taxed. As early as the 1720s, liquor taxes made up 11 percent of government revenues; the percentage had almost doubled by midcentury. In 1767 liquor monopolies in central Russia were sold to contractors and, except for a brief period of state monopoly in the 1820s, liquor farmers controlled the trade in central Russia until 1863. The farmers operated small drinking places scattered in the villages and towns. Their profits, although extensive, were reduced by the sums they paid the government for their local monopolies and by bribes paid to officials of all ranks.

From 1863 until the 1890s the state again assumed a monopoly to raise additional revenues, after which free trade and an excise tax system were introduced. During the period from 1805 to 1913, receipts from alcohol sales, primarily vodka, averaged 31.4 percent of all state revenues. Free trade prevailed in the western provinces, keeping prices lower and, thus, consumption higher. In the early twentieth century, state production of a uniform product at relatively low cost also encouraged greater consumption.

Social commentators, doctors, church leaders, and sometimes even government officials displayed growing concern over alcoholism during the nineteenth and early twentieth centuries. Vodka was the problem, not *kvas* or beer. Russians consumed 40 times more alcohol in the form of spirits than as beer or ale. Indeed, per capita beer consumption in the 1850s was less than 2 liters a year, far below the roughly 20 liters in the Polish provinces or 50 liters in Britain. Yet per capita vodka consumption was no higher than the use of distilled spirits in other European countries. As in early-nineteenth-century America, the problem was binge drinking; drinking simply to get drunk.

Drinking remained, as in previous centuries, partially linked to social and religious rituals and to mutual-aid activities like barn raisings or group harvest efforts. Cultural restraints on alcohol consumption, however, tended to weaken in the countryside and were especially weak in the cities. Contemporary observers decried the impact of the taverns on family and economic life and on the health of heavy drinkers. Reform efforts were hampered by the crucial role that vodka played in state finance. But concern was clearly rising, and in 1914 Russia embarked on a widely ignored experiment in prohibition.

The Soviet Period

The revolutions of 1917 inaugurated several years of severe food shortages. The new Bolshevik regime inherited food production and distribution difficulties as well as the alcohol problem from its Tsarist predecessor. These were compounded by World War I, the bloody Civil War, and the flounderings of the new regime. Despite many drastic policy changes, Russian patterns of eating and drinking showed substantial continuity with the past.

The industrial north continued to be a grain-deficit region with cities and rural dwellers that had to be supplied from the south and, increasingly, from Kazakhstan and Siberia. Improvements in internal transportation facilitated grain flows and allowed fruits and vegetables to reach European Russia from the Transcaucasian and central Asian republics. Much of central Asia, especially Uzbekistan, became a food deficit area with an economy based on cotton monoculture. Collectivization of agriculture, conducted during the 1930s at great human cost, did not solve the grain production problem, nor did the plowing of "virgin lands" or massive attempts to grow maize during the post-Stalin period.

Grain imports from the West have been necessary almost annually since the 1960s. Livestock production and meat consumption increased but continued to lag far behind Western norms, although in the years after World War II, efficient Russian fishing fleets roamed distant seas, providing more fish for Soviet consumption. Government policies kept food prices artificially low, with rationing and inflation masked by periodic shortages and long lines in shops.

Collective farmers were allowed to work small plots for their own profit. These intensively worked gardens produced a large proportion of the meat, eggs, milk, and fresh fruits and vegetables that appeared in urban markets. Armenian, Georgian, and central Asian entrepreneurs even found it profitable to bring melons and other produce from their sunny climes to the cold cities of northern Russia.

Rural diets did not begin to show major changes until after 1953, and even by 1960 there was remarkable continuity with prerevolutionary times. Table V.C.7.1, calculated from data presented by Basile Kerblay, demonstrates that (except for legumes, which are not shown), rural consumption levels in 1940 were still a little below averages prevailing at the end of the Tzarist rule. Cereals, potatoes, vegetable oils, sugar, meat, and fish were consumed in lower quantities in 1940 than before the revolution; people ate only marginally more vegetables, dairy products, and eggs.

In 1913, vegetable foods provided 84.2 percent of calories consumed by peasants, and 62.8 percent of the total came from cereals (Table V.C.7.2). In 1960 the comparable figures were 80 percent from plant sources, with 56 percent from grains. The most important change from 1940 to 1960 was the greater share of calories provided by vegetable oils and sugar. Consumption of foods of animal origin, especially fish and eggs, had increased significantly in the postwar years.

Official consumption data averaged for the entire population of the Soviet Union are shown for 1913, 1965, 1970, and 1976 in Table V.C.7.2. Quantities of meat, eggs, fish, dairy products, vegetables, fruits and berries, and sugar rose dramatically, with major gains in eggs and dairy products in the decade after 1965. Grains contributed less, with most of the decline coming before 1965. Government data paint a picture very much like those of Kerblay.

Table V.C.7.1. *Indexes of food consumption by collective farmworkers (1896-1915 = 100)*

	1940	1960
Cereals	63-71	58-66
Potatoes	85-91	104-12
Vegetables and fruit	96-114	132-58
Vegetable oils	76	214
Sugar	69	510
Meat, fat, and poultry	75-84	139-56
Fish	47-57	148-82
Milk and dairy products	110	149
Eggs	108	310

Source: Data from Kerblay (1962), p. 894.

Table V.C.7.2. *Consumption of major foods, 1913-1976 (kg/person/yr; except eggs)*

	1913	1965	1970	1976
Meat and meat products	29	41	48	55
Milk and dairy products	154	251	307	315
Eggs (units)	48	124	159	206
Fish and fish products	6.7	12.6	15.4	18.5
Sugar	8.1	34.2	38.8	40.4
Vegetable oils	–	7.1	6.8	7.7
Potatoes	114	142	130	119
Vegetables and melons	40	72	82	85
Fruits and berries	11	28	35	37
Bread and pasta	200	156	149	142

Source: Data from *Narodnoe khozyaistvo SSSR za 60 let* (1977), p. 511.

As in Tsarist Russia, members of the elite in the Soviet Union enjoyed a far greater variety and higher quality of foods and beverages than the bulk of the population. Ranking party officials and favored athletes, dancers, scientists, musicians, and other prominent persons had access to the finest domestic and foreign goods in special stores that were off-limits to workers and peasants. Such privileges marked a new elite and gave them excellent reasons to conform to the system.

Although food prices were heavily subsidized for most of the Soviet period, Russians continued to devote a substantial, though declining percentage of their incomes to food. Data for urban workers and employees of collective farms, presented for the period from 1940 to 1990 in Table V.C.7.3, show steady declines for both groups. It is interesting to note that the poorly paid farmers had to spend a higher proportion of their incomes for food than did urban contemporaries. Many toiled on farms that specialized in grain or cotton production, but even those who raised crops for themselves on private plots still had to buy much of their food.

Urbanization has been a major theme in the twentieth-century history of Russia, and urban diets have undergone somewhat more change than those of rural areas. Most of the improvements have come since the late 1940s, following the horrors of collectivization, forced industrialization, and World War II. City dwellers do consume a wider variety of foodstuffs than in the past, and the amount of foods of animal origin has increased significantly. Indeed, greater livestock production became a major goal

with Stalin's successors. Still, travelers and medical observers continue to describe a diet heavy in starches and low in fresh vegetables and fruits. Throughout the post-1945 period, production problems and a primitive distribution system have meant periodic shortages and long lines in shops. Meat and poultry remain expensive and of low quality. Sausage is a major component of meat consumption. Fat intake has risen and is, along with alcohol, implicated in rising rates of cardiovascular morbidity and mortality.

The Soviet regime never solved the alcohol problem it inherited from Tsarist times. Prohibition collapsed during the war, and with the establishment of stability in the early 1920s, old drinking habits reappeared. During the 1920s and 1930s there were intensive efforts to reduce drinking both in cities and in the countryside, but these had little impact. Officials decried the adverse effects of excess drinking on production and health, but the state continued to reap huge revenues from liquor sales. For example, during the 1960s and 1970s, taxes on alcohol produced about 10 percent of the state's income. Home distillation began in earnest during the Soviet period, as people coped with high prices and poor-quality state production and evaded periodic temperance campaigns by making *samogon*. Normal vodka had an average alcohol content of 40 percent; the alcohol content in *samogon* ranged from 25 to 75 percent. In the late 1950s and early 1960s, however, ethanol shortages led many to consume stolen wood alcohol, with sometimes fatal results. Cheap sugar, available from Cuba from the early 1960s, was a boon to *samogon* producers.

Table V.C.7.3. *Food as a percentage of family expenditure, 1940-90*

	1940	1965	1970	1975	1980	1985	1990
Industrial workers and employees	53.8	37.9	35.7	32.9	35.9	33.7	29.9
Collective farmworkers	67.3	45.2	40.4	37.1	39.6	36.3	32.4

Sources: Data from *Narodnoe khozyaistvo SSSR za 60 let* (1977), pp. 490-1, and *Narodnoe khozyaistvo SSSR v 1990 g* (1991), pp. 113-4.

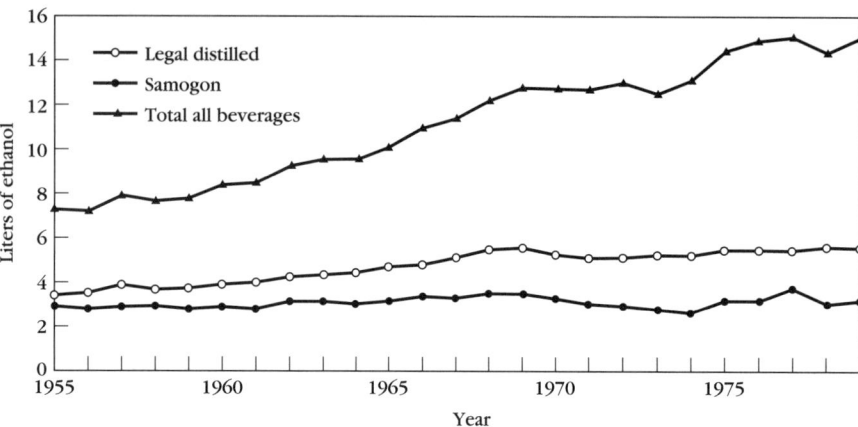

Figure V.C.7.1.1. Pure alcohol consumption per person over 15 years old, 1955–79. Total includes *samogon*, state-produced "strong" drinks, and state-produced wines and beers. Totals do not include home-brewed beer, *braga*, or wine, estimated by Treml as the equivalent of at least one additional liter of pure alcohol per person over 15 per year. Also excluded is consumption of stolen industrial alcohol. (Data from Treml, 1982, p. 68.)

Fig V : C : 7 : 1

Officials continued to decry the costs of alcohol abuse, and in the 1980s both Yuri Andropov and Mikhail Gorbachev attempted to control sales and enforce moderation in drinking habits, but their campaigns had little success. Indeed, as Figure V.C.7.1 shows, per capita alcohol consumption rose steadily and alarmingly in the years from 1955 to 1979, and it has remained high since then. Beer, *braga,* and wine consumption were clearly eclipsed by "strong" distilled beverages, although use of the former also rose. The heaviest drinkers were males in the Baltic and Slavic republics, especially Russia, Estonia, and Latvia. Per capita consumption was less in the traditional Islamic regions and in the wine-producing republics of Armenia and Georgia.

In 1970 it was estimated that Soviet citizens over the age of 15 spent an average of 13 percent of their incomes on state-produced alcoholic beverages. For Russia, the figure was 15.8 percent. These estimates do not include *samogon* or home-produced beer or wine. It is not surprising that health officials have placed much of the blame for high death rates among middle-aged and elderly Slavic males on alcohol abuse. Acute alcohol poisoning killed almost 40,000 people in 1976, a rate almost 90 times that of the United States. The impact of alcoholism on diseases of the liver and the cardiovascular system was also much greater than in the United States.

Famines

A final aspect of food history in Russia must be mentioned: famine. In Russia, as in most other preindustrial societies, bad weather and war often resulted in serious food shortages, sometimes over large regions. In contrast to the Western experience, however, famines continued to ravage Russia until the mid–twentieth century. Major famines have been recorded from the tenth century until 1946–7; even in the nineteenth century there were famines or serious, widespread food shortages in roughly one year out of five. Bad

weather, primarily cold in the north and drought in the south and in the Volga provinces, triggered many famines, but war and government policies frequently compounded or, sometimes, even created them.

Other factors made Russia particularly vulnerable to dearths. The deep poverty of most Russians meant that personal food reserves were usually inadequate to carry families over bad years. Many of the central provinces suffered serious rural overpopulation by the nineteenth century; seasonal labor migration to cities or richer agricultural areas and permanent migration to the Volga region and Siberia were inadequate safety valves. The Tsarist government made some efforts to monitor agricultural conditions and store grain for emergencies, yet lack of revenue and bureaucratic ineptitude hampered relief efforts. The government was usually too weak to control hoarding and speculation, even when it tried. But fortunately Russia was so large that the whole country could not be affected by the same adverse weather conditions or, usually, the same war or disorders, so there were always food surplus regions that could supply suffering provinces.

Large-scale movement of foodstuffs was, however, hindered by huge distances and a backward transportation system. Even the development of a national rail network in the late nineteenth century, although certainly helpful, was inadequate to meet needs. When frosts came too early or too late, or when the rains failed, peasants tightened their belts. They adulterated bread with a variety of wild plants and weeds, collected what they could from woods and fields as famine foods, and slaughtered their animals. Frequent dearths and the vagaries of the annual dietary cycle gave the peasants ample opportunity to learn to cope with food shortages.

Despite folk wisdom, peasant toughness, and relief efforts, the death tolls from famine were sometimes enormous. The 1891–2 famine killed roughly 400,000 people, despite government relief measures that were far more successful than critics of the regime would admit. Millions perished in 1921–2 when famine, caused by drought, the devastation of the Civil War, and ideologically driven state policies, swept the Volga provinces and part of the Ukraine. Only massive aid from the United States and Europe prevented a much greater catastrophe. The horrible famine of 1933-4, which ravaged most of the Ukraine and parts of the Volga basin and the northern Caucasus, was the direct result of Joseph Stalin's drive to collectivize agriculture and destroy the more prosperous stratum of the peasantry. Death tolls are currently being debated, but it is clear that several million perished. Similarly, the postwar famine of 1946-7, which killed at least several hundred thousand people, owed more to recollectivization of zones liberated from the Germans and government reconstruction priorities than to dry weather.

Conclusion

It would be wrong to conclude this survey on such a bleak note, especially as the Russian, Belarussian, and Ukrainian peoples are attempting to create new economic and political orders. Privatization of agriculture and free retail trade should bring better quality and more variety to grocery shelves. Russia is once again open to new dietary influences, ranging from McDonald's, Pepsi, and pizza to haute cuisine from France. By the same token, Russian foods, from caviar and beef Stroganoff to pirogi and borshch, have enriched the cuisines of many countries as Russian, Ukrainian, and Jewish migrants have brought them to Europe and North America.

K. David Patterson

Bibliography

Conquest, Robert. 1986. *The harvest of sorrow: Soviet collectivization and the terror-famine.* New York.

Dando, W. A. 1976. Man-made famines: Some geographic insights from an exploratory study of a millennium of Russian famines. *Ecology of Food and Nutrition* 4: 219-34.

Farley, Marta Pisetska. 1990. *Festive Ukrainian cooking.* Pittsburgh, Pa.

Herlihy, Patricia. 1991. Joy of the Rus: Rites and rituals of Russian drinking. *The Russian Review* 50: 131-47.

Hoch, Steven L. 1986. *Serfdom and social control in Russia: Petrovskoe, a village in Tambov.* Chicago.

Kerblay, Basile. 1962. L'évolution de l'alimentation rurale en russie (1896-1960). *Annales: Économies, Sociétés, Civilisations* 17: 885-913.

Matossian, Mary. 1968. The peasant way of life. In *The peasant in nineteenth-century Russia,* ed. Wayne S. Vucinich, 1-40. Stanford, Calif.

Narodnoe khozyaistvo SSSR v 1990 q. 1991. Finansy i statistika. Moscow.

Narodnoe khozyaistvo SSSR za 60 let. 1977. Tsentral'noe statisticheskoe upravlenie. Moscow.

Rabinovich, Michail G. 1992. Ethnological studies in the traditional food of the Russians, Ukrainians and Byelorussians between the 16th and 19th centuries: State of research and basic problems. In *European food history: A research review,* ed. Hans J. Teuteberg, 224-35. Leicester, England.

Smith, R. E. F., and David Christian. 1984. *Bread and salt: A social and economic history of food and drink in Russia.* Cambridge.

Toomre, Joyce. 1992. *Classic Russian cooking: Elena Molokhovets' A gift to young housewives.* Bloomington, Ind.

Treml, Vladimir G. 1982. *Alcohol in the USSR: A statistical study.* Durham, N.C.

V.D

The History and Culture
of Food and Drink in the Americas

V.D.1 ✑ Mexico
and Highland Central America

The diversity of the natural environment in Mexico
and highland Central America has influenced the
development of food and dietary patterns. From the
aridity of the great Sonoran Desert in the north,
through the temperate basins of the Valley of
Anahuac, to the tropical forests of the south, different
climates and soils have conditioned what and how
people ate. Within the larger regions, hundreds of
microregions have had their own environmental and
dietary characteristics, and for millennia cultures have
modified these environments to suit their food needs.
Three especially profound events that have influenced environment and diet are the emergence of
agriculture, the arrival of Europeans (1519), and the
technological and organizational changes of the twentieth century.

Early Diet

Before the advent of agriculture, hunting, fishing, and
gathering provided the nutrients for Mexican diets.
Most large mammals had become extinct by about
7200 B.C., and four plants in particular - mesquite,
nopal, maguey, and wild maize (teozinte) - increasingly complemented a diminishing amount of animal
protein provided by fishing and hunting. Even after
the rise of sedentary societies dependent on agriculture, food gathering continued to provide essential
nutrients for most indigenous groups. Densely populated communities in the central highland valleys and
seminomadic peoples in the arid north enriched their
food supply by collecting larvae, insects, and grubs, in
addition to small mammals and reptiles.

As food production became more abundant, the
quantity of collected foods declined, and it was on the
base of domesticated crops that Mexican civilization
rested. Maize, squash, beans, tomatoes, chillies, amaranth, several cactus varieties, and many fruits (among

them avocado and guava) constituted the diet of the
vast majority of Mexicans.

Maize was the main food of the sedentary peoples
of all of highland Middle America. In the highlands of
Guatemala one Quiché Maya word for maize is *kana,*
which means "our mother." Maize was so important to
some cultures that without it there was a cultural
sense of hunger, even if other foods were available
(Herrera Tejada 1987: 230-3). Maize is a particularly
fertile and nutritious plant, capable of providing abundant calories and nutrients. When it is eaten with
beans, another staple of the highland diet, the lysine,
isoleucine, and tryptophan deficiencies in maize are
overcome, and provides a pattern of amino acids similar to that of animal protein. Moreover, the traditional
preparation of maize, which involves soaking the
kernels in a lime (CaO) solution, releases niacin for
the consumer and provides significant amounts of
calcium.

Maize's centrality to the diet can be seen in the
diverse ways that it was prepared. First eaten raw for
its juices or toasted over a fire, its preparation as a
food gradually took many shapes and forms. When
ground finely and added to liquid, it formed the gruel
known variously as *atole, pozole,* or *pinole.* As a
masa, or dough, it was a food for the most versatile of
cooks. In addition to diverse tortillas (thin griddle
cakes) and tamales (dumplings steamed in corn
husks), maize was cooked in myriad other shapes
with such names as *peneques, pellizcadas, sopes,* and
tostadas. In addition, it could be popcorn, a preparation now well known the world over. Maize has
served as a plate to support other foods (as in a taco),
as the base for complicated dishes (for example, an
enchilada), and as a napkin.

Another important food for the sedentary people
of Mexico was squash, by which we mean a number
of plants belonging to the genus *Cucurbita,* which
includes pumpkins, squash, and zucchini, among others. All were fully employed as food sources. Their
stems constituted an ingredient of a soup now called
sopa de guias; the tasty yellow flowers have also long

been a part of soups, stews, and quesadillas, and the fruit itself can be boiled. In recent times, brown sugar and cinnamon have been added to form a thick syrup that transforms the boiled fruit into *calabaza en tacha,* the classical dessert for the *Día de los Muertos.* Pumpkin seeds are usually left to dry in the sun and then are toasted and eaten with a dash of salt. By weight, they have a higher content of isoleucine, leucine, lysine, methionine, phenylalanine, threonine, tryptophan, and valine than maize, beans, amaranth, and even egg whites. These seeds are also known as a medicine to get rid of tapeworms.

As already mentioned, many wild foods, some of them peculiar to Mexico's Central Valley region, were essential to the diet. *Tecuitlatl (Spirulina geitleri),* an algae collected from the surface of lakes in the valley, was particularly important as a source of protein, vitamins, and minerals. According to sixteenth-century reports, sufficient amounts of the algae were available to make it nutritionally significant.

Animal foods complemented the many plants that were the basis of the highland diet. Along with domesticated rabbits, dogs, and turkeys, the Aztecs enjoyed a variety of wild animals, birds, fish, reptiles, amphibians, and insects. Many of these food sources have remained parts of nutritional regimes into the twentieth century. Indeed, the turkey has subsequently gained greater importance in the cuisine. Despite the availability of wild fowl and then of domesticated ducks and chickens introduced by the Spaniards, the turkey survived as a culturally important food in Mexico. In contrast, Mexican hairless dogs *(xoloitzcuintli)* are no longer eaten.

The pre-Columbian diet of Middle America was also complex. The region dominated by the Maya had as much diversity as the central highlands. Along the coast and river estuaries, fish and shellfish provided essential nutrients. Cultivated maize was supplemented by plants such as *chaya (Cnidoscolus chayamansa)* and *ramón (Brosimum alicastrum). Ramón* may have been an especially significant foodstuff. Under cultivation, this tree produced large quantities of edible seeds that had a protein content between 11.4 and 13.4 percent, substantially higher than local grains (Puleston and Puleston 1979). Several root crops provided carbohydrates for the diet: *jícamas (Pachyrhizus erosus), camotes (Ipomoea batatas), yuca (Manihot esculenta),* and *malanga (Xanthosoma sp.)* (Vargas 1984: 278).

The quantity and quality of food in early diets remain open to interpretation. Anthropological evidence provides insights into specific sites during narrow time periods, but it does not help in the problem of generalizing for the region. One approach to the question of diet has been to analyze the carrying capacity of the land (population density versus potential food resources) on the eve of the arrival of Europeans. But even if it were possible to determine the precise carrying capacity of any region, it would not necessarily reveal how much people ate. Based on carrying capacity, estimates for the central region of Mexico range from 1,400 to 2,629 calories per person per day (Ortiz de Montellano 1990: 80).

One line of investigation that has revealed new insights into the quality of the diet has focused on Aztec cannibalism. The investigation took its modern form when Michael Harner published a widely cited article that emphasized protein deficiency as a reason for Aztec cannibalism (Harner 1977). According to his reasoning, the dense population of central Mexico, so dependent on a maize diet, lacked adequate numbers of domesticated animals, and hunting and gathering could not have supplied sufficient whole protein to compensate for its lack in the diet. Climatic uncertainties and recurring droughts in the late fifteenth century further contributed to deficiencies in the Aztec food supply.

Debate over such issues has led to different conclusions. One, which counters the protein-deficiency argument, stresses that the Aztec diet delivered plenty of good-quality protein. In addition, there is evidence showing that Aztecs suffered from gout, a condition associated with too much protein (Ortiz de Montellano 1990: 86, 121). Also useful in the debate is recognition of the success of Mesoamerican agricultural practices. Systems of terracing, irrigating, fertilizing, and the justly famous *chinampas* (artificial islands that could yield as many as four harvests a year), all combined to produce abundant quantities of food. Intercropping, or the growing of several crops together, was also beneficial. Intercropping was particularly useful when beans were planted with maize because the nitrogen-fixing beans helped increase maize yields (Ortiz de Montellano 1990: 94–7). In addition, the traditional *milpa* practice of planting squash and maize and letting edible wild herbs grow next to the latter served both to deter pests and to provide additional foods before the corn harvest, a time when there could have been scarcity.

Food preparation and consumption practices also contributed to good nutrition. As mentioned, maize, when prepared as a *masa* and eaten with beans and amaranth, delivers proteins comparable to those from animal sources. Other culinary staples added to the nutritional well-being of indigenous peoples as well. Chillies, full of vitamin C, were commonplace in the Aztec diet. So were tomatoes, as significant sources of minerals and vitamin C, and *quelites* (wild edible herbs), rich in vitamin A.

Far from being a monotonous and boring series of dishes, Mexican cuisine had great culinary variety, the result of an imaginative mixture of ingredients and methods of preparing them. Sauces or moles were common, and different combinations of chillies gave them different flavors. One such sauce is *pipián,* a thick mixture with a special texture made from ground squash seeds. A well-chosen combination of sauces could add different flavors to vegetables and meats while also providing more protein.

Mesoamericans also knew how to ferment several vegetable products, the best known of which is the sap of maguey *(agave),* used to produce the mildly alcoholic beverage *pulque.* They also fermented several maize products. *Pozol* was and is a popular preparation made with a combination of several varieties of corn, whereby the *masa* is made into small balls, which are covered with leaves and left to ferment. The balls are then dissolved in water to make the *pozol.* Mexican biologists and chemists (Cañas et al. 1993) have found that this kind of fermentation enhances the amount of protein the drink contains because of the growth of microorganisms.

Contact and Dietary Change

The arrival of the Spaniards in Middle America initiated dietary and cultural changes that have continued until today. The precise extent and pace of such changes remain subjects for research and interpretation, but the broad outlines of the process can be addressed.

Although the Spaniards expected to replicate their traditional food patterns in the New World, the extent to which they fulfilled this expectation depended on local geographic and cultural forces and on policies of trade and commerce. In the Caribbean, climate and culture hindered the establishment of Spanish alimentary regimes. There, Spanish culture survived through adaptation to local conditions and through an elaborate system of trade that supplied the islands. Wheat, the staple of the Spanish diet, was central to the trade.

In Mexico and the highlands of Central America, soil and climatic conditions encouraged the establishment of wheat production. The quantity and flavor of wheat grown in the valleys of the central highlands and in the broad plain of the *Bajío* became renowned throughout Middle America. Production of wheat often exceeded demand, and in the eighteenth century wheat exports fed soldiers and sailors garrisoned in Havana. As wars increased in frequency, the demand for wheat grew, and Mexico lost the Caribbean market to the United States, not because of insufficient grain for export but because of the higher cost of transporting Mexican grain.

Wheat was always a political issue in Mexico following the Conquest. In the late 1520s in Mexico City, legislation mentioned the importance of a supply of "white, clean, well-cooked and seasoned bread, free of barley and sand" *(Actas del Cabildo* 1889-1916, 1: 146-7). By the eighteenth century, when the capital city may have been consuming over 40 million pounds of bread a year, the problem of sufficient wheat bread had become considerably more complex. The quantity and quality of bread available was the result of the interaction among *hacendados* (wheat farmers), *molineros* (millers), *panaderos* (bakers), *pulperos* (small shopkeepers), and harried

public officials who tried to regulate prices and quality (Super 1982; García Acosta 1989).

Other grains, barley and rye in particular, were introduced to Mexico but assumed only regional importance. After wheat, rice probably had the most success of any of the imported grains among all ethnic and social groups in Middle America. By the middle of the seventeenth century, Panama was already producing enough of a surplus to support a small export trade to Peru (Castillero-Calvo 1987: 428). In Mexico, Indians came to depend on rice as a complement to or substitute for maize. External influences on the preparation of rice continued into the twentieth century. *Morisqueta,* rice prepared by a technique supposedly introduced by the Japanese, became common in the rural Mexican diet in the 1940s, and rice achieved even more fame as the basis for a drink known as *horchata,* prepared with rice flour, sugar, cinnamon, and ice (Horcasitas 1951: 162-3).

Even before they planted these grains, Spaniards introduced new sources of animal protein to Middle America. Pigs in particular were the animals of conquest – they were mobile, adaptable, and efficient producers of fat and protein. Their rapid proliferation presaged a century in which animal foods were more abundant than ever before or since. Sheep multiplied almost as rapidly. By the end of the sixteenth century, the Tlaxcala-Puebla region counted 418,000 head of sheep; Zimatlán-Jilotepec 360,000; and the Mixteca Alta 238,000 (Dusenberry 1948; Miranda 1958; Matesanz 1965).

Cattle followed pigs and sheep, transforming dietary patterns wherever they went. Enormous herds dominated the central and north-central regions of Mexico, where the landed estate system began to take shape in the late sixteenth century. Cattle were valuable for their hides; meat was of secondary importance, as reflected by the very low price of beef.

Meat-based diets were widespread throughout Mexico and Middle America, extending south to Panama. Indeed, meat may have been more abundant in the Panamanian diet than in that of the Mexican (Castillero-Calvo 1987: 432-4; Super 1988: 28-32). The period of abundant meat in the central areas, however, came to an end as the great herds exhausted the grasslands. But the period itself left a dietary legacy that continued through succeeding centuries. Fat from cattle had become the substitute for the European's olive oil and butter. Ignaz Pfefferkorn, a Jesuit very concerned with his stomach, summarized the situation in the eighteenth century: "The art of butter-making is as unfamiliar in Sonora as it is in all of America" (Pfefferkorn 1949).

Wheat and meat were the staples of the diet, providing the energy necessary for the establishment of Spanish society in Mexico. Along with the staples came scores of other foods, most of them basic to the Spanish diet at home. Among the vegetables common in the sixteenth century were onions, garlic, carrots, turnips, eggplants, and lentils; common fruits included peaches, melons, figs, cherries, oranges, lemons, limes, and grapefruit. Most of these foods had become regular items in the diet by the end of the sixteenth century and remain so today.

Olives and grapes did not follow this pattern. Both were essential to the Spanish diet, but neither had lasting success in Mexico. After an auspicious start, the cultivation of both was deliberately limited to ensure that southern Spain had a captive export market. Much olive oil and wine was still being imported at the end of the eighteenth century, but their dietary importance had declined because of Spanish mercantilist regulation and changing food preferences.

Sugar has a special place among the foods that came to the New World. In Mexico, Hernando Cortés was the first landholder to devote large areas to the cultivation of sugarcane. Production soon increased and sugar was exported; at the same time it became widely appreciated by the Mexican people. Its availability and price made it a good substitute for the relatively more expensive honey and the syrup fabricated by boiling the sap of the maguey plant. With a cheap and readily available sweetener, Mexicans were soon experts in preparing a wide variety of desserts and sweets that became characteristics of the cuisine (Zolla 1988).

Formation of the Creole Diet

The blending of indigenous and European foods and food techniques began immediately after the Conquest. The result was the emergence of a *comida novohispana,* which in turn became the basis of Mexican regional cuisines. Some elaborate dishes are elegant testimony to the fusion of the two food traditions. *Mole poblano* is one of the most highly regarded, with its chocolate base seasoned with different types of chillies and nuts. To this dish Europeans contributed foods and spices that they brought with them from the Old World: onions, garlic, cloves, cinnamon, and nutmeg. The fowl in the dish, almost secondary to its flavor, was either turkey (native to Mexico) or chicken (introduced into Mexico after the Conquest). Although dishes such as mole and *chiles en nogada* (chillies stuffed with minced meat and fruits, covered with a thick nut sauce) rightly deserve notice, an even more basic fusion was taking place. As mentioned, European livestock began providing the fat that native cuisine lacked, and fat from pigs, and then from cattle, was quickly absorbed into the Indian diet. Even dishes that might have seemed to be pure reflections of pre-Hispanic dietary regimes came quickly to depend for flavor on fat from Old World animals. *Frijoles refritos, gorditas,* quesadillas, and other traditional Mexican dishes were not prepared before the Conquest. The technique of frying itself was introduced only in the sixteenth century. Indeed,

most of the dishes so closely associated with Mexican cuisine – *carnitas, tortas,* tacos, and *tamales* – are prepared with animal fats, cheeses, onions, garlic, and bread, all of which were introduced by Europeans.

The diffusion of these foods among different indigenous groups has been a matter of some discussion. Chickens, pigs, and goats quickly became familiar parts of Indian economic activity and regular items in the diet. When prices were low enough, meat from cattle and bread from wheat were also eaten. But there are questions of how rapidly and to what extent beef and wheat were integrated into the diet of indigenous groups. A traditional interpretation is that there was little fusion of the different food traditions and that the "Indians continued their almost exclusively vegetarian diet: corn in liquid and solid form, beans, vegetables and chile; for bread, meat, and other foods were far too expensive for them" (Gamio 1926: 116). Recent research on the colonial period, however, suggests that fusion was much more extensive and that Native American diets did include wheat and meat, foods traditionally associated with a European diet (Castillero-Calvo 1987; Super 1988).

The development of a new diet did not necessarily require the addition of new foods. For example, *pulque,* already mentioned as the fermented juice of the maguey plant, emerged as the most widely consumed beverage of the central highlands because traditions that had limited its intake before the Conquest weakened in the sixteenth century. The resulting widespread consumption continued into the twentieth century. Although *pulque* provided needed carbohydrates, minerals, and vitamins to the diet, it also contributed to the image of widespread alcohol abuse among Indians and mestizos in Mexico.

Commercial production of this beverage spread with Spanish society and the emergence of the hacienda. The technology of *pulque* production remained essentially the same as before the Conquest, but new storage vessels of leather and wood made it possible to produce larger amounts of *pulque* more easily. Drinks from sugarcane (many different types of *aguardiente* were popular by the eighteenth century) were also accepted by indigenous cultures but did not replace *pulque* as a daily beverage. Of all the foods and beverages of indigenous cultures in Mexico, *pulque* remained the most politicized, sparking medical, moral, and economic controversy into the twentieth century (Calderón Narváez 1968; Leal, Rountee, and Martini 1978; Corcuera de Mancera 1990).

It is impossible to reduce the complex changes that took place in the diet during the colonial period to a series of statistics measuring calories and other nutrients. Nevertheless, the weight of the evidence suggests that the collision of cultures in the sixteenth century resulted in an initial improvement in nutrition among the poorer classes. The gains made were difficult to sustain as the colonial period drew to a close, and by the end of the eighteenth century the nutritional status of the individual was probably lower than it had been two centuries earlier (Borah 1979-89; Castillero-Calvo 1987; Super 1988). It is also important to note that until the late nineteenth century, Mexican regionalism was very pronounced, which encouraged the continued independent evolution of local cuisines.

The Nineteenth Century

Patterns of food production and distribution were disrupted by the struggle for independence and subsequent economic dislocations. But independence did not lead to the development of new alimentary regimes. Despite new influences affecting food preparation techniques for the wealthy (French food fashions, for example), most Mexicans continued to rely on diets that had changed very little from the colonial period.

The emergence of new agricultural and land-tenure patterns in the second half of the century may have reduced dietary quantity, but it is difficult to generalize for the entire region. Some of the prices for basic foods – maize, beans, rice, and chillies – did increase sharply, especially during the final years of the nineteenth century and the first few years of the twentieth. But such prices usually reflected trends in central Mexico that were not representative of the country as a whole. During the nineteenth century, regional variation continued to characterize food availability, prices, and consumption in rural Mexico.

As during earlier periods, the complex labor relationships of the haciendas influenced the availability of food. These in turn had regional variations. For example, in the Puebla-Tlaxcala region of central Mexico, although the *peones alquilados* (daily, weekly, or seasonal laborers) might have had high wages, they seldom received food rations. In contrast, the *peones acasillados* who lived on the haciendas often received fixed amounts of food and had the right to work a small amount of land, called a *pegujal,* for their own benefit. An interesting dimension of rural labor arrangements was the obligation of the *servicio de tezquiz,* whereby daughters and wives of rural workers prepared *atole* and tortillas for hacienda personnel. This, as with fieldwork, was paid for both in specie and in kind. In the latter case, the women received up to one *almud* (4.625 liters) of maize for performing this service (Coatsworth 1976; Cross 1978; Borah 1979-89; Nickel 1982: 125-48).

The traditional view is that a marked decline in nutrition occurred in the late nineteenth century. There is, however, some evidence to counter this view, which is based on wage and price data that can be misleading when local labor relationships are not understood. In many areas of rural Mexico, peasants continued to hold on to their land, producing for subsistence and then for the market. Workers who were entirely dependent on their employers often had access to rations that provided for their own – and their families' – basic caloric needs. Salaries, although low, were sufficient to buy some meat and nonessential foods. This is not to suggest that diets were good, or perhaps even adequate. But they were, it seems, not as bad as traditionally described.

The Twentieth Century

Like the struggle for independence that began the nineteenth century, the Mexican Revolution (1910-17) created disruptions in the production and distribution of food. As severe as these were in some areas, they were essentially transitory and had little lasting impact on food and diet.

More important were two gradual processes that would shape the history of food in the twentieth century. First was the continuing commercialization of food production, a process with origins in the advent of sixteenth-century European agricultural practices. It gained momentum during the colonial period and then surged under the rule of Porfirio Díaz (1876-1911) in the late nineteenth century as more and more land was devoted to agricultural products for an export market, particularly cattle, sugar, coffee, and two nonfood crops – cotton and henequen.

The latest step in this process has been the increase in the production of fruits, vegetables, and meats for the U.S. market, beginning in the 1960s. Related to this was the leap in the production of sorghum (used for cattle feed), which has become a leading crop in Mexico (Barkin 1987: 281). Similar to soya in Brazil, sorghum emerged to satisfy the demands of the export market rather than internal needs. One consequence has been increasing pressure on resources traditionally used to produce foods for local consumption.

The second process has been the industrialization of food production and distribution. The *molino de nixtamal,* a mill for maize flour, has had particularly far-reaching impact. Making tortillas by hand is a time-consuming process, once performed daily by homemakers, but with the introduction of the *molinos* in the early years of the twentieth century, and then of new methods of packaging and distributing tortillas, the traditional social roles of women changed. Freed from a daily four to six hours of labor with tortillas, women have had to adjust to new social and economic relationships. Cultural attitudes toward maize, still a sacred food among some highland Guatemala peoples, also changed as maize production was subjected to mechanization (Keremitis 1983; Herrera Tejada 1987; Vargas 1987).

The establishment of the *molino de nixtamal* is only one example of the growing consolidation of the processing and distribution of food. As in other societies experiencing rapid urbanization and industrialization, Mexico has seen its food systems undergo a profound alteration. National and transnational corporations influence everything about food from price to fashion, with the result that traditional foods and methods of preparation are giving way to national and global food processing and distribution systems. Such changes have also accentuated the loss of Mexican self-sufficiency in food production (Barkin 1987; Vargas 1987).

All of these changes have meant a new era in the history of Middle American food habits. Unfortunately, the new era has not yet shown the capacity to eliminate the nutritional problems that still plague many people, especially the poor in rural areas. Although malnutrition seldom reaches the level of starvation, high rates of infant mortality, low birth weights, and chronic illness and development problems afflict the poor. Average caloric intakes, some 2,600 per person per day in Mexico in the 1970s, obscure the regional inequalities in diet. People in rural zones of the south might consume less than 2,000 calories – an intake comparable to the poor of India, Kenya, or Vietnam (Pineda Gómez 1982: 104–7).

The Mexican government has created several programs to counter problems of malnutrition and the negative effects of the globalization of food production and distribution. It first directed its efforts toward the creation of a national marketing system, the *Compañía de Subsistencias Populares* (CONASUPO), whose mission has been to regulate the price and availability of food by intervening in national and international markets. A much heralded governmental effort was the *Sistema Alimentario Mexicano* (SAM), a program launched in 1980. SAM aimed to improve national nutritional well-being by focusing resources on the increased production and distribution of domestic foods. This was accomplished by providing technology, credit, and price supports to small producers, thereby encouraging them to contribute more effectively to satisfying national nutritional needs. On the heels of SAM came the *Programa Nacional de Alimentación* (PRONAL), an even more comprehensive effort that focused on creating an integrated national food system. New governmental policies that have favored free enterprise and international commerce have hindered public programs intended to increase food availability to the poor.

One solution to the problem of malnutrition is a reliance on the natural diversity and traditional foods of a region. The significance of traditional foods, such as *quelites* (cultivated and wild herbs), for example, has been increasingly recognized as a result of a classic 1946 study of the very poor Otomi Indians of the Mezquital valley. Despite the almost total absence of foods common to middle-class urban diets, especially meat, wheat bread, dairy products, and processed foods, the Otomi, who consumed *quelites,* showed few signs of malnutrition (Anderson et al. 1946).

Conclusion

Mexico's food system has suffered a long and complicated evolution. Elements of the past combine every day with those of the present on Mexican tables. Old Mesoamerican foods such as chillies, squash, beans, avocados, and all kinds of maize derivatives are considered necessary in a meal. These are enriched with foods from the Old World such as pork, beef, lettuce, rice, oranges, and coffee. Some of the old foods still have a special place in social gatherings. For instance, a traditional wedding deserves a *mole de guajolote* just as the typical breakfast on the day of a child's first communion is unthinkable without hot chocolate and *tamales.* Families going out at night patronize restaurants specializing in *pozole,* a stew with grains of corn, meat, and old and new spices. New foods appear continually: Coca-Cola is already a staple; hamburgers and hot dogs are everywhere; new Chinese restaurants and pizza parlors open every day. It is interesting to note that many of these foods become "Mexicanized." For example, the large hamburger restaurants offer chillies and Mexican sauces, and one can order a *pizza poblana* with long strands of green chilli and mole on it.

The increased modernization and internationalization of Mexican food and cuisine is clearly not without negative consequences. The variety of foods that characterized nutritional regimes in the past is declining; vast areas of land that once carried edible wild plants and animals have been cleared for agriculture, cattle raising, and expanding towns and cities. Packaged and processed foods, often less nutritious than their natural counterparts, are becoming more widespread, and there is still acute and chronic malnutrition in several parts of Mexico, even as obesity is a growing problem in affluent sectors of cities. Despite these problems, Mexico has a wide range of natural and cultural resources that may be called upon to help ensure a future where good diets are available to all.

John C. Super
Luis Alberto Vargas

Bibliography

Actas de cabildo de la ciudad de Mexico. 1889-1916. Mexico City.

Anderson, Richmond K., José Calvo, Gloria Serrano, and George C. Payne. 1946. A study of the nutritional status and food habits of Otomi Indians in the Mezquital valley of Mexico. *American Journal of Public Health* 36: 883-903.

Barkin, David. 1987. The end to food self-sufficiency in Mexico. *Latin American Perspectives* 14: 271-97.

Borah, Woodrow. 1979-89. Cinco siglos de producción y consumo de alimentos en el México central. *Memorias de la Academia Mexicana de la Historia, correspondiente de la Real de Madrid* 31: 117-44.

Calderón Narváez, Guillermo. 1968. Reflections on alcoholism among the pre-Hispanic peoples of Mexico. *Revista del Instituto Nacional de Neurología* 2: 5-13.

Cañas Urbina, Ana Olivia, Eduardo Bárzana García, et al. 1993. La elaboración del pozol en los Altos de Chiapas. *Ciencia* 44: 219-29.

Casillas, Leticia E., and Luis Alberto Vargas. 1984. La alimentación entre los Mexicas. In *Historia general de la medicina en Mexico*, Vol. 1, *Mexico antiguo*, ed. Fernando Martínez Cortés, 133-56. Mexico City.

Castillero-Calvo, Alfredo. 1987. Niveles de vida y cambios de dieta a fines del periodo colonial en América. *Anuario de Estudios Americanos* 44: 427-77.

Coatsworth, John H. 1976. Anotaciones sobre la producción de alimentos durante el Porfiriato. *Historia Mexicana* 26: 167-87.

Corcuera de Mancera, Sonia. 1990. *Entre gula y templanza. Un aspecto de la historia Mexicana*. Mexico City.

Cross, Harry. 1978. Living standards in rural nineteenth-century Mexico: Zacatecas, 1820-1880. *Journal of Latin American Studies* 10: 1-19.

Dusenberry, William H. 1948. The regulation of meat supply in sixteenth-century Mexico City. *Hispanic American Historical Review* 28: 38-52.

Gamio, Manuel. 1926. The Indian basis of Mexican civilization. In *Aspects of Mexican civilization*, ed. José Vasconcelos and Manuel Gamio. Chicago.

García Acosta, Virginia. 1989. *Las panaderías, sus dueños y trabajadores. Ciudad de México. Siglo XVIII.* Mexico City.

Harner, Michael. 1977. The ecological basis for Aztec sacrifice. *American Ethnologist* 4: 117-35.

Herrera Tejada, Clara. 1987. Cuando el maíz llora. *Revista de Indias* 47: 225-49.

Horcasitas de Pozas, Isabel. 1951. Estudio sobre la alimentación en el poblado de Acacoyahua. *Anales del Instituto Nacional de Antropología e Historia* 5: 153-77.

Keremitis, Dawn. 1983. Del metate al molino: La mujer mexicana de 1910 a 1940. *Historia Mexicana* 33: 285-302.

Leal, Juan Felipe, Mario Huacuja Rountee, and Mario Bellingeri Martini. 1978. La compañía expendedora de pulques y la monopolización del mercado urbano: 1909-1914. *Revista Mexicana de Ciencias Políticas y Sociales* 24: 177-241.

Matesanz, José. 1965. Introducción de la ganadería en Nueva España. *Historia Mexicana* 14: 533-65.

Miranda, José. 1958. Origenes de la ganadería indígena en la Mixteca. In *Miscellanea Paul Rivet. Octogenario dicata*, 787-96. Mexico City.

Nickel, Herbert J. 1982. The food supply of hacienda labourers in Puebla-Tlaxcala during the Porfiriato: A first approximation. In *Haciendas in central Mexico from late colonial times to the revolution*, ed. Raymond Buve, 113-59. Amsterdam.

Ortiz de Montellano, Bernard R. 1990. *Aztec medicine, health, and nutrition.* New Brunswick, N.J., and London.

Pfefferkorn, Ignaz. 1949. *Descripción de la provincia de Sonora*, trans. Theodore E. Trautlein. Albuquerque, N. Mex.

Pineda Gómez, Virginia. 1982. Estudio comparativo de la alimentación en México con la de otros países. *Anuario de Geografía* 22: 103-39.

Puleston, Dennis E., and Peter Oliver Puleston. 1979. El ramón como base de la dieta alimenticia de los antiguos mayas de Tikal. *Antropología e Historia de Guatemala* 1: 55-69.

Super, John C. 1982. Bread and the provisioning of Mexico City in the late eighteenth century. *Jahrbuch für Geschichte von Staat, Wirtschaft und Gesellschaft Lateinamerikas* 19: 159-82.

1988. *Food, conquest, and colonization in sixteenth-century Spanish America.* Albuquerque, N. Mex.

Vargas, Luis Alberto. 1984. La alimentación de los Mayas antiguos. In *Historia general de la medicina en Mexico*, Vol. 1, *Mexico antiguo*, ed. Fernando Martínez Cortés, 273-82. Mexico City.

1987. Mexico's food supply: Past, present and future. In *Food deficiency: Studies and perspectives*, 194-206. Bangkok.

Vargas, Luis Alberto, and Leticia E. Casillas. 1990. La alimentación en México durante los primeros años de la colonia. In *Historia general de la medicina en México*, Vol. 2, ed. Fernando Martínez Cortés, 78-90. Mexico City.

1992. Diet and foodways in Mexico City. *Ecology of Food and Nutrition* 27: 235-47.

Vasconcelos, José, and Manuel Gamio. 1926. *Aspects of Mexican civilization.* Chicago.

Zolla, Carlos. 1988. *Elogio del dulce. Ensayo sobre la dulcería mexicana.* Mexico City.

V.D.2 South America

The continent of South America has been a place of origin of many important food plants. Moreover, plant and animal introductions to the Americas made both before and after Columbus have provided an extraordinary diversity of food sources. Culinary traditions based on diverse foodstuffs show the imprint of indigenous, European, and African cultures. This is because food production and consumption in these lands stem from an environmental duality of both temperate and tropical possibilities. Moreover, throughout the twentieth century in South America, the binary distinction between food produced for commercial purposes and for subsistence needs has continued in a way that is unknown in North America. Contrasting nutritional standards and perturbations in supply add to the complexity of the total food situation in South America.

Domesticated Food Sources

The pre-Columbian peoples of South America domesticated more than 50 edible plants, several of which were such efficient sources of food that they subsequently have served as nutritional anchors for much of the rest of the world. The potato, manioc, and sweet potato, each belonging to different plant families, are among the top 10 food sources in the world today. The potato (*Solanum tuberosum* and related species) clearly originated in South America, where prior to European contact it was cultivated in the Andes through a range of 50 degrees of latitude. Archaeological remains of these tubers are scanty, but there is little doubt that Andean peoples have been eating potatoes for at least 5,000 years. The center of greatest morphological and genetic variability of potatoes is in southern Peru and northern Bolivia where they fall into five chromosome (ploidy) levels. That the potato is an efficient source of carbohydrates is well known, but it also provides not insignificant amounts of protein (in some varieties more than 5 percent), vitamins, and minerals. In the Andes, the tuber is traditionally boiled, but now it is also fried. *Chuño,* a dehydrated form of the fresh tuber, may have been the world's first freeze-dried food. Working at high elevation, Indians still go through the laborious process of exposing fresh potatoes to both above- and below-freezing temperatures before stepping on them with bare feet in order to make this easily stored form of food.

Manioc *(Manihot esculenta)* is another root crop from South America; it is grown and eaten in one form or another as far south as Corrientes Province, Argentina, and in the Andean valleys as high as about 2,000 meters above sea level. It is the top-ranking staple in the Amazon Basin where more uses and forms of processing are known than elsewhere. Its ability to grow in infertile soils, resistance to insect pests, and high caloric yield make it an attractive crop. The low protein (average of 2.5 percent) and the high levels of toxicity in certain varieties that force elaborate processing are its major disadvantages as human food.

The sweet potato *(Ipomoea batatas)* was known among early farming people of South America as far back as 4,000 years ago, but its origin is less understood than that of the potato because of the lack of plausible wild ancestors. The enlarged roots contain 25 to 28 percent carbohydrates, as well as about 5 percent sugar. In South America it is normally less of a staple than one might expect. Eaten usually in boiled form, it is also baked.

The rich array of South American root crops includes many scarcely known outside the continent. Probably domesticated before the potato in the Andes were *ullucu (Ullucus tuberosus), oca (Oxalis tuberosa),* and *añu (Tropaeolum tuberosum),* all three starchy additions to the stew pot. *Arracacha (Arracacia esculenta)* grows at lower elevations, primarily in Andean valleys from Venezuela to Bolivia. Its taste is reminiscent of parsnips. The tubers of jícama *(Pachyrhizus tuberosus)* and *ajipa (Pachyrhizus ahipa)* are typically eaten raw for their sweet flesh with a crunchy texture. *Achira (Canna edulis)* is a very starchy addition to the diet of some people in the Andean valleys. There are also several other tubers with very local distributions that are relics of a prior time and can be expected to become extinct.

Several "pseudo-cereals" survive as crops in the Andes, the most important being quinoa *(Chenopodium quinoa),* which is planted from Colombia to Chile and Argentina. Its average protein content of 13 percent is higher than that of wheat, and its high concentration of essential amino acids, especially lysine, has helped make it a staple for Andean people for at least two millennia.

The hardiest chenopod crop is *cañihua (Chenopodium pallidicaule),* now localized on the Altiplano of southern Peru and Bolivia. The tiny seeds are toasted or cooked in porridge, and the protein content is at least as high as that of quinoa. Growing in warm and dry valleys of the Andes as a relict crop is *kiwicha (Amaranthus caudatus).* Its nutritious seeds, sometimes popped, are usually eaten as a gruel.

Two leguminous seed plants are also among South America's contributions to the world's food inventory. The peanut *(Arachis hypogaea),* a major crop in Asia and Africa today, was probably domesticated in the zone circumscribed by Paraguay and southern Brazil. At least this is the region where the world's center of peanut diversity is found. This crop has both large amounts (25 to 35 percent) of protein and a high fat content (43 to 54 percent). The seeds have been eaten raw, boiled, and toasted, but the major use of the peanut today is for its oil. The other leguminous seed plant is the kidney bean *(Phaseolus vulgaris),* which may be of South American origin, although a wild relative is found as far north as Mexico. There is considerable diversity in the size, shape, and color of the kidney beans in South America, which are basic sources of vegetable protein for millions of people in South America and elsewhere in the world.

Several kinds of domesticated cucurbits are South American in origin. Crookneck squash *(Cucurbita moschata),* winter squash or *zapallo (Cucurbita maxima),* and *achokcha (Cyclanthera pedata)* are used in soups and stews.

Valuable fruit-bearing plants were domesticated in South America and in some cases have spread elsewhere in the tropics. The pineapple *(Ananas comosus)* had spread throughout the New World tropics by the time Columbus arrived, but it is certainly of South American origin. However, which one of the numerous wild-growing species of *Ananas* is the direct ancestor of this noble fruit has not yet been resolved. The fruit of this perennial, herbaceous plant is highly regarded around the world for the distinctive flavor of its sweet flesh and juice.

Papaya *(Carica papaya)* yields a more fragile fruit with a soft, sweet pulp around an inner mass of small round seeds. Its place of origin appears to be in warm eastern Andean valleys, but its earliest recorded use was in Central America.

Three South American members of the Solanaceae yield an edible fruit. One of these is the *pepino dulce* or melon pear *(Solanum muricatum),* with a sweet and juicy yellowish flesh reminiscent of cantaloupe. A second fruit in this family is the tree tomato *(Cyphomandra betacea),* yielding a red fruit the size and shape of an egg that tastes like an acid tomato. The third member is *naranjilla* or *lulo (Solanum quitoensis);* it comes from a bushy herb with seedy fruits that are the size of a small orange. Its vitamin-rich juice is greatly appreciated in Ecuador. Although no mention of this fruit appears in the historical record before the seventeenth century, much about it suggests that it was domesticated earlier.

Passiflora is a genus of edible fruits that grows on climbing herbaceous vines. The two major species, *Passiflora edulis (granadilla)* and *Passiflora quadrangularis (maracuja),* are grown for their sweet-tart juice containing 8 to 10 percent sugar. Cold fruit drinks and an ice cream flavor are made with the juice.

Colonial Transfer: Wheat and Olive Oil

The pre-Columbian inventory of crops and animals sustained the people who consumed it just as well as the late medieval food sources provided for Europeans. Nevertheless, when the potential of Spanish agriculture was added to the indigenous inventory, the nutritional possibilities were enhanced. Some of the European plants and animals fit into one or another ecological niche better than the native domesticates and gradually became indispensable.

Among Europeans in South America, the most desired of Old World foods was wheat. In addition to its flavor and texture, wheat bread had a strong symbolic identification with Spanish culture, whereas maize, after reaching Iberia, had a much lower standing as a food suitable to and for the Spanish palate. But within South America, wheat could not be successfully grown in warm, wet zones, thus eliminating the Amazon Basin, the Llanos, most of the Brazilian Planalto, the Guianas coast, and most other coastal plains in the tropical parts of the continent.

Hardtack *(bizcocho),* the earliest wheat food in South America, was imported from Spain. Wheat production was important in the Andes from Venezuela to Bolivia, and by the 1550s and 1560s, fresh bread was widely available. The grain was ground on gristmills turned by a horizontal waterwheel. In fact, wheat production, once important in the region, could become important again if imports were cut off. In the early 1980s, for example, Brazil imported almost as much wheat as it produced. But in 1988, this country achieved self-sufficiency in wheat, the result of paying Brazilian farmers three times the world price.

Another basic staple among the Iberians was olive oil, which was shipped to South America for more than a century in the early colonial period. Although other vegetable oils could readily substitute for olive oil, the latter had a particular flavor that Spaniards much appreciated. Starting an olive grove in the New World required patience; the trees did not begin to bear fruit profitably for 30 years, and they could only be grown in certain places. Olive trees require a climatic regime of winter rains and summer drought, and they tolerate no (or only very light) frost. These conditions could be found only in central Chile, although on the desert coast of Peru and in rain-shy western Argentina, olive trees would grow and yield fruit under irrigation. Elsewhere, olive growing was out of the question.

Common Prepared Foods

All of South America except Patagonia has granted to maize a place in the diet. In Colombia and Venezuela, corn is commonly ground into meal or flour to make an *arepa,* a bland undercooked ball of grilled corn dough. Wrapped in banana leaves and steamed, maize dough is made into tamales called *hallacas* in Colombia and Venezuela, and *humintas* in Ecuador, Peru, Bolivia, and Argentina. As in North America, boiled green corn on the cob is also eaten, especially in the Andean countries.

Wheat in the form of bread has continued to be much favored throughout South America, even in places where the grain cannot be successfully grown and supplies must be imported. Other ways of using it are in turnovers; filled with meat or cheese, they are much loved especially in Chile, Argentina, Bolivia, and Uruguay. Another wheat product, pasta, is now an important food in South America, and every country has semolina factories set up by Italian immigrants.

Unlike in Africa or Asia, no cultural barriers in South America have inhibited the consumption of meat, except that of the horse and the donkey. Beef, pork, and chicken are most widely consumed, though production of the latter has been industrialized only in this century. As in North America, the flesh of cattle is the preferred meat, with the difference being that South Americans willingly consume a wider range of the edible parts of the animal. The kidney, brain, and tripe that are processed into pet food in the United States are considered delicacies by many South Americans. Peruvians have such a special affinity for cubed, marinated, and skewered beef hearts *(anticuchos)* that they import substantial quantities of this organ from Argentina. Meat in South American butcher shops is sold mostly in slabs or chunks, not the particular cuts familiar to North American or European cooks. The four native domesticates – llama, alpaca, guinea pig, and Muscovy duck – are not major food sources. Wild game and land turtles, sold in markets, are still a source of meat in the Amazon Basin, although river fish supply most of the animal protein in this region. Saltwater fish form a basic element of diet in coastal towns and cities around the continent, somewhat more so on the Pacific side than on the Atlantic. Unlike in Europe, inland locales depend little on fish in the diet, a legacy in part of the poor transportation that has hindered its shipment.

Introduced fruit-bearing plants add to the wide range of produce that overflows markets from Bucaramanga to Brasília. But they have not necessarily turned adults into high per capita fruit eaters. Not infrequently, fruit production exceeds consumption, and much is left to rot. Bananas, including plantains, are nutritionally the most important fruit, and especially in tropical lowland locales, various kinds of bananas and plantains are a staple carbohydrate. Citrus is abundant in all countries, primarily as fresh fruit; a daily dose of orange juice is not yet part of Latin American custom. Mangoes are especially plentiful in hot, tropical areas with a pronounced wet and dry season. Avocados, native to Central America, are not as popular as one might expect, given a fat content (up to 30 percent) that is quite extraordinary for a fruit. The southern cone countries grow high-quality pome fruits; apples and pears from the Argentine valley of Rio Negro have long been exported to the tropical countries to the north.

Condiment use cannot be easily generalized. Most South Americans do not follow the Mexican pattern of the lavish use of chilli peppers. Yet, some local cuisines in western South America, for example those of Arequipa, Peru, make abundant use of capsicum, and are quite different from, say, the bland food that characterizes Florianópolis, Brazil, or Mendoza, Argentina. Generally, the more one goes into a diet focused on meat, the lower the seasoning profile. Heavy doses of onions and garlic often flavor food, and a good squirt from a lemon or lime cuts the grease in fried meats. Fresh coriander is a favorite cooking herb used in the Andean countries.

After the sixteenth-century introduction of sugarcane, honey was pushed into the background as a sweetener. Sweet desserts and liquids were one of the dietary outcomes of expansive sugar production and consumption. Brazilians prefer a sugary paste of guava or quince or a coconut-based sweet. In Hispanic countries, caramelized milk custard (flan) is the customary way to end a meal, clearly a transfer from Spain. Most people eat no cakes or pastries. As in Iberia, confections made with eggs, nuts, and sugar have been a specialty of convents. The nuns sell them to the public at designated times of the year. Beginning in this century, commercially manufactured candies featuring chocolate have satisfied the urban craving for sweets.

Forms of Preparation

Except for fruit, little food is eaten raw in South America. Salads of uncooked greens were rarely eaten before the twentieth century and still are not common in most diets. In Brazil, Japanese immigrants were the first people to commercialize salad vegetables seriously. Especially in São Paulo, Japanese-Brazilians grow and market fresh produce, an outgrowth of what was initially a desire to satisfy their own ethnic preferences.

Cooking methods vary regionally to some extent. Boiling is the traditional method of preparing many foods, and pre-Columbian peoples used ceramic pots for cooking. The Spaniards and Portuguese also had this tradition. Hearty soups and stews that combine meat, fat, and vegetables are found in different countries

under local names – *puchero* in Argentina, *cazuela* in Chile, *chupe* in Peru, and *ajiaco* in Colombia. Their warmth is especially welcome in the high-altitude chill or during the winter months in the south. Stew was first on the list of dishes in nineteenth-century Lima, Peru. Common ingredients marked a European tradition: beef, mutton, salt pork, sausage, pig's feet, cabbage, banana, rice, and peas; the native contribution was sweet potato, manioc, annatto and chilli pepper (Squier 1877). Because no major source of cooking oil existed in the pre-Columbian period, frying was introduced to South America by Europeans. Both frying and boiling are fuel-efficient ways to cook in fuel-deficient areas. Zones of high meat consumption feature roasting and barbecue.

Regional Dietary Traditions

Each national society and some areas within countries have their own dietary peculiarities. Brazil is especially characterized by the widespread acceptance of manioc, even among people of European origin. Wheat flour was often not available, and this alternative carbohydrate was close at hand and cheap. Brazilians consume much manioc in the form of a toasted flour *(farinha)*. Rice is another basic carbohydrate in Brazil because it grows well in tropical environments; when it is combined with black beans, whole protein is added to the diet. Thin slabs of meat, typically barbecued, form an element of the Brazilian diet, except among the very poor. *Feijoada,* a grand totemic dish of peasant origin, cuts across socioeconomic and ethnic boundaries. Although not recorded before the nineteenth century, *feijoada* has now come to symbolize Brazilian identity. This hearty concoction consists of rice, black beans, dried meats, sausage, and toasted manioc flour, and is garnished with kale and orange slices. Within Brazil, the northeast has the most original cookery. *Vatapá,* a famous dish of Bahia, combines shrimp and peanuts served with highly spiced coconut milk and palm oil. *Cuscuz paulista,* derived from the couscous of North Africa, uses cornmeal, not seminola, as the principal farinaceous ingredient.

The diets of the peoples of highland South America from Andean Venezuela through Bolivia are heavy in carbohydrates. The potato is a major element of the diet; maize is another staple food in this region. Meat is eaten much less in the highlands than in other parts of South America.

Carnivory has given the two Rio de la Plata countries a special nutritional cachet. With a developing-world income profile, Argentina and Uruguay have nevertheless a per capita meat consumption of more than 100 kilograms (kg) per year. Internal beef consumption has been so high at times that foreign demand has not always been adequately supplied. Fish resources are curiously underutilized. White bread is a staple food for this zone, the prime wheat-growing area of all of Latin America. The Mediterranean origin of the great majority of Argentines and Uruguayans partly explains the high-per capita wine consumption.

Chilean diets depend on seafood to a far greater extent than do diets elsewhere in Latin America. Markets are full of swordfish, oysters, mussels, shrimp, scallops, abalone *(locas),* and sea urchins. Fishing is rewarding in Chile's productive cold waters and is reinforced by the country's maritime orientation and limited extent of good livestock pasture. Within South America, the artichoke is a common vegetable only in Chile. Chileans are avid bread eaters and also have developed creative ways to use fruit.

The Guianas have non-Iberian food traditions. The complex ethnic patterns there range from African, East Indian, Amerindian, Javanese, Dutch, and British to French, making it difficult to generalize about cuisine in this zone of northern South America. The one dietary constant among most people in this region is an emphasis on rice.

Food specializations also give rise to a critical attitude and an inclination to make quality judgments. Argentines are cognoscenti in such questions as what quality of beef constitutes prime sirloin. Coastal-dwelling Chileans know the precise balance of ingredients that makes the most savory *chupe de mariscos.* Peruvians of all classes are knowledgeable about the culinary virtues of different varieties of potatoes. Paraguayans pass easy judgment on the right texture for *chipá,* a baked product made with manioc flour.

Nutritional Standards

Caloric intake within South America varies widely from more than 3,000 calories per day in Argentina to between 2,000 and 2,200 calories per day in Bolivia, Peru, and Ecuador. Throughout the 1980s, Argentina's animal protein consumption was more than three times that of Bolivia and Peru. Even in Venezuela, where per capita income is somewhat higher than in Argentina, the people enjoy less than half the protein intake. In spite of the country's developing-world economy, Argentina's has been one of the best-fed populations in the world. However, Argentina's cornucopian reputation has suffered as economic stagnation and hyperinflation have sharply reduced the purchasing power of the majority. In 1989, supermarkets in Rosario and elsewhere were mobbed by people who could not pay the inflated prices for staple items.

In analyzing South America as a whole in the late twentieth century, one must conclude that, despite the richness of the region's dietary patterns, many poor people have diets that can only be termed bad. Infants and children of poor families get insufficient protein for proper development. Milk consumption is low in South America, a result of various factors: non-availability in remote areas, the high cost of canned milk, and/or lack of education about its nutritional

importance. Lactose intolerance, especially among people of native and African origin, is also probably a very important factor in explaining low levels of milk intake.

Protein deficiencies seem especially incongruous in countries that have fishing industries. After World War II, for example, Peru exported fish meal to Europe largely as chicken feed. It was only with the revolutionary military regime of Juan Velasco, who came to power in 1969, that there was a serious attempt to get fish beyond the coastal ports to the highlands. By 1973, refrigerated fish depots began operating in several highland towns. Yet a decade later, these government-managed marketing channels were gone and fish consumption correspondingly dropped there. Peasants do not always eat the protein they produce themselves. Eggs and poultry in the Andes are often sold on the market rather than consumed at home, in part perhaps a legacy of the Spanish colonial period when eggs and live hens were a tribute item to government officials and payment in kind *(camarico)* to the local priest.

Food-Related Customs

South Americans have given special importance to the family-centered midday meal, a custom transferred from Mediterranean civilization. But in recent decades, the North American pattern of a quick, light lunch has made inroads in large South American cities where some business people have adopted a hectic "time is money" attitude. Evening meals in urban settings are typically late, especially in places where a collation is taken in the late afternoon. Snacking is common, fostered by food vending in public places. In most South American towns and cities, many poor people eke out a precarious living by preparing and selling foods on the street. Some rural folk in the Andean highlands follow a two-meal pattern that permits uninterrupted agricultural labor throughout the day. Among people with little formal education, food is often categorized as being either "hot" or "cold," referring not to its actual temperature but other, often ineffable, qualities. The result is a complicated etiquette determining which foods or drinks should accompany or follow others.

The eclecticism of food intake that characterizes present-day North America is less elaborated in South America where, because of a lack of many wide choices, monotony of diet is scarcely an issue. Only large cities offer exposure to foreign cuisines; moreover, many people are cautious about experimenting with new foods or food formats. The tradition of having domestic help and daily marketing reduces demand for canned and frozen foods in the diets of many people who could afford to buy them. The middle-class practice of hiring cooks of peasant origin reinforces culinary conservatism within families.

No national cuisine in Latin America completely

exploits the subtleties of flavor offered by its nutriments. Emile Daireaux, a Frenchman who traveled in Argentina in the 1880s, noted the splendid array of inexpensive food available, but the absence of epicurean discrimination. His explanation evoked the lack of a refined culinary tradition in southern Spain whence early Argentine settlers came (Daireaux 1888). Much more so than in Europe, large food portions became a measure of proper hospitality. Among the Latin American underprivileged, overweight has been a sign of well-being. Ideas about the links between diet and health are less developed than in the Puritan colossus to the north where cholesterol counting and vitamin content preoccupy consumers. Nonetheless, food movements such as vegetarianism and a preference for organic foods do exist in South America among small circles of urban people open to foreign influence.

Beverages and Drinks

Although coffee was hardly known in Latin America before the nineteenth century, it has subsequently become the outstanding hot beverage of the continent. Its preparation in the various countries meets very different standards (high in Brazil, low in Peru, for example). Many people in Uruguay, Paraguay, Argentina, and southern Brazil still prefer yerba maté, which in the late colonial period was also consumed in Bolivia and Peru.

Bottled beer, produced in commercial breweries started mostly by Germans, has become the preferred alcoholic beverage in South America. In hot climates such as Brazil, cold beer is especially popular, but even in the gelid Andes, bottled beer, imbibed at room temperature, is now the preferred vehicle for sociability. Partly due to intense propaganda *(beber cerveza es beber salud)* in this region, bottled beer has made deep inroads even in zones of traditional *chicha* consumption. The latter is a local fermented corn beverage of the Andes, often made under unsanitary conditions. Its popularity has waned in much the same way as has *pulque* in Mexico. Wine competes seriously with beer only in Argentina and Chile, doubtlessly because these countries both have major viticultural production. Carbonated, sweetened, and flavored soft drinks are wildly popular in South America and serve as a double foil for water loss in hot climates and impure water supplies. Much is bottled under license from multinational firms, such as Coca-Cola. In Brazil, native fruit flavors, such as the highly popular guaraná, expand the range of soft drinks.

Distilled beverages, led by rum, have been an important social lubricant among Latin Americans since the nineteenth century. A colonial reserve toward the popular consumption of these spirits broke down after independence was achieved in most countries. Much sugarcane is grown for rum; in some countries its only competitor is grape brandy,

called *pisco* in Peru and Chile, *singani* in Bolivia, and *aguardiente* in Argentina. Unlike the high value placed on sobriety in Mediterranean Europe, inebriation is a regular and rather shameless outcome of social drinking in South America.

Food Exports and Imports

Food sent to international markets has been a critical source of foreign exchange in South America, but it is no longer as central a trade item as it once was. In Venezuela, food exports are insignificant compared to the income generated by petroleum products. In Colombia, coffee is important, but less so than cocaine, which does not enter into trade statistics. Ecuador is still a leading banana exporter, but petroleum has relieved that country's dependency on that one fruit. Sugar production has greatly declined in Peru since the government turned the big estates into cooperatives. Bolivia cultivates less than one percent of its territory and exports hardly any foodstuffs.

Chile, on the other hand, has found an export niche in fresh fruit: Table grapes, peaches, nectarines, pears, plums, and kiwifruit now fill American supermarket produce displays from December to May at a time when domestic sources of these items are not normally available. By the late 1980s, the Chilean fruit industry employed some 250,000 people, earning 12 percent of the country's export income. Chile is also the world's leading exporter of fish meal and has enjoyed a large growth in fish farming in the south. Brazil exports soybeans, coffee, and sugar in large quantities and a number of specialty items, such as hearts of palm. Of all the South American nations, Argentina and Uruguay have depended most heavily on food export. Meat and wheat from these two countries helped to feed Europe during much of the twentieth century. Throughout the 1980s, food comprised more than half of all Argentine exports, far more in percentage terms than that of any other country of the continent. Nevertheless, in Argentina only 11 percent of the population was engaged in agriculture in 1987, compared to 43 percent in Bolivia and 38 percent in Peru.

Several South Americans countries have imported staples to cover food deficits. In Venezuela, processed foods, especially from the United States, dominated the middle- and upper-class market basket until the 1960s. But then Venezuela increasingly restricted these imports, favoring the Venezuelan subsidiaries of the North American–based firms (Wright 1985). Poor countries have been recipients of food aid, also largely from the United States. Under U.S. Public Law 480 ("Food for Peace"), passed in 1954, large quantities of wheat, powdered milk, and cheese were subsequently distributed, some sold for local currency ("Title 1") and some donated ("Title 2"). Brazil and Colombia formerly received this kind of food aid; Peru and Bolivia still do.

In 1990 the United States provided $85 million in food aid to Peru, which reached 13 percent of the population. But serious structural problems arise when city dwellers are able to buy imported food that is often sold cheaper than local farmers can produce it. Agriculture is undermined, exacerbating dependency on foreign food and intensifying the pattern of rural-to-urban migration. Regional self-sufficiency correspondingly declines. In the Peruvian and Bolivian Andes, the rice, sugar, wheat flour, noodles, and cooking oil brought from the coast or abroad have partially replaced the traditional staples, which used to be acquired by barter among peoples in different environmental zones.

Food Supply Problems

In most South American countries, food production has not kept pace with the growth of population. The slow rise or even decline in per capita agricultural output on the continent has several causes. Misuse of land resources is one such cause; many areas are seriously eroded, and this is reflected in declining yields. Ill-conceived agrarian reform programs have reduced the ability of countries to feed themselves. The breakup of large estates in Bolivia in the 1950s, Chile in the 1960s, and Peru in the 1970s each had this effect. At the same time, state and private investment in rural development has been sparse compared with investments that go to urban areas. The number of food producers in South America falls every year, a phenomenon that, however, is not matched by increases in productive efficiency. The meager return for unremitting hard work has accelerated rural-to-urban migration.

Natural hazards have periodically caused food shortages in South America. Droughts at distressingly frequent intervals in northeastern Brazil have shriveled standing crops, killed livestock, and brought mass starvation. During the "grande sêca" of 1877-9 in Ceará, between 200,000 and 500,000 people died, and most survivors were forced to migrate out of the region. The long history of famine in the Brazilian northeast prompted Josue de Castro to aim a Marxist critique at the problem in his book translated into several languages, including English as *The Geography of Hunger*. In 1955-6, a famine brought on by drought scourged the highlands of southern Peru. Food relief was not well timed or organized, with the result that some peasants starved, others were dispossessed, and some resorted to selling their children. The ability of modern South American governments to bring food relief to needy people has generally improved throughout the decades. But parts of the continent are still vulnerable to starvation if crops fail. In some ways, food production and distribution in South America reached its acme during the Inca Empire (A.D. 1200 to 1531). Surpluses of grains and chuño, moved by llama trains to specially constructed storehouses, were redistributed when regional or local food shortages occurred.

As one of the offshoots of Western civilization, South America shares some food characteristics and customs with Europe and North America. But tropical conditions, a strong indigenous presence, and weakly developed economies have greatly influenced the content of its food inventory, traditions, and nutritional profiles.

Daniel W. Gade

Bibliography

Brücher, Heinz. 1989. *Useful plants of neotropical origin and their wild relatives.* Berlin.
Cascudo, Luis de Câmara. 1967. *História da alimentação no Brasil.* 2 vols. São Paulo.
Daireaux, Emile. 1888. *La vie et les moeurs á La Plata.* 2 vols. Paris.
Estrella, Eduardo. 1986. *El pan de América: Etnohistoria de los alimentos aborígenes en el Ecuador.* Madrid.
Leonard, Jonathan Norton. 1968. *Latin American cooking.* New York.
Squier, Ephraim. 1877. *Peru: Incidents of travel and exploration in the land of the Incas.* London.
Super, John C. 1988. *Food, conquest, and colonization in sixteenth-century Spanish America.* Albuquerque, N. Mex.
Super, John C., and Thomas Wright, eds. 1985. *Food, politics, and scarcity in Latin America.* Lincoln, Nebr.
Weismantel, Mary J. 1988. *Food, gender, and poverty in the Ecuadorian Andes.* Philadelphia, Pa.
Wright, Eleanor Witte. 1985. Food dependency and malnutrition in Venezuela, 1958-74. In *Food, politics and society in Latin America,* ed. John C. Super and Thomas Wright, 150-73. Lincoln, Nebr.

V.D.3 ❧ The Caribbean, Including Northern South America and Lowland Central America: Early History

In writing the history of culinary practices, there is a tendency to emphasize the ethnic character of diets (González 1988). Yet nowhere are historical entanglements more apparent than in the international character of modern cuisine, even if explicit ethnic territories are strongly defended. Foods are often defined with apparent regard to national origin: Indian corn, Irish potatoes, Italian tomatoes, Dutch chocolate, and Hawaiian pineapple, to name but a few. However, the plants that form the basis of many European cuisines in fact originated in the Americas (Keegan 1992), and American diets were transformed in what Alfred Crosby (1986) has described as the creation of the neo-Europes.

"You call it corn, we call it maize." Contrary to the American television commercial in which a very Navaho-looking women makes that statement, the word is actually of Taino origin. Peter Martyr was among the first Europeans to describe this plant that the native West Indians called *maíz (Zea mays)* (Sauer 1966: 55). Other Taino words for plants and animals have also entered the English lexicon, including *cazabi* and *yuca (Manihot esculenta* Crantz), *guayaba (Psidium guajava* L.), *bixa (Bixa orellana* L.), *iguana,* and *manati (Trichechus manatus)* (Oviedo [1526] 1959: 13–16; Taylor 1977: 20–1).

Cultigens from the circum-Caribbean lowlands have also been of significant effect (Keegan et al. 1992). Tomatoes *(Lycopersicon esculentum* Mill.) were first encountered in coastal Mexico, where the Spanish were also treated to a drink called *chocolatl,* a blend of cacao *(Theobroma cacao* L.), peppers *(Capsicum* spp.), and other spices (including *Bixa orellana* L.). Cacao won immediate acceptance; together, it and vanilla *(Vanilla* spp.), a semidomesticated lowland orchid, have become the most important flavorings in the world. In contrast, the *tomatl* (tomato) languished under the specter of its membership in the "deadly" nightshade family of plants. First grown as an ornamental, and only much later as food, the tomato eventually reshaped Italian cuisine.

American foods have been reinterpreted in ever-changing dietary contexts since their "discovery" by Europeans. Maize, in particular, has been manipulated for use as a building material, lubricant, automobile fuel, and universal hardening additive. The objective of this review is to introduce a well-structured methodology for examining past diets, while at the same time providing comprehensive empirical coverage of the regions first reached by the Spaniards after 1492.

We begin with the native Tainos who occupied the Greater Antilles and Bahama Islands at the time of European contact (see Figure V.D.3.1). Their culinary practices are traced through the Saladoid expansion to their mainland South American origins. The earlier "preagricultural" Caribbean peoples, called Archaic in the regional parlance (Rouse 1986, 1992), are then briefly considered. Although little is known of Archaic diets, it has been suggested that the Tainos developed from the synergy of Archaic and Saladoid cultures (Chanlatte Baik and Narganes Storde 1990). The scope is then expanded to include pre-Columbian plant migrations into the circum-Caribbean.

Taino Diet and Nutrition

The study of prehistoric diet and nutrition in the Caribbean is a relatively recent phenomenon. Moreover, the investigators who have concerned themselves with these issues have approached the subject in a variety of ways. The earliest efforts involved the enumeration of plants and animals described in the contact-period chronicles (Fewkes 1907; Rouse 1948; Sturtevant 1961, 1969; Sauer 1966). More recently,

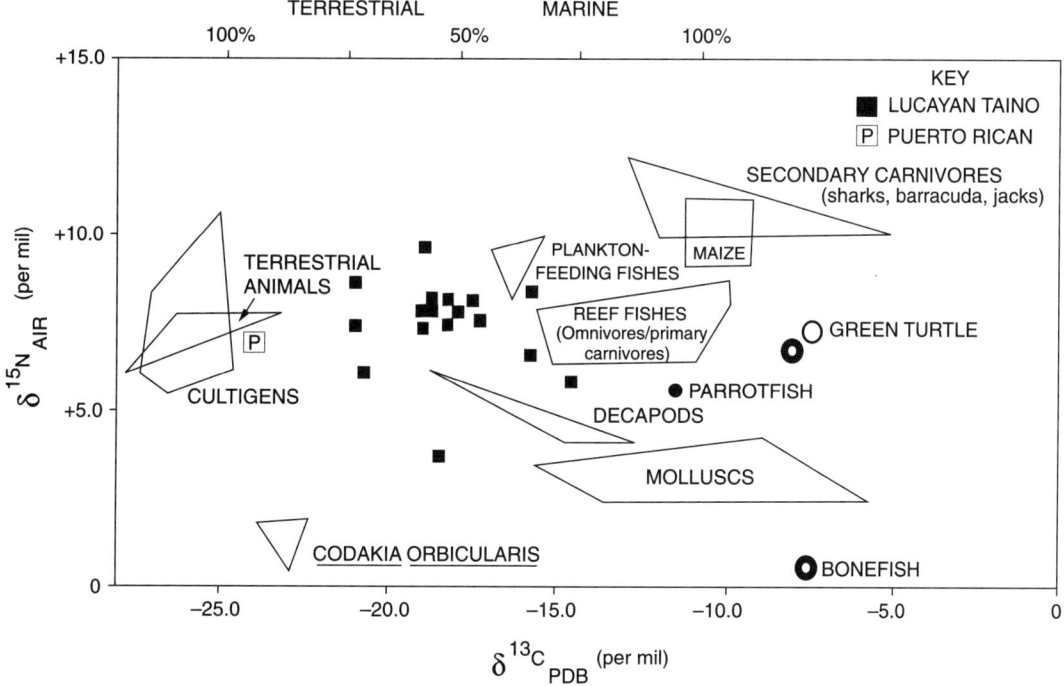

Figure V.D.3.1. Isotopic reconstruction of Lucayan consumption. (After Keegan and DeNiro 1988: Figure 2.)

attention has been drawn to the importance of diet and nutrition (Wing and Brown 1979). The analysis of animal remains in archaeological sites has been underway for some time (Wing and Reitz 1982; Wing and Scudder 1983). The investigation of archaeological plant remains has also been initiated. Although most of these studies are not yet published, they are investigating pollen, phytoliths, wood charcoal, and carbonized structures for the purposes of identifying cultigens, firewood, and modifications of the landscape (for example, Fortuna 1978; Pearsall 1985; Piperno, Bush, and Colinvaux 1990; Newsom 1993). Stable-isotope analysis has been used to investigate prehistoric diets (Keegan and DeNiro 1988; Klinken 1991), and studies of human skeletal remains have uncovered evidence of diet-related pathologies (Budinoff 1987).

Because different investigators approach questions of diet and nutrition from different perspectives, there has been a problem with the integration of their results. The author of this chapter has argued that diverse empirical studies need to be integrated in a well-structured research methodology (Keegan 1987; Keegan and DeNiro 1988). Such a methodology must include explanations for why people ate what they did, must predict what people should have eaten, and must incorporate techniques for determining the variety of foods people consumed.

The study of West Indian diets described here uses models developed in evolutionary biology under the title "Optimal Foraging Theory" (Winterhalder and Smith 1981; Smith 1983; Keegan 1986a; Smith and Winterhalder 1992). It was hypothesized that Caribbean diets would reflect the efficient capture of the aggregate nutritional currencies – calories and protein. The theory was examined with data derived from ethnological, ethnohistorical, zooarchaeological, paleobotanical, and other techniques, which specified what foods were eaten and the relative costs of obtaining these foods (Keegan 1985). Finally, osteochemical techniques were used to evaluate what food items were consumed from the record they left in the human skeleton (Keegan and DeNiro 1988). This three-tier approach provides a robust solution to questions of prehistoric diet and nutrition (see Bell 1992).

West Indian Food Items

The first task in reconstructing prehistoric diets involves compiling a list of the plants and animals that were consumed. Ethno-historic reports described the Taino in the Greater Antilles as practicing a mixed economy of root-crop horticulture and hunting-fishing-collecting (Fewkes 1907; Rouse 1948; Sauer 1966; Wing 1969; Wing and Reitz 1982).

The Spanish chroniclers reported that the Tainos cultivated manioc (*Manihot esculenta* Crantz),[1] sweet potatoes (*Ipomoea batatas* [L.] Lam.), yautía or cocoyam (*Xanthosoma sagittifolium* Schott), llerén

(*Calathea allouia* [Aubl.] Lindl.), peanuts (*Arachis hypogaea* L.), maize (*Zea mays* L.), beans (*Phaseolus* spp.), cucurbits (*Cucurbita* spp.), chilli peppers (*Capsicum frutescens* L. or *Capsicum annuum* L.), and fruit trees, including mamey (*Mammea americana* L.), jagua or genipop (*Genipa americana* L.), hicaco or cocoplum (*Chrysobalanus icaco* L.), guanábana or soursop (*Annona muricata* L.), bixa or annatto (*Bixa orellana* L.), guava (*Psidium guajava* L.), and cupey (*Clusea rosea*) (Fewkes 1907; Rouse 1948; Sturtevant 1961, 1969; Sauer 1966; Guarch 1974; Nadal 1981). Most of these cultigens were carried into the Antilles by the Island Arawak (see Ford 1984; Schultes 1984). A variety of wild or quasi-domesticated plants were also in use, including the stems of the cycad *Zamia*, primrose (*Oenothera* sp.), purslane (*Portulaca* sp.), masticbully (*Mastichodendron foetidissimum*), sapodilla (*Manilkara* sp.), cockspur (*Celtis iguanaea*), palm fruits, sea grapes (*Coccoloba uvifera*), pigeon plum (*Coccoloba diversifolia*), and panicoid grasses (*Setaria* spp.) (Sturtevant 1969; Fortuna 1978; Newsom 1993). The carbonized remains of maize, chilli peppers, palm fruits, and at least two unidentified tubers (probably manioc and sweet potato) are among the plant remains identified in West Indian sites (Newsom 1993).

As is the case with modern tropical horticulturalists, life revolved around garden cycles (Malinowski 1978; Johnson 1983). Garden plots (called *conucos* by the Tainos) of about one to two hectares per household were cleared at regular, possibly annual, intervals. Clearing involved the use of stone axes or shell tools to slash brush, fell trees, and girdle large trees so that they would drop their leaves. After clearing, the brush was left to dry and was then burned, releasing the nutrients stored in the vegetation.

Planting came next and was done with a sharpened digging stick. Manioc was planted in small mounds of loose earth, called *montones*. After planting, the gardens were weeded and the mature crops harvested; replantings were made on a continuous basis until the garden was abandoned. (Unlike temperate gardens that die in the winter, tropical gardens can be maintained for years.) After a few years, garden production was reduced to certain tree crops, and new gardens had to be prepared. The old garden was then left fallow until covered by at least secondary forest growth, at which time it might again have been cleared. The importance of the agricultural cycle is reflected in stone alignments, which were used to chart the summer solstice and the rising and setting of stars that were important in Native American agricultural calendars. The most notable examples are site MC-6 on Middle Caicos in the Turks and Caicos Islands and La Plaza de Chacuey in the Dominican Republic (Castellanos 1981; Aveni and Urton 1982; Alegría 1983).

Taino cultigens grew and matured at different rates. Consequently, the diet of the inhabitants changed continuously with the seasons. Nonbitter maniocs and other root crops would have been available throughout the year. Boiling was the usual method of cooking. Bitter maniocs, so-called because they contain toxic levels of cyanogenic glucosides, must be grated and squeezed before consumption (Roosevelt 1980: 129). The juice releases its toxins when exposed to air or cooked; the boiled juice, called *cassirepe*, is a base for pepper pots and manioc beer. The pulp is dried for use as starch (flour); it is also toasted to make farina or for use as an ingredient in tapioca. The reward for so much additional processing effort is indefinite storability (Roosevelt 1980: 129). Water is added to the starch to make pancake-like cassava bread that is baked on large, round, pottery griddles called *burénes*.

Manioc was the staple crop intensively cultivated on mounds at the time of European contact (Sturtevant 1969). Maize is reported to have been grown for roasting ears and, to some extent, for bread grain, but it was not a major foodstuff (Sturtevant 1961; Sauer 1966). Maize was apparently a late introduction and may have been the focus of agricultural intensification in the Greater Antilles at the time of Spanish contact (Keegan 1987; compare Lathrap 1987).

In addition to "outfield" garden plots, there were house gardens closer to and around the dwellings. House gardens contained new varieties of cultigens, herbs and spices, medicinal and narcotic plants, vegetable dyes, fruit trees, and other cultigens that required special attention or were needed frequently in small quantities (Lathrap 1977, 1987). A list of possible house-garden plants is given in Table V.D.3.1.

A meal without meat would not have been considered complete. As is typical of most islands, the West Indies have a depauperate terrestrial fauna (Keegan and Diamond 1987). Indigenous land mammals are limited to bats, rodents of the tribe Oryzomyini, spiny rat (Echimyidae), and small rodents (*Geocapromys* sp., *Isolobodon portoricensis, Plagiodontia* sp.). Opossum (*Didelphis virginiana*), agouti (*Dasyprocta aguti* L.), and armadillo (*Dasypus novemcinctus*) were introduced from the South American mainland (Eisenberg 1989). In addition, a type of small deer called brocket (*Mazama americana*) was known in Trinidad, which was connected to the mainland until the end of the Pleistocene (Wing and Reitz 1982). Other land animals include iguanas (*Iguana* sp., *Cyclura* spp.), crocodiles (*Crocodylus* sp.), a variety of small reptiles (e.g., *Anolis* sp.), land crabs (*Cardisoma guanhumi, Gecarchinus* sp.), numerous birds, and a land snail (*Caracolus* sp.) (Wing 1969; Wing and Reitz 1982; Wing and Scudder 1983; Steadman et al. 1984; Watters et al. 1984; Morgan and Woods 1986; deFrance 1988, 1989; Fandrich 1990). The Tainos kept domesticated Muscovy ducks (*Cairina moschata*) and dogs (*Canis familiaris*) (Sauer 1966; Wing and Scudder 1983). It is also likely that a variety of grubs and insects were consumed (see Johnson and Baksh 1987).

A number of these animals, such as *Isolobodon* (Reitz 1986), crocodile (McKinnen 1804; deFrance

1991), and iguana (Iverson 1979), suffered local extinctions after the arrival of Europeans (Olsen 1982; Morgan and Woods 1986).

The main component of prehistoric Antillean vertebrate faunal assemblages is marine fishes (Wing and Reitz 1982). In the Bahamas, marine fishes account for more than 80 percent of the estimated maximum vertebrate biomass in the sites with analyzed assemblages (Wing 1969; Wing and Scudder 1983; Keegan 1986b; deFrance 1991). A representative list of fish species identified in Lucayan sites is presented in Table V.D.3.2.

In addition to fishes, several large aquatic animals have also been identified in Antillean sites. These include marine turtles (mostly Chelonidae), porpoises (Delphinidae), West Indian monk seals *(Monachus tropicalis),* and manatees *(Trichechus manatus)* (Wing and Reitz 1982; Watters et al. 1984). These large reptiles and mammals have been emphasized in the subsistence activities of peoples throughout the circum-Caribbean (Nietschmann 1973; Davidson 1974; Campbell 1978; Wing and Reitz 1982; McKillop 1985).

The final category of subsistence remains is marine mollusks. Molluscan shell is the most abundant type of refuse in prehistoric sites in terms of both volume and mass. Despite this abundance, molluscan shell represents relatively small edible packages. The most important mollusks were queen conch *(Strombus gigas),* West Indian top shell *(Cittarium pica),* tiger lucine clams *(Codakia orbicularis),* chitons *(Chiton* spp.), and nerites (Keegan 1985; deFrance 1988).

Meats were roasted over a fire or barbecued ("barbecue" is derived from a Taino word). It has been suggested that the Lucayans may have used another traditional form of tropical-forest cooking called the "pepper pot." Pepper pots are stews, kept simmering over a low fire, to which meats and vegetables are added to replenish the pot. The large, thick clay pots made in the Bahamas and in the Lesser Antilles were well suited to this type of food preparation (Allaire 1984).

When viewed with regard to the number of different ways in which individuals could satisfy their hunger, the West Indies are noteworthy for the surfeit of options. It is difficult to imagine that anyone ever went hungry. Yet the fact that these people were selective in their food choices provides an important challenge. It is not sufficient simply to list the items that were, or may have been, eaten; rather, the criteria upon which dietary selections were based must be identified.

Because there is too much local variability to treat all West Indian diets as equivalent (deFrance 1988), the following study focuses on the subsistence decisions of the Lucayans. The Lucayans are of Taino ancestry. They occupied the Bahama archipelago between A.D. 600 and 1500 (Keegan 1992). Lucayan diet breadth is evaluated by comparison with an economic model of the diet that would result from the cost-efficient capture of nutritional currencies.

Table V.D.3.1. *Comparison of house-garden cultigens in native Amazonian and prehistoric West Indian gardens*

House garden plants	Native Amazonian house gardens		Prehistoric Antilles
	General	Machiguenga	
Agave sp. (sisal fiber)	-	-	St
Anacardium occidentale (cashew bush)	X	-	-
Anadenanthera peregrina (leguminous tree)	X	-	-
Ananas sp. (pineapple)	X	X	-
Annona sp. (soursop fruit)	-	X	St
Arachis hypogaea (peanut)	-	X	S, St
Bixa orellana (red dye)	X	X	S
Bocconia sp. (plume poppy)	-	-	F
Bromelia sp.	-	X	F
Bursera simaruba (gum elemi)	-	-	F
Capsicum sp. (pepper)	X	X	S, St
Carica papaya (papaya fruit)	X	X	F
Cassia sp.	-	-	X F
Cecropia peltata (mulberry)	-	-	F
Chenopodium ambrosoides (lamb's-quarters)	-	-	F
Chrysobalanus icaco (cocoplum fruit)	-	-	St
Chtysophyllum caimito (caimito fruit)	X	-	F
Crescentia cujete (calabash tree)	X	X	F, S
Cucurbita sp. (squash)	-	X	St
Cyperus sp. (sedge)	-	X	F
Datura sp. (moonflower, fish poison)	-	X	-
Digetaria sp. (grass)	-	-	F
Genipa americana (genipe, black dye)	X	-	S
Gossypium sp. (cotton)	X	X	S
Guazuma ulmifolia (chocolate)	-	-	F
Guilielma gasipaës (peach palm)	X	-	-
Helecho sp. (tree fern, fire box)	-	-	F
Inga sp. (guaba fruit)	X	X	F
Jacquemontia petantha (chainnindo)	-	-	F
Jatropha cura (psychic nut)	-	-	St
Lagenaria sp. (bottle gourd)	X	X	St
Mammea americana (fruit tree)	-	-	S
Nicotiana sp. (tobacco)	X	X	F, S
Peperonia sp.	-	-	F
Piptadenia peregrina (cahoba, narcotic)	-	-	S
Psydium guajava (guava fruit)	X	X	F
Puosopis juliglora	-	-	F
Ricinus comunis (castor bean)	-	-	F
Roystonea hispaniolana (palm)	-	-	F
Sapindus saponatia (soapberry)	-	-	F
Solanum sp.	X	X	F
Spondias mombin (cashew bush)	-	-	F
Syzysium jambas (jambolan plum)	-	-	F
Theobroma sp. (cacao)	X	X	-
Thrychilia hirta	-	-	F
Vetiveria alliacea	-	-	F
Wallenia sp.	-	-	F
Zamia debilis (cycad, starchy bread root)	-	-	F

Note: Native Amazonian lists are based on Lathrap's (1977) general list (column 1), and Johnson's (1983) list of minor cultigens in Machiguenga gardens (column 2). Prehistoric Antillean cultigens (column 3) are identifed in ethnohistoric reports (*S* = Sauer 1966; *St* = Sturtevant 1961) and in Fortuna's (1978) analysis (denoted by *F*) of pollen samples from Sanate Abajo, Dominican Republic (A.D. 1020). Many of these "cultigens" are actually managed, tended, and transplanted non- or quasi-domesticated species. (Johnson's [1983] longer list of 80 cultigens was shortened by deleting major cultigens [manioc, maize, beans], historic introductions [sugarcane], and plants that were not identified by their taxonomic name.)

Source: After Keegan (1987), Table 15-1.

Table V.D.3.2. *Fishes identified in Lucayan sites*

Fish genera (most common = >90% of genera)
Haemulon (grunt)
Sparisoma (parrot fish)
Lutjanus (snapper)
Acanthurus (surgeonfish)
Scarus (parrot fish)
Epinephelus (grouper)
Mulloidichthys (goatfish)
Pomocanthus (angelfish)
Calamus (porgy)
Albula vulpes (bonefish)

Other fish genera (<10% of genera)
Inshore-estuarine habitat
  Lactophrys (trunkfish)
  Gerreidae (mojarro)
  Eucinostomus (mojarro)
  Diodon (porcupinefish)
  Sphoeroides (puffer)
  Lachnolaimus (hogfish)
  Stronbylura (needlefish)
  Belonidae (needlefishes)
  Centropomus (snook)
  Sciaenidae (drums)
  Selene (lookdown)
Banks and reef habitats
  Halichoeres (wrasse)
  Elegatis (wrasse)
  Holocentrus (squirrelfish)
  Holocanthus (angelfish)
  Flammeo (squirrelfish)
  Chaetodon (butterfly fish)
  Serranidae (groupers)
  Ocyurus (yellowtail snapper)
  Gymnothorax (moray eel)
Two or more habitats
  Scorpaena (scorpion fish)
  Balistidae (triggerfish)
  Carangidae (jacks)
  Sphyraena (barracuda)
  Sharks and rays

Source: After Keegan (1986b).

Lucayan Diet Breadth

Lucayan diet can be described as consisting of inputs from five general sources: cultivated roots and tubers, maize, terrestrial animals, marine fishes, and marine mollusks (Sears and Sullivan 1978; Keegan 1992). These foods were obtained from the forest, the coastal strip, and the sea. To evaluate the Lucayan's behavior as cost-efficient foragers, the capture of foods in the three habitats is reviewed first. After identifying the foods and their associated costs, their return rates are compared by using a model derived from Optimal Foraging Theory. Finally, the diets predicted with the model are compared to the isotopic signatures in the bones of 17 individuals. The isotopic signatures reflect the foods that these individuals consumed.

Lucayan Food Procurement

The main component of the forest habitat was gardens. These were probably prepared in coastal accumulations of humic enriched sandy soil and would have followed the pattern of other tropical gardens (Ruddle 1974; Johnson 1983). Gardens were stable patches where output could be modified in response to changing needs. Root-crop horticulture provides high total and marginal rates of return. Average yields of manioc in Brazil are reported as 14.2 million calories per hectare (Roosevelt 1980: Table V.D.3.1). Using a generous estimate of human caloric needs (2,700 calories per day), 14 adults could have been supported on one hectare of land for an entire year. The availability of calories in other foods, which have higher net return rates, would have precluded the need for complete reliance on manioc production.

Because manioc does not require fertile soils for efficient tuber production, a single plot can be cultivated for many years. Long-term land use is not practiced in the tropical forest today because total human protein requirements also are met through garden production. The characteristics of maize make long-term, cost-efficient production on a single plot of land impossible (Keegan 1986a). Furthermore, yields from long-term manioc gardens can be increased by intercropping other cultigens (for example, sweet potatoes, cocoyams, fruit trees). These crops do not interfere with the growth of the manioc plants; rather, they increase yields per hectare for the additional investment of planting and harvesting, they aid in preventing weed growth, and they fill areas that would otherwise go unused (Ruddle 1974; Brierley 1985; Keegan 1986a). It is likely that the initial colonists planted small gardens with a diversity of crops, with garden size set by the caloric returns from manioc in relation to the caloric needs of the group. As population increased, garden size would have increased and other cultigens would have been added to the gardens.

The principal shortcoming of manioc is its low protein content (Roosevelt 1980). Since human nutritional requirements cannot be satisfied with manioc alone, other sources of protein had to be sought. In addition to animal protein sources, such cultigens as maize, beans, or ground nuts could have been added to the garden as protein supplements. These cultigens are more expensive in terms of harvesting and processing, contribute to a more rapid exhaustion of garden soils, and are available only during specific seasons.

Maize is the most cost-efficient of the high-protein cultigens. From Allen Johnson's (1983) studies it was estimated that maize has a marginal return rate of 20 grams of protein per hour of labor (Keegan 1986a). This return rate is higher than that for many other Lucayan foods. This would have promoted its acceptance when it became available after about A.D. 1100 (Keegan 1987). The disadvantages of maize production are the plant's need for fertile soils, its availability during only one season of the year, and the high cost of storing and processing maize when it is grown for use throughout the year. Thus, maize constituted only a partial solution to the problem of protein production.

Marginal return rates for animal species that inhabit the forest favor their use over horticulture. These animals (that is, hutia, iguana, and land crabs) could not, however, satisfy total needs. Their combined densities are equivalent to 1,861,950 calories per hectare, which could support only two individuals for a year if every animal was captured. But (in economic terms) intensive use would have rapidly reduced the frequency of encounters (that is, animals would not be seen very often), with the result a decline in the average return rate to a level below the marginal rate for other food sources (including horticulture). When this decline reached that level, those other foods would be added to the diet (Winterhalder and Smith 1981; Smith 1983). For the Lucayans, this other source of protein was the sea.

The inference from the economic model is that terrestrial animals were pursued whenever they were encountered. It is probable that game was taken in or near gardens (Linares 1976) and during visits to the coast. The forest is a difficult patch to traverse, and hunting trips in the forest were probably infrequent, especially after the decline of initially high prey densities. Since all of these small game were regular visitors to the coastal strip, the most efficient strategy would be to forage in this area. Travel along the coast is also less difficult, and other food sources would doubtless have been encountered (for example, wild plants, littoral mollusks).

The one exception to the forest-hunting proscription is land crabs, which congregate in the low areas that provide for moist burrows. These locations could be identified, and hunting could be accomplished with guaranteed results. But even land crabs can be taken on the coastal strip, especially when they congregate for mating (Gifford 1962; deFrance 1988).

The coastal strip is comprised of the beach patch and the rocky intertidal patch, and it provides access to marine habitats. The beach patch was the site of seasonal monk seal aggregations, turtle nesting grounds, and the accidental beaching of whales. In addition, terrestrial animals frequent this patch. Because settlements were located on the coast, the Lucayans were in a position to monitor activities on the beach.

The highest average return rate was available in the beach patch, although the highest return species were not available in all locations at all times (for instance, green turtles, monk seals, and whales). Turtles would have been available from April to July, and monk seals for about six weeks centered on December. Both would have been the focus of procurement efforts during their seasonal abundances.

The rocky intertidal patch supports dense aggregations of West Indian top shells, nerites, and chitons.

Top shells have a relatively high net return rate, and of the three they are the only ones used today with any frequency. However, the use of top shells is limited by two factors. Rocky intertidal zones are small, averaging less than three meters wide, and they are irregularly distributed. These snails also are easily exploited and would have rapidly disappeared following the start of human predation. The other common littoral mollusks have lower return rates. These low values suggest that they were exploited during periods of food shortage. In any case, chitons and nerites should have been among the last items added to the diet.

The marine environment is comprised of a tidal-flat patch and a reef patch. The tidal-flat patch can be further divided by procurement strategies into infaunal mollusk collecting (that is, in the mud–sand substrate), epifaunal mollusk collecting (that is, on the substrate), and fishing. These strategies are discussed in turn.

The tiger lucine clam, *Codakia orbicularis*, is the most commonly used infaunal mollusk species. They occur at high densities beneath shallow grass flats and would have provided a stable resource supply (Jackson 1972, 1973). In terms of weight, tiger lucine clams provided a more significant source of food than intertidal mollusks (Rose 1982). Yet, tiger lucine has low net return rates of both calories and protein. It is, however, possible that these rates have been underestimated in the present study. A study of pelecypod collecting in Australia indicated a caloric return rate that is twice that estimated for *Codakia orbicularis* (Meehan 1977). Historical evidence suggests that even if the return rates were underestimated, the ranking relative to other food items is accurate. Tiger lucine clams should therefore have also been one of the last items added to the diet.

The epifaunal gastropod *Strombus gigas* is the highest ranked marine resource. It is available at high densities on shallow grass flats (Doran 1958; Hesse and Hesse 1977) and was a significant component of the diet. The high return rates place *Strombus gigas* in the initial optimal diet. Foraging trips over the shallow grass flats would also have led to encounters with marine fishes, such as bonefish *(Albula vulpes)*.

The net return rate for fishes has been calculated as an average for all fishing strategies. Higher returns could have been obtained by pursuing particular strategies, such as the capture of fishes encountered during *Strombus gigas* collecting trips, but present evidence is not sufficient to discriminate the return rates for alternative strategies (Johannes 1981; Kirch 1982; Keegan 1986a). The average values for all fishing strategies places fishing just below rock iguana in the ranking of protein returns.

Optimal Horticulturalists

Having discussed the major habitats and their patches, attention is next focused on the food quest. In which patch should food be sought first? How much time should be devoted to the food quest in each patch? When should new foods be added to the diet? More complete information on time allocation and predation rates are needed before a quantitative solution for patch selection decisions can be calculated.

A qualitative solution can be proposed in the Lucayan case because the net return rates for the second through eighth ranked resources are sufficiently similar to analyze dietary change in a diet-breadth framework (Table V.D.3.3). This approach is based on the identification of horticultural production as part of the original subsistence endowment, and by the distribution of higher ranked resources in forest, coastal, and marine patches. Furthermore, the location of permanent settlements on the coast would eliminate significant differences in the time invested in traveling between patches.

The logic behind the use of the diet-breadth model, rather than the patch-selection model, is as follows. Although the patch-selection model compares average returns from different patches (including transportation time), while the diet-breadth model compares marginal returns to the overall foraging efficiency, the marginal return rates calculated for Lucayan food sources include some time investments that are better considered as search time. (Search time is a component of average return calculations.) This conflation of average and marginal returns results from the character of the information available to calculate those rates.

A second factor is that foraging from a central place should require similar investments in the time required to travel between patches. The high-ranked items in the Lucayan diet all have population densities that would have been rapidly depleted after the start of human predation. This reduction of animal densities would produce a reduction in the average return rates. Since the marginal rates for high-ranked items are similar, as is the time invested in traveling between patches, the marginal return rates should approximate the long-term decision-making problem. In other words, foraging decisions can be modeled as reflecting habitat selection based solely on short-term differences in resource distributions in each of the patches. This type of patch selection is so "fine-grained" (homogeneous) that it closely resembles and even operates like the diet-breadth model.

The diet-breadth model predicts that diet breadth will be expanded (in other words, items will be added to the diet) when the marginal return rate for a resource is equal to the average return rate for all higher-ranked resources. Because manioc cultivation was practiced when the Bahama archipelago was colonized, the higher-ranked resources would also have been in the original optimal set. These high-ranked resources are hutia, land crabs, queen conch, and rock iguana. This analysis suggests that despite their current absence in archaeological samples, green turtles and monk seals would have been captured during their seasonal availabilities. The food items mentioned

Table V.D.3.3. *Return rates and resource rankings of Lucayan foods*

Food Sources	Average weight/ individual (kg)	Kcal/ kg	Grams protein (kg)	Handling time (hr/kg)	Pop. density (kg/ha)	E/h	gP/h	Rank E/h	Rank gP/h
Green turtles (*Chelonia mydas*)	19.0	1300	2.2	0.026	2609	50,000	84	1	1
Hutia (*Geocapromys* sp.)	1.4	1500	1.5	0.12	21	12,500	13	2	5
Land crab (*Cardisoma* sp.)	0.2	900	1.7	0.10	2000	9,000	17	3	3
Queen conch (*Strombus gigas*)	0.17	800	1.3	0.09	850	8,889	14	4	4
Rock iguana (*Cyclura carinata*)	0.7	2000	2.4	0.24	15	8,333	10	5	6
Horticulture root crops	–	–	–	–	–	5,000	–	6	–
maize	–	–	–	–	–	–	20	–	2
All fishes	0.25	1000	1.9	0.22	–	4,545	9	7	7
West Indian top shell (*Cittarium pica*)	0.035	800	1.3	0.25	1750	3,200	5	8	8
Chiton sp.	0.005	800	1.3	0.5	500	1,600	3	9	9
Codakia orbicularis	0.01	800	1.3	1.39	4000	576	1	10	10
Nerites (*Nerita* sp.)	0.002	800	1.3	1.4	400	471	<1	11	11

Note: E/h is calories per handling hour; gP/h is grams of protein per handling hour.

Source: After Keegan (1985).

should have provided a diet sufficient to preclude the need to eat any other foods. One qualification to this is that high-ranked fishes, such as bonefish, were probably pursued when encountered during foraging on the tidal flats.

Terrestrial animals in the Bahamas are susceptible to overexploitation. Their availability would have rapidly declined after a short period of intense predation and as human population growth increased the demand for these foods (Iverson 1979; Jordan 1989). In addition, land clearance and other changes to the landscape would effect the survival of other species (Olsen 1982). The first response to a decline in high-ranked resources would be to migrate to previously unexploited habitats. Thus, the rapid decline in high-ranked terrestrial animals would have encouraged the rapid migration of people to unoccupied islands. When new areas were no longer available, then the intensification of foraging in the marine habitat should have occurred.

The redistribution of the human population was no longer a cost-efficient option when the presence of other settlements prevented people from moving into pristine areas. When such social circumscription occurred, the currency demands had to be satisfied in the vicinity of the village over a longer period of time. In response to the combined effects of increased demand due to population growth and declining returns due to long-term exploitation, the intensification of production could only focus on two options. These options were increased use of marine habitats and changes in garden breadth. The total contribution of land animals would have continued to decline as human population numbers increased. In marine habitats, sea turtles, *Strombus gigas,* and certain species of fish would have been the initial focus, with other fishes added to the diet as other fishing techniques were introduced, and ending with the highest-ranked littoral mollusk, *Cittarium pica,* the West Indian top shells. But this species would also have been rapidly exhausted in areas of human settlement.

During the final phase, the lowest-ranked foods (that is, nerites, chitons, and tiger lucine) would have been added in turn. *Strombus gigas* would have been sought at more distant locations, and a variety of more intensive fishing strategies would have been introduced. It is likely that fish traps were introduced early in this phase as the availability of such visible diurnal species as bonefish declined and as fishes had to be sought at more distant locations, such as along the barrier coral reef. Horticultural production would have been intensified with the addition of beans, groundnuts, and maize, all of which are high carbohydrate- and protein-producing cultigens. Fields might have been fallowed for shorter lengths of time, although the sandy soils may have supported production for longer periods than was possible on other tropical soils (as in the Yucatan Peninsula, Mexico; Roosevelt 1980). Nitrogen-fixing legumes could have

helped to maintain soil fertility. In the final phase, agriculture was intensified by the terracing of hillsides, the irrigating of fields, and the building of raised and drained fields (Zucchi and Denevan 1979).

The preceding discussion has served to identify three discrete diets. An initial diet was composed of root crops, land animals, and a few high-ranked marine species. This was followed by a second diet that included the consumption of more marine foods, a continuing contribution from root crops, and a precipitous decline in the contribution from land animals. In the third diet, land animals were reduced to a very minor level of use, marine production was further intensified, and horticulture was expanded to include higher-cost cultigens, such as maize and beans, which increased total protein and carbohydrate returns from the garden. It is this final pattern that is evident in the Lucayan faunal samples that have been analyzed to date (Wing and Reitz 1982; Wing and Scudder 1983; deFrance 1991).

Stable Isotope Analysis

The three diets just described were proposed on the basis of data gathered from ethnographic analogy, ethnohistoric reports, ethnobiological analyses, and formal economic models. To determine how well these diets reflect the actual subsistence practices of the Lucayans, a different analytical technique must be used to avoid circular reasoning. Stable-isotope analysis provides such a technique (Schoeninger and DeNiro 1984; Sealey 1986; Ambrose 1987, 1993; Keegan 1989c; Schoeninger et al. 1989; Sillen et al. 1989; see Stokes 1995 and de France et al. 1996 for new perspectives on this question.)

The Lucayan diet was evaluated by first measuring or estimating the carbon- and nitrogen-isotope compositions of food items and then measuring these in bone collagen extracted from 17 Lucayan skeletons. The results were then compared in order to determine the most likely components of the Lucayan diet.

An immediate division into marine and terrestrial food groups was observed in the carbon-isotope ratios. The marine group has an average delta^{13}C of −11 per mil, whereas the terrestrial group has an average delta^{13}C value of −25 per mil. Using these averages, the diet delta^{13}C values calculated for the Lucayan individuals can be interpreted. For instance, a diet delta^{13}C value of −11 per mil would suggest complete reliance on marine foods, a diet delta^{13}C of −25 per mil would suggest complete reliance on terrestrial foods, and a diet delta^{13}C value of −18 per mil would suggest equal contributions from both. Based on an estimated ±1 per mil uncertainty in the fractionation factor between diet and bone collagen, the diets of Lucayan individuals range from an estimated 71 ± 7 percent reliance on terrestrial foods (−21 per mil) to an estimated maximum of 74 ± 7 percent reliance on marine foods (−14.6 per mil).

If this interpretation is correct, the range in

delta[13]C values estimated for the diets of Lucayan individuals can be interpreted as reflecting a shift in consumption practices through time. The three most negative delta[13]C values (all around -20 per mil) match the first of the proposed diets in which land animals were abundant and only the highest-ranked marine organisms were consumed. The second dietary pattern would account for the majority of Lucayan individuals (n = 11), whose diet delta[13]C values of -18 ± 1 per mil reflects almost equal contributions from marine and terrestrial sources. The remaining three individuals exhibit ideal consumption patterns in the 66 to 74 ± 7 percent marine range (diet delta[13]C values of -15.2 ± .6 per mil). Such a strong reliance on marine foods is unlikely due to the relatively higher costs of marine fishing and collecting in relation to horticulture. An alternative interpretation is that the higher delta[13]C values indicate that maize was being consumed in substantial quantities during at least part of the year.

The carbon isotopes confirm the presence of three distinct diets. One explanation for these differences is that they represent changes in diet breadth through time. Unfortunately, the skeletons came from burials in caves and were not associated with materials that could be used to date them (Keegan 1982; Keegan and DeNiro 1988). Other explanations, such as the influence of more localized factors, must be entertained. Further investigations are needed to relate the isotopic study to expectations based on empirical studies and theoretical projections.

A second part of the isotopic study examined nitrogen-isotope distributions. Nitrogen-isotope values for marine and terrestrial food sources overlap, and so they cannot be used to distinguish among the contributions of land animals, cultivated roots and tubers, maize, and reef fishes in the Lucayan diet (Keegan and DeNiro 1988). When the isotopic signatures of Lucayan individuals are compared to this average, 76 percent of the individuals (n = 13) fall within ±1 per mil of this range.

Deviations from that average diet can be explained with reference to the lower values of mollusks and the higher values of pelagic fishes and marine mammals relative to other dietary components. One individual from Crooked Island had a higher dietary value, which suggests that pelagic fishes and/or marine mammals comprised a larger component of his diet and that mollusks made a relatively minor contribution. The location of this burial in an area where the barrier coral reef approaches the shore and the reef flat has a restricted range places this individual in the vicinity of marine habitats that are the most likely sources of such a dietary combination (Keegan 1982, 1986b).

The three individuals' diet values that are lower than the average probably reflect a stronger reliance on mollusks and perhaps a corresponding reduction in the consumption of higher-order carnivorous fishes. All three of these individuals are from islands with extensive *Thalassia* seagrass meadows (Grand Bahama Island and Great Abaco on the Little Bahama Bank, and Providenciales on the Caicos Bank). These shallow banks provide access to extensive mollusk populations while restricting access to reef-associated fishes (Wing and Reitz 1982; Wing and Scudder 1983; Keegan 1986b). Two of the individuals are less than 0.6 per mil below the average range, which reflects an increase in mollusk consumption to a level of less than 10 percent of total consumption. The other is 2.4 per mil below the average range, which suggests a reliance on mollusks and possibly other marine invertebrates approaching 40 percent of the diet.

The carbon- and nitrogen-isotope ratios are significant in their unequivocal rejection of commonsense interpretations of archaeological deposits. These deposits are largely composed of marine mollusk shells, the size and durability of which have led some investigators to propose that mollusks comprised as much as 95 percent of the meat protein in Lucayan diets. It is clear in the isotopic signatures of the 17 Lucayans that mollusks played a much more modest role in the diet. The same is true for the slave populations that followed them (Armstrong 1983).

The physical examination of the skeletons from the Bahamas indicates that the Lucayans enjoyed good health and nutrition (Keegan 1982). They certainly did not suffer from the nutritional and diet-related disorders of other prehistoric horticulturalists (Cohen and Armelagos 1984). They also lack the dental pathologies observed in Saladoid and Ostionoid burials at the Maisabel site, Puerto Rico. Linda Budinoff (1987), who analyzed the Maisabel skeletons, concluded that sand adhering to foods, exoskeleton and shell adhering to invertebrates, and a high percentage of carbohydrates in the diet conspired to destroy the teeth. One result was that middle-aged people had mouths more typical of old people.

In sum, the preceding examination of Lucayan diet has drawn together evidence from a variety of sources. On a general level, the empirical findings are consistent with the expectations derived from the formal model. There is every reason to believe that the Lucayans, and by extension other Tainos, were efficient, even optimal, horticulturalists.

Culinary Origins of the Tainos

The origins of the Tainos are conveniently traced to the banks of the Orinoco River in Venezuela (Rouse 1989a). As early as 2100 B.C., villages of horticulturalists who used pottery vessels to cook their food had been established along the Middle Orinoco. During the ensuing two millennia, their population increased in numbers, and they expanded downriver and outward along the Orinoco's tributaries (Lathrap 1977, 1987; Roosevelt 1980; Sanoja Obediente and Vargas 1983). One path of expansion led these people to the coast of the Guianas (Rouse 1992). From the Guianas, the opening of the West Indies awaited only the discovery of Grenada, which is separated from Trinidad by the widest gap in the chain of islands leading to Puerto Rico.

The movement of these people down the Orinoco River and through the Lesser Antilles to Puerto Rico is well documented (Roosevelt 1980; Sanoja Obediente and Vargas 1983; Zucchi, Tarble, and Vaz 1984; Rouse 1986). It is easily traced because these people manufactured a characteristic type of pottery known as Saladoid after the archaeological site of Saladero, Venezuela, at which it was first described (Rouse and Allaire 1978). In particular, the use of white-on-red painted decorations has facilitated the identification of the path along which this population expanded. Another indicator of migration is the presence of certain animals in the island archaeological remains.

The Saladoid expansion into the Antilles occurred at a rapid pace. The earliest Ceramic-Age settlements in the West Indies date to about 400 B.C. (Rouse 1989b; Haviser 1991; Siegel 1991). Saladoid settlements appear simultaneously on Puerto Rico and the islands of the Lesser Antilles (Rouse 1992). Given what is known of human reproductive potentials and the time that elapsed between departure from the mainland and colonization of Puerto Rico, the inescapable conclusion is that only the very best locations on a few of the Lesser Antilles were settled at this time. The most likely scenario is that most islands were settled temporarily and were then abandoned in favor of more abundant food resources on other islands. Only those few locations with superior resource concentrations were settled for a period that could be considered permanent (Watters 1982; Keegan and Diamond 1987; Haviser 1991). This practice of establishing temporary settlements that were moved in response to resource availability is typical of extensive horticulturalists, which the Saladoid peoples are believed to have been (Conklin 1968; Ruddle 1974; Johnson 1983).

Since paleobotanical studies have only recently been attempted, the composition of the Saladoids peoples' gardens has been hypothesized from ethnohistoric and ethnological descriptions of cultivations (Sturtevant 1961; Roosevelt 1980), and from the presence of certain food-processing artifacts. It has been proposed that manioc was the staple, but that a variety of other cultigens were also grown. The hypothesized importance of root crops is consistent with the results obtained from stable isotope analysis.

The earliest known villages in the Lesser Antilles follow the riverine settlement pattern of the mainland. On Grenada, Antigua, St. Martin, Vieques, St. Croix, and St. Kitts, the villages were located inland on river terraces, which provided access to the best setting for gardens (Haviser 1991; compare Siegel 1991). The shifting, extensive character of gardening practices is evident from the absence of deeply stratified sites and from settlement patterns in which different components are arranged in horizontal and sometimes overlapping relationships (Watters 1982).

Shortly after the initial colonization of the Antilles, there was a rapid and almost complete shift from inland to coastal settlement locations. Although horticulture continued as the primary source of foodstuffs, the change in settlement patterns was accompanied by a shift in midden deposits from terrestrial to marine animal remains. At the earliest sites, the remains of land crabs predominate in archaeological deposits. However, following the shift to coastal villages, the shells of marine mollusks and bones of marine fishes are the main components of archaeological deposits (Carbone 1980a; Goodwin 1980; Jones 1985; deFrance 1988, 1989; Keegan 1989b; Fandrich 1990). Stable isotope analysis has confirmed this strong initial reliance on terrestrial foods. One individual from the Hacienda Grande site (Rouse and Alegría 1990), an initial-period Saladoid settlement on Puerto Rico (around A.D. 100), has been analyzed. This individual exhibits a 93 ± 7 percent reliance on terrestrial foods (Keegan and DeNiro 1988).

Two explanations have been suggested to account for this shift from an emphasis on land resources to one on marine resources. The first proposed that a growing human population soon depleted the availability of terrestrial resources, which resulted in the shift to marine resources (Goodwin 1979). The second explanation proposed that changes in climate resulted in drier conditions, which acted to reduce population densities of the humidity-sensitive land crabs (Carbone 1980a, 1980b). Both are possible, but the first seems to have had the larger effect.

The examination of subsistence change on the mainland is instructive. In her study of Saladoid peoples on the Orinoco River of Venezuela, Anna Roosevelt (1980: 230–3) projected a population growth rate in Parmana that is exactly the same as the rate estimated for St. Kitts (Goodwin 1979). This coincidence suggested the question: As a shift in protein sources occurred when the population density doubled from about 1.5 to 3.0 persons per square kilometer in Parmana, did anything similar happen on St. Kitts? In Parmana, there was a shift in protein sources to an emphasis on maize in the diet (Roosevelt 1980; Merwe, Roosevelt and Vogel 1981); on St. Kitts, it has been estimated that the shift from land crabs to marine mollusks occurred at an equivalent population doubling point (Keegan 1989b).

In sum, Saladoid peoples expanded from northeastern Venezuela and the coast of the Guianas through the Lesser Antilles and Puerto Rico to establish a frontier in eastern Hispaniola. The initial migration through the Lesser Antilles to Puerto Rico took place in less than one century (Keegan 1995), a period that was insufficient for the establishment of permanent communities on every island in the Lesser Antilles. One stimulus to this rapid expansion was the small size of these islands and their limited terrestrial resource bases (Harris 1965). These constraints are apparent in the rapid and almost complete shift from terrestrial to marine sources of animal protein at the same time that the shift to coastal settlement locations provided ready access to the marine environment. The completion of this transformation of a riverine people to an island people was the economic foundation on which Taino societies developed.

Archaic West Indians

Archaeological investigations have documented the presence of human groups in the Greater Antilles by 4000 B.C. (Rouse and Allaire 1978; Veloz Maggiolo 1971-72). By most accounts, these groups were aceramic, preagricultural hunter-fisher-gatherers whose lifeways emphasized the gathering of wild plants and the exploitation of marine resources (Rouse 1948; Veloz Maggiolo and Vega 1982; Sanoja Obediente and Vargas 1983; Keegan 1994). G. J. van Klinken's (1991) stable-isotope study of 24 individuals from Aruba, Bonaire, and Curaçao, in the Netherlands Antilles, indicated a diet of C_4 grasses and marine animals from seagrass and coral-reef habitats. Dave Davis (1988: 181) has pointed out that the assumed lack of cultigens is based on the weakest of evidence. Lee Ann Newsom's (1993) study of plant remains from archaeological sites has led her to propose that "preagricultural" West Indians (Archaic peoples) were managing, and possibly cultivating, a suite of indigenous seed-bearing plants. Such incipient cultivation is now well documented among foragers (Ford 1985; Vaquer et al. 1986).

In reconstructing Archaic subsistence, it is usually assumed that a population of hunter-gatherers called Guanahatabey (or erroneously, Ciboney) survived in western Cuba until European contact (Rouse 1948). The author of this chapter has recently shown that there is not sufficient evidence to support that belief (Keegan 1989a; compare Rouse 1992). Therefore, ethnohistoric reports of Guanahatabey subsistence cannot be used to illuminate Archaic diets.

Paleobotanical evidence for the Archaic is limited. Only the starchy stem of the wild cycad Zamia and a fruit known as cupey (Clusea rosea) have been recovered in excavations (Nadal 1981; Veloz Maggiolo and Vega 1982). Both of these plants were cultivated by the Tainos, and it is possible that other Taino cultigens (for example, soursop, sweetsop, hogplum, guava, pineapple) were also eaten (Davis 1988: 181). The most common fauna in Archaic sites

are mollusks and reef fishes from shallow offshore habitats.

Marcio Veloz Maggiolo and Bernardo Vega (1982) propose an initial "adaptation" model of archaic subsistence in the Caribbean commencing around 9000 B.C. on the western coast of the United States and extending through Panama around to Trinidad. Trinidad was connected to the mainland until about 6000 B.C., with the Banwari-type occupation dating between 5500 to 3500 B.C. The diet was based on gathered plants and mollusks, with an emphasis on mangrove swamps, along with the hunting of small-to-middle-size game. Archaeological sites in the Dominican Republic date from between 2000 and 1500 B.C. Zamia and cupey were already present by this time, and land snails (Polydontes sp., Caracolus sp.), oyster (Crassostrea rizhoporae), intertidal gastropods (Cittarium pica), land crabs (Geocarcinus lateralis), marine cockroach (Acanthopleura sp.), parrot fishes (Scaridae), iguana (Cyclura sp.), and medium-size rodents (Heteropsomys sp., Isolobodon sp., and Nesophontes sp.) were also eaten.

The second adaptation, called Barrera-Mordan, dates to around 3000 B.C. in Cuba, Puerto Rico, and the Dominican Republic, and shows affinities with sites in the Colombian lowlands and Venezuela. This occupation was characterized by a more specialized emphasis on mollusks from sandy beaches (for instance, Arca spp., Codakia orbicularis), and the disappearance of mortars and pestles, suggesting a decline in the use of seeds, roots, and berries.

The third adaptation was based on fishing and mollusk gathering from beaches and mangrove swamps. It is distinguished by the high frequency of shell tools and occurs in Sambaqui-type shell mounds in northern Venezuela, including the offshore islands of Cubagua and Manicuare, Trinidad, Cuba, and the Dominican Republic (Sanoja Obediente and Vargas 1983). These sites date to around 4000 B.C. in Venezuela and 2000 to 1200 B.C. in Cuba and the Dominican Republic.

These relationships among the peoples whose material remains have been used to characterize these adaptations await further specification. It is interesting to note that in contrast to the horticultural Saladoid peoples, whose earliest adaptation seems to have emphasized terrestrial resources, the Archaic peoples had a more pronounced emphasis on the marine environment. Davis (1988) has commented on the absence of land crabs in Archaic sites, given the importance of land crabs in early Saladoid sites. It is likely that the availability of an efficient calorie producer (manioc) allowed the early Saladoids to pursue the higher-ranked but less abundant animals of the interior, whereas the Archaic peoples had to emphasize calorie capture in coastal habitats. The shift to marine resources by Saladoid peoples shows a convergence in diet with regard to protein capture that would reflect the decline in terrestrial animals.

When Old Met New

The arrival of the Spanish brought dramatic changes to the circum-Caribbean (Keegan 1996). The most notable change was the rapid decline in the native population due to warfare, disease, and abuse. Prior to their demise, the native peoples were the major suppliers of food for the European colonists. By 1497 the five major *cacicazgos* (regions ruled by a paramount *cacique* or chief) were providing tribute in the form of food and labor, a practice that mirrored tribute made to Taino caciques (Moscoso 1986). Manuel García-Arevalo (1990: 272) has noted that "dietary patterns and foodways were among the most important of the Taino contributions to be integrated into colonial culture" and that "cassava bread came to be known as the 'bread of the conquest.'"

The Spanish also introduced a variety of animals into these depauperate islands. Cattle *(Bos taurus)*, which were brought from the Canary Islands multiplied in unprecedented fashion on Hispaniola (Reitz 1986: 319, 1988), where cattle ranching became a significant occupation (Ewen 1990). In addition, pigs *(Sus scrofa)*, goats and sheep, horses *(Equus* sp.), chickens *(Gallus gallus)*, and rats and mice *(Rattus norvegicus, R. rattus, Mus musculus)* were introduced, the latter as unintended stowaways (Crosby 1972, 1986; Reitz 1986). It is interesting to note that the Spanish presence in early contact-period sites is more often identified by the occurrence of pig and rat bones than by European objects (Deagan 1988). Cattle, pigs, goats, and chickens adjusted to the climate. Pigs were so well adjusted that they were released on islands to form feral herds that could be hunted when needed. As Charles Ewen (1991: 108–9) expressed it, "[T]he diet of the colonists [showed] a mixture of the Iberian barnyard complex of peninsular Spain and the mixed hunting-fishing strategies of the indigenous peoples."

In colonizing the circum-Caribbean, the initial Spanish objective was to recreate their Iberian homeland (Crosby 1972, 1986). The colonists who founded St. Augustine in Florida brought seed stock for planting wheat and other cereals, cuttings for vineyards, and animals for breeding stock. They soon learned that the climate and soils were unsuited to this economy. Cereals withered on the stock, olives and grapes failed to grow, and their preferred meat source, sheep, did not thrive (Scarry and Reitz 1990: 344). In addition to raising cattle, the Spaniards introduced sugarcane as a cash crop. By 1545, there were 29 sugar mills belonging to prominent people on Hispaniola (García-Arevalo 1990: 275). Sugar was the magnet for the next invasion (Mintz 1985).

Subsistence practices in the sixteenth-century Spanish colonies mirrored those of the native economies that preceded them. The major change was the use of domesticated animals as a meat source, comprising from 20 to 50 percent of the vertebrate taxa (Reitz 1986: 319). In addition, peaches, melons, and watermelons produced well (Scarry and Reitz 1990: 350). Lastly, the Spanish continued to import Old World foodstuffs that would not grow in the colonies, including wheat, olives, and wine, but these supplies were rare and unreliable (Sauer 1966). According to Margaret Scarry and Elizabeth Reitz (1990: 344–5): "One soldier testified [in 1573] that rations were often short and that 'when there was nothing they ate herbs, fish and other scum and vermin.'"

British and African Arrivals

The British colonies pursued two very different types of plantation economies. In Jamaica and the Lesser Antilles, sugarcane was grown by slave labor for export, whereas in the Bahamas, cotton, utilizing far fewer slaves, was the main commodity (Craton 1978; Riley 1983; Saunders 1985; Craton and Saunders 1992). In both areas the vegetable portion of the meal was grown largely on provision grounds, although wheat flour and locally unavailable foodstuffs were imported. Indian corn *(Zea mays)* was the staple. In addition, true yams *(Dioscorea* sp.), sweet potatoes, eddoes *(Colocasia* sp.), okras *(Hibiscus esculentus)*, pigeon peas *(Cajanus cajan)*, red peas or cowpeas, black-eyed peas, snap beans, cabbage, pumpkins, castor oil, and Guinea corn (sorghum) were also grown (Farquharson 1831–2; Handler and Lange 1978). The new additions to this list were imported from Africa and Asia in the course of the slave trade. Kimber (1988) provides a remarkable discussion of plant introductions and use on the island of Martinique.

Some livestock and fowl were raised on the plantations, but most of the meats that were consumed were imported. Imports included salt beef and salt pork. It is ironic that salt fish, imported from North America, was a staple. In the study of faunal remains at Drax Hall, Jamaica, Douglas Armstrong (1983) detected little in the way of fresh fish, mollusks, or other sorts of wild game. However, following emancipation, there was a strong reliance on rocky intertidal mollusks.

Although foodstuffs were usually distributed to slaves for cooking, a main meal was sometimes served from a central kitchen on Barbadian plantations in the nineteenth century (Handler and Lange 1978). Slaves prepared their meals on an open fire by roasting or boiling. Jerome Handler and F. W. Lange suggest that meals were nutritious and monotonous, and that food allowances were often of insufficient quantity. As a result, the theft of food was common, and it was not considered wrong to steal from the master.

Slaves were also given allowances of rum, one effect of which was a condition called "dry bellyache." Handler and colleagues (1986) have shown that dry bellyache was caused by lead poisoning. Lead was the "demon" in rum; it was used in the equipment in which rum was distilled.

D. Gail Saunders (1985: 166) and others have noted that African foods such as accara, foo-foo, agedi, and my-my are remembered and still cooked in the Bahamas today. She describes accara as being a patty made with black-eyed peas, okras, onion, red peppers, flour, thyme leaves, tomato, and salt. With emancipation, what was remembered of African foodways was mapped onto the local environment.

Garifuna Diet

All of the preceding examples find their ultimate expression in the Garifuna. The Garifuna, often referred to as Black Caribs, presently occupy the coast of Central America from Belize to Nicaragua. They developed from intermixture of the Island Caribs and Africans in a social environment that was manipulated by white Europeans. By 1700, a new society that was racially and culturally distinct from the Island Caribs had developed on St. Vincent (Kirby and Martin 1972). What is striking about the Garifuna is that their diet reflects "the various exotic cultural influences experienced over the past 400 years" (González 1988: 98).

The best-known item in the Island Carib diet is human flesh. It was in reference to the Island Caribs that the term "cannibal" originated. More recently, investigators have questioned whether the Island Caribs did, in fact, consume human flesh or whether this practice was ascribed to them in order to permit their capture as slaves under Spanish law (Myers 1984; Davis and Goodwin 1990; Wilson 1990). The present consensus is that anthropophagy was practiced in ritual settings, perhaps even as a display of

fierceness, but that it never served as a source of dietary protein as has been suggested for the Aztecs (Harner 1977; compare Garn 1979).

It is likely that many of the cultigens attributed to the Tainos were also cultivated by the Island Caribs. The staples of their diet were cassava bread made from bitter manioc, and fish. They also cultivated sweet potatoes, chilli peppers, peanuts, beans, guava, soursop, and mamey. Pineapple (*Ananas comosus* [L.] Merr.) is described as having been fermented into wine (Rouse 1948; Sturtevant 1969), an activity still practiced by the Garifuna.

Oranges, citrons, grapefruits, figs, rice, bananas, and plantains were introduced from the Mediterranean by the Spanish (González 1988: 101). Cacao was introduced from the mainland because of its importance as a European trade item, an importance it maintains today. The introduction of coconut, the most important source of oil for the Caribs, is not recorded. The Spanish also introduced fowl and pigs. Feral pig herds achieved substantial numbers following their release. Okra, akee (*Blighia sapida* Konig), pigeon peas, marijuana, senna (*Cassia italica*), yams (*Dioscorea* sp.), sorghum, and plantains accompanied slaves from Africa (Sturtevant 1961; Grimé 1979; González 1988: 101). Finally, mangoes, sugarcane, coffee, and arrowroot (*Maranta arundinacea*) were introduced at an early date, the latter by the Tainos (Sturtevant 1969; Handler 1971; González 1988: 101; Newsom 1993). Nancie González's (1988: Table 5.1) summary of modern ceremonial foods by probable date of introduction neatly summarizes the successive waves of culinary influence (Table V.D.3.4).

Table V.D.3.4. *Garifuna ceremonial foods and the probable time of their introduction*

	Prehistoric	Sixteenth century	Nineteenth century	Twentieth century
Uwi	Fish Iguana Crab Fish roe	Chicken Eggs Pork	Lobster White cheese	Bologna
Breadkind	*Areba* Malanga Cassava gruel Sweet potato pudding Sweet manioc	–	Plantains Tamales Green bananas Rice and beans Banana fritters Tomato slices Rice gruel	Spaghetti White bread Cabbage
Sweets	–	Mangoes Watermelon	Coconut candy Cashew fruit	Cookies Hard candy
Beverages	*Hui*	–	Rum Coconut water	Kool-Aid Coca-Cola Orange pop Beer

Source: After González (1988), Table 5.1.

Through the eyes of the Garifuna, Nancie González (1988) describes the progressive homogenization of tropical diets among peoples of African ancestry. The pepper pot of the Island Caribs has today been replaced by *falmou,* a concoction of fish, tubers, and coconut milk. Both *Capsicum* (chilli peppers) and *cassirepe* (boiled juice of bitter manioc) have fallen out of favor. Fish stews similar to *falmou* are also popular with the Miskitos and other Belizean creoles (Nietschmann 1973: 37). Bitter manioc continues as an important source of food, and it joins maize, rice, and wheat as ubiquitous starches, along with mango, papaya, and watermelon as ubiquitous fruits on both sides of the Atlantic (González 1988: 105-6). Yet despite this convergence in food items, the menus maintain their separate ethnic dimensions.

Summary

Caribbean diets were strongly influenced by the diffusion of domesticated plants and animals. The initial conditions were established more than 10,000 years ago as biogeographic processes shaped the indigenous vegetation and fauna (Watts 1987). With the arrival of humans, this landscape was irrevocably modified to serve human needs. It is possible that the earliest immigrants did not bring new plants or animals with them, and that their procurement strategies had little impact on the islands. They were, however, followed by extensive horticulturalists who slashed and burned the forests and introduced a suite of new plants. Every wave of immigrants brought new cultigens and new ways to process or prepare those that were already present. In the end, the more than 40 different cultigens have been mentioned in this review.

Animals were also introduced. The earliest introduction was the dog, and others, such as hutia, agouti, and guinea pig, had their insular distributions enlarged. The Spanish made the biggest impact, bringing cattle, chickens, goats, rats, sheep, horses, and donkeys. These animals helped transform luxuriant tropical vegetation into scrub forage. As some animals were introduced, others became extinct (Olsen 1982; Morgan and Woods 1986). Manatee, monk seal, and sea turtles are either extinct or nearly so, and even the ubiquitous queen conch is now in short supply (Hesse and Hesse 1977).

Today, most West Indians have forsaken agriculture and instead rely on imported foods. For instance, Ifill noted in his study of Grenada that "in 1974 the estimated daily calorie intake per capita was 1,958.4 of which 1,535.9 [was imported]. . . . With respect to protein per capita, daily intake was 46.03g, of which imported food supplied 31.72g" (quoted in Brierley 1985: 52). Despite this national reliance on imported foods, rural peoples remain dependent on local production on both provision grounds and kitchen gardens.

This infield (kitchen garden)-outfield (provision grounds) division finds its recent origins in the slave plantation economy, but it mirrors practices that can be traced to South America and Africa. Present-day kitchen gardens reflect both continuity with and a synthesis of the past. For example, J. S. Brierley's (1985: Table 2) list of 20 common plants in Grenadian kitchen gardens includes crops from South America, Africa, Asia, Europe, and Oceania, as well as the Caribbean (1985: Table 5). As Brierley (1985: 55) points out, these are not simply a random selection of available cultigens; rather, the "nutritional balance of [the] crops must be attributed . . . to traditional knowledge and a process of selection governed by the dietary needs and ecological potential of the region."

Despite repeated waves of new peoples and new dietary items, the climate and ecology have shaped culinary practices. Until the very recent reliance on a cash economy, diets have been shaped by the low-cost caloric productivity of root crops (manioc, sweet potato, yams, dasheen), the paucity or expense of terrestrial animals (hutias, iguanas, cattle, sheep, and goats), and abundant but labor-intensive marine organisms (fishes, turtles, queen conch). In some ways, the more things changed, the more they remained the same. One result is a convergence of diets throughout the tropics as cultigens and animals are shared around the world.

William F. Keegan

Notes

1. Manioc occurs in both bitter and nonbitter ("sweet") varieties, although these varieties are members of the same species.

Bibliography

Alegría, R. E. 1983. *Ball courts and ceremonial plazas in the West Indies.* New Haven, Conn.

Allaire, L. 1984. A reconstruction of early historical Island Carib pottery. *Southeastern Archaeology* 3: 121-33.

Ambrose, S. H. 1987. Chemical and isotopic techniques of diet reconstruction in eastern North America. In *Emergent horticultural economies of the eastern woodlands,* ed. W. F. Keegan, 87-107. Carbondale, Ill.

  1993. Isotopic analysis: Methodological and interpretive considerations. In *Elemental and isotopic analyses: Understanding diet and diseases in past populations,* ed. M. K. Sanford, 59-130. London.

Ambrose, S. H., and L. Norr. 1993. Relationship of carbon isotope ratios of dietary protein and energy to those of bone collagen and apatite. Paper presented at the 58th annual meeting of the Society for American Archaeology, St. Louis, Mo.

Armstrong, Douglas V. 1983. *The "old village" at Drax Hall plantation: An archaeological examination of an Afro-Jamaican settlement.* Ph.D. thesis, University of California, Los Angeles.

Aveni, A. F., and G. Urton, eds. 1982. *Ethnoastronomy and archaeoastronomy in the American tropics.* New York.

Bell, J. A. 1992. Universalization in archaeological explanation. In *Metaarchaeology: Reflections by archaeologists and philosophers,* ed. L. Embree, 143-64. Boston, Mass.

Boucher, P. P. 1992. *Cannibal encounters: Europeans and Island Caribs, 1492-1763.* Baltimore, Md.

Brierley, J. S. 1985. West Indian kitchen gardens: A historical perspective with current insights from Grenada. *Food and Nutrition Bulletin* 7: 52-60.

Budinoff, Linda C. 1987. An osteological analysis of the human burials recovered from Maisabel: An early ceramic site on the north coast of Puerto Rico. Paper presented at the Twelfth International Congress for Caribbean Archaeology, Cayenne, French Guyana.

Butt, Audrey J. 1977. Land use and social organization of tropical forest peoples of the Guianas. In *Human ecology in the tropics,* ed. J. P. Garlick and R. W. J. Keay, 1-17. London.

Campbell. David G. 1978. *The ephemeral islands.* London.

Carbone, V. A. 1980a. Some problems in cultural paleoecology in the Caribbean Area. *Proceedings of the Eighth International Congress for the Study of the Pre-Columbian Cultures of the Lesser Antilles,* 98-126. Tempe, Ariz.

1980b. The paleoecology of the Caribbean area. *Florida Anthropologist* 33: 99-119.

Castellanos, R. 1981. La plaza de Chacuey, un instrumento astronomico megalitico. *Boletin del Museo del Hombre Dominicano* 16: 31-40.

Chanlatte Baik, L. A., and Y. M. Narganes Storde. 1990. *La nueva arqueologia de Puerto Rico (su proyección en las Antillas).* Santo Domingo.

Clough, Garrett C. 1972. Biology of the Bahamian hutia, *Geocapromys ingrahami. Journal of Mammology* 53: 807-23.

Cohen, Mark Nathan, and George Armelagos. 1984. *Paleopathology at the origins of agriculture.* New York.

Conklin, Harold S. 1968. An ethnoecological approach to shifting agriculture. In *Man in adaptation: The cultural present,* ed. Y. A. Cohen, 126-31. Chicago.

Craton, Michael. 1978. *Searching for the invisible man.* Cambridge.

Craton, M., and G. Saunders. 1992. *Islanders in the stream.* Athens.

Crosby, Alfred W. 1972. *The Columbian exchange.* Westport, Conn.

1986. *Ecological imperialism.* Cambridge.

Davidson, William V. 1974. *Historical geography of the Bay Islands, Honduras.* Birmingham, Ala.

Davis, Dave D. 1974. Some notes concerning the Archaic occupation of Antigua. *Proceedings of the Fifth International Congress for the study of the Pre-Columbian Cultures of the Lesser Antilles,* 65-71. Antigua.

1988. Coastal biogeography and human subsistence: Examples from the West Indies. *Archaeology of Eastern North America* 16: 177-85.

Davis, D. D., and R. C. Goodwin. 1990. Island Carib origins: Evidence and non-evidence. *American Antiquity* 54: 37-48.

Deagan, Kathleen. 1988. The archaeology of the Spanish contact period in the Caribbean. *Journal of World Prehistory* 2: 187-233.

deFrance, Susan D. 1988. *Zooarchaeological investigations of subsistence strategies at the Maisabel site, Puerto Rico.* M.A. thesis, University of Florida, Gainesville.

1989. Saladoid and Ostinoid subsistence adaptions: Zooarchaeological data from coastal occupation on Puerto Rico. In *Early ceramic population lifeways and adaptive strategies in the Caribbean,* ed. P. Siegel, BAR International Series 506, 57-78. Oxford.

1991. *Zooarchaeological research on Lucayan Taino subsistence: Crooked Island, Bahamas.* Florida Museum of Natural History. Gainesville.

deFrance, S. D., W. F. Keegan, and L. A. Newsom. 1996. The archaeobotanical, bone isotope, and zooarchaeological records from Caribbean sites in comparative perspective. In *Case studies in environmental archaeology,* ed. E. J. Reitz, L. A. Newsom, and S. J. Scudder, 289-304. New York.

Doran, Edwin, Jr. 1958. The Caicos conch trade. *The Geographical Review* 48: 388-401.

Eisenberg, John F. 1989. *Mammals of the neotropics: The northern neotropics, Vol. 1: Panama, Colombia, Venezuela, Guyana, Suriname, French Guiana.* Chicago.

Ewen, Charles R. 1990. The rise and fall of Puerto Real. In *Columbian consequences, Vol. 2: Archaeological and historical perspectives on the Spanish borderlands east,* ed. D. H. Thomas, 261-8. Washington, D.C.

1991. *From Spaniard to Creole: The archaeology of cultural formation at Puerto Real, Haiti.* Tuscaloosa, Ala.

Fandrich, Judith. 1990. Subsistence at Pearls, Grenada, W.I. (A.D. 200). In *Miscellaneous project report number 44,* Florida Museum of Natural History, 14-47. Gainesville.

Farquharson, Charles. 1831-2. *A relic of slavery: Farquharson's journal for 1831-32.* Copied from the original by O. J. McDonald, 1957. Nassau, Bahamas.

Fewkes, J. W. 1907. The aborigines of Puerto Rico and neighboring islands. *Twenty-fifth annual report of the U.S. Bureau of American Ethnology, 1903-1904,* 35-281. Washington, D.C.

Ford, Richard I. 1984. Prehistoric phytogeography of economic plants in Latin America. In *Pre-Columbian plant migration,* ed. D. Stone, Papers of the Peabody Museum of Archaeology and Ethnology, Vol. 76, 175-83. Cambridge, Mass.

1985. *Prehistoric food production in North America.* Ann Arbor, Mich.

Fortuna, Luis. 1978. Analisis polinico de Sanate Abajo. *Boletin del Museo del Hombre Dominicano* 10: 125-30.

García-Arevalo, Manuel. 1990. Transculturation in contact period and contemporary Hispaniola. In *Columbian consequences, Vol. 2: Archaeological and historical perspectives on the Spanish borderlands east,* ed. D. H. Thomas, 269-80. Washington, D.C.

Garn, Stanley M. 1979. The noneconomic nature of eating people. *American Anthropologist* 81: 902-3.

Gifford, Charles A. 1962. Some observations on the general biology of the land crab, *Cardisoma guanhumi* (Latreille) in South Florida. *Biological Bulletin* 123: 207-23.

González, Nancie L. 1988. *Sojourners of the Caribbean: Ethnogenesis and ethnohistory of the Garifuna.* Urbana, Ill.

Goodwin, R. C. 1978. The Lesser Antilles archaic: New data from St. Kitts. *Journal of the Virgin Islands Archaeological Society* 5: 6-16.

1979. *The prehistoric cultural ecology of St. Kitts, West Indies: A case study in island archaeology.* Ph.D. Thesis, Arizona State University, Tempe, Ariz.

1980. Demographic change and the crab-shell dichotomy. *Proceedings of the Eighth International Congress for the study of the Pre-Columbian cultures of the Lesser Antilles,* 45-68. Tempe, Ariz.

Grimé, William E. 1979. *Ethno-botany of the Black Americans.* Algonac, Mich.

Guarch, J. M. 1974. *Ensayo de reconstrucción ethnohistórica del Taino de Cuba.* Havana.

Handler, J. S. 1971. The history of arrowroot and the origin of peasantries in the British West Indies. *Journal of Caribbean History* 2: 46–93.

Handler, J. S., A. C. Aufderheide, R. S. Corruccini, et al. 1986. Lead contact and poisoning in Barbados slaves: Historical, chemical, and biological evidence. *Social Science History* 10: 399–425.

Handler, J. S., and F. W. Lange. 1978. *Plantation slavery in Barbados.* Cambridge.

Harner, Michael. 1977. The ecological basis for Aztec sacrifice. *American Ethnologist* 4: 117–35.

Harris, David R. 1965. *Plants, animals and man in the outer Leeward Island, West Indies: An ecological study of Antigua, Barbuda, and Anguilla.* Berkeley, Calif.

Haviser, J. B., Jr. 1989. Preliminary results of test excavations at the Hope Estate Site (SM-026), St. Martin. *Proceedings of the Eleventh International Congress for Caribbean Archaeology,* eds. E. N. Ayubi and J. B. Haviser, 647–66, Curaçao.

1991. Development of a prehistoric interaction sphere in the northern Lesser Antilles. *New West Indian Guide* 65: 129–51.

Hesse, R. C., and K. O. Hesse. 1977. The conch industry in the Turks and Caicos Islands. *Underwater Naturalist* 10.

Hulme, P., and N. L. Whitehead. 1992. *Wild majesty: Encounters with Caribs from Columbus to the present day.* Oxford.

Iverson, J. B. 1979. Behavior and ecology of the rock iguana, *Cyclura carinata. Bulletin of the Florida State Museum* 24.

Jackson, J. B. C. 1972. The ecology of the mollusks of *Thalassia* communities, Jamaica, West Indies. II. Molluscan population variability along an environmental stress gradient. *Marine Biology* 14: 304–37.

1973. The ecology of the mollusks of *Thalassia* communities, Jamaica, West Indies. I. Distribution, environmental physiology, and ecology of common shallow-water species. *Bulletin of Marine Science* 23: 313–50.

Johannes, R. E. 1981. *Words of the lagoon.* Berkeley, Calif.

Johnson, Allen. 1983. Machiguenga gardens. In *Adaptive responses of Native Amazonians,* ed. R. B. Hames and W. T. Vickers, 29–63. New York.

Johnson, A., and M. Baksh. 1987. Ecological and structural influences on the proportions of wild foods in the diets of two Machiguenga communities. In *Food and evolution,* ed. M. Harris and E. B. Ross, 387–406. Philadelphia, Pa.

Jones, Alick R. 1985. Diet change and human population at Indian Creek, Antigua. *American Antiquity* 50: 518–36.

Jordan, Kevin. 1989. *The ecology of the Bahamian hutia (Geocapromys ingrahami).* Ph.D. Thesis, University of Florida, Gainesville.

Keegan, W. F. 1982. Lucayan cave burials from the Bahamas. *Journal of New World Archaeology* 5: 57–65.

1985. *Dynamic horticulturalists: Population expansion in the prehistoric Bahamas.* Ph.D. thesis, University of California, Los Angeles.

1986a. The optimal foraging analysis of horticultural production. *American Anthropologist* 88: 92–107.

1986b. The ecology of Lucayan Arawak fishing practices. *American Antiquity* 51: 816–25.

1987. Diffusion of maize from South America: The Antillean connection reconstructed. In *Emergent horticultural economies of the eastern woodlands,* ed. W. F. Keegan, 329–44. Carbondale, Ill.

1989a. Creating the Guanahatabey (Ciboney): The modern genesis of an extinct culture. *Antiquity* 63: 373–9.

1989b. Transition from a terrestrial to a maritime economy: A new view of the crab/shell dichotomy. In *Early ceramic population lifeways and adaptive strategies in the Caribbean,* ed. P. Siegel, BAR International Series 506, 119–28. Oxford.

1989c. Stable isotope analysis of prehistoric diet. In *Reconstruction of life from the skeleton,* ed. M. Y. Iscan and K. A. R. Kennedy, 223–36. New York.

1992. *The people who discovered Columbus: An introduction to the prehistory of the Bahamas.* Gainesville, Fla.

1994. West Indian archaeology. 1. Overview and foragers. *Journal of Archaeological Research* 2: 255–84.

1995. Modeling dispersal in the prehistoric West Indies. *World Archaeology* 26: 400–20.

1996. West Indian archaeology. 2. After Columbus. *Journal of Archaeological Research* 4: 265–94.

Keegan, W. F., and M. J. DeNiro. 1988. Stable carbon- and nitrogen-isotope ratios of bone collagen used to study coral-reef and terrestrial components of prehistoric Bahamian diet. *American Antiquity* 53: 320–36.

Keegan, W. F., and J. M. Diamond. 1987. Colonization of islands by humans: A biogeographical perspective. In *Advances in archaeological method and theory,* Vol. 10, ed. M. B. Schiffer, 49–92. San Diego.

Keegan, W., C. M. Porter, N. Silk, W. L. Stern, et al. 1992. *New World harvest: A teacher's manual.* Gainesville, Fla.

Kimber, C. T. 1988. *Martinique revisited: The changing plant geographies of a West Indian island.* College Station, Tex.

Kirby, I. E., and C. I. Martin. 1972. *The rise and fall of the Black Caribs of St. Vincent.* St. Vincent.

Kirch, P. V. 1982. The ecology of marine exploitation in prehistoric Hawaii. *Human Ecology* 10: 455–76.

Klinken, G. J. van. 1991. *Dating and dietary reconstruction by isotopic analysis of amino acids in fossil bone collagen – with special reference to the Caribbean.* Publications of the Foundation for Scientific Research in the Caribbean Region No. 128. Amsterdam.

Lathrap, D. W. 1977. Our father the cayman, our mother the gourd: Spinden revisited, or a unitary model for the emergence of agriculture in the New World. In *Origins of agriculture,* ed. C. A. Reed, 713–51. The Hague.

1987. The introduction of maize in prehistoric eastern North America: The view from Amazonia and the Santa Elena Peninsula. In *Emergent horticultural economies of the eastern woodlands,* ed. W. F. Keegan, 345–71. Carbondale, Ill.

Linares, Olga. 1976. "Garden hunting" in the American tropics. *Human Ecology* 4: 331–49.

Loven, S. 1935. *Origins of the Tainan culture, West Indies.* Göteborg, Sweden.

Malinowski, Bronislaw. [1935] 1978. *Coral gardens and their magic.* New York.

McKillop, Heather I. 1985. Prehistoric exploitation of the manatee in the Maya and circum-Caribbean areas. *World Archaeology* 16: 337–53.

McKinnen, Daniel. 1804. *Tour through the British West Indies, in the years 1802 and 1803 giving a particular account of the Bahama Islands.* London.

Meehan, Betty. 1977. Man does not live by calories alone: The role of shellfish in a coastal cuisine. In *Sunda and Sahul,* ed. J. Allen, J. Golsen and R. Jones. New York.

Merwe, Nikolaas J. van der, Anna Cartenius Roosevelt, and J. C. Vogel. 1981. Isotopic evidence for prehistoric subsistence change at Parmana, Venezuela. *Nature* 292: 536–8.

Mintz, Sidney W. 1985. *Sweetness and power.* New York.

Morgan, Gary S., and Charles A. Woods. 1986. Extinction and the zoogeography of West Indian land mammals. *Biological Journal of the Linnaean Society* 28: 167-203.

Moscoso, Francisco. 1986. *Tribu y Clase en el Caribe Antiquo.* Dominican Republic.

Myers, Robert A. 1984. Island Carib cannibalism. *Nieuwe West-Indische Gids* 158: 147-84.

Nadal, Joaquin E. 1981. El caimito, el copey y los chronistas. *Boletin del Museo del Hombre Dominicano* 16: 75-81.

Newsom, Lee Ann. 1993. *Native West Indian plant use.* Ph.D. thesis, University of Florida, Gainesville.

Nietschmann, Bernard. 1973. *Between land and water: The subsistence ecology of the Miskito Indians, eastern Nicaragua.* London.

Olsen, Storrs. 1982. Biological archaeology in the West Indies. *The Florida Anthropologist* 35: 162-8.

Oviedo, Gonzalo Fernández de. [1526] 1959. *Natural history of the West Indies,* ed. and trans. S. A. Stoudemire. Chapel Hill, N.C.

Pearsall, D. M. 1985. Analysis of soil phytoliths and botanical macroremains from El Bronce archaeological site, Ponce, Puerto Rico. Appendix B in *Archaeological data recovery at El Bronce, Puerto Rico. Final report, phase 2,* ed. L. S. Robinson, E. R. Lundberg, and J. B. Walker. Jacksonville, Fla.

Piperno, D. R., M. B. Bush, and P. A. Colinvaux. 1990. Paleoenvironments and human occupation in late-glacial Panama. *Quaternary Research* 33: 108-16.

Reitz, Elizabeth J. 1986. Vertebrate fauna from locus 39, Puerto Real, Haiti. *Journal of Field Archaeology* 13: 317-28.

  1988. Impact of animals introduced to the New World: The case of Puerto Real, Haiti. Paper presented at Rethinking the Encounter: New Perspectives on the Conquest and Colonization, 1450-1550. Gainesville, Fla.

Riley, Sandra. 1983. *Homeward bound.* Miami.

Roosevelt, Anna C. 1980. *Parmana: Prehistoric maize and manioc subsistence along the Amazon and Orinoco.* New York.

Rose, Richard. 1982. The Pigeon Creek site, San Salvador, Bahamas. *The Florida Anthropologist* 35: 129-45.

Rouse, Irving. 1948. The West Indies. In *Handbook of South American Indians, Vol. 4, The circum-Caribbean tribes,* ed. J. H. Steward, 497-503. Washington, D.C.

  1986. *Migrations in prehistory: Inferring population movements from cultural remains.* New Haven, Conn.

  1989a. Peopling and repeopling of the West Indies. In *Biogeography of the West Indies, past, present and future,* ed. C. A. Woods, 119-35. Gainesville, Fla.

  1989b. Peoples and cultures of the Saladoid frontier in the Greater Antilles. In *Early ceramic population lifeways and adaptive strategies in the Caribbean,* ed. P. E. Siegel, BAR International Series No. 506, 283-403. Oxford.

  1992. *The Tainos.* New Haven, Conn.

Rouse, I., and R. E. Alegría. 1990. *Excavations at Maria de la Cruz Cave and Hacienda Grande Village site, Loiza, Puerto Rico.* Yale University Publications in Anthropology No. 80. New Haven, Conn.

Rouse, I., and L. Allaire. 1978. Caribbean. In *Chronologies in new world archaeology,* ed. R. E. Taylor and C. Meighan, 431-81. New York.

Ruddle, Kenneth. 1974. The Yupka cultivation system: A study of shifting cultivation in Colombia and Venezuela. *Ibero-Americana* No. 52. Los Angeles.

Sanoja Obediente, Mario and Iraida Vargas. 1983. New light on the prehistory of eastern Venezuela. *Advances in World Archaeology* 2: 205-44.

Sauer, Carl O. 1966. *The early Spanish main.* Berkeley, Calif.

Saunders, D. Gail. 1985. *Slavery in the Bahamas, 1648-1838.* Nassau.

Scarry, C. Margaret, and Elizabeth J. Reitz. 1990. Herbs, fish, scum, and vermin: Subsistence strategies in sixteenth-century Spanish Florida. In *Columbian consequences, Vol. 2, Archaeological and historical perspectives on the Spanish borderlands east,* ed. D. H. Thomas, 343-54. Washington, D.C.

Schoeninger, M. J., and M. J. DeNiro. 1984. Nitrogen and carbon isotopic composition of bone collagen from marine and terrestrial animals. *Geochimica et Cosmochimica Acta* 48: 625-39.

Schoeninger, M. J., M. J. DeNiro, and H. Tauber. 1983. Stable nitrogen isotope ratios of bone collagen reflect marine and terrestrial components of prehistoric human diet. *Science* 220: 1381-3.

Schoeninger, M. J., K. M. Noore, M. L. Murray, and J. D. Kingston. 1989. Detection of bone preservation in archaeological and fossil samples. *Applied Geochemistry* 4: 281-92.

Schultes, R. E. 1984. Amazonian cultigens and their northward and westward migration in pre-Columbian times. In *Pre-Columbian plant migration,* ed. D. Stone, Papers of the Peabody Museum of Archaeology and Ethnology, Vol. 76, 19-37.

Sealey, J. C. 1986. *Stable carbon isotopes and prehistoric diets in the south-western Cape Province, South Africa.* Cambridge Monographs in African Prehistory. Cambridge.

Sears, William H., and Shaun D. Sullivan. 1978. *American Antiquity* 43: 3-25.

Siegel, Peter E. 1991. Migration research in Saladoid archaeology: A review. *The Florida Anthropologist* 44: 79-91.

Sillen, A., J. C. Sealey, and N. J. van der Merwe. 1989. Chemistry and paleodietary research: No more easy answers. *American Antiquity* 54: 504-12.

Smith, Eric Alden. 1983. Anthropological applications of optimal foraging theory: A critical review. *Current Anthropology* 24: 625-51.

Smith, Eric Alden, and Bruce Winterhalder. 1992. *Evolutionary ecology and human behavior.* New York.

Steadman, D. W., D. R. Watters, E. J. Reitz, and G. K. Pregill. 1984. Vertebrates from archaeological sites on Montserrat, West Indies. *Annals of the Carnegie Museum* 53: 1-29.

Stokes, A. V. 1995. Understanding prehistoric subsistence in the West Indies using stable isotope analysis. In *Proceedings of the 15th International Congress for Caribbean Archaeology,* ed. R. Alegría and M. Rodríguez, 191-200. San Juan.

Sturtevant, William C. 1961. Taino agriculture. *Anthropologica* Supplement No. 2: 69-82.

  1969. History and ethnography of some West Indian starches. In *The domestication and exploitation of plants and animals,* ed. P. J. Ucko and G. W. Dimbleby, 177-9. Chicago.

Taylor, Douglas. 1977. *Languages of the West Indies.* Baltimore, Md.

Vaquer, Jean et al. 1986. Gisement chasséen de la fosse de La Toronde à Cavanac (Aude). *Gallia préhistoire* 29: 173-92. Paris.

Veloz Maggiolo, Marcio. 1976. *Medioambiente y adaptacion humana en la prehistoria de Santo Domingo.* Santo Domingo.

Veloz Maggiolo, Marcio, and Bernardo Vega. 1982. The Antillean preceramic: A new approximation. *Journal of New World Archaeology* 5: 33-44.

Veloz Maggiolo, Marcio. 1971–72. Las Antillas precolombinas ecología y población. *Revista dominicana de arqueologia y antropologia* 2: 165–69. Santo Domingo.

Watters, David R. 1982. Relating oceanography to Antillean archaeology: Implications from Oceania. *Journal of New World Archaeology* 5: 3–12.

Watters, D. R., E. J. Reitz, D. W. Steadman, and G. K. Pregill. 1984. Vertebrates from archaeological sites on Barbuda, West Indies. *Annals of the Carnegie Museum* 53: 383–412.

Watts, David. 1987. *The West Indies: Patterns of development, culture and environmental change since 1492.* Cambridge.

Wilson, Samuel M. 1990. *Hispaniola: The chiefdoms of the Caribbean in the early years of European contact.* Tuscaloosa, Ala.

Wing, Elizabeth S. 1969. Vertebrate remains excavated from San Salvador Island, Bahamas. *Journal of Caribbean Science* 9: 25–9.

  1989. Human exploitation of animal resources in the Caribbean. In *Biogeography of the West Indies,* ed. C. A. Woods, 137–52. Gainesville, Fla.

Wing, Elizabeth S., and A. B. Brown. 1979. *Paleonutrition.* New York.

Wing, Elizabeth S., and Elizabeth J. Reitz. 1982. Prehistoric fishing communities of the Caribbean. *Journal of New World Archaeology* 5: 13–32.

Wing, Elizabeth S., and Sylvia J. Scudder. 1980. Use of animals by prehistoric inhabitants of St. Kitts, West Indies. *Proceedings of the Eighth International Congress for the Study of the Pre-Columbian cultures of the Lesser Antilles,* 237–45. Tempe, Ariz.

  1983. Animal exploitation by prehistoric people living on a tropical marine edge. In *Animals and archaeology. 2. Shell middens, fishes and birds,* eds. C. Grigson and J. Clutton-Brock, BAR International Series No. 183, 197–210. Oxford.

Winterhalder, B., and E. A. Smith, eds. 1981. *Hunter-gatherer foraging strategies.* Chicago.

Zucchi, A., and W. M. Denevan. 1979. *Campos elevados a historia cultural prehispanica en los llanos occidentales de Venezuela.* Caracas.

Zucchi, A., K. Tarble, and J. E. Vaz. 1984. The ceramic sequence and new TL and C^{14} dates for the Aguerito site of the Middle Orinoco. *Journal of Field Archaeology* 11: 155–80.

V.D.4 ❦ The Caribbean from 1492 to the Present

Following 1492, the Caribbean basin became a cultural meeting ground that remains unsurpassed for the variety of influences: European, Asian, African, and American. At times, the clash of cultures led to tragedy, such as the destruction of pre-Columbian Indians by European diseases or the centuries of African enslavement on sugar plantations. But the Caribbean people have also produced cultural triumphs, not the least of which are the tropical dishes of island cooking.

Cuisine can provide important insights into the process of cultural change. Each new group of immigrants to the Caribbean, from Taino "natives" (originally from South America) to Spanish conquistadors and from African slaves to Asian laborers, brought with them their knowledge of foods and how to prepare them. Island cuisine drew together maize and manioc from America, domesticated pigs and cattle from Europe, garden plants, such as okra and akee, from Africa, and citrus fruits and rice from Asia. Unfortunately, notwithstanding this rich variety of foods, poverty has made malnutrition a recurring problem in the region. Slaves (and many whites) suffered from a frightful variety of nutrition-related diseases, many of which have returned to haunt the impoverished masses of the twentieth century. Modernization has, meanwhile, threatened to replace traditional dishes with a processed and packaged uniformity of industrial foods. But island cooks have adapted to pressures, both economic and ecological, to create a genuinely global cuisine with a uniquely local taste.

The Columbian Exchange

The arrival of Europeans transformed the ecology of the Caribbean basin, but it did so in an uneven manner. Sixteenth-century Spaniards concentrated their colonizing efforts on the Greater Antilles, comprising Cuba, Hispaniola, Jamaica, and Puerto Rico. The newcomers brought with them the staples of Mediterranean life, including plants, animals, and diseases (the latter having a disastrous impact on the native population), but they made little effort to consolidate their hold over the region. The Lesser Antilles, stretching from the Virgin Islands just east of Puerto Rico to the Venezuelan coast, did not attract European attention until the seventeenth century, when British, French, Dutch, and Danish colonists began challenging the Iberian New World monopoly. These new settlers, although left with only smaller islands unsettled by the Spanish, soon built wealthy plantations based on sugar harvested by African slaves. By the eighteenth century, the sugar economy had spread to encompass virtually the entire Caribbean.

Culinary Encounters

Spanish settlers, having exhausted the Caribbean's scant gold deposits within a few decades, recognized that a different approach was necessary in order to make their fortunes in the New World. For a model, they looked to the Canary Islands, off the coast of Africa, which had fallen to Spaniards in the last two decades of the fifteenth century. The natives there had quickly disappeared, either through death from European diseases or through intermarriage with European settlers, and the conquerors had reshaped the islands' ecology by introducing Mediterranean plants and animals. Spanish settlers hoped to create still more of these island replicas of Europe in the Caribbean (Crosby 1986: 80–100).

The Taino inhabitants of the Caribbean consumed foods that were quite different from those of Europe.

Their staple crops were not grains but rather roots, such as manioc *(Manihot esculenta),* sweet potato *(Ipomoea batatas),* and tania *(Xanmthosoma* spp.). Maize *(Zea mays)* was also cultivated although it did not add significantly to the native diet. Islanders prepared cassava "bread" from the poisonous manioc by grating the root, squeezing out its toxic juice, pressing the meat into a flat bread, and baking it on a griddle. Native fruits and vegetables included pineapple *(Ananas comosus),* guava *(Psidium guajava),* mamey *(Mammea americana),* pawpaw *(Carica papaya),* cashews *(Anacardium occidentale),* common beans *(Phaseolus vulgaris),* and lima beans *(Phaseolus lunatis).* These plants occasioned different reactions from the Europeans, who ate some eagerly and fed others to pigs. The conquistadors marveled at the game eaten by the Indians – "all sorts of wild and poisonous beasts" – including dogs, snakes, rodents, raccoons, armadillos, lizards, tapirs, opossums, and spiders. Seafood was more to the Spaniards' taste, with such items as bagre (a catfish of Caribbean and South American waters), mullet, herring, mackerel, tunny, shark, rayfish, dogfish, crayfish, shrimp, mussels, clams, oysters, crab, conches, and turtles (Morison 1963: 216-19; Sauer 1966: 53-9; Newson 1976: 41-57).

Notwithstanding the bountiful native foods, European settlers yearned for more familiar fare. Their habitual Mediterranean cuisine consisted of three staple items: wheat bread, olive oil, and vinifera wine. Spaniards considered wheat *(Triticum aestivum)* essential for both body and soul. According to an eleventh-century papal edict, it was the only grain that could serve as the Holy Eucharist (Ross 1977: 61-9). Wine from grapes *(Vitis vinifera)* fulfilled an equally important role in the Catholic Mass as the blood of Christ. And although priests could proceed in their work without olives *(Oleo europea),* Spanish cooks certainly could not. Christopher Columbus brought wheat seeds on his second voyage in 1493, but the grain refused to grow in the tropical climate, and transplanted vine cuttings and olive seedlings fared no better. Even imported Communion wafers "did bend like to wet paper, by reason of the extreme humidity and heat" (Crosby 1972: 65; Newson 1976: 84-6).

European livestock, by contrast, multiplied rapidly in the islands. In 1493 Columbus introduced horses, cattle, pigs, goats, and sheep to the New World. The goats and sheep proved ill adapted to the humid Caribbean air, but the other animals prospered. Diego Velázquez claimed that by 1514, the pig population of Cuba had increased to 30,000. Puerto Rico became an important center of cattle raising and exported large quantities of jerked beef and prepared hides during the seventeenth century. Spanish sailors purposely turned breeding stock loose on islands so that future visitors would have access to pork and beef. Unfortunately, rats and other vermin, inadvertently carried by the Europeans, likewise became firmly established on the islands (Crosby 1972: 75-9; Newson 1976: 88-90; Dietz 1986: 8).

Caribbean gardens and orchards became much more diverse as a result of the Columbian exchange. Colonists planted cabbages *(Brassica* sp.), onions *(Allium cepa),* carrots *(Daucus carota),* lettuce *(Lactuca sativa),* radishes *(Raphanus sativus),* garlic *(Allium sativum),* and chickpeas *(Cicer arietinum).* Large numbers of Asian plants arrived in the New World during the sixteenth century. In some cases, they had previously been introduced to Spain by the Muslims; in other instances, they reached the Caribbean via the slave trade. Citrus fruits included lemons *(Citrus limon),* limes *(C. aurantifolia),* and sour oranges *(C. aurantium),* as well as the European sweet orange *(C. sinensis).* Other Asian plants that thrived in the Caribbean were muskmelons *(Cucumis melo),* pomegranates *(Punica granatum),* plantains and bananas *(Musa paradisiaca sapientium),* eggplants *(Solanum melongena),* ginger *(Zingiber officinale),* cinnamon *(Cinnamomum zeylanicum),* and rice *(Oryza sativa).* Coconuts *(Cocos nucifera),* of undetermined origin, were present on the Pacific Coast in pre-Columbian times, but Spaniards probably introduced them to the Caribbean. The most significant of the new arrivals, however, was sugarcane *(Saccharum officinarum),* which ultimately dictated the social structure of most of the region (Watson 1974: 8-35; Newson 1976: 46, 84-7).

These new crops gave little compensation to the natives for the destruction caused by European diseases and labor drafts. Conquistadors received grants of Tainos entrusted to their care *(encomienda),* ostensibly for conversion to Christianity, but certainly as a source of labor as well. Moreover, the Spanish crown condoned outright slavery in the case of Carib tribes because of their "warlike nature" and supposed cannibalistic practices. The harsh working conditions of both Tainos and Caribs alike would have precipitated high death and low birth rates. But epidemics, such as that of smallpox, which began in 1518, also joined in the slaughter because the Indians had little resistance to European diseases. Indeed, it was with only small exaggeration that Bartolomé de las Casas claimed in 1542 that the Caribbean natives had virtually disappeared. By 1570, Indians in the Spanish Antilles numbered 22,000, a fourth of the entire population of those islands. And having resisted enslavement for centuries, a handful of Caribs survive to the present on Dominica (Sauer 1966: 203-5; Newson 1976: 149, 170; Knight 1990: 41-3; Hulme and Whitehead 1992: 345).

Following the conquests of Mexico in 1521 and Peru in 1532, the majority of colonists proceeded to the mainland, hoping to make their fortunes from Indian labor and silver mines, and the Greater Antilles were left with only a few small settlements of people who subsisted on corn and cassava. Havana became the leading port because of its strategic location on the route of silver fleets returning to Spain. For the next two and a half centuries, Spain's Caribbean colonies served mainly as defensive outposts, guarding against incursions by rival European powers.

The Tyranny of Sugar

Spaniards established sugar mills on Hispaniola as early as 1515 and operated a thriving business in the mid-1500s, but by the end of the century production had stagnated. Portuguese plantations in Brazil then dominated New World sugar production until 1630, when the Dutch West India Company invaded the South American colony. After the Dutch were finally driven out, they carried the Brazilian techniques to French and English planters in their newly founded colonies in the Lesser Antilles.

Sugar monoculture first took root in Barbados and then spread to other British and (later) French islands. The initial settlers of Barbados had made a meager living growing low-quality tobacco and cotton on small estates. But the introduction of sugar by Dutch merchants, beginning in the 1630s, transformed the island. Thanks to Europe's developing sweet tooth, the new industry proved enormously profitable, causing land values to rise astronomically. Smallholders sold out to an emerging planter elite, who, in their hunger for land, cleared much of the remaining forests until most of the island's acreage was planted in cane or food crops to feed whites and their slaves. But Europeans on the islands soon became a minority as tens of thousands of African slaves were imported to work the plantations. By 1680, sugar estates had gained similar domination over the rest of the British Antilles. The French were slower to make the transition from small farms, where they grew tobacco and cotton, to large plantations devoted to sugarcane grown by slaves. Nevertheless, by the mid-eighteenth century, Saint-Domingue, Guadaloupe, and Martinique had become major centers of sugar production, and by the latter part of the century, Caribbean sugar production amounted to nearly a quarter of a million tons (Dunn 1972: 46-62; Mintz 1985: 32-5; Watts 1987: 296-300; Tomich 1990: 15).

Sugar exports from the Spanish Antilles did not revive until the mid-eighteenth century. Royal trade regulations prevented colonial producers from selling sugar to northern European markets and limited the supplies of African slaves. Tax reforms undertaken in the 1740s reversed this situation, and exports to Spain increased massively. This trend accelerated in 1762 after British forces had captured Havana and imported thousands of additional slaves. When the Spanish regained control of the island the following year, they allowed Britain to continue trading with the port, and delighted by the additional tax revenues, officials encouraged cane production on Puerto Rico and Hispaniola as well. By the mid-nineteenth century, following the revolution on Saint-Domingue, Cuba had become one of the most profitable colonies in the world (Hall 1971: 98-100; McNeill 1985: 162-70; Dietz 1986: 19-20; Watts 1987: 301-4).

One final element of the Columbian exchange that resulted directly from the labor demands of sugar plantations was the transportation to the New World of huge numbers of African slaves. Philip Curtin (1969: 265-9; 1976: 595-605) estimated that Caribbean planters imported almost 5 million slaves, fully half the total brought to the Americas. And with them came African foods. Plants introduced to the Americas via the slave trade included watermelons *(Colocynthis citrullus),* okra *(Hibiscus esculentus),* taro *(Colocasia esculenta* - called eddo in the West Indies), oil palms *(Elaeis guineensis),* pigeon peas *(Cajanus cajan),* and yams *(Dioscorea* spp.) (Harris 1965: 92-3, 115; Newson 1976: 161). But familiar foods notwithstanding, the journey to America made significant changes in the diets of enslaved Africans.

Plantation Nutrition

The food aboard slave ships provided an ominous portent of life in the New World. The standard fare consisted of a dreary soup of rice, yams, horsebeans, palm oil, and red peppers. Illness followed the slaves throughout the voyage, from the initial shock of seasickness to lingering bouts of dysentery and, finally, the bleeding gums of scurvy (Kiple 1984: 57-64). A slave who survived the trip could expect little improvement on the plantation because, as J. Harry Bennett (1958: 37) explained, "he ate from his master's purse, and every mouthful was measured in cash." Virtually every nutritional deficiency disease was experienced by slaves somewhere in the West Indies. But although the African population ate poorly, Europeans spared no expense on their own, often imported foods.

Slave Subsistence

Sidney Mintz (1985: 55-61) has demonstrated that Caribbean sugar plantations, although worked by slave labor, were managed as capitalist enterprises. Planters faced enormous risks in the fluctuating world sugar market and sought to minimize their operating expenses whenever possible. Although buying slaves represented a substantial fixed investment, feeding them offered endless opportunities for cost cutting. Thus, in the early years when sugar prices were high, many estate managers planted every available acre in cane and fed their slaves with imported grain and dried meat. But as competition drove prices down, planters economized by reducing rations and allowing slaves to cultivate subsistence crops, especially on mountain slopes unfit for sugar cultivation. But despite marginal lands and limited free time, slaves with their own fields consumed a better diet than those who worked exclusively in the cane fields.

In practice, plantation diets fell between the two extremes of entirely ration-fed slaves and those who had to be self-sufficient. But even on the most heavily planted sugar islands, such as Barbados, Antigua, and St. Kitts, slaves kept small kitchen gardens with herbs, squash, peppers, and okra, and certain fields called "Negro fields" or "Negro ground" were set aside for slave use. Conversely, on islands with large areas of mountainous terrain, such as Jamaica and Martinique, plantation managers often bought staples, including corn, rice, manioc, yams, plantains, and bananas, rather than allocating provision grounds and free time to the slaves. Moreover, slaves on virtually all of the islands depended for animal protein on imports of dried meat and salted fish (Kiple 1984: 67; Morrissey 1989: 51–7; Tomich 1990: 271).

Mercantile policies dictated that provisions for the Caribbean sugar islands come from within each empire. Thus, British merchants supplied their plantations with salt cod and corn from New England, jerked beef from Ireland, herring from the North Sea, and rice from South Carolina. Many smaller Jamaican estates with less-favorable lands also produced staple crops for sale to the sugar plantations (Milling 1951: 82; Dunn 1972: 210, 276; Kiple 1984: 69). The French settlements of Guadeloupe, Martinique, and Saint-Domingue, meanwhile, imported a significant portion of the codfish harvested off Newfoundland (McNeill 1985: 112). And as Spanish sugar production expanded in the nineteenth century, planters on Cuba and, to a lesser extent, Puerto Rico began importing large quantities of rice and jerked beef (Humboldt 1969: 305; Dietz 1986: 19–20). Yet despite the intentions of colonial officials, smugglers cut across imperial lines on a regular basis (Liss 1983: 77; Pérotin-Dumon 1991: 65).

Imperial regulations also attempted to assure that slaves received adequate rations. The French *Code Noir*, promulgated in 1685 by Finance Minister Jean-Baptiste Colbert, required masters to issue each adult slave two pounds of salted beef or three pounds of fish and six pounds of cassava bread or the equivalent of manioc flour. British slave codes were more concerned with preserving order than protecting slaves, and it was not until the late eighteenth and early nineteenth centuries that a standard ration of about three pounds of meat or fish per week began to be prescribed. Eighteenth-century Spanish authorities, likewise, made belated calls for a weekly meat ration of three pounds. But once again, plantation reality differed sharply from imperial regulations, and many managers admitted feeding their slaves half of the required amounts, and they were often in such a rancid state that most of the nutrients were gone. Although slaves responded by stealing food whenever possible, this expedient was no substitute for adequate rations (Dunn 1972: 239; Friedman 1982: 507; Kiple 1984: 68, 77; Dirks 1987: 61–7, 100; Stein 1988: 52).

Slaves prepared their rations using simple cooking techniques taken from their African homelands or borrowed from native Indians. Cassava bread was made by means of pre-Columbian procedures for removing the toxic juice and then baking the grated flesh into a flat bread. Slaves who grew their own maize on provision grounds preferred to roast whole ears and eat them on the cob. But as a ration, they typically received corn in the form of meal, which was made into a thin gruel called "loblolly" or "coo-coo." Other foodstuffs, including salted meat or fish, yams, plantains, and vegetables, were boiled together in an iron pot. The ingredients of these stews varied among the islands according to availability. For example, slaves on Antigua reportedly ate a breakfast of eddo (taro), okra, yams, and other vegetables. On Jamaica, the pepper pot contained greens, such as callaloo, starch from yams or plantains, red pepper, and bits of fish (Harris 1965: 115; Dunn 1972: 278–9; Kiple and Kiple 1980: 202; Dirks 1987: 53–4).

Even this simple fare was threatened in the late eighteenth century, however, when imperial warfare and natural disaster led to a major subsistence crisis. Trouble began in 1774 when the American Continental Congress resolved to stop exporting goods to British dominions, including the West Indies. By 1776, the revolutionaries succeeded in rendering the British sugar industry unprofitable, and famine appeared on Barbados, Antigua, and St. Kitts. At first, Jamaican slaves fared better because of the availability of provision grounds. But beginning in 1780, the islands were struck by a series of hurricanes that killed thousands and destroyed provisions. Even after the final storms of 1786, thousands more died from malnutrition, dysentery, and other epidemic diseases. The British government compounded the disaster by refusing to allow a resumption of trade with the newly independent United States (Sheridan 1976: 615–41; Dirks 1987: 80).

The decade-long crisis demonstrated the need to make the islands more self-sufficient. One response of the British government was to import new food crops to the islands. In 1778, slave ships brought the akee fruit *(Blighia sapida)* to Jamaica from West Africa. An Asian domesticate, the mango *(Mangifera indica)*, arrived a few years later, and both fruits became important for slave subsistence. In 1787, the Royal Navy dispatched HMS *Bounty* under William Bligh to bring the breadfruit *(Artocarpus incisa)* from Tahiti. Thwarted at first by a notorious mutiny, in 1793 Bligh succeeded in his mission with the HMS *Providence*, earning a handsome reward from the Jamaican assembly. Unfortunately, the Jamaican slaves refused to eat the unfamiliar fruit, and for the next fifty years it was fed to pigs (Parry 1955: 1–20).

A more important change came from the expansion of slave provision grounds and slave markets. Slaves in Jamaica and Saint-Domingue had long produced staple crops on their provision grounds, and they even dominated the island markets. Amelioration laws, issued in the British Antilles late in the eighteenth century, encouraged more slaves on other islands to grow their own provisions. French officials on Martinique likewise allowed provision grounds and free time to grow substitutes for the rations handed out by masters (Mintz 1974: 180–213; Kiple

1984: 67-71; Tomich 1990: 262-5). And slaves who produced their own foods ate substantially better diets. According to Barry Higman (1979: 373-86), better nutrition was the reason that American-born slaves grew taller in the Bahamas than on islands where sugar was the primary crop. But despite attempts at amelioration, slave diets contained grave deficiencies.

Diet and Disease

One of the most notable aspects of the West Indian sugar industry was the failure to develop a self-sustaining slave population. Caribbean planters, unlike their North American counterparts, had to import tens of thousands of workers each year to replace those who had died. This policy may have developed in the seventeenth century from the cold calculation that it was more expensive to maintain slaves in good health than to work them to death and import replacements. But planters did not see their work force reproduce even after the abolition of the slave trade in the nineteenth century. One of the primary reasons for the slaves' failure to reproduce was the inadequate levels of nutrition. Diet-related diseases ran the gamut from protein and vitamin deficiencies to hypertension and lead poisoning.

Kenneth Kiple (1984: 77-81) has shown that slave diets were nutritionally deficient even if slaves actually received the provisions specified by legal requirements. For example, prescribed rations of dried beef and fish would appear to have exceeded the modern recommended dietary allowance of protein, but in fact, the slaves received these foods in a less-than-ideal state. One observer described the fish as "little better than a mass of foetid matter, containing as little nutrition as the brine in which they lie" (Kiple 1984: 80). Beef likewise lost much of its protein from the curing process. Protein deficiency weakened the slaves' immune systems and led in turn to widespread outbreaks of tuberculosis, dysentery, and other infectious diseases. Poor sanitary conditions unquestionably contributed to these epidemics, but slaves could have resisted many of these diseases with adequate supplies of protein (Kiple 1984: 142-3; Dirks 1987: 85).

Kiple has also documented shortages of most important vitamins, as well as calcium and iron. The most serious problems resulted from deficiencies of vitamin B_1 (thiamine) and B_3 (niacin). Slaves subsisting on white rice were at risk of developing beriberi, a thiamine-deficiency disease that takes two distinct forms. Both wet beriberi, with symptoms including swelling of the limbs and cardiac failure, and dry beriberi, characterized by muscular deterioration and paraplegia, were common to the Caribbean under the names "dropsy" and *mal d'estomach*. Corn rations, meanwhile, led to pellagra, a niacin-deficiency disease that caused dermatitis, dysentery, dementia, and death. Requirements for other vitamins, such as A and C, might have been satisfied by tropical fruits and chilli peppers. Unfortunately, low quantities of dietary fat prevented full utilization of vitamin A, and as a result, night blindness often reached epidemic proportions. The incidence of scurvy symptoms, including bleeding gums, festering wounds, and frequent bruises, implies a similar deterioration of vitamin C, probably due to excessive cooking. Deficiencies of A and C also slowed the absorption of calcium and iron, leading in turn to rheumatism, periodontal disease, dental caries, and anemia, although iron cooking pots would have helped offset the latter problem (Kiple 1984: 76-103).

Nutritional diseases took their worst toll among young children. Malnourished mothers often gave birth prematurely, and even full-term infants were often significantly underweight. The mother's poor health continued to have an adverse effect on her children throughout nursing. Neonatal tetany, caused by calcium shortages in the mother's milk, killed large numbers of infants in the first few weeks of life. Thiamine deficiencies were also passed on to children in the form of infantile beriberi because slave mothers, who did not themselves display symptoms of beriberi, were often unable to provide sufficient quantities of thiamine to their children. Youngsters, even after surviving the critical first year, still faced great risk at the time of weaning. The gruel given to replace a mother's milk contained little protein, and physicians frequently reported the swollen bellies symptomatic of kwashiorkor. Infant mortality rates on Caribbean plantations were higher even than among slaves in the United States, which helps explain the much greater number of Africans imported to the islands (Kiple 1984: 113-34; Dirks 1987: 85).

With the numerous deficiencies in the slave diet, it is ironic that one potentially serious health problem may have resulted from excessive consumption of sodium. West Africa was a particularly salt-poor region, and the inhabitants apparently adapted to this shortage by naturally retaining sodium. Experiments, for example, have shown that the perspiration of Africans contains much less sodium than that of whites. But once in the Caribbean, African slaves frequently found themselves confronted with sodium in the form of salted beef and fish, and especially with a substantial ration of salt itself. Thomas Wilson (1987: 257-68) has estimated that slaves may have received 20 times the modern recommended amount of salt. The resulting hypertension, although difficult to diagnose without a blood pressure cuff, probably contributed to the incidence of death by "dropsy." To relieve this chemical imbalance along with other nutritional deficiencies, many slaves engaged in "dirt-eating" (pica). Planters often believed this practice to be a method of committing suicide, and they muzzled slaves suspected of it (Kiple 1984: 46; Dirks 1987: 86-7).

Some Caribbean slaves also suffered from acute lead poisoning from a wide variety of sources. Water channeled by lead gutters, and foods exposed to the lead glaze of earthenware pottery, were potential sources of lead, as were lead-lined boilers and gutters used in sugar refining. Worst of all, slaves who drank cheap rum could have taken in large amounts of lead in alcohol, which was distilled in equipment with lead pipes and fittings. The body retains this excess lead in soft tissue, such as the brain, producing disastrous effects, including headaches, paralysis, coma, and death. One prominent symptom of lead poisoning was the "dry bellyache" - extremely painful intestinal cramps accompanied by severe constipation - which a contemporary described as an "excruciating torture of the bowels" (Handler et al. 1987: 140–66). Sailors, soldiers, and other poor whites also experienced this malady.

Malnourished slaves seldom challenged the society that held them in bondage; what planters feared most was the sudden burst of energy that came with the harvest around Christmas. Robert Dirks (1987: 167–84) has described the effects of relief-induced agonism, a condition of extremely aggressive behavior exhibited by people allowed to eat plentifully after a long period of semistarvation. Slaves in the British West Indies consumed little during the fall months as both sugarcane and provision crops matured. In December, when the end of the hurricane season brought merchant ships and planters handed out special bonuses of sugar, rum, and fish, the slaves suddenly had an overabundance of food. They responded by indulging in orgiastic revels of drinking, dancing, and occasional rebellion. This "Black Saturnalia" provided a temporary reversal of roles in which planters cringed as slaves approached, but after a few days of release, the slaves' world returned to its grim normality.

Dining in the Great House

Some plantation owners, while limiting slave rations to save a few pennies, often spent outlandish sums to maintain their own extravagant lifestyles. For example, the governor of Barbados celebrated a 1688 holiday by setting a 250-foot table for the island's leading citizens and opening wine casks in the streets for less distinguished souls. Richard Dunn (1972: 263–4, 280) has speculated that this penchant for conspicuous consumption derived from the hierarchical significance attached to food and clothing in early modern Europe. Each social class had a distinctive style of diet and dress, and nouveaux riches planters adhered to these standards, regardless of the discomforts involved in eating heavy roasts on a humid afternoon or wearing woolen coats and trousers under the tropical sun. But notwithstanding the determination of sweaty, constipated settlers, the islands demanded some adaptation or creolization of European cuisine.

The essentials of proper British dining comprised beef, bread, and beer, but reproducing this diet proved difficult in the tropics. Fresh meat spoiled virtually overnight, and so planters had to rely on salted beef, pork, and fish, although the fish was mackerel and

salmon rather than the cheap cod fed to slaves. Wheat, likewise, tended to go bad on the long voyages from Bristol and Philadelphia; thus, planters consumed hard biscuits rather than the soft bread favored in England. Finally, beer proved highly perishable in the tropical climate, and so settlers slaked their thirst with rum, punch, fruit juices, and imported wines and brandy. But what the meals lacked in quality was made up for in quantity; dinner parties with heavily piled tables constituted the sine qua non of planter affluence. A guest at one such party was so impressed by a table with massive piles of meats, fruits, and cakes that she "kept her feet out from under the table for fear it would collapse" (Dunn 1972: 272–81; quotation from Dirks 1987: 45).

The Creole inhabitants of Cuba and Puerto Rico similarly sought to recreate traditional Spanish life in the tropics. Havana cooks used olive oil and garlic with a Mediterranean generosity that overwhelmed Fanny Calderón de la Barca (1966: 28), the Scottish wife of a Spanish minister, on her visit to the island in 1839. She did, however, take great pleasure from the custards, ices, meringues, and other Spanish sweets available on the island. Berta Cabanillas de Rodríguez (1973: 336) likewise emphasized the Spanish character of recipes in the anonymous 1849 volume *El Cocinero Puertorriqueño*. To satisfy the demand for Iberian foods, the islands imported large amounts of Mexican wheat flour and Spanish wines and liquors (Humboldt 1969: 300; Lipsett-Rivera 1990: 463).

Frenchmen living on Guadeloupe, Martinique, and Saint-Domingue were no less eager to enjoy the foods of their homeland. Dominican priest and bon vivant Père Jean-Baptiste Labat imported French wine to the Caribbean as early as 1693 and insisted on drinking a glass with dinner, even after he had been captured by the Spanish. A nineteenth-century visitor observed that French cooking in the Antilles was done in the style of Provence rather than Paris, with olive oil instead of cream, perhaps as a concession to the environment. But French bread remained an invariable staple, and bakeries on Martinique employed women to carry fresh loaves to country estates on a daily basis so that planters did not have to forgo this national treasure (Hearn 1970: 112, 350; Labat 1970: 57, 186).

Despite these links with metropolitan capitals, Europeans never escaped their dependence on African slaves. On the islands of Jamaica and Saint-Domingue, slaves dominated local markets with produce from their provision grounds. They reportedly drove very hard bargains, and even merchants complained that they could not afford fresh eggs, poultry, and produce. If having to buy groceries from slaves caused consternation among whites, the fear that the food might be poisoned provoked genuine terror. Mass hysteria swept Saint-Domingue in the 1780s, and a number of slaves suspected of using poison were put to death. A fear of the slaves was not unfounded, as demonstrated by a slave rebellion in the 1790s that destroyed the colony's sugar economy and threatened the entire Caribbean plantation society (Hall 1971: 68–72; Geggus 1991: 100).

Modern Diet and Nutrition

In 1789 the French declared liberty to be one of the "rights of man," and a short time later the slaves of Saint-Domingue launched their own revolution to attain this goal. After more than a decade of fighting, in 1804 Haiti finally gained independence; to preserve it, the former slaves systematically destroyed the island's sugar economy. Terrified of the Haitian revolution, Caribbean planters fought hard to prevent its spread. Emancipation came slowly to the region. It began in the British colonies in 1834 (followed by a so-called apprentice period) and culminated in Cuba in 1886. However, as emancipation proceeded, planters replaced the slaves with indentured servants from the Far East. Independence, likewise, remained elusive. As European empires retreated, the United States came to dominate the region. Cuban and Puerto Rican sugar plantations passed into the hands of companies like the American Sugar Refining Company, while the cane workers remained destitute. So, although the citizens of the islands long ago escaped slavery, they have subsequently gained only limited control over their destinies.

Asian Transplants

Even as European legislators debated slave emancipation in the early 1800s, Caribbean planters began searching for an alternate source of labor. Imperial expansion into the Far East offered the prospect of endless supplies of indentured Asians to replace the liberated African slaves. In 1838, the year in which slavery ended in the British Antilles, the first boatload of indentured servants arrived from India. Cuba, likewise feeling the pinch of British abolitionism because of the Royal Navy's war on the slave trade, began to encourage Chinese migration from ports opened after the first Opium War (1839–42). Indentured Asians suffered working conditions little better than those of African slaves, but fortunately, the period of servitude ended much more quickly. By 1920, when the last indenture contract was canceled, Asians had made a significant impact on Caribbean culture and cuisine.

The number of Asian workers who migrated to the West Indies, although fluctuating with the sugar market, totaled more than 500,000 by the end of the nineteenth century. The typical contract specified five- to seven-year terms of indenture and offered minuscule wages, but agents stationed in the ports of Calcutta and Madras had no trouble attracting workers from the impoverished Indian countryside. British Guiana and Trinidad received the majority of the Indian migrants, about 380,000 in all, while some 45,000 went to Jamaica and other British islands. In 1860 the British government allowed French agents to recruit 6,000 Indians annually to work in the West Indies, and a decade later the Dutch received a similar conces-

sion. Only about 18,000 Chinese migrants went to the British Antilles. Cuba was their preferred destination, and between 1847 and 1874, nearly 125,000 Chinese came to work on Spanish sugar plantations (Tinker 1974: 52–4, 99, 112; Look Lai 1993: 292).

Indenture contracts usually required workers to return to their homeland at the end of the term, but Asians nevertheless established permanent communities on a number of islands. East Indians in Trinidad took advantage of slumps in the sugar market to entrench themselves in the local economy by growing rice. Chinese immigrants, meanwhile, sought to establish a niche in the Caribbean grocery trade. Competition from these newcomers was often resented, and Chinese people living in Jamaica sometimes became the targets of racial violence. Another barrier to the formation of Asian communities in the Caribbean was the shortage of women. Planters contracted far greater numbers of East Indian men than women; nevertheless, by the end of World War I, additional migration had evened out the sex ratio among East Indians in Trinidad and Martinique. Chinese men faced an even greater imbalance, for Cuba accepted only 62 Chinese women in the nineteenth century. As a result, men tended to marry Creoles and became assimilated more thoroughly than did the East Indians (Tinker 1974: 34, 364, 372; Johnson 1987: 82–95; Look Lai 1993: 188–216).

Asians made significant contributions to the cuisine of the islands. Rice had already been established by Spaniards and Africans centuries before the first Asians arrived. But East Indians carried *massala,* the unique spice combinations that form the basis for curry. They also introduced ghee, the clarified butter essential for traditional Hindu cooking, and roti, a form of flat wheat bread often served with curry. Foods have fulfilled an important role as part of the Hindu *yagna* celebrations that propagate religious and ethnic values in Trinidad. Chinese immigrants were more generally assimilated along with their foods, such as steamed fish and stir-fried vegetables, which became an important part of Cuban cuisine (Lambert Ortiz 1986: 7, 352; Vertovec 1990: 89–111; Mackie 1991: 144).

New Peasants, Old Problems

Caribbean slaves, once freed from the plantations, proceeded to form what Mintz (1974: 132) has called a "reconstituted" peasantry. Across the Caribbean, tens of thousands of freedmen and their families abandoned the lowland estates to build new villages in the highlands where sugarcane did not grow. The new yeoman farmers enlarged their provision grounds and expanded the production of export crops, such as allspice *(Pimenta officinalis),* coffee *(Coffea arabica),* bananas, cotton, ginger, and arrowroot, which had been grown for the first time during the later slave period. Improved nutrition led to a dramatic fall in the infant mortality rate, and African-Americans in the Caribbean finally began to reproduce their numbers naturally. The population of Jamaica, for example, nearly doubled in the half century after emancipation.

And despite political turmoil, Haiti likewise recorded demographic growth in the nineteenth century, a clear indication that the revolution improved conditions for the island's black majority (Kiple 1984: 118; Watts 1987: 456-64, 507-15).

In the twentieth century, population growth accelerated to dangerous levels, however, as a result of government programs to control disease and improve nutrition. Mosquito eradication campaigns finally began to bring yellow fever and malaria under control around the turn of the century. Authorities acted more slowly to alleviate the problems of malnutrition; nevertheless, by the 1970s, most of the islands had begun educational campaigns aimed at promoting adequate childhood nutrition. After 1959, Fidel Castro brought Cuba to the forefront of the movement to improve the health of rural children. Unfortunately, these reforms stimulated Caribbean population growth at rates in excess of 3 percent annually from 1950 to 1970 – some of the highest rates in the world. And ever-increasing populations have placed enormous pressure on island ecology. For example, Haitian peasants now cultivate subsistence crops on mountain slopes so steep that they need ropes to support themselves. The resulting erosion makes it even more difficult to sustain agriculture on the island (May and McLellan 1973: 145, 174, 220; Kiple 1984: 175-87; Watts 1987: 518).

Dietary deficiency diseases continue to afflict children throughout the Caribbean. Statistics from the United Nations Food and Agriculture Organization (FAO) reveal that the inhabitants of several islands, particularly Hispaniola, consume significantly below the recommended dietary allowances of vitamins and minerals. And because these figures represent nationwide averages, the poorest segments of Caribbean society suffer serious malnutrition. In the 1970s, the FAO estimated that protein-calorie deficiency strikes 30,000 to 50,000 Jamaican children, with the most serious cases exhibiting symptoms of kwashiorkor and marasmus. Moreover, studies of childhood deaths on the island indicate that a majority are nutrition related, and fully a third may have resulted directly from malnutrition. A survey of children in the Dominican Republic found only 25 percent with adequate nutrition levels, and of those admitted to hospitals, 39 percent suffered from kwashiorkor and 90 percent from anemia. Haiti recorded one of the highest infant mortality rates in the world, with 146.5 deaths per 1,000 live births in the 1970s. And village surveys found Haitian children to be as seriously malnourished as those of the neighboring Dominican Republic (May and McLellan 1973: 125, 177, 225; Kiple 1984: 184-6).

The problems of food shortages have been exacerbated by government attempts to implement crash industrialization programs and reliance on imported food. Such a lack of self-sufficiency was not unusual; as early as the 1880s, the small island of St. Pierre had become so dependent on canned foods from the United States that an American steamer was called a "food ship." Nevertheless, industrialization programs further reduced the region's capacity to support itself, as Puerto Rico's "Operation Bootstrap" demonstrated, beginning in 1949. Although aggregate incomes rose dramatically, the problem of unemployment remained, and in 1974 the United States government was forced to extend the food stamp program to the island. This, in turn, distorted the local economy, creating black markets in goods and labor and ruining the island's small farmers. It meant not only that people bought rice from California instead of the countryside but also that they discarded traditional dishes in favor of sugar-laden processed foods. Elsewhere in the region, the urban poor could not afford expensive imports, leading to widespread malnutrition and, at times, political unrest, such as the 1984 food riots in the Dominican Republic (Hearn 1970: 294; Weisskoff 1985: 60-4; Dietz 1986: 27, 63, 122; Knight 1990: 323).

Socialist Cuba attempted to balance modernization with equality, but despite some initial success, by the 1990s hunger had become widespread. Prior to Castro's revolution, malnutrition had been a serious problem in the Cuban countryside, with the daily diet deficient by 1,000 calories. Although Castro created a successful rural health-care system, initial mistakes in agricultural development led to a reliance on subsidies from the Soviet Union. By the mid–1980s imports had fallen from one-third of total food consumption to below 20 percent, at the same time that per capita intake of calories and proteins increased. But just a few years later, the collapse of communism in Eastern Europe closed markets for Cuban sugar and ended the subsidized petroleum supplies. While ration cards had long been a fact of life, in the early 1990s hunger, again, became a serious problem (Zimbalist and Brundenius 1989: 103-9; Miller 1992: 130-3).

The failure of Caribbean industrialization has driven millions to flee the region in search of a better life. Puerto Ricans, taking advantage of their United States citizenship, have flooded into New York, particularly the South Bronx. New York has also become home to large numbers of Jamaicans, Haitians, and Dominicans, while Cuban refugees have turned Miami into the second largest Cuban city. Shortly before Dutch Guiana became the independent state of Suriname in 1975, nearly 40 percent of the population had migrated to the Netherlands. The human tragedy of such an exodus from the Caribbean is best illustrated by the boatloads of Haitians braving the sea to escape the successive dictatorships and intense poverty of their homeland (Richardson 1989: 203-28).

Transnational Cuisine

The Caribbean people have been relatively slow to adopt the concept of nationalism, either within individual island states or as a pan-Caribbean phenomenon. This has resulted, in part, from the lingering colonial presence of the United States and European powers. Most of the British Antilles did not gain their independence until the 1970s, and foreign rule persisted until recently in the Netherlands Antilles. The Virgin Islands and Puerto Rico are part of the United States, just as Guiana, Guadeloupe, and Martinique are French departments. None of these has achieved the status of an independent nation. The diversity of ethnic origins has likewise impeded the formation of Caribbean nationalism, as even basic definitions of "race" within the region defy easy explanation (Mintz 1974: 315–24). Finally, massive migration, both from the islands to former colonial capitals and among different islands, has diffused the pressure for unifying nationalist ideologies. Yet, for all the regional and ethnic diversity, it is nevertheless possible, as Mintz (1974) has shown, to identify a uniquely Caribbean culture and cuisine.

Of course, the Caribbean traveler could find many different styles of cooking, perhaps the least representative being that served in tourist hotels. A typical menu might include fresh grilled fish, garnished with tropical fruits and washed down with a rum cocktail. But for the majority of the people in the Greater Antilles, seafood has meant salt cod rather than fresh fish. Moreover, hotel restaurants import the majority of their foods; even the tropical fruits often come from Florida. And those "authentic" island recipes, generally, have little real connection with the foods of the common people. Bonham Richardson (1992: 109) noted that visitors "find the mock authenticity of tourist-oriented dinner menus appealing, but they probably would not tolerate the fare consumed by Caribbean working classes."

While tourists seek sanitized versions of local cuisine, the natives have turned in ever-greater numbers to processed foods from the United States and Europe. Each new import, from spaghetti and canned soups to Nescafé and Johnny Walker, gains gourmet status because of its high cost, and poor islanders suffer acute embarrassment if they cannot offer guests a can of Spam (Wilson 1973: 22, 107). The adoption of Western consumption patterns led one Bahamian housewife to declare that she had given up preparing meals because her family "snacks outside continuously" (May and McLellan 1973: 13). Big Macs and Kentucky Fried Chicken have become common on the islands, and even socialist Cuba has succumbed to the lure of pizza parlors. The 1989 opening of the first McDonald's in Barbados saw serious traffic jams as cars lined up to enter the drive-through lane (Kurlansky 1992: 98).

Despite the encroachment of processed foods, however, it is still possible to recognize a peasant-based, pan-Caribbean cuisine. The simultaneous diversity and continuity of this food can be seen in the ubiquitous meal of rice and beans. This combination appears in Spanish-speaking islands as *moros y cristianos* (Moors and Christians), among French dominions as *pois et riz* (beans and rice), and in Jamaica as rice and peas (although it is generally made with dried red beans instead of fresh pigeon peas). Regional variations exist, even within the larger islands. In Cuba, for example, the residents of Havana eat the small black beans of neighboring Yucatán, whereas people in Oriente Province prefer the red beans common to Jamaica and Puerto Rico. Many other methods exist for preparing the staple, rice, among the most extravagant of which are the Haitian favorite *riz au djon-djon* (rice with black mushrooms) and Venezuela's rich, caramel *arroz con coco* (rice with coconut milk). Nevertheless, rice with beans remains the basis of regional cooking (Lambert Ortiz 1986: 258–82; Mintz 1974: 227; Sokolov 1991: 64).

Although relatively expensive compared to such root crops as cassava and yams, beans and rice provide a source of protein that is much cheaper than that from animal products. Neither beans nor rice alone yields a high-quality protein because the former lacks the essential amino acids methionine and cystine, while the latter is deficient in lysine. But together, each offsets the deficiency in the other, creating a complete amino acid chain that allows the body to build tissue efficiently. This nutritional synergism seems all the more fortuitous given that the American bean did not encounter Asian rice until after 1492 (Sanjur 1970: 26).

Similar eclectic combinations abound throughout the Caribbean. Codfish and akee, the national dish of Jamaica, originated with slaves who mixed the salt fish rations provided by planters with the akee fruit, an African domesticate that did not arrive in the island until 1778. Another common dish dating back to the period of slavery is callaloo soup, which takes its name from the leaves of the taro, and also includes okra and salt pork. Tamales, corn confections originally from Mexico, are widely prepared in Cuba, Martinique, and Venezuela. The dish most commonly associated with the French islands of Martinique and Guadeloupe is, ironically, a curry, *le colombo*. Elizabeth Lambert Ortiz (1986: 2) has observed that the identification of a food with a particular island has little to do with the dish's origins because of the wide travels of gifted cooks. It is this constant migration of diverse peoples that has defined the culture and cuisine of the Caribbean.

Jeffrey M. Pilcher

Bibliography

Armstrong, Douglas V. 1990. *The old village and the great house: An archaeological and historical examination of Drax Hall Plantation St. Ann's Bay, Jamaica.* Urbana, Ill.

Bennett, J. Harry. 1958. *Bondsmen and bishops.* Berkeley, Calif.

Cabanillas de Rodríguez, Berta. 1973. *El puertorriqueño y su alimentación a través de su historia (siglos XVI al XIX).* San Juan.

Calderón de la Barca, Fanny. 1966. *Life in Mexico: The letters of Fanny Calderón de la Barca,* ed. Howard T. Fisher and Marion Hall Fisher. Garden City, N.Y.

Crosby, Alfred W., Jr. 1972. *The Columbian exchange: Biological and cultural consequences of 1492.* Westport, Conn.

1986. *Ecological imperialism: The biological expansion of Europe, 900-1900.* Cambridge.

Curtin, Philip D. 1969. *The Atlantic slave trade: A census.* Madison, Wis.

1976. Measuring the African slave trade once again: A comment. *Journal of African History* 17: 595-605.

Dietz, James L. 1986. *Economic history of Puerto Rico: Institutional change and capitalist development.* Princeton, N.J.

Dirks, Robert. 1987. *The Black Saturnalia: Conflict and its ritual expression on British West Indian slave plantations.* Gainesville, Fla.

Dunn, Richard S. 1972. *Sugar and slaves: The rise of the planter class in the English West Indies, 1624-1713.* Chapel Hill, N.C.

Friedman, Gerald C. 1982. The heights of slaves in Trinidad. *Social Science History* 6: 482-515.

Geggus, David. 1991. The major port towns of Saint Domingue in the later eighteenth century. In *Atlantic port cities: Economy, culture, and society in the Atlantic world, 1650-1850,* ed. Franklin W. Knight and Peggy K. Liss, 87-116. Knoxville, Tenn.

González, Nancie L. 1988. *Sojourners of the Caribbean: Ethnogenesis and ethnohistory of the Garifuna.* Urbana, Ill.

Goslinga, Cornelis Ch. 1971. *The Dutch in the Caribbean and on the wild coast, 1580-1680.* Gainesville, Fla.

1985. *The Dutch in the Caribbean and in the Guianas, 1680-1791.* Assen, the Netherlands.

Hall, Gwendolyn Midlo. 1971. *Social control in slave plantation societies: A comparison of St. Domingue and Cuba.* Baltimore, Md.

Handler, Jerome S., Arthur C. Aufderheide, Robert S. Corruccini, et al. 1987. Lead contact and poisoning in Barbados slaves: Historical, chemical, and biological evidence. In *The African exchange: Toward a biological history of black people,* ed. Kenneth F. Kiple, 140-66. Durham, N.C.

Harris, David R. 1965. *Plants, animals, and man in the Outer Leeward Islands, West Indies: An ecological study of Antigua, Barbuda, and Anguilla.* Berkeley, Calif.

Hearn, Lafacadio. 1970. *Two years in the French West Indies.* Upper Saddle River, N.J.

Higman, Barry W. 1976. *Slave population and economy in Jamaica, 1807-1834.* Cambridge.

1979. Growth in Afro-Caribbean slave populations. *American Journal of Physical Anthropology* 50: 373-86.

Hulme, Peter, and Neil L. Whitehead. 1992. *Wild majesty: Encounters with Caribs from Columbus to the present day.* Oxford.

Humboldt, Alexander. 1969. *The island of Cuba.* New York.

Johnson, Howard. 1987. The Chinese in Trinidad in the late nineteenth century. *Ethnic and Racial Studies* 10: 82-95.

Kiple, Kenneth F. 1984. *The Caribbean slave: A biological history.* Cambridge.

Kiple, Kenneth F. ed., 1988. *The African exchange: Toward a biological history.* Durham, N.C.

Kiple, Kenneth F., and Virginia H. Kiple. 1980. Deficiency diseases in the Caribbean. *Journal of Interdisciplinary History* 11: 197-215.

Knight, Franklin W. 1990. *The Caribbean: The genesis of a fragmented nationalism.* Second edition. New York.

Kurlansky, Mark. 1992. *A continent of islands: Searching for the Caribbean destiny.* Reading, Mass.

Labat, Jean Baptiste. 1970. *The memoirs of Père Labat, 1693-1705,* trans. John Eaden. London.

Laguerre, Michel S. 1990. *Urban poverty in the Caribbean: French Martinique as a social laboratory.* New York.

Lambert Ortiz, Elizabeth. 1986. *The complete book of Caribbean cooking.* New York.

Lewicki, Tadeusz. 1974. *West African food in the Middle Ages: According to Arabic sources.* London.

Lipsett-Rivera, Sonya. 1990. Puebla's eighteenth-century agrarian decline: A new perspective. *Hispanic American Historical Review* 70: 463-81.

Liss, Peggy K. 1983. *Atlantic empires: The network of trade and revolution, 1713-1826.* Baltimore, Md.

Look Lai, Walton. 1993. *Indentured labor, Caribbean sugar: Chinese and Indian migrants to the British West Indies, 1838-1918.* Baltimore, Md.

Mackie, Cristine. 1991. *Life and food in the Caribbean.* New York.

May, Jacques M., and Donna L. McLellan. 1973. *The ecology of malnutrition in the Caribbean.* New York.

McNeill, John R. 1985. *Atlantic empires of France and Spain: Louisbourg and Havana, 1700-1763.* Chapel Hill, N.C.

Miller, Tom. 1992. *Trading with the enemy: A yankee travels through Castro's Cuba.* New York.

Milling, Chapman J., ed. 1951. *Colonial South Carolina: Two contemporary descriptions.* Columbia, S.C.

Mintz, Sidney W. 1974. *Caribbean transformations.* Chicago.

1983. Caribbean marketplaces and Caribbean history. *Radical History Review* 27: 110-20.

1985. *Sweetness and power: The place of sugar in modern history.* New York.

Morison, Samuel Eliot. 1942. *Admiral of the Ocean Sea: A life of Christopher Columbus.* Boston, Mass.

1963. *Journals and other documents on the life and voyages of Christopher Columbus.* New York.

Morrissey, Marietta. 1989. *Slave women in the New World: Gender stratification in the Caribbean.* Lawrence, Kans.

Newson, Linda A. 1976. *Aboriginal and Spanish colonial Trinidad: A study in culture contact.* London.

Parry, John H. 1955. Plantation and provision ground: An historical sketch of the introduction of food crops in Jamaica. *Revista de Historia de America* 39: 1-20.

Pérotin-Dumon, Anne. 1991. Cabotage, contraband, and corsairs: The port cities of Guadeloupe and their inhabitants, 1650-1800. In *Atlantic port cities: Economy, culture, and society in the Atlantic world, 1650-1850,* ed. Franklin W. Knight and Peggy K. Liss, 58-86. Knoxville, Tenn.

Quintana, Epaminondas. 1942. El problema dietético del Caribe. *América Indígena* 2: 25-8.

Richardson, Bonham C. 1989. Caribbean migrations, 1838-1985. In *The modern Caribbean,* ed. Franklin W. Knight and Colin A. Palmer, 203-28. Chapel Hill, N.C.

1992. *The Caribbean in the wider world, 1492-1992: A regional geography.* Cambridge.

Ross, Oliver D. 1977. Wheat growing in northern Spain. *North Dakota Quarterly* 45: 61-9.

Sanjur, Diva. 1970. *Puerto Rican food habits: A socio-cultural approach.* Ithaca, N.Y.

Sauer, Carl O. 1966. *The early Spanish Main.* Berkeley, Calif.

Sheridan, Richard B. 1976. The crisis of slave subsistence in the British West Indies during and after the American Revolution. *William and Mary Quarterly* 33: 615-41.

Sokolov, Raymond. 1991. *Why we eat what we eat: How the encounter between the New World and the Old changed the way everyone on the planet eats.* New York.

Stein, Robert L. 1988. *The French sugar business in the eighteenth century.* Baton Rouge, La.

Super, John C. 1988. *Food, conquest, and colonization in six-teenth-century Spanish America.* Albuquerque, N. Mex.

Tinker, Hugh. 1974. *A new system of slavery: The export of Indian labour overseas, 1830-1920.* London.

Tomich, Dale W. 1990. *Slavery in the circuit of sugar: Martinique and the world economy, 1830-1848.* Baltimore, Md.

Vertovec, Steven. 1990. Oil boom and recession in Trinidad Indian villages. In *South Asias overseas: Migration and ethnicity,* ed. Colin Clarke, Colin Peach, and Steven Verotvec, 89-111. Cambridge.

Watson, Andrew M. 1974. The Arab agricultural revolution and its diffusion, 700-1100. *Journal of Economic History* 34: 8-35.

Watts, David. 1987. *The West Indies: Patterns of development, culture and environmental change since 1492.* Cambridge.

Weisskoff, Richard. 1985. *Factories and food stamps: The Puerto Rico model of development.* Baltimore, Md.

Wilson, Peter J. 1973. *Crab antics: The social anthropology of English-speaking Negro societies of the Caribbean.* New Haven, Conn.

Wilson, Thomas W. 1987. Africa, Afro-Americans, and hypertension: An hypothesis. In *The African exchange: Toward a biological history of black people,* ed. Kenneth F. Kiple, 257-68. Durham, N.C.

Zimbalist, Andrew, and Claes Brundenius. 1989. *The Cuban economy: Measurement and analysis of socialist performance.* Baltimore, Md.

V.D.5 ❧ Temperate and Arctic North America to 1492

In writing about the history of food and drink in pre-Columbian North America, one is reminded that for the temperate part of the continent, we are describing cultures primarily known only through archaeological and archival research. Very few native populations survived the events of the past five centuries, and those that did endured considerable cultural modifications. Nonetheless, many of the foods and drinks they used became important legacies to the new North American and global foodways that emerged after 1492, and certainly such foods were critical to the survival of the first European colonists who established permanent communities there.

Perhaps the most important of these were pumpkins, squash, beans, and maize (corn), and although few of these crops were originally domesticated in temperate North America, today they, as well as indigenous cultivation and preparation techniques, continue to be valued.

The practice of mixing maize, beans, and squash in gardens was developed by Native Americans, who also contributed many maize dishes, including hominy, grits and other gruels, breads made with corn flour, corn on the cob, and succotash (Hudson 1976: 498-9). Early North Americans gave sunflowers to the world's economy and contributed to the develop-

ment of modern strawberry, blackberry, raspberry, blueberry, cranberry, hickory, and pecan varieties (Trager 1970: 278-80; Hedrick 1972). Finally, such preservation techniques as drying fruits or vegetables and curing meat by smoking over hickory coals have Native American antecedents (Hudson 1976: 499).

Native North American cuisine is important to scholars for its contribution to knowledge about adaptations to tropical, temperate, and arctic environments. In the sixteenth century, the continent was not occupied by a single people making use of a limited suite of plants and animals. Instead, many different peoples wove the resources of their regions into complex and specialized strategies that were finely adapted to local environmental features.

Subsistence patterns in the northern portion of the continent may be broadly generalized into subarctic and arctic hunting traditions and temperate seed-gathering traditions (Spencer and Jennings 1965: 2). The latter were widespread, forming the basis for farming lifestyles that developed in many areas. A farming tradition was being widely practiced in the temperate eastern sector of the continent and in the Southwest when the first European explorers arrived. The farming traditions of the temperate Eastern Woodlands had a profound impact on the earliest European colonists; indeed, those who survived did so only because they adapted to North American conditions, melding their own foodways with native North American dietary traditions (Reitz and Scarry 1985). In the sixteenth century, the "transplanted Spaniard" either adapted, left the colony, or died.

Because of the importance of Eastern Woodlands farming traditions to sixteenth-century European colonization, this chapter focuses on that region and, for historical depth, traces Mississippian dietary practices from their antecedents in the nonhorticultural Paleo-Indian and Archaic cultures into the horticultural traditions of the Late Archaic and Woodland periods (Table V.D.5.1). It concludes with an examination of the impact of native foodways on sixteenth-century Spanish colonies. Common names are used throughout the text; however, scientific names of plants and animals frequently found in Eastern Woodlands sites are provided in Tables V.D.5.2 and V.D.5.3.

Table V.D.5.1. *General chronological sequence*

Period	Age
Contact	A.D. 1520-1700
Mississippian	A.D. 1000-1520
Late Woodland	A.D. 600-A.D. 1000
Middle Woodland	A.D. 1-A.D. 600
Early Woodland	700 B.C.-A.D. 1
Late Archaic	4000-700 B.C.
Early and Middle Archaic	8000 B.C.-4000 B.C.
Paleo-Indian	?-8000 B.C.

Source: Modified from Steponaitis (1986).

Table V.D.5.2. *List of scientific and common names for plants*

Scientific name	Common name	Scientific name	Common name
Wild fruits and berries		**Roots and tubers**	
Amelanchier spp.	Serviceberry	*Acorus calamus*	Sweet flag
Asimina triloba	Papaw	*Allium cernuum*	Wild onion
Celtis occidentalis	Hackberry	*Allium canadense*	Wild garlic
Crataegus spp.	Hawthorn	*Amphicarpa bracteata*	Hog peanut
Diospyros virginiana	Persimmon	*Apios americana*	Groundnut
Fragaria virginiana	Wild strawberry	*Camassia esculenta*	Wild hyacinth
Gaylussacia spp.	Huckleberry	*Dentaria* spp.	Toothwort
Gleditsia aquatica	Honey locust	*Helianthus tuberosus*	Jerusalem artichoke
Ilex verticilliata	Winterberry	*Ipomoea pandurata*	Wild sweet potato
Malus coronaria	Crabapple	*Medeola virginiana*	Indian cucumber
Morus rubra	Red mulberry	*Nelumbo lutea*	American lotus
Nyssa spp.	Black gum	*Orontium aquaticum*	Golden club
Opuntia spp.	Prickly pear	*Peltandra virginica*	Arrow arum
Passiflora incarnata	Maypop	*Sagittaria* spp.	Arrowhead
Physalis spp.	Groundcherry	*Scirpus validus*	Bulrush
Prunus americana	Plum	*Smilax* spp.	Greenbrier
Prunus serotina	Wild black cherry	*Typha* spp.	Cattail
Rhus spp.	Sumac	*Zamia* spp.	Coontie
Ribes spp.	Gooseberry	**Beverages and condiments**	
Rubus spp.	Blackberry-raspberry	*Acer* spp.	Maple
Sambucus spp.	Elderberry	*Ilex vomitoria*	Yaupon, black drink
Solanum americanum	Black nightshade	*Ilex cassine*	Dahoon holly
Vaccinium spp.	Blueberry	*Lindera* spp.	Spicebush
Viburnum spp.	Blackhaw	*Liquidamber styraciflua*	Sweet gum
Vitis spp.	Wild grape	*Persea borbonia*	Sweet bay
Yucca spp.	Common yucca	*Sassafras albidum*	Sassafras
Nuts		**Eastern Woodland cultivated or domesticated plants**	
Carya glabra	Pignut hickory	*Chenopodium berlandieri* ssp. *jonesianum*	Domestic chenopod
Carya illinoensis	Pecan		
Carya laciniosa	Shellbark hickory	*Cucurbita pepo* ssp. *ovifera* v. *ovifera*	Gourd-squash
Carya ovata	Shagbark hickory		
Carya tomentosa	Mockernut hickory	*Helianthus annuus* v. *macrocarpus*	Domestic sunflower
Castanea dentata	American chestnut		
Castanea pumila	Chinquapin	*Hordeum pusillum*	Little barley
Corylus spp.	Hazelnut	*Iva annua* v. *macrocarpa*	Domestic sumpweed
Fagus spp.	Beechnut	*Lagenaria siceraria*	Bottle gourd
Juglans cinerea	Butternut	*Phalaris caroliniana*	Maygrass
Juglans nigra	Black walnut	*Polygonum erectum*	Erect knotweed
Quercus alba	White oak	**Introduced tropical domesticated plants**	
Quercus coccinea	Scarlet oak	*Amaranthus hypochondriacus*	Pale-seeded amaranth
Quercus macrocarpa	Burr oak	*Capsicum* sp.	Chilli pepper
Quercus prinus	Chestnut oak	*Cucurbita argyrosperma* (formerly *C. mixta*)	Cushaw squash
Quercus rubra	Red oak		
Quercus velutina	Black oak	*Cucurbita pepo* ssp. *pepo*	Pumpkin-marrows
Edible seeds and greens		*Cucurbita moschata*	Moschata squash
Amaranthus spp.	Pigweed	*Phaseolus lunatus*	Lima bean
Ambrosia trifida	Giant ragweed	*Phaseolus vulgaris*	Common bean
Ambrosia cf. *artemisiifolia*	Common ragweed	*Zea mays*	Maize
Arundinaria gigantea	Large cane	**Introduced Old World cultigens**	
Arundinaria tecta	Small cane	*Citrullus vulgaris*	Watermelon
Chenopodium album	Lamb's quarter	*Corylus avellana*	Domestic hazelnut
Chenopodium berlandieri	Goosefoot	*Cucumis melo*	Melon
Echinochloa spp.	Cockspurgrass	*Ficus carica*	Fig
Euphorbia maculata	Spruge	*Pisum sativum*	Common pea
Impatiens spp.	Jewelweed	*Prunus persica*	Peach
Iva ciliata	Marshelder	*Triticum* spp.	Wheat
Leersia oryzoides	Rice cutgrass	*Vigna unguiculata*	Cowpea
Lepidium virginicum	Peppergrass	*Vitis vinifera*	Wine grape
Phaseolus polystachios	Wild bean	**Wild progenitors**	
Phytolacca americana	Pokeweed	*Cucurbita pepo* ssp. *ovifera* v. *texana*	Texas wild gourd
Plantago rugelii	Plantain	*Chenopodium berlandieri*	Wild goosefoot
Portulaca oleracea	Purslane	*Iva annua* v. *annua*	Wild sumpweed
Rumex spp.	Dock	**Fish poisons**	
Sabal palmetto	Cabbage palm	*Aesculus* spp.	Buckeye
Serenoa repens	Saw palmetto	*Tephrosia virginiana*	Devil's shoestring
Strophostyles helvola	Wild bean		
Vicia spp.	Vetch		

Table V.D.5.3. *List of scientific and common names for animals*

Scientific name	Common name	Scientific name	Common name
Crustacea		**Freshwater fishes**	
Penaeus spp.	Shrimp	*Acipenser* spp.	Sturgeon
Callinectes sapidus	Blue crab	*Lepisosteus* spp.	Gar
Menippe mercenaria	Stone crab	*Amia calva*	Bowfin
		Notemigonus crysoleucas	Golden shiner
Freshwater bivalves		*Carpiodes cyprinus*	Quillback
Actinonaias spp.	Mucket	*Catostomus* spp.	Sucker
Amblema spp.	Threeridge	*Ictiobus* spp.	Buffalo
Anodonta spp.	Floater	*Hypentelium* spp.	Hog sucker
Cyclonaias tuberculata	Purple wartyback	*Minytrema melanops*	Spotted sucker
Elliptio spp.	Spike	*Moxostoma* spp.	Redhorse
Fusconaia spp.	Pigtoe	*Ameiurus* spp.	Bullhead catfish
Lampsilis spp.	Mucket	*Ictalurus* spp.	Freshwater catfish
Lasmigona spp.	Heelsplitter	*Noturus* spp.	Madtom
Obovaria spp.	Hickorynut	*Pylodictis olivaris*	Flathead catfish
Pleurobmea spp.	Pigtoe	*Esox* spp.	Pike
Quadrula spp.	Pimpleback	*Exox masquinongy*	Muskellunge
Tritogonia verrucosa	Pistolgrip	*Lepomis* spp.	Sunfish
Uniomerus tetralasmus	Pondhorn	*Micropterus* spp.	Bass
		Pomoxis spp.	Crappie
Marine bivalves		*Perca flavescens*	Yellow perch
Brachidontes spp.	Mussel	*Aplodinotus grunniens*	Freshwater drum
Geukensia demissa	Ribbed mussel		
Anadara spp.	Ark	**Marine fishes**	
Glycymeris spp.	Bittersweet	*Acipenser* spp.	Sturgeon
Agropecten spp.	Scallop	*Albula vulpes*	Bonefish
Crassostrea virginica	Oyster	Clupeidae	Herring
Mactra fragilis	Eastern mactra	*Arius felis*	Hardhead catfish
Donax spp.	Coquina	*Bagre marinus*	Gafftopsail
Tagelus spp.	Tagelus	*Opsanus tau*	Oyster toadfish
Polymesoda carolinana	Marsh clam	*Centropomus* spp.	Snook
Chione spp.	Venus shell	*Morone* spp.	Temperate bass
Mercenaria spp.	Hard clam	*Centropristis* spp.	Sea bass
Protothaca spp.	Venus	*Pomatomus saltatrix*	Bluefish
		Caranx spp.	Jack
Freshwater gastropods		*Chloroscombrus chrysurus*	Atlantic bumper
Campeloma spp.	Campeloma	*Archosargus probatocephalus*	Sheepshead
Pomacea spp.	Applesnail	*Bairdiella chrysoura*	Silver perch
		Cynoscion spp.	Sea trout
Marine gastropods		*Leiostomus xanthurus*	Spot
Littorina irrorata	Periwinkle	*Menticirrhus* spp.	Kingfish
Strombus spp.	Queen conch	*Micropogonias undulatus*	Atlantic croaker
Crepidula spp.	Slipper-shell	*Pogonias cromis*	Black drum
Polinices duplicatus	Shark eye	*Sciaenops ocellatus*	Red drum
Busycon spp.	Whelk	*Mugil* spp.	Mullet
Melongena spp.	Crown conch	*Paralichthys* spp.	Flounder
Ilynassa obsoleta	Mud nassa	*Chilomycterus*	Burrfish
Nassarius spp.	Nassa	*Diodon histrix*	Porcupine fish
Fasciolaria spp.	Tulip shell		
Pleuroploca spp.	Horse conch	**Amphibians**	
		Siren lacertina	Greater siren
Sharks and rays		*Amphiuma means*	Two-toed amphiuma
Ginglymostoma cirratum	Nurse shark	*Rana catesbeiana*	Frog
Odontaspis taurus	Sand tiger shark		
Carcharhinus leucas	Bull shark	**Reptiles**	
Carcharhinus plumbeus	Sandbar shark	*Alligator mississippiensis*	Alligator
Galeocerdo cuvier	Tiger shark	*Chelydra serpentina*	Snapping turtle
Rhizoprionodon terraenovae	Sharpnose shark	*Macroclemys temmincki*	Alligator snapping turtle
Sphyrna mokorran	Great hammerhead shark	*Kinosternon* spp.	Mud turtle
Sphyrna tiburo	Bonnethead shark	*Sternotherus* spp.	Musk turtle
Sphyrna zygaena	Smooth hammerhead	*Chrysemys picta*	Painted turtle
Pristis pectinata	Smalltooth sawfish	*Deirochelys reticularia*	Chicken turtle
Dasyatis spp.	Stingray	*Graptemys* spp.	Map turtle
Aetobatis narinari	Spotted eagle ray	*Pseudemys* spp.	Cooter
Myliobatis spp.	Eagle ray	*Malaclemys terrapin*	Diamondback terrapin
Rhinoptera bonasus	Cownose ray	*Terrapene carolina*	Box turtle

Table V.D.5.3. *(continued)*

Scientific name	Common name	Scientific name	Common name
Trachemys spp.	Slider	*Strix varia*	Barred owl
Gopherus polyphemus	Gopher tortoise	Picidae	Woodpecker
Apalone spp.	Softshell turtle	Corvidae	Crow
Chelonidae	Sea turtle	Muscicapidae	Thrush
Colubridae	Nonpoisonous snake	Mimidae	Thrasher
Viperidae	Poisonous snake		
Birds		**Mammals**	
Gavia immer	Common loon	*Didelphis virginiana*	Opossum
Podilymbus podiceps	Pied-billed grebe	*Sylvilagus* spp.	Rabbit
Phalacrocorax auritus	Cormorant	*Sciurus* spp.	Squirrel
Ardea herodias	Great blue heron	*Tamias striatus*	Chipmunk
Botaurus lentiginosus	American bittern	*Marmota monax*	Woodchuck (groundhog)
Casmerodius albus	Great egret	*Geomys* spp.	Pocket gopher
Egretta tricolor	Tricolored heron	*Spermophilus* spp.	Ground squirrel
Aix sponsa	Wood duck	*Ondatra zibethicus*	Muskrat
Anas spp.	Dabbling duck	*Castor canadensis*	Beaver
Aythya spp.	Diving duck	*Erethizon dorsatum*	Porcupine
Branta canadensis	Canada goose	*Tursiops truncatus*	Bottle-nosed dolphin
Chen caerulescens	Snow goose	*Canis familiaris*	Dog
Cygnus spp.	Swan	*Canis latrens*	Coyote
Lophodytes cucullatus	Hooded merganser	*Canis lupus*	Gray wolf
Oxyura jamaicensis	Ruddy duck	*Urocyon cineroargenteus*	Gray fox
Mergus spp.	Merganser	*Ursus americanus*	Black bear
Spatula clypeata	Shoveler	*Ursus arctos*	Brown bear
Coragyps atratus	Black vulture	*Procyon lotor*	Raccoon
Buteo platypterus	Broad-winged hawk	*Lontra canadensis*	Otter
Colinus virginianus	Quail	*Mephitis mephitis*	Striped skunk
Meleagris gallopavo	Wild turkey	*Mustela frenata*	Long-tailed weasel
Rallus elegans	King rail	*Mustela vision*	Mink
Porzana carolina	Sora	*Spilogale putorius*	Spotted skunk
Fulica americana	Coot	*Taxidea taxus*	Badger
Grus canadensis	Sandhill crane	*Felis rufus*	Bobcat
Charadrius vociferus	Killdeer	*Felis concolor*	Cougar
Catoptrophorus semipalmatus	Willet	*Alces alces*	Moose
Galinago gallinago	Common snipe	*Cervus elaphus*	Elk or wapiti
Laridae	Gull	*Odocoileus virginianus*	White-tailed deer
Ectopistes migratorius	Passenger pigeon	*Rangifer tarandus*	Caribou
Zenaida macroura	Mourning dove	*Bison bison*	Bison or buffalo

Cultivation, Domestication, and Horticulture

Evidence of horticulture is lacking for some areas of the Eastern Woodlands, which may signify either that horticulture was not practiced everywhere or that plant use in some locations is still poorly studied. Likewise, evidence of a domesticated plant variety in one area does not mean that this variety was grown throughout the region at the same time or that it was grown universally at any time.

As Richard Ford (1985a) has observed, the paths from wild to domesticated plants and from foraging to farming were not direct. A continuum exists between the wild and domesticated states, and doubtless plants passed through stages when they were intentionally tended, tilled, transplanted, or sown, but were not fully domesticated (Ford 1985a). Domestication is difficult to demonstrate with archaeological materials unless a phenotypic change can be spied that corresponds with genetic changes reflecting human intervention. Changes in color, for example, are often associated with domestication in both plants and animals, but are not normally found in the archaeological record. "Cultivated" plants are found in the archaeological record – often in large numbers in some deposits – indicating that they were probably intentionally propagated. But morphological changes providing evidence of the domesticated state are not observed (Ford 1985a; Fritz 1990). Plants are considered "domesticated" when archaeological remains reveal those signs of phenotypic alteration that indicate that domestication did take place. A domesticated plant would not normally be found unassociated with humans and, in fact, they often cannot survive without human intervention.

In North America, both cultivated and domesticated plants were grown under horticultural rather than agricultural conditions. Entirely different energy inputs are required by these systems because agriculture involves domestic animals and horticulture does not (Kottak 1987: 269–71). Agricultural techniques must produce adequate calories not only for humans but also for a complex of domestic animals, whereas horticultural production only meets human nutritional needs.

Although domestic crops in the Eastern Woodlands were grown under horticultural conditions, this does not mean that farming was limited to temporary fields or small garden plots. Rather, plants were grown in many large fields (Riley 1987; Woods 1987) that were permanently maintained with digging sticks and hoes, classic horticultural implements, and not with the agricultural plow.

Because cultivation and domestication of plants is achieved gradually, it is unlikely that North American farmers completely abandoned the use of wild foods. Certainly this would have been the case in the Eastern Woodlands, where those proteins, fats, vitamins, and minerals derived from animals could only be obtained through foraging, trapping, hunting, and fishing.

The Eastern Woodlands

Most of temperate North America from the Gulf of Mexico and Atlantic seaboards westward beyond the Great Lakes region is characterized by extensive, mixed-deciduous forests (Map V.D.5.1). The northern boundary of the Eastern Woodlands is defined by a mean annual January temperature of –10° C and the western boundary by a line marking rainfall equal to 80 percent evaporation (Shelford 1974: 17). It is the southern half of the Eastern Woodlands that is most closely associated with the Mississippian tradition of the sixteenth century (Smith 1986). The northern border of the Southeastern Woodlands is around 38° north latitude, roughly corresponding with the farthest glacial advance, which occurred around 16,000 B.C.

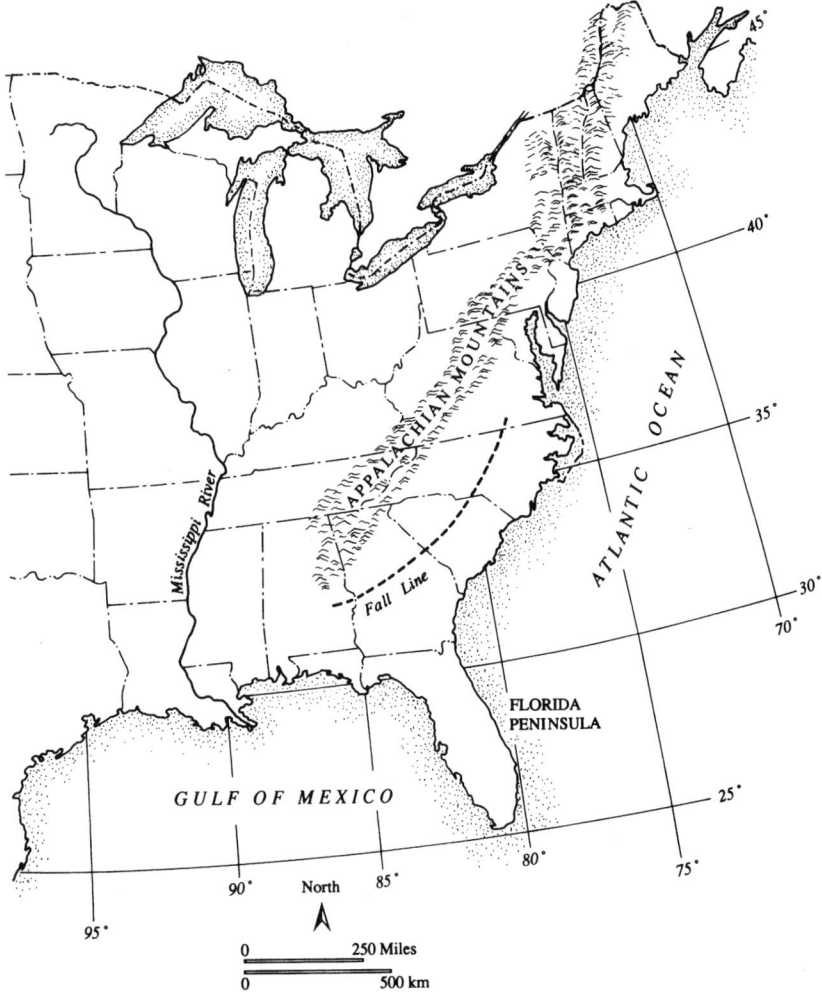

Map V.D.5.1. The Eastern Woodlands.

(Shelford 1974: 19; Delcourt and Delcourt 1981). Winters are relatively short and the growing season long. Annual rainfall varies from 100 to 150 centimeters (cm) and is greatest in the spring and summer, especially along the coasts and in the mountains (Shelford 1974: 56). The Southeastern Woodlands are well watered, with numerous rivers, floodplains, marshes, swamps, and lakes. Systems, such as that associated with the Mississippi River, drain vast portions of the continent. There are many smaller drainage systems throughout the region, particularly along the Atlantic and Gulf coasts.

Climate and vegetation in the Southeast were dynamic in the late Pleistocene and early Holocene (King and Lindsay 1976; Wright 1976; Delcourt and Delcourt 1981, 1983). During the late Pleistocene, the northern portion of the continent was covered by glaciers. At the peak of continental glaciation, about 16,000 B.C., boreal forests of spruce, jack pine, fir, and some deciduous trees covered much of the unglaciated interior plateau, whereas deciduous oaks and hickories mixed with southern pines were found on the coastal plain (Delcourt and Delcourt 1981, 1983; Smith 1986). At the same time, Gulf and Atlantic sea levels were 60 to 130 meters lower than today, and so the coastal plain was considerably broader (Blackwelder, Pilkey, and Howard 1979).

Temperate conditions began to replace boreal ones about 12,000 B.C., and by roughly 8000 B.C., temperate deciduous vegetation dominated most of the region between 34° and 43° north latitude (Delcourt and Delcourt 1981, 1983). South of this area there had generally been little change in vegetation since about 18,000 B.C. About 7000 B.C. the postglacial trend of rising temperatures culminated in a warm, dry period known as the Hypsithermal Interval (Deevey and Flint 1957; Wright 1976). Temperatures began to cool again after about 5000 B.C., and by 3000 B.C., an essentially modern climate prevailed, with forests achieving distributions similar to those of the sixteenth century (Wright 1976; Delcourt and Delcourt 1981). Important additional events at this time were a rise in sea level (with modern sea levels reached about 3000 B.C.) and changes in regional hydrology (Wright 1976: 586; Delcourt et al. 1980; Brooks and Sassaman 1990).

Origins of Mississippian Foodways

Humans probably came to the Eastern Woodlands sometime between 40,000 and 15,000 years ago, first crossing from Asia to North America while the floor of the Bering Strait was exposed by low Pleistocene sea levels (Dincauze 1985; Steponaitis 1986). Prey species important to humans, such as brown bear, moose, elk, white-tailed deer, and bison, had made a similar crossing somewhat earlier (Kurtén and Anderson 1980: 410, 416–17). Caribou probably originated on Beringia itself (Kurtén and Anderson 1980: 315).

Late Pleistocene conditions are associated with what is known in human terms as the Paleo-Indian period (Table V.D.5.1; Smith 1986; Steponaitis 1986). Information about subsistence in the Eastern Woodlands during this time is limited. Most people probably lived in small hunting and gathering bands using an impermanent residential pattern to take advantage of seasonal fluctuations in resources. From the limited evidence available, the foods commonly consumed by Paleo-Indians appear to have included hackberry, blackberry–raspberry, blueberry, hickory, walnut, goosefoot, bivalves, gastropods, fish, turtle, wild turkey, rabbit, squirrel, elk, and white-tailed deer (Adovasio et al. 1978). Although a number of now-extinct Pleistocene animals, such as giant land tortoise, ground sloth, mastodon, mammoth, horse, and tapir, lived in the Eastern Woodlands at this time, few remains have been found in contexts that conclusively prove that extinct animals were hunted by Paleo-Indians (Bullen, Webb, and Waller 1970; Wood and McMillan 1976; Clausen et al. 1979; Graham et al. 1981; Dincauze 1985; Grayson 1991).

Modern geological, climatic, and biological conditions are associated with the Archaic period, which began about 8000 B.C. (Table V.D.5.1). The Early and Middle Archaic periods were characterized by the use of modern animal species by peoples who employed a combination of gathering, hunting, and fishing techniques (Neusius 1986). The *atlatl*, or spear thrower, was used in hunting, whereas netsinkers and fishhooks indicate that fishing was part of the subsistence strategy. Nets could also have been used to capture reptiles, birds, and mammals. Grinding stones suggest that some foods were ground or pulverized.

Evidence for plant use in the Early and Middle Archaic is limited (Byrd and Neuman 1978; Yarnell and Black 1985; Neusius 1986). Seeds of fleshy fruits, such as papaw, hackberry, persimmon, plum, wild black cherry, elderberry, and wild grape, are abundant relative to other seeds throughout the Archaic period. Although walnut and acorn were commonly used in the Archaic, hickory is the most abundant nut found in archaeological deposits (Yarnell and Black 1985). However, Richard Yarnell and Jean Black (1985: 97) argue that in terms of nut food consumed, acorns were the most important plant food in the Southeast until the Mississippian period, at which time they were replaced by maize. Their estimates of dietary contribution suggest that acorns contributed 75 percent of the nut food consumed, whereas hickory nut comprised 20 percent (Yarnell and Black 1985). American chestnut, hazelnut, and beechnut were used in small amounts. Seeds of plants used for greens, such as pokeweed and purslane, are relatively abundant in some Early and Middle Archaic deposits (Yarnell and Black 1985). Some of the starchy-seed plants that later became important as cultivated and domesticated plants, such as goosefoot, may have been used for their leaves rather than for seeds during much of the Archaic period. This would account for their low numbers in Early and Middle Archaic deposits (Bye 1981; Yarnell and Black 1985).

The Late Archaic period is characterized by signs of demographic growth and sedentism in many parts of the Southeast (Steponaitis 1986). Large Late Archaic shell middens are characteristically found along streams and estuaries. There is evidence that residences in some aquatic and estuarine settings may have been multiseasonal, if not year-round (Reitz 1988). Elsewhere, dense midden deposits suggest increased and/or long-term use of specific locations. Large middens, as well as storage pits, indicate a higher degree of sedentism than earlier, although it has been suggested that subterranean storage facilities may indicate concealment of storable foods during periods when villages were abandoned (DeBoer 1988).

Cooking techniques such as stone boiling in baskets and stone bowls had probably been utilized throughout the Archaic period, but clay vessels reflect widespread adoption of food-preparation methods requiring containers that could be placed directly in or over fires and left to simmer unattended for long periods of time. Late Archaic fiber-tempered ceramics from the southeastern Atlantic coast are among the earliest known in the hemisphere (Smith 1986; Steponaitis 1986).

The Late Archaic is marked by changes in the use of plant resources. Nuts continued to be relied upon extensively, but starchy and oily seed use increased (Yarnell and Black 1985; Fritz 1990). Seeds found in large numbers in Late Archaic deposits include ragweed, goosefoot, wild beans, hog peanut, maygrass, and erect knotweed. The relative abundance of seeds from plants used for greens but not for seeds, such as pokeweed and purslane, declined from earlier Archaic levels and remained low until the Mississippian period (Yarnell and Black 1985). Yarnell and Black interpret this as evidence that starchy seeds contributing both greens and seeds, such as goosefoot, may have replaced plants that provided only greens, such as pokeweed and purslane (Yarnell and Black 1985). Seeds from such fruits as hackberry, persimmon, plum, blackberry-raspberry, elderberry, blackhaw, and wild grape are commonly identified in Late Archaic deposits, although the degree to which specific fruits and berries were used varied regionally (Kay, King, and Robinson 1980; Johannessen 1984; Watson 1985). Remains of American lotus at some sites indicate use of aquatic plants.

The Late Archaic is characterized by evidence for plant cultivation and domestication in some midlatitude, interior locations (Asch and Asch 1985; Cowan 1985; King 1985; Watson 1985, 1989; Smith 1989; Fritz 1990). Maygrass was probably a cultivated plant by 2000 B.C. (Cowan 1978; Yarnell and Black 1985). Domestication is first clearly demonstrated for the Eastern Woodlands with the identification of domestic chenopod, sunflower, and sumpweed at some Late

Archaic sites (Yarnell 1969, 1972, 1978; Marquardt 1974; Asch and Asch 1978; Conard et al. 1984; Heiser 1985; Smith 1985b, 1989; Yarnell and Black 1985; Fritz 1990). Important indigenous cultivated and domesticated plants suggest that the development of horticultural traditions in the Eastern Woodlands was not dependent upon introductions from tropical America (Yarnell and Black 1985). The increase in cultivated and domesticated plants is associated with an increase in pollen of species commonly found in disturbed habitats, such as garden plots (Delcourt 1987).

Occasional identifications of gourd-squash indicate the presence of this plant after 5000 B.C. at a few eastern locations, although its status is currently being debated (Ford 1981; Conard et al. 1984; Asch and Asch 1985; King 1985; Decker 1988; Decker and Newsom 1988; Watson 1989; Fritz 1990; Decker-Walters 1993). There is, however, growing evidence for domestication of some varieties of gourd-squash in the Late Archaic Eastern Woodlands (Kay et al. 1980; Ford 1981; Conard et al. 1984; King 1985; Yarnell and Black 1985; Smith 1987b, 1989; Decker 1988; Fritz 1990). Recent work suggests that a native wild plant closely related to the gourd-squash, the Texas wild gourd, was present in North America and might have been the source of domestic gourd-squash found in the Eastern Woodlands (Decker 1988; Smith 1989; Fritz 1990; Decker-Walters 1993). Gourd-squash includes acorn squash, scallop squash, fordhook, crookneck, and most of the ornamental gourds (King 1985), although the gourd-squash found in deposits about 2000 B.C. were probably woody varieties used for containers and oily seeds, rather than the fleshy vegetable found in the sixteenth century (Yarnell and Black 1985; King 1985).

The origin of bottle gourd is also in doubt (Heiser 1989; Smith 1989; Fritz 1990). Very small seeds and thin-walled fragments of bottle gourds found at two Eastern Woodlands deposits, dated between 5350 and 2300 B.C., suggest that they may have been used very early. Remains of bottle gourds that were clearly domesticated are found in contexts that date from around 1300 B.C. or a little before (Smith 1985b; Yarnell and Black 1985; Fritz 1990; Yarnell 1993). It is probable that the recovery of bottle gourd remains from contexts with early dates indicates that this plant reached the Eastern Woodlands serendipitously (Heiser 1989; Fritz 1990), perhaps by floating to the eastern seaboard from tropical America or Africa (Smith 1985b, 1989; Yarnell and Black 1985; Heiser 1989; Fritz 1990). It seems likely that bottle gourds were valued as containers, rather than as food (King 1985).

Although plant use was highly dynamic at the end of the Archaic period, use of animal resources seems to have remained stable at those few locations for which stratigraphic sequences are available. Archaic peoples consumed a broad range of animals, which suggests subsistence strategies making use of the most efficient resources available in a particular setting. In general, animal remains indicate strategies that combined white-tailed deer and a wide range of other species. Other taxa included bivalves and gastropods, gar, bowfin, sucker, catfish, sunfish, freshwater drum, snapping turtle, mud–musk turtle, box turtle, pond turtle, softshell turtle, snakes, opossum, rabbit, squirrel, woodchuck, pocket gopher, muskrat, beaver, black bear, raccoon, badger, and elk (Curren 1974; Stoltman 1974; Parmalee, McMillan, and King 1976; Neusius 1986). In some areas, migratory waterfowl were taken in season, but usually birds other than quail, wild turkey, and passenger pigeon were not a major part of Archaic diets. In coastal settings, this list becomes even more complex, with estuarine mollusks and fishes dominating the diet, whereas mammals, including white-tailed deer, were rarely consumed (Reitz 1988).

The Archaic is followed by the Woodland period, which began about 700 B.C. (Table V.D.5.1). In the Eastern Woodlands, extensive earthworks were constructed during this period; some of these assumed large geometric patterns, although many were conical earthen burial mounds. There were numerous villages of various sizes, of which some were occupied throughout the year. Villages were particularly common at coastal and aquatic settings, from which a complex of wetland, aquatic, and estuarine resources were used. Evidence for regional variation in diets is much stronger for the Woodland period than for the Archaic period, perhaps because more data are available.

During the Woodland period, there was an increase in the cultivation of starchy and oily seed crops and a corresponding decrease in reliance on nuts, although hickory and acorn continued to be important resources (Yarnell and Black 1985). Pawpaw, persimmon, wild strawberry, honey locust, maypop, plum, sumac, blueberry, wild grape, wild beans, and American lotus were also used (Watson 1969: 53; Munson, Parmalee, and Yarnell 1971; Byrd and Neuman 1978; Johannessen 1984; Yarnell and Black 1985; Gardner 1987). Seeds from greens are recovered from archaeological sites in low numbers, and remains of starchy seeds are notably more abundant in Woodland deposits than in Archaic ones (Yarnell and Black 1985).

The energy base for increased sedentism and mound construction in the interior upland areas of the Eastern Woodlands probably came from cultivated and domesticated plants (Yarnell and Black 1985; Fritz 1993). Little barley, maygrass, and erect knotweed were probably cultivated at this time, joining chenopod, sunflower, and sumpweed that had been domesticated in the Late Archaic (Ford 1981; Smith 1985b; Yarnell and Black 1985; Steponaitis 1986). This group of indigenous cultivated and domesticated grains comprises what is known as a starchy seed complex. Little barley and maygrass were summer-maturing starchy seeds, whereas erect knotweed and chenopod

were fall-maturing seeds (Smith 1985a), as were the oily seeds of sunflower and sumpweed. Yarnell (1993) estimates that at one site, starchy and oily seeds contributed as much as 76 percent of the plant foods in the diet, and starchy seeds may comprise as much as 90 percent of the seeds recovered from a Middle Woodland deposit (Yarnell and Black 1985). Domestic gourd–squash and bottle gourd were grown along with food crops in small gardens (Smith 1985b; Yarnell and Black 1985).

Maize is the only domesticated food plant of clearly tropical origin found in Middle Woodland deposits (Fritz 1990). It was introduced to the Eastern Woodlands from Mesoamerica sometime around A.D. 200 (Conard et al. 1984; Chapman and Crites 1987), although isotopic and other studies of human skeletal systems do not show that it was more than a minor component in the diet until many centuries later (Merwe and Vogel 1978; Bender, Baerreis, and Steventon 1981; Boutton et al. 1984; Ambrose 1987). A domesticated tropical pumpkin–marrow variety was introduced from Mesoamerica at the very end of the Woodland period, probably about A.D. 1000 (Smith 1989).

The increase in horticultural activities during the Woodland period is reflected in wood-charcoal and pollen studies in several locations. Late Archaic wood-charcoal assemblages at several sites are dominated by plants associated with floodplains, but in Middle Woodland samples, floodplain species drop to 10 percent of the wood spectrum (Johannessen 1984; Fritz 1990). Trees associated with disturbed habitats, such as pine, red cedar, tulip tree, and giant cane, increase during this same period (Fritz 1993). This evidence indicates that stream-terrace vegetation was cleared for planting (Chapman et al. 1982; Delcourt 1987; Smith 1987a; Fritz 1990). Many of the plant species used in the Eastern Woodlands also thrive in open or disturbed habitats, demonstrating this preference by living as commensal plants around human habitations (Yarnell 1982; Gremillion 1989).

Not all of these plants were grown throughout the Eastern Woodlands, although there is evidence for a Late Archaic–Woodland tradition that featured small starchy seeds in some portions of the region (Smith 1985a; Fritz 1993). One of the intriguing problems is that the starchy seed complex appears to have been of minor importance on the coastal plain. This may be because appropriate recovery techniques have not been used at archaeological sites below the fall line, or it might indicate that an entirely different complex of resources supported communities on the coastal plain and in the lower Mississippi River valley.

Evidence for Woodland animal use is much more abundant than for the Archaic period. It suggests, however, continuity rather than discontinuity in the animals harvested (Munson et al. 1971; Parmalee, Paloumpis, and Wilson 1972; Byrd and Neuman 1978; Springer 1980; Styles 1981; Kelly and Cross 1984;

Reitz, Marrinan, and Scott 1987; Reitz 1988; Reitz and Quitmyer 1988; Styles and Purdue 1991). This is surprising for two reasons. Sometime in the Woodland period, bows and arrows began to be used to hunt animals, augmenting the earlier spears. Additionally, the increased use of cultivated and domesticated plants might have called for an alteration of the strategies used to capture animals due to schedule conflicts or different opportunities to capture garden-raiding species. With more data we may find that subtle, site-specific changes did occur, but at present it would appear that there were no dramatic changes. All of the animals listed in Table V.D.5.3 have been found in most Woodland samples. The Archaic tradition of combining white-tailed deer with many other species continued into the Woodland period. Often those other species were aquatic or estuarine animals, which sometimes were used more frequently than land mammals, including white-tailed deer (Styles 1981; Reitz 1988; Reitz and Quitmyer 1988).

Mississippian Cuisine

Mississippian societies were among the most complex north of Mexico (Table V.D.5.1). The area associated with the Mississippian tradition includes most, although not all, of the Southeastern Woodlands (Smith 1986). It was densely populated in the sixteenth century by farmers who lived in villages organized into complex, hierarchical chiefdoms. The chief was a governing figure who inherited the role (Steponaitis 1986; Welch 1991). Many Mississippian communities had at least one flat-topped pyramidal earthen mound, and some of the larger towns had smaller subsidiary villages affiliated with them.

Chiefs who commanded large numbers of warriors collected tribute from vassal communities. This often took the form of goods, such as ceramic or copper objects, but it included maize, shell beads, bear canines, and deer hides as well (Welch 1991). Mississippian societies were not found universally throughout the Eastern Woodlands, but they had become widespread in the region after A.D. 1000, and in the sixteenth century, it was this lifestyle that was most frequently encountered by European explorers of the Southeast.

Mississippian cuisine included three types of resources: wild plants, wild animals, and cultivated and/or domesticated crops. A representative but incomplete list of some food resources and their scientific names is presented in Tables V.D.5.2 and V.D.5.3.

Wild Plants

Wild fruits, berries, and nuts were widely used in the Southeast (Medsger 1976; Byrd and Neuman 1978; Yarnell and Black 1985). Perhaps the most widely used fruit was persimmon, but many fruits and berries were included in Mississippian diets. In the sixteenth century, Old World watermelons, figs, and

peaches were added to the list. These fruits achieved such rapid acceptance by Native Americans that they preceded European explorers, who often thought them to be indigenous (Hudson 1976: 295). Such nuts as hickory, pecan, black walnut, and a wide variety of acorns were also frequent components of Mississippian meals.

Wild plants added a variety of greens, roots, tubers, and grains to the Mississippian diet. Large cane, wild beans, and vetch were often eaten by Mississippian peoples, depending on availability. Unfortunately, archaeological evidence for greens is limited unless seeds accompanied the leaves to be eaten, as in the case of ragweed. In addition, jewelweed, peppergrass, pokeweed, and purslane provided greens. Many of these plants are now considered weeds and are often found around human habitations, whereas others are abundant in low-lying damp locations, such as river valleys (Medsger 1976). Fungi may have been consumed, but little archaeological evidence survives for their use (Swanton 1946: 244).

Roots and tubers were an important wild resource for Mississippian peoples, although archaeological evidence is extremely rare due to preservation biases. From ethnographic evidence we know that sweet flag, wild onion, wild garlic, hog peanut, groundnut, wild hyacinth, toothwort, Jerusalem artichoke, wild sweet potato, Indian cucumber, greenbrier, and coontie were all used. Many of these plants are found in swamps, on marshy ground, and along lakes and streams (Medsger 1976). Some of the tubers and roots used are actually found in water, including American lotus, golden club, arrow arum, arrowhead, bulrush, and cattail.

Some plants provided condiments, beverages, and oil. Honey locust, maypop, sumac, maple, spicebush, sweet gum, and sweet bay were made into sweeteners and beverages (Hudson 1976: 309; Medsger 1976). Sassafras was used not only as a drink but also to thicken soups (Hudson 1976: 309). One of the most remarked upon drinks was cassina, made from yaupon holly. Yaupon could be made into a simple caffeinated beverage or into "black drink." Black drink had an emetic effect and was important in rituals on the coastal plain (Medsger 1976: 215-16; Hudson 1979; Welch 1991: 113-14). Plants, particularly the nuts, provided oil. Salt was obtained from salt licks as well as through trade with coastal peoples (Swanton 1946: 242, 268, 300-4; Hudson 1976: 316; Muller 1984), and some plants offered salt substitutes (Swanton 1946: 270, 303).

Wild Animals

Although many nutrients associated with plants could be obtained from either wild or cultivated–domesticated plants, sources of meat and animal-derived proteins, fats, minerals, and vitamins were almost entirely wild, with the possible exception of the dog, which may have been consumed in some locations (Hudson

1976: 289–90). Animals may be roughly divided into forest and aquatic–estuarine categories. In some respects this division is an artificial one because many animals that do not actually live in water are found in close proximity to it.

A wide range of forest animals were consumed by Mississippian peoples (Reitz 1982; Kelly and Cross 1984; Reitz et al. 1987; Carder 1989). Land resources often overlooked in discussions of Mississippian diets include box turtle, gopher tortoise, and snake. Quail, wild turkey, passenger pigeon, mourning dove, and a variety of small song birds were also sometimes included in Mississippian diets. Likewise, such mammals as opossum, rabbit, squirrel, woodchuck, black bear, raccoon, elk, and white-tailed deer were widely consumed.

Many Mississippian sites are found on river floodplains and bottomlands, and so it is not surprising that numerous aquatic animals were used by Mississippian peoples (Springer 1980; Hale 1984; Carder 1989). Where freshwater bivalves and gastropods were eaten, they accumulated into very large middens. However, the nutritional contribution of mollusks is uncertain (Parmalee and Klippel 1974).

Remains of fish are abundant in many deposits. In freshwater settings, fish may include gar, bowfin, sucker, catfish, pike, sunfish, and drum. Amphibians are not frequently found in Mississippian deposits, but sirens, amphiuma, and frogs were clearly eaten in some communities. A wide range of reptiles, including alligator, snapping turtle, mud turtle, musk turtle, map turtle, cooter, slider, softshell turtle, and snakes, were used. Wetland birds were used in large numbers only at sites located along important migration routes. At such sites heron, duck, and geese were consumed. In addition to these resources, such aquatic mammals as muskrat, beaver, and otter were eaten.

Coastal sites with access to estuarine settings form a special case. Archaeological evidence for use of a wide range of animal resources is abundant. This array includes crustacea, bivalves, gastropods, sharks, rays, and bony fish. Turtles were commonly consumed, particularly those found only in estuarine settings, such as diamondback terrapin. Evidence for use of sea turtle meat or eggs is very limited, as is evidence for widespread use of birds and land mammals. Remains of white-tailed deer, for example, are often nonexistent at coastal Mississippian sites (Reitz 1985, 1988; Reitz and Quitmyer 1988). Mammals restricted to marine settings, such as dolphins and manatees, were occasionally eaten, but at most villages they were probably not commonly used.

Cultivated and Domesticated Crops

Farming was a key Mississippian subsistence activity. Cultivated crops included little barley, maygrass, and erect knotweed, whereas domesticated ones included chenopod, gourd–squash, sunflower, sumpweed, and bottle gourd (Yarnell and Black 1985;

Steponaitis 1986; Fritz 1990). All were indigenous to the Eastern Woodlands, and in some communities starchy seeds contributed an average of 78 percent of the total identifiable seeds (Johannessen 1984). Although none of these plants individually constituted a complete protein source, their nutritional value was quite high and, when combined with other plants, would have provided a complete protein (Asch and Asch 1978; Cowan 1978; Crites and Terry 1984; King 1985). Maygrass is higher in protein than the other starchy seeds and is similar in protein density to fish (Crites and Terry 1984), although like all plants, it is inadequate in at least one essential amino acid (Asch and Asch 1978; Crites and Terry 1984). Sumpweed and sunflower seeds have a high oil content, with sunflower seeds yielding 20 percent oil (Medsger 1976). Chenopod, little barley, maygrass, and erect knotweed are high in carbohydrates (Crites and Terry 1984).

The domestic plants considered most characteristic of Mississippian diets, however, were introduced from tropical America. These included pale-seeded amaranth, pumpkin–marrow, the common bean, and maize (Fritz 1984; Yarnell and Black 1985). Tropical plants were introduced to the Eastern Woodlands just prior to or during the Early Mississippian period, but as already mentioned, maize was a minor crop throughout the Southeast for several centuries and only became important in most areas sometime between A.D. 800 and 1100 (Fritz 1990). At some sixteenth-century Mississippian sites, maize was clearly the most significant domesticated plant and had already become far more important than indigenous cultivated or domesticated plants. But at other sites, starchy seeds continued to be more abundant than maize (Scarry 1993a). The tropical common bean may have been added to the Mississippian diet as late as the 1400s (Fritz 1990).

Very little is known about either wild or domestic plant use by Mississippian peoples living in coastal settings. Although there have been lengthy discussions about the role of maize in coastal Mississippian economies, there has been little archaeological evidence of its importance (Yarnell and Black 1985; Reitz 1988, 1990).

Food Procurement Technology

The combination of wild fruits, nuts, tubers, seeds, and animals with maize and other crops provided a solid subsistence base characteristic of the Mississippian period. Such a base could have been exploited in a number of different ways to produce a surplus for storage and exchange. Many cultivated and domesticated crops were grown together in large, permanent fields, as well as in smaller gardens on river terraces (Swanton 1946: 304–10; Hudson 1976: 290–1; Smith 1985b; Riley 1987; Woods 1987).

Mississippian peoples living near large population centers appear not to have engaged in slash-and-burn or swidden cultivation, although people living in smaller communities may have done so. In some places, raised fields were constructed to improve drainage (Riley 1987; Woods 1987). The primary horticultural implements used were stone and bone hoes, stone axes, and digging sticks. Horticultural activities were largely the domain of women, although men participated in the initial clearing of the fields (Hudson 1976: 295).

Numerous techniques were used to acquire wild resources (Swanton 1946: 265-304, 310-44; Hudson 1976: 272-88), with many of these so sufficiently generalized that they could be applied to the acquisition of more than one resource. Wild berries, nuts, seeds, and tubers were gathered with the aid of beaters, skin bags, baskets, and digging sticks. Similar techniques and tools could have been used to collect most of the mollusks. Fish may have been captured using trotlines, gorges, spears, nets, weirs, and traps, and there is some evidence for the use of fish poisons (Swanton 1946: 246-7, 332-44; Rostlund 1952: 127-33). The latter are most effective in quiet waters, and many of the fish found in Mississippian sites are common in calm aquatic locations.

Fish were also caught with handlines or speared (Rostlund 1952: 113-26), and trotlines and traps would have been ideal for capturing aquatic turtles and mammals. Sirens, frogs, and snakes might also have been caught with such devices, and traps of various kinds, decoys, and snares would also have been useful for capturing most land animals (Swanton 1946: 328-32). Indeed, although larger animals, such as elk and white-tailed deer, could be hunted using spears, clubs, blowguns, and bows and arrows, traps and snares would have been considerably more efficient.

A particularly useful hunting strategy would have involved the careful visiting of gardens and fields each morning and evening in order to surprise garden-raiding animals (Linares 1976). Many of the birds and mammals commonly consumed by Mississippian peoples are attracted to crops, so that traps set in or near fields should have been productive. Hunting at night with torches would also have been effective, and communal surround drives were employed in some areas in the Southeast (Swanton 1946: 313; Hudson 1976: 275-6). Mississippian peoples may have burned forest underbrush in order to improve the growth of vegetation preferred by white-tailed deer. At the same time, this would have made more abundant the nuts and other plants that prefer open habitat (Yarnell 1982).

Foods were prepared in a number of ways (Swanton 1946: 351-72; Hudson 1976: 300). In addition to being consumed fresh, fruits, nuts, seeds, greens, roots, tubers, and meats were preserved by drying either through simple exposure to sun and air or by smoking. Mortar and pestle were employed to pulverize or grind foods to ready them for preservation, as well as for immediate consumption (Hudson 1976: 301, 307).

Maize was consumed in many forms. In addition to use as a vegetable (such as roasted "corn-on-the-cob"), it was treated with wood-ash lye and made into hominy. The lye treatment increases the amounts of the amino acid lysine and of the vitamin niacin available from maize (Katz, Hediger, and Valleroy 1974). From hominy, a number of maize dishes were made (Hudson 1976: 305). Hominy might be eaten whole or ground into flour for breads that were fried, boiled, or baked. In addition, maize was often combined with other foods, such as nuts and beans. Combinations of beans and maize were particularly common and are nutritionally interesting because each plant complements the limiting amino acids in the other, so that together they provide a complete protein source (Katz, Hediger, and Valleroy 1974).

Elsewhere in North America

Not all of the peoples living in North America in the sixteenth century were farmers. Two of the most distinct examples of nonhorticultural foodways were to be found on the Northwest Coast and in the Arctic. Although both of these areas had early contact with Europeans, it is probably significant that this contact was largely intermittent and did not lead to permanent sixteenth-century European settlements, such as those that developed on the Atlantic coast.

The Northwest Coast is a long, narrow area stretching along the Pacific coast of North America from, roughly, 60° to 42° north latitude. It has a relatively mild climate but a rugged topography and a temperate rain forest that is broken at frequent intervals by streams used by anadromous fish, especially members of the salmon family. The area is well known for its large sedentary villages, elaborate woodworking skills, and complex social organization supported without horticultural input (Stewart 1977; Isaac 1988; Suttles 1990b).

In large part, the reason for the lack of horticulture was a well-developed marine fishery, especially one associated with the vast, but highly seasonal, salmon runs into coastal rivers. Salmon, surf perch, rockfish, greenling, lingcod, sculpin, red Irish lord, and many other fish were the source of most of the meat in the diet (Mitchell 1988; Wessen 1988; Wigen and Stucki 1988; Suttles 1990b). But whales, porpoises, harbor and fur seals, sea lions, and sea otters were also consumed. Many of these mammals were high in fat, and a smelt, known as eulachon, provided an edible oil. Mussels and clams were taken from the marine environment, as was a wide range of ducks and other birds.

Freshwater fish and mammals, such as beaver and otter, were frequently eaten, although gastropods and bivalves were apparently seldom used in most areas. Land mammals, such as bear, raccoon, elk, deer, and caribou, were consumed, but not as commonly as marine resources. Inasmuch as many of these animals were only abundant seasonally, preservation techniques, including drying and smoking and the liberal use of oil as a preservative, were well developed.

Such an elaborate marine fishery has often obscured the fact that plants gathered but not cultivated played an important role in the diet (Spencer and Jennings 1965; Suttles 1990a). Many species of fruits and berries were consumed, including salmonberry, gooseberry, currant, red elderberry, huckleberry, salal, and cranberry (Suttles 1990a). These were dried and combined with oil and fish to form pemmican. Rhizomes, such as bracken, sword fern, lady fern, spiny wood fern, male fern, and licorice fern, were consumed, and rice-root lily, chocolate lily, camas, tiger lily, wild onion, fawn lily, wild hyacinth, and a tuber known as wapato were also eaten. Several marine algae were part of the diet, as was the edible cambium of spruce, pine, hemlock, alder, and cottonwood bark; tree lichen; and, in some locations, mushrooms (Suttles 1990a). Nuts were also consumed, but seeds were not widely used (Suttles 1990a).

In sharp contrast to the foodways of the Northwest Coast and the Eastern Woodlands were the Arctic hunting traditions developed in the far north of the continent by Eskimos, or Inuits (Damas 1984b). The southern boundary of the Arctic roughly corresponds with the tree line, where the boreal forest ends and the northern treeless region, or tundra, begins. This also marks the distribution of prey species significant in the hunting strategies practiced in the Arctic region (Damas 1984a: 1).

Both plant and animal resources have been limited in the Arctic, and prior to the sixteenth century, most peoples there specialized in a maritime strategy that focused on whales, walrus, and seals. But many also hunted hares, ground squirrels, and especially caribou, along with the flesh and the eggs of ducks, geese, sea birds, and ptarmigans. Fishing and mollusk gathering were also important activities. Since many of these resources were highly mobile, as well as markedly seasonal, Arctic peoples adapted their settlement patterns to correspond with the seasonal cycle of animals important to their diets. This unique inventory of animals was hunted with a highly complex technology (Balikci 1984).

Until recently, the Arctic diet was distinctive for its low content of plant resources, which meant little in the way of carbohydrates. In the absence of plant carbohydrates, humans can utilize protein only in the presence of fat; and an important characteristic of many of the animals consumed in the Arctic region was their high fat content (Freeman 1984: 45). Nonetheless, several plant foods were consumed in season. These included salmonberry, cranberry, crowberry, blueberry, cow parsnip, a lily bulb, licorice root, willow leaves, sourdock, cowslip, anemone greens,

parsnip, and kelp and other algae (Lantis 1984: 176; Ray 1984: 289).

Native Foodways and European Colonies

The first Europeans to maintain a permanent presence in temperate North America were the Spaniards. The Spanish colony of La Florida, which encompassed a portion of the Atlantic coastal plain and the Florida peninsula, was established in 1565 and lasted for 200 years. Unfortunately, very little archival evidence is available for Spanish diets in the Southeast during the sixteenth century. We do know that supply lines to La Florida were unsatisfactory and subject to interruptions. Natural disasters and attacks by a variety of human foes contributed to the unreliability of imported staples, munitions, and other supplies. Disease and other natural disasters further hampered efforts to develop the colony. In the records that are available, Spanish governors complained bitterly of starvation and of eating unwholesome foods. If we are to believe the official correspondence, sixteenth-century St. Augustinians, at the least, had very little to eat, and sometimes subsisted on extremely unpalatable foods, or even nonfoods.

Data on plant and animal use recovered from archaeological sites in Florida indicate, however, that complaints of food shortages in the colony were probably exaggerated (Reitz and Scarry 1985). This is not to deny that food might have been scarce occasionally. But there is nothing in the archaeological record to suggest that starvation of the sort reported by some Spanish governors was a common phenomenon or that inedible, nonnutritious resources were consumed often enough to become noteworthy.

Rather, what we have is evidence that the colonists adapted to North American conditions and blended their own foodways with native North American dietary traditions (Reitz and Scarry 1985). During the first few years of colonization, the plant and animal foods consumed by Spaniards and Native Americans were very similar (Reitz 1985; Scarry and Reitz 1990).

Domesticated and wild plants employed by indigenous Native Americans dominated the list of plants consumed by Spaniards in the sixteenth century (Reitz and Scarry 1985; Scarry and Reitz 1990). Squash, sunflower, beans, and maize comprised about half of the vegetable part of the diet, with nuts and wild fruits making up an additional third. The primary Old World domesticated crops in the diet were watermelon, melon, and peach (Reitz and Scarry 1985: 56). Efforts to grow wheat were generally unsuccessful. It is interesting to note that indigenous New World domesticated crops, such as chilli peppers, moschata squash, and lima beans, previously unknown in La Florida, were apparently imported from Mesoamerica by the Spaniards.

Sea and land animals used by Spaniards in the sixteenth century were mostly wild (Reitz and Scarry

1985; Scarry and Reitz 1990). Over a third of their meat came from sharks, rays, and bony fishes, with the most common the hardhead and gafftopsail catfish, sheepshead, Atlantic croaker, black drum, red drum, and mullet. A wide range of reptiles, including sea turtles, entered the diet, but predominating were the estuarine diamondback terrapin and freshwater turtles, such as the cooter and slider. Ducks, Canada geese, and turkeys were the most important of the wild birds that were harvested. Although opossum, rabbit, squirrel, and raccoon found their way to Spanish tables, deer and gopher tortoise were generally the most prevalent wild land animals. Domestic animals contributed less than half of the meat consumed by Spaniards: Beef was probably more common in the diet than either pork or chicken (the only domesticated bird); sheep and goats were very rare.

Archaeological data indicate that the Spaniards combined Eurasian and American foods into a locally viable cuisine, but like the Native Americans, Spaniards were heavily dependent upon indigenous crops and wild animals. To this complex of local resources they brought some Eurasian plants and animals that could do well on the coastal plain. In terms of animal resources, this strategy continued with little modification until the end of Spanish governance in the eighteenth century (Reitz and Cumbaa 1983).

Conclusion

A study of native North American subsistence strategies is important for the contribution it can make to our knowledge of foodways in temperate environments and for an understanding of the importance that such strategies had for European colonists. A survey of food and drink in North America shows that Native Americans employed the resources available to them in complex and specialized ways. The foodways of the Eastern Woodlands combined a wide range of wild, cultivated, and domesticated plants and many different wild animals into a mixed subsistence strategy. The resources used were primarily low-cost, calorically productive ones acquired from nearby fields, forests, and waterways. The archaeological record of the Eastern Woodlands suggests that patterns established in the Archaic continued with subtle modifications into the Mississippian period and even into the early years of European expansion. Over time, however, subsistence strategies came to include an increasingly diverse complex of crops and wild resources. The most significant changes that took place in foodways in the Eastern Woodlands were the development of indigenous cultivated and domesticated crops and the eventual addition of tropical cultigens to local farming traditions. These changes resulted in a cuisine that supported large numbers of people with complex political and economic systems.

The native foodways of the Eastern Woodlands had a profound impact on sixteenth-century Spanish colonists, who benefited from the well-established mixed economy practiced in the region. They altered indigenous practices primarily through the introduction of domestic animals and by adding a few of their plants to augment a diet based on American crops. Not only did this interchange enable European colonial efforts to succeed but it also ensured that many of the foods and drinks used by native North Americans would survive to be included in North American and global foodways in the twentieth century.

Elizabeth J. Reitz

I am grateful to Gayle J. Fritz, David R. Huelsbeck, and C. Margaret Scarry for their assistance in the preparation of this chapter. I am particularly pleased that Dr. Scarry was willing to share with me the text of the book she was editing while it was still in manuscript form. Errors in interpretation, however, are my own.

Bibliography

Adovasio, J. M., J. D. Gunn, J. Donahue, and R. Stuckenrath. 1978. Meadowcroft rockshelter, 1977: An overview. *American Antiquity* 43: 632–51.

Ambrose, Stanley H. 1987. Chemical and isotopic techniques of diet reconstruction in eastern North America. In *Emergent horticultural economies of the Eastern Woodlands,* ed. W. Keegan, Southern Illinois University, Center for Archaeological Investigations, Occasional Papers No. 7, 87–107. Carbondale.

Asch, David L., and Nancy B. Asch. 1978. The economic potential of *Iva annua* and its prehistoric importance in the lower Illinois Valley. In *The nature and status of ethnobotany,* ed. R. I. Ford, University of Michigan, Museum of Anthropology, Anthropological Papers No. 67, 300–41. Ann Arbor, Mich.

1985. Prehistoric plant cultivation in west-central Illinois. In *Prehistoric food production in North America,* ed. R. I. Ford, University of Michigan, Museum of Anthropology, Anthropological Papers No. 75, 149–203. Ann Arbor, Mich.

Balikci, Asen. 1984. Netsilik. In *Handbook of North American Indians: Arctic,* Vol. 5, ed. D. Damas, 415–30. Washington, D.C.

Bender, Margaret M., D. A. Baerreis, and R. L. Steventon. 1981. Further light on carbon isotopes and Hopewell agriculture. *American Antiquity* 46: 346–53.

Blackwelder, Blake W., Orrin H. Pilkey, and James D. Howard. 1979. Late Wisconsinan sea levels on the southeast U.S. Atlantic shelf based on in-place shoreline indicators. *Science* 204: 618–20.

Boutton, T. W., P. D. Klein, M. J. Lynott, et al. 1984. Stable carbon isotope ratios as indicators of prehistoric human diet. In *Stable isotopes in nutrition,* ed. J. R. Turnland and P. E. Johnson, *American Chemical Society Symposium Series* No. 258, 191–204.

Boyd, Donna C., and C. Clifford Boyd. 1989. A comparison of Tennessee Archaic and Mississippian maximum femoral lengths and midshaft diameters: Subsistence change and postcranial variability. *Southeastern Archaeology* 8: 107–16.

Bridges, Patricia. 1989. Changes in activities with the shift in agriculture in the southeastern United States. *Current Anthropology* 30: 385–94.

Brooks, Mark J., and Kenneth E. Sassaman. 1990. Point bar geoarchaeology in the upper coastal plain of the Savannah River Valley, South Carolina: A case study. In *Archaeological geology of North America,* ed. N. P. Lasca and J. Donahue, Geological Society of America Centennial Special Vol. 4, 183-97. Boulder, Colo.

Buikstra, Jane E., J. Bullington, D. K. Charles, et al. 1987. Diet, demography, and the development of horticulture. In *Emergent horticultural economies of the Eastern Woodlands,* ed. W. Keegan, Southern Illinois University, Center for Archaeological Investigations, Occasional Papers No. 7, 67-85. Carbondale.

Bullen, Ripley P., S. D. Webb, and B. I. Waller. 1970. A worked mammoth bone from Florida. *American Antiquity* 35: 203-5.

Bye, Robert A., Jr. 1981. Quelites - ethnoecology of edible greens - past, present, and future. *Journal of Ethnobiology* 1: 109-23.

Byrd, Kathleen M., and Robert W. Neuman. 1978. Archaeological data relative to prehistoric subsistence in the lower Mississippi River alluvial valley. *Geoscience and Man* 19: 9-21.

Carder, Nanny. 1989. Faunal remains from Mixon's Hammock, Okefenokee Swamp. *Southeastern Archaeology* 8: 19-30.

Chapman, Jefferson, and Gary Crites. 1987. Evidence for early maize *(Zea mays)* from the Icehouse Bottom site, Tennessee. *American Antiquity* 52: 352-4.

Chapman, Jefferson, Paul A. Delcourt, Patricia A. Cridlebaugh, et al. 1982. Man-land interaction: 10,000 years of American Indian impact on native ecosystems in the lower Little Tennessee River Valley, eastern Tennessee. *Southeastern Archaeology* 1: 115-21.

Clausen, Carl J., A. D. Cohen, C. Emiliani, et al. 1979. Little Salt Spring, Florida: A unique underwater site. *Science* 203: 609-14.

Conard, N., D. L. Asch, N. B. Asch, et al. 1984. Accelerator radiocarbon dating of evidence for prehistoric horticulture in Illinois. *Nature* 308: 443-6.

Cowan, C. Wesley. 1978. The prehistoric use and distribution of maygrass in eastern North America: Cultural and phytogeographical implications. In *The nature and status of ethnobotany,* ed. R. I. Ford, University of Michigan, Museum of Anthropology, Anthropological Papers No. 67, 263-88. Ann Arbor.

1985. Understanding the evolution of plant husbandry in eastern North America: Lessons from botany, ethnography, and archaeology. In *Prehistoric food production in North America,* ed. R. I. Ford, University of Michigan, Museum of Anthropology, Anthropological Papers No. 75, 205-43. Ann Arbor.

Crites, Gary D., and R. Dale Terry. 1984. Nutritive value of maygrass, *Phalaris caroliniana. Economic Botany* 38: 114-20.

Crosby, Alfred W., Jr. 1972. *The Columbian exchange: Biological and cultural consequences of 1492.* Westport, Conn.

Curren, Cailup B. 1974. An ethnozoological analysis of the vertebrate remains of the Little Bear Creek site (1 Ct° 8). *Journal of Alabama Archaeology* 20: 127-82.

Damas, David. 1984a. Introduction. In *Handbook of North American Indians: Arctic,* Vol. 5, ed. D. Damas, 1-7. Washington, D.C.

Damas, David, ed. 1984b. *Handbook of North American Indians: Arctic,* Vol. 5. Washington, D.C.

DeBoer, Warren R. 1988. Subterranean storage and the organization of surplus: The view from eastern North America. *Southeastern Archaeology* 7: 1-20.

Decker, Deena S. 1988. Origin(s), evolution, and systematics of *Cucurbita pepo* (Cucurbitaceae). *Economic Botany* 42: 3-15.

Decker, Deena S., and Lee A. Newsom. 1988. Numerical analysis of archaeological *Cucurbita pepo* seeds from Hontoon Island, Florida. *Journal of Ethnobiology* 8: 35-44.

Decker-Walters, Deena S. 1993. New methods for studying the origins of New World domesticates: The squash example. In *Foraging and farming in the Eastern Woodlands,* ed. C. M. Scarry, 91-7. Gainesville, Fla.

Deevey, Edward S., Jr., and R. F. Flint. 1957. Postglacial hypsithermal interval. *Science* 125: 182-4.

Delcourt, Helen R. 1987. The impact of prehistoric agriculture and land occupation on natural vegetation. *Trends in Ecology and Evolution* 2: 39-44.

Delcourt, Paul A., and H. R. Delcourt. 1981. Vegetation maps for eastern North America, 40,000 Yr B.P. to the present. In *Geobotany II,* ed. R. C. Romans, 123-65. New York.

1983. Late Quaternary vegetational dynamics and community stability reconsidered. *Quaternary Research* 19: 265-71.

Delcourt, Paul A., H. R. Delcourt, R. C. Brister, and L. E. Lackey. 1980. Quaternary vegetation history of the Mississippi embayment. *Quaternary Research* 13: 111-32.

Dincauze, Dena F. 1985. An archaeological evaluation of the case for pre-Clovis occupations. *Advances in World Archaeology* 3: 275-323.

Ford, Richard I. 1981. Gardening and farming before A.D. 1000: Patterns of prehistoric cultivation north of Mexico. *Journal of Ethnobiology* 1: 6-27.

1985a. The processes of plant food production in prehistoric North America. In *The nature and status of ethnobotany,* ed. R. I. Ford, Museum of Anthropology, University of Michigan, Anthropological Papers No. 67, 1-18. Ann Arbor.

Ford, Richard I., ed. 1978. *The nature and status of ethnobotany.* Museum of Anthropology, University of Michigan, Anthropological Papers No. 67. Ann Arbor.

1985b. *Prehistoric food production in North America.* Museum of Anthropology, University of Michigan, Anthropological Papers No. 75. Ann Arbor.

Freeman, Milton M. R. 1984. Arctic ecosystems. In *Handbook of North American Indians: Arctic,* Vol. 5, ed. D. Damas, 36-48. Washington, D.C.

Fritz, Gayle J. 1984. Identification of cultigen amaranth and chenopod from rockshelter sites in northwest Arkansas. *American Antiquity* 49: 558-72.

1990. Multiple pathways to farming in precontact eastern North America. *Journal of World Prehistory* 4: 387-435.

1993. Early and Middle Woodland period paleoethnobotany. In *Foraging and farming in the Eastern Woodlands,* ed. C. M. Scarry, 39-56. Gainesville, Fla.

Gardner, Paul S. 1987. New evidence concerning the chronology and paleoethnobotany of Salts Cave, Kentucky. *American Antiquity* 52: 358-67.

Gilbert, Robert I., Jr., and James H. Mielke, eds. 1985. *The analysis of prehistoric diets.* Orlando, Fla.

Gill, Steven J. 1983. *Plant utilization by the Makah and Ozette people, Olympic Peninsula, Washington.* Pullman, Wash.

Graham, R. W., C. V. Haynes, D. L. Johnson, and M. Kay. 1981. Kimmswick: A Clovis-Mastodon association in eastern Missouri. *Science* 213: 1115-17.

Grayson, Donald K. 1984. *Quantitative zooarchaeology: Top-*

ics in the analysis of archaeological faunas. Orlando, Fla.

1991. Late Pleistocene mammalian extinctions in North America: Taxonomy, chronology, and explanations. *Journal of World Prehistory* 5: 193-231.

Gremillion, Kristen Johnson. 1989. The development of a mutualistic relationship between humans and maypops (*Passiflora incarnata* L.) in the southeastern United States. *Journal of Ethnobiology* 9: 135-55.

Hale, H. Stephen. 1984. Prehistoric environmental exploitation around Lake Okeechobee. *Southeastern Archaeology* 3: 173-87.

Hastorf, Christine, and Virginia S. Popper, eds. 1988. *Current paleoethnobotany: Analytical methods and cultural interpretations of archaeological plant remains.* Chicago.

Hedrick, U. P., ed. 1972. *Sturtevant's edible plants of the world.* Reprint, New York.

Heiser, Charles B., Jr. 1985. Some botanical considerations of the early domesticated plants north of Mexico. In *Prehistoric food production in North America,* ed. R. I. Ford, University of Michigan, Museum of Anthropology, Anthropological Papers No. 75, 57-72. Ann Arbor, Mich.

1989. Domestication of Cucurbitaceae: *Cucurbita* and *Lagenaria.* In *Foraging and farming: The evolution of plant exploitation,* ed. D. Harris and G. Hillman, 471-80. London.

Hudson, Charles M. 1976. *The southeastern Indians.* Knoxville, Tenn.

Hudson, Charles M., ed. 1979. *Black drink: A Native American tea.* Athens, Ga.

Isaac, Barry L., ed. 1988. *Research in economic anthropology: Prehistoric economies of the Pacific Northwest Coast.* Greenwich, Conn.

Johannessen, Sissel. 1984. Paleoethnobotany. In *American Bottom archaeology,* ed. C. Bareis and N. Porter, 197-214. Urbana, Ill.

Johnson, A. Sidney, H. O. Hillestad, S. F. Shanholtzer, and G. F. Shanholtzer. 1974. *An ecological survey of the coastal region of Georgia.* National Park Service, Scientific Monograph Series No. 3. Washington, D.C.

Katz, S. H., M. L. Hediger, and L. A. Valleroy. 1974. Traditional maize processing techniques in the New World. *Science* 184: 765-73.

Kay, J., F. B. King, and C. K. Robinson. 1980. Cucurbits from Phillips Spring: New evidence and interpretations. *American Antiquity* 45: 806-22.

Keegan, William F., ed. 1987. *Emergent horticultural economies of the Eastern Woodlands.* Southern Illinois University, Center for Archaeological Investigations, Occasional Papers No. 7. Carbondale.

Kelly, Lucretia S., and Paula G. Cross. 1984. Zooarchaeology. In *American Bottom archaeology,* ed. C. J. Bareis and J. W. Porter, 215-32. Urbana, Ill.

King, Frances B. 1985. Early cultivated cucurbits in eastern North America. In *Prehistoric food production in North America,* ed. R. I. Ford, University of Michigan, Museum of Anthropology, Anthropological Papers No. 75, 73-97. Ann Arbor.

King, James E., and Everett H. Lindsay. 1976. Late Quaternary biotic records from spring deposits in western Missouri. In *Prehistoric man and his environments: A case study in the Ozark highland,* ed. W. R. Wood and R. B. McMillan, 63-78. New York.

Kottak, Conrad Phillip. 1987. *Anthropology: The exploration of human diversity.* New York.

Kurtén, Bjorn, and Elaine Anderson. 1980. *Pleistocene mammals of North America.* New York.

Kusmer, Karla D., Elizabeth K. Leach, and Michael J. Jackson. 1987. Reconstruction of precolonial vegetation in Livingston County, Kentucky, and prehistoric cultural implications. *Southeastern Archaeology* 6: 107-15.

Lantis, Margaret. 1984. Nunivak Eskimo. In *Handbook of North American Indians: Arctic,* Vol. 5, ed. D. Damas, 209-23. Washington, D.C.

Larsen, Clark Spencer. 1981. Skeletal and dental adaptations to the shift to agriculture on the Georgia coast. *Current Anthropology* 22: 422-3.

1982. The anthropology of St. Catherine's Island. III. Prehistoric human biological adaptation. *Anthropological Papers of the American Museum of Natural History* 57: 157-276.

1984. Health and disease in prehistoric Georgia: The transition to agriculture. In *Paleopathology at the origins of agriculture,* ed. M. N. Cohen and G. J. Armelagos, 367-92. Orlando, Fla.

Larsen, Clark Spencer, and D. H. Thomas. 1982. The anthropology of St. Catherine's Island. IV. The St. Catherine's period mortuary complex. *Anthropological Papers of the American Museum of Natural History* Part 4, 57.

Larson, Lewis H. 1980. *Aboriginal subsistence technology on the southeastern coastal plain during the late prehistoric period.* Gainesville, Fla.

Linares, Olga. 1976. "Garden hunting" in the American tropics. *Human Ecology* 4: 331-49.

Marquardt, William H. 1974. A statistical analysis of constituents in human paleofecal specimens from Mammoth Cave. In *Archeology of the Mammoth Cave area,* ed. P. J. Watson, 193-202. New York.

McMillan, R. Bruce. 1976. The Pomme de Terre study locality: Its setting. In *Prehistoric man and his environments: A case study in the Ozark highland,* ed. W. R. Wood and R. B. McMillan, 13-44. New York.

Medsger, Oliver Perry. 1976. *Edible wild plants.* New York.

Merwe, N. J. van der, and J. D. Vogel. 1978. [13]C content of human collagen as a measure of prehistoric diet in Woodland North America. *Nature* 276: 815-16.

Mitchell, Donald. 1988. Changing patterns of resource use in the prehistory of Queen Charlotte Strait, British Columbia. In *Research in economic anthropology: Prehistoric economies of the Pacific Northwest Coast,* ed. B. L. Isaac, 245-90. Greenwich, Conn.

Muller, Jon. 1984. Mississippian specialization and salt. *American Antiquity* 49: 489-507.

Munson, Patrick J., Paul W. Parmalee, and Richard A. Yarnell. 1971. Subsistence ecology of Scovill, A terminal Middle Woodland village. *American Antiquity* 36: 415-20.

Neusius, Sarah W., ed. 1986. *Foraging, collecting, and harvesting: Archaic period subsistence and settlement in the Eastern Woodlands.* Southern Illinois University, Center for Archaeological Investigations, Occasional Papers No. 6. Carbondale, Ill.

Parmalee, Paul W., and W. E. Klippel. 1974. Freshwater mussels as a prehistoric food resource. *American Antiquity* 39: 421-34.

Parmalee, Paul W., R. B. McMillan, and F. B. King. 1976. Changing subsistence patterns at Rodgers Shelter. In *Prehistoric man and his environments: A case study in the Ozark highlands,* ed. W. R. Wood and R. B. McMillan, 141-62. New York.

Parmalee, Paul W., Andreas A. Paloumpis, and Nancy Wilson. 1972. *Animals utilized by Woodland peoples occupying the Apple Creek site, Illinois.* Illinois State Museum, Reports of Investigations No. 23. Springfield.

Pearsall, Deborah M. 1989. *Paleoethnobotany.* San Diego, Calif.

Powell, Mary Lucas, P. S. Bridges, and A. M. W. Mires, eds. 1991. *What mean these bones?: Studies in southeastern bioarchaeology.* Tuscaloosa, Ala.

Ray, Dorothy Jean. 1984. Bering Strait Eskimo. In *Handbook of North American Indians: Arctic,* Vol. 5, ed. D. Damas, 285-302. Washington, D.C.

Reitz, Elizabeth J. 1982. Vertebrate fauna from four coastal Mississippian sites. *Journal of Ethnobiology* 2: 39-61.

  1985. A comparison of Spanish and aboriginal subsistence on the Atlantic coastal plain. *Southeastern Archaeology* 4: 41-50.

  1988. Evidence for coastal adaptations in Georgia and South Carolina. *Archaeology of Eastern North America* 16: 137-58.

  1990. Zooarchaeological evidence for subsistence at La Florida missions. In *Columbian consequences: Archaeological and historical perspectives on the Spanish borderlands east,* ed. D. H. Thomas, 543-54. Washington, D.C.

  1992. Zooarchaeological method and theory and their role in southeastern archaeological studies. In *The development of southeastern archaeology,* ed. J. Johnson, 230-50. Tuscaloosa, Ala.

Reitz, Elizabeth J., and Stephen L. Cumbaa. 1983. Diet and foodways of eighteenth-century Spanish St. Augustine. In *Spanish St. Augustine: The archaeology of a colonial Creole community,* ed. K. A. Deagan, 152-85. New York.

Reitz, Elizabeth J., Rochelle Marrinan, and Susan L. Scott. 1987. Survey of vertebrate remains from prehistoric sites in the Savannah River Valley. *Journal of Ethnobiology* 7: 195-221.

Reitz, Elizabeth J., and Irvy R. Quitmyer. 1988. Faunal remains from two coastal Georgia Swift Creek sites. *Southeastern Archaeology* 7: 95-108.

Reitz, Elizabeth J., and C. Margaret Scarry. 1985. *Reconstructing historic subsistence with an example from sixteenth-century Spanish Florida.* Society for Historical Archaeology, Special Publication No. 3. Tucson, Ariz.

Riley, Thomas J. 1987. Ridged-field agriculture and the Mississippian economic pattern. In *Emergent horticultural economies of the Eastern Woodlands,* ed. W. Keegan, Southern Illinois University, Center for Archaeological Investigations, Occasional Papers No. 7, 295-304. Carbondale.

Rostlund, Erhard. 1952. *Freshwater fish and fishing in native North America.* University of California, Publications in Geography, Vol. 9. Berkeley, Calif.

Ruff, Christopher B., Clark Spencer Larsen, and Wilson C. Hayes. 1984. Structural changes in the femur with the transition to agriculture on the Georgia coast. *American Journal of Physical Anthropology* 64: 125-36.

Scarry, C. Margaret. 1993a. Variability in Mississippian crop production strategies. In *Foraging and farming in the Eastern Woodlands,* ed. C. M. Scarry, 78-90. Gainesville, Fla.

Scarry, C. Margaret, ed. 1993b. *Foraging and farming in the Eastern Woodlands.* Gainesville, Fla.

Scarry, C. Margaret, and Elizabeth J. Reitz. 1990. Herbs, fish, scum, and vermin: Subsistence strategies in sixteenth-century Spanish Florida. In *Columbian consequences: Archaeological and historical perspectives on the Spanish borderlands east,* ed. D. H. Thomas, 343-54. Washington, D.C.

Shelford, Victor E. 1974. *The ecology of North America.* Urbana, Ill.

Smith, Bruce D. 1984. *Chenopodium* as a prehistoric domesticate in eastern North America: Evidence from Russell Cave, Alabama. *Science* 226: 165-7.

  1985a. *Chenopodium berlandieri* ssp. *jonesianum:* Evidence for a Hopewellian domesticate from Ash Cave, Ohio. *Southeastern Archaeology* 4: 107-33.

  1985b. The role of *Chenopodium* as a domesticate in pre-maize garden systems of the eastern United States. *Southeastern Archaeology* 4: 51-72.

  1986. The archaeology of the southeastern United States from Dalton to DeSoto (10,500 B.P.-500 B.P.). In *Advances in world archaeology,* Vol. 5, ed. F. Wendorf and A. E. Close, 1-92. Orlando, Fla.

  1987a. The economic potential of *Chenopodium berlandieri* in prehistoric eastern North America. *Journal of Ethnobiology* 7: 29-54.

  1987b. The independent domestication of indigenous seed-bearing plants in eastern North America. In *Emergent horticultural economies of the Eastern Woodlands,* ed. W. F. Keegan, Southern Illinois University, Center for Archaeological Investigations, Occasional Papers No. 7, 3-47. Carbondale.

  1989. Origins of agriculture in eastern North America. *Science* 246: 1566-71.

Smith, Bruce D., ed. 1990. *The Mississippian emergence.* Washington, D.C.

Spencer, Robert R., and Jesse D. Jennings, eds. 1965. *The Native Americans.* New York.

Springer, James Warren. 1980. An analysis of prehistoric food remains from the Bruly St. Martin Site, Louisiana, with a comparative discussion of Mississippi Valley faunal studies. *Mid-Continental Journal of Archaeology* 5: 193-223.

Steponaitis, Vincas P. 1986. Prehistoric archaeology in the southeastern United States, 1970-1985. *Annual Review of Anthropology* 15: 363-404.

Stewart, Hilary. 1977. *Indian fishing: Early methods on the northwest coast.* Seattle, Wash.

Stoltman, James B. 1974. *Groton plantation: An archaeological study of a South Carolina locality.* Harvard University, Peabody Museum, Monograph No. 1. Cambridge, Mass.

Styles, Bonnie Whatley. 1981. *Faunal exploitation and resource selection: Early Late Woodland subsistence in the lower Illinois Valley.* Evanston, Ill.

Styles, Bonnie Whatley, and James R. Purdue. 1991. Ritual and secular use of fauna by Middle Woodland peoples in western Illinois. In *Beamers, bobwhites, and bluepoints: Tributes to the career of Paul W. Parmalee,* ed. J. R. Purdue, W. E. Klippel, and B. W. Styles, Illinois State Museum, Scientific Papers No. 23, 421-36. Springfield.

Suttles, Wayne. 1990a. Environment. In *Handbook of North American Indians: Northwest Coast,* Vol. 7, ed. W. Suttles, 16-29. Washington, D.C.

Suttles, Wayne, ed. 1990b. *Handbook of North American Indians: Northwest coast,* Vol. 7. Washington, D.C.

Swanton, John R. 1946. *The Indians of the southeastern United States.* Smithsonian Institution, Bureau of American Ethnology, Bulletin No. 137. Washington, D.C.

Tannahill, Reay. 1973. *Food in history.* New York.

Taylor, Walter W., ed. 1957. *The identification of non-artifactual archaeological materials.* Washington, D.C. 1-64.

Trager, James. 1970. *The food book.* New York.

Watson, Patty Jo. 1985. The impact of early horticulture in the upland drainages of the Midwest and Midsouth. In *Prehistoric food production in North America,* ed. R. I. Ford, University of Michigan, Museum of Anthropology, Anthropological Papers No. 75, 99-147. Ann Arbor.

  1989. Early plant cultivation in the eastern woodlands of North America. In *Foraging and farming: The evolution of plant exploitation,* ed. D. Harris and G. Hillman, 555-71. London.

Watson, Patty Jo, ed. 1969. *The prehistory of Salts Cave, Kentucky*. Illinois State Museum, Reports of Investigations No. 16. Springfield, Ill.

Welch, Paul D. 1991. *Moundville's economy*. Tuscaloosa, Ala.

Wessen, Gary C. 1988. The use of shellfish resources on the Northwest Coast: The view from Ozette. In *Research in economic anthropology: Prehistoric economies of the Pacific Northwest Coast*, ed. B. L. Isaac, 179-207. Greenwich, Conn.

Wigen, Rebecca J., and Barbara Stucki. 1988. Taphonomy and stratigraphy in the interpretation of economic patterns at Hoko River rockshelter. In *Research in economic anthropology: Prehistoric economies of the Pacific Northwest Coast*, ed. B. L. Isaac, 87-146. Greenwich, Conn.

Wing, Elizabeth S., and Antoinette B. Brown. 1979. *Paleonutrition: Method and theory in prehistoric foodways*. Orlando, Fla.

Wood, W. Raymond, and R. Bruce McMillan, eds. 1976. *Prehistoric man and his environments: A case study in the Ozark highland*. New York.

Woods, William I. 1987. Maize agriculture and the late prehistoric: A characterization of settlement location strategies. In *Emergent horticultural economies of the Eastern Woodlands*, ed. W. F. Keegan, Southern Illinois University, Center for Archaeological Investigations, Occasional Papers No. 7, 275-94. Carbondale.

Wright, H. E. 1976. The dynamic nature of Holocene vegetation, a problem in paleoclimatology, biogeography, and stratigraphic nomenclature. *Quaternary Research* 6: 581-96.

Yarnell, Richard A. 1969. Contents of human paleofeces. In *The prehistory of Salts Cave, Kentucky*, ed. P. J. Watson, Illinois State Museum, Reports of Investigations No. 16, 41-54. Springfield.

  1972. *Iva annua* var. *macrocarpa*: Extinct American cultigen? *American Anthropologist* 74: 335-41.

  1978. Domestication of sunflower and sumpweed in eastern North America. In *The nature and status of ethnobotany*, ed. R. I. Ford, Museum of Anthropology, University of Michigan, Anthropological Papers No. 67, 289-99. Ann Arbor.

  1982. Problems of interpretation of archaeological plant remains of the Eastern Woodlands. *Southeastern Archaeology* 1: 1-7.

  1993. The importance of native crops during the Late Archaic and Woodland periods. In *Foraging and farming in the Eastern Woodlands*, ed. C. M. Scarry, 13-26. Gainesville, Fla.

Yarnell, Richard A., and M. Jean Black. 1985. Temporal trends indicated by a survey of Archaic and Woodland plant food remains from southeastern North America. *Southeastern Archaeology* 4: 93-106.

V.D.6   North America from 1492 to the Present

The food history of Native Americans before the time of Columbus involved ways of life ranging from big-game hunting to (in many cases) sophisticated agriculture. The history of foodways in North America since Columbus has been the story of five centuries of introduced foodstuffs, preparation methods, and equipment that accompanied peoples from Europe, Asia, and Africa, with the food culture of North America having been enriched by each addition.

The Sixteenth Century

Most narrative histories of North America give little attention to the sixteenth century, even though two earthshaking events took place during this time that were to alter the continent's history fundamentally. One was the demographic collapse of the native populations in the face of Eurasian diseases, such as smallpox. This made possible the second, which was the establishment of European settlements along the eastern seaboard without substantial native resistance.

The Native Americans

The peoples of North America, who numbered perhaps 20 million in 1492, dwelled in societies of many different types, with their cultures shaped by their foodways. Thus, those who depended on hunting and gathering usually lived in roaming bands, whereas maize agriculture normally implied settled life in villages or towns. In the north and west of the continent, the hunter-gatherer lifestyle still predominated in 1492. Game varied from bison on the Great Plains to rats in the deserts of the Southwest. Men hunted and women gathered in these usually nomadic, band-level societies. Some bands, like the Mi'kmaq of Nova Scotia, grew one crop, such as tobacco, and hunted and gathered the remainder of their food supply (Prins 1996). It is important to note that the European picture of Indians as primitives did not allow for such sophistication. The Mi'kmaq knew perfectly well what agriculture was but chose to obtain their food from the wild and to plant only tobacco, which the wild could not provide. Where a staple food could be collected easily, such as in parts of California (where acorns were the daily fare) or in northern Minnesota (where wild rice was the staple), the natives frequently formed settlements (Linsenmeyer 1976).

An agricultural complex had been developing for centuries in eastern North America when Ponce de León stepped ashore in 1513. Older staples, such as Jerusalem artichoke and sumpweed, had given way to Mexican maize, beans, and squash. Varieties of maize adapted to extreme conditions permitted horticulture to flourish as far north as the Dakotas.

In the Southeast and the Mississippi Valley, the area of the Mississippian culture, intensive agriculture supported cities resembling those of Mexico and Peru, with thousands of inhabitants, elaborate social systems, and multiple castes (Duncan 1995). Maize, beans, and squash, along with fish and game, fed the masses. A ceremonial beverage made from yaupon holly, called "black drink," was a caffeine-containing stimulant similar to tea or coffee (Hudson 1979). (It is strange that alcohol was almost unknown among North American natives, although some made a sort of ale from maize or maple sap; after European contact, however, alcoholism would become a serious problem for them.) The "Gentleman of Elvas," chronicler of Hernando De Soto's expedition (1539–42), described one Mississippian city – near the future site of Augusta, Georgia – that was ruled by a queen he called the "Lady of Cofachiqui" from a pyramidal mound topped by her large wooden house (Duncan 1995). Fields of maize stretched as far as the horizon. The surplus from the fields went into granaries to feed people in need – a mark of true civil society (Crosby 1986). Clearly, these people and others, like those who built the mounds at Cahokia in Illinois (Middle Mississippian ancestors of the Siouan-speaking Indians), had sophisticated state-level societies with governmental systems, long-distance trade, and complex religions.

Cofachiqui also had four huge barns wherein the dead from a smallpox epidemic were mummified, and by 1650, her elaborate society had vanished, likely because of further outbreaks of disease (Duncan 1995). Perhaps 90 percent of North America's native population died in a series of "virgin-soil" epidemics, and much knowledge of foodstuffs and other cultural traditions was lost forever in this immense demographic disaster (Crosby 1986).

In addition to their deadliness, the epidemics were demoralizing, as traditional religious and medical practices proved useless. Some Native Americans believed that the end of the world had come, and needless to say, diseases precipitated a great deal of migration: Tribes moved to escape the pathogens, to flee from enemies that they were too weak to resist, or to invade the territory of decimated foes. The map of aboriginal America was altered beyond the scholar's power to reconstruct. The Mississippian peoples vanished, and tribes having no knowledge of the origin of the great mounds took their places.

The Spanish Borderland Settlements

During the sixteenth century, Spanish priests and soldiers established several missions in the Southeast. St. Augustine was the most important, but others came into being along the coasts of Georgia, Carolina, and (briefly) Virginia. Both literary and archaeological evidence indicate that the Spanish imported a large amount of food, including wine and wheat flour (Milanich 1995). But more important for day-to-day survival were native foodstuffs, such as maize, yaupon, and wild game, provided by Indians living at the missions.

Spanish explorers also distributed wheat flour to native rulers and passed out European seeds as gifts to natives, with translated instructions for growing them; the peach orchards of the Mississippi Natchez stand as testimony to how far these plants spread (Farb 1968; Milanich 1995). In the warm climate, mis-

sion gardens yielded favorites brought from Europe, such as melons, figs, hazelnuts, oranges, chickpeas, greens, herbs, peas, garlic, barley, pomegranates, cucumbers, wine grapes, cabbage, lettuce, and even sugarcane. In addition, the Spanish carried the sweet potato of the Caribbean to Florida, where it was previously unknown (Milanich 1995).

Such plant transfers – not only from the Old World to the New but also from one area of the New World to another – resulted in confused, albeit enriched, foodways. Moreover, as Alfred Crosby (1986) has pointed out, Old World species exhibited an ability to edge out their New World counterparts, with "ecological imperialism" the result. Large numbers of wild horses, cattle, and hogs multiplied in an environment free of accustomed predators, and even the honeybee (native to Eurasia) thrived, while the pollen it spread about fertilized imported European plants that depended upon it. The result was an abundance of food in virtually all the neo-European societies of the New World – a situation that has continued to the present (Crosby 1986).

The Seventeenth Century

The Chesapeake Region

The seventeenth century saw the planting of permanent English colonies in North America, including the beginning of European settlement of the Chesapeake. Colonists usually brought provisions reflecting the diet of contemporary Britain, which was based on grains, meat, and milk products. Bread, the daily staple, ranged from the mixed-grain bread of the poor to the "white" bread of the wealthy. Luxurious meals for the upper classes included elaborate spicing, many pastries, and complex cooking methods reminiscent of those of the Near East, with copious use of rose water, almonds, and currants (Hess 1992). *Martha Washington's Booke of Cookery* (Hess 1981), a seventeenth-century manuscript recipe book (although some recipes in it are a good deal older) passed down in the Custis family of Virginia, provides a glimpse of this cuisine, with its profusion of custard curd dishes, rose water, garlic (later to be virtually forbidden), almond-scented meats, and practical hints on preserving foodstuffs (cherries, peas, turnips, and even oysters pickled in barrels) and distilling homemade medicines. Among other recipes is one for apple pie, foreshadowing its status as an American icon; oat "greats" (groats), soon to be replaced by American "grits" of corn (maize), are mentioned as well.

In the mid–1580s, English settlers landed on Roanoke Island in present-day North Carolina, but the first permanent British colony was Jamestown, Virginia, established in 1607 by 105 Englishmen, among whom there was but a single farmer. In an ensuing period of starvation, poisonous "Jimson" weeds, oysters, maize (stolen from the local Powhatan Indians), and even, apparently, human flesh kept the colonists from dying out completely (Smallzreid 1956). There-after, much more attention was paid to crops. British wheat did poorly in the climate of the Chesapeake, and the settlers came to depend on cornbread, grits, and pork. Their hogs ate maize, along with acorns and peanuts. "Ashcake" and "hoecake," baked in ashes on the blade of a hoe, were the staples of poor whites and, later, of black slaves, some of whom had known maize in Africa because of the slave traders, who imported the plant to feed slaves awaiting transport to the Americas. Bread was baked on coals or fried in pork fat, and meat was roasted, fried, or boiled (Fischer 1989). Cornbread was the food of the poor because of the ease with which maize could be grown, but the wealthy enjoyed its taste as well (Horry 1984). However, an overreliance on maize was to lead to malnutrition and vitamin deficiencies in the South, with poor health a consequence (Kiple and King 1981).

It is worth noting that some food historians attribute numerous American dishes, ranging from strawberry shortcake to Brunswick stew, and their means of preparation to the native peoples (Root and de Rochemont 1976). However, although the native origin of such foodstuffs as maize and venison is obvious, a survey of the foodways of the Powhatans of Virginia reveals that they contributed little that was exotic to the English settlers. For example, a feast prepared in 1607 at Arrohateck, Virginia, included mulberries and strawberries boiled with beans, cornbread, "meale," and a "land turtle" – hardly sophisticated fare (Rountree 1989). The truth of the matter was that the Indians of the Eastern Woodlands lacked salt and spices (even the hot peppers of Mexico and Peru), as well as frying pans and other iron utensils, ovens, wheat, sugar, dairy products, and all domestic animals save the dog. Thus, to assert that strawberry shortcake derives from an Indian dish that was nothing more than berries and maize or beans boiled together is, perhaps, something of an exaggeration. It is important not to confuse the Indians of North America with those of Central or South America: Although many have written that the native peoples of North America had, for example, the potato and the chilli pepper, as did, respectively, the Inca and the Aztecs, this was simply not the case.

New England

The Massachusetts area received its first white settlers with the *Mayflower* in late 1620. Following a harsh winter during which many of them died, the colonists learned from the Native American Wampanoags how to hunt and fish in the new land and how to plant crops. The following November established a landmark in American culinary history: the first "thanksgiving dinner," prepared by the Pilgrims and their Wampanoag hosts. In truth, the modern Thanksgiving holiday dates back only to Civil War times, and as for the Pilgrims' thanksgiving, there is no mention of the famous turkey.

In 1630, 1,000 colonists arrived on the 17 ships of the Winthrop fleet to found the Massachusetts Bay colony. Their provisions included cheese, salt fish, pork and beef, oatmeal, hard biscuit, bread and butter, peas, onions, raisins, prunes, and dates, with cider, beer, water, sweet wine, and small amounts of brandy, called "aqua vitae" (Smallzreid 1956). Because a virgin-soil epidemic had reportedly annihilated the local Indians in 1617, the landing of the settlers went unchallenged, and they proceeded to found a colony of self-sufficient farmers. They ate well, if somewhat monotonously; an average of 3,200 to 5,000 calories a day was the norm in New England (Derven 1984). As did their neighbors to the south, these settlers also consumed maize meal, both as porridge and as bread or "johnnycake," but the diet did not focus on "hog and hominy," as it did in Virginia.

The use of land for small farms meant that both rich people and poor were rare in New England (Lockridge 1985). The cold climate enabled rye to grow successfully, resulting in "rye'n'injun" ("rye and Indian," a bread baked with rye and maize meal) and "Boston brown bread," made from rye, wheat, and maize that was steamed over a kettle of beans cooking with pork and molasses. (The careful cook allowed the residual heat of the oven to keep beans warm for Sundays, when – for religious reasons – no cooking or other work was permitted.) Although yeast will not act well on any grain but wheat, the rye and maize breads of colonial America could be raised with "pearl ash" (potassium bicarbonate, made from wood ashes) or with beaten eggs (Hess 1992). The most ubiquitous dishes were pies, baked (like bread and beans) in wood-fired brick ovens modeled after those used in England. Indeed, a "Yankee" was to be defined as someone who ate pie for breakfast. The types of pies reflected the seasonal availability of fruits; and because the pie makers made use of first one fruit and then another throughout the year, there was a virtual calendar of pies (Fischer 1989).

Molasses was the usual sweetener (white sugar was expensive), and it was also employed in making rum. Drinking in New England centered on alcoholic beverages, with hard cider and some beer competing with rum. Although wine grapes would not grow, bees thrived, and a few settlers managed to make honey mead, which they had known in England (Wolcott 1971). Bread, cookies, and even beer could be made from pumpkins, which were a staple for New Englanders. In fact, the ease of growing pumpkins meant that "old Pompion was a saint," and "pumpkin sause [pumpkin stewed with butter, spices, and vinegar] and pumpkin bread" were on every table (Crawford 1914: 382; Wolcott 1971).

The Middle Region: Pennsylvania and New York

The New Amsterdam colony, which became New York, and the Quaker settlement in Pennsylvania were two other sites of seventeenth-century colonization, both settled by peoples whose foodways reflected diverse origins. In New Amsterdam, the Dutch relished heavy meals of meat and bread, washed down with tea (a Dutch favorite before it became popular in England) and followed by large amounts of rich pastry. Perhaps one-fourth of the houses in New Amsterdam sold beer, tobacco, or spirits (Booth 1971).

In seventeenth-century Pennsylvania, the colonists were a mixture of Quakers, other English settlers, and some Swedes (Nash 1968). David Hackett Fischer (1989) has claimed that the northern British origin of the Quakers encouraged a distinctive pattern of foodways, of which the consumption of apple butter and dried beef was typical. By contrast, Karen Hess (1992), who has examined the Penn family cookbook and other early American sources, found nothing unique about Quaker cookery, and it has also been pointed out that the distinctive cuisine of the north of England (including Yorkshire), based on grain porridge, oatcake, and ale, did not resemble Pennsylvania cooking (Brears 1987). Thus, there is little consensus about the cuisine of the Pennsylvania Quakers (Lea 1982), although perhaps its distinctiveness could be argued because of what was *not* consumed. The Quakers' wish to isolate themselves from the sinful world led to abstinence from many foodstuffs. Some, for example, refused to use sugar because it was made by slaves. Others rejected spices, saying that they altered the taste of food (Fischer 1989).

The Spanish Borderlands

By the 1600s, the Spanish settlements along the Carolina and Virginia coasts had been abandoned, although St. Augustine in Florida continued as home to a small Spanish colony that imported much of its food. Aside from game, the local foodstuffs consumed were maize and yaupon holly, from which was made the Indians' "black drink," containing caffeine. A priest explained that yaupon was drunk "every day in the morning and evening" and that "any day that a Spaniard does not drink it, he feels that he is going to die" (Sturtevant 1979: 150)

In the Southwest, which had been settled from Mexico during the sixteenth century, the traditional cookery of Native Americans came to include Spanish imports, such as domesticated food animals, sugar, tea, and coffee. As the hunter–gatherer Navaho and many other tribes became pastoralists, they adopted a diet of mutton, bread, and coffee (Driver 1961). Perhaps ironically, many Indian groups in the Southwest learned maize agriculture from the Spaniards, and beef and maize became the staples for many in this ranching land. Food was plentiful, if judged by a book on early California cooking that lists five daily meals. For dinner, a well-off family in Spanish California might have a selection of foods that mixed Iberian fruit preserves and wine, a salad of local pigweed, Mexican tortillas, beans, and succotash, and such European-influenced dishes as fried rice and coffee (Smallzreid 1956).

The Eighteenth Century

In America, the eighteenth century brought a "golden age" for the planters of the Chesapeake region. Cultural amalgamation among the several colonies meant the end of religious uniqueness for the New England Puritans and Pennsylvania Quakers. The Indians were forced beyond the Appalachian Mountains, and the colonies' political consolidation that began with the Albany Plan of Union ended with American independence and the Constitution of the United States. This political union meant that, in the long run, neither the Native Americans nor the Spaniards would retain their lands. The field of cookery also became "independent," as English cookbooks were succeeded by the first American cookbooks.

In all American societies, food availability depended on the seasons. Autumn saw an abundance, but late winter and early spring meant the "six weeks' want" (Farrington 1976). It was a time when greens and roots were used to relieve the monotony of stale meal and beans before the first garden vegetables came in. The southern colonies had longer growing seasons and thus less of an annual time of "want." However their warmer climate encouraged a hostile disease environment, with the result that New England families were larger and life spans longer (Fischer 1989).

It has been claimed that, in general, early Americans disliked, or at least seldom consumed, vegetables, and it was certainly the case that – in an age without refrigeration – green vegetables kept poorly. Moreover, without a marketing and transportation system, availability was limited; once the season for a particular food had passed, there would be no more of it until the following year. Perhaps most importantly, modern varieties of vegetables did not exist: There was no tomato designed to ripen slowly off the vine, nor a maize cultivar that stayed sweet. To obtain and cook vegetables required a certain tenacity, and in an age ignorant of vitamins and fiber, some people simply did not bother with them.

In spite of these factors, however, many Americans seem to have enjoyed vegetables and fruits. Amelia Simmons, in compiling her 1796 cookbook, evidently assumed that any good meal included vegetables (Simmons 1965). Vegetables were cooked for longer periods than they are today (in order to ensure their safety and edibility by those with few or no teeth) but were not necessarily boiled into mush, as is sometimes asserted. The eighteenth-century South Carolina housewife Sarah Rutledge, for example, boiled her cauliflower for only 15 minutes (Rutledge 1979).

Many people raised fruits and vegetables in abundance. An example comes from an 1806 gardening calendar kept by a Charleston lady who grew fruit trees, strawberries, gooseberries, currants, raspberries, thyme, savory, hyssop, peas, beans, cabbage, lettuce, endive, potatoes, artichokes, and Jerusalem artichokes (Tucker 1993). Thomas Jefferson and his Paris-trained slave-chef James Hemings kept a huge garden of peas, cauliflower, cabbage, lettuce, parsley, kale, tarragon, broccoli, spinach, "corn salad," endive, savory, turnips, carrots, beets, salsify, parsnips, radishes, onions, eggplant, melons, and beans (Tucker 1993). They even sprouted endive in the cellar to provide salads in wintertime.

New England

In the eighteenth century, the people of Massachusetts were suppliers of rum for slavers and ships for whaling and fishing. The colony was a hub of trade: Spices and foodstuffs from all corners of the globe passed through New England markets. However, its own cooking centered mostly, as before, on bread, beans, fish, and salt meat. The British habits of overcooking meat and greens persisted, as did such customs as brewing special beers for special occasions (Crawford 1914). Quilting bees ended with tea served in the English style, featuring sweets, "sage cheese" (flavored with that herb), and pastries (Crawford 1914). A favorite meal was the "boiled dinner" comprised of boiled meats and vegetables and, perhaps, boiled "bag pudding" for dessert (Farrington 1976).

Substantial meals were the rule, and pie for breakfast meant plenty of calories to start the day. A visitor to Boston in 1740 remarked on the abundance of poultry, fish, venison, and butcher's meat available. The ordination of a minister called for a celebratory meal of turkeys, pumpkins, cakes, and rum. Harvard students, however, ate meager meals of cold bread and hot chocolate (Crawford 1914). There was little opposition to alcohol consumption in early America, and pastor and congregation alike drank it before Sunday church services, as well as at every meal (Rorabaugh 1979). In addition to huge amounts of bread, porridge, and cheese, the average New Englander annually consumed some 32 gallons of hard cider, 15 pounds of butter, 40 gallons of milk, between 2 and 3 pounds of tea, more than 150 pounds of meat, 10 pounds of sugar, and 1 gallon of molasses (Derven 1984).

Trade made the merchant class wealthy in what had once been an egalitarian colony, and the menus of the wealthy could be elaborate. John Adams, certainly well-to-do, served a dinner of Indian pudding with molasses and butter, veal, bacon, neck of mutton (a dish also featured in Martha Washington's cookbook), and vegetables (Fritz, 1969). A Quaker friend outdid Adams with "ducks, hams, chickens, beef, pig, tarts, creams, custards, jellies, fowls, trifles, floating islands [a custard dish], beer, porter, punch, and wine" (Smallzreid 1956: 61). Nonetheless, despite such heavy eating habits, the old Puritan ideals died hard: Jokes had it that a New England family made the same roast gander serve as a main course for seven days in a row (Crawford 1914)!

The Middle Region

In the eighteenth century, Pennsylvania became home for large numbers of German settlers (later known as the "Pennsylvania Dutch"). Deemed not assimilable by many, they colonized the back country and prospered. Many joined the great migration southward along the Appalachian Mountains and ended up in Virginia and the Carolinas. Along with the iron cookstove, these Germans contributed waffles, "shoofly pie," scrapple, new kinds of sausage, vinegar, and more pastries – including doughnuts (Farrington 1976).

Technological innovations spread from the middle colonies. By 1750, a cast-iron pot – with a rim on the lid to hold coals – was in common use. Called a "Dutch oven," it was used to bake bread, roast meats, and make stews and other dishes; in modified form, it has remained in use to this day (Ragsdale 1991). The famous stove of inventor and ambassador Benjamin Franklin improved on German models. Franklin was perhaps the most famous vegetarian of his time, having been inspired by English vegetarian and pacifist Thomas Tryon (Spencer 1995). Franklin eschewed meat and beer in order to improve his health and drew up lists of vegetarian dishes for his landlady to prepare. Toward the end of his life, however, he returned to eating some meat.

As the century came to a close, the cosmopolitan city of Philadelphia had 248 taverns and 203 boardinghouses (Pillsbury 1990). Its diverse population of English, Germans, Swedes, and Africans contributed to a varied cuisine, including the famous "Philadelphia pepper pot," which, although attributed to George Washington's cook, is similar to a Caribbean dish of the same name.

Like Pennsylvania, New York contained a mixture of cultures. Foods in this port city included so much fish and fowl that servants (who apparently wanted more meat) complained if salmon was served more than once a week or heath hen (a bird now extinct) more than three times (Farrington 1976). Such an abundance of animal food on the table was unlike Old World cuisines, which relied on porridge, bread, and potatoes. Each year, two crops of peas and one of buckwheat came from the rich soil, which also produced rye, barley, maize, potatoes, and turnips (Tucker 1993). Food for the city of New York also arrived from the "garden colony" of New Jersey (Farrington 1976) and from what is now upstate New York, where Dutch and German settlers had introduced new kinds of plows and wagons to make their farms more productive. The "Dutch plow" or "Rotherham plow" (in fact, it originally derived from China) had a share and moldboard cast in one continuous piece (Temple 1986), and its advanced design greatly eased the task of plowing. The crops on Dutch farms were diverse, with those farms reflecting the intensive use of space typical of the Netherlands.

European fruits did well; farmers planted great orchards of apples to make cider, a favorite alcoholic beverage, which was often distilled into "Jersey lightning" by means of freezing it until a core of alcohol remained within the ice. But apples were also used in numerous other ways. For example, apple pie and milk were the nightly fare for "Hector St. John" (Michel G. J. de Crèvecoeur, author of *Letters from an American Farmer*) in the late eighteenth century (Sokoloff 1991). Long before the American Revolution, eating shops and taverns provided places to dine out in New York (Pillsbury 1990). One of these was the Queen's Head (soon known as Fraunces Tavern), which opened in 1770 and was still in business over a century later (Root and de Rochemont 1976). By the end of the eighteenth century, New York had 121 taverns and 42 boardinghouses that served food and drink (Pillsbury 1990).

The Chesapeake Region and the South

As mentioned, the eighteenth century was a "golden age" for some in the Virginia tidewater. The period saw a shift from tobacco monoculture to the mixed growing of tobacco and grain, although the former continued to dominate the region. Plantations worked by African slaves yielded an abundance of maize and other foodstuffs, and maize remained the staple for the slaves, as well as for poor whites. For others, there was either bread (made from dough that rose by the addition of beaten egg) or "beaten biscuit" (made with wheat flour) that was laid on a stump and struck repeatedly with an ax handle until it began to rise (Farrington 1976).

The predominance of maize in baking meant much cornbread, almost always eaten hot; when cornmeal was fried, the result was "hushpuppies." Maize was also fed to hogs, the principal source of meat in the South until the twentieth century. In addition, the mash made from maize was distilled into corn whiskey, which was popular even before the Revolution. Later, with rum from the British West Indies more difficult to obtain, corn whiskey became the liquid staple of what has been termed the "alcoholic republic" (Rorabaugh 1979). Rum or whiskey was mixed with water and sugar to become toddy; with fruit and sugar, it was punch (Farrington 1976). Some beer was drunk, including "Roger's best Virginia ale," brewed in Williamsburg (Hume 1970). But English beer yeasts spoiled in the American summer heat, and winter killed them, making beer brewing a difficult proposition (Rorabaugh 1979). Although Virginians also made cider and some wines in the colonial period, distilled spirits kept the best (Hume 1970).

Some of the gentry were voracious consumers of alcohol. When the governor of Virginia, Lord Norborne Berkeley Botetourt, died in 1770, he left behind more than 2,000 bottles of wine, brandy, and ale and many kegs of spirits (Hume 1970). Three years later, his successor, Lord John Murray Dunmore, ordered 15 dozen bottles of both ale and strong beer from England, as well as wine glasses, cloves, and 20 dozen packs of cards (Smallzreid 1956).

Wine, tea, coffee, and the spicy dishes of the early modern period figured prominently as the kitchens of the planters began to turn out the first high cuisine in British America (Fischer 1989). Much of this has been attributed to African cooks, who knew how to use flavorings and spices. Most plantations maintained kitchens in buildings separated from the main house (because of a fear of fire), as well as icehouses (where winter ice was stored in layers of straw), barns for grain and animals, springhouses (for storage of dairy products in cold water), and smokehouses (for preserving meat, such as the famous Virginia hams, by smoking).

Plantation dinners could be elaborate, multicourse affairs with abundant meats, hot breads, seasonal vegetables and fruits, and large amounts of alcohol. At Westover Plantation on the James River, blue-winged teal (duck), venison, asparagus, and garden peas were common on William Byrd's table (Fischer 1989). Other favorite dishes were "spoonbread" (a maize casserole), ham cooked in any of a dozen ways, oysters ("cooked any way"), fried chicken, fricassee of chicken, lamb, game, pies filled with meat or fowl, and the region's own peanut soup and peanut pie.

Foods in the South were preserved by drying, salting, and smoking, and although English cookbooks had long advised preserving fruits in brandy, this was a costly treat, available only for the rich. In general, for most in colonial Virginia, winter meant monotonous meals of cornbread, beans, and ham; variety in off-season meals had to await canning, which came with the Industrial Revolution.

English colonization spread farther south in the late seventeenth and early eighteenth centuries. In 1670, settlers and slaves from the crowded sugar island of Barbados had landed on the coast named "Carolana" for Charles I, with its capital city of Charleston, named for Charles II. By the early eighteenth century, Carolina was thriving, its semitropical economy based on the growing of indigo, hemp, sugar, and rice. The whites of Charleston drank beer and whiskey, both made from maize, and ate cornbread, but they also became – in that time, at least – the only society of English-speaking people to eat rice as a dietary staple (Rutledge 1979). They retained wheat for bread making, but meals were centered on rice, which even today is more prominent on Charleston tables than on many others in America.

Slaves, some of whom had known rice in Africa, provided much of the knowledge for planting, harvesting, and cooking it, although some innovations, such as the use of tidal flows to drive water into the rice paddies, were conceived by the whites (Dethloff 1988). Rice was generally prepared in the "Indian" or "African" manner, in which boiling was followed by steaming. Among the favorite rice dishes were "pilau," made with pork, "hoppin' John," made with black-eyed peas and ham hocks, and breads made with rice and wheat flour (Hess 1992). This rice-eating plantation society spread to coastal Georgia, and in both colonies, the isolation of African slaves on rice-growing sea islands led to the distinctive culture, language, and cookery of the African-American "Gullahs." Abundant seafood, rice, maize meal, and hot peppers were combined in such Gullah dishes as "down'ya stew" and shrimp-and-grits (Junior League of Charleston 1950).

Harriott Pinckney Horry, daughter of a prominent South Carolina Huguenot family, left a recipe book written at the end of the eighteenth century that provides some insight into the local cuisine. Her "journey cake" was made from either rice or maize; she also cooked with tomatoes, fresh ginger, and chilli peppers (Horry 1984). Clearly, her kitchen was the scene of good, and sometimes spicy, cooking.

Canada and American Independence

To the north, there was another society as different from Massachusetts as Massachusetts was from Virginia. In Quebec and Acadia, settlers from Normandy brought with them ways of cooking and bread making that persisted into the twentieth century. The center of their diets was the *pain de campagne,* or "bread of the countryside," made from a mixture of grains and baked in a wood-fired oven of clay or brick (Nightingale 1971). This bread – made in large loaves, four pounds being usual – was also the common bread of France during this period (so-called French bread was not made until the nineteenth century) (Boily-Blanchette 1979). Such dishes as meat pie (spiced with cinnamon or cloves) and yellow pea soup still survive in Quebec and Acadia (Gotlieb 1972).

Local ingredients modified the French-derived cookery of Quebec. Maple syrup found its way into everything from meat glazes to dessert pies, sometimes with disconcerting results, and hams were boiled in maple sap at sugar-making time (Benoäit 1970; Gotlieb 1972). The famous Oka cheese (similar to cheddar) also originated in this era (Gotlieb 1972), and American chillies were used to season pickled onions (Benoäit 1970).

British Canada's cooking was English in derivation, and plain dishes, such as boiled mutton and calf's head, as well as sweet custards, were common (Nightingale 1971). As in Massachusetts, entire meals were boiled in one iron pot; bacon, cod, and eggs, cooked together with potatoes and turnips, was one such sturdy meal (Nightingale 1971). Boiled "bag puddings," made with flour, eggs, and fruit, were often served for dessert (Benoäit 1970). As with other European colonies in North America, there was an abundance of foods. Oats grew well in Canada and went into oatmeal and bread; there were even "pilafs" made from oat groats instead of rice. "Grits" (Martha Washington's "greats") meant oat groats instead of corn, although "corn cake" did grace some Canadian tables (Benoäit 1970).

On the coast, oysters were a poor man's dish, and lobsters were so common as to be practically valueless, making people ashamed to eat them (Gotlieb 1972). Clams and cod went into pies, which in Canada were as popular as in New (and old) England (Benoäit 1970). Salt pork was so universal that it was even used in sweet cakes (Nightingale 1971). To accompany these dishes, Canadians made a variety of "wines" from all sorts of foodstuffs. Their "port wine," for example, was a concoction of whole wheat, currants, raisins, and potatoes that contained no grape juice. "Parsnip wine" and "beet wine" were other drinkables (Nightingale 1971). These country wines, like rum, owed their fermentation to sugar that Maritime settlers obtained from the sugar islands. Rum is still a preferred beverage in New Brunswick, where a "black rum" unknown in the United States is a favorite (Personal communication from Charles Morrisey 1996).

Canada and the colonies to the south were to be separated politically as well as in culinary matters. The American Revolution led to significant changes both on and off the table. American corn whiskey became more popular than rum, and it has been claimed that many drank coffee instead of tea as a show of loyalty to the new republic. But although tea was no longer available through British channels (as it had been before the Revolution), American traders began to obtain it directly from China. The switch from tea to coffee began in the early nineteenth century as Brazil began shipping more coffee to North America. This dramatically reduced prices and thus encouraged more widespread use of the beverage (Cummings 1940).

The Revolution affected the cooking of Canada, as thousands of loyalists fled the thirteen colonies to settle there. Some refugees from Virginia baked cornbread on the hearth or in a skillet (Nightingale 1971), although their "johnnycake" became decidedly Canadian with the addition of maple syrup. Fried chicken and "spoonbread," suggestive of a southern influence, were also enjoyed in Canada, and the chicken curry that came north was, as in South Carolina, called "country captain" and attributed to sea trade with India (to conform to local tastes, the Nova Scotian version of the dish called for only a single teaspoon of curry powder for a four-pound chicken) (Nightingale 1971). Yankee influence, in the form of Boston baked beans, was apparent in Nova Scotia as well (Benoäit 1970). Tea remained the preferred hot beverage, and teahouses were opened there as well as in other regions of Canada.

A Canadian cookbook of this period dealt apologetically with chilli peppers because they were a part of recipes from "Old Country people" and "Western dishes" for "a man's world" (Benoäit 1970: 86, 175, 182). On the other hand, "green tomato chow," a version of "chowchow" (a relish common in the American South), contained red peppers, and its apples and cucumbers link it, like chowchow, with the mixed fruit-and-vegetable pickles of medieval

England (Benoäit 1970). Perhaps Canada's most eccentric contribution to American cooking resulted from the resettlement of the Acadians, or Cajuns, in Louisiana. These exiled French-Canadians adopted the hot spices, rice, and seafoods of their new home and created a cuisine unlike any other (Root and de Rochemont 1976).

Cookbooks and Cooking

The first cookbook published in America was E. Smith's *The Compleat Housewife,* a 1742 reprint of a 1727 British volume (Smallzreid 1956). Other English cookbooks, such as Hannah Glasse's *The Art of Cookery,* were also printed in America but reached few readers in a land where many were illiterate and any kind of book ownership was rare. In 1796, Amelia Simmons, styling herself "an American orphan," published *American Cookery* in Hartford, Connecticut (1965). It was the first cookbook to include recipes employing such American staples as maize and pumpkins. For "johnnycake" or "hoecake" (the first recipe for cornbread in English), she instructed the reader to "scald 1 pint of milk and put to 3 pints of indian meal, and half pint of flour – bake before the fire" (Simmons 1965: 57). The author also included numerous recipes for vegetables and mentioned five kinds of cabbage and nine different beans. Kitchen gardens were apparently common in her world, as she supplied information on how to plant and harvest.

Simmons's book indicates how tastes had changed in Anglo-America since colonial times (for one thing, spicy dishes were no longer in favor) and also reveals several continuing trends in the food history of North America. First, there was still the immense abundance of food available that has already been noted. Second, cookery retained its English character, with minimal seasoning and meat as the center of the meal. Third, the authorities on cookery were not (as, for example, in France) a restaurant-trained elite but rather housewives and home cooks. Although Simmons herself was careful about cooking, the attention to quality of ingredients and cooking methods that later distinguished the *grande cuisine* of France were, on the whole, lacking in American cooking. It was apparent that, in cooking, America had inherited both the good and the bad from England.

The Nineteenth Century

During the nineteenth century, Native American populations continued to decline as European, African, and some Asian peoples filled the North American continent. Wild game, although still common, had been hunted to the point that several species, such as the passenger pigeon, beame as extinct as some of the Indian peoples who had once preyed on them (Root and de Rochemont 1976).

Three nineteenth-century trends combined to revolutionize the American diet. One was immigration, involving a mass of Europeans, as well as the arrival of the first Chinese immigrants in the west of the continent. The second (which created the first) was the Industrial Revolution. The third (made both possible and necessary by the first two) was the use of industrial technology to provide the growing population of European-Americans with a quantity and variety of foods undreamed of in previous ages. The quality of that food, however, was – and remains – questionable.

Regional Foodways of America

The North and urban squalor. Urban workers seldom enjoyed well-balanced meals. Americans who had migrated from rural regions crowded together with immigrants in the "slum" areas of northern cities, where fresh foods were largely unavailable, and hunting, fishing, and gardening were difficult, if not impossible. Consequently, as a rule, the diet of urban workers was inadequate in all but calories; fresh vegetables and fruit were almost absent from their tables, save for a few weeks in the summer and fall. Throughout the United States, the favorite vegetables were potatoes and cabbage, and the favorite fruit remained apples in their hundreds of local varieties (Levenstein 1988).

Southern and African-American foodways. The nineteenth century's antebellum epoch brought with it increasing polarization between North and South. As the nation lurched toward the Civil War, northern religious reformers and abolitionists attacked the institution of slavery, while southerners from the Chesapeake region, the "Rice Coast," the back country, and the western states of the newer South defended it. These disparate regions of the South became united, first by the slaveholding ideology, and then by the Confederate "Cause."

Southern cooking at this time was still marked by a preponderance of locally produced staples, such as maize, salt pork, and garden greens. Beef was little known and fresh milk almost nonexistent (Hilliard 1988). Whether or not the diet of black slaves was adequate has long been debated, but one conclusion is that although adequate in calories, it lacked sufficient protein and vitamins. Protein-calorie malnutrition and vitamin deficiencies are attested to by contemporary evidence (Kiple and King 1981). Some slaves kept garden plots or animals – a source of economic independence – but although a few could hunt or fish, most relied almost solely on rations. These provided a relatively monotonous diet of salt pork, maize meal, and, sometimes, molasses or sweet potatoes, although most slaves were given vegetables in season (Hilliard 1988). The use of fatty rather than lean pork for slaves was justified by the conviction that fat provided the energy needed for hard labor. The slaves' diet was the basis for modern "soul food."

For the planter class, excess was frequently the

rule. One of the most astounding of many extravagant dishes was the "Carolina wedding cake" made in 1850, which called for, among other things, 20 pounds each of butter, sugar, flour, and raisins, as well as 20 nutmegs and 20 glasses of brandy (Junior League of Charleston 1950). One author has estimated that it would have required 1,500 eggs and weighed a total of 900 pounds (Smallzreid 1956). Similar excesses were evident among cooks who deep-fried entire turkeys and garnished tables with great bowls of turtle steaks, merely to whet appetites (Hilliard 1988). One dinner on record featured ham, turkey, chicken, duck, corned beef, fish, sweet potatoes, "Irish" potatoes, cabbage, rice, beets, 8 pies, syllabub, jelly, "floating islands," and preserves (Rutledge 1979). Peach brandy and corn whiskey washed all of this down.

Virginians were as proud as South Carolinians of their reputation for gracious living. Tomatoes figured prominently in Mary Randolph's *The Virginia House-Wife,* originally published in 1828 but actually based on plantation cookery from the colonial era. Randolph, a relative of Thomas Jefferson, presented such recipes as hot-pepper vinegar, buttered okra, and stewed tomatoes, along with plenty of others for pork dishes and cornbread. Other writers, such as Letitia Burwell (1895), reveled in the colonial and antebellum past with exuberant nostalgia. Among her memories was afternoon tea with Robert E. Lee, who displayed the Custis silver of Mount Vernon at his table amid a truly English array of cakes and pastries. But such fondly recalled luxuries were not typical of Southern living, with its sharp polarization of the culture by class and race, at the table as well as in church and home.

Emancipation from slavery brought no freedom from a restricted diet, and after the Civil War, the poor – both black and white – lived on a regimen of cornbread, beans, grits, biscuits, and salt pork. Cornbread predominated over wheat bread even among those who could afford the latter: Southerners had come to prefer its distinctive taste (Hilliard 1988). The poorest chewed dirt, apparently to relieve the symptoms of hookworms, and frequently suffered from pellagra. This nutritional deficiency disease was the result of a diet lacking in niacin (one of the B vitamins) and progressed from diarrhea and dermatitis to dementia and death. Ingestion of any niacin source, such as fresh meat, was the cure (Cummings 1940). Poverty shaped the diet of the South in other ways. The poor used sorghum syrup to sweeten their coffee, pastries, and cornbread (because store-bought sugar was too expensive), and sorghum, an African plant, is still grown in the South to provide a flavorful sweetener (Cummings 1940). Similarly, the southern poor used cayenne *(Capsicum annuum),* which could be homegrown, instead of store-bought black pepper (Hess 1992).

The West and Hispanic foods. The foods of the Southwest added still another culinary experience for the American palate. During the second quarter of the nineteenth century, the United States expanded, by conquest and by land purchase, into this large area with its predominantly Hispanic population. The region's culinary heritage was rooted in part in the chilli-laced tamales and tortillas of the Aztecs and their predecessors and in part in the culture of Iberia. Shipments of olive oil, hams, wine, and even saffron arrived regularly from Spain (Linsenmeyer 1976). The last Spanish governor of California was inaugurated in 1816 with a gala affair featuring poultry, game birds, cordials, wine, fresh fruit, breads, and cakes (Linsenmeyer 1976). Salmon, crab, and pork were cheap in this new land, and the vines left by the Spanish friars formed part of the foundation for today's California wine industry (Lichine et al. 1982).

Cultures and foodways blended as time passed. A Texas landowner took stock of his garden in 1839. The fruits alone comprised peach, fig, raspberry, quince, plum, "sour orange," melon, pomegranate, and strawberry; in addition, there were 13 herbs and 22 kinds of vegetables (Tucker 1993). That he grew such Spanish favorites as quince and chilli peppers is worth noting, and clearly a blending of cultures took place at his table. By contrast, the early Anglo settlers of Arizona stuck to such familiar favorites as roast beef, sourdough bread, and rhubarb pie (DeWitt and Gerlach 1990).

Also in the nineteenth century, a spicy stew of meat, beans, and chillies received its name, *chile con carne.* In 1828, a writer mentioned it as the staple of the poor, and although no recipe was given, it is clear that the dish was prepared with ingredients similar to those that go into it today. Linked to cowboys (for whom beef and beans were staples), to Mexico (where similar dishes had been served for some time), and to the "chili queens" who served it from market stalls, *chile* soon became a regional favorite (DeWitt and Gerlach 1990). By 1896, an Army cookbook included "Spanish" recipes that were actually Mexican, such as tamales, tortillas, *chiles rellenos,* and refried beans with cheese (Levenstein 1988).

Before the Civil War, white settlers had moved into Oregon and Washington, where they found a potential culinary paradise. The Indians of the area had scorned agriculture because game and fish were so abundant. The salmon, abalone, and wild berries of the Northwest were supplemented by the white settlers with grain, meat animals, and fruit trees, all of which prospered in that climate (Root and de Rochemont 1976).

The Plains. The slaughter of the American bison (and of the Indians who depended on them) opened the Great Plains to white settlement. The artifact that increased the area's attractiveness was the steel plow, which enabled farmers to turn the tough sod of the plains and, thus, to grow wheat, with the result that wheat bread became available throughout the entire country (Root and de Rochemont 1976). A staple of these plains pioneers and others was sourdough bread, leavened by a yeast starter that was kept active by periodic feedings of water and flour. Known from California to the Canadian wilderness, it formed the basis of loaves of bread, pancakes, and even sweet desserts, and "sourdough" became the nickname of inhabitants of Alaska (Gotlieb 1972).

Pioneers also ate all kinds of game. Imaginative cooks made such dishes as stuffed moose heart and smoked gopher; others improvised French-style soups with fish from Canadian lakes (Gotlieb 1972). German and Czech pioneers brought one-pot casseroles to the region. A favorite on the trail was dried-apple pie: A cook rolled the crust out on the wagon seat, reconstituted the dried fruit by soaking, and had a pie ready to bake in the Dutch oven at day's end (Tannahill 1988).

No such treats characterized the foodways of the rapidly disappearing Indian population. Equipped with guns and horses, the Plains tribes had hunted the buffalo, using every part of it for food, implements, and shelter. But the wars against the whites ended with the natives confined on reservations and dependent for food on government handouts. Ruth Little Bear of the Blackfoot tribe recalled her grandmother's tales of food in a previous time, when buffalo tripe was stuffed with tenderloin, and neither spices nor utensils were used. She also provided recipes for fried bread, yeasted bread, and "bannock," the Scottish name for pan-baked bread, a staple among Indians subsisting on government-issued salt pork, flour, and rice (Hungry Wolf 1982). Other Indian dishes, dating from a time before the reservations, included a soup made from berries, "prairie turnip" (a wild root gathered by the tribes), and many kinds of smoked and boiled meat (Laubin and Laubin 1957).

Immigration

With the advent of steamships, the second half of the nineteenth century became a period when, for the first time, large numbers of non-English-speaking peoples poured into the United States to challenge the cultural dominance of the Anglo-Saxon "Old Americans." Of these, perhaps the most prominent in bringing new tastes were the Italians and the Chinese. Although immigrants from other areas also contributed ethnic dishes to the American repertoire, the Italians and Chinese founded the first "ethnic restaurants" and brought in new foods that Americans accepted, albeit after some initial misgivings.

European immigration. Irish settlers, fleeing the potato famine of the late 1840s, comprised the first wave of nineteenth-century immigrants. Like the English, the Irish had little tradition of refined cuisine, and those who were immigrants to hardscrabble Newfoundland continued to make such peasant dishes as "colcannon," a mixture of mashed potatoes, kale, and butter (Gotlieb 1972). In New York, Irish immigrants relied on bread, fried meats, pastries, and tea (Shapiro

1986). The Irish also brought Catholicism, with its insistence on Lenten fasts and meatless Fridays. However, despite their centuries-long experience in brewing and distilling, the Irish had little influence on American alcoholic beverages. American beer takes after German beer, and American whiskey was a unique maize product unknown in the British Isles until relatively recently.

Italians arrived toward the end of the century. Their traditions of cuisine, which stretch far back into history, were sophisticated, shaped in part by the variety of foods in sunny Italy and in part by the chronic scarcity in that country of fuel for fires, meaning that quickly cooked foods were cheaper to prepare. Their many contributions to American cuisine include pasta, olive oil, the versatile tomato, and wine. It is the case that as early as the time of Jefferson, some Americans were growing tomatoes and cooking pasta; indeed, Jefferson bought a pasta-making machine in Italy. But it was in the late nineteenth century that Italian immigrants inundated the Northeast, bringing with them a desire for fresh vegetables (especially tomatoes) and other staples of their Mediterranean homeland. During the depression of the early 1890s, the city of Detroit offered gardeners the use of vacant lots, and by 1896, this practice had spread to some 20 other cities, including New York. Reporters remarked on the lavish plots of tomatoes, peppers, and eggplant grown by Italians (Tucker 1993).

Immigration from Eastern Europe brought large numbers of Poles and Jews to America. Their culinary contributions included the dark rye breads of their homelands and the complex kosher dishes that were the stock-in-trade of the original Jewish delicatessens. Highly seasoned cold meats made the prohibition of cooking on the Sabbath more tolerable, and still do, although today such delicatessens, which are everywhere, are frequented by Jews and Gentiles alike.

The Jewish dietary laws that were cherished in the Old World, however, were frequently disregarded in the New. Jewish writers, such as Harry Golden (1958), have commented wryly that Chinese dishes, which nearly always included pork, were simply too much of a temptation for Jewish people. In fact, the Reform denomination of Jews set aside kosher dietary laws.

Other Eastern Europeans also came to America, in many cases settling in ethnic enclaves within large cities. Food festivals and church events helped to preserve the customs and dishes of such lands as Serbia, Lithuania, and Slovakia.

Chinese immigration. Far more exotic to Americans than the Eastern Europeans were the Chinese immigrants. The first Chinese came to America around 1820, and significant numbers followed during the California gold rush. Mostly Cantonese, they grew Asian vegetables in their garden plots and introduced stir-frying, the use of new seasonings, and above all, the Chinese restaurant (Linsenmeyer 1976; Tucker

1993). Preserved ginger, Chinese oranges, dried seafoods, and bean curd were imported, and each immigrant was allowed to carry in two jars of ginger for personal use (Linsenmeyer 1976). Shipping records show imports of foodstuffs as mundane as rice and as exotic as sharks' fins (Linsenmeyer 1976). Because of the southern Chinese origin of these immigrants, however, they did not bring with them the potted dishes and wheat breads of northern China, which remained unknown in America for another century and a half (Tropp 1982).

Restaurants

In the early decades of the nineteenth century, virtually no restaurants existed outside of the eastern cities with their grand hotels, although, of course, inns and taverns offered food (Root and de Rochemont 1976). But soon the excellent fare and low prices of Chinese restaurants made them a success despite an American apprehensiveness born of rumors that accused the Chinese of eating cats and dogs. Such "Chinese" dishes as "chop suey" and "chow mein" were actually invented in America and became American favorites; chop suey even made its way along with the Canadian Pacific railroad into the depths of that northern land (Smallzreid 1956; Benoäit 1970).

The most famous restaurant in the Northeast was Delmonico's in New York; first opened in 1825, it offered a menu and cooking style that were largely French, with some American concessions, such as "hamburger steak" (Pillsbury 1990). Eleven restaurants and three generations later, Prohibition caused the last Delmonico's to close in 1923 (Root and de Rochemont 1976), having served every president of the United States from 1825 to 1900; other clientele had ranged from Mark Twain to the Prince of Wales.

Toward the end of the century, Italians had also begun opening restaurants, and these joined other restaurants and saloons as welcome additions to the urban landscape of industrial America. In addition, industry and capitalism brought forth the first national chain restaurant, the Harvey House, founded in 1876 (Pillsbury 1990), which served standardized fare in locations along railway lines.

Food and Technology in the Nineteenth Century

The Industrial Revolution, which introduced mechanical power to produce consumer goods in quantity, brought widespread dietary changes, not least among them the advent of processed foods. By 1876, America was exporting yearly to Britain a million pounds of margarine, or "butterine," made from waste animal fat (Tannahill 1988). "Crisco," a mixture of fats, became a popular product that freed the housewife from having to render or strain hot grease, and powdered gelatin eliminated the labor of boiling calves' feet (Nightingale 1971). Roller mills manufactured white flour, which – despite its cheapness – kept longer, made loaves that rose higher, and was easier to digest

than brown flour (Tannahill 1988). In addition, it made much better sauces and pastries.

The Industrial Revolution also ushered new technology into the kitchen. The cast-iron stove meant that women no longer needed open fires for cooking, and the age-old risk of serious burns or even death for women who cooked at open hearths began to disappear (Smallzreid 1956). Refrigerated railcars and ships made fresh foods available far from their points of origin, and canning enabled the storage of large amounts of these and other foods for consumption out of season.

Fruits and vegetables had been preserved since Roman times by pickling or cooking with honey. With the 1809 development in France of "bottled" foods, and the later invention of the screw-top Mason and Ball jars in 1858, home "canning" became reliable and safe, and factory canning a multimillion-dollar industry (Root and de Rochemont 1976). The first tin cans were handmade, but the invention in 1849 of a machine that could produce them meant substantially lower prices for the food that they contained. The invention came just in time for the California gold rush, and by 1850 the miners were already eating large amounts of canned fish, shellfish, tomatoes, and peas (Root and de Rochemont 1976). The most significant food to be canned was milk, a process pioneered by Gail Borden and patented in 1856. His firm supplied large amounts of sugared, canned milk and juice to the Union army during the Civil War (Cummings 1940) and was still in business, although struggling, at the end of the twentieth century.

Recipe books provided instructions on canning for American housewives, who might each put up hundreds of jars of preserves each year, in addition to numerous crocks of pickles, relishes, "piccalilli," homemade catsup, and sauerkraut (Smallzreid 1956). Vegetables from the home garden and fruit from nearby orchards and farmers' markets were combined with spices in family recipes, and women often worked together to can as much as possible while a fruit or vegetable was in season.

Another method of keeping food was the icebox whose invention seems to have taken place in Maryland at the beginning of the nineteenth century – the broiling summers there doubtless the "mother" of this invention. But the ice had to be changed frequently, which would ultimately be remedied by home refrigeration. The discovery of the vapor-refrigeration principle and the invention of various compression machines were initial steps in this direction, and by the end of the Civil War, ice-making machines existed. By 1880 some 3,000 patents had addressed the topic of refrigeration – and some of these in turn led to a revolution in the meat industry.

The dominance of pork began to wane – even in the South – as southwestern cattle drives and the Chicago stockyards made available an enormous amount of beef (Levenstein 1993). Industrial workers' families, who had eaten only small amounts of fresh meat in the 1830s, consumed two pounds daily in 1851, and fresh meat was much more nutritious than the salted and preserved meats of colonial days. Milk consumption doubled, and the use of vegetables increased greatly (Cummings 1940).

Chicago's stockyards were modernized in the 1860s, and by 1875, manufacturers such as Swift and Armour, boasting of the cleanliness of their production facilities, had established their brands as leaders in the meat-packing industry, positions they still hold. In the 1870s and 1880s, railcars and ships, now equipped with refrigerators, carried meat to all parts of America (Root and de Rochemont 1976), and as Kathleen Ann Smallzreid (1956: 103) has noted, "refrigeration probably did more to change the flavor of the American meal than any other invention, and in doing so brought health as well as enjoyment to the table."

The newly mechanized stockyards used all parts of the animals they processed, including bone for china and glycerin for explosives (Smallzreid 1956). Unfortunately, federal inspection was negligible in the era of "robber barons"; sanitation was nonexistent, and by the turn of the century, conditions in Chicago meat-packing plants were horrific. When, in 1906, socialist writer Upton Sinclair published his eyewitness account of this situation, entitled *The Jungle,* the public was outraged. Meat sales dropped by half as people read of diseased animals, dirt, and excrement – as well as human body parts severed in accidents – being canned and sold along with the meat (Sinclair 1984). In reaction, President Theodore Roosevelt urged passage of the country's first Pure Food and Drug Law, mandating (among other things) inspection of meats sold in interstate commerce (Root and de Rochemont 1976). Despite this action, however, even as late as the 1970s, such foods as chicken pie were still being made under conditions considerably less than sanitary.

In addition to meat, trains carried fresh vegetables and fruits. Navel oranges from Bahia, Brazil, were planted in Florida in 1870 and in California in 1873. In 1887, California shipped 2,212 railcar loads of citrus fruit, mostly navel oranges. Five years later, that number had swollen to 5,871 carloads of oranges and 65 of lemons (Smallzreid 1956). Grapefruits were popular as well; in 1889, Florida shipped 400 tons of them. Bananas from Costa Rica were already arriving in quantity when in 1899 the United Fruit Company was founded. Thus began a monopoly of banana production in Central America and the Caribbean as well as a monopoly of distribution in the United States that would last throughout most of the twentieth century (Smallzreid 1956).

Sales of sugar doubled between 1880 and 1915 (Cummings 1940), and new sweets began to appear. Chocolate, once known to the Aztecs as a bitter spice and to the Spaniards as a beverage, was first made into candy in the second quarter of the nineteenth century. In 1876, "milk chocolate" was invented (Root and de Rochemont 1976). Cake making became easier – a result of improved baking powder – and ice cream, a rare treat before the invention of refrigeration, became available to all (Cummings 1940; Smallzreid 1956). In Canada, however, many rural areas saw almost no store-bought candy; even in the 1870s, candy was still made at home from maple syrup (Nightingale 1971).

The purchase of staples at stores was more typical as the century passed. The "New Woman" of the late nineteenth century was ready to give thought and action to such problems as women's rights, suffrage, and education because many household tasks had been eliminated. (It has recently been argued that mechanization increased housewives' workloads, but anyone who has cleaned clothes using lye soap and a boiler, or cooked a four-course meal over an open hearth, may appreciate why so many felt the immense appeal of the new technology.) As a rule, women no longer made soap, pickles, cheese, and cloth; nor grew vegetables, fruits, and medicinal herbs; nor butchered nor made beer at home (Smallzreid 1956).

Until the 1890s, the main meal ("dinner") was still eaten at noon, as it continued to be in much of rural America well into the twentieth century (Plante 1995). Typical meals in the late nineteenth-century Northeast might include a breakfast of corn muffins, fried potatoes, and fish, and a dinner might begin with macaroni soup and move on to duck salmi, baked potatoes, oyster salad, canned peas, and celery sauce, finishing with pumpkin pie. Supper, much lighter, could be muffins, dried beef, tea rusks, and baked apples (Smallzreid 1956).

Drinking in the Nineteenth Century
Drinking also changed drastically in the nineteenth century. The massive consumption of hard liquor in the early years peaked around 1840 at perhaps five gallons of alcohol annually per adult (Rorabaugh 1979). It subsequently declined for two reasons. The first was the rise of the American beer industry. German immigrants brought with them the knowledge of brewing lager, a much lighter beer than had previously been available to Americans, and the end result was the German-American beer of the twentieth century. The second reason had to do with the temperance movement. Its advocates railed against "Demon Rum" and urged its replacement by tea, coffee, or pure water (available for the first time in American cities).

Until the last decades of the century, coffee was usually made in the old way, by roasting beans over a fire or on the stove and grinding them at home; eggs and salt were used to get the coffee to settle (Smallzreid 1956). Inventors, however, had turned their attention to the improvement of coffee processing, and, in 1880, Joel Cheek of the Atlantic and Pacific Tea

Company developed a coffee roaster that allowed less flavor to escape during the roasting process. He marketed the coffee produced by this new method through his company's stores, naming the brand after the Maxwell House hotel in Nashville, where it was first served (Smallzreid 1956).

Ladies still met in the afternoon for tea, but this practice had nowhere near the popularity that it possessed in Canada and Australia, which had retained ties of tea and government with Great Britain. As late as 1834 in New York, tea (and coffee) was served in bowls as well as in cups, and into the twentieth century, some tea and coffee drinkers kept to the Chinese practice of pouring their drink from the cup into the saucer, from which they could sip it as it cooled (Pillsbury 1990).

Health, Nutrition, and Food Fads

The increase in the consumption of fruits and vegetables as well as meat and dairy products meant significant changes in the health of Americans. By the 1860s, life expectancy had lengthened, and Union soldiers during the Civil War (1861 to 1865) were, on the average, a half inch taller than soldiers had been in the period from 1839 to 1855 (Cummings 1940). Some researchers have claimed that average American stature subsequently decreased with the immigration of shorter peoples from southern and eastern Europe. In the 1880s, however, clothiers had to work from a scale of sizes larger than that previously in use, and a modern *corsetière* lamented that patterns from the nineteenth century were useless in the twentieth, indicating further increases in height and changes in body shape.

That nutritional improvements were taking place in America is borne out by the fact that health and stature did continue to increase as the turn of the twentieth century approached and passed. Harvard undergraduates in 1926, for example, were an inch taller than their fathers had been; the women of Vassar and Mount Holyoke were more than an inch taller than their mothers, and the width of their hips had decreased. In the same year, Boston schoolboys were three inches taller than boys of 1876 (Cummings 1940). Increasingly larger sizes of clothing at the end of the twentieth century suggested that, for better or for worse, Americans are continuing to get larger.

To return to the trend of the nineteenth century, however, it would seem that the presumed deleterious effects of using canned food, white flour, and too much sugar were more than offset by the abundance of fresh foods that Americans ate (Cummings 1940). Moreover, nutritional health was improving not only in spite of the increase in industrial food processing but also in the face of a number of faddish nutritional theories that, despite their shortcomings, enjoyed wide popularity.

The nineteenth century saw some strange food practices, with "Grahamism" perhaps the best-known example. Sylvester Graham combined a romantic admiration for "nature" with a fear of processed foods – especially roller-milled, white, bread flour – and preached that poor health could be remedied by regular bathing, drinking water instead of alcoholic beverages, exercise, vegetarianism, and avoidance of sexual activity.

Indeed, Graham took vegetarianism to a new extreme by rejecting sugar, mustard, catsup, pepper, and white bread, as well as meat (Root and de Rochemont 1976), and along with others of his ilk, he imagined that the classical Greeks and Romans had also been vegetarian, or at least partly so (Green 1986). "Grahamists" ate whole-wheat bread, dairy products, fruits, vegetables, and "Graham crackers," made with whole-wheat flour and molasses and invented by Graham, who claimed that such a diet would prevent illness and insanity and lessen sexual desire. Graham made many converts – despite hostility from butchers and bakers – and special boardinghouses opened to provide the food he recommended. Called "the prophet of brown bread and pumpkins," he counted among his disciples Sojourner Truth, Horace Greeley, and the entire sect of Shakers, who were vegetarians for about 10 years (Green 1986), although their rules later permitted some meat consumption.

Other nutritional theorists also linked religion, sex, and food. Mrs. Horace Mann, author in 1861 of a stern work on food and righteousness entitled *Christianity in the Kitchen,* argued that rich concoctions, such as wedding cake, suet-laced plum pudding, and thick turtle soup, were masses of indigestible material, which should never find their way to any Christian table, and that "there is no more common cause of bad morals than abuses of diet" (Shapiro 1986: 130; Tannahill 1988).

Another reformer, the Reverend Henry Ward Beecher (brother of Catherine Beecher and Harriet Beecher Stowe), feared processed flour as much as Graham did. Beecher argued that "the staff of life . . . has become a weak crutch," and his daughters held that store-bought white bread was "so much cotton-wool" (Root and de Rochemont 1976: 22).

New "health foods" were another legacy of Grahamism, with cold breakfast cereal the most prominent. The Seventh Day Adventists, members of a church founded in 1863, held that meat, spices, tea, coffee, tobacco, and alcohol were both unhealthy and immoral and that "foods of vegetable origin" paved the way to salvation and to "God-given health and happiness" (Smallzreid 1956: 150; Root and de Rochemont 1976). They therefore began to manufacture healthy and "moral" foods in Battle Creek, Michigan, where, in 1876, Dr. John H. Kellogg invented breakfast flakes made from wheat. C. W. Post, a client, joined the quest for "moral" foods. He began to sell "Postum" (a coffee substitute) in 1895 and "Grape Nuts" cereal in 1898 (Smallzreid 1956). "Shredded Wheat," another health-food favorite, was invented in 1891 by Henry Perkey, a non-Adventist entrepreneur (Smallzreid 1956). In all cases, commercial versions of these products, which incorporated a great deal of sugar, bore little resemblance to the ascetic foods envisioned by their inventors.

An even stranger fad than Grahamism was "mastication," the brainchild of Horace Fletcher. Fletcher believed that a "filtering organ" in the back of the mouth performed most digestion and that an inordinate amount of chewing was necessary to stimulate it. Chewing each bite of food 32 times was recommended, and college students were recruited to practice it. But because excessive chewing interfered with the pleasure of eating, the mastication theory was soon abandoned (Levenstein 1988).

A more important influence on American foodways in the late nineteenth and early twentieth centuries was that of "domestic science." Beginning in the last quarter of the nineteenth century, increasing numbers of women learned about cooking through classes centered on the application of science to the kitchen. Such women as Catherine Beecher, author of a book on "frugal housewifery," urged women to take control of the household economy in order to save money on food and other expenses (Shapiro 1986). But although the ideas that they learned (such as balancing protein and carbohydrates so as to provide nutritious and inexpensive meals) were good ones, the results of their application were not necessarily so. Breakfasts of fruit, stewed corn, baked potatoes, and hot water won approval, whereas hot bread and griddlecakes were abhorred (Shapiro 1986). "Manly" meals of beans, potatoes, and beef alternated with "ladies' luncheons" of salads, marshmallows stuffed with raisins, and "Dainty Desserts for Dainty People," which allegedly appealed to "delicate" feminine tastes (Shapiro 1986: 99).

Another product of the period's obsession with "science" was the work of Fannie Farmer. A teacher at the Boston Cooking School, she originated the concept of "level measurement," which was probably the first challenge in all of history to the slapdash practice of using a pinch of this and a smidgen of that. Farmer's 1896 *Boston Cooking-School Cook Book* incorporated cooking-school methods and level measures in the belief that anyone who read it could learn to cook. Every cookbook that gives exact measurements is a tribute to the tremendous impact of this woman (Farmer 1896). The use of cookbooks and level measurements and the influence of cooking schools and nutritional theories would come to predominate in American kitchens of the twentieth century.

The Twentieth Century

The twentieth century saw far-reaching changes in the foodways of America. The development of hybrid maize and other crops, the application of high technology to food processing and cooking, and the growth of such commercial interests as fast-food restaurant chains and supermarkets all contributed to these changes.

Although most Americans entered the century with their near-Puritanical distaste for "fancy cooking" well intact, this attitude coexisted alongside the allure of the exotic. "Theme restaurants," looking like Arabian tents or Southern mansions, arose to serve the same steak and lobster as more mundane establishments. The most popular place for lunch in the early twentieth century – as before – was the saloon, with its free food for customers who purchased alcoholic beverages.

The early part of the twentieth century saw a continuation of the gorging of the previous century. In 1913, a New York dinner hosted by Frank Woolworth (founder of the "five-and-ten" store chain) featured caviar, oysters, turtle soup, pompano with potatoes, guinea hen, terrapin, punch, squab, grapefruit-walnut salad, ice cream, cake, coffee, and wine (Levenstein 1988). But change was in the air, occasioned by an ever-growing interest in home economics and nutrition and an awareness of the lighter meals served in other parts of the world.

The diets of ordinary people were improved, as more and more could afford to take advantage of new technologies, such as refrigeration and canning. Certainly there was a greater abundance of vegetables consumed, as farmers' markets made them readily available during the season; preservation and storage for consumption later in the year had also become easier. Thus, in the early part of the century, steelworkers in Pennsylvania, for example, ate typical American suppers of meat, beans, potatoes, fruit, beets, and pickles. Other meals served by their wives included spinach, tomatoes, and eggplant (Levenstein 1988). Towns famous for particular fruits or vegetables began to hold festivals to celebrate their abundance of such crops as artichokes, or apples, or pumpkins, or pecans, or garlic (Levenstein 1993).

Like their eastern counterparts, midwestern farm families ate much meat, milk, vegetables, and fresh fruit in the early twentieth century (Cummings 1940). However, this was not true for many in the South. Kentuckians in 1919 and 1920 were relying on pork and maize meal augmented with white flour, and many in the Blue Ridge mountains had similarly restricted diets, with coffee and flour the only store-bought foods (Cummings 1940). When federal relief came to the South during the Great Depression, such foods as whole-wheat flour and grapefruit juice were as alien as coconuts to those in rural areas, who often ignored these introduced foods because they were unfamiliar (Cummings 1940).

The nutritionists of the early twentieth century failed on several counts. One problem was their belief that "mixed foods" were hard to digest. Thus, immigrants were pressured to give up nourishing ethnic dishes, such as Hungarian goulash, for pork chops and applesauce. Another problem was the contemporary enthusiasm for canned foods, even in preference to local, fresh ones, which meant that vitamins and minerals were often inadequate. A third problem was the continued hostility of the nutritionists toward spices and flavorings as well as "fancy cooking" (Shapiro 1986; Levenstein 1988). This often resulted in bland and insipid dishes that made it difficult to interest anyone in this "new nutrition." Even fresh, hot bread was frowned upon as indigestible by the experts, who advised immigrant families to buy their breakfast bread and pastries during the evening before they were to be eaten so as not to endanger their family's health (Shapiro 1986).

These same experts told black migrants from the South to abandon "corn pone" and pork in favor of codfish balls and Boston brown bread, although few of them actually did so (Shapiro 1986). Some immigrants also resisted the pressure to conform, most notably the Italians (Shapiro 1986), although the restaurants they established served Italians and others with Americanized versions of spaghetti, garlic bread, and more (Levenstein 1993).

A final problem with the new nutrition was the inconvenience of lengthy food preparation, such as the making of stews, which the nutritionists favored. But greater changes in working-class foodways were afoot. The same era that saw the failed efforts of the nutritionists also witnessed the birth of an American tradition when, in 1916, the nineteenth century's "hamburger steak" was made into a sandwich by the founders of the White Castle restaurant chain, Billy Ingram and Walter Anderson (Pillsbury 1990).

The Era of Prohibition

In 1919, the United States adopted Prohibition. The Volstead Act - a constitutional amendment outlawing the commercial manufacture and sale of alcoholic beverages - had its roots in the temperance movement that had arisen in reaction to the endemic drunkenness of the late eighteenth and early nineteenth centuries. Long unsuccessful at the national level, the movement had gained momentum during World War I, and suddenly the saloons and free lunches were no more. Prohibition also encouraged the conversion of bars to sandwich counters and hamburger "joints," while chains of "family restaurants," such as White Tower, its rival White Castle, and Howard Johnson's, spread across the nation (Pillsbury 1990).

Once Prohibition laws were in place, organized criminal syndicates and smugglers began providing illegal liquor and beer to those thirsty Americans who were not already making their own. But concern over the rise of crime and violence associated with Prohibition, as well as the onset of the Great Depression, ultimately combined to ensure the repeal of the Volstead Act.

The Great Depression and World War II

The crash of the stock market in late 1929 signaled the start of a decade of severe economic difficulties for the United States, as well as for the rest of the world's developed nations. Oral history and folklore recount stories of "making do," and the outright hunger and dietary changes brought about by the depression are reflected in national statistics of the time. Meat consumption dropped from an average of 130 pounds per person per year to 110 pounds. Americans ate an average of just under 10 pounds of dried beans to fill up; the average in 1920 had been just under 6 pounds (Brewster and Jacobson 1978).

The Great Depression was followed by World War II, which shaped the course of world history for the next 50 years. Both world wars had stimulated vigorous drives to persuade the public to eat perishables so that such staples as wheat and beef could be sent overseas to the troops. However, this was not necessarily a hardship. "Meatless days," the aim of a program established to restrict meat consumption, were bearable when Americans could eat salmon, lobster, or tuna instead (Levenstein 1988). Likewise, because candy companies received large rations of sugar, candy consumption went from 13 pounds per person in the 1930s to 21 pounds in 1944 (Brewster and Jacobson 1978). "Victory gardens" helped to ease the shortage of rationed foods, although, in terms of rationing, Americans were scarcely as deprived as their European counterparts (Tucker 1993). Campaigns prompted people to can foods, and pressure cookers were made available (often on loan from the government), with the average family putting up 165 jars of canned goods annually (Levenstein 1993). In 1941, wartime nutritionists drew up the first table of recommended dietary allowances (RDAs) for the chief nutrients. Flour and milk were quickly "fortified" with them (Levenstein 1993), with the augmentation viewed as an inexpensive way to attract consumers (Brewster and Jacobson 1978).

Changes in agricultural technology also began to affect the American diet. In the 1940s, the use of hybrid strains of maize had increased the U.S. maize yield from 30 bushels per acre to 40; by 1980, yields of 100 bushels per acre were the norm. Because hybrid seeds were produced by crossing parent strains, however, farmers who wanted the greater yields that hybrids made possible had to buy seed each year, instead of saving it, as had been the case in the past. Immense profits followed for seed companies as hybrid tomatoes, cotton, and other crops were developed (Kloppenburg 1988). One result has been that older, open-pollinated strains of maize and vegetables have been neglected and, in some cases, pushed to extinction. Another result, in the eyes of critics, is that because much of the increased maize yield has served as animal fodder and only reaches consumers secondhand in the meat they purchase, much energy and land is devoted to (and pollutants created by) what might be seen by some as waste on a massive scale.

"Convenience" Foods and the Homogenization of Tastes

With the 1950s, the new "consumer society" began to demand convenience in food preparation and consumption. Sales of fresh fruit dropped from 140 pounds per person in the 1940s to 90 pounds in the 1960s, whereas those of preserved fruit – loaded with sugar – increased (Brewster and Jacobson 1978). Intensive marketing of soft drinks (the amount consumed went from 90 servings per person per year in 1939 to 500 in 1969) led to a drop in coffee drinking, although the consumption of tea (mostly iced tea) increased very slightly (Brewster and Jacobson 1978). With the promise of more leisure time for cooks and their families, the proliferation of packaged foods put on the table such dishes as a so-called Welsh rarebit, made easier to prepare with Kraft's "Cheese Whiz" – a processed, foamy "cheese" product sprayed from an aerosol can – introduced in 1953 (Levenstein 1993). Another new food for many 1950s Americans was pizza, made by Italians in local restaurants, and a treat for Mom on her "night off" (Levenstein 1993). Pizza, as is true of many other Americanized foods, soon bore little resemblance to that made in the nation associated with it.

Local menus became more homogeneous in the twentieth century as canned and frozen foods, along with air-shipped fresh foods, increasingly meant that the same foods were available everywhere. As a result, it was (and is) easier for Virginians to buy kiwifruit (imported from New Zealand) than papaws (grown in their own state). Another consequence of the mass movement of staples was the establishment of fast-food restaurant chains. These differed from the chain restaurants of the nineteenth and earlier twentieth centuries in that the standardization of food preparation produced procedures that could be performed by low-paid, unskilled workers. McDonald's, perhaps the best known of the fast-food chains, began its rise in 1954, when Ray Kroc bought the McDonald brothers' restaurant and began to expand its hamburger business (Kroc 1977). By 1990, McDonald's had 8,000 outlets in the United States alone. Each served standardized foods, such as french fries made from Russet Burbank potatoes of uniform size, which were aged for a predetermined period to ensure that uniformity. The mid–1950s also saw the beginnings of Kentucky Fried Chicken, Burger King, Lums, and a number of other chains that soon followed (Pillsbury 1990).

These restaurants owed their success to several factors. First, identical portions of food could be refrigerated or frozen and shipped to any restaurant in the chain, ensuring that food that tasted the same could always be found under a familiar sign. Second, fried chicken and grilled hamburgers could easily be turned out in assembly-line style, with prices so low that local restaurants had great difficulty in competing. Third, diners generally served and cleaned up after themselves.

Fast food is almost always high in sugar and fat, and the nature of the business, until recently, made fresh fruit and vegetables unlikely offerings. However, in view of the health and environmental concerns of the 1990s, some chains have made salads and pasta available and have added lowfat products.

Revolutions in Food Technology and Distribution

Over the course of the twentieth century, American grocery shopping increasingly centered on large chain stores, which offered a vast variety of foods, ranging from fresh meats and fish to canned and baked goods to an ever-increasing array of frozen foods. Credit for the latter belongs to Clarence Birdseye, originator in the late 1920s of the brand of frozen foods that bears his name. He developed the "quick-frozen" method, along with cardboard packages that allowed food to freeze and thaw while maintaining an attractive appearance (Levenstein 1993). General Foods purchased his company and prospered, as many American households - even during the depression years - acquired refrigerators with freezing compartments. Others prospered as well; as early as 1941, there were already some 250 firms marketing frozen foods. Refrigerators in the home brought about a reduction in the consumption of canned condensed milk and a concomitant increase in the use of fresh milk (Brewster and Jacobson 1978).

The use of twentieth-century high technology in mass-production food processing was matched by technological advances in the kitchen at home. In general, however, the latter was more an adaptation of traditional cooking strategies to new technologies than the development of a truly new style of cooking. Thus, although the wood-fired ovens of the early nineteenth century were replaced by gas and electric ovens, the cook still put food inside and shut the door to bake, roast, or warm it. Pots were placed on gas or electric burners, just as they had been on wood stoves. Even "new" cooking methods that came into widespread use, such as stir-frying, were rooted in much older cooking techniques (Tropp 1982), while boiling, broiling, frying, and other methods of great antiquity continued to be basic.

Technology, however, has resulted in better and more convenient stoves, cooking "islands" in the kitchen, and a whole array of food processors, choppers, blenders, and toasters. One product of recent technology is the microwave oven, which was common by the 1980s despite widespread misconceptions that it emitted dangerous radiation and made food radioactive. The main advantage of the microwave oven is that it can heat food faster and with less energy than a conventional stove.

Advances in food technology and distribution, however, have not resolved the problems faced by those of low socioeconomic status. Since World War II, government food programs have aimed at not only promoting good nutrition but providing it. Food stamps feed a large number of needy Americans, and the Women, Infants, and Children Program (WIC) distributes nutritious foodstuffs to pregnant and nursing mothers and to children under age 5. This effort has resulted in measurably higher birth weights and a lower percentage of birth defects (Levenstein 1993). There is opposition to these and other aid programs, but they do provide even the poorest Americans with access to supermarket foodstuffs.

Health Concerns

The large amounts of meat in the American diet has increasingly become a matter of concern in a country whose people consume one-third of all the meat available in the world (Root and de Rochemont 1976). The same is true of sugar. In the 1970s, American sugar consumption reached 99 pounds per person per year, or more than 4 ounces per day (Root and de Rochemont 1976; Mintz 1985), while the consumption of carbonated beverages totaled 107 billion bottles per year. The American "sweet tooth" doubtless has much to do with such health problems as weight gain, rotten teeth, indigestion, and heart and pancreatic troubles, including hypoglycemia and diabetes. It is also arguable that the replacement of more nourishing vegetable foods by sugar is a cause of iron and calcium deficiency (Root and de Rochemont 1976). The fact that Americans in 1976 took in 125 percent of the fat, yet only 75 percent of the carbohydrates, that had been consumed in 1910 has also become a cause for worry, as heart disease, cancer, and hypertension are all believed to be linked to a fatty diet (Brewster and Jacobson 1978; Robertson, Flinders, and Godfrey 1976).

The nutritionists of the 1970s began to shift the emphasis to holistic health and lifestyle, as it seemed clear that cancer and heart disease involved factors other than diet, such as smoking, lack of exercise, and stress. Cholesterol, a fatty substance that accumulates in arteries, began to receive blame for heart attacks with the meat and milk consumption of the previous century viewed as the reason for high cholesterol levels (Levenstein 1993), and in 1977, alarmed by this news, many Americans started to alter their eating habits by consuming more chicken, fish, and vegetables and less red meat and butter (Levenstein 1993). In something of a contradiction, however, overall beef consumption actually increased, largely because of an increasing reliance on fast foods. Food companies have responded to health concerns by marketing lowfat dishes in frozen and fresh forms (Levenstein 1993), but, of course, lowfat and diet foods often contain a plethora of chemical additives (Belasco 1989).

Alcohol is often seen as posing another health problem. Drinking has had an uncertain status in America since the repeal of Prohibition, and liquor, in particular, has come under attack for its empty calories. On the other hand, since the advantages of moderate wine consumption in the prevention of heart disease were discovered in studies of the "Mediterranean diet," it has become clear that moderate consumption of any alcohol can be preventive.

Alcoholic beverages from America's past have been resurrected. The hard cider enjoyed by colonists returned in the 1990s, and two brands share popularity with a variety of "microbrewed" beers (some of which are reminiscent of the beers of yesteryear that were brewed in taverns and private houses) and their mass-produced competitors. Even colonial pumpkin beer has returned. In addition, regional wineries as far north as British Columbia have begun to flourish, using hybrid grape strains capable of producing wine of varying quality. It is unfortunate that many of these, and other, alcoholic beverages often depend for their flavor and consistent quality on chemical additives.

Suspicion has been focused on additives since the late 1950s, when scientists found that the hormones used to fatten chicken and cattle were carcinogenic. Such concerns have resulted in tougher labeling laws and in the banning of dangerous chemicals, such as DDT (Levenstein 1993). Because such bans are generally based on studies involving rats and mice, there are also jokes about how everything gives cancer to mice. Less humorous, however, is the possibility of risks they pose for humans, who consume unknown (but apparently considerable) amounts of additives and chemicals every year. In the eyes of some, food companies argued for years to their discredit that all their ingredients were "natural" before they bowed to consumer pressure for change (Belasco 1989).

Recent Developments in Foodways

The "counterculture" movement of the 1960s brought about an idealistic renewal of interest in vegetarian diets, gardening, and subsistence agriculture. In addition, rural, agricultural communes were formed to pursue "alternative" or "spiritual" ways of life, although most of them were not vegetarian, and many raised animals for consumption. Commune recipes collected in 1970 and 1971 exhibited a heavy use of soybeans and whole grains (Horton 1972).

Food cooperatives, begun in the 1960s, provided members with access to unusual, foreign, and organic foods in exchange for labor. The most famous of these, Berkeley's "Food Conspiracy," gave rise to others. A 1990s form of collective food buying was community-supported agriculture (CSA). Thirty or more members belonged to a collective and paid large annual fees (perhaps as much as $1,000) to support a family farm, the produce from which was then divided among its supporters (Iggers 1996). Another new and different way of acquiring food has involved delivery companies that send shipments of meat and other foods (usually frozen) to fill members' home freezers. Such a service could save substantial amounts of money for members who buy in bulk, as well as ensuring that, as a rule, the meat they consume is of better quality than that offered to the general public.

The emphasis on healthy eating begun in the 1960s continues, as do attempts at self-sufficiency. In the 1990s, about 29 million Americans kept gardens, 26 million fished, and 14 million hunted game (Tucker 1993). Surveys in 1994 and 1997 indicated that at least 2 million Americans were vegetarians; many more, perhaps 10 million, avoided red meat. An estimated 500,000 of these went beyond vegetarianism to become "vegans," those who eat no foods of animal origin, such as milk, eggs, or honey (Personal communication from the Vegetarian Resource Group 1997). Inspired by "reverence for life" and "animal rights" ideals, vegans hope to create a lifestyle devoid of cruelty to animals. There is a large and growing body of information and misinformation available for vegetarians. The most famous vegetarian cookbook, *Laurel's Kitchen,* a volume replete with nutritional information, vegetarian and vegan recipes, and moral exhortations, was compiled by members of a vegetarian collective in Berkeley, California (Robertson, Flinders, and Godfrey 1976). Like Sylvester Graham before them, the authors of *Laurel's Kitchen* abhor spices, white flour, and meat.

Laurel Robertson and her colleagues drew heavily on the influential work of Adelle Davis and Frances Moore Lappé. Davis was a key figure in Rodale Press's network of organic gardening cooks and writers. Accused in the late 1950s and early 1960s of providing readers with potentially harmful information on vitamins and minerals, as well as disquieting cooking and eating practices, she was labeled "potentially dangerous" long before her death from cancer – a disease that she believed her pattern of mineral and vitamin consumption would prevent. She also thought that it would prevent heart disease, yet her editor, J. I. Rodale, died of a heart attack (Levenstein 1993).

Lappé, author of *Diet for a Small Planet,* advocated replacing meat protein with "complementary" proteins found in grains and beans in order to lessen the stress placed on the world's environment by the feeding of grain to meat animals. Lappé's inspiration had been another fad diet, "macrobiotics," invented by George Ohsawa in Paris and allegedly based on Zen monastic cooking from Japan. This regime consisted of a series of diets, each more restrictive than the last. At first, converts partook of fish, noodles, clam sauce, and vegetables, according to the season (round food was eaten in winter, for example). But at the most restrictive level of macrobiotics, no food was permitted save brown rice and 8 ounces of liquid per day. The American Medical Association condemned macrobiotics, but this has only made it more attractive to "cranks" and conspiracy-minded "brown-ricers" (Levenstein 1993).

Then there have been fads, normally involving relatively small numbers of people, concerning cooking utensils. An example was the German *Römertopf* ("pot of the Romans"), an unglazed clay vessel used to bake meat and vegetables without the use of oil. Although capable of producing interesting results, the pot was difficult to use with many traditional recipes and proved to be a commercial failure in the United States (Tropp 1982). Another fad, backyard grilling, represents a considerable expansion of men's role in home cooking, which early in the twentieth century was limited to carving the meat (Levenstein 1993).

In a wider and somewhat contrasting development, the increase in career options for women has brought about a partial eclipse of regional and ethnic cooking traditions, as fewer families cook traditional meals "from scratch" at home. Although such meals were never fads, the often laborious preparation of such ethnic foods as tamales or raviolis is now generally confined to holidays. At the turn of the 1990s, only about 15 percent of American households regularly cooked and ate three meals a day at home (Belasco 1989).

Nonetheless, the appeal of the exotic is stronger than ever, with fads for ethnic cuisine coming and going much like technological fads such as home bread- and pasta-making machines. One important result has been to make exotic ingredients increasingly more available. Native American foods, such as Jerusalem artichokes and wild mushrooms, can be found in giant chain stores side by side with Thai lemongrass, fresh habanero peppers, Italian mushrooms, and sun-dried tomatoes. Honey mead, nowadays little known in the Western world, can generally be found in Ethiopian restaurants; "chicken Kiev" and fried rice, once rare treats, are now available in grocery stores in both frozen and unfrozen forms (Levenstein 1993).

Another exotic influence has to do with the latest influx of Spanish-speaking peoples to the United States during the latter half of the twentieth century, along with an increase in the number of Americans who speak Spanish. This trend has led to a nationwide acceptance of "Mexican" or "Tex-Mex" (meaning a combination of Texan and Mexican) foods. Chi-Chi's, Taco Bell, and other restaurant chains serve various versions of "Tex-Mex" cuisine to millions of customers, and burritos, tacos, and salsa are available in restaurants and supermarkets everywhere. Indeed, sales of salsa surpassed those of catsup in the 1990s.

The chilli pepper became a trend in itself in the 1990s. Catalogs listed hundreds of varieties of hot sauce, and representations of peppers decorated everything from china to underwear (DeWitt and Gerlach 1990). Monthly magazines and Internet Web sites listed enormous numbers of hot and hotter dishes; some incorporated explosive amounts of capsaicin (the chemical that produces the chilli's characteristic burning sensation), which is derived from specially bred varieties of peppers. Just one Red Savina, the hottest chilli pepper marketed in 1996, was alleged to be capable of producing spicy "heat" in 200 pounds of sauce!

Chilli peppers also figure prominently in the new cooking of Asian-Americans. The presence of Chinese people in California since the days of the gold rush has introduced the sophisticated culture and cookery of China to consumers. Changes in immigration laws in 1965 permitted a new wave of Asian immigrants, many of them Chinese, who found a tradition of Chinese-American cooking already in place. The 1980s fad for stir-frying induced supermarkets to carry Oriental vegetables, bean sprouts, soy sauce, and other Chinese sauces. Woks and Chinese steamers appeared in gourmet food stores, and earlier Cantonese restaurants were joined by Sichuan, Hunan, and "Peking"-style eateries. Ordinary Americans discussed and ate "pot-stickers" and other dim sum (a series of small portions of a variety of foods), and the availability of Asian foods – including Korean, Vietnamese, and Thai, among others – continues to grow.

Food writers and chefs, such as Julia Child, Craig Claiborne, James Beard, and Martin Yan also helped to introduce exotic cooking techniques and ingredients in their television programs and cookbooks. Child was perhaps the most influential in a drive to bring French cuisine to the American table; Yan's "Yan Can Cook" combined Chinese-American food with comedy and culture; and Beard's cookbooks are valuable resources for anyone studying gourmet cooking. The popularity of such books and programs has encouraged in Americans both a receptiveness to new ingredients and a demand for produce, meats, and seasonings that are absolutely fresh.

The Future

It is not easy to predict the future of foodways in America. Such major trends as preservation by freezing, dehydration, irradiation, and the use of additives will doubtless continue. The near future may bring "tissue culture," a technology that can produce coffee, spices, and drugs without growing entire plants (Kloppenburg 1988). The accelerating demand for speed and convenience in the 1990s that resulted in so many new time-saving products will probably also stay with us. Examples of really "fast" foods are packaged salads, sold with dressing so that the consumer simply opens the package and eats; microwave brownies, "baked" in a microwave oven; caramel topping that requires only pouring onto baked apples; "no-bake" cheesecake in machine-made pie crusts; and even ready-made omelettes that can be microwaved.

It seems clear that more and more processed foods of every kind, including those altered by biotechnology, will confront the consumers of the future. Probably we will also continue to witness the phenomenon of one ethnic food fad succeeding another, this accompanied by the marketing of ethnic foodstuffs in "Americanized" forms to satisfy desires for foods that are exotic but nevertheless familiar. Health and environmental concerns will doubtless lead to an increasing consumer insistence on accurate labeling and honest marketing procedures. As the planet becomes increasingly crowded in the twenty-first century, more efficient strategies will be required to feed growing numbers of people. America's vast bounty will likely be called upon, and it is to be hoped that the response will be both thoughtful and caring.

James Comer

Bibliography

Belasco, Warren J. 1989. *Appetite for change: How the counterculture took on the food industry.* Ithaca, N.Y.

Benoäit, Jehane. 1970. *The Canadiana cookbook: A complete heritage of Canadian cooking.* Toronto.

Boily-Blanchette, Lise. 1979. *The bread ovens of Quebec.* Ottawa.

Booth, Sally Smith. 1971. *Hung, strung & potted: A history of eating in colonial America.* New York.

Brears, Peter C. D. 1987. *Traditional food in Yorkshire.* Edinburgh.

Brewster, Letitia, and Michael F. Jacobson. 1978. *The changing American diet.* Washington, D.C.

Burwell, Letitia M. 1895. *A girl's life in Virginia before the war.* New York.

Crawford, Mary. 1914. *Social life in old New England.* New York.

Crosby, Alfred W. 1986. *Ecological imperialism: The biological expansion of Europe, 900–1900.* Cambridge.

Cummings, Richard Osborn. 1940. *The American and his food: A history of food habits in the United States.* Chicago.

Derven, Daphne. 1984. Deerfield foodways. In *Foodways in the northeast,* ed. Peter Benes and Jane Montague Benes, 47–63. Boston, Mass.

Dethloff, Henry C. 1988. *A history of the American rice industry, 1685–1985.* College Station, Tex.

DeWitt, David, and Nancy Gerlach. 1990. *The whole chili pepper book.* London.

Driver, Harold Edson. 1961. *Indians of North America.* Chicago.

Duncan, David Ewing. 1995. *Hernando de Soto: A savage quest in the Americas.* New York.

Farb, Peter. 1968. *Man's rise to civilization as shown by the Indians of North America from primeval times to the coming of the industrial state.* New York.

Farmer, Fannie Merritt. 1896. *The Boston Cooking-School cook book.* New York.

Farrington, Doris. 1976. *Fireside cooks and black kettle recipes.* Indianapolis, Ind.

Fischer, David Hackett. 1989. *Albion's seed: Four British folkways in America.* New York.

Fritz, Jean. 1969. *George Washington's Breakfast*. New York.

Golden, Harry. 1958. *Only in America*. Cleveland, Ohio.

Gotlieb, Sandra. 1972. *The gourmet's Canada*. Toronto.

Green, Harvey. 1986. *Fit for America: Health, fitness, sport, and American society*. New York.

Hess, Karen. 1992. *The Carolina rice kitchen: The African connection*. Columbia, S.C.

Hess, Karen, transcr. and annot. 1981. *Martha Washington's booke of cookery*. New York.

Hilliard, Sam. 1988. Hog meat and corn pone: Foodways in the antebellum South. In *Material life in America 1600-1860*, ed. Robert Blair St. George, 311-32. Boston, Mass.

Horry, Harriott Pinckney. 1984. *A colonial plantation cookbook: The receipt book of Harriott Pinckney Horry, 1770*, ed. Richard J. Hooker. Columbia, S.C.

Horton, Lucy. 1972. *The country commune cookbook*. New York.

Hudson, Charles M. 1979. Introduction. In *Black drink*, ed. Charles M. Hudson. Athens, Ga.

Hume, Rosemary. 1970. *Cordon bleu book of jams, preserves and pickles*. Chicago.

Hungry Wolf, Beverly. 1982. *The ways of my grandmothers*. New York.

Iggers, Jeremy. 1996. *The garden of eating: Food, sex, and the hunger for meaning*. New York.

Junior League of Charleston. 1950. *Charleston receipts collected by the Junior League of Charleston*, ed. Mary Vereen Huguenin and Anne Montague Stoney. Charleston, S.C.

Kiple, Kenneth, and Virginia Himmelsteib King. 1981. *Another dimension to the black diaspora: Diet, disease, and racism*. Cambridge.

Kloppenburg, Jack. 1988. *First the seed*. New York.

Kroc, Ray, with Robert Anderson. 1977. *Grinding it out: The making of McDonald's*. Chicago.

Laubin, Reginald, and Gladys Laubin. 1957. *The Indian tipi; its history, construction, and use*. Norman, Okla.

Lea, Elizabeth E. 1982. *A Quaker woman's cookbook: The domestic cookery of Elizabeth Ellicot Lea*, ed. William Woys Weaver. Philadelphia, Pa.

Levenstein, Harvey A. 1988. *Revolution at the table: The transformation of the American diet*. New York.

　　　1993. *Paradox of plenty: A social history of eating in modern America*. New York.

Lichine, Alexis, et al. 1982. *New encyclopedia of wines & spirits*. 3d edition. New York.

Linsenmeyer, Helen Walker. 1976. *From fingers to finger bowls*. San Diego, Calif.

Lockridge, Kenneth A. 1985. *A New England town: The first hundred years: Dedham, Massachusetts, 1636-1736*. Expanded edition. New York.

Milanich, Jerald T. 1995. *Florida Indians and the invasion from Europe*. Gainesville, Fla.

Mintz, Sidney W. 1985. *Sweetness and power: The place of sugar in modern history*. New York.

Nash, Gary B. 1968. *Quakers and politics: Pennsylvania, 1681-1726*. Princeton, N.J.

Nightingale, Marie. 1971. *Out of old Nova Scotia kitchens*. New York.

Pillsbury, Richard. 1990. *From boarding house to bistro: The American restaurant then and now*. Boston, Mass.

Plante, Ellen. 1995. *The history of the American kitchen*. New York.

Prins, Harald E. L. 1996. *The Mi'kmaq: Resistance, accommodation, and cultural survival*. Fort Worth, Tex.

Ragsdale, John. 1991. *Dutch ovens chronicled*. Fayetteville, Ark.

Randolph, Mary. [1828] 1984. *The Virginia house-wife*. Columbia, S.C.

Robertson, Laurel, Carol Flinders, and Bronwen Godfrey. 1976. *Laurel's kitchen: A handbook for vegetarian cookery & nutrition*. Berkeley, Calif.

Root, Waverley Lewis, and Richard de Rochemont. 1976. *Eating in America: A history*. New York.

Rorabaugh, W. J. 1979. *The alcoholic republic: An American tradition*. New York.

Rountree, Helen C. 1989. *The Powhatan Indians of Virginia: Their traditional culture*. Norman, Okla.

Rutledge, Sarah. [1847] 1979. *The Carolina housewife*. Facsimile edition. Columbia, S.C.

Shapiro, Laura. 1986. *Perfection salad: Women and cooking at the turn of the century*. New York.

Simmons, Amelia. [1796] 1965. *American cookery*. Grand Rapids, Mich.

Sinclair, Upton. [1906] 1984. *The jungle*. Cutchogue, N.Y.

Smallzreid, Kathleen Ann. 1956. *The everlasting pleasure: Influences on America's kitchens, cooks, and cookery, from 1565 to the year 2000*. New York.

Sokoloff, Raymond A. 1991. *Why we eat what we eat: How the encounter between the New World and the Old changed the way everyone on the planet eats*. New York.

Spencer, Colin. 1995. *The heretic's feast: A history of vegetarianism*. Hanover, N.H.

Sturtevant, William. 1979. Black drink and other caffeine-containing beverages among non-Indians. In *Black drink*, ed. Charles M. Hudson, 151-83. Athens, Ga.

Tannahill, Reay. 1988. *Food in history*. Revised edition. New York.

Temple, Robert K. G. 1986. *The genius of China: 3,000 years of science, discovery, and invention*. New York.

Tropp, Barbara. 1982. *The modern art of Chinese cooking*. New York.

Tucker, David. 1993. *Kitchen gardens in America*. Ames, Iowa.

Wolcott, Imogene, ed. 1971. *The Yankee cookbook: An anthology of incomparable recipes from the six New England states, and a little something about the people whose tradition for good eating is herein permanently recorded*. Revised edition. New York.

V.D.7 ❧ The Arctic and Subarctic Regions

Traditional foodways have played an intrinsic part in the daily lives of the Native American peoples in the Arctic and Subarctic. Unlike other Americans, whose visits to their local grocery stores for food are seldom memorable, the people of Minto could look at a piece of dried fish and remember where they caught it, the activity on the river, and congratulations received from family members. The point is that food is more intimate for those who catch, grow, or gather it than for those who simply drop it into a shopping cart. The procurement, processing, preparation, and serving of food unites such people with their history, their future, and each other. The use of local resources serves as a direct emotional and spiritual link to the environment on which they depend.

This chapter explores the prehistoric, historic, and current dietary patterns of Native Americans in Alaska, Canada, and Greenland. Because of the wide variety of cultures in the Subarctic and Arctic, this is necessarily a general discussion.

The People

The Native American groups of the Arctic and Subarctic consist of two major genetic and linguistic populations – the Northern Athapaskan Indians and the Eskimo. In Alaska and Canada, the Eskimo are generally coastal people who are believed to have entered North America some 9,000 years ago. The older denizens are the Northern Athapaskans, located for the most part in the interior of Alaska and Canada, who are thought to have crossed the Bering Strait about 15,000 years ago.

Environment

Subarctic

The Tanana people are Athapaskans who reside in the area of Minto Flats on the Alaska Plateau, which is dissected by the Yukon, Tanana, and Kuskokwim rivers. The landscape includes mountain ranges of 3,000 to 4,000 feet, rivers, streams, marshes, grassy fields, and islands.

There are four seasons in this Subarctic region. The winter – long, dark, windy, and very cold – is a time when minimal light and extreme cold limit travel. Spring is associated with the thawing of the rivers and boat travel, but frequent stops to warm up with tea and snacks are necessary to combat the cold. Spring weather is variable from day to day, with warm days and cold nights. Summer is short, warm, and without darkness, with rainy days often bringing concern about flooding rivers. These are the months that are associated with travel on the rivers and roads and, of course, with fishing and gathering. Autumn is marked by the gradual darkening of the night and colder days. By late autumn, the leaves have changed color or fallen, the snow has returned, and the focus is on moose and duck hunting.

A wide variety of flora are present in the Subarctic. Tree types include aspen, white spruce, birch, poplar, and willow. The spruce, birch, and willow are used for medicine, building materials, and fuel. Edible plants include wild rhubarb, Indian potato, wild onion, lowbush cranberry, highbush cranberry, blueberry, wild rose, and raspberry.

Animal populations that are hunted and trapped are mountain sheep, moose, bear, muskrat, rabbit, beaver, porcupine, and duck. A variety of fish are avail-

able, including salmon, burbot, grayling, whitefish, pike, and sucker.

All Northern Athapaskan populations practice a subsistence strategy of hunting, gathering, and fishing, which varies with location. It is a seminomadic subsistence strategy which, for some, involves moving from their villages to winter, summer, fall, and spring camps in order to take advantage of the local resources of each, although many now reside permanently in the winter camp.

There are, of course, regional variations. For example, the Tanaina, who reside in a lush coastal and riverine environment around the Cook Inlet in southern Alaska, have access to a wide variety of marine and inland resources. They are primarily hunters and fishers who procure mussels, crabs, seals, beluga, moose, caribou, and groundhogs. But their diet also incorporates a wide variety of plant resources during the spring, summer, and fall.

By contrast, more northerly populations, such as the Koyukon, live in a riverine environment considerably more mountainous. Like the Tanaina, these people also depend on hunting and fishing but rely more heavily on the latter throughout the year because of their access to the Yukon River. Salmon (chinook, chum, coho, and sockeye) has long been a primary resource for the Koyukon.

Arctic

The Arctic is designated as a high-altitude region, usually lying above the tree line. It includes a broad expanse of land stretching from western Alaska through Canada as well as Greenland. The ground is frozen year-round (permafrost), and minimal precipitation occurs.

The diversity of food sources in the Arctic is low compared to the Subarctic region. Eskimo populations throughout the Arctic depend mostly on marine species, including seals, whales, walrus, and fish (Freeman 1984). But inland fish are also procured, including char, trout, pike, grayling, and salmon (Freeman 1984). The most important land mammals that provide food are the caribou, arctic hare, and musk ox.

Precontact Subsistence

The majority of precontact Northern Athapaskan groups were interior populations of hunters, fishers, and gatherers, whose seasonal rounds were similar to the pattern seen today.

In winter – a time of minimal subsistence activity – large groups congregated at winter camps, where local resources were processed for food and clothing, and some celebrations were held. When the weather improved, from spring through fall, the larger groups divided into individual family groups that traveled to smaller camps, permitting greater access to food resources. Each family group tended to visit the same camp sites – loosely considered the group's own "territory" - every year. Some, such as the Upper Tanana people, were more dependent on large game, but they nonetheless fished the inland lakes and tributaries and the Tanana River. Spears, bows and arrows, fish traps, gill nets, dip nets, lures, and hooks were all employed in this seasonal harvest of protein, the storage of which was, obviously, important for the coming winter months (Sullivan 1942; VanStone 1974).

Throughout the spring, summer, and fall, the Northern Athapaskans dried, froze, and stored food in birchbark baskets above and below ground. The caches aboveground were small boxlike shelters on stilts with cutout openings or doors. Belowground the caches were dug into the permafrost and covered with wood to seal in the cold air and to protect against animals.

The mobility of the Northern Athapaskans allowed consistent access to food sources, yet their small groups were able to avoid depletion of such sources in any one subsistence area by having a variety of sites. The Tanana Valley people, for example, still continue to use a number of different sites during the year, moving from one to another by birchbark canoe or by snowshoe (Sullivan 1942; VanStone 1974).

In the spring and summer, the major foods obtained included whitefish, salmon, duck, and birds' eggs. Gathered products, such as blueberries and cranberries, were also stored during the late summer and fall months. The important foods during autumn were moose, caribou, duck, grouse, and rabbits. In the winter, stored foods were supplemented by trapping small game and by ice fishing.

Throughout the year, families spent considerable time exploiting other resources as well. Ducks were hunted in the spring as soon as the weather warmed and people could safely travel by boat. In the summer, berries and small animals were sought, in addition to fish, whereas larger mammals were hunted or trapped mostly during the fall. Such a pattern of seasonal subsistence was common for Indian populations, such as the Kutchin, Koyukon, Ingalik, Kolchan, Tanaina, and Ahtna (Clark 1981; De Laguna and McClellan 1981; Hosley 1981a; Slobodin 1981; Snow 1981; Townsend 1981).

In addition, some populations, such as the Ahtna and the Tanaina, who resided close to mountainous regions, could hunt Dall sheep (De Laguna and McClellan 1981; Townsend 1981). The Koyukon, who are northwest of the Tanana, actively traded with the Eskimo, which increased their subsistence region (Slobodin 1981), and some populations in the Subarctic, such as the Tanaina, hunted sea mammals along the coast of southern and western Alaska (Townsend 1981).

Almost all native Alaskan populations continued their seminomadic lifestyle until the turn of the twentieth century, when increased mining and fur-trading activities eventually brought about the development of permanent villages. But even today there are still many hunting and gathering populations that carry on in a traditional manner (Hosley 1981a; Berger 1985). Older members pass on subsistence knowledge to the rest of the population, which links the generations together (Berger 1985).

Contact and Chance in Subsistence and Diet

Prolonged contact with Western culture brought a dependence on trade goods, such as guns, iron chisels, knives, and axes and gradually led to the development of sedentary camps around the trading posts, which disrupted traditional subsistence activities (VanStone 1974; Martin 1978; McClellan 1981; Frank 1983; Newman 1985, 1987; Yerbury 1986).

In Canada, reliance on trade goods brought an increasing interdependence between Indians and trading-post inhabitants, as many of the former entered into economic relationships with traders. They hunted and fished for them, receiving trade items, such as guns, for their efforts.

One need only consider the disruption brought about when the Canadian Iroquois began, in the mid-seventeenth century, to hunt for furs instead of food. After depleting their own traditional hunting grounds of both food and fur-bearing animals, they began to encroach on the territories of neighboring groups. And as food resources continued to decline, they became increasingly more dependent on the trading posts. By the early 1800s, the moose and caribou had been overhunted and a dietary change had taken place, forcing the Indians to rely on hares, fish, and purchased food (Martin 1978). Yet even as food resources declined, sedentary life fostered Iroquois population growth, which considerably enhanced the risk of severe food shortages (Ray 1974).

To obtain goods to trade for food, many Alaskan natives turned to trapping in the late 1800s (McClellan 1981; Schneider 1986). The steel trap gained importance around 1900 and accelerated the pace of trapping animals for economic rather than subsistence reasons. Cash and trade relationships with the Alaska Commercial Company and the Western Fur and Trading Company, in particular, enabled Alaskan natives to purchase Western foods and products from trading posts and from Europeans moving through the region.

Animal populations declined as trapping increased and native human populations became more sedentary. Native trappers traveled ever farther away from these settlements in search of quality pelts, and it became necessary to leave family members behind, often for days. Moreover, as native populations continued to nucleate into fewer, and larger, settlements on the main rivers, the decrease in nomadic patterns led to a summer-winter dualism. By the middle to late 1930s, many families had established a pattern of occupying fishing camps during the summer and trapping and hunting from more permanent villages in the winter (Hosley 1981a). Finally, and obviously, an exchange of the traditional subsistence lifestyle for a kind of Western economic mode of living meant that increased sedentism also disrupted traditional dietary patterns.

Trade goods offered unique tastes in compact forms that were intriguing to the native populations. Foods high in carbohydrates, such as the white potato or crackers, infrequently found in the traditional diet, seemed attractive because they added variety. Other items, such as coffee, tea, flour, and sugar, quickly became staples to be purchased in bulk, and they are still bought in large quantities today. Coffee and tea quickly replaced the beverages decocted from local plants because they were easier to acquire than the traditional items.

The seductive appeal of trade goods reached out even as far as to the Greenland Eskimo (Freuchen 1935). Their participation in European whaling activities was rewarded with a variety of Western foods, such as tea, coffee, crackers, oatmeal, and chocolate (Freuchen 1935). The growing dependence on such foods was well documented by Peter Freuchen: "[T]he coffee beans they purchase raw and roast them to a crisp. To make them go a long way, the Eskimos mix the beans with rice or barley.... This form of coffee turns them into near-addicts. When they are without coffee, they say they feel worse than when they are starving" (1935: 109).

Disruption of traditional life by the fur trade was further exacerbated by the gold rush (1884 to 1920). Alaskan natives who had become dependent on Western products now encountered much difficulty in obtaining them. Competition for scarce food resources pushed the price of Western foods beyond their purchasing ability, and as a consequence, natives took jobs for wages in mining towns and on riverboats to increase their purchasing power. The trend toward sedentism that had begun with the fur trade accelerated, with some people abandoning all of their traditional subsistence activities as a result of the high wages to be obtained in the towns and on the rivers. And, as highways and roads were built in Alaska, the natives sought jobs associated with their construction.

Although such activity was generally destructive of old ways, such goods as firearms and dogsleds did help some people to adhere to traditional subsistence activities and diets. Certainly the rhythm of subsistence hunting was altered dramatically with the introduction of firearms, as hunting changed from a communal to an individual activity. It was the use of the rifle that ensured that moose and caribou would continue to be overhunted. Indeed, the caribou were ultimately decimated because they traveled in large herds, and with decreasing caribou, native populations focused their hunting strategies on the moose. Along with the greater access to food resources permitted by the rifle, hunters also increased their harvest of fur-bearing animals.

The adoption of sleds pulled by dogs was yet another factor that affected Indian lifestyle. Dogsleds permitted travel in the winter months, which extended the trapping season. In addition, as Robert A. McKennan (1981) points out, the introduction of the dog team increased both the need and the market for dried fish, an easily transportable dog food.

With an increased demand for fish, the Lower Tanana Indians adopted the use of the fishwheel, which meant larger quantities of fish for both human and animal populations. But because the fishwheel required deep and fast-moving water in order to be functional, Indian populations began moving away from the smaller rivers to the larger Tanana River.

Other dramatic changes came with the introduction of transportation based on fossil fuels (Cohen 1974), such as gasoline-powered boats, snowmobiles, and automobiles. Boats greatly increased access to local resources, especially during the fowl- and moose-hunting seasons. Water travel thus became more efficient, and winter and summer villages were able to be more widely separated (Hosley 1981a: 551).

Other gasoline-powered vehicles also allowed native people to move within their subsistence area faster and more frequently. In the 1960s, the Canadian Netsilik used snowmobiles to chase caribou. Unfortunately, it was this combined use of gasoline-powered vehicles and firearms that brought about the near total destruction of caribou in Canada (Neatby 1984). Another technological factor that encouraged this sort of overhunting was the home freezer, which led to the taking of more game and fish than could be immediately used.

Current Dietary Patterns

The Mix of Western and Traditional Foods
Current diets in the Subarctic and Arctic contain a mixture of traditional and Western foods. Many native populations eat such a combination because they are unable to obtain adequate foodstuffs by reliance on either traditional subsistence activities or Western resources alone. Traditional activities are frequently limited by participation in wage labor, yet many people are unable to afford the cost of Western foods on a daily basis.

This reliance on both subsistence foods and trade goods is aptly described by Kristin Borre (1991: 49) for an Inuit population of North Baffin Island, Canada. In this Arctic region, traditional hunting activities are of great importance, with children ages 7 to 15 contributing 40 percent, men 37 percent, and women 23 percent of the effort to capture most of the protein consumed. But despite a high level of traditional subsistence pursuits, the Inuit are also incorporating Western foods, purchased for immediate consumption, into their diet. Among other things, Western foods are increasingly attractive to younger members of the community.

A similar pattern can be observed among the Inupiat of Alaska's North Slope. Although many of the adult men work as wage laborers in the oil development at Prudhoe Bay, the Inupiat still need to rely on traditional food hunting and gathering for about 45 percent of foods consumed. Their increased income has resulted in the consumption of junk foods, especially soda pop and candy by the children (Kruse, Kleinfeld, and Travis 1982).

The uneasy juxtaposition of Western foods and traditional foods in the diet is evident in Richard K. Nelson's description of Athapaskan Alaskan life: "Sitting down for an evening meal, members of an Athapaskan family might find moose meat, bear grease, and wild berries on the table along with store-bought soup, bread and butter, and canned fruit. Before eating, someone may give a Christian blessing; and then a young daughter might be told not to eat a certain food because it is tabooed for a woman her age" (1986: 214).

Ceremonial Diet

Ceremonial food use, which also features a variety of traditional and Western foods, deserves consideration in any discussion of food and drink among current Subarctic and Arctic populations. Thus, the ensuing discussion highlights Alaskan Athapaskan potlatches observed by this author in 1987 and 1989, which illustrate the incorporation of both, along with comparative examples drawn from both Canada and Greenland.

Potlatches serve the important purpose of marking an event taking place or a stage of life. Such events include death, the memory of a person (and perhaps the making of a memorial song), a birthday, the first salmon catch of the season, a moose killed, a marriage, and important meetings. The largest potlatches are the funeral and memorial ceremonies. Family members give a memorial potlatch some one to five years after an individual's death. Memorial song potlatches are organizational ceremonies to create a song about the life of the person who died. Important meeting potlatches usually occur when a weighty decision has to be made concerning the village. The occasion may specifically involve an individual, or a family, but the holding of a potlatch often radiates out gradually to include the entire village, as well as other villages, due to the interrelationships existing within the population. The extensive quantity of food available during potlatches means that the Northern Athapaskan people understand them to be feasts as well.

Knowledge of an impending major potlatch, such as a birthday or a memorial, spreads quickly through villages in interior Alaska – especially the ones in proximity to Minto by river travel or to Fairbanks by air. People in different villages have developed close ties at potlatches, events that encourage them to reevaluate long-held traditions, relationships with friends, and village ties.

At another level, the potlatch is an occasion for distributing goods (Langdon and Worl 1981). During any type of potlatch, people who attend receive both food and gifts. The latter are given in respect and gratitude by the people hosting the potlatch. At a funeral potlatch, for example, some of the possessions of the deceased are given as presents, which makes them emotionally significant for the recipients.

Extensive quantities of food are common in ceremonies in the Subarctic and Arctic. One example is the Northern Alaskan Coast Eskimo Messenger Feast, which is a matter of competition among villages, with the village giving the feast attempting to "overwhelm a guest with food" (Spencer 1984).

A wide range of traditional foods, featuring both animal and plant items, is served at potlatches. Important animal dishes are moose, duck, salmon, beaver, and whitefish. Plant foods include a variety of berries, such as blueberries and highbush and lowbush cranberries, all boiled with water, flour, and sugar.

At a major potlatch, such as a funeral, the chiefs and other men receive the most highly desired portions of food, such as the large bones with moose meat still attached and the heads of salmon. Fish heads, considered a high-status food, are also served to the elder women.

Although moose meat is an important traditional food served at every potlatch, it obviously is of greatest importance at a first moose potlatch. After a family obtains its first moose of the season, its members hold a potlatch during which moose may be the only traditional food served.

The use of a traditional food as the primary dish also occurs at a first salmon potlatch, which is held in the village after someone catches the first salmon in the spring. Following the first catch, every effort is made to procure enough salmon for everyone. At the potlatch, the salmon is cooked in a variety of ways – boiled, in soup, and its eggs are also served.

Other protein foods, such as beluga, are important ceremonial foods for the MacKenzie Delta Eskimo. Marine animals are also used by the Iglulki to supplement "feasts of boiled meat . . . to which the whole camp was invited" (Mary-Rousseliere 1984: 440).

Western foods too are consumed at the potlatches, although these products are generally considered supplemental to traditional foods. Of all the village potlatches, the birthday ceremony contains the greatest variety of Western products, such as barbecued chicken, hot dogs, carrots, celery, green salad, fruit salad, white cake with frosting, deviled eggs, cauliflower, margarine, jam, and sweet soft drinks.

By contrast, at funeral potlatches mostly traditional foods are employed. Funeral potlatches have been a tradition of the Minto people for a long time, which explains the greater use of traditional foods, whereas birthday potlatches are relatively new (elders have indicated that they never used to celebrate the event). Thus, the presence of more Western foods corresponds with the newness of the birthday potlatch.

Current Dietary Patterns and Health

Traditional diets in both the Subarctic and Arctic provided much protein with a good ratio of unsaturated to saturated fats, and they were low in sugar and carbohydrates. But current Western foods incorporated into the diet do just the opposite in that they deliver high levels of saturated fats, sugar, and carbohydrates.

H. H. Draper (1977) discusses the contrasting health effects of traditional and Western foods in the diet of the Arctic Inuit. The traditional diet yielded much protein, and the consumption of the stomach contents of caribou, along with seasonal plant harvests, contributed important vitamins and minerals to the regimen. But the addition of dairy products, sugar, and carbohydrate-laden foods to the diet has created serious health problems. In the case of dairy products, Native American populations lack the ability to absorb lactose, and lactose malabsorption can produce cramping and diarrhea (Harrison 1975). There are other health difficulties that arise from the sugar and carbohydrates in the Western diet, ranging from tooth decay and obesity to diabetes and heart disease. In short, a departure from traditional diets to which they were well adapted has created a frequently life-threatening crisis of health for native peoples of the Subarctic and Arctic regions of the Americas. Alleviation of that crisis must begin with this realization.

Linda J. Reed

Bibliography

Ammitzboll, T., M. Bencard, J. Bodenhoff, et al. 1991. Clothing. In *The Greenland mummies,* ed. P. Jens, H. Hansen, Jorgen Meldgaard, and Jorgen Nordqvist, 116-49. Washington, D.C.

Berger, Thomas R. 1985. *Village journey: The report of the Alaska Native Review Commission.* New York.

Borre, Kristin. 1991. Seal blood, Inuit blood, and diet: A biocultural model of physiology and cultural identity. *Medical Anthropology Quarterly* 5: 48-62.

Bresciani, J., W. Dansgaard, B. Fredskild, et al. 1991. Living conditions. In *The Greenland mummies,* ed. P. Jens, H. Hansen, Jorgen Meldgaard, and Jorgen Nordqvist, 150-67. Washington, D.C.

Clark, A. McFadyen. 1981. Koyukon. In *Subarctic,* ed. J. Helm, 582-601. Washington, D.C.

Cohen, Yehudi A. 1974. Culture as adaptation. In *Man in adaptation: The cultural present,* ed. Y. A. Cohen, 45-68. Chicago.

Counter, S. Allen. 1991. *North pole legacy: Black, white and Eskimo.* Amherst, Mass.

De Laguna, Frederica. 1977. *Voyage to Greenland.* New York.

De Laguna, Frederica, and Catharine McClellan. 1981. Ahtna. In *Subarctic,* ed. J. Helm, 641-63. Washington, D.C.

Draper, H. H. 1977. The aboriginal Eskimo diet in modern perspective. *American Anthropologist* 79: 309-16.

Dumond, Don E. 1977. *The Eskimos and Aleuts.* London.

Ellestad-Sayed, J. J., J. C. Haworth, and J. A. Hildes. 1978. Disaccharide malabsorption and dietary patterns in two Canadian Eskimo communities. *American Journal of Clinical Nutrition* 31: 1473-8.

Frank, Ellen. 1983. *Moving around in the old days.* Fairbanks, Alaska.

Freeman, Milton M. R. 1984. Arctic ecosystems. In *Handbook of North American Indians,* Vol. 5, 36-48. Washington, D.C.

Freuchen, Peter. 1935. *Arctic adventure: My life in the frozen North.* New York.

Gullov, H. C., and Jorgen Meldgaard. 1991. Inuit and Norsemen. In *The Greenland mummies,* ed. P. Jens, H. Hansen, Jorgen Meldgaard, and Jorgen Nordqvist, 13-36. Washington, D.C.

Harrison, Gail G. 1975. Primary adult lactase deficiency: A problem in anthropological genetics. *American Anthropologist* 77: 812-35.

Hosley, Edward H. 1981a. Environment and culture in the Alaska plateau. In *Subarctic,* ed. J. Helm, 546-55. Washington, D.C.

1981b. Intercultural relations and culture change in the Alaska plateau. In *Subarctic,* ed. J. Helm, 618-22. Washington, D.C.

Joos, Sandra K. 1985. Economic, social, and cultural factors in the analysis of disease: Dietary change and diabetes mellitus among the Florida Seminole Indians. In *Ethnic and regional foodways in the United States: The performance of group identity,* ed. Linda Brown and Kay Mussell, 217-37. Knoxville, Tenn.

Kruse, John A., Judith Kleinfeld, and Robert Travis. 1982. Energy development on Alaska's North Slope: Effects on the Inupiat population. *Human Organization* 41: 97-106.

Langdon, Steve, and Rosita Worl. 1981. *Distribution and exchange of subsistence resources in Alaska.* Technical paper No. 55, University of Alaska. Fairbanks, Alaska.

Lippe-Stokes, Susan. 1980. Eskimo story-knife tales: Reflections of change in food habits. In *Food, ecology and culture: Readings in the anthropology of dietary practices,* ed. J. R. K. Robson, 75-82. New York.

Martin, Calvin. 1978. *Keepers of the game: Indian-animal relationships and the fur trade.* Berkeley, Calif.

Mary-Rousseliere, Guy. 1984. *Handbook of North American Indians,* Vol. 5, 431-46. Washington, D.C.

Maxwell, Moreau S. 1985. *Prehistory of the Eastern Arctic.* Orlando, Fla.

McClellan, Catharine. 1981. Tagish. In *Subarctic,* ed. J. Helm, 35-42. Washington, D.C.

McClellan, Catharine, and Glenda Denniston. 1981. Environment and culture in the cordillera. In *Subarctic,* ed. J. Helm, 372-86. Washington, D.C.

McKennan, Robert A. 1981. Tanana. In *Subarctic,* ed. J. Helm, 562-76. Washington, D. C.

Neatby, Leslie H. 1984. *Handbook of North American Indians,* Vol. 5, 377-90. Washington, D.C.

Nelson, Richard K. 1986. *Hunters of the northern forest: Designs for survival among the Alaskan Kutchin.* Chicago.

Newman, Peter Charles. 1985. *Company of adventurers.* New York.

1987. *The story of the Hudson's Bay Company.* New York.

Ray, Arthur J. 1974. *Indians in the fur trade. Their role as trappers, hunters and middlemen in the lands Southwest of Hudson Bay, 1660-1870.* Toronto.

Schaefer, Otto. 1971. When the Eskimo comes to town. *Nutrition Today* 8: 8-16.

Schneider, William S. 1986. On the back slough. In *Interior Alaska: A journey through time,* ed. Robert M. Thorson, Anchorage, Alaska.

Slobodin, Richard. 1981. Kutchin. In *Subarctic,* ed. J. Helm, 514-32. Washington, D.C.

Snow, Jeanne H. 1981. Ingalik. In *Subarctic,* ed. J. Helm, 602-17. Washington, D.C.

Spencer, Robert F. 1984. North Alaska Coast Eskimo. In *Handbook of North American Indians,* Vol. 5, 320-37. Washington, D.C.

Sullivan, R. J. 1942. *The Ten'A food quest.* Ph.D. thesis, Catholic University of America, Washington, D.C.

Townsend, Joan B. 1981. Tanaina. In *Subarctic,* ed. J. Helm, 623-40. Washington, D.C.

VanStone, James W. 1974. *Athapaskan adaptations: Hunters and fishermen of the Subarctic forests.* Chicago.

1984. Mainland Southwest Alaska Eskimo. In *Handbook of North American Indians,* Vol. 5, 224-42. Washington, D.C.

Vogt, Evon Z. 1972. The acculturation of American Indians. In *Perspectives on the North American Indians,* ed. M. Nagler, 2-13. Toronto.

Yerbury, J. C. 1986. *The Subarctic Indians and the fur trade, 1680-1860.* Vancouver, B.C.

V.E

The History and Culture of Food and Drink in Sub-Saharan Africa and Oceania

V.E.1 ◆ Africa South from the Sahara

Describing the principal sources of food for the inhabitants of Africa south from the Sahara is a relatively easy task. Most diets are dominated by products made from a single staple crop, and there are not all that many of them. Maize, sorghums, pearl or bulrush millet, and rice are the prominent grains, and cassava, yams, and bananas or plantains account for most of the vegetatively propagated varieties. Furthermore, their general geographies can be explained, for the most part, by annual totals and seasonality of rainfall. For example, near the dry margins of cropping, pearl millet makes its greatest dietary contribution, whereas the equatorial zone is where bananas and plantains come to the fore. Even adding in the role played by livestock, one that varies from insignificant to crucial, does not overly complicate the picture. Among farmers, fowl are fairly ubiquitous, while sheep, goats, and cattle are kept wherever diseases, especially sleeping sickness, do not prohibit them. When aridity intervenes to make crop cultivation too hazardous to rely upon, the herding of camels or cattle becomes the primary subsistence activity.

The problems come when attempting to go much beyond this level of generality. There is a plethora of other foods that are important to diets, including those from wild sources, and matters get even more difficult to sort out when issues of history, culture, and nutritional adequacy must be addressed. The region's human diversity is enormous, and most food systems display a complex interweaving of influences, ranging from the distant past to the present. Unfortunately, trying to understand what has happened through time is hindered by a dearth of information. The written record is sparse before the twentieth century, and archaeology, so far, has produced very few dates. As a result, temporal insights often must rely on somewhat less precise sources of information, such as paleobotany, historic and comparative linguistics, and cultural anthropology.

Our understanding of current diets and their adequacy is only slightly better informed. During recent decades, Africa south from the Sahara has replaced China and India as the "land of famine." Actual famine, however, has visited only restricted areas, such as portions of the Sahel, Somalia, and Mozambique. Elsewhere, people have not been starving, although only a few elites enjoy the luxuries of Western-like food abundance. Serious nutrition-related health problems clearly exist, especially among young children and reproductive-age women, and the food production data do point to an ever more precarious supply situation throughout much of the region. But surveys that allow for comparing diets and nutritional well-being are woefully inadequate.

As a result, the following presentation is offered in the spirit of being one best estimate. It begins with an overview of African "agricultural origins and dispersals," to borrow a title from Carl Sauer (1969), which, contrary to many earlier interpretations, were not all by-products of Egyptian influences. Other Africans engaged in their own domesticating processes, leading to the crops that provided the basic raw materials for the transition to food-producing ways of life. The most significant imports, the subjects of the next section, entered already existing agricultural systems. A brief discussion of food preparations and eating habits follows, and the final section is devoted to an assessment of what appear to be the most widespread diet-related disorders, excepting famine.

African Agricultural Origins

We can begin some 9,000 years ago when all Africans southward from the Sahara still gathered, hunted, and fished for their foods, with the particular dietary mix governed by what the local environment could provide. For example, on the vast savanna-covered plateaus, the abundance of game animals allowed meat to be eaten regularly, along with a variety of nuts, berries, roots, and tubers. Meat was harder to come by in more densely forested habitats, but freshwater fish were widely available as complements to vegetable foods, whereas along some coastal sections, extensive middens testify to the dietary importance of shellfish. Virtually all of the area appears to have been occupied, at least on a seasonal basis; exceptions were the higher elevations, the heart of the Sahara Desert (much less extensive then than now), the narrow strip of the Namib Desert, and the deeper recesses of the equatorial rain forest. For the most part, people lived in small, mobile bands exploiting territories that necessitated the use of tens of square kilometers to supply the subsistence needs of one adult.

By way of contrast, certain riparian habitats north and east of the equatorial rain forest supported higher population densities and more sedentary occupancy. They did so because of Late Stone Age technological advances that allowed people to use a diverse array of plants, including wild grass seeds, for foodstuffs, as well as to engage in an intensified exploitation of fish and waterfowl (Sutton 1977). The evidence to date points to such locales as these as having been at the forefront of domestication activities in Africa south from the Sahara, thus lending support to the agricultural origins models developed by D. Rindos (1984) and R. S. MacNeish (1992). Shortly thereafter, other movements in the direction of agriculture took place along the rain forest–savanna ecotone of western and central Africa and within what is now Ethiopia.

Whether there were broad zones or precise centers of domestication activity at the outset cannot be determined, but no matter which situation prevailed, the diffusion pattern evolved into one of multiple frontiers carrying a variety of crops and animals. And the pace of change varied considerably. In some instances, Stone Age economies seem to have given way quickly, but the norm was for agriculture to gain ascendancy over gathering, hunting, and fishing only very gradually.

Crops

The earliest signs of possible domestication come from two sites within the Sahara. One is at Nabta Playa in western Egypt, where a number of sorghum-type seeds have been found in deposits dated 8,100 years ago (Wasylikowa et al. 1993). Whether they were cultivated or gathered, however, cannot be determined. The other is in the Ahaggar and contains a seed, two pollen grains, and grain impressions, dated between 6,850 and 5,350 years ago, of what could be pearl millet *(Pennisetum glaucum)* (Muzzolini 1993). This is not much to go on, but the Ahaggar does fall within the biogeographical range of related wild varieties, while the timing corresponds to a moist episode that would have supported millet cultivation at favorable Saharan locales, such as in the highlands and along the shores of then fairly numerous lakes and rivers (Harlan 1989). Also dated to approximately the same time as the Nabta Playa and Ahaggar finds are Neolithic sites that have yielded

pottery, grindstones, and rubbers. Their presence by no means guarantees cultivation, but the large numbers of artifacts add extra fuel to the speculation that something of significance was indeed taking place (Camps 1982).

Farther south, events moved more slowly, although both botanical and linguistic research indicates that domestication processes were trending in the direction of agriculture within several different zones during the period from 5,000 to 4,000 years ago. One zone followed the Sahel–savanna country stretching from the upper Niger River valley, through the Lake Chad basin, to Dar Fur. Overall, the western half appears to have been more active, accounting for African rice *(Oryza glaberrima)*, fonio *(Digitaria exilis)*, guinea millet *(Brachiaria deflexa)*, watermelon *(Colocynthis citrullus)*, and Bambara groundnuts *(Voandzeia subterranea)*. The area east of Lake Chad was where the first sorghums *(Sorghum bicolor)* seem to have been cultivated. Later activities produced a variety of specialized sorghum races that would serve as the principle food source for peoples inhabiting the semiarid and subhumid regions of not only Africa but also India (Harlan 1989 and 1992).

So far, this vast zone to the south of the desert has yielded only two archaeological sites with substantiated evidence about the course of early crop cultivation. The oldest is Dhar Tichitt located in what is now south-central Mauritania, where P. J. Munson (1976) has documented a progression from an earlier riparian-type economy to a village-based one growing pearl millet by 3,100 years ago. No in-migration is indicated, thus pointing to diffusion from the Sahara as the likely source for the millet. The other site is Daima on the western side of Lake Chad. Here, excavations of earthen mounds have revealed the presence of a mixed economy involving fishing, hunting, gathering, herding, and crop cultivation centered on sorghums dating back to 2,500 years ago (Connah 1981). The agriculture practiced at Daima was advanced enough to support villages of more than 100 inhabitants and, therefore, must have been preceded by earlier developments that have not yet been unearthed.

Ever since the days of N. I. Vavilov (1926), the area within and around the Ethiopian highlands has been identified as a likely source of indigenous crop domestication. Now well established as coming from the cooler, seasonally rainy uplands of the center and east are teff *(Eragrostis tef)*, noog *(Guizotia abyssinica)*, and finger millet *(Eleusine coracana)*, whereas ensete *(Musa ensete)* and coffee *(Coffea arabica)* are ascribed to the warmer, wetter southwestern forests. Dates are unconfirmed, but opinion based on linguistic analyses favors something on the order of 5,000 years ago for the upland crops (Ehret 1979; Phillipson 1993). This date may be fairly accurate because when wheat and barley arrived from south Arabian sources, about 3,000 years ago, they seem to have been incorporated into already well established agricultural systems.

Finally, various African communities appear to have been experimenting with yam cultivation (primarily *Dioscorea rotundata* and *Dioscorea bulbifera*) along a wide front following the savanna–rain forest ecotone in western Africa (Alexander and Coursey 1969). How far back in time this goes cannot be determined, but it must have been by at least 5,000 years ago because of the association of yams with several major population migrations dated to around this time (Ehret 1982). Because of the workings of humid climates and acidic soils on a plant that is inherently perishable to begin with, archaeology is unlikely ever to shed much light on the origins of yam cultivation, and, thus, further insights will have to continue to be based primarily on advances in botanical and linguistic research.

Kersting's groundnuts *(Kerstingiella geocarpa),* cowpeas *(Vigna unguiculata),* and the oil palm *(Elaeis guineensis)* are other crops thought to derive from the same general ecotone environment (Harlan 1992), but so far only cowpeas have been archaeologically confirmed. These come from the several Kintampo sites focused on central Ghana, and are dated to around 3,800 years ago (Flight 1976). The inhabitants of Kintampo also made considerable use of oil palm kernels, but these probably came from the harvesting of stands of protected wild trees.

Livestock

Unlike its crops, Africa south from the Sahara has depended upon external sources for its most important livestock. No possible ancestors for sheep or goats existed on the continent. Instead they arrived in several waves, from southwestern and central Asian sources, and quickly became integral parts of agricultural systems developed in Egypt and the Maghreb. The first cattle also seem to have entered from the east, although it is possible that indigenous varieties of *Bos primigenius* were domesticated within the Sahara (Smith 1992). These were all humpless types from which the fully domesticated *Bos taurus* arose. Later, but at least by 2,500 years ago, came humped *Bos indicus* types that probably entered Africa both via Egypt and from seaborne contacts with India along the east coast. Eventually, *B. taurus* and *B. indicus* crosses produced several distinctive African breeds, such as the Fulani, Sanga, and Afrikander (Blench 1993; Clutton-Brock 1993).

One initial route of livestock diffusion went upstream along the Nile, as is evidenced at the archaeological sites of Kadero and Esh Shaheinab near the junction of the White and Blue Niles. Wheat and barley may have been grown here as well, but it was sheep, goats, and cattle that constituted the main additions to a preexisting riverine-based Stone Age economy by 7,000 years ago (MacNeish 1992). From here, livestock continued to spread inland, reaching the region of Ethiopia between 5,000 and 6,000 years ago (Ehret 1979).

Roughly contemporaneous with Kadero and Esh Shaheinab are signs of other emergent livestock-based economies within and around the Saharan highlands of Dar Fur, Tibesti, Air, and Ahaggar. The evidence includes animal skeletons, material cultural remains, and, most convincingly, rock art at the remarkable site of Tassili-n-Ajer (Lhote 1959). Preserved there since approximately 7,000 years ago are scenes of what clearly are domesticated, humpless, long-horn cattle, along with their herders (Camps 1982).

When camels first made their way to Africa remains unclear. The dromedary had been domesticated in the Arabian peninsula by at least 3,800 years ago, but it does not seem to have become important in Egypt and the Sahara until much later, perhaps not until Roman times. Rather than entering with caravans crossing via the Sinai, as most experts have tended to think, camels may have first reached Africa by being transported across the Red Sea, a route which would help to explain their seemingly greater antiquity among desert-dwelling nomads in this corner of the continent (Zeuner 1963).

Even more mystery surrounds the entry of the common fowl *(Gallus gallus)* into Africa. We know that they were present in Egypt over 3,000 years ago, but that is about all (Simoons 1961). The usual assumption is that they probably spread from here up the Nile Valley corridor, and it is possible that chickens could have been carried across the Sahara once they had reached the Maghreb. A still later introduction (about A.D. 500) may have been with Malayo-Polynesian voyagers, who touched at points along the Indian Ocean coast on their way to Madagascar. Today, chickens are kept by farmers virtually everywhere, although much of their popularity seems to be quite recent.

Africa can claim two animal domesticates, neither of which, however, became important sources of food. One is the ass *(Equus asinus),* for which the Nubian wild race seems to have provided most of the genetic material (Zeuner 1963). It was in use as a beast of burden in Egypt, and presumably in Nubia, by 5,000 years ago, and from there spread to Ethiopia, the Horn, and the Sahel/Sudanic zone of western Africa at uncertain dates. The other is the guinea fowl, derived largely from *Numidia meleagris galeata,* which appears to have been first raised in the savannas of western Africa. Appreciated more for its aesthetic qualities than anything else, it often cannot be easily differentiated from the wild varieties that are still found widely outside the rain forest zones (Donkin 1991).

These are the essential domesticates that supported the rise of food-producing economies in Africa south from the Sahara. Over a span of 4,000 to 5,000 years, they have been carried across the subcontinent's diverse environments by a complex mix of population migrations and technological diffusions.

Many of these, however, can only be speculated about.

Regional Agricultural Dispersals

Western Africa

The pace of agricultural development in the Sahelian and Sudanic zones of western Africa seems to have intensified under competition and population pressure from southward-drifting livestock herders seeking respite from the ever-worsening aridity that had set in by 4,000 years ago. The evidence points to their having been members of a rapidly diverging Nilosaharan language group, other members of which were also the likely first cultivators of pearl millet (Ehret 1993). The most attractive destinations would have been the water and grazing resources along the upper Niger River valley and its tributaries, the Senegal River valley, and Lake Chad, then much larger than it is now. The Lake Chad area seems to have been occupied by yet other Nilosaharans, in all probability growing sorghums. In the other two areas, however, the herders would have encountered members of the Mande and Atlantic branches of the Niger-Congo language group. It was among them that agricultural systems of production were developing around African rice, fonio, and guinea millet. From all appearances, the Nilosaharans were absorbed, but they did leave livestock as one of their legacies.

Eventually, pearl millet and sorghums spread throughout the Sahelian and Sudanic zones, cultivated either in the flood plain style known as *crue* and *decrue* or else on the interfluves as parts of land-extensive systems of shifting cultivation (Harris 1976). Cattle, sheep, and goats also spread throughout the region, although often herded by specialists, most notably the Fulbe or Fulani. Their origins are traceable to the Senegal River valley, where they may have arisen out of a synthesis of Nilosaharan herders and resident Atlantic-speaking cultivators (Smith 1992).

The Kintampo sites demonstrate that agriculture was on the fringes of the tropical forest zone of western Africa more than 3,000 years ago. Crops were probably still less important than gathered plant foods, but there is strong evidence that goats and sheep had achieved considerable economic importance (Stahl 1993). How long it took from the time of Kintampo for agriculture to reach into the forest itself cannot be determined, although it is unlikely that much of a move was made prior to 2,000 years ago. Then it arrived from two directions. In the west it accompanied the migrations of Atlantic- and Mande-speaking peoples who brought their African rice with them. Farther east, yams accompanied the expansion of other Niger-Congo speakers, this time affiliated with the Kwa and Ijoid families. Eventually, a line that still holds today at approximately the Bandama River in the Ivory Coast came to separate distinctive rice- and yam-eating zones.

A few domesticates from the tropical forest were added to the crop inventory as supplements to the staples. Those in most widespread use include okra *(Hibiscus esculentus),* kola *(Cola sps.),* akee *(Blighia sapida),* and the melegueta pepper *(Aframomum melegueta).* Also associated with the forest are dwarf varieties of humpless short-horn cattle that are somewhat tolerant of virtually ubiquitous sleeping sickness but yield very little milk. Most likely, they are adaptations of the types represented at Tassili (Blench 1993).

Ethiopia and the Horn

In general, the Ethiopian food crop domesticates remained rather narrowly confined to their original environments. The major exception is finger millet, which spread along with the migrations of Southern Cushites that began around 4,000 years ago. A branch of the Cushitic division of the Afroasiatic group that originated in Ethiopia, these people left their highland home for present-day Kenya and Tanzania (Ehret 1979). Taking with them livestock as well, the Southern Cushites were entering virgin agricultural country, but in such few numbers that most of it remained the province of hunter-gatherers until the arrival of later agriculturists.

Some other Cushites had become livestock specialists and claimed the semidesert and desert lands surrounding the Ethiopian highlands. The most ancient are the Beja (the Blemmeys of the Egyptians), who took possession of the lands astride the Red Sea coast. When their migrations first began is unclear, but they probably date to between 4,000 and 3,000 years ago. Camels were crucial to their advance through the desert, and if the time estimates are correct, they would have been Africa's original camel herders and the likely source for the animal's introduction into Egypt. Later, camels fueled the expansions of the Afar and Somali, who occupied the arid lands stretching from Djibouti to the Tana River in Kenya.

Equatorial Africa

The first agriculturists to approach the equatorial rain forest were proto–Central Sudanic (Nilosaharan group) speakers. They did not, however, enter the forest, remaining instead in the savanna and woodland country to the north, where they could cultivate sorghums and tend herds of cattle, sheep, and goats. Getting closer were Ubangian communities whose settlements reached the northern fringes of the forest (David 1982). Early yam–oil palm cultivators located in the Cameroon highlands, they had begun an expansion around 5,000 years ago that took them eastward through the lands straddling the watershed of the Nile and Congo rivers.

It was left to yet another group of yam-cultivating Niger-Congo speakers, the Bantu, to take food-producing economies into the rain forest proper. Originating in the vicinity of the Cross River valley of present-day Nigeria, they had entered the equatorial forest by

4,000 years ago (Ehret 1982). Avid fisher folk as well as farmers, the pioneers followed the Atlantic coast and river valleys west of the immense swamp along the lower reaches of the Ubangi River before it joins the Congo. Subsistence needs kept the frontier moving until advance communities eventually reached the forest's southern end. Some people then headed east and followed northward-flowing rivers back into the forest, completing a cycle by 2,000 years ago that created a linearlike pattern of Bantu-speaking fishing–farming villages surrounded by bands of pygmoid gatherer-hunters in the deeper forest recesses (Vansina 1990).

Eastern Africa

The transition of eastern Africa from a region of gatherer-hunters to agriculturists was linked to a complex interweaving of population migrations that spanned some 3,500 or more years. As noted, peoples of Southern Cushitic linguistic background introduced finger millet–based agriculture into parts of eastern Africa. Their migrations seem to have centered on better-watered upland areas, such as the slopes of mounts Kenya and Kilimanjaro (Nurse 1982).

At about the same time, or only slightly later, Central Sudanic agriculturists with sorghum and livestock entered the interlacustrine region of present-day Uganda, and may have eventually reached as far south as the Zambezi River valley. As with the Southern Cushites, their numbers were few, and they gave way between 3,000 and 2,000 years ago to Bantu migrants who had tracked through the equatorial forest following easterly rather than southerly routes. Adding Central Sudanic grain-farming and livestock-rearing technologies to their yam-based agriculture, the Bantu were set to claim most of eastern Africa's cultivable lands as their own (Ehret 1982). By 500 years ago, they had created a wide variety of agricultural systems, ranging from intensively irrigated ones to those using land-extensive methods of shifting cultivation.

The noncultivable lands of eastern Africa, ranging from semiarid to desert, fell to various herding peoples. The north of what is now Kenya was claimed by Cushitic-speaking Somali and Oromo, who (because of the aridity) emphasized camels, while cattle-oriented Nilotes (Nilosaharan group) took possession of the richer grassland and savanna habitats of the interior plateaus.

Southern Africa

As in equatorial and eastern Africa, food-producing economies reached the southern portions of the continent in the company of migrants. Some of them were Khoe-speakers, now called Khoikhoi (formerly Hottentot). They acquired (probably from Bantu sources) sheep and maybe goats, but not crops, somewhere in the vicinity of the middle portions of the Zambezi River valley about 2,000 years ago. From here they spread southward into the semiarid range lands bordering the Kalahari, and thence into the summer rainfall country from the Orange River valley to the Cape of Good Hope, either displacing or intermingling with bands of San (formerly Bushman)-speaking hunter-gatherers (Elphick 1977).

Following the Khoikhoi, but entering different environmental zones, were various communities of Bantu. Some were related to those who had moved through the equatorial rain forest. Continuing on a southward course, they entered the vast expanses of drought-prone and soil-poor brachystegia or miombo woodlands that stretch beyond the Zambezi River. Poorly suited to yam cultivation, at the outset the migrants were forced to rely on gathering, hunting, and fishing for subsistence. But then, sometime just prior to 1,500 years ago, sorghums and millets were acquired from yet other Bantu groups that had begun moving south from eastern Africa. With these crops, much of the area could support at least land-extensive forms of shifting cultivation. Although livestock also were introduced, their roles were restricted by the widespread prevalence of sleeping sickness.

Much better habitats were encountered by the eastern stream of Bantu. One favored route led around lakes Tanganyika and Nyasa and onto the Zimbabwe plateau, and thence to the high veld of South Africa. By A.D. 500, these areas, free from sleeping sickness and comparatively well watered, had been reached by advance communities with grain-growing and livestock-herding economies, although cattle do not seem to have been important until the advent of the New Iron Age after A.D. 1,000. Yet another route followed by Bantu agriculturalists went along the coast through Mozambique and into Natal, which also seems to have been reached by around 1,500 years ago (Hall 1990).

It thus took about 6,000 years from the signs of its first appearance for agriculture to make its way to the extreme southern end of the continent. To an almost exclusive degree, the crops involved were of African origin. However, some of the more important later developments were hinged to imports, and it is to these that the discussion now turns.

Later Imports

Plantains and Bananas

The first of the later imports to have widespread agricultural repercussions in Africa south from the Sahara were plantains and bananas *(Musa sp.).* Two routes of entry from their southeast Asian source of origin seem possible. The first could have brought them to Egypt over 2,000 years ago via trade with India; from Egypt they spread along the Nile to its headwaters in the Great Lakes region of eastern Africa. The second possibility involves Malayo-Polynesian voyages to the east coast on the way to settling Madagascar. Cuttings could have survived the long sea voyages, and therefore joined other crops, such as cocoyam *(Colocasia antiquorum)* and sugarcane *(Saccharum offici-*

narum), sometime during the second half of the first millennium A.D.

By whatever route, the adoption of bananas and plantains became crucial to the spread of agriculture through the lowland equatorial rain forest. People now had a high-yielding crop that allowed for relatively permanent villages to be established away from the river valleys and deeper into the forest proper. Bananas and plantains also played an important role in augmenting agricultural productivity throughout the moister zones of the Great Lakes region and in the uplands of eastern Africa, such as around the lower slopes of mounts Kenya and Kilimanjaro, thus helping to create some of Africa's most densely settled areas outside Egypt.

Asiatic Yams

It is possible that Asiatic yams (principally *D. alata* and *D. esculenta)* also reached Africa with the Malayo-Polynesian voyages. Their rise to prominence, however, seems mainly to have followed their importation by the Portuguese during the sixteenth century. Because of higher yields, they have largely replaced the indigenously developed varieties throughout the yam belt of western Africa and elsewhere, to the point where the latter serve more for ritual than staple-food purposes (Coursey 1976; Harris 1976).

Maize

Reports continue to circulate about the cultivation of maize having been widespread prior to the Columbian voyages, but it was only after the introduction of American varieties *(Zea maize)* that the crop became an important component of many African food systems. Although the evidence is far from definitive, it does point to the Portuguese as, once again, the carriers, and if this is true, then maize probably had many points of entry along the Atlantic and Indian Ocean coasts. Indeed, there is really no other way to explain its seemingly sudden appearance by the seventeenth century in places as far apart as the Senegal River valley, the Congo basin, the Natal coast of South Africa, and Zanzibar (Miracle 1966).

The frontiers of maize have been moving ever since, to the point where today its now numerous varieties have become the predominant staple for many people in Africa south from the Sahara. Areas where it is particularly important include the highlands of Kenya, Rwanda and Burundi, Malawi, the coastal savanna gap from eastern Ghana to Benin, the Bie Plateau of Angola, and the well-watered areas from Zambia to South Africa. The attractions of maize have been its high yields and invulnerability to bird attacks in comparison with millets and sorghums. About the only places where it does not show up among the list of important crops are in the lowland equatorial zone, the Sahel, and highland Ethiopia, and among rice growers in western Africa. Maize is Africa's most researched food crop, and the development of vari-

eties that are more drought resistant and that will grow in cooler highland climatic conditions has added to its attractions.

Cassava

There is little doubt about cassava *(Manihot utilissima* or *M. esculenta)* having been brought to Africa by the Portuguese. They found it growing in Brazil and, as with maize, seem to have taken it with them to many of their African landfalls. Initially, the most important of these was the Kongo Kingdom, located south from the Congo River below Malebo Pool. Cassava gained favor here early in the sixteenth century and rather quickly spread both north and south around the equatorial rain forest, apparently being welcomed as a high-yielding alternative to yams and sorghums (Jones 1959). As the slave trade intensified across this region, cassava became even more important. Harvesting could await the disappearance of the turbulence brought by slavers, and cassava flour could be made into cakes for storage and long-distance travel. As the demand grew, some peoples responded by forming their own slave-run plantations to grow cassava. Ironically, its appearance in central Africa probably kept populations growing sufficiently so that the slave trade and slavery could continue (Miller 1989).

A link to slavery may also partially explain cassava's importance in and around the Niger delta, although much of its spread there, and elsewhere in coastal West Africa, seems to have occurred after 1800 (Jones 1959). Commercial agriculture had begun to expand across the region from Ghana to Nigeria, and cassava's adoption may have been a response to a decline in other food crops as more land was given over to cacao *(Theobroma cacao),* another import from the Americas, and oil palm cultivation.

Cassava's tolerance to a wide range of soil types and moisture conditions, along with the ability to remain unharvested after ripening, made it a favorite of many colonial agricultural officials. They viewed cassava as an ideal famine-prevention food, and thus encouraged plantings in such areas as the upper Guinea Coast and interior eastern Africa where it had not found an earlier enthusiastic reception. Today cassava is tropical Africa's most widely planted crop, and the region has become the world's leading producer.

Two other American crop introductions need to mentioned. One is the groundnut *(Arachis hypogaea).* Groundnuts serve both as a food and cash crop for many Africans in the subhumid and semiarid parts of the continent, with the rural economies of Senegal and northern Nigeria particularly dependent on them. The second crop introduced from the Americas is the sweet potato *(Ipomoea batatas).* Although not really a staple anywhere in Africa, it is nevertheless an important secondary food source virtually everywhere it can be grown.

Food Preparation and Eating Habits

In Africa a staple food crop is just that – the principal item in the diet, eaten most days if not virtually every day. If a grain is used, most often it will be pounded into a flour, whereas root crops frequently are grated before being boiled. In either case, the end product is a stiff porridgelike substance that is normally formed into bite-size balls. These are then eaten with a variety of stews and soups. Greens of one kind or another will almost always be one of their ingredients, and onions are increasingly common. Otherwise, the additives will depend on local availability and preferences. Meat is always desired but is infrequent. Along coasts and rivers, small amounts of fish are commonly put into stews and soups, and oils, mostly from palms and groundnuts, are in regular use. Salt is a necessity, but the use of other spices varies considerably. In general, tastes tend to be on the bland side throughout most of eastern, central, and southern Africa, while in parts of western Africa and Ethiopia, the stews are often fired with chilli peppers.

Other kinds of preparations include roasting maize ears and steaming sliced cassava, plantains, and sweet potatoes in leaf wrappers. Rice is prepared in the usual boiled manner, and to an ever-increasing extent, imported varieties are preferred because of their higher quality. Such preferences are especially true of urban dwellers, who have created a demand for imported wheat flours to make leavened breads as well. Cassava flour is also used for bread, and in Ethiopia a flat bread made from teff or wheat is the staple source of carbohydrates for people living in the highlands.

All kinds of other foods, especially gathered ones, find their ways into African diets. By far the most common are greens of one kind or another; mushrooms are also widely eaten. Termites are popular, as are various caterpillars and mollusks. These days, game meats are increasingly uncommon, and the vast majority of people will never have occasion to eat them. In fact, game meats have fallen out of favor, even when made available as a part of government game-cropping schemes. Far preferred, if affordable, are beef, mutton, and goat. Vegetarianism by choice is not part of any African cultural tradition.

Contrary to what might be expected, pastoralists, such as the Fulbe and Maasai, also eat very little meat. They rely on fresh and soured milk, along with butter, as their staples, and slaughter animals only for special ceremonial occasions or when these become old and feeble. Milk products are uncommon for most other Africans, as is indicated by the high rates of lactose intolerance that exist, especially in western and equatorial Africa (Kretchmer 1977).

The normal pattern is for one large meal to be served each day. Both morning and evening meals tend to be more like snacks and often involve leftovers. Almost everywhere, men eat separately from women and young children and are served first. Individual plates are not used; rather, each person takes from common bowls and pots.

Meals are seldom accompanied by beverages, except if these are part of feasts. The drinking of alcoholic beverages, however, is virtually ubiquitous, except among Muslims. Traditional products are all basically variations of two themes. The most widespread is the fermentation of one of the crops into something beerlike. Finger millet is the grain generally employed by many eastern and central Africans, whereas maize is popular in South Africa. Also widely used are sorghums and bananas, with the higher sugars from the latter yielding greater alcohol content. A favored practice is to add honey to the fermentation to push the alcohol level even higher. The second theme is found mainly within the equatorial zone and along the coast. Here palm trees are topped to produce a sap that is turned into palm wine, which achieves greater strength than the beers.

In recent decades, commercially distilled spirits and brewed beers have become the alcoholic drinks of choice for many people. As a consequence, alcoholism is now a serious social and health problem, especially in Africa's rapidly growing cities.

Many food avoidances exist, the most widespread of which is attached to eggs. Some peoples, particularly in Kenya, eschew eggs altogether, equating them with excrement, but more often the restriction falls on girls and reproductive-age women. Reasons stated vary from eggs causing sterility or excessive sexuality to adversely affecting fetal development (Simoons 1961). Less widespread, but of considerable cultural and historical interest, is the avoidance of fish by peoples from Ethiopia southward through Kenya to Tanzania. They are all of Cushitic linguistic affiliation or others who have been heavily influenced by them (Murdock 1959). The reasons are lost in antiquity, but may relate to the low-caste status of fisher folk in the development of Cushitic society, one in which the vast majority of people are either farmers or herders.

Diet-Related Disorders

As a whole, Africa south from the Sahara has become characterized by a worsening food-supply crisis. This is illustrated by the sequence of famines, beginning with the Sahel and Ethiopia in the early 1970s and continuing to Somalia and Mozambique at the outset of the 1990s, and by a regionwide decline in per capita food production over roughly the same period of time. Only by the importation of more and more staple foodstuffs have famines and near famines been averted elsewhere.

Both because of their episodic nature and the coverage they have received, Africa's famines are not discussed here beyond a note of the complexity of their causes. Although natural events, particularly droughts, have often been involved, these have largely been triggers setting off deeper economic and political charges that initiate the famines. Attention is focused here, however, on more chronic diet-related disorders. These include the various syndromes of protein–energy malnutrition (PEM), vitamin A deficiency, anemias, and goiter.

Protein–Energy Malnutrition

There is very little doubt that, taken together, the syndromes of protein–energy malnutrition constitute the most widespread and serious diet-related disorders in Africa south from the Sahara. From the sketchy evidence available, it does seem that pure cases of kwashiorkor are rather rare today. Apparently, all of the earlier research on it has paid off, particularly with regard to recognizing kwashiorkor in its early stages and alerting parents to take children with symptoms to clinics and hospitals (Newman 1995). The current status of the other two clinical syndromes of marasmus and marasmic kwashiorkor is less certain. Early weaning onto inadequate breast-milk substitutes and exposure to bacterial contamination are still widespread, and in fact, the kinds of poverty, especially in urban areas, that favor this combination of health threats have been growing rather than declining. Unfortunately, the available medical and survey data are inadequate to the task of making any kind of reasonable statements about comparative frequencies.

Somewhat more can be said about the several growth measurements that are used to identify mild-to-moderate forms of PEM. Stunting, for example, is widespread, with rates for children under 5 years of age running from a low 16.6 percent in the Ivory Coast, to 47.8 percent in Burundi, to 53.7 percent in Malawi (Carlson and Wardlaw 1990). One can argue about the standards used for such determinations, but what we know from other sources about food availability in such places as Burundi and Malawi would confirm that many young children are suffering from chronic malnutrition that quickly can go from mild-to-moderate to clinical when infections strike.

Vitamin A Deficiency

Vitamin A deficiencies that lead to vision impairment are far more localized than PEM. They are almost completely absent from humid tropical regions, where sources of preformed vitamin A and beta-carotene are abundant. In contrast, these can be in short supply (especially seasonally) in drier environments, and this is where the problems are concentrated. Some fairly good studies of different time periods have come from Nigeria, and they document a north-to-south incidence gradient (Nicol 1949; Oke 1972). Similarly, the dry Luapula Valley is Zambia's trouble spot, with a recent study having recorded a deficiency rate of 75 percent among preschool children (Lubinga 1989).

The symptoms of severe vitamin A deficiency run a gamut from Bitot's spots, through night blindness, to keratomalacia. When the latter stage is reached, death usually follows within a short time because of the problems of caring for the blind in physically hazardous environments. Treatment of vitamin A deficiency is inexpensive and can easily prevent the occurrence of impaired vision, but sadly, access to treatment is still wanting in poorer, more remote areas (Sommer 1982).

Anemias

Two kinds of diet-related anemias seem to afflict many African women and are especially health threatening during their reproductive years. One is the megaloblastic variety, which develops from a severe deficiency of folic acid. The primary source for folic acid is green leafy vegetables, and most women do, in fact, ingest adequate quantities of these. However, seasonal shortages can occur, especially in more arid habitats, and during times of drought, greens may be almost totally unavailable.

A more widespread anemia stems from iron deficiency, although seldom is the cause dietary. Sometimes it results from metabolic malfunctioning that inhibits iron absorption, but much more common are cases associated with parasitic infestations, notably malaria, hookworm, and roundworm (Latham 1965).

Goiter

Goiters, resulting from a dietary deficiency of iodine, can be encountered in many parts of the continent where the ancient basement geological complex predominates as the bedrock. Because it lacks iodine, so, too, do the soils and, therefore, the plants. The center of endemicity seems to be Zaire, where incidences of up to 100 percent have been recorded within some communities (DeVisscher et al. 1961). Also possibly contributing to the high rates are goitrogenous agents in widely eaten cassava and cabbage. The majority of goiters occur to young women because of the thyroid stresses resulting from menstruation, pregnancy, and lactation. Most are temporary, having little or no health impact, although several studies have found a connection between community incidences of endemic goiter and cretinism (Bastinie et al. 1962; Delange and Ermans 1971).

James L. Newman

Bibliography

Adams, W. Y. 1977. *Nubia: Corridor to Africa.* Princeton, N.J.

Alexander, J., and D. G. Coursey. 1969. The domestication of yams. In *The domestication and exploitation of plants and animals,* ed. P. J. Ucko and G. W. Dimbley, 405–25. London.

Bastinie, P. A., A. M. Ermans, O. Thys et al. 1962. Endemic goiter in the Uele Region III. Endemic cretinism. *Journal of Clinical Endocrinology and Metabolism* 22: 187-94.

Blench, R. 1993. Ethnographic and linguistic evidence for the prehistory of African ruminant livestock, horses, and ponies. In *The archaeology of Africa: Food, metals, and towns,* ed. T. Shaw, P. Sinclair, B. Andah, and A. Okpoko, 71-103. London.

Butzer, K. W. 1976. *Early hydraulic civilization in Egypt: A study in cultural ecology.* Chicago.

Camps, G. 1982. The beginnings of pastoralism and cultivation in north-west Africa and the Sahara: Origins of the Berbers. In *The Cambridge history of Africa, Vol. 1: From earliest times to c. 500 B.C.,* ed. J. D. Clark, 548-623. Cambridge.

Carlson, B. A., and T. M. Wardlaw. 1990. *A global, regional and country assessment of child malnutrition.* New York.

Clutton-Brock, J. 1993. The spread of domestic animals in Africa. In *The archaeology of Africa: Food, metals, and towns,* ed. T. Shaw, P. Sinclair, B. Andah, and A. Okpoko, 61-70. London.

Connah, G. 1981. *Three thousand years in Africa.* Cambridge.

Coursey, D. G. 1976. The origins and domestication of yams in Africa. In *Origins of African plant domestication,* ed. J. R. Harlan, J. M. J. de Wet, and A. B. L. Stemler, 383-408. The Hague.

David, A. 1982. Prehistory and historical linguistics in central Africa: Points of contact. In *The archaeological and linguistic reconstruction of African history,* ed. C. Ehret and M. Posnansky, 78-103. Berkeley, Calif.

Delange, F., and A. A. Ermans. 1971. Role of a dietary goitrogen in the etiology of endemic goiter on Idjwi Island. *American Journal of Clinical Nutrition* 24: 1354-60.

DeVisscher, M., C. Beckers, H.-G. Van Den Schrieck et al. 1961. Endemic goiter in the Uele Region (Congo Republic) I. General aspects and functional studies. *Journal of Clinical Endocrinology and Metabolism* 21: 175-88.

Donkin, R. A. 1991. *Meleagrides: An historical and ethnographic study of the Guinea fowl.* London.

Ehret, C. 1979. On the antiquity of agriculture in Ethiopia. *Journal of African History* 20: 161-77.

⸻ 1982. Linguistic inferences about early Bantu history. In *The archaeological and linguistic reconstruction of African history,* ed. C. Ehret and M. Posnansky, 57-65. Berkeley, Calif.

⸻ 1993. Nilo-Saharans and the Saharo-Sudanese Neolithic. In *The archaeology of Africa: Food, metals, and towns,* ed. T. Shaw, P. Sinclair, B. Andah, and A. Okpoko, 104-25. London.

Elphick, R. 1977. *Kraal and castle: Khoikhoi and the founding of white South Africa.* New Haven, Conn.

Flight, C. 1976. The Kintampo culture and its place in the economic prehistory of West Africa. In *Origins of African plant domestication,* ed. J. Harlan, J. M. J. de Wet, and A. B. L. Stemmler, 211-21. The Hague.

Frend, W. H. C. 1978. The Christian period in Mediterranean Africa, c. A.D. 200 to 700. In *The Cambridge history of Africa, Vol. 2: from c. 500 B.C. to A.D. 1050,* ed. J. D. Fage, 410-89. Cambridge.

Hall, M. 1990. *Farmers, kings, and traders: The peopling of Southern Africa, 200-1860.* Chicago.

Harlan, J. R. 1989. The tropical African cereals. In *Foraging and farming: The evolution of plant exploitation,* ed. D. R. Harris and G. C. Hillman, 335-43. London.

⸻ 1992. Indigenous African agriculture. In *The Origins of*

agriculture: An international perspective, ed. C. W. Cowan and P. J. Watson, 59-70. Washington, D.C.

Harris, D. R. 1976. Traditional systems of plant food production and the origins of agriculture in West Africa. In *Origins of African plant domestication,* ed. J. R. Harlan, J. M. J. de Wet, and A. B. L. Stemler, 311-56. The Hague.

Hillman, G. C. 1989. Late Palaeolithic plant foods from Wadi Kubbaniya in upper Egypt: Dietary diversity, infant weaning, and seasonality in a riverine environment. In *Foraging and farming: The evolution of plant exploitation,* ed. D. R. Harris and G. C. Hillman, 207-39. London.

Jones, W. O. 1959. *Manioc in Africa.* Stanford, Calif.

Kretchmer, N. 1977. The geography and biology of lactose digestion and malabsorption. *Postgraduate Medical Journal* 53: 65-72.

Latham, M. 1965. *Human nutrition in tropical Africa.* Rome.

Lhote, H. 1959. *The search for the Tassili frescoes.* London.

Lubinga, D. 1989. Valley of the blind. *IDRC Reports, n. 18.* Ottawa.

MacNeish, R. S. 1992. *The origins of agriculture and settled life.* Norman, Okla.

Miller, J. C. 1989. *Way of death: Merchant capitalism and the Angolan slave trade, 1730-1830.* Madison, Wis.

Miracle, M. P. 1966. *Maize in tropical Africa.* Madison, Wis.

Munson, P. J. 1976. Archaeological data on the origins of cultivation in the southwestern Sahara and the implications for West Africa. In *Origins of African plant domestication,* ed. J. R. Harlan, J. M. J. de Wet, and A. B. L. Stemler, 187-209. The Hague.

Murdock, G. P. 1959. *Africa: Its peoples and their culture history.* New York.

Muzzolini, A. 1993. The emergence of a food-producing economy in the Sahara. In *The archaeology of Africa: Food, metals, and towns,* ed. T. Shaw, P. Sinclair, B. Andah, and A. Okpoko, 227-39. London.

Newman, J. L. 1995. From definition, to geography, to action, to reaction: The case of protein-energy malnutrition. *Annals of the Association of American Geographers* 85:233-45.

Nicol, B. M. 1949. Nutrition of Nigerian peasant farmers with special reference to the effects of riboflavin and vitamin A deficiency. *British Journal of Nutrition* 3: 25-43.

Nurse, D. 1982. Bantu expansion into East Africa: Linguistic evidence. In *The archaeological and linguistic reconstruction of African history,* ed. C. Ehret and M. Posnansky, 199-222. Berkeley, Calif.

Oke, O. L. 1972. A nutrition policy for Nigeria. *World Review of Nutrition and Dietetics* 14: 1-47.

Phillipson, D. W. 1993. The antiquity of cultivation and herding in Ethiopia. In *The archaeology of Africa: Food, metals and towns,* ed. T. Shaw, P. Sinclair, B. Andah, and A. Okpoko, 344-57. London.

Rindos, D. 1984. *The origins of agriculture: An evolutionary perspective.* Princeton, N.J.

Sauer, C. O. 1969. *Agricultural origins and dispersals.* Second edition. Cambridge, Mass.

Simoons, F. J. 1961. *Eat not this flesh: Food avoidances in the old world.* Madison, Wis.

Smith, A. B. 1992. *Pastoralism in Africa: Origins and development ecology.* London.

Sommer, A. 1982. *Nutritional blindness: Xeropthalmia and keratomalacia.* New York.

Stahl, A. B. 1993. Intensification in the West African late stone age: A view from central Ghana. In *The archaeology of*

Africa: Food, metals and towns, ed. T. Shaw, P. Sinclair, B. Andah, and A. Okpoko, 261–73. London.

Sutton, J. E. G. 1977. The African Aqualithic. *Antiquity* 51: 25–34.

Vansina, J. 1990. *Paths in the rain forest.* Madison, Wis.

Vavilov, N. I. 1926. Studies on the origins of cultivated plants. *Bulletin of Applied Botany and Plant Breeding* 16: 1245.

Wasylikowa, K., J. R. Harlan, J. Evans, et al. 1993. Examination of botanical remains from early neolithic houses at Nabta Playa, Western Desert, Egypt, with special reference to sorghum grains. In *The archaeology of Africa: Food, metals and towns,* ed. T. Shaw, P. Sinclair, B. Andah, and A. Okpoko, 154–64. London.

Zeuner, F. E. 1963. *A history of domesticated animals.* London.

V.E.2 ⧫ Australia and New Zealand

Australia and New Zealand are Pacific Rim countries situated on the southwestern edge of that vast ocean. But although Australia has been peopled for at least 50,000 years (some now say 70,000), and New Zealand for just over 1,000, the dominant foodways of both have been shaped over just the last 200 years – since the beginning of British settlement in Australia in 1788. The indigenous people, the Aborigine in Australia and the Maori in New Zealand, are now minorities in their own lands (Aborigines comprise less than 2 percent of Australia's population and Maori about 15 percent of New Zealand's), and the foods and beverages they consume have been markedly influenced by food and drink of British origin. Indeed, from a contemporary perspective, food and drink in Australia and New Zealand – the lands "down under" – predominantly derive from the strong British heritage.

In this chapter, the environments of Australia and New Zealand are briefly described, not only because they are notably unique but also because they were so amenable to "ecological imperialism" (Crosby 1978). The food systems of the indigenous peoples, although now vastly altered, are also outlined, but the bulk of the chapter is devoted to the processes that produced contemporary patterns of food and drink consumption among both the immigrants and the indigenous peoples.

Natural Environments

Australia

Because of its transitional position between the low and middle latitudes, about 40 percent of Australia is located within the tropics. However, the southwestern and southeastern littoral zones lie within the midlatitudes and have temperature and rainfall regimes somewhat similar to those of western and Mediterranean Europe and, consequently, have proven conducive to the naturalization of European flora and fauna. The continent is an ancient and stable one. Large parts of it have an aspect of sameness, with almost monotonous expanses of flat land and sweeping vistas (McKnight 1995), and only in the Eastern Highlands is there great topographical variety.

Climatically, two features stand out: aridity and tropicality. Central and western Australia are arid, and well over half of the continent receives less than 15 inches of rainfall a year. By contrast, northern Australia (away from the east coast) has a monsoonlike climate, which brings abundant moisture between November and March, followed by a seven- or eight-month dry season. The northeastern coast is humid and hot, but the southeast has true midlatitude conditions with adequate precipitation, although the summers are hotter than in comparable latitudes in the Northern Hemisphere. The southwest enjoys a subtropical dry-summer/wet-winter situation – a "Mediterranean-type" climate.

The flora and fauna that developed in Australia and provided the subsistence for its indigenous people are unique, primarily because of nearly 100 million years of isolation, during which the present biota evolved and diversified without interference from immigrant species. About 80 percent of Australia's 25,000 species of plants are endemic, with two genera, the eucalypts or "gums" (*Eucalypt* spp.) and the acacias or "wattles" (*Acacia* spp.) overwhelmingly dominant. Furthermore, much Australian flora exhibits pronounced xerophytic (drought-resistant) characteristics. Only over the last few million years has there been a limited exchange of biota between Australia and (the biotically rich) Southeast Asia. In the past 200 years, the introduction of new species, mostly of European origin, has dramatically impacted the landscapes, especially of temperate Australia.

Australia's assemblage of terrestrial animal life is also unique. The more familiar placental animal groups are absent, their place being taken by marsupials, the majority of which are herbivores, including the macropods (kangaroos and wallabies, rat kangaroos, wombats, phalangers, "possums," and koala). There are also a number of carnivorous marsupials ("mice," "moles," "cats," and "devils") and a group of numbats (anteaters), as well as omnivorous marsupials called bandicoots. Additionally, Australia has two monotremes (egg-laying mammals), the duck-billed platypus (*Ornithorhynchus anatinus*) and the spiny anteater (*Tachyglossus aculeatus*). Placental mammals are recent arrivals, which until the introduction of European species after 1788 were mostly rats, mice, and bats from Southeast Asia. Australia also has a wide variety of reptilian fauna, an exceedingly varied and singular avifauna, and abundant insects and arthropods but limited amphibian and freshwater fish life.

New Zealand

In contrast to Australia, New Zealand is characterized by sloping land, true midlatitude climates, and dense vegetation. It is located along the "Pacific Rim of Fire," and vulcanism is evident in the North Island; alpine mountains dominate parts of the South Island. Everywhere else, hill country and small valley plains dominate, except in the eastern part of the South Island where the Canterbury Plain, New Zealand's largest lowland, is located.

Overall, the climate can be characterized as "marine west coast," dominated by air from the oceans, especially from the west. Some parts of the east (leeward) side of major mountains are relatively dry, but in most of the country, the precipitation averages between 30 and 60 inches annually, with mountain regions receiving more. Temperatures are moderate (50° F to 80° F in summer and 30° F to 70° F in winter), again except for the mountains.

Prior to human occupation, the islands were heavily forested, with more than 75 percent of the total area covered with what the early British settlers called "bush." Much of this was actually a sort of temperate rain forest, which had evolved in relative isolation under unstable (volcanic and glacial) environmental conditions. The fauna inhabiting this environment was conspicuous by the lack of land mammals (other than a species of bat) and was dominated by bird life, a distinctive feature of which was the relatively high degree of flightlessness. The kiwi, New Zealand's national emblem, shares this characteristic, along with a variety of rails, woodhens, and other species.

The most notable nonflying birds were the two dozen species of moa – ostrichlike birds, now extinct, some of which were very large. Various types of waterfowl, parrots, and innumerable "bush birds," large and small, were also present in abundance, along with some species of lizards, but there were no amphibians save for a few species of frogs. A rich marine-mammal population included fur seals, sea lions, leopard seals, elephant seals, dolphins, and many species of whales, as well as an abundance of fish and mollusks.

Indigenous Food Systems

Australia

The unique and remote Australian environment provided a home for the Australian Aborigines, who comprised a distinctive society of hunters, gatherers, and fishers. Arriving from what is now Southeast Asia possibly as many as 70,000 years ago, over the subsequent millennia they spread across and occupied all parts of the continent at varying densities, depending on local environmental conditions. Mostly they led a seminomadic existence, but their movements were not helter-skelter (Davis and Prescott 1992). It is thought that there may have been from 500 to 600 tribes or tribelets, with each recognizing the territoriality of others.

Within each tribe there were usually several clans of a few dozen people each. Although there is no evidence of formal agriculture, the gathering and distribution of seed, the management of natural vegetation by fire, and the rudimentary cultivation of yams (*Dioscorea* spp.) in certain areas indicate some degree of plant husbandry. There were no domesticated animals except the dog. The total population of Aborigines at the time of European contact is not known. The most widely accepted estimate is about 300,000, although some authorities place the number as high as 1.5 million (McKnight 1995). Geographic distribution, density, and mobility were closely related to the availability of food, water, and other resources (Berndt and Berndt 1988).

Most Aboriginal languages had special terms for vegetable foods, as distinct from terms for the flesh of animals, birds, reptiles, fish, mollusks, and insects. Generally, foods from vegetable sources fell into three main categories: roots and tubers, fruits, and seeds (although some plants produced more than one type of food item, and, in a few instances, it was the pith of the plant that was consumed). There were considerable differences in the importance of various types of plant foods between ecological zones. In the vast desert and semiarid areas, Aborigines utilized between 60 and 100 edible species of plants (Latz and Griffin 1978; Peterson 1978). However, this extensive list could be reduced to about a dozen staples. (A staple is a plant species that singly or in combination with another accounts for at least 50 percent of the diet during the period it is consumed.)

Principal staples were the roots of various species of *Ipomoea* (convolvulus), *Vigna lancelota*, and *Portulaca oleracea* ("pigweed"); the fruits of *Solanum* (for example, the "bush tomato"), *Ficus*, and *Santalum* (the "quandong") species; and *Leichardtia australis* (the "bush banana"). Other principal staples were the seeds of various *Acacia* species ("wattles"); grasses, such as those of the genus *Panicum;* and herbs, such as *Rhyncharrhena linearis* (the "bush bean") (Peterson 1978; Palmer and Brady 1991). It is estimated that plants provided some 70 to 80 percent of the diet (in terms of bulk) consumed by desert Aborigines (Gould 1969).

In the more humid southeast, about 140 species of plants were eaten (Flood 1980). These included the roots and tubers of various lilies (such as *Aguillaria minus,* the "vanilla lily"); at least 20 species of terrestrial orchids (for example, *Gastrodia sesamoides,* the "potato orchid"); bulrushes *(Typha orientalis* and *Typha domingensis);* and the bracken fern *(Pteridium esculentum).* Also consumed were the roots and tubers of various dandelionlike plants, including the "yam daisy" *(Micoseris scapigera),* the "native carrot" *(Geranium solanderi),* and the "Australian carrot" *(Daucus glochidiatus).* Seasonal fruits, such as the "native cherry" *(Exocarpus cuppressiformis),* "native raspberries" *(Rubus triphyllus),* currants *(Coprosma quadrifida),* and the "kangaroo apple" *(Solanum linearifolium)*, entered the diet. The pith of tree ferns *(Dicksonia antarctica* and *Cyathea* spp.) was also consumed. More plant foods were eaten in the coastal regions of the southeast than in the highlands, but on the plains of the eastern interior, grass seed, especially the native millet *(Panicum decompositum)*, was the staple plant food.

In the tropical north, there were also a large number of plant foods. One study has identified 47 species of root crops and 49 of fruit or seed used by Aborigines (Crawford 1982), although the staples varied between coastal regions and river valleys and the interior (Turner 1974; Levitt 1981). Among the roots and tubers eaten, various yam species (for example, *Dioscorea transversa,* the "long yam," and *Dioscorea bulbifera,* the "round yam") were the most important, but the tubers of various convolvulus species *(Ipomoea* spp.), lilies (for example, the "blue water lily," *Nymphaea gigantica*), the "swamp fern" *(Blechnum indicum)*, and the "wild kapok" *(Cochlospermum gregorii)* were also consumed.

Seeds from numerous trees, including various *Acacia* species (Levitt 1981), as well as seeds from some species of *Sorghum* were consumed in the north, along with a large number of nuts – from the Zamia palm *(Cycas angulata)*, the Pandanus *(Pandanus spiralis)*, and the "nut tree" *(Terminalia grandiflora)*. Fruits included several species of *Ficus,* the "jungle plum" *(Buchaninia arborescens)*, the "native gooseberry" *(Physalis minima)*, the "big green plum" *(Planchonella pohlmaniana)*, the red "wild apple" *(Syzygium suborbiculare)*, and the "wild prune" *(Pouteria sericea)* (Davis and Prescott 1992).

Considerable variation also existed in the types of flesh eaten. Snakes and lizards, especially two species of "monitor" lizard or goanna *(Varunus varius* and *Varunus giganteus)*, were commonly consumed, as were a number of small marsupials and rodents (Peterson 1978; Flood 1980). In wetter areas, "possums" (phalangers) were frequently a part of the diet (either the "brushtail possum," *Trichosurus vulpecula,* or the "mountain possum," *Trichosurus canicus)*, along with various gliders (for example, the "squirrel glider," *Petaurus norfolcensis,* and the "greater glider," *Schoinobates volans)*, the koala *(Phascolarctos cinereus)*, and various types of "flying foxes" *(Pteropus* spp.).

Bandicoots *(Perameles* spp.) and other marsupial "rats" and "mice" (for example, *Antechinus* spp. and *Sminthopsis* spp.) served as food, as did rodents of various types (for example, the "broad-toothed rat," *Mastocomys fuscus,* and the "bush rat," *Rattus fuscipes)*. In addition, larger marsupials contributed to the human diet, although in arid and semiarid areas they were relatively limited, and even in wetter areas were problematic to hunt, requiring cooperative ventures that involved considerable numbers of hunters. The latter generally used fire (Peterson 1978), but in the New England tablelands, large permanent nets were employed (Flood 1980). The red kangaroo *(Macropus rufus)*, the "Euro" *(Macropus robustus)*, and the gray kangaroo *(Macropus fuliginosus)*, as well as numerous wallaby species (for example, the "red-necked wallaby," *Macropus rufogriseus*) were all hunted. In the wetter areas, wombats *(Vombatus ursinus)* became important dietary items.

It has been estimated that in coastal and riverine regions, fish, shellfish, and crustaceans made up perhaps as much as 40 percent of the diet (Flood 1980). In the southeast, fish – caught by line, net, trap, or spear – included mullet (mainly *Mugil cephalus)*, snapper *(Chrysophrys auratus* and *Trachichthodes affinus)*, and various types of wrasses (for example, parrot fish and red cod, *Pseudolabrus* spp.). Such shellfish as the pipi *(Paphies australis)*, cockles *(Chione stutchburyi)*, mussels *(Perna canaliculus* and *Mytilus edulis)*, the catseye *(Lunella smaragda)*, and the mudsnail *(Amphibda crenata)* were very important food items, as were crayfish *(Jassus* spp.), gathered along rocky shorelines.

In the coastal areas of the tropical north, a diversity of marine resources was enjoyed. Green sea turtles *(Chelonia mydas)* were hunted and their eggs gathered. The dugong *(Dugong dugon)*, a herbivorous marine mammal, was another valuable source of animal protein, especially in the Torres Strait region and off the coasts of Arnhem Land (Turner 1974). There is no question, however, that in the coastal regions of the north, where they were obtainable throughout the year, fish were the staple food.

Other marine resources that made important contributions to the diet in some areas included freshwater fish, shellfish, and crustaceans. In the watershed of the Murray-Murrumbidgee system (Flood 1980), the Murray cod *(Maccullochella macquariensis)*, the "trout cod" *(Maccullochella mitchelli)*, the silver perch *(Bidyanus bidyanus)*, crayfish, mussels, and the platypus *(Ornithorhynchus anatinus)* were captured and consumed. In the far north during the monsoon, the barramundi *(Lates calcarifer)*, a large, tasty fish, was hunted with spears across the inundated floodplains (Davis and Prescott 1992). Rivers flowing to the Tasman Sea throughout the southeast of the continent contained eels *(Anguilla* spp.).

Birds constituted an important source of food, although in very dry areas they were probably only substantial food items following the infrequent heavy rains (Frith 1978). On the more humid plains of the north, east, and southwest, emu *(Dromiceius novaehollandie)* were plentiful and available throughout the year, but they were difficult to catch (Flood 1980). Ducks, such as the "mountain duck" – *Tadorna tadornoides* – of the southeast, were abundant in swamps and lagoons and along the rivers, as were black swans *(Cygnis atratus)* and a variety of other waterfowl. Wild turkeys (the Australian bustard, *Eupodotis australis)* were another excellent source of food on the open plains, and smaller birds were probably an important source of protein because they could be hit with stones relatively easily (Flood 1980). Eggs also provided food and, in some places, were seasonally very important. For example, in the Daly River country, just south of Darwin, the goose-egg season could be counted on for an abundant harvest (Berndt and Berndt 1988).

Valuable contributions to the diet were made by various types of insects, with perhaps the most widely utilized the larvae of various moths, collectively called "witchetty grubs" (Peterson 1978). Among these, probably the most important were the larvae of the Cossidae family, especially *Xyleutes lencomochla,* which feed on the roots of certain acacias. In the southeast, especially in the granite peaks of the highlands, another moth, the bogong *(Agrotis infusa),* was important. During the spring and early summer, these moths migrated to the mountains, where they occupied fissures, clefts, and caves in summit rocks and could be collected and eaten in vast numbers (Flood 1980).

The primary beverage of the Aborigines appears to have been water. It does not seem that there were any intoxicating beverages, although in some areas, plants (for example, wild honeysuckle and pandanus fruit), honey, and such insects as crushed green ants were mixed with water (Massola 1971). In the more tropical parts of the continent, the Aborigines chewed the leaves of three plants *(Nicotiana gossei, Nicotiana excelsior,* and *Duboisia hopwoodi)* (Berndt and Berndt 1988), and on the north coast, tobacco was introduced by Makassan traders sometime after the sixteenth century (Berndt and Berndt 1988).

The seasonal distribution of edible plants and the movements of fish and animals imposed seasonal patterns of diet, as well as patterns of movement over territories (Crawford 1982). Any single Aborigine territory encompassed a variety of ecological systems and, thus, was capable of producing a variety of food supplies throughout the year.

In general, during the dry season (the winter in the north and the summer in the southwest), the Aborigines lived in the river valleys, and those in the Kimberleys, for example, started exploiting the first of the roots reaching maturity when the rains ceased around April or May (Crawford 1982). By June and July, they were digging up root plants in the alluvium along the banks of creeks and rivers, and at this time, they began burning spinifex and cane-grass to stimulate the regrowth that attracted kangaroos. Water lily tubers were harvested in August and September when water levels were low, and as the weather became hotter, ephemeral pools were poisoned for fish.

When the rains came in December, the camps were moved onto higher ground, although fruits and seeds were still gathered in the valleys. In the rich coastal areas of the southeast, seasonal movement was less than that elsewhere, but it did involve getting food from the bush during the winter and from the

rivers and coasts during the summer (McBryde 1974). People in the highlands and tablelands had a more nomadic existence, moving away from the higher land in the winter. Tribal territories were generally much smaller in the humid areas than in semiarid and desert areas.

Apart from knowing the right season, the right times for certain foods, and the right places to find them, obtaining them involved the use of implements and tools (Berndt and Berndt 1988). For plant foods, gathered almost exclusively by women, the most important tool was the digging stick. Men knew how to interpret the spoors of various creatures and to decoy animals and birds, and they had to be adept at spear throwing. Fire was commonly used in both hunting and food gathering (Latz and Griffin 1978). People were conscious of the abundance of food plants after burning but attributed this phenomenon to associated ceremonies performed to increase rain and food. The effect of frequent burning was to produce a series of small patches – at different stages of recovery from fire – that sustained different plant and animal communities.

Culinary practices were fairly rudimentary. Some fruits and tubers required no preparation and were usually eaten when and where they were found. Most roots, however, were cooked for some minutes in hot ashes or sand. The more fibrous roots were pulverized, and bitter or poisonous tubers were sliced, soaked, and baked, often several times (Crawford 1982). Grass seed was crushed in a stone mortar and mixed with water, with the resultant "dough" baked in hot ashes (Massola 1971). Small animals were cooked in hot ashes, and larger ones in earth ovens. Sometimes foods were mixed to improve their flavors and to make them more palatable; additives included gums from acacia trees, water sweetened with honey, and crushed green ants (Crawford 1982).

New Zealand

The first humans to settle in New Zealand (who came to be called Maori in the early nineteenth century) were Polynesians who arrived between 1,000 and 2,000 years ago (Davidson 1984). The precise dates are unknown, but there is no hard evidence of settlement before A.D. 800, and recently, dates of A.D. 1000 to 1200 have been suggested (Anderson 1989). Like the eastern Polynesian societies from whence they came, Maori obtained their food by gardening, raising domestic animals, hunting (particularly fowling), fishing and shellfish gathering, and gathering uncultivated and semicultivated plants (see Nancy Davis Lewis, chapter V.E.3.). However, in this temperate, midlatitude land, gardening (as practiced elsewhere in Polynesia) was at best marginal and at worst impossible. Indeed, there is now considerable evidence to suggest that even in regions most amenable to horticulture, gardens may have contributed only about 50 percent of the means of subsistence (Jones 1995).

Thus, the food quest in some communities can truly be described as "hunting-and-gathering."

Two aspects of Maori foraging and farming have dominated discussions of prehistoric subsistence (Davidson 1984). Hunting for *moa* has captured both popular and scientific interest for more than a century. But more recently, scholars have been equally impressed by the Maori achievement of adapting the sweet potato or kumara *(Ipomoea batatas)* to an annual cycle in a temperate climate. Moreover, it has been recognized that Maori moa hunting was merely one aspect of more general hunting activities, and that the use of other plants, particularly the bracken-fern root, or *aruhe,* also constituted very important adaptations in some areas (Young 1992).

Of the range of tropical crops that the Polynesian settlers must have tried to introduce, only six species survived until early European times: the sweet potato, taro *(Colocasia esculenta),* yam or *ubi (Dioscorea alata* and *Dioscorea esculenta),* the "bottle gourd" or *hue (Lagenaria siceraria),* the "paper mulberry" or *aute (Broussonetia papyrifera),* and a species of "cabbage tree" or *ti (Cordyline terminalis).* In 1769, Captain James Cook and his companions identified all six, but soon thereafter the yam and the paper mulberry seem to have died out (Davidson 1984).

The three main cultivated food plants were sweet potatoes, taro, and the bottle gourd, of which sweet potatoes were by far the most important. Indeed, the whole question of the introduction of horticulture in New Zealand has been bedeviled by controversy, which has centered on the sweet potato, because to grow it in New Zealand required both its adaptation to new climatic conditions and the protection of the plant and its fruits from extremes of temperature and heavy winter rains. The Maori developed an array of pits in which to store tubers – a departure from methods used elsewhere in Polynesia, where the plants grew perennially and were planted from shoots, and the tubers remained in the ground until required. Exactly how the sweet potato – an American plant – reached New Zealand (and the rest of Oceania, for that matter), let alone how its cultivation and storage came to be, remains a subject of speculation. We do know that by the twelfth century, sweet potato cultivation seems to have expanded from the northern part of the North Island into the southern part and, soon thereafter, into the northern South Island.

The species of cabbage tree, *Cordyline terminalis,* was brought to New Zealand from the tropics, but other cabbage trees *(Cordyline pumilio, Cordyline australis,* and *Cordyline indivisa)* are natives and were also exploited for food. The white inner trunk of young trees and the fleshy taproot were both used. Roots, often a meter in length, were split in two and cooked in an earth oven, and the trunks were prepared in the same manner (Young 1992).

Like cabbage trees, the *karaka (Corynocarpus laevigatus)* was also "semicultivated," yielding bounti-ful crops of plum-size, oval berries that turned orange when ripe. The outer flesh of this fruit is tasty, but the bulk of the food value is in the kernel, which is highly poisonous if eaten raw. Ripe berries were gathered from the ground and trod upon with bare feet to work off the outer flesh (Burton 1982). Next, the kernels were steamed in an earth oven for 24 hours, steeped in running water for a lengthy period to extract the bitter alkaloid poison, then preserved by drying in the sun; subsequently, they were stored in baskets.

Between the gardens and the bush lay areas where the bracken fern *(Pteridium aquilinum* var. *esculentum)* grew. The tips of the new fronds can be eaten raw or boiled, but the roots *(aruhe* in Maori) were the major parts of the plant that were consumed. This fern was usually dug up in the spring, at a time when the roots are about an inch thick and break crisply to reveal a white interior with a few black fibers. They were dried on shaded platforms by the wind, then roasted, scraped, the inner flesh pounded, and baked into small loaves.

Truly "wild" foods were secured from the forest. There are at least 190 edible native plants found in New Zealand (Crowe 1997), and Maori used most of them. A variety of roots were utilized, including those from two species of bindweed *(Calystegia* spp.); terrestrial orchid tubers (examples include those of the "potato orchid," *Gastrodia cunninghamii,* the "onion orchid," *Microtes unifolia,* and the "sun orchid," *Thelymitra longifolia);* the roots of the bulrush or *raupo (Typha orientalis);* and the rock lily *(Arthropodium cirratum).*

Shoots and leaves from a wide range of other species were used as greens. Important among these were the young fronds of a number of ferns, such as the curling buds of the hen-and-chicken fern, *Asplenium bulbiferum* (which taste like asparagus) and especially the "sow thistle" or *puha (Sonchus asper).* An introduced species, *Sonchus oleraceus,* is still eaten today. Like the pith of the cabbage tree, that of the black tree fern of the forest *(Cyathea medullus)* was baked for several hours on hot embers, then peeled and eaten, or, alternately, steamed in an earth oven, sliced, and dried on sticks.

The berries of numerous trees were consumed, but those of the *hinau (Elaeocarpus denatus),* the *tawa (Beilschmiedia tawa),* and the *tutu (Coriaria* spp.) underwent elaborate processing. *Hinau* berries, for example, were pounded and sifted to remove the hard kernels, and the meal was then kneaded into a paste and formed into dark brown, oily cakes that were cooked and could be stored. A somewhat simpler procedure subjected the kernels of *tawa* berries to roasting in hot ashes or steaming in an earth oven. Perhaps *tutu* berries underwent the most complex processing. The only part of these that was not deadly poisonous was the purple juice of the sepals enclosing the fruits. That juice was first sieved, with any vestiges of seeds, stalks, or leaves discarded, after which it was permitted to set until it became a relish, or it was boiled with the pith of tree fern or with pieces of bull kelp *(Durvillea antarctica)* to form jellies.

A large number of other trees supplied insignificant amounts of small berries, but these were not staple foods. They were often called "children's food," although many were regarded as delicacies. Sweeteners also were obtained from the bush, mainly from the nectar of flowers and from certain vines, such as the *rata (Metrosideros fulgens)*. A very important food item in some areas was the pollen of the *raupo (Typha orientalis)*, which was dried, stripped from the stems, sifted, mixed with water, then made into loaves and steamed.

Of the Polynesian domestic animals (the pig, *Sus scrofa*, the chicken, *Gallus gallus*, and the dog, *Canis canis*) described by Nancy David Lewis (chapter V.E.3.), only the dog seems to have survived the journey to New Zealand. Dogs were kept as food animals as well as for hunting birds, and their dietary importance varied from place to place. They were probably seldom a major source of protein but always a steady and reliable one (Davidson 1984). In addition, the small Polynesian rat *(Rattus exulans)* accompanied humans to New Zealand, and although it can hardly be viewed as a domesticated animal, it was a scavenger around settlements and a fruit-eating forest dweller that was esteemed as a delicacy. "Rat runs," where snares were laid, were so valuable that they were virtually "owned" by families, or by individuals.

There were also numerous hunted animals, particularly the fur seal *(Arctocephalus forsteri)*, and a wide variety of birds to capture, including the large flightless moa, already mentioned. The importance of the fur seal in the pre-European diet has only recently been appreciated. When Polynesians first arrived, the fur seals bred prodigiously, and as one seal represents an enormous amount of meat, they were probably as important in the diet as moa. They were gradually reduced in number and driven from their northern breeding grounds before the arrival of the Europeans, but they remained important in the south. Other marine mammals, such as sea lions, leopard and elephant seals, dolphins, and whales, were eaten when they were occasionally captured or, in the case of whales, washed up on beaches.

Although moa may not have dominated the early human diet in New Zealand as once thought, they were an important food item everywhere. While the dates of the final disappearance of moa from different parts of the country are not established, the birds seem to have survived in some localities until about the fifteenth century. Apart from moa, the most important birds eaten were shags, penguins (especially the Little Blue), ducks (particularly the Grey, *Anas gibberifrons*, and the Paradise, *Tadorna variegata*), the sooty shearwater (the "mutton bird" of later times), and various rails.

A variety of "bush" birds were eaten as well. These included the *kaka (Nestor meridonalis)*, the pigeon *(Hemiphaga novaeseelandiae)*, the *tui (Prosthermadera novaeseelandiae)*, the *kiwi (Apteryx* spp.), the *kakapo (Strigops habroptilus)*, parakeets *(Cyanoramphus* spp.), wattled birds, albatrosses, mollyhawks, and various gulls.

Birds were captured or killed with nets, spears, and snares, and by hand collection of the young. Bush birds were most commonly snared and speared in the autumn and early winter when berries were ripe or when nectar was in the flowers early in the summer. Bird carcasses were preserved in fat in airtight containers made from either gourds or bull kelp (Belich 1996).

Shellfish formed a very important item of Maori diet, especially by the eighteenth century and in the northern part of the country, where the most productive shellfish beds were located (Davidson 1984). Shellfish gathering was largely women's work, as was the gathering of crabs, sea urchins, and *kina*. In contrast, the catching of fin fish was largely done by men (Young 1992). Hook-and-line fishing, as well as various types of nets and traps, were used to catch snapper, red cod, barracouta, trevally, yellow-eyed mullet, and various wrasses. Many other fish were also caught and consumed, but there was considerable regional variation in the most important species. In the north, snapper dominated, but in the south it was barracouta and red cod. A considerable quantity of the fish caught was baked and hung from poles and racks to dry for future use. Seaweed, especially a type called *karenga (Porphyra columbina)*, was also consumed, as was bull kelp *(Durvillaea antarctica*, which served additionally to make storage containers for other foods) and sea lettuce *(Ulva lactuca)*.

Inland dwellers utilized small freshwater fish, such as the *kokopu* (a native trout), grayling, postlarval young trout returning upstream (known as *inanga* or whitebait), and a species of lamprey. Freshwater crayfish and mussels were consumed, but the most important freshwater creatures were eels, taken in basketwork traps. In some locations, elaborate weirs were constructed to channel eels during their migrations.

Although methods of preserving and preparing food have been mentioned, the latter deserve further comment. The earth oven (a circular hole in the ground about 2 feet in diameter and about 1 foot deep), called either a *hangi* or an *umu*, was the principal method of cooking (Crowe 1997). A fire was made in the hole, and a layer of stones laid upon it; these, when heated, were removed, and the embers cleaned out. The heated stones were returned to the hole, covered with green leaves, and sprinkled with water; then more leaves were added, and food baskets or leaf-wrapped food placed on this layer. The food was covered with still more leaves, wet flax mats, old baskets, and the like, and the whole sprinkled liberally with water and covered with earth so that the steam could not escape. A family's food would normally cook in an hour or less, although larger amounts took longer. In addition, some food was doubtless roasted in hot ashes. Another technique, stone boiling, was also in common usage. Water and food were placed in a wooden trough, and red-hot stones added to bring the water to a boil.

Finally, a comment upon cannibalism is necessary. Human flesh did constitute part of the diet (at least of eighteenth-century males) (Davidson 1984), but the practice seems to have been a form of revenge *(utu),* desecrating the victims beyond the grave by turning them into cooked food (Belich 1996). Although it fascinated and revolted early European observers, the preponderant evidence indicates that those cannibalized were enemies captured or killed in war, and cannibalism was primarily an ultimate way of subjugating adversaries (Hanson and Hanson 1983).

By way of summary then, broadly speaking, New Zealand in the eighteenth century was divided into three areas in terms of the mix of foods consumed (Cumberland 1949; Lewthwaite 1949). In the northern area, horticulture was most successful, and the many harbors and estuaries contained rich fish and shellfish resources. Along the coasts of the southern North Island and northern South Island, and in the interior of the North Island, horticulture was more marginal, and hunting and gathering much more significant. Apart from the northern fringe, people in the South Island depended on hunting, fishing, and the gathering of wild plants.

The period between A.D. 1350 and 1600 was one of transition. The early settlers had exploited the premium game animals, such as moa and seals, to the point of exhaustion, and this led people to move into areas suitable for gardening, particularly in the north; it also resulted in an increased reliance on fishing and gathering throughout the islands. Large-scale marine fishing seems to have increased in importance after 1600, but the hunting of smaller birds and the trapping of eels were also significant. Gardening certainly dominated in the north, but elsewhere the "semicultivated" plants also grew in importance in the diet.

After European contact, the Maori were quick to adopt a variety of European plants, in part to vary the diet in those areas where traditional horticulture had been practiced, and in part to create a new dimension in economics where traditional horticulture had been impossible. More vigorous varieties of sweet potatoes and taro were introduced, as was the white potato *(Solanum),* which probably dates from the early 1770s. Because it was easier to grow than the sweet potato and provided a higher yield, it rapidly gained popularity everywhere (Burton 1982; Belich 1996). Less popular European vegetables introduced in the eighteenth century were carrots, pumpkins, cabbages, turnips, and parsnips (Burton 1982) – although fruit trees, especially peaches, were welcomed. Maize was the first cereal to gain acceptance; wheat was adopted only during the 1840s and 1850s.

Of the European animals, the pig – well established and running wild by the early nineteenth century – was the earliest and most successful introduction. No other animal in New Zealand yielded such a large quantity of meat, and pork became an important source of protein. In fact, pork and white potatoes joined native *puha* (sow thistle) and sweet potatoes, foods from the sea, and birds from the forest as the Maori diet in the early decades of the nineteenth century. At first, all of these new introductions may have contributed to an improvement in nutrition, but once Maori began selling land and losing access to the resources of the bush and water, the quality of the diet diminished (Pool 1991).

From Colonies to Nations

The British Heritage

Although numerous Dutch, Portuguese, French, Spanish, and British explorers had touched the shores of Australia and New Zealand from the late sixteenth century onward, it was only in the late eighteenth century that European colonization of these lands commenced. The 1769 voyage of Captain Cook initiated this process, and the establishment by the British of a penal colony at Botany Bay in 1788 (soon moved to Sydney Harbour) marked the beginning of their (since then) permanent – and largely unchallenged – presence in these southern lands.

Several other penal colonies and one free-settler colony (South Australia) were established by 1840, but in the early years it was Sydney that dominated British affairs in the South Pacific. Among other things, Sydney was the base from which New Zealand's resources – enumerated as flax, timber, whales, seals, sex, and souls by James Belich (1996) – were exploited, and it was not until after 1840 that the direct settlement of New Zealand proceeded. Even then, Australian influences remained strong, especially with regard to food and beverage habits.

The free settlers (both working- and middle-to-upper class) who went to Australia and New Zealand after 1840 were from very similar socioeconomic backgrounds, and not surprisingly, the economies of the two countries developed in very similar ways. Australia was a little more Irish (and Catholic) than New Zealand because in Australia's formative years, more than one-third of the settlers (both convicts and assisted migrants) were from Ireland. In New Zealand, by contrast, approximately one-quarter of the settlers were Scots, and only 19 percent were Irish. Nonetheless, according to Michael Symons (1982), the Irish influence on antipodean food included a strong preference for potatoes, the method of cooking them (boiling in a cauldron), and a liking for strong drink consumed away from home at pubs.

English settlers comprised barely a half of those arriving in the colonies, and the overall mixed British – in contrast to purely English – character of the population also had considerable influence on eating and drinking in the region. Indeed, the food and beverage habits carried to Australia, and later to New Zealand, were basically those of Britain's burgeoning urban underclass: potatoes, bread, and tea, with a little sugar, milk, and occasionally bacon (see Colin Spencer, chapter V.C.4.).

On the other hand, some of the assisted migrants, from the working and lower-to-middle classes, were from rural backgrounds and accustomed to a bit more diversity in their diets (potatoes, bread, cheese, butter, bacon, milk, tea, sugar, peas, turnips, and a little meat). Moreover, the officers and officials of the Australian penal colonies and, later, the wealthier settlers in both Australia and New Zealand brought with them the food habits of a middle class, sometimes with upper-class aspirations. Colin Spencer (chapter V.C.4.) describes a late-eighteenth-century middle-class meal in England as consisting of three boiled chickens, a haunch of venison, a ham, flour-and-suet pudding, and beans, followed by gooseberries and apricots. As a rule, large amounts of meat were consumed by those who could afford it, and such vegetables as cabbages, carrots, spinach, Brussels sprouts, and turnips were common. Beer and ale were the most popular drinks until distilled spirits, such as gin and crude rums, took over during the eighteenth century.

Pastoral Economies

In both Australia and New Zealand, the early years of settlement were characterized by a failure to establish successful farms and achieve self-reliance in food production. The area around Sydney was poor farming country, and in the early nineteenth century, sheep farming for wool production became the lifeblood of Australia. Sheep reached New Zealand a bit later (1833), pastoralism expanded in the 1840s, and by the late 1850s, wool was also central to the New Zealand economy.

In Australia, a lasting dependence upon imported foodstuffs developed. New Zealand also depended on imports, but in addition, such settlements as Auckland, Wellington, New Plymouth, and Nelson came to rely on a flourishing Maori agriculture for their supplies of potatoes, maize, onions, cabbages, peaches, sweet potatoes, pumpkins, grapes, melons, apples, and quinces, as well as flour (milled in Maori mills), fish, chickens, geese, turkeys, and goats (Belich 1996). It was only in the late 1850s that settlers began to produce much of their own food and the role of the Maori as food providers began to decline.

The last half of the nineteenth century brought stunning transformations to Australia and New Zealand. The gold rushes that began in both countries during the 1850s precipitated rapid social and economic changes, including the growth of urban areas, so that by 1900, these areas encompassed about 50 percent of the population (Symons 1982). In addition, railway networks opened up areas for the production

of food of all types, not only for local consumption but also for export. After the 1870s, and especially after the inauguration of refrigerated shipping in 1882, both Australia and New Zealand became producers of meat (mutton, lamb, and beef), dairy products, and later fruit, for the British market. By the late nineteenth century, livestock ranching and the growing of both temperate and tropical cereals, fruits, and vegetables were all well established in areas suited to them, and in Australia, irrigated farming was developing along the Murray-Murrumbidgee river system. In well-watered, temperate New Zealand, the native vegetation was largely replaced by exotic pasture grasses to feed the introduced animals (Crosby 1978), and in southeastern Australia and along the northeastern coast (where the growing of sugar and tropical fruits came to dominate), the landscapes were transformed as well.

One outcome of the success of pastoralism was that Australia and New Zealand became nations of meat eaters. Up through the 1870s, there was no overseas market for meat, which, as a consequence, was inexpensive relative to people's incomes (Burton 1982). Meat in large amounts was eaten at every meal: beefsteaks or mutton chops at breakfast, cold beef at luncheon, and roast or boiled beef or mutton at dinner (Symons 1982; Walker and Roberts 1988).

"Rations" and "Crew Culture"

Convicts (under sentence of "transportation" to Australia) along with their guards, working-class settlers bound for New Zealand, and assisted migrants to both countries (not to mention the crews of the ships carrying them all) were all provided with "rations." The voyage from the British Isles was a long one, with three to six months the norm (the "First Fleet" to Australia in 1787 and 1788 took eight-and-a-half months), and although officers and cabin passengers enjoyed a satisfactory diet, the rations for the rest – which were not satisfactory – remained remarkably the same for more than 70 years.

By way of illustration, the weekly rations for each of the Royal Marines aboard during the First Fleet's voyage to Botany Bay were 7 pounds of bread, 2 pounds of salt pork, 4 pounds of salt beef, 2 pounds of peas, 3 pounds of oatmeal, 6 ounces of butter, three-quarters of a pound of cheese, and a half-pint of vinegar, along with 3 quarts of water a day (Symons 1982); the convicts' rations were two-thirds those of the marines. More than a half-century later, during the 1840s, New Zealand Company settlers were provided with 3.5 pounds of salt meat and 5.25 pounds of biscuit weekly, supplemented with rice, flour, oatmeal, dried peas, dried potatoes, raisins, butter, sugar, coffee, and tea.

Nor did the issuance of rations necessarily end when one stepped ashore. In Australia, the convicts and guards from the First Fleet had to subsist on rations for nearly three years, because agriculture had not yet developed (Walker and Roberts 1988). In the early settlements in New Zealand, ordinary migrants lived on New Zealand Company rations so long as the Company's money lasted (Belich 1996). But it was sheep farming that firmly entrenched the "ration mentality" in Australian and New Zealand food culture.

Sheep grazing required complements of shepherds as well as gangs to shear the sheep, usually made up of itinerant males, who were the founders of many working-class traditions in both countries. Shepherds were partially paid in rations; handed out on Saturday nights and supplemented with spirits and a paycheck, this food eventually earned the name "Ten, Ten, Two, and a Quarter" because it usually included 10 pounds of flour, 10 pounds of meat, 2 pounds of sugar, a quarter-pound of tea, and salt (Symons 1982).

"Ten, Ten, Two, and a Quarter" was the monotonous diet of the rural workforce until well into the twentieth century, and it was very characteristic of the diet of "crews" of coastal seamen, soldiers, sawyers, mill-workers, construction workers, road and railway builders, miners, gum diggers, and farmhands. The "crew culture" was a factor in quite a few industries, and despite the many different kinds of work, involved a number of common characteristics: The work was dangerous; the crews lived in rough conditions; they used similar slang; most members were single; most spent their money on binges; and most ate a ration-style diet.

Basically, then, for the first half century, the majority of Australians were reared on what might be called prison rations – a practice that was transferred to New Zealand. In both countries, crew culture was reinforced by the dominant means of cooking: an open fire, whether at a campsite or in a hut or cottage. With the necessary implements – hatchet, knife, quart-pot (the "billy can"), and frying pan – the standard rations made a "damper," a fry of meats, and pots of tea. The "damper" was flour and water, cooked in the ashes of the fire; the meat was salt pork, corned beef, or freshly slaughtered mutton; the tea, although taken with plenty of sugar, usually lacked milk. Its abundance meant that meat was consumed at every meal.

More Genteel Food Habits

In contrast to the diets of the lower classes, the foodways carried to these new lands by the more genteel folk reflected the social differences of the Great Britain they had just left. Cabin passengers breakfasted on rolls, toast, cold meat, and hot chops. At luncheon, the fare was ham, tongue, beef, pickles, bread, and cheese, and in the evening they dined on preserved salmon, soup, goose, saddle of mutton, fowls, curry, ham, plum puddings, apple tarts, fruit, and nuts, all of this washed down with stout, champagne, sherry, and port (Belich 1996).

Once ashore, these elite few endeavored to maintain their notions of genteel dietary regimes. Thus, as early as 1789, it is recorded that the governor of New South Wales, the senior officers of the regiment guarding the convicts, and the senior officials of the civil administration sat down to several courses of fish, meat, and game (Clements 1986). Or again, in New Zealand of the 1850s, the meal served at an elegant dinner party might have included local fish, beef, sweet potatoes, Irish pork, Lancashire ham, and Cheshire cheese (Burton 1982). Indeed, just a few years later, an upper-class "colonial banquet" in Australia consisted of asparagus, turtle soup, trumpeter (a local fish) with butter sauce, lamb *à la poulette,* roast kangaroo, Australian blue cheese, wines, and liqueurs with coffee (Symons 1982). Later in the century, a suggested menu for a dinner party included oysters, turtle soup, baked barramundi, "beef olives" and chicken cream, roast fillet of beef, roast turkey and bread sauce, asparagus on toast, "angel food" cake, cherries in jelly, fruit, olives, and deviled almonds (Symons 1982).

Generally speaking, middle-class meals were enormous. Breakfast consisted of porridge, bacon and eggs or lamb cutlets, and perhaps curry or fish (Burton 1982). Luncheon might feature soup, a roast joint, vegetables, and cooked pudding or fruit. Four- or five-course family dinners were not uncommon, beginning with an "appetizer" of soup or fish, continuing with a roast, vegetables, and a pudding, and topped off with fruit and cheese.

Diet and Modernization

Food habits were considerably influenced by late-nineteenth-century technological developments, such as urbanization, railroads that rapidly transported products, and breakthroughs in food processing and preservation (including refrigeration). Australia and New Zealand were becoming modern, mass-consumption societies.

Giant roller mills producing refined white flour began to appear in the 1860s, and from this time on, workers, like their counterparts in Britain, began to enjoy a cornucopia of biscuits, macaroni, jams, confectionery, cordials, pickles, condiments, and snacks. These products, with their brand names, were advertised extensively and commonly sold in the emerging grocery shops. Also in the 1860s, beer (now "bottom fermented" and thus capable of longer-term storage and long-distance transportation) was brewed, and by 1900, today's major brewery corporations were already in existence.

Cooking technology also changed. At the beginning of the nineteenth century, cooking was mostly done over an open fire, where meats were roasted and stewpots suspended. One refinement at this time was the "Dutch oven" or "camp oven," a round pot with legs and a handle so that it could either stand or hang. By the middle of the nineteenth century, the "Colonial oven," a simple cast-iron box with a door in front that sat in the fireplace, had come into widespread use. Cast-iron ranges were imported beginning in the 1850s, and by the 1870s, locally manufactured stoves had entered the market (Burton 1982). This was at about the same time that the first gas stoves were introduced, permitting better control of the cooking process.

By the early twentieth century, a new array of processed and packaged foods – that supplemented the basic bread, mutton, beef, pork, milk, eggs, fruit, vegetables, and tea – were in common use. As Symons (1982) has noted, tea was the national beverage, and alcohol was not usually drunk with meals (other than by the upper classes), but rather was imbibed separately in hotel bars (Wood 1988). By the time of World War I, both Australia and New Zealand had seen the development of strong temperance movements, which proved powerful enough to persuade governments to hold referendums on the outright prohibition of alcoholic beverages, and some of the voting was very close. During the war, hotel bar hours were curtailed (Symons 1982), with closing time usually at 6:00 P.M., leading to the infamous "six o'clock swill."

During the 1920s, numerous developments further standardized eating habits. Fresh fruits and nuts were heavily promoted, as were pasteurized milk and ice cream (Symons 1982). Bread – a staple in urban areas since the time of early settlement – was baked mostly in mechanized bakeries, and to see it wrapped for sale in grocery stores was becoming common in Australia. Iceboxes were now widespread, and by the 1920s, wealthier housewives were looking forward to owning their own refrigerators.

The 1920s also saw an increased American influence on food, as sundae shops and soda fountains arrived and such big American food companies as Heinz, Kellogg, and Kraft moved in. These, along with such others as Nestlé (Switzerland) and Cadbury (England), came to dominate Australian and New Zealand eating and drinking habits. They pushed early "convenience" foods, defined as those that needed no cooking outside of the factory, which simplified breakfast and provided after-school and bedtime snacks. One product epitomizes this era. "Vegemite," made from brewery waste (spent yeast), became a runaway success after its alleged health attributes were extensively advertised during the 1930s and 1940s (Symons 1982). The post–World War II baby boom created a huge new market for "Vegemite, the family health food."

At this time, too, food companies and women's magazines promoted a more dainty cuisine aimed at the afternoon tea market: "Lamingtons" (chocolate-and-coconut-coated cubes of cake), "Anzac biscuits" (made of coconut, rolled oats, and golden syrup), and especially the "Pavlova" (made of whipped egg whites, corn flour, vinegar, sugar, a few drops of vanilla essence, and a pinch of cream of tartar, baked and topped with whipped cream and fruit – especially passionfruit and, today, kiwifruit). Pavlova,

named after the famous ballerina ("It is as light as Pavlova"), is alternatively said to have originated in both Australia and New Zealand (Symons 1982).

World War II had much influence upon food and beverage habits. Rationing was introduced, which curtailed the use of sugar, tea, flour, and meat. However, the demand for more fruit and vegetables created by the presence of U.S. military forces in Australia and New Zealand brought about an increase in the acreage planted with both. Vegetables were also increasingly canned and, later, dehydrated to provide the military with preserved food. The meat-processing industry was compelled to upgrade its standards and put out new canned meats, such as *chile con carne,* luncheon meats, "Spam," and Vienna sausage (Symons 1982). Coca-Cola came with the American troops and stayed after they left.

Until the 1960s in both Australia and New Zealand, bread, milk, vegetables, groceries, and meat were all delivered. But with the advent of relatively inexpensive automobiles (first in Australia and quite a bit later in New Zealand) and universal ownership of refrigerators, supermarkets began to control food sales, all of which had the effect of furthering the trend toward nationally standardized and distributed food. Supermarket giants came to dominate food marketing with "prepackaging," bright labels, and an emphasis on low prices rather than on quality. These chain-store companies did not like dealing with small producers and growers. Because they preferred products with long shelf life, they tended to offer canned, dried, and frozen rather than fresh foods, processed by industrial-size producers who could guarantee regular supply, consistent quality, and steady prices.

By identifying gaps on the supermarket shelves, such producers brought forth a new array of foodstuffs, many of a "convenience" nature, such as "Muesli," reconstituted orange juice, teabags, pizza, frozen fruits and vegetables, and the like. Foods of this sort were marketed as "labor-saving," were usually aimed at target groups after extensive market research, and were given scientific credence through the endorsement of "home economists" and "nutrition experts" (Symons 1982). This was especially characteristic of the frozen-food industry, which included such internationally known brand names as Birdseye (owned by Unilever in Australia and New Zealand), as well as local processors (for example, Watties in New Zealand) that began freezing peas, corn, berry fruits, Brussels sprouts, beans, and asparagus during the 1950s and later expanded into fish products, "TV dinners," frozen chips, cakes, poultry, and meats.

As has been the case in developed countries elsewhere, recent decades have also witnessed the sacrifice of family farms to agribusiness, monoculture, the intensive use of fertilizers and pesticides, and the arrival of scientifically "engineered" fruits and vegetables, made possible by agricultural research and funded by both governments and private corporations (Symons 1982). Recently, however, new "alternative" farming ventures have also arisen that produce organic fruit and vegetables and market them directly to consumers through resurrected city markets. At the same time, the "back to the earth" movement has supplemented the limited information prevailing in industrial societies concerning the imitation of developing-world cuisine (Symons 1982). In Australia, the food items of the original inhabitants have begun to be noticed again, but as yet in New Zealand, there has not been the same level of interest in "Maori" food other than breads, seafoods *(kai moana),* and foods cooked in the traditional earth oven (Osborne 1989; Paul 1996).

Eating Out

Eating establishments have existed since the beginnings of settlement in Australia, and in fact, in 1800 the Freemason's Arms in Sydney served excellent French-style food. More commonly, early eating houses and taverns dished out boiled mutton and broths, but both the Australian and New Zealand colonies had numerous eating houses with reputations for excellent "British cookery" (Symons 1982). The belle epoque for fine restaurants was between 1890 and World War I, when in all of the major cities, gourmet restaurants served a wide range of continental cuisines. Following the war, however, gourmets could lament that the two countries had only one diet: steaks, chops, beef, mutton, potatoes, and gravy, with suet pudding and slabs of cheese (Symons 1982).

For the less wealthy, "fourpenny" and "sixpenny" restaurants, serving basic meats and vegetables, had come into being at about the middle of the nineteenth century (Symons 1982). The fish-and-chip shop, a feature of Australian and New Zealand life that has remained, albeit modified, to the present day, arrived somewhat later. Another such feature is the ubiquitous meat pie brought by the British, which evolved over a long period to become the standardized dish common since the 1920s (Symons 1982). Men commonly ate meat pies at sporting events and as a counter lunch item in hotel bars. By World War II, the meat pie had become a "national dish" in both countries. The New Zealand Food and Drug Regulations of 1973 state that meat pies shall be encased in a pastry shell and contain not less than 25 percent cooked or manufactured meat (Burton 1982).

Until recently, "going out to dinner" for many Australians and New Zealanders meant the fish-and-chip shop or the "pie cart," a mobile, trailerlike café parked at a convenient location, which served meat pies with various accompaniments (for example, mashed potatoes and peas, known all together as "pea, pie, and pud"), as well as various other types of portable food to its customers (Burton 1982). Even as late as the 1960s, the only alternatives to the fish shop and the pie cart were the dining rooms of hotels and exclu-

sive private clubs, both of which served a very standard antipodean cuisine: steak and chips, roast meats and vegetables, bread and butter, tea, and ice cream with passion fruit (Symons 1982).

By the late 1960s, however, the pie carts and the fish-and-chip shops began receiving stiff competition from American-style fast-food outlets. Kentucky Fried Chicken was the first, in 1968, and McDonald's and Pizza Hut were not far behind. A decade later, such fast-food franchises were everywhere, although their products did not completely replace fish-and-chips and meat pies, and many of the traditional fish-and-chip shops have recently expanded their "takeaway" (carry-out) menus to include Chinese food as well as a variety of European fast foods, such as gyros and kebabs. Fast-food outlets of this type, often operated by recent immigrants, have contributed significantly to the diversification of foodways in Australia and New Zealand.

Of even more importance, however, has been the recent explosive growth of all types of restaurants. Some of this growth can be attributed to the influence of immigrants from Europe soon after World War II and, more recently, from Asia and the Pacific region. But as affluence grew in both Australia and New Zealand, more people began to visit Europe and other places around the world, and as they did so, they discovered that there was more to the "good life" than steak-and-eggs and chips.

Contemporary Food and Beverage Ways

Migrants, overseas travel, the window to the world opened by television, affluence, and the continuing globalization of food have all contributed to the diversification of Australian and New Zealand diets. Another significant change has been in drinking habits. An accompaniment to the growth of diversified, quality eating places has been the proliferation of locally produced wines, some of fine quality, some not. Although Australians and New Zealanders were and are beer drinkers, they have also historically drunk sweet wines, characteristically "screw-topped Riesling" (Symons 1982).

Grapes have long been grown, since 1791 in Australia and 1819 in New Zealand (de Blij 1985). Wine making developed early in Australia: By the 1820s, it was successful around Sydney and had expanded to the Hunter Valley. In the 1830s and 1840s, viticulture and wine making began in Victoria and South Australia, and a solid market for sweet and fortified wines developed. During the 1960s and the years that followed, the industry was transformed, with new, high-quality cultivars planted; technological and wine-making improvements led to a vastly expanded and diversified array of wines to meet developing consumer tastes.

Large-scale wine making is much more recent in New Zealand, which had only 200 acres planted with wine grapes in 1945. But the industry expanded enormously after 1960, with white varietals initially dominating. Today, red varietals have also come into their own, and there are more than 140 vineyards marketing wine in New Zealand. Some are owned by large corporations; yet there are also many small producers making excellent wines.

"One Continuous Picnic"?

Symons (1982) has characterized eating and drinking in Australia since 1788 as "one continuous picnic," and the contention here is that the same has been true in New Zealand. Both peoples were dispatched to the antipodes with packed provisions – "rations" – of salt pork and ship's biscuits. Pastoralists were paid in rations of flour (for damper), "billy tea," and slabs of meat, and the indigenous peoples learned their new foodways from the "crews" who were transforming their lands. The railways sent Australians and New Zealanders jaunting off with a litter of tins and bottles. More recently, semitrailer trucks have brought in Coca-Cola, frozen puff pastry, and "Big Macs." The concept of a picnic highlights the most essential character of Australian and New Zealand food right from the beginning: portability. Even the penchant for outdoor barbecuing (the "put-another-shrimp-on-the-barbie" syndrome) can be interpreted in this light. Broiling meat and seafood over hot coals harks back – nostalgically? – to an earlier age, when men (and women, when they were present) cooked their rations over open fires with a minimum of equipment.

Brian Murton

Bibliography

Altman, J. C. 1987. *Hunters and gatherers today. An aboriginal economy in North Australia.* Canberra.

Anderson, Atholl. 1989. *Prodigious birds: Moas and moa-hunting in prehistoric New Zealand.* Cambridge.

Belich, James. 1996. *Making people. A history of the New Zealanders from Polynesian settlement to the end of the nineteenth century.* Auckland.

Berndt, Ronald M., and Catherine H. Berndt. 1988. *The world of the first Australians. Aboriginal traditional life: Past and present.* Canberra.

Burton, David. 1982. *Two hundred years of New Zealand food and cookery.* Wellington.

Clements, Fredrick W. 1986. *A history of human nutrition in Australia.* Melbourne.

Crawford, I. M. 1982. *Traditional aboriginal plant resources in the Kalumburu area. Aspects of ethno-economics.* Perth.

Crosby, Alfred W. 1978. Ecological imperialism. *The Texas Quarterly* 21: 10–22.

Crowe, Andrew. 1997. *A field guide to the native edible plants of New Zealand.* Auckland.

Cumberland, Kenneth B. 1949. Aotearoa Maori: New Zealand about 1780. *Geographical Review* 39: 401–24.

Davidson, Janet. 1984. *The prehistory of New Zealand.* Auckland.

Davis, S. L., and J. R. V. Prescott. 1992. *Aboriginal frontiers and boundaries in Australia.* Melbourne.

de Blij, Harm. 1985. *Wine regions of the Southern Hemisphere.* Totowa, N.J.

Flood, Josephine. 1980. *The moth hunters. Aboriginal prehistory of the Australian Alps.* Canberra.

Frith, H. J. 1978. Wildlife resources in central Australia. In *The nutrition of Aborigines in relation to the ecosystem of central Australia,* ed. B. S. Hetzel and H. J. Frith, 87–93. Melbourne.

Gould, R. A. 1969. *Yiwara. Foragers of the Australian desert.* New York.

Hanson, F. Allan, and Louise Hanson. 1983. *Counterpoint in Maori culture.* London and Boston, Mass.

Jones, Kevin. 1995. *Archaeology of the eastern North Island, New Zealand.* Wellington.

Latz, P. K., and G. F. Griffin. 1978. Changes in aboriginal l and management in relation to fire and food plants in central Australia. In *The nutrition of the Aborigines in relation to the ecosystem of central Australia,* ed. B. S. Hetzel and H. J. Frith, 77–86. Melbourne.

Levitt, Dulcie. 1981. *Plants and people: Aboriginal uses of plants on Groote Eylandt.* Canberra.

Lewthwaite, Gordon R. 1949. Human geography of Aotearoa about 1790. Unpublished M.A. thesis, University of Auckland.

Massola, Aldo. 1971. *The Aborigines of south-eastern Australia as they were.* Melbourne.

McBryde, Isabel. 1974. *Aboriginal prehistory in New England. An archaeological survey of northeastern New South Wales.* Sydney.

McKnight, Tom. 1995. *Oceania. The geography of Australia, New Zealand, and the Pacific islands.* Englewood Cliffs, N.J.

Osborne, Christine. 1989. *Australian and New Zealand food and drink.* New York.

Palmer, Kingsley, and Maggie Brady. 1991. *Diet and dust in the desert. An aboriginal community, Maralinga Lands, South Australia.* Canberra.

Paul, Joanna. 1996. *The Maori cookbook.* Auckland.

Peterson, N. 1978. The traditional pattern of subsistence to 1975. In *The nutrition of Aborigines in relation to the ecosystem of central Australia,* ed. B. S. Hetzel and H. J. Frith. Melbourne.

Pool, Ian. 1991. *Te Iwi Maori. A New Zealand population past, present, and projected.* Auckland.

Symons, Michael. 1982. *One continuous picnic. A history of eating in Australia.* Adelaide.

Turner, David H. 1974. *Tradition and transformation. A study of Aborigines in the Groote Eylandt area, northern Australia.* Canberra.

Walker, R. B., and D. C. K. Roberts. 1988. Colonial food habits: 1788–1900. In *Food habits in Australia. Proceedings of the First Deakin/Sydney Universities Symposium on Australian Nutrition,* ed. A. Stewart Truswell and Mark L. Wahlqvist, 40–59. Richmond, Victoria.

Wood, Beverley. 1988. Food and alcohol in Australia: 1788–1938. In *Food habits in Australia. Proceedings of the First Deakin/Sydney Universities Symposium on Australian Nutrition,* ed. A. Stewart Truswell and Mark L. Wahlqvist, 157–77. Richmond, Victoria.

Young, Jeffrey M. 1992. A study of prehistoric Maori food. M.A. research essay, Department of Anthropology, University of Auckland.

V.E.3 ❧ The Pacific Islands

In the Pacific Islands (or Oceania) great distances, distinct island environments, and successive waves of peoples reaching island shores have all shaped foodways, including gathering, hunting, and fishing, agricultural practices and animal husbandry, and modern food distribution systems.

The peoples of Oceania (which was subdivided by Eurocentric cartographers into Melanesia, Polynesia, and Micronesia) arrived at their island homes over a span of many thousands of years. The various islands have substantial differences in natural resources, and the inhabitants have had different experiences with explorers, colonizers, and missionaries. But since the 1960s, many of the peoples and lands of Oceania have had in common their own decolonization and integration into the global economy. What follows is a description of the history and culture of food and nutrition in the Pacific Islands that recognizes diversity yet also attempts to leave the reader with an impression of the whole.

The Pacific Region

In the vastness of the Pacific Ocean are some of the world's smallest nations and territories. Politically there are 22 states, excluding both Hawaii and New Zealand. The region's giant is Papua New Guinea. With a total land area of 462,000 square kilometers, it is over five times larger than all the other Pacific states combined. This nation, inhabited for many thousands of years longer than the rest of the region, is also home to over 60 percent of the region's population of 6 million individuals, whose diversity is illustrated by the more than 800 languages spoken in Papua New Guinea alone. Fiji is the only other Oceanic territory with a population of more than 500,000. By contrast, Tokelau, a territory of New Zealand, is made up of three coral atolls with a combined land area of 10 square kilometers and a population of 1,600. Cultural definitions of the region, however, incorporate New Zealand as well as Hawaii. New Zealand is treated elsewhere in this work, but for comparative purposes, this chapter includes several references to its original inhabitants, the Maori.

The Environment

The island types of Oceania range from the large, mountainous eastern half of the island of New Guinea, which the nation of Papua New Guinea shares with Indonesian Irian Jaya, to tiny coral atolls dispersed across the central and eastern Pacific. The dominant tectonic feature of the region is the Pacific Plate, which is moving slowly to the northwest and underthrusting the Asian land mass. Its western boundary forms the Pacific "Rim of Fire," characterized by volcanism and earthquake activity. In broad outline, the region presents a continuum of environments, from larger continental islands, extensions of the Asian land mass, and andesitic volcanoes in the western Pacific to basaltic volcanic islands and coral atolls in the north and east.

There are three major island types: continental, volcanic, and coral atolls. The islands in the west, many of which are continental islands, tend to be larger and geologically complex. Typically they include intrusions of andesitic volcanic rock and are surrounded by fringing and barrier reefs. These islands have a varied topography, contain metal-bearing ores, and can develop diverse soil types, rendering large areas suitable for agricultural development. The volcanic islands, produced by andesitic, explosive volcanoes west of the Andesite line and basaltic shield volcanoes in the Pacific Basin, are much more homogeneous. Weathering produces islands with steep, rugged interiors. Fertile soils may develop on weathered slopes and in the rich alluvial deposits on valley floors.

Coral islands are the third major island type in the region. Some cultures of the Pacific are found exclusively on these resource-limited islands. Most islands in the tropical Pacific are surrounded by barrier or fringing reefs. As the final stage in the evolution of these islands, only the coral remnants remain, leaving either an atoll, a ring of coralline islets surrounding a central lagoon, or a raised coral reef. Several variations of these two main types exist. Coral islands have a more limited agricultural potential, although the upraised limestone islands may develop fertile soils under some conditions. Water is often a limiting factor because of a lack of orographic precipitation and limited storage capacity.

The Climate

Whereas almost all the islands fall within the tropics and have high year-round temperatures, these conditions are moderated by oceanic location and offshore winds. In the eastern Pacific, north of the equator, the dominant trade winds are from the northeast; south of the equator, they are from the southeast. But in the western Pacific, seasonal monsoons influence weather patterns. The northwest monsoon reaches as far east as Papua New Guinea, the Solomons, and the Carolines, bringing storms and rain in the winter. During the rest of year, the dry southwest monsoon often brings drought. Trobriand islanders refer to this as the *molu,* or hunger season.

Between the two trade-wind belts are the doldrum areas, the largest of which extends as far west as the Solomons. The doldrums are characterized by low wind velocities, high humidity, cloudiness, and high temperatures. There, atolls with no orographic precipitation, especially those close to the equator, such as the Northern Line Islands in the eastern Pacific, can be subject to extreme drought. On high islands in the trade-wind belts there is significant dissymmetry between wet windward and dry lee shores. Typhoons (hurricanes) are also a threat throughout the region.

In addition to influencing climate, the ocean currents of the Pacific have played a major role in determining flora and fauna of Oceania. Those currents, along with prevailing wind patterns, also set the parameters for long-distance sea voyaging. Oceanic peoples with sophisticated navigational techniques and maritime skills reached these remote islands in the Pacific to complete humankind's occupation of the globe about a thousand years ago.

Flora and Fauna

The flora and fauna of the island Pacific are products of their distance from Asia and, to a lesser degree, from Australia. They are also products of the great distance between islands in the eastern Pacific and North and South America. Other variables include rainfall, altitude, soil, soil salinity, groundwater, insolation, and human activity (Oliver 1989). Terrestrial plants had to have reproductive parts capable of being carried by wind or birds or humans, or of surviving immersion in salt water. Generic diversity drops significantly as one moves from west to east. As the water gaps become larger, this tendency is increased, producing a significantly more depauperate flora and fauna in the eastern Pacific.

D. Oliver (1989) has listed the natural vegetation complexes encountered in the region. Seacoast or strand vegetation, confined to narrow coastal areas, is found on most islands. Additional lowland vegetation types include mangrove forest, swamp, and rain forest found on both continental and volcanic mountainous islands. Lowland rain forest, the most widespread vegetation type in the Pacific, provides important resources for food, medicines, fiber, and building materials. But population pressure and the search for exploitable resources such as lumber have led to encroachment and environmental degradation.

Other vegetation types are more restricted in their distribution. With increasing altitude or distance from the equator, for example, at 3,000 feet in equatorial Papua New Guinea and at 900 feet in Fiji, high montane cloud forests are found. Alpine vegetation is encountered only on the highest islands – extensively only on Papua New Guinea and Hawaii and in patches on the Solomons. Finally, grasslands and savanna woodlands, resulting from either insufficient rain or anthropomorphic processes such as burning, occur on New Guinea and lee areas on some of the other islands of Melanesia (including Viti Levu), on Hawaii, and on Easter Island in Polynesia.

The fauna is equally depauperate. West to east, there is a severe attenuation of terrestrial vertebrate genera. When the Polynesians first reached Hawaii's shores, the only mammals they found were the hoary bat (Lasiurus) and the Hawaiian monk seal (Monaachus). A similar attenuation can be seen with land birds. There are 869 species in Papua New Guinea and only 17 in Tahiti. This pattern is also evident in freshwater fauna. Marine species are more widely distrib-

uted; however, the marine biota is also less diverse in the eastern Pacific than in the west. For example, there are 60 species of cowries in the Marianas Islands in western Micronesia and only 35 in Hawaii.

Peoples of the Pacific

The complex history of the Oceanic peoples is less well understood than the region's natural environment, and it is a history that is continually being revised as archaeologists, linguists, ethnobotanists, and geneticists uncover new evidence.

In discussing the interplay of productive practices and social systems, the geographer B. Currey (1980) borrowed from earlier ethnographic depictions to characterize the Melanesians as gardeners, some of whom developed complex systems (revolving around the raising of pigs) in which status was more individually than communally derived, and leaders were seen as "Big Men." Polynesians were depicted as gardeners and fishermen, with societies built on group solidarity and relatively equal access to food (although some highly stratified societies developed, especially in Tahiti and Hawaii). The Micronesians were described as traders who developed interisland trading networks and various forms of class stratification. Although this is a gross generalization, for our purposes it is a useful one. But where did these people come from?

It is now evident that Pacific Island peoples, and most of their domesticated plants and animals, originated in Southeast Asia. Between 60,000 and 8,000 years ago, two distinct "races" of modern-type humans inhabited the islands to the west of New Guinea: Mongoloids in the north and west and Sundanoids (also known as Australoids or old Melanesians) in the south and east (Oliver 1989). By 40,000 years ago, during periods of lowered sea level, Sundanoids moved into New Guinea and the Sahul shelf of Australia (Bellwood 1979). The earliest occupation of New Guinea, however, was probably even earlier, although permanent sites were not established in the highlands until 25,000 years ago (Gorecki 1986).

Oliver (1989) has suggested that between 10,000 and 5,000 years ago, four important introductions reached the Pacific Islands: (1) genes carrying Mongoloid traits, (2) languages of the Austronesian family, (3) objects relating to animal domestication and plant cultivation, and (4) knowledge to improve seagoing craft and boat handling. The latter began an era in which the far reaches of the Pacific were discovered and inhabited.

By 5,000 years ago, most of the Sundanoid peoples of Southeast Asia had been replaced or absorbed by others with different traits, such as lighter skin, straighter hair, rounder crania, and flatter brow ridges. These pioneers began to move into the Pacific Islands, possibly from the region bordering the Celebes Sea. They reached western Micronesia (Palau and the Marianas Islands) about 3,600 years ago, having crossed open ocean distances of some 500 miles. At about the same time, another group that was more or less Mongoloid moved along the north coast of New Guinea to the Solomons, Vanuatu, and Fiji.

These eastward-moving peoples were farmers and fishermen, who kept dogs and pigs, developed sophisticated fishing techniques, and also hunted. Their cultivated crops included taro, yams, bananas, sugarcane, breadfruit, coconut, the aroids (*Cyrtosperma* and *Alocasia*), sago, and, probably, rice, although at the time of European contact rice was found only in the Marianas.

The absence of rice in most of the Pacific Islands is one of prehistory's most tantalizing questions. Works by Peter Bellwood (1979) and J. Clark and K. Kelly (1993) suggest that rice was somehow lost from the horticultural complex and that sagos and taros replaced it in swampy areas, whereas yams and tree crops were grown in dry fields and swamp-garden margins. But in another interpretation, M. Spriggs (1982), who posited a Southeast Asian origin for Pacific agriculture, has argued that the techniques used for irrigated taro reached the Pacific before rice was established as a staple in Southeast Asia.

Some 3,500 to 3,300 years ago, a wave of Mongoloid-featured, Austronesian-speaking migrants moved southeast across the Pacific and rapidly established settlements in Fiji, and then in Tonga and Samoa. Those who arrived in Samoa and Tonga were the ancestors of present-day Polynesians. They brought with them Lapita ware – a type of stamped and incised pottery that probably originated in the Admiralty Islands and the Bismarck archipelago. They had a well-developed maritime technology, were expert fishermen, and also were horticulturalists who raised pigs and chickens. They developed sophisticated exchange networks, transporting goods across long distances. Some 600 years later, another migratory group from the west, with different traits, reached Fiji to mix with the islanders and become ancestors of the Fijians (Oliver 1989).

From Tonga and Samoa, the rest of Polynesia was settled over time with differentiation in language and other aspects of culture. Spriggs and A. Anderson (1993) have argued for settlement dates of A.D. 300 to 600 for the Marquesas, sometime after A.D. 750 for the Society Islands, and A.D. 600 or later for Hawaii. Anderson (1991) has suggested dates of A.D. 1000 to 1200 for New Zealand and the end of the first millennium for Easter Island.

There has been less research for Micronesia, in part because it presents a more difficult environment for archaeological investigation. As mentioned previously, the Marianas were settled by Austronesian-speaking Mongoloids at least 3,600 years ago. Recent evidence suggests that descendants of the first inhabitants of Palau and the Marianas moved east into the Caroline Islands before Oceanic-speaking peoples migrated to Micronesia via the Solomons, Gilberts,

and Marshalls (Oliver 1989). Migrants had reached the southern Gilberts by 3,500 to 3,000 years ago.

Plant Foods of the Pacific

Because they share a tropical and subtropical climate, as well as a flora and fauna with common origins, it should be no surprise that there are many similarities in the history and culture of food and nutrition among the peoples of the Pacific. Some plants have been identified as specifically Pacific cultivars, notably the fruited pandanus, sugarcane, and the *Australimusa* banana. The coconut may have had multiple domestication sites (Sauer 1971). The major staple root crops, yams (*Dioscorea*) and taros (*Colocasia esculenta*, *Cyrtosperma chamissonis*, and *Alocasia macrorrhiza*), are from Southeast Asia, as is the *Areca catechu* palm (Lebot, Merlin, and Lindstrom 1992). Bellwood (1979) has discussed evidence of gardening and pig raising in the central highlands of New Guinea from 5,500 to 6,000, and possibly as many as 9,000, years ago. More recent evidence suggests that agricultural techniques appeared independently in Papua New Guinea 9,000 years ago, possibly predating their development in neighboring Southeast Asia. There is evidence of 9,000-year-old domestication and cultivation from the Kuk Swamp in Upper Wangi, New Guinea (Gorecki 1986), but it seems likely that intensive and continuing horticulture was not established in highland Papua New Guinea until about 4,000 years ago.

D. Yen (1991), the preeminent Pacific ethnobotanist, has recently proposed a model that attempts to explain the diffusion of agricultural crops across the Pacific: Agriculture began with the independent early domestication of endemic species in the New Guinea region about 10,000 years ago. It was accelerated by the introduction of species from Southeast Asia (about 6,000 years ago), and again by the advent of crop plants from the Americas, most notably the sweet potato. These arrived in Polynesia in prehistoric times but were not introduced into western Melanesia, including Papua New Guinea, until Western contact.

The timing of the introduction of the sweet potato and its role in the development of highland New Guinea's complex agricultural systems, which supported very large populations, has been the subject of considerable academic speculation. A parallel controversy surrounds the timing of the precontact introduction of the sweet potato into eastern Polynesia (see the discussion under "Root Crops").

Root Crops

Taro. Taro refers to four members of the Araceae family, *Alocasia macrorrhiza* (giant taro), *Cyrtosperma chamissonis* (giant taro or swamp taro, grown largely on atolls), *Xanthosoma* sp., (kong kong taro or American taro, a post-Columbian introduction from South

America), and *Colocasia esculenta* (true taro). The last is the most widely distributed, and in many places in Oceania, it was the favored staple. Ancient Hawaiians, perhaps Oceania's most sophisticated agriculturalists, recognized between 150 and 175 distinguishable varieties of taro (Murai, Pen, and Miller 1958). Taro was the main staple of Hawaiians and Samoans.

Colocasia taro is believed to have been among the first root crops to be domesticated (Pollock 1992). Traditionally, it was found from South Asia through Indonesia to the Pacific. Recent evidence suggests widely distributed multiple sites for the domestication of taro, with one of those sites being highland Papua New Guinea (Yen 1993). Polynesian taro, however, could be derived from a narrower genetic base that had its origins in Indonesia, although New Guinea may have been the immediate area of domestication (Yen 1991). Archaeologist Spriggs (1982), relying in part on similarities in the irrigation technologies of New Guinea and island Southeast Asia, argued that taro originated in Southeast Asia and diffused from there into the Pacific.

Recent evidence suggests human use of *Colocasia* 28,000 years ago in Kilu Cave, a Pleistocene site in the Solomon Islands. This discovery supports the hypothesis that the natural distribution area of *Colocasia*, and perhaps other aroids, included Australia, New Guinea, and the northern Solomons (Loy, Spriggs, and Wickler 1992). *Colocasia* (true taro), whose corm and leaves are both eaten, grows best in shady, well-watered settings, such as lowland and montane rain forests to about 7,000 feet (Oliver 1989). As was the case in Indonesia and Melanesia, *Colocasia* was also produced in sophisticated valley terrace systems in the Cook Islands, in eastern Polynesia, and with a system of aqueducts in Hawaii.

Cyrtosperma taro grows in coastal freshwater marshes. It is a much larger tuber that remains edible in the ground for several years and was an important crop in Micronesia because of its tolerance of stagnant, brackish water. Shoots of the rootstock are also planted, with compost and soil, in pits dug into coral to reach the freshwater lens. *Cyrtosperma* is labor-intensive, and some island peoples have surrounded its production with much secrecy while growing huge specimens for ceremonial exchange. *Alocasia* taro requires the least moisture and is the hardiest, but the edible starchy stem contains oxylate crystals and must therefore be processed prior to consumption. Usually a subsidiary food, it is highly valued in Samoa and Tonga.

Yams. *Dioscorea* are grown throughout the tropical world, and the relationship of those in the Pacific to those in Africa, tropical America, and Asia has not been fully established. *Dioscorea alata* and *Dioscorea esculenta,* the most common Pacific species, may well have been domesticated in Southeast Asia. In order to produce a large tuber, *D. alata* needs a prolonged dry season and, thus, in the Pacific tends to be an upland rather than a lowland crop. Yams also need deep planting in light, well-drained soil; where good drainage is wanting, the technique of mounding is employed, with the vines trained to climb poles or trees.

The tubers, which can reach 9 feet in length and more than 100 pounds in weight, are often prized for size rather than food value, as the flesh of such large specimens is too coarse to eat. Their production, like that of *Cyrtosperma* taro, is often surrounded with much ritual and secrecy. Farmers gain prestige for their skill as gardeners, and yam production is at the center of a number of Melanesian societies. In Fiji, where yams were the focus of the diet, the calendar revolved around their growing season. The tubers can be left in the ground or stored for months. Traditional yam storage houses are sometimes very elaborate, as those in the Trobriand Islands.

Sweet potato. As already noted, the presence of the sweet potato *(Ipomoea batatas),* like the absence of rice, has been the subject of much speculation by those concerned with the history of Oceania. This is because at the time of European contact, the sweet potato (an American plant) was found in almost every high-island archipelago, and those who suggest a New World origin for Pacific human populations have made the plant a part of their argument.

Yen (1974), citing botanical and linguistic evidence, has suggested that the sweet potato reached the Pacific from South America in three separate introductions, all via human agency, because the sweet potato does not propagate after lengthy immersion in seawater. According to this hypothesis, the plant was first introduced into the Marquesas, in the eastern Pacific, between A.D. 400 and 800. This took place after the first settlement of the Marquesas and before the subsequent settlement of Hawaii and Easter Island. From there the sweet potato was carried to other parts of Polynesia and eastern Melanesia. What this implies for proponents of eastward or westward voyaging is one of the intriguing dilemmas of Oceanic prehistory. Another hypothesis posits a second post-Columbian Portuguese introduction, in which the sweet potato supposedly traveled (via Africa and India) through Indonesia to New Guinea and New Britain during the sixteenth century. Finally, it is believed that in the seventeenth century, still another introduction took place in the Manila Galleons from Mexico to the Philippines; after that, sweet potatoes were carried to the Marianas and East Asia.

Sweet potatoes grow in a wide range of conditions and can be cultivated at high elevations. They are fairly tolerant of dry, sandy soils and typically are grown in mounds. Sweet potatoes were part of the highly complex agricultural systems that evolved in Papua New Guinea and were also important in Hawaii and Easter Island. Because of the difficulty of production in cooler climates, they became a valued luxury in temperate New Zealand.

Tree Crops

A large array of fruit and nut crops are found in Melanesia, but they become fewer in the more restricted environments that occur as one moves to the east. Only the main food tree crops – coconut, sago, breadfruit, pandanus, and banana – are discussed here; *Areca catechu* (betel nut) is treated along with kava and toddy in a later section.

Coconut. Perhaps the Pacific region is associated more with the coconut palm, found along the littoral of most tropical islands, than with any other plant. *Cocos nucifera* is widespread, but because of temperature requirements, it is not found in New Zealand above about 1,000 feet, and it has been extinct on Easter Island for over 600 years. Although considerable debate has surrounded the role of humans in the distribution of the coconut palm, and although the plant can propagate itself, most stands have been planted by humans (Oliver 1989). It is a very important supplement to starchy staples throughout the region.

As a result of centuries of selection and propagation, Pacific Islanders recognize many horticultural varieties of the coconut. The immature nut is filled with liquid, which, over time, turns into a layer of hard, white meat. The meat is often eaten as a snack, and it is also scraped and pressed to produce coconut "cream," an important component of Pacific dishes. At full development, the center of the nut contains a spongy, jellylike mass of embryo known as "spoon meat," which is sometimes fed to infants or to those who are ill. The "milk" of immature nuts ("drinking nuts") is an important source of liquid when water is in short supply. Coconut oil can be extracted after grating the meat and exposing it to the sun for several days.

The production of copra (dried coconut meat) for export has been a mainstay of Pacific economies since the 1860s, as it can be stored on and transported from the most remote of island locations. Copra, however, is an intermediate commodity; the ultimate product is coconut oil for food and industrial purposes. Unfortunately, global economic changes, transportation costs, the increasing use of substitute oils, and alleged health risks associated with consuming coconut oil have rendered copra an increasingly marginal export commodity.

Sago. Metroxylon sp. is a pinnate-leafed palm that reaches 30 to 50 feet tall and grows in swampy areas as far east as Samoa and the Caroline Islands. The trunk is filled with a starch that the plant employs to nourish its inflorescence; thus, the tree is commonly harvested just before flowering (at about 8 to 15 years of age). Sago palms are high-yielding, producing about 300 pounds of starch per tree. The tree is felled, split, and the pulp pulverized. The starch is then washed out of the fiber and allowed to dry, producing sago "flour," which keeps for months. The flour is made into pancakes, cooked as a porridge, and can also be used as a

thickener for other dishes. Sago has been a staple for many groups in Papua New Guinea and a dietary supplement for others there and in the Solomons and Vanuatu, although it is not now as widely exploited as it once was (Connell and Hamnett 1987). It was rarely used in Polynesia or Micronesia.

Breadfruit. Artocarpus sp., with origins in the Malay archipelago, is a handsome tree growing to 60 feet in height, with large, shiny, lobed leaves. It does especially well in the Marquesas Islands, where it provides the staple food. William Dampier, who found breadfruit on Guam in 1686, may have given it its English name (Murai et al. 1958). One hundred years later, Captain William Bligh's fateful voyage of the *Bounty* began as an effort to carry breadfruit from Tahiti to the West Indies. The plant was successfully transported there in 1792 but did not become a food for slaves as was originally intended. They refused to eat it.

Artocarpus altilis and *Artocarpus incisus* are both seedless, whereas *Artocarpus mariannensis,* the variety found in Papua New Guinea, contains seeds. The fruit, cultivated primarily in Micronesia and Polynesia, is round or elliptical and reaches up to 10 inches in diameter. Breadfruit tolerates less salt than both coconut and pandanus and, hence, is more restricted in its coastal distribution. It is also drought-intolerant. The fruit is eaten cooked, but the seeds may be consumed raw. Where it is an important staple, the fruit is traditionally preserved for months or years at a time in a covered pit, in which it ferments, producing a distinctive and, to Pacific Islanders, delicious flavor. Production is seasonal, with a large summer harvest and a smaller winter one.

Pandanus. Pandanus sp. (also called the "screwpine") is an Indo-Pacific genus with several species. It has long, narrow, prickly leaves and aerial roots. Both edible and inedible varieties grow in the Pacific region. In some parts, cultivated and semicultivated plants are a primary food source, most notably among some groups in Papua New Guinea and on the coral islands of Micronesia and Polynesia. In the latter areas, a number of parts of *Pandanus tectoris* are eaten: the "heart" or terminal bud of the branch, young leaves, the tips of aerial roots, and the seeds and fleshy portion of the fruit (Oliver 1989). In cultivated varieties, the fruits can weigh as much as 30 pounds, with 50 or more phalanges or keys with seeds at the end.

Pandanus is high in sugar, carbohydrates, and vitamin A. It can be eaten raw, but it is also cooked and made into a flour or a paste, both of which can last for months. In some parts of the Pacific, the paste is wrapped in plaited pandanus leaves and tied with coconut cord. In former times, these bundles could reach up to 6 feet in length and 1 foot in diameter (Murai et al. 1958). Pandanus is a major staple on coral atolls and once provided an important food source for long-distance voyaging.

Banana. Before European contact, the bananas of Oceania were either "cooking bananas" or plantains, and not the sweet ones eaten raw, although *Musa paradisiaca* (sweet bananas) and *Musa troglodytarum* (cooking bananas) are both of Southeast Asian origin and have a number of cultivars. In most cases, bananas were a supplement to the diet rather than a staple. Today, some of the varieties introduced by Europeans are preferred in the green stage for cooking, as in Samoa. In Polynesia, bananas were grown both as part of shifting cultivation and as perennial herbs in gardens and around settlements.Western perceptions to the contrary, the traditional diets of Pacific Islanders were not complemented by an abundance of fresh fruits. Citrus fruits and pineapple were introduced to Oceania by Westerners. Pacific fruits like the papaya were typically given away or, in modern times, sold. Both papayas and mangoes are fed to pigs.

Other Crops

Sugarcane. Saccharum officinarum, which when chewed satisfies both hunger and thirst, and *ti (Cordyline fruticosa, Cordyline terminalis),* with a root very high in sugar, were among the plants that Polynesians carried with them on their voyages, and both became widely established species. The former is best known in Oceania as a plantation crop on Hawaii and Fiji.

Manioc (cassava). Manihot esculenta or *Manihot utilissima,* an American plant, was introduced early into the Pacific by the Spaniards, but it did not become widespread as a food until the middle of the twentieth century. Since then, it has become an important staple in the Pacific, as elsewhere in the developing world. In Fiji, manioc superseded taro decades ago in total area under cultivation (Thaman 1990). Sometimes perceived as a lazy man's crop because of its ease of cultivation, it has been planted in areas where cash crops have captured the most productive land. With long, thin, tuberous, edible roots, most varieties contain toxic hydrocyanic acid and must be processed before consumption. Manioc grows best in wet climates, but it can survive dry periods. Usually baked or boiled, it can be processed and stored like flour. It is high in starch but low in vitamins and minerals, and, hence, its widespread displacement of traditional staples is decried by some nutritionists.

Food Production Systems

Oliver (1989) has noted that a major generalization which could be made about food production in Oceania is that individual plants have been planted and tended there, in contrast to the sowing of large quantities of seed. Fire, adzes, and axes were used to clear the land, and digging sticks were employed for planting. Weeds and pigs were common problems, and

islanders appealed to the supernatural for protection against crop pests and diseases. During recent research in Fiji, an Indian farmer suggested to me that it was still much better to pray than spray.

Agriculture

Agricultural production systems are closely tied to land tenure, which in most Pacific societies was, and to a large degree remains, communal. Land itself has a deep spiritual meaning in Pacific societies (Bonnemaison 1984). P. Cox and S. Banack (1991) have noted that in much of Polynesia, land and most equipment was the common property of descent groups and was allocated at the lowest unit of the group.This practice was modified in the most highly stratified societies, as in Hawaii, where at the time of Western contact, chiefs directly controlled the land. Many groups in Oceania had access to several microenvironments, such as strand and swamp.Typically, in Polynesia, the units of land tenure were pie-shaped wedges, from mountaintop to outer reef, that spanned four or five ecological zones.These lands were used both for production and for hunting and gathering (Oliver 1989).

Writing of Polynesia, P. Kirch (1991) has argued that the range of production systems reflected an adaptation not only to the wide range of environments that the islanders encountered but also to demographic and sociopolitical circumstances such as expansion and intensification.The agronomic complex of any location was also influenced by other factors. Not all food plants and animals made or survived voyages to new islands, and the voyagers themselves may not have been vested with all the agronomic lore of their home islands.

As already mentioned, there is a west-to-east decline in numbers of cultivated and husbanded species of plants and animals that mirrors, to a degree, the decline of indigenous flora and fauna but may also reflect the attrition wrought by long voyages. Moreover, as islanders moved from high to low islands, there were many adaptations in food production that reached their extreme in temperate New Zealand, where most tropical crops did not thrive. Taro could be grown in the north, but not very successfully, and other important crops, such as coconut, breadfruit, and banana, did not become established. The edible fern, *Pteridium esculentum,* became an important staple, and New Zealand Maori were highly dependent on both the rich avifauna and marine species.

In general, according to Oliver (1989), extended kin groups (those who slept together and ate together) constituted food-producing units, except in societies where gender segregation dictated eating and sleeping patterns. In Melanesia, males were primarily responsible for site preparation, climbing high trees, and felling sago palms. Females were usually, although not universally, responsible for weeding, planting, and harvesting. Kirch (1991) wrote that in

Polynesia most agricultural labor was done by males, with assistance from women in weeding, mulching, harvesting, and carrying crops. But in other societies, especially where dry-field cultivation was the norm (as on the islands of Hawaii and Maui), more female labor may have been required. Even in the 1990s, the role of women's labor in agricultural production was underestimated. Women's roles in gardening and pig rearing in Melanesian societies also had implications for women's roles in political and ritual life in these societies (Manderson 1986).

Types of production systems. Kirch (1991) described five types of agricultural systems in Polynesia, and these can be modified for Oceania as a whole. The initial phase in most high-island locations was shifting cultivation with aroids and yams. It was often succeeded by arboriculture and field rotation.

The second, dry-field cultivation, developed out of the intensification of shifting cultivation. Both shifting cultivation and dry-field cultivation are practiced today.

Water control, a third system, included inundated fields created by terracing, drained garden systems in swampy areas, and pit cultivation. The most highly developed forms include the miles of intricate drainage systems for sweet potato gardens on the marshy valley floors in highland New Guinea and the sophisticated taro drainage and irrigation systems found in New Caledonia, Fiji, Hawaii, and elsewhere in Polynesia. Yen (1991) has noted that irrigation has been the most commonly used method of raising *Colocasia* taro. Growing taro under irrigation is highly productive, resulting in considerable surplus, and Kirch (1984) has argued that such surpluses were important to the rise of Polynesian chiefdoms in late precontact Hawaii.

Arboriculture, the fourth system, was typical of lowland Melanesia with a mix of fruit- and nut-bearing species. Although arboriculture declines to the east, monocropping of breadfruit (*Artocarpus* sp.) did develop in Polynesia, especially in the Marquesas. Other important tree crops include the almost ubiquitous coconut, *Spondias dulcis -vi* or Kafika apple, and *Inocarpus fagifer,* the Tahitian chestnut.

Kirch identified animal husbandry as a fifth system in his classification and noted that pigs, dogs, and chickens (the Southeast Asian triad) were the three species raised in Polynesia, although one or more may have been absent in marginal eastern Polynesia and on some atolls. Most were found on Pacific islands at the time of Western contact, although chickens were absent in much if not most of Melanesia. In some New Guinea societies, wild cassowaries were captured and raised for food (Oliver 1989). Dogs were more marginal than pigs in most Pacific societies and usually survived by scavenging, except in Hawaii, where they were tended and fed. The chicken *(Gallus gallus)* was also a scavenger, although it was carefully husbanded on Easter Island (where the dog and the pig were absent), and there it served some of the ceremonial purposes that pigs did on other islands. Dogs were used in hunting where there were sufficient ground animals, as in Melanesia and New Zealand, but also served as food themselves in Hawaii and the Society Islands (Oliver 1989).

Pigs played a central role in many of the cultures of Oceania, especially in Melanesia. They were probably introduced to New Guinea from Indonesia as early as 5,000 years ago, but their range did not extend to Micronesia or, as noted, Easter Island, and they were not found in New Caledonia or New Zealand at the time of Western contact (Oliver 1989).

These pigs (*Sus scrofa*) were thin, long-legged "razorbacks," unlike today's much larger and fatter domestic pigs. Different husbandry strategies for pigs evolved, such as letting them forage exclusively, or feeding them occasionally, or constraining and feeding them all the time. In parts of Melanesia, much attention was lavished on pigs; their births were surrounded with ceremony, and they were suckled (as were dogs in some places), bathed, and fed premasticated food. They were a very important symbol of wealth and central to ritual, social relationships, and political power. In highland New Guinea, sweet potato gardens supported the production of large numbers of pigs, typically for ceremonial exchange (Megitt 1974), although many pigs were also slaughtered for ceremonial purposes (Oliver 1989) and consumed by kin and other social groups.

Hunting and Gathering

Hunting, gathering, and fishing in coastal and riverine locations were the only food-producing activities of humans in Oceania for the first 20 or so millennia (Oliver 1989). In most traditional societies (exceptions were a few in Papua New Guinea), hunting, although an important source of protein, did not provide the bulk of calories, which came from wild plants, grubs, insects, and, especially, marine foods.

Because of the paucity of mammals on the islands to the east, the hunting of avifauna, for both food and feathers, was well developed. In New Zealand, the arrival of the earliest inhabitants rapidly led to the extinction of 11 species of *moa* – giant flightless birds – and other species as well. In many parts of Oceania, the gathering of seabird and turtle eggs supplemented the diet, and fruit bats were hunted as far east as Samoa and Tonga.

It bears repeating, however, that the major constraint on hunting and gathering in the islands of the eastern Pacific was the severe attenuation of indigenous species of both plants and animals. E. S. C. Handy and E. G. Handy (1972) listed the wild species used in Hawaii as six species of ferns, six of roots or tubers, eight of nuts and berries, two of tree fruits, four of leaves, numerous species of seaweed, and many species of birds, but only one insect, the grasshopper.

Fishing

There is also an attenuation of both freshwater and marine fish species from west to east. Marine foods were a key to the peopling of the Pacific, and fishing was and remains a very important food-securing activity in the region, especially on the high islands and atolls of the central and eastern Pacific. Traditional fishing methods were many and varied. Relatively sessile marine creatures, such as mollusks and sea urchins and other slow-moving animals, were caught by hand in the inshore waters. Harvesting sea turtles was also common in many locations. On the reef and in the lagoon, stupefacients were used, as well as mesh nets, draft nets, spears, nooses (for eels and, in Hawaii, sharks), traps and snares, and lines for angling (Oliver 1989). The fishhooks of Oceania reveal a fascinating array of special-purpose applications.

The collection of *limu* (seaweed) has been particularly important in Polynesia, as was documented in the extensive work of I. Abbott (1991). There are 63 Hawaiian names for edible marine and freshwater plants, representing about 30 separate species. Hawaiians considered *limu* and *poi* a particularly satisfying dish. Elsewhere in Polynesia, *limu* was typically consumed with coconut cream or grated coconut, and the fact that *limu* was not eaten with coconut in Hawaii has been used to argue for a relatively late arrival of the coconut there (Handy and Handy 1972).

Culinary Practices

Beginning with the early explorers, discussions of the meaning of food and of meals in Oceania have been confused by Western preconceptions. For example, Nancy Pollock (1986, 1992), using evidence from Fiji, Hawaii, Tahiti, and elsewhere, has noted that the concept of a "meal" is less important than it is in Western societies (although the meaning of meals may be changing with the fast-food culture in the West). Typically, meals, as defined by Westerners, were consumed once or twice a day and consisted of a starch and an accompaniment, with perhaps a condiment, such as salt, mashed shellfish in brine, crushed insects, or seaweed.

Oliver (1989) has described the main meal, usually freshly cooked, as generally eaten in the late afternoon after the day's work was over. The first meal of the day might have been a light one consisting of leftovers from the previous day, and lunch was often foodstuffs collected and cooked during work, such as breadfruit roasted over an open fire. Oliver (1989) has also made some interesting generalizations about the various food habits of the region, which, although diverse, share many similarities. The peoples of Polynesia and Micronesia have tended to have more food recipes, even though they had fewer nonmarine food resources, than those of Melanesia, and oven baking has been more common in Polynesia and Micronesia. Polynesians and Micronesians also had more food-

preparation instruments – pounders, graters, spitters, and fire tongs. The implements used in eating included breadfruit or *ti*-leaf "plates," sharpened sticks, and sometimes wooden bowls, baskets, and seashells. Fingers also served as eating implements.

Food Preparation

Some Oceanic foods were eaten raw – small fish, marine invertebrates, pandanus "keys," coconut, and some fruits – although, as already noted, the adult diet typically did not include much fruit (Oliver 1989).

Cooking methods included broiling over fire or on hot ashes or stones, with the food either uncovered or leaf-wrapped, and sometimes hot stones were put in the body cavity of an animal. Where clay pots were part of the material culture, foods were sometimes boiled. In the early 1800s, whalers and missionaries introduced boiling pots and frying techniques.

The most distinctive cooking style, and one that is indigenous to Oceania, involves the use of the earth oven or *umu*. There are both household and communal ovens (Pollock 1992), with the latter a significantly larger version of the former. There were variations in the oven preparation, but generally a pit was dug and lined with stones upon which a fire was lit. Following this, the heated ash was brushed aside, some of the stones removed, and the remaining stones covered with green leaves. The foods to be cooked were placed on the stones, then covered with hot rocks and ash, leaves, fronds, perhaps earth, and, today, a burlap sack. Although such a slow-cooking technique is laborious, it persists in the region, particularly for feasts and Sunday meals.

No regionwide survey of cooking responsibilities has been carried out, but examples from 21 societies in Oceania revealed situations where women did all the cooking, others where women did the daily cooking and men cooked for feasts (which may be the most common), still others where both men and women cooked daily and for feasts, and the example of Truk, where men did most of the cooking on a daily basis as well as for festive occasions. In at least one society (Yap) each gender regularly cooked for itself, and in Tahiti there was some prohibition against women eating foods cooked by men (Oliver 1989).

Preservation

The storage of food, especially for times of natural disaster or human conflict, was well developed in parts of Oceania, perhaps especially so in the more environmentally sensitive areas. Pollock (1992) has argued that this practice developed not only for times of shortage but also because of a preference for the added taste of fermentation, as in *poi*, the taro dish of Hawaii, or in fermented breadfruit. In the famine-prone Marquesas, breadfruit was traditionally prepared by young men (it was believed that it would store longer if the men were virgins), fermented, and placed in *ti*-lined wooden vessels, and the *ma* was stored in underground pits for months or years. Similarly, taro and breadfruit paste were left to ferment and, sometimes, stored for 10 years or more.

Polynesian arrowroot and, more recently, manioc were preserved as flour. Sago starch was dried, fish were dried and/or salted, and bananas could also be dried or stored in tightly wrapped packets. Well-aired storage houses were used for yams, and food was also preserved by not harvesting it. As already noted, *Cyrtosperma* taro grown in pits can survive in swampy areas for a number of years, and both *Dioscorea* yams and manioc can be left in the ground.

Feasting and Ceremonies

Because they figure so predominantly in Pacific life, feasts have received a great deal of ethnographic attention. They were often dictated by political motives and defined by structured social relationships and religious considerations. They were also important mechanisms for exchange and had considerable economic significance.

Feasts, surrounded with rules and rituals, usually involved large numbers of individuals and a great amount and variety of food. In some societies, all food was prepared and eaten at the location where the feast took place; in others, cooked or uncooked food was given to guests for later consumption (Oliver 1989).

In Melanesia, feast preparations might have included the slaughter of hundreds of pigs. As mentioned previously, there and elsewhere, as in Pohnpei in Micronesia, gardeners would jealously and often secretly raise huge yams. No longer edible, these tubers nonetheless displayed the agriculturalist's prowess and earned credit in ceremonial exchange. Often an enormous amount of food was prepared – much more than could be consumed – and this also carried ceremonial and sociopolitical significance.

Food Taboos

Throughout Oceania, eating was governed by taboos based variously on age, sex, marital status, pregnancy, social grouping and rank, illness, and bereavement. According to Oliver (1989), the most widespread prohibitions were those based on totemism whereby groups would not eat food items (including many wild species) with which they were perceived to have a spiritual relationship. Food taboos for women in Oceania were common, and in ancient Tahiti, women were generally prevented from eating pig, dog, turtle, albacore, shark, dolphin, whale, and porpoise – all foods highly valued or in short supply (Manderson 1986).

Jocelyn Linnekin's book *Sacred Queens and Women of Consequence* (1990) has described a situation in Hawaii in which the dichotomies between chief and commoner or male and female defined social reality. Women were prohibited from eating with men, and cooking was men's work. The choicest foods were offered to chiefs and sacrificed to the

gods. Such foods were prohibited to women, although female chiefs were exempt from punishment (which could be death) for infractions.

Further light is shed on food taboos for women in Polynesia by Pollock (1992), who cited J. Williams's (1838) comments about the Cook Islands:

> Females at Rarotonga were treated as inferiors. They were neither allowed to eat certain kinds of food which were reserved for the men and the gods, nor to dwell under the same roof with their tyrannical masters, but were compelled to take their scanty meal of inferior provisions at a distance while the "lords of creation" feasted upon the "fat of the land" and the "abundance of the sea." (Williams 1838: 180)

Women typically had even more restricted food choices during pregnancy, as the maternal diet and development of the fetus were directly associated (Manderson 1986). A woman might, for example, have avoided eating a fish with a displeasing appearance for fear that her child might resemble the fish. Taboos were not, however, exclusive to women. Pork, a highly valued food, was prohibited to women in a number of Pacific societies, but in a few others, for example among the Etoro of New Guinea, the situation was reversed. For men, pork consumption was believed to deplete strength (Rappaport 1968). In the stratified societies of Polynesia, chiefs also imposed prohibitions on certain foods (e.g., pork, specific fishes, or food crops) for sociopolitical reasons, to assure the supply or protect the resource. Feasts might accompany the lifting of such prohibitions.

Eating and Body Size

In most of the societies of Polynesia, and especially among the nobility, large stature and obesity were highly regarded in both men and women. Large size was associated with status and hospitality; thus, a fat chief signified a wealthy society. Moreover, in some societies, such as that of Tahiti, obesity meant increased sexual attractiveness (Oliver 1989). There are numerous accounts of individuals of chiefly rank consuming seemingly impossible quantities of food and achieving a size that rendered them largely immobile. But even ordinary individuals took great pleasure in gorging on huge quantities of food, especially in Polynesia. One explanation for this practice is that it was a response to the seasonal availability of food. Pollock (1992) has noted that if taro was plentiful, it was not unusual for an adult to eat 5 to 10 pounds of it at a sitting.

Oliver (1989), though, referring to the work of M. Young (1971), pointed out a contrasting example, the Kalauna people of Goodenough Island in southeastern New Guinea, whose goal was "full gardens and small bellies." The latter was associated with physical beauty and was attained by hunger-suppressing magic and willpower.

Cannibalism

The role that cannibalism played in the Pacific has probably been exaggerated, and in fact there is evidence to suggest that in some instances, tales of cannibalism were fabricated by islanders to shock naive Europeans. Labeling enemies as cannibals was probably also a popular strategy. There are, however, credible reports of the practice of cannibalism in New Guinea, the Bismarcks, the Solomons, the New Hebrides, New Caledonia, Fiji, New Zealand, the Marquesas, the Gambiers, and Easter Island (Oliver 1989).

The practice was most prevalent in Melanesia (although not all Melanesians were cannibals), to which the appellation "Cannibal Isles" was applied. Oliver (1989), with some reservations about attributing motive, distinguished three categories of cannibalism. In the first, the purpose was to obtain meat (or, specifically, human meat); the second involved punishment, usually of a foreigner or, less commonly, of a local offender, and the practice also was used as a gesture of extreme contempt toward the victim. The third category invoked the realm of magic: In this case, the eating of an enemy, friend, or relative was done to absorb one or more of his or her important attributes. In this latter case, only specific parts of the body, such as the brain, the eye, the heart, the liver, or the genitals, were consumed.

Cannibalism for the purpose of punishment seems to have been the most widely practiced form, and cannibalism for magic ends was more common in Polynesia than Melanesia. In Micronesia, the only evidence we have of cannibalism has been the consumption of token parts of deceased relatives in Truk. A similar practice in highland New Guinea, where parts of the brain were consumed, especially by women and children, led to the transmission of the slow viral disease *kuru*. Cannibalism in the region probably reached its height in Fiji and the western Solomons after firearms were introduced. In the Solomons, firearms rendered raiding and head-hunting more efficient, and in eastern Viti, Levu chiefs imposed a levy of human bodies for consumption. The material culture of Fiji included special wooden cannibal forks, which today are reproduced for sale as tourist "art."

To Drink and Chew

Kava

With a few localized exceptions in the western Pacific, Oceania has had only two traditional drug plants, kava and betel, but only kava, a narcotic infusion of the pulverized root of *Piper methysticum*, is indigenous to the region. V. Lebot, M. Merlin, and L. Lindstrom (1992) have argued that kava was domesticated in the northern islands of Vanuatu about 3,000 years ago. Although kava is not technically classified as a drug because it does not promote addiction or dependence, its active ingredients, kavalactones, have mild narcotic, soporific, and diuretic properties. It is also a muscle relaxant.

The origin of kava is a prominent theme in Oceanic mythology (Lebot et al. 1992). Uprooted after several years of growth, the roots are dried or, less frequently, prepared green. The preparation of kava is often surrounded by highly ritualized ceremonies, and it is an integral part of religious and social life, especially in Tonga, Fiji, Pohnpei, and Samoa.

Two traditional patterns of kava use can be distinguished. In Samoa, Tonga, Fiji, Rotuma, Futuna, Uvea, and Vanikoro, the primary use has been ceremonial and the effects mild. The dry roots are prepared with a substantial quantity of water. But in Hawaii, eastern Polynesia, Vanuatu, Choiseul, and parts of New Guinea, where drinking has tended to be a more individual activity, green roots were often employed with less water added. This mixture was more potent and often resulted in sleep and paresis of the lower limbs.

Whereas kava consumption has generally been and remains a male activity, some age and gender restrictions have been relaxed, and practices are not uniform throughout Oceania. In Fiji, it is believed that drinking moderate amounts of kava when pregnant is good for the fetus and that it will ease childbirth. The drinking of kava during breast feeding is thought to favor the production of milk. In other Pacific societies, infertility has been attributed to kava, and it was also used as an abortifacient. In addition to its ceremonial role, kava has a more general place in Pacific societies. Laborers in rural areas share kava after a hard day's work, and in the towns, others gather at bars for the same purpose (Lebot et al. 1992).

In recent years, kava has become a cash crop in several Pacific countries, and it is now exported from Vanuatu, Tonga, and Fiji to other island countries and nations with Pacific Island populations. There is also an increasing market to meet the demands of the European pharmaceutical industry.

Betel

Betel is the other traditional Pacific drug, although betel chewing is more restricted than the consumption of kava and is found primarily in parts of Melanesia and western Micronesia, notably Palau, the Marianas, and Yap. Betel is employed in exchange and has some ceremonial significance, but its use is not nearly as ritualized as that of kava. It is not usually prohibited to women, although it is more commonly chewed among men.

The shorthand term "betel" refers to a combination of the hot and acrid nut of the *Areca catechu* palm, the bean or stem of the *Piper betel* vine (of the same family as kava), and slaked lime (from either seashells, coral, or mountain lime). There are various methods of using betel, but typically the ingredients are made into a wad, chewed in the mouth, and pressed against the cheek, irritating the mucous membrane and producing a localized sensation. The red fibers and juices are expectorated. The alkaloid arecoline is a stimulant with nicotine-like properties, and betel chewers believe it increases work capacity. As a rule, users of betel have darkened teeth and red stains around the mouth.

Toddy

Another drug used in some Pacific societies, most notably in Micronesia, is palm wine or "toddy," made from the sap of the coconut palm. The practice of collecting the sap from incisions made in the bound spathe of the palm's inflorescence probably originated in the Philippines. The sweet, milky-white sap is high in vitamin B and is consumed fresh. It is considered an ideal food for infants, the sick, and the elderly; it is also used as a flavoring agent in cooking and is boiled as a confection. Processed, it was sometimes stored as a famine food, but left to ferment for several days, it becomes an alcoholic drink.

Alcohol

Alcohol use has become common in the Pacific, although patterns of consumption vary throughout the region. In places where ceremonial kava drinking was traditional, the use of alcohol (usually beer) tends to be a social rather than a solitary activity, and drinks are consumed quickly – an entire bottle of beer in one draft, akin to drinking the entire bowl of kava.

By contrast, in his studies in Papua New Guinea, M. Marshall (1982) found that beer drinking tended to be patterned more on the Australian "mateship" and egalitarian model. Although per capita consumption of alcohol is less than it is in developed nations, high levels of individual intake are common, with drunkenness the major goal, especially among young men.

The Contemporary Pacific

Dietary Colonialism?

In most Pacific Island societies, explorers, whalers, and ships' crews stopping for provisions provided the earliest contact with the West. Later, the economic history of the Pacific came to be dominated to varying degrees by colonization, missionary influences, land alienation, and the production of primary products for export. At first it was the production of copra that altered patterns of daily life and land use in much of the region. Following this it was sugar, bananas, cacao, coffee, oil palm, pineapple, and other tropical export crops.

In Fiji and Hawaii in particular, such activities also altered the ethnic composition of the population, which has influenced the cuisines that we find in those places today. For example, beginning in the 1880s, East Indians were brought to Fiji as indentured laborers for the sugar plantations, and today approximately half the population is East Indian. No wonder that curries are common there.

At the northeastern anchor of the Polynesian triangle, in Waikiki, one can, if so inclined, order rice and Portuguese sausage at McDonald's. This offering, however, is but a pale example of the diversity of cuisines available on almost any business street in Honolulu, largely a legacy of the successive waves of immigrants – Chinese, Japanese, Portuguese, and Filipino - who began arriving in the 1850s to labor on the sugar and pineapple plantations of Hawaii. Later immigrants, the largest numbers from Korea and Southeast Asia, have added to the rich tapestry of ethnic cuisines. In the 1990s, chefs of Hawaii blended the culinary techniques and flavors inherited from the Pacific, Asia, California, and Europe to create their own versions of the new regional cuisines (Henderson 1994).

The Political and Economic Context

Although the Pacific's most international cuisines are found in Hawaii, some foods and foodstuffs from distant places have long been available to those in the urban and port areas throughout Oceania. The salt beef, weevil-laden flour, stale cabin biscuits, and moldy apples that were the fare of the earliest missionaries have been supplanted by tinned fish, frozen meats (including lamb flaps and turkey tails – leftovers from the livestock and poultry industries of Australia and New Zealand), rice, soft drinks, and "cheese twists." In addition to Western food staples, elements of a simplified Chinese-style cuisine, such as dried fish imported from Asia, rice, and condiments, are found in the many parts of the Pacific with Chinese immigrants, and one can find "take-aways" selling "chop suey" in Apia, Western Samoa, whereas "chicken longrice" (rice noodles) and *lomi lomi* salmon (an adaptation from the salt salmon of sailing ships) have become part of the typical "traditional" Hawaiian luau.

Nonetheless, although by the 1990s the island states of the Pacific were, to a greater or lesser degree, integrated into the global economy, in many ways they continue to occupy its fringes, or, as a prominent geographer has suggested, "the Earth's Empty Quarter" (Ward 1989). Although the majority are politically independent or self-governing, true economic independence eludes most, and this marginal role in the global economy can (with remoteness and a continued dependence on agricultural exports) influence contemporary diets in complex ways. The agricultural mosaic that one finds in the Pacific has been strongly influenced by the colonial experience, when economic activities focused on the production and export of primary crops produced on plantations, either through myriad cooperative schemes or as cash crops. But despite the beginning of decolonization in the early 1960s, this pattern has continued, with development officials and international aid agencies strongly urging the production of export crops, hailing such activity as the "road to development."

Consequently, prime garden lands were often converted to the production of cash crops, and subsistence plots were moved to more distant and more marginal land. Especially in Melanesia (Hau'ofa and Ward 1980), where women are the primary subsistence gardeners, such events increased the workload of women, demanding more of their time and energy, which may in turn have had a negative nutritional impact on the entire family, or at least on the young children.

By the early 1980s, as the nutritional and economic fallacy of cash-crop dependence became increasingly apparent, a more balanced approach, stressing food self-sufficiency and the production of indigenous crops, was adopted. This new approach reflected general changes in development thinking, but it was also the result of the efforts of academics, nutritionists, and others (Parkinson 1982) who advocated changes in government policy. The shift took place at a time when Pacific nations began to gain their political independence, and advocating food self-sufficiency became an important symbolic component of the process.

The production of food and other agricultural products remains the dominant economic activity for most of the population of Oceania. Yen wrote in 1980 that a mix of subsistence production and cash-cropping was the most common form of agriculture in Oceania, and this was probably still true in the 1990s. Pollock (1992), using data from 1980 to 1985, noted that foodstuffs constituted approximately 25 percent of total imports by value, but thought that this proportion was beginning to drop, perhaps because of efforts at food self-sufficiency. Data from eight of the countries in the region in the mid-1970s indicated that from 15 to 26 percent of total import dollars was spent on food, with the average somewhat under 20 percent (Lewis 1981). More recent data have suggested rates closer to 15 percent, especially for the more populous countries like Papua New Guinea, Fiji, and the Solomon Islands. But there are exceptions such as American Samoa, whose people spend 62 percent of total import dollars on food (South Pacific Economic and Social Database 1993) and a few islands where virtually all food is imported.

Urban and Rural Diets

Approximately 30 percent of the population in the Pacific can be classified as "urban," although this is a relative concept in the region. Many families produce some garden crops in periurban and urban areas, and many also receive produce through members of their extended families who reside in rural areas. It is no surprise that there tends to be a continuum from traditional to Western (or modern) diet as one moves from rural to urban areas and, for that matter, from the less "developed" parts of the region, like highland Papua New Guinea, to the more developed, as for example, Guam.

Families in rural areas are more dependent on locally produced foodstuffs, both because less imported food is available and because they have less money with which to purchase it. But it would be a mistake to assume that today's rural diets are the same as precontact diets (Pollock 1992). Rural producers in periurban areas may also have diets dominated by imported staples. Employing a household strategy designed to meet an increasing need for cash, rural producers may sell a truckload of taro and other produce and then, at considerably lower cost, purchase enough rice and flour to feed their families. The diet may be less expensive and less nutritious, but cash will be available for other needs.

Moreover, although the situation is beginning to change, in part as a response to government policy and incentives, it is not uncommon, depending on the season in urban markets, to find traditional staples, such as yams, taro, or sweet potatoes, and fish priced beyond what many urban consumers can afford (except, perhaps, for special occasions).

What People Eat

Since their earliest encounters with the West, Pacific peoples have been introduced to new foods, and these have become part of both the regular diet and, in some cases, the status food employed for ceremonial exchange. It is thought that the first canned product encountered by the Samoans was canned pea soup *(pisupo)* – a term used today for another imported and highly valued product, corned beef. Not only is *pisupo* common fare in Samoa, but kegs of beef in brine and case upon case of canned fish make up part of the exchange that accompanies ceremonial occasions.

As already noted, a rough continuum with respect to diet exists in the region, although only rural peoples in Melanesia and, perhaps to a lesser degree, remote parts of Fiji, Polynesia, and Micronesia have diets similar to those eaten by their forebears. In urban areas, people eat a mélange of traditional and Western foods on a daily basis and also patronize "take-aways" and fast-food establishments. At one time, the McDonald's in Guam was the largest in the world, and although it has lost this distinction, there are now three McDonald's franchises on that island. But for ceremonial occasions, and perhaps on Sundays (particularly in Polynesia), urban dwellers, like their rural counterparts, prepare a traditional meal and share it with the extended family.

Although one might decry the dietary change, the reasons for it are not difficult to understand. Foremost among them are the cost, degree of availability, and preparation time required for many traditional foodstuffs, as well as the influences of advertising and changing tastes. Certainly the highly refined imports of flour and rice, sugar, soft drinks, frozen meats, and high-fat corned beef make up a large part of the urban diet. Probably the most likely to be malnourished are the poor, often recent migrants to the towns, who have the least access to garden produce and the least cash to buy nutritionally sound foodstuffs. They may also be living in circumstances that do not facilitate food preparation.

Pacific Markets

Urban markets have existed, often in the same location, since colonial times, as products of the introduced cash economy. In one section there will be mounds of root and tree crops – yams, taro, sweet potatoes, cassava, coconuts, bananas, breadfruit, and other traditional foodstuffs. In another section, tables are piled with market garden produce and vegetables – greens, cabbages, squash, onions, and pumpkins. Fish and marine products are displayed in yet another section, whereas in still another, partly in response to increasing tourism, handicrafts may be found – woven pandanus and coconut-frond mats, baskets, hats, and fans, tapa, shells, shell and tortoiseshell jewelry, and wooden carvings of varying quality. In a central market there may be booths that sell a limited assortment of grains and canned or processed food. In Suva or Lautoka, Fiji, there are stalls selling *yaqona* (both kava root and the powdered form), and others with burlap bags overflowing with tumeric, chillies, and garam masala, the colorful Indian spices. In addition, prepared food and drink is often available.

Larger urban centers have supermarkets that sell fresh, frozen, and canned imported products and, sometimes, a limited selection of local ones. Some of these stores are modern versions of the old Burns Philp's or Morris Headstrom outlets of the colonial Pacific. But there are also smaller, less well-stocked groceries.

Rural stores tend to be small and often precarious business operations. In remote areas, tinned meats or fish, flour, rice, cabin biscuits, cooking oil, and tea may or may not be available. More prosperous operations may have a freezer with fish and meat, but the frozen food is often of questionable quality given the vagaries of electricity and appliance repair.

Health and Nutrition

A great deal has been written about diet, health, and nutrition in the Pacific, with much of the focus on the nutritional and health consequences that have resulted from incorporation into the global economy. This transition has been accompanied by an "epidemiological transition" (Omran 1971), in which dietary change and concomitant obesity have emerged as causal factors (Taylor, Lewis, and Levy 1989), and chronic and noncommunicable diseases have taken the lead as causes of death in the more modernized or "Westernized" parts of the Pacific.

Early studies of hypertension, such as that of more than 30 years ago by I. Prior and F. Davidson (1966), found that blood pressure did not increase with age in some traditional Pacific societies. But more recent studies show increases in blood pressure with modernization: Examples include elevated blood pressure (above 160/95) in 36 percent of males in Nauru and 34 percent of male Chamorros in Guam. Elevated blood pressure is also found in 7 percent of urban Fijians, as compared with 2 percent of rural Fijians

(Coyne 1984). Hypertension is more common in the more developed Polynesian and Micronesian societies than those of less developed Melanesia. That lifestyle appears to play a significant role was made clear by P. Baker and J. Hanna (1981), who found blood pressures among the lowest in the world in a traditional Western Samoan village and among the highest in the world among Samoans in Hawaii.

Researchers have also found some of the world's highest rates of diabetes mellitus II (DM) in the Pacific. Prevalence rates in the region ranged from none in highland Papua New Guinea to 30.3 percent in adults in Nauru and were generally higher among females than males, as is typical elsewhere (Taylor and Bach 1987). The DM rates in Nauru rival those of the Pima Indians of the United States, previously thought to have the highest rates in the world. Other studies found elevated rates (over 12 percent) in both urban and rural Fijian Indians, Western Samoans in San Francisco, urban dwellers in Papua New Guinea, and Wallasians living in New Caledonia (Lewis 1988). Recent data for Hawaii give age-adjusted DM rates of 46.2/1,000 for Hawaiians and 22.5/1,000 for non-Hawaiians (State of Hawaii 1992). In the over-65 population, rates for Hawaiians are almost three times those of non-Hawaiians. A number of risk factors have been identified, including genetic predisposition, obesity, diet, levels of activity, and more subtle effects of modernization.

Baker (1984) has elaborated on the "thrifty gene hypothesis" proposed by J. Neel (1962) to suggest that long-distance voyaging and bouts of acute short-term starvation following natural disasters (trials endured by those who settled the remote Polynesian and Micronesian islands) produced genotypes suited to such conditions. With the adoption of modern lifestyles, however, these genotypes may be predisposed to elevated blood pressure, obesity, and diabetes mellitus.

The role of diet in shaping contemporary health patterns in Oceania is complex and much remains to be discovered. Pollock (1992) calls researchers to task for equating "traditional diets" with modern rural diets in urban–rural studies. There are also important biological differences between populations, and such studies have employed a Western biomedical framework of analysis that largely ignores the meaning of food in Pacific societies.

Unfortunately, undernutrition as well as overnutrition is a problem (and an increasing one) in the Pacific, particularly, but not exclusively, in urban areas. As elsewhere, it is the nutritionally vulnerable young children and, sometimes, the elderly who suffer the most severe consequences. Throughout the region, the high cost of imported goods, a lack of knowledge about healthful diets, and a lack of gardening land in urban areas have served to undermine nutrition. In the Solomon Islands, a national survey found malnutrition affects 22 percent of children aged 0 to 4. In the Marshall Islands, 11 percent of urban children are underweight, and one-third of all deaths are of children under age 5. At the other end of the nutritional spectrum, 30 percent of the urban population over age 15 have diabetes (Republic of the Marshall Islands 1990, cited in Bryant 1993).

Summary

We have only an incomplete understanding of the role of diet in health and disease in the Pacific region. We have a somewhat better, but still incomplete, picture of what people are eating. It is a mix of foods that tends to more closely mirror traditional diets in the less developed and more rural parts of the region, although these diets are certainly not unmodified. But in other parts of the Pacific, especially in urban areas, diets are made up of imported foods, often of poor nutritional quality. However, traditional meals and feasts are still important in the Pacific.

There are cultural as well as economic and nutritional reasons for reexamining traditional diets within a framework that is relevant for the populations involved. Food remains an important cultural symbol and can be an important component of cultural identity. The Waianae Diet Program, a community-based program developed in response to high rates of obesity and chronic disease among native Hawaiians, is founded on traditional diets and cultural values and includes group support and a weight-loss protocol that is not calorie-restricted. Short-term results indicate significant reductions in weight, blood pressure, serum lipids, and serum glucose (Shintani et al. 1994). Although long-term research is needed and the positive results for individuals may be difficult to maintain over time, this culturally sensitive program is an example of the efforts being made to reassess and encourage traditional Pacific diets.

Holo i'a ka papa, kau 'ia e ka manu. This Hawaiian proverb, literally translated, means: "When the shoals are full of fish, birds gather over them" - a familiar and welcome sight to island fishermen. Its proverbial meaning is that where there is food, people gather (Puki 1983). The sharing of food – for ceremonial or merely social purposes – remains a dominant thread in the complex, rich fabric of culture in the Pacific. The thread and fabric will continue to evolve and change as they have done over the course of history, as the islands and islanders, increasingly less isolated, nonetheless continue to reassert their Pacific identities in a rapidly changing modern world.

Nancy Davis Lewis

Bibliography

Abbott, I. 1991. Polynesian uses of seaweed. In *Islands, plants and Polynesians: An introduction to Polynesian ethnobotany,* ed. P. Cox and S. Banack, 135-45. Portland, Ore.

Anderson, A. 1991. The chronology of colonization in New Zealand. *Antiquity* 65: 767-95.

Baker, P. 1984. Migration, genetics and the degenerative diseases of South Pacific islanders. In *Migration and mobility,* ed. A. Boyce, 209-39. London.

Baker, P., and J. Hanna. 1981. Modernization and the biological fitness of Samoans: A project report on a research program. In *Migration, adaptation and health in the Pacific,* ed. C. Fleming and I. Prior, 14-26. Wellington, New Zealand.

Baker, P., J. Hanna, and T. Baker, eds. 1986. *Changing Samoans: Behavior and health in transition.* New York.

Barrau, J. 1956. *Polynesian and Micronesian subsistence agriculture.* Noumea, New Caledonia.

1958. Subsistence agriculture in Melanesia. *Bernice P. Bishop Museum Bulletin* 219: 1-111. Honolulu, Hawaii.

1961. Subsistence agriculture in Polynesia and Melanesia. *Bernice P. Bishop Museum Bulletin* 223. Honolulu, Hawaii.

Bellwood, P. 1979. *Man's conquest of the Pacific: The prehistory of Southeast Asia and Oceania.* New York.

Blumer, R. 1968. The strategies of hunting in New Guinea. *Oceania* 38: 302-18.

Bonnemaison, Joel. 1984. The tree and the canoe: Roots and mobility in Vanuatu. *Pacific Viewpoint* 25: 117-51.

Brookfield, H. C. 1989. Global change and the Pacific: The coming half century. *The Contemporary Pacific* 1/2: 1-18.

Bryant, J. 1993. *Urban poverty and the environment in the South Pacific.* Armidale, New South Wales.

Casswell, S. 1986. *Alcohol in Oceania.* Auckland, New Zealand.

Clark, J., and K. Kelly. 1993. Human genetics, paleoenvironments and malaria: Relationships and implications for the settlement of Oceania. *American Anthropologist* 95: 612-30.

Clark, W. C. 1971. *Place and people: An ecology of a New Guinea community.* Berkeley, Calif.

Connell, J., and M. Hamnett. 1987. Famine or feast: Sago production in Bougainville. *Journal of Polynesian Society* 87: 231-41.

Cox, P., and S. Banack, eds. 1991. *Islands, plants, and Polynesians: An introduction to Polynesian ethnobotany.* Portland, Ore.

Coyne, T. 1984. *The effect of urbanization and Western diet on the health of Pacific island populations.* South Pacific Technical Paper 186. Noumea, New Caledonia.

Currey, B. 1980. Famine in the Pacific: Losing the chances for change. *Geojournal* 4: 447-66.

Doumenge, J. P., D. Villenave, and O. Chapuis. 1988. *Agriculture, food and nutrition in four South Pacific archipelagos.* Bogor, Indonesia.

Etkin, N., and M. Ross. 1982. Food as medicine and medicine as food: An adaptive framework for interpretation of plant utilization among the Hausa of northern Nigeria. *Social Science and Medicine* 16: 1559-73.

Firth, R. 1967. *The work of gods in Likopia.* Melbourne.

Frenk, Julio. 1992. Balancing relevance and excellence: Organizational responses to link research with decision making. *Social Science and Medicine* 35: 1397-1404.

Gorecki, P. 1986. Human occupation and agricultural development in the Papua New Guinea highlands. *Mountain Research and Development* 2: 159-66.

Handy, E. S. C., and E. G. Handy, with M. Pukui. 1972. *Native planters in old Hawaii.* This manuscript was published as the *Bernice P. Bishop Museum Bulletin* 233 by the Bishop Museum Press. Honolulu, Hawaii.

Hau'ofa, E., and R. G. Ward. 1980. The social context. In *South Pacific agriculture: Choices and constraints,* ed. R. G. Ward and A. Proctor, 49-71. Canberra, Australia.

Henderson, B., L. Kolonel, R. Dworsky, et al. 1985. Cancer incidence in the islands of the Pacific. *National Cancer Institute Monograph* 69: 73-81.

Henderson, J. 1994. *The new cuisine of Hawaii.* New York.

Johannes, R. E. 1981. *Words of the lagoon: Fishing and marine lore in the Palau district of Micronesia.* Berkeley, Calif.

Kahn, M. 1986. *Always hungry, never greedy: Food and the expression of gender in a Melanesian society.* Cambridge and New York.

Kirch, P. 1984. *The evolution of Polynesian chiefdoms.* Cambridge.

1986. Rethinking Polynesian prehistory. *Journal of Polynesian Society* 95: 9-40.

1991. Polynesian agricultural systems. In *Islands. plants, and Polynesians,* ed. P. Cox and S. Banack, 113-34. Portland, Ore.

Kofe, S. 1990. *Household food security in selected Pacific island countries.* Noumea, New Caledonia.

Lebot, V. 1991. Kava. In *Islands, plants and Polynesians,* ed. P. Cox and S. Banack, 169-201. Portland, Ore.

Lebot, V., M. Merlin, and L. Lindstrom. 1992. *Kava: The Pacific drug.* New Haven, Conn.

Lewis, N. 1981. Ciguatera, health and human adaptation in the island Pacific. Ph.D. thesis, University of California, Berkeley, Calif.

1986. Disease and development: Ciguatera fish poisoning. *Social Science and Medicine* 23: 983-93.

1988. Modernization, morbidity and mortality: Noncommunicable diseases in the Pacific Islands. *Pacific Islands Development Program.* Honolulu, Hawaii.

Lindstrom, L. 1987. *Drugs in western Pacific societies.* Landham, Md.

Linnekin, Jocelyn. 1990. *Sacred queens and women of consequence: Rank, gender and colonialism in the Hawaiian islands.* Ann Arbor, Mich.

Loy, T., M. Spriggs, and S. Wickler. 1992. Direct evidence for human use of plants 28,000 years ago: Starch residues on stone artifacts. *Antiquity* 66: 898-912.

Malinowski, B. 1936. *Coral gardens and their magic.* 2 vols. London.

Manderson, L., ed. 1986. *Shared wealth and symbol: Food, culture and society in Oceania and Southeast Asia.* Cambridge and New York.

Marshall, M. 1991. The second fatal impact: Cigarette smoking, chronic disease, and the epidemiological transition in Oceania. *Social Science and Medicine* 33: 1327-42.

ed. 1982. *Through a glass darkly: Beer and modernization in Papua New Guinea.* Monograph 18, Institute of Applied Social and Economic Research. Boroko, Papua New Guinea.

Marshall, M., and L. Marshall. 1975. Opening Pandora's bottle: Reconstructing Micronesians' early contacts with alcoholic beverages. *Journal of the Polynesian Society* 84: 441-65.

Megitt, M. J. 1974. "Pigs are our hearts!" The exchange cycle among the Mae Enga of New Guinea. *Oceania* 44: 165-203.

Murai, M., F. Pen, and C. Miller. 1958. *Some tropical South Pacific island foods.* Honolulu, Hawaii.

Neel, J. 1962. Diabetes mellitus: A thrifty genotype rendered detrimental by "progress." *American Journal of Human Genetics* 14: 353-62.

Oliver, D. 1974. *Ancient Tahitian society.* 3 vols. Honolulu, Hawaii.

1989. *Oceania: The native cultures of Australia and the Pacific Islands,* Vols. 1 and 2. Honolulu, Hawaii.

Omran, A. R. 1971. The epidemiological transition: A theory of epidemiology and population change. *Milbank Memorial Fund Quarterly* 44: 509-38.

Parkinson, S. 1982. Nutrition in the South Pacific – past and present. *Journal of Food and Nutrition* 39: 121.

Pawley, A., ed. 1991. *Man and a half: Essays on Pacific anthropology and ethnobiology in honor of Ralph Bulmer.* Auckland.

Pirie, P. 1994. *Demographic transition in the Pacific Islands: The situation in the early 1990s.* East West Center Working Paper No. 5. Honolulu, Hawaii.

Pollock, N. 1974. Breadfruit or rice? Dietary choice on a Micronesian atoll. *Ecology of Food and Nutrition* 3: 107-15.

1986. Food classification in three Pacific societies: Fiji, Hawaii and Tahiti. *Ethnology* 25: 107-17.

1992. *These roots remain: Food habits in the islands of the central and eastern Pacific since Western contact.* Honolulu, Hawaii.

Prior, I., and F. Davidson. 1966. The epidemiology of diabetes in Polynesians and Europeans in New Zealand and the Pacific. *New Zealand Medical Journal* 65: 373-83.

Puki, M. K. 1983. *O' lelo no'eau Hawaiian: Proverbs and poetic sayings.* Honolulu, Hawaii.

Rappaport, R. 1968. *Pigs for the ancestors: Ritual ecology in a New Guinea people.* New Haven, Conn.

Ravuvu, A. 1991. A Fijian cultural perspective on food. In *Food and nutrition in Fiji,* ed. A. Janese, S. Parkinson, and A. Robertson, 622-36. Suva, Fiji.

Reinman, F. 1967. *Fishing; an aspect of oceanic economy: An archaeological approach.* Chicago.

Sahlins, M. 1976. *Culture and practical reason.* Chicago.

Sauer, D., in Yen, D. 1971. A reevaluation of the coconut as an indicator of human dispersal. In *Man across the sea,* ed. C. L. Riley, J. C. Riley, C. W. Pennington, and R. L. Rand, 309-13. Austin, Tex.

Shintani, T., S. Beckham, H. O'Connor, et al. 1994. The Waianae Diet Program: A culturally sensitive, community-based obesity and clinical intervention program for the native Hawaiian population. *Hawaii Medical Journal* 53: 134-5.

South Pacific Economic and Social Database. 1993. *Western Samoa statistical compendium.* Canberra, Australia.

Spriggs, M. 1982. Taro cropping systems in the Southeast Asian Pacific region. *Archeology in Oceania* 17: 7-15.

Spriggs, M., and A. Anderson. 1993. Late colonization of eastern Polynesia. *Antiquity* 67: 200-17.

State of Hawaii. 1992. *Native Hawaiian health data book.* Honolulu, Hawaii.

Taylor, R. 1985. Mortality patterns in the modernized Pacific island nation of Nauru. *American Journal of Public Health* 75: 149-55.

Taylor, R., and F. Bach. 1987. *Proportionate hospital morbidity in Pacific island countries circa 1980.* Noumea, New Caledonia.

Taylor, R., N. Lewis, and S. Levy. 1989. Societies in transition: Mortality patterns in Pacific island populations. *International Journal of Epidemiology* 18: 634-43.

Thaman, R. 1988. Health and nutrition in the Pacific Islands: Development or underdevelopment? *Geojournal* 16: 211.

1990. The evolution of the Fiji food system. In *Food and nutrition in Fiji,* ed. A. Janese, S. Parkinson, and A. Robertson, 23-107. Suva, Fiji.

Ward, R. G. 1989. Earth's empty quarter? The Pacific Islands in a Pacific century. *The Geographical Journal* 155: 235-46.

Whistler, W. A. 1991. Polynesian plant introductions. In *Islands, plants, and Polynesians: An introduction to Polynesian ethnobotany,* ed. P. Cox and S. Banack, 41–66. Portland, Ore.

Williams, J. 1838. *A narrative of missionary enterprises in the South Sea Islands.* London.

Wilson, A., R. Taylor, G. Nugumi, et al. 1983. *Solomon Islands oral cancer study.* South Pacific Commission Technical Paper No. 183. Noumea, New Caledonia.

Yen, D. 1974. The sweet potato and Oceania. This monograph was published as the *Bernice P. Bishop Museum Bulletin* 236 by the Bishop Museum Press. Honolulu, Hawaii.

    1980. Pacific production systems. In *Pacific production systems,* ed. R. G. Ward and A. Proctor, 74–106. Canberra, Australia.

    1985. Wild plants and domestication in the Pacific Islands. In *Recent advances in Indo-Pacific prehistory,* ed. V. N. M. Misra and P. Bellwood, 315–26. New Delhi.

    1991. Polynesian cultigens and cultivars: The question of origins. In *Islands, plants and Polynesians: An introduction to Polynesian ethnobotany,* ed. P. Cox and S. Banack, 67–98. Portland, Ore.

    1993. The origins of subsistence agriculture in Oceania and the potentials for future tropical crops. *Economic Botany* 47: 3–14.

Young, M. 1971. *Fighting with food: Leadership, values, and social control in a Massim society.* Cambridge.

V.F

Culinary History

Since the 1970s, historical studies of food in particular cultures have emerged as a new field, "culinary history." Culinary history studies the origins and development of the foodstuffs, equipment, and techniques of cookery, the presentation and eating of meals, and the meanings of these activities to the societies that produce them. It looks at practices on both sides of the kitchen door, at the significance of the food to the cook and to those who consume it, and at how cooking is done and what the final product means. Consequently, culinary history is widely interdisciplinary. Studies make connections between the sciences – medical, biological, and social – and the humanities and draw heavily on anthropology, economics, psychology, folklore, literature, and the fine arts, as well as history. These multidisciplinary perspectives are integrated along geographic and temporal dimensions, and as a consequence, culinary history encompasses the whole process of procuring food from land or laboratory, moving it through processors and marketplaces, and finally placing it on the stove and onto the table. It emphasizes the role that food-related activities play in defining community, class, and social status – as epitomized in such fundamental human acts as the choice and consumption of one's daily bread.

Culinary history can also be defined by what it is not. It is not, for example, simply a narrative account of what was eaten by a particular people at a particular time. Nor is it a matter of rendering entertaining stories about food, or telling anecdotes of people cooking and eating, or surveying cookbooks. But it *is* informed analysis of how food expresses the character of a time, place, society, and culture. Put plainly, culinary history goes beyond anecdotal food folklore and descriptions of cuisine and cooking at a particular point in time to incorporate historical dimensions.

Times, Places, and Themes

Culinary history can (and should) be part of a number of avenues of investigation, such as social history, women's history, and anthropological analyses of food habits, systems, folklore, and material culture. There follows a brief examination of each of these.

Culinary History As Social History
In Europe, which has been the dominant geographic focus of culinary historians, there are basically three strands of investigation: First, there are the cuisines of the prosperous classes, including traditions of court and aristocracy; second, there is the food of middle and lower classes in urban settings; and third, there are the cuisines of rural societies of all classes. The presence or absence of haute (high) cuisine is itself a socially significant part of culinary history (Goody 1982).

Culinary history also plays an important role in regional and, later, national social histories, such as those of England, France, Spain, Germany, and Italy (Toussaint-Samat 1992; Brillat-Savarin 1995). French "*Annales* School" publications on food in social history (Braudel 1966), annual Oxford Food History Symposia, and historical analyses of European food folklorists are examples (Fenton 1986; Teuteberg 1993; Mennell 1996).

Thematic studies examine such topics as the historical significance of agricultural stresses in classical Greece (Garnsey 1990); the culinary impact of sugar and cooking ideas brought by North Africans to Spain and Italy (Peterson 1980); the insatiable demand for spices, which led Portuguese and Italian explorers – and, ultimately, Columbus – to search for new sources of supply (Laurioux 1985, 1989); the importance of the North Atlantic fisheries and their related salt fish industries; and the determinants and consequences of European demands for exotic food items, such as sugar, coffee, tea, and chocolate (Lippmann 1929; Mintz 1985; Coe and Coe 1996).

The impact of the "Columbian exchange" on both sides of the Atlantic has been told through the histories of food plants, their agricultural modes of production, and the techniques of food processing (Crosby 1972; Long 1996). The new foods and their impact on production, processing, and marketing – and on regional, national, and local cuisines – have been traced by European historians and food ethnologists, who follow evidence of introductions and diffusions through herbals, agricultural or botanical histories, food trade records, and other literary or documentary sources (Arnott 1976; Fenton and Owen 1981; Kaneva-Johnson 1995).

The diffusion and adoption of New World foods such as potatoes, maize, and chilli peppers – and the cultural, social, nutritional, and demographic changes occasioned by this – also created new food economies and cultures in Asia and Africa as these foods supplanted numerous older ones (Miracle 1966; Anderson 1988; Hess 1992). The shifts from traditional coarse grains (such as sorghums and millets) to maize in East Africa and from yams to cereal grains or cassava in Central and West Africa, as well as the commercialization of livestock, provide fine examples of the ways in which social history can be traced in terms of culinary history. Colonization and subsequent internationalization of food economies permanently affected gender and age relations in production, consumption, and cuisine.

Another significant watershed is the Industrial Revolution, which in Britain was driven in part by a widespread availability of sugar calories from the New World (consumed in relatively new beverages such as tea, coffee, and cacao) (Mintz 1985) and calories from the highly productive New World potato, which also fueled wars of nationalism in Germany (Salaman 1985). A history of caffeinated beverages from this period can tie together vastly changing food patterns all over the globe as well as economic issues of social history, like changing landholding and cropping patterns, slavery, and imperialism.

In the Western Hemisphere, European colonization resulted in the blending of foods of New and Old World origins. Later watersheds in the culinary history of the United States include the Civil War and its aftermath, with the growth of large industrial agribusinesses (Levenstein 1988); ethnic migrations from Europe in the nineteenth and twentieth centuries, and from Asia after the 1950s; and post–World War II migrations of African-Americans from the predominantly rural southern states to the urban northern states (Jerome 1980). The resulting cuisines have been analyzed in terms of "acculturation" or "changing food habits" of the ethnic populations (Mead 1964; National Research Council 1981) and in terms of their food components, formats, and cycles (see Goode 1989). In the case of Jewish-Americans, for example, their use of food is seen as a principal element in struggles either to maintain or reshape identities (Joselit, Kirshenblatt-Gimblett, and Howe 1990; Roden 1996).

All such phenomena, however, are presented within the larger context of a changing American culinary mosaic. Such national and regional analyses of culinary practices in relation to significant changes in the social order can also be found in the literature of the food habits of Europe (Fenton and Owen 1981; Rotenberg 1981), India (Katona-Apte 1976; Appadurai 1988), and China (Chang 1977; Anderson 1988; Simoons 1991). All interlink major temporal divides or points of transition with the construction of new cuisines.

Culinary History As Women's History

Culinary history, especially in the United States, has emerged, albeit slowly, out of women's history. In the past, feminist historians' analyses of women's domestic work (private sphere) – as contrasted with wage work (public sphere) – tended to focus more on child rearing and other household tasks (Strasser 1982; Cowan 1983). These scholars avoided looking at cooking, allegedly because the kitchen symbolized submission to the oppression of patriarchy, whereas their goal was to elucidate the historical sources and contexts of women's empowerment.

Important linkages of kitchen concerns to the public sphere, however, are found in Catharine Beecher's writings (and schools) of domestic science (Beecher 1869; Sklar 1973) and in the New England Kitchen, established by Ellen Richards and her Boston associates as a place where immigrants could learn to cook and enjoy Yankee cuisine as one dimension of their American assimilation (Levenstein 1988). In their eagerness to hasten the assimilation of immigrants, the New England Kitchen reformers overlooked the reluctance of groups to give up traditional foods in exchange for unfamiliar ones. As a result, this "noble experiment" was a failure.

Serious scholarly attention to domestic culinary arts has grown with the maturation and acceptance of women's history as an academic field and with the recognition that cookbooks, diary descriptions of food acquisition and eating events, and kitchen material culture are important dimensions of that history. Gender analysis, applied to the preparation and consumption of food, reveals cultural differences influencing what male and female cooks prepare, as well as changes over time and place. As a case in point, nineteenth- and twentieth-century cookbooks provide evidence that men and women were expected to eat differently. Such books make distinctions between "men's" (heavy meat dishes) and "women's" (lighter) foods. They also show that gender biases against domestic cooking by men have tended to lessen in later suburban contexts of backyard grilling. Moreover, connections made between meat and fat consumption and heart disease have significantly altered notions about the appropriateness of the "heavy" foods for males (Shapiro 1986).

Cookbooks published by women's voluntary associations often provide obvious links between women's history and culinary history. The tradition of these books began in the United States just after the Civil War, when women formed groups to aid veterans or their widows and orphans (e.g., Ladies Relief

Corps 1887). Since that time, thousands of such books have been published by groups of women all over the United States and sold to support churches, synagogues, schools, museums, and other community institutions, or to memorialize the favorite recipes of multigenerational families or groups of friends. In most cases, such books are the only records these groups left behind. They offer a unique resource for examining women's roles as community builders, especially where they contain chapters on the history of their communities, with particular attention given to the history and accomplishments of their own organizations (Brown and Brown 1961; Cook 1971; Wheaton 1984).

Culinary History As Nutritional Anthropology

Culinary history has also grown out of (but goes beyond) the study of cultural cuisines, defined as the culturally elaborated and transmitted body of food-related practices of any given culture. The latter includes descriptions of characteristic foods and their flavorings and textures, along with their symbolic combination in meals, menus, formats, and seasonal or lifetime cycles of ritual foods and eating (Rozin 1973; Messer 1984; Goode 1989). Nutritional anthropology, however, considers the distances and means by which food ingredients travel over time; the origins and diffusions of processing techniques; and the routes of commercial or customary distribution of foods from sites of production to final consumption destinations. The discipline adds to historical studies a biological dimension that probes the significant coevolution of cultural culinary components and cuisines and human populations. Evolutionary biocultural studies of the consumption of milk (McCracken 1971) and sugar (Messer 1986) are two examples of the types of anthropological studies of foodways that also fit the category of culinary history (Ritenbaugh 1978).

Biological anthropologists have tried to understand the evolution of favorable nutritional patterns – the mechanisms by which traditional peoples "unlock" potential nutritional values in their staple foods through cooking methods and dietary preferences. Studies have analyzed the significance of culinary techniques (such as the alkali processing of maize or the calcium/magnesium-salt processing of soy) in optimizing the nutritional quality of dietary food staples. Additionally, researchers have assessed the ways in which combinations of food components, such as maize with beans and squash seeds, or rice with soybeans, enhance nutritional values and have charted the distribution and diffusion of processing techniques, dietary combinations of foods, and dietary staple foods from their traditional areas to new locales (Katz 1987).

Moreover, anthropologists connect the history of diet with the history of disease. Their studies examine age- or gender-related dietary beliefs and practices, the impact of these practices on infant and child mortality (as well as pregnancy outcomes), and the circumstances under which such beliefs and practices change. Nutritional anthropological studies also analyze the so-called diseases of civilization (diabetes, coronary heart disease, hypertension, and various types of cancers) that seem to have accompanied dietary "Westernization" (including increased fat consumption) in most places where it has occurred (reviewed in Messer 1984).

Comparisons of recent with earlier ethnographic data on food systems and diets in Latin American, Asian, and African localities provide excellent opportunities for tracking changing relationships between food and the social order and elucidating the range of forces – from local to global – that influence such changes. One current of change has been proposed by cultural materialists, who view diet as shaped mainly (or exclusively) by ecological and political–economic ("material") conditions (Harris 1979).

Another current has been illuminated by symbolic or structural anthropologists, who emphasize how food and cooking express ideological–structural dimensions of social groups and their interrelationships. Notions of "purity and pollution" dominate Hindu rules, regulations, and rites surrounding all aspects of food, its preparation and serving, and social behavior (e.g., Khare 1976). M. Douglas discerned a structural logic of "pure" versus "anomalous" categories operating as the basis of food avoidances among the African Lele and then extended that principle to "The Abominations of Leviticus" (Douglas 1966). She moved on to decipher the social meanings of meals in European society (Douglas 1972) and food and the social order across cultures (Douglas 1984).

Claude Levi-Strauss's three-volume analysis of indigenous South American mythologies demonstrates how food and the "cooking" idiom are key to understanding social organization and cosmology (Levi-Strauss 1969, 1973, 1978). All of these analyses demonstrate that eating, cooking, and thinking are essentially philosophical operations, although most culinary studies tend to focus on sensory, technical, or instrumental dimensions of nutrition (Curtin and Heldke 1992).

In summary, anthropologists analyzing changes in foodways or food systems (culinary history) employ a combination of mental and material dimensions and approaches (Messer 1984, 1989). Anthropological approaches to understanding traditional cuisines and dietary change range from the social-structural, cognitive, and symbolic to the psychological, ecological, economic, and political, and to the relationships between nutrition and health. Studies go far back in time to elucidate culinary techniques beginning with elementary hunting, digging, processing, and use of fire (Gordon 1987; Stahl 1989) and extend forward through the present to the food of the future (Messer 1996b). Ethnographers, in the course of fieldwork, may increase their understanding by actively engaging in culinary activities of the past. Archaeologists, too, use experimental ("hands-on" or experiential) approaches, especially to increase their understanding of stone-tool manufacture, the use of such tools, and food-related artifacts in the archaeological record.

"Hands-on" Approaches to Culinary History

Culinary historians share some of the same pleasures and problems experienced by art historians and musicologists. Theory is an important dimension of such studies, but historical discussion must be tempered with a thorough understanding of the craft in order to interpret sources accurately. For culinary historians and the curators of living-history museums, this means researching and producing period meals that employ traditional techniques and authentic ingredients (within the limits of availability) (Noel Hume and Noel Hume 1978; Oliver 1995; Scully and Scully 1995; Dalby and Grainger 1996). Sometimes, substitutions must be made for ingredients no longer known or available, such as the replacement of silphium by celery seed in recipes for a Roman banquet (Arndt 1993). But the ingredients used must be appropriate to the period rather than to modern culinary conventions; for example, mushrooms or walnuts – not tomatoes – go into a catsup recipe from eighteenth-century North America. As with the written mode, such active culinary research compares food-related activities at different times and places using truly interdisciplinary frameworks and methods of analysis.

Museums have joined the enterprise with increasingly well-informed displays of their collections. Among these are reconstructions of cooking and dining venues such as the exhibitions of tables set in the modes of historical eras at the Historical Museum in Stockholm, the Alimentarium at Vevy in Switzerland, the Musée de l'homme in Paris, and the royal tables at Versailles (Musées Nationaux 1993), along with reenactments of cooking and dining, all of which illuminate the uses of culinary space and materials (see, for example, Deetz 1996).

Sources and Venues

Culinary historical scholarship draws on conventional documentary sources, such as diaries, letters, and travelogues, and also on less conventional sources, such as cookbooks and anthropological data.

Manuscript Sources

Diaries, account books, and letters are rich in data that can provide culinary understanding of peoples and periods. Samuel Pepys's diaries abound in accounts of meals. Lady Mary Wortley Montague took note of what she ate. The letters of Voltaire (François-Marie Arouet), too, show his tastes in food (and friends): Inviting a friend to dinner, he offered "a truffled turkey as tender as a squab and as fat as the bishop of Geneva." Felix Platter, a sixteenth-century

Swiss medical student at Montpelier, described the pungent foods served him and how he, a Protestant, evaded the rigors of the Lenten fast by cooking eggs over a candle in his room (Wheaton 1983).

Diaries and letters can be accessed by first consulting annotated bibliographies, then turning to specific texts or collections of letters. Examples with numerous food references include *Jane Austen's Manuscript Letters in Facsimile* (Carbondale, Ill., 1990); *Boswell's Journal of a Tour to the Hebrides with Samuel Johnson, LL.D.* (New York, 1936); *Mary Chesnut's Civil War* (New Haven, Conn., 1981); and *The Diary of a Country Parson: The Reverend James Woodforde* (London, 1924–31).

In addition, unpublished correspondence and other personal papers of leading American culinary figures such as Julia Child, Irma Rombauer, and M. F. K. Fisher are available in the manuscript collections of the Schlesinger Library at Radcliffe College.

Printed Literature

Travel literature. Travelers often describe food acquisition, preservation, and preparation, as well as meals. Such descriptions, however, should be used cautiously, because national, religious, class, and personal prejudices all work against dispassionate reporting. Sentimentalism, naivete, and ignorance are additional problems, because travelers without linguistic competence must frequently depend on interpreters and native informants who, whether reliable or not, may not be completely understood. Moreover, travelers have been known to copy from one another's accounts and to exaggerate – if not lie about – what they have seen. To this we might add that the memories of travelers are not infallible, and they are sometimes very gullible. Marco Polo, for example, is credited with having introduced pasta into Italy because he speaks of eating noodles during his travels in China. However, vermicelli was being produced on a commercial scale in Sicily a full century before his birth (Perry 1981). Culinary legends, once started, are hard to eradicate.

The use of travelers' accounts and diaries as sources for culinary history is usually a two-stage process. Annotated bibliographies are useful for pointing to accounts that contain relevant material. For descriptions of Russia, for example, one might begin with H. W. Nerhood's *To Russia and Return: An Annotated Bibliography of Travelers' English-Language Accounts of Russia from the Ninth Century to the Present* (1968). This in turn can lead to individual accounts, such as *The Russian Journals of Martha and Catherine Wilmot* (not published until 1934) and *Russia . . . and the Interior of the Empire* by Johann G. Kohl (1842), which are replete with descriptions of Russia's nineteenth-century foods. Examples of such works for other locales are those by P. Gerbod (1991 edition) for eighteenth-century France; W. Mayer (1961 edition) for early European travel in Mexico;

A. Tinniswood (1989) and W. Matthews (1967) for England; L. Arksey, N. Pries, and M. Reed (1983-7) for the United States; and J. Robinson (1990) on the subject of women travelers. The periodical *La Vie Quotidienne* (published in Paris since the 1930s) draws on travel diaries kept in many times and places.

Science and medicine. Travel literature is also a useful entry point for exploring food and nutritional health beliefs and practices. From Herodotus and Pliny the Elder onward, classic travel or "natural history" accounts influenced medieval and later European "epitomizers" and "cosmographers," whose often fanciful anecdotes of food customs lived on in the herbals and materia medica of both the Renaissance and the early modern period. Herbals and bestiaries contain information about how different kinds of plants and animals were believed to affect the human mind and body; they were one of the principal venues through which the nutritional and medical theories of antiquity and of the Islamic world were conveyed to a larger audience (Arber 1953, 1990; Anderson 1977).

Medical histories and encyclopedias of materia medica trace the diffusion of humoral health and nutritional theory from the classical and Islamic worlds into Europe (Siraisi 1990). Excellent comprehensive histories of the technology of the Old World are the eight-volume *A History of Technology* (1954-8), by C. Singer and colleagues, and J. Needham's *Science and Civilization in China* (1954-88); both works include extensive information on agricultural sciences.

Agricultural and cooking technology. Farm books offer insights into household and commercial agriculture, food processing, and storage technologies and demonstrate how rural estates were managed (Serres 1804; Markham 1986). They provide one class of information on the larger topic of cooking technologies that controlled and varied the character of local cuisines over time (Toomre 1992). Cooking arrangements set limits on what could be cooked. Shifts from hearths to freestanding cookstoves and ovens, as well as changes in fuel types, provide historical indicators of social standing (Cowan 1983) and also show up as a nutritional constraint where the cost of fuel is a major cooking expense, as it continues to be in contemporary developing countries.

Cooks used the heat of both kitchen fires and the sun to dry fruits and vegetables for winter storage and, occasionally, to preserve fruit in sugar. The milder warmth of the kitchen dried herbs, and the steady temperature of the earth preserved foods where cellars provided the only refrigeration. Even in the nineteenth century, ice houses were a luxury for most people. The culinary history of developing countries includes efforts by food technologists to overcome constraints on the seasonal availability of vitamin- and mineral-rich fruits and to encourage more economical

food purchases through improved storage and preservation methods (Riddervold and Ropeid 1988; see also occasional publications of the Program against Micronutrient Malnutrition, based in Atlanta, Georgia).

Watersheds in the history of technology, in addition to enclosed-firebox stoves and gas-powered stoves, include running water, electricity, refrigeration, home freezing, the food processor, and the microwave oven (Drummond and Wilbraham 1991). The works by Singer and colleagues (1954-8) and Needham (1954-88) offer a treasure trove for exploring culinary technology the world over (see also Forbes 1955-65 and the following citations). Changes in European cooking technologies can be gleaned through histories of domestic science instruction (McBride 1976; Davidson 1982; Attar 1987) and also through histories of the changing roles of domestic servants (Maza 1983; Fairchilds 1984).

Legal documents. Legal frameworks constitute another category of historical data revealing what were generally elite understandings of food qualities. From Roman times onward, governments usually attempted to supervise and control the quality and price of the principal staple - in the case of Europe, either flour or bread (McCance and Widdowson 1956; Kaplan 1976).

Governments also have regulated consumption of food and drink through control of the grain trade, sumptuary laws, and taxes on commodities such as salt, tea, and alcoholic beverages. Some regulations, such as the classical Athenian ban on speculation in grain, were intended to prevent hoarding of scarce food supplies. Others were meant to maintain class distinctions and to minimize trade deficits. Thus, in Renaissance Florence, wedding banquets of the bourgeois class were limited to three courses, and in eighteenth-century Sweden, coffee consumption was restricted to limit the importation of this expensive foreign product. Such efforts, however, were usually not very successful: The Florentine cooks invented delicacies that circumvented the course limit imposed, and the flavor of coffee became so desirable in Sweden that it was - and still is - used in making pot-roast gravy. In the 1560s, French sumptuary laws limiting the size of meals were simply ignored (Braudillart 1878-80).

Famine and food relief (or the history of hunger) is also a growing field of inquiry. The field includes global, regional, and period-specific studies (Newman 1990) that trace the ecological and political (trade and aid) causes of food shortages and analyze the motivations and relative effectiveness of emergency and other assistance. J. Drèze and A. Sen (1989) and R. Huss-Ashmore and S. Katz (1989, 1990) have produced analytical frameworks and case studies for the period during and following World War II. Although most emergency food aid is conceived to be humanitarian, M. Wallerstein (1980) has demonstrated how, during the Cold War, food aid was mostly political, intended to reward and to influence the behavior of friendly nations.

In developing countries, objectives of food aid have also included the development of tastes, and thereby markets, for the products of developed countries. This is a process connected to macroeconomic policies favoring the production of cash (export) over subsistence crops and the importation of cheap food (Lappe and Collins 1978). The recent history of food relief can be gleaned through the biannual *Hunger Report* of the Brown University World Hunger Program (Messer 1996b), the annual *Disasters Report* of the International Federation of Red Cross–Red Crescent Societies, and research publications of the Institute of Development Studies, Sussex (Maxwell and Buchanan-Smith 1994).

Dictionaries and encyclopedias. Dictionaries, lexica, and encyclopedias are rich sources for understanding food names, distributions, and associated lore. In both the New and Old Worlds, many contain entries on both individual ingredients and cuisines as a whole (see Brokgauz and Efron 1898; Rodinson 1949; Lewis, Pellat, and Schart 1965; Yule and Burnell 1968; *Kodansha Encyclopedia of Japan* 1983; Long 1996). New World "deadly nightshades" (tomato and potato) in Europe, for example, were labeled dangerous "apples" associated with lust, illness, or evil, which retarded their acceptance (Wheaton 1983). Word lists tend to highlight in special ways those foods that are most culturally important. For example, it was recorded – in sixteenth-century Spanish lists of words of the Aymara, a South American people – that the Aymara calculated time in terms of how long it took to boil a potato (Coe 1994).

Lexica also offer period-linked data on plant and animal food names, culturally recognized flavors and aromas, and other sensory or cultural qualities by which people in particular times and places ranked foods and food processing (see, e.g., Johns 1990). Word lists also document judgments of similarity and dimensions of difference between old and new foods; for example, New World "maize" was initially glossed "turkie wheat" (that is, foreign wheat) by the English (*Oxford English Dictionary*).

Folklore. Folklore, myth, and legend also tend to feature food and the quest for it (Darnton 1984). The European story of Hansel and Gretel, in which children deprived of food become prey to some wicked monster but then are able to overcome such evil by trickery or the help of some animal companion, has variants the world over. Children's literature instructs the young; cultural mythologies offer archetypes of how staple foods came to be and describe their cultural association with heroes or gods and their relationship with other cosmological elements, such as sun, wind, and rain.

Knowledge of fermentation and associated culinary techniques are also embedded in folklore. Indigenous Mexican folklore celebrates (and people imbibe) the effervescent products of fermented maguey in weddings and saints' rituals (see essays in Long 1996). In the Near East, wheat and barley – leavened into beer and bread – also leavened social life and carried their own mystique. The festival of the unleavened bread separated the new from the previous year's grain in ancient Middle Eastern cultures, a ritual later transmitted to modern times as the Jewish Passover. Unleavened bread (matzo) lately finds its greatest folkloric elaboration in factories in Brooklyn, New York (run by ultra-Orthodox Jewish sects), that squeeze operations for each cake of matzo into a magical 18 minutes to avoid any (unlucky and forbidden) fermentation (Jochnowitz 1996). Folklorists also record and analyze food ceremonies marking yearly and human life cycles and map distributions of food usages and terminologies (Hoefler 1908; Bächtold-Stäubli 1927–42; Gennep 1927; Wildhaber 1950).

Fiction, plays, and poetry. Since the time of Homer, descriptions of food have been used in literature to advance plot, characterize place or setting, and describe characters. Greek and Roman writings depict eating by both gods and humans and are mines of useful culinary information (Gowers 1993). Gastronomy appears as a major theme in Molière's comedy *Jean-Baptiste Poquelin* (Tobin 1990) and in *Dead Souls,* the work of Gogol. Careful descriptions of what people were eating are also part of the great literature of Charles Dickens and James Joyce (Armstrong 1992).

Visual Materials
Moving pictures. A modern media analogue to folklore, although more for entertainment than moral message, are films featuring food. Although many earlier films (such as *Gone with the Wind* and *Tom Jones*) featured blockbuster food-preparation and eating scenes, the 1980s and 1990s have witnessed an explosion of films principally devoted to the sensory and social dimensions of culinary arts. *Tampopo, Babette's Feast, Like Water for Chocolate,* and *Eat, Drink, Man, Woman* are four key examples. Even the violent satire *Pulp Fiction,* although principally a gangster story, interspersed some of its bloodier episodes with eating scenes that spoofed commercial food advertising and restaurant scenes from other films.

Food documentaries are the other major category of video that depict food culture. Special topics in the United States include the economic significance of restaurants and markets for immigrant groups (e.g., Cambodian-run donut shops) and documentaries about authentic preparation of ethnic foods (chicken soup, gefilte fish, Italian bread, Asian noodles). Food films increasingly are collected and shown at "ethnographic film" festivals, and food preparation is a growing theme for television. Public television stations around the country devote considerable airtime to cooking programs.

Still pictures. More conventionally, "still" pictures – drawings, paintings, photographs, and prints – provide period records, although, as with written sources, they must be used with care (Fare 1976; Henisch 1985; Bergstrom 1989). Sources include cookbooks and herbals, as well as more conventional art. Unfortunately, until the nineteenth century, most cookbooks did not include illustrations; exceptions are Bartolomeo de Scappi's *Cuoco Secrete di Papa Pio Quinto* (Cooking Secrets of Pope Pius V) (Venice, 1570), and Marx Rumpolt's *Ein Neu Kockbuch* (Frankfurt, 1581). From the seventeenth century, herbals offer increasingly naturalistic plant representations, and at all times there are eating scenes in ritual texts and paintings. Culinary historians who use works of art as source materials must be aware of the many conventions that dictate what is represented. For example, European still-life paintings focus in loving detail on foodstuffs both raw and prepared. Meats, fish, and the humbler vegetables appear in kitchen and market scenes. More luxurious vegetables, as well as fruit, confectionery, baked goods, and game, are shown in dining rooms and out-of-doors on terraces. Usually, readily recognizable foodstuffs are depicted, such as poultry roasting on a spit in eighteenth-century English genre scenes or pancakes being fried in the seventeenth-century Low Countries.

Some iconographical themes are especially good sources for pictures of food and food uses. Among Biblical topics, one finds everything from the miraculous fall of manna in the desert and the first Passover in the Old Testament to the wedding at Cana and the miraculous feeding of the five thousand in the New Testament. The "Seven Works of Mercy" (from Christ's Sermon on the Mount) include feeding the poor, caring for the sick, and giving drink to the thirsty. Secular subjects feature public rituals such as the Lord Mayor's banquet in London, coronation feasts, soup kitchens, and, by the nineteenth century, restaurants and genre paintings. Family portraits and conversation pieces often show gatherings around tables. Vincent Van Gogh's *Potato Eaters* (1885) is one of a number of household eating scenes by European oil painters that document the increasing significance of the humble tuber (Tilborgh 1993), and art criticism surrounding this and Jean-François Millet's earlier *Potato Planters* reveals much about the lingering snob appeal of bread versus potatoes in European diets and class structures (Murphy 1984).

Kitchen representations can be supplemented by works on architecture that offer ideas about how kitchens were laid out, as well as by examination of surviving cooking rooms, kitchens, and equipment (l'Orme 1567; Musée des Augustins 1992; Landesdenkmalamt Baden-Württemberg und der Stadt Zürich 1992). Archaeological and anthropological evidence also contributes useful findings that can amplify or modify evidence from visual and written sources.

Anthropological Evidence

Archaeological reports and dietary reconstructions detail histories and movements of food components and associated modes of preparation, storage, and distribution. Recent findings and analyses of the intestinal remains of well-preserved human "bog" specimens provide spectacular information about the diets and nutritional deficiencies of yesteryear. More routinely, skeletal and bone mineral analyses indicate seasonal or chronic malnutrition, particularly over periods of transition from foraging to farming (see essays in Harris and Hillman 1989). To determine culinary histories of particular sites and regions, archaeological reconstructions use the material remains of plants and animals, along with cooking and storage implements and architectural remains.

Ethnographic reports include descriptions of dietary life that become benchmarks for historical and cross-cultural comparison. Anthropological studies also draw on linguistic and literary sources, matching them to material remains and documentary evidence, which together allow the reconstruction of cuisines at particular points in and over time. Semiotic analyses of symbol, myth, and ritual, such as Levi-Strauss's *The Raw and the Cooked,* provide particularly rich metaphorical constructs for linking culinary practices to cultural transformations and patterns of migration, along with the ways in which the significance of particular food plants or animal species, or specific manners of preparation, are marked in myth and ritual and change over cultural time and space.

Ethnographic data also document changing food preferences and tastes and link them to major changes in food and political–economic systems and nutritional–health beliefs and practices. Anthropologists extend the dicta "tell me what you eat and I'll tell you who you are" (from the French) and "you are what you eat" (from the German) from the food itself to its preparation, distribution, and consumption, which are cultural and social markers as well. Recent studies explore how major transformations in agricultural technologies and available plant varieties, such as "Green Revolution" grains and the expansion of world agricultural trade and aid, can influence nutrition, health, and culture in developing areas. Among the results of such changes is increasing worldwide literacy and, consequently, the availability of written recipes from nonlocal sources (Appadurai 1988).

Cookbooks and Cooking Journals

Cookbooks provide specific information about ingredients, equipment, and techniques that cannot be found elsewhere. Some also contain information about daily life, gender roles, regional and economic differences in diet and literacy, and the development of a culinary language. They must, however, be seen in the context of the time and place in which they were produced and in the context of their relationship to other cookbooks (Toomre 1992). For example, most cookbooks published in the United States in the early twentieth century were addressed to women cooking at home, whereas most published in France before the middle of the nineteenth century were addressed to men cooking for patrons from among the wealthiest segments of society.

Bibliographies of cookery books from Europe and the United States include Theodor Drexel, *Katalog der Kochbücher-Sammlung* (Frankfurt-am-Main, 1885); Georges Vicaire, *Bibliographie Gastronomique* (Paris, 1890); Katherine Golden Bitting, *Gastronomic Bibliography* (San Francisco, 1939); Arnold W. Oxford, *English Cookery Books to the Year 1850* (London, 1913); Elizabeth Driver, *A Bibliography of Cookery Books Published in Britain, 1875–1914* (London, 1989); Virginia Maclean, *A Short-Title Catalogue of Household and Cookery Books Published in the English Tongue, 1701–1800* (London, 1981); Dena Attar, *A Bibliography of Household Books Published in Britain, 1800–1914* (London, 1987); Eleanor Lowenstein, *Bibliography of American Cookery Books, 1742–1860* (Worcester, Mass., 1972); Richard M. T. Westbury, *Handlist of Italian Cookery Books* (Florence, 1963); and Jacqueline Newman, *Chinese Cookbooks: An Annotated English-Language Compendium Bibliography* (New York, 1987).

Scholarly Societies and Symposia

Culinary history is being pursued on a worldwide basis in many different venues – in museums, libraries, and universities, and by scholars working outside of any formal academic institutional framework. *Petits Propos Culinaires* (essays and notes on food, cookery, and cookery books) and *Food and Foodways* are publications dedicated to culinary history, as was (to a lesser extent) the *Journal of Gastronomy,* which was published for several years by the American Institute of Wine and Food. In addition, the Foodways Section of the American Folklore Society, with partial support from the Michigan Traditional Arts Program, publishes the biannual journal *Digest: An Interdisciplinary Study of Food and Foodways.* Scholars of culinary history meet at conferences, the most long-standing of which is the biannual or triannual International Ethnological Food Research Congress.

Oxford Symposia on Food and Cookery have been published by Prospect Books (London), and the proceedings of one-day conferences held at the Brotherton Library in Leeds were published in six volumes of *Food and Society* by Edinburgh University Press. The Schlesinger Library of Radcliffe College and the Culinary Historians of Boston (CHB) cosponsored and published proceedings from a conference, *Current*

Research in Culinary History: Sources, Topics, and Methods (Cambridge, Mass., 1985).

Madison, Wisconsin, was the site of the 1997 joint meeting of the Agriculture, Food, and Human Value Society (AFHVS) and the Association for the Study of Food and Society (ASFS) – the latter a 12-year-old international interdisciplinary organization dedicated to studying the complex relationship between food and society. The meeting attracted several hundred food scholars – organic farmers, sociologists, chefs, medical historians, anthropologists, and nutritionists. Occasional conferences on specialized food topics have multiplied in recent years. In 1982, the Dublin Seminar for New England Folklife chose "Foodways of the Northeast" as the topic of its annual conference and later published the papers as its *Annual Proceedings 1982*. The Russian Research Center at Harvard University sponsored a conference in 1993 entitled "Food in Russian History and Culture," the papers of which appeared in a book of the same name (Glants and Toomre 1997). The University of New Hampshire held an interdisciplinary conference on food and culture; Boston University sponsored its sequel in 1995.

Additional venues are "living-history" museums, pioneering examples of which are Skansen in Stockholm, Sweden, and the Netherlands Open-Air Museum in Arnhem. In the United States, Sturbridge Village, Plimoth Plantation, and Colonial Williamsburg regularly sponsor programs in culinary history that include both lectures and demonstrations of culinary implements and hearthstone cooking. In conjunction with the Quincentenary (1992), museums on both sides of the Atlantic sponsored exhibits and conferences on the "Columbian exchange," such as the Smithsonian Institution exhibit and conference "Seeds of Change" (Viola and Margolis 1991). In Texas, the George Ranch, outside of Houston, emphasizes the history of black cowboys and chuck-wagon cooking, whereas the Jordan-Bachmann farm in Austin focuses on nineteenth-century German influences in the area, including regional foodways.

Scholarly and professional societies publish various materials of interest. The London Classical Society hosted *Food in Antiquity: Studies in Ancient Society and Culture* (Wilkins, Harvey, and Dobson 1995). Food and nutrition panels are featured at the annual meetings of major academic professional societies such as the American Anthropological Association (Huss-Ashmore and Katz 1989, 1990; Sharman et al. 1991), the American Studies Association, and the American Sociological Association (Maurer and Sobal 1995; Whit 1995). Food history panels are also found at the Eighteenth Century Society, the French Language Association, the American Historical Association, the American Association for the Advancement of Slavic Studies, and the Society for French Historical Studies. The breadth of interest in the field is shown by the wide range of scholarly and trade journals that publish food articles emphasizing cultural, social, historical, or literary themes, with special issues devoted to food topics in history, art history, regional foodways, literature, or films.

Since 1980, Boston has become a center for the study of culinary history. The Schlesinger Library of Radcliffe College, which is devoted to women's history, houses a growing culinary collection of over 12,000 volumes on food and, since 1990, has hosted monthly meetings of the CHB and a professional chefs' forum. Other active groups of culinary historians in the United States are located in the cities of Ann Arbor, Michigan, New York, Houston, Texas, Honolulu, Hawaii, and Washington, D.C., as well as in various cities of California. Activities are also expanding in Mexico, where scholars from the fields of history, anthropology, and biology orchestrated a symposium marking 500 years of European-New World food encounters (Long 1996), and where ethnobiologists and food anthropologists sponsor lectures and publications predominantly on food history topics, including an "Antropologia y Alimentacion" section of *Antropologicas,* a periodical of the Instituto de Investigaciones Antropologicas of the National Autonomous University of Mexico (UNAM).

Conclusion

Culinary history is emerging as an academic specialty. Programs at Boston University's Metropolitan College, courses taught at the Radcliffe College Seminars, and courses within the New York University (NYU) Food Studies Program combine culinary history with cultural studies and, at NYU, nutrition. Apart from these more humanistic approaches, histories of crop plants, agricultural and food processing technologies, and food commerce offer a growing literature on food within the history and sociology of science and technology. Ingredients and technology play off each other to create change in cuisine. Illustrative are the modern varieties of grains and tubers that since the 1970s have been changing the basic foods people eat in developing countries. Another example is the new enzyme processing, which is leading to the replacement of cane sugar by corn syrup in processed foods and, consequently, is influencing sugar- and corn-based economies all over the world. Yet another example - about which much will be written in coming years - concerns the history of foods formulated and aggressively marketed by transnational corporations such as Coca Cola and McDonald's, along with the nutritional and cultural consequences for populations that consume these products rather than other foods. These are but three illustrations of the ever-expanding list of aspects of food and nutrition that culinary historical perspectives help elaborate.

In addition, we can expect growing interest in culinary history on at least four fronts. The first is a growing medical interest in the history of food, diet, and nutritional health, prompted by concern about the extent to which diets play an etiologic role in coronary heart disease, hypertension, cancers, and diabetes. This avenue of investigation seeks to understand the sources of dietary variation and the circumstances under which food habits have changed in the past. The second is a growing agricultural-biological interest in the diversity of food species (and varieties) and their histories. This interest forms part of a global effort to conserve biodiversity. The third is the growing interest in culinary arts in the humanities, both as a part of women's history and also as a special area of literature and the fine arts. Finally, many with political-economic and ethnic-studies perspectives within anthropology, political science, economics, sociology, and history are becoming increasingly interested in the history of food and cuisine for the ways these shape - and are shaped by - social forces. Culinary history will continue to have numerous disciplinary voices.

Ellen Messer
Barbara Haber
Joyce Toomre
Barbara Wheaton

Bibliography

Anderson, E. 1988. *The food of China.* New Haven, Conn.

Anderson, F. J. 1977. *An illustrated history of herbals.* New York.

Appadurai, A. 1988. Cookbooks and cultural change: The Indian case. *Comparative Studies in Society and History* 30: 3-24.

Arber, A. 1953. From medieval herbalism to the birth of modern botany. In *Science, medicine, and history: Essays in the evolution of scientific thought and medical practice written in honor of Charles Singer,* ed. E. A. Underwood, 317-26. London.

 1990. *Herbals: Their origins and evolution. A chapter in the history of botany, 1470-1670.* Second edition. Cambridge.

Arksey, L., N. Pries, and M. Reed. 1983-7. *American diaries: An annotated bibliography of published American diaries and journals.* 2 vols. Detroit, Mich.

Armstrong, H. 1992. *The joyce of cooking.* Dublin.

Arndt, A. 1993. Silphium: Spicing up the palate. *Proceedings of the Oxford Symposium on Food and Cookery,* 28-35. London.

Arnott, M., ed. 1976. *Gastronomy: The anthropology of food habits.* The Hague.

Attar, D. 1987. *A bibliography of household books published in Britain, 1800-1914.* London.

Bächtold-Stäubli, Hanns, ed. 1927-42. *Handwörterbuch des deutschen Aberglaubens.* 10 vols. Berlin and Leipzig.

Beecher, C. E. 1869. *The American woman's home, or principles of domestic science.* New York.

Bergstrom, I. 1989. *Still life of the golden age. Northern European paintings from the Heinz family collection.* Washington, D.C.

Braudel, F. 1966. *La Méditerranée et le monde en l'époque de Philippe II.* Second edition. Paris.

Braudillart, H. 1878–80. *Histoire du luxe privée et public de l'antiquité jusqu'à nos jours.* 4 vols. Paris.

Brillat-Savarin, J. A. 1995. *The physiology of taste, or meditations on transcendental gastronomy,* trans. M. F. K. Fisher. Washington, D.C.

Brokgauz, F. A., and I. J. Efron, eds. 1898. *Entsiklopedicheski slovar'.* St. Petersburg.

Brown, E., and B. Brown. 1961. *Culinary Americana.* New York.

Chang, K. C., ed. 1977. *Food in Chinese culture: Anthropological and historical perspectives.* New Haven, Conn.

Coe, S. 1994. *America's first cuisines.* Austin, Tex.

Coe, S., and M. Coe. 1996. *The true history of chocolate.* New York.

Cook, M. 1971. *America's charitable cooks: A bibliography of fundraising cook books.* Kent, Ohio.

Cowan, R. S. 1983. *More work for mother. The ironies of household technology from the open hearth to the microwave.* New York.

Crosby, A. 1972. *The Columbian exchange. Biological and cultural consequences of 1492.* Westport, Conn.

Curtin, D. W., and L. M. Heldke, eds. 1992. *Cooking, eating, thinking. Transformative philosophies of food.* Bloomington, Ind.

Dalby, A., and S. Grainger. 1996. *The classical cookbook.* Los Angeles.

Darnton, R. 1984. *The great cat massacre and other episodes in French cultural history.* New York.

Davidson, C. 1982. *A woman's work is never done: A history of housework in the British Isles, 1650–1950.* London.

Deetz, J. 1996. *In small things forgotten: An archaeology of early American life.* Revised and expanded edition. New York.

Douglas, M. 1966. *Purity and danger.* Baltimore, Md.
   1972. Deciphering a meal. *Daedalus* 101: 61–81.
   ed. 1984. *Food and the social order.* New York.

Drèze, J., and A. Sen. 1989. *Hunger and public action.* New York.

Drummond, J. C., and A. Wilbraham. 1991. *The Englishman's food.* Second edition, rev. D. Hartley. London.

Fairchilds, C. 1984. *Domestic enemies: Servants and their masters in old regime France.* Baltimore, Md.

Fare, M. 1976. *La vie silencieuse en France: La nature morte au XVIIIe siècle.* Freiburg, Germany.

Fenton, A. 1986. *Food in change: Eating habits from the Middle Ages to the present.* Atlantic Highlands, N.J.

Fenton, A., and T. M. Owen, eds. 1981. *Food in perspective. Proceedings of the Third International Conference on Ethnological Food Research, in Cardiff, Wales, 1977.* Edinburgh.

Forbes, R. J. 1955–65. *Studies in ancient technology.* 9 vols. Leiden, the Netherlands.

Garnsey, P. 1990. Responses to food crisis in the ancient Mediterranean world. In *Hunger in history: Food shortage, poverty, and deprivation,* ed. L. Newman, 126–46. New York.

Gennep, A. van. 1927. *Manuel de folklore Français contemporain.* Paris.

Gerbod, P. 1991. *Voyages au pays des mangeurs de grenouilles: La France vue par les Britanniques du XVIIIe siècle à nos jours.* Paris.

Glants, M., and J. Toomre, eds. 1997. *Food in Russian history and culture.* Bloomington, Ind.

Goode, J. 1989. Cultural patterning and group-shared rules in the study of food intake. In *Research methods in nutritional anthropology,* ed. G. Pelto, P. Pelto, and E. Messer, 126–61. Tokyo.

Goody, J. 1982. *Cooking, cuisine, and class: A study in comparative sociology.* New York.

Gordon, K. 1987. Evolutionary perspectives on human diet. In *Nutritional anthropology,* ed. F. E. Johnston, 3–46. New York.

Gowers, E. 1993. *The loaded table: Representations of food in Roman literature.* New York.

Harris, D. R., and G. C. Hillman. 1989. *Foraging and farming. The evolution of plant exploitation.* London.

Harris, M. 1979. *Cultural materialism. The struggle for a science of culture.* New York.

Hemardinquer, J. J. 1970. *Pour une histoire de l'alimentation.* Paris.

Henisch, B. 1985. Unconsidered trifles: The search for cooking scenes in medieval sources. *Schlesinger Library-Culinary Historians of Boston proceedings: Current research in culinary history: Sources, topics, and methods,* 110–21. Cambridge, Mass.

Hess, K. 1992. *The Carolina rice kitchen: The African connection.* Columbia, S.C.

Hocquet, J. C. 1989. *Le sel de la terre.* Paris.

Hoefler, M. 1908. *Gebildbrote der Faschings-, Fastnachts- und Fastenzeit.* Vienna.

Huss-Ashmore, R., and S. Katz, eds. 1989, 1990. *African food systems in crisis. Part 1: Microperspectives. Part 2: Macroperspectives.* Langhorne, Pa.

Jerome, N. 1980. Diet and acculturation: The case of black American immigrants. In *Nutritional anthropology,* ed. N. W. Jerome, R. Kandel, and G. Pelto, 275–325. New York.

Jochnowitz, E. 1996. Making sense of matzoh: History, meanings, and message. Presentation to the Culinary Historians of Boston, December 12. Boston, Mass.

Johns, T. 1990. *With bitter herbs they shall eat it.* Tucson, Ariz.

Joselit, J. W., B. Kirshenblatt-Gimblett, and I. Howe. 1990. *Getting comfortable in New York: The American Jewish home, 1880–1950.* New York.

Kaneva-Johnson, M. 1995. *The melting pot: Balkan food and cookery.* London.

Kaplan, S. 1976. *Bread, politics, and political economy in the reign of Louis XV.* The Hague.

Katona-Apte, J. 1976. Dietary aspects of acculturation: Meals, feasts, and fasts in a minority community in South Asia. In *Gastronomy: The anthropology of food habits,* ed. M. Arnott, 315–26. The Hague.

Katz, S. 1987. Food and biocultural evolution: A model for the investigation of modern nutritional problems. In *Nutritional anthropology,* ed. F. E. Johnston, 47–66. New York.

Khare, R. 1976. *Hindu hearth and home.* Durham, N.C.

Kodansha encyclopedia of Japan. 1983. Tokyo.

Ladies Relief Corps of South Framingham. 1887. *Tested recipes for the inexperienced housewife.* Framingham, Mass.

Landesdenkmalamt Baden-Württemberg und der Stadt Zürich, ed. 1992. *Stadtluft, Hirsebrei, und Bettelmönch. Die Stadt um 1300.* Zurich and Stuttgart.

Lappe, F. M., and J. Collins. 1978. *Food first. Beyond the myth of scarcity.* New York.

Laurioux, B. 1985. Spices in the medieval diet: A new approach. *Food and Foodways* 1: 43–76.
   1989. *Le moyen age à table.* Paris.

Levenstein, H. 1988. *Revolution at the table. The transformation of the American diet.* New York.

Levi-Strauss, C. 1969, 1973, 1978. *The raw and the cooked; From honey to ashes; The origin of table manners,* trans. J. Weightman and D. Weightman. New York.

Lewis, B., Ch. Pellat, and J. Schart. 1965. *Encyclopedia of Islam*. Leiden, the Netherlands.

Lippmann, E. von. 1929. *Geschichte des Zuckers seit den ältesten Zeiten bis zum Beginn der Rübenzuckerfabrikation*. Second edition. Berlin.

Long, J., ed. 1996. *Conquista y comida: Consecuencias del encuentro de dos mundos*. Mexico City.

l'Orme, P. de. 1567. *Le premier tome de l'architecture*. Paris.

Markham, G. 1986. *The English housewife*, ed. M. Best. Kingston, Ontario.

Matthews, W. 1967. *British diaries: An annotated bibliography of British diaries written between 1442 and 1942*. Gloucester, Mass.

Maurer, D., and J. Sobal, eds. 1995. *Eating agendas. Food and nutrition as social problems*. Hawthorne, N.Y.

Maxwell, S., and M. Buchanan-Smith, eds. 1994. *Linking relief to development*. IDS Bulletin No. 25. Sussex.

Mayer, W. 1961. *Early travelers in Mexico, 1534-1816*. Mexico City.

Maza, Sarah C. 1983. *Servants and masters in eighteenth-century France: The uses of loyalty*. Princeton, N.J.

McBride, T. M. 1976. *The domestic revolution: The modernization of household service in England and France, 1820-1920*. New York.

McCance, R. A., and E. M. Widdowson. 1956. *Breads, white and brown: Their place in thought and social history*. Philadelphia, Pa.

McCracken, R. D. 1971. Lactase deficiency: An example of dietary evolution. *Current Anthropology* 12: 479-517.

Mead, M. 1964. *Food habits research: Problems of the 1960s*. National Academy of Sciences, National Research Council, Publication No. 1225. Washington, D.C.

Mennell, S. 1996. *All manners of food: Eating and taste in England and France*. Second edition. Urbana, Ill.

Messer, E. 1984. Anthropological perspectives on diet. *Annual Review of Anthropology* 13: 205-49.

1986. Some like it sweet. Estimating sweetness preferences and sucrose intakes from ethnographic and experimental data. *American Anthropologist* 88: 637-47.

1989. Methods for studying determinants of food intake. In *Research methods in nutritional anthropology*, ed. G. Pelto, P. Pelto, and E. Messer, 1-33. Tokyo.

1996a. Food wars: The use of hunger as a weapon in 1994. In *The hunger report: 1995*, ed. E. Messer and P. Uvin, 19-48. The Netherlands.

1996b. Visions of the future: Food, hunger, and nutrition. In *The hunger report: 1995*, ed. E. Messer and P. Uvin, 211-28. The Netherlands.

Mintz, S. 1985. *Sweetness and power*. New York.

Miracle, M. 1966. *Maize in tropical Africa*. Madison, Wis.

Murphy, K. 1984. *Millet*. Boston, Mass.

Musée des Augustins, Toulouse. 1992. *Plaisirs et manières de table aux XIVe et XVe siècles*. Toulouse, France.

Musées Nationaux. 1993. *Réunion des Musées Nationaux*. Paris.

National Research Council, Committee on Food Consumption Patterns. 1981. *Assessing changing food consumption patterns*. Food and Nutrition Board, U.S. National Research Council. Washington, D.C.

Needham, J. 1954-88. *Science and civilization in China*. 6 vols. Cambridge.

Nerhood, H. W. 1968. *To Russia and return: An annotated bibliography of travelers' English-language accounts of Russia from the ninth century to the present*. Columbus, Ohio.

Newman, L. F., ed. 1990. *Hunger in history: Food shortage, poverty, and deprivation*. Cambridge, Mass.

Noel Hume, A., and I. Noel Hume. 1978. *Food*. Colonial Williamsburg Archaeological Series No. 9. Williamsburg, Va.

Oliver, S. 1995. *Saltwater foodways: New Englanders and their food at sea and ashore*. Mystic, Conn.

Perry, C. 1981. The oldest Mediterranean noodle: A cautionary tale. *Petits Propos Culinaires* 9: 42-5.

Peterson, T. 1980. The Arab influence on western European cooking. *Journal of Medieval History* 6: 317-40.

Riddervold, A., and A. Ropeid. 1988. *Food conservation: Ethnological studies*. London.

Ritenbaugh, C. 1978. Human foodways: A window on evolution. In *The anthropology of health*, ed. E. E. Bauwens, 111-20. St. Louis, Mo.

Robinson, J. 1990. *Wayward women: A guide to women travelers*. New York.

Roden, C. 1996. *The book of Jewish food: An odyssey from Samarkand to New York*. New York.

Rodinson, M. 1949. Recherches sur les documents arabes relatifs la cuisine. *Revue des Études Islamiques*: 95-165.

Rotenberg, R. 1981. The impact of industrialization on meal patterns in Vienna, Austria. *Ecology of Food and Nutrition* 11: 25-35.

Rozin, E. 1973. *The flavor principle*. New York.

Salaman, R. [1949] 1985. *The history and social influence of the potato*, ed. J. Hawkes. Cambridge and New York.

Scully, D. E., and T. Scully. 1995. *Early French cookery: Sources, history, original recipes, and modern adaptations*. Ann Arbor, Mich.

Serres, O. de. [1600] 1804. *Le théâtre d'agriculture*. Paris.

Shapiro, L. 1986. *Perfection salad: Women and cooking at the turn of the century*. New York.

Sharman, A., J. Theophano, K. Curtis, and E. Messer, eds. 1991. *Diet and domestic life in society*. Philadelphia, Pa.

Simetti, M. T. 1989. *Pomp and sustenance. Twenty-five centuries of Sicilian food*. New York.

Simoons, F. 1991. *Food in China: A cultural and historical inquiry*. Boca Raton, Fla.

Singer, C., E. J. Holmyard, A. R. Hall, and T. I. Williams. 1954-8. *A history of technology*. 8 vols. Oxford.

Siraisi, N. G. 1990. *Medieval and early Renaissance medicine: An introduction to knowledge and practice*. Chicago.

Sklar, K. K. 1973. *Catharine Beecher: A study in American domesticity*. New Haven, Conn.

Stahl, A. B. 1989. Plant-food processing: Implications for dietary quality. In *Foraging and farming. The evolution of plant exploitation*, ed. D. R. Harris and G. C. Hillman, 171-94. London.

Strasser, S. 1982. *Never done. A history of American housework*. New York.

Teuteberg, H. J. 1993. *Kulturthema Essen: Ansichten und Problemfelder*. Berlin.

Tilborgh, L. van. 1993. *The potato eaters by Vincent Van Gogh*. Zwolle, the Netherlands.

Tinniswood, A. 1989. *A history of country house visiting: Five centuries of tourism and taste*. Oxford.

Tobin, R. W. 1990. *Tarte à la crème: Comedy and gastronomy in Molière's theater*. Columbus, Ohio.

Toomre, J. 1992. *Classic Russian cooking: Elena Molokhovets' "A gift to young housewives."* Bloomington, Ind.

Toussaint-Samat, M. 1992. *A history of food*, trans. A. Bell. Oxford.

Viola, H. J., and C. Margolis, eds. 1991. *Seeds of change: A quincentennial commemoration.* Washington, D.C.

Wallerstein, M. 1980. *Food for war - food for peace.* Cambridge, Mass.

Wheaton, B. 1983. *Savoring the past: The French kitchen and table from 1300 to 1789.* Philadelphia, Pa.

  1984. The cooks of Concord. *Journal of Gastronomy* 1: 5-24.

Whit, W. C. 1995. *Food and society: A sociological approach.* New York.

Wildhaber, R. 1950. *Schneckenzucht und Schneckenspeise.* Basel.

Wilkins, J., D. Harvey, and M. Dobson, eds. 1995. *Food in antiquity.* Exeter, England.

Yule, H., and A. C. Burnell. [1903] 1968. *Hobson-Jobson: A glossary of colloquial Anglo-Indian words and phrases, and of kindred terms, etymological, historical, geographical and discursive, by Henry Yule and A. C. Burnell,* ed. William Crooke. Second edition, reprint. New Delhi.

PART VI

History, Nutrition, and Health

Part VI takes up questions of food and nutrition that have historical as well as contemporary relevance. It begins with two chapters that continue a now decades-long debate over the extent to which improved nutrition may be responsible for reduced mortality within populations – a debate that has centered on, but certainly has not been limited to, the circumstances surrounding the population increases of the countries of Europe since the eighteenth century.

These are followed by a group of chapters that, although not specifically addressing matters of mortality decline, do help to illuminate some of its many aspects. An elaboration of the concept of synergy, for example, emphasizes the important role that pathogens (or their absence) play in the nutritional status of an individual, whereas the chapter on famine reveals the circumstances within which synergy does some of its deadliest work.

Stature, discussed next, is increasingly employed by historians as a proxy for nutritional status, and final adult height can frequently be a function of the nutrition of the mother before she gives birth and of the

infant and child following that event – a subject treated in the following chapter. A chapter on adolescent nutrition and fertility, harking back to matters of population increase, is succeeded by another concerned with the linkage between the nutrition of a child and its mental development.

By way of a transition to a second group of chapters in Part VI focusing on culture and foods is a chapter on the biological and cultural aspects of human nutritional adaptation. This discussion is followed by chapters that scrutinize food choices, food fads, food prejudices and taboos, and social and cultural food uses. Probably since humans first set foot on earth, they have believed in the magical properties of some foods and the medicinal qualities of others; both of these aspects of eating are examined in chapters on foods as aphrodisiacs (and anaphrodisiacs) and as medicines.

Not necessarily unrelated is the subject of vegetarianism, both condemned and embraced as a way of life, not to mention as a dietary regimen. Because of the controversial nature of vegetarianism we have both pro and con chapters on the matter to close out Part VI.

VI.1 ✎ Nutrition and the Decline of Mortality

Together with economic growth and technological advances, improvements in health and longevity are the typical hallmarks of a population's transition to modern society. Among the earliest countries to undergo such experiences were England and France, where mortality rates began declining steadily during the eighteenth century. Elsewhere in western and northern Europe, health and longevity began to improve during the nineteenth century. In the twentieth century, this pattern has been replicated in developing countries throughout the world.

Understanding the causes that underlie this pattern of mortality decline is important not only as a matter of historical interest but also because of the practical implications for policies that aim to improve life in developing countries, and for forecasting changes in mortality in developed countries. Accordingly, there has been much interest in identifying the causes of patterns of mortality decline and measuring their impact. By the 1960s, a consensus had emerged that the factors underlying mortality trends could be delineated within four categories, as reported in a study by the United Nations (UN) (1953): (1) public-health reforms, (2) advances in medical knowledge, (3) improved personal hygiene, and (4) rising income and standards of living. A later UN study (1973) added as an additional category "natural causes," such as a decline in the virulence of pathogens.

McKeown's Nutrition Hypothesis

Against this consensus view, the British epidemiologist Thomas McKeown argued in a series of influential articles and books from 1955 to the mid-1980s that the contribution of medicine to the decline of mortality before the twentieth century had been relatively small. Rather, relying on a residual argument that rejected other factors as plausible explanations, he proposed that improvement in nutrition was the primary cause of the mortality decline.

McKeown's view was best set forth in his 1976 book, *The Modern Rise of Population.* In it, he argued that the modern growth of population was attributable to a decline of mortality rather than to changes in fertility, and he sought to identify what had brought about death-rate reductions since the eighteenth century. His investigation relied heavily – indeed, almost exclusively – on cause-of-death information, which had been nationally registered in England and Wales since 1837. McKeown himself was aware that his evidence was geographically limited and did not fully cover the time period during which mortality had declined. Nevertheless, he believed that his findings could be generalized to explain the modern mortality experience of other European countries.

McKeown's analysis of causes of death in England and Wales during the period from 1848–54 to 1971 led him to the conclusion that the reduction of the death rate was associated predominantly with infectious diseases. Of the decline in mortality during that period, 40 percent resulted from a reduction in airborne diseases, 21 percent from reduction in water- and foodborne diseases, and 13 percent from reduction in other types of infections. The remainder (26 percent) was attributable to a lesser incidence of noninfective conditions. Thus, McKeown found that three-quarters of the mortality decline since the mid–nineteenth century could be explained by the reduction in infectious diseases. He further reasoned that despite sketchy historical evidence from the period before the beginning of cause-of-death registration, this trend could be extrapolated backward to the start of the modern mortality decline around the beginning of the eighteenth century. By his reckoning, 86 percent of the reduction in death rates from then until 1971 had resulted from a decline in mortality from infectious diseases. For McKeown, then, this conclusion was the central feature of mortality decline and constituted evidence against which the merits of alternative explanations of mortality decline would be judged.

McKeown methodically classified possible reasons for the lesser incidence of mortality from infectious diseases into four categories: (1) changes in the character of the diseases themselves, (2) advances in medical treatment, or the prevention and treatment of diseases by immunization and therapy, (3) reduced general exposure to disease, and (4) increased general resistance to disease because of improved nutrition. Taking these categories one at a time, he systematically considered each of the major disease groups (airborne infections, water- and foodborne infections, and other infections) in turn, and concluded that the only category that satisfactorily explained the decline in mortality was increased disease resistance resulting from improved nutrition.

In examining changes in the character of diseases as a possible explanation of mortality decline, McKeown found little reason to believe that this had been responsible for a substantial reduction in deaths from infectious diseases. By changes in the character of diseases he meant changes in the interaction between the infectious microorganism and the human host and whether such changes meant a decline in the virulence of the pathogen or an increased resistance in the human host through natural selection.

Although he acknowledged that a change in the character of scarlet fever did result in a reduction of deaths from that disease in the latter half of the nineteenth century, McKeown thought it "frankly incredible" that the other major airborne diseases of the period, which included tuberculosis, influenza, and measles, had all undergone such fortuitous changes simultaneously. On the contrary, he pointed out that tuberculosis, for example, continues to have devastating effects on populations not previously exposed to it. Nor did he think it likely that natural selection could have increased people's resistance to such diseases, leading to a decline in mortality. For such genetic selection to have occurred, McKeown pointed out that certain deleterious effects of early industrialization and urbanization, such as crowding, should have produced high mortality in the eighteenth century. Through natural selection, that experience would have left a population with greater resistance to the airborne diseases, which would account for lower mortality rates later on. However, McKeown believed that death rates during the eighteenth century had simply been too low to support such a theory.

Water- and foodborne diseases warranted a similar conclusion. McKeown did not altogether rule out the possibility that changes in the character of those diseases could have played some role in the reduction of mortality associated with them. But he thought that improved hygiene, leading to reduced exposure, was a much more convincing explanation. As for vectorborne diseases, typhus was mentioned as one that might have been affected by a change in its character. However, the contribution of the decline of this disease to the fall of mortality over the past three centuries was small.

The next possible reason for a decline in mortality from infectious diseases that McKeown dealt with was medical advances, and it is here that his arguments impressively marshaled historical evidence. He built his case against a significant role for medical treatment by examining the temporal pattern of death rates of the most lethal diseases. He first took care to point up the distinction between the interests of the physician and those of the patient. Although since the eighteenth century many important advances have been made in medical knowledge and institutions, such advances were not always immediately effective against diseases; they often required considerable intervals before becoming of practical, demonstrable benefit to the patient. In making this distinction, McKeown contended that whether different preventive measures and treatments in history had been effective could not be judged reliably from contemporary assessments; instead, their efficacy would best be determined in light of critical present-day knowledge.

Tuberculosis, the largest single cause of death in the mid–nineteenth century and the decline of which was responsible for a fifth of the subsequent reduction in mortality, served as a case in point. The identification of the tubercle bacillus by Robert Koch in 1882 was an important event in the progress of medical knowledge, but its immediate contribution to reducing tuberculosis was minimal. In addition, of the numerous treatments that were tried in the nineteenth and early twentieth centuries, none could be judged by modern medical knowledge to have been effective against the disease. Rather, McKeown suggested that effective treatment actually began only with the introduction of streptomycin in 1947 and *bacille Calmette-Guérin* (BCG) vaccination on a large scale in England and Wales from 1954. By these dates, however, mortality from tuberculosis had already fallen substantially. Roughly 60 percent of the decline since 1848–54 had already taken place by the turn of the twentieth century, and this decline continued up to the introduction of effective chemotherapy around 1950. If the medical contribution was meaningful only after 1950, it was therefore impossible for medical advances against tuberculosis to have been a major factor in the mortality decline, most of which had taken place by then.

Similarly, when the temporal patterns of mortality decline from the other major airborne diseases of the nineteenth century were compared with the dates of introduction of effective treatment or immunization against them, McKeown found that most of the fall in the death rates they produced had also occurred before effective medical measures became available. An exception to this was smallpox, the decline of which since the mid–nineteenth century was thought to be the result of mass vaccination. But McKeown pointed out that the reduction in smallpox mortality was associated with only 1.6 percent of the reduction in the death rate from all causes. McKeown also doubted that the rapid decline of mortality from diseases spread by water and food since the late nineteenth century owed much to medical measures. He thought that, in many cases, immunization was relatively ineffective even at the time he wrote, and that therapy of some value was not employed until about 1950.

Finally, reduced exposure to infection was considered as a possible explanation of mortality decline. In the case of airborne diseases, McKeown once again found little reason to think that reduced exposure had been a major factor in their decline. Indeed, he thought that the fall in deaths from measles and scarlet fever owed very little to reduced exposure, and although he allowed that reduced exposure did play a role in the decline of other airborne diseases such as tuberculosis, whooping cough, diphtheria, and smallpox, he believed that this was only a secondary consequence of other influences that lowered the prevalence of disease in the community.

In the case of water- and foodborne diseases, McKeown conceded that reduced exposure had played a greater role in reducing mortality than it had with airborne diseases, especially during the second half of the nineteenth century. Purification of water, efficient disposal of sewage, provision of safe milk, and improved food hygiene all contributed to the decline of mortality. He also felt that personal hygiene, particularly regular bathing, may have encouraged the abatement of typhus in the eighteenth and nineteenth centuries.

In summary, McKeown dismissed the ability of both changes in the character of infectious diseases and advances in medical treatment to account for the modern mortality decline. He thought the contribution of sanitation and hygiene had been somewhat more significant but still of limited scope and primarily confined to the second half of the nineteenth century. Therefore, advances in general health based on improved nutrition constituted the only possibility left that could explain the mortality decline, and, in McKeown's view, it was also the most credible explanation.

In support of his circumstantial case for nutrition, which he had arrived at by a process of elimination, McKeown offered some pieces of positive evidence. First, he pointed out that the great expansion of the English and Welsh populations during the eighteenth and early nineteenth centuries had been accompanied by an important increase in domestic food production. However, as McKeown conceded, the central question for the nutritional argument was whether the amount of food per capita, rather than total food consumption, had increased during that period. He found that evidence to settle the matter directly was unavailable and chose instead to consider the relationship between malnutrition and infection. Thus, as the second piece of evidence in support of nutrition, he pointed to the situation in developing countries, where malnutrition contributes largely to the high level of infectious deaths. Malnourished populations are more susceptible to infections and suffer more seriously when they are infected. McKeown also emphasized the dynamic interaction that exists between nutrition and infection, frequently characterized as synergism. Since infections adversely affect nutritional status, a vicious cycle between disease and malnutrition often results - a cycle characteristic of poverty and underdevelopment.

Reaction to the McKeown Thesis

McKeown's thesis drew the attention of scholars from a wide spectrum of disciplines. As it provided a theoretical framework that wove together such themes as industrialization, urbanization, rising standards of living, changing health, and shifting demographic patterns, it could hardly have failed to attract the interest of social scientists, especially demographers and economic historians. A number of studies extended McKeown's argument to the history of mortality rates in the United States (Meeker 1972; Higgs 1973, 1979; McKinlay and McKinlay 1977). In all probability, the contemporary interest in McKeown's nutritional thesis was also in part a consequence of great public concern over the "population bomb" - the fear that the explosive worldwide population increase in the post–World War II period would eventually lead to catastrophic shortages of food and other natural resources. It is not difficult to understand that an audi-ence constantly reminded, and so vividly, of the Malthusian link between food supply and population growth would have been receptive to McKeown's argument giving primacy to nutrition as the factor explaining the decline of mortality.

Reaction to the McKeown thesis, however, was by no means uniformly favorable. Although acknowledging that nutrition had played a role in mortality decline, many scholars nevertheless felt that McKeown had greatly overstated its importance. Of particular concern to critics of the nutrition hypothesis were the gaps in historical evidence. McKeown himself had freely conceded that the basic data were inadequate, but he had still believed that enough pieces existed to "cover the canvas" with a sketch or a comprehensive interpretation, the details of which could be filled in later as data and methodology improved. Not surprisingly, much of the research that countered his viewpoint addressed this evidential gap: Some offered differing interpretations of the sparse existing data, whereas others unearthed new evidence. Whatever the merits of McKeown's own arguments, there is no question that the debate he ignited over the role of nutrition in the modern decline of mortality was productive in that it defined the issues to be researched and spurred the search for new evidence.

Some critics were skeptical that an insufficient supply of food had been responsible for the high mortality rates in preindustrial societies. P. E. Razzell (1974), for example, questioned the food-supply hypothesis, citing the absence of a significant mortality differential between social classes. If nutrition was the critical factor, one would expect the aristocracy to enjoy lower mortality levels than the poor. Yet, in what came to be known as the "peerage paradox," he found that there was little difference in the mortality rates among the peerage and those of the laboring classes in England before 1725, and although presumably the poorer classes should have benefited more from any overall improvement in diet, the reduction in mortality after 1725 was greater among the aristocracy. Moreover, M. Livi-Bacci (1991) noted that in several other European countries as well, the aristocracy had not enjoyed any advantage in mortality over the lower classes. Furthermore, his examination of the European experience from the time of the Black Death to the era of industrialization led him to doubt whether nutritional improvement had shown any long-term interrelationship with mortality rates.

Other criticisms of the McKeown thesis were mainly directed against his underestimation of the role of public health. S. H. Preston and E. van de Walle (1978) concluded that, at least in France, water and sewage improvements had played a major role in urban mortality decline during the nineteenth century. Similarly, S. Szreter (1988) and A. Hardy (1993) argued that in England, preventive public-health initiatives had made significant contributions to the decline in prevalence and severity of a number of diseases, including smallpox, typhoid fever, typhus, and tuberculosis. In addition, purification of milk was thought specifically to have contributed to the fall in infant mortality (Beaver 1973).

McKeown's heavy reliance on English and Welsh data may also have caused him to overstate the case for nutrition. In an analysis of changes in mortality patterns among 165 populations, Preston (1976) pointed out that the English and Welsh experience was exceptional. Between 1851-60 and 1891-1900, decreased mortality from respiratory tuberculosis accounted for 44 percent of the drop in age- and sex-standardized death rates in England and Wales, whereas the normal reduction in other countries had been 11 to 12 percent. Similarly, a decrease in deaths from other infectious and parasitic diseases accounted for 48 percent of the mortality decline in England, compared to the standard 14 percent elsewhere. Preston (1976: 20) concluded that "the country with the most satisfactory early data appears to offer an atypical account of mortality decline, a record that may be largely responsible for prevailing representations of mortality reduction that stress the role of specific and readily identified infectious diseases of childhood and early adulthood."

During several decades of often heated debate over the nutrition hypothesis, virtually all aspects of McKeown's argument have been examined in great detail by critics and supporters alike. The points on which there is agreement after such prolonged and extensive investigation are certainly worth noting. That nutrition did play a role in the mortality decline is not disputed; the disagreement is over the magnitude of its contribution. Although McKeown was generally not receptive to criticisms of his thesis, in a later work (1988) he did acknowledge that the contribution of public-health measures had been greater than he had originally concluded. One important point of McKeown's that has survived intact is that specific therapeutic medical treatments had little impact on mortality reduction.

Generalizing the last point, some critics have commented that no single factor by itself – including nutrition – appears able to account for the mortality decline. Preston (1976) found that nutrition, as proxied by income levels, accounted for only about 20 percent of the fall in mortality between the 1930s and the 1960s. In fairness to McKeown, however, it should be noted that the period covered by Preston's study coincides with the era of antibiotics, whereas McKeown's arguments relied on the trends of mortality patterns before that time.

Diet versus Nutritional Status

In the debate over the role of nutrition in mortality decline, a great deal of confusion has been caused by differences in the ways the term "nutrition" has been understood and used by different investigators. Some have interpreted nutrition to mean food supply or diet, whereas others have followed epidemiologists or nutritionists by taking it to mean nutritional status, or net nutrition, which is the balance between the intake of nutrients and the claims against it. McKeown, the original proponent of the nutrition hypothesis used the term in both senses, although his writings indicate that he was aware of the difference between the two concepts. Lately, R. W. Fogel (1986, 1993, 1994) has suggested that when nutrition is mentioned in connection with food, the terms "diet" or "gross nutrition" be used. He advocated that the term "nutrition" itself be reserved for use in the sense of net nutrition – the balance of nutrients that becomes available for cellular growth – to avoid any further confusion.

There are clear advantages to adopting such a definition, not least of which is that it clarifies and suggests new avenues of research (as discussed shortly). However, as this new definition of nutrition is still not completely free of some pitfalls that could lead to further misunderstanding, it is worth considering in some detail what it actually means. That is, what are the determinants of nutritional intake, and what factors count as claims against that intake?

In a broad sense, nutritional intake may be taken to mean food supply, as has often been assumed in the debate over the historical role of nutrition. But complications exist even in the quantification of this relatively simple measure. Leaving aside the difficulty of obtaining reliable figures for gross food production in the past, one must also face the tricky issue of how to estimate the losses in nutrients that occur because of different, and often inefficient, food-storage, preparation, and preservation technologies.

These considerations, in turn, immediately suggest that quality, as well as quantity, is an important aspect of nutrition, a fact that may go far in explaining the peerage paradox. McKeown (1976) maintained that the peerage must have been eating unhealthy, or even infected, food, in which case the larger quantities they consumed could hardly be taken as grounds for expecting better health than that found among the lower classes. Fogel (1986) has also pointed out that toxic substances in the diet of the aristocrats, such as large quantities of salt and alcohol, would have had negative effects on their health and mortality. He has emphasized that the impact on the overall mortality rate of the peerage would have been especially large if it showed up mainly as high infant mortality, possibly because of adverse effects on the fetuses of mothers who apparently imbibed huge quantities of wine and ale on a daily basis. Moreover, Fogel has noted that the decline in infant and child mortality among the peerage after 1725 was paralleled by a gradual elimination of the toxic substances from the aristocratic diet between 1700 and 1900.

Another important way in which nutritional intake can be significantly influenced is through the pres-

ence of diseases that affect the body's ability to
absorb nutrients. This ability can be measured as
Atwater factors – food-specific rates at which the
energy value of a person's food intake is transformed
into metabolizable energy. Atwater factors are usually
in the 90 to 95 percent range for healthy populations,
but they can be as low as 80 percent among undernourished populations in which recurrent episodes of
acute diarrhea may impair the absorption of nutrients
(Molla et al. 1983).

Against the nutritional intake, all claims on nutrients must be deducted in order to arrive at the figure for nutritional status, or the balance that can be
metabolized for cellular growth. The claims on nutrients can be broadly classified into three categories
of energy expenditures: the energy required for
basic maintenance of the body, the energy for occupational and discretionary activities, and the energy
to fight infections. The first of these categories, basic
maintenance, accounts for most of the body's energy
usage and consists mainly of the Basal Metabolic
Rate (BMR). BMR is the energy required to maintain
body temperature and to sustain the normal functioning of organs, including heart and respiratory
action. Roughly speaking, it is equivalent to the
energy expended during rest or sleep and can be
considered the default cost of survival in terms of
energy.

Although there is some variation among individuals, BMR varies mainly by age, sex, and body weight. In
particular, the association with body weight is strong
enough that within any age/sex category, BMR can be
predicted by a linear equation in body weight alone
(WHO 1985). The BMR for an adult male, aged 20 to
39 and living in a moderate climate, ranges between
1,350 and 2,000 kilocalories (kcal) a day, which
would amount to somewhere between 45 and 65 percent of his total daily energy intake. It should be
noted that BMR does not allow for such basic survival
activities as eating, digestion, and minimal personal
hygiene.

Occupational and discretionary activities account
for most, if not all, of the energy requirements
beyond basic maintenance. Discretionary activities
include walking, recreation, optional household
tasks, and exercise. The pattern of energy expenditure among these categories will necessarily vary
with individual activity patterns, which are influenced greatly by age, sex, occupation, culture, and
technology. A World Health Organization (WHO)
report (1985) estimated the energy requirements of a
young male office clerk to be 1,310 kcal for basic
maintenance (51 percent), 710 kcal for work (28 percent), and 560 kcal for discretionary activities (22
percent). The energy usage of a young subsistence
farmer with a moderate work level in Papua New
Guinea was given as 1,060 (40 percent), 1,230 (46
percent), and 390 (15 percent) kcal over the same
expenditure categories. In yet another pattern of

energy usage, a young housewife in an affluent society requires 1,400 (70 percent), 150 (8 percent), and
440 (22 percent) kcal, respectively.

The adverse effects of infections on nutrition go
far beyond their impact on the body's ability to
absorb nutrients. Fever directly increases metabolic
demands, and the excess energy expenditure so
induced by an infection therefore constitutes a separate, additional claim on nutrients. Other effects of
infections that are similarly harmful include the loss
of nutrients resulting from vomiting, diarrhea,
reduced appetite, or restrictions on diet. For instance,
R. Martorell and colleagues (1980) estimated that during an episode of diarrhea, the loss of total energy
intake from reduced food intake alone can be as
much as 40 percent. Malnutrition also has the effect
of weakening the immune system and, thus, making
the body more susceptible to infections, which can
have further negative effects on nutrition in a deteriorating cycle.

The preceding discussion shows that nutritional
balance is jointly determined by nutritional intake
and various claims on that intake. Both intake and
claims comprise a great range of factors, which
appears to be broad enough to include almost every
determinant of health and mortality. There is obviously a great difference between nutrition in the
sense of diet and such a broadly inclusive concept as
that of net nutrition. For some, it may seem natural to
question whether the precision in the definition of
nutritional status actually masks a vagueness in practical usability.

As a hypothetical example, suppose a new medical
therapy is introduced that effectively cures a certain
infectious disease, and that this therapy has the effect
of substantially improving nutritional status by saving
nutrients that would formerly have been lost to prolonged infection. If the overall result is a reduction in
mortality, credit ought to go to the new medical treatment, but by definition, it can also be said that the
lower death rate is the result of improved nutrition.
Similarly, an effective public-health measure that lowers the prevalence of some infectious disease could
still be considered a case in which improved nutrition
leads to mortality decline.

Evidently the different causes of mortality decline
can no longer be considered mutually exclusive when
nutrition is defined as net nutrition, and it is no longer
clear what to make of statements that compare the
contribution of nutrition to that of medical treatment
or public-health measures. This ambiguity is perhaps
especially noticeable and problematic to those who
continue to think about the role of nutrition in the
context of the debate initiated by McKeown.

A related difficulty that follows from the new definition is that, even today, nutrition as a net balance is
quite difficult to measure accurately. Estimating how
nutritional status has changed throughout the past
several centuries is even harder. In order to calculate

claims against the intake of nutrients, the determinants of those claims – such as a population's body weight distribution (from which BMR is derived), its members' activity levels in work and leisure, and the prevalence, severity, and duration of infections suffered by them – all must be taken into account. Once again, the new definition does not appear to be very helpful for those interested in applying it directly to resolve issues raised by the nutrition hypothesis of mortality decline.

It should be noted, however, that ambiguity and difficulty of measurement are not problems newly introduced by the adoption of a definition of nutrition as net nutritional balance. Instead, the new definition serves to highlight the fact that the debate over the role of nutrition has lacked agreement on the exact meaning of nutrition. The view of nutrition as the balance between nutrient intake and energy expenditure also suggests that influences on health and longevity cannot be easily or even meaningfully sorted into discrete, measurable categories. Rather, health and mortality outcomes are now viewed as the joint result of several different processes that continually interact to determine health and aging.

In recent years, such a reassessment of the relationship between nutrition, health, and mortality has led some researchers, notably Fogel and his colleagues, to shift their focus away from the original debate over McKeown's nutrition hypothesis to other aspects of nutrition and mortality. The balance of this chapter briefly considers these new developments.

Anthropometric Measures

The difficulty of measuring or estimating nutritional status – especially with regard to the potential data deficiencies in historical research or in studies of developing countries – has prompted investigators to search for other measures that can be used as proxies for nutrition. Fortunately, there exists a class of measures that are comparatively easily observed (often even far back into the past) and are also known to be sensitive to variations in nutritional status. These are anthropometric measures, especially those of body height and body weight. Since weight is positively correlated to height, a measurement of weight-for-height is usually used, the most popular being the Body Mass Index (BMI), also known as the Quetelet index. It is derived as body weight in kilograms (kg) divided by the square of height in meters (m), or kg/m^2.

Height and BMI reflect different aspects of a person's nutritional experience. Adult height is an index that represents past cumulative net nutritional experience during growth. Studies in developing countries have shown that nutrition in early childhood, from birth to about age 5, is especially important in determining final adult height (Martorell 1985). Malnutrition among children of this age causes growth

retardation, which is known as stunting. Although it is possible for some "catch-up" growth to occur later, this is unlikely to happen in an impoverished environment that was probably responsible for the malnourishment and stunting in the first place. BMI, in contrast, primarily reflects a person's current nutritional status. It varies directly with nutritional balance; a positive balance increases body mass, and a negative balance indicates that the body is drawing on its store of nutrients.

Interest in height and BMI as proxy measures for nutrition has, in the context of research on nutrition and mortality, naturally been directed to their association with morbidity and mortality. Although anthropometric measures had previously been used as predictors of the risks of morbidity and mortality for young children, H. Th. Waaler's (1984) large-scale study of Norwegian adults was among the first to show that height and weight could be used to predict morbidity and mortality risks for adults as well. When Waaler analyzed age- and sex-specific risks of dying by height classes among 1.8 million Norwegian adults between 1963 and 1979, he found that there was a stable relationship between adult height and mortality risk that could be characterized as a J-shaped curve. Within each age/sex group, mortality risk was highest among the shortest group of people and declined at a decreasing rate as height increased. This negative association between height and mortality risk has received much attention in historical research, which has sought to tie the increasing secular trends in the mean heights of different populations to parallel improving trends in their health and life expectancies (Fogel 1986; Floud, Wachter, and Gregory 1990; Komlos 1994; Steckel 1995).

Waaler also found a stable relationship between BMI and mortality risk, which can be characterized as a U-shaped curve. Risk is unresponsive to weight over a wide range, from about 20 to 28 BMI, but it increases sharply at either tail beyond that range. As historical data on weight distribution are harder to come by than data on height, little research making use of this risk–BMI relationship has yet been done. However, in an interesting development, some attempts have been made to use height and BMI simultaneously to predict mortality risk, rather than using each anthropometric measure separately (Fogel 1993, 1994; Kim 1996).

As height represents an individual's early nutrition and BMI his current nutritional status, the resulting height-weight-risk surface makes better use of all nutritional information than the height-risk or BMI-risk curves. Fogel (1994) used such a surface to suggest that the combined effect of increases in body height and weight among the French population can explain about 90 percent of the French mortality decline between 1785 and 1870, but only about 50 percent of the actual mortality decline since then. Another study, using a similar surface to track secular changes in height, weight, and the risks of old-age morbidity in the United States, also has found that factors other than height or BMI explain a larger share of elderly health improvement from 1982 to 1992 than during the period from 1910 to the early 1980s (Kim 1996).

In closing this chapter, it seems appropriate to devote a bit more attention to recent methodologies that may help to shed more light on the relationship between nutrition and mortality decline. For example, in addition to height and BMI, waist-to-hip ratio (WHR) is another anthropometric measure that has gained acceptance as a predictor of chronic diseases, especially for coronary heart disease and non-insulin-dependent diabetes mellitus (Bjorntorp 1992; Hodge and Zimmet 1994; Baumgartner, Heymsfield, and Roche 1995). Although BMI and WHR are generally correlated and are therefore both linked to the risk of chronic diseases associated with obesity, a weakness of BMI is that it does not indicate body composition such as lean body mass versus total body fat, nor is it indicative of the distribution of fat within the body.

By contrast, WHR, as a measure of central adiposity, has been found in a number of studies to have predictive power independent of BMI. J. M. Sosenko and colleagues (1993) have reported that WHR was significantly higher among diabetic women and also among men (although not as markedly as among women), whereas BMI failed to differentiate between diabetics and nondiabetics. Similarly, A. R. Folsom and colleagues (1994) examined Chinese men and women aged 28 to 69 from both urban and rural areas and found that abdominal adiposity – represented by an elevated WHR – was independently associated with cardiovascular risk factors. Although BMI was also associated in a similar direction with most of these risk factors, the mean level of BMI in this study was relatively low, ranging from 20.1 to 21.9 among 4 sex- and age-groups, confirming that WHR is useful as a predictor of cardiovascular disease even among a lean Asian population. S. P. Walker and colleagues (1996) found in a five-year follow-up study of 28,643 U.S. male health professionals that BMI was only weakly associated with stroke risk, but that WHR was a much better predictor even when BMI, height, and other potential risk factors were taken into account. Yet although these studies suggest that there is a strong case for using WHR in conjunction with or perhaps as a substitute for BMI, it should be remembered that data on BMI are often more easily obtained or reasonably estimated, making BMI useful as a predictor or proxy for health or nutritional status in studies involving historical populations or in other situations in which detailed anthropometric data are lacking.

The preceding discussion on the role of adult height as a predictor of morbidity and mortality in middle or old age, combined with the theory that nutrition during the very early stages of life is a major determinant of adult height, suggests the possibility that the roots of some later-in-life diseases can be found very early in life, and intriguing research carried out by D. J. P. Barker and others (Barker 1993, 1994) has made this possibility seem a probability. In focusing on events surrounding birth for explanations of diseases in later life, Barker and his colleagues located United Kingdom birth records from Hertfordshire, Sheffield, and Preston, all of which contained detailed information on the infants. The Hertfordshire records covered births between 1911 and 1930 and included birth weight, weight at 1 year of age, number of teeth, and other details. The records from Sheffield and Preston covered roughly the same period but were even more detailed, and their inclusion of length from crown to heel, head circumference, biparietal and other head diameters, placental weight, and (after 1922) chest and abdominal circumferences allowed the computation of various body proportions. Linking these birth records with those still surviving as adults and with the records of those who had since died made it possible to investigate any relationship between at-birth measurements and health events in later life.

This research, compactly summarized by Barker (1994), has uncovered numerous associations between various birth measurements and disease in later life, including hypertension, excessive levels of blood cholesterol, non-insulin-dependent diabetes, and death rates from cardiovascular disease. Among men, low birth weight and weight at 1 year of age were associated with premature death from cardiovascular disease. Females whose weight was low at birth but above average as adults also experienced increased death rates. Other measurements at birth that indicate slow fetal growth have also been found to predict higher death rates from cardiovascular disease. These include thinness (as measured by the ponderal index – birth weight/length^3), small head circumference, short length, low abdominal circumference relative to head size, and a high placental-weight-to-birth-weight ratio. As slow growth in utero is often followed by slow growth afterward, these findings suggest one pathway through which nutrition, adult height, and mortality in old age may be related (cf. Barker, Osmond, and Golding 1990).

From birth records linked to survivors rather than to death records, Barker and his colleagues were also able to analyze the connection between measurements at birth and chronic diseases or their risk factors among the survivors. Babies who were small for date or with a higher ratio of placental weight to birth weight, both of which indicate undernutrition in utero, were found to have higher systolic and diastolic blood pressure as children and as adults. These findings were independent of, or dominated, the effects of the later-life environment, including the current weight, alcohol consumption, and salt intake of the subjects. The blood pressure of the mother was also found to be a nonfactor. Reduced liver size, as measured by abdominal circumference, was associated with raised serum concentrations of total and LDL cholesterol levels in both men and women. Based on these findings, Barker has suggested that impaired liver growth in late gestation may permanently alter the body's LDL cholesterol metabolism, resulting in an increased risk of coronary heart disease later in life. In both men and women, low birth weight predicted higher rates of non-insulin-dependent diabetes and impaired glucose tolerance.

British birth records have also been useful in establishing a link between infectious disease in childhood and chronic disease in later life. A follow-up study of men from the Hertfordshire records, which recorded illnesses periodically throughout infancy and early childhood, showed that death rates from chronic bronchitis were higher among those who had low birth weights and low weights at 1 year of age (Barker et al. 1991). In addition, S. O. Shaheen and colleagues (1995) have reported that among survivors represented in the Hertfordshire and Derbyshire records, men who had suffered bronchitis or pneumonia in infancy had significantly impaired lung function as measured by mean FEV_1 (forced expiratory volume in one second). These findings support the hypothesis that lower-respiratory-tract infections in early childhood lead to chronic obstructive pulmonary disease in late adult life.

The relationship of maternal (and thus fetal) nutrition – and that of infants – with diseases of later life was one, of course, that McKeown did not examine. That such a relationship seems to exist is one more powerful example of the complex nature of nutrition on the one hand and mortality on the other.

John M. Kim

Bibliography

Barker, D. J. P. 1994. *Mothers, babies, and diseases in later life.* London.
ed. 1993. *Fetal and infant origins of adult disease.* London.
Barker, D. J. P., K. M. Godfrey, C. Fall, et al. 1991. Relation of birthweight and childhood respiratory infection to adult lung function and death from chronic obstructive airways disease. *British Medical Journal* 303: 671-5.
Barker, D. J. P., and C. Osmond. 1986. Infant mortality, child nutrition, and ischaemic heart disease in England and Wales. *Lancet* 1986i: 1077-81.
Barker, D. J. P., C. Osmond, and J. Golding. 1990. Height and mortality in the counties of England and Wales. *Annals of Human Biology* 17: 1-6.
Baumgartner, R. N., S. B. Heymsfield, and A. F. Roche. 1995. Human body composition and the epidemiology of chronic disease. *Obesity Research* 3: 73-95.
Beaver, M. W. 1973. Population, infant mortality, and milk. *Population Studies* 27: 243-54.
Bjorntorp, P. 1992. Abdominal fat distribution and disease: An overview of epidemiological data. *Annals of Medicine* 24: 15-18.
Floud, R., K. Wachter, and A. Gregory. 1990. *Height, health, and history.* Cambridge.
Fogel, R. W. 1986. Nutrition and the decline in mortality since 1700. In *Long-term factors in American economic growth,* ed. S. L. Engerman and R. E. Gallman, 439-555. Chicago.
1993. New sources and new techniques for the study of secular trends in nutritional status, health, mortality, and the process of aging. *Historical Methods* 26: 5-43.
1994. Economic growth, population theory, and physiology: The bearing of long-term processes on the making of economic policy. *American Economic Review* 84: 369-95.
Folsom, A. R., Y. Li, X. Rao, et al. 1994. Body mass, fat distribution and cardiovascular risk factors in a lean population of South China. *Journal of Clinical Epidemiology* 47: 173-81.
Hardy, A. 1993. *The epidemic streets: Infectious disease and the rise of preventive medicine, 1856-1900.* Oxford.
Higgs, R. 1973. Mortality in rural America, 1870-1920: Estimates and conjectures. *Explorations in Economic History* 10: 177-95.
1979. Cycles and trends of mortality in eighteen large American cities, 1871-1900. *Explorations in Economic History* 16: 381-408.
Hodge, A. M., and P. Z. Zimmet. 1994. The epidemiology of obesity. *Baillieres Clinical Endocrinology and Metabolism* 8: 577-99.
Kim, J. M. 1996. The economics of nutrition, body build, and health: Waaler surfaces and physical human capital. Ph.D. dissertation, University of Chicago.
Komlos, J., ed. 1994. *Stature, living standards, and economic development: Essays in anthropometric history.* Chicago and London.
Livi-Bacci, M. 1991. *Population and nutrition: An essay on European demographic history,* trans. Tania Croft-Murray. Cambridge and New York.
Martorell, R. 1985. Child growth retardation: A discussion of its causes and its relationship to health. In *Nutritional adaptation in man,* ed. K. Blaxter and J. C. Waterlow, 13-30. London.
Martorell, R., C. Yarbrough, S. Yarbrough, and R. E. Klein. 1980. The impact of ordinary illnesses on the dietary intakes of malnourished children. *American Journal of Clinical Nutrition* 33: 345-50.
McKeown, T. 1976. *The modern rise of population.* New York.
1979. *The role of medicine.* Princeton, N.J.
1988. *The origins of human disease.* Oxford.
McKeown, T., and R. G. Brown. 1955. Medical evidence related to English population changes in the eighteenth century. *Population Studies* 9: 119-41.
McKeown, T., R. G. Brown, and R. Record. 1972. An interpretation of the modern rise of population in Europe. *Population Studies* 26: 345-82.
McKinlay, J., and S. McKinlay. 1977. The questionable contribution of medical measures to the decline of mortality in the twentieth century. *Milbank Memorial Fund Quarterly* 55: 405-28.
Meeker, E. 1972. The improving health of the United States, 1850-1915. *Explorations in Economic History* 9: 353-73.
Molla, A., A. M. Molla, S. A. Sarker, and M. Khatun. 1983. Whole-gut transit time and its relationship to absorption of macronutrients during diarrhoea and after recovery. *Scandinavian Journal of Gastroenterology* 18: 537-43.

Preston, S. H. 1976. *Mortality patterns in national populations.* New York.

Preston, S. H., and E. van de Walle. 1978. Urban French mortality in the nineteenth century. *Population Studies* 32: 275-97.

Razzell, P. E. 1974. An interpretation of the modern rise of population in Europe: A critique. *Population Studies* 28: 5-17.

Shaheen, S. O., D. J. P. Barker, and S. T. Holgate. 1995. Do lower respiratory tract infections in early childhood cause chronic obstructive pulmonary disease? *American Journal of Respiratory and Critical Care Medicine* 151: 1649-51.

Sosenko, J. M., M. Kato, R. Soto, and R. B. Goldberg. 1993. A comparison of adiposity measures for screening non-insulin dependent diabetes mellitus. *International Journal of Obesity and Related Metabolic Disorders* 17: 441-4.

Steckel, R. H. 1995. Stature and the standard of living. *Journal of Economic Literature* 33: 1903-40.

Szreter, S. 1988. The importance of social intervention in Britain's mortality decline, c. 1850-1914. A reinterpretation of the role of public health. *Social History of Medicine* 1: 1-37.

UN (United Nations). 1953. *The determinants and consequences of population trends.* New York.

    1973. *The determinants and causes of population trends.* New York.

Waaler, H. Th. 1984. Height, weight, and mortality: The Norwegian experience. *Acta Medica Scandinavica* 679 (Supplement): 1-51.

Walker, S. P., E. B. Rimm, A. Ascherio, et al. 1996. Body size and fat distribution as predictors of stroke among US men. *American Journal of Epidemiology* 144: 1143-50.

WHO (World Health Organization). 1985. *Energy and protein requirements.* Technical Report Series, No. 724. Geneva.

VI.2 ❧ Nutrition and Mortality Decline: Another View

The importance of nutrition to the preservation of human health cannot be reasonably denied. However, the extent of its power may have been overstated in recent years. For millions of Americans, "natural foods and vitamins" are seen as almost magical preservers of health, beauty, and longevity. Indeed, claims for the healing properties of nutrients have become an integral part of the post–World War II "baby-boomer" generation's vision of the world. For many, "faith" in the power of proper nutrition is part of a secular religion that comes close to denying the inevitability of aging and death. Vitamin C is considered a panacea one day and beta-carotene the next, as are such foods as broccoli and garlic. With such a cornucopia of natural "medicines," who would ever think that the history of humankind would reveal so much disease and ill health?

Although such popular exaggerations of the benefits of various nutriments are easily dismissed by serious scholars, other more scholarly claims are not. One suggestion dealing with the historical importance of nutrition has received remarkably widespread support in academic circles and, among historians, has become the orthodox explanation for understanding a key aspect of the modern world: increased longevity.

The McKeown Thesis

The classic formulation of this explanation was provided by the medical historian Thomas McKeown (1976, 1979), who argued that the reasons for the decline of mortality in the Western world over the last three hundred years have been largely the result of rising living standards, especially increased and improved nutrition. Equally important, the decline was not the result, as so many had rather vaguely believed, of any purposeful medical or public-health interventions.

Such a theory, of course, was not long confined to historical debates because of its clear policy implications for the allocation of resources in the developing (and the developed) world today. If the historical decline of mortality in the West occurred independently of science and medicine, then the high death rates in the developing world could best be combated by vigorously pursuing higher living and nutritional standards. Not only was money expended on high-technology hospitals and doctors ill spent, but even funds for immunization campaigns were a waste of limited resources. As McKeown put it: "If a choice must be made, free school meals are more important for the health of poor children than immunization programmes, and both are more effective than hospital beds" (McKeown 1979).

This revolutionary theory has a number of emotional and intellectual attractions. First, it constitutes a devastating attack on the legitimacy and claims of societal "authority," represented in this case by the medical profession and, to a lesser extent, the public-health and scientific establishments. The "experts" who claim the right to guide and control society and its inhabitants, based upon their past accomplishments, are revealed as self-deluded, if not as outright frauds. Such a critical position resonates very well in an era characterized by relentless attacks on all types of authority and one in which the delegitimization of social institutions is a daily affair.

What radical social critic could have better put what many regard as an imperious medical profession in its place than McKeown, who wrote (in an attempt to dispel the "erroneous belief" that he was hostile to the medical profession): ". . . if medical intervention is often less effective than most people, including doctors, believe, there is also a need . . . for greater emphasis on personal care of the sick (the pastoral role of the doctor) . . ." (McKeown 1979: ix). (Later in the same work [p. 112], he stated that the key advance in personal medical interventions in the past was the control of cavities by the dental profession.)

Second, McKeown's view of the nature of health is also very congenial to the post–World War II generation's view of life, death, and aging: "Most diseases, including the common ones, are not inevitable.... [Modern medicine is based on a different idea.] It assumes we are ill and must be made well, whereas it is nearer to the truth to say that we are well and are made ill" (McKeown 1979: 117–18). In addition, his work has an appeal to earlier generations, especially his claim that persons in their 70s who lived a healthy life would be as vigorous and capable as they were in their 30s! What the thesis seems to promise is eternal youth, if not eternal life, completely under the control of the careful and concerned individual without the messy intervention of doctors and other self-proclaimed experts. Such a view, when coupled with impressive scholarship, is very persuasive by itself, and the fact that the medical profession had indeed severely exaggerated its performance historically has also made it easier for many to embrace the argument.

Third, the McKeown thesis can be and has been profitably used by people representing a wide variety of political and ideological positions. In the West, it can be aimed at established authority figures in attempts to delegitimize basic Western institutions. The supposed accomplishments of science, medicine, and the public-health service, which bolster the West's claims to superiority as a civilization, can be denied.

For leftists in the developing world, the McKeown thesis could free their countries from dependence on Western medical and scientific expertise and technology. Better a homegrown political upheaval with land redistribution than a measles shot or a CAT scan machine. Since good health is promised as a natural by-product of a rising standard of living and better nutrition, its eventuality depends on radical politics, not on "imperialistic" science or medicine (Muraskin 1995).

But the Right also has had reasons to be attracted to the McKeown thesis, which lends support to deemphasizing expensive medical care for the "masses," both at home and abroad. If medicine and technology are not the key to lower mortality, why waste money on them in a time of escalating, and certainly threatening, medical costs? If the poor are underserved by doctors, maybe they are better off than their richer neighbors who are plagued by ineffective medical personnel and their iatrogenic interventions.

Despite the appeal of the McKeown thesis to so many political sectors, there are a number of reasons for criticism, not the least among them that McKeown reached his conclusion about the importance of nutrition in the mortality decline through the process of elimination of possible alternatives. If all the other possibilities are false, then the last standing explanation is the correct one.

Almost all of those who have questioned McKeown's argument have been struck by this methodology. For such a procedure to be effective, it is mandatory that all possible alternatives be presented and adequately explored. But this is impossible because history, science, and medicine are full of unknowns. Thus, although such a procedure may be suggestive and help generate a useful hypothesis, strong direct evidence must be presented to make an adequate case.

McKeown postulated that there were only five possible reasons for the decline of mortality in the West:

1. Medical intervention (including immunizations).
2. Public-health measures (for example, better sanitation, water purification, and food hygiene).
3. Changes in the nature and virulence of microorganisms.
4. Reduced contact with microorganisms.
5. Increased and improved nutrition.

He then proceeded to argue that until recently, it was assumed that "medical" interventions were the primary cause of increased life expectancy. This term, however, tended to include both personal medical care and public-health policies – two types of activities that must be separated for purposes of analysis.

The main thrust of his argument was aimed at the claims of personal medical care. He demonstrated that the decline in mortality was well advanced long before medical science developed effective forms of disease therapy or prevention. His proofs were elaborate and rather convincing. Unquestionably, McKeown has clearly, and probably permanently, deflated the claim that personal medical care played a major role in increasing longevity in the West. But such a claim could exist only because of the ahistorical nature of most public discourse in the West.

If most laypeople and doctors felt that modern medicine had performed miracles, very few of them, if challenged, would have insisted that medicine's effectiveness went back much before the advent of antibiotics in the 1940s or sulphonamides in the 1930s. Although there were great scientific minds, like Robert Koch or Louis Pasteur, in the late nineteenth century, there was no adequate control over infectious diseases. For most, modern medicine was probably viewed as so miraculous specifically because the nineteenth century (and the first third of the twentieth century) was seen as so bleak and unhealthy. Thus, McKeown's debunking of a tendency to view earlier medicine with lenses of the present was, in fact, an easy victory.

His larger thesis, however, required similar attacks on other possible causes of mortality decline. He disposed of the importance of immunizations (which he grouped with personal medical care rather than public-health activities) by arguing, on the one hand, that they occurred significantly later than the decline in mortality for the various diseases they were created to treat[1] and, on the other hand, that vaccinations did little or no good in the absence of better nutrition.

He gave considerably more credit for the lowering of mortality to public-health measures, especially clean water and safe food, than he gave to personal medical care, but as with immunizations, he argued that these measures were put in place long after mortality had already significantly declined.

McKeown next considered the possibility that a decline in the natural virulence of microorganisms or a decrease in exposure of the general population to dangerous pathogens led to the decline of mortality in the West. His discussion of these possibilities, however, was far more cursory than his argument about the ineffectiveness of personal medical care. In short, his convincing argument against much of a role for clinical medicine in the improvement of life expectancy did not carry over into an analysis of the other possibilities he set forth. Thus, one could argue that McKeown presented a fascinating and stimulating hypothesis that somehow came to be understood as an established truth.

Attacks on the McKeown Thesis

One of the most interesting assaults on the credibility of the McKeown thesis originated with a Danish anthropologist, Dr. Peter Aaby. His extensive research on measles mortality in Guinea-Bissau, West Africa, provided a unique opportunity for such an attack because McKeown used the World Health Organization's (WHO) position on measles to support his argument for the importance of nutrition over immunization in the decline of mortality. McKeown (citing WHO) claimed that vaccination of an underfed child is not protective, whereas a well-nourished child does not need vaccination to survive the disease. In other words, another bowl of rice is preferable to a measles shot.

Aaby claimed to have shared such a view until his discoveries in Guinea-Bissau no longer supported it. He wrote that there are three general ways of looking at measles mortality:

1. Emphasizing "host factors" (malnutrition, age of infection, genetics).
2. Emphasizing "transmission factors" (greater exposure, more virulent strains, synergism between infections).
3. Emphasizing "treatment and medical care factors" (ineffective treatment or neglect of effective treatments). (Aaby 1992: 155–6)

Certainly, most of the emphasis has been on host factors. In the case of measles, which kills about one and half million children a year in the developing world, "[t]hose who die are seen as somehow weaker than other individuals," and "severe measles has been explained particularly with reference to [host factors such as] malnutrition, the age at infection, genetic susceptibility and underlying disease" (Aaby 1992: 156).

Such an interpretation, Aaby maintained, easily leads to the implication that severe measles is a disease of the weak who are on the road to death, if not from this disease then from another. The implication for policy is that little is accomplished by immunization because of the phenomenon of "replacement mortality." Thus, the solution to preventing death from measles is not to fight the disease but to fight general malnutrition. Clearly, this is a position strongly supportive of McKeown's own view.

Aaby, however, found that the situation in Guinea-Bissau was not so supportive. The children who died were not noticeably different in nutritional level from those who survived. Moreover, the general level of nutrition in the country was quite adequate – better, in fact, than in countries (such as Bangladesh) with much lower rates of mortality from measles. Instead of nutrition, according to Aaby, the factor differentiating those who died and those who did not was whether the child was an "index case" or a "secondary case" in a family.

Index cases (the first persons infected) were usually exposed outside the home. By contrast, secondary cases were usually the siblings of those index cases who had brought the infection into the home. The difference in mortality risk between the two groups was striking, with secondary cases much more likely to succumb to the illness. The apparent reason for the disparity was that the index cases had experienced much less exposure to the virus (contracted in social interactions outside the home) than the secondary cases – who were continuously exposed by actually living with an infected sibling. The key, according to Aaby, was not nutritional status in the face of measles, but rather the degree of exposure to the illness.

Aaby also compared rates of measles mortality between different countries. He found that Bangladesh had significantly lower rates than Guinea-Bissau despite poorer levels of nutrition. But in Guinea-Bissau, fully 61 percent of the children under 3 years old were secondary cases (with the case fatality rate [CFR] a horrifying 25 percent), whereas in Bangladesh, secondary cases were only 14 percent, and the CFR was 3 percent.

The reason proposed for the extreme variance was that "[l]arger families and a high incidence of polygamy mean[t] that children in West Africa h[ad] a much greater risk of becoming secondary cases . . ." because there were large numbers of young, susceptible siblings living at home (Aaby 1992: 160). This factor also seemed to account for the lower mortality rates Aaby found among East Africans when compared to West Africans – that is to say there were fewer wives and fewer children in East Africa.

In addition, Aaby observed that the severity or mildness of the disease in the index case correlated with the likelihood of mortality and secondary cases. In other words, the more severe the index case, the higher the rate of death in secondary cases; and the milder the index case, the lower the death rate of subsequent cases. There also seemed to be an "amplification phenomenon" in which severe cases brought into a household (or institution or military camp) created waves of infection, each more severe than the last.

The Guinea-Bissau research also uncovered other unexpected transmission factors that correlated with significantly higher levels of measles mortality. The most surprising finding was that infection by a member of the opposite sex produced a noticeably greater chance of death than infection by someone of the same gender. Studies in other developing countries have found a similar cross-gender transmission factor, and Aaby, doing historical research, discovered that such a situation existed in Copenhagen at the turn of the twentieth century (Aaby 1992: 162).

In addition, this concentration on transmission factors, rather than host factors, brought to light a "delayed impact," which constitutes a long-term measles effect. Most studies deal with acute measles death (that is to say within one month of the appearance of the rash). But in Guinea-Bissau, "children who had been exposed to measles at home during the first six months of their lives had a mortality [rate] between ages six months and five years which was three times higher than community controls (34 percent vs. 11 percent)" (Aaby 1992: 164).

When background factors were taken into account, "the mortality hazards ratio was 5.7 times higher . . . among the exposed children than the controls" (Aaby 1992: 164). The "delayed excess mortality" existed both among children who had measles and among those without clinical symptoms. In light of this finding, it seems possible that the total mortality from measles infection is far higher in the developing world than is assumed.

Aaby has speculated on the possible meanings of this delayed mortality. One is "some form of persistent infection and immuno-suppression" at work. In addition, community studies in Nigeria, Guinea-Bissau, Senegal, Zaire, Bangladesh, and Haiti have shown that children immunized against measles have experienced major drops in overall mortality in the years after vaccination:

> In all studies the reduction in mortality was greater than expected from the direct contribution of measles death to over all mortality. For example, in Bangladesh, the reduction in mortality between 10 and 60 months of age was 36% although measles accounted only for 4% of all deaths among the controls . . . Thus measles immunization seems to be highly effective in preventing both acute and delayed mortality from the disease. (Aaby 1992: 167)

Aaby believed that what he learned from Guinea-Bissau and other developing countries sheds light on the historical decline of mortality in the West. He suggested that transmission factors, rather than improved nutrition (or age of infection), can best account for the decline of measles mortality in the developed world. In summing up his detailed argument he wrote:

> It seems likely that the most important causes of measles mortality decline were social changes which diminished the risk of intensive exposure within the family. Chief among these were the fall in family size [that is to say fewer susceptible siblings at home to infect] and greater social contact among young children which increased the risk [and benefits] of infection outside the home. Furthermore, the continual reduction in the numbers of fatal cases has reduced the risk of transmission of measles in a severe form [and thus eliminated the amplification effect]. (Aaby 1992: 170–1)

This conceptualization of the decline of measles mortality in terms of transmission rather than nutrition, Aaby believed, provides a model that can be used for other diseases as well. For example, he maintained that McKeown severely underestimated the importance of smallpox vaccination to the decline of mortality in the West, and he suggested that smallpox (which struck the well nourished and malnourished alike) may have had the same kind of delayed mortality effect as measles. Thus, people weakened by smallpox may have been more vulnerable to tuberculosis (TB) or other diseases. He speculated that the decline of smallpox may have led the way to the decline of TB, and the latter, McKeown maintained, was the key to the decline of mortality in the developed world (Aaby 1992: 178).

The significance for us of Aaby's work is that transmission factors such as severity of exposure, size of family, cross-sex infection, and delayed mortality were not discussed and then successfully eliminated by McKeown's analysis. Thus, it would seem that whether Aaby is right or wrong about other diseases, or even about the decline of measles in the West, he has made the point that McKeown's nutrition thesis is vulnerable and, perhaps, has been embraced too readily.

A second attack was made by Simon Szreter, a specialist in British history, who challenged McKeown's work not simply on its relevance to other countries but even on its accuracy for Great Britain. He stated his thesis very succinctly:

> It will be urged that the public health movement working through local government, rather than nutritional improvements through rising living standards, should be seen as the true moving force behind the decline of mortality in [the late nineteenth century]. (Szreter 1988: 2)

Szreter pointed out that although McKeown explicitly recognized the positive role that hygiene improvements in public-health measures involving municipal sanitation played in saving lives, he nevertheless maintained that "their impact and effects were . . . very much of a secondary and merely reinforcing kind" (Szreter 1988: 3) compared to better nutrition. It is interesting to note that Szreter believed that the effect of McKeown's emphasis on nutrition and his "devastating case against the pretension of the 'technocratic' section of the post-war medical profession" has led to the belief that "organized human agency in general had remarkably little to do with the historical decline of mortality in Britain . . ." (Szreter 1988: 3).[2]

This belief, in turn, led Szreter to criticize McKeown for his failure to carefully assess "the *independent* role of those socio-political developments which were responsible for such hard-won improvements as those in working conditions, housing, education, and various health services" (Szreter 1988: 11). Moreover, given McKeown's emphasis on the role of food it might have been expected that he would look closely at the history of the fight against food adulteration, but he did not. Rather, McKeown treated political, social, and cultural changes that were also arguably important in the mortality decline as a simple "automatic corollary of changes in a country's per capita real income" (Szreter 1988: 11).

According to Szreter, though, in the last third of the nineteenth century, after the "heroic age" of public-health activism in Britain had ended without much success on the national level, countless underpaid and overworked officials fought bitterly but successfully for better sanitation and increased disease prevention at the local level. There was nothing automatic about either their struggles or their victories – though historians, said Szreter, have missed the importance of such activities by focusing on the apparent ineffectiveness of the *national* sanitation reform movement during the middle decades of the nineteenth century and the decline of that movement after 1871 (Szreter 1988: 21–5).

McKeown, however, contended that the key to the decline of mortality in Britain was the decline of TB, which is caused by an airborne pathogen that does not respond to public-health measures but does respond to improved nutrition, and that, in any event, the decline of the disease predated effective medical or public-health measures. In addition, he alleged that TB was in decline before most other major diseases. This chronology is important, because if TB declined after public-health interventions, or if other diseases declined first, then those previous events, rather than improved nutrition, might account for the fall in TB mortality.

McKeown claimed that TB declined in Britain from 1838 onward (that is to say quite early). However, Szreter contended that there was actually a fluctuation in TB mortality, which rose once more after 1850 and did not decline again until after 1866–7. Moreover, Szreter, like Aaby, pointed out that smallpox mortality had declined considerably earlier than TB; thus,

even if tuberculosis had started to decline as early as 1838, McKeown would still have underestimated the possible effects of that prior decline on tuberculosis mortality (Szreter 1988: 15).

In addition, McKeown placed his emphasis on the decline in airborne diseases (as opposed to water- and foodborne diseases) because airborne diseases were not amenable to public-health interventions. Thus, their decline would seem to indicate an alternative source of amelioration. However, the airborne disease category that McKeown highlighted included not only TB, which did decline, but also a composite group – bronchitis, pneumonia, and influenza – that constituted the second most important cause of death in the mid–nineteenth century. That group of airborne diseases *increased* until after 1901, becoming the single most common cause of death and a greater killer than TB had been in 1850 (Szreter 1988: 13).

According to Szreter, one of the major effects of dividing the airborne diseases into two categories – TB and bronchitis/pneumonia/influenza – is that when the increased mortality of the latter group is set against the lower mortality of the former, it leaves the decline in food- and waterborne diseases as the most important reason for the decline of mortality, which does not support McKeown's argument. Yet Szreter pointed out that the almost complete elimination of smallpox, cholera, and typhoid during the late nineteenth century is proof of the effectiveness of public-health interventions, and that the rise of mortality for the bronchitis/pneumonia/influenza group "may well be evidence that in those areas . . . where preventive legislation and action was *not* forthcoming," problems occurred (Szreter 1988: 27). It is significant that clean air was an issue neglected by Victorian reformers, and the resulting urban smog probably goes far to help explain the high incidence of respiratory disease.

Szreter also indicated that infants did not benefit from the late-nineteenth-century decline of mortality in Britain; yet, after 1901, infant mortality fell rapidly. This reduction of infant mortality required the intervention of social services and the willingness of families to allow middle-class social workers to enter homes to instruct in hygienic food preparation (Szreter 1988: 28–31).

Thus, for Szreter, "[t]he invisible hand of rising living standards, conceived as an impersonal and ultimately inevitable by-product of general economic development, no longer takes the leading role as historical guarantor of the nation's mortality decline" (Szreter 1988: 34–5).

A third attack on the McKeown thesis comes from Leonard Wilson, an American historian. If Szreter argued that McKeown exaggerated the significance of the decline in TB mortality, Wilson directly challenged McKeown on the reason for TB's decline, which Wilson attributed not to improved nutrition but rather to segregation of those who had the disease.

In support of his position, Wilson highlighted a fact

that exposes one of the more glaring weaknesses in McKeown's argument: Tuberculosis was widespread among persons of the upper classes, who were, of course, the most likely to be well nourished. McKeown, however, claimed that despite adequate nutrition, their defenses were overwhelmed by constant contact with the lower classes – among whom the bacteria was ubiquitous. Wilson pointed out that the problem with this line of reasoning is that it acknowledges that the key to infection for the upper classes was their degree of exposure, which is one of the possible alternatives to the theory of improving nutrition (Wilson 1990). Thus, at the very least, the McKeown thesis turns out to be a dual theory of the decline of TB: a nutrition theory for the poor and an exposure theory for the rich, which seems to render the nutrition thesis considerably less persuasive.

The thesis that Wilson advanced is that the decline of TB mortality was closely linked to the degree to which individuals with TB were segregated during the periods they were most infectious. He argued that in Great Britain the provision of poor relief in workhouses (rather than at home) and the establishment of sanatoria led to a decline in the TB death rate compared to other societies that allowed infectious individuals to live freely in the community in close contact with their families. He contended that McKeown underestimated the importance of these segregating institutions because most individuals spent only limited time in them, and they did not cure individuals with the disease. But Wilson suggested that some segregation, although less helpful than a lot of separation, was still better than none and was sufficient to account for the declining mortality rate. The failure to cure tubercular individuals, although a tragedy for them, was less important than preventing transmission to others.

To test this thesis, Wilson compared the experience of a number of countries and ethnic groups. He found, for example, that Ireland experienced both declining food prices and rising incomes in the years after 1870, but experienced no significant decline in TB mortality.

Yet during the same period, Ireland did enjoy a decline in the typhus death rate, which no one claims was nutritionally related. Typhus-infected individuals were segregated and the contagion was controlled. By contrast, tuberculosis victims, after being reduced to poverty, as were almost all TB victims, were given home relief, which allowed them to live surrounded by family members whom they continued to infect. But in England, in contrast to Ireland, relief was restricted to poor-law infirmaries and workhouses, which kept infectious individuals out of the community and away from their families during the period when they were most intensively infectious. Those segregating institutions also taught the infected how to dispose of their sputum and lower the danger of spreading the infection when they were again free to go home (Wilson 1990: 384).

According to Wilson, before the advent of antibiotics, the segregation of contagious individuals was a necessity if diseases like TB or typhus were to be controlled. He pointed out that leprosy also declined, in both England and continental Europe, with the isolation of lepers. An exception, however, was Norway, where lepers were not segregated, and there the disease not only failed to decline but actually increased during the nineteenth century (Wilson 1990: 384–5).

Wilson accused McKeown of dismissing the importance of the discoveries of Koch and others in the decline of tuberculosis mortality because no therapies came out of those scientific breakthroughs for generations. Such a view, he asserted, ignores the fact that many nations and municipalities instituted segregation and isolation procedures soon after the cause of TB was discovered. For example, in New York City after 1889, the Health Department emphasized the danger of contagion and pushed for sanitary disposal of sputum, disinfection of rooms, and the opening of special hospitals for TB patients. Vigorous policing helped maintain the long and steady decline of tuberculosis in the city from 1882 to 1918, at which point three large TB hospitals were built.

Thus, Wilson argued that the decline in tuberculosis was not the result of a rising standard of living but rather of reduced opportunities for patients to spread the infection, and he pointed out that the recognition of the importance of segregation came directly from Koch's discoveries (Wilson 1990: 381).

In another study by Wilson, this time of tuberculosis in Minnesota, he was able to look directly at the effect of standard of living on the decline of the disease and to test the relationship between nutrition (or at least standard of living) and TB in a kind of "natural laboratory" which existed in that state.

For many decades, Minnesota had the reputation of having a remarkably healthy climate – with a very low tuberculosis rate. This changed as European immigrants reached the state, many of them suffering from the disease. The Irish immigrants had the highest rate – in keeping with conditions in their native land, where home relief allowed ill individuals to remain with their families. In Minnesota, the Irish still continued to live at home if infected and, consequently, infected their relatives. Scandinavian immigrants also had high rates of tuberculosis, as did the countries from which they came. However, German immigrants had a low rate of TB, similar to conditions in their homeland.

These different groups settled in Minneapolis, where their social and economic conditions were remarkably uniform. There was no major difference in their standard of living, only in their TB rates, which reflected their countries of origin, not their current conditions. What ultimately brought those rates down for the Irish and Scandinavians was not better food and housing but the decision to build sanatoria and segregate infectious individuals (Wilson 1992).

Thus, Wilson argued, McKeown ignored the key role played by public-health measures in lowering the TB death rate by finding the source of infection and working to prevent its transmission. Going beyond Szreter, Wilson suggested that medical men, from Koch down to doctors in the sanatoria, were vital elements in this process.[3]

The scholarly articles of Wilson, Szreter, and Aaby go a long way toward a successful undermining of the claims that McKeown has made about the pivotal role of nutrition in the decline of mortality in the West. Their arguments have been significantly advanced by the publication of Anne Hardy's book, *The Epidemic Streets: Infectious Disease and the Rise of Preventive Medicine, 1856-1900* (1993), a detailed study of disease in London during the last half of the nineteenth century. Hardy looked intensively at the history of eight major infectious diseases of the period (whooping cough, measles, scarlet fever, diphtheria, smallpox, typhoid, typhus, and tuberculosis) but did not restrict herself to the relatively superficial level of citywide sources. She focused instead on the district level, and on many occasions provided elaborate quantitative analyses of disease incidence street by street in particularly unhealthy areas. What she illustrated is the incredible complexity of the disease situation that broad-based national and city sources obscure. Hardy skillfully integrated quantitative and qualitative materials, and by doing so, enabled the reader to appreciate the immense amount of ambiguity and confusion involved in questions of disease etiology.

Hardy's discussion required her to investigate the myriad social, cultural, economic, political, and biological factors that influenced the morbidity and mortality rate for each disease. For example, tuberculosis rates were determined by the nature and location of housing, the extent of overcrowding, culturally shaped fears of fresh air, medical and folk-nursing practices, occupational hazards, class-based food preferences, and the synergistic effects of simultaneous infections – to name just a few.

Hardy also discussed "high risk" occupations in which workers were exposed to filth and foul air in closed and unventilated rooms. These included not only tailors and furriers but also such well-paid (and well-fed) workers as printers and clerks. The growth, decline, and geographic concentration of different trades directly influenced the local TB rates. Popular fears of fresh air and night chills led to nursing practices that kept the sick in closed rooms where family members were exposed to concentrated doses of pathogens. Ethnic groups in London (Jewish, Irish, Italian) differed in their cleanliness and general hygienic practices, and in methods of child rearing; this differentially affected their disease rates – independent of their generally inadequate incomes.

Hardy made it quite clear that before investigators can generalize about infectious disease in broad fashion, they must have a firm knowledge of the complexities and subtleties of the ways in which people actually live. In her work, Hardy did what professional historians are best at doing: puncturing those grand theories that social scientists and historical amateurs sometimes produce.

Of course, the confusion and ambiguity of real history is less intellectually satisfying than sweeping theories of cause and effect. Hardy's detailed discussions often make the reader cry out for simplicity and certainty, but neither history nor Hardy is able to oblige. Nevertheless, Hardy was willing to present some broad conclusions from her study. In looking at the major infectious diseases that afflicted the people of London, she commented:

> The epidemiological record clearly suggests ... that it was not better nutrition that broke the spiral of deaths from infectious disease after 1870, but intervention by the preventive authorities, together with natural modifications in disease virulence, which reduced exposure to several of the most deadly infections.... McKeown was a scientist speculating on historical phenomena, ... and [he was] unfamiliar ... with historical realities. (Hardy 1993: 292-3)

Like Szreter, Hardy found that the power of preventive medicine did not derive from national governmental policy but was rooted "in the persevering implementation of local measures based on local observation by a body of professional men whose sole responsibility was to their local community" (Hardy 1993: 292). As England's population was "above the critical threshold of under-nutrition below which resistance to infection is affected," it was consciously planned human intervention, not improved nutrition, that was the key to lower mortality rates (Hardy 1993: 292).

In summing up her survey of the eight major diseases she studied, Hardy pointed out the significant difference between those that affected children and those that affected adults. The latter were responsive to preventive actions, whereas the former were not. And it was among the adult diseases that the major drop in mortality in the late nineteenth century actually occurred:

> The impact of smallpox, typhoid and typhus, and (more arguably) of tuberculosis, was significantly reduced through the activities of the preventive administration ... The reduction in deaths from both typhoid and typhus through diligent local activity and public-health education was a major achievement of the Victorian preventive administration. And for tuberculosis, similarly, general sanitary improvements, in the sense of slum-clearances, new housing, constant water supplies, and the growing emphasis on domestic cleanliness, were probably important.

Environmental and occupational factors were clearly of considerable importance . . . and the Victorian evidence suggests that these were more potent . . . than . . . nutritionally satisfactory diet. (Hardy 1993: 290–1)

Hardy did not claim that her work ends the historical discussion of the role of nutrition in the decline of infectious disease in the West, but she has clearly moved the debate to a higher level by demonstrating, as did Szreter, that accurate knowledge of infectious disease requires intensive study of local materials.

Investigators of the modern developing world have also contributed to the search for explanations of mortality declines other than that of a rising standard of living and improved nutrition. John Caldwell, for example, has argued for the importance of "cultural, social and behavioral determinants of health" in the developing world (Caldwell 1993: 125). He reported on a major 1985 conference that looked closely at a group of health "success stories," in which poor countries achieved high life expectancy rates despite severely limited resources (for example, the Indian state of Kerala [66 years; per capita income $160–270], Sri Lanka [69 years; $320], Costa Rica [74 years; $1,430], China [67 years; $310]). The conference organizers concluded that "the exercise of 'political will'" by China, and of both "political and social will" by Kerala, Sri Lanka, and Costa Rica were keys to their success. They placed their "emphasis on comprehensive and accessible health programmes with community involvement and the importance of education, especially female schooling" (Caldwell 1993: 126).

Caldwell carried out additional analysis of the conference material, combined it with other data from high-achieving/low-income countries, and found that the strongest correlation with reduced mortality was the educational level of women of maternal age. He contended that the most efficacious of the noncommunist countries have benefited from a historical "demand for health services and education, especially the all-important schooling of girls, arising from the long-existing nature of the societies, particularly the independence of their women, [and] an egalitarian-radical-democratic tradition . . ." (Caldwell 1993: 126). These positive factors, however, although ultimately vital, could not bear fruit until modern health services became available: "When health services arrived here and elsewhere mortality fell steeply because of a symbiotic relationship between an educated independent population determined to use them and make them work, and readily available health services" (Caldwell 1993: 126).

Caldwell concluded from his research that mortality levels similar to those of industrial societies could be reached in the developing world within two decades if all children were educated through elementary school. Education and modern medicine interact as a potent combination. Thus, if Caldwell and

his colleagues provided no direct evidence to undermine McKeown's claim that the standard of living and nutrition was the key to the decline of mortality in the West, they nevertheless undercut his argument for the relevance of such a notion for the developing world today.[4]

Clearly, Szreter, Caldwell, Wilson, and Aaby were not in agreement as to the reasons for either past or present declines in mortality. But they did agree on the conclusion that the importance of nutrition and rising standards of living has been substantially overstated. Each one of them provided a provocative and plausible alternative explanation that was either unknown to McKeown and his supporters or given insufficient attention. The work of these researchers and others (Christopher Murray and Lincoln Chen 1993) has kept alive the debate over the role of improving nutrition in the decline of mortality in the West.

William Muraskin

Notes

1. McKeown made a number of exceptions, such as smallpox, polio, and diphtheria antitoxin. However, he claimed that most of the decline in mortality resulted from lower rates of other diseases, especially tuberculosis, which did not have a vaccine or drug therapy until comparatively late.

2. Szreter said that the belief that the public-health movement in Britain had little effect on mortality is even accepted by British historians of public health. Interestingly enough, he believed that the McKeown thesis is clearly not relevant to other countries but only to Britain, and, thus, he does not discuss the "grander" McKeown thesis. He based his view on the work of Samuel H. Preston, whose work, dealing with countries other than Britain, he considered definitive (see, for example, Preston 1975). Szreter characterized Preston's position by saying that "it has been upward shifts in the level of medical technology and services available and the successful introduction of public health measures which has been markedly more significant than rising per capita incomes [i.e., general standard of living] . . . in accounting for their falling levels of mortality" (Szreter 1988: 4).

   Preston's views have not had as far-reaching an effect on the general view of the issue as Szreter believed. In fact, his key research was published in the 1970s, *before* the McKeown thesis became the established view. This is not to say that it is not useful for a critique of McKeown, but only that it has not been as successfully used for that purpose as Szreter believed.

3. Wilson's argument flies in the face of much of the new research on tuberculosis presented in such studies as Linda Bryder's *Below the Magic Mountain: A Social History of Tuberculosis in Twentieth-Century Britain* (1988) and Francis Smith's *The Retreat of Tuberculosis, 1850–1950* (1988). However, most of that work was written under the influence of the McKeown thesis and has a strong antimedicine and anti-public-health (at least insofar as it was represented by sanatoria) emphasis. Interestingly enough, however, Smith saw segregation of infectious individuals in English workhouses as important in the decline of tubercu-

losis – just as Wilson did. Nancy Tomes, in her excellent review of the new tuberculosis literature, commented on the tendency to ignore the importance of the new bacteriological research in creating the concept of disease communicability and preventability. It was, she said, also medical science that created the tuberculin test, a tool that made the tracking of TB possible, thus permitting contemporaries to discover the social and economic conditions that favored the spread of the disease (see Tomes 1989).

4. Whereas Caldwell suspected that maternal education would also explain the decline of mortality in the West during the early twentieth century, he accepted the work of Preston as proving that to be untrue. For Caldwell, the reason for the difference between the West and the developing world was that sufficient effective health knowledge and practical applications to counteract the effects of broad economic forces were simply not available to educated mothers. Fortunately, such knowledge was available for the developing world after World War II. Caldwell was especially impressed with the power of education to convince people that they can and should collaborate to reduce mortality. Such education is "essentially Western education, and it carries a powerful Western pro-science message" that overcomes many of the indigenous beliefs that prevent effective action by parents.

Bibliography

Aaby, Peter. 1992. Lessons for the past: Third World evidence and the re-interpretation of developed world mortality decline. *Health Transition Review* 2 (Supplementary issue): 155–83.
Bryder, Linda. 1988. *Below the magic mountain: A social history of tuberculosis in twentieth-century Britain*. New York.
Caldwell, John. 1993. Health transition: The cultural, social and behavior determinants of health in the Third World. *Social Science and Medicine* 36: 125–35.
Hardy, Ann. 1993. *The epidemic streets: Infectious disease and the rise of preventive medicine, 1856-1900*. Oxford.
McKeown, Thomas. 1976. *The modern rise of population*. New York.
  1979. *The role of medicine: Dream, mirage or nemesis*. Princeton, N.J.
Muraskin, William. 1995. *The war against hepatitis B: A history of the International Task Force on Hepatitis B Immunization*. Philadelphia, Pa.
Murray, Christopher, and Lincoln Chen. 1993. In search of a contemporary theory for understanding mortality change. *Social Science and Medicine* 36: 143–55.
Preston, Samuel. 1975. The changing relation between mortality and level of economic development. *Population Studies* 29: 231–48.
Smith, Francis. 1988. *The retreat of tuberculosis, 1850-1950*. New York.
Szreter, Simon. 1988. The importance of social intervention in Britain's mortality decline c. 1850-1914: A re-interpretation of the role of public health. *Social History of Medicine* 1: 1–37.
Tomes, Nancy. 1989. The white plague revisited. *Bulletin of the History of Medicine* 63: 467–80.
Wilson, Leonard. 1990. The historical decline of tuberculosis in Europe and America: Its causes and significance. *Journal of the History of Medicine and Allied Sciences* 43: 366–96.
  1992. The rise and fall of tuberculosis in Minnesota: The role of infection. *Bulletin of the History of Medicine* 66: 16–52.

VI.3 ❧ Infection and Nutrition: Synergistic Interactions

The interactions of malnutrition and infection are synergistic, with each modifying the other in ways that cannot be predicted from studying just one condition or the other (Scrimshaw, Taylor, and Gordon 1968). The superimposed infection is more likely to be responsible for nutritional disease than a shortage of food alone. During recovery from infectious disease, however, the quantity and quality of food available is usually the limiting factor. Moreover, the frequency and severity of infections is increased for individuals whose nutritional status is poor. Although this increase depends in part on the social and environmental circumstances frequently associated with malnutrition, more important is the reduced resistance to infection directly associated with nutrient deficiency. This chapter examines the reasons why diseases are often more common and severe in the malnourished and discusses the metabolic and other functional consequences of infections.

Nutrition and Disease Morbidity and Mortality

The high frequency of diarrheal and respiratory diseases among young children in developing countries is both a major contributor to malnutrition and a consequence of lowered immunity in a poor sanitary environment combined with unsatisfactory personal hygiene (Mata 1978; Guerrant et al. 1983; Black, Brown, and Becker 1984). Furthermore, in both developing and industrialized countries, nosocomial infections (those originating in hospitals) are responsible for worsening the nutritional status of patients and thereby increasing overall morbidity and case fatality rates (Gorse, Messner, and Stephens 1989; Scrimshaw 1989).

In children whose nutritional status is poor, episodes of any of the common communicable diseases of childhood tend to be more severe and to have more secondary complications. In Guatemala, 50 percent of children with whooping cough require more than 12 weeks, and 25 percent more than 25 weeks, to recover the weight lost because of the disease (Mata 1978). In addition, there is recent evidence for a striking reduction of mortality after vitamin A supplementation was given to populations of underprivileged children in Indonesia (Sommer, Tarwotjo,

Table V1.3.1. *108 Acute infections among 32 children ages 2 to 9 years observed in a "model" convalescent home in Guatemala City for 90 days*

Disease	Total no. of episodes
Infectious hepatitis	2
Measles	2
Bronchopneumonia	3
Bronchial asthma and asthmatic bronchitis	15
Gastroenteritis	5
Amebiasis	9
Parotitis	4
Chicken pox	3
Gonococcal vaginitis	11
Purulent otitis media	4
Acute tonsillitis	7
Upper respiratory infection	15
Fever of unknown origin	9
Urinary infection	1
Impetigo and cellulitis	13
Skin allergy	5

Source: Unpublished INCAP data.

Hussaini et al. 1983, Sommer, Tarwotjo, Djunaedi et al. 1986) and India (Rahmathullah et al. 1990) and, in general, to poorly nourished children who acquire measles (Barclay, Foster, and Sommer 1987; Hussey and Klein 1990; Coutsoudis et al. 1992).

Even under relatively favorable institutional conditions, morbidity rates for children or the elderly can be very high. Table VI.3.1 lists 108 infections over a 90-day period among 32 well-fed children 2 to 9 years old in late recovery from malnutrition in a model convalescent home in Guatemala City (unpublished data from the Institute of Nutrition of Central America and Panama [INCAP], Guatemala City, Guatemala). Similar reports have come from orphanages in other countries. Under the less favorable conditions of open pediatric wards in developing countries, cross-infections among children are increased by low resistance and add to the duration of morbidity and to mortality rates.

Malnutrition, Infection, and Growth

Many studies confirm a reciprocal relationship between morbidity from diarrhea and other infectious diseases and growth (e.g., in the Gambia, Rowland, Cole, and Whitehead 1977; in Uganda, Cole and Parkin 1977; in Mexico, Condon-Paloloni et al. 1977; in Bangladesh, Black et al. 1984; in Sudan, Zumrawi, Dimond, and Waterlow 1987). Significant negative correlation of young child growth with diarrheal and other infections is a constant finding (e.g., Kielman, Taylor, and Parker 1978; Lutter et al. 1989; Martorell, Rivera, and Lutter 1990). In children whose nutritional status is marginal, measles will strongly reduce growth in ensuing weeks (in India, Reddy et al. 1986;

in Kenya, Duggan and Milner 1986; in Guatemala, Mata 1978). Even immunizations can affect the growth of poorly nourished children (Kielman et al. 1978). However, in the Guatemalan, Colombian, and Mexican studies, the negative effect of diarrhea on growth was prevented by a nutritious supplement. Thus, when the diet is adequate, the impact of acute infections on growth is usually transient (Lutter et al. 1989).

The Impact of Malnutrition on Resistance to Infection

It appears that every known nutrient deficiency can affect disease resistance if it is sufficiently severe, and this is also true for many nutrient excesses. A review of the logarithmic increase in research on nutrition and immunity clearly reveals that the same common mechanisms are affected by many different nutrients. The main mechanisms are still those identified in the 1968 World Health Organization (WHO) monograph, *Interaction of Nutrition and Infection* (Scrimshaw et al. 1968). These include physical barriers that depend on epithelial and other tissue integrity; phagocytosis; cell-mediated immunity; some forms of nonspecific resistance; and antibody formation. Recent advances in immunologic research and understanding have greatly enhanced knowledge of the mechanism of nutritional effects on both humoral and cell-mediated immunity.

One class of lymphocytes, the B cells, develop immunoglobulins or antibodies as integral proteins on their surface. The immunoglobulins are divided into five classes, A, D, E, G, and M, which vary in their susceptibility to nutritional deficiencies. Some lymphocytes function as memory cells for the production of large numbers of specific antibody-containing cells when the host is exposed to subsequent challenge or infection of the same kind. There is evidence that large numbers of these memory cells are attracted by the mammary gland when the mother develops an infection and contribute appropriate antibodies to breast milk (Hansen 1992).

Cell-mediated immunity offers a number of different stages in T-cell differentiation and function that can be affected by nutrient deficiencies. Both B cells and T cells recognize antigens and other mitogens, but the latter do not secrete antibodies. Some T cells have helper or suppressor cell functions through membrane surface receptors. Another subpopulation is that of the natural killer (NK) cells that function even before the other T cells respond and that can lyse particular cells without being previously sensitized. NK cells may be activated by interferon and influenced by eicosanoid-derived essential fatty acids (Byham 1991). The proliferation of both T and B cells in response to mitogens is impaired with various deficiencies that may include that of vitamin B_6 in the elderly (Meydani et al. 1990).

Humoral Immunity

Humoral immunity is lost in kwashiorkor (Olarte, Cravioto, and Campos 1956; Budiansky and da Silva 1957; Reddy and Srikantia 1964; Brown and Katz 1966), but once dietary treatment is initiated, antibody formation is restored (Pretorius and de Villiers 1962). M. G. Wohl, J. G. Reinhold, and S. B. Rose (1949) studied the antibody response to typhoid immunization in a Philadelphia hospital and found a markedly slower response in adult patients with albumin levels below 4.0 grams (g) per 100 milliliters (ml) and an improvement when those patients were given a protein supplement. R. E. Hodges and colleagues demonstrated conclusively that severe pantothenic acid and pyridoxine deficiency can interfere with antibody response to typhoid antigen, but it required a combination of deficient diets and metabolic antagonists to each of the vitamins (Hodges et al. 1962a, 1962b). Correcting the deficiencies returned the responses to normal. In experimental animals, it has been shown that sufficiently severe deficiencies of almost any essential nutrient can interfere with antibody formation (Scrimshaw et al. 1968). Although few of these experimental studies have public-health significance in human populations, they may be relevant to patients with metabolic and neoplastic disease and to some therapeutic regimens.

Phagocytosis

Phagocytic cells include both circulating leukocytes and the fixed macrophages in the reticuloendothelial system. A reduced phagocytic response with severe protein malnutrition was documented in the previously mentioned WHO monograph (Scrimshaw et al. 1968), but no other nutrients were mentioned in this regard. The phagocytic response in marasmus was reported to be normal, presumably because in marasmus (but not in kwashiorkor) amino acids are mobilized from skeletal muscle and are available for protein synthesis. Since 1968, much has been learned about nutritional interference with phagocyte function. Table VI.3.2 lists the

Table VI.3.2. *Antimicrobial systems in the neutrophil*

Oxygen dependent	Oxygen independent
Myeloperoxidase dependent MPO plus halide plus H_2O_2	Acid environment Cationic proteins
Myeloperoxidase independent	Lactoferrin
Hydrogen peroxide (H_2O_2)	Lysosomal hydrolases
Hydroxyl radical (OH·)	Lysozyme proteases
Singlet oxygen ($^1O_2$)	Neutral proteases
Superoxide anoin (O_2·)	Sequestration of phagocytic vacuole

Source: Stinnet (1983).

antimicrobial systems that have been identified in the neutrophil (Stinnett 1983). Phagocytes contain a collection of neutral proteases and lysozyme, an enzyme that hydrolyzes bacterial walls, as well as lactoferrin. Most of these mechanisms for killing infectious agents have been found susceptible to deficiency of one or more specific nutrients.

Delayed Cutaneous Hypersensitivity

The delayed cutaneous hypersensitivity response is a sensitive indicator of poor nutritional status. It is based on a combination of sequential processes involving sensitization of T lymphocytes against a macrophage-processed antigen, the production of soluble mediators (lymphokines), and an inflammatory response when sensitized T cells recognize and interact with an intradermally injected antigen. Lymphokines released at the local site produce the dermal induration characteristic of the response.

Children with a subnormal rate of growth due to protein deficiency show an impaired delayed hypersensitivity response to tuberculin (Jayalakshmi and Gopalan 1958; Harland 1965; Chandra 1972, 1977; Neumann, Stiehm, and Swenseid 1977). This is illustrated in Figure VI.3.1, in which serum transferrin serves as an indicator of protein depletion (Chandra and Newberne

Figure VI.3.1. Cutaneous delayed hypersensitivity to 5 t.u. tuberculin related to serum transferrin concentration in patients with pulmonary tuberculosis. A positive Mantoux test, induration 10 mm, was generally observed in individuals with serum transferrin level of ≥ 162 mg. Patients studied through the courtesy of Dr. H. B. Dingley, Tuberculosis Hospital, New Delhi. (From Chandra and Newberne 1977.)

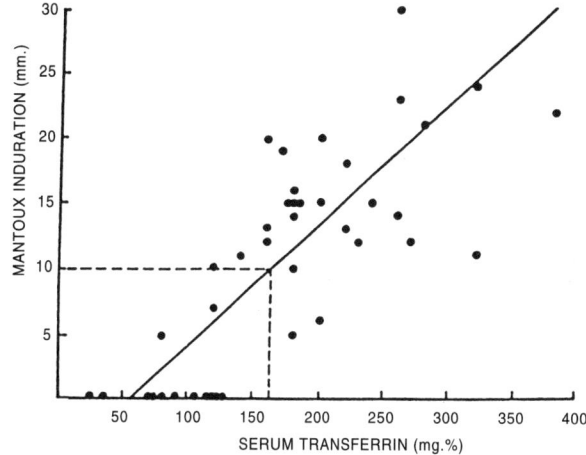

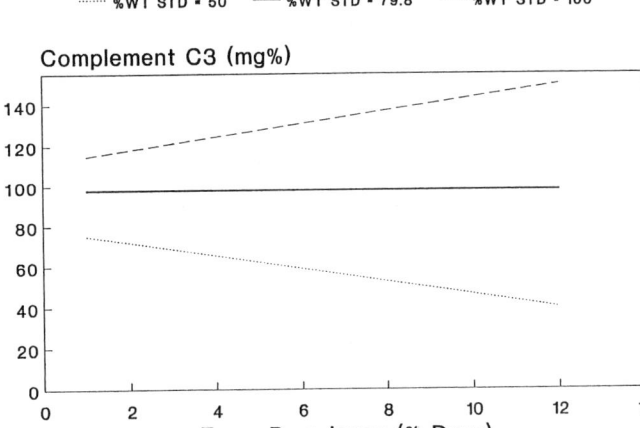

Figure VI.3.2. Serum C3 levels correlated with infection-morbidity indicated by the number of days of fever. Three weight categories in reference to the standard are shown. In well-nourished children, C3 concentration increases with infection. In the undernourished, C3 levels generally decrease. (From Kielman et al. 1976.)

1977). The failure to produce a response in malnourished children with the strong sensitizing agents 2,4-dinitrochlorobenzene and 2,4-dinitroflurobenzene has been reported by many authors (e.g., Smythe et al. 1971; Feldman and Gianantonio 1972; Chandra 1974; Schlesinger and Stekel 1974; Dutz et al. 1976; Smith et al. 1977). The case is similar with malnourished adults (Law, Dudrick, and Abdou 1973). Patients with iron-deficiency anemia also have a reduced delayed cutaneous hypersensitivity (Joynson et al. 1972).

Complement

Complement is a heat-labile opsonin in normal serum that can promote the lysis of other cells. It is a system of 17 protein compounds in two different pathways that sequentially activate specific proteases that deposit complement-3 on a particle to make it capable of being phagocytositized or lysed (Stinnett 1983). Complement-3 is susceptible to protein–energy deficiency (Sirisinha et al. 1973; Chandra 1975; Suskind et al. 1976; Neumann et al. 1977). Figure VI.3.2 presents data from India relating complement response to percentage of standard weight (Kielman et al. 1976).

Iron Withholding

Although, as indicated previously, iron deficiency is associated with increased morbidity and mortality from infections, it is a paradox that biological mechanisms for withholding iron from infectious agents appear to be an important means of inhibiting their replication. Both circulating transferrin and lactoferrin released by macrophages have an affinity for iron that is greater than that of bacterial sideophores. With infection, a rapid transfer of circulating iron to an intracellular compartment is mediated by the cytokine interleukin (Keusch 1990).

Other Mechanisms

Although included for completeness, nutritionally induced changes in tissue integrity are least important in explaining increased susceptibility to infection.

Nevertheless, epithelial tissues and mucous membranes are barriers to the direct penetration of infectious agents. Examples are the dermatosis associated with kwashiorkor and pellagra, the spongy gums of scurvy, and the epithelial lesions of vitamin A deficiency. When the skin is affected, the epithelial layers of the respiratory and intestinal tracts are usually also affected. Wound healing, fibroblast response, and collagen formation are other processes affected.

The clearest evidence that intestinal flora play a role in resistance to some infections is the decrease of Escherichia coli infections among breast-fed infants (Ross and Dawes 1954; Gyllenberg et al. 1957; György, Dhanamitta, and Steers 1962). Endocrine changes, whether the result of nutritional or other causes, can also affect any of the aforementioned resistance mechanisms.

Antagonisms between Nutrient Deficiencies and Infections

The 1968 WHO monograph (Scrimshaw et al.) reported 40 studies in experimental animals in which diets that were severely deficient in one or more B vitamins inhibited infections, compared with 70 in which similar diets worsened them. In 14 studies examining low-protein diets, antagonism was observed and compared with 94 in which synergism was the outcome. The 3 studies that involved iron deficiency reported a synergism between iron deficiency and hookworm in rats, dogs, and cats. Because the degree of deficiency in human populations always seemed to be associated with synergism, these reports of antagonism between malnutrition and infection in some experimental studies were not deemed to be important to public health.

There have, however, been studies that reported giving large doses of iron to severely iron-deficient children with kwashiorkor (McFarlane et al. 1970; Murray et al. 1978b) and to severely anemic refugees in Somalia (Bullen 1976; Murray et al. 1978a), which resulted in overwhelming infections. Moreover, the principle of withholding an essential nutrient from an infectious agent or a tumor cell underlies modern antibiotic therapy and chemotherapy.

How Infections Worsen Nutritional Status

Anorexia

Even when efforts are made to maintain a constant food intake during illness, anorexia will generally lead to a consistent decrease in food consumption even with infections as mild as that produced by immunization against yellow fever (Gandra and Scrimshaw 1961). Anorexia reduces the intake not only of protein and calories but also of most other nutrients. This effect contributes to precipitating clinically evident deficiencies of any nutrients that are already limiting.

Cultural and Therapeutic Practices

When young children experience febrile infections and diarrhea there is a strong tendency of the caregiver to withdraw solid food. Commonly, a thin starchy or sugary gruel that is low in protein and energy density is substituted (Hoyle, Yunus, and Chen 1980; Khan and Ahmad 1986). In field studies it is not possible to separate the effects of anorexia from those of deliberate withdrawal of food for cultural reasons. R. Martorell and C. Yarborough (1983) described an average reduction of 19 percent in dietary energy intake with various infections in Guatemalan children. Intakes were consistently less in children with diarrhea than in those without at all periods from 15 to 60 weeks (Mata et al. 1977; Martorell, Yarborough, et al. 1980; Martorell, Rivera, et al. 1990). Energy intakes in children under 5 years of age in Bangladesh were more than 40 percent less during acute diarrhea than after recovery (Hoyle et al. 1980). In Peru they decreased from 10 to 86 percent among breast-fed children with diarrhea (Bentley et al. 1991).

Despite a decrease in both intake and absorption of nutrients due to anorexia accompanying an infection, these losses are very much less than when food is withheld (Chung 1948; Chung and Viscorova 1948). Although consumption of food is reduced by anorexia, purposeful withholding of food may have a much greater impact. The clinical and public-health lesson is that food should not be withdrawn during diarrheal and other infections.

Malabsorption

In addition to the decrease in food intake with diarrhea, protein absorption is commonly reduced by 10 to 30 percent and occasionally by as much as 40 percent. A. W. Chung and B. Viscorova (1948) reported that the absorption of nitrogen in four children with diarrhea varied from 40 to 74 percent, and absorption of fat varied from 39 to 67 percent. Data from the International Center for Diarrheal Disease Research, Bangladesh (ICDDRB), on patients with diarrhea due to rotavirus show average absorption rates of 43 percent for nitrogen, 42 percent for fat, 74 percent for carbohydrate, and 55 percent for total energy. Slightly higher averages are managed by patients with diarrhea due to enteropathogenic E. coli and Shigella (Molla et al. 1982). E. D. Moyer and M. C. Powanda (1983) have summarized additional literature indicating a range of malabsorption for subjects with diarrhea of about 40 percent for proteins, 23 to 50 percent for fats, and 73 to 77 percent for carbohydrates. The high incidence of diarrheal disease in young children makes this malabsorption especially important for them.

Bacterial, viral, and protozoan enteritides cause similar malabsorption, as do intestinal parasites such as hookworm, fish tapeworm, ascaris, and Strongyloides, and it is also observed in systemic disorders such as measles, tuberculosis, malaria, and streptococcal infections. The mechanisms of malabsorption with these infections include shortened intestinal transit time, physical blocking of mucosal surfaces, and mesenteric blood flow.

Some children with acute diarrheal disease of nonspecific origin develop a persistent carbohydrate intolerance and experience a much more severe and prolonged nutritional deficit (Rosenberg and Scrimshaw 1972). In addition, between 30 percent and 50 percent of individuals living in an unsanitary environment in warm climates develop tropical jejunitis with chronic changes in the intestinal epithelium that include flattening of the villi and loss of microvilli (Klipstein and Falaiye 1969; Keusch, Plaut, and Troncale 1970; Bayless, Swanson, and Wheby 1971; Lindenbaum, Harmon, and Gerson 1972). This phenomenon undoubtedly occurs in most developing countries, which include Haiti (Klipstein et al. 1968), India (Gorbach et al. 1970; Baker 1972), Thailand (Sprinz et al. 1962; Keusch 1972), Bangladesh (Lindenbaum, Gerson, and Kent 1971), Colombia (Ghitis, Tripathy, and Mayoral 1967; Mayoral et al. 1967), and Puerto Rico (Lugo-de-Rivera, Rodriguez, and Torres-Pinedo 1972). In addition, I. Rosenberg, N. W. Solomons, and R. E. Schneider showed in 1977 that most rural Guatemalans had reduced absorption of protein and carbohydrates.

Catabolic Losses

A catabolic response occurs with *all* infections, even when they are subclinical (Beisel 1972, 1975, 1977; Beisel and Wannemacher 1980; Keusch and Farthing 1986). This is true even for yellow fever immunizations (Gandra and Scrimshaw 1961) and asymptomatic Q-fever infections (Beisel 1977). Once an infection is established, the breakdown of skeletal muscle protein begins and alanine and glutamine are synthesized and transported to the liver, where they are used for gluconeogenesis. This process occurs whether or not the infection causes fever. Increased losses of vitamin A, B-vitamins, ascorbic acid, and iron are also observed.

The stimulus for these changes comes from the release of interleukin-1 when macrophages break down, and from the resulting endocrine changes (Wannemacher 1977). More than two-thirds of the negative nitrogen balance of a young man with tularemia was due to this metabolic response, and the remainder to a spontaneous decrease in food intake (Beisel et al. 1967). Even an individual with completely asymptomatic Q fever can have an increasingly negative cumulative nitrogen balance for as long as 21 days (Beisel 1977).

Anabolic Losses

There is a marked increase in nitrogen retention following chicken pox, despite only a modest decrease in retention during the period of the rash (Wilson, Bressani, and Scrimshaw 1961). During an infection, amino acids are diverted from normal pathways for the synthesis of immunoglobulins, lymphokines, C-reactive proteins, and a variety of other proteins, including key liver enzymes (Wannemacher 1977). This diversion accounts for the finding that the extra nitrogen retained during the recovery period in metabolic balance studies exceeds that accounted for by the magnitude of the negative balance measured during the acute phase of an infection.

Fever

Whatever its benefits in increasing resistance to infection-induced disease, fever has a metabolic cost. The regulation of normal body temperature within a narrow range is a complex phenomenon. It is modified by the endogenous pyrogenic activity of interleukin-1 released by mononuclear leukocytes in response to infection. The resulting fever increases the basal metabolic rate 13 percent for each rise in temperature of 1 degree Celsius (DuBois 1937). During a period of high fever, metabolism may increase by nearly one-third. There is a relationship between basal metabolic rate and temperature measured in various infections. The increase varies between 30 and 60 percent for a 3-degree rise.

Additional Intestinal Losses

Although difficult to measure separately from malabsorption, a significant contributor to malnutrition in some infections is the direct loss of nutrients into the gut. Protein-losing enteropathy has been described for measles (Axton 1975; Dosseter and Whittle 1975; Sarker et al. 1986), diarrhea (Waldman 1970; WHO 1980; Rahaman and Wahed 1983), and especially shigellosis (Rahaman, Alam, and Islam 1974). Alpha 1-antitrypsin is a simple and useful quantitative marker for estimating the loss of protein into the gut in diarrheal disease (Rahaman and Wahed 1983), and it should be used for this purpose in studying the effects of other kinds of infections.

In ICDDRB studies, nearly two-thirds of patients with enterotoxigenic *E. coli* (ETEC) and 40 percent of those with rotavirus diarrhea were also found to have an excessive loss of protein in the feces (Molla et al. 1983). Between 100 and 500 ml of serum was lost in the feces each day by shigellosis patients due to protein-losing enteropathy. Bleeding into the intestine from *Schistosoma mansoni* (hookworm) also represents a loss of energy, iron, and other nutrients.

Reduced Growth and Weight Loss

As described earlier, children subjected to frequent infections and borderline diets show reduced growth. The result is a decrease in nutrient requirements that is proportionately larger for protein than for dietary energy. This loss is because the requirement for average daily growth of a 2-year-old child is about 12 percent of the total protein requirement, only about 2 percent of total energy needs. The savings from growth impairment are generally not sufficient to avoid actual weight loss, an almost inevitable consequence of infection.

Infectious Diseases and Nutrient Requirements

Bacterial, Viral, and Protozoal Infections

As already emphasized, the metabolic consequences of systemic infections depend not on the specific causative organism but rather on a common sequence of metabolic events.

Parasitic Infections

As an acute febrile illness, malaria has the same consequences as other acute systemic infections (Barr and DuBois 1918; McGregor 1982; Tomkins et al. 1983). This is also true for febrile episodes associated with toxoplasmosis, onchocerciasis, leishmaniasis, and trypanosomiasis. However, there may be additional local effects from parasitic infections. Reduced intestinal absorption of nitrogen can occur in malaria as a consequence of reduced mesenteric blood flow (Migasena and Mae-Graith 1969). Anemia is a common sequel to *Plasmodium falciparum* infection and to a lesser extent in the other malaria types (McGregor et al. 1966), which is due in part to an increased iron loss because of hemolysis. Immunologic destruction of unparasitized erythrocytes may also occur (Zuckerman 1966).

Giardia lamblia has been well documented as a common cause of chronic malabsorption, including wasting, hypoalbuminemia, diarrhea, steatorrhea (Chauduri 1943; Amini 1963; Solomons 1982), and malabsorption of fats and carbohydrates (Veghelyi 1938; Palumbo, Scudmore, and Thompson 1962; Kluska 1972; Riis 1975; Khosla, Sharma, and Srivastava 1978). Poor absorption of vitamin A is seen in giardiasis (Chesney and McCoord 1934; Katsampes, McCowd, and Phillips 1944; Mahalanabis et al. 1979). Several investigators have reported evidence of ileal malabsorption of vitamin B_{12} as a result of this infection (Peterson 1957; Antia et al. 1966; Notis 1972). Low serum folate levels in patients with *Giardia* infections have also been described.

Intestinal helminths, such as ascaris (Venkatachalam and Patwardhan 1953; Tripathy et al. 1972; Gupta et al. 1977; Brown et al. 1980; Taren et al. 1987), hookworm (Layrisse et al. 1964), *Strongyloides* (Milner et al. 1965; O'Brien 1975; Carvalho Filho 1978), *Trichuris* (Jung and Beaver 1951; Layrisse et al. 1967), and heavy infections of *Trichocephalus,* may also reduce intestinal absorption of protein and other nutrients (Crompton 1986). Careful metabolic balance studies generally fail to detect a significant effect of mild to moderate worm burdens on intestinal absorption, although appetite may be reduced (Bray 1953; Kotcher et al. 1966; El-Mawla, Abdallah, and Galil 1966). Vitamin A malabsorption has been described with ascariasis (Sivakumar and Reddy 1972). *Ascaris* and *Chlonorichis* can also cause biliary and pancreatic obstruction (Rosenberg and Bowman 1982).

Of the hookworms, *Necator americanus* causes a loss of about 0.03 ml of blood per worm per day (Roche et al. 1957a, 1957b; Roche and Perez-Gimenez 1959), whereas *Ancylostoma duodenale* causes a 5 to 10 times greater blood loss per worm (Farid et al. 1965). Although approximately half of the iron is reabsorbed (Roche and Perez-Gimenez 1959; Giles, Watson Williams, and Ball 1964), the loss in heavily infected patients ranged from 14 to 45 ml of blood per day. Surprisingly, even with severe hookworm anemia, adequate dietary iron can fully compensate for these losses without removal of the worms. L. S. Stephenson, D. W. T. Crompton, M. C. Latham, and colleagues (1980) described growth impairment with *Ascaris* infection, and, later, Stephenson, Latham, K. M. Kurz, and colleagues (1989) showed that active antihelminth treatment improved the growth of Kenyan schoolchildren with combined hookworm, trichuris, and ascaris infection.

The massive bleeding from the intestinal tract, sometimes seen in *Schistosoma mansoni,* may require surgical intervention. This parasite can also obstruct lymphatic return and thereby interfere with fat absorption. Other reported nutritional consequences of heavy *S. mansoni* infections in human clinical studies include daily loss of albumin, zinc, and vitamin A; elevated fecal fat and glucose intolerance; and subnormal levels of serum carotene (Waslien, Farid, and Darby 1973). Most of the protein in the blood entering the gut due to intestinal bleeding in hookworm infection is reabsorbed, but in heavily infected patients, increased fecal protein loss may occur (Blackman et al. 1965). Individuals with *Schistosoma hematobium* lose blood in the urine and are also at increased risk of iron deficiency.

Because of their aggregate bulk, some parasites compete with the host for some of the nutrients essential to both. Where the Scandinavian custom of consuming marinated raw freshwater fish persists, massive infection of the fish tapeworm *Diphyllobothrium latum* is associated with megaloblastic anemia due to competition for vitamin B_{12} (Von Bonsdorff

1948, 1956, 1964). This effect (and that of *G. lamblia*) may also partially be caused by hypochlorhydria or achlorhydria in the stomach (Hoskins et al. 1967), which interferes with vitamin B_{12} absorption.

Effects of Infections on Specific Nutrients

Protein
All of the mechanisms for the impact of infection worsen protein status, and as a result, clinical protein deficiency is often precipitated in individuals whose nutritional status is borderline. Powanda (1977) has summarized data for a wide variety of acute infectious diseases in adults by adding the total nitrogen losses and dividing them by the number of days over which these losses occurred. For all infections, the average loss of 0.6 grams of protein per kilogram per day (g/kg/day) is equal to the mean estimated protein requirement for adults. Diseases associated with diarrhea or dysentery produced an average protein loss of 0.9 g/kg/day. Higher losses were observed with typhoid fever and other severe infections, reaching 1.2 g/kg/day.

Measurements of the catabolic response in infection using urinary 3-methylhistidine as a measure of muscle protein catabolism in the septic patient suggest an average additional protein loss in the urine during sepsis to be the equivalent to 1.14 g/kg/day (Long et al. 1977). None of these calculations include energy expended for the multiple anabolic responses or make allowances for dietary change or for nutrient malabsorption.

Both metabolic and field observations suggest that even with an optimum diet, it may take two to three times longer to replete than to deplete an individual. If the diet is not sufficient for a maximum rate of recovery, daily improvement is correspondingly reduced and the time required for complete recovery increased. The more severe and closely spaced the episodes of infection, the more likely that full recovery will not occur and that the adverse effects will become cumulative.

Infections are likely to precipitate clinical protein deficiency in children whose nutritional status is borderline. Diarrhea is reported from many countries to be the most common contributory cause of kwashiorkor (Scrimshaw et al. 1968). This is the case even when the episode is not necessarily severe, because it may be only the latest in a long series of diarrheal, respiratory, and other infections that are progressively depleting, when there is neither sufficient food nor time for complete recovery between episodes. Kwashiorkor has been reported to follow measles, chicken pox, German measles, whooping cough, and other common communicable diseases of childhood. Measles has a particularly strong impact on nutritional status, causing a sharp drop in serum albumin (Dosseter and Whittle 1975), lean body mass (unpublished data from Fernando Viteri, Institute of Nutrition of Central America and Panama [INCAP], Guatemala City, Guatemala), and growth rates (Mata 1978).

Table VI.3.3. *Intake of calories in acute state (A), and 2 weeks (R₁) and 8 weeks (R₂) after recovery (mean ± SD)*

Etiology	A	R_1	R_2
Cholera	74.9 ± 36.20	111.1 ± 35.4	109.59 ± 31.7
Rotavirus	68.5 ± 22.6	87.2 ± 26.2	115.0 ± 20.2
ETEC	70.7 ± 37.9	90.97 ± 28.4	114.9 ± 19.0
Shigella	70.0 ± 28.2	100.5 ± 27.8	109.3 ± 18.8

Source: Molla et al. (1983).

Energy

Obviously, the severity of an energy deficit is related to the duration and magnitude of malabsorption in each individual situation; rarely does such a condition pose a major threat to nutrition unless infection is chronic or recurrent. For most respiratory diseases the energy cost is minimal, but for diarrheal diseases and the common communicable diseases of childhood, it can add significantly to a chronic energy deficit. Food intake is observed to drop during acute infection and then to increase during recovery to above normal levels if the diet is sufficient. Table VI.3.3 shows the large increase in caloric intake during convalescence from diarrhea in Bangladesh when a good diet is available ad libitum (Molla et al. 1983).

Vitamin A

Vitamin A blood levels are appreciably reduced in pneumonia, rheumatoid arthritis, acute tonsillitis, and infectious hepatitis (May et al. 1940; Shank et al. 1944; Harris and Moore 1947; Jacobs et al. 1954). Vitamin A is not normally found in the urine but does appear there in at least some infectious diseases (Moore 1957; Goldsmith 1959). Lower serum carotene and vitamin A levels have been reported with hookworm disease (Rodgers, Dhir, and Hosain 1960).

The capacity of infections to precipitate xerophthalmia and keratomalacia in individuals already marginally deficient in vitamin A is well established (Oomen 1959; McLaren 1963; Sommer 1982; Sommer et al. 1983; Sommer, Katz, and Tarwotjo 1984; Stanton et al. 1986; Tielsch et al. 1986; De Sole, Belay, and Zegeye 1987). The effect is particularly severe with measles (Sommer et al. 1984). A significant drop in serum vitamin A levels has been observed in children with acute respiratory infection, gastroenteritis, and measles; levels return to normal after recovery (National Institute of Nutrition 1980).

The adverse effect of intestinal parasitic infections on vitamin A absorption has already been described. Enteric infections of bacterial and viral origin also have this effect (Nalin et al. 1980; West and Sommer 1985), as do systemic febrile illnesses (Heymann 1936; Shank et al. 1944; Lala and Reddy 1970; Sivakumar and Reddy 1975). B. Sivakumar and V. Reddy (1972) reported that only 30 to 70 percent of ingested vitamin A is absorbed by children with acute diarrhea and respiratory infections. Although infec-

tion clearly impairs both dietary carotene and vitamin A absorption (West, Howard, and Sommer 1989), sufficient amounts of supplementary vitamin A can still be absorbed orally for effective treatment of corneal xerophthalmia.

Ascorbic Acid

Ascorbic acid levels decrease in plasma and increase in the urine of infected individuals compared to noninfected persons living under comparable conditions. This is seen even with the common cold and with immunization against smallpox and measles (Scrimshaw et al. 1968; Hume and Weyers 1973). Historically, infections are associated with the onset of florid scurvy in individuals already on a borderline diet (Scrimshaw et al. 1968).

B-Vitamins

The classic nutritional diseases of beriberi and pellagra, caused respectively by deficiencies of thiamine and niacin, were known to be precipitated in vulnerable individuals by a variety of infections. This finding is of more than historical interest because alcoholics frequently consume diets low in B-vitamins, and infections increase the likelihood of clinically significant deficiencies of the B complex. Given the frequency with which infections occur in indigent alcoholics, physicians treating them should be aware of this connection. W. R. Beisel and colleagues (1972) have reported a marked increase in riboflavin excretion with infection.

Minerals

Iron. When anemia is present at the time of an infection (or even moderate iron deficiency without anemia) a number of normal resistance mechanisms are compromised. Impaired processes include phagocytic killing power; delayed cutaneous hypersensitivity, T-cell proliferation, and T-killer cell activity; and if the anemia is sufficiently severe, impaired antibody formation.

Yet when individuals compromised in this way are given parenteral iron or large doses of oral iron the result may be an overwhelming infection, as described for children with kwashiorkor (Baker et al. 1981; Lynch et al. 1984; Picciano, Weingartner, and Erdman 1984; Beard et al. 1988) and for severely malnourished adults (Murray et al. 1975, 1978a, 1978b; Barry and Reeve 1977; Bercroft, Dix, and Farmer 1977; Weinberg 1978, 1984). This occurs because the infective agent is supplied with iron before the host immune system has had time to recover. However, field studies have shown that iron fortification (supplementation of poorly nourished adults with up to 100 milligrams [mg] of iron daily, and proportionately less for children) always results in *decreased* morbidity from infectious disease (Scrimshaw 1990b).

Copper and zinc. Careful metabolic studies by C. Castillo-Duran, P. Vial, and R. Uauy (1988) have documented the impact of diarrhea on zinc and copper status. Metabolic balances of the minerals were strongly negative during the period of acute diarrhea, compared with strongly positive balances in the control subjects. During the recovery period, zinc balances became positive (405.3 ± 20.4 mg/kg/day), but copper balance remained negative, although less so (-21.5 ± 46.7 mg/kg/day).

The mechanism for the loss is wastage from the gastrointestinal tract through malabsorption and excessive endogenous losses. Since the normal state for the growing infant is net retention of these minerals, the true magnitude of such losses is somewhat greater. Clearly, the inevitable combination of reduced oral intake and increased fecal losses of minerals should be taken into account in the management of prolonged diarrhea. These losses cannot be predicted from serum levels because copper levels often increase during infections as a result of stimulation of the hepatic production of cerruloplasm (Kampschmidt et al. 1973).

It is noteworthy that in a study by R. F. Kampschmidt and colleagues (1973) serum copper levels were significantly lower in diarrhea cases than in control cases. Conversely, plasma zinc levels often decline during acute infections because of an internal redistribution of the metal to the liver. The reduced retention of zinc during diarrhea thus interacts with the redistributional influence of the infection. On the basis of this study, it is reasonable to suggest that treatment regimens for diarrhea should contain supplemental amounts of copper and zinc, but whether this addition would make a detectable difference in therapeutic results remains to be demonstrated.

Nutrient Allowances for Infectious Disease Morbidity

Although it is important to provide a nutritious diet and encourage adequate nutrient intakes during an acute infection, some decrease resulting from anorexia is almost inevitable, and it is generally useless to attempt to increase food intake *during* illness. For the multiple reasons discussed in this chapter, persons are normally depleted to a greater or lesser degree during an infection. However, during the *recovery* period, there is a metabolic window in which appetite is increased and the rate of retention, at least for protein, may be as much as nine times the average daily requirement.

A 1979 United Nations University report calculated that a malnourished 1-year-old child depleted by an infectious episode lasting 7 days would need approximately 136 kilocalories (kcals) (569 kilojoules [kjoules]) per kilogram per day, and 2.56 grams of protein per kilogram per day, for repletion in 30 days. It should be noted that the same weight deficit without infection would have required less than one-third the amount of protein per kilogram per day but approximately the same amount of energy. Despite

clear evidence of the heavy burden of infection on the populations of developing countries, and the increased nutrient needs above normal requirement levels during convalescence from episodes of infectious disease, this issue is not dealt with quantitatively in national and international recommended nutrient allowances. The comment of a "Consultation on Energy and Protein Requirements" (FAO/WHO/UNU 1985) is illustrative of such vagueness: "[T]he increased requirement average of a population of school children would not be large." The report goes on to emphasize the need for preventing infections, rather than simply meeting increased requirements for recovery resulting from them. This emphasis is important but not helpful to the hundreds of thousands of children in developing countries whose diets are already deficient or borderline.

R. G. Whitehead (1977) recommended a 30 percent increase in energy and a 100 percent increase in protein to optimize nutritional repletion of young children depleted by infection. This recommendation is consistent with data summarized by Powanda (1977) and N. S. Scrimshaw (1977). Moyer and Powanda (1983) discuss the basis for significantly increased nutrient requirements during convalescence without arriving at quantitative recommendations. However, a task force report (Rhode et al. 1983) utilizing this and other information concluded that children should be offered 50 percent more than their usual diet for two to four times the duration of the illness *or* fed extra food daily until the weight prior to illness is regained or exceeded. Unfortunately, the diet of most infants and young children (and some adults) in developing countries is commonly too marginal to permit repletion before another episode of infection further depletes the individual.

The *energy* cost of depositing a gram of protein is estimated to be 24 kcal (100 kjoules), or about 6 kcal (25 kjoules) of total weight gain (United Nations University 1979). If this figure is applied to the observed protein losses previously summarized, average energy losses suggest a loss from this source alone of between 4 and 5 kcals (17 to 21 kjoules) per kilogram per day. This would correspond to 14, 22, and 29 kcal (59, 92, and 121 kjoules) per kilogram in children or adults. This loss appears to be minor, but it represents from 14 to 29 percent of the requirements of a 1-year-old child.

The energy cost of growth of children recovering from protein–energy malnutrition was found to be in the range of 4 to 5 kcal (17 to 21 kjoules) per gram of weight gain, with 40 percent of this amount considered to be fat tissue and 60 percent protein tissue (Jackson, Picou, and Reeds 1977). The energy cost of synthesizing a gram of lost protein is 7.5 kcal (31 kjoules) per gram and for replacing a gram of fat 11.6 kcal (49 kjoules). During the recovery period, this loss must be made up, together with deficits arising from malabsorption, infection-stimulated catabolism, and internal synthesis in reaction to infection. Such an increase in energy requirement during the convalescent period is difficult to quantify, however, because it is so variable.

Summary

The interactions of malnutrition and infection in human populations are almost always synergistic in the sense that each worsens the other. Deficiencies of protein, iron, and vitamin A are particularly likely to be responsible for an increase in morbidity and mortality from infectious diseases in underprivileged young children. In hospitalized patients, malnutrition often contributes to the severity of nosocomial infections. Mechanisms for increased susceptibility to infection with malnutrition include altered tissue integrity, impaired antibody formation, and many aspects of cell-mediated and nonspecific immunity. These include T-cell proliferation, killer T cells, helper T cells, complement C-3, phagocytic killing power, immunoglobulins G and E, delayed cutaneous hypersensitivity, and other parameters of cell-mediated immunity. Although iron deficiency interferes with several of these parameters of cell-mediated immunity, it can impair replication of some infectious agents. Severely iron-deficient individuals should receive supplementary iron to restore immunity, but never in high doses.

The mechanisms whereby systemic infections worsen nutritional status include anorexia, cultural withdrawal of solid food, increased metabolic losses, decreased intestinal absorption, and internal diversion of nutrients for immune proteins. The practical significance of these effects depends on the prior nutritional status of the individual, the diet during the infection, and the adequacy of the diet for prompt recovery. Intestinal parasitic infections, when sufficiently heavy, interfere with absorption of nutrients and have a variety of additional adverse effects that depend on their specific nature. Individuals who live in environments with frequent enteric infections develop chronic intestinal mucosal changes that impair nutrient absorption. Food intake should be maintained to the extent possible during an infection despite anorexia, and then increased during the convalescent period.

Nevin S. Scrimshaw

Bibliography

Amini, F. 1963. Giardiasis and steatorrhoea. *Journal of Tropical Medicine and Hygiene* 66: 190-2.

Antia, F. P., H. G. Desai, K. N. Jeejeebhoy, et al. 1966. Giardiasis in adults. Incidence symptomatology and absorption studies. *Indian Journal of Medical Sciences* 20: 471-7.

Axton, J. H. M. 1975. Measles: A protein-losing enteropathy. *British Medical Journal* 3: 79-80.

Baker, E. C., G. C. Mustakas, J. W. Erdman, Jr., and L. T. Black. 1981. The preparation of soy products with different levels of native phytate for zinc availability studies. *Journal of the American Oil Chemists Society* 58: 541-3.

Baker, S. J. 1972. Tropical sprue. *British Medical Bulletin* 28: 87-91.

Barclay, A. J. G., A. Foster, and A. Sommer. 1987. Vitamin A supplements and mortality related to measles: A randomised clinical trial. *British Medical Journal* 1: 1067-8.

Barr, D. P., and E. F. DuBois. 1918. Clinical calorimetry XXVII: The metabolism in malarial fever. *Archives of Internal Medicine* 21: 627-58.

Barry, D. M. J., and A. W. Reeve. 1977. Increased incidence of gram-negative neonatal sepsis with intramuscular iron administration. *Pediatrics* 60: 908-12.

Bayless, T. M., V. L. Swanson, and M. S. Wheby. 1971. Jejunal histology and clinical status in tropical sprue and other chronic diarrheal disorders. *American Journal of Clinical Nutrition* 24: 112-16.

Beard, J. L., C. M. Weaver, S. R. Lynch, et al. 1988. The effect of soybean phosphate and phytate content on iron availability. *Nutrition Research* 8: 345-52.

Beisel, W. R. 1972. Interrelated changes in host metabolism during generalized infectious illness. In *Malabsorption and nutrition,* ed. I. Rosenberg and N. S. Scrimshaw, 1254-60. Bethesda, Md.

1975. Metabolic response to infection. *Annual Review of Medicine* 26: 9-20.

1976. The influence of infection or injury on nutritional requirements during adolescence. In *Nutritional requirements in adolescence,* ed. J. McKigney and H. N. Munro. Cambridge, Mass.

1977. Magnitude of the host nutritional response to infection. *American Journal of Clinical Nutrition* 30: 1236-47.

Beisel, W. R., Y. F. Herman, H. E. Sauberlich, et al. 1972. Experimentally induced sandfly fever and vitamin metabolism in man. *American Journal of Clinical Nutrition* 25: 1165.

Beisel, W. R., W. D. Sawyer, E. D. Ryll, and D. Crozier. 1967. Metabolic effects of intracellular infections in man. *Annals of Internal Medicine* 67: 744-79.

Beisel, W. R., and R. W. Wannemacher. 1980. Gluconeogenesis, ureagenesis, and ketogenesis during sepsis. *Journal of Parenteral and Enteral Nutrition* 4: 277-85.

Bentley, M. E., R. Y. Stallings, M. Fukumoto, and J. A. Elder. 1991. Maternal feeding behavior and child acceptance of food during diarrhea, convalescence, and health in the Central Sierra of Peru. *American Journal of Public Health* 81: 43-7.

Bercroft, D. M. O., M. R. Dix, and K. Farmer. 1977. Intramuscular iron-dextran and susceptibility of neonates to bacterial infections. *Archives in Diseases of Childhood* 52: 778-81.

Black, R. E., K. H. Brown, and S. Becker. 1984. Effects of diarrhea associated with specific enteropathogens on the growth of children in rural Bangladesh. *Pediatrics* 73: 799-805.

Blackman, V., R. D. Marsden, J. Banwell, and M. H. Cragg. 1965. Albumin metabolism in hookworm anaemias. *Transactions of the Royal Society of Tropical Medicine and Hygiene* 59: 472-82.

Bray, B. 1953. Nitrogen metabolism in West African children. *Proceedings of the Nutrition Society* 7: 3-13.

Brown, K. H., R. H. Gilman, M. Khatum, and M. G. Ahmed. 1980. Absorption of macronutrients from a rice-vegetable diet before and after treatment of ascariasis in children. *American Journal of Clinical Nutrition* 33: 1975-82.

Brown, R. E., and M. Katz. 1966. Failure of antibody production to yellow fever vaccine in children with kwashiorkor. *Tropical and Geographic Medicine* 18: 125-8.

Budiansky, E., and N. N. da Silva. 1957. Formação de anticorpos na distrofia pluricarencial hidropigenica. *Hospital* 52: 251.

Bullen, J. J. 1976. Acute diarrhoea in childhood. In *Ciba Foundation Symposium*, 149-62. Amsterdam.

Byham, L. D. 1991. Dietary fat and natural killer cell function, *Nutrition Today* 1: 31-6.

Carvalho Filho, E. 1978. Strongyloidiasis. *Clinics in Gastroenterology* 7: 179-200.

Castillo-Duran, C., P. Vial, and R. Uauy. 1988. Trace mineral balance during acute diarrhea in infants. *Journal of Pediatrics* 113: 452-7.

Chandra, R. K. 1972. Immunocompetence in undernutrition. *Journal of Pediatrics* 81: 1194-200.

1974. Rosette-froming T lymphocytes and cell-mediated immunity in malnutrition. *British Medical Journal* 3: 608-9.

1975. Serum complement and immunoconglutin in malnutrition. *Archives in Diseases of Childhood* 50: 225-9.

1977. Cell-mediated immunity in fetally and postnatally malnourished children from India and Newfoundland. In *Malnutrition and the immune response*, ed. R. Suskind, 111-15. New York.

Chandra, R. K., and P. M. Newberne. 1977. *Nutrition, immunity and infection: Mechanisms of interactions.* New York.

Chauduri, R. N. 1943. A note on giardiasis with steatorrhea. *Indian Medical Gazette* 78: 284-5.

Chesney, J., and A. B. McCoord. 1934. Vitamin A of serum following administration of Haliver oil in normal children and in chronic steatorrhea. *Proceedings of the Society of Experimental Biology* 31: 87.

Chung, A. W. 1948. The effect of oral feeding at different levels on the absorption of food stuffs in infantile diarrhea. *Journal of Pediatrics* 33: 1-13.

Chung, A. W., and B. Viscorova. 1948. The effect of early oral feeding versus early oral starvation on the course of infantile diarrhea. *Journal of Pediatrics* 33: 14-22.

Cole, T. J., and J. M. Parkin. 1977. Infection and its effect on the growth of young children: A comparison of the Gambia and Uganda. *Transactions of the Royal Society of Tropical Medicine and Hygiene* 71: 196-8.

Condon-Paloloni, D., J. Cravioto, F. E. Johnston, et al. 1977. Morbidity and growth of infants and young children in a rural Mexican village. *American Journal of Public Health* 67: 651-6.

Coutsoudis, A., P. Kiepiela, M. Broughton, and H. M. Coovadia. 1992. Nutritional and immunological consequences of measles treated with vitamin A or placebo in young African children. In *Nutrition and immunology*, ed. R. K. Chandra, 143-62. St. John's, Newfoundland, Canada.

Crompton, D. W. 1986. Nutritional aspects of infection. *Transactions of the Royal Society of Tropical Medicine and Hygiene* 80: 697-705.

De Sole, G., Y. Belay, and B. Zegeye. 1987. Vitamin A deficiency in southern Ethiopia. *American Journal of Clinical Nutrition* 45: 780-4.

Dinarello, C. A. 1984. Interleukin-1 and the pathogenesis of the acute-phase response. *New England Journal of Medicine* 311: 1413-18.

Dosseter, J. F. B., and H. C. Whittle. 1975. Protein-losing enteropathy and malabsorption in acute measles enteritis. *British Medical Journal* 2: 592-3.

DuBois, E. F. 1936. *Basal metabolism in health and disease.* Philadelphia, Pa.

1937. *The mechanism of heat loss and temperature regulation.* Stanford, Calif.

Duggan, M. B., and R. D. G. Milner. 1986. Composition of weight gain by Kenyan children during recovery from measles. *Human Nutrition, Clinical Nutrition* 40C: 173-83.

Dutz, W., E. Rossipal, H. Ghavami, et al. 1976. Persistent cell mediated immune deficiency following infantile stress during the first 6 months of life. *European Journal of Pediatrics* 122: 117.

El-Mawla, N. G., A. Abdallah, and N. Galil. 1966. Studies on the malabsorption syndrome among Egyptians. 5. Faecal fat and D-xylose absorption tests in patients with ascariasis and taeniasis. *Journal of the Egyptian Medical Association* 49: 473.

FAO/WHO/UNU. 1985. *Energy and protein requirements.* Technical Report Series 724. Geneva.

Farid, Z., J. H. Nichols, S. Bassily, and A. R. Schulert. 1965. Blood loss in pure *Ancylostoma duodenale* infection in Egyptian farmers. *American Journal of Tropical Medicine and Hygiene* 14: 375.

Feldman, G., and C. A. Gianantonio. 1972. Aspectos immunologicos de la desnutrición en el niño. *Medicina* 32: 1-9.

Gandra, Y. R., and N. S. Scrimshaw. 1961. Infection and nutritional status. II. Effect of mild virus infection induced by 17-D yellow fever vaccine on nitrogen metabolism in children. *American Journal of Clinical Nutrition* 9: 159-63.

Ghitis, J., K. Tripathy, and G. Mayoral. 1967. Malabsorption in the tropics. II. Tropical sprue versus primary protein malnutrition: Vitamin B_{12} and folic acid studies. *American Journal of Clinical Nutrition* 20: 1206-11.

Giles, H. M., E. J. Watson Williams, and P. A. J. Ball. 1964. Hookworm infection and anaemia. *Quarterly Journal of Medicine* 33: 1-24.

Goldsmith, G. A. 1959. *Nutritional diagnosis.* Springfield, Ill.

Gorbach, S. L., J. G. Banwell, B. Jacobs, et al. 1970. Tropical sprue and malnutrition in West Bengal. I. Intestinal microflora and absorption. *American Journal of Clinical Nutrition* 23: 1545-58.

Gorse, G. J., R. L. Messner, and N. D. Stephens. 1989. Association of malnutrition with nosocomial infections. *Infection Control and Hospital Epidemiology* 10: 194-203.

Guerrant, R. L., L. V. Kirchoff, D. S. Shields, et al. 1983. Prospective studies on diarrheal illness in northeastern Brazil: Patterns of disease, nutritional impact, etiologies, and risk factors. *Journal of Infectious Diseases* 148: 986-97.

Gupta, M. C., S. Mithal, K. L. Arora, and B. N. Tandon. 1977. Effect of periodic deworming on nutritional status of ascaris infected pre-school children receiving supplementary food. *Lancet* 2: 108-10.

Gyllenberg, H., and P. Roine (with H. Unkila and M. Rossander). 1957. The value of colony counts in evaluating the abundance of 'Lactobacillus' bifidus in infant feces. *Acta Pathology Microbiology Scandinavica* 41: 146.

György, P., S. Dhanamitta, and E. Steers. 1962. Protective

effects of human milk in experimental staphylococcus infection. *Science* 137: 338.

Hansen, L. A. 1992. Immunity of breast feeding. In *Nutrition and immunology,* ed. R. K. Chandra, 45–62. St. John's, Newfoundland, Canada.

Harland, P. S. E. G. 1965. Tuberculin reactions in malnourished children. *Lancet* 1: 719–21.

Harris, A. D., and T. Moore. 1947. Vitamin A in infective hepatitis. *British Medical Journal* 1: 553.

Heymann, W. 1936. Absorption of carotene. *American Journal of Diseases in Childhood* 51: 273–83.

Hodges, R. E., W. B. Bean, M. A. Ohlson, and R. E. Bleiler. 1962a. Factors affecting human antibody response. III. Immunologic responses of men deficient in pantothenic acid. *American Journal of Clinical Nutrition* 11: 85.

    1962b. Factors affecting human antibody response. IV. Pyridoxine deficiency. *American Journal of Clinical Nutrition* 11: 180.

Hoskins, L. C., S. J. Winawer, S. A. Broitman, et al. 1967. Clinical giardiasis and intestinal malabsorption. *Gastroenterology* 53: 265–79.

Hoyle, B., M. Yunus, and L. C. Chen. 1980. Breast feeding and food intake among children with acute diarrhoeal disease. *American Journal of Clinical Nutrition* 33: 2365–71.

Hume, R., and E. Weyers. 1973. Changes in leucocyte ascorbic acid during the common cold. *Scottish Medical Journal* 18: 3.

Hussey, G. D., and M. Klein. 1990. A randomized, controlled trial of vitamin A in children with severe measles. *New England Journal of Medicine* 323: 160–4.

Jackson, A. A., D. Picou, and P. J. Reeds. 1977. The energy cost of relating tissue deficits during recovery from a protein energy malnutrition. *American Journal of Clinical Nutrition* 30: 1514–17.

Jacobs, A. L., Z. A. Leitner, T. Moore, and I. M. Sharman. 1954. Vitamin A in rheumatic fever. *Journal of Clinical Nutrition* 2: 155.

Jayalakshmi, V. T., and C. Gopalan. 1958. Nutrition and tuberculosis. I. An epidemiological study. *Indian Journal of Medical Research* 46: 87–92.

Joynson, D. H. M., A. Jacobs, D. M. Walker, and A. E. Dolby. 1972. Defect of cell-mediated immunity in patients with iron-deficiency anaemia. *Lancet* 2: 1058–9.

Jung, R. C., and P. C. Beaver. 1951. Clinical observations on *Tricocephalus trichiurus* (whipworm) infestation in children. *Pediatrics* 8: 548–57.

Kampschmidt, R. F., H. F. Upchurch, C. L. Eddington, and L. A. Pulliam. 1973. Multiple biological activities of partially purified leukocytic endogenous mediator. *American Journal of Physiology* 224: 530–3.

Katsampes, C. P., A. B. McCowd, and W. A. Phillips. 1944. Vitamin A absorption test in cases of giardiasis. *American Journal of Diseases of Children* 67: 189–93.

Keusch, G. T. 1972. Subclinical malabsorption in Thailand. I. Intestinal absorption in Thai children. *American Journal of Clinical Nutrition* 25: 1062–6.

    1990. Immunity and infection in iron deficiency. In *Functional significance of iron deficiency,* ed. C. O. Enwonwu, 81–92. Nashville, Tenn.

Keusch, G. T., and M. J. G. Farthing. 1986. Nutrition and infection. *Annual Review of Nutrition* 6: 131–54.

Keusch, G. T., A. G. Plaut, and F. J. Troncale. 1970. The interpretation and significance of the xylose tolerance test in the tropics. *Journal of Laboratory and Clinical Medicine* 75: 558.

Khan, M. U., and K. Ahmad. 1986. Withdrawal of food during diarrhoea; major mechanisms of malnutrition following diarrhoea in Bangladesh children. *Journal of Tropical Pediatrics* 32: 57–61.

Khosla, S. N., S. V. Sharma, and S. C. Srivastava. 1978. Malabsorption in giardiasis. *American Journal of Gastroenterology* 69: 694–700.

Kielman, A. A., C. E. Taylor, and R. L. Parker. 1978. The Narangwal nutrition study: A summary review. *American Journal of Clinical Nutrition* 31: 2040–52.

Kielman, A. A., I. S. Uberoi, R. K. Chandra, and V. L. Mehra. 1976. The effect of nutritional status on immune capacity and immune responses in preschool children in a rural community in India. *WHO Bulletin* 54: 477–83.

Klipstein, F. A., and J. M. Falaiye. 1969. Tropical sprue in expatriates from the tropics living in the continental United States. *Medicine* 48: 475–91.

Klipstein, F. A., I. M. Samloff, G. Smarth, and E. A. Schenk. 1968. Malabsorption and malnutrition in rural Haiti. *American Journal of Clinical Nutrition* 21: 1042.

Kluska, J. 1972. Carbohydrate absorption disorders in the course of lambliosis. *Wiadomosci Parazytologiczne* 18: 43–55.

Kotcher, E., M. Miranda, R. Esquivel, et al. 1966. Intestinal malabsorption and helminthic and protozoan infections in the small intestine. *Gastroenterology* 50: 366.

Lala, V. R., and V. Reddy. 1970. Absorption of beta-carotene from green leafy vegetables in undernourished children. *American Journal of Clinical Nutrition* 23: 110–13.

Law, D. K., S. J. Dudrick, and N. I. Abdou. 1973. Immunocompetence of patients with protein–caloric malnutrition. *Annals of Internal Medicine* 79: 545–50.

Layrisse, M., L. Aparcedo, C. Martinez-Torres, and M. Roche. 1967. Blood loss due to infection with *Trichuris trichura. American Journal of Tropical Medicine and Hygiene* 16: 613–19.

Layrisse, M., N. Blumenfeld, L. Carbonell, et al. 1964. Intestinal absorption tests and biopsy of the jejunum in subjects with heavy hookworm infection. *American Journal of Tropical Medicine and Hygiene* 13: 2.

Lindenbaum, J., C. D. Gerson, and T. H. Kent. 1971. The recovery of small intestinal structure and function after residence in the tropics. I. Studies in Peace Corps volunteers. *Annals of Internal Medicine* 74: 218.

Lindenbaum, J., J. W. Harmon, and C. D. Gerson. 1972. Subclinical malabsorption in developing countries. *American Journal of Clinical Nutrition* 25: 1056–61.

Long, C. L., W. R. Schiller, W. S. Blakemore, et al. 1977. Muscle protein ataboism in the septic patient as measured by 3-methylhistidine excretion. *American Journal of Clinical Nutrition* 30: 1349–52.

Lugo-de-Rivera, C., H. Rodriguez, and R. Torres-Pinedo. 1972. Studies on the mechanism of sugar malabsorption in infantile infectious diarrhea. *American Journal of Clinical Nutrition* 25: 1248–53.

Lutter, C. K., J. O. Mora, J. P. Habicht, et al. 1989. Nutritional supplementation: Effects on child stunting because of diarrhea. *American Journal of Clinical Nutrition* 50: 1–8.

Lynch, S. R., J. L. Beard, S. A. Dassenko, and J. D. Cook. 1984. Iron absorption from legumes in humans. *American Journal of Clinical Nutrition* 40: 42–7.

Mahalanabis, D., T. W. Simpson, M. L. Chakraborty, et al. 1979. Malabsorption of water miscible vitamin A in children with giardiasis and ascariasis. *American Journal of Clinical Nutrition* 32: 313–18.

Martorell, R., J. Rivera, and C. K. Lutter. 1990. Interaction of diet and disease in child growth. In *Breastfeeding, nutrition, infection, and infant growth in developing and emerging countries,* ed. S. A. Atkinson, L. A. Hanson, and R. K. Chandra, 307-21. St. John's, Newfoundland, Canada.

Martorell, R., and C. Yarborough. 1983. The energy cost of diarrheal diseases and other common illnesses in children. In *Diarrhea and malnutrition: Interactions, mechanisms, and interventions,* ed. L. D. Chen and N. S. Scrimshaw, 125-42. New York.

Martorell, R., C. Yarborough, S. Yarborough, and R. E. Klein. 1980. The impact of ordinary illnesses on the dietary intakes of malnourished children. *American Journal of Clinical Nutrition* 33: 345-50.

Mata, L. J. 1978. *The children of Santa Maria Cauque: A prospective field study of health and growth.* Cambridge, Mass.

Mata, L. J., R. A. Kromal, J. J. Urrutia, and B. Garcia. 1977. Effect of infection on food intake and the nutritional state: Perspectives as viewed from the village. *American Journal of Clinical Nutrition* 30: 1215-27.

May, C. D., K. D. Blackfan, J. F. McCreary, and F. H. Allen, Jr. 1940. Clinical studies of vitamin A level. *Journal of the American Medical Association* 123: 1108.

Mayoral, L. G., K. Tripathy, F. T. Garcia, et al. 1967. Malabsorption in the tropics: A second look. I. The role of protein malnutrition. *American Journal of Clinical Nutrition* 20: 866-83.

McFarlane, H., S. Reddy, K. J. Adcock, et al. 1970. Immunity, transferring and survival in kwashiorkor. *British Medical Journal* 4: 268-70.

McGregor, I. A. 1982. Malaria: Nutritional implications. *Review of Infectious Disease* 4: 798-803.

McGregor, I. A., K. Williams, W. Z. Billewicz, and A. M. Thomson. 1966. Hemoglobin concentration and anaemia in young West African (Gambian) children. *Transactions of the Royal Society for Tropical Medicine and Hygiene* 60: 650-67.

McLaren, D. S. 1963. *Malnutrition and the eye.* New York.

Meydani, S. N., J. D. Ribaya-Mercado, R. Russell, et al. 1990. The effect of vitamin B-6 on the immune response of healthy elderly. In *Micronutrients and immune functions,* ed. A. Bendich and R. J. Chandra. *Annals of the New York Academy of Science* 587: 303-6. New York.

Migasena, P., and B. G. MaeGraith. 1969. Intestinal absorption in malaria. I. The absorption of an amino acid (AIB-1-^{14}C) across the gut membrane in normal and plasmodium knowlesi-infected monkeys. *Annals of Tropical Medical Parasitology* 63: 439.

Milner, P. F., R. A. Irvine, C. J. Barton, et al. 1965. Intestinal malabsorption in *Strongyloides stercoralis* infestation. *Gut* 6: 574.

Molla, A., A. M. Molla, A. Rahim, et al. 1982. Intake and absorption of nutrients in children with cholera and rotavirus reinfection during diarrhoea and after recovery. *Nutrition Research* 2: 232-42.

Molla, A. M., A. Molla, S. A. Sarker, and M. M. Rahaman. 1983. Food intake during and after recovery from diarrhea in children. In *Diarrhea and malnutrition: Interactions, mechanisms, and interventions,* ed. L. D. Chen and N. S. Scrimshaw, 113-23. New York.

Moore, T. 1957. *Vitamin A.* London.

Moyer, E. D., and M. C. Powanda. 1983. Diarrhea and nutrient requirements. In *Diarrhea and malnutrition: Interactions, mechanisms, and interventions,* ed. L. C. Chen and N. S. Scrimshaw, 161-76. New York.

Murray, M. J., A. B. Murray, C. J. Murray, and M. B. Murray. 1975. Refeeding-malaria and hyperferraemia. *Lancet* 1: 653-4.

1978a. The certain adverse effect of iron repletion on the course of certain infections. *British Medical Journal* 2: 1113-15.

1978b. Diet and cerebral malaria: The effect of famine and refeeding. *American Journal of Clinical Nutrition* 31: 57-61.

Nalin, D. R., R. Russell, H. Greenberg, and M. M. Levine. 1980. Reduced vitamin A absorption after enteric infections. In *Current chemotherapy and infectious disease.* Proc. 11th CC 19th ICAAC American Society of Microbiology, 947-8. Washington, D.C.

National Institute of Nutrition. 1980. Effect of infection on serum vitamin A levels. In *Annual report,* 79-82. Hyderabad, India.

Neumann, C. G., E. R. Stiehm, and M. Swenseid. 1977. Complement levels in Ghanaian children with protein-calorie malnutrition. In *Malnutrition and the immune response,* ed. R. M. Suskind, 191-4. New York.

Notis, W. M. 1972. Giardiasis and vitamin B$_{12}$ malabsorption. *Gastroenterology* 63: 1085.

O'Brien, W. 1975. Intestinal malabsorption in acute infection with *Strongyloides stercoralis. Transcript of the Royal Society for Tropical Medicine and Hygiene* 69: 69-77.

Olarte, J., J. Cravioto, and B. Campos. 1956. Inmunidad en el niño desnutrido. I. Producción de antitoxina diftérica. *Boletin Médico Hospital Infanta* 13: 467.

Oomen, H. A. P. C. 1959. Nutrition and some disorders of the eye in the tropics. *Tropical and Geographical Medicine* 11: 66.

Palumbo, P. J., H. H. Scudmore, and J. H. Thompson, Jr. 1962. Relationship of infestation with *Giardia lamblia* to intestinal-malabsorption syndromes. *Proceedings of the Mayo Clinic* 37: 589.

Peterson, G. M. 1957. Intestinal changes in *Giardia lamblia* infestation. *American Journal of Rontgenerentology* 77: 670-7.

Picciano, M. F., K. E. Weingartner, and J. W. Erdman, Jr. 1984. Relative bioavailability of dietary iron from three processed soy products. *Journal of Food Science* 49: 1558-61.

Powanda, M. C. 1977. Changes in body balances of nitrogen and other key nutrients: Description and underlying mechanisms. *American Journal of Clinical Nutrition* 30: 1254-68.

Pretorius, P. J., and L. S. de Villiers. 1962. Antibody response in children with protein malnutrition. *American Journal of Clinical Nutrition* 10: 379-83.

Rahaman, M. M., A. K. M. J. Alam, and M. R. Islam. 1974. Leukemoid reaction, hemolytic anaemia, and hypoproteinaemia in severe *Shigella dysenteriae* type-1 infection. *Lancet* 1: 1004.

Rahaman, M. M., and M. A. Wahed. 1983. Direct nutrient loss and diarrhea. In *Diarrhea and malnutrition: Interactions, mechanisms, and interventions,* ed. L. C. Chen and N. S. Scrimshaw, 155-60. New York.

Rahmathullah, L., B. A. Underwood, R. D. Thulasiraj, et al. 1990. Reduced mortality among children in southern India receiving a small weekly dose of vitamin A. *New England Journal of Medicine* 323: 929-87.

Reddy, V., P. Bhaskaran, N. Raghuramulu, et al. 1986. Relationship between measles, malnutrition, and blindness: A prospective study in Indian children. *American Journal of Clinical Nutrition* 44: 924-30.

Reddy, V., and S. G. Srikantia. 1964. Antibody response in

kwashiorkor. *Indian Journal of Medical Research* 52: 1154-8.

Rhode, J. E., R. A. Cash, R. L. Guerrant, et al. 1983. Therapeutic interventions in diarrhea. In *Diarrhea and malnutrition: Interactions, mechanisms, and interventions,* ed. L. C. Chen and N. S. Scrimshaw, 287-98. New York.

Riis, P. 1975. Giardiasis: A cause of intestinal malabsorption. *Journal of the Royal College of Physicians* 10: 61-6.

Roche, M., and M. E. Perez-Gimenez. 1959. Intestinal loss and reabsorption of iron in hookworm infection. *Journal of Laboratory and Clinical Medicine* 54: 49.

Roche, M., M. E. Perez-Gimenez, M. Layrisse, and E. D. Prisco. 1957a. Gastrointestinal bleeding in hookworm infection. Studies with radioactive Cr^{51}; report of 5 cases. *American Journal of Digestive Diseases* 2: 265.

1957b. Study of urinary and fecal excretion of radioactive chromium Cr^{51} in man, its use in the measurement of intestinal blood loss associated with hookworm infection. *Journal of Clinical Investigation* 36: 1183.

Rodgers, F. C., P. K. Dhir, and A. T. M. Hosain. 1960. Night blindness in the tropics. *Archives of Opthalmology* 63: 927.

Rosenberg, I. H., and B. B. Bowman. 1982. Impact of intestinal parasites on digestive function in humans. *Federation Proceedings* 43: 246-50.

Rosenberg, I., and N. S. Scrimshaw. 1972. Workshop on malabsorption and nutrition. *American Journal of Clinical Nutrition* 25: 1045-1289.

Rosenberg, I., N. W. Solomons, and R. E. Schneider. 1977. Malabsorption associated with diarrhea and intestinal infections. *American Journal of Clinical Nutrition* 30: 1248-53.

Ross, C. A. C., and E. A. Dawes. 1954. Resistance of the breast-fed infant to gastro-enteritis. *Lancet* 1: 994.

Rowland, M. G. M., T. J. Cole, and R. G. Whitehead. 1977. A quantitative study into the role of infection in determining nutritional status in Gambian village children. *British Journal of Nutrition* 37: 441-50.

Sarker, S. A., M. A. Wahed, M. M. Rahaman, et al. 1986. Persistent protein losing enteropathy in post measles diarrhoea. *Archives of Diseases of Children* 61: 739-43.

Schlesinger, L., and A. Stekel. 1974. Impaired cellular immunity in marasmic infants. *American Journal of Clinical Nutrition* 27: 615.

Scrimshaw, N. S. 1977. Effect of infection on nutrient requirement. *American Journal of Clinical Nutrition* 30: 1536-44.

1989. Malnutrition and nosocomial infection (Editorial). *Infection Control Hospital Epidemiology* 10: 192-3.

1990a. Energy cost of communicable diseases in infancy and childhood. In *Activity, energy expenditure and energy requirements of infants and children,* ed. B. Schurch and N. S. Scrimshaw, 215-38. Lausanne.

1990b. Functional significance of iron deficiency: An overview. In *Functional significance of iron deficiency,* ed. C. O. Enwonwu, 1-14. Nashville, Tenn.

In press. Effect of infection, including parasitic diseases, on nutrient requirements. In *International nutrition,* ed. O. Galal.

Scrimshaw, N. S., C. E. Taylor, and J. E. Gordon. 1968. *Interactions of nutrition and infection.* Geneva.

Shank, R. E., A. F. Coburn, L. V. Moore, and C. L. Hoagland. 1944. The level of vitamin A and carotene in the plasma of rheumatic subjects. *Journal of Clinical Investigation* 23: 289-95.

Sirisinha, S., R. Suskind, R. Edelman, et al. 1973. Complement and C3 proactivator levels in children with protein-calorie malnutrition and effect of dietary treatment. *Lancet* 1: 1016-20.

Sivakumar, B., and V. Reddy. 1972. Absorption of labelled vitamin A in children during infection. *British Journal of Nutrition* 27: 299-304.

1975. Absorption of vitamin A in children with ascariasis. *American Journal of Tropical Medicine and Hygiene* 78: 114-15.

Smith, N. J., S. Khadroui, V. Lopez, and B. Hamza. 1977. Cellular immune response in Tunisian children with severe infantile malnutrition. In *Malnutrition and the immune response,* ed. R. M. Suskind, 105-9. New York.

Smythe, P. M., G. G. Breton-Stiles, H. J. Grace, et al. 1971. Thymolymphatic deficiency and depression of cell-mediated immunity in protein-calorie malnutrition. *Lancet* 2: 939-43.

Solomons, N. W. 1982. Giardiasis: Nutritional implications. *Review of Infectious Diseases* 4: 859-69.

Sommer, A. 1982. *Nutritional blindness: Xerophthalmia and keratomalacia.* London.

Sommer, A., J. Katz, and I. Tarwotjo. 1984. Increased risk of respiratory disease and diarrhoea in children with pre-existing mild vitamin A deficiency. *American Journal of Clinical Nutrition* 40: 1090-5.

Sommer, A., I. Tarwotjo, E. Djunaedi, et al. 1986. Impact of vitamin A supplementation on childhood mortality: A randomized controlled community trial. *Lancet* 1: 1169-73.

Sommer, A., I. Tarwotjo, D. Hussaini, and D. Susanto. 1983. Increased mortality in children with severe vitamin A deficiency. *Lancet* 2: 582-8.

Sprinz, H., R. Sribhibhadh, E. J. Gangarosa, et al. 1962. Biopsy of the small bowel of Thai people. *American Journal of Clinical Pathology* 38: 43.

Stanton, B. F., J. D. Clemens, B. Wojtyniak, and T. Khair. 1986. Risk factors for developing mild nutritional blindness in urban Bangladesh. *American Journal of Diseases of Children* 140: 584-8.

Stephenson, L. S., D. W. T. Crompton, M. C. Latham, et al. 1980. Relationships between *Ascaris* infection and growth of malnourished preschool children in Kenya. *American Journal of Clinical Pathology* 33: 1165-72.

Stephenson, L. S., M. C. Latham, K. M. Kurz, et al. 1989. Treatment with a single dose of Albendazole improves growth of Kenyan schoolchildren with hookworm *Trichuris trichiura* and *Ascaris lumbricoides* infections. *American Journal of Tropical Medicine and Hygiene* 41: 78-87.

Stinnett, J. D. 1983. *Nutrition and the immune response.* Boca Raton, Fla.

Suskind, R., R. Edelman, P. Kulapongs, et al. 1976. Complement activity in children with protein-calorie malnutrition. *American Journal of Clinical Nutrition* 103: 226.

Taren, D. L., M. C. Neshiem, D. W. T. Crompton, et al. 1987. Contribution of ascariasis to poor nutritional status of children from Chiriqui Province, Republic of Panama. *Parasitology* 45: 1466-91.

Tielsch, J. M., K. P. West, Jr., J. Katz, et al. 1986. Prevalence and severity of xerophthalmia in southern Malawi. *American Journal of Epidemiology* 124: 561-8.

Tomkins, A. M., P. J. Garlick, W. N. Schofield, and J. C. Waterlow. 1983. The combined effects of infection and malnutrition on protein metabolism in children. *Clinical Science* 65: 313–24.

Tripathy, K., E. Duque, O. Bolanos, et al. 1972. Malabsorption syndrome in ascariasis. *American Journal of Clinical Nutrition* 25: 1276.

United Nations University. 1979. Protein–energy requirements under conditions prevailing in developing countries: Current knowledge and research needs. *Food and Nutrition Bulletin.* Supplement 1, Tokyo.

Veghelyi, P. V. 1938. Giardiasis in children. *American Journal of Diseases of Children* 56: 1213–41.

Venkatachalam, P. S., and V. N. Patwardhan. 1953. The role of *Ascaris lumbricoides* in the nutrition host: Effects of ascariasis on digestion of protein. *Transactions of the Royal Society of Tropical Medicine and Hygiene* 47: 169.

Von Bonsdorff, B. 1948. Pernicious anemia caused by *Diphyllobothrium latum* in the light of recent investigations. *Blood* 3: 91–102.

    1956. Parasitological reviews: *Diphyllobothrium latum* as a cause of pernicious anemia. *Experimental Parasitology* 5: 207.

    1964. The fish tapeworm, *Diphyllobothrium latum;* a major health problem in Finland. *World Journal of Medicine* 11: 170.

Waldman, T. A. 1970. Protein-losing enteropathy. In *Modern trends in gastroenterology,* ed. W. I. Card and B. Creamer, 125–42. London.

Wannemacher, R. W. 1977. Key role of various individual amino acids in host response to infection. *American Journal of Clinical Nutrition* 30: 1269–80.

Waslien, C. I., Z. Farid, and W. J. Darby. 1973. The malnutrition of parasitism in Egypt. *Southern Medical Journal* 66: 47–50.

Weinberg, E. D. 1978. Iron and infection. *Microbiology Review* 42: 45–66.

    1984. Iron withholding: A defense against infection and neoplasia. *Physiology Review* 64: 65–102.

West, K. P., G. R. Howard, and A. Sommer. 1989. Vitamin A and infection: Public health implications. In *Annual Review of Nutrition,* ed. R. E. Olson, E. Beutler, and H. P. Broquist, 63–86. Palo Alto, Calif.

West, K. P., Jr., and A. Sommer. 1985. Delivery of oral doses of vitamin A to prevent vitamin A deficiency and nutritional blindness. *Food Review International* 1: 355–418.

Whitehead, R. G. 1977. Protein and energy requirements of young children living in the developing countries to allow for catch-up growth after infections. *American Journal of Clinical Nutrition* 30: 1536.

Wilson, D., R. Bressani, and N. S. Scrimshaw. 1961. Infection and nutritional status. I. The effect of chicken pox on nitrogen metabolism in children. *American Journal of Clinical Nutrition* 9: 154–8.

Wohl, M. G., J. G. Reinhold, and S. B. Rose. 1949. Antibody response in patients with hypoproteinemia – with special reference to the effect of supplementation with protein or protein hydrolysate. *Archives of Internal Medicine* 83: 402.

WHO (World Health Organization). 1980. Parasite related diarrhoeas. *WHO Scientific Working Group, WHO Bulletin* 58: 819–30.

Zuckerman, A. 1966. Recent studies on factors involved in malarial anemia. *Military Medicine* 131: 1201–16.

Zumrawi, F. Y., H. Dimond, and J. C. Waterlow. 1987. Effects of infection on growth in Sudanese children. *Human Nutrition, Clinical Nutrition* 41C: 453–61.

VI.4 ❧ Famine

Despite swelling populations around much of the globe, the enormous expansion of agricultural productivity, the rapid development of transport facilities, and the establishment of globally interlinked market networks have made it theoretically possible to provide adequate food for all. Yet famine and hunger still persist and, indeed, proliferate in some parts of the world. Their durable character represents a perplexing and wholly unnecessary tragedy (Drèze and Sen 1989; Watts and Bohle 1993b). Although the extent of hunger in the world will never be known with precision (Millman 1990), it has been estimated that in the early 1990s, more than 500 million adults and children experienced continuous hunger and even more people were deemed vulnerable to hunger, with over 1 billion facing nutritional deficiencies (WIHD 1992).

The community concerned with world hunger is far from unanimous in its understanding of the situation. S. Millman (1990) likens the situation to the parable of the elephant and the blind men, whereby hunger is perceived differently by those encountering different aspects of it. It is significant that these varying perceptions correspond to particular disciplinary or professional orientations, leading to different diagnoses of the nature of the problem and its underlying causes and implying distinct foci for policy interventions.

Problems of food supply, then, are among the most bewildering, diffuse, and frustrating of humankind's contemporary dilemmas. Within the lifetime of each of us, official views of the world food situation have oscillated from dire predictions of starving hordes to expectations of a nirvana of plentiful food, then back to impending doom. One expert states that famine is imminent, whereas another declares that our ability to adequately feed the world's people is finally within reach.

The term "famine" is one of the most powerful, pervasive, and (arguably) emotive words in our historical vocabulary. This in itself makes it all the more difficult to isolate its meaning and wider significance. But to this end, the ensuing chapter addresses the following topics: A brief review of famine in history; a definition of famine and its various dimensions; the identification and description of a range of cultural and social famine coping practices in traditional societies; an examination of the literature on the causes of famine, along with some of the recent attempts to model famine vulnerability and the famine process; and, finally, a focus on past and present attempts to develop famine policies.

Famine in History

Famines are woven into the fabric of history; indeed, as D. Arnold (1988) has pointed out, they are important historical markers, often used by chroniclers and historians in search of points in time when the normal rhythms of human life were interrupted, or when momentous developments appeared to have a discernible beginning or end. In singling out famines in this way, historians have done rather more than just seize upon convenient dates by which to slice up history into manageable portions. They have also followed the perceptions and traditions of the people themselves. In preliterate societies, particular famines, along with other collective catastrophes, served as a common means of recording and recovering the experience of the past.

We know that famines have led to untimely deaths for at least 6,000 years, which makes it necessary to simplify the enormously complex array of data and sources concerning them. W. A. Dando (1980) has identified a system of world famine regions for the period from 4000 B.C. to A.D. 1980. The first region, for the period from 4000 to 500 B.C., is Northeast Africa and West Asia, where the earliest authentic records of famine have been found, including several from the Nile Valley dated as early as 4247 B.C. The famine in Egypt of Joseph's day (1708 B.C.), recorded in the Old Testament, appears to have been part of a much more widespread scarcity throughout West Asia. Until 500 B.C., the literature of this area continued to be studded with accounts of famines.

In the thousand years after 500 B.C., the heaviest concentration of accounts mentioning famine are found in the region that became the Roman Empire. Imperial Rome may have brought order and organization to subjugated peoples, but Mediterranean Europe still experienced at least 25 major famines during this period. After A.D. 500, western Europe emerged as the region to which the extant accounts of famine most frequently refer. Up to A.D. 1500, the British Isles suffered from at least 95 famines, France suffered 75, and other famines or severe food shortages were recorded throughout these territories as well.

Indeed, famines are a much discussed part of the European experience until the nineteenth century. However, both the incidence and extent of major European famines seem to have begun to decline in the seventeenth and eighteenth centuries (Grigg 1985). Thus, the last major famine in England occurred in A.D. 1620, in Scotland in the 1690s, in Germany, Switzerland, and Scandinavia in 1732, and in France in 1795. During the nineteenth century, many parts of Europe were afflicted with harvest failure and high prices in 1816, and the 1840s were also a period of acute food shortage, including the "Great Famine" in Ireland (1846–51). But in general, even localized food crises diminished in Europe after the eighteenth century, and although until the mid-1800s most Europeans remained in a chronic state of undernourishment (Cipolla 1976), at least western Europe had shaken off the specter of famine.

The fourth famine region was eastern Europe, whose various sectors experienced more than 150 recorded famines between A.D. 1500 and 1700. Expanding the time frame a little, in Russia at least 100 hunger years and 121 famine years were recorded between A.D. 971 and 1974 (Dando 1980). Famine occurrence in imperial Russia reached its high point in the nineteenth century, but even after the revolution of 1917, the scourge of famine could not be eliminated. In 1921 and 1922, approximately 9 million people starved to death; in 1933 and 1934, the number was between 4 and 7 million, and in 1946 and 1947, it was nearly 2 million. The famines of 1921 and 1922 resulted from the breakdown of order associated with civil war, and those of the 1930s reflect Stalin's forced collectivization of agriculture. The famine of 1946–7 was also man-made. A decision to rigorously restore the provisions of the collective farm charter, which had been relaxed during World War II, coupled with a drought and the use of scarce grain in other segments of the world to promote communist goals, produced this famine (Dando 1980).

From A.D. 1700 to 1970, Asia emerged as the world's foremost famine area. In South Asia, legends and records document more than 90 major famines over the last 2,500 years, two-thirds of them after 1700, but most were localized (Kulkarni 1990), with only an occasional one (like the Durga Devi famine of the late fourteenth century in the Deccan) that covered a large area. Although all of India suffered to some extent in the early eighteenth century, without question the late eighteenth and nineteenth centuries were that country's time of famines. They devastated Bengal in 1770, the Ganges Valley, western India, the Deccan, and Madras in 1783, and almost all of the peninsula in 1790. In the first half of the nineteenth century, major famines took place from 1802 to 1804, in 1806 and 1807, in 1812, 1824, and 1825 and 1826, from 1832 to 1834, in 1837 and 1838, and in 1854. Most of these, however, were limited in their extent, although they did cause intense suffering and death regionally.

But the period between 1860 and 1880 in India was one in which five major famines and three local scarcities followed each other in rapid succession (Kulkarni 1990). The famines were widespread, but after 1880 there was a period when only local scarcities occurred and no famines. Then, in 1895, perhaps the most disastrous famine of the century began in the middle and upper Ganges Valley and spread, in 1896, to the whole South Asian region. This was followed by the famine of 1899 and 1900, which devastated a large area of the peninsula and the northwest as well.

There have also been a number of famines in the twentieth century in South Asia. In 1907 and 1908, one descended on the middle and upper Ganges Valley, but thereafter, although there were scarcities, no famine occurred until that of Bengal in 1943. Nor did scarcity and famine cease after India gained its independence in 1947. There was widespread scarcity (and probably starvation, despite denials of this by the

Indian central government and various state governments) in 1952 and 1953, and again between 1965 and 1967, 1970 and 1973, and in 1986 and 1987. In addition, Bangladesh was severely affected by famine in 1974.

Over the past 2,000 years, China has recorded perhaps as many as 90 famines per century. But, as in South Asia, the nineteenth century saw China's most devastating famines. Droughts, floods, locusts, hurricanes, and earthquakes were natural disasters that induced crop failures, but the breakdown of civil society and warfare also were important factors. Four of these famines alone (in 1810, 1811, 1846, and 1849) are reported to have claimed 45 million lives. Nine million died in the famine from 1875 to 1878 in northern China. Other severe famines were recorded in 1920 and 1929, and there was a particularly harsh one between 1958 and 1961, when it is estimated that between 14 and 26 million (and perhaps even as many as 40 million) people died (Kane 1988; Article Nineteen 1990).

Elsewhere in Asia there have been localized famines in many places over the past 200 years or so, and of late, areas such as Timor and Kampuchea have been afflicted. In the latter country, the decade of the 1970s was one of continuous food crisis, deepening into famine in 1975 and 1979; the latter has been described as the "most catastrophic famine in the history of the Khmer people" (Ea 1984).

Even North and South America, as well as the Pacific, have not escaped unscathed from famine. For example, in the middle of the fifteenth century, a four-year sequence of frosts and droughts produced a terrible famine in central Mexico (Townsend 1992), and famines, caused by a combination of drought and lack of political and economic cohesion, have been frequent in northeast Brazil (Cunniff 1996). Even in the lush, tropical Caribbean islands, famines were common during the seventeenth and eighteenth centuries, through a combination of physicoenvironmental, biological, and socioeconomic circumstances (Watts 1984). In the Pacific, small islands, vulnerable to environmental and societal perturbations, have always been susceptible to food shortages and famine (Currey 1980). Indeed, even in Hawaii, since European contact, famines have occurred on average every 21 years (Schmitt 1970).

Although famines have struck many parts of the world in the past two decades, sub-Saharan Africa has been especially hard hit and has afforded the contemporary world some extremely powerful and distressing visions of famine. However, famine in Africa is not a new phenomenon. Oral traditions from many areas mention numerous occurrences in precolonial times (Arnold 1988b), and colonial records document many more (Hill 1977; Watts 1983). Yet, as late twentieth-century events in Bosnia-Herzegovina reminded us, no place is free from famine, and one of its contemporary faces is worn by victims of war.

Nevertheless, although nearly 200 million people each year continue to be plagued by hunger, the trend in famines since the end of World War II has clearly been a downward one (Kates et al. 1988). This trend reflects both a lessening of famine generally and a major shift in incidence from populous Asia to less populous Africa. The Alan Shawn Feinstein World Hunger Program at Brown University, using data averaged for 7-year periods beginning in 1950, has found that the average number of people residing in countries in which *The New York Times* reported famine was 790 million annually from 1957 to 1963, but declined to an average of 265 million in the period from 1978 to 1984. Since that time, the average has dropped below 200 million.

Definitions and Dimensions of Famines

Millman (1990) has identified three hunger-related situations in the world today: food shortage, food poverty, and food deprivation. These situations are distinguished from one another primarily by the level of human organization (from an entire population to households to the individual) at which scarcity is manifested. "Food shortage" indicates a situation in which total food supplies within a bounded region are insufficient to meet the needs of its population. "Food poverty" refers to the situation in which a household cannot obtain enough food to meet the needs of all of its members. "Food deprivation" refers to insufficient food availability for an individual. At each level, the commonly used term "food security" can be taken to mean an ability to avoid the corresponding hunger situation. Food shortage is among the causes of food poverty, which in turn is among the causes of food deprivation. However, other factors may operate to cause food poverty when there is no food shortage, and food deprivation where there is no food poverty.

Thus, hunger is not a single, uniform experience. Its manifestations range from vulnerability resulting from dietary traditions that mesh imperfectly with variations in need over the life cycle, to household food insecurity rooted in poverty, to aggregate food-supply shortfalls, which, when they worsen, can become the massive hunger crises affecting large numbers within specified regions and generating substantial increases in mortality. The latter, in popular thinking, are called "famines." Certainly, the most poignant manifestations of hunger are famines, which we have become accustomed to thinking of as "disasters" of a particularly horrific kind, replete with human misery on a massive, almost unimaginable, scale.

Famine: A Subjective Window on Poverty and Hunger

One of the debates over famine that has emerged involves the question of whether it is a discrete event or merely the tip of an iceberg of underlying social, economic, and political processes (Currey 1992). Many writers (e.g., Mellor and Gavian 1987) have defined famine as a discrete event, separate from chronic hunger. Furthermore, the World Bank (1986) has separated transitory food insecurity from chronic food insecurity, and the World Food Programme has focused most of its attention on nutrition in times of disaster. B. Currey (1992), however, has questioned whether such crisis management is the most cost-effective means of reducing world hunger and has suggested that more efforts be directed toward building resilient agricultural systems and long-term monitoring of rural development.

Such differences in approach highlight one of the problems with famine, which, as a concept and as a historical phenomenon, presents us with a fundamental paradox: It is both event and structure (Arnold 1988). On one hand, it is clearly an "event." There may be widely different opinions as to exactly when a particular famine begins or ends, but there is common agreement that it occupies a finite span of historical time and human experience. Basically, famine signifies an exceptional (if periodically recurring) event – a collective catastrophe of such magnitude as to cause social and economic dislocation. It generally results in abnormal levels of destitution, hunger, and death. It can lead to the complete disintegration of customary patterns of work and subsistence and can greatly disrupt customary norms of social behavior, not to mention levels of mortality.

And yet, at the same time, famine cannot be meaningfully considered in isolation from the economic, social, and political structures of a specific society. Occasionally, we document a specific disaster, resulting in a famine, in a society that is otherwise relatively secure in its provisioning. More commonly, however, famine acts as a revealing commentary upon a society's deeper and more enduring difficulties. In other words, famine can be viewed as a subjective window on poverty and hunger. The proximate cause of a famine may lie in some apparently unpredictable "natural disaster," like a flood or drought, or in a human calamity like a civil war or invasion (Arnold 1988). But these are often no more than "triggering" events, intensifying or bringing to the fore a society's already extant vulnerability to food shortages and famine. Any historical understanding of famine must, therefore, be alert to its structural causes and to its social and cultural parameters, as well as to what happened during the crisis itself.

This approach to famine, as a meeting and intermingling of event and structure, partially derives from a perspective that sees history not as simply a narrative sequence of great events and personalities but as a search for underlying structures and recurrent patterns, famines among them (Arnold 1988). In a similar manner, it has been recognized among social scientists that individual action or agency is constrained by the relationship between agency and structure, and this dialectic takes place not only locally but on a world scale (Wisner 1993). Thus, although a famine

can arise locally, the constraints on humans that create their vulnerability to it can originate in the influence of structures located on other continents.

Famines As History

Famines form an integral part of formal attempts to record and recall the past in many parts of the world. Among other things, they act as an aid to recall, as a reminder of their terrifying consequences, and, sometimes, as a key to their putative meanings. The practice of naming famines is one indication that in the popular memory at least, all famines were far from identical, whatever similarities they might bear for outside observers. For example, India's famines commonly bore the title of the Hindu calendar year in which they occurred. Others were named after vengeful deities or were seen as marking the onset of the *Kali Yuga,* the Hindu age of suffering, corruption, and human misery. In Africa, rural people have often named famines after what they exchanged or sold to get food, or after what people ate.

Such examples highlight the fact that famines are "hitching posts" of history (Shipton 1990) and the poles around which experiences and impressions are organized and collected. Thus, famine forms a link between the world of personal memory and the broader domain of collective consciousness, despite the fact that many academic historians have been skeptical about the authenticity of famine accounts found in folklore, oral history, and even chronicles.

In the past, as famines touched the lives of millions deeply and directly, they lived on in collective memory, and terror of their return kept them alive in that memory. We should remember that it has only been in the last century or so that people in Western societies have felt themselves immune to famine and discarded such cumulative folk experience as redundant. Perhaps it is this lack of fear of famine that most critically divides us from our own past and from the lives of a large part of the world's peoples today (Arnold 1988).

Famine As Demographic Crisis

One of the ways in which famines impress themselves upon collective memory and experience is through the colossal and devastating mortality involved. However, mortality statistics can give only a rough impression of a famine's magnitude, and it would be unrealistic to credit such data with any real precision. Until the last century or two, few governments kept reliable and detailed records of vital data. Historians who have attempted to reconstruct famine mortality in the remote past have tried to compensate for this deficiency by using parish records, tax returns, and similar sources. But these records seldom provide a dependable picture of mortality trends over a wider area, and even where there was some form of birth and death registration, famine mortality was often grossly underreported. Local officials themselves fell ill, died, or deserted their posts. The deaths of villagers who wandered off elsewhere in search of food passed unrecorded. Thus, it is not surprising that our understanding of the relationships between demographic processes and famine is extremely limited (Hugo 1984).

Indeed, although mortality is viewed as one of famine's major effects and is, in fact, an integral part of many of its definitions, there is surprisingly little data to precisely quantify the impact of famine on mortality rates, even in modern times; the famines of the 1970s and 1980s stand out as examples (Hugo 1984). Accounts of famines in preindustrial societies usually paint pictures of death on a massive scale. P. A. Sorokin (1942, 1975), one of the earliest writers to systematically summarize the demographic impacts of famine on mortality, has suggested that in affected areas, death rates sometimes reached 200, 500, or even 800 for every 1,000 people, as compared with normal rates of 10 to 30. He maintains that in the Soviet famine of 1921, for example, regional death rates reached 600 per 1,000.

The concept of "excess deaths" has been found to be useful in examining the impact of contemporary famines on mortality. "Excess deaths" refers to the "number of deaths over and above those that would have occurred if previous nutritional conditions had prevailed" (Bongaarts and Cain 1981). Very few studies have employed this concept. One of these, by A. K. Sen (1980), makes several reasonable corrections to the existing mortality data for the 1943 Bengal Famine and concludes that the total figure for excess mortality associated with that famine was 3 million. Another, by J. C. Caldwell (1975), estimates that the excess mortality for the entire Sahelian region during the famines of 1970 to 1974 was no more than 250,000, despite massive publicity that insisted that many more people were dying, and M. Alamgir (1980), in a third study, estimates the excess mortality for Bangladesh in 1974 and 1975 as 1,500,000.

Famines also seem to have distinct phases of mortality response (Ruzicka and Chowdhury 1978; Bongaarts and Cain 1981). There appears to be an initial phase during which mortality rates respond immediately to the food crisis. This is followed by a second phase that sees mortality rates at least twice as high as normal, and a third involving a gradual rate decline. Finally, there is a phase in which mortality rates are actually lower than "normal" because the most vulnerable groups in the population have already been severely pruned.

Demographers have also tended to neglect the differential mortality within subgroups in populations during famines. Best documented are excess death rates among infants and children. Illustrative is the Bangladesh Famine of 1974 and 1975, during which there was a 70 percent increase in the infant mortality rate in a sample of 228 villages containing 120,000 people, which meant 529 deaths per 1,000 live births (Ruzicka and Chowdhury 1978). A study of the 1980 famine in Daramoja, Uganda, measured an infant mortality rate of 607 per 1,000 live births.

The elderly also are especially vulnerable to excess mortality in times of famine (Chen and Chowdhury 1977), as are pregnant and lactating women (Bongaarts and Cain 1981). In addition, there is no doubt that famine mortality disproportionately affects poor and landless people. For example, in Bangladesh, the 1975 crude death rate among landless families was three times higher than among those with at least three acres of land (Chen and Chowdhury 1977). It also is clear that in the 1943 Bengal Famine, the most affected group in terms of excess mortality was that of agricultural laborers (Mukherji 1965).

Although discussion of the demographic impact of famine has concentrated on assessments of mortality, another important dimension is its impact on fertility (the demonstrated capacity of women for reproducing) and fecundity (a predisposition or latent capacity for reproducing). There is considerable evidence to suggest that fertility, as demonstrated by birth rates, follows a distinctive pattern during famines (Bongaarts and Cain 1981). Birth rates initially remain at prefamine levels, then rapidly decline, some nine months after the famine's onset, to rates only 30 to 75 percent of those that are normal (depending on the severity of the famine). The low point in birth rates usually occurs nine months after the end of the crisis. But following this point, the conception rate recovers quickly, and the famine-induced period of depressed fertility is followed by one in which the birth rate exceeds prefamine levels for up to three years. Reasons for this pattern are varied. Fecundity is decreased by minimal nutrition and psychological stress. Hunger also tends to diminish the frequency of intercourse, and spouses are often separated by temporary migration during famines. In addition, there is an increase in voluntary birth control, sexual abstinence, abortion, and, historically at least, infanticide (Sorokin 1942; Connell 1955; Ruzicka and Chowdhury 1978).

As yet, there is little information on socioeconomic differentiation in the pattern of fertility response to famine, but the scattered evidence suggests that it is the poor and landless who most reduce their rate of conception during such a crisis (Stein et al. 1975; Ruzicka and Chowdhury 1978).

A third important demographic feature of famine is migration, which in traditional societies has historically been one of the most important ways that people have coped with famine. Although migration should be studied in relationship to mortality and fertility, in this chapter it will be considered with other coping strategies.

Famine and Disease

Assessments of the demographic impact of famine are greatly complicated by the disease factor because, in most famines, mortality from epidemic disease has greatly exceeded that from actual starvation. For example, during the course of the Bengal Famine of 1943, starvation was identified as the cause of death in only about 5 percent of cases; cholera, malaria, and smallpox accounted for the great majority of the 3 million deaths. Moreover, in the 1940s, just as in the nineteenth century, the colonial administration in India was loath to acknowledge starvation as a cause of death. This situation has continued since 1947 because famine mortality in India has remained a political matter.

The reasons for the intertwining of epidemics and famine appear to be both physiological and social. Malnutrition can weaken the body's immune responses, creating a diminished resistance to infection and a reduced capacity to recover from it. Further, migration has the effect of spreading disease to areas not directly affected by hunger. During times of famine, personal hygiene also tends to be neglected. Debilitated people may fail to wash, and they may drink filthy or contaminated water. They may consume "famine foods" (unripe grain, grass, or roots) in an attempt to suppress hunger; this sometimes causes diarrhea and vomiting, which results in a further weakening of the body and a greater risk of spreading disease. The high level of famine mortality, in other words, is partially a consequence of the nature of the expedients people adopt to try to escape from hunger and partly one of the disruption created by famine in customary patterns of social behavior.

Famine Chronology

All famines have their own internal chronology. Because hunger seldom kills outright and immediately, the symptoms of growing hunger may not be apparent to outsiders until destitution and debilitation have already reached an advanced stage. Thus, the duration of famine can be reckoned according to a variety of different criteria, and definitions made by those actually subject to the famine may differ greatly from those made by officials. Those experiencing a famine might date its onset from the first warning signs of approaching calamity, such as the delayed arrival of the rains and the first withering of standing crops. Officials, by contrast, might see a famine as beginning only when food prices climb to abnormal heights or when the signs of distress among the starving poor are given governmental recognition. Equally, an official definition of famine might end with the closing of state-managed relief work, though this may occur well before survivors of the famine feel themselves free of its grip.

Traditional Cultural and Social Coping Practices

"Coping" is the manner in which people act, within the constraints of existing resources and the range of expectations of a situation, to achieve various ends (Blaikie et al. 1994). In general, such action involves no more than "managing resources," but more specifically, it usually means how this management is accomplished under unusual and adverse circumstances. Thus, coping can include defense mechanisms, active ways of solving problems, and methods for handling stress. Resources for coping with famine include labor power, land, tools, seed for crops, livestock, draft animals, cash, jewelry, other items of value that can be sold, and, of course, storable food stocks, as well as skills and specialized knowledge. In order for tangible resources to be mobilized, people must be entitled to command them, which may be achieved in many ways. Among them are using the market, exercising rights, calling upon obligations (of household members, kin, patrons, friends, and the general public, by appeals to moral duty as in alms and charitable giving), stealing, or even committing violence. In many cases, specialized knowledge is required with certain resources, for instance, in locating wild foods, determining the moisture capacity of certain soils, discovering water sources, or finding wage labor in distant cities or plantations.

Although the range of strategies to prevent or minimize the risk of famine is enormous, two generalizations can be made. First, the objective of many of these strategies is to secure necessities, such as access to a minimum level of food, shelter, and physical security, rather than to increase income. Second, maintaining command of these basic needs in a risky environment usually implies employing multiple, varied methods of access to resources. These include diversifying production strategies, setting up nonagricultural income sources, strengthening or multiplying social support networks, and developing a demographic strategy aimed at the creation, maintenance, and mobilization of human labor.

Diversification is one strategy, and the production of farming people is usually diversified, involving mixed cropping, intercropping, the cultivation of non-staple crops, and the use of kitchen gardens. The result is often a "normal surplus" in good years because it is planned on the basis of meeting subsistence needs even in bad (but not the worst conceivable) years. Because planting a greater variety of crops provides the best chance of an optimum yield under all variations of weather, plant disease, and pest attack, it represents one of the most important precautionary strategies for coping with food shortages (Klee 1980; Wilken 1988).

Another important preventive/mitigating strategy involves the development of social support networks. These include a wide variety of rights and obligations among members of the same household (for example, wives and husbands, parents and children), within the extended family, and within other groups with a shared identity, such as clan, tribe, and caste. Parents may try to make strategic choices of marriage for children into comparatively wealthy families, which might increase their ability to call on resources in difficult times (Caldwell, Reddy, and Caldwell 1986). Within the household and family, successfully securing resources in potentially disastrous times depends upon the implicit bargaining strength of its members and on their "fallback" positions (Agarwal 1990) or "breakdown" positions, if cooperation in this bargaining position should fail (Sen 1988, 1990).

It has also been argued that in societies where people habitually live in the shadow of hunger, those people develop, or are the beneficiaries of, social and cultural practices that ensure that even the poorest will not starve to death. Such practices are based on ideas of "shared poverty" and "mutual assistance," which some writers term the "moral economy of the poor" (Scott 1976). Under circumstances of famine, those who have food share it with destitute kinsmen and needy neighbors. These noneconomic relations in times of hardship include those between patrons and clients and between rich and poor. They offer a minimum subsistence and a margin of security, and they constitute a "subsistence ethic" based on reciprocity. There are many examples of this type of relationship (see Bhatia 1963 on India and Scott 1976 on Southeast Asia).

Although most examples are drawn from the past, it would seem that this "moral economy" has not completely broken down in the contemporary world. For example, reports indicate that during the drought and period of extreme food shortage from 1980 to 1983 in southern India, the support system worked well, at least for the aged (Caldwell et al. 1986). Further, A. Gupta (1988) goes so far as to say that the continued existence of such support in present-day India is responsible for the retention of people in the countryside. In Nepal, it has been found that the wealthy are encouraged to avoid reducing daily wages for agricultural work in difficult times and to refrain from selling grain outside the village (Prindle 1979).

In general, it seems that when the outcome of a season is still uncertain, landlords and patrons make some provision for laborers and the poor. But once signs of a famine are evident, landowners respond by reducing their number of field hands. As the crisis deepens, workers in other sectors of an agrarian society, such as fishermen, artisans, and a range of rural dependents, become affected by the lack of patronage and support from the wealthy as well, a situation that has been documented in many parts of the world (Arnold 1988).

Rural households try to build up stores of food and salable assets. However, the first is difficult to achieve for people who are involved in a web of impoverishment and exploitation that is a normal and continuing part of life. In many parts of Africa, Asia, and Latin America (and in Europe in the past), even in "normal years," most households experience shortfalls in production for their own consumption. Furthermore, some staples, like potatoes (which simply cannot be kept for as long as a year – or until the next harvest),

rot and become inedible. Hence the historical attractiveness of cereal crops, because they can be stored for long periods. However, most people do have a range of salable assets (e.g., furniture, cooking utensils, jewelry, farm implements, livestock, and land) that can be converted to food as necessary.

Another strategy to mitigate the potential impact of famine is that of having a large number of children, thus improving security by increasing possible future family income. This strategy is an important one in places like Bangladesh, where children are considered to be a less risky investment than land (Cain 1978).

Once famine has begun, precautionary mechanisms are put into practice. There are others, which cannot be developed in advance but which also come into play as the famine unfolds. When there is a potential food shortage and possible famine, the period during which stress develops can be long, allowing for a succession of strategies. A review of a number of major studies of coping mechanisms in the face of famine (Watts 1983b; Corbett 1988; Rahmoto 1988; Waal 1989; Agarwal 1990; Brown 1991; O'Brien and Gruenbaum 1991) clearly identifies a sequence of activities. These include religious rituals and ceremonies, identification of scapegoats, reduction of the amount of food consumed and a longer spacing out of meals, substitution of lower-quality and wild foods, and calling for resources from others (especially family and kin), along with generating household income by wage labor, petty commodity production, and the sale of easily disposable items (as long as such sales do not undermine future productive capacity). But as the food crisis deepens, loans from moneylenders and the sale of important items, such as draft animals, agricultural implements, and livestock, become common. Finally, if all preceding strategies have failed to maintain minimum food levels, migration often ensues. But let us now examine some of these coping mechanisms in more detail.

The cultural context of famine has everywhere been reflected in religion, and one of the first responses to famine in any society has likely been an intensification of ritual. Prayers offered up in churches, mosques, and temples are supplemented by special rituals and ceremonies in streets, fields, and public places. Deities, saints, even plants and animals, are invoked.

When rituals fail to bring relief, more divisive or desperate responses can follow. Sometimes, scapegoats are sought out. Other times, the physical and spiritual anguish brought on by famine and pestilence has bred religious fanaticism. In some instances, the persistence of famine has caused doubts about the gods of the established pantheon. For example, in the famines of the late 1870s in India and China, Western missionaries won converts by pointing to the apparent failure of local deities to protect worshipers from want. In some societies, however, the people place great faith in divine will and believe it blasphemous to question their gods' purposes and intentions.

As a famine marches remorselessly onward, societies respond more materially. For example, the planting of a crop might be delayed, crop varieties with shorter growing seasons or lower water requirements might be planted, parts of farms might be abandoned and effort focused on better locations, or seed grain might be consumed rather than sown. While this is happening, households might reduce the amount of food consumed at each meal and space meals out over longer and longer intervals (just as they do during the "hungry gap," a period of seasonal food shortage that is a part of normal life; during this time, people know that they will lose some weight and then recover) (see Garine 1991).

In order to eke out food supplies, adulteration of staples often occurs. As a crisis deepens further, wild, "famine" foods replace staples. Different items fall into this category in different parts of the world. In Niger, for example, the pith of palm trees and lily roots are used, and in nineteenth-century Ireland, it was nettles, berries, fungi, seaweed, frogs, and rats. In China, people have eaten grass, bark, and even earth to quell hunger. As "famine" foods were often found on communal lands, continuing access to such lands today can be especially significant in densely populated regions (Blaikie, Harriss, and Pain 1985; Agarwal 1990; Chambers, Saxena, and Shah 1990).

At this stage, people usually sell the few assets they have to buy food, especially once food resources available from family and kin have been exhausted, along with other sources of family income such as wage labor, petty commodity production, and artisanal work. Houses are stripped of their furniture, doors, and window frames. Women sell cooking utensils and jewelry, and finally, farm animals and implements are sold, thus jeopardizing prospects of agricultural recovery after the famine ends. People may try to borrow money, but often moneylenders and even banks are loath to give credit in years when there is no harvest to lay claim to. As a last resort, land might be sold, which (along with migration) is one of the unmistakable signs of acute and deepening crisis. In Bengal in 1943, for example, over 250,000 households sold all their land, and 600,000 more sold part of their holdings. Considering the importance of land, such sales are a sign of desperation. As in the past, losing land as a result of famine is still one way in which property holders sink into the residual class of landless laborers. The sale brings short-term relief from starvation but has the net effect of increasing vulnerability.

While all of this is happening, those in the worst-hit portion of the population frequently begin to contest their deprivation. Laborers and tenants petition landlords, patrons, and governments, demanding to be fed. In the past, and in some places today, a lack of response to such pleas for relief has led to the looting of grain stores, market stalls, warehouses, carts, trucks, and barges. It is at such moments of mounting tension, anger, and fear that the idea of the poor having a right to food is most forcefully evinced (Thompson 1971). But food riots in most places and times have not lasted indefinitely; rather, they died away once provision was made for the basic needs of the hungry or, more often, the situation deteriorated further until no food was to be had by any means.

One common alternative has been recourse to what officialdom and the propertied elites have seen as "crime"; like food riots and looting, this measure has been a characteristic and almost universal way of coping with famine. Famine crime has assumed many forms, ranging from an intensification of normal banditry, sheep stealing, and petty theft, to murder. Usually, as society fractures under famine's pressure, crimes against property and persons soar.

When all attempted strategies have failed to maintain minimum food levels, migration occurs. Although this can be considered a demographic response to famine, it is also an important coping strategy. Much famine migration has been short-term and over relatively short distances, and once conditions have improved, people return to their homes and farms. This was true in Europe in the past (Sorokin 1942), and it certainly has been the case in a variety of other places in the world. During the Indian famines of the nineteenth century, there were many such movements to unaffected areas, and to the cities, in search of relief. In Brazil, the northeast has witnessed temporary flights to the towns in 1878, in 1915, from 1930 to 1932, in 1942, and in 1958. The Sahelian crisis from 1970 to 1974 also produced large-scale population movement (Caldwell 1975), much of which focused on refugee camps. There was also much short-distance local migration, some of it to the cities.

But famine-induced migration also has a permanent dimension, which is one of the more enduring demographic consequences of famine. It can be documented from preindustrial Europe, where this type of "forced" migration resulted in the colonization of new agricultural areas. Perhaps the most spectacular famine-induced migration out of any area in Europe was associated with the Irish famine from 1846 to 1851, when about 1 million people migrated to the United States and England. Between 1852 and 1916, another nearly 5 million Irish left, three-quarters of them bound for the United States. During the Sahelian crisis, much of the famine-induced urbanization, especially of pastoralists, was permanent (Colvin 1981). The sequence of famines in the Brazilian northeast has produced a permanent migration of peasants to the tropical rain forests of Amazonia and to São Paulo and Rio de Janeiro. In the nineteenth century, famine was one of the impelling forces behind the Indian diaspora to Natal, Mauritius, Malaya, Fiji, Guyana, and nearby Sri Lanka (then Ceylon). The exodus from southern India to the tea and coffee plantations of Sri Lanka reached its peak during the 1870s, a time when a high level of labor demand was matched by famine in Madras.

Women and Famine

The burden of famine has fallen, and in many developing-world societies continues to fall, with exceptional severity on women. One reason for this is that, in many parts of the world, women traditionally either have been the main agricultural producers or have constituted a substantial part of the agrarian workforce. Colonial regimes often had no practical interest in developing opportunities for women. Education and new employment opportunities were directed toward men, who took up work in the mines, on the plantations, and in the cities, often far from their home villages, weakening their commitment to subsistence labor, which, more often than not, was left to the women. Thus, the onset of a famine hits women directly. Their food production dwindles, and when field laborers are dismissed or left without employment, they lose cash and in-kind income as well.

The burden of famine also has fallen heavily on women because of their customarily low status in patriarchal societies. In many societies there is a cultural expectation that women will sacrifice their food and, ultimately, their lives to enable their husbands and sons to survive. Women normally eat after the men, and when food is in short supply, female children tend to be neglected and resources concentrated on male children. There is a great deal of historical and contemporary evidence to show that part of the burden of hunger and suffering has been transferred to women through neglect, starvation, abandonment, and sale into prostitution. Women, in short, have been victimized in the interests of male survival.

Famines, therefore, impose enormous physical and emotional suffering upon women. Women have often killed their children; marital relationships can be strained to the point of divorce and abandonment; and hunger can drive women into prostitution and slavery. They have been sold by landowners, moneylenders, and other males with authority over them, for money and for food. Further, in many parts of the world, even today, one of the commonest responses to famine has been the sale of children, especially girls. Thus, the devaluing of life that occurs in a famine has often further favored male power and ascendancy.

Conflicting Ideas about Famine Causation

An enormous literature has grown up to explain why famines occur. Once, "acts of God" and "freaks of nature" were seen as self-sufficient explanations for why people hungered and died. Warfare, blockades, and deliberate hoarding of grain have also been commonly used to explain why famine happened. Today, writers on the causes of famine are more disposed to see these as only precipitating or contributory factors, and, increasingly, famine has come to be regarded as a complex phenomenon, more a symptom than a cause.

One of the main sources of confusion about the subject arises from the multiple causes of famines and their great variety in space and time. Some of the literature makes a distinction between "general and predetermining factors," or the time–geographic dimensions of famine (long-term, intermediate, and immediate), and the trigger mechanism of the actual famine (Currey 1979, 1980; Murton 1980). W. I. Torry (1986) uses similarly distinct "ultimate" and "proximate" causes of famine, and P. M. Blaikie and colleagues (1994) employ the terms "root causes" and "underlying pressures," which create "unsafe conditions." It is also important to acknowledge that if there are many combinations of factors and mechanisms that bring about famine, then each famine is unique. Indeed, the task of building theories of famines is particularly difficult because of the complexity of each specific case. Any theory will involve an understanding not only of the existing systems of production but also the distribution of food in terms of access to land and inputs, as well as the operation of the market, the determination of prices, and the behavior of traders in food staples (Canon 1991). Government policies with regard to food production and distribution (and famine relief) may also play a profound role. Then there is always a series of contextual events peculiar to each famine, a "sequence of events" (Alamgir 1981), or in Currey's (1984) parlance, a "concatenation."

Two main (and largely competing) types of famine explanation, based on differing sets of causal mechanisms, can be identified. Many commentators have assumed that a famine arises out of an actual shortfall in the means of subsistence, or as it is commonly labeled, a food availability decline (often abbreviated to FAD). Either some natural disaster occurs, causing a crop failure to reduce the aggregate amount of food available, or population in the long term outstrips the quantity of food available. The other mechanism involves the decline in some people's entitlements to food (abbreviated to food entitlement decline, or FED). According to this explanation, first articulated by Sen (1981), famine is a result of the ways in which access to food is reduced because of the operation of social and political processes that deny or lessen "entitlement" to food.

These processes may involve a deterioration in the ability of people to grow their own food or to buy it through various forms of exchange. To this context should be added the impact of various hazards that may not reduce the overall amount of food but instead affect the success of different groups of people in fulfilling their entitlements. This type of explanation focuses much more firmly on relations of power within a society that may account for the distribution of assets and income (unequal in "normal" times) that become a matter of life and death in times of famine. This model tends to reduce the causal importance of natural events, which although they may be limited to a decline in the aggregate supply of food (with the impact of drought, flood, or pest attack), are analyzed in the context of the political economy of root causes and predetermining factors. In other words, people are made vulnerable to the impact of a natural hazard by their place in the economic, political, and social processes that affect their exchange entitlements.

Food Availability Decline (FAD)

The school of thought that attributes famine to an aggregate decline in the supply of food is clearly linked to explanations of famine in terms of natural events. In particular, drought has been identified as a major immediate cause of crop failure and, therefore, of a decline in food supply. It is difficult to find pure supply-side explanations of famine in the recent literature, but between the decline in aggregate food supplies and its immediate causes (such as drought) on one side, and the detailed mechanisms that actually precipitate famines on the other, the emphasis is usually on the former (Blaikie et al. 1994).

In addition to analyses of recent famines, the historical literature contains considerable discussion of the long-term shifts of climate that have appeared to gradually undermine a society's apparently secure subsistence base. Generally, whereas most historians have been wary of embracing the type of "climatic determinism" posited by Ellsworth Huntington (1915, 1919) and have tended to see climatic variations as too short-term and peripheral to provoke major subsistence crises, others have acknowledged that a substantial number of historical famines in many parts of the world were preceded by partial or complete failure of the rains (Arnold 1988).

Unfortunately, much of the writing also tends to subtly argue that if famines could be attributed to natural causes, they could be explained in terms of exceptional events and not by continuing and normal social processes (Hewitt 1983b). K. Hewitt (1983a) even argues that a previous generation of academics and practitioners virtually ostracized those who sought explanations that went deeper than the impact of the natural hazard. Given the dominance of science and technology in the modern era, the publication of any analysis of causes that failed to suggest that hazards could be modified and responded to by technology resulted in the exile of its authors from the mainstream social explanation.

Another important element in the food availability decline approach has been the "overpopulation" thesis. Deeply rooted in Western thought, the thesis is most commonly identified with the writings of Thomas Malthus (Turner 1986), who believed that the food supply was relatively inelastic, increasing at best by arithmetical progression, whereas population rose in geometrical leaps and bounds. In periodically sweeping away the excess population, famines maintained a rough equilibrium between population and subsistence. However, this thesis was to prove untenable for Britain (and Europe generally), where a transformation of industry and commerce improved agricultural productivity and transportation and led to the increased importation of foodstuffs. Not only did rapid population growth fail to trigger famine, but standards of living rose. Increasing prosperity and material security, however, were also accompanied by a growing practice of birth control through various means.

Although Malthus's thesis seemed to square with nineteenth- and early-twentieth-century reality only in places like India and China, since the 1950s, famines and food crises in Africa and Asia have led to a strong revival of interest in his ideas. Population in the developing world has risen sharply, largely as the result of improved medical services and sanitation. Food production is frequently, but not altogether accurately, assumed to have not kept up, and with too little food to go around and too many mouths to feed, famine has been predicted on a global scale by numerous "prophets of doom," as for example, Paul Erlich (1968), and W. and P. Paddock (1967). But very often these dire predictions are based on simple measurements of global food supply stocks versus rising population rates, without taking into account high levels of wasteful food consumption in the West, the nature of foodstuffs produced, and the unequal nature of food distribution (between nations, and within states, classes, and even families).

Food Entitlement Decline (FED)

In *Poverty and Famines* (1981), the Indian economist Amartya Sen challenges the view that famines are caused by food availability decline. As already noted, he views famine as the result of the many and complex ways in which people's access to food is reduced because of the operation of social and political processes that deny or lessen their "entitlement" to food. Such an approach distinguishes between aggregate availability or supply of food and an individual access to, or ownership of, food. People obtain food through five different types of "entitlement relationships" in private-ownership market economies (Sen 1981; Drèze and Sen 1989, 1990): (1) There is production-based entitlement, which is the right to own food that one produces with one's own or hired resources; (2) there is trade-based entitlement, which describes the rights associated with ownership when they are transferred through commodity exchange; (3) there is own labor entitlement, which is the trade-based and production-based entitlement when one sells one's own labor power; (4) there is inheritance and transfer entitlement, which is the right to own what is given by others (gifts) and what is transferred by the state, such as pensions; (5) there are extended entitlements, which are entitlements that exist outside legal rights (for example, ownership) and are based on legitimacy and expectations of access to resources.

Such entitlements are not fixed and equal but vary according to an individual's position within a wider system of production, exchange, control, and distribution. Entitlements are either owned by a person or can be exchanged by that person for other commodities. People are vulnerable to starvation if their endowment does not contain adequate food or resources to produce food and their capacity to exchange labor or other goods and services cannot be translated into enough food. This situation can occur without a decline in aggregate food supply and without any disruption or malfunction of the market.

The food entitlements decline approach just discussed recognizes the relations of power within a society that may account for the distribution of assets and income and that become a matter of life and death in times of famine. It also acknowledges the importance of changes in purchasing power. Further, it disaggregates regional food production and availability and follows through how food is distributed to individuals (it permits analysis of intrahousehold food allocation and explains why the rich never die in famines and why some classes benefit from them). This approach involves the regional, national, and world economy in the analysis and draws attention to the possible prevention of famines by food imports.

There have, of course, been criticisms of the food entitlement decline approach. First, there is a scale and boundary problem: If the analysis is stretched to include a big enough area, there is always enough food to avert a famine. Second, some famines clearly have had their origins in food availability decline, and although it may be incorrect to identify this as an ultimate or even most important cause, it is inescapable that a fall in the amount of locally produced food (because of war, drought, or longer-term environmental decline) hinders the ability of people to find alternative sources of food. Third, initially, entitlements, as well as resources (endowments), were conceived of as static and given. But recent research (Watts 1991) has pointed out that they are fought over and constitute the terrain of struggle within societies in which group interests (defined by class, caste, gender, age, ethnicity) are in contradiction.

In conclusion, the entitlements approach to the analysis of famine has released famine study from theoretical constraints. However, this pursuit of a single theory of the mechanisms of famine has diverted attention from multiple causality and the possibility of famines at different times in the same place being caused by a mix of factors. This concern has led to the further development of the concept of famine vulnerability, to which the food entitlements decline approach alludes but fails to pursue in depth.

Famine Vulnerability Models

Two models have recently been proposed that attempt to take into account the multiplicity of factors that make people vulnerable to famine. The first, developed by M. Watts and H. G. Bohle (1993a, 1993b), argues that the locally and historically specific configuration of poverty and hunger defines what they call a "space of vulnerability." These researchers set out to provide a theoretical means by which this space can be "mapped" with respect to its social, political, economic, and structural–historical coordinates. They endeavor to radically extend the concept of entitlements, not simply in a social or class sense but in a political and structural sense, to take account of (1) the particular distribution of entitlements and how they are reproduced in specific circumstances; (2) the larger arena of rights in which entitlements are defined, fought over, contested, and won and lost (that is, empowerment or enfranchisement); and (3) the structural properties (what they call "crisis proneness") of the political economy that precipitate entitlement crises.

Watts and Bohle review the extensive literature relating to "entitlement and capability," "empowerment and enfranchisement," and "class and crisis." They emphasize that these processes can be grasped only relationally (as congeries of social relations), and they develop a tripartite structure that defines the space of vulnerability through the intersection of the three causal powers: command over food (entitlement); state–civil society relations seen in political and institutional terms (enfranchisement/empowerment); and the structural–historical form of class relations within a specific political economy (surplus appropriation/crisis proneness).

The intersection of these causal powers produces three parallel analytical concepts; economic capability, property relations, and class power. Economic capability emerges from particular configurations of entitlement and empowerment, property relations from the intersection of entitlement and political economy, and class power from specific forms of political economy and empowerment. The three causal powers or processes (entitlement, empowerment, political economy) are conceived of as accounting for mass poverty associated with specific long-term (structural) changes. Famine results from violent short-term changes in these same mechanisms.

The space of vulnerability also has an internal structure in which it is possible to locate vulnerable groups and regions. Because the concept of vulnerability is relational, the space and shape of vulnerability is given by its social relations. For example, if famine is described as a food entitlement problem, vulnerability is located in the realm of economic, and especially market, relations. If, conversely, famine resides in the powerlessness of individuals, classes, and groups to claim and enforce food entitlements, then vulnerability is determined by the power and institutional relations within civil society. Finally, if famine is driven by processes of exploitation and surplus appropriation, it accordingly occupies a location within the space of vulnerability that lies in the realm of class relations.

It is also possible to place both vulnerable groups (social) and vulnerable regions (spatial) within the space of vulnerability. In the former, vulnerable individuals, groups, and classes can be located according to the causal processes that present possibilities and constraints in the sphere of subsistence. Individuals and groups vulnerable to market perturbations and unable to cope with food entitlement decline because they are resource and/or asset poor, may be located in the "economic space" of vulnerability. If the likelihood of deprivation is rooted in politics that can be inscribed in gender (patriarchal politics), work (production politics), and the public sphere (state politics) - all of which may render individuals and groups powerless - their location in the "political space" of vulnerability is determined by power and institutional relations. Finally, if deprivation arises from processes of surplus extraction and appropriation, individuals and groups are located in the "structural–historical" space of vulnerability given by specific configurations of class relations. All these spaces obviously exist simultaneously. Determining the precise weighting becomes important in assessing the ways in which famine differs between Somalia, Kampuchea, or Bangladesh.

This social map of vulnerability has a geographic or spatial counterpart. Vulnerable regions can be located in relationship to the tripartite structure of causal processes. Economically marginal regions that regularly or sporadically experience fluctuation in productivity and prices are most liable to food entitlement crises (they occupy the "economic space" of vulnerability). Peripheral regions experience vulnerability through relations of dependency to a regional core that drains surpluses and resources away (they occupy the "political space" of vulnerability). Finally, regions shaped by endemic crises and conflicts (both economic and ecological) due to processes of commercialization, proletarianization, and marginalization are logically situated in the "structural–historical" space produced by class relations.

In summary, this modeling of the "spaces of vulnerability" integrates many of the factors identified by previous research on famine into a more logical and causal structure. It provides a way to integrate the intersections of structures, tendencies, and conjunctures as they impinge on the famine process. The specific content of the social space of vulnerability, the actual concatenation of events that might trigger famine, and the specific structural forces at work, although deriving from the abstract causal structure, will naturally be time- and place-specific.

Blaikie and colleagues (1994) also have produced a comprehensive dynamic framework, which they call an "access model." They focus on the way unsafe conditions arise in relation to the economic and political processes that allocate assets, income, and other resources in a society. Natural events are integrated into the model through a focus on how resources are allocated by social processes. "Access" involves the ability of an individual, family, group, class, or community to use resources that are directly required to secure a livelihood.

Access to those resources is always based on social and economic relations, usually including the social relations of production, gender, ethnicity, status, and age. Rights and obligations obviously are not equally distributed among all people, and it is argued that less access to resources leads to increased vulnerability. The model incorporates the notion of "trigger events": war, as in the case of Ethiopia (1984 and 1990), Angola, Chad, Sudan, and Mozambique (1984); or natural hazards, as in the case of the Sahel (1970-6), Sudan (1985), and Ethiopia (1973). The model analyzes the structures and processes of famine in relation to making a living in normal times. It is an iterative approach in which "external" shocks and triggers have their impact upon the structures and processes of political economy.

Famine Policy

Although an enormous literature has grown up to explain why famines occur and what to do about them, it is clear today that there is disjuncture between explanation and policy. Explanation is largely a product of the academic world. Policies for dealing with famine are a product of famine relief agencies, governmental advisers, and governments. The lack of affinity between the two types of literature is surprising. In an ideal world there should be a progressive and interacting relationship between theories of famine avoidance and relief and policy, but instead they are widely apart. The two sides are separated almost by a different language and are pervaded by different constraints and concerns.

Policy in the Past

Certainly, the fortunes of the state, whether in Europe, Africa, or Asia, have long been bound up with the containment or prevention of famine and, more generally, with provisioning the populace. Protecting its subjects from starvation and extreme want has for centuries been one of the primary functions of government and one of the principal expectations of the public. If we look for pre-twentieth-century evidence of the state as an agency of famine control and as a provider of famine relief, we can find it in places as far apart as China and Europe. In China, state paternalism, fostered by the ideology of the Confucian state, led to the protection of peasants from the worst effects of natural disasters, as well as measures for famine prevention and relief. But this system began to break down in the nineteenth century, and the situation remained chaotic until after 1949. Famine control was one of the first priorities of the new Communist state and, seemingly, one of its great successes, until the famine from 1958 to 1961 cruelly exposed the limitations of China's agrarian revolution.

In medieval times, European states did what little they could to avert the threat of famine. As Europe crossed the threshold from medieval to modern times, problems of provisioning (especially of the growing cities) increased, as did the problems of maintaining order in food-shortage situations. One response in England in the late sixteenth century was the issuing of orders, which became the bases for the English Poor Law, to counter the problem of vagrancy and destitution. In France, the provisioning of Paris received special attention from the government, and alarm over basic subsistence needs helped to make the revolution of 1789.

In Europe, however, as agriculture became more productive and increasingly market-oriented, governments sought to free themselves from the obligation to feed people and regulate markets. In France, attempts to make subsistence a matter of individual rather than state concern was short-lived, but in England, ideas of "free trade" gained increasing momentum in the late eighteenth century and the early years of the nineteenth. In 1814 and 1815 the Corn Laws, the last bastion of old protectionists and paternalists, were eroded, and in 1846, under Sir Robert Peel, they were finally swept away. By this time in Britain, policy-makers were imbued with the belief that market forces should not be tampered with and that self-reliance must not be weakened or local effort superseded by the activities of the government. This commitment to laissez-faire, and the notion that the state should not intervene in famines, was immediately tested in Ireland, where initially the state's role was seen as being strictly confined to providing employment on public works. Only in 1847 was emergency relief belatedly instituted.

The Indian Famine Codes
In India, the East India Company administration also strongly supported the new orthodoxy. Even during the famines and shortages of the early nineteenth century, the presidency and provincial governments adhered firmly to the principles of noninterference in the operation of the market and trade. But it became evident, particularly during the heavy mortality of the 1860s and 1870s, that a policy of laissez-faire alone would not meet the extreme recurrent crises of famine. A number of reports demonstrated that the government had lost enormous amounts of revenue by not investing in irrigation, other preventive works, and railways to stimulate production and to move food to food-shortage areas. Although the general principle of nonintervention in the grain trade remained inviolate until World War II, by the late 1870s there were moves, however hesitant, toward greater state responsibility for the Indian economy and for the welfare of the Indian people.

This change in policy resulted in the first coherently written explanation of famine, linked to policy recommendation. From the 1860s extensive reports were written on famine, and in 1878 the First Famine Commission was appointed (Brennan 1984). Its reports of 1880 led to the drafting of the Famine Codes of the mid-1880s by each of the provinces of India. The reports also contained much speculation about the causes of famine. The reports are especially instructive on the relation between the theories of famine causation and policies of prevention, relief, and rehabilitation.

Reasonably effective policies were formulated from these efforts. The Famine Codes reveal a professed dislike of interference in the operation of the market through price controls, and contain the belief that free trade is the best guarantee of satisfying effective demand. There is also an aversion to charity and free handouts and a strong ethic of "self-help." Thus, the backbone of famine relief was massive public works generating guaranteed employment, plus free assistance for those unable to work. That the latter breached ideology was accepted as necessary to prevent people from dying. Tests were established to ensure that only the deserving received relief. There were detailed instructions in the Codes about early warning signs of impending famine; the duties of the police, medical officers, and other local officials; wages and rations; famine relief works; and many other practical instructions. The codes were used by the British until 1947. Their effectiveness is still the subject of heated debate, with an overstated radical and nationalist critique on one extreme and an imperialist apologist defense on the other, but since 1947, the Codes have continued to form the basis of famine prevention and relief. Thus, the Maharashtra drought of 1970 to 1973 was effectively prevented from triggering a famine by an employment guarantee scheme similar to that found in the earlier Codes.

Contemporary Policy Directions
Contemporary policymaking recognizes that for each link in any explanation of a famine there are a range of policy measures. A key issue that must be addressed is the relationship of policy action to the level of a problem where it can be effectively altered. Although an integrated explanation of famine may be intellectually fulfilling, a policy has to be located at a level at which it can make a significant impact: There must be a short-run effectiveness, as human lives often depend on it. However, often a focus on the short term can lead to a loss of any sense of the real causes of vulnerability. This is the contradiction that faces the makers of famine policy: They are restricted by temporal and spatial scales at which they must work and to which they must fit their policies.

Food Security
At the international and national level, achieving aggregate food security has been an important policy goal. In particular, national food self-reliance is frequently seen as a defense against famine. However,

with global increases in flows of goods and information, localized and even national production failures have become increasingly remediable by imports of food, whether as trade or aid. At the global level, food supplies over the last couple of decades have been sufficient to provide an adequate (although near-vegetarian) diet to all, if distributed equitably. However, global food supplies are still not distributed according to need, and shortages at regional, national, and even subcontinental levels have continued.

During the 1980s and early 1990s, some shortages have been caused by the continuing difficulty that international humanitarian relief efforts have had in gaining access to affected populations caught up in civil wars. This has led to the discussion in a number of countries of when and how national sovereignty should yield to humanitarian care for people in disastrous situations. This problem is more than a relief policy issue, and it raises geopolitical and, above all, ethical concerns about the human right to food, shelter, and health care (Waal 1991).

The theoretical advances that Sen's entitlement theory has afforded have led to some reevaluation of the importance of food security at the national and international levels. The insights that form the theory also suggest that a disaggregated approach to food security is required, which has led to a growing policy concern for vulnerable groups at the local level and the promotion of the idea that entitlements should be strengthened. However, at the level of large regions and nations, concerns over food availability remain important, especially where agreements among countries to exchange grain are involved, as in the case of southern Africa.

Any discussion of food security must also consider the political and economic significance of food aid since World War II. The United States, as a major food surplus state, has used food aid as an important political tool. Food assistance has been withheld from Marxist-run governments but ensured to reliable and dependent allies. Yet, in addition to these political objectives, continuing food aid abroad has helped to save grain farmers from bankruptcy at home. Overseas aid has been vital to the U.S. economy as a safety valve for its domestic overproduction. In 1961 the Kennedy administration was faced with the greatest American food surplus in history, and it was this domestic situation, rather than humanitarian concern, that prompted massive grain shipments overseas in the following years, notably in 1966 when one-fifth of the entire U.S. wheat crop was sent to India to relieve the effects of famine in Bihar.

Food aid has accounted for 28 percent of U.S. overseas development assistance since 1946. The Agricultural Trade Development and Assistance Act of 1954 (Public Law 480) was debated and approved by Congress not for humanitarian reasons or for development ends, but in order to promote trade and dispose of existing surpluses. Food aid has served to open new markets for American farm products, especially in Africa and Asia, often to the detriment of local agriculture, and the threat of food withdrawal or denial has been used to put pressure on countries to accept other forms of American economic intervention and political control.

Relief and Development

The issue of food aid raises another very important question: Should famine prevention efforts be short-term, basically the giving of food relief, or long-term, and more of a developmental nature in scope? In many ways this is something of an academic question, because so long as there are food shortages and famines in the contemporary world and there are donors willing to provide food aid and cash, short-term relief assistance will continue to be important.

Today, in addition to relief provided by national governments in times of crisis, there are a number of United Nations agencies and numerous nongovernmental organizations involved in famine relief (see Busetto 1993; Cullinan 1993; Katona-Apte 1993; Longford 1993; Singer 1993). The earliest United Nations agency established to provide humanitarian relief was the United Nations International Children's Emergency Fund (UNICEF), set up in 1946 to help children in the aftermath of World War II. Various other agencies, such as the United Nations High Commission for Refugees, established in 1951, and the United Nations Relief and Works Agency, established in 1950, have been active in the provision of relief, but since 1963 the World Food Programme has been the primary international agency involved in food aid.

Over the past three decades, the World Food Programme has invested approximately $13 billion and has provided more than 40 million tons of food aid to combat world hunger and to promote economic and social development. Food aid has been used to assist more than 1,600 development projects and 1,200 emergency operations. Within the United Nations system, the World Food Programme is now the largest source of grant assistance to developing countries, the largest source of assistance for poor women, and the largest provider of grant assistance for environmental activities in developing countries. The agency is headquartered in Rome, and although it has employees in 85 countries, it spends less than 6 percent of its budget on administration.

From the outset, the agency aimed to serve as more than a mechanism for surplus disposal or a means of providing charity for the poor. Indeed, by the late 1980s, two-thirds of its resources were being spent on development activities. However, numerous emergencies since that time have channeled 60 percent of its current resources into relief operations, and in 1993, new development commitments received only $250 million, in contrast to $778 million in 1988. At present, the agency has at any one time about 5 million tons of food in transit on 50 chartered ships, but it is hoped that once present emergencies end it will again be able to emphasize development.

Throughout the world, there are also a very large number of nongovernmental organizations, such as Save the Children, Oxfam Lutheran World Federation, Red Cross, Africare, Food for the Hungry, and Catholic Relief, involved in relief activities. Although many have other objectives, because they operate at local levels they are well placed to provide famine relief, sometimes parallel to large-scale governmental and international aid and sometimes as a conduit for that aid. Many also endeavor to administer food relief in ways that strengthen local livelihoods in the long run. Basically, these groups are involved in both relief and development, as they realize that relief alone can create dependency. But the great number of such organizations can occasionally create the problem of "swamping" affected areas by official and nongovernmental organizations who frequently do not coordinate their activities and who often collectively provide excessive relief assistance but not enough help for long-term mitigation.

Longer-term mitigation involves less direct measures for preventing famine, and the most important policy requirement is the strengthening of rural livelihoods. Of course, these measures can have objectives other than famine prevention and have development goals that are justifiable as ends in themselves. For example, in India, the government has attempted land reform, improved agricultural production technology, encouraged better processing and storage, operated a fairly effective system of public distribution of food, and developed a well-tried decentralized emergency response mechanism. All of this means that a reasonably effective famine prevention strategy has emerged, although malnutrition is still widespread. Nevertheless, as we have seen, it is difficult anywhere to demonstrate the level of impact of general rural development policies in famine prevention because the causes of famine are conjunctional and always involve a complexity of factors.

Early Warning Systems

The Indian Famine Codes established the idea of warning indicators that could be used to predict the onset of famine. For long, they were the only "early warning system" in operation, but since the Sahelian famine of the early 1970s, a number of famine early warning systems have been established (Blaikie et al. 1994). There are many different approaches to such systems. Some involve the use of sophisticated technology, such as the Food and Agricultural Organization's Global Information and Early Warning System, developed in the 1970s, which predicts crop yields by establishing biomass from satellite imagery. Another comparable approach is the United States–funded Famine Early Warning System. Approaches like this are all based on the assumption that famines are pri-

marily caused by natural events and that technological solutions will be important mitigating elements. However, other early warning systems are much less complex and involve the collection and collation of local-level information on food stocks, prices, and such things as the sale of household assets.

Summary and Conclusion

Although there is considerable uncertainty regarding the nature and extent of the world's food problems, hunger is a contemporary reality, even within rich countries. Everyone must eat, and because of this simplest of all imperatives, famine is a subject of urgent contemporary concern. It casts a harsh but clear light on the nature and problems of the societies it afflicts and the world in which it exists. However, "famine" is a rather imprecise term normally used to describe events associated with natural hazards such as drought, floods, and pest infestations, and with political events such as war, malicious or inappropriate state policies, and ethnic prejudice. Famine is often (though not always) preceded by prolonged malnutrition and hunger, and part of the difficulty in defining it arises from the need to make a distinction between "ordinary" hunger and the phenomenon of famine. The latter term is generally reserved for situations in which starvation affects large numbers of people in a distinct area, which has been influenced by a natural or political event, leading to a larger number of deaths from starvation and illness than would normally be expected. By contrast, ordinary hunger is conventionally explained as a result of the imperfections of economic systems. Clearly, then, famine remains in danger of being explained as something caused by an exceptional political or natural factor – one that is abnormal and outside the responsibility of the usual operation of economic and political systems.

Fortunately, of late it has been recognized that natural hazards or political events are no more than immediate "triggers" or proximate causes. The "ultimate causes" must be sought out and understood in the normal economic and political sphere. Basically, a proper understanding of famine and all its dimensions requires an approach that does not merely deal with shortages of food but focuses instead on the inability of people to consume enough food. Thus, instead of treating famine as a shortage of food, it is preferable to analyze the different ways in which people are prevented (by natural or human events) from getting enough to eat. Using this alternative approach, it can be asked why certain groups of people are predisposed to famine before the impact of any trigger event, natural or political. Such a predisposition has been termed vulnerability, and the ultimate causes of famine can then be analyzed as those that create the conditions in which certain trigger events lead to the collapse in people's ability to acquire adequate nutrition.

This issue is not merely theoretical because the policy implications of understanding famine as inadequate consumption rather than inadequate availability are likely to be very different. When famine occurs even though food is available, or when famine affects some groups but not others, then food aid may be irrelevant. This issue is now at the core of the interpretation of famine and associated policy directions. It is one not of food security but of entitlement security and its corollary, the reduction of vulnerability among those who are the most vulnerable.

Brian Murton

Bibliography

Agarwal, B. 1990. Social security and the family: Coping with seasonality and calamity in rural India. *Journal of Peasant Studies* 17: 341-412.

Alamgir, M. 1980. *Famine in South Asia: Political economy of mass starvation.* Cambridge, Mass.

　1981. An approach towards a theory of famine. In *Famine: Its causes, effects, and management,* ed. J. Robson, 19-44. New York.

Arnold, D. 1988. *Famine: Social crisis and historical change.* Oxford.

Article Nineteen (International Centre on Censorship), ed. 1990. *Starving in silence: A report on famine and censorship.* London.

Bhatia, B. M. 1963. *Famines in India.* Bombay.

Blaikie, P. M., T. Cannon, I. Davis, and B. Wisner. 1994. *At risk; natural hazards, people's vulnerability, and disasters.* London.

Blaikie, P. M., J. C. Harriss, and A. Pain. 1985. *Public policy and the utilization of common property resources in Tamilnadu, India.* Report to Overseas Development Administrators, Research Scheme R3988. London.

Bongaarts, J., and M. Cain. 1981. *Demographic responses to famine.* The Population Council, Center for Policy Studies Working Paper. New York.

Brennan, L. 1984. The development of the Indian Famine Code. In *Famine as a geographical phenomenon,* ed. B. Currey and G. Hugo, 91-111. Dordrecht, the Netherlands.

Brown, E. P. 1991. Sex and starvation: Famine and three Chadian societies. In *The political economy of African famine,* ed. R. Downs, D. Kerner, and S. Reyna, 293-321. Philadelphia, Pa.

Busetto, B. J. 1993. WFP and UNICEF. Relying on each other's strengths. *World Food Programme Journal* 26: 17-19.

Cain, M. 1978. *The household life cycles and economic mobility in Bangladesh.* The Population Council, Center for Policy Studies Working Paper. New York.

Caldwell, J. C. 1975. *The Sahelian drought and its demographic implications.* Overseas Liaison Committee, American Council of Education, Paper No. 8. Washington, D.C.

Caldwell, J. C., P. H. Reddy, and P. Caldwell. 1986. Period high risk as a cause of fertility decline in a changing rural environment: Survival strategies in the 1980-1983 South Indian drought. *Economic Development and Cultural Change* 34: 667-701.

Canon, T. 1991. Hunger and famine: Using a food systems model to analyse vulnerability. In *Famine and food scarcity in Africa and Asia: Indigenous responses and external intervention to avoid hunger,* ed. H. G. Bohle, T. Canon, G. Hugo, and F. N. Ibrahim, 291-312. Bayreuth, Germany.

Chambers, R., N. Saxena, and T. Shah. 1990. *To the hands of the poor: Water and trees.* Boulder, Colo.

Chen, L. C., and A. K. M. A. Chowdhury. 1977. The dynamics of contemporary famine. In *Proceedings of Internal Union for the Scientific Study of Population,* Population Conference, Mexico, 1977. Liège, Belgium.

Cipolla, C. M. 1976. *Before the Industrial Revolution: European society and economy, 1000-1700.* New York.

Colvin, L. G., C. Ba, B. Barry, et al. 1981. *The uprooted of the western Sahel.* New York.

Connell, K. H. 1955. Marriage in Ireland after the famine: The diffusion of the match. *Journal of the Statistical and Social Inquiry Society of Ireland* 19: 82-103.

Corbett, J. 1988. Famine and household coping strategies. *World Development* 16: 1099-112.

Cullinan, S. 1993. The growth of WFP. *World Food Programme Journal* 25: 13-20.

Cunniff, Roger Lee. 1996. Drought region (Brazil). In *Encyclopedia of Latin American history and culture,* ed. Barbara A. Tenenbaum. New York.

Currey, B. 1979. Mapping areas liable to famine in Bangladesh. Ph.D. dissertation, University of Hawaii.

　1980. Famines in the Pacific: Losing the chances for change. *Geojournal* 4: 447-66.

　1984. Coping with complexity in food crisis management. In *Famine as geographical phenomenon,* ed. B. Currey and G. Hugo, 183-202. Dordrecht, the Netherlands.

　1992. Is famine a discrete event? *Disasters* 16: 138-44.

Cutler, P. 1984. Famine forecasting: Prices and peasant behaviour in northern Ethiopia. *Disasters* 8: 48-55.

Dando, W. A. 1980. *The geography of famine.* London.

Downs, R. E., D. O. Kerner, and S. P. Reyna, eds. 1991. *The political economy of African famine.* Philadelphia, Pa.

Drèze, J., and A. Sen. 1989. *Hunger and public action.* Oxford.

　eds. 1990. *The political economy of hunger.* 3 vols. Oxford.

Ea, M. 1984. War and famine: The example of Kampuchea. In *Famine as geographical phenomenon,* ed. B. Currey and G. Hugo, 33-47. Dordrecht, the Netherlands.

Erlich, Paul. 1968. *The population bomb.* New York.

Garine, I. de. 1991. Seasonal food shortage, famine and socio-economic change among the Massa and Mussey of northern Cameroon. In *Famine and food security in Africa and Asia: Indigenous responses and external intervention to avoid hunger,* ed. H. G. Bohle, T. Canon, G. Hugo, and F. N. Ibrahim, 83-99. Bayreuth, Germany.

Greenough, P. R. 1982. *Prosperity and misery in modern Bengal: The famine of 1943-44.* Oxford.

Grigg, D. 1985. *The world food problem 1950-1980.* Oxford.

Gupta, A. 1988. *Ecology and development in the Third World.* London.

Hewitt, K. 1983a. The idea of calamity in a technocratic age. In *Interpretations of calamity,* ed. K. Hewitt, 3-32. Boston, Mass.

　ed. 1983b. *Interpretations of calamity.* Boston, Mass.

Hill, P. 1977. *Population, prosperity and poverty. Rural Kano 1900 and 1970.* Cambridge and New York.

Hugo, G. 1984. The demographic impact of famine. In *Famine as geographical phenomenon,* ed. B. Currey and G. Hugo, 7-31. Dordrecht, the Netherlands.

Huntington, E. 1915. *Civilization and climate.* New Haven, Conn.

1919. *The pulse of Asia. A journey in central Asia illustrating the geographical history.* New York.

Kane, P. 1988. *Famine in China: Demographic and social implications.* London.

Kates, R. W., R. S. Chen, T. E. Downing, et al. 1988. *The hunger report 1988.* The Alan Shawn Feinstein World Hunger Program, Brown University. Providence, R.I.

Katona-Apte, J. 1993. Food aid fights malnutrition. *World Food Programme Journal* 25: 2-6.

Klee, G., ed. 1980. *World systems of traditional resource management.* New York.

Kulkarni, S. N. 1990. *Famines, droughts and scarcities in India.* Allahabad, India.

Longford, S. 1993. Delivering the food. *World Food Programme Journal* 25: 27-31.

Mellor, J. W., and S. Gavian. 1987. Famine: Causes, prevention and relief. *Science* 235: 539-45.

Millman, S. 1990. Hunger in the 1980s. Backdrop for policy in the 1990s. *Food Policy* 15: 277-85.

Mukherji, K. 1965. *Agriculture, famine and rehabilitation in South Asia.* Calcutta.

Murton, B. 1980. The temporal dimensions of famine vulnerability in Ganjam District in the mid-nineteenth century. *The Indian Geographical Journal* 55: 1-11.

O'Brien, J., and E. Gruenbaum. 1991. A social history of food, famine, and gender in twentieth-century Sudan. In *The political economy of African famine,* ed. R. Downs, D. Kerner, and S. Reyna, 177-203. Philadelphia, Pa.

Paddock, W., and P. Paddock. 1967. *Famine - 1975! America's decision: Who will survive.* Boston, Mass.

Prindle, P. H. 1979. Peasant society and famines: A Nepalese example. *Ethnology* 1: 49-60.

Rahmoto, D. 1988. *Peasant survival strategies.* Geneva.

Ruzicka, L. T., and A. K. M. A. Chowdhury. 1978. *Demographic surveillance system - Matlab.* Vol. 4, *Vital events and migration, 1975.* Dacca, Bangladesh.

Schmitt, R. C. 1970. Famine mortality in Hawaii. *Journal of Pacific History* 5: 109-15.

Schoepf, B. G. 1992. Gender relations and development: Political economy and culture. In *Twenty-first-century Africa: Toward a new vision of self-sustainable development,* ed. A. Seidman and A. Anong, 203-41. Trenton, N.J., and Atlanta, Ga.

Scott, J. C. 1976. *The moral economy of the peasant: Rebellion and subsistence in Southeast Asia.* New Haven, Conn.

Sen, Amartya K. 1980. Famine mortality: A study of the Bengal Famine of 1943. In *Peasants in history: Essays in honour of Daniel Turner,* ed. E. J. Hobsbawm, 144-220. Calcutta.

1981. *Poverty and famines: An essay on entitlement and deprivation.* Oxford.

1988. Family and food: Sex bias in poverty. In *Rural poverty in South Asia,* ed. T. N. Srinivasan and P. K. Bardhan, 453-72. New York.

1990. Gender and cooperative conflict. In *Persistent inequalities: Women and world development,* ed. I. Tinker, 123-49. Oxford.

Shipton, P. 1990. African famines and food scarcity: Anthropological perspectives. *Annual Review of Anthropology* 19: 353-94.

Singer, H. W. 1993. Food aid. A historical perspective. *World Food Programme Journal* 25: 7-10.

Sorokin, P. A. 1942. *Man and society in calamity.* New York.

1975. *Hunger as a factor in human affairs.* Gainesville, Fla.

Stein, Z., M. Lusser, G. Saenger, and F. Marolla. 1975. *Famine and human development: The Dutch hunger winter of 1944/45.* New York.

Thompson, E. P. 1971. Moral economy of the English crowd in the eighteenth century. *Past and Present* 50: 76-136.

Torry, W. I. 1986. Economic development, drought and famine. Some limitations of dependency explanations. *Geojournal* 12: 5-18.

Townsend, Richard F. 1992. *The Aztecs.* New York.

Turner, M., ed. 1986. *Malthus and his time.* Basingstoke, England.

Vaughan, M. 1987. *The story of an African famine: Gender and famine in twentieth-century Malawi.* Cambridge and New York.

Waal, A. de. 1989. *Famine that kills. Darfur, Sudan, 1984-1985.* Oxford.

1991. Famine and human rights. *Development in Practice: An Oxfam Journal* 1: 77-83.

Watts, D. 1984. Cycles of famine in islands of plenty: The case of the colonial West Indies in the pre-emancipation period. In *Famine as a geographical phenomenon,* ed. B. Currey and G. Hugo, 49-70. Dordrecht, the Netherlands.

Watts, M. 1983a. On the poverty of theory: Natural hazards research in context. In *Interpretations of calamity,* ed. K. Hewitt, 231-62. Boston, Mass.

1983b. *Silent violence: Food, famine and peasantry in northern Nigeria.* Berkeley, Calif.

1991. Entitlements or empowerment? Famine and starvation in Africa. *Review of African Political Economy* 51: 9-26.

Watts, M., and H. G. Bohle. 1993a. Hunger, famine and the space of vulnerability. *Geojournal* 30: 117-26.

1993b. The space of vulnerability. The causal structure of hunger. *Progress in Human Geography* 17: 43-67.

Wilken, G. 1988. *Good farmers. Traditional agricultural resource management in Mexico and Central America.* Boulder, Colo.

Wisner, B. 1993. Disaster vulnerability: Scale, power, and daily life. *Geojournal* 30: 127-40.

World Bank. 1986. *Hunger and poverty.* Washington, D.C.

WIHD (World Institute on Hunger and Development). 1992. *Second annual report on the state of world hunger.* Washington, D.C.

VI.5 ❧ Height and Nutrition

Scientists have long recognized that there is a close association between the height of a population and its nutritional status, and by the end of the nineteenth century governments were coming under increasing pressure to measure their citizens as a means of determining that status.[1] Many have done so in the twentieth century, as height and weight statistics have played an ever increasing role in health assessment programs (Tanner 1981). This chapter employs the data generated thus far to construct a general picture of changes in height and nutritional status in various countries during the course of the twentieth century.

The studies on which this chapter is based have taken a variety of forms. Most of the information about changes in average heights has been derived from school surveys, but a great deal of data on adult heights is also available. Many of these data have been derived from military recruiting records and are primarily concerned with the heights of adult men (Floud, Wachter, and Gregory 1990).

In addition, a number of investigations have focused on changes in the timing of growth spurts and in overall rates of growth. These investigations have tended to focus on the age of peak-height-velocity (PHV) in both males and females and the onset of menarche in girls (e.g., Matsumoto et al. 1980; Matsumoto 1982; Danker-Hopfe 1986). Some observers have also examined changes in the relative dimensions of different parts of the body, such as leg length and sitting height (Himes 1979; Tanner et al. 1982).

The relationship between social and economic changes and changes in height is both simple and complex. On the one hand, there is a clear association between the average height of a population and its standard of living. This is reflected in the unprecedented improvements in average height that have occurred in many parts of the world during the past one hundred years, and in the differences that continue to exist between the average heights of people from different socioeconomic backgrounds (e.g., Rea 1971; Rona, Swan, and Altman 1978; Jones, Nesheim, and Habicht 1985).

On the other hand, it is much more difficult to define the precise significance of different components of the "standard of living." Most observers, for example, would agree that the two most important environmental determinants of height are diet and disease, but it has proven extremely difficult to establish their relative importance (Roche 1979). Some have suggested that "health care may be more important than nutrition in the first year of life" and that "nutrition may be more important than health care" after the first year, but the evidence on which these suggestions are based is far from conclusive (Floud et al. 1990: 249).

Another area of difficulty concerns the relationship between environmental and genetic influences. There are evident differences among the heights and rates of growth of different ethnic groups, but the extent to which these differences are genetic or environmental in origin is not clear (Eveleth 1979: 388; Eveleth and Tanner 1991). However, it is reasonable to argue that changes in the average height of members of the same ethnic group over time reflect environmental and nutritional changes rather than changes in genetic potential (Floud et al. 1990). We can also seek to isolate the genetic determinants of growth by comparing the heights and weights of members of the same ethnic group in different circumstances and in different parts of the world (e.g.,

Moore 1970; Greulich 1976; Bindon and Zansky 1986).

It is important to remember that changes in social and economic conditions can affect heights and rates of growth in a number of different ways. In general, undernourished children who are subjected to repeated bouts of infection grow more slowly than children who are well nourished and live in a largely disease-free environment. Undernourished children experience the adolescent growth spurt at a later age, and although they continue to grow for a longer period, their final height is shorter. These differences mean that the gap between the heights of the two populations is at its greatest when the more favored children reach adolescence. The increase in the average value of children's heights has, therefore, been considerably greater than the increase in the average heights of adults (Floud et al. 1990; Eveleth and Tanner 1991).

The structure of this chapter follows that laid down in P. Eveleth and James Tanner's invaluable surveys of *Worldwide Variation in Human Growth* (1976, 1991). The first two parts examine the main trends in the average height of Europeans in Europe and the heights of Europeans outside Europe. This is followed by sections on the heights of Africans in Africa and the Americas; the heights of Asiatics in Asia and the Americas; the heights of Indo-Mediterraneans in the Near East; the heights of peoples in North Africa and India; and finally the heights of Australian Aborigines and Pacific Island peoples. The last section summarizes the evidence and considers some of the implications of that evidence for future health policy.

Europeans in Europe

Europeans living in Europe have been the subject of a particularly large number of anthropometric surveys. Many of the earlier investigations were concerned with the heights of adult male army recruits, but the present century has seen a growing concentration on the heights of schoolchildren. We also possess a considerable amount of data on the age at which European girls reach menarche, and there is some information about changes in European birth weights. The long history of anthropometric monitoring in Europe, combined with the availability of large amounts of data, has encouraged a number of investigators to use the heights of Europeans as "standards" against which to assess the growth of other population groups (e.g., Eveleth and Tanner 1976, 1991).

Studies of European heights provide some of the clearest evidence of the increase in average height that has occurred in most parts of the world during the course of the twentieth century. In 1991, for example, Eveleth and Tanner reported evidence of a secular trend toward increased adult height in

Table VI.5.1. *Changes in the heights of European army recruits circa 1900–1975*

Country	Period	Change in height (cm)
Belgium	1902/4–69	8.1
Denmark	1904/5–66/75	8.4
France	1900–60	7.5
Germany (Bavaria)	1900–58	4.2
Italy	1900–52	3.6
Netherlands	1907–75	11.1
Norway	1900-60	6.7
Spain	1903/6–55	3.1
Sweden	1900–74	8.1
Switzerland	1908/10–57	6.2

Source: Floud (1984).

Sweden, Finland, Norway, France, the United Kingdom, Italy, Germany, Czechoslovakia, Poland, Hungary, the Soviet Union, the Netherlands, Belgium, Switzerland, and Austria (Eveleth and Tanner 1991).[2] Similarly, in 1984 Roderick Floud showed that the average height of army recruits in 10 European countries increased by between 3.1 and 11.1 centimeters (cm) during the years 1900 and 1975 (Table VI.5.1).

Some investigators have attempted to infer changes in average height by comparing the average height of men and women of different ages at the same point in time. Thus in 1971 Erik Bjelke demonstrated that Norwegians who were born between 1920 and 1929 were between 1.7 and 1.8 centimeters taller than Norwegians who had been born a decade earlier (Bjelke 1971). In 1988, Mary Walker, A. Shaper, and G. Wannamethee compared the heights of 7,735 British men who were born between 1919 and 1939 and concluded that the average heights of successive birth cohorts had risen by approximately 1.3 centimeters per decade (Walker, Shaper, and Wannamethee 1988).

There have also been a large number of investigations into the heights of children. The average height of 5-year-old boys in London increased by 7.4 cm between 1905–12 and 1966, whereas the average height of 5-year-old girls increased by 7.5 cm (Cameron 1979). Even more dramatic was the average height increase of 12-year-olds in Oslo, which was 12 cm for boys and 12.5 cm for girls between 1920 and 1975 (Brundtland, Liestøl, and Walløe 1980). In Sweden, the average height of 12-year-old children increased by a similar amount between 1883 and 1965–71 (Ljung, Bergsten-Brucefors, and Lindgren 1974), and the average height of 13- to 14-year-old children in Holland increased by more than 20 cm between the mid–nineteenth century and 1965 (van Wieringen 1979).

In addition, there have been striking changes in the heights of children in central and eastern Europe.

For example, the average height of Czechoslovakian 12-year-olds increased by between 12.8 and 15.5 cm between 1895 and 1968–70 (Suchy 1972), whereas the average height of 14- to 18-year-olds in Moscow increased by between 3.6 and 5.7 cm between 1925 and 1965 (Vlastovsky 1966). Moreover, the average heights of 12-year-old girls and 14- to 15-year-old boys in Zagreb increased by 10 cm and 13 cm, respectively, between 1951 and 1982 (Prebeg 1984).

Secular changes in birth weights and rates of physical maturation have also been examined by a number of authors. Of the two, the history of birth weights has received rather less attention, but new data are slowly becoming available (e.g., Ward 1988, 1990). In 1966, V. Vlastovsky demonstrated that the average length of newborn boys in Kursk City rose between 1930 and 1939 and rose again after the end of the Second World War. However, babies born in 1959 were only 0.1 cm longer than boys born 20 years earlier. The average weight of newborn boys increased from 3.43 kilograms (kg) in 1930 to 3.49 kg at the end of the 1950s. In 1988 Margit Rosenberg revealed that the average birth weight of children in Oslo, Bergen, and Trondheim increased by approximately 0.2 kg between 1860 and 1980. However, these increases are much smaller than the increases in the heights (and weights) of older children and adults (Malina 1979a). In 1981 Tanner estimated that the average birth weight of full-term males born at the end of the nineteenth century was only 0.1 kg less than that of European children today.[3]

By contrast, changes in the rate of maturation and in age of menarche have been much more dramatic. In 1962 Tanner suggested that mean menarcheal age had declined by 4 years in Norway between 1840 and 1950; by 1.7 years in Sweden between 1890 and 1950; by 2.3 years in Finland between 1860 and 1940; and by 3.0 years in Germany over the same period (Tanner 1962, 1966; Steendijk 1966).[4] There is also evidence after the Second World War of a continuation in this secular trend in Austria, Belgium, Bulgaria, Denmark, Finland, France, Germany, Greece, Hungary, Italy, the Netherlands, Poland, Romania, Spain, Sweden, the United Kingdom, Yugoslavia, and the former Soviet Union (Danker-Hopfe 1986; see also Venrooij-Ijsselmuiden, Smeets, and van der Werff Ten Bosch 1976; Laska-Mierzejewska, Milicer, and Piachaczek 1982; Helm and Helm 1984, 1987).

Some writers have suggested that the trend toward earlier maturation may be slowing down and that in some areas it may have ceased or even been reversed (Eveleth and Tanner 1976, 1991; Vercauteren and Susanne 1985). However, in 1986 Heidi Danker-Hopfe compared the median menarcheal ages of girls in eight countries in the 1950s and 1960s with the median menarcheal ages of girls in the same areas in the 1970s and 1980s and found an average decline in menarcheal age of approximately three and a half months (Table VI.5.2).

Table VI.5.2. *Median menarcheal age of girls in various
European countries, 1950s–60s and 1970s–80s*

Country	Period	Change in median age at menarche (yrs)
Belgium	1965–80/1	–0.10
Croatia (Zagreb)	1964–82	–0.45
France (Paris)	1965/6–74	–0.22
Hungary (Szeged)	1958/9–81/2	–0.43
Italy (Florence)	1955/7–77	–0.58
Netherlands	1965–80	–0.15
Poland (Warsaw)	1965–76	–0.28
United Kingdom (N.E. England and Newcastle-on-Tyne)	1967–71/9	–0.06

Source: Danker-Hopfe (1986).

Europeans Outside Europe

Despite a wealth of information about the heights of Europeans in Europe, we know much less about the secular trend in the heights of European descendants in other parts of the world. The one obvious exception to this rule is the history of changes in the heights of European descendants in the United States. But there is also some information about long-term trends in the heights of European descendants in Australia, the Caribbean, and parts of South America. There have, however, been very few studies of the heights of European descendants in southern Africa.

The main trends in the heights of white Americans in the United States have been summarized on many occasions, including the work of Thomas Cone (1961), Howard Meredith (1963, 1976), Robert Fogel (1986), and Richard Steckel (1989, 1992). In 1986, Fogel revealed that the average heights of native-born white Americans rose steadily from the beginning of the eighteenth century up until the middle of the nineteenth century. This was, however, followed by a sharp decline in the heights of those born during the second half of the nineteenth century, although there was a resumption of the general upward trend in the first third of the twentieth century. Some writers have suggested that the secular trend ceased after World War II, but this suggestion was subsequently contradicted (Bakwin and McLaughlin 1964; Damon 1968). In 1989 R. Bock and R. Sykes demonstrated that the heights of people attending the Fels Institute in Ohio continued to increase after 1945, and T. Greiner and C. Gordon (1992) claimed that the average height of successive birth cohorts of white Americans increased by 0.7 cm per decade between 1910-14 and 1970-4 (Bock and Sykes 1989; Greiner and Gordon 1992).

In addition to studying the heights of adult Americans, a number of authors have also attempted to examine the heights of children. Cone, for example, showed that the average height of Boston children increased by between 3 and 7 centimeters

between 1877 and 1930-56, and Harry Bakwin suggested that this trend continued into the early 1960s (Cone 1961; Bakwin 1964). The most comprehensive survey of heights in the United States was carried out by Meredith in 1963, who found that there had been very little change in either the length or weight of newborn infants since the end of the nineteenth century, but that there had been substantial increases in the heights of children from the age of 1 onward.

It is unclear whether these increases have continued toward the present. Eveleth and Tanner found no evidence of any increase in the heights of children in the United States between 1963-70 and 1976-80, but D. Jones, M. Neshiem, and J.-P. Habicht claimed that there was an increase in the heights of poor children over the same period (Jones et al. 1985; Eveleth and Tanner 1991).

There have also been a number of investigations into changes in the age of menarche among U.S. girls. In 1962 Tanner suggested that the mean age of menarche in the United States fell from 14.2 to 13.0 years between 1900 and 1950. These results have been confirmed by Grace Wyshak and Madeline Goodman. In 1983 Wyshak demonstrated that the mean menarcheal age among women born before 1920 was 0.86 years greater than the mean menarcheal age of women born after 1940 (Wyshak 1983). Goodman studied the mean age of menarche of 3,205 Caucasian, Japanese, and Chinese women in Hawaii who had been born between 1900 and 1940. The menarcheal age of the Caucasian women declined by 2.28 months per decade, whereas that of the Japanese and Chinese women declined by 6.36 months and 5.24 months, respectively (Goodman 1983).[5]

In view of the available data, it is probably inevitable that the anthropometric history of European descendants outside Europe should tend to concentrate on the history of those in the United States. There is, however, some evidence of secular changes in the heights of European descendants in Australia, Cuba, Argentina, and Venezuela. In 1983, for example, Antonio Gordon found that the average height of Cuban men had increased by between 5 and 6 cm since the start of the century, although he denied that the nutritional condition of the Cuban population had improved during the course of this period.

In Argentina, H. Lejarraga and colleagues (1989) showed that the average height of 15-year-old children in Buenos Aires had increased by between 6.5 and 8.2 cm during the interval between 1938 and 1981, and that the average height of 15-year-olds in Entre Rios had increased by between 4.5 and 6 cm between 1950 and 1981. In 1981 N. Farid-Coupal, M. Contreas, and H. Castellano discovered that the mean menarcheal age of girls in the Carabobo district of Venezuela fell by 1.7 years between 1937 and 1969. Moreover, the average height of children in Carabobo increased by 1.6 cm between 1978 and 1987 (Blanco, Landaeta-Jiménez, and Castellano 1989).

We also possess a limited amount of information about the heights of European descendants in Australia and Mozambique. The average height of children in western Australia increased by between 2 and 6 cm between 1940 and 1971, and that of children in Sydney increased by between 2 and 4 cm between 1937 and 1965 (Blanksby et al. 1974). These increases are somewhat greater than those recorded among white children in Mozambique. The average height of 7-year-old children in Lourenço Marques increased by only 0.5 cm (boys) and 1.5 cm (girls) between 1930 and 1965 (Martins 1971).

Africans at Home and Abroad

There have been a number of investigations into the heights of African populations in recent years, but very few of these provide any clear opportunity for chronological comparison. The main source of information about secular trends in the heights of Africans and people of African ancestry has been the United States. The lack of information about secular changes in the heights of Africans in Africa, combined with the poor social and economic circumstances of most of the continent's countries, has made it difficult to construct normal standards for assessing the growth of African children. However, studies of well-off Africans and black populations in the United States have shown that black children grow more quickly than white children between the ages of circa 8 and 14 years and experience puberty at an earlier age. These studies also suggest that Africans and African-Americans are more long-limbed than Europeans and white Americans, but that there is little difference in their final heights (Eveleth and Tanner 1991).

In view of the long history of anthropometric measuring in the United States, it is not surprising that we should possess quite a lot of information about the heights of black Americans. In 1963 Meredith suggested that the average height of 1-year-old boys rose by 5.7 cm between 1918-19 and 1944-56, and that the average height of 6-year-old boys rose by 6.3 cm between 1896-8 and 1957-8. In a separate study, William Moore discovered that the average height of 12-year-old boys increased by 17.41 cm between 1890 and 1968, whereas that of 12-year-old girls increased by 19.57 cm over the same period (Moore 1970). It is not clear whether the heights of black Americans continued to increase after this date. In 1979 Eveleth, E. Bowers, and J. Schall claimed that the average height of black adolescents in Philadelphia had increased by approximately 3.3 cm between 1956-65 and 1977, but the most recent national survey suggests that there was no increase in the heights of black children between 1963-70 and 1976-80 (Eveleth and Tanner 1976, 1991; Jones et al. 1985).

The availability of separate information about the heights of blacks and whites in the United States provides a valuable opportunity to study the secular trend in the heights of different population groups in the same national environment, but it must be admitted that the overall results are somewhat unclear. In his 1963 paper, Meredith argued that black males experienced greater increases in average height between the ages of 0 and 3, whereas white children experienced greater rates of increase between the ages of 6 and 17 (Meredith 1963). Yet Meredith also argued that black men experienced a greater increase in average height during early adulthood, and Moore has claimed that the average height of 14-year-old black boys increased by 2.88 cm per decade between 1890 and 1968. Previous estimates, however, had placed the rate of increase among black and white boys at 1.95 cm and 1.92 cm, respectively (Moore 1970). By contrast, Greiner and Gordon's study of the heights of successive birth cohorts of U.S. army recruits contradicted both studies. They argued that the average height of black Americans born between 1910-14 and 1970-4 increased at less than half the rate achieved by white Americans during the same period (Greiner and Gordon 1992).

Despite such an abundance of information about the heights of African-Americans, we know rather less about secular changes in the heights of Africans in other parts of the world – including Africa itself. The most detailed information comes from southern Africa, where there have been a number of studies of the heights of South African blacks and Kalahari Bushmen. P. Tobias (1962, 1974) found that the average height of adult Bushmen (San) had increased by approximately 3.5 cm since the start of the century, and in 1985 A. Hausman and E. Wilmsen revealed that the heights of San children continued to increase between 1967-8 and 1979-80 (Tobias 1962, 1974; Hausman and Wilmsen 1985).

The situation regarding black populations in other parts of southern Africa is more unclear. Tobias (1975) has argued that most southern African populations "show either the absence of the secular trend . . . or a frankly reversed secular trend" (145), but A. Walker and B. Walker have claimed that the average heights of black children in South Africa rose by up to 6.9 cm between 1938 and 1976 (Tobias 1975; Tobias and Netscher 1976; Walker and Walker 1977).[6]

A number of other studies have focused on the secular trend in the heights of Africans and people of African ancestry in Gambia, Mali, Nigeria, and the Caribbean island of Aruba. In 1981 Elisabeth van Wering demonstrated that the average height of children aged 5 to 14 on Aruba had increased by between 0.7 and 5.8 cm between 1954 and 1974. In a 1979 study suggesting improving nutrition in Nigeria, G. Ucho and A. Okorafor found that the mean menarcheal age of girls had fallen by approximately four months per decade since the early 1960s. However, no evidence of a secular trend toward greater height has been found in either Mali or Gambia. In Mali, the average height of adult men increased by only 0.2 cm between 1902 and 1985 (Prazuck et al. 1988). A longitudinal study of the heights of adult men and women in Gambia between 1951 and 1975 indicated that there was a slight tendency for height to decrease with age, but this was attributed to improvements in measuring techniques rather than to any real improvement in the heights of later-born subjects (Billewicz and Macgregor 1982).

Asiatics in Asia and the Americas

The term "Asiatic" describes a wide range of peoples who are believed to have originated in what is now known as the "Far East." Thus present-day Asiatic populations include Mongols, Arctic Eskimos, American Indians, and Indonesian-Malays. The latter group alone includes the indigenous populations of Japan, China, Thailand, and the Philippines (Eveleth and Tanner 1976, 1991). So far as the secular trend in height is concerned, we have much information about the heights of Japanese people in Japan and the United States and about Chinese people in China and Hong Kong. There is a smaller amount of information about the heights of other Asiatic populations in the United States, South America, and Indonesia.

The Japanese are arguably the most-measured population group in the world. This is largely because Japanese authorities instituted a national program of anthropometric monitoring at the start of the twentieth century and have continued to publish the results ever since (Tanner 1986). In 1966 Eiji Takahashi showed that the average height of Japanese adolescents increased slowly but steadily between 1900 and 1937. Then there was a sharp fall in average heights during World War II, followed by an even sharper increase between 1945 and 1960. The average heights of Japanese adolescents continued to increase after 1960, and in 1982 Tanner and his colleagues found that the average heights of 12-year-old girls and 13-year-old boys had increased by 7.9 cm and 9.7 cm, respectively, between 1957 and 1977. The average height of Japanese adults increased by 4.3 cm (men) and 2.7 cm (women) over the same period (Takahashi 1966; Tanner et al. 1982; see also Meredith 1976).

Students of the growth of Japanese children have also examined changes in the rates of their ages of peak-height-velocity. In 1982 Kenji Matsumoto demonstrated that the age at which Japanese children achieved their peak-height-velocity had fallen steadily over the course of the twentieth century (Matsumoto 1982; see also Nagai et al. 1980). Matsumoto also noted that the age at which girls achieved their peak-height-velocity had fallen particularly rapidly since the end of World War II, and he attributed this change to the dramatic improvement in the nutritional status of Japanese women during that period (Matsumoto et al. 1980). These conclusions correspond closely to those reached by students of the age of menarche. The mean menarcheal age of Japanese girls fell from

15.0 years for those born between 1896 and 1900 to 12.5 years for those born between 1966 and 1970 (Hoshi and Kouchi 1981; Nakamura et al. 1986).

In addition to the Japanese data, there is also a growing body of information about the height of Chinese people in both China and Hong Kong. In 1984 Alan Piazza found that the average height of Chinese boys remained roughly constant between 1915–25 and 1951–8, but rose very sharply between 1951–8 and 1979. He was unable to locate representative data for Chinese girls in the earlier period, but he was able to show that their heights rose equally sharply from 1951 onward.[7] There have also been significant changes in the heights of Chinese children in Hong Kong. J. Ling and N. King found that the average heights of 12-year-old boys increased by 6.7 cm and those of 12-year-old girls increased by 4.2 cm between 1961–3 and 1982–4 (Ling and King 1987: 187; see also Leung et al. 1987). The mean menarcheal age of South Chinese children in Hong Kong fell from 12.85 years in 1961–3 to 12.59 years 16 years later (Low, Kung, and Leong 1982).

We also have some information about the heights of Asiatic peoples in the southern United States, South America, and Indonesia. Pierre van der Eng has argued that the average heights of Indonesian and Indo-European children probably increased between 1911 and the late 1930s, but he was unable to find evidence of any further change between the late 1930s and 1973 (Eng 1995). Robert Malina and A. Zavaleta (1980) have indicated that the average heights of Mexican-American children aged 6 to 8 in the southern United States remained unchanged between 1929–31 and 1968–72, but small increases were recorded in the heights of those aged 8 to 15. The average height of Mexican-American children increased at all ages and at a greater rate between 1968–72 and 1982, but the overall rate of increase still lagged behind that of other U.S. groups. Malina, R. Martorell, and F. Mendoza (1986) concluded that the low rate of secular increase among Mexican-Americans reflected their failure to benefit from social and economic improvements, but their data may have been distorted by the inclusion of an influx of new migrants from Mexico and other South American countries.[8]

It is interesting to compare the heights of Mexican-Americans in the United States with those of Asiatic peoples in South America. In 1974, Eveleth, F. Salzano, and P. de Lima studied the heights of 363 Xingo Indians in Brazil between the ages of 20 and 50 and found no evidence of any increase in the average height of successive birth cohorts (Eveleth, Salzano, and de Lima 1974). In 1982 G. Gonzales, I. Crespo-Retes, and R. Guerra-Garcia claimed that the average height of Puno Indians between the ages of 7 and 20 had increased substantially between 1945 and 1980, but they could find no evidence of any increase in adult heights (Gonzales, Crespo-Retes, and Guerra-Garcia 1982). The findings for adults, but not for children, were echoed by John McCullough in his study of the heights of Yucatec Maya between 1895 and 1968. McCullough concluded that the majority of Mesoamerican populations had failed to experience the secular increase in height that had been observed in most parts of the world since the beginning of the twentieth century (McCullough 1982).

Indo-Mediterraneans of the Near East, North Africa, and India

The term "Indo-Mediterraneans" is used to describe the indigenous populations of the "Near East," North Africa, and India. It includes a wide range of diverse groups, including Hamites, Indo-Dravidians, Egyptians, Kuwaitis, and Libyans, but we know comparatively little about the secular trend in their growth or development. The majority of the relevant published studies concentrate on the populations of different parts of India, but it is possible to supplement these with some observations about possible trends in the heights of people in Ethiopia, Egypt, and Turkey.

Although there have been a number of studies focusing on different aspects of growth and stature in various parts of India, no consistent picture has emerged. It would appear that the pattern of change has varied considerably both between periods and between regions. In 1976 P. Ganguly examined secular changes in the height of 60 population groups and concluded that the dominant trend was toward a diminution of height rather than an increase (Ganguly 1977). This conclusion was reinforced by a study carried out in Hyderabad in 1977, but other investigations contradict it (Shatrugna and Rao 1987). In 1982 L. Sidhu, L. Bhatraga, and A. Dubey argued that the average height of well-off boys attending the Yadvindera Public School in Patiala increased by 7.5 cm between 1948-52 and 1973-7, and S. Singh and P. Malhotra contended that the mean menarcheal age of girls in Patiala fell by 0.65 years between 1974 and 1986 (Sidhu, Bhatraga, and Dubey 1982; Singh and Malhotra 1988). In 1981 D. P. Kaur and R. Singh compared the heights of Gujarati parents with those of their adult offspring and found that the children's heights exceeded their parents' by an average of 2.2 cm (Kaur and Singh 1981).

In view of the uncertainty surrounding the secular trend in the heights of Indians, it is interesting to compare the results of a number of different surveys carried out at different points in time between 1938 and 1982-3. In 1938 A. Chatterjee examined the average heights of more than 33,000 Bengali schoolboys, and the results were republished by W. M. Krogman in *Growth of Man* in 1941. These figures can be compared with the heights of the Indian boys whose measurements were reproduced in Eveleth and Tanner's two volumes in 1976 and 1991. The results suggest that the average height of Indian boys may have declined between 1938 and 1956-65 and then increased sharply between 1956-65 and 1982-3 (Table VI.5.3). However, it is important to note that

these surveys were carried out in different (although partly overlapping) areas and that they may have included different social groups.

One should also be mindful of such caveats when examining the secular trend in the height of other Indo-European populations. In the case of Egypt, information is available about the heights of 10- to 12-year-old boys in the whole of Egypt from 1956 to 1965 and about 10- to 12-year-old boys in East Cairo in circa 1981. The data show that the second group of children were between 3 and 4 cm taller than the first group, but this does not necessarily mean that the East Cairo children were taller than children from the same area or social background in the earlier study.

There is a similar problem with the data for Ethiopia, which show that "Ethiopian and Eritrean" children were between 5.2 and 6.7 cm shorter in 1958 than children in Addis Ababa and other urban areas 7 years later. In the case of Turkey, we can see that 13-year-old girls and 15-year-old boys in Ankara in 1950 were between 3.4 and 14.3 cm shorter than "poor" and "well-off" children in Istanbul in 1970. The figures suggest that average heights may have increased over time, but the difference between Ankara children in 1950 and poor children in Istanbul in 1970 is much less than the difference between the poor children and their well-off contemporaries.

Australian Aborigines and Pacific Island Peoples

This section reviews the available evidence regarding secular changes in the heights of the indigenous inhabitants of Australia, New Zealand, and the Pacific Islands. There have been a number of such studies of Aboriginal children, and in addition, a comparative study has been conducted of the heights of different groups of Samoan children. Insights can also be gained into the pattern of secular change by comparing the results of various surveys of the heights of people in Papua New Guinea.

The most detailed published effort examining Australian Aborigines in order to investigate the extent and nature of secular changes was that carried out by M. Barrett and T. Brown in 1961-9. They found that the adult heights of Aborigines in the central-western part of the Northern Territory were about 5.5 cm greater than the heights of comparable groups of Aborigines 30 years earlier (Barrett and Brown 1971). It is not clear, however, whether the experience of this group was typical of that of other Aborigines or whether the trend toward increased height has continued up to the present day.

In 1991 Eveleth and Tanner compared the heights of children in Barrett and Brown's survey with those of Aboriginal children in western Australia in 1983, and they found that the heights were almost identical. But, as they themselves pointed out, it was impossible to say whether this meant that the secular trend had been halted or merely obscured by cross-sectional

Table VI.5.3. *Average heights of selected groups of Indo-Mediterranean children at different periods*

Country	People or place	Period of study	Source	Height at age 13 (cm)
1. Males				
India	Bengal	<1938	Krogman 1941	147.9
India	India	1956–65	Eveleth & Tanner 1976	141.5
India	Calcutta	1982–3	Eveleth & Tanner 1991	151.5
Egypt	Egypt	1962–3	Eveleth & Tanner 1976	146.3
Egypt	East Cairo	<1981	Eveleth & Tanner 1991	149.0
2. Females				
Ethiopia	Ethiopia & Eritrea	1958	Meredith 1969	142.8
Ethiopia	Urban	1965	Eveleth & Tanner 1976	148.0
Ethiopia	Addis-Ababa	1965	Eveleth & Tanner 1976	147.1
Turkey	Ankara (urban)	1950	Meredith 1969	144.5
Turkey	Istanbul (well-off)	<1973	Eveleth & Tanner 1976	155.6
Turkey	Istanbul (poor)	<1973	Eveleth & Tanner 1976	147.9

Country	People or place	Period of study	Source	Height at age 15 (cm)
1. Males				
India	Bengal	<1938	Krogman 1941	161.3
India	India	1956–65	Eveleth & Tanner 1976	153.0
India	Calcutta	1982–3	Eveleth & Tanner 1991	162.4
Egypt	Egypt	1962–3	Eveleth & Tanner 1976	159.7
Egypt	East Cairo	<1981	Eveleth & Tanner 1991	167.5
Ethiopia	Ethiopia & Eritrea	1958	Meredith 1969	152.2
Ethiopia	Urban	1965	Eveleth & Tanner 1976	158.5
Turkey	Ankara (urban)	1950	Meredith 1969	152.7
Turkey	Istanbul	<1973	Eveleth & Tanner 1976	167.0
Turkey	Istanbul (poor)	<1973	Eveleth & Tanner 1976	159.9

regional variations (Eveleth and Tanner 1976, 1991; see also Abbie 1967, 1968).[9]

In addition to these investigations, we can also examine a more recent inquiry into the heights of three different groups of Samoans. In 1975–7 J. Bindon and S. Zansky compared the heights of children in a "traditional" community of Western Samoa with those of children in two more "modern" communities in American Samoa and Hawaii. They found that there was little difference between the American Samoan children and the Samoan children on Hawaii, but both were consistently taller than the "traditional" children in Western Samoa (Bindon and Zansky 1986). The heights of the Hawaiian Samoans were also considerably greater than those of native Hawaiian children who were measured almost half a century earlier. The average height of native Hawaiian children who were measured before 1930 was approximately 7 cm less than that of Hawaiian Samoan children in the mid-1970s (Krogman 1941).

Insights into the pattern of secular change among Pacific Island peoples can also be gained by comparing the results of a number of recent surveys of the heights of the Bundi and Manus peoples of Papua New Guinea. The Bundi, for example, were among the smallest people in the world when they were first measured by L. A. Malcolm in 1958–60, but their heights had increased considerably by the time a second survey was carried out in 1983–4 (Malcolm 1970; Zemel and Jenkins 1989).

There is also some evidence of an increase in the heights of Manus girls between 1966–8 and 1982, although the heights of Manus boys remained virtually unchanged (Heath and Carter 1971; Schall 1989). In view of the discrepancy between the data for boys and girls and the small number of children involved, it would probably be unwise to reach any firm conclusions about trends in the height of this population at the present time (Eveleth and Tanner 1976, 1991).

Conclusions

This chapter has shown that the average height of people in most parts of the world has increased since the beginning of the twentieth century and that most population groups are probably taller now than at any time in the recent past (Kates and Millman 1990). However, the secular trend toward greater height has been neither universal nor rectilinear (Roche 1979). The average height of populations has increased much more rapidly in Europe and the United States than in many parts of Africa, Asia, and South America, and even those countries that have registered the greatest increases in height have also experienced periods in which the secular trend has either been arrested or reversed (Takahashi 1966; van Wieringen

1979). Moreover, the distribution of heights in virtually all parts of the world continues to be marked by social and economic inequalities (Eveleth and Tanner 1991). This finding suggests that even within the "developed" world large numbers of children do not experience the nutritional and environmental conditions necessary for the achievement of their full height potential (Jones et al. 1985; Whincup, Cook, and Shaper 1988).

A number of writers have attempted to account for the secular trend and for the variations within it. Malina (1979b) attributed the trend to improvements in nutrition and sanitation, urbanization, industrialization, reduced family size, genetic selection, and heterosis. Eveleth and Tanner (1991) have credited improvements in nutrition, the control of infectious diseases, reduced family size, better health care, and population mobility. Other scholars who have examined the consequences of the secular trend have associated it with the reduction of mortality, the lengthening of the female reproductive span, changes in the relationship between children and adults, and increases in physical performance and efficiency (Himes 1979; Malina 1979a, 1979b; Waaler 1984; Eveleth and Tanner 1991).

Several writers have examined the relationship between changes in height (and other anthropometric indicators) and economic growth. In 1984 Floud concluded that variations in Gross Domestic Product (GDP) per head and in infant mortality rates explained "about 96 per cent of the observed variation in heights between and within western European populations since 1880," and that "an increase of one U.S. dollar (at constant 1970 prices) in GDP per capita has been accompanied by an increase in the average height of the population of 0.003 centimeters" (Floud 1984: 18). In 1988 H. Brinkmann, J. Drukker, and B. Slot argued that there was a close association between changes in GDP and the height of Army conscripts in Holland, and K. Liestøl found evidence of a similar relationship between changes of GDP and mean age of menarche in Norway (Liestøl 1982; Brinkmann, Drukker, and Slot 1988; but see also Mandemakers and van Zanden 1993). In 1988 L. A. Schmitt and G. A. Harrison concluded that "affluence" was the most important single cause of the differences that they observed in the average heights of 58 populations whose heights had been recorded in *Human Biology* and *Annals of Human Biology* over the previous 20 years (Schmitt and Harrison 1988).

Although economic growth is probably a necessary precondition for the long-term improvement of health and nutrition, it is not the only factor that has influenced trends in average height over the past 200 years. Both John Komlos and Floud have demonstrated that it is possible for the average height of a population to decline even when its GDP is increasing. In 1989 Komlos showed that soldiers who grew up in the economically more developed regions of

the Hapsburg Empire during the second half of the eighteenth century were shorter than soldiers who grew up in the less developed regions, and Floud revealed that the average height of successive birth cohorts of British soldiers declined during the middle years of the nineteenth century (Komlos 1989; Floud et al. 1990). In 1983 Steckel concluded that differences between the average heights of 22 contemporary populations were attributable to variations in national income, income inequality, and welfare provision (Steckel 1983). These findings are reinforced by the dramatic increases in average height in China and those that have been achieved in some parts of India and Sri Lanka since the end of World War II (Drèze and Sen 1989; Kates and Millman 1990).

Bernard Harris

Notes

1. For example, in 1904 the British Interdepartmental Committee on Physical Deterioration urged the government to institute a national program of anthropometric monitoring as a means of providing accurate information about the health and physique of the British population (see Harris 1989).
2. There is also evidence of a secular trend toward greater adult height among the Skolt Lapps of northern Finland (see Lewin, Jürgens, and Louekari 1970).
3. Bakwin (1964) has demonstrated that the weight of Scottish newborns increased by several hundred grams in the 85-year period between 1850-60 and 1935-45. But this appears to be the exception rather than the rule so far as European studies are concerned.
4. It is likely that Tanner overestimated the decline in mean menarcheal age in Norway. More recent estimates suggest that the actual age of menarche in 1840 was between 15.6 and 16.0 years. This would mean that the decline in mean menarcheal age between 1840 and 1950 was between 2.4 and 2.8 years (see Bruntland and Wallø 1976; Brudevoll, Liestøl, and Wallø 1979, 1980).
5. Goodman interviewed 1,291 Caucasian women, 1,519 Japanese women, and 395 Chinese women. Results were based on personal recall (Goodman 1983).
6. It is important to note that the average height of black South Africans remained well below that of more affluent black populations elsewhere in the world, as well as that of white children in the same country (Walker and Walker 1977).
7. The average height of Chinese children between the ages of 7 and 14 increased by approximately 8.04 cm between 1951-8 and 1979. The rate of increase was greater than that of any European population and roughly equal to that of Japanese children in this period (Piazza 1984).
8. These findings contrast with those of Greiner and Gordon (1992), who claim that the increase in the average height of successive birth cohorts of Hispanic-Americans was greater than that of any other ethnic group. However, they also claim that the overall rate of increase for Hispanic-Americans, for a range of 22 bodily dimensions, was generally below that of the white population.
9. W. J. Fysh and colleagues (1977) compared the birth weights of infants at Cherborg and Palm Island Aboriginal settlements in 1953, 1963, and 1972. There was a small increase in the birth weights of male infants at Cherborg set-

tlement between 1953 and 1963 but a sharp decline between 1963 and 1972. By contrast, the birth weights of male infants at Palm Island settlement increased between 1963 and 1972. The birth weights of female infants remained unchanged in both settlements.

Bibliography

Abbie, A. 1967. Skinfold thickness in Australian Aborigines. *Archaeology and Physical Anthropology in Oceania* 2: 207-19.

    1968. The homogeneity of Australian Aborigines. *Archaeology and Physical Anthropology in Oceania* 3: 223-31.

Bakwin, H. 1964. The secular change in growth and development. *Acta Paediatrica* 53: 79-89.

Bakwin, H., and S. McLaughlin. 1964. Secular increase in height: Is the end in sight? *Lancet* 2: 1195-6.

Barrett, M., and T. Brown. 1971. Increase in average height of Australian Aborigines. *Medical Journal of Australia* 2: 1169-72.

Billewicz, W., and I. Macgregor. 1982. A birth-to-maturity longitudinal study of heights and weights in two West African Gambian villages, 1951-75. *Annals of Human Biology* 9: 309-20.

Bindon, J., and S. Zansky. 1986. Growth patterns of height and weight among three groups of Samoan preadolescents. *Annals of Human Biology* 13: 171-8.

Bjelke, E. 1971. Variation in height and weight in the Norwegian population. *British Journal of Preventive and Social Medicine* 25: 192-202.

Blanco, M., M. Landaeta-Jiménez, and H. Castellano. 1989. Secular trend in height and weight: Carabobo, Venezuela. In *Auxology '88: Perspectives in the science of growth and development,* ed. J. Tanner, 207-10. London.

Blanksby, B., L. Freedman, P. Barrett, and J. Bloomfield. 1974. Secular change in the heights and weights of Western Australian primary schoolchildren. *Annals of Human Biology* 1: 301-9.

Bock, R., and R. Sykes. 1989. Evidence for continuing secular increase in height within families in the United States. *American Journal of Human Biology* 1: 143-8.

Brinkman, H., J. Drukker, and B. Slot. 1988. Height and income: A new method for the estimation of historical national income series. *Explorations in Economic History* 25: 227-64.

Brudevoll, J., K. Liestøl, and L. Walløe. 1979. Menarcheal age in Oslo during the last 140 years. *Annals of Human Biology* 6: 407-16.

Brundtland, G., K. Liestøl, and L. Walløe. 1980. Height, weight and menarcheal age of Oslo schoolchildren during the last sixty years. *Annals of Human Biology* 7: 307-22.

Brundtland, G., and L. Walløe. 1976. Menarcheal age in Norway in the nineteenth century: A reevaluation of the historical sources. *Annals of Human Biology* 3: 363-74.

Cameron, N. 1979. The growth of London schoolchildren 1904-66: An analysis of secular trend and intra-county variation. *Annals of Human Biology* 6: 505-25.

Cone, T. 1961. Secular acceleration of height and biologic maturation in children during the past century. *Journal of Pediatrics* 59: 736-40.

Damon, A. 1968. Secular trend in height and weight within old-American families at Harvard 1870-1965. *American Journal of Physical Anthropology* 29: 45-50.

Danker-Hopfe, H. 1986. Menarcheal age in Europe. *Yearbook of Physical Anthropology* 29: 81-112.

Drèze, J., and A. Sen. 1989. *Hunger and public action.* Oxford.

Eng, P. van der. 1995. An inventory of secular changes in human growth in Indonesia. In *The biological standard of living on three continents: Further explorations in anthropometric history,* ed. J. Komlos, 175-90. Boulder, Colo.

Eveleth, P. 1979. Population differences in growth: Environmental and genetic factors. In *Human growth,* Vol. 3, ed. F. Falkner and J. Tanner, 373-94. London.

Eveleth, P., E. Bowers, and J. Schall. 1979. Secular change in growth of Philadelphia black adolescents. *Human Biology* 51: 213-28.

Eveleth, P., F. Salzano, and P. de Lima. 1974. Child growth and adult physique in Brazilian Xingu Indians. *American Journal of Physical Anthropology* 41: 95-102.

Eveleth, P., and J. Tanner. 1976. *Worldwide variation in human growth.* First edition. Cambridge and New York.

    1991. *Worldwide variation in human growth.* Second edition. Cambridge and New York.

Farid-Coupal, N., M. Contreras, and H. Castellano. 1981. The age at menarche in Carabobo, Venezuela, with a note on the secular trend. *Annals of Human Biology* 8: 283-8.

Floud, R. 1984. The heights of Europeans since 1750: A new source for European economic history. *National Bureau of Economic Research Working Papers,* No. 1318, Cambridge, Mass.

Floud, R., K. Wachter, and A. Gregory. 1990. *Height, health and history: Nutritional status in the United Kingdom 1750-1980.* Cambridge.

Fogel, R. 1986. Nutrition and the decline in mortality since 1700: Some preliminary findings. In *Long-term factors in American economic growth,* ed. S. Engerman and R. Gallman, 439-555. Chicago.

Fysh, W., R. Davidson, D. Chandler, and A. Dugdale. 1977. The weights of Aboriginal infants: A comparison over twenty years. *Medical Journal of Australia Special Supplement* 1: 13-15.

Ganguly, P. 1977. The problem of human adaptation: An overview. *Man in India* 57: 1-22.

Gonzales, G., I. Crespo-Retes, and R. Guerra-Garcia. 1982. Secular change in growth of native children and adolescents at high altitude: I. Puno, Peru 3,800 metres. *American Journal of Physical Anthropology* 58: 191-5.

Goodman, M. 1983. Letter to the editor – Secular changes in recalled age at menarche. *Annals of Human Biology* 10: 585.

Gordon, A. 1983. The nutriture of Cubans: Historical perspective and nutritional analysis. *Cuban Studies* 13: 1-38.

Greiner, T., and C. Gordon. 1992. Secular trends of 22 body dimensions in four racial/cultural groups of American males. *American Journal of Human Biology* 4: 235-46.

Greulich, W. 1976. Some secular changes in the growth of American-born and native Japanese children. *American Journal of Physical Anthropology* 45: 553-68.

Harris, B. 1989. Medical inspection and the nutrition of

schoolchildren in Britain, 1900-50. Ph.D. thesis, University of London.

Hausman, A., and E. Wilmsen. 1985. Economic change and secular trends in the growth of San children. *Human Biology* 57: 563-71.

Heath, B., and J. Carter. 1971. Growth and somatotype patterns of Manus children, Territory of Papua and New Guinea: Application of a modified somatotype method to the study of growth patterns. *American Journal of Physical Anthropology* 35: 49-67.

Helm, P., and S. Helm. 1984. Decrease in menarcheal age from 1966 to 1983 in Denmark. *Acta Obstetricia Gynecologica Scandinavica* 63: 633-5.

1987. Uncertainties in designation of age at menarche in the nineteenth century: Revised means for Denmark, 1835. *Annals of Human Biology* 14: 371-4.

Himes, J. 1979. Secular changes in body proportions and composition. In *Secular trends in human growth, maturation and development*. Monographs of the Society for Research in Child Development 44 (Serial no. 179, nos. 3-4): 28-58.

Hoshi, H., and M. Kouchi. 1981. Secular trend of the age at menarche of Japanese girls with special regard to the secular acceleration of the age at peak height velocity. *Human Biology* 53: 593-8.

Jones, D., M. Nesheim, and J.-P. Habicht. 1985. Influences in child growth associated with poverty in the 1970s: An examination of HANESI and HANESII cross-sectional US national surveys. *American Journal of Clinical Nutrition* 42: 714-24.

Kates, R., and S. Millman. 1990. On ending hunger: The lessons of history. In *Hunger in history: Food shortage, poverty and deprivation,* ed. L. Newman, W. Crossgrove, R. Kates, et al., 389-407. Oxford.

Kaur, D., and R. Singh. 1981. Parent–adult offspring correlations and heritability of body measurements in a rural Indian population. *Annals of Human Biology* 8: 333-9.

Komlos, J. 1989. *Nutrition and economic development in the eighteenth-century Habsburg monarchy.* Princeton, N.J.

ed. 1995. *The biological standard of living on three continents: Further explorations in anthropometric history.* Boulder, Colo.

Krogman, W. M. 1941. *Growth of man.* The Hague, the Netherlands.

Laska-Mierzejewska, T., H. Milicer, and H. Piechaczek. 1982. Age at menarche and its secular trend in urban and rural girls in Poland. *Annals of Human Biology* 9: 227-34.

Lejarraga, H., I. Meletti, S. Brocca, and V. Alonso. 1989. Secular trend and environmental influences on growth at adolescence in Argentina. In *Auxology '88: Perspectives in the science of growth and development,* ed. J. Tanner, 211-19. London.

Leung, S., Y. Lam, S. Lui, et al. 1987. Height, weight and head circumference in Shatin children 3-7 years of age: Further evidence for secular changes. *Hong Kong Journal of Paediatrics* 4: 43-51.

Lewin, T., H. Jürgens, and L. Louekari. 1970. Secular trend in the adult height of Skolt Lapps: Studies in 1915, 1934 and 1968 of stature changes at population and familial level in a genetic isolate. *Arctic Anthropology* 7: 53-62.

Liestøl, K. 1982. Social conditions and menarcheal age: The importance of early years of life. *Annals of Human Biology* 9: 521-37.

Ling, J., and N. King. 1987. Secular trends in stature and weight in southern Chinese children in Hong Kong. *Annals of Human Biology* 14: 187-90.

Ljung, B., A. Bergsten-Brucefors, and G. Lindgren. 1974. The secular trend in physical growth in Sweden. *Annals of Human Biology* 1: 245-56.

Low, W., L. Kung, and J. Leong. 1982. Secular trend in the sexual maturation of Chinese girls. *Human Biology* 54: 539-51.

Malcolm, L. 1970. Growth and development of the Bundi children of the New Guinea highlands. *Human Biology* 42: 293-328.

Malina, R. 1979a. Secular changes in growth, maturation and physical performance. *Exercise and Sports Sciences Review* 6: 203-55.

1979b. Secular changes in size and maturity: Causes and effects. In *Secular trends in human growth, maturation and development.* Monographs of the Society for Research in Child Development 44 (serial no. 179, nos. 3-4): 59-102.

Malina, R., R. Martorell, and F. Mendoza. 1986. Growth status of Mexican-American children and youths: Historical trends and contemporary issues. *Yearbook of Physical Anthropology* 29: 45-79.

Malina, R., and A. Zavaleta. 1980. Secular trend in the stature and weight of Mexican-American children in Texas between 1930 and 1970. *American Journal of Physical Anthropology* 52: 453-61.

Mandemakers, C., and J. L. van Zanden. 1993. The height of conscripts and national income: Apparent relations and misconceptions. *Explorations in Economic History* 30: 81-97.

Martins, D. da Costa. 1971. Height, weight and chest circumference of children of different ethnic groups in Lourenço Marques, Moçambique, in 1965, with a note on the secular trend. *Human Biology* 43: 253-64.

Matsumoto, K. 1982. Secular acceleration of growth in height in Japanese [children] and its social background. *Annals of Human Biology* 9: 399-410.

Matsumoto, K., Y. Kudo, H. Takeuchi, and S. Takeda. 1980. Secular trend in age of maximum increment in mean height of Japanese children born from 1887 to 1965. *Wakayama Medical Reports* 23: 99-106.

McCullough, J. 1982. Secular trend for stature in adult male Yucatec Maya to 1968. *American Journal of Physical Anthropology* 58: 221-5.

Meredith, H. 1963. Change in the stature and body weight of North American boys during the last eighty years. *Advances in Child Development and Behaviour* 6: 69-114.

1969. *Body size of contemporary youth in different parts of the world.* Monographs of the Society for Research in Child Development 34 (serial no. 131, no. 7).

1976. Findings from Asia, Australia, Europe and North America on secular changes in mean height of children, youths and adults. *American Journal of Physical Anthropology* 44: 315-26.

Moore, W. 1970. The secular trend in physical growth of North American Negro schoolchildren. *Monographs of the Society for Research in Child Development* 35: 62-73.

Nagai, N., K. Matsumoto, T. Mino, et al. 1980. The secular trends in the menarcheal age and the maximum growth age in height for Japanese schoolgirls. *Wakayama Medical Reports* 23: 41-5.

Nakamura, I., M. Shimura, K. Nonaka, and T. Miura. 1986. Changes of recollected menarcheal age and month among women in Tokyo over a period of ninety years. *Annals of Human Biology* 13: 547-54.

Piazza, A. 1984. *Food consumption and nutritional status in the People's Republic of China.* Boulder, Colo.

Prazuck, T., A. Fisch, E. Pichard, and Y. Sidibe. 1988. Lack of secular change in male adult stature in rural Mali West Africa. *American Journal of Physical Anthropology* 75: 471-5.

Prebeg, Z. 1984. Secular trend in growth of Zagreb schoolchildren. In *Human growth and development,* ed. J. Borms, R. Hauspie, C. Sand, et al., 201-7. New York.

Rea, J. 1971. Social and economic influences on the growth of pre-school children in Lagos. *Human Biology* 43: 46-63.

Roche, A. 1979. Introduction. In *Secular trends in human growth, maturation and development.* Monographs of the Society for Research in Child Development 44 (serial no. 179, nos. 3-4): 1-2.

Rona, R., A. Swan, and D. Altman. 1978. Social factors and height of primary schoolchildren in England and Scotland. *Journal of Epidemiology and Community Health* 32: 147-54.

Rosenberg, M. 1988. Birth weight in three Norwegian cities, 1860-1984: Secular trends and influencing factors. *Annals of Human Biology* 15: 275-88.

Schall, J. 1989. Fat patterns and blood pressure among the Manus of Papua New Guinea: A migrant study. *American Journal of Physical Anthropology* 78: 296.

Schmitt, L., and G. Harrison. 1988. Patterns in the within-population variability of stature and weight. *Annals of Human Biology* 15: 353-64.

Shatrugna, V., and K. Rao. 1987. Secular trends in the height of women from the urban poor community of Hyderabad. *Annals of Human Biology* 14: 275-7.

Sidhu, L., B. Bhatraga, and A. Dubey. 1982. Secular trends in height and weight of Punjabi boys. *Anthropologischer Anzeiger* 40: 187-92.

Singh, S., and P. Malhotra. 1988. Secular shift in menarcheal age of Patiala India schoolgirls between 1974 and 1986. *Annals of Human Biology* 15: 77-80.

Steckel, R. 1983. Height and per capita income. *Historical Methods* 16: 1-7.

   1989. Heights and health in the United States 1710-1950. In *Auxology '88: Perspectives in the science of growth and development,* ed. J. Tanner, 175-85. London.

   1992. Stature and living standards in the United States. In *American economic growth and standards of living before the Civil War,* ed. R. Gallman and J. Wallis, 265-308. Chicago.

Steendijk, R. 1966. The secular trend in growth and maturation. *Tijdschrift voor sociale Geneeskunde* 44: 518-23.

Suchy, J. 1972. Trend of physical development of Czech youth in the twentieth century. *Review of Czechoslovak Medicine* 18: 18-27.

Takahashi, E. 1966. Growth and environmental factors in Japan. *Human Biology* 38: 112-30.

Tanner, J. 1962. *Growth at adolescence, with a general consideration of the effects of hereditary and environmental factors upon growth and maturation from birth to maturity.* Second edition. Oxford.

   1966. The secular trend towards earlier physical maturation. *Tijdschrift voor sociale Geneeskunde* 44: 524-38.

   1981. *A history of the study of human growth.* Cambridge and New York.

   1986. Growth as a mirror of the condition of society: Secular trends and class distinctions. In *Human growth: A multidisciplinary review,* ed. A. Demirjian, 3-34. London and Philadelphia, Pa.

Tanner, J., T. Hayashi, M. Preece, and N. Cameron. 1982. Increase in length of leg relative to trunk size in Japanese children and adults from 1957 to 1977: Comparison with British and with Japanese Americans. *Annals of Human Biology* 9: 411-23.

Tobias, P. 1962. On the increasing stature of the Bushmen. *Anthropos* 57: 801-10.

   1974. Growth and stature in southern African populations. In *The human biology of environmental change: Proceedings of a conference held in Blantyre, Malawi, April 5-12, 1971,* ed. D. Vorster, 96-104. London.

   1975. Stature and secular trend among South African Negroes and San Bushmen. *South African Journal of Medical Sciences* 40: 145-64.

Tobias, P., and D. Netscher. 1976. Evidence from African Negro skeletons for a reversal of the usual secular trend. *Journal of Anatomy* 121: 435-6.

Ucho, G., and A. Okorafor. 1979. The age at menarche in Nigerian urban schoolgirls. *Annals of Human Biology* 6: 395-8.

van Venrooij-Ijsselmuiden, M., H. Smeets, and J. van der Werff Ten Bosch. 1976. The secular trend in age at menarche in the Netherlands. *Annals of Human Biology* 3: 283-4.

Vercauteren, M., and C. Susanne. 1985. The secular trend of height and menarche in Belgium: Are there any signs of a future stop? *European Journal of Pediatrics* 144: 306-9.

Vlastovsky, V. 1966. The secular trend in the growth and development of children and young persons in the Soviet Union. *Human Biology* 38: 219-30.

Waaler, H. 1984. Height, weight and mortality: The Norwegian experience. *Acta Medica Scandinavica,* Supplementum 679: 1-51.

Walker, A., and B. Walker. 1977. Studies on increases in growth rate of South African black schoolchildren and their significance to health. *South African Medical Journal* 51: 707-12.

Walker, M., A. Shaper, and G. Wannamethee. 1988. Height and social class in middle-aged British men. *Journal of Epidemiology and Community Health* 42: 299-303.

Ward, J. 1990. Weight and length at birth in Edinburgh, 1847-1920. Paper presented to the Tenth International Economic History Congress, University of Leuven, August.

Ward, W. 1988. Birth weight and standards of living in Vienna, 1865-1930. *Journal of Interdisciplinary History* 19: 203-29.

Wering, E. van. 1981. The secular growth trend on Aruba between 1954 and 1974. *Human Biology* 53: 105-15.

Whincup, P., A. Cook, and A. Shaper. 1988. Social class and height. *British Medical Journal* 297: 980-1.

Wieringen, J. van. 1979. Secular growth changes. In *Human growth,* Vol. 2, ed. F. Falkner and J. Tanner, 445-73. London.

Wyshak, G. 1983. Secular changes in age at menarche in a sample of United States women. *Annals of Human Biology* 10: 75-7.

Zemel, B., and C. Jenkins. 1989. Dietary change and adolescent growth among the Bundi (Gende-speaking) people of Papua New Guinea. *American Journal of Human Biology* 1: 709-18.

VI.6 ⟋ The Nutrition of Women in the Developing World

There are at least two reasons why the nutritional status of women should be distinguished from that of men. The first is that a woman's nutritional status has a direct impact on her children. Better-nourished mothers lead to better-nourished infants by virtue of prepregnancy nutritional status, weight gain during pregnancy, and diet during lactation. This approach to women's nutritional status encapsulates the traditional "breeder and feeder" view.

The second reason is that women exhibit certain nurturing and allocative behaviors, reflecting societal roles, that enhance the food and nutrition security of the entire household and of children in particular. This behavior is most commonly demonstrated in the way women allocate their time and their own income and is particularly visible in certain types of female-headed households. Through both the direct and indirect links, women are the "gatekeepers" of the food and nutritional status of their household's members.

The objective of this chapter is to summarize the literature underlying such links between gender and nutrition within a conceptual framework. Eight main links are identified and discussed in turn, although it should be recognized that this organization is merely a convenient representation of the issues, and that there is considerable overlap across links.

Link 1. Mother's Nutritional Status, Infant and Child Health, and Supplementary Feeding

Birth weight is the single most important determinant of neonatal and infant mortality and of child growth to the age of 7. A number of maternal factors have been shown to be significant determinants of birth weight; most important is the mother's progravid weight and weight gain during pregnancy. Women entering pregnancy with a low preconception weight are several times more likely to produce a low-birth-weight baby (one less than 2,500 grams). Mean birth weight increases, and the incidence of low birth weight decreases, as the preconception weight of the mother increases (Lechtig et al. 1975).

Birth weight and maternal weight gain during pregnancy are also highly correlated, in part, because prenatal weight gain is associated with a decrease in the incidence of prematurity (gestational age less than 37 weeks). If nutritional status before pregnancy, as judged by low progravid weight, is less than adequate, weight gain during pregnancy becomes even more important in influencing neonatal outcomes.

Unfortunately, data indicate that weight gain during pregnancy in developing countries is typically suboptimal. In developed countries the average weight gain during pregnancy is 10 to 12 kilograms, but in developing countries it is 2 to 7 kilograms (Ghassemi 1990). Moreover, for many women in developing countries, negative weight gains are common during pregnancy. Part of the reason for this is a tendency to either not increase food intake or, in some cases, to decrease the amount of food consumed – a phenomenon labeled "eating down" during pregnancy (Brems and Berg 1988).

Although limiting calorie consumption during pregnancy is practiced by some women, in many areas a high level of physical activity, uncompensated by additional calories, is the more common reason for low weight gain during pregnancy. For example, a study in Gambia showed that birth weights were decreased only after the peak period of agricultural labor; during nonpeak seasons, birth weights were close to international norms (Lawrence and Whitehead 1988). Such data indicate that when agricultural labor demands are high, women are unable to cope with pregnancy solely by increasing caloric consumption.

Certain types of illness patterns during pregnancy can also have an adverse effect on the development of the fetus and the neonate. The incidence of low birth weight is known to increase following rubella, and the early onset of labor is common for women with hepatitis and measles. Some maternal infections can cause intrauterine growth retardation, and these infections are more common where poor hygiene is prevalent, as is the case in many low-income areas of developing countries. Thus, a study in four villages in Guatemala indicated high rates of maternal infections during pregnancy and consequently intrauterine exposure of the fetus to infectious agents (Lechtig et al. 1974).

In more general terms, the morbidity of mothers also correlates with a higher incidence of low birth weight. Classification of women in the four Guatemalan villages into high or low morbidity groups found that 33 percent of infants born to those in the high morbidity group were low birth weight compared to 10.5 percent of infants from women of low morbidity (Lechtig et al. 1974). The authors also found that those in the high morbidity group tended to come from homes with low calorie availability; they interpreted this to mean that morbidity during pregnancy is likely to be associated with a low energy consumption.

These maternal characteristics often occur in combination with each other. In other words, women who begin pregnancy with a low progravid weight often gain inadequate weight and have a high incidence of infection during pregnancy.

Dietary supplementation schemes targeted to high-risk women have been one type of intervention aimed at reducing adverse outcomes of pregnancy. A number of investigations in developing countries have indicated that calorie supplementation during pregnancy results in improved birth weight, decreases rates of prematurity, increases weight gain of the mother, and decreases incidence of anemia and toxemia in program participants (Iyenger 1967; Lechtig et al. 1975; Kielmann, Taylor, and Parker 1978). However, not all programs have been successful, and some researchers have criticized supplementation schemes as being too expensive for the benefits produced (Beaton and Ghassemi 1982). Those deemed successful have certain characteristics in common; typically a large ration is targeted to nutritionally vulnerable women, usually in combination with prenatal health services (Kennedy and Knudsen 1985).

Now, however, maternal dietary supplementation schemes are a less popular type of nutrition intervention. Irregular participation because of little time for such an activity was a major factor limiting effectiveness. A more promising approach to improving women's nutritional status, including that of pregnant women, is to decrease their physical activity – particularly during the last trimester of pregnancy. This approach appears more culturally acceptable than promoting maternal weight gain in many developing countries.

Link 2: Women's Nutritional Status, Time Allocation, and Energy Expenditure: Output Effects

The general assumption is that better-nourished individuals will be more productive. However, the empirical literature that deals with the effects of improved nutritional status on physical and cognitive productivity in developing countries is relatively thin. The evidence is strongest for men, because male labor force data are most readily available. An example of the short-term impact of calorie intake on productivity and capacity may be found in E. Kennedy's 1989 study of women in the south Nyanza district of rural Kenya. There, increases in household income (in both female- and male-headed households), due to agricultural commercialization, raised female calorie intake but did not improve female nutritional status (according to anthropometric measures) or health status. Female body mass index actually declined during a time of rising calorie intake, suggesting that the energy intensity of female activities was increasing disproportionately.

Short-run income-enhancing attempts to alleviate the time constraint of women may not succeed, even if a woman is prepared to place her nutritional needs above those of her family. A 1988 study by S. Kumar and D. Hotchkiss of Nepalese hill districts found that because of low agricultural productivity, new land needed to be cleared to maintain household basic needs. However, the subsequent deforestation increased the time allocated by women to collect fuel. This meant less time for female agricultural labor input, which led to fewer calories from this income source, which, in turn, increased the need for deforestation, and so on, in a downward spiral.

Link 3: Women's Share of Household Income and Household Food Security: Roles, Preferences, and Constraints

Household food security has been defined as the access of all people at all times to sufficient food for an active and healthy life (World Bank 1986). Two of the biggest determinants of household food consumption are income and prices. Rising income and falling food prices increase a household's ability to obtain an adequate diet. However, an accumulating body of evidence now suggests that it is not simply the *level* of household income but *who earns* that income that is important in improving a household's food intake.

Income controlled by women, particularly in Africa, is more likely to be spent on food than is male-controlled income (Braun and Kennedy 1994). At similar levels of income, households with more women-controlled income are more likely to be food secure. Evidence for the positive influence of female control of income on household food expenditure (Haddad and Hoddinott 1991), calorie intake (Garcia 1991), and anthropometric indicators (Thomas 1990) is increasing in both Africa and Asia.

This influence may be explained by a number of factors: (1) societal gender roles that cast women in the role of "gatekeepers"; (2) different preferences (women may prefer to spend more on children's food because they spend more time with them); (3) different constraints (women may spend more on food when more income is earned because of a need to purchase more expensive calories that take less time to prepare); or (4) different transaction costs (women earn money in flows that are more easily spent on food). Whatever the reason, getting income into the hands of women seems to be one way of enhancing the household's food security.

Link 4: Women's Time Allocation, Energy Expenditure, and Household Food Security: The Value of Women's Time

During times of economic hardship, women tend to act as "shock absorbers" for the welfare of the household, reflecting the undervalued nature of their time. There is a certain invisibility to the economic contribution of women outside the home as measured by censuses and International Labor Organization (ILO) statistics. R. B. Dixon (1982) documented this invisibility for a number of countries by comparing data from ILO, the Food and Agricultural Organization of the United Nations (FAO), and national agricultural census estimates of the percentage of the agricultural labor force that is female. For many North African and South Asian states, these three sets of statistics are widely divergent, and the formal censuses tend to cloak secondary and tertiary female economic activities.

An example of this shock-absorber behavior has been characterized in Latin America as the "feminization" of poverty (Buvinic 1990). During economic crises that result in less male employment, women enter the labor force to bolster household income and food security. But because women are less well educated, they tend to accept jobs that men would not and are paid very low wages for those jobs because the supply of female labor outweighs the demand for it.

Link 5: Household Food Security and Preschooler Food Security: Intrahousehold Allocation of Food

The identification of pockets of malnutrition and poverty within otherwise "better-off" households is one indication that household resources are not always allocated equitably or according to need. A survey of 45 developing countries found that in all but two of these girls die at a higher rate than boys between the ages of 1 and 4 (MacCormack 1988).

Part of this gender disparity in mortality is because of intrahousehold resource allocation. There are strong indications that female children are discriminated against in the allocation of food and other resources in South Asia (Carloni 1981; Chen, Huq, and d'Souza 1981; Harriss 1986). In sub-Saharan Africa, however, evidence for the maldistribution of food and other resources away from girls is not as clear. A recent review of nutrition studies in Africa by P. Svedberg (1990) did not find girls disfavored relative to boys in terms of anthropometric indicators. One interpretation of these findings is that the economic value of girls to households is more explicit and obvious in Africa than in Asia.

Another point, however, is that young children – whether boys or girls – seem to be generally disfavored in the allocation of family food. In recent studies from Kenya and the Philippines, preschool-aged children had a lower level of dietary energy adequacy than the household as a whole. In Kenya, average household calorie adequacy was 94 percent of requirements, but the energy adequacy of the child's diet was only between 60 and 70 percent, depending on age. Similarly, in the Philippines, although household calorie adequacy was in the 85 to 95 percent range, it was only 70 percent for preschoolers (Kennedy and Haddad 1992).

It is important to note, however, that the allocation bias of food tends to disappear for boys as they get older, but not for girls. Females tend to meet a smaller percentage of their energy requirements than do males in the same households (McGuire and Popkin 1990), in part because of a biased allocation of food away from women, and in part because of the energy intensity of women's activities.

This combination of women's reproductive role, heavy workload, and inadequate diet contributes to a series of nutritional problems for developing-country females, not least among them that they live shorter lives by about 10 years when compared to women in the industrialized world (Ghassemi 1990). A majority of the world's women are anemic; nonpregnant women are 2 to 3 times more likely to be anemic than men, whereas pregnant women are 20 times more likely to be anemic (McGuire and Popkin 1990).

To some extent, the poor nutritional status of women is due to differences in bargaining power and productivity across household members. For instance, if one individual in a household has better nutritional status than the remaining household members, is this attributable to his or her superior bargaining power, or is it simply an efficient allocation of resources to the individual best able (now or later) to raise household income? The primary determinants of bargaining power and productivity are cultural phenomena on the one hand (discrimination in, for example, education, time burdens, health care) and randomly distributed initial endowments of physical and cognitive abilities on the other hand.

Link 6: Women's Time Allocation and Preschooler Nutritional Status: Female-Headed Households

In many countries, the pattern of bias in the allocation of food to young children is influenced by the gender of the head of household. Recent studies in Kenya, Malawi, and the Dominican Republic, for example, find that at very low levels of income, some types of female-headed households – those in which the male head of household is absent for more than 50 percent of the time – have lower levels of preschooler malnutrition than male-headed households at comparable income levels (Kennedy and Peters 1992). This finding tends to buttress our earlier assertion that women may allocate proportionately more of their incomes to food and more of the household calories to children.

Other types of time-intensive nurturing behavior, such as feeding children more frequently, are also more common in some types of female-headed households. Such behavior is important to understand, because interventions that can promote appropriate nurturing behavior for children may be quite effective in enhancing nutritional status.

The successful food security and nutrition coping mechanisms exhibited in some types of female-headed households have limits, however. The growing number of female-headed households in developing countries is of concern because these households tend to be more vulnerable to poverty, and in Latin America, a growing number of women and children are living in poverty because of the increase of such households (Buvinic 1990). Women in female-headed households tend to be poorer because they have less access to labor, land, credit, and government resources (Rosenhouse 1989). In addition, as already mentioned, where women can participate in the labor force, they tend to do so with low-paying jobs (Buvinic 1990).

Link 7: Preschooler Nutritional Status and Women's Time Allocation: Intergenerational Effects

The nutritional status and morbidity levels of preschoolers will help determine the transmission of nutritional status across generations. Studies cited under Link 4 demonstrate the importance of early nutrition on later physical and cognitive performance. An additional pathway is through role-model formation and expectation setting. Better-educated parents, who promote better nutritional status for their children, will tend to expect enhanced school performance, which, in turn, will promote enhanced adult productivity. This is one way of breaking the intergenerational cycle of poverty and poor nutritional status.

Evidence of intergenerational transmission effects is provided by M. Buvinic (1990): Abandoned mothers in Santiago, Chile, tend to come from female-headed households. Moreover, D. Thomas (1991) has shown, with data from Ghana, the United States, and Brazil, that the intergenerational effects tend to run along gender lines: The father's education has a stronger effect on the son's anthropometric status, and the mother's education has a stronger effect on the daughter's anthropometric status.

Other intergenerational effects include (1) the impact healthier infants have on reduced health expenditures later in life and (2) the improved provision of old-age security for parents from healthier children.

Link 8: Women's Nutritional Status and Their Time Allocation and Energy Expenditure: A Zero-Sum Game?

Non-income-mediated pathways may be as important, or in some cases more important, than income alone in improving or maintaining child nutritional status. Almost all the non-income links to nutritional status are time-intensive. Links 2, 4, and 6 discuss the impact of women's time allocation decisions on household income, household food security, and preschooler nutritional status. Link 8 suggests that these relationships are not without cost (and are, therefore, unsustainable) in terms of women's nutritional status.

Time allocation studies indicate that, on average, women in developing countries put more hours per day into nonleisure activities than do men (Juster and Stafford 1991). Not only are women actively engaged in agriculture and wage-generating activities, but a substantial amount of their day is devoted to home production activities such as getting water and fuel wood, preparing meals, and child care. In many rural areas, domestic activities account for the largest proportion of women's time in any given day. Unfortu-

nately, low-income women have even longer working days than their higher-income counterparts, further exacerbating the poverty–malnutrition cycle.

In addition, many of the health-promoting strategies advocated as part of the child survival revolution – breast feeding, growth monitoring, oral rehydration therapy – add to the time constraints of women. Indeed, the low level of utilization of these child survival strategies may be related to the lack of time of the mother (Leslie 1989).

Women's time constraints have a negative effect on their own nutritional status. As already indicated in the previous section, biased allocation of food away from women in many countries, particularly in South Asia, combine with long hours of labor to work a decidedly negative impact on women's nutritional status. Thus, the few studies on women's nutritional status that exist indicate that malnutrition is more common in women than in men (McGuire and Popkin 1990).

Conclusions

The major links between women's nutritional status, household food security, and infant–child nutritional status have been discussed. In the past great attention has been focused on the effect of nutritional status during pregnancy and lactation on neonatal and perinatal nutritional status. Yet the prepregnant weight of the mother influences birth weight more than weight gain during pregnancy. Unfortunately, few interventions have addressed nutritional status issues related to nonpregnant women. A potentially cost-effective nutrition intervention, however, would be one aimed at improving the nutritional status of high-risk female adolescents.

Any intervention designed to improve the nutrition of women must take their time constraints into consideration. Failure to ensure regular participation of women was one reason for the lack of any robust effects of prior dietary supplementation schemes. Time-saving, and thus energy-saving, programs offer a greater potential than other types of interventions for improving women's nutrition. Since the greatest portion of the day for rural women is devoted to home production activities – getting water and fuel, housework, cooking, and so forth – any program that can decrease this time may have a significant nutrition benefit.

Much of the discussion in the literature stresses the improvement of women's nutrition as an equity issue. However, there are strong efficiency reasons why policy makers would want to improve women's nutrition. Better-nourished women are more economically productive. Thus, because women are major actors in developing-country agriculture – particularly in Africa – interventions that improve their nutritional status also offer the potential of ensuring a more productive agricultural sector.

Eileen Kennedy
Lawrence Haddad

Bibliography

Alba, M. 1991. Early childhood factors as determinants of education and earnings: The case of four rural villages in Guatemala. Ph.D. dissertation, Food Research Institute, Stanford University.

Beaton, G., and H. Ghassemi. 1982. Supplementary feeding programs for young children in developing countries. *American Journal of Clinical Nutrition* 34 (Supplement 1982): 864-916.

Braun, J. von, and E. Kennedy, eds. 1994. *Commercialization of agriculture: Poverty and nutritional effects.* Baltimore, Md.

Brems, S., and Alan Berg. 1988. *"Eating down" during pregnancy: Nutrition, obstetric, and cultural considerations in the Third World.* Washington, D.C.

Buvinic, M. 1990. The feminization of poverty. In *Women and nutrition,* United Nations Administrative Committee on Coordination/Subcommittee on Nutrition Symposium Report, Nutrition Policy Discussion Paper No. 6. Geneva.

Carloni, A. S. 1981. Sex disparities in the distribution of food within rural households. *Food and Nutrition Bulletin* 7: 3-12.

Chen, L., E. Huq, and S. d'Souza. 1981. Sex bias in the family allocation of food and health care in rural Bangladesh. *Population and Development Review* 7: 55-70.

Chung, K. 1991. Nutritional status and work productivity. Ph.D. dissertation, Food Research Institute, Stanford University.

Deolalikar, A. 1988. Nutrition and labor productivity in agriculture: Estimates for rural South India. *Review of Economics and Statistics* 703: 406-13.

Dixon, R. B. 1982. Women in agriculture: Counting the labor force in developing countries. *Population and Development Review* 8: 539-66.

Garcia, M. 1990. Resource allocation and household welfare. Ph.D. dissertation, Institute of Social Studies, The Hague.

　　1991. Impact of female sources of income on food demand among rural households in the Philippines. *Quarterly Journal of International Agriculture* 30: 109-24.

Ghassemi, H. 1990. Women, food, and nutrition – issues in need of a global focus. In *Women and nutrition,* United Nations Administrative Committee on Coordination/Subcommittee on Nutrition Symposium Report, Nutrition Policy Discussion Paper No. 6. Geneva.

Haddad, L., and H. Bouis. 1991. The impact of nutritional status on agricultural productivity: Wage evidence from the Philippines. *Oxford Bulletin of Economics and Statistics* 531: 45-68.

Haddad, L., and J. Hoddinott. 1991. Gender aspects of household expenditures and resource allocation in the Côte d'Ivoire. Applied Economics Discussion Paper 112. Institute of Economic Studies Working Paper, Oxford University.

Harriss, B. 1986. The intrafamily distribution of hunger in South Asia. In *Hunger and public policy,* ed. J. Drèze and A. K. Sen. Oxford.

Iyenger, L. 1967. Effect of dietary supplementation late in pregnancy on the expectant mother and her newborn. *Indian Journal of Medical Research* 55: 85-9.

Juster, F. T., and F. P. Stafford. 1991. The allocation of time: Empirical findings, behavioral models, and problems of measurement. *Journal of Economic Literature* 24: 471-522.

Kennedy, E. 1989. *The effects of sugarcane production on food security, health and nutrition in Kenya: A longitudinal analysis.* International Food Policy Research Institute Research Report 78. Washington, D.C.

Kennedy, E., and L. Haddad. 1992. Food security and nutrition 1971-1991: Lessons learned and future priorities. *Food Policy* 17: 2-6.

Kennedy, E., and O. Knudsen. 1985. A review of supplementary feeding programmes and recommendations on their design. In *Nutrition and Development,* ed. Margaret Biswas and Per Pinstrup-Andersen, 77-96. New York.

Kennedy, E., and P. Peters. 1992. Household food security and child nutrition: The interaction of income and gender of household need. *World Development* 20: 1077-85.

Kielmann, A., C. E. Taylor, and R. L. Parker. 1978. The Narangwal nutrition study: A summary review. *American Journal of Clinical Nutrition* 31: 2040-52.

Kumar, S., and D. Hotchkiss. 1988. *Consequences of deforestation for women's time allocation, agricultural production, and nutrition in hill areas of Nepal.* International Food Policy Research Institute Research Report 69. Washington, D.C.

Lawrence, M., and R. G. Whitehead. 1988. Physical activity and total energy expenditure of child-bearing Gambian village women. *European Journal of Clinical Nutrition* 42: 145-60.

Lechtig, A., L. J. Mata, J.-P. Habicht, et al. 1974. Levels of immunoglobulin M (Igm) in cord blood of Latin American newborns of low socioeconomic status. *Ecology of Food Nutrition* 3: 171-8.

Lechtig, A., C. Yarbrough, H. Delgado, et al. 1975. Influence of maternal nutrition on birth weight. *American Journal of Clinical Nutrition* 28: 1223-33.

Leslie, J. 1988. Women's work and child nutrition in the Third World. *World Development* 16: 1341-70.

　　1989. Women's time: A factor in the use of child survival technologies? *Health Policy and Planning* 4: 1-16.

MacCormack, C. 1988. Health and the social power of women. *Social Science and Medicine* 26: 678.

Mayatech. 1991. *Gender and adjustment.* Silver Spring, Md.

McGuire, J., and B. Popkin. 1988. The zero-sum game: A framework for examining women and nutrition. *Food and Nutrition Bulletin* 10: 27-32.

　　1990. Beating the zero-sum game: Women and nutrition in the Third World. In *Women and nutrition,* United Nations Administrative Committee on Coordination/Subcommittee on Nutrition Symposium Report, Nutrition Policy Discussion Paper No. 6, 11-65. Geneva.

Rosenhouse, S. 1989. Identifying the poor: Is headship a useful concept? Living Standards Measurement Study Working Paper 58. Washington, D.C.

Svedberg, P. 1990. Undernutrition in sub-Saharan Africa: Is there a gender bias? *Journal of Development Studies* 26: 469-86.

Thomas, D. 1990. Intrahousehold resource allocation: An inferential approach. *Journal of Human Resources* 25: 635-64.

　　1991. *Gender differences in household resource allocations.* Living Standards Measurement Survey Working Paper 79. Washington, D.C.

World Bank. 1986. *Poverty and hunger: Issues and options for food security in developing countries.* A World Bank Policy Study. Washington, D.C.

VI.7 ᔧ Infant and Child Nutrition

Infant Feeding in Prehistory

Prehistoric patterns of human infant feeding are important for understanding the forces that have shaped the nutritional requirements of today's infants and the biological capacities of their mothers to satisfy these requirements through lactation. The primary sources of data to reconstruct such patterns are observational studies of nonhuman primates in the wild, particularly the great apes, and ethnographic studies of contemporary peoples whose nomadic lifestyle and level of material culture probably approximate those of the first humans.

As a mammalian class, virtually all primates – prosimians, monkeys, and apes, as well as humans – follow a *k*-strategy of reproduction. That is, they have a small number of infants, most born as singletons, in whom considerable parental attention and effort are invested. The consequence is that a relatively high number of offspring live to adulthood, with the success of such a strategy depending on close physical contact for protection. Thus, nonhuman primate parents carry, rather than cache, their infants – a constant contact that is reinforced by primate milks. These are uniformly high in sugar and low in satiety-producing fat – a milk composition more suited to a frequent-snacking pattern of eating than to one of large, isolated meals. Frequent nursing episodes enhance the amount and, possibly, the energy density of milk (Quandt 1984a). They also delay the return of ovulation, leading to longer birth intervals. Such a biobehavioral complex involving infant feeding, infant care, and birth spacing was doubtless encouraged by the selection process in primate evolution, and consequently, infant feeding became an integral part of the reproductive process, as is demonstrated by studies of human foragers.

The infants of the latter are normally kept in skin-to-skin contact with the mother, and nursing takes place frequently upon demand. Observational studies of the !Kung San of the Kalahari Desert, for example, show that mothers nurse their infants only briefly, but as often as four times per hour during the daytime for an average of two minutes per feeding. Cosleeping of mothers and infants is the rule, and infants also nurse at will during the night (Konner and Worthman 1980). Birth intervals in this noncontracepting group average 44 months (Lee 1979). Weaning among hunter-gatherers is generally gradual, with complete severance not occurring until the next child is born. Premasticated foods are gradually added to the diet, because there are few available foods that can be otherwise managed by very small children.

Infant Feeding in the Historical Period

From the Neolithic to the Renaissance

The Neolithic Revolution brought significant alterations in infant- and child-feeding practices. This transition from a foraging subsistence base to one that incorporated a variety of food production techniques began some 8,000 to 10,000 years ago and was first accomplished in at least six places, including Egypt, Mesopotamia, highland Peru, Mesoamerica, the Indus Valley, and China. Accompanying these changes in food sources were the origins of urbanism, stratified social organization, and writing and record-keeping, along with a host of other cultural traits that joined to comprise what we regard as civilization.

Data on infant-feeding practices come from a variety of artifacts of these civilizations. In addition to archaeological data, there are documentary sources, including art, inscriptions, and early writings. Interpretation of these data is aided by ethnographic analogy with contemporary nonindustrialized societies.

Food production, as opposed to foraging, brought two major changes in the feeding of young children. One of these was the addition of starchy, semisoft foods to the infant diet as a complement to breast milk. Food production meant that the grains or tubers from which such foods could be made were now dependable staples. Cooked into gruels of varying consistency, these foods offered infants and young children relatively innocuous flavor, readily digestible carbohydrate composition, and concentrated energy. Such foods, however, could lead to infectious diseases when contaminated and to equally serious undernutrition, as vegetable foods are deficient in essential amino acids. Consequently, if they were given in place of breast milk, they made for a protein-deficient diet.

With the second change, which came with the domestication of such animals as cows, sheep, goats, and camels, nonhuman milks became available to supplement or even to replace breast milk and to serve as nutrient rich foods for children after weaning. Although there is no record of such milks in the New World or in the civilizations of eastern Asia, their use is well documented elsewhere.

Together these changes in feeding were closely linked to the population explosion that accompanied the Neolithic. The newly available infant foods could shorten the period of intensive breast feeding, leading to shorter periods of postpartum infecundability and, thus, shorter intervals between births. The latter requires substitute foods for infants abruptly displaced from the breast by subsequent newborns, and the milks and cereals were such substitutes.

This does not, of course, mean that breast feeding was abandoned. Early civilizations of the Near East (c. 3000 B.C.) left abundant evidence of their infant-feeding attitudes and practices. Sculptures, paintings, and inscriptions all indicate that mothers were highly regarded and that breast feeding was practiced. For

Egypt, medical papyri from about 1550 B.C. contain remedies and recommendations for a variety of nursing problems still addressed today. These include ways to increase milk supply, to ease breast pain, and to evaluate milk quality. Ointments, incantations, and magico-religious spells are also included.

Wet nursing seems to have been a well-accepted practice in Egypt and Mesopotamia. Among the ancient Egyptian royalty, wet nursing was apparently the usual method of feeding highborn infants, with the nurses accorded high status in the royal court (Robins 1993). During periods of Greek and Roman rule in Egypt, the practice changed so that wet nursing became even more widespread and was frequently performed by slave women. In addition to wet nursing, there is pictorial evidence of infants being fed animal milks from horn-shaped and decorated vessels. We cannot know how frequently such artificial feeding was practiced, but it seems likely that most infants were breast-fed. In the case of wet nursing, there were contracts that specified how long a wet nurse should suckle a child and how the child should be weaned before being returned to the parents (Fildes 1986).

Near Eastern texts also prescribed the weaning diet of young children. After several months of exclusive breast feeding, it was recommended that animal milks and eggs be added to the diet and that animal milks become the principal food after weaning, which occurred at 2 to 3 years of age. Other foods were not introduced until teeth were cut, and these were primarily fruits and vegetables. The feeding of corn and pulses to weaning infants is described in the Old Testament.

There is limited mention of infant feeding in the writings of the philosophers of ancient Greece. These make it clear that infants were breast-fed, usually from the first day after birth, but there is no indication if this initial feeding was done by the mother or another woman. (In this connection, Aristotle noted that the early milk is salty.) Wet nurses were used by the wealthy, but there was regional and temporal variation in whether they resided with the family and whether they were slaves. We have little evidence to indicate when children nursed by their own mothers were weaned or how, although it is probable that animal milks, cereals, and honey were employed in the task. Pottery feeding vessels of various designs have been found that were probably used during and after weaning to feed animal milks to children.

Roman physicians from the first and second centuries A.D. were the first to focus significant attention on the health of infants. The most influential of these, Soranus of Ephesus, wrote on gynecology in the second century, and his works were translated and circulated throughout Europe during medieval times (Atkinson 1991). The writings of Soranus and his contemporaries indicate some controversy over whether new arrivals should be given the mother's breast immediately, or whether a wet nurse should substitute until the mother's mature milk came in. There was also disagreement about whether or not newborns should be given purgatives to help remove the meconium.

Physicians discussed the personal qualities of wet nurses in their writings because there was widespread belief that those qualities could be transmitted via the nurses' milk. Thus, Spartan nurses were highly valued for their ability to transmit stamina and good physical and mental health (Fildes 1986). Despite the recommendation of physicians that other foods be withheld until teeth were cut, their writings indicate that women were feeding cereals to infants as young as 40 days. Writers disagreed over giving wine to infants, as well as over the value of prechewed foods. Although the literary sources do not mention their use, feeding vessels are common artifacts from Roman times. Ages recommended for weaning ranged from 2 to 3 years (deMause 1974).

Ancient Ayurvedic medical texts from the second millennium B.C. through the seventh century A.D. contain clear and consistent discussions of pediatrics and infant feeding in India. Practices in the first few days of life were ritualized and quite similar to those still employed in India and among those of Indian heritage elsewhere. These included the feeding of ghee (clarified butter) and honey mixed with other substances in a specific order and at regular intervals over three days. On the fourth day, milk was expressed from the mother's breasts, and then the infant was put to nurse. As in other civilizations, a wet nurse was employed if the mother was unable to nurse, and there is mention in the texts of the use of cow's and goat's milk if breast milk was insufficient. However, no feeding vessels are mentioned in the literature or have been found as artifacts from ancient India, so the extent (and method) of artificial feeding is unknown.

The concept of balance is found throughout the Ayurvedic writings on infant feeding. A wet nurse, for example, was to be neither fat nor thin, neither fickle nor greedy (Fildes 1986). The quality of milk could be disturbed by extreme emotions and could be brought back into balance with a specific diet. The first nonmilk baby food in India was rice. The timing of this feeding varied, but in many cases coincided with the eruption of teeth. Weaning from the breast occurred in the third year.

Although the texts from ancient civilizations do not link feeding practices to infant health, some of those mentioned, such as giving infants cereals or animal milks within the early weeks of life, must have led to illnesses. Contamination of these foods probably occurred with some frequency, as climates were hot and sanitary practices for food storage were not well developed. Preference for spring weaning in some places, for example, was probably based on seasonal patterns of disease and the known association of weaning and disease.

Careful study of populations undergoing the change from foraging to food production elsewhere indicate that an epidemiological transition also took place. The skeletal sequence from the Dickson Mounds, Illinois (A.D. 950 to 1300), for example, shows evidence of lower life expectancy at birth with the shift to food production (Goodman et al. 1984). Skeletons and dentition of adults bear evidence of infectious disease episodes and some deficiency diseases (Cassidy 1980). These same nutrition-related health difficulties probably characterized many populations of settled horticulturalists, with greater problems present among those who were most crowded and whose resources were seasonally strained.

From the Renaissance to the Eve of Industrialization

Most data bearing on infant and child nutrition during the centuries spanning the Renaissance and the beginning of industrialization are from Europe and its colonies. During this period, Europe was characterized by changing medical knowledge, social divisions, and cultural patterns. At the same time, great portions of the rest of the world were changed by the diffusion of European customs, much of this occurring within the context of slavery and colonial domination. In Europe and in the colonies, most infants of the sixteenth century were breast-fed by their mothers, and when mothers could not or did not nurse, wet nurses were employed. There were class differences in feeding practices throughout the period, with change coming sometimes from the upper and sometimes from the lower classes. There were regional differences as well, which make generalizations difficult and trends hard to describe in a simple fashion.

Neonatal feeding focused on the use of purgatives to help remove the fetal meconium from the intestines. It was believed that the consumption of milk before purging the meconium could lead to a dangerous coagulation in the bowels. The use of substances for purges such as almond oil, butter, and honey was continued from ancient times, and wine, pharmaceutical purges (such as castor oil), and others, like salt water or soap, became popular in the late seventeenth century. These were administered at regular intervals over the first few days of life, a period during which women were advised not to breast-feed their infants.

In fact, the period of withholding breast milk could range from a few days up to a month. This was in part because a mother was believed to need time to recover from the delivery and, also, to become "clean" after the vaginal discharge had stopped. But in addition, the infant was thought to be at risk of harm from the mother's impure colostrum and, as already mentioned, from the coagulation of colostrum and

meconium (Fildes 1986). The effect of this delay in breast feeding was to deprive the infant of the immune properties of the colostrum and to cause dehydration and weight loss. In addition, it disrupted the supply and demand nature of lactation, so that mothers might lack sufficient milk to feed their babies properly.

But such ideas began to change in the mid-seventeenth century following the publication of a number of medical and midwifery texts that advocated the feeding of colostrum, although it doubtless took some time for such new notions to be put into practice. A major impetus for such change came from English lying-in hospitals, where, by 1750, purgative use was discouraged and breast feeding of infants within 24 hours was advocated to reduce the incidence of breast abscesses and infections, both of which were major causes of maternal mortality. However, an important by-product of this practice was a marked decline in infant mortality as well (Fildes 1980).

These lying-in hospitals were used by poor women for delivery and were the site of medical training for both physicians and midwives who became advocates of early breast feeding. At the same time, upper-class women were beginning to read and to be influenced by treatises on infant care that incorporated the new medical ideas about early feeding. These changes in neonatal feeding were probably more responsible for the decline in infant mortality observed in England from the late preindustrial to the industrial period than any other factor (Fildes 1980).

During the preindustrial era, maternal breast feeding was practiced by most mothers after the neonatal period. They nursed infants with no supplemental foods for at least one year and usually continued breast feeding well into the second year of life until the infant was capable of consuming the family diet. Weaning from the breast was sometimes gradual and sometimes abrupt, with bitter substances smeared on the breast to deter the child; or the child was sent to stay with friends until weaning was accomplished (Treckel 1989).

The actual timing of weaning was dictated by the seasons and by the dental development of the child. The fall and spring were believed to be the best seasons for severance from the breast, and weaning in the summer and winter months was discouraged. This was because of presumed dangers of summer infections and the perils of winter cold. Children were also believed to be at risk of illness and death until most of their teeth had erupted, and so weaning was postponed until this had occurred. Nipple shields were sometimes used to reduce discomfort for mothers.

Until the late seventeenth century, upper-class women were more likely to employ wet nurses than to breast-feed children themselves. Although this practice was rationalized by women as avoiding a delay in feeding the infant because of the avoidance of colostrum, it was probably mostly the result of ideas about sexuality and gender roles held by upper-class women. Because sexual intercourse was believed to hasten the resumption of menstruation and to impair both the quality and quantity of breast milk, sexual abstinence until weaning was encouraged by medical authorities. The employment of a wet nurse avoided this issue, and husbands were normally responsible for the decision to seek a wet nurse. In so deciding, husbands were able to assert patriarchal authority and establish "ownership" of the child. In other words, having a wet nurse rather than the mother feed the child (especially when the child was sent away to be nursed) focused attention on the woman as wife and diminished her identity as mother (Klapisch-Zuber 1985).

If wet nursing solved some problems, however, it brought with it others. Because breast milk was believed to transmit the characteristics of the woman who produced it, care had to be taken in choosing and supervising a wet nurse. The possibilities for the transmission of influences ranged from temperament to physical attributes such as hair color and complexion. It was best if a boy's wet nurse had herself borne a boy, and a girl's borne a girl, so that appropriate gender demeanor would be transmitted.

Earlier in this period, there was general acceptance throughout Europe of women who employed wet nurses, although many physicians and moralists condemned the practice. But after the Reformation, there was considerably more sentiment against wet nursing. Indeed, mothers who did not breast-feed were portrayed as evil and self-indulgent in both popular tracts and in sermons (Lindemann 1981), and there was concern that the practices of upper-class women might spread to the lower classes. In the American colonies, wet nursing was deplored because of the Puritan ethic, which encouraged women to devote themselves to motherhood and not indulge their sensual urges. Women who placed their infants with wet nurses were criticized for being vain and sinful (Treckel 1989).

Such sentiments apparently also resulted in a reduced use of wet nurses among members of the stricter Protestant sects in England and in some countries on the Continent (Lindemann 1981; Fildes 1986). However, in other places, most notably France, wet nursing continued at all levels of society. Elsewhere, by the late eighteenth century, upper-class women had begun to nurse their own infants. But in France, the use of wet nurses began to spread from the upper to the lower social strata, resulting in an increasing reliance on rural wet nurses by the lower and working classes of growing urban populations (Sussman 1982; Fildes 1988). Infants were sometimes sent a considerable distance into the countryside to live with a wet nurse, not returning until the prescribed age of weaning, which could be several years of age. This brought with it considerable infant mortality, as there was little supervision of wet nurses to ensure that infants were fed and cared for.

It is the case, however, that perhaps because of its prevalence wet nursing was more regulated in France than elsewhere. Starting in the seventeenth century, a number of *recommandaresses* were authorized in Paris by local judiciaries to require registration of those wet nurses who took infants home with them to rural parishes. These *recommandaresses* were later consolidated and regulations added to protect the lives of the children in question. For example, nurses were forbidden to take on more than two infants at a time, and still later, additional regulations set the prices for wet nursing. In 1769, the *recommandaresses* were abolished and replaced with a single authority that was designed to enhance communication between parents and nurses and to enforce the payment of the wages to the nurse. Although the intentions of these regulations may have been good, the wet-nursing business was, in fact, highly entrepreneurial, with individuals contracting to bring infants to nurses in the countryside, competing against one another to do so, and more concerned with profits than with the welfare of parents, nurses, or infants. Infant mortality rates were extremely high.

One of the reasons wet nursing flourished in France was the doctrine of the Catholic Church, which solved the problem of the taboo on sexual intercourse during breast feeding by recommending that infants be placed with a wet nurse so that husbands could enjoy the conjugal relations they felt were owed to them. Other factors also contributed to the extensiveness of wet nursing. As we just noted, by the eighteenth century, large numbers of urban Frenchwomen had entered the workforce, and their work as artisans, shopkeepers, and domestics for upper-class families provided little opportunity to care for a baby. The crowded nature of living and working conditions in cities also made nursing a baby difficult, and a lack of safe breast milk substitutes left wet nursing as the only alternative.

The decline in wet nursing in France and elsewhere has been attributed to a number of factors. The foremost cultural theory – that of the "discovery of childhood" – has been the subject of considerable debate (Bellingham 1988). Philippe Aries (1962) has argued that in the past, child mortality was so high that adults invested little money or interest in children, who were frequently neglected or abused; wet nursing was, according to Aries, one form of such neglect. However, Edward Shorter (1976) has viewed the maternal investment in children less than 2 years of age as a product of modernization. As Enlightenment philosophers and physicians began to attack wet nursing and other child-care practices, upper-class mothers began to devote themselves to feeding, rearing, and caring for their own children. Such concerns for the welfare of the child gradually trickled down to the lower classes.

Infant Feeding in the Industrial Era

The Industrial Revolution of the nineteenth century brought dramatic changes in lifestyle that had drastic effects on infant-feeding practices. People flowed from traditional towns and villages to large urban communities, and with the concentration of the population in cities came overcrowding, contaminated water and milk supplies, and infectious diseases spawned by poor sanitation and crowded living conditions. Women entered the labor force in large numbers and, for both men and women, work was no longer based at home.

Enhanced access to education increased the literacy level of the population, and magazines, newspapers, and books became widely available. Included among these were infant-care manuals and numerous advertisements for infant foods, all of which heightened public demand for new products and services that would benefit their children (Fildes 1991). Moreover, improvements in the recording of vital statistics in the second half of the nineteenth century increased awareness of high infant-mortality rates, and – as inadequate nutrition was seen as a cause of disease and death – this also stimulated interest in infant feeding.

Research-oriented physicians and scientists developed theories of infant nutrition, and both practitioners dealing with breast-fed infants who were not thriving and mothers having problems with breast feeding sought nutritional solutions (Apple 1987). Although mothers' milk was recognized as the best food for infants, that milk had to be of optimal quality, and this, both physicians and mothers believed, was not always the case. Breast milk quality might be compromised by the mother's health, her behavior, even her disposition. Factors alleged necessary to the production of adequate milk ranged from consuming a good diet and getting sufficient rest to avoiding strong emotions and physical labor. Because these factors were thought to compromise the milk of wet nurses as well as mothers, wet nursing increasingly fell into disfavor.

Because wet nurses were used less, and women were working outside the home in large numbers, infants were fed foods other than breast milk by their caretakers (often, young girls) during the working day. Paps and porridges were made, frequently with bread and water flavored with a little milk and sugar, and kept warm all day on the stove to be fed as needed. When this food failed to soothe an infant, commercial baby tonics were given. Containing laudanum, these were probably very successful at quieting a hungry or fretful baby.

The infant-feeding practices of working-class Europe spread to other parts of the world as populations came under the economic domination of England and the other colonizing countries. Plantation systems and other labor-intensive industries needed a constant supply of workers, and returning mothers to work as soon as possible after giving birth was in the interest of the dominating powers. In the English-speaking Caribbean, for example, the African practice of prolonged breast feeding was discouraged among slaves. After returning to work, mothers left their infants in creches where they were fed paps and panadas by elderly caretakers in between nursing breaks (King and Ashworth 1987). These early supplemental foods were very similar to those fed in England at the time (Fildes 1986).

Such economic and social changes in the last half of the nineteenth century, as well as research into the chemical composition of milk in Europe and the United States, paved the way for the use of artificial milks or formula milks. Certainly, women were ready to adopt such milks. Most middle-class households could not afford a servant to breast-feed infants while the mother was engaged in activities outside the home, and working-class women had to wean their infants at a very young age to enter the labor force.

The earliest scientists to make a substantial impact on feeding practices through the development of formulas were Philip Biedert in Germany and Arthur Meigs in Philadelphia (Wood 1955). Biedert was the first to suggest modification of cow's milk, noting its high protein content and hard-curd consistency relative to human milk. He recommended the addition of cream, whey, and sugar to make cow's milk more digestible for human infants. Meigs published nutrient analyses of human and cow's milk in 1884, which showed the higher carbohydrate and lower protein and fat content of human milk. He was able to demonstrate that the protein of human milk formed a softer curd than cow's milk and thought that the addition of lime water was important to make cow's milk more alkaline. In combining the work of Biedert with his own, Meigs was able to produce what was to be one of the most popular formulas for the transformation of cow's milk into an approximation of human milk.

The problem of infant diarrhea provided the research impetus for therapeutic artificial milks, and two schools of thought developed. In the United States, that thought was complex, as Thomas Morgan Rotch (a professor of pediatrics at Harvard University) and his followers developed the "percentage method," based on Meigs's recommendations. Rotch advocated individualized infant-formula prescriptions that required considerable mathematical calculation and a hospital laboratory to produce.

In Europe at the same time a "caloric method" was developed by Heinrich Finkelstein, who hypothesized that infant diarrhea resulted from the fermentation of carbohydrates in the intestine. This theory led to the invention of "Eiweissmilch," a low-carbohydrate, high-protein milk produced by a process of sieving curdled casein back into artificially soured milk. In contrast to Finkelstein, Adalbert Czerny concluded that infant diarrhea resulted from an intolerance of milk fat. Almost simultaneously, he developed a mixture of butter and flour that was added to milk.

By 1910, the percentage method had fallen into disfavor, and pediatricians were noting a disturbing number of occurrences of deficiency diseases, such as scurvy, among infants fed the artificial milks. These infants also suffered high rates of mortality (Levenstein 1983). Reformers advocated a series of different measures, ranging from educating the poor to breast-feed to regulating the milk supply so as to guarantee its cleanliness. But while physician-scientists were developing formulas that could be prescribed to mothers for home preparation, chemists were devising other alternatives to breast milk, and the success of these products indicated the existence of a previously unrecognized market. The subsequent commercial marketing of formulas, in contrast to their prescription by physicians, once again gave control of infant-feeding decisions to mothers, as in the past when they had decided between breast-feeding or employing wet nurses. By the end of the nineteenth century, mothers could choose from viable alternatives to breast feeding, and in the twentieth, their preferences made artificial feeding a cultural norm.

Such changes in infant feeding were part of the transformation of medicine into a scientific profession, and at the turn of the century, science was highly valued and viewed as the key to resolving numerous important problems (Rosenberg 1976). As physicians obtained more and more scientific knowledge, they became increasingly regarded as experts with privileged information (Apple 1987).

The "Scientific" Era

Infant feeding in the 1930s and 1940s differed somewhat from earlier practices; there was a general acceptance of simpler infant formulas, and researchers themselves were involved in the commercialization of formulas. Thereafter, as the dangers and difficulties of artificial feeding lessened, the flurry of research on infant nutrition declined as well (Apple 1987). By the middle of the twentieth century, most babies in the United States were bottle-fed with artificial milks, as were a high percentage of babies in the industrialized countries of Europe and in those under European influence. The belief was that artificial feeding, with its scientific basis and medical direction, was equal or superior to breast feeding.

No wonder then that survey data from the United States, Europe, and European-influenced countries showed a consistent decline in breast feeding during the twentieth century. The number of breast-fed infants born in the United States dropped from 77 percent between 1936 and 1940 to 25 percent by 1970. Duration of breast feeding also declined from a 1930s average of 4.2 months to 2.2 months in the late 1950s (Meyer 1958, 1968; Hirschman and Hendershot 1979; Hendershot 1980, 1981).

There were striking demographic patterns of

Table VI.7.1. *Percentage of first-born infants ever breast-fed between 1951 and 1970 in the United States, by ethnic group and education*

Category	1951–5	1956–60	1961–5	1966–70
Ethnic group				
White	49	43	39	29
Black	59	42	24	14
Hispanic	58	55	39	35
Education				
< 9 yrs	62	53	40	32
9–11 yrs	50	40	29	17
12 yrs	45	40	32	23
13–15 yrs	57	48	50	35
>15 yrs	46	50	69	57

Source: From Hirschman and Hendershot (1979).

breast feeding during this period (Table VI.7.1). Although breast feeding was more common among blacks than whites earlier in the twentieth century, its subsequent decline was greater among blacks so that only 14 percent breast-fed by 1970, compared with 29 percent of whites and 35 percent of Hispanics. The relationship of education to breast feeding changed as well. In the early 1950s, the practice was most common among women with lower educational levels; better-educated mothers were less likely to breast-feed. But this trend was reversed by the 1970s – a phenomenon interpreted as a "trickling down" of values and behaviors from upper- to lower-class women (Salber, Stitt, and Babbott 1958; Meyer 1968). The incidence of breast feeding in the United States reached a low of 22 percent in 1972 – a downward trend paralleled in England (Newson and Newson 1963) and elsewhere.

Although recommendations from professional medical groups stressed breast feeding throughout this period, a variety of factors worked against it. One was the continued high value placed on science and technology and their applications to medicine (Apple 1987), as physicians and nurses learned more and more about artificial feeding and less and less about breast feeding. Moreover, birth became more of a medical event, and mothers who delivered in hospitals frequently stayed as long as two weeks. During that time, infants were often artificially fed because they were separated from their mothers and only brought to them to be nursed at fixed intervals. Mothers were instructed to wear face masks while breast-feeding, their nipples were washed before feeding, and they were not allowed to hold their babies afterward. All these practices virtually guaranteed that mothers' milk supplies would be inadequate and that their babies would require formula to supplement or replace breast milk.

That such hospital practices contributed to breast-feeding problems was recognized by some physicians (for example, Aldrich 1942). However, professional medical journals included recommendations from other practitioners who advised mothers to feed thickened cereal and other foods from an early age (Clein 1943; Stewart 1943). Others advocated feeding schedules, and some even recommended reducing the number of feedings to match family mealtimes (Clein 1943), reflecting cultural themes of regimentation and discipline applied to the infant (Millard 1990).

As already noted, by the 1970s the downward trend in breast feeding was reversed in the United States. More mothers initiated breast feeding, and they breast-fed for longer periods of time (Martinez and Nalezienski 1979; Hendershot 1981). This return to breast feeding paralleled the earlier decline, although now it was women of higher socioeconomic status who rediscovered the practice. As with the development of formula in the first half of the century, popular books and pamphlets stressed the scientific aspects of the "new" feeding method, which with breast feeding focused on greater disease resistance, prevention of allergies, and enhanced mother–infant bonding.

The return to breast feeding in Western countries in the 1970s was fueled by growing health activism and advocacy by women. As women discovered that they knew relatively little about their bodies and that they were dependent on the largely male medical community, lay efforts of women educating women grew (Boston Women's Health Book Collective 1976). La Leche League had been founded in 1956 as an organization focused on providing mothers with practical knowledge of breast feeding (La Leche League International 1963). The league filled a void. Few physicians had received any training in breast feeding, and lay breast-feeding knowledge had been lost as women turned to bottle feeding.

Breast feeding as promoted by La Leche League clashed sharply with other aspects of American culture. The League's promotion of extended breast feeding until a child weaned itself, often at 2 or 3 years of age, was at odds with cultural values of fostering independence. Infant-centered feeding patterns, with frequent nursing during the day and nighttime nursing, contrasted with the prevailing norm of scheduled feedings and use of the clock (Millard 1990). Comparing studies of League and non-League mothers shows the sharp contrast in feeding styles. Whereas League mothers nursed an average of 15 times per day (Cable and Rothenberger 1984), non-League mothers averaged only 7 (Quandt 1986).

The upward trend in breast feeding reached a peak in 1982 with 61 percent of newborns breast-fed and two-thirds of those still breast-feeding at 3 months of age (Martinez and Krieger 1985). But as the decade wore on, interest in breast feeding once again eroded, and by its end only 52 percent of newborns and 18 percent of 6-month-olds were breast-fed. The decline in initiation and duration was greatest among nonwhite mothers, younger mothers, and those with less

education (Ryan et al. 1991). A similar decline in breast feeding was recorded in Great Britain for the same period (Emery, Scholey, and Taylor 1990).

There are several possible explanations. Alan S. Ryan and colleagues (1991) suggest that there was a decline in attention given breast feeding in the public press at the same time that manufacturers of formula began to aggressively market their products through television and direct mailings to new parents. Economic pressures may also have contributed, because mothers in the labor force breast-fed less (Ryan and Martinez 1989). Indeed, even those not working outside the home expressed the need to be unencumbered by breast feeding if the need or opportunity to work arose (Wright, Clark, and Bauer 1993).

In addition to this cultural explanation of a decline in breast feeding, other scientists combined biological and behavioral perspectives into explanatory models that drew on rapid advances (during the 1980s) in knowledge of the hormonal control of milk production and milk volume (Stuart-Macadam and Dettwyler 1995). They pointed to the need for frequent stimulation of the nipple to maintain milk production (Quandt 1984b) and for baby-led feeding schedules to allow infants to regulate their own hunger and satiety levels through fat intake (Woolridge 1995). Sara A. Quandt (1984b) demonstrated that the introduction of beikost (nonmilk foods) to the diet of infants in the first 3 months of life resulted in declines in the number of breast feeds per day and, ultimately, in the duration of breast feeding. Thus, shorter durations of nursing at the population level appear to have a biobehavioral basis and are not simply the result of marketing of formula or women working outside the home.

Twentieth-Century Infant Feeding in the Developing World

In the second half of the twentieth century, considerable concern arose over changes in infant-feeding patterns occurring in developing countries. This was especially the case with changes thought to be the result of the marketing malpractice of multinational corporations (Chetley 1986). Scores of reports documented the promotion and sale of infant formula in developing countries, often to mothers who could not afford formula and who lived in circumstances where it could not be hygienically prepared. As a result, it was charged, low-income families were spending a large proportion of their incomes on products that were actually dangerous to the health of infants and also, because of the availability of breast milk, unnecessary. Indeed, dependence on formula meant erosion of breast-feeding knowledge and practices and increased poverty and infant mortality. Horror stories of "bottle babies" fed contaminated and overdiluted formula drew international attention, and pictures of infant graves marked by nursing bottles aroused anger toward the companies promoting the products.

After the publication, in 1974, of *The Baby Killer* (Muller 1974) and its German translation, Nestlé filed a libel suit against the Third World Action Group responsible for the translation. Although the group was found guilty of misrepresenting the formula manufacturer, it was assessed only a nominal fine, whereas the conduct of the formula manufacturer drew considerable public outcry. A number of public action groups joined to form the Infant Formula Action Coalition (INFACT), and in 1977, INFACT began to promote a consumer boycott of all Nestlé products. The boycott was extremely successful, with participation by large numbers of citizens as well as governmental agencies in the United States and Canada (Van Esterik 1989). In 1981, the World Health Organization (WHO) and the United Nations International Children's Emergency Fund (UNICEF) adopted a code of marketing with which Nestlé agreed to abide. INFACT called off the boycott in 1984.

Scientific research on infant-feeding patterns in developing countries, however, provides a more complex picture than that conveyed by the problems arising from the simple substitution of bottled formula for breast feeding. In some areas, new feeding modalities and products were added to existing breast-feeding practices. The contents of infant-feeding bottles were highly varied. There was inter- and intracultural variation in how breast feeding was practiced before the promotion of formula by multinational corporations. For example, mixed breast and artificial feeding had been common in the Caribbean for centuries, whereas extended breast-feeding had been the norm in Africa and Asia (King and Ashworth 1987).

Data gathered around 1980 from large, nationally representative samples for the World Fertility Survey in 17 countries make possible some tentative generalizations about the state of breast-feeding practices in the second half of the twentieth century (Popkin et al. 1983). In Asia and the Pacific Islands, the practice continued to be very common, with virtually all mothers initiating breast feeding. Over 90 percent of infants were still breast-fed at 3 months of age and between 60 and 90 percent at 12 months. Breast feeding was slightly more common and of longer duration in rural than in urban areas. Supplementation of breast feeding was often delayed until after 12 months.

In Latin America, by contrast, as many as 20 percent of infants were never breast-fed, and by 6 months of age, less than 60 percent were breast-fed. The vast majority were weaned by 12 months. Rural–urban differences were pronounced, with more and longer duration of breast feeding in rural areas.

African breast-feeding rates were intermediate between those of Asia and Latin America. Overall, these findings indicate that a general decline in breast-feeding duration, but not breast-feeding inci-

dence, had occurred. This change is probably tied to overall patterns of modernization (for example, changes in women's participation in the labor force and changes in postpartum sex taboos) and not exclusively to the promotional effects of formula manufacturers.

International interest in infant-feeding practices in developing countries stems from a broader and long-standing concern about child survival and the effects of malnutrition on the long-term functional development of children (Mosley and Chen 1984). The link of breast feeding of short duration and abrupt weaning to kwashiorkor and extended, unsupplemented breast feeding to marasmus was established by the 1960s (Williams 1955; McLaren 1966; Cravioto et al. 1967) and attributed to a variety of adverse biological and social factors. Both human and animal studies demonstrated that the long-term consequences of these severe forms of protein–energy malnutrition included impaired mental development (Pollitt 1969; Winick 1969). More recently, a series of intervention and observational studies has shown that even marginal malnutrition results in growth stunting in early life and continued functional impairments later in life (Allen 1995). The results of such studies make it clear that achieving adequate nutrition for infants is the foundation for optimal health in whole populations.

Sara A. Quandt

Bibliography

Aldrich, C. Anderson. 1942. Progress in pediatrics: Ancient practices in a scientific age - feeding aspects. *American Journal of Diseases of Childhood* 64: 714–22.

Allen, Lindsay H. 1995. Malnutrition and human function: A comparison of conclusions from the INCAP and nutrition CRSP studies. *Journal of Nutrition* 125 (Supplement 4): 1119S–1126S.

Apple, Rima D. 1987. *Mothers and medicine: A social history of infant feeding, 1890–1950*. Madison, Wis.

Aries, Philippe. 1962. *Centuries of childhood. A social history of family life*, trans. Robert Baldick. New York.

Atkinson, Clarissa W. 1991. *The oldest vocation. Christian motherhood in the Middle Ages*. Ithaca, N.Y.

Bellingham, Bruce. 1988. The history of childhood since the "invention of childhood": Some issues in the eighties. *Journal of Family History* 13: 347–58.

Bostock, John. 1962. Evolutional approach to infant care. *Lancet* 1 (7238): 1033–5.

Boston Women's Health Book Collective. 1976. *Our bodies, ourselves*. Second edition. New York.

Cable, T. A., and L. A. Rothenberger. 1984. Breastfeeding behavioral patterns among La Leche League mothers: A descriptive survey. *Pediatrics* 73: 830–5.

Cassidy, C. M. 1980. Nutrition and health in agriculturalists and hunter-gatherers. In *Nutritional anthropology: Contemporary approaches to diet and culture,* ed. Norge W. Jerome, Randy F. Kandel, and Gretel H. Pelto, 117–45. Pleasantville, N.Y.

Chetley, A. 1986. *The politics of baby food*. London.

Clein, Norman W. 1943. Streamlined infant feeding: A feeding routine utilizing earlier addition of solid foods and fewer feedings. *Journal of Pediatrics* 23: 224–8.

Cravioto, J., H. G. Birch, E. R. DeLicardie, and L. Rosales. 1967. The ecology of infant weight gain in a preindustrial society. *Acta Paediatrica Scandinavica* 56: 71–84.

deMause, Lloyd. 1974. The evolution of childhood. In *The history of childhood,* ed. Lloyd deMause, 1–73. New York.

Emery, J. L., S. Scholey, and E. M. Taylor. 1990. Decline in breast feeding. *Archives of Diseases of Childhood* 65: 369–72.

Fildes, Valerie. 1980. Neonatal feeding practices and infant mortality during the 18th century. *Journal of Biosocial Science* 12: 313–24.

  1986. *Breasts, bottles and babies. A history of infant feeding.* Edinburgh.

  1988. *Wet nursing from antiquity to the present.* New York.

  1991. Breast-feeding practices during industrialisation, 1800–1919. In *Infant and child nutrition worldwide: Issues and perspectives,* ed. Frank Falkner, 1–20. Boca Raton, Fla.

Goodman, A. H., J. Lallo, G. J. Armelagos, and J. C. Rose. 1984. Health changes at Dickson Mounds, Illinois (A.D. 950–1300). In *Paleopathology at the origins of agriculture,* ed. Mark N. Cohen and George J. Armelagos, 271–306. New York.

Hendershot, G. E. 1980. *Trends in breast feeding.* National Center for Health Statistics, Public Health Service. U.S. Department of Health, Education, and Welfare Publication No. 80-1250. Hyattsville, Md.

  1981. *Trends and differentials in breast feeding in the United States, 1970–75.* Working Paper Series No. 5, Family Growth Survey Branch, National Center for Health Statistics, Public Health Service, U.S. Department of Health, Education, and Welfare. Hyattsville, Md.

Hirschman, C., and G. E. Hendershot. 1979. *Trends in breast feeding among American mothers.* Vital and Health Statistics, Series 23, No. 3. DHEW Publication No. (PHS) 79-1979. National Center for Health Statistics, Public Health Service, U.S. Department of Health, Education, and Welfare. Hyattsville, Md.

Hopkins, Eric. 1994. *Childhood transformed: Working-class children in nineteenth century England.* Manchester, England.

King, Jean, and Ann Ashworth. 1987. Historical review of the changing pattern of infant feeding in developing countries: The case of Malaysia, the Caribbean, Nigeria, and Zaire. *Social Science and Medicine* 25: 1307–20.

Klapisch-Zuber, Christiane. 1985. *Women, family and ritual in Renaissance Italy.* Chicago.

Konner, Melvin, and Carol Worthman. 1980. Nursing frequency, gonadal function, and birth-spacing among !Kung hunter-gatherers. *Science* 207: 788–91.

La Leche League International. 1963. *The womanly art of breastfeeding.* Franklin Park, Ill.

Lee, Richard B. 1979. *!Kung San: Men, women, and work in a foraging society.* New York.

Levenstein, Harvey. 1983. "Best for babies" or "preventable infanticide"? The controversy over artificial feeding of infants in America, 1880–1920. *Journal of American History* 70: 75–94.

Lindemann, M. 1981. "Love for hire": The regulation of wet nursing business in 18th century Hamburg. *Journal of Family History* 6: 379–95.

Martinez, Gilbert A., and Fritz W. Krieger. 1985. Milk-feeding patterns in the United States. *Pediatrics* 76: 1004–8.

Martinez, Gilbert A., and John P. Nalezienski. 1979. The recent trend in breast-feeding. *Pediatrics* 64: 686–92.

McLaren, S. D. 1966. A fresh look at protein–calorie malnutrition. *Lancet* 2: 485–8.

Meyer, Herman F. 1958. Breast feeding in the United States: Extent and possible trends. *Pediatrics* 22: 116–21.

  1968. Breast feeding in the United States; report of a 1966 national survey with comparable 1946 and 1956 data. *Clinical Pediatrics* 7: 708–15.

Millard, Ann V. 1990. The place of the clock in pediatric advice: Rationales, cultural themes, and impediments to breastfeeding. *Social Science and Medicine* 31: 211–21.

Mosley, W. Henry, and Lincoln C. Chen, eds. 1984. *Child survival - strategies for research.* Cambridge and New York.

Muller, M. 1974. *The baby killer.* London.

Newson, John, and Elizabeth Newson. 1963. *Infant care in an urban community.* New York.

Pollitt, Ernesto. 1969. Ecology, malnutrition, and mental development. *Psychosomatic Medicine* 31: 193–200.

Popkin, Barry M., Richard E. Bilsborrow, John S. Akin, and Monica E. Yamamoto. 1983. Breast-feeding determinants in low-income countries. *Medical Anthropology* 7: 1–31.

Quandt, Sara A. 1984a. Nutritional thriftiness and human reproduction: Beyond the critical body composition hypothesis. *Social Science and Medicine* 19: 177–82.

  1984b. The effect of beikost on the diet of breast-fed infants. *Journal of the American Dietetic Association* 84: 47–51.

  1986. Patterns of variation in breast feeding behaviors. *Social Science and Medicine* 23: 445–53.

Robins, Gay. 1993. *Women in ancient Egypt.* Cambridge, Mass.

Rosenberg, C. E. 1976. *No other gods: On science and American social thought.* Baltimore, Md.

Rotch, Thomas Morgan. 1907. An historical sketch of the development of percentage feeding. *New York Medical Journal* 85: 532–7.

Ryan, Alan S., and Gilbert A. Martinez. 1989. Breast-feeding and the working mother: A profile. *Pediatrics* 83: 524–31.

Ryan, Alan S., David Rush, Fritz W. Krieger, and Gregory E. Lewandowski. 1991. Recent declines in breast-feeding in the United States, 1984 through 1989. *Pediatrics* 88: 719–27.

Salber, E. J., P. G. Stitt, and J. C. Babbott. 1958. Patterns of breast feeding: Factors affecting the frequency of breast feeding. *New England Journal of Medicine* 259: 707–13.

Shorter, Edward. 1976. *The making of the modern family.* New York.

Stewart, Chester A. 1943. The use of cereal-thickened formulas to promote maternal nursing. *Journal of Pediatrics* 23: 310–14.

Stuart-Macadam, Patricia, and Katherine A. Dettwyler, eds. 1995. *Breastfeeding: Biocultural perspectives.* Chicago.

Sussman, George D. 1982. *Selling mothers' milk. The wet-nursing business in France 1715–1914.* Urbana, Ill.

Treckel, Paula A. 1989. Breastfeeding and maternal sexuality in colonial America. *Journal of Interdisciplinary History* 20: 25–51.

Van Esterik, Penny. 1989. *Beyond the breast-bottle controversy.* New Brunswick, N.J.

Williams, Cicely D. 1955. Factors in the ecology of malnutrition. In *Proceedings of the Western Hemisphere Nutrition Congress.* American Medical Association. Chicago.

Winick, Myron M. 1969. Malnutrition and brain development. *Journal of Pediatrics* 74: 667-79.

Wood, Alice L. 1955. The history of artificial feeding of infants. *Journal of the American Dietetic Association* 31: 474-82.

Woolridge, Michael W. 1995. Baby-controlled breastfeeding: Biocultural implications. In *Breastfeeding: Biocultural perspectives,* ed. Patricia Stuart-Macadam and Katherine A. Dettwyler, 217-42. Chicago.

Wright, Anne L., Clarina Clark, and Mark Bauer. 1993. Maternal employment and infant feeding practices among the Navaho. *Medical Anthropology Quarterly* 7: 260-80.

VI.8 ❧ Adolescent Nutrition and Fertility

The relationship between nutrition and adolescent fertility has been a topic of much discussion in recent research on human biology. The apparent increase in the incidence of teenage pregnancy in Western societies has led some researchers to wonder whether there are biological as well as cultural factors that influence this phenomenon (Vinovskis 1988). Studies of adolescents in different geographic and socioeconomic settings have demonstrated that the age at which sexual maturity is reached is not fixed but is heavily shaped by numerous influences, such as fatness at adolescence, physique, health status, genetics, degree of physical activity, and socioeconomic status (Maresh 1972; Johnson 1974; Short 1976; Zacharias, Rand, and Wurtman 1976; Frisch 1978; Meyer et al. 1990; Moisan, Meyer, and Gingras 1990; Wellens et al. 1990).

Since the reproductive process requires energy, reproductive ability is curtailed in times of food scarcity or when calories burned through physical exertion or exercise exceed the amount provided by food intake. Undernourished women, for example, reach menarche later and experience menopause earlier than do well-nourished ones. Poorly nourished women also have higher frequencies of irregular menstruation and anovulatory menstrual cycles, with menstruation and ovulation disappearing entirely if malnutrition is severe. During pregnancy, malnourished women have a greater likelihood of miscarriage, and if they do carry the infant to term, they experience a longer period of lactational amenorrhea. In men, severe malnutrition leads to loss of libido, a decrease in prostate fluid and in sperm count and mobility, and, eventually, the loss of sperm production altogether. For children and adolescents, undernutrition delays the onset of puberty in both boys and girls, and

limits the fecundity of those who have achieved sexual maturity (Frisch 1978).

Researchers disagree, however, on the precise way to measure adequate nutritional status. Some, most notably Rose Frisch (1978), argue that achievement of a critical weight is the major factor in achievement of sexual maturity. Others argue that body composition, particularly the percentage of body fat, is the most important determinant of sexual maturity (Crawford 1975).

Much more is known about the effects of nutrition on adolescent fertility in girls than in boys (Boyd 1980). Fertility in girls is usually based on age at menarche, although even this event is not a foolproof measure because adolescent girls experience a number of anovulatory cycles before establishing regular menstruation (Short 1976). Nevertheless, researchers have clearly established that poorly nourished girls, female athletes, and girls with anorexia nervosa and other eating disorders reach menarche at later ages, have higher incidences of amenorrhea, and have a greater frequency of anovulatory cycles than do girls who have adequate dietary intake relative to calories expended (Frisch 1978; Wyshak and Frisch 1982).

Fertility in boys, however, is much harder to determine. The main indicator of male fertility is spermatogenesis, determined by measuring the amount of sperm contained in the seminal fluid. But data on the beginning of spermatogenesis is more difficult to obtain because there is no clearly visible sign, as is the case in menarche. Moreover, it is not clear whether the appearance of spermatozoa in the urine is a reliable measure of fertility in adolescent boys (Baldwin 1928; Short 1976). Some researchers have attempted to use age of first ejaculation (Kinsey 1948) as an indicator of male fertility, but this, too, is unreliable (Brown 1966; Short 1976). Consequently, less is known about the factors that influence adolescent male fertility.

The Secular Trend in Sexual Maturity

One of the more controversial issues in the history of adolescent sexuality is whether the age of sexual maturity has declined over time. Nearly all of the discussion in this area centers around the apparent declining age of menarche, particularly among young women in Europe and the United States. G. von Backman (1948) and J. M. Tanner (1962) were among the first to suggest that the age of menarche has declined precipitously over the past several hundred years, from a high of 17 or 18 in early modern times to an average age of 12 in contemporary Western societies.

Most historians and researchers in human biology have accepted this model of a secular trend in age at menarche (Zacharias et al. 1976; Frisch 1978; Shorter 1981). Some scholars, however, have questioned the methodology employed in determining the age of menarche in the past. It has been argued that the evidence for Tanner's secular trend is based on extremely small samples of young women, and some have questioned whether these findings can be applied to larger populations (Brown 1966; Bullough 1981). In addition, others have pointed out that the way in which age at menarche is usually determined is flawed, for it relies on the recollected memory of women who were interviewed much later in life. It has been suggested that during the nineteenth century, an early age of menarche was often associated with sexual promiscuity and/or working-class status. Therefore, some women may have stated a higher age of menarche than they actually experienced, in order to maintain an image of middle-class respectability (Brown 1966; Bojlén and Bentzon 1968; Diers 1974; Bullough 1981). Even Tanner admitted that "the early studies of age of menarche suffered from disadvantages of both sampling and technique" (Tanner 1968, 1973, 1981b).

Another troubling aspect of historical research on the secular trend is the fact that age of menarche appears to be younger in both ancient and medieval times than in the nineteenth century. Reviews of Greek and Roman textbooks, for example, indicate that the average age of menarche in the ancient world was about 13.5 years (Amundsen and Diers 1969; Diers 1974), and evidence from medieval textbooks indicates that the age of menarche varied from 13 to 15 years (Post 1971; Amundsen and Diers 1973; Diers 1974). Researchers are cautious about this evidence, however, because it comes from medical textbooks, rather than from direct observations of young women (Diers 1974).

Some historians have even suggested that there might be ideological reasons for placing so much faith in a secular trend in age at menarche. Both Vern L. Bullough (1981) and Maris A. Vinovskis (1988), for example, have argued that the secular trend is often linked with the increasing problem of teenage pregnancy in contemporary American society and is used to justify very stringent policies regarding teenage sexuality.

Despite these criticisms, however, most researchers do agree that there has been some decrease in the age of menarche over time. Even Bullough states: "Undoubtedly there has been some drop in menarcheal age in the United States since the 19th century, to under 13 in the 1980s" (Bullough 1981: 366). The consensus in recent research on the secular trend is that there has been a statistically significant decline in age at menarche, but the drop has been much less precipitous than that suggested by Tanner and Backman (Frisch 1978; Wyshak and Frisch 1982; Golub 1983).

The History and Geography of Studies on Adolescents

Scientific interest in the fertility and growth of young men and women dates back to at least ancient Greece. Aristotle was among the first to observe the negative effect of excessive training and undernutrition on young boys. He also warned of the dangers of precocious sexuality, claiming that "the physique of men is also supposed to be stunted when intercourse is begun before the seed has finished its growth" (quoted in Tanner 1981a: 8).

During Roman imperial times, Soranus noted that vigorous exercise could inhibit menstruation, but he stated that this was normal and did not require intervention. Like Aristotle, Soranus noted that precocious "excretion of seed is harmful in females as well as males," and that "men who remain chaste are stronger and bigger than others" (quoted in Tanner 1981a: 10). As a result of these warnings about precocious sexuality, Roman law linked the age of marriage with the age of puberty, which was believed to be 14 for boys and 12 for girls (Amundsen and Diers 1969; Tanner 1981a).

In the Middle Ages, the Renaissance, and the early modern period, medical texts tended to echo the writings of ancient authors on the subject of adolescent growth and development. Among them, as among the ancient authors, there seems to have been at least some understanding that the onset of puberty, and particularly the onset of menarche, was linked with nutritional status. G. Marinello, for example, observed in the sixteenth century that some girls menstruated earlier than others. He stated that "the cause of variation is [differences in] the natural composition of the body, or complexion or habits; thin and long girls [menstruate] later[,] fat and strong ones earlier" (Marinello 1574, quoted in Tanner 1981a: 21). Similarly, Hippolytus Guarionius (1571–1654), a contemporary of Francis Bacon, noted that peasant girls in seventeenth-century Germany menstruated later than the daughters of townsfolk or aristocracy. Guarionius noted that "the cause seems to be that the inhabitants of the town consume more fat (moist) foods and drink and so their bodies become soft, weak, and fat and come early to menstruation, in the same way as a tree which one waters too early produces earlier but less well-formed fruit than another" (quoted in Tanner 1981a: 29).

During the eighteenth and nineteenth centuries, ideas about adolescent growth and development shifted as a result of contemporary debates about the place of so-called inferior races in the natural order. The egalitarian rhetoric of the Enlightenment called into question earlier ideas of racial inferiority, implying that the "natural rights of man" applied to men and women of all races, classes, and ethnic origins. But many scientists at this time endorsed racist ideas about human difference and looked for physical traits that would demonstrate that working-class Europeans, Africans, Asians, and Native Americans were inferior to white, middle-class Europeans (Stepan 1982; Schiebinger 1993). One of the physical signs that was used to "prove" the inferiority of nonwhite and working-class individuals was early age of menstruation and physical maturity, because such traits seemed to place these groups closer to animals.

Scientists attributed the allegedly early age of puberty in nonwhite and lower-class individuals to two causes: precocious sexual activity and warm climate. Both of these factors, it was argued, caused a buildup of heat in the body. Because many believed that heat was the engine of growth, anything that caused an accumulation of heat would lead to an early age of puberty. Albrecht von Haller (1775), for example, claimed that girls in the southerly regions of Asia, where the climate was warm, were marriageable in their eighth year and gave birth in their ninth or tenth year; conversely, women in Arctic regions did not menstruate until age 23 or 24. This view was shared by other eighteenth-century writers, most notably J. F. Freind (1738), Herman Boerhaave (1744), and Montesquieu (1751). Similarly, Martin Schurig (1729), a Dresden physician, noted that bodily maturation in girls could be accelerated by indulging in conversations with men, kissing, and other sorts of sexual encounters. Schurig claimed that indulgence in sexual activity was why prostitutes and lower-class women had an earlier age of menarche than did gentlewomen (Tanner 1981a).

To be sure, some authors, most notably George-Louis Leclerc de Buffon (1749–1804) and John Roberton (1832, 1845), continued to argue that nutritional status was the most important factor in determining age of puberty. During the middle-to-late nineteenth century, Charles Darwin (1868) also tried to postulate a relationship between food supply and fertility, observing that domestic animals with a regular, plentiful food supply were more fertile than corresponding wild animals. Moreover, reformers who were interested in improving the plight of the laboring classes argued strongly against the idea that lax morals caused an early age of puberty among working-class girls. On the contrary, they argued that difficult living conditions delayed puberty in the working classes (Whitehead 1847).

Climatic theories about puberty persisted well into the twentieth century. As late as the 1950s, some medical writers were still claiming that women from the tropics matured much earlier than those from temperate or cold climates (Peters and Shirkande 1957; Shaw 1959).

As a result of the views described above, middle-class parents in Europe and the United States viewed precocious puberty with a certain degree of alarm. Nineteenth-century medical-advice literature cautioned mothers to prevent all children, but especially daughters, from masturbating, reading romantic novels, and indulging in any activity that might excite the sexual passions (Neuman 1975). Many physicians also believed that too much consumption of meat contributed to precocious sexual longings and sexual development in young girls and could even cause insanity and nymphomania. Doctors, therefore, advised

mothers to restrict their daughters' intake of meat in order to prevent such disasters (Brumberg 1988). In retrospect, this advice may have contributed to the perceived secular trend in the age of menarche.

During the mid–twentieth century, a number of developmental studies uncovered the methodological flaws in earlier studies of the effect of sexual activity and climate on age of puberty. Tanner (1962), for example, demonstrated that many of the studies of adolescents from tropical regions were performed on girls and boys from wealthy families who had access to abundant sources of protein-rich foods and, therefore, did not represent the average age of puberty in these societies. Moreover, researchers noted that the age of menarche in Eskimo girls was actually earlier than that of western European girls, a phenomenon that resulted from the Eskimos' meat-rich diet (Bojlén and Bentzon 1968).

The most definitive studies on the relationship between nutrition and adolescent fertility were performed during and after World War II. Studies of children who had experienced famine, illness, and other harsh conditions during the war years showed a definite link between poor nutrition and age of physical maturity (Ellis 1945; Markowitz 1955; Krali-Cercek 1956; Maresh 1972; Wellens et al. 1990; Murata and Hibi 1992). Likewise, cross-cultural studies of women in both Western and non-Western countries have demonstrated that socioeconomic status and, hence, nutrition, are much more important than climate in determining age of puberty (Kolata 1974; McBarnette 1988; Brink 1989; Riley, Huffman, and Chowdhury 1989). These discoveries have completely undermined earlier notions about the effect of climate or sexual activity on age of puberty and have established once and for all that nutritional status is the determining factor in age of sexual maturation.

Heather Munro Prescott

Bibliography

Amundsen, D. W., and C. J. Diers. 1969. The age of menarche in classical Greece and Rome. *Human Biology* 41: 125–32.
1973. The age of menarche in medieval Europe. *Human Biology* 45: 363–9.
Aristotle. 1948. *Politics,* trans. E. Barker. Oxford.
Backman, G. von. 1948. Die beschleunigte Entwicklung der Jugend. *Acta Anatomica* 4: 421–80.
Baldwin, B. T. 1928. The determination of sex maturation in boys by a laboratory method. *Journal of Comparative Psychology* 8: 39–43.
Boerhaave, Herman. 1744. *Praelectiones academicae in proprias institutiones rei medicae,* with notes by Albrecht von Haller. 3 vols. Göttingen.
Bojlén, K., and M. W. Bentzon. 1968. The influence of climate and nutrition on age at menarche: A historical review and modern hypothesis. *Human Biology* 40: 69–85.
Boyd, Edith. 1980. *Origins of the study of human growth,*

based on unfinished work left by Richard E. Scammon, ed. Bhim Sen Savara and John Frederick Schilke. Portland, Ore.

Brink, Pamela J. 1989. The fattening room among the Annang of Nigeria. *Medical Anthropology* 12: 131–43.

Brown, P. E. 1966. The age at menarche. *British Journal of Preventive Social Medicine* 20: 9–14.

Brumberg, Joan Jacobs. 1988. *Fasting girls: The emergence of anorexia nervosa as a modern disease.* Cambridge, Mass.

1993. "Something happens to girls": Menarche and the emergence of the modern hygienic imperative. *Journal of the History of Sexuality* 4: 99–127.

Buffon, Georges-Louis Leclerc de. 1749–1804. *Histoire naturelle, générale et particulière avec la description du Cabinet du Roi.* Paris.

Bullough, Vern L. 1981. Age at menarche: A misunderstanding. *Science* 213: 365–6.

Crawford, John D. 1975. Body composition and menarche: The Frisch-Revelle hypothesis revisited. *Pediatrics* 56: 449–58.

Darwin, C. 1868. *The variation of plants and animals under domestication.* New York.

Diers, Carol Jean. 1974. Historical trends in the age at menarche and menopause. *Psychological Reports* 34: 931–7.

Duncan, J. M. 1884. *On sterility in women.* Philadelphia, Pa.

Ellis, Richard W. B. 1945. Growth and health of Belgian children during and after the German occupation (1940–44). *Archives of Diseases in Childhood* 20: 97–109.

Freind, J. F. 1738. *Emmenologia,* trans. M. Devaux (first published Oxford 1703). Paris.

Frisch, Rose E. 1978. Population, food intake, and fertility. *Science* 199: 22–30.

Golub, Sharon. 1983. *Menarche: The transition from girl to woman.* Lexington, Mass.

Guarionius, Hippolytus. 1610. *Die Greuel der Verwüstung menschlichen Geschlechts.* Ingolstadt, Germany.

Haller, Albrecht von. 1775. *Herrn Albrecht von Hallers Anfangsgründe der Phisiologie des menschlichen Körpers.* Berlin.

Johnson, F. E. 1974. Control of age at menarche. *Human Biology* 46: 159–71.

Kinsey, A. C. 1948. *Sexual behavior in the human male.* Philadelphia, Pa.

Kolata, G. B. 1974. !Kung hunter-gatherers: Feminism, diet and birth control. *Science* 185: 932–24.

Krali-Cercek, Lea. 1956. The influence of food, body build, and social origin on the age at menarche. *Human Biology* 28: 393–406.

Maresh, Marion M. 1972. A forty-five year investigation for secular changes in physical maturation. *American Journal of Physical Anthropology* 36: 103–10.

Marinello, G. 1574. *Le medicine partenenti alle infermita delle donne.* Venice.

Markowitz, Stephen D. 1955. Retardation in growth of children in Europe and Asia during World War II. *Human Biology* 27: 258–73.

McBarnette, Lorna. 1988. Women and poverty: The effects on reproductive status. *Women and Health* 12: 55–81.

Meyer, François, Jocelyne Moisan, Diane Marcoux, and Claude Bouchard. 1990. Dietary and physical determinants of menarche. *Epidemiology* 1: 377–81.

Moisan, Jocelyne, François Meyer, and Suzanne Gingras. 1990. Diet and age at menarche. *Cancer Causes and Control* 1: 149–54.

Montesquieu, C. L. de Sede. 1751. De l'esprit des lois. *Oeuvres*

complètes (Bibliothèque de la Pléiade), Vol. 7, Book 16. Dijon.

Murata, Mitsunori, and Itsuro Hibi. 1992. Nutrition and the secular trend of growth. *Hormone Research* 38 (Supplement 1): 89–96.

Neuman, R. P. 1975. Masturbation, madness, and the modern concepts of childhood and adolescence. *Journal of Social History* 8: 1–27.

Osler, David C., and John D. Crawford. 1973. Examination of the hypothesis of critical weight at menarche in ambulatory and bedridden mentally retarded girls. *Pediatrics* 51: 675–9.

Peters, H., and S. M. Shirkande. 1957. Age at menarche in Indian women. *Fertility and Sterility* 8: 355.

Post, J. B. 1971. Age at menarche and menopause: Some medieval authorities. *Population Studies* 25: 83–7.

Potter, Robert G. 1975. Changes of natural fertility and contraceptive equivalents. *Social Forces* 54: 36–51.

Richardson, Barbara D., and Linda Pieters. 1977. Menarche and growth. *American Journal of Clinical Nutrition* 30: 2088–91.

Riley, A. P., S. L. Huffman, and A. K. M. Chowdhury. 1989. Age at menarche and postmenarcheal growth in rural Bangladeshi females. *Annals of Human Biology* 16: 347–59.

Roberton, John. 1832. An inquiry into the natural history of the menstrual function. *Edinburgh Medical and Surgical Journal* 38: 227.

1845. On the period of puberty in Hindu women. *Edinburgh Medical and Surgical Journal* 64: 156.

Schiebinger, Londa. 1993. *Nature's body: Gender and the making of modern science.* Boston, Mass.

Schurig, Martin. 1729. *Parthenologia historico-medica, hoc est viginitatis consideratio, qua ad eam pertinens pubertates et menstruatio, item varia de insolitis mensium viis, nec non de partium genitalium miliebrium pro virginitatis custodia.* Dresden.

Shaw, W. 1959. *Textbook of Gynecology.* Seventh edition. London.

Short, R. V. 1976. The evolution of human reproduction. *Proceedings of the Royal Society of London* 195: 3–24.

Shorter, Edward. 1981. L'age des Premières Règles en France, 1750–1950. *Annales: Économies, Sociétés, Civilisations* 36: 495–511.

Smith, W. T. 1855. *On the causes and treatment of abortion and sterility.* London.

Soranus. 1950. *Gynecology,* trans. O. Temkin. Baltimore, Md.

Stepan, Nancy. 1982. *The idea of race in science: Great Britain 1800–1960.* Hamden, Conn.

Tanner, J. M. 1962. *Growth at adolescence.* London.

1968. Earlier maturation in man. *Scientific American* 218: 2–8.

1973. Growing up. *Scientific American* 229: 34–43.

1981a. *A history of the study of human growth.* London.

1981b. Menarcheal age. *Science* 214: 604–5.

Vinovskis, Maris A. 1988. *An "epidemic" of adolescent pregnancy? Some historical and policy considerations.* New York.

Wellens, Rita, Robert M. Malina, Gaston Beunen, and Johan Lefevre. 1990. Age at menarche in Flemish girls: Current status and secular change in the 20th century. *Annals of Human Biology* 17: 145–52.

Whitehead, J. 1847. *On the causes and treatment of abortion and sterility. . . .* London.

Wyshak, Grace, and Rose E. Frisch. 1982. Evidence for a secular trend in age of menarche. *New England Journal of Medicine* 306: 1033–5.

Zacharias, Leona, William M. Rand, and Richard J. Wurtman. 1976. A prospective study of sexual development and growth in American girls: The statistics of menarche. *Obstetrical and Gynecological Survey* 31: 325-37.

VI.9 ❧ Nutrition and Mental Development

Most research on nutrition and human mental development has focused on protein–energy malnutrition (PEM), which consists of deficits in energy and protein as well as other nutrients (Golden 1988). But there is also an extensive literature on the importance to mental development of trace elements and vitamins, as well as the impact of short-term food deprivation. Thus, although the bulk of this essay focuses on PEM and mental development, we begin with an examination of these other areas of concern.

Vitamins and Trace Elements

General Vitamin and Mineral Deficiencies

It is well understood that severe vitamin deficiencies may have drastic effects on mental development. Serious thiamine and niacin deficiencies, for example, as well as those of folic acid and vitamin B_{12}, can cause neuropathy (Carney 1984). But milder, subclinical vitamin deficiencies are much more common, and thus their influence on mental development is presumably of much greater importance. Unfortunately, the extent to which multivitamin and mineral supplements influence intelligence in schoolchildren remains unknown, although this question has been the subject of at least five clinical trials (Schoenthaler 1991).

One study of 90 Welsh children using a multivitamin–mineral supplement over a nine-month period indicated that supplementation produced an increase in nonverbal IQs (Benton and Roberts 1988). A similar study of 410 children in the United States over 13 weeks also revealed an overall increase in nonverbal IQs (Schoenthaler 1991). However, in a Belgian study of 167 children who were supplemented for five months, only boys whose diets had previously been nutritionally deficient showed an increase in verbal IQs (Benton and Buts 1990). Other studies, one in London and the other in Scotland, reported no significant effects of supplementation (Naismith et al. 1988; Crombie et al. 1990).

Reasons for inconsistent findings may have to do with differences in the duration of the programs or may lie in the nature of the children's normal diets. Because supplementation is most likely to benefit children whose diets are deficient in one or more of the chief nutrients, more consistent results might have been obtained if the subjects had been restricted to children with deficient diets. Another problem with these studies is that a variety of vitamins and trace elements were administered in the supplements. Thus, it is not possible to single out those nutrients that may have played key roles in raising nonverbal IQs.

Trace Elements

Among the trace elements there are two that have been the subject of much research and are known to have a substantial influence on mental development.

Iodine. One is iodine, which is required for the production of thyroxine. Iodine deficiency during pregnancy can cause deficits in fetal brain maturation, resulting in cretinism. There are two types of cretinism, neurological and myxedematous; mental retardation is a symptom of both. Other symptoms of neurological cretinism include spastic diplegia and deaf-mutism, whereas dwarfism is symptomatic of myxedematous cretinism.

Cretinism, however, is not the only manifestation of iodine deficiency, and a number of others have been identified. These are referred to as iodine-deficiency disorders (IDD) (Hetzel 1983) and include goiter, neuromotor delays, deaf-mutism, and an increase in both pre- and postnatal mortality rates (Stanbury 1987).

Cretinism seems to be the extreme in a spectrum of cognitive and psychomotor deficits caused by iodine deficiency. Studies in Indonesia and Spain have indicated that village children living in iodine-deficient regions had poorer levels of mental and motor development than other village children who did not live in such areas (Bleichrodt et al. 1987). It may be that other disparities between the villages played a role in the differences. But, in a village in Ecuador, iodine supplementation of pregnant mothers reportedly led to improved motor development of the children, in comparison with children in a nonsupplemented village (Fierro-Benitez et al. 1986). Similar results were derived from a clinical trial conducted in Zaire (Thilly et al. 1980).

Yet in other studies, iodine supplementation seems to have been less effective. One of these, conducted in Peru, reported no effect on the development of the infants of mothers supplemented during pregnancy (Pretell et al. 1972). Two other studies involved schoolchildren. One, carried out in Bolivia, revealed no changes in school achievement and development despite iodine supplementation (Bautista et al. 1982), and a Spanish study discovered no effect on the mental or psychomotor development of supplemented children (Bleichrodt et al. 1989).

Clearly, more research of a conclusive nature is needed. There are some 800 million persons at risk of iodine deficiency in Asia, Africa, and Latin America;

close to 200 million persons in the world suffer from goiter, and more than 3 million are cretins (Hetzel 1987). This is especially tragic because iodine deficiency is so easily prevented by the consumption of iodized salt or iodized oil, or by iodine injection.

Iron. Iron is the second of the trace minerals that play a decided role in mental development. Its deficiency is the main cause of anemia, an important nutritional problem in both developed and developing countries. Because anemia symptoms include listlessness and lassitude, iron deficiency can and does negatively affect the cognitive processes.

Early investigations indicated associations between iron-deficiency anemia and poor levels of cognition in children. However, there were problems in eliminating social factors that could also be causal (see, for example, Webb and Oski 1973). Subsequent studies on iron-deficient children suggest, among other things, that the adverse effects of iron deficiency on the cognitive processes are most apparent when the deficiency is severe enough to cause anemia.

Age has much to do with such findings, as does the duration of the periods of iron supplementation. For example, in five studies, supplementation was given for periods of less than two weeks, and developmental levels assessed on infant scales were used as outcome measures. No significant gains from supplementation were discovered in four of the studies, which were conducted in Guatemala (Lozoff et al. 1982), Costa Rica (Lozoff et al. 1987), Chile (Walter et al. 1989), and North America (Oski and Honig 1978). A fifth study, in Chile, did find an improvement in developmental levels, although the absence of a placebo group compromised the results (Walter, Kovalskys, and Stekel 1983).

In another group of studies, however, children under two years of age were supplemented for longer periods. Two such studies were preventive trials in which high-risk children were supplemented from the age of 2 to 3 months and then tested at 12 months. In Chile, such supplementation produced better development (Walter et al. 1989), and in Papua New Guinea, supplemented children had longer fixation times than the controls (Heywood et al. 1989). On the other hand, in the United Kingdom, a group that underwent two months of supplementation did not produce better development scores than a placebo group, although a greater number of treated children achieved normal rates of development (Aukett et al. 1986). In Costa Rica, after three months of supplementation, children who experienced complete recovery of their iron status clearly benefited from the supplements (Lozoff et al. 1987). However, a study in Chile found no effect after three months of supplementation (Walter et al. 1989).

It appears that, as a rule, the longer the duration of treatment, the more likely there will be benefits in developmental levels. It has been suggested that iron

deficiency affects such development because it reduces a child's span of attention (Pollitt et al. 1982). But children under two years of age are difficult to assess, and only one study thus far has attempted to look at the matter (Heywood et al. 1989).

Results seem to be more positive in children over two years of age. Indeed, 10 studies have reported improvement in mental functions after iron supplementation. Three of these were conducted in Indonesia, and improvements in both cognitive functions and school achievement levels were reported after two or three months' treatment (Soemantri, Pollitt, and Kim 1985; Soemantri 1989; Soewondo, Husaini, and Pollitt 1989).

In India, two studies found improved cognitive functions after three months of supplementation (Seshadri and Gopaldas 1989); another, in Egypt, reported the same after four months of treatment (Pollitt et al. 1985). In India, two additional clinical trials showed improvements in IQ scores after three months of supplementation with both iron and folic acid (Seshadri and Gopaldas 1989). In the United States, the results of two studies, which were not true clinical trials, indicated that supplementation produced improvements in the cognitive functions of anemic children (Pollitt, Leibel, and Greenfield 1983a), and similar conclusions were reached in Guatemala (Pollitt et al. 1986). But two other studies, in the United States and Thailand, showed no apparent improvements with iron supplementation (Deinard et al. 1986; Pollitt et al. 1989).

From the foregoing, then, it would seem that there is good evidence to indicate that iron-deficiency anemia has detrimental effects on the mental development of children over the age of two, and that supplementation will erase those effects. In younger children, however, the evidence is less conclusive. In fact, there is little or no evidence of benefits with supplementation lasting less than two weeks, and although investigations with longer-term treatment have yielded more positive findings, such findings are inconsistent.

Nonetheless, the evidence generated by such investigations is of vital importance because about 51 percent of preschool-age and 38 percent of school-age children in developing countries, and 10 percent of preschool-age and 12 percent of school-age children in developed countries, are anemic (DeMaeyer and Adiels-Tegman 1985).

Short-Term Food Deprivation

Although improvement in school achievement is one of the goals of school feeding programs, there have been few well-designed evaluations of their effectiveness (Pollitt, Gersovitz, and Gargicilo 1978). The best results are most likely to be derived from such programs in developing countries where the prevalence of undernutrition is greater. But, unfortunately, most investigations conducted in these countries have tended to be poorly designed (Levinger 1986).

One exception was a small Jamaican study using a matched control group. It related improvements in school achievement to the school feeding plan, but not to improvements in nutritional status as such (Powell, Grantham-McGregor, and Eston 1983). It was speculated that the mere alleviation of hunger during school hours produced improvements in cognitive functions and behavior.

The most sensitive method of examining the effects of short-term food deprivation on mental functions involves studies in which children are used as their own controls and in which their performance is compared with and without breakfast. Four such studies (including three from the United States) have reported detrimental effects on mental functions when breakfast was omitted. In one of these, the omission of breakfast showed a deterioration in cognitive functions only in children with low IQs (Pollitt, Leibel, and Greenfield 1981). When the investigation was replicated, deterioration was found in the cognitive functions of all children (Pollitt et al. 1983b). Another study indicated that the detrimental effect on cognitive functions became worse as the period of deprivation increased (Conners and Blouin 1983).

In Jamaica, an investigation into the effects of missing breakfast among both undernourished and adequately nourished children discovered that the cognitive functions of undernourished children deteriorated with the omission of breakfast, whereas those of adequately nourished children did not (Simeon and Grantham-McGregor 1989).

The reason for the impact of short-term food deprivation on cognitive functions is not clear. However, it likely has a metabolic basis, which may result in changes in arousal levels (Pollitt et al. 1981) or in neurotransmitter levels (Wurtman 1986). The relationship between arousal levels and performance is complex (Kahneman 1973) and varies with the nature of the task (Hebb 1972) and the subjects (Eysenck 1976).

It does seem clear that undernourished children are more susceptible to cognitive function impairment resulting from short-term food deprivation than are adequately nourished children. It is possible that malnutrition may serve to sensitize the children to the stress of the omission of food. In other words, they may appraise the situation as being more threatening than do better-nourished children (Barnes et al. 1968; Smart and Dobbing 1977). But the response of malnourished children may also be due to abnormalities in carbohydrate metabolism. Illustrative is the fact that, during severe PEM, children have low fasting glucose and insulin levels (James and Coore 1970; Alleyne et al. 1972).

In concluding this discussion of short-term food deprivation and cognitive functions, we should note

that although the impact of such deprivation appears to be small, there may be important consequences. If, for example, food deprivation occurs frequently over a long period, the effects may be cumulative and lead to poor levels of development and school achievement. Indeed, food deprivation, which is hardly uncommon in malnourished children, may play a significant role in the low levels of mental development generally found in such children.

Protein–Energy Malnutrition

There have been three major classifications of PEM, with the Gomez classification being the first (Gomez et al. 1955): Children suffering from PEM were described as being mildly, moderately, or severely malnourished, depending on their deficits in weight compared to reference values for their sex and age. However, a second classification – the Wellcome classification – takes into account the presence of edema as well as weight deficits (Wellcome Trust Working Party 1970).

These two classifications are generally used in the identification of children with severe PEM. But the use of weight and age alone is not very useful in discriminating between different types of mild-to-moderate PEM. For example, a child with a low weight-for-age may be tall and thin or short and fat. To address this problem, J. Waterlow (1976) introduced a third classification, which employs height expressed as a percentage of the expected value for age and sex, and employs weight as a percentage of the expected value for the height and sex of an afflicted child. Low height-for-age, or stunting, is thought to reflect long-term PEM, whereas low weight-for-height, or wasting, is believed to reflect recent nutritional experiences.

The prevalence of mild-to-moderate PEM in developing countries ranges from 7 to 60 percent, whereas that of severe PEM is between 1 and 10 percent (Grant 1990). PEM has a decided impact on mental development, and with an estimated 150 million children suffering from the affliction worldwide, its potential cost in human, as well as social and economic, terms is staggering.

Mild-to-Moderate PEM

A number of observational studies have associated mild-to-moderate PEM with poor mental development. Yet PEM tends to occur amid economic deprivation that has its own deleterious effects on development. Because it is not possible to control for many of these factors, the most effective way to determine the impact of PEM lies in the use of experimental study designs.

Unfortunately, there have been only a few experiments in which at-risk children have been supplemented and their mental development compared with that of controls. What follows is a brief summary of the findings of observational studies and experimental studies, although only those in which there was statistical control of confounding background variables are mentioned.

Observational studies. Investigations examining associations between mild-to-moderate PEM and the mental development of preschool-age children have been conducted in Colombia (Christiansen et al. 1977), Guatemala (Lasky et al. 1981), and Jamaica (Powell and Grantham-McGregor 1985). The results of the three studies indicated that PEM was associated with poor development.

Another seven studies involved school-age children. Undernutrition in children was associated with poor school achievement levels in the Philippines (Popkin and Lim-Ybanez 1982; Florencio 1988), Nepal (Moock and Leslie 1986), and India (Agarwal et al. 1987), and with low IQs in Jamaica (Clarke et al. 1991). In Guatemala, a study showed a close association between undernutrition and low IQs, whereas in Kenya, malnutrition was correlated with poor levels of cognitive functions (Johnston et al. 1987; Sigman et al. 1989).

Experimental studies. There are two types of supplementation investigations: preventive and remedial. The former focuses on high-risk mothers who are supplemented during pregnancy, and on their offspring who are supplemented in early childhood to prevent them from becoming undernourished. By contrast, in remedial studies, the focus is on already undernourished children who are supplemented to improve their nutritional status.

The findings of experimental studies in developed countries are especially likely to be inconsistent. In one preventive investigation, carried out in North America, supplementation during pregnancy provided the infant with only small advantages in play, and none in development, during its first year of life (Rush, Stein, and Susser 1980). Two other trials revealed no apparent benefits for the infants whose mothers had received supplements (Osofsky 1975; Pencharz et al. 1983). In a fourth study in which supplementation began during pregnancy and continued during the first year of life, children experienced large gains in development, compared with their older siblings (Hicks, Langham, and Takenaka 1982).

One reason for the inconsistency in the findings of these four studies is that in a developed region like North America, the children under scrutiny would probably not have become malnourished, regardless of whether they had supplemented mothers.

A fifth supplementation study in the developed world was remedial. Carried out as a clinical trial in England (Lucas et al. 1990), it investigated the effects of an enriched formula on the development of small preterm children. Marked benefits were shown at 18 months, especially in motor development.

It is the case, however, that studies conducted in developing countries where malnutrition is endemic are much more useful in determining whether the association between PEM and mental development is causal. One from Colombia, in which the supplementation was preventive, produced evidence of beneficial effects, first in motor development (Mora et al. 1979) and later in language (Waber et al. 1981). In Taiwan, supplementation of pregnant mothers, but not of children, led to benefits in motor development when the children were eight months old, although there was no effect on mental development (Joos et al. 1983). Supplementation of both mothers and children, however, resulted in gains in mental and motor development in Mexico (Chavez and Martinez 1982), and in cognitive functions in Guatemala (Freeman et al. 1980).

As for remedial studies, in one conducted in Colombia, both malnourished and adequately nourished children were supplemented for one year. Only those who had been malnourished improved in their development (Mora et al. 1974). In a second such investigation in Colombia, a supplementation–stimulation program was found to encourage mental development and a subsequent improvement in school performance. Moreover, such positive effects increased with the duration of the program. However, supplementation alone had no effect on development (McKay et al. 1978).

Jamaica was the site of a third remedial study, in which children ages 9 to 24 months, with low heights-for-age, were given nutritional supplementation for two years. There was a beneficial effect on development. Locomotor development was affected first, followed by mental functions. This clinical trial also had a stimulation component, and the effects of supplementation and stimulation were additive and not interactive (Grantham-McGregor et al. 1991).

To sum up, in developing-world countries, improvement in mental development was found in studies in which supplementation was preventive. This was also the case in two of the three remedial investigations. There were design flaws in some of the investigations, but considering the consistency of the findings across developing countries, the evidence indicates that both remedial and preventive supplementation encourage development. In general, however, the benefits are small, perhaps because the gains in growth were also small in the supplemented children. Indeed, the actual levels of supplementation were less than intended because of the problems of food sharing and substitution that occur in supplementation studies (Beaton and Ghassemi 1982).

Finally, the importance of the cumulative effect of mild-to-moderate undernutrition (or its absence) throughout childhood cannot be accurately assessed in supplementation programs lasting a relatively short period of time and producing only small improvements in growth.

Severe PEM

The most common method of defining severe PEM in children is the Wellcome classification, which includes those suffering from marasmus, kwashiorkor, or marasmic-kwashiorkor.

Because it is not ethical to conduct experimental studies with severely malnourished children, investigations have been observational, and most of the children studied were treated in hospital in the acute stage. Early studies reported poor levels of mental development in children with severe PEM (see, for example, Gerber and Dean 1956). There followed a series of cohort studies of school-age children who survived severe PEM in early childhood.

As in examinations of mild-to-moderate PEM, a main problem was that the poor socioeconomic environment in which the victims lived tended to confuse the relationship between PEM and poor mental development. The use of well-matched controls was therefore essential and improved over time. Two strategies were employed to control for social background. The first was the use of siblings of the index children as controls, and the second included the use of children from similar socioeconomic backgrounds.

These strategies, of course, have inherent problems. Although it is reasonable to assume that both the index child and the sibling have lived under similar socioeconomic conditions, there are unavoidable biases when siblings are used as controls. It is not possible, for example, to control for age and birth order, both of which affect development. In addition, it is possible that a child who has become severely malnourished has not been treated the same way as a sibling who was not malnourished. Most importantly, it is probable that the siblings were also malnourished and, consequently, had lowered levels of mental development themselves. Finally, there is evidence that long-term PEM may have greater negative effects on mental development than an episode of severe PEM (Grantham-McGregor, Powell, and Fletcher 1989). Therefore, the true effects of severe PEM are likely to be worse than those determined from studies using sibling comparisons.

The use of nonsibling controls from the same socioeconomic class also presents problems. Families of children with severe PEM tend to be poorer (Richardson 1974) and to have less stimulating home environments (Cravioto and DeLicardie 1972) than their control comparisons, and both of these factors can affect mental development. In the following discussion, research on the effects of severe PEM on mental development during its acute phase will be discussed first, followed by a look at investigations of its long-term sequelae. Finally, the effects of severe PEM, as demonstrated by studies conducted in developed countries, will be reviewed.

Acute stage. In early reports, children suffering from severe PEM were described as apathetic (Williams 1933) and having poor levels of mental development

(Cravioto and Robles 1965; Yatkin and McLaren 1970; Monckeberg 1979). Although there was some evidence of improvement after clinical recovery, these studies had no controls. But, in a controlled study in Jamaica, severely malnourished children were found to have lower levels of mental development when compared with controls hospitalized for other illnesses. The developmental levels of both groups improved during their hospital stay. However, the malnourished group failed to reduce their deficit relative to the controls. The children who had suffered from PEM were also less active, more apathetic, and less exploring than the controls (Grantham-McGregor et al. 1990).

Long-term effects with nonsibling controls. In examining the long-term effects of PEM, eight studies were identified in which school-age children who had previously suffered from the illness were compared with nonsibling controls. In seven of these efforts, the malnourished children had lower levels of mental development than the controls. One, conducted in India, indicated that the index children had lower scores in perceptual, abstract, and verbal abilities, as well as in memory and sensory integration (Champakam, Srikantia, and Gopalan 1968).

Two other studies were conducted in Jamaica. In the first, the index children were found to have lower IQs (Hertzig et al. 1972) and lower school achievement levels (Richardson, Birch, and Hertzig 1973) than controls. The second Jamaican study also found deficits in IQs (Grantham-McGregor, Schofield, and Powell 1987) and school achievement (Powell and Grantham-McGregor 1990). In Barbados, children who had previously been severely malnourished were found to have lower IQs than controls (Galler et al. 1983b), and more behavior problems (Galler et al. 1983a), learning disabilities (Galler, Ramsey, and Solimano 1984a), and motor delays (Galler et al. 1984b).

In Uganda, severe PEM was also found to be associated with deficits in mental and motor development (Hoorweg and Stanfield 1976), and in Nigeria, children who had been severely malnourished had lower scores in a number of tests of cognitive functions (Nwuga 1977). Similarly, in South Africa, children who had previously suffered from severe malnutrition had lower IQs, lower levels of school achievement, and more behavior problems than controls (Stoch and Smythe 1976). Another South African study, however, was the only one of the eight under discussion that reported no difference in development between survivors of severe PEM and controls (Bartel et al. 1978).

Long-term effects and sibling controls. The long-term effects of PEM have also been examined in eight studies in which the development of school-age children who had previously been severely malnourished was compared with that of their siblings. Five of these studies revealed deficits in development. In Nigeria, index children were found to have lower IQs than their siblings (Nwuga 1977), whereas in India they had poorer levels of school achievement (Pereira, Sundaraj, and Begum 1979). In Mexico, boys who were previously severely malnourished had lower IQs than their siblings, although no difference was found with girls (Birch et al. 1971). In Jamaica, index children had lower verbal IQs (Hertzig et al. 1972) and more behavior problems (Richardson et al. 1973) than siblings, but there was no difference in school achievement levels. In South Africa, there was no difference in IQs between previously severely malnourished children and their siblings. However, the index children showed lower school achievement and produced lower scores on a drawing test (Evans, Moodie, and Hansen 1971).

Yet, severe PEM was found to have no effect on children's school achievement in Peru (Graham and Adrianzen 1979), and none on motor development in South Africa (Bartel et al. 1978). Another South African study examined the impact, on young adults, of severe PEM in early childhood. No difference was found in school attainment or in social adjustment when compared with their siblings (Moodie et al. 1980).

Developing countries. As we have mentioned, in studies conducted in developing countries, it is difficult to separate the effects on mental development of severe PEM from those of poor environment. Therefore, investigations using subjects from developed countries can be helpful. Unlike the situation in developing countries, where poverty is the primary cause of malnutrition, children in developed countries generally become malnourished because of diseases, such as cystic fibrosis. Since the children's developmental state tends not to be associated with deprived social conditions, such cases present an opportunity to view the long-term effects of severe PEM from a fresh angle.

The results of these studies have been inconsistent. Small deficits in children's development were demonstrated in some instances (Klein, Forbes, and Nader 1975; Winick, Meyer, and Harris 1975; Carmona da Mota et al. 1990), but no deficits were found in others (Lloyd-Still et al. 1974; Valman 1974; Ellis and Hill 1975). It is possible that the findings in developed countries have not been as consistent as those in developing countries because the children in the former tended to have less severe episodes of PEM that continued for shorter periods.

It is also possible that the environments in which the children were raised after the episode of PEM had a modifying effect. Psychosocial stimulation can improve the development of severely malnourished children. Such improvements were only transient in the wake of short-term programs (McLaren et al. 1973; Cravioto and Arrieta 1979) but lasted for several years following a three-year program (Grantham-

McGregor et al. 1987). This effect is consistent with animal studies in which stimulation has decreased the adverse effects of severe PEM on development (Levitsky 1979).

Clearly, then, there are problems with inferring a causal relationship between severe PEM and poor mental development on the basis of nonexperimental studies. Nonetheless, the results of the studies reviewed indicate that children who are severely malnourished in early childhood and are raised in deprived conditions usually have lower levels of mental development than similarly deprived children who are not severely malnourished. The effects have been more consistent in studies in which malnourished children were compared with nonsibling controls rather than with siblings. This may be because of overmatching in the latter studies.

The mechanism linking PEM to poor mental development is not clearly established, but there are several hypotheses that assume a causal relationship. Children who died from severe PEM have been found to have smaller brains than comparison children (Winick and Rosso 1969; Rosso, Hormazabal, and Winick 1970; Dickerson, Merat, and Yusuf 1982), and it is certainly possible that impairments in brain growth may have adverse effects on mental development. Although findings from animal studies indicate that the anatomical changes due to PEM are persistent (Bedi 1987), it is not clear if this is the case in humans. In addition, it is not known if children with mild-to-moderate PEM also experience impaired brain growth.

The brain function of severely malnourished children has also been investigated by using evoked brain potentials. However, here the findings have proven inconsistent. In Mexico, abnormal auditory evoked potentials were found in severely malnourished children when compared with matched controls, and the abnormality persisted after clinical recovery (Barnet et al. 1978). In South Africa, the results of electroencephalograph (EEG) measurements indicated that children who had previously been severely malnourished had delays in brain development when compared with their siblings, but there was no difference when compared with nonsibling controls (Bartel et al. 1979). On the other hand, two other South African studies found no difference in EEGs when previously severely malnourished children were compared either with their siblings (Evans et al. 1971) or with nonsibling controls (Stoch and Smythe 1976).

It has been speculated that malnourished children are less active, explore their environments less, and thus acquire skills more slowly than adequately nourished ones. It may well be that in addition, their caretakers become less responsive to them, thus exacerbating poor development. Yet, although malnourished children have been shown to have lower activity levels and poorer developmental levels than adequately nourished children (Chavez and Martinez 1982; Meeks Gardner et al. 1990), there is no evidence showing that reduced activity precedes poor development (Grantham-McGregor et al. 1990).

In conclusion, it seems clear that various nutritional deficiencies have adverse effects on mental development. There are concurrent deficits in development in the face of mild-to-moderate PEM, severe PEM, short-term food deprivation, and iron-deficiency anemia. Maternal iodine deficiency has long-term effects on development, and severe PEM, usually, has long-term effects on mental development, if the children live in poor environments. But it has not yet been established that less severe PEM has long-term sequelae.

Donald T. Simeon
Sally M. Grantham-McGregor

Bibliography

Agarwal, D., S. Upadhyay, A. Tripathi, and K. Agarwad. 1987. Nutritional status, physical work capacity and mental functions in schoolchildren. *Nutrition Foundation of India, Scientific Report No. 6.*

Alleyne, G., P. Trust, H. Flores, and H. Robinson. 1972. Glucose tolerance and insulin sensitivity in malnourished children. *British Journal of Nutrition* 27: 585-92.

Aukett, M., Y. Parks, P. Scott, and B. Wharton. 1986. Treatment with iron increases weight gain and psychomotor development. *Archives of Disease in Childhood* 61: 849-57.

Barnes, R., C. Neeling, E. Kwong, et al. 1968. Post-natal nutritional deprivations as determinants of adult rat behavior toward feed, its consumption and utilization. *Journal of Nutrition* 96: 467-76.

Barnet, A., I. Weiss, M. Sotillo, and E. Ohlrich. 1978. Abnormal auditory evoked potentials in early infancy malnutrition. *Science* 201: 450-1.

Bartel, P., R. Griesel, L. Burnett, et al. 1978. Long-term effects of kwashiorkor on psychomotor development. *South African Medical Journal* 53: 360-2.

Bartel, P., R. Griesel, I. Freiman, et al. 1979. Long-term effects of kwashiorkor on the electroencephalogram. *American Journal of Clinical Nutrition* 32: 753-7.

Bautista, A., P. Barker, J. Dunn, et al. 1982. The effects of iodized oil on intelligence, thyroid status and somatic growth in school-age children from an area of endemic goiter. *American Journal of Clinical Nutrition* 35: 127-34.

Beaton, G., and H. Ghassemi. 1982. Supplementary feeding programs for young children in developing countries. *American Journal of Clinical Nutrition* 35 (Supplement): 863-916.

Bedi, K. 1987. Lasting neuroanatomical changes following undernutrition. In *Early nutrition and later achievement,* ed. J. Dobbing, 1-49. London.

Benton, D., and J.-P. Buts. 1990. Vitamin/mineral supplementation and intelligence. *Lancet* 335: 1158-60.

Benton, D., and G. Roberts. 1988. Effect of vitamin and supplementation on intelligence of a sample of schoolchildren. *Lancet* 1: 140-3.

Birch, H., L. Pineiro, E. Alcalde, et al. 1971. Relation of kwash-iorkor in early childhood and intelligence at school age. *Pediatric Research* 5: 579-85.

Bleichrodt, N., F. Escobar del Rey, G. Morreale, et al. 1989. Iodine deficiency, implications for mental and psychomotor development in children. In *Iodine and the brain,* ed. G. Delong, J. Robbins, and P. Condliffe, 269-87. New York.

Bleichrodt, N., I. Garcia, C. Rubio, et al. 1987. Developmental disorders associated with severe iodine deficiency. In *The prevention and control of iodine deficiency disorders,* ed. B. Hetzel, J. Dunn, and J. Stanbury, 65-84. Amsterdam.

Carmona da Mota, H., A. Antonio, G. Leitao, and M. Porto. 1990. Late effects of early malnutrition. *Lancet* 335: 1158.

Carney, M. 1984. Vitamin deficiencies and excesses: Behavioral consequences in adults. In *Nutrition and behavior,* ed. J. Galler, 193-222. New York.

Champakam, S., S. Srikantia, and C. Gopalan. 1968. Kwashiorkor and mental development. *American Journal of Clinical Nutrition* 21: 844-52.

Chavez, A., and C. Martinez. 1982. *Growing up in a developing community.* Guatemala City.

Christiansen, N., L. Vuori, J. Clement, et al. 1977. Malnutrition, social environment and cognitive development of Colombian infants and preschoolers. *Nutrition Reports International* 16: 93-102.

Clarke, N., S. Grantham-McGregor, and C. Powell. 1991. Nutrition and health predictors of school failure in Jamaican children. *Ecology of Food and Nutrition* 26: 47-57.

Conners, C., and A. Blouin. 1983. Nutritional effects on behavior of children. *Journal of Psychiatric Research* 17: 193-201.

Connolly, K., P. Pharoah, and B. Hetzel. 1979. Fetal iodine deficiency and motor performance during childhood. *Lancet* 1: 1149-51.

Cravioto, J., and R. Arrieta. 1979. Stimulation and mental development of malnourished infants. *Lancet* 2: 899.

Cravioto, J., and E. DeLicardie. 1972. Environmental correlates of severe clinical malnutrition and language development in survivors from kwashiorkor or marasmus. In *Nutrition, the nervous system and behavior,* Scientific Publication No. 251, 73-94. Washington, D.C.

Cravioto, J., and B. Robles. 1965. Evolution of adaptive and motor behavior during rehabilitation from kwashiorkor. *American Journal of Ortho-Psychiatry* 35: 449-64.

Crombie, I., J. Todman, G. McNeil, et al. 1990. Effect of vitamin and mineral supplementation on verbal and nonverbal reasoning of schoolchildren. *Lancet* 335: 744-7.

Deinard, A., A. List, B. Lindgren, et al. 1986. Cognitive deficits in iron-deficient and iron-deficient anaemic children. *Journal of Pediatrics* 108: 681-89.

DeMaeyer, E., and M. Adiels-Tegman. 1985. The prevalence of anemia in the world. *World Health Statistics Quarterly* 38: 302-16.

Dickerson, J., A. Merat, and H. Yusuf. 1982. Effects of malnutrition on brain growth and development. In *Brain and behavioral development,* ed. J. Dickerson and H. McGurr, 73-108. Glasgow.

Dickie, N., and A. Bender. 1982. Breakfast and performance. *Human Nutrition: Applied Nutrition* 36A: 46-56.

Dwyer, T., M. Elias, J. Warram, and F. Stare. 1972. Effects of a school snack program on certain aspects of school performance. *Federal Proceedings* 31: 718.

Ellis, C., and D. Hill. 1975. Growth, intelligence and school performance in children with cystic fibrosis who have had an episode of malnutrition during infancy. *Journal of Pediatrics* 87: 565-8.

Evans, D., A. Moodie, and J. Hansen. 1971. Kwashiorkor and intellectual development. *South African Medical Journal* 45: 1413-26.

Eysenck, M. 1976. Arousal, learning and memory. *Psychological Bulletin* 83: 389-404.

Fierro-Benitez, R., R. Casar, J. Stanbury, et al. 1986. Long-term effects of correction of iodine deficiency on psychomotor development and intellectual development. In *Towards the eradication of endemic goiter, cretinism and iodine deficiency,* ed. J. Dunn, E. Pretell, C. Daza, and F. Viteri, 182-200. Washington, D.C.

Florencio, C. 1988. *Nutrition, health and other determinants of academic achievement and school-related behavior.* Quezon City, Philippines.

Freeman, H., R. Klein, J. Townsend, and A. Lechtig. 1980. Nutrition and cognitive development among rural Guatemalan children. *American Journal of Public Health* 70: 1277-85.

Galler, J., F. Ramsey, and G. Solimano. 1984a. The influence of early malnutrition on subsequent behavioral development. III. Learning disabilities as a sequel to malnutrition. *Pediatric Research* 18: 309-13.

Galler, J., F. Ramsey, G. Solimano, and W. Lowell. 1983a. The influence of early malnutrition on subsequent behavioral development. II. Classroom behavior. *Journal of the American Academy of Childhood Psychiatry* 22: 16-22.

Galler, J., F. Ramsey, G. Solimano, et al. 1983b. The influence of early malnutrition on subsequent behavioral development. I. Degree of impairment of intellectual performance. *Journal of the American Academy of Childhood Psychiatry* 22: 8-15.

1984b. The influence of early malnutrition on subsequent behavioral development. IV. Soft neurologic signs. *Pediatric Research* 18: 826-32.

Gerber, M., and R. Dean. 1956. The psychological changes accompanying kwashiorkor. *Courier* 6: 6-15.

Golden, M. 1988. The role of individual nutrient deficiencies in growth retardation of children as exemplified by zinc and protein. In *Linear growth retardation in less developed countries,* ed. J. Waterlow, 143-64. New York.

Gomez, F., R. Galvan, J. Cravioto, and S. Frenk. 1955. Malnutrition in infancy and childhood with special reference to kwashiorkor. *Advances in Pediatrics* 7: 131-69.

Graham, G., and B. Adrianzen. 1979. Status at school of Peruvian children severely malnourished in infancy. In *Behavioral effects of energy and protein deficits,* ed. J. Brozek, 185-94. Washington, D.C.

Grant, J. 1990. *The state of the world's children.* New York.

Grantham-McGregor, S., J. Meeks Gardner, S. Walker, and C. Powell. 1990. The relationship between undernutrition, activity levels and development in young children. In *Activity, energy expenditure and energy requirements of infants and children,* ed. B. Schurch and N. Scrimshaw, 361-83. Geneva.

Grantham-McGregor, S., C. Powell, and P. Fletcher. 1989. Stunting, an episode of severe malnutrition and mental development in young children. *European Journal of Clinical Nutrition* 43: 403-9.

Grantham-McGregor, S., C. Powell, S. Walker, and J. Himes. 1991. Nutritional supplementation, psychosocial stimulation, and mental development of stunted children: The Jamaican study. *Lancet* 338: 1-5.

Grantham-McGregor, S., W. Schofield, and C. Powell. 1987.

Development of severely malnourished children who received psychosocial stimulation: Six year follow-up. *Pediatrics* 79: 247-54.

Hebb, D. 1972. *Textbook of psychology.* Philadelphia, Pa.

Hertzig, M., H. Birch, S. Richardson, and J. Tizard. 1972. Intellectual levels of school children severely malnourished during the first two years of life. *Pediatrics* 49: 814-24.

Hetzel, B. 1983. Iodine deficiency disorders (IDD) and their eradication. *Lancet* 2: 1126-9.

1987. An overview of the prevention and control of iodine deficiency disorders. In *The prevention and control of iodine deficiency disorders,* ed. B. Hetzel, J. Dunn, and J. Stanbury, 7-31. Amsterdam.

Heywood, A., S. Oppenheimer, P. Heywood, and D. Jolley. 1989. Behavioral effects of iron supplementation in infants in Madang, Papua New Guinea. *American Journal of Clinical Nutrition* 50: 630-40.

Hicks, L., R. Langham, and J. Takenaka. 1982. Cognitive and health measures following early nutritional supplementation. *American Journal of Public Health* 72: 1110-8.

Hoorweg, J., and J. Stanfield. 1976. The effects of protein–energy malnutrition in early childhood on intellectual and motor abilities in later childhood and adolescence. *Developmental Medicine and Child Neurology* 18: 330-50.

James, W., and H. Coore. 1970. Persistent impairment of insulin secretion and glucose tolerance after malnutrition. *American Journal of Clinical Nutrition* 23: 386-9.

Johnston, F., S. Low, Y. de Baessa, and R. McVean. 1987. Interaction of nutrition and socio-economic status as determinants of cognitive development in disadvantaged urban Guatemalan children. *American Journal of Physical Anthropology* 73: 501-6.

Joos, S., E. Pollitt, W. Mueller, and D. Albright. 1983. The Bacon Chow study: Maternal nutritional supplementation and infant behavioral development. *Child Development* 54: 669-76.

Kahneman, D. 1973. *Attention and effort.* Englewood Cliffs, N.J.

Keister, M. 1950. Relation of mid-morning feeding to behavior of nursery school children. *Journal of the American Dietetic Association* 26: 25-9.

Klein, P., G. Forbes, and P. Nader. 1975. Effects of starvation in infancy (pyloric stenosis) on subsequent learning abilities. *Journal of Pediatrics* 87: 8-15.

Laird, D., M. Levitan, and V. Wilson. 1931. Nervousness in school children as related to hunger and diet. *Medical Journal Records* 134: 494-9.

Lasky, R., R. Klein, C. Yarbrough, et al. 1981. The relationship between physical growth and infant behavioral development in rural Guatemala. *Child Development* 52: 219-26.

Levinger, B. 1986. *School feeding programs in developing countries: An analysis of actual and potential impact.* AID Evaluation Special Study No. 30. Washington, D.C.

Levitsky, D. 1979. Malnutrition and the hunger to learn. In *Malnutrition, environment and behaviour: New perspectives,* ed. D. Levitsky, 161-79. Ithaca, N.Y.

Lloyd-Still, J., I. Hurtwitz, P. Wolf, and H. Shwachman. 1974. Intellectual development after severe malnutrition in infancy. *Pediatrics* 54: 306-11.

Lozoff, B., G. Brittenham, F. Viteri, et al. 1982. The effects of short-term oral iron therapy on developmental deficits in iron-deficient anaemic infants. *Journal of Pediatrics* 100: 351-7.

Lozoff, B., G. Brittenham, A. Wolf, et al. 1987. Iron deficiency anemia and iron therapy effects on infant developmental test performance. *Pediatrics* 79: 981-95.

Lucas, A., R. Morley, T. Cole, et al. 1990. Early diet in preterm babies and developmental status at 18 months. *Lancet* 335: 1477-81.

McKay, H., L. Sinisterra, A. McKay, et al. 1978. Improving cognitive ability in chronically deprived children. *Science* 200: 270-8.

McLaren, D., U. Yatkin, A. Kanawati, et al. 1973. The subsequent mental and physical development of rehabilitated marasmic infants. *Journal of Mental Deficiency Research* 17: 273-81.

Meeks Gardner, J., S. Grantham-McGregor, S. Chang, and C. Powell. 1990. Dietary intake and observed activity of stunted and non-stunted children in Kingston, Jamaica. Part II: Observed activity. *European Journal of Clinical Nutrition* 44: 585-93.

Meyers, A., A. Sampson, M. Weitzman, et al. 1989. School breakfast program and school performance. *American Journal of Disease of Children* 143: 1234-9.

Monckeberg, F. 1979. Recovery of severely malnourished infants: Effect of early sensory-affective stimulation. In *Behavioral effects of energy and protein deficits,* ed. J. Brozek and B. Schurch, U.S. Department of Health, Education, and Welfare Publication No. 79-1906, 121-230. Washington, D.C.

Moock, P., and J. Leslie. 1986. Childhood malnutrition and schooling in the Terai region of Nepal. *Journal of Development Economics* 20: 33-52.

Moodie, A., M. Bowie, M. Mann, and J. Hansen. 1980. A prospective 15-year follow-up study of kwashiorkor patients. Part II. Social circumstances, educational attainment and social adjustment. *South African Medical Journal* 58: 677-81.

Mora, J., A. Amezquita, L. Castrol, et al. 1974. Nutrition, health and social factors related to intellectual performance. *World Review of Nutrition and Dietetics* 19: 205-36.

Mora, J., J. Clement, N. Christiansen, et al. 1979. Nutritional supplementation, early stimulation and child development. In *Behavioral effects of energy and protein deficits,* ed. J. Brozek and B. Schurch, U.S. Department of Health, Education, and Welfare Publication No. 79-1906, 225-69. Washington, D.C.

Naismith, D., M. Nelson, V. Burley, and S. Gatenby. 1988. Can children's intelligence be increased by vitamin and mineral supplements? *Lancet* 2: 335.

Nwuga, V. 1977. Effect of severe kwashiorkor on intellectual development among Nigerian children. *American Journal of Clinical Nutrition* 30: 1423-30.

Oski, F., and A. Honig. 1978. The effects of therapy on the developmental scores of iron-deficient infants. *Journal of Pediatrics* 92: 21-5.

Osofsky, H. 1975. Relationships between pre-natal medical and nutritional measures, pregnancy outcome, and early infant development in an urban poverty setting. I. The role of nutritional intake. *American Journal of Obstetrics and Gynaecology* 123: 632-90.

Pencharz, P., A. Heller, A. Higgins, et al. 1983. Effects of nutritional services to pregnant mothers on the school performance of treated and untreated children. *Nutrition Research* 3: 795-803.

Pereira, S., R. Sundaraj, and A. Begum. 1979. Physical growth and neuro-integrative performance of survivors of pro-tein-energy malnutrition. *British Journal of Nutrition* 212: 165-71.

Pharoah, P., K. Connolly, B. Hetzel, and R. Ekins. 1981. Maternal thyroid function and motor competence in the child. *Developmental Medicine and Child Neurology* 23: 76-82.

Pollitt, E., M. Gersovitz, and M. Gargicilo. 1978. Educational benefits of the United States school feeding program: A critical review of the literature. *American Journal of Public Health* 68: 477-81.

Pollitt, E., P. Hathirat, N. Kotchabhakdi, et al. 1989. Iron deficiency and educational achievement in Thailand. *American Journal of Clinical Nutrition* 50: 687-97.

Pollitt, E., R. Leibel, and D. Greenfield. 1981. Brief fasting, stress and cognition in children. *American Journal of Clinical Nutrition* 34: 1526-33.

1983a. Iron deficiency and cognitive test performance in preschool children. *Nutrition and Behaviour* 1: 137-46.

Pollitt, E., N. Lewis, C. Garcia, and R. Shulman. 1983b. Fasting and cognitive function. *Journal of Psychiatric Research* 17: 169-74.

Pollitt, E., C. Saco-Pollitt, R. Leibel, and F. Viteri. 1986. Iron deficiency and behavioral development in infants and pre-school children. *American Journal of Clinical Nutrition* 43: 555-65.

Pollitt, E., A. Soemantri, F. Yunis, and N. Scrimshaw. 1985. Cognitive effects of iron-deficiency anemia. *Lancet* 1: 158.

Pollitt, E., F. Viteri, C. Saco-Pollitt, and R. Leibel. 1982. Behavioral effects of iron deficiency anemia in children. In *Iron deficiency: Brain biochemistry and behavior,* ed E. Pollitt and R. Leibel, 195-208. New York.

Popkin, B., and M. Lim-Ybanez. 1982. Nutrition and school achievement. *Social Science and Medicine* 16: 53-61.

Powell, C., and S. Grantham-McGregor. 1985. The ecology of nutritional status and development in young children in Kingston, Jamaica. *American Journal of Clinical Nutrition* 41: 1322-31.

1990. Selective review of studies on the behavioral effects of childhood malnutrition. In *Child nutrition in southeast Asia,* ed H. Visser and J. Bindels, 125-40. Dortrecht, the Netherlands.

Powell, C., S. Grantham-McGregor, and M. Elston. 1983. An evaluation of giving the Jamaican government schoolmeal to a class of children. *Human Nutrition: Clinical Nutrition* 37C: 381-8.

Pretell, E., T. Torres, V. Zenteno, and M. Cornejo. 1972. Prophylaxis of endemic goiter with iodized oil in rural Peru. *Advances in Experimental Medicine and Biology* 30: 249-65.

Richardson, S. 1974. The background histories of schoolchildren severely malnourished in infancy. *Advances in Pediatrics* 21: 167-95.

Richardson, S., H. Birch, and M. Hertzig. 1973. School performance of children who were severely malnourished in infancy. *American Journal of Mental Deficiency* 77: 623-32.

Rosso, P., J. Hormazabal, and M. Winick. 1970. Changes in brain weight, cholesterol, phospholipid and DNA content in marasmic children. *American Journal of Clinical Nutrition* 23: 1275-9.

Rush, D., Z. Stein, and M. Susser. 1980. A randomized controlled trial of pre-natal nutritional supplementation in New York City. *Pediatrics* 65: 683-97.

Schoenthaler, S. 1991. Brains and vitamins. *Lancet* 337: 587-8.

Seshadri, S., and T. Gopaldas. 1989. Impact of iron supplementation on cognitive functions in pre-school and school aged children: The Indian experience. *American Journal of Clinical Nutrition* 50: 675-86.

Sigman, M., C. Neumann, and A. Jansen. 1989. Cognitive abilities of Kenyan children in relation to nutrition, family characteristics and education. *Child Development* 60: 1463-74.

Simeon, D., and S. Grantham-McGregor. 1989. Effects of missing breakfast on the cognitive functions of schoolchildren of differing nutritional status. *American Journal of Clinical Nutrition* 49: 646-53.

Smart, J., and J. Dobbing. 1977. Increased thirst and hunger in adult rats undernourished in infancy: An alternative explanation. *British Journal of Nutrition* 37: 421-30.

Soemantri, A. 1989. Preliminary findings on iron supplementation and learning achievement of rural Indonesian children. *American Journal of Clinical Nutrition* 50: 698-702.

Soemantri, A., E. Pollitt, and I. Kim. 1985. Iron deficiency anemia and educational achievement. *American Journal of Clinical Nutrition* 42: 1221-8.

Soewondo, S., M. Husaini, and E. Pollitt. 1989. Effects of iron deficiency on attention and learning process in preschool children: Bandung, Indonesia. *American Journal of Clinical Nutrition* 50: 667-74.

Stanbury, J. 1987. Iodine deficiency disorders: Introduction and general aspects. In *The prevention and control of iodine deficiency disorders*, ed. B. Hetzel, J. Dunn, and J. Stanbury, 35-47. Amsterdam.

Stoch, M., and P. Smythe. 1976. 15-year developmental study on the effects of severe undernutrition during infancy on subsequent physical growth and intellectual functioning. *Archives of Disease in Childhood* 51: 327-36.

Thilly, C., G. Roger, R. Lagase, et al. 1980. Fetomaternal relationship, fetal hypothyroidism, and psychomotor retardation. In *Role of cassava in the etiology of endemic goiter and cretinism,* ed A. Ermans, N. Mbulamoko, F. Delange, and R. Ahluwalia, 111-20. Ottawa.

Upadhyay, S., D. Agarwal, K. Agarwal, et al. 1988. Brief fasting and cognitive functions in rural school children. *Indian Pediatrics* 25: 288-9.

Valman, H. 1974. Intelligence after malnutrition caused by neonatal resection of ileum. *Lancet* 1: 425-7.

Waber, D., L. Vuori-Christiansen, N. Ortiz, et al. 1981. Nutritional supplementation, maternal education and cognitive development of infants at risk of malnutrition. *American Journal of Clinical Nutrition* 34: 807-13.

Walter, T., I. de Andraca, P. Chadud, and C. Perales. 1989. Iron deficiency anemia: Adverse effects on infant psychomotor development. *Pediatrics* 84: 7-17.

Walter, T., J. Kovalskys, and A. Stekel. 1983. Effect of mild iron deficiency on infant mental development scores. *Journal of Pediatrics* 102: 519-22.

Waterlow, J. 1976. Classification and definition of protein energy malnutrition. In *Nutrition in preventative medicine,* ed. G. Beaton and J. Bengoa, World Health Organization Monograph Series, No. 62, 530-55, Geneva.

Webb, T., and F. Oski. 1973. Iron deficiency anemia and scholastic achievement in young adolescents. *Journal of Pediatrics* 82: 827-30.

Wellcome Trust Working Party. 1970. Classification of infantile malnutrition. *Lancet* 2: 302.

Williams, C. 1933. A nutrition disease of childhood associated with a maize diet. *Archives of Disease in Childhood* 8: 423-33.

Winick, M., K. Meyer, and R. Harris. 1975. Malnutrition and environmental enrichment by early adoption. *Science* 190: 1173-5.

Winick, M., and P. Rosso. 1969. Head circumference and cellular growth of the brain in normal and marasmic children. *Science* 190: 1173-5.

Wurtman, R. 1986. Ways that food can affect the brain. *Nutrition Reviews* 44 (Supplement): 2-6.

Yatkin, V., and D. McLaren. 1970. The behavioral development of infants recovering from severe malnutrition. *Journal of Mental Deficiency Research* 14: 25-32.

VI.10 ❧ Human Nutritional Adaptation: Biological and Cultural Aspects

The extraordinary diversity of aboriginal food cultures testifies to the capacity of many combinations of foodstuffs to sustain human health and reproduction. From this diversity it is apparent that humans have no requirement for specific foods (with the qualified exception of breast milk, which can be replaced by the milk of other mammals but with less satisfactory results). Modern nutritional science has demonstrated that good health is dependent upon the consumption of a discrete number of biochemical compounds that are essential for normal metabolism but cannot be synthesized de novo in the body. These compounds or their metabolic precursors can be obtained from many different combinations of foods.

It is possible that there are still unidentified trace elements required in such small amounts that it has not yet been possible to demonstrate their essentiality, although it is unlikely that they are of any clinical importance in human nutrition. It is probable that current perceptions of the amounts of some nutrients required for optimal health – such as the relative amounts of various fatty acids necessary for the prevention of cardiovascular disease – will undergo further change, but the present state of nutritional knowledge is adequate as a basis for evaluating the quality of different food cultures in terms of their ability to provide the nutrients required for nutritional health.

This chapter evaluates two contrasting food cultures: the carnivorous aboriginal diets of the Arctic Inuit and the traditional cereal-based diets consumed by the inhabitants of Southeast Asia and of Central and South America. Also, the current nutritional health of these populations is evaluated in terms of their adaptation to a modern diet and lifestyle.

Biological Adaptation to the Intuit Diet

Although nutritional anthropologists have concluded that the diets of most hunting and gathering societies were more varied than those of early agricultural societies, this clearly was not true of the aboriginal diet of the Inuit inhabitants of the high Arctic. Although berries and the leafy parts of edible plants were available in the Subarctic region, the diet of the Inuit residing 300 miles above the Arctic Circle was, for all practical purposes, carnivorous (that is, they were hunters but not gatherers).

Current diet recommendations in industrial societies promote the consumption of a mixture of foods belonging to four or more food groups: cereals, fruits and vegetables, meat and fish, and dairy products. The native diet of the Arctic Inuit – caribou, seal, and whale meat, augmented with lesser amounts of fish, birds, eggs, and the meat of other land mammals – is composed of foods belonging to only one of these groups.

Meat consumption in modern societies is being discouraged because of its propensity to cause cardiovascular disease. Yet, when the Inuit were first examined by ships' doctors, they were found to be virtually free not only of vascular disease but of renal disease, hypertension, and diabetes as well (Thomas 1927; Robinhold and Rice 1970; Mouratoff and Scott 1973). These conditions are the main manifestations of malnutrition in modern societies. The factors underlying the successful adaptation of the Inuit to their extraordinarily narrow food base have been discussed elsewhere (Draper 1977) and are further examined in the context of current knowledge in the following sections.

Sources of Metabolic Fuel

The Inuit native diet frequently is characterized as being high in protein or high in fat, but from the standpoint of metabolic adaptation, its most important feature is its low content of carbohydrate. In the absence of plant sources of starch and sugars, carbohydrates in the diet were limited to small amounts of glycogen and the sugar moieties of the glycoproteins and glycolipids present in animal tissues.

The postprandial energy state following consumption of the modern mixed diet, in which carbohydrates constitute the main source of energy, is marked by the conversion of excess glucose to fat for energy storage. The postprandial state following consumption of a carnivorous diet is marked by the obligatory synthesis of glucose, which is essential for brain function and other metabolic processes. Inasmuch as fatty acids, the main source of energy in the diet, cannot be converted to glucose, most of the glucose required must be obtained from gluconeogenic amino acids. Glycerol, the backbone of dietary triglycerides (fat) and of phospholipids, is an additional but minor metabolic source of glucose.

Because of its low carbohydrate content, the native Inuit diet had to be sufficiently high in protein, not only to supply the amino acids required for the synthesis of body proteins but to maintain normoglycemia as well. In some Inuit food subcultures, such as that of the caribou eaters of the Arctic tundra, pro-

tein (rather than fat) probably constituted the main source of energy in the diet, because caribou is much lower in fat than is modern beef.

The high rate of gluconeogenesis in the Inuit requires large amounts of enzymes (which consist mainly of proteins) for the conversion of amino acids to glucose and for the conversion of waste amino acid nitrogen to urea. These processes, respectively, account for the large livers and urine volumes long associated with Arctic Inuit. Increased enzyme synthesis in response to an increase in substrate concentration (so-called feed forward regulation of enzyme reactions) is a major form of metabolic adaptation to changes in diet composition.

Sources of Vitamins

The vitamins of the large B-complex group function as cofactors for enzymes involved in the metabolism of many biochemical compounds, including amino acids, fatty acids, and glucose. Consequently, there is a natural association between the amounts of these vitamins and the amounts of enzyme proteins present in the tissues of animals. Most of the protein in the liver, where many of these transactions occur, consists of enzyme proteins. This association is most apparent in the case of vitamin B_6, which functions exclusively in enzymatic transformations of amino acids, such as the aminotransferase reactions required to remove their nitrogen groups before their conversion to glucose.

As a result, the requirement for this vitamin is proportional to protein intake. Although the high-protein Inuit diet generates a high B_6 requirement, the risk of B_6 deficiency fails to increase with protein intake because of the strong association between this vitamin and protein in the diet. There is a similar, though less strong, association between other B vitamins and dietary protein. In contrast to cereal-based food cultures, there is no history of deficiencies of the B-complex vitamins among carnivores. The adequacy of the aboriginal Inuit diet in these nutrients was further ensured by their custom of eating food in the fresh, frozen, or lightly cooked state.

The nutriture of the Inuit with respect to vitamin C, a vitamin generally associated with fruits and vegetables, has long held a fascination for nutritionists. As for other apparent mysteries about Inuit nutrition, however, their freedom from vitamin C deficiency is readily explicable in terms of current knowledge relative to the amount of vitamin C required for the prevention of scurvy, its concentration and stability in the diet, and the capacity for storage. Prevention of scurvy requires 10 milligrams (mg) or less per day, an amount available from the fresh or frozen raw tissues of animals that synthesize it. The liver of land and sea mammals, often eaten fresh while still warm, is a good source of vitamin C. Seal liver, an Inuit delicacy, contains about 35 mg per 100 grams (g), an amount sufficient to provide for significant storage (Geraci and Smith 1979).

The epidemics of scurvy among Europeans in the eighteenth and nineteenth centuries were caused by the oxidation of vitamin C in grains and salt meats during long sea and land voyages and by its leaching from foods during cooking in water. Further, it is not necessary, as a recent advertisement claims, "to get your vitamin C every day." The amount of vitamin C stored by a typical adult in the United States or Canada is sufficient to prevent a deficiency, in the absence of any intake, for about 30 days (Baker et al. 1971).

The need to envelop the body in heavy clothing against the cold during the long winter night deprives the Arctic Inuit of solar radiation, the main source of vitamin D in temperate and tropical climates. The Inuit experience demonstrates that at least in some environments, there is an absolute dietary requirement for vitamin D, a nutrient that some have proposed be reclassified as a hormone because it can be synthesized in adequate amounts in the skin with sufficient exposure to sunlight. The high concentrations of vitamin D in the oils of fish and fish-eating sea mammals make up for limited synthesis of vitamin D in the skin during the Arctic winter, as demonstrated by the lack of historical evidence of rickets in Inuit children and of osteomalacia in adults consuming the native diet. These oils also provide an abundance of vitamin A. The occurrence of toxic amounts of vitamin A in polar bear liver, accumulated through the fish and seal food chain of this species, forms the basis of one of the strongest Inuit food taboos.

The vitamin E nutriture of the Inuit is unusual because their carnivorous diet contains no cereal oils, the main source of vitamin E in the modern mixed diet. Further, the high concentration of polyunsaturated fatty acids from fish and marine mammals in this diet generates a high requirement for vitamin E to maintain their oxidative stability in the tissues. Nonetheless, analysis of the blood plasma of Northern Alaskan Inuit has revealed concentrations of vitamin E similar to those of the general U.S. population (Wo and Draper 1975).

The explanation for this finding lies in a difference in the forms of vitamin E present in carnivorous and mixed diets. Although the total amount of vitamin E present in the mixed diet is substantially higher than in the carnivorous diet, only about one-quarter of the total occurs in the form of alpha-tocopherol; the rest is present mainly as gamma-tocopherol, which has only about 10 percent as much biological activity. In contrast, animal tissues contain almost exclusively alpha-tocopherol. Consequently, the amount of vitamin E in the Inuit native diet, expressed as biological activity, is comparable to that in the mixed diet.

As is evident from the pungent odor of volatile products of lipid peroxidation that permeates Inuit villages in summer, the concentration of vitamin E in the highly unsaturated oils of aquatic species is inadequate to protect them from oxidative rancidity when they are exposed to an air environment, even though it is sufficient at the reduced oxygen tension and temperature of their natural aquatic environment. In general, the concentration of vitamin E in plant oils and animal fats is proportional to the amount necessary to stabilize the unsaturated fatty acids they contain. For example, the inheritance of vitamin E and polyunsaturated fatty acids in maize is genetically linked, so that varieties high in polyunsaturated fatty acids are also high in vitamin E (Levy 1973). Fish, seal, and whale oils, on the other hand, impose a burden on the vitamin E requirement that must be borne by other food sources of the vitamin. Although Canadian Indians consuming a diet high in fish have been found to have a plasma vitamin E level below that of the general population (Desai and Lee 1974), dietary vitamin E deficiency has not been documented.

Sources of Inorganic Nutrients

Human requirements for inorganic nutrients (often loosely referred to as minerals) are qualitatively similar to those of other mammalian species. Hence, the carcasses of animals are a good source of these nutrients in human diets, provided they are eaten in their entirety, as they were (less the skin and compact bone) by the Arctic Inuit. The inorganic elements most frequently at risk of deficiency in human diets are iron and iodine. Iron deficiency, often precipitated by intestinal infections and diarrhea, is most prevalent among malnourished consumers of low-protein vegetarian diets. Iron is accumulated in animal tissues in the iron-binding liver proteins hemosiderin and ferritin, which, together with hemoglobin and other iron-containing proteins, provide an abundance of bioavailable iron in a carnivorous diet. Risk of iron deficiency is reduced by an adaptive feedback mechanism that increases the efficiency of iron absorption on a low-iron diet. This mechanism also serves to prevent iron toxicity on the high-meat Inuit diet by suppressing the absorption of excess dietary iron.

Iodine deficiency is a prevalent problem in various human populations, arising in some cases from its deficiency in the soil (for example, the "goiter belt" around Hudson's Bay) and in other cases from the ingestion of plant goitrogens. Neither of these circumstances applies to the Inuit native diet, which is devoid of goitrogens and is high in iodine from foods of aquatic origin. This diet also contains an abundance of zinc, which is present in marginal amounts in cereal diets high in phytin, a component of fiber that inhibits zinc absorption.

Meat has a very low calcium content, and in the absence of dairy foods, which supply about 75 percent of the calcium in the food supply of most industrialized societies, the spongy trabecular bone of land and sea mammals and the soft bones of fish are an essential source of this element in the native Inuit diet. Bone chewing, a nutritional as well as a social custom, is now nearly extinct, and a low consumption of dairy products has resulted in a calcium intake among the Inuit that is both below the historic level and below intake level currently recommended in the United States for optimal development of the skeleton during growth and for its stability during aging. However, the intake is comparable to the amount delivered by cereal-based diets, and there is no clear evidence that the lowered intake results in a state of calcium deficiency.

The body has an ability to adapt to a range of calcium intakes by modulating the efficiency of calcium absorption from the intestine. This ability, which serves to protect against both calcium deficiency and toxicity, is one of the best understood of metabolic adaptations to a change in nutrient intake. It involves an increase in the synthesis of parathyroid hormone in response to a small decline in serum calcium concentration caused by a decrease in calcium intake. This hormone effects an increase in the renal synthesis of 1,25-dihydroxycholecalciferol, the active form of vitamin D, which, in turn, enhances the synthesis of a calcium transport protein in the intestinal epithelium that is required for the active absorption of calcium.

The result is an increase in the efficiency of calcium absorption following a reduction in intake that restores serum calcium homeostasis. Whether this mechanism is fully successful in enabling adequate amounts of calcium to be absorbed to maximize skeletal development during growth and minimize bone loss during aging is a question of current interest with respect to the relationship between calcium intake and the incidence of osteoporosis.

The Inuit of Northern Alaska and Canada undergo a more rapid rate of aging bone loss, a risk factor for osteoporosis, than Caucasians consuming the mixed diet (Mazess and Mathur 1974, 1975). The high-protein, high-phosphorus, low-calcium content of the native diet has been implicated in this phenomenon. However, the high rate of aging bone loss in the Inuit does not appear to be associated with a high incidence of osteoporotic bone fractures.

This may be explained by a difference in bone morphology between the Inuit and Caucasians; the shorter, thicker bones of the Inuit may have a greater weight-bearing capacity than the longer, thinner bones of Caucasians. The rapid bone loss in the Inuit, nevertheless, may have relevance for the high incidence of fractures among elderly consumers of the "Western diet," which contains about twice as much protein as necessary to meet the protein requirement and an excess of phosphorus arising from a natural association of this element with protein and from the widespread use of phosphate food additives.

Oxidation of excess sulfur amino acids present in high-protein diets generates hydrogen ions and sulfate (sulfuric acid) that is excreted in the urine. On a high-protein (usually high-meat) diet the urine consequently is acid, whereas on a low-protein (usually high-cereal) diet it is near neutrality or slightly alkaline. Unopposed acidification of the renal filtrate decreases the reabsorption of calcium and increases its loss in the urine.

In experiments on adults fed purified proteins, this loss was found to amount to 300 mg per day, indicative of rapid bone loss, at a daily protein intake of 95 g, an amount well within the range of intakes on the mixed diet and low by Inuit standards (Linkswiler, Joyce, and Anand 1974). The protein intake of aboriginal Inuit adults in northwest Greenland has been estimated at nearly 400 g per day (Bang, Dyerberg, and Sinclair 1980). On a high-protein diet composed of normal foodstuffs, however, the decrease in calcium reabsorption by the proximal renal tubules caused by urine acidification is not unopposed.

The increased intake of phosphorus on high-protein diets results in a depression of serum calcium and a consequent increase in the synthesis of parathyroid hormone, which stimulates calcium reabsorption from the renal tubules and thereby counteracts the calciuretic action of excess dietary protein. Whether these opposing effects of dietary protein and phosphorus on urinary calcium excretion are always fully offsetting is not clear. However, it has become apparent that the most important nutrient ratio, from the standpoint of bone homeostasis, is not the ratio of calcium to phosphorus, which has received most attention, but the ratio of protein to phosphorus, which is fundamental to the maintenance of calcium balance on a high-protein diet. Whether the increased rate of bone resorption associated with excess dietary phosphate and protein observed on the Inuit diet and on the high-protein modern diet (Calvo, Kumar, and Heath 1988) results in increased bone loss and risk for osteoporosis is still controversial.

Metabolic Adaptation to Dietary Lipids

Danish studies on nutritional adaptation among the Inuit of northeast Greenland undertaken in the late 1960s and early 1970s led to an explanation for their low incidence of cardiovascular disease and to important innovations in methods for its prevention and treatment in modern societies. These studies revealed a protective effect of the unusual fatty acids present in the fish and marine mammal oils consumed in large quantities by the Inuit. Such oils contain polyunsaturated fatty acids with extremely long carbon chains (up to 22 carbon atoms) and unusually large numbers of double bonds (up to 6), characteristics that confer on them a low melting point that enables aquatic species to maintain membrane fluidity at the temperature of their environment. In contrast, the polyunsaturated fatty acids of cereal oils, the main source of fat in the modern mixed diet, contain up to 18 carbon atoms and up to 3 double bonds.

Another important difference is that the first double bond in most of the highly unsaturated fatty acids in the Inuit diet occurs between the third and fourth carbon atoms (n-3 fatty acids), whereas the first double bond in most of the fatty acids in cereals occurs between the sixth and seventh carbon atoms (n-6 fatty acids). The metabolic significance of this distinction is that the n-3 and n-6 fatty acids are precursors of two distinct groups of hormones, the prostacyclins and the prostaglandins, that have significantly different effects on the metabolism of blood lipids. They therefore also differently affect the risk of heart attack. Prostacyclins reduce the plasma triglyceride (fat) level, as well as the propensity of the blood to clot (and hence the risk of an embolism). A negative effect of the high n-3 fatty acid content of the Inuit diet is its tendency to cause nosebleeds (Fortuine 1971).

As a result of these findings, increased consumption of fish has been recommended as part of the Western diet, and concentrates of n-3 fatty acids prepared from fish oil are used in the clinical management of cardiovascular disease. The n-3 fatty acids have become recognized as dietary essentials for both children and adults, and official recommendations have been issued relative to their desirable level of intake (National Research Council, U.S. Academy of Sciences 1989; Health and Welfare Canada 1990). This series of events serves as an example of the value of cross-cultural research as a source of information relevant to the nutritional health of all human societies.

There is little doubt that hypercholesterolemia is a risk factor for heart attacks, and a plasma cholesterol level of 200 mg per deciliter or less has been selected as a desirable goal. Diet recommendations for the prevention of heart disease in modern societies call for a reduction in cholesterol intake to 300 mg per day or less (National Research Council, U.S. Academy of Sciences 1989; Health and Welfare Canada 1990). In light of these recommendations, the rarity of cardiovascular disease among the Inuit (Thomas 1927), whose traditional diet is extraordinarily high in cholesterol, seems anomalous.

Electrocardiographic recordings made on Northern Alaskan Inuit adults in the 1970s (by which time only about 50 percent of their calories were derived from native foods) revealed an incidence of abnormalities only half that recorded in a reference population of U.S. Caucasian adults (Colbert, Mann, and Hursh 1978). Indigenous foods in the partially acculturated diet of a cohort of adult Inuit living in the northwest Alaskan village of Point Hope in 1970 averaged 918 mg per day (range 420 to 1650 mg) (Feldman et al. 1978).

Studies on the epidemiology of hypercholesterolemia carried out between 1937 and 1961 showed "a strong tendency towards normocholesterolemia . . . among the unacculturated Eskimo groups but increased rates of elevated serum cholesterol among modernized Eskimos" (Feldman et al. 1978: 174). It is noteworthy that the plasma cholesterol levels of the Inuit during that period were similar to those of adults in the general population of the

United States, despite a twofold difference or more in cholesterol intake.

The explanation for this discrepancy has been provided by epidemiological and laboratory research on the relationship between the intake of cholesterol in the diet and the level of cholesterol in the plasma. The Inuit experience is consistent with the conclusion of A. Keys, J. T. Anderson, and F. Grande (1965), the originators of the connection between dietary fat and heart disease, and with the observations of subsequent investigators: In the normal, healthy, adult population, the level of cholesterol in the diet has only a minor influence on blood cholesterol.

The current public preoccupation with dietary cholesterol and the promotion of "cholesterol-free" foods is attributable to a seemingly logical assumption that lowering cholesterol intake should lower plasma cholesterol. This is often true in patients with clinical hypercholesterolemia, a condition associated with genetic and various metabolic disorders, including diabetes and obesity, in which the metabolic control mechanism that normally downregulates the synthesis of cholesterol in the body in response to a high intake in the diet is impaired.

This is, however, weak justification for imposing a limit of 300 mg per day on the intake of cholesterol by "the generally healthy population" for whom diet recommendations are issued (National Research Council, U.S. Academy of Sciences 1989; Health and Welfare Canada 1990). The "cholesterol free" label on foods has been used as a "red herring" to attract attention away from the more important characteristics of foods from the standpoint of their effect on plasma cholesterol, namely the amount and composition of the fat they contain.

Current nutrition recommendations in industrialized countries include a call for a reduced consumption of "red meat" as a means of lowering the risk of cardiovascular disease. This edict seems paradoxical in view of the reported absence of this disease among Inuit consumers of the native meat diet. It is aimed at the consumption of beef, which bears the stigma (no longer fully justified) that it is high in fat and saturated fatty acids and low in polyunsaturated fatty acids. (The term "red meat" itself seems anomalous, since the redder meat is, the lower it is in fat.)

Contrary to the general impression that all animal tissues are high in saturated and low in polyunsaturated fatty acids, the tissues of the fish and of the land and sea mammals that constituted most of the Inuit diet are the reverse. The lipids of seal, whale, walrus, and polar bear meat contain 15 to 25 percent polyunsaturated fatty acids, consisting mostly of fatty acids of the n-3 type (Wo and Draper 1975). In contrast to beef, caribou meat is so low in fat that the Inuit dip it in seal oil to improve its palatability. The lipids of caribou muscle have been found to contain 5.6 percent arachidonic acid and 15.4 percent linoleic acid of the n-6 polyunsaturated fatty acid series.

In contrast, values of 0.5 percent arachidonic acid and 2.5 percent linoleic acid have been reported for beef muscle (Link et al. 1970). Most of the polyunsaturated fatty acids in both caribou and beef muscle are located in the phospholipids of cell membranes. The phospholipids of beef muscle have a level of polyunsaturates comparable to that in caribou muscle (Link et al. 1970), but have been swamped by saturated fatty acids as a result of selection of beef animals for "marbling" with intramuscular fat to increase the palatability of their meat.

Current diet recommendations in the United States and Canada also call for a reduction in fat intake to 30 percent of calories or less as a further means of reducing the risk of cardiovascular disease (National Research Council, U.S. Academy of Sciences 1989; Health and Welfare Canada 1990). The experience of the Inuit, however, indicates that it is the composition of dietary fat, rather than its level in the diet, that is of primary importance in the prevention of heart disease.

This view is supported by the low incidence of cardiovascular disease among consumers of the "Mediterranean diet," which contains a preponderance of monounsaturated fatty acids derived mainly from olive oil used in cooking. These acids replace more saturated than polyunsaturated fatty acids in the diet, thereby shifting the ratio in favor of polyunsaturates. The role of this ratio is also indicated by an analysis of changes in the composition of dietary fat in the United States from the 1960s through the 1980s, an interval during which the death rate from heart disease declined by about 25 percent (Stephen and Wald 1990).

The data show that there was an increase in the ratio of polyunsaturated to saturated fatty acids in the diet over this period from about 0.25 to 0.50. This increase was due mainly to a decrease in the intake of total fat, which entailed a discrimination against "visible fat" (such as the peripheral fat around the outside of steak) that consists mostly of saturated fatty acids. These observations further indicate that it is the composition of dietary fat, rather than the amount of fat consumed, that is of prime importance in the prevention of cardiovascular disease. Reducing total fat intake, however, is the only practical means of increasing the ratio of polyunsaturated to saturated fatty acids in the modern diet of industrialized countries.

The ratio of polyunsaturates to saturates in the native Inuit diet is difficult to estimate with accuracy and is highly variable, but it clearly exceeds the ratio of 0.50 calculated for the U.S. diet in the 1980s (Stephen and Wald 1990) and probably exceeds the 1.0 ratio proposed in modern diet recommendations. Inuit diets in northwestern Greenland in 1976 were estimated to have a ratio of 0.84, compared to a ratio of 0.24 in the diet of Danes (Bang et al. 1980). In addition to a reduction in total fat consumption to 30 percent of energy intake, current recommendations call

for a 1:1:1 ratio of polyunsaturates to saturates to monounsaturates (Health and Welfare Canada 1990). The protection from cardiovascular disease afforded by the profile of fatty acids in the native Inuit diet is encouragement that implementation of these recommendations will confer a similar benefit on modern societies.

Adaptation to Dietary Sugars

The Inuit of western Greenland and northwestern Alaska are uniquely susceptible to congenital primary sucrase-isomaltase deficiency, a condition presumably related to the absence of sucrose in their traditional diet over many centuries (McNair et al. 1972; Raines, Draper, and Bergan 1973). Its epidemiology is familial, and studies on Greenland Inuit have indicated that it is due to a deficiency of an autosomal recessive gene. Its incidence was estimated to be about 3 percent in northwestern Alaska and 10 percent in a sample of hospital patients and staff in northeast Greenland.

This deficiency has a major effect on the capacity of those Inuit affected to deal with the modern diet. For example, children are unable to eat an ice-cream cone or drink a bottle of carbonated beverage unless it contains a synthetic sweetener in place of sucrose. In this respect, sucrase deficiency differs from lactase deficiency, in which lactase production declines during growth but persists at a reduced level in adulthood. Sucrase deficiency, a recently recognized cause of diarrhea in Inuit children, is present in acute form from birth.

The options available for dealing with it include replacing sucrose with other sugars (such as invert sugar in honey), using synthetic sweeteners, or taking oral sucrase preparations made from the intestinal juices of animals. Sucrase-isomaltase deficiency appears to be absent among Alaskan Inuit residents of the Subarctic, where the traditional diet has contained sucrose present in fruits and berries.

As in most societies (excepting mainly those of northern European origin), Inuit children undergo a progressive decrease in the intestinal synthesis of lactase during growth to a level that limits the amount of milk and milk products that can be digested in adulthood (Kretchmer 1972). Based on the results of a standard lactose tolerance test – which involves administering 50 g of lactose (the amount present in a liter of cow's milk), measuring the subsequent rise in plasma glucose, if any, and recording any adverse clinical reactions, such as abdominal cramps or diarrhea – about 70 percent of Inuit adults have been characterized as "lactose intolerant" (Gudmand-Hoyer and Jarnum 1969). However, if given a dose of 10 g of lactose (the amount present in a cup of milk), a large majority of Inuit adults experience no adverse symptoms and, therefore, from a nutritional standpoint, may be regarded as "lactose tolerant."

With respect to their ability to digest lactose, the Inuit resemble a majority of the world's population.

Alaskan Inuit children routinely consume milk or other dairy products as part of a school lunch program. The breakpoint in lactose tolerance in adults typically falls between 10 and 20 g (Raines et al. 1973); intakes in this range can be repeated after an interval of several hours. Hence, for most individuals, lactose intolerance is not a serious impediment to the acquisition of the calcium and other nutrients present in dairy foods.

Adaptation to the Modern Diet

Historically, the greatest threat to the nutritional status of the Arctic Inuit was famine, triggered by failure to catch a bowhead whale or by the failure of the caribou to run. In such exigencies, seals were the most reliable dietary staple. The Inuit population was kept in balance with its food supply by periodic famines, by a high infant mortality, by an extremely high rate of fatal accidents among adults pursuing the hunting culture, and if necessary, by infanticide. They had no nutrition education and no need for it. Their custom of eating animals almost in their entirety provided them with all the nutrients necessary for nutritional health, assuming their foods were available in sufficient amounts. There were no "junk foods" in their diet. Food not eaten fresh was preserved in the frozen state in the ice cellars that are still prevalent in Arctic Inuit villages. The central nutritional imperative was simply to get enough to eat.

For the first time since they migrated across the Bering Strait several thousand years ago, the Inuit in the twentieth century have been confronted with the necessity of making significant food choices in order to be well fed. Fractionation of primary foodstuffs by the modern food-manufacturing industry has generated multitudes of products of highly variable nutritional quality that must be reassembled in specific combinations to ensure a balanced diet. This necessity has led to the development of a set of rules for selecting proper combinations of foods that are inculcated into children by their parents and teachers and communicated to the public through nutrition education programs. To assist consumers in following these rules, a list of the nutrients that processed foods contain must be put on their labels, including the contribution of one serving to the recommended daily intake of each nutrient. A large government bureaucracy is devoted to ensuring that foods actually contain the amounts of nutrients listed on the label, and another agency is responsible for determining whether claims made for their efficacy in the prevention of disease are valid.

To primitive peoples whose only previous nutritional imperative was to get enough to eat, dealing with the complexities of the modern diet presents serious problems of nutritional adaptation. These problems are reflected in the poor nutritional status of Inuit and Amerindian inhabitants of the urban centers of Alaska and Canada. The nutritional health of urban Inuits is inferior to that of their forebears, as

well as to that of their Arctic contemporaries who still maintain a semblance of the traditional diet and lifestyle (Colbert et al. 1978).

The younger generation of Inuit, like younger generations of most other native minorities, has abandoned the traditional diet almost entirely. The incidence of obesity, hypertension, and cardiovascular disease among Alaskan Inuit follows an increasing gradient from the high Arctic to the Subarctic to the modern cities of the south (Colbert et al. 1978). The incidence of diabetes is also increasing, but is still substantially lower than in Caucasians (Thouez et al. 1990; Young et al. 1990).

The decline in the nutritional status of the Inuit in the second half of the twentieth century has more to do with psychosocial factors than with a lack of nutritious foods. Educational and technical deficiencies, loss of social status in the community, deterioration of cultural values, lack of a sense of community, and discrimination in employment are factors in their poor nutritional status. The modern Inuit are at a watershed in social acculturation, unwilling to revert to their traditional lifestyle, yet unable to cope successfully with the complexities of an industrialized society.

Metabolic Adaptation to Cereal-Based Diets

The cereal-based diets consumed by the inhabitants of Southeast Asia and of Central and South America are in direct contrast to those consumed by the Inuit; that is, they are high in carbohydrates and low in protein and fat, rather than vice versa. Consequently, the bioenergetic transformations imposed by this diet, are also reversed. Fat stored in the adipose tissues is formed primarily by lipogenesis from glucose released in carbohydrate digestion, rather than by the fatty acids released by fat digestion. As polyunsaturated fatty acids cannot be synthesized in the body, fat formed from glucose consists mainly of saturated and monounsaturated fatty acids. In contrast to the massive conversion of excess amino acids to glucose on the Inuit diet, most of the limited amounts of amino acids in cereal diets are used for the synthesis of tissue proteins.

In addition to food shortages caused by crop failures, cereal-based food cultures have been subject to epidemic deficiencies of specific nutrients, notably beriberi caused by thiamine deficiency in the case of rice diets and pellagra caused by niacin deficiency in the case of maize diets. These diseases have created a prevalent impression that cereal diets are low in nutritional quality, but, in fact, these afflictions were the result of a disruption of native food cultures by foreign influences or the failure of foreigners to adopt the native culture.

Replacement of brown rice with more prestigious polished rice, a minor food in Europe but the staple food in Southeast Asia, removed most of the thiamine from the diet and resulted in a classic example of so-called cultural malnutrition. The traditional method of preparing maize practiced by the Mexican Indians, which entailed grinding it in lime water, was not followed by the black and "poor white" populations of African and European origin who inhabited the southern United States.

Their maize diet had several nutritional liabilities. The niacin in maize is present in complex forms from which it must be released by some type of hydrolysis, which in the native Indian culture took the form of alkaline hydrolysis effected by grinding with lime water. Further, maize protein is low in tryptophan, an amino acid that can be converted to niacin in the body. Although pellagrins consumed substantial amounts of pork, it consisted mostly of fat ("sowbelly") that contained little niacin, protein, or tryptophan. The Indian practice of grinding maize in lime water presumably arose out of experience. Not only was it instrumental in protecting them from the ravages of pellagra but it also contributed substantially to their intake of calcium, which is low in cereal grains.

Cereal diets are lower in protein than modern mixed diets and tend to be associated with protein-deficiency diseases, such as kwashiorkor, a severe condition affecting impoverished children during the postweaning period. It is marked by an edema that wrongly gives the impression that the children are of normal weight. When their serum protein level is restored by providing enough dietary protein, the edema dissipates, revealing severe emaciation (marasmus) caused by inadequate energy intake. This condition of protein–calorie malnutrition can be prevented by providing an adequate cereal-based weaning diet, indicating that the main etiological factor is a lack of food, rather than a lack of protein specifically.

When sufficient calories are supplied to prevent the utilization of dietary amino acids for energy production, these acids become available for the synthesis of tissue proteins. Most cereal-based diets, particularly if they contain (as they usually do) small amounts of animal products, such as fish, chicken, eggs, or meat, provide enough protein to satisfy the requirement for this nutrient. Diets based on cassava, a root vegetable with no redeeming nutritional qualities other than as a source of calories, are an exception to this generalization.

Vitamin B$_{12}$ occurs only in foods of animal origin, which, therefore, must be included in all so-called vegetarian food cultures. Strict vegetarian diets, such as that of the "vegans," can result in macrocytic anemia and irreversible neurological damage caused by a deficiency of this vitamin. On the other hand, most of the B-complex vitamins and vitamin E are plentiful in the bran and germ of cereal grains. The vegetables and fruits that normally constitute a major part of vegetarian diets provide folic acid, vitamin C, and vitamin K and are good sources of beta-carotene, a precursor of vitamin A in the body. Yet, until programs of vitamin A supplementation were instituted in the mid–twentieth century, vitamin A deficiency was the main cause of blindness among children in Indonesia and other Southeast Asian localities, despite the fact that edible plants capable of preventing it were readily available.

Cereal diets have been of particular interest from the standpoint of mineral nutrition. Phytin, a component of the fiber of cereals (particularly wheat), binds dietary zinc, preventing its absorption and, at high intakes, precipitating a zinc deficiency. Dwarfism among poor Middle Eastern children, long presumed to be of congenital origin, was found to be due to chronic zinc deficiency caused by the consumption of large quantities of unleavened wheat bread (Prasad et al. 1963). Yeast fermentation degrades phytin and, thereby, prevents zinc deficiency, a relationship that evidently escaped recognition in this food culture for generations, even though the relationship between fermentation and the production of alcohol (presumably a higher priority) was known and exploited. Phytin also binds calcium, but to a lesser extent, and the capacity to adapt to a low intake of this element aids in the prevention of calcium deficiency.

Unlike carnivorous diets, which in general contain adequate amounts of essential trace elements to meet human requirements (because these elements are also essential in the diet of food animals), the trace element content of plants often reflects the content of the soil on which they were grown. Keshan disease, an acute cardiomyopathy among children in the Keshan district of China, is caused by an extremely low concentration of selenium in local soils and, consequently, in the cereals grown on these soils. Locally grown plant foods constitute the bulk of the diet in this area. Such deficiencies are less likely to occur on mixed diets, which contain plant foods grown on a variety of soils, as well as foods of animal origin.

The low calcium content of cereal diets is of current interest with respect to the role of this element in the prevention of osteoporotic bone fractures in elderly adults. Paradoxically, the incidence of hip fractures associated with the cereal-based food cultures of Japan and other Asian countries appears to be lower than it is in Western countries where calcium intake, derived mainly from dairy foods, is substantially higher (Fujita 1992). Whether this apparent anomaly reflects a minor role of calcium in the prevention of hip fractures, a high calcium requirement generated by the high-protein Western diet, a difference in lifestyle, a difference in the incidence of falls, a genetic involvement, or the effect of some unidentified factor is a question raised by cross-cultural studies on the epidemiology of osteoporotic bone disease.

Adaptation to Dietary Toxins

Plants did not evolve with the idea that they should be good to eat. In fact, the synthesis by plants of substances toxic to their predators (humans, animals, insects, and microbes) has been a major factor in survival to the present day. Humans and animals have eaten them at their own peril, sorting out those that, based on experience, could be safely added to their diet. A. C. Leopold and R. Ardrey (1972) have developed the thesis that the presence of toxins in plants was an important determinant of the dietary habits of primitive societies.

In addition to natural insecticides and substances poisonous to animals, plants contain a multitude of compounds that make them unsafe for human consumption: hemagglutinins, enzyme inhibitors, cyanogens, antivitamins, carcinogens, neurotoxins, and allergens, among others. Accounts of their occurrence have been given elsewhere (Ory 1981; Lampe 1986). L. S. Gold and colleagues (1992) have argued that nearly all the carcinogens in the diet are of natural rather than – as widely perceived – industrial origin. Although rigorous toxicological testing of food additives on laboratory animals is required before they are approved for human consumption, no such tests have been applied to the natural toxins present in the diet. Broadening of testing for carcinogenicity to include these compounds recently has been recommended (Gold et al. 1992).

Compounds toxic to humans are more likely to be encountered in foods of plant origin because they have not been subjected to toxicological screening by first having been consumed by animals. Many toxins that are not overtly toxic to animals are at least partially catabolized by enzymatic detoxification systems present in animal tissues, notably the microsomal mixed-function oxidase system in the liver. Some toxins in plants are destroyed by cooking, but this method of food preparation appears to have been practiced only during the last 20 percent of human existence (Grivetti 1981).

Removal of toxins from plants by selective breeding and food processing has made it possible to add many new foods to the modern mixed diet. In addition, commerce in foodstuffs has diluted the high concentrations of toxins present in plants grown in specific localities. For example, the soil in some areas of the western United States contains high levels of selenium, an element that is accumulated in the seed of wheat and other cereals. When these locally grown grains constitute the bulk of the diet fed to farm animals, they can cause severe symptoms of selenium toxicity and even death. It must be presumed that they also caused at least mild toxicity among the early settlers in the same areas, for whom locally grown grains made up a major part of the diet. Modern commerce in foodstuffs has resulted in dilution of high-selenium foods and removed the risk of toxicity among consumers of the mixed diet.

Numerous substances have been added to the modern diet to improve its nutritional quality and safety. The required listing of these supplementary nutrients and additives on the label of processed foods has created a prevalent impression among consumers that some products consist mainly of synthetic industrial chemicals of questionable safety. In fact, nearly all food supplements and additives are either natural substances or exact replicas of natural substances already present in the diet or in the body (Branen, Davidson, and Salminen 1989). Most cases of food poisoning in modern societies are caused by microbial toxins formed as a result of careless handling and preservation in the home.

The few additives of purely synthetic origin have been subjected to the exhaustive life-cycle testing on laboratory animals required by food safety laws. Two such substances are the lipid antioxidants, BHA and BHT, used to prevent the oxidation of polyunsaturated fatty acids in foods, a widespread problem in the food industry resulting in flavor deterioration and the formation of products that pose a possible health risk. The synthetic sweeteners used in low-calorie beverages were approved only after years, or even decades, of safety evaluation. As indicated, there are several grounds upon which the modern diet can be criticized, but the common impression that it is less safe, in toxicological terms, than so-called natural diets is without foundation. Indeed, the reverse is the case.

The epidemiology of cancer in modern societies shows correlations of uncertain interpretation with diets high in fat and protein, but none with the use of food additives (Doll 1992; Lutz and Schlatter 1992). There are correlations, probably signifying causation, between the presence of certain substances in the diet and a high incidence of specific cancers. These include stomach cancer among Japanese and other Asians who consume large quantities of heavily salted foods, and liver cancer in Madagascans who consume moldy peanuts containing the potent carcinogen aflatoxin B_1. There is no current information as to the possible role of natural chemicals in the estimated 35 percent of cancers in industrialized societies that are "diet related" (Doll 1992). W. K. Lutz and J. Schlatter (1992) have pointed out that this figure is "provocatively close" to the prevalence of overnutrition (that is, obesity) in these societies.

There remain a number of toxicological risks associated with the modern diet that are preventable or avoidable: formation of microbial toxins in poorly preserved foods; overdosing or accidental poisoning with synthetic vitamins; ingestion of harmful bacteria, residual plant enzymes, and antinutrients resulting from inadequate cooking; consumption of carcinogenic amino acid derivatives produced by overcooking meats; and ingestion of natural toxicants in such foods as mushrooms. There are also numerous allergens present in foods that seriously affect food selection by individuals but which do not have an important influence on general food cultures. The occurrence of immunological toxicants in foods has been discussed by L. W. Mayron (1981).

Cultural Factors in Nutritional Adaptation

There are many dietary practices that are not explicable in terms of environmental, nutritional, or toxicological (that is, biological) determinants. They are attributable to traditions (religious, societal, and familial) that often distinguish one food culture from another, even when their practitioners share other common influences on food choices, such as food economics, social class, and occupational status. Traditional ceremonies surrounding the procurement of food are still in evidence among some hunting cultures, as exemplified in the ceremony held by the Arctic Inuit on the eve of the annual whale hunt, even though this hazardous undertaking is no longer necessary to meet their nutritional needs.

Religious prohibitions affect the consumption of beef, pork, dairy products, and fish, as well as processed foods that contain substances of animal origin. Adherents to some food cultures would rather starve than consume foods that are a common item in other cultures (for example, dog meat and insects). Food fads, prevalent in modern societies, have a major, but usually short-term, influence on food practices. The role of cultural factors as determinants of traditional and modern food habits is discussed in several reviews and books (Wing and Brown 1979; Grivetti 1981; Axelson 1986; Gordon 1987; Kittler and Sucher 1989).

Notwithstanding the strength of cultural traditions, studies on intersocietal migrants and aboriginal societies undergoing acculturation have shown that changes in food habits can occur relatively rapidly, particularly among the young. A diet survey conducted on the inhabitants of an Arctic Inuit village in the early 1970s showed that about 50 percent of calories were still derived from native foods in the diet of adults, compared to only about 25 percent in the diet of children, even though all foods were eaten at home (Raines and Heller 1978). A similar generation gap in the acceptance of new foods has been observed among Chinese immigrants to the United States (Axelson 1986).

Adaptation to a new food culture often begins with the preparation of new foods by traditional methods and by selection of commercially prepared facsimiles of traditional foods, such as prepared tortillas by Mexican Americans (Axelson 1986). P. G. Kittler and K. Sucher (1989) compared the traditional food cultures of Native Americans, that of the original European settlers, and that of recent immigrants from other countries. Further, they traced the changes in native and foreign food cultures that have taken place to the present time. They concluded that the modern mixed diet reflects a strong influence of European food traditions on the dietary habits of all segments of the population, but that there is also clear evidence of an influence of all the major food cultures brought to America, except those brought by blacks. Consumption of traditional Native American foods is confined mainly to Indian reservations. The decimation of the Amerindian food culture is reflected in an extraordinarily high incidence of diseases that are the modern hallmarks of malnutrition in America.

Paradoxically, overnutrition in industrialized societies is more prevalent among the poor than among the affluent. Analysis of the disposal of family income in the United States indicates that expenditures for food are not closely related to income (Popkin and Haines 1981). This finding is attributable to the low cost of food, which makes it possible for even the poor to conserve family income by buying inexpensive food items.

The relationship between the cost of food and its nutritional quality is also weak. The poor nutritional status of blacks and Native Americans is not due in any major degree to an inability to buy nutritious food. It is, more importantly, a reflection of a lack of education that precludes understanding the health risks associated with obesity, a low social status lacking the peer pressure to maintain normal body weight that prevails among the middle and upper classes of society, and incomplete emergence from the agrarian culture of the nineteenth and early twentieth centuries. It was only some 50 years ago that obesity was regarded as a sign of good health and a source of energy that could be called upon in times of ill health. Popular figures in Western social culture (Shakespeare's Falstaff and Santa Claus, for example) are portrayed as jolly, fat men. It is understandable, therefore, that the opposite perception of obesity has not yet permeated all levels of American society.

H. H. Draper

Bibliography

Axelson, M. L. 1986. The impact of culture on behavior. *Annual Reviews in Nutrition* 6: 345-63.

Baker, E. M., R. E. Hodges, J. Hood, et al. 1971. Metabolism of ^{14}C- and ^{3}H-labelled L-ascorbic acid in human scurvy. *American Journal of Clinical Nutrition* 24: 444-54.

Bang, H. O., J. Dyerberg, and H. M. Sinclair. 1980. The composition of the Eskimo food in northwestern Greenland. *American Journal of Clinical Nutrition* 33: 2657-61.

Branen, A. L., P. M. Davidson, and S. Salminen, eds. 1989. *Food additives*. New York.

Calvo, M. S., R. Kumar, and H. Heath. 1988. Elevated secretion and action of serum parathyroid hormone in young adults consuming high phosphorus, low calcium diets assembled from common foods. *Journal of Clinical Endocrinology and Metabolism* 66: 823-9.

Colbert, M. J., G. V. Mann, and L. M. Hursh. 1978. Clinical observations on nutritional health. In *Eskimos of northwest Alaska. A biological perspective*, ed. P. L. Jamison, S. L. Zegura, and F. A. Milan, 162-73. Stroudsburg, Pa.

Desai, I. D., and M. Lee. 1974. Plasma vitamin E and cholesterol relationship in western Canadian Indians. *American Journal of Clinical Nutrition* 27: 334-8.

Doll, R. 1992. The lessons of life: Keynote address to the Nutrition and Cancer Conference. *Cancer Research* (Supplement) 52: 2024s-9s.

Draper, H. H. 1977. The aboriginal Eskimo diet in modern perspective. *American Anthropologist* 79: 309-16.

Feldman, S. A., A. Rubinstein, C. B. Taylor, et al. 1978. Aspects of cholesterol, lipid, and carbohydrate metabolism. In *Eskimos of northwestern Alaska. A biological perspective*, ed. P. L. Jamison, S. L. Zegura, and F. A. Milan, 174-83. Stroudsburg, Pa.

Fortuine, R. 1971. The health of the Eskimos, as portrayed in the earliest written accounts. *Bulletin of the History of Medicine* 45: 97-114.

Fujita, T. 1992. Comparison of osteoporosis and calcium intake between Japan and the United States. *Proceedings of the Society for Experimental Biology and Medicine* 200: 149-52.

Geraci, J. R., and T. G. Smith. 1979. Vitamin C in the diet of Inuit hunters from Holman, Northwest Territories. *Arctic* 32: 135-9.

Gold, L. S., T. H. Slone, B. R. Stern, et al. 1992. Rodent carcinogens: Setting profiles. *Science* 258: 261-5.

Gordon, K. D. 1987. Evolutionary perspectives on human diet. In *Nutritional anthropology*, ed. F. E. Johnston, 3-40, New York.

Grivetti, L. E. 1981. Cultural nutrition: Anthropological and geographical themes. *Annual Reviews in Nutrition* 1: 47-68.

Gudmand-Hoyer, E., and S. Jarnum. 1969. Lactose malabsorption in Greenland Eskimos. *Acta Medica Scandinavica* 186: 235-7.

Health and Welfare Canada. 1990. *Nutrition recommendations.* Ottawa.

Keys, A., J. T. Anderson, and F. Grande. 1965. Serum cholesterol responses to changes in diet. II. The effect of cholesterol in the diet. *Metabolism* 14: 759-65.

Kittler, P. G., and K. Sucher. 1989. *Food and culture in America.* Florence, Ky.

Kretchmer, N. 1972. Lactose and lactase. *Scientific American* 227: 70-8.

Lampe, K. F. 1986. Toxic effects of plant toxins. In *Toxicology.* Third edition, ed. C. D. Klassen, M. O. Amdur, and J. Doull, 757-67. New York.

Leopold, A. C., and R. Ardrey. 1972. Toxic substances in plants and food habits of early man. *Science* 176: 512-14.

Levy, R. D. 1973. Genetics of the vitamin E content of corn grain. Ph.D. thesis, University of Illinois at Urbana-Champaign.

Link, B. A., R. W. Bray, R. G. Cassens, and R. G. Kaufman. 1970. Fatty acid composition of bovine skeletal muscle during growth. *Journal of Animal Science* 30: 726-31.

Linkswiler, H. M., C. L. Joyce, and C. R. Anand. 1974. Calcium retention of adult males as affected by level of protein and calcium intake. *Transactions of the New York Academy of Sciences,* Series II 36: 333-40.

Lutz, W. K., and J. Schlatter. 1992. Chemical carcinogens and overnutrition in diet-related cancer. *Carcinogenesis* 13: 2211-16.

Mayron, L. W. 1981. Food and chemicals as immunologic toxicants. In *Antinutrients and toxicants in foods,* ed. R. L. Ory, 117-41, Westport, Conn.

Mazess, R. B., and W. Mathur. 1974. Bone mineral content of northern Alaskan Eskimos. *American Journal of Clinical Nutrition* 27: 916-25.

1975. Bone mineral content of Canadian Eskimos. *Human Biology* 47: 45-63.

McNair, A., E. Gudmand-Hoyer, S. Jarnum, and L. Orrild. 1972. Sucrose malabsorption in Greenland. *British Medical Journal* 2: 19-21.

Mouratoff, G. J., and E. M. Scott. 1973. Diabetes mellitus in Eskimos after a decade. *Journal of the American Medical Association* 226: 1345-6.

National Research Council, U. S. Academy of Sciences. 1989. *Recommended dietary allowances.* Washington, D.C.

Ory, R. L., ed. 1981. *Antinutrients and natural toxicants in foods.* Westport, Conn.

Popkin, B. M., and P. S. Haines. 1981. Factors affecting food selection: The role of economics. *Journal of the American Dietetic Association* 79: 419-25.

Prasad, A. S., A. Miale, Jr., Z. Farid, et al. 1963. Zinc metabolism in patients with syndrome of iron deficiency anemia, hepatosplenomegaly, dwarfism and hypogonadism. *Journal of Laboratory and Clinical Medicine* 61: 537-49.

Raines, R. R., H. H. Draper, and J. G. Bergan. 1973. Sucrose, lactose, and glucose tolerance in northern Alaskan Eskimos. *American Journal of Clinical Nutrition* 26: 1185-90.

Raines, R. R., and C. A. Heller. 1978. An appraisal of the modern north Alaskan diet. In *Eskimos of north Alaska. A biological perspective,* ed. P. L. Jamison, S. L. Zegura, and F. A. Milan, 145-56. Stroudsburg, Pa.

Robinhold, D., and D. Rice. 1970. Cardiovascular health of Wainwright Eskimos. *Arctic Anthropology* 7: 83-5.

Stephansson, V. 1936. Adventures in diet. Reprinted from *Harper's Magazine* by the Institute of Meat Packers. Chicago.

Stephen, A. M., and N. J. Wald. 1990. Trends in individual consumption of dietary fat in the United States, 1920-1984. *American Journal of Clinical Nutrition* 52: 457-69.

Thomas, W. A. 1927. Health of a carnivorous race. *Journal of the American Medical Association* 88: 1559-60.

Thouez, J-P., J. M. Ekoe, P. M. Foggin, et al. 1990. Obesity, hypertension, hyperuricemia and diabetes mellitus among the Cree and Inuit of northern Quebec. *Arctic Medical Research* 49: 180-8.

Wing, E. S., and A. B. Brown. 1979. *Paleo-nutrition.* New York.

Wo, C. K. W., and H. H. Draper. 1975. Vitamin E status of Alaskan Eskimos. *American Journal of Clinical Nutrition* 28: 808-13.

Young, T. K., E. J. E. Szathmary, S. Evers, and B. Wheatley. 1990. Geographic distribution of diabetes mellitus among the native population of Canada: A national survey. *Social Science and Medicine* 31: 129-39.

VI.11 ❧ The Psychology of Food and Food Choice

We can think of the world, for any person, as divided into the self and everything else. The principal material breach of this fundamental dichotomy occurs in the act of ingestion, when something from the world (other) enters the body (self). The mouth is the guardian of the body, a final checkpoint, at which the decision is made to expel or ingest a food.

There is a widespread belief in traditional cultures that "you are what you eat." That is, people take on the properties of what they eat: Eating a brave animal makes one brave, or eating an animal with good eyesight improves one's own eyesight (reviewed in Nemeroff and Rozin 1989). "You are what you eat" seems to be "believed" at an implicit level, even among educated people in Western culture (Nemeroff and Rozin 1989). It is an eminently reasonable belief, since combinations of two entities (in this case, person and food) usually display properties of both. Thus, from the psychological side, the act of eating is fraught with affect; one is rarely neutral about what goes in one's mouth. Some of our greatest pleasures and our greatest fears have to do with what we eat.

The powerful effect associated with eating has a strong biological basis.[1] Humans, like rats, cockroaches, raccoons, herring gulls, and other broadly omnivorous species, can thrive in a wide range of environments because they discover nutrients in many sources. But although the world is filled with sources of nutrition, there are two problems facing the omnivore (or generalist). One is that many potential foods contain toxins. A second is that most available (nonanimal) foods are nutritionally incomplete. An apt selection of a variety of different plant foods is required for the survival of omnivorous animals to the extent that they cannot find sufficient animal foods. Animal foods tend to be complete sources of nutrition, but they are harder to come by because they are less prevalent and because they are often hard to procure (for example, they move). Hence, the omnivore must make a careful selection of foods, avoiding high levels of toxins and ingesting a full range of nutrients. Any act of ingestion, especially of a new potential food, is laden with ambivalence: It could be a good source of nutrition, but it might also be toxic.

Specialist species, such as those that eat only insects, can identify food as small moving things; specialists that eat only one species or group of plants may identify food by some common chemical property of these plants. There is no simple, genetic way to program an omnivorous animal to identify food by its sensory properties, because anything might be food and anything might contain toxins (or harmful microorganisms). Hence, omnivores must basically learn what is edible and what is not and what constitutes a good combination of edibles. This learning is facilitated by a few biologically (genetically) based biases:

1. An innate tendency in many species (including rats and humans) to ingest things that taste sweet (correlated with the presence of calories in nature) and to avoid things that taste bitter (correlated with the presence of toxins in nature [Garcia and Hankins 1975]).
2. Conflicting tendencies to be interested in new foods and a variety of foodstuffs but to fear anything new. This results from what I have called the generalist's (omnivore's) dilemma; the importance of exploring new foods to obtain adequate nutri-

tion across different areas and seasons and, yet, the dangers of ingesting toxins in doing so. The conflicting tendencies are manifested as a cautious sampling of new foods and a tendency to eat a number of different foods in any day.
3. Special abilities to learn about the consequences of ingestion. Here omnivores face a difficult challenge, because both the positive and negative effects of foods occur many minutes to hours or even days after ingestion. But omnivores, like rats and humans, can learn to associate a food with the consequences of ingestion even if they occur some hours later (Garcia, Hankins, and Rusiniak 1974; Rozin 1976).
4. A few special preprogrammed food selection systems. These include systems that signal to an animal that it is in need of energy (what we loosely call "hunger"), water ("thirst"), and sodium ("sodium appetite"). The sodium system, at least for the rat, is linked to an innate recognition of the taste of the needed nutrient. As shown originally by the great food selection psychologist, Curt Richter, rats deprived of sodium for the first time in their lives show an immediate preference for the taste of sodium (salt) (Richter 1956; Denton 1982; Schulkin 1991). There is some evidence for something that may resemble an innate sodium-specific hunger in humans (Beauchamp, Bartino, and Engelman 1983; Shepherd 1988).

The psychology of human food-related behavior falls naturally into two areas. One is concerned with how much is eaten (the starting and stopping of eating, defining the meal). Almost all psychological research is devoted to understanding what determines how much people and animals eat and the disorders of this process (such as obesity and anorexia). These issues are discussed elsewhere in this work. But this chapter focuses on the second area, what is eaten, that is, on food selection.[2]

The Human Omnivore

Food selection can be accomplished by genetic programming (for example, the avoidance of bitter tastes), by individual experience with foods (for example, learning that a certain food causes adverse symptoms), or by social transmission. Social transmission obviously has the virtue of sparing an organism the efforts and risks of discovering what is edible and what is not. In nonhuman animals, there is social transmission that can be called inadvertent; that is, animals may learn to eat what their parents or conspecifics eat by some sort of exposure to the conspecifics when eating (see Galef 1988, for a review). Humans, however, have two other powerful modes of transmission of food preferences and information (see Rozin 1988, for a review). One is an indirect social effect: social institutions, cuisines, and technological advances that make certain varieties of nutritious foods easily available (for instance, by agriculture or importation) and reduce the likelihood of contact with harmful potential foods (such as poisonous mushrooms). The second effect is explicit teaching about food preferences by example or by transmission of information (for example, "don't eat wild-growing mushrooms"). There is no firm evidence for any nonhuman species of explicit (intentional) teaching about appropriate foods (Galef 1988).

Humans share with animals both the nutritive need for food and the derivation of pleasure from ingestion. However, humans supplement these two functions of food with others as well (Rozin 1990b). Food and eating can serve a social function by providing an occasion for the gathering of kin at mealtimes. Food also acts as a vehicle for making social distinctions (as in serving certain foods to indicate high regard for a guest) and as culture-wide social markers (as when cuisines serve as distinctive characteristics of different groups). In the form of cuisine, food also produces an aesthetic response that extends well beyond animal pleasure. And finally, for many people in the world, most particularly Hindu Indians, food is a moral substance; eating certain foods and avoiding others is a means of preserving purity, avoiding pollution, and leading a proper life (Appadurai 1981). The multiple functions of food for humans make the understanding of human uses of food and attitudes to food an extremely complex task.

The Psychological Categorization of Food

We are accustomed to biological/taxonomic (species) and nutritional classifications of foods. But for a psychology of food, the important distinctions are those made in the human mind, and these are only weakly related to scientific classifications of foods.

The simplest approach to human food choice is to determine, for any group of people, the types and amounts of foods consumed (or more easily, purchased). We can call this measure food *use*. It is of special significance from the point of view of economics, but it has a major shortcoming as a measure of human food selection, since much food use is determined by its cost and availability. It would certainly be inaccurate to assume that because a group consumes more of X than Y, that they prefer X, when it may be that X is simply more available or less costly.

A more appropriate psychological measure is *preference,* which indicates, with price and availability controlled, which foods a person or group chooses. Yet it would be a mistake to assume that preference is a direct and infallible measure of liking for particular foods. A dieter, for example, might like ice cream better than cottage cheese but prefer (choose) cottage cheese. *Liking,* then, is a third way of describing food selection. It usually refers to attitudes about the sensory properties of foods, most particularly the oral sensations (tastes, aromas [flavors], "mouth feel"). Thus, a psychology of human food choice must address the question of why particular humans or groups of humans use, prefer, and like particular foods.

Further analysis suggests that there is a richer psychological categorization of foods for humans. Of all the potential edibles in the world (which essentially means anything that can be gotten into the mouth), a first simple division is between items that are accepted and those that are rejected by any individual or group. However, acceptance or rejection can be motivated by any of three reasons (or any combination of these) (see Table VI.11.1; Rozin and Fallon 1980; Fallon and Rozin 1983).

One reason is "sensory-affective." This has to do with liking or disliking the sensory properties of a food. Foods that are accepted or rejected primarily on sensory-affective grounds can be called "good tastes" or "distastes," respectively. If X likes lima beans and Y does not, the reason is almost certainly sensory-affective. Most of the differences in food likes within a well-defined cultural group have to do with differences in sensory-affective responses.

A second reason for rejecting a food is anticipated consequences. One may reject a food (which we call

Table VI.11.1 *Psychological categorization of acceptance and rejection*

	Rejections				Acceptances			
Dimensions	Distaste	Danger	Inappropriate	Disgust	Good taste	Beneficial	Appropriate	Transvalued
Sensory-affective	–			–	+			+
Anticipated consequences		–				+		
Ideational		?	–	–		?	+	+
Contaminant		–		–				+
Examples	Beer Chilli Spinach	Allergy foods Carcinogens	Grass Sand	Feces Insects	Saccharin Favorite foods	Medicines Healthy foods	Ritual foods	Leavings of heroes, loved ones, or deities

Source: From Fallon and Rozin (1983).

a dangerous food) because one believes ingestion will be harmful (it may be high in fats, or may contain carcinogens). Or one may accept a food (which we call a beneficial food) because it is highly nutritive or curative (perhaps a vitamin pill or a particular vegetable).

A third, uniquely human reason for food acceptance or rejection is what we call ideational; it is the nature of the food and/or its origin that primarily determines our response. Thus, we reject a very large number of potential foods because we have learned simply that they are not food: paper, tree bark, stones. These (inappropriate) entities may not be harmful and may not taste bad; they simply are not food. This inappropriate category is very large, yet there is a much smaller (appropriate) category on the positive side: foods that we eat just because they are food. Certain ritual foods might fall into this category.

We have now used three reasons to generate three categories of acceptance (good tastes, beneficial, and appropriate) and three of rejection (distaste, danger, and inappropriate). There remains one more major category of rejection that represents, like inappropriate, a fundamentally ideational rejection. We call this category disgust: Although it is primarily an ideational rejection, disgusting items are usually believed to taste bad and are often believed to be harmful. Feces seems to be disgusting universally; in American and many other Western cultures, insects fall within this category as well.

Disgusting items have the unique property that if they touch an otherwise acceptable food, they render that food unacceptable; we call this psychological contamination (Rozin and Fallon 1987). The category of disgusts is large. The opposite positive category, which we call transvalued foods, is very small. These are foods that are uplifting for ideational reasons and which are often thought to be beneficial and tasty. A good example is "prasad" in Hindu culture. Food that has been offered to the gods, and is subsequently distributed to worshippers who believe it to have been partly consumed by the gods, is considered especially desirable (Breckenridge 1986).

A psychological account of food choice would have to explain how foods come to be in any of the eight categories we have generated.

Accounting for Food Preferences and Likes

It must be true that human food attitudes result from some combination of three sources of information or experience: biological heritage (that is, our genes), cultural environment, and unique individual experience. I shall examine each of these contributing causes, with emphasis on the last, most psychological of the three. Of course, the distinction among genetic, cultural, and individual-psychological origins of human preferences is somewhat arbitrary, and there is a great deal of interaction among these forces. Nonetheless, the distinction is very useful.

Genetic Aspects of Food Selection

By their nature, omnivores carry into the world little specific information about what is edible and what is not. I noted taste biases, suspicion of new foods with an opposing tendency to seek variety, and some special abilities to learn about the consequences of food. However, there are individual differences among people that have genetic bases and that influence food selection. The small minority of these directly affect the nervous system and food choice. The best-investigated example is an inherited tendency to taste (or not to taste) a certain class of bitter compounds (identified by one member of this category, phenyl-thiocarbamide or PTC). This ability is inherited as a simple, single-locus, Mendelian recessive trait (Fischer 1967) and probably has some modest effect on preferences for certain bitter substances, such as coffee. The incidence of PTC tasting differs in different cultural groups.

More commonly, genetic differences in metabolism affect the consequences that different foods have and, hence, whether they might enter the beneficial or harmful category for any individual. A well-investigated example is lactose intolerance, but others include a sensitivity to wheat protein (gluten) and sensitivity to a potential toxin in fava beans (see Katz 1982; Simoons 1982, for reviews). In the case of lactose intolerance, the inability of most human beings to digest milk sugar (lactose) as adults (a genetically determined trait) accounts for the absence or minimal presence of raw milk and other uncultured milk products in the majority of the world's cuisines. Those who are lactose intolerant can develop lower gastrointestinal symptoms (cramps, diarrhea) upon ingestion of even relatively moderate amounts of uncultured milk.

The fact remains that although there are genetic influences on food choice, they are rather minor, at least at the individual level. An indication of this is that the food preferences of identical twins are not much (if at all) more similar than are the preferences of fraternal twins (Rozin and Millman 1987).

Culture and Food Selection: Cuisine

Although it has never been directly demonstrated, it seems obvious that the major determinant of any individual's food preferences is his or her native cuisine. Put another way, if one wanted to guess as much as one could about a person's food attitudes and preferences, the best question to ask would be: What is your native culture or ethnic group? Not only would this response be very informative but there is also no other question one could ask that would be remotely as informative. In terms of the taxonomy of food acceptances and rejections (Table VI.11.1), cultural forces generally determine the ideational categories and strongly influence the good tastes–distastes and danger–beneficial categories.

This influence, obviously acquired in childhood, can be generally described as a body of rules and practices that defines what is appropriate and desirable food and how it is to be eaten. The most systematic description of the food itself comes from Elisabeth Rozin's (1982, 1992) analysis of cuisine. She posits three components that give a characteristic ethnic quality to any dish: The staple ingredients, the flavor principles (for example, the recurrent soy sauce, ginger root, rice wine combination in Chinese food), and the method of processing (for example, stir-frying for many Chinese foods).

Furthermore, cuisines specify the appropriate ordering of dishes within a meal (Douglas and Nicod 1974) and the appropriate combinations and occasions on which particular foods are consumed (Schutz 1988). All of these factors, along with rules about the manner and social arrangement of eating and the importance and function of food in life, are major parts of the human food experience and are basically part of the transmission of culture. That these cultural forces are strong is indicated by the persistence of native food habits, sometimes called the conservatism of cuisine in immigrant groups. Generations after almost all traces of original-culture practices are gone, the basic food of the family often remains the native cuisine (see, for example, Goode, Curtis, and Theophano 1984).

Psychological Determinants of Food Selection

Within the minimal constraints of biology and the substantial constraints and predispositions imposed by culture, any individual develops a set of culture-appropriate, but also somewhat unique, food preferences. I shall now address what little we know about how this happens.

Early Childhood: Milk and Weaning

Humans and other mammals begin life with one food: milk. It is both nutritive and associated with maternal nurturance. A first trauma in life is weaning away from this "superfood," which is accomplished in culturally variable ways. There is no evidence for special attachments that humans develop to this earliest food, although such a permanent attachment (liking) has been documented with respect to species recognition in a number of species: Exposure to a member of the species (usually a parent) at a critical period in development leads to a permanent attachment to and preferential recognition of that object. But this process of imprinting would be highly maladaptive for early food for mammals because they would then spend their lives seeking an unattainable food. Milk, for example, only became available as a food for some humans after infancy with the development of

dairying, which occurred relatively recently in human history (see Rozin and Pelchat 1988, for further discussion).

Neophilia and Neophobia

As omnivores, humans show both a tendency to be interested in new foods and a fear of new foods. Both tendencies have benefits and risks. The neophilic (attraction to new food) tendency manifests itself not only in an interest in genuinely new foods but also in a desire for variety in the diet. Thus, humans (and other animals) tend to come to like a food less if they eat it almost exclusively (boredom effect) and tend to eat more when confronted with a variety of foods. This general phenomenon has been called sensory specific satiety and has been subjected to systematic analysis by B. J. Rolls and her colleagues (Rolls et al. 1985).

Below the age of about 2 years, children seem to have little neophobia and, quite willingly, put almost anything into their mouths (reviewed in Rozin, 1990c). Presumably, parental monitoring of their food access controls this otherwise dangerous tendency. After 2 years of age, at least in American culture, children sometimes enter a neophobic phase, in which they refuse all but a few types of food. We do not know the origin or adaptive value (if any) of this pattern. In American culture, some adults also find an extremely limited range of foods acceptable, though most children with this extreme neophobia recover from it. Neophobia varies greatly across individuals in North America, and a scale has been developed to measure this tendency in both children and adults (Pliner and Hobden 1992).

Food Preferences and the Adult Taxonomy

We know very little about how, within any culture and individual, specific foods become categorized in accordance with the taxonomy presented in Table VI.11.1. I review here what is known.

Acquired dislikes. Best understood is the origin of the distinction between the danger and distaste categories. Generally, if a relatively new food is consumed, and this is followed within hours by unpleasant symptoms that include nausea, the food comes to be a distaste. However, if nausea is not a part of the symptoms, the result is usually that the food enters the danger category; that is, it is avoided because of anticipated harm, but is not distasteful (Pelchat and Rozin 1982). The taste-aversion learning originally described in rats by J. Garcia and his colleagues (1974) seems to be an example of acquired distaste mediated by nausea. Hence, nausea appears to be a magic bullet, producing distastes. This is not, however, to say that this is the only way in which distastes can be produced. There is evidence, for example, that when a food is accompanied by a bad taste (for example, when a bitter taste is added to a food), the food itself becomes distasteful, even when the originally unpleasant taste is removed (Baeyens et al. 1990).

Acquired likes. So far as we know, there is no magic bullet like nausea on the negative side that makes a potential food into a good taste (a liked food). However, this happens very frequently. There is evidence for three processes that contribute to acquired likes.

One of these is mere exposure. That is, simple exposure to a food (meaning its ingestion) is usually accompanied by an increased liking for the food (Pliner 1982). The mechanism for this may be nothing other than mere exposure. The effects of mere exposure on liking have been shown in many domains other than food (Zajonc 1968).

A second process that accounts for acquired likes is classical (Pavlovian) conditioning. That is, if an already liked entity (called an unconditioned stimulus) is paired with (that is, is contingent with) a relatively neutral potential food, the potential food tends to become more liked. This process of change in liking for a stimulus as a result of contingent pairing in humans has been called evaluative conditioning (Martin and Levey 1978; Baeyens et al. 1990). One example involves pairing of a flavor (conditioned stimulus) with the pleasant experience of satisfaction of hunger (unconditioned stimulus). In a laboratory setting, humans have been shown to increase liking for a food the ingestion of which is followed by satiety (Booth, Mather, and Fuller 1982).

Another example involves presentation (contingent pairing) of one flavor of herbal tea (conditioned stimulus) with sugar (unconditioned stimulus) and another flavor of tea without sugar. After a number of presentations, subjects tend to prefer the flavor of the tea that was paired with sweetness, even when that flavor is presented without sugar (Zellner et al. 1983).

Within the context of evaluative conditioning, it is likely that the major class of potent (unconditioned) stimuli that influence food likes is social. In particular, the perception (often, perhaps, by facial expression) of positive affect in another (respected) person in conjunction with consumption of a particular food probably makes that food more liked by the "observer." Recently, a first study has shown such an effect in the laboratory. Subjects who observe a person indicating pleasure in drinking a beverage from a glass of a particular shape (as opposed to other shapes) come to prefer that particular glass shape (Baeyens et al. 1994).

A third process that influences liking is also social, but it does not operate through conditioning. Rather, the perception of liking or value in a respected other operates more directly to influence one's own attitudes. For example, when a respected other uses a food as a reward (indicating that he/she values the food), a child tends to come to prefer (like) that food more (Birch, Zimmerman, and Hind 1980). Furthermore, there is evidence, both from the general litera-

ture in social psychology (Lepper 1983) and the development of food preferences (Birch et al. 1982), that the perception that the self or others consume a food for clear personal gain (nutrition, social advantage) is destructive to the development of liking. That is, when children perceive that a food preference (in themselves or others) is "instrumentally" motivated, that is, connected to a specific reward, they tend not to shift their liking for the food in question.

Reversal of Innate Aversions
Humans are almost unique among mammalian (if not all) generalists in developing strong likes for foods that are innately unpalatable. These include such common favorites as the oral or nasal irritants in chilli peppers, black pepper, ginger, horseradish, and alcoholic beverages or tobacco, and the bitter tastes in certain fruits, tobacco, most alcoholic beverages, coffee, chocolate, burnt foods, and so forth. Reversals of innate aversions seem to occur in all cultures (cuisines). They might well be accounted for in terms of the operation of the factors (mere exposure, evaluative conditioning, social influence) that have already been identified. But there are also some special mechanisms of acquired liking that require an initially negative response. Two have been identified, with particular reference to the acquisition of a liking for the innately negative oral burn of chilli pepper (Rozin 1990a).

In the service of maintaining the body at an optimum level of function, humans and other species seem to have compensatory mechanisms, which neutralize disturbances by producing, internally, events that oppose the original event. These internally generated events are called opponent processes (Solomon 1980). For example, it is widely believed that endorphins, natural opiatelike substances, are released in the brain to reduce a chronic pain experience. R. L. Solomon (1980) and others have suggested that opponent processes become more potent as they are repeatedly stimulated and have used this feature to account for the basic process of addiction. Normally, when one experiences something painful, one withdraws and avoids the situation in the future. However, in the case of the chilli pepper and other culturally supported innately negative entities, there is a strong cultural force that reintroduces the aversive experience. Thus, children end up repeatedly sampling the unpleasant burn of chilli pepper, permitting the development of a strong opponent process, which may grow to the extent that it overcompensates for the pain and produces net pleasure (perhaps by oversecretion of endogenous opiates) (Rozin 1990a). Hence, the negativity of an innately aversive substance may provide the conditions for an acquired liking.

A more cognitive account of the reversal of innate aversions engages a uniquely human interest in mastering nature. The signals sent to the brain from innately unpalatable substances impel the organism to reject them; they are adaptively linked to a system that rids the organism of harmful entities. But many innately unpalatable substances are not harmful, at least in modest doses (chilli pepper, ginger, coffee). Though chilli pepper makes the novice feel as if his palate will peel away, it is, in fact, harmless. It is possible that the realization that a substance–experience elicits bodily defensive mechanisms, but is actually safe, is a source of pleasure. We call this pleasure that comes from mastery over nature benign masochism (Rozin 1990a). A more striking instance is the unique human activity of enjoying bodily manifestations of fright (as opposed to pain): People presumably enjoy roller coasters because their body is frightened, but they know that they are actually safe.

Disgust: The Food-Related Emotion

The strongest reaction to a potential food is surely the revulsion associated with disgusting entities (Table VI.11.1). The emotion of disgust elicited in these situations is characterized by withdrawal, a sense of nausea, and a characteristic facial expression. According to our analyses (Rozin and Fallon 1987; Rozin, Haidt, and McCauley 1993), following on the seminal contributions of Charles Darwin (1872) and A. Angyal (1941), disgust is originally a food-related emotion, expressing "revulsion at the prospect of oral incorporation of offensive substances. The offensive substances are contaminants, that is, if they contact an otherwise acceptable food, they tend to render that food unacceptable" (Rozin and Fallon 1987: 23). Our analysis holds that disgust originates from distaste (and shares, to some extent, a facial expression with distaste), but is in fact quite distinct from distaste in adults. For example, the idea of a distasteful entity in one's stomach is not upsetting, but the idea of a disgusting entity in one's stomach is very upsetting.

The intensity of the disgust experience derives, in part, from the "you are what you eat" principle, since, by this principle, one who ingests something offensive becomes offensive. Virtually all food-related disgust entities are of animal origin. We have proposed that the core disgust category is all animals and their products (Rozin and Fallon 1987). In line with Angyal's suggestion (1941), we agree that feces is the universal disgust substance, and almost certainly the first disgust, developmentally. The potency of disgust elicitors is evidenced by the contamination property, a feature that seems to characterize disgust cross-culturally.

Disgust provides an excellent example of how a food system becomes a template or model for more elaborated systems. The emotion of disgust seems, through cultural evolution, to have become a general expression of anything offensive, including nonfoods. Our analysis suggests that principal elicitors of disgust cross-culturally include reminders of our animal origin (such as gore, death), a wide range of interpersonal contacts (such as wearing the clothing of undesirable persons), and certain moral offenses often involving purity violations or animality (Rozin et al. 1993).

Transmission of Food Preferences and Attitudes

Most available models for the acquisition of food preferences would predict a rather high correlation between the food preferences of parents and those of their children. For the first years of life, parents are the primary teachers and exemplars of eating and food choice for children. In addition, to the extent that there are individual differences in preferences that have genetic contributions, one would expect parent-child resemblances. Yet, the literature (reviewed in Rozin, 1991) indicates very low correlations between the food preferences of parents and their children (in the range of 0 to 0.3), whether the younger generation in the studies is one of preschoolers or of college age. There is no reasonable account for these low correlations; they do not result from the fact that the parents have different preferences for the foods under study, so that the child gets "mixed messages." Parent-child correlations remain low even when the parents are very similar in their preferences for the foods under study (Rozin 1991). Alternative sources of influence on children include peers and siblings (for whom there is evidence of some substantial resemblance [Pliner and Pelchat 1986]), and the media. The effectiveness and mode of operation of these and other influences has yet to be evaluated.

The low parent-child correlation for food preferences is part of what has been called the family paradox (Rozin 1991). The paradox is extended by the fact that there is no consistent evidence that mothers (as principal feeders and food purveyors) show higher child resemblance than do fathers, nor that same-sex parents have greater influence than opposite-sex parents - as views about identification might suggest (Pliner 1983; Rozin 1991).

The puzzling lack of parent-child resemblance for food (and other) preferences contrasts with much higher parent-child resemblance for values (Cavalli-Sforza et al. 1982; Rozin 1991). Apparently, values (such as religious or political attitudes) are more subject to parental influence. In this regard, it is of interest that food preferences may, under some circumstances, become values. Food is intimately related to moral issues in Hindu India, such that a leading scholar of this area has described food in Hindu India as a "biomoral substance" (Appadurai 1981). But even in Western cultures, specific foods may enter the moral domain. For example, vegetarianism for some has moral significance. It would be interesting to see if parental influence is greater on children for whom a preference has been moralized than for those for whom the preference is not moralized.

Attitudes and Choice: An Alternative Approach

The framework I have provided for examination of human food selection emphasizes the psychological categorization of foods and the combined influences of biological, psychological, and cultural factors on food selection. The emphasis has also been on the developmental history of food preferences. There are alternative formulations from within both psychology and marketing. A particularly prominent approach, based on the study of attitudes and their relation to behavior, examines the factors currently influencing selection of a particular food, independent of the ultimate origin of these causes. In other words, this approach models what would be going on in the head of a person in a supermarket faced with a choice between two products. For convenience, the forces acting on a person at a time of choice can be categorized as those attributable to the food and its properties, the person, and socioeconomic factors (Shepherd 1988).

The theory of reasoned action (Ajzen and Fishbein 1980) has probably been the most successful framework for analysis of choices in terms of the action of contemporary forces. According to this approach, the principal cause of a behavior (for instance, selecting a particular food) is the intention to behave in such a manner, and the principal predictors of the intention are personal attitudes to the behavior (for instance, whether it is seen as good or bad) and subjective norms (the perceived opinions of significant others about whether the behavior should be performed). Personal attitudes are themselves a function of a set of beliefs about the outcome of the behavior (food choice) in question (will it promote overweight, will it produce a pleasant taste?) and the evaluation of that outcome (is it good or bad?). A set of salient beliefs is determined, and the sum of the product of each belief and its evaluation composes the attitude score. The subjective norm is predicted in the same manner by the sum of normative beliefs about whether specific relevant people or groups think that the target person should perform the behavior, each norm multiplied by the motivation to comply with it.

A number of studies (see Tuorila and Pangborn 1988; Towler and Shepherd 1992) have applied the Ajzen-Fishbein model to food choices, with some success, in terms of prediction of consumption from (usually) questionnaire data on beliefs, evaluations of beliefs, subjective norms, and motivation to comply with those norms. Target foods have included a variety of dairy products, meats, and other high-fat foods. The results, on subjects from the Western-developed world, show a tendency for personal attitudes to be better predictors of choice than subjective norms. They also suggest that taste of food is the most important predictor of attitudes, with health effects often the second-best predictor (see Shepherd 1989b for a general discussion).

Food Selection Pathology in America

Throughout history, food has been viewed as not only the principal source of sustenance but also a major source of pleasure. In the United States, a surfeit of food, a developing concern about long-term harmful effects of certain foods, and a standard of beauty for women (at least among the white middle class in the United States) that is much thinner than the average woman have all contributed to an ambivalent, sometimes negative attitude to food (Polivy and Herman 1983; Rodin et al. 1985; Becker 1986; Rozin 1989; Rodin 1992).

Consumption of foods, especially those that are highly tasty and fattening, becomes for many a source of fear and guilt, rather than pleasure. The focal group for this (what I will call) pathology of food is white middle-class American women, among whom there is considerable concern about obesity and, consequently, considerable efforts aimed at dieting (Rodin 1992). One consequence of this is that eating disorders, such as anorexia nervosa and various forms of bulimia, are increasing in American women, whereas such disorders are at much lower levels in American males and virtually absent in developing countries (McCarthy 1990).

One cause of this hyperconcern about food, as mentioned, is the standard of thinness accepted by American women; unlike American men, American women see themselves as substantially overweight (Rozin and Fallon, 1988). Furthermore, white middle-class American women are more worried about being above ideal weight than are men; that is, even when men recognize that they are overweight, food is less likely to become a source of fear and guilt for them.

Although food is obviously a necessity for survival, potentially harmful effects on health of certain foods have come to be a matter of concern for many Americans. This recent concern results from a number of factors:

1. The reduction in death from infectious diseases has produced a corresponding increased incidence of death from degenerative diseases. This changes the focus of food risk from acute to chronic effects.
2. Epidemiological evidence on harmful effects of food, which is accumulating at a rapid rate, is conveyed to a public fascinated with such information in a salient – even sensational – way by the media.
3. Americans have become obsessed with longevity, or perhaps, immortality.
4. Americans (and others) are unprepared to deal with and evaluate the constant wave of food (and other) risk information to which they are exposed. They have never been taught cost–benefit analysis or interpretations of very low probabilities and have beliefs about food that are often incorrect. For example, many believe that if something is thought to be harmful at high levels, then it is also

harmful at trace levels. Such dose insensitivity causes some to shun even traces of salt, fats, or sugars (Rozin, Ashmore, and Markwith 1996). In addition, many Americans falsely believe that "natural" foods are invariably healthy, and processed foods are likely to be harmful. In fact, over the short term, the opposite is clearly true (that is, acute illness is more likely to be caused by natural foods), and there is reason to believe that in many cases, the long-term risks posed by the consumption of natural foods are higher than those posed by processed versions of the same foods (Ames et al. 1987). The centrality of food in life and the great concern about putting things in the mouth and body probably causes people to overestimate long-term food risks in contrast to other risks, such as driving.

The result is that eating, which is one of the greatest sources of pleasure and health that humans can experience, has become a nightmare for some and, in fact, threatens to become an American cultural nightmare. We can only hope that this obsessive concern does not, like so many other attitudes and beliefs of Americans, spread around the world.

Paul Rozin

Notes

1. See Rozin (1976) and Rozin and Schulkin (1990) for more detailed discussions of the biological and psychological frameworks for human food selection.
2. More extended reviews of the area covered in this chapter can be found in the volumes of collected papers by Barker (1982), Dobbing (1988), Shepherd (1989a and 1989b), and Thomson (1988); in books by Fischler (1990) and Logue (1991); and in specific review articles by Birch (1986), Blundell (1983), Booth (1982), Krondl and Lau (1982), Meiselman (1988), Pangborn (1980), P. Rozin (1982), Rozin and Schulkin (1990), Rozin and Vollmecke (1986), and Schutz and Judge (1984). Major historical summaries of basic points of view on food selection include those by Mead (1943), Richter (1943), and Young (1948).

Bibliography

Ajzen, I., and M. Fishbein. 1980. *Understanding attitudes and predicting social behavior.* Englewood Cliffs, N.J.

Ames, B. N., R. Magaw, and L. S. Gold. 1987. Ranking possible carcinogenic hazards. *Science* 236: 271–80.

Angyal, A. 1941. Disgust and related aversions. *Journal of Abnormal and Social Psychology* 36: 393–412.

Appadurai, A. 1981. Gastro-politics in Hindu South Asia. *American Ethnologist* 8: 494–511.

Baeyens, F., P. Eelen, O. Van den Bergh, and G. Crombez. 1990. Flavor-flavor and color-flavor conditioning in humans. *Learning and Motivation* 21: 434–55.

Baeyens, F., B. Kaes, P. Eelen, and P. Silverans. 1994. Observational evaluative conditioning of an embedded stimulus element. *European Journal of Social Psychology* 26: 15–28.

Bakwin, H., and R. M. Bakwin. 1972. *Behavior disorders in children.* Philadelphia, Pa.

Barker, L. M., ed. 1982. *The psychobiology of human food selection.* Bridgeport, Conn.

Beauchamp, G. K., M. Bertino, and K. Engelman. 1983. Modification of salt taste. *Annals of Internal Medicine* 98: 763–9.

Becker, M. H. 1986. The tyranny of health promotion. *Public Health Review.* 14: 15–25.

Birch, L. L. 1986. Children's food preferences: Developmental patterns and environmental influences. In *Annals of child development,* Vol. 4., ed. G. Whitehurst and R. Vasta. Greenwich, Conn.

Birch, L. L., D. Birch, D. W. Marlin, and L. Kramer. 1982. Effects of instrumental eating on children's food preferences. *Appetite* 3: 125–34.

Birch, L. L., S. I. Zimmerman, and H. Hind. 1980. The influence of social-affective context on the formation of children's food preferences. *Child Development* 51: 856–61.

Blundell, J. E. 1983. Problems and processes underlying the control of food selection and nutrient intake. In *Nutrition and the brain,* Vol. 6, ed. R. J. Wurtman and J. J. Wurtman, 163–231. New York.

Booth, D. A. 1982. Normal control of omnivore intake by taste and smell. In *The determination of behavior by chemical stimuli. ECRO symposium,* ed. J. Steiner and J. Ganchrow, 233–43. London.

Booth, D. A., P. Mather, and J. Fuller. 1982. Starch content of ordinary foods associatively conditions human appetite and satiation, indexed by intake and eating pleasantness of starch-paired flavors. *Appetite* 3: 163–84.

Breckenridge, C. 1986. Food, politics and pilgrimage in South India, A.D. 1350–1650. In *Food, society, and culture: Aspects of South Asian food systems,* ed. R. S. Khare and M. S. A. Rao. Durham, N.C.

Cavalli-Sforza, L. L., M. W. Feldman, K. H Chen, and S. M. Dornbusch. 1982. Theory and observation in cultural transmission. *Science* 218: 19–27.

Darwin, C. R. 1872. *The expression of emotions in man and animals.* London.

Denton, D. 1982. *The hunger for salt.* Berlin.

Dobbing, J., ed. 1988. *Sweetness.* London.

Douglas, M., and M. Nicod. 1974. Taking the biscuit: The structure of British meals. *New Society* (December 19): 744–7.

Fallon, A. E., and P. Rozin. 1983. The psychological bases of food rejections by humans. *Ecology of Food and Nutrition* 13: 15–26.

Fischer, R. 1967. Genetics and gustatory chemoreception in man and other primates. In *The chemical senses and nutrition,* ed. M. Kare and O. Maller, 61–71. Baltimore, Md.

Fischler, C. 1990. *L'Homnivore.* Paris.

Galef, B. G., Jr. 1988. Communication of information concerning distant diets in a social central-place foraging species: Rattus norvegicus. In *Social learning: A comparative approach,* ed. T. Zentall and B. G. Galef, Jr., 119–40. Hillsdale, N.J.

Garcia, J., and W. G. Hankins. 1975. The evolution of bitter and the acquisition of toxipohobia. In *Fifth international symposium on olfaction and taste,* ed. D. Denton and J. P. Coghlan, 1–12. New York.

Garcia, J., W. G. Hankins, and K. W. Rusiniak. 1974. Behavioral regulation of the milieu interne in man and rat. *Science* 185: 824–31.

Goode, J., K. Curtis, and J. Theophano. 1984. Meal formats, meal cycles and menu negotiation in the maintenance of an Italian-American community. In *Food in the social order,* ed. M. Douglas, 143-218. New York.

Katz, S. H. 1982. Food, behavior and biocultural evolution. In *The psychobiology of human food selection,* ed. L. M. Barker, 171-88. Westport, Conn.

Krondl, M., and D. Lau. 1982. Social determinants in human food selection. In *The psychobiology of human food selection,* ed., L. M. Barker, 139-51. Westport, Conn.

Lepper, M. R. 1983. Social control processes and the internalization of social values: An attributional perspective. In *Social cognition and social development,* ed. E. T. Higgins, D. N. Ruble, and W. W. Hartup, 294-330. New York.

Logue, A. W. 1991. *The psychology of eating and drinking.* Second edition. New York.

Marriott, M. 1968. Caste ranking and food transactions: A matrix analysis. In *Structure and change in Indian society,* ed. M. Singer and B. S. Cohn, 133-71. Chicago.

Martin, I., and A. B. Levey. 1978. Evaluative conditioning. *Advances in Behavior Research and Therapy* 1: 57-102.

McCarthy, M. 1990. The thin ideal; depression and eating disorders in women. *Behavior Research and Therapy* 28: 205-15.

Mead, M. 1943. The problem of changing food habits. *Bulletin of the National Research Council* 108: 20-31.

Meiselman, H. L. 1988. Consumer studies of food habits. In *Sensory analysis of foods,* ed. J. R. Piggott, 267-334. London.

Nemeroff, C., and P. Rozin. 1989. An unacknowledged belief in "you are what you eat" among college students in the United States: An application of the demand-free "impressions" technique. *Ethos. The Journal of Psychological Anthropology* 17: 50-69.

Pangborn, R. M. 1980. A critical analysis of sensory responses to sweetness. In *Carbohydrate sweeteners in foods and nutrition,* ed. P. Koivistoinen and L. Hyvonen, 87-110. London.

Pelchat, M. L., and P. Rozin. 1982. The special role of nausea in the acquisition of food dislikes by humans. *Appetite* 3: 341-51.

Pliner, P. 1982. The effects of mere exposure on liking for edible substances. *Appetite* 3: 283-90.

1983. Family resemblance in food preferences. *Journal of Nutrition Education* 15: 137-40.

Pliner, P., and K. Hobden. 1992. Development of a scale to measure the trait of food neophobia in humans. *Appetite* 19: 105-20.

Pliner, P., and M. L. Pelchat. 1986. Similarities in food preferences between children and their siblings and parents. *Appetite* 7: 333-42.

Polivy, J., and C. P. Herman. 1983. *Breaking the diet habit.* New York.

Richter, C. P. 1943. Total self regulatory functions in animals and human beings. *Harvey Lecture Series* 38: 63-103.

1956. Salt appetite of mammals: Its dependence on instinct and metabolism. In *L'instinct dans le comportement des animaux et de l'homme,* 577-629. Paris.

Ritson, C., L. Gofton, and J. McKenzie, ed. 1986. *The food consumer.* Chichester, England.

Rodin, J. 1992. *Body traps.* New York.

Rodin, J., L. Silberstein, and R. Striegel-Moore. 1985. Women and weight: A normative discontent. In *Psychology and gender. Nebraska Symposium on Motivation,* ed. T. B. Sonderegger. Lincoln, Neb.

Rolls, B. J., M. Hetherington, V. J. Burley and P. M. van

Duijvenvoorde. 1985. Changing hedonic responses to foods during and after a meal. In *Interaction of the chemical senses with nutrition,* ed. M. R. Kare and J. G. Brand, 247-68. New York.

Rozin, E. 1982. The structure of cuisine. In *The psychobiology of human food selection,* ed. L. M. Barker, 189-203. Westport, Conn.

1992. *Ethnic cuisine* (original 1983 title: *The flavor principle cookbook*). New York.

Rozin, P. 1976. The selection of foods by rats, humans, and other animals. In *Advances in the study of behavior,* Vol. 6, ed. J. Rosenblatt, R. A. Hinde, C. Beer, and E. Shaw, 21-76. New York.

1982. Human food selection: The interaction of biology, culture and individual experience. In *The psychobiology of human food selection,* ed. L. M. Barker, 225-54. Westport, Conn.

1988. Social learning about foods by humans. In *Social learning: A comparative approach,* ed. T. Zentall and B. G. Galef, Jr., 165-87. Hillsdale, N.J.

1989. Disorders of food selection: The compromise of pleasure. *Annals of the New York Academy of Sciences Series* 38: 63-103.

1990a. Getting to like the burn of chili pepper: Biological, psychological and cultural perspectives. In *Chemical irritation in the nose and mouth,* ed. B. G. Green, J. R. Mason, and M. L. Kare, 231-69. Potomac, Md.

1990b. Social and moral aspects of food and eating. In *Cognition and social psychology: Essays in honor of Solomon E. Asch,* ed. I. Rock, 97-110. Potomac, Md.

1990c. Development in the food domain. *Developmental Psychology* 26: 555-62.

1991. Family resemblance in food and other domains: The family paradox and the role of parental congruence. *Appetite* 16: 93-102.

Rozin, P., M. B. Ashmore, and M. Markwith. 1996. Lay American conceptions of nutrition: Dose insensitivity, categorical thinking, contagion, and the monotonic mind. *Health Psychology* 15: 438-47.

Rozin, P., and A. E. Fallon. 1980. Psychological categorization of foods and non-foods: A preliminary taxonomy of food rejections. *Appetite* 1: 193-201.

1987. A perspective on disgust. *Psychological Review* 94: 23-41.

1988. Body image, attitudes to weight, and misperceptions of figure preferences of the opposite sex: A comparison of males and females in two generations. *Journal of Abnormal Psychology* 97: 342-5.

Rozin, P., J. Haidt, and C. R. McCauley. 1993. Disgust. In *Handbook of emotions,* ed. M. Lewis and J. Haviland, 575-94. New York.

Rozin, P., and L. Millman. 1987. Family environment, not heredity, accounts for family resemblances in food preferences and attitudes. *Appetite* 8: 125-34.

Rozin, P., and M. L. Pelchat. 1988. Memories of mammaries: Adaptations to weaning from milk in mammals. In *Advances in psychobiology,* Vol. 13, ed. A. N. Epstein and A. Morrison, 1-29. New York.

Rozin, P., and J. Schulkin. 1990. Food selection. In *Handbook of behavioral neurobiology,* Vol. 10: *Food and water intake,* ed. E. M. Stricker, 297-328. New York.

Rozin, P., and T. A. Vollmecke. 1986. Food likes and dislikes. *Annual Review of Nutrition* 6: 433-56.

Schulkin, J. 1991. *Sodium hunger. The search for a salty taste.* New York.

Schutz, H. G. 1988. Beyond preference: Appropriateness as a measure of contextual acceptance of food. In *Food acceptability,* ed. D. M. H. Thomson, 115-34. London.

Schutz, H. G., and D. S. Judge. 1984. Consumer perceptions of food quality. In *Research in food science and nutrition*. Vol. 4: *Food science and human welfare*, ed. J. V. McLoughlin and B. M. McKenna, 229-42. Dublin.

Shepherd, R. 1988. Sensory influence on salt, sugar and fat intake. *Nutrition Research Reviews* 1: 125-44.

    1989a. Factors influencing food preferences and choice. In *Handbook of the psychophysiology of human eating*, ed. R., Shepherd, 3-24. Chichester, England.

Shepherd, R., ed. 1989b. *Handbook of the psychophysiology of human eating*. Chichester, England.

Simoons, F. J. 1982. Geography and genetics as factors in the psychobiology of human food selection. In *The psychobiology of human food selection*, ed. L. M. Barker, 205-24. Westport, Conn.

Solomon, R. L. 1980. The opponent process theory of acquired motivation. *American Psychologist* 35: 691-712.

Steiner, J. E. 1979. Human facial expressions in response to taste and smell stimulation. In *Advances in child development and behavior*, Vol. 13, ed. H. W. Reese and L. P. Lipsitt, 257-95. New York.

Thomson, D. M. H., ed. 1988. *Food acceptability*. London.

Towler, G., and R. Shepherd. 1992. Application of Fishbein and Ajzen's expectancy-value model to understanding fat intake. *Appetite* 18: 15-27.

Tuorila, H., and R. M. Pangborn. 1988. Behavioural models in the prediction and consumption of selected sweet, salty and fatty foods. In *Food acceptability*, ed. D. M. H. Thomson, 267-79. London.

Young, P. T. 1948. Appetite, palatability and feeding habit: A critical review. *Psychological Bulletin* 45: 289-320.

Zajonc, R. B. 1968. Attitudinal effects of mere exposure. *Journal of Personality and Social Psychology* 9 (Part 2): 1-27.

Zellner, D. A., P. Rozin, M. Aron, and C. Kulish. 1983. Conditioned enhancement of human's liking for flavors by pairing with sweetness. *Learning and Motivation* 14: 338-50.

VI.12 ∞ Food Fads

The term "food fad" often refers to socially deviant, cultlike eating behavior. Examples include diets that contain massive amounts of supposedly healthy foods, such as garlic; those that prohibit the consumption of allegedly hazardous products, such as sugar or white bread; and those that emphasize natural foods and question the purity of goods available in supermarkets (Fieldhouse 1986). Charlatans claiming to have discovered nutritional fountains of youth and cures for cancer become best-selling authors overnight, only to disappear shortly afterward. But they are not the only promoters of culinary fads. The *Webster's Third New International Dictionary* defines *fad* as "a pursuit or interest followed usu. widely but briefly with exaggerated zeal. . . ." Sophisticated diners who flock to Ethiopian restaurants one month and to Thai restaurants the next thus qualify as faddists but not necessarily as deviants.

That a food or group of foods is especially health promoting serves as the most characteristic claim of food faddists, both wild-eyed cult leaders and bottom-line business executives. Nevertheless, profit and power often provide unspoken motivations behind the crusades of both groups. Moreover, the nutritional science used to back assertions of healthfulness has developed in a halting, incomplete, and often contradictory manner. This chapter evaluates the validity of many of these nutritional claims while it examines a wide range of food fads that have appeared throughout the world, particularly in the last two centuries, in the contexts of the spread of industrial capitalism, the concern for moral standards, and the creation of social identity.

Food and Industry

Prior to the age of industrial capitalism, fads of any sort were limited to a small elite. Peasants living at the edge of subsistence simply could not afford to experiment with fashions that were soon discarded. With the rise of mass production, however, disposable goods became not only a possibility but almost a necessity: Planned obsolescence, for example, allowed auto makers to continue producing cars although virtually everyone already owned one. The imperatives of food marketing led to product differentiation as manufacturers sought to market ever greater quantities of food, and culinary fashions changed with startling speed in the restaurant industry's fiercely competitive environment. Food fads have also spread throughout the world in recent decades as multinational corporations have cultivated markets in developing countries.

Cuisine and Capitalism

The rise of European industrial capitalism depended on a surplus of workers, which required a corresponding surplus of food. Quantitative increases in the food supply resulted from an eighteenth-century agricultural revolution, but at the same time, European diets underwent qualitative changes as well. Anthropologist Sidney Mintz (1985) has shown that refined sugar from Caribbean colonies became an essential part of British working-class diets. Whether drunk with tea or eaten in jam, sugar provided the cheapest possible source of energy for workers and thus helped hold down industrial wages. The role of sugar continued to grow as food manufacturers expanded their control over world markets. In ongoing efforts to increase sales, advertisers have launched countless new food fads in the hope that they would become cultural icons.

Sociologist Jack Goody (1982) has identified four basic components in the industrial transformation of food: improvements in preservation, mechanization, transportation, and retailing. Salt, sugar, and vinegar had long been used to preserve food, but modern canning dates only to 1795, when French chef Nicolas Appert combined pressure cookers with glass bottles to help supply Napoleon's armies. Nineteenth-century technological improvements allowed the substitution of cheaper tin cans for bottles and permitted the mass marketing of canned fish, meat, vegetables, condensed milk, and prepared foods. At the same time, artificial freezing of meats became widespread, although frozen vegetables remained impractical until the early-twentieth-century development of moisture-proof cellophane wrapping.

Mechanization, in turn, allowed the mass production of canned and frozen foods, which the steadily improving transportation methods, such as steamships and railroads, carried to distant markets. Finally, these foods were distributed to consumers through a nineteenth-century revolution in retailing. Grocers, who formerly had specialized in small-scale, nonperishable luxury goods, such as spices, tea, and sugar, took over the trade in canned goods. As this market grew, such grocers as Thomas Lipton built chains of stores and, ultimately, incorporated butchers, bakers, and other traditional food suppliers into new supermarkets.

The food-processing industry made its most dramatic advances in the 1950s, a decade when food scientists seemed to have discovered the legendary philosopher's stone. These modern alchemists could grant virtual immortality to foods, and if they failed to create gold, Twinkies came pretty close. With chemical preservatives, breads lasted longer, vegetables maintained their color, and fats did not go rancid. At the same time, vitamins, hormones, and antibiotics increased livestock productivity. Artificial flavors and colors even made it seem possible to do away with plants and animals entirely: A General Foods researcher claimed that there were not enough strawberries grown in the world to meet the demand for Jell-O (Levenstein 1993).

Demand for industrial food products, such as strawberry Jell-O, derived largely from modern marketing techniques, including branding, packaging, and advertising. An early pioneer in this field was the National Biscuit Company, which came to dominate the soda-cracker industry at the turn of the twentieth century. Nabisco packaged its crackers in waxed-paper wrapping to convey a sanitary image quite different from that of the crushed and moldy crackers available in general stores' cracker barrels. In 1899, the company adopted a distinctive, if rather corny, brand name, the "Uneeda" cracker, and with heavy advertising, it captured 70 percent of the American cracker market. Imitators came up with similar names, such as "I wanta cracker" and "Hava cracker," but lacking Nabisco's enormous advertising budget, they proved commercial failures (Levenstein 1988).

Marketing techniques have become more sophisticated with the growth of mass media. Children in particular are the targets of television advertisements for junk foods, such as Chocolate Frosted Sugar Bombs. A recent study found that the odds of a child's being overweight go up by 2 percent for every hour per day spent watching television (O'Neil 1994). Although obesity is not solely a function of watching television, modern marketing techniques can be enormously successful in creating a demand for new foods. For example, Pringles "newfangled" potato chips, made by Procter and Gamble in a Tennessee factory from dehydrated potato mash and shipped across the country in tennis ball cans, seemed a particularly unlikely commercial venture. Nevertheless, with the assistance of a $15 million advertising campaign, the product captured 10 percent of the national market despite the fact that it tasted, as a company executive admitted, "more like a tennis ball than a potato chip" (Levenstein 1993: 197).

Retailers, likewise, contributed to the proliferation of new products. Supermarket chains, in their ongoing effort to maximize sales, stocked ever greater numbers of manufactured foods. Trendy new items were displayed in conspicuous places – at eye level on shelves and at the ends of aisles – where they were more likely to be purchased. Marketing research also found that simply having a superabundance of foods on hand encouraged people to buy more. This "virtuous circle" has seemed to fulfill the capitalist dream of production feeding consumption in never-ending succession. Perhaps the greatest threat to supermarket sales has come not from declining consumption of processed foods but, rather, from the ever-greater convenience offered by fast-food restaurants (MacClancy 1992).

The Rise of Restaurants

Culinary legend credits the French Revolution with having launched the modern restaurant industry. With noblemen fleeing the country or facing the guillotine, great chefs supposedly offered their services to the newly ascendant bourgeoisie by opening restaurants. But in fact, restaurants had already existed for centuries in England and had even begun to spread to the Continent before 1789 (Mennell 1985). Given the French stereotype of being a nation of cooks, it is not surprising that they have claimed the restaurant as their own invention. With more recent trends in fast-food chains, however, it seems only just that history returns the birthplace of the restaurant to its native "nation of shopkeepers."

There may be some truth in the French claim, however, for French haute cuisine reached its highest peaks in nineteenth-century Paris. Chef Antonin Carême (1784–1833) developed an architectural approach to cuisine, not only in the sculpting of elaborate centerpieces but also in the harmonious blending of multiple flavors. He constructed his dishes meticulously from the *fonds* up, adding, extracting, reducing, and garnishing, yet arriving in the end at a simple and unified whole. His successor, Auguste

Escoffier (1846–1935), codified these techniques in the 1902 *Guide Culinaire,* which provided a standard reference work for future chefs.

The consumers of this haute cuisine consisted exclusively of the rich, for no one else could afford its costly ingredients and rarefied preparations. Carême spent his final years working for the Baron James de Rothschild, whereas Escoffier and his partner, César Ritz, founded some of Europe's finest hotels. Their wealthy clients demanded more than refined cuisine; they also wanted constant novelty, preferably in the form of new dishes named in their honor, such as Escoffier's melba toast, named for Austrian opera singer Nellie Melba. Constantly searching for new recipes, chefs often turned for inspiration to traditional peasant dishes, which they transformed by substituting expensive truffles and caviar for more rustic ingredients. The results of this faddish search for novelty are cataloged in Escoffier's *Guide Culinaire,* with its almost 3,000 recipes (Mennell 1985).

It is no oxymoron to speak of a haute cuisine fad, for although few could afford to eat at the great hotels, their cooking styles were followed widely by lesser restaurants in late–nineteenth-century Paris. Jean-Paul Aron (1979) has shown that expensive cuisine became affordable to the masses through the creative use of leftovers. Paris supported thriving networks for distributing secondhand foods, and as the meats and vegetables got older, the sauces covering them got thicker. Fraudulent restaurants displayed counters full of fresh fruits, meats, and vegetables, but these foods were only rented, and clients actually received nothing but leftovers. Even the wine was bad, pressed as it was from the bloated grapes of over-fertilized vines, blended with grain alcohol for added bite, then adulterated with plaster to deepen the color (Loubère 1978).

Concern about impure food in the United States led to perhaps the most important development in the modern restaurant industry, the franchise system. Chains, such as the Fred Harvey System, had long catered to traveling Americans, but although they offered reliable service, the corporate owners often had difficulty finding managers who could turn a profit. Howard Johnson, a Massachusetts businessman, solved this problem in the 1930s by creating a franchise system in which individual owner-operators managed the restaurants and paid royalties to the parent company. Gleaming orange porcelain tile not only advertised the restaurants' cleanliness but was also visible to motorists miles away. Franchising truly came of age in the 1950s, when "Ronald McDonald" became surrogate uncle to the baby-boom generation. McDonald's appealed to suburban families by offering immediate service, made possible by assembly-line grills and drive-through windows. But competing chains soon appeared, and just as the great chefs of Europe struggled to create new dishes, McDonald's, Burger King, and Kentucky Fried Chicken marketed count-

less food fads, from the now-extinct Hulaburger to the seemingly immortal Egg McMuffin (Love 1986; Levenstein 1993).

While fast-food chains sprouted across the landscape, and even gourmet restaurants began using frozen vegetables, a new trend appeared at the highest levels of the restaurant universe. The *nouvelle cuisine* of the 1970s insisted on the use of only the freshest ingredients in the kitchen. Inspired by the great Fernand Point (1897–1955), who shunned Paris to operate a small restaurant in Vienne, the *nouvelle cuisiniers* became chef proprietors in provincial towns. What made their style unique was not the artful decoration of plates borrowed from the Japanese, or the minuscule portions, which led to confusion with the haute dieting of Michel Guérard's *cuisine minceur.* Instead, as Raymond Sokolov (1991) notes, the new recipes parodied rules laid down at the turn of the century by Escoffier. The salmon scaloppine with sorel sauce of Jean and Pierre Troisgros followed the procedure for pounding veal into thin scallops but resulted in a different, more delicate taste. Such chefs as Paul Bocuse eventually rose to become globe-trotting show-business stars, although from that status it was a quick tumble to obscurity.

The nouvelle cuisine attracted perhaps its most devoted following in California, which has always been a natural location for restaurant fads. Trendy chefs wore the spokes off their exotic-ingredient wheels of fortune in the 1980s, and enterprising restaurateurs were willing to invest in any theme, no matter how bizarre. Such places as the Bombay Bicycle Club, Orville Bean's Flying Machine, and Thank God It's Friday each had appropriate wall decor, if not menus. Meanwhile, Ed Debevic's, an upscale version of greasy-spoon diners, demonstrated the powerful appeal of restaurant nostalgia. Owned by Chicago's Lettuce-Entertain-You Restaurant Corporation, Debevic's attempted to recreate the "Happy Days" of the 1950s, but at least one skeptical patron had to ask her gum-smacking waitress: "Is this place fun, or is it just pretending to be?" (Belasco 1993: 241; Gutman 1993; Levenstein 1993).

Coca-Colonization

Critics might question the ambience of restaurants like Debevic's, but no one could doubt the profitability. With annual revenues of more than $4 million per restaurant, the only question for executives was how to grow further, and the answer seemed to lie in global expansion. Food manufacturers had been building international networks for more than a century. Kellogg's shipped breakfast cereals to Europe, Hormel marketed Spam in Latin America, Nestlé sold baby formula in Africa, and Coca-Cola distributed its bottles just about everywhere. But it was not until the 1970s that McDonald's led fast-food franchises into a search for global markets. Once the process had begun, golden arches sprang up in large cities everywhere, and the Big Mac seemed destined to become the culinary standard for middle-class consumers across the planet.

The success of international food marketing derived largely from the prestige value of its Western origins. In peasant societies around the world, the high cost of canned spaghetti and Spam gave these products status appeal far beyond their intrinsic culinary value (Kalčik 1984). Fast-food chains purposely resisted adapting to foreign tastes, calculating that their American origins would maximize sales. Kentucky Fried Chicken, for example, boosted sales in Japan with clever advertisements showing Americans eating the Colonel's chicken for Thanksgiving dinner. One Japanese executive even claimed that "if we eat McDonald's hamburgers and potatoes for a thousand years, we will become taller, our skin will become white, and our hair blonde" (Love 1986: 426).

Not all Japanese wanted white skin and blond hair, however. Many people rejected the foreign products and assumed ultranationalistic attachments to domestic foods, such as rice. More commonly, non-Western nations created industrialized versions of their own native cuisines. Japanese children ate tuna-fish crackers, while their Mexican counterparts munched pork-rind–flavored chips. Coke and Pepsi competed in Asia against local brands of ginseng cola. Unlike McDonald's, they increased sales by reformulating their syrup to suit indigenous tastes, typically by making them even sweeter than the American versions. So even as international capitalism worked to create a homogeneous world cuisine, it also contributed to ethnic diversity.

Food and Morality

Connections between diet and morality are common throughout world history. Jewish and Moslem dietary laws, for example, defined pork as unclean and prohibited its consumption. Many followers of Buddha went further and, out of a belief in reincarnation, abstained from all animal products. Confucius laid down social rather than religious rules for the correct preparation and consumption of foods. Because of their ancient heritage, none of these beliefs qualify as fads. Yet modern advocates of dietary restrictions – branded charlatans, and often with good reason – make similar claims that certain foods must be avoided as either polluted or sacred.

Victorian Movements

Sylvester Graham (1794–1851) originated modern food fads in the United States. About 1830, this Presbyterian minister from Connecticut developed a theory of health and morality he called "the Science of Human Life." He claimed that "natural" living was the secret to happiness and was the only way to avoid the menace of "dyspepsia" or indigestion, at the time a widely feared affliction. The two greatest dangers to a

natural life were an improper diet and sexuality. Graham warned his followers to avoid highly seasoned food, rich pastries, and, especially, meat. These foods stimulated the body, provoked sexual activity, and led to irritation, inflammation, and debility. Physical excitement, in turn, impaired spiritual health; vegetarianism, thus, became vital to personal salvation. Graham lectured up and down the Atlantic coast, building a loyal following and providing a model for future food faddists.

Historian Stephen Nissenbaum (1980) has found the key to Graham's crusade in his namesake bread. Graham decried the widespread consumption of commercially baked white bread and called for a return to coarse, homemade, whole wheat "Graham" bread (very different, despite its name, from the modern "Graham cracker"). The problem lay not in the loss of nutrients from removing the bran; instead, he concluded, white bread was too nutritious for the human body to digest. The additional bulk of whole wheat helped to balance the diet and prevent the alarming excesses caused by the consumption of white bread. According to Nissenbaum, the true concern was not the type of flour but, instead, the rising commercialization of production and the imminent breakdown of family life in Jacksonian America. Graham bread represented a return to a simpler subsistence lifestyle, sheltered by family values from the vagaries of the market economy.

The future of Graham's bread lay, ironically, in the breakfast cereal industry. Dr. James C. Jackson (1811–95), a recovered dyspepsia patient, created the first of these breakfast foods in 1863. "Granula," as he called it, consisted of Graham flour and water, formed into thin sheets and baked, then ground and baked again. The product proved a commercial failure, however, because it had to be reconstituted overnight in milk to provide an edible consistency. This drawback was later overcome by Dr. John Harvey Kellogg (1852–1943), a member of the Seventh-Day Adventist Church, who had adopted Sylvester Graham's dietary doctrines. Kellogg served "Granola" at the Adventist's sanitarium in Battle Creek, Michigan, to patients who included John D. Rockefeller, Theodore Roosevelt, and Amelia Earhart. However, a copyright infringement suit by Jackson prevented him from marketing the product. In 1895, Kellogg and his younger brother Will Keith (1860-1951), who actually founded the eponymous corporation, perfected a ready-to-eat breakfast cereal of wheat flakes, then proceeded to develop corn and rice flakes. But what ultimately made Battle Creek's breakfast cereal industry successful was not the convenience of Kellogg's corn flakes but rather the advertising genius of rival Charles W. Post (1854-1914), who made millions selling his own brand of wheat flakes with outlandish patent medicine claims (Carson 1957).

The Reverend Graham and Dr. Kellogg shared their vegetarian doctrines with European counterparts, such as the German clergyman Eduard Baltzer (1814–87). Influenced by Christoph Wilhelm Hufeland's 1796 work, *Makrobiotik*, which described magical forces for prolonging life, Baltzer published his four-volume *Die natürliche Lebensweise* (The natural way of life), a treatise on vegetarianism, from 1868 to 1872, and also founded Germany's first vegetarian club (Kühnau 1970).

The Victorian preoccupation with dyspepsia gave health advocates an enormous concern for regular bowel movements. Kellogg and others considered three trips to the lavatory a daily minimum. To assure this routine, young boys, in particular, received enemas and mineral oil, for cleansing the body was believed to be the only way of preventing less healthy outlets, such as masturbation. British Prime Minister William E. Gladstone himself stated that to assure proper digestion (and, presumably, regularity), he chewed each bite of food 32 times, once for each tooth. American businessman Horace Fletcher (1852–1919) took this advice to the extreme and chewed food until it dissolved in his mouth. He considered 32 chews sufficient for a piece of bread but claimed that a shallot had once required 720 chews. Although mistaken in his belief that digestion took place in the back of the throat, Fletcher produced remarkably odor-free stools, which he distributed freely by mail. Despite such promotional efforts, the chewing fad quickly passed, but the dream of healthy bowels lives on with the popularity of high-fiber bran cereals (Levenstein 1988; MacClancy 1992).

Nineteenth-century food faddists, although they seem absurd to modern science, nevertheless made a number of sound points. Vegetarian diets with large quantities of whole grains contrasted favorably with the carnivorous appetites of wealthy Victorians. Frequent complaints of indigestion and constipation seem quite understandable among people who consumed beefsteak, mutton chops, corned beef hash, scrambled eggs, fried potatoes, and hot cakes for breakfast (Levenstein 1988).

Science, Reform, and Fads

Elite banquet tables attracted the criticism of scientists as well as faddists. Harvey Levenstein, in a pathbreaking, two-volume social history of food in the United States (1988, 1993), examined how nutritional science affected American diets. Beginning in the late nineteenth century, home economists, the extension agents of this new science, attempted to transform the nation's eating habits. They particularly deplored the diets of newly arrived immigrants, such as Italians, Slavs, and Jews, but immigrant cooks clung tenaciously to their Old World recipes. And contrary to the reformers' expectations, popular awareness of nutrition opened fertile ground for a new generation of food faddists.

Chemists Wilbur Atwater and Ellen Richards initiated the study of domestic science in the United States in the 1880s. Using nutritional methods developed several decades earlier by German researcher Justus von Liebig, they attempted to determine the most efficient way to feed people the required proteins, carbohydrates, and minerals. The ideal diet, they concluded predictably, consisted of New England dishes, such as pressed meat, creamed codfish, boiled hominy, baked beans, and Indian pudding. The only acceptable seasoning was a bland white sauce. Home economists, seeking to gain scientific respectability, distanced themselves from mere cooking teachers, a field in which they perhaps recognized their own incompetence. As a result, they emphasized accuracy over taste, giving students scientifically precise recipes and warning them never to improvise in the kitchen (Shapiro 1986; Levenstein 1988).

Although middle-class housewives dutifully followed their textbook recipes for white sauce, no amount of coaching sufficed to persuade immigrants to give up their ethnic foods. Social workers tried in vain to convince Italian women of the inefficiency of paying high prices for imported pasta and cheeses. They had greater luck in changing the eating habits of children eager to fit in with their peers, even though the milk in school lunches often caused problems for lactose-intolerant ethnic groups. But these children counted as triumphs for the dietary reformers, who were more concerned about assimilating foreigners than improving their diets. Not until World War I, when Italy allied with the United States, did home economists concede that pastas offered an economical source of nutrition at a time of meat shortages (Levenstein 1988).

Dietary reform also became an important program for Mexican leaders around the turn of the twentieth century. They accepted the Victorian idea that spicy foods provoked immorality, and they blamed the disorderly behavior of the working classes on the consumption of chilli peppers. Mexican reformers, like their North American counterparts, established schools of domestic science to inculcate bourgeois family values among poor women. Educational kitchens took as their model diet the bland food of Britain, a drastic change indeed, and one that never caught on among Mexican cooks (Pilcher 1993).

The language of science appealed not only to elite reformers attempting to transform popular behavior but also to food faddists seeking to justify their outlandish claims. Dr. William Howard Hay, for example, used the difference between carbohydrates and proteins to explain eating disorders. This City University of New York medical school graduate developed a theory for the proper combination of foods. He believed that carbohydrates and proteins should never be eaten at the same meal because the body uses alkaline enzymes to digest carbohydrates whereas acids work on proteins. Thus, if a person ate both types of foods together, the alkalines and acids would neutralize one another, the stomach would be unable to digest anything, and the food would simply rot in the intestines. This posed a dilemma, for most foods contain both proteins and carbohydrates. Fortunately, although Hay's combining rules gained great popularity in the 1920s and 1930s, his theory was exposed as flawed because the alkaline enzymes operate in one part of the intestine and the acids in another (Pyke 1970; Deutsch 1977).

Hay's ideas about acids and alkalines, however, were carried to even greater extremes by Alfred W. McCann (1879-1931). A journalist in the muckraking tradition, McCann crusaded against food-processing firms with dramatic headlines that attracted both a wide popular following and numerous libel suits. He also predicted the imminent depletion of world food supplies and advocated the slaughter of all cattle to make grain cheaper. But his most outlandish claim was that Americans suffered from an epidemic of "acidosis." The causes of this supposed acid overdose ranged from improperly combined carbohydrates and proteins to eating meat and processed foods. The deadly effects, as McCann preached tirelessly in the press and on the radio, included "kidneycide" and heart attacks. In 1931, following a radio broadcast warning the public of the dangers of acidosis, McCann himself died of a heart attack (Deutsch 1977).

As with Graham, the food industry ultimately had the last laugh by turning McCann's crusades into advertising copy. The California Fruit Growers, for example, asserted that Sunkist brand citrus fruits actually had a beneficial alkaline effect despite their apparent acidity (Levenstein 1993). By the 1950s, food manufacturers had seemingly conquered American supermarkets with their myriad frozen, condensed, dehydrated, preserved, and otherwise processed products. But a backlash soon developed that revived many of the food fads of the nineteenth century.

The Counterculture Strikes Back

Like Upton Sinclair, who intended his 1906 book *The Jungle* as a radical call for socialism and instead contributed to a middle-class crusade for pure food, the late-1960s counterculture's attempt to overthrow industrial capitalism left one of its deepest imprints on the American diet. Food made an appealing medium of protest, both for its basic role in human life and because of the enormous changes effected by the food-processing industry. The radicals denounced such technological marvels as Wonder Bread, Minute Rice, and instant mashed potatoes, and echoing Sylvester Graham, they called for a return to natural foods, including whole wheat bread, brown rice, and wildflower honey. And although the majority of hippies ultimately abandoned their communes and reincorporated themselves into the society they had condemned, they did bring health foods and herb teas back with them into the mainstream (Belasco 1993).

The counterculture's pure-food protests grew out of news stories concerning the health hazards of pesticides and additives. In her 1962 book *The Silent Spring,* Rachel Carson warned that the pesticide DDT accumulated in the fatty tissue of both humans and animals with potentially fatal results. The U.S. Department of Agriculture insisted that the pesticide posed no danger; nevertheless, within a decade additional studies had confirmed Carson's claim, and the government banned DDT. And this was only the first wave in a flood of media revelations proclaiming the hazards of mercury in tuna, hormones in beef, arsenic in chickens, and carcinogens in bacon (Belasco 1993; Levenstein 1993).

Food-industry spokesmen, with the support of the U.S. Food and Drug Administration (FDA), responded by denying all charges against additives. Working on the theory that anything carbon was natural, they defended the use of petrochemicals as preservatives. They also observed that all foods contained carcinogens, which was true but begged the question of whether additives were in fact harmful in the quantities found in processed foods. Food lobbies' credibility suffered when the public learned of ties between scientific experts and the food industry. Frederick Stare, for example, founder of Harvard's Department of Nutrition and a leading crusader against food fads, testified in support of Kellogg's, Carnation, and other food corporations that donated large sums to his school (Levenstein 1993).

To avoid potential hazards in foods, the counterculture turned for guidance to organic gardening and to health-food experts, such as Jerome Irving (J. I.) Rodale (1899-1971). Rodale had founded the magazine *Organic Gardening and Farming,* in 1940, but had made little money because of the limited interest in compost fertilizers and natural insecticides. Another of his magazines, *Prevention,* was constantly accused of quackery by the medical establishment. By about 1969, however, such abuse by the medical establishment actually benefited Rodale; although by this time his son Robert had taken over editorial duties, hippies who rejected conventional authorities began to follow the Rodale gospel. Wilderness survivalist Euell Gibbons (1911-75) and vitamin supplement advocate Adelle Davis (1904-74) also enjoyed revivals. Perhaps the most persuasive arguments for the vegetarian cause came from Frances Lappé's bestselling *Diet for a Small Planet* in 1971. She relied on science, not mysticism, and based her diet on protein complementarity, those combinations of grains and legumes that supply the full range of amino acids needed for protein utilization. At the same time, her observations about beef cattle displacing peasants resonated with the moral outrage then being expressed by Vietnam War protesters (Deutsch 1977; Belasco 1993; Levenstein 1993).

Counterculture members, in search of social revitalization and alternate methods of health maintenance, often joined groups that were following natural and even mystical lifestyles. The most dedicated withdrew to agrarian communes, but the goal of independence proved elusive, and many survived poor harvests with the help of food stamps. Health-food stores and co-ops boomed during the early 1970s by offering more convenient sources of organically grown products. At the same time, large numbers of people formed communal kitchens, many of which grew into health-food restaurants. Mystical religious groups, such as the Hare Krishna and Divine Light, also contributed to the spread of health foods (Kandel and Pelto 1980; Belasco 1993).

Zen macrobiotics became one of the most controversial of the mystical health-food movements. Created by Japanese philosopher George Ohsawa (early in the twentieth century), macrobiotics applied the principles of yin and yang to food. Animal foods, such as meats and eggs, stood at the yang end of the spectrum while sugar and chemicals tended toward yin. The center included vegetables, fruits, and whole-grain cereals, and a diet of these foods represented the path to harmony with nature. Brown rice formed the exact midpoint, and this alone constituted the ideal macrobiotic diet. Unfortunately, nutritional-deficiency diseases began appearing in the Berkeley area, and in 1965, a young woman starved to death while seeking enlightenment. Nevertheless, macrobiotic restaurants attracted large audiences even among nonbelievers (Fieldhouse 1986; Levenstein 1993).

Other fads, such as the vitamin craze, penetrated deep into mainstream society. Megavitamin advocates claimed that when taken in sufficient quantities, vitamin C cured colds and other infections, whereas vitamin E improved sexual performance. Faddists even invented new vitamins, such as B_{15}, supposedly found in apricot kernels and capable of curing cancer. Scientific support for vitamins came from Nobel Prize–winning scientists Albert Schweitzer and Linus Pauling, and by 1969, half of all Americans regularly took vitamin supplements. Nevertheless, megavitamins provided questionable benefits. Excessive quantities – and some people advocated consuming hundreds of times the recommended daily allowances – of vitamins were simply eliminated by the body (Deutsch 1977; Levenstein 1993).

The health-food movement, considered a fad in the late 1960s and early 1970s, had become an important part of nutritional orthodoxy by the 1990s. Breakfast cereal manufacturers, some of the worst abusers of consumers' nutritional health, reformulated such products as Fruit Loops, Sugar Pops, and Cocoa Krispies to give them nutritional respectability. Meanwhile, artisanal bakers of crusty whole grain breads, although still no threat to the makers of Wonder Bread, have appeared throughout the country. And Alice Waters parlayed a communal kitchen for Berkeley radicals into Chez Panisse – one of the country's most innovative and respected restaurants (Thorne 1992; Belasco 1993; Levenstein 1993).

Food and Identity

Jean-Anthelme Brillat-Savarin (1755–1826), one of the pontiffs of French cuisine, affirmed the connection between cuisine and identity in his often abbreviated phrase, "Tell me what you eat, and I'll tell you who you are." One wonders how the venerable French gourmet would respond to modern food faddists recounting their gastronomic experiences. Certainly, he would find kindred souls among the new generation of globe-trotting gourmets, constantly seeking out variety among diverse ethnic cuisines. The legions of dieters starving themselves to attain fashion-model figures might be more difficult for him to comprehend. But most baffling of all would be the culinary changes wrought by modern technology and mass advertising.

The Obsession with Weight

Historian Hillel Schwartz (1986) dates the origins of the modern obsession with weight to the turn of the twentieth century. Although Victorian dyspepsia cures often resembled contemporary reducing diets, adherents hoped to gain a *feeling* of lightness, rather than to transform their outward appearance. But with the *fin de siècle,* fat went out of fashion. The husky men of Gilded Age banquets were condemned for their conspicuous consumption, while the voluptuous women portrayed in impressionist paintings turned to diets and exercise. Once the general trend toward slimness had begun, it proved difficult to stop. Feminine ideals fluctuated – the boyish flappers of the 1920s gave way to more rounded figures in the 1930s – but the overall trend headed ever downward, and by the 1960s, many considered film stars Marilyn Monroe and Jayne Mansfield to be overweight. The increasingly impossible standards of physical beauty encouraged countless fad diets.

Patent-medicine hucksters quickly saw the potential profits from dieting. Some were relatively benign, such as Jean Down's "Get Slim," which was simply pink lemonade, and Dr. W. W. Baxter's "phytolacca," a purgative found in the pokeberry, and supposedly eaten by overweight migratory birds. Other formulations proved more hazardous, such as "Helen's Liquid Reducer Compound," which promised in the 1930s that you could "Gargle your fat away!" with a compound of peppermint, bleach, and hydrogen peroxide. One of the most dangerous patent medicines of all was an obesity tablet marketed about 1910 that contained strychnine and arsenic (Deutsch 1977; Schwartz 1986).

As scientific knowledge advanced and the FDA's enforcement powers increased, patent medicines were replaced by liquid diets and prescription drugs. The former consisted of food powders mixed with water and taken in place of breakfast and lunch. Beginning in the 1930s with Dr. Stoll's Diet Aid, these milkshake-like concoctions have returned regularly to later generations under the names "Metrecal," "Natur-slim," "Herbalife," and "Slimfast." The 1930s also marked the discovery of amphetamines as appetite suppressants. Although widely prescribed since the 1950s, often with barbiturates to offset the jitters, amphetamines lose their effectiveness after six to ten weeks. Pharmaceutical companies have nevertheless continued to search for dieting drugs, one of the latest being a fat-blocking pill that attempts to prevent the body from absorbing dietary fats (Schwartz 1986).

The diet industry has offered seemingly endless opportunities for market growth and product differentiation. In the 1950s and 1960s, dieters could turn for help to group therapy in TOPS (Take Off Pounds Sensibly), Overeaters Anonymous, and Weight Watchers. The latter company, founded in 1964 by Brooklyn housewife Jean Nidetch, had built revenues of $39 million in little more than a decade. By the 1980s, food manufacturers had focused much of their chemical wizardry on producing an amazing array of "lite" foods, including diet colas, low-calorie "spreads," low-fat cheese foods, light beers and wines, and diet frozen dinners (Schwartz 1986; Belasco 1993).

Self-proclaimed diet experts also kept a constant eye out for new gimmicks, in the process reviving many food fads from the past. Harvey and Marilyn Diamond, for example, in the 1985 best-seller *Fit for Life,* advocated a "natural" life of vegetarianism and Fletcher-style chewing and warned against the mixing of proteins and carbohydrates. Dr. Robert Atkins, meanwhile, had rediscovered the high-protein, low-carbohydrate diet first made famous by Englishman William Banting (1798–1878). *Dr. Atkin's Diet Revolution,* published in 1972, not only sold millions of copies but also served as advertising for his extremely lucrative weight-loss clinic. Susan Powter, author of the 1992 *Stop the Insanity,* reversed this plan and called for a high-carbohydrate, low-fat diet. Best known for her white, crew-cut hair, Powter also marketed highly successful aerobic exercise videos.

The dieting mania dramatizes the continued importance of food in the social construction of identity. Diet and exercise fanatics considered a fashionable body image, rather than health, the ultimate goal. And as the anorexia nervosa epidemic of the 1970s demonstrated, the pursuit of such a fashionable body can ultimately prove hazardous to the health. Actress Jane Fonda admitted that she had suffered from bulimia, making her both advocate and victim of the culture of slimness. It seems appropriate that such a culture first appeared in advanced capitalist countries because the contradictions inherent in this search for perfection have alienated large numbers of people from their own sources of nourishment.

The Ethnic Revival

Food helps define the identity not only of individuals but also of groups. Just as progressive dietary reformers used cooking classes as a means of assimilating immigrants in turn-of-the-century America, people in the postcolonial world have sought to counter Western capitalist hegemony by forging national cuisines. This culinary ethnic revival eventually began to colonize the United States through the combined efforts of talented immigrant cooks and adventuresome American eaters. The resulting mixtures have enriched the diets and tastes of both groups.

Cookbooks defining national cuisines have recently emerged throughout the postcolonial, postindustrial world, and in some places, middle-class women, searching for a national identity to replace colonial ideologies, have often turned to indigenous folk traditions. In Mexico, such traditions have revived the popularity of peasant foods (for example, maize tortillas and tamales), which had formerly been snubbed as Indian foods by both Spanish and Creole elites. Following the revolution of 1910 and the resulting search for Mexico's indigenous roots, an emerging middle class embraced tamales as national symbols. In much the same way, Egyptians proclaimed their patriotism by eating *ful medames,* a peasant bean dish, while Brazilians honored *feijoada,* a combination of meats, beans, and rice similar to African-American "soul food" (Roden 1972; Oliven 1984; Pilcher 1993). In India, the national revival did not seek out lower-class traditions because of strict caste laws about purity. Instead, as Arjun Appadurai (1988) notes, cookbooks allowed middle-class women to experiment with regional recipes and thus eliminate ethnic barriers to Indian nationalism.

As national cuisines appeared in many countries, gastronomic pluralism gained new acceptance in the United States. Historian Donna Gabaccia (1998) shows how ethnic businesses packaged Chinese, Mexican, Italian, and other foreign foods for mainstream American consumers. These enterprises often began as neighborhood restaurants and grocery stores, and although catering at first to immigrant communities, they had to adapt to produce available in the United States. Chow mein, for example, was invented in San Francisco by an immigrant Chinese cook. Recipes often needed further alterations to attract wider audiences, as Italians found when they sold more tomato sauce by limiting the garlic, which most Americans found distasteful. Such modified ethnic foods often gained great popularity; salsa sales recently surpassed those of catsup in the United States. Ethnic identities themselves became blurred by constant mixing as the culinary melting pot produced such hybrids as taco pizza.

Many consumers rejected this trend and sought out more authentic versions of foreign cuisines. Sophisticated diners in the 1960s and 1970s, led by Craig Claiborne of the *New York Times* and Gael Greene of *New York Magazine,* discovered new dialects of French, Italian, and Chinese in the regional cuisines of Provence, Lombardy, and Sichuan. From there it was a small step to the foods of Thailand,

Turkey, Ethiopia, and Argentina. In the 1980s, residents of New York City, Washington, D.C., and San Francisco had to work full time just to keep up with the latest fads in Afghan, Moroccan, and Peruvian restaurants. And those bold enough to seek out ethnic grocers could reproduce exotic dishes at home with the help of cookbooks by Diana Kennedy, Claudia Roden, Ken Hom, and Paula Wolfert or the excellent series by Time-Life Books. Alternately, cooks could follow Jane and Michael Stern across the interstate highway system to sample the regional foods of the United States (Barr and Levy 1984; Levenstein 1993).

The search for ethnic and regional variety eventually percolated down to that culinary lowest common denominator, the fast-food franchise. Taco Bell, the most successful example, mass-marketed a bowdlerized version of border cuisine, while the Golden Wok and Teriyaki Express served up Asian-style fast foods, and Wienerschnitzel claimed German ancestry for its hot dogs. Meanwhile, the drive-through menus of major chains featured regional American dishes, such as McDonald's southern-barbecue–inspired McRib sandwich, and Arby's Philadelphia steak and cheese sandwich. Perhaps the greatest variety in ethnic fast food can be found, appropriately, in the food court of any neighborhood shopping mall. Adolescents searching out new styles in clothes or the latest in music can now take a break for the most recent food fad.

The Meal Is the Message

The pursuit of fashion, whether in food, dress, music, or automobiles, preoccupies many in modern society. People spend enormous sums keeping up with the latest trends, investing not only their money but also their personal identity in constantly changing commodities. For fashionable elites, being seen in the newest restaurant is more important than the meal itself, while the success of a dinner party depends on serving food that the guests have never before tasted. Fashion's arbitrary whims, likewise, facilitate contradictions, such as "lite" foods that are low in fat but high in sodium. As fads come and go, social norms seem increasingly arbitrary, and moral behavior, ultimately, loses all meaning (Finkelstein 1989).

Roland Barthes (1979) notes further that mass-marketed food has expanded far beyond the dining room, invading all aspects of modern life. Snack foods and TV dinners have made eating a part of the media experience; drive-through windows have transformed dashboards into lunch counters (Levenstein 1993). At the same time, the social implications of eating have changed as fast-food combo meals and individually packaged frozen dinners have replaced the traditional family dinner pot. Each person seemingly has greater freedom of choice, yet choices are actually often determined by marketing executives in corporate offices (Mintz 1985).

Important changes have occurred in the production as well as the consumption of food. The alienation of cook from food had already become apparent by the 1950s when cake-mix manufacturers changed the recipe on the boxes to include eggs and oil – at first they required only water – so that people would feel they were actually doing something (Levenstein 1993). But more fundamentally, as John Thorne (1992) has pointed out, the oral culture of the kitchen is being replaced by the written word, and with it an artisanal approach to cooking is giving way to science. Microwave ovens and food processors have taken over the demanding skills needed at the cutting board and over the stove, while cookbooks with fixed recipes, exact measures, and precise times have obviated tasting, smelling, or even watching what is going on in the kitchen. Ironically, a rapid growth in cookbook sales has coincided with a sharp decline in the number of meals eaten at home (Shapiro 1994). Cookbooks have gone from utilitarian kitchen manuals to glossy coffee-table books, travel guides, and parodies, such as the 1989 *Manifold Destiny: The Only Guide to Cooking on Your Car Engine* and *The Bubba Gump Shrimp Co. Cookbook,* which appeared in 1994.

These changes do not necessarily herald the culture of annihilation predicted by Umberto Eco (1968). Mass culture, according to Eco, relies on simple, repetitive formulas, such as commercial jingles, that deny consumers any form of participation in producing and interpreting the message. Yet even, or perhaps especially, small children are far from the defenseless consumers assumed by Eco. Recall the oft-repeated tale of Pop Rocks, a candy that fizzes in the stomach like carbonated water. Some nameless youth of urban legend supposedly ate a bag of Pop Rocks, washed them down with a cola, and then exploded. This story, in its very childishness, reveals a world far different from that of television's Pepsi Generation.

Food has long provided rich material for anthropologists seeking to interpret societies, and in the modern world this symbolic wealth is particularly great in the recent fad of food movies. The darkest fears of Barthes and Eco are played out in the film *Age of Innocence* (1993), where lavish depictions of Delmonico's haute cuisine have more appeal than do the repressed members of Gilded Age high society. Nevertheless, food can also serve as a means to personal fulfillment, both spiritual, in *Babette's Feast* (1987), and sexual, in *Like Water for Chocolate* (1992); both in the workplace, as in *Tampopo* (1987), and at home, as in *Eat, Drink, Man, Woman* (1994). The meaning of food fads, whether they annihilate individual judgment or facilitate culinary expression, must ultimately be decided anew as each philosopher gazes into his or her Cuisinart.

Jeffrey M. Pilcher

Bibliography

Appadurai, Arjun. 1988. How to make a national cuisine: Cookbooks in contemporary India. *Comparative Studies in Society and History* 23: 3–24.

Aron, Jean-Paul. 1979. The art of using leftovers: Paris, 1850–1900. In *Food and drink in history: Selections from the Annales: Économies, Sociétés, Civilisations,* Vol. 5, ed. Robert Forster and Orest Ranum, trans. Elborg Forster and Patricia M. Ranum, 98–108. Baltimore, Md.

Barr, Ann, and Paul Levy. 1984. *The official foodie handbook: Be modern - worship food.* New York.

Barthes, Roland. 1979. Toward a psychosociology of contemporary food consumption. In *Food and drink in history: Selections from the Annales, économies, sociétés, civilisations,* ed. Robert Forster and Orest Ranum, 166–73. Baltimore, Md.

Belasco, Warren J. 1993. *Appetite for change: How the counterculture took on the food industry.* Ithaca, N.Y.

Carson, Gerald. 1957. *Cornflake crusade.* New York.

Deutsch, Ronald M. 1977. *The new nuts among the berries.* Palo Alto, Calif.

Eco, Umberto. 1968. *Apocalipticos e integrados ante la cultura de masas.* Barcelona.

Fieldhouse, Paul. 1986. *Food and nutrition: Customs and culture.* London.

Finkelstein, Joanne. 1989. *Dining out: A sociology of modern manners.* Washington Square, N.Y.

Gabaccia, Donna R. 1998. *We are what we eat: Ethnic food and the making of Americans.* Cambridge, Mass.

Goody, Jack. 1982. *Cooking, cuisine and class: A study in contemporary sociology.* Cambridge.

Gutman, Richard J. S. 1993. *American diner: Then and now.* New York.

Herbert, Victor. 1980. *Nutrition cultism: Facts and fictions.* Philadelphia, Pa.

Kalčik, Susan. 1984. Ethnic foodways in America: Symbol and performance of identity. In *Ethnic regional foodways in the United States: The performance of group identity,* ed. Linda Keller Brown and Kay Mussell, 39–65. Knoxville, Tenn.

Kandel, Randy F., and Gretel H. Pelto. 1980. The health food movement: Social revitalization or alternative health maintenance system? In *Nutritional anthropology: Contemporary approaches to diet and culture,* ed. Norge W. Jerome, Randy F. Kandel, and Gretel H. Pelto, 327–63. Pleasantville, N.Y.

Kühnau, Joachim. 1970. Food cultism and nutrition quackery in Germany. In *Food cultism and nutrition quackery,* ed. Gunnar Blix, 59–68. Uppsala.

Levenstein, Harvey A. 1988. *Revolution at the table: The transformation of the American diet.* New York.

  1993. *Paradox of plenty: A social history of eating in modern America.* New York.

Loubère, Leo. 1978. *The red and the white: A history of wine in France and Italy in the nineteenth century.* Albany, N.Y.

Love, John F. 1986. *McDonald's: Behind the arches.* New York.

MacClancy, Jeremy. 1992. *Consuming culture: Why you eat what you eat.* New York.

Mennell, Stephen. 1985. *All manners of food: Eating and taste in England and France from the Middle Ages to the present.* Oxford.

Mintz, Sidney. 1985. *Sweetness and power: The place of sugar in modern history.* New York.

Nissenbaum, Stephen. 1980. *Sex, diet, and debility in Jacksonian America: Sylvester Graham and health reform.* Chicago.

Oliven, Ruben George. 1984. The production and consumption of popular culture in Brazil. *Latin American Perspectives* 11: 103–15.

O'Neil, Patrick M. 1994. Saturday morning commercials short on veggies, long on sugar. *Charleston Post and Courier.* December 18.

Pilcher, Jeffrey M. 1993. ¡Vivan tamales! The creation of a Mexican national cuisine. Ph.D. thesis, Texas Christian University, Fort Worth.

Pyke, Magnus. 1970. The development of food myths. In *Food cultism and nutrition quackery,* ed. Gunnar Blix, 22–9. Uppsala.

Roden, Claudia. 1972. *A book of Middle Eastern food.* New York.

Schwartz, Hillel. 1986. *Never satisfied: A cultural history of diets, fantasies, and fat.* New York.

Shapiro, Eben. 1994. Thousands of cookbooks in search of some cooks. *Wall Street Journal.* March 2, Sec. B, p. 1.

Shapiro, Laura. 1986. *Perfection salad: Women and cooking at the turn of the century.* New York.

Sokolov, Raymond. 1991. *Why we eat what we eat: How the encounter between the New World and the Old changed the way everyone on the planet eats.* New York.

Tannahill, Reay. 1988. *Food in history.* New York.

Thorne, John. 1992. *Outlaw cook.* New York.

Young, James Harvey. 1989. *Pure food: Securing the Federal Food and Drugs Act of 1906.* Princeton, N.J.

VI.13 ❧ Food Prejudices and Taboos

Over the past 2,000 years, scholars have produced a vast literature on food prejudices and taboos. This literature, however, is complicated by confusing etymology and indiscriminate or inconsistent application of several terms, such as food aversions, avoidances, dislikes, prejudices, prohibitions, rejections, and taboos/tabus.

The term *aversion* is used by food-habit researchers primarily in the context of disliked or inappropriate foods, whereby individuals elect not to consume items because of specific, defined, biological or cultural criteria. Some human food aversions, for example, are immediate as when foods are tasted and disliked because of sensory properties of odor, taste, and texture. Other foods are avoided because of biological-physiological conditions posed by nausea and vomiting, "heartburn" or "acid stomach," intestinal distress associated with flatulence, or acute diarrhea. Still other food aversions are cultural or psychological in origin, as evidenced when individuals report that they dislike specific foods even though the items have never been consumed by them. In such instances, anticipation triggers avoidance or aversive behavior, and merely the color, shape, or images of the food source itself are enough to elicit aversion and the individual decision not to eat.

The word *taboo* or *tabu,* in contrast, implies a moral or religious context of foods or food-related behavior. Taboo, the Polynesian concept to "set apart," includes the suggestion that some human activities, and eating behavior specifically, may be either protective or deleterious to the environment, to the consumer, or to society at large. Food-related taboos in this context are identical to dietary prohibitions, whereby foods and food-related behaviors are forbidden for specific positive or negative reasons.

Attached to food prohibitions and taboos are a broad range of ecological, economic, religious, and social attributes that define intake restriction. Thus, consumption of prohibited foods may produce serious consequences for individuals, groups, and societies at large, and as a result, violators may face personal and social condemnation. Some taboos may be imposed to protect food crops at specific periods of the growth cycle, whereas other food-related practices may be instituted to distribute economic gain more effectively among individuals or groups in society. Most food-related taboos, however, are religious in nature and are imposed to provide structure and to regulate individual and social behavior.

Although individual food dislikes may lead to food rejection and, ultimately, to food prejudice, food dislikes are not dietary prohibitions or taboos. Nor are food aversions. Taboos, in essence, have their basis in behavioral, ecological, and religious strictures. Accordingly, all food-related taboos result in avoidance behavior – but food-related avoidance patterns may not result in taboos.

Approaches, Paradigms, and Themes

Scholars interested in the origins, development, and evolution of food prejudices and taboos range from professionals in the humanities to researchers in the biological and medical sciences (Frazer 1935; Gaster 1955; Simoons 1961, 1978; Douglass 1977; Grivetti 1978a, 1981a). The literature presented within this broad spectrum poses a basic conflict. Anchored at one end are representative descriptive studies where explanations for food-avoidance behavior and dietary taboos are set within concepts of folklore and mythology and where magic and superstition play important interpretive roles.

In opposition to this approach are studies by researchers who reject such empiricism and seek scientific understanding of and validation for human food-related behavior. Some scholars argue that there is logic in the so-called protective magic of food taboos, whereas others seek the rationale for dietary prohibitions in causal relationships between ingestion and manifestation of disease.

A review of food-habit literature from antiquity to the twentieth century reveals that scholars have advanced at least 11 hypotheses to explain the origins of dietary codes (Grivetti and Pangborn 1974; Grivetti 1980):

1. Aesthetics: Prohibitions are instituted because the appearance, behavior, source, or origin of certain foods is aesthetically revolting, contaminating, or polluting to humans (Douglas 1966).
2. Compassion: Prohibitions are intended to demonstrate human compassion toward specific animals that might otherwise serve as food resources (Scott 1866; Chadwick, 1890).
3. Divine commandment: Prohibitions have their origins in instructions directly to humans by a god, priestly intermediaries, or other cultural authorities. Adherents reject twentieth-century attempts at scientific enquiry and explanation (Singer 1907).
4. Ecology: Prohibitions evolve because of logical interrelations between human economic systems and the environment that ultimately determine which foods will be favored or rejected (Harris 1972, 1973).
5. Ethnic identity: Prohibitions are instituted to strengthen ethnic bonds that reinforce cultural identification by setting practitioners apart from food-related practices of other societies (Mays 1963).
6. Health and sanitation: Prohibitions reflect religious or medical insights on causal associations between ingestion and disease or illness (Arrington 1959).
7. Literary allegory: Prohibitions are not directed toward food, per se, but serve instead as oblique references to other behavioral, cultural, or political nonfood practices (Novatian 1957; Ginzberg 1961).
8. Natural law: Food-related behaviors and prohibitions are instituted to reinforce concepts of compassion and to identify abominations and define "unnatural" appetite gratification (Mackintosh 1959; Cook 1969).
9. Self-restraint/denial: Prohibited foods, once highly desired, are forbidden by priests or other cultural authorities to reduce gastronomic pleasure and to teach and reinforce moral discipline (Kellogg 1899).
10. Staple conservation: Prohibitions and taboos are established to conserve and extend the food supply, thereby improving human survival potential during periods of environmental crisis or conflict (Thompson 1949).
11. Sympathetic magic: Food prohibitions are related to specific behavioral or physical characteristics of animals and qualities that humans wish to avoid (Frazer 1935; Gaster 1955).

Although there have been thousands of descriptions of food and food-related taboos from antiquity into the twentieth century, contemporary analysis of how and why dietary prohibitions have evolved and how taboos and practices stabilize social and ethnic groups stems from the classic studies of food patterns and human food-related behavior in southern African societies (Richards 1932, 1939; Willoughby 1932).

Regarding thematic approaches taken by researchers on food prejudices and taboos, the most attractive and recognized theme has been religion, given the extensive literature on the dietary taboos of the major world faiths as exemplified by (1) Judaism (Kaufman 1957; Korff 1966; Cohn 1973; Dresser 1979; Regenstein and Regenstein 1979, 1988, 1991); by (2) Christianity (Hehn, 1885; Simoons 1961; Knutsson and Selinus 1970; Bosley and Hardinge 1992; Pike 1992); by (3) Islam (Roberts 1925; Sakr 1971, 1975; Grivetti 1975; Rahman 1987; Twaigery and Spillman 1989; Chaudry, 1992); and by (4) Hinduism (Harding 1931; Prakash 1961; Grivetti 1991a; Kilara and Iya 1992).

Gender and age are perhaps the second most common theme, and especially the question of how dietary prohibitions or taboos reinforce sex roles in society and characterize rites of passage, such as birth, coming of age, marriage, and death (Frazer 1935; Gaster 1955; Douglas 1966, 1977; Garine 1972).

A third common theme involves protection and takes two directions. One of these focuses on the question of whether dietary prohibitions are protective medically or nutritionally to humans (Bolton 1972; Jelliffe and Jelliffe 1978). The second has to do with whether dietary taboos protect the cultural-ecological setting of different societies and provide a balance to human use of environmental resources (Heun 1962; McDonald 1977).

Religion

Many religious practices that developed in antiquity and still regulate human behavior and social activities are known from accounts written in ancient Egypt and also stem from the religious practices and dietary codes of Judaism, Christianity, Islam, and Hinduism.

Ancient Egypt

The Nile Valley civilizations present a rich archaeological record and literature that reveal food-related practices, cooking, dining, and food patterns, and dietary prohibitions (Loret, 1892; Keimer 1924; Emery 1962; Darby, Ghalioungui, and Grivetti 1977). Although numerous dietary taboos are known from ancient Egypt, only two are reviewed here.

Cattle and beef. Herodotus (*The Histories* 11:41), writing in the fifth century B.C., stated that local Egyptian priests abstained from beef, especially the flesh of cows, and that this dietary pattern extended beyond the geographical limits of Egypt westward into Libya. Such a taboo attached to beef was also described in the fourth century B.C. by Philochorus

of Athens, who attempted to explain the practice when he wrote that

> at one time, also when there was a dearth of cows, a law was passed, on account of the scarcity, that they [the Egyptians] should abstain from these animals since they wished to amass them and fill up their numbers not be slaughtering them (Philochorus, cited in Athenaeus 1927–41, 9:375:C).

Porphyry (1965, 2:11), writing in the third century A.D., provided a relatively late glimpse of what might be taken as the impact of the beef prohibition in ancient Egypt when he stated that: "[w]ith the Egyptians . . . any one would sooner taste human flesh than the flesh of a cow."

Greek and Roman texts notwithstanding, the archaeological evidence emphatically disputes the presence of a sweeping beef taboo throughout ancient Egypt. Tomb and temple art throughout the dynastic period, 3200–341 B.C., provides abundant pictorial evidence of bovine slaughter and butchering. Indeed, thousands of carvings and paintings depict the capture and killing of cattle, butchers at work cutting up the carcasses, the display of beef haunches and organ meats in shops, and boiling and roasting beef (Darby et al. 1977).

It is true that specific types of bulls were worshiped at the urban sites of Heliopolis, Hermonthis, and Memphis, and that cows were worshiped throughout the Nile Valley as the incarnation of the goddesses Hathor and Isis. But such deification did not inhibit beef consumption throughout the Nile Valley of ancient Egypt at all geographical localities (Monet 1958).

Other writers, however, have readily accepted the Greek texts, ignored the archaeological data, and attempted explanations for Egyptian beef avoidance. J. G. Wilkinson, for example, wrote that "by a prudent foresight, in a country possessing neither extensive pasture lands, nor great abundance of cattle, the cow was held sacred and consequently was forbidden to be eaten" (Wilkinson 1854).

Yet deification of bulls and cows in ancient Egypt was not related to available pasture land or threatened extinction but to specific physical characteristics of individual bulls and cows (Darby et al. 1977). Furthermore, given the wide range of texts that clearly identify offerings of meat from bulls, bullocks, calves, and cows, it is erroneous to conclude that there was a sweeping beef prohibition associated with Egyptians of all periods. It may be that a more limited beef prohibition was intact during late- and postdynastic times, but it is not possible to state, categorically, whether the prohibition applied to all varieties of beef, or specifically to cows, or perhaps to female calves, or to other bovine categories (Darby et al. 1977).

Another aspect of the late dynastic beef prohibition deserves attention since it relates not to meat, per se, but to the Egyptian manner of butchering. Herodotus (*The Histories* 4:1) commented that "[n]o native of Egypt, whether man or woman . . . will use the knife of a Greek . . . or taste the flesh of an ox, known to be pure, if it has been cut with a Greek knife." Because the ancient Egyptian standard method of butchering was to cut the throat, then drain and collect the blood for food, it may be that this passage indicates some significant differences in butchering techniques between Egyptians and Greeks. It could also, of course, be taken as evidence of (or it possibly reflected) an Egyptian aloofness and sense of superiority over the Greeks (Darby et al. 1977).

Fish. Fish held a dual position throughout the dynastic period of ancient Egyptian history. Texts and tomb art document geographical locations where (and historical periods when) fishing was an accepted occupation and eating fish was acceptable. Indeed, Egyptian kings regularly supplied beef, fish, and vegetables to soldiers as military rations and sometimes presented fresh and dried fish as temple offerings. But other passages and depictions indicate that priests abstained from fish, that fishing as a profession was abhorrent, and that fish eaters were ceremonially impure (Darby et al. 1977).

Five specific varieties of Nile fish figured prominently in Egyptian religion and were widely rejected as food: the latus *(Lates niloticus;* perhaps *Tilapia nilotica),* the lepidotus *(Barbus bynni),* the maeotes (possibly a siluride), the oxyrhynchus *(Mormyrus* spp.), and the phagrus (identification uncertain; possibly *Hydrocyon forskalii).* The latus was worshiped at the site of Esna where thousands of mummified examples have been discovered, but reverence and dietary avoidance of this species at Esna did not preclude its widespread consumption elsewhere along the Nile.

The lepidotus was revered throughout the Nile Valley and thus widely rejected as food. The maeotes was worshiped near Aswan where it was rejected as food because it was considered a harbinger of the Nile flood. The oxyrhynchus was universally avoided as food for two distinctive reasons: The fish was associated with the god Seth, whose followers rejected it out of respect, whereas the followers of Osiris avoided oxyrhynchus because this species reportedly fed upon the phallus of their deity and, therefore, was an abomination. The phagrus was rejected for two reasons: (1) because its appearance also signaled the Nile flood, and (2) because it, too, had fed upon the phallus of Osiris (Darby et al. 1977).

Judaism

Two central texts present the Jewish dietary traditions and laws. The Torah stems from ancient oral traditions and was codified in its present literary form by, perhaps, the sixth century B.C. The Talmud, pro-

duced in Babylon and Jerusalem in the sixth century A.D., provides guidelines for Jewish moral conduct and incorporates numerous discussions and critical assessments of food and food-related issues.

Study of the Torah and Talmud suggests the development and evolution of Jewish dietary codes through seven stages:

Stage One: In Genesis 1:29–31, all products on earth are clean.

Stage Two: In Genesis 1:29–31, plant food constituted the initial diet of humans.

Stage Three: At the time of the flood, in Genesis 7:1–2, clean and unclean animals are differentiated, but not identified or specified.

Stage Four: In Genesis 7:1–2, both clean and unclean animals are saved and brought into the ark.

Stage Five: In Genesis 9:3–4, Noah and his descendants are permitted all food except blood after the biblical flood. An appropriate human diet is defined as a combination of plant and flesh foods.

Stage Six: Clean and unclean flesh foods are identified and specified, other forbidden foods and food-related behaviors are codified:

A. Clean meats were specified in Leviticus 11:2–3, 9, 21–2; and Deuteronomy 14:4–6, 9, 11, 20.

B. Unclean meats are discussed in Leviticus 11:4–8, 10–20, 23–31, 41–4; and Deuteronomy 14:7–8, 10, 12–19.

C. Blood was prohibited in Genesis 9:3–4; Deuteronomy 12:16, 23–4, and 15:23; 1 Samuel 14:32–4; and Ezekiel 44:7, 15.

D. Carrion was prohibited in Exodus 22:31; Leviticus 11:39–40, 17:15–16, 22:8; Deuteronomy 14:21; and Ezekiel 4:14.

E. Fat was prohibited in Exodus 29:13, 22; Leviticus 3:3–4, 9–10, 17, 23–5, and 9:19–20; 1 Samuel 2:15–16; and 2 Chronicles 7:7.

F. Meat offerings to idols were prohibited in Exodus 34:15.

G. Sinew was prohibited in Genesis 32:32.

H. Food contaminated by dead animals was prohibited in Leviticus 11:37–8.

I. Seed contaminated by dead animals was prohibited in Leviticus 11:37–8.

J. Food from the inside of a house where a person has died was prohibited in Numbers 19:14–15.

Stage Seven: Regulations forbidding mixing meat and milk products (Epstein 1948) are believed to stem from the commandment not to seeth a kid in its mother's milk in Exodus 23:19, 34:26; and Deuteronomy 14:21.

Clean-unclean food lists. The form, structure, and content of the clean and unclean food lists of Leviticus and Deuteronomy have remained the subject of considerable interest and debate since the early years of the Christian era (Barnabas 1961). If the clean and unclean food lists are examined in light of twentieth-century archaeological data and linguistic advances, two basic questions emerge. These concern translation accuracy and assignment rationale.

Taking up the question of translation accuracy first, an examination of Table VI.13.1 reveals linguistic consistency throughout the centuries for a number of specific forbidden foods, among them *arnevet* (hare), *gamal* (camel), and *hazir* (pig). The translations of other terms for forbidden foods, however, have not been consistent, and through the years some have been quite variable. The term *a'nakah,* for example, has been translated variously as ferret or gecko; *'aiyah* as crow, falcon, hawk, kite, and vulture; *homet* as lacerta, lizard, sand lizard, snail, and winding lizard; and *tinshemet* has been rendered variously as barn owl, chameleon, maldewerp, and mole.

Most identification and translation problems concern amphibians, birds, and reptiles. The difficulty lies with honest attempts at zoological identification based upon incomplete linguistic evidence, set within a wide range of possible eastern Mediterranean faunal representatives. Such linguistic difficulties were compounded in recent centuries when Christian missionaries translated the Old Testament into languages far removed from the origins of Judaism, where Mediterranean animals did not exist.

In the area of assignment rationale, the question of why foods became listed as clean or unclean has also been the subject of considerable debate. Seven of the eleven hypotheses discussed in the section "Approaches, Paradigms, and Themes" have been employed by various authors to support the origins of the Jewish dietary codes. Only three, however, can be critically examined: health or sanitation, ethnic identity, and ecological arguments (Grivetti and Pangborn 1974).

Table VI.13.1. *Selected forbidden foods: Leviticus (Hebrew source with English translations)*

	Chapter-verse with Hebrew term								
	Selected consistent translations				Selected inconsistent translations				
English source	11:4 gamal	11:5 shofan	11:6 arnevet	11:7 hazir	11:14 'aiyah	11:18 ka'at	11:30 a'nakah	11:30 homet	11:30 tinshemet
Lexicons									
Alcalay, 1962	Camel	Rock badger	Hare	Swine	Hawk	Pelican	Ferret	Lizard	Chameleon
Einspahr, 1977	Camel	Coney	Coney	Pig	Falcon	Night bird	Ferret	Lizard	Barn owl
		Dassie	Hare	Swine	Hawk	Pelican			Chameleon
		Rabbit	Rabbit		Vulture				
Torah									
1962	Camel	Rock badger	Hare	Swine	Falcon	Pelican	Gecko	Sand lizard	Chameleon
Bibles									
1530	Camel	Coney	Hare	Swine	Vulture	Pelican	Hedgehog	Snail	Mole
1560	Camel	Coney	Hare	Swine	Kite	Pelican	Rat	Stellio	Mole
1609	Camel	Cherogrillus	Hare	Swine	Vulture	Bittern	Shrew	Lizard	Mole
1611	Camel	Coney	Hare	Swine	Kite	Pelican	Ferret	Snail	Mole
1782	Camel	Coney	Hare	Swine	Kite	Pelican	Ferret	Snail	Mole
1805	Camel	Coney	Hare	Swine	Kite	Pelican	Hedgehog	Snail	Mole
1850	Camel	Cirogrille	Hare	Swine	Crow	Swan	Mygal	Lacerta	Maldewerp
1897	Camel	Coney	Hare	Swine	Falcon	Swan	Ferret	Winding lizard	Mole
1950	Camel	Rock badger	Hare	Pig	Falcon	Water hen	Ferret	Sand lizard	Chameleon
1953	Camel	Coney	Hare	Swine	Kite	Pelican	Ferret	Snail	Mole
1965	Camel	Coney	Hare	Swine	Falcon	Swan	Gecko	Sand lizard	Chameleon
1966	Camel	Hyrax	Hare	Pig	Buzzard	Ibis	Gecko	Chameleon	Tinshemet
1970	Camel	Rock badger	Hare	Pig	Black kite	Pelican	Fanfoot gecko	Sand lizard	Chameleon
1970	Camel	Rock badger	Hare	Pig	Falcon	Desert owl	Gecko	Skink	Mole
1973	Camel	Rock badger	Hare	Hog	Buzzard	Pelican	Ferret	Snail	Mole
1973	Camel	Rock badger	Hare	Swine	Falcon	Pelican	Gecko	Sand lizard	Chameleon
1976	Camel	Rock badger	Hare	Pig	Falcon	Horned owl	Gecko	Great lizard	Chameleon
1978	Camel	Coney	Rabbit	Pig	Black kite	Desert owl	Gecko	Skink	Chameleon
1981	Camel	Coney	Hare	Swine	Kite	Pelican	Gecko	Snail	Chameleon
1981	Camel	Coney	Rabbit	Pig	Black kite	Desert owl	Gecko	Skink	Chameleon
1989	Camel	Rock badger	Hare	Pig	Kite	Desert owl	Gecko	Sand lizard	Chameleon
1990	Camel	Rock badger	Hare	Pig	Kite	Desert owl	Gecko	Sand lizard	Chameleon

In the matter of *health and sanitation,* however, it is not logical to presume that the ancients were more observant and astute medically than nineteenth- and twentieth-century scientific physicians. Furthermore, few foods on the forbidden or unclean list pose direct health threats to consumers, whereas some foods on the clean list are vectors for anthrax, brucellosis, and various parasitic diseases.

Explanations based on *ethnic identity* presume that foods on the unclean list were once the dietary prerogatives of the ancient Egyptians, Canaanites, or other societies among whom the ancient Israelites lived or whom they had as geographical neighbors. Such explanations also hold that foods on the Jewish clean list once were prohibited or forbidden to non-Jews in the Mediterranean region. Analysis reveals that the ancient Egyptians in certain geographical areas and during certain historical periods ate pork, and they also consumed bustard, hare, locust, and ostrich. Moreover, several other animals on the Jewish unclean food list were worshiped by the ancient Egyptians, among them egret, hawk, heron, and vulture. But some meats on the clean list, such as beef, goat, and lamb, were also consumed, and cattle, goats, and sheep were worshiped by the ancient Egyptians (Darby et al. 1977).

The *ecological* hypothesis applied to pork avoidance suggests that pigs in the Mediterranean region could not compete economically with sheep and goats because they offered no hair products or milk, posed herding difficulties, and were ill suited to Middle Eastern heat. Supporters also state that as swine were in direct competition for scarce water and food resources, forbidding pork as food would not have been likely to cause sociocultural difficulties (Harris 1972, 1973). Archaeological evidence, however, can be used to counter these arguments because pigs were raised in Egypt for more than 5,000 years and, thus, were hardly ill suited to the region (Darby et al. 1977).

Ritual slaughter. The Judaic preparation of meat is characterized by a highly structured ritual that regulates slaughter, butchering, meat preparation, and cooking. Common explanations for the religious laws governing these practices suggest that compliance assures that meat products will be religiously suitable, that ritual requirements for human consumption will be met, and that meats prepared in such a manner will be safe for consumption (Levin and Boyden 1940; Maimonides 1956, 1967).

Within Judaism, meats are divided into two categories: *kosher,* or fit and suitable for human consumption, and *terephah,* or forbidden and unsuitable. Both kinds of meats are found in the food lists of Leviticus and Deuteronomy. In essence, terephah animals and meat products always are forbidden and never suitable as human food, whereas kosher meats and products may become terephah if ritual law is not followed.

The butcher must be an Orthodox Jew and in normal practice is a rabbi or a trained rabbinical designate. The butcher is responsible for inspecting animals prior to slaughter and declaring whether or not all accepted religious criteria are met. Thus, animals selected must be certified alive just before slaughter; a knife and no other instrument must be used. The cut must be made without hesitation or pause, in a straight line directly across the throat, with a motion that severs both gullet and windpipe.

Once the throat has been cut, the animal is suspended and bled. The cut is inspected carefully by the butcher, and if any minor lacerations are detected along the cut line, the meat is declared terephah. Similarly, after the carcass is skinned and muscle tissues inspected, there must be no ruptured blood vessels. Next, the lungs are inflated, placed under water, and inspected for any bubbles that might appear; if detected, the meat is declared terephah. Internal organs, including gall bladder, heart, kidney, liver, intestines, spleen, and stomach, are also examined for a wide range of critical signs that determine whether or not meat from the carcass will be classified as fit or unfit (Levin and Boyden 1940).

After inspection and certification, only the forequarters of the animal can be used as food; hindquarters are terephah. Rejection of the hindquarters is symbolic and linked with the account in Genesis 32:32 of Jacob's wrestling with an angel who touched Jacob on the ischiatic nerve.

In modern times, if the carcass meat must be held in a cooler for more than 72 hours, or if transportation of the carcass will exceed 72 hours, the meat must be ritually washed, otherwise kosher status is lost and the meat is reclassified terephah (Lipschutz 1988).

Because the eating of blood is prohibited, several food preparation and cooking techniques have been devised through the centuries that separate Orthodox Jews from others. Kosher meats are soaked in tap water, salted on all surfaces, then placed on a slanted drain board. They are rinsed twice to remove the salt. Rare meat is terephah and so all meats must be cooked thoroughly. As a consequence, cooking techniques, such as broiling and boiling, became institutionalized in order to meet the religious law and maintain kosher designation (Grunfeld 1972; Lipschutz 1988).

Meat and milk. Within the Jewish food tradition, kosher foods are assigned one of three categories: *fleishig* (meat and meat products), *milchig* (milk and dairy products), and *parveh* (neutral foods, defined as all other permitted foods). A wide range of laws govern the cooking and blending of these three categories: Fleishig and milchig foods can never be blended or combined, whereas parveh items, because of their neutral status, may be mixed with either meat or milk and dairy items. This strict observance of not mixing meat with milk is called *basar be halab.*

Yet the Jewish injunction against mixing meat and milk is not specifically defined in the Torah. Scholars searching for the basis of the *basar be halab* law consider three oblique Torah references with the common admonition found in Exodus 23:19, 34:26; and Deuteronomy 14:21: "Thou shall not seeth a kid in its mother's milk." But examination of the Torah also reveals that Jews once readily consumed meat and milk together at the same meal. And in Genesis (18:7–8) it is written that "Abraham ran unto the herd, and fetcht a calf tender and good, and gave it unto a young man; and he hastened to dress it. And he took butter, and milk, and the calf which he had dressed, and set it before them; and he stood by them under the tree, and they did eat."

Nonetheless, the laws and regulations that govern the dietary separation of meat and milk products are outlined in a wide range of Talmud texts, as noted by Akiba ben Joseph (A.D. 50–132), who stated that every kind of flesh is forbidden to be cooked in milk (Epstein 1948, 8:104a).

Talmud discussions define that which constitutes meat and milk, along with the concept of mixing (Grivetti 1980). The ancient rabbis agreed that beef certainly was meat but differed as to the definitions of poultry and fish. Most Orthodox Jews, both historically and in modern times, have considered poultry to be fleishig, but a minority view, championed by Rabbi Jose of Galilee (first to second century A.D.), held that poultry should be designated parveh and, thus, permitted to be mixed with either milchig or fleishig foods. Jose's semantical and biological argument was based on the premise that it was impossible to seeth poultry in "mother's milk"; although fowl could be mothers, they were incapable of producing milk (Mishayoth 8:4 in Blackman 1964).

What constitutes milk was easily answered in the ancient Mediterranean world: Permitted milks could come only from mammals on the clean-food lists. The definition of milk, however, has become less clear during the twentieth century with the use of nondairy cream substitutes prepared from soy-based products. Some nondairy creamers, for example, contain the milk protein sodium caseinate, which would make the product milchig; soy-based milks, however, would be parveh and permitted to be mixed with fleishig products (Freedman 1970).

Definitions for mixing involve less obvious considerations. It seems clear that foods blended during the preparation or cooking process would be classified as mixed, but Orthodox Jewish tradition presents expanded, broader definitions that allude to concepts of proximity and touching.

Consider, for example, that two people, not related to each other, sit at the same table but dine separately: One wishes to consume roast beef, the other cheese. If both persons sitting at the table are Orthodox Jews, the law governing mixing of meat and milk is broken. But if one is Orthodox and the other gentile, the law

is maintained and differentiation is based upon proximity and the probability of social exchange: If the two were Orthodox they would experience the temptation to share food because of ethnic affiliation or because of friendship (Epstein 1948, 8:107b).

Mixing presents other difficulties as well. Suppose that an Orthodox Jew wishes to purchase meat and cheese from different sections of the same store. When purchased, the products are wrapped separately, then placed inside a shopping bag. In this case, the law is not broken because fleishig and milchig products cannot touch physically (Epstein 1948, 8:107b). But when both categories of wrapped food are carried into the consumer's house, and then unwrapped, the law is precise: Fleishig and milchig products must be placed inside separate pantries. Furthermore, in the modern era of electricity, both categories of food must be kept inside separate refrigerators, and specific parveh foods must not be interchanged with the other refrigerator; otherwise all such items become terephah. Food preparation and cooking of meat or milk products must be done independently, using separate sets of utensils and appliances for fleishig and milchig products. Similarly, meat and milk dishes must be baked, broiled, or otherwise cooked inside separate ovens (Korff 1966; Grunfeld 1972).

Mixing meat and milk also includes the question of time. How long, for example, should consumers wait before dining on the other food class so that the two food categories do not mix inside the human body? Rabbi Hisda (third century A.D.) stated that the order of consumption determined the law: Meat could be eaten immediately after cheese, but one day had to pass if the order was reversed. In contrast, Rabbi Ukba (third to fourth century A.D.) argued that the order of consumption was unimportant and that one day must pass before consuming any food from the other category (Epstein 1948, 8:105a). By the twelfth century A.D., however, a compromise had been reached: a wait of six hours between meals of either food class (Kaufman 1957; Maimonides 1967).

Cultural-religious manifestation of the dietary separation of meat and milk are readily observable in Orthodox Jewish homes, less so in Conservative Jewish homes, and not usually apparent in Reform Jewish homes. Among the Orthodox, the following conditions are required when keeping the law: separate sets of table linen, separate pantries for food storage, separate electrical appliances and food preparation utensils, separate ovens (and microwave ovens) for cooking fleishig and milchig meals, separate condiment containers for meat and dairy dishes, and separate dishwashers (Frazer 1919; Gaster 1955; Natow, Iteslin, and Raven 1975).

Basar be halab. A wide range of arguments have been advanced to explain the law of *basar be halab.* Several have argued that the Torah passages are mistranslated, or that the law originally did not forbid boiling or preparing meat and milk together, but was intended to apply to cooking or mixing meat with blood (Cheyne 1907; Smith 1969). Others feel that the basis was one of "Natural Law and Divine Order," that cooking a kid in the milk of its mother would be an abomination and contrary to nature (Scott 1866; Mackintosh 1959; Cook 1969). Still others have explained the law using the argument that the ancient Jews were a compassionate people, not prone to acts that would lead to a baby goat's being boiled in the fluid intended for its own nourishment (Chadwick 1890).

Early writers such as Philo (1954, 4:16:97, 4:17:111, 4:24:124) offered still another explanation when he wrote that the meat-milk codes were instituted because the two foods in combination were stimulating and pleasure giving to the consumer and, therefore, should be denied to demonstrate self-restraint.

Other commentators have suggested that the reason might have to do with sympathetic magic, specifically the belief that animals could control their milk after humans had obtained it. In this case, the boiling or heating of milk would have been tantamount to applying fire to cattle udders. These writers suggest that the code was a part of widespread cultural practices adopted to protect herds, lest the cattle be damaged (Frazer 1907a, 1907b, 1919; Schmidt 1926).

Still other writers conclude that the basis for the dietary separation of meat and milk was based upon considerations of food spoilage and bacterial contamination. They have argued that given the hot, desert conditions found throughout the Middle East, although both meat and dairy products spoil, they spoil more quickly if blended. This view, however, may be easily rejected since blended foods, in fact, do not spoil more rapidly than meat or milk products served alone (van den Heever 1967).

Within Judaism, meat and milk are forbidden in combination - yet meat and milk dishes are highly esteemed within Islam. Middle Eastern Muslims, in turn, reject dietary combinations of fish and milk - yet fish and milk dishes are desirable within Judaism. These acceptable and forbidden patterns of mixing foods clearly have separated Jews and Muslims in the Middle East since at least the seventh century A.D. when Muslim forces invaded and occupied the lands of ancient Palestine. Since that time, the meat-milk and fish-milk prohibitions have served as ethnic markers and as a clear means of religious and cultural separation (Grivetti 1975, 1980).

Other food-related issues. A wide range of Jewish dietetic rules codified in the Torah and Talmud have been reviewed and summarized by modern scholars (Preuss 1978). One important Talmud directive encourages eating in moderation with the saying, "More people have died at the cooking pot, than have been victims of starvation" (Shabbach 33a). Salt and yeast are identified as harmful to consumers if eaten in large quantities (Berachoth 34a).

Numerous rabbis cited in the Talmud present arguments well beyond those governing the clean and unclean food lists of Leviticus and Deuteronomy. Rabbi Abaye (A.D. 280–339) argued that Jews should abstain from fish, fowl, and salted meat, and argued further that consumption of fish was detrimental to human eyesight (Nedarim 54b). Rabbi Mar bar Rav Ashi (fifth century A.D.) suggested that fish and meat, in combination, should not be salted and that the consumption of this mixture resulted in leprosy (Pesachim 112a). Rabbi Rab (second century A.D.) considered fish that had been chewed upon by other sea creatures; he concluded that in such cases where the fish already were dead, the dietary law could be kept by merely cutting away the chewed-upon portions (Jerushalmi Terumoth 8:46a).

Other Talmud passages discuss foods thought to be life threatening. Among them were peeled garlic, peeled onions, peeled eggs, and any diluted liquid kept overnight and exposed to the air (Niddah 17a). The Talmud also ponders the problem of honey and the law: Since the bee is an insect not on the clean list, how could honey be allowed as a food fit for human consumption? Various rabbis argued that bee honey should be permitted since the insect "expels unchanged that which it sucketh out of blossoms." By contrast, the rabbis viewed honey obtained from hornets or wasps as a type of saliva (ri'r), and thus a product expressly forbidden as food (Bechoroth 7b; Tosefta Bechoroth 1:8).

Further evolution of Jewish dietary codes is seen in the sixteenth-to-eighteenth-century health and dietary compendium called *The Book of God's Deeds* or *Sefer Mif'alot Elokim*. This text is important because it bridges the period between ancient and modern health-related issues and diet and contains several specific food and food-related prohibitions. It forbids almonds, hazelnuts, and walnuts (unless eaten after meals), enjoins the faithful from reading or studying while eating, and provides the strict instruction never to eat bread unless the loaf has been well baked (Ba'al Shem and Katz 1936).

Christianity

Early food taboos. Dietary prohibitions and taboos associated with Christianity developed in response to a classic philosophical schism: Should all foods be allowed, or should portions of the dietary codes of Judaism be incorporated by Christians? The early position regarding dietary taboos was Christian repudiation of earlier Jewish food laws and the concept that all foods were acceptable (Mark 7:18-21; Acts 10:8-16, 11:5-10; 1 Corinthians 6:12-13, 10:23, 25-7; 1 Timothy 4:3-5; Titus 1:14-15).

Subsequent debate, however, resulted in Christian reevaluation that permitted converts to maintain their earlier dietary restrictions. This, ultimately, led to the development of three Christian dietary taboos that have not been enforced throughout the centuries: blood (Acts 15:20, 29; 21:25), carrion and "things strangled" (Acts 15:20, 29 and 21:25), and foods previously offered or dedicated to idols (Acts 15:20, 29; 21:25; 1 Corinthians 8:1, 10, 28). Subsequent New Testament texts, however, advise only: "Whether, therefore ye eat, or drink, or whatsoever ye do, do all to the glory of God" (1 Corinthians 10:31).

Subsequent food taboos and concerns. Such a laissez-faire attitude regarding dietary matters within the church continued toward the present. One notable flurry of debate erupted in the second century concerning marine species of fish. Although fish were widely consumed by Mediterranean Christians at this time, concern was expressed that marine species might feed upon the bodies of mariners and soldiers buried at sea. In this case, was the human consumption of such fish tantamount to cannibalism? A second concern had to do with the "essence" of the human body incorporated into fish tissue, which was viewed as an impediment to the reconstitution of the deceased for resurrection, and from this concern flowed another. If the soul of a sailor became part of fish tissue, it would pass directly into the consumer's body. Yet two souls could not occupy the same human body. Clearly, argued the opponents of marine fish consumption, such a food should be avoided.

Fortunately for fish lovers, however, Athenagoras, an Athenian Christian apologist, ably presented a number of positive counterarguments that succeeded in ensuring that the Christian faithful could continue dining on Mediterranean fish.

If there was little proscribing of foods in the history of early Christianity, there was much concern over foodstuffs that centered on physical, in contrast to spiritual, health. For example, John Chrysostom (later Saint John, 345?–407), an important fourth-century Christian leader and author of numerous religious tracts, also wrote extensively on diet. One of his major themes was that reduced food intake and regular fasting were important for Christians. In his words (Homily 22):

> frugality and a simple table are the mother of health.... Now if abstinence is the mother of health, it is plain that eating to repletion is the mother of sickness and ill health, and brings forth diseases ... caused by gluttony and satiety.... Abstinence [from food], in truth, as it is the mother of health, is also the mother of pleasure.

In like fashion, the fifth-century Greek physician Anthimus, in his work on *The Dietetics,* advised Christians to be moderate in their eating and drinking habits. In addition, he cautioned that foods consumed should be readily digestible, and he warned against eight items: bacon rind, aged cheese, hard-boiled eggs, fish that were not fresh, mushrooms, oysters, pickled meats, and pigeons (Gordon 1959).

Such warnings may also be found in the thirteenth-century text *Regimen Santitatas Salernitatum,* which is a blend of Christian and Muslim dietary traditions. Foods specifically identified to be avoided were those supposed to engender the formation of black bile. Other foods, described as "enemies of the sick," were also to be avoided by Christians. These offenders were: apples, cheese, goats, hares, salted meats, milk, peaches, pears, veal, and venison (Temkin 1953; Harrington 1957; Arano 1976).

Absolute food prohibitions within Christianity, however, are a relatively recent phenomenon, initiated by newly formed denominations. The Seventh-Day Adventists, for example, maintain the dietary prohibitions of the Jews against foods on the unclean lists found in Leviticus and Deuteronomy. They also abstain from alcohol consumption and frown upon "hot" spices and condiments, specifically, chilli pepper and black pepper. Aged cheeses (Limburger and Roquefort) are also discouraged. Moreover, the faithful are cautioned:

> Those who indulge in meat eating, tea drinking, and gluttony are sowing seeds for a harvest of pain and death.... A diet of flesh meat tends to develop animalism. . . . Flesh meats will depreciate the blood. Cook meat with spices, and eat it with rich cakes and pies, and you have a bad quality of blood.... Tea is poisonous to the system. Christians should let it alone. The influence of coffee is in a degree the same as tea, but the effect on the system is still worse.... Never take tea, coffee, beer, wine, or any spirituous liquors (Counsels on Diet and Foods 1938).

Members of the Church of Jesus Christ of Latter-day Saints, the Mormons, also reject alcohol and so-called hot drinks, defined as coffee and tea (Word of Wisdom in Smith 1833). In fact, many Mormons have extended this "hot drink" prohibition to any food or beverage that contains caffeine (Pike 1992).

Islam

Muslim dietary prohibitions are documented in two sources, the Koran and the Hadith. The Koran, the divine word of God revealed to the Prophet Mohammed, divides food into two basic categories: halal, or permitted, and haram, or forbidden. The Koran specifically forbids six foods or food categories: blood, carrion, pork, intoxicating beverages prepared from grapes *(khmr),* intoxicating drugs, and foods previously dedicated or offered to idols (Roberts 1925; Sakr 1971). The Hadith, or the collected traditions and sayings attributed to the Prophet Mohammed, contains a broad range of food-related passages.

A wide assortment of human behaviors relating to

food and the food quest are carefully coded in both the Koran and the Hadith. Muslims, for example, may not hunt when on religious pilgrimage to Mecca (Koran 99). At the time of slaughter of permitted animals, the name of God must be mentioned, specifically the phrase: "In the Name of God, the Compassionate, and the Merciful," or *Bisimallah er Rahman er Rahim*. The throat of the animal must be cut in front with a knife, with the exception of two allowed foods: fish, because their throat already is cut (that is, gills), and locusts, because they spring upward and aspire to heaven. If the butcher is distracted and the name of another person or deity is mentioned during slaughter or while butchering the carcass, the flesh of that animal is designated haram, forbidden. If meat is slaughtered correctly, but not permitted to bleed out, the flesh also is designated haram. Meat slaughtered by Christians and Jews may or may not be permitted; meat from animals slaughtered by atheists is always forbidden (Sakr 1971).

Because conservative Muslims living beyond the boundaries of the Middle East frequently do not know the religious orientation of butchers who prepare meat for sale in markets, some turn to vegetarianism during their time abroad or butcher their own animals on specific feast dates (Grivetti, unpublished data).

Local traditions also dictate food prohibitions. In Egypt, for example, some birds consumed elsewhere in the Middle East and Mediterranean region by Muslims are not killed because the bird call resembles pious, religious phrases. The dove (*Streptopelia* spp.) may be avoided as food in Egypt because its call is said to imitate the words: "Oh, all merciful; Oh, all merciful," or *Ya Rahman; Ya Rahman*. Other prohibited birds include the hoopoe *(Upupa epops),* who produces the sound: "Oh, all pitiful; Oh, all pitiful," or *Ya Raouf; Ya Raouf,* and the stone curlew *(Burhinus oedicnemus),* whose cry is said to mimic: "The Universe is Yours, Yours, Yours, Oh, master of the Universe," or *Al-Moluk lak lak lak Ya Sabib al- Moluk* (Darby et al. 1977).

The Hadith also delineates specific kinds of animals to be avoided as food. Among them are all quadrupeds that seize their prey with their teeth. Expressly identified are hyenas, foxes, and elephants. All birds with talons are prohibited. Specifically forbidden (without talons) is the pelican (Guillaume 1924).

The prominent medieval Persian physician Ibn Sina wrote, regarding prohibited foods, that fish should not be taken after laborious work or exercise because it undergoes decomposition and then decomposes the humors (*The Canon* No. 767). Elsewhere, he wrote on prohibited combinations of food:

Certain rules must be noted in regard to combinations of food: milk must not be taken with sour foods; fish must not be taken with milk for in that case chronic ailments such as leprosy

(juzam) may develop; pulses must not be taken with cheese or radishes or with the flesh of flying birds; barley-meal should not follow a dish of rice and sour milk (Ibn Sina 1930).

Other texts by Ibn Sina document still more inappropriate food combinations: milk with acid food, Indian peas with cheese, and fine flour with rice and milk ("Advice on Foods," cited in Kamal 1975).

Hinduism

The most ancient known Hindu document that considers food and dietary prohibitions is the Caraka-Samhita, written about 1500 B.C. and attributed to the physician Caraka. Specific passages in this important text (Caraka 1981) identify dietary principles, permitted and prohibited foods, and regimens for various diseases. Ancient Hindu diet was perceived as consisting of two types: immobile (plants) and mobile (animals). Diet patterns were classified according to four manners of intake: beverages, eatables, chewables, and lickables. Each of these intake categories was further based upon six types of taste: astringent, bitter, pungent, salty, sour, and sweet. Innumerable variations of diet resulted that were based upon 12 categories of food and factors of abundance, combination, and preparation (Grivetti 1991a).

The Caraka-Samhita (Caraka 1981) identifies food items designated as unwholesome and to be avoided by the majority of people. Among them are black gram bean (pulse category); rainy season river water (water category); beef (animal meats category); young dove (bird and fowl category); frog (animals living in holes category); sheep milk (animal milks category); and elephant fat (fats of plant-eating animals category).

Included elsewhere in the Caraka-Samhita (Caraka 1981) are other foods to be avoided:

Meat from animals who die natural deaths, are emaciated, too fatty, too old, too young, any animal killed by poison, not maintained on pasture [land], and meat from all animals bitten by snakes or tigers. . . . Vegetables affected by insects, wind, or sun; vegetables that are dried, old, unseasonable or not cooked with fat. . . . Fruits that are old, unripe, damaged by insects, animals, by snow, or sun, [all vegetables that] grow in unnatural places or [at] unnatural times, or are rotted.

A further development and expansion of Hindu food-related codes is embodied later in texts collectively called the Dharma-Sutra. These law codes, derived from oral tradition that date perhaps to 1500 B.C., had been collected, edited, and presented in written form by the sixth century B.C. The texts are divided into separate tracts: Apastamba (Müller 1896a), Baudhayana (Müller 1882a), Gautama (Müller 1896b), and Vasishtha (Müller 1882b). The document called Manu (1896c), or Laws of Manu, is a subsequent summary and synthesis that probably dates from the third century A.D.

The Hindu dietary prejudices and taboos presented in the Dharma-Sutra are subsumed under five broad rubrics that reflect aspects of human occupation, food location, human and animal behavior, and animal morphology. The fifth category identifies specific proscribed items (Apastamba 1896, 1:5.16:1–1:6:19:15; Baudhayana 1896, 1:5:9:1–2:7:12:12; Gautama 1896, 17:1–38; Manu 1896, 4:205–25; 5:5–56; Vasishtha 1896, 14:2–48; Grivetti 1991a):

Prohibitions associated with human professional and physiological status: All foods offered by an actor, artisan, basket maker, blacksmith, carpenter, cobbler, dyer, eunuch, goldsmith, harlot, hermaphrodite, hunter, hypocrite, informer, jailer, leaser of land, manager of a lodging, menstruating woman, miser, musician, paramour of a married woman, person who is ill, physician, police officer, prisoner, ruler of a town, seller of intoxicating beverages, spy, tailor, thief, trainer of hunting dogs, usurer, weapons dealer, or woman with no male relative.

Prohibitions associated with food location: All foods stored inside the house where a relative has died, all foods served from a wooden platform or table, items eaten while standing, and all foods prepared out of sight and sold by street vendors.

Prohibitions associated with human behavior and contact: All foods received directly from the hand of another person, any food sneezed upon or touched accidentally by a human garment or human foot, any item that contains a hair or insect, all foods specifically prepared for another person, and any consumables that have remained overnight in contact with air that subsequently have soured.

Prohibitions associated with animal behavior and contact: All foods sniffed at by a cat or smelled by a cow, meat from any animal that died after being worried by dogs, meat from any animal that behaved in a solitary manner, and all birds that scratch with their feet or thrust forward with their beak.

Prohibitions associated with animal morphology: All meats or milk products from animals with a single hoof, five toes, double rows of teeth, excessive hair, or no hair; any mammal with young that has recently died, milk or meat from any cow that has suckled a strange calf, and any permitted animal that has delivered twins.

Prohibitions associated with specific foods: Specifically identified prohibited foods fit three broad categories:

1. Plants and plant products: garlic, leek, mushroom, onion, turnip, young sprouts, tree resin, and red juice or sap extracted from any plant.
2. Animals: alligator, crab, crocodile, fish with misshapen heads; cormorant, crow, dove, duck, egret, falcon, flamingo, heron, ibis, osprey, parrot, black partridge, pigeon, raven, sparrow, starling, swan, vulture, and woodpecker; village pig and other tame village animals; black antelope, flying fox, and porpoise.
3. Beverages: milk from any buffalo, cow, or goat within 10 days after calving; any milk from camels, sheep, or wild deer; and water that accumulates at the bottom of a boat.

Prohibitions by Gender and Age

Numerous dietary prohibitions within a society are universal, applying to males and females of all ages. In other instances, however, taboos may be instituted at specific ages or associated with one gender. Dietary taboos practiced in the Republic of Botswana by the baTlokwa ba Moshaweng, a Tswana agro-pastoral cattle-keeping society of the eastern Kalahari Desert, offer examples of both.

General Prohibitions

Female and male baTlokwa of all ages reject antbear or aardvark (*Orvcheropus afer afer*) as food because they consider it inappropriate to kill and eat their tribal totem animal (see Table VI.13.2 for a list of

Table VI.13.2. *BaTlokwa ba Moshaweng: Foods restricted by gender and age*

	Females		Males	
	Characteristic or permitted	Prohibited or restricted	Characteristic or permitted	Prohibited or restricted
Death				
-	Eggs	Antbear	Eggs	Antbear
-	Meat: chin	Insects	Honey	Insects
Elderly	Meat: nose	-	Francolin	Small birds
Adults	Meat: placenta	-	Kidney	Small mammals
			Meat: stillborn calf	
			Tortoise	
Menopause or activity decline				
-	Liver	Antbear	Eggs, heat	Antbear
Active	-	-	Lung, rumen	Insects
Adults	-	-	Meat: forelegs & hindlegs	Small birds
				Small mammals
				Stillborn calf
Puberty				
-	Fish	Antbear	Eggs	Antbear
-	Insects	Eggs	Fish	Francolin
Childhood	-	Francolin	Insects	Honey
		Honey	Small birds	Tortoise
		Tortoise	Small mammals	
Weaning/off breast				
-	Breast milk	Beans	Breast milk	Beans
-	Donkey milk	Eggs	Donkey milk	Meat
Infancy	-	Solid food	-	Solid food
Birth				

foods restricted by age and gender). Pork is also not consumed by males and females of all ages for other reasons. Many state that pork is a disgusting food and offer explanations, such as that pigs are dirty, smelly, and disgusting in appearance and that they consume feces and even their own young. Still others reject pork because they say that the meat is too fatty for human consumption. BaTlokwa who break their universal taboo and eat pork, however, still may reject specific portions of the carcass: In contrast with the bones of acceptable animals, those of pigs are never cracked and chewed to extract marrow, lest the consumer become deaf (Grivetti 1976).

Several agro-pastoral Tswana societies living in the eastern Kalahari Desert do not eat locally grown oranges in the belief that the first maturing fruit is poisonous. Respondents state that it is impossible to determine precisely which orange ripens first. Therefore, locally grown oranges are all rejected, and oranges that are consumed are imported from South Africa.

Some baTlokwa, however, believe that planting orange trees is unnatural and possibly dangerous because this tree is not native to the eastern Kalahari. Other baTlokwa explain their prohibition using an analogy with another local Kalahari tree, *Melia azsedarach:* Although baTlokwa men and women readily dig up wild plants from surrounding bushlands and transplant them into their household gardens, they never experiment with *Melia azsedarach* in the belief that transplanting it will cause the death of all family members except the gardener, who then must suffer a life of loneliness (Grivetti 1976).

The baKwena, linguistic and cultural relatives of the baTlokwa who occupy territory southwest of the baTlokwa homelands, also reject oranges as food for still another reason. Documentation exists that the nineteenth-century missionary David Livingstone was the first to import orange trees into the Kalahari Desert in baKwena territory, and he is suspected of initiating the orange taboo to curtail theft from his orchard (Grivetti 1978b).

Age-Gender Matrix

The baTlokwa ba Moshaweng exhibit a well-structured pattern of food prohibitions reflecting dual themes of age and gender. But those dietary taboos and prohibitions that reinforce gender identification at specific periods of the human physiological cycle are balanced by other foods that are characteristically associated with the consumer's age and gender.

Infancy. Certain baTlokwa food-related behaviors regulate infant feeding practices. Parents must eat before feeding their infants, as it is forbidden to hold or allow the infant to sit on the parent's lap while the adult is eating. They believe that to do so makes the infant greedy. Furthermore, widows and widowers are discouraged from feeding infants. But if they do, the

infant must be held facing away from the adult to avoid eye contact (Grivetti 1978b).

Childhood. Seven foods expressly taboo to baTlokwa children are dietary prerogatives of elderly men. These foods include two types of honey, tortoise, and five birds: dikkop *(Burbinus capensis),* francolin *(Francolinus* spp.), guinea fowl *(Numida meleagris),* horn-bill *(Tockus* spp.), and red-crested korhaan *(Lophotis ruficrista).* The baTlokwa associate these seven items with memory and believe that their consumption exacerbates forgetfulness: Because elderly men are perceived as forgetful anyway, and memory should be developed in children, these seven foods are critical markers for age (Grivetti 1978b).

Other food taboos of childhood are associated with food remnants, especially sorghum porridge that sticks to wooden serving spoons. Boys are told that if they lick porridge from such utensils, they will develop breasts and resemble women (cultural reference to gynecomastia). Girls, on the other hand, are cautioned that such behavior will delay breast development (Grivetti 1976).

The actions of children at mealtime are also regulated. BaTlokwa children are forbidden to touch the floor with the left hand while eating as this is interpreted as a sign of laziness. Furthermore, children are not allowed to speak during mealtime because of a widely held conviction that "a talking child becomes lean" (Grivetti 1976).

When baTlokwa children are ill, mothers prepare a special sorghum beer called *bojalwa jwa tlhogwana,* to be drunk by all family members in the belief that this practice hastens recovery. While the tlhogwana is being prepared, no one in the family is allowed to sample it at any stage of the brewing process or to taste the sediment at the bottom of the clay or iron beer pot. To do so, reportedly, will make the child's illness acute (Grivetti 1976).

Adolescence. After baTlokwa children mature sexually and enter their reproductive years, other food-related prohibitions and taboos become operative. Teenage girls are prohibited from consuming eggs, a restriction that differentiates them sharply from male counterparts, who may eat eggs with impunity. The adolescent female egg prohibition is explained at several levels. Some respondents state that the prohibition is linked to the undesirable condition of adolescent pregnancy. It is thought that girls who eat eggs will become sexually overactive, possibly promiscuous, and, consequently, might conceive at an age when they would be unable to care properly for their babies. Others think that adolescent girls who eat eggs will experience difficult labor, and should the mother and child survive, the neonate will likely die soon after delivery because of impaired breathing. Adolescent women should also avoid eggs because even if they deliver healthy children, the latter will cry regularly and wake the family in the early morning in silly attempts to mimic roosters (Grivetti 1976).

Adult/mature years. Three cuts of beef are prohibited to baTlokwa pregnant women in the belief that they cause difficult labor and delivery. These are the fourth stomach *(ngati);* the large intestine *(mongopo);* and both meat and marrow extracted from lower leg bones *(ditlhako tsa kgomo).* Also forbidden during pregnancy are the meat, fat, and skin located under the belly of an ox *(mofufu wa kgomo),* thought to make the child greedy, or to promote the development of a large stomach (Grivetti 1976).

Commercial candy, available to the baTlokwa since the late nineteenth century, is proscribed during pregnancy. Its consumption is thought to cause the ensuing newborn to drool and spit up saliva. Similarly, sour milk *(madila)* is forbidden to the mother during pregnancy in the belief that it will later cause the newborn to vomit copiously (Grivetti 1978b).

After delivery, baTlokwa mothers enter a period of confinement for 3 to 6 months. During this period the mother is not permitted to eat with her bare hands. All foods must be cut, then transferred to the mouth with a utensil; otherwise it is believed that the mother's supply of breast milk will be adversely affected (Grivetti 1978b).

Elderly pattern. Elderly baTlokwa men and women are released from all previous culturally imposed dietary prohibitions and may eat any available food.

Gender, Pregnancy, and Allopathy

Throughout the Old and New Worlds, millions of people follow allopathic practices that specifically encourage or prohibit various foods during illness and during changes in physiological status, such as pregnancy and lactation. Allopathic systems emerged initially in India and subsequently spread to China and westward into the Mediterranean basin to influence Greek, Roman, Byzantine, and Jewish, Christian, and Muslim medical practices. Such practices became global during the fifteenth- and sixteenth-century era of exploration, and influenced the development of medicine in North, Central, and South America, as well as those portions of Africa and Asia colonized by Europeans (Grivetti 1991a).

At the core of allopathic medicine is the concept that illness and disease may be classified as hot or cold, and wet or dry, and that foods available to consumers are, likewise, hot (heating) or cold (cooling). Health in this system is perceived as a state of balance, whereby healthy individuals are neither too hot nor too cold; illness, accordingly, is perceived as a state of imbalance, and cures aim at restoring balance by treating with opposites. Thus, hot diseases are treated with cold foods, dry diseases with wet foods, and so forth (Grivetti 1991a, 1991b, 1991c, 1992).

Chinese Yang–Yin
Of specific interest to the study and evaluation of food prohibitions and taboos is the question of how concepts of hot or cold remain constant or shift, depending upon the consumer's gender and, in the case of women, whether or not they are pregnant or lactating. Traditional Chinese allopathic practitioners explain that pregnancy produces a physiological state of extreme heat (yang), which requires a cooling (yin) diet in order to restore balance. Dietary management during pregnancy has been considered in a wide range of works by ancient and medieval Chinese physicians.

Among them are texts on diet and food prohibitions by Chang Chi (A.D. 142–220), Hsü Chih-Ts'asi (A.D. 510–90), Sun Ssu-Mo (A.D. 581–682), Chen Tzu Ming (perhaps A.D. 960–1027), and Chu Chen-Heng (A.D. 1281–1358). In addition to these classical Chinese texts, numerous social scientists and physicians of the past 50 years also have written on hot–cold foods, and especially foods that are encouraged or prohibited during pregnancy and lactation (Platt and Gin 1938; Read 1976, 1977a-e; Pillsbury 1978; Anderson 1980, 1984; Tan and Wheeler 1983; Wheeler and Tan 1983; Hsu et al. 1986).

A review of both ancient and modern sources reveals that Chinese dietary prohibitions during pregnancy generally fit eight food categories (Grivetti 1991c).

1. The first and largest category is that of *meats and eggs.* Here prohibited items include: beef, bullfrog, carp, carp roe, chicken, crab, deer fat, dog, donkey, duck (wild and domesticated types), eel, eggs, elk, frog, gecko, goat (both meat and liver), horse, mule, pheasant, rabbit, sheep (mutton and liver), shellfish, sparrow brain, toad, and turtle.
2. Under the category of *cereals,* only barley is prohibited.
3. In the *legumes and seeds* group, almonds, amaranth, beans, and soybeans are prohibited.
4. Prohibitions on *vegetables* include bean leaf and mushrooms.
5. Among the *fruits,* banana, litchi, pear, pineapple, and watermelon are taboo.
6. In the category of *spices and flavorings,* garlic and ginger are forbidden.
7. Proscribed *beverages* include beer, soda pop, tea, and wine.
8. Among the *miscellaneous foods,* all frozen items are prohibited, along with malt, seaweed, and sloughed snake skin (used medicinally).

Set within the hot-cold paradigm, which encourages cooling foods, there seem to be three primary categories of explanation for these food prohibitions (Grivetti 1991c): Some of the foods are viewed as likely to cause *potential miscarriage or spontaneous abortion.* Among these are almonds, amaranth, banana, barley, beans, beer, eggs and salt, frozen foods, horse meat, pineapple, seaweed, and soybeans. Another group of foods is implicated in *transverse presentation, difficult delivery,* and *postpartum bleeding.* These are alcoholic beverages, crabs, donkey meat, duck, horse meat, mule meat, pheasant, sheep liver, shellfish, and tiger bones.

A final group of foods is believed to have a *negative impact on the neonate.* Birthmarks, for example, can be the work of beef, sparrows, or soybean paste, whereas deer fat, elk meat, or sparrow brain can cause blindness or other eye diseases. Boils, sores, and other skin lesions are associated with carp, carp roe, and shellfish, a deformed neck with turtles, and an early death (or during childhood) with frogs. Epilepsy in the child can be caused by either mushrooms or sheep (mutton). The latter is also held responsible for fever. A hoarse voice is linked to toads, jaundice to bananas, muteness or a hare lip to bullfrogs, chickens, dogs, ducks, eels, goats, rabbits, and turtles, whereas fresh ginger can trigger polydactyly (an extra digit).

Still other dietary prohibitions during pregnancy are related to the notion that the foods in question will produce specific undesirable behaviors once the child has grown to maturity. Chinese traditionalists believe, for example, that should women consume sparrow cooked in alcohol or wine during pregnancy, the child will exhibit lewd, licentious behavior as an adult (Grivetti 1991c).

The focus is upon cooling foods (yin) during pregnancy, and yin foods are commonly low in protein and energy. Consequently, dietary reliance upon these items during pregnancy often results in a low-birth-weight baby – but an easier delivery for the mother.

After delivery, the Chinese allopathic system classifies lactating women as strongest yin. Consequently, diet at this time is based upon hot (yang) foods that are high in protein and energy, thus providing a sound nutritional basis for postpartum recovery and breast milk production (Pillsbury 1978).

Taboos as Protective for Society and the Individual

Dietary taboos and prohibitions have also been considered from the viewpoint of protection. In some instances, such practices protect local and regional ecology or agricultural crops during various phases of their growth cycle; in other cases, they have to do with human health and disease.

Crop Protection

As residents of the arid Kalahari Desert of eastern Botswana, the baTlokwa face uncertainties of unseasonable weather, specifically uneven rainfall and drought, hail, and desiccating winds. The baTlokwa attempt to minimize these uncertainties by instituting a range of taboos and prohibitions in a cultural attempt to regulate weather.

The appearance and timing of rainfall in the Kalahari is critical to growing crops, and three specific taboos are instituted in the conviction that enforcement will assure rain. If the following taboos are broken, however, traditionalists believe that the rain clouds will be driven away:

1. Salt must never be thrown into a cooking fire or accidentally spilled onto flames or embers.
2. During their one-year mourning period, widows and widowers cannot wash their body during daylight and are forbidden to walk about the village during the heat of midday.
3. Pregnant or menstruating women are not allowed to walk across agricultural fields, or to touch agricultural equipment, such as plow blades, harnesses, and yokes, lest the heat of their bodies burn the earth or render the ground sterile (Grivetti 1981b).

Health Protection

There is also much in the way of literature that suggests that the origin and development of many dietary taboos may lie in attempts to maintain human health and reduce disease.

Pigs and pork. In ancient Egypt, swine played a role in both religious and dietary practices. In some historical eras, at specific geographical localities, pork was a highly favored food, but during other periods and at other locations pork was forbidden.

Before 3200 B.C., Egypt consisted of two distinctive geographical-cultural entities: a pork-consuming north or Lower Egypt, and a pork-avoiding south or Upper Egypt (Menghin and Amer 1932). Shortly after 3200 B.C., however, both regions were united politically when the South conquered the North. One result of this conquest was a broadly based pork avoidance throughout the Egyptian Nile Valley and Delta that predates the Jewish pork prohibition by more than 2,000 years.

Pigs in the ancient Egyptian pantheon were associated with Seth, the evil brother of Osiris. During political periods when Osiris worship dominated, pork was avoided, but when Seth gained ascendancy, pork was widely consumed. Certainly pork was an important food during the reign of Amenhotep III (about 1405–1370 B.C.), who offered pigs to the temple of Ptah at Memphis. Seti I, father of Ramses II (about 1318–1298 B.C.), allowed pigs to be raised inside the temple of Osiris at Abydos (Newberry 1928: 211). That swine were eaten by Egyptians during the Ramessid Period is confirmed by the large numbers of pig bones found in refuse-trash heaps associated with the workman's village of Deir-el-Medina at Thebes (Kees 1961).

By late dynastic times and during the subsequent Greek and Roman periods, however, literary and pictorial evidence for pork consumption or avoidance in

Egypt reveals the same kind of curious dichotomy that was noted previously for beef. On the one hand, a wide range of sources document pork consumption. One description, dating from the third century B.C., indicates that Egyptian priests at the city of Naucratis in the Egyptian delta were served pork (Hermeias, cited by Athenaeus *Deipnosophists* 4, 149:F). Moreover, numerous Greek and Roman writers commented on the widespread presence of pigs throughout Egypt. Pliny (*Natural History,* 13:50) reported that swineherds fed their animals dates and lotus stems, and Polynaeus (*Stratagems of War* 4:19) noted that herds of swine were raised near Memphis. Heliodorus's Ethiopian history (1587: 130) described herds of pigs at Aswan.

There are also, however, Greek and Roman writers who indicate that there was a strong dietary avoidance of pork in Egypt. Indeed, both Plutarch (*Isis and Osiris* 353: 5) and Aelian (*Characteristics of Animals* 10: 16) stated that pork was forbidden as food throughout Egyptian territory, and Sextus Empiricus (*Outlines of Pyrrhonism* 3: 233) wrote that Egyptian priests would sooner die than eat swine's flesh.

This ancient Egyptian pork avoidance, which dates from about 3200 B.C., predates the Mosaic codes against pork by more than 200 years. Yet, as we have seen in Egypt, pork avoidance was not associated with any relationship between ingestion and disease, but rather was instituted by the followers of Osiris because the pig was the cult animal of Seth (Darby et al. 1977).

It is true that one frequently mentioned reason for pork avoidance links pork consumption with trichinosis (Sakr 1991; Chaudry 1992). But although pork taboos have been instituted in Africa and the Middle East for at least 5,200 years, the relationship between eating pork and contracting trichinosis was not established until the nineteenth century (Hilton 1833; Owen 1835; Zenker 1860; Paget 1866).

Moreover, although associations between parasitism and disease would have been readily apparent in cattle, goats, sheep, and a wide range of fish and fowl, dietary taboos in Judaism, Christianity, and Islam do not exist for these animals. Further, there are no formalized, coded taboos in these three faiths for toxic mushrooms, or such plants as aconite or datura, which are lethal and clearly more deadly than eating pork infected with *Trichina (Trichinella) spiralis.*

Carrion. Meat from an animal that "dies of itself" is proscribed by each of the monotheistic faiths that developed in the Mediterranean region. For Jews, the injunction is repeated six times (Exodus 22:31; Leviticus 11:39–40, 17:15–16, and 22:8; Deuteronomy 14:21; and Ezekiel 4:14); for Christians, three times (Acts 15:20, 29, 21:25); and for Muslims, four times (Koran: The Cow, 168; Koran: The Table, 4; Koran: Cattle, 145; Koran: The Bee, 115).

The rejection of carrion as human food is hardly universal, however. Many societies readily consume carrion and "rancid meat" as dietary staples. Indeed, dietary use of carrion by circumpolar Arctic societies has been reviewed extensively (Borgoras 1909; Eidlitz 1969), and consumption of carrion by European Gypsies has been well documented, especially the use of animals burned to death by brush and forest fires (Petrovic 1939).

All of this brings up the question of whether religious prohibitions against carrion are in fact protective. Clearly, the potential for disease transmission exists if humans consume infected carrion, but to reject carrion as human food merely upon the *potential* for disease transmission is illogical, given that humans consume fish, fowl, meats, and plant foods that can and do create serious health problems after consumption.

In fact, it could be argued that eating carrion is protective in that it has helped millions of people survive periods of food shortages, wartime famines, and climatic stress. Indeed, droughts of recent decades in the southern African Kalahari Desert region severely challenged regional agro-pastoralists, who suffered loss of their herds but maintained their dietary and nutritional status by consuming carrion. When cattle and other livestock died of thirst or environmental stress, the baTlokwa butchered the carcasses and the carrion was steamed, with leaves of *Croton gratissimus* used to remove "off" odors. Such meat then was sun-dried and jerked and could be readily stored as a suitable famine food (Grivetti 1976, 1978b).

It is interesting to note that most baTlokwa agropastoralists are animists or moderate Christians; in contrast, most agro-pastoralists of the drought-stricken Sahel are Muslim. Both Christianity and Islam prohibit carrion consumption, but there are distinctive regional and cultural differences in keeping "the law."

Harmful foods not prohibited. Returning to a question posed earlier, if health considerations lie at the root of the carrion (and other food) prohibitions, then it might be asked why there are no codified prohibitions in Buddhism, Christianity, Hinduism, Islam, or Judaism for moldy grain (manifest as the human disease ergotism), or for fava beans (favism), or for field vetch (lathyrism).

To employ another example, human poisoning from eating European migratory quail *(Coturnix coturnix)* is manifest as the human illness coturnism. This food-related problem, documented since biblical times (Numbers 11:31–4), was known to Greek and Roman naturalists, among them Aristotle (*On Plants* 820: 6–7), Lucretius (*On the Nature of Things* 4: 639–40) and Pliny (*Natural History* 10: 33). However, no dietary codes were instituted to protect consumers. Furthermore, subsequent medieval Jewish and Muslim physicians described human poisoning from quail, among them Maimonides (*Commentary*

Epidemiarum 6: 5), Ibn Sina (*The Canon* 2:2:2:5), Qazwiny (*Kitab Aga'il* 2: 250), and al-Demiri (*Hayat al-Hayawan al Kubra* 1: 505). Nonetheless, not only were potentially toxic quail not proscribed but they have also remained a favorite food of Middle Eastern Jews, Christians, and Muslims throughout the centuries (Kennedy and Grivetti 1980).

Concluding Comments

The literature on food prohibitions and taboos is ancient and voluminous, and most certainly reflects human interest in understanding how and why specific foods have been proscribed throughout the ages. More than 10 hypotheses have been advanced to explain the origins and development of food-related taboos, and evidence in support of them and against them can be marshaled for each.

Some who study food-related taboos have worked for decades to identify unifying concepts that would explain ancient as well as contemporary human behavior toward food. Some have attempted scientific explanations; others have sought meaning in nonscientific descriptions. Most accounts have stressed the cultural-religious aspects of food prejudices in Christianity, Hinduism, Islam, or Judaism. Beyond religion, however, lie still other categories of food prohibitions associated with the consumer's age and gender, ecological protection, and medical-nutritional themes. But within this enormous body of literature, there remains a single concept that has been expressed in two ways: *Food for one is not food for all,* and *One man's meat is another's poison.*

Louis E. Grivetti

Bibliography

Aelian. 1958-9. *On the characteristics of animals,* trans. A. F. Scholfield. 3 vols. Cambridge, Mass.

Alcalay, R. 1962. *The complete English-Hebrew dictionary.* Hartford, Conn.

al-Demiry [Kamal ed-Din Mohammad Ibn Moussa]. 1957. *Hayat al-Hayawan al Kubra.* Third edition. Cairo.

Anderson, E. N. 1980. "Heating" and "cooling" foods in Hong Kong and Taiwan. *Social Science Information* 19: 237-68.

  1984. "Heating" and "cooling" foods re-examined. *Social Science Information* 23: 755-73.

Arano, L. C. 1976. *Tacuinum sanitatis: The medieval health handbook,* trans. L. C. Arano. New York.

Arberry, A. J., trans. 1955. *The Koran interpreted.* London.

Aristotle. 1955. On plants. In *Aristotle: Minor works,* trans. W. S. Hett. London.

Arrington, L. R. 1959. Foods of the Bible. *Journal of the American Dietetic Association* 35: 816-20.

Athenaeus, of Naucratis. 1927-41. *The Deipnosophists,* trans. C. B. Gulick. 7 vols. New York.

Athenagoras. 1956. The resurrection of the dead. In *The ante-Nicene fathers: Translations of the writings of the fathers down to A.D. 325,* Vol 2. *Fathers of the second century: Hermas, Tatian, Athenagoras, Theophilus, and Clement of Alexandria,* ed. A. Roberts and J. Donaldson. Grand Rapids, Mich.

Ba'al Shem, J., and N. Katz. 1936. Medical excerpts from Sefer mif'alot elokim [The book of God's deeds]. *Bulletin of the History of Medicine* 4: 299-331.

Bible. [1530] 1992. *Tyndale's Old Testament.* New Haven, Conn.

  [1560] 1969. *The Geneva Bible.* Madison, Wis.

  [1609] 1963. *The Holy Bible: Translated from the Latin Vulgate and diligently compared with Hebrew, Greek, and other editions in diverse languages and first published at the English College at Douay, Anno 1609.* Edinburgh.

  [1611] 1968. *The Holy Bible: The authorized or King James version of 1611 now reprinted with apocrypha.* New York.

  [1782] 1968. *The Holy Bible as printed by Robert Aiken and approved and recommended by the Congress of the United States of America in 1782.* New York.

  1805. *The Holy Scriptures, faithfully and truly translated by Myles Cloverdale, Bishop of Exeter.* Second edition. London.

  1850. *The Holy Bible containing the Old and New Testaments . . . in the earliest English version made from the Latin Vulgate by John Wycliffe and his followers.* Oxford.

  1897. *The Emphasised Bible: A new translation by J. B. Rotherham,* Vol. 1. Genesis-Ruth. Cincinnati, Ohio.

  1950. *The Basic Bible: Containing the Old and New Testaments in basic English.* New York.

  1953. *King James edition.* London.

  1965. *The amplified bible.* Grand Rapids, Mich.

  1966. *The Jerusalem Bible,* ed. A. Jones. Garden City, N.Y.

  1970a. *The New American Bible: Translated from the original languages, with critical use of all the ancient sources by members of the Catholic Biblical Association of America.* New York.

  1970b. *New World translation of the Holy Scriptures.* Brooklyn, N.Y.

  1970c. *The New English Bible with apocrypha.* New York.

  1973. *The Holy Bible: Revised Standard Version consisting of the Old and New Testaments. . . . Being the version set forth A.D. 1611, revised A.D. 1881-1885 and A.D. 1901.* New York.

  1978. *New International Version.* Grand Rapids, Mich.

  1981a. *The New Layman's Parallel Bible (King James Version, New International Version, Living Bible, Revised Standard Version).* Second edition. Grand Rapids, Mich.

  1981b. *The NIV Triglot Old Testament.* Grand Rapids, Mich.

  1989. *The Holy Bible: New Revised Standard Version.* New York.

  1990. *Life Application Bible.* Iowa Falls, Iowa.

Blackman, P., trans. 1964. Mishayoth. In *Order kodashum: Chullin.* Second edition. New York.

Bolton, J. M. 1972. Food taboos among the Orang Asli in west Malaysia: A potential nutritional hazard. *American Journal of Clinical Nutrition* 25: 789-99.

Borgoras, W. 1909. The Chuckchee. Material Culture. *Memoirs of the American Museum of Natural History* 11: 193-208.

Bosley, G. C., and M. G. Hardinge. 1992. Seventh-Day Adventists: Dietary standard and concerns. *Food Technology* 46: 112-13.

Bush, L. E. 1990. The word of wisdom in early nineteenth-century perspective. In *The Word of God: Essays on Mormon Scripture*, ed. D. Vogel, 161–85. Salt Lake City, Utah.

Caraka. 1981. *Caraka-Samhita: Agnivesa's treatise refined and annotated by Caraka and redacted by Drdhabala*, Vol. 1. *Sutrasthana to Indriyasthana*. ed. and trans. Priyavrat Sharma. Delhi.

Chadwick, G. A. 1890. *The book of Exodus: The Expositor's Bible*, ed. W. Robertson Nicoll. London.

Chang Chi. 1990. *Chin kuei yuao lueh* [Important principles from the golden treasure chest], redacted by Ching Chun. Taipei.

Chaudry, M. M. 1992. Islamic food laws: Philosophical basis and practical implications. *Food Technology* 46: 92–3, 104f.

Chen Tzu Ming. 1977. *Fu jen liang fang* [Excellent formulas for women]. Taipei, Taiwan.

Cheyne, T. K. 1907. *Traditions and beliefs of Ancient Israel*. London.

Chu Chen-Heng. 1984. *Tan chi hsin fa* [Methods from tan chi]. Taipei, Taiwan.

Cohn, J. 1973. *The royal table: An outline of the dietary laws of Israel*. New York.

Cook, S. A. 1969. Notes to the third edition. In *Lectures on the religion of the Semites: The fundamental institutions*. ed. W. R. Smith, 576–7. New York.

Counsels on Diet and Foods. 1938. *Counsels on diets and foods: A compilation from the writings of Ellen G. White*. Washington, D.C.

Crysostum (See John Chrysostum)

Darby, W. J., P. Ghalioungui, and L. E. Grivetti. 1977. *Food: The gift of Osiris*. 2 vols. London.

Douglas, M. 1966. *Purity and danger: An analysis of concepts of pollution and taboo*. London.

1977. Structure of gastronomy. In *Russell Sage Foundation annual report for the year 1976–1977*, 41–57. New York.

Dresser, M. 1979. Kosher catering: How and why. *Cornell Hotel Restaurant Administration Quarterly* 20: 83–91.

Ehrman, A., ed. 1965. *The Talmud with an English translation and commentary*. Jerusalem.

Eidlitz, K. 1969. Food and emergency food in the circumpolar area. *Studia Ethnographica Uppsaliensia* 32: 108–62.

Einspahr, B. 1977. *Index to Brown, Driver, and Briggs: Hebrew lexicon*. Chicago.

Emery, W. B. 1962. *A funerary repast in an Egyptian tomb of the archaic period*. Leiden, the Netherlands.

Epstein, I., ed. 1948. *Seder Kodashim: II (Hullin)*, trans. E. Cashdan. London.

Frazer, J. G. 1907a. Folklore in the Old Testament. In *Anthropological essays presented to Edward Burnett Tylor*, 101–74. Oxford.

1907b. Not to seethe a kid in its mother's milk. *Man* 7: 166.

1918–19. *Folklore in the Old Testament: Studies in comparative religion, legend, and law*. 3 vols. London.

1935. *The golden bough: A study in magic and religion*. Third edition. 12 vols. New York.

Freedman, S. E. 1970. *The book of Kashruth: A treasury of Kosher facts and frauds*. New York.

Garine, I. de. 1972. The socio-cultural aspects of nutrition. *Ecology of Food and Nutrition* 1: 143–63.

Gaster, T. H. 1955. *Customs and folkways of Jewish life*. New York.

Ginzberg, L. 1961. *The legends of the Jews*, Vol. 1. trans. H. Szold. Philadelphia, Pa.

Gordon, B. L. 1959. *Medieval and Renaissance medicine*. New York.

Grivetti, L. E. 1975. Flavor and culture: The importance of flavors in the Middle East. *Food Technology* 29: 38–40.

1976. Dietary resources and social aspects of food use in a Tswana tribe. Ph.D. dissertation, University of California, Davis.

1978a. Culture, diet and nutrition: Selected themes and topics. *BioScience* 28: 171–7.

1978b. Nutritional success in a semi-arid land: Examination of Tswana agro-pastoralists of the eastern Kalahari, Botswana. *American Journal of Clinical Nutrition* 31: 1204–20.

1980. Dietary separation of meat and milk: A cultural-geographical inquiry. *Ecology of Food and Nutrition* 9: 203–17.

1981a. Cultural nutrition: Anthropological and geographical themes. *Annual Review of Nutrition* 1: 47–68.

1981b. Geographical location, climate and weather, and magic: Aspects of agricultural success in the eastern Kalahari, Botswana. *Social Science Information: Human Societies and Ecosystems* 20: 509–36.

1991a. Nutrition past – nutrition today: Prescientific origins of nutrition and dietetics. Part 1. Legacy of India. *Nutrition Today* 26: 13–24.

1991b. Nutrition past – nutrition today: Prescientific origins of nutrition and dietetics. Part 2. Legacy of the Mediterranean. *Nutrition Today* 26: 18–29.

1991c. Nutrition past – nutrition today: Prescientific origins of nutrition and dietetics. Part 3. Legacy of China. *Nutrition Today* 26: 6–17.

1992. Nutrition past – nutrition today: Prescientific origins of nutrition and dietetics. Part 4. Aztec patterns and Spanish legacy. *Nutrition Today* 27: 13–25.

Grivetti, L. E., S. J. Lamprecht, H. J. Rocke, and A. Waterman. 1987. Threads of cultural nutrition: Arts and humanities. *Progress in Food and Nutrition Science* 11: 249–306.

Grivetti, L. E., and R. M. Pangborn. 1974. Origin of selected Old Testament dietary prohibitions. *Journal of the American Dietetic Association* 65: 634–8.

Grunfeld, D. I. 1972. *Dietary laws regarding forbidden and permitted foods, with particular reference to meat and meat products*, Vol. 1, *The Jewish dietary laws*. New York.

1972. *Dietary laws regarding plants and vegetables, with particular reference to the produce of the Holy land*, Vol. 2, *The Jewish dietary laws*. New York.

Guillaume, A. 1924. *The traditions of Islam. An introduction to the study of Hadith by A. Guillaume*. Oxford.

Harding, T. S. 1931. Food prejudices. *Medical Journal and Record* 133: 67–70.

Harrington, J. 1957. *The School of Salernum: Regimen Sanitatis Salerni*. Rome.

Harris, M. 1972. Riddle of the pig. *Natural History* 81: 32–6.
1973. Riddle of the pig II. *Natural History* 82: 20–5.

Hehn, V. 1885. *The wanderings of plants and animals from their first home*, ed. J. S. Stallybrass. London.

Heliodorus. 1587. *An Aethopian historie written in Greek by Heliodorus no less wittie than pleasaunt*, trans. T. Underdowne. London.

Heun, E. 1962. Nutrition and abstention in primitive peoples. *Medical Mirror* 1: 1–4.

Hilton, J. 1833. Notes on a peculiar appearance observed in human muscle, probably depending upon the formation of very small cysticerci. *London Medical Gazette* 11: 605.

Hsu, H-Y., Y-P. Chen, S-U Shen, et al. 1986. *Oriental materia medica: A concise guide.* Long Beach, Calif.

Ibn Sina [Abu Husayn Ibn Abdullah Ibn Sina]. 1930. *A treatise on the canon of medicine of Avicenna: Incorporating a translation of the first book,* trans. O. C. Gruner. London.

Jelliffe, D. B., and E. F. P. Jelliffe. 1978. Food habits and taboos: How have they protected man in his evolution? *Progress in Human Nutrition* 2: 67-76.

John Chrysostom. 1957. Homily 22 on John 2:4-10. In *Saint John Chrysostom: Commentary on Saint John the Apostle and Evangelist,* Vol. 33, The Fathers of the Church: A New Translation, trans. T. A. Goggin, 212-21. New York.

Kamal, H. 1975. *Encyclopedia of Islamic medicine: With a Greco-Roman background.* Cairo.

Kaufman, M. 1957. Adapting therapeutic diets to Jewish food customs. *American Journal of Clinical Nutrition* 5: 676-81.

Kees, H. 1961. *Ancient Egypt: A cultural topography,* ed. T. G. H. James, trans. I. F. E. Morrow. London.

Keimer, L. 1924. *Die Gartenpflanzen im alten Aegypten.* Hamburg.

Kellogg, S. H. 1899. The book of Leviticus. In *The Expositor's Bible,* ed. W. R. Nicholl, 277-304. London.

Kennedy, B. W., and L. E. Grivetti. 1980. Toxic quail: A cultural-ecological investigation of coturnism. *Ecology of Food and Nutrition* 9: 15-42.

Kilara, A., and K. K. Iya. 1992. Food and dietary habits of the Hindu. *Food Technology* 46: 94-104.

Kleist, J. A., trans. 1961. The epistle of Barnabas. In *Ancient Christian Writers,* Vol 6. London.

Knutsson, K. E., and R. Selinus. 1970. Fasting in Ethopia: An anthropological and nutritional study. *American Journal of Clinical Nutrition* 23: 956-69.

Korff, S. L. 1966. The Jewish dietary code. *Food Technology* 20: 76-8.

Levin, S. I., and E. A. Boyden. 1940. *The Kosher code of the orthodox Jew: Being a literal translation of that portion of the sixteenth-century codification of the Babylonian Talmud which describes such deficiencies as render animals unfit for food (Hilkot Terefor Shulhan 'Aruk); To which is appended a discussion of Talmudic anatomy in the light of science of its day and of the present time.* New York.

Lipschutz, Y. 1988. *Kashruth: A comprehensive background and reference guide to the principles of Kashruth.* Brooklyn, N.Y.

Loret, V. 1892. *La flore pharonique d'après les documents hiéroglyphiques et les spécimens découverts dans les tombes.* Paris.

Lucretius. 1910. *On the nature of things,* trans. C. Bailey. Oxford.

Mackintosh, C. H. 1959. *Notes on the Pentateuch.* New York.

Maimonides. 1956. *The guide for the perplexed.* Second edition, trans. M. Friedländer. London.

　　1967. *Sefer ha-mitzvoth,* trans. C. B. Chavel. 2 vols. London.

　　1970-1. *The medical aphorisms of Moses Maimonides,* ed. S. Munter, trans. F. Rosner. New York.

　　1987. *Maimonides' commentary on the aphorism of Hippocrates,* trans. F. Rosner. Haifa, Israel.

Mays, J. L. 1963. The book of Leviticus; The book of Numbers. In *The Layman's Bible Commentary,* Vol. 4, ed. D. H. Kelly, D. G. Miller, A. B. Rhodes, and D. M. Chalmers, 49. Richmond, Va.

McDonald, D. R. 1977. Food taboos: A primitive environmental protection agency (South America). *Anthropos* 72: 734-48.

Menghin, O., and M. Amer. 1932. *The excavations of the Egyptian University in the neolithic site of the Maadi: First preliminary report.* Cairo.

Monet, P. 1958. *Everyday life in Egypt in the days of Ramses the Great,* trans. A. R. Maxwell-Hyslop and M. S. Drower. London.

Müller, F. M., ed. 1882a. Baudhayana. In *The Sacred Laws of the Aryas: As taught in the schools of Apastamba, Gautama, Vasishtha, and Baudhayana,* Part 2. Vasishtha and Baudhayana, Vol. 14, *The Sacred Books of the East,* trans. G. Buhler. Second edition. Oxford.

　　1882b. Vasishtha. In *The Sacred Laws of the Aryas: As taught in the schools of Apastamba, Gautama, Vasishtha, and Baudhayana,* Part 2. Vasishtha and Baudhayana, Vol. 14, *The Sacred Books of the East,* trans. G. Buhler. Second edition. Oxford.

　　1896a. Apastamba. In *The sacred laws of the Aryas: As taught in the schools of Apastamba, Gautama, Vasishtha, and Baudhayana,* Part 1. Apastamba and Gautama, Vol. 2, *The Sacred Books of the East,* trans. G. Buhler. Second edition. Oxford.

　　1896b. Gautama. In *The Sacred Laws of the Aryas: As taught in the schools of Apastamba, Gautama, Vasishtha, and Baudhayana,* Part 1. Apastamba and Gautama, Vol. 2, *The Sacred Books of the East,* trans. G. Buhler. Second edition. Oxford.

　　1896c. Manu. In *The laws of Manu: Translated with extracts from seven commentaries,* Vol 25, *The sacred books of the East,* trans. G. Buhler. Oxford.

Natow, A. B., J. Iteslin, and B. C. Raven. 1975. Integrating the Jewish dietary laws into a dietetics program. *Journal of the American Dietetic Association* 67: 13-16.

Newberry, P. 1928. The pig and the cult animal of Set. *Journal of Egyptian Archaeology* 14: 211-25.

Novatian. 1957. On the Jewish meats. In *The Ante-Nicene Fathers,* Vol. 5, ed. A. Roberts and J. Donaldson. trans. R. E. Wallis, 645-50. Grand Rapids, Mich.

Owen, R. 1835. Description of a microscopic entozoon infesting the muscles of the human body. *Transactions of the Zoological Society of London* 1: 315-24.

Paget, J. 1866. On the discovery of Trichina. *Lancet* 1: 269-70.

Petrovic, A. 1939. Contributions to the study of the Serbian Gypsies. Part 2: The eating of carrion. *Journal, Gypsy Lore Society* (3rd Series) 18: 24-34.

Philo. 1954. On the special laws. In *The collected works of Philo,* Vol. 8, trans. E. H. Colson, 7-155. London.

Pike, O. A. 1992. The church of Jesus Christ of Latter-Day Saints: Dietary practices and health. *Food Technology* 46: 118-21.

Pillsbury, B. L. K. 1978. "Doing the month": Confinement and convalescence of Chinese women after childbirth. *Social Science and Medicine* 12: 11-22.

Platt, B. S., and S. Y. Gin. 1938. Chinese methods of infant feeding and nursing. *Archives, Diseases of Childhood* 18: 343-54.

Pliny. 1919-1956. *Natural history,* trans. H. Rackham and W. H. S. Jones. 8 vols. Cambridge, Mass.

Plutarch. 1936. Isis and Osiris. In *Moralia,* Vol. 5, trans. F. C. Babbitt. Cambridge, Mass.

Polynaeus. 1793. *Stratagems of War,* trans. R. Shepherd. London.

Porphyry. 1965. *On abstinence from animal food,* trans. Thomas Taylor. London.

Prakash, O. 1961. *Food and drinks in ancient India: From earliest times to c. 1200 A.D.* Delhi.

Preuss, Julius. 1978. *Julius Preuss' Biblical and Talmudic medicine,* ed. and trans. F. Rosner. New York.

Qazwiny [Zakaria ibn Mohammed ibn Mahmoud]. 1957. *Kitab aga'il el-makhlouquat wa ghara'ib el-mawgoudat.* 2 vols. Cairo.

Rahman, F. 1987. *Health and medicine in the Islamic tradition: Change and identity.* New York.

Read, B. E. 1976. *Chinese materia medica: Animal drugs.* Taipei.

   1977a. *Chinese materia medica: Avian drugs.* Taipei.

   1977b. *Chinese materia medica: Dragon and snake drugs.* Taipei.

   1977c. *Chinese materia medica: Fish drugs.* Taipei.

   1977d. *Chinese materia medica: Insect drugs.* Taipei.

   1977e. *Chinese materia medica: Turtle and shellfish drugs.* Taipei.

Regenstein, J. M., and C. E. Regenstein. 1979. An introduction to the kosher dietary laws for food scientists and food processors. *Food Technology* 33: 89-99.

   1988. The kosher dietary laws and their implementation in the food industry. *Food Technology* 42: 86, 88-94.

   1991. Current issues in kosher foods. *Trends in Food Science and Technology* 2: 50-4.

Richards, A. I. 1932. *Hunger and work in a savage tribe: A functional study of nutrition among the southern Bantu.* London.

   1939. *Land, labor and diet in northern Rhodesia: An economic study of the Bemba tribe.* Oxford.

Roberts, R. 1925. *The social laws of the Qorân: Considered and compared with those of Hebrew and other ancient codes.* London.

Sakr, A. H. 1971. Fasting in Islam. *Journal of the American Dietetic Association* 67: 17-21.

   1975. Dietary regulation and food habits of Muslims. *Journal of the American Dietetic Association* 58: 123-6.

   1991. *Pork: Possible reasons for its prohibition.* Lombard, Ill.

Schmidt, N. 1926. The numen of Penuel. *Journal of Biblical Literature* 45: 260-79.

Scott, T. 1866. *The Holy Bible containing the Old and New Testaments according to the authorized version with explanatory notes, practical observations, and copious marginal references.* New edition. 2 vols. London.

Sextus Empiricus. 1933. *Outlines of Pyrrhonism,* Vol 1, *Sextus Empiricus,* trans R. G. Bury. New York.

Simoons, F. J. 1961. *Eat not this flesh: Food avoidance in the Old World.* Madison, Wis.

   1966. The geographic approach to food prejudices. *Food Technology* 20: 274-6.

   1978. Traditional use and avoidance of foods of animal origin: A cultural historical review. *BioScience* 28: 178-84.

Singer, I. 1907. *The Jewish encyclopedia,* Vol 4. New York.

Smith, Joseph. [1833] 1869. A word of wisdom, for the benefit of the council of high priests, assembled in Kirtland, and church, and also the saints in Zion. In *The book of doctrine and covenants of the Church of Jesus Christ of Latter-Day Saints; Selected from the revelations of God by Joseph Smith, president.* Sixth European edition, 240-1. London.

Smith, W. R. 1969. *Lectures on the religion of the Semites: The fundamental institutions.* Third edition. New York.

Sun Ssu-Mo. 1980. *Ch'ien-chin i-fang [Formulas worth a thousand thals of gold].* Third edition. Taipei, Taiwan.

Tan, S. P., and E. Wheeler. 1983. Concepts relating to health and food held by Chinese women in London. *Ecology of Food and Nutrition* 13: 37-49.

Temkin, O. 1953. Greek medicine as science and kraft. *Isis* 44: 213-26.

Thompson, L. 1949. The relations of men, animals and plants in an island community. *American Anthropologist* 51: 253-76.

Torah. 1962. *The Torah: The five books of Moses.* Philadelphia, Pa.

Twaigery, S., and D. Spillman. 1989. An introduction to Moslem dietary laws. *Food Technology* 43: 88-90.

van den Heever, L. W. 1967. Some public health aspects of meat and milk. *South African Medical Journal* 41: 1240-43.

Wheeler, E., and S. P. Tan. 1983. From concept to practice: Food behavior of Chinese immigrants in London. *Ecology of Food and Nutrition* 13: 51-7.

Wilkinson, J. G. 1854. *A popular account of the ancient Egyptians.* 2 vols. New York.

Willoughby, W. C. 1932. *Nature-worship and taboo: Further studies in "The soul of the Bantu."* Hartford, Conn.

Zenker, F. A. 1860. Ueber die Trichinen-Krankheit des Menschen. *Virchows Archiv für pathologische Anatomie und Physiologie und für klinische Medizin* 18: 561-72.

VI.14 ✒ The Social and Cultural Uses of Food

Food is what Marcel Mauss (1967) called a "total social fact." It is a part of culture that is central, connected to many kinds of behavior, and infinitely meaningful. Food is a prism that absorbs a host of assorted cultural phenomena and unites them into one coherent domain while simultaneously speaking through that domain about everything that is important. For example, for Sardinians, bread is world (Counihan 1984). In the production, distribution, and consumption of bread are manifest Sardinian economic realities, social relations, and cultural ideals. An examination of foodways in all cultures reveals much about power relations, the shaping of community and personality, the construction of the family, systems of meaning and communication, and conceptions of sex, sexuality, and gender. The study of foodways has contributed to the understanding of personhood across cultures and historical periods (see Messer 1984).

Every coherent social group has its own unique alimentary system. Even cultures in the process of disintegration reveal their plight in the ways they deal with and think about eating.[1] Cultures articulate and recognize their distinctiveness through the medium of food. The English call the French "Frogs" because of their habit (wildly barbarian to the English) of eating the legs of that creature (Leach 1964: 31). In the Amazon region, Indian tribes that appear alike in the eyes of an outsider nonetheless distinguish themselves from one another in part through their different habits, manners, and conceptions of eating. Maligned other groups are defined as those who eat people and animals thought disgusting, as for example, "frogs and snakes and mice" (Gregor

1985: 14). Food systems are, of course, intimately related to the local environment, but in most cultures "only a small part of this edible environment will actually be classified as potential food. Such classification is a matter of language and culture, not of nature" (Leach 1964: 31). The study of foodways enables a holistic and coherent look at how humans mediate their relationships with nature and with one another across cultures and throughout history.

Food and Power

David Arnold (1988: 3) suggests that "food was, and continues to be, power in a most basic, tangible and inescapable form." Frances Moore Lappé and Joseph Collins (1986) make a strong argument that there is no more absolute sign of powerlessness than hunger, since hunger means that one lacks the control to satisfy the most basic subsistence need. Food is a central concern in the politics of nation states. Whereas Piero Camporesi (1989: 137) argues that chronic hunger and malnutrition were part of a calculated strategy of early modern political elites to maintain their power by keeping the poor debilitated and dazed, Arnold (1988) and others[2] point out that extreme hunger can bring about popular protest that may seriously weaken a government's stability. According to Arnold (1988: 96), "The fortunes of the state, whether in Europe or in Africa or Asia, have long been closely bound up with the containment or prevention of famine and, more generally, with provisioning the populace."

In stratified societies, hunger – like poverty – is far more likely to strike people in disadvantaged and devalued social categories: small children, the mentally ill, the handicapped, women, people of color, and the elderly (Physicians Task Force on Hunger in America 1985; Brown 1987; Brown and Pizer 1987; Arnold 1988; Glasser 1988). Food scarcity mirrors and exacerbates social distinctions; famine relief goes first to groups with power, and in times of economic crisis, the rich get richer by buying the land and other resources of the poor as the latter give them up in the struggle to eat.

A person's place in the social system can be revealed by what, how much, and with whom one eats. As Jack Goody (1982: 113) says, "the hierarchy between ranks and classes takes a culinary form." In India, caste is marked quite conspicuously by different food habits and rules prohibiting eating with those of lower caste (Goody 1982: 116 ff.; Khare and Rao 1986). Different consumption patterns are one of the ways the rich distinguish themselves from the poor (Bennett 1943; Fitchen 1988; Weismantel 1988). For example, according to Carol J. Adams (1990: 30), the consumption of meat protein reveals "the white Western world's enactment of racism. . . . The hierarchy of meat protein reinforces a hierarchy of race, class, and sex." Sugar was at first only a food of the rich, who used it to (among other things) create fabulous, ostentatious sculptures that proclaimed their wealth and power through extravagance with the precious and desirable commodity (Mintz 1985).

As sugar became more plentiful, however, the poor were increasingly able to eat it, which they did, in part, in an effort to emulate the rich and achieve a like status. Sugar consumption conveyed "the complex idea that one could *become* different by *consuming* differently" (Mintz 1985: 185). But to eat sugar, the poor sacrificed other foods, and their diet suffered, whereas the rich who could eat sugar *and* other foods simply chose new ways of proclaiming their difference. According to Stephen Mennell:

> Likes and dislikes are never socially neutral, but always entangled with people's affiliations to class and other social groups. Higher social circles have repeatedly used food as one of many means of distinguishing themselves from lower rising classes. This has been manifested in a succession of styles and attitudes towards food and eating (Mennell 1985: 331–2).

Class distinctions are also manifest through rules about eating and through the ability to impose rules on others (Counihan 1992). For example, we live in a culture that values thinness.[3] The dominant culture – manifest in advertising, fashion, and the media – projects a belief that thinness connotes control, power, wealth, competence, and success (Dyrenforth, Wooley, and Wooley 1980). Research has revealed that obesity for women varies directly with class status and ethnicity. Greater wealth and whiteness go along with thinness; poor Puerto Rican, black, and Native American women have lower status and greater obesity rates than well-off Euro-American women (Garb, Garb, and Stunkard 1975; Beller 1977; Stunkard 1977; Massara and Stunkard 1979; Massara 1989; Sobal and Stunkard 1989). The standard of thinness upholds a class structure where men, whites, and the rich are superior to women, people of color, and the poor.

Food and Community

Manners and habits of eating not only display the complex intricacies of the social hierarchy but also are crucial to the very definition of community, the relationships between people, interactions between humans and their gods, and communication between the living and the dead. In many societies, communal feasts involve a periodic reaffirmation of community "based upon primal conceptions of the meaning of eating and drinking in common. To eat and drink with someone was at the same time a symbol and a confirmation of social community and of the assumption of mutual obligations" (Freud 1918: 174).

Sharing food ensures the survival of the group both socially and materially. A companion is literally a person one eats bread with (Farb and Armelagos 1980: 4). Refusal to share food is a sign of enmity and hostility; as Marcel Mauss (1967: 58) reports of Brahmans, "A man does not eat with his enemy." For eating together is a sign of kinship, trust, friendship, and in some cultures, sexual intimacy, as we shall discuss further.

On a day-to-day basis, food exchanges are crucial in maintaining good relations between individuals. The message of the following Sardinian proverb (Gallini 1973: 60) is relevant in many cultures:

> Si cheres chi s'amore si
>   mantenzat
> prattu chi andet, prattu
> chi benzat.

> If you want love to be
>   maintained
> for a plate that goes,
> let a plate come back.

Mauss (1967) has shown the pervasive cultural power of the gift that keeps individuals constantly indebted to each other and continuously engaged in positive interaction through giving. In his interpretation of Mauss, Marshall Sahlins has said, "The gift is alliance, solidarity, communion, in brief, peace" (1972: 169). Food is an extremely important component of reciprocal exchanges, more so than any other object or substance (Mauss 1967). As Sahlins says: "By comparison with other stuff, food is more readily, or more necessarily shared" (1972: 215).

Bronislaw Malinowski (1961: 168–72), Miriam Kahn (1986, 1988), and Michael Young (1971) have explicitly demonstrated how in Melanesia, feasting both joins people in community and establishes power relations. Kahn (1986, 1988) describes two different kinds of feasts held by the Wamirans of Papua New Guinea, the T-mode (transaction) feast that serves to reinforce power ranks and the I-mode (incorporation) feast that strengthens community solidarity; "both types of exchanges are equally necessary" (Kahn 1986: 125). Similarly, in the Sardinian community of Tresnuraghes (Counihan 1984), the annual St. Mark celebration involves a collective feasting on mutton, donated by wealthy shepherds, and bread, donated by villagers seeking or repaying divine assistance. This redistributive feast serves simultaneously to bring the community together, to make abundant food available to the poor, and to display the wealth and prestige of those able to sponsor the feast. Similar redistributive celebrations occur in a wide range of peasant and tribal societies and are central to the maintenance of community and political organization.[4]

In many cultures, food is instrumental in maintaining good relations between humans and their gods. In Christianity, a central symbol is the consumption of bread, both by Christ and his disciples at the Last Supper, and regularly by the faithful in the Communion ritual (Feeley-Harnik 1981; Bynum 1987). The bread, or host, is the body of Christ; it stands for redemption, holiness, and salvation. The faithful literally eat their God, and, in so doing, incorporate the values and messages of their religion. Ancient Greeks, and many other peoples, use food sacrifices as a means of propitiating their gods (Mauss 1967; Detienne and Vernant 1989). Tibetan Buddhist Sherpas consciously cajole their gods with food offerings and say, "I am offering you the things which you eat, now you must do whatever I demand" (Ortner 1975: 147). By consciously employing the mechanisms of hospitality with the gods that facilitate human interaction, Sherpas hope that "aroused, pleased, and gratified, the gods, like one's neighbors, will feel 'happy' and kindly disposed toward the worshippers/hosts and any requests they might make" (Ortner 1975: 146–7).

Offerings of food to the deceased are a common cultural means of ensuring good relations with them (Frazer 1951; Goody 1962; Huntington and Metcalf 1979; Nutini 1988). On All Souls' Day or Eve, throughout the Christian world, people make food offerings and sometimes prepare entire meals for the dead. Some Sicilians eat fava beans; others consume cooked cereals (De Simone and Rossi 1977: 53–4). In Bosa, on All Souls' Day, Sardinians prepare *sa mesa*, literally, "the table," which is a meal for the deceased that they lay out as they are going to bed (Counihan 1981: 276–9). They always include spaghetti and *pabassini*, a special cookie made for All Souls' Day, as well as many other foods, including bread, nuts, fruit, and sometimes wine, beer, Coca-Cola, juice, coffee, snuffing tobacco, or cigarettes. The meal is destined specifically for one's own dead relatives, and often the optional food items reflect a specific deceased person's preferences in life. The meal serves to communicate and maintain good relations with the dead, just as food exchanges regularly do with the living.

In some cultures, the living actually eat the dead to honor them and gain some of their powers (Arens 1979; Walens 1981; Sanday 1986). Sigmund Freud argued that consumption of the deceased is based on the belief that "by absorbing parts of the body of a person through the act of eating we also come to possess the properties which belonged to that person" (1918: 107). The Yanomamo Indians of the Venezuelan Amazon eat the ashes of their deceased loved ones to ensure a successful afterlife. When ethnographer Kenneth Good was deathly sick with malaria, his informants expressed their affection by assuring him, "Don't worry, older brother. Don't worry at all. We will drink your ashes" (Good and Chanoff 1991: 133). Consumption establishes connection between the living and the dead, between humans and their gods, among neighbors and kin, and, in particular, among family members.

Food and Family

Feeding is one of the most important channels of infant and child socialization and personality formation.[5] In fact, the Pacific Atimelangers studied by Cora Du Bois believe that the original creation of human beings was from food; they were "created from molded rice and corn meal" (1941: 278–9). Food and the manner of giving it make the child. As Margaret Mead said, "It seems probable that as he is fed every child learns something about the willingness of the world to give or withhold food, to give lavishly or deal out parsimoniously" (1967: 70).

According to Freud, the child's earliest experiences of eating are the stage for important developmental processes and shape his or her lifelong personality: "The first and most important activity in the child's life, the sucking from the mother's breast," introduces the child to sexual pleasure and prefigures later adult sexuality (Freud 1962: 43; see also Malinowski 1927). Furthermore, breast feeding becomes part of the process of individuation for the child. As it recognizes gradually that the mother is other, and that its source of food is outside of itself, the child begins to establish an autonomous and bounded identity.

In some cultures, the family may be most effectively conceptualized as those people who share a common hearth (Weismantel 1988: 169). As Janet Siskind says of the Sharanahua Indians of the Peruvian Amazon, "Eating with people is an affirmation of kinship" (1973: 9). So important is feeding to the establishment of parent–child relations in Kalauna, Goodenough Island, that "fosterage . . . is wholly conceived in terms of feeding" (Young 1971: 41). Young goes on to note that this same "identification is buried in our own language: Old English 'foster' means 'food'" (1971: 41). In Kalauna, the father establishes his paternity by providing food for his pregnant wife. Young says:

> While the role of the mother in producing the child is self-evident, the father must reinforce his own role by feeding his wife during pregnancy. This is explicitly seen as nurturing the foetus, and it is a principal element in the ideology of agnatic descent (1971: 40).

Problematic feeding can lead to personality disturbances in children, and dysfunctional families may have members who suffer from eating problems (Palazzoli 1971; Bruch 1973). Anna Freud suggests that disturbed eating patterns may be "symbolic of a struggle between mother and child, in which the child can find an outlet for its passive or active, sadistic or masochistic tendencies towards the mother" (1946: 121).

Dorothy N. Shack (1969) and William A. Shack (1971) attribute a host of personality characteristics of the Gurage of Ethiopia to their inconsistent early-childhood feeding habits and later patterns of want and glut that reveal severe "dependency-frustration" (W. Shack 1971: 34). Gurage children are often neglected when hungry and then finally fed to excess after crying for hours (D. Shack 1969). Adults eat sparingly and quickly on normal occasions, but occasionally find themselves forced to eat when not hungry at feasts or as guests (W. Shack 1971). D. Shack argues that such eating patterns contribute to the development of personality traits that include "selfishness," "emotional detachment," "unrelatedness," "passivity," "dependency," and feelings of worthlessness (1969: 298).

W. Shack suggests that because the food supply is particularly unreliable for low-status men, they are susceptible to *awre* (spirit possession), marked by "loss of appetite, nausea and intermittent attacks of severe stomach pains" (1971: 35). The affliction is cured through a collective ritual in which the victim is covered by a white shawl, seated in a smoky room, and given special food called *bra-brat*. With this, he "begins greedily and ravenously stuffing his mouth" and continues to do so until the spirit, "speaking through the possessed person, utters with a sigh, several times – '*tafwahum*' – 'I am satisfied'" (W. Shack 1971: 36). The rite of *awre*-spirit exorcism allows a low-status man deprived of both food and prestige to gain both. It is a temporary overcoming of the dependency frustration embedded in the cultural foodways that produces a chronic anxiety in those most often hungry. The Gurage exemplify how feeding patterns can influence personality formation and show how different cultures have distinct ways of ensuring that people get fed.

Food as Meaning, Symbol, and Language

In every culture, foodways constitute an organized system, a language, which – through its structure and components – conveys meaning and contributes to the organization of the natural and social world. According to Roland Barthes (1975: 49–50), "Food . . . is not only a collection of products that can be used for statistical or nutritional studies. It is also a system of communication, a body of images, a protocol of usages, situations and behavior." Foodways are a prime domain for conveying meaning because eating is an essential and continuously repeated activity; foods are many; there are different characteristics of texture, taste, color, and modes of preparation of food that are easy labels for meaning; food constitutes a language accessible to all; and eating is extremely pleasurable.

In examining the meaning of food, social scientists have studied *cuisine,* the food elements used and rules for their combination and preparation; *etiquette and food rules,* the customs governing what, with whom, when, and where one eats; *taboos,* the prohibitions of and restrictions on the consumption of certain foods by certain people under certain conditions; and *symbolism,* the specific meanings attributed to foods in specific contexts.[6] There is of course much overlap between these four domains. For example, the study of Jewish dietary law[7] involves examination of foods eaten and not eaten and the legitimate bases of their combination (cuisine). But it also concerns the study of meals, the arrangement and sequence of foods, peoples' roles in the preparation and serving of food, and their placement at the table (etiquette). In addition, it includes the study of foods not eaten and why (taboo). And finally, to make sense out of all this, it involves the study of the complex and multivocal meanings of the foods and the behaviors centered around them (symbolism).

Food functions effectively as a system of communication because human beings organize their foodways into an ordered system parallel to other cultural systems and infuse them with meaning: "The cuisine of a people and their understanding of the world are linked" (Soler 1973: 943, my translation). It is to this cultural association between food and meaning that Claude Lévi-Strauss (1963a: 89) was referring in his oft-quoted statement that certain animal species are chosen as totems "not because they are 'good to eat' but because they are 'good to think.'" Foods have and convey meanings because they are part of complex systems; "food categories . . . encode social events" (Douglas 1974: 61). Jean Soler suggests that a food taboo "cannot be understood in isolation. It must be placed in the center of the signs of its level, with which it forms a system, and this system must itself be connected to systems of other levels, with which it articulates to form the socio-cultural system of a people" (1973: 946, my translation).

Structuralists (for example, Lévi-Strauss 1966; Verdier 1969) emphasize the dual nature of food and cuisine, which both stand between and mediate nature and culture. The process of naming a wild product as food and transforming it into something edible involves the "culturizing" of nature. And cuisine, because it is a "means of transformation, must facilitate at least metaphorically all transformation" (Verdier 1969: 54). Hence, foods are very often used in rites of passage (see Goody 1982: 79–81).

Among the Mehinaku, initiation ceremonies for girls involve the ritual of first menses, for boys the ear-piercing ceremony. These rituals and the related blood flow are seen as parallel and involve the same restrictions on eating:

> Both boys and girls must follow certain food taboos to ensure the rapid cessation of the flow of blood and a favorable dream. Initially, the children are subject to a fast; they are allowed to drink water after twenty-four hours. . . . Following the fast, they may eat all foods but fish, which would prolong the blood flow. "Fish," it is said, "eat other fish and therefore are filled with blood." Monkeys and birds eat only fruit and have a "different kind of blood" and are there-

fore acceptable to "menstruating" boys and girls. . . . With the total cessation of the flow of blood, a ceremony reintroduces fish to the diet. The boys are led outside, taste a small amount of fish, and spit it onto a fiber mat. The girls follow the same ritual inside the house. . . . Fish are now permissible . . . (Gregor 1985: 189).

Here food is used to signify the transformation of boys to men and girls to women while it simultaneously marks the similarity of the maturation of boys and girls (see also S. Hugh-Jones 1979 and C. Hugh-Jones 1979, especially chapter 5).

Food can be used metaphorically to convey just about any imaginable condition, thought, or emotion. American college students, for example, express feelings of love, anger, anxiety, depression, sorrow, and joy through their eating habits (Counihan 1992). After a satisfying meal, Sardinians say, "consolada(o) soe" – "I am consoled" – and imply the metaphorical and physical overlap between good food and good feelings (Counihan 1981). Because of the strong visceral pleasure of eating and pain of hunger, food readily adopts powerful connotations and is a rich symbol in written and oral literature.

Food in Folklore and Literature

Food meanings are paramount in Lévi-Strauss's (1963b, 1966, and 1969) monumental study of mythology. He is concerned with understanding, through mythology, the structure of the human mind. According to Lévi-Strauss, binary oppositions are embodied in our brains and appear in many levels of our thinking. The oppositions in the human relationship to nature mediated through food (for example, "the raw and the cooked," nature and culture, or animal and human) reveal universals in human thinking.

In stories told to children, proper eating represents humanness and effective socialization, whereas out-of-control eating and cannibalism stand for wildness and incomplete socialization. The widely known European folktale "Hansel and Gretel" is a good example of these themes; it "is about conflicting family loyalties expressed in terms of sharing and hoarding food" (Taggart 1986: 435). Bruno Bettelheim interprets the food themes of the story as being about children's struggle to outgrow oral dependency and symbiosis with the mother (1975: 159-66). Hansel and Gretel are forced from home due to food scarcity and they, subsequently, gobble up the candy house without thought or restraint.

This regression to "primitive incorporative and hence destructive desires" only leads to trouble, as they are trapped by the wicked witch, "a personification of the destructive aspects of orality" (Bettelheim 1975: 160, 162). Eventually, the children use reason to dominate their oral urges and refuse food so as to be able to kill the witch. Then they inherit her jewels and become reunited with their family in a new status: "As the children transcend their oral anxiety, and free themselves of relying on oral satisfaction for security, they can also free themselves of the image of the threatening mother – the witch – and rediscover the good parents, whose greater wisdom – the shared jewels – then benefit all" (Bettelheim 1975: 162). Their struggle with food, in essence, represents stages in their maturation.

The same theme about the power of food in family relations is beautifully depicted in Maurice Sendak's Caldecott Medal–winning children's story *Where the Wild Things Are* (1963). The tale, which many have placed in the category of superb children's literature, goes something like this: Once upon a time there was an energetic little boy, Max, who put on his wolf costume and pretended to be a ferocious animal. He annoyed his mother so much with his rambunctious behavior that she called him a "wild thing." When in response he threatened to eat her up, she made him go to bed without his supper.

While Max was lying in the dark, his room turned into a dense forest, and a boat arrived. He boarded it and it took him to the land where the wild things lived. He "tamed" them, and they liked him so much that they crowned him their king, which began a boisterous and rowdy time for all.

After a while Max became annoyed by all the commotion and wanted it to stop. As their king he called an end to the rumpus and sent everyone to bed without supper. By now he missed his family and their love for him, and he detected a wonderful aroma that could only be the good food at his house. Very homesick now, he decided to give up his crown and leave the kingdom. He told the wild things that he wanted to go home.

His unruly subjects, however, were not willing to let him leave. They first claimed to love him too much to let him go; in fact, they said that they loved him so much they would rather eat him up than see him leave. But when he insisted, they acted ferociously toward him, making horrible sounds and showing their fangs, and their eyes were evil and menacing. The boy relinquished his kingdom nonetheless and boarded the boat from which he waved good-bye. The way home was a very long journey. It seemed to the little boy to take over a year – but when he finally arrived back in his room, a meal was laid out to greet him. It was still warm.

Sendak's story shows how food is a source of love, power, socialization, and connection between parents and children. In the story, Max is a "wild thing," an incompletely socialized child. His wildness is shown by the wolf suit and his desire to eat his mother up, a desire that simultaneously expresses the incomplete separation of the child from the mother. This theme of eating as incorporation is recreated later in the story when the wild things want to eat Max up, to keep

him from leaving them. But Max does not stay with the wild things; he feels the pull of love in the smells of "good things to eat" that come from the place "where someone loved him best of all." He follows a long journey home where love awaits him in the form of the supper that was previously denied him because of his bad behavior. The fact that "it was still hot" symbolizes the mother's love that persists and is there to facilitate his socialization.

Food, Gender, Sex, and Sexuality

One of the most significant domains of meaning embodied in food centers on the relation between the sexes, their gender definitions, and their sexuality:

> Wives are like mothers. When we were small our mothers fed us. When we are grown our wives cook for us. If there is something good, they keep it in the pot until we come home. When we were small we slept with our mothers; when we are grown we sleep with our wives. Sometimes when we are grown we wake in the night and call our wives 'mothers' (Du Bois 1944: 96).

Eating is a sexual and gendered activity throughout life. Food may stand for sex; as Thomas Gregor says of the Mehinaku Indians, "A literal rendering of the verb to have sex might thus be 'to eat to the fullest extent.' . . . The essential idea is that the genitals of one sex are the 'food' of the other's" (1985: 70). Food and sex are metaphorically overlapping: Eating may represent copulation; foods may stand for sexual acts. The poet George Herbert captured this relation in the early seventeenth century: " 'You must sit down,' says Love, 'and taste my Meat.' / So I did sit and Eat" (quoted in Starn 1990: 78). In many cultures, particularly those with food scarcity, food gifts may be an important path to sexual liaisons (Holmberg 1969: 126; Siskind 1973).

In all cultures there are associations between eating, intercourse, and reproduction.[8] These activities share certain biopsychological attributes – particularly their contributions to life and growth, their passing in and out of the body, and their mingling of discrete individuals – that endow them with metaphorical and symbolic identity. Food and sex are analogous instinctive needs (Freud 1962: 1), and there is a lifelong connection between oral pleasure and sexual pleasure (Freud 1962: 43). Eating together connotes intimacy, often sexual intimacy or kinship (Freud 1918: 175; Siskind 1973: 9). Hence, both eating and copulation could be seen as effecting social merging.

Precisely because eating and intercourse both involve intimacy, they can be dangerous when carried out with the wrong person or under the wrong conditions. Hence, food consumption and sexual activity are surrounded with rules and taboos that regulate them and also reinforce beliefs about gender basic to the social order (see especially Meigs 1984). Food and sex both have associated etiquette about their appropriate times, places, and persons; often people with whom one can eat are those with whom one can have sex and vice versa (see, for example, Tambiah 1969). Among the Trobriand Islanders, a man and woman announce their marriage by eating yams together in public; before this they must never share a meal (Weiner 1988: 77).

Maleness and femaleness in all cultures are associated with specific foods, and rules exist to control their consumption (see Frese 1991 and Brumberg 1988: 176-8). For example, the Hua of New Guinea have elaborate conceptions about *koroko* and *hakeri'a* foods. The former are cold, wet, soft, fertile, fast-growing foods associated with females; the latter are hot, dry, hard, infertile, and slow-growing foods associated with males. Women can become more like men by consuming *hakeri'a* foods, which, it is believed, help minimize menstrual flow. Men, on the other hand, proclaim publicly that female foods and substances are "not only disgusting but also dangerous to the development and maintenance of masculinity." Secretly, however, they eat foods associated with females to gain vitality and power (Meigs 1984).

In general, the association between food and sex is deeper, more extensive, and more intimate for women than it is for men (see, for example, Bynum 1987: xiv). In all cultures, women's primary responsibilities involve food provisioning and the bearing and rearing of children (D'Andrade 1974; Moore 1988). Although these activities are undertaken with widely ranging amounts of autonomy, prestige, and control, they are nonetheless universally linked to womanhood. Women *are* food to the fetus and infant: The breasts can be sources of both sexual pleasure and food. As Mead noted, for women but not for men, both food and sex involve a posture of inception: "[T]he girl finds that the reinterpretation of impregnation and conception and birth fits easily into her early experience with the intake of food" (1967: 143). Where women are valued, their parallel experiences of eating, intercourse, and birth are likely to be positive, but where women are devalued, these activities can be a source of shame and subordination.

In the United States, for example, female college students report that they feel ashamed to eat in front of men with whom they have a romantic involvement (Counihan 1992). They fear fat with obsession and terror (Orbach 1978; Millman 1980; Chernin 1981), and report that men denigrate and gain power over them by saying they eat too much or are too fat (Millman 1980; Counihan 1992). In gender-stratified cultures as diverse as England (Charles and Kerr 1988), Italy (Counihan 1988), and Andean Ecuador (Weismantel 1988), men control women by claiming the authority to judge the meal the latter have cooked for them.

The power relations around food mirror the power of the sexes in general.[9] Whereas men gain power in some cultures by controlling money, and hence food purchasing power (Charles and Kerr 1988), women exert considerable power in all cultures by their control of food preparation and consumption. Adams (1990) argues that patriarchal power in Western society is embodied in the practice of eating meat, which involves the linking of women and animals and their objectification and subordination. Women can rebel through vegetarianism, which from this perspective is a political statement: a rejection of patriarchal power and values, an expression of feminism, and a claiming of female power over self and nature.

Among the Zumbaguan Indians of Andean Ecuador, the senior female is in charge of preparing and serving meals (Weismantel 1988: 28-9). This gives her the ability to determine hierarchies by the order in which she serves people and the contents of the plate she gives them (Weismantel 1988: 182). A woman can even punish an errant husband who finally returns from a drinking spree by serving him massive quantities of rich food that the husband, by force of etiquette, eats, with extremely unpleasant physical results.

In Western societies, for at least eight centuries, some women have used food in symbolic ways as a path to power.[10] Today, modern anorexics starve themselves, sometimes to death, to achieve physical and spiritual perfection. Their behavior is strikingly similar to that of medieval holy women in the fourteenth, fifteenth, and sixteenth centuries, although the cultural contexts of their behaviors are rather different (Bell 1985; Bynum 1987; Brumberg 1988; Counihan 1989). Medieval holy women fasted for religious and spiritual perfection (that is, holiness): They used eating or fasting as a path to reach God and to circumvent patriarchal, familial, religious, and civil authority. Some women achieved sainthood by virtue of the spirituality they revealed, primarily through fasting and other food-centered behaviors, such as multiplying food in miracles, exuding holy oils or milk from their own bodies, and giving food to the poor (Bynum 1987). Contemporary anorexics attempt to achieve perfection through self-control and thinness. They receive pitying recognition from family, friends, and medical professionals, and may die unless they find a path to the self-esteem, sense of control, and autonomy they so desperately seek through fasting (Bruch 1973, 1978; Lawrence 1984; Brumberg 1988).

Between men and women, food is a means of differentiation, as well as a channel of connection. By claiming different roles in regard to food and distinct attributes through identification with specific foods, men and women define their masculinity and femininity, their similarities and differences. They use food and food metaphors to achieve the most intimate union, as witnessed through language that equates eating with sexual relations and through practices that equate the exchange of food – whether with candlelight dinners in four-star restaurants or with baked taro on Trobriand verandas (Weiner 1988) – with sexual intimacy.

Conclusion

Food, although essential to biological survival, takes on myriad meanings and roles in contributing to "the social construction of reality" (Berger and Luckmann 1966). As humans construct their relationship to nature through their foodways, they simultaneously define themselves and their social world (Berger and Luckmann 1966: 180–3). Through the production, distribution, and consumption of food, they act out their most important relationships: with their family, with their own and the opposite sex, with the community, with the dead, with the gods, and with the cosmos. Food orders the world and expresses multiplex meanings about the nature of reality. The social and cultural uses of food are many and they provide much insight into the human condition.

Carole M. Counihan

Notes

1. The following sources treat social responses to food shortages and famine: Richards 1932, 1939; Firth 1959; Holmberg 1969; Turnbull 1972, 1978; Laughlin and Brady 1978; Colson 1979; Prindle 1979; Dirks 1980; Young 1986; Vaughan 1987; Messer 1989; Newman 1990.
2. See, for example, Tilly 1971; Hilton 1973; Kaplan 1976, 1984, 1990; Barry 1987; Mackintosh 1989.
3. Some works that explore the U.S. value on thinness are the following: Powdermaker 1960; Bruch 1973, 1978; Boskind-Lodahl 1976; Stunkard 1977; Orbach 1978; J. R. Kaplan 1980; Millman 1980; Styles 1980; Boskind-White and White 1983; Counihan 1985, 1989; Schwartz 1986; Sobal and Stunkard 1989.
4. Perhaps the most well-known redistributive ritual is the potlatch of the Northwest coast Indians, a feast that involves enormous conspicuous consumption in a competition between tribes to establish prestige and power relations, debts, social congress, and communion with the gods. See Benedict 1934; Codere 1950; Mauss 1967: 31–7; Piddocke 1969; and Harris 1974.
5. Some sources on feeding as a form of socialization and personality formation are the following: Du Bois 1941, 1944; Bossard 1943; A. Freud 1946; S. Freud 1962; Mead 1963, 1967; Holmberg 1969; D. Shack 1969; W. Shack 1971; Bruch 1973; Farb and Armelagos 1980.
6. The following sources have material on the meaning of food through the study of symbolism, taboo, etiquette, and/or cuisine: Lévi-Strauss 1966; Holmberg 1969: 78–81, 173–5; Lehrer 1969, 1972; Verdier 1969; Firth 1973; Murphy and Murphy 1974: 162–3; Ortner 1975; C. Hugh-Jones 1979, especially chapters 5 and 6; S. Hugh-Jones 1979; Farb and Armelagos 1980; Goody 1982; Laderman 1983; Mennell 1985; Manderson 1986.
7. On Jewish dietary law see Douglas 1966; Soler 1973; Alter 1979; Feeley-Harnik 1981; Fredman 1981; Harris 1985.
8. Works that have abundant material on the overlap between food, sex, and sexuality are Tambiah 1969; Verdier 1969; Murphy and Murphy 1974; Farb and Armela-

gos 1980; Meigs 1984; Gregor 1985; Pollock 1985; Kahn 1986; Herdt 1987; Frese 1991.
9. Some sources that focus explicitly on food and the power relations between men and women are the following: Charles and Kerr 1988; Counihan 1988; Weismantel 1988; Babb 1989; McIntosh and Zey 1989.
10. There is an enormous literature on what Jane R. Kaplan (1980) has called "the special relationship between women and food." In Western culture, women have variously used compulsive eating, obesity, fasting, or the symbolic value of food as a means of expressing themselves and coping with the problems of achieving a meaningful place in a world where they are defined as subordinate. Some sources dealing with women's complicated relationship to food are the following, in alphabetical order: Bell 1985; Beller 1977; Boskind-Lodahl 1976; Boskind-White and White 1983; Bruch 1973, 1978; Brumberg 1988; Bynum 1987; Charles and Kerr 1988; Chernin 1981, 1985; Counihan 1985, 1988, 1989, 1992; Gordon 1988, 1990; J. Kaplan 1980; Lawrence 1984; Massara 1989; Millman 1980; Orbach 1978; Palazzoli 1971; Schwartz 1986; Styles 1980; Thoma 1977; Waller, Kaufman and Deutsch 1940.

Bibliography

Adams, Carol J. 1990. *The sexual politics of meat: A feminist-vegetarian critical theory.* New York.

Alter, L. 1979. A new theory of *Kashrut. Commentary* 68: 46–52.

Arens, William. 1979. *The man-eating myth.* New York.

Arnold, David. 1988. *Famine: Social crisis and historical change.* New York.

Babb, Florence E. 1989. *Between field and cooking pot: The political economy of marketwomen in Peru.* Austin, Tex.

Barry, Tom. 1987. *Roots of rebellion: Land and hunger in Central America.* Boston, Mass.

Barthes, Roland. 1975. Toward a psychosociology of contemporary food consumption. In *European diet from pre-industrial to modern times,* ed. Elborg Forster and Robert Forster, 47–59. New York.

Bell, Rudolph. 1985. *Holy anorexia.* Chicago.

Beller, Anne Scott. 1977. *Fat and thin: A natural history of obesity.* New York.

Benedict, Ruth. 1934. *Patterns of culture.* Boston, Mass.

Bennett, John. 1943. Food and social status in a rural society. *American Sociological Review* 8: 561–9.

Berger, Peter, and Thomas Luckmann. 1966. *The social construction of reality: A treatise in the sociology of knowledge.* New York.

Bettelheim, Bruno. 1975. *The uses of enchantment: The meaning and importance of fairy tales.* New York.

Boskind-Lodahl, Marlene. 1976. Cinderella's stepsisters: A feminist perspective on anorexia nervosa and bulimarexia. *Signs* 2: 342–56.

Boskind-White, Marlene, and William C. White. 1983. *Bulimarexia: The binge/purge cycle.* New York.

Bossard, James H. S. 1943. Family table talk: An area for sociological study. *American Sociological Review* 8: 295–301.

Brown, J. Larry. 1987. Hunger in the U.S. *Scientific American* 256: 37–41.

Brown, J. Larry, and H. F. Pizer. 1987. *Living hungry in America.* New York.

Bruch, Hilde. 1973. *Eating disorders: Obesity, anorexia nervosa and the person within.* New York.

1978. *The golden cage: The enigma of anorexia nervosa.* New York.

Brumberg, Joan Jacobs. 1988. *Fasting girls: The emergence of anorexia nervosa as a modern disease.* Cambridge, Mass.

Bynum, Caroline Walker. 1987. *Holy feast and holy fast: The religious significance of food to medieval women.* Berkeley, Calif.

Camporesi, Piero. 1989. *Bread of dreams: Food and fantasy in early modern Europe,* trans. David Gentilcore. Chicago.

Charles, Nickie, and Marion Kerr. 1988. *Women, food and families.* Manchester, England.

Chernin, Kim. 1981. *The obsession: Reflections on the tyranny of slenderness.* New York.

1985. *The hungry self.* New York.

Codere, Helen. 1950. *Fighting with property: A study of Kwakiutl potlatches and warfare 1792-1930.* Monographs of the American Ethnological Society, 18. New York.

Colson, Elizabeth. 1979. In good years and bad: Food strategies of self-reliant societies. *Journal of Anthropological Research* 35: 18-29.

Counihan, Carole. 1981. Food, culture and political economy: Changing lifestyles in the Sardinian town of Bosa. Ph.D. dissertation, University of Massachusetts.

1984. Bread as world: Food habits and social relations in modernizing Sardinia. *Anthropological Quarterly* 57: 47-59.

1985. What does it mean to be fat, thin, and female in the United States? *Food and Foodways* 1: 77-94.

1988. Female identity, food, and power in contemporary Florence. *Anthropological Quarterly* 61: 51-62.

1989. An anthropological view of Western women's prodigious fasting. *Food and Foodways* 3: 357-75.

1992. Food rules in the U.S.: Individualism, control and hierarchy. *Anthropological Quarterly* 65: 55-66.

D'Andrade, Roy G. 1974. Sex differences and cultural institutions. In *Culture and personality, contemporary readings,* ed. Robert A. Le Vine, 16-39. New York.

De Simone, Roberto, and Annabella Rossi. 1977. *Carnevale si chiamava vincenzo.* Rome.

Detienne, Marcel, and Jean-Pierre Vernant. 1989. *The cuisine of sacrifice among the Greeks,* trans. Paula Wissing. Chicago.

Dirks, Robert. 1980. Social responses during severe food shortages and famine. *Current Anthropology* 21: 21-44.

Douglas, Mary. 1966. *Purity and danger.* London.

1974. Deciphering a meal. In *Myth, symbol and culture,* ed. Clifford Geertz, 61-81. New York.

Du Bois, Cora. 1941. Attitudes towards food and hunger in Alor. In *Language, culture, and personality: Essays in memory of Edward Sapir,* ed. L. Spier, A. I. Hallowell, and S. S. Newman, 271-81. Menasha, Wis.

1944. *The people of Alor.* 2 vols. New York.

Dyrenforth, Sue R., Orland W. Wooley, and Susan C. Wooley. 1980. A woman's body in a man's world: A review of findings on body image and weight control. In *A woman's conflict: The special relationship between women and food,* ed. J. R. Kaplan, 29-57. Englewood Cliffs, N.J.

Farb, Peter, and George Armelagos. 1980. *Consuming passions: The anthropology of eating.* New York.

Feeley-Harnik, Gillian. 1981. *The Lord's table: Eucharist and Passover in early Christianity.* Philadelphia, Pa.

Firth, Raymond. 1959. *Social change in Tikopia: Restudy of a Polynesian community after a generation.* New York.

1973. Food symbolism in a pre-industrial society. In *Symbols: Public and private,* ed. Raymond Firth, 243-61. Ithaca, N.Y.

Fitchen, Janet M. 1988. Hunger, malnutrition and poverty in the contemporary United States: Some observations on their social and cultural context. *Food and Foodways* 2: 309-33.

Frazer, James G. 1951. *The golden bough: A study in magic and religion.* New York.

Fredman, Ruth Gruber. 1981. *The Passover seder: Afikoman in exile.* Philadelphia, Pa.

Frese, Pamela. 1991. The union of nature and culture: Gender symbolism in the American wedding ritual. In *Transcending boundaries: Multi-disciplinary approaches to the study of gender,* ed. P. R. Frese and J. M. Coggeshall, 97-112. New York.

Freud, Anna. 1946. The psychoanalytic study of infantile feeding disturbances. *The psychoanalytic study of the child. An annual,* 2: 119-32.

Freud, Sigmund. 1918. *Totem and taboo.* New York.

1962. *Three contributions to the theory of sex,* trans. A. A. Brill. New York.

Gallini, Clara. 1973. *Dono e Malocchio.* Palermo.

Garb, Jane L., J. R. Garb, and A. J. Stunkard. 1975. Social factors and obesity in Navajo children. *Proceedings of the First International Congress on Obesity,* 37-9. London.

Glasser, Irene. 1988. *More than bread: Ethnography of a soup kitchen.* Tuscaloosa, Ala.

Good, Kenneth, and David Chanoff. 1991. *Into the heart: One man's pursuit of love and knowledge among Yanomama.* New York.

Goody, Jack. 1962. *Death, property and the ancestors: A study of the mortuary customs of the Lodagaa of West Africa.* London.

1982. *Cooking, cuisine, and class: A study in comparative sociology.* Cambridge.

Gordon, Richard A. 1988. A sociocultural interpretation of the current epidemic of eating disorders. In *The eating disorders,* ed. B. J. Blinder, B. F. Chaiting, and R. Goldstein, 151-63. Great Neck, N.Y.

1990. *Anorexia and bulimia: Anatomy of a social epidemic.* Cambridge.

Gregor, Thomas. 1985. *Anxious pleasures: The sexual lives of an Amazonian people.* Chicago.

Harris, Marvin. 1974. Potlatch. In *Cows, pigs, wars and witches,* ed. Marvin Harris, 111-30. New York.

1985. The abominable pig. In *Good to eat: Riddles of food and culture,* ed. Marvin Harris, 67-87. New York.

Herdt, Gilbert. 1987. *The Sambia: Ritual and gender in New Guinea.* New York.

Hilton, Rodney. 1973. *Bond men made free: Medieval peasant movements and the English rising of 1381.* New York.

Holmberg, Allan R. 1969. *Nomads of the long bow: The Siriono of Eastern Bolivia.* Prospect Heights, Ill.

Hugh-Jones, Christine. 1979. *From the Milk River: Spatial and temporal processes in northwest Amazonia.* Cambridge.

Hugh-Jones, Stephen. 1979. *The palm and the Pleiades: Initiation and cosmology in northwest Amazonia.* Cambridge.

Huntington, Richard, and Peter Metcalf. 1979. *Celebrations of death. The anthropology of mortuary ritual.* Cambridge.

Kahn, Miriam. 1986. *Always hungry, never greedy: Food and the expression of gender in a Melanesian society.* Cambridge.

1988. "Men are taro" (They cannot be rice): Political aspects of food choices. *Food and Foodways* 3: 41-58.

Kaplan, Jane Rachel, ed. 1980. *A woman's conflict: The special relationship between women and food.* Englewood Cliffs, N.J.

Kaplan, Steven L. 1976. *Bread, politics and political economy in the reign of Louis XV.* The Hague.

1984. *Provisioning Paris: Merchants and millers in the grain and flour trade during the eighteenth century.* Ithaca, N.Y.

1990. The state and the problem of dearth in eighteenth-century France: The crisis of 1738-41 in Paris. *Food and Foodways* 4: 111-41.

Khare, R. S., and M. S. A. Rao. 1986. *Food, society and culture: Aspects in South Asian food systems.* Durham, N.C.

Laderman, Carol. 1983. *Wives and midwives: Childbirth and nutrition in rural Malaysia.* Berkeley, Calif.

Lappé, Frances Moore, and Joseph Collins. 1986. *World hunger: Twelve myths.* New York.

Laughlin, Charles, and Ivan Brady, eds. 1978. *Extinction and survival in human populations.* New York.

Lawrence, Marilyn. 1984. *The anorexic experience.* London

Leach, Edmund. 1964. Anthropological aspects of language: Animal categories and verbal abuse. In *New directions in the study of language,* ed. E. H. Lenneberg, 23-63. Cambridge, Mass.

Lehrer, Adrienne. 1969. Semantic cuisine. *Journal of Linguistics* 5: 39-56.

1972. Cooking vocabularies and the culinary triangle of Lévi-Strauss. *Anthropological Linguistics* 14: 155-71.

Lévi-Strauss, Claude. 1963a. *Totemism.* Boston, Mass.

1963b. The structural study of myth. In *Structural anthropology,* ed. Claude Lévi-Strauss, 202-28. New York.

1966. The culinary triangle. *Partisan Review* 33: 586-95.

1969. *The raw and the cooked: Introduction to a science of mythology,* trans. John Weightman and Doreen Weightman. New York.

1973. *From honey to ashes: Introduction to a science of mythology,* trans. John Weightman and Doreen Weightman. New York.

Mackintosh, Maureen. 1989. *Gender, class and rural transition: Agribusiness and the food crisis in Senegal.* London.

Malinowski, Bronsilaw. 1927. *Sex and repression in savage society.* Chicago.

1961. *Argonauts of the western Pacific.* New York.

Manderson, Lenore, ed. 1986. *Shared wealth and symbol: Food, culture and society in Oceania and Southeast Asia.* Cambridge.

Massara, Emily B., and Albert J. Stunkard. 1979. A method of quantifying cultural ideals of beauty and the obese. *International Journal of Obesity* 3: 149-52.

Massara, Emily Bradley. 1989. *Que Gordita. A study of weight among women in a Puerto Rican community.* New York.

Mauss, Marcel. 1967. *The gift: Forms and functions of exchange in archaic societies.* New York.

McIntosh, William Alex, and Mary Zey. 1989. Women as gatekeepers of food consumption: A sociological critique. *Food and Foodways* 3: 317-22.

Mead, Margaret. 1963. *Sex and temperament in three primitive societies.* New York.

1967. *Male and female: A study of the sexes in a changing world.* New York.

Meigs, Anna S. 1984. *Food, sex, and pollution: A New Guinea religion.* New Brunswick, N.J.

Mennell, Stephen. 1985. *All manners of food: Eating and taste in England and France from the Middle Ages to the present.* Oxford.

Messer, Ellen. 1984. Anthropological perspectives on diet. *Annual Review of Anthropology* 13: 205-49.

1989. Small but healthy? Some cultural considerations. *Human Organization* 48: 39-52.

Millman, Marcia. 1980. *Such a pretty face: Being fat in America.* New York.

Mintz, Sidney. 1985. *Sweetness and power: The place of sugar in modern history.* New York.

Moore, Henrietta. 1988. *Feminism and anthropology.* Minneapolis, Minn.

Murphy, Yolanda, and Robert Murphy. 1974. *Women of the forest.* New York.

Newman, Lucile, ed. 1990. *Hunger in history: Food shortage, poverty, and deprivation.* New York.

Nutini, Hugo. 1988. *Todos Santos in rural Tlaxcala: A syncretic, expressive, and symbolic analysis of the cult of the dead.* Princeton, N.J.

Orbach, Susie. 1978. *Fat is a feminist issue: The anti-diet guide to permanent weight loss.* New York.

Ortner, Sherry B. 1975. Gods' bodies, gods' food: A symbolic analysis of a Sherpa ritual. In *The interpretation of symbolism,* ed. R. Willis 133-69. New York.

Palazzoli, Maria Selvini. 1971. Anorexia nervosa. In *The world biennial of psychiatry and psychotherapy,* Vol. 1, ed. Silvano Arietti, 197-218. New York.

Physicians Task Force on Hunger in America. 1985. *Hunger in America: The growing epidemic.* Middletown, Conn.

Piddocke, Stuart. 1969. The potlatch system of the southern Kwakiutl: A new perspective. In *Environment and cultural behavior,* ed. Andrew P. Vayda, 130-56. Garden City, N.J.

Pollock, Donald K. 1985. Food and sexual identity among the Culina. *Food and Foodways* 1: 25-42.

Powdermaker, Hortense. 1960. An anthropological approach to the problem of obesity. *Bulletin of the New York Academy of Medicine* 36: 286-95.

Prindle, Peter H. 1979. Peasant society and famine: A Nepalese example. *Ethnology* 18: 49-60.

Richards, Audrey I. 1932. *Hunger and work in a savage tribe: A functional study of nutrition among the southern Bantu.* London.

1939. *Land, labour and diet in northern Rhodesia: An economic study of the Bemba tribe.* London.

Sahlins, Marshall. 1972. *Stone Age economics.* New York.

Sanday, Peggy. 1986. *Divine hunger: Cannibalism as a cultural system.* Cambridge.

Schwartz, Hillel. 1986. *Never satisfied: A cultural history of diets, fantasies and fat.* New York.

Sendak, Maurice. 1963. *Where the wild things are.* New York.

Shack, Dorothy N. 1969. Nutritional processes and personality development among the Gurage of Ethiopia. *Ethnology* 8: 292-300.

Shack, William A. 1971. Hunger, anxiety, and ritual: Deprivation and spirit possession among the Gurage of Ethiopia. *Man* 6: 30-45.

Siskind, Janet. 1973. *To hunt in the morning.* Oxford and New York.

Sobal, Jeffrey, and Albert J. Stunkard. 1989. Socioeconomic status and obesity: A review of the literature. *Psychological Bulletin* 105: 260-75.

Soler, Jean. 1973. Sémiotique de la nourriture dans la Bible. *Annales: Économies, Sociétés, Civilisations* 28: 943-55.

Starn, Frances. 1990. *Soup of the day: A novel.* New York.

Stunkard, Albert J. 1977. Obesity and the social environment: Current status, future prospects. *Annals of the New York Academy of Sciences* 300: 298-320.

Styles, Marvalene. 1980. Soul, black women and food. In *A woman's conflict: The special relationship between women and food,* ed. J. R. Kaplan, 161-76. Englewood Cliffs, N.J.

Taggart, James M. 1986. "Hansel and Gretel" in Spain and Mexico. *Journal of American Folklore* 933: 435-60.

Tambiah, S. J. 1969. Animals are good to think and good to prohibit. *Ethnology* 8: 423-59.

Thoma, Helmut. 1977. On the psychotherapy of patients with anorexia nervosa. *Bulletin of the Menninger Clinic* 41: 437-52.

Tilly, Louise. 1971. The food riot as a form of political conflict in France. *Journal of Interdisciplinary History* 2: 23-57.

Turnbull, Colin. 1972. *The mountain people.* New York.

    1978. Rethinking the Ik: A functional non-social system. In *Extinction and survival in human populations,* ed. C. Laughlin and I. Brady, 49-75. New York.

Vaughan, Megan. 1987. *The story of an African famine: Gender and famine in twentieth-century Malawi.* Cambridge.

Verdier, Yvonne. 1969. Pour une ethnologie culinaire. *L'Homme* 9: 49-57.

Walens, Stanley. 1981. *Feasting with cannibals: An essay on Kwakiutl cosmology.* Princeton, N.J.

Waller, J. V., R. Kaufman, and F. Deutsch. 1940. Anorexia nervosa: A psychosomatic entity. *Psychosomatic Medicine* 2: 3-16.

Weiner, Annette B. 1988. *The Trobrianders of Papua New Guinea.* New York.

Weismantel, M. J. 1988. *Food, gender, and poverty in the Ecuadorian Andes.* Philadelphia, Pa.

Young, Michael. 1971. *Fighting with food: Leadership, values and social control in a Massim society.* Cambridge.

    1986. "The Worst Disease": The cultural definition of hunger in Kalauna. In *Shared wealth and symbol: Food, culture and society in Oceania and Southeast Asia,* ed. L. Manderson, 111-26. New York.

VI.15   Food as Aphrodisiacs and Anaphrodisiacs?

According to the first edition of the *Encyclopaedia Britannica* (1771), aphrodisiacs are "medicines which increase the quantity of seed, and create an inclination for venery." Since the twentieth-century advent of sexual endocrinology, the definition of an aphrodisiac has become restricted to "a substance which excites sexual desire" (*Steadman's Medical Dictionary,* 25th edition, 1990). The search for aphrodisiacs is rooted in universal anxieties about sexual performance and fertility. In many instances since ancient times, a distinction has been made between substances that were alleged to improve fertility (quantity of seed) and those that only stimulate the sex drive (inclination to venery). Some authorities held that the latter could only be achieved by achieving the former.

The scope of this essay is limited geographically to Europe and the Near East and, so far as possible, to foods and their preparation. Adequate nourishment has always been recognized as a requirement for health and a normal level of sexual activity, although the norm for the latter undoubtedly varies somewhat among cultures.

In ancient medical practices, when and by what indications nutritive and medicinal qualities of foods were differentiated is uncertain. A rather clear distinction, however, was made by Heracleides of Tarentum, a Greek physician in the first century B.C. In writing about aphrodisiacs, he said that "bulbs, snails, eggs and the like are supposed to produce semen, *not because they are filling,* but because their very nature in the first instance has powers related in kind to semen" (Athenaeus 1951: 275).

Another nagging question had to do with whether plant and animal products that ordinarily are not foods should be considered medicines or just special foods. Andrew Boorde (died 1549), a London physician, exemplified the vagueness of dietary-medicinal distinctions: "[A] good cook is half a physician. For the chief physic (the counsel of a physician excepted) does come from the kitchen: wherefore the physician and the cook for sick men must consult together for the preparation of meate [foods] for sick men" (1870: 227).

According to ancient literature, aphrodisiacs and their opposite, anaphrodisiacs, were generally simple rather than multi-ingredient prescriptions. This pattern gradually changed, and the most elaborate prescriptions were written in sixteenth- and seventeenth-century Europe (and much earlier in the Near East). Table VI.15.1

Table VI.15.1. *Ancient sexual stimulants and depressants*

Aegina	Pliny	Dioscorides	Paul
Aphrodisiacs			
Anise	–	+	–
Basil	+	–	–
Carrot	–	+	–
Clary (Salvia)	–	+	–
Gladiolus root	+	*	–
Orchid bulbs			
Major orchis bulb	+	+	+
Erythraicon bulb	+	–	–
Satyrion bulb	+	+	+
Pistachio nuts	+	+	–
Rocket	+	+	+
Sage	–	+	–
Sea fennel	+	–	+
Turnip	+	–	+
Skink flesh	+	+	+
River snails	+	–	–
Anaphrodisiacs			
Agnus castus	x	x	x
Dill	–	x	–
Gladiolus root	–	**	–
Lentil	–	x	–
Lettuce	–	x	–
Nasturtium (cress)	x		
Minor orchis bulb	x	x	–
Rue	x	x	x
Water lily	x	x	

*Upper gladiolus root.

**Lower gladiolus root.

Sources: Pliny (1963); Gunther (1959); Adams (1847).

lists the substances that were cited as aphrodisiacs and anaphrodisiacs by three ancient authorities, Pliny and Dioscorides from the first century A.D. and Paul of Aegina from the seventh century. The former two listed more substances than did Paul because they, and especially Pliny, sought to record every one they encountered and did not necessarily vouch for each. All three concurred about only three aphrodisiacs: varieties of orchid bulbs, leaves and seeds of rocket (Eruca sativa), and the flesh of the skink (a North African lizard). They agreed on only two anaphrodisiacs: the seed and, presumably, leaf decoction (tea) of Vitex agnus castus (also called the chaste tree), and parts of rue (Ruta graveolens), an evergreen shrub (Adams 1847, 3; Gunther 1959; Pliny 1963: Vols. 7 and 8).

A Western philosophical association between dietary gratification and sexual stimulation was enunciated most clearly by St. Thomas Aquinas (died 1274) in his Summa Theologica. The biological aspects of the explanation were those of Galen, and they remained unchallenged for almost three more centuries. According to Thomas, the most urgent of the carnal vices was lust, with gluttony the second. Both were viewed as vices because they distracted from intellectual pursuits that brought men close to God. Moreover, certain foods both provided sensual gratification and created great incentive to lust. Such potentially lust-inducing foods and the qualities by which they could be identified should be learned so as to avoid them.

Procreation, according to Thomas, who did not distinguish this from "lust," required the participation of three components: heat, vital spirit, and humor. Whatever enhanced the production of any of the three might be sexually stimulating. Substances that heated the body, such as wine, would stimulate the production of more heat. Flatulent foods, in turn, were part of the production of the vital spirit. Meat, the most nutritious food, was needed to produce humor. Lust, however, was kindled more by drinking wine than by eating meat. The more an animal resembled humans, the greater pleasure and nutrition it offered as food: "Animals which rest on the earth and breathe air and also their products, such as milk. Because of these resemblances to mankind, when they are eaten they produce a greater surplus of the seminal matter which is the immediate inciter of lust" (Aquinas 1932, 9: 189; 13: 71-2).

This definition, however, fails to explain the selection of one particular lizard and is inconsistent with the aphrodisiacal properties that, by the Middle Ages, were attributed to birds' eggs, roe, and fowl. A final peculiarity shown in Table VI.15.1 is that different parts or combinations of the same sources were accorded opposite effects. A bifid root might have stimulant properties assigned to one segment and inhibitory effects to another. The small quantity of flesh adjacent to the skink's kidneys was deemed especially stimulating because of its proximity to an excretory organ. However, if this was mixed with lentils or lettuce seed, the opposite effect was achieved (Gunther 1959: 108).

The reputation of several ancient remedies can be attributed to their alleged physical resemblance to genitalia. Illustrative is the association of double orchid bulbs with testes, with the very names of these bulbs revealing their perceived application: Orchis means testicle, and a single bulb variety was called satyrion (the mythological sexually aggressive satyr) (Brondegaard 1971). But orchid bulbs, along with carrots, turnips, and the like (which possibly bear some genital resemblances), were not ordinarily considered aphrodisiacal. Rather, the quality nearest to a common denominator that ancient aphrodisiacs supposedly possessed was that they presumably stimulated urine flow.

Some ancient aphrodisiacal attributions were based on mythology. Aphrodite, the goddess of love, for example, was said to consider sparrows sacred because of their "amorous nature" and, thus, they were included in some love potions. Although both bird and fish eggs were prescribed, among birds a predilection for the eggs and (especially) the brains of sparrows persisted at least through the Middle Ages. Geoffrey Chaucer in 1390 in The Canterbury Tales described the Summoner to be "as hot and lecherous as a sparrow" (1952: 42). Sparrows also were distinguished from other small birds by allegedly being "hard of digestion" (Chaucer 1952: 270). Yet this quality would, for most authors, have disqualified sparrows as aphrodisiacs.

Because the anatomic and physiological ideas expounded by Galen (A.D. 129–210) reigned unchallenged from the third to at least the sixteenth century, their relationship to the identification of supposed aphrodisiacs requires some scrutiny. According to Galenic humoral principles, the effects of nutrients on sexual function, most clearly that of the male, were governed both by their inherent humoral qualities and by the responses they elicited when consumed. To be effective as an aphrodisiac, a nutrient had to be "warm and moist." Substances that were "cold and dry" had the opposite effect. The production of semen and erectile potency were differentiated. Although both required warm and moist nutrients for nonspecific stimulation, semen production needed particularly nourishing foods. Improvement of erectile potency demanded foods that generate "windiness" because "the penis is tensed . . . when the hollow nerve [corpus cavernosus] is filled with pneuma" (Galen 1968: 656-60). Thus, the English anatomist Thomas Vicary (died 1562) could write: "This member has three holes. Through one passeth insensible pollution and wind that causes the penis to rise. The other two holes . . . are for the sperm and . . . for urine" (1888: 81-2). "Insensible pollution" was the pneuma, which in this location was viewed as an inflator. "Wind" provided the expulsive force for semen and other excreta. Consequently, foods reputed to be flatulent were also thought to stimulate the emission of semen, provided the diet was sufficiently nutritious for an adequate amount to have been produced.

Earlier, the influential medical translator and commentator Constantinus Africanus (Constantine of Carthage, 1015-87) had concurred that the ideal aphrodisiac is nutritious, warm, and moist and that it generates windiness. And it was because few substances were reputed to contain all of the required humoral qualities that later prescriptions tended to become much more complex than they had been in the more ancient, particularly pre-Galenic, writings. Constantine, for example, prescribed "a tested electuary which increases lust" containing 19 ingredients. One of these, which remained popular for several centuries, was *linguae avis* (Delany 1970: 55-65), which in this case did not mean birds' tongues, but rather was the name for ash seeds. It is interesting to note that in *The Merchant's Tale,* Constantine was cursed because his "book" *De Coitu* apparently revealed aphrodisiacal recipes (Chaucer 1952: 36-7).

The Spice Trade

Spices were vital ingredients in the formulation of aphrodisiacs, rendering many such recipes dependent on imported materials. While the Roman Empire was in existence, spices doubtless reached Europe from Asia Minor via Roman legions, and probably supply was never interrupted entirely after its collapse. By the ninth century or so, Arab traders were supplying parts of Europe with spices from as far away as India and China. However, a great increase in the quantity and variety of spices for Europe was initiated in 1499 when the Portuguese navigator, Vasco da Gama (died 1524), rounded the Cape of Good Hope to reach India and returned to Lisbon with a cargo of pepper. A round-trip between Lisbon and the west coast of India in the late sixteenth century took about 18 months but could produce great profits. One hundred pounds of pepper, purchased in Calicut for 3 ducats, wholesaled in Lisbon for 25 ducats, and then retailed for 80 ducats in Venice.

Spices were the predominant Asiatic import, and pepper, used also as a food preservative, was the most important. Illustrative is the inventory of four ships that returned to Lisbon from India in 1580. It revealed a total cargo weighing 2,695,100 pounds, of which 97.6 percent was spices (Guerra 1965). Spain, the other Iberian nation, also got into the spice business following its conquest of Mexico in 1521. The Americas not only had indigenous spices to offer but also provided locations to cultivate spices previously grown only in Asia. Thus, ginger (the first transplanted spice crop) was introduced into Mexico in 1530; by 1587 Spain was importing 2¼ million pounds of ginger, ten times that carried by the Portuguese from India.

All of this activity in spices made a big business out of spice retailing, the practitioners of which since the Middle Ages had not only filled prescriptions but also supplied cooks with spices. Indeed, guilds of "pepperers" and "spicers" had been formed from the twelfth to the fourteenth centuries, and in England in 1617, a separate guild of apothecaries that distinguished them from grocers was created by royal edict (Kremers and Urdang 1951: 83-4, 136-40).

Semitic Influences

One of the tales from *The Book of the Thousand Nights and One Night* [The Arabian Nights], which probably is at least a thousand years old, contains an early example of the complexity that aphrodisiacal prescriptions achieved quite early in the Near East. The story of "Beautyspot" pertains to a merchant whose marriage has been childless for 40 years. This was cured by a prescription that consisted of spices and foods. Different translations vary in some of the ingredients, but two versions agree on six of the spices. Richard Burton's version also includes opium, skink meat, frankincense, and coriander (1885: 30-2). These were to be mixed in honey and consumed after a meal of hotly spiced mutton and pigeon. In another text, musk and roe are added as final ingredients. But before consuming this prescription, a special aphrodisiacal diet had to be adhered to for three days; it was limited to hotly spiced roasted pigeons, male fish with intact genitalia, and fried rams' testicles.

Another ancient ingredient that found its way into some European prescriptions was mandragora, or mandrake. Dioscorides said obscurely that "the root seems to be a maker of love medicines" (Gunther 1959: 473-4). Pliny, on the other hand, made no claim for a sexual effect (Pliny 1963, 7: 241-3). Both referred to a white male and a black female variety, but neither suggested that the plant might resemble human form as did later writers. They agreed that ingesting it induced sleep, that it could be used for surgical anesthesia, and that an overdose was fatal.

It is interesting that mandrake differs from most plants alleged to affect sexual function in that it actually has demonstrable physiological effects. It is related to deadly nightshade, or belladonna, and its content of hyoscyamine makes it potentially lethal. Yet it had a long-standing reputation in the Near East for encouraging female fertility. In Genesis 30:14-21, for example, Leah, who had become infertile, was given mandrake (manner unspecified), after which she conceived three more children.

Although most claims that mandrake corrects female infertility derived from this biblical reference, in the seventeenth century decoctions of the "white male" variety were alleged to overcome impotence as well (Thorndyke 1958: 10-13). Yet in 1771, the medicinal demise of mandrake was announced in an entry of the first edition of the *Encyclopaedia Britannica:*

"Authors have spoken very largely and idly of the virtues of this plant. The most common quality attributed to it, is that of rendering barren women fruitful: but we have no tolerable foundation for this: what we certainly know of it is, that is has a soporific virtue like that of opium."

A leading medieval writer who expounded the aphrodisiacal qualities of various foods was Rabbi Moses ben Maimon, or Maimonides (1135-1204). A Talmudic scholar who became physician to Sultan Saladin of Egypt, Maimonides was medically a follower of Galen and of Avicenna. He differed from others of the period in regard to aphrodisiacs mainly in placing greater emphasis on meats and organs, although not ignoring vegetables and spices. Maimonides was blunt about the relative aphrodisiacal merits of foods and medicines, insisting that nutriments were of much greater value than medications. However, one needed to be selective. Foods (and medications) that moistened and warmed the body (that is, had the Galenic qualities of heat and humidity) were deemed to some degree aphrodisiacal, whereas those that were cooling and drying were to be avoided because of their anaphrodisiacal effects.

In addition to the guidance provided by Galenic qualities, symbolism also played a role in identifying other substances (Rosner 1974: 18-29). For example, one of Maimonides's "very special" prescriptions required one to: "[t]ake the penis of an ox, dry it and grind it. Sprinkle some of this on a soft-boiled egg, and drink in sips" (Rosner 1974: 29).

The desired stimulation was sometimes transmitted through an intermediate. According to an Indian recipe some two centuries after the foregoing: "Boil the penis of an ass together with onions and a large quantity of corn. With this dish feed fowl, which you then eat" (Burton 1964: 242).

During the late sixteenth century in Europe, the compounding of ingestible phallic symbols varied only slightly from some of the prescriptions of Maimonides. For example:

A man whose conjugal ardor has cooled should take the penis of a stag that has been killed while in rut, dry it and grind it into a powder. He should take 5 gm. of this and a dram of black pepper, mix these together in a drink of malmsey, and take it in the morning. Taken several days in a row it will make him right again (Mattioli 1590: 447b).

The Doctrine of Signatures

It is clear that symbolism has been used in the assignment of aphrodisiacal properties to plants and animal parts since pre-Christian times. But the delineation of a philosophy based on analogizing the appearance of natural objects with their perceived utility was delayed until the sixteenth century. It sprang from the ideas of the anti-Galenic itinerant Swiss physician

Paracelsus (1493-1541) and was popularized by some of his followers. One of the best known of the latter was German physician Oswald Croll (about 1560-1609). In the introduction to his *Basilica Chymica* (original 1609, English 1670) he stated the belief most clearly:

If he so desireth to be an expert physician, and to have knowledge of those things which point to Medicine, by that Art, which Nature externally proposeth by Signes, he may understand that those internally signify: for every thing that is intrinsical, bares the external figure of its occult property, as well in insensible as sensible Creatures. Nature as it were by certain silent notes speakes to us, and reveals the ingenuity and manners of every Individual. . . . As our intimate manners from external figures of the Body may be found out, so from the exteriour Signatures of Plants, Man may be admonished of their interiour Vertues. For Plants do as it were in occult words, manifest their excellency, and open the Treasures of hidden things to sickly Mortalls; that Man, of all Creatures the most miserable, may learn in grievous Diseases, where to find relief (Croll 1670: 3).

Herbals in the Sixteenth and Seventeenth Centuries

The complexity of European aphrodisiacal prescriptions in the sixteenth century is particularly well illustrated by concoctions called *diasatyrion* (so named because although they were based on an orchid bulb, they had additional ingredients as well). The following directions for the preparation of a diasatyrion were published in 1536:

Take male orchid bulb, satyrion bulb, parsnip, sea holly, nutmeg, pistacio nuts, and pine nuts, 12 drams each, carnation, ginger, anise, ash seed, and rocket seed, each 5 drams, and musk 7 grains. Compound with a sufficient amount of honey.
    Grate orchid bulbs and parsnip and cook for a short time while stirring with a spatula. Then add the pine nuts and pistacios, also grated. After brief cooking, remove from the fire and add the other ingredients, except for the musk. The latter is added the very last, [diluted] in rosewater (Schumacher 1936: 98-9).

Judging by the contents of herbals, which were the principal textbooks of materia medica of the time, the number of botanicals to which aphrodisiacal properties were attributed reached their peak between the late sixteenth and the late seventeenth centuries. The 1554 herbal of Pietro Mattioli (1500-77), in its expanded German edition of 1590, contained 39 such entries, about two-thirds of which would ordinarily be considered vegetables, spices, or edible nuts

Table VI.15.2. *Most commonly cited aphrodisiacs, 1546-1710*

Orchis, cynosorchis, dog-stones	8
Carrot	8
Mustard	7
Anise	6
Asparagus	6
Nettles	6
Claire, scarlet sage (Salvia)	5
Ladies bedstraw (Galium verum)	5
Ash seed (Lingua avis)	4
Rampion	4
Rocket	4
Sweet pea	4
Terebinth seed (Pistacia terebinthus)	4

(1590: 28). Yet most of the time the various herbalists failed to agree on the foods that had aphrodisiacal qualities, and even in comparing the 1597 and 1636 editions of the herbal of John Gerarde (1545-1612), one discovers numerous changes. For example, 35 substances in the earlier edition but only 30 in the later are said to be sexual stimulants. Moreover, only 24 were endowed with such a virtue according to both texts (Gerarde 1597; 1636).

A survey of eight herbals published between 1546 and 1710 found 13 substances (see Table VI.15.2) with alleged aphrodisiacal properties that are identified in at least four of them (Bock 1546; Dodoens 1578; Mattioli 1590; Gerarde 1597, 1636; Parkinson 1640; Theodorus 1664; Salmon 1710). The list was led by the double orchid bulb (8) and the carrot (8) (now gaining in aphrodisiacal reputation), followed by mustard seed (7), and anise, asparagus, and nettles (6 each).

It is difficult to explain the aphrodisiacal reputation of some foods in terms other than those having to do with their remote origin or their initial scarcity. The reception of the American potato in Europe serves as a good example.

The English word "potato" is derived from the generic term for the sweet potato, *Ipomoea batatas.* The sweet potato was a staple food in the West Indies and was among the plants that Columbus brought back from his first voyage. It was planted in Spain, but because it requires a warm climate, it did not do well in northern Europe, where it became a scarce, imported item. The white potato probably reached Spain no later than 1570 and it may have been introduced in England by Francis Drake in 1586. During the first half of the seventeenth century, the "common potato" and the "Virginia potato" were the names of the sweet and the white potato, respectively (Salaman 1949: 130-2, 142-8, 424-33).

The sweet potato, at least in sixteenth- and seventeenth-century England, was eaten mainly as a candied delicacy. But in a late sixteenth-century description of English dietary customs, it was referred to as a "venereous root" (Harrison 1577: 129), and it repeat-

edly appears on the seventeenth-century stage as an aphrodisiac, by itself and in complex recipes. In *The Merry Wives of Windsor* (Shakespeare 1971) Shakespeare has Sir John Falstaff tell a lady before embracing her: "Let the sky rain potatoes; let it thunder to the tune of Green Sleeves; hail kissing comfits, and snow eringoes; let there come a tempest of provocation, I will shelter me here" (Act 5, Scene 4).

In modern terms, Falstaff fantasized being inundated with sweet potatoes and candied fruit or vegetables (which could be a reference to the preferred preparation of the sweet potato), and candied sea holly, which was also recognized as an aphrodisiac. According to Gerarde's herbal:

> The roots [of eringoes, which is the same as sea holly] preserved with sugar . . . are exceeding good to be given unto old and aged people that are consumed and withered with age. . . . It is also good for other sorts of people that have no delight or appetite to venery, nourishing and restoring the aged, and amending the defects of nature in the younger (1597: 1000).

In the mid–seventeenth century, as potatoes became more available (although still expensive), it is probably this tuber that was now being referred to in various recipes and theatrical comments. The entry on the potato in the 1710 herbal by the English physician William Salmon (1644-1712) combines its nutritive quality with its alleged effect on libido and fertility:

> They stop fluxes of the bowels [diarrhea], nourish much, and restore a pining Consumption [tuberculosis]. Being boiled, baked, or rosted [sic], they are eaten with good Butter, Salt, Juice of *Oranges* or *Limons,* and double refined Sugar, as common Food: they encrease Seed and provoke Lust, causing Fruitfulness in both sexes, and stop all sorts of Fluxes of the Belly. (1710:)

In 1805, however, Sir Joseph Banks (1743–1820), then president of the Royal Society of London, called quasi-official attention to the fallacious use of these vegetables:

> [T]he sweet potatoe was used in England as a delicacy long before the introduction of our potatoes; it was imported in considerable quantities from Spain and the Canaries, and was supposed to possess the power of restoring decayed vigor. The kissing comfits of *Falstaff,* and other confections of similar imaginary qualities, with which our ancestors were duped, were principally made of these, and of eringo roots.

The potatoes themselves were sold by itinerant dealers, chiefly in the neighborhood of the Royal Exchange, and purchased when scarce at no inconsiderable cost, by those who had faith in their alleged properties (Banks 1805, 1: 8-12).

Although potatoes and sweet potatoes are examples of foods that lost their aphrodisiacal reputation quite early, that of the oyster has persisted from ancient times into the twentieth century. The Roman author Juvenal (second century A.D.), in a satire on the unrestrained behavior of contemporary women, associated loss of sexual decorum with alcoholic intoxication and the eating of "giant oysters at midnight" (Ramsay 1940: 107). Oysters, however, appeared infrequently among the aphrodisiacs in medical texts, and their folkloric popularity has been better reflected in literature. For example, in a comedy staged in 1611 by the London playwright George Chapman (died 1634), a "lover" in preparation for seduction is to be strengthened with "a banquet of Oyster-pies, Potatoes, Skirret rootes, Eringoes, and divers other whetstones of venery" (Act 2: 31). And it is interesting that in the nineteenth century, Jonathan Pereira (1804-53), professor of materia medica in London, in his authoritative textbook on medications merely commented: "An aphrodisiac property is usually ascribed to oysters" (1846: 47).

A hypothesis for the stimulatory reputation of oysters harkens back to the doctrine of signatures with their influence due to a resemblance to the female pudenda. But even if correct, it does not explain why, as therapeutics gradually became more rational, oysters maintained their aphrodisiacal reputation.

In the twentieth century, Havelock Ellis (1859-1939), the pioneer English sexologist, returned to the ancient principle that an aphrodisiac must foremost be nutritious. He speculated that "oysters and other shellfish . . . in so far as they have an action whatsoever on the sexual appetite, only possess it by virtue of their generally nutritious and stimulating qualities." He therefore concluded that because it is nutritious and easily digestible, "[a] beefsteak is probably as powerful a sexual stimulant as any food." Since it required relatively little energy to digest, more energy was available for other activities, including those that were sexual (Ellis 1906: 174). This is reminiscent of Galen's concept that to effect spermatogenesis, foods must be particularly nutritious.

Beverages and Anaphrodisiacs

A glimpse of the ancient ambivalence about the role of wine in sexual matters can be found in the Old Testament story of Lot's daughters, who each intoxicated their aged father with wine in order to be impregnated by him (Genesis 19:32-6). Perhaps the role of wine in this case was not that of an aphrodisiac but rather a sedative to overcome the taboo against incest. In the ancient world wine was consumed extensively, in part as medicine, but seemingly not as a sexual stimulant.

By the time of the Middle Ages this had changed. Maimonides, for one, strongly advocated wine as a sexual stimulant:

> Drinking honey water promotes erections, but even more effective in this regard than all medicines and foods is wine. . . . [I]t arouses the erections all the more when one enjoys the wine with desire, and after the meal and after the bath, because then its effect is far greater than that of anything else (Rosner 1974: 20-1).

About two centuries later, the Catalan physician Arnaldus de Villanova (1236-1311) wrote a manuscript on wine that, in 1478, became the first book on the subject to be printed. He believed that many specific varieties of wine exerted a restorative effect in the face of certain ailments. Thus "[w]ine made from fennel seeds stimulates sexual urge, consumes dropsy and leprosy. . . . It increases milk and the natural sperm" (1943: 39).

Later in the fourteenth century, Chaucer had one of his female characters voice the understanding that wine may affect both sexes similarly:

> Whenever I take wine I have to
> think of Venus, for as cold engenders hail
> A lecherous mouth begets a lecherous tail.
> A woman in her cups has no defense,
> As lechers know from long experience (1952: 295).

Yet if inebriation could leave a woman defenseless, it could also render a male incapable of taking advantage of her. This was expressed especially well by the French physician-novelist, François Rabelais (died 1553):

> When I say that wine abateth lust, my meaning is wine immoderately taken; for by intemperance, proceeding from the excessive drinking of strong liquor, there is brought upon the body . . . a chillness in the blood, a slackening in the sinews, a dissipation with a pervasive wryness and convulsion of the muscles, all which are great lets and impediments to the act of generation. . . . Wine nevertheless, taken moderately, worketh quite contrary effects, as is implied in the old proverb which saith: Venus taketh cold when not accompanied by Ceres and Bacchus. [Love is suppressed when it is not accompanied by food and drink] (1931, Book 3: 540).

The best-known literary comment on such contradictory effects of alcohol emanates from Shakespeare (Macbeth, Shakespeare 1971): "Lechery, sir, it provokes, and unprovokes; it provokes the desire, but it takes away the performance. Therefore much drink may be said to be an equivocator of lechery" (Act 2, Scene 3).

Most discussions of the sexual effects of alcohol have pertained to wines and, more recently, to liqueurs.

An exception is found in the herbal of Jacobus Theodorus (died 1590), a southern German physician who was enthusiastic about another beverage:

> Beer brewed from wheat, above all as a beverage, but also when used in food: on soups, sauces, and porridge, increases the natural seed, straightens the drooping phallus up again, and helps feeble men who are incapable of conjugal acts back into the saddle (1664: 641).

Nothing substantial has been added to an understanding of the behavioral effects of alcohol in the twentieth century. Clinicians who wrote extensively on sexual matters, such as the Swiss psychiatrist August H. Forel (1848-1931) and the German venereologist Iwan Bloch (1872-1922), both expounded on the pseudoaphrodisiacal effects that may occur when inhibitions are suppressed by small amounts of alcohol and the increasing anesthetic effect of gross intoxication.

Bloch speculated that moderate quantities of alcohol exert a dual effect, as "general psychic stimulant" and as a specifically sexual stimulant. But with a more protracted consumption of alcohol, the "psychic stimulation" deteriorates into "psychic paralysis" (loss of inhibition or judgment) before sexual excitement also wanes, leaving a gap of unrestrained sexual excitation. He concluded: "For the normal individual alcohol is not a means for the increase of sexual potency, but the reverse" (1919: 293, 444).

Other writers, biased by the temperance movement, were more outspoken. Thus, according to Forel:

> The drink habit corrupts the whole of sexual life.... Most narcotics, especially alcohol (either fermented or distilled) have the peculiarity of exciting the sexual appetite in a bestial manner, thereby leading to the most absurd and disgusting excesses, although at the same time they weaken the sexual power (1926: 332, 503).

Moving to nonalcoholic beverages, cacao (or cocoa), imported to Spain from the Caribbean islands, became a popular drink by 1580, after it had been modified into chocolate by the addition of sugar and milk. Although it was designated as "cold and dry," chocolate gained some reputation as an aphrodisiac. The reasons for this are uncertain. One mid–eighteenth-century French author implied that chocolate "promotes Venery" due to its nutritive quality. Because it is also a stimulant, its consumption is desirable as a restorative for old and phlegmatic people, while it should be avoided by "young people of a hot and bilious Constitution" (Lemery 1745: 364, 366).

Another reference work of the period states that cacao is cooling and yet "stimulates to Venery causing Procreation and Conception, facilitates Delivery, preserves Health, helps Digestion, makes people inclinable to seed" (Pomet 1748: 131-2). Yet in the seventeenth century, it had also become customary to mix various traditionally aphrodisiacal spices, such as pepper and cinnamon, with cacao. Proportions were adjusted to taste or according to the medicinal purpose. Hence, cacao may have been used by some to modify the potency of more traditional aphrodisiacs, and not actually accorded much potency of its own.

Although introduced to Europe toward the end of the sixteenth century, coffee did not become a popular beverage until about the middle of the seventeenth century - somewhat later than chocolate. As the popularity of coffee spread, so too did a rumor from its source in the Near East that, at least when consumed in excess, it suppressed sexual desires. Yet coffee was (correctly) recognized as having the ability to stimulate urine production, and since there had been an association between diuretics and aphrodisiacal properties since ancient times, any easy acceptance of the rumor seems inconsistent. Indeed, an English author felt the need to point out (published posthumously, 1746) that it is "an egregious Mistake, not only among the Persians, but also among most other Nations, to think that the Seed which when toasted is called Coffee ... is of so cooling a Quality as to produce Impotence, even in those who use it frequently; for it dries them (Paulli 1746: 138-9).

In the nineteenth century, some settled for the same explanation that had been offered for the dual effects of alcohol. For example, M. Lallemand, a member of the Montpellier medical faculty, declared that coffee "augments the venereal desires, favors erections, and accelerates ejaculations; taken in excess, however ... they are diminished and even completely extinguished." His explanation was that "what passed in the urinary organs is a good index of what is going on in the spermatic; the secretion of semen was increased as well as that of urine" (1866: 199-200). The implication was that although coffee is primarily an aphrodisiac, impotence eventually results from gonadal exhaustion caused by the protracted spermatorrhea-inducing stimulus.

Half a century later, Bloch continued to insist that coffee in sufficient volume induced impotence, which persisted as long as excessive coffee consumption continued (1919: 444). And an author in 1928, who still accepted that coffee ordinarily was an anaphrodisiac, recommended that in cases of impotence due to depression, it could act as a sexual stimulant by counteracting the symptom of fatigue (Loewe 1928: 184-6).

Anaphrodisiacs

As indicated in the discussion of coffee, save for alcohol consumed in excess, the list of dietary anaphrodisiacs is rather short and ambiguous. Among generally accepted foodstuffs, however, lettuce has had the most durable reputation - one probably originating in Greek mythology. The beautiful youth Adonis, killed by a wild boar, was laid out on a bed of lettuce by his lover, Venus (*Larousse Encyclopedia of Mythology* 1959: 81-2). Alternatively, he was killed in a field of wild lettuce (Athenaeus 1951: 301-3), or Venus threw herself on a bed of lettuce to lull her grief and repress her desires (Paris 1828: 9). In any event, the transient survival of a mortal, even when loved by a deity, became equated with the rapid withering of lettuce, which, in turn, became associated with impotence. Thus, according to Dioscorides, lettuce "is somewhat in virtue like unto Poppy. . . . [I]t is in generall soporiferous and easing of Paine" (Gunther 1959: 177). Such a notion is readily associated with the obviously anaphrodisiacal effect of sedation. According to Boorde, who wrote in the sixteenth century, lettuce "doth extynct veneryous actes, yet it doth increase mylke in a womans breste" (1870: 281).

One of the simpler seventeenth-century anaphrodisiacal recipes was a salad of lettuce, purslane, and mint with vinegar (Plater, Cole, and Culpeper 1662: 172). A contemporaneous prescription combined the alleged chemical and mineral anaphrodisiacal magic of many plants. Its ingredients were conserves of water lilies and of mint, candied lettuce and coolwort, seeds of Agnus castus (chaste tree), rue, coral, crystal, and camphor, made into an electuary with syrup of purslane.

Complex prescriptions were in demand, in part, at least, because of the paradoxical response of some persons to any one ingredient. In this regard, Nicolas Venette (1633-98), a French physician, informed his readers:

> Lettice and Succory, for Example, prevents the Generation of seed in most Men. But I know that in some it produces such a Plenty, especially if they eat it at Nights, as to subject them to Nocturnal Pollutions. This same experience teaches us, that Pepper and Ginger [usually aphrodisiacal] diminish the Seed, and dissipate Winds that are necessary to the action of Love (1906: 174-5).

Although most sexually inhibiting advice pertained to men, in the seventeenth century anaphrodisiacs were also prescribed to control "womb-furie." This was a manifestation of an "immoderate desire for carnal copulation [which] is able to master the Rational faculty [resulting in] Love-melancholy." The ailment was attributed mainly to virgins, young widows, and wives of impotent husbands. Thus a diagnosis of "immoderate desire" was doubtless based, at times, on some quite overt symptoms (Riverius 1655: 417-18).

Relevant prescriptions resemble those for the control of male lust, which were "cooling and sedating." Foodstuffs made up a minority of the ingredients, but among them, the leaves, stalks, and seeds of lettuce were the most common. Their alleged sedative effect was fortified by the inclusion of poppy seeds among the dozen or so ingredients (Riverius 1655: 417-8).

Disbelievers

Over the centuries, doubts about the effectiveness, mechanism of action, and the very existence of aphrodisiacs were occasionally raised, although most were limited or ambiguous. The Roman poet Ovid (43 B.C.-A.D. 18), who may have been the first recorded doubter, wrote in his *Ars Amatoria* (The Art of Love):

> There are, that strong provoking potions praise
> and nature with pernicious med'cines raise:
> Nor drugs nor herbs will what you fancy prove,
> And I pronounce them pois'nous all in love.
> Some pepper bruis'd, with seeds of nettles join,
> And clary steep in bowls of mellow wine:
> *Venus* is most adverse to forc'd delights
> Extorted flames pollute her genial rites.
> With fishes spawn thy feeble nerves recruit,
> And with eringo's hot salacious root.
> The goddess worship'd by th' *Erycian* swains,
> *Megara's* white shallot, so faint, disdains.
> New eggs they take, and honey's liquid juice,
> And leaves and apples of the pine infuse.
> Prescribe no more my muse, nor med'cines give,
> Beauty and youth need no provocative
> (1776, Book 2: 55-6).

Clearly, Ovid has provided a fine list of aphrodisiacal ingredients. But he warns that youth and beauty are sufficiently strong attractants that artificial stimulants are not only superfluous but counterproductive because artificially induced passion ("extorted flames") destroys true love.

Disagreement had always existed about the substances that affect sexual function and in which ways, but because the concept of objective therapeutic evaluation had yet to be devised, authors tended to ignore, rather than attack, claims with which they disagreed. But this situation gradually began to change at the end of the sixteenth century, with mandrake the first target. Gerarde, who acknowledged numerous botanical aphrodisiacs, disparaged anyone who would prescribe this root:

> Mandrake is called of the Graecians *Circea* of Circe the Witch, who by Art could procure love: for it hath beene thought that the roote heere of serveth to winne love. . . . There have been many ridiculous tales brought up of this plant, whether of olde wives or some runnegate surgeons or phisickmongers, I know not . . . , but sure some one or moe [sic] that sought to make themselves famous in skillful above others were first brochers of that errour I spake of (1597: 280-2).

Mandrake also came under attack in a larger effort aimed at the demolition of the doctrine of signatures by Sir Thomas Browne (1605-82). Although he did not mention aphrodisiacs as such in his *Pseudodoxia epidemica* (1646), his argument is relevant because "signatures of nature" were so important in the identification of these substances. Browne denounced as a "false conception" the notion that bifurcated root resembled human thighs. He pointed out that mandrake did not necessarily have a bifid root, and when it did, the two were often interwoven, destroying any human resemblance. Furthermore, bifid roots were not unique to this plant, and thus it made no sense to ascribe powers to mandrake because of a natural signature and not ascribe the same to a bifid carrot or a parsnip. In addition, such a notion gave rise to fraud because roots of other plants were carved to imitate bifid mandrake "to deceive unfruitful women" (1927: 285-99).

The waning of the conviction that the physical appearance of a natural object offered clues to its medicinal value did not, however, foster skepticism about substances believed to have a genital effect. But it did shift the focus to their intrinsic qualities. According to *A Golden Practice of Physick,* a well-known English medical text of 1662:

> [I]t is our opinion that such medicines [aphrodisiacs] work by a manifest quality, rather than by stretching the Yard [penis] with Wind as some say (which cannot be) besides their secret hidden quality which was observed by the first teachers of such things, from the whiteness of the flesh, fruits, and roots, resembling seed: Or because Taken from Leacherous Creatures; or from their shape resembling Stones [testicles] as the Satyrions or plants called Dogstones; or like a rough wrinkled Cod [scrotum], as Toad-stools or Mushrooms (Plater, Cole, and Culpeper 1662: 172).

Having disposed of both the pneuma mechanism of erection and a doctrine of signatures, the authors proceeded to provide a lengthy list of animals, animal products, vegetables, and seeds that would serve as sexual stimulants. Meats were best because they nourish well and produce much blood. Species to be selected should have white tissue, such as brain, testicles, and much marrow, particularly when these were obtained from "the most lecherous Beasts." The latter were cocks, quail, and the ever-present sparrow, along with beaver flesh and, in the case of the fox, just his testicles.

The sea creatures on the list were exclusively invertebrate, and were followed by nuts, grains, and vegetables. But at this point, without explanation, the authors veer away to conclude that the preparation of sexual stimulants was more important than the ingredients. All of these foods had the same effect, but "especially if they be peppered and salted: for Pepper stimulateth and provoketh Venery, and we suppose that when such things are so eaten it comes rather from the sauce than the meat" (Plater, Cole, and Culpeper 1662: 172).

Hermann Boerhaave (1668-1738), a famous professor of medicine at Leiden, wrote somewhat hesitantly regarding "generators of seed." These were the various botanicals, mammalian and rooster testicles and brains that "are commended by the Ancients; but these are doubtful, and perhaps vain" (1740: 152).

Later in the eighteenth century, however, the very existence of aphrodisiacs was clearly denied for the first time, with the credit going to William Cullen (1710-90), a leading physician of Edinburgh. Among the terms he defined in his *Treatise on the Materia Medica* (1789) we find:

> *Aphrodisiaca.* Medicines supposed to be suited to excite the venereal appetite, or to increase the venereal powers. I do not know that there are any medicines of specific power for these purposes; and therefore the term seems to have been for the most part improperly employed (1808: 107).

Nevertheless, despite Cullen's influential reputation, and the increasing skepticism of science, the popularity of aphrodisiacal prescriptions and recipes did not lose their popularity.

Lay Literature

Until recently, physicians saw only a minority of medical problems and were not consulted at all by large segments of the population. Medical advice, however, still reached many through a genre of "domestic medicine" books that began to appear in the vernacular in the seventeenth century. They became particularly popular toward the end of the eighteenth century and continue to be published today. And until the middle third of the twentieth century, far more people were likely to have been influenced by the recommendations in these popular books than by any personal contact with physicians.

Because these publications focused on actions that could be taken without the intervention of a physician, dietary advice was prominent, and as late as the nineteenth century, the problems that diets were intended to correct were "acidity" and "wind" (gas formation). Acids were deemed to irritate the urinary passages, thereby stimulating sexual sensations, and gaseousness stimulated the urge to expulsion, that is, ejaculation. Substances that induced either were generally considered aphrodisiacal, and those that counteracted them were anaphrodisiacal.

Thus, a domestic-advice book from 1800 recommended that to increase seminal fluid, the diet should emphasize milk, eggs, and tender and nutritious meats, as well as herbs and roots that were mild, spicy, and diuretic. Conversely, to inhibit passion, one was advised to resort to a diet that was less nutritious, to avoid spices, and to abstain from alcoholic beverages. "Cooling" nourishment, such as lettuce and cucumbers, was seen to be beneficial (Willich 1800: 557-61).

A similar volume in the latter part of the nineteenth century relied more on medicines than on diet to counteract impotence. In regard to nutrition, the reader was told only to rely on "plain, simple, easily digested, and nourishing food." Much greater attention, however, was paid to "spermatorrhea" (involuntary seminal emissions), as well as, implicitly, those voluntary emissions resulting from the sin of masturbation. The dietetic component of this therapy for spermatorrhea consisted of the avoidance of carbohydrates because they were thought to readily ferment, producing gas in the stomach and acid in the intestines. Such acids were then absorbed, and they acidified the urine, "causing great irritation of the lining surface of the bladder and urinary passages, greatly increasing and perpetuating the disease." More specifically, fruits and vegetables were to be eaten sparingly and milk was to be avoided. Distilled spirits were preferable to beer, wine, and other fermented liquors, although water and black tea were viewed as the safest beverages. Coarse, well-baked wheat bread, fresh eggs, and various meats, stewed or boiled to tenderness, formed the most curative diet. The author conceded that it did not afford much variety, but "it offers the most abundant nutrition, and aids materially in the cure of this ailment" (Gleason 1873: 454-60).

In a book written in 1894, Dr. J. Harvey Kellogg (1852-1943), the inventor of corn flakes, taught that the sole cause of almost all impotence was sexual excess of some kind. Consequently, controlling spermatorrhea prevented impotence. Such control required avoidance of all stimulation, dietetically including "tea and coffee, spices and other condiments, and animal food [because they] have a special tendency in this direction" (1894: 267-77, 319, 613). Other (and earlier) widely used books, such as those by S. A. Tissot (1769) and H. Buchan (1778), had avoided sexual matters other than pregnancy.

The Early Twentieth Century

The observation of Havelock Ellis (1906) that high nutritive value and ease of digestion are the only criteria for a dietary aphrodisiac coincided with a shift, at least in the medical literature, away from the notion that some foods could exert a specifically sexual effect. In texts of materia medica published between 1891 and 1911, the only real food item to which aphrodisiacal powers were attributed was in a work by the American physiologist Roberts Bartholow (1831-1904). He wrote: "Carrot seems . . . to produce diuresis, augment menstrual flux, and cause aphrodisiac effects in the male" (1903: 791). Some newer herbs, such as *damiana*, were recommended, as were metals reminiscent of Paracelsian teachings, among them gold chloride, iron arsenite, and zinc phosphide (Bartholow 1903: 297, 175, 135).

With the disappearance of aphrodisiacal foods from (at least) *scientific* discussion in the twentieth century, however, there remains only the question of vitamins to be dealt with, and of these the only ones shown to be specifically relevant to any aspect of sexual function are vitamins A and E. The American biochemist Herbert M. Evans (1882-1971), who discovered vitamin E in 1922 (Evans and Bishop 1922), subsequently found with collaborators that a lack of this substance from the diet of male rats resulted in sterility due to deterioration of the seminiferous tubules, but not to a loss of the sex drive. Females did not become sterile, but they did abort their fetuses. Vitamin A deficiency also resulted in male sterility (Evans 1932a, 1932b).

Rodent experiments such as these were misunderstood or distorted by the lay press and by charlatans touting the "anti-sterility vitamin" as a cure for all sorts of sexual dysfunctions of men and women. Some published case reports suggested that vitamin E might assist those women who have had spontaneous abortions to carry a pregnancy to term (American Medical Association Council on Pharmacy and Chemistry 1940: 2214-18). However, habitual abortion is not the result of vitamin E deficiency, and the reliability of vitamin E administration for such a problem has not been proven. Vitamin deficiencies, unless they are a part of starvation, seem to have no effect on human sexual activity.

Conclusion

According to modern science, the only substances in the realm of food and drink that can be considered to have a potentially aphrodisiacal effect are alcoholic beverages in quantities sufficiently small to reduce inhibitions without overtly sedating. There are no positive sexual stimulants and no inhibitors other than sedating amounts of alcoholic beverages. Circumstances surrounding the consumption of food or drink may, of course, exert a positive or negative psychological influence on sexual desire, which is another way of saying that the alleged sexual effects of foods are culturally determined, psychological factors. And the desire of the public for aphrodisiacal foods to exist continues to support the publication of books with titles such as *Aphrodisiac Culinary Manual* (Heartman 1942), *Venus in the Kitchen* (Douglas 1952), *The Virility Diet* (Belham 1965), and *Lewd Food* (Hendrickson 1974).

Thomas G. Benedek

Bibliography

Adams, Francis, trans. 1847. *The seven books of Paulus Aegineta*, Vol. 3. London.

American Medical Association Council on Pharmacy and Chemistry. 1940. The treatment of habitual abortion with vitamin E. *Journal of the American Medical Association* 114: 2214-18.

Aquinas, St. Thomas. 1932. *The "Summa Theologica" of*

St. Thomas Aquinas, Vols. 9, 13, trans. Fathers of the English Dominican Province. London.

Arnaldus de Villanova. 1943. *The earliest printed book on wine,* trans. Henry E. Sigerist. New York.

Athenaeus. 1951. *The Deipnosophists,* trans. C. B. Gulick. Cambridge, Mass.

Banks, J. 1805. An attempt to ascertain the time when the potato (Solanum tuberosum) was first introduced into the United Kingdom. *Transactions of the Horticultural Society* 1: 8–12.

Bartholow, R. 1903. *A practical treatise on materia medica and therapeutics.* Eleventh edition. New York.

Belham, G. 1965. *The virility diet.* London.

Bloch, I. 1919. *The sexual life of our time.* London.

Bock, H. 1546. *Kreuter Buch.* . . . Strasbourg.

Boerhaave, H. 1740. *A treatise on the powers of medicines,* trans. J. Martin. London.

Boorde, A. 1870. Compendyous regyment or a dyetary of helth. In *Andrew Boorde's introduction and dyetary,* ed. F. J. Furnivall. London.

Brondegaard, V. J. 1971. Orchideen als Aphrodisiaca. *Sudhoffs Archiv für Geschichte der Medizin* 55: 22–57.

Browne, T. 1927. *The works of Sir Thomas Browne,* ed. C. Sayle. Edinburgh.

Buchan, W. 1778. *Domestic medicine, or, the family physician.* Norwich, England.

Burton, R. F. 1885. *The book of the thousand nights and one night,* Vol. 4. London.

Burton, R. F. trans. 1964. *The perfumed garden of the Shayk Nefzawi.* New York.

Chapman, G. 1611. *May-day, a witty comedie.* London.

Chaucer, G. 1952. *The Canterbury tales,* trans. N. Coghill. Baltimore, Md.

Croll, O. 1670. *Treatise of signature of internal things.* London.

Cullen, W. 1808. *Treatise on the materia medica.* Third American edition. Philadelphia, Pa.

Delany, P. trans. 1970. Constantinus Africanus' *De coitu. Chaucer Review.* 4: 55–65.

Dodoens, R. 1578. *A niewe herball; or histories of plantes,* . . . trans. H. Lyte. London.

Douglas, Norman. 1952. *Venus in the Kitchen or, Love's Cookery Book.* London.

Ellis, H. 1906. *Studies in the psychology of sex,* Vol. 3. Philadelphia, Pa.

Evans, H. M. 1932a. Testicular degeneration due to inadequate vitamin A in cases where E is adequate. *American Journal of Physiology* 99: 477–86.

1932b. Vitamin E. *Journal of the American Medical Association* 99: 469–75.

Evans, H. M., and K. S. Bishop. 1922. Existence of a hitherto unknown dietary factor essential for reproduction. *Journal of the American Medical Association* 81: 889–92.

Forel, A. 1926. *The sexual question,* trans. C. F. Marshall. Brooklyn, N.Y.

Galen. 1968. *On the usefulness of the parts of the body,* trans. M. T. May. Ithaca, N.Y.

Gerarde, J. 1597. *The herball; or, generall historie of plantes.* London.

1636. *The herball; or, general historie of plantes,* amended by T. Johnson. London.

Gleason, C. W. 1873. *Everybody's own physician.* Philadelphia, Pa.

Guerra, F. 1965. Drugs from the Indies and the political economy of the sixteenth century. In *Analecta Medico-Historica,* ed. M. Florkin, 29–54. New York.

Gunther, R. T. 1959. *The Greek herball of Dioscorides,* trans. John Goodyear. New York.

Halban, J., and L. Seitz. 1924. *Biologie und Pathologie des Weibes,* Vol. 2. Berlin.

Harrison, W. 1577. *The description of England,* ed. G. Edelen. Ithaca, N.Y.

Heartman, C. F. 1942. *Aphrodisiac culinary manual.* New Orleans, La.

Hendrickson, R. 1974. *Lewd food.* Radnor, Pa.

Kellogg, J. H. 1894. *Plain facts for old and young: Embracing the natural history hygiene of organic life.* Burlington, Iowa.

Kremers, E., and G. Urdang. 1951. *History of pharmacy.* Second edition. Philadelphia, Pa.

Lallemand, M. 1866. *A practical treatise on the causes, symptoms, and treatment of spermatorrhoea,* trans. H. J. McDougall. Fifth American edition. Philadelphia, Pa.

Larousse encyclopedia of mythology. 1959. New York.

Lemery, M. L. 1745. *A treatise of all sorts of foods,* trans. D. Hay. London.

Loewe, S. 1928. Praktische Therapie mit Aphrodisiaka. *Deutsche Medizinische Wochenschrift* 54: 184–6.

MacDougald, D. 1961. Aphrodisiacs and anaphrodisiacs. In *The encyclopedia of sexual behavior,* Vol.1, ed. A. Ellis and A. Abarbanel. New York.

Mattioli, P. 1590. *Kreuterbuch,* . . . trans. and enlarged J. Camerarium. Frankfurt am Main.

Ovid. 1776. *The art of love,* trans. anon. London.

Paris, J. A. 1828. *Pharmacologia.* American edition. New York.

Parkinson, J. 1640. *Theatrum botanicum: The theater of plants, or a universal and compleate herball.* London.

Paulli, S. 1746. *A treatise on tobacco, tea, coffee, and chocolate,* trans. Dr. James. London.

Pereira, J. 1846. *The elements of materia medica and therapeutics,* Vol. 1. Second American edition. Philadelphia, Pa.

Plater, F., A. Cole, and N. Culpeper. 1662. *A golden practice of physick.* London.

Pliny. 1963. *Natural history,* Vols. 7, 8, trans. W. H. S. Jones. Cambridge, Mass.

Pomet, P. 1748. *A complete history of drugs.* Fourth edition. London.

Rabelais, F. 1931. *The works of Francis Rabelais,* ed. A. J. Nock and C. R. Wilson. New York.

Ramsay, G. G., trans. 1940. *Juvenal and Persius.* Cambridge, Mass.

Riverius, L. 1655. *The compleat practice of physick,* trans. N. Culpeper, A. Cole, and W. Rowland. London.

Rosner, F. 1974. *Sex ethics in the writings of Moses Maimonides.* New York.

Salaman, R. 1949. *The history and social influence of the potato.* Cambridge.

Salmon, W. 1710. *The English herbal or history of plants.* London.

Schumacher, B., trans. 1936. *Das Luminare majus von Joannes Jacobus Manlius de Bosco, 1536.* Mittenwald, Bavaria.

Shakespeare, W. 1971. *William Shakespeare: The Complete Works.* London.

Steadman's medical dictionary. 1990. Twenty-fifth edition. Baltimore, Md.

Theodorus, Iacobus (Tabernaemontani) 1664. *Neuw Vollkommentlich Kreuterbuch.* . . . Basel.

Thorndyke, L. 1958. *A history of magic and experimental science,* Vol. 7. New York.

Tissot, S. A. 1769. *Advice to people in general with respect to health.* Fifth edition. Dublin.

Venette, N. 1906. *The mysteries of conjugal love reveal'd.* Paris.

Vicary, T. 1888. *A profitable treatise of the anatomie of man's body, . . .* ed. F. J. Furnival and P. Furnivall. London.

Willich, A. F. 1800. *Lectures on diet and regimen . . . for the use of families.* London.

VI.16 ✎ Food as Medicine

Definitions

The eminent medical historian Henry E. Sigerist once noted that "[t]here is no sharp borderline between food and drug," and that both dietetic and pharmacological therapies were "born of instinct" (Sigerist 1951: 114–15). Today we tend to focus our studies of food on its nutritive values in promoting growth and health and in preventing disease, but for many centuries past, food had an additional, specifically medical role – as a remedy for illness.

The United States Food, Drug, and Cosmetic Act, signed into law June 27, 1938, provides no clearer differentiation between "food" and "drug" than Sigerist could. According to the current wording of that legislation, which updated the Pure Food and Drug Act of 1906, "the term 'food' means (1) articles used for food or drink for man or other animals, (2) chewing gum, and (3) articles used for components for any other such article," whereas "the term 'drug' means (A) articles recognized in the official United States Pharmacopoeias [and several other compendia]; and (B) articles intended for use in the diagnosis, cure, mitigation, treatment, or prevention of disease in man or other animals; and (C) articles (other than food) intended to affect the structure or any function of the body of man or other animals; and (D) articles intended for use as a component of any articles specified in clause (A), (B), or (C)." Under clause (B) above, many items that have traditionally been considered foods might also be regarded as drugs under federal law, although they seldom are. The Food and Drug Administration (FDA) can intervene in cases involving food only when it judges an item to be misleadingly labeled as a "food"; it specifically excludes vitamins from the category "drugs."

The Foundation for Innovation in Medicine recently coined the word "nutraceutical" to signify "any substance that can be considered a food and provides medical and health benefits, including the prevention and treatment of disease. Such products include traditional foods, isolated nutrients, dietary supplements, genetically engineered 'designer' foods, herbal products and processed foods" (*Tufts Journal* 1992: 10). However, the very concept of nutraceuticals seems to sidestep even the vague definitions with which the FDA is tethered. Indeed, it is probably not possible to differentiate foods from drugs with mutually exclusive definitions. The ambiguity, troublesome as it may be in some contexts, has deep historical roots. Until the early twentieth century, physicians routinely prescribed specific foods and diets for their medical – that is, curative or preventive – value. The reader should also keep in mind that nonprofessional healers, such as wives and mothers, have employed the same food remedies for similar purposes.

Rarely is it possible to pinpoint the putative healing roles of specific components of traditional foods, such as the oils that confer distinctive tastes on several botanical flavors and spices, or extracts with known pharmacological properties, such as the active principles of coffee, tea, and cocoa. Similarly, we are not concerned with toxins or biological contaminants of foods, such as the ergot alkaloids produced by a fungus that sometimes infects bread made with rye (Hofmann 1972) or the anticoagulant found in spoiled sweet-clover fodder for domestic cattle. Nor does this chapter deal with foodstuffs that only incidentally provide raw starting materials for synthesizing what are unmistakably drugs – for example, the yams from which are extracted the diosgenins that are used as starting material in the manufacture of steroids.

Medical Dietetics

Its Roots in the Ancient World

Beginning with the premise that "[m]an knew only too well that he could not live without food, that food sustained life," Sigerist postulated: "Physiology began when man . . . tried to . . . correlate the actions of food, air, and blood" (Sigerist 1951: 348–9). Ancient Egyptians, for instance, developed an ingenious theory to account for the transformation of food and air into the substance of the human body and to explain disease. Not only did they recognize the hazards of an inadequate food supply but they also knew when to prescribe a normal diet for the sick or injured, and their physicians used many items in the ordinary diet as remedies that would become common in later European cultures (Estes 1989; Manniche 1989).

The Egyptians' major sweetening agent, honey, was perhaps the most effective of all their medicines. Its efficacy as a wound dressing, attributable chiefly to the desiccating effect on bacteria of its 80 percent sugar content, probably led to its further use in many oral remedies because of its ability to prevent infection; Egyptian medical theory associated even superficial infections with internal disturbances. Modern laboratory studies have shown that honey could, indeed, have inhibited the growth of the bacteria that often contaminate wounds until normal immunological and tissue repair processes had been completed (Estes

1989: 68–71). Because it has the same effect on bacteria as honey, a thick paste of ordinary granulated sugar is sometimes applied to infected wounds today (Seal and Middleton 1991), but honey is unlikely to have been selectively effective as an antimicrobial agent when taken internally.

Although some of the Egyptians' speculative pathophysiological concepts can be recognized among the Greeks' explanations of health and disease, it was the latter that directly shaped many aspects of the relationship between food and health that survived for the next 2,500 years. As early as the sixth century B.C., the philosopher-physician Alcmaeon of Croton recognized that the body's growth depends on its food intake. A century later, the Hippocratic school of physicians described food as one source of the body's energy and its heat (Winslow and Bellinger 1945). Other sixth-century Greek thinkers tried to explain the conversion of food to parts of the body. Thales of Miletus, for example, in Asia Minor, thought that its primary substance was water, whereas Anaximenes, also of Miletus, argued that it was air. In the fifth century, the Sicilian philosopher Empedocles said that the four irreducible elements – fire, water, earth, and air – were the basic components of both food and body. He and his contemporary Anaxagoras, the first major philosopher to live in Athens, agreed with Alcmaeon that each foodstuff contains particles that are assimilated to specific parts of the body; Empedocles said that each assimilated particle fits exactly into the body part that takes it up (King 1963: 56–68; Leicester 1974: 9).

In the fourth century B.C., Aristotle followed Empedocles and Anaxagoras when he postulated that the four elements are blended from four "qualities" – hot, cold, moist, and dry – that are reciprocally paired in each element. He also held that the primary "chemical" reaction of the body is *pepsis,* a word that has historically been translated into English as "coction," from the Latin *coquere,* to cook. In both Latin and English forms, coction implies heating and ripening (of both fruit and morbific matter), and it was associated in English medical texts with perfecting something via natural processes. Aristotle used pepsis in the same way, describing it as the changes a foodstuff undergoes as it is prepared in the gastrointestinal tract for assimilation into the body. In short, both the Greek "pepsis" and the English "coction" were taken to mean "digestion." Hence, the diagnosis of dyspepsia was a synonym for indigestion. According to Aristotle, normal coction of foods, fueled by the body's innate heat, thickens the body's fluids. By contrast, coction is incomplete in the sick, resulting in abnormally thin, or watery, fluids (Leicester 1974: 15–18, 33–5).

In the second century A.D., the physician whose teachings came to dominate Western medical thought for seventeen centuries, Galen of Pergamum, in Asia Minor, reemphasized the teachings of Hippocrates, and postulated that all physiological activity depends on balances described by Aristotle (Winslow and Bellinger 1945; King 1963: 56–68; Leicester 1974: 9). According to Galen's medical configuration of Aristotle's physiological model, blood is associated with heat and moisture, phlegm is associated with moisture and cold, black bile is associated with cold and dryness, and yellow bile with dryness and heat.

Moreover, each humor was associated with one of the seasons, just as Posidonius of Rhodes, in about 100 B.C., had associated each with a corresponding temperament (Leicester 1974: 30–2). Blood was now associated with spring and the sanguine temperament, water with winter and the phlegmatic temperament, black bile with autumn and melancholy, and yellow bile with summer and the choleric or bilious temperament. (These terms for the temperaments, however, were not introduced until the twelfth century A.D., by Honorius of Autun.) The humoral theory satisfactorily explained the physiological clues to the balances that had to be rectified in order to restore health and stability to the sick body. At the same time, it permitted the construction of a pragmatic approach to the principles of medical therapy, including dietetics.

These principles were based on the premise that imbalances among the humors could be corrected by administering drugs – or foods – with appropriately opposite properties. Thus, because bilious fevers were associated with dryness and increased body heat, they should be treated with moist, cool remedies in order to rebalance the blood and yellow bile – the humors most disturbed in such patients. Similarly, dropsy, the accumulation of water in the tissues, should be treated with remedies that dried them, such as diuretics. Obviously, many foods could correct imbalances as well as doctors' drugs could. Cool, moist vegetables, for example, like cucumbers, were well suited to the needs of bilious fever patients.

The Hippocratic texts show that physicians of the fifth century B.C. recognized the influence of nourishment on human health. This was almost certainly not a new idea even then, but these are the earliest such writings to have survived. The *Regimen for Health* focuses on the therapeutic value of food, whereas the first section of the *Aphorisms* describes diet with special reference to illness. It teaches that proper nourishment, because of its influence on digestion, is more important to the sick patient than drugs (Lloyd 1978: 206–10, 272–6). Other authorities added that a carefully chosen diet can rectify disturbances in the balances of heat, cold, dryness, and moisture caused by exhaustion of the energy normally derived from the diet, or by changes in one's external circumstances, such as sudden wealth or poverty. Remedies were classified medically by the proportions of the same four qualities in each, and foods were further categorized as to whether they were wild or domesticated (Edelstein 1987, orig. 1931). In short, foods, like drugs, were prescribed in order to correct imbalances among the humors or to modify digestive processes that would themselves influence the humors, as far as ancient physicians could tell.

Dietetic instructions were designed to ensure optimum digestion, in order to minimize the amount of undigestible residues that could accumulate in the alimentary tract. Hence, in a physiological echo from the banks of the Nile, Diocles of Carystus, an Athenian physician of the fourth century B.C., cautioned: "The chief meal is to be taken when the body is empty and does not contain any badly digested residues of food" (Sigerist 1987: 238-40, orig. 1961), which, in the Egyptian tradition, were major causes of illness (Estes 1989: 80-91).

Hellenistic medical writers went beyond the Hippocratics when they asserted that a healthy diet is more important than post hoc healing of the sick. But emphasis on merely maintaining a healthy lifestyle receded when it became less feasible in the rapidly changing world of the Roman Empire. And by then, physicians were giving increased attention to diet as a coequal branch of their practice along with drugs and manual operations, such as bleeding – a differentiation that dominated the structure of professional medicine well past the Middle Ages (Siraisi 1981: 252; Edelstein 1987).

Early in the first century A.D., the Roman encyclopedist Celsus again echoed the Egyptian preoccupation with the intestines when he wrote that "digestion has to do with all sorts of troubles." His dietary guide, in the time-honored Aristotelian tradition, included lists of drugs that heat or cool; those that are least and most readily digested; those that move the bowels or constrict them; those that increase urine output, induce sleep, and draw out noxious materials that cause disease; and those that suppress illness with or without simultaneously cooling the patient. Celsus, however, concluded his pages on dietetics on a note of skepticism: "But as regards all these medicaments, . . . it is clear that each man follows his own ideas rather than what he has found to be true by actual fact" (Celsus 1935, 1: 77, 207-15).

A century later, Galen taught that most illnesses are caused by "errors of regimen [including diet], and hence avoidable." He went on to explain how appropriate attention to food, drink, and air can preserve and restore health (Temkin 1973: 40, 154-6). Indeed, his *Therapeutic Method* required that the physician understand precisely how the four basic physiological qualities of life were mixed in every foodstuff, as well as in every drug (Smith 1979: 103).

The complexities involved are evident in the *Materia Medica* by Celsus's near contemporary Dioscorides, a peripatetic Greek physician from Asia Minor (Dioscorides 1934). His book remained the fountainhead of European therapeutics – and dietetics – for 15 centuries, and traces of its influence can be detected even today. Over the years, but especially in the Middle Ages, Dioscorides's descriptions were altered and expanded by commentators who, as Celsus had feared, relied as much on what they thought was true as on what was evident to the senses. An anonymous sixth-century author cited Hippocrates and Dioscorides in his book on the nutritional medical uses of plant foods, but he, too, found it difficult to differentiate clearly between "foods" and "drugs" (Riddle 1992, orig. 1984).

Dietetics in Medieval Europe

Diet retained its position as one of the three major modes of therapy, along with medicine and surgery, throughout the Middle Ages (Siraisi 1990: 121, 137). Although emphasis on the healthful properties of diet was first systematized by Greek writers, much of it was transmitted back to Europe in Arabic texts of the ninth to eleventh centuries that preserved Hippocratic and Galenic principles (Levey 1973: 33-5).

For instance, the *Canon of Medicine*, written about A.D. 1000 by the Persian physician Avicenna, made its initial impact on Europe when it was translated into Latin in the twelfth century at Toledo, by Gerard of Cremona. It had become a medical text at Montpellier by at least 1340, which helped to ensure the diffusion of Avicenna's ideas throughout Europe.

Avicenna perpetuated the Egyptian notion that excess food tends to putrefy, and its Greek corollary that it promotes indigestion and alimentary obstruction. He expanded the teachings of Greek, Roman, and Indian writers with his assertion that foods have medicinal properties that are unrelated to their hot, cold, moist, or dry qualities, while recognizing that some foods have therapeutic properties even when they have no nutritional value. His *Canon* classifies foods as of rich or poor quality, light or heavy, and wholesome or unwholesome, and includes dietary rules applicable to both health and disease, as well as a diet for the aged (Shah 1966: ix-x, 182-7, 309-20, 338-40, 359-61).

Avicenna simplified Galen's description when he explained how food is subjected to its first coction in the stomach, resulting in chyle, which passes, via the portal veins, to the liver. There a second coction turns it into yellow bile, black bile, and blood, while its aqueous residue is carried to the kidneys for eventual release from the body. At the same time, the residue of the first, gastric, coction is discharged, partly as phlegm, into the lower intestinal tract. The blood alone is subjected to a third coction, when the heart converts it to what Aristotle had called the vital spirit, and a fourth, in the brain, where it is further transformed into a psychic spirit (Leicester 1974: 59). This satisfying explanation facilitated the physician's choice of appropriately therapeutic drugs – or foods.

Constantinus Africanus, who died 50 years after Avicenna, translated many Arabic texts at Salerno (site of the first major medical school in Europe) and

Monte Cassino. His *Book of Degrees* complicated therapeutic procedures when he described gradations in the heat, cold, dryness, and moisture of foods and medicines: A food is hot in the first degree if its heating power is less than that of the human body; it is hot in the second degree if its heating power equals that of the body; in the third degree if its heat exceeds that of the body; and in the fourth degree if it is simply unbearably hot. In his translation of a commentary on a book by Galen, Constantinus summarized current thinking about the dietary approach to therapy: "Good food is that which brings about a good humor and bad food is that which brings about an evil humor. And that which produces a good humor is that which generates good blood" (Thorndike 1923, 1: 751; Leicester 1974: 62-5).

By the thirteenth century, Latin translations of Galen's specifically dietary works, such as *De Alimentorum Facultatibus* and *De Subtiliante Dieta,* along with translations of pseudo-Galenic works on the same subjects, such as *De Nutrimento* and *De Virtutibus Cibariorum,* had joined the works of Avicenna and other Arabic writers, and the dietary works of a ninth-century Egyptian writer, Isaac Judaeus, in many medical curricula. One of the most widely consulted late medieval medical manuals was by Peter the Spaniard, or Petrus Hispanus, of Paris (later Pope John XXI, for a year until his accidental death in 1277). His scholastic commentaries on Isaac's *Universal Diets* and *Particular Diets* led him to pose such questions as: "Why does nature sustain a multitude of medicines, but not of foods? . . . Is fruit wholesome? . . . Are eggs or meat better for convalescents? . . . Should paralytics eat fried fish? Are apples good in fevers? . . . Why do we employ foods hot in the fourth degree and not those cold in the same degree?"

Peter answered such queries with syllogisms premised on gradations in the four basic qualities of foods. At the same time, he disputed the ancient idea that foods could be fully assimilated into the structure of the body (Thorndike 1923, 2: 488–507). However, Peter was not alone in rationalizing medical dietetics. As late as the 1570s, medical faculty and students at Montpellier debated such theses as "[w]hether barley bread should be eaten with fruit," "whether it was safe for persons with kidney trouble or fever to eat eggs," and "whether dinner or supper should be the more frugal meal" (Thorndike 1941, 6: 222-3).

The prominent attention given to diet in the fourteenth century is exemplified by the physician among the tale spinners who accompanied Chaucer's pilgrimage to Canterbury:

> He was well-versed in the ancient authorities;
> In his own diet he observed some measure;
> There were no superfluities for pleasure,
> Only digestives, nutritives and such (Chaucer
>   1960: 31).

It was not only physicians who were concerned with the relationship of diet to health in the Middle Ages, however. Medical authorities from Hippocrates to Avicenna were cited in many manuscripts designed for lay use (Thorndike 1940; Bullough 1957), such as several late medieval *Tacuina Sanitatis* (Handbooks of Health) based on the works of the eleventh-century Arabic physician Ibn Botlân. These manuscripts aimed, among their medical goals, to teach "the right use of food and drink," the "correct use of elimination and retention of humors," and how to moderate the emotions associated with each humor (Arano 1976: 6-10).

By the late Middle Ages, the therapeutic benefits of food had entered into the everyday planning of at least the grand households, the only ones for which evidence has survived. Spices, for example, were regarded as both aids to digestion and evidence of a host's wealth. Medieval herbals and dietaries listed the health-giving properties of foods in the classical humoral tradition. They classified foods and medicines by their degrees of heat, cold, moisture, and dryness. Thus, melons, obviously cold and moist, were suitable for treating patients with fevers. But it may be that this new order resulted from a misreading of the original texts, inasmuch as later writers did not retain it.

Largely under the influence of the *Regimen of Health,* which codified the prescripts for healthy living taught at Salerno in the eleventh century, physicians devised diets appropriate to both Aristotelian physiology and specific illnesses. Thus, Taddeo Alderotti, professor of medicine at Bologna in the late thirteenth century, recommended to many patients (probably chiefly those with fevers) that they avoid hot bread, cheese, fruits, beef, and pork, in favor of less-stimulating foods. However, in many instances, it is difficult to differentiate between his culinary and medical directions (Siraisi 1981: 293).

The patient's age was another determinant of therapeutic diets. In 1539, for example, a moderately moist and warm diet was still being recommended for young children, who were viewed as phlegmatic (that is, as very moist and cold). As they grew older, they were thought to become more sanguine or choleric, which meant that they would now benefit from much moister and colder foods. And as their strength declined in old age, they needed foods that were only as moderately moist and warm as those that had benefited them in childhood. Indeed, many foods were more closely associated, in medieval thinking, with illness than with their gustatory effects, although taste was a major clue to the presumed Galenic properties of any drug or food (Drummond and Wilbraham 1958: 65-77; Teigen 1987). In short, the medical correlates of food permeated many aspects of medieval life, from the preparation of patients for surgery to the choice of menus for banquets and bathing establishments (Cosman 1978).

Dietetics during the Scientific Revolution

The rudiments of modern chemistry were beginning to influence medical ideas in the late Middle Ages through the writings of alchemical physicians. In the late fifteenth century, for example, Conrad Heingartner of Zurich cautioned his readers to chew food thoroughly, in order to maximize its digestibility, and not to eat too many courses at one meal, because some foods are more readily digested than others. He also urged that the principal meal be taken at night, because the cold night air aids digestion by forcing the body heat necessary for its completion to stay deep inside the body (Thorndike 1934, 4: 377-8).

It is clear that Heingartner's concept of the physiology of digestion owed much to Hippocratic–Galenic medical concepts, but the latter were about to disappear in favor of more explicitly chemical explanations. The experimental science that began emerging in the late sixteenth century began, however slowly, to replace the classical Greek and Islamic traditions that had heretofore dominated European thought.

By the late seventeenth century, a major new hypothesis was beginning to hold sway over medical thinking. It postulated that illness represents imbalances not only in the classical four humors but also in the tone – the innate strength and elasticity – of the solid fibrous components of blood vessels and nerves. Both organs were considered to be hollow tubes that propelled their respective contents through the body with forces proportional to the tone of their constituent fibers. That is, the body was healthy when blood or "nerve fluids" could circulate freely, or when sweat, urine, and feces could be expelled freely, and so forth.

Thus, a fast pulse was the distinguishing hallmark of fever, which was interpreted as the result of excessive arterial tone, requiring depletive therapy to bring it under control. Conversely, a slow pulse was interpreted as evidence of a weakness that required stimulant therapy (Estes 1991a). Historians have labeled the new hypothesis as the "solidist theory," to distinguish it from the older humoral theory. The two concepts were by no means mutually exclusive, however, and most therapeutic effects were interpreted within the frameworks of both. Nevertheless, the older Hippocratic–Galenic focus became progressively less prominent in medical texts.

Dietetics fitted into the new theory as well as into humoralism. By the time solidism had taken hold in medical thinking, the specifically therapeutic role of diet had been clarified by categorizing daily menus as full, moderate (or middle), or low (or thin). As Thomas Muffett wrote in 1655: "The first increaseth flesh, spirits, and humors, the second repaireth only them that were lost, and the third lessenth them all for a time to

preserve life" (Drummond and Wilbraham 1958: 121-2). That is, full diets are appropriate, if not necessary, for maintaining growth and strength in vigorous younger people, whereas moderate diets are more suitable for middle age, and low diets for old age or during illness at any age. Muffett's description would surely have been recognizable to Aristotle, but within the solidist framework, the low diet was said to be depletive, "sedative," or antiphlogistic (that is, antifebrile), suitable for reducing excessive tone of the arteries and nerves, whereas the stronger diets were said to be stimulating.

Although the discovery of the Americas put new foods on European tables, medical properties were initially ascribed only to sassafras, sarsaparilla, and the pleasurable stimulating beverages – coffee and chocolate. When John Josselyn returned to London from New England, he reported that American watermelons were suitable for people with fevers, and cranberries for those with scurvy and "to allay the fervour of hot Diseases" (Josselyn 1672: 57, 65-6). Yet such foods could not survive the transatlantic crossing to European markets. Immigrants to colonial New England harvested both "meate and medicine" in their gardens, sometimes from the same plant, in the tradition they had learned before leaving home. Many relied on herbals for descriptions of each plant's medical properties, which closely followed those of Dioscorides (Leighton 1970: 134-7).

Early in the eighteenth century, Ippolito Francesco Albertini, professor of medicine at Bologna, echoed Avicenna when he wrote that his mother should not eat a food, such as meat, "that is easily converted into blood." At about the same time, Albertini's brother-in-law, Vincenzo Antonio Pigozzi, also a physician, directed a correspondent to strengthen his patient's stomach with food and medicine because, as Celsus had said, it was "apt to be weak in students and other diligent and well-behaved persons," so that "their daily food, on account of its coldness, is poorly purified and digested" (Jarcho 1989: 99, 177).

Eighteenth-century British hospitals developed standard diets based on humoral and solidist precepts. A 1782 London hospital dietary mandated the same breakfast for patients on both low and full diets: water-gruel or milk porridge (made of 1.25 ounces of oatmeal, and raisins, in a pint of water or milk). The supper menu was the same, supplemented by the addition of a pint of broth (made by boiling a leg of lamb or other meat for 1.5 hours) four times a week, or a quarter pound of cheese or butter during the week. The full and low diets differed chiefly in their midday dinner menus.

Febrile patients on the low diet received rice milk twice a week. Also twice a week they were served bread pudding (made by soaking a half pound of bread crumbs in one pint of milk overnight and then adding two or three eggs before the mixture was boiled in a bag for a hour or so). Lamb or other meat broth was also on the menu twice a week, or plumb broth (made by boiling six ounces of meat or bone with a half pint of peas and a half ounce of oats in water). A quarter pound of boiled beef or mutton, or roast veal, was added to the menu twice a week, and a 14-ounce loaf of bread was served every day.

By contrast, patients on a full diet received rice milk once a week. A half pound of boiled pudding appeared weekly (made by boiling a mixture of one pound of flour, a quarter pound of suet or meat or eels, and fruits, in 13 ounces of water, for one to two hours). A half pound of beef or mutton was served with greens four times weekly, and a loaf of bread daily. In addition, patients on the low diet received one pint of small beer daily, while those on the full diet were allowed four times as much. The presumed medical qualities of the two diets differed chiefly with respect to the stimulating property of red meat; their total mass was nearly the same (Estes 1990: 66-7). Such diets perpetuated the ancient admonition to "feed a cold and starve a fever," whose origins are in the Hippocratic texts, and it has remained a guiding therapeutic principle down to our own time.

In 1772, Dr. William Cullen of Edinburgh lamented that although dietetic prescriptions were among the most valuable of all therapies, they had fallen out of regular medical use in recent years (Risse 1986: 220). He might have been surprised when, a few years afterward, his colleague, Dr. Andrew Duncan, Jr., increased the proportions of stimulating foods served to his febrile or otherwise debilitated patients, chiefly by increasing their meat allowances (Estes 1990: 65-8). In fact, by the end of the century, Dr. William Heberden of London was complaining that "[m]any physicians appear to be too strict and particular in the roles of diet and regimen," and he urged that the sick be allowed to choose their own diets, according to their own tastes (Heberden 1802: 1-5).

In the meantime, experimental chemistry had begun to shed new light on the physiology of digestion and on the respiratory processes involved in the conversion of food into energy, carbon dioxide, and the tissues of the body. Early in the seventeenth century, Jan Baptista Van Helmont, who lived near Brussels, showed that gastric juice is acid, and that it is necessary for the digestion of food. He may even have identified hydrochloric acid as its chief component, but it was not until 1752 that this was proved by René Antoine Ferchault, Sieur de Réamur, in France. Although Van Helmont's concept of digestion contained some Aristotelian elements, he did show that the acid in gastric juice is neutralized in the duodenum by bile from the liver. However, it was in 1736 that Albrecht von Haller, at Göttingen, established that bile emulsifies fats. Haller's teacher, Hermann Boerhaave of Leiden, had already laid the groundwork for differentiating what were later named proteins (in 1838) and carbohydrates (in

1844). Haller added the last major food class, fats. But Boerhaave and Georg Ernst Stahl, professor of medicine at Halle, both leading proponents of solidism, denied that gastric juice was acid. Instead, they favored the ancient concept that digestion was a putrefactive or fermentative process, which eventually was abandoned in the face of Réamur's proof that digestion represents the dissolution of foodstuffs in gastric acid (Drummond and Wilbraham 1958: 232-55; Leicester 1974: 96-7, 118-27; Estes 1991a).

Between 1700 and 1850, when modern experimental pharmacology began to be applied to the study of drug effects on living organisms, physicians trained in the European medical tradition used as drugs about 500 botanical remedies, and 170 chemical compounds and other materials. Any given eighteenth-century physician employed some 125 different botanical remedies in his standard repertoire, depending on his training and experience. Save for the few botanical remedies that had been introduced from the New World by then, the majority of plants prescribed in the eighteenth century had also been used by healers in the ancient Mediterranean world, including most of the medically important foodstuffs shown in the seven tables that follow (Estes 1990). They illustrate the specifically therapeutic roles of familiar culinary ingredients, while reemphasizing the difficulty of discriminating between foods and drugs. These tabulations may not be all-inclusive, and several items could have been included in more than one list. Most of these foods are more fully described elsewhere in this work.

Comments on Table VI.16.1

Many of these foodstuffs, familiar in both the kitchens and apothecary shops of the eighteenth and nineteenth centuries, had been used as medicines for at least 2,000 years. As in the Middle Ages, their tastes were the most valuable clues as to how they could benefit the sick. Although some had clear-cut effects, especially the stronger cathartics, others were more speculative, as dictated by humoral and solidist theory, than verifiable.

One need not wonder that physicians prescribed these or any other time-tested remedies for as long as they did. Because 90 to 95 percent of adult patients recovered following treatment, whatever it was, their physicians had no reason not to conclude that their prescriptions benefited their patients. The double-blind controlled clinical trials on which we rely today to *prove* the therapeutic efficacy of putative remedies were not developed until the mid–twentieth century (Estes 1991a). Thus, although a few items listed above might have moved the bowels to a modest extent, most of their other effects, such as those on body tone, digestion, or uterine function, were only presumed to occur, in accord with prevalent pathophysiologic theories.

Table VI.16.1 *Past and present medicinal uses of flavorings and spices*

Angelica: Weak cathartic, tonic, carminative.
Anise: Tonic, pectoral, carminative; lactagogue.
Assafoetida: Antispasmodic, expectorant, emmenagogue, diuretic, diaphoretic, mild cathartic, anthelmintic.
Canella: Stomachic, gentle tonic.
Capers: Weak cathartic, diuretic, deobstruent.
Caraway: Stomachic, carminative, diuretic.
Cardamom: Carminative, diaphoretic.
Chocolate: Stomachic, antidysenteric.
Cinnamon: Tonic, stomachic, carminative, astringent.
Cloves: Tonic, mild styptic.
Coriander: Carminative.
Cumin: For plasters.
Dill: Carminative.
Fenugreek: Aphrodisiac; for emollient plasters.
Garlic: Tonic, diaphoretic, expectorant, diuretic, carminative, emmenagogue, rubefacient.
Ginger: Tonic; rubefacient.
Horse radish: Tonic, diuretic, diaphoretic.
Hyssop: Expectorant, antitussive, pectoral, carminative.
Juniper: Carminative, stomachic, diuretic, diaphoretic, emmenagogue.
Licorice: Cathartic, expectorant.
Marjoram: Tonic, cephalic, expectorant, errhine.
Mustard: Stomachic, digestive, diuretic, diaphoretic, emetic, mild cathartic, antiscorbutic; blistering agent.
Nutmeg–mace: Tonic, narcotic, stomachic, antiemetic, astringent.
Parsley: Carminative, aperient, diuretic, emmenagogue.
Peppermint: Tonic, carminative, antispasmodic.
Peppers: Stimulant, digestive, antispasmodic.
Pimento: Tonic, carminative.
Rosemary: Antispasmodic, sedative, cephalic, emmenagogue.
Saffron: Cordial, narcotic, antispasmodic, emmenagogue.
Sage: Astringent, carminative, stomachic, nerve tonic.
Sarsaparilla: Antirheumatic, antivenereal, demulcent, diaphoretic.
Sassafras: Weak cathartic, tonic, blood purifier, diuretic, diaphoretic, antirheumatic, antisyphilitic.
Sesame: Mild cathartic.
Spearmint: Carminative, stomachic, antispasmodic, antiemetic, anti-icteric.
Thyme: Analgesic for toothache.
Tumeric: Tonic, weak cathartic, emmenagogue, anti-icteric.
Wintergreen: Astringent, antidiarrheal, emmenagogue, lactagogue.

Interesting and odoriferous compounds, some of which have biological effects in animals or man, have been extracted from several of these flavorings and spices, but most cannot be related to the clinical effects listed. The few extracts that might have modest pharmacological activity include the gingerols isolated from ginger (they can stimulate cardiac action); the terpinem-4-ol in juniper (which can increase renal glomerular filtration and irritate the uterus); the mildly cathartic glycerrhizin in licorice; the apiol in parsley (which may promote diuresis and stimulate the uterus); the weak smooth-muscle relaxant menthol in the mints; and the extremely potent irritant capsicin in peppers. Safrole, which is responsible for the taste of sassafras, has been banned in the United States because it is carcinogenic to animals when administered in high doses; like nutmeg, it has mild stimulating effects in man (*Lawrence Review* 1987–91). Still, many of these items can be found in modern grocery stores and among over-the-counter remedies.

Comments on Table VI.16.2

It is difficult to discover how these fruits and nuts entered common medical usage, although it seems likely that their adoption followed the discovery of their gustatory merits. A few have a mild cathartic effect, oranges and strawberries might well appear cool to the taste, and the slightly bitter taste of others might make them seem astringent, but no consistent pattern seems to associate these foods medically.

Comments on Table VI.16.3

Lettuce and endive produce a cooling sensation, but the other alleged properties of lettuce probably owe more to its confusion with another lettuce species that was rarely prescribed by physicians. Several compounds have been extracted from chicory, including its aromatic principle, acetophenone, but none has any ascertainable role in the effects listed for it in this table. The oxalic acid in the sorrels might have contributed to their reputations as refrigerants and antiscorbutics at a time when acids were deemed appropriate for the treatment of scurvy (Estes 1979), but the irritating (and potentially dangerous) acid is unlikely to have had any true therapeutic effect (*Lawrence Review* 1987–91).

Table VI.16.2. *Past and present medicinal uses of fruits and nuts*

Almond milk: Diluent; mild cathartic; counteracts blisters.
Blackberries: Slightly astringent.
Cherries: Tonic, slightly narcotic, anthelmintic, antiseptic.
Currants: For sore throat.
Damsons: Tonic, astringent, cathartic, emetic.
Dates: Emollient, slightly astringent.
Elderberries: Cathartic, deobstruent, diuretic, diaphoretic.
Figs: Mild cathartic.
Lemons: Stomachic, antiseptic; antiscorbutic (after the 1790s).
Olive [oil]: Demulcent cathartic; antidote to rattlesnake venom.
Oranges: Tonic, refrigerant, antispasmodic, stomachic, carminative, antiseptic, antiscorbutic (after the 1790s).
Peaches: Cathartic, sedative, anthelmintic.
Pokeberries: Emetic, cathartic, mild narcotic.
Pomegranate: Cathartic, astringent, antidiarrheal, anthelmintic.
Raspberries: Refrigerant, stomachic, diuretic, diaphoretic.
Strawberries: Refrigerant, tonic, diuretic, cathartic.
Tamarinds: Cathartic, refrigerant.
White walnut: Anti-inflammatory, cathartic.

Table VI.16.3. *Past and present medicinal uses of vegetables*

Asparagus: Diuretic, weak cathartic, deobstruent.
Cabbage: Cathartic, emollient (Sauerkraut: antiscorbutic).
Celery: Weak cathartic, carminative.
Chicory: Cathartic, gastrointestinal tonic, stomachic, refrigerant.
Endive: Cooling weak cathartic.
Lettuce: Cooling sedative narcotic, antidiarrheal, antitussive.
Onion: Stomachic, diuretic, diaphoretic, expectorant.
Sorrel: Refrigerant, diuretic, weak cathartic, antidiarrheal, antiscorbutic.
Watercress: Weak cathartic, antiscorbutic.

Table VI.16.4. *Past and present medicinal uses of beverages*

Alcohol: Tonic, carminative, digestive; rubefacient.
Chocolate: See under flavorings and spices in Table VI.16.1
Coffee: Astringent, antiseptic, strong tonic, digestive; to stay awake.
Milk: To stimulate natural secretions; antiscorbutic.
Tea: Diluent, diuretic, diaphoretic.
Wine: Stomachic, diaphoretic, tonic, digestive, astringent.

Comments on Table VI.16.4

Alcohol and wine were among the first remedies subjected to quantitative experimental studies which, in the end, merely validated their age-old use as tonics. The major active ingredients in chocolate, coffee, and tea are, respectively, theobromine, caffeine, and theophylline, which share several pharmacological properties, such as diuresis and central nervous system stimulation, although to varying degrees. Theophylline is a mainstay of bronchodilator therapy for patients with asthma and related diseases, whereas caffeine still has a minor role as a stimulant, chiefly in a few over-the-counter painkillers (Estes 1991a).

Comments on Table VI.16.5

Barley water had been a common drink for the sick since antiquity, especially in low diets for fever patients. Barley, bread crumbs, and wheat or wheat flour contributed their soothing and gluten-based binding and stiffening qualities to plasters and wound dressings. The bran in oatmeal does increase stool bulk, but before the twentieth century, no medical use could have been made of oat bran's ability to bind cholesterol in the intestinal tract, which can help lower cholesterol concentrations in the blood. Ergot first entered medical usage as a result of its contamination of bread

Table VI.16.5. *Past and present medicinal uses of grains*

Barley: Refrigerant, demulcent.
Bread crumbs: For gastrointestinal symptoms; in plasters, to stimulate suppuration.
Ergot, on rye: For postpartum care.
Oats: Cathartic.
Wheat: Visceral tonic; paste for plasters.

Table VI.16.6. *Past and present medicinal uses of gums and roots*

Jujubes: Deobstruent, decongestant.
Manna: Cathartic, expectorant, carminative.
Marshmallow: Emollient, demulcent.
Slippery elm: Emollient, expectorant, antidiarrheal; demulcent dressing.

made from its agricultural host, rye. It was recommended for obstetrical use in Germany in 1582, and reintroduced for that purpose in 1787. In 1807, Dr. John Stearns of New York promoted its use for hastening birth, and in 1824 Dr. David Hosack of the same city recommended it for the control of postpartum bleeding (Estes 1990: 175), but such use remained controversial (Berman 1992). It is now well established that the alkaloids extracted from ergot are potent constrictors of blood vessels; they have been used to control postpartum bleeding in the twentieth century.

Comments on Table VI.16.6

None of these gummy plant extracts is known to contain pharmacologically active principles. They probably owe their roles in medicine to their soothing qualities. The slippery, or red, elm entered medical usage largely through the works of Samuel Thomson, the botanical physician who stimulated the practice of do-it-yourself medicine in the United States early in the nineteenth century (Estes 1992). Later in the century, New England Shakers, who had adopted Thomson's medical system, made and promoted a flour derived from the tree's bark (Estes 1991b).

Comments on Table VI.16.7

Although burned eggshells might well be presumed to neutralize acids, it is doubtful that they would have provided an efficient remedy for the hyperacidity that was frequently diagnosed after Réamur's discovery of hydrochloric acid in the stomach. It was probably a remedy that evolved out of the discovery that the calcium oxide produced by burning eggshells was chemically equivalent to the alkaline quicklime made by similar techniques. Egg whites, on the other hand, can help neutralize toxic metal ions in the stomach. The cathartic effect of yolks is arguable, but their reputation as a cure for jaundice most likely stems simply from the fact that they are yellow. The properties associated with honey in the eighteenth century were

Table VI.16.7. *Past and present medicinal uses of miscellaneous foodstuffs*

Eggs: Burned shells, as antacid; whites, as an antidote for copper and mercury poisoning; yolks, as cathartic or anti-icteric.
Honey: Weak cathartic, detergent, expectorant.
Rapeseed: Attenuating, detergent, antiseptic, diaphoretic.

probably speculative, and we do not know if it was used in ways similar to those of the Egyptian physicians. Rapeseed oil, now called canola oil, contains nothing that might have led physicians to deduce the properties with which they credited it.

Dietetics and Modern Food Sciences

By about 1900, medical dietetics assumed new forms and goals in the wake of experimental laboratory investigations that permitted physicians to incorporate the concept of metabolic needs into their professional thinking. Although the identification and isolation of vitamins over the following three decades nearly completed that story, daily requirements for carbohydrates, fats, proteins, minerals, and vitamins are still being debated and modified. Many of today's medical concerns about foods are related to their statistical associations with specific illnesses. While such topics are explored elsewhere in this work, consideration of the transition from old to new concepts of medical dietetics is pertinent here.

The first foods to provide a true cure of any disease were citrus fruits, but the ready response they elicited in scurvy patients was not, at first, recognized as the result of replacing a substance that was missing from their diet. Indeed, James Lind's celebrated experiment with oranges and lemons on HMS *Salisbury* in 1747 was not the negatively controlled clinical trial it is often said to have been: He was only comparing six acids, including the fruits, because scurvy was thought to be a kind of fever and, therefore, treatable with almost any cooling acid. Some thought that excess alkalinity caused scorbutic fever, which led to the same therapeutic conclusion. Moreover, Lind did not argue that citrus fruits were the best protection against scurvy; indeed, he continued to recommend several other acids. Marine surgeons had recognized the antiscorbutic value of lemons by at least 1617, but not until 1795 did the British navy adopt limes as standard protection against scurvy (the U.S. Navy followed suit in 1812), as evidence of their efficacy continued to accumulate. Even so, navy surgeons knew only that lemons, limes, and oranges could prevent or cure the disease, not that they replenished the body's stores of a vital principle. When, in 1784, the Swedish chemist Karl Wilhelm Scheele discovered citric acid in lemons, he erroneously assumed that it was the active therapeutic principle, and it was not until the 1920s that the true antiscorbutic principle, ascorbic acid, was isolated and identified as essential to life (Estes 1979, 1985, 1990: 49, 116).

Studies of the physiology of digestion provided essential stepping-stones to the development of modern dietetic therapeutics early in the nineteenth century. In England, William Prout classified foods into the three major groups that are, in retrospect, recognizable as carbohydrate, protein, and fat. Friedrich Tiedemann and Leopold Gmelin reported from Heidelberg,

in 1826, that the ingestion of any kind of food increased the amount of acid in the stomach, and that the acid could dissolve all foods. Some investigators continued to argue that lactic acid was the active principle of digestion, but in 1852 Friedrich Bidder and Carl Schmidt of the German university at Dorpat, Estonia – then emerging as the first academic center for the study of pharmacology – showed that the free hydrochloric acid discovered by Réamur was the only acid in gastric juice (Leicester 1974: 147, 161–3).

The experiments on gastric function performed by U.S. Army surgeon William Beaumont led him to conclude, in 1833, that although animal and grain products are easier to digest than most vegetable foods, the differences are attributable only to the relative sizes of their constituent fibers, not to their other properties. He emphasized this by pointing out that the action of the hydrochloric acid in gastric juice is the same on all foodstuffs (Beaumont 1833: 275–8), as Tiedemann and Gmelin had shown.

By the 1840s, digestive enzymes had been found in saliva, gastric juice, and pancreatic juice, and by 1857 Claude Bernard had demonstrated that the glucose that provides the body's energy is released from glycogen that has been synthesized and stored in the liver (Leicester 1974: 165–9). It was probably these discoveries that permitted the eventual abandonment of dietetic therapies that had originated in the ancient world, especially when it became apparent that food itself does not alter normal gastric acid or digestive enzyme secretion, although both were eventually shown to be altered in specific diseases.

In 1816, François Magendie of Bordeaux found that dietary sources of nitrogen, especially meat, are essential for health in dogs, and that all the nitrogen necessary to sustain life comes from food, not air (Leicester 1974: 146). His work prompted the studies of Justus von Liebig, of Giessen, in Germany, which by 1840 had laid the foundations for the study of metabolism and other aspects of human nutrition. He showed, for instance, that the nitrogenous substances present in meat and some vegetable foods are assimilated into animal tissues, while carbohydrates like starch and sugar are consumed during oxidative respiration. Liebig's work began to elucidate the complex chemical interactions of foodstuffs with the fabric of the body (Drummond and Wilbraham 1958: 285–6, 345; Holmes 1973). In 1866, his pupil Carl von Voit showed that carbohydrates and fats supply all the energy used by the body, while its chief nitrogenous components, the proteins, are themselves derived from dietary protein of both plant and animal origin (Leicester 1974: 192).

Perhaps with these discoveries in mind, in 1865 Liebig began to promote an "Extract of Meat" he had devised as a medicine for specific illnesses, such as typhoid fever and inflammation of the ovaries. He marketed it both as a proprietary remedy and, in Germany (but not Britain or the United States), as a prescription drug. Although it was shown almost immediately to lack meat's nutritive elements, the extract was a success in European, British, and American kitchens for many years afterward, especially when Liebig redirected its advertising toward over-the-counter consumers instead of physicians and pharmacists, who were unconvinced of its therapeutic value. The extract also prompted development of the first commercial formulations of infant foods, which were advertised as promoting growth and preventing disease (Apple 1986; Finlay 1992).

Like Liebig's Meat Extract and many botanical drugs, several foods were medically important in the eyes of nineteenth-century laymen, even if not in those of contemporary physicians. Some dietary lore was pure mythology, such as the aphrodisiacal properties imputed to nutmegs, tomatoes, quinces, and artichokes (Taberner 1985: 204-6, 60-3). However, many over-the-counter remedies or their ingredients had the imprimatur of regular medicine, as is evident in British and American home-medicine texts.

Such books evaluated not only the nutritive value of foods but also their specific physiological effects in health and disease. By way of example, when J. S. Forsyth prepared the twenty-second edition of William Buchan's *Domestic Medicine*, he moved the chapter on diet from near the end to the very beginning, and incorporated into it ideas he had developed in his own *Natural and Medical Dieteticon* (Buchan 1809: 413-31, 1828: 19-40). Forsyth began by explaining that the "constant use of bread and animal substances excites an unnatural thirst, and leads to the immoderate use of beer and other stimulating liquors, which generate disease, and reduce the lower orders of the people to a state of indigence" (Buchan 1828: 19). Moreover, he said: "The plethoric . . . should eat sparingly of animal food. It yields far more blood than vegetables taken in the same quantity, and, of course, may induce inflammatory disorders. It acts as a stimulus to the whole system, by which means the circulation of the blood is greatly accelerated" (Buchan 1828: 20). In other words, although a meat diet is best suited to the physiological needs of laborers, it predisposes them to intemperance and poverty.

Forsyth differentiated vegetables and meat in terms of their acidity and alkalinity. He said that plant foods are more acidic and lighter in the stomach; in addition, they mix more readily in the stomach with other foods, and are more constipating, than meat. By contrast, he thought that animal foods display the "greater tendency to alkalescency and putrefaction," which meant that they might cause diarrhea and dysentery, even if only rarely. Although in Forsyth's opinion they mixed less well with other foods during digestion, they did help keep the bowels regular. He concluded by pointing out that meat produces "a more dense stimulating elastic blood" than does a veg-

etable diet, because animal food "stretches and causes a greater degree of resistance in the solids, as well as excites them to stronger action" (Buchan 1828: 39-40). This explained the value of meat to the health of the workingman within the contexts of contemporary chemical knowledge and of the humoral and solidist medical traditions.

Although Buchan and his posthumous editor wrote for British readers in the first instance, their work found receptive audiences in the United States, where do-it-yourself medicine flourished more than in England. In 1830, John Gunn of Knoxville, Tennessee, explained to the people of America (he dedicated his book to President Andrew Jackson) that "[f]ood . . . is intended to support nature" (Gunn 1830: 124). According to Gunn, because the most nourishing food is of animal origin, it can overheat and exhaust the body, unlike vegetable foods. In this respect he went beyond Forsyth's caveats. Inasmuch as plant foods cause stomach acidity, flatulence, and debility if they are the only items in the diet, Gunn recommended a diet with balanced amounts of meat and vegetables.

Guides to diet as a way to health proliferated throughout the nineteenth century. Some were mixed with exhortations against alcohol or doctors' drugs, while others promoted the benefits of physical culture. Gymnastics enthusiast Dio Lewis, for example, published books specifically related to gastrointestinal health, including *Talks about People's Stomachs* (Boston, 1870) and *Our Digestion; or My Jolly Friend's Secret* (Philadelphia, 1874). The latter title alone suggests that the book focuses on how to avoid the unpleasant sour feeling that characterizes dyspepsia. Similar titles appeared in England, such as W. T. Fernie's *Meals Medicinal: . . . Curative Foods From the Cook; In Place of Drugs From the Chemist* (Bristol, 1905).

Some British writers had been promoting meatless diets for a century before Dr. William Lambe claimed, in 1806, that such diets are not hazardous, and could even cure tuberculosis. His work seems to have prompted Percy Bysshe Shelley, at the age of 21, to write a vegetarian tract that was republished many times between 1813 and 1884. But most physicians, a conservative lot, argued that plant foods are hard to digest, and would have agreed with Forsyth that meat is essential for maintaining strength and vitality (Green 1986: 46-7; Nissenbaum 1988: 45-9).

Thus, by the end of the nineteenth century, scientific studies of the chemistry of foods were being translated into professional texts and domestic health guides written by physicians. Most of the foodstuffs used as medicines during the 25 centuries between the era of Hippocrates and the discovery of pathogenic microbes in the 1870s quietly disappeared from pharmacopoeias in the early twentieth century, as did the vast majority of historic drugs. From then on, until the recent emergence of medical nutrition as a clinical subspecialty, regular medicine nearly abandoned the therapeutic application of diet to disease, save for patients with specific biochemical defects of intermediary metabolism or those with vitamin deficiencies.

In the meantime, however, some of the newly emerging information about foods (and distortions of it) was being exploited by promoters who functioned outside the mainstream of regular medicine, but who well understood the needs of mainstream Americans. They and their followers liked to think of themselves as innovators or "reformers."

Alternative Dietetics

A number of nineteenth-century American health reformers – many of them energetic entrepreneurs – mounted effective populist attacks on both traditional and modern medical ideas simultaneously. Their chief selling point was that their ideas were more prophylactic than curative, a highly liberal position in a proud new republic in which regular medicine was dominated by political conservatives.

The allure of do-it-yourself medicine for the traditionally self-reliant American public was quickened by Samuel Thomson, an itinerant New England healer who, beginning in 1805, found that his system of botanical medicine was more profitable than farming. Although the curative focus of his system revolved around a relatively small number of remedies made from indigenous plants, Thomson also emphasized the importance of proper diet for health. His own version of the Hippocratic concept of the humors presumed that all disease arises from disordered digestion, resulting in insufficient heat for maintaining normal body function (Estes 1992).

Regular physicians were privately incensed at the economic competition inherent in Thomson's system – one of his marketing slogans was "Every man be his own physician" – but in public they could only charge him with unscientific reliance on a single dogma, his insistence that all disease was caused by cold. Such notions were not entirely new. In 1682 an anonymous French writer who thought the large intestine was the primary seat of all disease had urged his readers to be their own physicians, and to use botanical remedies that grew in their own country (Thorndike 1958, 8: 409). But in the 1680s, such suggestions must have been seen as only adding to the surfeit of emerging medical ideas and not as heresy or competition.

The true fountainhead of the healthy diet in America was Sylvester Graham, a Presbyterian clergyman who preached the physiological benefits of abstinence from alcohol and sex, as well as dietary reliance on homegrown and homemade whole wheat bread. His medical notions were not entirely original, however. They stemmed largely from those of François-Joseph-Victor Broussais, a physician in Napoleonic France who had taught that all disease was caused by an irritation in the gastrointestinal tract. Therefore, said Broussais, almost any illness can be cured by removing the responsible stimulating irritation with bleeding and his version of a low diet.

Because of the historical association of meat eating with potentially pathogenic stimulation, vegetarian writers such as Graham associated avoidance of animal foods, alcohol, and sexual arousal with physical, moral, and spiritual health. The ideal diet he began advocating in the 1830s consisted of two small meatless meals daily that included whole wheat bread and cold water. Graham said that his regimen would preclude the exhaustion and debility that usually follow excessive stimulation (Nissenbaum 1988: 20, 39–49, 57–9, 126–7, 142–3).

His influence has persisted to the present in several guises. Graham certainly fostered the notion that a meat diet was the major cause of dyspepsia (Green 1986: 164). The self-sufficient Shakers, who farmed and sold medicinal herbs, adopted his teachings along with those of Thomson, and sold flour made to Graham's specifications. However, although the Shakers believed that dyspepsia was the quintessential disease of postwar America, they were not vegetarians themselves (Green 1986: 30–1; Estes 1991b).

The Grahamite proselytizing of Dr. Russell T. Trall has had the most lasting impact of all. He emerged in the 1840s as an energetic and prolific promoter of hydropathy, the water-cure techniques introduced in Austria by Vincenz Preissnitz, who, like Thomson, found healing more lucrative than farming (Armstrong and Armstrong 1991: 81–2). Preissnitz did not preach vegetarianism, but his American disciple did. Trall rationalized his therapeutic methods by updating the ancient four temperaments in what he said was a more "practical" classification.

He associated the nervous temperament with the nervous system, and the sanguine temperament with the arteries and lungs. He explained that these two temperaments were more active, or irritable, than the bilious temperament, which he paired with the veins and musculoskeletal system, or the lymphatic temperament, paired with the abdominal viscera. Thus, Trall described the gastrointestinal tract as torpid and incapable of irritation in persons with a lymphatic temperament (Trall 1852: 287–90).

Although he cited Liebig's differentiation of nitrogenous from non-nitrogenous foods, Trall based much of his dietary argument on his own reading of Genesis 1:29: "Behold, I have given you every herb bearing seed, which is upon the face of all the earth, and every tree in which is the fruit of a tree yielding seed; to you it shall be for meat." From this, Trall concluded that "the vegetable kingdom is the ordained source of man's sustenance" (Trall 1852: 399).

He went on to adduce anatomical, physiological, and "experimental" (actually, testimonial) evidence for the medical efficacy of a vegetable diet. He stated that the secretions of vegetable eaters are "more pure, bland, and copious, and the excretions . . . are less offensive to the senses," and that their blood is "less prone to the inflammatory and putrid diatheses." As a result, their "mental passions are more governable and better balanced," a conclusion that Graham would have seconded, although he might not have accepted Trall's association of any temperament with a nonirritable intestinal tract (Trall 1852: 410–12). Neither would Graham have tolerated Trall's opinion that certain boiled or broiled meats, white fish, and an occasional egg were acceptable. Still, the major item on the menu at Trall's water-cure establishments was unleavened bread made of coarse-ground, unsifted meal like Graham's (Trall 1852: 421–4).

Ellen G. White, who began the Seventh-Day Adventist movement in the late 1840s, at the time Graham and Trall were achieving fame, was interested in the teachings of both. The Adventists' continuing adherence to a vegetable diet today is presumed to be responsible, in large measure, for their lesser risk of major degenerative diseases (Webster and Rawson 1979).

In 1866, Mrs. White opened the Western Health Reform Institute in Battle Creek, Michigan, as an Adventist retreat that served its guests two vegetarian meals a day, modeled on those advocated by Russell Trall, along with the full range of water cures. Ten years later, Dr. John Harvey Kellogg became the Institute's medical director. There he invented and prescribed the original versions of "Granola" and peanut butter, and the rolled breakfast cereals that he developed in collaboration with his younger brother, Will Keith Kellogg. Not only were cereals nutritious, said the brothers, but they would also counteract the autointoxicants then being accused of causing many illnesses, and facilitate bowel movements.

Charles W. Post, a former patient at the Battle Creek Sanitarium (as J. H. Kellogg renamed it), followed suit with his own "Postum" (1895), "Grape-Nuts" (1898), and "Post Toasties" (1908). The Kelloggs had set up a company to manufacture their products, but it was after the brothers had parted ways that W. K. Kellogg in 1906 introduced "Corn Flakes." Although the Kelloggs and Post had many competitors among health-food manufacturers in the Battle Creek area alone, their products still dominate the marketplace for breakfast cereals. Their initial success was attributable largely to their advertised medical uses. Like other bran foods, W. K. Kellogg's "All-Bran" was first marketed as a relief from constipation. In 1931 Nabisco's "Shredded Wheat," a competing product, was proclaimed to offer "Strength in Every Shred" (Green 1986: 305–12; Whorton 1988; Armstrong and Armstrong 1991: 99–119).

A few other foods entered the realm of medical usage outside the framework established by Sylvester Graham. The most visible was probably the tomato, one of the most fleeting therapeutic discoveries in the history of medicine. Many Europeans had regarded it as inedible or poisonous after it was brought from the New World in the 1540s, because it belongs to the same family as the deadly nightshade. Its therapeutic value was reported in London as early as 1731, but when sent to North America soon afterward, it was only as an ornamental plant (Smith 1991).

In 1825, Dr. Thomas Sewall reported, in Washington, D.C., that tomatoes could cure bilious disease, probably because they have particles that are yellow, as is jaundice, produced by the accumulation of yellowish bile pigments in the skin as a result of liver or gall bladder disease. Then, in 1835, a brazen medical entrepreneur, John Cook Bennett, began telling Americans that tomatoes could cure diarrhea and dyspepsia. He claimed that Indians used them to promote diuresis, while others said they were good for fevers. The agricultural press spread Bennett's enthusiasm, and within five years several extracts of tomato had been marketed as typical panaceas (Smith 1991).

An 1865 advertisement claimed that "Tomato pills, will cure all your ills." However, reports of the hazards of tomatoes, as well as their lack of therapeutic efficacy, had already begun to resurface. Although the merits of tomatoes were being debated as late as the 1896 annual meeting of the American Medical Association, they had long since lost their medical appeal – but by then they had become firmly established in American cookery (Smith 1991).

The role of food as therapy is still central to several modern alternative-healing systems. Naturopathic healers (also known as naturists) cite Samuel Thomson as their chief source of authority, declaring that the "Naturist will be both dietician and herbalist." They, too, look on the stomach as "in almost every instance the seat of disease," and like Russell Trall, they cite Genesis 1:29 (Clymer 1960: 12, 33, orig. 1902). Some naturopathic regimens include coffee enemas, administered at two-hour intervals, to cleanse the intestines.

Occasionally, a small number of people will use a food for medical reasons despite evidence of the dangers of such usage. For example, unpasteurized milk has been promoted neither by advertising nor by any organization – its use seems to be inspired chiefly by folklore, supported by its consumers' supposition that it is a matter of freedom of choice. Those who persist in using raw milk, sometimes illegally, claim that it has more nutritive value than pasteurized milk, that it increases their resistance to disease and enhances their fertility, and that it contains unidentified substances, such as an "antistiffness factor" that helps prevent rheumatism (Potter et al. 1984).

When the word "macrobiotic" entered English usage in the early eighteenth century, it signified a diet or other rules of conduct that would prolong life. Its modern usage appeared in the early 1960s, when a Japanese, Georges Ohsawa, introduced a new concept in dietary therapy. He began with the premise that there is "no disease that cannot be cured by 'proper' therapy." His idea of "proper" therapy, which originated in ancient Chinese ideas of the balance between the complementary forces of yin and yang, was based on white grain cereals and on avoiding fluids. As much as 30 percent of the diet could be meat when the patient began the prescribed regimen, but by the time he or she had progressed through the entire ten-step sequence, which Ohsawa called the "Zen macrobiotic diet," the patient would be eating only grain products. In the 1970s, Michio Kushi revised Ohsawa's diet after its inventor had died, but without its meatless extremes. In addition, Kushi developed a cadre of "counselors" whose special training permits them alone to make diagnoses within the system. Many do so by iridology, which associates segments of the iris with specific parts of the body (iridology has also been practiced by chiropractors, among others). Because Ohsawa had said that the macrobiotic diet could cure any disease, it is sometimes resorted to by victims of cancer, who are instructed to chew each mouthful 150 times, to enhance the food's strengthening yang properties and to preclude overeating; healthy people need chew only 50 times (Macrobiotic diets 1959; AMA Council 1971; Simon, Wortham, and Mitas 1979; Cassileth and Brown 1988).

In the 1920s, a German physician, Max Gerson, developed a dietary cure for cancer based on his belief (which accorded with the pioneering studies of intermediary metabolism by Otto Warburg) that the rate of cancer cell growth depends on imbalances in the aerobic and anaerobic metabolic reactions of the malignant cells. Gerson said his diet would restore those balances to normal by, among other things, increasing potassium intake. It resembles the diet served at Russell Trall's water-cure establishments, with the addition of calves' liver, a mixture of special fruit juices, and coffee enemas. Gerson refined his regimen after emigrating to the United States, and it is still available from his heirs in Tijuana, Mexico (American Cancer Society 1990; Green 1992).

Other clinics in Tijuana offer diets that are said to cure cancer by strengthening the immune system and minimizing the intake of potential toxins. Such programs are often accompanied by vitamins, minerals, enzymes, and gland extracts and by stimuli to moral and religious health that are reminiscent of the activities provided at the Battle Creek Sanitarium (American Cancer Society 1991). Several diets and dietary supplements have been marketed without any medicalized rationalization beyond that used to promote five products sold by United Sciences of America, Inc.: "to provide all Americans with the potential of optimum health and vital energy" (Stare 1986).

Modern foods that originated in nineteenth-century efforts to improve the American diet are as healthful as their nutritional content allows. Nevertheless, today many of them - especially breakfast cereals

- are fortified with vitamins and minerals, often to enhance their presumed acceptability to consumers. But no one has yet discovered a food or devised a diet that can be proved to cure diseases, such as arthritis, cancer, or any other illness that is not the result of a specific nutritional deficit.

Dietetics in Other Cultures

Important discoveries in the biochemistry of food began to appear in the twentieth century, many of them soon after the discovery of vitamins. Eventually they led to the somewhat contentious discussions of the influence of specific foods on human illness that are a recurrent feature of American culture today. We have few written records that permit detailed comparisons of the dietary medicine practiced in cultures other than those whose roots were in ancient Egypt, Greece, and Rome. But the broad outlines of medical dietetics in a few other cultures can be ascertained.

Among North American Indians
There is evidence that at least some Indian groups of North America had specific ideas of what constituted a proper diet, and that they took dietary precautions when they were sick, such as starving a fever. Colonists reported that New England Indians remained healthy so long as they continued to eat their usual foods, and that they rejected some English foods even when, as hunter-gatherers, they were at the mercy of an uncertain food supply (Vogel 1970: 251-3).

Several Indian societies put plant foods to differing therapeutic uses. Pumpkins were used by the Zunis to treat the skin wounds made by cactus spines, but by the Menominees as a diuretic. New England Indians thought that sarsaparilla was useful as food when they were on the move, whereas the Iroquois used it to treat wounds. The Penobscots of the East Coast and the Kwakiutls of the West Coast used sarsaparilla as a cough remedy, and the Ojibwas applied it to boils and carbuncles (Vogel 1970: 356-61). It seems clear that such uses were as much based on the *post hoc ergo propter hoc* fallacy as were those in the Hippocratic-Galenic tradition. The Aztecs found some uses for the indigenous flora of Mexico that resembled those of their unrelated neighbors north of the Rio Grande. Thus, both Aztecs and the Indians who lived in Texas used the pods and seeds of edible mesquite as a remedy for diseased eyes (Ortiz de Montellano 1990).

In the Far East
The Chinese diet was even more rigidly associated with physiological concepts than that of the Graeco-Roman tradition. Balance between the classical complementary forces of yin and yang dominated the structure and function of the body, and was as important to health as were balances among the Hippocratic

humors. The basic digestive processes described in Chinese texts resemble those postulated by Aristotle, although only the latter based some of his conclusions on dissections. The Chinese assumed that food passes from the stomach to the liver, where it yields its vital forces to the muscles, and its gases to the heart (the origin of both blood and animal heat), while its liquid components move to the spleen, then the lungs, and finally the bladder (Leicester 1974: 45–9).

According to the teachings of Huang Ti, the mythical Yellow Emperor said to have reigned about 2600 B.C., but probably not written down before 206 B.C., proper medical treatment includes foods that can correct the patient's "mode of life." Because the Chinese recognized five elements – water, fire, wood, metal, and earth – the number five recurs throughout Chinese thought: They associated each of the five major organs – liver, heart, lungs, spleen, and kidneys – with one of the "five grains," the "five tree-fruits," the "five domesticated [meat] animals," and the "five vegetables," in terms of any organ's nourishment. In ancient China, as in the medieval European tradition, taste was correlated with a food's action, but within a different framework: Sweet foods were appropriate to the health of the liver, sour foods to the heart, bitter foods to the lungs, salty foods to the spleen, and pungent foods to the kidneys (Veith 1949: 1–9, 55–8).

The canonical sweet foods of Chinese dietetics (rice, dates, beef, and mallows) were believed to enter the body through the spleen, to produce a slowing effect. Sour foods (small peas, plums, dog meat, and leeks) enter via the liver, and produce an astringent, or binding, effect. Bitter foods (wheat, almonds, mutton, and scallions) enter via the heart, and strengthen, or dry, the body. Salty foods (large beans, chestnuts, pork, and coarse greens) enter through the kidneys, with a softening effect. And, finally, pungent foods (millet, peaches, chicken meat, and onions) disperse the smallest particles of the body after entering it via the lungs. One important precept that followed from these complex relationships was that a patient should avoid foods of the correlative taste whenever he or she had a disease in the organ through which that taste enters the body (Veith 1949: 199–207). The traditional Ayurvedic medical practices of India share many concepts with those of China, although their professional literatures differ in their underlying cosmological premises (Leicester 1974: 51–2).

Chinese medical dietetics loosened its adherence to strict rules as the centuries passed. For instance, although Ko Hung (under the nom de plume Pao-p'u Tzu) described basic principles for constructing healthy diets in about A.D. 326, he did not prescribe specific foods as cures, even if he did maintain that a patient's blood supply can be increased simply by eating more food (Huard and Wong 1968: 19–23). Yet eventually, as European dietary and medical notions penetrated the Far East, many traditional Chinese remedies disappeared – but not all of them.

By contrast, the medical lore of neighboring Tibet did not succumb to external influence. Along lines that Galen might have approved, Tibetan healers classified patients, in the first instance, as wind-types, bile-types, or phlegm-types, and, secondarily, by habitus, complexion, powers of endurance, amount of sleep, personality, and life span. For each patient type and subtype – they were all mutually exclusive – doctors prescribed specific medicines and foods, although their prescriptions show that they recognized more mixtures of the basic types than might have been supposed from their texts alone (Finckh 1988: 68–73).

Food or Drug? The Example of Garlic

Therapeutic descriptions by medical authorities since Dioscorides are still being cited in order to market some foods that were used as medicine in the ancient world. Such foods are not advertised as remedies; if they were in the United States, at least, they would be subject to the proofs of efficacy and safety required by the Food and Drug Administration. Nevertheless, they illustrate the continuing difficulty of devising mutually exclusive definitions of foods and drugs. The long history of garlic as a medical remedy is not only a case in point; it also exemplifies historical changes in medical theory.

Garlic in Ancient and Medieval Medicine

Garlic is the bulb of *Allium sativum,* a member of the lily family; the Romans derived the Latin genus name from a Celtic word for pungent bitterness. Ancient Egyptians did not use garlic as a remedy, but they did include it in a foul-smelling amulet designed to keep illness away from children (Sigerist 1951: 283). It was also found among Tutankhamen's burial goods – as a seasoning (Block 1985; Manniche 1989: 70–1). Modern Sudanese villagers, like some ancient Egyptians, place garlic in a woman's vagina to determine if she is pregnant; if she is, the characteristic odor will appear in her breath the next day (Estes 1989: 117). Ancient Mesopotamians prescribed garlic for toothache and painful urination and incorporated it in amulets against disease, as did the Egyptians (Levey 1966: 251). Traditional Chinese medicine associated garlic with the spleen, kidneys, and stomach, while Ayurvedic practitioners in India considered it a panacea, even if its specific actions were understood in the humoral and solidist traditions (Hobbs 1992).

The first-century testimonies of Dioscorides and Pliny the Elder provide similar pictures of the use of garlic in Graeco-Roman practice. The nearly complete text of its description by Dioscorides is given here because his book was the bedrock of virtually all herbal lore and prescription writing for the next 15 centuries. The translation is from the first – and still only – English version (1655) of his *Materia Medica:*

It hath a sharp, warming biting qualitie, expelling of flatulencies, and disturbing of the belly, and drying of the stomach causing of thirst, & of puffing up, breeding of boyles in ye outsyde of the body, dulling the sight of the eyes. . . . Being eaten, it drives out the broade wormes, and drawes away the urine. It is good, as none other thing, for such as are bitten of vipers, or of the Haemorrhous [hemorrhoids], wine being taken presently after, or else that being beaten small in wine, & soe dranck. It is applyed also by ye way of Cataplasme [a watery poultice] both for the same purposes profitably, as also layd upon such as are bitten of a mad dogge. Being aten, it is good against the chaunge of waters. . . . It doth cleare the arteries, & being eaten either raw or [boiled], it doth assuage old coughes. Being dranck with decoction of [oregano], it doth kill lice and nitts. But being burnt, and tempered with hon[e]y it doth cure the sugillationes oculorum [black eyes], and Alopeciae [bald spots] being anointed [with it], but for the Alopeciae (it must be applyed) with unguentum Nardinum [an extract of *Nardostachys jatamansi*]. And with salt & oyle it doth heale [papular eruptions]. It doth take away also the Vitiligenes, & the Lichenes, & the Lentigenes, and the running ulcers of the head, and the furfures [purpural spots], & ye Lepras [other spots, not leprosy], with hon[e]y. Being boiled with Taeda [pine tar] and franckincense, & kept in the mouth it doth assuage the paine of ye teeth. And with figge leaves & [cumin] it is a Cataplasme for such as are bitten of the Mygale [shrew-mouse]. But the leafes decoction is an insession [insertion into the vagina] that brings downe the Menstrua & the Secundas. It is also taken by way of suffumigation [fumigation, in which the patient stands over the burning medicine so that its fumes rise into her vagina] for ye same purpose. But the stamping that is made of it and ye black olive together, called Myrton, doth move the urine & open ye mouths of ye veines & it is good also for the Hydropicall [edematous] (Dioscorides 1934: 188–91).

In short, Dioscorides says that garlic expels intestinal worms and skin parasites, protects against venomous animals, neutralizes internal and external inflammations of many kinds, relieves toothaches and coughs, reduces hemorrhoids, and stimulates menstruation. Most important of all for later writers, garlic removes excess fluid from the body by dilating blood vessels and stimulating the kidneys.

Pliny, on the other hand, was an inquisitive encyclopedist, not a physician. In his *Natural History* he lists many of the same uses for garlic. But whereas only Dioscorides says that it can move the urine, Pliny adds that garlic can cure epilepsy, cause sleep, stimulate the libido, and neutralize the poisonous effects of

aconite and henbane (although such antidotal effects are unlikely) (Manniche 1989: 70–1; Hobbs 1992). Together, he and Dioscorides dictated the therapeutic uses of garlic for centuries.

Thus, al-Kindi, a royal tutor in ninth-century Baghdad, transmitted lessons he had learned from Greek and Roman sources when he said that garlic was good for inflamed ears (Levey 1966: 251). As Arabic works became available in European languages, ancient remedies were systematized within an increasingly rigid humoral framework. Consequently, the entry for garlic in a late–fourteenth-century *Tacuinum Sanitatis* says: "*Nature:* Warm in the second degree, dry in the third. *Optimum:* The kind that does not have too pungent a smell. *Usefulness:* Against poisons. *Dangers:* For the faculty of expulsion, and the brain. *Neutralization of the Dangers:* With vinegar and oil" (Arano 1976, plates 96–7). Such information changed from time to time, perhaps as doctors changed their minds, but also perhaps because of errors in transcribing manuscripts: A slightly later version of the same health handbook says exactly the same things about garlic, but describes it as warm in the fourth degree.

The most famous surgeon in sixteenth-century Europe, Ambroise Paré, based his therapeutic assessments on his own observations, perhaps because he had not learned his profession by scholastic disputation in a university. He thought garlic's major value was as a preventive against serious contagions:

Such as by the use of garlick have not their heads troubled, nor their inward parts inflamed, as Countrey people, and such as are used to it, to such there can bee no more certain preservative and antidote against the pestiferous fogs or mists, and the nocturnal obscurity, than to take it in the morning with a draught of good wine; for it being abundantly diffused presently over all the body, fils up the passages thereof, and strengtheneth it in a moment (Paré 1634: 823–4, 1031).

Paré's therapeutic reasoning is obscure; he seems to have presumed an analogy between garlic and onions, both of which he classified among the hottest of all remedies, those warm in the fourth degree. Surgeons who agreed with his Galenic assumptions quickly adopted an onion poultice Paré had invented on the premise that onions "attract, draw forth, and dissipate the imprinted heate" (Sigerist 1944).

Throughout the seventeenth century, physicians and laymen alike employed garlic as a diuretic and for virtually all the other uses listed by Pliny and Dioscorides, as well as for its ability to protect against contagious diseases (Leighton 1970: 306–7; Hobbs 1992). It was the major ingredient in one of more than 50 prescriptions recommended by the eminent London physician Thomas Willis for treating serious respiratory disease, especially consumption (Willis

1692: 86). As late as the early nineteenth century, physicians still relied on the properties that Dioscorides had ascribed to garlic, as revealed by its description in an influential 1794 compendium of medical practice:

> The root applied to the skin inflames. . . . Its smell is extremely penetrating and diffusive; when the root is applied to the feet, its scent is soon discovered in the breath; and taken internally, its smell is communicated to the urine, or the matter of an issue, and perspires through the pores of the skin. This pungent root stimulates the whole body. Hence, in cold leucophlegmatic habits, it proves a powerful expectorant, diuretic, and if the patient be kept warm, sudorific; it has also been supposed to be emmenagogue. In catarrhous disorders of the breast, flatulent cholics, hysterical, and other diseases proceeding from laxity of the solids, it has generally good effects: it has likewise been found serviceable in some hydropic cases. . . . The liberal use of garlick is apt to occasion headachs, flatulencies, febrile heats, inflammatory distempers, and sometimes discharges of blood from the haemorrhoidal vessels. In hot bilious constitutions, where there is already a degree of irritation, and where there is reason to suspect an unsound state of the viscera, this stimulating medicine is manifestly improper [contraindicated], and never fails to aggravate the distemper. Garlick made into an ointment with oils, &c. and applied externally, is said to resolve . . . cold tumors, and has been greatly esteemed in cutaneous diseases. It has likewise been sometimes employed as a repellent. When applied in the form of a poultice to the pubis, it has sometimes proved effectual in producing a discharge of urine, when retention has arisen from a want of due action of the bladder; and some authors have recommended, in certain cases of deafness, the introduction of a single clove, wrapt in thin muslin or gauze, into the meatus auditorius [ear canal] (*Edinburgh New Dispensatory* 1794: 87–8).

The *Dispensatory,* which reflects contemporary therapeutic practices at the Royal Infirmary of Edinburgh, also points out that garlic has been reported to be an effective treatment for malaria and smallpox. William Buchan of Edinburgh described a garlic ointment for whooping cough that could be prepared at home:

> by beating [it] in a mortar . . . with an equal quantity of hog's lard. With this the soles of the feet may be rubbed twice or thrice a day; but the best method is to spread it upon a rag, and apply it in the form of a plaster. It should be

renewed every night and morning at least, as the garlic soon loses its virtue (Buchan 1809: 212).

James Thacher presented selected aspects of the Edinburgh professors' views of garlic in his influential *American New Dispensatory* (Thacher 1813: 135–6). The first U.S. *Pharmacopoeia* (1820), which owed much of its content to its Edinburgh counterpart, included garlic among the remedies accepted by the American medical profession. Its 1905 edition listed it for the last time, but garlic as a recommended remedy remained in the United States as late as the 1936 edition of the *National Formulary* (Vogel 1970: 306–7).

Garlic during the Scientific Revolution

Solidist theories of pathophysiology melded well with the emergence of experimental chemistry in the eighteenth century. In 1822, Jacob Bigelow, a professor of medicine at Harvard, based much of his brief description of garlic's effects on those of its active principle, recently isolated as an oil:

> Garlic and other plants of its genus have a well known offensive odour and taste, which, however, in a weakened state, render them an agreeable condiment with food. These qualities depend on a thick, acrid, yellowish, volatile oil, which may be separated by distillation, leaving the bulbs nearly inert. Garlic is stimulant, expectorant and diuretic. It is given in the form of syrup in chronic coughs, and the secondary stages of pneumonia; also, in combination with other medicines, in dropsy. Externally the bruised bulbs, in the form of a poultice, act as rubefacients (Bigelow 1822: 58).

An important reference text published 50 years later describes the effects of garlic much as both Dioscorides and Bigelow had, but within the more explicit context of solidist physiology:

> Its effects on the system are those of a general stimulant. It quickens the circulation, excites the nervous system, promotes expectoration in debility of the lungs, produces diaphoresis or diuresis according as the patient is kept warm or cool, and acts upon the stomach as a tonic and carminative. It is also said to be emmenagogue. . . . Moderately employed, it is beneficial in enfeebled digestion and flatulence. . . . It has been given with advantage in chronic catarrh, and other pectoral affections in which the symptoms of inflammation have been subdued, and a relaxed state of the vessels remains. . . . If taken too largely, or in excited states of the system, garlic is apt to occasion gastric irritation, flatulence, hemorrhoids, headache, and fever. As a medicine, it is at present more used externally than inwardly. Bruised, and applied to the feet, it acts very beneficially, . . . in disorders of the

head; and is especially useful in the febrile complaints of children, by quieting restlessness and producing sleep. Its juice . . . is frequently used as a liniment in infantile convulsions, and other spasmodic or nervous affections in children (Wood and Bache 1874: 87–9).

Although garlic was not among the materia medica of Thomson (Estes 1992), one of his followers, the prominent eclectic physician John King, described its efficacy as a gastric tonic, as an anthelmintic, and in respiratory illnesses, especially those of children (Hobbs 1992). Despite the Shakers' unreserved reliance on Thomson's teachings, they recommended garlic as a stimulating tonic to promote expectoration in upper respiratory conditions, and to promote both diuresis and bowel movements. They also applied it externally to relieve pulmonary symptoms, just as Willis and the doctors of Edinburgh had done (Miller 1976: 177).

Modern herbalists preserve some indications for garlic inherited from the ancient world, including its use in love potions and prophylactic amulets. Others also prescribe it for effects not recognizable among those mentioned in medical works of the past, such as for "life-prolonging powers," and improved memory and mental capacity (Huson 1974: 32–3, 53–4, 252, 279, 312).

Garlic in the Modern Laboratory

In 1844, Theodor Wertheim, a German chemist, distilled a strongly pungent substance from garlic oil. He called the chemical group associated with the characteristic odor "allyl," from the plant's scientific name. Exactly 100 years later, Chester J. Cavillito and his colleagues at Sterling-Winthrop Company laboratories in Rensselaer, New York, discovered the chemical structure of allicin, the compound in garlic that produces its odor.

Four years later, in 1948, Arthur Stoll and Ewald Seebeck, at Sandoz Company laboratories in Basel, isolated alliin (0.9 percent of fresh garlic), the molecule that is biotransformed to allicin (0.1–0.5 percent of fresh garlic, up to 0.9 percent of garlic powder), which represents a doubling of the alliin molecule. The reaction is mediated by the enzyme allinase (in association with the coenzyme pyridoxal phosphate, or vitamin B_6). Garlic does not emit its typical odor until it is crushed. Stoll and Seebeck found that crushing releases allinase from the bulb's cells, permitting it to act on alliin to produce the odoriferous allicin (as well as ammonia and pyruvate ion).

Finally, in 1983, Eric Block of New York and workers at the University of Delaware and at the Venezuelan Institute of Scientific Investigations in Caracas established the structure of ajoene (*ajo* is the Spanish word for garlic), formed by the condensation of two molecules of allicin in garlic cloves. Ajoene cannot be detected in proprietary preparations of garlic, only in fresh cloves (Block 1985; *International Garlic Symposium* 1991: 10–11).

Several potentially therapeutic effects have been attributed to garlic oil and its chemical constituents since the early 1980s. Some preparations reduce plasma concentrations of cholesterol, triglycerides, and low-density lipoproteins to a modest extent, while increasing high-density lipoproteins. These effects seem to be secondary to inhibition of an enzyme necessary for cholesterol synthesis (hydroxy methyl glutaryl coenzyme A reductase), and may be associated with the ability of the same preparations to reduce blood pressure in hypertensive animals and men. An aqueous extract of garlic has been reported to inhibit angiotensin converting enzyme; modern drugs that selectively inhibit that enzyme are highly effective as antihypertensive medicines. Garlic and its extracts also inhibit thrombosis by inhibiting platelet aggregation, decreasing blood viscosity, dilating capillaries, and triggering fibrinolysis (clot breakdown). Ajoene, which is about as potent as aspirin as an antithrombotic compound, blocks platelet fibrinogen receptors. Indeed, it is probably the major antithrombotic factor in garlic juice (Block 1985; *Lawrence Review* 1988; Auer et al. 1990; Kiesewetter et al. 1990; Mader 1990; Vorberg and Schneider 1990; *International Garlic Symposium* 1991: 9, 19–44).

In 1858 Louis Pasteur found that garlic has antibacterial properties. Later studies have shown that a highly diluted solution of its juice can inhibit the growth of several important pathogenic bacteria, including *Staphylococcus, Streptococcus, Bacillus,* and *Vibrio cholerae,* as well as pathogenic yeasts and other fungi. Since then, garlic has been reported to inhibit the in vitro growth of several species of fungi, gram-positive and gram-negative bacteria, and the tuberculosis bacillus, and to reduce the infectivity of viruses, such as influenza B. Because it is the malodorous allicin that is responsible for garlic's antimicrobial effects, it is no surprise that the Sandoz Company decided not to develop it as an anti-infective drug following the discoveries of Stoll and Seebeck.

Other studies have demonstrated garlic's antineoplastic activity in rodents, but this effect may be associated with the trace elements germanium and selenium, rather than with allicin or its metabolites. Finally, recent evidence suggests that garlic decreases plasma concentrations of thyroxine, thyroid stimulating hormone, and glucose (and increases the concentration of insulin) (Block 1985; *Lawrence Review* 1988; Horowitz 1991; *International Garlic Symposium* 1991: 28–39; Farbman et al. 1993).

Several preparations of garlic are available in the United States as "health foods," although no clinical indication other than "goodness" is advertised for them – thus exacerbating the problem inherent in the coined word "nutraceutical." Most research on the therapeutic effects of garlic has been carried out in Great Britain and Europe, where garlic's medical value is more widely proclaimed. Some commercial garlic preparations are said to lack the characteristic odor, which means they are probably incapable of the potentially beneficial effects that have been attributed to alliin, allicin, and ajoene. Moreover, even though garlic has been used for culinary purposes for many centuries with no known toxic effects, it is possible that concentrated preparations might have deleterious effects in patients with diabetes or those taking anticoagulant drugs, but no reports of such effects seem to have been published (*Lawrence Review* 1988). Several sulfur-containing compounds found in fresh garlic have been held responsible for the acute gastroenteritis that ingestion of large amounts of its buds may induce in young children, while chronic ingestion of garlic has been reported to produce goiter by inhibiting iodine uptake by the thyroid gland (Lampe and McCann 1985: 28-9).

Whatever the eventual fate of garlic in pharmacological therapeutics, its history well illustrates how medical concepts have often been adapted to fit newly emerging ideas, even in the absence of any validation of the revised medical notions – other than the evidence implicit in the average adult patient's 95 percent chance of recovering from any nondevastating illness. Until the twentieth century, physicians had no better evidence on which to base dietetic prescriptions and recommendations. As Marie-François-Xavier Bichat said about two centuries ago: "The same drugs were successively used by humoralists and solidists. Theories changed, but the drugs remained the same. They were applied and acted in the same way, which proves that their action is independent of the opinion of doctors" (Estes 1990: ix). Clearly, Bichat would have included foods – even garlic – within the meaning of his word "drugs."

J. Worth Estes

Appendix: Definitions of Drug Properties

Anthelmintic: A drug that expels worms from the intestines.

Antidysenteric: Relieves dysentery.

Antihysteric: A form of antispasmodic used to treat several conditions regarded as "hysteric."

Anti-icteric: For treatment of jaundice *(icterus)*.

Antiseptic: To prevent putrefaction *(sepsis)*.

Antispasmodic: Reduces spasms (including fast heart rate), but without inducing insensibility (as narcotics do).

Antitussive: Cough suppressant.

Aperient: A weak cathartic.

Astringent: Strengthens a body that is too relaxed, or reduces excessive evacuations; also see *Styptic*.

Attenuating: Thins and divides the humors into smaller particles.

Carminative: Expels gas from the intestines, especially in dyspepsia.

Cathartic: A drug that promotes defecation, or increases fluid secretion from the intestinal lining.

Cephalic: For disorders of the head.

Demulcent: Lubricates organ surfaces (especially of intestines).

Deobstruent: Removes obstructions to the free flow of urine, sweat, feces, phlegm, bile, and blood.

Detergent: Cleanses or purges.

Diaphoretic: A drug that increases sweating, by stimulating blood vessels in the skin.

Digestive: Improves digestion and, therefore, nutrition.

Diluent: Dilutes blood, facilitating diuresis and diaphoresis.

Diuretic: A drug that promotes urine by stimulating the kidneys.

Emetic: A drug that induces vomiting.

Emmenagogue: Promotes menstruation.

Emollient: Reduces tension in rigid or distended organs, and warms and moistens them.

Errhine: Increases discharge from the nose; induces sneezing.

Expectorant: Promotes secretion and ejection of mucus from the lungs and trachea.

Lactatogue: Stimulates lactation.

Laxative: A gentle cathartic.

Narcotic: Affects the brain, by sedating *or* stimulating it.

Nervine: In seventeenth century, an emollient unguent for the sinews; from the eighteenth century, a stimulating tonic for weak nerves.

Pectoral: For disorders of the chest and lungs; often an antitussive and/or expectorant.

Rubefacient: Reddens or irritates the skin.

Stomachic: Warms and strengthens the stomach.

Styptic: An astringent for external use.

Tonic: Strengthens the body by increasing the force of the circulation, animal heat, secretions, digestion, or muscular activity, especially in debilitating illness.

Bibliography

American Cancer Society. 1990. Gerson method. *Ca* 40: 252-6.

　　1991. Questionable cancer practices in Tijuana and other Mexican border clinics. *Ca* 41: 310-19.

AMA (American Medical Association). Council on Foods and Nutrition. 1971. Zen macrobiotic diets. *Journal of the American Medical Association* 218: 397.

Apple, Rima D. 1986. "Advertised by our loving friends": The infant formula industry and the creation of new pharmaceutical markets. *Journal of the History of Medicine and Allied Sciences* 41: 3-23.

Arano, Luisa Cogliati. 1976. *The medieval health handbook "Tacuinum Sanitatis."* New York.

Armstrong, David, and Elizabeth Metzger Armstrong. 1991. *The great American medicine show.* New York.

Auer, W., A. Eiber, E. Hertkorn, et al. 1990. Hypertension and hyperlipidaemia: Garlic helps in mild cases. *British Journal of Clinical Practice* 44, no. 8, supplement 69: 3-6.

Beaumont, William. 1833. *Experiments and observations on the gastric juice and the physiology of digestion.* Plattsburgh, N.Y.

Berman, Paul. 1992. Obstetrical practice in south central Massachusetts from 1834 to 1845. *Proceedings of the Dublin Seminar for New England Folklife* 15: 185-90.

Bigelow, Jacob. 1822. *A treatise on the Materia Medica.* Boston, Mass.

Block, Eric. 1985. The chemistry of garlic and onions. *Scientific American* 252 (March): 114-19.

Buchan, William. 1809. *Domestic medicine.* Edinburgh.
   1828. *Domestic medicine.* Exeter, N.H.

Bullough, Vern L. 1957. The medieval medical university at Paris. *Bulletin of the History of Medicine* 31: 197-211.

Cassileth, Barrie R., and Helene Brown. 1988. Unorthodox cancer medicine. *Ca* 38: 176-86.

Celsus. 1935-38. *De medicina,* trans. W. G. Spencer. 3 vols. Cambridge, Mass.

Chaucer, Geoffrey. 1960. *The Canterbury tales,* trans. Nevill Coghill. Harmondsworth, England.

Clymer, R. Swinburne. [1902] 1960. *The medicine of nature.* Quakertown, Pa.

Cosman, Madeleine Pelner. 1976. *Fabulous feasts: Medieval cookery and ceremony.* New York.
   1978. Machaut's medical world. *Annals of the New York Academy of Science* 314: 1-36.

Dioscorides. 1934. *The Greek herbal,* trans. John Goodyer, ed. Robert T. Gunther. Oxford.

Drummond, J. C., and Anne Wilbraham. 1958. *The Englishman's food. A history of five centuries of English diet.* Revised edition. London.

Edelstein, Ludwig. 1987. The dietetics of antiquity. In *Ancient medicine: Selected papers of Ludwig Edelstein,* ed. Owsei Temkin and C. Lilian Temkin, 303-16. Baltimore, Md.

Edinburgh new dispensatory. 1794. Fourth edition. Edinburgh.

Estes, J. Worth. 1979. Making therapeutic decisions with protopharmacologic evidence. *Transactions and studies of the college of physicians of Philadelphia* n.s. 1: 116-37.
   1985. A naval surgeon in the Barbary Wars: Dr. Peter St. Medard on *New York* 1802-3. In *New aspects of naval history,* ed. Department of History, U.S. Naval Academy. Baltimore, Md.
   1989. *The medical skills of ancient Egypt.* Canton, Mass.
   1990. *Dictionary of protopharmacology. Therapeutic practices, 1700-1850.* Canton, Mass.
   1991a. Quantitative observations of fever and its treatment before the advent of short clinical thermometers. *Medical History* 35: 189-216.
   1991b. The Shakers and their proprietary medicines. *Bulletin of the History of Medicine* 65: 162-84.
   1992. Samuel Thomson rewrites Hippocrates. *Proceedings of the Dublin Seminar for New England Folklife* 15: 113-32.

Farbman, Karen S., Elizabeth D. Barnett, Gilles R. Bolduc, and Jerome O. Klein. 1993. Antibacterial activity of garlic and onions: A historical perspective. *Pediatric Infectious Disease Journal* 12: 613-14.

Finckh, Elisabeth. 1988. *Studies in Tibetan medicine.* Ithaca, N.Y.

Finlay, Mark R. 1992. Quackery and cookery: Justus von Liebig's extract of meat and the theory of nutrition in the Victorian age. *Bulletin of the History of Medicine* 66: 404-18.

Green, Harvey. 1986. *Fit for America: Health, fitness, sport, and American society.* New York.

Green, Saul. 1992. A critique of the rationale for cancer treatment with coffee enemas and diet. *Journal of the American Medical Association* 268: 3224-7.

Gunn, John. 1830. *Gunn's domestic medicine, or poor man's friend.* Knoxville, Tenn.

Heberden, William. 1802. *Commentaries on the history and cure of diseases.* London.

Hobbs, Christopher. 1992. Garlic - the pungent panacea. *Pharmacy in History* 34: 152-7.

Hofmann, Albert. 1972. Ergot - a rich source of pharmacologically active substances. In *Plants in the development of modern medicine,* ed. Tony Swain, 235-60. Cambridge, Mass.

Holmes, F. L. 1973. Justus von Liebig. In *Dictionary of scientific biography,* Vol. 8, ed. Charles Coulston Gillispie, 329-50. New York.

Horowitz, Janice M. 1991. Wonders of the vegetable bin. *Time,* September 2: 66.

Huard, Pierre, and Ming Wong. 1968. *Chinese medicine,* trans. Bernard Fielding. New York.

Huson, Paul. 1974. *Mastering herbalism.* New York.

International garlic symposium: Pharmacy, pharmacology and clinical application of Allium sativum. 1991. Berlin.

Jarcho, Saul. 1989. *Clinical consultations and letters by Ippolito Francesco Albertini, Francesco Torti, and other physicians.* Boston, Mass.

Josselyn, John. 1672. *New-England's rarities discovered.* London.

Kiesewetter, H., F. Jung, C. Mrowietz, et al. 1990. Effects of garlic on blood fluidity and fibrinolytic activity: A randomised, placebo-controlled, double-blind study. *British Journal of Clinical Practice* 44, no. 8, supplement 69: 24-9.

King, Lester S. 1963. *The growth of medical thought.* Chicago.

Lampe, Kenneth F., and Mary Ann McCann. 1985. *AMA handbook of poisonous and injurious plants.* Chicago.

Lawrence review of natural products. 1987-91. St. Louis, Mo.

Leicester, Henry M. 1974. *Development of biochemical concepts from ancient to modern times.* Cambridge, Mass.

Leighton, Ann. 1970. *Early American gardens: "For meate or medicine."* Boston, Mass.

Levey, Martin. 1973. *Early Arabic pharmacology: An introduction based on ancient and medieval sources.* Leiden.

Levey, Martin, trans. 1966. *The medical formulary or aqrabadhin of al-Kindi.* Madison, Wis.

Lloyd, G. E. R., ed. 1978. *Hippocratic writings.* Harmondsworth, England.

Macrobiotic diets for the treatment of cancer. 1959. *Ca* 39: 248-51.

Mader, F. H. 1990. Treatment of hyperlipidaemia with garlic-powder tablets. *Arzneimittelforschung/Drug Research* 40: 3-8.

Manniche, Lise. 1989. *An ancient Egyptian herbal.* London.

Miller, Amy Bess. 1976. *Shaker herbs, a history and compendium.* New York.

Nissenbaum, Stephen. 1988. *Sex, diet, and debility in Jacksonian America.* Westport, Conn.

Ortiz de Montellano, Bernard. 1990. *Aztec medicine, health, and nutrition.* New Brunswick, N.J.

Paré, Ambroise. 1634. *The workes of that famous chirurgion Ambrose Parey,* trans. Thomas Johnson. London.

Potter, Morris E., Arnold F. Kaufmann, Paul A. Blake, and Roger A. Feldman. 1984. Unpasteurized milk. The hazards of a health fetish. *Journal of the American Medical Association* 252: 2048-52.

Riddle, John M. 1992. The pseudo-Hippocratic *Dynamidia.*

No. 11 in *Quid pro quo: Studies in the history of drugs.* Hampshire, England.

Risse, Guenter B. 1986. *Hospital life in enlightenment Scotland. Care and teaching at the Royal Infirmary of Edinburgh.* Cambridge.

Seal, D. V., and K. Middleton. 1991. Healing of cavity wounds with sugar. *Lancet* 338: 571-2.

Shah, Mazhar J., trans. 1966. *The general principles of Avicenna's Canon of Medicine.* Karachi.

Sigerist, Henry E. 1944. Ambroise Paré's onion treatment of burns. *Bulletin of the History of Medicine* 15: 143-9.

   1951. *A history of medicine. I. Primitive and archaic medicine.* New York.

   1987. *A history of medicine. II. Early Greek, Hindu, and Persian medicine.* New York.

Simon, Allie, David M. Wortham, and John A. Mitas II. 1979. An evaluation of iridology. *Journal of the American Medical Association* 242: 1385-9.

Siraisi, Nancy G. 1981. *Taddeo Alderotti and his pupils. Two generations of Italian medical learning.* Princeton, N.J.

   1990. *Medieval and early renaissance medicine: An introduction to knowledge and practice.* Chicago.

Smith, Andrew F. 1991. Tomato pills will cure all your ills. *Pharmacy in History* 33: 169-77.

Smith, Wesley D. 1979. *The Hippocratic tradition.* Ithaca, N.Y.

Stare, Frederick J. 1986. Marketing a nutritional revolutionary "breakthrough": Trading on names. *New England Journal of Medicine* 315: 971-3.

Taberner, Peter V. 1985. *Aphrodisiacs: The science and the myth.* Philadelphia, Pa.

Teigen, Philip M. 1987. Taste and quality in 15th- and 16th-century Galenic pharmacology. *Pharmacy in History* 29: 60-8.

Temkin, Owsei. 1973. *Galenism: Rise and decline of a medical philosophy.* Ithaca, N.Y.

Thacher, James. 1813. *The American new dispensatory.* Boston, Mass.

Thorndike, Lynn. 1923-58. *A history of magic and experimental science.* 8 vols. New York.

   1940. Three tracts on food in Basel manuscripts. *Bulletin of the History of Medicine* 8: 355-69.

Trall, R. T. 1852. *The hydropathic encyclopedia.* New York.

Tufts Journal. 1992. Editors' Commentary. December: 10.

Veith, Ilza, trans. and ed. 1949. *Huang ti nei ching su wen: The yellow emperor's classic of internal medicine.* Baltimore, Md.

Vogel, Virgil J.. 1970. *American Indian medicine.* Norman, Okla.

Vorberg, G., and B. Schneider. 1990. Therapy with garlic: Results of a placebo-controlled, double-blind study. *British Journal of Clinical Practice* 44, no. 8, supplement 69: 7-11.

Webster, Ian W., and Graeme K. Rawson. 1979. Health status of Seventh-Day Adventists. *Medical Journal of Australia* 1: 417-20.

Whorton, James C. 1988. Patient, heal thyself: Popular health reform movements as unorthodox medicine. In *Other healers: Unorthodox medicine in America,* ed. Norman Gevitz, 52-81. Baltimore, Md.

Willis, Thomas. 1692. *The London practice of physick.* London.

Winslow, C.-E. A., and R. R. Bellinger. 1945. Hippocratic and Galenic concepts of metabolism. *Bulletin of the History of Medicine* 17: 127-37.

Wood, George B., and Franklin Bache. 1874. *Dispensatory of the United States of America.* Thirteenth edition. Philadelphia, Pa.

VI.17 ∽ Vegetarianism

Human populations often have been obliged to subsist on an all-vegetable diet because of a poverty or scarcity of animal foods. The term "vegetarianism," nevertheless, is usually reserved for the practice of voluntary abstention from flesh on the basis of religious, spiritual, ethical, hygienic, or environmental considerations. These in turn have led to still finer distinctions regarding exactly what nonmeat articles of diet are permissible, resulting in the fragmentation of vegetarians into several groups. The great majority of adherents are "lacto-ovo" vegetarians, who reject flesh but find dairy products and eggs acceptable. Smaller groups include "vegans," who admit no animal products whatsoever into their diet; "lacto-vegetarians," who consume milk but not eggs; "ovo-vegetarians," who allow eggs but not milk; "fruitarians," who eat only fruits and nuts; "raw foodists"; and "natural hygienists," who scorn even vegetable foods if these have been processed or refined. And because – for all those classes – vegetarianism implies a concern to persuade others to adopt meatless diets, the history of vegetarianism is, at core, the history of the development of arguments used to justify and to proselytize for a vegetable diet.

Vegetarianism in Eastern Religion

The most notable examples of a religious basis for vegetarianism are to be found in Asian culture. Hinduism, though not requiring a strictly vegetable diet, has fostered a significant tradition of vegetarianism among certain believers for more than two millennia. The practice is still more widespread in Buddhism, where the doctrine of ahimsa, or nonviolent treatment of all beings, forbids adherents to kill animals for food. Many Buddhists do, nevertheless, eat meat, supporting the indulgence with the argument that the animal was killed by others. Jainism, likewise, espouses ahimsa and specifically denies meat to any practitioners of the faith (Barkas 1975; Akers 1983: 157-64).

Vegetarianism has continued as a common practice down to the present in Asia, especially in India. In Western societies, religion has also been a factor in the history of vegetarianism, but there it has played a relatively minor role compared to philosophical and scientific influences. The Western rationale for a vegetable diet is, in truth, the result of a considerably more complicated evolution shaped by a variety of cultural forces, which are outlined in this chapter (Whorton 1994).

Vegetarianism in Antiquity

The term "vegetarianism" was coined relatively recently, in the mid–nineteenth century, as the consumption of a flesh-free regimen began to assume the form of an organized movement. As a practice, however, it dates to much earlier times. No later than the third century A.D., in fact, Porphyry could describe the doctrine as already "ancient," as well as characterize the self-image vegetarianism had long embraced and would retain: It was "a dogma . . . dear to the Gods" (Porphyry 1965: 22).

The antiquity of the dogma can be traced to Pythagoras, the Greek natural philosopher of the sixth century B.C., who founded a religious community in southern Italy in which vegetarianism is reputed to have been part of the rule of life. Pythagoras scorned the eating of meat because of his belief in the Orphic concept of the transmigration of souls: If human spirits were reborn in other creatures, animal souls must be of the same quality as human souls, and animals must be as deserving of moral treatment as people. The killing of an animal was equivalent to murder, and the eating of it akin to cannibalism (Dombrowski 1984; Spencer 1993).

Additional justifications of vegetarianism with arguments dear to the gods were forwarded by several authors in later antiquity. During the first two centuries of the Christian era, Ovid and Plutarch both denounced slaughter as vicious treatment of innocent animals: "O horrible cruelty!" the latter remonstrated, that "for the sake of some little mouthful of flesh, we deprive a soul of the sun and light, and of that proportion of life and time it had been born into the world to enjoy" (Plutarch 1898: 6). Plutarch's essay "Of Eating of Flesh," in fact, provided the most comprehensive yet concise statement against conventional diet to be penned before the Renaissance and offered several objections that would become stock components of the vegetarian rationale on to the present day. These included physical arguments to complement the spiritual ones.

Flesh foods, Plutarch asserted, "by clogging and cloying" the body, "render [men's] very minds and intellects gross" (Plutarch 1898: 9). People, furthermore, could not have been intended by nature to be meat eaters, "for a human body no ways resembles those that were born for ravenousness" (Plutarch 1898: 7); it lacks fangs, claws, and all the other predatory equipment of carnivores. Finally, meat was prejudicial to health, causing "grievous oppressions and qualmy indigestions," and bringing "sickness and heaviness upon the body" (Plutarch 1898: 14).

The last vegetarian treatise from antiquity was the third-century work of the neo-Platonist Porphyry, *On Abstinence from Animal Food,* an elaboration of earlier authors' objections to meat, with particular emphasis on vegetable diet for spiritual purification: "The eye of the soul will become free, and will be established as in a port beyond the smoke and the waves of the corporeal nature" (Porphyry 1965: 53). Nevertheless, as Plutarch had recognized, "it is indeed a hard and difficult task . . . to dispute with men's bellies, that have no ears" (Plutarch 1898: 10).

The despair of vegetarians throughout the centuries has been that, in most people, the stomach speaks more loudly than the conscience, and it demands flesh. Nor did the rise of Christianity to cultural dominance strengthen the voice of conscience in support of animal welfare. Although the medieval church harbored vegetarian sects such as the Manichees, the orthodox position was that presented by Aquinas, that humankind had been granted dominion over the animal creation to use to suit their needs. Aquinas's insistence on rationality as a requirement for the extension of moral consideration to a being overrode the notion of kinship between people and animals that had been put forward by ancient vegetarians (Aquinas 1989: 146, 188). To be sure, individual church luminaries – Saints John Chrysostom and Benedict, for example – forswore the consumption of meat; but their motivation was primarily the wish to suppress their own carnal appetites rather than to extend compassion to the animal creation (Dombrowski 1984).

The Seventeenth and Eighteenth Centuries

Not until the seventeenth century was there to be any expansion of the brief against meat eating, but then one encounters, in the works of Thomas Tryon, the most broad-based argument yet for the virtues of a vegetable diet (that an Englishman should revive vegetarianism was prophetic, for England would serve as the fountainhead of vegetarian thought well into the nineteenth century). In *The Way to Health, Long Life and Happiness* (1683: 447), this dissenting religionist-cum-health-reformer and sometime poet begged readers to consider,

> How shall they but Bestial grow,
> That thus to feed on Beasts are willing?
> Or why should they a long Life know,
> Who daily practice KILLING?

In those two couplets is expressed much of the modern rationale for a vegetarian diet. The killing of animals must be discountenanced both because it inflicts pain and death on "fellow creatures" and because scripture indicates that the original diet appointed by God for humankind was meatless (Gen. 1:29). Those who feed on meat will grow bestial in both mind and spirit, whereas those who actually carry out the slaughter of animals for food will become so hardened to suffering as to lose compassion for fellow humans as well, and even to commit crimes against them.

But Tryon's case against flesh food is most significant for raising the issue of physical health to a new level of emphasis. He did not merely declare that meat eaters would not know a long life or would in other ways suffer infirmity. Tryon proposed a distinct physical mechanism for flesh food's mischief, observing that "nothing so soon turns to Putrifaction" as meat, then adding that "'tis certain, such sorts of food as are subject to putrifie before they are eaten, are also liable to the same afterwards" (Tryon 1683: 376).

Meat, in other words, because it is highly putrescible even after ingestion, must "breed great store of noxious Humours" (Tryon 1683: 377). There was the pathological justification for Tryon's charge that had it not been for the adoption of a carnivorous diet, "Man had not contracted so many Diseases in his Body" (Tryon 1683: 446). Indeed, flesh eating produced so much sickness, and vice as well, that if it were abandoned, he suggested, society would have no need for physicians or lawyers (Tryon 1683; Ryder 1979).

Both the medical and the moral strains would remain central to vegetarian philosophy throughout the 1700s. Toward the end of that century, moreover, each would take on additional import. Greater attention to the moral implications of diet was encouraged by developments in two areas of inquiry in particular: physiology and religion. The former discipline had been dragged into the arena of philosophical dispute in the mid-seventeenth century by the physiological theories of René Descartes.

The Cartesian proposal that beasts were mere automata, utterly lacking in consciousness and sensation, had focused scientists' and philosophers' attention on the question of animal pain and provoked extensive debate over the morality of slaughter, vivisection experiments, and other uses of animals for human benefit (Cottingham 1978). It was generally agreed that Descartes had erred, that animals truly do experience pain; but it was also suggested that their pain is not felt as keenly as that of humans, and that, in any event, people are justified in using lower creatures to realize their own desires.

During the eighteenth century, however, studies of the nervous system demonstrated close structural similarities between humans and higher animals, sharply increasing the probability that brutes suffered pain as severely as people: "Answer me, mechanist," Voltaire sneered at the Cartesian physiologists, "Has nature arranged all the springs of feeling in this animal in order that he should not feel? Has he nerves in order to be unmoved?" (Voltaire 1962: 113). At the same time, and in England especially, several intellectual currents were fostering a stronger feeling of relationship to animals. The Enlightenment's promotion of natural rights and humanitarian sympathy for the less fortunate encouraged a heightened sensitivity to physical pain and abhorrence of cruelty that was being occasionally extended to lower creatures by the later 1700s.

Jeremy Bentham, the founder of utilitarianism, expressed the new solicitude for animal welfare in his refutation (1789) of the argument that brutes do not deserve kindness because they are not rational beings. "The question," he insisted, "is not, Can they *reason?* nor, Can they *talk?* but, Can they *suffer?*" (Bentham 1961: 380-1). That point was not necessarily an endorsement of vegetarianism; as Bentham observed, a butcher might give an animal a quicker and less painful death than it could expect from nature (implying that meat eating was actually the more humane diet) (Bentham 1961).

Nevertheless, every animal had a right – the word is Bentham's – not to be tormented. This concept of animal rights was, meanwhile, being advanced by several other Enlightenment authors, some of whom included the right not to be used as food. Simultaneously, English religious thought was entertaining the supposition that animals have souls and even a heaven, thereby at least suggesting a neo-Pythagorean condemnation of flesh eating (Stevenson 1956; Turner 1980: 1-14).

The Nineteenth Century

Regard for animal welfare was intensified still further at the beginning of the nineteenth century by a more politically directed religious movement. Evangelicalism, the outgrowth of John Wesley's determination to make Christianity a "social gospel," was dedicated through aggressive political action to relieving the miseries of society's downtrodden and exploited. Evangelicals succeeded in moving Parliament to legislate against the slave trade, child labor, Britain's barbaric penal code, and numerous other injustices. Among Evangelical good works was an animal protection campaign that attacked the mistreatment of animals used for labor or sport and resulted in Western society's first animal welfare legislation, a law passed in 1822 to protect work animals from abuse (Turner 1980: 15-38).

The new climate of distaste for animal cruelty gave vegetarianism added appeal, of course; and though it would remain the doctrine of a small fringe group, membership in the fold did increase significantly around the turn of the nineteenth century. Vegetarian literature grew apace, no longer just an occasional volume from an isolated eccentric but now a steady flow of treatises voicing outrage at the cruel ravages visited upon defenseless creatures. The title of the first major work in this new genre captures its prevailing sentiment perfectly: *The Cry of Nature,* as John Oswald named his book, *Or, an Appeal to Mercy and to Justice, on Behalf of the Persecuted Animals* (1791). Romantic sensitivity to the beauty and innocence of nature gushed through such volumes; Oswald's frontispiece, for example, portrayed a slaughtered fawn spilling its blood upon the earth while its mother tearfully called on it to rise. Nearby, an unclothed child of nature hid her face in shame. "Come," Oswald invited, "approach and examine with attention this dead body. It was late a playful fawn, which, skipping and bounding . . . awoke, in the soul of the feeling observer, a thousand tender emotions. But the butcher's knife hath laid low the delight of a fond dam, and the darling of nature is now stretched in gore upon the ground" (Oswald 1791: 22-3).

If the moral hideousness of slaying animals for food was the dominant theme of early-century vegetarianism, the physical repulsiveness of flesh food was hardly overlooked. Oswald requested readers to gaze upon the scene of carnage a second time: "Approach, I say, . . . and tell me, tell me, does this ghastly spectacle whet your appetite? Delights your eyes the sight of blood? Is the steam of gore grateful to your nostrils, or pleasing to the touch, the icy ribs of death? . . . or with a species of rhetoric, pitiful as it is perverse, will you still persist in your endeavour to persuade us, that to murder an innocent animal, is not cruel nor unjust; and that to feed upon a corpse, is neither filthy nor unfit?" (Oswald 1791: 22–3).

Filthy and unfit are moral terms, of course, but they have physiological connotations as well. What one sees here, and can find expressed still more overtly in subsequent vegetarian literature, is the suggestion that the revulsion produced by the sight of blood and the smell of gore is not simply an aesthetic reaction; it is also a physiological response to physical filth and physical unfitness, an indication that the human body is not designed to receive such food as nutriment.

Vegetarianism, Science, and Medicine

The physiological superiority of a vegetable diet was an especially critical point to demonstrate by the beginning of the nineteenth century. Enlightenment philosophy had elevated science to the position of an indispensable method of investigation and proof. Therefore, if the newly energized vegetarianism of the early 1800s was to legitimate itself in society's eyes, it had to prove itself nutritionally as well as spiritually.

It had to be demonstrated, first of all, that one could survive in reasonable health without flesh foods. It was generally assumed that meat, being most closely akin chemically to human muscle, must be more easily digested and assimilated than plants and provide greater strength and endurance. An all-vegetable diet, this reasoning supposed, must be debilitating, and surely self-preservation carried greater moral weight than kindness to other species.

Two English physicians were especially influential for presenting evidence that vegetarianism was not, after all, a form of slow suicide. The first was George Cheyne, one of the most widely read health writers of the eighteenth century. A high liver in his younger days, Cheyne turned to lacto-vegetarianism in the 1720s in order to reduce his now bloated and unwieldy 32-stone frame. But not only did he manage to shed considerable weight on his diet of milk and vegetables; various other complaints that had nagged him for years (headache and depression, for example) disappeared as well. Through subsequent observations of "my own crazy Carcase" (1734: xvi), as well as of numerous patients, Cheyne became convinced that flesh food "inflames the Passions, and shortens Life, begets chronical Distempers, and a decrepid Age"

(Cheyne 1734: 94). His several guidebooks to health were the first to recommend vegetarianism almost exclusively for reasons of physical well-being and to back claims of health with clinical cases.

Still more clinical evidence of the healthfulness of a vegetable diet was presented in 1809 by another London practitioner, William Lambe. Lambe had relieved himself of long-standing illness three years earlier by removing meat from his table. He had then applied that diet to the care of his patients and succeeded in curing, he believed, numerous cases of asthma, tuberculosis, and other chronic complaints, including cancer. Although he insisted that "a strict vegetable regimen" was an "absolute necessity" in the management of chronic illness, he was less forceful in his advocacy of vegetarianism for the healthy. He proposed only that meat was unnecessary, and that "what is unnecessary cannot be natural, [and] what is not natural cannot be useful" (Lambe 1815: 172).

Lambe's branding of meat as unnatural food for humans did sway several individuals well known in English society to convert to vegetarianism. Most prominent of all among these was the Romantic poet Percy Shelley, who in 1813 produced an emotionally charged pamphlet titled *A Vindication of Natural Diet*. In this work, logic was subjected to a fair amount of violence, yet the *Vindication* did achieve a certain balance by assigning roughly equal weight to both the moral and the physical objections to a flesh diet.

On the one side, the bloody excesses of the French Revolution and the tyranny of Napoleon were credited to the Gallic appetite for rare meat. But on the other, there was the assurance that "the bile-suffused cheek of Buonoparte, his wrinkled brow, and yellow eye, the ceaseless inquietude of his nervous system" were incontrovertible proof that he had not "descended from a race of vegetable feeders" (Shelley 1884: 17). Meat, Shelley declared bluntly, is "demonstrably pernicious" (20), as clear a demonstration as any being the "easiness of breathing" (24) acquired by vegetarians, granting them "a remarkable exemption from that powerful and difficult panting now felt by almost everyone after hastily climbing an ordinary mountain" (24).

Realistically, of course, the uphill battle had to be fought by vegetarians. Not only was the weight of medical opinion still on the side of meat, so was public opinion and, even more important, popular taste: "The forbidding of animal food," Lambe had despaired, is "an injunction that sounds more unwelcome to English ears than any perhaps that could be given" (Lambe 1815: 130). For such prejudice to be overcome, meat had to be transformed into a positive menace by the construction of physical arguments that were more sophisticated than were warnings that flesh eaters make poor alpinists. The elevation of physiology to primacy in the ongoing formulation of a rationale for vegetarianism, however, was the work of American theorists rather than English or other European ones.

Vegetarianism in America

Vegetarianism was brought to the United States toward the end of the 1810s by William Metcalfe, an envoy of the Bible Christian Church. The first organization in modern times to make vegetarianism one of the requirements of membership, the Church had been founded in Manchester, England, in 1807 by the Swedenborgian minister William Cowherd (there is a Dickensian irony in the names of the vegetarian leaders of the early 1800s – Cowherd, Metcalfe, and Lambe all conjuring up visions of chops and roasts). Though motivated in part by humanitarian sentiment, Cowherd had been equally impressed by the writings of Cheyne, and he forbade his congregation meat (and alcohol too), largely for reasons of health (Forward 1898: 7).

The Bible Christian sect would continue in existence in England until the 1880s at least, but its greatest impact came early in the century and on American soil. About 1830, in the process of organizing a New World branch of his church in Philadelphia, Metcalfe caught the attention of Sylvester Graham, a Presbyterian minister turned temperance lecturer. Graham, at that time, was in the process of expanding temperance into an all-inclusive program of physical and moral reform, and Metcalfe's understanding of the virtues of a vegetable diet was in perfect philosophical harmony with the American's own view of health behavior generally.

Graham's popular health reform movement, the first stage of what would become an enduring tradition of hygienic extremism in America, operated on the assumption that the laws of health were as much the dictates of God as the Ten Commandments, and, therefore, the two sets of rules could not conflict: Physiology must be congruent with morality. Acting from this certainty, that any behavior that tarnished the soul must also injure the body, Graham and his health reform comrades bombarded the public of the 1830s to 1850s with health injunctions against alcohol, extramarital sex, late-night entertainments, and sundry other practices both hateful and hurtful; included among these, by necessity, was the consumption of meat (Whorton 1977, 1982).

Graham hardly labored alone in erecting more extensive physiological supports for vegetarianism. Numerous health reformers participated, most notably William Andrus Alcott, who in the late 1830s supplanted Graham as commander of the forces of health reform. One of the most prolific self-help writers of the entire nineteenth century, Alcott contributed an 1838 volume under the title *Vegetable Diet,* specifying in his subtitle that vegetarianism was *Sanctioned by Medical Men and by Experience in All Ages.* The book was intended, in short, to show that science corroborated Christian moral principles

(or at least his interpretation of the spirit of compassion of the New Testament). Comparative anatomy was one of the sciences applied to the task, though the similarity of human teeth and intestines to those of herbivores had been pointed out by any number of earlier authors. Rather it was the still emerging science of nutrition that seemed to offer the most up-to-date demonstration that meat was a poison, and Alcott, Graham, and other health reformers mobilized an impressive array of entirely new nutrition-based arguments to prove their point.

The arguments were impressive, that is, for their quantity. Qualitatively, however, they were completely inadequate and scientifically invalid, both because of the period's severely limited understanding of nutrition and biochemistry and because of health reformers' determination to force science into the straitjacket of their moral preconceptions. The latter was facilitated by the adoption of the theory of pathology that had recently been formulated by French physician François Broussais, a theory that attributed all illness to overstimulation of body tissues, especially those of the digestive tract.

As stimulation was already a loaded word morally – to the Victorian mind, arousal of carnal appetites and animal passions was the root of all evil – Broussais's pathology offered an ideal foundation for the construction of a health reform version of vegetarianism. Consequently, stimulation arguments too numerous to recount were advanced by health reform apologists for vegetable diets throughout the antebellum period.

One effort, for example, interpreted the famous in vivo digestion experiments performed in the 1820s by William Beaumont on a man with a gastric fistula. Beaumont's studies included measurement of the digestion times required by various foods, accomplished by tying food samples to a string, introducing them into the stomach, and retrieving them hourly for inspection. Beaumont's conclusion was that, "generally speaking, vegetable aliment requires more time, and probably greater powers of the gastric organs, than animal" (Beaumont 1833: 36).

Graham objected, maintaining that greater speed of digestion is clearly an indication of a more intense response by the vital powers to the stimulus of food. The more intense a response, he reminded, the more intense the stimulus must be, so meat must be more stimulating – pathologically stimulating – than vegetables. There was additional evidence in the feeling of warmth experienced after a meal rich in meat. A later generation would attribute this to the specific dynamic action of protein, but for health reformers it was a "digestive fever" in which, according to Alcott, "the system . . . is inevitably worn into a premature dissolution, by the violent and unnatural heat of an over-stimulated and precipitate circulation" (Alcott 1840: 221).

Meat even stimulated itself, decomposing (as Tryon had noted two centuries earlier) in much less time than vegetables. It followed that human flesh constructed from the excessively stimulated molecules of meat must also be less stable and more subject to decay. That explained, in Alcott's opinion, why vegetarians smelled better. "The very exhalations of the lungs," he asserted, "are purer, as is obvious from the breath. That of a vegetable-eater," he had determined, "is perfectly sweet, while that of a flesheater is often as offensive as the smell of a charnel-house. This distinction is discernible even among the brute animals. Those which feed on grass . . . have a breath incomparably sweeter than those which prey on animals. Compare the camel, and horse, and cow, and sheep, and rabbit, with the tiger (if you choose to approach him), the wolf, the dog, the cat and the hawk. One comparison will be sufficient; you will never forget it" (Alcott 1838: 233–4).

Still more to the point, however, was that the unstable atoms of a carnivore's muscles must be subject to more rapid molecular turnover than a vegetarian's tissues and, hence, subject to accelerated aging and premature death. The mechanics of life could be summed up simply: "A man may not inaptly be compared with a watch – the faster it goes the sooner it will run down" (Cambell 1837: 291).

The condemnation of fast living was a double entendre, for try as they might to present their ideas as concrete science, health reform vegetarians could never stop moralizing. Alcott, for instance, immediately followed his alarm over the "violent and unnatural heat" of a flesh eater's digestive fever with the observation that a vegetable diet is cooling, and "has a tendency to temper the passions" (Alcott 1840: 221). Colleague Russell Trall was even more uneasy about untempered passions, warning that "no delusion on earth [is] so widespread [as] this, which confuses stimulation with nutrition. It is the very parent source of that awful . . . multitude of errors, which are leading the nations of the earth into all manner of riotous living, and urging them on in the road to swift destruction" (Trall 1860: 10).

To their credit, health reform vegetarians balanced their thrilling flights of theory with down-to-earth demonstrations by cases. The proof of the theory, after all, was in the state of health of those who practiced it, and history could offer robust vegetarians aplenty in evidence. The first to be recognized, predictably, were the antediluvians, those original folk whose simple diet kept them vigorous all the way to the end of their 900 years. But pagans could serve the cause as well, though, surprisingly, it was pagan soldiers, especially those of the Roman army, who were held up as paragons of hygiene, as they had marched to their greatest victories on plain vegetable rations.

The incongruity of the diet of gentleness and benevolence providing the strength for battlefield slaughter was missed by the health reformers in their excitement over the physical glory of the vegetarians of antiquity. Subsistence on vegetable food, according

to an agitated Graham, was "true of all those ancient armies whose success depended more on bodily strength and personal prowess, in wielding warclubs and grappling man with man in the fierce exercise of muscular power, and dashing each other furiously to the earth, mangled and crushed and killed" (Graham 1839: 188).

More recent, and less brutal, examples were more convincing and suitable. Alcott allotted nearly 200 pages of his book on vegetable diet to the presentation of testimonials, including such samples of prodigious vitality as Amos Townsend, a graminivorous bank cashier, who could "dictate a letter, count money, and hold conversation with an individual, all at the same time, with no embarrassment" (Alcott 1838: 75–6).

The Establishment of Vegetarian Societies

That American vegetarians' more pronounced orientation toward health impressed European counterparts is evident from the deliberations associated with the founding of the first national vegetarian organization. On September 30, 1847, meat abstainers from all parts of England gathered in Ramsgate, Kent, to form the Vegetarian Society. It was at this organizational meeting that the term "vegetarian" was coined, being taken from the Latin "vegetus": lively or vigorous. The founding members then pledged themselves "to induce habits of abstinence from the flesh of animals as food, by the dissemination of information upon the subject, by means of tracts, essays, and lectures" (Forward 1898, 22).

When they next enumerated the "many advantages" of vegetable diet that would be presented through literature and lecture, the traditionally favored advantage, morality, was pushed to a subsidiary position; again, vigor was the emphasis, their list beginning with "physical" improvements. The Society's monthly, *The Vegetarian Messenger*, was launched two years later and granted the same prominence to the physical in its messages; by 1853, 20 physicians and surgeons were included among the organization's membership of more than 800 (Forward 1898: 22, 33).

The new group's unorthodox philosophy immediately attracted ridicule. *Punch*, for instance, reported that "a prize is to be given [by the Society] for the quickest demolition of the largest quantity of turnips; and a silver medal will be awarded to the vegetarian who will dispose of one hundred heads of celery with the utmost celerity" ("Vegetarian Movement" 1848: 182). An organized movement of vegetarianism did spread with celerity. American vegetarians quickly followed the English lead, forming the American Vegetarian Society in 1850. As with its predecessor, the very first resolution adopted by this society recognized the value of a vegetable diet for health, declaring "that comparative anatomy, human physiology, and . . . chemical analysis . . . unitedly proclaim the position, that not only the human race may, but *should* subsist upon the products of the vegetable kingdom" ("Proceedings" 1851: 6). Morality did nevertheless follow close behind, with the next three resolutions adopted claiming biblical and ethical sanctions for vegetarianism.

In the meantime, vegetarianism was undergoing a similar development on the European continent. There, treatises such as *Thalysie: ou La Nouvelle Existence (Thalysie: Or the New Existence)* by Jean Antoine Gleizes (1840), and *Pflanzenkost, die Grundlage einer neuen Weltanschauung (Vegetable Diet, the Foundation of a New Worldview)* by Gustav von Struve (1861), slowly raised public awareness of the dietary alternative and attracted followers.

The first national organization of vegetarianism on the continent was established in Germany in 1866, under the leadership of Eduard Baltzer. Vegetarian journals and magazines appeared during the midcentury, beginning in England with the *Vegetarian Advocate* (1848) and the *Vegetarian Messenger* (1849) and continuing in the United States with the *American Vegetarian* (1851), published by the American Vegetarian Society. During the decade of the 1870s, vegetarian restaurants were established in major European and American cities; London could boast of a dozen by the end of the century (Forward 1898: 102). Finally, the first international organization was launched in 1908: The International Vegetarian Union.

Henry Salt

Britain and the United States remained the centers of vegetarian philosophy and practice into the twentieth century. In the former, the cause of vegetable diets was advanced with particular eloquence by Henry Salt (Mohandas Gandhi, among others, credited Salt for his conversion to vegetarianism). Author of numerous books calling for reform of social injustices, Salt was nevertheless best known (or most notorious) for his advocacy of *Animals' Rights Considered in Relation to Social Progress,* the title of an 1892 volume that attacked every form of exploitation of the brute creation. There, and in his later *The Logic of Vegetarianism* (1899), Salt employed a thoroughly unsentimental approach to argue that philosophy and science, alike, required abstention from meat.

Philosophy, his *logic* of vegetable diet posited, could not support the common assumptions that human beings have no moral relationship or obligation to other creatures and that the killing of animals for food is a law of nature. The latter idea had become an especially popular justification for meat eating in the wake of Charles Darwin's explanation of nature's rule of survival of the fittest. The response of Salt, and other late-century vegetarians, was that cooperation among animals was as common a strategy for survival as competition, and that human cooperation with other species was positively enjoined by Darwin's theory that people had descended from animal ancestors: How could one justify the slaughter of creatures with whom humans shared a "bond of consanguinity" (Salt 1892, 1899: 50)? Just such a bond had, in fact, been suggested by Darwin himself in *The Descent of Man;* there he presented a sizable body of evidence to demonstrate that "there is no fundamental difference between man and the higher mammals in their mental faculties.... The difference in mind between man and the higher animals, great as it is, certainly is one of degree and not of kind" (Darwin 1874: 74, 143).

The Twentieth Century

John Harvey Kellogg

Evolutionary kinship with livestock was also a significant element in the case constructed by America's most influential spokesman for vegetarianism in the early twentieth century. John Harvey Kellogg, however, gave greater emphasis to medical than to biological theory and propounded what was clearly the period's most persuasive argument against the consumption of meat. Kellogg was bred, if not born, a Grahamite by virtue of his family's membership in the Seventh-Day Adventist Church, an institution that gave allegiance to Graham's hygienic system on the basis of the divine, health-related visions experienced by spiritual leader Ellen White (Numbers 1976).

Kellogg also received training in hydropathy, an alternative system of medical practice that treated all conditions with applications of water and exhorted all patients to abide by Graham's rules of health. (Kellogg's mentor, and the leading figure in American hydropathy, Russell Trall, was a founding member and officer of the American Vegetarian Society, and the author of a volume titled *The Scientific Basis of Vegetarianism* [1860]).

Kellogg also completed a program of orthodox medical training and then, in 1875, returned to his native Battle Creek, Michigan, to assume the directorship of a struggling hospital and health-education facility operated by the Adventist Church. Not only did he quickly transform the Battle Creek Sanitarium into a thriving business, he built it into the most famous health institution in the country from the 1880s until World War II. As part of the Sanitarium's dietary program, Kellogg, along with his brother Will, created an assortment of meat substitutes and other vegetarian health foods, including the breakfast cereals that have immortalized the family's name (Schwartz 1970; Whorton 1982: 201–38).

Kellogg also lectured tirelessly, from coast to coast, and wrote voluminously. In addition to editing the popular periodical *Good Health,* he authored several dozen books, addressing every aspect of personal health behavior from *The Evils of Fashionable Dress,* to *Plain Facts about Sexual Life,* to *Colon Hygiene.* The last topic, the health of the large bowel, represented Kellogg's most significant contribution to the updating of the nutritional argument for vegetarianism. Here, he elaborated the dietary implications of one of the grand pathology fads of the turn of the twentieth century – intestinal autointoxication.

In the 1880s, laboratory scientists had isolated several substances produced in the intestinal tract through the bacterial putrefaction of undigested protein. The compounds were determined to be toxic when injected directly into the bloodstream in animals, and it was quickly supposed they might be absorbed from the colon into the human bloodstream and then circulated to play havoc throughout the body. Since these agents of self-poisoning were products of bacterial activity, the theory of autointoxication could be seen as an extension of medical bacteriology. Thus clutching the coattails of the germ theory, autointoxication swept into professional and popular awareness at the end of the nineteenth century (Chen and Chen 1989; Whorton 1991).

For Kellogg, autointoxication theory provided enough ammunition to support several book-length attacks on meat eating. In such works as *Autointoxication or Intestinal Toxemia* (1918), *The Itinerary of a Breakfast* (1919), and *The Crippled Colon* (1931), he expounded time and again on how the common diet contained so much protein from its flesh components as to encourage the growth and activity of proteolytic bacteria in the colon. As the microbes operated on undigested flesh food, the body would be "flooded with the most horrible and loathsome poisons" (Kellogg 1918: 131) and brought to suffer headache, depression, skin problems, chronic fatigue, damage to the liver, kidneys, and blood vessels, and other injuries totaling up to "enormous mischief." Anyone who read to the end of Kellogg's baleful list must have been ready to agree that "the marvel is not that human life is so short and so full of miseries, mental, moral, and physical, but that civilized human beings are able to live at all" (Kellogg 1918: 131).

"Civilized" referred to the fiber content of the ordinary diet, too. Modern people, Kellogg chided, ate too concentrated a diet, with insufficient bulk to stimulate the bowels to action. A vegetarian diet, he added for the unaware, was high in roughage. Its other advantage was that it was low in protein. The high-protein diet common to flesh eaters was ideal fodder for the putrefactive microorganisms of the colon, whereas its low-fiber content reduced its rate of movement to a crawl that gave the microbes time to convert all unabsorbed protein to poisons. In the meat eater's sluggish bowels, Kellogg believed, lay "the secret of nine-tenths of all the chronic ills from which civilized human beings suffer" (1919: 87), including "national inefficiency and physical unpreparedness," as well as "not a small part of our moral and social maladies" (Kellogg 1919: 93).

Morality could be merged with medicine in other ways. In *Shall We Slay to Eat*, Kellogg applied a bacteriologic gloss to the age-old objection to the cruelty of slaughter. Reminding readers of the gentleness of unoffending cows and pigs (animals with whom humans were bound by evolution), Kellogg then forced them, Oswald-like, to look upon the "tide of gore," the "quivering flesh," the "writhing entrails" of the butchered animals, and to listen to their squealing and bleating as they died (Kellogg 1905: 145–67). What he counted upon ultimately to move his readers, though, was the abominable filth through which the tide of gore flowed. The Augean nastiness of the typical abattoir (here nauseatingly detailed a year before the publication of Upton Sinclair's much more famous *The Jungle*) ensured that meat must be infested with every germ known: "Each juicy morsel," Kellogg revealed, "is fairly alive and swarming with the identical micro-organisms found in a dead rat in a closet or the putrefying carcass of a cow" (Kellogg 1923: 107).

Alexander Haig

Even biochemistry, just then blossoming as a laboratory science, was recruited to the vegetarian campaign. The other major pathology fad of the early twentieth century was uricacidemia, a disease-inducing state discovered by London physician Alexander Haig. Through a process too involved to be recounted here, Haig convinced himself during the 1880s that his migraine attacks were due to excess uric acid in his blood. As so often happens when an enthusiast discovers the source of his own health problems, Haig was soon blaming uric acid for everybody's problems. Through selective use of biochemical data and oversimplification of biochemical theory, Haig was able to propose mechanisms by which uric acid could cause every complaint from flatulence to cancer. His presentation of that thesis, a 900-page opus called *Uric Acid As a Factor in the Causation of Disease,* passed through seven editions in the 1890s and early 1900s. Haig's notions were soon disowned by his medical brethren, but the public's fear of uric acid carried into the 1920s and brought greater popular attention to bear on vegetarianism.

It was not necessarily approving attention, for the uric-acid-free diet Haig recommended was a highly restrictive system of eating. It required, after all, the elimination of every food containing either uric acid or purines that could be metabolized into uric acid. That rule eliminated not only all meat but many vegetables as well – beans, peas, asparagus, mushrooms, and whole-grain cereal products. Haig was thus left with milk, cheese, some vegetables, fruit, nuts, and – a unique position for a food reformer – white bread. Additional blandness was imposed by the prohibition of coffee and tea on the grounds that they contained methyl xanthines (it was later determined that caffeine and similar compounds are not metabolized into uric acid). And any rejoicing that at least alcoholic beverages were free of uric acid–producing substances was quickly squelched by Haig's assurance that his diet removed any need for stimulation and thus destroyed the taste for strong drink (Haig 1892).

The physical advantage of Haig's diet was demonstrated by the extraordinary success of several athletes who adopted it. Indeed, as early-twentieth-century society became captivated by competitive sports, vegetarians of every persuasion turned to athletic conquest for practical proof of the nutritional superiority of their regimen. As a result, a remarkable record of vegetarian victories in all sports was compiled in the 1890s and early 1900s, from the cycling records established by England's aptly named James Parsley to the championships won by the tug-of-war team of the unfortunately named West Ham Vegetarian Society. (Among the flesh-abstaining champions was Haig's son Kenneth, who won prizes as an Oxford rower but eventually was removed from his boat for fear that "his diet would demoralize . . . the rest of the crew.") Carnivorus competitors refused to acknowledge the vegetarians' athleticism, however, crediting their triumphs not to diet but to the dedication and competitiveness bred by fanaticism (Whorton 1981).

The "Newer Nutrition"

If full-fledged vegetarianism was still being taken lightly, the early twentieth century did foster a new respect for the nutritional value of vegetables; though few accepted vegetable foods as wholly sufficient for a healthful diet, all did come to see the consumption of vegetables as necessary to health. The critical development was the growth of understanding of vitamins over the first two decades of the century, accompanied by the realization that vitamin-rich fruits and vegetables were badly neglected at most tables. The most prominent representative of the so-called newer nutrition, vitamin discoverer Elmer McCollum, estimated in 1923 that "at least 90 per cent" of the food eaten by most American families was restricted to the old standards of white bread and butter, meat, potatoes, sugar, and coffee. His call for nationwide dietary reform aimed at educating and converting the public to replace much of the traditional diet with what he called the "protective foods."

The resultant dietary education campaign made the 1920s as truly the decade of newer nutrition as of bathtub gin and jazz. Food educators bombarded the public through lectures, newspapers, magazines, textbooks, and comic strips and were gratified to see the national consumption of fruits and vegetables increase markedly. To note one of the more extraordinary examples, between 1925 and 1927, the spinach intake of schoolchildren in Fargo, North Dakota, grew tenfold (Whorton 1989).

Public consciousness of the nutritional virtues of plant foods was not limited to vitamin awareness. Another dominant health theme of the 1920s was the lack of bulk in modern society's diet of refined and processed foods. Bulk foods were needed, of course, to prevent constipation, and ultimately autointoxication, still an unsettling threat in the public mind. The Kelloggs, Charles W. Post, and other manufacturers of bran-containing breakfast cereals fostered popular anxiety over torpid intestines with grossly exaggerated advertising warnings, giving the 1920s as pronounced a fiber consciousness as any more recent decade. But there was also the disinterested promotion of a higher-fiber diet by altruistic health reformers, some of them physicians and scientists.

At the head of this group was Britain's archenemy of autointoxication, the renowned surgeon Sir William Arbuthnot Lane. Convinced that the upright posture and soft lifestyle of civilized people weakened the colon and produced "chronic intestinal stasis," Lane surgically removed the colons of hundreds of patients during the 1910s in order to save them from autointoxication. The risks of surgery, as well as criticism from his professional colleagues, forced Lane to stop doing colectomies in the 1920s. But he remained convinced that constipation was the fundamental disease of civilization and was responsible for a host of illnesses, including colon cancer and other neoplasms. Consequently, in 1926, he organized the New Health Society in London and dedicated the last 17 years of his life to lecturing and writing on the dangers of intestinal stasis. Through Lane, the New Health Society, and the magazine *New Health,* British and American consumers were repeatedly harangued about the importance of fruits and vegetables for maintaining bowel regularity and preventing more serious diseases (Whorton 1991).

Vegetarianism and Health

Frequently included in Lane's presentations were anecdotal reports of the relative freedom from autointoxication diseases enjoyed by the vegetarian populations of less-developed nations. But it was not until the late 1940s, after Lane had died and autointoxication had disappeared from orthodox medical theory, that epidemiological studies of so-called developing-world cultures began to verify Lane's anecdotes by demonstrating statistical correlations between a high intake of dietary fiber and low incidences of hemorrhoids, gallstones, colon cancer, and various other "Western diseases" (Trowell 1981). Although some of the specific conclusions associated with the dietary fiber hypothesis have sparked debate, not to say controversy, among nutritionists and other health scientists, fiber has been officially recognized as an essential dietary component, and the general public has clearly been impressed with the health benefits of a diet high in unrefined vegetable foods.

Highly publicized studies linking cholesterol and saturated fats with cardiovascular disease have similarly conditioned society to associate vegetarianism with health and have motivated physicians and nutritionists to study heart disease and longevity in vegetarian groups such as Seventh-Day Adventists and Trappist monks. Those studies, conducted from the 1950s onward and too numerous to cite specifically, have largely confirmed what early-nineteenth-century vegetarians initially proposed, that a vegetable diet not only is capable of sustaining health but may actually improve it as well (Hardinge and Crooks 1963; Amato and Partridge 1989: 10–15).

Vegetarianism and Ethics

Running parallel with the twentieth-century growth of medical support for vegetarianism has been the expansion of the diet's moral rationale. Until recently, this argument has been aimed almost exclusively at the pain inflicted on animals at the time of slaughter and the injustice of depriving them of life. Some attention has also been directed to the discomforts endured by livestock being driven or transported to market; this issue was introduced into deliberations in the mid–nineteenth century, as animals began to be shipped in crowded boxcars and ship holds. Although both types of objections continue, discussion has widened since the middle of the twentieth century to take in the treatment of meat animals throughout their lives.

The transformation of farming into agribusiness, including the adoption of economies of scale in stock raising, fostered a system of more intensive rearing methods – "factory farming" – that confined animals in unnatural environments from birth. Ruth Harrison's 1964 *Animal Machines* first directed public attention to the raising of chickens in overcrowded coops and the packing of pigs into "Bacon Bin" fattening houses. Photographs of veal calves penned in narrow wooden cages all the days of their short lives soon became a common feature in vegetarian appeals (outdone in emotional impact only by the pictures of bludgeoned baby seals used in anti-fur advertisements). The maintenance of hens under similar conditions has encouraged lacto-ovo vegetarians to give up eggs; some have abandoned milk products as well in protest of the dairy industry's practice of separating calves from their mothers soon after birth (and the subsequent transformation of those calves into veal). Thus, the ranks of vegans have grown considerably in the later twentieth century (vegans are sometimes referred to as "pure" vegetarians, but there is some question about the applicability of the term, since the word "vegetarian" was minted to refer to a diet that includes eggs and milk). Even meat eaters have been affected by the critique of factory farming, a sizable number now selecting "free range" animal products whenever they are available.

The Animal Rights Movement

Bentham's proposal that slaughtering an animal for food saves it from a more painful and protracted death in the wild has lost its cogency in the age of the factory farm; now an animal's entire existence might be seen as one long death. The morality of imposing such an existence on any creature has been raised to a higher level of discussion, moreover, by the animal rights movement of the last quarter century. Peter Singer's 1975 work, *Animal Liberation,* the chief catalyst of the movement, is a work in which the heavily sentimental tone of traditional vegetarian moralism is set aside in favor of a rigidly philosophical analysis that recognizes animals as sentient beings, capable of experiencing pain and pleasure, and concludes that they should, therefore, be accorded the same respect as humans in areas where their interests are affected. Various violations of those interests are attacked by Singer (and they are much the same as the ones assailed by Salt nearly a century before) – for example, the use of animals in experimental research and the raising of animals for fur.

Because of the sheer numbers involved, however, the worst example of "speciesism" – the practice of moral discrimination purely on the basis of biological species – is the raising and killing of animals for food: "the most extensive exploitation of other species that has ever existed" (Singer 1975: 92; Regan 1975). The most significant element in such exploitation, however, is regarded not as the unnatural conditions of life imposed upon livestock or even their physical suffering. Fundamental to the animals' rights analysis is the affirmation of a right to life for every creature. Thus, even if the animal is allowed a free-range existence and is slaughtered painlessly, the simple act of killing it for food constitutes an unjustifiable moral offense.

The arguments of Singer, Tom Regan, and other advocates of equal moral consideration for animals have elicited a serious response from the philosophy community. Over the past two decades, professional journals and conferences have given an extraordinary amount of attention to the issue of animal rights and its practical applications, including vegetarianism. To be sure, much of the reaction among philosophers has been critical. The Singer analysis has been faulted on grounds of logic and even attacked as a trivialization of civil rights, women's rights, and other movements promoting more moral treatment of fellow human beings (Francis and Norman 1978).

Yet a good bit of the discussion has supported the animal rights arguments, endorsing both the abstract proposition of an animal's right to life and older sentiments such as an intuitive appreciation that eating animals with whom people sense a bond of kinship is wrong (Diamond 1978). Speciesism has acquired an odious taint as well from the human exploitation of wild animals that has pushed many species to the brink of extinction, and by studies of communication in other mammals that have strengthened our feeling of relation to the rest of the animal kingdom.

Vegetarianism and the Environment

Not only have the moral and medical defenses of a vegetable diet grown stronger individually over the twentieth century, they have been buttressed in recent decades by environmental arguments. This is not an entirely new approach – eighteenth- and nineteenth-century vegetarians occasionally pointed out that less land would be needed for agriculture if people were fed on grain rather than meat – and it is a frequently cited truism in vegetarian literature today that 16 pounds of grain are required to produce 1 pound of meat. But with the twentieth century's rapid increase of human population, the ceaseless conversion of arable land into housing developments and shopping malls, and the dramatic expansion of industry and the spread of industrial pollution, the degradation of the environment has become an object of grave scientific and public concern. As attention has been focused ever more sharply on the multitudinous threats to the fragile environment of our shrinking globe, a flesh diet has been recognized as a significant contributor to environmental decline.

The ecology of meat eating was first explored thoroughly by Frances Moore Lappé, whose 1971 best-seller *Diet for a Small Planet* examined livestock farming's toll on the land, water, and air. Since Lappé, it has become commonplace for vegetarian literature to detail the soil erosion associated with the cultivation of livestock food crops; the excessive demands on water supplies to irrigate those crops; the pollution of waterways by field and feedlot runoff; the large amounts of fossil fuel energy expended in raising meat animals; even the contribution to global warming made by the methane released in cattle flatulence. Lately, the destruction of the tropical rain forest to provide more grazing land for beef cattle has been singled out as flesh diet's greatest threat to the viability of "spaceship earth." And in the end, ecology has returned to ethics. In the twentieth-anniversary edition of *Diet for a Small Planet* (1991), Lappé concentrated her criticisms on the immorality of growing grain for the fattening of cattle while millions of people worldwide starve.

A final characteristic of contemporary vegetarianism is its accomplishment of a joining of East and West. The Western counterculture's fascination with Asian religious traditions has been an important contributor to the growth of vegetarianism over the past quarter century, with vegetarian religious sects such as the International Society for Krishna Consciousness now widely distributed through North America and Europe. Voluntary vegetarianism remains the practice of a small minority of the world's population, of course; the number of practitioners, nevertheless, has risen to a historic high due to the combination of spiritual, ethical, medical, and environmental preoccupations resident in the mentality of the late twentieth century. In the United States, there are now approximately 9 million people identifying themselves as vegetarians, whereas another 40 million claim to have decreased their flesh food intake for reasons of health, morals, or ecological concern (Amato and Partridge 1989).

James C. Whorton

Bibliography

Akers, Keith. 1983. *A vegetarian sourcebook.* New York.

Alcott, William. 1838. *Vegetable diet: As sanctioned by medical men, and by experience in all ages.* Boston, Mass.
    1840. Animal and vegetable food. *Library of Health* 4: 220-2.

Amato, Paul, and Sonia Partridge. 1989. *The new vegetarians.* New York.

Aquinas, Thomas. 1989. *Summa theologiae: A concise translation,* ed. Timothy McDermott. London.

Barkas, Janet. 1975. *The vegetable passion.* New York.

Beaumont, William. 1833. *Experiments and observations on the gastric juice, and the physiology of digestion.* Plattsburgh, N.Y.

Bentham, Jeremy. 1961. *An introduction to the principles of morals and legislation.* Garden City, N.Y.

Cambell, David. 1837. Stimulation. *Graham Journal of Health and Longevity* 1: 290-1.

Chen, Thomas, and Peter Chen. 1989. Intestinal autointoxication: A medical leitmotif. *Journal of Clinical Gastroenterology* 11: 434-41.

Cheyne, George. 1734. *An essay of health and long life.* London.

Cottingham, John. 1978. "A brute to the brutes?": Descartes' treatment of animals. *Philosophy* 53: 551-9.

Darwin, Charles. 1874. *The descent of man.* New York.

Diamond, Cora. 1978. Eating meat and eating people. *Philosophy* 53: 465-79.

Dombrowski, David. 1984. *The philosophy of vegetarianism.* Amherst, Mass.

Forward, Charles. 1898. *Fifty years of food reform.* London.

Francis, Leslie, and Richard Norman. 1978. Some animals are more equal than others. *Philosophy* 53: 507-27.

Graham, Sylvester. 1839. *Lectures on the science of human life.* Boston, Mass.

Haig, Alexander. 1892. *Uric acid as a factor in the causation of disease.* London.

Hardinge, Mervyn, and Hulda Crooks. 1963. Non-flesh dietaries. *Journal of the American Dietetic Association* 43: 545-9.

Harrison, Ruth. 1964. *Animal machines.* London.

Kellogg, John Harvey. 1905. *Shall we slay to eat?* Battle Creek, Mich.
    1918. *Autointoxication or intestinal toxemia.* Battle Creek, Mich.
    1919. *The itinerary of a breakfast.* Battle Creek, Mich.
    1923. *The natural diet of man.* Battle Creek, Mich.

Lambe, William. 1815. *Additional reports on the effects of a peculiar regimen.* London.

Lappé, Frances Moore. 1971. *Diet for a small planet.* New York.

Numbers, Ronald. 1976. *Prophetess of health: A study of Ellen G. White.* New York.

Oswald, John. 1791. *The cry of nature.* London.

Plutarch. 1898. Of eating of flesh. In *Plutarch's miscellanies and essays,* Vol. 5, trans. William Goodwin, 3-16. Boston, Mass.

Porphyry. 1965. *Porphyry on abstinence from animal food,* trans. Thomas Taylor. London.

Proceedings. 1851. *American Vegetarian* 1: 6.

Regan, Tom. 1975. The moral basis of vegetarianism. *Canadian Journal of Philosophy* 5: 181-214.

Ryder, Richard. 1979. The struggle against speciesism. In *Animals' rights - a symposium,* ed. David Patterson and Richard Ryder, 3-14. Fontwell, England.

Salt, Henry. 1892. *Animals' rights considered in relation to social progress.* London.

1899. *The logic of vegetarianism.* London.

Schwartz, Richard. 1970. *John Harvey Kellogg, M.D.* Nashville, Tenn.

Shelley, Percy Bysshe. [1813] 1884. *A vindication of natural diet.* London.

Singer, Peter. 1975. *Animal liberation: A new ethics for our treatment of animals.* New York.

Spencer, Colin. 1993. *The heretic's feast.* London.

Stevenson, Lloyd. 1956. Religious elements in the background of the British anti-vivisection movement. *Yale Journal of Biology and Medicine* 29: 125-57.

Trall, Russell. 1860. *The scientific basis of vegetarianism.* Philadelphia, Pa.

Trowell, Hugh. 1981. *Western diseases, their emergence and prevention.* Cambridge, Mass.

Tryon, Thomas. 1683. *The way to health, long life and happiness.* London.

Turner, James. 1980. *Reckoning with the beast.* Baltimore, Md.

The vegetarian movement. 1848. *Punch* 15: 182.

Voltaire. 1962. *Philosophical dictionary,* Vol. 1, trans. Peter Gay. New York.

Whorton, James. 1977. "Tempest in a flesh-pot": The formulation of a physiological rationale for vegetarianism. *Journal of the History of Medicine and Allied Sciences* 32: 115-39.

1981. Muscular vegetarianism: The debate over diet and athletic performance in the progressive era. *Journal of Sport History* 8: 58-75.

1982. *Crusaders for fitness: The history of American health reformers.* Princeton, N.J.

1989. Eating to win: Popular concepts of diet, strength, and energy in the early twentieth century. In *Fitness in American culture: Images of health, sport, and the body, 1830-1940,* ed. Kathryn Grover, 86-122. Amherst, Mass.

1991. Inner hygiene: The philosophy and practice of intestinal purity in Western civilization. In *History of hygiene. Proceedings of the 12th international symposium on the comparative history of medicine - east and west,* ed. Y. Kawakita, S. Sakai, and Y. Otsuka. Tokyo.

1994. Historical development of vegetarianism. *American Journal of Clinical Nutrition* 60 (Supplement): 1103-9.

VI.18 ❧ Vegetarianism: Another View

Early Humankind

Vegetarianism is a cultural and social, rather than a biological, phenomenon. Anatomically and physiologically, the digestive organs of the human species are designed for both animal and plant foods. Moreover, a global cross-cultural survey demonstrates the fact that all cultures, past and present, have revealed a preference for at least some form of animal fat and protein and that none have ever been totally vegetarian (Abrams 1987b: 207-23).

Current paleoanthropological research indicates that humans have been on this earth for some 3 to 4 million years. For over 99 percent of that time, humans were hunters and gatherers (Cohen 1977: 15; Johanson and White 1979: 321-30). From the Australopithecines to the inception of agriculture, humans gradually developed more efficient tools to obtain food, especially for hunting game. *Homo erectus* pursued large game, and early *Homo sapiens,* the late Paleolithic humans, were even more dedicated in this regard.

Indeed, the availability of game may well have dictated human settlement patterns. As population pressure mounted in Africa, the original home of humankind, herds of game dwindled, forcing people further afield to follow other herds. This ultimately led to human settlements in Asia, Europe, the Americas, and Australia - in all of the continents except Antarctica.

About 10,000 years ago, beginning in the Middle East, people finally started to raise plant foods because of their own growing number, on the one hand, and because so many game animals were scarce or had been hunted to extinction, on the other. And with sedentary agriculture came political organization and formal religions.

Religion and Diet

As people settled into sedentary agriculture, meat-eating prohibitions gradually became part of the tenets of some of their religions, such as Hinduism. Ultra-orthodox Hindus and Jains, for example, are strict vegetarians, but as anthropologist Marvin Harris points out, in earlier times the Hindus were beef eaters. Later, beef eating was restricted, primarily, to the Brahman caste; and finally, the practice became prohibited for all Hindus.

Harris has argued that such a prohibition was the result of human population growth. Because cows were valuable as draft animals and as providers of milk and dung (as fuel for cooking), it was wasteful to use them for meat. In fact, Harris argues that the consumption of certain animals is prohibited in many cultures for pragmatic reasons (Harris 1977: 129-52) and that compliance is more likely when such prohibitions are codified as tenets of religion (Dwyer et al. 1973: 856-65; Mayer 1973: 32; Todhunter 1973: 286).

Other religious groups that today adhere to some type of vegetarianism include Buddhists, Seventh-Day Adventists, and orders such as the Roman Catholic Trappist monks. Justification of vegetarianism on religious grounds may be because it is more spiritual, or because it is more in harmony with nature, or because of the conviction that all animal life is sacred (Abrams 1980: 53–87).

Modern-Day Vegetarianism

A phenomenal escalation of vegetarianism, which began in the 1960s, has occurred in the Western world and has had little to do with religion (Erhard 1973: 4–12; Sonnenberg and Zolber 1973). The new vegetarians include a wide variety of individuals with concerns ranging from what animals are fed and injected with to environmental problems and world hunger to the indictment of cholesterol and animal fats as causative factors in the development of vascular diseases, cancers, and premature deaths.

There is also considerable variation in the practice of vegetarianism. At one extreme are the vegans, who exclude all types of animal protein from their diet and subsist solely on vegetables, seeds, nuts, and fruits. Moreover, their dietary beliefs are extended to other daily activities. Vegans shun clothing made of animal products such as wool, silk, leather, fur, or pearl (Erhard 1974: 20–7). They abstain from using consumer goods, such as soap or cosmetics made with animal fat or brushes of animal hair, and they refuse immunization from animal-derived sera or drugs, or toiletries whose safety has been determined by animal testing.

Vegetarians toward the middle of the continuum choose a wider variety of foods and include certain animal protein foods in their diets. Lacto-vegetarians, for example, use dairy products; ovo-vegetarians, eggs; pollo-vegetarians, poultry; and pesco-vegetarians, fish. Some will use more than one type of animal protein foods, such as lacto-ovo vegetarians, who consume dairy products and eggs along with other foods.

Opposite to the vegans on the vegetarian continuum are the red-meat abstainers, who consume all animal protein foods except beef, lamb, and pork (Fleck 1976: 408–27).

Extreme Vegetarianism and Health

One form of extreme vegetarianism is the final stage of the Zen macrobiotic diet. This vegetarian phenomenon attained some popularity in the Western world during the 1960s but has declined since its founder's death. The diet encompasses a life philosophy based on a loose reading of Buddhist symbolism and the ancient Chinese dualistic concept of yin and yang (Dwyer 1979: 1–2). Allegedly, humans achieve harmony in all of life's manifestations by reaching a balance between the cosmic forces of yin and yang, which oppose while they complement one another (Keen 1978), such as male/female; contraction/expansion; and fire/water. In terms of food, such dualities are manifested in complements such as animal versus vegetable; mineral versus protein and fat; bitter and salty versus sweet.

According to the philosophy behind the macrobiotic persuasion, disease results from yin/yang imbalances, which can be restored by an ideal diet. The individual must follow 10 stages of an elaborate dietary regimen, with the final stage consisting solely of brown rice, salt, and fluids such as herbal teas. Reaching this final stage, presumably, assures attainment of perfect health, freedom from all disease, and spiritual enlightenment. In this latter connection, macrobiotics has been especially popular. Some individuals have embraced it in a search for an alternative to drug experimentation in order to experience a "natural high" (Keen 1978).

Yet one account, *The Death Diet* (Christagu 1967: 43–7), has described the tragedy suffered by a young couple upon reaching the tenth stage of the macrobiotic diet. The health of the male was impaired severely, and the woman died. Her death certificate read, "Multiple vitamin and protein deficiencies precipitated the chain of events leading to her death" (Mayer 1975).

Total vegetarians are likely to suffer deficiencies of many of the chief nutrients, among them vitamin B_{12}. All foods of animal origin contain vitamin B_{12}, yet plant sources for this vitamin are unreliable. The human body stores at least a thousand times the Recommended Dietary Allowance (RDA) of vitamin B_{12}, which is an amount sufficient to maintain serum levels in some people for up to five years, although there are a wide range of serum levels associated with the deficiency. Thus, deficiency may not be apparent for some time while reserves of the vitamin are gradually being tapped (Ellis and Mumford 1967: 205; Ellis and Montegriffo 1970: 249). It can be difficult to detect vitamin B_{12} deficiency because of the high folic acid intake of vegetarians, which frequently masks symptoms of the condition (Brown 1990: 175). All of this is particularly unfortunate because early detection of the deficiency is vital to avoid irreversible neurological impairment.

Some vegetarians, although aware of the risk of vitamin B_{12} deficiency, depend nonetheless on plants for this vitamin, despite the unreliability of such foods as a source. When found in plants, vitamin B_{12} is present only because of bacteria growing on the plant or because the plant has been contaminated by bacteria, especially from fecal matter. Spirulina and tempeh, used frequently by vegetarians as vitamin B_{12} sources, have virtually none and in fact provide B_{12} analogues that actually block the metabolism of functional vitamin B_{12} (Bailie 1987: 98–105).

Vitamin B_{12} deficiency can result in megaloblastic anemia, a grave condition. In the mid-1970s, a high incidence of megaloblastic anemia was reported among orthodox Hindus who had emigrated from India to England. The phenomenon was puzzling. The orthodox Hindus did not have vitamin B_{12} deficiency while they lived in India, nor after they first emigrated, but developed the deficiency during their residence in England. Their diet was similar in both countries. But investigations revealed that the cause stemmed from differences in growing, processing, and packaging foods in the two countries.

In India, where crops had minimal applications of costly pesticides, many plants were insect-contaminated, and the insects, or their eggs and larvae, contributed a supply of vitamin B_{12} to the diet. Additional opportunities for insect contamination were provided by minimally processed or packaged food. Thus, in India, the orthodox Hindus had adventitiously obtained sufficient vitamin B_{12} to prevent deficiency, a finding that helps to explain why extreme vegetarians in other developing countries may escape it as well. But ironically, the privileged in those countries, who can afford to purchase imported foods that are highly processed and protectively packaged, may suffer from an inadequate vitamin B_{12} intake (Rose 1976: 87).

In addition to lacking vitamin B_{12}, extreme vegetarian diets are often deficient in adequate proteins and even calories. Moreover, total vegetarian diets tend to be low in calcium and riboflavin (Raper and Hill 1973). Certain coarse, green leafy vegetables may be high in calcium, but the calcium is not well absorbed because of the high fiber content of the diet, and other minerals, including zinc, phosphorus, and iron, may also be poorly absorbed (Haviland 1967: 316–25; Reinhold et al. 1976: 163–80; Bodzy et al. 1977: 1139; Freeland, Ebangit, and Johnson 1978: 253).

Calcium absorption is also impaired by certain green leafy vegetables, such as spinach and Swiss chard, that contain oxalates. These compounds bind with calcium during digestion to form insoluble calcium oxalate, which is not utilized, and the calcium is excreted in the feces (Albanese 1980). Moreover, whole grains, frequently consumed in large quantities by many vegetarians, are high in phytates, and these substances, like the oxalates, interfere with calcium absorption (Hegsted 1976: 509). Similarly, vegetarians may have low zinc levels due to phytates and oxalates in their diets. In contrast, foods from animal sources provide dietary zinc, but they do not contain the inhibiting phytate and oxalate compounds (Prasad 1966: 225–38).

Zinc insufficiency is one of the greatest but least-known dangers of vegetarianism, according to the late Carl C. Pfeiffer, who commented wryly that "the light headed feeling of detachment that enshrouds some vegetarians can be caused by hidden zinc hunger, rather than by some mystical quality of the brown rice or other food consumed" (Pfeiffer 1975: 103). Among other things, low zinc levels are related to male infertility. In one study, mild zinc depletion in nine male volunteers resulted in decreased fertility, and the sperm count of the men fell to an infertility level after the men intentionally ate a zinc-deficient diet for about six months (Prasad 1982).

Obtaining sufficient iron can also be a problem for vegetarians, and women on strict vegetarian diets, especially during child-bearing years, may have real difficulties in this regard (Mayer 1973: 32). As with zinc, foods of animal origin are reliable iron sources, whereas foods of plant origin are not. Moreover, heme iron from foods of animal origin is absorbed and utilized far more efficiently than nonheme iron from plant foods: 10 to 30 percent can be absorbed from animal foods, compared with only 2 to 10 percent from plant foods; and finally, phytates and oxalates interfere with iron absorption (Finch 1969: 3).

Normal plasma estrogen levels are necessary for women's menstrual regularity. Because nutrition can affect hormone levels, dietary differences may affect menstrual patterns, as was shown in a study of evenly matched nonvegetarian and vegetarian premenopausal women at the Milton S. Hershey Medical Center in Hershey, Pennsylvania: Only 4.9 percent of the nonvegetarians experienced menstrual irregularities, whereas 26.5 percent of the vegetarians had difficulties. The probability of menstrual regularity was associated positively with protein and cholesterol intake and negatively with dietary fiber and magnesium intake (Pedersen, Bartholomew, and Dolence 1991: 879–85). Such results are consistent with the hypothesis that premenopausal vegetarian women have circulating estrogen concentrations (Lloyd, Schaeffer, and Walter 1991: 1005–10) and that these women may also have decreased reproductive capacity (Pedersen et al. 1991: 879–85). Another study at the Hershey Medical Center reveals that the frequency of menstrual irregularity was significantly higher in a lacto-ovo vegetarian group of women than in a matched group of nonvegetarian women (Lloyd et al. 1991: 1005–10).

Infants and children may suffer the most from extreme vegetarian diets. Commenting on this issue, the pediatrician George Kerr observed that "history has many examples of parents abusing children for the very best intention. . . . Specifically, should we start considering reporting these cases of growth failure on vegan diets to the authorities involved with child abuse?" (Kerr 1974: 675–6).

Infants breast-fed by women who are strict vegetarians have been found to be deficient in vitamin B_{12}, and such lactating women are advised both to take a vitamin B_{12} supplement and to include soybean milk or fermented soybean foods in their diets (Dwyer 1979: 1–2). Vegetarian infants and children tend to be smaller and to grow at a slower rate than do children from the general meat-eating population. One factor may be the high-bulk/low-calorie content characteristic of vegetarian diets (Erhard 1973: 11).

Pediatricians have expressed concerns about the vulnerability of infants and growing children who are especially at risk from extreme vegetarianism. "Kokoh," a special macrobiotic infant-feeding formula, was found to be capable of inducing kwashiorkor, one form of protein–energy malnutrition. Moreover, the

American Academy of Pediatrics (ACP) has reported that infants fed solely on this formula from birth usually are underweight within a few months and below average in total body length (Abrams 1980: 57).

Other research and clinical observations have also shown that infants fed no animal protein fail to grow at a normal rate and may develop kwashiorkor. Infants who are breast-fed and then placed on vegan diets do not grow or develop as normal infants, nor do they do as well as infants fed vegetarian diets supplemented with cow's milk (Erhard 1973: 10–12).

Vegetarianism and Chronic Diseases

Ancel Keys's seminal reports (Keys 1956: 364; Keys, Anderson, and Grande 1957: 959), followed by others, suggested a direct relationship between diet, especially animal fats, heart disease (Connor, Stone, and Hodges 1964: 1691–1705; West and Hayes 1968: 853; Anderson, Grande, and Keys 1976: 1184), and colon cancer (Burkitt 1971: 3, 1973: 274; Berg, Howell, and Silverman 1973: 915; Reiser 1973: 524, 1978: 865; Hill 1975: 31; Howell 1975; Nichols et al. 1976: 1384; Truswell 1978: 977–89). Conclusions drawn from these studies, however, remain controversial, and many other studies take issue with them (Mann et al. 1961: 31; Mann 1977: 644; Enstrom 1975: 432; Lyon, Klauber, and Gardner 1976: 129; Enig, Munn, and Keeney 1978: 2215; Glueck and Connor 1978: 727).

Nonetheless, the public has been led to believe that foods that contain saturated fat and cholesterol, such as eggs and red meats, are related to heart disease and colon cancer. In fact, some alarmed individuals have embraced a limited or total vegetarian diet in the belief that such measures will ward off these illnesses (Hardinge and Stare 1954: 83; West and Hayes 1968: 853; Ruys and Hickie 1976: 87; Sanders, Ellis, and Dickerson 1978: 805).

In truth, however, research has produced contradictory and puzzling findings. Seventh-Day Adventists, for example, have an educational health program for their members that advocates a well-balanced diet, including milk and eggs, along with other foods. In other words, these lacto-ovo vegetarians eat adequate amounts of animal protein foods, although they exclude red meats. Additionally, Seventh-Day Adventists have been found to have lower rates of cancer and coronary artery disease than the general American population (Wynder, Lemon, and Bross 1959: 1016–28). For cancer, they experience a 50 to 70 percent lower mortality incidence than the general population (Phillips 1975: 3513). For coronary heart disease, mortality was lower in males under 65 years of age than in the general population but not in males over 65, nor in females of any age (Phillips et al. 1978: S191).

Because Seventh-Day Adventists are red-meat abstainers, it was assumed that such abstention accounted for their lower incidence of heart disease than that of the general public. But other confounding factors may play important roles in preventing these diseases. For example, Seventh-Day Adventists abstain from tobacco, alcohol, and caffeinated beverages (Dwyer 1979: 1–2).

Members of the Church of Jesus Christ of Latter Day Saints (Mormons) provide another homogeneous group for study. Mormons are not red-meat abstainers, but the church urges moderation in lifestyle. Compared to the American average, Utahan Mormons were found to have a 22 percent lower incidence of cancer in general and a 34 percent lower incidence of colon cancer (Lyon et al. 1976: 129). However, Puerto Ricans, who eat large amounts of animal fats, especially pork, have very low rates of colon and breast cancers (Enig et al. 1978: 2215). Such contradictions practically leap off the pages of a comparative study of the incidence of breast and colon cancers conducted in Finland and the Netherlands. People in these two countries eat similar levels of animal fats per person per day, but despite this similarity, the incidence of breast and colon cancer in the Netherlands was nearly double that of Finland (Enig et al. 1978: 2215).

Nor are such contradictions confined to cancer. A study in western Australia has contradicted the notion that a high serum cholesterol level increases the risk of heart attack. Three groups of mothers and children were studied: those with high, those with medium, and those with low cholesterol levels. The groups had no significant differences in their daily dietary intake of proteins, fats, and carbohydrates, and obesity was ruled out as a factor, because cholesterol levels did not differ between the obese and the nonobese.

The conclusion reached was that diet did not appear to account for differences in cholesterol levels in a culturally homogeneous group. Furthermore, the "correlation between habitual diet and the average serum cholesterol level is good between contrasting populations (for example, people of Japan and Finland)" but "within a given culture, people eating the same kind of food can have different serum lipids. Those who develop coronary heart disease do not necessarily eat differently from those who do not" (Hitchcock and Gracey 1977: 790).

More recently, additional confounding evidence has been contributed by the so-called French Paradox. The eating habits of people in Gascony, in the southwest of France, were studied for 10 years. This area is noted as the world's leading producer of cholesterol-laden foie gras. People in Gascony consume goose and duck fat liberally, snack on dried duck skin, and eat more than twice as much foie gras as other French people and 50 times as much as Americans. Yet they were found to have the lowest incidence of death from cardiovascular disease in all of France. In Gascony, of 100,000 middle-aged men, about 80 die annually of heart attack, compared with 145 elsewhere in France and 315 in the United States (O'Neill 1991: 1, 22).

Fats

Because of the negative publicity that fats have received of late, we sometimes tend to forget that fat is essential for proper growth and development, even for life itself. Fat provides essential fatty acids necessary for cell membrane structure and for prostaglandins; it also acts as a carrier for the fat-soluble vitamins. Humans require different types of fats for different purposes, both structural and storage. Structural fats make possible the growth of the brain and the central nervous system and maintain cell membrane integrity. Structural fats are found inside the cell. Cell membranes are not mere envelopes but active parts of the cell, arranged as an orderly production line, creating some things, breaking down others, and transferring raw materials (nutrients) as needed from one place to another. Storage fats, no less important, are used for energy (Crawford and Marsh 1989: 120).

Vegetable Oils

It may be unfortunate that millions of people have been persuaded to change their choices of fat in the belief that oils from plants containing predominantly polyunsaturated or monounsaturated fatty acids are good, and fats from animals are bad. There is an argument that large amounts of polyunsaturated oils in the diet may be detrimental to health (Lyon 1977: 28–31). Although vegetable oils have been offered with promises of risk reductions for cardiovascular diseases, some authorities find these claims to be misleading and inaccurate (Pinckney and Pinckney 1973: 31–8; Moore 1989: 40–95).

Eggs and Cholesterol

Cholesterol has also gotten a bad press, which tends to obscure its vital roles in human health. It is needed for the transmission of nerve impulses throughout the body, and, in fact, the nervous system cannot function properly with insufficient cholesterol. In addition, cholesterol is needed to produce sex hormones. Indeed, it may well be because cholesterol is so crucial that the human body does not depend solely on dietary sources but also manufactures cholesterol. If dietary cholesterol is insufficiently supplied, then the body manufactures more to meet its requirements. Thus, Roger J. Williams turned current wisdom on its head when he observed that "anyone who deliberately avoids cholesterol in his diet may be inadvertently courting heart disease" (Williams 1971: 73).

In response to public concern about eggs and their cholesterol content, food processors have countered by concocting products that contain egg white (the noncholesterol component) but no yolk (the cholesterol-containing component). These products were intended for omelets and scrambled egg dishes. M. K. Navidi and F. A. Kummerow of the Burnsides Research Laboratory, University of Illinois, undertook an experiment to determine the nutritional value of such replacer eggs. They fed one group of lactating rats exclusively on fresh eggs and another group on Egg Beaters. They intended to run the experiment for 40 days, but all the rats on the egg substitute were dead in 17 days. They were underweight, were severely stunted in growth, and had mottled hair. All the rats on fresh whole eggs were healthy and normally sized (Navidi and Kummerow 1974: 565).

Diet and Primitive Societies

In using the term "primitive," we would note at the outset that there are no primitive peoples. The term, when used by anthropologists, denotes the development of technology used by cultures.

Not many hunting and gathering societies have survived to the present, and those that have are rapidly becoming acculturated. Yet the few still in existence have been extensively studied, with such efforts contributing considerably to our knowledge of the diet and health of past peoples.

Among other things, such knowledge disputes vegetarians who defend their practice with the claim that individuals in primitive societies (and presumably our ancestors) were herbivores who lived primarily on plant foods. The evidence is that most hunting-and-gathering peoples consume large amounts of meat and other types of animal protein whenever it is available.

The Eskimos constitute a classic example. They lived almost entirely on a traditional diet of raw sea and land mammals, fish, and birds, and so long as the traditional diet was followed, Eskimos remained in excellent health. Indeed, the raw meat and organs of these animals, including the liver and the adrenal glands, even provided an ample supply of vitamin C, so long as the meat was raw or cooked only a little. Being heat-sensitive, vitamin C is destroyed in meats by normal cooking (Stefansson 1960: 58).

Although it was obvious that Eskimos could thrive on a diet of raw meat (Stefansson 1937), the notion persisted that such a diet would probably harm Europeans, which led to an interesting experiment. Under the auspices of the Russell Sage Institute of Pathology at Bellevue Hospital (an affiliate of the Cornell University Medical College of New York), the anthropologist Vilhjalmur Stefansson and his colleague Karsten Anderson volunteered to eat a ratio of 2 pounds of raw lean meat to a half pound of raw fat and nothing else daily for a year. Both men thrived. After the year was up, Stefansson, who had previously lived for years on the Eskimo diet, continued on it for decades more and enjoyed sound health until his death at age 83. Similarly, Anderson was found to be in better physical condition after eating the traditional Eskimo diet for the year than when he began the experiment (Stefansson 1957: 60–89).

The Eskimo diet, then, also tends to confound the notion that meat and fats undermine human health. Paul Martin, for example, who spent years in the Arctic, discovered that although Eskimos consumed large amounts of animal fats, whale blubber, and seal oil, they did not have problems with cholesterol and, in fact, were remarkably free of degenerative diseases, especially those related to heart and to blood pressure (Martin 1977: 25-8).

Another observer of indigenous Eskimo culture concluded that the native diet of raw land and sea mammals and fish provided all the nutrients needed for excellent health (Schaefer 1971: 8-16). Unfortunately, with their adoption of industrialized foods since World War II, consisting mainly of refined carbohydrates (sugar and white flour), chemically altered fats, and other highly processed foods, the Eskimos began to suffer from those degenerative diseases common to the modern industrialized world (Schaefer 1971: 8-16).

George V. Mann, of Vanderbilt University Medical College, who challenged Keys's fat hypothesis, initiated several studies with the few available primitive societies still living largely on animal foods. He reasoned that if a high fat and cholesterol intake really did cause heart disease, then hypercholesteremia and coronary heart disease ought to characterize the health of groups of people living on high fat and cholesterol diets.

Mann first studied the Pygmies in the African rain forest. Almost untouched by civilization, these people have continued on a traditional diet of large amounts of meat, supplemented with plant foods. But Mann discovered that despite a high level of meat consumption, adult male Pygmies had the lowest cholesterol levels yet recorded (Mann et al. 1961).

Next, Mann observed the Masai of Tanganyika, a nomadic pastoral people living almost exclusively on meat, cow's blood, and milk. His examination of 400 Masai adult males revealed very little cardiovascular disease and no signs of arteriosclerotic disease. As a result of his investigation, Mann concluded that the widely held notion that meat and milk cause coronary heart disease is unsupported by the evidence (Mann 1963: 104).

Modern Nutrition and Tooth Decay

Tooth decay has been known throughout human history, but only in relatively modern times has it become endemic. The evidence shows that tooth decay was rare throughout the Paleolithic period, which spanned some 3 to 4 million years.

When the hunting-and-gathering way of life gave way to stable agriculture, though, the switch led, among other things, to increased tooth decay. And it would seem that dependence on high-carbohydrate foods, such as grains and other plant foods, began to seriously undermine the health of those who did not

find a way to maintain a favorable dietary balance between high-quality animal protein foods and lower-quality plant protein foods (Page and Abrams 1974: 188-203, 214-26; Abrams 1976: 102-12, 1978: 41-55).

Skeletal remains of European populations reveal a slow, steady increase in tooth decay from the Neolithic period when agriculture first began until the present, when it escalated (Wells 1964; Abrams 1976: 102-12, 1978: 41-55). Such a deterioration in teeth is also vividly portrayed in the experience of the Lapps (Sami) of northern Europe, who until recently had hunted in a manner similar to that of the late Paleolithic age and lived mainly on reindeer meat. They consumed about a pound of meat per person each day and were renowned for their healthy teeth. Eighteenth-century skeletal remains show a cavity rate of only 1.5 percent in Lapp teeth. But gradually, Lapps adopted the industrialized diet, with the result that their cavity rate has soared to 85 percent (Pelto and Pelto 1979: 292-301).

Examination of the skulls of the ancient Norse, who subsisted almost entirely on fish, seafood, and animals, also showed that dental decay was rare (Page and Abrams 1974: 188-203, 214-26). But skeletal remains of prehistoric Indians in the California area, whose diet was primarily vegetarian, revealed that 25 percent of the population had some tooth decay (Pelto and Pelto 1979: 292-301). Substantially worse were the teeth of prehistoric Indians in New Mexico, whose diet was based on corn (maize), supplemented with a few other plant foods and small amounts of animal protein. Tooth decay was a problem for 75 percent of that population (Pelto and Pelto 1979: 292-301).

Such relationships between diet and dental decay, as well as other degenerative diseases, has also been well documented by Weston A. Price's pioneering efforts around the globe. He found, for example, that so long as the Australian Aborigine, Polynesian, Eskimo, and other peoples followed their traditional diets, consisting of animal foods and unrefined, unprocessed plant foods, they had an exceptionally low incidence of caries and other health problems. But after adopting an industrialized diet these same peoples developed rampant tooth decay and other degenerative diseases, as well as malformations in offspring (Price 1989: 59-72).

Animal experiments have yielded similar results that underscore observations on human populations. Protein-malnourished rat pups developed more caries than when protein was amply supplied. Rats fed adequate calories but no protein also had a high incidence of tooth decay (DiOrio, Miller, and Navia 1973: 856-65; Menaker and Navia 1973: 680-7; Navia 1979: 1-4). Clearly, such findings suggest that humans, especially infants and children, are more susceptible to tooth decay if deprived of adequate animal protein foods.

Diet and the Lower Primates

It is sometimes argued that the basic human diet should be plant food because closely related species of primates such as monkeys and apes are vegetarian. Yet, since World War II, ethological studies on primates in the wild have shown that monkeys and apes, despite a predominantly vegetarian diet, nonetheless seek out small animals, insects, insect eggs, and larvae as food (Abrams 1980: 75).

Marmosets and squirrel monkeys are especially fond of crickets and flies (Abrams 1980: 75). Baboons actively hunt, kill, and eat a variety of wild animals, and zoo marmosets have failed to mate until animal foods were added to their diets (Abrams 1978: 42-50). Jane Goodall has witnessed chimpanzees in the wild fashioning crude tools to gather termites as food and has observed them killing and eating arboreal monkeys, baby baboons, and other small animals (Goodall 1971).

Gibbons often eat rodents, birds, and small antelopes. Orangutans feed on larvae, beetles, nesting birds, and squirrels. And in captivity, gorillas show a preference for meat over vegetarian fare (Perry 1976: 165-85). In this connection, it should be noted that the desire of chimpanzees to eat meat does not stem from a lack of plant foods, which are abundant and constitute most of their diet (Eimerl and De Vore 1968: 142-52; Goodall 1971).

Such findings have made it necessary to reclassify monkeys and apes. Rather than being herbivores, these animals are now recognized as omnivores, and the reason that they do not eat more animal food than they do may be the result of a limited ability to provide it in great abundance. But in seeking the animal foods that they do consume, monkeys and apes are most likely driven by a basic need to meet nutritional requirements that are available only from animal protein (Abrams 1980: 76).

The tree shrew, the most primitive of all the living primates, is closest in structure to the fossil ancestors of the first primates, who date from about 70 million years ago. The tree shrew is almost exclusively an insectivore (Berg et al. 1973: 915). Such findings about the primate progenitors of humans strongly suggest that all primates, including humans, have a basic need for some animal protein in the diet (Abrams 1980: 76).

In moving away from lower primates to humans, we find that available paleontological and archaeological data can tell us much about the diet of humans for most of their time on earth.

Humans as Hunters

Fossil remains of *Australopithecus,* the first humans (Dart 1969: 42-189; Leakey 1971: 215-90), have been found over the savannas of South and East Africa (Leakey 1971: 215-90). They ate their food raw, but unlike other primates, they made and utilized crude stone tools to collect more food per unit of time. Their diet consisted of insects and small animals and plant foods that could be eaten raw as found in nature (Biegert 1975: 717-27). They scavenged, eating the remains of any large carcass they found, and apparently were able to obtain surprisingly large amounts of meat (Schaller and Lowther 1969: 307-34).

Through mutations and natural selections, about a million years ago a more advanced human, *Homo erectus,* evolved. These people developed far more efficient tools and techniques for hunting large animals and spread from Africa into Asia and southern Europe (Constable 1973: 29-37, 70).

Between 35,000 and 70,000 years ago, modern *Homo sapiens* evolved. The late Paleolithic *Homo sapiens* is exemplified by Cro-Magnon man (Prideaux 1973). *Homo sapiens* continued to improve hunting techniques and followed game from Africa to the far north of Europe and, finally, to Siberia, the Americas, and Australia. Cro-Magnon's religion and magic, reflected in extraordinary cave art, centered around the theme of the hunt for large game.

Both archaeological excavations and cave art reveal the variety of meat available. In Europe and Asia, for example, Cro-Magnon hunted for bear, cave lion, hyena, wild horse, bison, woolly rhinoceros, reindeer, chamois, ibex, woolly mammoth, and deer. In the Americas, the quarry became the dire wolf, mammoth, giant beaver, giant sloth, American camel, and more than 100 other species (Prideaux 1973: 12, 14, 42-78). But beginning about 40,000 years ago, many of the large animal species began to die out worldwide, and by approximately 10,000 years ago, numerous animals had been hunted to extinction (Martin 1967: 32-8). Anthropologist Sherwood L. Washburn has postulated that the quest for game was a significant factor in the evolution and intellectual development of humans. Beginning with the *Australopithecines* and continuing over eons until the domestication of plants and animals, humans increasingly learned to be ever more efficient hunters, to devise better and better strategies, and to invent and improve better and more effective tools as well as techniques for using them. That humans were forced to shift from hunting and gathering to sedentary agriculture because of a decreasing supply of large animals suggests that they were too successful in perfecting their hunting techniques (Washburn 1961: 299).

Nutrients in Plants and Animals

It should be clear by now that our ancestors, both of the lower primates and of humans, consumed much in the way of animal food and with good reason, for nutrients in meat are much more highly concentrated and are utilized more efficiently than those from plant foods. For example, venison provides 572 calories/100 grams of weight, compared with only 100 calories from a similar amount of fruits and vegetables (White and Brown 1973: 68–94). Humans, then, developed an ability not only to hunt an animal efficiently but also to digest it efficiently. Through natural selection both of these abilities afforded humans an adaptive advantage for survival in a changing environment (Bronowski 1972: 42–56).

A full day of foraging is required to obtain the amount of food value from plants that is found in one small animal. By eating animals that lived on grasses and leaves, humans could obtain a highly concentrated and complete food, converted from plants into meat. When humans moved into the cold regions of northern Europe and Asia, they had to rely on meat even more. Edible plant foods were available only seasonally, whereas game was available throughout the year (Campbell 1976: 253–302). Moreover, game did not need to be cooked, whereas many plant foods had to be prepared in this fashion to be edible. *Homo erectus* may have used fire to a very limited extent some 300,000 years ago, but the evidence is sparse and questionable. Fire's general use, according to both paleontological and archaeological records, began only about 40,000 to 50,000 years ago (Abrams 1976: 102–12).

The use of fire, extended to food preparation, resulted in a great increase and variety of plant food supply. All of the major basic domesticated plant foods, such as wheat, barley, rice, millet, rye, and potatoes, require cooking before they are suitable for human consumption. In fact, in a raw state, many plants contain toxic or indigestible substances or antinutrients. But after cooking, many of these undesirable substances are deactivated, neutralized, reduced, or released; and starch and other nutrients in the plants are rendered absorbable by the digestive tract. Thus, the use of fire to cook plant foods doubtless encouraged the domestication of these foods and, thus, was a vitally important factor in human cultural advancement (Abrams 1986: 24–9).

In summary, it seems clear that the natural diet of humans is an omnivorous one and that proteins from animal sources are vital to health and well-being. This is because proteins differ in quality, depending on the amino acids from which they are built. Some amino acids ("nonessential" or "dispensable") can be synthesized in the human body; others ("essential" or "indispensable") must be supplied by food. For optimal protein quality, all amino acids must be present and in optimal ratios with one another. No individual plant meets these requirements, whereas all foods of animal origin do.

The egg represents the ideal quality protein against which all other proteins are measured in terms of its protein efficiency ratio (PER). At the top of the PER scale, the egg is followed closely by proteins from other animal sources, both organ and muscle meats. The PERs for plant foods such as legumes, grains, and seeds are much lower on the scale because all are limited by a low level of one or more of the amino acids, which are not in good balance with each other. To obtain an amount sufficient to meet human requirements, one would need to consume enormous quantities of a plant food, and the total diet would become imbalanced.

Perhaps in the future, with genetic engineering and other scientific and technological advances, it will become possible to develop plant foods that will supply, in ideal balance, all the amino acids and other nutrients required for optimal health. Meanwhile, it seems prudent to keep the traditional dietary wisdom of our predecessors and apply it, insofar as possible, to modern life, meaning that humans should eat a varied, balanced diet consisting of both animal and plant foods, all in moderation.

H. Leon Abrams, Jr.

Bibliography

Abrams, H. Leon. 1976. *Inquiry into anthropology.* New York.
　　1978. A diachronic preview of wheat in hominid nutrition. *Journal of Applied Nutrition* 30: 41–55.
　　1980. Vegetarianism: An anthropological/nutritional evaluation. *Journal of Applied Nutrition* 32: 53–87.
　　1986. Fire and cooking as a major influence on human cultural advancement: An anthropological/botanical/nutritional perspective. *Journal of Applied Nutrition* 38: 24–9.
　　1987a. Hominid proclivity for sweetness: An anthropological view. *Journal of Applied Nutrition* 39: 35–41.
　　1987b. The preference for animal protein and fat: A cross-cultural survey. In *Food and evolution: Toward a theory of human food habits,* ed. Marvin Harris and Eric B. Ross, 207–23. Philadelphia, Pa.
　　1989. The relevance of Paleolithic diets in determining contemporary nutritional needs. *Journal of Applied Nutrition* 31: 43–59.
Albanese, A. A. 1980. *Nutrition for the elderly.* New York.
Anderson, Joseph T., Francisco Grande, and Ancel Keys. 1976. Independence of the effects of cholesterol and degree of saturation of the fat in the diet on serum cholesterol in man. *American Journal of Clinical Nutrition* 29: 1184–9.
Bailie, I. E. 1987. The first international congress on vegetarian nutrition. *Journal of Applied Nutrition* 39: 97–105.
Berg, J. W., M. A. Howell, and S. J. Silverman. 1973. Dietary hypotheses and diet-related research in the etiology of colon cancer. *Health Services Reports* 88: 915–24.
Biegert, J. 1975. Human evolution and nutrition. *Progress in Food and Nutrition Science* 1: 717–27.
Bodzy, Pamela W., Jeanne N. Freeland, Margaret A. Eppright, and Ann Tyree. 1977. Zinc status in the vegetarian. *Federation Proceedings* 36: 1139.
Bronowski, Jacob. 1972. *The ascent of man.* Boston, Mass.
Brown, Myrtle L., ed. 1990. *Present knowledge in nutrition.* Sixth edition. Washington, D.C.
Burkitt, Denis P. 1971. Epidemiology of cancer of the colon and rectum. *Cancer* 28: 3–13.
　　1973. Some diseases characteristic of modern Western civilization. *British Medical Journal* 1: 274–8.
Campbell, Bernard G. 1976. *Humankind emerging.* Boston.

Campbell, Sheldon. 1978. Noah's ark in tomorrow's zoo: Animals are a'comin' two by two. *Smithsonian* 8: 42–50.

Christagu, R. 1967. The death diet. *Fact* 4: 43–7.

Cohen, Mark Nathan. 1977. *The food crisis in prehistory.* New Haven, Conn.

    1989. *Health and the rise of civilization.* New Haven, Conn.

Connor, William E., Daniel B. Stone, and Robert E. Hodges. 1964. The interrelated effects of dietary cholesterol and fat upon human serum lipid levels. *Journal of Clinical Investigation* 41: 1691–1706.

Constable, G. 1973. *The Neanderthals.* New York.

Crawford, Michael, and David Marsh. 1989. *The driving force: Food, evolution, and the future.* New York.

Dart, R. 1969. *Adventures with the missing link.* New York.

DiOrio, Louis P., Sanford A. Miller, and Juan M. Navia. 1973. The separate effects of protein and calorie malnutrition on the development and growth of rat bones and teeth. *Journal of Nutrition* 103: 856–65.

Dwyer, Joanna. 1979. Vegetarianism. *Contemporary Nutrition* 4: 1–2.

Dwyer, Joanna, Laura D. V. H. Mayer, Randy Frances Kandel, and Jean Mayer. 1973. The new vegetarians. *Journal of the American Dietetic Association* 62: 503–9.

Eimerl, S., and Irven De Vore, eds. 1968. *The primates.* New York.

Ellis, Frey R., and V. M. E. Montegriffo. 1970. Veganism, clinical findings and investigations. *American Journal of Clinical Nutrition* 23: 249–55.

Ellis, Frey R., and P. Mumford. 1967. The nutritional status of vegans and vegetarians. *Proceedings of the Nutrition Society* 26: 205–12.

Enig, Mary G., Robert J. Munn, and Mark Keeney. 1978. Dietary fat and cancer trends – a critique. *Federation Proceedings* 37: 2215–20.

Enstrom, J. E. 1975. Colorectal cancer and consumption of beef and fat. *British Journal of Cancer* 32: 432–9.

Erhard, Darla. 1973. The new vegetarians. Part I. *Nutrition Today* 8: 4–12.

    1974. The new vegetarians. Part II. *Nutrition Today* 9: 20–7.

Finch, Clement A. 1969. Iron metabolism. *Nutrition Today* 4: 3.

Fleck, H. 1976. *Introduction to nutrition.* Third edition. New York.

Freeland, Jeanne H., M. Lavone Ebangit, and Pamela Johnson. 1978. Changes in zinc absorption following a vegetarian diet. *Federation Proceedings* 37: 253.

Glueck, Charles J., and William E. Connor. 1978. Diet-coronary heart disease relationships reconnoitered. *American Journal of Clinical Nutrition* 31: 757–37.

Goodall, Jane V. L. 1971. *In the shadow of man.* Boston.

Hardinge, Mervyn G., and Fredrick J. Stare. 1954. Nutritional studies of vegetarians: 2. Dietary and serum levels of cholesterol. *Journal of Clinical Nutrition* 2: 83–8.

Harner, Michael J. 1977a. The ecological basis of Aztec sacrifice. *American Ethnology* 4: 117–35.

    1977b. The enigma of Aztec sacrifice. *Natural History* 86: 46–51.

Harris, Marvin. 1977. *Cannibals and kings, the origins of cultures.* New York.

Haviland, W. A. 1967. Stature at Tikal, Guatemala: Implications for ancient Maya demography and social organization. *American Antiquity* 32: 316–25.

Hegsted, D. Mark. 1976. Energy needs and energy utilization. Reprinted in *Nutrition Reviews' present knowledge in nutrition.* Fourth edition. New York.

Hill, M. J. 1975. The etiology of colon cancer. *Critical Reviews in Toxicology* 4: 31–82.

Hitchcock, Nancy E., and Michael Gracey. 1977. Diet and serum cholesterol. An Australian family study. *Archives of Disease in Childhood* 52: 790–3.

Howell, M. A. 1975. Diet as an etiological factor in the development of cancers of the colon and rectum. *Journal of Chronic Diseases* 28: 67.

Hunter, Beatrice Trum. 1978. *The great nutrition robbery.* New York.

Johanson, D. C., and T. D. White. 1979. A systematic assessment of early African hominids. *Science* 203: 321–30.

Keen, S. 1978. The pure, the impure, and the paranoid. *Psychology Today* 12: 67–8, 73–4, 76–7, 123.

Kerr, G. 1974. Babies who eat no animal protein fail to grow at normal rate. *Journal of the American Medical Association* 228: 675–6.

Keys, Ancel. 1956. Diet and development of coronary heart disease. *Journal of Chronic Diseases* 4: 364.

Keys, Ancel, Joseph T. Anderson, and Francisco Grande. 1957. Prediction of serum-cholesterol responses of man to changes in fats in the diet. *Lancet* 2: 959–66.

Laughlin, W. S. 1968. Huntington: An integrative biobehavior system and its evolutionary importance. In *Man the hunter,* ed. R. B. Lee and I. Devore, 304–20. Chicago.

Leakey M. D. 1971. *Olduvai gorge,* Vol. 3. Oxford.

Lloyd, T., J. M. Schaeffer, and M. A. Walter. 1991. Urinary hormonal concentrations and spinal bone densities of premenopausal vegetarian and nonvegetarian women. *American Journal of Clinical Nutrition* 54: 1005–10.

Lyon, J. L., M. R. Klauber, and J. W. Gardner. 1976. Cancer incidence in Mormons and non-Mormons in Utah, 1966–1970. *New England Journal of Medicine* 294: 129–33.

Lyon, N. 1977. Cholesterol – is just one heart threat. *Science Digest* 81: 28–31.

Mann, George V. 1963. Diet and disease among the milk and meat eating Masai warriors of Tanganyika. *Food and Nutrition* 34: 104.

    1977. Diet-heart: End of an era. *New England Journal of Medicine* 297: 644–50.

Mann, George V., O. L. Roeis, D. L. Price, and J. M. Merrill. 1961. Cardiovascular diseases in African Pygmies. *Journal of Chronic Diseases* 15: 341.

Mann, George V., E. M. Scott, and L. M. Hursh. 1962. The health and nutritional status of Alaskan Eskimos, a survey of the interdepartmental committee on nutrition for national defense – 1958. *American Journal of Clinical Nutrition* 11: 31–76.

Martin, P. S. 1967. Pleistocene overkill. *Natural History* 76: 32–8.

    1977. Eskimos, shocking example to us all, primitive diet vs. junk food. *Let's Live* 45: 25–8.

Mayer, Jean. 1973. Can man live by vegetables alone? *Family Health* 5: 32–4.

    1975. An extreme case of self starvation. *Daily News* August 27.

Menaker, Lewis, and Juan M. Navia. 1973. Effect of undernutrition during the perinatal period on caries development in the rat: II. Caries susceptibility in underfed rats supplemented with protein or caloric additions during the suckling period. *Journal of Dental Research* 52: 680–7.

Moore, Thomas J. 1989. *Heart failure.* New York.

Navia, Juan M. 1979. Nutrition, diet and oral health. *Food and Nutrition News* 50: 1–4.

Navidi, Meena Kasmall, and Fred A. Kummerow. 1974. Nutritional value of Egg Beaters™ compared with "farm fresh eggs." *Pediatrics* 53: 565–6.

Nichols, Allen B., Catherine Ravenscroft, Donald E. Lamphiear, and Leon D. Ostrander, Jr. 1976. Daily nutritional intake and serum lipid levels: The Tecumseh study. *American Journal of Clinical Nutrition* 29: 1384-92.

O'Neill, Molly. 1991. Can foie gras aid the heart? A French scientist says yes. *New York Times,* November 17, pp. 1, 22.

Page, Melvin E., and H. Leon Abrams. 1974. *Your body is your best doctor.* New Canaan, Conn.

Pedersen, Ann B., M. J. Bartholomew, and L. A. Dolence. 1991. Menstrual differences due to vegetarian and nonvegetarian diets. *American Journal of Clinical Nutrition* 53: 879-85.

Pelto, G. H., and P. J. Pelto. 1979. *The cultural dimensions of the human adventure.* New York.

Perry, R. 1976. *Life in forest and jungle.* New York.

Pfeiffer, Carl C. 1975. *Mental and elemental nutrients.* New Canaan, Conn.

Phillips, Roland L. 1975. Role of life-style and dietary habits in risk of cancer among Seventh-Day Adventists. *Cancer Research* 35: 3513-22.

Phillips, Roland L., Frank R. Lemon, Lawrence Beeson, and Jan W. Kusma. 1978. Coronary Heart Disease mortality among Seventh-Day Adventists with differing dietary habits: A preliminary report. *American Journal of Clinical Nutrition* 31: S191-8.

Pinckney, Edward R., and Cathy Pinckney. 1973. *The cholesterol controversy.* Los Angeles.

Prasad, Amanda, ed. 1982. *Clinical, biochemical, and nutritional aspects of trace elements.* New York.

  1966. *Zinc metabolism.* Springfield, Ill.

Price, Weston A. 1989. *Nutrition and physical degeneration.* Seventh edition. New Canaan, Conn.

Prideaux, T. 1973. *Cro-Magnon man.* New York.

Raper, N. R., and M. M. Hill. 1973. *Nutrition Program News* n.v.: 4.

Reinhold, J. G., B. Faradji, P. Abadi, and F. Ismail-Beigi. 1976. Decreased absorption of calcium, magnesium, zinc and phosphorus by humans due to increased fiber and phosphorus consumption as wheat bread. *Journal of Nutrition* 106: 493-503.

Reiser, Raymond. 1973. Saturated fat in the diet and serum cholesterol concentration: A critical examination of the literature. *American Journal of Clinical Nutrition* 26: 524.

  1978. Oversimplification of diet: Coronary heart disease relationships and exaggerated diet recommendations. *American Journal of Clinical Nutrition* 31: 865-75.

Rose, M. 1976. Serum cholesterol and triglyceride levels in Australian adolescent vegetarians. *Lancet* 2: 87.

Ruys, J. J., and B. Hickie. 1976. *British Medical Journal* 2: 87.

Sanders, T. A. B., Frey R. Ellis, and J. W. T. Dickerson. 1978. Studies of vegans: The fatty acid composition of plasma choline phosphoglycerides, erythrocytes, adipose tissue, and breast milk, and some indicators of susceptibility to ischemic heart disease in vegans and omnivore controls. *American Journal of Clinical Nutrition* 31: 805-13.

Schaefer, Otto. 1971. When the Eskimo comes to town. *Nutrition Today* 6: 8-16.

Schaller, G. B., and G. Lowther. 1969. The relevance of carnivore behavior to the study of early hominids. *Southwest Journal of Anthropology* 25: 307-41.

Shaper, A. G. 1962. Cardiovascular studies in the Samburu tribe of Northern Kenya. *American Heart Journal* 63: 437-42.

Shaper, A. G., Mary Jones, and John Kyobe. 1961. Plasmalipids in an African tribe living on a diet of milk and meat. *Lancet* 2: 1324-7.

Sonnenberg, L. C., and V. D. Zolber. 1973. Food for us all, the vegetarian study kit. *Journal of the American Dietetic Association* 62: 93.

Stefansson, Vilhjalmur. 1937. Food of the ancient and modern Stone Age man. *Journal of the American Dietetic Association* 13: 102-29.

  1957. *The fat of the land.* New York.

  1960. *Cancer: Disease of civilization?* New York.

Todhunter, E. Neige. 1973. Food habits, food faddism, and nutrition. *World Review of Nutrition and Diet* 16: 286-317.

Truswell, A. S. 1978. Diet and plasma lipids – a reappraisal. *American Journal of Clinical Nutrition* 31: 977-89.

Washburn, S. L. 1961. *Social life of early man.* New York.

Wells, C. 1964. Bones, bodies, and disease: Evidence of disease and abnormality in early man. New York.

West, Raymond O., and Olive B. Hayes. 1968. Diet and serum cholesterol levels: a comparison between vegetarians and nonvegetarians in a Seventh-Day Adventist group. *American Journal of Clinical Nutrition* 2: 853-62.

White, E., and D. Brown. 1973. *The first men.* Waltham, Mass.

Williams, Roger J. 1971. *Nutrition against disease.* New York.

Wynder, Ernest L., Frank R. Lemon, and Irwin J. Bross. 1959. Cancer and coronary artery disease among Seventh-Day Adventists. *Cancer* 12: 1016-28.

PART VII

Contemporary
Food-Related Policy Issues

The concern of Part VII is with the impact of economics, governments, politics, and special interest groups on diet in the twentieth century. It begins with the attention that nationalistic governments in the West belatedly paid to the nutritional health of their citizens at the turn of the twentieth century – the health of women, who provided offspring to strengthen the state demographically, and the health of men, who were called upon to fight for it. Mostly, however, Western governments have stopped short of active intervention in ensuring the food supply of individuals, and as the chapters on food entitlements and subsidies for infants and children make clear, such intervention – save for helping the very young – continues to be viewed with sufficient hostility that it is only grudgingly (and only partially) undertaken.

If governments are reluctant to underwrite food entitlements, however, they are much more willing to ensure the dissemination of nutritional guidelines, such as those discussed in the chapter dealing with recommended daily allowances of the chief nutrients and another treating recent food labeling requirements. Yet governments do not act in a vacuum, and the chapter on food lobbies in the United States (and elsewhere by implication) demonstrates the enormous ability of special interests to influence food policy, including the content of much of the nutritional information aimed at informing the public.

The question of the desirability of more or less government involvement in food matters runs deeply

through the next few chapters. That food biotechnology may turn out to be a blessing, a curse, or both is a concern of considerable magnitude, and rightfully so, as the chapter on its politics and implications for policy makes evident. However, in what is becoming a roller-coaster look at new food technology, the chapter that follows on biotechnology and food safety seems more reassuring.

The chapter on food additives, which opens a window on the past and present of this fascinating world, is succeeded by another that portrays substitute foods and ingredients, such as margarine and artificial sweeteners, as superfluous at best and health hazards at worst. The author of the chapter on nonfoods as dietary supplements critically evaluates them by describing the history of three – bioflavonoids, dietary fiber, and carnitine – whereas the question of food safety is revisited one last time in the penultimate chapter with a look at the food toxins and poisons imparted by microorganisms.

The last chapter in Part VII takes us full circle by discussing a hypothesis much in the news from time to time – namely, that we modern humans need to be more mindful of the diets consumed by our Paleolithic predecessors so as to reduce our risk of cancer, coronary problems, and other chronic diseases. After all, so the message reads, in the short span of the 10,000 or so years that separates us from them, we have not had much of an opportunity to make biological adjustments so as to utilize foods obtained by farming as well as those secured by foraging.

VII.1 ❧ The State, Health, and Nutrition

Overview

The science of nutrition has influenced consumers in their choices about the kinds and optimal amounts of food to eat, but there are other influences as well, such as prosperity levels within a given population, the efficiency of transportation and distribution systems, and the standards of hygiene maintained by food producers, processors, and retailers.

One factor, however, that has not received much scholarly attention is the increased role of the state, either through direct or indirect means, in the production, distribution, and consumption of food. Only recently have historians addressed the development of food policies (mostly those in Europe) in order to understand the state's role in controlling and monitoring food supplies.

In early modern European societies, the maintenance of public order and the control of food supply were intimately related; religious and secular authorities alike had a vested interest in ensuring that production met the demands of consumption. The actions of these authorities (the distribution of food or price-fixing, for example) were largely responses to localized crises. What distinguishes modern food policies from their early modern antecedents are the intended goals of these policies, as well as the scientific nature of their implementation.

The rise of industrialization and urbanization in the nineteenth century prompted new concerns about food supplies. The competitive nature of an industrialized, capitalist food market increased popular anxieties about adulteration; one of the more important roles of the state was to regulate the hygienic quality of food supplies. The economic conditions of the nineteenth century provoked greater concern with population's risking dietary deficiencies and, therefore, poor health. Social reformers and scientific experts took a more active and deliberate interest in monitoring the health of the laboring classes through the measurement of food consumption levels.

It is not mere coincidence that the rise of modern European food policies paralleled the development of the science of nutrition. As physiologists and social scientists explored both the content of foods and the uses which consumers made of them, state policies utilized this information to safeguard public health, thereby increasing the productivity and longevity of the population. This chapter provides a schematic, comparative overview of state intervention in popular diet throughout the nineteenth and early twentieth centuries, a period when there was an increased recognition of the extent and effects of dietary deficiencies but no cohesive state programs to guarantee proper nutrition for all.

It was often for the sake of military strength that European governments showed interest in the nutritional status of their populations, but even then much of the burden for improving diets was placed on the nutritional education of housewives. World War I, as a contest of industrial and military strength, made necessary the efficient management of resources, including food. Governments were thrown into the roles of suppliers and distributors of foodstuffs, and much of food policy formation was piecemeal, at times chaotic, in nature.

Then, after the states had assumed new regulatory powers over food supplies, the question of whether continued intervention was necessary, or even desirable, formed the basis for interwar debates over the link between food policies, civilian health, and greater economic productivity. Although military and economic competition between nations continued to make civilian health important to national well-being, questions of degrees of state intervention to safeguard health were never adequately resolved. What was clear by the time of World War II, however, was that European states had become increasingly interested parties in matters of food consumption as they related to public health.

The Nineteenth Century

Throughout the nineteenth century, the twin processes of industrialization and urbanization brought dramatic changes to European food consumption habits. Decreased opportunity for domestic agricultural production placed populations, particularly urban ones, at the mercy of price fluctuations. Public discontent over food issues shifted away from riots and disturbances over food availability and toward forms of protest over wages, prices, and standards of living. The division of labor and the monetary economy in industrial capitalist societies brought the rise of commercial middlemen concerned with profits rather than increasing food supplies. This new business ethic spread fears of food adulteration and unscrupulous business practices for the sake of greater profits. Social scientists and reformers observed that in industrialized areas, the poorer segments of the laboring classes suffered from malnutrition, staving off their hunger with cheap carbohydrates such as those provided by bread, potatoes, liquor, and sugar.

Nonetheless, the nineteenth century can be characterized as one in which the quality and variety of diet slowly improved. In addition to sugar, new foodstuffs like wheaten flour, margarine, coffee, and chocolate became urban dietary staples as industrializing nations experienced what Hans Teuteberg has termed "the democratization of dietary gratification" (Teuteberg 1975: 79). By the latter half of the nineteenth century, the rationalization of agriculture, decreasing transport costs, and the industrial mass production of foodstuffs reduced food prices. In Germany, as household incomes rose, families consumed a richer diet and shifted their preferences from potatoes and grain to dairy products and meat, allotting less income for subsistence in relation to other expenditures (Offer 1989: 40).

This is not to say, of course, that meat was regularly consumed by everyone. Rural consumers might have eaten meat only once a week or on holidays. It is interesting to note, however, such changes in consumption patterns signaled new criteria for evaluating diet. In Great Britain, for example, the increase in meat and sugar consumption was seen as a shift to more energy-producing foods and therefore as more desirable for the average worker (Burnett 1966; Mennell 1985; Shammas 1990).

It was in the late nineteenth century that members of scientific communities began to shape dietary evaluation criteria. The science of physiology broke foods down into the essential components of carbohydrates, proteins, and fats. Social scientists, charitable organizations, and parliamentary committees documented the consumption habits of the laboring classes while evaluating standards of living and health. The scientific community also scrutinized some of the troubling effects of industrialization on dietary patterns. Levels of concern and scientific conclusions depended, of course, on national context. Italian physiologists, observing the effects of late-nineteenth-century industrialization on the population, noted that at the same time consumers could afford more nutritious foods, they could also afford alcohol, tobacco, sugar, and coffee, all of which could cancel out the beneficial effects of an improved diet (Helstosky 1996).

The term "diet," distinct from food or food consumption, indicated that there were new criteria for evaluating the place of food in everyday life. Diet implied a certain level of adequacy in food consumption patterns, whether measured by the emerging body of scientific knowledge about calories and nutrients or evaluated in terms of food's capacity to fuel laborers. Therefore, diet was simultaneously a prescriptive and descriptive term, denoting both current habits and a nutritional goal set by members of the scientific community. Statistical knowledge about actual dietary practice relied largely upon concrete records of consumption habits in the form of family budget studies. These studies ranged from government-funded inquests of large populations to studies of smaller groups, sometimes a single family, funded by universities and charitable concerns.

Generally, the period between 1850 and 1910 in western Europe was characterized by a broad range of state and private investigations into the living standards of agricultural and industrial workers (Porter 1986; Hacking 1990). One of the most influential of these, Frederic Le Play's *Enquete agricole* – commissioned by the French Ministry of Agriculture, Commerce, and Public Works – was published in 36 volumes between 1869 and 1870. In Le Play's analysis, dietary habits constituted only a small part of the standard of living; other factors such as literacy, wage rates, housing conditions, and delinquency, for example, also were given analytic leverage.

The European social scientific community followed Le Play's lead in structuring their own monographs; food consumption habits and spending were only parts of detailed works encompassing a wide array of social problems. Data on working-class family budgets from Belgium became the basis upon which the German statistician Ernst Engel formulated his famous law: The proportion of outgo used for food, other things being equal, is the best measure of the material standard of living of a population; the poorer the individual, family, or people, the greater must be the percentage of the income necessary for the maintenance of physical sustenance (Engel 1895).

Nineteenth-century determinations of living standards underscored the centrality of experts and the use of scientific criteria to define social problems. Such determinations also had the effect of emphasizing the importance of the relationship between dietary practice and the physical and social condition of a given population.

By the turn of the century, concrete budget studies of the laboring classes became the basis from which physiologists made nutritional recommendations for dietary intake. There was, however, little agreement over such recommendations. German physiologists like Carl von Voit and Jacob Moleschott defended high levels of dietary protein (between 100 and 130 grams per day), whereas American physiologist Russell Chittenden claimed the body could function adequately on only 60 grams of protein per day (Offer 1989: 39–44). There is no question that scientific recommendations reflected prevailing habits and consumption levels that varied from nation to nation. Uniform nutritional standards were not formulated until the Interallied Scientific Commission met in 1917 and recommended a daily intake of 145 grams of protein, 75 grams of fat, 490 grams of carbohydrates, and 3,300 calories for the average man of 154 pounds working at least an eight-hour day ("Scientists and the world's food problems" 1918: 493).

Debates over what did constitute an adequate intake of nutrients and calories, combined with tabulations of consumption habit by class and region, naturally led to questions of how to improve the nutritional quality of diet and who was to be responsible for such improvements. To some extent, European social scientists and physiologists looked to their governments to take a more active role in guaranteeing better nutrition for all. National governments sponsored investigations into living standards, and on the municipal and national levels, social welfare policies ameliorated poor living conditions through housing reform, consumer cooperatives, and health education programs.

There were no national food policies in the nineteenth century. There were, however, governmental actions that had the effect of improving nutritional standards, such as the adoption of standardized supervision against food falsifications and fraud, as well as assistance for specific populations at risk of dietary deficiencies. The first of these interventions, the regulation of the food market, was arguably one of the most important means of protecting public health. Yet most European governments were reluctant to intervene in the food market, even though in Great Britain, for example, works detailing fraudulent practices ranged from chemist Frederick Accum's *Treatise on the Adulterations of Food* (1820) to Henry Mayhew's *London Labour and the London Poor* (1861).

Such works provoked vigorous political and scientific debates over regulation, but in England there was no governmental attempt to intervene between producer, retailer, and consumer until the enactment of adulteration legislation in 1870 (Burnett 1966). Similarly, in Germany, controls for milk, one of the most commonly adulterated foods, were slow to develop, and it was not until 1879 that uniform food controls and punishments for adulteration were passed (Teuteberg 1994).

In Italy, regulations governing fraudulent retail practices were instituted in 1890 only to be judged ineffectual by the scientific community. As physiologist Adolfo Zerboglio noted in 1897, "[I]t is common knowledge that the poor are obliged to stave off their hunger with spoilt food . . . everyone knows how certain merchants will push poor quality food onto the poor, so as not to keep it in stock" (Zerboglio 1897: 12).

Similarly, governmental interventions to assist populations at risk, such as infants and children, were not fully organized and implemented until the turn of the twentieth century. Diet had improved for many as a result of the increased consumption of fresh fruits and vegetables, butter, and eggs. This was particularly true for Italy and Germany, where the effects of later industrialization were making themselves felt.

In Britain, the inadequate height of military recruits for the Boer War spawned a national debate focused on civilian health and fears of racial degeneration. The minimum height requirement for infantry recruits was lowered from 5 feet 6 inches to 5 feet 3 inches in 1883, and to 5 feet in 1902 (Drummond and Wilbraham 1939: 484-5). Although the stunted growth and malnourished physiques of urban dwellers was of considerable concern, more attention

in the ensuing scientific and political debates was given to housing and sanitary conditions than to the influence of inadequate nutrition on public health. The Royal College of Surgeons and Royal College of Physicians were both reluctant to undertake an inquiry into the nutritional status of the population. However, an interdepartmental Committee on Physical Deterioration finally concluded that poor nutrition was in fact playing a role in the continued physical degeneration of the British people. The committee's findings, issued in 1904, focused considerable attention on the preference for refined, white bread among the working classes, but also concentrated on the feeding of infants and children; working-class mothers were found to be poorly nourished and therefore unable to breast-feed properly (Drummond and Wilbraham 1939: 485-7; Winter 1980).

Mercantilist demographic pressures, coupled with the growing fear of national degeneration, led to a more focused educational campaign to raise the nutritional status of the family. Both charitable organizations and eugenics societies undertook to instruct British women on infant nutrition. These efforts, however, generated feelings of anxiety and inadequacy among working-class mothers faced with the task of juggling household budgets to procure better-quality foods when the formidable appetites of their families demanded quantity (Davin 1978). Social scientists and reformers frequently noted that working-class mothers sacrificed their own health in order to feed their families properly, and pregnant women, younger mothers, and children often subsisted on a diet of bread with margarine and tea (Ross 1993).

Similarly, European-wide campaigns to increase infant birth weight (and reduce infant mortality) focused on the health of the mother without making positive contributions toward maternal nutrition. By the late 1870s, doctors had come to recognize that poor maternal health (including nutrition), as well as short intervals between pregnancies, contributed to low birth weights and consequently to low levels of infant health, and by the end of the century the practice of weighing and measuring newborns in hospitals had become common. Policy suggestions in Switzerland, Germany, the Netherlands, and France, however, focused not on improving maternal nutrition but rather on the importance of a period of rest for mothers before giving birth to increase birth weight and reduce infant mortality (Ward 1993: 24-5).

In Britain, concern for the physical health of the population continued through World War I because of the size and health of military recruits and resurfaced once again during the "hungry thirties" (Winter 1980; Mayhew 1988). During this period, scientific documentation of poor physical stature associated individual health with living conditions, whereas public debates over state intervention linked standards of living to national economic health and military strength.

Great Britain was by no means the exception; across Europe in the early twentieth century, solutions to the problem of popular welfare were debated at national and international conferences on population, eugenics, hygiene, infant mortality, and social work.

Such concerns may be understood as characteristic of modernity (Horn 1994: 3–5) and must be seen within a broader context of national and local governmental efforts to "regulate the social" (Steinmetz 1993). But state intervention to improve housing conditions and sanitation was less controversial than efforts to improve diets. European governments were fundamentally uneasy with direct interventions in the everyday life of the family, and any policy that sought to redress nutritional deficiencies for entire populations was not easily reconciled with either liberal democratic governments or capitalist markets.

Even nutritional assistance to populations at risk – infants, schoolchildren, and the poor – was fraught with tension. At the municipal level, assistance was meted out with few problems. In the northern regions of Italy, where pellagra was prevalent, municipal governments worked in conjunction with charitable societies to organize and extend soup kitchens to those consuming the monotonous, maize-based diet that caused the disease (Porisini 1979). And in Germany, socialist and women's organizations pressured municipal governments to experiment with consumer cooperatives and other means of making food more affordable for the working classes (Steinmetz 1993: 4).

On the national level, however, intervention to provide more nutritious foods for those in need was limited to the provision of school meals and milk. School feedings were justified on both economic and eugenic grounds: to guarantee proper nutrition to the neediest so as to ensure the health of future generations.

Under pressure from school boards, school feedings were incorporated into national education acts on the grounds that improperly nourished children could not perform well. In France, free and subsidized meals for children were considered to be an integral part of the school system, and in Norway, breakfast was offered to all children, rich or poor. In the Netherlands, however, the School Act of 1900 contained provisions that food and clothing be supplied to needy children – a policy judged less successful precisely because school feeding was linked to poverty and therefore tainted by paternalism and charity (den Hartog 1994: 71).

In Great Britain, school-feeding policies grew out of charitable initiatives like the Destitute Children's Dinner Society (1864), but the government was long reluctant to act on a national level for fear that the poor would become dependent on the state for sustenance and other material needs. National intervention, however, was finally justified by the turn-of-the-century debate over health, efficiency, and empire

triggered by the small stature of many who served in the Boer War (1899–1902).

In twentieth-century Europe, such an extension of state responsibility for assuring nutritional adequacy has often resulted from military (rather than economic or social) considerations. School meals were no exception. As John Burnett recently observed, "War, the fear of it and the retreat of the danger of it, has been a major influence throughout the history of school meals" (Burnett 1994: 55). But although the state increasingly justified intervention on the grounds of national survival, local officials and others continued to view the provision of free or cheap meals and milk as an act of charity.

World War I

The circumstances of World War I dramatically altered the attitude of European governments toward promoting civilian health through food policies. They literally were forced by wartime conditions to provide enough food to keep their populations fit for military and civilian service. If the war was a watershed in the history of modern food policy, it was not because governments were able to promote scientific principles of nutrition. Although scientific knowledge about vitamins and other nutrients in food was developing, it was difficult to incorporate this into wartime policies based on expediency.

Within both belligerent and occupied nations, the consumption of proteins and fats declined, and food shortages developed even in the postwar period. In western Europe, malnutrition aggravated mortality from tuberculosis, nephritis, and pulmonary diseases, especially in Germany and Belgium.

Within the Allied nations, World War I further spread the "democratization of dietary gratification" by narrowing dietary distinctions between socioeconomic classes. The homogenization of consumption patterns has been an overall trend in the twentieth century; however, "the principal agency in narrowing the gap between the rich and the poor was the social effect of the war" (Oddy 1990: 262). Full employment provided regular as well as increased incomes, and the extension of state control over food modified the division of food on the basis of price. To some extent, food consumption levels improved in the Allied nations because military provisioning made more nutritious foods available to soldiers. In the case of Great Britain, "the nation which went to war in 1914 was still so chronically undernourished that for millions of soldiers and civilians wartime rations represented a higher standard of feeding than they had ever known before" (Burnett 1966: 217). There is little doubt that this was the case for soldiers, but to make a similar argument for civilians would be a more complicated matter.

Indeed, a comparison between Great Britain and Italy during the war demonstrates that food policies aimed at civilians had a complex effect on living standards and consumption habits. In both nations, histories of popular diet published after the war claimed that living standards had been so miserable that wartime rationing actually improved the nutrition of many (Bachi 1926; Drummond and Wilbraham 1939). But if these assertions were true, it was for different reasons: The malnourished in Britain comprised the urban poor and the industrial working class, whereas in Italy it was the rural "backwards" peasantry that was in the worst dietary shape. In both nations, full employment and higher wages were the most significant factors in improving living standards. Rationing policies sought to make more food available to all. However, as price was still the limiting factor in working-class consumption, allowances for more expensive goods like meat did not make much difference if consumers could not afford a full ration. And as one history of British food policy points out, scientific experts still used calories to judge the adequacy of diet, so it was entirely possible that experts would not detect an actual decline in nutritional standards based on food substitution (Barnett 1985: 180–1).

In Great Britain and Italy, bread was never rationed but made available in varying weights and consistencies at different, sometimes subsidized, prices. Yet ensuring the availability of cheap bread, as a matter of wartime food policy, made a significant difference in working-class consumption habits. Not only were consumers able to stave off hunger with as much bread (barring occasional shortages) as they could eat, but subsidized bread freed up more of the household budget to purchase other necessity and non-necessity items. Non-necessity items in these cases were often modest: a few extra eggs, dairy products, coffee, or alcohol.

Moreover, even after the war had ended, the public furor ignited by the termination of the Italian bread subsidy in 1919 demonstrates that consumers had come to view cheap staple foods as an entitlement. The postwar bread riots and disturbances in Italy differed from those of earlier times; consumers still clamored for cheap bread, but they did so now in order to afford more coffee, tobacco, and wine (Helstosky 1996). Thus, food policies in Britain and Italy did not transform consumption habits among the lower classes all that dramatically, although there were subtle dietary changes that were significant for those who experienced them. The increased consumption of eggs and dairy products and of refined wheat-flour bread were critical indicators of an improved living standard.

Although the war's duration called for tightly organized systems of food controls, food policies in Europe progressed on a piecemeal basis, were sometimes chaotic in organization, and mixed private voluntarism with state bureaucracy. The aim was to ensure the health of the labor and military forces, and even in the absence of legal governments, as in the case of Belgium, a national committee (the *Comité national de secours et d'alimentation*) attempted to coordinate food aid at different levels to guard the welfare of Belgian labor and thus assure future economic security (Scholliers 1994: 40–1).

Whereas national governments coordinated food imports, requisitioning, and shipments of food out to military forces, municipal governments were usually the first to institute policies important for consumers. In Italy, the national government responded to, and coordinated, prefectoral initiatives on price ceilings, rationing, and domestic trade controls. In wartime Berlin, the municipal government acted to control commercial practice in the interests of consumers and preserving domestic order (Davis 1993).

If the implementation of consumer-oriented policies had its origins in local politics, however, such policies branched out into national politics after 1917, when war weariness on both sides demanded a greater equalization of experience within populations, especially in terms of resource sharing and sacrifice. The most commonly discussed example of the shift from producer-oriented, paternalistic policies to consumer-oriented ones has been that of Germany (Kocka 1984; Offer 1989; Davis 1993). Increasing civil annoyance with the uneven distribution of food led to bitter criticism of food policies and mechanisms of distribution. Consumers chafed at the Reich's calls for a domestic truce *(Burgfrieden)* when they perceived disparities in the distribution and acquisition of food between regions and classes. The hardships experienced during the "turnip winters" of 1917 and 1918 led to civil unrest and attacks on commercial middlemen and contributed to a more generalized criticism of governmental war aims and military policy (Kocka 1984: 53–4).

As the war dragged on, Allied governments paid increased attention to consumption issues, primarily to keep civilian workers content and productive. Moreover, because the Allies borrowed both money and food from the United States, some consideration had to be given to managing consumption in order to extend food supplies. Voluntary measures urging austerity were common; wartime ministries resorted to rationing only as a last resort. Austerity campaigns forged a new bond between citizens, particularly women, and government. Budget management and providing the family with a more nutritious diet were tasks that fell upon the housewife, whether or not she worked. During the war, "economy could now be urged upon the housewife all the more strongly because it was justified on social rather than private grounds" (Mennell 1984: 249). It is likely that propaganda slogans like "food wasted is another ship lost" publicly reinforced women's intermediary roles as food preparers and paved the way for future negotiations between state and housewife for provisioning responsibilities.

The amount of food that Allied nations were able

to conserve was never enough in the eyes of Herbert Hoover, U.S. Food Administrator after August 1917 (and later the director of U.S. relief efforts). Following the advice of his "diet squad" of American physiologists, Hoover suggested that Europeans do more to curtail consumption by reducing their intake and substituting foods (Offer 1989: 377). It was during the negotiations between U.S. food administrators and European officials that the idea of transforming scientific findings directly into food policies was debated.

The nutritional studies of American scientists claimed that a general reduction in calories lowered individual body weight and basal metabolism, leading to a more economical working of the body. Hoover and others urged a general reduction in food consumption in order to reduce Allied wheat consumption by one-fourth, thereby easing the wartime strain on U.S. grain stocks (Offer 1989: 378). The British Royal Society soundly rejected such a proposal, noting that any such policy of forced reduction would risk both industrial efficiency and political stability.

Wartime conditions brought about a contradictory situation with respect to popular diet. Although the salaries of workers rose to allow for increased consumption, shortages of supplies and pressure from the United States acted to deny it, and whether consumers were able to purchase more nutritious foods with their additional money is open to question. After the war, the Carnegie Foundation sponsored research that examined changes in living standards and food supplies that had occurred during the war. Authors of these books – mostly economists and agricultural experts – observed mixed results. Economist Riccardo Bachi's study of wartime Italy, for example, concluded that the war improved the nutritional quality of diet primarily because prewar consumption levels were so low (Bachi 1926). Italian physiologists, however, contradicted Bachi's findings, asserting that consumers used higher wages to purchase non-nutritive goods like tobacco, coffee, and wine, thus succumbing to what one scientist termed "alimentary sensualism" (D'Alfonso 1918: 28).

Dr. M. Demoor of Belgium's *Académie Royale de Médecine* rejected the possibility of any objective and scientific study of alimentation during the war: The incomplete documentation of living standards meant that nothing but speculation was possible (Henry 1924: 195). In France, the continuation of subsidized prices for special groups like pregnant women, families with more than two children, and the aged indicated that rations were still not adequate for all segments of the population (Augé-Laribé and Pinot 1927: 258-9). It is difficult, then, to generalize about the nutritional content of diet during and immediately after the war. There were few detailed monographs written on living standards, and those that were usually addressed the situation of workers in industrialized areas.

It is also difficult to generalize about the impact of state policy on food consumption habits, given the wide variation in national experience. Assessments of policy have as much to do with social scientific observations of living standards (which are sorely lacking in many cases) as they do with public perceptions of policy efficacy. Consumers in Germany, where essential foods were rationed and often unavailable, interpreted the effects of food policies far differently from the way that consumers did in Britain, where only sugar and meat were rationed and most goods were continuously available for purchase.

Despite the sometimes chaotic nature of food policy development, what seems clear is that European governments assumed a greater responsibility for civilian health over the course of the war. Whereas state intervention prior to the war was limited to the regulation of food distribution and assistance for the few, wartime policies sought to control the mechanisms of production, distribution, and consumption. The few scientific observations of changing living standards during the war, combined with the standardized nutritional recommendations of the Interallied Scientific Commission, led to an even greater awareness of dietary "averages" to be met as policy goals for the interwar period. There was no question that European governments had become more involved in matters of food consumption as a result of the war; the questions open for debate during the interwar period were whether intervention should continue and for what purposes.

The Interwar Years into World War II

Wartime consumption patterns – more dairy products, meat, fruits, and vegetables, as well as further increases in wheat consumption – were consolidated during the prosperous 1920s and reversed in the following decade of economic crisis. Generally, with the continued development of food processing and retailing in the interwar period, all social classes were enjoying a greater variety of foods. These included industrially created foods like margarine, breakfast cereals, preserves, and meat or fish pastes, along with canned fruits and vegetables. Scientific knowledge about food continued to advance, and vitamins as well as minerals were pronounced essential components of diet. Recommendations for caloric intake, however, fell slightly during this period because greater numbers of people were living more sedentary lifestyles.

Feeding populations at risk became more closely related to the promotion of commercial concerns. The "Milk for Schoolchildren" program in Britain, for example, was sponsored by the National Milk Publicity Council. Similarly, nutritional education programs for housewives and mothers, as well as domestic economy literature, counseled women to buy only standardized, commercial products they could trust (such as foods from Nestlé and Leibig or brand-name products such as Bovril or Kellogg's Corn Flakes). This was probably useful advice for many housewives, especially wherever consumers patronized local shops with less than ideal hygienic practices.

In terms of broader food policies, the most interesting changes in the interwar period reflected the wide-ranging turbulence created by competing systems of political economy. This was the era when both liberal democracies and authoritarian regimes alike took a greater interest in popular health, although their concerns manifested themselves differently. In Great Britain, dietary standards were debated in an effort to address chronic poverty, although, typically, the state ultimately balked at the idea of assuming broader powers of intervention. In Fascist Italy and Nazi Germany, by contrast, food production and consumption were more carefully controlled so that the dictatorships could successfully implement policies of greater economic self-sufficiency. The economic crisis of the 1930s sharpened both the impulse toward autarky and the debate over state responsibility for minimal versus optimal health.

In Great Britain, the publication of John Boyd-Orr's *Food, Health and Income* in 1936 and B. Seebohm Rowntree's *Poverty and Progress* in 1941 pushed the issues of dietary standards and civilian health into the political forefront. Boyd-Orr's study found that 10 percent of the working population during these depression years earned wages that were insufficient to purchase a nutritionally adequate regime. Moreover, he determined that half of the general population consumed a diet that satisfied hunger but was deficient in the nutrients that would maintain what he called optimal health (Boyd-Orr 1937: 8). Lower than optimal dietary standards, he believed, were a financial drain on the state, and he argued for greater state intervention in nutritional matters. Both the findings and the conclusions of Boyd-Orr, however, were roundly criticized in both political and scientific circles for having greatly exaggerated dietary deficiencies in the general population.

Politically, the debate focused on whether the state should work to ensure dietary improvements for all or simply continue protecting populations at risk, such as children. Fear of creeping socialism prevented drastic intervention, but both sides of the political spectrum agreed to focus on improving child nutrition, the left in the hopes of extending state welfare and the right because of eugenic concerns with degeneration (Oddy 1990: 276). The scientific debate over popular nutrition centered upon whether income or food preparation played a more important role in determining the nutritional quality of diet. Scientists were divided on whether malnutrition was a product of ignorance or insufficient income (Mayhew 1988: 450). Despite Boyd-Orr's calls for greater state involvement, responsibility for proper nutrition ultimately was shifted to consumers; as physiologist E. P. Cathcart of the University of Glasgow stated, "It has been our experience, as a result of repeated dietary studies, that one of the most prominent contributory factors toward defective and deficient dietaries is not so much the inadequacy of income as its faulty expenditure" (Pike 1985: 36).

Thus, Britain did not undertake more drastic measures to improve the overall quality of diet. Governmental involvement remained limited to the continued nutritional education of mothers, school feedings, and interventions to meet the needs of the economic crisis.

With economic and agricultural crisis also came more action from European governments to protect domestic agriculture. These interventions assumed the primary form of tariffs, and when tariffs alone were insufficient, the second line of defense consisted of import quotas and milling requirements for domestic grains. Great Britain abandoned laissez-faire agricultural policies by adopting import duties and creating marketing boards. France organized marketing boards for agricultural staples like wheat and wine; Denmark introduced domestic market supports; Nazi Germany instituted a comprehensive organization of production, marketing, and trade; Italy intensified domestic grain production and tightened controls over imports (Tracy 1989).

Such protectionist policies had indirect effects on food consumption habits in the sense that they made domestic staples like wheat more expensive. If staple goods came to occupy a greater portion of the household food budget, this meant that less money was available for the non-necessity items consumers had become accustomed to purchasing during and after the war.

The effect of economic policies on food consumption habits seems particularly important in light of the fact that an adequate standard of living was tied intimately to the promotion of economic and political systems. In Fascist Italy, for example, the regime founded the Committee to Study the Problem of Alimentation in 1928. One of the Committee's responsibilities was to organize, conduct, and publicize grand inquests into the living standard, in order to prove to the rest of the world that fascism as an economic system was leading the nation out of its backward status.

By contrast, sociologists in Belgium worked to measure the nutritional standard of the working classes and, as Peter Scholliers has observed, "[t]heir writings had ideological aims, stressing the fact that the capitalist system was, in the long run, capable of ensuring a decent standard of living for all people" (Scholliers 1992: 73). Although authoritarian regimes in Italy and Germany worked to exert tighter controls over food production, distribution, and consumption, the primary goal of such policies was not to improve nutritional standards. Rather, the motive was to ensure that populations could survive on less food, should there be another war or invasion.

The experience of World War II threw European governments back into the roles of providers and coordinators of food supplies. Rationing was implemented earlier and, because of the duration and severity of the conflict, was imposed on more food items than during the previous war. The struggle for adequate sustenance was a more difficult one in many areas, as exemplified by the extension of the black market in foodstuffs and the use of goods as viable currency throughout the continent. As in the case of World War I, European governments again acted out of expediency, making it difficult to ensure proper nutrition through a rationalized program of food controls. It would not be until after the war and well into the economic miracle Europeans experienced in the 1950s and 1960s that consumers in some nations would experience the culture of superabundance and confront for the first time the health problems associated with overconsumption.

Summary

State intervention in matters of nutrition during the nineteenth and early twentieth centuries in Europe can be characterized by a hesitancy and a reluctance to assume greater responsibilities for the overall health of the population. Governmental concern over popular diet had as much to do with mercantilist and militarist anxieties as it did with a growing public awareness about the importance of nutrition in building and maintaining health. Even when limited interventions – such as the feeding of schoolchildren – sought to safeguard the economic and military future of European nations, these actions were rooted in the voluntaristic paternalism that characterized charity in earlier periods. Pressure to guarantee optimal health for entire populations came mostly from the scientific and social-scientific communities, but it was only under wartime conditions that states acted with such broad measures to guarantee a minimal subsistence for all.

This is not to say, however, that state activities did not influence patterns of food consumption. Direct and indirect intervention in food markets affected the allocation of household budgets and therefore the nutritional composition of diets. Over the course of the nineteenth and early twentieth centuries, European governments demonstrated an increasing interest in safeguarding the health of populations through food consumption; but their limited range of activities demonstrates the political and economic constraints under which they functioned. Prior to the formation of the post-1945 welfare state, which ideally regarded optimal health as a right of citizenship, decisions to implement food policies as a means of building labor productivity, reducing mortality, or satisfying eugenic concerns depended upon economic and political circumstances as much as they did on the scientific knowledge of nutrition.

Carol F. Helstosky

Bibliography

Augé-Laribé, Michel, and Pierre Pinot. 1927. *Agriculture and food supply in France during the war.* New Haven, Conn.

Bachi, Riccardo. 1926. *L'alimentaztione e la politica annonaria in Italia.* Bari, Italy.

Barnett, L. Margaret. 1985. *British food policy.* Boston, Mass.

Boyd-Orr, John. 1937. *Food, health and income: Report on a survey of adequacy of diet in relation to income.* Second edition. London.

Burnett, John. 1966. *Plenty and want: A social history of diet in England from 1815 to the present day.* London.

    1994. The rise and decline of school meals in Britain, 1860–1990. In *The origins and development of food policies in Europe,* ed. J. Burnett and D. Oddy, 55–69. Leicester, England.

D'Alfonso, N. R. 1918. *Il problema dell'alimentazione come problema educativo.* Milan.

Davin, Anna. 1978. Imperialism and motherhood. *History Workshop Journal* 5: 222–49.

Davis, Belinda. 1993. Home fires burning: Politics, identity and food in World War I Berlin. Ph.D. thesis, University of Michigan.

den Hartog, Adel P. 1994. Feeding schoolchildren in the Netherlands: Conflict between state and family responsibilities. In *The origins and development of food policies in Europe,* ed. J. Burnett and D. Oddy, 70–89. Leicester, England.

Drummond, J. C., and Anne Wilbraham. 1939. *The Englishman's food: A history of five centuries of English diet.* London.

Engel, Ernst. 1895. *Die Lebenskosten belgischer Arbeiter-Familien früher und jetzt.* Dresden.

Hacking, Ian. 1990. *The taming of chance.* Cambridge and New York.

Helstosky, Carol. 1996. The politics of food in Italy from liberalism to fascism. Ph.D. thesis, Rutgers University.

Henry, Albert. 1924. *Le Ravitaillement de la Belgique pendant l'occupation Allemande.* Paris.

Horn, David G. 1994. *Social bodies: Science, reproduction and Italian modernity.* Princeton, N.J.

Hurt, John. 1985. Feeding the hungry schoolchild: The first half of the twentieth century. In *Diet and health in modern Britain,* ed. D. Oddy and D. Miller, 178–206. London.

Kocka, Jürgen. 1984. *Facing total war: German society, 1914–1918,* trans. B. Weinberger. Cambridge, Mass.

Mayhew, Madeleine. 1988. The 1930s nutrition controversy. *Journal of Contemporary History* 23:445–64.

Mennell, Stephen. 1985. *All manners of food: Eating and taste in England and France from the Middle Ages to the present.* London.

Oddy, Derek J. 1990. Food, drink and nutrition. In *The Cambridge social history of Britain, 1750–1950,* ed. F. M. L. Thompson, Vol. 2, 251–78. Cambridge and New York.

Offer, Avner. 1989. *The First World War. An agrarian interpretation.* Oxford.

Pike, Magnus. 1985. The impact of modern food technology

on nutrition in the twentieth century. In *Diet and health in modern Britain,* ed. D. Oddy and D. Miller, 32–45. London.

Porisini, Giorgio. 1979. *Agricoltura, alimentazione e condizioni sanitarie. Prime ricerche sulla pellagra in Italia dal 1880 al 1940.* Geneva.

Porter, Theodore M. 1986. *The rise of statistical thinking, 1820–1900.* Princeton, N.J.

Ross, Ellen. 1993. *Love and toil: Motherhood in outcast London, 1870–1918.* Oxford.

Scholliers, Peter. 1992. Historical food research in Belgium: Development, problems and results in the 19th and 20th centuries. In *European food history: A research review,* ed. H. J. Teuteberg, 71–89. Leicester, England.

  1994. The policy of survival: Food, the state and social relations in Belgium, 1914–1921. In *The origins and development of food policies in Europe,* ed. J. Burnett and D. Oddy, 39–53. Leicester, England.

Scientists and the world's food problems. 1918. *National Food Journal* 1: 492–4.

Shammas, Carol. 1990. *The pre-industrial consumer in England and America.* Oxford.

Steinmetz, George. 1993. *Regulating the social. The welfare state and local politics in imperial Germany.* Princeton, N.J.

Teuteberg, Hans J. 1975. The general relationship between diet and industrialization. In *European diet from pre-industry to modern times,* ed. E. Forster and R. Forster. New York.

  1994. Food adulteration and the beginnings of uniform food legislation in late nineteenth-century Germany. In *The origins and development of food policies in Europe,* ed. J. Burnett and D. Oddy, 146–60. Leicester, England.

Tracy, Michael. 1989. *Government and agriculture in western Europe, 1880–1988.* Third edition. New York.

Ward, Peter M. 1993. *Birth weight and economic growth. Women's living standards in the industrializing West.* Chicago.

Winter, J. M. 1980. Military fitness and civilian health in Britain during the First World War. *Journal of Contemporary History* 15: 211–44.

Zerboglio, Adolfo. 1897. *Le basi economiche della salute.* Alessandria, Italy.

Zimmerman, Carle C. 1936. *Consumption and standards of living.* New York.

VII.2 ❧ Food Entitlements

Throughout the world there is enough food to feed every human being. Yet hunger and malnutrition persist. "Food security" – that is, access to culturally acceptable nutriments, through normal channels, in quantities sufficient for daily life and work – should be among the most basic of universal human rights. Hunger, poverty, and marginalization are caused by political and economic forces and decisions, which result in entitlement failures that undermine food security at the household level.

Having enough to eat depends upon access to at least a minimum "floor" level of the means of subsistence. In one sense, human history may be viewed as a gradual expansion of a sense of responsibility for others, which helps to secure that minimum "floor" for ever-increasing numbers of people. The concept of an entitlement to subsistence for households within one's own clan has been accepted for ages. Such "food security" became available to citizens of Greece and Rome thousands of years ago and was extended to most Europeans beginning about 200 years ago (Kates and Millman 1990: 398–9).

In spite of this record of progress, however, hundreds of millions of people throughout the world suffer unnecessarily from hunger and malnutrition, and, although the proportion of hungry people is diminishing, their total number continues to grow. Between 1990 and 2000, the absolute number of hungry people was projected to continue to increase and then gradually decline to a level of about 3 percent of the world's population in 2050. "In the meantime, half of the world's women who carry the seeds of our future may be anemic, a third of the world's children may be wasted or stunted in body or mind, and perhaps a fifth of the world's people can never be sure of their daily bread, chapati, rice, tortilla, or ugali" (Kates and Millman 1990: 405). Today, some 1 billion children, women, and men daily confront chronic hunger and, consequently, the specters of starvation, undernutrition, deficiencies of iron, iodine, and vitamin A, and nutrient-depleting diseases (Kates 1996: 4–6).

Among the shades of hunger, starvation is the most arresting to the observer and receives major, if often belated, coverage by news media when it occurs. In the latter twentieth century, the plight of refugees in central Africa has been a current and recurrent example. Famine-related food shortages threaten roughly 1 percent of the world's population with starvation every year.

Undernutrition, the most widespread form of hunger, is especially dangerous for children. It affects their ability to grow, their cognitive development, and their susceptibility to illness. Even relatively mild "chronic undernutrition," the typical form of hunger in the United States, can permanently retard physical growth and brain development and can reduce the ability of children to concentrate and perform complex tasks.

Nutritional anemia (a condition in which a lack of dietary iron causes a shortage of red blood cells) can cause an impaired capacity for work and intellectual performance as well as a decreased resistance to disease and an increased susceptibility to lead poisoning. Nearly one-fifth of pregnant women in the United States suffer from this condition.

A lack of vitamin A in the diet permanently blinds 250,000 children throughout the world each year and increases the chances that millions more will suffer from the three leading child killers – diarrheal disease, measles, and pneumonia. Iodine deficiency results in the birth of 120,000 brain-damaged children annually; millions more grow up stunted, listless, mentally retarded, or incapable of normal speech, hearing, or both. In addition, nutrient-depleting diseases such as diarrhea, measles, malaria, and parasitic infestations prevent millions of people from fully benefiting from the nutrients contained in the nutriments they do manage to take in.

Rights, Entitlements, and the Right to Food

Virtually every society develops a social compact – a set of values and behavior standards – that defines the rights and responsibilities of its members. From the sixteenth through the early nineteenth centuries, survival was considered in European societies to be largely an individual or family-based responsibility, with food and other necessities procured through work. But assistance was available for some of those not able to achieve self-reliance through work, and the various European nations enacted strikingly similar laws that separated needy people into two distinct categories – those who were deemed worthy and those considered unworthy of public aid.

In England, for example, only children, the blind, the disabled, and those elderly persons who could not work were thought worthy of relief under the Poor Laws. Destitute but able-bodied unemployed persons risked savage treatment at the hands of local authorities. They could be consigned indefinitely to workhouses or prisons. Adults and children were severely punished, sometimes even executed, for stealing food (Dobbert 1978: 187).

Today, in the United States and other industrialized countries, able-bodied persons are expected to earn their livelihoods. Often, there is debate over the extent to which the state should meet the needs of those who cannot work – whether because of age, or physical or mental infirmity, or because jobs paying a livable wage are unavailable. For some who cannot attain self-reliance through work, the condition is temporary, and only transitional support is needed. For others, age or infirmity makes the attainment of self-reliance unrealistic; these persons require lasting support.

Human Rights

Human rights are "enforceable claims on the delivery of goods, services, or protection by others" – meaning that people in need can insist upon the delivery of assistance, with recourse, if necessary, to legal or moral enforcement of their demand (Eide, Oshaug, and Eide 1991: 426). Such rights are based on social obligations that are accepted by all persons without reference to distinctions of race, gender, nationality, language, religion, or socioeconomic class. Human rights may be promulgated globally but must be implemented locally within nationally determined limits (Barker 1991: 105, 203; Eide et al. 1991: 415).

Some analysts separate such rights into two categories: civil/political rights and social/economic/ cultural rights. Civil and political rights are basic "rights recognized in democratic constitutions, such as life, liberty, and personal security; freedom from arbitrary arrest, detention, or exile; the right to fair and public hearings by impartial tribunals; freedom of thought, conscience, and religion; and freedom of peaceful association" (Barker 1991: 105). Social, economic, and cultural rights include "the right to work, education, and social security; to participate in the cultural life of the community; ... to share in the benefits of scientific advancement and the arts" (Barker 1991: 105), *and the right to eat.*

The protection of vulnerable groups, such as the poor, those with handicaps, and endangered indigenous peoples, is a major aim of social, economic, and cultural rights. Taking these rights seriously requires grappling with issues of social integration, solidarity, equality, and distribution of wealth. Perhaps as a consequence, although civil and political rights have received considerable attention, social, economic, and cultural rights have been relatively neglected at both the international and national levels (Eide and Rosas 1995: 17).

Those who separate human rights into two distinct categories argue that civil and political rights emphasize "freedom from" state interference; they are absolute, are immediately realizable at little financial cost to governments, and are capable of being adjudicated in court. In contrast, social, economic, and cultural rights are seen as claims on the state for protection and assistance; these are relative to the circumstances of one's society, are only gradually realizable at substantial financial cost to governments, and are dependent upon politics rather than the courts for such realization. Other analysts, however, view the two categories of rights as interrelated and as addressing "different aspects of the same three basic concerns: integrity, freedom, and equality of all human beings" (Eide 1995a: 21–2; Eide and Rosas 1995: 17).

Humans require basic necessities such as food, clothing, and housing (depending on the cultural conditions in which they live) to enable them to participate fully – without shame or unreasonable obstacles – in the everyday life of their communities. The right to a standard of living that supports such participation is, therefore, a basic social right (Eide 1995b: 90).

The three major components of such a standard of living are adequate food, care, and the prevention and control of disease. As a basic social right, this standard of living is a necessary foundation for an effective social compact, but it is not a solely sufficient one, as the compact must also provide for other social, economic, and cultural rights, as well as for civil and political rights. Thus, the right to adequate food is an essential – and perhaps the most important – building block in the foundation of a satisfactory social compact.

"Adequate food" means that every household can depend upon the availability of a stable supply of culturally acceptable, uncontaminated, good-quality food, which provides all necessary energy, nutrients, and micronutrients (such as vitamins and iodine). Food adequacy implies economic and social (as well as environmental) sustainability, which entails access to food through a combination of fair wealth distribution and effective markets, together with various forms (public and private, formal and informal) of supports and "safety nets" (Eide 1995b: 90–1).

According to the United Nations Administrative Committee on Co-ordination, Subcommittee on Nutrition, "care is the provision in the household and the community of time, attention and support to meet the physical, mental and social needs of the growing child and other family members" (Eide 1995b: 91). Such care implies, among other things, access to primary health care, protection from infection, medical assistance during illness, and assistance to meet the needs of disability and old age. Adequate care is necessary for everyone but is especially important for vulnerable groups such as young children, pregnant and lactating women, and the elderly (Eide 1995b: 91–3).

Adequate prevention and control of disease is essential to a satisfactory standard of living because of the close connection between disease and malnutrition. Therefore, immunization and breast-feeding campaigns, oral rehydration child survival programs, nutrition education, sanitation programs, and the like are important contributions to living standards (Eide 1995b: 93).

Entitlements and "Entitlement Failure"

An entitlement is a societal obligation to provide support as a right when people have insufficient resources to live in conditions of health and decency (Melnick 1994: 54–6). Entitlement to food is the ability to command food through the various forms of exchange relationships to which one has access (Sen 1981). Amartya Sen describes three basic forms of food entitlement: "(a) access to resources to collect or to produce food, (b) the exchange of resources (property, money, labor power) for food, and (c) the receipt of gifts or grants of food or the resources to procure food" (Sen 1981; Kates and Millman 1990: 397). An entitlement approach to food security "requires a shift in thinking from *what exists?* to *who can command what?*" (Eide 1995b: 95).

Many other rights interact with and affect the entitlement to food. The right to property supports the right to food both because ownership of land makes it possible to grow food and because ownership of assets makes it possible to produce items that can be exchanged for food. As property is often unevenly distributed, the right to work at a living wage is directly related to the right to the income necessary to purchase food, and, of course, the right to work is in turn affected by the right to an education. If a person lacks property and is unable to work because of age, disability, illness, lack of skill or training, scarcity of appropriate jobs, or because available work does not pay a living wage, a right to social security becomes necessary to secure access to food (Eide 1995b: 95–6).

Sen's three basic forms of entitlement have not changed over time. What has changed "is the mix: from a primary emphasis on household self-provision, to slave, servant, or serf status where labor is appropriated in return for minimal entitlement, to market exchange of labor and production, and most recently to the development of extensive safety-nets of food security" (Kates and Millman 1990: 398).

Sen's conceptualization of "entitlement failure" (Sen 1981; Drèze and Sen 1990a, 1990b, 1990c, 1991) has provided a powerful analytical tool with which to understand and intervene in the political economy of hunger. Most important, the concept helps avoid the pitfall of assuming that per capita food supplies that on average seem adequate will result in universal food security. Just as it is possible to drown in a stream that averages only an inch deep, it is possible to starve in a world, nation-state, region, or even household in which there is a seemingly sufficient average food supply.

When some people thrive but others do not – whether in the presence of food or faced with food shortages – one must ask *why* some have access to sufficient food and thrive, whereas others, lacking access, sicken or die. For Sen, "entitlement failure" is the central cause of hunger, starvation, and famine. People suffer malnutrition and die of starvation because of an inability to claim access to sufficient food resources to meet their nutritional needs. Such entitlement failure is a consequence of choices made publicly and privately at the international, national, state, community, and household levels.

Household Food Security

For a right to food to have meaning, it must be implemented where food is actually consumed, by individuals at the household level. The presence of food supplies in a nation or region is no guarantee of food security if households lack access to them. Household food security depends upon a household's "access to a basket of food which is nutritionally adequate, safe, and culturally acceptable, procured in a manner consistent with the satisfaction also of other basic human needs, and obtained from supplies, and in ways, which are sustainable over time" (Eide et al. 1991: 455).

Even if a household has access to a supply of food that, if equitably shared, could meet the needs of all of its members, that food may or may not be available according to individual needs. In many societies, for example, men and boys eat first, and women and girls wait to eat whatever the males leave.

Strategies for Food Security

Jean Drèze and Sen (1990a: 22–6) describe two contemporary strategies for replacing persistent want and hunger with food security: "growth-mediated security" and "support-led security." Growth-mediated security is based upon rapid economic expansion, with benefits shared through new jobs and higher wages, and use of growth-generated resources "to expand public support of health, nutrition, education, and economic security for the more deprived and vulnerable" (Drèze and Sen 1990a: 22). The "trickle-down" economics promoted by some politicians in the United States and the structural adjustment policies promulgated by the World Bank and the International Monetary Fund both assume the creation of growth-mediated benefits, but whether such benefits are shared with poor and marginalized people is a matter of public policy choices.

By contrast, support-led security involves providing "public support measures without waiting for the country to become rich through economic growth" (Drèze and Sen 1990a: 24). China, Sri Lanka, Costa Rica, Cuba, Chile, Jamaica, and the state of Kerala in India are all examples of governments that have followed the support-led strategy with considerable benefit to marginalized citizens.

Although there is a significant difference between the two approaches, public support plays an important role in each. "Indeed, in the absence of public involvement to guarantee that the fruits of growth are widely shared, rapid economic growth" can have a negative impact on the entitlements that secure sufficient food and other necessities of life. It is, according to Drèze and Sen (1990a: 26), essential to replace "unaimed opulence" with growth benefits targeted to the needs of the marginalized.

Moreover, Asbjørn Eide has argued that it is a mistake to assume that governments must have the primary responsibility to provide food to needy people through costly, potentially overgrown state bureaucracies. Instead, governments should work to maximize the capability of individuals to provide food for themselves and their households through their own resources and efforts (Eide 1995a: 36–8). This goal involves three levels of obligation. First, governments must respect individual freedoms and resources; for example, government actions to ensure the land rights of endangered indigenous peoples and to clarify smallholders' titles to their land enable such people to maximize self-reliance and their ability to earn an adequate living. Second, governments must protect the rights of less-powerful people against more powerful interests that may exploit them and reduce their ability to be self-reliant. Third, when no other possibilities exist, governments must fulfill rights by direct action, such as providing for basic needs through programs of food aid or social security (Eide 1995a: 36–8).

The Evolution of an International Entitlement to Food

The development of a right to food is the culmination of several centuries of struggle to affirm human rights and then extend them to people without property,

such as former slaves, and women. The human rights from which the right to food has emerged are grounded in the philosophy of John Locke and Jean-Jacques Rousseau, in the 1690–1 British Bill of Rights, in the 1776 U.S. Declaration of Independence, and in the 1779 French Declaration on the Rights of Man and the Citizen (Dobbert 1978).

Until World War II, international law provided no basis for a right to food. The right could be claimed only by groups such as members of the armed forces (entitled to food in exchange for their willingness to fight) or the inmates of penitentiaries, almshouses, and similar public institutions, who were prevented from self-provision. Attitudes toward human rights, however, were fundamentally altered by the events surrounding World War II. The acute food shortages experienced by war-torn countries in Europe and elsewhere led to the emergence of the concept of a right to food as a universal right (Dobbert 1978: 188–9).

In 1941, in his well-known "Four Freedoms" State of the Union address, U.S. President Franklin D. Roosevelt introduced the concept of "freedom from want" into modern political discourse. Later that year, the Atlantic Charter – framed by Roosevelt and British Prime Minister Winston Churchill – called for international economic collaboration to secure "improved labor standards, economic advancement and social security" for all. Finally, in his 1944 State of the Union message, Roosevelt proposed an international "Economic Bill of Rights" recognizing that "true individual freedom cannot exist without economic security and independence." "People," he said, "who are hungry and out of a job are the stuff of which dictatorships are made" (Eide 1995a: 29).

International Conventions and Covenants

The Universal Declaration of Human Rights (UDHR), adopted by the General Assembly of the United Nations (UN) on December 10, 1948, is the foundation upon which efforts to realize an international right to food are based. In order to foster global freedom and democracy, the UDHR envisions worldwide human rights – to be monitored internationally and implemented nationally – for all people. Article 25(1) anticipates the right to food: "Everyone has the right to a standard of living adequate for the health and well-being of himself and his family, including food, clothing, housing and medical care and necessary social services" (Dobbert 1978: 192).

The UN Commission on Human Rights, which drafted the declaration, could not obtain the agreement of the United States and other nations of the industrial West to include both civil/political and social/economic/cultural rights in a single, legally binding convention. But subsequently, in 1966, 18 years after the promulgation of the UDHR, separate international covenants on civil/political rights and social/economic/cultural rights were adopted by the

UN General Assembly (Eide and Rosas 1995: 15). By 1995, 120 nations had ratified the international Covenant on Civil and Political Rights (CCPR).

The evolution of the international Covenant on Economic, Social and Cultural Rights (CESCR) has been more controversial. Article 11 contains the language most relevant to a right to food. By 1957, when most of the substantive language of the CESCR had been accepted, Article 11 stated simply that the nations party to the covenant "recognize the right of everyone to adequate food, clothing and housing" (Dobbert 1978: 191). In 1964, following a call by Dr. B. R. Sen, Director-General of the Food and Agriculture Organization of the United Nations, for a strengthening of the covenant, compromise language was adopted providing for a right to an adequate standard of living based on universal subsistence rights to adequate food and nutrition, clothing, housing, and necessary conditions of care (Dobbert 1978: 191–4). By 1995, the CESCR had been ratified by 118 nations. But although the U.S. government signed the covenant in 1976, it had still not been ratified by the U.S. Senate some 20 years later.

The actual enjoyment of these theoretically universal social, economic, and cultural rights still eludes many people throughout the world. Nevertheless, paying at least "lip service" to them provides an opportunity for advocates in all countries to press for their extension and implementation.

The Role of Intergovernmental Organizations

Several intergovernmental organizations (IGOs) have played important roles related to food security and contributed significantly to the conceptual evolution of a right to food but have been less successful in ensuring its realization. These include the Food and Agriculture Organization of the UN (FAO), the World Food Programme (WFP), the World Food Council (WFC), the International Fund for Agricultural Development (IFAD), the United Nations International Children's Emergency Fund (UNICEF), and the UN's World Health Organization (WHO) (Eide et al. 1991: 437–8).

The Food and Agriculture Organization was conceived during World War II and established in 1945, before the war ended. After the war, FAO made its headquarters in Rome, housed in the offices from which Italian dictator Benito Mussolini had hoped to rule an empire. The organization functions as a clearinghouse for scientific information on food and agriculture, but when it addresses structural causes of hunger, such as regulation of the world grain trade or issues of land reform, FAO risks conflict with its sponsoring governments.

FAO's role in promoting the right to food has varied from virtual inactivity to strong support, depending upon the bent of its directors. Although it was not until 1965 that the preamble to the FAO Constitution was amended to include "humanity's freedom from hunger," FAO played an important role in strengthening the CESCR. It was instrumental, too, in founding the World Food Programme and in initiating the 1974 International Undertaking on World Food Security, which recognized (paragraph I.1) "that the assurance of world food security is a common responsibility of the entire international community." In addition, the FAO worked to create the 1975 Food Security Assistance program to help developing countries implement national food-stock and reserve programs and was important in negotiating the nonbinding World Food Security Compact in 1985 (Tomasevski 1987; Eide et al. 1991). In 1996, FAO sponsored the International Food Summit in Rome.

The World Food Programme was founded by FAO and the United Nations in 1961. The WFP administers the food aid pledged by members of the United Nations for emergencies and development projects. When administered with careful attention to its effects on exchange entitlements, food aid can be very successful; by contrast, poorly targeted food aid can wreak havoc on entitlement relationships. The WFP has stressed the right to food "as the most fundamental of human rights, and a precondition to development" (Eide et al. 1995: 442–3).

The World Food Conference in Rome (held from November 5 to 16, 1974) focused global attention on the idea that hunger and malnutrition are solvable problems. It adopted the Universal Declaration on the Eradication of Hunger and Malnutrition, which proclaimed: "Every man, woman, and child has the inalienable right to be free from hunger and malnutrition in order to fully develop and maintain their physical and mental facilities" (Tomasevski 1987: 343). The declaration set a goal of eliminating hunger worldwide within 10 years and was subsequently endorsed by the UN General Assembly. Further activities intended to implement the declaration and the 22 resolutions of the conference included the establishment of the World Food Council, the FAO Committee on World Food Security, the International Fund for Agricultural Development, and the United Nations Administrative Committee on Co-ordination, Sub-Committee on Nutrition (ACC/SCN) (Tomasevski 1987).

The World Food Council was established by the UN General Assembly in December 1974 to coordinate the work of UN agencies related to "food production, nutrition, food security, food trade and food aid" (Tomasevski 1987: 346–7). In 1977, the WFC adopted the Manila Communiqué, an action program to eliminate hunger and malnutrition, and in 1979, it adopted the Mexico Declaration, which proposed, among other things, that countries "consider practical ways and means to achieve a more equitable distribution of income and economic resources so as to ensure that food production increases result in a more equitable pattern of food consumption" (Tomasevski 1987: 39–40). The ability of the WFC to serve as the UN's conscience on food security is, however, limited by its practice of operating on consensus, which precludes serious consideration of the more radical structural analyses offered by various country-groups. The WFC Secretariat has shown only moderate interest in promoting legal approaches to the right to food (Eide et al. 1991: 415).

The International Fund for Agricultural Development was established in 1976 with initial funding of $1 billion for programs to increase food production, reduce rural poverty, and improve nutrition in developing countries. IFAD gives priority to the poorest food-deficient countries and attempts to strengthen the entitlements of small and landless farmers. IFAD, then, is the IGO that works directly to reduce poverty among the most severely marginalized groups. Food security is now a major focus of its work.

The United Nations International Children's Emergency Fund was established in 1946 to promote health, education, and social services for children in developing countries and is actively employing in its work the Convention on the Rights of the Child (CRC), which was adopted by the UN General Assembly in November 1989. The CRC addresses rights to health (Article 24) and to social security (Article 25), whereas Article 27 recognizes "the right of every child to a standard of living adequate for the child's physical, mental, spiritual, moral and social development." The 1990 World Summit for Children sponsored by UNICEF to promote the CRC was attended by more than 70 heads of state, and by 1995, the convention had been ratified by 150 nations (Eide 1995a and 1985b). Until then, the United States was the sole major nonsignatory of the convention, and although the U.S. government at last signed the CRC (as a memorial to UNICEF executive director James Grant), it had not yet ratified the document by the end of the following year.

The World Health Organization, in response to worldwide activism against the irresponsible marketing of infant formulas, has worked to create awareness of infants' right to adequate nutrition. Its Code of Marketing of Breast Milk Substitutes was adopted by the World Health Assembly in 1981.

U.S.-Based Nongovernmental Organizations

During the 1970s and 1980s, a growing public awareness of the problem of hunger resulted in the establishment of a large number of antihunger nongovernmental organizations (NGOs). National and international NGOs based in the United States that have played substantial roles in the struggle to develop food security or the right to food include Oxfam America, Food for the Hungry, and the Campaign for Human Development (founded in 1970); Bread for the World (1974); Food First and World Hunger Year (1975); World Hunger Education Service (1976); the Hunger Project (1977); and Results (1980).

By 1985, the more economically developed countries supported an estimated 2,000 NGOs – mostly

focused on development and self-help – throughout the world. Some were quite large; World Vision, for example, had 750,000 subscribers and raised an international budget of $300 million annually. Catholic Relief Services had a 1990 budget of $220 million, CARE $294 million, Lutheran World Relief $49 million, and Church World Service $43 million (Beckman and Hoehn 1992: 20–1).

Millions of U.S. residents have participated in episodic, short-term, hunger-relief activities in response to famines – such as aid concerts, "Hands across America," and the like (Millman et al. 1990: 326). In 1991, for example, "334,580 people participated in Church World Service 'CROP Walks' to raise money for anti-hunger efforts" (Beckman and Hoehn 1992: 15–18).

Development aid from the governments of developed countries increased from $7 billion to $48.1 billion between 1970 and 1988. "But most of this 'aid' is tied to political and commercial interests of the Northern governments, and often hurts rather than helps poor people in Southern hemisphere countries" (Beckman and Hoehn 1992: 22). Although the majority of U.S.-based NGOs focus on relief or development activities, Bread for the World and Results have mobilized substantial grass-roots constituencies lobbying for changes in U.S. public policy that will support food security.

Bread for the World (BFW) is an interdenominational Christian organization in the United States with about 40,000 members. BFW members lobby the U.S. Congress on policies that affect domestic and global hunger. In 1974, BFW mobilized its members to pressure the U.S. Congress to enact a "Right-to-Food Resolution." (H.R. 737 was passed in the U.S. House of Representatives with a vote of 340 to 61; S.R. 138 was passed in the U.S. Senate by voice vote.) The resolution by the House stated the sense of Congress as follows:

(1) the United States reaffirms the right of every person at home and abroad to food and a nutritionally adequate diet;
(2) the need to combat hunger shall be a fundamental point of reference in the formulation and implementation of United States policy in all areas that bear on hunger;
(3) the United States should seek to improve domestic food assistance programs for Americans in need, to ensure that all eligible recipients have the chance to obtain a nutritionally adequate diet;
(4) the United States should increase substantially its assistance for self-help development among the poorest people of the world with particular emphasis on increasing food production and encouraging improved food distribution and more equitable patterns of economic growth; this

assistance should be coordinated with expanded efforts by international organizations, donor nations, and recipient countries to provide a nutritionally adequate diet for all. (U.S. House of Representatives 1976b)

Among its lobbying efforts, BFW has led successful attempts to increase U.S. allocations for intergovernmental child survival programs that save millions of lives annually. Through its Transforming the Politics of Hunger project, BFW is encouraging those in the voluntary feeding movement to take a more active role in affecting governmental antihunger policy (Beckman and Hoehn 1992).

The Results organization is a hard-headed, policy-focused spin-off of the Hunger Project begun in 1977, which seeks "to empower people to take actions against hunger" (Millman et al. 1990: 327). By 1987, the Hunger Project claimed to have enrolled more than 5 million members in 152 countries (Millman et al. 1990: 327). Mobilization efforts by Results have included generating support in the United States and several other countries for the World Summit for Children and the Convention on the Rights of the Child.

International Nongovernmental Efforts

There are several international efforts to strengthen and implement the right to food that should be mentioned. An October 1981 meeting – organized in Gran, Norway, by the United Nations University – resulted in the 1984 publication of *Food As a Human Right* (Eide et al. 1984). The book emphasized (p. ix) that human food supplies are "filtered through socioeconomic processes which deny an adequate supply of food to many while delivering a large over-dose to a 'lucky' few" and that meaningful intervention "will probably require deep structural changes" that will generate conflict.

The World Institute for Development Economics Research (WIDER) was established by the United Nations University in 1984. The following year, it began its program, "Hunger and Poverty: The Poorest Billion," and in 1986, it sponsored (in Helsinki) a Food Strategies Conference to identify feasible opportunities for affecting world hunger. The conference pursued an entitlement approach emphasizing public intervention to improve literacy rates, life expectancy, and infant mortality in low-income nations. Follow-up activities to the WIDER conference included publication of the three-volume work *The Political Economy of Hunger* (Drèze and Sen 1990a, 1990b, 1990c).

In June 1984, the Right to Food Project of the Netherlands Institute for Human Rights (SIM), with cosponsorship by the Norwegian Human Rights Project, brought together "42 lawyers, nutritionists, and development experts, from all parts of the world, and from both nongovernmental and intergovernmental organizations" (Alston and Tomasevski 1984:

215). Participants in the conference, "The Right to Food: From Soft to Hard Law," criticized discussions of world hunger as frequently oversimplified. Instead of being defined simply in terms of calorie/protein requirements, hunger, they contended, should be analyzed "in terms of economic, social, political, cultural, and other structural factors, which deprive some people of access to land, work and food" (Alston and Tomasevski 1984: 217). A wide range of discussions focused on causes (for example, land tenure and access to work and food), rather than on manifestations, of hunger. The conference proceedings were published as *The Right to Food*, which attempted, "for the first time, to make hunger a prominent issue on the human rights agenda and to put the right to food on the agenda of national and international human rights agencies" (Alston and Tomasevski 1984: 7).

The SIM conference called for a translation of the "soft law" norms of human rights into "hard law" capable of adjudication. Conferees proposed monitoring the implementation of the right to food through (1) an international system based on cooperation among the relevant UN agencies, (2) a redesign of the CESCR reporting system, and (3) an NGO network using an Amnesty International–style "mobilization of shame" approach (Alston and Tomasevski 1984: 220). The greatest need, according to the SIM conferees, was for:

a network of support by and among NGOs which would include the mobilization of other private sector groups such as professional organizations of lawyers and doctors and churches in the fight against hunger. This network could strengthen existing NGOs, building and using human rights law and developing a concrete, realistic program of action on the right to food. (Alston and Tomasevski 1984: 220)

Five years later, in 1989, "a group of 24 planners, practitioners, opinion leaders, and scientists," brought to Bellagio, Italy, by the World Hunger Program of Brown University, adopted "The Bellagio Declaration: Overcoming Hunger in the 1990s." Its signers represented national or international agencies, organizations, universities, and research institutes in 14 countries, both northern and southern.

Whereas some advocates approach ending hunger incrementally, and others envision more fundamental structural changes, the Bellagio Declaration sought a "common middle ground" in which half of the world's hunger could be ended in a decade by appropriately applying the "better and the best" of current programs throughout the world. The Bellagio strategy included: (1) eliminating deaths from famine, (2) ending hunger in half of the poorest households, (3) cutting malnutrition in half for mothers and small children, and (4) eradicating iodine and vitamin A deficiencies (Kates and Millman 1990).

In December 1992, preceding the International Conference on Nutrition in Rome, a Task Force on Children's Nutrition Rights was established under the aegis of the World Alliance on Nutrition and Human Rights. The task force encouraged national workshops "designed to launch locally-based long-term campaigns to strengthen children's nutrition rights, giving attention to both their articulation in the law and the effective implementation of that law." Workshops were held in Guatemala and Mexico in 1993 and are being planned in several additional countries (Kent 1993a).

The Task Force on Children's Nutrition Rights is collaborating with the Foodfirst Information and Action Network (FIAN), an "international human rights organization for the right to feed oneself" (Kent 1993b: 10), which has chapters in several countries. At the June 1993 World Conference on Human Rights in Vienna, FIAN took the lead in advocating an optional protocol for the CESCR that would empower individuals to bring human rights complaints to the UN Committee on Economic, Social, and Cultural Rights (Kent 1993b).

In the 1990s, poor weather conditions reduced world grain reserves to a perilously low level and caused the price of grain to rise. Although this was a boon to farmers in grain-exporting countries like the United States, it played havoc with the economies of grain-importing countries throughout the developing world. Concurrently, total annual commitments of external assistance to agriculture in developing countries fell from about $16 billion in 1988 to about $10.7 billion in 1993.

Prompted by widespread food insecurity, the FAO made plans for the World Food Summit in Rome in 1996 to deal with problems of hunger and malnutrition. The summit, the first global conversation in 22 years that was focused specifically on food and hunger adopted the Declaration on World Food Security and Plan of Action, which reaffirmed the right to be free from hunger through universal access to safe and nutritious food and pledged to reduce the number of hungry people to 400 million by the year 2015.

The retreat from the 1974 World Food Conference goal of ending hunger worldwide in 10 years to the 1996 World Food Summit goal of reducing hunger by half in 20 years reflected diminished support by the United States and other developed countries for a legal right to food. During the two years of negotiations on the 1996 summit documents, U.S. representatives repeatedly expressed concern that a right to food could expose producing countries to lawsuits and trade complaints from the developing world. In opposition to the 1996 declaration, the U.S. delegation to the summit contended that the right to food is only an "aspiration" that creates no international obligation for governments.

Entitlement Failure: And the Right to Food

In light of this chapter's recitation of the resolutions, conventions, declarations, protocols, visions, and down-to-earth efforts of IGOs and NGOs to nurture recognition of the right to food and to implement food security, one might be tempted to ask why hunger and malnutrition persisted as the twentieth century came to a close. Is there any reason for hope that the right to food will become as commonly accepted as, say, entitlement to public education, and that the global right to food will become as commonly accepted as civil and political rights? Where must we go from here in order to attain the basic social justice reflected in a universal, implementable right to food security?

To speak only about the United States, the challenge seems especially daunting during a time in which public programs are under attack. Even with the present food-security safety net relatively intact, 4 million U.S. children under age 12 experience hunger, and every year another 9.6 million are at risk of hunger. In fact, 29 percent of U.S. children live in families that experience food shortage problems year after year (FRAC 1995: v–vi), and poor children in the United States have less access to food than poor children in 15 other industrial nations (Bradsher 1995). The U.S. welfare "reform" legislation of 1996, which replaced the entitlement to public assistance of families with dependent children with a time-limited, work-based program, might well push more than 1 million additional children below the U.S. poverty threshold.

The human costs of slow progress are great. The demise of hunger is not guaranteed. But hunger can be ended, if we choose. R. W. Kates and Sara Millman (1990: 404) describe the progress that has been made and the challenges we still face:

> In global terms, there is enough food to go around. In the 1960s the earth passed the first threshold of theoretical food sufficiency (enough to provide a near-vegetarian diet for all if distributed according to need) and [is] approaching a second threshold of improved diet sufficiency (enough to provide 10 percent animal products). But we are still a long way from a third threshold of a full but healthy diet with the choices available in industrialized nations. Projecting world food demand, under alternative assumptions of both diet and population growth, indicates that nearly three times the present level of production might be required for an improved diet and almost five times for a full, but healthy, diet, some 60 years from now.

In other words, there is cause for hope. Reduced contributions for development aid will harm, yet not cripple, development efforts. The dramatic strengthening of civil society in some developing countries is one of the major causes for hope.

Moreover, there is a deep-seated tradition in a number of the industrialized nations of caring for one's poorer neighbors. Widespread public opinion in the United States holds that no one should go hungry. Perhaps BFW and its antihunger-movement allies will succeed in transforming the politics of hunger and in energizing the feeding movement to affect the direction of national aid policies. A reenergized, populist, antihunger movement throughout the world, armed with appreciation of entitlement failure as the key to understanding the political economy of hunger, may yet succeed in transforming "soft" concern about hunger into the "hard law" of an enforceable, adjudicatory right to food.

William H. Whitaker

An earlier version of this chapter was presented at the Fourth International Convention in Social Work, "Redesigning the Future: New Answers in Response to Current Challenges," Universidad Nacional Autónoma de México, Escuela Nacional de Trabajo Social, October 2–4, 1996, Mexico City.

Bibliography

Alston, P., and Katarina Tomasevski. 1984. *The right to food.* The Hague.
Barker, R. L. 1991. *The social work dictionary.* Second edition. Washington, D.C.
Beckman, D., and Richard Hoehn. 1992. *Transforming the politics of hunger.* Washington, D.C.
Bradsher, Keith. 1995. Low ranking for poor American children: U.S. youth among worst off in study of 18 industrialized nations. *The New York Times,* August 14, p. A9.
Dobbert, J. P. 1978. Right to food. In *The right to health as a human right,* ed. René-Jean Dupuy, 184–213. The Hague.
Drèze, Jean, and Amartya Sen. 1990a. *The political economy of hunger.* Vol. 1, *Entitlement and well-being.* Oxford.
   1990b. *The political economy of hunger.* Vol. 2, *Famine prevention.* Oxford.
   1990c. *The political economy of hunger.* Vol. 3, *Endemic hunger.* Oxford.
   1991. Public action for social security: Foundations and strategies. In *Social security in developing countries,* ed. E. Ahmad, J. Drèze, J. Hills, and A. Sen, 1–40. Oxford.
Eide, Asbjørn. 1995a. Economic, social and cultural rights as human rights. In *Economic, social, and cultural rights: A textbook,* ed. A. Eide, C. Krause, and A. Rosas, 21–40. Boston, Mass.
   1995b. The right to an adequate standard of living including the right to food. In *Economic, social, and cultural rights: A textbook,* ed. A. Eide, C. Krause, and A. Rosas, 89–105. Boston, Mass.
Eide, A., W. B. Eide, S. Goonatilake, et al., eds. 1984. *Food as a human right.* Tokyo.
Eide, A., A. Oshaug, and W. B. Eide. 1991. Food security and the right to food in international law and development. *Transnational Law and Contemporary Problems* 1: 415–67.
Eide, A., and Allan Rosas. 1995. Economic, social, and cultural rights: A universal challenge. In *Economic, social, and cultural rights: A textbook,* ed. A. Eide, C. Krause, and A. Rosas, 15–19. Boston, Mass.
Food Research and Action Center (FRAC). 1995. *Community childhood hunger identification project: A survey of childhood hunger in the United States.* Washington, D.C.
Hellman, J. A. 1994. *Mexican lives.* New York.
Kates, R. W. 1996. Ending hunger: Current status and future prospects. *Consequences* 2: 3–11.
Kates, R. W., and Sara Millman. 1990. On ending hunger: The lessons of history. In *Hunger in history: Food shortage, poverty, and deprivation,* ed. L. F. Newman, 389–407. Cambridge, Mass.
Kent, George. 1993a. Children's right to adequate nutrition. *International Journal of Children's Rights* 1: 133–54.
   1993b. Nutrition and human rights (United Nations Administrative Committee on Coordination, Subcommittee on Nutrition [SCN]). *SCN News* 10: 9–12.
Melnick, R. Shep. 1994. *Between the lines: Interpreting welfare rights.* Washington, D.C.
Messer, Ellen. 1996. The human right to food (1989–1994). In *The hunger report: 1995,* ed. E. Messer and P. Uvin, 65–82. Amsterdam.
Millman, S., S. M. Aronson, L. M. Fruzzetti, et al. 1990. Organization, information, and entitlement in the emerging global food system. In *Hunger in history: Food shortage, poverty, and deprivation,* ed. L. F. Newman, 307–30. Cambridge, Mass.
Sen, A. 1981. *Poverty and famines: An essay on entitlement and deprivation.* Oxford.
Tomasevski, K., ed. 1987. *The right to food: A guide through applicable international law.* Boston, Mass.
U.S. House of Representatives, Committee on International Relations, Subcommittee on International Resources, Food, and Energy. 1976a. *Hearings on H. Con. Res. 393, the right-to-food resolution.* Washington, D.C.
   1976b. *Right to food resolution.* Report 94–1543, Part 1. Washington, D.C.

VII.3 ❧ Food Subsidies and Interventions for Infant and Child Nutrition

One hundred and fifty million children, or one in three, in the developing world are seriously malnourished (United Nations Development Program 1990). This includes 38 million children underweight, 13 million wasted, and 42 million stunted. In addition, 42 million children are vitamin A–deficient (West and Sommer 1987), 1 billion people, including children, are at risk of iodine-deficiency disease (Dunn and van Der Haar 1990), and 1.3 billion have iron-deficiency anemia (United Nations 1991).

Malnutrition, whether undernutrition per se or a specific micronutrient deficiency, is usually the result of an inadequate intake of food because households do not have sufficient resources. In a review of the income sources of malnourished people in rural areas, J. von Braun and R. Pandya-Lorch (1991) found that among households with a per capita income below $600 (U.S.), there was a close relationship between household food security and the nutritional status of children.

The problems associated with nutritional deprivation are compounded when access to sanitation is limited, because poor sanitation and hygiene results in increased morbidity. This condition is often accompanied by a reduction in food intake at the very time when energy and nutrient requirements are high. About one-third of the populations of developing countries has access to sanitation, and just over half have access to safe water, but there are large urban–rural differences. Ease of access to water is 48 percent lower in rural areas than urban areas, and overall access to sanitation is 77 percent lower in rural areas (United Nations Development Program 1990).

Although urban populations may appear better off than rural ones, the plight of the urban poor is getting worse. The average annual growth rate of urban populations in developing countries is 3.7 percent, whereas that of rural ones is 0.9 percent (Hussain and Lunven 1987). However, in urban slums and squatter settlements, the population of which represents one-quarter of the world's "absolute poor," the growth rate may exceed 7 percent per annum. This rapidly expanding population comprises people who often lack the resources to obtain an adequate diet for either themselves or their children.

There are also gender, social, and cultural inequalities in addition to urban–rural disparities. In the rural areas of Africa and the urban slums of Latin America, women commonly head the household. In many cases, these women are compelled to be employed, but in general their remuneration is low because they tend to work in subsistence agriculture or in the informal sector, where women's wages are lower than those of men. Social and cultural inequalities also often favor males over females, which is manifested in, for example, better health care and nutrition for males and neglect of female education. Irrespective of the environmental and political situation, social, economic, and cultural interactions exist that make improving the nutritional status of the poor a formidable task.

Targeting interventions so that those most nutritionally vulnerable, especially children, can benefit is important not only from an economic perspective but also in terms of the nutritional impact of the intervention program. Thus, although policy makers may be interested in improving the nutritional status of preschoolers, to focus solely on this age group is neither realistic nor practical (Berg 1986; Beaton and Ghassemi 1987). Indeed, in order to improve the nutritional status of infants and young children, it is more cost-effective to use programs that would bene-fit the entire household. The objective of a food-policy program aimed at the poor should be to improve their nutritional status by improving their access to food. However, unless nutritional considerations are explicitly stated in a food policy, it cannot be considered a food policy (Berg 1986).

Food policies can be based on *economic* and *nutrition* interventions. Specific economic interventions, which aim to stabilize food prices, may include those to increase agricultural and livestock production, to commercialize agriculture, to hold buffer stocks, and to subsidize consumer food prices. In addition to food policies, there are also other macroeconomic policies that influence the availability and consumption of food. An overvalued foreign exchange rate, for example, may discourage farmers from producing food because imported food can be cheaper. Similarly, food production can decline when industrial development is carried out at the expense of agricultural development.

Nutrition interventions, however, include food fortification, the use of formula foods, supplementary feeding programs, food-for-work and food-for-cash programs, and nutrition education. The boundaries between economic and nutrition interventions are not always distinct. Supplementary feeding and food-for-work programs, for example, can be considered as consumer food-price subsidies or as income transfers.

This chapter reviews the different economic and nutrition interventions that are used as policy tools to increase the energy and nutrient intakes of the poor, thereby increasing their household food security and the nutritional status of their infants and young children.

Economic Interventions

Agricultural and Livestock Production

Increased agricultural and livestock production are often prerequisites for food security because they generate additional amounts of both food and income. Increasing productivity, however, entails changing or modifying an existing production system to make it more cost-effective. This may be achieved in a number of ways: first, by increasing yields per unit of land area or worker; second, by ensuring the availability of sufficient inputs – fertilizer, pesticides, and so forth; and last, by establishing price relationships that can act as an incentive to both innovation and the mobilization of resources (Mellor undated).

Improved technology. The Green Revolution, through the use of improved technology, was instrumental in expanding world food production during the 1970s – in particular that of rice and wheat in Asia. Similar approaches are needed for the staple food crops grown in other parts of the world, especially in Africa. Specifically, attention needs to be given to root crops as well as to the more drought-tolerant cereals, such as sorghum and millet.

Expanding the area under cultivation and increasing cropping intensity are the means of increasing agricultural production, be it for home consumption or for sale. Outside of Africa, there is little scope to expand the area under cultivation. However, through the wider use of those improved crop varieties that are more resistant to pests and diseases, farm yields could be stabilized. The greater use of early-maturing varieties, which shorten the growing season, would also allow for multiple cropping. Intercropping, too, increases overall yields, stabilizes production, and allows food to be grown throughout a longer season. Management issues such as pest and disease control, the use of crop residues and animal manure as fertilizer, and soil conservation also help to augment yields and at the same time to lower the costs of production. Livestock productivity can be increased through better disease and parasite control. This not only results in farmers' getting a better yield of milk and a better price for their dairy products or meat but also improves the work performance of draft animals and thus the asset value of the animals themselves. An increase in agricultural and livestock production can result in an improvement in the nutritional status of households through increasing household food security, which can in turn reduce the risk of infants and young children from becoming undernourished.

Land reform. There is a great deal of evidence to show that small farmers are more productive per unit of land than are large farmers (Lipton 1985). This is because small farmers depend on family labor to grow high-value or double crops, to improve land in the slack season, to reduce fallow lands in area and duration, and to enhance yields through better cultivation practices. Large farmers tend to use imported machinery as a labor-displacing strategy, and such machinery depends on imported fuel and spare parts (Norse 1985; Longhurst 1987).

The inequality in both land ownership and tenure systems is the primary cause of poverty in the rural areas of Asia, Latin America, and, to a lesser extent, Africa (Norse 1985). Access to land clearly determines access to food and income (Braun and Pandya-Lorch 1991). Landless households that depend on the sale of their labor for survival are nutritionally the most vulnerable group. Sharecroppers and tenant farmers, who give part of their crop or work at peak agricultural times in lieu of rent, and very small farmers, are also extremely vulnerable nutritionally.

Availability of inputs and services. Unless soils are replenished, the production potential of land slowly declines as soil nutrients are depleted. Inputs, particularly fertilizer and water, are needed in order to maintain production levels. The money needed to finance these inputs, generated through credit, as well as an advisory service in the form of agricultural extension services, must be available. Both inputs and services should be available to women as well as to men because a great number of women are already involved in agriculture and dependence upon women's earnings increases as employment for men falls (Mencher 1986).

In addition to inputs and services, it is essential that the reliability and efficiency of the marketing infrastructure for both food and nonfood commodities be improved if farm income levels are to be raised. Distortions in policies that adversely affect the availability of agricultural inputs and services to the small farmer will limit any improvement in agricultural production and, ultimately, influence income and the nutritional status of young children.

Commercialization of Agriculture

The integration of small farmers into a market economy entails a shift from subsistence food crop to cash crop production. However, increasing the production of cash crops at the expense of domestic food crops can disrupt traditional economic and social relationships. This, in turn, may have an adverse impact on the income, food consumption, and nutritional status of the poor (Senauer 1990). The evidence to support this theory, however, is mixed, with some studies showing commercialization having a positive effect on nutritional status (Braun and Kennedy 1986; Braun 1989) and others showing either no effect (Kennedy and Cogill 1987) or a negative one (Pinstrup-Anderson 1985; Kennedy and Alderman 1987).

Commercialization of agriculture need not necessarily be detrimental to nutritional status for two reasons. First, even though the promotion of cash crop production may decrease domestic food production, the foreign exchange generated from agricultural exports can more than offset the cost of importing food for the domestic market. Second, nutritional problems are not necessarily the result of a lack of food, but may be caused by a lack of access to sufficient food, which in itself is determined by income levels and food prices. Thus, increasing the income of poor farmers, whether from food or nonfood crops, rather than simply increasing production, should be a priority for agricultural production programs.

In general, part of any increase in income is spent on food. Among the poor, the additional proportion spent on food may be quite high. This does not, however, necessarily mean that more energy will be consumed, because families may diversify their diet rather than increase the absolute quantity of the foods they already eat (Braun and Kennedy 1986). Thus, an increase in income alone will not necessarily result in better nutrition, and other interventions, such as nutrition education, are also needed.

Another aspect of commercialization is that income flow, as opposed to total income, is important in determining the impact of income on nutritional status. A lump sum of money, such as that generated from growing cash crops, is more likely to be spent on nonfood items such as school fees or housing, whereas continuous income is more likely to be spent on food (Kennedy and Alderman 1987).

The status of the person who controls the household's money may also be important. In many developing countries, the income generated from commercial crops is viewed as belonging to men, whereas that from food crops goes to women (FAO 1987). When women have some decision-making power, they are more likely than men to purchase food and health care (Kennedy and Cogill 1987). In some countries, such as India, the money earned by mothers has been found to have a greater impact on child nutrition than that from other income sources (Kumar 1979). Braun and Pandya-Lorch (1991) have claimed that women spend more of their income on food, whereas men spend their income according to personal taste on either food or nonfood items. This observation has important implications for programs that encourage expanding the cultivation of a particular crop that can change the way in which a household's land is allocated for food and nonfood crops. Any program that reduces the amount of land available for food production without altering the control and use of income can adversely affect nutritional status.

Type of income can also influence consumption patterns. In India, S. Kumar (1979) found that payment in kind, rather than in cash, was used for consumption. Likewise, J. Greer and E. Thorbecke (1983) noted that in Kenya, income from food production rather than from off-farm work was associated with increased food intake. E. Kennedy and H. Alderman (1987) suggested that income from home gardens and home production was more likely to increase household food intake than was an equivalent amount of cash income. This interpretation emphasizes the importance of the role of women in agricultural programs, given that, in general, they control the food produced for household consumption and the income generated from the sale of food crops. Obviously, their position has important implications for child nutrition.

Buffer Stocks

Buffer stocks are strategic food stores that are used to meet fluctuations in demand, or to accommodate fluctuations in supply, when there are no alternative sources of food. Buffer stocks are primarily used to stabilize prices – for example, at times of harvest failure or just prior to the harvest season when supplies are low.

In order to stabilize prices, buffer stocks should be released onto the market and sold at a controlled, or intervention, price once a predetermined consumer "ceiling price" has been reached. Over time, the intervention price, paid by the consumer, needs to fall, as does the producer price. In order to avoid a decline in production associated with the use of buffer stocks, grain has to be bought up when the producer price on the free market falls below a predetermined "floor price."

The margin between the floor price paid to farmers and the ceiling price paid by consumers is crucial to the stabilization desired from the use of the buffer stock. If the range is wide, so that the floor price is low and the ceiling price high, then net flows of food will be small and infrequent. This situation will allow stock levels to be relatively small, but the effect on the market will also be small. In contrast, if the margin is too narrow, then the floor price may rise above the producer price or the ceiling price below the consumer price. This will cause stock levels to fluctuate wildly. Thus, the narrower the margin the larger the food stock required to maintain it, but the greater the stability in prices.

Political pressure – from farmers (to increase producer prices) and from urban consumers (to keep consumer prices low) – can undermine a buffer-stock scheme, as can private commodity dealers. For buffer stocks to be effective in stabilizing prices, the operators must have foresight and knowledge about the different types of price fluctuations (regional, seasonal, annual, inflationary, and so forth). In addition, the administration of buffer stocks should be independent so as to resist political pressure. Finally, storage costs of the buffer stock should be low (Streeten 1987).

Buffer stocks are both difficult to administer and expensive to maintain. For example, 1 ton of buffer-stock wheat held in the Sahel can cost $500 (U.S.), as compared with a price of $200 (U.S.) per ton (including freight) for wheat purchased on the world market (Streeten 1987). Aside from capital costs (such as warehouses, staff training, and the initial cost of the grain) and recurrent costs (wages, pesticides, building maintenance, and so forth), buffer stocks incur such additional costs as the interest on the funds tied up in the stock, the value of losses caused by pests, and losses resulting from deterioration in quality. S. Maxwell (1988) suggests that these additional costs may be larger than the capital or maintenance costs, although they are rarely included in estimates of buffer-stock costs. In Sudan, for example, these additional costs were equivalent to 40 percent of the purchase price of sorghum.

Buffer stocks have been used as a means to get grain to food-deficient areas in Indonesia (Levinson 1982) and as a famine reserve in Ethiopia (Maxwell 1988). These programs were implemented with the assumption that the poor, who are the most nutritionally vulnerable, would not suffer from any further deterioration in nutritional status.

Consumer Food-Price Subsidies

Consumer food-price subsidies are essentially income transfer policies that enable consumers to buy food at a lower price. They exist because cheap food is often regarded as a nutritional as well as a political necessity (Pinstrup-Anderson 1985, 1988).

Food subsidies have been found to have a positive impact on nutritional status in a number of countries (Pinstrup-Anderson 1987). This impact has been achieved in three ways. First, food subsidies increase the purchasing power of households because their members can buy more food for the same price. Second, they may reduce the price of food relative to the price of other goods, thus encouraging households to buy more food. Third, they may make certain foods cheaper relative to others and thereby change the composition of the diet.

Food subsidies, however, are not necessarily the most economic means of increasing the food intake of the poor. This is because they benefit all income levels: The rich, who do not need the subsidy, gain more than the poor because the rich can afford to buy more of the subsidized food. In addition, households do not necessarily increase their intake of the subsidized food; they may instead use the savings from its availability to buy other food or nonfood items that may be of limited nutritional benefit.

There is evidence, however, that food subsidies do increase the real income of the poor. In one study, food subsidies represented the equivalent of 15 to 25 percent of total incomes of poor people (Pinstrup-Anderson 1987). Because poor households spend between 60 and 80 percent of their income on food, the economic benefit of subsidized food as a proportion of current income is larger for the poor than for the rich, even if the absolute value of the subsidy is greater for the rich.

Food-subsidy programs have also been found to increase energy intakes at the household level, although the effect at the individual level is not always apparent. In Kerala, India, Kumar (1979) found that the subsidized ration resulted in an increase in energy intake by the lowest income group of 20 to 30 percent.

Food subsidies are often considered more beneficial to urban than to rural populations. Alderman and Braun (1986) learned that the Egyptian subsidies on bread benefited the urban population more than did subsidies on wheat flour. However, the opposite was true in rural areas where there were fewer bakeries to sell subsidized bread. R. Ahmed (1979), in Bangladesh, found that although only 9 percent of the population lived in urban areas, two-thirds of the subsidized cereal went to urban consumers. In Pakistan, B. Rogers and colleagues (1981) discovered that ration shops, which sold rationed subsidized wheat flour, had no significant effect on the energy intake of the rural population, whereas that of the urban population was increased by 114 calories per capita. Clearly, the transportation and administrative costs involved in serving a scattered rural population may limit the extent of a subsidy network. In addition, the threat of political unrest in urban areas is often a reason for governments to pursue food-price subsidies.

The political and economic climate invariably determines who benefits from a food subsidy program and how the program is implemented. The effect of food subsidies on household food consumption and, ultimately, on the nutritional status of children will depend, in part, on whether there is a *general* food subsidy, a *rationed* food subsidy, or a *targeted* food subsidy. In addition, the choice of the food to be subsidized is important.

General food subsidy. A general food subsidy is one in which the subsidized price of a specified food (or foods), in the market is below that of supply. Although politically very popular, such programs may not be the most efficient or effective way to improve the nutritional status of the poor. General price subsidies are costly and may divert financial resources from other programs, such as employment creation and wage increases, that would increase the purchasing power of the poor (Reutlinger 1988). In addition, in order to help pay for the subsidy, the programs themselves may cause increases in the prices of other foods that are important in the diet of the poor.

Yet a number of countries have implemented general food subsidy programs, which, in spite of their costs, have benefited the poor. For example, wheat flour and bread are subsidized throughout Egypt at ration shops, with no restrictions on the amount that may be purchased. Oil, sugar, and rice are also subsidized, but the supply of these is rationed. In addition, there are government-controlled cooperatives that sell subsidized frozen meat, poultry, and fish. Alderman and Braun (1984) have reviewed the Egyptian program, in which over 90 percent of the population derived benefits. In 1980, the subsidies cost the government some $1.6 billion, which was equivalent to 20 percent of concurrent government expenditure. But along with the cost burden of the general subsidy, there were noticeable nutritional gains, as shown in the fact that per capita energy intake in Egypt was greater than that in any of the countries having a per capita gross national product (GNP) up to double that of Egypt.

Access to subsidized food, however, was biased toward the rich in Egypt for a number of reasons (Alderman, Braun, and Sakr 1982). First, the lack of refrigeration facilities in rural areas precluded cooperatives from operating there, although ration shops were omnipresent. Second, the wealthier neighborhoods of Cairo appeared to have better supplies of the subsidized commodities, such as rice, than did the poor areas. In addition, although subsidized rationed commodities, such as oil, were not always rationed in the rich neighborhoods, oil was not even always available in the poor areas. Third, in addition to the regular cooperatives, civil servants and workers had their own workplace cooperative shops (in locations where more than 200 people were employed), which received extra allocations of subsidized meat and poultry. Fourth, wealthier households could afford to employ servants to fetch and queue for the subsidized food. Last, wealthier households could afford to pay bribes to ensure preferential access to subsidized food.

The Egyptian study found that although there were large variations in access to the subsidized food and also inequalities in the distribution system, the poor did benefit from an effective increase in purchasing power as a result of access to cheap food. Indeed, food subsidies accounted for 12.7 percent of expenditures for the lowest income quartile in urban areas and 18 percent of total expenditures of the poorest households in rural areas.

Rationed food subsidies: Dual prices. A dual price system is one in which certain quantities of food are rationed at a subsidized fixed price, and unlimited quantities are available at the prevailing market price. Typically, a household's quota for a rationed food is less than the total amount required by the household, and the difference is made up from purchases in the open market, where prices are higher. This arrangement effectively allows households to increase their expenditure on food.

Dual price systems, utilizing ration shops, have been implemented in India for wheat, rice, and small amounts of coarse grains (Scandizzo and Tsakok 1985) and in Pakistan for the wheat flour known as "atta" (Alderman, Chaudhry, and Garcia 1988). The ration price in India was 60 percent, and that in Pakistan 51 percent, of the open market price.

Targeted food subsidies: Food stamps. A food-stamp program is one in which coupons are sold to a selected target group who may then buy specific foods of a stated value in authorized stores. The store cashes in the coupons at a bank and the bank is reimbursed by the government. The rationale behind food stamps, in contrast to cash transfers, is that households are more likely to increase food intake with transfers in kind rather than in cash (Kumar 1979). In other words, "leakage," meaning the purchase of nonfood items or more expensive "prestigious" food, is lower. Kennedy and Alderman (1987) noted that unless the value of the food stamps is more than that which a household would normally spend on food, there is no reason to expect the nutritional effect to be greater than that of giving a direct cash transfer. If, however, the cost of the coupons is close to that which the household would normally spend on food but the quantity of food that can be purchased with the coupons is higher, then the nutritional effect would be larger than that of a cash transfer. This is because, in addition to the income effect, food is cheaper at the margin. An example frequently cited is that of the U.S. food-stamp program, which until 1979 enabled a household to spend, say, $100 (U.S.) to receive $150 (U.S.) worth of food stamps.

Although it has been argued that food-stamp programs are costly to implement, S. Reutlinger (1988) has pointed out that the direct costs of administering a food-stamp program could be small because it brings in customers, so there would be no need for shops or banks to charge for processing the coupons. In addition, marketing costs may fall, which could lead to lower food prices because of an increased volume of shop sales. Thus, the only administrative costs are for printing the coupons, handling the distribution, and regulating against abuses.

As with all food-distribution programs, identifying the target group is not easy. Colombia, for example, has had a program in which only households in low-income regions with young children and pregnant or lactating women were eligible to participate. Coupons were distributed through health centers, where growth monitoring and nutrition education were carried out concurrently. The value of the food stamps was 2 percent of average income, but there was no evidence that the nutritional status of the target group improved (Pinstrup-Anderson 1987). In Sri Lanka, only households whose "declared" incomes were below a specified level could receive food stamps. However, this restriction meant that wage-earning workers on the tea estates where hunger was present did not qualify for food stamps even though they were one of the nutritionally most needy groups (Edirisinghe 1987).

In order to increase food intake and, thus, the nutritional status of the poor, the value of the food stamps must be indexed to inflation. This was not done in Sri Lanka, and so, over a four-year period, the value of the food stamps declined to 56 percent of their original value. The net result was that the already low total energy intake of the poorest 20 percent of the population declined by 8 percent.

Like other food-price subsidy programs, coupons do not necessarily result in increased consumption if the food issued does not meet the perceived needs of the household. The latter will depend on a household's composition and food preferences. In Colombia, for example, the foods that could be purchased with food stamps included highly processed foods not normally consumed by the poor.

In addition, the need for cash to buy the coupons often discriminates against the neediest households, which do not always have a regular source of cash. Moreover, even when a household does have income, it may not be sufficient to cover the cost of the coupons. But unfortunately, setting up a progressive program in which the price of the coupons is based on what a household can pay is not feasible in many societies (Pinstrup-Anderson 1987).

Choice of subsidized food. Most programs subsidize a staple cereal, and when the entire population consumes significant quantities of that staple, the cost can become prohibitive. In order to cover the costs and ensure that the poorest sections of the population benefit, the selection of the food to be subsidized is critical, particularly where more than one food is considered a staple. In Brazil, for example, C. Williamson-Gray (1982) found that subsidizing wheat bread resulted in a decrease in the energy intake of the poor. This was because the poor substituted the still more expensive subsidized bread for rice and other foods, thus decreasing their total intake of food. Williamson-Gray suggested that subsidizing cassava, rather than wheat, would have been better. Such a subsidy would have effectively increased the income of the poor because cassava is not prominent in the diet of the rich.

It has been pointed out that where "inferior" foods are subsidized, the subsidy program becomes self-targeting toward the group that consumes the "inferior" food. For this to happen, however, the "inferior" food must be consumed by a large proportion of the targeted population. Various studies cited by P. Pinstrup-Anderson (1988) indicate that subsidizing highly extracted wheat flour benefits the poor more than the rich largely because the latter perceive such flour as lower in quality because of its physical appearance.

As can be seen, a range of economic policies have been used, directly or indirectly, to improve food security among the poor. Undernutrition is inexorably linked with poverty, and unless poor households have the ability and resources to feed themselves, their infants and young children will suffer. For this reason, the focus of food-related economic policies has been at the household level.

Nutrition Interventions

Like economic interventions, nutrition interventions can be targeted or nontargeted. Once implemented, nontargeted interventions, such as food fortification, protect the entire population against a specific nutrient deficiency from an early age. Targeted interventions, such as the use of formula foods, feeding programs, and nutrition education, attempt to focus specifically on infants and young children, although many also include pregnant and lactating women. This section reviews the most commonly used nutrition interventions: food fortification, formula foods, supplementary feeding programs, and nutrition education.

Food Fortification

Food fortification is the addition of specific nutrients to foods. It can be used to restore nutrients lost in processing or to increase the level of a specific nutrient in a food. Examples of fortified food commonly consumed in developing countries include milk containing vitamin D (originally introduced to prevent infantile rickets) and salt to which iodine is added (to prevent goiter).

To ensure that the most vulnerable members of the population benefit from food fortification, the vehicle for fortification must be a staple food consumed throughout the year by a large proportion of people with relatively little inter- and intraindividual variation. Intake levels must be self-limiting to minimize the possibility of toxicity. The level of fortification must be such that it contributes significantly to nutritional requirements without altering the taste, smell, look, physical structure, or shelf life of the food vehicle. Because control and monitoring procedures must be adopted at the manufacturing level to ensure that fortification levels are adequate, legislation may be necessary (International Nutritional Anaemia Consultative Group 1977, 1981; Bauernfeind and Arroyave 1986; Arroyave 1987).

The advantages of food fortification are many. Such a procedure is socially acceptable; it does not require the active participation of the consumer; it requires no changes in food purchasing, cooking, or eating habits; and the fortified food remains the same in terms of taste, smell, and appearance. Because the product to be fortified should already be marketed and have a widespread distribution system, fortified food can be introduced quickly; its benefits are readily visible; legislation for compliance is possible; its use is relatively easy to monitor; it is the cheapest intervention for a government; and it is the most effective sustainable method of eliminating a micronutrient deficiency (International Nutritional Anaemia Consultative Group 1977, 1981; Bauernfeind and Arroyave 1986; Venkatesh Mannar 1986; Arroyave 1987).

The main disadvantage of food fortification is that although it is applied to a food that is processed and marketed throughout a society, only those who consume that food will benefit. Fortification, for example, will not benefit people who use only locally produced or unprocessed foods. Other disadvantages are that fortified food reaches nontargeted as well as targeted individuals and may not be the most economical way to reach the target group. Moreover, when the cost of fortification is passed on to the consumer, purchasing patterns may change adversely among those most intended to benefit. Fortification also involves recurring costs. Finally, political will, legislation, and mechanisms to enforce decisions to fortify foods are necessary to ensure the success of such programs (Bauernfeind and Arroyave 1986; Arroyave 1987).

Among the nutritional deficiencies of children for which the use of fortified foods has been advocated in the developing world are the control of xerophthalmia, or night blindness (International Vitamin A Consultative Group 1977), goiter (Dunn and van der Haar 1990), and nutritional anemia (International Nutritional Anaemia Consultative Group 1977, 1981; United Nations 1991). One example of the use of a specific commodity as a vehicle for vitamin A fortification to control xerophthalmia is sugar in Guatemala (Arroyave 1986, 1987). Another is the use of vitamin A–fortified monosodium glutamate in the Philippines (Latham and Solon 1986) and Indonesia (Muhilal et al. 1988), although large-scale programs have not been implemented. Iodization of salt to control goiter has been successfully introduced in China, India, and 18 countries in Central and South America, although in the latter case, some countries have had a recurrence of iodine deficiency due to a lack of continuous monitoring and control measures (Venkatesh Mannar 1986). Fortification of wheat flour with an iron salt to control nutritional anemia is being implemented in Grenada. Trials on other nonfortified foods have been implemented in a number of developing countries. In Thailand, for example, fish sauce, a widely used condiment, is fortified with an iron salt (WHO 1972). In South Africa, curry powder has been fortified with iron EDTA (ethylenediaminetetraacetic acid) (Lamparelli et al. 1987), and in Chile, reconstituted lowfat milk is fortified with an iron salt, whereas wheat biscuits have been fortified with bovine hemoglobin (Walter 1990).

Formula Foods

Formula foods are premixed foods made from unconventional sources. They may be made by combining a local cereal grain with a vegetable/pulse protein rich in the amino acids deficient in the cereal. Originally, formula foods were developed as low-cost milk substitutes to be fed to weaning children. Two classic examples are a milk substitute made from corn and cottonseed flour (INCAPARINA), and corn-soya-milk (CSM). CSM is an important food-aid commodity and a major staple of many ongoing supplementary feeding programs.

The advantages of formula foods are that they are cheaper than conventional sources of animal protein, vitamins, and minerals and can be formulated to meet the specific nutritional needs of a target group while providing energy at the same time. In addition, they do not require cold storage.

The disadvantages are that although the costs are less than those of animal protein supplements, they are higher than those of cereal staples because of manufacturing and distribution costs. The main beneficiaries of formula foods tend to be urban populations because the formula foods are generally sold through commercial channels and can become prohibitively expensive in rural areas. B. Popkin and M. C. Latham (1973) estimated that formula foods were priced at between 8 and 40 times the cost of homemade traditional foods on a nutrient-per-dollar basis. In addition, a lack of familiarity with formula foods may result in low levels of acceptability. Thus, on balance, the use and potential of such foods appear to be somewhat limited in terms of developing countries, particularly in rural areas.

Supplementary Feeding Programs

Supplementary feeding programs are conducted at health centers, schools, or community facilities, which have the advantage of keeping capital outlays low by using existing institutional infrastructures. They also facilitate decisions on intrahousehold food distribution in situations when food and income are limited. Politically, such programs are acceptable because they often generate support among the recipients.

There are, however, disadvantages involved in feeding programs. First and foremost is their cost. Apart from the possible cost of the food (which may or may not be donated food aid), there are the administrative and operational expenses of the program. These include those of transport, storage, wages, overhead, physical plant, fuel, and cooking utensils. In addition, the operation of feeding programs in health centers or schools imposes extra work on the staff, which may be detrimental to the institution's core concerns and thus is itself a hidden cost. Further questions include whether the intended beneficiaries actually participate in and benefit from the program, whether a feeding program based on imported food aid encourages black marketeering, whether the food is used for political ends, and whether feeding programs create psychological, nutritional, and political dependence.

Participation in any feeding program depends upon a number of factors, which ultimately determine the success of the program when that success is measured in terms of an improvement in nutritional status. Criteria for success include the quality and quantity of food reaching the recipients, the regularity of supply, the timing of meals, the nutritional status of the participants, and the degree of targeting.

The quality of foods served in a feeding program is important in enhancing the overall quality of the diet provided. For example, powdered milk fortified with vitamins A and D is preferable to unfortified milk. Where premixes are employed, the addition of sugar to an oil/cereal base or oil to a sugar/cereal base not only increases the energy density of the food but also renders it more palatable and, thus, increases the likelihood of its being eaten. The use of premixes has both advantages and disadvantages. On the positive side, leakage of one of the commodities (sharing or selling the commodity) is restricted, especially if a high value is put on a particular food. On the other hand, although premixes may be made up of foods that are consumed locally, the appearance and consistency of a cooked premix may be alien to the intended beneficiaries.

The quantity of food each participant receives is critical to the success of any feeding program. In general, "average" rations are based on the extent to which the general diet is deficient in both energy and specific nutrients. But no allowances are made for individual variation or for leakage. Thus, Kennedy and Alderman (1987), for example, cite a CARE review finding that in four feeding programs, 62 to 83 percent of the total energy gap was the fault of the supplementary foods. In yet another feeding program in India, sharing reduced the amount of the ration consumed by child beneficiaries by 50 percent.

Minimizing leakage through the use of increased rations, or by having on-site feeding programs, will inevitably add to costs, but these measures are more likely to encourage attendance and produce viable results (Kennedy and Knudsen 1985). One difficulty encountered in all supplementary feeding programs, regardless of leakage, is ensuring that children actually eat an adequate amount of food. Undernourished children are often anorexic. Their total intake is likely to be greater if they are fed on a "little and often" basis rather than at set meals. This means that on-site feeding centers need to operate beyond conventional working hours and may require additional staff.

The regularity of supply of supplementary food is essential for it to have an impact. Regularity, however, can be impaired by transportation and bureaucratic constraints. Any uncertainty in supply can result in a reluctance on the part of local administrators to invest either time, personnel, or resources in a supplementary feeding program. Uncertainty in supply may also jeopardize existing programs by generating ill will among the recipients, especially if they have to travel or wait for food that fails to arrive.

The timing of the issuance of supplementary meals is also important for two reasons. First, it influences how much food a child will eat, and second, it may determine the extent to which the supplementary meal is considered as a substitute for the home meal. A meal served early in the morning is unlikely to be fully eaten by a participant if the individual has already eaten at home. At the same time, it may deter a mother from giving her child an adequate meal first thing in the morning if she knows there will be one at the feeding center. The same consideration applies to other supplementary meals given near the times that meals would normally be eaten in the home. To overcome this effect, feeding programs in some countries (for example, Guatemala) changed the time at which the food was distributed so that it was perceived as a "snack" rather than a meal (Anderson et al. 1981; Balderston et al. 1981).

The initial nutritional status of the participants in a feeding program influences the success of the program. Indeed, the greatest benefit from a supplementary feeding program ought to be seen among the most undernourished children (Beaton and Ghassemi 1987). For this reason the "targeting" of feeding programs becomes very important (Kennedy and Knudsen 1985; Kennedy and Alderman 1987).

Yet targeted programs are often politically difficult to implement because they involve singling out one group of people, which may not be socially or culturally acceptable. Conversely, groups not in nutritional danger, who want to benefit from what is perceived

as a "free handout," should be excluded. In order to target successfully, there must be some criteria with which to identify the intended beneficiaries (Anderson 1986). All too often, the data for doing this are limited (Cornia 1987).

Where undernutrition is widespread, feeding programs that are well targeted geographically can be effective in reaching the nutritionally disadvantaged population. This type of targeting is generally used in drought situations – for example, in Sudan and Ethiopia between 1984 and 1986. Geographic targeting is appropriate for areas in which there is a concentration of intended beneficiaries. Kennedy and Alderman (1987) have suggested that if less than 20 percent of households or children in an area are nutritionally needy, then geographic targeting on its own is unlikely to be an effective tool.

Once vulnerable individuals have been identified, targeting at the community level can be directed at households or individuals. This will largely depend on whether the program aims to improve the energy intake of vulnerable households or only that of vulnerable children and women. At the community level, targeting often relies on some arbitrary cutoff point using nutritional criteria such as weight-for-height, weight-for-age, and in some cases, middle-upper-arm circumference. Children are enrolled in and discharged from feeding programs based on nutritional status criteria. Once a child reaches and maintains an acceptable level of nutrition for a specified time period (at least one month), he or she can be discharged from the program.

Because undernutrition often involves not only a simple food deficit but also problems of sanitation and hygiene, it is important to address these factors as well so as to reduce the likelihood of children being caught in the undernutrition–morbidity cycle that inevitably ends in their being readmitted into a feeding program.

A feeding program must not overlook the importance of maintaining an improved nutritional status once it has met its objectives, and the causes of undernutrition have been removed (Pinstrup-Anderson 1987). G. H. Beaton and H. Ghassemi (1987) have suggested that although the implementation of a feeding program may improve nutritional status, it may also disrupt the equilibrium between a community and its environment. Because of this, when a feeding program is terminated, it is essential that it be phased out over a period of time in order to ensure that the positive results of the program are not lost and that the circumstances that led to the establishment of the program in the first place do not occur again.

Supplementary feeding programs fall into four categories: on-site, take-home, school, and community programs. Each of these can also be used as a vehicle for nutrition education, which is an essential component of any feeding program that hopes to modify nutritional behavior.

On-site and take-home feeding programs. On-site and take-home feeding programs are generally aimed at children 6 months to 5 years old, women in the last trimester of pregnancy, and women in the first six months of lactation. On-site programs involve the beneficiaries' attendance at a feeding center once or twice a day to receive food rations, whereas take-home programs distribute rations at regular intervals.

As previously mentioned, on-site programs tend to cost more than take-home programs, and although the beneficiaries of the former are more likely to consume the food themselves, the coverage of such programs is usually limited in both area and numbers. In addition, there is some evidence that the supplementary food is more likely to serve as a substitute (rather than a supplement) for the food that would otherwise be eaten at home (Beaton and Ghassemi 1987). Kennedy and Alderman (1987) point out that because a household operates as an economic unit, it attempts to promote the well-being of all its members. A child who receives food at a feeding center may be considered to have been fed already and is thus given less food at home, with a resulting net energy intake that is considerably lower than intended by the planners of supplementation. There is also the danger that when the responsibility for feeding a child is removed (albeit temporarily) from the mother, undernutrition may come to be regarded as a disease to be cured through outside interventions, rather than through a reallocation of resources within the household.

Take-home programs have more scope for leakage than do on-site programs because the food may be shared among the whole household or sold. M. Anderson and colleagues (1981) compared supplementary feeding programs in five countries and found that 79 to 86 percent of children attending on-site feeding centers ate their ration, whereas only 50 percent of children receiving a take-home ration did so.

Distributed food is more likely to be shared if it is a food that is widely accepted by the local population as appropriate for consumption. Indeed, Beaton and Ghassemi (1987), in their review of over 200 reports on feeding programs, found that sharing accounted for 30 to 60 percent of the food distributed, and the overall net increase in food intake of the target population was only 45 to 70 percent. The investigators concluded that on-site and take-home programs are not effective in reaching children less than 2 years of age, although such children are nutritionally a very vulnerable group. The reasons cited for failing to enroll children younger than 2 years included the use of unfamiliar weaning foods that are considered inappropriate by mothers, as well as the mothers' lack of knowledge about feeding children of this age.

Because of the time often required for travel to a feeding center, feeding programs may suffer from low participation and low attendance and have difficulties in reaching the most vulnerable groups. In their review of feeding programs, Beaton and Ghassemi (1987) found that participation rates were 25 to 80 percent of the intended level of distribution. Low participation and attendance result in part from the fact that mothers are often working, either domestically (collecting water or firewood, preparing food, looking after a large family, and so forth), or on their land, or in the informal sector. Participating children left with older siblings do not always benefit from the feeding program because the older children may not know how to prepare the supplementary food or not understand its importance. Indeed, experience in Sudan showed that older children were more interested in playing than in bringing an undernourished child to a feeding center on time or in attempting to feed a child who was anorexic.

School feeding programs. School feeding programs have been widely adopted in many countries. Such programs encourage school enrollment and attendance and improve school performance and cognitive development (Freeman et al. 1980; Jamison 1986; Moock and Leslie 1986). Many, however, operate only during the school year. School meals may replace, rather than supplement, meals eaten at home, although in situations when the mother is not at home during the day, it is questionable whether the child would get a midday meal anyway. In the latter situation, the advantage of the school meal outweighs the disadvantage of its possibly being a replacement meal. In India, school feeding programs were found to influence household expenditure patterns because school meals were cereal-based, which allowed households to spend less money on cereals and more on milk, vegetables, fruits, and nonvegetarian foods (Babu and Hallam 1989).

Among the poor, however, school-age children are often required to work to augment the household's meager income or to look after younger siblings while the adults work. Indeed, in many situations, children from the most vulnerable households are the least likely to be at school and, thus, the least likely to benefit from a school feeding program.

Community feeding programs. Strictly speaking, community feeding programs provide replacement or substitute rather than supplementary meals. Community-organized mass feeding programs, known as *comedores,* have been implemented in Lima, Peru (Katona-Apte 1987). There, members of a group of women take turns preparing morning and midday meals. Standardized portions are sold at set prices to participants, whose entitlement depends on household size. The money collected is used to purchase foods additional to those contributed by donor agencies. Households pay for meals depending upon their circumstances, although the *comedor* does limit the number of free meals it issues each day.

The advantage of community feeding programs is that they benefit from economies of scale. Thus, not only the quantity but the quality of the meals will most likely be nutritionally superior to that of meals that would have been prepared at home. Communal kitchens also afford participating mothers more time for other activities, and yet one more benefit of a community-based program is that it gives women the opportunity to interact with and help each other.

The disadvantages of community-based feeding programs are that they do not allow for individual food preferences and that they take the control and responsibility of feeding the family away from the household. This runs the risk of child undernutrition coming to be perceived as a problem that the household cannot solve.

Food-for-Work and Food-for-Cash Programs

Food-for-work (FFW) and food-for-cash (FFC) programs are indirect nutrition interventions involving labor-intensive employment programs. Such programs effectively subsidize labor through the provision of either food or wages as remuneration, thereby improving a household's access to food and reducing the risk of child undernutrition. The short-term outcome of such programs is the creation of employment for the poor, whereas the long-term one is income generation for both poor and nonpoor through the development of an asset base (Biswas 1985; Stewart 1987; Braun, Teklu, and Webb 1991; Ravallion 1991).

The participation and involvement of both the local community and government in the design and implementation of the program is essential if the poorest people, who generally have no power base, are to participate in and benefit from it. Payment, whether in cash or as food, must be determined by the prevailing food-market conditions (Braun et al. 1991). Poor people already spend a large proportion of their income on food, and any increase in income is generally translated into further food purchases (Alderman 1986; Braun and Kennedy 1986). In order to ensure that this change takes place, the existing food market must be such that it can cope with the increased demand without price increases that will negate some positive effects of the program.

There are numerous advantages to FFW or FFC programs in terms of improving household food security and, thus, nutritional status. First, because of their relatively low level of remuneration, they do tend to reach the poor and are, consequently, self-targeting. Second, they are relatively low-cost in relation to the jobs they create. Third, they develop and improve a much needed infrastructure. Fourth, they increase local purchasing power. Fifth, they increase food demand through the generation of income for the poor, which will stimulate the local market. Sixth, there is no notion of charity. Seventh, they enable communities to be involved in their own asset creation, including that of environmental sanitation,

thereby reducing the morbidity–undernutrition risk. Eighth, they can be implemented in the slack agricultural season, thereby reducing seasonal fluctuations in income and, thus, dependency on moneylenders in rural areas (Biswas 1985; Stewart 1987; Braun et al. 1991).

The constraints of FFC and FFW programs are that many developing countries – particularly in Africa – do not have the institutional capabilities to set up, monitor, and maintain them. In many situations, it is not easy to determine the wage rate or to identify suitable small-scale infrastructural projects. In addition, the quality of the work carried out may be poor because of insufficient funds or inadequate work performance. Finally, the programs depend not only on the existence of surplus labor but also on the willingness of the laborers to be mobilized (Braun et al. 1991; Ravallion 1991).

Funds for FFW or FFC programs are generated through food aid, which can be used directly or indirectly, with the latter meaning that the food is sold and the proceeds are used to subsidize the program. As a result of administrative costs, food aid has been estimated to cost between 25 and 50 percent more than purely financial aid (Thomas et al. 1975; World Bank 1976), and food aid is not appropriate in rural areas with surplus agricultural production because it can depress local prices and incomes.

Nutrition Education

The main purpose of nutrition education is to change behavior patterns that determine the distribution of food within a household so as to reduce any intra-household inequality in nutritional status. However, without a proper understanding of the problems and constraints that households face, nutrition education on its own will have little impact. For example, if income is the most limiting factor, then education to reallocate income or food within the household is unlikely to be effective (Pinstrup-Anderson 1987). Indeed, nutrition education is likely to be useful only when households are capable of responding – for example, when a large proportion of the budget is spent on nonessential goods.

The most widely used themes in nutrition education are the encouragement of breast feeding; the introduction of appropriate food supplements for breast-fed infants between the ages of 4 and 6 months; the best use of scarce money to purchase the cheapest combination of nutritious food; the minimization of food wastage through improved food preparation and preservation; safer food preservation procedures; and ways to cook more efficiently, thereby saving on fuel costs (Manoff 1987). However, each theme cannot be treated as a discrete educational entity. For example, the promotion of breast feeding is related to the nutrition of both pregnant and lactating women, the introduction of weaning foods, the prevention and control of diarrheal disease, the adverse marketing practices of commercial breast milk substitutes, changes in hospital practices, and changes in policies such as paid maternity leave and provision of nurseries at the workplace.

Nutrition education techniques have relied largely on mass media campaigns and face-to-face communication through maternal-child-health clinics, women's groups, agricultural extension agents, and so forth. Few, however, involve the community, although R. C. Hornik (1987) and R. K. Manoff (1987) have suggested that unless communities develop the messages and undertake the administrative and financial responsibility for nutrition education programs on their own, it is unlikely that nutrition education will be effective on a large scale. If people pay for a service, however, they will use it and change their behavior.

Although the mass media has the potential to inform a large number of people, the number of people who can be reached in the lowest economic strata - nutritionally the most vulnerable - is generally not large. Irrespective of literacy levels, the majority of people in developing countries do not have access to newspapers, and there are only about 170 radios and 40 televisions per 1,000 people in the entire developing world (United Nations Development Program 1990). Moreover, in many developing countries there are multiple languages and dialects, as well as differing religious beliefs, ethnic groups, and cultural practices. Nationalized mass media messages may, therefore, not be very appropriate.

Women comprise the majority of the 870 million illiterate adults in the developing world (United Nations Development Program 1990). But mothers are not the only ones to whom messages need to be directed in order to effect a change in behavior. The medical profession, too, could play a much larger role than it currently does. In addition, schoolchildren, religious leaders, and the members of any institutionalized program have a role to play in nutrition education. If behavior is to be truly changed, however, the focus must be on ways to educate and communicate both relevant and appropriate nutrition advice.

The preceding sections show the range of nutrition policies that may be used to improve the nutritional status of infants and young children. Each policy has been analyzed in terms of its benefits and constraints, but it is difficult to ensure that the most nutritionally vulnerable children do, indeed, benefit from an intervention. For this reason, it is more appropriate to identify the vulnerable groups - that is, poor households with specific characteristics - than the vulnerable children. In short, to improve the nutritional status of infants and young children, economic and nutrition interventions must be aimed at poor households.

Penelope Nestel

Bibliography

Ahmed, R. 1979. *Foodgrain supply, distribution, and consumption policies within a dual pricing mechanism: A case study of Bangladesh.* International Food Policy Research Institute Research Report No. 8. Washington, D.C.

Alderman, H. 1986. *The effect of food price and income changes on the acquisition of food by low-income households.* Washington, D.C.

Alderman, H., and J. von Braun. 1984. *The effects of the Egyptian food subsidy system on income distribution and consumption.* International Food Policy Research Institute Research Report No. 45. Washington, D.C.

  1986. Egypt's food subsidy policy: Lessons from the past and options for the future. *Food Policy* 11 (3): 223-7.

Alderman, H., J. von Braun, and S. A. Sakr. 1982. *Egypt's food subsidy and rationing system: A description.* International Food Policy Research Institute Research Report No. 34. Washington, D.C.

Alderman, H., G. Chaudhry, and M. Garcia. 1988. *Household food security in Pakistan: The ration shop system.* International Food Policy Research Institute Working Papers on Food Subsidies No. 4. Washington, D.C.

Anderson, M. 1986. Targeting food-aid from a field perspective. In *Nutritional aspects of project food-aid,* ed. M. Forman, A21-37. Rome.

Anderson, M., J. E. Austin, J. D. Wray, and M. F. Zeitlin. 1981. *Nutrition interventions in developing countries, study 1: Supplementary feeding.* Cambridge, Mass.

Arroyave, G. 1986. Vitamin A deficiency control in Central America. In *Vitamin A deficiency and its control,* ed. J. C. Bauernfeind, 405-23. Orlando, Fla.

  1987. Alternative strategies with emphasis on food fortification. In *Delivery of oral doses of vitamin A to prevent vitamin A deficiency and nutritional blindness: A state-of-the-art review,* ed. K. P. West and A. Sommer, 87-91. (United Nations Subcommittee on Nutrition, Administrative Committee on Co-ordination. Subcommittee on Nutrition); Nutrition policy discussion paper no. 2. Rome.

Babu, S. C., and J. A. Hallam. 1989. Socioeconomic impacts of school feeding programs: Empirical evidence from a South Indian village. *Food Policy* 14: 58-66.

Balderston, J., A. B. Wilson, M. E. Freire, and M. S. Simonen. 1981. *Malnourished children of the rural poor.* Boston, Mass.

Bauernfeind, J. C., and G. Arroyave. 1986. Control of vitamin A deficiency by the nutrification food approach. In *Vitamin A deficiency and its control,* ed. J. C. Bauernfeind, 359-84. Orlando, Fla.

Beaton, G. H., and H. Ghassemi. 1987. Supplementary feeding programs for young children in developing countries: A summary of lessons learnt. In *Food policy: Integrating supply, distribution, and consumption,* ed. J. P. Gittinger, J. Leslie, and C. Hoisington, 413-28. Baltimore, Md.

Berg, A. 1986. Integrating nutrition in food policy analysis. In *Food policy: Frameworks for analyses and action,* ed. C. K. Mann and B. Huddleston, 50-4. Bloomington, Ind.

Biswas, M. 1985. Food-aid, nutrition, and development. In *Nutrition and development,* ed. M. Biswas and P. Pinstrup-Anderson, 97-119. Oxford.

Braun, J. von. 1989. *Commentary: Commercialization of smallholder agriculture - policy requirements for capturing gains for the malnourished poor.* International Food Policy Research Institute Report 11 (2): 1-4.

Braun, J. von, and E. Kennedy. 1986. *Commercialization of subsistence agriculture: Income and nutritional effects in developing countries.* International Food Policy Research Institute Working Papers on Commercialization of Agriculture and Nutrition No. 1. Washington, D.C.

Braun, J. von, and R. Pandya-Lorch. 1991. *Income sources of malnourished people in rural areas: Microlevel information and policy implications.* International Food Policy Research Institute Working Papers on Commercialization of Agriculture and Nutrition No. 5. Washington, D.C.

Braun, J. von, T. Teklu, and P. Webb. 1991. *Public works for food security: Concepts, policy issues, and review of experience in Africa.* International Food Policy Research Institute Working Papers on Food Subsidies No. 6. Washington, D.C.

Cornia, G. A. 1987. Social policymaking: Restructuring, targeting, efficiency. In *Adjustment with a human face: Protecting the vulnerable and promoting growth,* ed. G. A. Cornia, R. Jolly, and F. Stewart, 165-82. Oxford.

Dunn, J. T., and F. van der Haar. 1990. *A practical guide to the correction of iodine deficiency.* International Council for Control of Iodine Deficiency Disorders Technical Manual No. 3. Amsterdam.

Edirisinghe, N. 1987. *The food stamp scheme in Sri Lanka: Costs, benefits, and options for modification.* International Food Policy Research Institute Research Report No. 58. Washington, D.C.

FAO (Food and Agriculture Organization). 1987. Women in African food production and food security. In *Food policy: Integrating supply, distribution, and consumption,* ed. J. P. Gittinger, J. Leslie, and C. Hoisington, 133-40. Baltimore, Md.

Freeman, H. E., R. E. Klein, J. W. Townsend, and A. Lechtig. 1980. Nutrition and cognitive development among rural Guatemalan children. *American Journal of Public Health* 70: 1277-85.

Greer, J., and E. Thorbecke. 1983. *Pattern of food consumption and poverty in Kenya and effects of food prices.* Ithaca, N.Y.

Hornik, R. C. 1987. Nutrition education: An overview. In *Food policy: Integrating supply, distribution, and consumption,* ed. J. P. Gittinger, J. Leslie, and C. Hoisington, 429-35. Baltimore, Md.

Hussain, A. M., and P. Lunven. 1987. Urbanization and hunger in the cities. *Food and Nutrition Bulletin* 9: 50-61.

International Nutritional Anaemia Consultative Group. 1977. *Guidelines for the eradication of iron deficiency anaemia.* Washington, D.C.

  1981. *Iron deficiency in women.* Washington, D.C.

International Vitamin A Consultative Group. 1977. *Guidelines for the eradication of vitamin A deficiency and xerophthalmia.* Washington, D.C.

Jamison, D. T. 1986. Child malnutrition and school performance in China. *Journal of Development Economics* 20: 299-309.

Katona-Apte, J. 1987. Food-aid as communal meals for the urban poor: The *comedor* program in Peru. *Food and Nutrition Bulletin* 9: 245-8.

Kennedy, E., and H. Alderman. 1987. *Comparative analyses of nutritional effectiveness of food subsidies and other food-related interventions.* Washington, D.C.

Kennedy, E., and B. Cogill. 1987. *Income and nutritional effects of the commercialization of agriculture in southwestern Kenya.* International Food Policy Research Institute Research Report No. 63. Washington, D.C.

Kennedy, E., and O. Knudsen. 1985. A review of supplementary feeding programs and recommendations on their design. In *Nutrition and development,* ed. M. Biswas and P. Pinstrup-Anderson, 77-96. Oxford.

Kennedy, E., and P. Pinstrup-Anderson. 1983. *Nutrition-related policies and programs: Past performances and research needs.* Washington, D.C.

Kumar, S. 1979. *Impact of subsidized rice on food consumption and nutrition in Kerala.* International Food Policy Research Institute Research Report No. 5. Washington, D.C.

Lamparelli, R. D., A. P. MacPhail, T. H. Bothwell, et al. 1987. Curry powder as a vehicle for iron fortification: Effects on iron absorption. *American Journal of Clinical Nutrition* 46: 335-40.

Latham, M. C., and F. S. Solon. 1986. Vitamin A deficiency in the Philippines. In *Vitamin A deficiency and its control,* ed. J. C. Bauernfeind, 425-43. Orlando, Fla.

Levinson, F. 1982. Towards success in combating malnutrition: An assessment of what works. *Food and Nutrition Bulletin* 4: 23-44.

Lipton, M. 1985. *Land assets and rural poverty.* World Bank Staff Working Paper No. 616. Washington, D.C.

Longhurst, R. 1987. Policy approaches towards small farmers. In *Adjustment with a human face: Protecting the vulnerable and promoting growth,* ed. G. A. Cornia, R. Jolly, and F. Stewart, 183-96. Oxford.

Manoff, R. K. 1987. Nutrition education: Lessons learned. In *Food policy: Integrating supply, distribution, and consumption,* ed. J. P. Gittinger, J. Leslie, and C. Hoisington, 436-42. Baltimore, Md.

Maxwell, S. 1988. *Food security study: Phase 1.* Brighton.

Mellor, J. W. Undated. *The emerging world food situation and challenges for development policy.* International Food Policy Research Briefs No. 1. Washington, D.C.

Mencher, J. 1986. Women and agriculture. In *Food policy: Frameworks for analyses and action,* ed. C. K. Mann and B. Huddleston, 39-49. Bloomington, Ind.

Moock, P. R., and J. Leslie. 1986. Childhood malnutrition and schooling in Terai region of Nepal. *Journal of Development Economics* 20: 35-52.

Muhilal, D. Permeisih, Y. R. Idjradinata, Muherdiyantiningsih, and D. Karyadi. 1988. Vitamin A-fortified monosodium glutamate and health, growth, and survival of children: A controlled field trial. *American Journal of Clinical Nutrition* 48: 1271-6.

Norse, D. 1985. Nutritional implications of resource policies and technological change. In *Nutrition and development,* ed. M. Biswas and P. Pinstrup-Anderson, 20-42. Oxford.

Pinstrup-Anderson, P. 1985. The impact of export crop production on human nutrition. In *Nutrition and development,* ed. M. Biswas and P. Pinstrup-Anderson, 43-59. Oxford.

  1987. Nutrition interventions. In *Adjustment with a human face: Protecting the vulnerable and promoting growth,* ed. G. A. Cornia, R. Jolly, and F. Stewart, 241-56. Oxford.

  1988. The social and economic effects of consumer oriented food subsidies: A summary of current evidence. In *Food subsidies in developing countries,* ed. P. Pinstrup-Anderson, 3-20. Baltimore, Md.

Popkin, B., and M. C. Latham. 1973. The limitations and dangers of commerciogenic nutritious foods. *American Journal of Clinical Nutrition* 26: 1015-23.

Ravallion, M. 1991. On the coverage of public employment schemes for poverty alleviation. *Journal of Development Economics* 34: 57-79.

Reutlinger, S. 1988. Urban malnutrition and food interventions. *Food Policy* 10: 24-8.

Rogers, B., et al. 1981. *Consumer foodprice subsidies.* Cambridge, Mass.

Scandizzo, P. L., and I. Tsakok. 1985. Food price policies and nutrition in developing countries. In *Nutrition and development,* ed. M. Biswas and P. Pinstrup-Anderson, 60-76. Oxford.

Senauer, B. 1990. Household behavior and nutrition in developing countries. *Food Policy* 15: 408-17.

Stewart, F. 1987. Supporting productive employment among vulnerable groups. In *Adjustment with a human face: Protecting the vulnerable and promoting growth,* ed. G. A. Cornia, R. Jolly, and F. Stewart, 197-217. Oxford.

Streeten, P. 1987. *What price food? Agricultural price policies in developing countries.* Ithaca, N.Y.

Thomas, J. W., S. J. Burki, P. C. Davies, and R. M. Hook. 1975. *Employment and development: A comparative analysis of the role of public works programs.* Cambridge, Mass.

United Nations. 1991. Controlling iron deficiency. United Nations Administrative Committee, Coordination-Subcommittee on Nutrition Policy Discussion Paper No. 9. Geneva.

United Nations Development Program. 1990. *United Nations development report.* Oxford.

Venkatesh Mannar, M. G. 1986. Control of iodine deficiency disorders by iodination of salt: Strategy for developing countries. In *The prevention and control of iodine deficiency disorders,* ed. B. S. Hetzel, J. T. Dunn, and J. B. Stanbury, 111-26. Amsterdam.

Walter, T. 1990. Combating iron deficiency in Chile: A case study. In *Combating iron deficiency anemia through food fortification technology.* International Nutritional Anemia Consultative Group. Washington, D.C.

West, K. P., and A. Sommer. 1987. *Delivery of oral doses of vitamin A to prevent vitamin A deficiency and nutritional blindness: A state-of-the-art review.* (United Nations Administrative Committee on Co-ordination. Subcommittee on Nutrition). Policy discussion paper no. 2. Rome.

Williamson-Gray, C. 1982. *Food consumption parameters for Brazil and their application to food policy.* International Food Policy Research Institute Research Report No. 32. Washington, D.C.

World Bank. 1976. *Public works programs in developing countries: A comparative analysis.* Staff Working Paper No. 224. Washington, D.C.

WHO (World Health Organization). 1972. *Nutritional anaemias.* Technical Report Series No. 503. Geneva.

VII.4 ❧ Recommended Dietary Allowances and Dietary Guidance

To view this topic in perspective, we need answers at the outset to two questions: "What are Recommended Dietary Allowances (RDA)?" and "What purpose do they serve?" RDA are a set of *dietary standards;* they are *reference values* for the amounts of essential nutrients and food sources of energy that should be present in human diets. Standards of this type, based on the best available scientific knowledge, are needed by policy administrators, public-health officials, physicians, dietitians, and educators who have responsibility for establishing food and health policy; for providing the public with reliable dietary advice; for planning nutritionally adequate food supplies for large groups of people; and for assessing the adequacy of diets consumed by individuals or populations.

Definition of RDA
RDA for essential nutrients are defined differently from RDA for food sources of energy. For essential nutrients, the RDA values are amounts judged to be high enough to meet the known physiological needs of practically any healthy person in a group that has been specified by age and sex. They exceed average requirements to ensure that few, if any, individuals who are consuming amounts of nutrients equivalent to the RDA will have inadequate intakes. In contrast, RDA values for food sources of energy are the *average* amounts needed by the members of each group. RDA are not, in themselves, general dietary recommendations, but as standards, they serve as the scientific basis for many aspects of practical nutrition and food and health policy (FNB 1989b).

Nomenclature
The name "Recommended Dietary Allowances" for these reference values was proposed by the Food and Nutrition Board (FNB) of the U.S. National Research Council (NRC) in 1941 when it first established a dietary standard (ADA 1941). As the term "RDA" was more and more widely used, it became evident that its meaning was not well understood. It was frequently used as a synonym for requirements or with the implication that RDA were dietary recommendations for use directly by the public. The response of the FNB was to increase the specificity of the definition in subsequent RDA reports and to include an introductory section explaining the uses of RDA (FNB 1974).

In an effort to distinguish more clearly between reference values and general dietary recommendations, some national and international committees have used other names for their dietary standards. A Canadian committee called its values simply a "Dietary Standard" (CCN 1940). The Food and Agriculture and World Health Organizations of the United Nations (FAO/WHO) have usually entitled their reports "Nutrient Requirements," with the dietary standards derived from the average requirements being designated as "Recommended Daily Intakes" (FAO/WHO 1970) or "Safe Levels of Intake" (FAO/WHO 1985). The United Kingdom adopted the term "Recommended Daily Amounts of Nutrients" (DHSS 1985). Canada (HWC 1983) and Australia (NHMRC 1990) have used "Recommended Nutrient Intakes." Recently, the United Kingdom adopted the terms "Dietary Reference Values for Food Energy and Nutrients" and "Reference Nutrient Intakes" (DHSS 1991). These are the clearest and most specific terms proposed. It is hoped that they will be widely accepted and thereby reduce misunderstanding about the meaning of dietary standards.

About 40 countries have established national dietary standards; at least 10 national committees have adopted the term "RDA," and several others the FAO/WHO standards (Truswell 1987, 1990). Although definitions of dietary standards differ slightly from one organization to another, and values for some nutrients differ from one national standard to another, the various sets of reference values (regardless of the names used for them) have all been designed for the same purposes. The term "RDA" is used for the most part in this chapter, but the equivalence of this and other terms for dietary standards should be kept in mind.

Historical Perspective

Prehistoric Knowledge of Food and Health

The essentiality of specific constituents of foods for human health and survival was discovered only during the nineteenth and early twentieth centuries. The concept of dietary standards and programs of dietary guidance based on knowledge of human needs for individual nutrients are, thus, of recent origin. However, as food is a basic biological necessity, our early ancestors undoubtedly learned through observation and much trial and error how to identify safe sources of nutriment from among the vast array of natural products available to them.

They discovered that some of these products were toxic and caused illness and even death. At the same time, they learned how to cope with several potentially dangerous foods and other dietary problems. For example, the indigenous peoples of the Amazon Basin found that the poisonous cassava root could be converted into a wholesome, edible product by steeping it in water, and peoples in the Arctic region discovered that scurvy, the debilitating and often fatal disease caused by a lack of ascorbic acid (vitamin C), was prevented or cured if they consumed extracts of evergreen needles (Clark 1968). Thus, the human species learned early to distinguish among natural products that were valuable sources of food, those that had medicinal properties, and those that contained poisons (Harper 1988). Oral transmission of such information can be viewed as the earliest form of dietary guidance.

In recent prehistoric times (12,000 to 5000 B.C.), the domestication of certain plants (especially cereal grains and legumes) and animals (sheep, goats, pigs, cattle) to provide safe and dependable sources of food (Cowan and Watson 1992) was undoubtedly based on this knowledge. Also, observations about the effects of certain foods and other natural products in treating diseases expanded and, by early historic times (3000 to 500 B.C.) in Egypt, Babylonia, India, and China, had become intimately associated with an organized practice of medicine. In all of these civilizations, extensive lists of prescriptions (pharmacopoeias) were compiled, and an immense number of natural materials, especially herbs (some of which have since been shown to contain effective medicinal components) but also some traditional foods, were used as remedies for a variety of ailments.

In Egypt, for example, the onion, a good source of ascorbic acid, was recommended as a cure for a disease resembling scurvy. At the same time, much of the accumulated knowledge about the use of natural products for the treatment of illnesses was subjective and unreliable and was intertwined with mythical and magical beliefs. Major diseases were attributed mainly to supernatural causes and restoration of health to the magical or supernatural powers of the remedy or the healer (Ackerknecht 1982). Apart from improved methods of obtaining a dependable supply of food and increased knowledge of the medicinal properties of natural products, concepts of foods and nutriture during the early historic period differed little from those of the prehistoric period.

Medical Dietetics – Hippocrates to the Renaissance

In Greece, a new attitude toward food and health began to emerge between 600 and 400 B.C. Physicians of the Hippocratic school of medicine in Cos rejected the belief that magical and supernatural influences determined human well-being. They accepted the viewpoint of the Ionian philosophers that the only reliable way to learn about the natural world was through direct observation and logical reasoning. Those physicians described the symptoms of their patients and the course of diseases in great detail with remarkable accuracy, and they recognized the recuperative powers of the body and the importance of food in maintaining or restoring health. They observed: "Growing bodies have the most innate heat; they therefore require the most food for otherwise their bodies are wasted. . . . In old persons the heat is feeble and they therefore require little fuel" (Adams 1952: 131).

Diet loomed large in both their diagnosis and treatment of diseases. The Greek physicians were concerned with what to feed, along with when, how much, and how often, and developed a complex system of dietetic medicine (Fidanza 1979). Despite their many astute observations, however, they believed that health depended upon the appropriate balance of four mystical humors – blood, phlegm, black bile, and yellow bile – and their associated qualities: warm, cold, moist, and dry. They believed that imbalances among these humors caused diseases (Ackerknecht 1982). They further believed that the basic elements of matter were fire, water, earth, and air – a concept proposed by Empedocles (490 to 430 B.C.) that remained the basis of theoretical chemistry until the eighteenth century (Brock 1993) – and that foods contained only a single source of nutriment: "aliment" (McCollum 1957: 63). These erroneous concepts of chemistry and human biology and reliance on subjective observations without controlled experimental studies prevented the early Greek physicians from achieving an understanding of the chemical nature of foods, the process of nutrition, and objective knowledge of relationships between diet and disease.

The Greek era of medicine culminated with Galen, who in the second century A.D. compiled an extensive record of Greek medical knowledge and his own contributions to it. He used the experimental method to establish that urine was formed in the kidney, not in the bladder, and recognized that food must undergo transformation in the body before it can be used to form tissues. But he, too, was limited by the chemical and biological concepts of the times. Of pertinence to the present topic, however, he codified rules of personal hygiene, of healthful living. He identified health-influencing factors over which the individual could exert some control – air, food and drink, activity, rest, sleep, evacuation, and passions of the mind – and he recommended moderation in all things (Whorton 1982).

Hippocratic and Galenic concepts dominated medicine in Europe until the seventeenth century, but they were gradually discarded as science progressed. The rules for healthful living, however, persisted and were a stimulus for many health movements in the eighteenth and nineteenth centuries (Burnham 1987), probably because they were compatible with the theology of the times in providing a moralistic solution for the sins of gluttony, sloth, and intemperance to which illness was attributed. Present-day dietary guidelines are a modern version of some of these rules. The objective remains the same – guidance for healthful living with moralistic overtones – but is now bolstered by scientific observations.

Knowledge of foods, nutrition, and relationships between diet and health advanced little for over 1,500 years following the death of Galen. With the decline of the Roman Empire and the rise of Christianity, interest shifted from the body to the soul; the social and religious environment was no longer conducive to investigations of natural phenomena. The concepts and teachings of the Greek philosophers and physicians became ossified, and it was only toward the end of the Renaissance that resistance to authoritarian doctrines and a rebirth of the scientific attitude opened the way for a new era of critical inquiry.

The nature of the transition is illustrated by the career of Paracelsus (1493-1541), a Swiss physician, alchemist, magician, and necromancer (Pachter 1951). He rejected the Galenic belief that diseases were caused by an imbalance of humors and proposed that they were caused by improper diet or defective body function. He taught that foods were sources of aliment, medicine, and poison, and asserted: It is the dose that makes the poison. Despite his enlightened approach, however, he accepted the magical "doctrine of signatures," the belief that potential remedies exhibited signs of the conditions for which they were effective – the shape of the leaves of the liverwort, for example, indicated its value for treating diseases of the liver. Thus, reading the efforts of Paracelsus to express his concepts of biological processes without knowledge of basic chemistry is reminiscent of viewing Michelangelo's unfinished statues, in which the partially formed figures appear to be struggling to break out of the blocks of marble.

The Enlightenment: The Impact of Science on Nutrition

By the beginning of the eighteenth century, the power of the scientific method to expand knowledge of natural phenomena had been demonstrated in the physical sciences through the investigations of Galileo Galilei (1564-1642) and Isaac Newton (1642-1727). The essentiality of a component of air for respiration had been established by Robert Boyle (1627-91) and his colleagues. The mystical elements assumed by the Greeks – Empedocles and Aristotle – and by the alchemists to be the basis of matter were being questioned. The anatomical observations of Andreas Vesalius (1514-64) had begun to undermine the authority of Galen, and William Harvey (1578-1657) made discoveries about the nature of blood circulation that opened up new approaches to the study of respiration (Wightman 1953). Yet knowledge of food and nutrition had advanced little. The Hippocratic belief that the state of health was determined by the balance of humors was still dominant in medicine, as was the concept that foods contained only a single source of nutriment.

There were, however, a few observations of links between foods, diet, health, and disease made during the seventeenth and eighteenth centuries that may be taken as harbingers of progress to come in nutrition (McCollum 1957; Guggenheim 1981). The effectiveness of citrus fruits and fresh vegetables as cures for scurvy was reported on several occasions during the seventeenth century (Carpenter 1988). Investigations of this disease by James Lind (1716-94) in 1753 led some 40 years later to the inclusion of citrus juice in the rations of sailors in the British Navy. Earlier Thomas Sydenham (1624-89), a prestigious London physician, had observed (in the 1670s) that a tonic of iron filings in wine produced clinical responses in anemic patients. Pellagra was noted by Gaspar Casal (1679-1759) to be associated with consumption of a poor diet, and in Germany, C. A. von Bergen noted in 1754 that liver, later found to be a good source of vitamin A, had been recommended in several places as a treatment for night blindness. But although Sydenham's observations could be taken as early evidence of the essentiality of iron (McCollum 1957), and the formal action of requiring citrus juice in the rations of British sailors as the initial example of a dietary standard (Leitch 1942), they were not recognized as such at the time, probably because success in treating diseases with foodstuffs was attributed to their content of medicinal substances.

The scientific contributions of Antoine-Laurent Lavoisier (1743-94) to our knowledge of the nature of gases, the process of oxidation, and the chemical structure of matter, which built on the discoveries of many of his predecessors and colleagues (Brock 1993), finally opened the way for an understanding of the composition of foods and the functions of individual food constituents in nutrition. After Lavoisier had shown that during combustion, various metals and carbon combined with oxygen and released heat, he and Pierre Simon de Laplace demonstrated (between 1770 and 1790) that respiration by guinea pigs and human subjects was an analogous process and that oxidation of carbon compounds by the body was accompanied by the release of heat (Lusk 1964). Foods, it was now evident, were not just a source of building materials for body substance but were also a source of energy for physical activity and other body functions.

In 1816, Françoise Magendie (1783-1855) concluded, from the results of experiments on dogs fed on diets that contained only carbohydrate or fat, that food was the source of nitrogen for the body. Although his experiments were less definitive than is often assumed (Carpenter 1994), his work led to the recognition that protein was an essential dietary constituent. During this time, the major constituents of foods had been separated and identified and, in 1827, William Prout (1785-1850), a London physician and scientist, proposed that the nutrition of higher animals was to be understood through consideration of the three major food components – carbohydrates, fats, and proteins. By 1850, largely through animal-feeding studies in Europe, particularly those conducted by Jean Baptiste Boussingault (1802-87) in France, five mineral elements – calcium, phosphorus, sodium, chloride, and iron – were known to be required in the diets of animals (McCollum 1957; Guggenheim 1981). The foundation for a science of nutrition had now been laid.

Nutrients As the Basis for Dietary Advice

After these advances, making dietary recommendations based on the chemical composition of foods was a concept finally approaching reality. During the 1830s, Boussingault in France, Gerrit Mulder (1802-80) in Holland, and Justus von Liebig (1803-73) in Germany had all proposed that the nitrogen content of a food could serve as an indicator of its nutritive value. Liebig began to teach that the "plastic" (nitrogen or protein) and "fuel" (carbohydrate plus fat) constituents of foods, together with a few minerals, represented the essentials of a nutritionally adequate diet. During the 1840s, Liebig and his colleagues in Giessen prepared extensive tables for predicting relative nutritive values of foods from their content of protein and energy-yielding constituents.

Mulder probably deserves credit for proposing the first dietary recommendations for a specific nutrient. In 1847, based on studies of Dutch army rations, he recommended 100 grams of protein daily for a laborer and 60 grams for a sedentary person (Todhunter 1954). In selecting a higher value for laborers, he was conforming with Liebig's erroneous belief that muscle protein was degraded during physical activity and was replaced by proteins from foods. During the 1850s, Lyon Playfair (1818-98), a professor of chemistry at Edinburgh who also accepted Liebig's hypothesis that muscular work involved breakdown of muscle protein, undertook extensive surveys of the diets consumed by men doing different types of work as a way of assessing protein needs. He took the results of his surveys (that laborers doing heavy physical work consumed much more protein than those who were less active) as support for Liebig's hypothesis. His results were not surprising. If food is readily available, individuals doing hard work will eat more than those working less vigorously and will therefore consume more protein whether or not they need it. Nonetheless, in 1865 he concluded that healthy adults should consume 119 grams of protein daily in a diet providing about 3,000 kilocalories of energy (Munro 1964).

This approach of basing dietary recommendations on estimates of the amounts and types of foods consumed by a generally healthy segment of the population was continued throughout the century. In Germany, Carl von Voit, a colleague of Liebig, on the basis of surveys of the diets of German workers in different occupations, reached essentially the same conclusions as Playfair, as did Wilbur Atwater (1844-1907), who had worked with Voit and later studied the diets of workers in the United States. But these recommendations were not actually dietary standards; all were based only on observed intakes of active healthy people, not on measured needs.

An exception was one set of recommendations by Edward Smith (1819-74), a British physician and scientist who had done extensive experimental studies of energy expenditure and nitrogen excretion by human subjects. During the depression of the 1860s, he was requested by the medical officer of the British Privy Council to determine the quantity and quality of food that would avoid "starvation-diseases" among the unemployed (Leitch 1942). He concluded from his experimental observations that a nutritionally adequate diet for working men should provide about 80 grams of protein and about 3,000 kilocalories of energy and recommended about 10 percent less for women. His recommendations were the first true dietary standards based on experimental evidence of human requirements (Todhunter 1961).

Throughout the nineteenth century, dietary recommendations were directed exclusively toward meeting needs for protein and energy, in large measure because of the prestige of Liebig, who had asserted strongly that protein and energy-yielding nutrients (fats and carbohydrates), together with a few minerals, were the essentials of a nutritionally adequate diet. This concept was the basis for dietary advice provided to the public by the U.S. Department of Agriculture (USDA) between 1890 and 1905. Yet, as early as 1849, J. Pereira (1804–53), a British physician and Fellow of the Royal Society, had questioned the validity of Liebig's views on the grounds that diets providing adequate quantities of protein and energy, but lacking variety, were associated with the occurrence of scurvy. Subsequently, several investigators in France, Britain, and Switzerland provided strong circumstantial evidence that foods contained many other unidentified substances essential for health (McCollum 1957; Guggenheim 1981). But it was only in the second decade of the twentieth century that Liebig's concept of a nutritionally adequate diet was generally acknowledged to be untenable. This came after experiments had demonstrated that modifications of diet or provision of dietary supplements could cure diseases such as beriberi in humans and scurvy in guinea pigs, and that supplements of small amounts of milk or egg could prevent growth failure in rodents fed a diet consisting of purified proteins, carbohydrates, fats, and minerals.

Evidence that several diseases associated with the consumption of poor diets were caused by nutritional deficiencies (MRC 1932) began to affect dietary recommendations toward the end of World War I. A Food Committee of the British Royal Society, besides recommending 70 to 80 grams of protein and 3,000 kilocalories of food energy for the "average man," stated that every diet should include "a certain proportion" of fresh fruits or green vegetables and that diets of all children should contain "a considerable proportion of milk" to protect against unknown dietary deficiencies (Leitch 1942). In response to this "newer knowledge of nutrition," the USDA in 1916 developed a food guide based on five food groups and recommended that diets be selected from a wide variety of foods to ensure that both known and unknown nutrients would be consumed in adequate amounts (Hertzler and Anderson 1974).

Between 1925 and 1935, the importance of consuming protective foods was also emphasized in reports of the British Medical Association (BMA) (1933) and a League of Nations committee on nutrition-related policy issues (1937). The objective of dietary recommendations prior to this time had been, first, to prevent starvation and malnutrition during periods of economic depression and, second, to maintain the working capacity of those in the labor force

and the army (Leitch 1942). The new recommendations were designed to improve the health of the entire population but were framed only in general terms because knowledge of human requirements for specific nutrients was sparse.

Dietary Standards – A New Concept

During the depression years from 1929 to 1935, E. Burnet and W. R. Aykroyd (1935) prepared a report on diet and health for the League of Nations. In it they emphasized the inadequate state of knowledge of human nutrition and the importance of investigating human needs for nutrients to provide a reliable base for dietary recommendations. An important outcome of the discussion of their report by the Assembly of the League was a statement calling attention to the need for, among other things, public education about the principles and practice of nutrition and the need to establish dietary standards (Harper 1985). This was the first time that a clear distinction was made between recommendations that represented food and nutrition policy and standards to establish that policy.

Between 1920 and 1940, rapid progress was made in advancing knowledge of the newly discovered essential nutrients. Chemical structures of some of the vitamins were determined, the effects of several vitamin and mineral deficiencies were described, and human needs for essential nutrients were investigated (McCollum, Orent-Keiles, and Day 1939; Rosenberg 1945). The knowledge needed for establishing dietary standards was becoming available.

Hazel Stiebling of the USDA, who had been a U.S. representative at meetings of League of Nations committees on food and nutrition problems, proposed the first set of standards for ensuring that diets used in feeding programs during the depression of the 1930s would be nutritionally adequate (Stiebling 1933). This standard for several essential nutrients – vitamins A and C, calcium, phosphorus, and iron – was subsequently expanded to include values for the vitamins thiamine and riboflavin (Stiebling and Phipard 1939). The values were derived from estimates of human requirements (USDA 1939). It is noteworthy that Stiebling and E. F. Phipard made separate recommendations for children of various ages and that they set their recommended intakes 50 percent above the average requirement to allow for variability among the requirements of individuals.

During this time, the League of Nations Technical Commission on Nutrition (1938) published recommended intakes for calcium and iron in addition to energy and protein. The commission did not make quantitative recommendations for vitamins but emphasized consumption of "protective foods" – meat, milk, leafy vegetables, fruits, eggs, organ meats, and fish – as important sources of vitamins and minerals and included specific recommendations for pregnant and lactating women. In 1939, the Canadian Council on Nutrition (CCN) (1940) proposed a "Canadian Dietary Standard" that included reference values for energy, protein, fat, calcium, iron, iodine, and vitamins C and D. Thus, by 1940 the principles for developing dietary standards had been established.

In 1940, at the request of the U.S. government, the NRC established a Committee on Food and Nutrition, which, a year later, was given permanent status as the Food and Nutrition Board (FNB). One of the first actions of the FNB in fulfilling its obligation of advising the federal government on problems relating to national defense was to prepare a set of dietary standards for adequate intakes of essential nutrients. The process by which this was done has been described by Lydia Roberts (1944, 1958), chair of the committee that was assigned this task. The set of values for nine essential nutrients adopted by the FNB, and designated as Recommended Dietary Allowances, was approved by the American Institute of Nutrition (the professional nutrition society of the United States) and subsequently accepted at a national conference on nutrition convened at the request of President Franklin Roosevelt in 1941. The reference values for seven of the nine essential nutrients included in this standard did not differ appreciably from those proposed by Stiebling and Phipard; the other two nutrients, niacin and vitamin D, were new additions.

The RDA publication has been revised nine times since 1941; the tenth edition was published in 1989. The number of nutrients for which RDA or safe and adequate intakes are established has expanded from 9 (ADA 1941) to 26 (FNB 1989b). Changes in the first seven editions have been summarized by Donald Miller and Leroy Voris (1969). The International Union of Nutritional Sciences has compiled detailed information on many national and international dietary standards (Truswell 1983).

The Process for Establishing Dietary Reference Values

The process by which dietary standards are established is described in the various RDA reports and has been discussed by Gordon Young (1964), Alfred Harper (1987a, 1994), Stewart Truswell (1990), Roger Whitehead (1992), and others cited by these authors. It involves appointment of a committee that assumes responsibility for selecting age-sex groups for which RDA are needed, evaluating information about human requirements for nutrients, and then establishing procedures for deriving appropriate recommended intakes from knowledge of the requirements for, and utilization of, nutrients.

Committees on Dietary Standards
In the United States, a committee appointed by the NRC and reporting to the FNB is assigned the task of setting RDA. In most other countries, committees to establish Recommended Nutrient Intakes are appointed by departments of health. The committees

usually consist of 8 to 12 scientists with both a broad general knowledge of nutrition and expertise in one or more special areas. In brief, in the United States, individual members or subcommittees prepare background papers on one or more nutrients based on a critical evaluation of the scientific literature on human requirements. These papers are reviewed by the entire RDA committee at several meetings over a period of three years, and problems are identified and resolved, sometimes with the aid of consultants or workshops. After revisions, the final draft of the report is submitted to the NRC for further review and revision before the final version is published.

The international agencies – FAO and WHO – follow a different procedure. Their reports deal with only a few nutrients at a time. One report, for example, may be on energy and protein (FAO/WHO 1985), whereas another may discuss vitamin A, iron, folate, and vitamin B_{12} (FAO/WHO 1988). The two organizations jointly appoint a committee of from 12 to as many as 20 scientists from various nations and a secretariat, consisting mainly, but not exclusively, of members of their staffs, to coordinate and facilitate the work of the committee. Its members (and those of the secretariat) prepare background papers on different aspects of requirements for the nutrients under consideration; they then meet together for about 10 days to discuss and resolve problems and prepare a draft report. This is circulated to the members for comment, after which a subgroup of the committee and the secretariat prepare the final report for publication.

Age-Sex Groups
The first step in setting RDA is to select age ranges and age-sex groups for which separate RDA values are needed and to specify body weights appropriate for each group. Most RDA reports currently include values for some 15 age-sex groups and for gestation and lactation. This number of groups is necessary for two reasons – first, because requirements for nutrients per unit of body weight decline as the growth rate declines and, second, because RDA for essential nutrients are expressed as amounts recommended daily per person in the specified group rather than as amount per unit of body weight. The range of ages included within a group must, therefore, be narrow during early life, when requirements per unit of body weight are high, and during adolescence, when body size is increasing rapidly. Also, requirements per person for females differ from those for males, mainly, but not exclusively, because of differences in body size, so that, except at young ages, separate groups are also employed for the two sexes. The age ranges and weights for groups frequently differ from one country to another, making exact comparisons among values from different reports difficult.

For individuals or groups whose weights deviate considerably from the specified weights, RDA should be adjusted on the assumption that they are proportional to body weight. For those judged to be substantially overweight, adjustment on the basis of lean body mass is thought to be more appropriate. Body weights for the age-sex groups are currently based on information obtained in national health surveys. They are not "ideal" or "desirable" weights. In the United States, the values are the median weights observed for the population (FNB 1989b); in Britain they correspond with the fiftieth percentile for body weight (DHSS 1991).

Establishing RDA for Essential Nutrients

The objective in establishing RDA for essential nutrients is to identify a level of intake high enough to ensure that the tissues of virtually all individuals in the population will contain enough of the nutrient to prevent impairment of health even if intake is inadequate for some period of time. The time differs from one nutrient to another, owing to differences in the ability of the body to store and conserve them. To accomplish this objective, the usual procedure is, first, to assemble and evaluate the information on human requirements for the different age-groups that have been studied; second, to estimate the variability among requirements of individuals; and, third, to assess the effects of various factors that influence nutrient needs, such as efficiency of absorption and utilization in the body, the bioavailability of the nutrient from major foodstuffs, and the contributions of precursors of nutrients in the food supply. The extent to which the last group of factors influences RDA differs from nutrient to nutrient and depends upon the nature of the foods consumed.

Estimation of Requirements

Methods that can be used for estimating requirements differ from one nutrient to another, and there is not always agreement as to the most appropriate criteria for establishing when a requirement has been met. Maintenance of a satisfactory rate of growth is accepted generally as an appropriate criterion for establishing that the requirements of infants and young children have been met. The amounts of nutrients consumed by infants growing well on a diet of human milk or a formula of proven quality are generally viewed as satisfactory, but not necessarily minimal, estimates of infant requirements.

With adults, several approaches have been used. In the case of nutrients for which naturally occurring dietary deficiencies have been encountered, the amounts needed to prevent or cure deficiency signs have been estimated both in practical studies and experimentally. These include thiamine, niacin, vitamins A and C, iron, and iodine. Experimental studies in which human subjects have been depleted of a nutrient until they develop signs of deficiency and then are replenished with different amounts until the signs disappear have been used to estimate require-

ments for ascorbic acid, vitamins A, E, and B_6, riboflavin, and folic acid. These methods are based on the assumption that body reserves are adequately restored when deficiency signs disappear. Balance studies have been used to estimate requirements for protein, calcium, magnesium, and zinc. In these the minimal amount of nutrient required to just prevent loss from the body is estimated from measurements of intake of the nutrient and excretion of the nutrient or its metabolites by human subjects whose intakes are increased incrementally.

The body content (usually called the body pool) of a few nutrients, for example, vitamin B_{12}, ascorbic acid, and iron, can be measured directly by isotopic methods; then, relationships among intake, rate of loss, and the development of signs of deficiency can be established. For several others, an indirect measure of the state of body reserves can be estimated from measurements made while intake is varied, of the rate of excretion of the nutrient or one of its metabolites in urine (niacin, vitamin B_6), the concentration in blood (vitamin A), or the activity of an enzyme or other protein of which the nutrient is a component (thiamine, selenium).

Confidence in estimates of requirements is increased when there is reasonable agreement between values obtained by two or more methods. With all of these methods, however, an element of judgment is required in selecting the point at which the requirement is met. What, for example, is the appropriate body pool size, blood level, or enzyme activity to equate with an adequate intake, especially when the responses to increasing or decreasing intakes of nutrients are characteristically curvilinear and do not have clear inflection points?

Appearance of deficiency signs is clear evidence of an inadequate intake and, thus, prevention of these signs provides a guide to the minimal amount required. But it is a matter of judgment when it comes to how much the body pool, blood level, or metabolic indicator should be above the value associated with the prevention of signs. As intake of most nutrients is increased, excretion of the nutrient or of its metabolic products increases, and a sharp rise in body losses serves as an indicator that intake is in excess of needs. But as intake of some nutrients (vitamins A and D, for example) is increased, they continue to accumulate to a point at which toxic reactions can occur.

The total numbers of subjects studied in experiments on requirements, and the total amount of information available, is less than desirable. For many nutrients, values for intermediate age-groups must be obtained by interpolation from what is known about the requirements of infants and young adults; this is because few subjects at other ages have been studied. Differences in the judgments of various national committees lead to differences in estimates of the requirement. For a few nutrients, such as ascorbic acid and calcium, such differences in judgment are wide. But as a rule, the similarity of the values determined by different committees is impressive.

Individual Variability of Requirements

Individuals differ considerably in their requirements for essential nutrients owing to genetic differences among them. Stiebling and Phipard (1939) originally suggested that an intake of 50 percent above the average requirement should meet the needs of those with the highest requirements. L. B. Pett, C. A. Morrell, and F. W. Hanley (1945) assumed that requirements follow a Gaussian distribution, so RDA values would have to exceed average requirements by about three times the standard deviation of the mean in order to meet the needs of all individuals in the population. M. H. Lorstad (1971) subsequently proposed that a value two standard deviations above the average requirements (which would cover 97 to 98 percent of the population) would be an appropriate practical dietary standard. His proposal was adopted by FAO/WHO and has since been accepted generally. In view of the tendency of RDA committees to be generous rather than parsimonious in the selection of values for requirements, and of the ability of the body to conserve nutrients if intake is somewhat below the requirement without impairment of health, this would seem to be an acceptable approach.

In practice, for many nutrients there are not enough individual values to permit reliable estimates of the variability of requirements. In the case of nutrients for which the procedure has been applied, requirements follow a Gaussian distribution with coefficients of variation (the standard deviation expressed as a percentage of the mean) of about 15 (10 to 20) percent (Beaton 1994). If it is assumed that requirements for other nutrients follow a similar pattern, increasing the average requirement by about 30 percent should give an acceptable estimate for setting RDA generally (FAO/WHO 1988; Beaton 1991). Iron requirements of menstruating women, which are skewed toward the upper end of the range, are an exception.

Other Considerations in Setting RDA

RDA are the amounts of nutrients that should be present in foods as they are eaten. Losses of nutrients that occur during processing and preparation are not taken into account in setting RDA, but factors that influence the utilization of nutrients in the food ingested are. These include the digestibility of the foods, the biological availability of the nutrient from the food, absorption, and the presence in foods of precursors of certain nutrients. The requirement for protein, for example, is a composite requirement for nine essential amino acids and for a nonspecific source of nitrogen. The requirement for protein, thus, depends upon the digestibility of the protein and the proportions of amino acids it contains. RDA for protein are based on requirements for protein of the highest quality.

Many plant foods contain carotenoids, precursors of vitamin A (retinol) that differ in vitamin A value. To take this into account, RDA for vitamin A are expressed as retinol equivalents. The contributions from the vitamin and its precursors will depend upon the nature of the food supply. The amino acid tryptophan is a precursor of the vitamin niacin, so the need for this vitamin will depend upon the tryptophan content of the protein consumed. Thus, the RDA is expressed as niacin-equivalents.

The biological availability of iron may range from as low as 3 percent for foods of plant origin to 20 percent for foods of animal origin; hence, RDA for this nutrient will depend upon the proportions of plant and animal products in the food supply. Differences in the biological availability of nutrients in national food supplies account for some of the differences in RDA for essential nutrients among countries. There is no evidence to suggest that physiological requirements for different racial groups differ significantly.

RDA for Food Sources of Energy

The RDA for energy, expressed as kilocalories or megajoules per day (1,000 kilocalories equal 4.184 megajoules), are actually requirements for the components of the diet that, upon oxidation in the body, yield energy – carbohydrates, fats, and proteins. Ordinarily the amount of food consumed by most healthy individuals is controlled spontaneously by the body, over time, to an amount that will provide just enough energy to balance the amount expended and maintain body weight relatively constant – often for a period of years. If the RDA for energy were set, as for essential nutrients, at the upper end of the requirement range, it would be a recommendation for overconsumption and, hence, overweight for most people, because intakes in excess of the amount needed are not excreted but stored. The RDA values for energy are, therefore, average requirements for each group, not reference values for each individual in the group.

Energy requirements of individuals can be estimated from knowledge of their resting (basal) energy expenditure, energy expended for physical activity, and energy lost as heat from the stimulation of metabolism after a meal (thermogenesis). Resting energy expenditure varies with body weight, age, and sex. It can be estimated from equations derived empirically from relationships among basal metabolic rate, body weight, age, sex, and height, which are based on measurements of energy expenditures determined directly by calorimetry. Energy required for activity is estimated using factors that are multiples of the resting expenditure appropriate for each activity, and then multiplying these by the amounts of time spent in different activities (HWC 1990; Warwick 1990). The total of energy required for activity and resting energy expenditure, with an allowance for thermogenesis, yields the final value. The amount of food energy consumed daily, averaged over a period of several days, provides a reasonable estimate of the energy requirements of adults who are maintaining a stable body weight.

Uses of RDA

The original purpose of RDA was to "serve as a goal for good nutrition" – to act as reference values for planning nutritionally adequate food supplies and diets for large groups of people, and for devising dietary guidance systems based on sound scientific principles for the public. They have since been used in many other ways, some of which they were not designed for and for which they have limitations that are not always recognized. The uses can be separated into two general categories: (1) "standards for dealing with practical applications of nutrition," and (2) "guidelines for food and nutrition regulations and policies." This distinction is somewhat arbitrary because practical applications may arise from, or even be the basis for, policy decisions. Uses of RDA have also been grouped in another, more technical, way. Those related to planning food supplies and diets, offering dietary guidance, and serving as standards for food regulations and economic assistance programs have been categorized as *prescriptive* uses. Those related to assessment of the adequacy of nutrient intake, diets, and food supplies have been termed *diagnostic* (Beaton 1994). The former classification seems more appropriate for the present purpose, even though the separation between the categories is less distinct.

In using RDA as reference values for different purposes a question arises as to whether they apply equally well to individuals and groups. For energy, the situation is clear. RDA for energy are average values for groups; for applications involving individuals, energy needs of each person must be estimated separately. For essential nutrients the situation is more complex. RDA for essential nutrients exceed the requirements of nearly all persons in the specified groups, so a food supply that meets the RDA should be adequate for an individual and, provided it is distributed equitably, for all members of a group as well. But when RDA are employed as standards for assessing the adequacy of essential nutrient intakes, the answer is less clear. The problems that arise are considered in the following sections.

Uses Related to Practical Applications of Nutrition

Planning food supplies and diets. The RDA are used to estimate the amounts of foods needed to provide large groups of people, such as the armed forces or populations of institutions, with nutritionally adequate diets. For this purpose, information is needed about the proportions of the population in various age-sex categories and about the composition of the available foods. The RDA for energy, being average requirements for each age-sex group, can be used to

calculate directly the total amount of energy sources needed, as about half of the individuals in the group should consume more and half less than the RDA. The RDA for essential nutrients are then used as reference values to assure that foods selected and diets formulated provide the requisite amounts of essential nutrients. Allowance must also be made for losses that occur during food preparation. A similar procedure is used by international agencies to estimate the adequacy of both the quantity and quality of food supplies of nations in meeting the nutritional needs of their populations (FAO/WHO 1985).

It should be emphasized that the objective in planning food supplies and diets is not merely to provide amounts of essential nutrients needed to meet RDA. Diets should be composed of a wide variety of palatable and acceptable foods so that they will meet psychological and social needs and be eaten in the required amounts over long periods of time. In trying to accomplish this, the amount of vitamin A provided, for example, will ordinarily vary greatly from one day to another because relatively few foods are rich sources of this vitamin. Although RDA are specified as daily amounts, this kind of day-to-day variability in the provision of individual nutrients need not be of concern as long as the total amount of each nutrient, averaged over several days, meets the RDA.

Nutrition education. RDA are employed effectively by health professionals for planning nutritionally adequate diets, but they are not designed for use by the public. For people with limited knowledge of nutrition, RDA for nutrients must be translated in terms of foods. A common way of doing this is by first separating familiar foods into a few groups on the basis of the essential nutrients of which they are good sources, and then, using the RDA as reference values, estimating the number of servings from each food group that must be eaten daily to meet essential nutrient needs.

This has been the basis for a food guide, developed by Louise Page and Esther Phipard (USDA 1957), designed to explain how to obtain the required amounts of essential nutrients from a specified number of servings selected from four familiar groups of foods. The number of servings required by adults to obtain the foundation for a nutritionally adequate diet provided only 1,200 to 1,600 kilocalories daily and allowed for obtaining the needed extra energy from additional servings of any of a variety of foods.

The number and selection of servings were modified for children. Estimates of the nutrient content of model diets based on this food guidance system demonstrated that the principles underlying it are sound. The system has been widely used in nutrition education programs for teaching the principles of a nutritionally adequate diet. Many modifications have been proposed in order to adapt it for groups with different cultural backgrounds, lifestyles, and incomes (King et al. 1978). More recently, a modified version based on five food groups – the "food pyramid" (USDA 1992) – was designed as a guide for the total diet and for limiting fat consumption.

Therapeutic nutrition. Although RDA are standards for nutrient intakes of healthy people, they serve equally well as a guide to the nutritional needs of persons with medical problems that do not affect food consumption or nutrient utilization. They also provide a baseline for modifying diets to meet the special nutritional needs of individuals who are ill. Loss of appetite, associated with many types of illness, can result in the wasting of tissues and depletion of body stores of nutrients that must be replenished. Infections of the gastrointestinal tract, disorders that cause malabsorption, systemic infections, injuries, renal failure, certain inborn errors of the metabolism, and many other health problems alter nutritional needs in different ways and to different degrees, owing to the impairment of absorption or excretion or to increased metabolic wastage of nutrients. Dealing with the specific nutritional needs resulting from these conditions requires specific clinical and dietary management.

Designing new or modified foods. RDA are employed in formulating new food products composed of highly purified constituents, foods for special dietary purposes, or products designed as meal replacements, such as special diets for weight reduction, so as to ensure that these will provide appropriate amounts of essential nutrients. When RDA are used for this purpose, it is essential to remember that they are standards for amounts of nutrients to be consumed daily. In the case of products that are total diet replacements, especially those for weight reduction that provide restricted amounts of energy sources, the daily allotment should contain amounts of nutrients that meet the entire RDA.

Foods for general use should contain essential nutrients in reasonable proportion to the amount of energy derived from the product. The concept of "nutrient density" – the amounts of nutrients in the product expressed per 1,000 kilocalories – provides the basis of a method for accomplishing this goal (Hansen, Wyse, and Sorenson 1979). To provide a set of standards, RDA are expressed as units of nutrient required per 1,000 kilocalories of energy sources required. The quantities of nutrients in the product can then be adjusted to correspond with the standard.

Some shortcomings of this procedure should be recognized. In establishing standards for nutrient density, only a single RDA value is used for each nutrient – usually the value for the age-sex group with the highest requirement. For other groups, the standards therefore deviate in varying degrees from the RDA. Nutrient density values have also been proposed as guides to the relative nutritive values of foods. Caution should be exercised, however, in employing the nutrient density concept to compare the nutritive values of foods. The contributions of foods to meeting nutritional needs depend not just on differences in their nutrient content but also on differences in the amounts consumed. Two foods may have the same nutrient density, but if one is eaten in an amount only 10 percent that of the other, their contributions to meeting nutrient needs will differ by tenfold.

Assessing the adequacy of nutrient intakes – individuals. The amounts of essential nutrients consumed by individuals can be estimated from records of the quantities of different foods they eat and tables of food composition. The amounts of nutrients consumed can then be compared with the RDA. Unfortunately, comparisons of this type permit few firm conclusions about the adequacy of intakes. Because RDA exceed the requirements of most people, the probability of nutritional inadequacy is obviously remote for those whose intakes equal or exceed the RDA. But because requirements of individuals differ widely, it is not valid to conclude that an intake below the RDA is inadequate. All that can be said is that the further the intake falls below the RDA, the greater is the probability that the intake is inadequate. This is not a shortcoming of the RDA; dietary standards generally are not meant to be used for this purpose. The adequacy of essential nutrient intakes of individuals can be evaluated accurately only by clinical and biochemical assessment, not by comparing intakes with the RDA or with any other standard.

Inability to quantify the degree of nutrient inadequacy from knowledge of intakes below the RDA has, however, stimulated efforts to apply statistical methods (and the risk concept) as an alternative procedure for assessing the adequacy of essential nutrient intakes. Application of probability analysis, using information about *requirements* (not RDA) and intakes of essential nutrients, has been proposed as a way of obtaining a quantitative estimate of the *risk* of nutritional inadequacy (FNB 1986; FAO/WHO 1988; Beaton 1991, 1994).

From plots of the cumulative percentage distribution of *requirements* (assuming they are normally distributed) against intake, the probability that an intake below the highest requirement is inadequate can be estimated; for example, the probability that an intake equal to the average requirement is inadequate is 50 percent. Although a quantitative estimate of the probability (risk) of a particular intake being inadequate is obtained through this type of analysis, it does not establish whether the intake actually is inadequate. But it can help in deciding if an individual should be referred for specific biochemical tests.

Uses Related to Food and Nutrition Policy

Nutritional standards are needed both for many food and nutrition programs and regulations and to provide a reliable scientific basis for interpreting the nutrient intake information that is employed to establish food and nutrition policy. For some of these uses, RDA are appropriate standards, but for others they are too complex and must be modified, or they are too limited in scope and must be used in conjunction with other standards.

Assessment of nutritional adequacy – populations. Information about the adequacy of essential nutrient intakes in a population is used to identify potential health problems. In assessing the adequacy of intakes in a population, one must take into account not only the variability of requirements but also the variability of intakes. Food and, hence, nutrient intakes of individuals vary widely. Even in developed countries, where the average nutritional intake of the population exceeds the RDA, those of many individuals are found to be less – and some much less – than the RDA (USDHHS/USDA 1986). This may occur for many reasons, such as poverty, illness, and ignorance, but the point is that even if the average intake of a population is in excess of the RDA, there is no assurance that all individuals within that population are meeting their requirements. Moreover, the problem of estimating the proportion of persons who have inadequate intakes remains unresolved.

From the results of dietary surveys of representative samples of large populations, the proportions of the population with different intakes can be determined. Then, with this information about the distribution of intakes, the same type of analysis that is used to assess the risk of inadequacy for an individual can be employed to assess the probable incidence (risk) of inadequate intakes in the population (FNB 1986; FAO/WHO 1988). This problem has been analyzed in detail by G. H. Beaton (1994), who concluded that only if the average intake of a population exceeds the *average requirement* by more than twice the coefficient of variation of the *average intake* will the probability of inadequate intakes in the group be low. This raises a question as to whether RDA for groups should be higher than those for individuals. The answer is not clear, but because the problem is important in relation to policy decisions, it is important to be aware of it. The actual prevalence of nutritional inadequacy in a population, as in an individual, can be assessed accurately only through clinical and biochemical observations, not by comparing the average population intake with a standard.

It seems not to be sufficiently appreciated, as Beaton (1994) has emphasized, that estimates of the probability of intake being inadequate are based on the observed distribution of individual *requirements* around the mean. Inclusion of a table of average requirements in RDA reports would be more useful than the table of RDA for assessing the adequacy of nutrient intakes by probability analysis. As all committees use essentially the same information for establishing requirements, a higher degree of agreement might

be anticipated in establishing average requirements than in establishing RDA. Having both sets of values published together would also draw attention to the need for a critical assessment of criteria, both for establishing when a requirement has been met and for evaluating the process used to derive RDA from requirements.

Difficulties in trying to assess the adequacy of nutrient intakes using RDA as standards have also stimulated interest in alternative standards. Separate standards that represent the lower limits of acceptable nutrient intake have been developed in New Zealand, Norway, and Australia. These are to be used only for evaluating the adequacy of nutrient intakes (Truswell 1990). The FAO and WHO (1988) have published separate reference values for "basal requirements" and "safe levels of intake" (essentially RDA) for iron and for vitamin A.

The major problems in evaluating the adequacy of nutrient intakes from dietary information are not resolved by establishing new standards. Conclusions about inadequacy can still be drawn only in terms of probability or risk. Moreover, individuals cannot be identified as having inadequate intakes from dietary assessment alone, but as Truswell (1990) notes, intakes below the lower standard are more likely to be associated with deficiency than are intakes at some arbitrary level below the RDA.

Food labeling. To provide consumers with information about nutrient contributions of foods, the U.S. Food and Drug Administration (FDA) established a standard based on the RDA. To use the RDA directly for this purpose would be unwieldy and complicated; in order to devise a standard with a single set of values for food labeling, the FDA selected the highest values from among the RDA for 20 nutrients and called these U.S. Recommended *Daily* Allowances (NNC 1975). Nutrient contributions of products have been listed on labels as percentages of the U.S. RDA per serving. (The different meanings of the terms "U.S. RDA" and "RDA" had created a measure of confusion.)

There are differing views about the purpose of food labels: According to one, the label should provide information that can readily be related to nutritional needs, and thereby serve as a tool for nutrition education; according to another, the main purpose of having nutrition information on the label is to enable the purchaser easily to compare the nutrient contributions of different products. The U.S. RDA are not useful guides to nutrient needs of the various age-sex groups for which RDA are set other than for the adult male. They do serve effectively, however, for the primary purpose for which they were designed – to provide an easy and simple standard for comparing products as to the per-serving percentages of the U.S. RDA that they contain. U.S. RDA are also appropriate standards for programs that fortify foods with nutrients judged to be low in the food supply.

The FDA has recently established new standards for food labeling and regulations. The basic standard for essential nutrients – Reference Daily Intake – is a population-weighted average of the 1989 RDA values for age-sex groups beyond 4 years of age. The amount of nutrient provided by a food product may be included on the label as a percentage of the Daily Reference Value – the amount of the nutrient that should be provided by a diet that yields 2,000 kilocalories. This system will permit simple comparisons of the nutrient contributions of different foods just as the earlier system did, but the values will not relate closely to the RDA. It is essentially a modified form of the nutrient density concept and, as such, may eventually find a niche in nutrition education programs.

Food assistance and welfare programs. Most economic assistance programs of government agencies in the United States are direct or indirect food assistance programs. They include programs such as school lunches, supplementary food for women, infants, and children, and nutrition for the elderly. RDA are used as reference values for many of these programs. To assure that foods or meals supplied through these programs will be of high nutritional quality, it is required that they contain specified proportions of the RDA for certain nutrients. RDA are appropriate standards for meeting needs for essential nutrients, but they are not appropriate as the sole standards for planning meals or diets. As mentioned in relation to diet planning generally, planning meals requires, in addition, consideration of palatability, acceptability, and variety of the food supply, so that diets will be eaten and enjoyed over prolonged periods of time.

Meeting RDA has been an important consideration in developing the food plan that has served as the basis for allotting coupons in the food-stamp program, for licensing and certifying nursing homes and day-care centers, and for establishing the poverty level of income. RDA are appropriate standards for meeting needs for essential nutrients, but even though they are employed in conjunction with other standards, their use in this way has resulted in economic assistance programs being viewed as nutrition programs. It may make such programs more politically acceptable, but it also diverts attention from the need for broader and more comprehensive standards for them. It also has led to efforts to include use of RDA for economic assistance programs as part of the basis for setting RDA values, a procedure that, if accepted, would undermine their scientific validity as dietary standards.

Dietary guidance for the public. The RDA-based food guide system, employed in teaching the principles of a nutritionally adequate diet in nutrition education programs, was developed originally by the USDA as part of that agency's response to the policy of providing dietary guidance for the public. Many aspects of such guidance, however, extend beyond the scope of RDA, such as desirable proportions in the diet of carbohydrates, fats, and other sources of food energy; maintaining a healthful body weight; and associations between diet and disease. These topics ordinarily are discussed in only broad terms in RDA publications, and some are addressed in dietary guidelines adopted jointly (as part of current health policy) by the USDA and the U.S. Department of Health and Human Services (USDHHS) (1990), by Canada (HWC 1992), and by many other countries (Truswell 1987).

To comply with current health policy, a modified food guide system for selecting the *entire* diet from five food groups and emphasizing food selections that will reduce fat and cholesterol consumption (USDA 1992) has been substituted for the earlier one, which provided *partial* guidance in selecting only 1,200 to 1,800 kilocalories from four food groups as a basic diet – to be supplemented with other selections. This new system represents a shift in public dietary guidance in the United States, whereas in Canada, the four-food-group system, with an emphasis on meeting essential nutrient needs, has been retained (albeit with new guidelines for reduced fat consumption) (HWC 1992). RDA continue, nonetheless, to serve as the scientific basis for selecting a nutritionally adequate diet in programs of dietary guidance.

RDA and Changing Health Policy

During the past 30 years, emphasis in health policy in the United States and many other developed nations has shifted toward the prevention of chronic and degenerative diseases. This shift has been accompanied by changes in dietary guidance that require a different base of knowledge from that for guidance based on the RDA. When the nature of the changes is examined, it is evident that this has implications for the concepts of RDA.

Changing Emphasis in Food and Nutrition Policy

Changing health status. Health has improved dramatically in the United States during the twentieth century while dietary advice has been based on the RDA (USDHEW 1979). Nutritional deficiency diseases have been virtually eliminated; mortality from infectious diseases has declined sharply; the proportion of infants born who live to age 65 or older has increased from less than 40 percent to 80 percent or more; height at maturity has increased; and life expectancy has risen from less than 50 to about 75 years. These improvements have occurred in association with improved sanitation, diet, and medical care and a higher standard of living. The extent to which they are attributable to better diets cannot be established, but increased infant and childhood survival and increased growth rates and height at maturity could not have occurred unless diets had been nutritionally adequate (Harper 1987b).

A consequence of the high rate of survival of the young to old age, with a stable, then declining, birth rate, is that the proportion of people 65 years of age or older in the population has increased from 4 to 12 percent. Such aging of the population has been accompanied in most developed countries by an increase in the proportion of deaths from cardiovascular diseases and cancer, from about 20 percent of total deaths during the early 1900s to about 70 percent today.

New directions in dietary advice. The emergence of chronic and degenerative diseases as the major causes of death, coupled with the perception that alterations in diet may increase life expectancy by delaying the onset of such diseases (the causes of which are poorly understood), has brought about a striking change in food, nutrition, and health policy. Much greater attention is now being given to dietary guidance for the "prevention" of diseases associated with aging than to advice on how to select a nutritionally adequate diet (USDHHS 1988; USDA/USDHHS 1990).

This change in policy evolved over a period of more than two decades (Truswell 1987), mainly in response to reports of associations between the type and quantity of fat in the diet and mortality from heart disease. Conclusions drawn from these associations and accepted as the bases for changes in health policy have, nonetheless, been controversial (FNB 1980), and skeptical views have been expressed by numerous experts.[1] Later observations that high intakes of vegetables and fruits are associated with lower mortality from certain cancers expanded interest in diet modification as a disease prevention measure (USDHHS 1988; FNB 1989a). The underlying bases for these associations have not been established, and claims that certain known plant constituents (such as carotenoids) may be among the effective agents have led to further controversy. Despite this, however, the recommendation for increased consumption of vegetables and fruits is accepted generally, on several grounds, as appropriate nutrition policy.

In 1980, as the culmination of an effort to achieve consensus among conflicting views over the role of diet in delaying the onset of chronic and degenerative diseases, the USDA and USDHHS jointly adopted (and later revised) a set of "Dietary Guidelines for Americans" (USDA/USDHHS 1990). Two of the seven guidelines – "Eat a variety of foods" (a nutritionally adequate diet), and "Maintain healthy body weight" – are the essence of the RDA-based dietary guidance initiated decades ago for variety and moderation in food consumption. The others, recommending a diet low in fat (and especially in saturated fat and cholesterol), with plenty of vegetables, fruits, and grains (providing fiber) and only moderate use of sugars, salt, and alcohol, were proposed as guidelines for reducing the risk of developing chronic and degenerative diseases, as is emphasized in the text of the publication.

The purpose of these guidelines is distinctly different from those based on the RDA. They are uniform dietary recommendations for the entire population, adopted to institute a health policy for the control of diseases that are not products of nutritional deficiencies and to which individuals differ greatly in susceptibility. They deal mainly with foods and food constituents that are not essential nutrients (energy sources, fiber, cholesterol) and are based on information that is beyond the scope of the RDA – indirect evidence of associations that cannot be accurately quantified. RDA, in contrast to these guidelines, are quantitative reference values for intakes of essential nutrients. They are part of the information base employed in developing programs to institute a policy of encouraging consumption of diets containing adequate amounts of nutrients, deficits of which will cause diseases in all individuals in the population. In a recently published revision of *Dietary Guidelines for Americans* (USDA/USDHHS 1995), although the guidelines themselves remain essentially the same, the text has been modified considerably. Much more emphasis has been placed on dietary guidance for maintaining health and much less on diet as a disease prevention measure. This change has improved the balance between dietary guidance based on well-established knowledge of the effects of essential nutrients (the RDA) and guidance based on evidence, much of it indirect, of probable health benefits from other components of foods (including unidentified substances).

The adoption of a policy that emphasizes dietary modification as a means of disease prevention has led to proposals that the RDA concept be modified to conform with the new direction in health policy (Hegsted 1993; Lachance 1993; IM 1994). To accomplish this, the RDA would be expanded to include all dietary constituents shown to influence susceptibility to chronic and degenerative diseases; some examples are carotenoids (plant pigments, some of which are precursors of vitamin A), cholesterol, and fiber (Lachance 1993, 1994). Moreover, observations that high intakes of certain vitamins (especially those that can function as antioxidants, such as vitamins E and C) may reduce the risk of heart disease and some cancers have given rise to proposals that such information be used in setting values for the RDA (IM 1994). Controversy over issues of this type delayed revision of the tenth RDA report for several years (Pellett 1988).

If the basis for setting RDA is modified to include consideration of the effects of substances (such as fiber) that cannot be quantified accurately, and of medicinal or pharmacological effects of vitamins or other nutrients (which require amounts well in excess of those that can be obtained from diet), the RDA will cease to be reliable reference values for meeting basic physiological needs (Truswell 1990; Harper 1994; Rosenberg 1994). Such a change would represent modification of a standard (the RDA) to conform with policy. The RDA, which are set on the basis of critical scientific evaluation, would become a vehicle for dietary guidance comparable to dietary guidelines, which are established by consensus. To maintain the independence and integrity of sources of information employed in making policy decisions, it is essential that the process of evaluating information used in setting policy be separated clearly from the process used to develop programs to institute policy. Continuing the approach used in most countries of maintaining a clear separation between the process for establishing dietary guidelines and that for setting dietary standards (Reference Nutrient Intakes; RDA) will accomplish this. Separate publication of dietary guidelines also provides an appropriate mechanism for presenting information about the potential health benefits (even tentative ones) of foods and food constituents independently of the RDA. Adoption of the British approach of calling the dietary standards "reference values" would be a further contribution toward maintaining such separation.

Alfred E. Harper

Note

1. These experts include E. H. Ahrens, Jr. (1985); G. J. Brissom (1981); Harper (1987b); S. B. Hulley, J. M. B. Walsh, and T. B. Newman (1992); D. Kritchevsky (1992); J. McCormick and P. Skrabanek (1988); M. F. Muldoon, S. B. Manuck, and K. E. Matthews (1990); M. F. Oliver (1986); R. E. Olson (1986); R. L. Smith and E. R. Pinckney (1988, 1991); W. E. Stehbens (1989); and W. C. Taylor and colleagues (1987).

Bibliography

Ackerknecht, E. H. 1982. *A short history of medicine.* Baltimore, Md.

Adams, F., trans. 1952. Hippocratic writings. In *Great books of the Western world,* Vol. 10, ed. R. M. Hutchins. Chicago.

Ahrens, E. H., Jr. 1985. The diet-heart question in 1985: Has it really been settled? *Lancet* 1: 1085-7.

American Dietetic Association (ADA). 1941. Recommended allowances for the various dietary essentials. *Journal of the American Dietetic Association* 17: 565-7.

Beaton, G. H. 1991. Human nutrient requirement estimates. *Food Nutrition and Agriculture* 1: 3-15.

1994. Criteria of an adequate diet. In *Modern nutrition in health and disease.* Eighth edition, ed. M. E. Shils, J. A. Olson, and M. Shike, 1491-1505. Philadelphia, Pa.

Brissom, G. J. 1981. *Lipids in human nutrition.* Englewood, N.J.

British Medical Association (BMA). 1933. Committee on nutrition. *British Medical Journal,* Supplement 25.

Brock, W. H. 1993. *The Norton history of chemistry.* New York.

Burnet, E. T., and W. R. Aykroyd. 1935. Nutrition and public health. *Quarterly Bulletin of the Health Organization of the League of Nations* 4: 1-52.

Burnham, J. C. 1987. *How superstition won and science lost.* New Brunswick, N.J.

Carpenter, K. J. 1988. *The history of scurvy and vitamin C.* New York and Cambridge.

1994. *Protein and energy.* New York and Cambridge.

CCN (Canadian Council on Nutrition). 1940. The Canadian dietary standard. *National Health Review* 8: 1-9.

Clark, F. Le G. 1968. Food habits as a practical nutrition problem. *World Review of Nutrition and Dietetics* 9: 56-84.

Cowan, C. W., and P. J. Watson, eds. 1992. *The origins of agriculture.* Washington, D.C.

DHSS (Department of Health and Social Security) (U.K.). 1985. *Recommended daily amounts of food energy and nutrients for groups of people in the United Kingdom.* London.

1991. *Dietary reference values for food energy and nutrients for the United Kingdom.* London.

FAO/WHO (Food and Agriculture Organization and World Health Organization of the United Nations). 1970. *Requirements of ascorbic acid, vitamin D, vitamin B12, folate and iron.* WHO Technical Report Series No. 452. Geneva.

1985. *Energy and protein requirements.* WHO Technical Report Series No. 724. Geneva.

1988. *Requirements of vitamin A, iron, folate and vitamin B12.* FAO Food and Nutrition Series No. 23. Rome.

Fidanza, F. 1979. Diets and dietary recommendations in ancient Greece and Rome and the school of Salerno. *Progress in Food and Nutritional Sciences* 3: 79-99.

FNB (Food and Nutrition Board). 1974. *Recommended dietary allowances.* Eighth edition. Washington, D.C.

1980. *Toward healthful diets.* Washington, D.C.

1986. *Nutrient adequacy: Assessment using food consumption surveys.* Washington, D.C.

1989a. *Diet and health.* Washington, D.C.

1989b. *Recommended dietary allowances.* Tenth edition. Washington, D.C.

Guggenheim, K. Y. 1981. *Nutrition and nutritional diseases.* Lexington, Mass.

Hansen, R. G., B. W. Wyse, and A. W. Sorenson. 1979. *Nutritional quality index of foods.* Westport, Conn.

Harper, A. E. 1985. Origin of the recommended dietary allowances – an historic overview. *American Journal of Clinical Nutrition* 41: 140-8.

1987a. Evolution of recommended dietary allowances – new directions. *Annual Review of Nutrition* 7: 509-37.

1987b. Transitions in health status: Implications for dietary recommendations. *American Journal of Clinical Nutrition* 45: 1094-1107.

1988. Nutrition: From myth and magic to science. *Nutrition Today* 23 (January/February): 8-17.

1994. Recommended dietary intakes: Current and future approaches. In *Modern nutrition in health and disease.* Eighth edition, ed. M. E. Shils, J. A. Olson, and M. Shike, 1475-90. Philadelphia, Pa.

Hegsted, D. M. 1993. Nutrition standards for today. *Nutrition Today* 28: 34-6.

Hertzler, A. A., and H. L. Anderson. 1974. Food guides in the United States. *Journal of the American Dietetic Association* 64: 19-28.

Hulley, S. B., J. M. B. Walsh, and T. B. Newman. 1992. Health policy on blood cholesterol. *Circulation* 86: 1026-9.

HWC (Health and Welfare Canada). 1983. *Recommended nutrient intakes for Canadians.* Ottawa.

1990. *Nutrition recommendations.* Ottawa.

1992. *Food guide.* Ottawa.

IM (Institute of Medicine). 1994. *How should the recommended dietary allowances be revised?* Washington, D.C.

King, J. C., C. G. Cohenour, C. G. Corruccini, and P. Schneeman. 1978. Evaluation and modification of the basic four food guide. *Journal of Nutrition Education* 10: 27-9.

Kritchevsky, D. 1992. Unobserved publications. In *Human nutrition: A continuing debate,* ed. M. Eastwood, C. Edwards, and D. Parry, 51-60. London.

Lachance, P. 1993. *Proceedings of a workshop on future recommended dietary allowances.* New Brunswick, N.J.

   1994. The RDA concept: Time for a change. *Nutrition Reviews* 52: 266-70.

League of Nations. 1937. *Final report of the Mixed Committee of the League of Nations on the relation of nutrition to health, agriculture and economic policy.* League of Nations Official No. 13, II, A.

   1938. Report by the Technical Commission on Nutrition on the work of its third session. *Bulletin of the League of Nations Health Organization* 7: 461-82.

Leitch, I. 1942. The evolution of dietary standards. *Nutrition Abstracts and Reviews* 11: 509-21.

Lorstad, M. H. 1971. Recommended intake and its relation to nutrient deficiency. *FAO Nutrition Newsletter* 9: 18-24.

Lusk, G. 1964. Early history of nutrition. In *Milestones in nutrition,* ed. S. A. Goldblith and M. A. Joslyn, 19-94. Westport, Conn.

McCollum, E. V. 1957. *A history of nutrition.* Baltimore, Md.

McCollum, E. V., E. Orent-Keiles, and H. G. Day. 1939. *The newer knowledge of nutrition.* New York.

McCormick, J., and P. Skrabanek. 1988. Coronary heart disease is not preventable by population interventions. *Lancet* 2: 839-41.

Miller, Donald F., and Leroy Voris. 1969. Chronological changes in recommended dietary allowances. *Journal of the American Dietetic Association* 54: 109-17.

MRC (Medical Research Council) (U.K.). 1932. *Vitamins: A survey of present knowledge.* London.

Muldoon, M. F., S. B. Manuck, and K. E. Matthews. 1990. Lowering cholesterol concentrations and mortality: A quantitative review of primary prevention trials. *British Medical Journal* 301: 309-14.

Munro, H. N. 1964. Historical introduction: The origin and growth of our present concepts of protein metabolism. In *Mammalian protein metabolism,* ed. H. N. Munro and J. B. Allison, 1-29. New York.

NHMRC (National Health and Medical Research Council) (Australia). 1990. *Recommended nutrient intakes: Australian papers,* ed. A. S. Truswell. Sydney.

NNC (National Nutrition Consortium). 1975. *Nutrition labeling.* Bethesda, Md.

Oliver, M. F. 1986. Prevention of coronary heart disease - propaganda, promises, problems, and prospects. *Circulation* 73: 1-9.

Olson, R. E. 1986. Mass intervention versus screening and selective intervention for prevention of coronary heart disease. *Journal of the American Medical Association* 255: 204-7.

Pachter, H. M. 1951. *Magic into science.* New York.

Pellett, P. L. 1988. Commentary: The R.D.A. controversy revisited. *Ecology of Food and Nutrition* 21: 315-20.

Pett, L. B., C. A. Morrell, and F. W. Hanley. 1945. The development of dietary standards. *Canadian Journal of Public Health* 36: 232-9.

Roberts, Lydia J. 1944. Scientific basis for the recommended

dietary allowances. *New York State Journal of Medicine* 44: 59-66.

   1958. Beginnings of the recommended dietary allowances. *Journal of the American Dietetic Association* 34: 903-8.

Rosenberg, H. R. 1945. *Chemistry and physiology of the vitamins.* New York.

Rosenberg, I. H. 1994. Nutrient requirements for optimal health: What does that mean? *Journal of Nutrition* 124 (Supplement): 1777-9.

Smith, R. L., and E. R. Pinckney. 1988. *Diet, blood cholesterol, and coronary heart disease.* Vol. 1, *A relationship in search of evidence.* Santa Monica, Calif.

   1991. *Diet, blood cholesterol, and coronary heart disease.* Vol. 2, *A critical review of the literature.* Santa Monica, Calif.

Stehbens, W. E. 1989. The controversial role of dietary cholesterol and hypercholesterolemia in coronary heart disease and atherogenesis. *Pathology* 21: 213-21.

Stiebling, H. K. 1933. *Food budgets for nutrition and production programs.* USDA Miscellaneous Publication No. 183. Washington, D.C.

Stiebling, H. K., and E. F. Phipard. 1939. *Diets of families of employed wage earners and clerical workers in cities.* USDA Circular No. 507. Washington, D.C.

Taylor, W. C., T. M. Pas, D. S. Shepard, and A. L. Komaroff. 1987. Cholesterol reduction and life expectancy: A model incorporating model risk factors. *Annals of Internal Medicine* 106: 605-14.

Todhunter, E. N. 1954. Biographical notes on the history of nutrition - Gerrit Jan Mulder. *Journal of the American Dietetic Association* 30: 1253.

   1961. Biographical notes on the history of nutrition - Edward Smith. *Journal of the American Dietetic Association* 39: 475.

Truswell, A. Stewart. 1983. Recommended dietary intakes around the world. *Nutrition Abstracts and Reviews* 53: 939-1015, 1075-1119.

   1987. Evolution of dietary recommendations, goals, and guidelines. *American Journal of Clinical Nutrition* 45: 1060-72.

   1990. The philosophy behind recommended dietary intakes: Can they be harmonized? *European Journal of Clinical Nutrition* 44 (Supplement 2): 3-11.

USDA (U.S. Department of Agriculture). 1939. *Food and life. Yearbook of agriculture.* Washington, D.C.

   1957. *Essentials of an adequate diet.* USDA Home Economics Research Report No. 3. Washington, D.C.

   1992. *Food guide pyramid.* Home and Garden Bulletin No. 249. Washington, D.C.

USDA/USDHHS (U.S. Department of Agriculture and U.S. Department of Health and Human Services). 1990. *Nutrition and your health: Dietary guidelines for Americans.* Home and Garden Bulletin No. 232, Third edition. Washington, D.C.

   1995. *Dietary Guidelines for Americans.* Washington, D.C.

USDHEW (U.S. Department of Health, Education, and Welfare). 1979. *Healthy people - the Surgeon General's report on health promotion and disease prevention.* USDHEW Publication No. 79-55071. Washington, D.C.

USDHHS (U.S. Department of Health and Human Services). 1988. *The Surgeon General's report on nutrition and health.* USDHHS (PHS) Publication No. 88-50210. Washington, D.C.

USDHHS/USDA (U.S. Department of Health and Human Services and U.S. Department of Agriculture). 1986. *Nutri-*

tion monitoring in the United States. USDHHS (PHS) Publication No. 86-1255. Washington, D.C.

Warwick, P. M. 1990. Predicting food energy requirements from estimates of energy expenditure. In *Recommended nutrient intakes: Australian papers,* ed. A. S. Truswell, 295-320. Sydney.

Whitehead, Roger G. 1992. Dietary reference values. *Proceedings of the Nutrition Society* 51: 29-34.

Whorton, J. C. 1982. *Crusaders for fitness.* Princeton, N.J.

Wightman, W. P. D. 1953. *The growth of scientific ideas.* New Haven, Conn.

Young, E. Gordon. 1964. Dietary standards. In *Nutrition: A comprehensive treatise.* Vol. 2, *Vitamins, nutrient requirements, and food selection,* ed. G. H. Beaton and E. W. McHenry, 299-325. New York.

VII.5 ❧ Food Labeling

In the United States, the past three decades have witnessed tremendous changes in the way the public views the foods it buys. Unlike counterparts in the developing world, where problems of food availability and food quantities still dominate, consumers in the United States (and the West in general) have become increasingly interested in the nutritional quality of the foodstuffs they are offered. As a consequence, nutrition labeling has emerged to play a key role in government regulation of the food supply, in informing consumers about the constituents of the foods they eat, and in the formulation and marketing of food products by the manufacturers.

The importance of food labels has come about in spite of the fact that during the last 20 years or so, policy decisions regarding the implementation of nutrition labeling have been made in a political environment that emphasizes nonintervention in the operation of market economies. Recent legislation in industrialized countries has taken, for the most part, a minimalist approach to the regulation of nutritional quality. But although still controversial, labeling is seen as an acceptable "information remedy" that requires relatively little market intervention, and most Western nations have established some form of legislative guidelines for the regulation of nutrition labeling. With the adoption of the Nutrition Labeling and Education Act (NLEA) in 1994 (Caswell and Mojduszka 1996), the United States is currently in the forefront of establishing a mandatory and comprehensive national nutrition labeling policy.

The growing interest in nutrition policy reflects the understanding that foods represent major potential risks to public health because of such factors as foodborne organisms, heavy metals, pesticide residues, food additives, veterinary residues, and naturally occurring toxins. But although these are very real health hazards, scientists believe that the risks associated with nutritional imbalances in the composition of the diet as a whole are the most significant in the longer run, particularly in industrialized countries, where the high percentage of fat in daily diets seems to significantly threaten public health (Henson and Traill 1993). The recognition of nutritional quality as a value in itself has led to a separation of the nutritional from other food safety issues and a growing tendency to develop legislation targeted specifically at nutrition.

The latter, along with a perceived need for nutrition labels, is a reflection of the social changes that are influencing how, where, and when, as well as what, people eat (Wilkins 1994). Perhaps the most important change is the growing number of households that consist of two working parents or a single parent. With such a change in family structure, more meals are consumed in restaurants, more foods are eaten at home that have been prepared elsewhere, and convenience items predominate among foods prepared at home. In addition, the traditional three meals per day are often replaced with ad hoc meals as consumers employ an even greater variety of "heat and eat" foods. As a result, the consumption of traditional staple foods, such as cereals and potatoes, has decreased, and in most industrialized countries, the consumption of meat, milk, and milk products has markedly risen. The percentage of fat in the diets of citizens in industrialized countries has thus grown substantially in the last half century. Whereas regional variations persist, these current trends in eating patterns have generally meant a much greater intake of fats as a percentage of calories, which many view as a major factor in increasing morbidity and mortality from so-called chronic diseases such as cancer and coronary artery disease (Helsing 1991).

Such linkages between diet and health, and the communication of this knowledge to the general public, have led to an increased demand for higher quality, to which producers and retailers have responded by extending the variety of foods offered for sale. The nutritional composition of many foods has improved as well as their labeling; this, in turn, has stimulated an even more intensive marketing of the nutritional attributes of food products, as producers have recognized that an informed public will pay for better nutrition. Thus, as growing numbers of scholarly studies show, nutrition labels have become vital to public knowledge about food and, consequently, to improving public health (Caswell 1991).

The Evolution of Labeling Regulation

Despite the recent importance that labeling has achieved, concerns with labeling food products according to safety and purity have a long history. For example, throughout the medieval and early modern periods, foods of all kinds were identified by origin and grade, and regulatory "marks" on bread go back at least to the reign of Henry III in thirteenth-century

Britain. Indeed, they were one of the most common forms of control imposed on food producers in the Middle Ages. Manufacturers also recognized the profitability of such regulation; the German "Brewing Purity Law" of 1516, imposed by the Bavarian court but readily adopted by German brewers, stands as an example that continues to this day as a marketing tool for beer.

The history of food regulation in its current form has its roots in aspects of late-nineteenth-century modernization and industrialization. Scientific chemical experimentation in the early 1800s made possible the sophisticated adulteration of food as well as tests of its quality. The later growth of international markets and transportation networks contributed to a decline of reliance on fresh food and advanced the increasingly impersonal aspects of food markets. The key to such markets was food durability, and as processing capabilities evolved through packaging, bottling, and canning in the nineteenth, and freezing in the twentieth century, so interests in marking and labeling food products by brand name and contents became increasingly important.

Because they presumably carried assurances of quality and consistency in an impersonal market, brand names substituted to some degree for the lack of face-to-face contact in modern retailing, and by 1900 food labels showing brand names were well established in the industrialized Western nations. In the United States, major brands dating from the late nineteenth century include those created by Joseph Campbell, H. J. Heinz, and P. D. Armour. By 1920, producers recognized that brand names were a significant factor in trade and worth protecting legally as the important "public face" of a company's product line (Wilkins 1994). Beyond displaying brand names that promoted company reputation and increased consumer recognition, food labels sometimes included frequently specious claims about the content, quality, and healthfulness of their products.

During the late nineteenth century, there was a growing government interest in regulating the food supply through inspection and control of such deceptive labeling. To some extent this was a response to varying national standards for the import of meat products, but it was also because of an increasing public recognition of the potential health hazard of processed food. In the United States, public and government concerns with food purity helped propel the outspoken Dr. Harvey Wiley, a chemist from Purdue University, into work on food safety with the Department of Agriculture in 1883. As leader of the Bureau of Chemistry, the forerunner of the U.S. Food and Drug Administration (FDA), Wiley worked on a variety of food- and health-related issues.

The Pure Food and Drug Act of 1906 for which he had labored long and hard (FDA 1993) marked a major step toward labeling regulation and offers a classic example of how interactions between con-

sumers, government, and industry shape the food regulatory environment. Various attempts to pass food and drug legislation had languished in Congress for over 15 years, while food poisoning scandals and investigative reports appearing in the scientific and popular press called growing attention to abuses in the food industry. And public outcry against the unsanitary conditions in the meat-packing industry in Chicago was inspired by the publication of Upton Sinclair's 1905 novel, *The Jungle.*

All of this activity encouraged President Theodore Roosevelt to back legislation authorizing federal oversight of the food industry. The provisions of Wiley's Pure Food and Drug Act, along with an accompanying Beef Inspection Act, authorized the federal inspection of meat-processing plants, established controls on food additives and preservatives, and tightened controls on food labels (FDA 1993). The latter, in a major step forward, were now required to correctly identify the producer so as to facilitate consumer complaints. Food labels were also to honestly list package contents; descriptive superlatives, such as "best" or "superfine," had to be removed if the manufacturer could not prove the claim. If producers had products tested and registered by the Department of Agriculture, an official label could be used on these packages.

This provision, however, was weakened by the lack of postregistration oversight: Unless a consumer complained, producers could use official labels with impunity, even though product composition might have changed since initial registration. Thus, in a progression that became typical of industry reception of new food regulations, the powerful Chicago "Beef Trust" at first resisted the new legislation but then publicly adopted the federal stamp of approval in an effort to revive public confidence and increase flagging demand for its meat products (FDA 1993).

Other important regulatory measures were adopted in the United States during the following decades. In 1938 a new U.S. Food, Drug, and Cosmetic Act updated the 1906 Pure Food and Drug Act and tightened labeling regulations considerably. In addition to prohibiting statements that were false or misleading, the law prescribed that labels on all processed and packaged foods had to include the name of the food, its net weight, and the name and address of its manufacturer or distributor. A detailed list of ingredients was also required on certain products. The Food, Drug, and Cosmetic Act was subsequently updated, and in 1950, an Oleomargarine Act required clear labels on margarine spreads to distinguish them from butter. In 1957, the Poultry Act authorized the labeling of poultry products.

In 1969, the White House Conference on Food, Nutrition, and Health (FDA 1993) investigated dietary deficiencies in the United States and recommended that the federal government take a more active role in identifying the nutritional qualities of food, which set the stage for the differentiation of food safety from nutrition regulation. The 1970s saw an explosion of public interest in healthful foods, as fears of pesticides, food radiation, and mercury poisoning in fish, on the one side, and the rise of "health food," organic farming, and consumer watchdog groups, on the other, encouraged a more activist approach to nutrition policy and food labeling.

Recent Labeling Regulation in the United States

The United States, as the world leader in the regulation of nutrition labeling, moved from partial controls in the 1970s and 1980s on voluntary provision of nutrition information (on product labels) to mandatory nutrition labeling in the 1990s. No other Western nation has similar mandatory labeling regulations. This move was, in part, a response to heightened public awareness of nutrition-related health issues in the United States. But it represented, as well, an acknowledgment on the part of federal health agencies that a significant portion of the population had poor diets. At the same time, manufacturers discovered that nutritional claims on packaging labels could be powerful marketing tools.

In 1973 the FDA had issued rules requiring nutrition labeling on all packaged foods to which one or more nutrients had been added or on foods whose advertising included claims about their nutritional qualities and/or their importance in the daily diet. But for almost all other foods, nutrition labeling was voluntary. Voluntary nutrition labeling went into effect in 1975; if producers wished to include nutritional information on their packaging they could, but they were required to use a standardized, federally designed label, which remained in use until 1994.

From 1975 to 1984, food health claims for marketing purposes were prohibited; after 1984, however, some claims were allowed, following case-by-case review by the FDA for nutrient content and health claims (FDA 1993). However, this review process was lax, and little enforcement against deceptive claims took place, virtually inviting industry abuses. Examples included Salisbury steaks that were labeled "lowfat," even though the meat product derived 45 percent of its total calories from fat, and labels on potato chips that concealed high levels of cholesterol-elevating saturated fat.

In 1988, Surgeon General C. Everett Coop released a report on nutrition and health in which, for the first time, the federal government formally recognized the role of diet in the etiology of certain chronic diseases and proposed labeling policies. And after 1989, growing public interest in nutrition, and several publicized cases of label disinformation, led to stricter state and federal scrutiny of nutrient content and health claims on food labels. In 1990, negotiation between the FDA and the United States Department of Agriculture (USDA), often made tense by lobbying on the part of special-interest groups, led to the enactment by Congress of the Nutrition Labeling and Education Act (NLEA) (Gorman 1991). This legislation, which went into effect in 1994, makes nutrition labeling mandatory and strictly regulates nutrient content and health claims. Nutrition labeling, however, remained voluntary for raw foodstuffs (primarily fruits, vegetables, and meats), though grocery stores were allowed to post general nutrition information at the point of sale. Other exempted products from labeling included those destined for consumption away from home, as, for example, in restaurants, hospitals, and other institutions. Small producers, with annual gross sales under $500,000 or food sales under $50,000, were also exempt.

NLEA regulations changed the nutrients that must be listed on the redesigned "Nutrition Facts" panel, which appears on the back side of product packaging. The new list emphasizes fats, sodium, and cholesterol – nutrients that most consumers worry about having too much of rather than too little – and requires that manufacturers indicate percentages of the following macro- and micronutrients on food labels: total calories, calories derived from fat, total fat, saturated fat, cholesterol, total carbohydrates, sugars, dietary fiber, protein, sodium, vitamins A and C, calcium, and iron. Information on the content of these nutrients is presented in quantitative amounts and as percentages of standardized dietary reference values, stated as "Percent of Daily Value." Other nutrition labeling is permitted on a voluntary basis, including information on calories derived from saturated fat and polyunsaturated fat and listings on soluble fiber, insoluble fiber, potassium, and other essential vitamins and minerals.

The percentages given in the "Nutrition Facts" panel are based on standardized serving sizes to help consumers understand and compare the nutritional values of different foods. In fact, according to the NLEA, serving sizes are supposed to be consistent across product lines and close to the amounts people actually consume; the number and amounts of nutrients labeled is based on the serving or portion size supposedly eaten by an "average person" over the age of 4 and must be given in common household and metric measures. Packages that contain less than two servings are considered single-serving containers, and their nutrient contents have to be declared on the basis of the contents of the entire package.

In order to control the manipulation of food descriptors, the FDA has developed consistent and uniform definitions of nine nutrient content claims that expressly or implicitly characterize the level of a nutrient present in a product (such as the Quick Quaker Oats front label, which claims, in eye-catching yellow, that the product is a "lowfat food," a "good source of fiber," a "sodium-free food, and a "cholesterol-free food"). These nutrient content claims are allowed on a voluntary basis, but manufacturers can use them only when a food meets particular nutritional standards.

The nine descriptor terms include: free, low, high, source of, reduced, light (or lite), less, more, and fresh. Because these are key advertising terms and typically appear in marketing tag lines on product front labels, NLEA has encouraged producers to either reformulate their products or drop deceptive nutrient descriptors.

Until 1984, a food product making a claim about the relationship between a nutrient and a disease on its label was treated as a drug (FDA 1993). But in a major shift in nutrition regulatory policy, the NLEA, for the first time, allowed food labels to include voluntary health claims, linking a nutrient or food to the risk of specific diseases or health conditions. For example, within carefully defined limits, food labels are allowed to cite links between calcium and osteoporosis, sodium and hypertension, fat and cardiovascular disease, and fat and cancer (thus, the Quick Quaker Oats back label states in part that "[t]his product is consistent with the American Heart Association dietary guidelines" and that "diets low in saturated fat and cholesterol and high in fiber-containing grains . . . may reduce risk of heart disease").

Recognizing that labels were of limited value without an informed and educated consumer who could understand them, the FDA has also begun a multiyear food labeling education campaign that involves participation by consumer advocates, industry groups and corporations, and other government agencies. Its purpose is to increase consumers' knowledge and to assist them in making sound dietary choices in accordance with the USDA-designed "Dietary Guidelines for Americans." The latter promotes a diet balanced between basic food groups and is usually represented in the form of a food pyramid.

The FDA estimates that in the United States the new food label will cost food processors between $1.4 and $2.3 billion over the next 20 years. But measured in monetary terms, the potential benefits to the public may well exceed the costs; health benefits potentially include decreased rates of coronary heart disease, cancer, osteoporosis, obesity, high blood pressure, and allergic reactions to food (FDA 1993).

Thus, the effects of nutrition labeling go far beyond serving as a shopping aid for consumers. The NLEA is also expected to have a significant impact on the functioning and performance of the food industry because manufacturers will redesign food nutritional profiles to meet changing consumer demands. In other words, for food companies the implementation of mandatory labeling requirements is likely to have important effects on both consumer demand and the marketing of foods (Caswell and Mojduszka 1996).

Nutrition Labeling in Europe

In post–World War II Europe, agricultural and food industry policies were mainly shaped by criteria such as the welfare of industrial workers, economic implications for farmers, national employment, and military security. So long as nutrition experts advised Ministry of Agriculture officials in various European countries on the best crops to cultivate to overcome food shortages in the immediate postwar years, health and nutrition issues were rarely central considerations in agricultural planning but instead were seen as primarily relevant to developing countries.

In 1974, however, the World Food Conference stressed the need for all countries to adopt food safety and nutrition policies, regardless of their stage of development. In Europe, Norway was the first industrialized country to adopt such a policy. By the mid-1980s, a number of health departments in European nations, including West Germany, France, and Great Britain, had issued reports on nutrition and diet, and international organizations such as the World Health Organization (WHO) and the Food and Agriculture Organization (FAO) – both offices of the United Nations – also called attention to the role of nutrients in human health in industrialized societies, citing dietary problems associated with oils and fats.

By 1990, seven countries in Western Europe had established food safety and nutrition policies similar to those in the United States before NLEA (Helsing 1991). But although the majority of these programs recognized that information and public education were key components of a national nutrition policy, they stopped short of requiring labeling on all processed food products.

The regulation of food and nutrition labeling in Europe has taken place within the context of attempts to establish a common European market. In 1979, the European Community (EC) issued rules on food safety and consumer protection based on the "Principle of Mutual Recognition," intended to standardize food health regulations to facilitate international trade. Under this rule, no EC country was to prevent the importation of a food product legally produced and sold in another country, even though the product might not be legally produced according to standards established by the importing country's own laws. Such a rule eased trade restrictions in the EC but presented risks of lowered food quality and safety in countries with more stringent quality standards.

To address these concerns, the EC expanded regulation in the 1980s with new rules on product definition, quality differentiation, and labeling. Under these directives food labels were required to display information on product characteristics, including quality, quantity, and origin of ingredients. Producers are prohibited from making health claims that link their product to the prevention or treatment of diseases. EC labeling policy was intended to supply European consumers with adequate information on nutrition and food quality to help them make informed choices in the grocery store without setting up rigid labeling regulations that might place burdens on individual national economies (Worley et al. 1994).

The variety of nutrition policies in Europe underscores the way variations in regional dietary patterns and differing political environments affect governments' willingness to establish nutrition regulations and is illustrated by a brief examination of food policy in Norway, Denmark, and Poland. In Norway, government planners chose a carefully activist nutrition policy, unique in the extent to which it relied on government intervention. Norway's readiness to adopt interventionist policies reflects in part the relative limits of the country's domestic agricultural sector, based heavily on dairy and beef production, and its dependence on foreign imports of sugar and grains.

Adopted in 1975, Norway's "Food Supply and Nutrition Policy" acknowledged the relationship between public-health objectives and food supply planning. The stated aims of the policy included encouraging healthy eating habits in the population, implementing the recommendations of the World Food Conference of 1974, and maximizing the domestic production of food to ensure the stability, security, and quality of the national food supply. Specific dietary changes recommended for the population – to reduce fat intake to 35 percent of total dietary energy, to increase the consumption of cereal and potatoes, to increase the proportion of polyunsaturated fat in the diet, and to increase the consumption of fish – reflected concerns over the dietary level of fat but also posed a potential threat to Norway's domestic agriculture.

Acting with support from a coalition of industry, consumer, and government representatives, the Norwegian government used a variety of consumer food subsidies (many were already in place) together with agricultural policies intended to slowly raise domestic production of grains while lowering consumer consumption of saturated fats, so as to protect both consumer and industry interests. Information controls forbade misleading advertising, particularly for foods with poor nutritional profiles such as ice cream, chocolate, and soft drinks. Educational programs were also launched and special attention was given to the nutritional content of school courses at the nursery, primary, secondary, and higher levels. Voluntary nutrition labeling of processed foods aimed to better inform the population on the nutritional content of food products. By 1990 fat consumption had dropped to the 35 percent target level and overall agricultural production rose as planned, demonstrating the success of Norway's combination of interventionist and information policies (Gormley, Downey, and O'Beirne 1987; Helsing 1991).

In Denmark, by contrast, food and nutrition policy came relatively late, and was poorly promulgated and coordinated. Acting in response to consumer interest in diet and health, the government adopted a formal nutrition policy in 1984. Unlike Norway, Denmark's policy did not formulate specific nutrition policy goals or assign responsibility for coordination of policy activities. Although the government helped establish several research institutes focused on nutrition issues, little attention was given to providing nutrition information to the public. In 1990, Denmark's nutrient pattern failed to show the same dramatic improvements that had been seen in Norway (Helsing 1991).

Poland's experience with nutrition policy offers an exemplary case of the problems countries on the geographical and economic periphery of the European Union (EU) face in achieving standards deemed important by the Union. In Poland, as in other Eastern European countries with command economies before 1989, nutrition policy lags behind and creates problems for public health and international trade. Though the right of Polish consumers to truthful disclosure of information about the quality of food products was presumably guaranteed when the Polish government accepted United Nations Organization directives in 1985, advertising became the main – and not very satisfactory – source of information about food quality for most Polish people after 1989.

In April 1995, the Federation of Polish Consumers issued a report on "The State of Realization of Consumer Rights in the Polish Food Market" that called attention to shortcomings in the Polish regulatory system. The report made it clear that despite growing public awareness of nutrition issues, laws then in place that dealt with the nutritional composition of foods and their advertising were not effective because the Polish government lacked the power to enforce them. Thus, for example, it became impossible to fine manufacturers that used deceptive advertising because there was no government office to evaluate the nutritional claims made by advertisements.

An ineffective nutrition policy also affects foreign markets for Poland's agricultural products, and it would seem that food labeling policy is necessary to make Polish food acceptable and competitive in international markets as well as competitive with imports reaching Poland. The regulation of nutrition labeling would give Polish manufacturers incentives to quickly come into compliance with higher standards. Such a step would also provide Polish consumers with knowledge to protect themselves from risks posed by foods and save them from buying costly products whose quality is misrepresented. Like other central and Eastern European nations where agriculture and food production are key sectors of the national as well as the export economy, Poland faces the need to put in place effective regulations and enforcement policies that ensure the quality of food products and the reliability and usefulness of information provided on food labels.

An international comparison of nutrition regulation can also underline the importance of food labeling, not only for its value in public education and for encouraging better health but also as an increasingly important component of international trade. The stiffer regulatory environment in the United States poses potential barriers to the import of food from other countries, even those in Western Europe, where regulations are less strict (Worley et al. 1994). As countries in both Eastern and Western Europe and North America transform their regulatory requirements to comply with international trade agreements, informational approaches to food regulation will play a more significant role and will likely lead toward the gradual convergence of international regulatory policies.

This is a slow-moving process, largely because labeling policies evolve in different political climates and in response to different regional diets, but also because food manufacturers typically oppose mandatory nutrition labeling of foods. Changes in national nutrition-labeling regulation have to be carefully negotiated between consumer, government, and industry representatives and involve important policy issues.

Nutrition Labeling and Policy Issues

Since a better awareness of linkages between diet and health has been achieved, governments of many countries have been forced to confront the issue of market intervention in order to regulate food quality. There are two main approaches to the implementation of nutrition policies by central governments. The first, called the minimalist approach, stresses the responsibility of the individual in the attainment of a healthful diet. The role of government is limited to the development and advocacy of dietary guidelines and to the provision and monitoring of information available to the consumer on the nutritional composition of foods. The planned interventionist approach, in contrast, maintains that government should actively intervene in many sectors of the economy to achieve optimum nutrition for all citizens.

With the exception of Norway, however, developed nations have thus far adopted minimalist approaches to nutrition regulation that rely on market forces to ensure the nutritional quality of food products and the nutritious diets of their populations. Governments have many reasons for hesitating to adopt planned interventionist programs. The most common can be grouped under the headings "scientific/philosophical" and "political." Scientific/philosophical reasons include a lack of confidence in the scientific basis of most nutrition theories and thus a hesitation to intervene in nutrition-related health issues without "absolute" scientific proof. When combined with philosophical beliefs in the sufficiency of the market and a reluctance to interfere with the individual's freedom of choice, these reasons join to make a compelling argument for a minimalist approach.

Political reasons for the unwillingness of governments to adopt interventionist policies center primarily on the relative importance of the agricultural and food processing industry sectors in different countries. For example, in nations with economically highly ranked agriculture and food processing industries, like Denmark, the Netherlands, Ireland, and Belgium, politicians may be unwilling to interfere with food availability and choice because of resistance from powerful producers and various lobbies and a lack of a clear support from the public. Public demands for action, however, may encourage elected officials to address such issues (Gormley et al. 1987).

As already noted, though, even the implementation of a minimalist government nutrition policy has been politically controversial, especially in the United States and Great Britain, where the agricultural and the food processing industries were concerned that government efforts to implement dietary guidelines could threaten their survival. In fact, a successful implementation of the ideal dietary guidelines would imply reduced demand for meat, dairy products (two well-organized producer groups in the United States), eggs, fats, and sweets and increased demand for vegetables, fruits, cereals, and vegetable oils. This would represent a major shift in the diets of the populations and could potentially disrupt the food production sector. Not surprisingly, the regulation of nutrition has often been resisted by meat and dairy producers and other agricultural interests.

Nevertheless, despite the potential economic dislocation feared by advocates of a "hands-off" approach, there are compelling arguments for government intervention in nutrition regulation. Even though a degree of scientific uncertainty exists, most researchers agree that public health is well served by increased knowledge of nutrition and by the availability of nutritionally sound foods. Yet although it is true that producers will readily supply food with a positive nutrition profile if it is profitable for them to do so, the cost is a likely deterrent. Consequently, without some form of regulation to control the truthfulness of label claims, producers who do market higher-quality food face unfair competition from others offering less expensive, lower-quality products.

Following the philosophical assumptions surrounding belief in the "free market," some economists, policy makers, and food manufacturers have argued that relatively unregulated markets provide adequate information to consumers on the nutritional quality of foods, making government regulation of information disclosure unnecessary. In a perfectly operating market, product price will, theoretically, transmit all the information the consumer needs to make a rational, informed choice. A variety of products with different levels of quality and risks would be offered for sale at a variety of prices; higher nutritional quality would be signaled by higher prices. In a theoretically "free market," consumers would choose among a variety of foods based on their preferences for products and the attributes of those products (Caswell and Mojduszka 1996).

The actual marketplace, however, is rarely free or perfect in the theoretical sense and typically fails to provide either accurate nutritional information or foods with good nutritional profiles. Manufacturers are better informed about the content and nutritional profiles of their products than consumers. Consequently, if information on the nutritional quality of food is inaccurate, or if public perceptions about the risks or hazards associated with certain food products are incorrect, then consumers are exposed to health risks far greater than they would have been willing to face if they were able to make informed decisions. These factors imply that government should intervene in the marketplace to ensure the provision of nutritious food and, thus, enhance consumer health.

Governments in market economies have three basic instruments that can be used to influence the nutritional quality of the food supply: providing the public with more reliable information about nutrition, enhancing production standards at processing plants, and confronting manufacturers with pecuniary measures, including taxes, subsidies, and fines (Kramer 1990). Because the political and philosophical climate of the last two decades has favored minimalist approaches to market intervention, government agencies have focused mostly on the first of these. Information remedies can take a variety of forms: the mandatory disclosure of information about the nature of products by manufacturers; controls on claims made for product promotion; provision of public information and education; government subsidies for the provision of information; and control of product names. Such measures are undertaken in an attempt to encourage people to demand foods with a high nutritional profile and, as we have already noted, to inspire manufacturers to produce higher-quality foods. As we have seen, the NLEA, as promulgated by the FDA, leans heavily on information remedies.

Policy experts consider information regulation appropriate, and particularly valuable, in the case of nutrition because without it, it is generally impossible for consumers to determine either the health safety or the nutritional quality of food, even after the product has been bought and consumed. Advocates of the minimalist approach also assume that the regulation of information will encourage consumers to purchase more healthful food bundles, in turn compelling producers to improve the nutritional formulation of their products without direct legislative intervention in the production process.

Though the FDA contends that food prices will show little change as a result of mandatory nutrition labeling, reliance on information remedies to regulate food nutrition does impose other costs on consumers by forcing them to spend time reading labels and, of course, learning about nutrition. This can be something of a problem because minimalist information remedies do little to control food advertising beyond limiting false or misleading claims, and even under the relatively stringent NLEA rules, producers and marketers are able to sometimes use vague nutrition-related claims to powerfully influence consumer food choice. Finally, critics of the minimalist approach maintain that its intent is often severely weakened by a lack of formal government commitment to action. For example, educational or enforcement programs may have inadequate funding.

The effects of labeling regulation are difficult to measure. A 1996 survey in the United States showed mixed results: Whereas 58 percent of consumers polled said that they always read the nutrition label before buying a product for the first time (up from 52 percent in 1991), and more than half said they were trying to eat less fat, 46 percent agreed with the statement that "there is so much conflicting information about which foods are good for me that I'm not sure what to eat anymore" (Howe 1996).

Information remedies clearly have limits, and interventionist approaches, despite their current unpopularity, may ultimately offer consumers greater health protection by directly requiring producers to improve the quality of their foods. In a political climate that favors a minimalist approach, however, government adoption of nutrition regulation focused on information remedies can influence product design, advertising, consumer confidence in food quality, and consumer education about diet and health. The implementation of nutrition labeling regulation thus offers real health benefits to the general population and potentially improves both economic efficiency and public welfare (Caswell and Padberg 1992).

Conclusion

Before World War II, rules for information disclosure on food labels were generally understood as one component of more general food safety policies. After the war, nutrition was increasingly seen as an important factor in its own right, and by the 1970s, most developed countries had established nutrition policies that included provisions for consumer information and food labeling. Perhaps ironically, concerns with nutrition are greater in countries where there is abundant food for most citizens and malnutrition is a result of poor dietary habits rather than food shortages. In less developed countries, where nutrition deficits are often the result of a lack of food, regulation of nutrition through labeling may appear superfluous or unnecessary until supply problems are solved; in addition, neither consumers nor governments can afford the relatively high costs associated with labeling programs.

Nutrition labeling is only one of the possible policy tools available to governments as part of a modern program of nutrition and food safety regulation, but in an economic environment stressing free trade and nonintervention, it has become increasingly important. Product labeling and information disclosure requirements act as an interface between government requirements, manufacturer response, and consumer demand that encourages nonpunitive market incentives with relatively limited government interference. Nutrition labeling policies continue to evolve in an increasingly international environment and are now seen as possible nontariff barriers to the flow of international trade. Among the strongest incentives to modify nutrition labeling policy in the twenty-first century will be concerns with the compatibility of regulatory regimes across national boundaries.

Nutrition labels can provide an important benefit to the health of certain groups of consumers, but they also impose costs on consumers, producers, and government. The use of labels can require expensive monitoring programs in regulating industry and educational programs to encourage public awareness; producers may also be forced to invest in product reformulation and new label design. Labels are also something of a double-edged sword and, at times, have been used by manufacturers to misrepresent the nutrition profiles of certain foods in marketing campaigns. In the end, the success of nutrition labeling depends on a number of interacting factors, making effectiveness difficult to measure without broad studies that focus on changes in consumer awareness and dietary patterns, as well as on the introduction of new foods with more healthful nutrition profiles and improvements in the nutritional quality of existing food products.

Eliza M. Mojduszka

Bibliography

Avery, F. 1984. Diet for a corporate planet: Industry sets world food standards. *Multinational Monitor* 14: 12–15.

Burton, Scott, and A. Biswas. 1993. Preliminary assessment of changes in labels required by the NLEA of 1990. *The Journal of Consumer Affairs* 27: 127–44.

Caswell, Julie A., ed. 1991. *Economics of food safety.* New York.

  1995. *Valuing food safety and nutrition.* Boulder, Colo.

Caswell, Julie A., and Eliza M. Mojduszka. 1996. Using informational labeling to influence the market for quality in food products. *American Journal of Agricultural Economics* 78: 1248–53, 1261–2.

Caswell, Julie A., and Daniel I. Padberg. 1992. Toward a more comprehensive theory of food labels. *American Journal of Agricultural Economics* 74: 460–8.

FDA (Food and Drug Administration). 1993. FDA consumer special report: Focus on food labeling. *FDA Consumer* 27 (May): 7–56.

Gorman, Christine. 1991. The fight over food labels. *Time* (July 15): 52–9.

Gormley, T. R., G. Downey, and D. O'Beirne. 1987. *Food, health, and the consumer.* London and New York.

Helsing, Elisabet. 1991. Nutrition policies in Europe: Background and organization. *Food Policy* 16: 371–83.

Henson, Spencer, and Wlodzimierz Sekula. 1994. Market reform in the Polish food sector: Impact upon food consumption and nutrition. *Food Policy* 19: 419–42.

Henson, Spencer, and Bruce Traill. 1993. The demand for food safety: Market imperfections and the role of government. *Food Policy* 18: 152–62.

Howe, Peter J. 1996. American's dilemma: What's for dinner? *Boston Globe,* June 27, p. 3.

Kennedy, E., and L. Haddad. 1992. Food security and nutrition, 1971–91. Lessons learned and future priorities. *Food Policy* 17: 2–6.

Kinsey, Jean. 1993. GATT and the economics of food safety. *Food Policy* 18: 163–76.

Kramer, Carol S. 1990. Food safety: Consumer preferences, policy options, research needs. In *Consumer demands in the market place: Public policies related to food safety, quality, and human health,* ed. K. L. Clancy, 74–87. Washington, D.C.

Swinbank, Alan. 1993. Industry note: Completion of the EC's internal market, mutual recognition, and the food industries. *Agribusiness* 9: 509–22.

Wilkins, Mira. 1994. When and why brand names in food and drink? In *Adding value: Brands and marketing in food and drink,* ed. G. J. Jones and N. J. Morgan, 15–40. London and New York.

Worley, C. T., R. J. Folwell, V. A. McCracken, and G. L. Bagnara. 1994. Changing labeling regulations: Implications for international food marketing. *Journal of Food Distribution Research* 25 (February): 21–5.

  1995. Food label regulations in the United States and the European Community: International trade facilitators or non tariff barriers. *Journal of International Food and Agribusiness Marketing* 7: 91–103.

Zarkin, G. A., and D. W. Anderson. 1992. Consumer and producer responses to nutrition label changes. *American Journal of Agricultural Economics* 74: 1202–7.

VII.6 ✎ Food Lobbies and U.S. Dietary Guidance Policy

In April 1991, the United States Department of Agriculture (USDA) withdrew from publication its *Eating Right Pyramid,* a new food guide for the general public. Despite official explanations that the guide required further research, its withdrawal was widely believed to have been prompted by pressure from meat and dairy lobbying groups who objected to the way the *Pyramid* displayed their products (Burros 1991b; Combs 1991; Sugarman and Gladwell 1991; Nestle 1993a).

This incident focused attention on a continuing political and ethical dilemma in American government: The rights of individuals guaranteed by the First Amendment to the Constitution versus the social good. In this case, the dilemma involved the inherent right of private industries to act in their own economic self-interests versus the best judgments of health authorities as to what constitutes good nutrition for the public. The *Pyramid* controversy also focused attention on the dual and potentially conflicting USDA mandates to protect U.S. agricultural interests and to issue dietary recommendations to the public (Nestle 1993b).

To address such dilemmas, this chapter reviews the history of dietary guidance and lobbying policies in the United States, describes the principal food lobbies, and presents examples of ways in which they have influenced - or have attempted to influence - federal dietary advice to the public. Finally, it discusses options for correcting improper, sometimes unconscionable, food lobby influence on U.S. nutrition policies.

U.S. Dietary Guidance

From its inception in 1862, the USDA was assigned two roles that have led to the current conflict of interest: to ensure a sufficient and reliable food supply, and to "diffuse among the people of the United States useful information on subjects connected with agriculture in the most general and comprehensive sense of that word" (USDA 1862). In the early 1890s, the USDA began to sponsor research on the relationship between agriculture and human nutrition and to translate new discoveries into advice for consumers. By 1917, the agency had produced at least 30 pamphlets that informed homemakers about the role of specific foods in the diet of children and adults.

The USDA's first dietary recommendations established principles that govern its policies to this day. The agency recommended no specific foods or combinations of foods. Instead, it grouped foods of similar nutrient content into five general categories - fruits and vegetables, meats, cereals, sugar, and fat (Hunt and Atwater 1917). Such a recommendation was intended to encourage the purchase of foods from the full range of American farm products, for by 1921, improvements in agriculture had led to greater availability of many different kinds of foods, any one of which was said to contribute to wholesome and attractive diets (Hunt 1921).

Thus, the recommendation was supported by food and agricultural producers who suspected that the market for their products was becoming limited as the U.S. food supply was already sufficient to provide adequate food to all of its citizens; consequently, any increase in use of one food commodity would have to occur at the expense of others (Levenstein 1988). During the next 35 years, the USDA produced many pamphlets based on the food group approach, all emphasizing the need to consume foods from certain "protective" groups in order to prevent deficiencies of essential nutrients (Haughton, Gussow, and Dodds 1987). The number of recommended food groups, however, varied over the years in no consistent pattern (Nestle and Porter 1990).

At least some of the variation in the number of food groups reflected concerns about the impact of dietary advice on consumer purchases. A Great Depression-era food guide, noting that producers want "to know how much of different foods may well appear in the diets of different consumer groups, and to what extent consumption may rise or fall as the economic situation changes," increased the number of food groups to 12 and included, for the first time, milk as a separate category (Stiebeling and Ward 1933).

In the 1950s, national nutrition surveys indicated that the diets of many Americans were below standard for several nutrients. To help the public choose foods more wisely, USDA nutritionists proposed a simplified guide based on four groups - milk, meats, vegetables and fruits, and breads and cereals - which, for the first time, would specify the number and size of servings.

Prior to its release, the USDA invited leading nutrition authorities to review the guide. Food industry representatives were also sent drafts because "it was felt that food industry groups would have a vital interest in any food guide sponsored by the government" (Hill and Cleveland 1970). Dairy organizations were pleased with the treatment given to milk and milk products, but "meat industry groups were unhappy about the serving size indicated for meat . . . [t]hey pointed out that this size is smaller than average" (Hill and Cleveland 1970). Despite these complaints, the controversial serving sizes (two daily portions of 2 to 3 ounces cooked meat) were incorporated unchanged into the final version of what became known as the *Basic Four* (USDA 1958). This guide remained the basis of USDA nutrition policies for the next 20 years (Figure VII.6.1). Except for the minor concern about portion size, food producer groups supported USDA efforts to promote consumption of more - and more varied - food products.

This relationship changed when policymakers became aware that nutritional deficiencies had declined in prevalence and had been replaced by chronic diseases related to dietary excesses and imbalances. Early reports on the role of dietary fat in atherosclerosis were published in the mid-1950s (Page, Stare, Corcoran et al. 1957), advice to reduce caloric intake from fat in 1961 (American Heart Association 1961), and recommendations for dietary changes and public policies to reduce coronary heart disease risk factors in 1970 (Inter-Society Commission 1970). These last recommendations called for significant reductions in overall consumption of fat (to 35 percent of calories or less), saturated fat (to 10 percent), and cholesterol (to 300 milligrams per day).

The 1977 Farm Bill (Public Law 95-113) specified that the USDA was to be responsible for a wide range of nutrition research and education activities, including dietary advice to the public. In 1988, in an effort to ensure that the federal government speak with "one voice" when it issues dietary recommendations, the House Appropriations Committee reaffirmed USDA's lead agency responsibility for this activity (U.S. House of Representatives 1988). As dietary recommendations shifted from "eat more" to "eat less," the USDA's dual responsibilities for protecting agricultural producers and advising the public about diet created increasing levels of conflict.

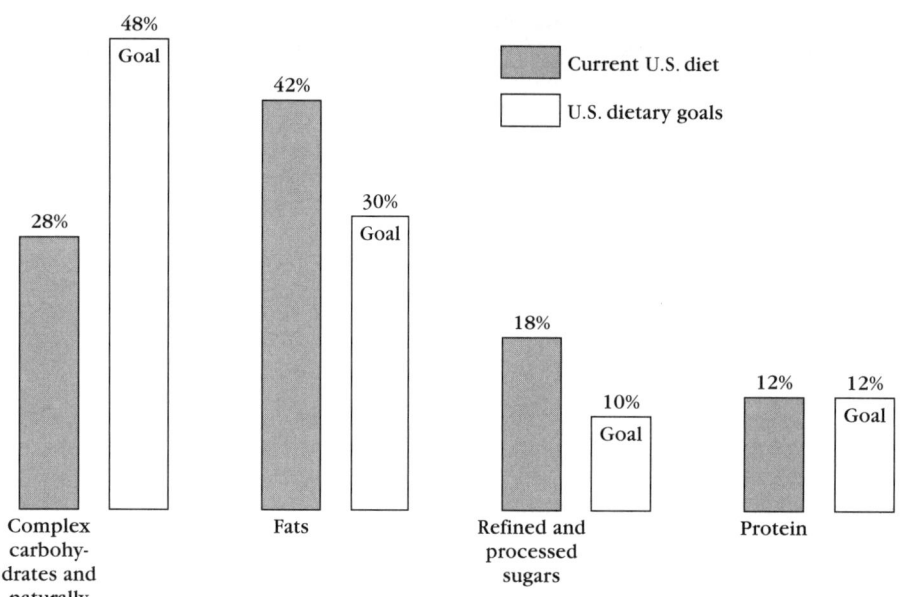

Figure VII.6.1. Meat and dairy groups approved as the 1958 *Basic Four*, as it emphasized the importance of their products in the U.S. diet. Meat producers complained, however, that the suggested portion sizes were too small. (From Hill and Cleveland 1970; USDA 1958.)

Although this conflict was often expressed in terms of the scientific validity of diet–disease relationships, it derived from the profound economic implications of dietary recommendations (Timmer and Nesheim 1979). Foods of animal origin – meat, dairy products, and eggs – have provided much of the total fat and saturated fat, and all of the cholesterol, in the U.S. food supply. In 1990, for example, meat provided 32 percent of the total fat and 40 percent of the saturated fat, and dairy products 12 and 20 percent, for a combined total of 44 and 60 percent, respectively (Raper 1991). Thus, advice to consume less fat and cholesterol necessarily translated into reduced intake of meat, dairy products, and eggs. By 1977, this message was well understood by nutrition scientists, dietitians, and consumer activists (U.S. Senate Select Committee 1977c) and was reflected in declining sales of whole milk and eggs (Putnam 1991). As these trends continued and as beef sales also began to decline, food producer lobbies became much more actively involved in attempts to discredit, weaken, or eliminate dietary recommendations that suggested using less of their products.

Lobbies and Lobbyists

In tribute to their level of influence, lobbies and lobbyists have been viewed as constituting a third house of Congress (Schriftgiesser 1951) or fourth branch of government (Berry 1984). But its members are appointed rather than elected, paid to represent private (and thus not always public) interests and to pursue those interests through activities that are often not in full view of the general public. Thus the actions of lobbies can and do raise concerns about their potential to corrupt democratic political processes (American Enterprise Institute 1980).

Definition of Lobbying
In the broadest possible sense, lobbying includes any legal attempt by individuals or groups to influence government policy or action; this definition specifically excludes bribery. All lobbying efforts involve three common elements: an attempt to influence governmental decisions, representation of the views of special interest groups, and communication with government officials or their representatives. Therefore, a lobbyist is an individual who communicates with a government official on behalf of a third party in the hope of influencing federal decisions. When surveyed, lobbyists have stated that their one common characteristic is similar to that of most others connected with the political process: They try to influence governmental decisions in some way (Milbrath 1963).

Lobbying in the United States
The history of attempts to control lobbying reflects basic tensions in the American political system. From its beginnings, this system has granted individuals the right to express political views publicly, to petition government regarding such views, and to organize on behalf of them. Elected officials of representative governments must listen to constituents, yet special interest groups constantly pressure the government to enact policies that may benefit relatively few constituents. Attempts to control such pressures, how-

ever, have been viewed as infringements of constitutionally guaranteed civil rights, and Congress has found it difficult to draft acceptable laws to curb lobbying abuses (Milbrath 1963). Despite substantial public and congressional concern about many lobbying activities, there is little consensus as to how such activities might be controlled (Berry 1984).

This dilemma appeared early in U.S. history. James Madison, writing of the "dangerous vice" of factions (the term he used for lobby groups), observed that they arise from causes inherent in human nature and in the unequal distribution of property. Relief from the "mischiefs of faction," according to Madison, would derive from the principles of majority rule proposed for the federal republic. A faction "may clog the administration, it may convulse the society," but under the terms of the Constitution, "it will be unable to execute and mask its violence" (Madison 1787: 45).

Indeed, from the earliest years of the new republic, public exposures of excessive and dishonest lobbying were followed by investigations and demands for regulation of interest groups. In response, Congress made sporadic attempts to control lobbying abuses. Proposed legislation typically passed in one house or the other but failed to become law. Congressional leaders were unable to agree on legislation that would curb dishonest lobbying yet permit individual rights to free speech and petition (Congressional Quarterly 1968).

Table VII.6.1 summarizes selected landmarks in the history of U.S. lobbying. As early as 1829, individuals who frequented the lobby of the state capitol in Albany in order to seek favors from New York legislators were called "lobby-agents." By 1832, Washington journalists were using the term "lobbyists" in the current meaning of the term. In 1877, frequent abuses led the state legislature of Georgia to declare lobbying to be a crime, and Massachusetts, Maryland, Wisconsin, and New York passed antilobby legislation between 1890 and 1905. Beginning in 1911, nearly every Congress attempted to probe and control lobbying and related activities. Between 1935 and the early 1940s, Congress enacted laws requiring employees of public utilities, the merchant marine, and foreign governments to register and report political contributions, and it prohibited labor unions from making such contributions. Such actions, however, failed to make any real progress in controlling lobbying abuses (U.S. Senate Special Committee 1957; Congressional Quarterly 1965).

Legislative Mandate

When Congress finally did address interest group practices, it made lobbying legal. The 1946 Federal Regulation of Lobbying Act protected lobbyists' rights and required only that persons paid to lobby, or the organizations paying them, disclose their identities and sources of funds. The act, which is still in force, requires lobbyists to register and to file with Congress sworn quarterly reports disclosing the amounts of

Table VII.6.1. *Selected landmarks in the history of U.S. lobbying*

1787	James Madison, in Federalist Paper No. 10, warns of the dangers of self-interested "factions" to government processes.
1792	First Amendment to Constitution guarantees right to free speech, assembly, and petition to Congress.
1829	The term "lobby-agent" is used to describe a person who frequents the lobby of the state capitol in Albany in order to seek special favors.
1832	Washington journalists first use the term "lobbyists."
1877	Georgia's constitution declares lobbying to be a crime.
1890–1900	Massachusetts, Maryland, Wisconsin, and New York pass anti-lobby legislation.
1907	Congress forbids corporations to make political campaign contributions in federal elections.
1919	Internal Revenue Service rules lobbying expenditures are not deductible from federal income taxes by businesses or individuals.
1935	Public Utilities Holding Company Act prohibits political contributions by utility companies and requires individuals who do make contributions to register and report.
1936	Merchant Marine Act requires similar registration and reporting.
1938	Foreign Agents Registration Act imposes registration and reporting requirements for political contributions.
1943	Smith-Connolly War Labor Disputes Act bars political campaign contributions in federal elections by labor unions during war emergency.
1946	Federal Regulation of Lobbying Act, adopted as Title III of the Legislative Reorganization Act of 1946 (P.L. 79-601), requires paid lobbyists to register and file financial reports.
1947	Taft-Hartley Act prohibits political campaign contributions by labor unions and corporations.
1954	Supreme Court upholds constitutionality of 1946 act in *U.S. v. Harriss;* limits law to individuals paid by a third party to communicate directly with members of Congress to influence legislation.
1956	In connection with a bribery attempt, Superior Oil Company attorneys become the first – and only – individuals to be convicted for failure to register under the 1946 act.
1957	Senate investigating committee finds 1946 act failing to achieve the disclosure aims that it was designed to accomplish.
1968	*Congressional Quarterly* lists 23 former senators and 90 former congressmen who have registered as lobbyists since 1946.
1974	Amendments to the Federal Election Campaign Act authorize the formation of Political Action Committees (PACs) to fund congressional campaigns.
1980	Congress attempts to revise the lobbying act.
1991	More than 7,000 individuals register as lobbyists.

Sources: Schriftgiesser (1951), U.S. Senate Special Committee (1957), Congressional Quarterly (1965, 1968), American Enterprise Institute (1980), and "Registered Lobbyists" (1991).

money they receive or spend, the individuals to whom they pay funds, the purposes of these payments, and the specific legislation that they are supporting or opposing (Schriftgiesser 1951; Congressional Quarterly 1965). This law, considered vague by virtually all authorities (U.S. Senate Committee 1991), was reduced further in coverage by challenges in federal courts. In a 1954 case, *U.S. v. Harriss,* the Supreme Court upheld the constitutionality of the act, albeit through a narrow interpretation; it limited the law's applicability only to individuals who solicited or received money for the purpose of lobbying members of Congress (Congressional Quarterly 1965).

These decisions leave much room for ambiguity; they can be interpreted as permitting interest groups to lobby congressional staff or officials and staff of cabinet departments and their agencies, and to decide for themselves whether and how much they need to report. The act defines no special enforcement procedures, even though it specifies criminal penalties for noncompliance. In its entire history, the act has resulted in only one conviction (Congressional Quarterly 1968). Despite repeated attempts to strengthen its provisions (American Enterprise Institute 1980), the 1946 act remains in force only as modified by *U.S. v. Harriss.* Thus, the view that lobbying legislation is unenforced, unenforceable, and widely ignored continues to prevail (U.S. Senate Committee 1991).

Registered Lobbyists

The extent to which the lobbying act may be ignored is uncertain. During the 20 years following its passage, an average of 400 lobbyists registered and reported contributions that amounted to $4 to $5 million annually, but these figures were considered low because of the many loopholes in reporting requirements (Congressional Quarterly 1968). The number of registrations grew rapidly from 1960 to 1980, partly in response to expansion in the size and complexity of government. In 1963, the government included 10 major cabinet departments and 70 major agencies, and Congress employed 7,700 aides. By 1991, these numbers had increased to 14, 140, and 20,062, respectively. The number of registered lobbyists doubled between 1976 and 1986 (Browne 1988). At the beginning of the 1990s, 7,000 to 8,000 individuals registered as lobbyists, many representing multiple organizations or causes (Registered lobbyists 1991; U.S. Senate Committee 1991).

The interests represented by lobbyists encompass every conceivable aspect of American corporate and private enterprise: banks; corporations; legal, public relations, and life insurance firms; educational institutions; professional societies; advocacy groups; city, state, and national governments; defense, health, computer, energy, drug, chemical, paper, tobacco, transportation, travel, and, of course, food industries. They all pay individuals to represent their interests to Congress. There is no industry too small, no group too iso-lated, and no opinion too extreme to lack a professional lobbyist. Lobbying is a multimillion-dollar industry with enormous impact on government decisions (U.S. Senate Committee 1991).

Food Lobbies

The Agricultural Establishment

By the end of World War II, farmers and food producers had come to view the USDA as their department and its secretary as their spokesman. Producers, together with USDA officials and members of the House and Senate Agricultural Committees, constituted the "agricultural establishment" and ensured that federal policies in such areas as land use, commodity distribution, and prices promoted their interests (Paarlberg 1964). The control exercised by producer groups over USDA and congressional actions was so complete that both the secretary of agriculture and the president were said to be excluded from any significant role in policy decisions (Kramer 1979).

The perpetuation of this system was guaranteed by the congressional seniority system and the strong representation on agriculture committees of members from farm states. Committee membership rarely changed hands. Allen Ellender (D-La), for example, chaired the Senate Agriculture Committee for a total of 18 years, and his successor, Herman Talmadge (D-Ga), held the chair for 10 more. Jamie Whitten (D-Miss), first elected to Congress when Franklin Roosevelt was president, chaired the House Agricultural Appropriations Subcommittee for so long that he was referred to as "the permanent secretary of agriculture" (Morgan 1978b); he was elected to his twenty-seventh term of office in 1992 and resigned the committee chair he had held since 1949 when he finally left office in 1994 (Binder 1995).

By the early 1970s, this system weakened as new constituencies demanded influence on agriculture policies. A combination of bad weather, poor harvests in foreign countries, and massive purchases of U.S. grain by the Soviet Union had led to increased food costs and consumer complaints (Kramer 1979). Agriculture was gaining in importance in the U.S. economy, and the food industry was expanding to include processors and marketers as well as producers (Morgan 1978b). Responsibility for providing food assistance to the poor was assigned to the USDA (Morgan 1978a). In response to demands from these constituencies, the House expanded the membership of its Agriculture Committee to include representatives from urban areas in 1974, and, in 1977, the agriculture committees of both houses were assigned jurisdiction for policies and programs related not only to agricultural production, marketing, research, and development, but also to rural development, forestry, domestic food assistance, and some aspects of foreign trade, international relations, market regulation, and tax policies (Knutson, Penn, and Boehm 1983).

Food Lobbyists

The number of food lobbying groups reflected the expansion in constituencies. In the 1950s, 25 groups of food producers dominated agricultural lobbying, but by the mid-1980s, 84 groups lobbied on food issues (Browne 1988). In the early 1990s, food lobbies included a multiplicity of groups, businesses, and individuals attempting to influence federal decisions. They represent producers, growers, marketers, processors, and distributors of every imaginable fruit, vegetable, cereal, baby food, diet aid, nutritional supplement, sweetener, and product grown or manufactured at the local, state, or national level. They also represent manufacturers of pesticides, feeds, and fertilizers; professional and health organizations; and food, nutrition, antihunger, and welfare activists (Registered lobbyists 1991). Table VII.6.2 lists specific examples of such groups. The number of active food lobbyists is uncertain. A 1977 study identified 612 individuals and 460 groups lobbying on food and agriculture issues (Guither 1980). A cursory review of current lobbyist registrations suggests that 5 to 10 percent of lobbyists are concerned with such issues.

Lobbying Methods

Personal Contacts

No matter whom they represent, all lobbyists use similar strategies to gain access and influence. Of these methods, lobbyists rank personal contacts as the most effective means of gaining access to government officials. These contacts are established through office visits, meetings, participation on advisory boards, testimony at hearings, social occasions, fundraising sessions, and performance of favors, as well as through the engagement of other individuals and groups to perform such favors. Lobbyists also organize meetings, provide technical advice, contribute to election campaigns, stage media events, employ public relations firms, organize public demonstrations, and encourage lawsuits (U.S. Senate Special Committee 1957; Milbrath 1963; Browne 1988).

Technical Expertise

Virtually all blueprints for successful lobbying emphasize the importance of knowledge and credibility (deKieffer 1981; Berry 1984). These attributes establish lobbyists as technical experts who provide Congress with well-researched advice on issues related to proposed legislation. The value of this expertise is, in part, responsible for a congressional reluctance to control lobbying activities.

Financial Contributions

Individual and corporate contributions and gifts to members of Congress are strictly regulated by the Federal Election Campaign Act. Small items such as lunches, books, awards, liquor, samples, and theater tickets are considered acceptable (deKieffer 1981). Also considered legal are very large payments for administrative costs, fundraising events, travel expenses, and honoraria. Thus in 1991 several food and agriculture corporations legally donated $100,000 or more each to the Republican Party (Babcock 1991).

An analysis of privately funded travel among members of the House of Representatives in 1989–90 identified nearly 4,000 trips sponsored by lobby groups, two-thirds of them corporations or trade associations.

Table VII.6.2. *Selected examples of food lobbying groups*

Commodity producer organizations
American Soybean Association
American Sugar Beet Growers Association
Florida Sugar Cane League
National Association of Wheat Growers
National Broiler Council
National Cattlemen's Association
National Corn Growers' Association
National Fisheries Institute
National Milk Producers' Federation
National Peanut Growers Group
National Pork Producers Council
Rice Millers' Association
United Egg Producers
United Fresh Fruit and Vegetable Association

Processing, manufacturing, and marketing organizations
American Frozen Food Institute
American Meat Institute
Chocolate Manufacturers' Association of the U.S.A.
Corn Refiners Association
Food Marketing Institute
Grocery Manufacturers of America
National Food Processors Association
National Frozen Food Association
National Soft Drink Association
Peanut Butter and Nut Processors' Association

Public interest groups and professional societies
American Cancer Society
American Dietetic Association
American Heart Association
American School Food Service Association
Center for Science in the Public Interest
Food Research and Action Center
Public Voice for Food and Health Policy
Society for Nutrition Education

Private food producers
Cargill
ConAgra
Archer-Daniels-Midland
Mars
Pizza Hut
Safeway Stores
Ralston-Purina

Sources: Guither (1980) and Browne (1988).

In particular, agriculture lobbies sponsored 390 trips and paid more than $500,000 in honoraria to House members during the 101st Congress; of these trips, 239 went to members of the House Agriculture and Appropriations Committees. The most frequent corporate-sponsored traveler was Charles Stenholm (D-Tex), a senior member of the Agriculture Committee. Of his 50 paid trips, agricultural interest groups sponsored 37; they also provided $38,250 in honoraria (McCauley and Cohen 1991).

Election Campaign Contributions

In 1974, amendments to the Federal Election Campaign Act authorized formation of Political Action Committees (PACs) by corporations and other groups to collect and disburse voluntary campaign contributions. Although the law limits the amount of money that can be contributed to any one candidate, it does not restrict the number of candidates to whom contributions can be made or the number of PACs that can contribute to any one candidate. In 1974-5, 608 PACs contributed $12.5 million to election campaigns; by 1982, 3,371 PACs, nearly half of them corporate, were contributing $83 million (Berry 1984); and by the election of 1989-90, nearly 4,700 PACs were contributing more than $370 million to candidates (Federal Election Commission 1991b).

The size of the contribution to any one candidate typically varied from $500 to $2,000; however, such contributions could add up to substantial amounts. In 1989-90, Senators Robert Dole (R-Kan), Jesse Helms (R-NC), and Tom Harkin (D-Iowa), all members of the Committee on Agriculture, Nutrition, and Forestry, received respectively $308,000, $790,000, and $1.5 million in PAC contributions. These amounts all derived from contributions of $5,000 or less (Federal Election Commission 1991a).

Relatively few PACs represent food and agriculture interests. In 1978, 82 such PACs were identified, 46 of them producer groups contributing a total of $1.4 million. The largest contributor was the Associated Milk Producers PAC, which distributed a total of $456,000 among 37 candidates for the Senate and 185 candidates for the House (Guither 1980). PACs representing the dairy industry remain relatively large contributors; an analysis by Common Cause of Federal Election Commission data found that dairy groups contributed nearly $1.8 million to candidates in 1989-90. In comparison, beef PACs contributed just over $326,000 in that election. In the period from 1985 to 1990, dairy PACs contributed a total of $5.5 million and beef PACs $864,000 to election campaigns, but these amounts were greatly exceeded by the $25, $23, and $12 million donated by the real estate and construction, insurance, and banking industries, respectively (Common Cause, personal communication).

In the 1989-90 election campaign, food and agriculture PACs, though still in the minority, were well represented. Contributions came from the sugar, meat, dairy,

egg, soft-drink, wine and liquor, rice, fruit, vegetable, seed, and snack food industries, as well as from PACs representing growers, distributors, manufacturers, and promoters. As an example, Table VII.6.3 provides a partial listing of food and agriculture PACs that contributed to the 1989-90 campaign of Senator Harkin. PACs representing consumer, health, or public interest groups are rare. As noted by Senator Dole in an earlier context, "there aren't any Poor PACs or Food Stamp PACs or Nutrition PACs or Medicare PACs" (Berry 1984).

Nevertheless, experts differ on whether the small amount of money contributed by any one PAC is sufficient to buy influence. Some political commentators believe that the power of PACs is overrated (Bowers 1991), whereas others view it as insidious, largely because members of the House and Senate who hold important positions on powerful committees become "... more beholden to the economic interests of their committee constituents than to the interests of their district residents or to the President or party" (Califano 1992).

Table VII.6.3. *A partial list of food and agriculture Political Action Committees (PACs) contributing to the 1989-90 election campaign of Senator Tom Harkin (D-IA), a member of the Appropriations and Agriculture, Nutrition and Forestry Committees*

Amalgamated Sugar Company
American Agriculture Movement
American Crystal Sugar Association
American Dietetic Association
American Meat Institute
American Sheep Industry
American Sugar Cane League
American Sugarbeet Growers
Archer-Daniels-Midland
Bakery, Confectionary, and Tobacco Workers
Dairymen Inc.
Diamond Walnut Growers
Florida Sugar Cane League
Food Marketing Institute
General Mills
Hawaiian Sugar Planters
Land O' Lakes, Inc.
Mid-America Dairymen
Milk Marketing Inc.
National Broiler Council
National Cattlemen's Association
National Farmers Union
National Pork Producers Council
National Restaurant Association
National Turkey Federation
Ocean Spray Cranberries
Peanut PAC of Alabama
Southern Wine and Spirits
Sunkist Growers
United Egg Association
United Fresh Fruit and Vegetable Association
Wheat for Congress
Wine Institute

Source: Federal Election Commission (1991b).

One study found that members of the House of Representatives who received dairy PAC funds were almost twice as likely to vote for legislation to maintain price supports as those who did not; that supporters of maintenance received 2.5 times more PAC funds than opponents; and that the more PAC money members received, the more likely they were to support such legislation (Public Citizens' Congress Watch 1982). Most experts agree that PACs give the appearance of purchasing influence, whether or not they actually do so.

Revolving Door

The transformation of government officials into lobbyists and of lobbyists into government officials is commonly known as the "revolving door." By 1968, at least 23 former Senators and 90 former Congressmen had registered as lobbyists for private organizations (Congressional Quarterly 1968). Job substitutions between food producer lobbies and the USDA have been especially frequent and noticeable. At the USDA, as many as 500 agency heads and their staff members are chosen on the basis of political party, support from key politicians, and other political criteria rather than expertise. Such appointments are strongly influenced by special interest groups (Knutson et al. 1983).

In 1971, for example, USDA secretary Clifford Hardin traded places with Earl Butz, who was director of the Ralston Purina Company; Butz became USDA secretary and Hardin went to Ralston Purina. One report identified several assistant secretaries, administrators, and advisers who joined the USDA from positions with meat, grain, and marketing firms or who left the agency to take positions with food producers (Jacobson 1974). The chief USDA negotiator arranging for private companies to sell grain to the Soviet Union in 1972 soon resigned to work for the very company that gained the most from the transaction (Solkoff 1985). More recently, the appointment of JoAnn Smith, a former president of the National Cattlemen's Association, as chief of the USDA's food marketing and inspection division raised questions about apparent conflicts of interest when she approved the designation "fat-reduced beef" for bits of meat processed from slaughtering by-products and opposed an American Heart Association proposal to put a seal of approval on certain meat products low in fat (McGraw 1991).

Generic Advertising (Checkoff Programs)

In an effort to counteract declining consumption trends, Congress passed a series of food promotion and research acts that require producers of 15 specific commodities – among them beef, pork, dairy products, milk, and eggs – to deduct or "checkoff" a fee from sales. These strictly enforced fees are then used to promote the commodities (Becker 1991). Through these and more than 300 state programs, about 90 percent of all U.S. producers contributed more than $530 million to promote about 80 farm commodities in 1986 (Blisard and Blaylock 1989).

The two largest national checkoff funds are dairy and meat; they generated $194 and $84 million, respectively, in 1986 (Blisard and Blaylock 1989). About half the funds are distributed to state commodity boards and the other half to national promotion and research boards. The beef checkoff began as a voluntary program generating $31,000 in 1922. In the 1970s, as beef consumption began to decline, the National Cattlemen's Association started lobbying for a compulsory program through a campaign that involved PACs, letter writing, and personal visits to members of Congress by hundreds of cattle farmers. The legislation passed in 1985; beef lobbies are especially effective because cattlemen are distributed among a great many states, and beef sales amount to nearly $22 billion annually (Wilde 1992). The beef checkoff generated nearly $90 million in 1991 (Cattlemen's Beef 1991).

The various checkoff boards collect and spend the funds, award contracts, and sponsor advertising, research, and education programs. Although the legislation prohibits use of the funds for lobbying, the distinction between promoting a product to consumers and to lawmakers can be subtle. The boards are closely affiliated with lobbying groups (Becker 1991), some even sharing office space. The Cattlemen's Beef Promotion and Research Board, for example, shared an address with the National Cattlemen's Association, and the National Pork Board shared offices, staff, and telephone services with the National Pork Producers Council. The legislation actually specifies that a certain percentage of checkoff funds must be allocated to the commodity groups who nominate members of the promotion boards to be appointed by the USDA (Cloud 1989).

Although checkoff funds are supposed to be used for research as well as advertising, only a small fraction is used for that purpose. Between 1986 and 1989, the Beef Board spent nearly $106 million, of which only about 5 percent went toward research and only 1.4 percent toward development of leaner products. At the same time, the board paid more than $1 million each to movie stars Cybill Shepherd and James Garner for participating in a beef advertising campaign (Parrish and Silverglade 1990).

Checkoff programs attempt to convince consumers to choose one type of food product over another (Becker 1991). The Meat and Beef Boards, for example, aim to build demand for red meats and meat products (National Live Stock and Meat Board 1987); encourage consumers to view beef as wholesome, versatile, and ever lower in cholesterol; and educate doctors, nurses, dietitians, teachers, and the media about the nutritional benefits of beef (Cattlemen's Beef 1990). Similarly, the Dairy Boards promote consumption of cheese, milk, butter, and ice cream as the best sources of calcium and other nutrients (Westwater 1988). For the most part, studies have shown a positive relationship between such campaigns and sales for a wide range of commodities. From 1984 to 1990, for example, generic advertising was associated with significant increases in consumption of milk and cheeses (Blisard, Sun, and Blaylock 1991). The Beef Board has attributed the industry's increased relative strength to the checkoff program (Cattlemen's Beef 1991).

Checkoff supporters maintain that these programs benefit farmers at little cost to the USDA and provide useful information to consumers. Of concern, however, is the potential of checkoff programs to increase food costs and competition between commodity groups and to promote products high in fat, saturated fat, and cholesterol. Of even greater concern is the ability of lobbying groups to use the millions of dollars available from check-off funds to influence food and nutrition policies (Becker 1991).

Brand Advertising

In 1991, the annual cost of all food product advertising was $8 billion (Becker 1991). In that year, food companies that were among the top 100 U.S. advertisers spent $3.9 billion to promote their products. Three billion dollars of this amount was spent on television commercials, one-third of them for snacks and soft drinks. The leading national advertiser, Procter and Gamble, which sells food products, among others, spent nearly $2.3 billion on advertising, and McDonald's, eighth in rank, spent more than $764 million ("The 100 Leading National Advertisers" 1991).

Academic and Professional Support

Food companies routinely fund academic departments, research programs, individual investigators, and meetings, conferences, journals, and other activities of professional societies. For example, at least 16 food or nutritional supplement companies provide funding for the *Journal of Nutrition Education;* 22 support educational activities of the American Society for Clinical Nutrition; and Kraft General Foods supports a consumer hot line staffed by the American Dietetic Association.

One survey of university nutrition and food science departments identified frequent food industry payments to faculty for consulting services, lectures, membership on advisory boards, and representation at congressional hearings. This same study noted several departments receiving significant portions of their research budgets from food company grants. These faculty and departments may disclose corporate connections willingly but are rarely required to do so; they are usually grateful for the support and deny that it affects their views in any way (Rosenthal, Jacobson, and Bohm 1976).

Such conflicts of interest are not confined to the United States; a British study found that 158 of 246 members of national committees on nutrition and food policy consulted for, or received funding from, food companies (Cannon 1987). Such relationships naturally raise questions about the ability of academic experts to provide independent opinions on policy matters that might affect their sources of funding.

Food Lobbies in Action

Dietary Goals for the United States

Aware of evidence that diets high in fat, saturated fat, cholesterol, sugar, and salt were associated with chronic diseases, the staff of the Senate Select Committee on Nutrition and Human Needs, chaired by George McGovern (D-SD), held hearings on dietary determinants of obesity, diabetes, and heart diseases in 1973, and produced a report on nutrition and chronic disease in 1974. In July 1976, the committee held further hearings on the role of American food consumption patterns in cancer, cardiovascular disease, and obesity (U.S. Senate Select Committee 1977e).

On the basis of evidence presented at these hearings, the staff produced the February 1977 report *Dietary Goals for the United States.* Consistent with American Heart Association recommendations, the report established six goals for dietary change: Increase carbohydrate intake to 55–60 percent of calories; decrease fat to 30 percent, saturated fat to 10 percent, and sugar to 15 percent of calories; reduce cholesterol to 300 milligrams per day and salt to 3 grams per day. To achieve these goals, the committee advised consumption of more fruits, vegetables, whole grains, poultry, and fish, but less meat, eggs, butterfat, whole milk, and foods high in fat (U.S. Senate Select Committee 1977a).

Many groups objected to one or another of these recommendations, but the advice to "eat less" brought immediate protest from the groups most affected – cattlemen, the dairy industry, and egg producers. The cattle industry, especially in McGovern's home state, pressured the committee to withdraw the report. "Here, after all, was the Congress of the United States telling the public not to eat their products" (Broad 1979). Meat and egg producers demanded and obtained additional hearings to express their views. In these hearings, a pointed exchange between Senator Robert Dole and Mr. Wray Finney, president of the National Cattlemen's Association, established the basis for compromise on the key recommendation (No. 2) to eat less meat:

> *Senator Dole:* I wonder if you could amend No. 2 and say "increase consumption of lean meat"? Would that taste better to you?
> *Mr. Finney:* "Decrease is a bad word, Senator." (U.S. Senate Select Committee 1977d).

Committee members who represented states with large producer constituencies demanded changes in the report. McGovern "said he did not want to disrupt the economic situation of the meat industry and engage in a battle with that industry that we could not win" (Mottern 1978). The report was revised to state, "choose meats, poultry, and fish which will reduce saturated fat intake" (U.S. Senate Select Committee 1977b). These statements and later versions of recommendations concerning meat intake are listed in Table VII.6.4.

When Nick Mottern, the staff member who wrote the original report, objected to the changes, he was asked to leave his position (Mottern 1978). Shortly thereafter, McGovern was quoted as saying about McDonald's and other fast-food companies that "on the whole, quick foods are a nutritious addition to a balanced diet," leading one reporter to suggest that "still another industry has thrown its weight around" (Broad 1979).

Despite such compromises, the *Dietary Goals* report established the basis of all subsequent dietary recommendations and altered the course of nutrition education in the United States. This contribution, however, was the Select Committee's last. Shortly after release of the report, the Senate abolished the committee and transferred its functions to the Nutrition Subcommittee of the newly constituted Committee on Agriculture, Nutrition, and Forestry as of the end of the year (Hadwiger and Browne 1978). In 1980, McGovern lost his bid for reelection.

Table VII.6.4. *Evolution of federal recommendations to reduce dietary fat through changes in meat consumption*

Year	Report, Agency	Recommendation
1977	*Dietary Goals*, U.S. Senate	Decrease consumption of meat
1977	*Dietary Goals*, 2d ed., U.S. Senate	Choose meats . . . which will reduce saturated fat intake
1979	*Healthy People*, DHEW	Relatively . . . less red meat
1979	*Food*, USDA	Cut down on fatty meats (2 servings of 2–3 ounces each)
1980	*Dietary Guidelines*, USDA and DHEW	Choose lean meat
1985	*Dietary Guidelines*, 2d ed., USDA and DHHS	Choose lean meat
1988	*Surgeon General's Report*, DHHS	Choose lean meats
1990	*Dietary Guidelines*, 3d ed., USDA and DHHS	Have 2 or 3 servings, with a daily total of about 6 ounces
1991	*Eating Right Pyramid*, USDA	Choose lean meat (2–3 servings or 5–7 ounces)

Healthy People

In 1979, reflecting the emerging consensus among scientists and health authorities that national health strategies should be "dramatically recast" to emphasize disease prevention, the Department of Health, Education, and Welfare (DHEW) issued *Healthy People*. This report announced goals for a 10-year plan to improve the health status of Americans. Its nutrition section recommended diets with fewer calories; less saturated fat, cholesterol, salt, and sugar; relatively more complex carbohydrates, fish, and poultry; and less red meat. The report, noting that more than half the U.S. diet consisted of processed foods rather than fresh agricultural produce, suggested that consumers pay closer attention to the nutritional qualities of such foods (USDHEW 1979).

Because dietary advice to restrict red meat and be wary of processed foods was certain to attract notice, *Healthy People* was released in July without a press conference as one of the final official acts of Joseph Califano, who had been fired from his position as DHEW secretary by President Carter the month before. Nevertheless, the report elicited a "storm" of protest from the meat industry. The president of the National Live Stock and Meat Board was quoted as saying, "The report begins with 'the health of the American people has never been better,' and we think it should have ended right there" (Monte 1979: 4).

Healthy People became the last federal publication ever to suggest that Americans eat less red meat. When later asked about this issue, Surgeon General Julius Richmond speculated that subsequent editions of this report might advise a switch to lean meat rather than a decrease in intake of red meat in general (USDA and USDHEW 1980).

USDA's Food Books

Because USDA nutritionists found diets that met the *Dietary Goals* to be "so disruptive to usual food patterns," they developed a series of publications under the generic title *Food* to inform the public about ways to modify the calorie, fat, sugar, and salt content of diets (Wolf and Peterkin 1984). This first USDA publication to address diet and chronic disease, *Food: The Hassle-Free Guide to a Better Diet*, was notable for its caution:

> Many scientists say the American diet is contributing to some of the chronic diseases that hit people in later life. . . . Other scientists believe just as strongly that the evidence doesn't support such conclusions. So the choice is yours. (USDA 1979)

USDA staff revised the Basic Four to display the food groups in a vertical format with the vegetable/fruit and bread/cereal groups located above the dairy and meat groups. At the bottom, they added a fifth group of foods – fats/sweets/alcohol – that keep bad "nutritional company" and are high in calories but low in essential nutrients and fiber. To reduce fat intake, they suggested, "cut down on fatty meats."

Food was the most requested USDA publication in 1979 (Carol Tucker Foreman, personal communication). After the 1980 election, however, under pressure from representatives of the meat, dairy, and egg industries who objected to the negative advice about fat and cholesterol and the placement of their products below fruits, vegetables, and grains, *Food* was not reprinted and all action on subsequent publications in the series was suspended. Eventually, the USDA gave its completed page boards for *Food II* to the American Dietetic Association, which published them as two separate booklets in 1982 ("ADA to Publish" 1982). *Food* became the last federal publication to use the phrase "cut down" in reference to meat (see Table VII.6.4).

1980 Dietary Guidelines

In February 1980, the USDA and DHEW announced joint publication of *Nutrition and Your Health: Dietary Guidelines for Americans.* The recommendations were to eat a variety of foods; maintain ideal weight; avoid too much fat, saturated fat, and cholesterol; eat foods with adequate starch and fiber; avoid too much sugar and too much sodium. Those who consume alcohol should do so in moderation (USDA and USDHEW 1980). Because these guidelines had replaced the unacceptable "eat less" phrases with the vague "avoid too much," agency officials did not expect objections from food producers. As stated by USDA secretary Bob Bergland during the press conference: "They feared we might issue edicts like eat no meat, or eggs, and drink less whole milk. They have been waiting for the other shoe to fall. There is no shoe" (Greenberg 1980).

Indeed, the Food Marketing Institute (FMI) commented that the *Guidelines* are "simple, reasonable and offer great freedom of choice," and the American Meat Institute (AMI) called them "helpful," noting that they provide "a continuing and central role for meat" (USDA and USDHEW 1980). But for certain food producers, especially the meat industry, even these mild recommendations went too far; they lobbied Congress to end funding for the publication (Broad 1981). One commentator observed that the purpose of the USDA is to make it easier for farmers to make money, a goal that is not well served by permitting federal agencies "to run loose on such politically sensitive matters as red meat, butter, and eggs" (Greenberg 1980).

On the eve of Appropriation Committee hearings on the *Guidelines,* called in July by Senator Thomas Eagleton (D-MO), a coalition of 104 consumer and health organizations criticized producer efforts to suspend distribution of the publication (Haas 1980). In part, this coalition had been created in response to an attack from the quasi-federal National Research Council (NRC). In May 1980, just three months after release

of the *Dietary Guidelines,* the NRC issued its belated response to the *Dietary Goals.* This report, called *Toward Healthful Diets,* immediately became notorious for its conclusion that advice to restrict intake of fat or cholesterol was unwarranted (NRC 1980). One explanation for this conclusion was that the report had been financed by food industry donations, and that at least 4 of the 15 Food and Nutrition Board scientists responsible for its development had been funded by egg, meat, or other food producers (Wade 1980). Shortly after the election, but before the Reagan administration assumed office, Congress established a committee to revise the *Guidelines.*

At this point, the demise of the *Guidelines* seemed virtually assured. The new USDA secretary, John Block, was an Illinois hog farmer who during his confirmation hearings had remarked that he was "not so sure government should get into telling people what they should or shouldn't eat" (Maugh 1982). Through the revolving door, two high-level USDA positions had been filled by a former executive director of the American Meat Institute and a lobbyist for the National Cattlemen's Association. In addition, one of Block's first acts had been to close USDA's Human Nutrition Center, a research unit remarkable for its promotion of consumer rather than producer interests and its linking of research to policies, such as the *Dietary Guidelines* (Broad 1981).

Further attacks on dietary recommendations followed the release of *Diet, Nutrition, and Cancer,* an NRC report that had been commissioned by the National Cancer Institute during the last year of the Carter administration (NRC 1982). Food producers objected to the recommendation to reduce fat to 30 percent of calories by decreasing intake of high-fat meats. Livestock prices had dropped following release of the report, leading one food industry representative to observe that advice on diet and cancer "could be very harmful long term to the meat industry" ("Livestock Prices Fall" 1982: 44). In response to a request from the National Pork Producers Council, seven members of Congress called for an investigation of the cancer report (U.S. General Accounting Office 1984), and USDA political appointees drafted a report rejecting the 30 percent fat recommendation (Zuckerman 1984).

1985 Dietary Guidelines

When the committee to revise the *Dietary Guidelines* was finally appointed, five of the six USDA nominees appeared to be closely connected to the food industry ("USDA Readies" 1983). When informed of the committee's composition, a prospective Department of Health and Human Services (DHHS) appointee threatened to resign, stating that he had "no intention of being part of a process that guts the guidelines" ("Dietary Guidelines Review" 1982: 6). To the surprise of critics, however, the committee eventually made only minor changes in the text (USDA and USDHHS 1985), and USDA secretary Block, joined by the National Cattlemen's Association, endorsed the *Guidelines,* admitting that "all of us have changed in our thinking" ("Reagan Administration" 1985: 2).

This change in views was principally the result of an increasing consensus on the scientific basis of diet and disease relationships, as expressed in three groundbreaking reports released in 1988 and 1989. The first was the NRC's *Designing Foods,* which recommended reducing fat intake to 30 percent of calories and challenged the meat industry to develop methods to raise leaner beef; remarkably, this report had been requested by the USDA and issued with the full cooperation of meat producers (NRC 1988). It was followed by the 1988 *Surgeon General's Report on Nutrition and Health* (USDHHS 1988) and the 1989 NRC *Diet and Health* study (NRC 1989). All three of these reports identified reduction of fat – particularly saturated fat – as the primary dietary priority. Because none of these reports elicited much critical comment, consensus on dietary recommendations appeared to have been achieved (Nestle and Porter 1990).

1990 Dietary Guidelines

Despite the apparent consensus among medical and scientific authorities, USDA political appointees argued that recent research had established a need to reexamine the *Dietary Guidelines.* Invoking the lead agency mandate, they pressed for and obtained appointment of a committee to write a third edition. As appointed, the new committee consisted of nine nutrition scientists and physicians with few apparent ties to the food industry. Of 13 groups who submitted written comments during committee deliberations, however, 10 represented food producers, trade associations, or organizations allied with industry (USDA 1990).

This process revealed that the current consensus on dietary recommendations had been achieved at the expense of clarity. To address concerns that certain foods are increasingly perceived as "bad" and unfit for inclusion in healthful diets, the committee altered the phrasing of the *Guidelines* to make their tone more positive. For the phrase, "avoid too much," it substituted, "choose a diet low in." For the phrase "choose lean meat . . . ," it substituted, "have two or three servings of meat . . . with a daily total of about 6 ounces." Its one significant achievement was to suggest upper limits of 30 percent of calories from fat and 10 percent from saturated fat – precisely those recommended by the 1977 *Dietary Goals.* Lest these figures appear too restrictive, however, the new edition emphasized:

[T]hese goals for fats apply to the diet over several days, not to a single meal or food. Some foods that contain fat, saturated fat, and cholesterol, such as meats, milk, cheese, and eggs, also contain high-quality protein and are our best sources of certain vitamins and minerals. (USDA and USDHHS 1990)

Unlike the previous two editions, the 1990 *Dietary Guidelines* elicited no noticeable complaints from food producers.

The Food Guide Pyramid

In 1991, the interference of food lobbies in dietary guidance policy again came to public attention, this time over a food guide with a simple, pyramid-shaped graphic. This project had originated a decade earlier in response to criticisms that consumers would have difficulty planning menus that met dietary recommendations (Peterkin, Kerr, and Shore 1978). In the heat of the controversy over the 1980 *Dietary Guidelines,* USDA nutritionists had rushed a menu guide into print just prior to President Reagan's inauguration (USDA 1981).

With the *Guidelines* under revision, the nutritionists began to develop a new guide that would specify the numbers and sizes of food servings needed to meet its recommendations. They presented this guide in a wheel format for use in an American Red Cross course in 1984 (Cronin, Shaw, Krebs-Smith et al. 1987). Food industry experts objected to the study guides prepared for the course and requested extensive changes in the text (Zuckerman 1984); the wheel also proved difficult for the public to understand. Thus, USDA staff initiated a consumer research study to identify a more useful format; they continued to use the portion sizes and numbers presented in the wheel in subsequent publications such as the 1990 *Dietary Guidelines.*

The research demonstrated that consumers preferred the *Pyramid* over many other designs. Its graphic displays grains and cereals at the wide base, vegetables and fruits in the band above, meats and dairy foods in the narrow upper band, and fats and sweets in the narrow peak. The band width represents the number of portions of each food group recommended by USDA. But unlike earlier graphics, the *Pyramid* format indicates that the daily diet should include more servings of grains, fruits, and vegetables than of meats, dairy products, and fats and sweets.

Preparation of the *Pyramid* graphic and accompanying brochure began in 1988. During the next two years, these materials were reviewed extensively, publicized widely, and fully cleared for publication; they were sent to the printer in February 1991 ("A Pyramid Topples" 1991). In April, representatives of the National Cattlemen's Association saw a *Washington Post* report on the *Pyramid* (Gladwell 1991) and joined other producer groups to protest that it "stigmatized" their products and should be withdrawn immediately (Burros 1991b; Combs 1991; Sugarman and Gladwell 1991). Two weeks later, the newly appointed USDA secretary, Edward Madigan, a former

Republican congressman from Illinois, announced that the *Pyramid* required further testing on children and poorly educated adults and postponed its publication. His explanation for this decision, however, was widely disbelieved ("A Pyramid Topples" 1991). Instead, observers attributed his actions to a direct response to pressures from meat producer lobby groups.

During the following year, the USDA issued a new and far more expensive contract to retest alternative designs on children and low-income adults. While this research was in progress, newspaper and magazine reporters wrote repeatedly of the *Pyramid* incident as an example of the conflict of interest created by the dual mandates of the USDA to protect American agricultural interests and to advise the public about food choices; they also used the incident as an illustration of the excessive and heavy-handed influence of lobbyists in federal policy decisions (Nestle 1993a).

The research tested the impact of alternative designs – particularly bowl shapes – that were preferred by most food industry representatives. When the messages conveyed by bowl designs were tested against those conveyed by pyramid designs, the results were nearly indistinguishable. At that point, the USDA was faced with a dilemma; the agency could choose the original *Pyramid* and risk embarrassment over the delay, additional costs, and continued opposition from food producers, or it could choose the bowl design for what might be interpreted as political rather than scientific reasons. Eventually, the USDA chose the pyramid design, perhaps because press reports kept public attention focused on the issue.

In April 1992, USDA released its *Food Guide Pyramid*. This publication seemed quite similar to the previous version. Its most significant difference concerned the numbers of recommended servings. These were relocated outside the triangle and reset in boldface type that two to three daily servings of meat and dairy foods were still recommended (USDA 1992). This change, which gave no indication that the servings were meant to be small and an upper limit, pleased food producers who made no further complaints about this publication (Nestle 1993a).

1995 Dietary Guidelines

Lobbying from meat and dairy groups was noticeably absent during preparation of the fourth edition of the *Dietary Guidelines* (USDA and USDHHS 1995). The recommendation for meat was similar to that offered in previous editions – "Choose two to three servings of lean . . . meats" – and the accompanying text suggested the benefits of eating moderately from the meat and beans group and avoiding sources of saturated fat in the diet. For the first time, the *Dietary Guidelines* recommended meals with rice, pasta, potatoes, or bread at the center of the plate and included a section on vegetarian diets. Nevertheless, release of this report elicited no comments from meat

producers, perhaps because the meat serving was defined as 2 to 3 ounces, in effect extending the recommended intake range to 9 ounces per day.

Concluding Comments

Classic studies have viewed lobbying as a healthy influence within the political system that keeps Congress informed about issues, stimulates public debate, and encourages participation in the political process. These views find undue lobby influence unlikely, as "it is virtually impossible to steal or buy a public policy decision of any consequence in Washington" (Milbrath 1963).

Nonetheless, the history of dietary guidance policy records the increasing involvement of food lobbies – and the incorporation of their views – into federal recommendations for chronic disease prevention. In 1956, USDA staff drafted the *Basic Four* and, as a courtesy, permitted industry representatives to review it. But since 1980, food industry representatives increasingly have participated in the design of dietary guidance materials as well as in their review. This change in role occurred as the goal of dietary recommendations shifted from prevention of nutrient deficiencies to prevention of chronic diseases and from "eat more" advice to "eat less," and as food lobbies more vigorously defended their products against such advice.

Through their connections in Congress and the USDA, and use of their strong financial base, food lobbies successfully convinced government policymakers to alter advice about meat, a principal source of dietary fat, from "eat less" to "choose lean" to "have 2–3 portions." Yet this policy shift occurred concurrently with increasing scientific consensus that reduced fat intake would improve the health of the public, that the 30 percent target level has been a political compromise, and that evidence all along has supported a level of 20 to 25 percent or less (Burros 1991a; Wynder, Weisburger, and Ng 1992). To some extent, it seems likely that contradiction between scientific consensus and federal advice is responsible for Americans' failing to reduce their fat intake (McGinnis and Nestle 1989; Putnam 1991; Nestle 1995).

It must be emphasized that lobbying strategies are entirely legal and available to consumer groups as well as to food producers. What should be clear from this discussion, however, is that producer groups possess far greater resources for lobbying activities than do either consumer groups or the federal government. The hundreds of millions of dollars available to the meat and dairy lobbies through checkoff programs, and the billions of dollars spent on food advertising, far exceed the $1.3 million spent by the USDA on dietary guidance and research in 1991 (USDA 1991). As one commentator stated, it is unfortunate that "good advice about nutrition conflicts with the interests of many big industries, each of which has more lobbying power than all the public-interest groups combined" (Jacobson 1974).

The controversy over the *Eating Right Pyramid* demonstrates that the connections between members of Congress, USDA officials, and food lobbies must continue to raise questions about the ability of federal officials to make independent policy decisions. Individuals concerned about such issues might consider whether the USDA's conflicts of interest have so impaired its ability to educate the public about diet and health that such functions should be transferred to an agency less tied to food industry groups. Also worth consideration is more forceful advocacy of consumer perspectives to Congress, reform of lobbying laws, reduced dependence on PAC expenditures, tighter restrictions on the revolving door, disclosure of funding sources by members of advisory committees, and education of the public on the extent of lobbying influence.

Marion Nestle

Bibliography

ADA to publish Food II magazine as separate booklets. 1982. *CNI Weekly Report* 12: 1–2.

American Enterprise Institute. 1980. *Proposals to revise the lobbying law.* Washington, D.C.

American Heart Association. 1961. Dietary fat and its relation to heart attacks and strokes. *Circulation* 23: 133–6.

Babcock, C. R. 1991. $100,000 political donations on the rise again. *The Washington Post,* September 30, pp. A1, A4.

Becker, G. S. 1991. Farm commodity promotion programs. *Congressional Research Service Report for Congress,* 91–151 ENR. Washington, D.C.

Berry, J. M. 1984. *The interest group society.* Boston, Mass.

Binder, D. 1995. Jamie Whitten, who served 53 years in House, dies at 85. *The New York Times,* September 10, p. 53.

Blisard, W. N., and J. R. Blaylock. 1989. *Generic promotion of agricultural products.* USDA Economic Research Service Agricultural Information Bulletin No. 565. Washington, D.C.

Blisard, W. N., T. Sun, and J. R. Blaylock. 1991. *Effects of advertising on the demand for cheese and fluid milk.* USDA Economic Research Service Staff Report No. AGES 9154. Washington, D.C.

Bowers, J. 1991. *Political action committees: Selected references, 1989–1991.* Congressional Research Service report for Congress 91–382 L. Washington, D.C.

Broad, W. J. 1979. The ever-shifting dietary goals. *Science* 204: 1177.

    1981. Nutrition research: End of an empire. *Science* 213: 518–20.

Browne, W. P. 1988. *Private interests, public policy, and American agriculture.* Lawrence, Kan.

Burros, M. 1991a. Eating well. Experts agree on one thing at least: Even less fat is better. *The New York Times,* July 31, p. C4.

    1991b. U.S. delays issuing nutrition chart. *The New York Times,* April 27, p. 9.

Califano, J. A. 1992. Throw the rascals out sooner. *The New York Times Book Review,* September 27, p. 7.

Cannon, G. 1987. *The politics of food.* London.

Cattlemen's Beef Promotion and Research Board. 1990. *The beef board annual report.* Englewood, Colo.

    1991. *The beef board annual report: A new direction.* Englewood, Colo.

Cloud, D. S. 1989. When Madison Avenue talks, farm-belt members listen. *Congressional Quarterly* 3047–51, November 11.

Combs, G. F. 1991. What's happening at USDA. *AIN Nutrition Notes* 27: 6.

Congressional Quarterly Service. 1965. *Legislators and the lobbyists.* Washington, D.C.

    1968. *Legislators and the lobbyists.* Second edition. Washington, D.C.

Cronin, F. J., A. M. Shaw, S. M. Krebs-Smith, et al. 1987. Developing a food guidance system to implement the dietary guidelines. *Journal of Nutrition Education* 19: 281–302.

deKieffer, D. E. 1981. *How to lobby Congress: A guide for the citizen lobbyist.* New York.

Dietary guidelines review. 1982. *CNI Weekly Report* 12 (48): 6.

Federal Election Commission. 1991a. *Candidate index of supporting documents.* September 26. Washington, D.C.

    1991b. *PAC activity falls in 1990 election.* Press release, March 31. Washington, D.C.

Gladwell, M. 1991. U.S. rethinks, redraws the food groups. *The Washington Post,* April 13, pp. A1, A7.

Greenberg, D. S. 1980. Nutrition: A long wait for a little advice. *Science* 302: 535–6.

Guither, H. D. 1980. *The food lobbyists: Behind the scenes of food and agri-politics.* Lexington, Mass.

Haas, E. 1980. *Community Nutrition Institute press release: Over 100 organizations protest industry efforts to suppress national dietary guidelines.* July 15. Washington, D.C.

Hadwiger, D. G., and W. P. Browne, eds. 1978. *The new politics of food.* Lexington, Mass.

Haughton, B., J. D. Gussow, and J. M. Dodds. 1987. An historical study of the underlying assumptions for United States food guides from 1917 through the basic four food group guide. *Journal of Nutrition Education* 19: 169–75.

Hill, M. M., and L. E. Cleveland. 1970. Food guides – their development and use. *USDA Nutrition Program News* July/October: 1–6.

Hunt, C. L. 1921. *A week's food for an average family.* USDA Farmers' Bulletin No. 1228. Washington, D.C.

Hunt, C. L., and H. W. Atwater. 1917. *How to select foods. I. What the body needs.* USDA Farmers' Bulletin 808. Washington, D.C.

Inter-Society Commission for Heart Disease Resources. 1970. Primary prevention of the atherosclerotic diseases. *Circulation* 42: A55–98.

Jacobson, M. 1974. *Nutrition scoreboard,* 197–8. New York.

Knutson, R. D., J. B. Penn, and W. T. Boehm. 1983. *Agricultural and food policy.* Englewood Cliffs, N.J.

Kramer, J. 1979. Agriculture's role in government decisions. In *Consensus and conflict in U.S. agriculture,* ed. B. L. Gardner and J. W. Richardson, 204–41. College Station, Tex.

Levenstein, H. 1988. *Revolution at the table: The transformation of the American diet.* New York.

Livestock prices fall after report ties fat in diet to cancer. 1982. *The Wall Street Journal,* June 17, p. 44.

Madison, J. 1787. The federalist no. 10. In *The federalist papers,* by A. Hamilton, J. Madison, and J. Jay, ed. G. Wills, 42-9. New York.

Maugh, T. H. 1982. Cancer is not inevitable. *Science* 217: 36-7.

McCauley, M., and A. Cohen. 1991. *They love to fly . . . and it shows: An analysis of privately-funded travel by members of the U.S. House of Representatives 101st Congress (1989-1990).* Washington, D.C.

McGinnis, J. M., and M. Nestle. 1989. The Surgeon General's report on nutrition and health: Policy implications and implementation strategies. *American Journal of Clinical Nutrition* 49: 23-8.

McGraw, M. 1991. A case of "very vested interest." *Kansas City Star,* December 10, p. A6.

Milbrath, L. W. 1963. *The Washington lobbyists.* Chicago.

Monte, T. 1979. The U.S. finally takes a stand on diet. *Nutrition Action* 6: 4.

Morgan, D. 1978a. "Plain, poor sister" is newly alluring. *The Washington Post,* July 4, pp. A1, A8.
    1978b. Trying to lead the USDA through a thicket of politics. *The Washington Post,* July 5, p. A8.

Mottern, N. 1978. Dietary goals. *Food Monitor.* March/April: 8-10.

National Live Stock and Meat Board. 1987. *The meat board: Who? What? Why?* Chicago.

NRC (National Research Council). 1980. *Toward Healthful Diets.* Washington, D.C.
    1982. *Diet, nutrition, and cancer.* Washington, D.C.
    1988. *Designing foods: Animal product options in the marketplace.* Washington, D.C.
    1989. *Diet and health: Implications for reducing chronic disease risk.* Washington, D.C.

Nestle, M. 1993a. Dietary advice for the 1990s: The political history of the Food Guide Pyramid. *Caduceus* 9: 136-53.
    1993b. Food lobbies, the food pyramid, and U.S. nutrition policy. *International Journal of Health Services* 23: 483-96.
    1995. Dietary guidance for the 21st century: New approaches. *Journal of Nutrition Education* 27: 272-5.

Nestle, M., and D. V. Porter. 1990. Evolution of federal dietary guidance policy: From food adequacy to chronic disease prevention. *Caduceus* 6: 43-67.

The 100 leading national advertisers. 1991. *Advertising Age* (September 25).

Paarlberg, D. 1964. *American farm policy: A case study of centralized decision-making.* New York.

Page, I. H., F. J. Stare, A. C. Corcoran, et al. 1957. Atherosclerosis and the fat content of the diet. *Circulation* 16: 163-78.

Parrish, R. D., and B. Silverglade. 1990. *Testimony on the beef and pork promotion and research programs before the Committee on Agriculture, Subcommittee on Livestock, Dairy, and Poultry, U.S. House of Representatives.* Washington, D.C.

Peterkin, B. B., R. L. Kerr, and C. J. Shore. 1978. Diets that meet the dietary goals. *Journal of Nutrition Education* 10: 15-18.

Public Citizens' Congress Watch. 1982. *An ocean of milk, a mountain of cheese, and a ton of money: Contributions from the dairy PAC to members of Congress.* Washington, D.C.

Putnam, J. J. 1991. Food consumption, 1970-90. *FoodReview* 14: 2-11.

A pyramid topples at the USDA. 1991. *Consumer Reports* 56: 663-6.

Raper, N. 1991. Nutrient content of the U.S. food supply. *FoodReview* 14: 13-17.

Reagan administration OK's dietary guidelines. 1985. *CNI Weekly Report,* September 26, p. 2.

Registered lobbyists. 1991. *Congressional Record* 137 (122): HL 287-372, August 15.

Rosenthal, B., M. Jacobson, and M. Bohm. 1976. Feeding at the company trough. *Congressional Record* H8974-8977, August 26.

Schriftgiesser, K. 1951. *The lobbyists.* Boston, Mass.

Solkoff, J. 1985. *The politics of food.* San Francisco.

Stiebeling, H. K., and M. M. Ward. 1933. *Diets at four levels of nutritive content and cost.* USDA Circular No. 296. Washington, D.C.

Sugarman, C., and M. Gladwell. 1991. Revised food chart killed. *The Washington Post,* April 17, p. A1.

Timmer, C. P., and M. C. Nesheim. 1979. Nutrition, product quality, and safety. In *Consensus and conflict in U.S. agriculture,* ed. B. L. Gardner and J. W. Richardson, 155-92. College Station, Tex.

USDA and HEW unveil guidelines for healthy eating. 1980. *CNI Weekly Report* 10 (6): 1-2.

USDA readies to carve up the dietary guidelines. 1983. *Nutrition Action* 10: 3-4.

USDA (U.S. Department of Agriculture). 1862. *Department of Agriculture Organic Act* 12 Stat. 317, May 15.
    1958. *Food for fitness: A daily food guide.* Leaflet No. 424. Washington, D.C.
    1979. *Food: The hassle-free guide to a better diet.* Home and Garden Bulletin No. 228. Washington, D.C.
    1981. *Ideas for better eating: Menus and recipes to make use of the dietary guidelines.* Washington, D.C.
    1990. *Report of the Dietary Guidelines Advisory Committee on the dietary guidelines for Americans.* No. 261-463/20444. Washington, D.C.
    1991. *1990 report on USDA human nutrition research and education activities: A report to Congress.* Washington, D.C.
    1992. *The Food Guide Pyramid.* HG-249. Hyattsville, Md.

USDA and USDHEW (U.S. Department of Agriculture and U.S. Department of Health, Education, and Welfare). 1980. *Nutrition and your health: Dietary guidelines for Americans.* Washington, D.C.

USDA and USDHHS (U.S. Department of Agriculture and U.S. Department of Health and Human Services). 1985. *Nutrition and your health: Dietary guidelines for Americans.* Second edition. Washington, D.C.
    1990. *Nutrition and your health: Dietary guidelines for Americans.* Third edition. Washington, D.C.
    1995. *Nutrition and your health: Dietary guidelines for Americans.* Fourth edition. Washington, D.C.

USDHEW (U.S. Department of Health, Education, and Welfare). 1979. *Healthy people: The Surgeon General's report on health promotion and disease prevention.* DHEW (PHS) 79-55071. Washington, D.C.

USDHHS (U.S. Department of Health and Human Services). 1988. *The Surgeon General's report on nutrition and health.* Washington, D.C.

U.S. General Accounting Office. 1984. *National Academy of Sciences' reports on diet and health - Are they credible and consistent?* GAO/RCED-84-109. Washington, D.C.

U.S. House of Representatives. 1988. *Rural development, agriculture, and related agencies appropriations bill, 1989: Report No 100-690.* June 10, p. 107. Washington, D.C.

U.S. Senate Committee on Governmental Affairs. 1991. *The federal lobbying disclosure laws: Hearings before the*

Subcommittee on Oversight of Government Management, S-Hrg. June 20, July 16, September 25, pp. 102–377.

U.S. Senate Select Committee on Nutrition and Human Needs. 1977a. *Dietary goals for the United States.* February. Washington, D.C.

    1977b. *Dietary goals for the United States.* Second edition. December. Washington, D.C.

    1977c. *Dietary goals for the United States - Supplemental views.* November. Washington, D.C.

    1977d. *Diet related to killer diseases. III. Hearings in response to dietary goals for the United States: re meat.* March 24. Washington, D.C.

    1977e. *Final report.* December. Washington, D.C.

U.S. Senate Special Committee to Investigate Political Activities, Lobbying, and Campaign Contributions. 1957. *Final Report.* Washington, D.C.

Wade, N. 1980. Food Board's fat report hits fire. *Science* 209: 248–50.

We feel compelled to break relations. 1980. *CNI Weekly Report* 10 (24): 4–5.

Westwater, J. J. 1988. Dairy farmers are pioneers in promotion. In Marketing U.S. agriculture, ed. Deborah Takiff Smith. *The . . . Yearbook of Agriculture,* 271–5. Washington, D.C.

Wilde, P. 1992. No "meating" of minds: Are federal agriculture and health departments heading for a showdown? *Vegetarian Times* 174 (February): 58–62, 97.

Wolf, I. D., and B. B. Peterkin. 1984. Dietary guidelines: The USDA perspective. *Food Technology* 38: 80–6.

Wynder, E. L., J. H. Weisburger, and S. K. Ng. 1992. Nutrition: The need to define "optimal" intake as a basis for public policy decisions. *American Journal of Public Health* 82: 346–50.

Zuckerman, S. 1984. Killing it softly. *Nutrition Action* (January–February): 6–10.

VII.7 ❧ Food Biotechnology: Politics and Policy Implications

Food biotechnology – the use of recombinant deoxyribonucleic acid (rDNA) and cell fusion techniques to confer selected characteristics upon food plants, animals, and microorganisms (Mittal 1992; Carrol 1993) – is well understood as a means to increase agricultural productivity, especially in the developing world. The great promise of biotechnology is that it will help solve world food problems by creating a more abundant, more nutritious, and less expensive food supply. This theoretical promise is widely appreciated and beyond dispute (Rogers and Fleet 1989; U.S. Congress 1992).

Nonetheless, food biotechnology has elicited extraordinary levels of controversy. In the United States and in Europe, the first commercial food products of genetic engineering were greeted with suspicion by the public, vilified by the press, and threatened with boycotts and legislative prohibitions. Such reactions reflect widespread concerns about the safety and environmental impact of these products, as well as about their regulatory status, ethical implications, and social value. The reactions also reflect public fears about the unknown dangers of genetic engineering and deep distrust of the biotechnology industry and its governmental regulators (Davis 1991; Hoban 1995).

Biotechnology industry leaders and their supporters, however, dismiss these public concerns, fears, and suspicions as irrational. They characterize individuals raising such concerns as ignorant, hysterical, irresponsible, antiscientific, and "troglodyte," and they describe "biotechnophobia" as the single most serious threat to the development, growth, and commercialization of the food biotechnology industry (Gaull and Goldberg 1991: 6). They view antibiotechnology advocates as highly motivated and well funded and believe them to be deliberately "interweaving political, societal and emotional issues . . . to delay commercialization and increase costs by supporting political, non-science-based regulation, unnecessary testing, and labelling of foods" (Fraley 1992: 43).

In the face of this controversy, industry leaders have concluded that their most important challenge is to find ways to allay public fears (U.S. Congress 1991a) and to "assure the public that the new food technologies are not only beneficial to society, but safe" (Gaull and Goldberg 1991: 9).

This divergence in industry and public viewpoints can be traced to the conflict inherent in the two basic goals of the food biotechnology industry: (1) to benefit the public by developing agricultural products that will solve important food problems, and (2) to benefit the industry itself through the successful commercial marketing of these products. Although development of genetically engineered food products might well be expected to meet both goals, such is not always the case. One problem is the lack of a viable market, which experts view as a major barrier to research on food problems of the developing world (Hodgson 1992). Another centers on industry needs for rapid returns on investment; such needs constitute a driving force in decisions about research and development and cause industry leaders to view legitimate public questions about the use, safety, or social consequences of particular food products as threats to the entire biotechnology enterprise.

This chapter examines the reasons why so potentially useful an application of molecular techniques to food product development has elicited so great a level of controversy in the United States and elsewhere. Using the situation in the United States as a case study, it reviews key issues of economics, marketing, and risk that have affected the development and implementation of regulatory policies for the commercial products of food biotechnology, particularly those that affect food safety, allergenicity, environmental impact, and intellectual property rights. It also addresses issues that have influenced public perceptions of these products and describes how these issues have affected industry and public responses to the first genetically engineered food products released in the United States. Finally, it suggests implications of the present controversy for future product development, industry actions, and public policies.

The Promise

There seems little doubt that biotechnology holds great promise for addressing world food problems, most notably the overall shortfall in food production now expected early in the twenty-first century (Fraley 1992). No theoretical barriers impede the use of the techniques of molecular and cellular genetics to improve the quantity and quality of the food supply, to increase food safety, and to reduce food costs (Reilly 1989; U.S. Congress 1992; Hayenga 1993). Table VII.7.1 lists the wide range of potential applications of food biotechnology that as of the mid-1990s were under investigation or are theoretically possible. Such applications could greatly increase world food production, especially given the conditions of poor climate and soil typical of many developing countries (Swaminathan 1982).

Table VII.7.1. *Theoretical and current applications of food biotechnology*

Improve the flavor, texture, freshness, or nutrient content of fruit and vegetables.
Modify seed storage proteins to increase their concentration of limiting amino acids such as lysine or tryptophan.
Alter the chain length and degree of saturation of plant seed oils.
Increase plant production of specialty chemicals such as sugars, waxes, phytooxidants, or pharmaceutically active chemicals.
Increase levels of vitamins and other nutrients in plant food crops.
Decrease levels of caffeine or other undesirable substances in plant food crops.
Increase resistance of crops to damage by insect or microbial pests.
Increase resistance of crops to "stress" by frost, heat, salt, or heavy metals.
Develop herbicide-resistant plants to improve weed control.
Enable crop plants to be grown under conditions of low input of fertilizers, pesticides, or water.
Enable major crop plants to fix atmospheric nitrogen.
Develop plant foods containing antigens that can vaccinate humans against disease.
Increase the efficiency of growth and reproduction of food-producing animals.
Create disease-resistant animals.
Develop animal veterinary vaccines and diagnostic tests.
Allow cows to produce milk containing recombinant human milk proteins that can be used in infant formulas.
Create microorganisms, enzymes, and other biological products useful in food processing.
Develop microorganisms capable of converting environmental waste products – plastics, oil, pesticides, or PCBs – into usable animal feeds.

The potential for such improvements in the food supply constitute the principal basis for industry and government conclusions that "biotechnology is the most important scientific tool to affect the food economy in the history of mankind" (Gaull and Goldberg 1991: 150), that "biotechnology promises consumers better, cheaper, safer foods" ("Biotechnology Promises" 1990: 1), and that "genetic engineering and biotechnology will create miracles to help us feed a hungry world efficiently and economically" (Sullivan 1991: 97).

Such promises, however, have not yet been fulfilled, nor are they likely to be realized in the immediate future (Messer and Heywood 1990), principally because many of the applications listed in Table VII.7.1 pose biological and technical problems of formidable complexity (Barton and Brill 1983; American Medical Association 1991). For example, many hundreds of as yet uncharacterized genes appear to be involved in the reproduction of corn (Kilman 1994b), and the more than 350 varieties of cassava (manioc) grown throughout the world seem especially resistant to transgenic transformations (Beachy 1993). But the slow progress of biotechnology in addressing world food problems should not imply that such problems cannot be solved. Given sufficient time, commitment, and funding support, the technical barriers almost certainly can be overcome.

Economic Issues

Costs and Benefits
Technical problems, however, are not the most important barriers to the application of food biotechnology to world agricultural productivity. Instead, the greatest barrier derives from the need of the industry to recover the costs of research and development and to maximize return on investment (Harlander 1989). Research costs are not trivial: The average genetically modified plant requires about $10 million (U.S.) to develop and about six years to become marketable (Ollinger and Pope 1995). Thus, the expected returns on such an investment need to be substantial (U.S. Congress 1991a). Although no products had as yet been brought to market, food biotechnology was considered in the early 1990s to have "a huge potential to make money" (Kim 1992a: B1). At that time some experts suggested that the value of the industry would increase to at least $50 billion by the year 2000 (Leary 1992a) and that the prices of biotechnology stocks would rise by 25 percent annually well into the 1990s (Somerville 1993).

To date, however, stock market returns have not reflected such projections. Although the biotechnology industry increased in sales, revenues, and numbers of companies and employees from 1989 to 1993, net losses also increased steadily during that period (Waldholz 1994). One notable exception has been the Monsanto Company; its stock prices gained 75 percent in 1995 (Fritsch and Kilman 1996) and another 70 percent in 1996 (Wadman 1996). Monsanto officials estimated that their products of plant biotechnology would earn $2 billion by the year 2000 and that sales would grow to $6 or $7 billion by 2005 and to $20 billion by 2010 (Feder 1996).

The generally poor performance of other food biotechnology stocks has been attributed to uneven management, corporate shortsightedness, and product failures (Hamilton 1994). It also has been attributed to lack of government investment. Although overall federal investment in biotechnology research exceeded $4 billion in 1994, only 5 percent of these funds supported agricultural projects; in contrast, 41 percent were applied to drug development (Caswell, Fuglie, and Klotz 1994). By the mid-1990s, only a few products had come to market, and their degree of acceptability was as yet unknown. The resulting uncertainties in profitability explain industry preoccupation with issues of federal regulation, intellectual property, and public perception (Fraley 1992).

The need for return on investment has encouraged the industry to focus on the development of products that are most technically feasible, rather than those that might be most useful to the public or to developing countries. To date, food biotechnology research has tended to concentrate on agronomic traits that most benefit agricultural producers and processors. These include control of insects, weeds, plant diseases, and ripening, and production of crops that will resist insects and tolerate herbicides (Office of Planning 1988; Olempska-Beer et al. 1993). Research also has focused on the development of foods that will last longer on the shelf and cost less to process (U.S. Congress 1991a; Barnum 1992). A 1988 survey of 74 food processing firms that used biotechnology methods found that of their research projects, 27 percent were devoted to enzymes (such as those used in cheese manufacture), 15 percent to sweeteners, 11 percent to flavors, fragrances, and colors for prepared food products, and 10 percent to better detection of contaminants; the remaining 37 percent were concentrated on product development and processing methods (Reilly 1989). A more recent study reported that chemical and pesticide companies have obtained 41 percent of all permits for field testing of genetically engineered plants (Ollinger and Pope 1995).

In 1990, the leading 36 agrochemical and agricultural biotechnology companies together spent nearly $400 million on such research and development, but an order of magnitude less ("puny" by comparison) on projects designed to address agricultural problems of the developing world (Hodgson 1992: 49). Such problems – and their biotechnological solutions – are well defined (Bokanga 1995; Knorr 1995). Although many sources of private and public funding are available to support biotechnology projects in developing countries (Chambers 1995), these are fragmented, poorly coordinated, and often promote donors' priorities rather than those of the recipients (Messer 1992). One well-established research institute dedicated to improving crops in developing countries reports little success in obtaining industry financing or support beyond the permission to use patent-protected techniques "for specific crops under certain circumstances" (Beachy 1993: 61). Such observations have led commentators to conclude: "Nearly 20 years into the gene-splicing revolution, the industry has ballooned to well over 1,000 public or private companies that have raised about $20 billion. Yet no one has cured cancer or produced a bioengineered miracle of loaves and fishes for a hungry Third World. The industry is still peddling dreams . . ." (Hamilton 1990: 43).

Marketing Barriers

To assure adequate returns on investment, the biotechnology industry must create and sell new products. These products, however, compete with other products in a market that is already highly competitive because the United States vastly overproduces food (Stillings 1994). In 1990, for example, the U.S. food supply made available an average of 3,700 kcal/day for every man, woman, and child in the country (Putnam and Allshouse 1996), even though adult men require two-thirds that amount, women about half, and children even less (National Research Council 1989). Because the amount of energy that any one person can consume is finite, such overproduction implies that a choice of any one food product will preclude choice of another.

Food marketers compete for consumer purchases through two principal means: advertising and new product development. Retail sales of food generated $791 billion in 1994. In the same year, food marketers spent $9.8 billion on direct consumer advertising and about twice that amount on retail promotion in trade shows, product placements, point-of-purchase campaigns, and other incentives. From 1984 to 1994, food companies introduced 125,000 new products into U.S. markets, more than 15,000 of them in 1994 alone (Economic Research Service 1994; Gallo 1995). Nevertheless, such efforts have failed to improve overall growth in the food processing sector, which has increased at less than 1 percent per year since the late 1940s, a rate considered stagnant by comparison to other industries. In so competitive an environment, biotechnology is seen as a crucial force for development of new products that will increase the country's overall economic productivity (Reilly 1989).

Risk Issues

Tryptophan Supplements

From the standpoint of the biotechnology industry and its supporters, genetically engineered foods are no different from foods produced by conventional genetic crosses. Therefore, industry supporters argue that any risks associated with these foods are extremely small and greatly outweighed by their benefits (Gaull and Goldberg 1991; Miller 1991; Falk and Bruening 1994). Critics, however, insist that food biotechnology raises safety concerns that in the absence of prior experience are difficult to define, predict, or quantify. They point, as an example, to the case of tryptophan supplements to illustrate the unknown hazards of commercial biotechnology.

In 1989, health officials linked tryptophan supplements from a single manufacturer to an unusual syndrome of muscle pain, weakness, and increased blood levels of certain white cells (eosinophils), a constellation of symptoms termed eosinophilia-myalgia syndrome (Centers for Disease Control 1989). Eventually, more than 1,500 cases of illness and nearly 40 deaths were attributed to the use of such supplements as a self-medication for insomnia and other conditions (Roufs 1992; Mayeno and Gleich 1994). Because tryptophan is a normal amino acid component of all proteins, investigators believed that toxic contaminants must have developed during the manufacturing process. This process involved the creation of a strain of bacteria genetically manipulated to produce high levels of tryptophan and extraction of this amino acid through a series of purification steps (Fox 1990).

To date, characterization of the toxic components remains incomplete (Mayeno and Gleich 1994). Although it appears unlikely that the genetic engineering methods were directly at fault (Philin et al. 1993), their use to modify a bacterial strain created a situation in which toxic products were formed, albeit inadvertently (Aldhous 1991). This example suggests that concerns about the unknown hazards of biotechnology have some basis in experience.

Allergenicity

Because genes encode proteins, and proteins are allergenic, the introduction of allergenic proteins into previously nonallergenic foods could be another unintended consequence of plant biotechnology. In a finding described as "Another shadow . . . cast over the agricultural biotechnology industry . . ." (Winslow 1996: B6), researchers have now demonstrated that an allergenic protein from Brazil nuts can be transferred to soybeans, and that people with demonstrable allergies to Brazil nuts react similarly to soybeans that contain the Brazil-nut protein (Nordlees et al. 1996).

The Brazil-nut soybeans were developed as a means to increase the content of the amino acid methionine in animal feeds, which must otherwise be supplemented with methionine to promote optimal growth. The Brazil-nut protein is especially rich in methionine and its gene was a logical choice as a donor. Nuts, however, are often allergenic, and the investigators happened to have collected serum samples from people known to be allergic to Brazil nuts. Thus, they had in place all the components necessary to test for allergies to Brazil-nut proteins. Such compo-

nents are rarely available for testing other potentially allergenic proteins, however.

Adverse reactions to food proteins can be documented in just 2 percent of adults and 8 percent of children (Sampson and Metcalfe 1992), but many more people are expected to develop food sensitivities as proteins are increasingly added to commercially prepared foods. Soy proteins, for example, already are very widely used in infant formulas, meat extenders, baked goods, and dairy replacements. Most biotechnology companies are using microorganisms rather than food plants as gene donors. Although these microbial proteins do not appear to share sequence similarities with known food allergens (Fuchs and Astwood 1996), few of them have as yet entered the food supply. At the present time, their allergenic potential is uncertain, unpredictable, and untestable (Nestle 1996).

As discussed in the following section, allergenicity raises complicated regulatory issues. Under a Food and Drug Administration (FDA) policy established in 1992, the manufacturer of the Brazil-nut soybeans was required to – and did – consult the FDA about the need for premarket testing. Because testing proved that the allergenic protein had been transmitted, the company would have been required to label its transgenic soybeans. Because the company had no simple method in place to separate soybeans intended for animal feed from those intended for human consumption, it withdrew its transgenic soybeans from the market. This action was interpreted by supporters of the FDA policy as evidence of its effectiveness.

Others, however, viewed this event as further evidence that the FDA policy could not protect consumers against lesser-known transgenic allergens to which they might be sensitive and, therefore, favored industry. The lack of a requirement for labeling was of particular concern, as avoidance is often the only effective way to prevent allergic reactions. In 1993, the FDA requested public comment on whether and how to label food allergens in transgenic foods (FDA 1993). Then, in 1994, the FDA drafted a rule that would require companies to inform the agency when developing new transgenic foods, in part to help resolve safety issues related to allergenicity. Implementation of such a rule seemed unlikely, however, especially because the biotechnology industry demanded that any such requirement be limited in scope and "sunset" after three years ("Bio Favors" 1994). To date, the FDA has not reported or acted on the public comments related to labeling of transgenic allergens.

Policy Issues

Regulation

Current debates about the regulation of food biotechnology center on a conflict between issues of safety on the one hand and a broad range of ecological, societal, and ethical issues on the other. For the industry and its supporters, safety is the only issue of relevance. Because the safety of most genetically engineered products is well supported by science, regulations appear to create unnecessary barriers to further research and economic growth (Gaull and Goldberg 1991; Miller 1991). For critics, however, regulations must be designed to protect the public not only against known safety risks but also against those that cannot yet be anticipated (Mellon 1991). In addition, as discussed in the next sections, critics view safety as only one component of a far broader range of concerns about the impact of biotechnology on individuals, society, and the environment – issues that might also demand regulatory intervention. For government officials, regulation of food biotechnology must find the proper balance between oversight of the industry and encouragement of its efforts to develop and market new food products (U.S. General Accounting Office 1993). Thus far, the balance achieved by existing regulatory policies has satisfied neither the industry nor consumer groups.

Table VII.7.2 outlines key historical events in the development of policies for regulation of food biotechnology. This history has resulted in current regulatory policies that affect three key areas of concern: food safety, environmental protection, and intellectual property rights.

Table VII.7.2. *Key events in the history of the commercialization of food products of biotechnology in the United States*

1930	Congress passes Plant Patent Act, extending protection to distinct, asexually propagated varieties.
1970	Plant Variety Protection Act extends patent rights to new sexually propagated plant varieties.
1973	Cohn and Boyer clone insulin gene using rDNA technology.
1975	Asilomar Conference suggests guidelines for rDNA research.
1976	Genentech established as the first company dedicated to exploitation of rDNA technology. NIH publishes safety guidelines for rDNA research.
1980	U.S. Supreme Court rules that microorganisms may be patented (*Diamond v. Chakrabarty*); first patent issued for rDNA construction to Cohn and Boyer. Genentech stock sets Wall Street record (share price rises from $35 to $89 in 20 minutes). Congress passes amendments to Patent Acts allowing nonprofit institutions and small businesses to retain titles to patents developed with federal funds.
1982	Recombinant insulin approved for use. Transgenic plant prodcued using *agrobacterium* transformation system.
1983	A plant gene is transferred from one species to another. Executive order permits large businesses to hold title to patents developed with federal funds.
1985	The Environmental Protection Agency (EPA) issues use permit to Advanced Genetic Sciences for release of organisms genetically engineered to lack ice-nucleation proteins. Patent Office extends protection to corn with increased levels of tryptophan (*ex parte* Hibberd). FDA authorizes sales of meat and milk from cows treated with recombinant bovine somatotropin (rbST); reaffirms safety of these foods in 1988, 1989, and 1990.
1986	Office of Science and Technology Policy issues Coordinated Framework for the Regulation of Bio-Technology, partitioning regulatory responsibility among USDA, EPA, FDA, and, to a lesser extent, NIH (51 FR 23302, June 26). Congress passes Technology Transfer Act permitting companies to commercialize government-sponsored research. USDA develops transgenic pigs carrying the gene for human growth hormone.
1987	Tomatoes with a gene for insect resistance are field-tested. USDA requires field-testing permits only for genetically engineered organisms that present risks to plants (52 FR 22892, July 16).
1988	Patent Office extends patent protection to genetically engineered animals.
1990	Food and Drug Administration (FDA) approves recombinant chymosin (rennet) as generally recognized as safe (GRAS). NIH issues statement that rbST is safe.
1992	FDA announces policy on foods derived from new plant varieties (57 FR 22984, May 29). USDA grants Calgene, Inc. permision to field-test the Flavr Savr tomato.
1993	FDA requests data and information on labeling issues related to foods derived from biotechnology (58 FR 25837, April 28); approves rbST for commercial use (58 FR 59946, November 12); requests public comment on whether and how to label food allergens in transgenic foods. Congress issues moratorium on use of rbST. Patent Office resumes granting patents on genetically engineered animals.
1994	Congressional moratorium on rbST expires.
	USDA reaffirms policies that genetically engineered livestock and poultry are subject to existing regulations for slaughter, research, and inspection (59 FR 12582, March 17).
	FDA publishes interim guidance on voluntary labeling of milk from cows treated with rbST and forbids statements such as "rbST-free" (59 FR 6279, February 10); concludes consultation with Calgene, Inc., finding no significant difference between the Flavr Savr and other tomatoes with a history of safe use (59 FR 26647, May 23); approves use of aminoglycoside 3'-phosphotransferase II (the kanamycin-resistance gene) for use in developing new varieties of tomatoes, oilseed rape, and cotton (59 FR 26700, May 23); concludes consultation approving seven other genetically altered plants, including tomatoes, squash, potato, cotton, and soybeans.
	EPA announces that federal pesticide laws will apply to toxins and other substances introduced into crop plants through genetic engineering (59 FR 60496, November 23).
1996	Congress requires USDA to discontinue its advisory committee on food biotechnology and close its Office of Agricultural Biotechnology.
	Allergen from Brazil nuts is transmitted to transgenic soybeans; transgenic herbicide resistance is transmitted to weeds, raising environmentalist concerns.
	Monsanto plants Bt cotton, herbicide (Roundup)-resistant soybeans. Ciba-Geigy plants herbicide-resistant corn. Both encounter consumer resistance in Europe. The European Union approves the soybeans, requires committee discussion of the corn, approves the corn but requires labeling of transgenic crops.

Table VII.7.3. *Safety issues raised by food biotechnology*

Unanticipated health effects resulting from genetic manipulations.
Increase in levels of naturally occurring toxins or allergens.
Activation of dormant toxins or allergens.
Introduction of known or new toxins, allergens, or antinutrients.
Adverse changes in the composition, absorption, or metabolism of key nutrients.
Increase in antibiotic-resistant microorganisms through use of antibiotic marker genes.
Transmission of herbicide resistance to weeds.
Adverse changes in the nutrient content of animal feed.
Increased levels of toxins in plant by-products fed to animals.

Food Safety

From the first, gene cloning experiments elicited safety concerns, mainly focused on the potential hazards of releasing new organisms with unknown properties into the environment. At a conference in 1975, scientists suggested stringent guidelines for research studies employing recombinant DNA techniques. The following year, the National Institutes of Health required researchers to follow similar guidelines. In subsequent years, as understanding of the techniques improved, concerns about safety diminished and the guidelines were modified accordingly. Nevertheless, common genetic methods for food modification involving, for example, bacteria that cause crown gall (a plant disease), marker genes for

antibiotic resistance, and insertion of genes from one living species into another, continued to elicit debate about the known and unknown hazards of such techniques (International Food Biotechnology Council 1990). Table VII.7.3 summarizes the principal safety issues that have been raised by the use of food biotechnology.

In 1986, the White House Office of Science and Technology Policy (OSTP) developed a "Coordinated Framework" for regulating biotechnology based on the premise that its products were no different from those developed through conventional techniques, and that existing laws and agencies were sufficient for their regulation. OSTP specified the distribution of regulatory responsibility among the various federal agencies. Under laws then in effect, responsibility for the regulation of food biotechnology involved no less than three offices reporting directly to the president; four major federal agencies; eight centers, services, offices, or programs within agencies; and five federal committees – all operating under the authority of 10 distinct acts of Congress (U.S. Congress 1992).

As might be expected, critics immediately identified a substantial lack of coordination, duplication of effort, overlapping responsibility, and gaps in oversight in this regulatory framework (Mellon 1988; Fox 1992). Because the principal laws affecting food safety were written before biotechnology became an

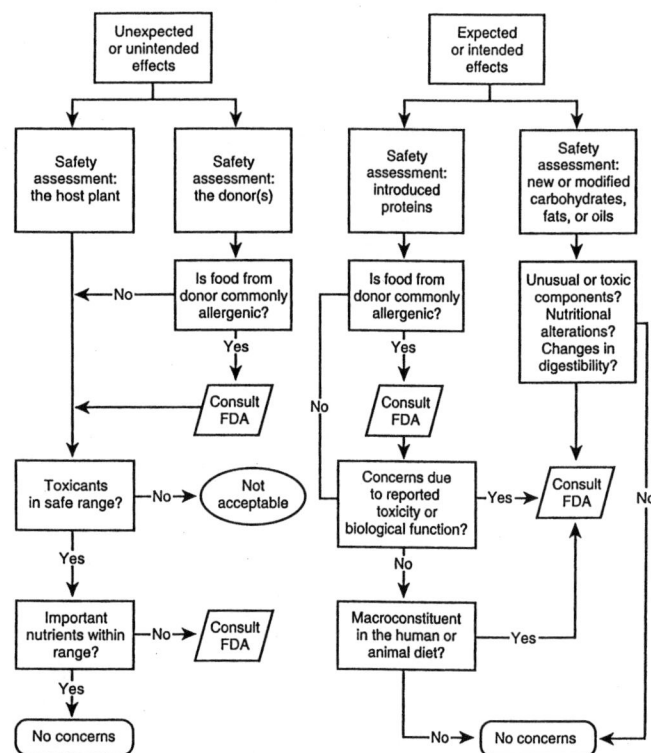

Figure VII.7.1. Food and Drug Administration Policy guidelines for regulation of foods developed through biotechnology. (From Food and Drug Administration 1992.)

issue, they did not necessarily apply to the new methods (Browning 1992). Thus, the confusing and uncertain regulatory status of recombinant products stimulated the food biotechnology industry to demand more precise guidance from the FDA. The President's Council on Competitiveness, a group dedicated to reducing regulations that impede industry, strongly supported such demands (Leary 1992b).

In response, the FDA developed a formal policy for the regulation of plant foods produced through biotechnology (FDA 1992). The agency designed this policy to be "scientifically and legally sound and . . . adequate to fully protect public health while not inhibiting innovation" (Kessler et al. 1992: 1832). This policy framework is summarized in Figure VII.7.1. The policy presumed that foods produced through rDNA techniques raised no new safety issues and could be regulated by the FDA's postmarket authority for foods "Generally Recognized as Safe" (GRAS). Therefore, safety evaluation would focus on changes in the "objective characteristics" of foods – new substances, toxins, allergens, or nutrients – and not on the techniques used to produce them. Under this policy, the FDA would invoke its testing requirements for new food additives, and would require industry consultation, only if the transgenic foods contained unusual or potentially toxic components (e.g., allergens). This new biotechnology policy required no premarket safety evaluation, premarket approval by the FDA, or special labeling of the new foods.

The response of the industry to these "election-year efforts by the White House to provide . . . as much regulatory relief as possible," was enthusiastic and viewed as "a very strong incentive for investment in the agricultural/food biotechnology area" (Ingersoll 1992: B1). One investment analyst summarized the new policy as an "assurance that after all a company's planning for a picnic, the government won't rain on it" (Kim 1992b: B3).

By contrast, consumer groups criticized the policy as inadequate to protect public safety and threatened to respond with mail campaigns and legal challenges (Hoyle 1992). A group of leading chefs in New York City called for an international boycott of genetically engineered foods, with one quoted as saying:

> I don't want a biotechnician in a lab coat telling me it's a better tomato . . . I think mother nature does a great job on her own. These people are tampering with the ecosystem and will cause problems. But what is most disturbing to me is the idea of selling the food without a label. ("Chefs Urge Boycotting" 1992: C6)

Critics of the policy were especially concerned about the lack of requirements for premarket testing and labeling (Hopkins, Goldburg, and Hirsch 1991). Commentators wondered whether this policy of "least regulatory resistance" actually might increase public suspicion of genetically engineered foodstuffs

(Hoyle 1992), especially in light of increasing press attention to "Frankenfoods" (O'Neill 1992). In response to such concerns, a federal study recommended formal review of the entire federal regulatory framework for food biotechnology in order to establish a better regulatory balance between promotion of the industry and protection of the public (U.S. General Accounting Office 1993).

Despite the controversy, the FDA implemented its policy. By late 1994, the agency had approved the marketing of tomatoes genetically engineered to reach optimal ripening after they were picked, milk from cows treated with a recombinant growth hormone, a virus-resistant squash, an insect-resistant potato, an herbicide-resistant cotton (used to make seed oil for animal feed), and herbicide-resistant soybeans (Associated Press 1994).

Environmental Impact

The "Coordinated Framework" affirmed that the U.S. Department of Agriculture (USDA) and the Environmental Protection Agency (EPA) were the primary agencies responsible for regulating agricultural biotechnology (see Table VII.7.2). Under the authority of two laws – the Federal Insecticide, Fungicide, and Rodenticide Act (FIFRA) and the Toxic Substances Control Act (TSCA) – the EPA was authorized to regulate genetically engineered organisms used to control insects and other pests, including those viral and bacterial, as well as any genetically engineered chemicals that might be hazardous to humans or to the environment. The EPA classified rDNA as such a substance and began to require biotechnology companies to obtain permits prior to the manufacture or release of their agricultural products (Caswell et al. 1994).

EPA policies were designed to address concerns that widespread agricultural use of new kinds of living species might present direct risks to human health. Such risks, however, are seen as minimal by environmentalists as well as by experts sympathetic to the industry (Mellon 1988; Miller 1994). Instead, the chief concern of environmental advocates is that agricultural biotechnology poses uncertain – but potentially grave – ecological risks. They offer considerable evidence to support the possibility that biotechnological organisms might displace existing plants and animals, create new plant pathogens, disrupt ecosystems, reduce crop diversity, and change climate patterns (Mellon 1988; Rissler and Mellon 1993). In addition, environmentalists are even more concerned about the impact of biotechnology on ongoing efforts to promote more widespread use of sustainable agricultural practices. They note, for example, that a large proportion of agricultural biotechnology research is dedicated to the development of herbicide-resistant crops, and that such research stimulates reliance on chemical herbicides to manage pests (Goldburg et al. 1990).

Thus, the EPA's 1994 decision to apply federal pesticide laws to toxins and other pesticidal substances introduced into crop plants through rDNA techniques was especially controversial. The biotechnology industry opposed it as an anachronistic and scientifically indefensible decision and noted that the EPA should instead have considered a risk-based regulatory system focusing on the organisms themselves rather than on the processes by which they were created. For the industry, the EPA decision would undoubtedly "exert a profoundly negative effect" on research into biological pest management strategies, particularly those unlikely to provide a sufficient financial return (Miller 1994: 1817).

Environmental advocates, although "pleased that EPA plans to regulate such crops the way it regulates traditional chemical pesticides," were also dissatisfied; they noted that the EPA rules focused "too narrowly on the development of genetically engineered, toxin-producing crops," and were insufficiently attentive to the potential hazards of herbicide-resistant crops that were virtually certain to bring about increases in the use of potentially damaging herbicides (Environmental Defense Fund 1994: 1). The marketing by the Monsanto Company of soybeans genetically engineered to be resistant to Roundup, a widely used herbicide also produced by that company, has only heightened such concerns (Feder 1996; Fritsch and Kilman 1996).

Environmentalist doubts about the adequacy of EPA regulatory policies were further stimulated by two events in 1996. That year, farmers planted 2 million acres with cotton engineered by the Monsanto Company to contain Bt *(Bacillus thuringiensis)*, a soil bacterium that produces a compound toxic to cotton bollworms and other common insect pests. Bt has long been a key component of pest management in sustainable agricultural systems. When the Bt crop failed to protect thousands of acres of cotton against bollworms, observers feared that so large a planting had induced selection for insects resistant to Bt, thereby rendering the toxin useless for sustainable or any other type of agriculture (Kaiser 1996). EPA officials were reported to have asked Monsanto to test the surviving bollworms for Bt resistance, but to have admitted ". . . that further evaluation of the crop is entirely dependent on Monsanto's own reporting" (Benson, Arax, and Burstein 1997: 68).

Also in 1996, researchers reported that oilseed rape (canola) plants genetically engineered to resist herbicides readily transmitted herbicide resistance to related weed plants – plants that could reproduce rapidly (Mikkelsen, Anderson, and Jorgensen 1996). This report led critics to charge that transgenic crops could lead to the creation of "superweeds" and, therefore, to "ecological catastrophe." Despite this charge, federal officials continued to argue that monitoring of herbicide resistance should not be their responsibility: ". . . it is the developer of the product that has the interest in assuring that resistance does not build up"

(Kling 1996: 181). Well before the time this statement was published, however, Congress had removed the USDA from involvement in biotechnology policy by eliminating funding for its advisory committee on biotechnology research and its Office of Agricultural Biotechnology (Fox 1996).

Intellectual Property Rights

United States intellectual property laws grant rights to patent owners to exclude everyone else from making, using, or selling the protected product for at least 17 years. Patents were first granted to plant varieties developed through asexual propagation in 1930. In 1970, Congress extended these rights to new varieties of plants developed through traditional genetic methods of sexual propagation. In 1980, the Supreme Court granted patent rights to microorganisms developed through rDNA techniques, and the Patent Office issued the first patent for such an organism. Patent rights were further extended to genetically engineered plants in 1985 and to animals in 1988 (U.S. Congress 1989, 1991a).

The patenting of biotechnological microorganisms and plants provided a major incentive for the growth of the food biotechnology industry, and patent rights are believed to have greatly stimulated such growth during the 1980s. Within just a few years, however, patent awards were challenged by industry and government officials in the United States, Canada, and Europe. By 1995, the U.S. Patent Office had issued 112 patents for genetically engineered plants. Among these were exclusive patent rights to one company for all forms of bioengineered cotton and to another for all uses of the "antisense" genes that were used to create the Calgene tomato (see later section on the "Flavr Savr" tomato). The breadth of such patents ". . . stunned the agricultural biotechnology community . . . It was as if the inventor of the assembly line had won property rights to all mass-produced goods . . . ," and numerous lawsuits were soon filed (Stone 1995: 656).

The patenting of animals has generated even greater debate, particularly from animal-rights organizations and other groups concerned that the genetic engineering of farm animals might adversely affect family farmers, be cruel to animals, and endanger other living species (U.S. Congress 1989). The principal arguments for and against the patenting of transgenic animals are summarized in Table VII.7.4 (U.S. Congress 1991a).

Perhaps in response to concerns about such issues, the Patent Office ceased issuing patents for transgenic animals in 1988. In 1993, it resumed processing of the 180 animal patent applications that had accumulated during this "self-imposed moratorium" (Andrews 1993). By that time, far fewer companies were attempting to patent farm animals, largely because persistent technical problems and concerns about costs had encouraged them to shift to more

Table VII.7.4. *The principal arguments for and against the patenting of transgenic animals*

Arguments for patenting transgenic animals
Patent laws regulate inventiveness, not commercial uses.
Patenting is an incentive to research and development.
Patenting enables the biotechnology industry to compete in international markets.
Patenting is preferable to trade secrets.
Patenting rewards innovation and entrepreneurship.

Arguments against patenting transgenic animals
Metaphysical and theological considerations make patenting untenable.
Patenting involves inappropriate treatment of animals.
Patenting reflects inappropriate human control over animal life.
Patenting disturbs the sanctity and dignity of life.
Most other countries do not permit patenting of animals.
Patenting could cause adverse economic effects on developing countries.
Patenting promotes environmentally unsound policies.
Animal patents will increase costs to consumers and producers.
Animal patents will result in further concentration in agricultural production.
Patent holders will derive unfair benefits from royalties on succeeding generations of patented animals.

Sources: U.S. Congress (1989) and Fox (1992).

profitable areas of research. But lobbyists against animal patents, such as Jeremy Rifkin, a leading antibiotechnology advocate, continued to protest Patent Office policies on both philosophical and economic grounds:

> We believe the gene pool should be maintained as an open commons, and should not be the private preserve of multinational companies . . . this is the Government giving its imprimatur to the idea that there is no difference between a living thing and any inert object . . . it's the final assault on the sacred meaning of life and life process. (Andrews 1993)

International Trade
Soybeans are used in more than 60 percent of all the processed foods sold in European markets (Wolf 1997). Transgenic, herbicide-resistant soybeans constituted 2 percent of the 59 million tons grown in the United States in 1996, their first year of production (Ibrahim 1996). Corn exports to Europe were valued at $500 million in 1995 (Wadman 1996). Transgenic Bt corn, also herbicide-resistant, was expected to account for half of the nearly $25 billion in annual sales in the United States within just a few years (Wolf 1997). Clearly, any action interfering with acceptance of transgenic crops would have grave economic consequences.

But European consumers were highly resistant to the idea of transgenic foods. This resistance has been attributed in part to memories of Nazi eugenics during World War II (Dickman 1996), in part to concerns that the antibiotic-resistance marker gene used in constructing the corn might spread to animals and to people, and in part to fears generated by the 1996 food-safety crisis over "mad cow" disease in England. The transmission of antibiotic-resistant bacteria from animals and milk to people had been demonstrated some years earlier (Holmberg et al. 1984; Tacket et al. 1985) but did not involve plants. The transmission of "mad cow" disease, although poorly understood, also did not appear to involve plants (Smith and Cousens 1996). European consumers, however, also were reacting to broader issues related to what they viewed as the arrogance of American officials who were claiming the superiority of their food safety criteria and were attempting to control trading policies through sanctions against European countries conducting business with Iran, Libya, or Cuba.

The transgenic soybeans and corn were approved as safe by the governments of the United States, Canada, and Japan. The European Union (EU) approved the import and processing of transgenic soybeans in April 1996. It referred the approval of the transgenic corn to scientific committees in June, thus raising the possibility that Europe might refuse corn from the United States and thereby cause a "corn war" (Wadman 1996). In October, Jeremy Rifkin announced the initiation of a worldwide boycott of genetically engineered crops produced in the United States. Rifkin was joined in this effort by an official of EuroCommerce, a trade association representing a large number of retail and commerce groups in 20 European countries, who called for separation and labeling of products using these grains so that European consumers could decide whether to buy them (Jones 1996). As the official later explained:

> Our message from our customers is that for whatever reason they would prefer not to have it in their foodstuffs . . . I am telling the American exporters to please, in this season, if you are wise, don't ship those soybeans to Europe because you may trigger a lasting reaction. And, if you must, separate and label them. (Ibrahim 1996: D1)

Surveys reported that 85 to 90 percent of European consumers wanted genetically engineered foods to be labeled as such (Ibrahim 1996: D24). Labeling, however, would require strict separation of genetically engineered from the usual varieties of corn or soybeans. Producers considered such separation impractical. If consumers refused to buy transgenic corn, or the European Union banned its import, U.S. producers would lose more than half a billion dollars in corn sales alone. This situation generated "tremendous interest" in a small company in Iowa that was marketing a test that could identify soybeans, corn, and other plants that had been genetically engineered (Wadman 1996). In December, the EU approved the genetically modified corn, leading the biotechnology industry to be "... optimistic that Europeans will come around to the benefits of genetically engineered crops" (Wolf 1997: 8).The EU ruling required labeling of genetically modified foods, however: "We must not miss this opportunity to repeat our clear signal that better labeling is one of the ways forward in this area" ("EU Approves" 1997: 1).

In Canada, a proposal to establish a central biotechnology regulatory agency met with opposition from farm, consumer, and industry groups, all of which viewed the current system of joint regulation by the departments of health and agriculture as satisfactory. Industry groups were especially concerned that government policies provide explicit regulations for the development and introduction of new plant varieties. Consumer proposals for labeling were opposed by the Canadian Federation of Agriculture:

> Canada must be in step with our major partners to ensure that Canada's labeling policy does not conflict ... and thereby reduce the competitiveness of Canadian producers ... The development of labeling regulations must recognize that the imposition of a labeling regime that is not based on science would have a negative trade implication for Canada. (Elliott 1996: 3)

Public Perceptions

Because food is overproduced in the United States and the West generally, and because the food industry is so competitive, biotechnology industry leaders view consumer acceptance of their products as an issue of critical importance: "Both the industrial and scientific communities have lagged in their understanding of the importance of the public's attitude toward biotechnology ... It is the consumer – the poorly informed and uninitiated average individual – who holds the key to our future" (Walter 1995: 216).

Consumer surveys do indeed document a fundamental public misunderstanding of basic food safety issues. Many surveys have reported a large proportion of respondents to be deeply concerned about the hazards of pesticides or irradiation, whether or not they believe these hazards to be more important (Food Marketing Institute 1994) or less important (Lynch and Lin 1994) than the far greater dangers of microbial contamination.

Because of the importance of consumer attitudes to the future of the industry and to federal regulatory efforts, various agencies in the United States and Canada have conducted surveys designed specifically to reveal consumer perceptions of food biotechnology.The methods used to obtain this information have varied among the surveys, and their results are not strictly comparable. Nevertheless, the results of such surveys have proven remarkably consistent over time, and they reveal an internally consistent logic of considerable predictive value.

At least three surveys have examined public attitudes toward agricultural biotechnology in the United States. In 1986, the Office of Technology Assessment commissioned the Harris organization to conduct focus groups and to administer a telephone survey of a national probability sample of 1,273 adults on perceptions of science, genetic engineering, and biotechnology (U.S. Congress 1987). In 1992, the USDA commissioned a telephone study of the attitudes of 1,228 consumers, along with a series of focus groups (Hoban and Kendall 1993; Zimmerman et al. 1994). In addition, Rutgers University researchers conducted a telephone survey of 604 New Jersey residents in May of 1993 (Hallman and Metcalfe 1993).

The results of these surveys are summarized in Table VII.7.5. Despite differences in method, population, and year, they yielded virtually identical responses that provide a consistent picture of public attitudes toward food biotechnology. Although respondents to all three surveys displayed a limited understanding of science and technology, they expressed high levels of interest in those fields, as well as high expectations that food biotechnology would produce benefits for them and for society as a whole. The respondents were concerned about the potential and unknown dangers of genetically engineered foods, but they believed that the benefits of biotechnology outweighed any risks, and they strongly supported continued federal funding of food biotechnology research.

It is especially noteworthy that the survey participants preferred some genetically engineered food products to others. They were most likely to accept products that appeared to be beneficial to health or society, to save money or time, to be safe, or to improve the environment.

Safety considerations, although often the focus of biotechnology debates (Hopkins et al. 1991), did not emerge in these surveys as the most important public concern. Instead, survey respondents appeared most troubled by ethical issues related to food biotechnology. Thus, they were more willing to accept genetically engineered foods that involved plants rather than animals, that did not harm animals, and that did not involve the transfer of animal genes into plants. These views derived from value systems that encompassed issues extending far beyond food safety (see Table VII.7.4), and the importance of such value systems to consumer perceptions of biotechnology cannot be overestimated:

> Whatever the actual saliency of these ethical charges and critiques, obviously fundamental social, cultural, and religious values are at stake, arising out of broad cultural traditions and interests. Animal biotechnology, coupled to the engines of corporate economics, is felt to threaten fundamental and traditional moral, religious, and cultural orientations (Donnelley, McCarthy, and Singleton 1994: S21).

Table VII.7.5. *Public perceptions of food biotechnology*

Respondents express	U.S. Congress (1987)	Hoban and Kendall (1993)	Hallman and Metcalfe (1993)
Great interest in food biotechnology	✓	✓	✓
Limited understanding of science and techniques	✓	✓	✓
Expectations that food biotechnology will benefit them and society	✓	✓	✓
Concerns about unknown risks	✓	✓	✓
Expectations that benefits will outweigh risks	✓	✓	✓
Belief that government should continue to fund food-biotechnology research	✓	✓	✓
Greater willingness to accept products that			
Directly benefit health, consumers, or society	✓	✓	✓
Save money or time	–	✓	✓
Are safe	✓	✓	✓
Help improve the environment	✓	✓	✓
Involve plants rather than animals	✓	✓	✓
Do not harm animals	✓	–	✓
Do not involve transfer of animal genes into plants	–	✓	–
Distrust of government credibility related to science and technology	✓	✓	✓
Distrust of government regulatory ability	✓	✓	✓
Distrust of the biotechnology industry	✓	✓	✓
Belief that food biotechnology should be regulated	✓	✓	✓
Belief that biotechnology-derived food products should be labeled	✓	✓	✓

All three surveys confirmed substantial public distrust of government credibility in scientific and technical safety matters and in the ability of government to regulate food biotechnology appropriately. Respondents were equally skeptical of the ability of the biotechnology industry to make decisions in the public interest. For these reasons, all three surveys indicated that the large majority of respondents wanted genetically engineered food products to be labeled as such. A 1993 survey conducted in Canada reported similar results (Walter 1995).

Industry leaders have tended to interpret such results – scientific misunderstanding, fear of unknown dangers, concern about animal welfare, distaste for transgenic experiments, and demand for regulation and food labeling – as evidence for public irrationality (Gaull and Goldberg 1991; Walter 1995). They and others further interpret these survey results as strongly supporting the need for comprehensive education campaigns to inform consumers about the safety and benefits of biotechnology (Bruhn 1992; Hoban and Kendall 1993; Walter 1995).

Such interpretations miss the most strikingly useful conclusion to be drawn from these surveys: Consumer acceptance of food biotechnology is entirely product-specific. The survey results clearly demonstrate that the public will readily accept genetically engineered products that are perceived as filling important needs: "People appear to be far more focused on the characteristics of products than the process used to create those products. People may be willing to overlook their objections to genetic engi-

neering if its products produce specific benefits" (Hallman and Metcalfe 1993: 3).

The results of the Canadian survey further support this conclusion:

The Canadian public tends to consider biotechnology products individually, based mainly on their potential benefits. For example, the general concept of transferring genetic material from one plant to another was accepted by 51% of the respondents. This support jumped to 70% if the transfer improved plant nutritional value, though it slid to only 36% if the transfer only improved plant color ... Products with laudable goals were strongly supported, while those with dubious benefit were rejected. (Walter 1995: 216)

Such results demonstrate that the key issue in consumer acceptance of genetically engineered foods is the value of the specific product to public health and welfare. The implication of these results is equally clear: If the food biotechnology industry wants consumers to accept its products without protest, it must market products worthwhile to the public as well as to the industry.

Predictive Implications: U.S. Case Studies

The survey results also suggest an analytical framework for predicting the degree of difficulty with which a given genetically engineered food is likely to achieve public acceptance in the United States. This

Table VII.7.6. *Analytical framework for predicting public acceptance of a food product of biotechnology*

1. Is the food valuable? Will it
   Increase nutrient content?
   Increase food availability?
   Decrease food cost?
   Improve food taste?
   Grow better under difficult conditions?
   Reduce use of herbicides and pesticides?
2. Is the food safe for people and for the environment?
3. Is the food ethical? Does it avoid
   Harm to animals?
   Insertion of animal genes into plants?

analysis presumes that consumer acceptance is predicated on the importance of a product, its safety, and its ethical value. To predict whether a product will be acceptable, one need only ask the questions listed in Table VII.7.6. If the answers to all three questions are affirmative, the product is highly likely to be accepted by the great majority of consumers. To the extent that the answers are negative or equivocal, consumer resistance is likely to increase. Consumer responses to the genetically engineered products that have been approved for marketing in the United States constitute case studies that illustrate the predictive value of such questions.

Pharmaceuticals

By the early 1990s, the FDA had approved at least 15 recombinant drugs for use in human subjects. Recombinant insulin, for example, was the first to receive approval, in 1982. This drug is of unquestioned utility (U.S. Congress 1991a). It solves problems of scarcity and quality, as it can be produced in unlimited quantities. Its amino acid structure is identical to that of human insulin, and it is, therefore, superior to insulin obtained from the pancreas of pigs or cows. It is safe and raises no ethical issues. Recombinant insulin readily meets all three criteria for consumer acceptance, and it is neither surprising nor inconsistent that activists against biotechnology in the United States have never protested its use.

Chymosin

Recombinant enzymes used in food manufacture also have been accepted readily. Chymosin, an enzyme used to coagulate milk to make cheese, was traditionally extracted from the stomachs of calves and sold as part of a mixture called rennet. The enzyme was difficult to extract, varied in quality, and was scarce and expensive. Through rDNA techniques, the gene for chymosin was transferred to bacteria that can be grown in large quantities. Chymosin derived from this process was approved for food use in 1990 (U.S. Congress 1991a). This action elicited no noticeable complaints from biotechnology critics, not only because the manufacturer saw "little to gain from waving the

biotech flag," but also "because the alternative is slaughtering baby calves" (Kilman 1994b: R7). This product also meets the three criteria for consumer acceptance: It is more useful, more ethical, and just as safe as the product it replaced.

The "Flavr Savr" Tomato

Americans have come to expect tomatoes to be available on a year-round basis. The market for fresh tomatoes was estimated at between $3 and $5 billion annually in the early 1990s (Fisher 1994; Hilts 1994). In 1993, American farmers produced nearly 16 pounds of fresh tomatoes per capita and another 77 pounds per capita for processing (Putnam and Allshouse 1994). But supermarket tomatoes, bred for disease resistance, appearance, and durability, have long been the bane of consumers longing for "backyard" taste and freshness (Mather 1995).

Beginning in the mid-1980s, Calgene, a California-based biotechnology company, invested $25 million and eight years of effort to develop a tomato with a reversed (and, therefore, blocked) gene for ripening. This process was designed to permit it to be picked and marketed at a more mature stage of ripeness and taste (U.S. Congress 1991a). Calgene expected this "Flavr Savr" tomato to capture at least 15 percent of the market for fresh tomatoes as soon as it became available (Kim 1992b). The company planned to market – and label – the tomato as genetically engineered to taste better.

As the first company to develop such a food, Calgene voluntarily sought FDA guidance on the tomato's regulatory status in 1989, long before it was ready to market. In 1990, Calgene requested an FDA advisory opinion as to whether the gene for resistance to the antibiotic kanamycin, used as part of the genetic engineering process, could be used as a marker in producing tomatoes and other crops. The following year, Calgene requested a more formal FDA "consultation" on whether the Flavr Savr would be subject to the same regulations as conventional tomatoes, and, in 1992, the company published a comprehensive report on the tomato's safety and nutrient content (Redenbaugh et al. 1992).

The following year, Calgene filed a petition with the FDA to approve the kanamycin-resistant gene as a food additive. The FDA reviewed this request under its 1992 policy and also requested an opinion from its Food Advisory Committee (FDA 1994a; Hilts 1994). In its review, and during the committee hearings, the FDA insisted that the discussion focus exclusively on safety questions. Consumer and other representatives on the committee said they were ". . . frustrated by a debate that, to them, ignores other key issues that affect consumers' preferences for foods, such as religious, ethical, or aesthetic criteria . . . They also say that such foods should carry labels" (Fox 1994: 439).

The FDA decision, in 1994, that "all relevant safety questions about the new tomato had been resolved"

(FDA 1994a) was greeted as "terrific news for the industry," and the price of Calgene stock increased slightly (Fisher 1994: B7). Consumer groups, however, charged that the FDA review of the tomato had been an anomaly because the approval system had been entirely voluntary. Certain antibiotechnology advocacy groups threatened picket lines, "tomato dumpings," boycotts, and legal challenges (Leary 1994). Most analysts, however, believed that consumers would accept the tomato if they perceived its improved taste to be worth what it would cost (O'Neill 1994). Although the price was originally expected to be twice that of conventional varieties (Sugawara 1992), the cost of the tomato was reduced in test markets to compete with locally grown products (Biotech 1994). By the summer of 1996, however, supplies of the tomato were still too limited to determine its level of acceptance.

From the answers to the questions in Table VII.7.6, some consumer resistance should be expected. Although the Flavr Savr is demonstrably safe, it raises issues related to its impact on small tomato growers. Its benefit to the public is restricted to taste. Perhaps most important, its higher costs identify the Flavr Savr as a luxury product targeted to an upscale market.

To Calgene, however, the tomato was well worth the huge investment of time, money, and effort; indeed, it was said that part of the effort involved providing members of Congress with bacon, lettuce, and Flavr Savr sandwiches (Stix 1995). FDA approval of the tomato paved the way for subsequent approval of the company's seed oils, herbicide-resistant cotton, and other genetically engineered crops, raising hopes that Calgene would at last obtain a return on its investment. The company was reported to have lost more than $80 million since its formation in the early 1980s (McMurray 1993), and it continued to report losses during 1994. In June 1995, Monsanto, the manufacturer of recombinant bovine somatotropin (see next section), purchased 49.9 percent of Calgene, thus becoming the leading supplier of fresh tomatoes in the nation (Fisher 1995).

Bovine Somatotropin

The story of recombinant bovine somatotropin (rbST), the first food product to be approved by the FDA under its 1992 policy, best illustrates how issues of societal benefit, safety, and ethics contribute to consumer resistance to biotechnology. The product, a growth hormone that increases milk production in cows by at least 10 to 20 percent (Pell et al. 1992), has elicited an extraordinary level of debate. Its very name is controversial: Most proponents use its scientific name, rbST, whereas critics tend to use its more readily understandable common name, Beef (or Bovine) Growth Hormone, abbreviated rBGH (Daughaday and Barbano 1990). For purposes of consistency, this chapter employs the term rbST.

The Monsanto Company developed rbST in the mid-1980s and promoted it as a means to make dairy farming more efficient. Although such efficiency would seem to be of great benefit to consumers, critics soon raised questions about the product's effects on human health, animal welfare, and the economic viability of small dairy farms (U.S. Congress 1992). They also raised issues related to consumers' freedom of choice in the marketplace: When the FDA ruled that milk from cows treated with rbST cannot be so labeled.

For the industry and its supporters, concerns about factors other than safety were seen as irrelevant and highly threatening to the future of agricultural biotechnology; if rbST failed in the marketplace, the entire industry would be in jeopardy (Schneider 1990). Accordingly, this hormone and an equivalent product for pigs were extolled as:

> Biotechnological miracles that would give consumers more for their money at less cost to the environment. Yet these and other long-tested products . . . are likely to be mired in continuing controversies instigated more by ignorance, nostalgia and a Luddite view of technology than by understanding and actual fact . . . whether such improvements will ever reach the marketplace will depend largely on how well consumers accept BST (Brody 1993: C17).

Yet rbST was controversial almost from its inception. By 1989, during periods of testing on commercial farms and research centers in nearly every major dairy state (Schneider 1989, 1990), rbST had become the target of groups concerned about family farms as well as of those suspicious of genetic engineering (Sun 1989). As a result, supermarket chains announced that they would not carry milk from rbST-treated cows, and dairy companies such as Ben and Jerry's stated that their products would carry label statements that opposed the use of rbST (Schneider 1989). The state legislatures of Wisconsin and Minnesota temporarily banned the sale of rbST, an action considered extraordinary in the case of a product not yet approved for commercial use (Schneider 1990). By 1992, four major supermarket chains, two large manufacturers of dairy products, and the nation's largest dairy cooperative had joined the boycott (Miller 1992), as had many small farmers, dairy cooperatives, and groceries (Day 1994). Such a level of protest might easily have been anticipated, as rbST raised many of the issues suggested by the questions in Table VII.7.6.

Safety issues. Bovine somatotropin stimulates milk production, and the natural hormone is always present in cow's milk in low concentrations. Milk from rbST-treated cows contains both the natural hormone and rbST; these are almost identical and cannot easily be distinguished, complicating efforts to require labeling. The hormone is unlikely to be harmful to humans, even though its concentration is higher in milk from treated cows. Its protein structure differs from that of the human hormone and it is biologically inactive in humans. Moreover, like all proteins, the cow hormone is largely broken down in the human intestinal tract. The hormone had been tested on 21,000 cows, and described in more than 900 research papers by 1992, with no indication of untoward effects on human health (Miller 1992).

Despite this evidence, critics continued to raise doubts about safety because of concerns about two factors that might be present in rbST milk: insulin-like growth factor-I (IGF-I) and antibiotics (Blayney 1994). Treatment with rbST increases concentrations of IGF-I in cows' milk, raising concerns that this factor might stimulate premature growth in infants and cancers in adults. Proponents of rbST argue that the factor appears to be relatively inactive in rats, is denatured in infant formulas, and seems unlikely to be absorbed by the human digestive tract in sufficient amounts to be harmful (Juskevich and Guyer 1990). A federal study has confirmed that IGF-I concentrations are indeed higher in rbST-treated cows but concluded that more research would be needed to determine whether the higher levels posed any risk (U.S. General Accounting Office 1992b).

The second concern arose because cows treated with rbST develop udder infections (mastitis) more frequently than untreated cows. Such infections are treated with antibiotics that can appear in milk and meat and, theoretically, contribute to human antibiotic resistance. Although federal regulations require testing for antibiotic residues in milk, the FDA tests for only a small fraction of animal drugs in common use – just 4 out of 82 in one study – leading to charges that the agency lacks a comprehensive strategy for monitoring animal drugs (U.S. General Accounting Office 1992a). These concerns led yet another federal committee to recommend discontinuation of rbST marketing until antibiotic risks could be evaluated; at the same time, the committee called for development of a feasibility study of rbST labeling to provide information to the public (U.S. General Accounting Office 1992b). As discussed here, these recommendations were not implemented.

In 1990, Monsanto-sponsored scientists reported in a leading medical journal that rbST milk was safe for human consumption and that FDA studies had answered all safety questions (Daughaday and Barbano 1990). That same year, FDA scientists reviewed more than 130 studies of the effects of rbST on cows, rats, and humans and concurred in the conclusion that the hormone did not affect human health (Juskevich and Guyer 1990). The publication of this last report in a prestigious scientific journal was judged "unprecedented," as it gave the appearance of a conflict of interest: The FDA seemed to be acting as a proponent of a drug that it had not yet approved (Gibbons 1990). Critics viewed the report as "part of a

campaign by the four companies developing the drug and portions of the dairy industry to calm the public's concern. . . . The review could not have been conducted without the permission of the manufacturers to disclose their own confidential studies on the safety of the drug" (Schneider 1990: A18). Nevertheless, a panel of experts recruited by the National Institutes of Health (NIH) also concluded that milk from rbST-treated cows was essentially the same – and as safe – as milk from untreated cows (Office of Medical Applications 1991).

Animal welfare. Because treatment of cows with rbST increases milk production, concerns have also been expressed about the effect of the drug on the health and reproductive ability of the animals. In addition to increasing cases of mastitis, injections of rbST have been reported to produce localized reactions at the injection sites in some cows (Pell et al. 1992; U.S. General Accounting Office 1992b). Despite FDA and industry assertions that appropriate herd-management practices can minimize such problems, they are nonetheless regularly reported. Between March 1994 and February 1995, for example, more than 800 farmers filed complaints with the FDA about animal health problems related to the use of rbST. Yet, according to the FDA, such reports "raise no new animal health concerns" ("Over 800 Farmers" 1995: 6).

Dairy farming. In the opinion of many, arguments about the safety of rbST have tended to obscure "the real issue – the economic impact of BGH once it hits the market" (Sun 1989: 877). For years, dairy production has exceeded demand, resulting in large surpluses of milk, butter, and other dairy products; such surpluses are purchased by the government to maintain prices (Schneider 1989). Common use of rbST will almost certainly increase milk production, but the effects of this increase on prices to farmers and costs to consumers and the government are difficult to predict. One estimate has suggested that the use of rbST will lead to a 2 percent decrease in prices paid to farmers and, therefore, to a 1 percent decline in farm income by 1999 (U.S. Congress 1991b). Any decline in milk consumption, coupled with increasing supplies, might be expected to accelerate trends toward the elimination of small dairy farms (Schneider 1994b). Federal spending on dairy price supports might also increase, although such an increase could be offset by the lower costs of federal commodity distribution programs (Blayney 1994).

Whether rbST milk will cost less is uncertain. The industry contends that the use of the hormone will reduce farm production costs because equivalent amounts of milk can be produced by fewer cows. Although it might seem logical that creation of milk surpluses would lead to lower prices, any price decline stimulates higher levels of federal spending to protect farm incomes (Kilman 1994b). Most commentators – but not all (U.S. Congress 1991b) – believe that at least some dairy farmers will be forced out of business.

Regulation. In 1985, the FDA permitted Monsanto to use the drug on an experimental basis (Schneider 1989). The agency reaffirmed the safety of rbST milk and meat in 1988, 1989, and again in 1990 (Miller 1992), as did the NIH in 1990 (Office of Medical Applications 1991) and the Office of Technology Assessment in 1991 (U.S. Congress 1991b). FDA approval of rbST as a new animal drug product appeared imminent (Miller 1992), but in August 1993, Congress enacted a 90-day moratorium on rbST sales. In fact, the Senate, concerned about the fate of small dairy farms, had approved a moratorium lasting an entire year, but House opposition forced this compromise ("BGH Moratorium" 1993).

After lengthy deliberations, advisory committee consultations, and public hearings, the FDA approved Monsanto's rbST as a new animal drug in November 1993. In announcing the decision, the FDA commissioner stated: "There is virtually no difference in milk from treated and untreated cows . . . in fact, it's not possible using current scientific techniques to tell them apart . . . we are confident this product is safe for consumers, for cows and for the environment" (Schneider 1993: 1).

FDA approval applied only to the Monsanto product, although approval of products from other companies was expected to follow ("FDA Approves" 1993). Industry representatives hailed the FDA decision as a strong signal that the administration intended to reduce regulatory barriers, as a victory for Monsanto, and as a "banner day for agricultural biotechnology" (Schneider 1993: 9). The actual effect of the ruling, however, would not be seen until the moratorium on sales ended. In the meantime, Monsanto was reported to be giving the product to farmers at no cost ("FDA Approves" 1993).

Because dairy companies, concerned about consumer reactions to rbST, had been labeling their products as "BGH-free," industry groups requested FDA guidance on the labeling of dairy products derived from untreated cows. In February 1994, the FDA stated that it did not have the authority to require special labeling and ruled that companies might voluntarily inform customers that they were not using rbST, provided "that any statements made [we]re truthful and not misleading." Because all milk contains some bST, milk could not be labeled as "BGH-free." Because bST and rbST are indistinguishable, milk also could not be labeled as "rBGH-free." However, these designations could be used if accompanied by a statement that put them in proper context: "[N]o significant difference has been shown between milk derived from rbST-treated and non-rbST-treated cows" (1994b: 6280).

Nevertheless, the state of Vermont passed legislation requiring the labeling of milk from rbST-treated cows, in conflict with FDA rulings: "Vermonters have the right to know what is in the food they eat . . . In particular, there is a strong public interest in knowing whether or not rbST has been used in the production of milk and milk products" (Schneider 1994d: A16). By 1996, however, industry groups had successfully challenged this law in the courts ("Court Strikes Down" 1996).

Moreover, two major milk marketers launched new brands certified as coming from untreated cows. In response, Monsanto warned dairy companies that such labels were misleading and "might create the impression that something is wrong with milk from treated cows" (Kilman 1994a: B7). By May 1994, Monsanto had sued at least two dairy companies to force them to comply with the FDA ruling. Because the dairies lacked resources as extensive as Monsanto's, they seemed certain to lose the suits. As one report stated, "Everyone is terrified of Monsanto . . . it is quite ominous" (Burros 1994: C4).

International implications. The European Community (EC) has long been skeptical about the use of growth hormones in cattle. This is the result of 1980 incidents in which consumption of baby foods containing veal from cows treated with diethylstilbestrol was associated with cases of premature sexual development in infants. Despite such skepticism, in 1987 Monsanto Europe requested approval of rbST from the EC's Committee for Veterinary Medicinal Products (Vandaele 1992). The following year, however, the EC banned nontherapeutic use of hormones in the domestic livestock industry and soon extended the ban to countries that exported meat to the EC.

This action raised trade issues related to the use of rbST (Krissoff 1989). In 1991, the Veterinary Products Committee decided that rbST met requirements for quality, efficacy, and safety and posed no risk to consumers or cows. But this decision was overruled by the EC Directorates General, an action seen as a "blow to agricultural biotechnology" (Vandaele 1992: 148). Indeed, the EC executive committee proposed a seven-year ban on rbST use because it feared that the hormone might undermine efforts to reduce farm surpluses.

Thus, rbST became caught in a "policy paradox"; it would be manufactured by Monsanto in Europe, where it could not be sold, and then exported to the United States, where its use was permitted (Aldhous 1993). In 1995, the United States successfully persuaded the EC to declare that all Codex Alimentarius international standards for food additives, including animal drugs, should be based on science (i.e., biological safety). This was clearly an effort to force the EC to permit the use of rbST-derived milk and meat. But a straightforward motion by the United States for EC approval of rbST as posing no health risk fared less well; it was postponed until the Codex meeting scheduled for 1997 (Leonard 1995).

Industry actions. As early as 1987, rbST was expected to become agricultural biotechnology's first billion-dollar product (Sun 1989). In 1989, the market for rbST was estimated at $100 to $500 million annually (Schneider 1989); more recent estimates have been somewhat higher (Millstone, Brunner, and White 1994; Schneider 1994a). The potential for such a large return on investment helps to explain Monsanto's unusually aggressive sales tactics (Feder 1995) and heavy-handed political actions to protect and promote this and its other products (Benson et al. 1997). Certainly the company took full advantage of its connections in government. FDA employees with ties to Monsanto played key roles in the agency's review of rbST (Schneider 1994e; U.S. General Accounting Office 1994), and Monsanto enlisted an influential former congressman, to whom the secretary of agriculture owed his appointment, to encourage the USDA to prevent Congress from studying the economic effects of rbST (Engelberg 1994).

Monsanto leveled charges of plagiarism against independent researchers who had used company data to analyze counts of white blood cells ("pus," according to critics) in rbST-treated milk, thereby preventing publication of their report (Millstone et al. 1994). The company used legal and political strategies to resist demands for labeling and recruited dairy industry executives to help persuade the FDA to establish favorable labeling guidelines. In addition, Monsanto was reported to have recruited at least two Washington law firms to monitor dairies for advertising and labeling violations and to instigate legal action against milk processors who had "inappropriately" misled customers (Schneider 1994c).

To some extent, these efforts succeeded. By March 1995, Monsanto claimed to have sold 14.5 million doses of rbST during the previous year and stated that 13,000 dairy farmers, or 11 percent of the potential market, were customers (Feder 1995). Sales were said to be especially strong in the state of New York, with 10 percent of dairy farmers reported to be using rbST. But in Wisconsin, where milk is the foundation of a $10 billion dairy industry, only 5 percent of the state's 29,000 dairy farmers were said to be using the hormone (Schneider 1994c), and 90 percent were reported as hoping that the drug would never be widely adopted. Overall sales for the first year were estimated at $70 million, far short of what had been anticipated (Feder 1995).

Consumer responses. The degree of consumer acceptance of rbST was also uncertain in 1995. A telephone survey of 1,004 adults suggested that use of rbST would have no impact on milk consumption, as most respondents had never heard of the drug. However, the phrasing of the survey questions, which used the term somatotropin rather than "growth hormone," and emphasized safety rather than issues of ethics and values, may have led respondents to more favorable answers. For example, respondents answered positively (scoring 6.18 on a scale where 10 is strongly positive) to this question:

> The National Institutes of Health, the American Medical Association, and several other independent medical groups have found milk from cows that receive BST is unchanged, safe, and nutritionally the same as milk currently on grocery store shelves. Given this information, how acceptable do you find the use of BST. . . ? (Hoban 1994: 8)

The lack of labeling of rbST dairy products complicates understanding of consumer acceptance. Despite FDA rulings, surveys demonstrate overwhelming consumer support for special labeling of rbST products (Blayney 1994). Supporters of rbST have argued that the marketplace should be allowed to decide the commercial fate of the hormone (Sun 1989), but without labeling, consumers cannot easily make their opinions known.

Implications. Public skepticism about rbST relates to nearly all of the areas of concern listed in Table VII.7.6. Given the strength of these concerns, this product seems an unfortunate first choice for commercialization. United States farmers already overproduce milk, and rbST offers no clear benefit to consumers in availability, price, or quality. It will not even create more manufacturing jobs, as most rbST will be made and packaged in Europe (Hansen and Halloran 1994). That the product affects milk itself is also unfortunate: "Is there any product in the world that has tried harder to sell itself as wholesome and pure than milk? . . . It is a food for innocent, trusting children, culturally laden with symbolism. Any adulteration of milk . . . is seen as taboo" (Kolata 1994: E13).

The primary gainers from rbST, therefore, appear to be its manufacturers and the large dairy farmers who can best exploit its use. As summarized by the head of a dairy company that refuses to use rbST:

> We do know that the use of BGH will increase the supply of milk at a time when we already have a tremendous surplus. It does not make any sense to exacerbate this problem with a product about which there are so many legitimate doubts, a product whose principal beneficiaries will be chemical companies and corporate agribusiness. (Cohen 1993: 1)

Policy Implications

This history indicates that the controversy over food biotechnology derives from the conflict between the industry's need to be profitable and the desire of consumers for products that are economically and socially valuable, as well as safe. Therefore, to frame the debate about food biotechnology in terms of rational science versus an irrational public is to do a disservice to both.

Biotechnology is not inherently dangerous, and it is capable of doing much good. The public is not inherently irrational and is quite capable of judging whether genetically engineered products are worth buying. Few consumers demand that biotechnology "pack up its test tubes"; they support industry efforts to impart to food plants desirable qualities such as resistance to diseases and pests to food plants. At the moment, however, many view the great promise of biotechnology as having been betrayed (Hamilton 1990: 43).

Thus, the open contempt of policymakers and industry leaders for public misunderstanding of science and technology misses an important point. As this analysis has indicated, public views of biotechnology in the United States are product-specific and, as such, are logical, consistent, and predictable. Analysts of biotechnology policy who are aware of this logic recommend that regulators and the public decide the risks and benefits of each new product on a case-by-case basis (Davis 1991). They agree with industry that the marketplace should be allowed to determine the success of these products. They suggest that the products be labeled so that the public can make informed decisions in that marketplace and believe that if industry is producing valuable products, the label will encourage the public to purchase them.

Although it is always useful to educate the public about the benefits of science and technology, education alone will not solve problems of consumer acceptance. The analysis presented here suggests that it will continue to be difficult to convince the public that genetically engineered food products are necessary or safe as long as the principal beneficiary of food biotechnology is the industry itself. If the food biotechnology industry wants to convince the public that its products are beneficial, it will need to place far greater emphasis on the development of truly useful products, those that foster sustainable agriculture, drought- and pest-resistance, and improved nutrient quality.

This analysis also argues in favor of the development of federal regulatory mechanisms capable of addressing a much broader range of issues than just food safety. As noted by one commentator, regulations should be based on a comprehensive analysis of policy and assessment of technology that examines the full range of social and environmental consequences of technological change (Brown 1991).

That the agricultural biotechnology industry would benefit from such an analysis is evident from recent events. Developing-world countries are moving quickly to develop recombinant crops that will solve their local food problems. These efforts, which

derive directly from the need to produce more food, are focusing on improvements in disease resistance and nutritional quality, especially among native plant species (Moffat 1994; Bokanga 1995). Such efforts deserve much support and should encourage food biotechnology companies in industrialized nations to focus research and development efforts on products that will benefit individuals and societies as well as the companies' investors.

Marion Nestle

Bibliography

Aldhous, P. 1991. Yellow light on L-tryptophan. *Nature* 353: 490.
  1993. Thumbs down for cattle hormone. *Science* 261: 418.
American Medical Association, Council on Scientific Affairs. 1991. Biotechnology and the American agricultural industry. *Journal of the American Medical Association* 265: 1429-36.
Andrews, E. L. 1993. U.S. resumes granting patents on genetically altered animals. *The New York Times*, February 3, pp. A1, D5.
Associated Press. 1994. Seven engineered foods declared safe by FDA: Some scientists question biotech standard. *The Washington Post*, November 3, p. A11.
Barnum, A. 1992. Brave new foods: Bioengineered crops could meet consumer resistance. *San Francisco Chronicle*, June 15, pp. B1, B6.
Barton, K. A., and W. J. Brill. 1983. Prospects in plant genetic engineering. *Science* 219: 671-6.
Beachy, R. 1993. Transferring genes. In *Symbol, substance, science: The societal issues of food biotechnology*, conference proceedings, ed. W. S. Burke, 45-51, 61-2. Research Triangle Park, N.C.
Benson, S., M. Arax, and R. Burstein. 1997. A growing concern: As biotech crops come to market, neither scientists – who take industry money – nor federal regulators are adequately protecting consumers and farmers. *Mother Jones* 21: (January/February): 36-43, 66, 68, 71.
BGH moratorium. 1993. *Nutrition Week* (August 6): 5.
BIO favors limited notification on biotech food 3-year sunset. 1994. *Food Chemical News* (May 16): 7-8.
Biotech. 1994. *Nutrition Week* (August 26): 7.
Biotechnology promises consumers better, cheaper, safer foods. 1990. *Food Insight Reports* (March/April): 1.
Blayney, D. P. 1994. Milk and biotechnology: Maintaining safe, adequate milk supplies. *FoodReview* 17: 27-31.
Blayney, D. P., R. G. Fallert, and S. D. Shagam. 1991. Controversy over livestock growth hormones continues. *FoodReview* 14: 6-9.
Bokanga, M. 1995. Biotechnology and cassava processing in Africa. *Food Technology* 49: 86-90.
Brody, J. E. 1993. Of Luddites, cows, and biotechnology miracles. *The New York Times*, November 17, p. C17.
Brown, G. 1991. Recent American agricultural history. In *New technologies and the future of food and nutrition*, ed. G. E. Gaull and R. A. Goldberg, 25-36. New York.
Browning, Graeme. 1992. Biotech politics. *National Journal* (February 29): 511-14.
Bruhn, C. M. 1992. Consumer concerns and educational strategies: Focus on biotechnology. *Food Technology* 45: 80, 95, 97.

Burros, M. 1994. More milk, more confusion: What should the label say? *The New York Times,* May 18, pp. C1, C4.

Carrol, W. L. 1993. Introduction to recombinant-DNA technology. *American Journal of Clinical Nutrition* 58 (Supplement): 249s–258s.

Caswell, M. F., K. O. Fuglie, and C. A. Klotz. 1994. *Agricultural biotechnology: An economic perspective.* USDA Agricultural Economic Report No. 687. Washington, D.C.

Centers for Disease Control. 1989. Eosinophilia-myalgia syndrome - New Mexico. *Journal of the American Medical Association* 262: 3116.

Chambers, J. A. 1995. Creating new partnerships in global biotechnology. *Food Technology* 49: 94–6.

Chefs urge boycotting new foods. 1992. *The New York Times* (June 3): C6.

Cohen, B. 1993. *Ben & Jerry's testifies before FDA in favor of BGH labeling.* Press Release. Waterbury, Vt.

Court strikes down Vermont BGH dairy labeling law. 1996. *Nutrition Week* 26: 2.

Daughaday, W. H., and D. M. Barbano. 1990. Bovine somatotropin supplementation of dairy cows: Is the milk safe? *Journal of the American Medical Association* 264: 1003–5.

Davis, B. D., ed. 1991. *The genetic revolution: Scientific prospects and public perceptions.* Baltimore, Md.

Day, K. 1994. Where did the milk come from? Tracking dairy hormone may prove impossible. *The Washington Post,* February 13, pp. A1, A22.

Dickman, S. 1996. Germany joins the biotech race. *Science* 274: 1454–5.

Donnelley, S., C. R. McCarthy, and R. Singleton, Jr. 1994. *The brave new world of animal biotechnology.* Special supplement to the *Hastings Center Report* 24: S1–31.

Economic Research Service. 1994. *Food marketing review, 1992–93.* USDA Agricultural Economic Report No. 678. Washington, D.C.

Elliott, I. 1996. Proposed Canadian biotech agency opposed. *Feedstuffs* (November 11): 3, 6.

Engelberg, S. 1994. Democrats' new overseer is everybody's Mr. Inside. *The New York Times,* August 19, pp. A1, A16.

Environmental Defense Fund. 1994. *EDF cautiously praises EPA's proposed genetic engineering rule.* Press Release. New York.

EU approves Bt corn, but it must be labeled. 1997. *Genetically Modified Foods Market Intelligence* (January 8): 1–2.

Falk, B. W., and G. Bruening. 1994. Will transgenic crops generate new viruses and new diseases? *Science* 263: 1395–6.

FDA approves biotech milk hormone, will not require BGH labeling. 1993. *Nutrition Week* (November 12): 1–2.

Feder, B. J. 1995. Monsanto has its wonder hormone. Can it sell it? *The New York Times,* March 12, p. 8.

    1996. Out of the lab, a revolution on the farm: New genetic weapons to battle bugs and weeds. *The New York Times,* March 3, Sect. 3, pp. 1, 11.

Fisher, L. M. 1994. Developer of the new tomato expects a financial bonanza. *The New York Times,* May 19, p. B7.

    1995. Monsanto to acquire 49.9% of biotechnology company. *The New York Times,* June 29, p. D3.

FDA (Food and Drug Administration). 1992. Statement of policy: Foods derived from new plant varieties; notice. *Federal Register* 57: 22984–23005.

    1993. Food labeling: Food derived from new plant varieties. *Federal Register* 58: 25837–41.

    1994a. *Biotechnology of food.* Washington, D.C.

    1994b. Interim guidance on the voluntary labeling of milk and milk products from cows that have not been treated with recombinant bovine somatotropin. *Federal Register* 59: 6279–80.

Food Marketing Institute. 1994. *Trends in the United States: Consumer attitudes and the supermarket, 1994.* Washington, D.C.

Fox, J. L. 1990. Tryptophan production questions raised. *Bio/Technology* 8: 992.

    1994. FDA nears approval of Calgene's Flavr Savr. *Bio/Technology* 12: 439.

    1996. USDA downplays closing of biotech advisory programs. *Nature Biotechnology* 14: 261.

Fox, M. W. 1992. *Superpigs and wondercorn.* New York.

Fraley, R. 1992. Sustaining the food supply. *Bio/Technology* 10: 40–3.

Fritsch, P., and S. Kilman. 1996. Huge biotech harvest is a boon for farmers - and for Monsanto. *The Wall Street Journal,* October 24, pp. A1, A10.

Fuchs, R. L., and J. S. Astwood. 1996. Allergenicity assessment of foods derived from genetically modified plants. *Food Technology* 50: 83–8.

Gallo, A. E. 1995. *The food marketing system in 1994.* USDA Agricultural Information Bulletin No. 717. Washington, D.C.

Gaull, G. E., and R. A. Goldberg, eds. 1991. *New technologies and the future of food and nutrition.* New York.

Gibbons, A. 1990. FDA published bovine growth hormone data. *Science* 249: 852–3.

Goldburg, R., J. Rissler, H. Shand, and C. Hassebrook. 1990. *Biotechnology's bitter harvest: Herbicide-tolerant crops and the threat to sustainable agriculture.* Biotechnology Working Group. Washington, D.C.

Hallman, W. K., and J. Metcalfe. 1993. *Public perceptions of agricultural biotechnology: A survey of New Jersey residents.* Ecosystem Policy Research Center, Rutgers University, and New Jersey Agricultural Experiment Station, Cook College. New Brunswick, N.J.

Hamilton, J. O'C. 1990. A tempest in a cottonfield: Are Calgene's herbicide-resistant seeds a boon or a biohazard? *Business Week* (April 9): 43.

    1994. Biotech: An industry crowded with players faces an ugly reckoning. *Business Week* (September 26): 84–92.

Hansen, M. K., and J. M. Halloran. 1994. Make them label it. Letter to the Editor. *The New York Times,* February 21, p. A16.

Harlander, S. K. 1989. Biotechnology opportunities for the food industry. In *Biotechnology and the food industry,* ed. P. L. Rogers and G. H. Fleet, 1–16. New York.

Hayenga, M. L. 1993. Food and agricultural biotechnology: Economic implications. *American Journal of Clinical Nutrition* 58 (Supplement): 313s–316s.

Hilts, P. J. 1994. Genetically altered tomato moves toward U.S. approval. *The New York Times,* April 9, p. 7.

Hoban, T. J. 1994. *Consumer awareness and acceptance of bovine somatotropin (BST).* Unpublished survey conducted for the Grocery Manufacturers of America.

    1995. The construction of food biotechnology as a social issue. In *Eating agendas: Food and nutrition as social problems,* ed. D. Maurer and J. Sobal, 189–212. New York.

Hoban, T. J., and P. A. Kendall. 1993. *Consumer attitudes about food biotechnology: Project summary.* Raleigh, N.C.

Hodgson, J. 1992. Biotechnology: Feeding the world? *Bio/Technology* 10: 47–50.

Holmberg, S. D., M. T. Osterholm, K. A. Senger, and M. L. Cohen. 1984. Drug-resistant Salmonella from animals fed antimicrobials. *New England Journal of Medicine* 311: 617-22.

Hopkins, D. D., R. J. Goldburg, and S. A. Hirsch. 1991. *A mutable feast: Assuring food safety in the era of genetic engineering.* New York.

Hoyle, R. 1992. FDA's slippery food policy. *Bio/Technology* 10: 956-9.

Ibrahim, Y. M. 1996. Genetic soybeans alarm Europeans. *The New York Times,* November 7, pp. D1, D24.

Ingersoll, B. 1992. New policy eases market path for bioengineered foods. *The Wall Street Journal,* May 26, pp. B1, B6.

International Food Biotechnology Council. 1990. Biotechnologies and food: Assuring the safety of foods produced by genetic modification. *Regulatory Toxicology and Pharmacology* 12 (Supplement): S1-196.

Jones, H. C. 1996. Rifkin launches latest boycott. *Feedstuffs* (October 14): 3.

Juskevich, D. C., and C. G. Guyer. 1990. Bovine growth hormone: Human food safety evaluation. *Science* 249: 875-84.

Kaiser, J. 1996. Pests overwhelm Bt cotton crop. *Science* 273: 423.

Kessler, D. A., M. R. Taylor, J. H. Maryanski, et al. 1992. The safety of foods developed by biotechnology. *Science* 256: 1747-9, 1832.

Kilman, S. 1994a. Dairy-food concerns launch products from cows not treated with hormone. *The Wall Street Journal,* May 2, p. XX. Sec B, p. 7.

1994b. Growing pains: Genetic engineering's biggest impact may eventually be in agriculture. The key word: eventually. *The Wall Street Journal,* May 30, p. R7.

Kim, J. 1992a. Biotech firms design food for thought. *USA Today,* April 28.

1992b. Genetic agriculture gets go-ahead. *USA Today,* May 27, p. B3.

Kling, J. 1996. Could transgenic supercrops one day breed superweeds? *Science* 274: 180-1.

Knorr, D. 1995. Improving food biotechnology resources and strategies in developing countries. *Food Technology* 49: 91-3.

Kolata, G. 1994. When the geneticists' fingers get in the food. *The New York Times,* February 20, p. E13.

Krissoff, B. 1989. The European ban on livestock hormones and implications for international trade. *National Food Review* 12: 34-6.

Leary, W. 1992a. Cornucopia of new foods is seen as policy on engineering is eased. *The New York Times,* May 27, p. A1.

1992b. Gene-altered food held by the F.D.A. to pose little risk. *The New York Times,* May 26, pp. A1, C9.

1994. F.D.A. approves altered tomato that will remain fresh longer. *The New York Times,* May 19, pp. A1, B7.

Leonard, R. E. 1995. Codex at the crossroads: Conflict on trade, health. *Nutrition Week* 25 (July 14): 5-6.

Lynch, S., and C.-T. J. Lin. 1994. Food safety: Meal planners express their concerns. *FoodReview* 17: 14-18.

Mather, R. 1995. *A garden of unearthly delights: Bioengineering and the future of food.* New York.

Mayeno, A. N., and G. J. Gleich. 1994. Eosinophilia-myalgia syndrome and tryptophan production: A cautionary tale. *Trends in Biotechnology* 12: 346-52.

McMurray, S. 1993. New Calgene tomato might have tasted just as good without genetic alteration. *The Wall Street Journal,* January 12, p. B1.

Mellon, M. 1988. *Biotechnology and the environment.* Washington, D.C.

1991. An environmentalist perspective. In *The genetic revolution: Scientific prospects and public perceptions,* ed. B. D. Davis, 60-76. Baltimore, Md.

Messer, E. 1992. Sources of institutional funding for agrobiotechnology for developing countries. *Advanced Technology Assessment Systems* 9: 371-8.

Messer, E., and P. Heywood. 1990. Trying technology: Neither sure nor soon. *Food Policy* 15: 336-45.

Mikkelsen, T. R., B. Anderson, and R. B. Jorgensen. 1996. The risk of crop transgene spread. *Nature* 380: 31.

Miller, H. 1991. Regulation. In *The genetic revolution: Scientific prospects and public perceptions,* ed. B. D. Davis, 196-211. Baltimore, Md.

1992. Putting the bST human-health controversy to rest. *Bio/Technology* 10: 147.

1994. A need to reinvent biotechnology regulation at the EPA. *Science* 266: 1815-18.

Millstone, E., E. Brunner, and I. White. 1994. Plagiarism or protecting public health? *Nature* 371: 647-8.

Mittal, G. S. 1992. *Food biotechnology.* Lancaster, Pa.

Moffat, A. S. 1994. Developing nations adapt biotech for own needs. *Science* 265: 186-7.

National Research Council. 1989. Recommended Dietary Allowances. 10th edition. Washington, D.C.

Nestle, M. 1996. Allergies to transgenic foods – questions of policy. *New England Journal of Medicine* 334: 726-8.

Nordlee, J. A., S. L. Taylor, J. A. Townsend, et al. 1996. Identification of a Brazil-nut allergen in transgenic soybeans. *New England Journal of Medicine* 334: 688-92.

Office of Medical Applications of Research. 1991. *Bovine somatotropin: National Institutes of Health Technology Assessment Conference statement, December 5-7, 1990.* Washington, D.C.

Office of Planning and Evaluation and Center for Food Safety and Applied Nutrition. 1988. *Food biotechnology: Present and future.* 2 vols. Washington, D.C.

Olempska-Beer, Z. S., P. M. Kuznesof, M. DiNovi, and M. J. Smith. 1993. Plant biotechnology and food safety. *Food Technology* 47: 64-72.

Ollinger, M., and L. Pope. 1995. *Plant biotechnology: Out of the laboratory and into the field.* USDA Agricultural Economic Report No. 697. Washington, D.C.

O'Neill, M. 1992. Geneticists' latest discovery: Public fear of "Frankenfood." *The New York Times,* June 28, pp. A1, A14.

1994. Tomato review: No substitute for summer. *The New York Times,* May 19, p. B7.

Over 800 farmers report problems related to rBGH. 1995. *Nutrition Week* (June 2): 6.

Pell, A. N., D. S. Tsang, B. A. Howlett, et al. 1992. Effects of a prolonged-release formulation of Sometribove (n-methionyl bovine somatotropin) on Jersey cows. *Journal of Dairy Science* 75: 3416-31.

Philin, R. M., R. H. Hill, W. D. Flanders, et al. 1993. Tryptophan contaminants associated with eosinophilia-myalgia syndrome. *American Journal of Epidemiology* 138: 154-9.

Putnam, J. J., and J. E. Allshouse. 1996. *Food consumption, prices and expenditures, 1970-95.* USDA Statistical Bulletin No. 928. Washington, D.C.

1994. *Food Consumption, Prices and Expenditures 1970-95.* USDA *Statistical Bulletin.* Washington, D.C.

Redenbaugh, K., W. Hiatt, B. Martineau, et al. 1992. *Safety assessment of genetically engineered fruits and vegetables: A case study of the Flavr Savr tomato.* Boca Raton, Fla.

Reilly, J. M. 1989. *Consumer effects of biotechnology.* USDA

Agricultural Information Bulletin No. 581. Washington, D.C.

Rissler, J., and M. Mellon. 1993. *Perils amidst the promise: Ecological risks of transgenic crops in a global market.* Washington, D.C.

Rogers, P. L., and G. H. Fleet, eds. 1989. *Biotechnology and the food industry.* New York.

Roufs, J. B. 1992. Review of L-tryptophan and eosinophilia-myalgia syndrome. *Journal of the American Dietetic Association* 92: 844–50.

Sampson, H. A., and D. D. Metcalfe. 1992. Food allergies. *Journal of the American Medical Association* 268: 2840–4.

Schneider, K. 1989. Stores bar milk produced by drug: Five big chains take action – U.S. calls process safe. *The New York Times,* August 24, pp. A1, A18.

　1990. F.D.A. defends milk-producing drug in study. *The New York Times,* August 24, p. A18.

　1993. U.S. approves use of drug to raise milk production: Gain for biotechnology. *The New York Times,* November 6, pp. 1, 9.

　1994a. Farmers eager to test drug to get more milk. *The New York Times,* February 5, p. 6.

　1994b. Grocers challenge use of new drug for milk output. *The New York Times,* February 4, pp. A1, A14.

　1994c. Lines drawn in a war over a milk hormone. *The New York Times,* March 9, p. A12.

　1994d. Maine and Vermont restrict dairies' use of a growth hormone. *The New York Times,* April 15, p. A16.

　1994e. Question is raised on hormone maker's ties to F.D.A. aides. *The New York Times,* April 18, p. A9.

Smith, P. G., and S. N. Cousens. 1996. Is the new variant of Creutzfeldt-Jakob disease from mad cows? *Science* 273: 748.

Somerville, C. R. 1993. Future prospects for genetic modification of the composition of edible oils from higher plants. *American Journal of Clinical Nutrition* 58 (Supplement): 270s–275s.

Stillings, B. R. 1994. Trends in foods. *Nutrition Today* 29: 6–13.

Stix, G. 1995. A recombinant feast: New bioengineered crops move toward market. *Scientific American* 273: 38–9.

Stone, R. 1995. Sweeping patents put biotech companies on the warpath. *Science* 268: 656–8.

Sugawara, S. 1992. For the next course, "engineered" entrees? "Genetic" tomato may launch an industry. *The Washington Post,* June 10, p. F1.

Sullivan, L. W. 1991. The link between nutrition and health. In *New technologies and the future of food and nutrition,* ed. G. E. Gaull and R. A. Goldberg, 97. New York.

Sun, M. 1989. Market sours on milk hormone. *Science* 246: 876–7.

Swaminathan, M. S. 1982. Biotechnology research and Third World agriculture. *Science* 218: 967–72.

Tacket, C. O., L. B. Dominguez, H. J. Fisher, and M. L. Cohen. 1985. An outbreak of multiple-drug-resistant *Salmonella* enteritis from raw milk. *Journal of the American Medical Association* 253: 2058–60.

U.S. Congress, Office of Technology Assessment. 1987. *New developments in biotechnology – background paper: Public perceptions of biotechnology.* OTA-BP-BA-45. Washington, D.C.

　1989. *New developments in biotechnology: Patenting life – special report.* OTA-BA-370. Washington, D.C.

　1991a. *Biotechnology in a global economy.* OTA-BA-494. Washington, D.C.

　1991b. *U.S. dairy industry at a crossroad: Biotechnology and policy choices – special report.* OTA-F-470. Washington, D.C.

　1992. *A new technological era for American agriculture.* OTA-F-475. Washington, D.C.

U.S. General Accounting Office. 1992a. *Food safety and quality: FDA strategy needed to address animal drug residues in milk.* GAO/RCED-92-209. Washington, D.C.

　1992b. *Recombinant bovine growth hormone: FDA approval should be withheld until the mastitis issue is resolved.* GAO/PEMD-92-26. Washington, D.C.

　1993. *Food safety and quality: Innovative strategies may be needed to regulate new food technologies.* GAO/RCED-93-142. Washington, D.C.

　1994. *Letter from Acting General Counsel Robert P. Murphy to the Honorables George E. Brown, Jr., David Obey, and Bernard Sanders.* B257122. Washington, D.C.

Vandaele, W. 1992. bST and the EEC: Politics vs. science. *Bio/Technology* 10: 148–9.

Wadman, M. 1996. Genetic resistance spreads to consumers. *Nature* 383: 564.

Waldholz, M. 1994. An industry in adolescence. Think of biotechnology as a teenager: Lots of promise, lots of headaches. *The Wall Street Journal,* May 20, p. R4.

Walter, R. 1995. We must boost public acceptance of biotech. *Bio/Technology* 13: 216–17.

Winslow, R. 1996. Allergen is inadvertently transferred to soybean in bioengineering test. *The Wall Street Journal,* March 14, p. B6.

Wolf, J. 1997. Europe turns up nose at biotech food: Lacking EU rules for modified crops, farm sector could suffer. *The Wall Street Journal,* January 2, p. 8.

Zimmerman, L., P. Kendall, M. Stone, and T. Hoban. 1994. Consumer knowledge and concern about biotechnology and food safety. *Food Technology* 48: 71–7.

VII.8 ❧ Food Safety and Biotechnology

The ready availability of safe, wholesome food is often taken for granted by citizens of modern societies. However, maintaining the safety of a large, diverse food supply is a challenging undertaking that requires coordinated effort at many levels. In this chapter, the principles of food safety are discussed first with regard to traditional foods and then again as they concern novel foods developed through genetic modification.

Definitions and Priorities

The term "food safety," as used today, encompasses many diverse areas, including protection against food poisoning and assurance that food does not contain additives or contaminants that would render it unsafe to eat. The term evolved mainly in the context of preventing intoxication by microbial poisons that act quickly (within hours to a day or two of exposure) and often induce such serious symptoms as convulsive vomiting and severe diarrhea, or respiratory failure and death (Cliver 1990). An example of the former is staphylococcal food poisoning, caused by the proteinaceous enterotoxins of the pathogenic bacterium *Staphylococcus aureus* (Cliver 1990). Botulism is an example of the latter, caused by the neurotoxins synthesized by *Clostridium botulinum* (Cliver 1990).

Both staphylococcal food poisoning and botulism result from ingesting toxins that are preformed in the implicated foods. For illness to ensue, it is necessary only to ingest the toxin, not the microbe itself. Food poisoning may also follow the ingestion of certain pathogenic bacteria, such as *Salmonella,* which produce gastrointestinal (GI) infections, and *Escherichia coli* 0157:H7, which produces an infection and a potent toxin within the GI tract (Cliver 1990). The infection results in bloody diarrhea, while the toxin enters the bloodstream and induces kidney damage.

Given the foregoing, it should come as no surprise that the Food and Drug Administration (FDA), the lead federal agency charged with ensuring the safety of the food supply in the United States, considers foodborne microbial pathogens and the toxins they produce to be the most important of the various food safety risks (Table VII.8.1). Unfortunately, evidence indicates that the public often tends to focus too much on pesticide residues and food additives, wrongly believing that the risk from these materials is as great as that from pathogenic microorganisms (Pariza 1992c).

Table VII.8.1. *Ranking food safety risks*

1. Food-borne disease.
2. Environmental contaminants.
3. Naturally occurring toxins.
4. Food additives.
5. Pesticide residues.

Source: Young (1989).

Table VII.8.2. *Summary of reported food-borne disease outbreaks in the United States, 1983–7*[a]

Etiologic agent	Percentage of cases	Percentage of outbreaks[b]
Pathogenic bacteria[c]	92	66
Viruses[c]	5	5
Parasites[c]	<1	4
Chemical agents[d]	2	26

[a]During this time period, 91,678 cases and 2,397 outbreaks of foodborne illness were reported to the Centers for Disease Control (CDC). The etiologic agent was identified in 38 percent of the outbreaks. These data are summarize in this table.

[b]An outbreak is the occurrence of two or more cases of illness transmitted by a single food.

[c]Pathogenic bacteria, viruses, and parasites are all classified as microorganisms.

[d]Some instances of chemical poisoning were actually due to chemical toxins produced by microorganisms. No instances of illness traced to synthetic chemicals were identified in the report.

Source: Bean et al. (1990).

Microbial Foodborne Illness

Table VII.8.2 shows a summary of foodborne illness in the United States, compiled by the Centers for Disease Control (CDC), from 1983 to 1987 (Bean et al. 1990). But according to both the CDC and the FDA, the reported cases and outbreaks account for only a tiny fraction of the total foodborne illnesses that occurred during that period. It is estimated that several million cases of microbial food poisoning actually occur in the United States each year (Archer and Kvenberg 1985).

Foodborne illness is caused by a relatively small number of bacterial species. All raw foods contain microorganisms, some of which may be pathogens. Whether or not this becomes a problem is determined largely by how the food is handled prior to consumption. Pathogen growth depends on a number of factors. The most important of these are (1) the levels of salt and other electrolytes present in the food; (2) the types and amount of acid in the food; (3) the amount of available water; (4) the presence of microbial inhibitors (both naturally occurring and synthetic); (5) storage conditions; and (6) cooking conditions. Safe food processing depends on understanding these factors and effectively utilizing the basic principles of microbiology as they apply to foods.

In addition to precipitating illness and soaring medical costs, foodborne illness can also bring economic devastation for producers of an implicated product (Todd 1985). A dramatic example occurred in 1982, when two Belgians developed botulism after sharing a can of Alaskan salmon. One of them subsequently died of the illness.

The problem was traced to a can press that was used at the processing plant to form the can in question. The press was defective and had produced a tiny rupture in the wall of the implicated can. The rupture, which was virtually invisible, nonetheless permitted a small amount of nonsterile water to be drawn into the can during the cooling step that followed heat processing. The water was contaminated with spores of *Clostridium botulinum* which, once inside the can, germinated and produced the toxin that induced the illness. Fears that other cans might have been similarly damaged prompted voluntary recalls of much of the canned Alaskan salmon produced that year. In all, 60 million cans were recalled and discarded (Hayes 1983).

Foods provide a medium for the growth of specific pathogens, but they can also be passive carriers for virtually any pathogen capable of producing infection via the oral route. In this case the pathogens do not actually have to grow in the food. They need only to survive. Good examples are the foodborne viruses, such as the virus that causes hepatitis A. These cannot grow in the foods that carry them, yet illness follows ingestion of the contaminated food.

It should be noted that food spoilage and food safety are not related in a direct manner. A food may be spoiled but nonetheless safe. Alternatively, however, a food can contain bacterial toxins at deadly levels yet appear perfectly "normal." And finally, it is important to recognize that not all microbes in food are bad. Rather, harmless microorganisms are an integral part of many traditional foods. One could not produce bread, cheese, yoghurt, soy sauce, sauerkraut, beer, or wine without specific yeasts, bacteria, and molds. Such microorganisms are needed to induce desirable changes in the food through a process called "fermentation." Besides providing characteristic flavors, fermentation is also an important, effective method of food preservation. The harmless fermentation microorganisms produce microbial inhibitors and otherwise change the ecology of the food in ways that discourage subsequent pathogen growth.

Risks from Synthetic Chemicals

The data summarized in Table VII.8.2 indicate that the risk of developing foodborne microbial illness is far higher than the risk of becoming ill because of exposure to toxic chemicals in food. The instances of chemical poisoning reported in Table VII.8.2 represent almost exclusively naturally occurring toxins or contaminants. Only one approved food additive (monosodium glutamate) was reported as possibly causing illness in two outbreaks that occurred in 1984, involving a total of seven persons. In no instance was a synthetic chemical identified in the CDC report as a cause of illness (Bean et al. 1990). The data summarized in Table VII.8.2 refer to clinical illness, almost all of which is acute (that is, there is only a short time interval between exposure and onset of symptoms). Of course, questions about risks from "chemicals" in food often center on chronic effects, such as cancer, which in humans takes many years to develop.

The causes of chronic illness are much more difficult to determine because of the long time intervals between initial exposure and the onset of symptoms. Nonetheless, there is an extensive toxicology data base against which hypotheses can be tested. For example, based on these data, one may conclude that it is highly unlikely that synthetic pesticide residues or food additives pose a cancer risk to consumers (Ames, Profet, and Gold 1990; Pariza 1992a, 1992b).

Risks of Naturally Occurring Pesticides

Plants lack the defenses that animals possess (mobility, claws, and teeth), and so they must rely on passive defenses that are effective in situ. Accordingly, evolution has provided plants with the ability to synthesize naturally occurring toxins. In a very real sense, plants are practitioners of chemical warfare against potential predators.

The natural toxins that plants produce are usually nonspecific in nature; that is, they act against a variety of potential pests, including mammals as well as insects. The pathways regulating the synthesis and expression of these toxins tend to be under general control, meaning that any number of stresses, from insect infestation to drought, can "turn on" the entire spectrum of chemical and biological defenses that a plant possesses.

In this context, crop breeding can be seen as a means of controlling unwanted wild traits, such as toxin production, in plants destined for the table. Experience has shown that this is a relatively easy matter, even without any knowledge of the underlying science, doubtless because toxin production is not an inherent part of the growth and reproductive processes. Humans select and artificially propagate variants that would not otherwise survive but that nonetheless exhibit desirable traits. Because of the genetic linkage within the generalized protective mechanism pathways, increased expression of traits that humans deem desirable will usually be accompanied by decreased toxin expression (International Food Biotechnology Council 1990).

Unfortunately, selected traits that make a plant desirable as human food also make it desirable to insects. This, in fact, is why synthetic pesticides are used: They replace the naturally occurring pesticides and related survival traits that have been bred out of food plants.

Yet, although the natural pesticide levels of food plants have been lowered considerably through breeding, they have not been totally eliminated. Rather, the data in Table VII.8.3 show that many commonly consumed food plants and plant products contain naturally occurring pesticidal carcinogens. Moreover, unlike synthetic chemicals, which must be rigorously tested before regulatory agencies will approve them for food-related use, the toxins made naturally by plants are not ordinarily subjected to any sort of testing (Ames et al. 1990). For some individuals, however, it is unsettling to learn that many of those substances that have been tested have proved to be carcinogenic in rat or mouse feeding studies.

Yet it is important to put these findings into perspective by a consideration of (1) the relative exposure of the public to natural versus synthetic carcinogenic pesticide residues, and (2) the relative risk of cancer from these exposures.

With regard to exposure, FDA data indicate that the average daily intake of synthetic pesticides per person in the United States is 0.09 milligrams (mg) (Ames et al. 1990). About half of this intake (0.04 mg) comes from four chemicals that were not carcinogenic in high-dose rodent feeding studies. Thus, assuming that all of the remaining exposure is to carcinogenic pesticides (an unlikely assumption), the maximum exposure to synthetic carcinogenic pesticide residues is 0.05 mg per person per day.

Table VII.8.3. *Some natural pesticidal carcinogens in food*

Rodent carcinogen	Plant food	Concentration, ppm
5-/8-methoxypsoralen	Parsley	14
	Parsnip, cooked	32
	Celery	0.8
	Celery, new cultivar	6.2
	Celery, stressed	25
ρ-hydrazinobenzoate	Mushrooms	11
Glutamyl r-hydrazinobenzoate	Mushrooms	42
Sinigrin (allyl isothiocyanate)	Cabbage	35–590
	Collard greens	250–788
	Cauliflower	12–66
	Brussels sprouts	110–1560
	Mustard (brown)	16000–72000
	Horseradish	4500
Estragole	Basil	3800
	Fennel	3000
Safrole	Nutmeg	3000
	Mace	10,000
	Pepper, black	100
Ethyl acrylate	Pineapple	0.07
Sesamol	Sesame seeds (heated oil)	75
α-methylbenzyl alcohol	Cocoa	1.3
Benzyl acetate	Basil	82
	Jasmine tea	230
	Honey	15
Catechol	Coffee (roasted beans)	100
Caffeic acid	Apple, carrot, celery, cherry, eggplant, endive, grapes, lettuce, pear, plum, potato	50–200
	Absinthe, anise, basil, caraway, dill, marjoram, rosemary, sage, savory, tarragon, thyme	>1000
	Coffee (roasted beans)	1800
Chlorogenic acid (caffeic acid)	Apricot, cherry, peach, plum	50–500
	Coffee (roasted beans)	21600
Neochlorogenic acid (caffeic acid)	Apple, apricot, broccoli, brussels sprouts, cabbage, cherry, kale, peach, pear, plum	50–500
	Coffee (roasted beans)	11600

Source: Ames, Profet, and Gold (1990).

By comparison, it is estimated that Americans consume 1.5 grams of natural pesticides per person per day, or about 15,000 times more than the amount of synthetic pesticides. Moreover, many of these natural pesticides are also carcinogenic in high-dose rodent feeding studies (Table VII.8.3). Clearly, the public is exposed to far higher levels of naturally occurring pesticides, and, in fact, when compared to naturally occurring pesticides, synthetic pesticide exposure is trivial (Ames et al. 1990).

Moreover, toxicology is not just about exposure levels to toxic substances, because animals, including humans, have numerous biochemical and physiological resources to defend against such exposure. These defenses include enzymes that detoxify toxins and repair toxin-induced damage to DNA and other important biological structures, as well as the continual shedding of cells at epithelial surfaces that are most exposed to toxic insult (that is, cells at the surface of skin, eyes, and gastrointestinal tract). In short, humans have layer on layer of protection against the toxic dangers of "natural" environments.

Because of the immense number and variety of potential toxins, the defense systems must by necessity be general in nature. In this regard, there is nothing unique about synthetic pesticides. The protective mechanisms that act against naturally occurring toxins also act against synthetic toxins. These protective mechanisms are, of course, even more effective when the dose is exceedingly low as is the case with exposure to synthetic pesticide residues on produce. Moreover, it is important to note that the biological effects produced in animals by naturally occurring pesticides and other potential toxins are not always adverse. Rather, paradoxically, many of the substances shown in Table VII.8.3 that cause cancer when fed to rodents at excessively high levels seem to protect against cancer when fed at the lower, more realistic levels encountered in a normal diet (Pariza 1993).

One implication of this paradox is that unrealistically high dose cancer tests have been responsible for indicting the naturally occurring substances shown in Table VII.8.3. In fact, this consideration has led many experts to reexamine the entire framework through which we detect and regulate "carcinogens" (Ames et al. 1990; Pariza 1992c; National Research Council 1993).

The Safety of Novel Foods

There are many kinds of novel foods. In the simplest sense, a food may be novel in one locale and a dietary staple in another. Examples include the many foods that crossed the Atlantic Ocean between Europe and the Americas in the years following Columbus's voyages (Goldblith 1992). Corn, potatoes, tomatoes, and cacao (chocolate), which today are common throughout the world, were novelties for everyone on earth, save the Native Americans, just 500 years ago.

At the other end of the spectrum are novel foods developed by using recombinant DNA technology (for example, Calgene's flavr savr tomato). The recombinant DNA process is defined as "cutting and recombining DNA molecules to remove segments from or otherwise modify an organism's genetic material, or to combine segments of DNA from different types of organisms" (International Food Biotechnology Council 1990:).

Discovered and refined only since the 1970s, recombinant DNA methods represent a revolutionary means of controlling the introduction of new traits into plants, animals, and microorganisms. It should be stressed, however, that the "revolution" is not the process itself. There is ample evidence that gene transfer between different species has occurred throughout the history of life on this planet (International Food Biotechnology Council 1990). Rather, the revolution is that humans are able to control the process. For the first time in history, it is possible to direct the transfer of DNA from one species to another. It is also possible to create entirely new genes that, seemingly, have not existed before and transfer them into living hosts where the new genes will then replicate along with the host's genetic material.

The incredible power of this technology has led some to conclude that to prevent misuse, the process itself must be carefully regulated. Others argue that the process is simply a scientific tool and that the focus of regulation should be on the products of biotechnology, not on the process.

With specific regard to food, most experts agree that the focus of safety evaluation should be on the novel foods themselves, and not on the process whereby novel foods are developed (International Food Biotechnology Council 1990; Kessler et al. 1992). The rationale for this reasoning is that recombinant DNA technology is no less safe than plant breeding or any other traditional means of genetic manipulation. In all cases, one is (or should be) concerned with the expression of genetic information.

For example, in traditional plant breeding, one should determine if unexpected traits that bear on safety are expressed by the new cultivar. Such unexpected traits may arise directly from the genetic material itself that has been transferred in the cross may result because the transferred genetic material affected a regulatory element, thereby inducing the expression of an undesirable new trait (for example, the expression of a toxin).

In any attempt to establish the safety of a novel food, the same procedures should be followed to assure that the gene being transferred produces a safe product and that the gene does not induce changes in the recipient that bear on health and safety issues.

Addressing the first concern (whether the gene that is being transferred produces a safe product) is a relatively straightforward matter. This is because the gene can be completely defined. If the gene codes for a protein, it, too, can be completely defined and studied directly for toxigenic potential.

The second concern (whether the transferred gene induces changes in the recipient that bear on health and safety issues) is somewhat more problematic, as it is with traditional methods of genetic modification.

For example, the data of Table VII.8.3 indicate that many food plants naturally produce potentially carcinogenic compounds. As already discussed, the expression of such natural pesticides does not occur at a constant rate irrespective of other considerations. Rather, these substances are under genetic control, which in turn is influenced by environmental factors, such as insect infestation and drought. A pertinent example shown in Table VII.8.3 concerns celery.

Celery produces a class of natural pesticides called psoralins, which are light-activated mutagenic carcinogens. Ordinarily, the concentration of psoralins in celery is about 0.8 parts per million, which is too low to produce evidence of adverse effects in persons who consume the vegetable. However, through the use of traditional breeding methodology, an insect-resistant celery cultivar was developed that contained about 10 times the concentration of psoralin typically found (Table VII.8.3). This level was sufficiently high to produce skin irritations in consumers (Ames et al. 1990). Ordinary celery, subjected to stress, contains still higher levels of psoralin.

The increased psoralin content of the new celery cultivar was the result of genetic manipulation via traditional crop breeding techniques. It represents a reversal of the more commonly observed trend of decreased levels of naturally occurring toxicants in plants as they are "domesticated" through crop breeding (International Food Biotechnology Council 1990). In this particular case, however, the breeder's goal was to select for enhanced insect resistance so as to minimize the need for synthetic pesticides. Hence, the outcome of increased levels of psoralin (celery's natural insecticide) is not surprising. It should be noted that when the excessive psoralin problem was discovered, the cultivar was quickly withdrawn from the market (Ames et al. 1990).

This example offers insight into the evaluation of the safety of novel foods. The issue is whether introducing the new gene into the recipient triggers a response by the recipient that bears on health and safety. One of the main considerations is the possibility of increased synthesis of a toxicant synthesized naturally by the recipient plant (such as psoralin in a hypothetical novel celery).

There is considerable information on naturally occurring toxicants that are produced by food plants (International Food Biotechnology Council 1990). Such information can provide the framework for comparing the natural toxin levels in a novel food with those in its traditional (unmodified) counterpart – for instance, the psoralins in the hypothetical novel celery versus those in ordinary celery. A given plant species produces only a limited number of the known naturally occurring toxicants (usually restricted to a specific chemical class). Hence, it is not necessary to analyze each plant for every known, naturally occurring toxin. Rather, effort can be concentrated on the potential toxicants with which the plants in question are known to be associated. Such assays can take the form of specific chemical analyses, possibly coupled with judicious, limited animal testing (International Food Biotechnology Council 1990; Kessler et al. 1992).

The concept of comparative toxicology – assessing safety of a novel food by comparing it with its traditional counterpart – is central to the food safety assessment schemes developed by the International Food Biotechnology Council, a food and biotechnology industry-sponsored group (International Food Biotechnology Council 1990) and the FDA (Kessler et al 1992). In addition to assays for specific toxins, one should also consider changes in composition that might affect pathogen growth (Pariza 1992b).

Conclusion

With the advent of biotechnology, the production and availability of food is entering a new era of great promise for improved human welfare. Procedures and methodologies are available to ensure the safety of the novel foods that have been and will be developed through biotechnology (International Food Biotechnology Council 1990; Kessler et al. 1992). These procedures and methodologies are not fundamentally different from those used now to assure the safety of traditional foods developed though traditional means of breeding and improvement.

Michael W. Pariza

Bibliography

Ames, B. N., M. Profet, and L. S. Gold. 1990. Dietary pesticides (99.99% all natural). *Proceedings of the National Academy of Science* 87: 7777–81.

Archer, D. L., and J. E. Kvenberg. 1985. Incidence and cost of foodborne diarrheal disease in the United States. *Journal of Food Protection* 48: 887–94.

Bean, N. H., P. M. Griffin, J. S. Goulding, and C. B. Ivey. 1990. Foodborne disease outbreaks, 5-year summary, 1983–1987. *Morbidity Mortality Weekly Report* 39(SS-1): 1–23.

Cliver, D. O., ed. 1990. *Foodborne Diseases.* New York.

Goldblith, S. A. 1992. The legacy of Columbus, with particular reference to foods. *Food Technology* 46: 62–85.

Hayes, A. H., Jr. 1983. The Food and Drug Administration's role in the canned salmon recalls of 1982. *Public Health Report* 98: 412–15.

International Food Biotechnology Council. 1990. Biotechnologies and food: Assuring the safety of foods produced by genetic modification. *Regulatory Toxicology and Pharmacology* 12: S1–196.

Kessler, D.A., M. R. Taylor, J. H. Maryanski, et al. 1992. The safety of foods developed by biotechnology. *Science* 256: 1747–9, 1832.

National Research Council. 1993. *Issues in Risk Assessment.* Washington, D.C.

Pariza, M. W. 1992a. A new approach to evaluating carcinogenic risk. *Proceedings of the National Academy of Science* 89: 860–1.

  1992b. Foods of new biotechnology vs traditional products: Microbiological aspects. *Food Technology* 46: 100–2.

  1992c. Risk assessment. *Critical Reviews in Food Science Nutrition* 31: 205–9.

  1993. Diet and Cancer: Where do matters stand? *Archives of Internal Medicine* 153: 50–6.

Todd, E. C. D. 1985. Economic loss from foodborne disease and non-illness related recalls because of mishandling by food processors. *Journal of Food Protection* 48: 621–33.

Young, F. E. 1989. Weighing food safety risks. *FDA Consumer* September: 8–13.

VII.9 ❧ Food Additives

Foods are biological products and, therefore, incorporate complex physical and biochemical systems. Many vegetables, fruits, and (sometimes) meat and fish are eaten raw, but in general they are cooked. And cooking induces profound chemical and physical changes. Some changes, such as the denaturation of protein and the gelation of starch, render food more digestible and are beneficial; others, by improving appearance, color, flavor, and texture, are also desirable. But some that cause heat damage to proteins, the loss of vitamins, or the formation of carcinogens on the surfaces of roast and barbecued meats are deleterious. Cooking leads to the use of one system, or a component of it, in the establishment of another. An example would be the role of egg yolks in emulsifying oil and water (vinegar) to make mayonnaise and to color it. Cooking also permits the use of major and minor ingredients and, thus, infinite variation in the final dish, but it also opens the way for the entry into food of nonfood substances derived from utensils and containers, and from the kitchen itself.

Food processors operate highly organized and sophisticated kitchens, and they apply detailed scientific knowledge of the raw materials to the production and packaging of products in response to market demands for variety, safety, wholesomeness, nutrition, and reasonable price. In effect, food processors are "super-cooks," but if in making mayonnaise they use lecithin (emulsifier) and beta-carotene (color) instead of egg yolk, or if they add acetic or citric acids instead of vinegar, then they are using additives.

Put simply, a food additive is a substance deliberately added to food by the processor to facilitate processing or to improve appearance, texture, flavor, keeping quality, or nutritional value. By contrast, any unwanted substance that finds its way into food is a contaminant. This may be defined even more widely as a substance that is not normally present in that food in its natural form; or is present in concentrations not normally found; or is not permitted under the food regulations to be present; or, being an additive as defined under the regulations, exceeds the concentration permitted.

Unfortunately, practice denies such simplicity, and the Codex Alimentarius Commission uses the following definition:

> "Food additive" means any substance not normally consumed as food by itself or not normally used as a typical ingredient of the food, whether or not it has nutritive value, the intentional addition of which to food for a technological (including organoleptic) purpose in the manufacture, processing, preparation, treatment, packing, packaging, transport or holding of such food results, or may be reasonably expected to result, (directly or indirectly) in it or its by-products becoming a component of or otherwise affecting the characteristics of such foods. The term does not include "contaminants" or substances added to food for maintaining or improving nutritional qualities (Codex Alimentarius Commission 1979).

There are gaps and uncertainties in such a definition. The key word in the Codex definition is "intentional." This excludes substances in which residues are inevitably present that are legitimately used in the production and processing of food. Strictly speaking, these residues are contaminants, but they are variously described as adventitious, indirect, incidental, or unintentional additives and are treated by most regulatory authorities in the same way as substances added for functional purposes to the food itself. They include pesticide residues, processing aids, sanitizers,

boiler water additives, and packaging migrants and are quite different in kind, and often in concentration, from industrial contaminants, such as the notorious mercury contamination of the fish in Minimata Bay, Japan, and polychlorinated biphenyls (PCBs). For the purposes of this discussion, then, substances permitted by the Codex definition, together with such nutrients as vitamins and minerals, will be considered to be additives.

Food Additives in History

There is nothing new about the concept of food additives. The ancient Chinese unknowingly used traces of ethylene and propylene from burning paraffin to ripen fruit, although additives were probably used originally simply to preserve food. Smoking is an ancient method of food preservation, usually for meat or fish, which relies partly on drying and partly on the preserving chemicals in the smoke.

Similarly, the resins added to Greek wine act as mild preservatives, and in classical times, the pitch linings of amphorae contributed substances that helped to preserve the wine carried in them. More recently, the practice of burning sulfur in empty wine barrels not only fumigated the barrel but also adventitiously ensured that the wine filling the barrel would be treated with sulfur dioxide, still the preservative of choice in the industry.

It is possible, however, that the first additive deliberately used to preserve foods was salt. Salted foods, especially fish, were known in antiquity. Salt was used lavishly as a preservative; the Romans made a fish sauce, liquamen, in which the fermentation, as well as the keeping quality, was controlled by adding salt. Salt is, however, so familiar and is used so much in such proportions that we now think of it as an ingredient, in contrast to an additive.

The same could be said of sugar, which emerged much later, possibly from India. Salt, however, is a simple inorganic chemical, whereas cane (or beet) sugar is a rather more complex organic molecule. White granulated sugar is a very pure chemical of great value in food preparation, whether in the home or factory. In honey and dried fruits, the sugar present acts as a preservative as does cane sugar in jams – the value of sugar as a flavoring is obvious. Sugar is a functional additive, but today, like salt, it too is thought of as an ingredient. However, saltpeter (sodium nitrate), which has been used from ancient times as a preservative, is *not* considered an ingredient but is firmly classified as an additive and is subject to continuing scrutiny.

Fermentation was long used as an empirical method of preservation. Alcoholic fermentation is itself a kind of preservation, and alcohol, in the form of brandy, was used in brandied wines as an additive. The production of lactic acid by fermentation, as in cheese, yoghurt, certain cured sausages, and sauerkraut, is another historical example of the formation of a preservative in situ by fermentation. And the acetic acid of vinegar was used by the Romans as a preservative for fruits and vegetables. A modern parallel is the surface treatment of meat with acetic acid to prolong shelf life.

The use of spices as flavorings is very old, as is the Western spice trade with the East. Even if the popularity of spices in Europe was really the result of an efficacy in masking the flavors of salted and tainted meats, the demand for them was established, and it is now known that they also act as mild preservatives. Some 600 years ago, hops were added to beer as a flavoring, which was not at first appreciated; but it was then noted that hopped beer kept better than unhopped ale. Hop resins, too, function as preservatives, but both spices and hops also are today classified as ingredients.

Before the factory production of food, preservation and flavor seem to have been more important than color. Nonetheless, saffron was used as a food color in ancient Egypt, and upper-class Romans had a preference for white bread, which was produced for them by sieving the flour and then adding alum, a practice that persisted until the end of the nineteenth century. Food coloring became popular in medieval times but was confined to the kitchens of the castles and great houses whose chefs used many colors of plant origin. These included indigo, alkanet from the root of borage, sanders from sandalwood, saffron from crocuses, marigold, and turmeric; greens came from the chlorophyll of sage and spinach, and pinks, blues, mauves, and violets from petal extracts.

In the seventeenth century, cochineal (from the dried insect *Coccus cacti*) and annatto (from the seeds of the shrub *Bixa orellana*) reached Europe from the New World. The latter was used to color butter and cheese, although in the eighteenth century butter was colored with saffron. In addition, the greening of vegetables by cooking in copper vessels was well known. No food-processing industry existed, however, and additives were confined to the kitchen and to farmhouse and village technology – that is, to butter, cheese, wine, and cider making, and to brewing, baking, and milling. Because there was no food industry, there were no processing aids, sanitizers, boiler water additives, or packaging migrants; nor were there any agricultural chemicals. But there was lead, an outright contaminant that came from the pipes of water systems; from cooking, eating, and drinking utensils; and from ingredients.

The Romans employed lead for collecting and distributing water, and their methods persisted. Even today lead pipes are used for water reticulation in many old houses and buildings in Britain and Europe. In the ancient world, food was cooked and stored in vessels of lead, leaded bronze and brass, and pewter and was served on lead and pewter plates and dishes. The Romans lacked sugar and, for a sweetener, used grape juice concentrated by boiling in lead vessels, because of the extra sweetness derived from the lead salts (Nriagu 1983).

So high was the lead content of the food and drink (especially wine) consumed by the upper-class Romans that lead poisoning has been confidently proposed as one of the major causes of the decline of the Roman Empire (Gilfillan 1965; Nriagu 1983).

Lead acetate ("sugar of lead") itself, and other lead compounds, were used as sweeteners in wine well into the nineteenth century (Christison 1835; Johnson 1989). In 1767 the disease "Devonshire colic" was identified as lead poisoning and traced to lead fittings on cider presses and lead-lined tanks to hold the apple juice, which, because of the malic acid content, readily picks up lead (Baker 1767, cited in Smith 1986; MAFF 1983). Also during this period, warnings were issued about the danger of the solution of lead from the glazes on earthenware (Drummond and Wilbraham 1957), but as late as the 1870s, lead salts, especially chromate, were being added as colors to confectionery (Dunn 1878). Thus, by 1905, when the Australian state of Victoria introduced food regulations, the first of those regulations included the prohibition of lead in or in contact with food.

The attempts of governments, however, to regulate food additives had a long history. In the late Middle Ages, for example, saffron was used by pastry cooks to simulate eggs, and by the seventeenth century, butter was being colored with annatto. But in 1574 the authorities in the French city of Bourges acted to prohibit egg simulation, and in 1641 Amsterdam prohibited annatto coloring in order to protect May butter, which, because of its color, enjoyed a premium (Meijer 1961; Truhaut and Souverain 1963).

In England in the eighteenth century, claims that chalk and ground bones were added to bread to whiten it were successfully refuted (Drummond and Wilbraham 1957). But there is no doubt that alum was used in this capacity. Calcium carbonate in the form of marble, chalk, or shells was added to beer and cider to counteract acidity; bean flour and isinglass were used as clarifiers; and copperas (iron sulfate) was added to produce a "head" (Drummond and Wilbraham 1957).

With the emergence of factories during the Industrial Revolution, adulteration increased dramatically. Most of this had to do with cheaper substitutes, but some of it involved what would now be called additives: colors, flavors, thickeners, and so forth. In 1820, F. Accum, for example, reported among other things the whitening of bread with alum, the greening of pickles with copper salts, the coloring of Gloucester cheese with red lead, and the flavoring of beer with *Cocculus indicus*. By midcentury, alum, black lead, Prussian blue, lead chromate, copper carbonate, red lead, vermilion, and copper arsenite were all being used in food and confectionery (Mitchell 1848; Hassall 1855; Campbell 1990). One example of such usage involved spent tea leaves that were "faced" with a mixture of Prussian blue and turmeric to permit their resale as green tea (Cochran 1870).

At least as early as the 1840s, sodium nitrate was employed to preserve butter (Anon. 1843). From the 1830s to the 1870s, attempts were made in Australia to preserve meat with sulfites, phosphoric and lactic acids, acetates, nitrates, and nitrites for shipment to Britain (Farrer 1980). Boric and salicylic acids emerged later in the century as flavored preservatives for sausages, milk, and cordials, and in the United States, this led eventually to the "Poison Squad" of volunteers set up by H. H. Wiley, Chief Food Chemist of the U.S. Department of Agriculture, to test the safety of preservatives then in use.

Similar concerns had surfaced elsewhere. In Canada, a report to a meeting of the British Medical Association in Toronto in 1905 resulted in the Adulteration Act, under which the first list of additives prohibited for use in food was published (Pugsley 1959). In Australia, a report by the Victorian Government Analyst covered (among other things) colors, preservatives, flavors, saccharin, and alum. This led at the end of 1905 to the aforementioned Pure Food Act (Farrer 1980).

In 1856 William Perkin's accidental discovery of mauveine initiated the dyestuffs industry, which by the beginning of the twentieth century made available a large number of synthetic colors, some 80 of which were being used in food (Noonan and Meggos 1980). Their tinctorial properties were such as to require only very small concentrations to obtain the desired result, and thus they were perceived to be, and were, much safer than the lead, copper, and even arsenic salts that had been used for so long. In 1906, the United States listed 7 colors permitted to be used in foods, and in the interests of commercial rationalization, the number of dyes of "food grade" were soon limited elsewhere by manufacturers. In the period up to World War II, the American list was extended, and lists of colors permitted to be used in foods were adopted by various other countries.

Also in the early years of the twentieth century, borates and salicylates fell into disuse as preservatives and were largely replaced with sulfites and benzoates. For thickening and stabilizing, regular flour was employed (that is, the starch in it), along with corn flour, gelatin, and gums, and the natural lecithin of egg yolk was a common emulsifier. Changes came only after the World War II, when the carcinogenicity of additives and even of ingredients became an issue, and when large numbers of new functional additives became available.

Food Additives in Processing

The appearance, flavor, texture, and keeping quality of foods have always been important, and as noted, additives have long been used to improve them all.

By enabling food to be presented in new, attractive, stable, and convenient ways, modern food additives have raised consumers' expectations to the extent that the demand for the advantages that food additives confer may be said to be sociological rather than technological.

Some may argue that it is the food technologist who has created such a demand, but at best this would be only half true. Colors, flavors, and preservatives have been used for centuries. Gelatin for jelly making, for example, was laboriously prepared in medieval times, and no doubt earlier, from calves' feet and hartshorn. Chemical aerators for baked goods have been dated from 1842 when Abel Conant obtained a patent for a baking powder. The role of the food technologist has been to simplify the preparation of many of the traditional additives and to offer better, more reliable, and safer alternatives to other older additives, while simultaneously providing and responding to the demand for greater variety, more convenience, and better keeping quality in the food products themselves.

Functional Additives

Table VII.9.1 is by no means a complete summary of food additives and the functions they perform, and it is readily apparent that some of them serve more than one purpose. The discussion that follows will concentrate not so much on the additives themselves as on the properties modified by them.

Organoleptic properties: Color and flavor. Color has a great deal to do with food selection and appreciation, and thus the argument in favor of the addition of food colors to processed foods is primarily aesthetic. Nonetheless, there are three technological justifications: (1) to intensify natural colors considered by manufacturer and consumer to be too weak; (2) to smooth over color variations in the raw material and thus to ensure standardization of the product in the marketplace; and (3) to replace color lost during processing by heating, chemical reaction (for example, bleaching with sulfur dioxide used as a preservative), or light.

Although all three justifications could be considered extensions of the aesthetic argument, they are part of the fulfillment of consumer expectations and therefore of importance to both manufacturer and consumer. Many natural colors are included in the various permitted lists; some are synthetic but their number is slowly diminishing.

No matter how tempting a food may look, however, if its flavor is found to be unacceptable it will not be bought a second time. Apart from confectionery and beverages (specifically, soft drinks), which are special cases, the arguments for the addition of flavors to foods are the same as those for adding colors. In addition, there is a fourth justification, which is (4) to make flavorful and attractive an otherwise unin-

Table VII.9.1. *Food additives and their functions*

Additives	Appearance	Texture	Keeping quality	Flavor	Nutritive value
Acidulants, alkalis & buffers	-	-	X	X	-
Aerators	X	X	-	-	-
Anticaking & free-running agents	X	X	-	-	-
Antioxidants	-	-	X	-	-
Colors	X	-	-	-	-
Emulsifiers, gums & stabilizers	X	X	-	-	-
Enzymes	-	X	-	X	-
Flavors	-	-	-	X	-
Humectants	-	X	X	-	-
Minerals	-	-	-	-	X
Preservatives	-	-	X	-	-
Sequestrants	--	X	-	-	
Sweeteners	-	-	-	X	-
Vitamins	-	-	-	-	X

Source: Farrer (1987).

teresting formulated product, such as a meat analogue from spun vegetable protein.

Natural flavorings have always been used, and by far the largest proportion of food flavors employed today are of natural origin. Because of the chemical complexity of flavors and the low concentrations normally required, it has been difficult to classify and control them, but they are generally recognized as falling into a few categories: (1) aromatic, but natural, raw materials of vegetable or animal origin, such as spices and meat extract; (2) natural flavors that are concentrates of materials in the first category; and (3) natural flavoring substances isolated from them. Then there are (4) flavoring substances that are synthesized or isolated; and finally, (5) artificial flavoring substances that simulate natural flavors but are not found in them. All flavors in the first three categories contain dozens, sometimes hundreds, of separate, naturally present, and identifiable chemical compounds.

Flavorings are sold in solution, and the *solvents* used, very often alcohol, are subject to the same scrutiny as the flavors themselves. *Flavor enhancers* are compounds that, apart from salt, have little flavor of their own but have the property of intensifying other flavors. Monosodium glutamate (MSG), possibly the best known of these, was identified early this century from a seaweed preparation known in antiquity for its property of intensifying other flavors.

Some *enzymes* are very useful in establishing flavor profiles. These substances are of natural origin and are able, among many other things, to split fats, proteins, and carbohydrates. Those associated with flavor development are usually lipases ("fat splitters") and proteinases ("protein splitters"). They are, perhaps, most obviously active in cheese. Some, in purified form, may be used to develop flavor in other products. Food acids, *acidulants,* have long been known in the form of vinegar (acetic acid), lemon juice (citric acid), and the juices of other fruits, such as verjuice from grapes and the malic acid of apples.

Their influence on flavor is well known, and many products are flavored with, say, citric or acetic acids.

Nonnutritive sweeteners (as distinct from sugars) are a special group of flavors. The oldest is saccharin, which is hundreds of times sweeter than cane sugar but leaves a slightly bitter aftertaste. More recently, the cyclamates and aspartame were introduced, but the former, probably unfairly, fell under a cloud of suspicion. The latter is now well established, and although these compounds cannot exactly duplicate the taste of sugar, they are valuable in making a useful range of products available to diabetics and people on weight-reduction diets.

Pouring and slicing: Texture. Many different substances are variously classified as *modifiers and conditioners.* Between them they contribute to all the qualities of food except nutritive value – especially to appearance and texture. They ensure that emulsions do not break, that salad dressings pour satisfactorily, that baked products do not collapse in crumbs, that crystals of ice, salt, or phosphate, do not form where they are not wanted, and so forth.

Emulsifiers facilitate the dispersion of water and oil in each other to form the emulsions of such things as cake batters, salad dressings, ice cream, processed cheese, and some meat products. Gums of vegetable origin and thickeners and stabilizers, such as gelatin, starches, and modified starches, are then used to stabilize the systems. *Humectants* maintain the texture of such items as fruitcake and Christmas puddings, by preventing them from drying out, and *anticaking agents* ensure that salt, milk powders, and the like will run freely when poured.

Aerators have been used traditionally in baked goods to establish the desired texture, in this case, crumb structure, and in so doing have contributed to appearance. Yeasts, as well as yeast food to stimulate fermentation, make up a biological system of aeration, but chemical aerators also are common. They consist

VII/Contemporary Food-Related Policy Issues

of slow-acting acidulants and baking soda and are designed to liberate carbon dioxide slowly enough to enable the desired texture to develop. *Enzymes* are used to modify texture in many products, and the oldest application may well be the use of rennet to set the curd for cheese making. Other applications are the tenderizing of meat, modification of gluten in dough making, digestion of pectin in fruit products to reduce gelling, and reduction of haze in beer.

Shelf life: Preservatives and antioxidants. Food, by its very nature, is perishable because it supports the growth of microorganisms, such as molds, yeasts, and bacteria. As they grow, these organisms can destroy food and render it unfit for human consumption. Yet sometimes, before its unfitness is apparent, such food can be positively dangerous to health. The empirical *preservatives* of history – salt, sugar, wood smoke, burning sulfur, and the alcohol and acid of fermentation – have been discussed, as have the chemical preservatives that came into use during the nineteenth century.

Modern methods of food processing, especially heat processing and refrigeration, have greatly reduced the need for chemical preservatives, although it is sometimes necessary to include one to protect a product once the container has been opened. This is particularly the case in tropical countries where many do not have home refrigeration. In addition, some modern packaging techniques rely on preservatives. For example, the flexible packaging material used for cheese frequently carries the antimycotic, sorbic acid, to inhibit the growth of the mold spores that are inevitably present on cheese surfaces.

Preservatives are also important in some processes. When meat, for example, is comminuted (as in the making of sausage), heat is generated in it, and the inclusion of a preservative, usually a sulfite, is necessary to stop the growth of microorganisms. Wine making is more difficult without the help of sulfur dioxide to control unwanted microbial growth, and for the same reason this preservative is used frequently in fruit juices.

Nitrates have long been associated with the preservation of meat, and it is now understood that nitrate reduces readily to nitrite, which inhibits the growth of *Clostridium botulinum,* the most deadly of all food-poisoning organisms. It is also the case that nitrates, via the nitrites, may give rise to nitrosamines that have proved carcinogenic in rats. Yet the benefit of the inhibition of *Cl. botulinum* outweighs the very low risk associated with nitrosamine formation.

That oils and fats develop rancidity is well known. This is a common flavor defect caused by oxidation that can also produce unacceptable colors and textures. These oxidation defects may be delayed (but not corrected or ultimately prevented) by the addition of *antioxidants,* and these compounds can, thus,

be regarded as a special class of preservatives. In addition, because rancidity is promoted by traces of copper and iron, it is sometimes beneficial to add a *sequestrant* to an oil, which locks up such trace metals and eliminates their catalytic effect.

Some antioxidants, such as ascorbic acid (vitamin C), the tocopherols (vitamin E), and natural phospholipids (lecithin, for example), occur naturally in fruit and vegetables, whereas others, like the gallates, are synthetic compounds. Antioxidants may be used in oils and fats, as well as in other food products where their use has been shown to prolong shelf life. Also it has been suggested that some antioxidants in food may offer protection against certain forms of cancer of the alimentary tract.

The acidity (or alkalinity) of a biological system is an extremely important property, usually expressed as pH within a range from 1 (very acid) through 7 (neutral) to 14 (very alkaline). *Acids,* such as the vinegar used in salad dressings, send the pH down, whereas *alkalis* move it up. If it is necessary to hold the pH steady, a *buffer* is added. This is a substance that has the ability to "soak up" the acidity or alkalinity. Phosphates are the most common buffers used in food systems. The pH of most phosphates ranges from about 3 (some salad dressings) to about 8. Low pH (high acidity) inhibits microbial growth; conversely, higher pH, either slightly acid or on the alkaline side of neutral, favors such growth, meaning that meats and some cheeses are more vulnerable to microbial spoilage than, say, tomato products. Clearly then, the keeping quality of food products may frequently be improved by lowering the pH.

Nutritive value. Vitamins and minerals are added to foods for a number of reasons, the most important being to protect or improve nutritive value. The invention of margarine in 1870 introduced a new product that lacked the vitamins A and D of butter. This deficiency was not, of course, discerned until after the discovery of vitamins early in the twentieth century, and when eventually sources of A and D were commercially available, it became obligatory for the margarine manufacturers to add them to their products. This is a good example of the addition of a nutrient to a substitute (or analogue) in order to match the concentration found in the natural product.

A fine example of the rectifying of processing losses that could otherwise endanger the health of whole communities is found in the addition of B vitamins (especially thiamine) to rice after it is stripped of a vitamin-rich husk in a polishing process intended to improve keeping quality. Similar examples include the addition of calcium to the British national loaf in wartime; the addition of vitamin D to milk; the addition of iodine to salt or to bread for the prevention of goiter; and the addition of fluoride to water for the prevention of dental caries. All are illustrative of government additive programs in the interests of their constituents.

Rather different, however, was the addition of nutrients for purely commercial reasons – an initiative that dated from the late 1940s, when vitamins became freely available as ordinary items of commerce. A rash of advertising claims were made to the effect that the addition of large "unnatural" concentrations of vitamins, and some minerals, made products more "healthy." As a result of such exaggerated claims, some countries now limit the addition of vitamins and minerals to specific products and in specific concentrations.

During the processing of food, it is inevitable that (as in the kitchen) vitamins and minerals will be lost to a greater or lesser extent. The example of polishing rice is a special case, but in both kitchen and factory, losses resulting from leaching and heat are common, which is the reason for the addition of sufficient quantities of vitamins to replace these losses. Similarly, the concentrations of some vitamins will fall during storage, and additions ensure that at the end of the stated shelf life of the product the vitamin activity claimed or expected will still be present. There might also be reason to standardize a product made from variable raw material, so that it contains the level of a vitamin or a mineral that would normally be expected of it.

Indirect Additives

Additives from the field. Many chemicals are used in agriculture, horticulture, and animal husbandry, and it is inevitable that traces of them will find their way into foods. Because of this result, some regulatory authorities subject such chemicals to the same close scrutiny as is given to additives proper. Of these substances, the most important are pesticides, which are used directly on food products. Traces large or small, usually depending on the way in which instructions for harvesting are observed, will be found on almost all raw food materials, and regulations governing the concentrations of pesticides permitted in food offered for sale have been introduced throughout the world since the 1950s. It is fortunate that the development of the wide range of chemical pesticides available today coincided quite closely with the discovery and application of modern methods of chemical analysis, which permit the measurement and detection of pesticides in very low concentrations.

Additives from the factory. Many substances are legitimately used in the food factory to facilitate processing and to clean and sanitize both plant and equipment, and these may be found in foods in minute amounts. For example, traces of boiler water additives to prevent the buildup of scale in steam boilers can be transferred in droplets of water in wet steam. Processing aids that may enter foods include flocculants and clarifying agents, enzymes, lubricants (such as

medicinal paraffin on packaging machinery), and talc (on certain types of confectionery), along with quick-release agents in the baking industry. In addition, because cleanliness and the highest hygienic standards are essential, detergents (which sometimes must be quite specialized) and sanitizers used daily in food factories, can also enter foods.

Additives from the package. The first packages in modern food technology were Nicolas Appert's glass jars of the 1780s, which were followed by tin cans in 1810. The former contribute little to the food packed in them. But the latter may transfer tin, iron, and (in the past) even lead from the solder used to seal the can, although recent concern over lead in food has resulted in the development of the welded can (to eliminate the soldered side seam). Canned foods inevitably pick up some tin. This metal has not been a cause of significant concern, but the amount that might reach the consumer has been reduced, even though it occasionally imparts a desirable flavor, as with canned asparagus.

The wide use of plastics, both rigid and flexible, in the packaging of food products has focused attention on traces of residual monomers, plasticizers, colors, and so forth that may find their way from the package into the food, especially oily and fatty products. Some of these substances are potentially dangerous, and industry worldwide has collaborated with regulators to develop strict guidelines for plastics that come into contact with foods.

Control of Food Additives

The English "Assize of Bread," which remained in force from 1266 until the Bread Act of 1822, controlled weight and price but not additives. The French "Livres des Métiers" of 1268 sought to protect both the pocket and the health of the consumer and touched upon additives by forbidding the flavoring of beer. The appointment of German wine inspectors for Swabia and Alsace dates from 1488, and measures were taken at about this time by companies in England, the Netherlands, and France to protect their good names by controlling the misuse of certain additives.

In 1701, the government of Denmark issued an order against food that was tainted or unwholesome or that could cause sickness. This was a vague regulation with only the faintest implication of additive control, but a list of colors permitted for use in food was issued in Denmark in 1836, well before the first dye was synthesized. In 1887 the use of harmful colors in foods was forbidden by the German "Color Act" (Hinton 1960; Uhl and Hansen 1961; Hamann 1963; Truhaut and Souverain 1963).

In England, additive control was inextricably linked with the control of adulteration. Accum's 1820 treatise dealt primarily with adulteration, and only with modern eyes can it be seen as an indictment of the abuse of additives. Similarly, the search for pure food in the United Kingdom, which has been well documented by I. Paulus (1974), was only incidentally related to additive control. Regulations under the Victoria (Australia) Pure Food Act of 1905 and those flowing from the American Pure Food and Drug Act of 1906 were not primarily directed at additives, although as noted, concern over lead incidentally finding its way into food was a factor. The French, too, early in the twentieth century, accepted the possibility of dangerous metals (lead, zinc, arsenic, antimony) entering the food from utensils or kitchen equipment (Truhaut and Souverain 1963), and up to World War II many countries placed limitations of one kind or another on colors, preservatives, and heavy metals in foodstuffs.

Concern over food additives, first by governments and then by consumers, began to intensify in the 1950s. There were four reasons:

1. Results from animal tests in the late 1930s strongly suggested that a so-called coal tar dye used to color butter and margarine was carcinogenic; this finding converged in the late 1940s with a growing awareness of environmental links with some forms of cancer, and a 1952 lecture by A. F. J. Butenandt on the carcinogenicity of some food colors was taken up by the press (Hamann 1963).
2. Food technology had emerged during the war as an important new subject of study, and industry was offering a range of substances that could simplify the preparation of many existing products and permit the formulation and manufacture of new ones.
3. Analytic chemistry was on the threshold of enormous advances, and the detection and measurement of additives and the like was fast becoming easier.
4. There were new needs and, through United Nations agencies, new opportunities for the international regulation of food.

Governments in a number of countries appointed committees and developed mechanisms to study and propose regulations for food additives. In 1956, the United Nations Food and Agriculture and World Health Organizations set up a Joint Expert Committee on Food Additives (JECFA) for the same purpose. JECFA adopted a set of principles as follows:

- Food additives should not be used to disguise faulty processing or handling techniques, nor to deceive the consumer with regard to the nature or quality of the food.
- Special care should be exercised in the use of additives in foods that may form a major part of the diet of some sections of the community, or that may be consumed in especially large quantities at certain seasons.
- The choice of food additives should be related to the prevailing dietary patterns within a community. The availability of essential nutrients and their distribution in the various foods consumed should be taken into account before the true significance of making a further addition of a particular nutrient (e.g., calcium or phosphorus) or of using an additive that may change the pattern of nutrients in a food (e.g., an oxidizing agent) can be assessed.
- The specifications needed for each food additive have been compiled with three main objectives in mind: to identify the substance that has been subjected to biological testing; to ensure that the substance is of the quality required for safe use in food; to reflect and encourage good manufacturing practice (JECFA 1957).

In 1953, Australia had adopted similar principles (Farrer 1990). In Canada, the Adulteration Act of 1884 had included four general principles related to food additives, and in 1906 a report to the Canadian government made six recommendations, which, though directed specifically at preservatives, were the first related to the use of food additives (McGill 1906). The four general principles called for toxicological safety, technological need, labeling, and, where there is no provision for their use, exclusion. In effect, these are the principles that govern the use of food additives today.

Expert committees in many developed countries and the Scientific Committee for Food (SCF) of the European Community (EC) gather and assess information from many sources before deciding whether to recommend a specific additive for use in food and, if so, under what conditions. In some countries the technological need for a given additive in a given product must be demonstrated. But the SCF makes the questionable assumption that a request for permission to use an additive is prima facie evidence of technological need and concerns itself only with toxicological safety. In both cases, if there is any doubt about the toxicological safety of the additive in the way it is to be used, it will not be recommended. JECFA has a key role in establishing toxicological safety, and the information it seeks is detailed and stringent. Full details of the substance are required: how it is made, likely impurities, its method and rate of use, what happens to it in food, its effect on nutrients, and the substitute additives available.

Much detailed toxicological and pharmacological information about the additive also is sought: the no-observable-effect level (NOEL) of additives – that is, the concentration in the diet expressed as mg/kg of body weight that may be consumed over several generations without producing any discernible effect;

acute and chronic toxicity; the results of studies on carcinogenicity, mutagenicity, and teratogenicity, and of changes induced in cells and the nervous system; and whether the additive triggers or exacerbates an effect caused by another substance or alters the balance between naturally occurring substances. The 1980s saw a heightened awareness of the allergenic properties of some additives, and it is possible that in the future, more questions will be asked about neurotoxicity. The results obtained from all these studies are important, but equally important are the methodologies, which also must be reported.

From all the information generated by these investigations and using a safety factor of, usually, 100, JECFA calculates an Acceptable Daily Intake (ADI). This is "the amount of a chemical which may be ingested daily, even over a lifetime, without appreciable risk to the consumer in the light of all the information available at the time of the evaluation" (JECFA 1957). *Without appreciable risk* is taken to mean the practical certainty that injury will not result after a lifetime exposure (Vettorazzi 1975). If the data are insufficient to satisfy the committee, a "Temporary ADI" may be adopted, or it may be a case of "No ADI Allocated." Substances of very low toxicity are classified as "ADI not Specified," and the designations "Not to be used" and "Decision postponed" speak for themselves. JECFA assessments are very thorough, and its recommendations count for a great deal with both national and international regulatory authorities. They are reflected in the International Standards of Codex Alimentarius, which are of increasing importance in the world trade of food products.

In some countries, permitted additives have been listed for use in all foods, as, for example, substances classified in the United States as GRAS (Generally Recognized as Safe). In others, such as the United Kingdom, the tendency has been to let the courts decide what is "harmful," although the Public Health Regulations 1925 (Preservatives etc. in Food) limited preservatives to sulfur dioxide, sulfites, benzoic acid, and benzoates, and their use to 20 categories of food (nitrates were excluded from the definition of "preservative").

The trend now is to limit additives to specified products and limit them up to specified concentrations. These limitations combine the concepts of technological need and toxicological safety-in-use. In addition, former blanket labeling provisions (for example, the general statement "Artificially Colored") are being replaced by explicit requirements for the naming of each additive, or at least inclusion on the label of identifiable codes, such as the numbering system used in Europe and elsewhere. These requirements make it possible for persons who show idiosyncratic responses to avoid substances that are safe-in-use for the vast majority of people.

Because the evidence relating to substances proposed for use as food additives is freely available all over the world, lists of permitted additives and their concentrations are very similar. Nevertheless, there are differences, most of which reflect likes, prejudices, cultural differences, and politics. In the latter case, the range is from the influence of pressure groups (those of both consumers and industry) to the widespread effect of the American "Delaney Clause." Enacted by the U.S. Congress in 1958, this clause prohibits the use in food of any substance that has been shown to cause cancer when ingested by humans or any animal.

Ostensibly unchallengeable, this clause has caused untold difficulty in America and in many other countries as well. It takes into account no qualifying circumstance, such as dose levels (that is, amount of substance in a serving), variations in the responses of different animal species, the size of the animal, the frequency of consumption of the substance, and so on. Moreover, in the words of one commentator, "this clause has generated much controversy because of recognition by most scientists that the continued existence of mankind is silent witness to the fact that low levels of carcinogens can be tolerated" (Wodicka 1980). Fortunately, no other country is so legally constrained as the United States. There was recourse to the principle of *de minimis non curat lex* ("the law is not concerned with trifles"), which enabled some scientific evaluations to be made (Middlekauf 1985), but only for a few years. In 1992 a court decision in the United States ruled that the Delaney Clause meant *no* levels of carcinogens were permissible (Winter 1993). Because of the extreme sensitivity of modern methods, this definition has created a difficult (some would say, impossible) situation.

Food Additives in Popular Culture

Late–twentieth-century food-additive usage has a foundation of scientific evaluation that is not readily apparent to the casual observer. Newspaper articles, radio and television programs, books, even school teachers, inveigh against food additives as "chemicals added to our food." Some individuals class as contaminants certain substances that add quality to processed food products, and reject additives without any understanding of their functions. Nor is it generally understood that more fearsome substances occur naturally in foods than are ever added by humans.

Some food manufacturers have sought to profit from public uneasiness by advertising their products as free from all, or at least free from stipulated classes of, additives. One result has been to reinforce many consumers' uncertainties while creating unjustified suspicion of other products.

For many people, the most damning thing about food additives is that they are "chemicals," and chemicals are perceived as something to be avoided. Unfortunately, the chemical nature of food and of life itself is generally unappreciated. The body contains thousands of chemicals from the simple, such as water and salt (sodium chloride), to the complex, such as hemoglobin and cholesterol, and all are necessary for life itself. Water, salt, and many others must be supplied in the food, whereas hemoglobin and thousands more such compounds are made by the body as required. In addition, there are substances such as cholesterol, which is both manufactured in vivo and supplied in foods, such as eggs. And then, there is monosodium glutamate (MSG), which is naturally present in some foods, manufactured in the body from others, *and* also used as an additive.

For generations, cooks have used potassium hydrogen tartrate and sodium hydrogen carbonate. Better known as cream of tartar and baking soda, respectively, both are chemicals and both are food additives. There are many such examples of additives with familiar names; but there are others, known only by intimidating chemical names, that are no less safe. Similarly, many examples could be given of chemical reactions that occur in food during cooking and processing and of others that go on continuously in the body to permit such simple operations as breathing or typing these words.

Late-twentieth-century opponents of food additives cite several concerns. A major one relates to possible long-term and cumulative effects of their consumption, and the further possibility of interactions in vivo of additives with each other, with other food constituents, and with body components. Another concern is that toxicologically innocuous substances may cause nutritional imbalance or the physical obstruction of some biological process. Certainly, none of these possibilities should be unequivocally dismissed, but the detailed and exhaustive testing of substances proposed as food additives is intended to ensure that in the circumstances in which they are eventually permitted to be used, they will be safe; that is, they will be "safe-in-use."

Early in the sixteenth century, the Renaissance physician Paracelsus wrote that all substances are poisons and it was the right dose that differentiated a poison from a remedy. This truth is the clue to the understanding and acceptance of food additives. It is a statement of what is now called dose–response, of which probably the most familiar modern example is the effect of alcohol. For each person there is a limited number of drinks ("units" of alcohol) that produce no visible response in his or her behavior, but once that limit is passed there is a clearly visible response.

Put another way, given time, it is conceivable that the body can cope with any dose, but some substances can quickly swamp the body's capability to deal with them. Cyanide is well known as a deadly poison, but marzipan contains cyanide. It is, however, in such a small concentration that the body can deal

with it without visible response, and in some countries, cyanide is specifically permitted by regulation to be present in marzipan up to a specified (very low) level. Dose–response, knowingly or not, is considered by everyone who drinks fermented liquids, and it is at the heart of food-additive usage. So, too, is risk–benefit analysis.

Certainly there is risk in food consumption, but the greatest risk is not that of food additives but, rather, that of food poisoning. This is a microbial risk, and it is increasing as people eat out more often and as an increasing number of housewives work and find themselves taking shortcuts in the kitchen. It has been calculated that the risk of food poisoning is 100,000 times greater than any risk from food additives (Truswell et al. 1978).

Nonetheless, the community has the right to expect that food-additive usage is fully explained and is as safe as it can be. And government, industry, and food technologists have the responsibility to see that it is.

K. T. H. Farrer

Bibliography

Accum, F. 1820. *Treatise on the adulteration of foods and culinary poisons.* London.
Anonymous. 1843. *Belfast News Letter.* April 14.
Baker, G. 1767. *Medical tracts read at the College of Physicians between 1767 and 1785.* London.
Begley, S. 1991. The contrarian press. *Food Technology* 45: 245-6.
Campbell, W. A. 1990. Vermilion and verdigris – not just pretty colours. *Chemistry in Britain* 26: 558-60.
Christison, R. 1835. *A Treatise on poisons in relation to medical jurisprudence, physiology and the practice of physic.* Third edition. Edinburgh.
Cochran, W. 1870. Exhausted tea leaves. *The Food Journal* 1: 161.
Codex Alimentarius Commission (1979). *Guide to the safe use of food additives.* Rome.
Drummond, J. C., and Anne Wilbraham. 1957. *The Englishman's food: A history of five centuries of English diet.* London.
Dunn, F. 1878. Confectionery analysis. *Industrial and Technological Museum Laboratory Notes and Museum Record* 1: 5-9.
Farrer, K. T. H. 1979. Adulterations of all descriptions. *Food Technology in Australia* 31: 340-9.
    1980. *A settlement amply supplied: Food technology in nineteenth century Australia.* Melbourne.
    1987. *A guide to food additives and contaminants.* Carnforth, Lancashire, England.
    1990. The Australian Food Additives Committee 1953-1963. 1. Cutting the pattern with colours. *Food Australia* 42: 146-50.
Feingold, B. F. 1975. *Why your child is hyperactive.* New York.
Gilfillan, S. C. 1965. Lead poisoning and the fall of Rome. *Journal of Occupational Medicine* 7: 53-60.
Hamann, V. 1963. *Food additive control in the Federal*

Republic of Germany. FAO Food Additive Control Series No. 7. Rome.

Hassall, A. H. 1855. *Food and its adulterations.* Reports of the *Lancet* Analytical Sanitary Commission. London.

Hinton, C. L. 1960. *Food additive control in the United Kingdom.* FAO Food Additive Control Series No. 2. Rome.

ILSI Australia. 1991. The scientific facts about MSG. Papers and discussion of a symposium held in Sydney, 31 July under the auspices of the International Life Sciences Institite, Australian Chapter. *Food Australia* 43 (Supplement): S2–19.

Johnson, H. 1989. *The story of wine.* London.

JECFA (Joint Expert Committee on Food Additives) 1957. *First Report: General principles governing the use of food additives.* Geneva.

Loblay, R. H., and A. R. Swain. 1985. Adverse reactions to tartrazine. *Food Technology in Australia* 37: 508–10.

Lockey, S. D. 1959. Allergic reactions due to F. D. and C. Yellow No. 5 tartrazine, an aniline dye used as a coloring and identifying agent in various steroids. *Annals of Allergy* 17: 719–21.

MAFF. 1983. U.K. Ministry of Agriculture, Fisheries and Food. *Food additives and contaminants committee report on the review of metals in canned foods.* FAC/REP/38. London.

McGill, A. 1906. Legislation regarding food preservatives. *British Medical Journal* 2: 858–86.

Meijer, W. 1961. *Food additive control in the Netherlands.* FAO Food Additive Control Series No. 3. Rome.

Middlekauf, R. D. 1985. Delaney meets de minimis. *Food Technology* 39: 62–9.

Miller, K. 1982. Sensitivity to tartrazine. *British Medical Journal* 285: 1597–8.

Mitchell, J. 1848. *Treatise on the falsification of food and the chemical means used to detect them.* London.

National Advisory Committee on Hyperkinesis and Food Additives. 1980. *Final report to the Nutrition Foundation.* New York.

Noonan, J. E., and H. Meggos. 1980. Synthetic food colors. In *Handbook of food additives,* Vol. 2, second edition, ed. T. E. Furia, 339–83. Boca Raton, Fla.

Nriagu, J. O. 1983. *Lead and lead poisoning in antiquity.* New York.

Paulus, I. 1974. *The search for pure food: A sociology of legislation in Britain.* London.

Pugsley, L. I. 1959. *Food additive control in Canada.* FAO Food Additive Control Series No. 1. Rome.

Smith, M. 1986. Lead in history. In *The lead debate,* ed. R. Lansdown and W. Yule, 7–24. London.

Truhaut, R., and R. Souverain. 1963. *Food additive control in France.* FAO Food Additive Control Series No. 6. Rome.

Truswell, A. S., N.-G. Asp, W. P. T. James, and B. MacMahon. 1978. Food and cancer: Special report. *Nutrition Reviews* 36: 313–14.

Uhl, E., and S. C. Hansen. 1961. *Food additive control in Denmark.* FAO Food Additive Control Series. No. 5. Rome.

Vettorazzi, G. 1975. The safety evaluation of food additives: The dynamics of toxicological decision. *Lebensmittelwissenschaft und Technologie* 8: 195–201.

Winter, C. K. 1993. Pesticide residues and the Delaney Clause. *Food Technology* 57: 81–6.

Wodicka, V. O. 1980. Legal considerations on food additives. In *Handbook of food additives,* Vol. 2. Second edition, ed. T. E. Furia, 1–12. Boca Raton, Fla.

VII.10 ❧ Substitute Foods and Ingredients

Substitute Foods

Substitute foods mimic their traditional counterparts: margarine as butter; nondairy products as milk, cream, and cheese; or extruded soybean mixes as bacon, beef, poultry, or fish. But although substitute food products may resemble their traditional counterparts, they are also likely to be composed of substances from totally different sources. The substitutes are partitioned and restructured, whereas the traditional foods are intact.

In the past, substitute foods were frequently developed as inexpensive replacements for more costly primary foods. An example is a cheese replacer. However, in recent years, substitute foods have been introduced and promoted for health reasons associated with reducing the intake of saturated fat, cholesterol, and calories. Examples are nonfat frozen desserts, egg replacers, and reduced-calorie baked goods.

On occasion, a substitute food, first launched as an inexpensive replacer, has become more expensive than its traditional counterpart. An example is margarine, originally offered as an inexpensive substitute for butter. But later it was promoted as more healthful than butter, and some special margarines became more expensive than butter (Sanford 1968).

Margarine as a Paradigm

Margarine was the first successful substitute food. A search for a butter substitute began in the early 1800s, and commercial production of margarine was launched in 1873.

Normally, the predominantly unsaturated oils used in margarine manufacture would soon oxidize and turn rancid when exposed to air. But the process of hydrogenation employed in its manufacture modifies the oils and makes them more saturated and durable. The raised melting point improves the fat's consistency and color for the deep-frying of foods, and it protects both the fats and the foods made with them from developing off-flavors. These qualities made hydrogenated oils suitable for the manufacture of margarine and other solid shortenings and for use in numerous processed foods.

Although hydrogenation serves a technological purpose, there are biological and nutritional consequences. Hydrogenation converts the *cis* form of fatty acids, naturally present in oils, to a trans form. The original molecular pattern is rearranged, and the biological quality has become nutritionally inferior. Normally, trans isomers are not present in human tissues. If present, they are less well utilized in the human body. They do not circulate in the blood, nor do they move through the tissues as liquids. They may disrupt the permeability characteristics of the membranes of the body's cells and prevent normal transport of nutrients into and out of cells (Emken 1984).

By the mid–1950s, warnings were sounded about the health risks of consuming hydrogenated fats and oils. A leading article in the *Lancet* predicted that "[t]he hydrogenation plants of our modern food industry may turn out to have contributed to the causation of a major disease" (Fats and Disease 1956: 55).

Shortly thereafter, Dr. Hugh Sinclair, at Oxford University's Laboratory of Human Nutrition, reported that hydrogenation of fats produced a deficiency of essential fatty acids (EFAs) by destroying them, or resulted in abnormal toxic fatty acids with an antiEFA effect both in animal experiments and with clinical human studies. Sinclair demonstrated that a deficiency of EFAs is "a contributory cause in neurological diseases, heart disease, arteriosclerosis, skin disease, various degenerative conditions such as cataracts and arthritis, and cancer" (Sinclair 1957: 33).

Additional reports and critical assessments of trans fatty acids in margarine and processed foods containing hydrogenated fats and oils were made by others (Bicknell 1960; Kummerow et al. 1974; Enig, Munn, and Keeney 1978; Enig et al. 1983; Keeney 1981; Enig, Budowski, and Blondheim 1984).

By the 1980s, a Canadian government task force had noted the apparent cholesterol-raising effects of trans fatty acids (Beardsley 1991). The group recommended that margarine manufacturers should reduce the amounts by modifying the hydrogenation process.

A turning point was reached in 1990, when a study directed attention to the hypercholesterolemic effect of trans fatty acids in margarine (Mensink and Katan 1990). The researchers found that these isomers raised levels of unfavorable low-density lipoproteins (LDLs) and lowered levels of favorable high-density lipoproteins (HDLs) to an even greater extent than did saturated fat. Trans fatty acids increased the lipoprotein risk profile. The researchers recommended avoidance of trans fatty acids by those at risk of atherosclerosis.

Additional incriminating evidence was revealed. At an epidemiology conference in 1993 sponsored by the American Heart Association, a team of Harvard University researchers reported the results of a survey of 239 heart attack patients and 282 healthy controls. After having analyzed the eating patterns of their subjects, the investigators had calculated the trans fatty acid intake. Even after adjustments for numerous factors, the association of trans fatty acids with heart attacks remained highly significant. Individuals who consumed more than two and a half pats of margarine daily had a nearly two and a half times greater risk of heart attack than did those who never used margarine (Ascherio 1993).

Release of the Nurses Health Study in 1993 corrob-orated these findings (Willett et al. 1993). For eight years, 85,000 nurses had been monitored for margarine intake. Women who ate products that contained hydrogenated fats and oils had increased their risks of heart attack by 70 percent. Those who ate more than four teaspoons of margarine daily in all products, and especially in white breads and cookies, were at far greater risk of coronary heart disease (CHD) than those who consumed margarine less than once a month. The researchers noted that as a result of pressure from well-intentioned but unenlightened activists, fast-food restaurants had switched from beef tallow to partially hydrogenated vegetable oils for deep-fat frying. The quantity of trans isomers in beef tallow is 3 to 5 percent; in hydrogenated vegetable oils, it is 30 percent.

The history of margarine can serve as a paradigm for the risk inherent in the use of all substitute foods. Indeed, the European Community Commission has proposed that novel foods and ingredients be regulated. At a toxicology forum, members described the need to evaluate them as a "burning and timely issue. . . . We need to look at them from both toxicological and nutritional viewpoints. It's a whole new era" (Somogyi 1993: 18).

Substitute Ingredients

Similar to substitute foods, ingredients, too, have been developed as inexpensive replacements for more costly or scarce ingredients. Examples are imitation vanillin, substituted for vanilla flavoring; inexpensive trash fish used in making surimi "sea legs" to simulate lobster; or the simulated maple taste in pancake blend syrup, in lieu of maple syrup.

In recent years, many substitute ingredients, like substitute foods, have been developed in response to concerns regarding certain health risks inherent in the industrialized diet, such as undesirable high levels of calories, fat, cholesterol, and sodium, or undesirable low levels of dietary fibers. One such effort has been to find a substitute for sugar.

Sugar Substitutes

The search for sugar substitutes has been driven by forces that involve health considerations. At first, the search was to meet a medical need: an acceptable sweetener that was tolerated by diabetics. Later, the driving forces were for sugar substitutes that were noncariogenic (to avoid tooth decay) and noncaloric or low caloric (to control weight).

Gradually, these specific health considerations became more generalized. A recent survey found that the main incentive for consumers to choose low-caloric products was to maintain overall health, rather than merely to reduce weight (Wilkes 1992).

In 1978, some 42 million Americans consumed low-calorie foods and beverages. By 1986, the number had more than doubled, to 93 million; and in 1991, it reached 101 million. In 1993, a national survey disclosed that the number had risen to 136 million, and low-calorie foods and beverages were being consumed by 73 percent of the total U.S. adult population (Fat Reduction in Foods 1993). The most popular low-calorie foods and beverages are soft drinks, consumed by 42 percent of all adults; sugar substitutes in other beverages and foods, consumed by 31 percent; sugar-free gums and candies, used by 28 percent; and sugar-free gelatins and puddings, eaten by 18 percent (Wilkes 1992).

Saccharin: An early substitute. Saccharin, an early sugar substitute, has been in continuous use as a noncaloric sweetener since the turn of the twentieth century. At present, however, it competes against more recently introduced noncaloric and low-caloric sweeteners. In fact, it was saccharin's beleaguered history of use in the United States that gave impetus to the development of alternatives (National Academy of Sciences 1975). In 1977, saccharin was found to be carcinogenic in rats, and the Food and Drug Administration (FDA) attempted to ban its use under the Delaney Clause in the 1958 Food Additives Amendment to the 1938 Food, Drug, and Cosmetic Act (U.S. House of Representatives 1977). However, the U.S. Congress enacted a moratorium on the ban, and the moratorium was renewed several times. Then, in 1991, the FDA announced its decision to withdraw the proposed 1977 ban. Thus, saccharin continues to be used in the United States food supply, and currently, it is also employed in more than 90 other countries (Wilkes 1992; Dillon 1993; Giese 1993).

Aspartame: A low-caloric substitute. Aspartame, approved by the FDA in 1981 for table use, represented the first sugar substitute approved in America in more than 25 years. Aspartame consists of two amino acids, L-phenylalanine and L-aspartic acid, and is 180 to 200 times sweeter than sucrose. Hence, it can be used at such a low level that it contributes only 4 calories per gram, and is regarded as a low-caloric sweetener (also known as a high-intensity sweetener).

Soft drinks account for 80 percent of aspartame's use in the United States. However, since aspartame's original approval, its use has been extended to thousands of food and beverage products, including carbonated soft drinks, refrigerated fruit juices, milk beverages, ready-to-drink teas, and frozen desserts, puddings, fillings, and yoghurt products, in addition to its use as a table sweetener (Wilkes 1992; Dillon 1993; Giese 1993).

The United States now accounts for approximately 80 percent of the global market for aspartame, although it is predicted that worldwide consumption will more than double by the end of the twentieth century. Aspartame is approved for use in more than 90 countries and is available, worldwide, in more than 5,000 products (Wilkes 1992).

Like saccharin, aspartame has been indicted for producing various adverse health effects, especially among heavy users (U.S. Senate 1987). These include numerous central nervous system and digestive system disturbances (Centers for Disease Control 1984; Monte 1984; Yokogoshi et al. 1984; Wurtman 1985; Drake 1986; Walton 1986; Koehler and Glaros 1988; Lipton et al. 1989; Potenza and El-Mallakh 1989; McCauliffe and Poitras 1991).

In 1984, the Centers for Disease Control conducted a four-month review of 517 consumer complaints relating to aspartame usage. The conclusions were that the complaints "do not provide evidence of the existence of serious widespread adverse health consequences attendant to the use of aspartame." However, further monitoring was advised (Centers for Disease Control 1984: 607).

Acesulfame K: A low-caloric substitute. The most recently introduced low-caloric sugar substitute is acesulfame K. Presently, it is used in about 600 food products in more than 50 countries. In 1988, the FDA approved its use for tabletop sweeteners, chewing gums, dry beverage bases, and dry dessert bases. Future approvals may be extended for confectionery products, baked goods, soft drinks, and other liquid beverages (Giese 1993).

Glycyrrhizin: Flavorant and sweetener. Glycyrrhizin, in the root of the licorice plant, is an intensely sweet triterpenoid saponin. It is from 50 to 100 times sweeter than sucrose. Extracts are used to flavor and sweeten confectionery products (Cook 1970). Glycyrrhizin is on the FDA list of GRAS (Generally Recognized as Safe) substances as a flavorant but not as a sweetening agent. However, food manufacturers have increasingly been using glycyrrhizin for its sweetening quality.

Metabolic studies have shown that glycyrrhizin can be hydrolyzed by human intestinal microflora to release glucuronic acid, a sugar that is almost completely metabolized. Moreover, glycyrrhizin has corticoid activity, influencing steroid metabolism to maintain blood pressure and volume and regulate glucose–glycogen balance. At high levels, glycyrrhizin is capable of producing a variety of health problems, including hypokalemia, high blood pressure, and muscular weakness (Chamberlain 1970; Robinson, Harrison, and Nicholson 1971; Blachley and Knochel 1980; Edwards 1991; Farese et al. 1991).

Other available sugar substitutes. Numerous low- or noncaloric sugar substitutes are in use elsewhere in the world but await approval in the United States. Sucralose, for example, was approved in 1991 for use in Canada, and shortly thereafter in Australia, Mexico, and Russia. Sucralose is 600 times sweeter than sucrose, and it does not break down in the body. It is manufactured by a multistep process that involves the selective chlorination of sucrose. Although a food-additive petition for sucralose use in 15 food and beverage categories was submitted to the FDA as early as 1987, the data are still under review. Applications are pending also in the United Kingdom and the European Community (Lite Sweeteners Maneuver 1989; Canada First Country 1991; Canada Clears Sucralose 1991; U.S. Department of Agriculture 1991).

Alitame, a low-caloric sugar substitute awaiting FDA approval, is 2,000 times sweeter than sucrose. It is formed by two amino acids, L-aspartic acid and D-alanine, and 2,2,4,4-tetramethylthietanyl, a novel amine. The aspartic acid component is metabolized normally; the alanine amide goes through the body with minimal metabolic changes. In the United States, a petition was filed for use of alitame in a broad spectrum of food products as early as 1986. But although alitame has been approved for use in Australia, New Zealand, and Mexico, the FDA is still reviewing the data (Alitame 1990; U.S. Department of Agriculture 1991).

Oligofructosaccharides (FOS) are natural sugar polymers that are potential sugar replacers. They contribute only 1.5 calories per gram and can be manufactured from sucrose by means of a fungal enzyme. They are reported to stimulate the growth of healthy bifidobacteria in the human intestine. At present, they are used in Japan (Mitsuoka 1990; Modler, McKellar, and Yaguchi 1990; Fat Reduction in Foods 1993). In the United States, interest in FOS is focused more on their value as dietary sweeteners than on their therapeutic benefits.

Potential botanical substitutes. Numerous substitute sweeteners can be derived from botanicals. Many have had a long history of use elsewhere but lack regulatory approval in the United States.

Dihydrochalcones are derived from two flavones, naringin and neohesperidin, found in citrus peels, and are several hundred times sweeter than sucrose. Many studies have confirmed their safety. The Scientific Committee for Food of the Commission of the European Community has allocated for dihydrochalcones an Acceptable Daily Intake (ADI) of 5 milligrams per kilogram of body weight. Currently, this sugar substitute is approved for use in Belgium and Argentina. The FDA has requested additional toxicological tests (New 'Super Sweeteners' 1970; McElheny 1977).

Stevia *rebaudiana* is a South American plant that yields several sweet compounds. Purified glycoside components of this plant have been employed for many years in South America. Currently, the main consumers of steviosides are the Japanese. Dental research suggests that *S. rebaudiana* may suppress the growth of oral microorganisms (Shock 1982).

The red serendipity berry (*Dioscoroephyllum cuminsii* Diels) from Africa contains a sweet component, monellin. A sweet herb from Mexico *(Lippia dulcis)* has hernandulcin, an intensely sweet sesquiterpene. Some plants commonly grown in the United States also have sweet constituents. Leaves of the herb, sweet cicely *(Myrrhis odorata),* known as the candy plant, have been used as a sweetener and flavor enhancer in conserves and to sweeten tart foods. The dried leaves of the big-leafed hydrangea (*Hydrangea macrophylla* var. Thunbergii) and the rhizomes of the common fern (*Polypodium vulgare* L.) also contain sweet constituents.

A final sweetener from botanicals is *Lo Han Kao* (*Momordica grosvenori* Swingle), a fruit from southern China. The purified sweetener from the dried fruit is about 400 times sweeter than sucrose (Inglett 1981).

Alternative approaches for substitutes. One innovation in the search for sugar substitutes is the utilization of molecules that are mirror images. Natural sugars usually occur in the so-called D-form, which is metabolized. The mirror image, which rarely occurs in nature, is in the L-form and is not metabolized. This feature makes L-sugars attractive candidates as noncaloric sugar substitutes. Currently, 3 of the 10 known L-sugars have been selected for safety testing and scale-up production studies (Process Yields No-Cal 1981; The Use of Sucrose 1982; L Sugars 1989; Giese 1993).

Another approach is to attach small molecules of sweeteners that are normally absorbed to much larger polymer molecules that are not absorbed. The sweetening agent leached to the polymer passes intact through the intestinal tract and is excreted unabsorbed (In the 1980s 1979).

The introduction of noncaloric and low-caloric sugar substitutes has not lessened the consumption of caloric sweeteners. On the contrary, there has been a steady increase in the use of *all* types of sweeteners – caloric, noncaloric, and low caloric (U.S. Department of Agriculture 1988). By 1993, the annual consumption of caloric sweeteners had reached 144.8 pounds per person in the United States (U.S. Department of Agriculture 1993).

Concomitantly, obesity continues as one of the most common and important medical conditions in the United States. More than one-third of all adults in the population are significantly overweight (Najjar and Rowland 1987; Sichieri, Everhart, and Hubbard 1992). The prevalence of obesity in some minority groups, especially Native Americans, African-Americans, and Hispanic women, reaches as high as 50 percent of these populations (Williamson et al. 1990). Although the problem of obesity is multifactorial, caloric intake is an important aspect. Clearly, the sweetening substitutes have not alleviated this problem; rather, they offer increased possibilities for food technologists to create a range of highly processed foods and beverages that further encourage poor food choices.

Fat Substitutes

The growing interest in fat and cholesterol reduction gained impetus in the 1980s and led to a multiplicity of developments for partial and total fat substitutes. In 1989 some 450 new food products introduced in the U.S. marketplace were labeled "low fat" or "nonfat." By 1992, 519 new low-fat or low-cholesterol products had been launched. Fully one-third of these products were dairy foods. Others included baked goods, condiments, meats, and snacks (Mancini 1993).

By 1993, more than two-thirds of all American adults were consuming low- or reduced-fat foods and beverages, and they expressed the desire to have still others available. It was predicted that, eventually, a low-fat version of virtually every type of food would become available (Mancini 1993).

Hydrocolloid-based fat substitutes. Many partial fat substitutes are made from cellulosics. Some are hydrocolloid stabilizers, such as cellulose gel from microcrystalline cellulose (MCC) isolated from plants (Cellulose Gel Helps 1990); powdered cellulose, a by-product of the pulp paper industry (Powdered Cellulose Reduces 1990); and semi- or totally synthetic celluloses that are nonabsorbable (Klose and Glicksman 1968).

Carbohydrate-based hydrocolloid fat substitutes consist of water-soluble polymers from vegetable gums, such as carrageenan and guar (Starches Replace Fat 1989; Fat Substitutes 1990). The polymers are also derived from plant starches, such as those from potato and corn (Potato Starch Replaces 1989); from dextrins, such as those in tapioca (Potato Starch Replaces 1989); and from maltodextrins, such as those in hydrolyzed cornstarch (Get Rid of Unwanted Fat 1989). Some of these complex carbohydrates are absorbable, whereas others are not (Klose and Glicksman 1968).

One cereal-based fat substitute, "oatrim," has notable characteristics as a fat substitute. It is derived from soluble oat fiber and from beta-glucans – complex carbohydrates contained in oat and other cereal grains – that have been found useful in lowering cholesterol. Thus, oatrim not only serves as a fat substitute but also as a cholesterol reducer.

Oatrim is made by treating oat bran and oat flour with alpha amylases. The starches are converted to amylodextrins, which, along with the beta-glucans, go into solution. The process yields a smooth, bland, white gel that can be used in numerous types of foods, such as extra-lean ground-beef mixtures, luncheon meats, cookies, muffins, and nonfat cheeses.

Consumption of oat bran had been promoted because of its ability to reduce cholesterol. However, it was found that the amounts needed were too great and could lead to gastrointestinal problems. In contrast, oatrim retains the cholesterol-reducing properties of oats and can be useful for this purpose at realistic levels of consumption (McBride 1993; American Chemical Society 1990).

Oatrim has been honored as being among the hundred most significant new technologies of 1993 (Hardin 1993). George E. Inglett and his associates at the U.S. Department of Agriculture's National Center for Agricultural Research at Peoria, Illinois, patented Oatrim in 1991. Several national and multinational food companies have obtained licenses to manufacture and use oatrim in food products.

Microparticulated protein. Several protein-based low-fat substitutes have been developed. The first to win FDA approval (1990) was Simplesse, developed by NutraSweet, a subsidiary of Monsanto. Simplesse contains only 1.3 calories per gram of food, compared to 9 calories in traditional fats. It is composed primarily of milk and egg white proteins, with added vegetable gum, lecithin, sugar, acid, and water. The molecules of the proteins are rearranged in a process called microparticulation. The resulting proteins consist of extremely small spherical particles, about one-thousandth of a millimeter in diameter. In this shape and size, the particles roll over one another, are perceived as being fluid, and mimic the mouthfeel and appearance of real fat (Fat Substitutes on the Horizon 1988).

Although the FDA concluded that Simplesse is safe because it consists of common food components, such an assumption has been challenged. The decreased particle size and homogenization of milk and egg white proteins may influence free cholesterol absorption. The technique creates stereochemical changes of amino acids and peptides, which could alter ratios of neurotransmitters and induce hyperinsulinemic responses (Roberts 1989).

In addition, concerns have been expressed about the potential sensitizing properties of Simplesse for individuals who have egg and/or milk intolerance. Dr. Ronald A. Simon, a member of FDA's Ad Hoc Advisory Committee on Hypersensitivity, warned of the possibility of unique antigens in Simplesse that might be sensitizing and induce allergenicity. He urged that careful studies be conducted prior to sanctioning Simplesse for general use to determine what reactivity-sensitivity there might be, and encouraged allergenicity tests for both the product and any metabolic breakdown products (Allergy Specialist Expresses Concern 1988; see also Zikakis 1974 and Roberts 1989).

Another fat substitute based on egg and milk is under FDA review. Kraft General Foods has petitioned for approval of its product Trailblazer, which is a modified protein texturizer. It consists of a mixture of dried egg white and whey protein concentrate or skim milk, changed in form, and combined with xanthan gum and food-grade acid. Vitamin A, normally present in milk fat, is absent from this mixture, and Kraft announced that it would add vitamin A to any frozen dessert products made with Trailblazer (Dziezak 1989).

Emulsifier-based fat substitutes. Emulsifiers to reduce fat levels were introduced as early as the 1930s, in "superglycerated" shortenings. In recent years, the application of emulsifier technology, in conjunction with other functional ingredients, has made it possible to achieve greater fat reduction (Fat Reduction in Foods 1993).

Emulsifiers themselves may be fat derivatives, with mono- and diglycerides constituting a major category. By changing the positions on the glyceride molecule, emulsifiers can be made to function differently in the body (Richard 1990). Every emulsifier has both hydrophilic and lipophilic portions, which makes the characteristic oil-and-water interface possible. The hydrophilic-lipophilic–based emulsifiers have a fat-derived component, usually one or more fatty acids attached to the hydrophilic portion of such substances as glycerine, sorbitol, sucrose, or propylene glycol. These emulsifiers, usually combined with water, can replace fat in food products. Some, such as the polyglycerol esters (PGEs), with or without added fat, offer the mouthfeel of fat. The PGEs have been used to provide about one-third fewer calories than traditional fats in food products (Richard 1990).

Due to their chemical composition or molecular weight, some of the emulsifiers (although fat derived), are poorly metabolized and absorbed. Similarly, some PGEs, which are complex molecules of glycerine and fatty acids, may be so large that they are hydrolyzed only partially in normal fat metabolism. Thus, they are not absorbed fully by the body (Richard 1990). Medium-chain triglycerides (MCTs) are metabolized by a different pathway, and normally are not stored in the body. Rather, they are burned as energy (Richard 1990).

Future synthetic fat substitutes. Sucrose polyester (SPE) functions and tastes like fat. Its molecules are too large to be broken down by the body's enzymes, and so it is neither digested nor absorbed. SPE is a mixture of hexa-, hepta-, and octa-esters that form when sucrose is esterified with long-chain fatty acid molecules derived from a fat, such as soy oil (Inglett 1981). Under development for several decades, SPE was accidentally discovered by researchers at Procter and Gamble (P&G) who were searching for fatty acids more easily digestible by premature infants than were those found in milk. It was patented by P&G in 1971 (The Use of Sucrose 1982).

In 1987, P&G petitioned the FDA to approve its SPE product (Olestra) for use as a fat substitute to replace up to 35 percent of traditional oils and shortenings for home and commercial uses, such as grilling; seasoning of vegetables, meats, and fish; and making doughnuts, sauces, and salad oils. It also replaces up to 75 percent of traditional oils and shortenings used in deep-fat frying in food-service outlets. Another use is in the commercial manufacture of snack foods, such as potato chips (McCormick 1988).

Researchers have suggested that in addition to such SPE features as its escape from digestion and absorption, other characteristics may also prove beneficial. By interfering with cholesterol absorption, SPE might lower blood cholesterol and prevent or retard the development of atherosclerosis and bowel cancer. Moreover, it was thought that SPE might help block absorption of such toxins as DDT (dichlorodiphenyltrichloroethane) and other harmful compounds that remain in the body's fatty tissues for long periods, and might also help to expedite the excretion of such toxins from the body (Glueck, Mattson, and Jandecek 1979; Progress with Sucrose Polyester 1980; The Use of Sucrose 1982; Mellies et al. 1983; Sucrose Polyester 1983).

In human tests, however, SPE produced some adverse effects, such as gastrointestinal distress, including bloating, flatulence, nausea, diarrhea, soft oily stools, anal leakage, and increased urgency or frequency of bowel movements (Mellies et al. 1983). To avoid these problems, researchers modified the product's chemical structure. Another problem was that SPE blocked absorption of vital fat-soluble vitamins, especially A and E. Thus SPE could produce serious vitamin deficiencies (Mattson, Hollenbach, and Kuehlthau 1979).

The FDA classified Olestra as a food additive, and, legally, this classification required P&G to demonstrate that the substance was safe under conditions of its intended use (Definition of the Term 1985). After this classification, safety questions were raised by a panel of a dozen scientists organized by the Medatlantic Research Foundation, a private research group. The panel requested the FDA to require additional studies on the long-term health effects of Olestra and its possible absorption by humans (Swasy 1989). In 1989, P&G initiated additional safety tests to avoid having the FDA delay any further review by several years and secured approval for Olestra in 1996.

Meanwhile, other fatty acid–based fat substitutes are being developed. Among them is phenylmethylpolysiloxane (PS), a polymeric liquid oil that is chemically inert and nonabsorbable (Braco, Baba, and Hashim 1987). Another is dialkyl dihexadecylmalonate (DDM), a synthetic fat substitute with potential applications for high-temperature use with fried snack foods. DDM is reported to be minimally digested and absorbed (Fat Substitute Menu 1990; Spearman 1990).

In addition, work is proceeding on an esterified propoxylated glycerol (EPG) nonabsorbable fat substitute intended for cooked and uncooked food products (Dziezak 1989). Under investigation are alkyl glycoside fatty acid polyester (AGFAP) (Schiller, Ellis, and Rhein 1988); raffinate polyesters (trisaccharide fatty esters) (Schiller et al. 1988); and trialkoxytricarballylate (TATCA) (Fat Substitute Menu 1990), a nonhydrolyzable noncaloric oil-like compound.

Fat substitutes and safety concerns. The prospect of many food products with fat substitutes raises safety concerns. Many of the fat substitutes, such as SPE, are regarded by the FDA as food additives, and, as a rule, a food additive represents only a very small percentage of a food product, at most only 1 or 2 percent. But with synthetic fat substitutes, the percentage is far higher. As replacers of fat – a macronutrient in the diet – these substances might replace up to 40 percent of calories consumed daily.

In this event, it seems clear that present safety tests are inadequate, and new ones need to be devised that go beyond the traditional guidelines, which in this instance would mean guidelines that address more than 100 percent of the test diet. For widely used fat substitutes, the traditional margins of safety – between no effect levels in animals and estimated exposure levels in many humans – may need to be reduced. The FDA needs to find ways of modifying the traditional safety factor and, at the same time, to assure that food additives are safe (Scarbrough 1989).

Fat substitutes and nutritional concerns. It has been suggested that low-fat diets might compromise the intake of adequate amounts of certain nutrients, including essential fatty acids, calcium, iron, and zinc (Rizek, Raper, and Tippett 1988). Unfortunately, few feeding studies have been conducted with fat substitutes. Some trials suggest that they are ineffective for weight control, because individuals fed a meal that contained a lower than usual amount of caloric fat tended to compensate by eating more food at the next meal (Stark 1988).

Similarly, in animal studies, decreased carbohydrate intake made the subjects more hungry and resulted in an increased total food intake (Gladwell 1990). All of this, of course, raises the question of whether a decreased fat intake will result in a similar compensatory mechanism if fat substitutes gain widespread use.

Many health professionals are wary about the trend toward extensive use of fat substitutes. For years, public health programs have attempted to modify dietary habits. Americans have been encouraged, repeatedly, to increase consumption of nutrient-rich vegetables, fruits, whole-grain products, and lean foods of animal origin, while decreasing consumption of high-fat and high-sugar foods.

Thus, some health professionals are concerned that the availability of numerous low-fat and nonfat products (as well as those with low-caloric and noncaloric sweeteners) will lure consumers away from healthful nutrient-dense foods to poorer selections. A spokesperson for the American Heart Association cautioned that Simplesse, the first of the newly approved fat substitutes, "may do little but reinforce the country's taste for high-fat foods" (Fat Substitute Rolled Out 1990: 39).

Food products made with fat substitutes may follow a consumption pattern similar to that of the sugar substitutes. The latter originally were hailed as the great hope for banishing obesity. However, this condition is more of a problem than ever. Will the fat substitutes, which offer a similar promise, also prove ineffective?

Beatrice Trum Hunter

Bibliography

Alitame. 1990. *Chilton's Food Engineering* 62: 31.

Allergy specialist expresses concern about Simplesse sensitivities. 1988. *Food Chemical News* 30: 36.

Alper, Joseph. 1982. Finding a sugar replacement. *What's Happening in Chemistry?*, Vol. 31.

American Chemical Society. 1990. *Oat gel replaces fat, lets frozen desserts reduce your cholesterol.* Press release, April 24.

Ascherio, A. 1993. Epidemiology conference, American Heart Association (Poster Session). Santa Fe, New Mexico. March 19, 1993. *Food Chemical News* 35: 22-3.

Aspartame critics persist, recommend avoidance during pregnancy. 1984. *Medical World News,* Psychiatry edition. February 29, pp. 11-12.

Beardsley, T. 1991. *Trans* fat: Does margarine really lower cholesterol? *Scientific American* 264: 34.

Best, D. 1987. Conference unveils new ingredient technologies. *Prepared Foods* 156: 165.

Bicknell, F. 1960. *Chemicals in food and in farm produce: Their harmful effects.* London.

Blachley, J. D., and J. P. Knochel. 1980. Tobacco chewer's hypokalemia: Licorice revisited. *The New England Journal of Medicine* 302: 784-5.

Blakeslee, S. 1990. New light being shed on early mechanisms of coronary heart disease. *The New York Times.* March 27, p. C3.

Braco, E. F., N. Baba, and S. A. Hashim. 1987. Polysiloxane: Potential noncaloric fat substitute; effects on body composition of obese Zucker rats. *American Journal of Clinical Nutrition* 46: 784-9.

Calorie Control Council. 1993. *Fat reduction in foods.* Technical Report of the Calorie Control Council. Atlanta.

Canada clears sucralose use in a range of foods, beverages. 1991. *Food Chemical News* 33: 35-6.

Canada first country to approve sucralose. 1991. *Calorie Control Commentary* 13: 1.

Cellulose gel helps trim the fat. 1990. *Dairy Foods* 91: 76.

Centers for Disease Control. 1984. Evaluation of consumer complaints related to aspartame use. *Morbidity and Mortality Weekly Report* 33: 605-7.

Chamberlain, T. J. 1970. Licorice poisoning, pseudoaldosteronism and heart failure. *Journal of the American Medical Association* 213: 1342.

Cook, M. K. 1970. Ammoniated glycyrrhizin: A useful natural

sweetener and flavour potentiator. *The Flavour Industry* 1: 831-2.

Definition of the term "food additive." 1985. Item 201(a) in *Federal Food, Drug and Cosmetic Act, as Amended, and Related Laws, 4.* Washington, D.C.

Dillon, P. M. 1993. Sweet options. *Chilton's Food Engineering* 65: 101-4.

Drake, M. E. 1986. Panic attacks and excessive aspartame ingestion. *Lancet* 328: 631.

Dziezak, J. D. 1989. Fat substitutes. *Food Technology* 43: 66-74.

Edwards, C. R. W. 1991. Lessons from licorice. *The New England Journal of Medicine* 325: 1242-3.

Emken, E. A. 1984. Nutrition and biochemistry of *trans* and positional fatty acid isomers in hydrogenated oils. *American Review of Nutrition* 4: 339-76.

Enig, M. G., P. Budowski, and S. H. Blondheim. 1984. Trans-unsaturated fatty acids in margarines and human subcutaneous fat in Israel. *Human Nutrition: Clinical Nutrition* 38C: 223-30.

Enig, M. G., R. J. Munn, and M. Keeney. 1978. Dietary fat and cancer trends - a critique. *Federation Proceedings* 2215-20. Federation of American Societies for Experimental Biology (FASEB). Bethesda, Md.

Enig, M. G., L. A. Pallansch, J. Sampugna, and M. Keeney. 1983. Fatty acid composition of the fat in selected food items with emphasis on *trans* components. *Journal of the American Oil Chemists' Society* 60: 1788-95.

Enig, M. G., L. A. Pallansch, H. E. Walker, et al. 1979. Trans fatty acids: Concerns regarding increasing levels in the American diet and possible health implications. *Proceedings: Maryland Nutrition Conference for Feed Manufacturers* 9-17. Baltimore, Md.

Farese, R. V., E. G. Biglieri, C. H. L. Shackleton, et al. 1991. Licorice-induced hypermineralocorticoidism. *The New England Journal of Medicine* 325: 1223-7.

Fats and disease. 1956. *Lancet* 270: 55.

Fat substitute menu: Under development and review. 1990. *Calorie Control Commentary* 12: 5.

Fat substitute rolled out. 1990. *American Medical News* 33: 39.

Fat substitutes. 1990. *Chilton's Food Engineering* 62:69.

Fat substitutes on the horizon. 1988. *Calorie Control Commentary* 10: 3.

Get rid of unwanted fat with GPC's maltrin/Maltodextrins. 1989. Advertisement in *Dairy Foods* 90: 27.

Giese, J. H. 1993. Alternative sweeteners and bulking agents. *Food Technology* 47: 114-26.

Gladwell, M. 1990. Does fake fat pose diet risk? *The Washington Post.* April 15: A18.

Glueck, C. J., F. H. Mattson, and R. J. Jandecek. 1979. The lowering of plasma cholesterol by sucrose polyester in subjects consuming diets with 800, 300, or less than 50 mg of cholesterol per day. *American Journal of Clinical Nutrition* 32: 1636-44.

Hardin, B. 1993. *Oatrim wins new technology award.* U.S. Department of Agriculture, Office of Public Affairs, Press Release. Washington, D.C.

Inglett, G. E. 1981. Sweeteners - a review. *Food Technology* 35: 37-8, 40-1.

Ingredient notes. 1993. *Prepared Foods* 162: 46.

In the 1980s: Nonabsorbable polymer-leached additives. 1979. (In special section "Foods of Tomorrow.") *Food Processing* 12(F): 22-3.

Keeney, M. 1981. Comments on the effects of dietary trans-fatty acids in humans. *Cancer Research* 41: 3743-4.

Klose, R. E., and M. Glicksman. 1968. Sodium carboxymethyl-cellulose. In *Handbook of food additives,* ed. T. E. Furia, 338-41. Cleveland, Ohio.

Koehler, S. M., and A. Glaros. 1988. The effect of aspartame on migraine headache. *Headache* 28: 10-14.

Kummerow, F. A., T. Mizuguchi, T. Arima, et al. 1974. Swine as an animal model in studies on atherosclerosis. *Federation Proceedings* 33: 235. Federation of American Societies for Experimental Biology (FASEB). Bethesda, Md.

Lipton, R. B., L. C. Newman, J. S. Cohen, and S. Solomon. 1989. Aspartame as a dietary trigger of headache. *Headache* 29: 90-2.

Lite sweeteners maneuver for heavyweight title. 1989. *Prepared Foods* 158: 92.

L sugars under development. 1989. *Food Technology* 43: 138.

Mancini, L. 1993. Low fat comes of age. *Chilton's Food Engineering* 65: 149-58.

Mattson, F. H., E. J. Hollenbach, and C. M. Kuehlthau. 1979. The effects of a non-absorbable fat, sucrose polyester, on the metabolism of vitamin A by the rat. *Journal of Nutrition* 109: 1688-93.

McBride, J. 1993. Two thumbs up for Oatrim. *Agricultural Research* 41: 4-7.

McCauliffe, D. P., and K. Poitras. 1991. Aspartame induced lobular panniculitis. *Journal of the American Academy of Dermatitis* 24: 298-300.

McCormick, R. 1988. Sucrose esters. *Prepared Foods* 4: 120-1.

McElheny, V. K. 1977. An alternative sweetener in focus. *The New York Times.* March 16: 42.

Mellies, M. J., R. J. Jandacek, J. D. Taulbee, et al. 1983. A double-blind placebo-controlled study of sucrose polyester in hypercholesterolemic outpatients. *American Journal of Clinical Nutrition* 37: 339-46.

Mensink, R. P., and M. B. Katan. 1990. Effects of dietary *trans* fatty acids on high-density and low-density lipoprotein cholesterol levels in healthy subjects. *The New England Journal of Medicine* 323: 439-44.

Mitsuoka, T. 1990. Bifidobacteria and their role in human health. *Journal of Industrial Microbiology* 6: 263-8.

Modler, H. W., R. C. McKellar, and M. Yaguchi. 1990. Bifidobacteria and bifidogenic factors. *Journal of the Canadian Institute of Food Science and Technology* 21: 29-41.

Moffat, A. 1990. Fiber fracas at FASEB. *Science* 3: 1442.

Monte, W. C. 1984. Aspartame: Methanol and the public health. *Journal of Applied Nutrition* 36: 42-54.

Najjar, M. F., and M. Rowland. 1987. Anthropometric reference data and prevalence of overweight. *Vital Health Statistics* 2. No. 238. National Center for Health Statistics. Hyattsville, Md.

National Academy of Sciences. 1975. *Sweeteners: Issues and uncertainties,* 127-74. Washington, D.C.

New "super sweeteners" made from citrus peel. 1970. (In special section "Foods of Tomorrow.") *Food Processing* 3 (Summer F): 4-6.

Pfizer moves in a new direction. 1991. (In section "Industry Report.") *Chilton's Food Engineering* 63: 17.

Potato starch replaces fats and oils. 1989. *Prepared Foods* 158: 91.

Potenza, D. P., and R. S. El-Mallakh. 1989. Aspartame: Clinical update. *Connecticut Medicine* 53: 395-400.

Powdered cellulose reduces fat content in fried foods. 1990. *Chilton's Food Engineering* 61: 40.

Process yields no-cal "left-handed" sugars. 1981. *Food Development* 15: 10.

Progress with sucrose polyester. 1980. *Research Resources Reporter* 4: 8-9.

Richard, W. D. 1990. Lower calorie food formulations using lipid-based ingredients. Symposium in *Fat and Fiber*. Calorie Control Council/George Washington University School of Medicine. Washington, D.C.

Rizek, R. L., N. R. Raper, and K. S. Tippett. 1988. Trends in U.S. fat and oil consumption. *Journal of the American Oil Chemists' Society* 65: 722-3.

Roberts, H. J. 1989. The licensing of Simplesse. An open letter to the FDA. *Journal of Applied Nutrition* 41: 42-3.

Robinson, H. J., F. S. Harrison, and J. T. L. Nicholson. 1971. Cardiac abnormalities due to licorice intoxication. *Pennsylvania Medicine* 74: 51-4.

Sanford, D. 1968. Unmilk, cowing the consumer. *New Republic.* August 10, pp. 11-3.

Scarbrough, F. E. 1989. Safety and testing of fat substitutes and replacements. Annual Meeting, American Dietetic Association. In *Fats, Nutrients or Nuisance?,* 72. Kansas City, Mo.

Schiller, Z., J. E. Ellis, and R. Rhein. 1988. NutraSweet sets out for fat-substitute city. *Business Week.* February 15, pp. 100-3.

Shock, C. C. 1982. Rebaudi's stevia: Natural noncaloric sweeteners. *California Agriculture* 37: 4-5.

Sichieri, R., J. E. Everhart, and V. S. Hubbard. 1992. Relative weight classifications in the assessment of underweight and overweight in the United States. *International Journal of Obesity* 16: 303-12.

Sinclair, H. 1957. Sees essential fatty acid lack causing degenerative disease. *Drug Trade News* 32: 33, 50.

Somogyi, A. 1993. Dietary effects in toxicity testing: When do physiological effects become toxic manifestations? Panel Discussion, Toxicology Forum, Aspen, Colorado. *Food Chemical News* 35: 16-18.

Spearman, M. E. 1990. Malonate esters: Thermally stable non-nutritive oil for snack food use. Symposium in *Fat and Fiber*. Calorie Control Council/George Washington University School of Medicine. Washington, D.C.

Specialty starches function as fat and oil replacements. 1990. *Chilton's Food Engineering* 62: 30.

Starches replace fat. 1989. *Prepared Foods* 158: 102.

Stark, C. 1988. Fake fats raise real issues. *Professional Perspectives* 4: 4. Nutritional Science, Cornell University, Ithaca, New York.

Sucrose polyester for hypercholesterolemia. 1983. *Anabolism, Journal of Preventive Medicine* 2: 1-2.

Swasy, A. 1989. P&G fat substitute moves sluggishly toward market. *Wall Street Journal.* April 24, p. 1.

U.S. Department of Agriculture, Economic Research Service. 1988. *Sugar and sweetener, situation and outlook yearbook,* Table 25: 57. Washington, D.C.

U.S. Department of Agriculture, Economic Research Service. 1991. World and U.S. high intensity sweeteners. *Sugar and sweetener, situation and outlook report* 16: 25. Washington, D.C.

U.S. Department of Agriculture, Economic Research Service. 1993. *Sugar and sweetener, situation and outlook yearbook,* Table 44: 79. Washington, D.C.

The use of sucrose polyester in weight reduction therapy. 1982. *Journal of the American Medical Association* 248: 2963-4.

U.S. House of Representatives. 1977. *Proposed saccharin ban: Hearings before the Subcommittee on Health and the Environment of the Committee on Interstate and Foreign Commerce.* Washington, D.C.

U.S. Senate. 1987. *"NutraSweet" - health and safety concerns: Hearings before the Subcommittee on Labor and Human Resources.* Washington, D.C.

Walton, R. G. 1986. Seizure and mania after high intake of aspartame. *Psychosomatics* 27: 218-20.

Wilkes, A. P. 1992. Expanded options for sweetening low-calorie foods. *Food Product Design* 2: 58-69.

Willett, W. C., M. J. Stampfer, J. E. Manson, et al. 1993. Intake of *trans* fatty acids and risk of coronary heart disease among women. *The Lancet* 341: 581-5.

Williamson, D. F., H. S. Kahn, P. L. Remington, and R. F. Anda. 1990. The 10-year incidence of overweight and major weight gains in U.S. adults. *Archives of Internal Medicine* 150: 665-72.

Wurtman, R. J. 1985. Aspartame: Possible effects on seizure susceptibility. *Lancet* 326: 201.

Yokogoshi, H., C. H. Roberts, B. Callabero, and R. J. Wurtman. 1984. Effects of aspartame and glucose administration on brain and plasma levels of large neutral amino acids and brain S-hydroxyindoles. *American Journal of Clinical Nutrition* 40: 1-7.

Zikakis, J. P. 1974. Homogenized milk and atherosclerosis. Letter in *Science* 183: 472-3.

VII.11 ~ Nonfoods as Dietary Supplements

Food: A substance (of natural origin) ingested to maintain life and growth.

Diet: The habitual pattern of consumption of food and drink.

Supplement: That which supplies a deficiency or fulfills a need.

The semantically inclined will, no doubt, perceive an element of inconsistency in the title of this contribution. Any food(stuff) ingested for a nutritional purpose is, it could be argued, ipso facto a dietary component. To refer to "nonfood dietary supplements" would, therefore, be meaningless.

On the other hand, foods are often defined in traditional-historical terms, and it is apparent that there are a substantial number of "nutritionally significant" substances which, although not ordinarily components of a diet, may nevertheless be ingested in special circumstances. Whether such "foreign" substances are then described as food(stuffs) or as dietary nonfood(stuffs) is very much a matter of opinion.

The issue is further clouded by a tendency to regard foods as being of natural origin, whereas certain dietary supplements, although having a clearly definable nutritional role, may nevertheless have a "nonnatural" (synthetic) origin. And whereas "true" foods are rarely challenged in terms of potential toxicity, this is not the case with supplements - as evidenced, for example, by the American report on the safety of amino acids used as dietary supplements (Anderson, Fisher, and Raiten 1993).

Again, one must distinguish between nonfoods as dietary supplements and nonfoods as dietary components. Geophagists, picaists, and drug addicts may, in certain circumstances, ingest large amounts of nonfood materials, but these fall outside the scope of this discussion. Supplementation implies that the additional material is introduced intentionally for an avowedly dietary reason and is a substance that could not, in normal circumstances, be supplied by realistic dietary manipulation.

Since the purpose of dietary supplementation is to improve the nutritional status of the subject (thus distinguishing dietary supplements from pharmacological treatments), its practice must be congruous with generally accepted nutritional thought – which, in turn, implies that the intentional use of dietary supplements is a development of fairly recent origin. Consequently, the significance attributed to many nonfood supplements has, in recent years, ebbed and flowed, thereby reflecting the kaleidoscopic nature of orthodox nutritional thought itself.

By the same token, it is equally apparent that the concept of nonfood dietary supplements is a relative one, with the lines of categorization shifting from community to community. Thus dietary fiber, a widely advocated nonfood dietary supplement in the Western European diet, would have no such status in many African communities. Equally difficult to define is the distinction between the use of a supplement in a dietary capacity and its use as a pharmacological agent. Megadoses of ascorbic acid (vitamin C) may, in this respect, be contrasted with the more moderate levels used for orthodox dietary supplementation; and the use of arginine to modify immunity and intestinal carrier systems could, it may be argued, reflect a pharmacological, rather than a nutritional, role for supplementation (Hirst 1993; Park 1993).

By the late nineteenth century, the categorization of foods in functional terms had progressed considerably. Foods were described as "body-building" (nitrogenous) or "energy-forming" (nonnitrogenous), and there was, consequently, a tendency to simplify dietary concepts and to limit precepts to recognizably bona fide members of these two groups. However, by the turn of the century, the recognition of the role of vitamins – nonfoods in a quantitative sense – and the blurring of the lines of demarcation between "energy" and "growth" foods provided a more flexible conceptual framework for the proliferation of ideas about the usefulness of nonfood supplementation.

This chapter therefore deals with substances that, without falling into the conventional categories of dietary components (protein, energy sources, vitamins, and minerals), are nevertheless believed to enhance dietary effectiveness. They would not, in normal circumstances, be supplied by customary dietary components – either because the foods containing them are ingested in supposedly inadequate amounts (as in the case of dietary fiber in certain communities) or because the substance in question is not readily available from food(stuff) sources. This latter category is, in evolutionary terms, less likely to exist and, it could be argued, implies more of a pharmacological relationship than a nutritional one. Perhaps with this in mind, Michele Sadler, in a recent discussion of dietary supplements, has referred to them as "Functional Foods" and has defined them as lying between foods and pharmaceuticals (1993).

Three examples of "nonfood" dietary supplements are discussed below. All have achieved, at different times, some significance as supplements during the last 40 years or so, and they represent three "etiologically" different categories.

Bioflavonoids

The term "bioflavonoids" has been widely used to refer to those flavonoids that are believed to have pharmacological or nutritional properties. They have no apparently essential role in nutrition and, consequently, no daily requirement can be specified. Nevertheless, for a period of some 30 years they were held to have an "adjuvant" role in maintaining good health – possibly by enhancing the activity of vitamin C.

The flavonoids are a large group of plant compounds based on a $C_6C_3C_6$ skeleton. They are of widespread distribution in the plant kingdom, being virtually ubiquitous in angiosperms and also existing in more primitive groups, such as green algae, and Bryophyta, including Hepaticae. It has been estimated that in the West, the average per capita daily intake of bioflavonoids is approximately 1 gram (g) (Middleton 1988). Higher animals have, perforce, evolved in an environment in which, of necessity, their feeding habits exposed them to a wide range of flavonoid material, ingested as "secondary" components of foodstuffs. It is, therefore, quite conceivable that this evolutionary exposure to a wide range of flavonoids has elicited physiological and biochemical responses in higher animals. Certainly some bioflavonoid features, such as their ability to chelate with metals and the antioxidant activity associated with hydroxyl groups, indicate a considerable potential for biochemical involvements.

Bioflavonoids first attracted the attention of nutritionists in the 1930s when Hungarian workers reported that certain vegetables and fruits (notably citrus) contained substances capable of enhancing the antiscorbutic properties of ascorbic acid (vitamin C) and even of partially substituting for it. It was claimed that "the age-old beneficial effect of fruit juice is partly due to its vitamin P *[sic]* content" (Bentsáth, Rusznyák, and Szent-Györgyi 1937: 327); it was also suggested that "citrin," a flavonoid preparation, could prolong the survival period of scorbutic guinea pigs and that extracts of *Citrus limon* and *Capsicum annuum* could correct capillary fragility – a condition characteristic of ascorbic acid deficiency (Bentsáth, Rusznyák, and Szent-Györgyi 1936). The new factor(s) was regarded as separate from vitamin

C and was designated "vitamin P" (Rusznyák and Szent-Györgyi 1936), and sometimes was named, primarily by French workers, the "C_2" factor. However, the true nature of the relationship (if any) between the bioflavonoids and vitamin C was unclear, and later work indicated that some of the earlier results were probably attributable to traces of vitamin C in the flavonoid preparations. Nevertheless, by the late 1930s the bioflavonoids had acquired a niche, albeit a minor one, in the annals of vitaminology. But considerable reservations remained about their real nutritional significance (Harris 1938: 28).

In 1949 Harold Scarborough and A. L. Bacharach published an important review article summarizing the work done between 1935 and 1949, and dismissing any suggestion that vitamin P could generally substitute for vitamin C. They centered their attention on the influence of bioflavonoids on capillary resistance and quoted with approval an earlier statement that "guinea pigs placed on a scorbutic diet supplemented with adequate amounts of ascorbic acid show a decline in capillary strength . . . restorable by vitamin P" (Scarborough and Bacharach 1949: 11).

The consensus of opinion in 1950 was that flavonoids were of physiological significance and that their main influence (on capillary resistance) was mediated independently of vitamin C. Nevertheless, the Joint Committee on Biochemical Nomenclature (United States) recommended in 1950 that the term "vitamin P" be replaced by the designation "bioflavonoids"; and in 1980 the (U.K.) Committee on Dietary Allowances of the Food and Nutrition Board (COMA) indicated that the bioflavonoids should be regarded as pharmacological, rather than as nutritional, agents.

Interest in the possible nutritional significance of bioflavonoids forged ahead during the 1950s (see Table VII.11.1), with a continuing emphasis upon their possible adjuvant relationship with vitamin C. It is interesting to note that almost half of the bioflavonoid papers published during the period from 1948 to 1957 dealt with the specific bioflavonoid rutin (quercetin-3-rutinoside).

Table VII.11.1. *Publications during 1930–90 relating to the nutritional significance of (a) bioflavonoids and (b) carnitine*

	Bioflavonoids	Carnitine
1930–9	29 [53]	0
1940–9	51 [102]	0
1950–9	60 [172]	9 [25]
1960–9	35 [132]	9 [35]
1970–9	19 [85]	23 [104]
1980–9	7 [30]	93 [384]

Source: Based on papers abstracted in *Nutrition Abstracts and Reviews* and expressed per 20,000 total nutrition papers; the figures in brackets refer to the "uncorrected" total number of publications on bioflavonoids and carnitine, respectively.

Rutin was widely used at the time in model experimental systems and is still sold as a dietary supplement, sometimes in the form of extracts of buckwheat *(Fagopyrum esculentum),* one of its principal natural sources. Other specific compounds to receive attention by nutritionists were quercetin and hesperidin.

Work on bioflavonoids was extended in the 1950s and 1960s to include a wide range of supposed physiological and biochemical involvements. Possibly for historical reasons, workers in Eastern European countries were particularly active in this respect. K. Böhm, in his 1968 monograph, cited some 40 definable influences of flavonoids in humans – although the evidence for many of these was weak and sometimes contradictory. M. Gabor, in his 1972 monograph, dealt almost exclusively with one of these suggested areas, namely the supposed anti-inflammatory effect of flavonoids. Other, and more overtly nutritional, areas where bioflavonoids were believed to have a role were hepatic detoxication and lipid utilization (Hughes 1978).

Nonetheless, by the 1960s, interest in a nutritional role for bioflavonoids had peaked, along with their associated use as dietary supplements (see Table VII.11.1). Thereafter the main nutritional interest in bioflavonoids centered on their supposed synergistic relationship with vitamin C and their possible role as antioxidants. There was substantial evidence that bioflavonoids could "enhance" the ascorbic acid status of hypovitaminotic C guinea pigs, and much work in the 1960s and 1970s was aimed at elucidating the nature of this relationship. Discussions centered on whether bioflavonoids could actually substitute for (or synergistically assist) vitamin C in some of its roles, or whether they increased the availability of vitamin C either by protecting it from oxidative breakdown in the tissues or by enhancing its absorption from the gastrointestinal tract (Hughes and Wilson 1977).

Two aspects of flavonoid metabolism attracted some attention – their antioxidant capacity and, in some cases, an apparent mutagenicity. But studies of the nutritional significance of these features gave inconsistent and difficult-to-interpret results. For example, one study dealing with mice indicated that, whereas a dietary supplement of quercetin shortened life span, a flavonoid-rich extract of black currants (containing quercetin together with other flavonoids) extended it (Jones and Hughes 1982). Moreover, none of these studies provided any incontrovertible evidence of an essential role for bioflavonoids in nutrition, and a recent reviewer opined that their function in health and disease as natural biological response modifiers still needed to be determined (Middleton 1988). M. M. Cody, in a contribution to the *Handbook of Vitamins,* dealt with bioflavonoids under the heading "Substances without vitamin status" (Cody 1984: 578–85).

Nonetheless, there remains a certain amount of residual evidence favoring the use of bioflavonoids as a dietary supplement to enhance the absorption of vitamin C from the gastrointestinal tract and, possibly, its subsequent retention by the tissues (Hughes and Wilson 1977). As a consequence, to advocate the ingestion of "natural" vitamin C (as, for example, in the form of bioflavonoid-rich black currant juice) – rather than the synthetic "tablet" form of the vitamin – by persons otherwise recalcitrant to vitamin C absorption (such as the elderly) is not entirely without experimental basis.

For the decade 1980–9, however, only 30 "nutritionally orientated" bioflavonoid publications could be identified, and general interest in the erstwhile suspected nutritional role of bioflavonoids and in their consequent use in dietary supplementation would now appear to be waning.

The recent COMA report dismissed them as an "unnecessary substance" and made no recommendation for their use as a supplement.

Dietary Fiber

There were many "latent" references to dietary fiber before it was identified and characterized as a specific dietary component. Early writers on diet, such as Thomas Elyot (*The Castel of Helth …* [1541]), Ludovicus Nonnius (*De Re Cibaria* [1645]), and Thomas Moffet (*Health's Improvements* [1655]), who referred to the laxative property of whole-meal bread (when compared with lower-extraction-rate breads), were in reality commenting on the fiber content.

Thomas Cogan, the Elizabethan dietitian, wrote in his *The Haven of Health:* "Browne bread made of the coursest of wheate floure, having in it much branne . . . shortly descendeth from the stomacke [and] . . . such as have beene used to fine bread, when they have beene costive, by eating browne bread and butter have been made soluble" (1612: 25).

Similarly, Thomas Venner, the Bath physician, wrote of whole-meal bread in his *Via Recta ad Vitam Longam* that

> by reason of some part of the bran which is contained in it, it doth sooner descend and move the belly, for there is a kind of abstersive [laxative] faculty in the bran: wherefore for those that are healthy, and yet subject to costiveness, and also for such as would not wax grosse, it is most profitable (1638: 25).

This comment is curiously congruous with the standpoint adopted by present-day fibrophiles.

Hugh Trowell, in his extensive bibliography *Dietary Fibre in Human Nutrition* (1979), mentions a paper written in 1919 as the earliest to deal with definable fiber (cellulose) per se. Arthur Rendle-Short, a British surgeon, argued in the 1920s that epidemiological evidence suggested a relationship between lack of dietary cellulose and the incidence of appendicitis. The earliest title in Trowell's bibliography to contain the term "fibre" was one by M. A. Bloom, published in 1930.

It was not until the 1970s, however, that a wide interest emerged in the nutritional significance of what had been regarded, until then, merely as dietary "roughage," or waste material. Three names are usually associated with this phase in the history of fiber. One is that of T. L. Cleave, a British naval doctor, who argued (1974) that a number of pathological conditions were probably attributable to an increased intake of refined sugar and starch. Although Cleave did not emphasize the mirror image of his thesis – namely, that an increasingly refined diet was in reality a low-fiber one – he has, nevertheless, been widely, and somewhat incorrectly, hailed as a pioneer of current dietary fiber hypotheses.

A more overt and direct link between fiber lack and disease was promulgated in the 1970s by Hugh Trowell (1979; see also 1985) and by Denis Burkitt (1971), and the genesis of modern fiber studies has become almost synonymous with their names. Burkitt himself, in tracing the early history of thought on fiber, has included a fourth name, that of A. R. Walker of South Africa. The number of identifiable publications on the subject of dietary fiber rose from an annual average of 10 in the late 1960s to 125 in the early 1970s; 10 years later (in 1983), the average had risen to well over 500. Trowell's original thesis (1960) stemmed from his observation that a number of diseases that appeared to be characteristic of affluent Western technological communities were rare or absent in the more "primitive" parts of Africa with which he was familiar. He drew particular attention to the differential incidence of diseases of the gastrointestinal tract and suggested that a high consumption of fiber-rich foods was protective against noninfective diseases of the large bowel. Similarly, and independently, Burkitt (in 1971) published his evidence that dietary fiber might be protective against colorectal cancer.

At that time, however, there was no generally accepted definition of dietary fiber, and much confusion stemmed from the use of values for "crude" fiber (the residue left after serial extraction with acid and alkali). This was a measure that excluded the bulk of the cellulose and hemicellulose material, both important components of dietary fiber. The problem of definition was, of course, inextricably linked to difficulties in the development of a method for the accurate determination of fiber (Englyst and Cummings 1990). Trowell, in 1971, defined dietary fiber as the plant cell material that was resistant to digestion by the gastrointestinal enzymes, and this became the accepted definition. More recently the term "dietary fiber" has been displaced by the resurrected form "nonstarch polysaccharide material," which reflects current analytic procedures.

The original "dietary fiber hypothesis" was soon extended by other workers to embrace suggested relationships between dietary fiber and nongastrointestinal diseases, particularly cardiovascular disorders (for example, Judd 1985; Kritchevsky 1988). Epidemiological studies indicated a negative correlation between fiber intake and the incidence of cardiovascular disease, and experimental studies showed that certain types of dietary fiber were potent hypocholesterolemic agents. However, relationships of this type posed a problem. By definition, dietary fiber was a substance that did not leave the gastrointestinal tract. How then could one explain its supposed "extragastrointestinal" effects?

Nor was it always easy to distinguish between a direct protective effect of fiber and a displacement effect on "harmful" dietary components. Mechanisms based on a fiber-mediated inhibition of cholesterol absorption or an increased bile acid excretion were among those mooted. But much of the epidemiological work related to fruit and vegetable intake and not to intake of fiber per se. M. L. Burr and P. M. Sweetnam (1982), however, found that in Wales, a vegetarian lifestyle could be correlated with a reduced incidence of heart disease, but fiber intake could not.

The picture was further complicated by the interrelationships now known to exist between dietary fiber and the intestinal flora. This is a complex two-way relationship. Not only are certain types of fiber subject to degradation by colonic bacteria, but there is also increasing evidence that fiber itself may, in turn, modify the nature and metabolic activity of the colonic flora, with consequent modifications to the formation and absorption of a wide range of metabolites. Considerations of this type have led to suggestions that dietary fiber may modify the estrogen status in females, with consequent implications for a protective role for fiber in breast cancer and, possibly, other cancers (Hughes 1990;Adlercreutz 1991).

The current consensus would appear to favor an increased fiber intake in the Western-type diet, but an optimal intake has yet to be clearly delineated. Appeals to primitive dietary patterns are of little help in this respect, as the fiber intake of humans has fluctuated substantially during their stay on earth. Estimates based on coprolite analysis have indicated substantially higher ingestion of dietary fiber by primitive peoples than by their present-day descendants, with daily intakes of 100 to 200 grams occurring at certain periods. In addition, there have been significant changes in fiber intake at critical points in the socioeconomic development of humanity, such as during the "neolithic transition" (Eaton 1990).

Fifteen years after the birth of the fiber hypothesis, Rodney H. Taylor, in a leading article in the *British Medical Journal* (1984), questioned the prophylactic usefulness of high-fiber diets except for improving colonic function and alleviating constipation. Recent dietary precepts are almost equally noncommittal in their advocacy of dietary fiber. The most recent COMA recommendation (1991) echoed Taylor's doubts. Although advocating an increase in NSP (nonstarch polysaccharides) from the current average intake of 13 g/day to 18 g/day to improve bowel function, the committee was unable to find sufficient evidence for a direct mediating influence of fiber in other suggested areas, such as diabetes and cardiovascular disease. Moreover, the increased intake, it was suggested, should be attained by dietary manipulation, rather than by overt supplementation. It is possible that after a quarter of a century of often frenzied investigative activity, the dietary fiber movement is beginning to disintegrate.

Carnitine

Carnitine was discovered at the beginning of this century when its presence in Liebig's meat extract – at the time a popular dietary supplement – was reported. Twenty years later its structure was elucidated, and it was shown to be (beta-hydroxy-gamma-(trimethylamino)-butyric acid. But it attracted little biochemical or nutritional attention until the late 1950s when its role in the metabolism of fats was described. Reviewing the situation at that time, G. Fraenkel and S. Friedman wrote that "a small amount of evidence has been pieced together indicating that carnitine may be active in the metabolism of fats or their derivatives" (1957: 104).

Subsequent, in vivo studies with labeled fatty acids confirmed this conclusion, and within a few years the role of carnitine in stimulating the mitochondrial oxidation of fatty acids was generally accepted (Olson 1966). Subsequent investigations revealed the nature of the mechanism of this stimulation when it was shown that carnitine acts as a transport molecule for the movement of long-chain fatty acid molecules into the mitochondrial matrix. A number of situations in which carnitine has a derived or secondary role as a buffering agent for acyl groups have also been described (Cerretelli and Marconi 1990).

A lack of carnitine, or a reduced or defective activity of one or more of the transport enzymes, would therefore reduce the availability of fat as a source of energy. This could be significant in cases where it is believed that a substantial proportion of the energy metabolism is derived from fat – as in the newly born infant or in cardiac muscle metabolism. It would appear, however, that in the short term, substantial falls in carnitine are required before an impairment of fatty acid oxidation becomes apparent (Carroll, Carter, and Perlman 1987).

The body is able to biosynthesize carnitine, and by the 1980s the biosynthetic pathway had been elucidated. It was shown that the precursor molecules were lysine and methionine, two essential dietary amino acids. The lysine is methylated by the methionine to form the protein-bound trimethyllysine, which is then hydroxylated to form beta-hydroxy-N-trimethyllysine. This is converted, first to gamma-butyrobetaine and then to carnitine (Rebouche and Paulson 1986).

Carnitine deficiency diseases, resulting from a defect in the biosynthetic pathway, have been described. Such a condition was first reported by A. G. Engel and C. Angelini in 1973, and since then a number of apparently different types of carnitine deficiency have been noted and discussed in the literature. Two basic types are sometimes recognized – systemic carnitine deficiency (characterized by a general reduction of carnitine in the tissues, including the liver) and muscle or myopathic deficiency, in which the reduction in carnitine occurs in the muscles. In such cases, carnitine replacement therapy is a recognized mode of treatment; supplementation must take the form of L-carnitine, the DL/D form being ineffective and, in some cases, further exacerbating the condition.

There are also a number of secondary or noncongenital syndromes that respond to treatment with carnitine, some of which are side effects of other clinical conditions (Rebouche and Paulson 1986; Smith and Dippenaar 1990). Carnitine levels are, in general, lower at birth than in adulthood, and there is evidence that some newly born infants may have a reduced capacity for carnitine biosynthesis. At birth, too, fatty acids become increasingly important as an energy source (Smith and Dippenaar 1990), and it has been suggested that all infants should receive carnitine supplements at least until the end of their first year of life (Olson, Nelson, and Rebouche 1989; Giovannini, Agostoni, and Salari 1991). A recent COMA report accepted that carnitine supplements could be necessary "for low birth weight or preterm infants" (Committee on Medical Aspects of Food Policy 1991: 135). Barbara Bowman, in a recent review, has pointed out that carnitine "appears to be a conditionally essential nutrient in malnutrition and in newborns, pregnant and lactating women, patients receiving dialysis or total parenteral nutrition, and patients with liver disease" (1992: 142).

Many of these examples of carnitine supplementation presumably stem from the correction of an abnormal feature of carnitine metabolism or by restoring a defective carnitine status to normal. Others are more overtly pharmacological than nutritional in nature. A striking example of the pharmacological use of [acetyl]carnitine was the report of a double-blind, randomized, controlled clinical trial in which the progression of Alzheimer's disease was significantly delayed by the ingestion of 2 grams of acetylcarnitine daily for a year (Spagnoli et al. 1991).

Whether carnitine supplementation has a role in normal or "nonclinical" nutrition is more debatable. Much of the discussion in this respect has centered on the possibility of using carnitine supplements to enhance aerobic power and the capacity for physical exercise (Cerretelli and Marconi 1990). Theoretically, such supplementation could be advantageous in a situation characterized by an increased demand for "physical energy" and, more specifically, in circumstances characterized by (1) an increased use of fatty acids as an energy source, and (2) a depression in the biosynthetic capacity of the body.

A depressed biosynthetic capacity might, in turn, result from a reduced availability of the essential nutrients involved in the biosynthetic pathway. This latter consideration – the influence of other dietary factors on carnitine status – could be of some significance and is central to the concept of carnitine as a conditionally essential nutrient.

The hydroxylation reactions in the formation of carnitine from lysine and methionine require ascorbic acid (vitamin C) as a cofactor; in addition, two members of the vitamin B complex (niacin and pyridoxine) are involved, as is iron. The endogenous formation of carnitine, therefore, involves the participation of six obligatory dietary components – a requirement that places it in a "high risk" category with respect to inadequate supporting diets. A review has underlined this point:

> If the exogenous supply of carnitine is temporarily cut off, and provided the subject is not suffering from protein hypo- or malnutrition (as may happen in vegetarianism) plasma carnitine concentrations do not shift . . . [but] however, drop sharply if the co-factors essential for carnitine synthesis are lacking (Giovannini, Agostoni, and Salari 1991: 88).

Of the essential cofactors, lysine (often the limiting amino acid in poor-quality diets and frequently present in a physiologically unavailable form [Helmut 1989]) and ascorbic acid (vitamin C) are probably the most critically important ones. There is evidence, both experimental and circumstantial, that a reduced availability of one or both of these essential nutrients results in a fall of carnitine and possibly a reduction of carnitine-mediated energy release. Thus, the intake of three compounds – preformed carnitine, lysine, and vitamin C (the three forming the "carnitine base") – will determine the carnitine status of an individual, and one can point to a number of historically significant situations where a reduced carnitine base has resulted in the emergence of a stage consistent with what we now know to be the physiological consequences of carnitine deficiency: primarily a reduced capacity for sustained muscular exercise (Hughes 1993).

Thus, there are grounds for believing that the fatigue and lassitude, invariably present in the early stages of scurvy, could have resulted from the impairment of carnitine synthesis, which in turn would have resulted from a deficiency of vitamin C (Hughes 1981, 1993; see also Figures VII.11.1 and VII.11.2). It is tempting to speculate that the lowered aptitude for physical

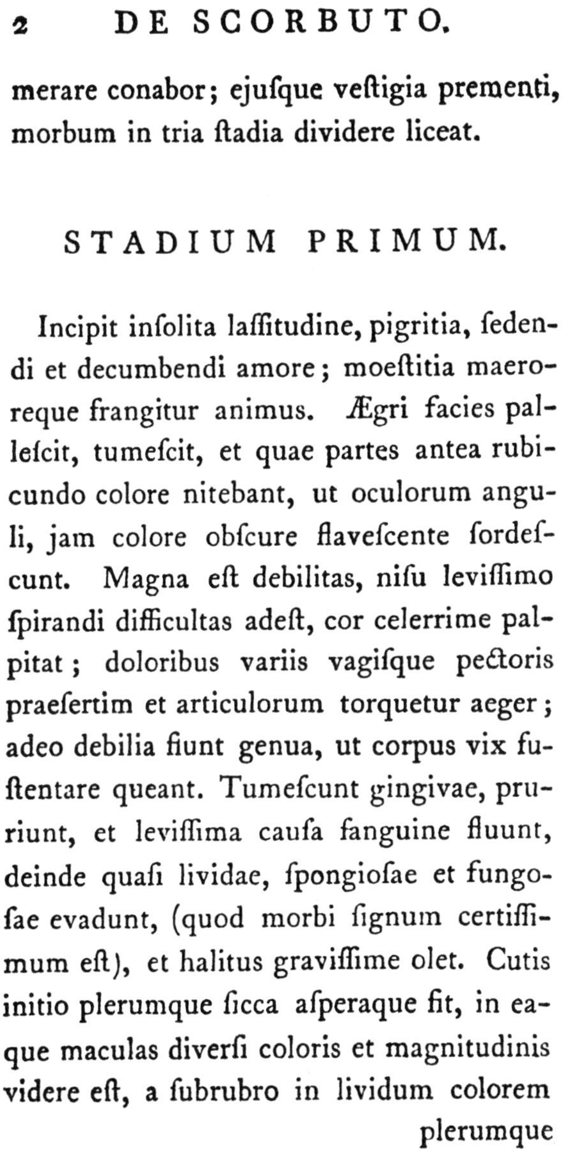

2   DE SCORBUTO.

merare conabor; ejufque veftigia prementi, morbum in tria ftadia dividere liceat.

STADIUM PRIMUM.

Incipit infolita laffitudine, pigritia, fedendi et decumbendi amore; moeftitia maeroreque frangitur animus. Ægri facies pallefcit, tumefcit, et quae partes antea rubicundo colore nitebant, ut oculorum anguli, jam colore obfcure flavefcente fordefcunt. Magna eft debilitas, nifu leviffimo fpirandi difficultas adeft, cor celerrime palpitat; doloribus variis vagifque pectoris praefertim et articulorum torquetur aeger; adeo debilia fiunt genua, ut corpus vix fuftentare queant. Tumefcunt gingivae, pruriunt, et leviffima caufa fanguine fluunt, deinde quafi lividae, fpongiofae et fungofae evadunt, (quod morbi fignum certiffimum eft), et halitus graviffime olet. Cutis initio plerumque ficca afperaque fit, in eaque maculas diverfi coloris et magnitudinis videre eft, a fubrubro in lividum colorem plerumque

Figure VII.11.1.   Eighteenth-century description of scurvy which includes fatigue and lassitude. (From Kiernan 1783.)

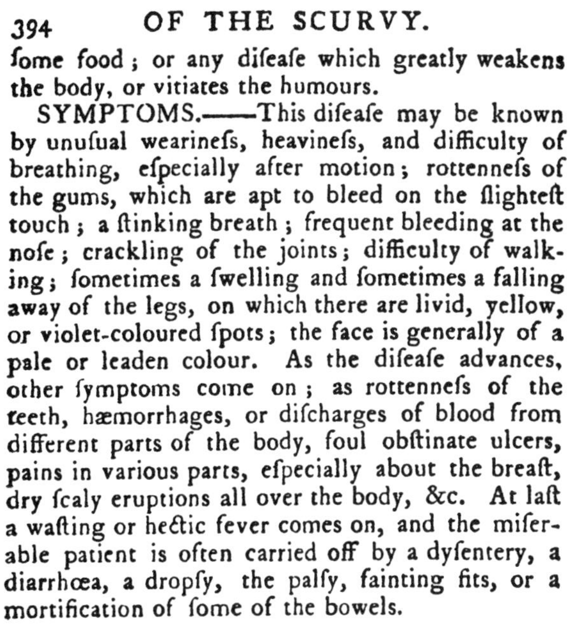

labor displayed by potato-eating Irish and by vegetable-eating French peoples and commented on by a number of observers in the last century was, at least in part, attributable to a reduced carnitine base (Young 1780; Lewes 1859; Bennet 1877; Williams 1885). A diet that centered almost exclusively on potatoes (as was eaten in Ireland during the nineteenth century) would contain virtually no preformed carnitine. Moreover, 20 pounds of potatoes would have to be eaten to obtain the amount of lysine present in half a pound of meat.

394   OF THE SCURVY.

fome food; or any difeafe which greatly weakens the body, or vitiates the humours.

SYMPTOMS.——This difeafe may be known by unufual wearinefs, heavinefs, and difficulty of breathing, efpecially after motion; rottennefs of the gums, which are apt to bleed on the flighteft touch; a ftinking breath; frequent bleeding at the nofe; crackling of the joints; difficulty of walking; fometimes a fwelling and fometimes a falling away of the legs, on which there are livid, yellow, or violet-coloured fpots; the face is generally of a pale or leaden colour. As the difeafe advances, other fymptoms come on; as rottennefs of the teeth, hæmorrhages, or difcharges of blood from different parts of the body, foul obftinate ulcers, pains in various parts, efpecially about the breaft, dry fcaly eruptions all over the body, &c. At laft a wafting or hectic fever comes on, and the miferable patient is often carried off by a dyfentery, a diarrhœa, a dropfy, the palfy, fainting fits, or a mortification of fome of the bowels.

Figure VII.11.2.   Another eighteenth-century description of scurvy suggestive of carnitine deficiency. (From Buchan 1791.)

The remarks of George Henry Lewes in 1859 are interestingly pertinent in this respect. Describing the relative capacities of the French and the English for physical work he wrote:

> It is worth noting that the popular idea of one Englishman being equal to three Frenchmen, was found by contractors to be tolerably accurate, one Englishman really doing the work of two and a half men; and M. Payen remarks that the consumption of mutton in England is three times as much as that in France. . . . [B]y giving the Frenchmen as ample a ration of meat as that eaten by the Englishman, the difference was soon reduced to a mere nothing (1859, 1: 174).

Lewes's reference to mutton was, in this respect, a strikingly apt one, for of all meats and fishes analyzed to date, mutton has by far the highest carnitine concentration (Smith and Dippenaar 1990).

The belief in a positive correlation between animal protein intake and capacity for physical work was a central feature of dietary thought until disproved by the biochemical reductionism of the post-Liebigean era. H. Letheby summarized some of this anecdotal evidence in his Cantor Lectures in 1868:

> [T]here is always a relation between the amount of nitrogen contained [in] the food and the labor value of it. Carnivorous animals, for

example, are . . . stronger and more capable of prolonged exertion than herbivores. . . . The bears of India and America, says Playfair, which feed on acorns, are mild and tractable whilst those of the polar regions, which consume flesh, are savage and untameable. The Peruvians whom Pizarro found in the country at its conquest were gentle and inoffensive in their habits, and they subsisted chiefly on vegetable food; whilst their brethren in Mexico, when found by Cortes, were a warlike and fierce race, feeding for the most part on animal diet. . . . The Hindoo navvies also who were employed in making the tunnel of the Bhore Ghat Railway, and who had very laborious work to perform, found it impossible to sustain their health on a vegetable diet; and being left at liberty by their caste to eat as they pleased they took the common food of the English navigators, and were then able to work as vigorously (1870: 79).

About seventy years later, Robert McCarrison (also in a series of Cantor Lectures) made almost the same point by comparing the diets and physical capabilities of different Indian races (McCarrison 1944). In general, however, by the beginning of the twentieth century, advances in our knowledge of muscle biochemistry were beginning to undermine the belief in a necessary relationship between animal protein intake and physical activity (Hutchinson 1902: 38).

It is interesting to note that the same biochemical reductionism that dismissed the supposed relationship between activity and a "strong" (animal protein) diet now prompts us to reconsider this anecdotal evidence from the standpoint of "carnitine base" status. Many of the "weak" or "poor" diets referred in this section would almost certainly be found wanting in this respect. By the same token, it has been suggested that certain significant socioeconomic changes could imply a change in carnitine base availability. Thus the "Neolithic transition," although leading to an improved supply and availability of food, almost certainly resulted in a reduction in dietary quality and, particularly, in that of the "carnitine base" (Cohen 1990; Hughes 1993).

Such considerations are of direct interest vis-à-vis carnitine supplementation. In more general terms, they underline the importance in supplementation studies of considering each situation on its own merits. Any reduction in one or more of the components of the dietary carnitine base could indicate a need for carnitine supplementation. A sudden fall in the animal protein intake or in the availability of the lysine component or in vitamin C intake (as would appear to occur in the institutionalized elderly where the tissue concentrations of vitamin C are significantly below those believed to be functionally desirable in younger subjects) could result in a reduction in endogenously formed carnitine (Hughes 1993).

General Observations

The entire issue of dietary supplementation is clouded by adventitious circumstances and considerations. Thus it will be apparent that certain intellectual environments or passing paradigms of scientific thought can be particularly favorable to the concept of dietary supplementation. The burgeoning interest in bioflavonoids in the late 1940s and 1950s (and in fiber in the 1970s) was probably not unassociated with two acceptable features of nutritional thought at the time: (1) the belief in "subclinical" manifestations of deficiency diseases (which, in some undefined way, were believed to exist despite a normal intake of accepted nutrients); and (2) the conviction that supplementation of foodstuffs with micronutrients was nutritionally appropriate – a belief that, in cases such as the supplementation of low-extraction flour, carried the seal of government approval.

It is true that there have always been those who advocated supplementation for scientifically inadequate reasons. Such persons belong to the same category as those who, also for nonscientific reasons (such as folklore or romantic naturalism), favored brown (whole-meal) bread rather than low-extraction breads (McCance and Widdowson 1956). Where arguments for supplementation stem from external sources of this nature and are, consequently, difficult to accommodate within the current framework of scientific thought, they should always be treated with proper scientific skepticism and subjected to the appropriate scientific scrutiny. If it turns out that the advocacy of a supplement is consonant with current biochemical thought, then the arguments for its use can be that much more convincing.

The three examples outlined in this essay represent, in this respect, cases of dietary supplementation with three quite different origins. The suggested use of bioflavonoids stemmed, in essence, from a mixture of folklore and weak anecdotal evidence, supported originally by unconfirmed laboratory reports, and was enthusiastically embraced by believers in the value of natural foods as contrasted with manufactured ones. There are many other erstwhile dietary supplements that belong to this category – "vitamin B_{15}" (pangamic acid), "vitamin B_{17}" (laetrile), sea salt, and a host of herbal preparations. These supplements, for the most part, entered the nutritional field, as it were, from "outside" and for nonscientific reasons. Their alleged efficacy was, consequently, more easily disproved by accepted experimental and statistical techniques, and their use was frequently subjected to criticism and, sometimes, ridicule by scientifically orientated "establishment" nutritionists (see, for example, Bender 1985).

Fiber belongs to a somewhat different category of nonfood supplements, as its appearance as a candidate for dietary status was the consequence of epidemiological studies, although it must be admitted that in a nutritional context, it is not always easy to distinguish between "strong anecdotal evidence" (as presented, for example, by Trowell in his early studies) and statistically acceptable epidemiological evidence. Unlike the bioflavonoids, however, dietary fiber has achieved a foothold in current nutritional thought mainly because of strong correlative evidence coupled with the results of some experimental studies. Dietary intervention studies with fiber have been somewhat less successful, and accommodating the purported advantages of fiber supplementation within the current ambit of biochemical thought still poses considerable problems.

Carnitine represents a third etiologic category of potential dietary supplements. Its emergence as a factor of possible nutritional significance, in contrast to the two other examples discussed, was an "internal" event; it was not thrust upon nutritional thought, as it were, from the outside. Arguments for its acceptance in certain circumstances as a dietary supplement placed no conceptual strain on contemporary nutritional thought. In scientific terms it belongs, therefore, to a more acceptable category than the other two examples discussed. Other putative supplements whose emergence has reflected the current state of the art, rather than external and unrelated circumstances are taurine (which, alongside carnitine, receives conditional acceptance as a supplement in the current COMA report), inositol, para-amino benzoic acid, and specific amino acids. In all such cases of putative dietary supplements, the final verdict must await extensive experimental work and intervention studies.

This brief survey of the recent history of three "nonfood" dietary supplements should serve to illustrate three important and cautionary facts. First, it is useful, as far as possible, to distinguish between a pharmacological role and a nutritional role for supplements. Second, one should exercise caution before accepting claims based on anecdotal evidence or derived from statements or arguments external to (and sometimes in open contradiction to) current scientific thought. Third, and most importantly, dietary supplementation must be defined in terms of lacunae and imbalances in the existing dietary pattern, rather than in terms of absolute requirements – the concept of "conditional essentiality."

Classical nutrition derived much of its strength (and lately, some of its weaknesses) from generalizations based on an essentially reductionist and unitary approach to dietary components. A necessary condition for its success was the virtual exclusion of any conceptually extraneous matter, such as the possible importance of nonobligatory dietary components, the significance of dietary interactions, and the importance of the changing balance between tissue demands and nutrient availability. There are signs that current nutritional thought is shedding at least some of its traditional absolutism (Hughes 1993: 40-1). Future studies will presumably be designed not so much to prove in absolute terms the usefulness of specific supplements but to define the nutritional circumstances in which such conditionally essential nutrients as carnitine and fiber would be deemed to be necessary.

R. E. Hughes

Bibliography

Because of the wide range of topics covered, the references cited in this article are, for the most part, restricted to (1) historically important ones and (2) general review articles wherein references to more specific papers may be located.

Adlercreutz, H. 1991. Diet and sex hormone metabolism. In *Nutrition, toxicity and cancer,* ed. I. R. Rowland, 137-195. Boca Raton, Fla.

Anderson, S. A., K. D. Fisher, and D. J. Raiten. 1993. Safety of amino acids used as dietary supplements. *American Journal of Clinical Nutrition* 57: 945-6.

Bender, A. E. 1985. *Health or hoax.* Goring-on-Thames, England.

Bennet, J. H. 1877. *Nutrition in health and disease.* London.

Bentsáth, A., S. Rusznyák, and A. Szent-Györgyi. 1936. Vitamin nature of flavones. *Nature* 138: 798.

1937. Vitamin P. *Nature* 139: 326-7.

Bloom, M. A. 1930. Effect of crude fibre on calcium and phosphorous retention. *Journal of Biological Chemistry* 89: 221-33.

Böhm, K. 1968. *The flavonoids.* Aulendorf, Germany.

Bowman, Barbara A. B. 1992. Acetyl-carnitine and Alzheimer's disease. *Nutrition Reviews* 50: 141-4.

Buchan, William. 1791. *Domestic medicine.* Twelfth edition. London.

Burkitt, D. P. 1971. Possible relationships between bowel cancer and dietary habits. *Proceedings of the Royal Society of Medicine* 64: 964-5

Burr, M. L., and P. M. Sweetnam. 1982. Vegetarianism, dietary fibre and mortality. *American Journal of Clinical Nutrition* 36: 873-7.

Carroll, J. E., A. L. Carter, and S. Perlman. 1987. Carnitine deficiency revisited. *Journal of Nutrition* 117: 1501-3.

Cerretelli, P., and C. Marconi. 1990. L-carnitine supplementation in humans. The effects on physical performance. *International Journal of Sports Medicine* 11: 1-14.

Cleave, T. L. 1974. *The saccharine disease.* Bristol, England.

Cody, M. M. 1984. *Handbook of vitamins,* ed. L. J. Machlin, 578-85. New York.

Cogan, Thomas. 1612. *The haven of health . . .* London.

Cohen, M. N. 1990. *Hunger in history,* ed. Lucile F. Newman, 56-97. Oxford.

Committee on Medical Aspects of Food Policy. 1991. *Dietary reference values for food energy and nutrients for the United Kingdom.* London.

Eaton, S. B. 1990. Fibre intake in prehistoric times. *Dietary Fibre Perspectives* 2: 27-40

Engel, A. G., and C. Angelini. 1973. Carnitine deficiency of human skeletal muscle with associated lipid storage myopathy; a new syndrome. *Science* 179: 899-902

Englyst, H., and J. Cummings. 1990. Dietary fibre and starch; definition, classification and measurement. *Dietary Fibre Perspectives 2,* 3-26.

Fraenkel, G., and S. Friedman. 1957. Carnitine. *Vitamins and Hormones* 15: 73-118

Gabor, M. 1972. *The anti-inflammatory action of flavonoids.* Budapest.

Giovannini, M., C. Agostoni, and P. C. Salari. 1991. Is carnitine essential in children? *Journal of International Medical Research* 19: 88-102

Harris, L. J. 1938. *Vitamins and vitamin deficiencies.* London.

Helmut, F. E. 1989. Factors influencing uptake and utilisation of macronutrients. In *Nutrient availability,* ed. D. A. T. Southgate et al., 330-9. London.

Hirst, B. H. 1993. Dietary regulation of intestinal nutrient carriers. *Proceedings of the Nutrition Society* 52: 315-24.

Hughes, R. E . 1978. Fruit flavonoids: Some nutritional implications. *Journal of Human Nutrition* 32: 47-52.

　　1981. Recommended daily amounts and biochemical roles – the vitamin C, carnitine, fatigue relationship. In *Vitamin C,* ed. J. N. Counsell and D. H. Hornig, 75-86. London.

　　1990. Dietary fibre and female reproductive physiology. *Dietary Fibre Perspectives* 2: 76-86.

　　1993. *L-carnitine: Some nutritional and historical perspectives.* Basel.

Hughes, R. E., and H. K. Wilson. 1977. Flavonoids: Some physiological and nutritional consequences. *Progress in Medicinal Chemistry* 14: 285-301.

Hutchinson, R. 1902. *Food and the principles of dietetics.* London.

Jones, E., and R.E. Hughes. 1982. Quercetin, flavonoids and the life-span of mice. *Experimental Gerontology* 17: 213-17.

Judd, P. A. 1985. Dietary fibre and gallstones. *Dietary Fibre Perspectives* 1: 40-6.

Kiernan, Richard. 1783. *De scorbuto.* Edinburgh.

Kritchevsky, D. 1988. Dietary fibre. *Annual Review of Nutrition* 8: 301-28.

Letheby, H. 1870. *On food.* London.

Lewes, George Henry. 1859. *The physiology of common life.* 2 vols. Edinburgh and London.

McCance, R. A., and E. M. Widdowson. 1956. *Breads white and brown.* London.

McCarrison, R. 1944. *Nutrition and national health.* London.

Middleton, E. 1988. Some biological properties of plant flavonoids. *Annals of Allergy* 61: 53-7.

Olson, J. A. 1966. Lipid metabolism. *Annual Review of Biochemistry* 35: 559-98.

Olson, A. L, S. E. Nelson, and C. J. Rebouche. 1989. Low carnitine intake and altered lipid metabolism in infants. *American Journal of Clinical Nutrition* 49: 624-8.

Park, K. G. M. 1993. The immunological and metabolic effects of L-arginine in human cancer. *Proceedings of the Nutrition Society* 52: 387-401.

Rebouche, C. J., and D. J. Paulson. 1986. Carnitine metabolism and function in humans. *Annual Review of Nutrition* 6: 41-66.

Rusznyák, S., and A. Szent-Györgyi. 1936. Vitamin P: Flavonols as vitamins. *Nature* 138: 27.

Sadler, Michele. 1993. Functional foods: Foods of the future. *Nutrition and Food Science* 4: 11-13.

Scarborough, Harold, and A. L. Bacharach. 1949. Vitamin P. *Vitamins and Hormones* 7: 1-55.

Smith, K. A., and N. G. Dippenaar. 1990. Carnitine: A review. *South African Journal of Food Science and Nutrition* 2: 28-34.

Spagnoli, A., U. Lucca, G. Nenasce, et al. 1991. Long-term acetyl-L-carnitine treatment in Alzheimer's disease. *Neurology* 41: 1726-32.

Taylor, Rodney H. 1984. Bran yesterday . . . bran tomorrow? *British Medical Journal* 289: 69-70.

Trowell, Hugh C. 1960. *Non-infective disease in Africa.* London.

　　1979. *Dietary fibre in human nutrition: A bibliography.* Bristol.

　　1985. Dietary fibre: A paradigm. *Dietary fibre, fibre-depleted foods and disease.* London.

Venner, Tobias. 1638. *Via recta ad vitam longam, or A Plain Philosophical Demonnstration of the Nature . . . of all things as by way of nourishment. . . .* London.

Williams, W. M. 1885. *The chemistry of cookery.* London.

Young, A. 1780. *A tour in Ireland,* Vol 2. London.

VII.12 ⁓ Food Toxins and Poisons from Microorganisms

The Processes Affecting Toxicity

Rather than undertaking a categoric examination of the myriad toxins in food, this essay highlights various considerations that should provide a sense of perspective in viewing toxins as a whole. It is important to realize that toxic substances must negotiate the various degradation and propulsive properties of a gastrointestinal tract in order to be absorbed and exert a harmful effect on the body. The ability of the toxin to be absorbed helps determine the amount of a substance that must be ingested before toxic effects become manifest. Moreover, the handling of ingested toxins by an immature gastrointestinal tract of a premature or term newborn infant may be different from that of the fully developed gastrointestinal tract.

Development of the tract begins during the first 12 weeks of gestation as it matures from a straight tube to one that is progressively convoluted, and the surface area for absorption increases. Over the next six months, the gut acquires a sophisticated immune system and the capacity to digest complex carbohydrates, fats, and proteins. Not all of these mechanisms, however, are fully functional until several months after birth.

The extent to which ingested substances, including food and toxins, are absorbed by the intestine is dependent on the capabilities it has developed to deal with carbohydrates, fats, proteins, water, and ions. These are highly complex issues about which varying amounts of information are understood. Nevertheless, a general concept of how absorption occurs may help put the discussion of food toxins in context.

Carbohydrates constitute the nutrients that provide the largest proportion of calories in the Western diet. Carbohydrate intake, in an adult diet, is approximately 400 grams per day. The major ingested carbohydrates are starch, sucrose (table sugar), and lactose (milk sugar) as 60 percent, 30 percent, and 10 percent, respectively, of the total digestible carbohydrates.

Starch is broken down by enzymes acting within the lumen or tube of the small intestine. The smaller molecules of sugar are digested (broken down) to molecules consisting of one to a few linked sugar molecules, and most are transported across the intestinal wall and into the blood by an energy-requiring "pump" enzyme system in the cell membrane (Van Dyke 1989).

Proteins undergo initial digestion in the stomach and are broken down further by pancreatic enzymes in the small intestinal lumen until they become either individual amino acids or small multiamino acid units called oligopeptides. The intestine has evolved separate transport mechanisms for absorption of different types of amino acids as well as oligopeptides.

Digestion of fat begins in the mouth but is primarily accomplished in the upper small intestine where bile acids from the gallbladder emulsify the fat, permitting the efficient action of the pancreatic enzyme lipase to break down the fats into free fatty acids. Because fats are poorly soluble in water, they are transported by micelles, made of bile acids and fat, to the surface of the upper small intestinal wall where they are absorbed as free fatty acids across the intestinal wall. There they enter either the blood, bound to proteins, or the lymphatic system. Many of the toxic substances in food are absorbed by the protein or fat digestion mechanism (Van Dyke 1989).

Other than the processes of digestion and absorption, intestinal factors that may affect the toxicity of substances in foods include the rapid turnover and sloughing of the intestinal epithelial cells in direct contact with toxins. Persons with intestines in which cell turnover has been slowed, as with those in developing countries suffering from protein–energy malnutrition, may be at greater risk of absorbing toxins from dietary staples.

Another factor is the motility of the gastrointestinal tract. Rapid transit, such as in diarrhea, may minimize the contact of foreign substances with the small intestine and thus reduce the opportunities for absorption (Silverman and Roy 1983). An additional consideration that has not been well studied is the presence of a variety of ingested substances in the intestinal lumen that may interfere with the ability of a toxic substance to come into contact with the intestinal absorptive surface. Thus, for example, the ingestion of phytates from various crops may interfere with the absorption of metals, such as zinc and calcium (Alpers 1989; Wallwork and Sandstead 1990).

Sometimes the ingestion of large quantities of one metal can inhibit the absorption of another. Such an inverse relationship exists between copper and zinc (Li and Vallee 1980). Furthermore, the porosity of the gastrointestinal tract is greater in young infants than in older children and adults (Silverman and Roy 1983). This allows the direct passage of intact proteins, and perhaps other substances as well, from the intestinal lumen into the blood, which could make infants more vulnerable to various toxins than older individuals.

The Concept of Bioavailability

Collectively, those factors that regulate intestinal absorption of toxic substances in foods, as well as of required nutrients, determine the *bioavailability* of the toxin. Although the bioavailability of many of the food toxins has not been clearly defined, it is important to consider this aspect of food toxins, because bioavailability will influence the amount of a substance that must be ingested before its toxicity becomes manifest. It is also a consideration in devising specific therapies for the ingestion of known toxins, such as the use of activated charcoal to bind a toxin in the intestinal lumen or the induction of vomiting to empty the stomach of a potential toxin.

An example of how bioavailability influences the degree to which toxic substances can produce harm is that of aluminum. Aluminum is the third most abundant element on earth and is a contaminant of many foods and medicinal products (Alfrey 1983). When it enters patients as a contaminant of solutions used for hemodialysis or intravenous feeding (total parenteral nutrition), it accumulates in bones, causing reduced bone formation and mineralization (Klein 1990). In addition, it interferes with hemoglobin synthesis, producing anemia, and in patients with kidney failure, it can accumulate in the brain causing progressive dementia and convulsions (Alfrey 1983). By contrast, oral intake of aluminum in normal individuals without damaged kidneys is well tolerated.

Excessive aluminum ingestion, as with long-term consumption of aluminum-containing antacids, may bind phosphate in the intestine and produce phosphate deficiency (Klein 1990). However, ingestion of aluminum in quantities present in normal Western diets (Alfrey 1983) or in currently manufactured infant formulas (Sedman et al. 1985) poses no threat to health so long as the kidneys function normally. The reason for this appears to be that the intestinal absorption of aluminum is very poor, probably less than 0.5 percent of intake, and the kidneys are efficient in eliminating that which is absorbed, leaving very little to accumulate in tissues (Klein 1990). Thus, oral intake of even large quantities of aluminum is not generally harmful because the bioavailability of aluminum in food is very low.

Metabolism

Once ingested, toxins that are absorbed are metabolized. The substances in question undergo biochemical transformation, largely in the liver, by a series of enzymes known as microsomal mixed function oxidases. Some of the reactions involving processes such as oxidation, reduction, or hydrolysis may increase or decrease the activity of the substances.

Other reactions, termed conjugation, involve coupling between the toxin and an endogenous molecule, such as a carbohydrate or an amino acid. These conjugation reactions often result in inactivation (Goodman and Gilman 1980). The fate of the particular toxin in the body will be determined by the relative rates of increased activation and inactivation. The enzymes involved in these reactions are subject to a wide range of individual variability in which genetics, age, body temperature, and nutritional status play important roles.

In general, very young children have a reduced quantity of microsomal enzymes, compared to older individuals. An increase in body temperature produces an increase in all aspects of metabolism, including microsomal enzyme activity, and protein–energy malnutrition depresses the activity of microsomal enzymes (Goodman and Gilman 1980).

The substances themselves may alter the activity of selected microsomal enzymes. Thus, such metals as aluminum, cadmium, and lead have been reported to reduce selectively some microsomal enzyme activity, although these same metals may increase the activity of some conjugating enzymes (Bidlack et al. 1987). Therefore, the variability resulting from the interaction of all the factors influencing metabolism of ingested toxins makes it extraordinarily difficult to predict the fate of any individual substance once absorbed.

It should be evident that both the bioavailability and metabolism of food toxins are very poorly understood variables, and the ensuing discussion of the nature of food toxins must be viewed in light of the highly complex response of the body to these substances, either alone or in combination.

Food Toxins

Food toxins can be generally categorized as plant pesticides (natural and synthetic), mycotoxins, metals, and animal toxins, as well as toxins present in foods as the result of industrial contamination. Each category is considered in turn in this section.

Plant Pesticides

Plant pesticides may be synthetic or natural. In recent years, synthetic pesticides have aroused public concern about possible health effects, especially carcinogenicity. Data gathered by the U.S. Food and Drug Administration (FDA) and reported by B. Ames, M. Profet, and L. Gold (1990a) showed that the average dietary intake of synthetic pesticide residues was 0.09 milligrams (mg) per person per day, compared to 1.5 grams per person per day of natural pesticides. Of the 0.09 mg, four chemicals not carcinogenic in rodents – ethylhexyl diphenyl phosphate, chloroprophan, malathion, and dicloran – constitute approximately half the intake, leaving 0.05 mg synthetics, primarily polychlorinated biphenyls (PCBs), as the only possible carcinogens consumed.

FDA monitoring for pesticides in food samples for a one-year period between 1986 and 1987 revealed that exposure of the American population to PCBs and other synthetic pesticides was consistently less than limits set by the U.S. Environmental Protection Agency (EPA), with less than 1 percent of samples containing pesticide residues exceeding the regulatory limits imposed by the FDA (Ames, Profet, and Gold 1990a).

In 1981, R. Doll and R. Peto estimated that approximately 35 percent of cancer cases could be attributed to the human diet. If true, and if synthetic pesticides account for such a small quantity of dietary intake, it is reasonable to cast suspicion, as do Ames, Profet, and Gold (1990b) and R. Beier (1990), on the natural pesticides.

These phytotoxins, as they are called, constitute a wide variety of chemical compounds produced by plants in response to injury from insects, fungi, climate, animal predators and physical damage. Although synthetic pesticide residues may be present in plants in the parts per billion range, natural pesticides may be present in plants in the parts per million or even parts per thousand range. Thus, they are present in much greater concentration than are the synthetic residues.

As an example, glucobrassicin, a polycyclic hydrocarbon, has a breakdown product called indole carbinol. Glucobrassicin is found in large quantities in vegetables, such as broccoli and Brussels sprouts. When these vegetables are chewed (cooked or raw), they release an enzyme that breaks down the glucobrassicin to indole carbinol. This substance acts biochemically in a manner similar to dioxins, some of which may be a carcinogenic synthetic residue. However, although the EPA has set an acceptable human dose limit for dioxin of 6 mg per kilogram (kg) per day, 100 mg of broccoli is estimated to contain 5 mg of indole carbinol (0.1 mg/kg/day) (Ames et al. 1990a).

Despite the large number of natural pesticides, relatively few have been tested for toxicity. Ames and colleagues (1990a, 1990b) estimate that they abound in the tens of thousands, existing in every edible vegetable and fruit to varying degrees. Yet it has also been estimated that only about 2,800 chemicals have been tested in laboratory animals, mainly rodents, for toxicity (Ames et al. 1990b).

The main categories of toxicity include (1) the potential to cause chromosome breakage in vitro, (clastogenicity); (2) the potential to cause genetic mutations (mutagenicity); (3) the potential to produce birth defects (teratogenicity); and (4) the potential to produce tumors (carcinogenicity). The vast majority of tests done using laboratory animals are carried out in rodents and at "maximum tolerated" (near-toxic) doses given chronically. B. N. Ames and colleagues (1990a) cite data showing that of 340 natural pesticides administered to rodents in conventional chronic high-dose protocols, approximately 70 percent were either carcinogens, mutagens, or both. Yet data on toxicity of these natural pesticides for humans are sparse. In addition, some of these natural pesticides (phytoalexins) have other properties that cause more acute toxicity in humans and animals without necessarily being carcinogenic.

Examples of natural chemicals that are harmful to humans include those found in a variety of Asian herbs containing pyrrolizidine alkaloids, which can be toxic to the liver. Thus, Indian herbal teas are known to cause hepatic veno-occlusive disease. Similarly, comfrey tea, made of the leaves and roots of the Japanese comfrey herb, are hepatocarcinogenic in rats, although insufficient data are available for humans. However, as much as 26 mg of pyrrolizidine alkaloids could be consumed in a cup of comfrey tea (Beier 1990).

Another instance of natural pesticides being harmful to human beings is the case of the white potato. Introduced into the Western diet as a result of the Spanish conquest of Peru, the white potato contains two major glycosteroid alkaloids, alpha solanine and alpha chaconine. Both are cholinesterase inhibitors, and thus have the potential to interfere with autonomic nervous system function.

Several outbreaks of a syndrome resembling gastroenteritis with a headache have been attributed to these alkaloids when the concentration of alpha solanine ranged from 100 to 400 micrograms per gram (μg/g) potato. Since not only the consumption of potatoes but also that of their skins (the site of peak alkaloid concentration) is increasing in restaurants, and at least one company is manufacturing a potato chip made from skins, it is possible that further outbreaks of alpha solanine poisoning will be seen. This is of special concern because these alkaloids appear to be resistant to cooking and frying. Some snack foods contain more than 7 times the safe limit of glycoalkaloids (limit of 200 μg/g potato) (Beier 1990).

Potatoes also contain nitrates with an average level of 119 μg/g fresh weight. Nitrates can react with various amine compounds to form N-nitroso compounds, which are carcinogenic and mutagenic in rodents. Potatoes supply 14 percent of the per capita ingestion of nitrates in the United States (Beier 1990).

In addition, there is epidemiological evidence suggesting that the glycoalkaloids in potatoes may be teratogenic in human beings. Attempts to breed strains more resistant to the potato blight fungus have led to an increase in the amount of natural pesticides produced by new strains of potato. L. Penrose (1957) has pointed out that Ireland has weather conducive to the growth of the blight fungus and also the world's highest incidence of anencephaly (congenital absence of the cranial vault) and spina bifida. Other areas of the world that have developed varieties of potato more resistant to blight have undergone as much as a doubling of the frequency of anencephaly (Beier 1990).

The risk of anencephaly is not eliminated by avoiding the consumption of potato during pregnancy. That the theoretical risk remains is suggested in the report by R. Beier (1990) that solanium, the aglycone derivative of alpha solanine, is stored in the body for a long time and could possibly be released during periods of increased metabolic demand, such as pregnancy. Although evidence supporting a role of the potato glycoalkaloids in the pathogenesis of anencephaly is only circumstantial, a case can surely be made for the need to determine more definitively the relationships of these natural pesticides to human birth defects.

The example of celery being harmful to humankind is more clearly established than that of the potato. The parsley plant group, most prominently celery, contains phytoalexins known as furanocoumarins. These are photosensitizing toxins that will cause both contact dermatitis and photodermatitis. Grocery workers subject to repeated handling of apparently healthy celery have experienced photodermatitis.

The problem stems from attempts to breed a more naturally pest-resistant form of the plant that have produced an elevation in its furanocoumarin content (Beier and Oertli 1983). In the epidemic of photodermatitis in grocery store workers, the linear furanocoumarin content was 14 times higher in the celery in question than in other celery varieties; psoralen, the most photosensitizing of the linear furanocoumarins, was 19 times higher than in other varieties of celery (Beier 1990).

Other evidence of harm to humans done by photosensitizing furanocoumarins are anecdotal. Psoralen ingestion followed by ultraviolet light exposure can produce cataracts in animals and humans (Lerman 1986). Severe, even fatal burns may occur in individuals ingesting psoralen and then visiting tanning parlors (Beier 1990).

These same linear furanocoumarins also are found in citrus and fig plants, which contain furanocoumarin in the peels that are used as flavorings for candies, soft drinks, and baked goods. D-limonene, a psoralen and coumarin derivative, is sold as an insecticide to control pests on household pets (Beier 1990). Fig photodermatitis is seen in fig handlers: In Turkey, 10 percent of fig handlers reportedly contract it (Beier 1990).

In addition, some crops are cultivated in developing countries because they are hardy and do not need the protection of expensive synthetic pesticides. However, they do require extensive processing to detoxify them. For example, much of the cassava root in South America and Africa contains cyanide in high concentrations and is edible only following washing, grinding, scraping, and heating (Beier 1990). Ataxia, or neuromuscular incoordination, due to chronic cyanide poisoning is prevalent in many of the areas of

Africa where cassava is consumed (Cooke and Cock 1989). Similarly, in India the pest-resistant grain *lathyrius sativas* is grown with its seeds containing a potent neurotoxin, B-N-oxalyl-amino alanine, the cause of a crippling nervous system disorder, neurolathyrism (Jayaraman 1989).

As an alternative to plant breeding and use of synthetic pesticides, "organic" farmers claim to use only natural pesticides from one plant species against pests that attack a different species. Thus, phytoalexins, such as rotenone, employed in India as a fish poison, or pyrethrins from chrysanthemum are used. These naturally derived pesticides have not been studied in sufficient detail to determine carcinogenicity in rodents (Ames et al. 1990a, 1990b).

Inasmuch as there are so many natural pesticides in virtually all our edible produce, one might wonder how it is that we are protected against them. Given the complexities in evaluating the effects of bioavailability and tissue metabolism of these toxins, this becomes a very difficult question. But it does seem that what is true for rodents may not be true for humans. Thus, species differences in the bioavailability and metabolism of naturally occurring toxins may account for differences not only in the minimum ingested quantity but also in the time course necessary to produce toxicity in humans. It is possible that humans rapidly metabolize natural pesticides to nontoxic metabolites or are not so susceptible to their toxic actions as laboratory rodents.

Secondly, even within the scope of rodent testing, doses of phytoalexins lower than the maximum tolerated dose may be protective or anticarcinogenic. Examples of this include limonene, caffeic acid found in coffee bean and potatoes, and indole carbinol (Ames et al 1990a). Often, feeding rodents large quantities of cruciferous vegetables, such as broccoli, cabbage, and Brussels sprouts, before their exposure to known carcinogens, such as aflatoxin, decreases the incidence of tumors and increases the rate of survival (Ames et al. 1990b). In contrast, if the experiment is performed in reverse and rodents are given the carcinogen prior to feeding on cruciferous vegetables, the incidence of tumors is increased.

Thus, in summary, the naturally occurring phytoalexins in our foods and medicinal herbs have not been subject to the same intensive scientific scrutiny as have the synthetic pesticides. But the public's current health concerns, the United States government recommendations that more fiber and starch be included in the American diet, and the popularity of "natural" foods and remedies sold in health-food stores combine to make mandatory an increasing amount of scientific study of the safety of such chemicals in the Western diet.

Furthermore, the continued prescription of herbal remedies without scientific basis, on the one hand, and consumption of agricultural staples high in natural pesticides by people in developing countries, on the other hand, pose both real and potential hazards of global dimensions.

Mycotoxins

Perhaps the reverse of the production of natural pesticides by plants responding to infestations and physical damage is the manufacture of toxic metabolic products by the invaders of the plants (that is, fungi). One example is the production of fungal toxins or mycotoxins. Mycotoxin poisoning was noted in ancient times in China and Egypt, and an epidemic identified by some as ergotism (one form of such poisoning) was recorded in Sparta in 430 B.C. (Beier 1990).

The mycotoxin thought to be most responsible for human disease is aflatoxin. Some others also implicated in human toxicity are ochratoxin A, trichothecenes, zearalenone, deoxynivalenol, citrinin, stergmatocytin, and ergot. These mycotoxins are relatively small molecules, with which humans most likely come in contact through contaminated foods.

The Food and Agriculture Organization of the United Nations (FAO) has estimated that 25 percent of the world's food crops are contaminated by mycotoxins, including 10 to 50 percent of the grain crops in Africa and the Far East (Mannon and Johnson 1985). Aflatoxins are primarily found in corn, peanuts, cottonseed, and tree nuts; ergot alkaloids, in rye and wheat; ochratoxin and T-2 toxin, in a variety of grains including barley, oats, corn, soybeans, wheat, and rice; penicillic acid, in corn and dried beans; and zearlenone, in corn and wheat (Beier 1990). Of all the fungi producing mycotoxins, only *aspergillus flavus* and *aspergillus parasiticus* produce aflatoxin, which is the most highly publicized fungal toxin affecting human health (Beier 1990).

Acute aflatoxicosis in humans has been reported from Taiwan and Uganda (U.S. Council for Agricultural Science and Technology 1989). The syndrome is manifested by abdominal pain, vomiting, liver necrosis, and fatty infiltration, as well as the accumulation of fluid in the lungs (pulmonary edema).

In 1974 in western India, unseasonal rains and food scarcity were responsible in over 200 villages for the consumption of corn contaminated with aflatoxin as high as 16 parts per million. Of 994 patients examined there were 97 fatalities (mostly due to gastrointestinal bleeding). However, the presence of other mycotoxins in the corn could not be ruled out, and consequently the epidemic may have been the work of multiple mycotoxins.

This example, along with other reported cases among children in Thailand, combine to suggest a serious risk of acute aflatoxicosis in developing countries where contaminated grain is more likely to be marketed for human consumption than in developed countries. A report by the U.S. Council for Agricultural Science and Technology (1989) suggests that acute aflatoxicosis poses a low risk in Western diets due to the apparent rarity of heavily contaminated grain in the food supply.

Conversely, aflatoxin B_1 has produced liver tumors in several species of experimental animals and is listed as a probable human carcinogen by the International Agency for Research on Cancer (U.S. Council for Agricultural Science and Technology 1989). Thus, there is concern about chronic low-level exposure of humans to aflatoxin despite the low risk of massive doses. The 1989 report by the U.S. Council for Agricultural Science and Technology has reviewed epidemiological studies from both Asia and Africa and concluded that the incidence of liver cell cancer is higher in regions where there is high chronic exposure to aflatoxin. However, there is no evidence that this correlation represents cause and effect.

In fact, a study of rural white males from different sections of the United States (Stoloff 1983) found that despite an estimated 1,000-fold difference in the intake of aflatoxin among men in different regions, the risk of death from liver cell cancer was only 6 to 10 percent higher in the most exposed population. Moreover, Chinese males living in the United States have a high incidence of liver cell carcinoma despite a low likelihood of exposure to aflatoxin (Stoloff 1983). Therefore, the risk of aflatoxin B_1 to humans as a probable carcinogen is still uncertain, at least with consumption of Western diets.

In addition to the encouragement of proper harvesting, drying, and storing methods, attempts are currently being made with a variety of techniques to degrade or otherwise chemically alter aflatoxin in grains (Beier 1990). Thus, as with aflatoxins, other mycotoxins probably pose a greater threat to human health in developing countries than in the more developed countries. In the former, the scarcity of food and the increased likelihood of grain contamination combine to magnify the likelihood of human consumption of tainted food products. Nevertheless, contaminated grains that may, from time to time, enter Western markets constitute at least a theoretical risk and mandate continued vigilance by governmental regulating agencies over national food supplies.

Fish Toxins

Endogenous toxins produced by fish may be less of a public health problem than industrial contaminants entering the food chain via fish or other foods. However, ciguatoxin, saxitoxin, and tetrodotoxin are acknowledged food hazards, and mention of them should be made. Ciguatera poisoning was described as early as the 1600s in the New Hebrides (now Vanuatu), and in 1774, the British navigator Captain James Cook reported an outbreak of apparent ciguatera poisoning in New Caledonia (Hokama and Miyahara 1986).

Ciguatoxin is of low molecular weight and belongs to a class of organic compounds called polyethers. It is one of the most potent toxins known, yet associated with few fatalities because its concentration in fish flesh is very low (Tachibana et al. 1987). The toxin is synthesized by a species of flagellate called *Gambierdiscus toxicus* and is passed through the aquatic food chain from herbivorous to carnivorous fish and then to humans, usually by consumption of certain reef fishes encountered around islands in the Caribbean and in the Pacific (Hokama and Miyahara 1986).

The onset of toxic symptoms may begin 10 minutes to 24 hours after consumption with gastrointestinal symptoms, such as diarrhea, vomiting, and abdominal pain. Neurological symptoms are caused by ciguatoxin's disruption of ion transport mechanisms that aid in the transmission of impulses along nerve axons (Hokama and Miyahara 1986). The symptoms include increased sensitivity to cold, which produces a painful tingling sensation, dilatation of the pupils, weakness, unsteady gait (ataxia), and abnormalities in deep tendon reflexes. With a large dose of ciguatoxin, respiratory depression may occur, and neurological symptoms can persist for months. Cardiovascular effects of ciguatoxin include abnormalities in blood pressure and heart rate, initially low, then sometimes too high, with an occasional irregular heart rhythm. These effects usually disappear within 48 to 72 hours. Of interest and concern, however, is that multiple poisonings of an individual generally increase his or her sensitivity to the toxin, resulting in more severe clinical effects with repeated ingestion.

Saxitoxin, like ciguatoxin, is produced by one or more species of flagellates (Valenti, Pasquini, and Andreucci 1979). These toxins, however, are often found in mollusks, which concentrate them. Saxitoxin is found, for the most part, in the Alaska butter clam and in mussels and scallops, especially during the warm months of the year. An epidemic of saxitoxin poisoning that occurred in Italy in October 1976 was attributable to the consumption of contaminated shellfish (Valenti et al. 1979).

Like ciguatoxin, saxitoxin is an organic compound of low molecular weight that acts as a neurotoxin by blocking the channels for sodium ion to cross the membranes of excitable nerve cells, thus blocking transmission of neuromuscular impulses. Symptoms usually appear within 30 minutes of ingestion. These include numbness around the mouth, lips, face, and extremities; a broad-based gait with neuromuscular incoordination, accompanied by nausea and vomiting and diarrhea; loss of voice; impaired swallowing; and respiratory impairment, which can lead to death within 12 hours.

A lethal dose of saxitoxin is reported to be 1 to 2 milligrams, whereas the concentration for saxitoxin in affected mollusks consumed in Italy ranged from 556 to 1479 micrograms per 100 grams pulp. Thus, there must be individual variation in the susceptibility to the effects of saxitoxin, because very large quantities of pulp are normally consumed.

Tetrodotoxin was first isolated in 1894 from the fugu (also called puffer) fish. It is found primarily in fish inhabiting the waters of Japan, China, and Polynesia and is one of the most potent toxins known. Ingestion of 2 grams of fish eggs can kill a person (Valenti et al. 1979). Female fish appear to produce greater amounts of toxin than males. Balloon fish, shellfish, toad fish, and globe fish also are known to produce tetrodotoxin. Like saxitoxin, tetrodotoxin is a rapid-acting sodium-ion channel poison that blocks neuromuscular conduction (Valenti et al. 1979).

The onset of symptoms occurs between 10 and 50 minutes following ingestion, with vomiting, spreading numbness, voice loss, swallowing difficulty, and respiratory depression. In Japan, more than half the victims die within an hour of ingestion, and 100 percent of those that die do so within 24 hours. Those ingesting only a minimal amount of tetrodotoxin recover without residual problems (Valenti et al. 1979).

The fugu fish is considered a delicacy by the Japanese, and restaurant chefs must have a special license from the government to prepare it in such a way that tetrodotoxin is inactivated. There are some anecdotal reports in the medical literature claiming that rapid administration of anticholinesterase drugs, such as edrophonium, can immediately reverse the paralytic effects of tetrodotoxin (Torda, Sinclair, and Ulyatt 1973; Chew et al. 1984).

Food Poisoning from Microorganisms and Their Toxins

Food poisoning is, regrettably, more than an occasional public health problem, usually resulting from either unhygienic food preparation or food storage or both. Spoiled food is contaminated primarily by toxins produced by strains of clostridium and staphylococcus. Salmonella may itself contaminate certain foods, but it does not produce a toxin, according to present knowledge. The causative organism for anthrax is among a group of other microorganisms found in spoiled food. The disease results from the ingestion of contaminated undercooked meat and is manifested by bloody diarrhea, pain, and occasionally shock. Anthrax is seldom a problem in the West and is more often encountered in underdeveloped countries (American Academy of Pediatrics 1991).

Bacillus cereus, a spore-forming gram-positive rod, may be present in a variety of foods. In fried rice (where it frequently occurs) it causes vomiting, and in meat and vegetables it causes diarrhea. The spores are relatively heat resistant, and the organism can grow and produce toxins in the intestine. The course is usually mild and resolves spontaneously within 24 hours (American Academy of Pediatrics 1991).

Two forms of clostridial food poisoning are noteworthy, that originating from *Clostridium botulinum* (botulism) and that generated by *Clostridium perfringens.* Botulism is a neurological disorder pro-

duced by neurotoxins A, B, E, and F of *Clostridium botulinum.* The toxins create a flaccid paralysis of the muscles of swallowing and phonation, as well as double vision, blurred vision, and slurred speech. Infant botulism, which occurs primarily in those less than 6 months old, is manifested by constipation, loss of muscle tone, a weak cry, poor feeding, a diminished gag reflex, and ocular palsies.

The neurotoxins are found in improperly preserved foods, especially those that are home processed and canned (American Academy of Pediatrics 1991). Illness occurs when the neurotoxins in unheated food are consumed. Most cases of infant botulism do not have a known source for the clostridial spores. However, honey is one identified source, corn syrup another. The American Academy of Pediatrics (1991) recommends withholding honey and, perhaps, corn syrup from an infant's diet for the first 6 months of life.

The cramping abdominal pain and watery diarrhea that develop 8 to 24 hours following ingestion of beef, poultry, gravy, and, notoriously, Mexican food usually result from a heat-labile enterotoxin produced by type A *C. perfringens.* The infection is generally acquired at places where food is prepared in large quantities and kept warm for long periods. Thus schools, camps, caterers, restaurants, and public markets where cooking is done would be typical sources of the infection. As in the case of infection by *B. cereus,* the symptoms usually resolve spontaneously within 24 hours (American Academy of Pediatrics 1991).

Caliciviruses are RNA viruses that can cause gastroenteritis-like symptoms lasting approximately four days. Outbreaks have been reported in children in institutional settings in Japan and the United Kingdom. Contaminated shellfish and cold foods are thought to be vehicles of transmission (American Academy of Pediatrics 1991).

Campylobacter jejuni, one of the most common organisms causing bloody diarrhea, has been isolated from the feces of turkeys and chickens. Transmission occurs by intake of contaminated food, including unpasteurized milk and improperly cooked poultry (American Academy of Pediatrics 1991).

Vibrio cholerae and its toxin can be acquired from ingestion of contaminated shellfish. The recent cholera epidemic in Peru and other parts of South America was originally attributable to "ceviche" (raw fish treated with lime juice) that was contaminated by *V. cholerae.* Adequate cooking eradicates the organism from foodstuffs.

Listeria monocytogenes is a cause of neonatal and perinatal infection. During outbreaks it has been traced to maternal intake of unpasteurized cheese or contaminated cole slaw, and milk has also been implicated.

Norwalk viruses can produce a gastroenteritis along with muscle aches, fever, and crampy abdominal pain. These RNA viruses are implicated in epidemics of gastroenteritis, and outbreaks are associated with eating contaminated shellfish and salads (American Academy of Pediatrics 1991).

Salmonellosis, or gastroenteritis produced by nontyphoid strains of salmonella, can be contracted from improperly processed meat or unpasteurized milk. Food handlers who carry salmonella are additional sources of outbreaks (American Academy of Pediatrics 1991).

Staphylococcus aureus and, occasionally, staphylococcus epidermitis can produce a variety of heat-stable enterotoxins: A, B, C_{1-3}, D, E, and F. The enterotoxins, if present in such foods as egg and potato salads, cream-filled pastries, poultry, and ham can produce abdominal cramping pain, nausea, vomiting, and diarrhea from 30 minutes to 7 hours after ingestion. The symptoms are severe but self-limited (American Academy of Pediatrics 1991).

Yersinia enterocolitica, an infection that may mimic other gastrointestinal diseases, including Crohn's disease (a chronic inflammatory bowel disease) and lymphoma, may be contracted by the consumption of contaminated food, especially uncooked pork and unpasteurized milk (American Academy of Pediatrics 1991).

Finally, one of the routes of transmission of toxoplasmosis, caused by a multi-organ protozoan pathogen with multiple disease manifestations, is by the consumption of poorly cooked meat. The same is true for trichinosis, caused by the nematode *Trichinella spiralis*. It too can cause anything from mild gastroenteritis to severe multiorgan disease and death.

Contamination of Food by Industrial Products

Industrial human-made toxins that contaminate foods include the heavy metals, such as lead, cadmium, and mercury, as well as lighter metals such as aluminum, dealt with in the section "The Concept of Bioavailability." Other industrial contaminants include halogenated hydrocarbons used as pesticides. The following section cites several examples of these contaminants as industrial disasters, as well as potential hazards.

Metal Contamination

Cadmium. In the Japanese prefecture of Toyama in the Jinzu River basin, postmenopausal women became ill after eating cadmium-contaminated rice. The illness, known as "itai-itai disease" was characterized by bone pain, osteoporosis, X-ray appearance of bone thickening overlying an incomplete fracture, and kidney disease as manifested by protein and sugar in the urine. Cadmium ingestion has also been the result of leaching from cadmium-plated containers by acidic drinks, such as fruit juices. These types of containers are now prohibited by law in many parts of the United States (Klein and Snodgrass 1993).

Cadmium may be deposited in soil and water near industrial plants that utilize it in metallurgy, plastics stabilizers, nuclear reactor rods, battery plants, and semiconductors. Because cadmium concentration in the soil can be high in these areas, crops grown in such soil may have high cadmium levels (Klein and Snodgrass 1993). Such may have been the case with itai-itai disease. Cadmium can also enter the aquatic food chain, especially through plankton, mollusks, and shellfish.

Mercury. Two major disasters have been reported as a result of epidemic mercury ingestion. One of these, in Japan, involved two episodes of methyl mercury ingestion as a result of waste dumping by an acetaldehyde manufacturing plant that discarded mercury into Minimata Bay. In 1956 and again in 1965, many infants of mothers from the cities surrounding the bay were born with brain malformations. They, and older individuals, developed irreversible neurological disease known in the literature as "Minimata disease."

In Iraq, a similar set of neurological problems developed following the 1971 consumption of bread made from wheat contaminated by a mercury-containing fungicide. The neuropathies resulted from degeneration of the nervous tissue caused by the mercury. Symptoms in exposed infants included cerebral palsy, psychomotor retardation microcephaly, spastic or flaccid paralysis, visual disorders, and convulsions. In older individuals, muscle weakness and visual and hearing impairment were prominent (Klein and Snodgrass 1993).

Lead. Although there are no recent major disasters on record for lead such as those reported for cadmium and mercury, it is now recognized that ingestion of even small quantities of lead, especially by children, may result in both behavioral and learning disorders. This finding is the work primarily of H. L. Needleman and colleagues (1990). The main source of lead ingestion by children has been lead-based paint that chips off the walls in run-down inner-city housing. However, it is apparent that other sources of lead ingestion include foods. In many cases, this is because agricultural vehicles, which are not required to use unleaded gasoline, release lead-containing exhaust onto crops, and lead accumulates most prominently in green, leafy vegetables. In addition, acidic foods can leach lead from the lead solder in cans (Klein and Snodgrass 1993).

Aluminum. Aluminum contaminates many foods in our diet, with the average adult consuming from 2 to 5 milligrams per day (Alfrey 1983). The Joint Food and Agriculture Organization/World Health Organization Expert Committee (1989) has indicated that a provisional tolerable weekly intake is around 7 mg per kilogram body weight.

Aluminum accumulation in bone has been associated with reduced bone formation and mineralization, in some cases leading to fractures and severe skeletal pain (Alfrey 1983, Klein 1990). It has also been implicated in a progressive dementia affecting uremic patients (Alfrey 1983). As we mentioned, the intestinal absorption of dietary aluminum is very low, about 0.5 percent (Klein 1990).

In recent years, the detection of large quantities of aluminum in some infant formulas has caused concern (Sedman et al. 1985). This has prompted the American Academy of Pediatrics to caution against the use of soy-based formulas (which have a high content of aluminum) for premature infants because of their immature kidney function (American Academy of Pediatrics Committee 1986). The source of the aluminum contamination in these soy formulas is the calcium and phosphate salts added to them, as well as the soy-protein isolate itself. The calcium and phosphate salts make up the chief sources of aluminum contamination of intravenous feeding solutions in use in hospitals (Sedman et al. 1985).

Chlorinated Hydrocarbons
There are numerous reports of halogenated, primarily chlorinated hydrocarbons contaminating the food chain, either via intake by fish or contamination of livestock feed. According to several reports, fish have been contaminated with DDT (dichlorodiphenyltrichloroethane) and other organic compounds, such as PCB (polychlorinated biphenyls), resulting in high human adipose tissue concentration of these chemicals (Kreiss et al. 1981; Ansari et al. 1986). It is also clear that these chlorinated hydrocarbons can concentrate in human breast milk to levels that may reach 20 times their concentration in cow's milk, with large dosing of infants a potential result (Fytianos et al. 1985).

Although all of the health implications (including carcinogenicity) of these ingestions are not understood, there is a report of more than 3,000 patients who developed porphyria in southeast Turkey following ingestion of hexachlorobezene fungicide added to wheat seedlings. Many of the breast-fed infants in this exposure under 1 year of age died as a result (Cripps et al. 1984).

In Michigan in 1973-4, there was a large environmental exposure because of the erroneous mixing of approximately one ton of polybrominated biphenyls (PBBs), a commercial flame retardant, into livestock feed. By mid-1974 virtually every Michigan resident had been exposed to these polybrominated biphenyls by consuming contaminated meat, milk, eggs, and other dairy products. Approximately 300 farm family members who consumed contaminated products from their own farms were followed for study (Anderson et al. 1979; Meester 1979).

Although no specific disease was identified, many of the exposed individuals complained of fatigue, visual problems, skin rashes, reduced resistance to infection, reduced tolerance of alcoholic beverages, and reduced libido. Several individuals complained of migratory arthritis, and one patient had aplastic anemia. The amount of polybrominated biphenyls in the subcutaneous fat did not correlate with symptoms, nor was there any kind of a dose–response relationship. The potential for carcinogenicity is uncertain although animal data suggest this is a risk in high-dose, long-term exposure (Groce and Kimbrough 1984). Furthermore, G. Lambert and colleagues (1990) have found that the hepatic microsomal enzymes of individuals exposed to PBBs remain activated up to 10 years following exposures. These activated enzymes are capable of producing carcinogenic metabolites from drugs and other organic compounds.

Conclusion

This chapter is intended to point out the variability of human defenses against the toxic substances we ingest; to illustrate the scope of our dietary exposure to toxins and putative toxins; to suggest our relative ignorance of the potential for harm caused by the myriad chemicals we consume with our food; to indicate that the majority of these are natural and not synthetic; and to show that industrial mishaps can indeed affect our food supply.

Although the public generally has confidence in the food with which it is supplied, there is a need for further scientific study of the effects of natural chemicals on our health, as well as a need for vigilance on the part of both industry and government to ensure that our food supply is neither needlessly nor irresponsibly contaminated.

Finally, in less-developed areas of the world, where the food available for human consumption is scarce and less subject to official scrutiny, the problem of toxic ingestion is magnified and its true extent probably unknown at the present time.

Gordon L. Klein
Wayne R. Snodgrass

The authors would like to express appreciation to Douglas E. Goeger, assistant professor of preventive medicine and community health at the University of Texas Medical Branch at Galveston, for the provision of key references as well as helpful comments. They would also like to thank Wilma L. Nance for manuscript preparation.

Bibliography
Alfrey, A. C. 1983. Aluminum. *Advances in Clinical Chemistry* 23: 69-91.
Alpers, D. H. 1989. Absorption of vitamins and divalent minerals. In *Gastrointestinal disease: Pathophysiology, diagnosis, management,* ed. M. H. Sleisinger and J. S. Fordtran, 1057-8. Philadelphia, Pa.

American Academy of Pediatrics. 1991. *Report of the Committee on Infectious Diseases,* 1-670. Elk Grove Village, Ill.

American Academy of Pediatrics, Committee on Nutrition. 1986. Aluminum toxicity. *Pediatrics* 78: 1150-4.

Ames, B. N., M. Profet, and L. S. Gold. 1990a. Dietary pesticides (99.99% all natural). *Proceedings of the National Academy of Sciences of the United States of America* 87: 7777-81.

  1990b. Nature's chemicals and synthetic chemicals: Comparative toxicology. *Proceedings of the National Academy of Sciences of the United States of America* 87: 7782-6.

Anderson, H. A., A. S. Wolff, R. Lilis, et al. 1979. Symptoms and clinical abnormalities following ingestion of polybrominated biphenyl-contaminated food products. *Annals of the New York Academy of Sciences* 320: 684-702. New York.

Ansari, G. A. S., G. P. James, L. A. Hu, and E. J. Reynolds. 1986. Organochlorine residues in adipose tissue of residents of the Texas Gulf Coast. *Bulletin of Environmental Contamination and Toxicology* 36: 311-16.

Beier, R. 1990. Natural pesticides and bioactive components in food. *Reviews of Environmental Contamination and Toxicology* 113: 47-137.

Beier, R. L., and E. H. Oertli. 1983. Psoralen and other linear furocoumarins as phytoalexins in celery. *Phytochemistry* 22: 2595-7.

Bidlack, W. R., R. C. Brown, M. S. Meskin, et al. 1987. Effect of aluminum on the hepatic mixed function oxidase and drug metabolism. *Drug-Nutrient Interactions* 5: 33-42.

Chew, S. K., L. S. Chew, K. W. Wang, et al. 1984. Anticholinesterase drugs in the treatment of tetrodotoxin poisoning. *Lancet* 2: 108.

Cooke, R., and J. Cock. 1989. Cassara crops up again. *New Scientist* 122: 63-8.

Cripps, D. J., H. A. Peters, A. Grocner, and I. Dogranaci. 1984. Porphyria turcica due to hexachlorobenzene: A 20 to 30 year follow-up study on 204 patients. *British Journal of Dermatology* 111: 413-22.

Doll, R., and R. Peto. 1981. The causes of cancer: Quantitative estimates of avoidable risks of cancer in the United States today. *Journal of the National Cancer Institute* 66: 1171-1308.

Fytianos, K., G. Vasilikotis, L. Weil, and N. Laskaridis. 1985. Preliminary study of organochlorine compounds in milk products, human milk and vegetables. *Bulletin of Environmental Contamination and Toxicology* 34: 504-8.

Gilman, Alfred Goodman, Louis S. Goodman, Alfred Gilmar, et al. 1980. *The pharmacological basis of therapeutics.* Sixth edition. New York.

Groce, D. F., and R. D. Kimbrough. 1984. Stunted growth, increased mortality, and liver tumors in offspring of polybrominated biphenyl (PBB) dosed Sherman rats. *Journal of Toxicology and Environmental Health* 14: 695-706.

Hokama, Y., and J. T. Miyahara. 1986. Ciguatera poisoning: Clinical and immunological aspects. *Journal of Toxicology and Toxin Reviews* 5: 25-53.

Jayaraman, K. S. 1989. Neurolathyrism remains a threat in India. *Nature* (London) 339: 495.

Joint Food and Agriculture Organization/World Health Organization Expert Committee on Food Additives. 1989: 33rd Report. *Evaluation of certain food additives and contaminants.* World Health Organization Technical Report No. 776, 1-64. Geneva.

Klein, G. L. 1990. Nutritional aspects of aluminum toxicity. *Nutrition Research Reviews* 3: 117-41.

Klein, G. L., and W. R. Snodgrass. 1993. The toxicology of heavy metals. In *Encyclopedia of food science, food technology and nutrition,* ed. R. Macrae, R. Robinson, and M. Sadler. London.

Kreiss, K., M. M. Zack, R. D. Kimbrough, et al. 1981. Cross-sectional study of a community with exceptional exposure to DDT. *Journal of the American Medical Association* 245: 1926-30.

Krishnamachari, K. A., R. V. Bhal, V. Nagaraja, and T. B. G. Tilak. 1975. Hepatitis due to aflatoxicosis. An outbreak in Western India. *Lancet* 1: 1061-3.

Lambert, G. H., D. A. Schoeller, H. E. B. Humphrey, et al. 1990. The caffeine breath test and caffeine urinary metabolite ratios in the Michigan cohort exposed to polybrominated biphenyls: A preliminary study. *Environmental Health Perspectives* 89: 175-81.

Lerman, S. 1986. Photosensitizing drugs and their possible role in enhancing ocular toxicity. *Ophthalmology* 93: 304-18.

Li, T.-K., and B. L. Vallee. 1980. The biochemical and nutritional roles of other trace elements. In *Modern nutrition in health and disease,* ed. R. S. Goodhart and M. E. Shils, 408-41. Philadelphia, Pa.

Mannon, J., and E. Johnson. 1985. Fungi down in the farm. *New Scientist* 105: 12-16.

Meester, W. D. 1979. The effects of polybrominated biphenyls on man: The Michigan PBB disaster. *Veterinary and Human Toxicology* 21 (Supplement): 131-5.

Needleman, H. L., A. Schell, D. Bellinger, et al. 1990. The long-term effects of exposure to low doses of lead in childhood. An 11-year follow-up report. *New England Journal of Medicine* 322: 83-8.

Penrose, L. S. 1957. Genetics of anencephaly. *Journal of Mental Deficiency Research* 1: 4-15.

Sedman, A. B., G. L. Klein, R. J. Merritt, et al. 1985. Evidence of aluminum loading in infants receiving intravenous therapy. *New England Journal of Medicine* 312: 1337-43.

Silverman, Arnold, and Claude C. Roy. 1983. *Pediatric clinical gastroenterology.* Third edition. St. Louis, Mo.

Stoloff, L. 1983. Aflatoxin as a cause of primary liver cell cancer in the United States: A probability study. *Nutrition and Cancer* 5: 165-86.

Tachibana, K., M. Nukina, Y.-G. Joh, and P. J. Scheuer. 1987. Recent developments in the molecular structure of ciguatoxin. *Biological Bulletin* 172: 122-7.

Torda, T., E. Sinclair, and D. B. Ulyatt. 1973. Puffer fish (tetrodotoxin) poisoning: Clinical record and suggested management. *Medical Journal of Australia* 1: 599-602.

U.S. Council for Agricultural Science and Technology. 1989. *Mycotoxins: Economic and health risks.* Task Force Report No. 116. Ames, Iowa.

Valenti, M., P. Pasquini, and G. Andreucci. 1979. Saxitoxin and tetrodotoxin intoxication: Report of 16 cases. *Veterinary and Human Toxicology* 21 (Supplement): 107-10.

Van Dyke, R. W. 1989. Mechanisms of digestion and absorption of food. In *Gastrointestinal disease: Pathophysiology, diagnosis, management,* ed. M. H. Sleisinger and J. S. Fordtran, 1062-88. Philadelphia, Pa.

Wallwork, J. C., and H. H. Sandstead. 1990. Zinc. In *Nutrition and bone development,* ed D. J. Simmons, 316-39. Oxford.

VII.13 ❦ The Question of Paleolithic Nutrition and Modern Health: From the End to the Beginning

A conviction has been growing among some observers that contemporary human health could be substantially improved if we would just emulate our hunter–gatherer ancestors in dietary matters. A look at this contention seems an appropriate way to bring this work to a close because the subject takes us full circle - linking contemporary issues of food and nutrition with our Paleolithic past. In addition, it offers an opportunity for some summary, and, finally, it provides a chance to remind ourselves of how ephemeral food and nutritional dogma can be.

In fact, in retrospect we call such fleeting tenets "Food Fads" (see the treatment by Jeffrey M. Pilcher, this work chapter VI.12), and in the United States at least, it was not very long ago that vitamin E capsules were being wistfully washed down in the hope of jump-starting sluggish libidos (Benedek, this work chapter VI.15). Not long before that, the egg was enshrined as the "perfect" food, with milk in second place, and cholesterol, now an apparently significant ingredient in the gooey deposits that plug heart arteries, was not a word in everyday vocabularies (Tannahill 1989).

In those "B.C." (before cholesterol) days, meat was in, and the starchy foods (potatoes, breads, and pastas), although full of fiber, were out - considered bad for a person's waistline and health, not to mention social standing. Garlic had a similarly dismal reputation - only foreigners ate it - and only winos drank wine. Who could have foreseen then that we would soon toss all of that nutritional lore that guided us into the ash heap of history and embrace its polar opposite - the "Mediterranean Diet" (Keys and Keys 1975; Spiller 1991; see also Marion Nestle, chapter V.C.1).

This, however, leads us back to the just-mentioned "growing conviction" among some students of current science and distant history that a fundamental flaw in our present approach to nutrition is a failure (or refusal) to realize that our diets were programmed at least 40,000 years ago and thus we are, to a very important extent, what our ancestors ate. Moreover, these same students believe that it is our obliviousness to the obvious that will prove most baffling of all to future observers of our nurture and nature (Eaton, Shostak, and Konner 1988a, 1988b; Nesse and Williams 1994; Profet 1995).

The purveyors of *The Paleolithic Prescription* (Eaton et al. 1988a; see also their "Stone Agers in the Fast Lane" [1988b]) belong to a group that subscribes to what has been labeled "Darwinian medicine" - a school of thought that has called into question many of the notions we have about nutriments and nutrients, as well as many practices in the practice of medicine.

Illustrative is the medical treatment of fever, routinely but perhaps mistakenly lowered with pain relievers. Fever, it is argued, is a part of a highly evolved defense system for combating pathogens. When fever is artificially lowered, that system is impaired, and recovery may take longer and be less perfect (Kluger 1979).

Another example is "morning sickness," said to arise from a mechanism evolved in the distant past to produce sufficient queasiness in newly pregnant women that they avoid foods - like slightly overripe meat, or cruciferous vegetables - that could be mildly toxic and, therefore, harmful to fetuses, which are especially vulnerable during the first trimester of pregnancy. If such ideas are correct, then it is possible that treating this Stone Age condition with modern nausea-preventing drugs increases the risk of birth defects (Profet 1995).

A final example from the medical side of the Darwinian thinkers' agenda has to do with what have become alarmingly high rates of breast and ovarian cancer. The Darwinians suggest that contemporary women endure an estimated three times more days with menstrual cycles than their hunter–gatherer ancestors because the latter averaged more children over a lifetime and breast-fed each for about three years - all of which suppressed menstrual cycles. The condition of modern women means three times the exposure to surges of estrogen that occur during those cycles - and estrogen has been implicated in the generation of female cancers (Nesse and Williams 1994).

No less disturbing are the nutritional implications that emerge from similar lines of reasoning that reach back into Paleolithic times. As we saw in Part I of this work, written by bioanthropologists, our hunter–gatherer forebears may have enjoyed such variety in viands that they fared better nutritionally than any of their descendants who settled down to invent agriculture; indeed, in terms of stature, it would seem that they did better than practically everyone who has lived ever since (see Mark Nathan Cohen 1989 and this work chapter I.6; Clark Spencer Larsen, this work chapter I.1).

Data on both stature and nutrition indicate that human height began to diminish with the transition from collecting to growing food, finally reaching a nadir in the nineteenth century. It has only been in the twentieth century that humankind, at least in the West, has started to measure up once again to our ancestors of at least some 25,000 to 10,000 years ago (Eaton et al. 1988a; Harris, this work chapter VI.5).

Proof of the early decline in stature and health, along with soaring rates of anemia and infant and child mortality, lies mostly in the skeletal remains of those who settled into sedentary agriculture. Such remains also bear witness to deteriorating health through bone and tooth lesions – caused on the one hand by an ever-more-circumscribed diet and on the other by the increased parasitism that invariably accompanied sedentism (Larsen 1995).

Paradoxically, then, enhanced food production, made possible by the switch to herding and growing, resulted in circumscribed diets and nutritional deficiencies. Thus it would seem that the various Neolithic revolutions of the world, which invented and reinvented agriculture and are collectively regarded as the most important stride forward in human history, were actually backward tumbles as far as human health was concerned. Moreover, when we remember that the superior nutritional status of the hunter-gatherers over that of their sedentary successors was achieved and maintained without two of the food groups – grains and dairy products – that we now call "basic" but which only came with the Neolithic Revolution, the hunter-gatherers' superiority seems downright heretical in the face of current nutritional dogma.

In longitudinal terms, humans have been on the earth in one form or another for a few million years, during which time they seem to have perpetuated themselves with some efficiency. About 1.5 million years ago, they shifted from a diet of primarily unprocessed plant foods to one comprised of increasing amounts of meat, some of which was scavenged. Approximately 700,000 years ago, humans began the deliberate hunting of animals, and Homo sapiens, who some 100,000 years ago had brains as large as ours today, became expert at it, judging from the frequent discoveries of abundant large-mammal remains at ancient sites (Larsen, this work chapter I.1). Meat may have constituted as much as 80 percent of the diet of those proficient at hunting, but they also ate wild vegetables and fruits; and certainly, as the Darwinists point out, it was these foods – meat, vegetables, and fruits – that constituted the diet from 25,000 to roughly 10,000 years ago (Eaton et al. 1988a).

In light of this nutritious past, it can be argued that humans are best adapted to these "old" food groups. Certainly, one piece of evidence in such an argument seems to be that humans are among the very few animal species that cannot synthesize their own vitamin C – an ability made superfluous by the great amounts forthcoming from the fruits and vegetables in the diet, and apparently lost along the evolutionary trail (Carpenter 1986; see also R. E. Hughes, this work chapter IV.A.3).

The other side of that coin, however, is that humans may not be well adapted to the "new" foods – dairy products and grains – and it is worth noting that from a nutritional standpoint, hunter-gatherers seem to have gotten along better nutritionally without these two food groups than the sedentary folk who created them and have used them ever since.

Recently, of course, meat – one of the old food groups – has become a primary suspect in the etiol-

ogy of chronic illnesses, especially that of coronary artery disease, and it has been pointed out that modern-day hunter-gatherers (for example, the !Kung San in and around Africa's Kalahari desert) take in much more meat and, thus, more cholesterol than medicine today recommends. The traditional !Kung San and other modern-day hunter-gatherers, however, have very low blood-cholesterol levels and virtually no heart disease. Similarly, the Inuit of the Arctic and Subarctic, until recently at least, consumed mostly animal foods with the same lack of deleterious effects. It has only been with their switch to the foods the rest of us eat that their health has begun to deteriorate (Eaton et al. 1988a; see also Harold H. Draper, this work chapter VI.10; Linda Reed, this work chapter V.D.7).

It is true that hunted animals as a rule have only a fraction (about one-seventh to one-tenth) of the fat of their domesticated counterparts, along with a better ratio of polyunsaturated to saturated fats. Consequently, it has been estimated that our hunter-gatherer ancestors got only about 20 percent of their calories from fats, whereas fats deliver about 40 percent of the total calories in modern diets. But because the amount of cholesterol in meat is little affected by fat content, it would seem that our ancestors, like the !Kung San, also consumed more cholesterol than we do today and more than is recommended by nearly all medical authorities (Eaton et al. 1988a; see also Stephen Beckerman, this work chapter II.G.10).

It is interesting that a group of researchers in the United Kingdom has argued that cholesterol may not be the culprit – or at least not the only culprit – in bringing about coronary artery disease. Their search for its causes entailed the systematic and painstaking gathering, in all of Europe, of data on diets and deaths from heart disease, and analysis of this data has revealed one positive correlation: People living in the four European countries with the highest rates of heart disease (all in northern Europe) take in far more calcium than people in the four countries with the lowest rates (all in southern Europe) (see Stephen Seely, this work chapter IV.F.4).

Of course, that which is a significant correlation to some is merely an interesting speculation to others. But it may be the case that calcium can be harmful, depending on its source. During hunting-and-gathering times, calcium came mostly from plant foods, and bone remains indicate that our ancestors got plenty of it. Since the Neolithic, however, dietary calcium has increasingly been derived from dairy products, such as cheese and yoghurt – and milk, for those who can tolerate it.

Indeed, "tolerate" is the key word as far as milk is concerned, and, presumably, much of the reason for the difference in calcium intake between northern and southern Europeans is that the latter are less likely to consume milk after weaning because they are more likely to be lactose intolerant (cheese and yoghurt are less of a problem because when milk is fermented, lactose is converted to lactic acid) (Kretchmer 1993; see also K. David Patterson, chapter IV.E.6). Northern Europeans, by contrast, collectively constitute a lactose-tolerant enclave in a largely lactose-intolerant world, and, not incidentally, the point is made that white North Americans, whose ancestral homeland was northern Europe, are also able to tolerate milk and also suffer high rates of coronary artery disease (Seely, this work chapter IV.F.4).

One might then argue that in an evolutionary scheme of things, dairy products are newfangled: Allergies to cow's milk are common among children, and milk-based formulas can be deadly for infants (Fauve-Chamoux, this work chapter III.2). It may be true that lactose intolerance is Nature's way of preventing the consumption of much in the way of dairy foods that can calcify the arteries, and the heart attacks suffered by adult northern Europeans and their progeny in other parts of the world are the price of overcoming this trait. It is interesting to note that areas in Europe where oats are consumed are also those with the highest rates of coronary disease, and oats contain a great deal of calcium (Seely, this work chapter IV.F.4), which moves us to grains - the other "new" food group.

As with dairy products, it may be that humans are not well adapted to grains either. People with celiac disease - caused by the proteins in wheat and some other grains - most certainly are not. And perhaps significantly, this relatively rare genetic condition has its highest frequency in those regions that spawned the most recent major wheat-producing societies (see Donald D. Kasarda, this work chapter IV.E.2). Is it, therefore, possible that celiac disease is a holdover from earlier times, when the body evolved a mechanism to prevent the consumption of toxic wild grains? One trouble with such an argument, of course, is the need to explain how it was that the Neolithic Revolution ever got off the ground in the first place if people were genetically incapable - at least initially - of digesting the crops they grew.

One answer that has been proposed is that grains were not originally grown because of a need for food but, rather, because of a taste for alcohol (Katz and Voigt 1986; see also Phillip A. Cantrell, this work chapter III.1). It appears that barley-ale was being produced at least 7,500 years ago, and the records of the ancient Sumerians, for example, show that a staggering (no pun intended) 40 percent of their grain production went into brewing (Tannahill 1989). And ale making did precede bread making, so perhaps there was a time when grains were mostly for drinking, and only later was there a shift toward eating them.

The rise to prominence of grains that tended to narrow the diet - wheat in temperate Asia and Europe, rice in tropical and semitropical Asia, millet and sorghums in Africa, and maize in the Americas - was perhaps the most important factor in the previously mentioned decrease in human stature and significant deterioration of dental and skeletal tissues. This is because these so-called "super" foods are super only in the sense that they have sustained great numbers of people; they are far from super nutritionally. Almost all are poor sources of calcium and iron; each is deficient in essential amino acids, and each tends to inhibit the activities of other important nutrients (Larsen, this work chapter I.1, upon which the following paragraph also is based).

Rice, for example, inhibits the activity of vitamin A, and if its thiamine-rich hulls are pounded or otherwise stripped away, beriberi can be the result. The phytic acid in wheat bran chemically binds with zinc to inhibit its absorption, which, in turn, can inhibit growth in children. Zein - the protein in maize - is deficient in three essential amino acids, which, if not supplemented, can also lead to growth retardation; moreover, because the niacin contained in maize is in bound form, many of its consumers have suffered the ravages of pellagra. In addition, maize (along with some other cereals) contains phytates that act against iron absorption and also has sucrose, which - we are continually reminded - exerts its own negative impact on human health (significantly, dental caries were exceedingly rare in preagricultural societies). In short, it is arguable that humans may not be programmed for the newfangled grains either.

Much firmer ground, however, is reached with the assertion that humans are definitely not programmed for the quantities of sodium chloride many now take in. Even the most carnivorous of our ancestors, on an 80 percent meat diet, would have ingested less than half of the average per capita daily salt intake in the United States, and of course, excessive dietary salt has been linked with stomach cancer and hypertension, the latter disease a major contributor to heart attacks, kidney failure, and especially strokes. Modern-day hunting-and-gathering populations that consume little sodium (meaning amounts comparable to those of our hunter-gatherer forebears) suffer no hypertension - not even, it is interesting to note, the age-related increase in blood pressure that medicine has come to believe is "normal" (Cohen, this work chapter I.6).

In the case of sodium chloride, as in that of lactose absorption, western Europeans, once again, pioneered in the attempt to reprogram the Stone Age metabolism, although in this case they were joined by East Asians. All mammals normally consume less sodium than potassium, which complements bodily mechanisms that strive to conserve sodium, because the mineral is, after all, crucial to life itself. But not the Europeans - at least not after salt became an inexpensive commodity some 1,000 years ago. They preserved foods with salt, cooked them in salt, then added more salt at the table, with the result that over the ages, their bodies seem to have learned to some extent to rid themselves of sodium with brisk efficiency through urine and perspiration (Kiple 1984;

Eaton et al. 1988a; see also Thomas W. Wilson and Clarence E. Grim, this work chapter IV.B.7).

By contrast, it has been argued that those not of western European (and probably eastern Asian) ancestry and, thus, without a long history of heavy salt consumption, such as African-Americans (whose ancestral lands were poor in salt, whose ancestral cooking habits did not call for it anyway, and whose bodies seem still to treat the mineral as something precious to be conserved), are in considerable peril in cultures where sodium is routinely added at almost every step in food preservation, processing, preparation, and consumption (Wilson 1987; Wilson and Grim, this work chapter IV.B.7). Moreover, because potassium is progressively leached out during these procedures, people in affluent countries have now turned the Stone Age potassium-to-sodium ratio upside down and are consuming some 1.5 times as much sodium as potassium (see David S. Newman, this work chapter IV.B.6). Modern-day hunter-gatherers, by contrast, are said to have potassium intakes that exceed sodium by 10 times or more (Eaton et al. 1988a).

Another controversial, but fascinating, avenue of investigation traveled by some of the Darwinian thinkers has to do with iron, an essential mineral found in all cells in the body and a key component of hemoglobin, wherein can be found about 70 percent of all our iron. The remaining 30 percent is stored in the spleen, the liver, and especially in bone marrow, where it can be called upon as needed. Iron-deficiency anemia is the most common form of anemia worldwide and is especially prevalent in developing countries, where the diet is likely to contain little meat (from which iron is most efficiently absorbed) but much vegetable food (from which iron is poorly absorbed). Moreover, some dietary substances in vegetable foods, such as oxalic acid and tannic acid, actually interfere with iron absorption (Eaton et al. 1988a; Bollet and Brown 1993).

As a few of the authors in the present work point out, however, the presence of pathogens also affects iron levels, and the impact of this presence is more profound than that of dietary imbalance. Helminthic parasites, such as the hookworm, make their living on human blood and the iron it contains, and they frequently cause anemia when they prosper to the point that they become too many, taking too much advantage of a good thing (see Susan Kent, this work chapter IV.D.2; Kent and Patricia Stuart-Macadam, this work chapter IV.B.3; Nevin S. Scrimshaw, this work chapter VI.3).

What is of interest in addition to helminthic parasites, however, is a recently demonstrated and much more subtle interaction of iron and smaller parasites. Bacteria and viruses also need iron to multiply. To forestall such multiplication, or at least to slow it down, our bodies have developed the knack of reacting to pathogenic presence by drawing down the iron supply in the blood and putting it in storage – in

effect, starving the pathogens – until the danger has passed, whereupon iron levels in the blood are permitted to rise again (Kent, this work chapter IV.D.2). But it would seem that only a small percentage of physicians are aware of this phenomenon, with the result that they may mistake bodily defenses for anemia and issue prescriptions for iron that can hurt the patients while helping the pathogens (Kent, this work chapter IV.D.2; see also Nesse and Williams 1994).

Moreover, studies in Polynesia, New Guinea, and West Africa have demonstrated that infants given iron have a much higher incidence of serious infectious diseases than those who are not given iron, and that discontinuing the administration of iron in itself lowers the incidence of infections. Thus, it is urged that health workers be reeducated to understand that, in many instances, the high incidence of anemia in the developing world does not mean a dietary failure that requires iron administration; rather, it means that an important bodily defense is at work, combatting high rates of parasitism (Nesse and Williams 1994; Kent, this work chapter IV.D.2).

In the developed world, the argument continues, the extent to which iron may be a threat to health is compounded, and the body confounded, by the indiscriminate and massive iron fortification of many cereal products and the regular use of iron supplements. This may be especially serious in countries like the United States, where elderly men and postmenopausal women have the highest incidence of anemia – which, it is contended, is really anemia defending against the chronic diseases to which these groups are most vulnerable, including neoplastic cells that, like pathogens, also need iron for multiplication. In addition, evidence is accumulating that high iron levels play a significant role in coronary artery disease (Kent, this work chapter IV.D.2).

Another recently recognized bodily mechanism that evolved with humans has to do with an unfortunately tenacious ability of the body to maintain a certain level of fat, even if it is an unhealthy level. A recent Rockefeller study (Leibel, Rosenbaum, and Hirsch 1995) indicates that the body has a preset level of fat that it strives to maintain by changing the efficiency with which it metabolizes food, so that it can either reduce or increase the amount of fat going into storage. What this means – to put the Rockefeller study together with the so-called thrifty-gene theory first advanced by the geneticist James Neel (1962) – is that those who try to lose weight seem to be up against Stone Age "thrifty genes" that probably evolved during the glacial epochs. Then, nutrition under harsh climatic conditions often would have been a matter of feast and famine, and individuals who, during times of feasting, could most efficiently store excess calories as fat to ride out famines would have enjoyed a considerable survival advantage over those lacking this ability (see Leslie Sue Lieberman 1993 and this work chapter IV.E.7).

Today, however, these thrifty genes are blamed

directly for diabetes and gallstones and indirectly for all conditions in which obesity is a contributing factor. Apparently, here is another Stone Age mechanism that is troubling modern humans, particularly when today's diets give us calories in such compact forms that we can easily get more than we need before ever feeling comfortably full. It has been estimated that, in hunter–gatherer days, 5 pounds of food were required to provide 3,000 calories; today, 5 pounds of food may deliver upwards of 9,000 calories – some 3 times as many (Eaton et al. 1988a; Lieberman 1993).

Such a caloric conundrum presents an especially serious hazard to some groups of humans in transition. Studies of Native Americans, Australian Aborigines, Pacific islanders, and Alaskan Eskimos all have reported precipitous declines in health, suffered upon the abandonment of traditional diets and patterns of exercise (Lieberman 1993; Kunitz 1994). North American Indians, along with Polynesians, Micronesians, and native Hawaiians, have some of the highest rates of diabetes mellitus in the world. In sub-Saharan Africa, hypertension rates are rising alarmingly in the cities, where salt-laden prepared foods are replacing the foods of the villages. And coronary artery disease and hypertension are becoming commonplace in the Pacific, where just decades ago they were unknown (Wilson 1987; Lieberman 1993; Kunitz 1994; Draper, this work chapter VI.10; see also Nancy Davis Lewis, this work chapter V.E.3).

By way of concluding, it remains to be seen how much blame for current chronic diseases can be laid on Paleolithic nutritional adaptations. Another factor, of course, is that to some extent, humans have also been shaped by the requirements of more recent ancestors. Those who settled into cold and damp places, for example, chose diets that were rich and fatty and that helped build fat to insulate against the weather. In warm climates, where evaporating perspiration served to cool the body, strong herbs and spices that encouraged sweating were consumed; and much liquid was drunk to replace lost fluids. Today, central heating obviates the need for a fatty diet, and air conditioning reduces the need to sweat. But there are many dietary holdovers from those old days, too, that do humans no good and, in tandem with Stone Age genetic mechanisms, perhaps a great deal of harm. For example, it was not all that long ago that the author of a late-eighteenth-century cookbook picked a quarrel with a competing writer who called for 6 pounds of butter to fry 12 eggs. One-half that amount of butter was plenty, she primly assured her readers (Tannahill 1989).

Yet, hardly anybody wants to return to a hunting-and-gathering lifestyle. And although history sheds no light on an ideal diet, it does, in a way, defend those grains and dairy products that have just been examined and which, it can be argued, at least have been consumer tested for the past 8,000 to 10,000 years.

Nonetheless, what our authors and others have had to say on matters of Paleolithic nutrition has been well researched, well reasoned, and well received in many quarters. In other words, their work is not wild speculation, and their point, namely that natural selection has not had time to revise our bodies to cope with modern diets, is a good one. But about all Darwinian nutrition can actually do for us at this point is to remind us of the wisdom of moderation in food consumption and nutritional supplementation from yet one more perspective.

Kenneth F. Kiple

Bibliography

Beckerman, Stephen. Game. This work chapter II.G.10.

Benedek, Thomas. Food as aphrodisiacs and anaphrodisiacs? This work chapter VI.15.

Bollet, Alfred J., and Audrey K. Brown. 1993. Anemia. In *The Cambridge world history of human disease,* ed. Kenneth F. Kiple, 571-7. Cambridge and New York.

Cantrell, Phillip A., II. Beer and ale. This work chapter III.1.

Carpenter, Kenneth J. 1986. *The history of scurvy and vitamin C.* Cambridge and New York.

Cohen, Mark Nathan. 1989. *Health and the rise of civilization.* New Haven, Conn.

History, diet, and hunter-gatherers. This work chapter I.6.

Draper, Harold H. Human nutritional adaptation: Biological and cultural aspects. This work chapter VI.10.

Eaton, S. Boyd, Marjorie Shostak, and Melvin Konner. 1988a. *The Paleolithic prescription.* New York.

　1988b. Stone Agers in the fast lane: Chronic degenerative diseases in evolutionary perspective. *American Journal of Medicine* 84: 739-49.

Fauve-Chamoux, Antoinette. Human breast milk and artificial infant feeding. This work chapter III.2.

Harris, Bernard. Height and nutrition. This work chapter VI.5.

Hughes, R. E. Vitamin C. This work chapter IV.A.3.

Kasarda, D. Celiac disease. This work chapter IV.E.2.

Katz, Solomon H., and Mary Voigt. 1986. Beer and bread: The early use of cereals in the human diet. *Expedition* 28: 23-34.

Kent, Susan. Iron-deficiency and anemia of chronic disease. This work chapter IV.D.2.

Kent, Susan, and Patricia Stuart-Macadam. Iron. This work chapter IV.B.3.

Keys, A., and M. Keys. 1975. *How to eat well and stay well, the Mediterranean way.* New York.

Kiple, Kenneth F. 1984. *The Caribbean slave: A biological history.* Cambridge and New York.

Kluger, Matthew J. 1979. *Fever; its biology, evolution, and function.* Princeton, N.J.

Kretchmer, Norman. 1993. Lactose intolerance and malabsorption. In *The Cambridge world history of human disease,* ed. Kenneth F. Kiple, 813-17. Cambridge and New York.

Kunitz, Stephen. 1994. *Disease and social diversity: The European impact on the health of non-Europeans.* New York.

Larsen, Clark Spencer. 1995. Biological changes in human populations with agriculture. *Annual Review of Anthropology* 24: 185-213.

Dietary reconstruction and nutritional assessment of past peoples: The bioanthropological record. This work chapter I.1.

Leibel, R. L., M. Rosenbaum, and J. Hirsch. 1995. Changes in energy expenditure resulting from altered body weight. *New England Journal of Medicine* 332: 621-8.

Lewis, Nancy Davis. The Pacific islands. This work chapter V.E.3.

Lieberman, Leslie Sue. 1993. Diabetes. In *The Cambridge world history of human disease,* ed. Kenneth F. Kiple, 665-76. Cambridge and New York.

Obesity. This work chapter IV.E.7.

Matzen, Richard N., and Richard S. Lang, eds. 1993. *Clinical preventive medicine.* St. Louis, Mo.

Neel, J. V. 1962. Diabetes mellitus: A "thrifty" genotype rendered detrimental by "progress." *American Journal of Human Genetics* 14: 353-62.

Nesse, Randolph M., and George C. Williams. 1994. *Why we get sick: The new science of Darwinian medicine.* New York.

Nestle, Marion. The Mediterranean (diets and disease prevention). This work chapter V.C.1.

Newman, David S. Potassium. This work chapter IV.B.6.

Patterson, K. David. Lactose intolerance. This work chapter IV.E.6.

Pilcher, Jeffrey M. Food fads. This work chapter VI.12.

Profet, Margie. 1995. *Protecting your baby-to-be: Preventing birth defects in the first trimester.* New York.

Reed, Linda. The Arctic and Subarctic regions. This work chapter V.D.7.

Sandford, Mary K., ed. 1993. *Investigations of ancient human tissue.* Amsterdam.

Scrimshaw, Nevin S. Infection and nutrition: Synergistic interactions. This work chapter VI.3.

Seely, S. The cardiovascular system, coronary artery disease, and calcium: An hypothesis. This work chapter IV.F.4.

Spiller, Gene A., ed. 1991. *The Mediterranean diets in health and disease.* New York.

Tannahill, Reay. 1989. *Food in history.* New York.

Wilson, Thomas W. 1987. Africa, Afro-Americans, and hypertension: An hypothesis. In *The African exchange: Toward a biological history of black people,* ed. K. F. Kiple, 257-68. Durham, N.C., and London.

Wilson, Thomas W., and Clarence E. Grim. Sodium. This work chapter IV.B.7.

PART VIII

A Historical Dictionary
of the World's Plant Foods

This final portion of the book is perhaps the most ambitious. It was initially conceived of as a dictionary of the exotic plants mentioned in the text, which our authors would otherwise be called upon to identify in their chapters and, in so doing, interrupt their narratives.

The expansion of Part VIII began when it was decided to include entries on *all* plant foods mentioned in the text and continued when it became apparent that the various fruits of the world do not lend themselves to generalized essays, because many have been mostly seasonal items in the diets of relatively few – and often unrelated – people. For example, the ancient Malaysians ate the "Java apple" (*Eugenia javanica*) when it was ripe, whereas, on the other side of the world, Native Americans of Brazil did the same with their "pitanga" (*Eugenia uniflora*). The plants that produce these two fruits are both in the same genus of the family Myrtaceae, but there is little that historically connects their human consumers (unlike the consumers of maize or wheat or potatoes). Thus, save for a few staples (bananas and plantains, for example), fruits really did not seem to belong in the earlier parts of the work dealing with staple foods, and when it was decided to treat fruits in individual dictionary entries – and not as botanical families, or even, as a rule, as genera – there seemed no question that these entries should be included in Part VIII.

More expansion ensued when our students, researching the gathered foods mentioned in a number of the chapters (such as those dealing with hunters and gatherers, early North America, the ancient Near and Middle East, and Australia and New Zealand), began making their own discoveries of gathered foods not covered in those chapters. These were subsequently included as entries in the dictionary, with the result

that Part VIII also offers a glimpse of the myriad wild foods that sustained our hunting-and-gathering ancestors during almost all of humankind's time on earth – a glimpse of especial interest to those of us whose diets are generally limited to a relatively few commercialized plant foods. Among other things, these dictionary entries might be viewed as collectively questioning the wisdom of the progressive limiting of viand variety in the human diet that began with the invention of agriculture.

A final effort, which also expanded the size of Part VIII, was an attempt to include as many as we could identify of the common names (and synonyms) for food plants in English (and some in other languages). We hope that this labor will help researchers in sorting out items mentioned in the world's various spice trades; others who might find it useful to know that words like "colewort" (in Old English texts) would today mean cabbage (with "coleslaw" a reminder of the earlier name); and still others who might be interested to learn, for example, that "pigweed" can mean amaranth, goosefoot, lamb's-quarter, purslane, *quelites,* and quinoa (which in turn is also "quinua" and begins another long list of common names).

We have, in addition, attempted to provide something of the history of the more than 1,000 plant foods treated in Part VIII whenever such information was available. However, much of such history remains speculative, because although individual species may have evolved in discrete locations, many plants were moving across continents and even oceans – on their own or with human help – long before the dawn of recorded history.

Plant names constitute perhaps the single most daunting obstacle to an enterprise like Part VIII. Obviously, different languages and cultures have assigned their own common names to plants, so that well-traveled plants will generally have a host of them, and much-used names may well refer to multiple plants – as the previously mentioned example of "pigweed" illustrates. Scientific names – generally Latinized botanical terms drawn from Greek and Latin – were intended to remedy this problem so that at least the scientific community concerned with plants could speak the same language despite differences in plants' common names. But languages change, and change can be vexing. Disagreements about classification mean that equivalents are frequently used in the realm of scientific names designating genus and species (we indicate this with an equals sign [=] whenever we have turned up the information). Illustrative are some plants of the genus *Eugenia* that have also been assigned to the genus *Syzygium,* so that, for example, the fruit with the common name "rose apple" is both *E. jambos* and *S. jambos.* In addition, new scientific names may have come into use

that were not employed by the sources we consulted. It was only at the last minute, for example, that we became aware that *Lens culinaris* was now an acceptable designation for lentils, previously called *Lens esculenta* (hence, *Lens esculenta = L. culinaris*). We have dealt as best we could with such taxonomic tribulation, but because we are not botanists, we have doubtless misunderstood, misinterpreted, and mistreated such information at various points, and for this we apologize.

Virtually all of the entries in Part VIII were written "in-house" by the editors, with plenty of research help from the members of our staff, led by Stephen V. Beck, all of whom are credited in the work's general acknowledgments. At this point, however, we would like to acknowledge and thank Charles B. Heiser, who contributed the entry on the "Jerusalem Artichoke," and Jeffrey M. Pilcher, who wrote some of our Mesoamerican entries. Both of these scholars also made contributions elsewhere in this work, and we are most grateful for their extra effort.

Abalong - *see* **COCOYAM**
Abata kola - *see* **KOLA NUT**
ABIU - A native of lowland South America, the abiu (*Pouteria cainito*) is a relative of the sapodilla, the mamey sapote, and the canistel. The abiu is a small yellow fruit, which grows on a tree that can reach upward of 30 feet in height. Like its better-known relatives, the abiu contains a sticky latex within its skin. Although the fruit is appreciated locally, it is generally not commercially exploited in its homeland; however, some varieties that have been introduced into South Asia and Australia reportedly have commercial possibilities.

Abóbora - *see* **CALABAZA (SQUASH)**
Abyssinian banana - *see* **ENSETE**
ACACIA - There are a number of species of (chiefly tropical) trees belonging to the genus *Acacia,* with some (especially *A. senegal*) exuding from their trunks a gum - called "gum arabic" - that has a wide variety of commercial uses, including many in food manufacturing and processing. In much of the tropical world, the gum as well as the leaves, pods, and seeds of acacia trees have food uses. The pods and seeds are dried and ground into a flour used for bread-making. In Mexico, the pods of the prairie acacia (*A. angustissima*) were consumed by Native Americans, as were those of the catclaw acacia (*A. greggii*) in what is now the southwestern United States. Acacia has a multitude of other names, including "wattle," "mimosa," and "Egyptian thorn."
Common names and synonyms: Catclaw acacia, Egyptian thorn, mimosa, prairie acacia, wattle(s).
ACEITUNA - Also called "olivo" and "paradise tree," the aceituna (*Simarouba glauca*) is a tree native to tropical America. It is prized for its oil seeds and for its edible fruit pulp, which is normally eaten raw. The aceituna is found in most produce markets of Central America, especially in El Salvador, where the trees are grown commercially. In addition to Central America and Mexico, the tree can be found throughout the Caribbean region, in Florida, and in Hawaii.
Common names and synonyms: Olivo, paradise tree.
ACEROLA (*see also* **CHERRY**) - Also known as the "Barbados cherry" and the "West Indian cherry," the acerola is so called because of its supposed resemblance to the Mediterranean azarole. The original habitat of the best-known species of acerola (*Malpighia glabra*) included the Caribbean region, southern Texas, Mexico, and Central America; today, however, it can be found in South America and throughout the southern United States as well. The fruit is borne on thick, quick-growing bushes and trees that reach from 6 to 25 feet in height. With its small size and bright red coloring, it bears a superficial resemblance to a cherry. Unlike a cherry, however, the acerola contains three seeds and has vertical grooves in its skin. Rich in vitamin C, the unripe

acerola far surpasses all other fruits as a source of this nutrient, containing an incredible 20 times the ascorbic acid of an orange. Too tart for consumption as a fresh fruit, it finds many uses in the preparation of jellies, jams, preserves, and baby foods (in combination with other fruits to increase the amount of vitamin C), as well as in the pharmaceutical industry.
Common names and synonyms: Barbados cherry, *huesito,* Surinam cherry, West Indian cherry.
Acha - *see* **FONIO**
Achee - *see* **ACKEE**
Achiote - *see* **ANNATTO**
ACHIRA - Plants of the genus *Canna* are most often cultivated for ornamental use. The fleshy rhizomes of the achira (*Canna edulis*), however, produce a yellow starch that has long been a foodstuff consumed in the Andean region. It probably originated in the area that is now Peru, where remains of the plant - dating back to 2500 B.C. - have been excavated. Today, *C. edulis* is grown and marketed for human consumption in an area ranging from Chile to Venezuela in South America, on some islands in the Caribbean, to a lesser extent in Java and northern Australia, and, finally but not least, in Vietnam, where, during the past three decades, large areas have been devoted to its cultivation in order to make the highly prized transparent noodles that are an indispensable part of that country's cuisine. The plant has also been cultivated in subtropical Hawaii as a feed for cattle and pigs.
Common names and synonyms: Australian arrowroot, canna, gruya, Queensland arrowroot, *tous-les-ois.*
Achis - *see* **AMARANTH**
Achita - *see* **AMARANTH**
Achokcha - *see* **KORILA**
Achotillo - *see* **SOUARI NUT**
ACKEE - A West African plant, the ackee (*Blighia sapida*) reached the West Indies during the latter part of the eighteenth century and spread from there to most of tropical America. Some have credited its introduction to Captain William Bligh (hence the genus name *Blighia*), but most agree that it reached the Caribbean aboard slave ships. In fact, the presence of ackee in Jamaica has been dated from 1778, when the first known ackee slips were purchased from the captain of a slave ship by a local physician/botanist. In any event, the plant's introduction was a welcome one, as it occurred during a period in which warfare and hurricanes had triggered a desperate search for new foodstuffs for the slaves on English plantations. The large, shrublike ackee tree grows almost anywhere in the tropics, bears red- or orange-colored fruits in its fourth year, and will then bear fruit twice a year for the next half century or so. Despite the tree's West African origin, the main focus of ackee cultivation, consumption, and exportation today is in the West Indies. When cooked, the fruit has an appearance and taste that have been

compared to those of a fine omelette – or brains (a nickname is "vegetable brains"), depending on the point of view. The classic use of ackee is in its famous gastronomical marriage with salted codfish. The fruit, which splits open when ripe, consists of pink pods, black seeds, and a fluffy yellow pulp. Only the yellow pulp is edible, however; the pink tissue contains a toxic peptide. All unopened (and thus unripe) ackees are toxic. Historically, this toxicity has been responsible for a number of deaths among Jamaican children, who ate fallen fruit picked up from the ground. Because of its potential danger to the unwary, ackee is generally only available in cans outside of the regions where it is grown. The fruit is a good source of beta-carotene and vitamin C.

Common names and synonyms: Achee, akee, vegetable brains.

ACORN – Technically, an acorn is the fruit of any oak tree (genus *Quercus,* of which there are some 400 to 500 species). The oak is native to all the continents except Australia, and edible acorns may be found in Europe and Asia as well as in North America. Yet even the so-called sweet acorns have a high content of tannic acid, meaning that all acorns are best leached and roasted before eating. In North America, sweet acorns from the white oak (*Q. alba*) have been the most popular. Today, acorns – which constitute an annual crop larger than all other nut crops put together – constitute a vastly underexploited resource that is utilized mostly as feed for hogs. In the past, however, acorns have been a staple food for many people (they were doubtless among the wild foods that humans gathered over many millennia), and they are still widely eaten in southern Europe. In North America, acorns sustained many Native American groups, who exploited some 20 species and ground the nuts to make breads and porridges, thereby supplementing diets composed largely of smoked fish and meat. Throughout the Middle Ages and since, acorns have been extensively used for meat production, and hogs were annually herded into forests during the oak mast. Acorns entered the diets of the first Europeans to reach North American shores, and during the Civil War, when blockades and wartime conditions in general made coffee scarce, ground acorns were discovered to be a serviceable substitute. Very sophisticated methods of employing acorns can be found in the areas around the Mediterranean from Turkey to Spain, as well as in Japan. The nuts have a high carbohydrate content and are relatively high in protein. It is interesting to note that some acorns are technically (and correctly) referred to as "beechnuts."

Common names and synonyms: Beechnut.

ACORN SQUASH (*see also* **SQUASH AND PUMP-KIN**) – An American native – and one of the most familiar squashes in North America – the acorn squash (*Cucurbita pepo*) is so called because it is shaped something like an acorn. It is a winter

squash with a hard, ridged rind which makes it difficult to peel, but it is easily cut in half for stuffing and is excellent for baking. The acorn squash has a mild, nutty flavor and delivers a good deal of calcium but (in view of its orange-colored flesh) surprisingly little beta-carotene.

See in addition: "Squash," Part II, Section C, Chapter 8, and "Squash and Pumpkin" in this section.

Adam's-needle - *see* **YUCCA**
Adlay millet - *see* **JOB'S-TEARS**
Advance - *see* **LOQUAT**
Adzuki bean - *see* **AZUKI BEAN**
Aerial yam - *see* **AIR POTATO**
African bitter yam - *see* **BITTER YAM**
African horned cucumber - *see* **KIWANO**
African horned melon - *see* **KIWANO**

AFRICAN LOCUST – The genus *Parkia* – named for Mungo Park, the famous late-eighteenth-century explorer of West Africa – is comprised of a number of leguminous trees of tropical Africa. Among them is the African locust (*Parkia africana*), which has pods containing edible seeds that are generally roasted. A close relative is *P. biglandulosa,* which bears very rich seeds that are usually boiled and made into cakes.

AFRICAN LOCUST BEAN – A tall tree of the West African tropics, the African locust bean (*Parkia filicoidea*) has leaves that are cooked and used as a vegetable. When the seeds are ripe, they are considered by some to be an aphrodisiac. The seeds are also pressed for a cooking oil.

African pumpkin - *see* **OYSTERNUT**

AFRICAN RICE (*see also* **RICE**) – African rice (*Oryza glaberrima*) is one of the two cultigens of the genus *Oryza.* The other, of course, is common or Asian rice. Although the two are similar in many respects, the latter has been far more successful in terms of consumer appeal and as a market commodity of global proportions.

It has been theorized that *O. glaberrima* was domesticated from the wild annual *O. barthii,* which grew in the flood basin of the central Niger delta, and that cultivation of the crop was under way as early as 3,500 years ago. From the Niger delta, it was introduced into other parts of West Africa, where farmers further developed the grain into diverse cultivars that could thrive in deepwater basins, water holes in savannas, forest zones, swampy areas, or dry highlands.

African rice, like its better-known relative, is an outstanding source of energy and important vitamins and minerals. It surpasses whole wheat and maize in terms of protein, is devoid of cholesterol, and is low in sodium and fat. Most varieties have a reddish color, which is perhaps one of the reasons that the more polished, white, Asian types have largely replaced *O. glaberrima* – even in regions where for many centuries it was both an important component of cherished rituals and an essential food. Another reason is that the Asian types of rice are more easily produced, harvested, and milled. Those who continue the cultivation of African rice are generally small-scale farmers, frequently in remote areas, who prefer the grain's distinctive taste, aroma, and coloring; consequently, the crop is grown mostly for local use. Such cultivation occurs on the "floating fields" of the flood plains of Nigeria, in Mali on the Niger's inland delta, and, to a lesser extent, on the hills near the Ghana–Togo border and in Sierra Leone.

African rice is prepared in the same manner as Asian rice, but traditional African uses include fermenting the grain to make regionally popular beers, as well as converting it to flour to make a variety of baked goods. The rice also still figures prominently in a number of West African rituals.

See in addition: "Rice," Part II, Section A, Chapter 7.

African spinach - *see* **AMARANTH**

African tea - *see* **KHAT**

AFRICAN YAM BEAN - Also known as the "wild yam bean," the African yam bean (*Sphenostylis stenocarpa*) is cultivated in West Africa and equatorial Central Africa and grows wild in the African tropics. The pods, seeds, and tubers of the African yam bean are all eaten, and its leaves are cooked as a vegetable.

Common names and synonyms: Wild yam bean.

AGAR (*see also* **SEAWEED**) - Called "agar-agar" in the past, agar is a gelatin obtained from seaweed – especially seaweeds belonging to the genera *Euchema* and *Gelidium*. It has reportedly been used in China since A.D. 300, and perhaps somewhat later in Japan (where it is called *kanten*). Many kinds of jellied sweets that are sold in tropical Asia retain their firmness because of agar, which is employed to thicken other foods as well. Agar also finds its way into vegetable dishes and salads and, in addition, has a number of medical uses.

Common names and synonyms: Agar-agar, *kanten.*

See also: "Algae," Part II, Section C, Chapter 1.

Agar-agar - *see* **AGAR, LAVER, SEAWEED**

Agati - *see* **SESBAN**

AGAVE - Any of numerous American plants of the genus *Agave* go by this name as well as "maguey" or "century plant." The latter term implies longevity and is the name of one variety (*A. americana*) that is common in the deserts of northern Mexico and the southwestern United States. This plant flowers only after 20 to 30 years of life, and then dies. Agaves are evergreens with fleshy, lance-shaped leaves. They were used as food by Native American peoples, who roasted the leaves and grilled the "heart" of the plant. In fact, remains found in the caves of Tehuacán indicate that agave was already an important food source by 6500 B.C. The 2-meter-long leaves also served as shelter material and as fuel, but perhaps the most common use of the plant was the fermentation of the sweet liquid

that accumulates inside (up to 1,200 liters in a single plant) to make a thick alcoholic beverage called *pulque.* Later, the fermented juice was distilled by Spanish settlers to make *mescal* and tequila. Current Mexican law stipulates that tequila must be made from blue agave plants (*A. tequilana*) grown in the state of Jalisco, where the town of Tequila is located. The agave worm (also called the maguey worm or *gusano*) was formerly added to bottles of tequila to provide a measure of quality and potency – a weak alcohol content allowed the worm to rot. Nowadays, however, the outrageous prices offered for *gusanos* have forced small distillers to substitute slivers of maguey or sugarcane.

Common names and synonyms: Blue agave, century plant, maguey.

Agnus castus - *see* **CHASTE TREE**

Aguacate - *see* **AVOCADO**

Ague bark - *see* **HOPTREE**

Aguweed - *see* **BONESET**

Ahipa - *see* **AJIPA**

Ahuacatl - *see* **AVOCADO**

Ahuyama - *see* **CALABAZA (SQUASH)**

Aibika - *see* **SUNSET HIBISCUS**

Airelle de myrtille - *see* **CRANBERRY**

AIR POTATO (*see also* **YAMS**) - A native of South Asia that later spread to the South Pacific region and is now cultivated throughout the world's tropics and subtropics, the "air potato" (*Dioscorea bulbifera*) is also called the "potato yam" and the "aerial yam." Its name derives from the fact that its edible, potato-like tubers do not all form underground; instead, many are produced at the junction of the leaves and the stem of this tall, climbing herb.

Common names and synonyms: Aerial yam, potato yam.

See in addition: "Sweet Potatoes and Yams," Part II, Section B, Chapter 5.

Aiwain - *see* **AJOWAN**

AJÍ (*see also* **CHILLI PEPPERS**) - This chilli pepper (*Capsicum baccatum*) is of the Andes region of South America, where it is understandably known as *ají* because (in western South America and the West Indies) the word *ají* means chilli. The pepper called *ají* is - at least when fresh - a thin, tapered chilli, some 3 to 4 inches in length, with green or red flesh, which provides considerable heat for salsas and cooked dishes. When dried, the pepper is known as *ají mirasol* or *ají amarillo,* because its ripe red color turns yellowish. In this form, the pepper is used in a variety of sauces and also to make *ceviche* in Peru. Another pepper called *ají* is *ají panca,* a mild pepper that dries to a chocolate brown color and is used to make chilli sauces and various cooked dishes - generally featuring fish.

Common names and synonyms: Ají amarillo, ají mirasol, ají panca.

See in addition: "Chilli Peppers," Part II, Section C, Chapter 4.

Ají amarillo - *see* **AJÍ**

AJÍ DULCE (*see also* **CHILLI PEPPERS**) - In western South America and the Caribbean, the word *ají* frequently connotes all chilli peppers - and *dulce* would seem to suggest a sweet pepper. But this member of the genus *Capsicum* (*C. chinense* Jacq.) is not the mild-mannered chilli pepper its name implies. Rather, it is an aggressive Venezuelan relative of the fiery habanero pepper (also of the species *C. chinense*), which it resembles somewhat in shape, although it is quite a bit larger.
  See in addition: "Chilli Peppers," Part II, Section C, Chapter 4.

Ají mirasol - *see* **AJÍ**

AJIPA (*see also* **LEGUMES**) - Like jícama, ajipa (*Pachyrhizus ahipa*) is a legume that develops swollen roots. Also called a "yam bean," it is unknown outside of South America, where it was grown by ancient Native Americans. The white tubers are often eaten raw in salads, to which they add a crispness and a sweet taste. The tubers are also boiled or steamed like potatoes.
  Common names and synonyms: Ahipa, yam bean.

Ají panca - *see* **AJÍ**

AJOWAN - A native of southern India, ajowan (*Carum ajowan*) is also grown in an area that extends westward from Afghanistan, across Iran, and into Egypt - and doubtless has been for thousands of years. Although its whole or ground seeds have a taste similar to that of thyme, the plant is actually related to caraway and is used in much the same way as the latter in breads and pickles and with legumes.
  Common names and synonyms: Aiwain, ajwain, bishop's-weed, *omam, omum.*
  See also: "Spices and Flavorings," Part II, Section F, Chapter 1.

Ajwain - *see* **AJOWAN**

Aka-suguri - *see* **CURRANT(S)**

Akee - *see* **ACKEE**

Alcachofa - *see* **ARTICHOKE**

Alecost - *see* **COSTMARY**

ALEXANDER - There are a number of plants called alexander, alexanders, or alexander buds. One is *Smyrnium olusatrum* - a European plant with the name of "alexanders" that resembles celery and was cultivated in the past as a potherb. Alexanders is also a name that was applied in the past to various members of the parsley or carrot family (Umbelliferae). Finally, alexanders can mean any plant of the genus *Zizia,* especially golden alexanders (*Z. aurea*), a native of eastern North America. This plant has yellow flowers and can be found in moist woods and meadows. The young umbels of the flowers were eaten by Native Americans just as they began to bud.
  Common names and synonyms: Alexander buds, alexanders, golden alexanders.

Alexander buds - *see* **ALEXANDER**

Alexanders - *see* **ALEXANDER**

ALFALFA - A native of Eurasia, alfalfa (*Medicago sativa*) is a tall, cloverlike plant belonging to the pea family. It is now grown in North America (frequently as a cover crop to reduce erosion) and used for fodder. Its other uses are also mostly non-culinary: The fiber is employed in the production of paper; the drying oil derived from the seeds goes into paints; and the plant is a commercial source of chlorophyll. After the introduction of alfalfa into the New World, its tiny seeds were consumed by some Native American groups and are still used for sprouting by many concerned with health foods. The seeds are high in the minerals calcium, magnesium, and potassium, and the leaves (also edible) are high in vitamins A, C, D, E, and K.
  Common names and synonyms: Lucerne, sativa.

Algae - *see* **SEAWEED**

Algarroba - *see* **ALGARROBO, CAROB, MESQUITE**

ALGARROBO - A native of Peru and Ecuador, the algarrobo (*Prosopis pallida* - also called "algarroba") is a tree that has been naturalized in Puerto Rico and Hawaii (where it is called "kiawe"). Its sweet pods are made into a syrup used in various drinks. The algarrobo blanco (*Prosopis alba*), which is found in subtropical Argentina, Uruguay, Paraguay, and southern Brazil, has pods that have been toasted to make a coffee substitute and are also used to make other beverages as well as flour.
  Common names and synonyms: Algarroba, algarrobo blanco, ibope, igope, kiawe, tacu, white algarrobo.

ALICANTE BOUSCHET (*see also* **GRAPES**) - A cross between Grenache and Petite Bouschet, the Alicante Bouschet grape (*Vitis vinifera*) is deep purple in color with a thick skin. The latter attribute made these grapes extremely popular during the days of Prohibition in the United States, because they could withstand rough handling when shipped to the homes of aspiring private wine makers. The Alicante Bouschet is used primarily for blending.
  See in addition: "Wine," Part III, Chapter 13.

ALKANET - A European plant, alkanet (*Alkanna tinctoria*) yields a dye from its roots that is used to color some cheeses and improve the color of inferior ports and other wines.

Alligator pear - *see* **AVOCADO**

Allouya - *see* **GUINEA ARROWROOT**

ALLSPICE - Unlike most spices (which are indigenous to the tropics of southern China, southern India, and the East Indies), allspice (*Pimenta dioica*) is a berry of the New World, native to the West Indies and Central America. A member of the myrtle family, allspice was used by the Taino and Carib Indians (and quite possibly also by those of the Mesoamerican mainland) long before the Europeans reached the Americas. The small, aromatic, tropical tree and its berries were among the many early "discoveries" of Spanish explorers, who mistook the pea-sized berries for peppercorns. In fact, even today the Spanish word *pimenta* refers to all-spice. The Spaniards introduced the spice into Europe in the sixteenth century, and in both whole and ground forms it has subsequently become a part of the cuisines of many peoples across the globe. Allspice, which begins as a purple berry but turns brown when sun-dried, acquired its English-language name because of its versatility: Its taste is like a combination of nutmeg, cinnamon, and clove. It is best in sweet and savory dishes and is used frequently in mulled wines and for pickling, not to mention in fruitcakes and spice cakes. Commercially, allspice is important in the production of catsup, sauces for meats, sausages, and cured meats. Today, allspice remains American – it is grown exclusively in the Western Hemisphere, especially in Jamaica (where it still thrives in the wild). That island, with its limestone soils, is the biggest allspice producer, and the Jamaicans also use the berries to make a kind of rum.

Common names and synonyms: Jamaica pepper, myrtle pepper, *pimenta*, pimento.

See also: "Spices and Flavorings," Part II, Section F, Chapter 1.

ALMOND (*see also* **CUDDAPAH ALMOND, JAVA ALMOND, MALABAR ALMOND**) – Almonds are the fruit seeds of *Prunus dulcis* (formerly *P. amygdalus*) = *Amygdalus communis*, a tree closely related to the peach and the plum, and are said to be native to the Mediterranean region and western Asia, where (like many other wild nuts) they doubtless helped to sustain our hunting-and-gathering forebears. Perhaps the oldest, as well as the most widely known, of the world's nut crops, almonds were first cultivated in Europe by the Greeks, are mentioned frequently in the Old Testament, and were a favorite of the Romans, whose sugared almonds may have been among the first sweetmeats in history. Recipes incorporating almond "flour" date from the Middle Ages in Europe, a period when almond "milk" was also used – as a liquid substitute for milk and eggs on days of fasting. The Spaniards brought the almond to the New World, where it is now grown extensively in California, and that state has joined Spain and Italy as a leading producer of the most important nut in the world nut trade. There are two types of almonds: sweet and bitter. Nuts of the latter type contain prussic acid and thus are toxic when raw; these must be blanched and roasted before being processed into an oil, a paste, or an extract that is used to flavor liqueurs and some confections. Sweet almonds, by contrast, are eaten whole, as well as blanched, slivered, chopped, diced, and ground for pastries and for meat and vegetable dishes. Almond paste is the soul of macaroons and marzipan. An almond tree will bear nuts for a half century or more, producing between 25 and 40 pounds annually. Almonds contain more calcium

than any other kind of nut and are also a source of the B vitamins and vitamin E. They provide a small amount of protein and are high in fat.

ALOCASIA (*see also* **TARO**) – As members of a genus belonging to the family Araceae, *Alocasia* species are related to taro (*Colocasia esculenta*). These plants are cultivated in tropical areas throughout Asia, and their roots are starchy and nutritious. The "giant taro" or "giant alocasia" (*A. macrorrhiza*) and the "Chinese taro" (*A. cucullata*) have tubers that are eaten as cooked vegetables, whereas *A. indica* is used in Indian curries.

Common names and synonyms: Ape, Chinese taro, elephant-ear plant, giant alocasia, giant taro, *pai.*

See in addition: "Taro," Part II, Section B, Chapter 6.

Alpine strawberry – *see* **WILD STRAWBERRY**

Alverja – *see* **PIGEON PEA**

AMALAKA – Also known as "emblic," the amalaka (*Phyllanthus emblica*) is a large tree, native to Malaya but cultivated throughout South and Southeast Asia and now grown in Puerto Rico as well. It produces small, walnut-sized, green-to-yellow fruits, which are sour and are generally used for jams, pickles, and chutneys. The fruits are very high in vitamin C.

Common names and synonyms: Amalaki, emblic, Indian gooseberry, Malacca tree, myrobalan.

Amalaki – *see* **AMALAKA**

Amarante – *see* **AMARANTH**

AMARANTH (*see also* **CHENOPODIUM, CHINESE AMARANTH**) – Hernando Cortés, the Spanish conqueror of Mexico, prohibited the cultivation of the amaranth grown in Mesoamerica (*Amaranthus hypochondriacus* and *A. cruentus* – a third species, *A. caudatus,* was cultivated in the South American Andes) because it was used for religious as well as culinary purposes. The result is that this legendary plant of the Aztecs, which they called *huautli,* has only recently been rediscovered by the West, although it has long been grown in India and tropical Africa – in fact, in most of the world's tropical areas – and the Mexican descendants of the Aztecs have continued its cultivation on their *chinampas.* Because the tiny, usually yellowish (but sometimes red) amaranth grains do not come from a member of the grass family, they are technically not grains at all. Rather, the plant is a member of the chenopod family – related to lamb's-quarter and tumbleweed – and grows well (to about 6 feet in height) in hot and sunny locations. But whether it is a weed or not, the sesame-like amaranth seed, with its pleasant nutty flavor, is packed with calcium, magnesium, and iron, delivers a considerable amount of folacin and riboflavin, and has a high protein content. In addition to the seeds, the leaves are also eaten (much like spinach) wherever amaranth is extensively cultivated. Amaranth seeds are usually boiled and eaten as a porridge or used as an ingredient in soups and stews. In addition, they can be popped and used to make *alegría,* a popular sweet in Mexico. Amaranth sprouts are also good to eat.

Common names and synonyms: Achis, achita, African spinach, amarante, *bledos,* bondue, bush greens, *ckoito, coimi, coyo, cuime,* green leaf, *huautli,* Indian spinach, Joseph's-coat, kiwicha, livid amaranth, love-lies-bleeding, *millmi,* pale-seeded amaranth, pigweed, princess-feather, purple amaranth, quintonil, redroot, spinach-grass, Surinam spinach, wild beet, wild blite.

See in addition: "Amaranth," Part II, Section A, Chapter 1.

Amarelle - *see* **CHERRY**

Ambarella - *see* **GOLDEN APPLE**

Amber - *see* **AMBERSEED**

AMBERCANE (*see also* **SORGHUM**) - Grown especially in South Africa, ambercane (*Sorghum dochna* or *S. bicolor*) is a grain crop much like millet and is used in much the same manner.

See in addition: "Sorghum," Part II, Section A, Chapter 9.

AMBERSEED - Also called "ambrette" and "musk seed," amberseed is the seed of the abelmosk (*Hibiscus Moscheutos*), which is a bushy herb. Native to tropical Asia and the East Indies, amberseed has long been used as a flavoring in coffee and in perfumery.

Common names and synonyms: Amber, ambrette, musk seed.

See also: "Spices and Flavorings," Part II, Section F, Chapter 1.

Ambrette - *see* **AMBERSEED**

American angelica - *see* **PURPLESTEM ANGELICA**

American beech (tree) - *see* **BEECHNUT**

AMERICAN BITTERSWEET - Also known as "false bittersweet," "climbing bittersweet," and a host of other common names, American bittersweet (*Celastrus scandens*) is a woody vine that grows on trees and fences. It has clusters of greenish flowers and a yellow fruit in the form of a yellow capsule, neither of which is edible - in fact, the entire plant is toxic. But the twigs and inner bark were used as food by Native Americans, who discovered that boiling eliminated the poison.

Common names and synonyms: Bittersweet, climbing bittersweet, false bittersweet. American black walnut - *see* **WALNUT**

American horsemint - *see* **BEE BALM, BERGAMOT**

AMERICAN LINDEN - Also called "basswood" and other common names, the American linden (*Tilia americana*) is a forest tree that is especially common in mountainous terrain from Canada to Georgia. Native Americans harvested its sap for a beverage and ate its inner bark. The young leaves can be made into a salad, cooked as a vegetable, and added to soups and stews. The red berries of the tree are also edible, making it a year-round food source.

Common names and synonyms: Basswood, linden, whitewood.

American mandrake - *see* **MAYAPPLE**

American storax - *see* **SWEET GUM**

American styrax - *see* **SWEET GUM**

American taro - *see* **MALANGA**

American wormseed - *see* **EPAZOTE**

Amra - *see* **HOG PLUM**

ANAHEIM (*see also* **CHILLI PEPPERS**) - This member of the genus *Capsicum* (*C. annuum*) is named for the city of Anaheim, California, where the pepper was first grown at the beginning of the twentieth century. Another name, "California chilli," honors its home state. It is actually, however, a "New Mexican chilli," which is another of its aliases, along with "long green chilli" and "long red chilli." The Anaheim is a relatively mild pepper (although some can be hot), is frequently seen in produce markets, and is one of the most commonly used peppers in the United States. As its various names imply, the Anaheim pepper is green while still maturing and red after it has matured. It is eaten in both forms (the red is the sweeter of the two), is often roasted or pickled, and - when stuffed - is the star of the Mexican classic *chillis rellenos.* Anaheims are also dried and made into a powder called *chilli colorado.* A *pasado* is a red Anaheim that has been roasted, peeled, and dried.

Common names and synonyms: California chilli, Chile Colorado Anaheim, Chile Verde Anaheim, *chilli colorado,* long green chilli, long red chilli, New Mexican chilli, *pasado,* Red Chile Anaheim.

See in addition: "Chilli Peppers," Part II, Section C, Chapter 4.

Anana - *see* **PINEAPPLE**

Anana del monte - *see* **POSHTE**

Ananás - *see* **PINEAPPLE**

Ananas de Mexico - *see* **MONSTERA**

Anato - *see* **ANNATTO**

Ancho - *see* **POBLANO**

ANDEAN LUPIN (*see also* **BEANS, LEGUMES**) - Known also as the "South American lupin" and "lupino," as well as a number of other names such as *chocho* and *tarvi,* the Andean lupin (*Lupinus mutabilis*) is a leguminous plant with large seeds (as a rule, bigger than lima beans) that served as food for ancient, pre-Incan peoples of the central Andean region. The Andean lupin is still widely cultivated there, even though the seeds contain alkaloids that must be leached out by a complex procedure. As with so many other poisonous plants, one can only wonder how the Andean lupin ever came to be widely used - or even used at all. The seeds are rich in protein and oil, are used in soups and stews, and can be made into a flour.

Common names and synonyms: Chocho, lupino, South American lupin, *tarvi.*

ANEMONE GREENS - Some greens from plants of the genus *Anemone* are used for food and medicinal purposes. The leaves of *A. flaccida* are eaten in Japan and China, whereas Eskimos eat the leaves of *A. narcissiflora* raw, fermented, or in oil. The crushed leaves of *A. hepatica* yield anemone camphor, which is used as a tonic. × *A. hupehensis* Hort. Lemoine var. *japonica* is cultivated in China for its roots, which are believed to be useful in treating heart disease. When collected during flowering, the dried plant *A. patens* is used to increase appetite and restore digestion.

ANGELICA (*see also* **PURPLESTEM ANGELICA**) – One of the tallest growing of the herbs, angelica (*Angelica archangelica*) provides stems as well as roots and leaves that are boiled and eaten as a vegetable. Angelica has a long history of use for medicinal purposes – indeed, its name (Latin for "angel") was assigned because of its healing properties. Angelica was one of the so-called scurvy grasses that were thought either to drive the disease away or to keep it at bay, and (until well into the twentieth century) after long winters, Icelanders dug up the roots to cure their bleeding gums. Today, oil from the roots and seeds is used for flavoring liqueurs, and the herb is used mostly in candied form. The stems are crystallized with sugar and employed in fruitcakes, as a flavoring in jams, and as a decoration for pastries.

Common names and synonyms: European angelica, garden angelica, Japanese angelica, scurvy grass, wild angelica.

Angel's-trumpet – *see* **MOONFLOWER**

ANGLED LUFFA – Also called "Chinese okra" because it is shaped like okra, the angled luffa (*Luffa acutangula*) is a dark green cucurbit native to India and has been grown (often on trellises) for many thousands of years for its tasty young fruits (the mature fruits become bitter). It is used mostly in China as a vegetable. Another more fibrous species, *L. aegyptiaca,* is dried and its fibrous skeleton used as a sponge. The United States is a major consumer of luffas and imports millions each year. But although it is called the "sponge gourd," *L. aegyptiaca* is also a food, and its flowers, buds, leaves, and young fruits are all eaten.

Common names and synonyms: Chinese okra, loofah, smooth loofah, sponge gourd, vegetable sponge.

ANGOSTURA – The bitter and aromatic bark of either of two Brazilian trees (*Galipea officinalis* and *Cusparia trifoliata* = *C. febrifuga*) is used to make a tonic called "angostura," named after a river town in Venezuela that is now called Ciudad Bolívar. "Angostura" is also the name of a proprietary brand of bitters made in Trinidad.

Common names and synonyms: Bitters.

ANISE (*see also* **CICELY, FENNEL, STAR-ANISE, SICHUAN PEPPERCORN**) – Also called aniseed, anise (*Pimpinella anisum*) is a native of the Mediterranean region (it grows wild in Greece and Egypt) and is one of the oldest of the spices. Anise was used by the ancient Greeks, Romans, and Hebrews, who viewed it as a powerful medicine, and today is grown in an area extending from southern Russia across South Asia, as well as in Mexico. Anise is a relative of dill, chervil, coriander, and cumin and has a licorice-like taste (after the seeds are dried) that is used to flavor liqueurs such as the Pernod of France, the ouzo of Greece, the anisette enjoyed in Spain, and the arrack of the eastern Mediterranean. Oil of anise has medicinal properties and is employed in cough syrups and lozenges. As a spice in the kitchen, anise is added to salads, pastries, fruit dishes, sauces, meat dishes, and fish and shellfish.

Common names and synonyms: Aniseed, *jintan,* sweet cumin.

See in addition: "Spices and Flavorings," Part II, Section F, Chapter 1.

Aniseed – *see* **ANISE**

Anise-pepper – *see* **SICHUAN PEPPERCORN**

Anise root – *see* **CICELY**

ANISILLO – A member of the New World genus *Tagetes* (which includes the garden marigold), anisillo (*T. minuta*) is an annual herb that grows to a height of from 3 to 6 feet. Throughout much of Latin America, it is dried and used to make a tealike beverage that is flavorful both hot and cold and is also thought of as a medicine. The dried plant is also added to rice dishes and stews for flavoring.

Common names and synonyms: Chilca, chinchilla, chiquilla, suico, wild marigold.

Anjou (pear) – *see* **PEAR**

ANNATTO – The bright red or yellow-brown fruits of the annatto plant (*Bixa orellana*), an American spice, have been employed more for their color than their flavor. Indeed, Native Americans of the Caribbean and Mesoamerica decorated their bodies with dyes made from the pulp that surrounds the seeds of this rough, berry-like fruit. The seeds are used – whole or ground – to color (and flavor) dishes such as Jamaica's famed ackee-fish-and-rice and the popular Mexican chilli powders. Annatto was carried by the Manila galleons to the Philippines, where the seeds have become important in many dishes. In Europe, annatto is used to color cheeses, butter, and oils.

Common names and synonyms: Achiote, anato, arnato, bija, bijol, *bixa,* lipstick tree, roucou.

See also: "Spices and Flavorings," Part II, Section F, Chapter 1.

Annual bunch grass – *see* **TEF**

Anon – *see* **SWEETSOP**

Anona – *see* **CHERIMOYA, CUSTARD APPLE**

Anona blanca – *see* **ILAMA**

Anu – *see* **MASHUA**

Ao-Togarashi (chilli pepper) – *see* **ASIAN CHILLIES**

Ape – *see* **ALOCASIA**

Apio – *see* **ARRACACHA**

APIOS – Also called "potato bean" and "groundnut" (but not to be confused with the peanut), apios (*Apios americana* or *A. tuberosa*) is a legume native to and found throughout eastern North America. Its edible underground tubers, roots, and seeds were gathered and widely consumed by Native Americans long before the Europeans arrived, but the plant was probably never cultivated. Apios is a twining vine with flowers ranging in color from pink to purple. It may have been taken to Europe as an ornamental as early as the end of the sixteenth century, and – later – there were thoughts of employing it as a potato substitute during the mid-nineteenth-century Irish potato famine. The idea was dropped, however, as disease-resistant lines of potatoes were developed. Among tubers, apios is very high in protein as well as carbohydrates, with a crude protein content about three times that of the potato. In addition, apios is unique among root and tuber crops for its ability to fix nitrogen. It nonetheless remains a neglected crop.

Common names and synonyms: Bog potato, groundnut, Indian potato, potato bean, Virginia potato, wild bean, wild potato.

Appalachian tea - *see* **WINTERBERRY**

APPLE (*see also* **CRAB APPLE**) - This fruit of legends – ranging from the tale of an apple as the cause of the Trojan War to the steady hand and eye of William Tell – is classified, along with the pear, as a pome fruit (meaning one with a compartmented core), and in fact "pome" means apple in Latin. Over 7,000 varieties of the apple (*Pyrus malus* or *Malus domestica*) are grown worldwide, and no wonder, for apple trees are valued not only for their fruit but also for their beauty in gardens and on lawns. Once the tree begins to bear fruit (after some 5 to 10 years for regular trees, but only 2 to 3 years for dwarf trees), it will continue to do so for upward of a century. Cultivated apples are descendants of wild or crab apples and are believed to have originated in Southwest Asia and the region around the Mediterranean. However, because crab apples still grow wild in Central Asia and Europe, some would widen the area of origin. Evidence indicates that this fruit, reputed to be the forbidden fruit of the Garden of Eden, was being cultivated and stored at least 5,000 years ago, and probably long before that. Apples were grown by the Etruscans, the Egyptians, the Greeks, and the Romans and, as with so many other food plants, were spread about Europe within the Roman Empire and thus have been cultivated there for at least 2,000 years. Apples reached the Americas in the seventeenth century with the early colonists, and today about 2,500 varieties are grown in the United States alone. Only 16, however, account for over 90 percent of the total U.S. production, about half of which goes into apple products such as cider, juice, applesauce, and the like. The leading 8 of the top 16, which account for 80 percent of U.S. production, are as follows:

• Golden Delicious, which when ripe is yellow and is the most widely consumed apple in the world. It was developed by accident in West Virginia toward the end of the nineteenth century.

• Granny Smith, a pale green apple, originated in Australia at about the middle of the nineteenth century. It is good eaten raw, is used for juice, and is suitable for general baking, for stuffing, for chutneys, and for salsas.

• Jonathan, a dark red and juicy apple, is used for juice and applesauce as well as for baking and stuffings.

• McIntosh is a greenish red apple that is good eaten raw and is used for juice and applesauce.

• Red Delicious, a red apple with crisp, juicy flesh, is the most popular apple in the United States.

• Rome Beauty, a red or red-striped apple, is favored for baking but is a bit mealy for eating out of hand.

• Stayman is a purplish apple for all-purpose use.

• York, also called York Imperial, is another good baking apple. It has a pink skin.

Other apples have somewhat specific uses. The Gravenstein is used mostly for applesauce; the Northern Spy is good for pies; the Winesap is a favorite for making cider. The sour crab apple is used for making jellies.

Most apples have a high sugar content, are low in tannin, and are slightly acidic. They are only a fair source of minerals, but they provide some vitamin A and have a good measure of vitamin C in their peels. Because apples are high in sugar, they are also high in carbohydrates.

Common names and synonyms: Cider apple, cooking apple, crab (wild) apple, dessert apple, Golden Delicious, Granny Smith, Gravenstein, Jonathan, McIntosh, Northern Spy, pippin, pome(-fruit), Red Delicious, Rome Beauty, Rome Delicious, Russet, Stayman, Winesap, Yellow Delicious, York, York Imperial.

Apple banana - *see* **BANANA**

Apple cactus - *see* **CACTUS APPLE**

Apple mint - *see* **MINT**

Apple-of-love - *see* **EGGPLANT**

Apple pear - *see* **ASIAN PEAR**

Apricock - *see* **APRICOT**

APRICOT - A sweet-sour fruit, the apricot (*Prunus armeniaca*) was long viewed as a kind of plum – and one that came from Armenia. In truth, it is a stone fruit (a drupe) of the same family as the peach, plum, almond, nectarine, and cherry and apparently originated (despite its scientific name) in China, where it has been cultivated for some 5,000 years. From China, the apricot traveled by way of northern India, finally reaching the Near East. After this, both Alexander the Great (356–323 B.C.) and, later, Roman legionnaires are credited with carrying the fruit to Europe. From Greece and Rome, apricots spread throughout Europe, and the Spaniards introduced them to the New World, where today they grow from Chile to California, with the latter area accounting for most North American production. In Europe, Spain is the leading producer of apricots. These walnut-sized fruits, which resemble peaches with their copper-colored flesh, are versatile in that they can be eaten fresh, dried, or canned and may be worked into rolls (apricot "sheets"), made into jelly, grilled, and poached. The kernels are a source of oil (although those of some varieties are poisonous), and the leaves can serve as fodder for sheep and goats. Apricots are an excellent source of beta-carotene, vitamin C, and potassium; when dried, they also are a good source of iron.

Common names and synonyms: Apricock.

Apricot vine - *see* **MAYPOP**

Arabian tea - *see* **KHAT**

ARAÇÁ-BOI - A fruit that is practically unknown outside of the Amazon Basin, the *araçá-boi* (*Eugenia stipitata*) has a pleasant appearance. It is also sweet smelling but has such a fiercely sour taste that its juice must be sweetened before consumption.

ARAÇÁ-PERA (*see also* **GUAVA**) - A wild guava of the Amazon, the *araçá-pera* (*Psidium angulatum*) provides a sour juice that must be both diluted and sweetened to make it palatable.

Arbor-vitae - *see* **CEDAR**

Archiciocco - *see* **ARTICHOKE**

Areca nut palm - *see* **BETEL NUT**

ARGAN - An evergreen tree native to North Africa (probably Morocco), the argan (*Argania sideroxylon*) has fruits with a high oil content. About the size of plums, they are pressed for an oil much appreciated by the Moroccans for its aroma and as a cooking medium. The oil can be found in specialty stores in the United States, but at a considerable price.

ARMENIAN CUCUMBER (*see also* **CUCUMBER**) - With other common names like "snake melon" and "snake cucumber," the Armenian cucumber (*Cucumis melo*) is - not surprisingly - very long (up to 3 feet) and very narrow (up to 3 inches in diameter). But it is not a cucumber. Rather, it is a melon, like the muskmelon (also *C. melo*), and a native of the Old World tropics. The Armenian cucumber, however, is not eaten as a melon but is used mostly for preserves.

Common names and synonyms: Japanese cucumber, snake cucumber, snake melon.

See in addition: "Cucumbers, Melons, and Watermelons," Part II, Section C, Chapter 6.

Arnato - *see* **ANNATTO**

AROIDS (*see also* **COCOYAM, TARO**) - The inclusive common name for all plants belonging to the Araceae family, the term "aroids" denotes over 1,000 genera and approximately 2,000 species, 90 percent of which are tropical in origin and grown largely as ornamentals. The exceptions are staple crops such as cocoyam and taro (genus *Colocasia*), which are cultivated in Southeast Asia, Malaysia, and the Pacific Islands. *Poi,* a Hawaiian dish, is made from taro. Monstera fruits, also part of the Araceae family, are edible as well.

Arracach - *see* **ARRACACHA**

ARRACACHA - A root of the Andean region of South America, arracacha (*Arracacia xanthorrhiza* or *A. esculenta*) is a staple for many of the Native Americans living there and, indeed, may be one of the oldest of the cultivated plants in that region. It stands in place of the potato in the diet and, in fact, was domesticated prior to the potato. Also called the "Peruvian carrot," arracacha is related to celery and - aboveground - resembles it. But belowground it has carrotlike roots that are boiled. Their flavor, according to expert Noel Vietmeyer, combines the tastes of celery, roasted chestnuts, and cabbage. No longer confined to the Andean region, arracacha is consumed throughout much of Latin America.

Common names and synonyms: Apio, arracach, arracacia, fecula, Peruvian carrot, Peruvian parsnip, r'accacha, white carrot.

Arracacia - *see* **ARRACACHA**

ARROW ARUM - A hardy North American perennial marsh plant, arrow arum (*Peltandra virginica*) is also called "green arrow arum," "Virginian tukahoe," "Virginian wake-robin," and "tukahoe." Native Americans in what is now the eastern United States ate the roots, stems, and flowers as vegetables.

Common names and synonyms: Green arrow arum, tukahoe, Virginian tukahoe, Virginian wake-robin.

ARROWHEAD - Arrowhead plants (genus *Sagittaria*) are widespread in the shallow waters of ponds, streams, and marshes, and those that are edible have roots that are cooked like potatoes or dried for flour. Some Native Americans used *S. latifolia* extensively, often acquiring it by discovering caches of the plants stored away by muskrats. *Sagittaria sinensis* is cultivated extensively in parts of China and Japan. Its root is similar to a lily bulb in appearance, has a bland, sweet taste, and is used in the same way as a potato.

Common names and synonyms: Arrowleaf, duck potato, swamp potato, wapata, wapato, wapatoo.

Arrowleaf - *see* **ARROWHEAD**

ARROWROOT - A perennial plant of the American tropics, arrowroot (*Maranta arundinacea*) is native to South America and the Caribbean and has been naturalized in southern Florida. It is also cultivated in Southeast Asia, Australia, and South Africa. The plant grows to a height of 3 to 5 feet, has long, very pointed leaves and small white flowers, and is cultivated for its starchy roots, which yield an edible starch that makes both a flour and a very smooth jelly or paste. The flour is almost all starch, is easily digested, is often employed as a thickener, and is prized by many chefs for making sauces. Both flour and jelly are used in infant foods, puddings, ice cream, and arrowroot biscuits, as well as in the manufacture of cosmetics and glue. Because Native Americans believed that the root absorbed poison from arrow wounds (hence its name), the plant has long been thought to have medicinal properties.

Starchy products from other plants are often subsumed under the general rubric of the term "arrowroot," and some can substitute for arrowroot. *Tacca leontopetaloides,* for example, is known as "Polynesian arrowroot."

Common names and synonyms: Polynesian arrowroot, tapioca, yuquilla.

Arrugula – *see* ARUGULA

Artichaut – *see* ARTICHOKE

ARTICHOKE – Although at least three vegetables are called artichokes, the globe or French artichoke (*Cynara scolymus*) has little relationship to either the Jerusalem artichoke or the Chinese artichoke. This is fortunate, because there is confusion enough created by the numerous varieties of the globe artichoke grown around the world. In Europe, the leaves are often reddish in color, but in the United States the only variety normally encountered in produce departments is the Italian Green Globe, with most of these grown in California. The artichoke appears to have originated in North Africa (where it still exists in a wild state). It subsequently became a wild thistle in Sicily, where its bitter leaves as well as its flower heads were gathered for food. The Greeks and Romans began its cultivation, and the parts of the immature flower head – artichoke leaves (tender and fleshy at the base) and bottoms ("hearts") – have been enjoyed at least since Roman times. The artichoke became an important part of Italian gastronomy and was subsequently imported to France by Queen Catherine de Médicis. Artichokes did not reach the United States until the nineteenth century. Today, the Spaniards, French, and Italians are the most fervent artichoke enthusiasts on the European continent, and California, Belgium, France, and the Mediterranean countries are the vegetable's most prolific producers. Similar to a miniature cabbage in appearance, the artichoke has leaves that are steamed and eaten with a dipping sauce, and the "hearts" and "bottoms" are sautéed, steamed, pickled, and cut into salads. Artichokes may be purchased fresh, frozen, and canned, and "baby" artichokes are frequently available marinated in jars. Artichokes are a good source of vitamin C and dietary fiber.

Common names and synonyms: Alcachofa, archiciocco, artichaut, articiocco, baby artichoke, *carciofo,* French artichoke, globe artichoke, Italian Green Globe, *karzochy.*

Articiocco – *see* ARTICHOKE

ARUGULA – Also known as "rocket" and "garden rocket," this native of Europe and western Asia (*Eruca sativa*) is a cruciferous plant that has long provided tender, slightly bitter, mustard-flavored greens for the salad bowls of southern Europeans and Italian-Americans. Lately, it has become widely available in the United States, where it has been naturalized. Its leaves resemble those of the radish, which

is a close relative. The seeds of arugula are also eaten, and they yield an oil that is used for culinary purposes, as a lubricant, and in medicines. Arugula is loaded with vitamins A and C and – like many greens – provides much iron and calcium as well.

Common names and synonyms: Arugula, garden rocket, jamba oil, Mediterranean rocket, rocket, rocket salad, roka, roquette, rucola, rugala, rugela, rugula.

See also: "Cruciferous and Green Leafy Vegetables," Part II, Section C, Chapter 5.

Aruhe – *see* BRACKEN FERN

Arvi – *see* COCOYAM

ASAFETIDA – Asafetida (ass-uh-feh-TEE-da; *asa* from the Persian "gum" and *foetida* from the Latin "stinking") is a spice made from a notoriously bad-smelling plant (*Ferula assa-foetida*) of the carrot family, which can grow to 10 or even a dozen feet in height. The plant is a native of Iran and Afghanistan, is related to fennel, and is commonly used in Indian and – to a lesser extent – other Asian and Middle Eastern cuisines. Because of its fetid odor (some say it is like that of garlic), the Germans called it *Teufelsdreck,* which can be translated as "devil's-dung." But in the past asafetida was worn around the neck as an amulet to ward off disease and during medieval times to ward off witches. Asafetida was also prized in the ancient world for its alleged contraceptive powers, and the Romans regarded it as a substitute for silphium, an herb that became extinct about the time of Nero. Fortunately, the plant's odor, caused by sulfur compounds, disappears during cooking, and the leaves and stems are eaten as a vegetable. The spice, made from the milk-like juice of asafetida, usually comes in ground form and is added very sparingly to dishes such as meatballs and to pickles for its truffle-like flavor. It is also an ingredient in the venerable Lea & Perrins Worcestershire sauce.

Common names and synonyms: Asafoetida, assafetida, assafoetida, devil's-dung, food-of-the-gods, *hing,* stinking gum, *Teufelsdreck.*

See also: "Spices and Flavorings," Part II, Section F, Chapter 1.

Asafoetida – *see* ASAFETIDA

Assafetida – *see* ASAFETIDA

Assafoetida – *see* ASAFETIDA

ASAM GELUGUR – A fruit from a tall tree that is native to Burma and Malaya, *Garcinia atroviridis* is orangish to yellow when ripe, round, about 3 inches in circumference, and very tart. As a rule, the fruit is sun-dried and used in curries. Immature fruits are incorporated in chutneys.

ASIAN CHILLIES (*see also* CHILLI PEPPERS) – Although all members of the genus *Capsicum* are native to the Americas, Asian peoples have enthusiastically adopted chilli peppers (which first reached Asia via the trading empires of Spain and Portugal) and incorporated them into the respective cuisines of the region. Many of the chillies, such as jalapeños, serranos, and Anaheims, would be familiar to Westerners, but others, now associated firmly with Asian cooking, would not. Among these are the tiny, red or green "bird's-eye" or "bird" chillies, which (frequently in dried form) give Thai cuisine its well-deserved reputation for fiery tastes. Another chilli, called "Thai" (this one about an inch and a half in length, and pointed), is also often dried, comes in green and red, and delivers significant heat (that lingers). A close relative of the Thai pepper is the Korean chilli, which is employed to put a bit of bite in *kimchee*. *Togarashi* chillies (often called by the Spanish *Japonés* in markets) are the Japanese equivalent of the Thai bird's-eye and, like it, are intensely hot. By contrast, the small, green *Ao-Togarashi* chillies have a mild flavor, as do the long, deep red Kashmiri chillies, which are employed for their color.

Common names and synonyms: Ao-Togarashi, bird chilli, bird's-eye, *Japonés,* Kashmiri chilli, Korean chilli, Thai chilli, Tien-tsin, *Togarashi.*

See in addition: "Chilli Peppers," Part II, Section C, Chapter 4.

ASIAN PEAR (*see also* **PEAR**) - A wide variety of seemingly different fruits are called "Asian pears" (*Pyrus ussuriensis* or *Pyrus pyrifolia*). Many of these now grow in the western part of the United States - having been brought there by Chinese immigrants during the nineteenth century - but have been widely marketed only in the past few decades. Among these are "apple pears," "sand pears," "Chinese pears," and "Oriental pears" that range in size from very small to quite large. These fruits often resemble a cross between an apple and a pear and come in a wide variety of colors. But all are juicy and so crisp that they can be sliced very thinly. Like other pears, they are eaten raw as well as cooked. There are more than 25 varieties of Asian pears in U.S. markets (where the most popular one is the "Twentieth Century") and more than 100 varieties available in Japan. Asian pears are a good source of vitamin C and fiber.

Common names and synonyms: Apple pear, Chinese pear, Japanese pear, *nashi,* Oriental pear, salad pear, sand pear.

Asiatic aubergine - *see* **EGGPLANT**

Asiatic yam - *see* **LESSER YAM, WATER YAM**

ASPARAGUS - A member of the lily family (which includes leeks, garlic, onions, and other relatives of the grasses), this perennial (*Asparagus officinalis*) was doubtless an important gathered food for our Stone Age ancestors. There are about 300 species of asparagus native to a region that extends from Siberia to southern Africa (and possibly species native to South America as well). Some, mostly of African origin, are poisonous and are grown only for ornamental purposes; these include the ubiquitous "asparagus fern" or "florist's fern." Wild asparagus

grows like a weed on English seacoasts, in the southern parts of eastern Europe, and on the steppes of the tundra, where horses and cattle graze on the vegetable. Asparagus has long been praised for both its culinary merit and its alleged medicinal properties, especially in the case of the kidneys. It has been cultivated since at least the time of the ancient Greeks and was a favorite of the Romans.

Asparagus can be green or white; the latter is the product of a method whereby soil is heaped on the growing stalks so as to block the sunlight necessary for chlorophyll production. White asparagus, with a stronger and somewhat more bitter flavor, is much more appreciated in Europe (especially in Spain and certain parts of France) and Argentina than in the United States, where commercial growers are mostly concerned with green asparagus. Although asparagus has a fairly short growing season in the United States, fresh spears can be purchased year-round because of South American production. France and Italy are also large producers. Frozen and canned asparagus is available, with the frozen close to the fresh in taste and nutritional value. The fresh green spears and green spears with white butts are frequently braised but are also excellent when steamed. Most canned asparagus is blanched white. Fresh asparagus has a large amount of vitamin C, although much can be lost during storage and preparation as well as during canning procedures. Asparagus is also high in vitamins A and E. Asparagus seeds have served as a substitute for coffee.

Common names and synonyms: Asparagus fern, florist's fern, garden asparagus, green asparagus, special bean, white asparagus, wild asparagus.

Asparagus bean - *see* **COWPEA, WINGED BEAN**

Asparagus broccoli - *see* **CALABRESE, CAULIFLOWER**

Asparagus lettuce - *see* **LETTUCE**

ASPARAGUS PEA - A native of southern Europe, the asparagus pea (*Lotus tetragonolobus*) is frequently confused with Africa's winged bean (*Psophocarpus tetragonolobus*) because of its winged pod. Asparagus peas are enjoyed as young edible pods that have an asparagus-like flavor and are prepared and served much like asparagus.

ASSAM AUR AUR - A native of Malaysia, and a fruit that has long grown wild in Southeast Asia, assam aur aur (*Garcinia hombroniana* Pierre) is now regarded as a candidate for cultivation as a specialty fruit. It is a close relative of the mangosteen, and its major culinary use involves its dried, crimson-colored rind - used as a relish in curries. In the past, the pulp of assam aur aur was fermented into a vinegar.

Assam - *see* **TEA**

Assfoot - *see* **COLTSFOOT**

ATEMOYA - A delicious dessert fruit that was created in the American tropics and subtropics, the atemoya (genus *Annona*) is a hybrid resulting from a cross between the cherimoya and the sweetsop. The fruit, which grows on small trees, is cultivated in southern Florida, the West Indies, and Central and South America in the New World. It has spread to Australia, New Zealand, and the Philippines in Oceania and to India, Israel, and South Africa in the Old World. The fruit looks somewhat like an artichoke on the outside; inside, it is pudding-like, creamy, and sweet. The taste of the atemoya resembles that of vanilla custard. It is a fine source of vitamins C and K as well as potassium.

Aubergine – *see* **EGGPLANT**

Auguweed – *see* **BONESET**

Australian arrowroot - *see* **ACHIRA**

AUSTRALIAN BLUE SQUASH (*see also* **SQUASH AND PUMPKIN**) - Although all squashes and pumpkins have an American origin, the Australian Blue squash (*Cucurbita maxima*) was developed in Australia. Also called the Australian Queensland pumpkin, it looks like a blue-gray-green pumpkin that is flat on both ends. Its soft flesh and mild flavor contribute to its frequent use in soup and bread making.

Common names and synonyms: Australian Queensland pumpkin.

See in addition: "Squash," Part II, Section C, Chapter 8.

AUSTRALIAN CARROT - A wild, dark-rooted carrot – native to Australia - the Australian carrot (*Daucus glochidiatus*) belongs to the same genus as the common carrot, which is domesticated in much of the rest of the world. The Australian version of the vegetable was one of the many foods gathered by the Aborigines.

AUSTRALIAN CHESTNUT - Also known as the "Moreton Bay chestnut" and the "bean tree" (because its fruits come in long pods), this big, evergreen, leguminous tree belongs to the pea family. The Australian chestnut (*Castanospermum australe*) produces large brown seeds that have long been an important food for the Aborigines. Like true chestnuts, these seeds are generally roasted before consumption.

Common names and synonyms: Bean tree, Moreton Bay chestnut.

Australian corkscrew tree – *see* **SESBAN**

AUSTRALIAN CURRANT - A small tree or shrub, *Leucopogon richei* is native to Australia and has white, edible fruits. These were among the many gathered fruits that sustained the Aboriginal population.

Australian desert kumquat – *see* **AUSTRALIAN DESERT LIME**

AUSTRALIAN DESERT LIME - Also known as the Australian desert kumquat, the Australian desert lime (*Eremocitrus glauca*) is a fruit - related to the orange - that grows on a shrub (an Australian native) about 8 to 10 feet in height. The pale yellow fruits are egg shaped and are made into beverages, jams, and preserves.

Common names and synonyms: Australian desert kumquat.

Australian nut – *see* **MACADAMIA NUT**

Australian Queensland pumpkin - *see* **AUSTRALIAN BLUE SQUASH**

Autumn olive – *see* **ELAEAGNUS**

Avens - *see* **HERB BENNET**

AVOCADO - The avocado (*Persea americana*) apparently originated in Central America, where it was cultivated as many as 7,000 years ago. It was grown some 5,000 years ago in Mexico and, by the time of Christopher Columbus, had become a food as far south as Peru, where it is called *palta.* Legend has it that Hernando Cortés found avocados flourishing around what is now Mexico City in 1519. The English word "avocado" is derived from the Aztec *ahuacatl,* which the Spaniards passed along transliterated as *aguacate.* Other names for the avocado are "alligator pear" and "butter pear," probably because of its green, leathery rind and buttery-, nutty-tasting flesh. Avocados are classified into three races, Guatemalan, Mexican, and West Indian, among which the Mexican is the least popular. Avocados have been grown in California and Florida since the middle of the nineteenth century, and – although there are more than 20 varieties of avocados on the market – for North Americans, they basically fall into two categories: those from California (a Guatemalan–Mexican hybrid and others of the Guatemalan race) and those from Florida (the West Indian race). Among those from California are Bacon, Zuttano, and Fuerte, and especially the Hass variety (by far the most abundant and, many say, the best tasting), a darker, bumpy-skinned, and considerably smaller fruit than the green, smooth-skinned Florida kinds (such as Lulu, Booth, and Waldin), which can look like pale green melons. The Florida avocados are lower in fat and calories than those grown in California but also have less texture and taste. Because avocados (along with olives and coconuts) contain high amounts of oil (avocado oil is similar to olive oil), their green, white, or yellow flesh doubtless played an important role in the otherwise lowfat diets of pre-Columbian peoples. Indeed, a recipe for guacamole - mashed avocados with spices - comes to us from the Aztecs. The Spaniards ate avocados with sugar, salt, or both, and introduced them into other parts of the Americas as well as other tropical parts of the world. But until the end of World War II, avocados were virtually unknown in Europe. This is no longer the case, however, as advertising has paved the way for their entrance into European produce markets everywhere. Today, avocados are considered a "fruit-vegetable," meaning that they go with both fruit and vegetable salads, are great with poultry and pasta, and make a nice sandwich as well. Avocado orchards stretch from California to Florida and from the Caribbean to Peru in the Americas. Avocados are grown in West Africa, in the countries surrounding the Indian Ocean, and in Israel, which supplies much of the European demand. In addition to its fat content, the avocado is fairly high in beta-carotene, is poor in vitamin C, is high in the B vitamins, and delivers a number of minerals.

Common names and synonyms: Aguacate, ahuacatl, alligator pear, avocado pear, *avocat,* Bacon, Booth, butter pear, Fuerte, Guatemalan avocado, Hass, Lulu, Mexican avocado, *palta,* Waldin, West Indian avocado, Zuttano.

Avocado pear - *see* AVOCADO

Avocat - *see* AVOCADO

AZAROLE - Native to North Africa and the Middle East, the azarole tree (*Crataegus azarolus*) is also known as the "Spanish pine," and its fruit as the "Neapolitan medlar" – both names suggesting its popularity in the Latin countries. By contrast, the fruit reached England in 1640 but never caught on there or in northern Europe. Azarole fruits range from red to yellow in color, are about the size of a crab apple, and make excellent preserves and marmalade as well as wine. The tree's flowers were once used to make a liquor, and its young buds and leaves are ingredients in salads. Azarole fruits are high in vitamin C and the B complex.

Common names and synonyms: Neapolitan medlar, Spanish pine.

AZUKI BEAN (*see also* **BEANS**) - This small, red bean (*Phaseolus angularis* - also known as the adzuki bean) is almost square in shape. It is native to China, where - as in Japan and Korea as well - it is grown extensively. Azuki beans are mostly dried and prepared by boiling, but they are also available canned in many countries around the world. The beans are generally used in dessert dishes. They are made into a paste for stuffing pastries, and pureed, they become a part of ice cream.

Common names and synonyms: Adzuki bean.

See in addition: "Beans, Peas, and Lentils," Part II, Section C, Chapter 3.

B

BABACO (*see also* **PAPAYA**) - A native of Ecuador, the babaco (*Carica pentagona*) - a close relative of the papaya (*Carica papaya*) - is a cross between the mountain papaya (*C. pubescens*) and the chamburo (*C. stipulata*). We have, however, no idea of the antiquity of the fruit, which was discovered in the 1920s by European botanists. It is oblong in shape and has a yellowish green edible skin and pale yellow flesh. In the early 1970s, the fruit was introduced into New Zealand, where it has become yet another South American adoptee. Babaco is very high in vitamin C.

Babricorn bean - *see* SWORD BEAN

Bachang - *see* HORSE MANGO

Bachelor's-button - *see* CORNFLOWER

Bacon - *see* AVOCADO

Bactrian typha - *see* MAIZE

BACURÍ - A South American native, the bacurí (*Platonia esculenta* or *P. insignis*) is a yellow fruit that grows on a tall timber tree. A relative of the mangosteen, the fruit has creamy, white, and sweet flesh. The bacurí is commercially grown – and rather intensively so – in the Amazon Basin.

Common names and synonyms: Bacury, bakuri.

BACURIPARI - A small tree, native to the Amazon region of South America, the bacuripari (*Rheedia macrophylla*) produces a fruit of the same name that is somewhat like the mangosteen, a close relative. Its flesh is white and creamy, with a fine flavor, quite similar to that of the bacurí.

Bacury - *see* BACURÍ

Badian anise - *see* STAR-ANISE

BAEL FRUIT - Also known as the "bel-fruit" and "Bengal quince," the bael fruit grows on the bael tree (*Aegle marmelos*), a native of India that is now grown throughout much of South and Southeast Asia. The tree reaches about 40 feet in height, and its fruits are generally about 2 to 5 inches across. The Portuguese called them *marmelos* because they have the flavor of marmalade and can be eaten raw. Bael fruits are also used to make a refreshing beverage.

Common names and synonyms: Bael tree, bel-fruit, Bengal quince, Indian bael, *marmelo.*

Bahama whitewood - *see* WHITE CINNAMON

Bajra - *see* MILLET

Bakeberry - *see* CLOUDBERRY

Baked-apple berry - *see* CLOUDBERRY

BAKUPARI - Also known as *pacura,* the bakupari (*Rheedia brasiliensis*) is a Brazilian tree that produces an edible, orange-colored fruit with snow-white flesh. The fruit is slightly acid and is eaten out of hand as well as made into jellies and jams.

Common names and synonyms: Pacura.

Bakuri - *see* BACURÍ

BALANITES - Members of *Balanites,* a small genus of Old World tropical trees that is part of the family Zygophyllaceae, are cultivated from Africa to Burma for the acorn-like drupes they produce. The nuts are sometimes used for food but are mostly employed for the production of an oil used in cooking.

Balata - *see* MIMUSOPS

Balazo - *see* MONSTERA

Balloonberry - *see* STRAWBERRY-RASPBERRY

Balm mint - *see* LEMON BALM

Balm-of-Gilead tree - *see* BALSAM FIR

BALSAM APPLE - A tropical vine, native to the Old World, the balsam apple (*Momordica balsamina*) has yellow flowers and a warty, orange fruit that is eaten raw, boiled, and fried. Also called the "wonder apple," it grows in the tropics of India, New Guinea, and the Philippine Islands.

Common names and synonyms: Wonder apple.

BALSAM FIR - A North American tree that provides an inner bark once used by Native Americans for food, the balsam fir (*Abies balsamea*) is also known as the "Canada balsam" and the "balm-of-Giliad tree." The balsam or pith was also eaten, but the bark - often used to make a kind of bread - was so important to some tribes that it could almost be called a staple.

Common names and synonyms: Balm-of-Giliad tree, Canada balsam.

Balsam herb - *see* COSTMARY

Balsam pear - *see* BITTER MELON

BAMBARA GROUNDNUT (*see also* LEGUMES) - This leguminous plant (*Voandzeia subterranea* or *Vigna subterranea*) develops underground, nutlike fruits. Similar to peanuts, the fruits are encased in pods and are rich in starch and protein. Grown in the arid lands of Africa, Asia, and South America, they are most popular in Zambia and Madagascar. Bambara groundnuts are eaten fresh or boiled and have a taste similar to peas. They are also dried, ground into flour, and used for baking.

Common names and synonyms: Bambarra, Bambarra nut, Congo goober, ground pea, voandzou.

Bambarra nut - *see* BAMBARA GROUNDNUT

Bamboo - *see* BAMBOO SHOOT(S), WATER BAMBOO

BAMBOO SHOOT(S) - Plants of the bamboo tribe (*Bambusaceae*) are among the tallest of the grass family, occasionally reaching heights of 100 feet. Bamboo "shoots" are their young stems. Bamboo plants and their shoots are native to the warmest parts of Africa, the Americas, and, of course, Asia. As any zoo aficionado knows, these are the favorite (and practically the only) food of China's pandas. Bamboo is also important in the cuisines of Asia's humans, who add the shoots to dishes for a crunchy texture and also pickle and candy them. Outside of Asia, the shoots are generally available only in canned form, although they can be found in some Asian-style markets. Fresh bamboo shoots deliver good amounts of thiamine, potassium, and vitamin B_6, but the canning process robs them of most of their nutrients.

Common names and synonyms: Takenoko, tung sun.

Bamia - *see* OKRA

BANANA (*see also* **BANANA FLOWER, ENSETE, PLANTAIN**) - The various forms of the banana (*Musa paradisiaca*) are probably native to South and Southeast Asia and doubtless helped feed hunter-gatherers for hundreds of thousands of years. The banana is among the oldest plants that humans have used, was one of the first to be cultivated, and today constitutes one of the most important food crops in the world. The identity of the exact homeland of the banana has been blurred by the plant's ability to spread rapidly throughout the tropics. By way of an example, when bananas reached the tropical New World (apparently with Spanish explorers), they propagated with such rapidity that some of the earliest chroniclers thought that the fruit was an American native. And bananas apparently reached tropical Africa and Polynesia much earlier (c. A.D. 500 and 1000, respectively) than they did the New World.

The banana "tree" is really a giant herb that can grow to 20 or more feet in height in only a year, even though it sprouts from a rhizome or corm. Suckers rise in clumps from the rhizome and, as they grow, form groups of flowers that can become bunches (called "hands") of bananas. One "hand" may consist of as many as 400 bananas, but that is all the plant will ever produce; after producing one bunch, it dies, although another sucker may grow from the rhizome to take its place. Bananas did not become commercially important for export until the nineteenth century (with the advent of refrigerated ships), and today Brazil is the biggest exporter and the United States the biggest importer of the fruit. But most bananas - about 80 percent - are consumed in their respective African, Asian, Caribbean, or Central and South American regions of production, where the fruit is often an important staple food.

Bananas - with some 200 varieties - come in different shapes, sizes, and colors. *Manzanos* (also called finger or apple bananas) are about the length of a finger and turn from yellow to black when ripe. Saba and Brazilian bananas are medium-sized, tart, and straight rather than curved, whereas red bananas are sweeter. The Cavendish, with its color ranging from green through yellow to black (indicating its degree of ripeness), is the banana most commonly encountered in the produce markets of North America. Other common varieties are the Martinique, the Jamaica, the Gros Michel, and the Bluefield. Bananas can be baked, fried, and grilled, although roughly one-half of those produced are simply peeled and eaten out of hand. Bananas are easily digestible, can be used at various stages of ripeness, and are an excellent source of carbohydrates, potassium, and vitamins A and C.

Common names and synonyms: Apple banana, Bluefield, Brazilian banana, Cavendish, dwarf banana, finger banana, Gros Michel, Jamaica, *manzano,* Martinique, *pisong jacki,* red banana, Saba, Silk Fig.

See in addition: "Bananas and Plantains," Part II, Section B, Chapter 1.

Banana chilli - *see* WAX PEPPERS

Banana de brejo - *see* MONSTERA

BANANA FLOWER (*see also* BANANA) - The banana fruit is not the only edible part of the banana plant (*Musa paradisiaca*). The male flowers - the compact, purple, pointed heads at the end of a forming bunch of bananas - are also eaten, often on the site where the bananas are grown. They are used as a vegetable and garnish in the countries of Southeast Asia, where they are available in local markets.

Common names and synonyms: Banana blossom, banana bract, banana bud, banana heart(s), *jantung pisang,* Silk Fig.

See in addition: "Bananas and Plantains," Part II, Section B, Chapter 1.

Banana heart(s) - *see* **BANANA FLOWER**

Banana pepper - *see* **WAX PEPPERS**

BANANA SQUASH (*see also* **SQUASH AND PUMPKIN**) - A sometimes huge squash, weighing upward of 30 pounds, the banana squash (*Cucurbita maxima*) is often sold in smaller pieces at produce counters. It is perhaps the most bland of this American species that was domesticated in South America. The banana squash has an orange flesh that is high in beta-carotene as well as vitamin C.

See in addition: "Squash," Part II, Section C, Chapter 8.

BAOBAB - A huge tree, native to tropical Africa, the baobob (*Adansonia digitata*) is famous for its trunk, which often reaches 30 feet in diameter. Also grown in India, the tree has an edible-fleshed fruit sometimes called "monkey-bread." The fruit is about 9 inches in length, oval, and hard-shelled, and has a fibrous, floury white pulp. Its juice is also consumed - after sweetening - and in the past was used to treat tropical fevers. The leaves of the tree are eaten as a vegetable.

Common names and synonyms: Monkey-bread.

Barbados cherry - *see* **ACEROLA**

Barbados eddoe - *see* **COCOYAM**

BARBADOS GOOSEBERRY (*see also* **BERRIES**) - A member of the large cactus family, the Barbados gooseberry (*Pereskia aculeata*) is native to the West Indies. Its edible yellow fruit resembles the gooseberry in appearance and has a fine taste. Also called the "lemon vine," this cactus has leaves that are edible as well; they are usually consumed raw.

Common names and synonyms: Leafy cactus, lemon vine.

Barbary fig - *see* **PRICKLY PEAR**

Barbe de capucin - *see* **CHICORY**

BARBERRY (*see also* **BERRIES**) - There are numerous different species of shrubs of the genus *Berberis* that bear small orange or red berries similar to currants. They can be found in Asia, Europe, North Africa, and North and South America, growing best where there is plenty of sunlight. A very popular barberry is *B. thunbergii,* a native of Japan, and there are other popular varieties native to Korea and Japan. In France, famous jams are made from the seedless barberry. The bright red berries ripen in the fall in North America and are especially abundant in New England. In the western United States, the barberry is called the "wild Oregon grape," or just "Oregon grape." The berries are generally very tart and are the basis of fine jellies and preserves. They were doubtless another food employed by hunting-and-gathering Native Americans, as were barberry leaves, which go nicely in salads and can be cooked as a vegetable.

Common names and synonyms: California barberry, holly-leaved barberry, Oregon grape, pepperidge, Rocky Mountain grape, seedless barberry, trailing mahonia, wild Oregon grape.

BARLEY (*see also* **WILD BARLEY**) - Barley (*Hordeum vulgare*) originated in western Asia, and, as our hunter-gatherer ancestors settled into sedentary agriculture during the Neolithic Revolution, it became one of the first grains to be cultivated. This grain has the advantage of a relatively short growing season and - because it matures quickly - has adapted to a considerable variety of environments. Barley was important in early Egypt and China but was displaced by wheat in ancient Rome. Like rye, it became a staple in northern Europe during the Middle Ages. Barley has also long been a source of drink as well as food. Malt is made from barley by soaking the seeds until they sprout. In the process, the proteins in the bran change into enzymes that convert starches - first into sugars and then into alcohol. As with other grains, barley is refined by milling to the point that many nutrients are stripped away. Pearl barley, for example, has had the entire outer husk removed. Pot or Scotch barley is much less refined and is good in soups. Barley flakes and grits are used in breakfast cereals. Barley has a nutlike flavor, is high in carbohydrates, and contains phosphorus, calcium, and some of the B-vitamin complex. In North America and Europe, most barley either is used for the production of beer, ale, and whiskey or becomes feed for animals. But in less-developed countries, such as many of those in Africa, barley is still an important part of the human diet, and it remains a staple in the Middle East.

Common names and synonyms: Barleycorn, barley flakes, barley grits, malt, naked barley, pearl barley, pot barley, Scotch barley, six-row barley, two-row barley.

See in addition: "Barley," Part II, Section A, Chapter 2; "Beer and Ale," Part III, Chapter 1.

BARREL CACTUS - There is some taxonomical dispute concerning the genera of these two cacti (*Ferocactus wislizenii* and *Echinocactus,* especially *E. grandis*) known as "barrel cactus." They are also called "visnaga." Both are natives of the southwestern United States. The barrel cacti provided stem pulp that served as food for Native Americans, as did their fruits.

Common names and synonyms: Fish-hook cactus, southwestern barrel cactus, visnaga.

Basil - An herb that is part of the mint family, is native to India (and possibly Africa as well), and is known as the tomato's best friend, basil (*Ocimum basilicum* = *O. americanum*) comes in many types - and more than a few colors - that are now distributed worldwide. Closing in on becoming the world's most popular herb, basil was virtually unknown outside of Europe 30 years ago. It is sometimes classified as either "sweet basil" or "bush basil." Sweet basil has a larger leaf that is more aromatic and flavorful. Bush basil (*Satureja vulgaris* or *Ocimum minimum* - also called "wild basil"), although native to the Old World, is widely naturalized in the Americas. Basil was used by the ancient Greeks, and the Greek word *basilikon,* meaning "royal," perhaps suggests that the herb was reserved for royalty. The Romans spread the herb around Europe, where basil's heart-shaped and aromatic leaves have long been a favorite of the Italians and the Provençals - indeed, in Italy the leaves are considered symbols of love. Basil is best fresh, is often used in soups and pâtés, is vital to Italian pesto, and is a natural companion for tomatoes in sauces and salads. Dried basil does not retain the same delicate flavor as the fresh leaves, but it is frequently added to sauces nonetheless. Many people preserve their fresh leaves in olive oil in a tightly sealed jar. Basil is also employed to flavor the liqueur Chartreuse.

Common names and synonyms: Basilic common, *basilico,* bush basil, sweet basil, wild basil.

See also: "Spices and Flavorings," Part II, Section F, Chapter 1.

Basilic common - *see* **BASIL**

Basilico - *see* **BASIL**

Basswood - *see* **AMERICAN LINDEN**

Batata dulce - *see* **SWEET POTATO**

Batavian endive - *see* **ENDIVE AND ESCAROLE**

BAYBERRY (*see also* **BERRIES**) - The shrubs *Myrica pensylvanica* and *M. cerifera* are North American plants that produce gray, waxy berries, which have historically been melted down into wax for candles. Bayberry leaves, however, have culinary applications. They are pickled and dried for use as a less pungent bay leaf in soups, stews, and the like.

Bay laurel - *see* **BAY LEAF**

BAY LEAF - The aromatic leaves of the bay laurel tree (*Laurus nobilis*) are regarded by many as an indispensable flavoring herb in the kitchen. The leaves come from a small evergreen that apparently was a native of Asia Minor but has been scenting the air of the Mediterranean region for so long that it is also thought of as native there. Indeed, the Romans used laurel leaves for fashioning garlands to honor soldiers, athletes, and poets - hence the term "laureate," which still persists to indicate preeminence. In earlier times, the laurel leaf also had a reputation for warding off evil. Aromatic bay leaves are among the most versatile herbs used in Mediterranean cooking and, in fact, are popular in most cuisines throughout the world. If used fresh, they are first crumbled; if dried, they can be used either whole, crumbled, or ground. Bay leaves are good (often with thyme) in almost any soup, stew, sauce, or meat dish (including pâtés) and are one of the principal ingredients in a bouquet garni. They are also important in pickling and are added to vinegars, marinades, and puddings. Laurel leaves are now produced in areas of North Africa and North America as well as in their traditional regions of cultivation.

Common names and synonyms: Bay laurel, Grecian laurel, laurel, sweet bay, sweet laurel.

See also: "Spices and Flavorings," Part II, Section F, Chapter 1.

BEACH PEA (*see also* **LEGUMES**) - A number of the fruits of the leguminous plants of the genus *Lathyrus* were used for food in the past by hunter-gatherers. Along the coasts of North America - including those of the Great Lakes - the immature seeds of the beach pea (*L. maritimus*) were eaten like sweet peas, and ripe ones were ground into a flour. The inflorescences of the sweet pea (*L. odoratus*), a popular garden flower originally from the Mediterranean region, may also have served as food in the past. Today, the plant is grown commercially for its flowers, which yield an essential oil used in perfumes. Other species have been used as food by Europeans and Asians over many millennia.

Common names and synonyms: Sweet pea.

See in addition: "Beans, Peas, and Lentils," Part II, Section C, Chapter 3.

BEACH PLUM (*see also* **PLUM**) - The beach plum (*Prunus maritima*) is a seacoast shrub that bears an edible plumlike fruit. This plant ranges along the east coast of North America from the province of New Brunswick in Canada to as far south as Virginia. It is a strange plant that frequents only seemingly infertile areas like sand dunes, and its fruit, which ranges from red and purple to yellow, can be sweet and delicious or so tart as to be inedible. The beach plum is used mostly for making a jelly that goes well with duck and venison.

Common names and synonyms: Shore plum.

Beaked hazel - *see* **HAZELNUT AND FILBERT**

Bean tree - *see* **AUSTRALIAN CHESTNUT**

BEANS (*see also* the various bean entries) - Beans were among the first (and most important) foods to be gathered. In Afghanistan, the Himalayan foothills, and central Asia, *Vicia faba* - the fava bean, broad bean, or Windsor bean - was food for hunter-gatherers tens of thousands of years ago, as was *Cicer arietinum* (the chickpea or garbanzo) - in western Asia. These were gradually brought under cultivation in an area encompassing much of Asia, the Middle East, and Egypt and had become staples in the diets of many long before the ancient Greeks employed them as counters for balloting. The Phoenicians are credited with carrying the chickpea to the western end of Europe, where "garbanzos" became entrenched in the diet of the Iberians and have continued as an important staple to this day. Moreover, in prehistoric times, three species of the genus *Lupinus* were brought under cultivation in the Mediterranean region and later embraced enthusiastically by the Greeks and Romans. These were the white lupine (*L. albus*), the blue lupine

(*L. angustifolius*), and the European yellow lupine (*L. luteus*). In addition to their splendid pink-and-blue flowers, lupines provide very nourishing seeds, but around the time of the Renaissance they began their disappearance from culinary use. To this day, however, large lupine seeds are preserved in brine by many peoples of the Mediterranean, who simultaneously strip them of their thick skins and pop them in the mouth, eating them as a snack.

Meanwhile, in the New World, a vast range of beans of the genus *Phaseolus* had, as in Europe, initially been gathered and later brought under cultivation. The first species to be domesticated was the common bean (*P. vulgaris*), which archaeological evidence from the Peruvian Andes suggests occurred about 8,000 years ago (findings from the Tehuacán Valley in central Mexico indicate domestication there about 1,000 years later). Varieties of the common bean were subsequently cultivated from southern South America to as far north as the St. Lawrence River. Among them were seeds we know today as turtle beans (black beans), kidney beans (including the white cannellini), Lamon beans, chili beans, cranberry beans, pinto beans, red beans, "great northern" beans, string (snap) beans, Romano (Italian green) beans, flageolets, and other round white beans ranging from the large marrow bean to the small pea or navy bean.

A second New World species is *P. lunatus*, comprised of the lima and sieva beans and so called because of the lunar - actually half-moon - shape of the seeds of some varieties. Archaeological evidence shows that, like common beans, lima beans (named after Peru's capital city) were in use in the Andean highlands some 8,000 years ago. However, they do not appear in the archaeological record of Mexico. The smaller sieva beans, by contrast, were apparently never in Peru but were grown in Mexico about 1,200 years ago, all of which has prompted the conclusion that the two varieties had a common ancestor but were domesticated independently by Andean and Mesoamerican farmers. In Peru, there is much evidence to indicate that lima beans were playing a major role in the diet 5,000 years ago. Today, the large lima beans are called "Fordhooks" or "butter beans," and the smaller sievas are called "baby limas." Other names for members of *P. lunatus* are "Madagascar bean" and "Towe bean."

The scarlet runner (*P. coccineus*), today often grown as an ornamental climber in the United States (but much appreciated at the table in Great Britain), is the third New World species. These beans were gathered about 9,000 years ago and were cultivated in Mexico at least 1,500 years ago (there is disagreement as to whether pods dating from about 4000 B.C. were gathered in the wild or were domesticated). Both the purple-seeded and white-seeded varieties are frequently cultivated

around poles (thus, "pole beans") to keep them from "running."

The fourth New World species of bean is the now obscure tepary bean (*P. acutifolius*). Of the four species, this one had the northernmost area of origin: Central Mexico, where teparies were cultivated about 5,000 years ago, and what is now the U.S. Southwest, which they reached by about 1,200 years ago. Apparently, the major use of teparies was to grind them into flour for more or less "instant" bean dishes.

The American beans began to travel after the arrival of the Iberians in the Americas. In the Far East, their reception was lukewarm because of local favorites such as the azuki bean (*P. angularis*), the mung bean (*P. aureus*), the cowpea (*Vigna unguiculata*), and, of course, the soybean (*Glycine max*) - today the most widely consumed bean in the world. Similarly, the West Africans had their own beans, such as the cowpea or black-eyed pea (actually a bean), and the winged bean (*Psophocarpus tetragonolobus*). But the American beans found ready acceptance in East Africa and in almost all of Europe.

Experimentation in bean breeding in Europe has produced considerable confusion. Native Americans probably consumed some beans as immature pods despite their stringiness, but the beans' major use was in the dried form, which was easily stored. The Europeans, however, sorted through the American beans and selected (and developed) many for use as snap beans. Thus, when the Europeans settled North America, they brought American beans back to their home hemisphere, but the green pods had become "French" beans - presumably because the French had given American beans the name *haricot*. In France, any bean of the genus *Phaseolus* is called an *haricot* whether fresh or dried, but in England "haricot" generally means a dried bean, whereas fresh pods are called French or green beans. Much breeding has finally removed the strings from string beans so that now they are known as "snap" beans, a category that includes green snap beans, green haricots, the Romano bean, the wax bean (the common name for the yellow snap bean), the purple wax bean, pole beans, scarlet runners, and even cowpeas when immature.

Some of the world's great dishes are based on beans. Among the first were the succotash of the Native Americans and the various "fabadas" (stews and soups made with fava beans) of Europe. Then there is the *cassoulet* of France, the *feijoada* of Brazil, the chile con carne of Texas, the "hoppin' John" of the U.S. South (and the three-bean salad of the United States in general), the hummus of the Middle East, the minestrone of Italy, the refried beans of Mexico, and, of course, Boston baked beans.

Beans are nitrogen-fixing, which means that when the plants are plowed under they become "green manure." Indeed, when beans are planted in rotation with wheat and barley, almost no fertilizer is required. Beans are cholesterol-free and high in vitamins, minerals, and soluble fiber. Long called "poorman's-meat," they are also very high in protein.

Common names and synonyms: Azuki bean, baby lima, black bean, black-eyed bean, black-eyed pea, blue lupine, broad bean, butter bean, cannellini, chickpea, chile bean, chili bean, common bean, cowpea, cranberry bean, European yellow lupine, *faba,* fava, flageolet, Fordhook, French bean, *garbanzo,* great northern bean, green bean, green haricot, green snap bean, *haricot,* Italian green bean, kidney bean, Lamon bean, lima bean, lupine, Madagascar bean, marrow bean, mung bean, navy bean, pea bean, pinto bean, pole bean, poor-man's-meat, purple-seeded pole bean, purple-seeded scarlet runner, purple wax bean, red bean, Romano bean, scarlet runner, sieva bean, snap bean, string bean, tepary bean, Towe bean, turtle bean, wax bean, white bean, white cannellini, white lupine, white-seeded pole bean, white-seeded scarlet runner, Windsor bean, winged bean, yellow lupine, yellow snap bean.

See in addition: "Beans, Peas, and Lentils," Part II, Section C, Chapter 3; "Soybean," Part II, Section E, Chapter 5.

BEAN SPROUTS (*see also* **BEANS, MUNG BEAN, SOYBEAN**) – Typically from mung beans (*Phaseolus aureus*) or soybeans (*Glycine max*), the early shoots of these plants are widely used in Asian cooking. The 1- to 2-inch-long sprouts are tender and rich in vitamin C. They are usually eaten raw, although they can be lightly cooked and still retain their nutritive value.

See in addition: "Beans, Peas, and Lentils," Part II, Section C, Chapter 3; "Soybean," Part II, Section E, Chapter 5.

BEARBERRY (*see also* **BERRIES, HEATHER**) – Also known as "kinnikinnick" and "crowberry," the red bearberry comes from several North American shrubs (genus *Arctostaphylos*) that have small evergreen leaves and white or pink flowers. The eastern black bear is said to be fond of them, and they were among the many wild foods gathered by Native Americans.

Common names and synonyms: Crowberry, kinnikinnic, kinnikinnick.

Bearss - *see* **LEMON**

Bear's-weed - *see* **YERBA SANTA**

BEE BALM (*see also* **BERGAMOT**) – There is considerable confusion surrounding bee balm, balm, and melissa. Balm is a Eurasian native known as *Melissa officinalis* or melissa, from the Latin and Greek meaning "bee" and from "honey" or *meli* (consider the word "mellifluous") – the whole suggestive of the attraction that the flowers of this plant have for bees. Confusion began with one of the early Spaniards in the New World, Nicolas Monardes, a physician and naturalist, who seems to have been the first European to describe a close relative,

Monarda didyma, an American native that was subsequently named for him. This plant is called bergamot but is very commonly named bee balm and melissa as well – hence the confusion. Both plants are sweet, herbal members of the mint family. In the case of the American native (the Eurasian cousin is now naturalized in North America), the leaves were used by the Oswego Indians to make a kind of tea, and when rebellious North American colonists could no longer obtain tea through British channels, they copied the Indians in making what they called "Oswego tea." In the case of the Eurasian plant, it is still used today to flavor liqueurs such as Benedictine and Chartreuse. The leaves of both "bee balms" are also used fresh and dried to flavor pork dishes, cooked vegetables, salads, stews, and poultry.

Common names and synonyms: American horsemint, balm, bee herb, bergamot, garden balm, horsemint, melissa, Oswego tea, wild bee balm.

Beech mast - *see* **BEECHNUT**

BEECHNUT – Beech trees (genus *Fagus*) belong to the family that also includes oak and chestnut trees. Their bark is smooth, light colored, and easily scratched or carved upon; consequently, the European beech (*F. sylvatica*), in particular, served as a "bulletin board" for eons prior to the advent of paper. In Europe, beechnuts (referred to as "mast" or "beech mast") were employed – historically as well as today – in fattening hogs and for oil. During both of the twentieth-century world wars, however, beechnuts were used extensively by humans as a survival food. The American beech (*F. grandifolia*) is native to the eastern part of the United States, where many consider its nut to be among the best tasting of all. The flavor of this small nut is somewhere between that of chestnuts and hazelnuts. It can be eaten raw and is also often roasted, made into nut "butter," and pressed to yield a fine oil. It is interesting to note that the nuts produced by certain kinds of oak trees are technically known as beechnuts rather than acorns.

Common names and synonyms: American beech, beech mast, European beech, mast.

Beech wheat - *see* **BUCKWHEAT**

Beefsteak fungus - *see* **MUSHROOMS AND FUNGI**

BEEFSTEAK PLANT – Also called *shiso* by the Japanese, the beefsteak plant (*Perilla arguts*) – a member of the mint family – is native to Burma, China, and the Himalaya Mountains. Both the red and green varieties are cultivated for garnishes, sprouts, and use as a vegetable.

Common names and synonyms: Shiso.

Beef tongue - *see* **MUSHROOMS AND FUNGI**

Bee herb - *see* **BEE BALM, LEMON BALM**

BEET (*see also* **MANGELWURZEL, SWISS CHARD**) – All of today's beets are descended from a wild forebear whose green tops doubtless nourished our own prehistoric forebears. Indeed, the first cultivated beets were apparently tended only for their leaves (eaten like spinach), and it was not until the early Christian era that their roots became appreciated. The commercially most important descendant of the wild beet (*Beta maritima*) is the European sugar beet (*B. vulgaris* L. ssp.), which was developed to produce sugar and became a serious competitor of sugarcane in the nineteenth century. However, the red, yellow, and white edible roots of some of the other native European *B. vulgaris* varieties (beetroots as they are called in the United Kingdom) find their way to the dinner table. The red garden beet, essential to borscht, is also the ingredient of the famous Harvard beets dish (named and perhaps created because of the university's crimson colors) and is prominent as a pickled vegetable as well. In much of Europe, however, the yellow variety has historically been prized because of a sweeter taste and greater suitability for pickling. The white-rooted beet is important for its leaves and stalks, which can be put to use as substitutes for, respectively, spinach and asparagus. Still another beet, the mangelwurzel, with a very large bulb, is employed as animal fodder. Unfortunately, many (especially middle- and upper-class Europeans) feel that *all* beets are essentially animal food – or, at best, peasant food. Beet greens are a source of riboflavin, iron, and vitamins A and C. The roots are high in folacin and vitamin C. Beets are available fresh, pickled, and canned.

Common names and synonyms: Beetroot, chad, chard, European sugar beet, garden beet, Harvard beet, mangel, mangelwurzel, red beet, red-beet leaf, red garden beet, spinach beet, sugar beet, Swiss chard, white-rooted beet, wild beet, yellow beet.

Beetle-bung - *see* **BLACK GUM**

Beggar's-button(s) - *see* **BURDOCK**

Beldobes - *see* **QUELITES**

Bel-fruit - *see* **BAEL FRUIT**

BELGIAN ENDIVE (*see also* **CHICORY**) - Also called "French endive," Belgian endive (*Cichorium endivia*) is known in Europe as *witloof* and is a relative of both escarole and chicory. It is a smooth, pale, elongated, and slightly bitter vegetable, which has been forced from roots that have been covered with soil and kept in darkness – hence its pale color. Belgian endive is used in salads and is braised as a vegetable.

Common names and synonyms: French endive, red Belgian endive, white endive, *witloof.*

BELIMBING - A relative of carambola, the belimbing (*Averrhoa bilimbi*) is also known as the "sour finger carambola" and the "cucumber tree." The fruit is light green to yellow in color, about 3 inches in length, and is much like a small, unripe mango in appearance. It is much too sour to eat raw, and in Malaysia, Thailand, Indonesia, and the Philippines, it is stewed and added to curries to impart a sour taste. Belimbings are very high in vitamin C.

Common names and synonyms: Bilimbi, blimbling, cucumber tree, sour finger carambola.

Beli Pinot - *see* **PINOT BLANC**

Bellflower - *see* **CAMPANULA**

Bell pepper - *see* **SWEET PEPPERS**

Bendi - *see* **OKRA**

Bengal bean - *see* **PIGEON PEA**

Bengal gram - *see* **CHICKPEA**

Bengal grass - *see* **MILLET**

Bengal quince - *see* **BAEL FRUIT**

Benne - *see* **SESAME**

Ben(n)iseed - *see* **SESAME**

Benjamin bush - *see* **SPICEBUSH**

BENOIL TREE - Although originally native to the Indian subcontinent, benoil trees (*Moringa oleifera* and *M. pterygosperma*) are now found throughout the Old World tropics. The leaves and roots of this tree taste like horseradish and, chopped up and mixed with water or milk, are made into a sauce that is thought to aid digestion. The seeds yield an oil that is used for industrial purposes and also contain a sweetening substance. In short, virtually all parts of this tree are eaten or used in some way. The young seedpods – long and slender like drumsticks, and probably the source of the nickname "drumstick tree" – are eaten as a vegetable or used in curries. The roots may easily substitute for horseradish. The leaves – perhaps one of the richest sources of calcium in the plant world, and rich as well in vitamins, minerals, and proteins – are cooked and served as a vegetable and are also used as a flavoring and an animal feed.

Common names and synonyms: Drumstick tree, drumstick vegetable, horseradish tree, moringa nut.

Ber - *see* **DESERT APPLE**

BERGAMOT (*see also* **BEE BALM**) - The fruit called bergamot fruit comes from a small spiny tree (*Citrus bergamia*). It is called the bergamot orange, or mellarosa, and is halfway between an orange and a lemon. It is sour, and its leaves, flowers, and pear-shaped fruits are used mostly in perfumery. However, the oils from the rind are also employed in flavoring liqueurs, and the fruit goes into an Italian preserve, *mostarde di frutta*. The bergamot orange is grown mostly in the southern Italian province of Calabria.

Another plant called bergamot is wild bergamot, a name given to the leaves of any of several American plants of the genus *Monarda*. These are also known as "bee balm" and "American horsemint" and are made into tea.

Common names and synonyms: American horsemint, bee balm, bergamot herb, bergamot orange, horsemint, mellarosa, wild bergamot.

Bergamot lemon - *see* **LEMON**

Bergamot orange - *see* **ORANGE**

BERRIES (*see also* the various berry entries) - Berries were, arguably, among the very first human foods. Certainly they were a sweet seasonal staple for our hunting-and-gathering ancestors for scores of millennia. And at some point in the past, humans learned to dry them and store them for use in the winter, to make them into various kinds of preserves, and to mix them with meats and fats to become pemmican, as did the Native Americans. Wild berry gathering remains a popular activity in Europe as well as North America, but most berries encountered in stores have been cultivated. There are several species of blackberries and raspberries (with segmented fruits) belonging to the genus *Rubus,* some of which have been cultivated since the seventeenth century or so. Smooth-skinned blueberries and cranberries are members of the genus *Vaccinium* that have been cultivated commercially for a century or more in the United States. Strawberries (*Fragaria* species), of course, are the most popular berries and are widely cultivated, as are currants (genus *Ribes*). Most berries are very rich in vitamin C and potassium. Berries come fresh, frozen, canned, and in some cases (for example, that of cranberries) as a juice.

BETEL NUT – The orange- to scarlet-colored fruit of a palm that is native to tropical Asia, betel nut (*Areca catechu*) is processed by boiling and drying, then mixed with betel leaves and lime and chewed by many people for its slight narcotic effect. Those who chew it believe that betel nut sweetens the breath, strengthens the gums, and promotes digestion.

Common names and synonyms: Areca, areca nut palm, betel(nut) palm, *catechu, pinang.*

Betel(nut) palm – *see* **BETEL NUT**

Bhindee – *see* **OKRA**

Bhindi – *see* **OKRA**

Bible leaf – *see* **COSTMARY**

Bible-leaf mace – *see* **COSTMARY**

Bigarade – *see* **ORANGE**

Bigarreau – *see* **CHERRY**

BIG GREEN PLUM (*see also* **PLUM**) – Known also as the wild plum, the big green plum (*Planchonella pohlmaniana*) is an edible fruit of Australia and one of the many that sustained its hunting-and-gathering Aboriginal population over millennia.

Common names and synonyms: Great green plum, wild plum.

BIG-LEAFED HYDRANGEA – A native of China, the deciduous shrub *Hydrangea macrophylla* is the ancestor of most of our garden hydrangeas. Its dried rhizomes and roots have been used as both a food and a medicine.

BIGNAY – Also called *buni,* "Chinese laurel," and "salamander tree," the bignay (*Antidesma bunius*) is a small tree – native to Australia and India – that is widely cultivated in Indonesia for its red and somewhat sour fruits (about half an inch in diameter) that grow in clusters. They are eaten raw as well as made into preserves, jellies, and syrups. They are also used to flavor brandies, and to make a sauce for fish.

Common names and synonyms: Buni, Chinese laurel, salamander tree.

Bija – *see* **ANNATTO**

Bijol – *see* **ANNATTO**

BILBERRY (*see also* **BERRIES**) – A European relative of the blueberry, the bilberry (*Vaccinium myrtillus* – also known as the whortleberry in Europe) seems its identical twin (the Australians call bilberries blueberries), save that they have differently shaped flowers and that the bilberry is a bit darker than the blueberry. Perhaps the result of a natural hybridization, the bilberry is the focus of northern European berry pickers as well as their counterparts in northern North America during the summer and fall months. But it also grows in California and the American Southwest, where it is wrongly called huckleberry as well as blueberry. Bilberries were an important food for many Native American tribes.

Common names and synonyms: Blueberry, huckleberry, *myrtille,* whortleberry, windberry.

Bilimbi – *see* **BELIMBING, CARAMBOLA**

Billion-dollar grass – *see* **JAPANESE MILLET**

Bilsted – *see* **SWEET GUM**

Bindi – *see* **OKRA**

Bindweed – *see* **ROUGH BINDWEED**

Bird chilli – *see* **ASIAN CHILLIES**

Bird pepper – *see* **BRAZILIAN MALAGUETA, TEPÍN CHILLIES AND RELATIVES**

Bird's-beak – *see* **CAYENNE PEPPER**

Bird's-eye – *see* **ASIAN CHILLIES**

Bird vetch – *see* **TUFTED VETCH**

BIRIBÁ – Native to northern South America and the West Indies, the biribá (*Rollinia deliciosa*) grows on a small tree and is most appreciated in northern Brazil, where it is grown commercially. It is a round, yellow, sweet, and juicy fruit that can weigh up to 3 pounds when mature. It is consumed fresh and made into juice.

Birthroot – *see* **TRILLIUM**

Bishop's-weed – *see* **AJOWAN**

Bistort – *see* **KNOTWEED AND SMARTWEED**

Bitter button(s) – *see* **TANSY**

Bitter cucumber – *see* **BITTER MELON**

Bitter gallberry – *see* **WINTERBERRY**

Bitter gourd – *see* **BITTER MELON**

BITTER MELON (*see also* **MELON**) – The fruit of a tropical vine, which is also known as "bitter cucumber," "balsam pear," and "bitter gourd," the bitter melon (*Momordica charantia*) originated in the Old World – possibly in Africa, but more likely in India – and was carried by the Portuguese to Brazil in the sixteenth or seventeenth century. Although now widespread in the tropical world from the Philippines to the Caribbean, the bitter melon is most highly regarded in much of Asia, where it is thought to have medicinal properties (it does contain quinine, which accounts for its bitter taste); it is believed to purify the blood and cool the body.

But the bitter melon is also cultivated as a food in China and South and Southeast Asia. The fruit has a skin that is light to bright green, wrinkled, and shiny, and it turns yellow as it ripens. Consumers look for the green skin because bitter melon is deemed best when it is immature. Like the cucumber, which it resembles, this fruit is usually prepared by halving it and scooping out the seeds. The Chinese braise or steam the bitter melon, whereas in India it is used in curries, pickled, frequently boiled and fried, and sometimes eaten raw after being steeped in water to remove the bitter taste.

Common names and synonyms: Balsam pear, bitter cucumber, bitter gourd, *kerela.*

See in addition: "Cucumbers, Melons, and Watermelons," Part II, Section C, Chapter 6.

Bitter oca - *see* OCA

Bitter orange - *see* ORANGE

BITTER POTATO (*see also* WHITE POTATO) - The bitter potato (*Solanum × juzepczukii* or *S. × curtilobum*) is an ancient food of the high Andean plateau spanning Peru and Bolivia, where its cultivation dates from at least 8,000 years ago. Early Spanish chroniclers mentioned potatoes that were processed by freezing, thawing, and drying to make *chuño* - a life-sustaining staple. Although bitter potatoes were not the only potatoes that were "freeze-dried" in this fashion, in their case such processing was essential to remove their glycoalkaloids. Both black and white versions of *chuño* are made; the former is a thoroughly dehydrated product that keeps well, and the more expensive white *chuño* is available in markets and consumed on festive occasions.

See in addition: "Potatoes (White)," Part II, Section B, Chapter 3.

Bitterroot - *see* VALERIAN

BITTER ROOT - A western North American plant, *Lewisia rediviva* was named for Meriwether Lewis of the Lewis and Clark expedition across the continent in 1806 and 1807. The plant has white flowers and fleshy, edible roots that were roasted or boiled and consumed by Native Americans in the western part of the country. They also dried and ground the roots into a meal.

Bitters - *see* ANGOSTURA

Bitter tomato - *see* LOCAL GARDEN EGG

BITTER VETCH (*see also* VETCH) - This Mediterranean herb (*Vicia ervilia* or *Ervum ervilia*) is widely cultivated as fodder for livestock. Care must be taken with bitter vetch, however, because its seeds are considered poisonous for pigs and dangerous when moist and mature. Occasionally, it is eaten in soups. Found in Europe, Asia, and the United States, bitter vetch is also known as ervil.

Common names and synonyms: Ervil.

Bitterweed - *see* RAGWEED

BITTER YAM (*see also* YAMS) - Also called "African bitter yam," the bitter yam (*Dioscorea dumetorum*)

is a native of tropical Africa, where it has remained because of the bitter taste its name proclaims. The reason that it is cultivated at all (mostly in Nigeria) is that it apparently has a higher yield than most other African yams. It is usually boiled in soups and stews.

Common names and synonyms: African bitter yam, cluster yam, trifoliate yam.

See in addition: "Sweet Potatoes and Yams," Part II, Section B, Chapter 5.

Bixa - *see* ANNATTO

Black alder - *see* WINTERBERRY

BLACKBERRY (*see also* BERRIES) - There are numerous species of blackberries (genus *Rubus*), which are divided into those that grow on brambles and those that grow on trailing vines; the latter are often called "dewberries" in the southern United States. Together, the blackberry and the dewberry constitute the most important of the wild berry crops in the United States. As a rule, these berries are indeed black or purplish black and outwardly resemble raspberries (also of the genus *Rubus*) in that each berry looks like a cluster of very tiny berries. Blackberries are an autumn crop that was harvested far back in prehistoric times. Their remains have been found in excavations of the earliest European habitations. Blackberries were known to the ancient Greeks and were another of the many gathered foods that sustained Native Americans, who may also have used them medicinally. The berries are said to be good blood cleansers and useful in combating dysentery as well as colds, and the leaves have been employed against sore throats. Some hybrid varieties of the blackberry, such as boysenberries, loganberries, and olallieberries, have been developed. Like all berries, the blackberry is a fine source of vitamin C. It also provides a good deal of iron.

Common names and synonyms: Boysenberry, bramble(s), dewberry, loganberry, olallieberry.

Black-cap - *see* RASPBERRY

Black caraway (seed) - *see* NIGELLA

Black cumin - *see* NIGELLA

BLACK CURRANT (*see also* CURRANTS) - Called *cassis* by the French, the black currant (*Ribes nigrum*) is employed to make the cordial *crème de cassis* and an aperitif called "Kir"; it is also used as a garnish with ice cream.

Common names and synonyms: Cassis, European black currant.

Black dhal - *see* MUNG BEAN

Black diamond (truffle) - *see* TRUFFLE(S)

Black drink - *see* YAUPON

Black-eyed pea - *see* BEANS, COWPEA

Black gram - *see* MUNG BEAN

BLACK GUM - Also called "sour gum," "pepperidge," and "tupelo," the black gum (*Nyssa sylvatica*) is a tree of eastern, central, and southern North America. It produces small, blue-black, plumlike fruits that were among the many foods gathered by Native Americans.

Common names and synonyms: Beetle-bung, pepperidge, sour gum, tupelo.

BLACK HAW (*see also* **BERRIES**) – Also known as "sweet haw," "sheepberry," "nannyberry," and "stagbush," these trees have two different scientific names depending on where they are found. On the east coast of the United States, the black haw is known as *Viburnum prunifolium,* whereas in the Midwest and on the Pacific coast it is *Crataegus douglasii.* The trees are usually planted for ornamental purposes, although their small, blue-black fruits can be made into preserves; the leaves, too, are edible, as Native Americans well knew. The black haw is also known for the medicinal uses of its bark. Containing the bitter resin viburnin, it is used as a sedative, uterine relaxant, and diuretic.

Common names and synonyms: Hawthorn, nannyberry, sheepberry, stagbush, sweet haw.

Black Indian hemp - *see* **HEMP DOGBANE**

BLACK MONKEY ORANGE – Native to southern Africa, *Strychnos madagascariensis* bears fruits that average a little over 3 inches in diameter and change from blue-green to yellow upon ripening. A thick shell protects the pulp, which is frequently made into a kind of jam by the Zulu people. In Zimbabwe, the pulp is dried in the sun or over a fire to serve as a nutriment during times of food shortage. The oil of the pulp is used as a medicine for dysentery.

Black nightshade - *see* **WONDERBERRY**

Black oyster-plant - *see* **SCORZONERA**

Black persimmon - *see* **BLACK SAPOTE**

Black salsify - *see* **SCORZONERA**

BLACK SAPOTE (*see also* **WHITE SAPOTE**) – A number of different fruits are called sapote (or sapota), which can produce considerable confusion. One might expect to find, for example, that the white sapote and the black sapote – both tropical American natives – are different-colored specimens of the same fruit. But they are not even of the same family: The white sapote belongs to the family Sapotaceae, and the black sapote to the family Ebenaceae. The black sapote (*Diospyros digyna* – a relative of the persimmon) does, however, resemble the sapodilla in form, although it has a sweet, soft, dark brown flesh. It is a highly prolific tree, grown throughout the New World tropics and subtropics, as well as in Hawaii and California, and the fruit is principally used in desserts.

Common names and synonyms: Black persimmon, black sapota, chocolate-pudding fruit, *zapte negro.*

Black snakeroot - *see* **WILD GINGER**

Black tamarind - *see* **VELVET TAMARIND**

Blackthorn - *see* **HAW, SLOE**

BLADDER CAMPION – There are a number of plants of the genus *Silene* that are called "campion" – especially "bladder campion" (*S. cucubalus = S. vulgaris*). It is a European green gathered in the spring for use as a potherb, particularly in the south of France.

Bladder weed - *see* **KELP, SEAWEED**

Blanc Fumé - *see* **SAUVIGNON BLANC**

Blé de Turquie - *see* **MAIZE**

Bledos - *see* **AMARANTH**

Blessed herb - *see* **HERB BENNET**

Blimbling - *see* **BELIMBING**

BLOOD ORANGE (*see also* **CITRUS FRUITS, ORANGE**) – A very large variety of sweet orange, the blood orange (*Citrus sinensis*) has juice that is usually of a burgundy hue, which along with the red color of its flesh, accounts for its name. Blood oranges (also called pigmented oranges) are a favorite in Europe (especially in countries along the Mediterranean coastline) but have not really caught on in the United States, although the "Ruby Blood" and "Moro" varieties are grown in California and Florida. Blood oranges come mostly from Spain and Italy; important European varieties include the Spanish *Sanguinella* and the "Maltese Blood." The English call these fruits "Maltese oranges," the French "*Maltaise oranges,*" and it is from the latter people that a hollandaise sauce – with the addition of the grated rinds of blood oranges – received the name "maltaise sauce." Like other oranges, the blood orange is a good source of vitamin C and provides some fiber as well. Its red color, however, does not come from carotene, which is one of the many exceptions to the rule that red and orange coloring of fruits and vegetables is a promise of beta-carotene.

Common names and synonyms: Maltaise orange, Maltese Blood, Maltese orange, Moro, pigmented orange, Ruby Blood, *Sanguinella.*

BLUEBERRY (*see also* **BERRIES, BILBERRY**) – Blueberries come from any of a number of shrubs of the genus *Vaccinium* that grow wild over much of the globe and can be found in the Western Hemisphere from Alaska to the jungles of South America. Those indigenous to North America are either highbush (especially *V. corymbosum* - also called the swamp blueberry) or lowbush (*V. angustifolium* - sometimes called the sweet blueberry). The former type has been commercially cultivated in the United States throughout most of the twentieth century and is considerably larger than its wild counterparts. Blueberries, which look almost the same as huckleberries, keep longer in storage than other berries – in both fresh and frozen forms. Blueberries were an important food for Native Americans, who used them in stews and dried and stored them for winter use. The Indians of Alaska have traditionally preserved them in seal oil for consumption in the winter. Blueberries are frequently eaten alone as a fruit, but are also popular in muffins, pies, cobblers, jams, and jellies and are made into wine. They are an excellent source of vitamins A and C as well as fiber.

Common names and synonyms: Highbush blueberry, huckleberry, late sweet blueberry, late sweet bush, lowbush blueberry, low sweet bush, rabbit-eye blueberry, swamp blueberry, sweet blueberry, whortleberry.

Blueberry elder - *see* **ELDERBERRY**

Bluebottle - *see* **CORNFLOWER**

BLUE COHOSH - A plant with a number of common names, such as "papoose root," "squawroot," and "blue ginseng" or "yellow ginseng," the blue cohosh (*Caulophyllum thalictroides*) is found in eastern North America and is especially common in the Allegheny region. Its seeds have been roasted and used as a substitute for coffee, and its large leaves consumed after boiling, but its blue berries are said to be poisonous. Its rootstock, which contains an alkaloid, is used medicinally.

Common names and synonyms: Blue ginseng, papoose root, squawroot, yellow ginseng.

Blue ginseng - *see* **BLUE COHOSH**

Blue lupine - *see* **BEANS**

Blue mountain tea - *see* **GOLDENROD**

BLUE-STEM - A grass of the western United States, blue-stem (*Andropogon furcatus*) is also called "blue-stem wheatgrass" and "western wheatgrass." Today it is used for hay; in the past both the stems and the seeds provided food for Native Americans; the plant also was used as a medicine for indigestion.

Common names and synonyms: Blue-stem wheatgrass, western wheatgrass.

Blue-stem wheatgrass - *see* **BLUE-STEM**

BLUE VERVAIN - A North American member of a genus that includes species scattered around the globe, blue vervain (*Verbena hastata*) grows as a weed throughout southern Canada and here and there in the United States – from Florida to Arizona. Native Americans processed the seeds of the plant by roasting and grinding them into a flour.

Common names and synonyms: False verbain, verbain, verbena, vervain, wild hyssop.

Blue water lily - *see* **LOTUS**

Bochweit - *see* **BUCKWHEAT**

Boechweite - *see* **BUCKWHEAT**

Bogbean - *see* **BOG MYRTLE**

BOG HEATHER - Also called cross-leaved heath and cross-leaf heath, bog heather (*Erica tetralix*) is a European shrub of bogs and marshes. Some varieties have dark, rose-red flowers with stems and petals that are said to be edible.

Common names and synonyms: Cross-leaf heath, cross-leaved heath.

BOG MYRTLE - Also called "Scotch gale" and "sweet gale," bog myrtle (*Myrica gale*) grows in bogs throughout the north temperate zone and has bitter-tasting leaves that are used as a potherb. In the past, before the use of hops, bog myrtle was widely employed in western Europe for flavoring beer, and it is still used on occasion for this purpose in England, where hopped beer has always met with some consumer resistance. Another plant known as bog myrtle and similarly used is the buckbean (*Menyanthes trifoliata*).

Common names and synonyms: Bogbean, buckbean, marsh trefoil, Scotch gale, sweet gale.

Bog potato - *see* **APIOS**

Bog rhubarb - *see* **COLTSFOOT**

BOK CHOY (*see also* **CABBAGE AND CHINESE CABBAGE**) - This member of the cabbage family is an East Asian native and a mainstay in the diets of the region. But bok choy (*Brassica rapa*) is also available in the markets of Europe and North America. It is sometimes called Chinese cabbage or Chinese mustard cabbage, which leads to confusion with the real Chinese cabbage (napa). In appearance, its nonheading stalks and leaves (both are eaten) resemble Swiss chard, or celery without the ribs. The taste of the stalks is something like that of romaine lettuce, whereas the leaves have a definite cabbage-like flavor. Bok choy is a favorite among the stir-fry vegetables and, in addition to being a fine source of vitamins A and C, also provides some calcium.

Common names and synonyms: Celery cabbage, Chinese cabbage, Chinese mustard cabbage.

See in addition: "Cruciferous and Green Leafy Vegetables," Part II, Section C, Chapter 5.

BOLETE (*see also* **MUSHROOMS AND FUNGI**) - Several of the mushroom members of the genus *Boletus* are poisonous, but not *Boletus edulis,* also called *porcino,* cep, *cèpe de bolete,* and *cèpe de Bordeaux.* These are wild mushrooms – easily recognized by the presence of spongy tubes instead of gills under their brownish-colored caps – and are highly prized throughout much of Europe. Although this mushroom also grows in North America, it tends to be moldy and is often a prey of insects. But in the spring and again in the fall the Italians hunt and consume their *porcini* with gusto, as do the French their *cèpes,* and the Germans their *Steinpilze.* A delicious mushroom that is generally eaten fresh – but wonderful as well when dried – it is also powdered and preserved in oil. *Boletus edulis* provides some vitamin D and a little of the vitamin B complex. It is also a good source of fiber.

Common names and synonyms: Cep, *cèpe, cèpe de bolete, cèpe de Bordeaux,* king bolete, *porcini, porcino, Steinpilz.*

See in addition: "Fungi," Part II, Section C, Chapter 7.

Bonavist bean - *see* **HORSE GRAM**

Bondue - *see* **AMARANTH**

BONESET - Any of several plants of the genus *Eupatorium* - and especially *E. perfoliatum* - are called boneset, along with a host of other colorful names, such as "auguweed," "feverwort," and "sweating plant," all suggestive of past medicinal uses. Some species, like *E. dalea,* have been used as a vanilla substitute in the American tropics. The leaves and flowering tops of others are cooked as greens in Asia, and in North America, where *E. perfoliatum* is a common weed, these parts of the plant served Native Americans as a wild food. One North American species (*E. rugosum*) – called "white snakeroot" – is toxic. This is the infamous weed that caused trematol poisoning in the cattle that grazed on it and "milk sickness" in the humans who drank their milk – a surprisingly frequent cause of death in the early decades of the nineteenth century.

Common names and synonyms: Aguweed, auguweed, feverwort, sweating plant, white snakeroot.

BONIATO (*see also* **SWEET POTATO**) – In Cuba, *boniato* (*Ipomoea batatas*) means sweet potato. This term is not to be confused with the Puerto Rican *boniata,* which means sweet yuca. Yet even the Cuban meaning is hazy, because white-fleshed sweet potatoes are preferred on that island, so that *boniato* has come to signify only the light-colored varieties that spread from their American homeland to Europe and throughout Asia – the latter region now grows some 90 percent of the world's production. A kind of cross between the orange sweet potato and a white potato, the *boniato* is a fair source of vitamin C and the B-vitamin complex. The whiter-fleshed varieties are not, however, good sources of beta-carotene, and some contain absolutely none.

Common names and synonyms: Cuban sweet potato, sweet potato, white sweet potato, yam (U.S.).

See in addition: "Sweet Potatoes and Yams," Part II, Section B, Chapter 5.

Bonnet pepper - *see* **HABANERO AND SCOTCH BONNET PEPPERS**

Booth - *see* **AVOCADO**

BORAGE (*see also* **INDIAN BORAGE**) – A native of the Middle East and Mediterranean regions, where it still grows wild, borage (*Borago officinalis*) has azure, nectar-filled flowers that bees love. The name derives from the Latin *burra* – meaning "rough hair" – and refers to the "hairs" that protrude from the stems and leaves of the plant, which taste something like unripened cucumbers. The Chinese stuff the leaves of borage in much the same way that Greeks stuff grape leaves. In France and Italy, the leaves are employed fresh in spring salads, are added to stews, and are used as a base for borage soup. In Germany, borage is often used in salads with dill, and in Britain and North America the leaves and flowers are sometimes added to cold drinks. Borage is also an ingredient in Pimm's No. 1, a gin drink of England. The flowers are added to salads and are frequently crystallized.

Borassus palm - *see* **WINE PALM**

Boreal vetch - *see* **TUFTED VETCH**

Borecole - *see* **COLLARDS, KALE**

Botoko plum - *see* **GOVERNOR'S PLUM**

BOTTLE GOURD (*see also* **CALABASH, SQUASH AND PUMPKIN**) – Although apparently a native of Africa, the bottle gourd (*Lagenaria siceraria*) spread to both Asia and the Americas in prehistoric times. In Mexico, bottle gourd remains dating from 7000 B.C. have been found, but how the Atlantic crossing was achieved is one of the mysteries surrounding the movements of plants in the distant past. The bottle gourd is so called because, when dried, it can be scooped out and employed as a container; such gourds were probably among the first utensils used by some human groups and, of course, are still in use as dipper gourds today. Although not well known as a food plant, bottle gourds are regularly consumed in India, China, and Japan and are similar in taste and texture to summer squashes. In India, the bottle gourd is called *doodhi,* and its flesh is added to stews and curries. In Japan, it becomes *kampyo* – the flesh is cut into ribbon-like strips that are dried and used as edible ties for packaging sushi. Bottle gourds are also employed as food in some of the countries of Latin America.

Common names and synonyms: Doodhi, hue, kampyo.

Bounce berry - *see* **CRANBERRY**

Box thorn - *see* **MATRIMONY VINE**

BOYSENBERRY (*see also* **BERRIES, BLACKBERRY**) – The boysenberry (*Rubus loganobaccus*) is the creation of twentieth-century American horticulturalist Rudolph Boysen, who in about 1920 created this huge blue-black hybrid berry by crossing the loganberry, the raspberry, and the blackberry. The boysenberry resembles the latter two in taste and has been assigned to the genus *Rubus.*

BRACKEN FERN – Also known simply as bracken or brake, this fern (*Pteridium aquilinum*) is well distributed throughout the world's temperate and tropical regions and has found use in such diverse corners of the globe as North America, Europe, Asia, the South Pacific, and the Canary Islands. The fronds are used for thatching and as fodder, but young ones are also cooked and eaten as a vegetable and made into soups. The rhizomes of the plant are roasted and ground into flour used in bread making. Native Americans steamed the fern in fire pits.

Common names and synonyms: Aruhe, bracken, brake.

Brake - *see* **BRACKEN FERN**

BRAMBLE(S) (*see also* **BERRIES, BLACKBERRY, BOYSENBERRY, CLOUDBERRY, DEWBERRY, JAPANESE WINEBERRY, LOGANBERRY, RASPBERRY, SALMONBERRY**) – An overarching name for any prickly plant or shrub of the genus *Rubus* is "bramble" or "brambles," which embraces black-berries, boysenberries, loganberries, and rasp-berries as well as other lesser-known species and varieties.

Brazilian cherry - *see* **PITANGA**

Brazilian grape tree - *see* **JABOTICABA**

BRAZILIAN MALAGUETA (*see also* **CHILLI PEP-PERS**) - A small, greenish, tapered chilli pepper, the Brazilian malagueta (*Capsicum frutescens*) is not so narrowly confined as its name implies. It is actu-ally a widely grown pepper, and its territory reaches north through Central America as far as Louisiana, where a variety called tabasco is grown.

Common names and synonyms: Bird pepper, tabasco pepper.

See in addition: "Chilli Peppers," Part II, Section C, Chapter 4.

BRAZIL NUT - This three-sided nut (*Bertholletia excelsa*) with a hard, dark shell grows in bunches of from one to more than two dozen nuts inside coconut-like shells (called *cocos* in Portuguese) on evergreens that tower over the Amazon rain forest. These nuts, which are native to Brazil and Guiana, take about 14 months to ripen after the flowers fade, and one tree can yield more than a half ton of fruit. There are some Brazil-nut plantations, but most are still harvested in the wild. And because the trees attain a height of upwards of 150 feet, and the *cocos* weigh about 5 pounds, and they are gath-ered only after they fall to the ground, harvesting these missiles can be hazardous work. It it interest-ing to note that Brazil nuts are not much consumed in Brazil, save for medicinal purposes. Rather, fairly early in the nineteenth century, the country began exporting almost the entire crop, and Europe and the United States became and remain the major importers. Because attempts have failed to cultivate the tree elsewhere, Brazil has a monopoly on more than the name. Brazil nuts have a high oil content and, consequently, are high in calories. But they are also a good source of calcium, thiamine, vitamin E, selenium, and sulfur-containing amino acids.

Common names and synonyms: Cream nut, para nut.

BREADFRUIT - The breadfruit tree (*Artocarpus altilis* = *A. communis* = *A. incisus*), which grows to about 40 feet in height, is native to the East Indies and the tropics of the South Pacific. It was carried eastward as far as the Hawaiian Islands by migrating Polynesians and is known to have been cultivated for more than 2,000 years as a staple food for Pacific peoples. Breadfruit was first described (for Europeans) by the English navigator William Dampier, who found it growing on Guam in 1688. About a century later, Captain James Cook observed the plant in Tahiti. This occurred in the aftermath of the American Revolution, which had resulted in much French interdiction of England's shipping to its colonies in the Caribbean and, con-sequently, much hardship for slaves on English

sugar plantations. In 1787, the British government dispatched HMS *Bounty,* commanded by Captain William Bligh (who had been Cook's lieutenant), to Tahiti to collect breadfruit and other plants that might be useful for feeding slaves. The notorious mutiny on the *Bounty* prevented Bligh from accomplishing this first attempt at his mission, but later - in 1793 - he succeeded in carrying to the West Indies a cargo that included young breadfruit trees. The slaves, however, refused to eat breadfruit, which resembled nothing they had known in either West Africa (the "breadfruit" there is *Treculia africana*) or the West Indies, and for a half century or so the fruits of *A. altilis* were a food mostly for hogs. Yet following the end of slavery, breadfruit finally found its way into human diets in the Caribbean. Not really a fruit, the breadfruit comes in many varieties, some with seeds and some with-out. The seeded varieties are known as "breadnuts" and can be roasted like chestnuts. Breadfruit is baked, boiled, roasted, fried, and dried to make flour. When utilized as a completely green veg-etable, the breadfruit - which can attain the size of a cantaloupe - is hard like a raw potato; when a bit ripe (it does not keep well), it is more like a baked potato. Breadfruit absorbs the flavors of other foods and thus can stretch the taste of meats, fish, and fowl. Like cassava, however, it is lacking in most nutrients, save some calcium and vitamin C. Unfor-tunately, the latter is largely destroyed by the heat of cooking.

Common names and synonyms: Breadnut, *fruit à pain, pana de pepita, sukun.*

BREADNUT - Also called *ramón,* the breadnut is the fruit of *Brosimum alicastrum,* a tree native to the West Indies and Central America. The tree grows to some 75 feet in height and produces a heavy yield of edible fruit, either a large, somewhat flavorless, red variety or a smaller, better-tasting, yellow one. The Maya prepared the fruit in the same manner as maize - grinding it on a stone and patting it into a flat bread similar to a tortilla. The seeds were made into gruel after cooking in ash water to remove the bitterness of their latex outer coating. The Maya call the breadnut "food of the ancestors," and some experts believe it was the staple food of many Mesoamerican Indians before the Spanish con-quest. Its English name came about because the fruit is round and nutlike and can be ground to make a substitute for wheat flour. But the word "breadnut" is also used to describe the seeded vari-eties of breadfruit (not a relative), and it is impor-tant not to confuse the two. Today, the breadnut remains a part of certain Mayan religious rituals, but on an everyday basis it is usually fed to pigs.

Common names and synonyms: Ramon, *ramón.*

BREADROOT (*see also* **INDIAN TURNIP**) - Also called "prairie turnip," *tipsin,* "Indian breadroot," and "breadroot scurf pea," breadroot (*Psoralea* *esculenta*) is a North American native that can be found on the plains from the Northwest Territories of Canada to Texas. Its thick, brown, edible starchy root was a staple for Native Americans and later sustained explorers and immigrants.

Common names and synonyms: Breadroot scurf pea, Indian breadroot, Indian potato, Indian turnip, prairie potato, prairie turnip, *tipsin.*

Breadroot scurf pea - *see* **BREADROOT**
Brinjal - *see* **EGGPLANT**
Bristle grass - *see* **MILLET**
Broad bellflower - *see* **CAMPANULA**
Broad-leaved tea-tree - *see* **CAJEPUT**
BROCCOLI (*see also* **BROCCOLI RAAB, CABBAGE, CALABRESE, CAULIFLOWER, CHINESE BROCCOLI**) - A member of the mustard family, and doubtless a descendant of the wild cabbage (*Brassica oleracea*), broccoli (*Brassica oleracea* var. *italica*) began as a wild-growing native of the Mediterranean region. Like all cabbages, broccoli was originally eaten for its stems, with the flowering heads a later development. Although broccoli is believed to be the forerunner of cauliflower - a vegetable known in Europe by the sixteenth century - it trailed behind cauliflower by about a century in culinary usage, save perhaps in Italy. The Italians claim broccoli as their own: The name comes from the Italian *brocco,* meaning "sprout" or "shoot," which, in turn came from the Latin *brachium,* meaning "arm" or "branch" - a succinct description of this plant with its many thick and fleshy stalks. Broccoli was introduced into England (where the term "broccoli" refers to cauliflower) around 1720 and was probably brought to North America soon thereafter, during colonial times. However, although much of the latter region offers the abundant moisture and cool climate that broccoli thrives within, the vegetable was not commonly grown in the United States until the twentieth century and only became popular after World War II - when returning GIs, who had eaten broccoli abroad, created a demand. It has subsequently become one of the most important frozen foods in the world. The green, unopened flower end is the part that is generally eaten, usually after steaming or boiling, although the leaves and tender parts of the stem can also be consumed. Broccoli is packed with vitamins and minerals, is an especially good source of vitamins A and C, and, as a cruciferous vegetable, is thought to be in the front line of foods that fight cancer.

Common names and synonyms: Asparagus broccoli, calabrese, Italian asparagus, sprouting broccoli.

See in addition: "Cruciferous and Green Leafy Vegetables," Part II, Section C, Chapter 5.

BROCCOLI RAAB (*see also* **BROCCOLI, CABBAGE**) - A favorite of the Italians (who call it *rapini*), broccoli raab (*Brassica napus*) is related to the turnip (some call broccoli raab "turnip broccoli") as well

as being a member of the family that includes cabbage, cauliflower, and broccoli. It has dark green leaves, and its stalks resemble thin broccoli stalks. It is cooked and eaten like broccoli or kale; its taste, which is pungent and somewhat bitter, seems to encompass all of the most zesty flavors of its relatives and can certainly enliven bland foods. Like most greens, this especially aggressive representative is a good source of vitamins A and C as well as calcium and iron.

Common names and synonyms: Broccoli rab, broccoli rabe, broccoli rape, *brocoletti di rape, brocoletto,* Italian turnip, rape, *rapini,* turnip broccoli.

See in addition: "Cruciferous and Green Leafy Vegetables," Part II, Section C, Chapter 5.

Broccoli rab - *see* **BROCCOLI RAAB**
Broccoli rabe - *see* **BROCCOLI RAAB**
Broccoli rape - *see* **BROCCOLI RAAB**
Brocoletti di rape - *see* **BROCCOLI RAAB**
Brocoletto - *see* **BROCCOLI RAAB**
Broken Orange Pekoe Fannings - *see* **TEA**
BROMELIA - *Bromelia* is the type genus of the family Bromeliaceae, which comprises plants often subsumed under the genus *Ananas,* such as the pineapple and the pinguin.

BROOKLIME - Also known as brooklyme, brooklime is any of several species of the genus *Veronica,* such as the Eurasian *V. beccabunga* and the American *V. americana,* which are edible aquatic or semi-aquatic plants similar to watercress.

Common names and synonyms: Brooklyme, speedwell.

Brooklyme - *see* **BROOKLIME**
Broomcorn - *see* **SORGHUM**
BRUSH CHERRY - An Australian shrub or tree, the brush cherry (*Eugenia myrtifolia* or *Syzygium paniculatum*) is also called native myrtle (in Australia) and rose apple. Its edible red fruit has a sweet-tasting white flesh that is sometimes made into jelly. The fruit has helped to feed the Aborigines over many millennia.

Common names and synonyms: Native myrtle, rose apple.

BRUSSELS SPROUT(S) (*see also* **CABBAGE**) - Members of the mustard family that descended from the cabbage (*Brassica oleracea*) and were named for the capital of Belgium, Brussels sprouts (*Brassica oleracea* var. *gemmifera*) are immature buds, shaped like tiny cabbages, that cluster on the main stem of the plant they grow on. Although the cabbage is native to the Mediterranean region (where it has been cultivated for some 2,500 years), Brussels sprouts were developed in northern Europe (the cabbage was carried there by the Romans) around the fifth century - or perhaps even later. One source claims that the plant was cultivated near Brussels in the thirteenth century; another places the first recorded description of Brussels sprouts in 1587; still another claims that they have been widely grown in Europe only since the seventeenth century; whereas at least one more source insists that they have become popular in Europe only since World War I. Of course, these claims are not necessarily contradictory. But surely, in view of its name, the plant must have been grown around Brussels at some time. Brussels sprouts reached North America with French settlers, who grew them in Louisiana, but they have been popular in the United States only during the twentieth century, with most grown in the states of New York and California. Brussels sprouts brim with vitamins. They are an especially good source of vitamins A and C and, like other members of the cabbage family, enjoy a reputation for lowering low-density lipoprotein and for preventing cancer.

See in addition: "Cruciferous and Green Leafy Vegetables," Part II, Section C, Chapter 5.

Buckbean - *see* **BOG MYRTLE**

BUCKEYE - Also called "horse chestnuts," buckeyes come from any of several trees of the genus *Aesculus.* Although poisonous when raw (because they are rich in saponin), buckeyes become edible when roasted and leached with water for a few days – a procedure with which Native Americans were familiar. They also used buckeyes raw as a fish poison. The seeds of local species are still consumed in Asia today.

Common names and synonyms: Horse chestnut.

BUCKTHORN - A number of shrubs and trees of the genus *Rhamnus* are called "buckthorn." They have berry-like fruits, and these – along with the bark and sap of the plants – have been mostly used as purgatives. However, the fruits of *R. crocea* in what is now southern California were eaten by Native Americans, as were those of *R. caroliniana* in the southeastern portion of North America.

Common names and synonyms: Redberry.

BUCKWHEAT - Grown extensively in China for millennia (although thought to be a native of Manchuria and Siberia), "buckwheat" is any plant of the genus *Fagopyrum,* especially *F. esculentum.* It is neither a true cereal nor a grass but constitutes a family of its own. Buckwheat was introduced into Europe toward the end of the Middle Ages. It does well in areas where the climate is cool and moist and became important in some northern and eastern European areas that had not only such a climate but also soils in which other grains did not thrive. In the Netherlands, the plant was called *boechweite* or "beech wheat," perhaps because the grains are shaped a bit like beechnuts. The Dutch, in turn, carried the grain to the New World, where the name became buckwheat. Another name, *kasha,* acquired from the Slavic mediators between Asia and Europe, is today applied to roasted and cracked buckwheat. Finely ground buckwheat is called buckwheat grits, whereas buckwheat groats are whole kernels that are either unroasted and white, or roasted and brown. In addition, the grain is turned into buck-

wheat flour for pancakes. The plant also serves as an animal feed, and its flowers and leaves yield a substance used in the treatment of hypertension. Today, the countries of the former Soviet Union (especially Russia) are collectively the main producers of buckwheat, of which there are three major varieties: Silverhull, Tartary, and Japanese.

Common names and synonyms: Beech wheat, *bochweit, boechweite,* buckwheat grits, buckwheat groats, Japanese buckwheat, *kasha,* Silverhull, Tartary.

See also: "Buckwheat," Part II, Section A, Chapter 3.

Buddha's-hand - *see* **CHAYOTE**

BUFFALO BERRY (*see also* **BERRIES**) – Two North American shrubs, *Shepherdia argentea* and *S. canadensis,* yield the silver buffalo berry and the russet buffalo berry respectively. Resembling currants (and sometimes called "Nebraska currants") as well as barberries, buffalo berries have long been a part of the Native American diet on the Great Plains and in western North America. The shrubs grow wild along streams and are one of the few plants that do well in a dry and rocky environment. *Sheperdia canadensis* (also known as the Canadian buffalo berry) produces the smaller of the two berries and is relatively tasteless. The berries of *S. argentea,* by contrast, are flavorful and used in jellies. Buffalo berries are a fine source of vitamin C.

Common names and synonyms: Canadian buffalo berry, Nebraska currant, russet buffalo berry, silver buffalo berry.

BUFFALO GOURD (*see also* **SQUASH AND PUMPKIN**) – A large plant with a bad smell, the buffalo gourd (*Cucurbita foetidissima*) grows wild in the south-central and southwestern United States as well as in northern Mexico. The fruits were sometimes used as rattles by Native Americans and reportedly were cooked and eaten at times, although today they are considered inedible. The seeds, however, were regularly consumed, generally after roasting and grinding them into a kind of mush. Oil was also obtained from the seeds. The pulp of the fruits and the huge root (which can weigh over 200 pounds) of the buffalo gourd contain saponin and were therefore employed as soap.

Common names and synonyms: Calabazilla, Missouri gourd.

See in addition: "Squash," Part II, Section C, Chapter 8.

Bulbine lily - *see* **YAM DAISY**

Bulghur - *see* **WHEAT**

Bullace grape - *see* **MUSCADINE**

Bullace plum - *see* **DAMSON PLUM**

Bullbrier - *see* **GREENBRIER**

Bull-dog - *see* **TURKEY FRUIT**

Bullock's heart - *see* **CUSTARD APPLE**

Bullrush - *see* **BULRUSH**

Bullsfoot - *see* **COLTSFOOT**

BULRUSH - A versatile food source in the wilderness, bulrushes (genus *Scirpus*) are grassy sedges that grow in wet places. These wild marsh plants have young shoots and juicy stem bases that can be boiled as greens or consumed raw in salads. In addition, the rhizomes are edible (they were often dried and ground), and the pollen was gathered by Native Americans to mix with flours for porridges and cakes. The seeds of some species are also edible. Most bulrushes are American natives, but Europe and Asia also have their own species – indeed, a bulrush constituted the Old Testament papyrus – and in East Asia the young stems of *S. fluviatilis* are still consumed today. Bulrush, broadly speaking, can also mean cattail, especially in Britain.

Common names and synonyms: Bullrush.

Bunchberry - *see* **CORNUS**

BUNCHOSIA - *Bunchosia argentea* is called the "peanut butter fruit" for the excellent reason that its flesh has both the consistency and the flavor of peanut butter. It is a native of tropical South America and is also grown in Florida, but it is uncommon almost anywhere else. The trees grow to more than 30 feet tall and bear flowers and fruit almost all year long. The small fruits are yellow or red, are oblong, and hang in clusters. Their flesh is the color of cream and, although sweet, is often too tart to be enjoyed fresh. The fruit may be made into preserves, but it is more frequently employed as a flavoring.

Common names and synonyms: Ciruela, peanut-butter fruit.

Buni - *see* **BIGNAY**

Burbank's spineless - *see* **PRICKLY PEAR**

BURDEKIN PLUM (*see also* **PLUM**) – The fruits of the Australian trees *Pleiogynium timoriense* and *P. solandri* are called "Burdekin plums." Both are plum-sized and edible, but the fruit of *P. timoriense* is purple, whereas that of *P. solandri* is red. They are not sweet and today are used mostly in jellies and jams. However, the fruits have long served as food for the Aborigines.

BURDOCK – Also known as "great burdock" and originally from Siberia, burdock (*Arctium lappa*) is cultivated for its long (up to 4 feet), slender, carrot-shaped taproot. The Japanese, who use burdock as others do carrots, are its foremost producers and consumers, although it can also be found in the markets of Taiwan and Hawaii. The roots are grated or cut into pieces and stir-fried or added to various dishes – especially soups – to which they contribute a somewhat earthy taste. The plant grows wild in North America and Europe, producing burrs that attach themselves to the clothing of those who cross meadows. Nutritionally, burdock offers mostly minerals, such as potassium and magnesium, although it is not a bad source of folacin.

Common names and synonyms: Beggar's-button(s), clotbur, edible burdock, *gobo*, great burdock, harlock.

BURMA MANGROVE – An evergreen tree of the Old World tropics, the Burma mangrove (*Bruguiera gymnorhiza*) produces edible, berry-like fruits. In some places, the bark is used as a flavoring; in others, the leaves are cooked as a vegetable.

BURNET – The name "burnet" comes from the Middle English and Old French *brunette,* which describes the brownish red flowers of the several species of this European native, now also commonly found in North America. One kind of burnet, *Poterium sanguisorba,* with cucumber-tasting leaves, was once a popular herb but is not much used anymore save in a few Italian and French dishes. In the past, however, especially in Elizabethan England, its leaves were frequently added to salads and sauces. There is confusion between this burnet and great burnet (*Sanguisorba officinalis*), also known mistakenly as bloodwort because of its reputation for stopping bleeding. Asian burnet and Japanese burnet are also different species.

Common names and synonyms: Garden burnet, lesser burnet, pimpinel, salad burnet, small burnet.

Burning bush - *see* **DITTANY**

BUSH CURRANT – A small tree or shrub that is also called the "currant bush," the bush currant (*Antidesma ghaesembilla*) is a wild plant of Australia that produces small edible purple or black berries.

Common names and synonyms: Currant bush, gucil.

Bush greens - *see* **AMARANTH**

Bush okra - *see* **JEW'S-MALLOW**

BUTTERCUP SQUASH (*see also* **SQUASH AND PUMPKIN**) – So called because of their turbanlike caps, the orange-fleshed and green-skinned buttercup squash and other moderate-sized varieties of *Cucurbita maxima* are also sometimes referred to as Kabocha-type squashes. These include the Black Forest, the Hokkaido (also Red Kuri), and Honey Delight varieties, all of which make good purees, soups, and pies.

Common names and synonyms: Black Forest, Hokkaido, Honey Delight, Kabocha, Red Kuri.

See in addition: "Squash," Part II, Section C, Chapter 8.

BUTTERFLY WEED – A plant mostly of eastern North America, the butterfly weed (*Asclepias tuberosa*) is the only one of the milkweeds that does not contain milky juice. Its roots were baked and eaten by Native Americans, as were its orange flowers, shoots, and leaves.

Common names and synonyms: Indian posy, orange milkweed, orange root, pleurisy root, tuberroot.

BUTTERNUT - *see also* **WALNUT**

BUTTERNUT SQUASH (*see also* **SQUASH AND PUMPKIN**) – Along with the acorn squash, the butternut (*Cucurbita moschata*) is the most common squash on the tables of North America. It is a winter squash that generally weighs from 2 to 4 pounds and has a tan skin, a long neck, and a swollen bottom. This squash is usually roasted, and its yellow flesh is high in beta-carotene.

See in addition: "Squash," Part II, Section C, Chapter 8.

Butter pear - *see* **AVOCADO**

Butterweed - *see* **HORSEWEED**

CABBAGE (*see also* the various *Brassica* entries) – Sources indicate that the cabbage (*Brassica oleracea*) is an ancient vegetable of the European Old World, but cabbages in China were mentioned by Confucius (d. 497 B.C.), which suggests that the plant traveled quite widely in the distant past. Certainly the wild cabbage must long ago have provided sustenance for those of our hunting-and-gathering ancestors who sought the vegetables out. The wild cabbage was a small plant that grew around European coastal areas (especially those of the Mediterranean) and - like broccoli - was first eaten for its stem. But by the time of the Romans, the head had become larger and more rounded, and the subsequent encouragement of various characteristics has resulted in some 400 varieties, such as numerous head cabbages, broccoli, Brussels sprouts, cauliflower, collards, kale, and kohlrabi, to name but a few. Moreover, the various Oriental species of the cabbage family include the Chinese cabbage (napa) and bok choy.

In general, cabbages have trouble with hot weather, although the ability of some (such as the frost-resistant green and red varieties) to thrive in cool climates made them important long ago in central and eastern Europe. Legend has it, however, that the technique of pickling cabbage to preserve it (as sauerkraut) reached Europe from China via the Tartars. In light of such widespread use, it is interesting to note that cabbages have never been uniformly accepted nor very highly regarded. They were not a part of the diet in the Neolithic Near East and, although apparently appreciated by the Greeks and Romans (at least for alleged medicinal qualities), were subsequently viewed in Europe as an unsophisticated food that gave off a bad smell when cooked and provoked flatulence when eaten.

Today, however, this remarkable group of vegetables is said to promote health by lowering cholesterol, preventing cancer, and providing the consumer with fiber and a number of important vitamins and minerals, especially vitamin C. Round cabbages have traditionally been boiled with meats and potatoes or beans in countless cultural versions of the "boiled dinner," and, because these vegetables were called cole cabbage and colewort in the past, we continue to refer to another means of cabbage preparation as "coleslaw," often without knowing why. Round cabbages include white, green, and red varieties with smooth leaves, as well as those with wrinkled leaves, such as the Savoy cabbage. European spring cabbages are one example of pointed cabbages, as is Chinese cabbage. Brussels sprouts are cabbages with hypertrophied buds. An example of a cabbage with dense flowering is the cauliflower, and a cabbage with its flowering in spears is broccoli.

Common names and synonyms: Cole cabbage, coleslaw, colewort, common cabbage, European spring cabbage, green cabbage, head cabbage, pointed cabbage, red cabbage, round cabbage, sauerkraut, Savoy cabbage, wild cabbage.

See in addition: "Cruciferous and Green Leafy Vegetables," Part II, Section C, Chapter 5.

Cabbage palm - *see* **HEART(S) OF PALM**

CABBAGE TREE - "Cabbage trees" (*Cordyline terminalis* and other species) are shrubs or small trees that are cultivated in India and the Pacific Islands, where the plant is also known as *ti,* ti palm, and palm lily. In Hawaii, the roots - high in sugar content - are fermented to make a beverage, and the long, sword-shaped leaves are exploited for making skirts and for other decorative purposes. The leaves are also used to wrap foods for baking in Polynesia, and in New Zealand fibers from the leaves are employed as a source of twine. Finally, the leaves are also used as plates, and young leaves are eaten as a potherb.

Common names and synonyms: Palm lily, *ti,* ti leaf, ti palm, ti root.

Cabbage turnip - *see* **KOHLRABI**

CABERNET (*see also* **GRAPES**) - There are two varieties of the cabernet grape (*Vitis vinifera*) - Cabernet Sauvignon and Cabernet Franc - both of which are red grapes employed in making the fine wines of Bordeaux and California. Indeed, Cabernet Sauvignon is the most important red wine grape in the world and is also grown in Australia, South Africa, and New Zealand, as well as in other European countries besides France.

Common names and synonyms: Cabernet Franc, Cabernet Sauvignon.

See in addition: "Wine," Part III, Chapter 13.

Cabernet Franc - *see* **CABERNET**

Cabernet Sauvignon - *see* **CABERNET**

CACAO - The cacao tree (*Theobroma cacao*) produces the pods that yield the oblong beans that are dried, pressed, and ground to produce cocoa butter and a reddish brown powder, cocoa. That it has been a well-appreciated substance is evident from the tree's scientific name, which in Greek means "food for the gods." A member of the same family as the kola nut of West Africa, cacao is native to the American tropics (and still grows wild in the Amazon rain forest as well as in the forests of Central America) but is now raised commercially in many other tropical regions of the world. It was apparently the Maya who first domesticated the cacao tree. Columbus encountered the plant in the West Indies and took it to Spain at the end of his second voyage. Hernando Cortés, however, has been credited with properly introducing cacao in Europe because he knew what to do with it (mix the powder with vanilla), having learned from the Aztecs whom he had just conquered. Beginning in Spain and then throughout the rest of Europe, cocoa preceded coffee and tea as a stimulating drink (it contains caffeine), and by the end of the seventeenth century there were chocolate houses all over the Continent. The chocolate industry was under way, and the Spaniards began to spread cacao cultivation around the world. Plants were taken to the island of Fernando Po off the west African coast, after which they entered Africa. Cacao traveled west from Mexico via the Manila galleons to take root in the Philippines, and its cultivation was subsequently extended throughout the East Indies by the Dutch. Chocolate (as opposed to cacao) production began in North America in 1765, and in 1779 Dr. James Baker (whose name is practically synonymous with chocolate in the United States) entered the business. In 1828, the Dutch invented a press that would remove much of the cocoa butter, and a bit later the techniques for making chocolate bars were developed. In 1876, the Swiss, by mixing cocoa powder and powdered milk, developed milk chocolate (which is still considered the best chocolate), and in 1900 Milton Hershey introduced the first "Hershey Bars" in the United States. Soon afterward, he began construction of a chocolate factory near Harrisburg, Pennsylvania, and there quickly grew up a town that was named Hershey, Pennsylvania, in 1903. In addition to the culinary uses of cacao, cocoa butter is employed in the manufacture of cosmetics and pharmaceuticals. The shells – left over after processing the cacao beans – serve as a source of theobromine (a mild stimulant) and vitamin D and are often used as animal feed.

Common names and synonyms: Chocolate, cocoa.

See also: "Cacao," Part III, Chapter 3; "Spices and Flavorings," Part II, Section F, Chapter 1.

Cachira – *see* **ICE-CREAM BEAN**

CACTUS APPLE – A large, treelike, thorny cactus native to South America, the cactus apple (*Cereus peruvianus*) produces edible fruits that are known as *pitaya* fruits to Latin Americans. *Pitayas* range in color from yellow to red and have a white flesh with small edible seeds.

Common names and synonyms: Apple cactus, *pitaya* (fruit).

Cactus fig – *see* **PRICKLY PEAR**

Cactus pad – *see* **NOPALES**

Cactus paddle – *see* **NOPALES**

Cactus pear – *see* **PRICKLY PEAR**

Cactus-spoon – *see* **SOTOL**

Caihua – *see* **KORILA**

Cail – *see* **KALE**

Caimito (fruit) – *see* **STAR-APPLE**

Cajá – *see* **TAPEREBÁ**

CAJEPUT – An East Indian tree, the cajeput (*Melaleuca quinquenervia* or *M. cajuputi*) has a bark that has long been used for sacred writing, and it yields a pungent oil that some call "tea-tree oil," which has had myriad nonfood uses – from a painkiller in dentistry, to a killer of fleas and lice, to a mosquito repellent. But the oil is also used as a flavoring in foods ranging from baked goods through desserts to meat products and soft drinks.

Common names and synonyms: Broad-leaved tea-tree, punk tree, tea-tree oil.

CALABASH (*see also* **BOTTLE GOURD, XICALL**) – Also called the "tree gourd," this green fruit of the calabash tree (*Crescentia cujete*) has a hard outer rind that encloses a white pulp containing seeds. Probably both the sweetish fruit and the seeds have been eaten (and the pulp used medicinally), but the main use of the calabash has been as a container for food and beverages. In Africa, the name "calabash" has been applied to the bottle gourd (*Lagenaria siceraria*), which grows on a vine instead of a tree but has served many of the same functions as *C. cujete*.

Common names and synonyms: Bottle gourd, *calabaza, calebasse,* tree gourd.

CALABAZA (SQUASH) (*see also* **CALABASH, SQUASH AND PUMPKIN**) – *Calabaza* means "gourd" in Spanish, and the word is often intended to mean "calabash." But it has also come to mean a usually bright orange squash variety of the *Cucurbita moschata* species, which has flowers that – like its skin – range from creamy white to yellow to deep orange. This squash is a native American plant that can be found daily in the markets of the West Indies and Central and South America. Because it tends to grow to the size of a large pumpkin, it is often sold in pieces, but – like the pumpkin (a close relative) – the calabaza also comes in smaller sizes. Reportedly, this squash was an important food for the Indians of Florida when the Spaniards first reached that peninsula, and it has seemingly always been a favorite of Cubans and many other natives of the Caribbean islands. Calabaza goes well in stews, and pureed calabaza makes a fine soup. Many fry the raw squash in strips, and in Mexico pieces of young, green calabaza are sautéed with chicken. Calabaza is a fine source of vitamin A, folic acid, and potassium. Like pumpkin seeds, those of the calabaza are wonderful when toasted.

Common names and synonyms: Abóbora, ahuyama, crapaudback, Cuban squash, giraumon, toadback, West Indian pumpkin.

See in addition: "Squash," Part II, Section C, Chapter 8.

Calabazilla – *see* **BUFFALO GOURD, CABBAGE**

CALABRESE (*see also* **BROCCOLI**) – A variety of broccoli, calabrese (*Brassica oleracea* var. *italica*) is apparently named for Calabria, a region in the toe of Italy about to kick Sicily. Noted for its tightly packed green (or purple) flower heads, calabrese was introduced into France and England in the eighteenth century but was rare in the United States until after World War II. Today, however, California is a big producer of calabrese. The vegetable is high in vitamin C and some of the B vitamins as well as many of the trace minerals. Along with other members of the family Cruciferae, calabrese may be important in cancer prevention.

Common names and synonyms: Asparagus broccoli, sprouting broccoli.

See in addition: "Cruciferous and Green Leafy Vegetables," Part II, Section C, Chapter 5.

Calabur - *see* **CAPULIN**

Calalu - *see* **CALLALOO**

CALAMONDIN (*see also* **CITRUS FRUITS**) - Thought by many to be a naturally occurring hybrid between the Mandarin orange and the kumquat, the orange-hued calamondin grows on a small evergreen tree (now designated as × *Citrofortunella microcarpa,* although in the past it was called *Citrus mitis* or *Citrus reticulata*) and is also known as the "musk lime," "Panama orange," and "calamondin orange." The fruits are about 1.5 inches in diameter and look like tangerines. There is some debate as to whether the calamondin is a Philippine native or originated in China, but in any event it is today widely cultivated in the Philippines and also in Hawaii and Florida in the United States. Calamondins are made into marmalades, jellies, and beverages, are used to flavor teas, and are also eaten raw. They are a good source of vitamin C.

Common names and synonyms: Calamondin orange, China orange, musk lime, Panama orange, Philippine orange, to-kumquat.

Calamus - *see* **SWEET FLAG**

Calebasse - *see* **CALABASH**

California chilli - *see* **ANAHEIM**

CALLALOO (*see also* **COCOYAM, TARO**) - The name of a soup made in many islands of the Caribbean, callaloo is also the name of the large, wide, green leaves that go into it. One of these greens is amaranth (genus *Amaranthus*) - either "Surinam amaranth" (with an African origin) or "Chinese spinach" (which is probably native to the West Indies). The other kind of green is the leaves of dasheen or taro (*Colocasia esculenta*). Collectively called callaloo - and in some places "sagaloo" - the leaves resemble spinach or sorrel and are cooked as a vegetable dish. Fresh callaloo leaves can be found in West Indian markets in the summer months, and they are available canned throughout the year.

Common names and synonyms: Calalu, callalou greens, Chinese spinach, dasheen, sagaloo, Surinam amaranth, taro.

See in addition: "Amaranth," Part II, Section A, Chapter 1; "Taro," Part II, Section B, Chapter 6.

Caltrop - *see* **WATER CHESTNUT**

Calvance pea - *see* **CHICKPEA**

CAMAS - The bulbs of "camas" herbs (*Camassia scilloides* or *C. leichtlinii* and *C. quamash* or *C. esculenta*) constituted an important food for Native North Americans of the West and Northwest. Indeed, both were named by these peoples who originally roasted, baked, and boiled them. Their consumption required some caution, however, for camas bulbs can be confused with the "death camus" (*Zigadenus* spp.), which, as its common name suggests, is toxic and can be lethal. In fact, it frequently poisons grazing animals in the western United States. Camas is also called "wild hyacinth."

Common names and synonyms: Camash, camass, commas, common camass, quamash, sqamash, wild hyacinth.

Camash - *see* **CAMAS**

CAMBUCÁ - A rare fruit, the cambucá (*Marlierea edulis*) grows on a tree with a range that is mostly confined to the coastal forests of the Brazilian states of Rio de Janeiro and São Paulo. The cambucá is a relative of the guava and the jaboticaba, and its yellowish fruit has a good flavor. It is eaten raw and made into juice.

Camomile - *see* **CHAMOMILE**

Camote - *see* **SWEET POTATO**

CAMPANULA - The genus name for numerous species of plants known as "bellflowers" or "Canterbury bells" is *Campanula* (meaning "bell" and referring to the shape of the flowers). Found in temperate zones, especially in the Mediterranean and tropical mountains, three species have been used as food. In the past, the fleshy roots and leaves of *C. rapunculoides* were cultivated to be eaten in England, and the plant was carried to North America, where it is now naturalized. Rampion (*C. rapunculus*) - another European native - was also grown for its roots and leaves in centuries past. It has an edible root that is used in salads and shoots that are cooked like asparagus. In addition, the leaves of *C. versicolor* have been used in salads.

Common names and synonyms: Bellflower, broad bellflower, Canterbury bell(s), harebell, rampion.

Canada ginger - *see* **WILD GINGER**

Canada pea - *see* **TUFTED VETCH**

Canada snakeroot - *see* **WILD GINGER**

Canada sweetgale - *see* **SWEET FERN**

Canadian turnip - *see* **RUTABAGA**

Cañahua - *see* **CAÑIHUA**

Canary grass - *see* **MAYGRASS**

Candleberry - *see* **CANDLENUT**

CANDLENUT - Also called "candleberry" and "Indian walnut," the candlenut tree (*Aleurites moluccana*), native to tropical Southeast Asia, produces a seed kernel that is roasted and eaten. The seeds are more used, however, for their oil, which presumably at one time or another has been used for candle making.

Common names and synonyms: Candleberry, Indian walnut.

Candy plant - *see* **CICELY**

Canella - *see* **WHITE CINNAMON**

CAÑIHUA (*see also* **CHENOPODIUM, QUINOA**) - A native of the Andean regions of southern Peru and Bolivia, cañihua (*Chenopodium pallidicaule*) is a cold-resistant grain known also as "quañiwa" and "cañahua." It is used much like quinoa, but does better in high regions because it is tolerant of both

frost and drier soils. In addition, it has a higher protein content. Cañihua was first cultivated by ancient settlers in the region and continues to be grown today, but botanists think that its domestication is not yet complete. The grain is used to make a flour called *cañihuaco* and to make soups, stews, and desserts. It is even employed to flavor drinks.
Common names and synonyms: Cañahua, quañiwa.

CANISTEL - The fruit of a tropical tree, canistel (*Pouteria campechiana*) probably originated in Central America (Costa Rica or Belize) but has now spread throughout the Caribbean. It is sold in Florida and is a favorite in the markets of Havana and Nassau. The fruit is oval, hard, and green, changing to soft, orange, and glossy when ripe. The flesh has the texture of a hard-boiled egg (another of its names is eggfruit) and a taste similar to that of a sweet potato. It is eaten raw with lemon juice, is good in salads, and is made into custards and ice cream. It is extremely rich in beta-carotene.
Common names and synonyms: Eggfruit (tree).

Cankerroot - *see* **GOLDTHREAD**

Canna - *see* **ACHIRA, BERRIES**

CANNELLINI BEAN (*see also* **BEANS**) - Much used in Italian soups and stews and often appearing as an antipasto dressed with olive oil, the cannellini bean (*Phaseolus vulgaris*) is a "common bean" of American origin. It is, in fact, a white kidney bean that may have been developed in Italy. Cannellini beans are generally sold in canned form.
See in addition: "Beans, Peas, and Lentils," Part II, Section C, Chapter 3.

Canola oil - *see* **RAPE**

CANTALOUPE AND MUSKMELON (*see also* **MELONS**) - A variety of muskmelon, the cantaloupe (*Cucumis melo*) belongs to the squash family and is a member of the genus that includes cucumbers. The places of origin of most melons are uncertain, but Africa (the home of the watermelon), the Near East, and India appear to be the most likely candidates. The muskmelon (*Cucumis melo*) probably entered Europe from the Muslim world via Spain, and during the Renaissance, monks developed the cantaloupe from muskmelons in the garden of the papal villa at Cantalupo, located close to Rome. It was muskmelon seeds, however, that were carried to the New World by Columbus and later planted by the Spaniards in California - so that today it is muskmelons that are generally consumed by North Americans, even if they mistakenly call the fruits "cantaloupes." The cantaloupe, also known as the "sugar melon," has remained mostly a European melon, is somewhat larger than the muskmelon, and has a warty or scaly rind, in contrast to the raised netting that characterizes the rind of the muskmelon. The orange flesh of both provides plenty of beta-carotene and vitamin C as well as potassium.
Common names and synonyms: Sugar melon.

See in addition: "Cucumbers, Melons, and Watermelons," Part II, Section C, Chapter 6.

Cantarela - *see* **OKRA**

Canterbury bell(s) - *see* **CAMPANULA**

CAPE GOOSEBERRY (*see also* **BERRIES**) - Also called the "Peruvian cherry" and the "Peruvian groundcherry," the cape gooseberry (*Physalis peruviana*), with pale-yellow blooms, is a native of tropical America and very closely related to the tomatillo (*Physalis ixocarpa*), also American in origin. Nonetheless, it is named the "cape gooseberry" because of a round-the-world journey that took it to, among other places, South Africa, where it was cultivated at the Cape of Good Hope. When first introduced in Australia, it was called the cape gooseberry, and the name stuck. Long before this, however, the berries grew wild and were important to many Native American groups, who ate them fresh and also dried them for winter use. The cape gooseberry has additional relatives, such as the Chinese lantern plant and the groundcherry (and, indeed, any of the plants of the genus *Physalis,* all of which have a parchment-like husk). Cape gooseberries are yellowish and juicy and a good source of beta-carotene, vitamin C, the B complex, phosphorus, and iron. They are frequently made into jams and jellies.
Common names and synonyms: Goldenberry, golden husk, groundcherry, Peruvian cherry, Peruvian groundcherry, strawberry tomato, winter cherry.

Cape periwinkle - *see* **PERIWINKLE**

CAPER(S) - A spiny trailing shrub, the caper bush (*Capparis spinosa*) grows to between 4 and 5 feet in height. It is native to the Mediterranean region and possibly to the Middle East as well. Its flower buds, which are picked and pickled in vinegar, are the capers that have been used since at least the time of the ancient Greeks as a condiment to add a salty-sour flavor to sauces, cheeses, salad dressings, stews, and various other meat and fish dishes. The caper bush grows wild and thrives in southern Europe, where Italy and Spain are the biggest caper producers.
Common names and synonyms: Caper berry, caper bud, caperbush, caper fruit, *cappero, kápari,* smooth caper, spiny caper, *tapèra.*
See also: "Spices and Flavorings," Part II, Section F, Chapter 1.

Cappero - *see* **CAPER(S)**

Capucine - *see* **MASHUA**

Capuli - *see* **CAPULIN, CHERRY**

CAPULIN (*see also* **CHERRY**) - Both the Mexican tree *Prunus capuli* and the Central and South American tree *P. salicifolia* are called "capulin" or "capuli." *Prunus capuli* is sometimes thought to be a form of the black cherry (*Prunus serotina*). Its edible cherries are consumed raw and in jellies, and their pits are ground to make flour. *P. salicifolia,* also known as the "tropical cherry," has edible purple cherries, which are also eaten out of hand or in preserves. Another fruit called "capulin" is the downy groundcherry (*Physalis pubescens*), which is also edible. Still another "capulin" is the Mexican wild plum (*Prunus capollin*), which is eaten both raw and cooked and turned into a juice that is combined with cornmeal and fried as cornmeal cakes. All of these fruits were important in the diet of Native Americans long before the arrival of Columbus. A final "capulin" is the small red fruit of *Muntingia calabura,* also called "calabur," "Panama berry," and "Jamaican cherry." This capulin has culinary applications like the others, but in addition, its leaves can be used to make a refreshing tea.

Common names and synonyms: Calabur, capuli, downy groundcherry, Jamaican cherry, Mexican wild plum, Panama berry, tropical cherry.

Carageen - *see* **CARRAGEENIN**

CARAMBOLA - The carambola (*Averrhoa carambola*) is also known as the "star fruit," and with good reason. It has an elongated yellow (sometimes white) body with five ribs that produce star shapes when it is sliced. Its native region was probably Malaysia, but the fruit now belongs to the world. Averrhoës, whose name it bears, was a twelfth-century Arab philosopher and physician who translated the works of Aristotle into Arabic. The word "carambola," however, is a Native American name for the fruit, and today it is cultivated in Asia, the West Indies, Florida, Hawaii, and Central and South America. The carambola has a fragrance reminiscent of quince and crisp, juicy flesh that can be either sweet or sour: Both tastes work well when applied to the appropriate salads, cooked dishes, and drinks. The carambola is also delicious eaten raw and provides the consumer with plenty of vitamin C.

Common names and synonyms: Belimbing, bilimbi, Chinese star fruit, five-angled fruit, star apple, star fruit.

CARAUNDA - Also known as "karanda," the caraunda (*Carissa carandas*) is an evergreen shrub or small tree of the East Indies that has a somewhat acidic fruit. In India, these reddish berries are eaten raw when ripe and pickled when not mature.

Common names and synonyms: Karanda.

CARAWAY - An herb native to Europe and Asia, caraway (*Carum carvi*) still grows wild on both continents. It is also a plant closely associated with the Arab world, where it is called *karawya,* and has traveled sufficiently widely to have become naturalized in the Americas. Its slightly sharp- and peppery-tasting seeds, which are ready for harvesting when they turn brown, have been used as a spice for at least 5,000 years, and there is reportedly evidence of their culinary use even prior to the Neolithic Revolution. Caraway seeds were an ancient item of importance in the spice trade and have been much in demand for the preservation of foods such as sauerkraut. Caraway was once enormously popular in English cookery. Shakespeare

mentions "a dish of caraways," and at Trinity College, Cambridge, the tradition of serving roasted apples with caraway continues. Today, caraway is most frequently used in northern European - especially German and Austrian - cooking. The seeds are a common ingredient in rye breads, sauerkraut, potato salads, cabbage dishes, goulashes, cheeses, cakes, and the German liqueur *Kümmel,* the name of which means caraway.

Common names and synonyms: Jintan, karawya, Kümmel.

See also: "Spices and Flavorings," Part II, Section F, Chapter 1.

Carciofo - *see* **ARTICHOKE**

CARDAMOM - A member of the ginger family, cardamom (*Elettaria cardamomum*) is a plant native to South Asia, and the Cardamom Hills in India were named for the cardamom growing there. The seeds of the plant, which come in triangular capsules, have been used as a spice since ancient times. They found their way to Europe along the caravan routes and were an important commodity in the Greek spice trade with the East as early as the fourth century B.C. Cardamom was a popular spice in Rome and presumably radiated out from there to those other inhabitants of Europe who could afford it. Today, there are cardamom plantations in much of the tropical world, including Central America, although southern India remains the largest producing region. The biggest consumers of cardamom are the diverse peoples of Scandinavia and India. Scandinavians use the sweetness of the seeds to flavor fruit dishes, gingerbread, and Swedish meatballs. The Indians use the dried and ground seeds as one of the essential ingredients of curry powder. In addition, cardamom is crucial to the flavored coffees of the Arab world, and an oil derived from the plant is employed in flavoring liqueurs. "Cardamom" is also the name of an East Indian plant (*Amomum cardamomum*) whose seeds are used as a bad substitute for true cardamom seeds.

Common names and synonyms: Cardamon, cardamum.

See also: "Spices and Flavorings," Part II, Section F, Chapter 1.

Cardamon - *see* **CARDAMOM**

Cardamum - *see* **CARDAMOM**

Cardi - *see* **CARDOON**

Cardoni - *see* **CARDOON**

CARDOON - One of the edible thistles, the cardoon (*Cynara cardunculus*) is a relative of the globe artichoke. It is celery-like in appearance, with silvery gray stalks. The plant is native to the Mediterranean region, where it has been cultivated since the days of the Romans and where it remains a popular vegetable in Spain, France, and Italy. Cardoons were cultivated for a time in the United States but were never much appreciated save by Italian-Americans, in whose markets the vegetables can still be found. It is unfortunate that cardoons are not more widely known because they have an excellent flavor. They are frequently eaten raw in a sauce of olive oil, anchovies, and garlic; when cooked (usually blanched), the stalks taste bittersweet – something like celery and something like artichokes. Cardoons are a good source of potassium, iron, and calcium.

Common names and synonyms: Cardi, cardoni, common cardoon, Paris cardoon, red-stemmed cardoon, Spanish cardoon, Tours cardoon.

CAROB – Carob pods grow on a leguminous tree (*Ceratonia siliqua*) of the pea family that can rise upward of 50 feet above the ground. Carobs are native to the eastern Mediterranean region (and possibly western Asia as well), where they were grown in ancient times by the Greeks, who also introduced their cultivation into Italy. The pods (which are sweet and are enjoyed by animals and humans alike) are probably the proverbial "locusts" eaten by John the Baptist during his stay in the wilderness and thus are called "Saint-John's-bread." They were also a staple in the diet of the Duke of Wellington's cavalry during the Peninsular War. The pods grow up to a foot in length, dry on the tree, and are harvested when they fall to the ground. They contain seeds whose weight is believed to have been used by early jewelers to determine the carat. Today, the seeds are utilized to make locust gum, which is employed in the food industry as a thickener, in the preparation of cheese and meat products, and to stabilize ice cream. A pulpy material from the pod is dried to become carob powder, a substance that is roasted and used as a substitute for cocoa and chocolate as well as coffee. Carob has far fewer calories than chocolate or cocoa and does not contain caffeine or cause allergies.

Common names and synonyms: Algarroba, locust, locust bean, Saint-John's-bread.

Carolina tea-tree – *see* **YAUPON**

CAROLINA VANILLA – An herb of the southeastern United States that reaches 2 to 3 feet in height, Carolina vanilla (*Trilisa odoratissima*) has leaves that are employed in large amounts to flavor tobacco. The leaves, which have a pleasing vanilla odor, are also used to make a fragrant tea.

Common names and synonyms: Deertongue, vanilla leaf, vanilla plant.

See also: "Spices and Flavorings," Part II, Section F, Chapter 1.

CARRAGEEN AND CARRAGEENIN (*see also* **SEAWEED**) – Also called "Irish moss" and "pearl moss," carrageen (*Chondrus crispus*) is a type of purple seaweed that frequents the coasts of the North Atlantic from the British Isles on the European side to the Maritime Provinces and New England on the American side. Most is harvested commercially for a gelatin used in food processing. It has also been used for clarifying beer, and some carrageen is employed in thickening soups and chowders and

making jelly. Carrageenin is an extractive of carrageen and other red algae (such as *Gigartina mammillosa*), used mostly as a suspending agent in foods. It is also called "Irish moss extractive."

Common names and synonyms: Carrageen, carragheen, Irish moss, pearl moss.

See in addition "Algae," Part II, Section C, Chapter 1.

CARROT – A root vegetable of the Umbelliferae family – and thus related to parsley, dill, and celery – the carrot (*Daucus carota* ssp. *carota* when wild and ssp. *sativus* when domesticated), although originally native to Afghanistan, is now found all over the world in many shapes, sizes, and colors. It grows best in moist soils and mild climates, and its taproot is the edible portion of the plant. Early varieties were red, black, or purple, and today carrots in Asia can look much like beets to Westerners, who would also probably approach with caution one carrot variety in the Far East that grows up to 3 feet long. Carrots were cultivated by the Greeks and the Romans but not used very widely in Europe until the Middle Ages. In the sixteenth century, a yellow strain began to develop, and, in Holland of the seventeenth century, the orange type now familiar in the West arose. After the carrot reached the Americas, it frequently escaped cultivation to become the wild carrot known as "Queen-Anne's-lace." Like so many other vegetables from Europe, carrots became popular in the New World only after Americans had occasion to visit the Continent in large numbers and become familiar with the foods there. In the case of this vegetable, the occasion was World War I, after which Michigan and California became the biggest carrot producers in the United States. Carrots are available fresh, canned, frozen, dehydrated, and as a juice. They are eaten raw and often added to salads, as well as becoming an important ingredient in dishes such as carrot cake. Cooked, they make an excellent ingredient in stews and soups. In addition, the seeds contain an oil that is expressed for flavorings and for perfumes. The carrot has a great reputation as a source of beta-carotene (the precursor of vitamin A) and vitamin C, and it joins other vegetables as an apparent cancer fighter, cholesterol lowerer, and fiber provider.

Common names and synonyms: Queen-Anne's-lace.

CASABA (MELON) (*see also* **MELONS**) – Also spelled "cassaba," the name casaba designates a variety of winter melon (*Cucumis melo*) named for Kassaba, itself a former name of Turgutlu, Turkey. The fruit has a yellow rind and sweet, whitish flesh that contains much vitamin C.

Common names and synonyms: Cassaba, winter melon.

See in addition: "Cucumbers, Melons, and Watermelons," Part II, Section C, Chapter 6.

CASCABEL (*see also* **CHILLI PEPPERS**) – In Spanish, *cascabel* means to jingle or rattle – and when this green or red pepper (about the size and shape of a small tomato) is dried and turns a brownish red, it becomes translucent and its seeds rattle about inside. Rarely used fresh, the dried *cascabel* (*Capsicum annuum*) is prized for the rich, smoky heat that it imparts to any dish or sauce in which it is simmered. Cascabel peppers are grown in Mexico but are available in the United States.

Common names and synonyms: Chilli bola.

See in addition: "Chilli Peppers," Part II, Section C, Chapter 4.

CASHEW - A kidney-shaped nut that grows in a double shell at the end of a strongly sweet-smelling, pear-shaped fruit, the cashew (*Anacardium occidentale*) is a very unusual nut. The largest part of the fruit is the juicy, pear-shaped fruit called the cashew "apple," which is eaten raw or fermented to become alcohol. The nut itself grows at the lower end of the "apple," but one never sees cashews sold in the shell for a very good reason. The cashew is related to poison ivy and poison sumac, and the shells contain an irritating oil that must be gotten rid of by heating before the nut can be extracted. The tree is a native of South America, but in the sixteenth century the Portuguese introduced it in the East African and Indian parts of their empire, and these areas are today the biggest exporters of cashews. Although lower in total fat than most nuts, cashews are high in saturated fat. They are a good source of folacin, iron, protein, and vitamin C. The cashew apple is also high in vitamin C and is used in beverages and to make jelly.

Common names and synonyms: Cashew apple, cashew fruit, cashew nut.

Cashew apple - *see* **CASHEW**

Cassaba - *see* **CASABA (MELON)**

Cassabanana - *see* **CUCUMBER**

Cassava - *see* **MANIOC**

Cassia - *see* **CINNAMON AND CASSIA, INDIAN BARK, SAIGON CINNAMON**

Cassina - *see* **YAUPON**

Cassine - *see* **DAHOON HOLLY**

Cassis - *see* **BLACK CURRANT**

CASTORBEAN - A native of Africa, the castor-oil plant (*Ricinus communis*) produces the castorbean - a poisonous seed - from which oil is extracted. The tree now grows throughout the tropical world, and its oil has many valuable industrial uses, but save for doses of the infamous castor oil, it is not consumed by humans.

Common names and synonyms: Castor-oil plant.

Castor-oil plant - *see* **CASTORBEAN**

Cat - *see* **KHAT**

CATARINA (*see also* **CHILLI PEPPERS**) - Grown in Texas and northern Mexico, the catarina chilli (*Capsicum annuum*) is red, some 1 to 2 inches in length, and can be either tapered or broad and oblong. Like its relative the cascabel, when the catarina is dried, its seeds rattle. Its moderate heat makes it an excellent ingredient in salsas.

See in addition: "Chilli Peppers," Part II, Section C, Chapter 4.

CATAWBA (GRAPE) (*see also* **GRAPES**) - The catawba is an American wine grape (*Vitis labrusca*) used to make Catawba wines. Called "one of the most celebrated of native American wines, at the beginning of the twentieth century, at century's end these heavy and somewhat sweet wines were virtually unknown. Most Catawba wines were white, and the highest priced were of the "sparkling" type. Some red Catawba was made, along with "sweet Catawba," which was a rich, fortified wine.

See in addition: "Wine," Part III, Chapter 13.

Catbrier - *see* **GREENBRIER**

Catchweed - *see* **GOOSEGRASS**

Catclaw acacia - *see* **ACACIA**

Catechu - *see* **BETEL NUT**

CATJANG (*see also* **COWPEA**) - One of the cowpeas of the genus *Vigna,* the catjang (*V. unguiculata*) is a relatively primitive form, cultivated mostly in Asia but also in Africa. Its main use is as animal feed, but people also use the seeds for food in both fresh and dried forms.

Common names and synonyms: Catjang pea.

See in addition: "Beans, Peas, and Lentils," Part II, Section C, Chapter 3.

Catjang pea - *see* **CATJANG**

Catmint - *see* **CATNIP**

Catnep - *see* **CATNIP**

CATNIP - A perennial herb native to Eurasia, catnip (*Nepeta cataria*) is now widely naturalized in North America. Usually regarded as a weed, it has flowering tops, grows to about 3 feet in height, and has long been associated with cats, which are attracted by its odor. But the leaves and roots of catnip have also been used medicinally and as food for millennia. Indeed, they are still regularly consumed in parts of East Asia.

Common names and synonyms: Catmint, catnep.

Cat's-eye - *see* **LONGAN**

CATTAIL - A familiar roadside sight along drainage ditches, cattails - of the genus *Typha* - are marsh-dwelling plants that are scattered about the world, and their various parts have been used as food by hunter-gatherers since time immemorial. Native Americans, for example, ate the tender shoots and leaf bases raw, dried and ground the rhizomes into flour, and even roasted and ate the tops like corn on the cob. The seeds are also edible, and the flowers provide a pollen that can be added to flour. Cattails and bulrushes are sometimes lumped together, but they belong to different genera.

Common names and synonyms: Reed-mace.

Cattley guava - *see* **STRAWBERRY GUAVA**

CAULIFLOWER (*see also* **CABBAGE**) - The cauliflower (*Brassica oleracea* var. *botrytis*), another - and many would say the most elegant - member of the sprawling cabbage family, is a direct descendant of the original wild cabbage and a close relative of broccoli. The kind of cauliflower usually found in vegetable hors d'oeuvres has a white head, achieved by growers who cover the flower head in its outer leaves so as to block sunlight and, thus, prevent the formation of chlorophyll. There is also a purple type, called cauliflower broccoli. The cauliflower (the name is probably from the Italian *caolifiori,* meaning "cabbage flowers") was apparently known in much of Europe during the Middle Ages, but then disappeared and had to be reintroduced to the rest of the Continent in the sixteenth century. This was accomplished by the Italians, probably from Cyprus, where the plant had reached from Asia. In Europe, where much cauliflower is consumed, Italy has long been the major producer. The vegetable could be found in U.S. markets from the turn of the twentieth century onward but consumption only became significant following World War II. Cauliflowers are very low in calories but rich in vitamin C, the B complex, and vitamin K (which helps to clot blood).

Common names and synonyms: Asparagus broccoli, broccoli (British), cauliflower broccoli.

See in addition: "Cruciferous and Green Leafy Vegetables," Part II, Section C, Chapter 5.

Caulorapa - *see* **KOHLRABI**
Cava - *see* **KAVA**
Cawesh - *see* **POSHTE**
Cayenne - *see* **CAYENNE PEPPER**
Cayenne cherry - *see* **PITANGA**
CAYENNE PEPPER(*see also* **CHILLI PEPPERS**) - Today, the term "cayenne" is synonymous with red pepper and can mean any of the ground, hot, red chilli peppers of the *Capsicum* species that are native to the Americas. And recipes from areas as diverse as Mexico and China, Louisiana and India, call for it. Originally, however, the pepper in question (*C. annuum*) was ground into powder in Cayenne in French Guiana (it is also called the ginnie pepper and guine pepper), and the term "cayenne" was meant to signify the hottest ground red pepper available. Cayennes are very hot, bright red when mature, long (some 4 to 6 inches) and slender, and generally are dried. These pointed red pods make an excellent addition to sauces, and when green they are incorporated in salsas. But their major use is in the production of powdered cayenne pepper (also designated hot red pepper). In addition, cayenne peppers have long been the primary ingredient in all of the Louisiana hot sauces except the Tabasco brand. The *de árbol* is a close relative of the cayenne pepper (and looks like it) and also is ground into powdered form. Another, smaller (about an inch long) close relative is the red *Pico de Pajaro* or "bird's-beak" – so named because of its beaklike shape. Today, cayenne peppers are grown in Mexico; Louisiana; South, Southeast, and East Asia; and West Africa.

Common names and synonyms: Bird's-beak, cayenne, *de árbol,* ginnie pepper, guine pepper, hot red pepper, *Pico de Pajaro.*

See in addition: "Chilli Peppers," Part II, Section C, Chapter 4.

Caygua - *see* **KORILA**
Caymito - *see* **STAR-APPLE**
Cayua - *see* **KORILA**
Ceci - *see* **CHICKPEA**
CEDAR - The name "cedar" embraces a number of trees of various genera, including those of the genus *Thuja,* which helped to feed Native Americans. In the northwestern portion of North America, the inner bark of the giant or western red cedar, *T. plicata,* provided food in much the same fashion as the inner bark of the slippery elm. In the Northeast, it was the white cedar (*T. occidentalis* – also known as northern white cedar, yellow cedar, featherleaf cedar, and arbor-vitae) that provided young shoots and leaves that were cooked like vegetables and made into tea.

Common names and synonyms: Arbor-vitae, featherleaf cedar, giant cedar, northern white cedar, western red cedar, white cedar, yellow cedar.

Ceiba - *see* **KAPOK TREE**
Celeriac - *see* **CELERY AND CELERY ROOT**
CELERY AND CELERY ROOT (*see also* **CELERY SEED**) - A member of the parsley family, and native to the Mediterranean region and the Middle East, wild celery (*Apium graveolens*) was one of the first vegetables to appear in recorded history. From the writings of Confucius, we know that celery (probably wild) was in use in China before 500 B.C. The ancient Egyptians gathered the plant for its seeds – used as seasoning – as well as for its stalks and leaves, whereas in ancient Greece celery had a medicinal as well as a culinary reputation.

Two types of celery have subsequently been developed. One is the so-called true celery (*Apium graveolens* var. *dulce*), with green or blanched stems that are eaten raw, sliced into salads, and cooked as a vegetable, and the seeds of which are still used as seasoning. The most common variety is the medium-green Pascal celery, which was first cultivated in Italy and, by the seventeenth century, in France. In the United States, commercial cultivation of Pascal celery dates from 1874, when Dutch farmers near Kalamazoo, Michigan, passed out free samples to train passengers to popularize the vegetable. Celery comes in both blanched form (celery hearts) and green with large, fleshy ribs, the difference being that the former is kept away from the sun to ensure whiteness. Celery leaves are sometimes cut up and dried to be added as an herb to stews, soups, and other dishes. Celery is reputed to lower blood pressure, is very low in calories, and provides a respectable amount of vitamin C and folacin.

The other type of celery (*Apium graveolens* var. *rapaceum*), cultivated for its starch-storing root rather than for stalks, is commonly called celery root or celeriac. It appears as an ugly sort of foodstuff – a gnarled, turnip-like form with dangling rootlets – ranging in size from an orange to a cantaloupe. But its zesty taste of celery and parsley intermingled has long been a part of French salads (often with a remoulade sauce) as well as an important ingredient of soups, stuffings, purees, and the like in Russia and the countries of northern Europe. Also called "knob celery" and "turnip-rooted celery," the root is a fair source of iron and calcium and makes a small contribution to the B-vitamin intake.

Common names and synonyms: Celeriac, *céleri rave*, celery heart(s), Hamburg celery, knob celery, Pascal celery, true celery, turnip-rooted celery, wild celery.

Celery cabbage - *see* **BOK CHOY, CHINESE CABBAGE**

Celery mustard - *see* **PAKCHOI AND KAI CHOY**

CELERY SEED - Celery (*Apium graveolens* var. *dulce*) was developed in seventeenth-century Europe from its wild predecessor and was first recorded as a plant in 1623 in France. The tiny brown seeds from celery impart a mild celery flavor to dishes in which the use of the stalks would not be appropriate, such as bread dough and sauces and some soups, salads, stews, and potato salads. Ground celery seeds also flavor celery salt, salad dressings, and the like.

See also: "Spices and Flavorings," Part II, Section F, Chapter 1.

Celtuce - *see* **LETTUCE**

Century plant - *see* **AGAVE**

Cep - *see* **BOLETE, MUSHROOMS AND FUNGI**

Cèpe - *see* **BOLETE, MUSHROOMS AND FUNGI**

Cèpe de bolete - *see* **BOLETE**

Cèpe de Bordeaux - *see* **BOLETE**

Ceriman - *see* **MONSTERA**

Ceriman de Mexico - *see* **MONSTERA**

CEYLON GOOSEBERRY (*see also* **BERRIES**) - Also known as *ketembilla*, and *quetembilla*, the Ceylon gooseberry (*Dovyalis hebecarpa*) is a fruit of tropical Asia that grows on a bushy shrub. The berries are maroon to purple in color and resemble gooseberries in appearance and taste. Today, the berries are cultivated throughout tropical Asia, and especially in India. Ceylon gooseberries are also commercially cultivated on a small scale in Florida and California. They are eaten fresh and made into preserves and jellies.

Common names and synonyms: Ketembilla, quetembila.

Ceylon spinach - *see* **MALABAR SPINACH, TALINUM**

Chaco - *see* **CHAYOTE**

Chad - *see* **BEET**

Chago - *see* **MAUKA**

CHAMBURO (*see also* **PAPAYA**) - A relative of the papaya, and papaya-like in appearance, the chamburo (*Carica pubescens*) is a native of northern South America that is now cultivated along the Andes as far south as Bolivia at altitudes of about 3,000 feet. The yellow fruit is tart, even when mature, and is generally made into juice or preserved instead of eaten raw.

CHAMOMILE - The dried flowers of chamomile (*Anthemis nobilis*) are used as an herbal infusion for baths and tisanes. They deliver a pungent, grassy flavor, and chamomile (also camomile) is said to be good for the digestive system. Chamomile teas were much consumed by Victorian ladies hoping to restore vitality. The herb was also employed historically as a gargle for sore throats.

Common names and synonyms: Camomile.

Champignon d'Paris - *see* **MUSHROOMS AND FUNGI**

Chan - *see* **HYPTIS**

CHANTERELLE (*see also* **MUSHROOMS AND FUNGI**) - The yellow or golden (although occasionally black or white) trumpets of the chanterelle (*Cantharellus cibarius*), a wild mushroom of the woodlands, are found in both Europe and North America. This edible fungus is gathered in abundance in the Pacific Northwest but has been especially appreciated in Europe, where it is known by many names, including *chanterelle* (French), *Pfifferling* (German), and *girolle* (Italian). The chanterelle has yet to be cultivated and thus is only gathered. Its taste varies widely – from delicate to fairly intense. The chanterelle is a good source of vitamins A and D and makes a contribution to the intake of the vitamin B complex.

Common names and synonyms: Chantarelle, forest mushroom, *girolle,* golden chanterelle, *Pfifferling.*

See in addition: "Fungi," Part II, Section C, Chapter 7.

Chard - *see* **BEET, SWISS CHARD**

CHARDONNAY (*see also* **GRAPES**) - The great white Burgundian wines of France, such as the light and dry Pouilly Fuissé, are made almost exclusively with Chardonnay grapes (*Vitis vinifera*), which are now grown all over the world. In the climate of Oregon, this grape grows so well that the state has become well known for its Burgundy-style wines. In California and Australia, Chardonnay is used to make dry wines as well as serving as a base for sparkling wines. It is a very expensive grape.

See in addition: "Wine," Part III, Chapter 13.

Charnushka - *see* **NIGELLA**

CHASTE TREE - Cultivated in both the New and the Old Worlds, this aromatic shrub or tree (*Vitex agnus-castus*) has a reputation for anaphrodisiac qualities – hence its name. But it is also called "wild pepper" and "monk's-pepper," and its seeds have served as a spice. The leaves of other *Vitex* species are used for tea, and some produce fruits that are consumed throughout the world's tropical zones.

Common names and synonyms: Agnus castus, hemp tree, Indian spice, monk's-pepper tree, sage tree, wild pepper.

Chawa - *see* **SWEET PEPPERS AND WAX PEPPERS**

CHAYA - Also called the "spinach tree," chaya (*Cnidoscolus chayamansa*) is found throughout Mesoamerica and the West Indies. In Mexico, this plant, which can attain the height of a human, has large leaves that are boiled and eaten as a vegetable and used to wrap tamales. The leaves must be boiled to render harmless a toxin they contain, and many varieties have stinging hairs on the leaves, which makes some cooks less than enthusiastic about their preparation.

Common names and synonyms: Spinach tree.

CHAYOTE (*see also* **SQUASH AND PUMPKIN**) - A member of the gourd family (Cucurbitaceae), this well-traveled, spiny vegetable (*Sechium edule*) originated in the American tropics. Called *chayotli* in Nahuatl, it was domesticated in what is now Mexico, was spread throughout South America after the Spanish conquest, and is now found in places as diverse and distant as North Africa and Indonesia. Such peregrinations doubtless account for its myriad names, a few of which are vegetable pear, mirliton, *pepinella, xuxu,* christophene, *chocho,* custard marrow, and *sousous.* The taste of this usually green, pear-shaped, vine-growing vegetable resembles that of other cucurbits such as zucchini and the summer squashes; unlike these, however, the chayote must usually have its skin removed before cooking. Most parts of the plant are edible, and the leaves and vine tips are eaten as vegetables. The tuberous roots, which are generally peeled and boiled and taste similar to a Jerusalem artichoke, are an important source of starch. The fruit is used like a squash. It is boiled, baked, fried, steamed, stuffed, pureed in soups, and made into desserts; many consider the seed a delicacy as well. Chayote is a fair source of vitamin C and potassium.

Common names and synonyms: Buddha's-hand, *chaco, chayotli, chinchayote, chocho, choko,* christophene, christophine, *chuchu,* custard marrow, *guispui,* mango squash, mirliton, *pepinella, sousous, tallon, tallote,* vegetable pear, *xuxu.*

Chayotli - *see* **CHAYOTE**

CHE (*see also* **BERRIES**) - A native of eastern Asia that was long ago naturalized in Japan and more recently introduced in Europe and the United States, che (*Cudrania tricuspidata*) is related to the mulberry and is sometimes called the "Chinese mulberry." Its fruits are relatively large, develop a bright, reddish color when ripe, and are reportedly delicious. In China, che leaves serve to feed silkworms when there is a shortage of mulberry leaves.

Common names and synonyms: Chinese mulberry, cudrang, mandarin melon-berry.

Checkerberry - *see* **WINTERGREEN**

Chekkurmanis - *see* **SWEET-SHOOT**

CHEMPEDAK - Probably native to Indochina, the chempedak tree (*Artocarpus integer*) is an ancient cultivar. Its yellowish to brown, oblong fruits are large - reaching a foot or more in length. The custard-like pulp is sweet and eaten raw, and the seeds are consumed after boiling.

CHENOPODIUM (*see also* various *Chenopodium* entries) - A large genus of herbs, *Chenopodium* includes the goosefoots and other plants that are found throughout the world's temperate regions - today mostly as weeds. Species raised in the pre-Columbian Americas that are still in cultivation include quinoa (*C. quinoa*), mostly grown in Ecuador, Peru, and Bolivia, and *cañihua* (*C. pallidicaule*), confined to the high Andes. In addition, *C. bushianum* appears to have been cultivated by Native Americans in eastern North America prior to the arrival of the Europeans, and *C. nuttalliae* was domesticated in Mexico. Since 1492, *C. huauzontle* has also been domesticated in Mexico, and both the Mexican grains are called *chia.* All of these plants were (and are) cultivated primarily for their seeds, which are ground to make breads, gruels, and - in the Andean regions - *chicha,* a beer. This does not mean, however, that the green, fleshy parts of the plants were not consumed, and other chenopods - for example, lamb's-quarter (*C. album*) and the wild spinach "Good-King-Henry" (*C. bonus-henricus*) - were gathered for their flower buds and greens. Still others, such as *epazote* (*C. ambrosioides*), called "Mexican tea" in Mexico and *paiko* in Peru, have served for thousands of years as seasonings.

Common names and synonyms: Chenopod, *chia, epazote,* goosefoot, lamb's-quarter, *paiko,* quinoa.

CHERIMOYA - No wonder the cherimoya (*Annona cherimola*) is sometimes called a "custard apple." When ripe, this heart-shaped, scaly, pulpy fruit has smooth, cream-colored flesh and tastes like a custard made from tropical fruit. Although much smaller than a watermelon, it has similar large, black seeds. The cherimoya's name comes from the ancient Quecha language, and the fruit is of American (specifically, the South American highlands) origin but has been grown for many centuries in Central America and the Caribbean region for local use. It has also moved as far as Iberia to the east and to Australia, New Zealand, and Malaysia in other parts of the globe. In the United States, the cherimoya is grown in California and Florida. But because it does not keep well in shipping, it is not generally available in produce markets, and those who cannot find this fruit must order it through specialty catalogs for an exotic treat. The cherimoya, of the same family as the sweetsop and the sugar apple, provides a good measure of vitamin C and some iron.

Common names and synonyms: Anona, chirimoya, custard apple, sherbet-fruit.

Chermai - *see* **OTAHEITE GOOSEBERRY**

CHERRY (*see also* **CAPULIN, CHERRY LAUREL, CHIMAJA, CHOKECHERRY, SAND CHERRY, SOUR CHERRY**) - Cherries come from any of several trees that belong to the genus *Prunus* and are part of the rose family. The small, rounded fruits are - along with apricots, peaches, and plums - "stone fruits," or "drupes." The cherry originated in temperate Europe and Asia, and doubtless wild cherries played a role in the human diet eons before the invention of agriculture and the beginning of recorded history. Our Neolithic ancestors extracted - and presumably fermented - cherry juice before it was discovered how to make wine from grapes.

The sweet cherry (*Prunus avium*) and the sour cherry (*P. cerasus*) are the two main cultivated types; such cultivation apparently stretches back at least to the ancient Greeks. Cherries were very popular in Germany, France, and England toward the end of the Middle Ages, and they reached the Americas with early immigrants. The bulk of the world's cherries is still produced in Europe. One important exception is the sour cherry, which is mostly cultivated in North America despite its historical background in the world of Rome (it is named for Cerasus in Pontus, the city where the Roman general Lucullus defeated Mithradates and Tigranes, after which he took their cherry trees back to Italy).

Various cultures have provided many names for the hundreds of varieties of cherries that are consumed fresh, canned, and frozen and used (among other things) for candies, jams, tarts, pie fillings, liqueurs (especially kirsch), and flavoring medicines. In parts of the Old World, the powder of ground cherrystones has been employed as a spice.

The bing cherry is perhaps the best known of the sweet varieties in the United States, and the Montmorency the best known of the sour. In addition, of course, there are wild red and black cherries. The wild black cherry, also known as the chokecherry (*Prunus virginiana*), was exploited by Native Americans in the eastern part of North America for both food and medicine long before the Europeans arrived. In fact, this cherry is still used in both capacities; it is a principal ingredient in cough medications, including the venerable "Smith Brothers'" cough drops. Wild black cherries also find their way into some rums. Cherries are high in potassium and, like all red fruits, contain vitamins A and C along with B vitamins.

Common names and synonyms: Amarelle, Bigarreau, bing cherry, bird cherry, black cherry, capuli, Capulin, chokecherry, Gean, Guigne, klarbar, Mazzard, Montmorency, pie cherry, red cherry, sour cherry, sweet cherry, tart cherry, wild black cherry, wild red cherry.

Cherry birch - *see* **SWEET BIRCH**

CHERRY LAUREL (*see also* **CHERRY**) - An evergreen plant of Europe, and now naturalized in North America, the cherry laurel (*Prunus laurocerasus*) bears small black fruits that have little taste. But its thick, glossy leaves have a flavor like bitter almond and are used in cooking - especially for flavoring dessert puddings.

Cherry pepper - *see* **HUNGARIAN CHERRY PEPPER**

CHERRY PLUM (*see also* **PLUM**) - Also known as the "myrobalan plum," the cherry plum (*Prunus cerasifera*) is an Asiatic fruit now used extensively in Europe for stock to bud domestic varieties. The European plum (*P. domestica*) is thought to be a hybrid of the cherry plum and the sloe. Cherry plums are yellow, red, or purple; they are juicy but not especially tasty.

Common names and synonyms: Myrobalan plum.

Cherry tomato - *see* **TOMATO**

CHERVIL - There is an annual chervil (*Anthriscus cerefolium*) and a biennial (*Chaerophyllum bulbosum*); the latter is also called "turnip-rooted chervil." Both are related to the carrot family and to parsley (which the annual variety resembles). The latter is native to western Asia and the Balkans (it grows wild in Iran and southwestern Russia) and derives its name from a Greek word meaning "cheer-leaf." The Romans used chervil for its aromatic, parsley-tasting, anise-smelling leaves and are credited with introducing it into western Europe and then spreading it about the continent. Chervil has parsley-like leaves, used for seasoning, that were long popular in England and today are especially appreciated in France. It is one of the fines herbes (along with parsley, chives, and tarragon) employed in salads and as potherbs. In addition, chervil is used much in the same way as parsley in fish and shellfish dishes, omelettes, soups, and sauces. The leaves are available both fresh and dried. The biennial, which is native to Europe, is grown for its carrot-like root.

Common names and synonyms: Garden chervil, leaf chervil, salad chervil, sweet cicely, turnip chervil, turnip-rooted chervil.

See also: "Spices and Flavorings," Part II, Section F, Chapter 1.

CHESTNUT - Members of the beech family, chestnut trees are native to the world's temperate regions, and there are several trees of the genus *Castanea* that bear nuts enclosed in a prickly burr. The name, said to derive from a town - Kastanéa - in Asia Minor, has been preserved in most of the countries of Europe where chestnuts are enjoyed (*Kastanie* in German and *châtaigne* in French, for example), and the aroma of roasting chestnuts during the holiday season has long been an indelible memory for most city dwellers of Europe and North America. In the early twentieth century in North America, the native chestnut (*Castanea dentata*) was almost totally destroyed by a blight - a destructive fungal bark disease that may have killed 3 billion or more chestnut trees between the turn of the century and

1940. Because Asiatic varieties of the chestnut tree proved resistant to the blight, an attempt has been made to substitute Chinese trees (and European varieties), but thus far practically all chestnuts that are roasted or boiled and chopped into dressings to accompany birds and game in America have been imported from Europe. They are not, however, European "horse chestnuts" (*Aesculus hippocastanum*), which are bitter and mildly toxic, unlike the American and other European varieties, which have a mild, sweet, nutty taste. Chestnuts have a mealy consistency reminiscent of roasted cassava or potatoes. They were mentioned and used by the ancient Greeks and Romans and have served some people very much as a staple crop. Indeed, dried chestnuts were historically ground into flour for making breads, and in some places chestnuts constituted the most important food for whole populations. The chestnut is the only nut high in vitamin C, and it is also a good source of the B vitamins. A bonus is that it is low in fat and calories.

Common names and synonyms: American chestnut, *châtaigne,* Chinese chestnut, dwarf chestnut, European chestnut, European horse chestnut, Japanese chestnut, *Kastanie,* Spanish chestnut, sweet chestnut.

See also: "Chestnuts," Part II, Section D, Chapter 1.

Chestnut bean - *see* **CHICKPEA**

CHIA - A species of sage that produces pods filled with tiny seeds, chia (*Salvia columbariae*) long provided Native Americans of southwestern North America with a grain substitute. In addition, the Aztecs, farther south, used these seeds and those of a Mexican chia (*Salvia hispanica*) to make a refreshing drink. The seeds are gathered much like grain and are then parched and ground into meal for baking flat breads and making porridges. Chia seeds were also often stored for future use.

Common names and synonyms: California chia, ghia, Mexican chia.

Chiccory - *see* **CHICORY**

Chich-pea - *see* **CHICKPEA**

Chickling grass - *see* **CHICKLING VETCH**

Chickling pea - *see* **CHICKLING VETCH**

CHICKLING VETCH (*see also* **LEGUMES**) - Also known as "grass pea" and "European grass pea," chickling vetch (*Lathyrus sativus*) is a pea cultivated in Europe for its seeds and for animal forage.

Common names and synonyms: Chickling grass, chickling pea, European grass pea, grass pea.

See in addition: "Beans, Peas, and Lentils," Part II, Section C, Chapter 3.

Chickory - *see* **CHICORY**

CHICKPEA (*see also* **BEANS**) - Known as *garbanzo* in Spanish, *ceci* in Italian, "gram" in India, and often as just plain "pulse" across the globe, the chickpea (*Cicer arietinum*) is an ancient pulse that originated in western Asia and was domesticated there some 7,000 years ago. The tan, hazelnut-sized seeds, with their wrinkled surfaces, nutty flavor, and crisp texture, soon became popular from the Mediterranean to India (as culinary traditions make clear) and today are practically universal. In the Near East, the chickpea is the basic ingredient for hummus and falafel and is frequently incorporated in couscous. In India, as the country's most important legume, the chickpea is roasted, boiled, and fried, is made into flour, and is part of a *dhal*. In the Mediterranean region, the chickpea figures prominently in the "poor cuisine" – as a staple in the diet of poor people, a substitute for meat (and sometimes for coffee as well), and an ingredient in the boiled dinners (*cocidos*) of Iberia.

Exactly when the chickpea reached Spain and Portugal is unclear – perhaps with the Phoenicians, certainly with the Romans. The Portuguese call the chickpea *grão do bico* ("grain with a beak") because of the little horn on the pea. From Iberia, chickpeas traveled to the Americas, where they achieved fame in Cuban bean soup and in menudo. The vegetable has also become a standard item on practically every salad bar in North America, a region where it can also be purchased dried or canned (but seldom fresh) in markets. Like almost all legumes, the chickpea is high in protein and the B-vitamin complex. Moreover, the chickpea and others of its relatives have recently come to be viewed as cholesterol fighters.

Common names and synonyms: Bengal gram, calvance pea, *ceci,* chestnut bean, chich, chich-pea, dwarf pea, garavance, garbanza, *garbanzo,* gram, gram pea, *grão do bico,* pulse, yellow gram.

See in addition: "Beans, Peas, and Lentils," Part II, Section C, Chapter 3.

CHICKWEED - So called because they are eaten by chickens, chickweeds (any of the various plants of the genus *Stellaria,* especially the common chickweed, *S. media*) have enjoyed something of a reputation for medicinal use. In fact, a synonym, "stitchwort," was assigned because of an alleged ability to cure pains in the side. Native to Europe, *Stellaria* species were given the Latin word for star as a name in view of the shape of their flowers. Several species of chickweed are eaten in Japan. In North America, *S. media* (introduced from Europe) has a reputation for making an excellent salad with its tender leaves and stems. The seeds are also edible. Today, chickweeds are used mostly as a potherb, but because they are so hardy, growing even throughout the winter months, and because they can be cooked as a green, they doubtless served for millennia as food for hunter-gatherers and also for those caught in famine circumstances, even in the colder seasons. The term chickweed can also refer to plants of the genus *Cerastium.*

Common names and synonyms: Common chickweed, stitchwort.

Chicle (tree) - *see* **SAPODILLA**

Chico - *see* **SAPODILLA**

CHICORY (*see also* BELGIUM ENDIVE, ENDIVE AND ESCAROLE) – Semantic problems abound with chicory (*Cichorium intybus*) – also called succory, radicchio, and red chicory), endive (*Cichorium endivia*), and escarole, which is the broad-leafed variety of endive. All three are members of the dandelion family, but there the resemblance ends. *Cichorium endivia,* native to India, was the ancestor of endive and known to the Egyptians as well as to the ancient Greeks and Romans. By contrast, *C. intybus* is native to Europe, but the names nonetheless remain confused. In the United States, chicory is generally called Belgian endive, although this is also referred to simply as endive. The French, too, call it endive (and call endive *chicorée*), and radicchio is chicory's Italian name. The Flemish name for Belgian endive is *witloof* or "whiteleaf," because it was grown in cellars in dim light, which produced both the plant's whitish leaf color and its elongated leaves as they stretched out to seek light – indeed, modern methods of growing this pale, cigar-shaped vegetable follow the same principle. If part of the confusion is semantic, part also stems from the different uses of the plants. Chicory as well as endive roots are ground to become a natural coffee substitute (especially in France and French-influenced areas) or an addition to regular coffee for added flavor and reduced caffeine. However, the tight hearts of Belgian endive and radicchio are also attractive and slightly bitter ingredients in salads; in addition, their braised leaves can be a vegetable dish in their own right. Radicchio, although a relative newcomer to the U.S. culinary scene, is now grown domestically in New Jersey and California as well as in Italy and Mexico. Nonetheless, it remains a very expensive produce item.

Common names and synonyms: Asparagus chicory, *barbe de capucin,* Belgian endive, chiccory, chickory, endive, radicchio, *radicchio di castelfranco, radicchio di chiogga, radicchio di treviso, radicchio di Verona, radicchio rosso,* red chicory, red-leafed chicory, red treviso chicory, red Verona chicory, *rosso di Verona,* succory, *witloef, witloof.*

Chico sapote – *see* SAPODILLA

Chico zapote – *see* SAPODILLA

Chihli cabbage – *see* CHINESE CABBAGE

Chiku – *see* SAPODILLA

Chilaca – *see* PASILLA

Chilca – *see* ANISILLO

Chilean cranberry – *see* CHILEAN GUAVA MYRTLE

CHILEAN GUAVA MYRTLE – Also called the Chilean cranberry, the Chilean guava myrtle (*Myrtus ugni*) is a small evergreen shrub with delicious mahogany red, sphere-shaped fruits that are an inch or more in diameter. The plant is a native of Chile; its fruits are used for jelly, and its fragrant leaves as well as the fruits are employed in flavoring water and making perfumes.

Common names and synonyms: Chilean cranberry, *ugni.*

CHILEAN PINE – Also known as the "monkey-puzzle," the Chilean pine (*Araucaria araucana*) is a South American native. It bears the name of Native Americans (the Araucana) who fought the Spanish conquistadors to a standstill in what is now Chile, and the tree also bears nuts that are eaten raw as well as boiled or roasted.

Common names and synonyms: Monkey-puzzle (tree).

Chile caballo – *see* MANZANA

CHILHUACLE PEPPERS (*see also* CHILLI PEPPERS) – The three *chilhuacle* chillies (*Capsicum annuum*) are all grown only in southern Mexico (Oaxaca and Chiapas). The *rojo* (colored a deep red), the *negro* (oxblood to almost black in tone), and the *amarillo* (with a reddish yellow hue) average some 2 to 3 inches in length and appear like miniature bell peppers (which are members of the same species), although the *chilhuacles* can also taper somewhat. The *chilhuacles* are moderately hot, are almost always dried, and generally are employed in mole sauces. Of the three, the *chilhuacle negro* is the most highly prized and thus the most expensive.

Common names and synonyms: Chilhuacle amarillo, chilhuacle negro, chilhuacle rojo.

See in addition: "Chilli Peppers," Part II, Section C, Chapter 4.

Chilhuacle rojo – *see* CHILHUACLE PEPPERS

Chili (pepper) – *see* CHILLI PEPPERS

Chilli bola – *see* CASCABEL

Chilli colorado – *see* ANAHEIM, NEW MEXICO CHILLIES

Chilli negro – *see* PASILLA

CHILLI PEPPERS (*see also* SWEET PEPPERS) – All chilli peppers belong to the genus *Capsicum* and are mostly varieties of two species – *C. annuum* and the generally smaller and hotter *C. frutescens.* Chilli peppers are native to the Americas, where they were cultivated for many thousands of years as they spread from South America north to Mesoamerica, the Caribbean, and the North American Southwest. When the Europeans reached the New World, chillies were the most common spice used by Native Americans. But after this they were no longer a secret from the rest of the world. Columbus called them *pimientos* after the *pimienta* or black pepper he had hoped to find and carried them to Iberia, whereupon they began to spread. Peppers also radiated to the East via the Spaniards' Manila galleons (trading between Mexico and the Philippines) and traveled with the Portuguese, who introduced the plants into West and East Africa, India, and the East Indies. The wildfire spread of chillies took place so quickly in the sixteenth century, and they became so well naturalized, that many in Africa, India, East and Southeast

Asia, and elsewhere began to think of the plants as native to their own regions of the world. The "fire" of chillies, which comes from the alkaloid capsaicin, is imparted in dozens of hot sauces throughout the world from Thailand (*nam prik*) to Mexico (*salsa*) to Tunisia (*barissa*), and chillies are vital in the cuisines of China, India, and Africa – south as well as north of the Equator. Chillies are green, yellow, red, or black in color and range in shape from long, skinny, hot, green chillies - or Anaheims - to the squat habaneros and jalapeños, to the plump, elongated serranos and banana chillies, to name but a few. All of these come dried as well as fresh and are crushed and ground. In addition to sauces, chillies are made into powders, pickled, smoked, roasted, and canned whole as well as chopped. Chillies are very high in vitamin C and also provide a good measure of vitamin A.

Common names and synonyms: Capsicum (pepper), *chile* (pepper), chili (pepper), chilli(es), Japanese mustard (Korean), pepper, pepper of Calicut (archaic), *pimiento,* red pepper.

See in addition: "Chilli Peppers," Part II, Section C, Chapter 4; "Spices and Flavorings," Part II, Section F, Chapter 1.

Chilli pequeño - *see* **TEPÍN CHILLIES AND RELATIVES**

Chilli pequín - *see* **TEPÍN CHILLIES AND RELATIVES**

Chilli rocoto - *see* **MANZANA**

Chilli seco - *see* **SERRANO**

CHIMAJA (*see also* **CHERRY**) - Also called the "holly-leaved cherry," this wild cherry plant (*Prunus ilicifolia*) has roots and leaves that are dried, ground, and added to the dishes of Mexico (where it originated) and those of the southwestern United States. The sweet fruit is also eaten, and in the past Native Americans processed the kernel of the stone to make a kind of meal.

Common names and synonyms: Holly-leaved cherry.

China bean - *see* **COWPEA**

CHINABERRY (*see also* **BERRIES**) - An Asiatic tree, the chinaberry (*Melia azedarach*) has smooth, yellow, edible berries. The tree has become naturalized in the southern United States. A soapberry (*Sapindus saponaria*) of the desert Southwest and Mexico is also called "chinaberry."

China orange - *see* **CALAMONDIN**

China sweet orange - *see* **ORANGE**

Chinchayote - *see* **CHAYOTE**

Chinchilla - *see* **ANISILLO**

CHINESE AMARANTH (*see also* **AMARANTH**) - There are several species of *Amaranthus* cultivated in southwestern Asia, with Chinese amaranth (*A. tricolor*) probably the most important. It is an ancient food that is mentioned in early Chinese records, but despite its scientific name, the plant seems to sport only two colors. The green kind resembles spinach and is used in much the same way in vegetable

dishes, salads, and the like. The other is known as "red-in-snow" in China, because it grows early in the spring when the ground still has something of a snow cover. This type is eaten fresh and also pickled. Chinese amaranth is grown to a limited extent for the Chinese market in the United States.

Common names and synonyms: Chinese spinach, red-in-snow, *tampala.*

See in addition: "Amaranth," Part II, Section A, Chapter 1.

Chinese anise - *see* **STAR-ANISE**

Chinese apple - *see* **POMEGRANATE**

CHINESE ARTICHOKE - The Chinese artichoke (*Stachys sieboldii = S. affinis*) has nothing to do with the globe artichoke. Rather, it is a crisp, edible tuber, which resembles the Jerusalem artichoke in taste and is native to and grown in China and Japan. Also called the Japanese artichoke, in Europe it goes by the name of *crosne,* which – according to legend – was also the name of a small town in France where the Chinese artichoke was introduced in 1822. Chinese artichokes are usually boiled for a few minutes and then eaten as a cooked vegetable; they may also serve as an ingredient in other dishes, especially soups.

Common names and synonyms: Crosne, Japanese artichoke, Japanese potato.

CHINESE BROCCOLI (*see also* **CABBAGE**) - Also known as *gai-larn,* "Chinese kale," and *kailan,* Chinese broccoli (*Brassica alboglabra*) resembles Chinese flowering cabbage but has a flavor similar to kale. As in the case of the flowering cabbage, the tender green stems are of more interest to consumers than the leaves. The stems are steamed or braised and often served with oyster sauce. They are also used in soups and noodle dishes.

Common names and synonyms: Chinese kale, *gai-larn, kailan.*

See in addition: "Cruciferous and Green Leafy Vegetables," Part II, Section C, Chapter 5.

CHINESE CABBAGE (*see also* **CABBAGE**) - Also called napa, nappa, celery cabbage, and *pe-tsai,* this vegetable (*Brassica pekinensis*) is often confused with bok choy (*Brassica chinensis*), which is also sometimes called "Chinese cabbage." They resemble one another in their oblong or pointed (as opposed to round) form. The leaves of the Chinese cabbage, which look something like those of pale romaine lettuce, are crisp, tender, mild tasting, and certainly more delicate than those of round cabbages. Chinese cabbage has been an important dietary item in China since ancient times and is also consumed in other parts of Asia - especially in Japan and Korea, where it is stir-fried, boiled, pickled, or braised for use in a number of different dishes (the well known Korean pickle, *kimchee,* is made with Chinese cabbage). Chinese cabbages were virtually unknown in the West until the Israelis began to grow them, after which growers in California followed suit (hence napa or nappa cabbage, after the Napa Valley). Chinese cabbage is high in folic acid, vitamin A, and potassium.

Common names and synonyms: Celery cabbage, *chibli* cabbage, Chinese broccoli, Chinese leaf, *chou de chine, gay lon, hakusai,* Michihli, Napa, napa cabbage, nappa cabbage, Peking cabbage, *pe-tsai,* pointed cabbage, Shantung cabbage, Tientsin, *wong bok.*

See in addition: "Cruciferous and Green Leafy Vegetables," Part II, Section C, Chapter 5.

Chinese chard - *see* **PAKCHOI AND KAI CHOY**

Chinese chestnut - *see* **CHESTNUT**

CHINESE CHIVE(S) - Other names for Chinese chives (*Allium tuberosum*) - such as "Oriental garlic," "Chinese leeks," "garlic chives," and "flowering chives" - indicate that not only are the leaves employed as chives but the bulbs are also used much like garlic. Flowering chives are Chinese chives that are allowed to mature and grow an edible pointed flower. The Chinese also grow these chives without exposure to sunlight, whereupon they become "yellow chives."

Common names and synonyms: Chinese leeks, flowering chives, garlic chives, Oriental garlic, yellow chives.

See also: "The *Allium* Species," Part II, Section C, Chapter 2.

Chinese cinnamon - *see* **CINNAMON AND CASSIA**

Chinese date - *see* **JUJUBE**

Chinese eddoe - *see* **COCOYAM**

Chinese fig - *see* **PERSIMMON**

CHINESE FLOWERING CABBAGE (*see also* **CABBAGE**) - Also called *choy sum* and "mock *pak choy,*" Chinese flowering cabbage (*Brassica parachinensis*) has long, white-to-green stems, with rounded green leaves. *Choy sum* means "vegetable hearts," and it is the stems rather than the leaves that are sought after. They are generally cooked without peeling and served with an oyster sauce.

Common names and synonyms: Choy sum, mock *pak choy.*

See in addition: "Cruciferous and Green Leafy Vegetables," Part II, Section C, Chapter 5.

Chinese garlic - *see* **CHIVE(S)**

Chinese gooseberry - *see* **KIWI FRUIT**

Chinese kale - *see* **CHINESE BROCCOLI, KALE**

Chinese lantern - *see* **TOMATILLO**

Chinese laurel - *see* **BIGNAY**

Chinese leaf - *see* **CHINESE CABBAGE**

Chinese leeks - *see* **CHINESE CHIVE(S)**

Chinese mulberry - *see* **CHE, MULBERRY**

Chinese mustard cabbage - *see* **BOK CHOY**

Chinese okra - *see* **ANGLED LUFFA**

Chinese olive - *see* **CHINESE WHITE OLIVE**

Chinese parsley - *see* **CILANTRO, CORIANDER**

Chinese pea - *see* **SUGAR PEA**

Chinese pear - *see* **ASIAN PEAR**

Chinese potato - *see* **CHINESE YAM**

Chinese radish - *see* **DAIKON**

Chinese raisin tree - *see* **JAPANESE RAISIN TREE**

Chinese red date - *see* **JUJUBE**

Chinese snow pea - *see* **SUGAR PEA**

Chinese spinach - *see* **CALLALOO, CHINESE AMARANTH**

Chinese squash - *see* **FUZZY MELON**

Chinese star fruit - *see* **CARAMBOLA**

CHINESE TALLOW TREE - Known also as "Chinese vegetable tallow" or simply "vegetable tallow," the Chinese tallow tree (*Sapium sebiferum*) is a native of China and Japan but is now grown in other countries of East and South Asia and the southern United States. Also called the "white wax-berry," the tree is cultivated for these fruits about the size of peas, the seeds of which yield an oil with numerous industrial applications. However, the oil is used for cooking in Asia.

Common names and synonyms: Chinese vegetable tallow, tallow tree, vegetable tallow, white wax-berry.

Chinese taro - *see* **ALOCASIA**

Chinese vegetable marrow - *see* **FUZZY MELON**

Chinese vegetable tallow - *see* **CHINESE TALLOW TREE**

CHINESE WHITE OLIVE - Often mistakenly called the "Java almond," the Chinese white olive (*Canarium album*) is a large tree of South and Southeast Asia that belongs to a large genus of tropical trees. Many of these bear nuts sometimes called pilai nuts. In the case of the Chinese white olive, it bears a fruit with pulp that is preserved for use as a condiment.

Common names and synonyms: Chinese olive.

Chinese winter melon - *see* **FUZZY MELON, MELONS**

CHINESE YAM (*see also* **LESSER YAM, YAMS**) - A yam that is a native of China and widely cultivated there, the Chinese yam (*Dioscorea batatas*) is also called "Chinese potato" and, sometimes, "cinnamon vine" because the flowers smell of cinnamon. The tubers, which are also grown in Japan and other parts of East Asia, are mainly employed in sliced and grated form to add substance to various dishes, but they can also be fried, baked, or boiled like potatoes. This yam, along with others, has served as food for the peoples of China since the days of the hunter-gatherers.

Common names and synonyms: Chinese potato, cinnamon vine.

See in addition: "Sweet Potatoes and Yams," Part II, Section B, Chapter 5.

Chipiles - *see* **QUELITES**

Chipotle (chilli) - *see* **JALAPEÑO**

Chipotle grande - *see* **JALAPEÑO**

Chiquilla - *see* **ANISILLO**

Chirauli nut - *see* **CUDDAPAH ALMOND**

Chirimen - *see* **KABOCHA (SQUASH)**

Chirimoya - *see* **CHERIMOYA, POSHTE**

CHIVE(S) - The chive (*Allium schoenoprasum*) is of the lily family, is related to the onion, leek, and garlic, and has the most delicate taste of all of its close relatives. Chives are grown for their long, thin, grasslike, hollow stalks, which are used in salads, cheeses, soups, omelettes, and other dishes. Chives are also among the fines herbes – a traditional French blend of chervil, chives, parsley, and tarragon used for seasoning soups, salads, omelettes, and cottage and cream cheeses. The chive is an ancient herb. It is said to be native to the Mediterranean, but it was known by the Chinese some 5,000 years ago (varieties are called "Chinese onion" and "Oriental garlic") and grew wild in North America as well. Chives were enjoyed by the ancient Greeks but only reached the gardens of much of the rest of Europe in the sixteenth century. Chives are rich in vitamins A and C.

Common names and synonyms: Chinese garlic, Chinese onion, Oriental garlic.

See also: "The *Allium* Species," Part II, Section C, Chapter 2; "Spices and Flavorings," Part II, Section F, Chapter 1.

Chocho – *see* **ANDEAN LUPIN, CHAYOTE**

Chocolate – *see* **CACAO, MUTAMBA**

Chocolate-pudding fruit – *see* **BLACK SAPOTE**

Choctaw-root – *see* **HEMP DOGBANE**

CHOKEBERRY (*see also* **BERRIES**) – The chokeberry (*Aronia melanocarpa* or *A. arbutifolia*), like its fellow family (Rosaceae) member, the chokecherry (*Prunus virginiana*), is a very astringent fruit. Nonetheless, in eastern North America, the red, purple, or black fruits were gathered by Native Americans, who dried them for winter use. Around 1700, the plant was imported into Europe, where it was desired more for the ornamental appeal of the shrub than for its bitter fruit. However, the berries also make a useful substitute for black currants in areas where these cannot be grown. Chokeberries are very rich in vitamin C.

CHOKECHERRY (*see also* **CHERRIES**) – A member of the Rosaceae family, the chokecherry (*Prunus virginiana*), also called the wild black cherry, is a wild North American cherry and should not be confused with another family member, the chokeberry. With a name like chokecherry, one can be certain that the dark red or blackish fruit is very astringent. Nonetheless, chokecherries were gathered by Native Americans, who dried them and combined them with other fruits for winter storage. Later foragers have used them for jams and jellies, and they were even cultivated for a time in the southern provinces of Canada. Chokecherries were also employed for decades in cough remedies and were the principal ingredient in "Smith Brothers' " cough drops. Like other sour cherries, chokecherries are high in vitamin C and beta-carotene.

Common names and synonyms: Black chokecherry, capulin, western chokecherry, wild black cherry, wild cherry.

Choko – *see* **CHAYOTE**

Chopsuey greens – *see* **CHRYSANTHEMUM**

Chou de chine – *see* **CHINESE CABBAGE**

Chou-rave – *see* **KOHLRABI**

Choy sum – *see* **CHINESE FLOWERING CABBAGE, FLOWERING WHITE CABBAGE**

Christmas Rose (grape) – *see* **GRAPES**

Christmas tea-bush – *see* **YAUPON**

Christophene – *see* **CHAYOTE**

Christophine – *see* **CHAYOTE**

CHRIST'S-THORN FRUIT – Several prickly or thorny bushes of Palestine and the Near East are called "Christ's-thorn," especially *Ziziphus* (= *Zizyphus*) *spina-christi* and *Paliurus spina-christi*. They bear a small, red, edible fruit (a jujube), which is dried and eaten locally. Also called "Jerusalem thorn," this bush is popularly believed to have been used to fashion Christ's crown of thorns.

Common names and synonyms: Christ-thorn berry, Jerusalem thorn.

Christ-thorn berry – *see* **CHRIST'S-THORN FRUIT**

CHRYSANTHEMUM – "Japanese greens" (*Chrysanthemum coronarium*), also called "chopsuey greens," and the crown daisy or garland chrysanthemum (*C. spatiosum*) both have aromatic leaves that are cooked much like spinach in East Asia and are also used raw as garnishes.

Common names and synonyms: Chopsuey greens, crown daisy, edible-leaved chrysanthemum, garland chrysanthemum, Japanese greens.

Chu chi – *see* **MATRIMONY VINE**

Chuchu – *see* **CHAYOTE**

CHUFA – The edible roots of the weed "chufa" (*Cyperus esculentus*) are tubers that look somewhat like peanuts and, in the past, have been called "earth almonds" and "rush nuts." They can be eaten raw or cooked by boiling or roasting. They are also dried for later use and made into a flour, and chufa seeds can substitute for coffee. In Europe and the Middle East, desserts and drinks are made from the tubers. The plant, which is widespread geographically, is also of some antiquity. It was used by native North Americans on one side of the world and by the ancient Egyptians on the other side. Another common (and confusing) name for chufa is galingale, which is actually *Alpinia galanga*.

Common names and synonyms: Earth almond, galingale, nut(-)grass, purple nutgrass, rush nut, sedge, tigernut, yellow nutsedge, zula nut.

CICELY – Also known as "sweet cicely" – and sometimes as "sweet chervil" and even "myrrh" and "garden myrrh" – cicely (*Myrrhis odorata*) is an herb native to the Savoy region of France. Its pale green leaves and especially its ripe, glossy brown seeds have a licorice-like flavor that goes well with fruits and in salads and desserts. Cicely is so sweet that it can be added to stewed fruit dishes (such as rhubarb) and thereby considerably reduce the amount of sugar that is normally called for. In the past, cicely roots were boiled and eaten as a vegetable, but the plant is much less popular than it once was.

Common names and synonyms: Anise root, candy plant, European sweet chervil, garden myrrh, myrrh, Spanish chervil, sweet chervil, sweet cicely.

Cilantrillo - *see* **CILANTRO**

CILANTRO (*see also* **CORIANDER**) - Cilantro is a term that indicates the fresh green leaves of coriander (*Coriandrum sativum*), a plant whose seeds are also used as a spice (treated separately – along with the history of the plant – under the entry **Coriander**). Also called Chinese parsley, the pungent leaves of cilantro were long ago thought by some to smell delightfully peppery and by others to carry the odor of bedbugs. Nonetheless, cilantro has been acclaimed today as the most common flavoring herb in the world. The word cilantro comes from Spanish, but in Caribbean Spanish the term is *cilantrillo,* which can lead to confusion. Cilantro is available in bunches in produce departments and looks much like flat-leafed parsley. But there is also "culantro," which tastes like cilantro (although stronger) but looks like blades of grass. Cilantro is most important to the cuisines of Iberia, the Middle East, China, India, and many of the South American countries, and it is absolutely crucial to Mexican cookery, in which it appears as a green in many dishes, especially in salsas, guacamole, and with fish. Until recently, however, when Mexican food became more popular and widespread, cilantro was little known in the United States. The leaves deliver some vitamin A as well as vitamin C.

Common names and synonyms: Chinese parsley, *cilantrillo,* coriander, culantro, Mexican parsley, *yuen sai.*

Cimaru - *see* **TONKA BEAN**

Cinderella pumpkin - *see* **ROUGE VIF D'ÉTAMPES (PUMPKIN)**

Cinnamon - *see* **CINNAMON AND CASSIA, INDIAN BARK, SAIGON CINNAMON, WHITE CINNAMON**

CINNAMON AND CASSIA (*see also* **SAIGON CINNAMON**) - These ancient spices - cinnamon (*Cinnamomum zeylanicum = C. verum*) and cassia (*Cinnamomum cassia*) - are both derived from the dried inner bark of two related evergreen trees that belong to the laurel family. The trees are native to different parts of Asia (Sri Lanka and Burma, respectively), and, thus, cinnamon was an early - as well as vital - item in the spice trade that moved from the East to the West. Evidence exists to suggest that cinnamon was valued by the ancient Egyptians for witchcraft and embalming and, perhaps, for culinary purposes as well. It is mentioned in the Old Testament (along with cassia) and in Sanskrit manuscripts. In the East, cassia was cultivated by the Chinese as early as 2500 B.C., and may have been in use well before that. Cinnamon has been credited with magical ("love potions") as well as medicinal properties, and a drink prescribed for colds by a Roman physician – hot liquor and stick cinnamon – is still in use today. At one time cinnamon was viewed as more

precious than gold. Cinnamon has long been an essential ingredient in Moroccan and Greek chicken and beef dishes, and in the Middle East it is commonly used with meats, especially lamb. Europeans and North Americans tend to employ cinnamon mostly in sweets. Much of the cinnamon used in Europe is true cinnamon, whereas most of that reaching the United States is actually cassia. The difference is easy to spot: Cinnamon is tan, whereas cassia is reddish brown in color.

Common names and synonyms: Chinese cinnamon (cassia), cinnamon bark (both), false cinnamon (cassia), *kayu manis* (both), Seychelles cinnamon (cinnamon), sweet wood (both), true cinnamon (cinnamon).

See in addition: "Spices and Flavorings," Part II, Section F, Chapter 1.

Cinnamon bark - *see* **CINNAMON AND CASSIA**

Cinnamon vine - *see* **CHINESE YAM**

CINSAULT (*see also* **GRAPES**) - One of the important grapes of the southern Rhône Valley of France, the Cinsault (*Vitis vinifera*) is large, black, and used mostly to blend wines. A small amount is also produced in California.

See in addition: "Wine," Part III, Chapter 13.

Ciruela - *see* **BUNCHOSIA**

Citrange - *see* **CITRANGEQUAT**

CITRANGEQUAT (*see also* **CITRUS FRUITS, KUMQUAT, ORANGE**) - A cross between the orange relative *Poncirus trifoliata* and varieties of the sweet orange produced the hybrid known as a "citrange." Crossing the citrange with the kumquat has resulted in yet another hybrid, the "citrangequat" (involving three genera: *Citrus, Poncirus,* and *Fortunella*), which has a very sour fruit. Like the limequat and the orangequat, the citrangequat is the result of a breeding program - sponsored by the U.S. Department of Agriculture (USDA) - that is attempting to breed the cold-resistance of the kumquat into other plants.

CITRON (*see also* **CITRUS FRUITS, LEMON**) - A native of Southeast Asia, the citron (*Citrus medica*) was cultivated by the Chinese and Sumerians in very ancient times and in southern Italy, Corsica, and Sicily by around the fourth century B.C. It reached the Americas with the Europeans, and a small crop was finally grown in California at the beginning of the twentieth century. The citron is cultivated mostly for its thick, spongy rind, in appearance like the rind of a large lemon, which is candied and often chopped into fruitcakes. It is also used to make fruit syrups, liqueurs, and perfume. In the past, the citron was used medicinally, and it has enjoyed considerable religious significance. The unripe fruit is the "citron of the law" used by Jewish communities in ceremonies celebrating the harvest festival Succoth. The citron's principal areas of cultivation are Italy, Corsica, and Greece, and a variety came to be known as the "Leghorn citron" when the islands of Corsica and Sardinia shipped their crops to Leghorn, Italy, for processing.

Another fruit (*Citrullus lanatus* var. *citroides* – of the same species as the watermelon) is also called "citron" and, except for its bitter taste, resembles a small watermelon. That it is used somewhat in the same way as *C. medica* is suggested by another of its common names, "preserving melon." It is also called the "stock melon" because it is sometimes fed to hogs.

Common names and synonyms: Citron melon, Corsican citron, Diamante citron, esrog, ethrog, etrog, Leghorn citron, preserving melon, stock melon.

See in addition: "Cucumbers, Melons, and Watermelons," Part II, Section C, Chapter 6.

CITRUS FRUITS (*see also* the various citrus entries) – Save for recent hybrids (uglis, ortaniques, or tangelos, for example) and the grapefruit, all members of the citrus family (Rutaceae) originated in Southeast Asia (or – in the case of the sweet orange – China) and were first cultivated in China and India. Gradually they moved westward to Arabia and then to the countries surrounding the Mediterranean. The ancient Greeks apparently knew nothing of citrus fruits, and the Romans had only the citron. Oranges were recorded in Sicily at the beginning of the eleventh century and were reported as growing around Seville in Spain a couple of centuries later. The lemon was in the Near East by the tenth century or so and was being cultivated in Italy by the fifteenth century. Christopher Columbus and those explorers who followed in his wake scattered citrus seeds over much of the rest of the globe, discovering in the process the loose-skinned mandarin (tangerine) species that had long been cultivated in China and Japan. Grapefruits seem to have been born in the eighteenth century in the West Indies as a cross between the pomelo and the orange. The kumquat, a native of China and Japan, is not a citrus fruit but belongs to a similar genus.

Civet-cat fruit - *see* **DURIAN**

Ckoito - *see* **AMARANTH**

CLARY - An herb, clary (*Salvia sclarea*) is also called "clary sage." The taste of its flowering tops combines the flavors of sage and mint. In the past, clary was much employed in Europe as a seasoning for various foods and for wine. It is still used to enhance egg dishes and is one of the herbs that is used in making Italian vermouths.

Common names and synonyms: Clary sage.

See also: "Spices and Flavorings," Part II, Section F, Chapter 1.

Clear-up cactus - *see* **PITAHAYA**

Cleavers - *see* **GOOSEGRASS**

Clevner - *see* **PINOT BLANC**

Climbing bittersweet - *see* **AMERICAN BITTERSWEET**

Clotbur - *see* **BURDOCK**

CLOUDBERRY (*see also* BERRIES) - A creeping plant of northern climates, the cloudberry (*Rubus chamaemorus*) does best close to or even within the Arctic Circle, flourishing in the nearly 24-hour-long days of summer sunshine. The reddish orange to yellow fruit and white flowers of the cloudberry plant are found throughout the Scandinavian countries and Alaska. The Eskimos and Lapps collect the juicy, sweet berries in the fall and freeze them for winter consumption – the berries have doubtless done much over the centuries to provide vitamin C to peoples in a part of the world that is decidedly lacking in the usual fruits and vegetables. Cloudberries are also sold in northern Scandinavia for making preserves and baking pastries, and they are fermented to make vinegar. Like other berries, cloudberries are high in vitamin C.

Common names and synonyms: Bakeberry, baked-apple berry, *malka, Moltebeere,* salmonberry, *Torfbeere,* yellowberry.

CLOUD EAR (*see also* MUSHROOMS AND FUNGI) - The Tremellales, or the jelly fungi, are a group of gelatinous, edible wood fungi of which the cloud ears *Auricularia polytrica* and *A. auricula* are the species commonly eaten. They are brown to black gelatinous lobes that resemble human ears, are widely distributed in the world, and are found in the wild in clusters on logs. In China *A. polytrica* has been used in cooking for some 2,000 years. In the Pacific Northwest and Rocky Mountain regions of the United States they are often encountered near melting snow. Often consumed after being dried, cloud ears are most appreciated for their delicate flavor. In the Far East and in China, they are cultivated.

Common names and synonyms: Black (tree) fungus, Chinese mushroom, Jew's-ear, Judas('s) ear, *kikurage, mo-ehr, mook yee,* silver ear, tree ear, wood ear, *yun er.*

See in addition: "Fungi," Part II, Section C, Chapter 7.

CLOVE(S) - A pungent flavoring agent, the clove (*Syzygium aromaticum*) is another of those ancient spices that have an exotic past. Cloves are the dried buds of trees native to the Moluccas and provided one of the reasons those islands have long been called the Spice Islands. Centuries before the Christian era, cloves were used by the Chinese and became an important item in the spice trade with the West. The Egyptians, Greeks, and Romans were all familiar with cloves. Indeed, the name "clove" comes from the Latin word *clavus,* which means "nail" and aptly describes their appearance. The Portuguese were the first from the West to reach the Spice Islands and create a monopoly on the clove trade. At the beginning of the seventeenth century, they were succeeded by the Dutch, who established their own monopoly and limited production to just one of the islands. This monopoly was only broken at about the time of the American

Revolution, when a French diplomat managed to smuggle out some seedlings. Today, cloves are grown in Tanzania (which accounts for about half the world's production), Madagascar, Sri Lanka, and – in the New World – Grenada. Perhaps the first use of cloves was to freshen the breath, but it doubtless required little time to discover that their strong aroma and flavor went well with foods. Any meat dish, especially ham, can be enhanced with cloves. They are also called for in a multitude of recipes for spiced cakes, mincemeat, gingerbread, marinades, stewed-fruit dishes, any apple dish, and mulled-wine drinks. Cloves can be purchased dried, either whole or ground.

Common names and synonyms: Mother-of-clove(s).

See also: "Spices and Flavorings," Part II, Section F, Chapter 1.

CLOVER (*see also* **PRAIRIE CLOVER, SWEET CLOVER**) - Rarely used for human consumption except in times of famine, clover (genus *Trifolium*) is typically employed as fodder. Some exceptions are *T. repens, T. pratense,* and *T. campestre.* Icelanders boil *T. repens* (white Dutch clover, white clover) as a vegetable. In Europe, the young leaves of *T. pratense* (wild red clover) are eaten in salads and sandwiches, and the flowers are used to make a tea. A bitter variety, *T. campestre* (the "large hop clover") was used to flavor beer before the discovery of hops.

Common names and synonyms: Ladino clover, large hop clover, red clover, sweet clover, white clover, white Dutch clover, wild red clover.

Clusterbean - *see* **GUAR**

Cluster yam - *see* **BITTER YAM**

Cob - *see* **HAZELNUT AND FILBERT**

Cobnut - *see* **HAZELNUT AND FILBERT**

COCA - This shrub (*Erythroxylum coca*) is native to the Andean region of South America. The dried leaves yield a crystalline alkaloid substance known as cocaine. Taken internally, cocaine is a stimulant, whereas external use has the effect of a local anesthetic. The Indians of Peru and Bolivia chew the leaves to help them work long hours and ward off hunger, fatigue, and cold temperatures. This practice is comparable to the chewing of betel nut in Southeast Asia or kola nut in Africa. Some people make a coca "wine" from the leaves as well. Coca is also grown in Sri Lanka, Java, and Taiwan.

Common names and synonyms: Cocaine plant, spadic.

Cochineal plant - *see* **NOPALES**

COCKLEBUR - The seeds of the cocklebur (*Xanthium commune*) were used by Native Americans, who ground them into a meal. They may also have employed the shoots and leaves of *X. strumarium,* which others have reportedly boiled and eaten as a vegetable.

COCKSPUR (*see also* **BERRIES**) - A small tree of Colombia and Central America, *Celtis iguanaea*

produces edible, berry-like fruits that are green when immature and yellowish when ripe. They are generally eaten raw and have an excellent taste.

Cockspur thorn - *see* **HAWTHORN BERRY**

Coco - *see* **COCONUT**

Cocoa - *see* **CACAO**

Cocoaplum - *see* **COCOPLUM**

COCONA (*see also* **BERRIES**) - A berry native to northern South America, cocona (*Solanum topiro = S. sessiliflorum*) is edible, although many other species of the genus *Solanum* are poisonous. The berry is cultivated today from Trinidad to Costa Rica and, although not known in the wild, also "voluntarily" plants itself in abandoned plots and clearings. The berries are yellowish to red when ripe and are covered with a kind of fuzz that can be brushed off.

Common names and synonyms: Topiro.

COCONUT - Hunter-gatherers doubtless learned hundreds of thousands of years ago to crack open these fruit seeds of the coconut palm (*Cocos nucifera*) for the "milk" and "meat" contained therein, not to mention the usefulness of the shell as a drinking and eating vessel and as a scraping utensil. Truly, the coconut is one of the oldest of food plants. It originated in the Malayan Archipelago but long ago distributed itself throughout the world's tropics because it easily floats and, hence, can cross oceans. The coconut is mentioned in Sanskrit manuscripts, but it is said that Marco Polo (in his narratives of his travels in Asia) was the first European to describe it. During the Portuguese expansion of the fifteenth and sixteenth centuries, coconuts were carried back to Europe, and the Portuguese gave us the name we know the fruit by today. They called it *coco,* which meant "head" or "noggin." The hairy shell that encloses the fruit is itself enclosed by a greenish, fibrous husk. As the fruit ripens within this double seal – full ripening requires a year – more and more of the thin white liquid within (coconut "water") is converted to meat (called copra when dried), which is pressed for oil and made into various coconut foods and cosmetic products. Coconut cream is a blending of the coconut water and flesh. For the moment, at least, the coconut – especially its oil – is somewhat in disrepute because of its heavy concentration of saturated fat.

Common names and synonyms: Coco, cokernut.

See also: "Coconut," Part II, Section E, Chapter 2; "An Overview of Oils and Fats," Part II, Section E, Chapter 1.

COCOPLUM - Also known as cocoaplum, hicaco, and icaco, the cocoplum (*Chrysobalanus icaco*) is the fruit of a small tree native to tropical America. The fruit's color can be either white, black, or a combination of the two, and cocoplums are generally used for preserves.

Common names and synonyms: Cocoaplum, hicaco, icaco, icaco plum.

COCOYAM (*see also* **TARO**) – Often – and understandably – confused with taro and with malanga, from both of which it is practically indistinguishable, the cocoyam (*Colocasia esculenta*) is a variety of taro that is probably native to India but also possibly to parts of Southeast Asia. The problem is that the taxonomy of the cultivars of *Colocasia* remains a subject of investigation. These plants have clearly traveled, moving from India to Egypt some 2,000 years ago and from there to southern Europe. From Iberia, the cocoyam was carried to the Americas and then probably introduced into West Africa from the New World. It was successfully established in East Africa as well and moved eastward out of India to the Pacific. In these travels, the cocoyam picked up many names. Like taro and malanga, the cocoyam is also called "dasheen," "eddoe," and a dozen other names, including "taro." Moreover, in West Africa malanga is also called cocoyam. The plant was especially important in the West Indies for feeding slaves, and it continues to be a common part of the diet in many islands. Its young shoots and leaves serve as a cooked vegetable (callaloo), and the tubers are fried, roasted, or boiled. The leaves are a good source of vitamin A, calcium, and potassium; the corms brim with starch and, thus, energy.

Common names and synonyms: Abalong, arvi, Barbados eddoe, Chinese eddoe, curcas, dagmay, dalo, dasheen, eddo, eddoe, *keladi,* koko, kolkas, malangay, malangu, taioba, taro, *taro de chine, ya, ya bené, yu-tao.*

See in addition: "Taro," Part II, Section B, Chapter 6.

Cocozelle - *see* **ZUCCHINI**

COFFEE – Also called *kaffe, kahve,* and *kahwa,* coffee (*Coffea arabica*) is surrounded by myths and legends, especially those dealing with the discovery of the plant, which seems to have originated in both Yemen and southern Ethiopia (in the province of Caffa). One of the most pervasive legends has an Arab goatherd around A.D. 850 becoming curious about the lively behavior of his goats and subsequently discovering that the animals were nibbling the coffee berries of nearby evergreen trees. Apparently, the first human use of coffee was to emulate the goats by also chewing the "beans" to get a lift, but by around A.D. 1000 (or even earlier) coffee beans were being roasted and crushed to make a beverage. From this point to the cultivation of coffee trees was a short step, and the beans came to be monopolized by Arab merchants, who shipped them from the Yemeni port of Mocha. Coffee quickly became an important beverage for the Muslims, who were prohibited alcohol (although many fanatically condemned the new drink), and coffeehouses of a sort were established in cities and towns throughout the Islamic world.

Constantinople (Istanbul) has been put forward as the location of the world's first real coffeehouse, established at about the end of the fifteenth century (the dates given vary from 1474 to 1554), and at about the same time coffeehouses were also opened in Medina, Mecca, Cairo, Damascus, and Baghdad – all of the capitals of the Islamic world. The new social centers were viewed with suspicion by various sultans worried about sedition, and coffeehouses were closed from time to time, but never for long. Coffee drinking had become an entrenched part of Arab life.

Europe soon had a similar experience. Venice, heavily involved in the spice trade, was exposed to coffee as early as the fifteenth century, and its first coffeehouse was established around the middle of the sixteenth century – about the same time that Vienna got its first one. Another century elapsed, however, before the new beverage moved northward and westward. Coffeehouses were opened at Oxford in 1650, at Marseilles in 1671, and at Paris the following year, but it was only in 1686 that the Café Procope, the first true café in Paris, opened its doors (it still exists although at a different location). It may be doubted that the first of the coffeehouses in England were inundated with patrons because – as late as 1657 in London – coffee was advertised as a medicine for ills such as gout and scurvy. But the coffeehouses clearly were doing a brisk business by 1675 when, like the Islamic sultans, King Charles II issued a proclamation to suppress them on the grounds that they were hotbeds of sedition. The proclamation, however, was rescinded the following year, and over time coffeehouses in England developed into gentlemen's clubs, whereas in France they continued to be cafés (albeit also clubs at times).

Both the British and the Dutch East India Companies bought coffee at Mocha for import into Europe, but as decades passed and overseas empires developed, the Arab monopoly on coffee became a major irritant. As the eighteenth century got under way, the Dutch began growing their own coffee in Java and later introduced it into Sri Lanka, whereas the English planted coffee in their West Indian colonies – especially Jamaica and Guiana. The Portuguese in Brazil were also in the coffee business (after the plant was introduced there from Guiana in 1727), and the French planted coffee, first in their colony of Martinique and a bit later in San Domingue – which, by the end of the eighteenth century (when the revolution began that would lead to the new nation of Haiti), was producing almost two-thirds of the world's supply. Later, coffee would also be a Cuban crop, and throughout the Americas coffee production became inextricably linked with slave labor, until abolition finally came to Brazil and Cuba in the last decades of the nineteenth century. Sugar was also cultivated with slave labor, and increasing sugar production, in turn, was inextricably linked with the soaring consumption of coffee – along with tea and chocolate – in Europe.

In 1774, in the soon-to-be United States, colonists were increasing their consumption of coffee as a protest against British taxes on tea, and this trend continued as a tea-drinking people were converted to coffee drinking. By 1850 or so, average per capita consumption exceeded 6 pounds annually. Americans were accustomed to buying their coffee beans green and doing their own roasting and grinding, but after the Civil War, Folger's Coffee (established in San Francisco) began to give people a choice. The Folger's brand was soon followed by Chase and Sanborn (which in 1878 became the first company to pack roasted coffee in sealed cans), Hills Brothers, and Maxwell House (named for a Nashville hotel). In 1901, the first "instant" coffee was invented in Chicago, and in 1964, General Foods introduced "Maxim" freeze-dried instant coffee.

Coffee is ground in different ways for different purposes: "Coarse" and "medium" for use in percolators, urns, and the like; "drip" (which is finer than medium) for use in electric drip coffee makers; and "fine" for cone filters and drip pots. There is also the very fine espresso, for espresso machines, and the even more finely ground Turkish, for use in Turkish brewers. Almost 90 percent of the world's coffee is *C. arabica,* but another species, *C. canephora = C. robusta* and generally known as *Robusta,* is cultivated in Africa and India and – because it is cheaper and contains substantially more caffeine – is often a component of supermarket blends. Brazil produces about half of the world's coffee and has been the major U.S. supplier since the early days of the republic. Jamaican Blue Mountain, Hawaiian Kona, Java, and Mocha coffees are relatively rare and highly prized, followed by the Andean-grown Colombian coffee (the top grade is *supremo*).

Common names and synonyms: Colombian coffee, espresso, Hawaiian Kona, Jamaican Blue Mountain, Java, joe, *kaffe, kahve, kahwa,* Mocha, *Robusta, supremo* coffee, Turkish coffee.

See also: "Coffee," Part III, Chapter 4.

Coffee weed - *see* **SESBAN**

COHUNE PALM - A native of Central America and Mexico, the cohune nut palm (*Orbignya cohune* and *Attalea cohune*) produces nuts that yield an oil that can substitute for coconut oil. In addition, the tree's young leaf buds are cooked and eaten as a vegetable.

Coimi - *see* **AMARANTH**
Coines - *see* **QUINCE**
Coing - *see* **QUINCE**
Coinworth - *see* **PENNYWORT**
Cokernut - *see* **COCONUT**
Cola nut - *see* **KOLA NUT**
Cole cabbage - *see* **CABBAGE**

Colewort - *see* **CABBAGE**
Colicroot - *see* **WILD YAM**
Colirrambano - *see* **KOHLRABI**
COLLARDS (*see also* **CABBAGE, KALE**) - Called *couve* in Brazil and often regarded as a form of kale (which they are, differing mostly in the smoothness of their leaves), collards (*Brassica oleracea* var. *acephala*) constitute one of the oldest members of the cabbage family and probably originated in the Mediterranean region. However, collard greens subsequently spread over much of the tropical and subtropical world and are cultivated today in Southeast Asia (including southern China), East and West Africa, the West Indies, South America, and the southern United States. Collards probably reached the Americas from Africa via the slave trade and are mostly consumed in those regions that formerly harbored slave societies. The flavor of the vegetable is milder than that of kale, and the large, dark green leaves, which are a component of southern "soul food," are traditionally boiled with pork or fatback. Collards supply folic acid and vitamin A and are a rich source of calcium, potassium, and iron. In addition, as a cruciferous vegetable, collards are said to act as a preventive against certain cancers.

Common names and synonyms: Borecole, collard greens, *couve*, kale.

See in addition: "Cruciferous and Green Leafy Vegetables," Part II, Section C, Chapter 5.

Colocynth - *see* **EGUSI**
Colombian coffee - *see* **COFFEE**
COLTSFOOT - The wide leaves of this plant (*Tussilago farfara*) resemble horses' hooves, hence the name "coltsfoot," along with a variety of similar names such as "assfoot," "foalfoot," "horsefoot," "sowfoot," and just plain "hoofs." Coltsfoot is a European plant with roots that have been used medicinally since the days of the ancient Greeks. The plant is now naturalized in eastern North America. When young, the leaves can be eaten raw, whereas older ones are cooked as greens, and ashes from the leaves have been used as a salt substitute. The plant also has a yellow flower head that opens only in sunny weather, and this, along with its stalk, is also edible when raw. Coltsfoot is grown and widely used in Japan, where the celery-like flavor of its green stalks is especially appreciated.

Common names and synonyms: Assfoot, bog rhubarb, bullsfoot, coughwort, foalfoot, hoofs, horsefoot, sowfoot.

Colza - *see* **RAPE**
COMFREY - A somewhat hairy herb that is native to Eurasia, comfrey (*Symphytum officinale,* among some 25 other comfrey species) has long been employed by humans, but more for healing than for sustenance. Its roots and leaves were used historically to treat wounds, and in fact, the name comes from ancient Greek and means to grow together – which in this case refers to the edges of wounds

and broken bones (accounting for one of the plant's old names, "knit-bones"). But comfrey is also edible. It is frequently used to make a tisane, can be added to salads, and is cooked like spinach as a vegetable. *Common names and synonyms:* Knit-bones.

Comice - *see* **PEAR**

Comino - *see* **CUMIN**

Commas - *see* **CAMAS**

Common red ribes - *see* **CURRANT(S)**

COMMON REED - A plant widespread throughout the world, the common reed (*Phragmites communis* or *P. australis*) has rhizomes and roots that in Russia are harvested for their starch content. Native Americans also procured starch from the rootstock of the common reed and ate its young shoots. The stems - rich in sugar - have been ground into a sweet powder for use in baking. They also exude a gumlike substance that was highly regarded as a sweet by Native Americans.

Compass plant - *see* **SILPHIUM**

Concombre des Antilles - *see* **GHERKIN**

CONCORD GRAPE (*see also* **GRAPES**) - A variety of the fox grape, the North American Concord grape (*Vitis labrusca*) lacks sugar, which limits its use in wine making. But these grapes are much used for the production of grape juice and jellies. They come from a wild grape named after Concord, Massachusetts, by Ephraim Bull, who planted the vines there in 1843.

CONEFLOWER - Several plants are called coneflower. Those that are subsumed under the genus *Echinacea* are tall weeds with purple blossoms and grow throughout the prairie region of the United States. They have edible roots, leaves, and seeds that were used mostly for medicinal purposes by Native Americans. Another coneflower, *Ratibida columnifera,* is also a prairie plant, bearing leaves that Native Americans made into a tea. A final coneflower is *Rudbeckia laciniata,* of eastern North America, with leaves that were cooked as a vegetable.

Congo goober - *see* **BAMBARA GROUNDNUT**

Congo pea - *see* **PIGEON PEA**

Cook's-truffle - *see* **TRUFFLE(S)**

COOLWORT - An American plant also called false miterwort, toothwort, and foam flower, coolwort (*Tiarella cordifolia*) is a white-flowered herb of the woodlands and was reportedly used by Native Americans as a spice. The true miterwort (genus *Mitella*) is also called fairywort. *Common names and synonyms:* Fairywort, false miterwort, foam flower, miterwort, toothwort.

Coontie - *see* **ZAMIA**

Coptis - *see* **GOLDTHREAD**

CORAL BEAN - Cultivated in Central America and Mexico, the coral bean trees - *Erythrina berteroana* (called *pito*) and *E. rubinervia* (called *gallito*) - all have young shoots, leaves, and buds that have long been consumed in salads, stews, and various other dishes. Another species, *E. fusca,* is used in like fashion in India and the East Indies, whereas still another relative, *E. poeppigiana* (called *poro*), which serves as a shade tree for coffee bushes in Central and South America and the West Indies, has flowers that are used in salads and soups. The pretty (but poisonous) seeds of *pito* and *gallito* are used medicinally, as a toxin for rats and fish, and as beads that are strung together to make necklaces, bracelets, and the like. *Common names and synonyms: Gallito, macrette, pito, poro.*

Corazon - *see* **CUSTARD APPLE**

CORDIA - A flowering shrub or small tree of Asia and Australia, cordia (*Cordia myxa*) belongs to a large genus of mostly tropical plants that bear fleshy, often edible fruits. In the case of cordia, it produces yellowish, nutlike fruits that helped to sustain aboriginal populations.

CORIANDER (*see also* **CILANTRO**) - Also known as cilantro, culantro, and Chinese parsley, coriander (*Coriandrum sativum*) is an herb that is cultivated for its aromatic seeds and leaves. It is a member of the parsley family and closely related to caraway. Coriander is apparently a native of the Mediterranean region, and its dried seeds have been in use for some 7,000 years. They have been found in the tombs of ancient Egypt and were widely used by the Hebrews, Greeks, and Romans (who flavored their bread with coriander) of antiquity. The seeds contain an aromatic oil and are used to flavor liquors (such as gin), to season soups and pastries, and to spice up marinades in Scandinavia and Greece. Dried coriander seeds are generally more appreciated in northern than in southern Europe, and coriander is vital to the cuisine of India because of its crucial role as an ingredient in curry powder. *Common names and synonyms:* Chinese parsley, cilantro, culantro, *yuen sai.* *See in addition:* "Spices and Flavorings," Part II, Section F, Chapter 1.

Corkwood tree - *see* **SESBAN**

Corn - *see* **MAIZE**

Cornel - *see* **CORNUS**

Cornelian cherry - *see* **CORNUS**

CORNFLOWER - A garden plant native to Eurasia, the cornflower (*Centaurea cyanus*) - like corn-salad - is so called because it is found in fields of corn. It is also known as "bachelor's-button" and "bluebottle" because of its bold blue blossoms. These flowers were used in the past by pastry chefs to provide a blue color for creamy desserts. *Common names and synonyms:* Bachelor's-button, bluebottle.

CORN MINT - Found in temperate regions, this herb (*Mentha arvensis*) is cultivated commercially in China, Japan, and Brazil. The leaves yield an oil that is 60 percent menthol and is used to flavor pharmaceuticals, toothpaste, food products, cigarettes, and alcoholic beverages. The leaves can also be boiled and eaten or used as a condiment.

Common names and synonyms: Field mint, Japanese mint.

See also: "Spices and Flavorings," Part II, Section F, Chapter 1.

CORNSALAD - "Cornsalad," so named because these plants with small, bluish flowers grow in cornfields, actually refers to any of several plants of the genus *Valerianella,* especially *V. olitoria* and *V. locusta.* Also called "lamb's-lettuce," "field salad," "fat-hen," "lamb's-quarter," "marsh salad," "hog salad," and a variety of other names, these European natives – found throughout North America as well – provide slightly bitter-tasting leaves that are much appreciated in salads. The various types of cornsalad were considered weeds until the seventeenth century, when they began to be cultivated, and cultivation doubtless accounts for the different varieties now identified.

Common names and synonyms: European cornsalad, fat-hen, field salad, hog salad, lamb's-lettuce, lamb's-quarter, mache, *mâche,* marsh salad.

CORNUS - The genus *Cornus,* native to Europe, eastern Asia, and North America, includes a number of shrubs and trees that bear what is actually not a berry but a drupe. Among those in North America is *C. florida,* often called the "flowering dogwood," which is native to the eastern United States. This has edible fruits that (like the leaves) become scarlet-colored in the autumn. The "bunchberry" (*C. canadensis*) is a close relative, and Native Americans used this fruit for both food and medicine. The cornelian cherry (*C. mas*) is a European species, the fruit of which is eaten fresh and made into preserves and wine (*vin de corneulle*); at one time, it was widely cultivated.

Common names and synonyms: Bunchberry, cornel, cornelian cherry, dogberry, dog cherry, dogwood berry, dogwood cherry, dogwood tree, flowering dogwood, Siberian cherry, Tartar cherry.

Corsican citron - *see* **CITRON**

Cos - *see* **LETTUCE**

Coscushaw - *see* **CUSHAW (SQUASH)**

Costa Rican guava - *see* **WILD GUAVA**

Costeño - *see* **GUAJILLO AND PULLA CHILLIES**

COSTMARY - A plant that is native to Asia, was a popular herb in ancient Greece, and has seen both past and present use in England, costmary (*Chrysanthemum balsamita*) - with its leaves' hint of lemon and mint flavorings - is employed to season poultry as well as stuffings, soups, salads, and sauces. It was naturalized, and now grows wild, in North America, where it is known as "Bible leaf" because its long, narrow leaves were used in former times as page markers in Bibles. Costmary has also been known in the past as "alecost" because it was used in the production of home-brewed ale.

Common names and synonyms: Alecost, balsam herb, Bible leaf, Bible-leaf mace, mace, mint geranium.

See also: "Spices and Flavorings," Part II, Section F, Chapter 1.

COTTONSEED OIL - In 1887, Wesson Oil began as the Southern Cotton Oil Company in Philadelphia. The firm had cottonseed-crushing mills throughout the southern United States and quickly became the largest producer of cottonseed oil as well as the first U.S. manufacturer of vegetable shortening. Cottonseed oil (from cotton - genus *Gossypium*) was employed as an inexpensive substitute for olive oil in cooking and in salads prior to the advent of other oils, such as that from soybeans. Cottonseed oil has found continued use in the food-packing industry, as, for example, in the packing of sardines.

See also: "An Overview of Oils and Fats," Part II, Section E, Chapter 1.

Couch-couch - *see* **CUSH-CUSH YAM**

COUCH GRASS - Also known as "wheat grass" and a host of other names including "quack grass," couch grass (*Agropyron repens = Elytrigia repens*) is a Eurasian grass now naturalized in North America. It is generally used for grazing and hay production, but in medieval Europe the tender tips of its rhizomes were gathered in the spring to be eaten raw as a vegetable and the whole rhizome later dried to make a flour. Today, in England, the rhizomes are still gathered and dried (and sometimes exported to France and Italy) for making a tea and, when roasted, are used in Central Europe as a coffee substitute.

Common names and synonyms: Dogtooth, quack grass, quick grass, scutch, twitch grass, wheat grass.

Coughwort - *see* **COLTSFOOT**

Country almond - *see* **MALABAR ALMOND**

Courge - *see* **SQUASH AND PUMPKIN**

Courgette - *see* **SQUASH AND PUMPKIN, ZUCCHINI**

Cousee-cousee - *see* **CUSH-CUSH YAM**

COUVE (*see also* **CABBAGE, COLLARDS**) - Couve is a tall, dark green Portuguese cabbage that (like the 400-odd other cabbage varieties) is a member of the species *Brassica oleracea.* Couve has a taste that is something of a cross between turnip greens and kale, and it is the primary ingredient in *caldo verde,* the well-known soup of Portugal. Many Portuguese grow the cabbage in their yards; in Minho, it is often grown under trellised grape vines.

See in addition: Collards and "Cruciferous and Green Leafy Vegetables," Part II, Section C, Chapter 5.

Cowberry - *see* **LINGONBERRY**

Cow bitter(s) - *see* **TANSY**

COW PARSNIP - With a taste somewhat like that of asparagus, the leaves and stems of the European cow parsnip (*Heracleum sphondylium*), found in temperate areas of Europe and Asia, are cooked and consumed as a green vegetable, and its roots have been used as a condiment. In Lithuania and Poland, a home-brewed beer is made from the stems and seeds, and elsewhere in eastern Europe the cow parsnip was also employed to make borscht. The American cow parsnip (*H. lanatum*) has a much stronger taste and served Native Americans as a food. The roots were cooked, and the shoots and leaves were eaten both cooked and raw.

Common names and synonyms: American cow parsnip, European cow parsnip, Meadow parsnip.

COWPEA (*see also* **BEANS, LEGUMES**) – Also called "long bean," "asparagus bean," and "yard long bean" because of the length of its pods, the cowpea (*Vigna unguiculata* or *V. sesquipedalis* or *V. sinensis*) is, in fact, a bean. It has been cultivated since prehistoric times in tropical Asia (especially India) and is a relative of the mung bean and other Asian legumes, suggesting a South Asian origin for the plant. However, China has been proposed as another center of origin, and because the plant occurs in the wild in many parts of Africa, that continent may have been yet another cradle of the cowpea. It reached the New World via the slave trade and today is cultivated throughout the tropical and subtropical world.

The cowpea comes in a number of varieties. Black-eyed peas are perhaps the best known of these in the United States, where they are available fresh, dried, canned, and frozen. Crowder peas and field peas are other favorites, especially in the U.S. South. Prior to the Civil War, cowpeas were sometimes given to slaves but were used mostly for animal fodder. Today, they are one of the major constituents of "soul food."

Common names and synonyms: Asparagus bean, black-eyed bean, black-eyed pea, China bean, Crowder pea, field pea, long bean, red pea, southern pea, yard-long bean.

See in addition: "Beans, Peas, and Lentils," Part II, Section C, Chapter 3.

COWSLIP – Two plants are known by this name. The first is a European wildflower (*Primula veris*). Its sweet-smelling flowers are added to salads or used to make wine, vinegar, mead, and tea. The flower may also be candied. In the United States, however, "cowslip" refers to the marsh marigold, whose Latin name is *Caltha palustris*. This plant is found in the temperate regions of North America, Asia, and Europe. A hardy perennial herb, the entire plant is eaten as a vegetable. The leaves may also be used as a potherb, and the pickled flower buds can be substituted for capers.

Common names and synonyms: Kingcup, marsh marigold, may-bob, meadow-bright.

Cowtree - *see* **MIMUSOPS**

Cow vetch - *see* **TUFTED VETCH**

Coyo - *see* **AMARANTH**

Coyote melon - *see* **SQUASH AND PUMPKIN**

CRAB APPLE (*see also* **APPLE**) – There are several species of wild fruit trees of the genus *Malus* (espe-

cially *M. coronaria*) that produce small, brightly colored crab apples. The crab apple is the ancestor of cultivated apples and has been used as a food since prehistory, although the harsh, acidic taste of these fruits doubtless precluded eating them raw. Crab apples make excellent jellies and preserves.

Common names and synonyms: Sweet crabapple, wild apple.

Cramp bark - *see* **BERRIES, HIGHBUSH CRANBERRY**

CRANBERRY (*see also* **BERRIES, HIGHBUSH CRANBERRY, LINGONBERRY**) – Of the same genus as the blueberry, the cranberry (*Vaccinium macrocarpon*) is a North American shrub that is so named because its flower stamens resemble a beak – hence "crane berry," a name (which subsequently became "cranberry") assigned to it by the early European settlers in New England. The berries, which grew wild in New England, had long been used by Native Americans for pemmican (dried meats pounded into a paste and mixed with berries and fat). The early European settlers found cranberries too tart to eat by themselves but made them into pies, puddings, tarts, relishes, preserves, and cranberry sauce. Perhaps appropriately, it was in Massachusetts that commercial cranberry production was begun in the 1840s, and that state still supplies about half of the U.S. crop.

Cranberries are planted in sandy bogs that are irrigated, and harvesting entails loosening the berries so that they fall into the water, then sweeping the floating berries into processing machinery. Before being crushed, however, cranberries (also known as "bounce berries") are "bounced" to determine ripeness, meaning that they must clear a hurdle or are discarded.

Another, smaller cranberry (*V. oxycoccos*) is also native to North America as well as to northern Europe and Asia. It is seldom cultivated commercially, but the wild berries are picked for home consumption. The so-called lowbush cranberries are actually lingonberries. In addition, "highbush cranberries" are erroneously called cranberries. North American commercial cranberries have been introduced in the Scandinavian countries and Great Britain. Almost all of the commercial crop is made into juice or canned cranberry sauce. Cranberry juice is a recent (since 1959) development, representing a successful effort to diversify an industry that once did most of its business around the holidays, producing the indispensable accompaniment to turkey. Cranberries are very high in vitamin C and in the past have proven an effective cure for scurvy.

Common names and synonyms: Airelle de myrtille, American cranberry, bounce berry, crane berry, fen berry, large cranberry, small cranberry.

Cranberry bush - *see* **HIGHBUSH CRANBERRY**

Crane berry - *see* **CRANBERRY**

Crapaudback - *see* **CALABAZA (SQUASH)**

Cream nut - *see* **BRAZIL NUT**

Creeping myrtle - *see* **PERIWINKLE**

Creole mustard - *see* **HORSERADISH**

CREOSOTE BUSH - Also called the "little stinker" because of the resinous odor it gives off, the creosote bush (*Larrea tridentata = L. mexicana*) is a native of the desert Southwest of the United States and Mexico. It was used by Native Americans for medicinal purposes and as a wood for smoking foods. In addition, its flower buds have been consumed.
Common names and synonyms: Little stinker.

CRESS - "Cress" is a name applied to a number of greens belonging to the mustard family, especially garden cress (*Lepidium sativum*). The British are especially fond of cresses, which are grown in enormous quantities in market gardens around London. Young sprouts of garden cress are often mixed with mustard greens in salads. Another name for cress is "pepper-grass."
Common names and synonyms: Garden cress, pepper-grass.
See also: "Cruciferous and Green Leafy Vegetables," Part II, Section C, Chapter 5.

Crinkleroot - *see* **TOOTHWORT**

Crosne - *see* **CHINESE ARTICHOKE**

Cross-leaf heath - *see* **BOG HEATHER**

Crowberry - *see* **BEARBERRY**

Crowder pea - *see* **COWPEA**

Crown daisy - *see* **CHRYSANTHEMUM**

Cuachilote - *see* **CUAJILOTE**

CUAJILOTE - A tree native to Mexico and Central America, the cuajilote (*Parmentiera edulis = P. aculeata*) produces pointed, yellowish green fruits. They have a sweet taste and are eaten raw, cooked, and preserved (often as pickles).
Common names and synonyms: Cuachilote, guajilote.

Cubanelle pepper - *see* **SWEET PEPPERS**

Cuban spinach - *see* **PURSLANE**

Cuban squash - *see* **CALABAZA (SQUASH)**

Cuban sweet potato - *see* **BONIATO**

Cubeb - *see* **TAILED PEPPER**

Cuckoo flower - *see* **LADY'S SMOCK**

CUCUMBER (*see also* **GHERKIN, INDIAN CUCUMBER, SQUASH AND PUMPKIN**) - A native of southwestern Asia, the cucumber (*Cucumis sativus*) is a member of the squash family and has been cultivated since prehistoric times for its fruit. It is related to melons and, like melons, has a high water content, which means that it is always cool. The ancient Egyptians enjoyed cucumbers (and reputedly fed them to their Hebrew slaves), as did the Greeks and the Romans. The latter probably spread the cucumber about their empire (as was the case with so many foods), although at least one source states that the cucumber first reached France as late as the ninth century, and England only in the fourteenth century.

We know that the vegetable came to the Americas with the Spaniards, but a problem with keeping track of cucumbers historically is that there are so many related species. They range, for example, from the West Indian gherkin (*C. anguria*), a tropical American vine originally from Africa that reached the West Indies via the slave trade, to the snake or serpent cucumber (*C. melo* var. *flexuosus*), which is botanically a melon, to the African horned cucumber (*C. metuliferus*). Cucumbers are divided into three groups: the standard field-grown slicing cucumber, the new hothouse varieties (some of which are seedless), and the smaller pickling kinds.

The West Indian gherkin is perhaps the most widely used for this latter purpose, although, of course, all lend themselves well to pickling and to the relishes that are so prominent in Indian cookery. Cucumbers suffered a decline in popularity in Europe from the Middle Ages to the eighteenth century, as they fell under medical suspicion of being hard on the digestive system. They are low in calories but contain little in the way of important nutrients. Cucumbers can be baked, boiled, steamed, and braised as well as added to salads, and because of their high water content, they can also be used to make warm teas and cool drinks.
Common names and synonyms: American gherkin, cassabanana, cuke, gherkin, hothouse cucumber, lemon cucumber, Mandera cucumber, pickling cucumber, serpent cucumber, slicing cucumber, snake cucumber, West Indian gherkin.
See in addition: "Cucumbers, Melons, and Watermelons," Part II, Section C, Chapter 6.

Cucumber tree - *see* **BELIMBING**

Cucurutz - *see* **MAIZE**

CUDDAPAH ALMOND - Also called the "chirauli nut," the cuddapah almond (*Buchanania latifolia*) is a tree that provides food for the peoples of South and Southeast Asia and has also helped to feed the Aborigines of Australia. Moreover, the seeds, which are eaten, yield an edible oil used in cooking.
Common names and synonyms: Chirauli nut.

Cudrang - *see* **CHE**

Cuime - *see* **AMARANTH**

Cuke - *see* **CUCUMBER**

Culantro - *see* **CILANTRO, CORIANDER**

CUMIN - Known as *comino* in Spanish, cumin (*Cuminum cyminum*) seems to be a Mediterranean plant - as are most other members of the carrot family - although some think it originated in Asia, and it apparently has been cultivated in India, Egypt, and the Mediterranean region since time immemorial. Certainly cumin was prescribed in early Hindu medicine for a variety of ailments; it was also a popular spice in ancient Rome and is mentioned in both the Old and New Testaments of the Bible. Cumin seeds are aromatic and yield an oil used in the perfume industry. Whole or ground, they season many Mexican dishes and are a vital ingredient in *chile* powders. Similarly, cumin is also crucial to curry powder and many dishes of India. In addition, North African recipes call for cumin in marinades, couscous, and lamb dishes. Finally, cumin is used in baking – especially in rye breads.

Common names and synonyms: Comino, cummin, *jintan.*

See also: "Spices and Flavorings," Part II, Section F, Chapter 1.

Cummin - *see* CUMIN

Cumquat - *see* KUMQUAT

Cup plant - *see* SILPHIUM

CUPUASSU - A relative of cacao, *cupuassu* (*Theobroma grandiflorum*) is a fruit of the Amazon Basin that is generally available in local markets. It is used for making sweetened juice and frozen desserts.

Curcas - *see* COCOYAM

Curcas oil - *see* PHYSIC NUT

Curcuma - *see* TURMERIC

CURLED DOCK - A European plant that has become naturalized as a weed in North America, curled dock (*Rumex crispus*) has long provided food for gatherers. Its leaves and seeds are edible, as is its large and fleshy root, which is dug up in the fall and dried.

Common names and synonyms: Curly dock, narrow dock, sour dock, yellow dock.

CURRANT(S) (*see also* **BERRIES, BLACK CURRANT**) - There are three kinds of European currants that come in the colors red, white, and black. These berries of the genus *Ribes* were cultivated in northern Europe prior to the seventeenth century and subsequently brought to North America. In addition, there is a native North American red currant - *Ribes sanguineum*. The European red currant (*R. rubrum*), a small, tart, red- or scarlet-colored berry, is much used in northern Europe for making juice, jellies, cakes and other desserts, compotes, and mixed drinks. The black currant (*R. nigrum*), which is of greater commercial importance, is the basis for jelly, juice, sweet must, and the liquor crème de cassis, as well as a clear, biting alcoholic beverage that is much like schnapps. White currants (*R. sativum*) are made into a white wine but are generally less used than red or black currants, which are very rich in vitamins A and C. Currants were extremely important in the diet of Native Americans, who cooked them, ate them raw, and made them into pemmican. In recent years, currants have been utilized less in the United States.

Common names and synonyms: Aka-suguri, black currant, common red ribes, European black currant, European red currant, garden currant, North American red currant, northern red currant, red currant, white currant.

Currant bush - *see* BUSH CURRANT

Curri - *see* HAZELNUT AND FILBERT

CURRY LEAF - The small, shiny, pungent leaves of this Asiatic shrub (*Murraya koenigii*) are used for flavoring. The curry leaf tree is best associated with Sri Lankan cuisine, but it grows in most tropical Southeast Asian countries. The leaves are employed fresh, dried, and powdered.

CUSHAW (SQUASH) (*see also* **SQUASH AND PUMPKIN**) - The designation of various squashes as cushaws has led to some semantic confusion. "Cushaw" is sometimes intended to be synonymous with "calabaza" squash. But one of the crooknecks of *Cucurbita moschata* that is widely grown in the United States received its name from the Algonquian *coscushaw*. In general, however, the cushaw squashes are understood to be of the species *C. mixta*, which grows in an area ranging from Costa Rica north to the southern United States. This "mixed" squash type was originally included in *C. moschata* but later came to be regarded as a separate species.

Common names and synonyms: Cashaw, *coscushaw,* crookneck.

See in addition: "Squash," Part II, Section C, Chapter 8.

CUSH-CUSH YAM (*see also* **YAMS**) - A native of northern South America and the Caribbean, the cush-cush yam (*Dioscorea trifida*) was an important food for resident Native Americans and is still widely cultivated in this region today; it is also now cultivated to a limited extent in the tropics of Asia and West Africa. The cush-cush is a climbing vine that produces subterranean, yellow-skinned tubers. These yams are small but have an excellent flavor and are frequently baked or boiled. The vegetable is called a *ñame* (e.g., *ñame vino, ñame de la India*) as well as *mapuey* in the Spanish-speaking Caribbean, whereas English speakers name it "couch-couch."

Common names and synonyms: Couch-couch, couche-couche, cousee-cousee, *ñame, ñame mapuey,* yampi.

See in addition: "Sweet Potatoes and Yams," Part II, Section B, Chapter 5.

CUSTARD APPLE (*see also* **CHERIMOYA, PAPAW, SWEETSOP, WHITE SAPOTE, WILD CUSTARD APPLE**) - The term "custard apple" is a nickname for the cherimoya but also refers to its close relative, the fruit known around the world as custard apple (*Annona reticulata*). Also called "bullock's-heart," it is a native of the American tropics, grows on a small tree with yellow flowers, is almost round and up to 4 or 5 inches in diameter, and has a tough skin, which protects a creamy white flesh of thick custard-like consistency. Its flavor is not especially appreciated by many (some find it insipidly sweet), but it is nonetheless widely cultivated in the West Indies, tropical Africa, and Southeast Asia. The custard apple, although generally eaten raw, is also used as a flavoring for milk shakes and the like.

Common names and synonyms: Anona, bullock's-heart, *corazon,* nona, pawpaw, sugar apple.

Custard marrow - *see* **CHAYOTE**
Cut-eye bean - *see* **JACKBEAN**
Cycad - *see* **ZAMIA**
Cydonian apple - *see* **QUINCE**
Cymling - *see* **SQUASH AND PUMPKIN**

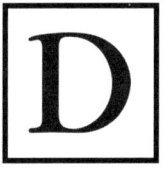

Dagmay - *see* **COCOYAM**
DAHOON HOLLY - A native of southeastern North America, dahoon holly (*Ilex cassine*) has leaves that - like those of its close relatives, yaupon holly and yerba maté - contain a substantial amount of caffeine. Native Americans used them to brew an emetic tea, which was consumed in purification rituals.
Common names and synonyms: Cassine, dahoon.

DAIKON - A native of Asia and also called the "Oriental radish," the daikon (*Raphanus sativus* spp.) bears little resemblance to round, red-skinned radishes. It is a very long root that averages about a foot in length (although in Japan there are more oblate varieties) and is white in color. Daikon is the Japanese name for this type of radish, which is called *mooli* in India and the West Indies. The daikon is an ancient vegetable that is grown throughout Asia but is probably most appreciated in Japan, China, and Korea. It has a pungent flavor, which the Koreans utilize in a type of *kimchee*. In Japan, daikon is often grated and used as a condiment in numerous dishes including sushi, and in China it is worked into a pudding and served raw at dim sum restaurants.

Two relatives (also *R. sativus*) of the daikon are of interest as well. One is the red-fleshed radish called *sing li mei*, which means "the heart is beautiful." These are eaten as a snack food and add color to salads. Another is the "green Oriental radish," which can grow to a size approaching that of its giant cousin and which is generally used in soups and dishes that are simmered. In addition, spicy sprouts, called *kaiware*, can be grown from daikon seeds. *Kaiware* are most commonly used in salads or for garnish.
Common names and synonyms: Chinese radish, giant white radish, green Oriental radish, Japanese radish, Japanese white radish, *kaiware, mooli,* Oriental radish, red-fleshed radish, *sing li mei, tsumamina.*
See also: "Cruciferous and Green Leafy Vegetables," Part II, Section C, Chapter 5.

Dalima - *see* **POMEGRANATE**
Dalo - *see* **COCOYAM**
DAMIANA - The dried leaf of damiana (*Turnera diffusa = T. aphrodisiaca*) was consumed in the past for its alleged aphrodisiacal properties and as a tonic. It is a plant found in the American tropics and in Texas and California.
DAMSON PLUM (*see also* **PLUM**) - The Damson plum (*Prunus insititia*) is the classic small, dark blue plum that ripens in August and has been virtually unaltered for thousands of years. It is named for the city of Damascus, from which the fruit traveled to reach Italy and then spread out across the rest of Europe, where it grows today both in the wild and in home orchards. The Damson plum is notable for its ability to resist disease and cold and to thrive with little or no care. It is tart and used mostly in preserves and in the production of liqueurs such as slivovitz.
Common names and synonyms: Bullace plum, tart Damson plum.

Dancy tangerine - *see* **MANDARIN ORANGE**
DANDELION - Although regarded as a nuisance by many whose lawns become infested with these "weeds," dandelions (*Taraxacum officinale*) have served as a versatile wild food in the Old World since the days of the hunter-gatherers. This bright spring flower was reported in seventeenth-century Massachussetts, and dandelions had entrenched themselves in Australia by the mid-nineteenth century. Today the plants are cultivated commercially - by the French and the Italians in particular - for their bitter, chicory-like flavor. Dandelion leaves are eaten raw in salads or cooked as greens, whereas the roots are also edible and can be boiled or ground and used as a coffee substitute. The white crowns are cooked as a vegetable, the flower buds are frequently pickled, and the flower heads have been used to make wine. The leaves are very high in vitamin A and, like most other greens, provide an abundance of calcium and iron, some thiamine and riboflavin, and, if not cooked too thoroughly, vitamin C as well.

Darjeeling - *see* **TEA**
Darnel - *see* **RYEGRASS**
Dasheen - *see* **CALLALOO, COCOYAM, MALANGA, TARO**
DATE - Arabs say that there are as many culinary and pharmaceutical ways of using dates (*Phoenix dactylifera*) as there are days in the year, which serves to underscore the importance of dates to desert peoples. The date tree grows in hot and arid regions where most plants cannot, and at its top are clusters of dates packing a high-energy-giving sugar content of 54 percent. The date palm is thought to be native to North Africa and Arabia - three-quarters of the world's date crop is still produced in the Middle East - and its cultivation stretches back in time some 7,000 years, beyond even the time of the Sumerians and Babylonians, who made it their sacred tree. The name is from the Greek *daktulos* (meaning "finger," from the shape of the fruit). Dates were also known to Mediterranean peoples from early times, and the Spaniards introduced them into the New World. Spanish missionaries carried dates to California, which today - along with Arizona - produces most of the U.S. crop.

There are soft, semisoft, and dry dates, depending on moisture content. The semisoft Deglet Noor variety dominates U.S. production. Elsewhere the semisoft Zahidi and Medjool are popular, along with the Bahri, a soft date. Dates are eaten fresh, naturally preserved, or dried, and they are ground into meal to make cakes. In addition, dates are pressed for juice to make *shekar* and alcoholic beverages. They are an ingredient in many dishes of the Middle East and wherever else they have been cultivated for a long time. Most dates available outside of their growing areas are soft, partly dried ones. The sap of the date palm is also employed as a beverage. Aside from the Middle East and the United States, dates are grown in India, Pakistan, northern Africa, and the Canary Islands. Dates are high in calories but supply much potassium and a fair amount of vitamin B_6, niacin, iron, and magnesium.

Common names and synonyms: Bahri date, date palm, Deglet Noor date, dry date, Medjool date, red date, semisoft date, soft date, Zahidi date.

Date palm - *see* **DATE**

Date plum - *see* **PERSIMMON**

Datura - *see* **MOONFLOWER**

DAYLILY - Any of the plants of the genus *Hemerocallis* are called daylilies. These natives of Eurasia reached North America as garden plants but subsequently "went native" there as well. In China, the buds of *H. fulva* in particular are cooked in slow-simmering dishes. But any daylily buds are good boiled or stir-fried as a vegetable. Plants of the genus *Hosta* - called plantain lilies - are also referred to as "daylilies" but do not appear to be consumed as a food.

Common names and synonyms: Plantain lily.

DE AGUA (*see also* **CHILLI PEPPERS**) - A chilli pepper of the genus *Capsicum,* this medium-hot variety looks a lot like a larger but more slender version of the jalapeño. It is much used in parts of Mexico for stuffing and in salsas, but is seldom found north of the border.

See in addition: "Chilli Peppers," Part II, Section C, Chapter 4.

De árbol - *see* **CAYENNE PEPPER**

Deer's-ears - *see* **GENTIAN**

Deertongue - *see* **CAROLINA VANILLA**

Deglet Noor date - *see* **DATE**

Delica - *see* **KABOCHA (SQUASH)**

DELICATA (SQUASH) (*see also* **SQUASH AND PUMPKIN**) - A small squash, generally about 7 or 8 inches long with a diameter of 2 to 3 inches, the delicata (*Cucurbita pepo*) has a taste and smell of, alternatively, butternut squash, corn, or sweet potato - the latter the reason for another of its names, "sweet-potato squash." Of American parents, this is a delicious squash, "human-made" by squash breeding. It is a great source of vitamins A and C along with iron and potassium.

Common names and synonyms: Bohemian squash, Jack-Be-Little, Munchkin, sweet-potato squash.

See in addition: "Squash," Part II, Section C, Chapter 8.

Demon walnut - *see* **WALNUT**

Dent maize - *see* **MAIZE**

DESERT APPLE - Also known as "Indian jujube" and "ber" as well as "desert apple," the small thorny tree this fruit grows on (*Ziziphus mauritiana*) may be of either African or Indian origin. The fruits, which smell like carob, are round or oblong, about the size of plums, and have a taste that is sweet to slightly acidic and suggests that of an apple. They are eaten raw, preserved, or dried. The desert apple is cultivated as a desert crop in India but has spread throughout tropical Southeast Asia as well. It does best, however, where the climate is not continually moist. The name "jujube" comes from the French for a lozenge, which the fruit was supposedly reminiscent of.

Common names and synonyms: Ber, Indian jujube.

Desert blazing star - *see* **MOONFLOWER**

Desert holly - *see* **SALTBUSH**

Desert jointfir - *see* **MORMON TEA**

Desert lavender - *see* **HYPTIS**

Desert-spoon - *see* **SOTOL**

Desert thorn - *see* **MATRIMONY VINE**

Devil-in-the-bush - *see* **NIGELLA**

Devil's-bones - *see* **WILD YAM**

Devil's-claws - *see* **UNICORN PLANT**

Devil's-dung - *see* **ASAFETIDA**

Devilwood - *see* **OSMANTHUS**

DEWBERRY (*see also* **BERRIES, BLACKBERRY**) - Blackberries grow upright, whereas the several forms of the dewberry (such as *Rubus hispidus* and *R. caesius*) trail on the ground. Otherwise, dewberries (although sometimes a little smaller) are practically identical to blackberries, are used for the same purposes, and are rich in vitamin C.

Diamante citron - *see* **CITRON**

Dihé - *see* **TECUITLATL**

Dijon mustard(s) - *see* **MUSTARD SEED**

DILL - This herb (*Anethum graveolens*), a member of the parsley family and more aromatic than fennel (a relative), has been pronounced native to central Asia and to southeastern Europe. The name, however, comes from the Norse word *dilla,* meaning "lull," apparently because the seeds were believed to be good for insomnia. Confusion over the plant's origin is probably inevitable because it grows wild in most temperate regions. The ancient Greeks used dill as a remedy for hiccups as well as for culinary purposes, and it has been a part of Mediterranean cuisines ever since. The Romans credited the plant with fortifying qualities and made certain that gladiators were well fortified with it. As their empire receded, dill remained behind to become seminaturalized in much of northern Europe, although it has to be cultivated in the Scandinavian countries. Today, both dill seed and dill weed are used as seasonings. The aromatic seed heads flavor pickles (their best-known use for most Americans is in dill pickles), sauces, and other foods such as fish, cheeses, and yoghurt. The feathery green leaves (dill weed) have a wonderful aroma when fresh and taste milder than the seeds. The fresh leaves go well in potato and tuna salads. Dried, the leaves lose all their aroma and most of their taste.

See also: "Spices and Flavorings," Part II, Section F, Chapter 1.

Dilly - *see* **SAPODILLA**

DITTANY - There are three herbs with the name dittany. One is an aromatic Old World plant called Crete dittany (*Origanum dictamnus*), a relative of marjoram and once believed to have the power to expel arrows from the body. The second is the so-called gas plant (*Dictamnus albus*), native to Eurasia and also named "burning bush" because it emits a vapor that can be ignited. The third is "stone mint" (*Cunila origanoides* - also known as Maryland dittany), an eastern North American plant that is a member of the mint family. True to its name, it grows in rocky places and was harvested by Native Americans to make a tea. Stone mint can also substitute for other herbs such as marjoram and thyme.

Common names and synonyms: Burning bush, Cretan dittany, Crete dittany, gas plant, Maryland dittany, stone mint.

Dock - *see* **SORREL**

Dogbane - *see* **HEMP DOGBANE**

Dogberry - *see* **CORNUS, WINTERBERRY**

Dog cherry - *see* **CORNUS**

Dog rose - *see* **ROSE HIP(S)**

Dogtooth - *see* **COUCH GRASS**

Dogwood berry - *see* **CORNUS**

Dogwood cherry - *see* **CORNUS**

Dogwood tree - *see* **CORNUS**

DOM PALM - Grown in Florida and the Nile region of Africa, the leaves of the plant *Hyphaene thebaica* are used for cordage, mats, and paper. The unripe seeds are eaten raw or made into sweetmeats or molasses. The outer husk or pulp is said to taste like gingerbread, thus encouraging its common names, "gingerbread palm" and "gingerbread tree."

Common names and synonyms: Doom palm, doum palm, Egyptian doum, gingerbread palm, gingerbread tree.

Doodhi - *see* **BOTTLE GOURD**

Doom palm - *see* **DOM PALM**

Douhé - *see* **TECUITLATL**

Doum palm - *see* **DOM PALM**

Downy groundcherry - *see* **CAPULIN**

Downy haw - *see* **HAWTHORN BERRY**

Dragon's-eye - *see* **LONGAN**

Dragon's-tongue - *see* **PIPSISSEWA**

Drumstick tree - *see* **BENOIL TREE**

Drumstick vegetable - *see* **BENOIL TREE**

DUAN SALAM - Also called "Indonesian bay" and "laurel leaf," duan salam (*Eugenia polyantha* or *Syzygium polyantha*) is a tall tree that seems to be a native of South Asia. Its aromatic leaves can be dried and used like bay leaves. When young, they are frequently cooked like greens, often with a bit of meat for flavoring.

Common names and synonyms: Indonesian bay, laurel leaf.

Duck potato - *see* **ARROWHEAD**

DUIKA - Called a wild mango - which it is not - the duika (*Irvingia gabonensis*) is a fruit that grows on trees of Central Africa. Its flavor is something like that of a mango but not very tasty. The seed, however, which is oily, provides cooking oil and is used to make Gabon chocolate.

Common names and synonyms: Wild mango.

Du jour - *see* **KALE**

Duku - *see* **LANGSAT**

DULSE (*see also* **SEAWEED**) - A coarse, reddish brown seaweed, dulse (especially *Rhodymenia palmata*) is found on North Atlantic coasts and is plentiful in New England waters and those of the British Isles. It is first dried in the sun, then used as a vegetable in salads and - in Scotland - as a condiment. Dulse is generally available in health-food stores.

Common names and synonyms: Dulce, sea moss.

See in addition: "Algae," Part II, Section C, Chapter 1.

DURIAN - A foul-smelling fruit with a spiked skin like that of a pineapple, the durian (*Durio zibethinus*) grows on a tall tree native to the Malaysian region but is now cultivated throughout Southeast Asia. When mature, the fruit is normally the size of a football and weighs about 5 pounds, although there have been reports of weights up to 100 pounds. The edible, cream-colored pulp has a delicious "figs-and-bananas" flavor - despite its obnoxious odor (some have likened it to that of Limburger cheese) - and is generally eaten raw, although unripe fruits can be boiled and eaten as a vegetable. The large seeds are roasted.

The fruit is also grown in East Africa, but, although introduced in the American tropics, did not become popular there. Because of their odor, durians are seldom available in fresh form. They are exported to Europe and the United States but few airlines will accept them for shipment. The fruit is also sold in cans and bottles, packed in sugar syrup. Durian is a fine source of potassium and fairly high in vitamin C.

Common names and synonyms: Civet-cat fruit, Lahong, Tutong.

Dutch durian - *see* **SOURSOP**

DUTCH RED PEPPER (*see also* **CHILLI PEPPERS**) - Understandably also known as the "Holland chilli," this member of the genus *Capsicum* is a fairly recently developed hybrid chilli pepper for the Dutch export trade in produce. It is red and hot and used in all the many ways - from stuffing to salsas to pickles - that other peppers have long been used.

Common names and synonyms: Holland chilli.

See in addition: "Chilli Peppers," Part II, Section C, Chapter 4.

Early Red - *see* LOQUAT

Earth almond - *see* CHUFA

EARTH NUT - In addition to serving as another synonym for peanut, the term "earth nut" can mean an Old World plant (*Conopodium denudatum* - also called "pignut") with small tubers that - in England at least - are often eaten raw. Another "earth nut," *Lathyrus tuberosus* (known as well as the "heath pea"), is also European in origin but is now naturalized in the United States. These tubers have been used as food and to flavor whiskey in Scotland and are now cultivated commercially in Holland. Both earth nuts reportedly have the flavor of chestnuts, and both have been mistakenly called chufa.

Common names and synonyms: Heath pea, pignut.

Ebisu - *see* KABOCHA (SQUASH)

Eboe yam - *see* WHITE YAM

Eddo - *see* COCOYAM, TARO

Eddoe - *see* COCOYAM, TARO

Eddy root - *see* TARO

Edible-pod pea - *see* PEA(S), SUGAR PEA

Eggfruit - *see* CANESTEL, LUCUMA

Eggfruit (tree) - *see* CANISTEL

EGGNUT - A little-known nut of the Amazon region, the eggnut (*Couepia longipendula*) has an extraordinarily hard shell that protects its oil-rich kernels. The nut is said to have an excellent flavor.

EGGPLANT - The size and color of the eggplant (*Solanum melongena*) range from the white, egg-shaped types of India (from whence the name derives) to a large, green or white variety of melon size, although the most common (in North America) remains the familiar dark purple, ovoid form sometimes called the "Japanese eggplant." In West Africa, eggplants - there called "garden eggs" - are small and round, with colors that run from white to yellow, whereas in the West Indies eggplants are often streaked with green and have a variety of names including "gully bean," "susumber," and "pea aubergine."

Known in much of the world as "aubergine" and in the Middle East as "poor-man's-caviar," the vegetable (technically a fruit) is native to southern and eastern Asia and was only introduced into Europe (by the Arabs via Spain) during the Middle Ages. It is a member of the nightshade family, which includes the potato, and has a reputation for bitterness, but is so versatile - it can be fried, grilled, boiled, baked, deep-fried, stuffed, or stewed - that its flavor changes with different methods of preparation, and in some cuisines (and diets) the eggplant, with its fleshy texture, takes the place of meat.

Eggplant is the star in many famous dishes, such as the moussaka of Greece and the eggplant parmigiana of Italy. Although not especially nutritious, the eggplant is a good source of folic acid.

Common names and synonyms: Apple-of-love, Asiatic aubergine, aubergine, baby eggplant, *brinjal,* garden egg, Guinea squash, gully bean, Italian eggplant, Japanese eggplant, melanzana, melongene, Oriental eggplant, pea apple, pea aubergine, poor-man's-caviar, susumber, *terong,* white eggplant.

EGUSI - The egusi (*Citrullus colocynthis*) is of the same genus as the watermelon and, like it, a native of tropical Africa. But the similarities end abruptly with taste, because the egusi is an extremely bitter fruit. Instead of the pulp, it is the seeds of the egusi that are utilized. Oil is extracted from them, and they are ground into powder for cooking purposes. They are also roasted for consumption.

Common names and synonyms: Colocynth.

See also: "Cucumbers, Melons, and Watermelons," Part II, Section C, Chapter 6.

Egyptian bean - *see* HYACINTH BEAN

Egyptian doum - *see* DOM PALM

Egyptian lotus flower - *see* LOTUS

Egyptian onion - *see* ONION TREE

Egyptian taro - *see* TARO

Egyptian thorn - *see* ACACIA

Egyptian tree onion - *see* ONION TREE

EINKORN (*see also* WHEAT) - This grain (*Triticum monococcum*) - a one-seeded wheat - is one (along with emmer) of the ancestral species of modern wheat and one of the founder grain crops of the Neolithic Revolution. Primitive varieties of einkorn such as *T. monococcum* spp. *boeoticum* originated in the Balkans, western Asia, and the eastern Mediterranean, and the transition to the cultivated variety (*T. monococcum*) probably took place in Anatolia. About 7,000 years ago, einkorn came to Europe, where it was grown until the nineteenth century, especially in barren regions where other crops were not successful. Primitive varieties still grow wild in the Balkans and West Asia. Although it is seldom cultivated as a cereal, einkorn is used as livestock feed and in the manufacture of beers and vinegars.

Common names and synonyms: One-grained wheat, wild einkorn, wild einkorn wheat.

See in addition: "Wheat," Part II, Section A, Chapter 10.

ELAEAGNUS (*see also* BERRIES) - There are a number of shrubs of the genus *Elaeagnus* that produce edible berries. *Elaeagnus umbellata,* the "autumn olive" of Asia, has small orange or red berries that are used like red currants or dried like raisins. *Elaeagnus angustifolia,* called the "Russian olive," "wild olive," or "oleaster," originated in Asia but is now a popular berry in southeastern Europe, its sweetness enjoyed raw or cooked. In the Philippines, the "lingaro" (*E. philippinenis*) - a large shrub - yields red berries that taste like cherries. Also in the East Asian neighborhood is the "silverthorn" (*E. pungens*), a spiny shrub or tree that has sweet red fruits. Finally, *E. commutata* - the "silverberry" - is a native of northwestern North

America with berries that helped to sustain Native Americans such as the Inuits.

Common names and synonyms: Autumn olive, lingaro, oleaster, Russian olive, silverberry, silverthorn, wild olive.

ELDERBERRY (*see also* **BERRIES**) – There are a number of shrubs and trees of the genus *Sambucus* (elder) that produce elderberries – some of the trees growing to upwards of 50 feet in height. A native of both the Americas (*S. canadensis* and *S. caerulea*) and the Old World (*S. nigra*), the elderberry has been gathered, dried, and cooked for millennia and its fragrant flowers added to salads and made into fritters. The berries vary considerably in color – ranging from blue to red to black – and also in taste. Popular wisdom holds that they should not be eaten raw in any quantity, and it is the case that the foliage and stems are slightly toxic. Native Americans employed elderberries as food and used the tree's vertical hollow stems for arrows and whistles and as taps for gathering maple sap. The ancient Greeks employed the stems for musical instruments called "sambuke." Elderberries are generally employed in tarts and pies and can be made into syrup, jelly, and wine. Although usually found in the wild, in Portugal elderberries are cultivated in large quantities and used to add a deep red color to port wine. Like all berries, elderberries are rich in vitamin C.

Common names and synonyms: American elder, American elderberry, blueberry elder, blue elderberry, eastern elderberry, red elderberry, western elderberry.

ELECAMPANE – A large herb of Eurasia, elecampane (*Inula helenium*) has been naturalized in North America. It has yellow flowers that are edible – as are its young leaves – but the major reason for the cultivation of elecampane, which has been going on since ancient times, is for its aromatic root, employed both medicinally and as a flavoring. The roots can be grated into a spice and added to any number of dishes. In the past they were candied; today their essential oil continues to flavor vermouth.

Elephant(-)apple – *see* **INDIAN WOOD-APPLE, QUINCE**

Elephant-ear plant – *see* **ALOCASIA**

Elephant's-ear – *see* **MALANGA, TARO**

Elk-weed – *see* **GENTIAN**

Emblic – *see* **AMALAKA**

EMMER (*see also* **WHEAT**) – A Eurasian wheat, and (along with einkorn) one of the ancestral species of modern wheat and a founder grain crop of the Neolithic Revolution, emmer (*Triticum dicoccum = T. dicoccon*) originated in the Middle East and western Asia at the dawn of the Neolithic Age. It is a winter or spring wheat and was used by the Babylonians and the Egyptians before it spread across Europe beginning about 5000 B.C., making

it one of the earliest grains to be cultivated there. But emmer, although hardy, was not suitable for bread making, and, slowly, crossbreeding with varieties of einkorn developed softer (and more productive) wheats that were suitable. Gradually, emmer gave way to these softer "bread wheats," although it is still grown in the United States for use as livestock feed and in breakfast cereals. Its starchy white flour is also favored for making fine pastries and cakes.

Common names and synonyms: Emmer wheat, German wheat, rice wheat, starch wheat, two-grained spelt, two-grained wheat, wild emmer wheat.

See in addition: "Wheat," Part II, Section A, Chapter 10.

Emu apple – *see* **SOUR PLUM**

ENDIVE AND ESCAROLE (*see also* **CHICKORY**) – This plant (*Cichorium endivia*) is a member of the daisy family and is cultivated for its crisp, succulent (if somewhat bitter) leaves that are used in salads and are also braised. It should not be confused with a relative – Belgian endive, called chickory in Europe. Its ancestor was wild chicory (probably native to India), but endive was domesticated early and grown in ancient Egypt, Greece, and Rome. It was introduced (or reintroduced) in Europe by the Dutch during the sixteenth century. The two principal types under cultivation are curly endive and broad-leafed or Batavian endive. The latter is also known as escarole (from the Old French *scariole* and Late Latin *escariola*) and has a bushy head with large, open, green and white leaves. The roots of this plant are ground, roasted, and added to coffee. Another variety, not bushy at all but rather blanched and spidery in appearance, is called *frisée*. Endive and escarole are fairly high in vitamin A and provide some vitamin C.

Common names and synonyms: Batavian endive, broad-leafed endive, *chicorée,* curly endive, *escariola, frisée, scariole.*

English tomato – *see* **KIWANO**

Enoki – *see* **ENOKITAKE, MUSHROOMS AND FUNGI**

ENOKITAKE (*see also* **MUSHROOMS AND FUNGI**) – Enokitake (*Flammulina velutipes = Collybia velutipes*) is a long-stemmed, tight-capped mushroom that is much appreciated in Japan, where it is cultivated. It grows wild in North America (where it is called the "winter mushroom"), but only the cultivated varieties are available in (usually Asian) markets. It is very white, has a somewhat sweet taste, and supplies a small quantity of the B-complex vitamins.

Common names and synonyms: Enoki, enok mushroom, golden mushroom, velvet stem, winter mushroom.

See in addition: "Fungi," Part II, Section C, Chapter 7.

Enok mushroom – *see* **ENOKITAKE**

ENSETE (*see also* **BANANA**) – Alternately called the "jungle banana," the "Abyssinian banana," and the "little red banana," this plant (*Musa ensete*) is now grown mostly as an ornamental because of its erect and bright green, broad leaves. Another fruit called "ensete" and closely related to the banana is *Ensete ventricosum,* which is grown as a staple in some of the higher altitudes of Ethiopia. The pulp is made into bread.

Common names and synonyms: Abyssinian banana, jungle banana, little red banana.

See in addition: "Bananas and Plantains," Part II, Section B, Chapter 1.

EPAZOTE (*see also* **CHENOPODIUM**) – Called *paiku* in Peru, this semicultivated green, epazote (*Chenopodium ambrosioides*) is traditional and necessary in Mexican and Central American cooking. The aromatic leaves (some would say the odor is foul, others find it pleasant) of this sweet and mild-flavored herb are found in markets on large green stalks as well as in chopped and dried forms. When added to dishes containing beans, epazote is believed to reduce gassiness, and it is also used to make "Mexican tea," which is another name for the plant. Epazote has a reputation for combating helminthic boarders in the body, and the leaves and tops of one variety (*C. ambrosioides* var. *anthelminticum*) are considered especially powerful in this regard. An essential oil is extracted from this plant for medicinal uses.

Common names and synonyms: American wormseed, Jerusalem oak, Mexican tea, wormseed.

Erigeron – *see* **HORSEWEED**
Eringo – *see* **SEA HOLLY**
Erosus yam bean – *see* **JÍCAMA**
Ervil – *see* **BITTER VETCH**
Eryngo – *see* **SEA HOLLY**
Escariola – *see* **ENDIVE AND ESCAROLE**
Escarole – *see* **ENDIVE AND ESCAROLE**
Espinaca acquatica – *see* **SWAMP CABBAGE**
Esrog – *see* **CITRON**
Ethrog – *see* **CITRON**
Etrog – *see* **CITRON**
European filbert – *see* **HAZELNUT AND FILBERT**
European grass pea – *see* **CHICKLING VETCH**
European sweet chervil – *see* **CICELY**
EVENING PRIMROSE – Native to North America, the various species of the genus *Oenothera* grow southward from British Columbia and Newfoundland and are found across most of the continental United States. The young shoots and leaves provided food for Native Americans, as did the boiled seeds and roots of some species. The evening primrose was one of the first American plants introduced as a food in Europe, where it was cultivated for both young shoots and roots. In France, *O. biennis* came to be known as *jambon du jardinier* or "gardener's ham."

Common names and synonyms: Gardener's ham, *jambon du jardinier.*

Evening star – *see* **MOONFLOWER**

EVERLASTING PEA – Any of several species of the genus *Lathyrus* – and especially *Lathyrus latifolius* – are called "everlasting pea." It is a native of southern Europe that is now consumed mostly in Asia, where the pods and shoots are boiled as a vegetable and the seeds are roasted.

Common names and synonyms: Perennial pea.

See also: "Beans, Peas, and Lentils," Part II, Section C, Chapter 3.

Exotic grape – *see* **GRAPES**

Faba – *see* **FAVA BEAN**
Fagara – *see* **SICHUAN PEPPER-CORN**
Fairywort – *see* **COOLWORT**
False bittersweet – *see* **AMERICAN BITTERSWEET**
False coriander – *see* **LONG CORIANDER**
False miterwort – *see* **COOLWORT**
False sandalwood – *see* **TALLOW WOOD PLUM**
False verbain – *see* **BLUE VERVAIN**
Fameflower – *see* **TALINUM**
Fanweed – *see* **PENNYCRESS**
Fat(-)hen – *see* **CORNSALAD, GOOD-KING-HENRY**
FAVA BEAN (*see also* **BEANS, LEGUMES**) – Known to the English as the "broadbean" or the "horse bean," the fava (*Vicia faba* – from *faba,* which means "bean" in many of the Romance languages) has a very long history, figuring in Chinese cuisine at least 5,000 years ago. Today, favas are very prominent in the cuisines of Mediterranean countries, the Middle East, Africa, South America, and China, but not, for some reason, in that of North America – perhaps because of the need to skin them, which is time-consuming. A remote potential difficulty with ingesting the beans, or even inhaling the pollen from the flowers, is hemolytic anemia, brought on by a type of enzyme deficiency – glucose-6-phosphate-dehydrogenase (G6PD) deficiency – that has developed among some of the people of the world as a protection against malaria. Like most beans, favas deliver protein and iron and, in addition, are a good source of vitamin A and a good provider of the B-vitamin complex.

Common names and synonyms: Broadbean, horse bean, tickbean, Windsor bean.

See in addition: "Beans, Peas, and Lentils," Part II, Section C, Chapter 3.

Fecula – *see* **ARRACACHA**
Feijão-prêto – *see* **TURTLE BEAN**
FEIJOA – The feijoa, a fruit (*Feijoa sellowiana*), is a native of Brazil with a Portuguese name suggestive of a bean (in Portuguese, *feijão*). But although it is unlikely that the kiwi fruit–sized berry of this ever-

green shrub would ever be confused with a bean, its common names – "pineapple guava" or even just "guava" – do tend to promote confusion. The feijoa has a green, bumpy skin and a jelly-like pulp surrounded by a whitish flesh with a delicious, tart taste that is something of a cross between the flavors of pineapple and strawberry and goes well in fresh fruit salads. Beginning at the end of the nineteenth century, the feijoa traveled from Brazil to be grown in and exported from southern Europe (1890) and California (1900) on one side of the in world and, more recently, New Zealand and Australia on the other. It is frequently eaten fresh or made into a jelly. When fresh, in particular, the feijoa is a good source of vitamin C.

Common names and synonyms: Guava, pineapple guava.

Felon herb - *see* **MUGWORT**
Fen berry - *see* **CRANBERRY**
FENNEL – Fennel (*Foeniculum vulgare*), a native of southern Europe, is often wrongly called "anise" or "sweet anise" because of its licorice flavor. However, that flavor is less pronounced in fennel than in anise, and the seeds (as well as the roots, leaves, and stalks) of fennel have been employed since ancient times as an ingredient in sauces, sausages, stews, and salads, as well as in breads and various meat, egg, and fruit dishes.

The herb was cultivated by the Egyptians and was popular with the ancient Greeks and Romans. According to Greek mythology, when humans received knowledge from Olympus, the gift came in the form of a fiery-hot coal within a fennel stalk. The name "fennel" derives from a Latin word that indicates a kind of sweet-smelling hay – a hay that was discovered to keep insects at bay. The use, as a vegetable, of the celery-like stalks and leaves of one variety, called "Florence fennel," is mostly seen in Italian cuisine (the root is especially vital in Sicilian cuisine), although fennel is also cultivated for its vegetable (in contrast to herbal) qualities in Greece, France, and the United States – in the latter case, largely because of an Italian-American demand.

Like the seed, the vegetable is licorice-like in taste and has long been associated in Europe with fish recipes. It is also employed raw in salads and appetizers and cooked in any number of dishes. The vegetable provides some vitamin A and niacin, and a little iron. The seed was called the "meetin' seed" by the early New England Puritans, who were accustomed to nibble them during church services. Fennel seeds are especially important in flavoring fish, shellfish, and fish sauces. They are also added to meat dishes, spaghetti sauces, and breads and pastries.

Common names and synonyms: Finocchio, Florence fennel, meetin' seed, Roman fennel, sweet anise, sweet fennel, wild fennel.

See also: "Spices and Flavorings," Part II, Section F, Chapter 1.

Fennel-flower - *see* **NIGELLA**
FENUGREEK – The leguminous seeds of fenugreek (*Trigonella foenum-graecum*), a Eurasian plant, are employed as a spice throughout the Mediterranean region, South Asia, and North Africa. Fenugreek was mentioned in the Ebers papyrus and was used by the ancient Egyptians to make a paste that, when applied to the body, was supposed to combat fevers. In Latin, the name means "Greek hay," presumably because the clover-like plant made good fodder for animals.

Fenugreek seeds have a bitter taste (which is removed by dry-roasting) and a yellow coloring, that they impart to other foods. Ground, they are an important ingredient in curry powders. In parts of Africa, the dried seeds are soaked and prepared like the legumes, which means they are rich in protein. The dried leaves (called *methi*) are mixed into vegetable dishes in Indian, Middle Eastern, and Asian cuisines. Other uses for fenugreek are as the most important flavoring in artificial maple syrup and in halvah, as well as an ingredient in some oral contraceptives. In addition to protein, fenugreek, like most other legumes, is high in the B-vitamins.

Common names and synonyms: Foenugreek, *methi*.

Fernbush - *see* **SWEET FERN**
Ferngale - *see* **SWEET FERN**
Fever bush - *see* **WINTERBERRY**
Feverwort - *see* **BONESET**
FIDDLEHEAD FERN – All ferns are "fiddleheads" when their new, tightly coiled, green shoots emerge from the earth – usually in the spring. After they uncoil into fronds, they are no longer edible, and as with certain mushrooms, there are questions about the edibility of some of the so-called fiddleheads which are suspected of being carcinogenic. However, the one usually marketed – the ostrich fern (*Matteuccia struthiopteris*) – is supposed to be safe. Fiddleheads grow in damp places and in North America are sought mostly in forests along the eastern seaboard, especially in New Brunswick, Maine, and Vermont. For some, their taste is akin to that of artichokes; for others, it is more like the flavor of asparagus. Although they are often added raw to salads, fiddleheads are best when (as with asparagus or artichoke hearts) they are lightly boiled and served with melted butter or some other appropriate dressing. The nutrients provided are vitamins A and C.

Common names and synonyms: Fiddlehead(s), fiddlehead greens, ostrich fern.

Fiddlehead greens - *see* **FIDDLEHEAD FERN**
Field horsetail - *see* **HORSETAIL PLANT**
Field mint - *see* **CORN MINT, MINT**
Field mushroom - *see* **MUSHROOMS AND FUNGI**
Field pea - *see* **COWPEA, PEA(S)**
Field pennycress - *see* **PENNYCRESS**

Field salad – *see* **CORNSALAD**

Field vetch – *see* **VETCH**

FIG – The common fig tree (*Ficus carica*) is a member of the mulberry family. Although a native of Southwest Asia, it long ago was growing wild around the Mediterranean basin, and its sweet, pear-shaped, and many-seeded fruit was picked up by hunter-gatherers. Figs have been cultivated for over 6,000 years, and nowadays practically every Mediterranean garden has its fig tree. When the fruits are ripe, the ground around becomes slippery with their pulp.

The fig was known to the Egyptians, the Greeks, and the Romans, who fed them to their gladiators for quick energy. The Greek word "sycophant," meaning "one who shows the fig," was first applied to the priests who declared that a fig crop was ripe and could be gathered. Later, it meant those who informed on individuals in the illegal fig trade from Greece. The common fig was brought to the Americas by the Spaniards around 1600 and was first planted in California by Franciscan friars around 1770. Commercial production there, however, only dates from about 1900. Today, California produces almost all of the U.S. crop. Other commercial producers are Italy, Turkey, Algeria, Greece, Spain, and Portugal.

In all, there are about 100 kinds of figs, such as the Smyrna fig; even the rubber and banyan trees are species of figs. Major varieties of the fruit are the Black Mission, with a black or purple skin; the Kadotta, with a yellow-green skin; a large fig, the Calimyrna, with a yellow-green skin; and the Brown Turkey, which has a somewhat purplish skin. The fruit is eaten fresh but is also stewed, canned, preserved, and dried. The latter form is the most nutritious, and for millennia dried figs have been a staple food in many parts of the world, where they were known as "poor-man's-food." Fig leaves are also eaten. Figs are a good source of carbohydrates, vitamin A, fiber, and potassium, as well as calcium, iron, and copper.

Common names and synonyms: Adriatic fig, Black Mission fig, Brown Turkey fig, Calimyrna fig, common fig, Kadotta fig, poor-man's-food, Smyrna fig, sycamore fig.

FIG-LEAFED GOURD (*see also* **SQUASH AND PUMPKIN**) – Unknown in the United States, although of American origin, the fig-leafed gourd (*Cucurbita ficifolia*) was cultivated at least 5,000 years ago in Peru. It is so called because the plant has leaves similar to those of the fig tree. Immature fruits are prepared and eaten like summer squashes, whereas the black seeds are roasted for consumption and are turned into a kind of gravy. In addition, the fruit of this versatile vegetable is candied for special occasions in Central American and Andean countries, and the flesh is also fermented to make beer.

Common names and synonyms: Malabar gourd.

See in addition: "Squash," Part II, Section C, Chapter 8.

Filbert – *see* **HAZELNUT AND FILBERT**

Filé – *see* **SASSAFRAS**

FINGER MILLET (*see also* **MILLET**) – Known as *ragi* in the dry areas of India and Sri Lanka, where it is a major grain, finger millet (*Eleusine coracana*) is generally made into flour, porridges, and flatbreads. It is also used for making beer. Higher in protein and fat than most other grains, finger millet is a very wholesome food.

Common names and synonyms: African millet, *ragi*.

See in addition: "Millets," Part II, Section A, Chapter 5.

Finocchio – *see* **FENNEL**

Fish-hook cactus – *see* **BARREL CACTUS**

Fitweed – *see* **LONG CORIANDER**

Five-angled fruit – *see* **CARAMBOLA**

Flag – *see* **IRIS**

Flageolet – *see* **BEANS**

Flag root – *see* **SWEET FLAG**

FLAX SEED – The fibers from a number of plants of the genus *Linum*, and especially the cultivated *L. usitatissimum*, have long been used to make fine linen, and for just as long the seeds of these plants have been crushed to make linseed oil. Indeed, flax is one of the oldest cultivated crops, dating back at least 7,000 years. The Egyptians raised it, and it was among the first crops in Syria and Turkey. Flax cultivation spread to Europe about 3,000 years ago. Although the oil is generally thought of as a drying oil – used in such products as paints and varnishes – one occasionally reads of it being employed as a cooking oil in the past. Flax seed has also been employed to make teas.

Common names and synonyms: Linseed (oil).

Florida arrowroot – *see* **ZAMIA**

Florida sago – *see* **ZAMIA**

Florist's fern – *see* **ASPARAGUS**

Flowering bean – *see* **MALOGA BEAN**

Flowering chives – *see* **CHINESE CHIVE(S)**

Flowering dogwood – *see* **CORNUS**

FLOWERING WHITE CABBAGE (*see also* **CABBAGE**) – A type of Chinese cabbage grown near Canton, the flowering white cabbage (*Brassica campestris*) is similar to broccoli and to bok choy, which seems to be a close relative. It is also called *choy sum* (which translates as "vegetable hearts"), and nearly all its parts are edible and highly nutritious.

Common names and synonyms: Choy sum.

See in addition: "Cruciferous and Green Leafy Vegetables," Part II, Section C, Chapter 5.

Flowery Orange Pekoe – *see* **TEA**

Fluted cucumber – *see* **OYSTERNUT**

FLUTED GOURD – Practically unknown in the United States, the fluted gourd (*Telfairia occidentalis*) is cultivated in West Africa, often on trellises. The fruit is not eaten, but the seeds are protein-rich and are roasted, boiled, and made into a powder for soups.

Common names and synonyms: Fluted pumpkin, oysternut.

Fluted pumpkin - *see* **FLUTED GOURD**
Foalfoot - *see* **COLTSFOOT**
Foam flower - *see* **COOLWORT**
Foenugreek - *see* **FENUGREEK**
FONIO - Fonio is perhaps the oldest of Africa's cereal crops. For thousands of years, fields of its barely knee-high stalks have stretched across the uplands of West Africa. White fonio (*Digitaria exilis*) is cultivated in an area that extends from the Atlantic coast to Chad. People on the central plateau in Nigeria call it *acha*. Black fonio (*Digitaria iburua*) is more likely found on the Jos-Bauchi Plateau of Nigeria and in northern Togo and Benin.

The history of the crop is little known, as scholars have yet to give it much attention. The seeds of both species are white, but black fonio (despite its lesser popularity) is nutritionally equal to its cousin. Their protein and fat contents are similar to those of wheat and fonio is very rich in several important amino acids.

Unlike some other ancient African cereals, fonio is still widely cultivated and serves as an important food for as many as 4 million people. No doubt one of the reasons for this is its excellent taste. Perhaps another reason is that the crop is particularly well suited to West Africa's semiarid savanna regions; it tolerates poor soil and often grows well where few other cultigens do. Moreover, a number of varieties mature very quickly, and hence provide food during normally lean times when other cereals are still far from being ready for harvest, giving rise to one of its many names - "hungry rice."

In many West African societies, fonio was (and still is) held in high esteem. At times, it was reserved for chiefs and royalty or saved for special festivities. In some cultures, it denoted part of the bride-price, and many feel that it is the best-tasting cereal of all. The kernels can be cooked as a porridge; they serve as a delicious base for couscous; and they are brewed into beer. Heated over a hot fire, they can be popped. Ground into flour, they are baked into breads or used as a substitute for semolina.

Common names and synonyms: Acha, black fonio, hungry rice, white fonio.

Food-of-the-gods - *see* **ASAFETIDA**
FOREST MILKBERRY - A tree of southern Africa, the forest milkberry (*Manilkara discolor*) ranges from 15 to over 50 feet in height and grows at many different altitudes. It bears flowers that are followed by tiny (less than a half inch in diameter) fruits that are fleshy and yellow to red in color.

Forest mushroom - *see* **CHANTERELLE, MUSHROOMS AND FUNGI**
Four-angled bean - *see* **WINGED BEAN**

Four-wing saltbush - *see* **SALTBUSH**
Foxberry - *see* **LINGONBERRY**
FOX GRAPE (*see also* **GRAPES**) - Originating in the New World, the fox grape (*Vitis labrusca*) was gathered by native peoples of eastern North America. Later, with the arrival of the Europeans, this purplish black fruit became the source of many cultivated grape varieties that were made into wine. These varieties are hardier and more disease resistant than grapes native to the Old World. Because the skin separates readily from the pulp, labrusca grapes are also called "slip-skin" grapes. The taste of these grapes made into wine has been defined as "foxy."

Common names and synonyms: Labrusca grape, slip-skin grape, wild grape.
See in addition: "Wine," Part III, Chapter 13.

Foxtail barley - *see* **WILD BARLEY**
Fremont screwbean - *see* **MESQUITE**
FRENCH COLOMBARD (*see also* **GRAPES**) - A high-yielding white grape, French Colombard (*Vitis vinifera*) is used in France mostly for making cognac. In California, it generally goes into bulk wines and is often marketed as chablis.

See in addition: "Wine," Part III, Chapter 13.

French endive - *see* **BELGIAN ENDIVE**
French peanut - *see* **MALABAR NUT**
French weed - *see* **PENNYCRESS**
Fresadilla - *see* **TOMATILLO**
FRESNO (*see also* **CHILLI PEPPERS**) - Another member of the genus *Capsicum,* the Fresno is a red pepper that resembles the jalapeño but is a bit wider (and hotter). It is grown in California and other places in the U.S. Southwest as well as in Mexico. In addition to their use in salsa, Fresnos are excellent when roasted.

See in addition: "Chilli Peppers," Part II, Section C, Chapter 4.

Frijol arroz - *see* **RICE BEAN**
Frijol negro - *see* **TURTLE BEAN**
Frisée - *see* **ENDIVE AND ESCAROLE**
Fruit à pain - *see* **BREADFRUIT**
Fruit-salad fruit - *see* **MONSTERA**
Fruta de Mexico - *see* **MONSTERA**
Frutillo - *see* **MATRIMONY VINE**
Fumé Blanc - *see* **SAUVIGNON BLANC**
Fuyu - *see* **PERSIMMON**
FUZZY MELON (*see also* **MELONS**) - Also called "hairy melon," "Chinese squash," "Chinese vegetable marrow," and "Chinese winter melon," the fuzzy melon (*Benincasa hispida = B. cerifera*) is a huge cucurbit that grows on a vine that spreads out over the ground like a pumpkin vine. Apparently native to southern China (and an ancient food of the Chinese), the fuzzy melon comes in two varieties; one is cylindrical in shape, whereas the other narrows at the middle like a dumbbell. Both have a splotchy green skin that is waxy (they are also called "wax gourds") and both are cov-

ered with white, fuzzy hairs. The flavor of their pale green flesh is reportedly delicious, and in addition to peeling them and eating them raw, fuzzy melons are braised, boiled, and used in stir-fries.

Common names and synonyms: Chinese squash, Chinese vegetable marrow, Chinese winter melon, hairy melon, *moqua,* wax gourd.

See in addition: "Cucumbers, Melons, and Watermelons," Part II, Section C, Chapter 6.

G

Gaai chow - *see* **PAKCHOI AND KAI CHOY**

Gaai choy - *see* **PAKCHOI AND KAI CHOY**

Gai chow - *see* **PAKCHOI AND KAI CHOY**

Gai choy - *see* **PAKCHOI AND KAI CHOY**

Gai-larn - *see* **CHINESE BROCCOLI**

Galanga - *see* **GALANGAL**

GALANGAL - Also called galingale, greater galangal (*Alpinia galanga*) is an aromatic root, native to Indonesia, that resembles ginger and is a close relative of the gingerroot family. It is joined in this relationship by both the lesser galangal (*A. officinarum*) and by galanga - *Kaempferia galanga.* In fact, greater galangal (also called laos) almost replaces gingerroot in much of the cooking of Southeast Asia. Lesser galangal and galanga are also eaten, but more as a cooked vegetable than a spice. At one time, galangal was widely used in Europe (for example, in England during the Middle Ages), where the root was sliced in both fresh and dried forms and added to dishes; it was also dried and ground. Now, however, galangal's principal use in the West is in making liqueurs and bitters.

Common names and synonyms: Galanga, galangale, galingale, greater galanga(l), laos, lesser galanga(l).

See also: "Spices and Flavorings," Part II, Section F, Chapter 1.

Galangale - *see* **GALANGAL**

Galega - *see* **GOAT'S-RUE**

Galingale - *see* **CHUFA, GALANGAL**

Gallberry - *see* **WINTERBERRY**

Gallito - *see* **CORAL BEAN**

GAMAY (*see also* **GRAPES**) - Grown in France, California, and elsewhere, Gamay grapes (*Vitis vinifera*) are used to produce the dry red table wines of the Beaujolais district of Burgundy. In California, two distinct types are grown: Napa Valley Gamay and Gamay Beaujolais. These names actually give a false impression. It seems that the Napa variety is the true Beaujolais grape, and the California Gamay Beaujolais is actually a variant of Pinot Noir - a famous grape of Burgundy.

Common names and synonyms: Gamay Beaujolais, Gamay Noir, Napa Valley Gamay.

See in addition: "Wine," Part III, Chapter 13.

Gamay Beaujolais - *see* **GAMAY**

Gamay Noir - *see* **GAMAY**

Gandul - *see* **PIGEON PEA**

Garavance - *see* **CHICKPEA**

Garbanzo - *see* **BEANS, CHICKPEA**

Garden balm - *see* **BEE BALM, LEMON BALM**

Garden egg - *see* **EGGPLANT, LOCAL GARDEN EGG**

Gardener's ham - *see* **EVENING PRIMROSE**

Garden huckleberry - *see* **WONDERBERRY**

Garden myrrh - *see* **CICELY**

GARLIC - A close relative of the onion, garlic (*Allium sativum*) is the common name for several small bulbous herbs of the lily family - among them British wild garlic (*A. oleraceum*), American wild garlic (*A. canadense*), and British and American field garlic (*A. vineale* - also known as "wild garlic"). *Allium sativum* is said by some to be a native of southern Europe; most, however, say central Asia.

Garlic was much appreciated by Egyptians, Hebrews, Greeks, and Romans, and by the time of the Middle Ages, was well entrenched in the cookery of southern Europe, where it remains to this day. Garlic may have somehow reached the Americas before the voyages of Christopher Columbus: The expedition of Hernando Cortés reportedly encountered it on its march into Mexico.

The term "garlic" comes from an old Anglo-Saxon word for "spear," after its spear-shaped leaves. Garlic is controversial - and not only because of "garlic breath." Throughout the ages, it has been regarded as a powerful medicine (even today it is viewed by some as protective against heart disease and cancer), an aphrodisiac, and a talisman for warding off demons and vampires. The bulb itself consists of bulblets or "cloves" grouped together between membranous scales and enclosed within a whitish or reddish skin. Recently, "elephant garlic," a hybrid of garlic and onion, has appeared in supermarkets - with its popularity the result of the current practice of garlic roasting. It is much larger than normal garlic bulbs (hence the name "elephant") and has a considerably milder flavor.

Common names and synonyms: American field garlic, American wild garlic, British field garlic, British wild garlic, elephant garlic, field garlic, *rocambole,* sand leek, wild garlic.

See also: "The *Allium* Species," Part II, Section C, Chapter 2; "Spices and Flavorings," Part II, Section F, Chapter 1.

Garlic chives - *see* **CHINESE CHIVE(S)**

GARLIC-MUSTARD - A tall weed that is native to Europe, garlic-mustard (*Alliaria officinalis* = *Sisymbrium alliarin*) has the odor of garlic (hence the scientific name, derived from "Allium"), tastes something like mustard seed, and can be used in salads. Also called "hedge garlic," the plant was much used in the past by Europeans as an herb. It is now naturalized in North America.

Common names and synonyms: Hedge garlic.

Garnacha - *see* GRENACHE

Garnacha Blanc - *see* GRENACHE

Gas plant - *see* DITTANY

Gbanja kola - *see* KOLA NUT

Gean - *see* CHERRY

Genip - *see* GENIPAP, SPANISH LIME

GENIPAP - The greenish or russet-brown fruit of *Genipa americana* is the size of a small orange and grows in clusters. Its acidic taste militates against its consumption raw, and its common use is in marmalade-like preserves. However, a cool drink known as *genipapado* is also made from the fruits, and the plant yields an indelible blue dye used as body paint. Genipap is found in Mexico, the West Indies, and South America, where it is also known as the "marmalade box."

Common names and synonyms: Genip, genipe, genipop, jagua, marmalade box.

Genipe - *see* GENIPAP, SPANISH LIME

Genipop - *see* GENIPAP

GENTIAN - There are numerous plants of the type genus *Gentiana*, some with large blue flowers. The dried rhizome and roots of a yellow-flowered European variety, yellow gentian (*G. lutea*), are sometimes used to make a tonic. Another plant of the Gentianaceae family is called deer's-ears, elk-weed, or green gentian (*Frasera speciosa* or *Swertia radiata*). Its roots were consumed by Native Americans in the American West.

Common names and synonyms: Deer's-ears, elk-weed, gentian root, green gentian, yellow gentian.

Gentle balm - *see* LEMON BALM

Gerasole - *see* JERUSALEM ARTICHOKE

German mustard - *see* HORSERADISH

German wheat - *see* EMMER

Gerrard vetch - *see* TUFTED VETCH

GEWÜRZTRAMINER (*see also* GRAPES) - In German, Gewürz means "spice" or "herb," which serves to indicate the aroma of the wine made from these grapes (*Vitis vinifera*) of the Rhine valley type. The region of Alsace produces most of the dry white wine made from Gewürz (also called Traminer, which is actually a cousin) grapes in Europe. In the United States, the grapes are also employed to make very creditable California "Rhine" wines.

Common names and synonyms: Traminer.

See in addition: "Wine," Part III, Chapter 13.

GHERKIN (*see also* CUCUMBER) - There are several varieties of small, rough-skinned cucumbers called gherkins (an English name for cucumber), and there exists some confusion about their origin. It was long believed in the West that the original gherkin was the so-called Jamaican gherkin or West Indian gherkin (*Cucumis anguria*) - a trailing herb also common in Brazil. But a kind of cucumber, which the English called "gherkin," has been eaten in India (where cucumbers are thought to have originated) for over 3,000 years and has been enjoyed in Europe since classical times. This was probably *C. melo* var. *conomon,* a native of India, commonly called the "Oriental pickling melon." The West Indian gherkin, by contrast, is a native of tropical Africa and thus must have reached the tropical New World from there, probably with the early-sixteenth-century slave trade. Soon afterward, it was carried back across the Atlantic and mentioned for the first time in Europe in a French publication of 1549. Immature gherkins are both cooked and eaten raw, but their general use is as pickles.

Common names and synonyms: Concombre des Antilles, Jamaican cucumber, Jamaican gherkin, Oriental pickling melon, *pepinito, pepino,* West Indian gherkin, West Indian gourd.

See in addition: "Cucumbers, Melons, and Watermelons," Part II, Section C, Chapter 6.

Ghia - *see* CHIA

Giant bladder weed - *see* SEAWEED

Giant cane - *see* LARGE CANE

GIANT GRANADILLA - A robust climbing vine that is a native of tropical South America, the giant granadilla (*Passiflora quadrangularis*) now grows throughout the tropical world. It has roundish, medium to dark green leaves that are 6 to 9 inches across, and pleasantly scented white flowers sometimes edged with pink. Its greenish yellow fruits can reach from 5 to 10 inches in length. Their shape is oblong, and their light-colored, firm flesh surrounds a cavity that is filled with numerous dark seeds embedded in a pink pulp. The juice is fragrant and slightly acidic and lends itself well to flavoring ice creams and other desserts and to making refreshing drinks. One such drink, known as a *marquesa* (or *markeesa*), is very popular in Indonesia. Unripe, the fruit may also be cooked and eaten as a vegetable. It contains considerable amounts of phosphorus and vitamin A.

GIANT HOLLY FERN - Known also as a "sword fern," which is the name given to several ferns of both the Old and the New Worlds, the giant holly fern (*Polystichum munitum*) is a plant of western North America. Native Americans ate the rhizome of this species, and those of other species are still consumed in Asia.

Common names and synonyms: Sword fern.

Giant sea kelp - *see* KELP, SEAWEED

Giant sunflower - *see* INDIAN POTATO, SUNFLOWER OIL AND SEED

Giant taro - *see* ALOCASIA

Giant white radish - *see* DAIKON

Gilliflower - *see* GILLYFLOWER

Gill-over-the-ground - *see* **GROUND IVY**

GILLYFLOWER - The term "gillyflower" (also spelled gilliflower) refers to any of several plants with fragrant flowers, generally of the genus *Dianthus,* an important Old World genus of herbs. Gillyflowers were used as herbs for flavoring food and especially beverages.

Common names and synonyms: Gilliflower.

Ginep - *see* **SPANISH LIME**

Gingelly - *see* **SESAME**

GINGER - The underground rhizome of a tropical flowering plant, gingerroot (*Zingiber officinale*) can be purchased fresh, dried, grated, ground, preserved in vinegar or syrup, and crystallized. If fresh, its tan skin must be removed before grating or slicing. The word *zingiber* means "horn-shaped" in Sanskrit and was applied to ginger because of the shape of its rhizomes. Ginger was used in China and India 7,000 years ago and was an important item in the spice trade that stretched overland and by sea from India to the ports of the eastern Mediterranean, and to Egypt via the Red Sea.

Although known to the Greeks and the Romans, ginger apparently only became popular in Europe during the Middle Ages. The Portuguese took it to Africa as they explored the western coast of that continent in the fifteenth century, and the Spaniards carried it to the New World in the following century. In fact, the latter encouraged the cultivation of ginger in the Americas as part of an effort to grow those exotic (and expensive) spices that usually were only available from the East.

Ginger requires fertile soil and a warm climate to grow properly, and Haiti and especially Jamaica became, and remain, major New World producers. In fact, it is said that the highest-quality ginger comes from the central mountain region of Jamaica. The sharp but sweet flavor of ginger goes well in Asian dishes, and the ground root is used extensively in baking - in gingerbread, spice cakes, and the like. It is also employed in making various alcoholic beverages.

Common names and synonyms: Gingerroot, Jamaica ginger.

See also: "Spices and Flavorings," Part II, Section F, Chapter 1.

Gingerbread palm - *see* **DOM PALM**

Gingerbread tree - *see* **DOM PALM**

Ginger bud - *see* **MYOGA GINGER, TORCH GINGER**

Ginip - *see* **SPANISH LIME**

GINKGO NUT - Also called the "maidenhair tree," the ginkgo nut (*Ginkgo biloba*) appears to be native to China. One says "appears" because the *Ginkgo* genus, with some of its representatives long extinct, includes members that are among the oldest plants on the planet. Their fanlike leaves basked in the same sunlight as the dinosaurs, and their fleshy, inedible, odoriferous, yellow fruit contains a plumlike, hard-shelled, cream-colored nut that must have provided food for humans since the beginning of their time on earth. Grown in China for thousands of years, the tree reached Japan about 1,000 years ago (presumably after first being introduced in Korea) and found its way to Europe during the early part of the eighteenth century. The tree is said to have first been planted in North America in 1784 in a garden outside of Philadelphia. The nuts are still widely used - after being roasted, grilled, steamed, or boiled - in Asian soups, appetizers, and desserts. Boiled and canned ginkgo kernels are imported from the Orient and are available in ethnic food stores.

Common names and synonyms: Ginkgo (tree), ginko nut (tree), maidenhair tree.

Ginnie pepper - *see* **CAYENNE PEPPER**

GINSENG (*see also* **BLUE COHOSH**) - There are a few plants of the genus *Panax* that are called ginseng (especially *P. quinquefolius* and *P. schinseng*) and are strongly associated with the Chinese, who credit their forked roots (which resemble the lower part of the human body) with health-giving and especially aphrodisiacal properties. Actually, however, *P. quinquefolius* is North American in origin, and its leaves were used by Native Americans to brew a kind of tea. They also consumed the roots of dwarf ginseng (*P. trifolius*) both raw and boiled. American ginseng is now cultivated in North America for export to China and for the health-food industry at home.

Common names and synonyms: American ginseng, dwarf ginseng.

Girasole - *see* **JERUSALEM ARTICHOKE**

Giraumon - *see* **CALABAZA (SQUASH)**

Girolle - *see* **CHANTERELLE, MUSHROOMS AND FUNGI**

Girsole - *see* **JERUSALEM ARTICHOKE**

GLASSWORT (*see also* **SAMPHIRE**) - Glasswort actually comprises a number of species, among them *Salicornia europaea* and *S. herbacea*, which are both edible and often called "samphire." A cousin, *S. stricta,* employed in the making of glass, may have provided the official name, although the crunching sound glasswort makes when stepped upon also sounds like glass being broken. The roots of these small plants grow wild along rocky seacoasts (even right through rocks) and have historically been much appreciated by the French and English, who pickled them. And today *S. europaea* is gathered commercially in France to be served raw with fish and pickled. Because the plant seems to flourish in the presence of salt, however, it also grows around salt marshes far away from the sea. The plant is crisp and salty tasting when young and can be used in salads as well as pickled. Glasswort is high in iron and vitamin C. In the United States, glasswort is generally but wrongly called samphire.

Common names and synonyms: Marsh samphire, *pousse-pied,* samphire, sea bean, seagrass, sea pickle.

Goa bean - *see* **WINGED BEAN**

GOAT CHILLI (*see also* **CHILLI PEPPERS**) - A cold-tolerant *Capsicum* variety, the goat pepper is said to belong to the species *C. pubescens* but cannot be crossed with any of its other members. It is grown in the high Andes, where its leaves as well as its dried fruit are used for seasoning.
Common names and synonyms: Goat pepper.
See in addition: "Chilli Peppers," Part II, Section C, Chapter 4.

Goat-nut - *see* **JOJOBA NUT**

Goat pepper - *see* **GOAT CHILLI**

GOAT'S-RUE - Also called "galega," goat's-rue (*Galega officinalis*) is a tall, bushy, blue-flowered European herb now cultivated as an ornamental but used in the past as a potherb.
Common names and synonyms: Galega.

Gobo - *see* **BURDOCK**

Golden alexanders - *see* **ALEXANDER**

GOLDEN APPLE - Not to be confused with the Golden Delicious apple, the golden apple (*Spondias cytherea* = *S. dulcis*) is not an apple at all, but rather a yellow fruit with a single large stone (something like the avocado) surrounded by flesh with a taste ranging from tart to sweet. It is a native of Polynesia but is widely grown in the West Indies. Golden apples are used for tall, sweet drinks and made into jam and chutneys. They are now available in many tropical markets.
Common names and synonyms: Ambarella, Jew plum, Otaheita-apple, vi-apple.

Goldenberry - *see* **CAPE GOOSEBERRY**

Golden button(s) - *see* **TANSY**

Golden chanterelle - *see* **CHANTERELLE, MUSHROOMS AND FUNGI**

GOLDEN CLUB - An aquatic plant native to the eastern United States, golden club (*Orontium aquaticum*) was exploited by Native Americans for food in a number of different ways. The roots were dried and made into flour, the seeds were also dried, and even the flowers were eaten.

Golden gram - *see* **MUNG BEAN**

Golden husk - *see* **CAPE GOOSEBERRY**

Golden mushroom - *see* **ENOKITAKE**

GOLDEN NUGGET (SQUASH) (*see also* **SQUASH AND PUMPKIN**) - The Golden Nugget (*Cucurbita maxima*) is a winter squash that - with its orange skin - looks like a miniature pumpkin. It is a product of plant breeding and has a pleasant squash taste. Generally baked or roasted, one Golden Nugget provides a single serving and delivers much in the way of vitamin A and iron.
Common names and synonyms: Gold Nugget.
See in addition: "Squash," Part II, Section C, Chapter 8.

Golden orange - *see* **KUMQUAT**

GOLDENROD - Native to central and eastern North America, one species of goldenrod (*Solidago odora*) is also known as "blue mountain tea" and "sweet goldenrod" because its fragrant leaves are made into a licorice- or anise-scented tea. The leaves of another species (*S. missouriensis*) were used as food by Native Americans, who ate them raw when young and cooked them as a vegetable.
Common names and synonyms: Blue mountain tea, sweet goldenrod.

Golden timothy (grass) - *see* **MILLET**

Gold Nugget - *see* **GOLDEN NUGGET (SQUASH)**

GOLDTHREAD - A small plant with shiny green leaves, native to both North America and northern Asia, goldthread (*Coptis trifolia*) is named for its long, slender, golden-colored roots. They are bitter but were apparently eaten by natives of the Northern Hemisphere. The roots have also been employed to flavor beer.
Common names and synonyms: Cankerroot, coptis, yellowroot.

Gombaut - *see* **OKRA**

Gombo - *see* **OKRA**

Goober (pea) - *see* **PEANUT**

GOOD-KING-HENRY (*see also* **CHENOPODIUM**) - A member of the goosefoot family, "Good-King-Henry" (*Chenopodium bonus-henricus*) is a Eurasian plant naturalized in North America and was said to be named for King Henry VII of England (reigned 1485-1509). But the truth seems to be that it was first named "Good-Henry" to distinguish it from a weed called "Bad-Henry," and "King" was added later. In England, the plant was also called "fat-hen" because chickens seemed to like it. Remains of the plant (a leafy green vegetable) have been found in Neolithic sites, but it was doubtless gathered by our Paleolithic forebears long before the dawn of agriculture. Good-King-Henry was cultivated as a potherb during the Middle Ages and the beginning of the modern period but afterward returned to the wild state in which it can be found (and gathered) today.
Common names and synonyms: Fat-hen, perennial goosefoot.

Goongoo pea - *see* **PIGEON PEA**

GOOSEBERRY (*see also* **BERRIES**) - The origin of the gooseberry (*Ribes grossularia* = *R. uva-crispa* - of the same genus as currants), and that of its name, is something of a mystery. The one that is cultivated is a Eurasian native that was apparently brought to France by the Normans in the tenth century. There - because it was made into a sauce to go with mackerel - the berry came to be known as *groseille à maquereau* ("currant for mackerel"). The English name is thought to have been the result of using the berry to stuff roasted goose and accompanying the dish with a relish of gooseberries as well. In Scandinavia, Hungary, and Russia, a soup is made with gooseberries. Over the past few centuries, the berry has been tinkered with by European farmers, so that now over 2,000 varieties exist that come in several shapes and sizes, almost all bigger and sweeter than the generally wild gooseberries that grow in the United States.

American gooseberries are apt to be rough and prickly. Although mostly greenish, they also come in shades of white and purple, and they vary in taste from sweet to sour, indicating the wide variety of species that provided Native Americans with food. Among the wild North American gooseberry species consumed by Native Americans were the "orange gooseberry" (*R. pinetorum*) and the "wolf currant" (*R. wolfii*); the latter is still in use in baking and making tart jellies. Where the gooseberry is cultivated in Europe – and now in New Zealand – the tree is often placed against brick or stone walls. In several areas of the United States and Canada, however, growing the fruit is prohibited because it is host to a disease called "white-pine blister-rust," which is deadly to white pine trees.

Common names and synonyms: English gooseberry, European gooseberry, *groseille à maquereau,* old gooseberry, orange gooseberry, wolf currant.

Gooseberry tree - *see* **OTAHEITE GOOSEBERRY**

GOOSEFOOT (*see also* **CHENOPODIUM, GOOD-KING-HENRY, QUINOA**) – The term "goosefoot" actually refers to a number of closely related plants of the genus *Chenopodium* that are also called "lamb's-quarter" and "pigweed." Some of these have arrived in the New World during the past few centuries from Europe, Asia, and elsewhere, but most are native to the Americas. Moreover, because "pigweed" is also a name for some members of genus *Amaranthus,* and "lamb's-quarter" another name for some members of genus *Valerianella,* we quickly sink into semantic quicksand. Goosefoot today is a weed with leaves that are sometimes gathered and eaten as a vegetable. In the pre-Columbian New World, goosefoot leaves were similarly gathered and used, but in Mesoamerica and the Andean region, the grains of another close relative, quinoa, were consumed as a cereal.

Common names and synonyms: Lamb's-quarter, pigweed.

GOOSEGRASS – A number of different grasses are named goosegrass, including several plants of the genus *Galium* (especially *G. aparine* – also called "cleavers" and "catchweed"), along with *Eleusine indica* and *Potentilla anserina,* among many others. The seeds of some were reportedly used for food by Native Americans.

Common names and synonyms: Catchweed, cleavers.

Gorget - *see* **POKEWEED**

Gota kola - *see* **PENNYWORT**

Gourd - *see* **PUMPKIN, SQUASH AND PUMPKIN**

GOVERNOR'S PLUM (*see also* **PLUM**) – Also called the "botoko plum" and "ramontochi," the governor's plum (*Flacourtia indica*) originated in South Asia and grows in tropical Africa but enjoys its greatest popularity in the West Indies. The plum is a small, purple fruit about the size of a large grape. High in vitamin C, governor's plums are regularly cooked and eaten with fish and make an excellent jelly.

Common names and synonyms: Botoko plum, ramontochi.

Gow kee - *see* **MATRIMONY VINE**

Goyave - *see* **GUAVA**

Grains-of-paradise - *see* **MELEGUETA PEPPER**

Gram - *see* **CHICKPEA**

Gram bean - *see* **MUNG BEAN**

Gram pea - *see* **CHICKPEA**

Granada - *see* **POMEGRANATE**

Granadilla - *see* **GIANT GRANADILLA, MAYPOP, PASSION FRUIT**

Granny's-bonnet - *see* **HABANERO AND SCOTCH BONNET PEPPERS**

Grão do bico - *see* **CHICKPEA**

GRAPEFRUIT (*see also* **CITRUS FRUITS**) – A large and tart member of the citrus family, the grapefruit (*Citrus × paradisi*) is so named because it grows in clusters like grapes. Its origins, however, are something of a mystery. All members of the citrus family (lemons, oranges, limes, etc.), save for the grapefruit, are native to Southeast Asia. The grapefruit, it seems, although of Southeast Asian parents, was born in the Americas. It is believed that one of its progenitors – the pomelo (*C. maxima*) – somehow crossed the Indian Ocean and moved about the Middle East, eventually reaching Europe and then sailing off to the West Indies. There, perhaps in the eighteenth century, it may be that either a mutation occurred or the pomelo was crossed with an orange, with the modern grapefruit the result.

But further confusing the picture was the arrival in the Americas around 1800 of a ship commanded by Captain James Shaddock, who brought a cargo of pomelos (or grapefruit), claiming that he had discovered them in the Fiji Islands. Consequently, the grapefruit was subsequently called "shaddock" in America. A variation on the story would have the captain taking the fruits to England, whereupon they were carried by the British to the Caribbean. A third version would have the pomelo reaching Florida, where it was hybridized with orange pollen for sweetness, and the grapefruit came into being. The Ruby Red grapefruit variety was definitely the result of a seed mutation in McAllen, Texas, in 1929. Certainly, the grapefruit has long been one of the most popular citrus fruits in North America, but it was only following World War II that it became a breakfast food in Europe – the result of American influence. Like all citrus fruits, the grapefruit is high in vitamin C.

Common names and synonyms: Marsh grapefruit, Ruby Red, shaddock, Thompson grapefruit, Webb grapefruit.

GRAPE LEAF – Greek and Middle Eastern recipes frequently call for young grape leaves (genus *Vitis*) to be wrapped around meat, rice, and other fillings, making little packages for poaching or steaming. The fresh leaves are generally first steamed or blanched. Grape leaves can also be purchased in cans.

GRAPES (*see also* **RAISIN**) - Botanically, the grape is a berry of any species of *Vitis,* the genus of the vine family that was growing wild over much of the earth long before there were humans about. In North America, the vines evolved toward the species *V. labrusca* - the fox grape, one variety of which is the Concord grape. But practically all of the world's wine comes from varieties of a single Old World species, *V. vinifera* - the vine that bears wine. It is thought to have originated in Asia Minor and, as people early discovered (to their delight) that grapes and their juice ferment, has been cultivated for some 6,000 years.

Perhaps the Egyptians initially exploited the grape on a large scale. New varieties were developed by the Greeks and, later, by the Romans, who first practiced grafting and who introduced the vines into the cooler regions of Europe, including what is now France. Over the centuries, human intervention has given rise to a great number of varieties, such as the Chardonnay, the Pinot Noir, and the Riesling, along with the many different grapes of Bordeaux, Burgundy, and the Rhineland, to name but a very few regions.

Although it is largely because of wine that the grape is one of the most heavily cultivated of all fruit crops, grapes are also eaten as fresh fruit. Until the beginning of the twentieth century, however, table grapes were not marketed but rather were consumed by those who grew them. (The grapes that make the best wine do not necessarily make the best dessert grapes.) Today, California table grapes include the Calmeria, the Christmas Rose, the Emperor, the Exotic, the Flame Seedless, the Perlette, the Red Globe (about the size of a small plum), the Ribier, the Ruby Seedless, the Superior, and the Thompson Seedless.

Table grapes that do not "measure up" to table-grape standards are made into juice and other nonalcoholic beverages. In 1869, "Welch's Grape Juice" was born in Vineland, New Jersey (but later moved to Watkin's Glen, New York), when prohibitionist Thomas Bramwell Welch developed a substitute for the wine used in his church's communion services. Grapes also become jellies and especially raisins, which have doubtless been eaten since humans discovered grapes. California is now the biggest producer of these wrinkly, sun-dried sweetmeats. In some cultures, the seeds of grapes have been consumed as well.

Common names and synonyms: Black grape, California grape, Calmeria, catawba, Christmas Rose, Concord grape, dessert grape, Emperor, European grape, Exotic, Flame Seedless, fox grape, green grape, muscadine, Perlette, Red Globe, Ribier, Ruby Seedless, scuppernong, southern fox grape, Superior grape, table grape, Thompson Seedless, wine grape.
See in addition: "Wine," Part III, Chapter 13.

Grass pea - *see* **CHICKLING VETCH**

Gravek-plant - *see* **TRAILING ARBUTUS**
Gray pea - *see* **PIGEON PEA**
Great angelica - *see* **PURPLESTEM ANGELICA**
Greater yam - *see* **WATER YAM**
Great green plum - *see* **BIG GREEN PLUM**
Grecian laurel - *see* **BAY LEAF**
Green bell pepper - *see* **SWEET PEPPERS**
Greenbriar - *see* **GREENBRIER**
GREENBRIER - A number of plants of the genus *Smilax* are called greenbrier, especially the prickly vine *S. rotundifolia,* found in the eastern United States. Its roots were used by Native Americans for starch, and the shoots were eaten both raw and cooked as a vegetable. Other species in Asia are still in use as food, including their berries. The roots of some American species, such as *S. aristolochiifolia,* provide sarsaparilla.
Common names and synonyms: Bullbrier, catbrier, greenbriar.

Greengage - *see* **PLUM**
Green gram - *see* **MUNG BEAN**
Green haricot - *see* **BEANS**
Green leaf - *see* **AMARANTH**
Green lemon - *see* **LIME**
Green mung bean - *see* **LENTIL(S)**
Green Oriental radish - *see* **DAIKON**
Green pepper - *see* **SWEET PEPPERS**
GREEN SAPOTE - Another of the sapotes, the green sapote (*Calocarpum viride = Pouteria viridis*) grows on a large, tropical, American evergreen tree. The fruits, each containing a single big seed, are ovoid and up to 6 inches long. The inner pulp of the fruit has a rich, sweet, creamy flavor.
Common names and synonyms: Injerto.

Green sloke - *see* **SEAWEED**
Green snap bean - *see* **BEANS**
Green Swiss chard - *see* **SWISS CHARD**
Green tea - *see* **TEA**
Green tomato - *see* **TOMATILLO**
GRENACHE (*see also* **GRAPES**) - There are both red and white Grenache grapes (*Vitis vinifera*), but unless white (Grenache Blanc or Garnacha Blanc) is specified, "Grenache" refers to the red version, Grenache Noir. The grape - the second most important in the world - is grown in Spain (there, it is called Garnacha) and California and is especially popular in the Rhône Valley of France. Grenache grapes have a high level of sugar and consequently can produce wines with a high percentage of alcohol.
Common names and synonyms: Garnacha, Garnacha Blanc, Grenache Blanc, Grenache Noir.
See in addition: "Wine," Part III, Chapter 13.

Grenache Blanc - *see* **GRENACHE**
Grenache Noir - *see* **GRENACHE**
Grenade - *see* **POMEGRANATE**
Grenadine - *see* **POMEGRANATE**
Groseille à maquereau - *see* **GOOSEBERRY**
Grosella - *see* **OTAHEITE GOOSEBERRY**
Ground bean - *see* **HAUSA GROUNDNUT**

Groundcherry – *see* **CAPE GOOSEBERRY**

GROUND IVY – Also called "gill-over-the-ground," ground ivy (*Glechoma hederacea*) is a Eurasian native. A creeping or trailing aromatic plant with small purple flowers, it has been used as a potherb and for making tisanes.

Common names and synonyms: Gill-over-the-ground.

Groundnut – *see* **APIOS, BAMBARA GROUND-NUT, HAUSA GROUNDNUT, PEANUT**

Ground pea – *see* **BAMBARA GROUNDNUT**

GRUMICHAMA – A Brazilian shrub, now grown in the West Indies and South Florida, the grumichama (*Eugenia dombeyi = E. brasiliensis*) has a very pleasant-tasting, purple-black fruit about the size and flavor of a cherry.

Gruya – *see* **ACHIRA**

Guaba – *see* **ICE-CREAM BEAN**

Guacimo – *see* **MUTAMBA**

Guaje – *see* **LEUCAENA**

GUAJILLO AND PULLA CHILLIES (*see also* **CHLLI PEPPERS**) – These two closely related chillies (*Capsicum annuum*) are very common in Mexico. Both grow to upward of 6 inches in length, are orange red in color, are tapered like an Anaheim, and are generally dried. The difference is mostly in the heat they produce. The *guajillo* is a relatively mild chilli that goes well in salsas and makes a fine chilli sauce. The *pulla* is used in the same ways but adds substantially more "fire" to dishes. Another relative, the *costeño,* is roughly the same color and also dried but is only about half as long and is even hotter than the *pulla.*

Common names and synonyms: Costeño.

See in addition: "Chilli Peppers," Part II, Section C, Chapter 4.

Guajilote – *see* **CUAJILOTE**

Guama – *see* **ICE-CREAM BEAN**

Guamochil – *see* **PITHECELLOBIUM**

Guanabana – *see* **SOURSOP**

GUAR (*see also* **LEGUMES**) – Also called "cluster-bean" because of the way its pods cluster together, the guar (*Cyamopsis tetragonolobus*) is a native of India. This drought-tolerant legume has long been cultivated there for use in vegetarian cooking. Its small, hairy pods, which resemble soybeans, are picked when very young for human consumption. The rest are employed for fodder or for their seeds, which contain a gum used as a thickening agent.

Common names and synonyms: Clusterbean, *Gwaar ki phalli.*

GUARANÁ – A Brazilian climbing shrub that yields seeds from which a dried paste is made, guaraná (*Paullinia cupana*) contains much caffeine and tannin. The paste is employed medicinally, but the most important use of guaraná is as a base for the guaraná beverage, which is an enormously popular soft drink in Brazil.

Guasima – *see* **MUTAMBA**

GUAVA (*see also* **FEIJOA, ICE-CREAM BEAN, STRAWBERRY GUAVA, WILD GUAVA**) – Easily identified by an intense tropical aroma, the guava (*Psidium guajava*) is native to Brazil and possibly the Caribbean region. Today, however, its many varieties are commercially produced in Hawaii, Australia, India, Colombia, Venezuela, Mexico, South Africa, and Southeast Asia. There are also guava groves in Florida and California. The guava is highly vulnerable to fruit-fly infestation and therefore is rarely a welcome import. The fruit is usually pear shaped but sometimes round, ranges in size from that of a small egg to that of a large orange, and can taste either sweet or sour. The skin is almost always yellow green or pale yellow, and the meaty flesh runs from white to yellow or from pinkish to red. Guavas are eaten whole, sliced into salads, and made into guava paste or jelly for spreading on bread and crackers; they are also employed to make syrup and vinegar and are even boiled down to become "guava cheese." Guavas are rich in vitamin A, the B complex, and vitamin C.

Common names and synonyms: Brazilian guava, common guava, goyave, *guayaba,* Guinea guava, guyaba, lemon guava, montain guava, purple guava, *waiawi-'ula'ula.*

Guava machete – *see* **ICE-CREAM BEAN**

Guavo-bejuco – *see* **ICE-CREAM BEAN**

Guayaba – *see* **GUAVA**

Gucil – *see* **BUSH CURRANT**

Güero – *see* **WAX PEPPERS**

Guiana chestnut – *see* **MALABAR NUT**

Guigne – *see* **CHERRY**

GUINEA ARROWROOT – This perennial (*Calathea allouia*) has been cultivated by indigenous farmers in its tropical American habitat for more than a millennium. In Brazilian Amazonia, the plant held an important place in the diet and culture of native peoples until as recently as the 1950s. Increasingly, however, it has been abandoned by its traditional growers in favor of other crops or food products from industrialized regions. The Guinea arrowroot, also known as "sweet-corm-root" or "leren" (and *lerenes* in Puerto Rico), has several relatively large leaves (2 to 4 feet long) and white flowers aboveground, but it is cultivated for its tubers, which (like the potatoes they resemble) grow underground.

These roots are a rich source of many essential amino acids and are valued for their texture (which remains crisp even after cooking) and for their flavor (said to resemble that of green maize). Now grown throughout many parts of the world, including various countries in South America, Africa, and Asia, and particularly in Puerto Rico and other Caribbean islands, the Guinea arrowroot enhances numerous salads, stews, and fish dishes.

Common names and synonyms: Allouya, leren, *lerenes,*
  llerén, llerenes, sweet-corm-root, *topee-tambu.*

Guinea corn - *see* **MAIZE, SORGHUM**

Guinea grains - *see* **MELEGUETA PEPPER**

Guinea squash - *see* **EGGPLANT**

Guinea yam - *see* **WHITE YAM, YELLOW YAM**

Guine pepper - *see* **CAYENNE PEPPER**

Güiro - *see* **XICALLI**

Guispui - *see* **CHAYOTE**

Gulfweed - *see* **SEAWEED**

Gully bean - *see* **EGGPLANT**

Gum arabic - *see* **ACACIA**

Gumbo - *see* **OKRA**

GUM PLANT (*see also* **YERBA SANTA**) - Also known
  as "gumweed," the gum plant (*Grindelia robusta* or
  G. squarrosa) is found in western North America. It
  grows to about 18 inches in height, and its name
  derives from a resinous substance that covers the
  entire plant. Native Americans made tea from its
  leaves, which they also chewed.

  Common names and synonyms: Gumweed.

Gum tree - *see* **MANNA GUM**

Gumweed - *see* **GUM PLANT**

Gungo pea - *see* **PIGEON PEA**

Gunpowder - *see* **TEA**

Guyaba - *see* **GUAVA**

Guyana chestnut - *see* **MALABAR NUT**

Gwaar ki phalli - *see* **GUAR**

**HABANERO AND SCOTCH BON-
NET PEPPERS** (*see also* **CHILLI
PEPPERS**) - The name habanero
implies that the first of these small,
lantern-shaped chillies (they look like
miniature, collapsed bell peppers) is a
native of Havana, which seems to be
contradicted both by its scientific name *Capsicum
chinense* (most chilli peppers are *C. annuum*) and by
the fact that it is most extensively cultivated and consumed in Central America and the Yucatán. It is
slightly larger than its very close relative the Scotch
Bonnet (it does look a bit like one), which is grown
mostly on Jamaica and other Caribbean islands, and
with which it is regularly confused. The confusion is
eminently understandable because they do resemble
each other, in their colors (red, green, orange, and yellow) and because they hold the distinction of being
the hottest domesticated peppers in the world.

In a very close second place, however, are two
other relatives. One is the Jamaican hot pepper,
which is always a bright red but is similar in shape
to both the habanero and the Scotch Bonnet. The
other is the Rocotillo (sometimes called rocoto or
squash pepper because of a resemblance to pattypan squash), a South American chilli that ranges
from red to pale yellow in color and is a frequent
addition to ceviches.

A major use of these peppers (save for the
Rocotillo) is in commercially prepared hot sauces
(now available in astounding variety), with the
Scotch Bonnet prevailing in Jamaican jerk sauces
and the Jamaican hot pepper foremost in
Caribbean chutneys and curries. Habaneros and
Scotch Bonnets are also much used in the preparation of numerous dishes as well as sauces in Central and South America and in West Africa, where, as
in the Caribbean, they are greatly appreciated.

Common names and synonyms: Bonnet pepper,
  Granny's-bonnet, Jamaican hot pepper, Jamaican
  Red, Rocotillo, rocoto, squash pepper.

See in addition: "Chilli Peppers," Part II, Section C,
  Chapter 4.

Habichuela - *see* **HYACINTH BEAN**

Hachiya - *see* **PERSIMMON**

HACKBERRY (*see also* **BERRIES**) - The genus *Celtis*
  encompasses a number of trees and shrubs that
  have a berry-like, often edible fruit that is sometimes called a "sugarberry." The hackberry was an
  important food gathered in late fall and early winter by Native Americans for thousands of years. As
  with the American persimmon, the berries are best
  after the first frost. Hackberry seeds have also
  served as a food.

  Common names and synonyms: Sugarberry.

Hakusai - *see* **CHINESE CABBAGE**

HAMBURG PARSLEY (*see also* **PARSLEY**) - Popular
  in central Europe, Hamburg parsley (*Petroselinum
  crispum* var. *tuberosum*) is a variety of parsley cultivated not for its leaves but for its edible root,
  which resembles a small parsnip. It has a strong
  taste that is appreciated in stews.

HANOVER KALE (*see also* **CABBAGE, KALE**) -
  Another member of the cabbage family, Hanover
  kale (*Brassica napus*) has leaves similar to those of
  spinach. They are used in salads and cooked as a
  vegetable.

  Common names and synonyms: Hanover salad,
    spring kale.

  See in addition: "Cruciferous and Green Leafy Vegeta-
    bles," Part II, Section C, Chapter 5.

Harebell - *see* **CAMPANULA**

Haricot - *see* **BEANS**

Haricot riz - *see* **RICE BEAN**

Harlock - *see* **BURDOCK**

Haselnuss - *see* **HAZELNUT AND FILBERT**

Hass - *see* **AVOCADO**

HAUSA GROUNDNUT - Also called "ground bean"
  and "Kersting's groundnut," the Hausa groundnut
  (*Kerstingiella geocarpa* = *Macrotyloma geocarpa*) is an herb cultivated in the drier portions
  of western Africa from Senegal to Nigeria. It produces pods that contain from 1 to 3 kidney-shaped
  seeds. The seeds are high in protein, and the leaves
  are also cooked as a vegetable. The Hausa groundnut is very similar to the more wide-ranging bambara groundnut.

Common names and synonyms: Ground bean, groundnut, Kersting's groundnut.

Hausa potato - *see* **KAFFIR POTATO, SUDAN POTATO**

Hautbois - *see* **WILD STRAWBERRY**

HAW (*see also* **BERRIES, BLACK HAW, HAWTHORN BERRY, SLOE**) - The reddish fruit of the hawthorn (genus *Crataegus*) is known as a haw. But in the United States the term has signified the bluish black, plumlike fruit of the blackthorn (*Prunus spinosa,* a Eurasian shrub) as well; this fruit is also called "sloe" and is used to flavor sloe gin. And the semantic confusion goes even further because the fruit of one of the hawthorns of southeastern North America (*C. uniflora*) is called both a "pear haw" and a "blackthorn." Haws were well utilized by Native Americans, who ate them raw and also dried them to make pemmican. The leaves of some species were eaten as well.

Common names and synonyms: Blackthorn, pear haw, sloe, stagbush.

Hawaiian Kona coffee - *see* **COFFEE**

HAWAIIAN PLANTAIN (*see also* **PLANTAIN**) - Perhaps better known as *hua moa,* the Hawaiian plantain (*Musa* × *sapientum*) is a common plantain of many Pacific Islands. In 1960, William F. Whitman brought the plant to the United States from Tahiti, and it has since found a comfortable niche in southern Florida and special favor with Cuban-Americans. The fruit is shorter but much thicker than the usual plantains and often looks as if two bananas were enveloped by the same skin. It is used like other plantains for frying and cooking in the unripe state but is also eaten out of hand when ripe.

Common names and synonyms: Hua moa.

See in addition: "Bananas and Plantains," Part II, Section B, Chapter 1.

Hawthorn - *see* **BLACK HAW, HAWTHORN BERRY**

HAWTHORN BERRY (*see also* **BERRIES**) - The genus *Crataegus* is comprised of a great number of thorny shrubs and trees that bear a reddish fruit called a haw. In England, the white to pink blossoms of the hawthorn, which appear in May, inspired the name of the ship *Mayflower.* The berry is actually a small pome fruit with a high sugar content. In the United States, those hawthorns that still have fruit in the winter help to sustain wildlife until spring. This "winter fruit" did the same for Native Americans.

Common names and synonyms: Cockspur thorn, downy haw, haw, hawthorn, haw tree (archaic), mayhaw, red haw, scarlet haw.

Haw tree - *see* **HAWTHORN BERRY**

HAZELNUT AND FILBERT - The term "hazelnut" has been used so interchangeably with "filbert" that the two are sometimes listed as synonymous in dictionaries - and no wonder, because they appear as practically identical, have the same sweet taste, and grow on shrubs or trees that are members of the birch family. But despite the German word *Haselnuss,* filberts come from Eurasian plants (*Corylus avellana,* the European filbert, and *C. maxima,* the giant filbert), whereas the hazelnut comes from an American shrub (*C. americana*). To add to the confusion, "hazelnut" (instead of "filbert") was apparently the name first given to this acorn-like nut in Europe because of its medium brown color (for example, the French word *noisette* means both the nut and the color). The name was later changed to filbert because St. Philbert's day falls on August 22, the day the nuts are supposedly finally ripe in France. The American hazelnut is found mostly in the eastern United States. In the Pacific states, imported filbert trees are cultivated. But, most of North America's hazelnuts are actually filberts imported from Turkey. For those who would dwell on the differences between hazelnuts and filberts, another has to do with the outer husks - those of hazelnuts are shorter, whereas the filbert husk extends beyond the nut. Like all nuts, hazelnuts and filberts alike provide some selenium, calcium, and iron, are rich in folacin, and supply vitamin E and the B complex.

Common names and synonyms: American hazelnut, beaked hazel, Chinese filbert, Chinese hazel, Chinese hazelnut, cob, cobnut, curri, European filbert, European hazel, giant filbert, *Haselnuss,* Himalayan hazel, Lambert's filbert, *noisette,* Siberian hazel, Tibetan filbert, Tibetan hazelnut, Turkish filbert, Turkish hazel.

Heartnut - *see* **WALNUT**

HEART(S) OF PALM - There are thousands of palm species in the world's tropics, all with edible "hearts," of which perhaps 100 have hearts large enough to be commercially valuable. In the United States the hearts have in the past often meant the terminal buds of the palmetto, a small palm (*Sabal palmetto* - called the "cabbage palm") that grows in Florida. More recently, the hearts have been the buds of South American (and especially Brazilian) members of the families Palmae and Arecaceae. The whole heart can weigh some 2 to 3 pounds and may be cut up and fried or boiled, as was the case in old Florida, where the vegetable was called "swamp cabbage." Most palm hearts today, however, are stripped of their tough husk, cut into small cylinders, and canned for use in salads or as a snack or appetizer served with a sauce. They have a delicate, asparagus-like flavor. Fortunately, the palms grow prolifically, because removing the heart kills the tree.

Common names and synonyms: Cabbage palm, palmetto, palm heart(s), swamp cabbage.

Heart snakeroot - *see* **WILD GINGER**

Heath - *see* **HEATHER**

HEATHER - Eurasian heather consists of *Calluna vulgaris* and several related plants of the genus *Erica.* Also called ling, heather grows in dense masses, with clusters of pink and purplish flowers. Heather ale - a traditional Scottish beverage - is made from the blossoms. In the southwest of North America, Native Americans have used the berries of the heather "manzanita" (*Arctostaphylos uva-ursi* - also called bearberry) for food and for making a beverage.

Common names and synonyms: Bearberry, heath, ling, pointleaf manzanita.

Heath pea - *see* **EARTH NUT**

Hedged gourd - *see* **KIWANO**

Hedge garlic - *see* **GARLIC-MUSTARD**

HEMLOCK - The soft inner bark of a few species of the evergreen trees of the genus *Tsuga* was used as food by Native Americans. That of western hemlock (*T. heterophylla*) and mountain hemlock (*T. mertensiana*) was shaped into loaves for baking. The bark of the eastern hemlock (*T. canadensis*) was also eaten, and its leaves were used to make a tea.

Common names and synonyms: Eastern hemlock, mountain hemlock, western hemlock.

HEMP DOGBANE - An American native that grows as a weed throughout the United States, hemp dogbane (*Apocynum cannabinum* - also known as Indian hemp) - has a rootstock that has long been used for medicinal purposes. The plant's leaves are poisonous, but its seeds were employed as food by Native Americans.

Common names and synonyms: Black hemp, black Indian hemp, Choctaw-root, dogbane, Indian hemp.

HEMP SEED - The seeds of hemp (*Cannabis sativa*), an Asiatic herb, yield a fatty oil that is used in cooking, mostly in Asia. The seeds have been cultivated for thousands of years and were often roasted for consumption. This plant that we know as marijuana has also long been a source of fiber for rope making.

Hemp tree - *see* **CHASTE TREE**

HERB BENNET - Also called the "blessed herb" and "avens," the herb bennet (*Geum urbanum*) is a European plant with yellow flowers and an odor of cloves. It has been grown or gathered as a potherb and has long been used to make a tea.

Common names and synonyms: Avens, blessed herb.

Herb-of-grace - *see* **RUE**

Hicaco - *see* **COCOPLUM**

HICKORY (*see also* **PECAN**) - Hickories (of the genus *Carya*) are American members of the walnut family that produce edible nuts. The only commercially important one of these nuts is the pecan (treated in a separate entry). Hickories are widespread throughout eastern and central North America and yield an incredible variety of nuts, the most abundant and popular of which come from the shagbark hickory (*C. ovata*).

Historically, these have been divided into thick-shell shagbarks and thin-shell shagbarks, with the latter nuts considered the most desirable because their meat is more easily obtainable. Native Americans of central and eastern North America made hickory nuts a regular part of their diet. Hickory nuts have a sweet flavor and are much used in baking. Chunks and chips of hickory wood are used to flavor barbecued and smoked meats. Hickory nuts provide calcium, potassium, iron, vitamin E, and the vitamins of the B complex.

Common names and synonyms: Shagbark, thick-shell shagbark, thin-shell shagbark.

HIGHBUSH CRANBERRY - A North American shrub, the highbush cranberry (*Viburnum trilobum*) has scarlet berries that are often mistakenly called "cranberries" and are used as a cranberry substitute in sauces. They were employed by Native Americans as a medicine and in stews, as well as for making teas and pemmican. The berries are low in calories and high in vitamin C and potassium.

Common names and synonyms: Cramp bark, cranberry bush, squaw bush, viburnum.

Higüero - *see* **XICALLI**

Hijiki - *see* **SEAWEED**

HINAU BERRY - The hinau (*Elaeocarpus dentatus*) is a New Zealand timber tree that produces an edible berry. The latter was one of the many gathered foods that sustained the Maori - the aboriginal people of New Zealand.

Hing - *see* **ASAFETIDA**

Hoarhound - *see* **HOREHOUND**

HOG PEANUT - Also called the wild peanut, the hog peanut (*Amphicarpaea bracteata*), a native of central North America, is a brown, edible seed. It comes in an underground pod, resembles a peanut, and is much appreciated by hogs. However, long before hogs arrived to root for these subterranean fruits, hog peanuts were being dug by Native Americans, for whom they were an important dietary item.

Common names and synonyms: Wild peanut.

HOG PLUM (*see also* **PLUM**) - Quite a few fruits go by the name of "hog plum." One is *Spondias pinnata*, a Malayan fruit also called *amra*. It is not much appreciated as it is said to smell of rotting apples. More popular in that part of the world is the "great hog plum" (*S. cytherea*), also known as *kĕdondong*, which has an oblong fruit that is yellow with whitish flesh when ripe. These fruits are eaten raw and stewed and also made into a jam or chutney. Other *Spondias* plants, such as *S. mombin* (the "yellow mombin") and *S. purpurea* (variously named "Spanish plum," "Jamaican plum," and "red mombin"), have edible fruits that resemble plum-sized mangoes and are called "hog plum" by some. In the United States, *Prunus americana* grows wild in its native Florida and South Carolina. Sometimes called a hog plum, it, too, is a small, oval-shaped fruit, which is generally made into jams and jellies.

Common names and synonyms: Amra, great hog plum, Jamaican plum, *kĕdondong,* red mombin, Spanish plum, yellow mombin.

Hog salad – *see* **CORNSALAD**
Hogweed – *see* **HORSEWEED**
Hoka – *see* **KABOCHA (SQUASH)**
Hokkaido – *see* **BUTTERCUP SQUASH**
Holland chilli – *see* **DUTCH RED PEPPER**
HOLLAND GREENS (*see also* **CABBAGE**) – Also known as "tyfon," Holland greens (*Brassica rapa* 'tyfon') are the greens of a new plant – a cross between the Chinese cabbage and the turnip. The new plant is tolerant of cold, grows vigorously, and is reluctant to bolt. Holland greens are used in the same fashion as turnip greens or mustard greens or collards – in salads and as a cooked vegetable.
Common names and synonyms: Tyfon.
See in addition: "Cruciferous and Green Leafy Vegetables," Part II, Section C, Chapter 5.
Holland pepper – *see* **SWEET PEPPERS**
Holly – *see* **DAHOON HOLLY, HOLLYBERRY, YAUPON, YERBA MATÉ**
HOLLYBERRY (*see also* **BERRIES**) – There are numerous trees and shrubs that we call holly, have bright red berries, and belong to the genus *Ilex*. Two are especially worthy of culinary comment. One is the American holly (*I. opaca*), native to the eastern United States, the berries of which yield an edible pulp that helped Native Americans with their vitamin C intake. The other is *I. paraguariensis,* native to Paraguay and Brazil in South America; its berries and leaves are employed to make yerba maté tea.
Common names and synonyms: American holly.
Holly-leaved barberry – *see* **BARBERRY**
Holly-leaved cherry – *see* **CHIMAJA**
Ho loan – *see* **SUGAR PEA**
HONEWORT – There are two related plants called honewort. One is *Cryptotaenia canadensis,* a native of North America; the other is a native of Japan – Japanese honewort (*C. japonica*), which is also called *mitsuba*. They are members of the carrot family, and the roots are often boiled and served with oil. The greens (which resemble flat Italian parsley) and stems have a distinctive flavor and are used as garnishes, eaten raw in salads, added to soups, and cooked as a vegetable. The Japanese variety is grown commercially in California for Japanese-Americans.
Common names and synonyms: Japanese honewort, Japanese parsley, *mitsuba*.
Honeyberry – *see* **SPANISH LIME**
HONEYDEW (MELON) (*see also* **MELONS**) – A winter melon (*Cucumis melo*), the honeydew has the advantage of keeping well for up to a month. As a consequence, these melons – about the size of large muskmelons, with a whitish rind and pale green flesh – are ubiquitous in produce markets.
Common names and synonyms: Winter melon.
See in addition: "Cucumbers, Melons, and Watermelons," Part II, Section C, Chapter 6.

HONEY LOCUST – A tall, usually spiny tree of eastern North America, the honey locust (*Gleditsia triacanthos*) bears long, twisted pods that resemble beans. These were cooked and eaten by Native Americans, even though they are reported to be mildly toxic. Because the pods have a sweetish pulp surrounding the seeds, the tree is also known as sweet bean, sweet locust, and honeyshuck.
Common names and synonyms: Honeyshuck, sweet bean, sweet locust.
Honey mushroom – *see* **MUSHROOMS AND FUNGI**
Honeyshuck – *see* **HONEY LOCUST**
HONEYSUCKLE – There are a number of species of the genus *Lonicera* – called honeysuckle – spread about the globe, and some are or have been used as food. Others, however, are toxic and can even cause death. Probably the edible ones have been consumed since the early days of the hunter-gatherers because they are sweet, whereas many (but not all) of the poisonous species are bitter. Native Americans enjoyed the sweetness of a few species, and in Japan, the young leaves of *L. japonica* (the Japanese honeysuckle) are still used as a vegetable.
Common names and synonyms: Japanese honeysuckle.
Honey tree – *see* **JAPANESE RAISIN TREE**
Hoofs – *see* **COLTSFOOT**
Hoogly – *see* **UGLI FRUIT**
HOP(S) – There are several twining vines of the genus *Humulus* – especially *H. lupulus*, a Eurasian-American vine – that have green, cone-like flowers. When dried, the flowers yield a bitter, aromatic oil used in brewing beer. Hop plants have been cultivated in Germany for about 1,000 years and were once used to prevent beer from spoiling. Hops also put out shoots in the spring that can be gathered and cooked and eaten like asparagus. Doubtless they were consumed by hunter-gatherers in Eurasia, as well as by Native Americans in the Western Hemisphere.
Common names and synonyms: Hop plant.
See also: "Beer and Ale," Part III, Chapter 1.
Hop plant – *see* **HOP(S)**
HOPTREE – A tall shrub of eastern North America, the hoptree (*Ptelea trifoliata*) is so called because its bitter fruits have been used as a substitute for hops in flavoring beer. Native Americans also ground them for use as a condiment, and after malaria was imported from Europe and Africa, the bark of the hoptree's roots was sometimes used like quinine against the disease.
Common names and synonyms: Ague bark, waferash.
HOREHOUND – The bitter extract of horehound (*Marrubium vulgare*) comes from an aromatic plant of the mint family. It is an Old World native now naturalized in North America. Horehound is used in candies, cordials, and cough medicines and has been culti-

vated since antiquity for other medicinal uses. It is also said to have been employed as a condiment.

Common names and synonyms: Hoarhound.

Horned melon - *see* **KIWANO**

Horse balm - *see* **HORSEWEED**

Horsebean - *see* **FAVA BEAN, JACKBEAN**

Horse chestnut - *see* **BUCKEYE**

Horsefoot - *see* **COLTSFOOT**

Horse grain - *see* **HORSE GRAM**

HORSE GRAM - Also called "horse grain" and "bonavist bean," the horse gram (*Dolichos biflorus*) is a native of the Old World tropics (probably India) that grows on a twining herb. The plant is generally cultivated for fodder in Asia, but its immature seeds are also used as food for humans.

Common names and synonyms: Bonavist bean, horse grain.

See also: "Beans, Peas, and Lentils," Part II, Section C, Chapter 3.

HORSE MANGO - Growing on a tree native to southern Asia that is some 70 feet in height, the horse mango (*Mangifera foetida*), reaches about 5 inches in length and about 3 inches in diameter. It is yellowish green when ripe and has a bright orange to yellow flesh. Unripe, the fruit contains a sap that irritates the skin and is not safe to eat. Even ripe the horse mango has a bad smell and consequently is seldom eaten raw. Instead, it is used in curries and made into chutney.

Common names and synonyms: Bachang.

Horsemint - *see* **BEE BALM, BERGAMOT**

HORSERADISH (*see also* **CABBAGE**) - A member of the cabbage family and a relative of the radish, horseradish (*Armoracia rusticana* = *A. lapathifolia*) is sometimes called "German mustard," perhaps because its strong, biting flavor derives from mustard oils that are released when the tissue of the root is cut. The latter is thick, white, and cylindrical, with a thin, brown skin, and is safe to eat even though the leaves and stems of the plant are said to contain a toxic substance.

Horseradish is native to southeastern Europe and western Asia (where it continues to grow wild) but is cultivated in most other parts of the world and has been naturalized in the northeastern United States and southern Canada. Traditionally, the root was peeled and grated in the home and served on the side with meats such as boiled beef. But grated horseradish became a commercial product in the first part of the nineteenth century. It was preserved in vinegar and bottled initially in brown bottles to disguise the turnip filler that was often included. In 1869, however, H. J. Heinz began his business at Sharpsburg, Pennsylvania, by packing processed horseradish in clear bottles.

Today, horseradish is generally bottled in combination with vinegar and salt, blended into a cream sauce, or mixed with mustard to become Creole mustard. Horseradish vinegar and horseradish powder are also horseradish products, as is red horseradish, which has had beet juice added to it. Horseradish is a good source of vitamin C.

Common names and synonyms: Creole mustard, German mustard, horse-reddish root (archaic), red horseradish.

See in addition: "Spices and Flavorings," Part II, Section F, Chapter 1.

Horseradish tree - *see* **BENOIL TREE**

HORSETAIL PLANT - Any of the various plants of the genus *Equisetum* are called horsetail. The field horsetail (*E. arvense*) of the United States and Canada produces brownish shoots that have been used medicinally, eaten as a vegetable, and made into tea. The plant also grows in Eurasia, where it long ago provided food for hunter-gatherers.

Common names and synonyms: Field horsetail.

HORSEWEED - Also called horse balm, butterweed, hogweed, mare's-tail, erigeron, and a host of other names, horseweed (*Erigeron canadensis* = *Conyza canadensis*) is a common herb found throughout North America. The boiled young seedlings served as food for Native Americans, and the plants were introduced in Japan, where they are still reportedly consumed. In addition, erigeron oil, which is used medicinally, is distilled from the plants.

Common names and synonyms: Butterweed, erigeron, hogweed, horse balm, mare's-tail.

Hot red pepper - *see* **CAYENNE PEPPER**

Huachinango - *see* **JALAPEÑO**

Hua moa - *see* **HAWAIIAN PLANTAIN**

Huautli - *see* **AMARANTH**

Huauzontle - *see* **QUINOA**

HUBBARD SQUASH (*see also* **SQUASH AND PUMPKIN**) - As old - as well as old-fashioned - squashes, the large Hubbards (*Cucurbita maxima*) are less popular today than in the past because they are indeed large, reaching 30 pounds or more, which frequently makes it necessary to sell them in pieces. The big Hubbards come in blue, orange, and green hues and generally have a wart-covered skin that can resist anything short of an axe in an attempt to carve them. Fortunately, there are now smaller Hubbards, such as the Baby Blue and Golden varieties, that come in a 5- to 15-pound range and are much easier to manage. Their flesh is a brilliant orange and has a superior taste.

Common names and synonyms: Baby Blue Hubbard, Golden Hubbard.

See in addition: "Squash," Part II, Section C, Chapter 8.

HUCKLEBERRY (*see also* **BERRIES**) - Any of a number of shrubs of the genus *Gaylussacia* bear huckleberries. They are American natives that traveled early to Europe. These blackish berries are often confused with blueberries (to which they are related) and are a great favorite of wildlife as well as humans, although they are not as sweet as blueberries. One of the many berries that were regular items in the diet of Native Americans, this berry also lent its name to the famous lad of literature, Huckleberry Finn. At one time, huckleberries were a staple food for Scottish Highlanders, who made them into – among other things – a wine. Huckleberries have become increasingly less popular with the commercial success of blueberries.

Common names and synonyms: Black huckleberry, common huckleberry, hurtleberry, whortleberry.

Hue – *see* **BOTTLE GOURD**

Huesito – *see* **ACEROLA**

HUITLACOCHE (*see also* **MUSHROOMS AND FUNGI**) – A maize-smut fungus, huitlacoche (*Ustilago maydis*) grows on cornstalks. It is a favorite in Mexico, where it can be found in restaurants and grocery stores, if only briefly during the summer. Huitlacoche is used in the same ways that mushrooms are used.

Common names and synonyms: Mexican corn fungus.

See in addition: "Fungi," Part II, Section C, Chapter 7.

HUNGARIAN CHERRY PEPPER (*see also* **CHILLI PEPPERS**) – A red and round pepper often encountered at salad bars, the Hungarian cherry pepper (*Capsicum annuum* L.) has numerous seeds and is generally sweet, although some can have a bit of a bite. The original area of domestication was probably Mexico, but these chillies are now distributed across the globe and are grown chiefly in California and eastern Europe, especially Hungary. Cherry peppers are often pickled and sold in jars. They are also dried to a mahogany color and used to flavor simmered dishes and to make sauces.

Common names and synonyms: Cherry pepper.

See in addition: "Chilli Peppers," Part II, Section C, Chapter 4.

Hungarian grass – *see* **MILLET**

Hungarian sweet chilli – *see* **SWEET PEPPERS**

Hungarian wax pepper – *see* **WAX PEPPERS**

Hungarian yellow wax pepper – *see* **WAX PEPPERS**

Hungry rice – *see* **FONIO**

Hurtleberry – *see* **HUCKLEBERRY**

Husk tomato – *see* **TOMATILLO**

HYACINTH BEAN (*see also* **BEANS**) – Also known as the "lablab bean," "Egyptian bean," and *habichuela*, the hyacinth bean (*Lablab niger* = *L. purpureus*) probably originated in tropical Asia but was introduced in tropical Africa about a thousand years ago and spread with the slave trade to the West Indies and Central and South America. The seeds are generally available in cans as well as fresh and dried forms. The immature pods, along with the young leaves, are cooked as a vegetable and contain much in the way of vitamin C.

Common names and synonyms: Egyptian bean, *habichuela*, lablab bean.

See in addition: "Beans, Peas, and Lentils," Part II, Section C, Chapter 3.

HYPTIS – There are several species of the genus *Hyptis,* the seeds of which were used as food by Native Americans and in some instances are still in use. One (*H. suaveolens*), a native of southern Mexico and Central America, is called "chan" or "wild spikenard"; its seeds, rich in linoleic acid, fed pre-Columbian peoples of the region. Two others, both called "desert lavender," are *H. albida* and *H. emoryi.* The former is a Mexican plant with leaves that are still used for flavoring foods. The latter, of the desert Southwest, provided seeds that were eaten whole, roasted, and ground into a meal. In addition, its minty leaves were used to make a tea.

Common names and synonyms: Chan, desert lavender.

Hyson – *see* **TEA**

HYSSOP – A venerable herb, native to the Mediterranean region and a member of the mint family, hyssop (*Hyssopus officinalis*) was employed by the ancient Greeks for medicinal purposes and is mentioned several times in the Bible (although some scholars believe that the "hyssop" of the Bible was not *H. officinalis*). The Arabs used it, and in the European Middle Ages hyssop was employed as a potherb. Its fresh leaves are aromatic, with a somewhat bitter taste, and are added to salads and pasta dishes. The dried leaves go well in soups and stews and are used in tisanes ("hyssop tea"). The purple hyssop flowers are also added to green salads, and hyssop oil flavors liqueurs such as the chartreuse and absinthe of France.

Common names and synonyms: Hyssop tea.

Hyssop tea – *see* **HYSSOP**

Hyuga – *see* **KABOCHA (SQUASH)**

I

Ibope – *see* **ALGARROBO**

Icaco – *see* **COCOPLUM**

Icaco plum – *see* **COCOPLUM**

ICE-CREAM BEAN – The ice-cream bean (*Inga vera*) apparently originated in Hispaniola, Jamaica, and Puerto Rico but has since joined *I. edulis* and other *Inga* species in Central and South America. The "beans" grow on evergreen trees that reach up to 60 feet in height and are widely used to shade coffee and cacao trees. The fruit is a hairy brown pod between 4 and 6 inches long that embraces a whitish pulp and several brown seeds. The pulp is eaten out of hand and used to flavor various desserts. In addition, Colombian Indians use the fruit to make *cachiri,* an alcoholic beverage. The blossoms are exceptionally rich in nectar and serve as a magnet for bees, thereby lending themselves to honey production.

Common names and synonyms: Cachira, guaba, guama, guava machete, guavo-bejuco.

Iceland lichen – *see* **ICELAND MOSS**

ICELAND MOSS - An edible lichen, Iceland moss (*Cetraria islandica*) is, as the name implies, found in northerly regions, frequently on heather moors. Its somewhat erect, reddish brown thallus lobes are boiled and dried before being ground into powder for use in baking.
Common names and synonyms: Iceland lichen, Island moss.

ICE PLANT - With a name like ice plant, it seems incongruous that this vegetable (*Mesembryanthemum crystallinum*) is a native of southern Africa and member of a family of some 600 species that are also mostly centered in that region. The name, however, has to do with its edible leaves, which are fleshy and seem to glint like ice crystals in the sunlight. They are cooked and eaten much like spinach.

Igope - *see* **ALGARROBO**

ILAMA - Another member of the family Annonaceae, the ilama (*Annona diversifolia*) is a fruit tree that grows on the Pacific slopes from Mexico to El Salvador but is most common in southwestern Guatemala. The fruit has a thin skin, which encloses flesh of a white to reddish color, and has the characteristically delicious, sweet flavor of the other "custard apples." Some find it better than the cherimoya; others think it inferior. The ilama is not, however, cultivated commercially on a large scale and is grown mostly by local peoples for their own consumption. Ilamas are eaten fresh and used as an ingredient in ice cream.
Common names and synonyms: Anona blanca.

IMBÉ - The trees of the imbé (*Garcinia livingstonei*) are grown mostly as ornamentals outside of their native habitat in East Africa. They are cultivated for fruit in Florida, but not commercially. The leaves are up to 6 inches in length and a glossy dark green; the fruits, which are yellow to orange in hue, are shaped somewhat like miniature apples and measure approximately 2 inches in diameter. They have a large seed covered by a small amount of juicy flesh and a thin, tender skin. The taste is pleasant but relatively tart, and imbé juice is noted for creating lasting stains. Most are eaten fresh, although some are employed in beverages.

Imbu - *see* **UMBÚ**

Imperial - *see* **TEA**

Inca wheat - *see* **QUINOA**

Indian almond - *see* **MALABAR ALMOND**

Indian bael - *see* **BAEL FRUIT**

Indian balm - *see* **TRILLIUM**

INDIAN BARK - Also known as "Indian cassia," Indian bark (*Cinnamomum tamala*) is a native of the Indian subcontinent and is grown extensively in northern India. Like its relatives, cassia and cinnamon, it is a tree cultivated for its bark, which is processed into a spice. In addition, its leaves are used as a flavoring in curries.
Common names and synonyms: Indian cassia.

See also: "Spices and Flavorings," Part II, Section F, Chapter 1.

INDIAN BORAGE - Probably a native of Indonesia (it grows wild in Malaysia), Indian borage (*Coleus amboinicus*) is grown in Southeast Asia and the West Indies for its aromatic leaves, which can substitute for sage. Indeed, the herb is used exactly like sage for seasoning stuffings, poultry, and other dishes.

Indian breadroot - *see* **BREADROOT**

Indian buchu - *see* **MYRTLE**

Indian cassia - *see* **INDIAN BARK**

Indian corn - *see* **MAIZE**

Indian cress - *see* **NASTURTIUM**

INDIAN CUCUMBER - Also known as "Indian cucumber root," this member of the lily family is a small herb (*Medeola virginica*) native to eastern North America. Native Americans enjoyed the plant's crisp and succulent white rhizomes, which have a texture and taste similar to that of cucumbers.
Common names and synonyms: Indian cucumber root.

Indian cucumber root - *see* **INDIAN CUCUMBER**

Indian date - *see* **TAMARIND**

Indian fig - *see* **PRICKLY PEAR**

Indian gooseberry - *see* **AMALAKA, OTAHEITE GOOSEBERRY**

Indian hemp - *see* **HEMP DOGBANE**

Indian jujube - *see* **DESERT APPLE, JUJUBE**

INDIAN LONG PEPPER - A native of South Asia, the Indian long pepper (*Piper longum*) is a member of the genus that includes the common black and white peppercorns. It is grown mostly in India and Indonesia for its berries, which are dried and used as a spice - generally by adding them whole to curries, pickles, and the like.

Indian mulberry - *see* **MORINDA**

Indian mustard - *see* **MUSTARD GREENS**

Indian nut - *see* **PINE NUT**

Indian pea - *see* **PIGEON PEA**

Indian pear - *see* **PRICKLY PEAR**

Indian posy - *see* **BUTTERFLY WEED**

INDIAN POTATO (*see also* **APIOS, BREADROOT**) - Any of several native American plants with edible tubers are called "Indian potatoes." One is the groundnut (apios; another is the breadroot; still another is the giant sunflower (*Helianthus giganteus*), which is a tall North American plant with edible tuberous roots. Finally, there is the "yamp" (or "yampa," or "yampah" - *Carum gairdneri* or *C. kelloggii*); also called the "squawroot," this plant, too, has fleshy, edible roots. Another "yampah" is "Parish's yampah" (*Perideridia parishii*), of the parsley or carrot family. Native to the southwestern United States, this plant provided roots that were an important food for Native Americans and pioneers, who frequently ground them into a flour.

Common names and synonyms: Giant sunflower, Parish's yampah, squawroot, yamp, yampa, yampah.

INDIAN PRUNE - Known as *rukam manis* in its native Malaysia, the Indian prune (*Flacourtia rukam*) belongs to a large family of mostly tropical trees. It produces a dark purplish red, plumlike fruit that is juicy and sweet when ripe. These fruits are generally eaten raw but are also used for jams and chutneys.

Common names and synonyms: Rukam, rukam manis.

Indian rice - *see* **WILD RICE**

Indian ricegrass - *see* **RICEGRASS**

Indian saffron - *see* **TURMERIC**

Indian soap - *see* **SOAPBERRY**

Indian sorrel - *see* **ROSELLE**

Indian spice - *see* **CHASTE TREE**

Indian spinach - *see* **AMARANTH, MALABAR SPINACH**

INDIAN TURNIP (*see also* **BREADROOT**) - There are quite a few plants with the name "Indian turnip." One, also called "jack-in-the-pulpit" (*Arisaema triphyllum*), has an acrid but edible tuber. Another is *Eriogonum longifolium,* the roots of which were consumed by Native Americans in the western United States. The tuberous roots of several species of the genus *Psoralea* (known collectively as "breadroots" as well as "Indian turnips") were also consumed, often after being dried and later ground into flour, but they could also be eaten raw. The leaves of some species were cooked and eaten as a vegetable.

Common names and synonyms: Breadroot, jack-in-the-pulpit.

Indian walnut - *see* **CANDLENUT**

INDIAN WOOD-APPLE - Also known as the "elephant-apple," the Indian wood-apple (*Feronia limonia = Limonia acidissima*) is probably a native of India but now grows throughout Southeast Asia. The fruit - borne on a medium-sized tree - has a woody shell, making it difficult to get at its pulp, which consists of many seeds surrounded by a red, gummy substance. The fruit can be eaten raw but is used mostly to make jelly, chutney, and a refreshing drink.

Common names and synonyms: Elephant-apple.

Indonesian bay - *see* **DUAN SALAM**

Injerto - *see* **GREEN SAPOTE**

Inkberry - *see* **POKEWEED, WINTERBERRY**

Intermediate wheatgrass - *see* **WILD TRIGA**

IRIS - Any of the various members of the *Iridaceae* genus are called "iris," which includes colorful, herbaceous plants that develop from rhizomes or bulbs. It is the rhizomes that serve as a food for humans, especially in East Asia. The roots of *I. germanica,* known as "orris root," are pulverized and used in perfumery, medicines, and as a flavoring in certain gins.

Common names and synonyms: Flag, orris root.

Irish moss - *see* **CARRAGEEN AND CARRAGEENIN, SEAWEED**

Irish potato - *see* **WHITE POTATO**

Irish shamrock - *see* **WOOD SORREL**

Island moss - *see* **ICELAND MOSS**

Italian asparagus - *see* **BROCCOLI**

Italian brown mushroom - *see* **MUSHROOMS AND FUNGI**

Italian parsley - *see* **LOVAGE, PARSLEY**

Italian squash - *see* **ZUCCHINI**

Italian turnip - *see* **BROCCOLI RAAB**

IVY GOURD (*see also* **TANDOORI**) - Not to be confused with the tandoori, which is also called "ivy gourd," this ivy gourd (*Coccinea cordifolia = C. grandis*) is a native of tropical Asia and Africa. Also called the "small gourd," the plant is cultivated today in India, Indonesia, and Sudan. Its leaves, roots, and immature fruits are cooked as vegetables.

Common names and synonyms: Small gourd.

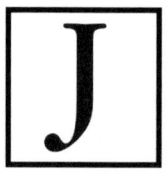

JABOTICABA - A member of the Myrtaceae family, the jaboticaba (*Myrciaria cauliflora*) is a very popular fruit in Brazil. It is also an unusual tree, because the fruit and flowers are borne on the trunk and on older branches. In color, it is a dark purple or nearly black fruit and its size - about a half inch in diameter - is that of a grape. Indeed, its pulp has the taste of a sweet grape, but the skin is tough and generally not eaten. The jaboticaba is consumed raw, used in salads, and made into jellies and wine.

Common names and synonyms: Brazilian grape, Brazilian grape tree.

Jaca - *see* **JACKFRUIT**

Jack - *see* **JACKFRUIT**

JACKBEAN (*see also* **BEANS**) - Also called the "horsebean" and the "cut-eye bean" and sometimes confused with the sword bean (a close relative), the jackbean (*Canavalia ensiformis*) originated in Central America and the Caribbean area but now is grown throughout much of the tropical and subtropical world. The young pods and seeds are employed as a cooked vegetable, and the seeds can be dried for later use.

Common names and synonyms: Cut-eye bean, horsebean, sword bean.

See in addition: "Beans, Peas, and Lentils," Part II, Section C, Chapter 3.

Jack-Be-Little - *see* **DELICATA (SQUASH)**

JACKFRUIT - Also called "jakfruit," "jak," "nangka," and a half dozen other names mostly derived from the Portuguese *jaca,* the jackfruit (*Artocarpus heterophyllus = A. integrifolius*) is a tropical fruit closely related to the breadfruit. The consensus is that it is likely a native of India, but because it is of ancient cultivation and has spread so widely throughout tropical Asia, its original home will probably never be known with certainty. In more recent times, the jackfruit has also been grown in Africa and in tropical America, including Florida.

Like the breadfruit, the jackfruit can be large, with a length of up to 2 feet and a weight of up to 20 and, on occasion, even as much as 60 pounds. Layers of flesh around the seeds are sweet and can be eaten raw, but other parts of the fruit contain latex and must be cooked before eating. Often the seeds are roasted and eaten as well, either on their own or as an added seasoning in other dishes, especially curries. The jackfruit is rich in carbohydrates but offers little in the way of other nutrients.

Common names and synonyms: Jaca, jack, jack hirsutus Lam, jak, jakfruit, nangka.

Jack hirsutus Lam - *see* **JACKFRUIT**

Jack-in-the-pulpit - *see* **INDIAN TURNIP**

Jagua - *see* **GENIPAP**

Jak - *see* **JACKFRUIT**

Jakfruit - *see* **JACKFRUIT**

Jalapa hybrid - *see* **JALAPEÑO**

JALAPEÑO (*see also* **CHILLI PEPPERS**) - Named for the Mexican town of Jalapa, the jalapeño pepper (*Capsicum annuum*) is probably the best known of the hot chilli peppers and is believed to have been domesticated in Mexico long before the Spaniards arrived. Generally, jalapeños are purchased to be consumed while still green, but mature red fruits (with a sweeter flavor) are also readily available in most produce markets. The jalapeño is a fairly hot pepper and stars in many salsa preparations as well as in cooked dishes. Additionally, jalapeños are pickled and canned, stuffed as a snack, and roasted. Moreover, the ripe (red) form is dried and smoked (which imparts a chocolate-like flavor), after which it becomes a chipotle chilli, and the *huachinango,* a large and highly prized jalapeño, is similarly treated to become a chipotle grande.

The dried fruits are dark brown to black in color, are much gentler on the palate (with less heat) than the fresh peppers, and are available in cans in a red adobo sauce. Chipotles are vital to Mexican cuisine - as well as to that of the southwestern United States - and are used in stews, soups, and salsas. Other types of jalapeños that are smoked and dried include the *mora* or *mora rojo,* the *morita,* and the *mora grande* - the names indicating the relative sizes of these chillies, which range from about 3 inches to about 1 inch in length. And finally there is a new jalapeño - the Jalapa hybrid - which is more productive than its predecessors. Jalapeños are grown chiefly in Mexico (especially the *mora*), Texas, and New Mexico.

Common names and synonyms: Chipotle (chilli), chipotle grande, *huachinango,* Jalapa hybrid, *mora* chilli, *mora grande, mora rojo, morita.*

See in addition: "Chilli Peppers," Part II, Section C, Chapter 4.

Jamaican Blue Mountain - *see* **COFFEE**

Jamaican cherry - *see* **CAPULIN**

Jamaican cucumber - *see* **GHERKIN**

Jamaican hot pepper - *see* **HABANERO AND SCOTCH BONNET PEPPERS**

Jamaican plum - *see* **HOG PLUM**

Jamaican Red - *see* **HABANERO AND SCOTCH BONNET PEPPERS**

Jamaican sorrel - *see* **ROSELLE**

Jamaica pepper - *see* **ALLSPICE**

Jamba oil - *see* **ARUGULA**

Jamberry - *see* **TOMATILLO**

JAMBOLAN (*see also* **JAMBOLAN PLUM, PLUM**) - A native of India and Java, the jambolan tree (*Eugenia cumini* or *Syzygium cumini*) has now spread throughout much of the world's tropics. Its fruits, green at first, turn purple as they ripen. They are about the size of a Damson plum and are mostly eaten raw, although in India a wine is made from the ripe ones and a vinegar from those that are still green.

Jambolana - *see* **JAMBOLAN PLUM**

JAMBOLAN PLUM (*see also* **PLUM**) - Also called the jambolan, the jambolana, and the Java plum, the jambolan plum (*Eugenia jambolana*) is the fruit of a large tree found mostly in the East Indies and Australia. The fruits are disappointing when eaten raw, and the seeds are very astringent. The bark of the tree is used medicinally.

Common names and synonyms: Jambolan, jambolana, Java plum.

Jambon du jardinier - *see* **EVENING PRIMROSE**

Jambos - *see* **JAVA APPLE, ROSE APPLE**

Jambu - *see* **JAVA APPLE, ROSE APPLE**

Jambu merah (tree) - *see* **MALAY APPLE**

Jantung pisang - *see* **BANANA FLOWER**

Japanese artichoke - *see* **CHINESE ARTICHOKE**

Japanese brown mushroom - *see* **MUSHROOMS AND FUNGI**

Japanese bunching - *see* **WELSH ONION**

Japanese cucumber - *see* **ARMENIAN CUCUMBER**

Japanese greens - *see* **CHRYSANTHEMUM**

Japanese horseradish - *see* **WASABI**

Japanese medlar - *see* **LOQUAT**

JAPANESE MILLET (*see also* **MILLET**) - A quick-growing cereal, Japanese millet (*Echinochloa frumentacea*) can be ready for harvesting in about six weeks. It is also called "billion-dollar grass," and its light brown to purplish grains are used as a food in India and the Far East and serve as a quickly grown substitute if the rice crop fails.

Common names and synonyms: Billion-dollar grass.

See in addition: "Millets," Part II, Section A, Chapter 5.

Japanese mint - *see* **CORN MINT**

Japanese parsley - *see* HONEWORT
Japanese pear - *see* ASIAN PEAR
JAPANESE PLUM (*see also* LOQUAT, PLUM) -
Thought to have originated in China - but domesticated in Japan - the Japanese plum (*Prunus salicina*) reached the United States around 1870 to become a popular fruit. It is relatively large for a plum (from 1.5 to 2 inches in diameter), reddish in color, and juicy when ripe. U.S. production is mostly in California.
Japanese potato - *see* CHINESE ARTICHOKE
Japanese pumpkin - *see* KABOCHA (SQUASH)
JAPANESE QUINCE - A native of China, the Japanese quince (*Chaenomeles speciosa*) is a small tree or shrub with scarlet flowers and widely grown as an ornamental. It produces a small fruit with a quince-like odor, which is generally made into jellies and jams.
Common names and synonyms: Japonica.
Japanese radish - *see* DAIKON
JAPANESE RAISIN TREE - Also called the "Chinese raisin tree," the Japanese raisin tree (*Hovenia dulcis*) is from both of these countries. A member of an Asiatic genus of trees and shrubs, it is a spicy-smelling plant that is grown for its sweet, swollen, reddish, edible flower stalks, which have a fruity taste.
Common names and synonyms: Chinese raisin tree, honey tree.
Japanese white celery mustard - *see* PAKCHOI AND KAI CHOY
Japanese white radish - *see* DAIKON
JAPANESE WINEBERRY (*see also* BERRIES) -
Although the Japanese wineberry (*Rubus phoenicolasius*) is a native of Southeast Asia, it now grows wild in the southern Appalachian region of the United States. There it is called the "strawberry-raspberry" and resembles the latter of the two in appearance. Despite its designation as a "wineberry," the fruit is not, as a rule, made into wine, but it does yield a good-tasting juice.
Common names and synonyms: Strawberry-raspberry, wineberry.
Japonés - *see* ASIAN CHILLIES, CHILLIES
Japonica - *see* JAPANESE QUINCE
JASMINE - Any of a number of plants with extremely sweet-smelling flowers are called "jasmine" (genus *Jasminum*). The flowers are mostly prized for their essential oils that are used in perfumery, but they are also combined with black tea to make jasmine tea.
Java - *see* COFFEE
JAVA ALMOND - A member of an extensive genus of tropical plants, the Java almond (*Canarium commune*) is a large tree of the East Indies that produces rich, oily nuts of the same name. These are pressed for oil and used as food.
Common names and synonyms: Kanari.

JAVA APPLE - A native of Indonesia, the Java apple (*Eugenia javanica*) is one of the jambu fruits and, because of a similarity in both scientific and common names, often is confused with the rose apple. The Java apple, which is also known by the names "wax-apple" and "jambos," has fruits that are usually green, although some are pink or red, and they appear a little like miniature bell peppers. Called the wax-apple because of a skin that feels waxlike, the fruit is usually eaten raw but is also made into a sauce.
Common names and synonyms: Jambos, jambu, wax-apple.
Java jute - *see* ROSELLE
JAVANESE LONG PEPPER - Another member of the genus *Piper*, which includes common black and white peppercorns, the Javanese long pepper (*P. retrofractum = P. officinarum*) yields berries that are dried and added whole to curries and pickles. The Javanese long pepper is very much like its close relative, the Indian long pepper.
Java pepper - *see* TAILED PEPPER
Java plum - *see* JAMBOLAN PLUM
Jelly melon - *see* KIWANO
JELLY PALM - Also known as the pindo palm, the jelly palm (*Butia capitata*) is a native of South America and is now found throughout the West Indies and the U.S. South as far north as Georgia. It has white flowers that bloom in the spring, and the tree produces large bunches of yellow, orange, or pinkish fruits that are used to make jelly - hence the name. It might also have been called the "wine tree" after yet another use of the fruit.
Common names and synonyms: Pindo palm.
Jenny-stonecrop - *see* STONECROP
JERING - A native of tropical Asia, *Pithecellobium jiringa* has seeds that are boiled or roasted for food. The tree's young shoots and seed pods are also eaten.
JERUSALEM ARTICHOKE (*see also* SUNFLOWER) - Although widely cultivated around the world, Jerusalem artichokes (*Helianthus tuberosus*), which are the tubers of the American sunflower, are nowhere a major crop. In many places, however, these tubers serve as a minor source of food for humans and livestock. This vegetable is rather unusual among root and tuber crops in that the reserve food is inulin rather than starch. The plant is a hexaploid. Some have thought that *Helianthus annuus* (the wild sunflower) is involved as one of the parents in its origin, but it seems more likely that only perennial species figured in its ancestry.
The wild Jerusalem artichoke is widespread in eastern North America, and Native Americans adopted it as a cultivated plant in prehistoric times. The first written notice of the plant was provided in 1605 by Samuel de Champlain in his observations on the area that is now Massachusetts. Shortly after, the plant appeared in France

and then spread throughout Europe. Its early reception as a food was favorable, one writer of the time stating that the tubers were "dainties for a Queene." Yet another was soon to state that they "caused the belly to be pained and [are] a meat more fit for swine, than man." But despite their flatulent properties, Jerusalem artichokes continue to be consumed, and in the United States in recent years they have enjoyed a renewed popularity. The tubers are generally eaten cooked, but they can be used raw in salads.

The name "Jerusalem artichoke" has generally been thought to be a corruption of the Italian *girasole articiocco*. The artichoke part is easily explained, for early writers found the taste to be similar to that of the more familiar globe (or French) artichoke. R. N. Salaman (1940), however, has suggested that Jerusalem is a corruption of Ter Neusen, a place in Holland from whence the tubers were imported into England.

Common names and synonyms: Gerasole, girasole, girsole, sunchoke.

See in addition: "Sunflower," Part II, Section E, Chapter 6.

Jerusalem oak - *see* **EPAZOTE**

JERUSALEM PEA (*see also* **BEANS, LEGUMES**) - A native of the East Indies but now cultivated mostly in West Africa, the Jerusalem pea (*Phaseolus trinervius*) is sometimes regarded as a variety of the mung bean. It grows wild in India, where it is considered a famine food. Each of the small pods of the Jerusalem pea contains about nine edible seeds.

See in addition: "Beans, Peas, and Lentils," Part II, Section C, Chapter 3.

Jerusalem thorn - *see* **CHRIST'S-THORN FRUIT**

Jesuit nut - *see* **WATER CHESTNUT**

JEWELWEED - Several American and Eurasian species of the genus *Impatiens* are known as jewelweed or "touch-me-not." Their leaves and stems are used as food in Asia, and the same parts of *I. capensis* were boiled and eaten by Native Americans in eastern and central North America.

Common names and synonyms: Touch-me-not.

Jew plum - *see* **GOLDEN APPLE**

Jew's-ear - *see* **CLOUD EAR, MUSHROOMS AND FUNGI**

JEW'S-MALLOW - Also known as "jute mallow," Jew's-mallow (*Corchorus olitorus*) is a native of India that now grows in most of the world's tropical and subtropical regions. This stout herb is cultivated in Egypt, Syria, South America, and the Caribbean as a potherb and in India for its jute fiber. The young, tender, green leaves of Jew's-mallow - which are edible (and palatable) raw as well as cooked - have been used for food since the days of the hunter-gatherers. In Egypt, they are used to make the country's national dish - a thick soup called *molokhia*. The greens are high in beta-carotene, calcium, and vitamin C.

Common names and synonyms: Bush okra, jute, jute mallow, long-fruited jute, Nalta jute, Spanish okra, tossa jute, tussa jute, West African sorrel.

JÍCAMA - A plant that provides both a root vegetable and beans, the jícama (*Pachyrhizus erosus = Dolichos erosus*) is also called "Mexican potato," "yam bean," and "potato bean." The jícama is an American native that - along with a closely related species, *P. tuberosus* (also called "yam bean" and ajipo) - was cultivated long ago by the Aztecs and the Maya. The young pods are eaten as a cooked vegetable. The root is cylindrical and has a rough, sandy-colored skin, the removal of which reveals a white interior. In the past, the roots were normally eaten raw and enjoyed for their cool crispness rather than their bland flavor. Today, jícama remains a popular snack food eaten with lime juice in Mexico as well as California, where it is also grown. It can be baked like a potato but is mostly pickled and included in salads and casseroles. Until recently, jícama was practically unknown in North America, but now it can be found in most produce departments. Asian-American cooks occasionally employ it as a substitute for water chestnuts.

Common names and synonyms: Erosus yam bean, *jícama de agua*, *jícama de leche*, Mexican potato, potato bean, yam bean.

Jícama de agua - *see* **JÍCAMA**

Jícama de leche - *see* **JÍCAMA**

Jicara - *see* **XICALLI**

Jimsonweed - *see* **MOONFLOWER**

Jintan - *see* **ANISE, CARAWAY, CUMIN**

JOB'S-TEARS (*see also* **MILLET**) - A grass probably native to Southeast Asia, "Job's-tears" (*Coix lacryma-jobi*) now grows throughout the world's tropics, where it is sometimes cultivated and sometimes regarded as a weed. At one time, it was a major cereal in India, where people pounded its large, nut-flavored grains into flour, cooked them in gruels and soups, ate them whole, and used them to make teas and fermented beverages. The grain remains a minor cereal in India and elsewhere, and the pearly white seeds of some ornamental varieties are often sold as beads and strung to make necklaces.

Common names and synonyms: Adlay, adlay millet, tear-grass.

See in addition: "Millets," Part II, Section A, Chapter 5.

Johannisberg Riesling - *see* **RIESLING**

Johnson grass - *see* **SORGHUM**

JOJOBA NUT - About the size of an acorn, the jojoba nut (*Simmondsia chinensis*) is - despite its scientific name - native to the North American Southwest and the Baja peninsula. The nuts grow on a bush, usually in a wild state, although today they are also cultivated for their oil, which is used in lubricants and medicines. In the past, however, Native Americans made a coffee-like beverage from the nuts.

Common names and synonyms: Goat-nut.

Joseph's-coat - *see* **AMARANTH**
Judas('s) ear - *see* **CLOUD EAR**
Juglans - *see* **WALNUT**
JUJUBE (*see also* **DESERT APPLE**) - A native of China with a French name meaning "lozenge," the jujube (*Ziziphus jujuba*) resembles a large, dark red cherry. The spiny tree that bears jujubes has been cultivated by the Chinese for more than 4,000 years and has been growing in the Mediterranean region for some 2,500 years. It has spread throughout East Asia and is also grown in parts of Africa. The jujube was introduced in the United States in 1837; better varieties were obtained from China in 1906, and they continue to thrive in the hot, dry climate of the U.S. Southwest, although they are not grown on a large commercial scale.

Also called "Chinese dates" and "Chinese red dates," jujubes were often cooked in traditional Chinese households with millet or rice to make a kind of sweet porridge, and the dried fruit has always been especially popular. There are other very similar and related fruits. One, called the Indian jujube (*Z. mauritiana*), produces a fruit with a color ranging from yellowish to orange and brown and is now grown in Florida. Another - a Mediterranean variety, *Z. lotus* - yields a fruit that is like a sweet olive. This is said to be the fruit of the lotus-eaters described by Homer in the *Odyssey*. The "Christ-thorn" berry (*Z. spina-christi*) is yet one more relative. Jujubes are eaten fresh but are also baked, boiled, stewed, and made into syrup. The juice of the fruit is employed in making the small candies that are called "jujubes." Jujubes (the fruit) are rich in vitamin C.

Common names and synonyms: Chinese date, Chinese jujube, Chinese red date, common jujube, cottony jujube, Indian jujube.

Jumbie bean - *see* **LEUCAENA**
Juneberry - *see* **SERVICEBERRY**
Jungle banana - *see* **ENSETE**
Jungle plum - *see* **LITTLE GOOSEBERRY TREE**
JUNIPER BERRY - The fruits of a small evergreen tree or shrub, juniper berries (*Juniperus communis*) are legendary in folklore for their supposed medicinal and magical properties. Their most important application, however, lies in the oil derived from the dried berries, which is added to the final distillation of gin for flavoring. The spicy taste of juniper is also added to other liquors and foods. In cooking, the dried and crushed (to release their full powerful flavor) berries work well with wild game and are added to sauerkraut, sausages, stuffings, and marinades as well. In Europe during the Middle Ages, juniper berries were used to flavor beef, pork, mutton, and especially venison. A bit later on, they were one of the ingredients employed to adulterate pepper.

Juniper berries grow wild in most of the world's temperate regions. In North America, they were used as food by some Native American groups, who ate them fresh and also dried and ground them to make a mush. Others have roasted juniper berries as a coffee substitute. But their flavor and especially their potency varies considerably. The best are said to come from southern Europe in general and the mountainous regions of Italy in particular.

Common names and synonyms: Common juniper.
See also: "Spices and Flavorings," Part II, Section F, Chapter 1.
JUNIPER MISTLETOE - A yellow-green mistletoe, juniper mistletoe (*Phoradendron juniperinum*) is parasitic to several species of juniper. It has translucent, globular berries that birds feed on, after which they carry the sticky seeds to other trees, thus spreading the parasite. At one time, the Navaho reportedly employed the berries for food, but today the juniper mistletoe is used only medicinally (by the Hopi Indians).

Common names and synonyms: Mistletoe.
Jute - *see* **JEW'S-MALLOW**
Jute mallow - *see* **JEW'S-MALLOW**

 **KABOCHA (SQUASH)** (*see also* **SQUASH AND PUMPKIN**) - The name "kabocha" designates a group of squashes (*Cucurbita maxima* or *C. moschata*) that were developed in Japan and are exceptionally sweet and flavorful. Weighing an average of 3 to 4 pounds, they generally have thick, green skins with pale stripes and a yellow-orange flesh. The Japanese - who consume large amounts of squash on a per capita basis - are big importers of kabocha during the off-season, when they cannot grow it themselves. New Zealand and Mexico are major producers. Like other winter squashes, the kabocha contains much in the way of vitamins A and C.

Common names and synonyms: Chirimen, Delica, ebisu, hoka, Home Delite, hyuga, Japanese pumpkin, Sweet Mama.
See in addition: "Squash," Part II, Section C, Chapter 8.
Kachun - *see* **PEPINO**
Kaffir corn - *see* **SORGHUM**
Kaffir date - *see* **KAFFIR PLUM**
KAFFIR LIME (*see also* **CITRUS FRUITS**) - A species of *Citrus* grown in Southeast Asia, the Kaffir lime (*C. hystrix*) is cultivated more for its leaves than for its fruit, although its juice is used as a flavoring. The leaves are employed both fresh and dried (like bay leaves) in soups, curries, sauces, and gravies. Powdered leaves of the Kaffir lime can be found in Asian markets, but these are not totally satisfactory as a substitute for the whole leaves.

Common names and synonyms: Papeda, wild lime.
Kaffir orange - *see* **MONKEY ORANGE**

KAFFIR PLUM - A tree of South Africa, the Kaffir plum (*Harpephyllum caffrum*) produces a sweet, red fruit a bit smaller than a plum - in fact about the size of a date (and the fruit is also called a "Kaffir date"). The tree is now grown in California and Florida as an ornamental.

Common names and synonyms: Kaffir date.

KAFFIR POTATO - An apparently close relative of the Sudan potato, with which it shares the common name "Hausa potato," the Kaffir potato (*Plectranthus esculentus*) is a native of tropical West Africa that today is cultivated in an area extending throughout Central Africa and into East Africa. The tubers, which have been food for Africans since prehistoric times, are generally boiled and frequently added to the many vegetables in the always-simmering family soup.

Common names and synonyms: Hausa potato, Livingstone potato.

KAI APPLE - Also known as "kau apple" and "kei apple," the kai apple (*Aberia caffra = Dovyalis caffra*) is a South African native. The "apple" grows on a thorny tree or bush and is a very acidic, yellowish fruit with the general shape of an apple. It is usually employed to make preserves.

Common names and synonyms: Kau apple, kei apple.

Kai choy - *see* **PAKCHOI AND KAI CHOY**

Kail - *see* **KALE**

Kailan - *see* **CHINESE BROCCOLI**

Kaiware - *see* **DAIKON**

Kaki - *see* **PERSIMMON**

KALE (*see also* **CABBAGE, COLLARDS, HANOVER KALE**) - A variety of cabbage with ruffled, crinkled leaves that form no head, kale (*Brassica oleracea* var. *acephala*) is an ancient vegetable. It is descended from the wild cabbage, which was native to the Mediterranean region, doubtless was enjoyed by Stone Age hunter-gatherers, and may have been the first form of cultivated cabbage. It was one of the many plants consumed by the Romans, who spread its cultivation throughout their empire. Kale is a hardy plant that can be left in the ground over the winter and thus has been especially appreciated when other greens are scarce.

Curly kale is the variety most frequently consumed, although local forms have been developed in specific areas. Of these, Scotch kale (which is very curly and somewhat prickly) and blue kale (which is less curly and a blue-green in color) are probably the most common types. Kale has coarse leaves, which can become very wide, and grows best in cool weather.

It is used in several different ways, most typically in soups and salads or as a steamed vegetable. In Portugal, a special kind of kale - called *couve* - is grown to make the country's famed *caldo verde*. Colored varieties of kale - sometimes called "salad savory" - are grown as ornamentals; in Japan, for example, they are often employed to enhance flower gardens. Kale is rich in vitamins A and C and fairly high in calcium and iron.

Common names and synonyms: Blue kale, borecole, cail, Chinese kale, *couve,* curly greens, curly kale, du jour, green cabbage, kail, marrow stem, Nagoya kale, ornamental kale, peacock kale, red flowering kale, red-on-green flowering kale, red Russian kale, salad savory, Scotch kale, thousand-headed, white flowering kale.

See in addition: "Cruciferous and Green Leafy Vegetables," Part II, Section C, Chapter 5.

Kalonji - *see* **NIGELLA**

Kampyo - *see* **BOTTLE GOURD**

KAMUT (*see also* **WHEAT**) - Kamut (*Triticum turgidum*) is regarded by some to be the ancestor of grains and, at the very least, the oldest relative of modern durum wheats. This is reflected in the name "kamut," which was the ancient Egyptian word for wheat. There is disagreement over the plant's biological classification, and a number of different subspecies have been proposed.

About a half century ago, kamut reached America, and it is now produced commercially on a small scale in both the United States and Canada, mostly for the health-food market. It has never been hybridized, and its kernels are about three times the size of most wheat. They have a pleasant, nut-like flavor and are used - in conjunction with wheat flour - mostly for making pastas, puffed cereals, crackers, and bread. Kamut is high in dietary fiber and rich in the B-vitamin complex; it also delivers good quantities of folic acid and iron.

See in addition: "Wheat," Part II, Section A, Chapter 10.

Kana - *see* **MAIZE**

Kanari - *see* **JAVA ALMOND**

KANGAROO APPLE - A yellow, mealy fruit with the shape of an egg, the kangaroo apple (*Solanum aviculare*) grows on shrublike trees in New Zealand and Australia. It contributed to the diets of the aboriginal peoples of both countries.

Kang kong - *see* **SWAMP CABBAGE**

Kang(-)kung - *see* **SWAMP CABBAGE**

Kanten - *see* **AGAR**

Kápari - *see* **CAPER(S)**

KAPOK TREE - Also called the "silk-cotton tree" because of the cotton-like substance surrounding its seeds (which is used in life preservers), the kapok tree (*Ceiba pentandra*) is an East Indian native (now grown in Florida) and a close relative of Africa's famous baobab tree. The young leaves of the kapok tree are often cooked as a vegetable.

Common names and synonyms: Ceiba, silk-cotton tree.

KARAKA - *Karaka,* a Maori word, refers to an orange-colored fruit (*Corynocarpus laevigata*) of New Zealand, and the same word also means the tree on which the fruit grows. The fruit has an edible pulp and poisonous seeds, but – interestingly – the seeds are the most valuable part of this plant. When cooked and dried, they become edible, and they have long been an important item in the Maori diet.

Karamta - *see* **SWAMP CABBAGE**

Karanda - *see* **CARAUNDA**

Karaschi - *see* **MUSTARD SEED**

Karawya - *see* **CARAWAY**

Karenga - *see* **SEAWEED**

Karzochy - *see* **ARTICHOKE**

Kasha - *see* **BUCKWHEAT**

Kashmiri chilli (pepper) - *see* **ASIAN CHILLIES, CHILLI PEPPERS**

Kastanie - *see* **CHESTNUT**

Kat - *see* **KHAT**

Katook - *see* **SWEET-SHOOT**

Katuk - *see* **SWEET-SHOOT**

Kau apple - *see* **KAI APPLE**

KAVA - Also known as cava and kava-kava, kava (*Piper methysticum*) is a shrub of the tropical Pacific Islands. Its roots and rhizomes are dried and used to make an intoxicating beverage, which has long been used both in ceremonies and to promote friendships.
Common names and synonyms: Cava, kava-kava.
See also: "Kava," Part III, Chapter 6.

Kava-kava - *see* **KAVA**

Kayu manis - *see* **CINNAMON AND CASSIA**

Kechapi - *see* **SENTUL**

Kĕdondong - *see* **HOG PLUM**

Keemum - *see* **TEA**

Keemun - *see* **TEA**

Kei apple - *see* **KAI APPLE**

Keladi - *see* **COCOYAM**

KELP (*see also* **SEAWEED**) - Any of the brown and olive-green seaweeds of the orders Laminariales and Fucales are called "kelp," including several large Pacific plants known as "giant kelp," such as *Macrocystis pyrifera* and *Laminaria japonica*. The Japanese, in particular, are skilled in preparing kelp (called *kombu*) as a food product by drying and shredding it. Kelp is used in soups, is boiled as a vegetable, and is especially important in making stocks for savory dishes. It is also burned to produce iodine.
Common names and synonyms: Bladder weed, giant kelp, *kombu*, sea kelp, tangle kelp.
See in addition: "Algae," Part II, Section C, Chapter 1.

Kerela - *see* **BITTER MELON**

Kersting's groundnut - *see* **HAUSA GROUNDNUT**

Ketembilla - *see* **CEYLON GOOSEBERRY**

Key lime - *see* **LIME**

KHAT - Also called kat, cat, qat, qhat, and African or Arabian tea, khat (*Catha edulis*) is a shrub cultivated by the Arabs for its leaves. These are either chewed or made into a tea for the narcotic effect they produce.
Common names and synonyms: African tea, Arabian tea, cat, kat, qat, qhat.
See also: "Khat," Part III, Chapter 7.

Kiawe - *see* **ALGARROBO**

Kikurage - *see* **CLOUD EAR**

Kingcup - *see* **COWSLIP**

King-of-fruits - *see* **MANGOSTEEN**

King-of-trees - *see* **OLIVE**

King's-cure - *see* **PIPSISSEWA**

King's-nut - *see* **MARULA PLUM**

Kin-kan - *see* **KUMQUAT**

Kinnikinnic - *see* **BEARBERRY**

Kinnikinnick - *see* **BEARBERRY**

KIWANO - A member of the cucumber family, the kiwano (*Cucumis metuliferus*) was long known as the "African horned melon," but New Zealand growers had so much success marketing the Chinese gooseberry after they changed its name to "kiwifruit" that they have pursued a similar course with this fruit. It is a colorful one, about the size and shape of a small cucumber, with a bright orange (and inedible) skin covered with little horns, and bright green flesh. The kiwano is eaten raw and makes a fine ingredient in salads. It is, however, very expensive, and although now beginning to appear in produce markets, it has in the past been available only through mail-order businesses specializing in exotic fruits.
Common names and synonyms: African horned cucumber, African horned melon, English tomato, hedged gourd, horned melon, jelly melon, melano, *metulon*.
See also: "Cucumbers, Melons, and Watermelons," Part II, Section C, Chapter 6.

Kiwicha - *see* **AMARANTH**

KIWIFRUIT - The kiwifruit (*Actinidia chinensis*) was a small, hard berry growing wild in China at the beginning of the twentieth century. It was subsequently cultivated in New Zealand, where it was known as the "Chinese gooseberry." But later, when China became Communist China, the name "kiwifruit" was applied, thus disassociating it from its homeland. In part, this was to facilitate marketing in the West, and in part, it was because of the fruit's supposed resemblance to New Zealand's kiwi, a small, flightless bird with brown, hairlike plumage. The new name provoked a remarkable marketing success, and during the 1950s, New Zealand acreage devoted to the fruit increased rapidly to meet the sudden demand. The kiwifruit – about the size of a large egg – is very juicy and usually sweet, although sometimes it has a tart flavor. The thin skin is hairy and brown, and the flesh is a bright green with very small black seeds that surround a creamy white core. In addition to appearing in salads as a fresh fruit, the kiwifruit is also processed into juice, jams, and jellies and is canned and frozen. The fruit is grown on trellises and provides much in the way of vitamins A and C.
Common names and synonyms: Chinese gooseberry, *yang tao*.

Klarbar - *see* **CHERRY**

Knit-bones - *see* COMFREY

Knol-kohl - *see* KOHLRABI

KNOTTED WRACK (*see also* SEAWEED) - A perennial brown algae, knotted wrack of the genus *Ascophyllum* attaches itself to rocks in sheltered areas of temperate seas. In the United States, it is used mostly for fertilizers, soil conditioners, and fodder as well as packing material for shipping live lobsters and clams. However, this "sea vegetable" is also ground into a meal that is consumed by humans.

Common names and synonyms: Rockweed.

See in addition: "Algae," Part II, Section C, Chapter 1.

KNOTWEED AND SMARTWEED - A number of plants of the genus *Polygonum* are called "knotweed" or "smartweed." Many species, such as the Japanese knotweed (*P. cuspidatum* - also known as "Mexican bamboo"), have been introduced into the New World from Eurasia. Others, like *P. coccineum*, are natives of North America, and still others, like *P. viviparum,* are native to both North America and Eurasia.

In some cases, such as that of the "bistort" or "smokeweed" (*P. bistorta* or *P. bistortoides*), it was the rhizomes of the plant that were eaten by gatherers in the northern portions of the continents. But the young shoots and leaves of most knotweeds are also edible, and Japanese knotweed is cultivated for its immature stems, which are employed in salads and as a potherb. *Polygonum persicaria* may have been employed as food in the past; it was certainly used for medicinal purposes by Native Americans. The seeds of some species are edible as well. Native Americans, for example, ground the seeds of *P. douglasii* into a meal, whereas the seeds of *P. convolvulus* have long been made into a kind of porridge. And finally, the smartweed, "water pepper" (*P. hydropiper*), yields an acrid, peppery juice that has been used medicinally and as a condiment.

Common names and synonyms: Bistort, Japanese knotweed, lady's-thumb, Mexican bamboo, smokeweed, water pepper.

KOHLRABI (*see also* CABBAGE) - Native to northern Europe, kohlrabi (*Brassica oleracea* Gongylodes Group) is of the mustard family. It is a relative newcomer to *Brassica,* the cabbage genus, having been developed from marrow cabbages some 400 to 500 years ago. It was first described in the sixteenth century and by the end of that century was known in Germany, England, Italy, and Spain. But it was only cultivated in the United States at the beginning of the nineteenth century.

The name comes from the German words *Kohl* (meaning cabbage) and *Rabi* (meaning turnip), and in fact, it is a type of cabbage with stems that swell into turnip-like bulbs - hence, "turnip cabbage" is another of its names. Kohlrabi grows best in cool climates. It is sweet and crisp when the bulbs are small but tough and bitter when they grow large.

This vegetable can be eaten raw but is usually cooked and is commonly used in soups. Some kohlrabi varieties are "Prague Special," "Purple Vienna," "Triumph of Prague," and "White Vienna."

Common names and synonyms: Cabbage turnip, caulorapa, chou-rave, colirrambano, knol-kohl, koolrabi, Prague Special, Purple Vienna, Triumph of Prague, turnip cabbage, White Vienna.

See in addition: "Cruciferous and Green Leafy Vegetables," Part II, Section C, Chapter 5.

Koko - *see* COCOYAM

KOLA NUT - Native to West Africa, the kola nuts - abata kola (*Cola acuminata*) and *gbanja kola* (*C. nitida*) - have been an important trade commodity in sub-Saharan Africa for thousands of years. *Cola nitida* is indigenous to Ashanti, the Ivory Coast, and Sierra Leone but is now cultivated extensively in Nigeria as well. *Cola acuminata* is native to Nigeria, Gabon, and the Congo Basin but is less cultivated.

The kola nut is a brownish, bitter seed about the size of a chestnut. The nuts grow on small trees and are enclosed - beanlike - in green, wrinkled pods. Because they contain caffeine, kolatine, and theobromine, kola nuts have a stimulating effect when chewed or otherwise utilized, as, for example, in flavoring cola soft drinks. Kola nuts are also credited with allaying thirst and promoting energy. In addition to Africa, kola nuts are cultivated in the West Indies, South America, and Indonesia.

Common names and synonyms: Abata kola, cola, cola nut, *gbanja kola, owe kola.*

See also: "Kola Nut," Part III, Chapter 8.

Kolkas - *see* COCOYAM

Kombu - *see* KELP, SEAWEED

Kong(-)kong taro - *see* MALANGA

Koolrabi - *see* KOHLRABI

Korean chilli (pepper) - *see* ASIAN CHILLIES

KORILA (*see also* CUCUMBER) - A cucurbit that may have originated in the Caribbean region (but more likely South America or Mesoamerica), korila (*Cyclanthera pedata* - also known as the "wild cucumber") is now cultivated in all of these regions and in parts of Southeast Asia as well. The Incas ate the young fruits raw and stuffed the mature ones - often with meat - after which they were dried and stored in warehouses for future use. Today, the pale green fruits are still eaten raw and are frequently stuffed with meat or fish and baked. The shoots are also consumed, but the seeds generally are not.

Common names and synonyms: Achokcha, caihua, caygua, cayua, wild cucumber.

KUDZU - A vine native to Japan, kudzu (*Pueraria thunbergiana* = *P. lobata*) has starchy roots that can be boiled and eaten or are processed into a thickener for sauces. The plant has also been appreciated since ancient times for its medicinal properties, which supposedly become active when the roots are dried and ground into a powder. Kudzu has joined the group of Asian plants now growing in the southern United States.

KUINI - The kuini (*Mangifera odorata*) is a tall tree, probably native to Malaysia. It bears green, oval-shaped fruits about the size of large oranges. Their flesh is orange in color, quite juicy, and very sweet. The fruits have a strong smell when ripe, which tells their consumers they are safe. Immature fruits with little odor contain a poisonous sap. The kuini is eaten raw and used to make chutney.

Common names and synonyms: Kuwini.

Kumara - *see* **SWEET POTATO**

Kümmel - *see* **CARAWAY**

KUMQUAT (*see also* **LIMEQUAT**) - Native to East Asia, the several varieties of the kumquat tree (genus *Fortunella*) belong to the family Rutaceae - the same family as citrus fruits. Kumquats are cultivated throughout the subtropics, including places like California and Florida in the United States. The most common varieties are Nagami (*F. margarita*), Meiwa (*F. crassifolia*), and Marumi (*F. japonica*). The edible skin resembles that of an orange, and in fact, the kumquat was thought to be a citrus fruit until early in the twentieth century, when it was decided that it belongs to a different - but related - genus. The bright-colored, orange-yellow fruit is about the size of a large olive or a small plum, varies in shape between round and oval, and ranges in taste from sweet to mildly acidic. Availability is best during the winter. Kumquats are cooked, candied, canned, made into preserves, and used in salads, but most are popped into the mouth whole and eaten raw. Kumquats are an excellent source of vitamin C.

Common names and synonyms: Cumquat, golden orange, *kin-kan, limau pagar,* Marumi, Meiwa, Nagami.

KUNDANGAN - An Indochina native, the kundangan (*Bouea macrophylla*) is yellow, about the size of a small orange, and soft when ripe. The mature fruits are made into chutneys and jams, and the young green fruits are pickled for curries. This tree-growing fruit is also known as Setar and star.

Common names and synonyms: Setar, star.

Kusaie - *see* **RANGPUR AND KUSAIE**

Kuwini - *see* **KUINI**

Lablab bean - *see* **HYACINTH BEAN**

Labrusca grape - *see* **FOX GRAPE**

LADY APPLE -Also known as the "red wild-apple," the lady apple (*Syzygium suborbiculare*) is a relative of the clove. A wild, reddish fruit of Australia, it is mentioned as one of the gathered foods of the Australian Aborigines.

Common names and synonyms: Red wild-apple.

Lady('s)-finger(s) - *see* **OKRA**

LADY'S BEDSTRAW - Also known as "yellow bedstraw" and "yellow cleavers" (because the barbed stems cleave to fur and clothing), lady's bedstraw (*Galium verum*) shares the common name "bedstraw" with a few other species of the genus *Calium*. The name came about because the plants were used as mattress stuffing, but they also have some food value; the seeds, for example, have served as a coffee substitute.

Common names and synonyms: Yellow bedstraw, yellow cleavers.

LADY'S SMOCK - Also called "cuckoo flower," lady's smock (*Cardamine pratensis*) is a bitter cress of North America and Europe. It finds use mostly as a condiment.

Common names and synonyms: Cuckoo flower.

Lady's-thumb - *see* **KNOTWEED AND SMART-WEED**

Lahong - *see* **DURIAN**

Lambert's filbert - *see* **HAZELNUT AND FILBERT**

LAMBRUSCO (*see also* **GRAPES**) - The vines that produce the Lambrusco variety, an Italian wine grape (*Vitis vinifera*) that originated in the Emilia-Romagna wine region, are still heavily planted in the clay soils of the Po Valley. The Lambrusco grape makes a sweet, light- to medium-bodied, sparkling red wine that has been popular in the United States. Lambrusco grapes are also used to make dry red and white wines.

See in addition: "Wine," Part III, Chapter 13.

Lamb's lettuce - *see* **CORNSALAD**

LAMB'S-QUARTER (*see also* **CHENOPODIUM, CORNSALAD, GOOSEFOOT**) - The leaves of lamb's-quarter (*Chenopodium album*) - also known as pigweed - a wild plant common in Europe and now naturalized in North America, taste something like spinach when they are cooked. When young, they are delicious raw. The seeds are also edible after the saponin they contain is leached out.

Common names and synonyms: Goosefoot, pigweed.

Lampong (pepper) - *see* **PEPPER(CORNS)**

LANGSAT - Natives of western Malaysia, both the langsat and the duku are classified under the same botanical name - *Lansium domesticum*. Their pale yellowish, berry-like fruits have been grown since ancient times. In the fifteenth century, Chinese voyagers saw these fruit trees in Java and attempted without success to grow them in China. The trees will not tolerate even the slightest cold, nor will they endure long dry spells, all of which means that they have remained typically Malaysian. Aside from a milky juice present in the langsat, the major difference between the duku and the langsat seems to be that the duku is somewhat larger (about 2 inches long in contrast to about 1.5 inches for the langsat) but has fewer fruits in a bunch. The fruits, which are generally eaten raw, are not very sweet, and some are slightly bitter (the seeds are extremely bitter). Both fruits are difficult to find, even in Asian markets.

Common names and synonyms: Duku, lanzone.

Lanzone - *see* **LANGSAT**

Laos - *see* **GALANGAL**

Lapsung Souchong - *see* **TEA**

LARGE CANE - Also called "giant cane," large cane (*Arundinaria gigantea*) is the tall grass that constitutes the canebrakes of the southern United States. Its succulent young shoots were gathered by Native Americans to cook as a vegetable.

Common names and synonyms: Giant cane.

Laurel - *see* **BAY LEAF**

Laurel leaf - *see* **DUAN SALAM**

LAVENDER - An Old World plant now grown for its scent - from the essential oil of its flowers - lavender (*Lavandula officinalis = L. angustifolia*) was popular in the past as a potherb and was used for flavoring jellies as well. Its sole remaining culinary use is to make a tisane.

See also: "Spices and Flavorings," Part II, Section F, Chapter 1.

LAVER (*see also* **AGAR, SEAWEED**) - Any of several seaweeds - mostly of the genus *Porphyra* - are called laver, including such species as *P. laciniata* or *P. vulgaris* (red laver) and *P. tenera* or *P. umbilicalis* (green, purple, and sea laver). In Japan, laver is called *nori* and is employed principally to obtain a gelatin to make agar-agar, which are sheets of dried and compressed laver used as sushi wrappers. But laver is also shredded into soups and other dishes. In Scotland and Ireland, where this "sea vegetable" has been named *sloak* or *slook,* laver is boiled and served with butter, or perhaps fried in bacon fat after boiling. Laver is also pickled.

Common names and synonyms: Agar-agar, green laver, *nori,* purple laver, red laver, sea laver, *sloak, slook.*

See in addition: "Algae," Part II, Section C, Chapter 1.

Lead tree - *see* **LEUCAENA**

Leaf beet - *see* **SWISS CHARD**

Leafcup - *see* **YACÓN**

Leaf mustard - *see* **MUSTARD GREENS**

Leaf pekoe - *see* **TEA**

Leafy cactus - *see* **BARBADOS GOOSEBERRY**

LEAFY SPURGE - A tall perennial Eurasian herb that has been naturalized in the northern United States and Canada, leafy spurge (*Euphorbia esula*) has stems that contain a milky juice. Formerly, this plant and other species of the genus *Euphorbia* were used as purgatives - hence the name spurge - although some also have served as food.

LECHEGUILLA - With a name that is the diminutive of the Spanish *lechuga* (meaning "lettuce"), lecheguilla (*Agave lecheguilla*) is a wild lettuce that can be toxic to sheep and goats that feed on it.

Nonetheless, it was reportedly consumed by humans in the past.

Common names and synonyms: Lechuguilla.

Lechuguilla - *see* **LECHEGUILLA**

Leechee - *see* **LITCHI**

LEEK(S) - A plant related to the onion, the leek (*Allium porrum*) looks like a giant scallion. It is native to the Mediterranean region, where it was apparently cultivated in prehistory and later enjoyed by the ancient Greeks. The Roman emperor Nero ate leeks regularly, and the Romans carried leeks to much of the rest of Europe, where the vegetable was especially popular during the Middle Ages. In Wales, leeks are the national emblem and regarded as the national vegetable. Legend has it that seventh-century Welsh troops - in battle with the Saxons - wore leeks in their hats to distinguish themselves from the enemy.

Leeks are most appreciated in Europe, where they are a favorite; France, Belgium, and the Netherlands are the leading producers. California, New Jersey, and Florida satisfy much of the U.S. market. The vegetable - known as "poor-man's-asparagus" in France - is used to make soups, and is a vital ingredient in many of the French *potage* standards, including vichyssoise (which was actually invented in New York City). The Welsh and the Scots both have famous leek soups as well.

Leeks are also boiled, blanched, or braised, and served perhaps with cheese or a dressing. Despite its warm-climate origin, the leek is a hardy plant that can survive the ice and snow of the cold months in temperate climates and thus is a winter vegetable. Leeks are a rich source of folacin and a good source of vitamin C and vitamin B_6.

Common names and synonyms: Poor-man's-asparagus.

See also: "The *Allium* Species," Part II, Section C, Chapter 2.

Leghorn citron - *see* **CITRON**

LEGUMES (*see also* **BEANS, PEAS**) - The legumes (peas, beans, and lentils), also called pulses, are members of the second most important family of plants in the human diet (after the grasses that have given us our grains). It was the Romans who decided that a legume is the edible seed in a pod that splits into two valves with seeds attached to the lower edge of one of the valves, all of which means that peas as well as beans belong to the family Leguminosae (Fabaceae). The family name derives from the Latin verb *legendus* or *legere* and the Greek *legein,* meaning to gather or collect, and doubtless wild legumes were gathered by humans long before they got around to domesticating them. The first wave of the latter activity probably took place in the Near East, with the lentil, pea, chickpea, and broadbean all domesticated between 7000 and 3000 B.C.

Bean domestication in the Americas took place at about this same time, which saw four species of beans brought under human control beginning around 6000 B.C. These, all of the genus *Phaseolus* and called *haricots* by the French, added considerably to the world's stock of beans. The tepary bean developed in the area that became Mexico and the southeastern United States. The scarlet runner was domesticated farther south in Mexico, and the lima bean even farther south in the Andean region (a smaller sieva bean of the same species was developed in Mexico). However, by far the most familiar and most widespread of the American beans was the common bean (*P. vulgaris*), several varieties of which were cultivated from the Great Lakes to Argentina. These have since been further developed, so that today there are hundreds of varieties of the common bean, including the black bean, navy bean, kidney bean, pinto bean, white bean, and great northern bean.

Somewhat later in Asia, perhaps around 1000 B.C., the mung bean, the azuki bean, and the winged bean were domesticated, although all were apparently preceded a bit in China by the soybean. More complicated and less certain are the dates for the domestication of African legumes. The cowpea may have been cultivated as early as 3000 B.C. Domestication of the pigeon pea and the yam pea were presumably somewhat later, although too little is known with certainty about the development of legumes in Africa. In fact, in many instances, it is difficult if not impossible to determine which ones may have been Asian transients.

Without doubt, there are many species of legumes that have disappeared, and others may still await discovery. Some legumes, such as the peanut (which is eaten as a nut), the carob bean (made into a cocoa substitute), and alfalfa and jackbeans (used for animal fodder), are treated in separate entries.

See in addition: "Beans, Peas, and Lentils," Part II, Section C, Chapter 3; "Peanuts," Part II, Section D, Chapter 2; "Soybean," Part II, Section E, Chapter 5.

LEMON (*see also* **CITRUS FRUITS**) – A native of Southeast Asia, the lemon (*Citrus limon*) was slow to leave that region. Although it reached China about 1900 B.C., it was not until the Middle Ages that the fruit entered Europe via trade with the Arabs, who spread it around the Mediterranean basin from Greece to Spain. The word *citron* (or some variation of it) became the name given to the lemon by many of the various European peoples, although not by the Iberians. The Spaniards called it *limón,* and the Portuguese named it *limão* and carried both the fruit and the name to the New World. Indeed, lemons were reported growing in the Azores as early as 1494, and the men of Christopher Columbus and those who followed in their wake must have been quick to scatter lemon seeds around the West Indies, because lemon trees were recorded in the Greater Antilles

in 1557; 30 years later, lemon orchards were seen in South America.

The most common lemons are the "Lisbon" and the "Eureka" – both yellow ovoids with a blunt nipple at the flower end and a characteristic acid taste. The Eureka is distinguished by a short neck at the stem end and may have a few seeds, whereas the Lisbon is seedless. In the United States, Florida-grown lemons (of the Lisbon variety) are called "bearss." The Meyer lemon – a cross between a lemon and a tangerine – is golden in color and sweet. Yet another lemon, the bergamot, is grown largely for its aromatic leaves and skin. In terms of food use, lemons are employed in a number of ways. The taste of seafoods is frequently enhanced with a squeeze of lemon juice, and lemons are also used to flavor salads, vegetable and meat dishes, drinks (especially lemonade), sauces, and desserts. In addition, lemon peel yields an essential oil with a number of culinary and industrial applications. Lemons brim with vitamin C and, like limes, have long had a reputation as a scurvy preventive as well as a cure. During the California gold rush, scurvy was so prevalent that miners would pay up to a dollar for a lemon.

Common names and synonyms: Bearss, bergamot lemon, *citron* (archaic), Eureka lemon, *limão, limón, limou amarillo,* Lisbon lemon, Meyer lemon.

LEMON BALM – Probably a native of the Middle East and Asia, lemon balm (*Melissa officinalis*) has been cultivated in the Mediterranean at least since the time of the ancient Greeks. In fact, the name comes from the Greek *melissa,* meaning honeybee, which this lemon-scented plant attracts in abundance. The aromatic leaves with a distinct lemon odor are used fresh and dried to flavor fish and poultry dishes. They are also employed in stuffings, salads, and soups, and they go well in egg dishes. In addition, lemon balm is used as a flavoring in many liqueurs.

Common names and synonyms: Balm, balm mint, bee herb, garden balm, gentle balm, melissa, sweet balm.

Lemon cucumber – *see* **CUCUMBER, MANGO MELON**

LEMONGRASS – There are two grasses of the genus *Cymbopogon* that are cultivated for lemongrass oil. One is West Indian lemongrass (*Cymbopogon citratus*), which has long, spear-shaped leaves and is now grown in many tropical and subtropical parts of the world. The other is *C. flexuosus,* or East Indian lemongrass. In both instances, in addition to providing lemongrass oil for making perfumes, the whole stalk, with a strong, lemon-like flavor, is used in many dishes. Indeed, this herb is a most important ingredient in Asian cuisines, especially those of Vietnam and Thailand, where it provides both the base and added flavorings for numerous soups, including its namesake, "lemongrass soup." Lemongrass also goes well in curries, stews, and casseroles.

LEMON VERBENA - A plant originally native to Chile and Argentina, lemon verbena (*Lippia citriodora*) gives off a lemon-like scent when cut. It was long ago carried by the Spaniards to Europe, where an essential oil distilled from its leaves was employed in making soaps and cosmetics. The leaves of lemon verbena are used both fresh and dried in tisanes, salads, soups, stews, fruit drinks, and as a substitute for lemongrass in Asian recipes.

Common names and synonyms: Verbena.

Lemon vine - *see* **BARBADOS GOOSEBERRY**

LENTIL(S) (*see also* **BEANS, LEGUMES**) - Probably the oldest of the cultivated legumes (which also includes peas and beans), the lentil (*Lens esculenta*) - a native of Southwest Asia that had grown wild in the Middle East and central Asia - was brought under cultivation by the first Neolithic peoples of India, Egypt, and the Middle East some 9,000 years ago. They were heavily consumed by the ancient Greeks and Romans. The Egyptians were and remained the chief lentil exporter of those (and later) times and the Romans the chief importer. Since then, Europeans have continued to consume these little, flat, disk-shaped, dried seeds - mostly in soups, stews, and the like. The European variety is greenish or brownish in color, but others are often bright red, yellow, black, or green, and in South Asia they can be narrow in shape like rice grains. In India, lentils are usually served as *dahl* - a side dish that accompanies almost every meal - and they continue as a staple in the Middle East and Eastern Europe. Beans, peas, and lentils become intertwined in the Indian subcontinent. The black lentil (*Phaseolus mungo*) - used for *dahl* - is considered to have the best flavor. The red mung bean and the green mung bean or green lentil (*Phaseolus aureus*) are also used to make *dahl* in India and are sprouted throughout much of the rest of Asia. Yellow lentils (*Pisum sativum*) are closely related to the garden pea and, in addition to being used for *dahl*, are dry-roasted and seasoned to make a snack. Lentils are an important source of protein, are rich in folacin, iron, and phosphorus, and are a fair source of thiamine and vitamin B_6.

Common names and synonyms: Black lentil, brown lentil, green lentil, green mung bean, large-seeded lentil, red mung bean, small-seeded lentil, wild lentil, yellow lentil.

See in addition: "Beans, Peas, and Lentils," Part II, Section C, Chapter 3.

Lentisk - *see* **MASTIC TREE**

Leren - *see* **GUINEA ARROWROOT**

Lerenes - *see* **GUINEA ARROWROOT**

Lesser burnet - *see* **BURNET**

Lesser galanga(l) - *see* **GALANGAL**

LESSER YAM (*see also* **YAMS**) - An ancient cultivar that, although native to Southeast Asia, has been cul-

tivated in China for some 2,000 years, the lesser yam (*Dioscorea esculenta*) now grows throughout the world's tropics. These yams are used in soups and stews, are boiled as a vegetable, and are also roasted and fried.

Common names and synonyms: Asiatic yam, Chinese yam, potato yam.

See in addition: "Sweet Potatoes and Yams," Part II, Section B, Chapter 5.

LETTUCE - The various lettuces are plants of the genus *Lactuca* and - along with endive and dandelions - members of the daisy family. Wild lettuce was gathered for millennia by hunter-gatherers and was still being gathered by humans at the time of the ancient Greeks. The latter probably began its cultivation, which was continued by the Romans. The first cultivated lettuce was *L. serriola,* which is native to the Mediterranean region.

There are four major lettuce varieties. One, *L. sativa* var. *crispa,* consists of the red and green loose-leafed lettuces (also called garden lettuce), easily grown by gardeners and generally used in salads. A second, which is essentially confined to romaine (also called "cos" by the English after that once-Greek island), is *L. sativa* var. *longifolia* - the latter referring to the elongated head, the leaves of which are featured in Caesar salads. Butterhead lettuces (*L. sativa* var. *capitata*) include the Boston and Bibb lettuces with their "buttery" flavors. Boston lettuce is loosely headed and larger than the more compact Bibb lettuce (also called "limestone"), a recent (nineteenth-century) development. A fourth group consists of the iceberg lettuce (*L. sativa* var. *capitata*), more properly called "crisphead," which is actually classified with the butterheads but is a relatively new variety that emerged at the hands of growers in just the last century or so.

In addition to use in salads, lettuces are sometimes braised and creamed; in some cultures, lettuce seeds have been eaten as well as the leaves. Romaine and loose-leaf lettuces contain far more vitamin C and beta-carotene than iceberg, which provides relatively little in the way of nutrients. All, however, deliver some magnesium - perhaps the reason lettuce has been credited by some with soothing properties.

Common names and synonyms: Asparagus lettuce, Bibb lettuce, Boston lettuce, butterhead lettuce, celtuce, cos, crisphead lettuce, curled lettuce, garden lettuce, green oak-leaf lettuce, green romaine lettuce, head lettuce, iceberg lettuce, limestone lettuce, lolla rossa, loose-leaf lettuce, Perella Red, red oak-leaf lettuce, red romaine lettuce, romaine lettuce, Tango lettuce.

LEUCAENA - Known also as the "wild tamarind," "jumbie bean," and (in Spanish) *guaje,* the leucaena (*Leucaena leucocephala*) probably originated in Mexico and Central America but now grows throughout the world's tropics. It is a tree that produces flower buds, foliage, young pods, and seeds, all of which have been foods for humans since prehistoric times.

Common names and synonyms: Guaje, jumbie bean, lead tree, wild tamarind.

Libyan lotus - *see* **LOTUS**

Lichee - *see* **LITCHI**

Lichen(s) - *see* **ICELAND MOSS, MANNA**

Lichi - *see* **LITCHI**

LICORICE - The Greek word *glykyrrhiza,* meaning "sweet root," gave rise to the Latin name (*Glycyrrhiza glabra*) for licorice, which is the condensed juice from the roots of this Old World plant. A native of the Middle East, licorice was employed by the ancient Egyptians in medicinal preparations. Today, it is used in candy, to flavor liquors, and in the manufacture of tobacco. In addition, there is American licorice, *G. lepidota,* a wild licorice of North America with roots that were cooked by Native Americans, who also nibbled on the raw roots as a treat.

Common names and synonyms: American licorice, licorice root, liquorice, wild licorice.

See also: "Spices and Flavorings," Part II, Section F, Chapter 1.

Lily - *see* **DAYLILY, TIGER LILY**

Limão - *see* **LEMON**

Limau pagar - *see* **KUMQUAT**

LIME (*see also* **CITRUS FRUITS, LIMEQUAT**) - Like most of the other members of the citrus family, the lime (*Citrus aurantiifolia*) is native to Southeast Asia. It was first cultivated in China and India, then introduced in southern Europe (probably during the Crusades), and carried much later by the Spaniards to the West Indies. The original lime – small, round, and quite tart – is today called the "Mexican," "West Indian," or "Key" lime, with its juice deemed essential to Key lime pies. The limes generally encountered in the produce departments of U.S. supermarkets, however, are "Persian" (sometimes called "Tahiti") limes. These are larger and – save for the green skin – quite lemon-like in appearance. Persian limes are a fairly recent development, apparently the result of a cross between the Key lime and the citron early in the twentieth century. The lime and lemon industry of Florida (which provides close to 90 percent of the limes grown in North America) got its start in the 1880s, declined after freezes in the 1890s, and revived after World War I. Limes are very high in vitamin C and figured prominently in warding off scurvy, the dread disease of seamen from the sixteenth through the nineteenth centuries. In the eighteenth century, the British navy issued lime juice to all seamen to keep the disease at bay – hence the nickname "limeys."

Common names and synonyms: Green lemon, Key lime, Mexican lime, Persian lime, sour lemon, Tahiti lime, West Indian lime.

LIMEBERRY (*see also* **BERRIES**) - A spiny shrub of Southeast Asia, the limeberry (*Triphasia trifolia*) is now naturalized in Florida and Mexico, where it is often used for hedges. Its fruit is a small, red berry, called the "miracle fruit" because, after it is eaten, all subsequent foods eaten for hours to come will seem to have a sweet, lime-like taste.

Common names and synonyms: Miracle fruit.

LIMEQUAT (*see also* **KUMQUAT, LIME**) - A hybrid resulting from a cross between the Key lime and the kumquat, the limequat (genera *Citrus* and *Fortunella*) has a limelike flavor, and some varieties have an edible rind like the kumquat. Along with the orangequat and citrangequat, the limequat is the result of a U.S. Department of Agriculture breeding program to introduce the cold-hardiness of the kumquat into other plants.

LIMETTA (*see also* **CITRUS FRUITS**) - Also known as "sweet lemon" and "sweet lime" (with good reason), the limetta (*Citrus limetta*) looks like a lemon but is sufficiently lacking in citric acid that it is not sour. In fact, when eaten raw, the limetta tastes like lemonade, although it can be insipidly sweet when ripe. The best known of the limetta varieties is the Millsweet, which is grown in Italy and in California. Egypt and other tropical countries also cultivate limettas. Because they do not travel well, limettas are seldom seen in produce markets.

Common names and synonyms: Millsweet limetta, sweet lemon, sweet lime.

Limón - *see* **LEMON**

Limu - *see* **SEAWEED**

Ling - *see* **HEATHER**

Lingaro - *see* **ELAEAGNUS**

Lingen - *see* **LINGONBERRY**

LINGONBERRY (*see also* **BERRIES**) - The lingonberry (*Vaccinium vitis-idaea*) is the red and somewhat acidic fruit of a creeping evergreen shrub native to the northern regions of the world. Related to the cranberry, lingonberries are very popular in the Scandinavian countries, where they are made into preserves and pastries and served to accompany meat dishes. They are also mentioned with frequency as one of the foods of native North Americans.

Common names and synonyms: Cowberry, foxberry, lingen, mountain cranberry, rock cranberry.

Linseed (oil) - *see* **FLAX SEED**

Lipstick tree - *see* **ANNATTO**

Liquorice - *see* **LICORICE**

LITCHI - Also called lichee, lichi, and lychee, the litchi nut (*Litchi chinensis*) is actually a white, sweet berry with a rough, red or pink outer shell. A relative of the longan, litchis grow on tropical and subtropical evergreen trees that are members of the soapberry family and native to southern China, where they have been cultivated for at least 2,000 years. Only the pulp of the ripe fruit is eaten; the skin and seeds are inedible. Peeled, litchis look like large white grapes and have a sweet fragrance and flavor. Their appearance in the Western world began in 1775, when they were introduced in Jamaica, and now litchis are cultivated in Hawaii, California, and Florida (Florida's first crop was in 1916), as well as other tropical and subtropical areas of the world. Litchis are eaten raw, are also preserved and canned, and are high in vitamin C. In addition, dried litchis are consumed for their smoky flavor. Often called litchi nuts or litchis, these are not the central seeds – which are never eaten – but rather the raisinlike pulp.

Common names and synonyms: Leechee, lichee, lichi, litchi nut, lychee, lychi.

Litchi nut - *see* **LITCHI**

Little barley - *see* **WILD BARLEY**

LITTLE GOOSEBERRY TREE - Also called the "jungle plum," the little gooseberry tree (*Buchanania arborescens*) produces a wild, plumlike fruit that has served as food in the Australian bush for millennia.

Common names and synonyms: Jungle plum.

Little red banana - *see* **ENSETE**

Little stinker - *see* **CREOSOTE BUSH**

Liver fistulina - *see* **MUSHROOMS AND FUNGI**

Livingstone potato - *see* **KAFFIR POTATO**

Llerén - *see* **GUINEA ARROWROOT**

Llerenes - *see* **GUINEA ARROWROOT**

LOCAL GARDEN EGG - A close relative of the eggplant, the "local garden egg" (*Solanum incanum* and *S. macrocarpon*) comes in two forms. These are both cultivated in West Africa, even though the plants are generally regarded as wild forms of the eggplant. *Solanum incanum* is also known as the "bitter tomato" and is used in soups and stews to add flavor. *Solanum macrocarpon* is utilized more like the eggplant in that it is sliced and fried or cooked as a vegetable.

Common names and synonyms: Bitter tomato.

LOCUST (*see also* **AFRICAN LOCUST, AFRICAN LOCUST BEAN, CAROB, HONEY LOCUST, MESQUITE**) - A tall tree of eastern North America, also known as the "black locust," the locust tree (*Robinia pseudoacacia*) provided much in the way of food for Native Americans. Its edible flowers were sweet treats that were also used to make a tea; the young pods were cooked as a vegetable; and the seeds were boiled and eaten.

Common names and synonyms: Black locust, honey locust.

Locust bean - *see* **AFRICAN LOCUST BEAN, CAROB**

LOGANBERRY (*see also* **BERRIES, BLACKBERRY**) - The loganberry (*Rubus loganobaccus*) was produced in 1881 (it is a hybrid) by Judge James H. Logan (1841–1928) in Santa Cruz, California, and was introduced commercially in 1882. The red berry (similar to a blackberry) grows on a prickly bramble shrub, and although its parentage has been a matter of some debate, it would seem that it is a hybrid of the blackberry and the red raspberry. At one time it was grown commercially in California and the Pacific Northwest but proved overly susceptible to disease. Now loganberries generally are grown only in home gardens.

LONGAN - Sometimes called "dragon's-eyes," longans (*Euphoria longan = Dimocarpus longan*) are related to litchis. They are native to Southeast Asia and popular in southern China but are not a major crop outside of Asia, although a small one is raised in Florida. The fruit grows in clusters in the depths of thick evergreen trees that can reach up to 36 feet in height and 40 or more feet in circumference. This sweet fruit ranges in size from that of a grape to that of a plum. It is covered by a brown shell and has a whitish, jelly-like fruit with a single dark seed in the middle. Longans are usually eaten raw and are very high in vitamin C. They are also available canned.

Common names and synonyms: Cat's-eye, dragon's-eye, long an, longyen, lungan.

Long an - *see* **LONGAN**

Long bean - *see* **COWPEA, WINGED BEAN**

LONG CORIANDER - Also called "false coriander" and "fitweed," long coriander (*Eryngium foetidum*) is an herb with long, stiff, green leaves that have serrated edges and give off a strong smell when crushed. The plant is probably a native of China, where it has been used for thousands of years as a medicine as well as a substitute for coriander – both as a garnish and in cooking. The Chinese carried the long coriander throughout Asia, and it is now cultivated in Malaysia and India. It reached Europe in the seventeenth century and is also grown there.

Common names and synonyms: False coriander, fitweed.

See also: "Spices and Flavorings," Part II, Section F, Chapter 1.

Long-fruited jute - *see* **JEW'S-MALLOW**

Long green chilli - *see* **ANAHEIM, NEW MEXICO CHILLIES**

Longleaf ephedra - *see* **MORMON TEA**

Long pepper - *see* **PEPPER(CORNS)**

Long-podded cowpea - *see* **WINGED BEAN**

Long red chilli - *see* **ANAHEIM**

Longyen - *see* **LONGAN**

Lontar palm - *see* **WINE PALM**

Loose-leaf lettuce - *see* **LETTUCE**

LOQUAT - A native of eastern Asia, the loquat (*Eriobotrya japonica*) is a small tree of the rose family (Rosaceae), with fragrant white flowers and is often grown as an ornamental. It bears a popular Asian fruit - sometimes called the Japanese medlar or plum - that resembles an apricot in its yellow coloring, shape (like a pear), and tart flavor. The loquat originated in China and, after its introduction in Japan, was expanded into 10 or more species. Many uses have been found for this fruit in pies, jams, and salads, and in the production of liquors. It is also eaten fresh, stewed, candied, and preserved. Today, the fruit is grown in California, Florida, Hawaii, southern Europe, and Israel as well as East Asia. Loquats, however, are delicate fruits that are difficult to ship because they bruise easily. Canned loquats preserved in syrup are probably more widely available. Loquats are a fine source of beta-carotene.

Common names and synonyms: Advance, Champagne, Early Red, Japanese medlar, Japanese plum, nispero, Premier, tanaka, thales.

LOTUS – There are about 90 species of the water-lily family (Nymphaeaceae), many of which have served as food. The "sacred lotus" (*Nelumbo nucifera*), for example, is a perennial aquatic plant of India that was carried to China and to Egypt, where it was consumed at least 4,000 years ago. The poor in Egypt frequently have eaten the seeds and rhizome of the Egyptian lotus (*Nymphaea lotus*), boiled, dried, and ground into flour. Native Americans employed the yellow American marsh lotus (*Nelumbo lutea*) in much the same fashion, and the women would gather the roots of plants of the genus *Nuphar* from the lairs of beavers and muskrats that had collected them for their own use. The Chinese have eaten the rhizome of their pink lotus (*Nelumbo nucifera*) since ancient times and have used lotus leaves for wrapping food. In India, lotus is employed in curries, and all Asians appreciate its crunchy texture and its appearance. The tuberous roots have air tunnels, so that, when sliced, the crisp round looks like a piece of Swiss cheese or – perhaps a better description – a lacy-patterned snowflake. Lotus roots are sliced, chopped, and grated for soups, salads, and stir-frying.

Common names and synonyms: American marsh lotus, blue lotus, blue water lily, Chinese pink lotus, Egyptian lotus flower, Hindu sacred lotus, Libyan lotus, lotus root, water lily, water-lily tuber.

Lotus root – *see* **LOTUS**

LOVAGE – As is the case with numerous herbs employed at least since the time of the ancient Greeks and Romans, many uses for the seeds, leaves, and roots of lovage (*Levisticum officinale*) have been long forgotten. The plant, a native of Europe, looks like angelica, and in fact, its stems are candied like those of angelica. The leaves, however, are parsley-like, which has given rise to other names such as "Italian parsley," "love parsley," and "wild parsley." Yet lovage tastes very much like celery, and in parts of Italy the roots are peeled and cooked like celery root. Most uses, however, involve the leaves, which can be obtained fresh or dried (those that are dried retain their strong flavor), and sometimes the dried seeds, which are added to soups, salads, stuffings, and stews.

Common names and synonyms: Common lovage, garden lovage, Italian lovage, Italian parsley, love parsley, smallage, wild parsley.

Lovegrass – *see* **TEF**

Love-in-a-mist – *see* **NIGELLA**

Love-in-winter – *see* **PIPSISSEWA**

Love-lies-bleeding – *see* **AMARANTH**

Love parsley – *see* **LOVAGE**

Lovi-lovi – *see* **THORNLESS RUKAM**

Lucerne – *see* **ALFALFA**

LUCUMA – A native of South America that is partial to the coolness of highlands, the lucuma (*Pouteria obovata*) is, as its species name suggests, an egg-shaped fruit, also called eggfruit. It is yellow when mature and has a yellow flesh that is sometimes eaten raw but more often made into a drink. In Chile and Peru, where the lucuma is a commercial crop of some importance, the fruits are normally dried and ground into a powder that is stirred into milk.

Common names and synonyms: Eggfruit.

Lulo – *see* **NARANJILLA**

Lulu – *see* **AVOCADO**

Lungan – *see* **LONGAN**

Lupine(s) – *see* **ANDEAN LUPIN, BEANS**

Lupino – *see* **ANDEAN LUPIN, BEANS**

Lychee nut – *see* **LITCHI**

Lychi – *see* **LITCHI**

MABOLO – A relative of the persimmon and native to the Philippines but uncommon elsewhere, this fruit (*Diospyros discolor*) is also called the "velvet apple" from the reddish brown, peachlike hair that covers its thin skin. In fact, its shape is much like that of a peach. The skin may be pink or brown and turn a brilliant red in late summer when the fruit is ripe. Then it is eaten mostly fresh, skin and all, after the hairy covering has been rubbed off. But the mabolo is also made into desserts. Its flesh is creamy, its taste is sweet and slightly acidic, and its aroma is said to be reminiscent of cheese. For some, the taste may have to be an acquired one.

Common names and synonyms: Mabulo, velvet apple.

Mabulo – *see* **MABOLO**

MACA – A turnip-like plant of the mustard family, maca (*Lepidium meyenii*) was one of the root crops of the ancient Incas and has been cultivated for at least 2,000 years. Its small leaves are edible, and the small roots can be roasted or made into a gruel. Today, the plant is cultivated only on small plots at high altitudes in Peru, where strong winds and cold temperatures limit other crops. Peasants there believe that eating maca will help infertile couples to have children.

MACADAMIA NUT - Always in demand even though they contain more fat and calories than any of their counterparts, macadamia nuts are actually divided into two species, *Macadamia integrifolia* and *M. tetraphylla*. They represent one of Australia's few contributions to the food plants of the world (they were first called "Queensland nuts" by early white settlers). The nuts of *M. integrifolia* come from an evergreen tree native to the rain forests of southeastern Queensland, whereas *M. tetraphylla* is found farther south - in the rain forests of New South Wales.

Until 1858, they were enjoyed almost exclusively by the Aborigines, who had gathered them every autumn for millennia. But in that year a German botanist engaged in collecting Australian botanical specimens encountered and described a new genus of trees, which he named *Macadamia* in honor of an Australian friend, Dr. John Macadam (d. 1865).

Macadamia trees were introduced into Hawaii in 1881 and after 1930 became the basis of a major industry there. Indeed, at one time Hawaii produced some 90 percent of the world's supply, and macadamias remain one of that state's most important crops. However, Australian efforts over the past 30 years have begun to threaten the Hawaiian dominance of world production, and the nuts are grown in California as well. Impossible to open without some kind of nutcracker, macadamias have a superb crunch and taste has recommend them to the rarefied world of the gourmet - with a corresponding price. The nuts are a good source of protein and carbohydrates and are fairly high in magnesium and thiamine as well as iron.

Common names and synonyms: Australian nut, Queensland nut.

MACAW PALM - The macaw palm is also called "macaw tree" and *macaúba,* and these names are used for several species of the genus *Acrocomia,* which provide fruits that yield both pulp and kernel oil. Macaw palms grow throughout Central and South America in dry regions, where African oil palms do not do well. In some instances, the violet-scented oil is used only in perfumery, but in others the oils produced are edible and used in cooking.

Common names and synonyms: Macaúba, macaw tree.

MACE (*see also* **NUTMEG**) - This spice tastes like strong nutmeg, which is understandable, as mace is the lacy covering (aril) of the nutmeg berry. The berry fruits on an evergreen (*Myristica fragrans* = *M. officinalis*) that is a native of the Moluccas in the Spice Islands. After harvesting (several times a year), the berries are put in the sun to dry, and the mace is removed by hand and flattened into "blades" to dry separately from the nutmeg. Mace and nutmeg moved slowly westward, apparently reaching the Byzantine court in the sixth century. In the eleventh century, the famous Arab physician Avicenna described the two spices, and, in the following century, they seem to have reached Europe via Arab traders. Initially, however, they were used for perfumes or in medicines and only gradually found culinary applications.

After the Portuguese moved into the Spice Islands, they established a monopoly on mace and nutmeg as well as on cloves. The Dutch succeeded them as monopolists and worked zealously to prevent the export of any nutmeg trees. But during the wars of the eighteenth and nineteenth centuries, the islands were shuttled back and forth between Dutch and English domination, and - to be on the safe side - the latter took the opportunity to remove some of the trees to Singapore and to the West Indies. Today, the island of Grenada produces about 40 percent of the world's mace and nutmeg, although the trees are also grown in Brazil, Colombia, Central America, and Madagascar. Mace is available whole in "blades" and in ground form. It is used mostly in puddings, cakes, and sauces, and in poultry and fish dishes.

See in addition: "Spices and Flavorings," Part II, Section F, Chapter 1.

Mache - *see* **CORNSALAD**

Mâche - *see* **CORNSALAD**

Macho pepper - *see* **TEPÍN CHILLIES AND RELATIVES**

Macrette - *see* **CORAL BEAN**

Madeira - *see* **MALVASIA**

Maggistan - *see* **MANGOSTEEN**

Maguey - *see* **AGAVE**

MAHAWASOO - A South American tree, the mahawasoo (*Vaupesia cataractarum*) produces toxic oilseeds that are rendered edible by boiling. In the past, the seeds served as a famine food for Native Indians in the northwestern Amazon Basin, who also consumed them in connection with various ceremonial rites.

MAHUA - Native to the Indian subcontinent, mahua (*Madhuca longifolia*) is an evergreen tree, the seeds of which yield an oil that substitutes for butter and is used in cooking. The tree's flowers are also eaten and employed in the production of liqueurs. India is the major producer of mahua.

Maidenhair tree - *see* **GINKGO NUT**

MAIZE - Maize (*Zea mays*), native to the Americas and now the second-largest cereal crop in the world, has been one of the most versatile cultivated food plants in human history. Hundreds of varieties of maize (or "corn," as it is generally called in the United States) thrive in an astonishing assortment of geographic regions and environmental conditions, and the crop is employed in a number of ways, ranging from its increasing role as a staple food for humans in certain developing areas, to its principal present use as a feed for livestock animals (largely but not solely in industrialized countries), to its growing importance as a raw material in food processing and nonfood manufacturing.

It is usually accepted that maize was growing in Mesoamerica by between 8000 and 5000 B.C. Reliable archaeological evidence of domesticated maize dates from as long ago as 3600 B.C. in what is now central Mexico, and it is thought that domestication of the crop first took place - doubtless at a much earlier date - in this general area. To the south, a separate domestication of maize may have been accomplished at about the same time by South American Indians in the central Andes, or the crop may simply have traveled to that area from its point of origin. To the north, however, there seems to be no doubt that domesticated maize arrived much later, with locally adapted varieties appearing in the Eastern Woodlands of North America around A.D. 200 and in the central portion of the continent by about A.D. 600.

Indigenous American societies intensively cultivated maize, and it became a principal staple of the Aztecs, the Inca, the Maya, and many groups of North American Indians - especially those in what is now the southeastern United States - for several centuries before the arrival of Europeans. All parts of the plant were used for food and other purposes; the Inca even made maize "beers," known collectively as *chicha*. It is interesting that New World natives and their forebears - the original cultivators and consumers of maize - did not suffer from pellagra, the dangerous nutritional deficiency disease (caused by a lack of niacin, one of the B-vitamins) that has plagued most of the world's maize-eating peoples for centuries. This apparent immunity caused much puzzlement among medical researchers until it was realized that the Native American customs of preparing maize grain in alkali solutions and frequently consuming the grain in combination with leguminous vegetables tended to increase both the niacin availability and the protein quality of maize, thus greatly improving its nutritional value. But when maize was adopted as a staple food by Old World populations, and by non-natives (blacks and whites) in North America, these customs failed to accompany it, with pellagra the result.

Christopher Columbus carried maize to Spain, where by 1500 or so it was under cultivation. Before many years had passed, maize was being grown throughout the Iberian and Italian peninsulas and had appeared as a garden vegetable in England and central Europe; it had also entered eastern Europe via the Balkans and areas along the Danube River. By the seventeenth century, maize had become an important European field crop and staple food, especially in those areas that now comprise northern Italy, Romania, Slovenia, Serbia, and Bulgaria, in addition to Spain; perhaps a century

later, it was a principal dietary item in Austria-Hungary and southern France as well.

As the new crop spread across Europe, its New World origins were largely forgotten, but in each locality people at least knew that it came from somewhere else, and it was called "Barbary corn," "Egyptian corn," "Guinea corn," and a host of other names. "Corn" was a generic word meaning simply "grain" in a number of European languages, so that its many aliases actually identified maize as "foreign grain," and the American usage of "corn" for maize grows out of such terminology - in this case, "corn" is the shortened version of the English term "Indian corn," by which the colonists meant, of course, "Indian grain," or maize.

During the sixteenth century, Portuguese traders carried the plant to East Africa and Asia, whereas Arab merchants were probably responsible for its introduction into North Africa. Somewhat later, maize reached West Africa from the Caribbean and was used on both sides of the Atlantic as an inexpensive means of provisioning the human cargoes of the slave trade. The crop spread rapidly throughout the African continent, greatly augmenting the food supply, had become a major staple by the end of the nineteenth century, and even increased in importance by the late twentieth century. In Asia, maize spread along trade routes from the Indian subcontinent, reaching points in China and Southeast Asia by the mid-sixteenth century. It was established in the Philippines and Indonesia during the seventeenth century, and during the eighteenth was much expanded as a crop in China. From there, it spread to Korea and Japan.

Meanwhile, in North America, the early English colonists as well as later immigrants (unlike their Spanish predecessors) had adopted maize as a staple food, and the grain later became the foundation of the U.S. diet and the country's agricultural economy. Countless American dishes and recipes testify to the early pervasiveness of "corn" in direct human consumption, and beginning about the turn of the nineteenth century, U.S. farmers and gardeners began to develop a number of varieties of sweet corn for use as a vegetable (sweet varieties had, however, existed long before this in South America). Moreover, from the mid-nineteenth century onward, U.S. agricultural scientists took the lead in creating hybrid maize varieties with greatly increased grain yields and other desirable characteristics, and with the growth of American livestock industries, the value of "corn" for feeding animals destined to become food themselves surpassed even its importance as a human staple.

Today, maize provides the basis for a number of commercial and industrial products as well as human foods, including starches, sweeteners, corn "flakes" and other packaged breakfast cereals, corn "chips," corn oil, corn syrup, whiskeys, beers, ethanol, plastics, and – most important – animal feed.

Maize is a good source of carbohydrates, and thus of calories and energy, and is high in protein and certain essential fatty acids. But its protein quality is marginal, with low levels of the essential amino acids tryptophan and lysine. It is also low in calcium, and white maize is low in vitamin A.

Common names and synonyms: Bactrian typha, Barbary corn, *blé de Turquie,* corn, cornmeal, *cucurutz,* dent maize, Egyptian corn, flint maize, floury maize, Guinea corn, Indian corn, Indian meal, *kana,* mealies, *milho,* popcorn, Roman corn, *sara chulpi,* Sicilian corn, Spanish corn, sweet corn, Syrian dourra, Turkie corne, Turkish wheat, Virginia wheat, waxy maize, Welsch corn, yellow maize.

See also: "Maize," Part II, Section A, Chapter 4.

Maja pahit - *see* **QUINCE**

MALABAR ALMOND - Also called the "Indian almond," the "country almond," and the "tropical almond," the Malabar almond (*Terminalia catappa*) is an evergreen tree of tropical Asia – probably a native of the Malay Peninsula, although it is now planted in North America and elsewhere as an ornamental. The fruit is about 2 inches long and red to green in color, and its pulp is eaten for its sweet flavor. The almond-shaped kernel inside the fruit is also eaten both raw and roasted, but first it is necessary to break its very tough shell.

Common names and synonyms: Country almond, Indian almond, tropical almond.

Malabar chestnut - *see* **MALABAR NUT**

Malabar gourd - *see* **FIG-LEAFED GOURD, SQUASH AND PUMPKIN**

MALABAR NUT - A nut known by a number of common names such as "Guyana chestnut" and "French peanut," the malabar nut also has two scientific names – *Bombax glabra* and *Pachira aquatica.* A native of the tropical estuaries in a region that stretches from southern Mexico to Guyana and northern Brazil, the malabar nut grows on an attractive evergreen tree. The fruit is a relatively large green pod (4 to 12 inches long and 2 to 2.5 inches in diameter), which contains the nuts until it finally bursts to spill them on the ground. Consumed fresh, the nuts have a flavor reportedly like that of peanuts; when roasted or fried, the taste resembles that of chestnuts. The nuts are also ground into flour for bread, and the young leaves and flowers of the tree are cooked as a vegetable. Another Malabar nut, *Adhatoda vasica,* comes from an East Indian shrub and is used medicinally.

Common names and synonyms: French peanut, Guiana chestnut, Guyana chestnut, Malabar chestnut, provision tree, saba nut.

MALABAR SPINACH - Also called "red vine spinach," malabar spinach (*Basella rubra = B. alba*) is a plant of the Asian tropics that has now spread around the world to be cultivated in most tropical and temperate regions. In the Western Hemisphere, malabar spinach is grown in Mexico and parts of North America for its succulent leaves that are used in the same ways as spinach – as a potherb and raw in salads.

Common names and synonyms: Ceylon spinach, Indian spinach, red vine spinach, vine spinach.

Malacca tree - *see* **AMALAKA**

Malagueta (pepper) - *see* **BRAZILIAN MALAGUETA, MELEGUETA PEPPER**

MALANGA - When the Spaniards arrived in the West Indies, one of the first native American plants they described was *yautía* – still the Puerto Rican name for malanga. However, this leads us straight into a semantic jungle, because the plant is also called "tania," "elephant's-ear," and a score of other names, including "cocoyam" (which it is not) in Africa. Contributing to the confusion are some 40 species of malanga, many of which are mixed up with taro (*Colocasia esculenta*).

Perhaps the most important distinction to be made is that between white malanga (*Xanthosoma sagittifolium = X. violaceum*) and yellow (*X. atrovirens*). White malanga is tania and *yautía* and was also called "dasheen" historically in the West Indies – a name that also is used to refer to taro. However, white malanga is not cultivated for its tuber (as taro is) but rather for its stem and heart leaves, known in the West Indies as callaloo.

Yellow malanga, in contrast, is cultivated for a corm that is shaped like a big yam and is cooked in much the same ways, by boiling, steaming, baking, frying, or roasting. In Africa, the corms are sometimes ground to make "foo-foo." Malanga most probably originated in South America and was brought to the Caribbean Islands by migrating Taino and Carib Indians. It made another leap when it was introduced into West Africa – to feed slaves bound for the Americas – and took root there as one kind of cocoyam. Today, malanga is also cultivated in Central America, the Pacific Islands, and tropical Asia. Malanga provides mostly energy in the form of carbohydrates, although the yellow variety does contain a little vitamin A.

Common names and synonyms: American taro, callaloo, cocoyam, dasheen, elephant's-ear, kong(-)kong taro, spoonflower, tania, tannia, white malanga, *yautía,* yellow malanga.

See also: "Taro," Part II, Section B, Chapter 6.

Malangay - *see* **COCOYAM**

Malangu - *see* **COCOYAM**

MALAY APPLE - A native of Indonesia, the jambu merah tree has been cultivated for millennia. In the past few centuries, the Portuguese spread its fruit, the Malay apple (*Eugenia malaccensis = Syzygium malaccense*), throughout the tropical Old World, and the English brought it to the West Indies in the New World. Malay apples are oblong, about the size of a large orange, and red or crimson when ripe. They are generally eaten raw.

Common names and synonyms: Jambu merah (tree), Tahiti apple.

Malay gooseberry - *see* **OTAHEITE GOOSEBERRY**

Malka - *see* **CLOUDBERRY**

MALLOW - Native to Europe, several herbs of the Malvaceae family are called mallows and are employed to flavor cheese. In the United States, the best known of the mallows is the marsh mallow (*Althaea officinalis*). The plant was so called because it was found in and around marshes near the sea, and it has been naturalized in the marshes of eastern North America. In past centuries, the roots of the marsh mallow were used to flavor candy "marshmallows," which are now made with sugar, corn syrup, gelatin, and starch, then dusted with a little powdered sugar.

Common names and synonyms: Marsh mallow.

Malmsey - *see* **MALVASIA**

MALOGA BEAN - Also called the "flowering bean," the maloga bean (*Vigna lancelota*) is an Australian tree whose roots served as food for the Aborigines.

Common names and synonyms: Flowering bean.

Malt - *see* **BARLEY**

Maltaise orange - *see* **BLOOD ORANGE**

Maltese Blood (orange) - *see* **BLOOD ORANGE**

Maltese orange - *see* **BLOOD ORANGE**

MALVASIA (*see also* **GRAPES**) - An ancient fruit of Greece, Malvasia grapes (*Vitis vinifera*) were used during the Middle Ages to make sweet dessert wines that were frequently shipped from the Greek port of Monemvasia. The name Malvasia is an Italian corruption of that city's name, just as *malvoisie* is a French corruption and "malmsey" an English one. Actually, the name "Malvasia" refers today to a complex of varieties; these are among Italy's most widely planted grapes and constitute an important part of the grape crop of Spain as well. Those planted are mostly white, but there are also red grapes, and both sweet and dry wines are made from them. In addition, the Malvasia lives on in Madeira wine, which has traditionally been based on this grape.

Common names and synonyms: Madeira, malmsey, *malvoisie.*

See in addition: "Wine," Part III, Chapter 13.

Malvoisie - *see* **MALVASIA**

MAMEY SAPOTE - Little known outside the American tropics, the mamey (also mammey) sapote (*Calocarpum sapota = Pouteria sapota*) is related to the sapodilla and is found chiefly in Central America, Mexico, northern South America, Cuba, Hispaniola, and the state of Florida. The light, coffee-colored fruit grows on medium-sized trees. It is a large fruit, weighing up to a pound, with a rough, brown skin. The flesh is salmon colored and surrounds a large avocado-like pit. It has a rich and distinctive flavor, not appreciated by everyone. The mamey sapote is a good source of vitamins A and C.

Common names and synonyms: Mammey sapote, sapota.

MAMMEE - The tropical American mammee (*Mammea americana*) is native to the West Indies (and its fruits are common in markets there) but is now grown in the tropics and subtropics around the world, including Florida. Also known as the mammee apple and the San Domingo apricot, the fruit grows on trees that can reach 60 feet in height. It is about the size of a small grapefruit and tastes something like a tart apple while still green and something like an apricot when it is ripe and stewed. The fruit is sometimes eaten raw and in salads but is generally cooked. Mammee flowers are used to make an aromatic liqueur called *eau de Créole.* The mammee is not related to the mamey sapote.

Common names and synonyms: Mammee apple, mammy apple, San Domingo apricot, South American apricot.

Mammee apple - *see* **MAMMEE**

Mammee sapota - *see* **SAPODILLA**

Mammey sapote - *see* **MAMEY SAPOTE**

Mammy apple - *see* **MAMMEE**

Mamoncilla - *see* **SPANISH LIME**

Mamoncillo - *see* **SPANISH LIME**

Manchurian wild rice - *see* **WATER BAMBOO**

Mandarin melon-berry - *see* **CHE**

MANDARIN ORANGE (*see also* **CITRUS FRUITS**) - Other citrus fruits that are very similar (or identical) to the Mandarin orange include the tangerine, the *satsuma,* and the "Clementine," all of which are identified as members of *Citrus reticulata* and orange varieties. The Mandarin - developed in China, or possibly Cochin China (southern Vietnam) - probably took its name from the yellow robes of the Chinese civil servants called Mandarins. It worked its way toward the Near East at a leisurely pace and reached Europe directly from China only at the beginning of the nineteenth century. By midcentury, Mandarin oranges were being grown around the Mediterranean, and they entered the United States at about the same time. Believed to have originated in Tangier, they came to be known as tangerines in North America.

The Clementine - a cross between the Mandarin and the bitter orange - originated in Algiers, whereas the *satsuma* is a seedless Japanese Mandarin. In the early 1870s, Florida orange grower Col. George L. Dancy pioneered commercial tangerine cultivation, and the Dancy tangerine became the most popular of the Mandarin oranges. Florida remains the largest tangerine producer, although the fruits are also grown in California, Texas, and Louisiana. In 1898, U.S. Department of Agriculture botanist Walter Tennyson Swingle developed the tangelo, a cross between a tangerine and a grapefruit. All fruits belonging to *C. reticulata* are small, sweet, easily peeled, and segmented.

Common names and synonyms: Clementine, Dancy tangerine, *satsuma,* tangelo, tangerine.

Mandioc - *see* **MANIOC**

Mandioca - *see* **MANIOC**

MANDRAKE (*see also* **MAYAPPLE**) - An herb of southern Europe and North Africa, the mandrake (*Mandragora officinarum*) has spherical yellow fruits that in the past were believed to have aphrodisiacal properties. This was doubtless because the plant has a long forked root that was believed to resemble the human body from the waist down and was the subject of much sexual superstition. It was also a narcotic. The root was ground and used to encourage a sense of well-being, and possibly of enhanced sexuality.

Manga - *see* **MANGO**

MANGABA - An interesting vine (*Hancornia speciosa*) of Brazil called *mangabeira* produces the mangaba fruits, which are plum-sized and red and have a sweet taste. The same plant also produces a latex that yields a rubber.

Common names and synonyms: Mangabeira.

Mangabeira - *see* **MANGABA**

Man-gay - *see* **MANGO**

Mangel - *see* **BEET**

MANGELWURZEL (*see also* **BEET**) - From the German *Mangold-Wurzel,* meaning "beet root," the mangelwurzel is a variety of the common beet (*Beta vulgaris*) that is chiefly produced for cattle feed, although the young beets are sometimes consumed by humans.

Common names and synonyms: Mangle, mangold, mangold-wurzel.

Mangetout - *see* **PEAS, SUGAR PEA**

Mangga - *see* **MANGO**

Manggis - *see* **MANGOSTEEN**

Manggusta - *see* **MANGOSTEEN**

Mangle - *see* **MANGELWURZEL**

MANGO (*see also* **DUIKA, HORSE MANGO**) - The mango tree (*Mangifera indica*) is an Asian evergreen that can attain a height of 100 feet or more. It is cultivated throughout the tropics of the world, most abundantly in India (where it may have originated and where the mango is connected with both folklore and religious ceremonies) for its greenish yellow fruit, much of which is made into chutney. Mango flesh surrounds a flat but rounded seed or stone and is sweet and golden, even though the skin is tough and inedible. Mangoes are eaten ripe and pickled when green.

All of the 40-some species of *Mangifera* are Southeast Asian in origin, and some may have been domesticated as early as 4,000 to 6,000 years ago. Exactly how they were subsequently dispersed around the world is a matter of conjecture. The Portuguese (who named the fruit *manga*) doubtless had a hand in this in the sixteenth century, taking the mango to islands of the Pacific, throughout the Indian Ocean, and to the east and west coasts of

Africa. Mangoes were planted in Brazil around 1700, were carried to the West Indies (where they remain extremely popular) at about the middle of the eighteenth century, and reached Florida (which now produces about 20 percent of the world's mangoes) in North America in the early nineteenth century.

Mangoes belong to the Anacardiaceae family, which includes poison ivy, and for those who are allergic, touching mango juice can cause the skin to swell and blister. For some reason, Midwesterners in the United States call sweet bell peppers "mangoes"; both are good sources of vitamin A and a great source of vitamin C and potassium, not to mention fiber. The mango kernel is also eaten after it is boiled or roasted.

Common names and synonyms: Manga, man-gay, mangga, man-kay.

Mangold - *see* **MANGELWURZEL**

Mangold-Wurzel - *see* **MANGELWURZEL**

MANGO MELON (*see also* **MELONS**) - The genus *Cucumis* embraces the different species of melons and cucumbers. The mango melon (*C. melo* var. *chito*) is a muskmelon that is mistakenly called a mango, and the fact that it is also known as a "lemon cucumber" further indicates a considerable popular ambivalence about this fruit's identity. It is a small melon – about the size of an orange, with a yellow skin and white flesh – and is cultivated primarily for making preserves and "mango pickles."

Common names and synonyms: Lemon cucumber.

See in addition: "Cucumbers, Melons, and Watermelons," Part II, Section C, Chapter 6.

Mango squash - *see* **CHAYOTE**

Mangostan - *see* **MANGOSTEEN**

MANGOSTEEN - This fruit, native to Malaya, enjoys a reputation among those who should know as the world's most delicious fruit. Actually a berry (and unrelated to the mango), the mangosteen (*Garcinia mangostana*) is the size of a small- to medium-sized orange, and at first glance with its purplish leathery skin looks something like a pomegranate. Its flesh is juicy, pink- or cream-colored, and somewhat tart; its taste blends the flavors of grape and strawberry by some accounts and those of peach and pineapple according to others.

The Portuguese called the fruit *manggusta* and later mangistão and *maggistan,* but by the seventeenth century it had become "mangostan" and eventually "mangosteen." It was described by Captain James Cook in 1770, was introduced in Ceylon (Sri Lanka) around 1800, and spread out from there. Today, the fruit is grown in parts of the southern United States, the West Indies, and Central America, as well as Southeast Asia, but nowhere on a commercial scale because it bruises too easily to ship well. A mangosteen is almost always eaten raw.

Common names and synonyms: King-of-fruits, *maggistan,* manggis, *manggusta,* mangostan, men-gu.

MANGROVE (*see also* **BURMA MANGROVE, TAGAL MANGROVE, NIPA PALM**) – The fruits and leaves of mangroves have long been used as food by indigenous peoples – especially during hard times. On the coasts of tropical America, West Africa, and the islands of Polynesia, the mangrove in question is the red mangrove (*Rhizophora mangle*), the fruit of which, with its starchy interior, can be eaten both fresh and preserved. Moreover, a light wine has been made from its fermented juice. In the Old World tropics (from South and East Africa to southern China, Australia, Melanesia, and Micronesia), the plant is the Asiatic mangrove (*R. mucronata*). This fruit would seem to be sweeter than its New World counterpart and, again, can be made into a light wine. Both plants have also long been a part of the pharmacopoeia of folk medicines.

Common names and synonyms: American mangrove, Asiatic mangrove, red mangrove.

Mani – *see* **PEANUT**

Manihot – *see* **MANIOC**

Manila bean – *see* **WINGED BEAN**

Manila tamarind – *see* **PITHECELLOBIUM**

Manilla bean – *see* **WINGED BEAN**

MANIOC – The name "manioc" (*Manihot esculenta*) comes from the Brazilian Indian word *mandioca,* but the plant is also known as cassava, yuca, and the tapioca-plant. A Brazilian native, it is a perennial shrub with long, narrow, starchy tubers. Manioc traveled in canoes with South American Indians migrating northward into the Caribbean and, later, in Portuguese ships from Brazil to Africa. Its advantages are that it requires little labor to cultivate yet produces more calories per acre than any other food plant, and it keeps in the ground until needed.

A disadvantage is that save for carbohydrates, it has little to offer in the way of nutrients. Another is that although sweet manioc varieties pose no threat, the roots of most varieties are bitter and can contain enough cyanide to be toxic. The poison must first be removed by pounding, scraping, and cooking. The vegetable is then boiled or baked like a potato, made into a flour for breads, and employed to thicken soup. The meal or flour is sprinkled onto most any dish. Tapioca is a kind of manioc flour.

Common names and synonyms: Cassava, mandioc, *mandioca,* manihot, tapioca-plant, yuca.

See also: "Manioc," Part II, Section B, Chapter 2.

Man-kay – *see* **MANGO**

MANNA – Some of the lichens of the genus *Lecanora* are called manna, presumably because one of them, *L. esculenta,* (a kind of moss containing a fungus that grows on trees, rocks, and stones and is blown about the desert), is reputed to be the manna that dropped out of heaven in ancient times to sustain the Israelites in their flight from Egypt. In the Middle East, lichen bread and manna jelly are made from it. Another "manna lichen" is *Gyrophora esculenta,* which is widely eaten in Japan.

Common names and synonyms: Manna lichen.

MANNA GUM – Also known as "manna eucalyptus" and "gum tree," the manna gum (*Eucalyptus viminalis*) is an Australian native (as are all eucalypts) that exudes a red gum or "manna" from punctures or cracks in the bark. This gum, along with the tree's aromatic leaves, was eaten by Australian Aborigines.

Common names and synonyms: Gum tree, manna eucalyptus.

Manna lichen – *see* **MANNA**

MANZANA (*see also* **CHILLI PEPPERS**) – Appearing very much like a small sweet bell pepper, the manzana, with black seeds that distinguish it as a member of *Capsicum pubescens,* has nothing sweet about it. Barely known to consumers in the United States, this pepper (like the other members of *C. pubescens*) originated in South America and migrated north, reaching Mexico and Central America, where it is now cultivated, perhaps as late as a century ago. This hot, deep yellow–colored pepper is frequently stuffed or used in salsas.

Common names and synonyms: Chile caballo, chilli rocoto, manzano.

See in addition: "Chilli Peppers," Part II, Section C, Chapter 4.

Manzanillo (olive) – *see* **OLIVE**

MAPLE SYRUP AND MAPLE SUGAR – Both maple syrup and maple sugar are made from the sap of several varieties of maple trees (*Acer* spp.) and especially from that of the sugar maple (*A. saccharum*). All of these trees are natives of the northern United States and Canada. The sap is collected by boring a tap-hole into the tree, then inserting a spout upon which a sap-bucket is hung. The collected sap is subsequently boiled down into syrup, and the granular residue left when all the liquid is gone is the sugar. Maple sugar (and syrup) was the only sweetener for Native Americans and continued to be the only one used in much of Canada and by some of those in the northeastern United States until fairly recently. The gathering season is in the early spring and ends when the trees begin to bud.

Common names and synonyms: Sugar maple (tree).

Mapuey – *see* **CUSH-CUSH YAM**

Maracuja – *see* **PASSION FRUIT**

Mare's-tail – *see* **HORSEWEED**

MARIGOLD – Although marigolds generally are thought of as members of the genus *Tagetes* and natives of tropical America, this familiar daisy-like flower (*Calendula officinalis*) – the "pot marigold" – is said to have originated in Europe. Its orange petals were used as one of the first coloring agents for cheeses and are sometimes employed as a substitute for saffron in rice dishes. Nowadays, the pot marigold is used much less frequently for seasoning foods than it was in the past, especially in the Middle Ages, when its cultivation began.

Common names and synonyms: Pot marigold, Scotch marigold.

MARJORAM AND OREGANO - Native to the Mediterranean region, oregano (*Origanum vulgare*) is actually a variety of wild marjoram. The name "oregano" comes from a Greek term meaning "joy of the mountains"; indeed, oregano thrives in mountainous terrain, and strongly flavored varieties of this herb - called *rigani* - grow in the mountains of Greece. Marjoram comes as pot marjoram (*O. onites*) and sweet marjoram (*O. majorana*). Both varieties have a flavor similar to, but more delicate than, that of oregano. Although marjoram and oregano have long played an important role in French, Greek, and especially Italian cuisines, it was only with the return of American GIs from Italy after World War II that the two spices became well known in the United States. They are available both fresh and dried and go well in tomato-based dishes. Oregano is the quintessential herb for pizza and is also an important ingredient in chilli powders.

Common names and synonyms: Knotted marjoram, pot marjoram, *rigani,* Spanish oregano, sweet marjoram, wild marjoram.

See also: "Spices and Flavorings," Part II, Section F, Chapter 1.

Marmalade box - *see* **GENIPAP**

Marmalade plum - *see* **SAPODILLA**

Marmelo - *see* **BAEL FRUIT**

MARROW - In the case of plant foods, the term "marrow" in its broadest sense can mean the pulp of any fruit. For the British in particular, "vegetable marrow" or "marrow squash" generally connotes summer squashes with white to green skins like the zucchini (*Cucurbita pepo*). In the eastern United States, however, "marrow" often indicates a huge orange winter squash (*C. maxima*) used in cooking.

Common names and synonyms: Marrow squash, vegetable marrow.

See also: "Squash," Part II, Section C, Chapter 8.

Marrow stem - *see* **KALE**

Marsh-elder - *see* **SUMPWEED**

Marsh mallow - *see* **MALLOW**

Marsh marigold - *see* **COWSLIP**

Marsh salad - *see* **CORNSALAD**

Marsh samphire - *see* **GLASSWORT**

Marsh trefoil - *see* **BOG MYRTLE**

Martynia - *see* **UNICORN PLANT**

MARULA PLUM - A large wild tree of southern Africa, the marula (*Sclerocarya caffra*) has plum-like fruits with a thick yellow peel and white, sweet-sour flesh. They are eaten raw, used to flavor alcoholic beverages, and made into juices and jams. In addition, the seeds of the fruits are eaten like nuts by aficionados, who are clearly enthusiastic about what they call the "king's-nut."

Common names and synonyms: King's-nut.

Marumi - *see* **KUMQUAT**

MASHUA - Also called *anu* (among other common names) and related to the ornamental nasturtium, the carrot- and potato-shaped tubers of mashua (*Tropaeolum tuberosum*) are an important staple in the Andean region, esprcially at altitudes where potatoes and other tubers cannot be grown successfully. The tubers of mashua are not eaten raw, but rather are cured in the sun, then freeze-dried and used like potatoes. The plant is also said to have medicinal properties.

Common names and synonyms: Anu, capucine, *ysaño.*

Mast - *see* **BEECHNUT**

Masterwort - *see* **PURPLESTEM ANGELICA**

MASTIC BULLY - *Sideroxylon mastichodendron* is a tree of South Florida and the West Indies with "iron-like" wood that in the past was useful for shipbuilding. The fruits of this and related species such as *S. foetidissimum* are edible although quite acidic.

MASTIC TREE - Also called "mastic shrub," the mastic tree (*Pistacia lentiscus*) is a small tree grown in southern Europe for mastic (also "lentisk") - a resin obtained by cutting into the tree. Mastic is used mostly for varnishes, paints, and the like, but the word "mastic" also designates an alcoholic beverage flavored with mastic. Another group of trees called mastic trees are South American "pepper trees" (genus *Schinus*), especially *S. molle,* a Peruvian evergreen that has small red drupes - the pink peppercorns that have recently been discovered to be potentially harmful. In the past, a good *chicha* (a beerlike drink) was made from the seeds of the tree they call *molle* in Peru.

Common names and synonyms: Lentisk, mastic shrub, *molle,* pepper tree.

Mat bean - *see* **MOTH BEAN**

Maté - *see* **YERBA MATÉ**

MATRIMONY VINE - Also called "box thorn," *gow kee,* and *chu chi,* the matrimony vine (of the genus *Lycium*) comprises *L. chinense* (originally from East Asia) and a number of species native to the southwestern United States and Mexico, such as *L. andersonii* - the "desert thorn." The tender leaves and shoots were eaten in the past by Native Americans and are still consumed in Asia. In addition, the plants produce red, juicy, oblong berries (known as *frutillos* in Mexico) that are edible but do not seem to excite much enthusiasm. They were put to use as a famine food by Native Americans.

Common names and synonyms: Box thorn, *chu chi,* desert thorn, *frutillo, gow kee.*

Matsutake (mushroom) - *see* **MUSHROOMS AND FUNGI**

Ma-tum - *see* **QUINCE**

MAUKA - Called *mauka* in Bolivia and *chago* (among other terms) in Peru, this plant (*Mirabilis expansa*) constitutes a seeming contradiction: It is a virtually unknown crop with a wide geographic distribution. Grown in the Andes region from Venezuela to Chile in small vegetable gardens, the cultivation of *mauka* was described for the first time only a quarter of a century ago. Both the tuberous roots and the leaves are consumed – the latter in salads and chilli sauces. The roots are used like manioc and are an ingredient in soups and stews.

Common names and synonyms: Chago.

MAVRODAPHNE (*see also* **GRAPES**) – Mavrodaphne is an eastern Mediterranean wine grape (*Vitis vinifera*), which the Greeks in particular have used to make sweet, portlike, dessert wines for many centuries. The name means "black laurel," and the grape is aromatic and powerful.

See in addition: "Wine," Part III, Chapter 13.

Maw seed – *see* **POPPY SEED**

Maya – *see* **PINGUIN**

MAYAPPLE (*see also* **MAYPOP**) – Because it was commonly known as the "American mandrake" or just plain "mandrake," many refrained from eating the mayapple (*Podophyllum peltatum*), fearing that like the mandrake of Europe, it too was poisonous. In fact, the roots, leaves, and seeds of this woodland plant of eastern North America *are* poisonous, but its lemon-shaped fruit is not and is often made into a marmalade. This wild-growing plant with its distinctive white flowers was surely also a food of Native Americans, who probably learned the hard way that only its fruit was edible.

Common names and synonyms: American mandrake, mandrake.

May-bob – *see* **COWSLIP**

Maycock – *see* **MAYPOP**

Mayflower – *see* **TRAILING ARBUTUS**

MAYGRASS – In North America, there are native species of maygrass (*Phalaris caroliniana*) as well as other species of the genus *Phalaris* that have been introduced from the Mediterranean region, from West Africa, and from the Canary Islands (the latter, *P. canariensis*, is called "canary grass"). Their seeds have been used as a grain and the young shoots eaten raw or cooked like a vegetable.

Common names and synonyms: Canary grass.

Mayhaw – *see* **HAWTHORN BERRY**

MAYPOP – A North American cousin to the South American passion fruit, the maypop (*Passiflora incarnata*) grows wild in the southeastern United States. Originally, the plant was called "maycock" after the Powhatan *machawq*, suggesting that Native Americans were familiar with it. The fruit is about the size of a small lemon, has a hint of a lemon taste, and has also been called "mayapple." In addition to the use of the fruit as a food, the leaves, stems, and yellow flowers of maypops have long been used medicinally.

Common names and synonyms: Apricot vine, granadilla, mayapple, maycock, wild passion-flower.

Mazzard – *see* **CHERRY**

Meadow-bright – *see* **COWSLIP**

Meadow fern – *see* **SWEET FERN**

Meadow mushroom – *see* **MUSHROOMS AND FUNGI**

Meadow parsnip – *see* **COW PARSNIP**

Meadow salsify – *see* **MOONFLOWER**

Mediterranean rocket – *see* **ARUGULA**

Medjool date – *see* **DATE**

MEDLAR – Originating in Persia (and possibly also in Europe), the medlar (*Mespilus germanica*) belongs to the apple family but is a small, round, brown fruit that looks like a plum. Medlars were known to the ancient Greeks, and Pliny wrote of the Romans having three kinds. Like so many fruits and vegetables, medlars were carried throughout the Roman Empire and afterward remained very popular in Europe. The fruit traveled with Europeans to North America, where medlar trees now grow from the southern United States to southern Canada. The medlar is interesting in that it is not edible until well after it has achieved ripeness – in fact when it has begun to decay. Its juice makes a fine cold drink, and although the pulp was once consumed raw, most medlars that are used nowadays go into jelly. Medlars are, in fact, becoming a forgotten fruit. This medlar should not be confused with the loquat, which is also called the Japanese medlar.

Meetin' seed – *see* **FENNEL**

Meiwa – *see* **KUMQUAT**

Melano – *see* **KIWANO**

Melanzana – *see* **EGGPLANT**

MELEGUETA PEPPER – Also known as "malagueta pepper" and "grains-of-paradise," melegueta pepper (*Aframomum melegueta*) is the pungent seed of a West African plant. Related to cardamom – and with a similar odor – the tiny grains have a hot and peppery taste and are used as a spice.

Common names and synonyms: Grains-of-paradise, Guinea grains, malagueta pepper.

See also: "Spices and Flavorings," Part II, Section F, Chapter 1.

Melilot – *see* **SWEET CLOVER**

Melissa – *see* **BEE BALM, LEMON BALM**

Melist – *see* **SWEET CLOVER**

Mellarosa – *see* **BERGAMOT**

Melloco – *see* **ULLUCO**

MELON CACTUS – Called "melon-thistle," "Turk's-cap," "Turk's-head," and *melon*, as well as melon cactus, about 35 species in the genus *Melocactus* in one form or another resemble melons and have a bristly crown filled with woolly fibrous matter. Many of these natives of the West Indies, Central America, and tropical South America (especially *M. communis* of Jamaica) bear small, pinkish, edible fruits.

Common names and synonyms: Melon, melon-thistle, Turk's-cap, Turk's-head.

Melon fruit – *see* **PAPAYA**

Melongene – *see* **EGGPLANT**

Melon pawpaw - *see* **PAPAYA**
Melon(-)pear - *see* **PEPINO**
MELONS (*see also* **PUMPKIN, SQUASH AND PUMPKIN,** and various melon entries) - Most melons are members of the extensive Cucurbitaceae or gourd family, along with such diverse relatives as the pumpkins and squashes of the New World and the cucumber of the Old World. Plant expert Charles B. Heiser, Jr., has pointed out that the Latin word *cucurbitare* means (or at least meant) "to commit adultery," and it is the case that melons have interbred so promiscuously that classification is difficult. What follows is a discussion of a few basic melon types.

Save for the watermelon, melons are like winter squashes in structure - with a thick rind and a seed-filled center. The watermelon, by contrast, resembles the cucumber in that its seeds are more evenly dispersed. Watermelons (*Citrullus lanatus = C. vulgaris*) are the first melons to show up in the historical record - about 6,000 years ago in Egyptian tomb art. However, it would appear from archaeological remains that they were in India much earlier - during prehistoric times - and unidentified melons were being cultivated in the Indus Valley about 4,000 years ago. This gives India a claim to be the cradle of melons, but Persia and tropical Africa have also been put forward as likely candidates. Most probably, tropical Africa was the home of the watermelon, and the other melons arose elsewhere - perhaps in both India and the Middle East. Certainly it was Africa that sent watermelons to the Americas via the slave trade, and now they are grown all around the globe.

The past of the other melons, all (along with the cucumber) closely related members of the genus *Cucumis,* is even more obscure. They seem to have been unknown to the ancients, and although Pliny in the first century A.D. apparently mentioned melons, it was not with much enthusiasm. Melons were still thought of as green vegetables - and not particularly good ones at that, unless they were cooked and eaten with plenty of spices. Nonetheless, melons were spread by the Romans throughout their empire; the Moors encouraged melon cultivation in Spain after their invasion in 711; and real enthusiasm for the fruits was expressed for the first time during the fifteenth century, when they became popular at the French court. Sweet melons seem finally to have been developed at this point - perhaps through the patience of Mediterranean gardeners in southern Europe, or perhaps in the Arab world - and were introduced into Europe via the Moors still holding Granada in Spain at the time.

And such development continued. The word for the melon known as cantaloupe (*Cucumis melo* var. *cantalupensis*) comes from Cantalupo, a papal garden near Rome where that variety of melon was born during the Renaissance. Christopher Colum-

bus reached the West Indies with melon seeds, and melons were reported growing in New Mexico by 1540. Later, the Spaniards began cultivating muskmelons in California. In fact, what North Americans call cantaloupes are actually descendants of these muskmelons - the difference basically being that the muskmelon (*Cucumis melo* var. *reticulatus*) has a netted skin, whereas the true cantaloupe of Europe has a scaly or warty rind. Both have flesh ranging in color from orange to green, and both are aromatic. The Persian melon - also aromatic - is a variety of the muskmelon. The winter melons (*Cucumis melo* var. *inodorus*), by contrast, are not aromatic. These include the honeydew (the sweetest of the melons) and the casaba - a melon that has been crossed with the Persian melon to produce the Crenshaw.

Chief among the Asian melons is the bitter melon (*Momordica charantia*) - bitter, among other reasons, because it contains quinine, which has doubtless helped many to live with malaria in the Asian tropics. The bitter melon is braised or steamed and sometimes cut up and stir-fried. The Chinese winter melon or "fuzzy melon" (*Benincasa hispida*) - one of the largest vegetables grown - is also cooked as a vegetable.

All melons are rich in vitamin C and potassium. Those with orange flesh are also a good source of beta-carotene.

Common names and synonyms: Bitter melon, cantaloupe, casaba, Chinese winter melon, Crenshaw (melon), fuzzy melon, honeydew, muskmelon, Ogen melon, Oriental melon, Persian melon, sweet melon, watermelon, winter melon.

See in addition: "Cucumbers, Melons, and Watermelons," Part II, Section C, Chapter 6.

Melonshrub - *see* **PEPINO**
Melon-thistle - *see* **MELON CACTUS**
Men-gu - *see* **MANGOSTEEN**
Merkel - *see* **MOREL**
MERLOT (*see also* **GRAPES**) - A red grape, the Merlot (*Vitis vinifera*) produces a wine that has been used mostly to blend with other wines but is now achieving an identity of its own. Until 1970 or so, Merlot grapes were grown almost exclusively in Europe. Since that time, however, they have become increasingly popular in California, where initially they were used to blend with Cabernets. In the process it was discovered that Merlot grapes yield a wine that can stand on its own.
See in addition: "Wine," Part III, Chapter 13.
MERTAJAM - A tree native to Indonesia, the mertajam (*Erioglossum rubiginosum*) has small, purple fruits about the size of large grapes. They grow in clusters and have a somewhat astringent taste. Not a commercial fruit, the mertajam is made into jams and syrups.
MESQUITE - Also called "algarroba" and "honey locust," mesquite comprises several members of the

genus *Prosopis* (especially *P. juliflora* var. *juliflora*), all of which are members of the pea family, Fabaceae. Mesquite plants are small trees or shrubs, native to the Americas and especially abundant throughout the southwestern United States and Mexico. The pods of *P. juliflora* var. *juliflora* are among the oldest known foods of humans in the New World and have long constituted a staple for Indians of the desert Southwest.

While still immature, the pods were eaten raw or cooked like a vegetable, and when ripe they yielded a sweetish pulp that was either eaten or fermented to make a mesquite wine. Generally, however, they were ground to make a meal called *pinole,* which was used to make a gruel, and today mesquite flour products are still popular. The branches also exude a sweet gum that can be eaten for dessert. The screwbean mesquite (*P. pubescens*), the western honey mesquite (*P. juniflora* var. *glandulosa*), and the velvet mesquite (*P. velutina*) were used in much the same fashion, with the latter also employed for medicinal purposes.

Common names and synonyms: Algarroba, Fremont screwbean, honey locust, screwbean, screwbean mesquite, screwpod mesquite, tornillo, velvet mesquite, western honey mesquite.

Mesta – *see* **OKRA**

Methi – *see* **FENUGREEK**

Metulon – *see* **KIWANO**

Mexi-Bell – *see* **SWEET PEPPERS**

Mexican apple – *see* **WHITE SAPOTE**

Mexican bamboo – *see* **KNOTWEED AND SMART-WEED**

Mexican breadfruit – *see* **MONSTERA**

Mexican corn fungus – *see* **HUITLACOCHE**

Mexican husk tomato – *see* **TOMATILLO**

Mexican parsley – *see* **CILANTRO**

Mexican potato – *see* **JÍCAMA**

Mexican strawberry – *see* **PITAHAYA**

Mexican tea – *see* **EPAZOTE**

Mexican wild plum – *see* **CAPULIN**

Michihli – *see* **CHINESE CABBAGE**

Mignonette pepper – *see* **PEPPER(CORNS)**

Milfoil – *see* **YARROW**

Milho – *see* **MAIZE**

Milkmaid – *see* **YAM DAISY**

MILKWEED – Most plants of the genus *Asclepias* have milky juice, especially *A. syriaca,* the "common milkweed" of eastern North America, which is also called "silkweed." It has clusters of purple blossoms and pointed pods that Native Americans dried and used to flavor foods.

Common names and synonyms: Common milkweed, silkweed.

MILLET (*see also* **FINGER MILLET, JAPANESE MILLET, JOB'S-TEARS, SORGHUM**) – Millet is a name applied to a variety of cultivated grasses (*Panicum* spp. and *Setaria* spp.) that are native to Asia and Africa. Millet was cultivated for food some 9,000

years ago at Thessaly in Greece (making it one of the oldest grains known to humans) and around 8,000 years ago in China (where it was considered one of the sacred plants). By the second century B.C. (and probably long before), millet was the most important cereal in Japan, and it was one of the first plants cultivated in Africa. It was an important crop in Europe during the Middle Ages and, much more recently, has been grown in the New World for hay.

Among the most important varieties are the "pearl," "finger," and "foxtail" millets. Despite the tiny size of millet grains (the smallest of all the grains), they have sustained huge numbers of people for millennia, and it is interesting to note that it was millet – not rice – that was first predominant in China. Early on, the significant centers of Chinese agriculture were in the north, where millet was an important staple. Because millets lack gluten, they are a particularly important food for those who must avoid that protein. However, the absence of gluten also means that millets cannot be used for making raised breads but only flatbreads. Pearl millet, the most important of the varieties grown for human consumption, is used for couscous and makes a fine hot cereal as well. Millet (available in health-food stores) provides the consumer with significant amounts of folacin, thiamine, and magnesium.

Common names and synonyms: Bajra, Bengal grass, bristle grass, bulrush millet, finger millet, foxtail millet, German millet, golden timothy (grass), guinea millet, Hungarian grass, Italian millet, *milho,* panic(oid) grass(es), pearl millet, *ragi,* Siberian millet.

See in addition: "Millets," Part II, Section A, Chapter 5.

Millmi – *see* **AMARANTH**

Millsweet limetta – *see* **LIMETTA**

Miltomate – *see* **TOMATILLO**

Mimosa – *see* **ACACIA**

MIMUSOPS – The *Mimusops* – within the family Sapotaceae – constitute a large genus (also called *Manilkara*) of tropical trees that are primarily used for timber but also yield a gum and bear edible fruits. Perhaps the best-known representative of the genus is the sapodilla (*Manilkara zapota*), but there are many others. One of these is *Mimusops parvifolia* of the Philippines and the southwestern Pacific area. Another is *Mimusops elengi,* a large East Asian tree called the "tanjong tree" (also the "Spanish cherry"), which has yellow berries that are eaten despite a floury consistency and also yield an oil from their seeds. The Brazilian cowtree (*Mimusops elata*) has fruits about the size of an apple, which yield a milky latex that is used in coffee. The naseberry (*Mimusops sieberii*) that grows in the southern United States and Mexico is eaten raw for its fine flavor. *Manilkara bidentata* (called "balata"), that grows in Trinidad and northern

South America, bears an oily, sweet fruit that is much appreciated by children. In addition, the young shoots of many of these trees are cooked and eaten with other vegetables, and the latex is chewed like gum.

Common names and synonyms: Balata, cowtree, naseberry, Spanish cherry, tanjong tree.

Miner's-lettuce - *see* **PURSLANE**

Miner's-salad - *see* **PURSLANE**

MINT (*see also* **CORN MINT**) - Some 600 perennial herbs of the genus *Mentha*, which are widely distributed throughout the world, fall under the rubric of mint - a name derived from the nymph Minthe, who was reputed to have turned into this plant. All apparently originated in the Mediterranean area and North Africa and have been used since ancient times for the flavor provide by the essential oils contained in their leaves. Perhaps the most ubiquitous of the mint plants is spearmint (*M. spicata*), which flavors a favorite tea in North Africa, mint juleps in the U.S. South (said to have been invented in 1809), and mint sauces or jellies to accompany lamb. A pungent offspring of spearmint is peppermint (*M. × piperita*), with its menthol-containing essential oil that adds flavor to many things from toothpaste to the liqueur crème de menthe and has dozens of pharmaceutical uses. Still another commonly grown variety is apple mint (*M. × rotundifolia*) – also called Bowles mint – which has the flavor of apples and is sweeter than other varieties. Mint is sold fresh or dried and goes well in herbal teas, salads, stews, and candies, and with fruit, poultry, meat, and fish dishes.

Common names and synonyms: Apple mint, Bowles mint, corn mint, field mint, pennyroyal, peppermint, red mint, Scotch spearmint, spearmint.

See in addition: "Spices and Flavorings," Part II, Section F, Chapter 1.

Mint geranium - *see* **COSTMARY**

MINTHOSTACHYS - The family Lamiaceae (Labiatae) comprises a great number of aromatic plants, many of which contain essential oils that are used for flavoring foods and teas. Among these are a dozen or so species of the genus *Minthostachys,* which are mintlike herbs native to a range in the Andean region stretching from Venezuela to Argentina. Piperina (*M. verticillata*), which grows in the latter country, is employed to make a popular tea called "Peperina." Tipo or poleo (*M. mollis*) and other species are also used to make beverages, and their minty flavor is employed as a condiment. Some of these herbs are added to potatoes in storage to inhibit sprouting.

Common names and synonyms: Piperina, poleo, tipo.

Mioga ginger - *see* **MYOGA GINGER**

Miracle berry - *see* **MIRACLE FRUIT**

MIRACLE FRUIT (*see also* **LIMEBERRY**) - Native to hot, tropical lowlands in West Africa, this fruit (*Synsepalum dulcificum*) is about the size and shape of an olive and has a single seed surrounded by white flesh and a deep red skin. The fruit is eaten fresh but did not derive its name from an exceptional sweetness. Rather, "miracle fruit" comes from its ability to affect the palate in a way that makes subsequently consumed sour or acidic foods appear sweet. This "miraculous berry" grows on bushes or trees reaching up to 18 feet in height in their native habitat, but in other areas they rarely achieve 5 feet. The leaves are elongated and a lush green (in some varieties the leaves are hairy); the flowers are small and white.

Common names and synonyms: Miracle berry, miraculous berry.

Miraculous berry - *see* **MIRACLE FRUIT**

Mirliton - *see* **CHAYOTE**

Mississippi chicken corn - *see* **SORGHUM**

Missouri gourd - *see* **BUFFALO GOURD**

Mistletoe - *see* **JUNIPER MISTLETOE**

Miterwort - *see* **COOLWORT**

Mitsuba - *see* **HONEWORT**

Mizuna - *see* **MUSTARD GREENS**

MOCAMBO - Of the same genus as cacao (from which chocolate is made), the mocambo (*Theobroma bicolor*) is a tree that is native to Central and South America and reaches some 30 feet in height. Its fruit is cone shaped, with a chocolate-colored interior, and is used mostly for making a beverage.

Mocha - *see* **COFFEE**

Mock pak choy - *see* **CHINESE FLOWERING CABBAGE**

Mo-ehr - *see* **CLOUD EAR**

Molle - *see* **MASTIC TREE**

Moltebeere - *see* **CLOUDBERRY**

Mombin - *see* **HOG PLUM, YELLOW MOMBIN**

MONGONGO - This large, deciduous tree (*Ricinodendron rautanenii*), growing wild in the arid soils of southern Africa, belongs to the Euphorbiaceae, a generally poisonous family of plants. However, the fruit from this particular tree is not only edible but is said to provide over half of the daily calories consumed by the !Kung San, a hunting-and-gathering people of the Kalahari Desert. The fruit's flesh is edible, as is its kernel, which is protected by a hard-shelled stone. This nut is high in both fat and protein. Mongongo nuts do not mature on the tree but fall when still green. Only then do they start the ripening process, with the skin changing to brown, the flesh softening, and the flavor developing.

Monkey-bread - *see* **BAOBAB**

Monkey nut - *see* **PEANUT**

MONKEY ORANGE - This small, thorny shrub (*Strychnos spinosa*) can be found throughout tropical and subtropical eastern and southern Africa, particularly on arid savannas and the lower ranges of mountain slopes. The skin of its brilliantly green fruit changes to yellow when ripening. The gelatin-like flesh, too, is yellow, but of a darker shade. Sweet yet acidic in taste, the fruits are frequently mixed with milk. They are also used to make an alcoholic beverage. Unripe fruits and the roots of the shrub serve as the basis of a snakebite antidote for some native African peoples. The seeds of *Strychnos spinosa* are poisonous.

Common names and synonyms: Kaffir orange, Natal orange.

Monkey-puzzle (tree) - *see* **CHILEAN PINE**

Monk's pepper tree - *see* **CHASTE TREE**

MONSTERA - A peculiar-looking fruit, the monstera (*Monstera deliciosa*) is native to Mexico and Guatemala, where it is called *ceriman.* Also called the "Swiss-cheese plant" and "Mexican breadfruit," it is in fact the fruit of the split-leaf philodendron, which is (in smaller size), a familiar houseplant. The fruit grows on large vines with leaves up to 3 feet wide. In shape, it resembles an elongated pinecone, covered as it is with many small kernels. When ripe, these kernels split apart to reveal a pale yellow, sweet pulp with a delicious taste seemingly a cross between the flavors of banana and pineapple. If the fruit is not allowed to ripen fully, however, it can irritate the mouth and the throat. In the United States, the monstera is grown in Florida and California, and some gourmet shops carry the fruit.

Common names and synonyms: Ananas de Mexico, balazo, banana de brejo, ceriman, ceriman de Mexico, fruta de Mexico, fruit-salad fruit, Mexican breadfruit, *pina anona,* Swiss-cheese plant.

Montmorency - *see* **CHERRY**

Mook yee - *see* **CLOUD EAR**

Mooli - *see* **DAIKON**

MOONFLOWER - A number of plants are called "moonflower." One is *Mentzelia pumila,* the "desert blazing star" (also "evening star"), which, in addition to bright yellow, star-shaped flowers, has a bullet-shaped seed capsule. Native Americans ground these seeds for meal. Another moonflower is the yellow salsify (*Tragopogon dubius*), which is also called meadow salsify. It is a perennial herb that was introduced from Europe and is now naturalized in the Americas. Native Americans used this plant for both food and medicine. Two more moonflowers are comprised of South American plants of the genus *Datura* - called "angel's-trumpets" - that are cultivated for their large, trumpet-like flowers. In the United States, "sacred datura" (*Datura meteloides*), also called jimsonweed and moon lily, is a dangerous plant: All its parts are extremely poisonous if ingested. However, sacred datura was one of the most important medicinal plants for Native Americans.

Common names and synonyms: Angel's-trumpet, *datura,* desert blazing star, evening star, jimsonweed, meadow salsify, moon lily, sacred datura, yellow salsify.

Moon lily - *see* **MOONFLOWER**

Moqua - *see* **FUZZY MELON**

Mora - *see* **JALAPEÑO**

MOREL (*see also* **MUSHROOMS AND FUNGI**) - Perhaps the best-known and most sought-after type of fungus, morel mushrooms (genus *Morchella*) come in many varieties - all edible - and are distinguished by their hollow stems and the irregular pits and ridges in their cone-shaped caps. Of all the various morels, probably the two most common are the true or yellow morel (*M. esculenta*), which is 2 to 6 inches tall (3 to 4 inches making up the length of the cap), and the white morel (*M. deliciosa*), which is slightly longer and is thought to be the best-tasting morel. Morels grow wild, often in wooded areas that have been burned-over, but they cannot (at least to this point) be cultivated. They are used in several different dishes. Morels were doubtless viewed as a springtime delicacy by countless generations of Native Americans; moreover, there are European species of morels that have also been consumed for millennia.

Common names and synonyms: Black morel, golden morel, merkel, morille, narrow-capped morel, pinecone mushroom, sponge mushroom, true morel, white morel, yellow morel.

See in addition: "Fungi," Part II, Section C, Chapter 7; "Mushrooms and Fungi," Part VIII.

Morella - *see* **WONDERBERRY**

Moreton Bay chestnut - *see* **AUSTRALIAN CHESTNUT**

Morille - *see* **MOREL**

MORINDA - Members of a large genus of East Indian tropical trees and shrubs, many *Morinda* plants produce an edible, pulpy fruit that is eaten raw and often used in chutneys and curries. One of these, called the "Indian mulberry" (*M. citrifolia*), now grows in the Florida Keys.

Common names and synonyms: Indian mulberry.

Moringa nut (tree) - *see* **BENOIL TREE**

Morita - *see* **JALAPEÑO**

MORMON TEA - Also called the "desert jointfir" and "teposote" among other appellations, "Mormon tea" was sometimes the longleaf ephedra shrub (*Ephedra trifurca*), sometimes *E. nevadensis,* and sometimes *E. viridis.* It received the name "Mormon tea" after Mormon settlers in Utah made tea from the dried twigs and stems of these plants. However, Native Americans preceded the Mormons in using the various species of *Ephedra* for tea making and also for treating illnesses.

Common names and synonyms: Desert jointfir, longleaf ephedra, teposote.

Moro (orange) - *see* **BLOOD ORANGE**

Mostarda - *see* **MUSTARD SEED**

Mostaza - *see* **MUSTARD SEED**

MOTH BEAN - Native to tropical Asia and also called the "mat bean," the moth bean (*Phaseolus aconitifolius = Vigna aconitifolia*) is a small, yellowish brown seed in a cylindrical pod that grows on vines which provide a matlike cover for the soil. The bean is used, especially in India, for human food. It is made into dhal and bean paste, and the immature pods are cooked as a vegetable.

Common names and synonyms: Mat bean.

See also: "Beans, Peas, and Lentils," Part II, Section C, Chapter 3.

Mother-of-clove(s) - *see* **CLOVE(S)**

MOUNTAIN ASH - A native of northeastern North America and the Appalachian region, the mountain ash (*Sorbus americana*) produces clusters of orange red berries. Although these are much too bitter to eat out of hand, Native Americans in the past dried them and ground them into a meal. The berries are also made into syrup, jams, and the like.

Mountain balm - *see* **YERBA SANTA**

Mountain cranberry - *see* **LINGONBERRY**

Mountain hemlock - *see* **HEMLOCK**

Mountain hollyhock - *see* **WASABI**

MOUNTAIN PAPAYA - A hardy member of the papaya family, the mountain papaya (*Carica candamarcensis = C. pubescens*) constitutes an exception to the tropical nature of its relatives by growing at elevations of 8,000 to 9,000 feet in Ecuador and Colombia. The price of such cold-resistance, however, is a small, tart fruit. Too acidic to eat raw, it is always cooked, and then only eaten when better fruits are unavailable.

Mountain plum - *see* **TALLOW WOOD PLUM**

MOUNTAIN SORREL - Mountain sorrel (*Oxyria digyna*), with its long-stemmed leaves, grows in an area ranging from Alaska and Greenland through British Columbia to the mountains of New Hampshire. Eskimos gather mountain sorrel and ferment it like sauerkraut. Mountain sorrel is also eaten raw in salads when the plants are young, whereas mature plants are used as a potherb. The plant is a valuable source of vitamin C in the far north, accounting for its nickname "scurvy grass."

Common names and synonyms: Scurvy grass.

Mountain spinach - *see* **ORACH**

Mountain sumac - *see* **SMOOTH SUMAC**

Mousseron - *see* **MUSHROOMS AND FUNGI**

Mousseron d'automne - *see* **MUSHROOMS AND FUNGI**

Moutarde - *see* **MUSTARD SEED**

Moxa - *see* **MUGWORT**

MUGWORT - The dried leaves of the perennial Eurasian plants of the genus *Artemisia* - and particularly *A. vulgaris* - are called mugwort and have long been used as an herb to flavor various dishes, especially those containing fatty foods such as goose or pork. Mugwort's aromatic, slightly bitter taste is also good for seasoning stews, stuffings, sweets, and ale. Some make a tea from mugwort that is believed to relieve the symptoms of rheumatism, and it is employed to flavor absinthe. A related plant - *A. verlotorum,* called Chinese mugwort - is used in the Far East to flavor rice and as a tobacco

substitute, and its young leaves are boiled and eaten in Japan.

Common names and synonyms: Chinese mugwort, felon herb, *moxa.*

See also: "Spices and Flavorings," Part II, Section F, Chapter 1.

Mulato - *see* **POBLANO**

MULBERRY (*see also* **BERRIES**) - Several trees of the genus *Morus* have edible mulberries. The red mulberry (*M. rubra*), which is native to eastern and central North America, has fruits that resemble blackberries. The white - or "Chinese" - mulberry (*M. alba*) is the one that the Chinese use to feed silkworms. It has whitish or purplish fruit. The Russian mulberry (*M. nigra*), also called the black mulberry, was introduced in the United States during the last quarter of the nineteenth century. All mulberries are quite sweet, with the white mulberry being the sweetest. More popular in Europe than in the United States, mulberries are quite perishable and thus are not grown for market. They are eaten fresh and made into pies and jellies.

Common names and synonyms: Black mulberry, Chinese mulberry, red mulberry, Russian mulberry, white mulberry.

Munchkin - *see* **DELICATA (SQUASH)**

MUNG BEAN (*see also* **BEANS, LEGUMES**) - Small and frequently green, mung beans (*Phaseolus aureus*) are generally used for bean sprouts and are especially important in the cooking of both China and Japan, where they are frequently stir-fried. Also known as "black grams" and in India as "green grams," mung beans are also boiled and eaten as a vegetable, used in curries, and made into flour. The bean also finds its way into soups and is the base for cellophane noodles. In the past, consumers had to sprout mung beans themselves, but bean sprouts have been sold commercially on an ever-increasing scale since the 1950s.

Common names and synonyms: Black dhal, black gram, black mung, golden gram, gram bean, green gram, red mung bean, urd.

See in addition: "Beans, Peas, and Lentils," Part II, Section C, Chapter 3.

Muntok (pepper) - *see* **PEPPER(CORNS)**

Murnong - *see* **YAM DAISY**

MUSCADINE (*see also* **GRAPES**) - A purple grape of the southeastern United States, the muscadine (*Vitis rotundifolia* - also called the "bullace grape" and the "scuppernong") serves mostly as a grape for the table and for making jellies, jams, and juices. But some wine is made from muscadine grapes, especially dessert wines that taste something like muscat wines. There are several dozen cultivars of muscadines, grown mostly for use in the home and for local markets.

Common names and synonyms: Bullace grape, scuppernong, southern fox grape.

See in addition: "Wine," Part III, Chapter 13.

MUSCAT (*see also* **GRAPES**) – Several varieties of sweet white grapes are called muscats (*Vitis vinifera*) and are used for making wines such as muscatels and sauternes. They are also used as raisins and as table grapes.

See in addition: "Wine," Part III, Chapter 13.

MUSHROOMS AND FUNGI – Mushrooms are found in almost all temperate parts of the world. Although often viewed as the plant itself, they are actually the fruit of a network of stems that remain underground. The mushroom aboveground is there to propagate the organism by diffusing spores to extend the underground network. As plants that have neither leaves nor roots, mushrooms cannot photosynthesize sugars and instead live on the rotting remains of other organisms. That they are successful in such parasitic activity seems clear enough when one learns that (depending on the authority consulted) mushrooms and fungi comprise between 40,000 and 120,000 species around the world, of which some 1,800 are recognized as edible.

One cannot imagine our hunter–gatherer ancestors not eating mushrooms, which have been described as "vegetable meat." However, it is downright painful to imagine the trial-and-error process that eventually separated those that were edible from those that were poisonous. Perhaps early foragers concentrated on a few species that were fairly easy to identify, such as puffballs (of the family Lycoperdaceae) with their ball-shaped fruiting bodies. In fact, puffball remains have been found in Paleolithic settlements. Yet it may be that our Stone Age forebears had a substantially more sophisticated knowledge of fungi than this. Observation of contemporary hunter-gatherers indicates that they know a great deal about mushrooms both edible and poisonous, and they consume the former while employing the latter to bring down game and bring up fish.

Mushrooms of the *Agaricus* genus are among the relatively few fungi that can be grown commercially, and some of these have been propagated since classical times. The *Champignon d'Paris,* or Paris mushroom (*Agaricus bisporus* and *A. campestris*), is the most common mushroom in produce markets today. It is also called the common white mushroom, and if small, a "button" mushroom, or in France a *mousseron,* from which the English "mushroom" was derived. This mushroom has been cultivated since the seventeenth century in France. During Napoleonic times, they were grown on so-called farms located in caves in the many stone quarries close to Paris. There, the mushrooms were nurtured in the dark coolness, where humidity and temperature were both controlled, on beds of horse manure mixed with straw and soil – a method that is continued today both commercially and in the corners of family basements, with the important difference that the horse manure is now sterilized and pasteurized. Most mushrooms that come sliced or whole in cans, or marinating in jars, are "button" mushrooms.

By the late 1800s, mushrooms were being grown commercially in other countries. Italian growers also cultivated the common mushroom but preferring the brown-capped variety, which are often called cremini mushrooms (or Italian brown) and have an earthy flavor that is fine for soups and stews and for stuffing. The large and beefy Portabello (also Roma) is actually a fully grown cremini, with dense and meaty flesh that lends itself nicely to grilling or roasting. Originally, cremini mushrooms were imported from Italy, but now they are cultivated in the United States.

Although many swear by the hearty flavor of the cultivated Portabello, wild mushrooms are generally regarded as significantly more flavorful than their domesticated counterparts, and wild varieties are becoming increasingly available in produce markets, in both fresh and dried forms. One of these is the chanterelle (*Cantharellus cibarius*) – the golden chanterelle (*girolle*) of France, and the *Pfifferling* of Germany – which has long been highly regarded as a "forest" mushroom in Europe but is now becoming increasingly popular in the United States, where it grows in forests from coast to coast. It is orange in color, funnel shaped, and has firm, light, yellowish flesh. There are numerous other chanterelles that come in colors ranging from red, brown, and gray to orange-and-yellow, and almost all are also ranked as delicious, although they are much more difficult to locate.

Also in the delicious category is *Boletus edulis,* which goes by the name of *Steinpilz* in Germany, *porcini* in Italy, and *cèpe* (also cep) in France and the United States, where it grows as well. Indeed, many consider these stout-stemmed fungi with their large brown, dry caps to be the finest tasting of all the wild mushrooms. Their rich flavor and firm texture make them ideal for soups, sauces, and stuffings.

Morel (*Morchella esculenta*) fanciers, however, would give the "best-tasting" ranking to their favorite fungus. Nicknamed the "pinecone mushroom" because of the elongated, dome-like shape of its whitish to light brown head, which is composed of chambers that make it appear a network of ridges and pits, the true morel appears only in the spring and thus commands a very high price throughout the year.

Many mushrooms that are originally from the Far East are not only available dried and canned but can also be found fresh in produce markets the world over. Perhaps the best known of these – and certainly the most available – is the Japanese brown mushroom or shiitake (*Cortinellus shiitake*). Once grown only in Japan by introducing spores to a local type of oak tree, this mushroom is now cultivated in the United States – on artificial logs. The shiitake is umbrella-like in shape, brown to black in color, and firmly textured; it has an assertive flavor that goes well in sautés. Its cousin, the Chinese black mushroom (*Lentinus edodes*), is actually brown to pale buff in color. Known as the "winter mushroom" in China (as is the shiitake, which is also grown there), it is like most other mushrooms in that its flavor intensifies with drying.

The enokitake (*Flammulina velutipes*), or sometimes just *enoki* (their home is on the stumps of the Chinese hackberry tree called *enoki*), are slender mushroom stalks with small bulbs at the top, which grow in clumps and reach upwards of 5 inches in length. Their delicate flavor is called for in many Asian dishes, but they are best appreciated when eaten raw in salads. Enokitake mushrooms are now cultivated in California. Another cultivated mushroom is the straw mushroom (*Volvariella volvacea*) that is small, globe-shaped, and grown on straw, from which it develops its distinctive earthy taste. These are only occasionally found fresh, and never dried, but are universally available in cans.

Rarely found outside of Japan is the matsutake (*Armillaria edodes*), a thick, meaty, and delicious mushroom that is very popular there and also very expensive. A final Asian fungus is the cloud-ear fungus (*Auricularia auricula* and *A. polytrica*), better known in the United States as "wood ear" but also as "tree ear," "Jew's-ear," and "black tree fungus." The cloud-ear fungus is highly regarded for supposed medicinal properties (it does seem to thin the blood) by the Chinese, who have also incorporated it into their cuisine for at least 1,500 years. It is found mostly in Asian markets in the United States.

Oyster mushrooms (*Pleurotus ostreatus*) are also called "tree mushrooms" because they grow (in clusters) on rotting trees in parts of every continent except Antarctica. Although a wild variety, they are easily cultivated and thus widely available. Of the same family is the most famous of the tree fungi, the beefsteak fungus (*Fistulina hepatica*). It is also known by a variety of other names, such as "liver fistulina," "oak tongue," "vegetable beefsteak," and "beef tongue" because of its rough, reddish surface – which suggests a beef tongue or steak or liver – and its reddish juice, not to mention a meaty taste when cooked. A final mushroom that lives on dead as well as living trees (in clusters) is the honey mushroom (*Armillariella mellea*) – the name describing the color of its cap rather than its taste, which is delicious nonetheless.

The field mushroom (*Agaricus campestris* – also "meadow mushroom" and "pink-bottom") is more or less the same as the "common" mushroom (discussed first in this entry) except that it is a wild version. Rodman's mushroom (*Agaricus rodmani*) with its white to yellowish cap is another that is

very similar (and closely related) to the common mushroom. Fairy-ring mushrooms (*Marasmius oreades*) are so called because of their tendency to grow in rings or circles. They appear mostly in the autumn and in France are called the *mousseron d'automne* or the false *mousseron* because of the resemblance of their caps to those of the button mushroom.

Mushrooms are far more nutritious than many people believe. In addition to a good deal of protein, they deliver essential minerals and substantial amounts of the B complex. Moreover, they contain various medicinal substances and some (such as the common mushroom) may provide a cancer preventive. Cooked fresh, mushrooms are considerably more nutritious than those that are available marinated and canned. As a rule, dried mushrooms have an intensely concentrated flavor (especially after they are reconstituted by soaking in hot water) and consequently are used more as a seasoning than as a vegetable. In the United States, Pennsylvania is the leading mushroom-producing state (accounting for about half the domestic crop), and most of this activity is accomplished in and around the little Pennsylvania town of Kennett Square. Michigan, California, and Florida are also important producers, and the countries of Italy, France, China, Japan, and Thailand all export mushrooms in large quantities.

Common names and synonyms: Beefsteak fungus, beef tongue, black tree fungus, brown-capped mushroom, button mushroom, cep, *cèpe, champignon d'Paris,* chanterelle, Chinese black mushroom, cloud-ear fungus, common mushroom, common white mushroom, cremini mushroom, English mushroom, *enoki,* enokitake, fairy-ring mushroom, false *mousseron,* field mushroom, forest mushroom, *girolle,* golden chanterelle, honey mushroom, Italian brown mushroom, Japanese brown mushroom, Jew's-ear, liver fistulina, matsutake, meadow mushroom, morel, *mousseron, mousseron d'automne,* oak tongue, oyster mushroom, Paris mushroom, *Pfifferling,* pinecone mushroom, pink-bottom, *porcini,* Portabello, puffball, Rodman's mushroom, Roma, shiitake, *Steinpilz,* straw mushroom, tree ear, tree mushroom, vegetable beefsteak, vegetable meat, wild mushroom, winter mushroom, wood ear.

See also: "Fungi," Part II, Section C, Chapter 7.

Musk lime - *see* CALAMONDIN

Muskmelon - *see* CANTALOUPE AND MUSK-MELON, MELONS

Musk seed - *see* AMBERSEED

Mustard cabbage - *see* PAKCHOI AND KAI CHOY

MUSTARD GREENS (*see also* CABBAGE, MUSTARD SEED) - A vegetable belonging to the cabbage family (and also called "leaf mustard" and "leaf mustard cabbage"), mustard greens (*Brassica juncea*) have a more delicate flavor than kale, but one that is, at the same time, more piquant. Most plants of the genus *Brassica,* are of Eurasian origin. *Brassica* *juncea,* however, is probably a native of Africa that spread into Asia, although the plant may have originated in China and spread outward from there. Mustard greens have an arching stalk and large green leaves, which grow in clusters. The leaves are generally eaten when young, because they become coarse with age. They can be cooked and eaten as a vegetable or used in salads. Mustard greens are fairly high in beta-carotene, vitamin C, and calcium.

Common names and synonyms: Brown mustard, Chinese mustard, curled mustard, Indian mustard, leaf mustard, leaf mustard cabbage, *mizuna,* Oriental mustard, rape(seed), red Asian mustard, southern curled mustard.

See in addition: "Cruciferous and Green Leafy Vegetables," Part II, Section C, Chapter 5.

MUSTARD SEED (*see also* **MUSTARD GREENS**) – There are three basic types of mustard that are all members of the cabbage family: black mustard (*Brassica nigra*); white mustard (*B. alba*); and brown mustard (*B. juncea*). The mustard plants were originally weeds, and some evidence suggests that our prehistoric ancestors may have utilized their seeds to chew with meat.

Mustard plants have been cultivated since ancient times and were highly valued for their oil content. The Greeks and Romans used mustard as a medicine and plaster for rheumatism and arthritis; it was also a part of the cuisine of the ancient Egyptians, Greeks, and Romans as a condiment; and mustard seed is mentioned several times in the New Testament.

Each country and region has subsequently developed mustards to accompany their own cuisines. Ground mustard seeds are mixed with a liquid medium (at which point a reaction of enzymes causes the seeds to become pungent), such as vinegar, wine, beer, or mayonnaise. One such medium was grape "must," hence the French *moutarde,* the Italian *mostarda,* the Spanish *mostaza,* and the English "mustard" – all from the Latin *mustum ardens,* meaning "burning must."

In China, white mustard seeds from the West (*B. alba* is a Mediterranean native) were being grown by the tenth century, but the hot Chinese mustard and the even hotter Japanese mustard (*karaschi*) are made from brown mustard seed. The English also have a preference for hot mustard, which goes well with sausages and rare roast beef. French mustards, such as those from Dijon, seem to go with French sausages, just as German mustards, such as Düsseldorf, are suited to the sausages of Germany. And what is a hot dog without the yellow (because of the turmeric added) mustard of the United States? In addition, mustard seeds and powder are used in cooking meats and vegetables, in pickling, and in the preparation of sauces, relishes, and salad dressings, and mustard seeds and oil are frequently added to dishes. Black mustard seeds, for example,

are vital to the cuisines (especially curries) of India, and many meats are dusted with mustard powder before cooking.

Common names and synonyms: Black mustard (seed), brown mustard (seed), Dijon mustard(s), Düsseldorf mustard, hot Chinese mustard, hot mustard, Japanese mustard, *karaschi, mostarda, mostaza, moutarde, mustum ardens,* white mustard (seed), yellow mustard.

See in addition: "Spices and Flavorings," Part II, Section F, Chapter 1.

Mustum ardens – *see* **MUSTARD SEED**

MUTAMBA – This native of both North and South America is a tall tree (*Guazuma ulmifolia*) with some 25 to 30 aliases ranging from "West Indian elm" and "mutambo" to "chocolate" and "guasima." The reason for the plethora of names is because it is known in many languages in a region stretching from Brazil to Peru to Mexico. The mutamba produces an edible fruit, but its major contribution has been to the herbal medicine practiced in all of the countries in which it is grown. The teas made from its bark, roots, and leaves have been used against everything from asthma to leprosy, often with such effectiveness that it has attracted the attention of medical science, and a number of studies have appeared on its usefulness against heart-related diseases and cancer.

Common names and synonyms: Chocolate, guacimo, guasima, mutambo, West Indian elm.

Mutambo – *see* **MUTAMBA**

MYOGA GINGER – A native of Japan, myoga (*Zingiber mioga*) is a member of the ginger family that is grown for its young shoots and buds. These are mostly used raw in salads and shredded as a garnish but are also added to soups and simmered dishes.

Common names and synonyms: Ginger bud, mioga ginger.

Myrobalan – *see* **AMALAKA**

Myrobalan plum – *see* **CHERRY PLUM**

Myrrh – *see* **CICELY**

Myrtille – *see* **BILBERRY**

MYRTLE (*see also* **CHILEAN GUAVA MYRTLE, PERIWINKLE**) – An evergreen aromatic shrub, native to the Mediterranean region and western Asia, myrtle (*Myrtus communis*) has blue-black berries that are sweet and pulpy and are dried for use as a condiment as well as eaten raw. Myrtle was enjoyed by the ancient Greeks, who also accorded it a role in their mythology (it was sacred to Aphrodite). Other myrtles are native to South America or New Zealand save for the North American native (*M. verrucosa*) called "stopper," which also has edible fruit.

Common names and synonyms: Indian buchu, "stopper."

MYRTLE APPLE – A wild shrub native to southern Africa, the myrtle apple (*Eugenia capensis*) provides both nourishment as a fruit and medicinal relief from diarrhea. It ranges in color from orange to red and looks like a tiny apple; on average, it reaches not quite 2 inches in diameter. Like the strawberries that they are said to resemble in taste, myrtle apples grow close to the ground and are ready for picking in summer. Their pulp is consumed as food, whereas the roots are used medicinally.

Myrtle flag - *see* **SWEET FLAG**
Myrtle-leafed orange - *see* **ORANGE**
Myrtle pepper - *see* **ALLSPICE**

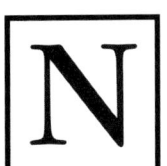

Nagami - *see* **KUMQUAT**
Nalta jute - *see* **JEW'S-MALLOW**
Ñame - *see* **CUSH-CUSH YAM**
Ñame mapuey - *see* **CUSH-CUSH YAM**
Nana - *see* **PINEAPPLE**
NANCE - A relative of the acerola and native to the West Indies, Central America, and much of South America, the nance (*Byrsonima crassifolia*) is a small tree with yellow fruits ranging from the size of a walnut to that of a lemon. The fruit is sweet and generally eaten raw but is also turned into a juice that is sometimes fermented to make an alcoholic beverage.

Nangka - *see* **JACKFRUIT**
Nannyberry - *see* **BLACK HAW**
Napa - *see* **CHINESE CABBAGE**
Napa Valley Gamay - *see* **GAMAY**
Nappa - *see* **CHINESE CABBAGE**
NARANJILLA - Found in Ecuador, Peru, Colombia, and Costa Rica, this small shrub (*Solanum quitoense*) bears bright orange, tomato-shaped, edible fruit at altitudes of 3,000 to 5,800 feet. Also called *lulo,* it has a juicy pulp that is used to make drinks, sherbet, preserves, and pies. The juice is rich in proteins and mineral salts. It does not travel well, but the fruit's popularity in sherbets has led to its commercial cultivation in Ecuador.
Common names and synonyms: Lulo.
Narrow-capped morel - *see* **MOREL**
Narrow dock - *see* **CURLED DOCK**
Naseberry - *see* **MIMUSOPS, SAPODILLA**
Nashi - *see* **ASIAN PEAR**
NASTURTIUM - The west coast of South America is the homeland of this creeping or climbing plant (*Tropaeolum majus*) also known as "Indian cress," which has a surprising number of culinary uses. Its leaves and young shoots have a hot, peppery flavor that goes well in salads and with eggs. The buds are pickled and can substitute as capers, and the flowers are chopped and added to rice and pasta dishes. From time to time, the nasturtium has been cultivated in Europe for its culinary properties, and it is used as a food in Peru today, as it has been for thousands of years. The plant is rich in vitamin C.
Common names and synonyms: Garden nasturtium, Indian cress.

Natal orange - *see* **MONKEY ORANGE**
NATAL PLUM (*see also* **SOUR PLUM**) - This large, thorny, South African shrub (*Carissa grandiflora = C. macrocarpa*), which is used for hedges in Natal, bears a fruit called the Natal plum. It is purple and plumlike and has a taste of gooseberry that goes well in pies and preserves. The Natal plum now also grows in frost-free areas of the United States, including Hawaii.
NATIVE CHERRY - A shrubby tree of Australia, the "native cherry" (*Exocarpos cuppressiformis*) produces a fruit that is a drupe, with a bright red, cherry-like appearance.
Native cucumber - *see* **PEPINO**
Native gooseberry - *see* **WILD GOOSEBERRY**
NATIVE GUAVA - The small tree or shrub of Australia called the "native guava" (*Rhodomyrtus psidioides*) bears an edible fruit that is remarkably similar to the tropical American guava (*Psidium guajava*). The former has been used as food for millennia by the Aborigines.
NATIVE LIME - Australia has two citrus trees that bear fruits called "native limes." One is designated *Citrus australis,* and the other is *Microcitrus australasica.* In both cases, the fruit is very acidic and quite high in vitamin C.
Native myrtle - *see* **BRUSH CHERRY**
Native peach - *see* **QUANDONG**
Native potato - *see* **WILD YAM**
NAVY BEAN (*see also* **BEANS**) - Also called the "pea bean," the navy bean is any of several varieties of the kidney bean (*Phaseolus vulgaris*) that are cultivated for their nutritious white seeds. The name "navy bean" recalls former times when the beans were among the standard provisions of warships of the U.S. Navy.
Common names and synonyms: Kidney bean, pea bean.
See in addition: "Beans, Peas, and Lentils," Part II, Section C, Chapter 3; "Legumes," Part VIII.
Neapolitan medlar - *see* **AZAROLE**
NEBBIOLO (*see also* **GRAPES**) - The best of the red wine grapes of the Italian Piedmont, Nebbiolo grapes (*Vitis vinifera*) were named from the Italian *nebbia,* meaning "fog," because they are harvested during a time when the Langhe hills of the Piedmont are covered with mist. The Nebbiolo is used to produce the famed Barolo and Barbaresco wines and also to blend with other grapes. Nebbiolo grapes are expensive because, like the Pinot Noir variety, they are very difficult to grow.
See in addition: "Wine," Part III, Chapter 13.
Nebraska currant - *see* **BUFFALO BERRY**
NECTARINE (*see also* **PEACH**) - There are over 150 varieties of nectarines, with the name apparently derived from the Greek *nektar,* meaning "drink-of-the-gods." The nectarine is itself a variety of peach (*Prunus persica*), which it resembles in every way save that it is smaller, sweeter, and fuzzless - mean-

ing that it looks more like a plum than a peach. The peach is an ancient fruit, but nectarines are hardly a newcomer to the dining table, having been known for more than 2,000 years. It is interesting, however, that little mention of nectarines can be found in the writings of the ancients.

In London in 1673, they were being grown for medicinal use by the Worshipful Society of Apothecaries, and by 1720, they were being cultivated among the peaches of Virginia. Like peaches, nectarines are either clingstone or freestone. They constitute one of the world's major fruit crops, with the United States and Italy the principal areas of cultivation. The fruit is grown in California, South America, and the Middle East for the American market, which makes them available year-round. Nectarines are eaten whole, made into juice, poached, baked, and grilled to accompany barbecued meats. Most are orange or yellow fleshed, but some are white fleshed. The orange-fleshed kinds in particular are an excellent source of vitamin A, and all are rich in vitamin C.

NEROLI (*see also* **CITRUS FRUITS**) – Also called "orange-flower water," neroli is the essential oil of bitter orange blossoms (*Citrus aurantium*), which is obtained by distillation. The oil is used in perfumery, and the perfumed essence is employed in making syrups and flavoring liqueurs. The process was introduced in France during the late seventeenth century by Anna Maria de la Trémoille, Princess of Neroli.

Common names and synonyms: Neroli oil, orange-flower oil, orange-flower water.

See in addition: "Spices and Flavorings," Part II, Section F, Chapter 1.

NETTLE(S) – Everyone knows these perennial herbs of the genus *Urtica* (especially *U. dioica*), which are naturalized worldwide. They bear "toothed" leaves that are covered with tiny, hollow hairs containing a number of irritating substances, which inflict a sting and a rash on those who accidentally touch them. But the young tips, picked as they broke through the ground in the spring, were frequently cooked and eaten as a vegetable by our foraging forebears, who may well have been on the lookout for greens to rid themselves of the first symptoms of scurvy after a winter of vitamin-C deprivation. The young leaves of nettles are often prepared much like spinach, are included in other dishes, and have been brewed into tea and even beer. Nettle seeds have been gathered for food as well. Indeed, many people still gather nettles today; the medicinal uses of the plant are as well known as its nutritional capacity. Nettles are rich in vitamins and minerals, particularly vitamin C, iron, sulfur, potassium, and sodium.

Common names and synonyms: Burning nettle(s), stinging nettle(s).

NEW MEXICO CHILLIES (*see also* **CHILLI PEPPERS**) – There are quite a number of chillies called New Mexico – all of the *Capsicum annuum* species, including the Anaheim, which is one of many New Mexico varieties. The major ones are the New Mexico Green (also called the "long green chilli") and the New Mexico Red (the mature form). Between 6 and 10 inches in length, and close to 2 inches in diameter, these peppers are only moderately hot and are favorites for roasting and stuffing. The red form is also used in a number of sauces, including barbecue sauces. When peeled and dried, New Mexico green and red chillies are sometimes called dried California chillies, and the red is also called *chilli colorado*. The latter is used to make chilli sauces and ground chilli powders. Other New Mexico chillies – the "NuMex" Eclipse, Sunrise, and Sunset – are, respectively, purple, goldish, and bright orange in color and are used mostly for decorative purposes, as are the newly developed New Mexico "Miniatures."

Common names and synonyms: Chilli colorado, dried California chilli, long green chilli, New Mexico Green, New Mexico Miniature, New Mexico Red, NuMex Eclipse, NuMex Sunrise, NuMex Sunset.

See in addition: "Chilli Peppers," Part II, Section C, Chapter 4.

NEW ZEALAND SPINACH – Although not actually a spinach (indeed, it is a member of a different botanical family), "New Zealand spinach" (*Tetragonia expansa*) has a spinach-like appearance and flavor, goes well in salads, and is also cooked like spinach. Native to New Zealand and Australia, this vegetable has diffused around the world and grows well in those warmer places where real spinach does not. Like spinach, New Zealand spinach is rich in beta-carotene, folacin, and other vitamins and minerals.

NIGELLA – A member of the buttercup family and native to the northern Himalayan mountains, the Middle East, and eastern Europe, nigella (*Nigella sativa*) consists of tiny dried black seeds, quite similar to black caraway seeds, with which they are sometimes confused. Today, the plant that yields them in swollen pods is most extensively cultivated in India, where nigella is used in numerous dishes. In the United States, it is carried in gourmet shops under the Indian name *kalonji* and, as in the Middle East, is sprinkled on breads. In fact, black nigella seeds are often encountered atop Jewish rye bread, pumpernickel, and the like.

Common names and synonyms: Black caraway, black cumin, black nigella, *charnushka,* devil-in-the-bush, fennel-flower, *kalonji,* love-in-a-mist, Russian caraway.

See also: "Spices and Flavorings," Part II, Section F, Chapter 1.

Niger – *see* **NIGER SEED**

NIGER SEED – Originating in West Africa and now grown extensively in Ethiopia and India, niger seed (*Guizotia abyssinica*) is cultivated as an oil crop, although the seeds are also used by humans as a condiment and as a food for birds. The oil has a number of industrial applications, but it is edible as well and is employed in the usual culinary ways – for cooking and in salads – especially in Ethiopia, where the seed is called "noog," and its oil is the most important edible oil in the country. In addition, niger-seed oil serves as an adulterant in other oils.

Common names and synonyms: Niger, nog, noog, nug, ramtil.

NIPA PALM – Palms of the genus *Nypa* (or *Nipa*) have leaves that are used locally for thatching, basket weaving, and making hats, whereas the stems are employed to fashion arrows. The Chinese eat the raw fruits of this tree for their sweetness or candy them as preserves. Sugar extracted from the fruit is used to make alcohol and vinegar, and the alcoholic beverage is also called "nipa."

Common names and synonyms: Mangrove, nypa palm.

Nispero - *see* **LOQUAT, SAPODILLA**
Nitta tree - *see* **PARKIA**
Noblecane - *see* **SUGARCANE**
No-eye pea - *see* **PIGEON PEA**
Nog - *see* **NIGER SEED**
Noisette - *see* **HAZELNUT AND FILBERT**
Nona - *see* **CUSTARD APPLE**
Noog - *see* **NIGER SEED**
Nopal - *see* **NOPALES, PRICKLY PEAR**
NOPALES (*see also* **PRICKLY PEAR**) – Also named *nopalitos* and "cactus pads," nopales are the leaves (called "paddles") of certain varieties of Mexican cacti (genus *Opuntia*). (In addition, the cochineal plant [*Nopalea cochenillifera = N. coccinellifera*] is called nopal, and its young joints are often sold as nopales.) These vegetables are fleshy yet slippery (they exude a mucilaginous substance similar to that in okra), have a crunchy texture, and when fresh have a delicate taste somewhere between that of green pepper and asparagus. Nopales can be eaten raw (once the spines are removed) but more often are cooked in boiling water until tender. They are frequently cooked with eggs, are often steamed for a vegetable dish, and (after cooling) can be added to salads. Nopales that are purchased in jars have a tart and pickle-like taste; they are called for in many "Tex-Mex" dishes. Nopales have been consumed by Native Americans of Mesoamerica and the southwestern portion of North America for millennia and have often served as a famine food. They are a fine source of beta-carotene, vitamin C, and some of the B-vitamins as well.

Common names and synonyms: Cactus pad, cactus paddle, cochineal plant, nopal, *nopalitos*.

Nopalitos - *see* **NOPALES**
Nori - *see* **LAVER, SEAWEED**
Northern pine - *see* **WHITE PINE**

Nug - *see* **NIGER SEED**
NuMex Eclipse - *see* **NEW MEXICO CHILLIES**
NuMex Sunrise - *see* **NEW MEXICO CHILLIES**
NuMex Sunset - *see* **NEW MEXICO CHILLIES**
Nut(-)grass - *see* **CHUFA**
NUTMEG (*see also* **MACE**) – A kernel of the fruit of a tropical tree (*Myristica fragrans*), the dried nutmeg berry is called "nutmeg" because of its nutlike appearance. Nutmeg and mace are the only spices that come from the same fruit, with mace the aril of the dried seed. The nutmeg berry can be as small as an apricot or as large as a peach. An ancient spice, nutmeg is native to the Moluccas (the "Spice Islands") and was employed in South Asian cuisines for many centuries before it found its way to Rome, where Pliny wrote of a tree that bore a nut with two different tastes. Its subsequent history is that of mace. Like mace, nutmeg has been used in the West primarily in sweet beverages and desserts. Many grate it at home, as needed, with a small grater. But nutmeg can also be purchased already ground. A sprinkle works well in stews and numerous sauces. The oil derived from nutmeg has medicinal applications and is also a component of nutmeg butter. Today, nutmeg is grown primarily in Grenada and Indonesia.

See in addition: "Spices and Flavorings," Part II, Section F, Chapter 1.

Nut pine - *see* **PINE NUT**
Nux gallia - *see* **WALNUT**
Nypa palm - *see* **NIPA PALM**

Oak tongue - *see* **MUSHROOMS AND FUNGI**

OAT(S) – One of the last of the wild grasses to be domesticated and cultivated, oats (*Avena sativa*) have served humans principally as a feed for domestic animals. Historically, oats achieved only a relatively minor status as a food for humans – perhaps because the crop was a latecomer among the domesticated grains – and today only about 5 percent of the world's crop is consumed in this way. Developed from wild grasses of eastern Europe and Asia, oats were despised by the Egyptians and others of the Middle East and were viewed as animal fodder by the Greeks and Romans. Indeed, it may be the case that the plant, which existed mostly as a weed in wheatfields, was not domesticated until after the Christian era had begun.

Some time after this, oats became a staple food in Scotland (mostly in the form of porridge) and by 1600 the grain was adapted as an important crop to the wet climate of northern Europe. By 1650, oats had crossed the Atlantic to be planted in Massachusetts, and in 1877 the Quaker Mill Company was founded in Ravenna, Ohio. Beginning in 1884, "Quaker Oats" – one of the first packaged foods to be marketed – were sold in the now-famous card-board canisters. "Steel-cut" oats are cracked-oat kernels, whereas "rolled" oats have been put through a roller to flatten them into thin flakes. Oats are a good source of manganese, folacin, iron, zinc, and vitamin E and an excellent source of dietary fiber. Oat bran is said to be an effective cholesterol reducer and thus was the focus of a health-food craze for a period in the latter part of the twentieth century. Today, we know that oats can help to lower LDL (the "bad" cholesterol), but not by enough to justify the claims of the faddists.

Common names and synonyms: Rolled oat(s), steel-cut oat(s).

See also: "Oat," Part II, Section A, Chapter 6.

OCA – An important crop in the Andean highlands, oca (*Oxalis tuberosa*) has edible leaves and young shoots, but its tubers are the most important parts nutritionally. They are wrinkled and come in a variety of sizes and shapes, not to mention colors, which range from red and orange to yellow and white. There are two kinds, sweet and bitter. The sweet variety is eaten raw, cooked, and dried (by the sun). More intensive drying produces a product that tastes like dried figs and has been used as a sweetener by native populations.

Bitter oca is freeze-dried and stored for later use. After the potato, it was oca that sustained Native American highland populations for millennia, and it remains a staple of Peruvian and Bolivian Indians living at high altitudes. Around 1830, oca reached the British Isles, where it served as a food, especially in Wales. In France, the plant grows wild and is gathered to make a dish called Peruvian soup. In the 1860s, oca was carried to New Zealand by an English immigrant who acquired some of the tubers in Chile, and the plant has recently become popular there as a misnamed "yam" that is boiled, baked, and fried.

Common names and synonyms: Bitter oca, occa, oka, sweet oca, ulluco.

Occa – *see* **OCA**

Ochro – *see* **OKRA**

OGEN MELON (*see also* **MELON**) – This cultivar of the green-fleshed muskmelon was developed in Israel. Smaller than most melons, the Ogen melon (*Cucumis melo*) averages from 3 to 4 pounds and has a golden yellow skin with attractive vertical green stripes. When ripe, its creamy flesh has an appealing aroma and is deliciously sweet, which may explain why the chefs of many acclaimed restaurants offer the melon on their menus. The Ogen melon is featured in appetizers, salads, and desserts, often in tandem with other fruits or sorbets. An enticing combination is Ogen melon, raspberries, and port.

See in addition: "Cucumbers, Melons, and Watermelons," Part II, Section C, Chapter 6.

OIL-BEAN TREE – A tropical West African native, the oil-bean tree (*Pentaclethra macrophylla*) has seeds that are rich in an oil (owala oil) used locally for cooking purposes. The seeds, high in protein, are also employed as a condiment.

Common names and synonyms: Owala-oil tree.

Oil nut – *see* **WALNUT**

Oil palm – *see* "An Overview of Oils and Fats," Part II, Section E, Chapter 1; "Palm Oil," Part II, Section E, Chapter 3

Oka – *see* **OCA**

OKARI NUT – This nut (*Terminalia okari*) belongs to the family Combretaceae. Native to Papua New Guinea, it is now grown in Southeast Asia as well as in Hawaii and Florida. The nut has a shiny dark outer skin but is white inside. It is eaten raw or roasted and is pressed into oil.

OKRA – A member of the mallow family, and called "gumbo" and "lady-fingers" along with a host of other common names, okra (*Abelmoschus esculentus* = *Hibiscus esculentus*) is often thought of as a vegetable but is actually a fruit. A native of Africa (most likely tropical Africa), okra was used by the Egyptians, was known to the Spanish Moors in the twelfth century A.D., and in the late seventeenth century was carried by slaves to the Americas. According to legend, okra was introduced in southeastern North America by the "Cassette Girls" – 25 young Frenchwomen who landed at Mobile in 1704 in search of husbands. They had with them okra that had been obtained from slaves in the West Indies, and which they used to invent "gumbo," which is a soup or stew thickened with okra. Okra has played a major role in the cuisines of ex-slave societies in the Americas, where it continues to be especially popular. It is also cultivated in Africa and East and South Asia. Okra has been commonly used in gumbo, but the pods are also cooked (especially fried) as a vegetable. The plant is often found in home gardens and produces seeds that can be saved and used the following year. Much of the okra crop is frozen and canned, and in Asia a dried okra powder is also used. Okra is a good source of calcium, magnesium, and potassium as well as vitamin C, folacin, and some of the other B-vitamins.

Common names and synonyms: Bamia, *bendi,* bhindee, bhindi, bindi, cantarela, gombaut, gombo, gumbo, lady('s)-finger(s), mesta, ochro, okro, quiabo, quimbambo, quingombo, rosenapfel, vendakai.

Okro – *see* **OKRA**

Olallieberry – *see* **BLACKBERRY**

Old-man – *see* **SOUTHERNWOOD**

Oleaster – *see* **ELAEAGNUS**

OLIVE (*see also* **ELAEAGNUS, OSMANTHUS**) – A very old fruit – actually a berry – the olive grows on gnarled and twisted evergreen trees (*Olea europaea*) that are apparently eastern Mediterranean in origin and were under cultivation by Semitic peoples some 5,000 years ago. Phoenician colonists, who carried olive trees to the Iberian Peninsula about 800 B.C., may have introduced them throughout much of Mediterranean Europe and Africa as well. Ancient Hebrew texts mention olives, and they were known in Greece by about 900 B.C. The olive tree – called the "king of trees" in the Bible – was further spread by the Romans about those regions of Europe that could grow it. In the first century A.D., Pliny recorded a number of varieties under cultivation as far away as Gaul (France) and Iberia, and any areas in the Mediterranean basin that the Romans may have missed were later filled in with olive trees by the conquering Arabs. Olives reached the New World with the Spaniards in the first decades of the sixteenth century and were later carried to California by the Franciscans, who planted the trees in San Diego. And just prior to the American Revolution, Thomas Jefferson tried unsuccessfully to grow olives at Monticello.

Olives have been cultivated mostly for their oil. Those that are consumed are too bitter to be eaten fresh and are first pickled – cured in lye, brine, or dry salt, with the majority brine-cured. Olives come in all shapes and sizes but are sometimes misleadingly categorized as "green" and "ripe." In fact, the green ones are actually the ripest, whereas the black, so-called ripe olives from California are really unripe green olives that have been processed with lye and oxidized to turn them brownish black. Black olives that have been picked when truly ripe will appear shriveled. Among the best-known olive varieties that are pickled are the Queen (especially the Sevillano of Spain), the Mission (California's most important variety), and the Manzanillo (an Old World variety), which is the largest of the pickling olives. In the United States, olives have long been stuffed with pimento and more recently with tiny onions, almonds, hot peppers, and anchovies. In Europe, olives have an important place in cooking, especially in the Mediterranean cuisines of Greece, Italy, and Provence in France. They are also frequently permitted to ferment a bit, then served as an appetizer. Spain, Italy, Greece, and Portugal are the world's leading olive producers. California accounts for about 5 percent of the world's crop. Delicious as olives can be, the reason they are pressed for oil is because they are loaded with fat. After processing, they are also loaded with sodium.

Common names and synonyms: Black olive, green olive, king-of-trees, Manzanillo, Mission, pickling olive, Queen, ripe olive, Sevillano.

See in addition: "An Overview of Oils and Fats," Part II, Section E, Chapter 1.

Olivo - *see* **ACEITUNA**

Olluco - *see* **ULLUCO**

Omam - *see* **AJOWAN**

Omum - *see* **AJOWAN**

ONION (*see also* **ONION TREE, RAKKYO, WELSH ONION, WILD LEEK(S)**) - Cultivated since prehistoric times, the onion (*Allium cepa*) is a native of central or western Asia that has become indispensable to cuisines the world over. This plant was used by the ancient Egyptians, Babylonians, Romans, and Greeks, who believed it to have curative powers. In addition, onions – along with garlic and chickpeas - reportedly made up the bulk of the food rations for the 100,000 or so laborers who built the Great Pyramid of Cheops around 2900 B.C. The ancients interpreted the layered internal structure of the onion as a symbol of eternity, and later the onion-shaped towers which became part of the architecture of Russia and Eastern Europe were so constructed to (hopefully) ensure that the buildings would stand forever. During the Middle Ages in Europe, physicians prescribed onions for people's ills, and even today they are a part of many home remedies.

The most common of the onions is the yellow onion, which accounts for more than 75 percent of the world's production. Sweet onions include the Spanish, the Bermuda, the California Italian Red, the Vidalia (from the area around Vidalia, Georgia), the Walla Walla (from Washington State), and the Maui (from Hawaii). "Scallions," used in salads and vegetable trays, are also called salad or green onions. Red onions (known to some as Italian red onions), purple onions, and tiny "pearl onions" (used for pickling and added whole to soups and stews) round out the list of the cultivated varieties.

In addition, there are many wild varieties around the world, including those of North America. Onions are common in salads, and both raw and fried onions are used in sandwiches and a great variety of other dishes. They are made into soups and are baked, boiled, and sautéed. Onions can be purchased frozen and canned, and they are also dehydrated to become onion flakes, onion powders, and onion salt. Onions are high in vitamin C and were long important to sea and desert travelers as a means of preventing scurvy.

Common names and synonyms: Bermuda onion, California Italian Red onion, common onion, green onion, Italian red onion, Maui onion, pearl onion, purple onion, red onion, salad onion, scallion, Spanish onion, spring onion, sweet onion, Vidalia onion, Walla Walla onion, white onion, wild onion, yellow onion.

See in addition: "The *Allium* Species," Part II, Section C, Chapter 2; "Spices and Flavorings," Part II, Section F, Chapter 1.

ONION TREE (*see also* **ONIONS**) - An unusual plant, the onion tree (*Allium cepa*) has no bulb at the base of the stem. Rather, the bulb, bulbils, or bulblets are located at the top of the plant, and as the top becomes too heavy for the stem, the latter bends - so that the bulbils may root several inches away from the main plant. Because of this, the onion tree is sometimes called a "walking onion." The top bulblets are generally pickled, but the stems and tops are also used as scallions.

Common names and synonyms: Egyptian onion, Egyptian tree onion, perennial onion, walking onion.

See in addition: "The *Allium* Species," Part II, Section C, Chapter 2.

ONZA (*see also* **CHILLI PEPPERS**) - Although called for in many soup and sauce recipes, the onza pepper (*Capsicum annuum*) is difficult to find even in its native Mexico. It is a small chilli that looks like a bright red jalapeño and delivers a medium amount of heat.

See in addition: "Chilli Peppers," Part II, Section C, Chapter 4.

Oolong - *see* **TEA**

ORACH - The various plants of the genus *Atriplex*, especially *A. hortensis*, are called orach. Orach has edible green leaves that resemble those of spinach and are used in the same ways. Although naturalized in America, orach is a Eurasian native that has doubtless been a quarry of foragers for millennia. It is also an ancient cultivar that continued to be widely grown until the eighteenth century. Today, however, like other plants such as "Good-King-Henry," orach has returned to the wild.

Common names and synonyms: Garden orach, green orach, mountain spinach, orache, red orach.

Orache - *see* **ORACH**

ORANGE (*see also* **BLOOD ORANGE, CITRUS FRUITS, MANDARIN ORANGE, TANGOR**) - One way to categorize this fruit of the genus *Citrus* is to distinguish bitter oranges (*C. aurantium*) from sweet oranges (*C. sinensis*). The bitter orange (also known as Sevilla, sour orange, and Bigarade) is a native of Southeast Asia and was cultivated in the Indus Valley some 6,000 years ago. The sweet orange (also known as the China sweet orange and - in India - the Malta orange) may also have originated in Southeast Asia, although many believe it to be a native of southern China, as is evidenced by its scientific name. Both fruits were slow to find their way to the Mediterranean basin; the bitter orange eventually arrived with the Arabs around A.D. 1000, but the Western advent of the sweet orange came more than 400 years later, perhaps with the help of Genoese traders or Portuguese explorers.

Sweet-orange trees were planted at Versailles in 1421, and later (1548) in Lisbon. Meanwhile, in 1493, the second voyage of Christopher Columbus is said to have carried sweet-orange seeds (along with lemon seeds) to Hispaniola, and Spaniards stationed in Florida were reportedly growing oranges there in 1565, the year St. Augustine was founded. A couple of centuries later, the Franciscans began planting orange groves at their mission of San Diego in California. In western North America, however, California trailed behind Arizona, which saw its first groves at the beginning of the eighteenth century. By the end of the Civil War, Florida was already shipping large quantities of oranges to the rest of the country, and today that state produces about 70 percent of the U.S. crop, practically all of which (some 90 percent) is made into juice.

Sweet oranges can be further divided into the varieties that have been developed. In the United States, only sweet oranges are grown commercially. The Valencia - a major representative of the sweet orange, sometimes called the "common orange" - accounts for about half of the oranges produced annually. The popular "navel oranges" constitute another variety that is easily identified by thick skins and navel-like scars. Most of California's orange crop is from Washington navel orange trees (which were developed in Bahia, Brazil, and ripen for Christmas holiday sales) or from those of the Valencia variety. Still other varieties are the virtually seedless Hamlins (grown mostly in Florida), "Pineapple oranges" (good for juicing but with many seeds), and Jaffa oranges (developed in Israel), which are sweeter than Valencias. Still other sweet oranges, such as the blood oranges and the Mandarin oranges (Clementine, Tangelo, Tangerine, Temple) are treated in separate entries in this work.

There is less to say about sour-orange trees, which are grown mostly as rootstock for other *Citrus* species, and produce fruits that are too sour to be eaten raw. Their major use is for marmalades and preserves, although the bergamot orange is grown for its oil, and others, such as the myrtle-leafed orange, have small fruits that are candied. Oranges contain much in the way of vitamin C, and in fact, orange juice is the most important supplier of this vitamin for many Americans.

Common names and synonyms: Bergamot orange, Bigarade, bitter orange, China sweet orange, Chinese orange, Clementine, common orange, Hamlin, Jaffa orange, Malta orange, Mandarin orange, myrtle-leafed orange, navel orange, Pineapple orange, Sevilla, sour orange, sweet orange, tangelo, tangerine, Valencia, Washington navel orange.

Orange-flower oil - *see* **NEROLI**
Orange-flower water - *see* **NEROLI**
Orange gooseberry - *see* **GOOSEBERRY**
Orange milkweed - *see* **BUTTERFLY WEED**
Orange pekoe - *see* **TEA**
ORANGEQUAT (*see also* **CITRUS FRUITS**) - A cross between the kumquat and the Mandarin orange, the orangequat (genera *Citrus* and *Fortunella*) is another hybrid resulting from a program of research, sponsored by the U.S. Department of Agriculture, designed to breed the resistance to cold of the kumquat into plants of other genera that have desirable qualities. The orangequat has a good, kumquat-like flavor.

Orange root - *see* **BUTTERFLY WEED**
Oregano - *see* **MARJORAM AND OREGANO**
Oregon grape - *see* **BARBERRY**
Organ-pipe cactus - *see* **PITAHAYA**
Oriental garlic - *see* **CHINESE CHIVE(S), CHIVE(S)**
Oriental melon - *see* **BITTER MELON, MELONS**

Oriental pear - *see* ASIAN PEAR
Oriental pickling melon - *see* GHERKIN
Oriental radish - *see* DAIKON
Orris root - *see* IRIS
OSMANTHUS - Also called "devilwood" and "wild olive," *Osmanthus* is a widely distributed genus of evergreen shrubs or trees with small, olive-like fruits that are softened in brine and used like green olives. In addition, the flowers of *O. americanus* are employed to add aroma to black teas.
Common names and synonyms: Devilwood, wild olive.
Ostrich fern - *see* FIDDLEHEAD FERN
Oswego tea - *see* BEE BALM
Otaheita-apple - *see* GOLDEN APPLE
OTAHEITE GOOSEBERRY - Also known as the "gooseberry tree," the Otaheite gooseberry (*Phyllanthus acidus*) is a small tropical tree, native to Africa and South Asia, that is now naturalized in the Caribbean and southern Florida. It produces a small, round, acidic fruit that is edible but is too sour to be eaten raw. Rather, it is pickled, made into chutney, and used to produce a syrup and jams.
Common names and synonyms: Chermai, gooseberry tree, grosella, Indian gooseberry, Malay gooseberry.
OTAHEITE ORANGE (*see also* CITRUS FRUITS) - Otaheite was the former name of Tahiti, and the Otaheite orange (*Citrus taitensis*) has retained the old name while also going by the name "Tahiti orange." The fruit is the size of an apple, has the shape of a lemon, and is colored like an orange. The pulp tastes something like pineapple.
Common names and synonyms: Tahiti orange.
Oudo - *see* UDO
Oval-leaf - *see* PEPEROMIA
Owala-oil tree - *see* OIL-BEAN TREE
Owe kola - *see* KOLA NUT
OYSTER MUSHROOM (*see also* MUSHROOMS AND FUNGI) - Raised mostly in California, Canada, and the southeastern United States, the oyster mushroom (*Pleurotus ostreatus*) grows in wooded areas and forms clusters on the stumps of dead trees. The 2- to 6-inch cap resembles a seashell and is moist and spongy; the color is usually brown to gray and fades with age. The gills run down the stem and are widely separated; they have a creamy beige or white color. The stem, which may be absent, is white, short, and firm (not as soft as the cap). The oyster mushroom is very much in demand but is only good as long as it is immature.
Common names and synonyms: Oyster fungus, pleurotte, shimeji, tree mushroom, tree oyster.
See in addition: "Fungi," Part II, Section C, Chapter 7.
OYSTERNUT - A native of tropical Africa and cultivated in East and Central Africa, the oysternut (*Telfairia pedata*), also called the "Zanzibar oil vine," is cultivated mostly for its large, edible, nut-like seeds, which are very high in protein. They are generally roasted before consumption and are also pressed to yield an oil similar to that from olives.

Common names and synonyms: African pumpkin, fluted cucumber, Zanzibar oil-vine.
Oyster-plant - *see* SALSIFY

Pacura - *see* BAKUPARI
Pai - *see* ALOCASIA
Paiko - *see* CHENOPODIUM, EPAZOTE
PAKCHOI AND KAI CHOY (*see also* CHINESE CABBAGE) - Both pakchoi (*Brassica chinensis*) and kai choy (*B. campestris*) are variations of Chinese cabbage with many synonyms. Pakchoi looks like tiny Swiss chard, whereas the leaves of kai choy are cupped.
Common names and synonyms: Celery mustard, Chinese chard, gaai chow, gaai choy, gai chow, gai choy, Japanese white celery mustard, mustard cabbage, pak choy, pak choy sum, pak toy, spoon cabbage.
See in addition: "Cruciferous and Green Leafy Vegetables," Part II, Section C, Chapter 5.
Pak choy - *see* PAKCHOI AND KAI CHOY
Pak choy sum - *see* PAKCHOI AND KAI CHOY
Pak toy - *see* PAKCHOI AND KAI CHOY
Palmetto - *see* HEART(S) OF PALM
Palm heart(s) - *see* HEART(S) OF PALM
Palm lily - *see* CABBAGE TREE
Palm oil - *see* "An Overview of Oils and Fats," Part II, Section E, Chapter 1; "Palm Oil," Part II, Section E, Chapter 3
Palmyra - *see* WINE PALM
PALOMINO (*see also* GRAPES) - A grape grown mostly in Spain, the Palomino (*Vitis vinifera*) accounts for 90 percent of the grapes planted to make sherry (*jerez*), the renowned fortified wine of that country.
See in addition: "Wine," Part III, Chapter 13.
Palta - *see* AVOCADO
Pana de pepita - *see* BREADFRUIT
Panama berry - *see* CAPULIN
Panama orange - *see* CALAMONDIN
PANDANUS - There are a number of species of palm-like trees and shrubs of the genus *Pandanus* (also called "screw-pines") that are found in southeastern Asia and the Pacific region. Most are utilized for fiber to weave mats and other such articles. Some, however, are used as a food source by Pacific Islanders in places like Papua New Guinea. The terminal bud of the branch, or "heart," is eaten along with the tips of roots, the young leaves, and the seeds and fleshy part of the fruit, which in cultivated varieties can weigh upwards of 30 pounds. In addition, the heart can be made into a flour that is high in carbohydrates. Eaten raw, pandanus is a good source of vitamins A and C.
Common names and synonyms: Fruited pandanus, pandanus fruit, pandanus heart(s), pandanus key(s), pandanus nut, screw(-)pine.

Panic(oid) grass(es) - *see* **MILLET**

Papa - *see* **WHITE POTATO**

PAPAW - Also called "pawpaw" and "custard apple," the papaw is a small, fleshy, edible fruit from the tree designated *Asimina triloba*. These trees reach from 30 to 40 feet in height and grow wild in North America along the East Coast of the United States and from New York State through the Midwest. The fruit, which is shaped like a thick, short banana, turns black as it ripens, at which point the yellowish pulp has the taste of an overripe cantaloupe. Papaws can be eaten raw, but many people find the taste more agreeable when the fruit is cooked. Generally mentioned as one of the many foods that sustained Native Americans, the papaw is central to a muddle of nomenclature because its names, "papaw" and "pawpaw," probably came from "papaya," a fruit to which it is not related. Nor is "custard apple" an appropriate nickname, because it is generally one of the names given to the cherimoya – also not a relative.

Common names and synonyms: Custard apple, paw(-)paw.

PAPAYA (*see also* **BABACO, CHAMBURO, MOUNTAIN PAPAYA**) - The papaya tree (*Carica papaya*) is an evergreen with a palmlike appearance. It is native to tropical Mesoamerica, is related to the gourd, melon, and pumpkin family, and may represent an ancient fusion of two or more species of the genus *Carica,* native to Mexico and Central America. The first Spaniards to reach Yucatán were welcomed by Mayans bearing gifts of fruit, among them papayas. At that time, the papaya was known only from Mexico to Panama, but shortly afterward, the Spaniards began moving the fruit via their Manila galleons westward across the Pacific to the Philippines and beyond, and the Portuguese carried it around the globe in the other direction.

The result is that the papaya is now cultivated throughout the tropical world – especially in Hawaii, Africa, and South Asia – for its fruit and for its milky latex. The latex contains the proteolytic enzyme papain, which is used as a meat tenderizer, to clear beer, and also for medical purposes. The yellow, orange, or pinkish somewhat sweet fruit is usually eaten raw (often for breakfast) but is also candied, converted into juice, put into pies and salads, and used to make sherbets. The unripe fruit is cooked like squash.

The papaya is sometimes wrongly called "pawpaw" or "papaw." Although papayas are grown throughout the world's tropical regions, most of those reaching U.S. consumers are the pear-shaped Solo varieties from Hawaii (introduced there from Barbados). These are about 6 inches in length and have either pink or yellow flesh. Papayas are a fine source of vitamin C.

Common names and synonyms: Green papaya, melon fruit, melon pawpaw, papaw, paw(-)paw, Solo (papaya).

Papdi - *see* **SUGAR PEA**

PAPER MULBERRY - This tree (*Broussonetia papyrifera*) is called "paper mulberry" because its bark is used to make paper in China and Japan. The tree also produces a sweet, red fruit, which is eaten raw, and leaves that are also edible. The paper mulberry is a native of East Asia that is now naturalized in southeastern North America.

Paper-reed - *see* **PAPYRUS**

Paper-rush - *see* **PAPYRUS**

Papoose root - *see* **BLUE COHOSH**

PAPRIKA (*see also* **CHILLI PEPPERS, SWEET PEPPERS**) - Because paprika, like cayenne, is made from dried American red peppers (*Capsicum annuum* and *C. frutescens*), it is a relative newcomer to the world's spice rack. As a rule, the chillies made into paprika are less potent than those used for cayenne. Chilli peppers were carried by the conquistadors from Mexico to Spain. The peppers subsequently found their way to Poland (the name "paprika" comes from the Polish *pierprzyca*) and then to Hungary, where they became a vital ingredient in Hungarian goulash – and, in due course, as the Hungarians perfected it, paprika became the national spice.

Paprika comes as sweet, mild, and hot (only the seeds are used for the mild type; the hot version is made from the whole fruit), and the best is made in Hungary; paprika made elsewhere is without much flavor and used mostly for the color it imparts. Paprika both flavors and adorns many Hungarian dishes, and it also spices and colors the sausages of Spain – another country that produces large quantities of paprika for its own national dishes.

Common names and synonyms: Paprika pepper, paprika plant.

See in addition: "Chilli Peppers," Part II, Section C, Chapter 4.

PAPYRUS - A tall sedge of the Nile Valley, papyrus (*Cyperus papyrus*) has also been called "paper-rush" and "paper-reed" because it was used by the ancient Egyptians, Greeks, and Romans to make a sheet or roll of material to write on. Practically forgotten is the food value of the plant, which provided tender shoots and rhizomes for the cooking pot.

Common names and synonyms: Paper-reed, paper-rush.

Paradise nut - *see* **SAPUCAIA NUT**

Paradise tree - *see* **ACEITUNA**

Paraguay(an) tea - *see* **YERBA MATÉ**

Para nut - *see* **BRAZIL NUT**

Paris mushroom - *see* **MUSHROOMS AND FUNGI**

Parish's yampah - *see* **INDIAN POTATO**

PARKIA - Named for the eighteenth-century Scottish explorer and surgeon Mungo Park, *Parkia* is a genus of leguminous, Old World tropical trees with pods that contain edible seeds and pulp. Among the species are the nitta tree (*P. biglobosa*) and the petai tree (*P. speciosa*). The latter has large, edible beans that hang down on the outside of the tree.

Common names and synonyms: Nitta tree, petai tree.

Parry pinyon pine - *see* **PINE NUT**

PARSLEY (*see also* **HAMBURG PARSLEY, LOVAGE**) - The aromatic leaves of parsley (*Petroselinum crispum*), a native of southern Europe, are employed for flavoring, although some parsley varieties are boiled and their roots consumed as a vegetable. The use of parsley dates from at least the time of the ancient Greeks, and because the plant has been introduced into most areas of the globe, it is one of the world's best-known herbs. According to the Sardinians, it is native to their island, although other regions also claim parsley as their own; regardless, it has been used in the Mediterranean region for thousands of years. The Greeks, who made crowns of it to honor athletes at ceremonies and themselves at banquets, also had medical uses for the herb. The Romans utilized parsley as an herb and introduced the plant throughout Europe.

There are three basic kinds of parsley. One is the familiar, bright-green curly parsley; another, sometimes called Italian parsley, has flat leaves and a stronger flavor than the curly type. The third is Hamburg parsley, also called turnip-rooted parsley, which is grown for its long white root, that when cooked tastes something like celeriac. Both curly and Italian parsley lend taste and eye appeal to salads and other dishes. Parsley also comes in dried flakes, but these have virtually no taste. The fresh kinds are rich in vitamins A and C, calcium, and iron.

Common names and synonyms: Curly parsley, Italian parsley.

See in addition: "Spices and Flavorings," Part II, Section F, Chapter 1.

PARSNIP - The parsnip (*Pastinaca sativa*), a native of Europe and western Asia, has been cultivated for its long, yellowish brown, carrot-shaped edible taproot since at least the time of the ancient Greeks. In the Middle Ages, physicians credited parsnips with medicinal properties, and in parts of England and Ireland (where parsnips have long enjoyed considerable popularity), many different ways of preparing the vegetable have evolved, and even a kind of wine has been made from its fermented roots.

Parsnips were introduced into the West Indies during the sixteenth century and North America at the beginning of the seventeenth century, whereupon their use spread rapidly among Native Americans. The vegetable also served as an important staple in the diet of the European colonists until the potato finally replaced it in the nineteenth century. Parsnips are usually boiled, then sometimes mashed or pureed, but they can also be fried and baked and go well in stews. The taste of parsnips is best only after the first frost; indeed, it was long customary to leave much of a crop in the ground over the winter to let the action of frost improve the flavor even more.

Such a practice, however, was not without controversy; some people insisted that parsnips became poisonous when left in the ground, whereas others held that the vegetable was not safe to eat until after it had weathered the first frost. Both sides have been pronounced wrong for various reasons, but very recently, medical science has suggested that parsnips may be toxic after all – because they contain psoralens, which have been linked to the development of cancer and mutations in laboratory animals. Unlike their relative the carrot, parsnips contain little beta-carotene, but they are rich in vitamin C.

Common names and synonyms: Wild parsnip.

Pasado - *see* **ANAHEIM**

PASILLA (*see also* **CHILLI PEPPERS**) - In Spanish, *pasa* means raisin, and thus *pasilla* translates as "little raisin." However, there is nothing raisin-like about the size of this chilli pepper (*Capsicum annuum*), which when fresh is called *chilaca* and averages about 6 inches in length. And even though it does have a wrinkled skin when dried, its other name, chilli negro, inspired by its dark color, seems more appropriate. Fresh *chilacas* are seldom available - in part, one suspects, because of the considerable demand for the dried fruit, which is regarded as crucial to many Mexican mole sauces. Other pasilla relatives that are smoked and dried are the *Pasilla de Oaxaca* (so called because it is grown only in Oaxaca) and the *Pátzcuaro,* both of which are relatively hot. *Pasillas* are also employed in salsas and are available in both dried and powdered forms. They are moderately hot.

Common names and synonyms: Chilaca, chilli negro, *Pasilla de Oaxaca, Pátzcuaro.*

See in addition: "Chilli Peppers," Part II, Section C, Chapter 4.

PASSION FRUIT - Native to southern Brazil, the passion fruit (*Passiflora edulis* or *P. quadrangularis*) is so named because early Spaniards in the New World thought that they saw in its flowers the symbols of the passion of Christ. However, they also called it a *granadilla,* representing the more mundane observation that the fruit resembled a small pomegranate. The fruits are yellow or purple berries, which can be either sour or sweet. They are eaten raw (including the edible seeds), the pulp is used to make cold drinks, and immature fruits are sometimes boiled as a vegetable.

Most passion fruits, however, become passion-fruit juice, which is used in numerous beverages and sauces. Passion fruits are grown commercially in California, Australia, South Africa, New Zealand, Hawaii, Kenya, and especially Colombia. There are some 350 other types of passion fruits, among them the "yellow granadilla" and the "wild water lemon" of Brazil and the "sweet granadilla" of Central America. Passion fruits are an excellent source of vitamins C and A and iron.

Common names and synonyms: Granadilla, mara-cuja, purple granadilla, purple passionfruit, sweet granadilla, wild passion-flower, wild water lemon, yellow granadilla, yellow passionfruit.

Patate aquatique - *see* **SWAMP CABBAGE**

PATAUÁ - A palm tree (*Jessinia bataua*) that is native to the Americas and is, indeed, the most common palm in the Amazon region, patauá has a huge fruit that provides both an edible oil (patauá oil) and a beverage. The oil, similar to olive oil, is used in cooking. The beverage, *chicha de seje,* tastes like chocolate.

Common names and synonyms: Seje ungurahuay.

Pátzcuaro - *see* **PASILLA**

Paw(-)paw - *see* **PAPAW, PAPAYA**

PEA(S) (*see also* **BEACH PEA, CHICKLING VETCH, LEGUMES, PEA LEAF, SUGAR PEA**) - Technically legumes, "peas" are the edible seeds enclosed in the elongated green pods of the vine *Pisum sativum.* Peas comprise a large group that can be divided into those that are "edible-podded" and those that are "tough-podded." Foremost among the latter are "green peas," also known as "garden peas" and "English peas" - the large, bulging sweet peas, fresh from gardens or found in produce markets. Other varieties - often canned or frozen - include baby green peas (*petits pois*) and the larger "early" or "June" peas. The edible-podded peas include "sugar" or "snow" peas, the sugar snap pea (*mange-tout*), and the Chinese pea pod. Historically, however, by far the most important peas in a nutrition sense were those that were preserved and consumed throughout the year.

Like so many of our foods, there is confusion over the origin of the pea, which may have occurred in central or southern Asia or in the Middle East. In any event, the wild forms must have been tasty seasonal items on the menus of hunter-gatherers, and peas were among the first plants to be domesticated - about 8,000 years ago (following the beginning of agriculture), after which they spread quickly to the Mediterranean region and to India and China.

Peas were an important food of the Egyptians, Greeks, and Romans - indeed, the word "pea" is from the Latin *pisum,* which was in turn derived from the Greek *pison.* The ancient Greeks mostly ate peas dried, as did the Europeans of the Middle Ages. The Old English *pise* became *pease* to remind us that "pease porridge" hot, cold, or nine days old was a bulwark of the English diet. In the sixteenth century, tender varieties of green peas (designed to be eaten fresh) entered the diet as the *mange-tout* or sugar pea was developed in Dutch gardens, and *petits pois* became a part of French cuisine.

Meanwhile, peas had made their way with the earliest settlers to the New World, becoming part of the diet of North America, and in 1870 the vegetable was among the first to be canned by what would become the Campbell Soup Company. And while dwelling on the subject of peas and their history, we should mention the famous experiments during the 1860s in which the Austrian monk Gregor Mendel employed peas to deduce two fundamental laws of genetic inheritance.

Chickpeas, black-eyed peas ("cowpeas"), and pigeon peas are not true peas and are treated in other entries.

Common names and synonyms: Baby green pea, chickling vetch, Chinese pea pod, early pea, edible-podded pea, English pea, field pea, garden pea, green pea, June pea, *mange-tout, petits pois,* snow pea, sugar pea, sugar snap pea, sweet pea, tough-podded pea.

See in addition: "Beans, Peas, and Lentils," Part II, Section C, Chapter 3.

Pea apple - *see* **EGGPLANT**

Pea aubergine - *see* **EGGPLANT**

PEACH - Apparently a native of China despite its scientific name, *Prunus persica,* the peach spread to the Middle East and then to Greece. The Romans introduced the fruit in Europe, and the Spaniards carried it to the New World. In fact, peaches were growing so widely in eastern North America by the time of the American Revolution that many assumed the fruit to be an American native. Peaches are one of the stone fruits (drupes) and are classified as freestone or clingstone, depending on how easily the flesh separates from the pit. Modern peaches, the result of centuries of selective breeding, have either white or yellow flesh. Yellow-fleshed freestone types are the most preferable, and the "Bonanza" is the most popular of these. Peaches that are sold fresh or frozen are almost always freestone (as, for example, the Rio Oso Gem); clingstones (like the Red Haven) are generally used for canning. Peaches are a fine source of vitamins A and C.

Common names and synonyms: Bonanza peach, clingstone peach, freestone peach, Red Haven peach, Rio Oso Gem peach.

Peach palm - *see* **PEJEBAYE**

PEA LEAF (*see also* **PEA**) - In China, the tender leaves of the garden pea (*Pisum sativum*) are prevented from flowering or fruiting, which allows them to grow. Sold fresh, they are stir-fried and used in soups, generally on special occasions.

See in addition: "Beans, Peas, and Lentils," Part II, Section C, Chapter 3.

PEANUT (*see also* **HOG PEANUT**) - Native to South America, the peanut (*Arachis hypogaea*) is actually not a nut but a legume that develops belowground (hence the name "groundnut") and is very soft before it is dried. Peanuts dating from around 800 B.C. have been found in archaeological excavations in Peru. Native Americans ate the nuts fresh as a vegetable but also roasted them and crushed them into a nutritious, oily paste. Peanuts were being grown by the Tainos on Hispaniola when the Spaniards first arrived in the West Indies, and were later carried to the Philippines and the East on the Spanish Manila galleons.

The Portuguese accomplished the same thing, heading in the other direction. From Brazil, they introduced peanuts into Africa, where the crop became an important staple almost immediately. They also carried them to India, which today is the largest producer of peanuts, followed by China and the United States (with Nigeria the biggest exporter). In fact, the peanut is now a crop of tremendous commercial importance the world over.

Until World War II, peanuts were used mostly as livestock feed, but since then their importance in the human diet has increased enormously, although peanut meal continues to be used for animal feed. Peanuts are salted in the shell by soaking in a brine solution. They are dry-roasted, boiled, and made into peanut butter (which accounts for about half of the U.S. crop) and peanut brittle. Peanuts are also pressed to yield an oil for cooking, preserving, and use at the table and are made into flour for bread baking. Indonesians, Indians, Africans, and the Chinese prepare wonderful dishes that include peanuts, but this is generally not the case in the plant's home hemisphere, save for the West African cookery of the Brazilian northeast. Peanuts are higher in protein than any other nut and are a fine source of the B-vitamins, magnesium, and iron.

Common names and synonyms: Earth nut, goober (pea), groundnut, *mani,* monkey nut, runner peanut, Spanish peanut, Valencia peanut, Virginia peanut.

See in addition: "Peanuts," Part II, Section D, Chapter 2; "An Overview of Oils and Fats," Part II, Section E, Chapter 1.

Peanut-butter fruit - *see* **BUNCHOSIA**

PEAR - Indicative not so much of the millennia over which the pear (*Pyrus communis*) has been cultivated but rather of grafting done over the past few centuries, there are now some 5,000 varieties of the fruit. Native to the Middle East, pears today also grow wild across much of Europe and Asia. They do not seem to have been known to the ancient Greeks or Egyptians, but were to the Romans, who spread pear cultivation throughout their empire.

Pear trees were brought by early European visitors to North America, where the bell-shaped, yellow-skinned Bartlett, a summer pear, has emerged as the most widely grown and a pear much used in canning. The Anjou is the most abundant winter pear. Other varieties that can be found in markets include the Bosc, which is firm and thus is good for cooking and baking; the Comice, perhaps the sweetest of pears; the tiny Seckel; the juicy, sweet Clapp; and the Nellis, a late-winter pear. A pome fruit, the pear is related to the apple, and like apples, pears are frequently baked or otherwise

cooked as well as eaten raw, especially as dessert pears. In addition, they are turned into cider ("perry"), although not so often today as in the past. Pears are also canned and made into pear nectar. Most of the vitamin C and fiber that raw pears supply in good quantity is contained in the skins.

Common names and synonyms: Anjou, Bartlett, Bosc, Clapp, Comice, common pear, Nellis, perry, pome(-fruit), Seckel, summer pear, Winter Nellis, winter pear.

Pear haw - *see* **HAW**

Pearl moss - *see* **CARRAGEEN AND CARRAGEENIN**

Pear(-)melon - *see* **PEPINO**

Pearson bean - *see* **SWORD BEAN**

PECAN - A North American nut (actually a kind of hickory nut) sometimes said to be a native of Oklahoma, the pecan (*Carya illinoinensis*) is really indigenous to an area extending from the U.S. Midwest throughout the South and Southwest into Mexico - a region where it still grows wild today. Pecans are commercially cultivated in the band of states running from Georgia west to New Mexico, as well as in Mexico, Brazil, and, outside of the Western Hemisphere, in Israel, South Africa, and Australia.

The first recorded instance of pecan cultivation is said to have been when Thomas Jefferson carried the trees from the Mississippi Valley back to Virginia and gave them to George Washington. But long before this - eons before the Europeans arrived - pecans were an important item in the diet of Native Americans living in the south-central region of North America. The name "pecan" comes from the Algonquian *paccan,* which is similar to the Ojibwa *pagân,* meaning "hard-shelled nut."

The shells of wild pecans are indeed hard, but those that are cultivated have been bred for thinner shells that are easier to crack. The nuts are eaten raw, roasted, dry-roasted, and fried. They flavor stuffings for poultry as well as numerous desserts, including pecan pie. Unfortunately, as a nut, the pecan is high in fat and low in protein, but it does deliver a respectable amount of the B-vitamins, vitamin E, and numerous minerals.

Common names and synonyms: Carya pecan.

PEDRO XIMÉNEZ (*see also* **GRAPES**) - The best of the grapes planted to make sherry, the Pedro Ximénez (*Vitis vinifera*) is named for Peter Siemons, who carried the grape from Germany to Spain. Pedro Ximénez grapes are also employed to make white wines.

See in addition: "Wine," Part III, Chapter 13.

PEJEBAYE - Also known as the "peach palm," the pejebaye (*Bactris gasipaës* = *Guilielma utilis* = *G. gasipaës*) is a palm tree of the western Amazon region that was domesticated by Native Americans. It bears a fruit (largely unknown outside of Brazil) that somewhat resembles an apricot, although it is triangular in form. It is cooked before eating - usually by roasting. In addition, the fruit is dried and ground into flour and is also pressed for vegetable oil. But the tree's main culinary function (at least recently) has been to provide fresh palm hearts for Latin American and North American markets.

Common names and synonyms: Peach palm.

Peking cabbage - *see* **CHINESE CABBAGE**

Pekoe souchong - *see* **TEA**

PENNYCRESS - Plants of the genus *Thlaspi* are called "pennycress" along with a host of other names. Their leaves are edible, and the seeds can be employed as a condiment, like mustard seed. There are native species in North America that were a part of the diet of Native Americans. In Asia, Eurasian pennycress species have also long been cultivated.

Common names and synonyms: Fanweed, field pennycress, French weed, penny grass, thoroughwort pennycress.

Penny grass - *see* **PENNYCRESS**

Pennyroyal - *see* **MINT**

PENNYWORT - Any of several plants of the genus *Centella* (and the closely related *Hydrocotyle*) are called "pennywort," including Indian pennywort (*C. asiatica*). Also known as "coinworth" and *gota kola,* Indian pennywort has round green leaves that historically have been considered a stimulant to brain activity in India. They are eaten raw, cooked as a vegetable, and made into tea. Sometime in the past, the plant reached the eastern United States, where it grows as a weed.

Common names and synonyms: Asiatic pennywort, coinworth, *gota kola,* Indian pennywort.

PEPEROMIA - A large genus of tropical herbs, *Peperomia* belongs to the family Piperaceae - the same family as *Piper nigrum,* which provides the white and black peppercorns used at the table. Today, species of *Peperomia* are grown as ornamentals, but in the past some, like "oval-leaf" (*Peperomia obtusifolia*), were cultivated for their leaves, which were eaten as a vegetable.

Common names and synonyms: Oval-leaf.

Pepinella - *see* **CHAYOTE**

Pepinito - *see* **GHERKIN**

PEPINO - Also called "melon-shrub," "melon-pear," and "pear-melon," and often mistaken for a melon because of its taste and shape, the pepino (*Solanum muricatum*) is a native of the Andean region of South America and, like peppers and tomatoes, a member of the nightshade family. It was domesticated in pre-Columbian times and was widely cultivated when the Spaniards first arrived. For reasons that remain obscure, they named it *pepino de la tierra,* or "native cucumber." Although the pepino comes in many varieties, none of them resemble a cucumber. The most common are reddish, with stripes of varying color. The fruit is quite sweet and watery, like the cantaloupe. Outside of the American tropics, pepinos are cultivated in California and

New Zealand, which together meet most North American demand.

Common names and synonyms: Kachun, melon (-)pear, melon(-)shrub, native cucumber, pear (-)melon, *pepino de la tierra, pepino dulce.*

Pepino de la tierra - *see* **PEPINO**

Pepino dulce - *see* **PEPINO**

Pepitas - *see* **PUMPKIN**

Pepo - *see* **SQUASH AND PUMPKIN**

Pepper - *see* **CHILLI PEPPERS, INDIAN LONG PEPPER, JAVANESE LONG PEPPER, MELEGUETA PEPPER, PEPPER(CORNS), SICHUAN PEPPERCORN, SWEET PEPPERS**

PEPPERCORN - *Piper nigrum* is a vine - native to the East Indies - that has a small berry-like fruit called a peppercorn. Peppercorns, from which pepper is ground, come in colors. Underripe berries are green. When the full-grown but unripe fruit is dried, it is black. If the berries are allowed to mature further, they turn red or pink. White pepper - which commands a higher market price - is the result of drying the ripe fruit, then removing the outer shell. Lampong and Tellicherry are black peppercorns; Muntok and Sarawak are white. These pungent condiments are among the most important of the East Indian spices that have been eagerly sought since ancient times.

The Greeks and Romans accepted peppercorns as tribute, and the spice was certainly the basis for much of the "lure of the East" that impelled first the Portuguese and then other European explorers around Africa toward the fabled Spice Islands. Although both are called "pepper," *Piper nigrum* should not be confused with the American chilli peppers of the *Capsicum* genus. Major producers of pepper(corns) today include Indonesia, India, Malaysia, and China; white pepper is preferred by the majority of people in the latter country. In addition, white pepper yields an oil that is used in perfumes and medicines.

Common names and synonyms: Black pepper(corn), green pepper(corn), Lampong, long pepper, mignonette pepper, Muntok, pepper, pink pepper(corn), *pippah,* red pepper(corn), Sarawak, Sichuan pepper(corn), Tellicherry, white pepper(corn).

See also: "Spices and Flavorings," Part II, Section F, Chapter 1.

Pepper(-)grass - *see* **CRESS**

Pepperidge - *see* **BARBERRY, BLACK GUM**

Peppermint - *see* **MINT**

Pepper of Calicut - *see* **CHILLI PEPPERS**

PEPPERONCINI (*see also* **CHILLI PEPPERS**) - An orange-red chilli that is also known as "pepperoncino," the pepperoncini (*Capsicum annuum*) is a favorite in Italy, Sicily, and Sardinia. When dried, it is wrinkled, curved, and about 2 to 3 inches in length. A moderately hot pepper, the pepperoncini is used in sauces and cooked dishes and is often bottled in olive oil. It is also grown in Louisiana for the production of hot sauces.

Common names and synonyms: Pepperoncino.

See in addition: "Chilli Peppers," Part II, Section C, Chapter 4.

Pepper-root - *see* **TOOTHWORT**

Pepper tree - *see* **MASTIC TREE**

Pequín - *see* **TEPÍN CHILLIES AND RELATIVES**

Perennial goosefoot - *see* **GOOD-KING-HENRY**

Perennial onion - *see* **ONION TREE**

Perennial pea - *see* **EVERLASTING PEA**

Périgord (truffle) - *see* **TRUFFLE(S)**

PERILLA - Native to the Himalayan mountains between India and China, perilla (*Perilla frutescens* and *P. ocimoides*) is a plant grown for its fruit and leaves. The fruit seeds contain an oil that is employed in cooking and has industrial applications as well. The leaves are dried and used as an herb in cooking.

PERIWINKLE - Periwinkle is comprised of several Old World vetchlike herbs of the genus *Vinca*. *Vinca major*, a trailing foliage plant, is called "large periwinkle," whereas *V. minor*, a trailing evergreen herb, is known as "common periwinkle," "myrtle," "running myrtle," and "creeping myrtle." A third plant – this of the Old World tropics – is *V. rosea* (= *Catharanthus roseus*), which is called "cape periwinkle," "red periwinkle," and "Madagascar periwinkle." These plants are cultivated mostly for fodder, but their seeds have also served humans as food, especially during times of hardship.

Common names and synonyms: Cape periwinkle, common periwinkle, creeping myrtle, large periwinkle, Madagascar periwinkle, myrtle, red periwinkle, running myrtle.

Perry - *see* **PEAR**

Persian lime - *see* **LIME**

Persian walnut - *see* **WALNUT**

PERSIMMON - Although there are persimmon trees that are native to North America, the orange-red persimmon (*Diospyros kaki*) that North Americans usually consume originated in Asia. This persimmon is native to China but is known as the Japanese persimmon because it has been cultivated mostly in Japan. Today, however, the fruit is also cultivated in the south of France and some of the Mediterranean countries, where it was introduced in the early nineteenth century, and in the southern United States and California, where it arrived in 1870.

The American persimmon (*Diospyros virginiana*) is native to the eastern and southern United States, and the name "persimmon" – deriving from the Algonquian *pessemin* – is American, too. The Algonquians ate persimmons raw and also dried the fruits for winter consumption. American persimmons are smaller than those from Japan, which are about the size of a tomato. Both varieties may be yellow, orange, or red, although the American persimmon can be a darker red, almost purple. The trees of the *D. kaki* species grow to between 20

and 30 feet in height, whereas *D. virginiana* reaches 30 to 60 feet. A mature tree will yield 75 to 100 pounds of persimmons annually.

The Hachiya variety, which accounts for the overwhelming bulk of the commercial crop in the United States (grown mostly in California), is an astringent variety, meaning that it is bitter until it is ripe. Another variety, Fuyu (crisper and lighter in color), is more common in Japan and Israel. When ripe, persimmons are soft, and their brown or orange pulp has a sweet taste. They are a good source of beta-carotene and potassium as well as vitamin C.

Common names and synonyms: American persimmon, Chinese fig, common persimmon, date plum, Fuyu, Hachiya, Japanese persimmon, *kaki*, Oriental persimmon.

Peruvian carrot - *see* **ARRACACHA**

Peruvian groundcherry - *see* **CAPE GOOSEBERRY**

Peruvian parsnip - *see* **ARRACACHA**

Petai tree - *see* **PARKIA**

Petanga - *see* **PITANGA**

PETITE SIRAH (*see also* **GRAPES**) - Not the true Syrah (also Shiraz) grape, the Petite Sirah (*Vitis vinifera*) makes a wine that is dark red to almost purple, with a peppery taste. Although in California the Petite Sirah grape was at one time believed to be the Syrah, it is now generally thought that it is the Durif Rhône grape, which is no longer grown in France. Once used to make a blending wine, the Petite Sirah has become an important varietal in the California wine industry.

See in addition: "Wine," Part III, Chapter 13.

Petits pois - *see* **PEA(S)**

Pe-tsai - *see* **CHINESE CABBAGE**

Pfifferling - *see* **CHANTERELLE, MUSHROOMS AND FUNGI**

PHALSA - Also known as "pharsa," phalsa (*Grewia asiatica*) is a shrubby tree of India and the East Indies. It produces a small red berry that is used to make sorbets and syrups but is too tart to eat out of hand.

Common names and synonyms: Pharsa.

Pharsa - *see* **PHALSA**

Philippine orange - *see* **CALAMONDIN**

Philippine spinach - *see* **TALINUM**

PHYSIC NUT - A small tree, originally of the American tropics, *Jatropha curcas* produces the "physic nut," which yields curcas oil. The oil has medicinal uses, especially as a purgative, but is toxic in high doses. When roasted, however, the nuts are said to be relatively harmless and are apparently consumed by many in India as well as the Americas. The young leaves of the tree are cooked like greens, and ashes of the burned root are used as a substitute for salt.

Common names and synonyms: Curcas oil, purging nut.

Piasa - *see* SUDAN POTATO
Pico de Pajaro - *see* CAYENNE PEPPER
Piedmont truffle - *see* TRUFFLE(S)
Pie-plant - *see* RHUBARB
Pigeon berry - *see* POKEWEED
PIGEON PEA (*see also* BEANS, LEGUMES) - Called
by literally scores of names including "Congo pea,"
"no-eye pea," "red gram," and "gandul," the pigeon
pea (*Cajanus cajan* or *C. indicus*) is probably
native to South Asia and perhaps tropical Africa.
Actually a bean that grows on a perennial shrub, it
is one of the oldest cultivated plants and now is
widespread throughout the tropical world, with
India a center of diversity. In the Americas, it is a
very important crop in Jamaica and is naturalized in
South Florida and Mexico.

The fresh leaves are often used as a vegetable, as
are the immature pods. The seeds are dried and
used in the same ways as lentils or split peas in
soups, stews, and so forth. Like other dried beans,
pigeon peas are rich in nutrients. They are high in
calcium, iron, protein, the vitamin-B complex, and
folacin.

Common names and synonyms: Alverja, Bengal bean,
Congo pea, dhal(l), gandul, goongoo pea, gray pea,
Gungo pea, Indian dhal, Indian pea, no-eye pea, pois
cajun, pois d'Angole, red gram, yellow dhal(l).
See in addition: "Beans, Peas, and Lentils," Part II, Section C, Chapter 3.
PIGEON PLUM (*see also* PLUM) - An American plant
that (like its close relative the sea grape) grows on
the seacoasts of the southern United States, Mexico,
and the Caribbean, the pigeon plum (*Coccoloba
diversifolia* = *C. floridana*) is a drupaceous fruit
that is quite astringent until ripe, after which it has a
pleasant sweet-and-sour taste. Additionally, there is
the edible fruit of an African tree (*Chrysobalanus
ellipticus*) that is also called "pigeon plum."
Common names and synonyms: Snailseed.
Pignoli - *see* PINE NUT
Pignolia - *see* PINE NUT
Pignon - *see* PINE NUT
Pignut - *see* EARTH NUT
Pigweed - *see* AMARANTH, CHENOPODIUM,
GOOSEFOOT, LAMB'S-QUARTER, PURSLANE,
QUELITES, QUINOA
PILI NUT - A tropical evergreen tree of the Philippines, the pili nut (*Canarium ovatum*) has a number of uses. Its nuts are eaten both raw and roasted
and in either case are said to have a very pleasant
flavor. Additionally, pili nuts are used in baked
goods and ice cream, and the kernel is pressed for
an edible oil of high quality. The pulp of its fruit is
also pressed for oil but can be eaten, as can the
young shoots, which frequently appear in salads.
Most of the nuts are harvested from trees growing
in the wild, which means that the crop has
remained a relatively minor one.
Pimenta - *see* ALLSPICE

Pimento - *see* ALLSPICE, SWEET PEPPERS
Pimiento - *see* SWEET PEPPERS
Pimiento - *see* CHILLI PEPPERS
Pimiento dulce - *see* SWEET PEPPERS
Pimiento morrón - *see* SWEET PEPPERS
Pimpinel - *see* BURNET
Piña - *see* PINEAPPLE
Pina anona - *see* MONSTERA
Pinang - *see* BETEL NUT
Pindo palm - *see* JELLY PALM
PINEAPPLE - A native of the New World, the pineap-
ple (*Ananas comosus*) is now cultivated in frost-
free areas around the world. The Tupi-Guarani Indi-
ans of South America have been credited with its
domestication, although this is in some dispute. It
would seem, however, that the origins of the
pineapple are definitely in lowland South America.
The earliest written references to the fruit were
made by Spanish chroniclers, including Christopher Columbus, who is alleged to have named the
fruit, calling it the "pine of the Indies" because of its
resemblance to a pinecone. It is still called *piña* in
Spanish today, whereas the Portuguese word for
"pineapple," *ananás* (also part of the scientific
name), derives from an Indian term for the fruit.

After their discovery, pineapples were used to
provision ships and spread from the Americas by
two routes: One was across the Pacific in Spain's
Manila galleons to the Philippines and from there
to China; the second was in Portuguese ships from
Brazil to Africa and beyond to India. Before the end
of the sixteenth century, pineapple cultivation had
spread across much of the tropical world, and the
plant had found its way to some of the Pacific
Islands. In the late eighteenth century, pineapples
were introduced in Hawaii, where they have since
become that state's most important fruit crop.
Pineapples are mostly canned and made into juice,
although some are eaten fresh. They are an excellent source of vitamins A and C and potassium.
Common names and synonyms: Anana, *ananás,*
Cayenne pineapple, Hawaiian pineapple, nana, *piña.*
Pineapple guava - *see* FEIJOA
Pineapple orange - *see* ORANGE
Pineapple quince - *see* QUINCE
Pinecone mushroom - *see* MOREL, MUSHROOMS
AND FUNGI
PINE NUT - Also called pignoli, pignolia, pignons,
piñon nuts, and Indian nuts, these ivory-toned seeds
come from the pinecones of several trees of the
genus *Pinus* and rank alongside macadamias and
pistachios as the most expensive nuts on the market. The European term for pine nuts is pignolia,
indicating that they come from the Italian stone
pine, which grows in Italy, Iberia, and North Africa.
They are especially used in Mediterranean cooking,
and Italian pignolia (from the Italian term for Pinoc-
chio) are a vital ingredient in making pesto. But
although the European pine nut has a higher oil

content and is the one most widely available in the United States, there are American varieties – and some from South America are much larger than their European counterparts. In the American Southwest, the piñon or Indian nut from the Colorado piñon tree has been consumed for thousands of years and was assiduously gathered and stored by many Native American tribes. Pine nuts go well in soups, salads, and desserts, in addition to pesto sauce, and they are also eaten roasted, salted, and raw. Like other nuts, pine nuts are a good source of thiamine, magnesium, and iron.

Common names and synonyms: Indian nut, Mexican nut pine, nut pine, Parry pinyon pine, pignoli, pignolia, pignon, pinolia, piñon (pine) (nut), pinyon (pine) (tree), silver pine, stone nut.

PINGUIN – A plant of the American tropics, and a relative of the pineapple, the pinguin (*Bromelia pinguin*) is used for hedges but also has a crowded head of berries that are plumlike and edible. Another of its names is "wild pineapple," and the fruit is employed mostly for juice. Similar fruits – such as *B. balansae* and *B. karatas* – also grow in South America. These, too, are used mostly for juice, although the yellow fruit of *B. karatas* is good to eat out of hand when ripe.

Common names and synonyms: Maya, piñuela, wild pineapple.

Pink-bottom (mushroom) – *see* **MUSHROOMS AND FUNGI**

Pink ginger-bud – *see* **TORCH GINGER**

Piñon (pine) (nut) – *see* **PINE NUT**

Pinot Bianco – *see* **PINOT BLANC**

PINOT BLANC (*see also* **GRAPES**) – A white wine grape grown mostly in the Alsace region of France, the Pinot Blanc (*Vitis vinifera*) yields an affordable, all-purpose, dry wine. It has been confused with the Chardonnay grape (which also makes a dry, white wine) to the extent that a number of Australian wines that are called Pinot Blanc are actually Chardonnay. Pinot Blanc grapes are also used in the production of sparkling wines and are grown in California.

Common names and synonyms: Beli Pinot, Clevner, Pinot Bianco, Weissburgunder, Weisserburgunder, Weisser Klevner.

See in addition: "Wine," Part III, Chapter 13.

PINOT MEUNIER (*see also* **GRAPES**) – A black wine grape that yields a white juice and is heavily planted in the Champagne region of France, Pinot Meunier (*Vitis vinifera*) is one of the three wine grapes (along with Chardonnay and Pinot Noir) used to make champagne. In the Australian state of Tasmania, Pinot Meunier grapes are now grown to fuel an ever-increasing production of sparkling wine "down under."

See in addition: "Wine," Part III, Chapter 13.

PINOT NOIR (*see also* **GRAPES**) – A black grape that yields a white juice and is sometimes regarded as the "headache" grape by growers because of the difficulties (fragility and genetic changeability) in working with it, the Pinot Noir grape (*Vitis vinifera*) is nonetheless the grape responsible for the revered red wines of Burgundy. Indeed, Appellation Contrôlée laws prescribe that all red burgundies (save for Beaujolais) be made from Pinot Noir grapes, which are also one of the three principal grapes used to fashion French champagne. Pinot Noir grapes have also been adapted for growing in California. Needless to say, because of the difficulties in growing them, wines made from these grapes are generally on the expensive side.

See in addition: "Wine," Part III, Chapter 13.

Piñuela – *see* **PINGUIN**

Pinyon (pine) (tree) – *see* **PINE NUT**

Piperina – *see* **MINTHOSTACHYS**

Pippah – *see* **PEPPER(CORNS)**

PIPSISSEWA – Plants with many more common names than uses, pipsissewa are two species of weeds, *Chimaphila umbellata* and *C. maculata,* that grow in northern and eastern North America, respectively. Found in wooded areas, they are small herbs with bitter leaves that have long been employed in folk remedies and to make teas. More recently, pipsissewa has been used as one of the ingredients in root beer. *Chimaphila maculata* is known, among other things, as the striped or spotted pipsissewa, ratsbane, and dragon's-tongue. *Chimaphila umbellata* is called common pipsissewa and, more colorfully, king's-cure and love-in-winter.

Common names and synonyms: Common pipsissewa, dragon's-tongue, king's-cure, love-in-winter, ratsbane, spotted pipsissewa, striped pipsissewa.

Pisong jacki – *see* **BANANA**

Pistache – *see* **PISTACHIO NUT**

PISTACHIO NUT – A native of central Asia and member of the cashew family, the pistachio nut (*Pistacia vera*) has been cultivated for some 3,000 years and has a long history of popularity in the Mediterranean world. But it was not until the 1930s, with the advent of vending machines, that pistachio nuts (also called pistache) imported from Italy became something of a rage in the United States as a snack food. Their red-dyed, bony shells split naturally, making them easy to crack by hand or with the teeth. Following World War II, the evergreen trees that bear pistachios were imported to California, and although the imported nuts are still dyed, most American-grown pistachios are sold without dye, in naturally tan shells. The name "pistachio" is the Italian version of the Persian word *pistah,* meaning "nut." In the Middle East, pistachio nuts are an accompaniment for roast lamb, and many Mediterranean dishes also call for them. The characteristically green kernels are a good source of thiamine and iron.

Common names and synonyms: Pistache.

PITAHAYA (*see also* **SAGUARO**) - The cerus type of cacti is divided into *pitayos* - tall columnar cacti (like the saguaro [*Carnegia gigantea*]) with large fruits called *pitayas* - and *pitahayos,* which are smaller cacti with smaller fruits (*pitahayas*). Pitahayas were a staple of Native Americans, have been cultivated commercially in Mexico and Central America since colonial times, and are today grown in Texas, Florida, and the desert Southwest of the United States.

The flavorful, generally red to purple fruits are eaten fresh, made into drinks, preserves, jams, ice cream, and other desserts, and frozen and dried for later reconstitution. Some of the fruits also contain a natural oil, which is thought to improve the functioning of the digestive tract. Pitahayas are regularly shipped to Europe, but the United States - for health reasons - prohibits entry to those grown in certain countries, save in the form of a frozen puree. Among the fruit-bearing cacti are the "tree cactus" (genus *Cephalocereus*) and, in the genus *Echinocereus,* the *pitahaya de Agosto* (*E. conglomeratus*), the "Mexican strawberry" "(*E. stramineus*), and the "clear-up cactus" (*E. triglochidiatus*). The pitahayo or *pitahayas de agua* (genus *Heliocereus*) is another, as are the *pitahaya* (*Hylocereus undatas*) and the *pitayo dulce* (*Lemaireocereus queretaroensis*), also called the "organ-pipe cactus."

Common names and synonyms: Clear-up cactus, Mexican strawberry, organ-pipe cactus, *pitahaya de Agosto, pitahayas de agua, pitahayo, pitayo dulce,* tree cactus.

Pitahaya de Agosto - *see* **PITAHAYA**
Pitahayas de agua - *see* **PITAHAYA**
Pitahayo - *see* **PITAHAYA**
PITANGA - Also known as the "Surinam cherry," pitanga (*Eugenia uniflora*) is native to Brazil but now can be found throughout the world's tropics and subtropics. Given room, the tree will reach 20 feet or so in height, but generally it is grown as a bush or shrub. The fruits vary in size, color, and flavor but are usually oblate and, when ripe, maroon or nearly black. The taste is tart, very much like that of a sour cherry. In addition to being simply popped in the mouth, the fruits are used in salads, jellies, and pies.

Common names and synonyms: Brazilian cherry, Cayenne cherry, petanga, pitanga cherry, Surinam cherry.

Pitanga cherry - *see* **PITANGA**
Pitaya - *see* **SAGUARO**
Pitaya - *see* **CACTUS APPLE**
Pitayo - *see* **SAGUARO**
Pitayo dulce - *see* **PITAHAYA**
Pitchiri - *see* **PITURI**
PITHECELLOBIUM - Some species of the genus *Pithecellobium,* such as *P. dulce* (otherwise known as the "Manila tamarind" and guamochil), are native to the Americas in general, whereas a few New

World species (like *P. flexicaule*) are native to North America (Texas, South Florida, and Mexico). Other species are native to tropical Asia. The young pods and shoots are edible and are cooked as a vegetable. The seeds are also eaten, after roasting, and the pulp that surrounds the seeds of *P. dulce* is made into a beverage.

Common names and synonyms: Guamochil, Manila tamarind.

Pito - *see* **CORAL BEAN**
PITOMBA - A relative of the guava, the pitomba (*Eugenia luschnathiana*) is a small yellow or orange fruit that grows on a small tree or bush. The fruit, a native of Brazil and grown almost exclusively there, is sometimes eaten raw but more often is made into juice and preserves.

PITURI - Of the family Solanaceae, pituri (*Duboisia hopwoodii*) is a perennial shrub of Australia. It produces a black berry, but its main use involves the leaves, which traditionally were dried, powdered, and mixed with other "power plants" by the Aborigines, then made into a quid and chewed. This preparation - called *pituri* or *pitchiri* - was commonly thought to be a narcotic by the first European visitors. A high nicotine content, however, seems to have been the reason for its use.

Common names and synonyms: Pitchiri.

PLANTAIN (*see also* **HAWAIIAN PLANTAIN**) - A herbaceous plant of the tropics, the plantain (*Musa × paradisiaca*) is a fruit similar to the banana (and a close relative), but it is larger, is green (although some varieties undergo the same changes of color as bananas), has more starch, and is not eaten raw. Plantains are believed to have originated in Southeast Asia but are now grown throughout the tropics of Asia, the New World, Africa, and the Pacific. They are fried, roasted, baked, boiled, and also dried and ground into a flour. In addition, in Africa plantains are used to make beer. Plantains (*plátanos*) are a favorite in the diets of many West Indian and Latin American populations, in which they replace potatoes or yams as the most important starch. Like bananas, plantains are a good source of potassium and vitamin C, and they are a better source of beta-carotene than bananas.

Another group of plants with the name "plantain" belongs to the genus *Plantago.* These are weeds with broad leaves that, when young, serve as a potherb. The plants were used by Native Americans for food and for medicine, and the leaves can also be boiled to make a tisane.

Common names and synonyms: Plátano.
See in addition: "Bananas and Plantains," Part II, Section B, Chapter 1.

Plantain lily - *see* **DAYLILY**
Plátano - *see* **PLANTAIN**
Pleurisy root - *see* **BUTTERFLY WEED**
Pleurotte - *see* **OYSTER MUSHROOM**

PLUM (*see also* **BEACH PLUM, CHERRY PLUM, DAMSON PLUM, JAPANESE PLUM, SLOE**) – A pitted fruit, or drupe, and related to peaches and apricots, the plum is the most widely distributed of all the stone fruits, growing on every continent save Antarctica. Certainly wild plums would have been a favorite of our hunting-and-gathering ancestors. Plums appear to have been cultivated by the ancient Egyptians and definitely were raised by the Romans, who encouraged the establishment of orchards throughout their empire.

Europeans brought their own plum (*Prunus domestica*) to the New World, with the result that American plum varieties have not been produced commercially. The plums of *P. domestica* are frequently dried (thus becoming prunes) and are also stewed and made into preserves. Then there is *P. salicina* – often called the "salicina" plum or the Japanese plum – which found its way from China to Japan about 300 years ago and subsequently reached North America. Salicina plums, with juicy, reddish to yellow flesh, are not turned into prunes but rather are eaten fresh, and a few varieties can be used in cooking. European plums, especially the California French variety with its high sugar content and firm flesh, make the best prunes. Plums that become prunes are generally freestone, and the drying process consolidates the nutrients, making the dried fruits a good source of vitamins A and E and a fair source of the vitamin-B complex. Prune juice is naturally very sweet, and pitted prunes are frequently cooked with poultry and lamb. Prunes, of course, are well known for their laxative properties, as is prune juice. Plums are a good source of vitamin C.

Common names and synonyms: California French, common plum, garden plum, greengage, Japanese plum, prune, prune plum, Red Beauty, red plum, Reine Claude, salicina plum, Santa Rosa, wild plum.

POBLANO (*see also* **CHILLI PEPPERS**) – Appearing something like a dark-green or almost black (or red in the mature form) bell pepper with a point, this member of the genus *Capsicum* is said to be one of the most popular peppers in Mexico, doubtless in no small part because of its versatility. Fresh, the poblano – a usually mild pepper – is often roasted, and its relatively large size makes it a favorite for stuffing (*chiles rellenos*). In addition, fresh poblanos are used in a number of cooked dishes. Dried, the poblano is called an ancho or a mulato. Ancho means "broad" or "wide" in Spanish and refers to the dried pepper's appearance, which is flat and wrinkled with a color ranging from oxblood to nearly black. The mulato is chocolate brown in color, and both impart a smoky flavor vital to mole sauces, with that of the mulato said to be superior.

Common names and synonyms: Ancho, mulato.

See in addition: "Chilli Peppers," Part II, Section C, Chapter 4.

Pocan – *see* **POKEWEED**

POHOLE – A fiddlehead fern native to Hawaii, the pohole (genus *Athyrium*) grows on the volcanic slopes of Maui, and its tender shoots have been a part of the Hawaiian diet for centuries. Their taste has been described as a blend of the flavors of asparagus and artichoke. Pohole shoots are steamed, sautéed, and added to salads.

Poi – *see* **TARO**

Pointed gourd – *see* **TANDOORI**

Pointleaf manzanita – *see* **HEATHER**

Pois cajun – *see* **PIGEON PEA**

Pois d'Angole – *see* **PIGEON PEA**

Poke – *see* **POKEWEED**

Pokeberry – *see* **POKEWEED**

Pokeroot – *see* **POKEWEED**

Poke salad – *see* **POKEWEED**

POKEWEED – Its blackish red berries are just one of the products of pokeweed (*Phytolacca americana*), a tall North American plant. In the U.S. South, the young shoots and tender tops of the plant are boiled to make "poke salad" in the early spring, and for many in the past – especially slaves – this dish was (despite the boiling) an important source of vitamin C after a winter of meat and meal. The root is poisonous but, with processing, has medicinal uses. The seeds of the berries are also toxic, but the flesh is not, and it is often pressed into a juice. The word "poke" comes from the Algonquian *pocan,* and doubtless the shoots, leaves, and berries of pokeweed were consumed by red men long before white and black men ever reached North America.

Common names and synonyms: Gorget, inkberry, pigeon berry, *pocan,* poke, pokeberry, pokeroot, poke salad, scoke, skoke, Virginian poke.

Polecat weed – *see* **SKUNK CABBAGE**

Poleo – *see* **MINTHOSTACHYS**

POLYNESIAN CHESTNUT – This edible kidney-shaped nut of the Polynesian chestnut tree (*Inocarpus edulis*) is called the Polynesian chestnut by everyone except the Maori of New Zealand (who call it *rata*) and others who prefer the name "Tahitian chestnut." The taste of the nuts is similar to that of chestnuts. They are boiled, roasted, and baked; in addition, some puree the seeds and flavor them with coconut cream.

Common names and synonyms: Rata, Tahitian chestnut.

POMEGRANATE – The pomegranate tree (*Punica granatum*), which reaches a height of 15 to 20 feet, is an ancient tree native to the Middle East (probably Iran). Along with olives, figs, dates, and grapes, the pomegranate was (some 5,000 to 6,000 or more years ago) among the first fruits to be cultivated. Because pomegranates are hardy and easily transported, they were widely known in early times, even in regions where they could not be grown. From Mesopotamia, the pomegranate spread out to be cultivated in ancient Egypt, India, Afghanistan, and China, and it reached Europe at a very early date. The fruit became important in ancient Greek mythology and was mentioned in early literature, including the Bible. It is now grown in all of the drier subtropical areas of Europe and Asia, and in the Americas from the warmer parts of North America (especially California) to Chile.

The name "pomegranate" translates literally as "apple with many seeds." The fruit is round and about the size of a large orange, with a smooth, leathery skin that varies in color from brownish yellow to red. Inside, the fruit is filled with edible, juicy pulp and hundreds of small seeds that are also edible. The rind is tough, which has permitted the pomegranate to serve as a kind of natural canteen for those navigating desert areas. The fruit is eaten fresh, made (including the seeds) into sauces, and is a part of various desserts. Pomegranate juice is highly regarded and is also used commercially to make grenadine syrup, which is employed around the world to flavor milk drinks, desserts, sodas, lemonades, and cocktails. The seeds (which some use as a meat tenderizer) figure prominently in the making of chutneys.

Common names and synonyms: Chinese apple, dalima, granada, grenade, grenadine.

POMELIT (*see also* **CITRUS FRUITS, GRAPEFRUIT**) – A cross between the pomelo and the grapefruit, the pomelit (genus *Citrus*) was developed in Israel for export. Its fruit is sweeter than the grapefruit and juicier than the pomelo.

POMELO (*see also* **CITRUS FRUITS, GRAPEFRUIT**) – The progenitor of the grapefruit, the pomelo (also pummelo) (*Citrus maxima* or *C. grandis*) probably originated in southeastern Asia, where it grew wild in the Indochinese peninsula and Indonesia (although the West Indies has also been proposed as a place of origin). The pomelo is the largest of the citrus fruits and is also known as "pumelo" and "shaddock" because it (or the grapefruit) was brought to the Caribbean by Captain James Shaddock. The aromatic fruit is very large and oval shaped with a thick skin. The pulp is sweet and a light-colored pink or red, the outside ranging from green to yellow to pink. Usually the pomelo is eaten raw, but in Asia the peel is candied, and an alcoholic beverage is made from the fruit. Today, pomelos are grown in California, China, and Japan. They differ from other kinds of citrus fruits in that the white pith is not edible. Pomelos have a high content of vitamin A and are a fine source of vitamin C.

Common names and synonyms: Chinese grapefruit, pumelo, shaddock, sweet pomelo.

Pomi di mori - *see* **TOMATO**
Pomme d'amour - *see* **TOMATO**
Pompion - *see* **PUMPKIN**
Poor-man's-asparagus – *see* **LEEK(S)**
Poor-man's-caviar – *see* **EGGPLANT**
Poor-man's-food – *see* **FIG**

Poor-man's-meat – *see* **BEANS**
Popcorn – *see* **MAIZE**
POPLAR – Mostly native to North America, poplar trees (genus *Populus*) grow from Alaska to the mountains of Kentucky and westward through the Rockies to California and Mexico. The inner bark of most species can be eaten raw, and the bark was also boiled or dried and ground into meal by Native Americans. In addition, the bark was used to make a tea and cut into strips to be cooked like noodles. Whites on the frontier learned to rely on the poplar for sustenance – even the sugary sap was collected and drunk. Because the use of the poplar provided much in the way of vitamin C, it was a scurvy preventive during the winter months.

POPPY SEED – The opium poppy (*Papaver somniferum*), which yields a latex that provides the drug opium (and the opiate derivatives morphine and codeine), has a botanical name that means "sleep-bearing." Fortunately for poppy-seed consumers, the latex comes from unripe seedpods, whereas the tiny, kidney-shaped, edible seeds form in ripe pods and thus have no narcotic effect. Asia Minor seems to be the plant's native region, and doubtless its "magical" effects attracted the attention of hunter-gatherers early on. Its medicinal properties have been put to work for humans at least since the time of the ancient Egyptians. Despite the minuscule size of the seeds – it takes close to a million of them to make a pound of weight on the scales – at some time in the distant past it was discovered that oil could be pressed from them. Their nutty taste was also appreciated, so that today poppy seeds are widely grown (the Netherlands is a major producer) and widely used in baked goods, from India through the Middle East to Europe and North America.

Common names and synonyms: Maw seed.
See also: "Spices and Flavorings," Part II, Section F, Chapter 1.

Porcini – *see* **BOLETE, MUSHROOMS AND FUNGI**
Porcino – *see* **BOLETE**
Poro – *see* **CORAL BEAN**
Portabello (mushroom) – *see* **MUSHROOMS AND FUNGI**
POSHTE – Perhaps the least known of the Annonaceae, the poshte (*Annona scleroderma*) is mostly cultivated in southwestern Guatemala and is prominent in the markets of that part of the world. Unlike its relatives – the cherimoya, the soursop, and the sugar apple – the poshte has a very tough skin, which means that it is less likely to be damaged in handling and transportation. But like the others it has a delicious pulp that is easily removed with a spoon.

Common names and synonyms: Anana del monte, cawesh, chirimoya.

Potato bean – *see* **APIOS, JÍCAMA**
Potato(es), sweet – *see* **SWEET POTATO**
Potato(es), white – *see* **WHITE POTATO**

Potato yam - *see* **AIR POTATO, LESSER YAM**
Pot marjoram - *see* **MARJORAM AND OREGANO**
Poussee-pied - *see* **GLASSWORT**
Prague Special - *see* **KOHLRABI**
PRAIRIE CLOVER - A number of species of the genus *Petalostemon* are called prairie clover, among them *P. candidum* (the white-tassel-flower) and *P. oligophyllum*. Native Americans ate the roots and young leaves as well as the flowers.
Common names and synonyms: White-tassel-flower.
Prairie potato - *see* **BREADROOT**
Prairie sunflower - *see* **SUNFLOWER OIL AND SEED**
Prairie turnip - *see* **BREADROOT**
Premier - *see* **LOQUAT**
Preserving melon - *see* **CITRON**
Prickly ash tree - *see* **SICHUAN PEPPERCORN**
PRICKLY LETTUCE - A wild Eurasian lettuce naturalized in North America, prickly lettuce (*Lactuca scariola* = *L. serriola*) reaches as many as 7 feet in height, with large lower leaves that can approach a foot in length. The upper ones are much smaller, but they, along with the bigger leaves, are eaten in salads and cooked as a vegetable.
Common names and synonyms: Wild lettuce, wild opium.
PRICKLY PEAR - The prickly pear is the edible fruit of various cacti of the genus *Opuntia*. Native to the Americas, where varieties can be found from South America to Canada, prickly pear cacti produce fruits that are pear shaped and bristle with sharp spines that require careful removal before eating or cooking. Also called cactus pears or Indian pears, the fruits (actually large berries) come in an estimated 300 species - often incredibly colored (inside and out) - with some sweet, some sour, some that can be eaten raw, and others that need cooking. About the size of large eggs, the berries contain a multitude of hard, black seeds.

The Aztecs used the berry juice to make an alcoholic beverage, and also boiled the juice down for its sugar. Indeed, the prickly pear was an important dietary item in Mexico long before the Spaniards arrived and until well into the twentieth century constituted the bulk of the diet of entire communities. When the Spaniards were adapting to their newly conquered Mexico, they called the pears *tunas* and delighted in encouraging new arrivals to eat one particular *tuna* that caused the urine of the consumer to turn bright red. Today, prickly pears are greatly appreciated for their sweet taste, and not just in Mexico and Central and South America but throughout much of the world, including all of the countries ringing the Mediterranean, southwestern Asia, Australia, and South Africa.

In the latter two areas, where the cacti were introduced by early European explorers, they had no natural parasites or competitors and have prospered to the point of becoming more nuisance than food. In Israel, the word *sabra* (meaning prickly pear) has given rise to the nickname "sabras" for the Israelis themselves - prickly on the outside, sweet on the inside! Prickly pears are crushed to make punches and cocktails, sliced into salads as well as eaten raw, and preserved or pickled with other fruits, such as lemons. The juice is sometimes used as a drink mixed with vodka or rum. In addition, prickly pears have served as a handy cattle feed in times of shortage. The prickly pear is a fine source of vitamin C, potassium, and fiber.
Common names and synonyms: Barbary fig, Burbank's spineless, cactus fig, cactus pear, Indian fig, Indian pear, *nopal*, *sabra*, spineless cactus, *tuna*.
Princess-feather - *see* **AMARANTH**
Princess pea - *see* **WINGED BEAN**
Proboscis-flower - *see* **UNICORN PLANT**
Provision tree - *see* **MALABAR NUT**
Prune - *see* **PLUM**
Puffball - *see* **MUSHROOMS AND FUNGI**
PULASAN - A tree native to the Malay Archipelago, pulasan (*Nephelium mutabile*) is related to the litchi. Pulasan trees grow wild. Those that are cultivated are grown mostly for their fruits, which are oblong, about 2 inches in length, and dark red when ripe. The skin is thin and leathery but not attached to the tart flesh, which comes out easily. The fruits are eaten raw and stewed, and made into jams and preserves.
Pulla chilli - *see* **GUAJILLO AND PULLA CHILLIES**
Pulse - *see* **CHICKPEA**
Pumelo - *see* **POMELO**
Pummelo - *see* **POMELO**
Pumpion - *see* **PUMPKIN**
PUMPKIN (*see also* **PUMPKIN SEED, ROUGE VIF D'ÉTAMPES [PUMPKIN], SQUASH AND PUMPKIN**) - Known in Old English as "pumpions" or "pompions," pumpkins (or calabazas) make up several species of the genus *Cucurbita*, and considerable confusion exists about the differences between them and winter squashes. From the standpoint of the consumer, pumpkins generally have orange-colored skins (although there are both black and white pumpkins as well) and are the more strongly flavored of the two. Pumpkins, which were domesticated in Mexico some 6,000 years ago, were probably initially cultivated for their edible seeds. Called *pepitos*, these were dried for consumption as a snack and also became vital ingredients in sauces, moles, and enchilada-type dishes.

Pumpkins spread northward and across North America long before the Europeans arrived to become one of the most important foods of the Native Americans of eastern North America. Later on, they were a chief factor in saving the Pilgrims of Plymouth Plantation from starvation during the winter of 1622-3. Today, pumpkins are far less important as a food than they were during colonial times, and in the United States the bulk of the pumpkin crop is grown for use at Halloween.

Most of the Halloween pumpkins belong to *C. pepo*, but *C. moschata* and *C. mixta* are also represented, as well as very large specimens of *C. maxima*. As a rule, those pumpkins used for decoration are too big and stringy to eat. How big? In 1900, a 400-pound pumpkin earned first prize at the World's Fair, but since then 800-pound pumpkins have been raised, which makes them the largest fruits of the plant kingdom. Such a behemoth would make quite a pie if used in this fashion, but it is generally the smaller and sweeter pumpkins (usually *C. pepo*) that are made into pie fillings and soups and used for other cooking purposes.

Perhaps the world's best pumpkin for use in this regard escaped from the Americas to be developed by the French. This is their famous *Rouge Vif d'Étampes* – also known as the "Cinderella pumpkin" – the flesh of which is very thick and is traditionally used for soups.

Pumpkin for cooking is available in canned (and frozen) form, which most people prefer to fresh. The taste is no different but there is considerably less mess. Pumpkin seeds are still eaten as a snack, and pumpkins themselves are cultivated worldwide.
Common names and synonyms: Calabaza, New England pie pumpkin, pepitas, pompion, pumpion, sugar pumpkin.
See in addition: "Squash," Part II, Section C, Chapter 8.

PUMPKIN SEED (*see also* **PUMPKIN, SQUASH AND PUMPKIN**) – The roasted and boiled seeds of other winter squashes as well as those of pumpkins (*Cucurbita pepo*) were a staple in the diets of Native American peoples for many millennia. In fact, pumpkins may well have started out as gourds raised for their edible seeds. Even today, pumpkin seeds are regarded as a tasty snack after they are dried, salted, and toasted – with a little oil – until golden brown. Indeed, on the street corners of Mexico City, *pepita* vendors are ubiquitous, as they are in many other cities of the world. Pumpkin seeds also yield an edible oil and are made into a paste used for thickening soups and other culinary purposes. In addition to their fine flavor, pumpkin seeds are low in fat, high in protein, and a good source of iron.
See also: "Squash," Part II, Section C, Chapter 8.

PUNCTURE VINE – Called the puncture vine because its prickly fruits can pierce tires, the feet of humans, and the hooves of livestock, this annual weed (*Tribulus terrestris*) is a Mediterranean native now naturalized in southwestern North America. The fruit separates into five nutlets that have been pounded into a meal for consumption during hard times. In addition, the leaves have been cooked as a vegetable.
Common names and synonyms: Punctureweed.

Punctureweed - *see* **PUNCTURE VINE**
Punk tree - *see* **CAJEPUT**

PUNTARELLE – A member of the genus *Cichorium* and a close relative of chicory, puntarelle (*C. intybus*) is an Italian vegetable with a name meaning "little points" – presumably because of the tiny points on its feathery leaves. Also known as "Roman chicory" or "wild Roman chicory," it is available only in the winter months. The typical head of puntarelle has bitter green leaves borne on less bitter, hollow, white stalks – the whole appearing much like endive. There is also a variety called "puntarelle red-rib," with bright red stalks and dark green leaves. Puntarelle stalks are used in salads (often with anchovy dressing), braised and eaten with fava beans, sautéed with garlic, and wilted in soups.
Common names and synonyms: Puntarelle red-rib, Roman chicory, wild Roman chicory.

Puntarelle red-rib - *see* **PUNTARELLE**
Purging nut - *see* **PHYSIC NUT**
Purple-goat's-beard - *see* **SALSIFY**
Purple granadilla - *see* **PASSION FRUIT**
Purple nutgrass - *see* **CHUFA**

PURPLESTEM ANGELICA – Also called "American angelica," "great angelica," and "masterwort," purplestem angelica (*Angelica atropurpurea*) is a North American native, found in the eastern half of that continent (as far west as Minnesota). It reaches from 4 to 6 feet in height and has an aromatic odor. Its roots (said to be poisonous when fresh) have been candied, and its stems and leaves were eaten by Native Americans and by early European settlers.
Common names and synonyms: American angelica, great angelica, masterwort.

Purple Vienna - *see* **KOHLRABI**

PURSLANE – Also called "pussley," purslane (*Portulaca oleracea*) is a trailing weed that has small yellow flowers, reddish stems, and leaves that are sometimes used in salads and stews and are also cooked like spinach as a side dish. Like okra, purslane has the ability to thicken dishes in which it is cooked. A relative – winter purslane (*Montia perfoliata*), also known as "miner's-lettuce" – is used in much the same manner.
Common names and synonyms: Cuban spinach, miner's-lettuce, miner's-salad, pigweed, pussley, winter purslane.

Pussley - *see* **PURSLANE**

Qat - *see* **KHAT**
Qhat - *see* **KHAT**
Quack grass - *see* **COUCH GRASS**
Quamash - *see* **CAMAS**
Quandang - *see* **QUANDONG**
QUANDONG – Also known as quondong, quandang, and native peach, the quandong tree (*Fusanus acuminatus* or *Elaeocarpus grandis*), of the family Santalaceae, is a

native of Australia. It produces round and red edible drupes, called "native peaches." The stone also contains an edible seed called the quandong nut. Both drupes and nuts were food for the Aborigines.

Common names and synonyms: Native peach, quandang, quandong nut, quondong.

Quañiwa - *see* **CAÑIHUA**

Queen-Anne's-lace - *see* **CARROT**

Queensland arrowroot - *see* **ACHIRA**

Queensland nut - *see* **MACADAMIA NUT**

QUELITES - The generic Spanish term *quelites* refers to a wide variety of edible greens gathered by the indigenous inhabitants of Mexico and Central America. Some prominent examples of the more than 2,000 species that have been identified are pigweed (genus *Amaranthus*), shrubby wound-wort (*Liabum glabrum*), violeta (*Anoda cristata*), chipiles (*Crotalaria pumila*), yerba de conejo (*Tridax coronopifolium*), and beldobes (*Galinsoga parviflora*). Native cultivators allowed these plants to grow freely in their *milpa* fields and harvested them young to eat raw, to boil in soups, or to spice mole sauces and tamales. Mature specimens were fed to animals along with maize leaves. Although many of these varieties are considered famine foods, used to extend maize after crop failures, they also provide an important source of vitamin A in the diets of many peasants. However, their consumption has declined in recent years in favor of European vegetables, which are considered more prestigious. The spread of modern agricultural methods, particularly the use of herbicides, has also decreased the importance of these herbs in Mexican diets.

Common names and synonyms: Beldobes, chipiles, pigweed (amaranth), shrubby wound-wort, *violeta*, *yerba de conejo.*

Quetembilla - *see* **CEYLON GOOSEBERRY**

Quiabo - *see* **OKRA**

Quick grass - *see* **COUCH GRASS**

Quihuicha - *see* **QUINOA**

Quimbambo - *see* **OKRA**

QUINCE - An aromatic fruit, quince (*Cydonia oblonga*) is yellow, small, and pear shaped, with very tough flesh. It is not eaten raw, but when cooked, its orange pulp turns a deep pink and becomes very sweet. The quince - a native of western Asia (Iraq and Iran) - grows on a small, twisted tree that rarely reaches a height of more than 12 to 15 feet. It is an old fruit that was very popular among the ancient Greeks and Romans (it was reportedly introduced in Rome in 65 B.C. by Pompey), and both Pliny and Columella were well acquainted with it.

Because of its sweetness, the quince became very popular around the Mediterranean during the Middle Ages. The Portuguese called the fruit *marmelo,* and the preserve they made from it *marmelada.* In fact, because of the great amount of pectin the

quince yields, it is ideal for marmalade, jelly, jam, and candies and shares with the guava, the apple, and a few others the distinction of being among the best jelly fruits. However, beginning with the advent of cane sugar (and continuing through the fairly recent loss of interest in preserving), the quince has been reduced from a near-essential item in Western kitchens to a specialty fruit. Quince production is now principally located in the United States and a few European countries. The quince is a good source of vitamin C and fiber.

Common names and synonyms: Coines, coing, Cydonian apple, elephant apple, maja pahit, ma-tum, pineapple quince, quitte, vilvam.

Quingombo - *see* **OKRA**

QUINOA (*see also* **CHENOPODIUM**) - Pronounced "keen-wah," quinoa (*Chenopodium quinoa*) is an annual herb of the tropical American highlands and a native of Chile and Peru. Also known as quinua and sometimes as "goosefoot," quinoa is and historically has been the most important of the cultivated chenopods. Like amaranth, it is technically not a grain, meaning that it is not one of the cultivated grasses. Also like amaranth, quinoa helped sustain a great American civilization - in this case the Incas. After maize, it was the most utilized grain in the Andes region at the time of the Spanish conquest. It was used to make beer (*chicha*) as well as soups, stews, and porridges, and its leaves were employed as a potherb.

Quinoa does well in poor soils at high altitudes; indeed, it flourishes at 13,000 feet above sea level. One reason for this is its content of saponin, a bitter, soaplike coating that discourages birds and insects and protects the seeds from the greater radiation of sunlight at high altitudes. A closely allied species called *huauzontle* (*C. nuttalliae* = *C. berlandieri*) was developed in pre-Columbian Mexico, and a third, less important chenopod - *cañihua* (*C. pallidicaule*) - was also cultivated in the Altiplano regions of Peru and Bolivia.

Quinoa is cultivated today throughout the Andes from Ecuador to Bolivia and at one time was grown in England, where the leaves were consumed as greens and the seeds given to poultry. It is superior to the true grains in nutritional quality, with a better yield of riboflavin, folacin, magnesium, and zinc. Quinoa is employed in soups and gruels and is also toasted and ground into flour for breads, cakes, and biscuits. Quinoa can be found in health-food stores and even supermarkets. The bitter - and perhaps toxic - saponin must be washed away before consumption.

Common names and synonyms: Goosefoot, *huauzontle,* Inca wheat, pigweed, *quihuicha,* quinua.

Quintonil - *see* **AMARANTH**

Quinua - *see* **QUINOA**

Quitte - *see* **QUINCE**

Quondong - *see* **QUANDONG**

R'accacha - *see* **ARRACACHA**

Radicchio - *see* **CHICORY**

RADISH (*see also* **DAIKON**) - Technically referring to any of a number of plants belonging to the genus *Raphanus* and the mustard family, the term "radish" is usually taken to mean the thickened edible ends of *R. sativus,* which are used in salads and eaten as snacks and appetizers. Radishes come in innumerable varieties, colors (especially red, white, purple, and black), and shapes (ranging from round, to oblong, to long and finger-like). The most common in U.S. produce markets are red and round and are eaten raw, often in salads. Black radishes, common in Eastern Europe and found in a number of Russian dishes, have a very strong flavor and consequently are usually mixed with other foods. The white varieties are sometimes cooked and eaten like the turnips they resemble in taste. Additionally, in East Asia there is a giant white radish called a daikon, which is grated and cooked and used in salads and stir-fries.

Common names and synonyms: Clover radish.

See in addition: "Cruciferous and Green Leafy Vegetables," Part II, Section C, Chapter 5.

Ragi - *see* **FINGER MILLET, MILLET**

RAGWEED - A group of mostly North American plants, viewed as chief culprits in emitting a profuse pollen that provokes allergenic symptoms among hay-fever and asthma sufferers, ragweeds nonetheless belong to a genus called *Ambrosia* - a term from ancient Greek mythology meaning "food for the gods." The weeds' more appropriate common name derives from the ragged shape of their leaves, although the plants are also called "tansy ragwort," "bitterweed," and just plain "ragwort." The plants do have a food use, however, because an edible oil (oil of ragweed) can be obtained from their achenes, and the leaves of some species have reportedly been used as a flavoring.

Common names and synonyms: Bitterweed, ragwort, tansy ragwort.

Ragwort - *see* **RAGWEED**

RAIN TREE - So called because of a belief that it somehow exudes water from its leaflets, the rain tree (*Pithecellobium saman*) is a native of the American tropics that now also grows in the Old World tropics. It is widely used as a shade tree for crops such as coffee, cacao, and nutmeg, but it also produces sweet-pulp pods that serve as cattle fodder as well as a snack food for humans, especially children. A beverage is also made from the pulp.

RAISIN (*see also* **GRAPES**) - Doubtless, wild grapes that had dried on the vine were consumed by our hunting-and-gathering ancestors for hundreds of thousands of years. These were the first raisins (genus *Vitis*). With vine cultivation came the more conscious process of picking grapes and spreading them out to be sun-dried. Raisins were an important item of trade in the Near East and were highly prized by the Romans, who introduced grapes and the knowledge of raisin making to the rest of Europe. The Spaniards brought grapes and raisin-making techniques to the New World, and Spanish missionaries introduced them in California, where today, in the San Joaquin valley, about half of the world's raisins are produced. Like prunes, raisins have concentrated nutrients and are a good source of the B-vitamins - thiamine and B_6 - along with iron.

RAKKYO (*see also* **ONION**) - A relative of the onion, rakkyo (*Allium chinense*) is a small onion bulb that resembles garlic. Rakkyo is cultivated in China, Japan, and Thailand (and by Asian-Americans in the United States) and is used mostly for pickling, although it is also occasionally employed in cooking. *See in addition:* "The *Allium* Species," Part II, Section C, Chapter 2.

RAMBAI - A widely cultivated native of Indonesia, the rambai tree (*Baccaurea motleyana*) is adorned with strings of rambai fruits that hang from its branches. The fruits are about the size of a hen's egg, brownish yellow, and soft to the touch when ripe. They are eaten fresh, stewed and made into jam.

Ramboutan - *see* **RAMBUTAN**

RAMBUTAN - A native of the Malay Archipelago, rambutan (*Nephelium lappaceum*) is a member of the soapberry family, a relative of the litchi and the longan, and one of the most common fruits of Southeast Asia. The fruit is bright red and oval, is about the size of a small egg, is covered with long, soft spines, and has a sweet, acid flesh that combines the tastes of pineapple and apricot. It grows on trees that can reach 60 feet in height and generally fruit twice a year. Rambutan has been cultivated in the Southeast Asian region since prehistoric times and figured prominently in early trade with the Arabs, who took the fruit to Zanzibar, where it is still cultivated. Rambutan is normally eaten raw but is also stewed and made into jams. Rambutans are high in vitamin C.

Common names and synonyms: Ramboetan, rambotan, ramboutan, rambustan, ramtum.

Ramón - *see* **BREADNUT**

Ramontochi - *see* **GOVERNOR'S PLUM**

Ramp - *see* **WILD LEEK(S)**

Rampion - *see* **CAMPANULA**

Ram's-horn - *see* **UNICORN PLANT**

Ramtil - *see* **NIGER SEED**

Ramtum - *see* **RAMBUTAN**

RANGPUR AND KUSAIE (*see also* **LIME**) - Both of these fruits are called "limes," but neither wholly deserves the name. Rather, both are probably hybrids of the Mandarin orange (*Citrus reticulata*) and the true lime (*C. aurantiifolia*). The rangpur develops a deep orange color that the kusaie does not. Both are acid in taste, although not so much as the lime, and the ease with which the segments separate is suggestive of the Mandarin orange. In the Western Hemisphere, the fruits are grown in the West Indies and California.

RAPE – An annual herb of European origin, rape (*Brassica napus*) looks like a cabbage but is cultivated mostly for its seeds, which yield an edible oil (rapeseed oil, called "canola oil" in the United States). The oil (also called "colza") is used for cooking and in salads, and the leaves of the young plants serve as a vegetable, in much the same way as spinach.

Common names and synonyms: Canola oil, colza, rapeseed oil.

See in addition: "An Overview of Oils and Fats," Part II, Section E, Chapter 1; "Cruciferous and Green Leafy Vegetables," Part II, Section C, Chapter 5.

Rapini – *see* **BROCCOLI RAAB**

RASPBERRY (*see also* **BERRIES**) – A number of shrublike, prickly plants of the genus *Rubus* have fruits that we call raspberries. Among them are *R. strigosus* (= *R. leucodermis*), which is a purple and black berry (the "black-cap") native to eastern North America, and *R. idaeus,* which is native to Europe. The latter species bears red raspberries, and most varieties cultivated today are a cross between the two. Pliny the Elder mentioned raspberries as a wild fruit, and they were probably not cultivated much before the seventeenth century. The apothecary and botanist John Parkinson – in his 1629 *Paradisi in sole paradisus terrestris* – wrote of red, white, and thornless varieties, indicating that some were under cultivation at that point.

The raspberry has a range that extends from the polar regions down through temperate North America, Asia, and Europe. One berry appears like a group of tiny berries lumped together. In addition to flavoring desserts and ice cream, raspberries are turned into wine, jams, and jellies, and the fruit is also used to flavor certain liqueurs. In the past, raspberries were among the berries gathered regularly and ritually by the Native Americans. Raspberries provide a good amount of vitamin C.

Common names and synonyms: American red raspberry, black-cap, black raspberry, purple raspberry, thimbleberry.

Rata – *see* **POLYNESIAN CHESTNUT, RATA VINE**

RATA VINE – A Maori word, *rata* indicates New Zealand trees of the genus *Metrosideros.* Some are hardwood trees that the Maori employed to make paddles and weapons such as war clubs. One (*M. fulgens*) has a vine that the Maori exploited as a sweetener. *Rata* can also mean the Polynesian chestnut.

Ratsbane – *see* **PIPSISSEWA**

Rattlebush – *see* **YELLOW WILD-INDIGO**

Red bell pepper – *see* **SWEET PEPPERS**

Redberry – *see* **BUCKTHORN**

Red-fleshed radish – *see* **DAIKON**

Red Globe – *see* **GRAPES**

Red gram – *see* **PIGEON PEA**

Red gum – *see* **SWEET GUM**

Red haw – *see* **HAWTHORN BERRY**

Red-in-snow – *see* **CHINESE AMARANTH**

Red Kuri (squash) – *see* **BUTTERCUP SQUASH**

Red pepper – *see* **CHILLI PEPPERS**

Red mombin – *see* **HOG PLUM, SPANISH PLUM**

Redroot – *see* **AMARANTH**

Red sorrel – *see* **ROSELLE**

Red vine spinach – *see* **MALABAR SPINACH**

Reed-mace – *see* **CATTAIL**

Rheumatism root – *see* **WILD YAM**

RHUBARB – Chinese rhubarb (*Rheum officinale*) is used mostly for medical purposes. Garden rhubarb (*R. rhabarbarum*) is grown for its edible stalks. The plant is native to southwestern Russia, southern Siberia, and China, where it was grown in ancient times for the alleged medicinal value of its roots. Rhubarb was cultivated in Europe from at least the seventeenth century and reached North America shortly after the American Revolution. The leaves are highly toxic, and only the reddish pink and celery-like stalk is consumed as a "fruit" in pies and sauces. Rhubarb, which has a bitter taste, contains much oxalic acid, which can adversely affect the absorption of calcium and iron.

Common names and synonyms: Chinese rhubarb, garden rhubarb, pie-plant, wild rhubarb.

Ribier – *see* **GRAPES**

RICE (*see also* **AFRICAN RICE, WILD RICE**) – Rice (*Oryza sativa*) is the most "super" of all the "superfoods" in that it helps to sustain more than half of the world's population. It is an ancient grain that has been cultivated for around 5,000 years and now comes in some 2,500 varieties. Most rice species are native to the Indian subcontinent – save for a minor species with red grains that is native to Africa. (The wild rice of North America is not actually a rice but rather an aquatic oat.) A plant of hot climates, rice only became important in China when agriculture developed in the southern provinces. Some have credited Alexander the Great with introducing the grain in Europe, but it was not until the eighth century that the Muslims grew large quantities of it in Spain. "Carolina rice" came into being in 1685, when rice was introduced into South Carolina.

Today, rice is divided into long-, medium-, and short-grained varieties, and various cultures prize one or another of these over the rest. Long-grained rice is preferred in most Western kitchens and in India. Medium-grained rice is more appreciated in some Asian countries, whereas short-grained rice, with its starch that makes the grains stick together, is the favorite of those who use chopsticks, such as the Japanese and Chinese.

In most industrialized countries, white rice is enriched to replace the nutrients stripped from the grain by milling. Brown rice is far more nutritious because it has only had the husk removed during milling and retains the bran on its outer coating. Parboiled or converted rice is soaked and steamed before milling to drive nutrients into the grain. Instant rice has been fully cooked and then dehydrated. In addition, there are special rices, such as Arborio, which absorbs much water as it cooks and plumps up well for dishes like Italy's specialty, risotto, and Spain's paella. *Basmati* rice, grown in India and Pakistan, elongates rather than plumps and is commonly featured in Indian cooking, whereas Jasmine rice is a traditional rice of Thailand.

Common names and synonyms: Arborio, *Basmati,* brown rice, Carolina rice, dry rice, *gohan,* hill rice, instant rice, Jasmine rice, long-grained rice, medium-grained rice, *meshi,* polished rice, short-grained rice, white rice.

See in addition: "Rice," Part II, Section A, Chapter 7.

RICE BEAN (*see also* **BEANS**) - A native of Asia, the rice bean (*Phaseolus calcaratus* = *Vigna umbellata*) grows wild from the Himalaya Mountains through central and southern China to Malaysia. It is cultivated to some extent in Asia and in the East Indies for its seed, although the young pods and leaves are also cooked as a vegetable. The seeds are generally eaten with rice, hence the name.

Common names and synonyms: Frijol arroz, haricot riz.

See in addition: "Beans, Peas, and Lentils," Part II, Section C, Chapter 3.

RICEGRASS - Also called "Indian ricegrass" because it was an important food for Native Americans, ricegrass (*Oryzopsis hymenoides* and *O. aspera*) is a bunch grass that grows throughout central North America. Its grain was ground into meal for bread and porridges.

Common names and synonyms: Indian ricegrass.

Rice wheat - *see* **EMMER**

RIESLING (*see also* **GRAPES**) - A white wine grape, the Riesling (*Vitis vinifera*) makes the great wines of Germany's Rhine and Mosel valleys as well as many of those from Alsace in France. The grape is also one of the two major white grapes grown in Washington State. In California, the grape is called Johannisberg Riesling. Oregon is also a major producer. Rieslings can vary from very dry to sweet, dessert-type wines, although most tend to the dry side.

Common names and synonyms: Johannisberg Riesling, white Riesling.

See in addition: "Wine," Part III, Chapter 13.

Rigani - *see* **MARJORAM AND OREGANO**

Robusta - *see* **COFFEE**

Rocambole - *see* **GARLIC**

Rock cranberry - *see* **LINGONBERRY**

Rocket - *see* **ARUGULA, YELLOW ROCKET**

Rocket salad - *see* **ARUGULA**

Rockweed - *see* **SEAWEED**

Rocky Mountain grape - *see* **BARBERRY**

Rocotillo - *see* **HABANERO AND SCOTCH BONNET PEPPERS**

Rocoto - *see* **HABANERO AND SCOTCH BONNET PEPPERS**

Roka - *see* **ARUGULA**

Roma - *see* **MUSHROOMS AND FUNGI**

Roman chicory - *see* **PUNTARELLE**

Roquette - *see* **ARUGULA**

ROSE (*see also* **ROSE HIPS**) - Roses (genus *Rosa*) are ancient plants that grew wild in Asia and have found culinary uses for thousands of years. The petals are used in salads, candied in desserts, and made into syrups and jams. Rose water (and rose essence, a more concentrated distillation of rose water) adds flavor and aroma to various dishes – especially curries and rice dishes – and has long been used to flavor milk drinks, desserts, and cakes.

Common names and synonyms: Rose essence, rose water, wild rose.

See in addition: "Spices and Flavorings," Part II, Section F, Chapter 1.

ROSE APPLE - Often confused with the Java apple because of similar scientific as well as common names, the rose apple (*Eugenia jambos* or *Syzygium jambos*) belongs to the family Myrtaceae, which includes myrtle, clove, and allspice. The fruits of an evergreen tree native to Southeast Asia, rose apples grow in clusters of four or more. When ripe, they are about 2 inches long, white or yellow with pink streaks, with a relatively large seed and the aroma of rose water (hence their name). The quality of the fruits varies considerably, and many are not juicy enough to deliver an excellent flavor. Those that are juicy are sometimes eaten raw, but as a rule rose apples are made into jams and jellies.

Common names and synonyms: Jambos, jambu, wax apple.

Rose-essence - *see* **ROSE**

ROSE HIP(S) (*see also* **ROSE**) - The red- to orange-colored, urn-shaped fruits of the rose that appear in late summer and early fall, rose hips (*Rosa canina* and *R. rugosa*) are actually the bases to which the flower's petals are attached. Once considered sacred, the hips were used by Catholic believers during the Middle Ages to count prayers or series of prayers – hence the name of the string of beads called a "rosary." Most rose hips are gathered from wild rose bushes and are utilized to make tea, jellies, and preserves and, in parts of Europe, a syrup used as a tonic. Rose hips are extremely high in vitamin C.

Common names and synonyms: Dog rose, wild rose.

Rosella - *see* **ROSELLE**

ROSELLE - Probably a native of West Africa (it is a close relative of okra), roselle (*Hibiscus sabdariffa*) is also called "rozelle," "Indian sorrel," "red sorrel," "Jamaican sorrel," and just plain "sorrel." The young shoots and leaves of the plant are eaten raw or as a cooked vegetable, and the flowers (actually the calyx), which constitute the main reason for the cultivation of roselle, are used to make beverages, jellies, sauces, preserves, and chutneys.

Roselle was introduced in Brazil in the seventeenth century but may have reached the West Indies even earlier – both of these introductions probably occurring via the slave trade. In addition, the plant has been under cultivation in Asia for some three centuries; extensive roselle cultivation was begun in Australia at the turn of the twentieth century and in the Dutch East Indies during the 1920s. Today, India, Java, and the Philippines are major producers.

Common names and synonyms: Indian sorrel, Jamaican sorrel, Java jute, red sorrel, rosella, rozelle, sorrel.

ROSEMARY – An aromatic herb, rosemary (*Rosmarinus officinalis*) is a Mediterranean native whose Latin name means "dew of the sea," presumably because it was frequently found growing close to the coast. The plant was known to the Romans, who used it mostly for medicinal purposes. Early in the Middle Ages, however, although its medical applications continued, rosemary joined a host of other herbs employed for culinary reasons, especially in the kitchens of the European royal and noble courts. Today, rosemary is more utilized in Italian cooking than in any of the other Mediterranean cuisines; in northern Europe, it is sometimes used in sausage making. The needle-like leaves of the rosemary plant are used both fresh and dried, but they have to be crushed, crumbled, or chopped to release their bold flavor and (especially in the case of fresh rosemary) to avoid spearing the consumer. Rosemary is wonderful with poultry, beef, lamb, and fish, and goes well in sauces. It is also used in salads, salad dressings, soups, and stews, and to make tisanes.

See also: "Spices and Flavorings," Part II, Section F, Chapter 1.

Rosenapfel - *see* **OKRA**
Rose water - *see* **ROSE**
Rosinweed - *see* **SILPHIUM**
Rosso di Verona - *see* **CHICORY**
Roucou - *see* **ANNATTO**
ROUGE VIF D'ÉTAMPES (PUMPKIN) (*see also* **PUMPKIN, SQUASH AND PUMPKIN**) – The French crafted this elegant pumpkin variety, the *Rouge Vif d'Étampes* (*Cucurbita maxima*), from more basic American stock. Also called the "Cinderella pumpkin," it is a heavily fleshed pumpkin that is generally regarded as the best of all pumpkins for baking, and especially for soup making.

Common names and synonyms: Cinderella pumpkin.
See in addition: "Squash," Part II, Section C, Chapter 8.
ROUGH BINDWEED – A European plant, rough bindweed (*Smilax aspera*) has roots that yield a kind of sarsaparilla.

Common names and synonyms: Bindweed, bindweed root.

ROUND GOURD – Known also as the "round melon," the round gourd (*Praecitrullus fistulosus*) is grown primarily in India and is practically unknown in the West. The round gourd is cooked as a vegetable while immature, and its seeds can be roasted.

Common names and synonyms: Round melon.
Round melon - *see* **ROUND GOURD**
ROWANBERRY (*see also* **BERRIES**) – The rowan tree (*Sorbus aucuparia*) is a small, attractive native of Europe and western Asia that produces orange-red rowanberries. The species name *aucuparia* means "bird-catching," referring to the trees' ancient use as bait. The berries have a long history of magical as well as culinary uses. Ancient northern Europeans comforted themselves with the belief that rowanberries guarded against the spells of witches, demons, and the like. The berries' juice makes a fine jelly that historically was eaten with game or cold meats. Rowanberries have also been fermented and used for distilling liquor. A similar species yields the whitebeam berry, which is like the rowanberry and was once used to make wine. Another, the service tree, yields serviceberries, which are now less common.

Common names and synonyms: Serviceberry, whitebeam berry.

Rozelle - *see* **ROSELLE**
Rucola - *see* **ARUGULA**
RUE – A Eurasian plant, rue (*Ruta graveolens*) has been used for many centuries in medicines and as a disease preventive. Indeed, rue was once credited with warding off the plague known as the Black Death and was called "herb-of-grace." The bitter, pungent leaves have also been employed as a potherb – first in Europe and later, after the plant became naturalized, in the southern United States.

Common names and synonyms: Herb-of-grace.
Rugala - *see* **ARUGULA**
Rugela - *see* **ARUGULA**
Rugula - *see* **ARUGULA**
Rukam - *see* **INDIAN PRUNE**
Rukam manis - *see* **INDIAN PRUNE**
Runner nut - *see* **PEANUT**
Running myrtle - *see* **PERIWINKLE**
Rush nut - *see* **CHUFA**
Russian caraway - *see* **NIGELLA**
Russian olive - *see* **ELAEAGNUS**
RUTABAGA – Closely related to the turnip, the rutabaga (*Brassica napobrassica*) is a relatively modern vegetable that resulted from a cross between a Swedish turnip and a cabbage. Called a "Swede," the rutabaga spread from Sweden to central Europe and had reached England by 1800. It was grown in the United States by the beginning of the nineteenth century. However, many rutabagas come to the United States from Canada, which has led to the nickname "Canadian turnip." The rutabaga's flesh is yellowish, and its taste is milder than that of the turnip.

Common names and synonyms: Canadian turnip, swede, Swedish turnip, yellow turnip.

See also: "Cruciferous and Green Leafy Vegetables," Part II, Section C, Chapter 5.

RYE – A native of central Asia, rye (*Secale cereale*) is a widely cultivated cereal grass with seeds that are used for flour, for making whiskey, and as livestock feed. The grain has been cultivated for millennia, but not always deliberately. Beginning some 4,000 years ago, rye started a westward movement, generally as a weed in fields of wheat (a close relative) and barley. Rye came to be appreciated when its hardiness kept it standing while the more valued crops failed. However, in the Mediterranean region, a mild climate prevented rye from displaying its quality of hardiness, and the grain was reportedly despised by the ancient Greeks.

Rye expanded during Roman times – but apparently not with the assistance of the Romans – and was cultivated mostly outside the empire, especially in northern Europe (from about the first century A.D.), where the climate was colder and the plant could grow in soils too poor for wheat. It was brought to North America by European colonists, and became an important staple in early New England, where it may also have played a disruptive role. Rye is especially prone to infection by ergot, a fungus that can cause hallucinations, convulsions, and even gangrene and death, and some historians suspect that ergot-poisoned rye may have been behind the strange behavior of the Salem "witches."

Certainly ergotism was a deadly disease in Europe for hundreds of years, and today rye is carefully inspected for the ergot fungus. Although generally thought of as "poor man's flour," rye remains popular in Scandinavia and eastern Europe. Rye flour is normally mixed with wheat flour to make rye bread. In addition, rye flakes, cracked rye, and whole rye "berries" are used in breakfast cereals, muffins, soups, and casseroles. A major product of rye over the last few hundred years has been the excellent malt it furnishes for the brewing and distillation of alcoholic beverages. The relatively small crop produced in the United States is divided between food and alcohol production on the one hand, and animal feed on the other hand.

See also: "Rye," Part II, Section A, Chapter 8.

RYEGRASS – Any of several species of the genus *Lolium* are called ryegrass. They are European plants that have become naturalized throughout North America. Some, such as Italian ryegrass (*L. multiflorum*), which is much used for hay, or English ryegrass (*L. perenne*) probably served as food for Old World humans in the past. In the New World, the grains of darnel (*L. temulentum*) were consumed by some Native American groups.

Common names and synonyms: Darnel, English ryegrass, Italian ryegrass.

Saba - *see* **BANANA**
Saba nut - *see* **MALABAR NUT**
Sabra - *see* **PRICKLY PEAR**
Sacred datura - *see* **MOON-FLOWER**

SAFFLOWER – A thistle-like herb, the safflower plant (*Carthamus tinctorius*) is native to Asia or perhaps Egypt but is now cultivated throughout the world. The plant has red and yellow flowers that were once used as a seasoning (a saffron substitute), whereas its seeds have served for millennia in India as the base of medicines, paints, and cosmetics. But the main use of the seeds is to press them for an oil employed in cooking. Safflower oil is light, with a neutral taste, and is used in salads and for stir-frying.

SAFFRON – This spice comes from a species of crocus (*Crocus sativus*), in the form of saffron "threads," which are the stigmas (the parts that catch pollen for the ovary) of the flower. It has been estimated that, at three stigmas per plant, upwards of 250,000 of these crocus flowers are required to yield a pound of saffron. These numbers, coupled with the fact that the work is all done by hand, serve as a powerful explanation for saffron's distinction as the world's most expensive spice.

Native to the eastern Mediterranean, saffron was used in cooking for thousands of years before the Romans built their empire. Indeed, some credit Phoenician traders with introducing it in Spain – the country that today is the leading producer for the commercial market.

The word saffron comes from the Arabic word for "yellow," and its distinctive color and taste grace Spanish, Cuban, French, and Indian cuisines, especially their rice dishes. It is a vital ingredient in an authentic bouillabaisse or paella as well as the saffron bread of a traditional Swedish feast. Saffron also goes well with poultry, in tomato-based sauces and stews, and in liqueurs such as Chartreuse. The spice is marketed as dried threads and in ground form. Unfortunately, much adulteration of ground saffron occurs, including its near-total replacement with turmeric – a crime that in fifteenth-century Germany drew a penalty of execution by burning or burying alive.

See also: "Spices and Flavorings," Part II, Section F, Chapter 1.

Sagaloo - *see* **CALLALOO**

SAGE – The aggressive flavor and smell of sage (*Salvia officinalis*) doubtless helped to convince numerous peoples – from the ancient Greeks, Arabs, and Romans to the Europeans of the Middle Ages – of its medicinal properties. There are numerous varieties of this small Mediterranean native, with its long and narrow, not to mention pungent, leaves. Exactly when sage became more important in cooking than curing is not clear. Its leaves were brewed into a tea that was used as a spring tonic, and during the Middle Ages the plant gained a reputation (and its common name) for imparting wisdom and improving memory.

But for many centuries, sage has also been flavoring Italian veal, German eels, and French sausages, along with other meats such as pork. In the United States, the herb is a vital ingredient in many seasoned poultry stuffings; fresh sage leaves are universally employed in flavoring pickles, salads, and cheeses and are sometimes made into a tisane. Sage can be purchased in whole leaves (fresh or dried), and in dried and crumbled form (rubbed sage). Today it is cultivated in eastern and western Europe, around the Mediterranean, in the United States, and to a limited extent in West Africa and the West Indies at altitudes of over 1,500 feet.

Common names and synonyms: Common sage, garden sage, rubbed sage.

See also: "Spices and Flavorings," Part II, Section F, Chapter 1.

Sage tree - *see* **CHASTE TREE**

SAGO - Sago is a starch taken in large quantities from several varieties of tropical (sago) palms of the genus *Metroxylon.* The palms grow wild in low-lying, swampy areas of Southeast Asia, Oceania, and northern South America. When mature (at about 10 to 15 years of age), the tree is felled, the trunk split open, and the pith scooped and rasped out to be made into a powdery starch. A single tree may yield from 600 to 800 pounds of starch, which is cooked like rice pudding (it resembles tapioca) and used as a food thickener. "Pearl" sago, produced by putting a sago paste through a sieve and then drying the "pearls," is often used for desserts. Pearl sago is generally the only kind of sago available outside of the tropics. Sago provides much in the way of carbohydrates but lacks most other important nutrients and must be supplemented with foods containing protein, such as fish and local vegetable foods.

Common names and synonyms: Pearl sago.

See also: "Sago," Part II, Section B, Chapter 4.

Sago fern - *see* **TREE-FERN**

SAGUARO (*see also* **PITAHAYA**) - A giant columnar cactus of northern Mexico and southern Arizona, the saguaro (*Cereus giganteus* or *Carnegiea gigantea*) served as a staple food for Native Americans of the region, who often gathered saguaro fruits that had fallen to the ground and had been naturally dried by the sun. These they stored for later use. The red pulp of the fruit can also be eaten fresh, pressed into juice, and made into a syrup. In addition, the seeds can be turned into a paste. The fruits are sometimes called *pitayas,* and the saguaro cactus a *pitayo.*

Common names and synonyms: Pitaya, pitayo.

SAIGON CINNAMON (*see also* **CINNAMON AND CASSIA**) - Like its relatives cinnamon and cassia, "Saigon cinnamon" (*Cinnamomum loureirii*) is a tree cultivated for its bark, which is processed into a spice. Probably a native of Southeast Asia, the tree is now grown primarily in China, Japan, and Java. Also known as "cassia" (which promotes some confusion), Saigon cinnamon is sold as cinnamon and is widely used in industrial baking and food processing in the United States.

Common names and synonyms: Cassia.

Saint-John's-bread - *see* **CAROB**

SAINT-JOHN'S-WORT - A Eurasian plant, now growing in North America and known throughout the world for its alleged antidepressant properties, "Saint-John's-wort" (*Hypericum perforatum*) produces lemon-scented leaves that have served humans as food for thousands of years and have also been used to make a tea. In addition, the flowers have been consumed, as have the flower buds and leaves of "great Saint-John's-wort" (*H. pyramidatum*).

Common names and synonyms: Great Saint-John's-wort.

Salad pear - *see* **ASIAN PEAR**

Salad savory - *see* **KALE**

SALAK - Salak (*Salacca edulis*) is the native name in Malaya for a fruit that grows on a palm, looks like a pear, and tastes like a pineapple.

SALAL - A close relative of wintergreen, salal (*Gaultheria shallon*) is a shrub of the northwestern Pacific coast of North America. It bears fruits that are dark, sweet, juicy, and about the size of the common grape. When these berries ripened in the autumn, they were consumed in great amounts by Native Americans of the region, who also dried them for use in the winter.

Salamander tree - *see* **BIGNAY**

SALEP - A starchy powder, ground from the dried roots of various Old World orchids of the genera *Orchis* and *Eulophia,* salep is employed in Asian cookery. When mixed with boiling milk, it makes a kind of pudding that is enjoyed by children. In a diluted form, salep was formerly sold on the streets to London laborers as an early-morning drink. Salep stalls, however, long ago gave way to coffee stalls.

SALMONBERRY (*see also* **BERRIES, CLOUD-BERRY**) - This edible berry grows on a prickly shrub (*Rubus spectabilis*) that is a native of the coastal regions of the U.S. Northwest. Actually a raspberry, the fruit is a yellow-pink "salmon" color, hence its name. Both the berries and the young shoots of the plants were eaten by Native Americans.

Common names and synonyms: Thimbleberry.

Saloop - *see* **SASSAFRAS**

SALSIFY (*see also* **SCORZNERA**) - A perennial plant, thought by some to have a taste similar to that of an oyster (and consequently nicknamed "oyster-plant" and "vegetable-oyster"), salsify (*Tragopogon porrifolius*) is native to the Mediterranean region, where it has been cultivated since at least the sixteenth century. It is a parsnip-like root vegetable with light brown skin and a whitish flesh that is much more appreciated in Europe than in the Americas, although the plant has existed in North America for a couple of centuries and is grown commercially there.

At the top of the seed heads of this interesting plant grows a fluffy tuft that has prompted another nickname – "purple-goat's-beard." (A black variety of salsify is known as *scorzonera*.) Salsify has edible leaves that grow upwards of 2 feet in length and are used in salads or cooked as a vegetable. After the roots (an excellent winter vegetable) are unearthed, they are normally scraped, then prepared – like parsnips – by steaming or parboiling and sautéeing. Salsify provides the consumer with some measure of the B-vitamins and vitamin C.

Common names and synonyms: Oyster-plant, purple-goat's-beard, vegetable-oyster, white salsify.

SALTBUSH – A member of the goosefoot family (Chenopodiaceae), the four-wing saltbush (*Atriplex canescens*) has foliage that tastes salty. Native Americans used its seeds for meal and ate the new shoots and leaves as greens. Several other species of *Atriplex* were similarly employed. Another plant called saltbush – desert holly (*A. hymenelytra*) – may or may not have ever served as human food.

Common names and synonyms: Desert holly, four-wing saltbush.

SAMPHIRE (*see also* **GLASSWORT**) – A plant that inhabits Old World coastal areas from the British Isles along the shores of western Europe to the Mediterranean, samphire (*Crithmum maritimum*) has fleshy leaves that are used in salads. A member of the parsley family, saphire is also called "glasswort." Another plant with the name samphire is *Philoxerus vermicularis,* which is common along the beaches of the southeastern United States. It also has fleshy, edible leaves.

Common names and synonyms: Glasswort.

SAND CHERRY (*see also* **CHERRY**) – One of the many wild cherries of eastern North America, the "sand cherry" (*Prunus pumila*) is a low-growing cherry that likes sandy soil. The fruit is black, with a taste that ranges from sweet to very acidic. Native Americans pounded sand cherries (including the pits) into a jelly-like mass that could be shaped, dried, and stored for the winter. There is also a "western sand cherry" (*P. besseyi*) – of western North America – which bears a large fruit that is generally quite sweet.

Common names and synonyms: Western sand cherry.

Sand leek - *see* **GARLIC**

San Domingo apricot - *see* **MAMMEE**

Sand pear - *see* **ASIAN PEAR**

SANGIOVESE (*see also* **GRAPES**) – A red wine grape of central Italy (especially Tuscany), the Sangiovese (*Vitis vinifera*) is the primary grape used to make Chianti – the most popular wine of Italy. It is also used to make some of the other Tuscan red wines as well as medium-bodied reds in California.

See in addition: "Wine," Part III, Chapter 13.

Santa Fe Grande - *see* **WAX PEPPERS**

SAPODILLA – A tropical American species, the sapodilla (*Manilkara zapota*) is a tree that seems to have had its origins in southern Mexico, Central America, and perhaps northern South America, but it is now widespread from the West Indies to the East Indies – and with good reason. The bark contains a milky latex, widely known as "chicle" (an ingredient of chewing gum), and the tree bears fruits that are both juicy and sweet when ripe. The latter (also called "naseberries") are small, round, and reddish brown, with a yellowish pulp that can be spooned out of the skin. In addition to being eaten out of hand, sapodillas are used in salads and desserts.

Common names and synonyms: Chicle (tree), chico, chico sapote, chico zapote, chiku, dilly, mammee sapota, marmalade plum, naseberry, nispero, zapote, zapotillo.

Sapota - *see* **BLACK SAPOTE, MAMEY SAPOTE, WHITE SAPOTE**

SAPUCAIA NUT – Several trees of the genus *Lecythis,* which are native to Brazil, Guiana, and Trinidad, produce sapucaia nuts. Also called the "paradise nut," it is a sweet, oily nut that resembles the Brazil nut in taste, although some find that of the sapucaia to be superior. Like Brazil nuts, sapucaia nuts are formed inside an urn-shaped container. But this vessel – commonly called a "monkey pot" – is considerably larger than that of the Brazil nut. The problem is that unlike Brazil nuts, the sapucaia is not protected by a hard shell, and at maturity the cap of the "monkey pot" loosens, scattering the nuts over the jungle floor to be consumed by monkeys and other animals, and those that are not consumed are difficult to find. Thus, only a very small portion of sapucaia nuts are ever consumed by humans, and those reaching U.S. markets tend to be expensive.

Common names and synonyms: Paradise nut.

Sara chulpi - *see* **MAIZE**

Sarawak (pepper) - *see* **PEPPER(CORNS)**

SARSAPARILLA – The dried roots of American tropical plants of the genus *Smilax* yield an extract that was used in London for one of the first "soft drinks" – "Dr. Butler's Ale," first made around the turn of the seventeenth century. Sarsaparilla was later a common base for soft drinks made in the United States.

Saskatoon berry - *see* **SERVICEBERRY**

Saskatoon serviceberry - *see* **SERVICEBERRY**

SASSAFRAS – The spicy bark of both the trunk and roots of the North American tree *Sassafras albidum* is dried and used for flavorings. Sassafras tea has long been employed for medicinal purposes, and "saloop" – a kind of sassafras tea – not only was considered a remedy for many ailments but also, like salep, was sold on the streets of London to working men, much as coffee is now. In addition, sassafras twigs and leaves contain much mucilaginous matter, which is utilized in filé to flavor and thicken gumbos and other soups.

Common names and synonyms: Filé, saloop, sassafras tea.

Sassafras tea - *see* **SASSAFRAS**

Sativa - *see* **ALFALFA**

Satsuma - *see* **MANDARIN ORANGE**

Sauerkraut - *see* **CABBAGE**

Sauvignon - *see* **SAUVIGNON BLANC**

SAUVIGNON BLANC (*see also* **GRAPES**) – Also called Fumé Blanc, Sauvignon Blanc is a white wine grape (*Vitis vinifera*) that is employed to make some of the great dry wines of the Graves region of Bordeaux and the Loire Valley (important wine-producing areas of France) as well as many that are produced in California and Washington State. The wine Pouilly Fumé, of the Loire Valley, is 100 percent Sauvignon Blanc, as is Sancerre, and the grape is a major variety used in the production of Sauternes. Sauvignon Blanc grapes have been grown in California for over a century. The name Fumé Blanc was an invention of California wine maker Robert Mondavi that was intended to stimulate sales of his Sauvignon Blanc wine. To say simply that he succeeded is a colossal understatement.

Common names and synonyms: Blanc Fumé, Fumé Blanc, Sauvignon.

See in addition: "Wine," Part III, Chapter 13.

SAVORY – Summer savory (*Satureja hortensis*) and winter savory (*S. montana*) are both herbs that are native to the Mediterranean region. Their leaves have served to flavor foods since the time of the ancient Romans. Both have a faintly peppery taste, but that of summer savory is milder. Savory leaves are available both fresh and dried and go well with tomato-based dishes, legumes, stuffings, fish, salads, sauces, and sausages – to name but a few of the various foods this herb enhances.

Common names and synonyms: Summer savory, winter savory.

See also: "Spices and Flavorings," Part II, Section F, Chapter 1.

Scallion - *see* **ONION**

Scariole - *see* **ENDIVE AND ESCAROLE**

Scarlet haw - *see* **HAWTHORN BERRY**

Scoke - *see* **POKEWEED**

SCORZONERA – This vegetable (*Scorzonera hispanica*) was once believed by the Spaniards to cure snakebites as well as to just make people feel happy. Scorzonera is native to central and southern Europe, where it has been cultivated since at least the sixteenth century. The root is shaped like a carrot and is black skinned with white flesh. The flowers are yellow and the oblong leaves are hairy. A member of the Compositae family, scorzonera can be either eaten raw (often in salads) or boiled as a vegetable. The taste is often described as being

similar to that of an oyster. Scorzonera is an annual plant and popular in Europe. It grows wild over much of the continent, from Spain in the south and west, north to Germany, and east to the Caucasus. Scorzonera is also commonly known as black salsify.

Common names and synonyms: Black oyster-plant, black salsify, viper-grass.

Scotch bonnet - *see* **HABANERO AND SCOTCH BONNET PEPPERS**

Scotch gale - *see* **BOG MYRTLE**

Scotch spearmint - *see* **MINT**

Screwbean - *see* **MESQUITE**

Screw(-)pine - *see* **PANDANUS, STRIPED SCREW-PINE**

Screwpod - *see* **MESQUITE**

Scuppernong - *see* **MUSCADINE, GRAPES**

SCURVY GRASS (*see also* **ANGELICA, MOUNTAIN SORREL**) – There are a number of plants called "scurvy grass." These plants were generally those that appeared early in the spring and were consumed by humans after a winter of vitamin-C deprivation. This "official" scurvy grass (*Cochlearia officinalis*) is a denizen of northern regions that has extremely bitter foliage. It is also called spoonwort because of the shape of its leaves; needless to say, it does contain some vitamin C.

Common names and synonyms: Spoonwort.

Scutch - *see* **COUCH GRASS**

Seabeach sandwort - *see* **SEA PURSLANE**

Sea bean - *see* **GLASSWORT**

SEA BUCKTHORN – A shrub found on the coasts of Europe and Asia, the sea buckthorn (*Hippophae rhamnoides*) has silver leaves and produces orangish red, edible berries.

SEA GRAPE – Also called the shore grape, the sea grape (*Coccoloba uvifera*) is a tropical American native found on sandy beaches from Florida throughout the West Indies to Venezuela. Not a grape (despite its name), the sea grape is a bushy, salt-tolerant, evergreen plant with clusters of purplish red fruits that are sweet. They are eaten raw, juiced, and made into jelly and wine.

Common names and synonyms: Shore grape.

Seagrass - *see* **GLASSWORT**

SEA HOLLY – A plant common in southeastern Europe (which has been introduced in North America) and credited over the centuries with medicinal properties, the sea holly (*Eryngium maritimum*) is also often called "eringo" or "eryngo." The plant was once believed to be an aphrodisiac. Its leaves were brewed to make a kind of tea, and the roots went into various concoctions. But the roots have served as a food, too; when cooked, they have a taste that is said to resemble that of chestnuts. The young shoots were also sometimes eaten. Candied sea holly roots are called "eryngo."

Common names and synonyms: Eringo, eryngo.

SEAKALE – A summer vegetable, seakale (*Crambe maritima*), which looks a bit like broccoli, grows wild along the coasts of western and northern Europe and has been cultivated in England and the United States. Despite its name, seakale is not related to the kale of the cabbage family. The stems and leaf tips are generally blanched, dipped into melted butter, and enjoyed like asparagus for their nutlike flavor.

SEA LETTUCE (*see also* **SEAWEED**) – Bright green seaweeds of the genus *Ulva* – especially *U. lactuca* – are collectively called "sea lettuce." These are gathered from rocks along seacoasts and added to soups, salads, and the like.

See in addition: "Algae," Part II, Section C, Chapter 1.

Sea moss – *see* **DULSE, SEAWEED**

Sea pickle – *see* **GLASSWORT**

SEA PURSLANE – Also called "seabeach sandwort," sea purslane (*Atriplex halimus* or *A. hastata*) has small edible leaves that are boiled and eaten as a vegetable. The plant is native to the Mediterranean, where its leaves have probably been consumed since the days of the hunter-gatherers.

Common names and synonyms: Seabeach sandwort.

Seaside plum – *see* **TALLOW WOOD PLUM**

Sea tangle – *see* **SEAWEED**

Sea vegetable(s) – *see* **SEAWEED**

Seaving – *see* **SOUARI NUT**

SEAWEED – Seaweeds – or more appetizingly, "sea vegetables" – consist of certain species of marine algae (belonging to genera like *Chondrus, Fucus, Macrocystis, Nereocystis, Laminaria,* and *Porphyra*) such as kelp, rockweed, gulfweed, and laver. When such algae are fresh, their taste is that of salty greens; when they are dried, however, the taste is just salty. Although (save for some people in the British Isles) Westerners from the time of the ancient Greeks have steadfastly ignored seaweed as a food, the Japanese have long appreciated it. They use kelp such as *nori* (in English, "laver" – *Porphyra laciniata, P. tenera,* and *P. umbilicalis*) for wrapping sushi; *kombu* (*Laminaria japonica* – known as giant sea kelp) for broths and stocks and for wrapping dried fish; *wakame* (*Undaria pinnatifida*) for soups and salads, and to sprinkle over rice dishes; *hijiki* (*Cystophyllum fusiforme*) for sautéing as well as deep-frying tempura; and agar as an agent for jelling. In the West, "Irish moss," or *carrageen*, is a seaweed that is the source of *carrageenin* and is instrumental in thickening salad oils, cottage cheese, and the like. Laver has been traditionally cooked into flatcakes (laverbread) by the Irish, and green laver is used as a cooked vegetable. In the past in the United States, one kind of edible kelp was called "bladder weed" because of its streamer-like leaves (or "giant bladder weed" when the streamers averaged 30 to 40 or more feet in length).

Depending on the variety, seaweed can be high in beta-carotene and vitamin C, and all types are packed with a host of minerals.

Common names and synonyms: Agar, alga(e), bladder weed, carrageen moss, dulse, giant bladder weed, giant sea kelp, green laver, green sloke, gulfweed, *hijiki,* Irish moss, *karenga,* kelp, *kombu,* laver, *limu, nori,* rockweed, sea lettuce, sea moss, sea tangle, sea vegetable(s), *tecuitlatl, wakame.*

See also: "Algae," Part II, Section C, Chapter 1.

Seckel – *see* **PEAR**

SEDGE – Plants of the sedge family (Cyperaceae) and of the genus *Carex* are called "sedges"; they resemble grasses but have sharp stems that are solid rather than hollow. Various species are found worldwide, and their stems, corms, and grains have served as food for many thousands of years. Examples include the tender, whitish bases of the leaves of *C. aquatilis,* a plant that grows in North America and Europe and has long been consumed. The grains of an East Asian species (*C. kobomugi*) are also eaten.

Seje ungurahuay – *see* **PATAUA**

SÉMILLON (*see also* **GRAPES**) – This white grape (*Vitis vinifera*) is used to produce dry white wines, usually in combination with another grape such as Sauvignon. However, it is also used to make sweet Sauternes wines and is found mainly in the Graves and Sauternes regions of France.

See in addition: "Wine," Part III, Chapter 13.

Seminole bread – *see* **ZAMIA**

Sencha – *see* **TEA**

SENNA – Any of the various plants of the genus *Cassia* are called senna. The leaves of many of these, such as *C. angustifolia,* have been used medicinally especially in Asia. In North America the leaves, young shoots, and green pods of others, such as *C. occidentalis,* were used as food by Native Americans and settlers.

SENTUL – The fruit of a tall tree native to Indonesia, the sentul (*Sandoricum koetjape* formerly *indicum*) is round, yellow, 2 to 3 inches in diameter, and sweet and juicy. The fruit is generally eaten raw but is also made into jam. In addition, there is a red sentul – called *kechapi* – that is smaller and sour tasting.

Common names and synonyms: Kechapi.

SERENDIPITY BERRY – An edible red berry, the serendipity berry (*Dioscoreophyllum cumminsii*) is found in west-central Africa. It belongs to a large genus of mostly tropical fruits and is a relative of both the American black sapote and the Japanese persimmon.

Serpolet – *see* **THYME**

SERRANO (*see also* **CHILLI PEPPERS**) – A very popular pepper in Mexico and the southwestern United States, the serrano (meaning "mountain" or "highland"), a *Capsicum annuum,* is a very hot pepper, about 1 to 2 inches in length, with a torpedo-like shape. Serranos come in the colors green and red; both kinds are used interchangeably in salsas and other dishes. They are also canned, pickled, and packed in oil. When dried, serranos are called *chilli seco* or *serrano seco,* remain intensely hot, and are available both whole and in powdered form.

Common names and synonyms: Chilli seco, serrano seco.

See in addition: "Chilli Peppers," Part II, Section C, Chapter 4.

SERVICEBERRY (*see also* **BERRIES, ROWANBERRY**) - Growing in most of the world's temperate zones on a number of small trees and shrubs of the genus *Amelanchier,* the serviceberry is also known in North America as "shadbush" (because its white flowers appeared at about the same time that shad did in the rivers) and as "juneberry." The brownish or purple to black serviceberries were an important food for Native Americans such as the Chippewa. This was especially true of the fruits of *A. alnifolia* (a plant of North America called "Saskatoon" in the Cree language) and the western serviceberry, which resembles the blueberry more than do other serviceberries. Serviceberries were of particular significance in the American West, where they were sometimes the only food available to nourish the Mormons and other pioneers. Today, the fruits are sought for their "serviceability" in pies, jams, jellies, and sauces. Serviceberry is also a name sometimes applied to closely related berries of the mountain ash family. Equally confusing is the name bilberry, sometimes given to serviceberries.

Common names and synonyms: Juneberry, Saskatoon berry, Saskatoon serviceberry, shadblow, shadbush, western serviceberry.

Sesaban - *see* **SESBAN**

SESAME - A small seed with a nutty flavor that comes in a variety of colors (white, black, red, and brown), sesame (*Sesamum indicum*) is far more important in other parts of the world than it is in North America, where the white or black seed is used mostly atop breads and buns. The plant is alternatively said to be native to East Africa and to India (as the Latin name would have it), but there is no reason that it cannot have originated in both locations. Sesame is probably the oldest crop grown for its oil: It was cultivated in the Tigris and Euphrates valleys some 5,000 years ago and has competed with olive oil in the Mediterranean and India ever since its production began.

Sesame oil is also the oil for many in Asia: The seeds are a basic ingredient in the *tahina* of the Middle East and the *halvah* of Turkey, and in the Far East pastry cooks have long mixed sesame seeds with wheat flour. The seeds traveled in the holds of slave ships to reach the New World and today are commercially grown in South America.

The darker, unhulled seeds (in contrast to the whitish, hulled seeds) are rich in calcium and iron.

Common names and synonyms: Benne, ben(n)iseed, gingelly, sim(-)sim, til(seed).

See also: "Sesame," Part II, Section E, Chapter 4; "Spices and Flavorings," Part II, Section F, Chapter 1.

SESBAN - Also known by numerous common names such as "sesaban," "sesnania," "white spinach," "West Indian pea," "corkwood tree," and "agati," sesban (*Sesbania grandiflora*) - now naturalized in the United States - is a small tree of Southeast Asia and Australia, where it is called the "Australian corkscrew tree." Its white wood is very soft, which lends it to the same uses as cork. The fruit is a green pod (growing up to 2 feet in length), which is cooked and eaten along with the leaves, the buds, and the very large, white flowers. In many cultures, the flower petals are battered and fried. The tree has provided nourishment for humans for thousands of years, and even today is cultivated in India as a food plant. A related North American plant is the "coffee weed" (*S. cavanillesii*), the roasted seeds of which have served Mexicans as a coffee substitute.

Common names and synonyms: Agati, Australian corkscrew tree, coffee weed, corkwood tree, sesaban, sesnania, West Indian pea, white spinach.

Sesnania - *see* **SESBAN**

Setar - *see* **KUNDANGAN**

Seychelles cinnamon - *see* **CINNAMON AND CASSIA**

Shadblow - *see* **SERVICEBERRY**

Shadbush - *see* **SERVICEBERRY**

Shaddock - *see* **GRAPEFRUIT, POMELO**

Shagbark - *see* **HICKORY**

SHALLOT(S) - Shallots, once thought to be a species (*Allium ascalonicum*) distinct from the onion (although related to it [as for example, are chives and garlic, also members of the genus *Allium*]), are now considered to be a variety of the onion species (*A. cepa*). In fact, because shallots do not exist in a wild state, they may actually be a mutation of the onion.

The name "shallot" comes from the Greek name of a trading town in southern Palestine (*Askalon*) that was associated with the vegetable, which was carried to western Europe by returning Crusaders. A shallot is generally the size of a large head of garlic, grows in clove form, has a flavor more subtle than onion, and is less pungent than garlic. Chopped fine, shallots are indispensable in numerous classic sauces; sliced, they are an ingredient in many fine dishes; and they are roasted whole as an accompaniment for meats and poultry. In the Far East, shallots are pickled for use in salads, as a snack, and as a side dish. In Louisiana, scallions are frequently (and incorrectly) called shallots, doubtless because the French settlers there substituted scallions for the shallots of their homeland.

Common names and synonyms: White shallot.
See also: "The *Allium* Species," Part II, Section C, Chapter 2.

Shantung cabbage – *see* **CHINESE CABBAGE**

Shattercane – *see* **SORGHUM**

Shea-butter – *see* **SHEA TREE**

SHEA TREE – A West African native, the shea tree (*Butyrospermum parkii*) has large seeds with kernels that yield a fat called "shea-butter." The fat is utilized locally in cooking and is also exported to Europe, where it is used to make margarine and employed as a cooking fat.

Common names and synonyms: Shea-butter.

Sheepberry – *see* **BLACK HAW**

Sheep sorrel – *see* **SORREL**

Sherbet-fruit – *see* **CHERIMOYA**

Shiitake – *see* **MUSHROOMS AND FUNGI**

Shimeji – *see* **OYSTER MUSHROOM**

Shiraz – *see* **SYRAH**

Shiso – *see* **BEEFSTEAK PLANT**

Shore grape – *see* **SEA GRAPE**

Shore plum – *see* **BEACH PLUM**

Shrubby wound-wort – *see* **QUELITES**

SHUM – A life-saving tree during India's great famine of 1868–9, the bark of the shum (*Prosopis cineraria*) was used to make a flour that kept many from starving to death.

Siberian cherry – *see* **CORNUS**

Siberian hazel – *see* **HAZELNUT AND FILBERT**

SICHUAN PEPPERCORN (*see also* **PEPPERCORN**) – An ancient spice in China but not actually a peppercorn, the "Sichuan peppercorn" (*Zanthoxylum piperitum*) was in use (especially in the province of Sichuan) long before true peppercorns arrived. It is a small, aromatic, reddish brown seed from the prickly ash tree and, when ground, is frequently blended with salt to make pepper-salt – a fragrant dip for grilled and fried foods – and is also blended with other ingredients as in China's "five spices." In Japan, the leaves of the prickly ash tree (which have a peppery-lemon taste) serve as a garnish.

Sicilian corn – *see* **MAIZE**

Silk-cotton tree – *see* **KAPOK TREE**

Silk Fig – *see* **BANANA, BANANA FLOWER**

Silkweed – *see* **MILKWEED**

Silphion – *see* **SILPHIUM**

SILPHIUM – An extinct plant of the genus *Ferula,* silphium was well known to the ancient Greeks and utilized as a condiment by the Romans. It was grown in North Africa and was used as a medicine as well as in cooking. There are other plants of a genus now called *Silphium* that have been employed as foods. One such food is the sap of an eastern North American plant (*S. laciniatum*) called "rosinweed" or "compass plant." Another is the roots of *S. laeve* (also called "compass plant"), which reportedly were consumed by Native Americans. These peoples also used the sap of the cup

plant (*S. perfoliatum*), but apparently mostly as a medicine.

Common names and synonyms: Compass plant, cup plant, rosinweed, silphion.

See also: "Spices and Flavorings," Part II, Section F, Chapter 1.

SILVANER (*see also* **GRAPES**) – A grape known as "sylvaner" in Austria and France, the Silvaner (*Vitis vinifera*) originated in eastern Europe and moved west to become well known in medieval Germany. It remained one of Germany's most important wine grapes until about the middle of the twentieth century but now accounts for only about 7 percent of that country's wine. It is regarded today as a specialty grape of Franken (Franconia) in western Germany, although it is also grown in Alsace.

Common names and synonyms: Sylvaner.

See in addition: "Wine," Part III, Chapter 13.

Silver beet – *see* **SWISS CHARD**

Silverberry – *see* **ELAEAGNUS**

Silver ear – *see* **CLOUD EAR**

Silver pine – *see* **PINE NUT**

Silverthorn – *see* **ELAEAGNUS**

Sim(-)sim – *see* **SESAME**

Sing li mei – *see* **DAIKON**

SKIRRET – A Eurasian herb, skirret (*Sium sisarum*) is a member of the parsley family. It was cultivated in the past for its small, sweet, fleshy, edible roots, which can be boiled and buttered and eaten like potatoes or parsnips.

Common names and synonyms: Skirret-root(s).

Skoke – *see* **POKEWEED**

SKUNK CABBAGE – An offensive-smelling, swamp-dwelling herb of eastern North America, "skunk cabbage" (*Symplocarpus foetidus*) has a host of less-than-elegant common names, such as "polecat weed," "swamp cabbage," and "stinking poke." Its purple flowers are among the first of the New Year to appear and announce the impending arrival of spring. Skunk cabbage has long been used medicinally and even – despite its rank smell – culinarily. Native Americans boiled its young shoots as a vegetable and also cooked the root, after which it could be dried and made into a flour.

Common names and synonyms: Polecat weed, stinking poke, swamp cabbage.

SLIPPERY ELM – A tree of eastern North America, the slippery elm (*Ulmus fulva* = *U. rubra*) has unappetizing leaves and a rough outer bark but a fragrant, mucilaginous inner bark. Native Americans ate the inner bark raw and boiled it as a vegetable in both fresh and dried form. The bark continues to be harvested and dried (generally under pressure so that it remains flat); when reconstituted, it is employed as a food for babies and for adults with digestive problems.

Slip-skin grape – *see* **FOX GRAPE**

Sloak – *see* **LAVER**

SLOE (*see also* **PLUM**) - Also called "sloes," "black sloe," and "blackthorn," the sloe (*Prunus spinosa*) is a Eurasian and North African plum that is sometimes viewed as the ancestor of the Damson plum and other cultivated varieties. The fruit is berry sized, pale blue to black in color, and - as a rule - too astringent to be eaten raw. It is, however, made into juice, jellies, syrups, and preserves. Perhaps the most notable use of sloes is in the flavoring of liquors and liqueurs such as "sloe gin."

Common names and synonyms: Black sloe, blackthorn, sloes.

Sloes - *see* **SLOE**

Slook - *see* **LAVER**

Smallage - *see* **LOVAGE**

Small gourd - *see* **IVY GOURD**

Smartweed - *see* **KNOTWEED AND SMARTWEED**

Smokeweed - *see* **KNOTWEED AND SMARTWEED**

Smooth loofah - *see* **ANGLED LUFFA**

SMOOTH SUMAC - Also known as "mountain sumac," "upland sumac," and "vinegar tree" (among other common names), the smooth sumac (*Rhus glabra*) is a shrub of eastern North America. It is a relative of poison oak, poison ivy, and poison sumac, but it produces edible red berries that were dried and used as food by Native Americans.

Common names and synonyms: Mountain sumac, upland sumac, vinegar tree.

Snailseed - *see* **PIGEON PLUM**

Snake bean - *see* **WINGED BEAN**

Snake cucumber - *see* **ARMENIAN CUCUMBER, CUCUMBER, SNAKE GOURD**

SNAKE GOURD - Also called "snake melon," the snake gourd has long been thought of in terms of two species (*Trichosanthes anguina* and *T. cucumerina*), but it is now generally acknowledged that both names refer to the same species. Yet, as the two names remain, so do distinctions. *Trichosanthes anguina* is mostly intended to mean wild snake gourds, whereas *T. cucumerina* ("cucumber-like") refers to the cultivated vegetable. Unquestionably, the suggestion of a snake-like appearance seems appropriate - at least for the wild gourds, which can grow up to 5 or even 6 feet in length, sometimes remaining straight, sometimes curling, but in either case resembling a snake. The snake gourd is most appreciated in India and southeastern Asia, where the immature fruits, with a zucchini-like taste, are usually harvested at 10 to 12 inches in length and are boiled to be eaten whole or used in curries. The mature fruits, which become bitter, are cut into pieces for soups.

Common names and synonyms: Snake cucumber, snake melon.

Snake melon - *see* **ARMENIAN CUCUMBER, SNAKE GOURD**

Snapping hazel - *see* **WITCH-HAZEL**

Snow pea - *see* **PEA(S), SUGAR PEA**

SOAPBERRY - Any of several (mostly tropical) plants of the genus *Sapindus,* which produce berries that lather like soap in water, are called "soapberries," especially *S. saponaria* (the southern soapberry). Indeed, the berries contain sufficient saponin that they are sold as soap in some places. There are, however, other species, like *S. marginatus,* which Native Americans employed as food.

Common names and synonyms: Indian soap, southern soapberry.

SOLOMON'S-SEAL - Plants of the genus *Polygonatum* are called "Solomon's-seal" because of the resemblance of scars on their rootstocks to that mystical symbol of two interlaced triangles that make a six-pointed star. The plants are native to both Europe and North America, where their rhizomes have served humans as food for millennia. However, those rootstocks are toxic and consequently required processing. Native Americans sometimes dried them, then ground them into flour. In Europe, the rhizome was boiled and the starch made into a bread. The rootstocks and fresh shoots of some species are still consumed in East Asia.

SONCOYA - As its scientific name indicates, the soncoya (*Annona purpurea*) is a close relative of the cherimoya. The tree - a native of tropical and subtropical America - is relatively small (rarely reaching more than 22 feet in height), but the brown fruit is large. Its pulp is orange and sweet, and some have likened the taste to that of a papaw. The fruit is mostly eaten fresh.

SORB APPLE - The astringent fruit of the service tree, the "sorb apple" (*Sorbus domestica*) is a native of Asia Minor that was once fairly popular but is now uncommon. Like medlars, sorb apples are made edible by "bletting" (storage until they are on the verge of decomposing). A frost also helps to improve the texture and taste of these pear- and apple-shaped, brownish green fruits. Rowanberries and serviceberries are close relatives of the sorb apple, and their names are sometimes used interchangeably.

SORGHUM (*see also* **MILLET**) - There are several varieties of this Old World grass (*Sorghum vulgare* = *S. bicolor*) that are cultivated for grain, for forage, and as a source of syrup. Sorghum is native to East Africa, where it was being cultivated around 5,000 to 6,000 years ago. Sometime in the distant past (at least 2,000 years ago), the grain crossed the Indian Ocean to India and subsequently made its way to China. More recently, various sorghums reached the New World via the slave trade. Today, grain sorghums are grown extensively in Africa and Asia for use as human food and in the Americas as animal food.

Some sorghums in North America - like "Johnson grass" and "Mississippi chicken corn" - probably arrived as the seeds of important cultivars, only to escape from cultivation and become annoying weeds. The juices of sorghums have provided humans with syrup for sweetening, and in Asia and Africa the plant supplies malt, mash, and flavoring for alcoholic beverages, especially beers. Sorghum grains are made into flour (for unleavened breads) and into porridges, and they are also prepared and consumed much like rice. In addition, they can be popped in hot oil like popcorn. Despite these many uses, however, when available, the major grains like wheat, rice, and maize are chosen before sorghum, which means that its major role has been that of a famine food.

Common names and synonyms: Broomcorn, grain sorghum, great millet, Guinea corn, Johnson grass, Kaffir corn, Mississippi chicken corn, shattercane, sorgo, Sudan grass, sweet sorghum.

See also: "Sorghum," Part II, Section A, Chapter 9.

Sorgo - *see* **SORGHUM**

SORREL (*see also* **ROSELLE, WOOD SORREL**) - Species of the genus *Rumex* are called either sorrel or "dock." Garden sorrel (*R. acetosa*), also known as "sheep sorrel," and French sorrel (*R. scutatus*) are the two most important species that are cultivated for use as vegetables or herbs. Another type, *R. patientia,* known as "spinach dock," is less widely used. The name "sorrel" is derived from a Germanic word meaning "sour"; the plant's oxalic acid content contributes to its sour or bitter taste. Sorrel is related to rhubarb.

Many species of sorrel were native to Eurasia, and it was an herb used by the ancient Egyptians, Greeks, and Romans. These Old World species subsequently became naturalized in North America alongside native species that had been employed as food by Native Americans and were often cultivated as a vegetable. *Rumex articus* is an Arctic species that is still utilized by the Inuit, who boil and eat the leaves and also ferment them for later use. "Water dock" (*R. hydrolapathum*) and several other species are simply sorrels that grow in wet places.

The French employ *R. scutatus,* which is somewhat less acidic than garden sorrel, for their sorrel soup and famous *soupe aux herbes.* Other uses are in salads and egg dishes, and sorrel was a key ingredient in the old English green sour sauces that accompanied a roasted goose or pig. Last, sorrel leaves are often cooked and eaten like spinach, which they resemble. Sorrel is very high in vitamins A and C and is a good source of potassium.

Common names and synonyms: Dock, French sorrel, garden sorrel, round(-leaved) sorrel, sheep sorrel, sour(-)dock, sour grass, spinach dock, water dock, wild sorrel.

SORVA (*see also* **SERVICEBERRY**) - A tree of South America, sorva (*Couma utilis*) yields an edible, sweet fruit that is sold in local markets. Its main product, however, is a latex that serves as a substi-

tute for chicle gum. "Sorva" is also a common name for the serviceberry.

SOTOL - Also known as the "spoonplant," "desert-spoon," and "cactus-spoon," the sotol (*Dasylirion wheeleri*) is a member of the agave family. Native Americans ate the heart and young stalks of the plant. Its head contains a sugary sap that when fermented becomes a potent beverage also called sotol.

Common names and synonyms: Cactus-spoon, desert-spoon, spoonplant.

SOUARI NUT - A native of Guiana, the souari nut (*Caryocar nuciferum* or *C. amygdaliferum* - also called "butternut") is an edible nut that grows on very tall trees that have been much used in shipbuilding. In addition to its consumption raw, the souari nut yields an oil used in cooking. This nut with white meat is seldom seen in North American markets.

Common names and synonyms: Achotillo, butternut, seaving.

Souchong - *see* **TEA**

SOUR CHERRY (*see also* **CHERRY**) - A member of the rose family, the sour cherry (*Prunus cerasus = Cerasus vulgaris*), a stone fruit, is mostly cultivated in North America but is said to be native to southwestern Asia. Its tree has been cultivated since antiquity. Indeed, there is a story that its Latin name refers to the city of Cerasus in Pontus, an ancient kingdom in the northeast of Asia Minor. After defeating its king, Mithradates, the Roman general Lucullus carried the tree back to Italy and called it *cerasus.*

The sour cherry tree is small and rarely reaches over 8 feet in height, but it is known to spread out quite a bit. Sour cherries, which are bright red to almost black in color, can be eaten raw and are often cooked in various dishes, most notably cherry pie. In addition, they yield a colorless juice, which can be used to advantage in certain culinary applications. There is also an Australian tree (*Eugenia corynantha*) with sour-tasting red fruits that are called "sour cherries." Both sour cherries are rich in vitamin C.

Sour(-)dock - *see* **CURLED DOCK, SORREL**
Sour finger carambola - *see* **BELIMBING**
Sour grass - *see* **SORREL**
Sour gum - *see* **BLACK GUM**
SOUR PLUM - *Ximenia caffra* is a small tree or shrub common in southern Africa. Its greenish blossoms are followed by oval orange to scarlet fruits that are about 1 inch in diameter. The fruit envelops a seed that yields an oil used in the tanning of leather. The pulp, rich in vitamin C and potassium, is made into jelly and marmalade.

Common names and synonyms: Emu apple, Natal plum.

SOURSOP - Native to the Caribbean region and now also grown in Madeira and the Canary Islands, the soursop (*Annona muricata*) is a spiny fruit with a white, tart, edible pulp. Also called "guanabana," it is a big fruit that can easily weigh 4 or 5 pounds. It is used for making syrups, it is often served as a frozen dessert resembling ice cream, and its juice is sold commercially as a soft drink. The soursop is a very close relative of the sweetsop (custard apple) and the cherimoya.

Common names and synonyms: Dutch durian, guanabana.

SOURWOOD - A tree of eastern North America, the sourwood (*Oxydendrum arboreum*) has longish and slightly sour-tasting leaves that, when young and tender, constituted one of the many wild foods gathered by Native Americans. Indigenous peoples also braved bees in seeking the honey made from the sourwood's small white flowers, which blossom in June and July.

Sousous - *see* **CHAYOTE**

South American apricot - *see* **MAMMEE**

South American lupin - *see* **ANDEAN LUPIN**

Southern curled mustard - *see* **MUSTARD GREENS**

Southern fox grape - *see* **GRAPES, MUSCADINE**

Southern pea - *see* **COWPEA**

SOUTHERNWOOD - A shrubby European wormwood sometimes called "old-man," southernwood (*Artemisia abrotanum*) has become naturalized in North America. In Europe, its leaves have been employed to flavor beers.

Common names and synonyms: Old-man, southern wormwood.

Southern wormwood - *see* **SOUTHERNWOOD**

Southwestern barrel cactus - *see* **BARREL CACTUS**

Sowfoot - *see* **COLTSFOOT**

SOW THISTLE - A number of coarse, often spiny herbs comprise the genus *Sonchus*. *Sonchus arvensis* (perennial sow thistle), *S. asper* (spiny sow thistle), and *S. oleraceus* (annual sow thistle) were known to the ancient Romans and doubtless to the hunter-gatherers who preceded them by thousands of years. Today, this plant, a native of Europe but now naturalized throughout the world, is a weed that grows best in cultivated soils. Its roots can be eaten raw or cooked, and the young shoots and leaves make a fine salad.

SOYBEAN (*see also* **BEANS, LEGUMES**) - Legumes are by far the best plant sources of protein, and soybeans (*Glycine max*) are the best of the legumes because they are the only plant food to contain a complete protein. Equally remarkable, the soybean is the most widely consumed plant in the world. According to legend, soybeans were under cultivation in China close to 5,000 years ago, and we know that the plant had emerged as a domesticate in the eastern part of northern China by about 3,000 years ago. The Chinese have had myriad uses for this green, pea-sized legume that comes in a hairy pod. It provides vegetable milk, vegetable oil, bean sprouts, meal, flour, paste, various sauces, a

curd (tofu) that substitutes for meat, and the beans themselves, which are eaten both fresh and dried.

Many of these uses were expanded with the widening range of the plant. In the sixth century, soybeans accompanied Chinese Buddhist missionaries to Korea and Japan and became a staple food and a nutritional cornerstone for the teeming populations of these parts of East Asia. Soybeans were also introduced (by the migration of tribes, and by trade along the Silk Road and by sea) into Indonesia, the Philippines, Vietnam, Thailand, Malaysia, and northern India. Through Portuguese, Dutch, and (later) English traders and travelers, the West was made aware of soybeans, but, aside from acquisitions by botanical gardens, there was little interest in the plant. Indeed, this attitude persisted even after the turn of the eighteenth century, when Engelbert Kaempfer, a medical officer of the Dutch East India Company who had lived in Japan, published a book that explained the varied foodstuffs made possible by soybean cultivation.

In 1765 and again in 1803, soybeans were introduced in North America from England, and later on, after U.S. naval officer Matthew Perry had opened Japan to the West in 1854, germ plasm was acquired directly from Japan (as well as from China and Korea). However, those who grew the crop in the United States did so mostly for forage, and it was only in the late nineteenth and early twentieth centuries that soybeans began to receive scientific evaluation. In 1922, the first major soybean processing plant was built in Decatur, Illinois, and when enough such plants had come into being (about a decade later), the National Soybean Processors Association was formed.

During World War II, soybean oil was employed to replace imported fats and oils, and the meal found use as a feed to help expand the production of meat animals. After the war, soybeans played a major role in feeding the destitute population of Europe. Soybean production in the United States skyrocketed, and the nation quickly became the world's leading producer. Production in 1940 had been 78 million bushels, and in 1945 it was 193 million bushels. But by 1984, U.S. production had hit almost 2 billion bushels annually and was still climbing a decade later. Much of the U.S. crop is used for cattle feed, but soybean oil is also a mainstay of margarines, vegetable oils, salad dressings, and a host of processed foods. In addition, soy flour has many food-processing uses.

See in addition: "Soybean," Part II, Section E, Chapter 5; "Beans, Peas, and Lentils," Part II, Section C, Chapter 3; "An Overview of Oils and Fats," Part II, Section E, Chapter 1; "Spices and Flavorings," Part II, Section F, Chapter 1.

Spadic - *see* **COCA**

SPAGHETTI SQUASH (*see also* **SQUASH AND PUMPKIN**) - Also called "vegetable spaghetti," the spaghetti squash (*Cucurbita pepo*) is an exception to the rule that stringiness in squash is bad. This relatively new squash variety – the origin of which is uncertain – is so stringy that it can be baked (or "microwaved") and then its flesh raked with a fork into spaghetti-like strands that can be eaten like pasta. Moreover, spaghetti squash packs far fewer calories than pasta. Recipes abound combining this vegetable – spaghetti-like – with garlic, with vinaigrette dressing, with meat sauce, and with any of the other favorite pasta toppings.

Common names and synonyms: Vegetable spaghetti.
See in addition: "Squash," Part II, Section C, Chapter 8.

SPANISH BAYONET – There are several plants of the genus *Yucca* (and especially *Y. aloifolia* = *Y. elephantipes*) that are called "Spanish bayonet" because of the formidable appearance of their stiff, pointed leaves. The plants have a redeeming feature, however, in an edible pod-like fruit that ripens in clusters and is generally cooked rather than eaten raw. These fruits were among the many that sustained Native Americans in the southern part of North America.

Spanish cherry – *see* **MIMUSOPS**
Spanish chervil – *see* **CICELY**

SPANISH LIME – Also called "ginep," and *mamoncilla* in Cuba, the Spanish lime (*Melicoccus bijugatus*) is a popular tropical American green berry, about an inch in diameter and resembling a plum in appearance, with a grape-like taste. The fruit is eaten raw, although its pulp must be popped out of its tough skin; it is also made into drinks and cooked. In addition, Caribbean peoples roast the seeds of the Spanish lime and eat them like chestnuts. The tree is grown as far north as southern Florida.

Common names and synonyms: Genip, genipe, ginep, ginip, honeyberry, *mamoncilla*.

Spanish okra – *see* **JEW'S-MALLOW**
Spanish pine – *see* **AZAROLE**

SPANISH PLUM (*see also* **HOG PLUM, PLUM**) – Also called the "red mombin," the Spanish plum (*Spondias purpurea*) is a native of tropical America and a distant relative of cashews and pistachios. It is a red, edible fruit that is both eaten raw and employed in cooking. In addition, its stone is sometimes roasted and eaten like a chestnut.

Common names and synonyms: Red mombin.

Speedwell – *see* **BROOKLIME**

SPELT (*see also* **WHEAT**) – The place of origin of spelt (*Triticum spelta*), a hardy wheat, is a matter of some debate, with some experts suggesting Iran about 6000 to 5000 B.C.; others arguing for two independent sites, one in Iran and the second in southeastern Europe; and still others who would have spelt emerging only in Europe and at a later date. In any case, spelt was cultivated throughout the Near East, Europe, and the Balkans during the Bronze Age (4000 to 1000 B.C.) and, along with

einkorn and emmer, it is another of the ancestors of modern wheat. Spelt was probably an important cereal of the ancient Egyptians and Greeks and seems to have been a staple of the Romans, in which case the latter people may have facilitated the grain's spread northward to Germany and Switzerland and westward to Spain, where it was still being grown at the beginning of the twentieth century.

Complicating the picture, however, are the finds of spelt remains dating from 3800 to 2800 B.C. in Neolithic sites in Spain, western Germany, the Netherlands, and Belgium – but whether these are the remains of domesticated spelt is another matter. Also confounding the problem is that invading Vandals have been credited with introducing spelt in Europe around the fifth century A.D.

But, whenever and wherever spelt was established, the grain became a major cereal crop in Europe and joined einkorn and emmer in sustaining multitudes during the Middle Ages. Around the middle of the nineteenth century (if not before), spelt was carried to North America, where production (much of it for fodder) peaked in the early decades of the twentieth century. Spelt is grown today on a small scale in isolated parts of Germany and Switzerland, and it seems to be making a comeback in the United States and Canada because of the health-food market.

See in addition: "Wheat," Part II, Section A, Chapter 10.

Spice birch – *see* **SWEET BIRCH**

SPICEBUSH – "Spicebush" refers to a number of plants but the name is mostly intended to mean the eastern North American spicebush (*Lindera benzoin*). Also called the "Benjamin bush," it produces red or yellow berries. Native Americans dried and powdered the berries and used them as a spice. The bark from the roots and stems – along with the leaves – were employed to make a tea.

Common names and synonyms: Benjamin bush.

Spikenard – *see* **UDO**

SPINACH – A green leafy vegetable, spinach (*Spinacia oleracea*) is a native of southwestern Asia. The plant reached China as a gift from Nepal during the first years of the Tang dynasty (the early seventh century A.D.) and was introduced in Sicily in 827 by invading Saracens from North Africa – they having first encountered the plant in Persia. However, spinach seems to have been in no hurry to spread out over the rest of Europe, although it may well have done so without recorded mention during those centuries of the Middle Ages that food historian Reay Tannahill has called "The Silent Centuries." The vegetable probably reached Spain with the invading Moors, but it was not until the very end of the Middle Ages that spinach showed up in a cookbook published anonymously in Nuremberg in 1485. After this it caught on rather quickly on the Continent, probably in no small part because spinach made its appearance in early spring, when other fresh vegetables were still scarce yet human bodies were desperate for vitamin C after a winter of deprivation. Spinach was first planted in England in 1568, and within a century it had become one of the few vegetables that appeared on the tables of the wealthy. Presumably, the plant was carried to North America long before 1806, when seed catalogs mentioned three varieties. However, it was only after another century had elapsed that a food encyclopedia stated that the vegetable was becoming "increasingly popular."

Part of the difficulty in tracing the history of spinach is that there are so many spinach-like vegetables (such as the amaranth of India and Japan, the kang kong or water spinach of Southeast Asia, and New Zealand spinach) that one is not always certain which "spinach" is being confronted, and even "real" spinach comes in two basic types. The fresh spinach encountered in most markets is the crinkle-leafed Savoy kind, but there is also the flat, smooth-leafed variety that is generally employed for freezing or canning. In addition, there is a sort of "semi-Savoy" spinach that is a cross between the two basic types. Young, tender spinach leaves make fine salads. Sautéing and steaming are great ways to prepare the vegetable so that it does not become overcooked and develop a characteristic limp and washed-out appearance. Spinach also makes splendid soufflés; oysters, broiled on the half shell with a mixture of spinach, some other ingredients, and a sauce become "Oysters Rockefeller"; and when foods are served on a bed of spinach, they are known collectively as *florentine*.

With apologies to "Popeye the Sailor-Man" (whose appearance as a cartoon character in 1929 increased spinach consumption by 33 percent among children), spinach is not a "miracle food" – not even a particularly good source of iron. But it is rich in beta-carotene, calcium, folacin, and a number of important minerals.

Common names and synonyms: Savoy spinach.

Spinach beet - *see* **BEET, SWISS CHARD**
Spinach dock - *see* **SORREL**
Spinach-grass - *see* **AMARANTH**
Spinach tree - *see* **CHAYA**
Spineless cactus - *see* **PRICKLY PEAR**
Spirulina - *see* **TECUITLATL**
Sponge gourd - *see* **ANGLED LUFFA**
Spoon cabbage - *see* **PAKCHOI AND KAI CHOY**
Spoonflower - *see* **MALANGA**
Spoonleaf yucca - *see* **YUCCA**
Spoonplant - *see* **SOTOL**
Spoonwort - *see* **SCURVY GRASS**
Spotted alder - *see* **WITCH-HAZEL**
Spring kale - *see* **HANOVER KALE**
SPRUCE - The young shoots as well as the inner bark of spruce trees (genus *Picea*) were eaten by Native Americans, and the shoots are still employed in

Europe for various dishes. In addition, the shoots of some species have served to make "spruce beer" (at one time thought to be effective against scurvy), and the leaves can be made into a tea. Finally, spruce trees have been a source of balsam used as "chewing gum" since Paleolithic times.

Sqamash - *see* **CAMAS**

SQUASH AND PUMPKIN (*see also* **PUMPKIN, SQUASH FLOWERS**) - Squashes, pumpkins, and some gourds are all American natives and members of the Cucurbitaceae. However, further division can sometimes be confusing, especially when a common name embraces more than one species. There are five species of the genus *Cucurbita* that were domesticated in the Americas, four of which subsequently became good food for people the world over. But squashes are gourds, and domestication probably came about initially at the hands of those seeking hard shells to employ as containers and utensils. From that point on, however, it was only a matter of time until the seeds and, later on, the flesh of the various squashes began playing an important role in the Native American diet.

Moving from north to south, *C. pepo* may have been domesticated in what is now the eastern United States as well as in Mexico, where it has reportedly been grown for over 7,000 years. Most varieties of this species, such as zucchini, yellow straightneck, yellow crookneck, and pattypan (also called cymling or scallop), fall under the rubric of summer squash. The summer squash are eaten while still soft and immature, as are winter varieties of *C. pepo* (like the acorn squash and most pumpkins), which otherwise mature into hard, starchy fruits (the very large pumpkins, however, belong to *C. maxima*). Chayote, although thought of as a summer squash, is another plant entirely, albeit "squashlike."

The other species of *Cucurbita* provide winter varieties. *Cucurbita mixta* is the cushaw or calabaza - a pear- or crookneck-shaped squash - developed in an area extending from the U.S. Southwest to Costa Rica. The species that came into being at the intersection between the Northern and Southern Hemispheres is *C. moschata,* the major representative of which is the Butternut squash. *Cucurbita maxima* was apparently domesticated in Peru, and out of this emerged the Hubbard and banana squashes, as well as varieties developed outside the Americas, like the Australian Blue and the *Rouge Vif d'Étampes* squashes. Native Americans, who cultivated squashes and pumpkins, ate the vegetables roasted or boiled and preserved the flesh as *conservas* in syrup. They also ate the young shoots, leaves, flowers, and especially the seeds. Since the arrival of the Europeans, usage has been expanded to include employing the flesh in pies, in soups (especially in France), and even as pickles.

A species that was domesticated in the Americas but did not travel to other lands (although it was long thought to be a native of Asia) is *C. ficifolia*, sometimes known as the Malabar gourd or the fig-leafed gourd. Of all the cucurbits, this is the only species adapted to high altitudes, and it is a food for many in the highlands of Mexico and South America, where its fruits, appearing on the outside like small watermelons, can often be seen on rooftops, drying in the sun. In addition, there are wild cucurbits with flowers and seeds that served Native Americans as food; these include the buffalo gourd (*C. foetidissima*) and the coyote melon (*C. palmata*), and in southern Florida *C. okeechobeensis,* named for the lake, was consumed by Native Americans.

The yellow and orange flesh of winter squashes (especially the Hubbard and the Butternut) is rich in beta-carotene and not a bad source of vitamin C and folacin. Summer squashes are high in water content and, consequently, low in calories. They, too, are a fair source of vitamin C and folacin.

Common names and synonyms: Acorn squash, Australian Blue, banana squash, buffalo gourd, Butternut, calabaza, courge, courgette, coyote melon, crookneck, cushaw, cymling, fig-leafed gourd, gourd, Hubbard, Malabar gourd, pattypan squash, *pepo,* pumpkin, *Rouge Vif d'Étampes,* scallop squash, straight crookneck, summer squash, turban squash, vegetable marrow, winter squash, yellow crookneck, yellow straightneck, zucchini.

See in addition: "Squash," Part II, Section C, Chapter 8.

Squash blossom(s) – *see* **SQUASH FLOWER(S)**

SQUASH FLOWER(S) (*see also* **SQUASH AND PUMPKINS**) – The orangish yellow, mostly male flowers (so the vines will still bear fruit) that appear on summer squash (*Cucurbita pepo*) vines are frequently picked for consumption. They are edible and considered a delicacy by many. In fact, it is probably no coincidence that they are available in the markets of Mexico and are added most to the dishes of that land, where many, perhaps most, of the squashes originated. Squash flowers are sometimes added to *quesadillas* and sautéed, but they are generally battered and deep-fried. The flowers are a good source of beta-carotene and also – if the cooking is brief – of vitamin C.

Common names and synonyms: Squash blossom(s).

See also: "Squash," Part II, Section C, Chapter 8.

Squash pepper – *see* **HABANERO AND SCOTCH BONNET PEPPERS**

Squaw bush – *see* **HIGHBUSH CRANBERRY**

Squawroot – *see* **BLUE COHOSH, INDIAN POTATO, TRILLIUM**

Squirrel-tail barley – *see* **WILD BARLEY**

Stagbush – *see* **BLACK HAW, HAW**

Star – *see* **KUNDANGAN**

STAR-ANISE – Despite the names "star-anise" and "Chinese anise," *Illicium verum* is not, in fact, a member of the magnolia family and not related to true anise. Doubtless, the reason for the "anise" part of its name is that it has a licorice-like flavor, very similar to that of anise. As the rest of its name implies, star-anise has star-shaped yellow flowers, with each point of the star containing a shiny, oval seed. The leaves and seeds (which have a taste somewhat stronger than that of anise) are dried and added whole, broken, or ground to various dishes, especially in the cuisines of China and Vietnam. This spice has never been much used in the West, save as a flavoring for liquors such as anisette.

Common names and synonyms: Badian anise, Chinese anise.

See also: "Spices and Flavorings," Part II, Section F, Chapter 1.

STAR-APPLE (*see also* **CARAMBOLA**) – A tropical American fruit of the sapodilla family, and native to the West Indies and Central America, the star-apple (*Chrysophyllum cainito*) is a purple-brown, sweet fruit about the size of an apple. It grows on a large evergreen tree and fascinated early Spanish explorers, who discovered that when it was cut in two, it had a star shape in the middle.

Common names and synonyms: Caimito (fruit), *caymito.*

Starch wheat – *see* **EMMER**

Starchy breadroot – *see* **ZAMIA**

Star fruit – *see* **CARAMBOLA**

Steinpilz(e) – *see* **BOLETE, MUSHROOMS AND FUNGI**

STEVIA – An herb of South America (especially southern Brazil and Paraguay), stevia (*Stevia rebaudiana*) has leaves that have long been employed locally as a natural sweetener. Dried and ground, they are said to be infinitely sweeter than sucrose, and one suspects that we will hear more of this plant as a sugar substitute.

Common names and synonyms: Sugar-leaf, sweet-herb-of-Paraguay.

See also: "Spices and Flavorings," Part II, Section F, Chapter 1.

Stinking gum – *see* **ASAFETIDA**

Stinking poke – *see* **SKUNK CABBAGE**

Stitchwort – *see* **CHICKWEED**

STONECROP – A number of species of the genus *Sedum* are collectively called "stonecrop." *Sedum roseum* of North America has fleshy roots that have served as food for millennia. In Europe, the young leaves and shoots of *Sedum reflexum* are eaten in soups and salads, especially by the Dutch. They may be consumed cooked or raw and have a slightly astringent taste. The sharp taste of *S. acre* is sometimes employed for seasoning in Asia. The plant is also known as "Jenny-stonecrop" and "ditch-stonecrop."

Common names and synonyms: Ditch-stonecrop, Jenny-stonecrop.

Stone mint – *see* **DITTANY**

Stone nut - *see* **PINE NUT**

Stopper - *see* **MYRTLE**

Straight crookneck (squash) - *see* **PUMPKIN, SQUASH AND PUMPKIN**

STRAWBERRY (*see also* **BERRIES, WILD STRAW-BERRY**) - The garden strawberry (*Fragaria ananassa*) is probably the best known of the berries and certainly the most versatile. It is a hybrid - between the Chilean berry (*F. chiloensis*) and *F. virginiana* of eastern North America that is now cultivated worldwide. There are myriad other strawberry species, however, that grow wild in the Americas and Eurasia. Indeed, although strawberries have been planted in gardens since Roman times, berries gathered from the wild were generally the only kind available to most people until the fifteenth century, when Europeans began to cultivate them in earnest. Most of the European names for these berries poetically suggest their fragrance, although the English name comes from the layers of straw that were placed around the plants to keep the berries off the ground. Strawberries were probably also cultivated by the Indians of North and South America, which may account for the fact that two of the American species produce the largest fruits.

Strawberries are now available fresh most of the year, making it possible to avoid frozen strawberries, which tend to disintegrate when thawed. Strawberries are mostly eaten raw but are also made into jams, preserves, and pies and are used to flavor everything from ice cream to chewing gum. They contain more vitamin C than any other berry.

Common names and synonyms: European strawberry, garden strawberry, Virginia strawberry.

STRAWBERRY GUAVA - Also known as the "Cattley guava," the strawberry guava (*Psidium cattleianum*) grows on a bush that is much more resistant to cold and frost than the common guava. But the reddish fruits are much smaller and lack the common guava's flavor. They are generally used for jelly.

Common names and synonyms: Cattley guava, purple guava.

STRAWBERRY-RASPBERRY (*see also* **JAPANESE WINEBERRY**) - This real "strawberry-raspberry" (*Rubus illecebrosus*), which is sometimes confused with the Japanese wineberry, is a low bramble that is frequently used in Japan as a ground cover to hold the soil on the banks of rivers and streams. It also produces showy, red, edible fruits that are generally made into preserves.

Common names and synonyms: Balloonberry.

Strawberry tomato - *see* **CAPE GOOSEBERRY**

STRAWBERRY TREE - A native of the Mediterranean region, the strawberry tree (*Arbutus unedo*) is a small evergreen tree with fruits that are strawberry-like in appearance but not in taste. The tree was known to the ancient Greeks, but its fruits have never really been developed. The most common variety is the "Killarney strawberry tree," whose berries are made into liqueurs, sherbets, confections and the like but are not eaten raw.

Common names and synonyms: Killarney strawberry tree.

Straw mushroom - *see* **MUSHROOMS AND FUNGI**

STRIPED SCREW-PINE - A native of the tropics of the Old World, and an important food tree for Pacific Islanders, the striped screw-pine (*Pandanus veitchii*) is also known as the "Veitch screw-pine." It has fruits and nuts that are both edible.

Common names and synonyms: Veitch screw-pine.

Succory - *see* **CHICORY**

Sudan grass - *see* **SORGHUM**

SUDAN POTATO - Also called "Hausa potato" and "piasa," the Sudan potato (*Coleus tuberosus = C. parviflorus = Solenostemon rotundifolius*) is a tuber - probably a native of tropical Africa - that is grown and used like a white potato. It is still cultivated in Africa and also in Southeast Asia. As a rule, the tubers (and sometimes the leaves) are boiled for consumption.

Common names and synonyms: Hausa potato, piasa.

Sugar apple (tree) - *see* **CUSTARD APPLE, SWEET-SOP**

Sugar beet - *see* **BEET, SUGARCANE**

Sugarberry - *see* **HACKBERRY**

SUGARCANE - There are several species of sugarcane (genus *Saccharum*) in Southeast Asia, which probably gave rise to cultivated cane (*S. officinarum*), with a juice or sap high in sugar. This giant grass was used as a medicine - and possibly to sweeten foods and beverages - in ancient India and China. Sugar became known to the Persians and probably to the Greeks around 500 B.C., when, during a foray into the Indus Valley, the Persian king Darius reported finding reeds that produced honey although there were no bees. A couple of centuries later, an emissary of Alexander the Great learned that the "honey" in question was actually cane juice evaporated by boiling, and sometime after that the Persians themselves began making sugar.

Sugarcane was introduced in southern Europe in the ninth and tenth centuries A.D. by the Arabs, who had captured Persia and revived its sugar industry. Venice became a "middleman" that imported sugar, then exported it again to central Europe and the Slavic countries, and plantations were established in the West by the Arabs around Valencia in Spain. Medieval Europeans called sugar "white salt" but never tasted it save in medications destined mostly for the wealthy. Yet demand was sufficient that in the fifteenth century, the Iberians transferred sugar cultivation to Madeira and the Canary Islands, and slaves were imported from nearby Africa to work in the fields - all a dreadful harbinger of things to come in the Americas in the wake of Christopher Columbus. By 1518, the Spaniards were operating a number of sugar plantations on Hispaniola, and in that year began the transatlantic slave trade.

Europe, however, was closer to the sugar of the Middle East than it was to that of the West Indies, and a voracious European demand for sugar (other than as a medicine) had to wait for the consumption of tea, coffee, and chocolate to become widespread, which it did during the course of the seventeenth and eighteenth centuries. The Dutch seized northeastern Brazil in 1635 and moved into the sugar industry there. After being driven out a few years later, they began providing the secrets of sugar production to English colonists on Barbados, along with the financing to help them switch from tobacco to sugar cultivation. Such behavior was hardly altruistic; the Dutch made great profits supplying Barbados with slaves from Africa and carrying the sugar away to Europe.

This activity at about the midpoint of the seventeenth century is generally viewed as the beginning of the "sugar revolution," during which on island after island in the Caribbean saw lands devoted to sugar monoculture and gathered into the hands of a relatively few whites, surrounded by huge black slave populations. The French island of Martinique was caught up in the sugar revolution in 1655 – the same year that the British seized Jamaica from Spain. By the end of the seventeenth century, Jamaica had emerged as a major sugar producer, but by the end of the following century French St. Domingue was producing about half of the world's sugar. The slave revolution in that country (which created the new nation of Haiti) and British abolition of first the slave trade and then slavery itself (during the first third of the nineteenth century) led next to the rise of Cuba as the Caribbean's biggest sugar grower and a competitor of Brazil for dominance of the world market – a competition that Cuba won because of the willingness of its planters to embrace railroads and other new technologies.

Meanwhile, in North America sugar had been grown in Louisiana by French colonists throughout most of the eighteenth century, albeit with little success until experts on the crop, fleeing from the revolution in Haiti, arrived to take a hand. By the time of the American Civil War, Louisiana sugar held a position of world importance that it would never regain after the war's end and the abolition of slavery.

Despite the avalanche of sugar from sugarcane that was reaching the Old World from the New, beet sugar had been experimented with, and during the Continental blockade around the turn of the nineteenth century, Napoleon ordered that thousands of hectares of French land be planted with sugar beets to avoid dependence on imports from the New World. Although French production faltered after the war in the face of resumed imports of cane sugar, beet-sugar production continued to constitute worrisome competition for cane-sugar producers, and by 1845 beet sugar had captured some 15 percent of the world market.

In the United States, sugar beets were being raised on a commercial scale in the last two decades of the nineteenth century but accounted for only a fraction of the country's sugar needs. It was at about this time (1878) that London sugar magnate Henry Tate introduced the sugar cube to the world. Its effect on demand is not known, but about a century later – during the last decades of the twentieth century – the world was producing more sugar than it could use, despite the heavy demands made by the food-processing and beverage industries. Thus, in addition to its use as a sweetener with myriad applications, its employment in raw form in many tropical countries, and its by-products, such as molasses, rums, and other cane spirits, there have been efforts to convert sugar into fuel for automobiles, and even into wax. In the face of health concerns as well as competition from artificial sweeteners (such as saccharin and aspartame, which are now in use, and a vast number of others on the horizon), the future of sugar, after four centuries or more of prosperity, seems uncertain.

Common names and synonyms: Noblecane, white salt.

See also: "Sugar," Part II, Section F, Chapter 2.

Sugar-leaf – *see* **STEVIA**

Sugar maple (tree) – *see* **MAPLE SYRUP AND MAPLE SUGAR**

Sugar melon – *see* **CANTALOUPE AND MUSK-MELON**

SUGAR PEA (*see also* **LEGUMES, PEA**) – Peas were domesticated about 6000 B.C. in the Near East, but the sugar pea (*Pisum sativum* var. *macrocarpon*) has only been around since the sixteenth century. Also known as the "snow pea," *mange-tout,* and "edible pod pea," the sugar pea is often said to have originated in China, but there is some evidence to indicate that the plant was first cultivated in Europe and taken to China by the Dutch. Moreover, the extent to which the sugar pea is employed in Asian cuisine today appears to be a matter of contention (in India there is a similar flat legume called *papdi*), although there is no question of its prominence in Asian dishes served in the West.

"Snow pea" seems something of a misnomer because the plant grows no earlier in the season than other peas. But the name "sugar pea" is quite appropriate, as it is a sweet legume. It appears similar to a garden pea except that it has a skin so thin and delicate that the entire pod can be eaten. Or at least this is the case if the sugar pea is picked when the immature peas inside are only just discernible, but if it reaches maturity, the pod becomes tough, and the sugar content decreases. The sugar snap pea, which has recently been developed, is an interesting legume that permits large sweet peas to grow inside a pod that remains sweet and edible. Sugar peas are high in vitamin C and iron.

Common names and synonyms: Chinese pea, Chinese pea pod, Chinese snow pea, edible-podded pea, edible pod pea, *ho loan, mange-tout, papdi,* podded pea, snow pea, sugar snap pea.

See in addition: "Beans, Peas, and Lentils," Part II, Section C, Chapter 3.

Suico - *see* **ANISILLO**

Sukun - *see* **BREADFRUIT**

Sultana - *see* **THOMPSON SEEDLESS (GRAPE)**

Sumac - *see* **SMOOTH SUMAC, SUMAC BERRY**

SUMAC BERRY (*see also* **BERRIES**) - There are countless varieties of shrubs and trees of the genus *Rhus,* with one in particular – "Sicilian sumac" (*R. coriaria*) – noted for its red, slightly sour-tasting berries that can impart a cherry color to dishes. These are dried and used whole, ground for sauces, or combined with other spices to sprinkle on meat dishes. The Romans employed sumac berries for their fruity sourness before lemons reached Europe, and they remain popular in the Middle East. In Europe, however, they are no longer in common use. In North America, *R. typhina* produces a sumac berry that was doubtless used by Native Americans for flavoring foods and liquids. Also doubtless, Native Americans quickly learned to stay clear of some other members of the sumac family, such as poison sumac, poison ivy, ;and poison oak.

SUMPWEED - A plant with an interesting history and a harsh name, sumpweed (*Iva annua*) has also been more pleasingly called the "marsh-elder." It is a weed that inhabits the central United States, is generally around 2 or 3 feet in height, and yields an oily seed that is as nutritious as the seeds of its domesticated relative, the sunflower. In fact, archaeobotanists have discovered that sumpweed was also domesticated some 2,000 years ago. Yet by the time the Europeans arrived, the plant had returned to the wild. The most likely explanation for this is that sumpweed was displaced by the maize-beans-and-squash triumvirate that had moved northward from Mexico and then across all of North America by A.D. 1200 or so.

Common names and synonyms: Marsh-elder.

Sunberry - *see* **WONDERBERRY**

Sunchoke - *see* **JERUSALEM ARTICHOKE**

SUNFLOWER OIL AND SEED (*see also* **JERUSALEM ARTICHOKE**) - The sunflower (*Helianthus annuus*), with its daisy-like head bristling with oil-rich seeds, is North America's only native plant to become a major world crop (the second most important oilseed crop in the world). Wild sunflower seeds were an important food gathered by Native Americans that could be dried and used throughout the winter. But many tribes in the western and especially the southwestern parts of what

is now the United States had gone beyond the gathering stage to domesticate and cultivate sunflowers long before the Europeans arrived. After that arrival, sunflowers – then thought of as a decorative plant – were carried to Europe around 1510, beginning what would be a world tour.

Two centuries later, the plants were being grown for their oil on a large scale in France and Bavaria, and following this development, they moved farther eastward into eastern Europe and especially Russia, where – as a previously unknown food – sunflower oil was not on the proscribed list for the many fasting days observed by the Orthodox church. As a result, today Russia is by far the world's largest producer of sunflower oil, accounting for about three-quarters of the total despite vast tracts of land given over to sunflowers in Argentina (which is a distant second), Uruguay, the United States, and some of the other eastern European countries. Turkey, Morocco, Tanzania, and Ethiopia are the most important producers in the tropics and subtropics.

With its low unsaturated-to-saturated fat ratio, sunflower oil has become ever more important as an oil for cooking, and the oilseeds (the black-shelled kind) are also popular as a feed for birds. Dried sunflower seeds make a fine snack that is high in protein, the B-vitamins, and calcium.

Common names and synonyms: Common sunflower, giant sunflower, prairie sunflower, single-headed sunflower.

See in addition: "Sunflower," Part II, Section E, Chapter 6; "An Overview of Oils and Fats," Part II, Section E, Chapter 1.

SUNSAPOTE - Native to the lowland tropics of central-northern South America, the sunsapote (*Licania platypus*) is a tall wild or semicultivated tree that produces a large fruit of the same name. The pulp of the fruit is sweet and generally is eaten raw. The sunsapote can be important locally but is not really a commercial crop.

SUNSET HIBISCUS - Also called "edible hibiscus" and "aibika," the sunset hibiscus (*Abelmoschus manihot = Hibiscus manihot*) is a relative of okra and probably a native of China. It is widely cultivated for its leaves in the islands of the South Pacific and in areas of tropical Asia. The usually sweet leaves are harvested when fully developed and are eaten raw, cooked as greens, and used in stews.

Common names and synonyms: Aibika, edible hibiscus.

Surinam amaranth - *see* **CALLALOO**

Surinam cherry - *see* **ACEROLA, PITANGA**

Surinam spinach - *see* **AMARANTH**

Susumber - *see* **EGGPLANT**

SWAMP CABBAGE (*see also* **HEART(S) OF PALM, SKUNK CABBAGE**) - Not to be confused with hearts of palm, which can also go by this name, this real swamp cabbage (*Ipomoea aquatica*) is a green-leafed vegetable and not a cabbage, grows in or near water, and is a member of the Convolvulaceae (sweet potato) family. "Kang kong" and "water spinach" are two common names for the plant, and both Africa and tropical Asia have been put forward as its place of origin. Swamp cabbage is grown throughout Southeast Asia, in some parts of Africa, and in Australia. A land form of the plant is grown in Indonesia. Both the water and land forms are raised for their tender stems and leaves, which are used in salads and cooked as a vegetable. The leaves are a good source of calcium and a fair source of vitamin C.

Common names and synonyms: Espinaca acquatica, kang(-)kong, karamta, kang kung, patate aquatique, swamp morning-glory, water convolvulus, water spinach.

Swamp morning-glory - *see* **SWAMP CABBAGE**
Swamp potato - *see* **ARROWHEAD**
Sweating plant - *see* **BONESET**
Swede - *see* **RUTABAGA**
Swedish turnip - *see* **RUTABAGA**
Sweet anise - *see* **FENNEL**
Sweet balm - *see* **LEMON BALM**
Sweet bay - *see* **BAY LEAF**
Sweet bean - *see* **HONEY LOCUST**

SWEET BIRCH - A tree that is native to eastern North America, the sweet birch (*Betula lenta*) is known to many as the "black birch." Its inner bark was eaten by Native Americans, who consumed it fresh and also dried it for later use. The twigs and leaves of the sweet birch (along with the inner bark) contain an oil similar to wintergreen and were used to brew a tea; the sap of the tree was also drunk. Later, European settlers made "birch beer" by steeping the bark in water.

Common names and synonyms: Black birch, cherry birch, spice birch.

SWEET CLOVER - This biennial herb (*Melilotus officinalis*) is native to Europe, temperate Asia, and North Africa. It was introduced into North America around 1700 and is grown for erosion control and for fodder. In Europe, it is often used as an herb. In France, sweet clover is an ingredient in the stuffing for a cooked rabbit. In Switzerland, the flowers and seeds of the plant are used to flavor Gruyère and Sapsago cheeses. The roots are also edible, and in Iceland they are cooked and eaten like other root vegetables. In many places throughout Europe, the leaves and flowers of sweet clover flavor soups, stews, and marinades. Its flowers are also a good source of nectar for honey production.

Common names and synonyms: Melilot, melist, yellow melilot, yellow sweet clover.

Sweet-corm-root - *see* **GUINEA ARROWROOT**
Sweet cumin - *see* **ANISE**
SWEET DUMPLING (SQUASH) (*see also* **SQUASH AND PUMPKIN**) - Like the Delicata and the Golden Nugget, the Sweet Dumpling squash (*Cucurbita pepo*) is a small squash that serves only one person. It is generally light colored with green stripes, and its sweet flesh makes a good soup. The small cavity of the squash can also be hollowed out for stuffing.

See in addition: "Squash," Part II, Section C, Chapter 8.

SWEET FERN - A shrub that grows throughout eastern North America, the sweet fern (*Comptonia peregrina*) has a pleasing, sweet-scented odor. Its leaves have been steeped to make a tea, and the leaves and tops can be chopped and used as a condiment.

Common names and synonyms: Canada sweetgale, fernbush, ferngale, meadow fern, sweet bush.

SWEET FLAG - Also known as "calamus," sweet flag (*Acorus calamus*) grows in eastern North America in moist areas such as swamps, the shores of lakes, and riverbanks. It has fernlike foliage and an aromatic root with a sharp taste, which in the past, at least, was sometimes candied. The rhizome is also used for flavoring alcoholic beverages, including beer, and has been sold commercially as a breath freshener. Native Americans ate the young shoots of the plant both raw and after cooking.

Common names and synonyms: Calamus, calamus root, flag root, myrtle flag.

Sweet gale - *see* **BOG MYRTLE**
Sweet granadilla - *see* **PASSION FRUIT**
SWEET GUM - The hardy tree *Liquidambar styraciflua* is native to North and Central America. Also known as "red gum," "American sweet gum," and "bilsted," the tree yields a resin that is called American styrax or storax. The resin has been chewed both to freshen the breath and to clean the teeth. It has also been used to flavor tobacco and beverages.

Common names and synonyms: American storax, American styrax, American sweet gum, bilsted, red gum.

Sweet haw - *see* **BLACK HAW**
Sweet-herb-of-Paraguay - *see* **STEVIA**
Sweet laurel - *see* **BAY LEAF**
Sweet-leaf bush - *see* **SWEET-SHOOT**
Sweet lemon - *see* **LIMETTA**
Sweet lime - *see* **LIMETTA**
Sweet locust - *see* **HONEY LOCUST**
Sweet pea - *see* **BEACH PEA, PEA, SUGAR PEA**
SWEET PEPPERS (*see also* **CHILLI PEPPERS**) - These Capsicums (*C. annuum* var. *annuum*) are called sweet because they do not impart the heat that their more aggressive relatives are noted for (although the "Mexi-Bell" - a cross between a sweet bell pepper and a hot pepper - has a bit of a bite). Bell peppers, which constitute one category of sweet peppers, are so called because of their bell-like shape. Although most commonly found in the color green, bell peppers also come in variations of red, yellow, orange, and black. Such variety makes bell peppers a colorful ingredient in salads and any

number of other dishes and sauces. They are also grilled, roasted, and in many cultures have traditionally been stuffed.

A large, dark, heart-shaped red pepper (although not actually a red bell pepper, with which it is often confused), grown in the U.S. South, in Spain, and in Hungary, is called variously a pimento (or pimiento), a *chilli pimiento,* a *pimiento dulce,* or a *pimiento morrón.* The flesh of this chilli is roasted to become pimento or pimiento (not allspice, which the Jamaicans call pimiento), which is packed in jars and can be used for decorating dishes such as paella. Its major uses, however, are in stuffing olives and the production of paprika. A similar pepper is the Hungarian sweet chilli, which is elongated in shape but fairly thick, crimson in color, and sweet, with a flavor quite like that of the pimento.

Cubanelle peppers (also called *chawa*) are also sweet and have more taste than bell peppers. They are relatively long (about 4 inches), tapered, and range in color from pale yellow to light green; in other words, they have the characteristics of the banana or Hungarian wax peppers, including just a touch of heat. Of the sweet peppers, which are all natives of the Americas, bell peppers are the most popular in the United States and are extensively grown in California and Mexico as well as in the Mediterranean countries, Hungary, and the Netherlands.

Holland peppers, grown hydroponically in the Netherlands for the Dutch export trade in specialty produce, come in all of the bell pepper's many colors and act as expensive substitutes. In addition, the "sweet purple pepper" is cultivated by the Dutch. Sweet peppers are a good source of vitamin C, and those that tend toward red in color are rich in beta-carotene.

Common names and synonyms: Bell pepper, *chawa, chile pimiento, chilli pimiento,* cubanelle pepper, green bell pepper, green pepper, Holland pepper, Hungarian sweet chilli, mango (pepper), Mexi-Bell, pimento, pimiento, *pimiento dulce, pimiento morrón,* red bell pepper, sweet purple pepper.

See in addition: "Chilli Peppers," Part II, Section C, Chapter 4.

SWEET POTATO (*see also* **BONIATO**) – Not to be confused with the potato of the genus *Solanum,* nor with the yam of the genus *Dioscorea,* the sweet potato (*Ipomoea batatas*), with the Caribbean Indian name *batata,* is a member of the morning-glory family and a native of tropical America (probably western South America but possibly also southern Mexico and Central America). It was cultivated in Peru some 5,000 years ago for its sweet and starchy tubers, while at the same time there were many other wild *Ipomoea* species whose tubers and leaves constituted gathered

foods for other Native Americans in North, Central, and South America.

But the sweet potato did not confine its range to the Western Hemisphere. Rather, it wandered far and mysteriously – reaching Australia, New Zealand, and Polynesia long before (about 1,500 years before) the Europeans stepped ashore in the New World. By the time Christopher Columbus arrived, sweet potato cultivation had spread over much of the Americas and certainly across the Caribbean, and sweet potatoes were among the items he carried back to Spain at the end of his first voyage. A few years later, Hernando Cortés reintroduced sweet potatoes in Spain, and in 1564 John Hawkins is said to have taken the tubers from the Caribbean to England. Unlike the potato, which took a while to catch on, the sweet potato was received enthusiastically from the beginning by Europeans, who appreciated its sweet taste and were titillated by the reputation it quickly acquired as an aphrodisiac.

From the New World, sweet potatoes traveled on the Manila galleons of Spain to the Far East, while the Portuguese also spread the plant about as they tended their empires in Africa and the East Indies. The sweet potato was a staple for many in colonial America, including those soldiers in the War for Independence against Great Britain. Today, sweet potatoes are widely cultivated in the world's tropics and subtropics, especially in Latin America, the southern United States, Southeast and East Asia, and Oceania.

Sweet potatoes come in moist- and dry- (or mealy-) fleshed forms. The moist-fleshed variety is the one often (and wrongly) called a yam. Most people in the United States eat sweet potatoes only on the Thanksgiving and Christmas holidays, which means that save for these special occasions, they are depriving themselves of one of the most nutritious of the world's foods. Sweet potatoes are an excellent source of vitamin A, the B-vitamins, and vitamin C. They can be boiled, baked, and fried – indeed, they are used in the same ways as white potatoes, which includes starring in potato salad. Sweet potatoes come canned and frozen as well as fresh, but those that are canned and frozen suffer a substantial loss of nutrients.

Common names and synonyms: Batata, batata dulce, camote, common potato (archaic), *kumara,* wild sweet potato.

See in addition: "Sweet Potatoes and Yams," Part II, Section B, Chapter 5.

SWEET-SHOOT – Found in Southeast Asia, the sweet-shoot (*Sauropus androgynus*) has leaves that are used to flavor soups and stews. They are also consumed as a vegetable, act as a green dye in pastries, and as an ingredient in the alcoholic beverage "brem bali." The fruits of the plant are made into sweetmeats.

Common names and synonyms: Chekkurmanis, katook, katuk, sweet-leaf bush.

SWEETSOP - The sweetsop is a tropical American tree (*Annona squamosa* - sometimes called the "sugar apple tree") with a sweet, edible, yellowish green fruit about the size of a baseball (often called a "sugar apple"). The tree can reach upwards of 20 feet in height and (like its relative the papaw) belongs to the custard-apple family - so called because the taste of their fruits resembles that of custard. Although widely cultivated in warm regions, where it is used for making jellies and preserves, the sweetsop is quite perishable and thus is far from commonplace in northern markets.

Common names and synonyms: Anon, custard apple, sugar apple (tree).

Sweet wood - *see* **CINNAMON AND CASSIA**

SWISS CHARD (*see also* **BEET**) - Also called chard, "silver beet," and "spinach beet," Swiss chard (*Beta vulgaris* var. *cicla*) is a kind of beet, native to the shores of the Mediterranean (it may have originated in Sicily), that is grown for its greens rather than its roots. The leaves of both red (the leaf stalks and veins are red) and green Swiss chard are large and fleshy and are used in salads or prepared like spinach. The thick white or, occasionally, red stalks that can reach between 1 and 2 feet in length not only may be eaten but, in some countries of Europe, are viewed as the best part of the plant and a very satisfactory asparagus substitute. The small root, however, is not edible. Like other greens, Swiss chard is high in vitamin C, calcium, and especially vitamin A.

Common names and synonyms: Chard, green chard, green Swiss chard, leaf beet, red chard, red Swiss chard, seakale beet, silver beet, spinach beet, white beet.

Swiss-cheese plant - *see* **MONSTERA**

SWORD BEAN (*see also* **BEANS, JACKBEAN**) - Sometimes called the "wonder bean" or "Pearson bean" in the United States, and the "Babricorn bean" in the West Indies, the sword bean (*Canavalia gladiata*) is a native of tropical Asia and Africa but is now cultivated throughout the tropical world. It is very similar to the jackbean - so similar, in fact, that a common ancestor is suspected. The young pods and seeds are eaten as a cooked vegetable, and the seeds are also used in dried form.

Common names and synonyms: Babricorn bean, Pearson bean, wonder bean.

See in addition: "Beans, Peas, and Lentils," Part II, Section C, Chapter 3.

Sword fern - *see* **GIANT HOLLY FERN**

Sylvaner - *see* **SILVANER**

SYRAH (*see also* **GRAPES**) - Not to be confused with Petite Sirah, the Syrah (*Vitis vinifera*) is a grape with a pepper-like taste that has long been grown in the northern Rhône valley of France and more recently in Australia (where the popular wine it yields is called "Shiraz"). In California, Syrah is used to make spicy red wines.

Common names and synonyms: Shiraz.

See in addition: "Wine," Part III, Chapter 13.

Szechwan pepper(corn) - *see* **SICHUAN PEPPERCORN**

Common names and synonyms: Anise-pepper, fagara, prickly ash tree.

See also: "Spices and Flavorings," Part II, Section F, Chapter 1.

TABASCO PEPPER (*see also* **CHILLI PEPPERS**) - In the aftermath of the American Civil War, a wild pepper from Mexico (presumably from the state of Tabasco) was brought to Avery Island, Louisiana, where it was put under cultivation to make the now-famous McIlhenny "Tabasco" brand sauce. This bright orange to red and very pungent variety of *Capsicum frutescens* (the species name means "brushy") is now grown commercially in Central America as well. In addition to serving as the base of "Tabasco" sauce, the dried tabasco goes well in stir-fries and makes a lively salsa.

See in addition: "Chilli Peppers," Part II, Section C, Chapter 4.

TACOUTTA - Known also as "wing sesame," tacoutta (*Sesamum alatum*) is a West African tree that yields oil-rich seeds. The oil is used in cooking, and the seeds are often ground into a flour.

Common names and synonyms: Wing sesame.

Tacu - *see* **ALGARROBO**

TAGAL MANGROVE - An evergreen tree of East Africa and South and Southeast Asia, the tagal mangrove (*Ceriops tagal*) provides a bark that has a multitude of uses in folk remedies. It also has a leathery, berry-like fruit that is edible if not very tasty.

Tahitian chestnut - *see* **POLYNESIAN CHESTNUT**

Tahiti apple - *see* **MALAY APPLE**

Tahiti lime - *see* **LIME**

Tahiti orange - *see* **OTAHEITE ORANGE**

TAILED PEPPER - Also called the "Java pepper" as well as "cubeb," the tailed pepper (*Piper cubeba*) is a native of the Indonesian islands, where it is grown mostly in Java. The "pepper" in question is a brownish berry that grows on a tree-like vine. The berry was a commodity in the early spice trade and became popular in the West as both a medicine and a spice (it substituted for the peppercorn) until about 1600. That popularity, however, began to dissipate as real peppercorns became more available, and today the tailed pepper is once more confined to its native habitat. A member of the same genus as the common black and white peppercorns, the tailed pepper does not have the same taste, but rather one more like that of allspice.

Common names and synonyms: Cubeb, Java pepper.

Taioba - *see* **COCOYAM**

Takenoko - *see* **BAMBOO SHOOT(S)**

TALINUM - One of the edible plants of the genus *Talinum* is the fameflower (*T. aurantiacum*), the roots of which were cooked and eaten by Native Americans in southwestern North America. Another (*T. triangulare*) is called both fameflower and waterleaf; although probably a tropical American native, it is also cultivated in tropical Asia and Africa. Its other common names, such as "Ceylon spinach" or "Philippine spinach," correctly suggest that the plant is grown for its leaves, which sometimes are cooked to be eaten alone as a vegetable but more frequently are added to soups and stews.

Common names and synonyms: Ceylon spinach, fameflower, Philippine spinach, waterleaf.

Tallon - *see* **CHAYOTE**

Tallote - *see* **CHAYOTE**

Tallow tree - *see* **CHINESE TALLOW TREE**

TALLOW WOOD PLUM - Also known as "false sandalwood," "seaside plum," and - somewhat contradictorily - "mountain plum," the tallow wood plum (*Ximenia americana*) is borne on a small, spiny, tropical tree or shrub. It grows in tropical and subtropical America but, despite its scientific name, seems to be a native of Africa. The "plums" in question are plumlike, edible, yellow to orange fruits, which are eaten both raw and cooked and sometimes pickled when unripe. Inside the fruit is a seed containing a nutlike kernel that is edible raw or roasted and also yields an oil sometimes used for cooking. The young leaves of this plant can be eaten as well, after cooking.

Common names and synonyms: False sandalwood, mountain plum, seaside plum.

Tamar - *see* **TAMARIND**

Tamar-hindi - *see* **TAMARIND**

TAMARILLO - Sometimes called the "tree tomato," the tamarillo (*Cyphomandra betacea*) is a member of the eggplant family. The fruit comes from an evergreen tree that was originally native to Peru or Brazil but has been grown commercially in Jamaica and is now cultivated mostly in New Zealand. The tamarillo is about the size of a small, oval-shaped tomato - and, in fact, is a very distant subtropical relative of the tomato - with a skin color ranging from yellowish to purple to crimson. Within the tough peel, which is not eaten, is an orange flesh and rows of purple seeds. The fruits, which tend to be sour, are generally stewed, although they can be eaten raw. The tamarillo tree is noted for the attractive fragrance of its foliage and flowers, and its fruit contains high amounts of vitamins A and C.

Common names and synonyms: Tomate de arbol, tree tomato.

TAMARIND - The tamarind, a basic ingredient in Worcestershire sauce, has a Latin name (*Tamarindus indica*) that certainly suggests an Indian origin, but East Africa also claims this plant. Its name, which comes from the Arabic *tamar-hindi,* means "Indian date." The tamarind has been cultivated since ancient times in India, where it retains a place in formal Hindu ceremonies. It must have reached Europe sometime before the Spaniards moved into the Americas, because they carried the plant to the West Indies and Mexico.

The tamarind is classified as a spice and looks like a fruit but is actually a "bean" that grows on a tree. Tamarinds can be acquired fresh, dried, and in concentrated and block form. Their sticky black pulp has a sour, acidic taste, is used in curries and chutneys, and is made into tamarind paste, which is much appreciated in the dishes of India. In addition, the flowers and leaves of the plant are eaten in salads, and the fruit pulp is sometimes made into a sherbet. The tamarind has a prominent place in many Caribbean and South American recipes as well.

Common names and synonyms: Indian date, *tamar, tamar-hindi.*

Tampala - *see* **CHINESE AMARANTH**

Tanaka - *see* **LOQUAT**

TANDOORI - Also called "ivy gourd," the tandoori (*Trichosanthes dioica*) seems to be native to South Asia. These vegetables look like miniature light or dark green cucumbers and are used in curries.

Common names and synonyms: Ivy gourd, pointed gourd, tindola, tindoori.

Tangelo - *see* **MANDARIN ORANGE, ORANGE**

Tangerine - *see* **MANDARIN ORANGE, ORANGE**

Tango - *see* **LETTUCE**

TANGOR (*see also* **CITRUS FRUITS**) - The most important American tangor is the "Temple" orange, which is a cross between the Mandarin orange (*Citrus reticulata*) and the sweet orange (*C. sinensis*). Tangors have segments that separate more easily than those of sweet oranges, which makes them an important hybrid.

Common names and synonyms: Temple orange.

Tania - *see* **MALANGA**

Tanjong tree - *see* **MIMUSOPS**

Tannia - *see* **MALANGA**

Tansey - *see* **TANSY**

TANSY - A wild-growing herb native to Europe, tansy (*Tanacetum vulgare*) has small, yellow flowers and very green, aromatic leaves with a bitter taste. Nonetheless, the leaves (always used fresh) can give a pleasant flavor to desserts and in the past were much used in confections. Tansy is also added sparingly to salads, omelettes, and ground meats.

Common names and synonyms: Bitter button(s), cow bitter(s), golden button(s), mugwort, tansey.

TANSY MUSTARD - Also called "mountain tansy mustard," this plant (*Descurainia pinnata*), a member of the mustard family, is found throughout the desert Southwest of the United States. It has bright yellow flowers and long, slender, seed-containing pods. Native Americans employed the seeds for making "pinole," a ground meal. Another species, *D. richardsonii,* was similarly used (and is also called "tansy mustard"); in addition, its leaves served Native Americans as a vegetable.

Common names and synonyms: Mountain tansy mustard.

Tansy ragwort - *see* **RAGWEED**

Tapèra - *see* **CAPER(S)**

TAPEREBÁ - Also known as cajá, taperebá (*Spondias lutea*) is a distant relative of cashews and pistachios and a very popular fruit in the Brazilian northeast. The pulp is generally sour, but it is readily turned into a sweetened juice of excellent flavor.

Common names and synonyms: Cajá.

Tapioca-plant - *see* **MANIOC**

Tara - *see* **TARO**

Tare vetch - *see* **VETCH**

TARO (*see also* **CALLALOO, COCOYAM, MALANGA**) - A tropical root, taro (*Colocasia esculenta* or *Colocasia antiquorum*) belongs to the arum family. It is a shaggy, large, brown-colored tuber that has a number of smaller (or side) tubers. The flesh is white and very starchy, with a nutty flavor, and is used much like that of potatoes. The origin of the plant was probably in South Asia, but it reached Egypt about 2,000 years ago. From there, taro was introduced into Europe, and the Spaniards carried it to the New World, and it probably reached West Africa from there. Meanwhile, taro had spread outward from India to the Pacific, and consequently this plant has long served as a common staple throughout much of Asia and the islands of the Pacific as well as in Africa and parts of the Americas. In Hawaii, taro is made into *poi,* a sticky, paste-like substance that has a lengthy tradition of use. In the West Indies, taro is known as "dasheen" or "eddo." Apparently, "dasheen" is a corruption of *de chine* ("from China") - the name deriving from the belief that the plant was imported from China into the West Indies to feed slaves. Taro remains important in many Chinese dishes, and in the West Indies taro leaves are called "callaloo." Given taro's plethora of names and geographic range, it is little wonder that it is frequently confused with malanga - and even with manioc. The so-called Egyptian taro (*C. antiquorum*), which is also apparently native to India, is regarded as inferior to other taro varieties.

Common names and synonyms: Callaloo, cocoyam, dasheen, eddo, eddoe, eddy root, Egyptian taro, elephant's-ear, *poi,* swamp taro, tara, tarro, tarrow, true taro.

See in addition: "Taro," Part II, Section B, Chapter 6.

Taro de chine - *see* **COCOYAM**

TARRAGON - French tarragon (*Artemisia dracunculus*) and Russian tarragon (*A. dracunculoides*) are two closely related forms of the same herb. Native to western Asia, tarragon reached Europe with Arab traders. The Arabs seem to have been the first to use the herb for cooking (in the thirteenth century), and by the fifteenth century it was in common use throughout Europe. Tarragon's scientific name, *dracunculus,* means "little dragon," and apparently the herb was so called because in the Middle Ages it was thought that tarragon was an antidote for the bites of poisonous snakes and insects. Like anise - and fennel, for that matter - tarragon has a licorice flavor; the French variety (now called "true tarragon") possesses the more delicate taste, whereas the Russian type is more pungent and bitter. In the West, most people prefer French tarragon, which makes a great contribution to flavoring vinegars, salad dressings, and cooked vegetables. The French use the herb to flavor numerous meat, egg, and fish dishes as well, not to mention classic sauces such as béarnaise.

Common names and synonyms: French tarragon, Russian tarragon, true tarragon.

See also: "Spices and Flavorings," Part II, Section F, Chapter 1.

Tarro - *see* **TARO**

Tarrow - *see* **TARO**

Tartar cherry - *see* **CORNUS**

Tarvi - *see* **ANDEAN LUPIN**

TAWA BERRY - Native to New Zealand, the fruits and seeds of the evergreen tree *Beilschmiedia tawa* (much used for timber) are among the many "bush foods" that have long sustained the Maori.

TEA - Tea (*Camellia sinensis*) - the most commonly consumed drink in the world after water - is an ancient beverage that was enjoyed in China for at least 1,600 years before Europeans ever tasted it (Chinese legend would have it almost 4,500 years). But it was only about 1,000 years ago, during the Song dynasty, that tea drinking started to become widespread and the government began to supervise the production of tea, regulate its trade, and collect tea taxes. Buddhist monks, who were not permitted alcohol and needed stimulation to stay awake during meditation, are given much credit for helping to popularize the beverage, as well as for carrying tea culture to Korea and Japan.

The Portuguese reached the South China coast in 1514 and become the first Europeans to gain the right to trade with China and the first to drink tea. They were also the first to introduce tea in Europe, and in the following century tea became one of the prizes sought in the three-way tug-of-war between the Portuguese, Dutch, and English for control of the China trade.

Tea - along with coffee and cacao - caught on in Europe during the seventeenth century, which in turn increased demand for slave-grown sugar to sweeten the new beverages. In London, "coffee-houses" that served these beverages began to multiply, and some – such as that owned by Edward Lloyd, which served a specialized clientele (in this case, individuals concerned with maritime shipping and marine insurance) – blossomed into other businesses like Lloyd's of London. Others, such as "Tom's Coffee House," opened by Thomas Twining, became major tea importers.

Tea was a staple of the English colonists in North America and, because of a British tax, became one more source of friction between the thirteen colonies and Parliament, which ultimately resulted in the Boston Tea Party – one in a succession of steps that seem to have led inexorably to the American Revolution.

It was only in the nineteenth century that Europeans discovered the secrets of tea cultivation, thus dispelling an ignorance that until then had meant monopoly for China. It was during the first half of that century that the British established the great plantations of Assam and Ceylon in India, and the Dutch created tea plantations in their East Indian colonies. But China nonetheless continued to dominate the markets of the world, and Britain continued to buy huge amounts of Chinese tea, even though, as a rule, the tea had to be paid for in specie. The stubborn insistence by the Chinese that they needed nothing from the West but precious metals had always been a major irritant to the English, who now saw opium (grown in British India and smuggled into China) as a solution to the trade imbalance. The Chinese government became increasingly outraged at the wholesale addiction of its people, and its attempt to stop the traffic triggered the Opium Wars (1840–2), during which Britain triumphed militarily and effectively "opened" China to the trade of the world while wrangling huge territorial and trade concessions for itself.

The half century or so following the Opium Wars saw much competition in the China trade, and, with a Western public convinced that the fresher the tea the better, speed in transport became critical. For a few romantic decades, that speed was supplied by the famous clipper ships, which could rush tea from China to London or New York in 90 to 120 days instead of the earlier 6 to 9 months – effectively cutting the sailing time in half.

Tea reached the height of its popularity in the 1880s, but subsequent events served to sustain demand for the beverage. One was the introduction of iced tea to a thirsty crowd at the St. Louis World's Fair of 1904, which, although hardly constituting the invention of the drink (as has been claimed), certainly did help to popularize it. Another such event was the inadvertent invention of the "tea bag" by Thomas Sullivan in 1908. Sullivan was a tea merchant who began distributing his samples in

hand-sewn silk bags rather than in tin boxes and was suddenly swamped with orders by customers who had discovered that they could brew the tea right in the bag.

It has been said that there are more kinds of tea in China than there are wines in France. To this it might be added that the classification of teas is every bit as complicated as that of wines. All tea starts as "green," and it must be rolled, withered, fired, and dried to deactivate an enzyme present in the leaves. If, however, the rolled and cut leaves are permitted to stand (and ferment) for one to three hours before heating, the tea becomes "black." If the leaves are semifermented, the tea is called "Oolong." Tea grading is by leaf size. Young, soft shoots make the best tea, and thus only the bud and the top leaves are plucked from the bush. With black tea, the leaf bud is called "pekoe tip"; the youngest fully opened leaf is "orange pekoe"; the next leaf is "pekoe," then "pekoe souchong"; and finally there is "souchong" – the largest leaves that are used. The corresponding green tea grades are "twanky" for the bud, then "gunpowder," "imperial," "young hyson," and "hyson." The very small pieces, called "dust," generally go into tea bags.

The most famous of China's black teas is Keemun (or Keemum), known for its winelike quality. Darjeeling tea, from the foothills of the Himalayas, is one of India's contributions to the ranks of rare and prestigious black teas. Assam tea (from the same region but a lower elevation) is another. The Ceylon teas, from Sri Lanka, run the gamut – from the mild Flowery Orange Pekoe to the full-bodied Broken Orange Pekoe Fannings. The highest-grade Oolongs and the smoky Lapsung Souchongs come mostly from Taiwan.

In truth, however, most commercial teas are blends of several of these individual teas. Green teas are consumed mostly in Japan and some of the Arab countries, whereas black teas constitute the overwhelming bulk of the tea drunk in the West.

Common names and synonyms: Assam, black tea, Broken Orange Pekoe Fannings, *ch'a,* Darjeeling, dust, Flowery Orange Pekoe, green tea, gunpowder, hyson, iced tea, imperial, Keemum, Keemun, Lapsung Souchong, leaf pekoe, Oolong, orange pekoe, pekoe souchong, pekoe tip, *sencha,* souchong, *tsocha,* twanky, women's-tobacco, young hyson.

See also: "Tea," Part III, Chapter 11.

Teaberry – *see* **WINTERGREEN**

Tear-grass – *see* **JOB'S-TEARS**

Tea-tree oil – *see* **CAJEPUT**

TECUITLATL – A blue-green algae (*Spirulina geitleri*), *tecuitlatl* grew profusely in pre-Hispanic times on the surface of Lake Texcoco and was harvested and eaten by the residents of Tenochtitlan, the island capital of the Aztec empire. The Indians used fine nets to gather it, then spread it out to dry. After a few days, they cut it into loaves, which kept for up to a year. The Spanish naturalist Francisco Hernández described *tecuitlatl* as being like cheese "with a certain muddy smell." The Indians ate it on tortillas, often spiced with tomato-and-chilli sauce.

Tecuitlatl is 70 percent protein, with a blend of amino acids similar to that in a chicken egg, and is also an excellent source of the B-vitamin complex. Some scholars have speculated that the profuse growth of *tecuitlatl* indicates that the Mexicans dumped raw sewage into Lake Texcoco, and consequently would have suffered widespread gastrointestinal disease. Other sources, however, relate that wastes from the island city were carried by canoe to fertilize the raised-field *chinampas* of Lake Chalco-Xochimilco. Following the Spanish conquest, the lakes of the central valley were drained and *tecuitlatl* gradually declined. The algae was recently rediscovered on the shores of Lake Chad in central West Africa, where it was called *dihe* and was harvested and eaten in much the same manner as in pre-Hispanic Mexico.

Common names and synonyms: Dihe, dihé, douhé, tecuitatl.

See also: "Algae," Part II, Section C, Chapter 1.

TEF – Tef (*Eragrostis tef = E. abyssinica*), a plant native to Ethiopia, is an ancient grain that was cultivated long before recorded history. It is the basic ingredient in *injera,* the popular unleavened bread that is a major component of Ethiopian cuisine. *Injera* is a large, round, somewhat sour-tasting, spongy, flat bread from which pieces are torn to pick up mouthfuls of the stews that are generally the main course of the meal.

Both the bread and the grains from which it is made are cherished. But tef is costly, and thus only those with sufficient means can enjoy the bread regularly. Tef is also an important ingredient in *kita* (a sweet bread), in *muk* (a nutritious gruel), and in a number of homemade beverages. In addition, it can serve as a thickener for all sorts of foods. Nutritionally, tef is a superior cereal. It is a good source of protein and is rich in lysine, iron, calcium, potassium, and phosphorus; moreover, because the entire kernel is consumed, none of the important nutrients are lost. Free of gluten, tef provides an attractive alternative for persons allergic to wheat.

Despite its immense popularity in Ethiopia, *Eragrostis tef* has been a neglected crop in most other parts of the world. Exceptions are Yemen, Kenya, Malawi, and India, where it has been included in the traditional diet, and Australia and South Africa, where it has been cultivated as animal fodder. This is likely to change, however, as more and more people around the globe (particularly in Western cultures) come in contact with tef and enjoy it either as an exotic ethnic food or as a nutritious health food, or both. Because the plant is ideally suited to grow in arid regions and under conditions in which many other plants fail, it is not surprising that other countries, including the United States, have started production, albeit on a small scale.

Common names and synonyms: Annual bunch grass, lovegrass, t'ef, teff, toff, warm-season annual bunch grass.

T'ef – *see* **TEF**

Teff – *see* **TEF**

Tellicherry (pepper) – *see* **PEPPER(CORNS)**

Temple orange – *see* **TANGOR**

TEMPRANILLO (*see also* **GRAPES**) – A red-wine grape grown mostly in Spain, the Tempranillo (*Vitis vinifera*) is the dominant grape in the Spanish wine regions of Rioja, Navarra, Toro, and Ribera del Duero.

See in addition: "Wine," Part III, Chapter 13.

Ten-months-yam – *see* **WATER YAM**

TEPARY BEAN (*see also* **BEANS**) – An annual twining bean, the tepary bean (*Phaseolus acutifolius*) is a native of the southwestern United States and Mexico. It has been cultivated since ancient times by Native Americans (especially the Papagos, who are known as the "bean people") and is now also grown by white farmers because of its adaptability to arid conditions. In the past, the green, immature pods were sometimes eaten raw or cooked as a vegetable, but the bean's main food use was as dried seeds that were ground or parched.

See in addition: "Beans, Peas, and Lentils," Part II, Section C, Chapter 3.

TEPÍN CHILLIES AND RELATIVES (*see also* **CHILLI PEPPERS**) – Present in the archaeological record of Mexico from some 8,000 years ago, the wild varieties of the *Tepín* chilli (*Capsicum annuum*) still exist in a region extending from the southern United States, through the West Indies and Central America, to northern South America, and they are still collected and sold in the markets of Central America, where they are called *chilli pequín*. These are tiny (about a quarter of an inch in diameter), orange-red, oval-shaped peppers, which pack a huge punch when used in salsas, soups, and other cooked dishes.

Chilli pequín is also the name of a cultivated pepper that looks like the wild variety but is somewhat elongated. A close relative is the Macho pepper, which is cultivated and, as the name implies, is extremely hot – indeed, it is a close second to the fiery Scotch Bonnet and Habanero in pungency. Machos are tiny like the *pequín,* are both green and red, are generally used fresh, and are grown almost exclusively in Mexico. Another type of *pequín* is the *tuxtla,* an orangish, pointed chilli that is slightly larger and slightly less hot than its fiery relatives. Collectively, these are also known as "bird peppers" because birds eat the fruits.

Common names and synonyms: Bird pepper, chilli pequeño, *chilli pequín,* Macho pepper, *pequín,* Tepín pepper, *tuxtla.*

See in addition: "Chilli Peppers," Part II, Section C, Chapter 4.

Teposote - *see* MORMON TEA
Terong - *see* EGGPLANT
Teufelsdreck - *see* ASAFETIDA
Thai chilli (pepper) - *see* ASIAN CHILLIES
Thales - *see* LOQUAT
Thick-shell shagbark - *see* HICKORY
Thimbleberry - *see* RASPBERRY, SALMONBERRY
Thin-shell shagbark - *see* HICKORY

THISTLE - There are many species of thistle (genus *Cirsium*) as well as plants of the genera *Carduus* and *Onorpordum*, some of which are natives of the New and others of the Old World. However, today, as the result of humans transporting them about, they are found mixed together all around the globe. Native Americans ate the boiled or roasted roots of many different kinds of these prickly plants, along with the stems, which were peeled and cooked like greens. Other species have been consumed in Asia and Europe since the days of the hunter-gatherers. The dried flowers are employed to curdle milk, and the seeds can be dried and roasted or ground into meal.

THOMPSON SEEDLESS (GRAPE) (*see also* GRAPES) - Originally a wine grape from Turkey called the "Sultana," and further named for William Thompson, the first person to grow Sultana grapes in California around the turn of the twentieth century, the Thompson Seedless (*Vitis vinifera*) has been giving ground to the French Colombard and Chenin Blanc grapes since 1983 and now is mostly a table grape. In the past, however, it was an important grape in the California wine industry.
Common names and synonyms: Sultana (grape).
See in addition: "Wine," Part III, Chapter 13.

THORNLESS RUKAM - The thornless rukam (*Flacourtia inermis*) is easier to work with than most trees of the genus *Flacourtia*, which are, as a rule, very thorny. It is a native of Malaysia (and perhaps also of India) that produces bright red fruits about the size of cherries. Although there are sweet varieties, most are sour and are used to make pies, jams, and chutneys.
Common names and synonyms: Lovi-lovi.

THYME - Thyme, a strongly flavored herb that comes in many varieties, has leaves that are used both fresh and dried. The three most important kinds of thyme are *Thymus vulgaris, T. × citriodorus,* and *T. serpyllum*. The first - common or garden thyme - grows as a bush and has tiny, dark green leaves. The second - lemon thyme - has a citrus-like aroma and flavor and spreads out by growing horizontally. The third kind - creeping thyme, also called *serpolet* - is a wild French thyme that flavors Provençal dishes.

Thyme is a Mediterranean plant that, like so many herbs, was put to use medicinally before it was employed for culinary purposes. The name comes from the Greek "to make a burnt offering," meaning presumably that the spice was burned as

a fumigant. But oil of thyme has been used since antiquity for gargles and mouthwashes as well. In culinary usage, thyme is one of the requisite herbs for a bouquet garni, and it joins sage in poultry stuffings and basil and oregano in tomato sauces. Thyme is an important ingredient in the Creole cookery of Louisiana as well as in the liqueur Benedictine.
Common names and synonyms: Common thyme, European wild thyme, French thyme, garden thyme, lemon thyme, *serpolet.*
See also: "Spices and Flavorings," Part II, Section F, Chapter 1.

Ti - *see* CABBAGE TREE
Tickbean - *see* FAVA BEAN
Tien-tsin (chilli pepper) - *see* ASIAN CHILLIES
Tientsin - *see* CHINESE CABBAGE

TIGER LILY - Native to East Asia, but now grown in gardens throughout the world for its black-spotted, reddish-orange flowers, the tiger lily (*Lilium tigrinum*) also has a starchy bulb that resembles a garlic bulb, cloves and all. Tiger lily bulbs are sold in both fresh and dried form and are added to simmered and stir-fried dishes.

Tigernut - *see* CHUFA
Ti leaf - *see* CABBAGE TREE
Til (seed) - *see* SESAME
Tindola - *see* TANDOORI
Tindoori - *see* TANDOORI
Tipo - *see* MINTHOSTACHYS
Tipsin - *see* BREADROOT
Tlilxochitl - *see* VANILLA
Toadback - *see* CALABAZA (SQUASH)

TOBACCO - An American herb, tobacco is a plant of the genus *Nicotiana,* now cultivated worldwide. Its leaves are dried and prepared for smoking, chewing, and "snuffing." Tobacco was used by the Indians of the Antilles when Christopher Columbus first reached them, and the word "tobacco" is probably from the Taino meaning a "roll of (tobacco) leaves." The name for the genus is in honor of Jean Nicot, who introduced tobacco plants at the French royal court. Tobacco use speeds up the metabolic processes and thus helps to hold down a person's weight, although at a considerable risk to health.

Tobacco-root - *see* VALERIAN
Toddy palm - *see* WINE PALM
Toff - *see* TEF
Togarashi (chilli pepper) - *see* ASIAN CHILLIES
To-kumquat - *see* CALAMONDIN
Tomate - *see* TOMATO
Tomate de arbol - *see* TAMARILLO
Tomate de bolsa - *see* TOMATILLO
Tomate de cascara - *see* TOMATILLO
Tomate verde - *see* TOMATILLO

TOMATILLO - A member of the tomato family, the tomatillo (*Physalis ixocarpa*) is a large berry (about the size of a cherry tomato) native to Mexico and used in a number of Mexican dishes including *salsa verde* and guacamole. Also called the "husk tomato," the tomatillo (which means "little tomato" in Spanish) has a compact, green pulp covered by a dry, parchment-like skin that is easily removed. The tomatillo has been cultivated in Mexico for thousands of years. The Aztecs used the term *tomatl* (meaning something round and plump) for several fruits, including a number of tomatoes of the Solanaceae family, which today are regarded as true tomatoes. But it was the tomatillo that was preferred, even after the tomato (*Lycopersicon esculentum*) – a South American native – reached Mexico to fit nicely into a system of cultivation already long established for *Physalis ixocarpa*. Indeed, even today in the Mexican highlands, the tomatillo is preferred for cooking, but it has only recently traveled out of Mexico to find a place in the cuisines of other cultures. Tomatillos can be grown in most gardens and can be purchased fresh or canned. Canned tomatillos work about as well in sauces as fresh ones. They are high in vitamins A and C.

Common names and synonyms: Chinese lantern, *fresadilla,* green tomato, husk tomato, jamberry, Mexican green tomato, Mexican husk tomato, *miltomate, tomate de bolsa, tomate de cascara, tomatillo enteros,* tomatillo ground cherry, *tomatitos verdes, tomatl, tomatoe verde.*

Tomatitos verdes – *see* **TOMATILLO**
Tomatl – *see* **TOMATILLO, TOMATO**

TOMATO – The tomato (*Lycopersicon esculentum*) is an American plant with an American name. In Nahuatl, the language of the Aztecs, *tomatl* indicates something round and plump, and this fruit (rather than vegetable) was almost certainly domesticated in Mexico, even though the presence of its numerous wild relatives (consisting of at least seven species) in South America suggests that it originated there. Apparently, however, tomatoes were not much used in the Andes region.

Meanwhile, to the north in Mexico, the tomatillo or "husk tomato" of the genus *Physalis,* which is also round and plump, was being cultivated, and as a consequence, there was already a cultivation tradition into which the newest round and plump fruit was fitted after its arrival. How the tomato made the voyage from South America to Mexico is not known with certainty, but it is probable that the seeds of wild tomatoes were carried by birds and that tomatoes began their career in Mexico as weeds in tomatillo fields. By the time Hernando Cortés reached Mexico in 1519, careful cultivation had brought forth a number of tomato varieties that were utilized for sauces, mixed with chillies, and eaten with beans along with numerous other dishes.

Before the sixteenth century was out, the tomato had been introduced in Europe, where its reception was far from enthusiastic. In part, this was because no one knew what it was or what to do with it, and nomenclature was such that no one could be certain that they were talking about the same plant. The sudden introduction of several American foods had left Europeans a bit confused about where all of these new items were coming from. As a rule, new foods had arrived from across the Mediterranean with the Moors. Thus, in a number of languages, the tomato became a *pomi di mori* ("apple of the Moors") or some variation thereof. In addition, there arose corruptions, such as the French *pomme d'amour* ("love apple") – although the tomato had no reputation as an aphrodisiac – and the Italian *pomodoro* ("golden apple"), which has wrongly been taken by some as an indication that the first tomatoes in Europe were of an orangish or yellowish variety. The Spanish, who continued to call the tomato a *tomate,* readily incorporated it into their diets and introduced it as well in their territories in Italy, where it was destined to make its largest impact.

However, tomatoes caught on more slowly elsewhere, probably in part because of the rank smell of the plant, in part because it was known to be a relative of "deadly nightshade," and partly because the tomato was adapted to warm climates, and new varieties were needed for northern climates. Thus, in Great Britain and the United States (even though Thomas Jefferson had grown tomatoes), the acceptance of the tomato was a late-nineteenth-century or even twentieth-century phenomenon. This was also the case in China and much of the East, even though tomatoes were introduced in Asia by the Spaniards and the Portuguese as early as the sixteenth century.

Tomatoes come in numerous varieties, ranging from bite-sized cherry tomatoes (used in salads and as appetizers); to egg-shaped plum tomatoes, also called Italian or Roma tomatoes (good for sauces, stews, and other cooked dishes); to round tomatoes (such as the "beefsteak" or "sunny") that are sliced and diced or left whole for everything from sandwiches to salads to stewing. Tomatoes are red or yellow in color when ripe but are also breaded when green for frying. In the past, tomatoes were stored in cellars to ripen for winter use.

In the United States, California produces most of the tomatoes (about 85 percent) to be used for processing. These are field grown and mechanically picked and result in catsup, salsa, juice, and any of the other tomato products, such as tomato paste, puree, sauce, and soup. Tomatoes destined for the table, however, are still picked by hand, and increasingly, those grown in greenhouses in either soil or water (hydroponically) have become available for home consumption. In addition, tomatoes are sun-dried, just as Native Americans processed them for storage centuries ago. Ripe tomatoes contain large quantities of vitamin C and respectable amounts of beta-carotene.

Common names and synonyms: Beefsteak tomato, cherry tomato, Italian tomato, plum tomato, *pomi di mori, pomme d'amour, pomodoro,* Roma tomato, sunny tomato, *tomate, tomatl.*

See also: "Tomatoes," Part II, Section C, Chapter 9.

TONKA BEAN - Also called *cimaru,* which is the name of the mostly wild tropical American tree that it grows on, the tonka bean (*Dipteryx odorata*) has been cultivated to a limited extent in Venezuela and Trinidad. The bean is used mostly to flavor tobacco and in perfumery, but it is also employed to flavor liqueurs and to make artificial vanilla extracts.

Common names and synonyms: Cimaru.

TOOTHWORT (*see also* **COOLWORT**) - "Toothwort" is a common name for members of the genus *Dentaria.* These are wildflowers with edible tubers that are native to Europe, Asia, and eastern North America. In the latter region, the roots of *D. diphylla* (known as well as two-leaved toothwort, pepper-root, and crinkleroot) also served Native Americans as a spice. The roots have a horseradish-like flavor and are employed in salads and eaten raw like radishes. In addition, the leaves were eaten, both raw and cooked as a vegetable. This toothwort is not to be confused with a European plant, *Lathraea squamaria,* which is parasitic on hazel and beech trees.

Common names and synonyms: Crinkleroot, pepper-root, two-leaved toothwort.

Topee-tambu - *see* **GUINEA ARROWROOT**

Topiro - *see* **COCONA**

TORCH GINGER - A perennial herb of the East Indies that probably originated in southern Asia, torch ginger (*Phaeomeria magnifica*) has thick stems that can reach 15 feet in height and are topped with red or pink flower heads in the shape of cones, all of which gives the impression of a cluster of "torches." The plant is cultivated for its young shoots, which are used to flavor curries in Indonesia and Malaysia, and for its edible buds, which are often shredded as a garnish and added to soups and salads.

Common names and synonyms: Ginger bud, pink ginger bud.

Torfbeere - *see* **CLOUDBERRY**

Tornillo - *see* **MESQUITE**

Tossa jute - *see* **JEW'S-MALLOW**

Touch-me-not - *see* **JEWELWEED**

Tous-les-ois - *see* **ACHIRA**

TRAILING ARBUTUS - A plant of eastern North America, the trailing arbutus (*Epigaea repens*) spreads on the ground. Fragrant, waxy, pink flower clusters appear in the spring, and these were eaten raw by Native Americans.

Common names and synonyms: Gravek-plant, mayflower.

Trailing mahonia - *see* **BARBERRY**

Traminer - *see* **GEWÜRZTRAMINER**

Trapa - *see* **WATER CHESTNUT**

TREBBIANO (*see also* **GRAPES**) - Said to be the most widely planted of the white grapes in Italy, Trebbiano (*Vitis vinifera*) is used in the production of Italian white wines and is one of only two white grapes that can be used in making Chianti. Trebbiano is also blended into other wines of Italy.

See in addition: "Wine," Part III, Chapter 13.

Tree cactus - *see* **PITAHAYA**

Tree ear - *see* **CLOUD EAR, MUSHROOMS AND FUNGI**

TREE-FERN - The genus *Cyathea* encompasses a number of Australian and New Zealand tree-ferns with stems that yield a starch that has been consumed by aboriginal peoples for millennia. In New Zealand, one of these, the black tree-fern - also called the silver tree-fern - was heavily exploited by the Maori.

Common names and synonyms: Black-stemmed tree-fern, black tree-fern, sago fern, silver tree-fern.

Tree gourd - *see* **CALABASH**

Tree mushroom - *see* **OYSTER MUSHROOM, MUSHROOMS AND FUNGI**

Tree oyster - *see* **OYSTER MUSHROOM**

Tree tomato - *see* **TAMARILLO**

TRIFOLIATE ORANGE (*see also* **CITRUS FRUITS**) - A native of central and northern China, the trifoliate orange tree (*Poncirus trifoliata*) is planted for its rootstock, which is used in grafting *Citrus* species. The tree produces small, intensely bitter fruits that cannot be eaten directly, but their rinds are employed to flavor beverages and desserts.

Trifoliate yam - *see* **BITTER YAM**

TRILLIUM - There are a number of plants of the genus *Trillium* that have served as food in the past, although the roots of most species have generally been employed medicinally. The roots of *T. pendulum,* for example, are known as "birthroots" and were used by Native Americans as an aid in childbirth. But these peoples also cooked the young leaves of *T. grandiflorum* as a vegetable. In addition, the reddish berries of some *Trillium* species were consumed in northwestern Asia. The many species of *Trillium* have an incredible number of common names, among them "wake-robin," "Indian balm," and "squawroot."

Common names and synonyms: Birthroot, Indian balm, squawroot, wake-robin.

TRITICALE - Triticale is a hybrid grain (*Triticum secale*), the result of cross-breeding wheat (genus *Triticum*) and rye (genus *Secale*). Such a cross was first attempted in 1875 by a Swedish botanist in an effort to develop a grain that would combine the baking qualities and high yield of wheat with the durability and protein content of rye. The few seeds that did germinate, however, were sterile, and it was only in the late 1930s that a fertile cross was achieved. This engineering of a brand new species that is hardier and more nutritious than both of its parent strains became part of the stimulus for the "Green Revolution." Triticale combines the taste of rye with the nutrition of wheat and has a better balance of amino acids than either of the two. It can be purchased cracked, in flakes, and as whole berries, most usually in health-food stores. The grain has not yet proven as useful or important as had been anticipated, and although it is increasingly employed in the baking industry, most triticale is used as livestock feed. It is a good source of the B-vitamins, thiamine, and folacin.

See also: "Rye," Part II, Section A, Chapter 8; "Wheat," Part II, Section A, Chapter 10.

Tropical almond - *see* **MALABAR ALMOND**

Tropical cherry - *see* **CAPULIN**

TRUFFLE(S) (*see also* **MUSHROOMS AND FUNGI**) - A number of fleshy subterranean fungi of the genus *Tuber* are called truffles, which today, depending on the kind, can cost between $800 and $1,500 a pound, ranking them among the most expensive food items in the world, and certainly making them the world's most expensive vegetable. Truffles are also among the oldest vegetables in the historical record. Food historian Reay Tannahill reports that they were known to the Babylonians and the Romans and that truffles were secured from the Arabian Desert in ancient times, just as today some of the richest truffle mines known are located in the Kalahari Desert.

Truffles gained European attention in fourteenth-century France, where they had developed a reputation as an aphrodisiac. In the late fifteenth century, their popularity as a flavoring agent was on the rise and by the seventeenth century, they were known in England. The late eighteenth and nineteenth centuries saw truffles become something of a rage - with their desirability considerably enhanced by French gastronome Jean-Anthelme Brillat-Savarin's declaration in 1825 that without them there could be no truly gastronomic meal.

In France, the truffle of note (and the most famous variety) is the Périgord (*Tuber melanosporum*), a truffle that is black both inside and out, which Brillat-Savarin called a "black diamond." Another truffle - black on the outside but white on the inside - is the so-called cook's-truffle (*T. aestivum*). As the name implies, this fungus, found in the United Kingdom, is not as highly regarded. By contrast, the white truffle of the Italian Piedmont (*T. magnatum*) is a serious rival of the French Périgord, especially in the minds of the Italians. Spain, although not known for it, joins France and Italy as a major truffle producer, and in a given year any of the three countries may outproduce the other two.

"Mysterious" is a word often used in writings on truffles. Truffles vary in size from that of a walnut to that of a fist (belying the species name of the Piedmont truffle), are round shaped, and have a rough exterior. They live in clusters close to (and on) the roots of a host tree - especially the *truffier* or truffle oak - and, like mushrooms, they use spores to propagate. Truffles are gathered from October to late fall on the Continent (in the United Kingdom, the season is in late spring). Actually they are hunted, because they never break ground and thus must be smelled out, although a clue to their presence is that little else grows near the host tree - the truffles in providing their chosen tree with so much in the way of important nutrients from the soil discourage other growth. A sow, straining on a leash held by her owner, is a vivid portrait of a truffle-hunting team provided by art - the sow sniffing them out apparently because of a musky chemical exuded by truffles that mimics a sex hormone given off by hogs. Dogs (and other animals) are also used to hunt truffles but must be more rigorously trained for a task that the sow does happily.

The quarry is equally mysterious as a comestible. All truffles have a distinctive and powerful odor (something like garlic), which some find unpleasant and others think wonderful - and the Piedmont truffles have a garlicky taste. Yet somehow both aroma and taste transfer to whatever they are cooked with and enhance those foods in unbelievable fashion.

This quality helps to account for the cost of truffles. Another reason is scarcity. At the beginning of this century, the most costly truffles imported into the United States sold for upwards of $4 a pound - expensive in those days but nothing like the $1,000 or more charged today. This increase in cost reflects both the loss of forest lands and the over-harvesting that make truffle production today only about 10 percent of what it was a century ago. In 1978, France harvested its first commercially cultivated truffles, but such production was fraught with so many difficulties that planned cultivation on a large scale remains a dream, and truffle prices continue to rise.

Because of the nearly prohibitive price of truffles (as well as the intense flavor they impart), they are used sparingly, frequently grated raw over hot foods (creamy fettuccine, for example) and employed to enliven the taste of pâté de foie gras. Truffles are also available canned and in tubes as a paste.

Common names and synonyms: Black diamond, cook's-truffle, Périgord, Piedmont truffle, white truffle.

See in addition: "Fungi," Part II, Section C, Chapter 7.

TRUMPET TREE - Also known as "trumpetwood," the trumpet tree (*Cecropia peltata*) has large leaves with hollow stems. It is native to the Caribbean, where its young buds have served the people of the region as a cooked vegetable for millennia. The tree also produces a sweet, edible fruit.

Common names and synonyms: Trumpetwood.

Trumpetwood - *see* **TRUMPET TREE**

Tsocha - *see* **TEA**

Tsumamina - *see* **DAIKON**

Tuberroot - *see* **BUTTERFLY WEED**

Tucum - *see* **TUCUMA**

TUCUMA - *Astrocaryum* is a genus of chiefly Brazilian palm trees, many species of which are found in the Amazon region. Some, especially *A. tucuma*, produce fruits that yield an edible oil. The fruits are also eaten for their pulp, but the taste is reportedly bitter and not much appreciated by people from outside of the region.
Common names and synonyms: Tucum, tucum palm.

TUFTED VETCH - A species of *Vicia,* tufted vetch (*V. cracca*) is cultivated locally in Europe and Asia and is now naturalized in the eastern United States. Like many other vetches, the tufted vetch has edible seeds, pods, shoots, and leaves. In the past, the plant was cultivated in Europe for its seeds, whereas other, New World species of *Vicia* served as a gathered food for Native Americans.
Common names and synonyms: Bird vetch, boreal vetch, Canada pea, cow vetch, Gerrard vetch.

Tuhu - *see* **TUTU**

Tukahoe - *see* **ARROW ARUM**

Tumeric - *see* **TURMERIC**

Tuna - *see* **PRICKLY PEAR, TUNA DE AGUA**

TUNA DE AGUA - This cactus of Mexico (*Pereskiopsis aquosa*) has fruits that are called "water tunas" or *tunas de agua.* They are used for making beverages and also are boiled to be eaten as a vegetable.
Common names and synonyms: Water tuna.

Tung sun - *see* **BAMBOO SHOOT(S)**

Tupelo - *see* **BLACK GUM**

TURKEY FRUIT - Sometimes called the "bull-dog," this wild, edible fruit of Australia (*Grewia retusifolia*) is a drupe, and red to red-brown when ripe. *Grewia* is a large genus of Old World tropical shrubs that produce such fruits.
Common names and synonyms: Bull-dog.

Turkish coffee - *see* **COFFEE**

Turkish wheat - *see* **MAIZE**

Turk's cap - *see* **MELON CACTUS**

Turk's head - *see* **MELON CACTUS**

TURMERIC - A major ingredient in curry powders, turmeric (*Curcuma longa*) is a member of the ginger family and, like ginger, is rhizomatous. Although it originated in India, the Chinese, Arabs, and Persians were all cultivating turmeric thousands of years ago. Turmeric was never very popular as a spice in western Europe, but its bright yellow color has been employed as a dye for clothing, margarine, and cheeses. Turmeric can be purchased whole or dried but - unlike ginger - is rarely available fresh. In addition to its use in curry powder, the spice goes well in chutneys, in rice and poultry dishes, and with cooked vegetables.
Common names and synonyms: Curcuma, Indian saffron, tumeric.

See also: "Spices and Flavorings," Part II, Section F, Chapter 1.

TURNIP AND TURNIP GREENS (*see also* **RUTABAGA**) - Members of the mustard family, wild turnips (*Brassica rapa*), which apparently are native to Asia Minor, were dug up and eaten by Old World hunter-gatherers millennia before such vegetables were cultivated - and they have been under cultivation in Eurasia for at least 4,000 years. Turnips, which are among the cruciferous vegetables, can grow in even poor soil and are so cheap to cultivate that they have often been grown for animal feed. Turnips were known to the Romans, became a staple of the European poor during the Middle Ages, and reached the Americas with colonists from both England and France. Turnip roots are generally white but can be other colors as well. They are used in stews and soups and are baked, fried, and boiled.

Perhaps more useful these days than turnip roots are the tops of turnips, eaten as a popular green, especially in Europe, the Orient, and the southern United States. They are tough and have very coarse leaves that are mostly light green, thin, and have a covering of hair. For tenderness and the best taste, turnip greens are harvested when they are very young. At one point in American history, this vegetable was a common part of the diet consumed by slaves and - consequently - today is a part of the cuisine called "soul food." Some varieties of turnips that are especially grown for their edible foliage are known as "Seven Top" and "Shogun."
Common names and synonyms: Seven Top, Shogun.
See in addition: "Cruciferous and Green Leafy Vegetables," Part II, Section C, Chapter 5.

Turnip broccoli - *see* **BROCCOLI RAAB**

Turnip cabbage - *see* **KOHLRABI**

Turnip chervil - *see* **CHERVIL**

Turnip-rooted celery - *see* **CELERY AND CELERY ROOT**

Turnip-rooted chervil - *see* **CHERVIL**

TURTLE BEAN (*see also* **BEANS**) - The turtle bean (*Phaseolus vulgaris*) is the small black bean that is the *frijol negro* of Mexico and of Cuba - indeed the main ingredient for the black-bean soup enjoyed by residents of that island and Cubans in Florida. Turtle beans are also much consumed in Brazil and are the foundation of that country's famous *feijoada.*
Common names and synonyms: Black bean, *Feijâo-prêto, frijol negro.*
See in addition: "Beans, Peas, and Lentils," Part II, Section C, Chapter 3.

Tussa jute - *see* **JEW'S-MALLOW**

Tutong - *see* **DURIAN**

TUTU BERRY - *Tutu* is a Maori word for a group of New Zealand shrubs or small trees of the genus *Coriaria.* Some, such as *C. ruscifolia,* produce a berry-like fruit that the Maori have made into a wine known as *tutu* or *tuhu*. Although the berries are edible, the rest of the parts of the tree (i.e., the shoots and seeds) are poisonous.

Common names and synonyms: Tuhu, wineberry.

Tuxtla - *see* **TEPÍN CHILLIES AND RELATIVES**

Twanky - *see* **TEA**

Tyfon - *see* **HOLLAND GREENS**

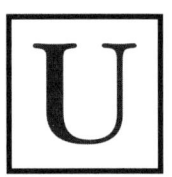

UDO - A stout Japanese herb, udo (*Aralia cordata*) is a perennial that annually produces edible shoots from its roots. Cultivation generally involves keeping the young shoots totally covered with soil to blanch them. The result is an asparagus-like vegetable that is briefly boiled to remove a resin, then added to salads or cooked further in various dishes.

Common names and synonyms: Oudo, spikenard.

UGLI FRUIT (*see also* **CITRUS FRUITS**) - A far-from-handsome fruit, as its name might suggest, the ugli fruit, of the genus *Citrus*, is a cross between the tangerine and the grapefruit. Also known as "hoogly," the fruit was developed in Jamaica but is now grown commercially in Florida as well. Although the ugli looks like a badly mistreated grapefruit, it has a delicious, sweet, and juicy taste, which seems to combine the flavors of grapefruit, bitter orange, and tangerine. Moreover, because it has the loose skin of the tangerine, it is easy to peel, and the orange-yellow pulp is practically seedless. Like all citrus fruits, the ugli fruit is high in vitamin C.

Common names and synonyms: Hoogly.

Ugni - *see* **CHILEAN GUAVA MYRTLE**

ULLUCO (*see also* **OCA**) - Also known as *olluco* and *ullucu*, ulluco (*Ullucus tuberosus*) is another of the ancient Andean root crops that have been cultivated for their edible tubers. A staple of the Inca diet, these multicolored (white, yellow, green, magenta) tubers are still grown commercially today and, indeed, are increasing in importance and thus in their geographic range, which now extends from Venezuela to Chile and northwestern Argentina. The plants, which form tubers both above and below the ground, are frost resistant and, along with potatoes, generally constitute a major source of carbohydrates for those who consume them. The tubers, which are used like potatoes, can be eaten fresh or dehydrated.

Common names and synonyms: Melloco, *olluco, ullucu*.

Ullucu - *see* **ULLUCO**

UMBÚ - A native of the Brazilian Northeast, the *umbú* (*Spondias tuberosa*) grows on a medium-sized tree. When ripe, the oval fruit is about 10 inches in length and has a sweet flesh that is almost liquid in consistency. The umbú is eaten raw and made into preserves and into juice - the latter is often mixed with

milk to become *imbuzada*. This drink of the Northeast has historically played an important role in the health of the people of the region.

UNICORN PLANT - Also called "martynia" and "devil's-claws," unicorn plants (*Proboscidea louisianica, P. parviflora,* and *P. fragrans*) are natives of the southern United States and Mexico. The elongated pods of these plants were eaten by Native Americans, and until recently people cultivated them in gardens and pickled the pods in much the same way as cucumbers are pickled.

Common names and synonyms: Devil's-claws, martynia, proboscis-flower, ram's-horn.

Upland cress - *see* **YELLOW ROCKET**

Upland sumac - *see* **SMOOTH SUMAC**

Urd - *see* **MUNG BEAN**

VALERIAN - A few plants of the genus *Valeriana* are called valerian. The "common valerian" (*V. officinalis*), a native of Europe and western Asia (and now naturalized in North America), has leaves that are used as greens and flowers that can flavor sauces. But its main use - and the reason for its cultivation in northern and eastern Europe - lies in its roots and rhizomes that have been used medicinally since the days of the Greeks. They contain an essential oil, which is employed mostly in the pharmaceutical industry but is also used to flavor beverages. Another valerian (this one a native of North America) called "tobacco-root" (*V. edulis*) has a large, fleshy, edible root, which was used as food by Native Americans.

Common names and synonyms: Bitterroot, common valerian, tobacco-root.

VANILLA (*see also* **CAROLINA VANILLA**) - Of the great number of orchid family members, *Vanilla planifolia* (= *V. fragrans*) is one of the few to be prized for something other than its flowers. The vanilla bean is the pod fruit of this climbing orchid, which is native to that part of the New World that also gave chocolate to the whole world. Indeed, when Hernando Cortés and his men first reached Mexico, the Aztecs offered them *chocolatl,* a chocolate drink flavored with *tlilxochitl* - the Aztec name for "vanilla" (the word "vanilla" itself is from the Spanish diminutive for *vaina,* which means "pod").

However, it was not the Aztecs who first discovered the secret of vanilla, which was one of nature's better-guarded secrets in that neither the vanilla flower nor its fruit have a telltale aroma that might have demanded further investigation. Rather, it was the Totonacs, in what has become the Mexican state of Vera Cruz, who discovered at least 1,000 years ago that if the initially tasteless beans were "sweated" in the sun for two or three weeks, and then slowly dried for several months, this process would force the development of *vanillin,* the major flavor component of the beans.

It is interesting to note that although the Totonacs were subsequently conquered by the Aztecs, they in turn joined forces with the newly arrived Spaniards to overturn the Aztec empire. And this meant that they continued to have a monopoly on vanilla. For although the Spaniards carried vanilla and chocolate back to Europe with them, and sugar produced in the New World became more and more plentiful (bringing on something of a revolution in beverages and desserts as well as baked goods), until the nineteenth century the Europeans were totally unsuccessful in growing vanilla elsewhere.

This was because of an intricate system of pollination involving hummingbirds, bees, ants, and butterflies within an ecosystem not found elsewhere in the world. But, during the eighteenth century, French colonists in Mexico cultivated vanilla, and in the nineteenth century the French introduced bees from Vera Cruz into their own tropical islands; combined with intensive hand-pollination techniques, this effort finally established vanilla production outside of Mexico. Recently, another plant (*V. tahitensis*) was promoted in French Polynesia to lessen reliance on the original vanilla orchid. And back in 1874, German chemists synthesized vanilla in an effort to free the flavor from the plant itself. Because of the high cost of real vanilla, there is plenty of false vanilla on the market today, although synthetic vanilla is easily detected because of a flat aroma and an unfortunate aftertaste. United States law insists that "vanilla extract" be true vanilla. In addition to extract, whole beans and powdered vanilla are available.

Common names and synonyms: Tlilxochitl.

See in addition: "Spices and Flavorings," Part II, Section F, Chapter 1.

Vanilla lily - *see* **YAM DAISY**

Vegetable beefsteak - *see* **MUSHROOMS AND FUNGI**

Vegetable brains - *see* **ACKEE**

VEGETABLE-FERN - The leaves of the vegetable-fern (*Diplazium esculentum*) are cooked and eaten as a vegetable in Java and other parts of tropical Asia.

Vegetable marrow - *see* **MARROW, SQUASH AND PUMPKIN, ZUCCHINI**

Vegetable meat - *see* **MUSHROOMS AND FUNGI**

Vegetable-oyster - *see* **SALSIFY**

Vegetable pear - *see* **CHAYOTE**

Vegetable spaghetti - *see* **SPAGHETTI SQUASH**

Vegetable sponge - *see* **ANGLED LUFFA**

Vegetable tallow - *see* **CHINESE TALLOW TREE**

Veitch screw-pine - *see* **STRIPED SCREW-PINE**

Velvet apple - *see* **MABOLO**

Velvet stem - *see* **ENOKITAKE**

VELVET TAMARIND - There are two trees of the genus *Dialium* that are called "velvet tamarind."

One is a large East Indian tree - *D. indicum* - that is used for timber and produces a small fruit with a blackish, velvety rind and a sweet pulp that is eaten raw. The other (also called the "black tamarind") is a West African tree - *D. guineense* - that produces velvety black pods that have an acid pulp. They are chewed to relieve thirst and are soaked in water to make a beverage.

Common names and synonyms: Black tamarind.

Vendakai - *see* **OKRA**

Verbain - *see* **BLUE VERVAIN**

Verbena - *see* **BLUE VERVAIN, LEMON VERBENA**

Vermont snakeroot - *see* **WILD GINGER**

VETCH (*see also* **BITTER VETCH, CHICKLING VETCH, LEGUMES, TUFTED VETCH**) - The common name vetch is the general label for the 150 species of *Vicia,* a genus of the legume family, the members of which are cultivated throughout the world. The most notable of the vetches is *V. faba* - the fava bean. Then there is the common vetch (*V. sativa*), native to the Mediterranean region and western Asia. Also known as "tare vetch" or "spring vetch," it is cultivated as a cover crop or for use as fodder. However, the young shoots as well as the pods and seeds of spring vetch, along with those of many other *Vicia* species, are edible. In North America, both *V. americana* and *V. gigantea* served as food for Native Americans.

Common names and synonyms: Common vetch, field vetch, spring vetch, tare vetch.

Viburnum - *see* **HIGHBUSH CRANBERRY**

Vilvam - *see* **QUINCE**

Vinegar tree - *see* **SMOOTH SUMAC**

Vine spinach - *see* **MALABAR SPINACH**

VIOGNIER (*see also* **GRAPES**) - A white grape from the Rhône valley of France, the Viognier (*Vitis vinifera*) is extremely susceptible to disease and thus difficult to grow. It is grown nonetheless because it yields a fine wine, and indeed, two of the most famous (and expensive) wines of the Rhône Valley are made from Viognier grapes. The grape has recently been planted in California, where presumably it will prosper and add even more diversity to the California wine industry.

See in addition: "Wine," Part III, Chapter 13.

Violeta - *see* **QUELITES**

Viper-grass - *see* **SCORZONERA**

Virginian poke - *see* **POKEWEED**

Virginian tukahoe - *see* **ARROW ARUM**

Virginian wake-robin - *see* **ARROW ARUM**

Virginia potato - *see* **APIOS, WHITE POTATO**

Virginia strawberry - *see* **STRAWBERRY**

Virginia wheat - *see* **MAIZE**

Visnaga - *see* **BARREL CACTUS**

Voandzou - *see* **BAMBARA GROUNDNUT**

Waferash - *see* HOPTREE
Waiawi-'ula'ula - *see* GUAVA
Wakame - *see* SEAWEED
Wake-robin - *see* TRILLIUM
Waldin - *see* AVOCADO
Waldmeister - *see* WOODRUFF
Walking onion - *see* ONION TREE

WALNUT - There are some 15 species of walnuts native to Asia, Europe, and the Americas, of which two - both with a green, leathery husk - are the best known. By far the most important of these commercially is the smooth-shelled and tan-colored Persian (or English, or Italian) walnut (*Juglans regia*), with its easy-to-crack shell. The Persian walnut was reportedly sent to ancient Greece by the Persians and found its way throughout Europe with the Romans. It is interesting to note that although one of its names is the English walnut, *wealhhnutu,* the Old English translation of the Latin *nux gallia,* means "Gaulish nut" or "foreigner's nut." Today, these nuts are grown in orchards and sold commercially, with California one of the leading producers. Historically, oil pressed from the Persian walnut has been highly prized. It was much used in the Middle Ages by those without a taste for - or access to - olive oil and was common in the cooking of central France until the middle of the nineteenth century. Today, some consider walnut oil to be one of the greatest salad oils because of its nutty flavor.

Another walnut is the black walnut (*J. nigra*), a North American native. It comes in a rough and very hard to crack shell but nonetheless is much used (in its native land, at least) in breads, cakes, candies, and ice cream. Still a third walnut is the little-known butternut (*J. cinerea*), another North American native, which many claim to be the best tasting of all nuts. Walnuts provide the consumer with some vitamin B_6 as well as iron, and the butternut has an incredibly high protein content - close to 30 percent.

Common names and synonyms: American black walnut, black walnut, butternut, California black walnut, Carpathian walnut, cordate walnut, demon walnut, eastern black walnut, English walnut, heartnut, Hind's walnut, Italian walnut, Juglans, *nux gallia,* oil nut, Persian walnut, Siebold walnut, walnut oil, *wealhhnutu.*

Walnut oil - *see* WALNUT

Wampee - *see* WAMPI

WAMPI - Native to southern China, the wampi (*Clausena lansium*) belongs to the family of plants that also includes oranges and lemons. Unlike these more familiar fruits, however, wampi are small and grow in clusters, much as grapes do. They are pale yellow and have a hard rind enclosing flesh with a consistency reminiscent of Jell-O. Their taste is sweet yet slightly acidic. Wampi are eaten as fresh fruit, made into preserves, used in desserts, and added to curries.

Common names and synonyms: Wampee.

Wapata - *see* ARROWHEAD
Wapato(o) - *see* ARROWHEAD
WASABI - A perennial crucifer, native to Japan and sometimes called "Japanese horseradish" or "mountain hollyhock," the wasabi plant (*Wasabia japonica*) has a gray-green-colored root that, when grated, becomes a searingly hot condiment used with dishes such as sushi and sashimi. A traditional but now very expensive seasoning in Japanese cuisine, wasabi is available fresh and in powdered form in most Asian markets. New Zealand now grows wasabi for the Japanese market and it is also cultivated in Oregon in the United States.

Common names and synonyms: Japanese horseradish, mountain hollyhock.

See also: "Spices and Flavorings," Part II, Section F, Chapter 1.

WATER BAMBOO - Also called Manchurian wild rice, water bamboo (*Zizania latifolia*) is a close relative of the wild rice (*Z. aquatica*) of North America. A gathered food in prehistoric times, water bamboo has been cultivated for its succulent stems since the beginnings of agriculture in paddy-like East Asian fields from Manchuria to Taiwan.

Common names and synonyms: Manchurian wild rice.

Water caltrop - *see* WATER CHESTNUT

WATER CHESTNUT - An Asian vegetable, the Chinese water chestnut (*Eleocharis dulcis*) is the edible bulb of a Chinese water plant that has been cultivated for thousands of years. The firm, white flesh is covered by a brown, shaggy coat that is not eaten. These bulbs are a paddy crop, grown in the mud, and require plenty of water. A similar but unrelated aquatic plant is the "caltrop" or European water chestnut (*Trapa natans*), which provided food for hunter–gatherer bands and has been fried, roasted, and made into flour in both Europe and Asia since antiquity. It is, however, the starchy and somewhat sweet Chinese water chestnut that provides crispness for so many Asian dishes.

Another vegetable called water chestnut is the water caltrop (*Trapa bicornis*), which is used like a water chestnut. Most water chestnuts available outside of Asia are canned, although they can be found fresh in some ethnic markets. There is also water-chestnut powder, available in many Chinese markets. Water chestnuts are a good source of carbohydrates as well as vitamin B_6 and riboflavin.

Common names and synonyms: Caltrop, Chinese water chestnut, European water chestnut, Jesuit nut, *trapa* nut, water caltrop, waternut.

Water convolvulus - *see* SWAMP CABBAGE

WATERCRESS - Native to Eurasia, watercress (*Nasturtium officinale*) is a cruciferous vegetable that now grows wild in freshwater ponds and streams the world over. But watercress is also produced commercially and is available in bunches in the produce sections of U.S. supermarkets as well as in the markets of Europe. The pungent, deep green leaves make a wonderful garnish and give a peppery taste to salads and sandwiches. Watercress is high in vitamin C and calcium.

See also: "Cruciferous and Green Leafy Vegetables," Part II, Section C, Chapter 5.

Water dock - *see* **SORREL**

WATERLEAF (*see also* **TALINUM**) - Any North American plant of the genus *Hydrophyllum* is called a waterleaf and is identifiable by its clusters of white or purplish flowers. The roots, leaves, and shoots of *H. canadense* served as food for Native Americans (and, later, white settlers) in the eastern part of the continent, whereas *H. occidentale* was similarly exploited in the West.

Water lily - *see* **LOTUS**

WATERMELON (*see also* **MELON**) - A native of Africa, this ground-hugging vine (*Citrullus lanatus* = *C. vulgaris*), cultivated for its melons, managed early on to get around the globe with a great deal of agility. It reached the Middle East, India, and what is now Russia in prehistoric times, was consumed in Egypt and ancient Persia some 6,000 years ago, and was later cultivated by the ancient Greeks and Romans. The Chinese were growing the fruit by the tenth century A.D.; it entered Europe through Spain with the Moors and reached the Americas via the slave trade.

Wild watermelons, which grow throughout Africa around water holes in the savannas and oases in the deserts, are not much larger than apples. Those that are cultivated (there are some 50 varieties) grow larger, ranging from "icebox" varieties that fit in the refrigerator to the "picnic" sizes that can be large enough to feed a crowd. Watermelons are cultivated worldwide in subtropical, tropical, and temperate climates; in the United States, they have flourished in the warm soils of the southern states as well as those of New Jersey. Most watermelons have red flesh, but some are orange and yellow fleshed, and all contain about 90 percent water and about 10 percent sugar. Watermelon rinds - especially those that are white inside - have traditionally been turned into sweet pickles. Juice from the fruit is bottled commercially and drunk fresh as well as reduced to syrup or sugar. Another use is as watermelon wine.

Watermelon seeds are consumed by humans after drying, roasting, and salting. In Iran and China, such snacks are thought to control hypertension. The seeds are 30 to 40 percent protein, are rich in the enzyme urease, and yield an edible oil (20 to 45 percent) that is used for cooking and illumination. Livestock animals are fed the expressed oilseed cakes and benefit from the high protein content. Like nuts, however, watermelon seeds are high in fat, whereas the flesh is low in calories. Seedless varieties have been developed and are very popular, although more expensive than the traditional seeded varieties. Watermelons provide their consumers with some vitamin C.

Common names and synonyms: American watermelon, Jubilee, seeded watermelon, seedless watermelon.

See in addition: "Cucumbers, Melons, and Watermelons," Part II, Section C, Chapter 6.

Waternut - *see* **WATER CHESTNUT**

Water oat(s) - *see* **WILD RICE**

Water pepper - *see* **KNOTWEED AND SMARTWEED**

Water spinach - *see* **SWAMP CABBAGE**

Water tuna - *see* **TUNA DE AGUA**

WATER YAM (*see also* **YAMS**) - Also called "white yam," "greater yam," "Asiatic yam," and "winged yam" (among numerous other common names), the water yam (*Dioscorea alata*) is a native of Southeast Asia but is now grown throughout the tropical regions of the world, including the Caribbean and especially Australia and Polynesia. The plant is a climbing vine usually planted at the beginning of the rainy season, and its tubers are generally mature by the season's end. The large tubers, with a fine white flesh, are baked or boiled as a vegetable or cooked with coconut milk, although they can also be roasted and fried.

Common names and synonyms: Asiatic yam, greater yam, ten-months-yam, white yam, winged yam.

See in addition: "Sweet Potatoes and Yams," Part II, Section B, Chapter 5.

Wattle(s) - *see* **ACACIA**

Wax(-)apple - *see* **JAVA APPLE, ROSE APPLE**

Wax gourd - *see* **FUZZY MELON**

WAX PEPPERS (*see also* **CHILLI PEPPERS, SWEET PEPPERS**) - Also known generically as banana chillies (and in Spanish as *güero* - meaning "blond"), wax peppers (genus *Capsicum*) include the banana pepper, the Hungarian yellow wax pepper, and the Santa Fe Grande. They are all relatively large - about 3 to 5 inches in length and about an inch and a half in diameter. As a rule, the banana pepper is sweet with a generally mild taste; Hungarian wax peppers are hotter; and the Santa Fe Grande has just a touch of heat. A problem is that all three may be generically labeled "yellow wax" in supermarkets, which gives no clue as to the degree of heat they might deliver. Another pepper with the characteristics and color of waxed peppers is the Chawa, which is found mostly in stores in California. Wax peppers go well in salads, are pickled, and are used to make yellow mole sauces.

Common names and synonyms: Banana chilli, banana pepper, Chawa, *güero*, Hungarian wax pepper, Hungarian yellow wax pepper, Santa Fe Grande, yellow wax pepper.

See in addition: "Chilli Peppers," Part II, Section C, Chapter 4.

Wealhhnutu - *see* **WALNUT**

Weissburgunder - *see* **PINOT BLANC**

Weisser Burgunder - *see* **PINOT BLANC**

Weisser Klevner - *see* **PINOT BLANC**

WELSH ONION (*see also* **ONION**) - An important ingredient in the cuisines of China and Japan, the Welsh onion (*Allium fistulosum*), also known as the "Chinese onion," grows in clusters, which accounts for another of its many common names, "Japanese bunching." Actually a kind of scallion, with dark green, hollow, cylindrical leaves and a white end that does not develop a bulb, the Welsh onion is widely used in stir-fries.

Common names and synonyms: Chinese onion, Japanese bunching, spring onion.

See in addition: "The *Allium* Species," Part II, Section C, Chapter 2.

West African sorrel - *see* **JEW'S-MALLOW**

Western wheatgrass - *see* **BLUE-STEM**

West Indian cherry - *see* **ACEROLA**

West Indian elm - *see* **MUTAMBA**

West Indian gherkin - *see* **GHERKIN**

West Indian pea - *see* **SESBAN**

Weymouth pine - *see* **WHITE PINE**

WHEAT (*see also* **EINKORN, EMMER, KAMUT, SPELT**) - The wheat now growing in vast fields stretching across the Great Plains of North America had its beginnings in the eastern Mediterranean region, where the wild grass *Triticum aestivum* originated to become one of the first of the domesticated grains and ultimately one of the world's two most important superfoods. Wheat was probably first domesticated in the Middle East many thousands of years ago. The ancient Egyptians made bread from it, but only later did the Greeks adopt wheat in preference to emmer. Later still, one of the reasons for the expansion of Rome was the need for wheat, and the Romans turned Egypt into a wheat-growing breadbasket for their empire.

Wheat reached northern China later than it reached the West, and in eastern Asia it joined millet as a major crop. The plant does poorly in warm and humid climates because it is very susceptible to disease. But although it likes cool climates, it does not grow as far north as do rye and oats. In Europe, wheat lost ground to other grains (such as barley and rye) after the fall of the Roman Empire and did not regain its prominence until the nineteenth century. The grain reached the Americas in the early seventeenth century with the Spaniards and was first planted on the Great Plains at about the time of the American Civil War.

Wheat comes in some 30,000 varieties, which in part is testimony to its longevity as a domesticated plant which people tinkered with. The varieties, however, can be fitted into a relatively few classifications, such as "hard red spring," "hard red winter," "soft red winter," "durum," and "white" wheat. The hard varieties (hardness measured according to the strength of the kernel) provide more protein and are most valued for the production of all-purpose and baking flours. The even harder durum wheat is employed for making semolina and pasta, whereas the soft wheats are preferred for flours utilized to bake pastries.

As a grain, wheat has a special characteristic that provides humankind with raised breads: When it is ground and combined with water, its protein forms gluten - a sticky, adhesive mass that can be rolled and pummeled yet still holds together and expands to contain rather than release the gases produced by yeast. Bulgur is made by steaming and drying whole wheat kernels, then cracking them. The coarsest wheat grains are used for pilafs, the medium for cereals, and the finest for the various forms of tabbouleh - a cold grain salad. Farina (also called "Cream of Wheat"), which has most of the bran and germ removed, usually comes as a breakfast cereal. Wheat can also be purchased as whole "berries," as cracked wheat, as rolled wheat, and as wheat flakes.

Common names and synonyms: Alaska wheat, bearded wheat, bread wheat, bulgur, common wheat, cone wheat, cracked wheat, durum wheat, English wheat, farina, hard wheat, macaroni wheat, Mediterranean wheat, non-bearded wheat, Poulard wheat, red wheat, river wheat, rivet wheat, rolled wheat, soft wheat, spring wheat, wheat flakes, white wheat, wild wheat, winter wheat.

See in addition: "Wheat," Part II, Section A, Chapter 10.

Wheat grass - *see* **COUCH GRASS**

Whitebeam berry - *see* **ROWANBERRY**

White beet - *see* **SWISS CHARD**

White carrot - *see* **ARRACACHA**

WHITE CINNAMON - An aromatic tree, the white cinnamon (*Canella alba* or *C. winteriana*) is native to southern Florida and the West Indies. It is also known as the wild cinnamon tree, and its bark, which is marketed rolled up in tubes, is referred to as "canella," "Bahama whitewood," and "white cinnamon," as well as "wild cinnamon." The bark's aromatic qualities make it useful as a spice. It is also employed to flavor tobacco and for medicinal purposes.

Common names and synonyms: Bahama whitewood, canella, wild cinnamon (tree).

See also: "Spices and Flavorings," Part II, Section F, Chapter 1.

WHITE PINE - Also known as the northern pine and the Weymouth pine, the white pine (*Pinus strobus*) - along with other species of *Pinus* - provides an inner bark that served as food for Native Americans of eastern North America. The bark was eaten fresh and was also dried over a fire, whereupon it was fashioned into cakes.

Common names and synonyms: Northern pine, Weymouth pine.

WHITE POTATO - An enlarged tip of an underground stem that stores energy in the form of starch, the potato (*Solanum tuberosum*) may have been domesticated in the highlands of Peru as many as 10,000 years ago. Certainly it was a well-established crop some 5,000 to 6,000 years ago and, along with other tubers, maize, and quinoa, served as the foundation of the Andean diet. There were hundreds of varieties – some sweet, some bitter, some red, some blue, and some black – that were baked, boiled, used in soups and porridges, and even eaten for dessert. In addition, the ancient Peruvians discovered how to preserve potatoes by a process of freezing and drying, with the resulting product called *chuño*.

Outside of the Andean region there were and are a great number of species of wild potatoes, the tubers and leaves of which served as food for other Native Americans from North through Central to South America. But apparently it was only in the Andes that the potato was domesticated, and the Spaniards reaching Peru in the 1530s who had never seen one before thought at first that potatoes were truffles. The Incas called the potato a *papa*, a name the Spanish adopted. However, because they also adopted the Caribbean Indian name for the sweet potato, *batata*, sufficient confusion ensued that the potato (*papa*) was eventually given the name of the sweet potato (*batata*).

Potatoes were carried back to Spain in 1539 by returning conquistadors and followed the same route as the tomato to reach Spanish territory in Italy, where a hungry peasantry quickly embraced them. They reached the British Isles more circuitously, bringing about even more semantic confusion in the process. The story is that the confusion began when Francis Drake in 1586 picked up some potatoes at Cartegena in the Caribbean, then went to Virginia before returning to England. This created the impression that the potato had originated in Virginia. It also gave rise to the name "Virginia potato," which received "scientific" blessing in John Gerard's *Herbal* of 1597, and neither the impression nor the name was fully dispelled until the 1930s work of Russian geneticist Nikolai Vavilov established or reestablished an American origin for the potato.

Hardy and easy to grow, potatoes were therefore an inexpensive food that caught on quickly enough that the poor of Ireland were planting them in "lazybeds" by the early 1640s. The timing was fortunate, because at the end of that decade the English, under Oliver Cromwell, began killing and transporting thousands of Irish, and those who survived the English depredations did so on potatoes. Potatoes were also planted for the poor relatively early on in England but were not much appreciated there. On the Continent, potatoes were regarded with even less enthusiasm because they were thought to cause leprosy – a suspicion that lingered on in France until well into the eighteenth century. Moreover, potatoes were denounced by religious fundamentalists because the vegetable had not been mentioned in the Bible. Nonetheless, beginning in

about 1650, potatoes started to gain acceptance in the Netherlands and then became widespread throughout the Low Countries by the middle of the following century.

Elsewhere, in Germany and Russia, rulers compelled the peasantry to plant potatoes, sometimes at gunpoint, and by the end of the eighteenth century even the French were eating them. Resistance to the tubers, however, continued well into the nineteenth century in Russia, where (in the aftermath of two famines) they were at last uniformly adopted. By the beginning of the twentieth century, Russia was among the leading potato-producing countries of the world, with a good bit of that production becoming vodka.

Meanwhile, the peripatetic potato, which had left the New World to become the "Virginia potato" in the British Isles, returned to the Americas as the "Irish potato," reaching Boston in 1718 with Irish immigrants. The following year, potatoes were planted in New Hampshire, although another century elapsed before they really caught on in North America. Elsewhere, the Spaniards and Portuguese had carried potatoes to Africa and disseminated them throughout the East. By the middle of the seventeenth century they were grown in even the most remote regions of China and, along with sweet potatoes, were helping to fuel a population explosion. Because potatoes produce far more calories per acre than cereal crops, they were also to some immeasurable extent responsible for the population explosion in Europe during the eighteenth and nineteenth centuries.

The Irish potato famine – which began in 1845 with the loss of half the potato crop and saw its total loss in 1846, causing the death or migration of millions – was, in retrospect, inevitable. The Irish potato crop had failed numerous times during the previous 100 years, each time encouraging tenant farmers to select potato varieties that were the highest yielding. But in so doing, they narrowed the genetic base and bred potatoes with little resistance to fungal diseases. Perhaps ironically, the fungus (*Phytophthora infestans*) that caused the potato famine reached Ireland from North America, probably on potatoes imported for breeding purposes.

The devastating blight that killed one million persons was a stark reminder of the dangers of too much reliance on a single crop, yet at the same time it galvanized plant breeders to develop potatoes that not only were disease resistant but also stored and shipped well. Unfortunately, their product has turned out to be not particularly tasty. The relatively few potato varieties available outside of the Andean region are often divided into the dry and mealy kinds, such as Idaho or russet potatoes, utilized for baking and mashing, and the moist and waxy kinds (new potatoes, for example), which are scalloped and made into potato salads.

In addition to these uses, there are french fries, born in the mid-nineteenth century on the streets of Paris, where they were peddled by pushcart vendors. Beginning in 1864, french fries were increasingly united with fried fish, on sale in London streets since the seventeenth century, to become the famous English "fish and chips." It is interesting to note that as U.S.-based restaurant chains such as McDonald's and Burger King have become worldwide operations, french fries are now known in many places as "American fries."

Potato chips, however, are the true American fries. They are said to have been invented in 1852 in Saratoga Springs by a chef mischievously responding with humor to a customer's complaint that his french fries were too thick. In 1925, an automatic potato-peeling machine was introduced, allowing potato-chip production on a massive scale, which in turn permits Americans to consume a per capita average of 6 pounds of potato chips annually. Other breakthroughs have seen potatoes dehydrated for "instant" products, and french fries, hash browns, and even mashed potatoes are now frozen. Consequently, almost 65 percent of the potatoes grown in the United States are used for these processed products, including, of course, potato chips.

Potatoes constitute the fourth most important crop in the world – after rice, wheat, and maize – and are by far the healthiest. Potatoes are a good source of vitamin C (in fact, they are a leading source in the American diet because of the vast quantities consumed), potassium, niacin, vitamin B$_6$, and iron.

Common names and synonyms: American fry (fries), common potato, European potato, french fry (fries), Idaho potato, Irish potato, new potato, *papa,* potato chip(s), red potato, round potato, Russet Burbank, russet potato, Virginia potato.

See also: "Potatoes (White)," Part II, Section B, Chapter 3.

White salt - *see* **SUGARCANE**

WHITE SAPOTE - The white sapote (*Casimiroa edulis*), a native of Central America and Mexico, is now cultivated in California (since the nineteenth century), Florida, Hawaii, and Puerto Rico. It is about the size of an orange with a green to yellow skin and white pulp. This fruit's sweet yet simultaneously bitter taste is not appreciated by some, which helps to explain why the white sapote has been a somewhat neglected fruit.

Common names and synonyms: Custard apple, Mexican apple, sapota, *zapote, zapote blanco.*

White snakeroot - *see* **BONESET**
White spinach - *see* **SESBAN**
White sweet potato - *see* **BONIATO**
White-tassel-flower - *see* **PRAIRIE CLOVER**

White Vienna - *see* **KOHLRABI**
White wax-berry - *see* **CHINESE TALLOW TREE**
WHITE WILLOW - A large tree of Eurasia and North Africa, the white willow (*Salix alba*) was long ago introduced into North America. Its inner bark is edible, as are its young shoots, leaves, and flower clusters. The leaves, which are rich in vitamin C, were doubtless discovered to be a scurvy preventive sometime in the distant past.

Whitewood - *see* **AMERICAN LINDEN**

WHITE YAM (*see also* **YAMS**) - One of several yams that long ago lured West Africans into the forests to cultivate the tubers in clearings, the white yam (*Dioscorea rotundata*) has other common names, such as "Guinea yam" and "Eboe yam," which speak to its West African origin. The white yam is considered by many to be the premier yam grown in the region, and it is this yam that generally is used to make "foo-foo," the famous West African dish.

Common names and synonyms: Eboe yam, Guinea yam, white Guinea yam.

See in addition: "Sweet Potatoes and Yams," Part II, Section B, Chapter 5.

Whortleberry - *see* **BILBERRY, BLUEBERRY, HUCKLEBERRY**
Wild angelica - *see* **ANGELICA**
Wild apple - *see* **CRAB APPLE**
WILD BARLEY - Barley (*Hordeum vulgare*) – a Middle Eastern native – was domesticated in early Neolithic times. But many other species of the genus *Hordeum* continued to grow wild. In the Americas, one of these wild species was "little barley" (*H. pusillum*), which was widespread in western and southern North America as well as tropical America. Another was "foxtail barley" or "squirrel-tail barley" (*H. jubatum*). Both provided food for Native Americans.

Common names and synonyms: Foxtail barley, little barley, squirrel-tail barley.

See also: "Barley," Part II, Section A, Chapter 2.

Wild bean - *see* **APIOS**
Wild black cherry - *see* **CHERRY, CHOKECHERRY**
Wild blite - *see* **AMARANTH**
Wild cherry - *see* **CHOKECHERRY**
Wild cucumber - *see* **KORILA**
WILD CUSTARD APPLE - Native to West Africa, the wild custard apple (*Annona senegalensis*) now enjoys a wide distribution across all of that continent's tropical regions. Although it does well even in poor, sandy soils of those hot climates, the small tree (or shrub) prefers low, moist places, such as along a stream or in a boggy wooded area. With such optimal conditions, it may grow to a height of 19 feet. The leaves, lush and green year-round, are enjoyed by monkeys and bushpigs. The tree bears fruits that are barely 2 inches in diameter. When young, they are green with light spots and, depending on the variety, turn yellow or red when ripe.

Opinions on their flavor range from "limited appeal" to "the best indigenous fruit in parts of tropical Africa." Some have likened their taste to that of an apricot and their aroma to that of a pineapple. Their sweet pulp is consumed fresh and the fruits are also pickled.

WILD GINGER - The reference here is not to the wild form (*Zingiber zerumbet*) of the Old World's common ginger (*Z. officinale*). Rather, it is to two species of the genus *Asarum* that are called "wild ginger." By far the best known is Canada wild ginger (*A. canadense*), which is also named "Canada snakeroot," "Vermont snakeroot," "heart snakeroot," and so forth. It is a small plant with kidney- or heart-shaped leaves and is found in the forests of and along roadsides in eastern North America. The other "wild ginger," *A. caudatum,* is a lesser-known denizen of western North America. Both have a fragrant, spicy-tasting rootstock – with a flavor somewhat reminiscent of ginger – that is used either fresh or dried and powdered as a spice. Native Americans made a tea from the roots. There is also a perennial Australian plant, *Alpinia coerulea,* which grows wild and is related to the common ginger.

Common names and synonyms: Black snakeroot, Canada ginger, Canada snakeroot, Canada wild ginger, heart snakeroot, Vermont snakeroot.

WILD GOOSEBERRY (*see also* **BERRIES**) - Also known as the "native gooseberry" – although it is not a true gooseberry (genus *Ribes*) at all – the wild gooseberry (*Physalis minima*) is an edible berry of Australia and one of the many foods that were gathered by the aboriginal populations.

Common names and synonyms: Native gooseberry.

Wild grape - *see* **FOX GRAPE**

WILD GUAVA (*see also* **GUAVA**) - Also known as the "Costa Rican guava," the wild guava (*Psidium friedrichsthalianum*) is a tree of Central America that produces greenish (or yellowish) fruit. As with other guavas, the flesh of the fruit (in this case, white in color) is good to eat raw if one does not mind the numerous hard seeds. The latter can, however, be ground into an edible paste. A refreshing beverage is derived from the juice of the fruit, and jellies and jams are made from it as well.

Common names and synonyms: Costa Rican guava.

Wild hyacinth - *see* **CAMAS**

Wild hyssop - *see* **BLUE VERVAIN**

WILD LEEK(S) (*see also* **ONION**) - Actually not a leek but rather a North American wild onion, the "wild leek" (*Allium tricoccum*) is one of about 500 members of the genus *Allium*. This plant – frequently called a ramp – resembles the leek, in that it has a long stalk and flat tapering leaves. But unlike the leek, which has a mild taste, the wild leek is noted for its strong, garlic-like flavor. Native Americans gathered ramps, and they are still eagerly sought out by many in springtime.

Common names and synonyms: Ramp.

See also: "The *Allium* Species," Part II, Section C, Chapter 2.

Wild lettuce - *see* **PRICKLY LETTUCE**

Wild lime - *see* **KAFFIR LIME**

Wild mango - *see* **DUIKA**

Wild marigold - *see* **ANISILLO**

Wild olive - *see* **ELAEAGNUS, OSMANTHUS**

Wild opium - *see* **PRICKLY LETTUCE**

Wild Oregon grape - *see* **BARBERRY**

Wild parsley - *see* **LOVAGE**

Wild passion-flower - *see* **MAYPOP, PASSION FRUIT**

WILD PEACH - The "wild peach" (*Landolphia kirkii*) is a member of the Apocynaceae family of mainly tropical trees, shrubs, and herbs. The fruit, highly esteemed by the Zulu people, grows on shrubs or woody climbers in southern Africa and matures between November and March. Rich in carbohydrates, it lends itself to the preparation of refreshing drinks and delicious jams.

Wild peanut - *see* **HOG PEANUT**

Wild pepper - *see* **CHASTE TREE**

Wild pineapple - *see* **PINGUIN**

Wild potato - *see* **APIOS**

Wild prune - *see* **WONGAY**

WILD RICE - This tall, annual, grain-producing aquatic grass (*Zizania aquatica*) is actually not a rice at all. Rather, it is a native of the northern Great Lakes region of North America, where it grows in the shallow water of marshes and lakes and along riverbanks. It has been harvested by Native Americans from their canoes for millennia. They used the ripened, dark brown grains – now considered a delicacy – as a staple food. Recently, however, commercial producers have begun growing "wild rice" in paddies and employing mechanical harvesters – making the grain considerably less wild, although (so far at least) not less expensive.

Common names and synonyms: Indian rice, water oat(s).

Wild Roman chicory - *see* **PUNTARELLE**

WILD STRAWBERRY (*see also* **BERRIES, STRAWBERRIES**) - Wild strawberries (*Fragaria vesca* and numerous other species) have been an important food collected by humans since the days of the hunter-gatherers. One of these fruits is the "alpine strawberry" (*F. vesca* var. *monophylla*), which grows in the northern latitudes of Asia, Europe, and North America right up to the Arctic Circle. The *hautbois* (*F. moschata*), a native of central Europe, is another important wild strawberry, as were several American species (such as *F. vesca* var. *americana,* the "woodland strawberry"; and *F. chiloensis*) that provided vitamins A, B, C, and E for Native Americans. Today, wild strawberries are gathered mostly for making jams and jellies.

Common names and synonyms: Alpine strawberry, *hautbois,* woodland strawberry.

Wild tamarind - *see* **LEUCAENA**

WILD TRIGA - Also called "intermediate wheatgrass" when used as a forage crop, wild triga (*Agropyron intermedium* × *A. trichophorum* or *Elytrigia intermedia* ssp. *barbulata*) is an Old World perennial grain that can be cooked whole as a cereal or ground into flour for baking. It is a relative of wheat and may have been a staple crop in western Asia in ancient times. Today, wild triga is grown commercially in North America and elsewhere for hay and forage.

Common names and synonyms: Intermediate wheatgrass.

Wild water lemon - *see* **PASSION FRUIT**

WILD YAM (*see also* **YAMS**) - Also known as the "native potato," "devil's-bones," "rheumatism root," and "colicroot," the wild yam (*Dioscorea villosa*) grows throughout what is now the eastern and central United States. The rootstock was usually gathered in the fall and was one of the many foods that carried Native Americans through the winter. It is probably not the case (as has been suggested) that the plant's various common names, indicating pain, were occasioned by the backbreaking pain involved in digging up these slender tubers because the plant was also used medicinally.

Common names and synonyms: Colicroot, devil's-bones, native potato, rheumatism root.

See in addition: "Sweet Potatoes and Yams," Part II, Section B, Chapter 5.

Wild yam bean - *see* **AFRICAN YAM BEAN**

WILLOW - The majority of the 300 species of the genus *Salix* have practical uses and are planted for erosion control, windbreaking, or ornamental purposes, or are grown for their flexible branches, which can be woven into baskets and employed in light construction. But in the culinary realm, the leaves of the white willow (*S. alba*) are edible raw and are used as a tea substitute, whereas the inner bark and the young shoots of some Alaskan species are consumed raw or with seal oil by Eskimos. The leaves contain a fair measure of vitamin C.

Windberry - *see* **BILBERRY**

Windsor bean - *see* **FAVA BEAN**

Wineberry - *see* **JAPANESE WINEBERRY, TUTU BERRY**

WINE PALM - "Wine palm" refers to any of the various palm trees that yield sap or juice from which wine is made. Mostly, however, the name is intended to mean *Borassus flabellifer*, which has other common names such as "toddy palm," "lontar palm," and "palmyra." The wine palm also serves as a source of sugar in the drier portions of tropical areas where it grows best, especially in parts of India. In addition to providing sugar and toddy, the nuts of this palm contain a liquid that makes a refreshing drink, and the kernel of the fruit is eaten as a vegetable.

Common names and synonyms: Borassus palm, lontar palm, palmyra, toddy palm.

WINGED BEAN (*see also* **BEANS, LEGUMES**) - An annual herb, with names like "winged pea," "four-angled bean," "asparagus bean," "Goa bean," and "Manila bean" among its many aliases, the winged bean (*Psophocarpus tetragonolobus*) is a very close relative of the cowpea. It is usually said to have originated in tropical Asia - probably in India, although China may have been another center of origin. But some believe the winged bean to be an African plant because it grows wild in many parts of that continent. One explanation for this, however, is that it originally reached Africa from the East as a cultivated food crop but some plants managed a return to the wild.

The winged bean is now cultivated in all of the world's tropics, including those of South America and the Caribbean, which it presumably reached via the slave trade. The leaves, pods, seeds, shoots, and tubers of the plant are all edible and high in protein. The young and tender pods, which grow to a much greater length than string beans, are usually green, are eaten like string beans, and are known for their asparagus-like flavor as well as for their four longitudinal wings.

Once the seeds of the winged bean have reached maturity, they are either dried or eaten after roasting. In many places, the flowers of the winged bean are fried and yield a taste similar to that of mushrooms. Winged beans are very important in the cuisines of many peoples of Southeast Asia and southern China. The vegetable not only is a good source of protein but also provides some calcium, iron, and a fair amount of the vitamin-B complex. Today, in addition to the uses already mentioned, parts of the winged bean plant can be dried and used as a cereal and as feed for livestock, and the oily seeds make a cooking oil.

Common names and synonyms: Asparagus bean, asparagus pea, four-angled bean, Goa bean, long bean, long-podded cowpea, Manila bean, princess pea, snake bean, vegetable cowpea, winged pea.

See in addition: "Beans, Peas, and Lentils," Part II, Section C, Chapter 3.

Winged pea - *see* **WINGED BEAN**

Winged yam - *see* **WATER YAM**

Wing sesame - *see* **TACOUTTA**

WINTERBERRY - Like yaupon, the winterberry is a member of the holly family (genus *Ilex*). The leaves of this evergreen shrub are widely used for tea. Common winterberry is comprised of the species *I. verticillata* and *I. glabra*. The former is also called black alder, dogberry, and fever bush; the latter is called gallberry, bitter gallberry, inkberry, and Appalachian tea. In addition to the use of the leaves for tea, the flowers of *I. glabra* are a good source of nectar, which, after the bees finish their work, becomes honey.

Common names and synonyms: Appalachian tea, bitter gallberry, black alder, common winterberry, dogberry, fever bush, gallberry, inkberry.

Winter cherry - *see* **CAPE GOOSEBERRY**

Winter cress - *see* **YELLOW ROCKET**

WINTERGREEN - A native of eastern North America, wintergreen (*Gaultheria procumbens*) has aromatic leaves and spicy, edible, red berries. Oil of wintergreen is extracted from the leaves for flavoring a variety of foods, candies, chewing gum, and drugs. The berry is also called "checkerberry" and "teaberry" and it exudes the wintergreen aroma as well.

Common names and synonyms: Checkerberry, teaberry.

See also: "Spices and Flavorings," Part II, Section F, Chapter 1.

Winter melon - *see* **CASABA (MELON), HONEYDEW (MELON), MELONS**

Winter mushroom - *see* **ENOKITAKE, MUSHROOMS AND FUNGI**

Winter squash - *see* **SQUASH AND PUMPKIN**

WITCH-HAZEL - This tall shrub (which can reach 25 feet in height) is a native of eastern North America. Historically, it has been known as the plant that provided witch-hazel extract to relieve the itching bites of insects, other skin irritations caused by plants, and even burns. But witch-hazel (*Hamamelis virginiana*) also has culinary uses. Its small, shiny, black seeds - contained in a seed capsule that bursts open - were reportedly eaten by Native Americans, who also used the leaves of the witch-hazel plant to make a tea.

Common names and synonyms: Snapping hazel, spotted alder, wych-hazel.

Witloef - *see* **CHICORY**

Witloof - *see* **BELGIAN ENDIVE, CHICORY**

Wolf currant - *see* **GOOSEBERRY**

Women's-tobacco - *see* **TEA**

Wonder apple - *see* **BALSAM APPLE**

Wonder bean - *see* **SWORD BEAN**

WONDERBERRY (*see also* **BERRIES**) - Also known as "garden huckleberry," "sunberry," "morella," and "black nightshade," the wonderberry (*Solanum nigrum*) is closely related to the poisonous nightshades. Nonetheless, the leaves of the plant - which is probably Eurasian in origin - are cooked and eaten in Asia and southern Europe. The fruits - ripe black berries - can be eaten raw but are more often used in pies and preserves. Wonderberries grow mostly wild (in Africa and the states of the U.S. South as well as Europe and Asia), although they have been cultivated on occasion.

Common names and synonyms: Black nightshade, garden huckleberry, morella, sunberry.

WONGAY - Also called the "wild prune," the wongay (*Pouteria sericea*) is an Australian fruit that grows wild and was one of many gathered foods of the Aboriginal population.

Common names and synonyms: Wild prune.

Wong bok - *see* **CHINESE CABBAGE**

Wood ear - *see* **CLOUD EAR, MUSHROOMS AND FUNGI**

Woodland strawberry - *see* **WILD STRAWBERRY**

WOODRUFF - Several plants of the genus *Asperula*, and especially *A. odorata* (= *Galium odoratum*), are called woodruff, *Waldmeister,* and sweet woodruff. Although a native of Eurasia, woodruff is naturalized in North America. It has small, white flowers with an aroma when dried that is used for flavoring May wine, other drinks, and in Europe a variety of foodstuffs as well.

Common names and synonyms: Sweet woodruff, *Waldmeister.*

WOOD SORREL - Any of the approximately 850 species of the genus *Oxalis* may be labeled "wood sorrel," although the term is technically limited to *O. acetosella* and *O. violacea*. A perennial herb found in Europe and North America, *O. acetosella* - also known as "European wood sorrel" or "Irish shamrock" - bears leaves that have been eaten as a vegetable. *Oxalis violacea,* also a perennial herb, and sometimes called "violet wood sorrel," is another American plant that was eaten by Native Americans.

Common names and synonyms: European wood sorrel, Irish shamrock, violet wood sorrel.

Wormseed - *see* **EPAZOTE**

WORMWOOD - There are a number of plants of the genus *Artemisia* called wormwood, especially *A. absinthium*. The latter is a native of Europe and is now naturalized in North America. Its leaves were employed in Europe in centuries past for flavoring sauces. The plant also yields a bitter extract used for flavoring vermouth. It was employed in making absinthe, which has been outlawed in many countries since World War I because the combination of wormwood's essential oil and alcohol was not only highly addictive but could and did produce hallucinations and convulsions that sometimes led to death.

See also: "Spices and Flavorings," Part II, Section F, Chapter 1.

Wych-hazel - *see* **WITCH-HAZEL**

XICALLI (*see also* **CALABASH**) - *Xicalli* is the Nahuatl name for a gourd of the tree *Crescentia cujete;* in Spanish, the gourd became *jicara* and the tree became *jicaro*. When the Spaniards first reached the New World, *xicalli* was used by the Aztecs to fashion vessels for drinking chocolate and bailing out canoes. Doubtless in the process of making such cups and pails, the seeds of the gourd were sometimes retained to be roasted, and perhaps even the pulp was consumed. It is probably the case, however, that these squashes were initially cultivated for the manufacture of liquid containers, and only later were the edible seeds and flesh exploited.

Common names and synonyms: Güiro, higüero, jicara, jicaro.

Xuxu - *see* **CHAYOTE**

Ya - *see* **COCOYAM**
Ya bené - *see* **COCOYAM**
YACÓN - Also called "leafcup," yacón (*Polymnia sonchifolia*) - like ajipa - is often confused with jícama and, in fact, is called jícama in parts of South America. The plant originated in the Andes, was domesticated long before the Europeans reached the New World, and today is cultivated from Venezuela to northeastern Argentina and in New Zealand and the United States as well. The plant's purple roots (which are orange colored on the inside) are sweet tasting and generally eaten raw, but only after several days of exposure to the sun, so that the peel shrivels.

Common names and synonyms: Leafcup.

YAM(S) (*see also* **AIR POTATO, BITTER YAM, BONIATO, CHINESE YAM, CUSH-CUSH YAM, LESSER YAM, WATER YAM, WHITE YAM, WILD YAM, YELLOW YAM**) - There are several species of yams (genus *Dioscorea*) grown in the world's tropical and subtropical regions, some of which are used solely for medicinal purposes. Among the most common edible species are the water yam or greater yam (*D. alata*), a native of Southeast Asia, and the yellow yam (*D.* × *cayenensis*) and white yam (*D. rotundata*), both of which are natives of Africa. In the New World, the major species is *D. trifida,* with common names such as Barbados yam, yampie, *ñame,* and cush-cush.

Yams evolved separately in Asia, Africa, and the Americas, and although they may have been cultivated as many as 10,000 years ago in Asia, for most who ate them they were a gathered food for many more years than that. Indeed, until relatively recently, the wild yam was a valued food for some Native American groups in North America. Yams are cultivated for their tubers, which are between 15 and 40 percent starch. These can reach upwards of 100 pounds in weight, and many average some 30 pounds, although most are about the size of the sweet potatoes they resemble.

Depending on the kind, flesh color can range from white to orange to orange-red to purple. Some Old World yams contain a poisonous alkaloid and must be carefully peeled and then boiled to be safe. In addition to use in stews and soups, yams are baked, fried, and boiled like potatoes. In Japan, yams are also battered and deep-fried.

See in addition: "Sweet Potatoes and Yams," Part II, Section B, Chapter 5.

Yam bean - *see* **AFRICAN YAM BEAN, AJIPA, JÍCAMA**

YAM DAISY - With daisy-like flowers aboveground and yam-like tubers below, it is not difficult to understand how the yam daisy (*Microseris lanceolata,* formerly *M. scapigera,* and also called *murnong*) got its name. The tubers constituted an important food of the southeastern Australian Aborigines, whose women dug up the roots with digging sticks, then roasted them in baskets in earth ovens. The appearance of the plant's flowers was the signal to the gatherers that the roots were fully developed. Other important flowering plants with roots that were dug and consumed by the Aborigines were the "bulbine lily" (*Bulbine bulbosa*), the "vanilla lily" (*Arthropodium milleflorum*), and the "milkmaid" (*Burchardia umbellata*).

Common names and synonyms: Bulbine lily, milkmaid, *murnong,* vanilla lily.

Yamp - *see* **INDIAN POTATO**
Yampa - *see* **INDIAN POTATO**
Yampah - *see* **INDIAN POTATO**
Yampi - *see* **CUSH-CUSH YAM**
Yang tao - *see* **KIWI FRUIT**
Yard-long bean - *see* **COWPEA**

YARROW - Known as "milfoil" in Europe, yarrow (*Achillea millefolium*) is a pungent Eurasian herb now widely naturalized in North America. Its strongly flavored leaves enliven salads and soups; a tisane is also made from the plant, and it has been employed to flavor beer. Yarrow's genus is named for Achilles, who was said to have discovered its healing powers, and its medicinal uses have subsequently been myriad. A variety called western yarrow (*A. millefolium* var. *lanulosa*), which grows in the desert Southwest of North America, was much used by Native Americans.

Common names and synonyms: Milfoil.

YAUPON - Also known as cassina, the "Christmas teabush," and the "Carolina tea-tree," this holly (*Ilex vomitoria*) is found throughout the southeastern United States. The plant is a woody shrub that reaches 5 to 10 feet in height, with gray bark, dark green leaves, and yellow or orange berries. Native Americans made a ceremonial tea from the leaves by first toasting and then boiling them. This was the "black drink," the consumption of which might be followed by vomiting. The Muskogee (Creek) Indians as well as the related Seminoles of Florida were enthusiastic users, and indeed, the name of the Seminole war chief Osceola (1804?-38), which translates as "black water," was given to him because of his ritual position in the black-drink ceremony. Europeans who drank the black drink, however, experienced no emetic effect, and tests done in the twentieth century have established that yaupon is not an emetic. Thus, the vomiting seems to have been the result of a cultural practice. But yaupon *is* a natural source of caffeine, similar to *Ilex paraguariensis,* the yerba-maté tea of South America. The white residents of North Carolina's Outer Banks continued to drink yaupon until the twentieth century, as did residents of Charleston, South Carolina. The Europeans who first encountered the tea sent some of the leaves back to Europe, but this and subsequent efforts to establish yaupon tea as a commercial product have met with no success.

Common names and synonyms: Black drink, Carolina tea-tree, cassina, Christmas tea-bush.

Yautía - *see* MALANGA

YEHIB - Native to the arid regions near the Horn of Africa, this evergreen shrub (*Cordeauxia edulis*) is now an endangered species. It produces pods embracing a seed that weighs between 2 and 3 grams. Rich in starch and sugars, the pleasant-tasting nut is used by nomads in the region as a staple food.

Yellow bedstraw - *see* LADY'S BEDSTRAW

Yellowberry - *see* CLOUDBERRY

Yellow chives - *see* CHINESE CHIVE(S)

Yellow cleavers - *see* LADY'S BEDSTRAW

Yellow dhal(l) - *see* PIGEON PEA

Yellow dock - *see* CURLED DOCK

Yellow ginseng - *see* BLUE COHOSH

Yellow gram - *see* CHICKPEA

Yellow granadilla - *see* PASSION FRUIT

Yellow melilot - *see* SWEET CLOVER

YELLOW MOMBIN - A native of northern South America and Central America, the yellow mombin (*Spondias mombin*) is now grown throughout most lowlands of tropical America, although not with much enthusiasm, and it is not highly commercialized. The fruits are oblong, average about 10 inches in length, and vary greatly in taste, with some sweet but others harsh and unpleasant. They are consumed raw, made into preserves, and used as a flavoring.

Yellow nutsedge - *see* CHUFA

YELLOW ROCKET - Although considered a weed by some, this biennial herb (*Barbarea vulgaris*) has leaves that, when young, have occasionally been used in salads, whereas older leaves have been cooked as a vegetable. Native to Europe, the plant can now be found in North Africa, Asia, North America, New Zealand, and Australia. It is also known as "rocket," "upland cress," and "winter cress" and is rich in vitamins A and C.

Common names and synonyms: Rocket, upland cress, winter cress.

Yellowroot - *see* GOLDTHREAD

Yellow salsify - *see* MOONFLOWER

Yellow turnip - *see* RUTABAGA

YELLOW WILD-INDIGO - An herb with countless common names, ranging from "American indigo" to "rattlebush," yellow wild-indigo (*Baptisia tinctoria*) is found across eastern and central North America,

its native territory. Its young shoots were cooked and eaten by Native Americans.

Common names and synonyms: American indigo, rattlebush.

YELLOW YAM (*see also* YAMS) - Also known as "Guinea yam" and "yellow Guinea yam," the yellow yam (*Dioscorea* × *cayenensis*) is a West African native that was carried to the West Indies via the early-sixteenth-century slave trade. It continues to be widely cultivated in West Africa, where it is perhaps the most important yam species. It is of much less importance in the Caribbean and is not grown in other tropical regions of the world. The yellow yam is one of those yams used to make the famous West African "foo-foo," and is also roasted, boiled, and fried.

Common names and synonyms: Guinea yam, twelve-months yam, yellow Guinea yam.

See in addition: "Sweet Potatoes and Yams," Part II, Section B, Chapter 5.

Yerba de conejo - *see* QUELITES

YERBA MATÉ - Also called maté and Paraguay(an) tea, yerba maté is a tea made from the dried leaves and young shoots of the evergreen tree *Ilex paraguariensis.* It is mildly stimulative and was being consumed throughout the day and evening by males in what is now Paraguay and Brazil long before the Spaniards and Portuguese ever arrived in the New World. Most likely, then as now, the natives were drinking the tea out of dried gourds – actually sucking it through a tube called a *bombilla* with a strainer attached.

Common names and synonyms: Maté, Paraguay(an) tea.

YERBA SANTA - Common along the Pacific coast from Oregon to California, yerba santa (*Eriodictyon californicum*) is an evergreen shrub with leaves that are covered with a fragrant resin. They have long been chewed to alleviate thirst and also are made into a tea.

Common names and synonyms: Bear's-weed, gumplant, mountain balm.

YOUNGBERRY (*see also* BERRIES) - Developed by B. M. Young, a twentieth-century fruit grower, the youngberry (genus *Rubus*) is a hybrid between a blackberry and a dewberry. A juicy and very large berry, the youngberry is mostly cultivated and available in the western United States.

Young hyson - *see* TEA

Ysaño - *see* MASHUA

Yuca - *see* MANIOC

YUCCA - There are various members of the genus *Yucca* with white flowers that in the American Southwest are sometimes added to salads. *Yucca filamentosa* has been a perennial favorite of the region and was exploited by Native Americans, who boiled or roasted its flower stalks and buds and ate its plumlike fruits.

Common names and synonyms: Adam's-needle, spoonleaf yucca.

Yuen sai - *see* **CILANTRO, CORIANDER**
Yun er - *see* **CLOUD EAR**
Yuquilla - *see* **ARROWROOT**
Yu-tao - *see* **COCOYAM**
YUZU - A golden yellow citron, the yuzu (*Citrus medica*) is about the size of a small orange. It is a very sour Japanese fruit, which is cultivated for its aromatic rind. The Japanese carve the rind into traditional shapes and use it as a garnish. The yuzu can sometimes be found in Asian markets in the United States.

Z

Zahidi date - *see* **DATE**
ZAMIA - Of the cycad family (and looking something like palm trees except for their fern-like as well as palmlike leaves), these tropical American members of the genus *Zamia* (including *Z. integrifolia* in southeastern North America) have underground roots that Native Americans of the West Indies and southern North America pounded, grated, dried, ground, boiled, mashed, washed with plenty of water, and drained and dried (again) to obtain starch for making bread and porridges. These rigorous methods were necessary to render the vegetable safe; without such efforts, the roots are toxic – even deadly. The seeds from the cone-like fruits, as well as the zamia stems, are also toxic and must be cooked or otherwise processed before they become edible. Almost from the time they reached the island of Hispaniola, Columbus and his men began dining on zamia bread prepared by the Taino Indians.
Common names and synonyms: Coontie, cycad, Florida arrowroot, Florida sago, Seminole bread, starchy breadroot.
Zanzibar oil-vine - *see* **OYSTERNUT**
Zapote - *see* **BLACK SAPOTE, SAPODILLA, WHITE SAPOTE**
Zapotillo - *see* **SAPODILLA**
ZINFANDEL (*see also* **GRAPES**) - This red wine grape (*Vitis vinifera*) has been something of a surprise in California, where it was earlier employed to make "jug" wines. In the past two decades, however, it has been developed into one of the best of the red varietal grapes and is the most widely grown grape in the state. Although the Zinfandel is of obscure European origin, it has become known as "California's grape," in part because it has been grown in that state since the late nineteenth century, and Zinfandel wines have been a major American contribution to the world of wine. There are both red and white Zinfandels (actually, the "white zinfandel" is a "blush" wine, and one only recently made available), or "Zins," as they are popularly known.
See in addition: "Wine," Part III, Chapter 13.
ZUCCHINI (*see also* **SQUASH AND PUMPKIN**) - Although winter squashes do not enjoy the popularity they once did, the same is not true for summer squashes, and especially not for the versatile zucchini. An American summer squash, the zucchini (*Cucurbita pepo*) bears an Italian name that is the diminutive of *zucca,* meaning "gourd." As a rule, this vegetable has a smooth, shiny, green, very thin rind – reminiscent of that of its cousin, the cucumber. But the flesh is firmer. The zucchini also comes with a deep yellow skin – this is called a "golden zucchini" – and there is another variety called "Italian squash" or *cocozelle.* Zucchini goes well with tomato sauce and is worked into numerous main and side dishes. On its own it can be steamed, fried, boiled, broiled, simmered, stuffed, and eaten raw as an appetizer and in salads.
Common names and synonyms: Cocozelle, courgette, golden zucchini, Italian squash, vegetable marrow.
See in addition: "Squash," Part II, Section C, Chapter 8.
Zula nut - *see* **CHUFA**
ZULU MILKBERRY - A southern African tree or shrub, *Manilkara concolor* varies in height from 9 to 23 feet and bears Zulu milkberries - egg-shaped fruits that range from yellow to bright red in color. Deliciously sweet, the fruits are good when eaten fresh but also are fermented to make alcoholic beverages. Zulu milkberries are highly prized and are frequently reserved for village chiefs.
Zuttano - *see* **AVOCADO**

Sources Consulted

Allen, Betty Molesworth. 1967. *Malayan fruits.* Singapore.

Andrews, Jean. 1984. *Peppers: The domesticated capsicums.* Austin, Tex.

Arbizu, C., and M. Tapia. 1994. Andean tubers. In *Neglected crops: 1492 from a different perspective,* ed. J. E. Hernándo Bermejo and J. León, 149-63. FAO Plant Production and Protection Series No. 26. Rome.

Arkcoll, David. 1990. New crops from Brazil. In *Advances in new crops,* ed. J. Janick and J. E. Simon, 367-71. Portland, Ore.

Ayerza, Ricardo, and Wayne Coates. 1996. New industrial crops: Northwestern Argentina Regional Project. In *Progress in new crops,* ed. J. Janick, 45-51. Alexandria, Va.

Bailey, L. H. 1976. *Hortus third: A concise dictionary of plants cultivated in the United States and Canada initially compiled by Liberty Hyde Bailey and Ethel Zoe Bailey.* Revised and expanded by the staff of the Liberty Hyde Bailey Hortorium. New York.

Bartlett, Jonathan. 1996. *The cook's dictionary and culinary reference.* Chicago.

Beauthéac, Nadine, ed. 1992. *The book of tea,* trans. Deke Dusinberre. Italy.

Bender, A. E., and D. Bender. 1995. *A dictionary of food and nutrition.* Oxford.

Brothwell, D., and P. Brothwell. 1969. *Food in antiquity: A survey of the diet of early peoples.* London.

Burkill, I. H. 1966. *A dictionary of the economic products of the Malay Peninsula.* 2 vols. Kuala Lumpur.

California Rare Fruit Growers. 1995. Online, CRFG Publications 1969-89, World Wide Web, Jan. 9, 1999.

Campbell, Richard J. 1996. South American fruits deserving further attention. In *Progress in new crops,* ed. J. Janick, 431-9. Alexandria, Va.

Cantwell, Marita, Xunli Nie, Ru Jing Zong, and Mas Yamaguchi. 1996. Asian vegetables: Selected fruit and leafy types. In *Progress in new crops,* ed. J. Janick, 488-95. Alexandria, Va.

Carpenter, Kenneth J. 1986. *The history of scurvy and vitamin C.* Cambridge, London, and New York.

1994. *Protein and energy: A study of changing ideas in nutrition.* Cambridge, New York, and Melbourne.

Chandler, William H. 1950. *Evergreen orchards.* Philadelphia, Pa.

Coe, Sophie D. 1994. *America's first cuisines.* Austin, Tex.

College of Agricultural Sciences. Ongoing project; last update Mar. 17, 1998. Commercial vegetable production guides. Online, Oregon State University, World Wide Web, Nov. 3, 1998.

Collins, Wanda W. 1993. Root vegetables: New uses for old crops. In *New crops,* ed. J. Janick and J. E. Simon, 533-7. New York.

Considine, John A. 1996. Emerging indigenous crops of Australia. In *Progress in new crops,* ed. J. Janick, 26-36. Alexandria, Va.

Couplan, François. 1998. *The encyclopedia of edible plants of North America.* New Canaan, Conn.

Densmore, Frances. 1974. *How Indians use wild plants for food, medicine and crafts.* New York.

Douglas, James A. 1993. New crop development in New Zealand. In *New crops,* ed. J. Janick and J. E. Simon, 51-7. New York.

Duke, James A. 1983. *Handbook of energy crops.* Online, Purdue University Center for New Crops and Plant Products, World Wide Web, Oct. 27, 1998.

Dunmire, William W., and Gail D. Tierney. 1997. *Wild plants and native peoples of the Four Corners.* Santa Fe, N. Mex.

Ensminger, Audrey H., et al. 1983. *Foods and nutrition encyclopedia.* 2 vols. Clovis, Calif.

Epple, Anne Orth, and Lewis E. Epple. 1995. *A field guide to the plants of Arizona.* Helena, Mont.

Facciola, Stephen. 1992. *Cornucopia, a source book of edible plants.* Second edition. Vista, Calif.

Felker, Peter. 1996. Commercializing mesquite, leucaena, and cactus in Texas. In *Progress in new crops,* ed. J. Janick, 133-7. Alexandria, Va.

Flowerdew, Bob. 1995. *The complete book of fruit.* New York.

Foster, Nelson, and Linda S. Cordell. 1992. *Chilies to chocolate: Food the Americas gave the world.* Tucson, Ariz., and London.

Freedman, Robert, comp. Ongoing project; last update March 10, 1998. Famine foods. Online, Purdue University Center for New Crops and Plant Products, World Wide Web, Oct. 19, 1998.

Giacometti, D., and E. Lleras. 1994. Subtropical Myrtaceae. In *Neglected crops: 1492 from a different perspective,* ed. J. E. Hernándo Bermejo and J. León, 229-37. FAO Plant Production and Protection Series No. 26. Rome.

Gray, Patience. 1987. *Honey from a weed: Fasting and feasting in Tuscany, Catalonia, the Cyclades and Apulia.* New York.

Griffith, Mark. 1994. *Index of garden plants.* Portland, Ore.

Grigson, Jane, and Charlotte Knox. 1986. *Cooking with exotic fruits and vegetables.* New York.

Hamilton, Philip, et al. Ongoing project; last update July 5, 1998. Edible fruit. Online, *UW Oykangand and UW Olkola dictionary,* World Wide Web, 1 Sept. 1998.

Harlan, Jack R. 1993. Genetic resources in Africa. In *New crops,* ed. J. Janick and J. E. Simon, 65-8. New York.

Heiser, Charles B., Jr. 1979. *The gourd book.* Norman, Okla., and London.

 1981. *The story of food.* San Francisco.

 1985. *Of plants and peoples.* Norman, Okla.

Hymowitz, Theodore. 1990. Grain legumes. In *Advances in new crops,* ed. J. Janick and J. E. Simon, 54-7. Portland, Ore.

Kiple, Kenneth F., ed. 1993. *The Cambridge world history of human disease.* New York and Cambridge.

Janson, H. Frederic. 1996. *Pomona's harvest: An illustrated chronicle of antiquarian fruit literature.* Portland, Ore.

Lamberts, Mary, and Jonathan H. Crane. 1990. Tropical fruits. In *Advances in new crops,* ed. J. Janick and J. E. Simon, 337- 55. Portland, Ore.

Mabberley, D. J., ed. 1997. *The plant book: A portable dictionary of the vascular plants.* Second edition. Cambridge and New York.

MacNeish, Richard S. 1991. *The origins of agriculture and settled life.* Norman, Okla., and London.

Magness, J. R., G. M. Markle, and C. C. Compton. 1971. *Food and feed crops of the United States.* Interregional Research Project IR-4, IR Bulletin 1 (Bulletin 828, New Jersey Agricultural Experiment Station). Online, Purdue University Center for New Crops and Plant Products, World Wide Web, Sept. 22, 1998.

Mahdeem, H. 1994. Custard apples. In *Neglected crops: 1492 from a different perspective,* ed. J. E. Hernándo Bermejo and J. León, 85-92. FAO Plant Production and Protection Series No. 26. Rome.

Margen, Sheldon, and the editors of the University of California at Berkeley. Wellness letter. 1992. *The wellness encyclopedia of food and nutrition.* New York.

Martin, Franklin W., Carl W. Campbell, and Ruth M. Ruberté. 1987. *Perennial edible fruits of the tropics: An inventory.* USDA Agriculture Handbook No. 642. Washington, D.C.

Matossian, Mary Kilbourne. 1989. *Poisons of the past: Molds, epidemics, and history.* New Haven, Conn., and London.

McGee, Harold. 1984. *On food and cooking: The science and lore of the kitchen.* New York.

McHargue, Lawrence T. 1996. Macadamia production in southern California. In *Progress in new crops,* ed. J. Janick, 458-62. Alexandria, Va.

McKean, Steve. Unpublished; ongoing project. Edible fruits of Zululand. Online, World Wide Web, Jan. 8, 1999.

Miller, Orson K., Jr. 1979. *Mushrooms of North America.* New York.

Mizrahi, Y., and A. Nerd. 1996. New crops as a possible solution for the troubled Israeli export market. In *Progress in new crops,* ed. J. Janick, 37-45. Alexandria, Va.

Mujica, A. 1994. Andean grains and legumes. In *Neglected crops: 1492 from a different perspective,* ed. J. E. Hernándo Bermejo and J. León, 131-48. FAO Plant Production and Protection Series No. 26. Rome.

Nagy, Steven, and Philip E. Shaw. 1980. *Tropical and subtropical fruits.* Westport, Conn.

National Research Council. 1996. *Lost crops of Africa.* Vol. 1: *Grains.* Washington, D.C.

Nerd, Avinoam, James A. Aronson, and Yosef Mizrahi. 1990. Introduction and domestication of rare and wild fruit and nut trees for desert areas. In *Advances in new crops,* ed. J. Janick and J. E. Simon, 355-63. Portland, Ore.

Ng, Timothy J. 1993. New opportunities in the Cucurbitaceae. In *New crops,* ed. J. Janick and J. E. Simon, 538-46. New York.

Noda, H., C. R. Bueno, and D. F. Silva Filho. 1994. Guinea arrowroot. In *Neglected crops: 1492 from a different perspective,* ed. J. E. Hernándo Bermejo and J. León, 239-44. FAO Plant Production and Protection Series No. 26. Rome.

Novak, F. A. 1966. *The pictorial encyclopedia of plants and flowers,* ed. J. G. Barton. London and New York.

O'Hair, Stephen K. 1990. Tropical root and tuber crops. In *Advances in new crops,* ed. J. Janick and J. E. Simon, 424-8. Portland, Ore.

Ortiz, Elisabeth Lambert. 1992. *The encyclopedia of herbs, spices and flavorings.* London.

Passmore, Jacki. 1991. *The encyclopedia of Asian food and cooking.* New York.

Peet, Mary. Last update Jul. 1, 1998. *Sustainable practices for vegetable production in the South.* Online, Hort Base, North Carolina State University, World Wide Web, Nov. 3, 1998.

Purseglove, J. W. 1968. *Tropical plants - dicotyledons.* London.

 1972. *Tropical crops - monocotyledons.* London.

Rhodes, David. Ongoing project; last update Oct. 2, 1998. Potatoes - general introduction. Online, Purdue University Center for New Crops and Plant Products, World Wide Web, 17 Nov. 1998.

 Ongoing project; last update Oct. 10, 1998. Squash, pumpkins and gourds - general introduction. Online, Purdue University Center for New Crops and Plant Products, World Wide Web, Nov. 3, 1998.

Roecklein, John C., and PingSun Leung. 1987. *A profile of economic plants.* New Brunswick, Canada.

Rosengarten, F. 1984. *The book of edible nuts.* New York.

Royse, Daniel J. 1996. Specialty mushrooms. In *Progress in new crops,* ed. J. Janick, 464-75. Alexandria, Va.

Saade, R. Lira, and S. Montes Hernández. 1994. Cucurbits. In *Neglected crops: 1492 from a different perspective,* ed. J. E. Hernándo Bermejo and J. León, 63-77. Plant Production and Protection Series No. 26, FAO. Rome.

Salaman, R. N. 1940. Why "Jerusalem artichoke." *Journal of the Royal Horticultural Society* 95: 338-48, 376-83.

Schneider, Elizabeth. 1986. *Uncommon fruits and vegetables: A commonsense guide.* New York.

Schneider, M. 1990. Acorns as a staple food - different types and change of exploitation through time. *Bodenkultur* 41: 81-8.

Sievers, A. F. 1930. *The herb hunters guide.* USDA Miscellaneous Publication No. 77. Washington, D.C.

Simmons, N. W., and J. Smartt, eds. 1995. *Evolution of crop plants.* Second edition. London.

Simon, J. E., A. F. Chadwick, and L. E. Craker. 1984. *Herbs: An indexed bibliography, 1971-1980. The scientific literature on selected herbs, and aromatic and medicinal plants of the temperate zone.* Hamden, Conn.

Stallknecht, G. F., K. M. Gilbertson, and J. E. Ranney. 1996. Alternative wheat cereals as food grains: Einkorn, emmer, spelt, kamut, and triticale. In *Progress in new crops,* ed. J. Janick, 156-70. Alexandria, Va.

Stephens, James M. 1994. Guar - *Cyamopsis tetragonolobus* (L.) Taub. Online, University of Florida Horticultural Sciences Department, World Wide Web.

Tannahill, Reay. 1988. *Food in history.* New York.

Terrell, Edward E., Steven R. Hill, John H. Wiersema, and William E. Rice. 1986. *A checklist of names for 3,000 vascular plants of economic importance.* USDA Agriculture Handbook No. 505. Washington, D.C.

Thames, Shelby F., and Thomas P. Schuman. 1996. New crops or new uses for old crops: Where should the emphasis be? In *Progress in new crops,* ed. J. Janick, 8-18. Alexandria, Va.

Tindall, H. D. 1983. *Vegetables in the tropics.* Westport, Conn.

Tous, Joan, and Louise Ferguson. 1996. Mediterranean fruits. In *Progress in new crops,* ed. J. Janick, 416-30. Alexandria, Va.

Toussaint-Samat, Maguelonne. 1992. *History of food,* trans. Anthea Bell. Cambridge, Mass.

Trager, James. 1995. *The food chronology.* New York.

Ukers, William H. 1936. *The romance of tea: An outline history of tea and tea-drinking through sixteen hundred years.* New York and London.

Uphof, J. C. Thomas. 1968. *Dictionary of economic plants.* New York.

Vaughan, J. G., and C. A. Geissler. 1997. *The new Oxford book of food plants.* Oxford, New York, and Tokyo.

Wagoner, Peggy. 1995. Wild triga intermediate wheatgrass. Online, New Crop Factsheet, Purdue University Center for New Crops and Plant Products, World Wide Web, Sept. 27, 1998.

Walton, Stuart. 1996. *The world encyclopedia of wine.* New York.

Ward, Artemas. 1848-1925. *The grocer's encyclopedia.* New York.

Watson, L., and M. J. Dallwitz. 1992 ff. The families of flowering plants: Descriptions, illustrations, identification, and information retrieval. Online, World Wide Web, May 8, 1998.

Westland, Pamela. 1987. *The encyclopedia of herbs and spices.* London.

Yamaguchi, Mas. 1990. Asian vegetables. In *Advances in new crops,* ed. J. Janick and J. E. Simon, 387-90. Portland, Ore.

Zohary, D., and M. Hopf. 1993. *Domestication of plants: The Old World.* Oxford.

Index of Latin Names

Abelmoschus esculentus - see **Okra**
Abelmoschus manihot - see **Sunset Hibiscus**
Aberia caffra - see **Kai Apple**
Abies balsamea - see **Balsam Fir**
Acacia angustissima - see **Acacia**
Acacia greggii - see **Acacia**
Acacia senegal - see **Acacia**
Acer saccharum - see **Maple Syrup and Maple Sugar**
Achillea millefolium - see **Yarrow**
Achillea millefolium var. *lanulosa* - see **Yarrow**
Acorus calamus - see **Sweet Flag**
Acrocomia, genus - see **Macaw Palm**
Actinidia chinensis - see **Kiwi Fruit**
Adansonia digitata - see **Baobab**
Aegle marmelos - see **Bael Fruit**
Aesculus, genus - see **Buckeye**
Aesculus hippocastanum - see **Chestnut**
Aframomum melegueta - see **Melegueta Pepper**
Agaricus bisporus - see **Mushrooms and Fungi**
Agaricus campestris - see **Mushrooms and Fungi**
Agaricus rodmani - see **Mushrooms and Fungi**
Agave americana - see **Agave**
Agave lecheguilla - see **Lecheguilla**
Agave tequilana - see **Agave**
Agropyron intermedium var. *trichophorum* - see **Wild Triga**
Agropyron repens - see **Couch Grass**
Aleurites moluccana - see **Candlenut**
Alkanna tinctoria - see **Alkanet**
Alliaria officinalis - see **Garlic-Mustard**
Alliaria petiolata - see **Garlic-Mustard**
Allium ascalonicum - see **Shallot(s)**
Allium canadense - see **Garlic**
Allium cepa - see **Onion, Onion Tree**
Allium cepa - see **Shallot(s) (mentioned)**
Allium chinense - see **Rakkyo**
Allium fistulosum - see **Welsh Onion**
Allium oleraceum - see **Garlic**
Allium porrum - see **Leek(s)**
Allium sativum - see **Garlic**
Allium schoenoprasum - see **Chive(s)**
Allium tricoccum - see **Wild Leek(s)**
Allium tuberosum - see **Chinese Chive(s)**
Allium vineale - see **Garlic**
Alocasia cucullata - see **Alocasia**
Alocasia indica - see **Alocasia**
Alocasia macrorrhiza - see **Alocasia**
Alpinia coerulea - see **Wild Ginger**
Alpinia galanga - see **Galangal**

Alpina officinarum - see **Galangal**
Althaea officinalis - see **Mallow**
Amaranthus, genus - see **Callaloo, Goosefoot, Quelites**
Amaranthus caudatus - see **Amaranth**
Amaranthus cruentus - see **Amaranth**
Amaranthus hypochondriacus - see **Amaranth**
Amaranthus tricolor - see **Chinese Amaranth**
Ambrosia, genus - see **Ragweed**
Amelanchier alnifolia - see **Serviceberry**
Amomum cardamomum - see **Cardamom**
Amphicarpa bracteata - see **Hog Peanut**
Amygdalus communis - see **Almond**
Anacardium occidentale - see **Cashew**
Ananas, genus - see **Bromelia**
Ananas comosus - see **Pineapple**
Andropogon furcatus - see **Blue-Stem**
Anemone flaccida - see **Anemone Greens**
Anemone hepatica - see **Anemone Greens**
Anemone hupehensis Hort. Lemoine - see **Anemone Greens**
Anemone narcissiflora - see **Anemone Greens**
Anemone patens - see **Anemone Greens**
Anethum graveolens - see **Dill**
Angelica archangelica - see **Angelica**
Angelica atropurpurea - see **Purplestem Angelica**
Annona, genus - see **Atemoya**
Annona cherimola - see **Cherimoya**
Annona diversifolia - see **Ilama**
Annona muricata - see **Soursop**
Annona purpurea - see **Soncoya**
Annona reticulata - see **Custard Apple**
Annona scleroderma - see **Poshte**
Annona senegalensis - see **Wild Custard Apple**
Annona squamosa - see **Sweetsop**
Anoda cristata - see **Quelites**
Anthemis nobilis - see **Chamomile**
Anthriscus cerefolium - see **Chervil**
Antidesma bunius - see **Bignay**
Antidesma ghaesembilla - see **Bush Currant**
Apios americana - see **Apios**
Apios tuberosa - see **Apios**
Apium graveolens - see **Celery and Celery Root**
Apium graveolens var. *dulce* - see **Celery and Celery Root, Celery Seed**
Apium graveolens var. *rapaceum* - see **Celery and Celery Root**
Apocynum cannabinum - see **Hemp Dogbane**
Arachis hypogaea - see **Peanut**

Aralia cordata – see **Udo**
Araucaria araucana – see **Chilean Pine**
Arbutus unedo – see **Strawberry Tree**
Arctium lappa – see **Burdock**
Arctostaphylos, genus – see **Bearberry**
Arctostaphylos uva-ursi – see **Heather**
Areca catechu – see **Betel Nut**
Argania sideroxylon – see **Argan**
Arisaema triphyllum – see **Indian Turnip**
Armillaria edodes – see **Mushrooms and Fungi**
Armillariella mellea – see **Mushrooms and Fungi**
Armoracia lapathifolia – see **Horseradish**
Armoracia rusticana – see **Horseradish**
Aronia arbutifolia – see **Chokeberry**
Aronia melanocarpa – see **Chokeberry**
Arracacia esculenta – see **Arracacha**
Arracacia xanthorrhiza – see **Arracacha**
Artemisia abrotanum – see **Southernwood**
Artemisia absinthium – see **Wormwood**
Artemisia dracunculoides – see **Tarragon**
Artemisia dracunculus – see **Tarragon**
Artemisia verlotorum – see **Mugwort**
Artemisia vulgaris – see **Mugwort**
Arthropodium milleflorum – see **Yam Daisy**
Artocarpus altilis – see **Breadfruit**
Artocarpus communis – see **Breadfruit**
Artocarpus heterophyllus – see **Jackfruit**
Artocarpus incisus – see **Breadfruit**
Artocarpus integer – see **Chempedak**
Artocarpus integrifolius – see **Jackfruit**
Arundinaria gigantea – see **Large Cane**
Asarum canadense – see **Wild Ginger**
Asarum caudatum – see **Wild Ginger**
Asclepias syriaca – see **Milkweed**
Asclepias tuberosa – see **Butterfly Weed**
Ascophyllum nodosum – see **Knotted Wrack**
Asimina triloba – see **Papaw**
Asparagus officinalis – see **Asparagus**
Asperula odorata – see **Woodruff**
Astrocaryum tucuma – see **Tucuma**
Athyrium, genus – see **Pohole**
Atriplex, genus – see **Orach**
Atriplex canescens – see **Saltbush**
Atriplex halimus – see **Sea Purslane**
Atriplex hastata – see **Sea Purslane**
Atriplex hortensis – see **Orach**
Atriplex hymenelytra – see **Saltbush**
Attalea cohune – see **Cohune Palm**
Auricularia auricula – see **Cloud Ear, Mushrooms and Fungi**
Auricularia polytrica – see **Cloud Ear, Mushrooms and Fungi**
Avena sativa – see **Oat(s)**
Averrhoa bilimbi – see **Belimbing**
Averrhoa carambola – see **Carambola**

Baccaurea motleyana – see **Rambai**
Bactris gasipaës – see **Pejebaye**
Balanites, genus – see **Balanites**
Baptisia tinctoria – see **Yellow Wild-Indigo**
Barbarea vulgaris – see **Yellow Rocket**
Basella alba – see **Malabar Spinach**
Basella rubra – see **Malabar Spinach**
Beilschmiedia tawa – see **Tawa Berry**
Benincasa cerifera – see **Fuzzy Melon**
Benincasa hispida – see **Fuzzy Melon, Melons**
Berberis thunbergii – see **Barberry**

Bertholletia excelsa – see **Brazil Nut**
Beta vulgaris L. ssp. *maritima* – see **Beet**
Beta vulgaris – see **Beet, Mangelwurzel**
Beta vulgaris var. *cicla* – see **Swiss Chard**
Beta vulgaris saccharifera – see **Beet**
Betula lenta – see **Sweet Birch**
Bixa orellana – see **Annatto**
Blighia sapida – see **Ackee**
Boletus edulis – see **Bolete, Mushrooms and Fungi**
Bombax glabra – see **Malabar Nut**
Borago officinalis – see **Borage**
Borassus flabellifer – see **Wine Palm**
Bouea macrophylla – see **Kundangan**
Brassica alba – see **Mustard Seed**
Brassica alboglabra – see **Chinese Broccoli**
Brassica campestris – see **Flowering White Cabbage, Pakchoi and Kai Choy**
Brassica chinensis – see **Pakchoi and Kai Choy**
Brassica juncea – see **Mustard Greens, Mustard Seed**
Brassica napobrassica – see **Rutabaga**
Brassica napus – see **Broccoli Raab, Hanover Kale, Rape**
Brassica nigra – see **Mustard Seed**
Brassica oleracea – see **Broccoli, Brussels Sprout(s), Cabbage, Couve**
Brassica oleracea var. *acephala* – see **Collards, Kale**
Brassica oleracea var. *botrytis* – see **Cauliflower**
Brassica oleracea var. *gemmifera* – see **Brussels Sprout(s)**
Brassica oleracea var. *gongylodes* – see **Kohlrabi**
Brassica oleracea var. *italica* – see **Broccoli**
Brassica oleracea var. *italica* – see **Calabrese**
Brassica parachinensis – see **Chinese Flowering Cabbage**
Brassica pekinensis – see **Chinese Cabbage**
Brassica rapa – see **Bok Choy**
Brassica rapa rapifera – see **Turnip and Turnip Greens**
Brassica rapa 'typhon' – see **Holland Greens**
Bromelia, genus – see **Bromelia**
Bromelia balansea – see **Pinguin**
Bromilia karatas – see **Pinguin**
Bromelia pinguin – see **Pinguin**
Bromelia trianae – see **Pinguin**
Brosimum alicastrum – see **Breadnut**
Broussonetia papyrifera – see **Paper Mulberry**
Bruguiera gymnorhiza – see **Burma Mangrove**
Buchanania arborescens – see **Little Gooseberry Tree**
Buchanania latifolia – see **Cuddapah Almond**
Bulbine bulbosa – see **Yam Daisy**
Bunchosia armeniaca – see **Bunchosia**
Burchardia umbellata – see **Yam Daisy**
Butia capitata – see **Jelly Palm**
Butyrospermum parkii – see **Shea Tree**
Byrsonima crassifolia – see **Nance**

Cajanus cajan – see **Pigeon Pea**
Cajanus indicus – see **Pigeon Pea**
Calathea allouia – see **Guinea Arrowroot**
Calendula officinalis – see **Marigold**
Calluna vulgaris – see **Heather**
Calocarpum sapota – see **Mamey Sapote**
Calocarpum viride – see **Green Sapote**
Caltha palustris – see **Cowslip**
Camassia esculenta – see **Camas**
Camassia leichtlinii – see **Camas**
Camassia quamash – see **Camas**
Camassia scilloides – see **Camas**
Camellia sinensis – see **Tea**
Campanula rapunculoides – see **Campanula**

Citrus paradisi - see **Grapefruit**
Citrus reticulata - see **Calamondin, Mandarin Orange, Rangpur** and **Kusaie** (mentioned), **Tangor**
Citrus sinensis - see **Blood Orange, Orange, Tangor**
Citrus taitensis - see **Otaheite Orange**
Clausena lansium - see **Wampi**
Cnidoscolus chayamansa - see **Chaya**
Coccinia cordifolia - see **Ivy Gourd**
Coccinia grandis - see **Ivy Gourd**
Coccoloba diversifolia - see **Pigeon Plum**
Coccoloba floridana - see **Pigeon Plum**
Coccoloba uvifera - see **Sea Grape**
Cochlearia officinalis - see **Scurvy Grass**
Cocos nucifera - see **Coconut**
Coffea arabica - see **Coffee**
Coffea canephora - see **Coffee**
Coffea robusta - see **Coffee**
Coix lacryma-jobi - see **Job's-Tears**
Cola acuminata - see **Kola Nut**
Cola nitida - see **Kola Nut**
Coleus amboinicus - see **Indian Borage**
Coleus parviflorus - see **Sudan Potato**
Coleus tuberosus - see **Sudan Potato**
Collybia velutipes - see **Enokitake**
Colocasia, genus - see **Aroids, Cocoyam**
Colocasia antiquorum - see **Taro**
Colocasia esculenta - see **Callaloo, Cocoyam, Malanga, Taro**
Comptonia peregrina - see **Sweet Fern**
Conopodium denudatum - see **Earth Nut**
Conzy canadensis - see **Horseweed**
Coptis trifolia - see **Goldthread**
Corchorus olitorius - see **Jew's-Mallow**
Cordeauxia edulis - see **Yehib**
Cordia myxa - see **Cordia**
Cordyline terminalis - see **Cabbage Tree**
Coriandrum sativum - see **Cilantro, Coriander**
Coriaria ruscifolia - see **Tutu Berry**
Cornus canadensis - see **Cornus**
Cornus florida - see **Cornus**
Cornus mas - see **Cornus**
Cortinellus shiitake - see **Mushrooms and Fungi**
Corylus americana - see **Hazelnut and Filbert**
Corylus avellana - see **Hazelnut and Filbert**
Corylus maxima - see **Hazelnut and Filbert**
Corynocarpus laevigata - see **Karaka**
Couepia longipendula - see **Eggnut**
Couma utilis - see **Sorva**
Crambe maritima - see **Seakale**
Crataegus, genus - see **Hawthorn Berry**
Crataegus azarolus - see **Azarole**
Crataegus douglasii - see **Black Haw**
Crataegus uniflora - see **Haw**
Crescentia cujete - see **Calabash, Xicalli**
Crithmum maritimum - see **Samphire**
Crocus sativus - see **Saffron**
Crotalaria pumila - see **Quelites**
Cryptotaenia canadensis - see **Honewort**
Cryptotaenia japonica - see **Honewort**
Cucumis, genus - see **Melons**
Cucumis anguria - see **Cucumber, Gherkin**
Cucumis melo - see **Armenian Cucumber, Cantaloupe and Muskmelon, Casaba (Melon), Honeydew (Melon), Ogen Melon**
Cucumis melo chito - see **Mango Melon**
Cucumis melo var. *flexuosus* - see **Cucumber**
Cucumis melo var. *cantalupensis* - see **Melons**
Cucumis melo var. *inodorus* - see **Melons**

Cucumis melo var. *reticulatus* - see **Melons**
Cucumis melo L. var. *conomon* - see **Gherkin**
Cucumis metuliferus - see **Cucumber, Kiwano**
Cucumis sativus - see **Cucumber**
Cucurbita, genus - see **Squash and Pumpkin**
Cucurbita ficifolia - see **Fig-Leafed Gourd, Squash and Pumpkin**
Cucurbita foetidissima - see **Buffalo Gourd, Squash and Pumpkin**
Cucurbita maxima - see **Australian Blue Squash, Banana Squash, Buttercup Squash, Golden Nugget (Squash), Hubbard Squash, Kabocha (Squash), Marrow, Pumpkin, Rouge Vif d'Étampes (Pumpkin), Squash and Pumpkin**
Cucurbita mixta - see **Cushaw (Squash), Pumpkin, Squash and Pumpkin**
Cucurbita moschata - see **Butternut Squash, Calabaza (Squash), Cushaw (Squash), Kabocha (Squash), Pumpkin, Squash and Pumpkin**
Cucurbita okeechobeenis - see **Squash and Pumpkin**
Cucurbita palmata - see **Squash and Pumpkin**
Cucurbita pepo - see **Acorn Squash, Delicata (Squash), Marrow, Pumpkin, Pumpkin Seed, Spaghetti Squash, Squash and Pumpkin, Squash Flower(s), Sweet Dumpling (Squash), Zucchini**
Cudrania tricuspidata - see **Che**
Cuminum cyminum - see **Cumin**
Cunila origanoides - see **Dittany**
Curcuma longa - see **Turmeric**
Cusparia trifoliata - see **Angostura**
Cyamopsis tetragonoloba - see **Guar**
Cyathea medullus - see **Tree Fern**
Cyclanthera pedata - see **Korila**
Cydonia oblonga - see **Quince**
Cymbopogon citratus - see **Lemongrass**
Cymbopogon flexuosus - see **Lemongrass**
Cynara cardunculus - see **Cardoon**
Cynara scolymus - see **Artichoke**
Cyperus esculentus - see **Chufa**
Cyperus papyrus - see **Papyrus**
Cyphomandra betacea - see **Tamarillo**
Cystophyllum fusiforme - see **Seaweed**

Dasylirion wheeleri - see **Sotol**
Datura meteloides - see **Moonflower**
Daucus carota var. *carota* - see **Carrot**
Daucus carota var. *sativus* - see **Carrot**
Daucus glochidiatus - see **Australian Carrot**
Dentaria diphylla - see **Toothwort**
Descurainia pinnata - see **Tansy Mustard**
Descurainia richardsoni - see **Tansy Mustard**
Dialium guineënse - see **Velvet Tamarind**
Dialium indicum - see **Velvet Tamarind**
Dianthus, genus - see **Gillyflower**
Dictamnus albus - see **Dittany**
Digitaria exilis - see **Fonio**
Digitaria iburua - see **Fonio**
Dimocarpus longan - see **Longan**
Dioscorea, genus - see **Yam(s)**
Dioscorea alata - see **Water Yam, Yam(s)**
Dioscorea batatas - see **Chinese Yam**
Dioscorea bulbifera - see **Air Potato**
Dioscorea cayenensis - see **Yam(s), Yellow Yam**
Dioscorea dumetorum - see **Bitter Yam**
Dioscorea esculenta - see **Lesser Yam**
Dioscorea rotundata - see **White Yam, Yam(s)**
Dioscorea trifida - see **Cush-Cush Yam, Yam(s)**

Dioscorea villosa - see **Wild Yam**
Dioscoreophyllum cumminsii - see **Serendipity Berry**
Diospyros digyna - see **Black Sapote**
Diospyros discolor - see **Mabolo**
Diospyros kaki - see **Persimmon**
Diospyros virginiana - see **Persimmon**
Diplazium esculentum - see **Vegetable-Fern**
Dipteryx odorata - see **Tonka Bean**
Dolichos biflorus - see **Horse Gram**
Dolichos erosus - see **Jícama**
Dovyalis caffra - see **Kai Apple**
Dovyalis hebecarpa - see **Ceylon Gooseberry**
Duboisia hopwoodii - see **Pituri**
Durio zibethinus - see **Durian**

Echinacea, genus - see **Coneflower**
Echinocactus grandis - see **Barrel Cactus**
Echinocereus conglomeratus - see **Pitahaya**
Echinocereus stramineus - see **Pitahaya**
Echinocereus triglochidiatus - see **Pitahaya**
Echinochloa frumentacea - see **Japanese Millet**
Elaeagnus angustifolia - see **Elaeagnus**
Elaeagnus commutata - see **Elaeagnus**
Elaeagnus philippinensis - see **Elaeagnus**
Elaeagnus pungens - Elaeagnus
Elaeagnus umbellata - see **Elaeagnus**
Elaeocarpus denatus - see **Hinau Berry**
Elaeocarpus grandis - see **Quandong**
Eleocharis dulcis - see **Water Chestnut**
Elettaria cardamomum - see **Cardamom**
Eleusine coracana - see **Finger Millet**
Eleusine indica - see **Goosegrass**
Elytrigia intermedia ssp. *barbulata* - see **Wild Triga**
Elytrigia repens - see **Couch Grass**
Ensete ventricosum - see **Ensete**
Ephedra nevadensis - see **Mormon Tea**
Ephedra trifurca - see **Mormon Tea**
Ephedra viridis - see **Mormon Tea**
Epigaea repens - see **Trailing Arbutus**
Equisetum arvense - see **Horsetail Plant**
Eragrostis abyssinica - see **Tef**
Eragrostis tef - see **Tef**
Eremocitrus glauca - see **Australian Desert Lime**
Erica, genus - see **Heather**
Erica tetralix - see **Bog Heather**
Erigeron canadensis - see **Horseweed**
Eriobotrya japonica - see **Loquat**
Eriodictyon californicum - see **Yerba Santa**
Erioglossum rubiginosum - see **Mertajam**
Eriogonum longifolium - see **Indian Turnip**
Eruca sativa - see **Arugula**
Ervum ervilia - see **Bitter Vetch**
Eryngium foetidum - see **Long Coriander**
Eryngium maritimum - see **Sea Holly**
Erythrina berteroana - see **Coral Bean**
Erythrina fusca - see **Coral Bean**
Erythrina poeppigiana - see **Coral Bean**
Erythrina rubinervia - see **Coral Bean**
Erythroxylum coca - see **Coca**
Eucalyptus viminalis - see **Manna Gum**
Euchema, genus - see **Agar**
Eugenia brasiliensis - see **Grumichama**
Eugenia capensis - see **Myrtle Apple**
Eugenia corynantha - see **Sour Cherry**
Eugenia cumini - see **Jambolan**
Eugenia dombeyi - see **Grumichama**
Eugenia jambolana - see **Jambolan Plum**

Eugenia jambos - see **Rose Apple**
Eugenia javanica - see **Java Apple**
Eugenia luschnathiana - see **Pitomba**
Eugenia malaccensis - see **Malay Apple**
Eugenia myrtifolia - see **Brush Cherry**
Eugenia polyantha - see **Duan Salam**
Eugenia stipitata - see *Acaçá-Boi*
Eugenia uniflora - see **Pitanga**
Eulophia, genus - see **Salep**
Eupatorium, genus - see **Boneset**
Eupatorium dalea - see **Boneset**
Eupatorium perfoliatum - see **Boneset**
Eupatorium rugosum - see **Boneset**
Euphorbia esula - see **Leafy Spurge**
Euphoria longana - see **Longan**
Exocarpus cuppressiformis - see **Native Cherry**

Fagopyrum esculentum - see **Buckwheat**
Fagus grandifolia - see **Beechnut**
Fagus sylvatica - see **Beechnut**
Feijoa sellowiana - see **Feijoa**
Ferocactus wislizenii - see **Barrel Cactus**
Feronia limonia - see **Indian Wood-Apple**
Ferula, genus - see **Silphium**
Ferula assa-foetida - see **Asafetida**
Ficus carica - see **Fig**
Fistulina hepatica - see **Mushrooms and Fungi**
Flacourtia indica - see **Governor's Plum**
Flacourtia inermis - see **Thornless Rukam**
Flacourtia rukam - see **Indian Prune**
Flammulina velutipes - see **Enokitake, Mushrooms and Fungi**
Foeniculum vulgare - see **Fennel**
Fortunella, genus - see **Citrangequat, Limequat, Orangequat**
Fortunella crassifolia - see **Kumquat**
Fortunella japonica - see **Kumquat**
Fortunella margarita - see **Kumquat**
Fragaria, genus - see **Berries**
Fragaria ananassa - see **Strawberry**
Fragaria chiloensis - see **Wild Strawberry**
Fragaria moschata - see **Wild Strawberry**
Fragaria vesca - see **Wild Strawberry**
Fragaria vesca var. *americana* - see **Wild Strawberry**
Fragaria vesca var. *momophylla* - see **Wild Strawberry**
Frasera speciosa - see **Gentian**
Fucus, genus - see **Seaweed**
Fusanus acuminatus - see **Quandong**

Galega officinalis - see **Goat's-Rue**
Galinsoga parviflora - see **Quelites**
Galipea officinalis - see **Angostura**
Galium aparine - see **Goosegrass**
Galium odoratum - see **Woodruff**
Galium verum - see **Lady's Bedstraw**
Garcinia atroviridis - see **Asam Gelugur**
Garcinia bombroniana - see **Assam Aur Aur**
Garcinia livingstonei - see **Imbé**
Garcinia mangostana - see **Mangosteen**
Gaultheria procumbens - see **Wintergreen**
Gaultheria shallon - see **Salal**
Gaylussacia, genus - see **Huckleberry**
Gelidium, genus - see **Agar**
Genipa americana - see **Genipap**
Gentiana lutea - see **Gentian**
Geum urbanum - see **Herb Bennet**
Gigartina mammillosa - see **Carrageen and Carrageenin**
Ginkgo biloba - see **Ginkgo Nut**

Glechoma hederacea - see **Ground Ivy**
Gleditsia triacanthos - see **Honey Locust**
Glycine max - see **Beans, Bean Sprouts, Soybean**
Glycyrrhiza glabra - see **Licorice**
Glycyrrhiza Lepidota - see **Licorice**
Gossypium, genus - see **Cottonseed Oil**
Grewia asiatica - see **Phalsa**
Grewia retusifolia - see **Turkey Fruit**
Grindelia robusta - see **Gum Plant**
Grindelia squarrosa - see **Gum Plant**
Guazuma ulmifolia - see **Mutamba**
Guilielma gasipaës - see **Pejebaye**
Guilielma utilis - see **Pejebaye**
Guizotia abyssinica - see **Niger Seed**
Gyrophora esculenta - see **Manna**

Hamamelis virginiana - see **Witch-Hazel**
Hancornia speciosa - see **Mangaba**
Harpephyllum caffrum - see **Kaffir Plum**
Helianthus annuus - see **Sunflower Oil and Seed**
Helianthus giganteus - see **Indian Potato**
Helianthus tuberosus - see **Jerusalem Artichoke**
Heliocereus, genus - see **Pitahaya**
Hemerocallis fulva - see **Day Lily**
Heracleum sphondylium - see **Cow Parsnip**
Hibiscus esculentus - see **Okra**
Hibiscus manihot - see **Sunset Hibiscus**
Hibiscus moscheutos - see **Amberseed**
Hibiscus sabdariffa - see **Roselle**
Hippophaë rhamnoides - see **Sea Buckthorn**
Hordeum jubatum - see **Wild Barley**
Hordeum pusillum - see **Wild Barley**
Hordeum vulgare - see **Barley, Wild Barley**
Hosta, genus - see **Day Lily**
Hovenia dulcis - see **Japanese Raisin Tree**
Humulus lupulus - see **Hop(s)**
Hydrangea macrophylla - see **Big-Leafed Hydrangea**
Hydrocotyle, genus - see **Pennywort**
Hydrophyllum canadense - see **Waterleaf**
Hydrophyllum occidentale - see **Waterleaf**
Hylocereus undatas - see **Pitahaya**
Hypericum perforatum - see **Saint-John's-Wort**
Hypericum pyramidatum - see **Saint-John's-Wort**
Hyphaene thebaica - see **Dom Palm**
Hyptis albida - see **Hyptis**
Hyptis emoryi - see **Hyptis**
Hyptis suaveolens - see **Hyptis**
Hyssopus officinalis - see **Hyssop**

Ilex cassine - see **Dahoon Holly**
Ilex glabra - see **Winterberry**
Ilex opaca - see **Hollyberry**
Ilex paraguariensis - see **Hollyberry, Yerba Maté**
Ilex verticillata - see **Winterberry**
Ilex vomitoria - see **Yaupon**
Illicium verum - see **Star-Anise**
Impatiens capensis - see **Jewelweed**
Inga vera - see **Ice-Cream Bean**
Inocarpus edulis - see **Polynesian Chestnut**
Inula helenium - see **Elecampane**
Ipomoea aquatica - see **Swamp Cabbage**
Ipomoea batatas - see **Boniato, Sweet Potato**
Iridaceae germanica - see **Iris**
Irvingia gabonensis - see **Duika**
Iva annua - see **Sumpweed**

Jasminum, genus - see **Jasmine**

Jatropha curcas - see **Physic Nut**
Juglans cinerea - see **Walnut**
Juglans nigra - see **Walnut**
Juglans regia - see **Walnut**
Juniperus communis - see **Juniper Berry**

Kaempferia galanga - see **Galangal**
Kerstingiella geocarpa - see **Hausa Groundnut**

Lablab niger - see **Hyacinth Bean**
Lablab purpureus - see **Hyacinth Bean**
Lactuca sativa var. *capitata* - see **Lettuce**
Lactuca sativa var. *crispa* - see **Lettuce**
Lactuca sativa var. *longifolia* - see **Lettuce**
Lactuca scariola - see **Prickly Lettuce**
Lactuca serriola - see **Lettuce, Prickly Lettuce**
Lagenaria siceraria - see **Bottle Gourd, Calabash**
Laminaria japonica - see **Kelp, Seaweed**
Landolphia kirkii - see **Wild Peach**
Laninaria, genus - see **Seaweed**
Lansium domesticum - see **Langsat**
Larrea mexicana - see **Creosote Bush**
Larrea tridentata - see **Creosote Bush**
Lathraea squamaria - see **Toothwort** (mentioned)
Lathyrus, genus - see **Everlasting Pea**
Lathyrus latifolius - see **Everlasting Pea**
Lathyrus maritimus - see **Beach Pea**
Lathyrus odoratus - see **Beach Pea**
Lathyrus sativus - see **Chickling Vetch**
Lathyrus tuberosus - see **Earth Nut**
Laurus nobilis - see **Bay Leaf**
Lavandula angustifolia - see **Lavender**
Lavandula officinalis - see **Lavender**
Lecanora esculenta - see **Manna**
Lecythis, genus - see **Sapucaia Nut**
Lemairocereus queretaroensis - see **Pitahaya**
Lens esculenta - see **Lentil(s)**
Lentinus edodes - see **Mushrooms and Fungi**
Lepidium meyenii - see **Maca**
Lepidium sativum - see **Cress**
Leucaena leucocephala - see **Leucaena**
Leucopogon richei - see **Australian Currant**
Levisticum officinale - see **Lovage**
Lewisia rediviva - see **Bitter Root**
Liabum glabrum - see **Quelites**
Licania platypus - see **Sunsapote**
Lilium tigrinum - see **Tiger Lily**
Limonia acidissima - see **Indian Wood-Apple**
Lindera benzoin - see **Spicebush**
Linum usitatissimum - see **Flax Seed**
Lippia citriodora - see **Lemon Verbena**
Liquidambar styraciflua - see **Sweet Gum**
Litchi chinensis - see **Litchi**
Lolium multiflorum - see **Ryegrass**
Lolium perenne - see **Ryegrass**
Lolium temulentum - see **Ryegrass**
Lonicera japonica - see **Honeysuckle**
Lotus tetragonolobus - see **Asparagus Pea**
Luffa acutangula - see **Angled Luffa**
Luffa aegyptiaca - see **Angled Luffa**
Lupinus albus - see **Beans**
Lupinus angustifolius - see **Beans**
Lupinus luteus - see **Beans**
Lupinus mutabilis - see **Andean Lupin**
Lycium andersonii - see **Matrimony Vine**
Lycium chinense - see **Matrimony Vine**
Lycopersicon esculentum - see **Tomato**

Prunus armeniaca – see **Apricot**
Prunus avium – see **Cherry**
Prunus besseyi – see **Sand Cherry**
Prunus capollin – see **Capulin**
Prunus capuli – see **Capulin**
Prunus cerasifera – see **Cherry Plum**
Prunus cerasus – see **Cherry, Sour Cherry**
Prunus domestica – see **Cherry Plum, Plum**
Prunus dulcis – see **Almond**
Prunus ilicifolia – see **Chimaja**
Prunus insititia – see **Damson Plum**
Prunus laurocerasus – see **Cherry Laurel**
Prunus maritima – see **Beach Plum**
Prunus persica – see **Nectarine, Peach**
Prunus pumila – see **Sand Cherry**
Prunus salicifolia – see **Capulin**
Prunus salicina – see **Japanese Plum, Plum**
Prunus serotina – see **Capulin**
Prunus spinosa – see **Haw, Sloe**
Prunus virginiana – see **Cherry, Chokeberry** (mentioned), **Chokecherry**
Psidium angulatum – see **Araçá-Pera**
Psidium cattleianum – see **Strawberry Guava**
Psidium friedrichsthalianum – see **Wild Guava**
Psidium guajava – see **Guava, Native Guava** (mentioned)
Psophocarpus tetragonolobus – see **Asparagus Pea** (mentioned)
Psophocarpus tetragonolobus – see **Beans, Winged Bean**
Psoralea, genus – see **Indian Turnip**
Psoralea esculenta – see **Breadroot**
Ptelea trifoliata – see **Hoptree**
Pteridium aquilinum – see **Bracken Fern**
Pueraria lobata – see **Kudzu**
Pueraria thunbergiana – see **Kudzu**
Punica granatum – see **Pomegranate**
Pyrus communis – see **Pear**
Pyrus malus – see **Apple**
Pyrus pyrifolia – see **Asian Pear**
Pyrus ussuriensis – see **Asian Pear**

Quercus alba – see **Acorn**

Raphanus sativus – see **Daikon, Radish**
Ratibida columnifera – see **Coneflower**
Rhamnus carolinianus – see **Buckthorn**
Rhamnus crocea – see **Buckthorn**
Rheedia brasiliensis – see **Bakupari**
Rheedia macrophylla – see **Bacuripari**
Rheum officinale – see **Rhubarb**
Rheum rhabarbarum – see **Rhubarb**
Rhizophora mangle – see **Mangrove**
Rhizophora mucronata – see **Mangrove**
Rhodomyrtus psidoides – see **Native Guava**
Rhodymenia palmata – see **Dulse**
Rhus corioria – see **Sumac Berry**
Rhus glabra – see **Smooth Sumac**
Rhus typhina – see **Sumac Berry**
Ribes, genus – see **Berries, Currant(s)**
Ribes grossularia – see **Gooseberry**
Ribes nigrum – see **Black Curran, Currant(s)**
Ribes pinetorum – see **Gooseberry**
Ribes rubrum – see **Currant(s)**
Ribes sanguineum – see **Currant(s)**
Ribes sativum – see **Currant(s)**
Ribes uva-crispa – see **Gooseberry**
Ribes wolfi – see **Gooseberry**

Ricinodendron rautanenii – see **Mongongo**
Ricinus communis – see **Castorbean**
Robinia pseudoacacia – see **Locust**
Rollinia deliciosa – see **Biribá**
Rosa canina – see **Rose Hip(s)**
Rosa rugosa – see **Rose Hip(s)**
Rosmarinus officinalis – see **Rosemary**
Rubus, genus – see **Berries, Blackberry Boysenberry, Bramble(s), Raspberry, Youngberry**
Rubus caesius – see **Dewberry**
Rubus chamaemorus – see **Cloudberry**
Rubus hispidus – see **Dewberry**
Rubus idaeus – see **Raspberry**
Rubus illecebrosus – see **Strawberry-Raspberry**
Rubus leucodermis – see **Raspberry**
Rubus loganobaccus – see **Boysenberry, Loganberry**
Rubus phoenicolasius – see **Japanese Wineberry**
Rubus spectabilis – see **Salmonberry**
Rubus strigosus – see **Raspberry**
Rudbeckia laciniata – see **Coneflower**
Rumex acetosa – see **Sorrel**
Rumex articus – see **Sorrel**
Rumex crispus – see **Curled Dock**
Rumex hydrolapathum – see **Sorrel**
Rumex patientia – see **Sorrel**
Rumex scutatus – see **Sorrel**
Ruta graveolens – see **Rue**

Sabal palmetto – see **Heart(s) of Palm**
Saccharum officinarum – see **Sugarcane**
Sagittaria latifolia – see **Arrowhead**
Sagittaria sinensis – see **Arrowhead**
Salacca edulis – see **Salak**
Salicornia europaea – see **Glasswort**
Salicornia herbacea – see **Glasswort**
Salicornia stricta – see **Glasswort**
Salix alba – see **White Willow, Willow**
Salvia columbariae – see **Chia**
Salvia hispanica – see **Chia**
Salvia officinalis – see **Sage**
Salvia sclarea – see **Clary**
Sambucus canadensis – see **Elderberry**
Sambucus coerulea – see **Elderberry**
Sambucus nigra – see **Elderberry**
Sandoricul indicum – see **Sentul**
Sandoricum koetjape – see **Sentul**
Sanguisorba officinalis – see **Burnet** (mentioned)
Sapindus marginatus – see **Soapberry**
Sapindus saponaria – see **Soapberry**
Sapium sebiferum – see **Chinese Tallow Tree**
Sassafras albidum – see **Sassafras**
Satureja hortensis – see **Savory**
Satureja montana – see **Savory**
Satureja vulgaris – see **Basil**
Sauropus androgynus – see **Sweet-Shoot**
Schinus molle – see **Mastic Tree**
Scirpus fluviatilis – see **Bulrush**
Sclerocarya caffra – see **Marula Plum**
Scorzonera hispanica – see **Scorzonera**
Secale, genus – see **Triticale**
Secale cereale – see **Rye**
Sechium edule – see **Chayote**
Sedum acre – see **Stonecrop**
Sedum collinum – see **Stonecrop**
Sedum reflexum – see **Stonecrop**
Sedum roseum – see **Stonecrop**
Sesamum alatum – see **Tacoutta**

Name Index

Subject Index

About This Index

All plant and animal species appear under both their common name and their scientific (Latin) name. For example, the common pea is listed under *pea(s)* as well as *Pisum sativum*. The page citations given under the common names are for the major discussions of the food. Detailed subentries are found under the common name only and generally will not be duplicated under the scientific name.

The common name for any one species, such as *pea*, may also refer to many other species that are not *Pisum sativum*. In these cases the species most widely known by the common name is indicated by the subheading *common* before the Latin name. For example, under the main entry *pea(s)* are also such subheadings as *beach (Lathryus maritimus)*, *blackeyed (Vigna* spp.), as well as the *common (Pisum sativum)*.

In addition, the index subsumes entries under both individual countries and geographical regions. Thus, there are entries for Italy as well as for Europe, southern. Regions may also sometimes overlap, such as *Oceania, Pacific Islands*, and *Hawaiian Islands*. This is because of differences in the way the various essays discussed geographical regions and also because of changes in the names and boundaries of geographical regions over time.

A

abaca fiber (*Musa textilis*), 176
abalone
    in Chile, 1258
    farming of, modern, 467
    in Japan, 464
        culture of, 462
    in Korean archeological sites, 1187
    in North America (post-Columbian), 1312
abalong (cocoyam, *Colocasia esculenta*), 1760. *See also* cocoyam
abata kola (kola nut, *Cola acuminata*), 1797. *See also* kola nut
Abbassids, 1143
Abelmoschus esculentus (okra), 1824. *See also* okra
Abelmoschus manihot (= *Hibiscus manihot*, sunset hibiscus), 1861
Abies balsamea (balsam fir), 1726

abiu (*Pouteria cainito*), 1713
abóbora (*calabaza, Cucurbita moschata*), 1742
abol, 205
Aboriginal Australians (Aborigines). *See* Australian Aborigines
abortion
    iodine deficiency and, 803–804
    spontaneous, vitamin E in, 772
Abrégé du dictionnaire des cas de conscience, 630
absorption, intestinal. *See* intestinal absorption
Abu Hureyra site (northern Syria), 84, 163
Abydos site, 397
Abyssinian banana (ensete, *Musa ensete*), 1771–1772
acacia (*Acacia* spp.), 1713
    in Australia, 1339
    seeds of, 1340
Acacia angustissima (prairie acacia), 1713

Acacia greggii (catclaw acacia), 1713
Acacia senegal (gum arabic), 1713
academic institutions, lobbyists on, 1636
Académie de Gastronome, 1213
Académie Française, 1213
Académie Royale de Médecine, 1582
Acanthopleura sp. (marine cockroach), 1271
Acanthuridae (surgeonfishes), 54
An Account of Foxglove and Some of its Medical Properties, 846
aceituna (*Simarouba glauca*), 1713
Acer spp. (maple syrup, maple sugar), 1810
    in North America
        post-Columbian, 1310
            19th cent., 1315
        pre-Columbian, 1289, 1296
Acer saccharum (sugar maple), 1810
acerola (*Malpighia glabra*, etc.), 1713. *See also* cherry
acesulfame K, 1679
Acetaria, a Discourse on Sallets, 1222

Algeria
cattle in, 492
wine in, 736
alginates, 233, 241
"Ali Baba and the Forty Thieves,"
415
Ali Kosh site, 84
Alicante Bouschet grape (*Vitis
vinifera*), 1716. *See also*
grape(s); wine
alimentary sensualism, 1582
alitame, 1680
"alkali disease," 861
alkali processing, of maize, 103, 108
alkaline phosphatase
magnesium on, 826
zinc on, 869
alkanet (*Alkanna tinctoria*), 1716
"All-Bran," 1545
allergies, food, 1022–1028,
1048–1054. *See also* food
allergies
Alliara petiolata (garlic mustard),
433. *See also* garlic mustard
Alliaria officinalis (= *Sisymbrium
alliarin*, garlic-mustard),
433, 1776–1777
allicin, 259, 1550
antimicrobial and antiviral actions
of, 261
on atherosclerosis, 259
on fibrinogen, 259–260
alligator (*Alligator mississippiensis*),
1290, 1297
eggs of, 499
alligator pear (avocado, *Persea americana*), 1724–1725. *See
also* avocado
alligator snapping turtle (*Macroclemys temmincki*), 1290
alliinase, 259
allithiamin, 259
Allium spp., 249–265. *See also* individual species, e.g., onion(s)
botany of, 249
Allium ascalonicum (shallot),
1851–1852. *See also* shal-
lot(s)
Allium canadense (American wild
garlic, wild garlic), 1776.
See also garlic
Allium cepa (onion), 250–256, 433,
1825. *See also* onion(s)
Allium cernuum (wild onion), 1825.
See also onion(s)
Allium chinense (rakkyo), 1842
Allium fistulosum. See also onion(s)
Chinese onion (Welsh onion),
1878
Japanese bunching onion (Welsh
onion), 1878

spring onion, 1878
in China, 250
Welsh onion, 1878
Allium longicuspis, 257
Allium nipponicum (water garlic),
256
Allium oleraceum (British wild garlic), 1776. *See also* garlic
Allium porrum (leek), 1799. *See
also* leek(s)
Allium sativum (garlic), 433, 1776.
See also garlic
Allium schoenoprasum (chives),
432, 1755–1756. *See also*
chives
Allium tricoccum (wild leeks), 1881
in Caribbean, 1716–1717
in Central America, 1716–1717
in Europe, 1717
in Jamaica, 1717
Allium tuberosum (Chinese chive),
1755. *See also* chives
Allium vineale (American field garlic, British field garlic, wild
garlic), 1776. *See also* garlic
allotriophagia, 969
allouya (guinea arrowroot, *Calathea
allouia*), 1782–1783
allspice (*Pimenta dioica*), 432,
1716–1717
in Caribbean (post-Columbian),
1284
Almanach des Gourmands, 1213
almond(s)
common (*Prunus dulcis*), 432,
1717
in British Isles (Roman period),
1218
in Europe
northern (Middle Ages),
1229
southern, 1209
Kosher law on, 1502
in North America (17th cent.),
1305
almond(s). *See also* Java almond; Malabar almond
cuddapah (*Buchanania latifolia*), 1765
earth (peanut, *Arachis
hypogaea*), 364–372
(*see also* peanut(s))
Java (*Canarium commune*), 1792
Terminalia catappa
country, 1807
Indian, 1807
Malabar, 1807
tropical, 1807
almond milk
in British Isles (Medieval), 1220
medicinal use of, 1540

alocasia (*Alocasia* spp.), 1717. *See
also* taro
in Asia, 1717
botanical features of, 219–221
giant (*A. macrorrhiza*), 1717
in India, 1717
in Pacific Islands, 1353
Alocasia cucullata (Chinese taro),
1717
Alocasia indica, 1717
Alocasia macrorrhiza (false taro,
giant taro, giant alocasia),
219, 1717. *See also* taro
in Asia, Southeast, 1154
in Pacific Islands, 1353
Alopochen aegyptiaca (Egyptian
goose), 529, 530
alpaca (*Lama pacos*), 555–559
as dairy animal, future, 558
distribution of, 555
as food, 555–556
meat of, commercialization of, 558
milk of, 558
nonmilking enigma of, 556–557
preservation of, 555
ritual uses of, 556, 557
alpha-kainic acid, in algae, 245
alpha solanine, 1697
alpha-tocopherol. *See also* tocopherols; vitamin E
in algae, 241
Alpinia coerulea, 1881
Alpinia galanga
galangal, 433, 1776
galingale, 1756
Alpinia officinarum (galangal, lesser
galinga), 433, 1776
Althaea officinalis (mallow), 1808
Alto Salaverry site, 231
aluminum, toxicity of, 1701–1702
bioavailability on, 1695
alverja (pigeon pea, *Cajanus cajan,
C. indicus*), 1834
amalaka (amalaki, *Phyllanthus
emblica* = *Emblica officinalis*), 1717
in Asia, South, 1717
for diabetes, 1079
Amanita caesarea, 316
Amanita muscaria (fly agaric), 330
amanitin, 330
amarante (amaranth, *Amaranthus
hypochondriacus, A. cru-
entus, A. caudatus*),
1717–1718. *See also* amaranth
amaranth (*Amaranthus* spp.),
75–81, 1717–1718
A. gangetaicus, 1157
in Africa, 80
West, 1717

cherry birch (sweet birch, *Betula lenta*), 1862
cherry laurel (*Prunus laurocerasus*), 1751. *See also* laurel
cherry pepper (Hungarian, *Capsicum annuum*), 1788
cherry plum (*Prunus cerasifera*), 1751
cherry tomato
Lycopersicon esculentum, 1870–1871
Lycopersicon esculentum var. *cerasiforme*, 352
chervil
Anthriscus cerefolium, 432, 1751
in Asia, 1751
in Balkans, 1751
in British Isles (Roman period), 1218
Chaerophyllum bulbosum, 1751
in Europe, 1751
in France (14th–18th cent.), 1211
in Roman empire, 1751
Spanish (cicely, *Myrrhis odorata*), 1756
sweet (cicely, *Myrrhis odorata*), 1756
Chesapeake region
17th cent., 1305–1306
18th cent., 1309–1310
Chester jar, 461
chestnut(s)
Australian, Moreton Bay (*Castanospermum australe*), 1724
common (*Castanea*), 1751–1752
American (*C. dentata*), 1751–1752
in North America (pre-Columbian), 1289, 1293
in British Isles (prehistoric), 1217
C. sativa, 359–363
consumers of, 361–362
cultivation of, 360–361
for fruit *vs.* wood, 359–360
decline of, 362–363
distribution of, 359
drying of, 361
flour from, 361
grinding of, 361
harvesting of, 361
in Mediterranean, 359
nutritive value of, 360
nuts of, 360
origin of, 359
peeling of, 361
planting of, 360
preparation of, 360
trees of, 359–360

Chinese, 1751–1752
in Europe, southern, 1209
European, 1751–1752
Japanese, 1751–1752
in Korea, 1185, 1187
Spanish, 1751–1752
sweet, 1751–1752
horse (*Aesculus*), 1739
A. hippocastum (buckeye), 1751–1752
European (*A. hippocastanum*), 1751–1752
Polynesian (*Inocarpus edulis*), 1837
Tahitian (*Inocarpus fagifer*), 1357
chestnut bean (chickpea, garbanzo, *Cicer arietinum*), 1752
chestnut oak (*Quercus prinus*), 1289
chevaline (horse, *Equus caballus*), 543–544. *See also* horse(s)
chevrotain (*Tragulus javanicus, Tragulus napu*), 1156
Chez Panisse, 1492
chi, 1079
Ch'i-Min-Yao-Shu, 141, 142, 250, 256, 263, 315
chia
Chenopodium huauzontle, 1750
Salvia columbariae, 1752
Salvia hispanica, 1752
chiang, 315
Chianti wine. *See also* grape(s); wine(s)
Sangiovese (*Vitis vinifera*), 1848
Trebbiano (*Vitis vinifera*), 1871
Chicago Assyrian Dictionary, 414
chiccory (chicory, *Cichorium intybus*), 1753
chich (chickpea, garbanzo, *Cicer arietinum*), 1752. *See also* chickpea(s)
chich-pea (chickpea, garbanzo, *Cicer arietinum*), 1752. *See also* chickpea(s)
chicha, 623, 1811
in South America, 1259
chicken(s) (*Gallus gallus, G. domesticus*), 496–498, 561. *See also* chicken egg(s)
in Africa, North, 497
in Africa, sub-Saharan, 497–498
introduction of, 1332
in Asia, Southeast, 496–497, 1156
in Asia, Southwest, 497
in Australia (colonial period), 1346
in British Isles
1485–1688, 1222
Roman period, 1218
in Caribbean (post-Columbian), 1272

in Central Asia, 497
coccidiosis in, 501
Cochin, 501
in divination and sacrifice, 500
in Europe, 497
southern, 1209
in France (Middle Ages), 1211
in Korea, 1188
in Mexico
post-Columbian, 1251
pre-Columbian, 1249
in New World, 498
nomenclature of, 498
in North America (Spanish colonial), 1300
in Oceania, 496–497
origins of, 496, 499–500, 561
in Pacific Islands, 1357
in Russia (early), 1241
show breeding of, 501
in South America, 1256
uses of, 496
chicken egg(s), 499–507, 561
air cell of, 503, 504
albumen of, 502–504, 505
chemistry of, 505
desugaring of, 507
in divination, 500
drying and dehydration of, 506–507
Easter eggs from, 500
formation of, 502–503
grading of, 504
hard-cooked, 507
history of, 499–501
homogenization of, 506
Lent and, 500
liquid egg industry and, 506–507
microbiology of, 505–506
nutritional value of, 501, 505
packaging of, 506
pasteurization of, 506
production of, world, 502
quality evaluation in, 504
quality preservation in, 504–505
Salmonella enteriditis in, 505, 1032
shell of, 504
industry for, 501–502
sizes of, 505
structure of, 503–504
USDA grading of, 504
white of, 505
yolk of, 502–504, 505
chicken turtle (*Deirochelys reticularia*), 1290
chickling grass (chickling vetch, *Lathyrus sativus*), 1752
chickling pea (chickling vetch, *Lathyrus sativus*), 279, 1752

coconut milk, 392
coconut oil (*Cocos nucifera*), 385
   extraction of, 390
   fatty acids in, 390
   as fuel, 391
   myristic acid in, 390
   nonfood uses of, 390
   in soap, 391, 394
   tocopherols in, 381, 390
coconut oleine, 390–391
coconut palm (*Cocos nucifera*), 385.
   See also coconut
coconut pollen, 395
coconut stearine, 390
coconut water, 392, 393
cocoplum (*Chrysobalanus icaco*),
   1759–1760
   in Caribbean (pre-Columbian),
     1262
Cocos nucifera (cocona, coconut,
   coconut oil), 385, 388–395,
   1759. *See also* coconut;
   coconut oil
cocoyam, 1154
   Colocasia, 1721
   Colocasia antiquorum (taro),
     1866
     dissemination of, 1334–1335
   Colocasia esculenta (taro), 1760,
     1866 (*see also* taro)
   Xanthosoma atrovirens
     (malanga), 1807
   Xanthosoma sagittifolium, 1262
cocozelle (zucchini squash, *Cucur-*
   bita pepo), 1886. *See also*
   squash
cod
   Atlantic, propagation and release of
     in Britain, 461
     in U.S., 460
   Murray (*Maccullochella mac-*
     quariensis), 1341
   in North America (18th cent.),
     1310
   red (*Pseudolabrus* spp.), 1341
   trout (*Maccullochella mitchelli*),
     1341
cod liver oil, 386–387
   for night blindness, 743
   tocopherols in, 381
   as vitamin D source, 765
Codakia orbicularis (tiger lucine
   clam)
   in Barrera-Mordan settlement, 1271
   in Caribbean (pre-Columbian),
     1263, 1266, 1267, 1268
Codd's bottle, 711
Code Noir, 1281
Codes des nourrices de Paris, 628
Codex Alimentarius Commission,
   1657–1658

on food additives, 1668
Codex Badianus, 316
Codex Elsers, 256
Codex Magliabecchi, 316
codfish
   in British Isles (1700-1900), 1223,
     1224
   in Caribbean, 1281, 1286
     on slave plantations, 1281
   in Europe, southern, 1209
   Gadus macrocephalus, in
     Alaskan Arctic, 55
Codium fragile
   in China (prehistoric), 232
   in Japan (premodern), 233
Cofachiqui, 1305
Coffea arabica (coffee), 641, 651,
   1760–1761. *See also*
   coffee
Coffea canephora (= *Coffea
   robusta*, coffee), 1761
Coffea liberica (coffee), 1163
Coffea robusta (= *C. canephora*, coffee), 1761
coffee, 639, 641–652, 1760–1761
   as aphrodisiac, 1529
   brewing of, 645, 1760
   and calcium absorption, 953–954
   Coffea arabica, 1760–1761
   Coffea canephora (= *Coffea
     robusta*), 1761
   Coffea liberica, 1163
   consumption of
     in British Isles (1485-1688),
       1223
     in Dutch Republic
       (1500-1800), 1235
     by Eskimos, 1326
     in Europe, 642–644, 1760
       northern, 1230
     Garifuna, 1273
     in Korea, 1189
     in Middle East, 1143
     in the Netherlands
       (1800-1960), 1237
     in North America, 1317
       17th cent., 1307
       18th cent., 1310
       19th cent., 1315–1316
     in Russia (18th cent.), 1242
     in South America, 1259
     by Sufis, 641
     in Turkey, 1147
     in United States, 644–647, 1761
     in world, 647
   decaffeinated, 647
   domestication of, 641, 1760
   exchanges and trading of, 645–646,
     1760
   freeze-dried, 1761
   gourmet, 646

government restrictions on, 1371
   grinds of, 1761
   instant, 647, 1760
   Java, 645, 646, 1761
   medicinal use of, 1541
   origins of, 641–642, 1760
   preparation of, early, 641, 1760
   production of
     in Africa, 651–652, 1760
       sub-Saharan, 1331
     in Arabia, 647–648, 1760
     in Asia, 648
       Southeast, 1163
     in Brazil, 649–650, 1259,
       1760–1761
     in Caribbean, 648–649, 1284,
       1760
     in Latin America, 652, 1760
     in Mexico, 1252
     Mocca (Mocha), 645, 646,
       1760, 1761
     and slave labor, 648–649
     and slavery, 1760
     Spanish-American, 650–651,
       1760
   prohibitions against, 1560
   roasting of, 645, 1761
     development of, 1315–1316
   socioeconomic aspects of,
     651–652
   soluble, 651–652
   standardization of, 646
   types and grades of, 651, 1761
   vacuum packing of, 645
coffee breaks, 646
coffee shops, 646
coffeehouses
   in British Isles (1485-1688), 1223
   in Dutch Republic (1500-1800),
     1235
   in Europe, 643–644, 1760
   origin of, 642, 1760
   in United States, 644
   Viennese, 643, 1760
coffeeweed (sesban)
   Sesbania cavanillesii, 1851
   Sesbania grandiflora, 1851
cognac, 656–657, 733
   from French colombard grapes,
     1775
cognitive performance, nutrition on,
   1442, 1458. *See also* mental development
cohosh, blue (*Caulophyllum thalic-*
   troides), 1735
cohune (nut) palm (*Orbignya
   cohune, Attalea cohune*),
   1761
coimi (amaranth, *Amaranthus hypo-*
   chondriacus, A. cruentus,
   A. caudatus), 1717–1718

1988

Subject Index

Cruciferae *(cont.)*
nutritional value of, 295–297
taxonomy of, 288–289
cruciferous and green leafy vegetables, 288–298
antioxidants in, 296
on cancer, 1698
as cultivated food source, 289–290
(see also Brassica)
disease prevention from, 296–297
nutritional value of, 295–297
taxonomy of, 288–289
crustaceans. *See also* individual
species, e.g., lobster
in Europe, southern, 1209
in North America (pre-
Columbian), 1297
paragonimiasis from, 1046
Cruÿdeboeck, 356, 989–990
The Cry of Nature, 1555
cryptosporidiosis, 1043–1044
Cryptosporidium parvum,
1043–1044
Cryptotaenia canadensis
(honewort), 1786
Cryptotaenia japonica (honewort),
1786
*cuajilote (Parmentiera edulis = P.
aculeata),* 1765
Cuba
animal foods in
mollusks, 1271
pig, 538, 1279
Barrera-Mordan settlement in,
1271
as colonial port, 1279
dietary liquids in
coffee, 1760–1761
production of, 649
rum, 660
emancipation in, 1284
indentured servants in, 1284
malnutrition in, 1285
plant foods in
black beans, 1286
calabaza, 1742
habanero chilli, 1783
red beans, 1286
sugar, 437, 660
sugarcane, 442, 443, 447, 1280
turtle bean, 1873
yam, 1736
Sambaqui-type shell mounds in,
1271
Cubagua, Sambaqui-type shell
mounds in, 1271
Cuban spinach (purslane, *Portulaca
oleracea*), 1840
Cuban squash *(calabaza, Cucurbita
moschata),* 1742. *See also*
squash

Cuban sweet potato (boniato, *Ipomoea batatas*), 1736
cubanelle pepper (sweet peppers,
Capsicum annuum var.
annuum), 1862–1863. *See
also* chilli pepper(s)
cubeb pepper (tailed pepper, *Piper
cubeba*), 1864–1865
cubebs, in British Isles (Medieval),
1220
cuckoo flower (lady's smock, *Cardamine pratensis*), 1798
cucumber(s), 300–303. *See also*
gherkin; melon(s); squash
in Africa, 1765
Armenian (*Cucumis melo*), 300,
302
bitter (*Momordica charantia*),
1158
Cucumis anguria (gherkin), 1777
West Indian gherkin (cucumber), 1765
botany of, 302
Cucumis melo var. *flexuosus*
serpent, 1765
snake, 1765
Cucumis metuliferus
African horned (kiwano), 1765
kiwano, 1796
Cucumis sativus, 1765
botany of, 300–301, 302, 303
Burpee Hybrid, 308
consumption of, 311
fresh-market, 302
history and ethnography of,
305
hothouse, 1765
in India, native, 305
lemon, 302, 1765
Mandera, 1765
nutritional composition of, 311
origin of, 305
pickling, 302, 1765
production of, 308–309
slicing, 1765
Spartan Dawn, 308
spread of, 305
taxonomy of, 299
uses of, 305
variety improvement in,
307–308
in Egypt (ancient), 1765
in Europe, 1765
southern, 1208
fluted (oysternut, *Telfairia
pedata*), 1827
in Greek city-states, 1765
Indian (*Medeola virginiana*),
1789
in North America (pre-
Columbian), 1289, 1296

Korea, 1185
native (pepino, *Solanum muricatum*), 1832
in Roman empire, 1765
in Russia
early, 1240
19th cent., 1242
spread of, 1813
Spanish empire in, 1305
wild (korila, *Cyclanthera
pedata*), 1797
cucumber tree (belimbing, *Averrboa
bilimbi*), 1731
Cucumerinae, 299
Cucumis anguria (gherkin), 1777.
See also cucumber
West Indian gherkin (cucumber),
1765
botany of, 302
Cucumis melo. See also melon(s);
muskmelon
C. melo var. *cantalupensis* (cantaloupe), 1813
C. melo var. *conomon* (gherkin),
1777
C. melo var. *flexuosus* (cucumber, serpent cucumber,
snake cucumber), 1765
C. melo var. *inodorus* (winter
melon), 1813
C. melo var. *reticulatus*
(muskmelon), 1813
cantaloupe (muskmelon), 1744
casaba, 1746
in Egypt (ancient), 1133
honeydew melon, 1786
in North America (pre-
Columbian), 1289
ogen melon, 1824
Cucumis metuliferus
African horned cucumber
(cucumber), 1765
kiwano, 1796
Cucumis sativus (cucumber), 299,
300–303, 305, 1765. *See
also* cucumber(s); gherkin;
squash
Cucurbita, 335–351, 1839–1840. *See
also* squash
in Caribbean (pre-Columbian),
1262
Cucurbita argyrosperma (= *C.
mixta,* cushaw squash),
336, 1766. *See also* squash
domestication of, 344
evolution of, 344–345
history of, 337, 344–345
in North America (pre-Columbian),
1289
origin of, 344
plant and fruit of, 337

H

habanero pepper (*Capsicum chinense*), 1716, 1783. *See also* chilli pepper(s)

habichuela (hyacinth bean, *Lablab niger* = *L. purpureus*), 1788

Hachiya (persimmon, *Diospyros kaki, D. virginiana*), 1833. *See also* persimmon

Hacienda Grande site (Puerto Rico), 1270

haciendas, in coffee production, 650

Hacinebi Tepe site (Turkey), 620

hackberry (*Celtis* spp.), 1783
  C. occidentalis, 1289, 1293, 1294

haddock
  in the Netherlands (1300-1500), 1233
  propagation and release of, in Britain, 461

Hadith, 1503-1504

Hadza (Tanzania), diet in, 64, 65

haidi (*Laminaria japonica*), in China, 232

hairy melon (fuzzy melon, *Benincasa hispida* = *B. cerifera*), 1775-1776

Haiti. *See also* San Domingue; St. Domingue
  dietary liquids in
    cacao, 638, 643
    coffee, production of, 652
    rum, 660
  infant mortality in, 1285
  malnourishment in, 1285
  pig in, 541
  plant foods in
    chilli pepper (pre-Columbian), 281
    ginger, 1778
    rice (post-Columbian), 1286
    sugar and rum, 660
  population growth in, post-colonial, 1285
  revolution for independence in, 1284

Hajji Firuz site, 730, 1126

hake, in British Isles (1700-1900), 1224

hakusai (Chinese cabbage, *Brassica pekinensis*), 1754-1755

Hallan Cemi site (Turkey), 537

Halmahera, sugarcane in, 438

Hamamelis virginiana (witch-hazel), 1883

Hamburg celery (celery, *Apium graveolens*), 1748-1749. *See also* celery

Hamburg parsley (*Petroselinum crispum* var. *tuberosum*), 1783. *See also* parsley

Hamlin orange (orange, *Citrus sinensis*), 1826. *See also* orange(s), common

Hamwith site (England), 519-520

Hancornia speciosa (mangaba), 1809

Handbook of Geographical and Historical Pathology, 917, 988

Handbook of Vitamins, 1687

Handlist of Italian Cookery Books, 1374

Hanover kale (*Brassica napus*), 1783. *See also* cabbage; kale

Hanover salad (Hanover kale, *Brassica napus*), 1783

Harappa site (Indus Valley), 413, 496, 497, 593

Haratua's pa site, 210

harbor seal, 1298. *See also* seal(s)

hard clam (*Mercenaria* spp.), 1290

hard wheat (wheat, *Triticum aestivum*), 1878. *See also* wheat

hardhead catfish (*Arius felis*), in North America
  pre-Columbian, 1290
  Spanish colonial, 1300

hare. *See also* rabbit
  arctic, 1324
  in British Isles (Roman period), 1218
  Christian prohibitions of, 1503
  as forbidden food, 1499
  in North America (pre-Columbian), 1299

harebell (campanula, *Campanula*), 1743
  in British Isles (prehistoric), 1217

haricot (beans, *Phaseolus* spp.), 1729, 1799-1800

haricot riz (rice bean, *Phaseolus calcaratus* = Vigna umbellata), 1844

harlock (burdock, *Arctium lappa*), 1740

Harpephyllum caffrum (kaffir plum), 1795

Harper Hybrid melon, 308

Harris lines, 22-23, 41

Harvard beet (beet, *Beta vulgaris*), 1730-1731. *See also* beet

Harvard growth standards, 984

Harvard University, 1374, 1491, 1678

harvest moon festival, in Korea, 1187

Haselnuss (hazelnut, *Corylus avellana, E. maxima*), 1784. *See also* hazelnut

Hass avocado (avocado, *Persea americana*), 1724-1725. *See also* avocado

Hastinapura site (India), 594

Haugh Units, 504

Hausa groundnut (*Kerstingiella geocarpa* = *Macrotyloma geocarpa*), 1783-1784

Hausa potato
  Plectranthus esculentus, 1795
  Sudan potato (*Coleus tuberosus* = C. parviflorus = Solenostemon rotundifolius), 1859

haute cuisine, southern European courtly, 1208

Haven of Health, 1688

Haversian canals, 22

haw (*Crataegus* spp., hawthorn berry), 1784. *See also* black haw; hawthorn berry; sloe

haw tree (hawthorn berry, *Crataegus* spp.), 1784

Hawaiian Islands
  diabetes mellitus in, 1363
  dietary colonialism in, 1361
  dietary liquids in, kava, 664, 665, 668
  famine in, 1413
  fish farming in, tribal, 457-458
  plant foods in
    banana, 178
    macadamia nut, 1805
    papaya, 1828
    pineapple, 1834
    rice, 139
    sugarcane, 444
    sweet potato (pre-Columbian), 210
    taro, 223, 224, 226, 227, 1866
    watermelon (post-Columbian), 306

Hawaiian Kona coffee (coffee, *Coffea arabica*), 1761. *See also* coffee

Hawaiian pineapple (pineapple, *Ananas comosus*), 1834

Hawaiian plantain (*Musa* × *sapientum*), 1784. *See also* plantain

hawk, broad-winged (*Buteo platypterus*), 1291

hawksbill turtle (*Eretmochelys imbricata*), 567

hawthorn
  black haw (*Viburnum prunifolium, Crataegus douglasii*), 1734
  Crataegus spp., 1784
  in North America (pre-Columbian), 1289

hawthorn berry (*Crataegus* spp.), 1784

I

K

kaai choi (*Brassica juncea*), 293
kabocha squash. *See also* squash
  Cucurbita maxima (buttercup squash), 1740, 1794
  Cucurbita moschata, 1794
  in Japan, 1794
  in Mexico, 1794
  in New Zealand, 1794
kachun (pepino, *Solanum muricatum*), 1832
Kadotta fig (fig, *Ficus carica*), 1774
Kaempferia galanga (galanga), 1776
kaffe (coffee, *Coffea arabica*), 644, 1760-1761. *See also* coffee
kaffir corn (sorghum, *Sorghum vulgare* = S. bicolor), 1853-1854
kaffir date (kaffir plum, *Harpephyllum caffrum*), 1795
kaffir lime (*Citrus hystrix*), 1794
kaffir orange (monkey orange, *Strychnos spinosa*), 1815-1816
kaffir plum (*Harpephyllum caffrum*), 1795
kaffir potato (*Plectranthus esculentus*), 1795
Kafika apple (*Spondias dulcis*), 1357
Kahlua liqueur, 661
kahve (coffee, *Coffea arabica*), 1760-1761. *See also* coffee
kahwa (coffee, *Coffea arabica*), 1760-1761. *See also* coffee
kahwe (coffee, *Coffea arabica*), 1761. *See also* coffee
kai choi (*Brassica chinensis*), 1827
kail (kale, *Brassica oleracea* var. *acephala*), 1795
kailan (Chinese broccoli, *Brassica alboglabra*), 1754. *See also* cabbage
kaiware (daikon, *Raphanus sativus*), 1767
kaka (*Nestor meridonalis*), 1344
kakapo (*Strigops habroptilus*), 1344
kaki (persimmon, *Diospyros kaki*), 1833
Kalahari Desert
  caloric intake in, 66
  carrion as food in, 1509
  diet and workload in, 64-65
  parasites in, 66
  watermelon in, 306, 307
kale, 1741. *See also* cabbage; collards
  Brassica alboglabra (Chinese kale, Chinese broccoli), 1754
  Brassica napus (Hanover kale, spring kale), 1783
  Brassica oleracea var. *acephala*, 290, 291, 1761, 1795

in Asia Minor, native, 291
in Japan, 1795
in Mediterranean, 1795
  native, 291
in Portugal, 1795
in Roman empire, 1795
in Brazil, 1257
in Europe, southern, 1209
in North America (post-Columbian), 1313
  18th cent., 1307-1308
kalonji (nigella, *Nigella sativa*), 1822
kampyo (bottle gourd, *Lagenaria siceraria*), 1736
kamut (*Triticum turgidum*), 164, 1795. *See also* wheat
kana (maize, *Zea mays*), 1805-1807
  in Guatemala, 1248
kanamycin, 1654
kanari (Java almond, *Canarium commune*), 1792
kang-kong (swamp cabbage, *Ipomoea aquatica*), 1861-1862
kang kung (swamp cabbage, *Ipomoea aquatica*), 1861-1862
kangaroo
  gray (*Macropus fuliginosus*), 1341
  red (*Macropus rufus*), 1341
kangaroo apple (*Solanum linearifolium*), 1340
kanten (agar, *Euchema* spp., *Gelidium* spp.), 1715. *See also* seaweed
kaoliang, 1184
kaolinite, 970
Kaopectate, 970
kápari (caper(s), *Capparis spinosa*), 1744
kape (giant taro, *Alocasia*), 219-221. *See also* taro
kapok tree (*Ceiba pentandra*), 1795
karaka (*Corynocarpus laevigatus*), 1343, 1795-1796
karamta (swamp cabbage, *Ipomoea aquatica*), 1861-1862
karanda (caraunda, *Carissa carandas*), 1745
karaschi (Japanese mustard), 1820
karawya (caraway, *Carum carvi*), 1745
karenga (seaweed, *Porphyra columbina*), 1344, 1850
Karmir Blur site (Yerevan), 413-414, 415
Kartoffelkrieg (potato war), 191
karzochy (artichoke, *Cynara scolymus*), 1722
kasabi (manioc, *Manihot esculenta*), 181
kaschiri, 623
kasha (buckwheat, *Fagopyrum*

esculentum, Fagopyrum spp.), 1739
  in Russia (19th cent.), 1242, 1243
Kashmiri chilli, 1723
Kastanie (chestnut, *Castanea*), 1751-1752
kat (khat, *Catha edulis*), 1796
Katalog der Kochbücher-Sammulung, 1374
katook (sweet shoot, *Sauropus androgynous*), 1863-1864
katsuo-bushi (dried bonito), 1178-1179
katuk (sweet shoot, *Sauropus androgynous*), 1863-1864
katy. See khat
Kaupokonui site, 210
kava drinking circle, 667
kava-kava (kava, *Piper methysticum*). *See* kava
kava lactones, 669
kava (*Piper methysticum*), 664-670, 1360, 1796
  alcohol and, 669
  botanical description of, 665
  commercial development of, 670
  distribution of, 665-666
  exchanges of root of, 668
  narcotic properties of, 669
  origin and spread of, 664-665
  processing of, 666-667
  ritual uses of, 666
  secular usage of, 668-669
kayu manis
  Cinnamomum cassia (cassia), 1757
  Cinnamomum zeylanicum (= C. *verum*, cinnamon), 1757
kayu manis (sweet wood), 1160
Kazakhstan, animal foods in
  camel's milk, 474
  sheep, 578
kechapi (sentul, *Sandoricum koetjape* = S. *indicum*), 1850
kĕdondong (hog plum, *Spondias cytherea*), 1785
Keemum tea (tea, *Camellia sinensis*), 1866-1867. *See also* tea(s)
keladi (cocoyam, *Colocasia esculenta*), 1154, 1760
Kellogg's products, 1348, 1488, 1491
kelp (Laminariales, Fucales), 1796. *See also* seaweed
  in Arctic, 1299
  Laminaria japonica, 1796, 1850
  Macrocystis pyrifera, 1796
  in North America (pre-Columbian), 1299
Kemp's ridley turtle (*Lepidochelys kempii*), 567, 572

leek(s)
  in British Isles, 263
    Medieval, 1219, 1221
  Chinese (*Allium ramosum*),
        263
  common (*Allium porrum*),
        263-264, 1799
    in Belgium, 1799
    chemistry of, 264
    cultivation of, 263
    in Europe, 1799
    in France, 1799
    in Greek city-states, 1799
    history of, 263
    in Mediterranean, 1799
    in Netherlands, 1799
    nutritive value of, 263
    origin of, 263
    in Roman empire, 1799
    in Scotland, 1799
    in Wales, 1799
  in Egypt and Greece (ancient),
        263
  in Germany, 250
  in Korea, 1185
  in Roman empire, 263
  sand (garlic, *Allium* spp.), 1776
  wild (*Allium tricoccum*), 1881
    in Caribbean, 1716-1717
    in Central America, 1716-1717
    in Europe, 1717
    in Jamaica, 1717
Leersia oryzoides (rice cutgrass),
        1289
legal documents, and culinary his-
        tory, 1371-1372
leghorn citron (citron, *Citrus med-
        ica*), 1757-1758. *See also*
        lemon
legume(s), 271. *See also* pulses; spe-
        cific types, e.g., lentil(s),
        Phaseolus
  in Africa, 1800
  in Americas, 1800
  amino acid composition of, 907,
        908
  in Asia, 1800
    Southeast, 1157
  botany of, 271-272
  in Europe, southern, 1208
  food allergies to, 1024
  in Mexico, 1800
  in Near East, 1799
  as phosphate source, 835, 836
  protein content of, comparative,
        887
  pulses (Fabaceae, Leguminosae),
        1752, 1799-1800
  in Roman empire, 1799
  in United States, 1800
  vetch (*Vicia*), 1875

Leichardtia australis (bush banana),
        1340
Leiostomus xanthurus (spot), 1290
lemon (*Citrus limon*), 433, 1800
  bergamot, 1800
  in Caribbean, 1279
  Eureka, 1800
  Lisbon, 1800
  in Mexico, 1251
  Meyer, 1800
  in Near East, 1758
  in North America, (19th cent.),
        1315
  for scurvy, 704-705, 993, 994
  in South America, 1257
lemon balm (*Melissa officinalis*),
        432, 1800
  in Europe, southern, 1209
lemon barley water, 708
lemon cucumber (cucumber,
        Cucumis sativus), 302,
        1765
lemon grass (*Cympobogon citratus*),
        433, 1161
lemon guava (guava, *Psidium gua-
        java*), 1782
lemon squash, 708
lemon thyme (thyme, *Thymus citri-
        odorus*), 1869
lemon verbena (*Lippia citriodora*),
        1801
lemon vine (Barbados gooseberry,
        Pereskia aculeata), 1727
lemonade, 704, 706-707
  efferverscent, 706
lemongrass (*Cymbopogon citratus,
        C. flexuosus*), 433, 1161,
        1800-1801
Lens culinaris (lentils), 1712
Lens culinaris ssp. *macrosperma*
        (lentil), 277
Lens culinaris ssp. *microsperma*
        (lentil), 277
Lens ervoides, 277
Lens esculenta (lentils), 1712, 1801
Lens nigricans, 277
Lens odemensis, 277
Lens orientalis, 277
  domestication of, 278-279
  seed dormancy in, 278
Lent
  eggs and, 500
  fasting during, 1203, 1204, 1205
  in the Netherlands (1300-1500),
        1232-1233
  in Russia, 428
    early, 1241
lentil(s)
  in Afghanistan, 273
  in Africa, North, 277
  anaphylaxis from, 1024

  in Asia, 1801
    Central, 1801
    South, 1801
  black, 1801
  botany of, 277-278
  in British Isles (Roman period),
        1218
  brown, 1712
  in China, 273
  domestication of, 277, 278-279
  dormancy in, 278
  in Egypt, 1801
    ancient, 1135
  in Europe, 1801
    eastern, 1801
    northern (Neolithic), 1228
  in France, 277
  in Greek city-states, 1801
  green, 1801
  in India, 273, 277, 1801
  large-seeded, 1801
  Lens culinaris, 277-279
  Lens culinaris ssp.
        macrosperma, 277
  Lens culinaris ssp. *microsperma*,
        277
  Lens ervoides, 277
  Lens esculenta, 277-279
  Lens nigricans, 277
  Lens odemensis, 277
  Lens orientalis, 277
    seed dormancy in, 278
  in Mexico (post-Columbian), 1251
  in Middle East, 1801
  in Near East, 277
    ancient, 277
  nomenclature for, 272
  origins of, 273
  Phaseolus aureus, 1801
  Phaseolus mungo, 1801
  Pisum sativum, 1801
  in Roman empire, 1801
  seed dormancy in, 278
  small-seeded, 1801
  in Spain, 277
  in Tadzhikistan, 273
  in Uzbekistan, 273
  wild, 1801
  yellow, 1801
lentil water, 631
Lentinus edodes (shitake, Chinese
        black mushroom), 315, 1819
Lentinus lepideus, 327
lentisk (mastic tree, *Pistacia lentis-
        cus*), 1811
leopard, 1344
Lepidium sativum (cress), 433, 1765
  in British Isles (Medieval), 1219
  in England, 1765
Lepidium virginicum (peppergrass),
        1289, 1296

motion pictures, and culinary his-
    tory, 1372–1373
motor development, protein in, 1460
Moturua Island site, 210
mountain ash (*Sorbus americana*),
    1817
mountain balm (yerba santa, *Eriodic-
    tyon californicum*), 1885
mountain cranberry (lingonberry, *Vac-
    cinium vitis-idaea*), 1802
mountain duck (*Tadorna
    tadornoides*), 1341
mountain hemlock (*Tsuga merten-
    siana*), 1785
mountain hollyhock (wasabi,
    Wasabia japonica), 1876
Mountain Lapps, 486
mountain papaya
    Carica candamarcensis (= *C.
        pubescens*), 1817
    Carica pubescens (papaya), 1725
mountain plum (tallow wood plum,
    Ximenia americana), 1865
mountain possum (*Trichosurus cani-
    cus*), 1341
mountain sheep, in Subarctic, 1324
mountain sorrel (*Xyria digyna*),
    1817
mountain spinach (orach, *Atriplex*
    spp.), 1826
mountain sumac (smooth sumac,
    Rhus glabra), 1853
mountain tansy mustard (tansy mus-
    tard, *Descurainia pin-
    nata*), 1865–1866
mourning dove (*Zenaida
    macroura*), 564
    in North America (pre-
        Columbian), 1291, 1297
mousseron d'automne, 1819
moutarde (mustard), 1820
moxa (mugwort, *Artemisia spp.*),
    1817
Moxostoma spp. (redhorse), 1290
Mozambique
    animal foods in
        chicken (prehistoric), 498
    plant foods in
        manioc, 184
        rice, 139
        yam, 215
    plant foods in (colonial)
        manioc, 184
        sweet potato, 209
mozarella di bufala cheese, 1209
*Mrs. Beeton's Book of Household
    Management*, 571
Mt. Olo (Samoa) site, 213
mucket, in North America (pre-
    Columbian)
    Actinonaias spp., 1290

Lampsilis spp., 1290
Mucor, in Chinese alcoholic bever-
    ages, 315
mud nassa (*Ilynassa obsoleta*), 1290
mud turtle (*Kinosternon* spp.),
    1290, 1295, 1297
mudsnail (*Amphibda crenata*), 1341
Mug House Ruin site (Arizona), 581
Mugil spp. (mullet, gray mullet), 1155
    in North America (pre-Columbian),
        1290
Mugil cephalus (mullet), 1341
mugwort
    Artemisia spp., 1817
    Artemisia vulgaris, 433, 1817
        in Korea, 1187
    Tanacetum vulgare (tansy), 1865
mulard duck (Muscovy/common
    duck hybrid), 560
mulato (*Capsicum*, poblano), 1837
mulberry
    Chinese (che, *Cudrania tricuspi-
        data*), 1750
    Indian (*Morinda*), 1816
    Morus spp., 1817
    paper (*Broussonetia papyrifera*),
        1828
    red (*Morus rubra*), 1817
        in North America (pre-
            Columbian), 1289
    in silk industry, 362
mullet
    in Australia, 1341
    in Caribbean (pre-Columbian), 1279
    in Europe, southern, 1209
    farming of, modern, 466
    grey (*Mugil* spp.), 1155
        farming of, 463
    Mugil spp., 463, 1155, 1290,
        1300
    Mugil cephalus, 1341
    in New Zealand, 1344
    in North America
        pre-Columbian, 1290
        Spanish colonial, 1300
    in Roman empire, 457
    in Taiwan, 464
    yellow-eyed, 1344
Munchkin (delicata, *Cucurbita
    pepo*), 1768
mung bean (*Phaseolus aureus*),
    1157, 1729, 1800, 1817
    black, 1817
    green, 1801
    in Korea, 1185
    red, 1801, 1817
    sprouts of, 426, 1730
Muntingia calabura (capulin, cal-
    abur, Panama berry, Jamaica
    cherry), 1745
Muntok (peppercorn(s), *Piper*

nigrum), 1832. *See also*
    peppercorn
Mureybit site (Euphrates River, Syr-
    ian steppe), 83, 1124
murlines (*Alaria esculenta*), 233
Murray cod (*Maccullochella mac-
    quariensis*), 1341
Murray River (Australia) site, 926, 1341
Murraya koenigii (curry leaf), 433,
    1766
Musa × sapientum (Hawaiian
    plantain), 1784. *See also*
    plantain(s)
Musa acuminata (banana, wild
    banana), 175, 177, 178,
    1158. *See also* bananas and
    plantains
Musa acuminata ssp. *malaccensis*
    (banana), 178
Musa balbisiana (banana), 175, 177,
    178
Musa corniculata (banana), 177
Musa ensete (ensete), 1771–1772. *See
    also* bananas and plantains
Musa nana (banana), 177
Musa paradisiaca (banana), 177,
    1726. *See also* bananas and
    plantains; banana flower;
    ensete; plantain(s)
    flower of, 1726–1727
Musa sapientum (banana), 177
Musa textilis (abaca fiber), 176
Musa troglodytarum (*fe'i* bananas),
    175, 176, 177, 179
Musa × paradisiaca (plantain), 1836
Musa × sapientum (Hawaiian plan-
    tain), 1784
muscadine grape (*Vitis rotundifo-
    lia*), 1781, 1817. *See also*
    grape(s); wine(s)
    in United States, 1817
Muscadiniae, 730
muscat grape (*Vitis vinifera*), 1818.
    See also grape(s); wine(s)
Muscicapidae (thrush)
    in Europe, southern, 1209
    in North America (pre-
        Columbian), 1291
muscle(s)
    calcium and, 948
    metabolism of, "conservation of
        energy" in, 884, 891
    potassium and, 845–846
    protein as fuel for, 883–884
Muscovy ducks (*Cairina moschata*),
    559–561
    in Caribbean, 582
        pre-Columbian, 1263
    distribution of, 559
    domesticated (*C. moschata
        domestica*), 560

myrtle flag (sweet flag, *Acorus calamus*), 1862. *See also* sweet flag

myrtle-leafed orange (orange, *Citrus aurantium*), 1826

myrtle (*Myrtus communis*), 433, 1820. *See also* Chilean guava myrtle; periwinkle

myrtle pepper (allspice, *Pimenta dioica*), 1716–1717. *See also* allspice

Myrtus communis (myrtle), 433, 1820

Myrtus ugni (Chilean guava myrtle), 1753

Myrtus verrucosa (myrtle, "stopper"), 1820

Mytilus spp. (mussels), 1156. *See also* mussel(s)

Mytilus edulis (mussels), 1341

myxomatosis, 567

N

Nabisco, 1487

Nabta Playa (Egypt) site, 1128–1129, 1331

Naga ed-Dar archaeological site, 117

nagami. *See* kumquat

Nagami kumquat (*Fortunella margarita*), 1798. *See also* kumquat

nagana disease, 493

Nagoya kale (kale, *Brassica oleracea* var. *acephala*), 1795

Nahal Hemar cave site (Judean Hills), 84

naked barley (barley, *Hordeum vulgare*), 1727

nalta jute (Jew's mallow, *Corchorus olitorus*), 1793

nam pla (fish soy), 1162

namasu, 1177

ñame. See also cush-cush yam
    Dioscorea trifida (yams), 1884

ñame mapuey. See cush-cush yam

Namibia, pearl millet in, 115

Nan Fang Ts'ao Mu Chuang, 202

nana (pineapple, *Ananas comosus*), 1834. *See also* pineapple

nanacatl (mushroom), 316

nance (*Byronima crassifolia*), 1821

nangka (jackfruit, *Artocarpus heterophyllus = A. integrifolius*), 1790–1791

nangoué, 684. *See also* kola nut

nannyberry (black haw, *Viburnum prunifolium, Crataegus douglasii*), 1734

napa cabbage
    bok choy (*Brassica rapa*), 1735, 1741
    Chinese cabbage (*Brassica pekinensis*), 1754–1755

Napa Valley Gamay grape (*Vitis vinifera*), 1776. *See also* grape(s); wine

nappa cabbage (Chinese cabbage, *Brassica pekinensis*), 1754–1755

naranjilla (*Solanum quitoense*), 1821
    in South America, 1255–1256

Nardostachys jatamansi, 1548

Narrative of a Journey through the Upper Provinces of India, 743

narrow-capped morel (*Morchella* spp.), 1816

narrow dock (curled dock, *Rumex crispus*), 1766

naseberry
    Manilkara zapota (sapodilla), 1848
    Mimusops sieberii, 1814

nashi (Asian pear, *Pyrus ussuriensis, P. pyrifolia*), 1723

nassa
    mud (*Ilynassa obsoleta*), 1290
    Nassarius spp., 1290

Nassarius spp. (nassa), 1290

nasturtium (Indian cress, *Tropaeolum majus*), 433, 1821

Nasturtium officinale (watercress), 289, 295, 434, 1876–1877
    in Europe, 1877
    native, 1876
    for scurvy, 993
    in United States, 1876

natal orange (monkey orange, *Strychnos spinosa*), 1815–1816

natal plum
    Carissa grandiflora, 1821
    Ximenia caffra (sour plum), 185

Natator depressus (Australian flatback turtle), 568

National Academy of Sciences, on potassium requirement, 847

National Adolescent Student Health Survey, 1073

National Agricultural Research Institute (INIA, Chile), 100

National Agricultural University (Peru), 100

National Autonomous University of Mexico (UNAM), 1375

National Biscuit Company, 1487

National Cancer Institute, 1638

National Cattlemen's Association, 1635, 1636, 1638

on *Food Guide Pyramid*, 1639–1640

National Center for Health Statistics (NCHS), child weight standards of, 979

National Corn Growers Association, 98

National Formulary, 1549

National Health and Medical Research Council of Australia, on iodized bread, 808

National Health and Nutrition Examination Survey (NHANES)
    cholesterol findings of, 1101
    First, 1062, 1072
    Second, 928

National Institute of Forestry and Agricultural Research (Mexico), 100

National Institutes of Health, 1656

National Milk Publicity Council, 1582

National Pellagra Remedy Company, 962

National Research Council
    on cholesterol and fats, 1103, 1106, 1638, 1639
    on dietary requirements, 1611

National Seed Storage Laboratory, 100

National Seminar on the Etiology of Keshan Disease, 941

National Soybean Processors Association, 1855

nationalism, and food preparation, 1121

Native Americans
    anemia in, 931–932
    diet of
        vs. European settlers, 1475
        watermelon in, 306
    medicinal foods of, 1546
    obesity in, 1063
    in 16th cent., 1304–1305

native carrot (*Geranium solanderi*), 1340

native cherry (*Exocarpos cuppressiformis*), 1340, 1821

native cucumber (pepino, *Solanum muricatum*), 1832

native gooseberry (wild gooseberry, *Physalis minima*), 1341, 1881

native guava (*Rhodomyrtus psidioides*), 1821

native lime (*Citrus australis, Microcitrus australasica*), 1821

native myrtle (brush cherry, *Eugenia myrtifolia, Syzygium paniculatum*), 1738

green, 1862–1863
green bell, 1862–1863
Holland, 1862–1863
Hungarian cherry pepper,
1788
in Hungary, 1863
mango, 1862–1863
in Mediterranean, 1863
Mexi-Bell, 1862–1863
in Mexico, 1863
in Netherlands, 1863
in North America, 1862–1863
pimento, 1862–1863
pimiento, 1862–1863
pimiento dulce, 1862–1863
pimiento morrón, 1862–1863
red bell, 1862–1863
in South America, 1862–1863
in Spain, 1863
sweet purple, 1862–1863
in United States, 1863
wax, 1877
tabasco, 1864
Capsicum frutescens (Brazilian malagueta), 1737
in Central America, 1864
tailed (*Piper cubeba*), 1864–1865
water (*Polygonum hydropiper*),
1797
wax (*Capsicum*), 1877
banana, 1877
chawa, 1877
güero, 1877
Hungarian wax, 1877
Hungarian yellow wax, 1877
Santa Fe Grande, 1877
pepper dulse (*Laurencia pinnatifida*), 233
pepper of Calicut (chilli pepper(s),
Capsicum annuum),
1753–1754. *See also* chilli
pepper(s)
pepper pots, 1263
pepper tree (mastic tree, *Schinus*
spp.), 1811
peppercorn(s)
common (*Piper nigrum*), 282,
433, 1160, 1832
black, 1832
in British Isles (Roman period),
1218
in Europe, southern, 1209
in Greek city states, 1832
green, 1832
native, 1832
in Roman empire, 1832
in Russia (early), 1241
in spice trade (ancient-
medieval), 1525
Sichuan (*Zanthoxylum piperitum*), 1852

in Korea, 1185
peppergrass
Lepidium sativum (cress), 1765
Lepidium virginicum, 1289, 1296
pepperidge
Berberis spp. (barberry), 1727
Nyssa sylvatica (black gum),
1733–1734
peppermint (*Mentha × piperita*),
1815
medicinal use of, 1540
peppermint water, 707
pepperroot (toothwort, *Dentaria
diphylla*), 1871
Pepsi-Cola, 709, 1489
Pepsico, potatoes and, 195
pequín (tepín chillies, *Capsicum
annuum*), 1868. *See also*
chilli pepper(s)
Perameles spp. (bandicoots), 1341
Perca flavescens (yellow perch),
1290
perch
in Europe
ancient-medieval, 458
southern, 1209
in the Netherlands (1300–1500),
1233
Nile, 1129
sea (*Lates clacarifer*), 1155
silver
Bairdiella chrysoura, 1290
Bidyanus bidyanus, 1341
surf, 1298
yellow (*Perca flavescens*), 1290
percolator, coffee, 645
Perella Red (lettuce, *Lactuca* spp.),
1801. *See also* lettuce
perennial goosefoot (Good-King-
Henry, *Chenopodium
bonus-henricus*), 1750,
1779
perennial onion (onion tree, *Allium
cepa*), 1825–1826
perennial pea (*Lathyrus latifolius*,
Lathyrus spp.), 1772
perennial sow thistle (sow thistle,
Sonchus arvensis), 1855
Pereskia aculeata (Barbados gooseberry), 1727
Pereskiopsis aquosa (tuna de agua),
1873
Perideridia parishii (Parish's yampah), 1789
Perigord truffle (black truffle, *Tuber
melanosporum*), 1872
flavor of, 327
perilla (*Perilla frutescens*, P. ocimoidesi), 1833
Perilla arguts (beefsteak plant), 1730
Perilla frutescens (perilla), 1833

Perilla ocimoidesi (perilla), 1833
periostitis, in prehistoric hunter-
gatherers, 67
periwinkle
Littorina irrorata (gastropod),
1290
Vinca spp. (plant), 1833
Perlette grape, 1781
permafrost, 1324
Perna canaliculus (mussel), 1341
pernicious anemia, 753–754
Peronospora destructor (downy
mildew)
on chives, 264
on onions, 252
Perrier water, 710
perry, 703
in British Isles (Medieval), 1220
Pyrus communis (pear), 1831
Persea americana (avocado),
1724–1725. *See also*
avocado
Persea borbonia (sweet bay), 1289,
1296
Persia
alchemy in (ancient-medieval),
655
chicken in, 500
plant foods in
onion, native, 250
watermelon, 1877
native, 1812
plant foods in (ancient-medieval)
rice, 139
sesame, 416
Persian empire, 1144–1145
Persian lime (lime, *Citrus aurantiifolia*), 1802
Persian melon, 300
Cucumis melo var. *reticulatus*,
1813
Persian walnut (walnut, *Juglans
regia*), 1876
Persian wild goat (*Capra aegagrus*),
532. *See also* goat
persimmon
Diospyros digyna (black persimmon, black sapote), 1734
Diospyros kaki (orange-red persimmon), 1833
Diospyros virginiana, 1833
in North America (pre-
Columbian), 1289,
1294, 1295, 1296
Peru
animal foods in
alpaca, 555
cattle, 1256
duck, Muscovy, 560
prehistoric, 560
llama, 555

Q

smoking. *See also* tobacco
and cardiovascular disease, 1113
and obesity, 1067
Smoot-Hawley Tariff, 424
smooth caper (caper(s), *Capparis
spinosa*), 1744. *See also*
caper
smooth hammerhead shark (*Sphyrna
zygaena*), 1290
smooth loofah (*Luffa aegyptiaca*),
1719
smooth muscle, potassium and,
845–846
smooth sumac (*Rhus glabra*), 1853
smudge, onion (*Collectotrichum
circinan*), 253
smut. *See also* rot
loose (*Ustilago avenae*), 124
onion (*Urocystis cepulae*), 253
and chives, 264
Smyrna fig (fig, *Ficus carica*), 1774
Smyrnium olusatrum (alexander),
432, 1716
snail(s)
in British Isles (Roman period),
1218
fasciolopsis from, 1045
in Korean archeological sites, 1187
land
Caracolus sp.
in Caribbean (pre-
Columbian), 1263
in Dominican Republic,
1271
Polydontes sp., 1271
trematodes from, 1045–1046
snailseed (pigeon plum, *Coccoloba
diversifolia* = C. floridana,
Chrysobalanus ellipticus),
1834
in Europe, southern, 1209
snake(s)
in Caribbean (pre-Columbian),
1279
in North America (pre-Columbian),
1291, 1295, 1297
nonpoisonous (Colubridae),
1291
poisonous (Viperidae), 1291
snake bean (winged bean, *Psophocarpus tetragonolobus*),
1882
snake cucumber
Cucumis melo (Armenian cucumber), 1721
Cucumis melo va. *flexuosus*,
1765
snake cucumber (snake gourd, *Trichosanthes anguina, T.
cucumerina*), 1853

snake gourd (*Trichosanthes anguina,
T. cucumerina*), 1853
snake melon, 300
Cucumis melo (Armenian cucumber), 1721
Trichosanthes anguina (snake
gourd), 1853
Trichosanthes cucumerina
(snake gourd), 1853
snakeroot, white (*Eupatorium rugosum*), 1735–1736
snap bean (common bean, *Phaseolus vulgaris*), 1729. *See
also* bean(s)
in Caribbean (post-Columbian),
1272
snapper
Chrysophrys auratus, 1341
Lutianus spp., 1155
in New Zealand, 1344
Trachichthodes affinus, 1341
snapping hazel (witch-hazel,
Hamamelis virginiana),
1883
snapping turtle
alligator (*Macroclemys
temmincki*), 1290
Chelydra serpentina, 1290, 1295,
1297
snipe (*Galinago gallinago*)
in British Isles (Medieval), 1220
in North America (pre-
Columbian), 1291
snook (*Centropomus* spp.), 1290
snow goose (*Chen caerulescens*),
1291
snow pea (sugar pea, *Pisum sativum
var. macrocarpon*),
1860–1861
soapberry (*Sapindus* spp.), 1853
S. saponaria, 1754
soba, 1176, 1181
Société des Mercredis, 1213
Society for French Historical Studies,
1374
Society for the Encouragement of
Agriculture, 445
Society Islands, taro in, 226
Society of St. Andrew, 199
sociopolitical/socioeconomic status
and anemia, 930–932
and anorexia nervosa, 1005
and diet, in Near East (ancient-
medieval), 1126, 1127
and obesity, 1067
and protein-energy malnutrition,
985
soda fountains, 707
soda water, 705–706
as elegant beverage, 706

as mixer, 707
sodium
-hunger pathway, 850
and calcium metabolism, 956
and hypertension, 848–854
current thinking on, 854
history of, 853–854
in human evolution, 851
physiology of, 850–851
salt in, dietary
in body, 848
deficiency of, 851–852
excess of, 852–853
historical use of, 848
physical need for, 849–850
measurement of, flame photometric method for, 850
sodium carbonate, 848
sodium chloride. *See* salt
sodium nitrate, 1670
sodium-potassium-ATPase pump,
844–845
sodium saccharin, and cancer, 1093
sodium-selenium, for Keshan disease,
941–942
sodium silicate, 863
soft date (date, *Phoenix dactylifera*),
1767–1768. *See also* date(s)
soft drinks, 702–711
artificial mineral waters, 705–706
aspartame in, 1679
as bottled product, 709
colas, 709–710
as concentrated syrups, 709
cordials and domestic drinks, 704
definition of, 702
draft, 711
elegant and refreshing beverages,
706–707
fruit drinks, 708–709
fruit-flavored drinks, 704
growing market in, 710
high-fructose corn syrup in, 448
in Japan, 710
low-calorie, 710
high-intensity sweeteners in,
448
mixer drinks, 707
in the Netherlands, 1238
new-age, 710
in North America, 709–710, 1320
packaging of, 710–711
in South America, 1259
sports and isotonic, 710
teas, iced, 710
temperance drinks, 707–708
in United States, 647, 1320
soft rot (*Erwinia carotovora*)
onion maggot and, 254
on onions, 253

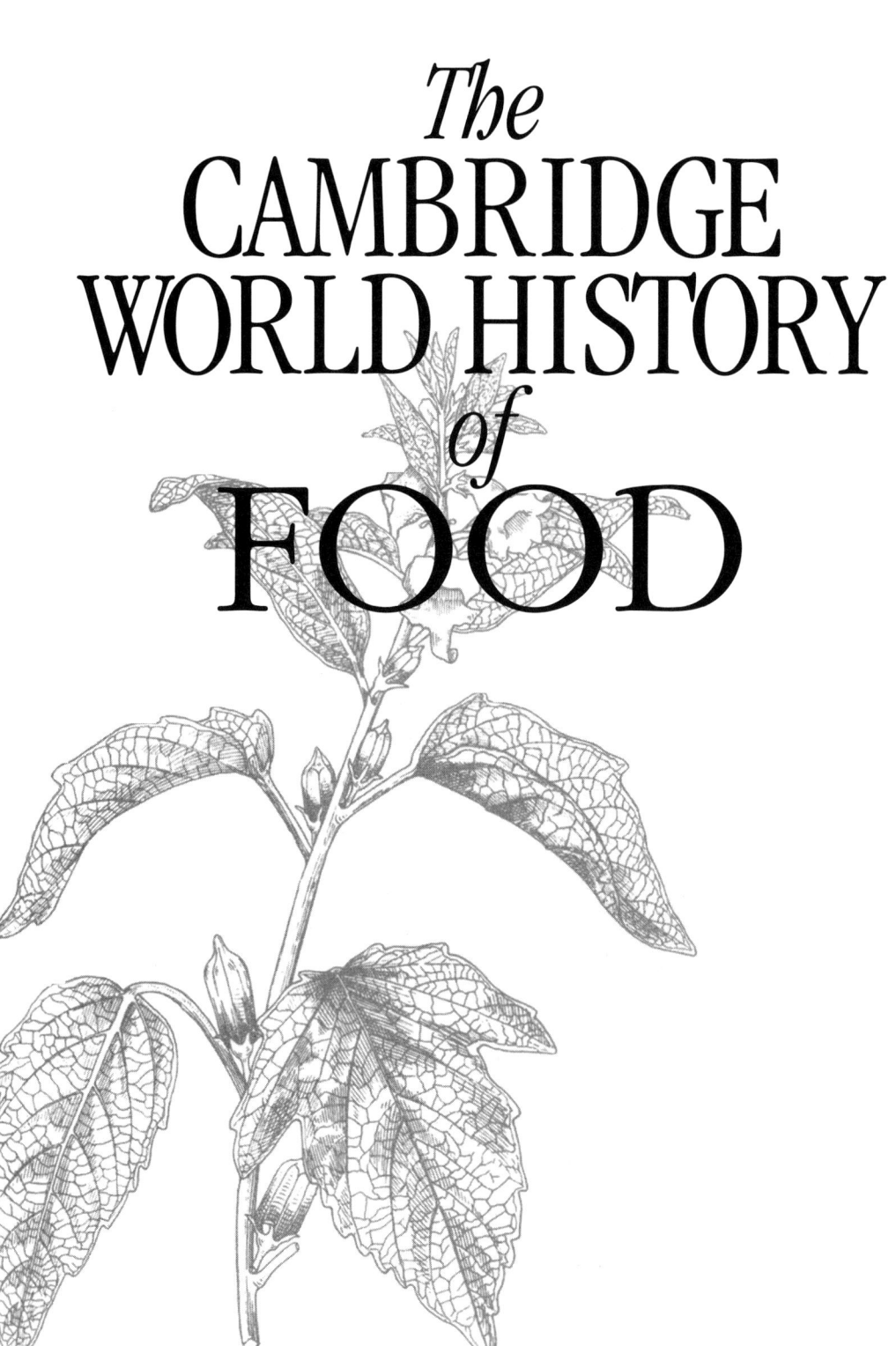

The
CAMBRIDGE
WORLD HISTORY
of
FOOD

The CAMBRIDGE WORLD HISTORY *of* FOOD

EDITORS

Kenneth F. Kiple
Kriemhild Coneè Ornelas

VOLUME ONE

CAMBRIDGE
UNIVERSITY PRESS

PUBLISHED BY THE PRESS SYNDICATE OF THE UNIVERSITY OF CAMBRIDGE
The Pitt Building, Trumpington Street, Cambridge, United Kingdom

CAMBRIDGE UNIVERSITY PRESS
The Edinburgh Building, Cambridge CB2 2RU, UK
40 West 20th Street, New York, NY 10011-4211, USA
10 Stamford Road, Oakleigh, VIC 3166, Australia
Ruiz de Alarcón 13, 28014 Madrid, Spain
Dock House, The Waterfront, Cape Town 8001, South Africa

http://www.cambridge.org

First published 2000
Reprinted 2000, 2001

Printed in the United States of America

Typeface Garamond Book 9.5/10.25 pt.   *System* QuarkXPress®   [GH]

The following illustrations in Part II are from the LuEsther T. Mertz Library, The New
York Botanical Garden, Bronx, New York: Corn, Sorghum.

The following illustrations in Parts II and III are from the General Research Division,
The New York Public Library, Astor, Lenox and Tilden Foundations: Banana plant,
White potato, Prickly sago palm, Taro, Early onion, Lentil, Cabbage, Brussels sprouts,
Cucumber, Watermelon, Field mushroom, Long white squash, Tomato, Chestnut,
Peanut, Sesame, Soybean, Coriander, Peking duck, Geese, Goat, Cacao, Kola.

The following illustrations in Parts II and III are from the Rare Book and Manuscript
Library, Columbia University: Oat, Olive, Sugar, Reindeer, Cattle, Turkey, Coffee.

A catalog record for this book is available from the British Library.

Library of Congress Cataloging in Publication Data

The Cambridge world history of food / editors, Kenneth F. Kiple, Kriemhild Coneè
Ornelas.
        p. cm.
    Includes bibliographical references and index.
    ISBN 0-521-40214-X (v. 1) – ISBN 0-521-40215-8 (v. 2) – ISBN 0-521-40216-6
(slipcase set)
    1. Food–History. I. Kiple, Kenneth F., 1939- II. Ornelas, Kriemhild Coneè.

TX353.C255 2000
641.3'09–dc21   00-057181

ISBN   0 521 40214 X (Volume 1)
ISBN   0 521 40215 8 (Volume 2)
ISBN   0 521 40216 6 (Set)

In Memory of
Norman Kretchmer
Richard P. Palmieri
James J. Parsons
Daphne A. Roe
and
K. David Patterson

CONTENTS

VOLUME ONE

Part II   Staple Foods: Domesticated Plants and Animals

VOLUME TWO

TABLES, FIGURES, AND MAPS

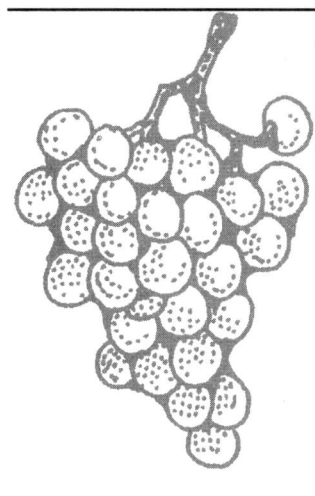

Maps

CONTRIBUTORS

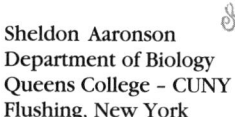

Sheldon Aaronson
Department of Biology
Queens College – CUNY
Flushing, New York

Edmund Abaka
Department of History
University of Miami
Miami, Florida

H. Leon Abrams, Jr.
Consulting Anthropologist
Bloomfield, New Jersey

Kenneth Albala
Department of History
University of the Pacific
Stockton, California

John J. B. Anderson
Department of Nutrition
University of North Carolina
Chapel Hill, North Carolina

Jean Andrews
Department of Botany
University of Texas
Austin, Texas

Allan W. Austin
Department of History
University of Cincinnati
Cincinnati, Ohio

J. Allen Barksdale
American Culture Studies
Bowling Green State University
Bowling Green, Ohio

Eva Barlösius
Institut für Agrarpolitik, Marktforschung und
    Wirtschaftssoziologie der Universität Bonn
Bonn, Germany

Stephen V. Beck
Department of History
Bowling Green State University
Bowling Green, Ohio

Stephen Beckerman
Department of Anthropology
Pennsylvania State University
University Park, Pennsylvania

Dorothea Bedigian
Antioch College
Yellow Springs, Ohio

Thomas G. Benedek
Department of Medicine
University of Pittsburgh School of Medicine
Pittsburgh, Pennsylvania

K. G. Berger
Technical Consultant – Oils and Fats
Chiswick
London, England

Roger Blench
Overseas Development Institute
London, England

Clarke Brooke
Department of Geography
Portland State University
Portland, Oregon

Phillip A. Cantrell, III
Department of History
West Virginia University
Morgantown, West Virginia

Kenneth J. Carpenter
Department of Nutritional Sciences
University of California, Berkeley
Berkeley, California

Te-Tzu Chang
International Rice Research Institute
Tamshui
Taipei, Taiwan

Peter R. Cheeke
Department of Animal Sciences
Oregon State University
Corvallis, Oregon

Mark N. Cohen
Department of Anthropology
State University of New York
Plattsburgh, New York

James Comer
Department of History
Bowling Green State University
Bowling Green, Ohio

Carole M. Counihan
Department of Sociology and Anthropology
Millersville University of Pennsylvania
Millersville, Pennsylvania

Deena S. Decker-Walters
The Cucurbit Network
P.O. Box 560483
Miami, Florida

J. M. J. de Wet
University of Illinois Champaign-Urbana
Urbana, Illinois

Harold H. Draper
Department of Nutritional Sciences
University of Guelph
Guelph, Ontario
Canada

Darna L. Dufour
Department of Anthropology
University of Colorado at Boulder
Boulder, Colorado

Frederick L. Dunn
Department of Epidemiology and Biostatistics
University of California School of Medicine
San Francisco, California

Jacqueline L. Dupont
Department of Nutrition
Florida State University
Tallahassee, Florida

Johanna Dwyer
Frances Stern Nutrition Center
New England Medical Center
Boston, Massachusetts

Colin Emmins
Freelance writer and researcher
West Ealing
London, England

J. Worth Estes
Department of Pharmacology and Experimental
    Therapeutics
Boston University School of Medicine
Boston, Massachusetts

K. T. H. Farrer
Consultant in Food Science and Technology
Chandler's Ford
Hants, England

Antoinette Fauve-Chamoux
Commission Internationale de Démographie Historique
Paris, France

Robert C. Field
Department of History
Bowling Green State University
Bowling Green, Ohio

Daniel W. Gade
Department of Geography
University of Vermont
Burlington, Vermont

J. H. Galloway
Department of Geography
University of Toronto
Toronto, Canada

Sally M. Grantham-McGregor
Institute of Child Health
University College London
London, England

Clarence E. Grim
Division of Cardiology
Medical College of Wisconsin
Milwaukee, Wisconsin

Louis E. Grivetti
Department of Nutrition
University of California, Davis
Davis, California

Barbara Haber
Curator of Books, Schlesinger Library
Radcliffe College
Cambridge, Massachusetts

Lawrence Haddad
Food Consumption and Nutrition Division
International Food Policy Research Institute
Washington, D.C.

Christopher Hamlin
Department of History
University of Notre Dame
South Bend, Indiana

John Derek Lindsell Hansen
Department of Paediatrics and Child Health
University of Witwatersrand
Johannesburg, Republic of South Africa

Alfred E. Harper
Department of Nutrtional Sciences
Department of Biochemistry
University of Wisconsin-Madison
Madison, Wisconsin

Hugh C. Harries
Centro de Investigación Científica de Yucatán AC
Cordemex, Merida
Yucatán, Mexico

Bernard Harris
Department of Sociology and Social Policy
University of Southampton
Southampton, England

Robert P. Heaney
John A. Creighton University Professor
Creighton University
Omaha, Nebraska

Susan L. Hefle
Department of Food Science and Technology
University of Nebraska
Lincoln, Nebraska

Charles B. Heiser, Jr.
Department of Biology
Indiana University
Bloomington, Indiana

Carol F. Helstosky
Department of History
University of Denver
Denver, Colorado

Basil S. Hetzel
International Council for the Control of Iodine Deficiency
    Disorders
Adelaide Medical Centre for Women and Children
North Adelaide, Australia

Robert Hoffpauir
Department of Geography
California State University
Northridge, California

Joel D. Howell
Clinical Scholars Program
University of Michigan
Ann Arbor, Michigan

R. Elwyn Hughes
School of Pure and Applied Biology
University of Wales at Cardiff
Cardiff, Wales

Beatrice Trum Hunter
Food Editor, *Consumer's Research*
Hillsboro, New Hampshire

Naomichi Ishige
National Museum of Ethnology
Osaka, Japan

Richard F. Johnston
Department of Biological Sciences
University of Kansas
Lawrence, Kansas

Glenville Jones
Department of Biochemistry
Queen's University
Kingston, Canada

Lawrence Kaplan
Department of Biology
University of Massachusetts
Boston, Massachusetts

Mary Karasch
Department of History
Oakland University
Rochester, Michigan

Donald D. Kasarda
U.S. Department of Agriculture
Western Regional Research Center
Albany, California

William F. Keegan
Department of Anthropology
Florida Museum of Natural History
University of Florida
Gainesville, Florida

Eileen Kennedy
International Food Policy Research Institute
Washington, D.C.

Susan Kent
Anthropology Program
Old Dominion University
Norfolk, Virginia

John M. Kim
Center for Population Studies
Graduate School of Business
University of Chicago
Chicago, Illinois

Kenneth F. Kiple
Department of History
Bowling Green State University
Bowling Green, Ohio

Gordon L. Klein
Pediatric Gastroenterology Division, Child Health Center
University of Texas Medical Branch
Galveston, Texas

Robert Kroes
Research Institute for Toxicology, Utrecht University
Utrecht, The Netherlands

Hansjörg Küster
Institut für Geobotanik
Universität Hannover
Hannover, Germany

Clark Spencer Larsen
Research Laboratory of Archaeology
Department of Anthropology
University of North Carolina
Chapel Hill, North Carolina

Nancy Davis Lewis
Department of Geography
University of Hawaii
Honolulu, Hawaii

Leslie Sue Lieberman
Department of Anthropology
University of Florida
Gainesville, Florida

Janet Long
Instituto de Investigaciones Históricas
Ciudad de la Investigación en Humanidades
Ciudad Universitaria
Mexico City, Mexico

Rosemary Luff
Department of Archaeology
University of Cambridge
Cambridge, England

Kevin C. MacDonald
Institute of Archaeology
University College London
London, England

Murdo J. MacLeod
Department of History
University of Florida
Gainesville, Florida

Lois N. Magner
Department of History
Purdue University
West Lafayette, Indiana

Susan M. Martin
Harpenden
Hertfordshire, England

David Maynard
Department of Sociology and Anthropology
Baruch College, City University of New York
New York, New York

Donald N. Maynard
Institute of Food and Agricultural Sciences
University of Florida
Bradenton, Florida

G. Mazza
Agriculture and Agri-Food Canada
Pacific Agri-Food Research Centre
Summerland, British Columbia
Canada

Will C. McClatchey
Department of Botany
University of Hawaii at Manoa
Honolulu, Hawaii

Joy McCorriston
Department of Anthropology
Ohio State University
Columbus, Ohio

Ellen Messer
World Hunger Program
Brown University
Providence, Rhode Island

Naomi F. Miller
The University Museum
University of Pennsylvania
Philadelphia, Pennsylvania

Eliza Mojduszka
Department of Resource Economics
University of Massachusetts
Amherst, Massachusetts

T. D. Mountokalakis
University of Athens Medical School
Athens, Greece

William Muraskin
Department of Urban Studies
Queens College, City University of New York
Flushing, New York

J. Paul Murphy
Department of Crop Science
North Carolina State University
Raleigh, North Carolina

Brian Murton
Department of Geography
University of Hawaii
Honolulu, Hawaii

Colin E. Nash
National Marine Fisheries Service (NOAA)
Seattle, Washington

Penelope Nestel
Demographic and Health Surveys
IRD/Macro Systems International, Inc.
Columbia, Maryland

Marion Nestle
Department of Nutrition, Food and Hotel Management
New York University
New York, New York

David S. Newman
Department of Chemistry
Bowling Green State University
Bowling Green, Ohio

James L. Newman
Department of Geography
Syracuse University
Syracuse, New York

Forrest H. Nielsen
Northern Plains Area Grand Forks Human Nutrition
   Center
U.S. Department of Agriculture
Grand Forks, North Dakota

Patricia O'Brien
Department of Sociology, Anthropology, and
   Social Work
Kansas State University
Manhattan, Kansas

Sean F. O'Keefe
Department of Food Sciences and Human Nutrition
University of Florida
Gainesville, Florida

Melissa Hendrix Olken
Department of Internal Medicine
St. Joseph Mercy Hospital
Ann Arbor, Michigan

Stanley J. Olsen
Department of Anthropology
University of Arizona
Tucson, Arizona

Donald J. Ortner
Department of Anthropology
National Museum of Natural History
Smithsonian Institution
Washington, D.C.

Anneke H. van Otterloo
Faculty of Political and Socio-Cultural Sciences
University of Amsterdam
Amsterdam, The Netherlands

Richard P. Palmieri†
Department of Geography
Mary Washington College
Fredericksburg, Virginia

Sujatha Panikker
Department of Medical Microbiology
University of Manchester Medical School
Manchester, England

Michael W. Pariza
Food Research Institute
Department of Food Microbiology and Toxicology
University of Wisconsin-Madison
Madison, Wisconsin

James J. Parsons†
Department of Geography
University of California, Berkeley
Berkeley, California

K. David Patterson†
Department of History
University of North Carolina
Charlotte, North Carolina

Peter L. Pellett
Department of Nutrition
School of Public Health and Health Sciences
University of Massachusetts
Amherst, Massachusetts

Judy Perkin
Department of Health Sciences
Santa Fe Community College
Gainesville, Florida

David M. Peterson
U.S. Department of Agriculture
Agricultural Research Service – Midwest Area
Cereal Crops Research Unit
Madison, Wisconsin

Julia Peterson
School of Nutritional Science and Policy
Tufts University
Medford, Massachusetts

Jeffrey M. Pilcher
Department of History
The Citadel
Charleston, South Carolina

Nancy J. Pollock
Department of Anthropology
Victoria University of Wellington
Wellington, New Zealand

Ananda S. Prasad
Harper-Grace Hospital
Wayne State University School of Medicine
Detroit, Michigan

Heather Munro Prescott
Department of History
Central Connecticut State University
New Britain, Connecticut

Sara A. Quandt
Department of Public Health Sciences
Bowman Gray School of Medicine
Wake Forest University
Winston-Salem, North Carolina

Ted A. Rathbun
Department of Anthropology
University of South Carolina
Columbia, South Carolina

Linda J. Reed
Archaeologist
Burns Paiute Tribe
Burns, Oregon

Elizabeth J. Reitz
Museum of Natural History
University of Georgia
Athens, Georgia

Daphne A. Roe†
Division of Nutritional Sciences
Cornell University
Ithaca, New York

Delphine Roger
Department of History
Université de Paris
Saint-Denis, France

Paul Rozin
Department of Psychology
University of Pennsylvania
Philadelphia, Pennsylvania

Françoise Sabban
École des Hautes Études en Sciences Sociales
Paris, France

Joy B. Sander
Department of Anthropology
University of Colorado
Boulder, Colorado

Ritu Sandhu
Frances Stern Nutrition Center
New England Medical Center
Boston, Massachusetts

Nevin S. Scrimshaw
Food and Nutrition Programme for Human and Social
    Development
United Nations University
Boston, Massachusetts

Stephen Seely
Department of Cardiology
The Royal Infirmary
University of Manchester
Manchester, England

Donald T. Simeon
Commonwealth Caribbean Medical Research Council
Port-of-Spain, Trinidad

Wayne R. Snodgrass
Department of Pediatrics
University of Texas Medical Branch
Galveston, Texas

Kristin D. Sobolik
Department of Anthropology
University of Maine
Orono, Maine

Thomas Sorosiak
American Culture Studies
Bowling Green State University
Bowling Green, Ohio

Colin Spencer
Freelance writer and researcher
Suffolk, England

Herta Spencer
Metabolic Research
Veterans Administration Hospital
Hines, Illinois

William J. Stadelman
Department of Food Science
Purdue University
West Lafayette, Indiana

Elizabeth A. Stephens
Department of Anthropology
University of Arizona
Tucson, Arizona

Patricia Stuart-Macadam
Department of Anthropology
University of Toronto
Toronto, Canada

John C. Super
Department of History
West Virginia University
Morgantown, West Virginia

H. Micheal Tarver
Department of History
McNeese State University
Lake Charles, Louisiana

Gretchen Theobald
Department of Anthropology
National Museum of Natural History
Smithsonian Institution
Washington, D.C.

Myrtle Thierry-Palmer
Department of Biochemistry
Morehouse School of Medicine
Atlanta, Georgia

Joyce Toomrey
Davis Center for Russian Studies
Harvard University
Cambridge, Massachusetts

Steven C. Topik
Department of History
University of California, Irvine
Irvine, California

Luis A. Vargas
Instituto de Investigaciones Antropológicas
Universidad Nacional Autonoma de México
Mexico City, Mexico

Keith Vernon
Department of Historical and Critical Studies
University of Central Lancashire
Preston, England

Terrence W. Walters
The Cucurbit Network
P.O. Box 560483
Miami, Florida

Margaret J. Weinberger
American Culture Studies
Bowling Green State University
Bowling Green, Ohio

John H. Weisburger
American Health Foundation
Valhalla, New York

Wilma Wetterstrom
Harvard Botanical Museum
Cambridge, Massachusetts

Barbara Wheaton
Honorary Curator of the Culinary Collection, Schlesinger
    Library
Radcliffe College
Cambridge, Massachusetts

William H. Whitaker
School of Social Work
Marywood University
Scranton, Pennsylvania

James C. Whorton
Department of Medical History and Ethics
School of Medicine
University of Washington
Seattle, Washington

Christine S. Wilson, Editor
Ecology of Food and Nutrition
Annapolis, Maryland

Thomas Wilson
Department of Epidemiology
Anthem Blue Cross/Blue Shield
Cincinnati, Ohio

Elizabeth S. Wing
The Florida State Museum
University of Florida
Gainesville, Florida

George Wolf
Department of Nutritional Sciences
University of California, Berkeley
Berkeley, California

Yiming Xia
Institute of Food and Nutrition
Chinese Academy of Preventive Medicine
Beijing, China

David R. Yesner
Department of Anthropology
University of Alaska
Anchorage, Alaska

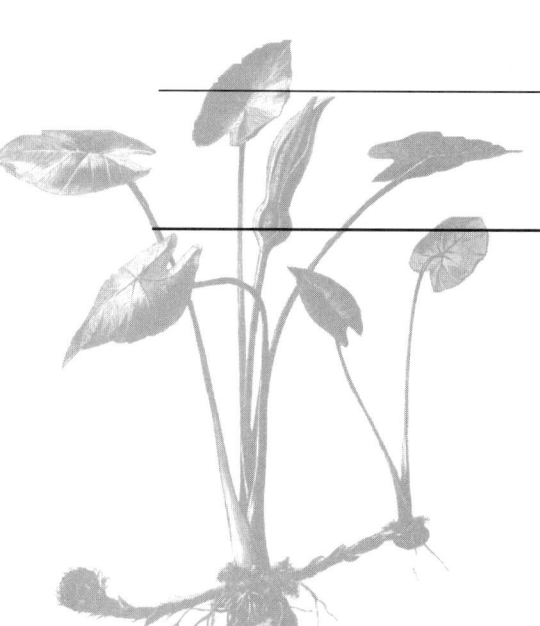

PREFACE

This work together with its predecessor, *The Cambridge World History of Human Disease,* represents an effort to encapsulate much of what is known about human health as a new millennium begins. As such the volumes should prove important to researchers of the future just as today many investigators find important August Hirsch's three-volume *Handbook of Geographical and Historical Pathology* that was translated and published in London during the years 1883 to 1886. We hope, however, that in light of the accelerating academic and public interest in the things we eat and drink and what they do for us (or to us) the present work will also find an appreciative audience here and now. It is, to our knowledge, the first effort to draw together on a global scale the work of scholars on both nutritional and food-related subjects and to endow the whole with a strong interdisciplinary foundation that utilizes a great number of approaches to food questions ranging from the anthropological to the zoological.

Many of these questions are policy-related and look at real and pressing problems such as poor nutrition among the young of the developing world, food additives and biotechnology in the developed world, and food entitlements in both worlds. Many others, however, are dedicated to determining what our ancestors ate in Paleolithic times; the changes – both dietary and physiological – brought on by the various Neolithic Revolutions and the domesticated plants and animals they nurtured; and what products of those Revolutions have been consumed in the various corners of the globe ever since.

Another broad set of questions employs nutritional science to evaluate the quality of diets, both past and present, and to indicate the diseases, defects, and disorders that can and have developed when that quality is low. A final focus is on the numerous psychological, cultural, and genetic reasons individual humans as well as societies embrace some foods and beverages yet reject others that counterparts find eminently satisfactory.

More implicit than explicit are two threads that loosely stitch together the essays that follow. One is the thread of food globalization, although by globalization we do not mean the current concern about world "burgerization" or even the process of menu homogenization – the latter which began in the aftermath of World War II and has been accelerating ever since. Rather, we mean the inexorable process of food globalization that started some eight to ten thousand or more years ago with the domestication of plants and animals. Although this first occurred in places such as Mesopotamia, the Indus Valley, Egypt, and China in the Old World and Peru and MesoAmerica in the New World, and the fruits of domestication were at first shared mostly by propinquous peoples, those fruits sooner or later spread out over the entire globe. They were carried by restless folk – initially by explorers, pioneers, and the like and then by merchants, missionaries, marauders, and mariners who followed on their heels.

The second thread has to do with the taxes that technological advances generally levy on human nutrition. Many believe that this process began in the distant past as hunter-gatherers devised tools which enabled them to become so efficient in hunting large animals that their growth in numbers and a decline in the amount of prey seriously jeopardized their food supply. This forced another technological advance – the greatest of all – which was the invention of agriculture. But with sedentism came even more population growth, circumscribed diets, and pathogenic prosperity. Such problems continue to curse many in the developing world today where the response to any technologically driven increase in the food supply has generally been an increase in the number who share that food. Meanwhile, in the developed world the response to ever more abundance – much of it in the form of new calorie-dense foods – has been a different kind of population growth as its citizens individually grow ever larger in an outward direction.

ACKNOWLEDGMENTS

This work is the offspring of the Cambridge History and Culture of Food and Nutrition project which, in turn, was the progeny of the Cambridge History of Human Disease project. As the latter effort neared completion in 1990, the former was launched. We are enormously grateful to the National Library of Medicine for providing one grant (1 RO1 LMO5320-01) to begin the effort and another (1RO1 LMOC574-01) to see it completed. In between, funding was provided by a Bowling Green State University History Department challenge grant from the State of Ohio, by grants from Cambridge University Press, and by various university budgets. In addition, Department of History chairpersons Gary Hess, Fujiya Kawashima, and Donald Nieman each ensured that the project was always staffed by graduate students who checked sources, entered manuscripts into the computer, and performed countless other duties. That some four generations of students worked on the project can be seen in the list of assistant editors whose names appear opposite the title page. We are indebted to all of them. In addition, we wish to thank the History Department secretaries Connie Willis and Judy Gilbert for the countless hours of their labor given cheerfully and generously.

Frank Smith, our editor at Cambridge University Press, was instrumental in launching this project. He collaborated in its conceptualization, worked with us in assembling the Board Members, encouraged us at every stage of the effort for a full decade, procured last-minute permissions, and took over the task of securing the decorative art. He has been a true partner in the project.

Rachael Graham, who served as executive editor of the disease project, retired with husband Jim shortly after the food and nutrition project began. She was succeeded by Mike Tarver (also a veteran of the earlier effort) – a computer whiz who propelled all of us in the direction of computer literacy while overseeing the daily office procedures of entering manuscripts into the computer and checking sources. But then he, too, left us (for "a real job" as we heard one of our assistant editors mutter under his breath), and Stephen Beck took over.

Steve was born for the job, and many of our authors, including myself, are in his debt for sentences that are now clearer and sharper (and in some instances far more coherent) than they were before. His grasp of the English language is also matched by a fine eye for details and a much appreciated ability to keep track of those details over months and even years. This is particularly apparent in Part VIII where he maintained an ever-growing list of the names of plant foods, both common and scientific, which prevented much repetition, not to mention duplication. In addition he and Coneè supervised the activities of the assistant editors on the project and finally, on numerous occasions (such as the pellagra essay, and some of the Part VIII entries), Steve also took on the tasks of researcher and author.

None of this is to imply that others had no hand in the editorial and production process. Kathi Unger and Steve Shimer compiled the very large indexes on the other end of this work both swiftly and competently. Kathie Kounouklos produced the handsome page layouts, and Mary Jo Rhodes steadfastly checked the manuscript and proof from beginning to end. Claire McKean and Phyllis Berk under the direction of Françoise Bartlett at G&H SOHO did a wonderful job of imposing order on a manuscript whose very size doubtlessly made it intimidating. In so doing they untangled and straightened out much that we thought we had untangled and straightened out. We are very grateful to them and to Cathy Felgar of Cambridge University Press who was ultimately in charge of the work's production.

However, despite the editorial exertions here and in New York, in the final analysis these volumes belong to its authors – in this case around 160 of them – of which fully a quarter represent some 15 countries in addition to the United States. We thank each one for what has become a magnificent collective achievement and apologize for the "extra" years that it took to get the work into print. As we have explained (or confessed) to the many who have inquired, the project just became so large that every one of its stages required considerably more time than estimates based on the earlier disease project allowed for.

The nearly 40 members of our Board of Editors have been a vital part of the project. Most of the suggestions for authors came from them, and every essay was read by them for scientific and historical accuracy. Especially active in this latter capacity were Thomas G. Benedek, Kenneth J. Carpenter, Alfred W. Crosby, Frederick L. Dunn, Daniel W. Gade, Jerome S. Handler, Clark Spencer Larsen, Leslie Sue Lieberman, Ellen Messer, Marion Nestle, James L. Newman, K. David Patterson, and Jeffrey M. Pilcher. In addition, Frederick J. Simoons not only read a number of essays with his characteristically painstaking care but made numerous and invariably sterling suggestions for authors that lightened our load considerably.

It should be noted, however, that we did not always take the suggestions of Board Members. In some cases this was because reports disagreed. In others it was because authors made good cases against proposed revisions. And at times it was because, rightly or wrongly, we decided that suggested revisions were not necessary. But this means only we and the authors bear final responsibility for the essays embraced by these volumes. In no way does it detract from the great wisdom (not to mention the great amount of time) so graciously donated by the members of our Board of Editors.

One of these individuals, K. David Patterson, died suddenly and prematurely during the latter stages of the project. Dave was a good friend as well as colleague who served both of our Cambridge projects as an energetic board member and enthusiastic author. He did everything from collaborating in their conceptualization to accepting huge writing assignments for each to the researching and writing of essays whose authors failed to deliver them. Yet, despite taking on so much, everything that he did reflected scholarship of the highest possible quality. Dave truly was a scholar in the best sense of the word, and we greatly miss him.

This work is dedicated to Dave and to four other individuals who died during this project. We did not personally know Norman Kretchmer, one of the board members, or authors Richard P. Palmieri, James J. Parsons, and Daphne A. Roe, but we knew them by their work and reputations. We know that they will be sorely missed in, among other fields, those of the Nutritional Sciences and Geography.

KENNETH F. KIPLE
KRIEMHILD CONEÈ ORNELAS

ABOUT THESE VOLUMES
AND HOW TO USE THEM

The history of the world's major staple foods – both animal and vegetable – along with supplementary foods that loom large in such diets – are dealt with at length in Part II. Shorter entries of these same staple plant foods also appear in Part VIII along with some 1,000 of the world's other fruits and vegetables.

These volumes were never intended to comprise an encyclopedia but rather to be a collection of original essays. Therefore, the chapters are far from uniform, and at times there is overlap between them, which was encouraged so that each essay could stand alone without cross-referencing. Bibliographies range from gargantuan to gaunt; most (but not all) authors employ in-text citations, and a few use end notes as well. Such disproportion was not considered a problem. Our authors represent many disciplines, each with his or her own manner of delivering scholarship, and, consequently, they were given considerably latitude in their style of presentation.

The table of contents, of course, is one way of navigating this work, and to help in its use the entries have been arranged in alphabetical order wherever it made sense to do so. But although the table of contents will direct readers to a major entry such as "Wheat," it is in the index where every mention of wheat in both volumes is indicated and the grain's geographic spread and historical uses can be discerned.

The capability for tracing foods longitudinally came with the preparation of a special subject index that was also geographically focused; hence, a food like manioc can be found both by subject and under the various areas of the world where it is, or has been, important, such as Brazil, the Caribbean, and West Africa. In addition, there is an index of all names mentioned in the text.

The entries in Part VIII are also represented in the subject index. This is the only part of the work that is cross-referenced, and it contains numerous synonyms that should prove useful to researchers and intriguing to linguists, including those no longer in use such as "colewort" (cabbage) or "pompion" (pumpkin). The synonyms appear twice: once in alphabetical order to direct readers to (in the case of the examples just used) "Cabbage" or "Pumpkin" and then again in a synonyms list at the end of these entries. Moreover, the Part VIII articles send the reader to related entries in that section and also to chapters in Parts II and III (in the case of cabbage or pumpkin to "Cruciferous and Green Leafy Vegetables" and "Squash," respectively).

We should note for the record that any discussion in these volumes of a foodstuff (or a nonfood for that matter) which might be consumed should not be taken as a recommendation that it be consumed, or that it is safe to consume. The new (and sometimes unfamiliar) foods that our authors state are edible doubtlessly are. But as many of the chapters that follow indicate, foods, especially plant foods, are generally toxic to some degree to help protect against predators.

A good example is bitter manioc whose tubers contain prussic acid – a poison that must be removed before consumption. But toxicity can vary with plant parts. Thus, the celery-like stalks of rhubarb are edible after cooking, but the rhizomes and leaves of the plant are so loaded with oxalic acid as to be deadly. Even the common white potatoes that many of us eat may contain solanine in their skins that can make a person sick.

Some plant foods – kava, khat, and coca, for example – are frequently illegal to possess; and still other potential foods, such as the numerous fungi and myriad other wild plants, require specialized knowledge to sort out the edible from the fatal.

Finally, the chapters on vitamins and minerals discuss the importance of these nutrients to human health both historically and today. In Part VIII "ball-park" nutrient values are provided for many of the foods listed there. But our authors on the nutrients warn against too much of a good thing, just as our ancient ancestors would have done. Caution and moderation in matters of food were vital to their survival and, by extension, to our presence.

Introduction

We began work on the Cambridge History and Culture of Food and Nutrition Project even as we were still reading the page proofs for *The Cambridge World History of Human Disease,* published in 1993. At some point in that effort we had begun to conceive of continuing our history of human health by moving into food and nutrition – an area that did more than simply focus on the breakdown of that health. For the history of disease we had something of a model provided by August Hirsch in his three-volume *Handbook of Geographical and Historical Pathology* (London, 1883–6). Yet there was no "Handbook of Geographical and Historical Food and Nutrition" to light the way for the present volumes, and thus they would be unique.

Fortunately, there was no lack of expertise available; it came from some 200 authors and board members, representing a score of disciplines ranging from agronomy to zoology. This undertaking, then, like its predecessor, represents a collective interdisciplinary and international effort, aimed in this case at encapsulating what is known of the history of food and nutrition throughout humankind's stay on the planet. We hope that, together, these volumes on nutrition and the earlier one on disease will provide scholars of the future – as well as those of the present – a glimpse of what is known (and not known) about human health as the twentieth century comes to a close.

Two of our major themes are embedded in the title. *Food,* of course, is central to history; without it, there would be no life and thus no history, and we devote considerable space to providing a history of the most important foodstuffs across the globe. To some extent, these treatments are quantitative, whereas by contrast, *Nutrition* – the body's need for foods and the uses it makes of them – has had much to do with shaping the quality of human life. Accordingly, we have placed a considerable array of nutritional topics in longitudinal contexts to illustrate their importance to our past and present and to suggest something of our nutritional future.

The word "Culture," although not in the book title, was a part of the working title of the project, and certainly the concept of culture permeates the entire work, from the prehistoric culture of our hunting-and-gathering ancestors, through the many different food cultures of the historical era, to modern "food policies," the prescription and implementation of which are frequently generated by cultural norms. Finally, there is "health," which appears in none of our titles but is – either explicitly or implicitly – the subject of every chapter that follows and the raison d'être for the entire work.

An Overview

Functionally, it seems appropriate to begin this overview of the work with an explanation of the last part first, because we hope that the entries in Part VIII, which identify and sketch out brief histories of vegetable foods mentioned in the text, will constitute an important tool for readers, especially for those interested in the chapters on geographic regions. Moreover, because fruits have seldom been more than seasonal items in the diet, all of these save for a few rare staples are treated in Part VIII. Most readers will need little explanation of foods such as potatoes (also treated in a full chapter) or asparagus but may want to learn more about lesser-known or strictly regional foods such as ackee or zamia (mentioned in the chapters that deal with the Caribbean area). On the one hand, Part VIII has spared our authors the annoyance of writing textual digressions or footnotes to explain such unfamiliar foods, and on the other, it has provided us with a splendid opportunity to provide more extensive information on the origins and uses of the foods listed. In addition, Part VIII has become the place in the work where synonyms are dealt with, and readers can discover (if they do not already know) that an aubergine is an eggplant, that "swedes" are rutabagas, and that "Bulgar" comes from *bulghur*, which means "bruised grain."

We now move from the end to the beginning of the work, where the chapters of Part I collectively constitute a bioanthropological investigation into the kinds and quantities of foods consumed by early humans, as well as by present-day hunter-gatherers. Humans (in one form or another) have been around for millions of years, but they only invented agriculture and domesticated animals in the past 10,000 years or so, which represents just a tiny fraction of 1 percent of the time humankind has been present on earth. Thus, modern humans must to some extent be a product of what our ancient ancestors ate during their evolutionary journey from scavengers to skilled hunters and from food gatherers to food growers.

The methods for discovering the diet (the foods consumed) and the nutritional status (how the body employed those foods) of our hunting-and-gathering forebears are varied. Archaeological sites have yielded the remains of plants and animals, as well as human coprolites (dried feces), that shed light on the issue of diet, whereas analysis of human remains - bones, teeth, and (on occasion) soft tissue - has helped to illuminate questions of nutrition. In addition, the study of both diet and nutrition among present-day hunter-gatherers has aided in the interpretation of data generated by such archaeological discoveries. The sum of the findings to date seems to suggest that at least in matters of diet and nutrition, our Paleolithic ancestors did quite well for themselves and considerably better than the sedentary folk who followed. In fact, some experts contend that the hunter-gatherers did better than any of their descendants until the late nineteenth and early twentieth centuries.

Part II shifts the focus from foraging to farming and the domestication of plants and animals. The transition from a diet of hunted and collected foods to one based on food production was gradual, yet because its beginnings coincided with the time that many large game animals were disappearing, there is suspicion that necessity, born of an increasing food scarcity, may have been the mother of agricultural invention. But however the development of sedentary agriculture came about, much of the blame for the nutritional deterioration that appears to have accompanied it falls on the production of the so-called superfoods - rice, maize, manioc, and wheat - staples that have sustained great numbers of people but only at a considerable cost in human health, in no small

part because diets that centered too closely on such foods could not provide the range of vitamins, minerals, and whole protein so vital to human health.

Part II is divided into sections, or groups of chapters, most of which consider the history of our most important plant foods under a number of rubrics ranging from "Grains," "Roots, Tubers, and Other Starchy Staples," through "Important Vegetable Supplements," to plants that are used to produce oils and those employed for flavorings. All of the chapters dealing with plants treat questions of where, how, and by whom they were first domesticated, along with their subsequent diffusion around the globe and their present geographic distribution. With domestication, of course, came the dependence of plants on humans along with the reverse, and this phenomenon of "mutualism" is explored in some detail, as are present-day breeding problems and techniques.

The historical importance of the migration of plant foods, although yet to be fully weighed for demographic impact, was vital - although frequently disruptive - for humankind. Wheat, a wild grass that flourished in the wake of retreating glaciers some 12,000 years ago, was (apparently) deliberately planted for the first time in the Middle East about 2,000 years later. By the first century B.C., Rome required some 14 million bushels per year just to feed the people of that city, leading to a program of expansion that turned much of the cultivable land of North Africa into wheatfields for the Romans. Surely, then, Italians had their pastas long before Marco Polo (1254?-1324?), who has been credited with bringing notions of noodles back with him from China. But it was only the arrival of the vitamin C-loaded American tomato that allowed the Italians to concoct the great culinary union of pasta and tomato sauce - one that rendered pasta not only more satisfactory but also more healthy. And, speaking of China, the New World's tomato and its maize, potatoes, sweet potatoes, and peanuts were also finding their respective ways to that ancient land, where in the aftermath of their introduction, truly phenomenal population increases took place.

Migrating American plants, in other words, did much more than just dress up Old World dishes, as tomatoes did pasta. Maize, manioc, sweet potatoes, a new kind of yam, peanuts, and chilli peppers reached the western shores of Africa with the ships of slave traders, who introduced them into that continent to provide food for their human cargoes. Their success exceeded the wildest of expectations, because the new foods not only fed slaves bound for the Americas but helped create future generations of slaves. The American crops triggered an agricultural revolution in Africa, which in greatly expanding both the quantity and quality of its food supply, also produced swelling populations that were drained off to the Americas in order to grow (among other things) sugar and coffee - both migrating plants from the Old World.

In Europe, white potatoes and maize caught on more slowly, but the effect was remarkably similar. Old

World wheat gave back only 5 grains for every 1 planted, whereas maize returned 25 to 100 (a single ear of modern maize yields about 1,000 grains) and, by the middle of the seventeenth century, had become a staple of the peasants of northern Spain, Italy, and to a lesser extent, southern France. From there maize moved into much of the rest of Europe, and by the end of the eighteenth century, such cornmeal mushes (*polenta* in Italy) had spread via the Ottoman Empire into the Balkans and southern Russia.

Meanwhile, over the centuries, the growth of cities and the development of long-distance trade – especially the spice trade – had accelerated the process of exploring the world and globalizing its foods. So, too, had the quest for oils (to be used in cooking, food preservation, and medicines), which had been advanced as coconuts washed up on tropical shores, olive trees spread across the Mediterranean from the Levant to the rim of the Atlantic in Iberia, and sesame became an integral part of the burgeoning civilizations of North Africa and much of Asia.

In the seventeenth century, invasion, famine, and evictions forced Irish peasants to adopt the potato as a means of getting the most nourishment from the least amount of cultivated land, and during the eighteenth century, it was introduced in Germany and France because of the frequent failures of other crops. From there, the plant spread toward the Ural Mountains, where rye had long been the only staple that would ripen during the short, often rainy summers. Potatoes not only did well under such conditions, they provided some four times as many calories per acre as rye and, by the first decades of the nineteenth century, were a crucial dietary element in the survival of large numbers of northern Europeans, just as maize had become indispensable to humans in some of the more southerly regions.

Maize nourished humans indirectly as well. Indeed, with maize available to help feed livestock, it became increasingly possible to carry more animals through the winters and to derive a steady supply of whole protein in the forms of milk, cheese, and eggs, in addition to year-round meat – now available for the many rather than the few. Thus, it has been argued that it is scarcely coincidence that beginning in the eighteenth century, European populations began to grow and, by the nineteenth century, had swollen to the point where, like the unwilling African slaves before them, Europeans began migrating by the millions to the lands whose plants had created the surplus that they themselves represented.

The last section of Part II treats foods from animal sources ranging from game, bison, and fish to the domesticated animals. Its relatively fewer chapters make clear the dependence of all animals, including humans, on the plant world. In fact, to some unmeasurable extent, the plant foods of the world made still another important contribution to the human diet by assisting in the domestication of those animals that – like the dog that preceded them – let themselves be tamed.

The dog seems to have been the first domesticated animal and the only one during the Paleolithic age. The wolf, its progenitor, was a meat eater and a hunter (like humans), and somewhere along the way, humans and dogs seem to have joined forces, even though dogs were sometimes dinner and probably vice versa. But it was during the early days of the Neolithic, as the glaciers receded and the climate softened, that herbivorous animals began to multiply, and in the case of sheep and goats, their growing numbers found easy meals in the grains that humans were raising (or at least had staked out for their own use). Doubtless, it did not take the new farmers long to cease trying to chase the animals away and to begin capturing them instead – at first to use as a source of meat to go with the grain and then, perhaps a bit later, to experiment with the fleece of sheep and the waterproof hair of goats.

There was, however, another motive for capturing animals, which was for use in religious ceremonies involving animal sacrifice. Indeed, it has been argued that wild water buffalo, cattle, camels, and even goats and sheep were initially captured for sacrifice rather than for food.

Either way, a move from capturing animals to domestication and animal husbandry was the next step in the case of those animals that could be domesticated. In southeastern Europe and the Near East (the sites of so much of this early activity), wild goats and sheep may have been the first to experience a radical change of lifestyle – their talent for clearing land of anything edible having been discovered and put to good use by their new masters. Soon, sheep were being herded, with the herdsmen and their flocks spreading out far and wide to introduce still more humans to the mysteries and rewards of domestication.

Wild swine, by contrast, were not ruminant animals and thus were not so readily attracted to the plants in the fields, meaning that as they did not come to humans, humans had to go to them. Wild boars had long been hunted for sacrifice as well as for meat and would certainly have impressed their hunters with their formidable and ferocious nature. Tricky, indeed, must have been the process that brought the domesticated pig to the barnyard by about 7000 to 6000 B.C.

Wild cattle were doubtless drawn to farmers' fields, but in light of what we know about the now-extinct aurochs (the wild ancestor of our modern cattle), the domestication of bovines around 6000 B.C. may have required even more heroic efforts than that of swine. Yet those efforts were certainly worth it, for in addition to the meat and milk and hides cattle provided, the ox was put to work along with sheep and goats as still another hand in the agricultural process – stomping seeds into the soil, threshing grain, and pulling carts, wagons, and (later on) the plow.

The last of today's most important animals to be domesticated was the chicken, first used for sacrifice and then for fighting before it and its eggs became food. The domesticated variety of this jungle bird was present in North China around 3000 B.C.; however, because the modern chicken is descended from both Southeast Asian and Indian wildfowl, the question of the original site of domestication has yet to be resolved. The wildfowl were attracted to human-grown grain and captured, as was the pigeon (which, until recently, played a far more important role in the human diet than the chicken). Ducks, geese, and other fowl were also most likely captivated by – and captured because of – the burgeoning plant-food products of the Neolithic. In other parts of the world, aquatic animals, along with the camel, the yak, and the llama and alpaca, were pressed into service by *Homo sapiens,* the "wise man" who had not only scrambled to the top of the food chain but was determinedly extending it.

The chapters of Part III focus on the most important beverages humans have consumed as accompaniment to those foods that have preoccupied us to this point. One of these, water, is crucial to life itself; another, human breast milk, has – until recently, at least – been vital for the survival of newborns, and thus vital for the continuation of the species. Yet both have also been sources of infection for humans, sometimes fatally so.

Hunter-gatherers, in general, did not stay in one place long enough to foul springs, ponds, rivers, and lakes. But sedentary agriculturalists did, and their own excreta was joined by that of their animals. Wherever settlements arose (in some cases as kernels of cities to come), the danger of waterborne disease multiplied, and water – essential to life – also became life-threatening. One solution that was sensible as well as pleasurable lay in the invention of beverages whose water content was sterilized by the process of fermentation. Indeed, the earliest written records of humankind mention ales made from barley, millet, rice, and other grains, along with toddies concocted from date palms and figs – all of which makes it apparent that the production of alcohol was a serious business from the very beginning of the Old World Neolithic.

It was around 3000 B.C. that grape wine made its appearance, and where there was honey there was also mead. The discovery of spirit distillation to make whiskeys and brandies began some seven to eight hundred years ago, and true beer, the "hopped" successor of ales, was being brewed toward the end of the Middle Ages (about 600 years ago). Clearly, humans long ago were investing much ingenuity in what can only be described as a magnificent effort to avoid waterborne illness.

Milk, one of the bonuses of animal domestication, was also fermented, although not always with desired outcomes. Yet over time, the production of yoghurts, cheeses, and butter became routine, and these foods – with their reduced lactose – were acceptable even among the lactose-intolerant, who constituted most of the world's population. Where available, milk (especially bovine milk) was a food for the young after weaning, and during the past few centuries, it has also served as a substitute for human milk for infants, although sometimes with disastrous results. One problem was (and is) that the concentrated nutrient content of bovine milk, as well as human antibodies developed against cow's-milk protein, make it less than the perfect food, especially for infants. But another was that bovine tuberculosis (scrofula), along with ordinary tuberculosis, raged throughout Europe from the sixteenth to the nineteenth centuries. Wet nurses were another solution for infant feeding, but this practice could be fraught with danger, and artificial feeding, especially in an age with no notions of sterile procedure, caused infants to die in staggering numbers before the days of Joseph Lister and Louis Pasteur.

Boiling water was another method of avoiding the pathogens it contained, and one that, like fermentation, could also produce pleasant beverages in the process. The Chinese, who had used tea since the Han period, embraced that beverage enthusiastically during the Tang dynasty (618–907) and have been avid tea drinkers ever since. The nomads of central Asia also adopted the drink and later introduced it into Russia. Tea use spread to Japan about the sixth century, but it became popular there only about 700 years ago. From Japan, the concoction was introduced into Indonesia, where much later (around 1610) the Dutch discovered it and carried it to Europe. A few decades later, the English were playing a major role in popularizing the beverage, not to mention merchandising it.

Coffee, although it found its way into Europe at about the same time as tea, has a more recent history, which, coffee-lore would have it, began in Ethiopia in the ninth century. By 1500, coffee drinking was widespread throughout the Arab world (where alcohol was forbidden), and with the passing of another couple of centuries, the beverage was enjoying a considerable popularity in Europe. Legend has it that Europeans began to embrace coffee after the Ottoman Turks left some bags of coffee beans behind as they gave up the siege of Vienna in 1683.

These Asian and African contributions to the world's beverages were joined by cacao from America. Because the Spaniards and the Portuguese were the proprietors of the lands where cacao was grown, they became the first Europeans to enjoy drinking chocolate (which had long been popular among pre-Columbian Mesoamericans). In the early decades of the sixteenth century, the beverage spread through Spain's empire to Italy and the Netherlands and, around midcentury, reached England and France.

Thus, after millennia of consuming alcoholic beverages to dodge fouled water, people now had (after a century or so of "catching on") an opportunity for relative sobriety thanks to these three new drinks, which all arrived in Europe at about the same time. But an important ingredient in their acceptance was the sugar that sweetened them. And no wonder that as these beverages gained in popularity, the slave trade quickened, plantation societies in the Americas flourished, and France in 1763 ceded all of Canada to Britain in order to regain its sugar-rich islands of Martinique and Guadeloupe.

Sugar cultivation and processing, however, added still another alcoholic beverage – rum – to a growing list, and later in the nineteenth century, sugar became the foundation of a burgeoning soft-drink industry. Caffeine was a frequent ingredient in these concoctions, presumably because, in part at least, people had become accustomed to the stimulation that coffee and tea provided. The first manufacturers of Coca-Cola in the United States went even further in the pursuit of stimulation by adding coca – from the cocaine-containing leaves that are chewed in the Andean region of South America. The coca was soon removed from the soft drink and now remains only in the name Coca-Cola, but "cola" continued as an ingredient. In the same way that coca is chewed in South America, in West Africa the wrapping around the kola nut is chewed for its stimulative effect, in this case caused by caffeine. But the extract of the kola nut not only bristles with caffeine, it also packs a heart stimulant, and the combination has proven to be an invigorating ingredient in the carbonated beverage industry.

In East Africa, the leaves of an evergreen shrub called khat are chewed for their stimulating effect and are made into a tealike beverage as well. And finally, there is kava, widely used in the Pacific region and among the most controversial, as well as the most exotic, of the world's lesser-known drinks – controversial because of alleged narcotic properties and exotic because of its ceremonial use and cultural importance.

In addition to the beverages that humans have invented and imbibed throughout the ages as alternatives to water, many have also clung to their "waters." Early on, special waters may have come from a spring or some other body of water, perhaps with supposed magical powers, or a good flavor, or simply known to be safe. In more recent centuries, the affluent have journeyed to mineral springs to "take the waters" both inside and outside of their bodies, and mineral water was (and is) also bottled and sold for its allegedly healthy properties. Today, despite (or perhaps because of) the water available to most households in the developed world, people have once more staked out their favorite waters, and for some, bottled waters have replaced those alcoholic beverages that were previously employed to avoid water.

Part IV focuses on the history of the discovery and importance of the chief nutrients, the nutritional deficiency diseases that occur when those nutrients are not forthcoming in adequate amounts, the relationship between modern diets and major chronic diseases, and food-related disorders. Paradoxically, many such illnesses (the nutritional deficiency diseases in particular), although always a potential hazard, may have become prevalent among humans only as a result of the development of sedentary agriculture.

Because such an apparently wide variety of domesticated plant and animal foods emerged from the various Neolithic revolutions, the phenomenon of sedentary agriculture was, at least until recently, commonly regarded as perhaps humankind's most important step up the ladder of progress. But the findings of bioanthropologists (discussed in Part I) suggest rather that our inclination to think of history teleologically had much to do with such a view and that progress imposes its own penalties (indeed, merely to glance at a newspaper is to appreciate why many have begun to feel that technological advances should carry health-hazard warnings).

As we have already noted, with agriculture and sedentism came diets too closely centered on a single crop, such as wheat in the Old World and maize in the New, and although sedentism (unlike hunting and gathering) encouraged population growth, such growth seems to have been that of a "forced" population with a considerably diminished nutritional status.

And more progress seems inevitably to have created more nutritional difficulties. The navigational and shipbuilding skills that made it possible for the Iberians to seek empires across oceans also created the conditions that kept sailors on a diet almost perfectly devoid of vitamin C, and scurvy began its reign as the scourge of seamen. As maize took root in Europe and Africa as well as in the U.S. South, its new consumers failed to treat it with lime before eating – as the Native Americans, presumably through long experience, had learned to do. The result of maize in inexperienced hands, especially when there was little in the diet to supplement it, was niacin deficiency and the four Ds of pellagra: dermatitis, diarrhea, dementia, and death. With the advent of mechanical rice mills in the latter nineteenth century came widespread thiamine deficiency and beriberi among peoples of rice-eating cultures, because those mills scraped away the thiamine-rich hulls of rice grains with energetic efficiency.

The discovery of vitamins during the first few decades of the twentieth century led to the food "fortification" that put an end to the classic deficiency diseases, at least in the developed world, where they were already in decline. But other health threats quickly took their place. Beginning in the 1950s, surging rates of cancer and heart-related diseases focused suspicion on the environment, not to mention food additives such as monosodium glutamate (MSG), cyclamates, nitrates and nitrites, and saccharin. Also coming under suspicion were plants "engineered" to make them more pest-resistant – which might make them more carcinogenic as well – along with the pesticides and herbicides, regularly applied to farm fields, that can find their way into the human body via plants as well as drinking water.

Domesticated animals, it has turned out, are loaded with antibiotics and potentially artery-clogging fat, along with hormones and steroids that stimulate the growth of that fat. Eggs have been found to be packed with cholesterol, which has become a terrifying word, and the fats in whole milk and most cheeses are now subjects of considerable concern for those seeking a "heart-healthy" diet. Salt has been implicated in the etiology of hypertension, sugar in that of heart disease, saturated fats in both cancer and heart disease, and a lack of calcium in osteoporosis. No wonder that despite their increasing longevity, many people in the developed world have become abruptly and acutely anxious about what they do and do not put in their mouths.

Ironically, however, the majority of the world's people would probably be willing to live with some of these perils if they could share in such bounty. Obesity, anorexia, and chronic disease might be considered tolerable (and preferable) risks in the face of infection stalking their infants (as mothers often must mix formulas with foul water); protein-energy malnutrition attacking the newly weaned; iodine deficiency (along with other mineral and vitamin deficiencies) affecting hundreds of millions of children and adults wherever foods are not fortified; and undernutrition and starvation. All are, too frequently, commonplace phenomena.

Nor are developing-world peoples so likely as those in the developed world to survive the nutritional disorders that seem to be legacies of our hunter-gatherer past. Diabetes (which may be the result of a "thrifty" gene for carbohydrate metabolism) is one of these diseases, and hypertension may be another; still others are doubtless concealed among a group of food allergies, sensitivities, and intolerances that have only recently begun to receive the attention they deserve.

On a more pleasant note, the chapters of Part V sketch out the history and culture of food and drink around the world, starting with the beginnings of agriculture in the ancient Near East and North Africa and continuing through those areas of Asia that saw early activity in plant and animal domestication. This discussion is followed by sections on the regions of Europe, the Americas, and sub-Saharan Africa and Oceania.

Section B of Part V takes up the history of food and drink in South Asia and the Middle East, Southeast Asia, and East Asia in five chapters. One of these treats the Middle East and South Asia together because of the powerful culinary influence of Islam in the latter region, although this is not to say that Greek, Persian, Aryan, and central Asian influences had not found their way into South Asia for millennia prior to the Arab arrival.

Nor is it to say that South Asia was without its own venerable food traditions. After all, many of the world's food plants sprang from the Indus Valley, and it was in the vastness of the Asian tropics and subtropics that most of the world's fruits originated, and most of its spices. The area is also home to one of our "superfoods," rice, which ties together the cuisines of much of the southern part of the continent, whereas millet and (later) wheat were the staples of the north-

ern tier. Asia was also the mother of two more plants that had much to do with transforming human history. From Southeast Asia came the sugarcane that would later so traumatize Africa, Europe, and the Americas; from eastern Asia came the evergreen shrub whose leaves are brewed to make tea.

Rice may have been cultivated as many as 7,000 years ago in China, in India, and in Southeast Asia; the wild plant is still found in these areas today. But it was likely from the Yangtze Delta in China that the techniques of rice cultivation radiated outward toward Korea and then, some 2,500 years ago, to Japan. The soybean and tea also diffused from China to these Asian outposts, all of which stamped some similarities on the cuisines of southern China, Japan, and Korea. Northern China, however, also made the contribution of noodles, and all these cuisines were enriched considerably by the arrival of American plants such as sweet potatoes, tomatoes, chillies, and peanuts – initially brought by Portuguese ships between the sixteenth century (China) and the eighteenth century (Japan).

Also characteristic of the diets of East Asians was the lack of dairy products as sources of calcium. Interestingly, the central Asian nomads (who harassed the northern Chinese for millennia and ruled them when they were not harassing them) used milk; they even made a fermented beverage called *kumiss* from the milk of their mares. But milk did not catch on in China and thus was not diffused elsewhere in East Asia. In India, however, other wanderers – the Aryan pastoralists – introduced dairy products close to 4,000 years ago. There, dairy foods did catch on, although mostly in forms that were physically acceptable to those who were lactose-intolerant – a condition widespread among most Asian populations.

Given the greater sizes of Sections C (Europe) and D (the Americas) in Part V, readers may object to what clearly seems to be something of a Western bias in a work that purports to be global in scope. But it is the case that foods and foodways of the West have been more systematically studied than those of other parts of the world, and thus there are considerably more scholars to make their expertise available. In most instances, the authors of the regional essays in both these sections begin with the prehistoric period, take the reader through the Neolithic Revolution in the specific geographic area, and focus on subsequent changes in foodways wrought by climate and cultural contacts, along with the introduction of new foods. At first, the latter involved a flow of fruits and vegetables from the Middle and Near East into Europe, and an early spice trade that brought all sorts of Asian, African, and Near Eastern goods to the western end of the Mediterranean. The expansion of Rome continued the dispersal of these foods and spices throughout Europe.

Needless to say, the plant and animal exchanges between the various countries of the Old World and the lands of the New World following 1492 are dealt with in considerable detail because those exchanges so profoundly affected the food (and demographic) history of all the areas concerned. Of course, maize, manioc, sweet potatoes and white potatoes, peanuts, tomatoes, chillies, and a variety of beans sustained the American populations that had domesticated and diffused them for a few thousand years in their own Neolithic Revolution before the Europeans arrived. But the American diets were lacking in animal protein. What was available came (depending on location) from game, guinea pigs, seafoods, insects, dogs, and turkeys. That the American Indians did not domesticate more animals – or milk those animals (such as the llama) that they did domesticate – remains something of a mystery. Less of a mystery is the fate of the Native Americans, many of whom died in a holocaust of disease inadvertently unleashed on them by the Europeans. And as the new land became depopulated of humans, it began to fill up again with horses, cattle, sheep, hogs, and other Old World animals.

Certainly, the addition of Old World animal foods to the plants of the New World made for a happy union, and as the authors of the various regional entries approach the present – as they reach the 1960s, in fact – an important theme that emerges in their chapters is the fading of distinctive regional cuisines in the face of considerable food globalization. The cuisine of the developed world, in particular, is becoming homogenized, with even natives of the Pacific, Arctic, and Subarctic regions consuming more in the way of the kinds of prepared foods that are eaten by everybody else in the West, unfortunately to their detriment.

Section E treats the foodways of Africa south of the Sahara, the Pacific Islands, and Australia and New Zealand in three chapters that conclude a global tour of the history and culture of food and drink. Although at first glance it might seem that these last three disparate areas of the planet historically have had nothing in common from a nutritional viewpoint, they do, in fact, share one feature, which has been something of a poverty of food plants and animals.

In Africa, much of this poverty has been the result of rainfall, which depending on location, has generally been too little or too much. Famine results from the former, whereas leached and consequently nitrogen- and calcium-poor soils are products of the latter, with the plants these areas do sustain also deficient in important nutrients. Moreover, 40 inches or more of rainfall favors proliferation of the tsetse fly, and the deadly trypanosomes carried by this insect have made it impossible to keep livestock animals in many parts of the continent. But even where such animals can be raised, the impoverished plants they graze on render them inferior in size, as well as inferior in the quality of their meat and milk, to counterparts elsewhere in the world. As in the Americas, then, animal protein was not prominent in most African diets after the advent of sedentism.

But unlike the Americas, Africa was not blessed with vegetable foods, either. Millets, yams, and a kind of African rice were the staple crops that emerged from the Neolithic to sustain populations, and people became more numerous in the wake of the arrival of better-yielding yams from across the Indian Ocean. But it was only with the appearance of the maize, peanuts, sweet potatoes, American yams, manioc, and chillies brought by the slave traders that African populations began to experience the substantial growth that we still witness today.

Starting some 30,000 to 40,000 years ago, waves of Pacific pioneers spread out from Southeast Asia to occupy the islands of Polynesia, Melanesia, and Micronesia. They lived a kind of fisher–hunter–gatherer existence based on a variety of fish, birds, and reptiles, along with the roots of ferns and other wild vegetable foods. But a late wave of immigrants, who sailed out from Southeast Asia to the Pacific Basin Islands about 6,000 years ago, thoughtfully brought with them some of the products of the Old World Neolithic in the form of pigs, dogs, chickens, and root crops like the yam and taro. And somehow, an American plant – the sweet potato – much later also found its way to many of these islands.

In a very real sense, then, the Neolithic Revolution was imported to the islands. Doubtless it spread slowly, but by the time the ships of Captain James Cook sailed into the Pacific, all islands populated by humans were also home to hogs, dogs, and fowl – and this included even the extraordinarily isolated Hawaiian Islands. Yet, as with the indigenous populations of the Americas, those of the Pacific had little time to enjoy any plant and animal gifts the Europeans brought to them. Instead, they began to die from imported diseases, which greatly thinned their numbers.

The story of Australia and New Zealand differs substantially from that of Africa and the Pacific Islands in that both the Australian Aborigines and (to a lesser extent) the New Zealand Maori were still hunter-gatherers when the Europeans first reached them. They had no pigs or fowl nor planted yams or taro, although they did have a medium-sized domesticated dog and sweet potatoes.

In New Zealand, there were no land mammals prior to human occupation, but there were giant flightless birds and numerous reptiles. The Maori arrived after pigs and taro had reached Polynesia, but at some point (either along the way to New Zealand or after their arrival) they lost their pigs, and the soil and climate of New Zealand did not lend themselves to growing much in the way of taro. Like their Australian counterparts, they had retained their dogs, which they used on occasion for food, and the sweet potato was their most important crop.

Thus, despite their dogs and some farming efforts, the Aborigines and the Maori depended heavily on hunting-and-gathering activities until the Europeans arrived to introduce new plant and animal species.

Unfortunately, as in the Americas and elsewhere in the Pacific, they also introduced new pathogens and, consequently, demographic disaster.

Following this global excursion, Part V closes with a discussion of the growing field of culinary history, which is now especially vigorous in the United States and Europe but promises in the near future to be a feast that scholars the world over will partake of and participate in.

Part VI is devoted to food- and nutrition-related subjects that are of both contemporary and historical interest. Among these are some examples of the startling ability of humans to adapt to unique nutritional environments, including the singular regimen of the Inuit, whose fat-laden traditional diet would seem to have been so perfectly calculated to plug up arteries that one might wonder why these people are still around to study. Other chapters take up questions regarding the nutritional needs (and entitlements) of special age, economic, and ethnic groups. They show how these needs frequently go unmet because of cultural and economic circumstances and point out some of the costs of maternal and child undernutrition that are now undergoing close scrutiny, such as mental decrement. In this vein, food prejudices and taboos are also discussed; many such attitudes can bring about serious nutritional problems for women and children, even though childbearing is fundamentally a nutritional task and growing from infancy to adulthood a nutritional feat.

A discussion of the political, economic, and biological causes and ramifications of famine leads naturally to another very large question treated in the first two chapters of Part VI. The importance of nutrition in humankind's demographic history has been a matter of some considerable debate since Thomas McKeown published *The Modern Rise of Population* in 1976. In that work, McKeown attempted to explain how it happened that sometime in the eighteenth century if not before, the English (and by extension the Europeans) managed to begin extricating themselves from seemingly endless cycles of population growth followed by plunges into demographic stagnation. He eliminated possibilities such as advances in medicine and sanitation, along with epidemiological factors such as disease abatement or mutation, and settled on improved nutrition as the single most important cause. Needless to say, many have bristled at such a high-handed dismissal of these other possibilities, and our chapters continue the debate with somewhat opposing views.

Not entirely unrelated is a discussion of height and nutrition, with the former serving as proxy for the latter. Clearly, whether or not improving nutrition was the root cause of population growth, it most certainly seems to have played an important role in human growth and, not incidentally, in helping at least those living in the West to once again approach the stature of their Paleolithic ancestors. Moreover, it is the case that no matter what position one holds with respect to the demographic impact of nutrition, there is agreement that nutrition and disease cannot be neatly separated, and indeed, our chapter on synergy describes how the two interact.

Cultural and psychological aspects of food are the focus of a group of chapters that examines why people eat some foods but not others and how such food choices have considerable social and cultural resonance. Food choices of the moment frequently enter the arena of food fads, and one of our chapters explores the myriad reasons why foods can suddenly become trends, but generally trends with little staying power.

The controversial nature of vegetarianism – a nutritional issue always able to trigger a crossfire of debate – is acknowledged in our pages by two chapters with differing views on the subject. For some, the practice falls under the rubric of food as medicine. Then there are those convinced of the aphrodisiacal benefits of vegetarianism – that the avoidance of animal foods positively influences their sexual drive and performance. For many, vegetarianism stems from religious conviction; others simply feel it is wrong to consume the flesh of living creatures, whereas still others think it downright dangerous. Clearly, the phrase "we are what we eat" must be taken in a number of different ways.

The closing chapters of Part VI address the various ways that humans and the societies they construct have embraced particular foods or groups of foods in an effort to manipulate their own health and well-being as well as that of others. Certain foods, for example, have been regarded by individuals as aphrodisiacs and anaphrodisiacs and consumed in frequently heroic efforts to regulate sexual desires. Or again, some – mostly plant – foods have been employed for medicinal reasons, with many, such as garlic, viewed as medical panaceas.

Part VII scrutinizes mostly contemporary food-related policy questions that promise to be with us for some time to come, although it begins with a chapter on nutrition and the state showing how European governments came to regard well-nourished populations as important to national security and military might. Other discussions that follow treat the myriad methodological (not to mention biological) problems associated with determining the individual's optimal daily need for each of the chief nutrients; food labeling, which when done fairly and honestly can aid the individual in selecting the appropriate mix of these nutrients; and the dubious ability of nonfoods to supplement the diet.

As one might expect, food safety, food biotechnology, and the politics of such issues are of considerable concern, and – it almost goes without saying – politics and safety have the potential at any given time for being at odds with one another. The juxtaposition is hardly a new one, with monopoly and competitive capital on the one hand and the public interest on the other. The two may or may not be in opposition, but the stakes are enormous, as will readily be seen.

First there is the problem of safety, created by a loss of genetic diversity. Because all crops evolved from wild species, this means that in Darwinian terms, that the latter possessed sufficient adaptability to survive over considerable periods of time. But with domestication and breeding has come genetic erosion and a loss of this adaptability – even the loss of wild progenitors – so that if today many crops were suddenly not planted, they would simply disappear. And although this possibility is not so alarming – after all, everyone is not going to cease planting wheat, or rice, or maize – the genetic sameness of the wheat or the maize or the rice that is planted (the result of a loss of genetic material) has been of some considerable concern because of the essentially incalculable risk that some newly mutated plant plague might arise to inflict serious damage on a sizable fraction of the world's food supply.

There is another problem connected with the loss of genetic material. It is less potentially calamitous but is one that observers nevertheless find disturbing, especially in the long term. The problem is that many crops have been rendered less able to fend off their traditional parasites (in part because of breeding that reduces a plant's ability to produce the naturally occurring toxicants that defend against predators) and thus have become increasingly dependent on pesticides that can and do find their way into our food and water supplies.

Genetic engineering, however, promises to at least reduce the problem of chemical pollution by revitalizing the ability of crops to defend themselves – as, for example, in the crossing of potatoes with carnivorous plants so that insects landing on them will die immediately. But the encouragement of such defense mechanisms in plants has prompted the worry that because humans are, after all, parasites as far as the plant is concerned, resistance genes might transform crops into less healthy or even unhealthy food, perhaps (as mentioned before) even carcinogenic at some unacceptable level. And, of course, genetic engineering has also raised the specter of scientists accidentally (or deliberately) engineering and then unleashing self-propagating microorganisms into the biosphere, with disastrous epidemiological and ecological effect.

Clearly, biotechnology, plant breeding, plant molecular and cellular biology, and the pesticide industry all have their perils as well as their promise, and some of these dangers are spelled out in a chapter on toxins in foods. But in addition, as a chapter on substitute foods shows, although these substitutes may have been developed to help us escape the tyranny of sugars and fats, they are not without their own risks. Nor, for that matter, are some food additives. Although most seem safe, preservatives such as nitrates and nitrites, flavor enhancers like MSG, and coloring agents such as tartrazine are worrisome to many.

As our authors make clear, however, we may have more to fear from the naturally occurring toxins that the so-called natural foods employ to defend themselves against predators than from the benefits of science and technology. Celery, for example, produces psoralins (which are mutagenic carcinogens); spinach contains oxalic acid that builds kidney stones and interferes with the body's absorption of calcium; lima beans have cyanide; and the solanine in the skins of greenish-appearing potatoes is a poisonous alkaloid.

From biological and chemical questions, we move to other problems of a political and economic nature concerning what foods are produced, what quantities are produced, what the quality is of these foods, and what their allocation is. In the United States (and practically everywhere else) many of the answers to such questions are shaped and mediated by lobbying groups, whose interests are special and not necessarily those of the public. Yet if Americans sometimes have difficulty in getting the truth about the foods they eat, at least they get the foods. There is some general if uneasy agreement in America and most of the developed world that everyone is entitled to food as a basic right and that government programs – subsidies, food stamps, and the like – ought to ensure that right. But such is not the situation in much of the developing world, where food too frequently bypasses the poor and the powerless. And as the author of the chapter on food subsidies and interventions makes evident, too often women and children are among the poor and the powerless.

To end on a lighter note, the last chapter in Part VII takes us full circle by examining the current and fascinating issue of the importance of Paleolithic nutrition to humans entering the twenty-first century.

We close this introduction on a mixed note of optimism and pessimism. The incorporation of dwarfing genes into modern plant varieties was responsible for the sensationally high-yielding wheat and rice varieties that took hold in developing countries in the 1960s, giving rise to what we call the "Green Revolution," which was supposed to end world hunger and help most of the countries of the world produce food surpluses. But the Green Revolution also supported a tremendous explosion of populations in those countries it revolutionized, bringing them face to face with the Malthusian poles of food supply and population.

Moreover, the new plants were heavily dependent on the petrochemical industry for fertilizers, so that in the 1970s, when oil prices soared, so did the price of fertilizers, with the result that poorer farmers, who previously had at least eked out a living from the land, were now driven from it. Moreover, the new dwarfed and semidwarfed rice and wheat plants carried the same genes, meaning that much of the world's food supply was now at the mercy of new, or newly mutated, plant pathogens. To make matters worse, the plants seemed even less able to defend themselves against existing pathogens. Here, the answer seemed to be a still more lavish use of pesticides (against which bitter assaults were launched by environmentalists) even as more developing-world farmers were being driven out of business by increasing costs, and thousands upon thousands of people were starving to death each year. Indeed, by the 1980s, every country revolutionized by the Green Revolution was once again an importer of those staple foods they had expected to produce in abundance.

Obviously, from both a social and political-economic as well as a biological viewpoint, ecologies had not only failed to mesh, they had seriously unraveled. However, as our earlier chapters on rice and wheat point out, new varieties from plant breeders contain variations in genes that make them less susceptible to widespread disease damage, and genetic engineering efforts are under way to produce other varieties that will be less dependent on fertilizers and pesticides.

Meanwhile, as others of our authors point out, foods such as amaranth, sweet potatoes, manioc, and taro, if given just some of the attention that rice and wheat have received, could help considerably to expand the world's food supply. But here again, we teeter on the edge of matters that are as much cultural, social, economic, and political in nature as they are ecological and biological. And such matters will doubtless affect the acceptance of new crops of nutritional importance.

As we begin a sorely needed second phase of the Green Revolution, observers have expressed the hope that we have learned from the mistakes of the first phase. But of course, we could call the first flowering of the Neolithic Revolution (some 10,000 years ago) the first phase and ponder what has been learned since then, which – in a nutshell – is that every important agricultural breakthrough thus far has, at least temporarily, produced unhappy health consequences for those caught up in it, and overall agricultural advancement has resulted in growing populations and severe stress on the biosphere. As we enter the twenty-first century, we might hope to finally learn from our mistakes.

The Editors

PART I

Determining What
Our Ancestors Ate

About 10,000 years ago, humans started changing the way they made a living as they began what would be a lengthy transition from foraging to farming. This transformation, known as the Neolithic Revolution, was actually comprised of many revolutions, taking place in different times and places, that are often viewed collectively as the greatest of all human strides taken in the direction of progress. But such progress did not mean better health. On the contrary, as the following chapters indicate, hunter-gatherers were, on the whole, considerably better nourished and much less troubled with illnesses than their farmer descendants. Because hunter-gatherers were mobile by necessity, living in bands of no more than 100 individuals they were not capable of supporting the kinds of ailments that flourished as crowd diseases later on. Nor, as a rule, did they pause in one spot long enough to foul their water supply or let their wastes accumulate to attract disease vectors – insects, rodents, and the like. In addition, they possessed no domesticated animals (save the dog late in the Paleolithic) who would have added to the pollution process and shared their own pathogens.

In short, hunter-gatherers most likely had few pathogenic boarders to purloin a portion of their nutritional intake and few illnesses to fight, with the latter also sapping that intake. Moreover, although no one questions that hunter-gatherers endured hungry times, their diets in good times featured such a wide variety of nutriments that a healthy mix of nutrients in adequate amounts was ensured.

Sedentism turned this salubrious world upside down. Because their livelihood depended on mobility – on following the food supply – hunter-gatherers produced relatively few children. By contrast, their sedentary successors, who needed hands for the fields and security in old age, reproduced without restraint, and populations began to swell. Squalid villages became even more squalid towns, where people lived cheek to jowl with their growing stock of animals and where diseases began to thrive, along with swarms of insects and rodents that moved in to share in the bounty generated by closely packed humans and their animals.

But even as pathogens were laying an ever-increasing claim to people's nutritional intake, the quality of that intake was sharply declining. The varied diet of hunter-gatherers bore little resemblance to the monotonous diet of their farmer successors, which was most likely to center too closely on a single crop such as wheat, millet, rice, or maize and to feature too little in the way of good-quality protein.

The chapters in Part I focus on this transition, the Neolithic revolutions, which although separated in both time and space, had remarkably similar negative effects on human health.

I.1. ❧ Dietary Reconstruction and Nutritional Assessment of Past Peoples: The Bioanthropological Record

The topics of diet (the foods that are eaten) and nutrition (the way that these foods are used by the body) are central to an understanding of the evolutionary journey of humankind. Virtually every major anatomical change wrought by that journey can be related in one way or another to how foods are acquired and processed by the human body. Indeed, the very fact that our humanlike ancestors had acquired a bipedal manner of walking by some five to eight million years ago is almost certainly related to how they acquired food. Although the role of diet and nutrition in human evolution has generally come under the purview of anthropology, the subject has also been of great interest to scholars in many other disciplines, including the medical and biological sciences, chemistry, economics, history, sociology, psychology, primatology, paleontology, and numerous applied fields (e.g., public health, food technology, government services). Consideration of nutriture, defined as "the state resulting from the balance between supply of nutrition on the one hand and the expenditure of the organism on the other," can be traced back to the writings of Hippocrates and Celsus and represents an important heritage of earlier human cultures in both the Old and New Worlds (McLaren 1976, quoted in Himes 1987: 86).

The purpose of this chapter is threefold: (1) to present a brief overview of the basic characteristics of human nutriture and the history of human diet; (2) to examine specific means for reconstructing diet from analysis of human skeletal remains; and (3) to review how the quality of nutrition has been assessed in past populations using evidence garnered by many researchers from paleopathological and skeletal studies and from observations of living human beings. (See also Wing and Brown 1979; Huss-Ashmore, Goodman, and Armelagos 1982; Goodman, Martin, et al. 1984; Martin, Goodman, and Armelagos 1985; Ortner and Putschar 1985; Larsen 1987; Cohen 1989; Stuart-Macadam 1989. For a review of experimental evidence and its implications for humans, see Stewart 1975.) Important developments regarding nutrition in living humans are presented in a number of monographic series, including *World Review of Nutrition and Dietetics, Annual Review of Nutrition, Nutrition Reviews,* and *Current Topics in Nutrition and Disease.*

Human Nutriture and Dietary History

Although as living organisms we consume foods, we must keep in mind that it is the *nutrients* contained in these foods that are necessary for all of our bodily functions, including support of normal growth and maturation, repair and replacement of body tissues,

and the conduct of physical activities (Malina 1987). Estimations indicate that modern humans require some 40 to 50 nutrients for proper health and well-being (Mann 1981). These nutrients are typically divided into six classes – carbohydrates, proteins, fats, vitamins, minerals, and water. Carbohydrates and fats are the primary energy sources available to the body. Fats are a highly concentrated source of energy and are stored in the body to a far greater degree than carbohydrates. Fats are stored in the range between about 15 and 30 percent of body weight (Malina 1987), whereas carbohydrates represent only about 0.4 to 0.5 percent of body weight in childhood and young adulthood (Fomon et al. 1982). Proteins, too, act as energy sources, but they have two primary functions: tissue growth, maintenance, and repair; and physiological roles.

The building blocks of proteins are chains of nitrogen-containing organic compounds called amino acids. Most of the 22 amino acids can be produced by the body at a rate that is necessary for the synthesis of proteins, and for this reason they are called nonessential amino acids. Eight, however, are not produced in sufficient amounts and therefore must be supplied to the body as food (essential amino acids). Moreover, all essential amino acids have to be present simultaneously in correct amounts and consumed in the same meal in order to be absorbed properly. As noted by W. A. Stini (1971: 1021), "a reliance on any one or combination of foods which lacks even one of the essential amino acids will preclude the utilization of the rest, resulting in continued and increased excretion of nitrogen without compensatory intake."

Vitamins, a group of 16 compounds, are required in very small amounts only. Save for vitamin D, none of these substances can be synthesized by the body, and if even one is missing or is poorly absorbed, a deficiency disease will arise. Vitamins are mostly regulatory in their overall function. Minerals are inorganic elements that occur in the human body either in large amounts (e.g., calcium and phosphorus) or in trace amounts (called trace elements: e.g., strontium, zinc, fluorine). They serve two important types of functions, namely structural, as in bone and blood production, and regulatory, such as proper balance of electrolytes and fluids. Water, perhaps the most important of the nutrients, functions as a major structural component of the body in temperature regulation and as a transport medium, including elimination of body wastes. About two-thirds of body weight in humans is water (Malina 1987).

Throughout the course of evolution, humans, by adaptation, have acquired a tremendous range of means for securing foods and maintaining proper nutriture. These adaptations can be ordered into a temporal sequence of three phases in the evolution of the human diet (following Gordon 1987). The first phase involved the shift from a diet comprised primarily of unprocessed plant foods to one that incorporated deliberate food-processing techniques and included significant amounts of meat. These changes likely occurred between the late Miocene epoch and early Pleistocene (or by about 1.5 million years ago). Archaeological and taphonomic evidence indicates that the meat component of diet was likely acquired through a strategy involving scavenging rather than deliberate hunting. Pat Shipman (1986a, 1986b) has examined patterns of cut marks produced by stone tools and tooth marks produced by carnivores in a sample of faunal remains recovered from Olduvai Bed I dating from 2.0 to 1.7 million years ago. In instances where cut marks and tooth marks overlapped on a single bone, her analysis revealed that carnivore tooth marks were *followed* in sequence by hominid-produced cut marks. This pattern of bone modification indicates that hominids scavenged an animal carcass killed by another animal.

The second phase in the history of human diet began in the Middle Pleistocene epoch, perhaps as long ago as 700,000 years before the present. This phase is characterized by deliberate hunting of animal food sources. In East Africa, at the site of Olorgesailie (700,000 to 400,000 years ago), an extinct species of giant gelada baboon (*Theropithecus oswaldi*) was hunted. Analysis of the remains of these animals by Shipman and co-workers (1981) indicates that although the deaths of many were not due to human activity, young individuals were selectively killed and butchered by hominids for consumption.

Some of the most frequently cited evidence for early hominid food acquisition is from the Torralba and Ambrona sites, located in the province of Soria, Spain (Howell 1966; Freeman 1981). Based on an abundance of remains of large mammals such as elephants, along with stone artifacts, fire, and other evidence of human activity, F. Clark Howell and Leslie G. Freeman concluded that the bone accumulations resulted from "deliberate game drives and the killing of large herbivores by Acheulian hunting peoples" (1982: 13). Richard G. Klein (1987, 1989), however, subsequently argued on the basis of his more detailed observations of animal remains from these sites that despite a human presence as evidenced by stone tools, it is not possible to distinguish between human or carnivore activity in explaining the extensive bone accumulations. First, the relatively greater frequency of axial skeletal elements (e.g., crania, pelves, vertebrae) could be the result of the removal of meatier portions of animal carcasses by either humans or the large carnivores who frequented the site. Second, the overabundance of older elephants could represent human hunting, but it also could represent carnivore activity or natural mortality. Thus, although hominids in Spain were quite likely acquiring protein from animal sources, the evidence based on these Paleolithic sites is equivocal. We know that early hominids acquired meat through hunting activity, but their degree of success in this regard is still unclear.

By later Pleistocene times (20,000 to 11,000 years ago), evidence for specialized hunting strategies clearly indicates that human populations had developed means by which larger species of animals were successfully hunted. For example, at the Upper Paleolithic site of Solutré, France, Howell (1970) noted that some 100,000 individuals of horse were found at the base of the cliff, and at Predmosti, Czechoslovakia, about 1,000 individuals of mammoth were found. Presumably, the deaths of these animals resulted from purposeful game drives undertaken by local communities of hominids. Virtually all faunal assemblages studied by archaeologists show that large, gregarious herbivores, such as the woolly mammoth, reindeer, bison, and horse, were emphasized, particularly in the middle latitudes of Eurasia (Klein 1989). But some of the best evidence for advances in resource exploitation by humans is from the southern tip of Africa. In this region, Late Stone Age peoples fished extensively, and they hunted dangerous animals like wild pigs and buffalo with considerable success (Klein 1989).

Because of the relatively poor preservation of plant remains as compared to animal remains in Pleistocene sites, our knowledge of the role of plant foods in human Paleolithic nutriture is virtually nonexistent. There is, however, limited evidence from a number of localities. For example, at the *Homo erectus* site of Zhoukoudian in the People's Republic of China (430,000 to 230,000 years before the present), hackberry seeds may have been roasted and consumed. Similarly, in Late Stone Age sites in South Africa, abundant evidence exists for the gathering of plant staples by early modern *Homo sapiens*. Based on what is known about meat and plant consumption by living hunter-gatherers, it is likely that plant foods contributed substantially to the diets of earlier, premodern hominids (Gordon 1987). Today, with the exception of Eskimos, all-meat diets are extremely rare in human populations (Speth 1990), and this almost certainly was the case in antiquity.

The third and final phase in the history of human diet began at the interface between the Pleistocene and Holocene epochs about 10,000 years ago. This period of time is marked by the beginning of essentially modern patterns of climate, vegetation, and fauna. The disappearance of megafauna, such as the mastodon and the mammoth, in many parts of the world at about this time may have been an impetus for human populations to develop new means of food acquisition in order to meet protein and fat requirements. The most important change, however, was the shift from diets based exclusively on food collection to those based to varying degrees on food production.

The transition involved the acquisition by human populations of an intimate knowledge of the life cycles of plants and animals so as to control such cycles and thereby ensure the availability of these nutriments for dietary purposes. By about 7,000 years ago, a transition to a plant-based economy was well established in some areas of the Middle East. From this region, agriculture spread into Europe, and other independent centers of plant domestication appeared in Africa, Asia, and the New World, all within the next several millennia.

It has been both the popular and scientific consensus that the shift from lifeways based exclusively on hunting and gathering to those that incorporated food production – and especially agriculture – represented a positive change for humankind. However, Mark N. Cohen (1989) has remarked that in game-rich environments, regardless of the strategy employed, hunters may obtain between 10,000 and 15,000 kilocalories per hour. Subsistence cultivators, in contrast, average between 3,000 and 5,000 kilocalories per hour.

More important, anthropologists have come to recognize in recent years that the shift from hunting and gathering to agriculture was characterized by a shift from generally high-quality foods to low-quality foods. For example, animal sources of protein contain all essential amino acids in the correct proportions. They are a primary source of vitamin B_{12}, are high in vitamins A and D, and contain important minerals. Moreover, animal fat is a critical source of essential fatty acids and fat-soluble vitamins (Speth 1990). Thus, relative to plant foods, meat is a highly nutritional food resource. Plant foods used alone generally cannot sustain human life, primarily because of deficiency in essential amino acids (see discussion in Ross 1976). Moreover, in circumstances where plant foods are emphasized, a wide variety of them must be consumed in order to fulfill basic nutritional requirements. Further limiting the nutritional value of many plants is their high fiber content, especially cellulose, which is not digestible by humans.

Periodic food shortages resulting from variation in a number of factors – especially rainfall and temperature, along with the relative prevalence of insects and other pests – have been observed in contemporary human populations depending on subsistence agriculture. Some of the effects of such shortages include weight loss in adults, slowing of growth in children, and an increase in prevalence of malaria and other diseases such as gastroenteritis, and parasitic infection (Bogin 1988).

Archaeological evidence from prehistoric agriculturalists, along with observation of living peasant agriculturalists, indicates that their diets tend to be dominated by a single cereal staple: rice in Asia, wheat in temperate Asia and Europe, millet or sorghum in Africa, and maize in the New World. These foods are oftentimes referred to as *superfoods,* not because of nutritional value but rather because of the pervasive focus by human populations on one or another of them (McElroy and Townsend 1979).

Rice, a food staple domesticated in Southeast Asia and eventually extending in use from Japan and Korea southward to Indonesia and eastward into parts of India, has formed the basis of numerous complex cultures and civilizations (Bray 1989). Yet it is remarkably deficient in protein, even in its brown or unmilled

form. Moreover, the low availability of protein in rice inhibits the activity of vitamin A, even if the vitamin is available through other food sources (Wolf 1980). Vitamin A deficiency can trigger xerophthalmia, one of the principal causes of blindness. White rice – the form preferred by most human populations – results from processing, or the removal of the outer bran coat, and consequently, the removal of thiamine (vitamin B_1). This deficiency leads to beriberi, a disease alternately involving inflammation of the nerves, or the heart, or both.

Wheat was domesticated in the Middle East very early in the Holocene and has been widely used since that time. Wheat is deficient in two essential amino acids – lysine and isoleucine. Most human populations dependent on wheat, however, have dairy animals that provide products (e.g., cheese) that make up for these missing amino acids. Yet in some areas of the Middle East and North Africa where wheat is grown, zinc-deficient soils have been implicated in retarding growth in children (Harrison et al. 1988). Moreover, the phytic acid present in wheat bran chemically binds with zinc, thus inhibiting its absorption (Mottram 1979).

Maize (known as corn in the United States) was first domesticated in Mesoamerica. Like the other superfoods, it formed the economic basis for the rise of civilizations and complex societies, and its continued domestication greatly increased its productivity (Galinat 1985). In eastern North America, maize was central in the evolution of a diversity of chiefdoms (Smith 1989), and its importance in the Americas was underscored by Walton C. Galinat, who noted:

> [By] the time of Columbus, maize had already become the staff of life in the New World. It was distributed throughout both hemispheres from Argentina and Chile northward to Canada and from sea level to high in the Andes, from swampland to arid conditions and from short to long day lengths. In becoming so widespread, it evolved hundreds of races, each with special adaptations for the environment including special utilities for man. (Galinat 1985: 245)

Like the other superfoods, maize is deficient in a number of important nutrients. Zein – the protein in maize – is deficient in lysine, isoleucine, and tryptophan (FAO 1970), and if maize consumers do not supplement their diets with foods containing these amino acids, such as beans, significant growth retardation is an outcome. Moreover, maize, although not deficient in niacin (vitamin B_3), contains it in a chemically bound form that, untreated, will withhold the vitamin from the consumer. Consequently, human populations consuming untreated maize frequently develop pellagra, a deficiency disease characterized by a number of symptoms, including rough and irritated skin, mental symptoms, and diarrhea (Roe 1973). Solomon H. Katz and co-workers (1974, 1975;

see also Katz 1987) have shown that many Native American groups treat maize with alkali (e.g., lye, lime, or wood ashes) prior to consumption, thereby liberating niacin. Moreover, the amino acid quality in alkali-treated maize is significantly improved. Most human populations who later acquired maize as a dietary staple did not, however, adopt the alkali-treatment method (see Roe 1973). Maize also contains phytate and sucrose, whose negative impact on human health is considered later in this chapter.

Dietary Reconstruction: Human Remains

Chemistry and Isotopy

Skeletal remains from archaeological sites play a very special role in dietary reconstruction because they provide the only *direct* evidence of food consumption practices in past societies. In the last decade, several trace elements and stable isotopes have been measured and analyzed in human remains for the reconstruction of diets. Stanley H. Ambrose (1987) has reviewed these approaches, and the following is drawn from his discussion (see also van der Merwe 1982; Klepinger 1984; Sealy 1986; Aufderheide 1989; Keegan 1989; Schoeninger 1989; Sandford 1993).

Some elements have been identified as potentially useful in dietary reconstruction. These include manganese (Mn), strontium (Sr), and barium (Br), which are concentrated in plant foods, and zinc (Zn) and copper (Cu), which are concentrated in animal foods. Nuts, which are low in vanadium (V), contrast with other plant foods in that they typically contain high amounts of Cu and Zn. Like plants, marine resources (e.g., shellfish) are usually enriched in Sr, and thus the dietary signatures resulting from consumption of plants and marine foods or freshwater shellfish should be similar (Schoeninger and Peebles 1981; Price 1985). In contrast, Br is deficient in bones of marine animals, thereby distinguishing these organisms from terrestrial ones in this chemical signature (Burton and Price 1990).

The greater body of research done on elemental composition has been with Sr. In general, Sr levels decline as one moves up the food chain – from plants to herbivores to primary carnivores – as a result of natural biopurification (a process called fractionation). Simply put, herbivores consume plants that are enriched with Sr contained in soil. Because very little of the Sr that passes through the gut wall in animals is stored in flesh (only about 10 percent), the carnivore consuming the herbivore will have considerably less strontium stored in its skeleton. Humans and other omnivores, therefore, should have Sr concentrations that are intermediate between herbivores and carnivores in their skeletal tissues. Thus, based on the amount of Sr measured in human bones, it is possible (with some qualifications) to determine the relative contributions of plant and meat foods to a diet.

Nonetheless, in addition to the aforementioned problem with shellfish, there are three chief limitations to Sr and other elemental analyses. First, Sr abundance can vary widely from region to region, depending upon the geological context. Therefore, it is critical that the baseline elemental concentrations in local soils – and plants and animals – be known. Second, it must be shown that diagenesis (the process involving alteration of elemental abundance in bone tissue while it is contained in the burial matrix) has not occurred. Some elements appear to resist diagenesis following burial (e.g., Sr, Zn, Pb [lead], Na [sodium]), and other elements show evidence for diagenesis (e.g., Fe [iron], Al [aluminum], K [potassium], Mn, Cu, Ba). Moreover, diagenetic change has been found to vary within even a single bone (e.g., Sillen and Kavanaugh 1982; Bumsted 1985). Margaret J. Schoeninger and co-workers (1989) have evaluated the extent of preservation of histological structures in archaeological bone from the seventeenth-century Georgia coastal Spanish mission Santa Catalina de Guale. This study revealed that bones with the least degree of preservation of structures have the lowest Sr concentrations. Although these low values may result from diet, more likely they result from diagenetic effects following burial in the soil matrix. And finally, pretreatment procedures of archaeological bone samples in the laboratory frequently are ineffective in completely removing the contaminants originating in groundwater, such as calcium carbonate, thus potentially masking important dietary signatures.

Valuable information on specific aspects of dietary composition in past human populations can also be obtained by the analysis of stable isotopes of organic material (collagen) in bone. Isotopes of two elements have proven of value in the analysis of diets: carbon (C) and nitrogen (N). Field and laboratory studies involving controlled feeding experiments have shown that stable isotope ratios of both carbon ($^{13}C/^{12}C$) and nitrogen ($^{15}N/^{14}N$) in an animal's tissues, including bone, reflect similar ratios of diet. Because the variations in isotopic abundances between dietary resources are quite small, the values in tissue samples are expressed in parts per thousand (o/oo) relative to established standards, as per delta (δ) values.

The $\delta^{13}C$ values have been used to identify two major dietary categories. The first category has been used to distinguish consumers of plants with different photosynthetic pathways, including consumers of C4 plants (tropical grasses such as maize) and consumers of C3 plants (most leafy plants). Because these plants differ in their photosynthetic pathways, they also differ in the amount of ^{13}C that they incorporate. Thus, C4 plants and people who consume them have $\delta^{13}C$ values that differ on average by about 14 o/oo from other diets utilizing non-C4 plants. Based on these differences, it has been possible to track the introduction and intensification of maize agriculture in eastern North America with some degree of precision (Figure I.1.1). The second cate-

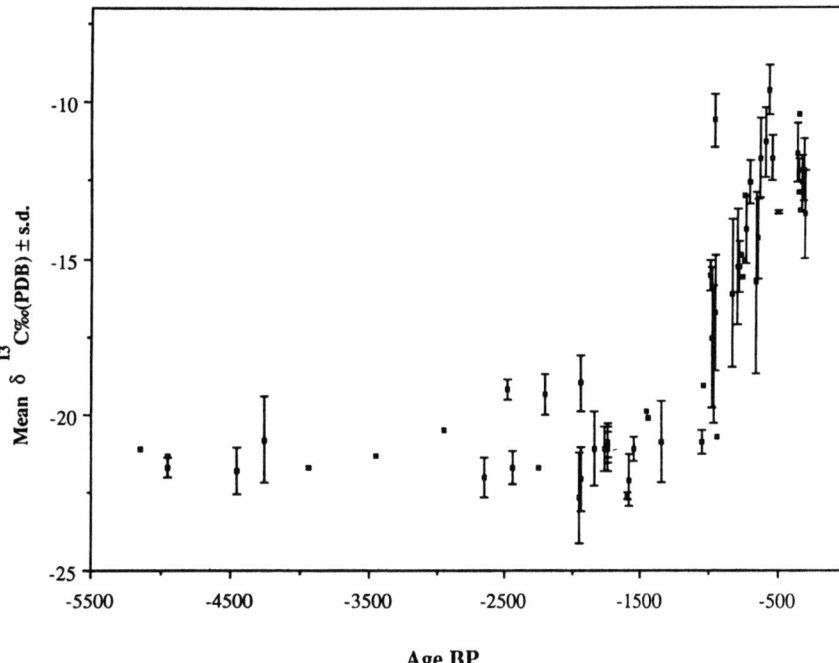

Figure I.1.1. Temporal changes in mean values of δ13C of prehistoric eastern North American Indians. The error bars represent one standard deviation. (From Ambrose 1987, in *Emergent Horticultural Economies of the Eastern Woodlands,* ed. W. F. Keegan; ©1987 the Board of Trustees, Southern Illinois University; reprinted by permission of the author and the Center for Archaeological Investigations.)

gory of dietary identification reflected by $\delta^{13}C$ values includes primarily marine foods. Marine fish and mammals have more positive $\delta^{13}C$ values (by about 6 o/oo) compared to terrestrial animals feeding on C3 foods, and less positive values (by about 7 o/oo) than terrestrial animals feeding on C4 foods (especially maize) (Schoeninger and DeNiro 1984; Schoeninger, van der Merwe, and Moore 1990).

Nitrogen stable isotope ratios in human bone are used to distinguish between consumers of terrestrial and marine foods. Margaret Schoeninger and Michael J. DeNiro (1984; see also Schoeninger et al. 1990) have indicated that in many geographical regions the $\delta^{15}N$ values of marine organisms differ from terrestrial organisms by about 10 parts per thousand on average, with consumers of terrestrial foods being less positive than consumers of marine foods. Recent research on stable isotopes of sulphur (i.e., $^{34}S/^{32}S$) suggests that they may provide an additional means of identifying diets based on marine foods from those based on terrestrial foods because of the relatively greater abundance of ^{34}S in marine organisms (Krouse 1987). A preliminary study of prehistoric populations from coastal Chile has supported this distinction in human remains representative of marine and terrestrial subsistence economies (Kelley, Levesque, and Weidl 1991).

As already indicated, based on carbon stable isotope values alone, the contribution of maize to diets in populations consuming marine resources is difficult to assess from coastal areas of the New World because of the similarity of isotope signatures of marine foods

and individuals with partial maize diets (Schoeninger et al. 1990). However, by using both carbon and nitrogen isotope ratios, it is possible to distinguish between the relative contributions to diets of marine and terrestrial (e.g., maize) foods (Schoeninger et al. 1990).

Stable isotopes (C and N) have several advantages over trace elements in dietary documentation. For example, because bone collagen is not subject to isotopic exchange, diagenetic effects are not as important a confounding factor as in trace elemental analysis (Ambrose 1987; Grupe, Piepenbrink, and Schoeninger 1989). Perhaps the greatest advantage, however, is that because of the relative ease of removing the mineral component of bone (as well as fats and humic contaminants) and of confirming the collagen presence through identification of amino acids, the sample purity can be controlled (Ambrose 1987; Stafford, Brendel, and Duhamel 1988). However, collagen abundance declines in the burial matrix, and it is the first substance to degrade in bone decomposition (Grupe et al. 1989). If the decline in collagen value does not exceed 5 percent of the original value, then the isotopic information is suspect (see also Bada, Schoeninger, and Schimmelmann 1989; Schoeninger et al. 1990). Therefore, human fossil specimens, which typically contain little or no collagen, are generally not conducive to dietary reconstruction.

Teeth and Diet: Tooth Wear
Humankind has developed many means of processing foods before they are eaten. Nevertheless, virtually all foods have to be masticated by use of the teeth to one

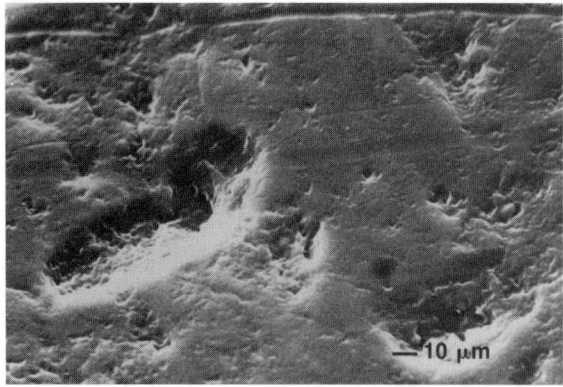

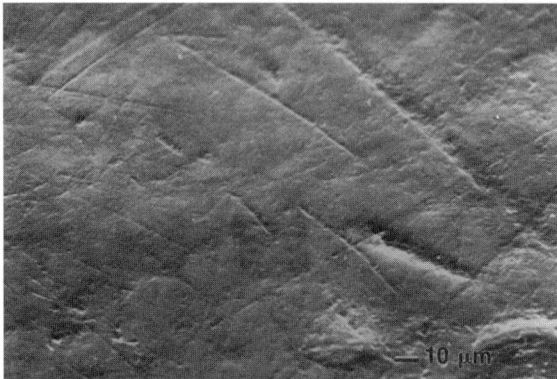

Figure I.1.2. Scanning electron micrographs (×500) of prehistoric hunter–gatherer molar (top) and historic agriculturalist molar (bottom) from the southeastern U.S. Atlantic coast. (From Teaford 1991, in *Advances in Dental Anthropology,* ed. Marc A. Kelley and Clark Spencer Larsen; ©1991; reprinted by permission of the author and Wiley-Liss, a division of John Wiley and Sons, Inc.)

extent or another before they are passed along for other digestive activities. Because food comes into contact with teeth, the chewing surfaces of teeth wear. Defined as "the loss of calcified tissues of a tooth by erosion, abrasion, attrition, or any combination of these" (Wallace 1974: 385), tooth wear – both microscopic and macroscopic – provides information on diets of past populations. The importance of tooth wear in the reconstruction of diet has been underscored by Phillip L. Walker (1978: 101), who stated, "From an archaeological standpoint, dietary information based on the analysis of dental attrition is of considerable value since it offers an independent check against reconstruction of prehistoric subsistence based on the analysis of floral, faunal and artifactual evidence."

Recent work with use of scanning electron microscopy (SEM) in the study of microwear on occlusal surfaces of teeth has begun to produce important data on diet in human populations (reviewed in Teaford 1991) (Figure I.1.2). Field and laboratory studies have shown

that microwear features can change rapidly. Therefore, microwear patterns may give information only on food items consumed shortly before death. These features, nevertheless, have been shown to possess remarkable consistency across human populations and various animal species and have, therefore, provided insight into past culinary habits. For example, hard-object feeders, including Miocene apes (e.g., *Sivapithecus*) as well as recent humans, consistently develop large pits on the chewing surfaces of teeth. In contrast, consumers of soft foods, such as certain agriculturalists (Bullington 1988; Teaford 1991), develop smaller and fewer pits as well as narrower and more frequently occurring scratches.

Macroscopic wear can also vary widely, depending upon a host of factors (Molnar 1972; Foley and Cruwys 1986; Hillson 1986; Larsen 1987; Benfer and Edwards 1991; Hartnady and Rose 1991; Walker, Dean, and Shapiro 1991). High on the list of factors affecting wear, however, are the types of foods consumed and manner of their preparation. Because most Western populations consume soft, processed foods with virtually all extraneous grit removed, tooth wear occurs very slowly. But non-Western populations consuming traditional foods (that frequently contain grit contaminants introduced via grinding stones) show rapid rates of dental wear (e.g., Hartnady and Rose 1991). Where there are shifts in food types (e.g., from hunting and gathering to agriculture) involving reduction in food hardness or changes in how these foods are processed (e.g., with stone versus wooden grinding implements), most investigators have found a reduction in gross wear (e.g., Anderson 1965, 1967; Walker 1978; Hinton, Smith, and Smith 1980; Smith, Smith, and Hinton 1980; Patterson 1984; Bennike 1985; Inoue, Ito, and Kamegai 1986; Benfer and Edwards 1991; Rose, Marks, and Tieszen 1991).

Consistent with reductions in tooth wear in the shift to softer diets are reductions in craniofacial robusticity, both in Old World settings (e.g., Carlson and Van Gerven 1977, 1979; Armelagos, Carlson, and Van Gerven 1982; y'Edynak and Fleisch 1983; Smith, Bar-Yosef, and Sillen 1984; Wu and Zhang 1985; Inoue et al. 1986; y'Edynak 1989) and in New World settings (e.g., Anderson 1967; Larsen 1982; Boyd 1988). In prehistoric Tennessee Amerindians, for example, Donna C. Boyd (1988) has documented a clear trend for a reduction in dimensions of the mandible and facial bones that reflects decreasing masticatory stress relating to a shift to soft foods. Although not all studies of this sort examine both craniofacial and dental wear changes, those that do so report reductions in both craniofacial robusticity and dental wear, reflecting a decrease in hardness of foods consumed (Anderson 1967; Inoue et al. 1986). Other changes accompanying shifts from hard-textured to soft-textured foods include an increase in malocclusion and crowding of teeth due to inadequate growth of the jaws (reviewed by Corruccini 1991).

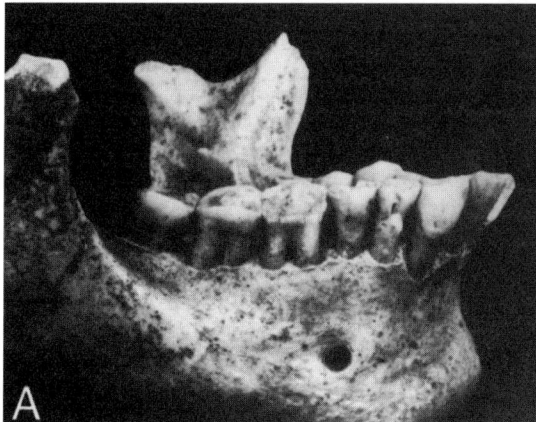

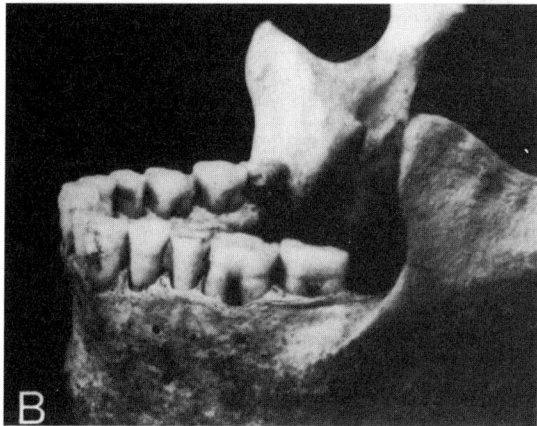

Figure I.1.3. Views of mandibular dentitions showing agriculturalist (A) and hunter–gatherer (B) wear planes. Note the angled wear on the agriculturalist's molars and the flat wear on the hunter-gatherer's molars. (From Smith 1984, in *American Journal of Physical Anthropology;* ©1984; reprinted by permission of the author and Wiley-Liss, a division of John Wiley and Sons, Inc.)

B. Holly Smith (1984, 1985) has found consistent patterns of tooth wear in human populations (Figure I.1.3). In particular, agriculturalists – regardless of regional differences – show highly angled molar wear planes in comparison with those of hunter-gatherers. The latter tend to exhibit more evenly distributed, flat wear. Smith interpreted the differences in tooth wear between agriculturalists and hunter-gatherers as reflecting greater "toughness" of hunter–gatherer foods.

Similarly, Robert J. Hinton (1981) has found in a large series of Native American dentitions representative of hunter-gatherers and agriculturalists that the former wear their anterior teeth (incisors and canines) at a greater rate than the latter. Agriculturalists that he studied show a tendency for cupped wear on the chewing surfaces of the anterior teeth. Because agriculturalists exhibit a relatively greater rate of premortem posterior tooth loss (especially molars), Hinton relates

the peculiar wear pattern of the anterior teeth to the use of these teeth in grinding food once the molars are no longer available for this masticatory activity.

Specific macroscopic wear patterns appear to arise as a result of chewing one type of food. In a prehistoric population from coastal Brazil, Christy G. Turner II and Lilia M. Machado (1983) found that in the anterior dentition the tooth surfaces facing the tongue were more heavily worn than the tooth surfaces facing the lips (Figure I.1.4.). They interpreted this wear pattern as reflecting the use of these teeth to peel or shred abrasive plants for dietary or extra-masticatory purposes.

Teeth and Diet: Dental Caries

The health of the dental hard tissues and their supporting bony structures are intimately tied to diet. Perhaps the most frequently cited disease that has been linked with diet is dental caries, which is defined as "a disease process characterized by the focal demineralization of dental hard tissues by organic acids produced by bacterial fermentation of dietary carbohydrates, especially sugars" (Larsen 1987: 375). If the decay of tooth crowns is left unchecked, it will lead to cavitation, loss of the tooth, and occasionally, infection and even death (cf. Calcagno and Gibson 1991). Carious lesions can develop on virtually any exposed surface of the tooth crown. However, teeth possessing grooves and fissures (especially posterior teeth) tend to trap food particles and are, therefore, more prone to colonization by indigenous bacteria, and thus to cariogenesis. Moreover, pits and linear depressions arising from poorly formed enamel (hypoplasia or hypocalcification) are also predisposed to caries attack, especially in populations with cariogenic diets (Powell 1985; Cook 1990) (Figure I.1.5).

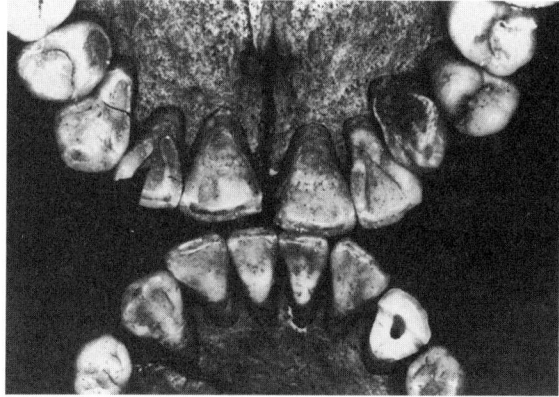

Figure I.1.4. Lingual wear on anterior teeth of prehistoric Brazilian Indian. (From Turner and Machado 1983; in *American Journal of Physical Anthropology;* ©1984; reprinted by permission of the authors and Wiley-Liss, a division of John Wiley and Sons, Inc.)

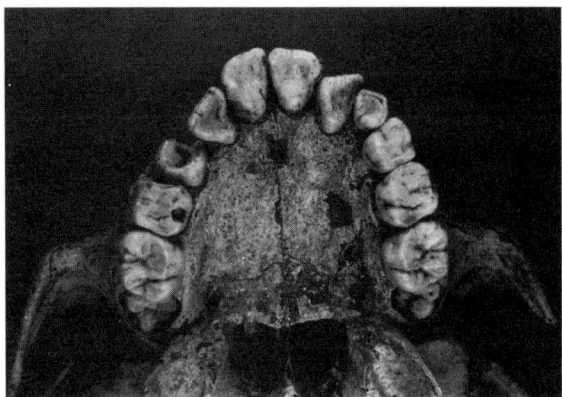

Figure I.1.5. Dental carious lesion in maxillary molar from historic Florida Indian. (Photograph by Mark C. Griffin.)

Dental caries is a disease with considerable antiquity in humans. F. E. Grine, A. J. Gwinnett, and J. H. Oaks (1990) note the occurrence of caries in dental remains of early hominids dating from about 1.5 million years ago (robust australopithecines and *Homo erectus*) from the Swartkrans site (South Africa), albeit at low prevalence levels. Later *Homo erectus* teeth from this site show higher prevalence than australopithecines, which may reflect their consumption of honey, a caries-promoting food (Grine et al. 1990). But with few exceptions (e.g., the Kabwe early archaic *Homo sapiens* from about 130,000 years before the present [Brothwell 1963]), caries prevalence has been found to be very low until the appearance of plant domestication in the early Holocene. David W. Frayer (1988) has documented one of these exceptions – an unusually high prevalence in a Mesolithic population from Portugal, which he relates to the possible consumption of honey and figs.

Turner (1979) has completed a worldwide survey of archaeological and living human populations whereby diet has been documented and the percentage of carious teeth has been tabulated. The samples were subdivided into three subsistence groups: hunting and gathering (*n* = 19 populations), mixed (combination of agriculture with hunting, gathering, or fishing; *n* = 13 populations), and agriculture (*n* = 32 populations). By pooling the populations within each subsistence group, Turner found that hunter-gatherers exhibited 1.7 percent carious teeth, mixed subsistence groups (combining hunting, gathering, and agriculture) exhibited 4.4 percent carious teeth, and agriculturalists exhibited 8.6 percent carious teeth.

Other researchers summarizing large comparative samples have confirmed these findings, especially with regard to a dichotomy in caries prevalence between hunter-gatherers and agriculturalists. Clark Spencer Larsen and co-workers (1991) compared 75 archaeological dental samples from the eastern United States. Only three agriculturalist populations

exhibited less than 7 percent carious teeth, and similarly, only three hunter–gatherer populations exhibited greater than 7 percent carious teeth. The greater frequencies of carious teeth in the agricultural populations are largely due to those people's consumption of maize (see also Milner 1984). The cariogenic component of maize is sucrose, a simple sugar that is more readily metabolized by oral bacteria than are more complex carbohydrates (Newbrun 1982). Another factor contributing to high caries prevalence in later agricultural populations may be due to the fact that maize is frequently consumed in the form of soft mushes. These foods have the tendency to become trapped in grooves and fissures of teeth, thereby enhancing the growth of plaque and contributing to tooth decay due to the metabolism of sugar by indigenous bacteria (see also Powell 1985).

High prevalence of dental caries does not necessarily indicate a subsistence regime that included maize agriculture, because other carbohydrates have been strongly implicated in prehistoric nonagricultural contexts. Philip Hartnady and Jerome C. Rose (1991) reported a high frequency of carious lesions – 14 percent – in the Lower Pecos region of southwest Texas. These investigators related elevated levels of caries to the consumption of plants high in carbohydrates, namely sotal, prickly pear, and lecheguilla. The fruit of prickly pear (known locally as tuna) contains a significant sucrose component in a sticky, pectin-based mucilage. The presence of a simple sugar in this plant food, coupled with its gummy nature, is clearly a caries-promoting factor (see also Walker and Erlandson 1986, and Kelley et al. 1991, for different geographical settings involving consumption of nonagricultural plant carbohydrates).

Nutritional Assessment

Growth and Development
One of the most striking characteristics of human physical growth during the period of infancy and childhood is its predictability (Johnston 1986; Bogin 1988). Because of this predictability, anthropometric approaches are one of the most commonly used indices in the assessment of health and well-being, including nutritional status (Yarbrough et al. 1974). In this regard, a number of growth standards based on living subjects have been established (Gracey 1987). Comparisons of individuals of known age with these standards make it possible to identify deviations from the "normal" growth trajectory.

Growth is highly sensitive to nutritional quality, especially during the earlier years of infancy and early childhood (birth to 2 years of age) when the human body undergoes very rapid growth. The relationship between nutrition and growth has been amply demonstrated by the observation of recent human populations experiencing malnutrition. These populations show a secular trend for reduced physical size of children and adults followed by increased physical size with improvements in diet (e.g., for Japanese, see Kimura 1984; Yagi, Takebe, and Itoh 1989; and for additional populations, Eveleth and Tanner 1976).

Based on a large sample of North Americans representative of different socioeconomic groups, Stanley M. Garn and co-workers (Garn, Owen, and Clark 1974; Garn and Clark 1975) reported that children in lower income families were shorter than those in higher income families (see also review in Bogin 1988). Although a variety of factors may be involved, presumably the most important is nutritional status.

One means of assessing nutrition and its influence on growth and development in past populations is by the construction of growth curves based on comparison of length of long bones in different juvenile age groups (e.g., Merchant and Ubelaker 1977; Sundick 1978; Hummert and Van Gerven 1983; Goodman, Lallo, et al. 1984; Jantz and Owsley 1984; Owsley and Jantz 1985; Lovejoy, Russell, and Harrison 1990) (Figure I.1.6). These data provide a reasonable profile of rate or velocity of growth. Della C. Cook (1984), for example, studied the remains of a group ranging in age from birth to 6 years. They were from a time-successive population in the midwestern United States undergoing the intensification of food production and increased reliance on maize agriculture. Her analysis revealed that individuals living during the introduction of maize had shorter femurs for their age than did individuals living before, as hunter-gatherers, or those living after, as maize-intensive agriculturalists (Cook 1984). Analysis of depressed growth among prehistoric hunter-gatherers at the Libben site (Ohio) suggests, however, that infectious disease was a more likely culprit in this context because the hunter–gatherers' nutrition - based on archaeological reconstruction of their diet - was adequate (Lovejoy et al. 1990).

Comparison of skeletal development, a factor responsive to nutritional insult, with dental development, a factor that is relatively less responsive to nutritional insult (see the section "Dental Development"), can provide corroborative information on nutritional status in human populations. In two series of archaeological populations from Nubia, K. P. Moore, S. Thorp, and D. P. Van Gerven (1986) compared skeletal age and dental age and found that most individuals (70.5 percent) had a skeletal age younger than their dental age. These findings were interpreted as reflecting significant retardation of skeletal growth that was probably related to high levels of nutritional stress. Indeed, undernutrition was confirmed by the presence of other indicators of nutritional insult, such as iron-deficiency anemia.

In living populations experiencing generally poor nutrition and health, if environmental insults are removed (e.g., if nutrition is improved), then children may increase in size, thereby more closely approximating their genetic growth potential (Bogin 1988). However, if disadvantageous conditions are sustained,

then it is unlikely that the growth potential will be realized. Thus, despite prolonged growth in undernourished populations, adult height is reduced by about 10 percent (Frisancho 1979). Sustained growth depression occurring during the years of growth and development, then, has almost certain negative consequences for final adult stature (Bogin 1988 and references cited therein).

In archaeological populations, reductions in stature have been reported in contexts with evidence for reduced nutritional quality. On the prehistoric Georgia coast, for example, there was a stature reduction of about 4 centimeters in females and 2 centimeters in males during the shift from hunting, gathering, and fishing to a mixed economy involving maize agriculture (Larsen 1982; Angel 1984; Kennedy 1984; Meiklejohn et al. 1984; Rose et al. 1984; and discussions in Cohen and Armelagos 1984; Larsen 1987; Cohen 1989). All workers documenting reductions in stature regard it as reflecting a shift to the relatively poor diets that are oftentimes associated with agricultural food production such as maize in North America.

Cortical Bone Thickness

Bone tissue, like any other tissue of the body, is subject to environmental influences, including nutritional quality. In the early 1960s, Garn and co-workers (1964) showed that undernourished Guatemalan children had reduced thickness of cortical (sometimes called compact) bone compared with better nourished children from the same region. Such changes were related to loss of bone during periods of acute protein energy malnutrition. These findings have been confirmed by a large number of clinical investigations (e.g., Himes et al. 1975; and discussion in Frisancho 1978).

Bone maintenance in archaeological skeletal populations has been studied by a number of investigators.

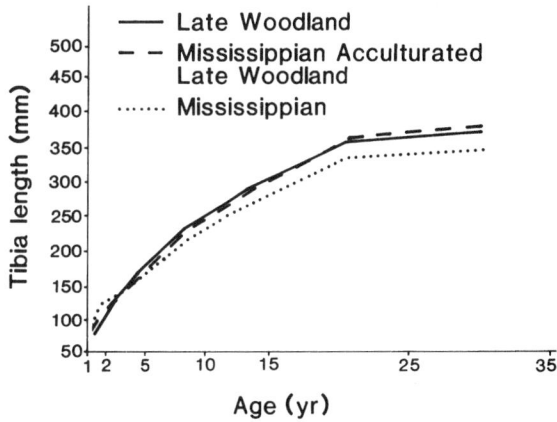

Figure I.1.6. Growth curves from Dickson Mounds, Illinois, Indian population. (Adapted from Lallo 1973; reproduced from Larsen 1987 with permission of Academic Press, Inc.)

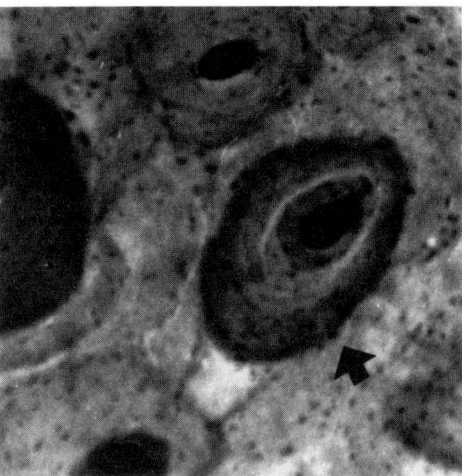

Figure I.1.7. Micrograph (×150) showing hypermineralized rings (dark zones) within an osteon from prehistoric Nubian. (Photograph courtesy of Debra L. Martin.)

Most frequently expressed as a ratio of the amount of cortical bone to subperiosteal area – or percent cortical area (PCCA) or percent cortical thickness (PCCT) – it has been interpreted by most people working with archaeological human remains as reflecting nutritional or health status (e.g., Cassidy 1984; Cook 1984; Brown 1988; Cohen 1989). It is important to note, however, that bone also remodels itself under conditions of mechanical demand, so that bone morphology that might be interpreted as reflecting a reduction in nutritional status may in fact represent an increase in mechanical loading (Ruff and Larsen 1990).

Cortical Bone Remodeling and Microstructure

An important characteristic that bone shares with other body tissues is that it must renew itself. The renewal of bone tissue, however, is unique in that the process involves destruction followed by replacement with new tissue. The characteristic destruction (resorption) and replacement (deposition) occurs mostly during the years of growth and development prior to adulthood, but it continues throughout the years following. Microstructures observable in bone cross sections have been analyzed and have provided important information about bone remodeling and its relationship to nutritional status. These microstructures include osteons (tunnels created by resorption and partially filled in by deposition of bone tissue), Haversian canals (central canals associated with osteons), and surrounding bone.

As with cortical thickness, there is a loss of bone mass that can be observed via measurement of the degree of porosity through either invasive (e.g., histological bone thin sections) or noninvasive (e.g., photon absorptiometry) means. With advancing age, cortical bone becomes both thinner and more porous. Cortical bone that has undergone a reduction in bone

mass per volume – a disorder called osteoporosis – should reflect the nutritional history of an individual, especially if age factors have been ruled out (Martin et al. 1985; Schaafsma et al. 1987; Arnaud and Sanchez 1990). If this is the case, then bone loss can affect any individual regardless of age (Stini 1990). Clinical studies have shown that individuals with low calcium intakes are more prone to bone loss in adulthood (Nordin 1973; Arnaud and Sanchez 1990; Stini 1990). It is important to emphasize, however, that osteoporosis is a complex, multifactorial disorder and is influenced by a number of risk factors, including nondietary ones such as body weight, degree of physical exercise, and heredity (Evers, Orchard, and Haddad 1985; Schaafsma et al. 1987; Arnaud and Sanchez 1990; Stini 1990; Ruff 1991; Lindsay and Cosman 1992; Heaney 1993).

Porosity of bone also represents a function of both the number of Haversian canals and their size (Atkinson 1964; Thompson 1980; Burr, Ruff, and Thompson 1990). Therefore, the greater the number and width of Haversian canals, the greater the porosity of bone tissue. The density of individual osteons appears to be related to nutritional quality as well. For example, the presence of osteons containing hypermineralized lines in archaeological human remains likely reflects periods of growth disturbance (e.g., Stout and Simmons 1979; Martin and Armelagos 1985) (Figure I.1.7).

Samuel D. Stout and co-workers (Stout and Teitelbaum 1976; Stout 1978, 1983, 1989) have made comparisons of bone remodeling dynamics between a series of hunter-gatherer and maize-dependent North and South American archaeological populations. Their findings show that the single agricultural population used in the study (Ledders, Illinois) had bone remodeling rates that were higher than the other (non-maize) populations. They suggested that because maize is low in calcium and high in phosphorus, parathyroid hormone levels could be increased. Bone remodeling is highly stimulated by parathyroid hormone, a disorder known as hyperparathyroidism.

In order to compensate for bone loss in aging adults (particularly after 40 years of age), there are structural adaptations involving more outward distribution of bone tissue in the limb bones. In older adults, such adaptation contributes to maintaining the biomechanical strength despite bone losses (Ruff and Hayes 1982). Similarly, D. B. Burr and R. B. Martin (1983; see also Burr et al. 1990) have suggested that the previously discussed material property changes may supplement structural changes. Thus, different rates of bone turnover in human populations may reflect mechanical adaptations that are not necessarily linked to poor nutrition.

Skeletal (Harris) Lines of Increased Density

Nonspecific markers of physiological stress that appear to have some links with nutrition status are radiographically visible lines of increased bone density, referred to as Harris lines (Figure I.1.8). These lines either partly or completely span the medullary cavities of tubular bones (especially long bones of the arms and legs) and trace the outlines of other bones (Garn et al. 1968; Steinbock 1976). These lines have been found to be associated with malnutrition in modern humans (e.g., Jones and Dean 1959) and in experimental animals (e.g., Stewart and Platt 1958). Because Harris lines develop during bone formation, age estimates can be made for time of occurrence relative to the primary ossification centers (e.g., Goodman and Clark 1981). However, the usefulness of these lines for nutritional assessment is severely limited by the fact that they frequently resorb in adulthood (Garn et al. 1968). Moreover, Harris lines have been documented in cases where an individual has not undergone episodes of nutritional or other stress (Webb 1989), and they appear to correlate negatively with other stress markers (reviewed in Larsen 1987).

Dental Development: Formation and Eruption
Like skeletal tissues, dental tissues are highly sensitive to nutritional perturbations that occur during the years of growth and development. Unlike skeletal tissues, however, teeth - crowns, in particular - do not remodel once formed, and they thereby provide a permanent "memory" of nutritional and health history. Alan H. Goodman and Jerome C. Rose (1991: 279) have underscored the importance of teeth in the anthropological study of nutrition: "Because of the inherent and close relationship between teeth and diet, the dental structures have incorporated a variety of characteristics that reflect what was placed in the mouth and presumably consumed" (see also Scott and Turner 1988).

There are two main factors involved in dental development - *formation* of crowns and roots and *eruption* of teeth. Because formation is more heritable than eruption, it is relatively more resistant to nutritional insult (Smith 1991). Moreover, the resistance of formation to environmental problems arising during the growth years is suggested by low correlations between formation and stature, fatness, body weight, or bone age, and lack of secular trend. Thus, timing of formation of tooth crowns represents a poor indicator for assessing nutritional quality in either living or archaeological populations. Eruption, however, can be affected by a number of factors, including caries, tooth loss, and severe malnutrition (e.g., Alvarez et al. 1988, 1990; Alvarez and Navia 1989). In a large, cross-sectional evaluation of Peruvian children raised in nutritionally deprived settings, J. O. Alvarez and co-workers (1988) found that exfoliation of the deciduous dentition was delayed. Other workers have found that eruption was delayed in populations experiencing nutritional deprivation (e.g., Barrett and Brown 1966; Alvarez et al. 1990). Unlike formation, eruption timing has been shown to be correlated with various measures of body size (Garn, Lewis, and Polacheck 1960; McGregor, Thomson, and Billewicz 1968). To my

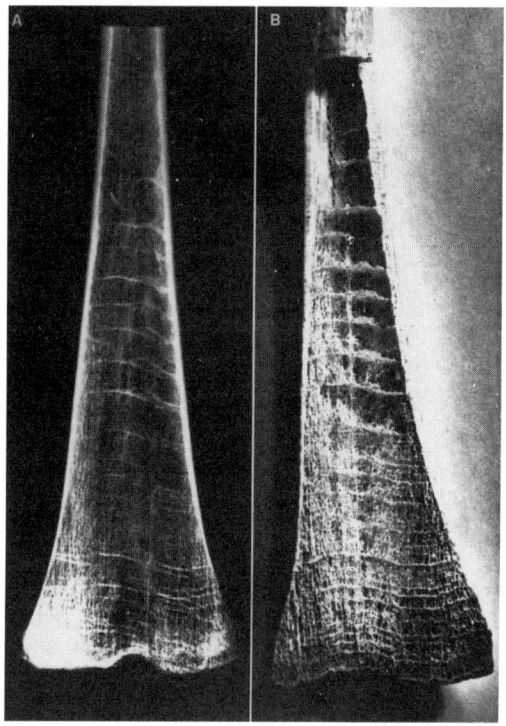

Figure I.1.8. Radiograph (A) and section (B) of prehistoric California Indian femur with Harris lines. (From McHenry 1968, in *American Journal of Physical Anthropology;* ©1968; reprinted by permission of author and Wiley-Liss, a division of John Wiley and Sons, Inc.)

knowledge, there have been no archaeological populations where delayed eruption timing has been related to nutritional status.

Dental Development: Tooth Size
Unlike formation timing, tooth size appears to be under the influence of nutritional status. Garn and co-workers (Garn and Burdi 1971; Garn, Osborne, and McCabe 1979) have indicated that maternal health status is related to size of deciduous and permanent dentitions. Nutrition and tooth size in living populations has not been examined. However, the role of nutrition as a contributing factor to tooth size reduction has been strongly implicated in archaeological contexts. Mark F. Guagliardo (1982) and Scott W. Simpson, Dale L. Hutchinson, and Clark Spencer Larsen (1990) have inferred that the failure of teeth to reach their maximum genetic size potential occurs in populations experiencing nutritional stress. That is, comparison of tooth size in populations dependent upon maize agriculture revealed that juveniles had consistently smaller teeth than adults. Moreover, a reduction in deciduous tooth size in comparison between hunter-gatherers and maize agriculturalists on the prehistoric southeastern U. S. coast was reported by Larsen (1983). Because

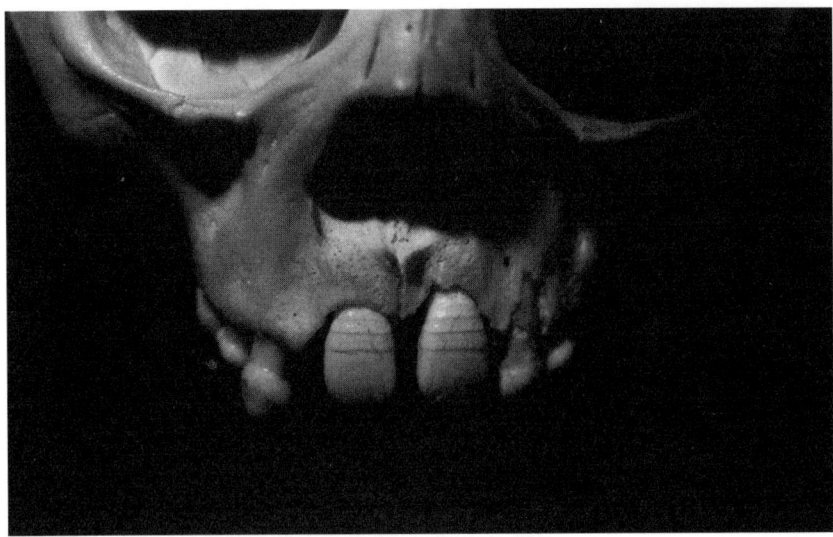

Figure I.1.9. Juvenile anterior dentition showing hypoplasias on incompletely erupted incisors. (Photograph by Barry Stark.)

deciduous tooth crowns are largely formed *in utero,* it was suggested that smaller teeth in the later period resulted from a reduction in maternal health status and placental environment.

Dental Development: Macrodefects

A final approach to assessing the nutritional and health status of contemporary and archaeological populations has to do with the analysis of enamel defects in the teeth, particularly hypoplasias (Figure I.1.9). Hypoplasias are enamel defects that typically occur as circumferential lines, grooves, or pits resulting from the death or cessation of enamel-producing cells (ameloblasts) and the failure to form enamel matrix (Goodman and Rose 1990). Goodman and Rose (1991) have reviewed a wide array of experimental, epidemiological, and bioarchaeological evidence in order to determine whether hypoplasias represent an important means for assessing nutritional status in human populations, either contemporary or archaeological. They indicate that although enamel hypoplasias arising from systemic (e.g., nutrition) versus nonsystemic factors (e.g., localized trauma) are easily identifiable, identification of an exact cause for the defects remains an intractable problem. T. W. Cutress and G. W. Suckling (1982), for example, have listed nearly 100 factors that have a causal relationship with hypoplasias, including nutritional problems. The results of a number of research projects have shown that a high frequency of individuals who have experienced malnutrition have defective enamel, thus suggesting that enamel is relatively sensitive to undernutrition. Moreover, it is a straightforward process to estimate the age at which individual hypoplasias occur based on matching the hypoplasia with dental developmental sequences (e.g., Goodman, Armelagos, and Rose 1980; Rose, Condon, and Goodman 1985; Hutchinson and Larsen 1988).

Studies based on archaeological human remains have examined hypoplasia prevalence and pattern (reviewed in Huss-Ashmore et al. 1982; Larsen 1987). In addition to determining frequency of enamel defects (which tends to be higher in agricultural populations), this research has looked at the location of defects on tooth crowns in order to examine age at the time of defect development. Contrary to earlier assertions that age pattern of defects are universal in humans, with most hypoplasias occurring in the first year of life (e.g., Sarnat and Schour 1941; see discussion in Goodman 1988), these studies have served to show that there is a great deal of variability in age of occurrence of hypoplasias. By and large, however, most reports on age patterning in hypoplasia occurrence indicate a peak in defects at 2 to 4 years of age, regardless of geographic or ecological setting (Hutchinson and Larsen 1988; Goodman and Rose 1991), a factor that most workers have attributed to nutritional stresses of postweaning diets (e.g., Corruccini, Handler, and Jacobi 1985; Webb 1989; Blakely and Mathews 1990; Simpson et al. 1990). Analyses of prevalence and pattern of hypoplasia in past populations have largely focused on recent archaeological populations. In this respect, there is a tendency for agricultural groups to show higher prevalence rates than nonagricultural (hunter-gatherer) populations (e.g., Sciulli 1978; Goodman et al. 1984a, 1984b; Hutchinson and Larsen 1988).

Unlike most other topics discussed in this chapter, this indicator of physiological stress has been investigated in ancient hominids. In the remains of early hominids in Africa, the Plio-Pleistocene australopithecines, P. V. Tobias (1967) and Tim D. White (1978) have noted the presence of hypoplasias and provided some speculation on relative health status. Of more importance, however, are the recent analyses of hypoplasias in European and Near-Eastern Neanderthal (Middle Paleolithic) populations. Marsha D. Ogilvie, Bryan K. Curran, and Erik Trinkaus (1989) have recorded prevalence data and estimates of developmental ages of defects on most of the extant Neanderthal teeth ($n = 669$ teeth). Their results indicate high prevalence, particularly in the permanent teeth (41.9 percent permanent teeth, 3.9 percent deciduous teeth). Although these prevalences are not as high as those observed in recent archaeological populations (e.g., Hutchinson and Larsen 1990; Van Gerven, Beck, and Hummert 1990), they do indicate elevated levels of stress in these ancient peoples. Unlike other dental series, age of occurrence of hypoplasias on the permanent dentition follows two distinct peaks, including an earlier peak between ages 2 and 5 years and a later peak between ages 11 and 13 years. The earlier peak is consistent with findings of other studies. That is, it may reflect nutritional stresses associated with weaning (Ogilvie et al. 1989). The later peak may simply represent overall high levels of systemic stress in Neanderthals. Because genetic disorders were likely eliminated from the gene pool, Ogilvie and co-workers argue against genetic agents as a likely cause. Moreover, the very low prevalence of infection in Neanderthal populations suggests that infection was an unlikely cause, leaving nutritional deficiencies, especially in the form of periodic food shortages, as the most likely causative agents.

Analysis of dental hypoplasia prevalence from specific Neanderthal sites confirms the findings of Ogilvie and co-workers, particularly with regard to the Krapina Neanderthal sample from eastern Europe (e.g., Molnar and Molnar 1985). With the Krapina dental series, Larsen and co-workers (in preparation) have made observations on the prevalence of an enamel defect known as hypocalcification, which is a disruption of the mineralization process following deposition of enamel matrix by ameloblasts. The presence of these types of enamel defects confirms the unusually high levels of stress in these early hominid populations, which is likely related to undernutrition.

Dental Development: Microdefects

An important complement to the research done on macrodefects has been observations of histological indicators of physiological stress known as Wilson bands or accentuated stria of Retzius (Rose et al. 1985; Goodman and Rose 1990). Wilson bands are features visible in thin section under low magnification ($\times 100$ to $\times 200$) as troughs or ridges in the flat enamel surface (Figure I.1.10). Concordance of these defects with hypoplasias is frequent, but certainly not universal in humans (Goodman and Rose 1990), a factor that may be related to differences in histology or etiology or both (Rose et al. 1985; Danforth 1989). K. W. Condon (1981) has concluded that Wilson bands may represent short-term stress episodes (less than one week), and hypoplasias may represent long-term stress episodes (several weeks to two months).

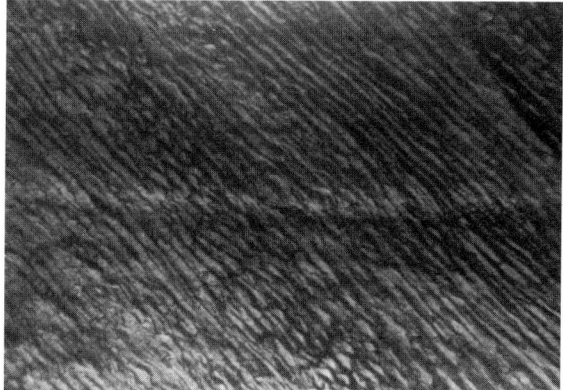

Figure I.1.10. Micrograph ($\times 160$) of canine tooth showing Wilson band from Native American Libben site. (Photograph courtesy of Jerome C. Rose.)

Jerome C. Rose, George J. Armelagos, and John W. Lallo (1978) have tested the hypothesis that as maize consumption increased and animal sources of protein consumption decreased in a weaning diet, there should be a concomitant increase in frequency of Wilson bands. Indeed, there was a fourfold increase in rate (per individual) in the full agriculturalists compared with earlier hunter-gatherers. They concluded that the declining quality of nutrition reduced the resistance of the child to infectious disease, thus increasing the individual's susceptibility to infection and likelihood of exhibiting a Wilson band. Most other studies on prehistoric populations from other cultural and geographic contexts have confirmed these findings (references cited in Rose et al. 1985).

Specific Nutritional Deficiency Diseases

Much of what is known about the nutritional quality of diets of past populations is based on the nonspecific indicators just discussed. It is important to emphasize that rarely is it possible to relate a particular hard-tissue pathology with a specific nutritional factor in archaeological human remains, not only because different nutritional problems may exhibit similar pathological signatures, but also because of the synergy between undernutrition and infection (Scrimshaw, Taylor, and Gordon 1968; Gabr 1987). This relationship has been succinctly summarized by Michael Gracey (1987: 201): "Malnourished children characteristically are enmeshed in a 'malnutrition-infection' cycle being more prone to infections which, in turn, tend to worsen the nutritional state." Thus, an episode of infection potentially exacerbates the negative effects of undernutrition as well as the severity of the pathological signature reflecting those effects.

Patricia Stuart-Macadam (1989) has reviewed evidence for the presence in antiquity of three specific nutritional diseases: scurvy, rickets, and iron-deficiency anemia. Scurvy and rickets are produced by respective deficiencies in vitamin C (ascorbic acid) and vitamin D. Vitamin C is unusual in that it is required in the diets of humans and other primates, but only of a few other animals. Among its other functions, it serves in the synthesis of collagen, the structural protein of the connective tissues (skin, cartilage, and bone). Thus, if an individual is lacking in vitamin C, the formation of the premineralized component of bone (osteoid) will be considerably reduced.

Rickets is a disease affecting infants and young children resulting from insufficiencies in either dietary sources of vitamin D (e.g., fish and dairy products) or, of greater importance, lack of exposure to sunlight. The insufficiency reduces the ability of bone tissue to mineralize, resulting in skeletal elements (especially long bones) that are more susceptible to deformation such as abnormal bending (Figure I.1.11).

Both scurvy and rickets have been amply documented through historical accounts and in clinical settings (see Stuart-Macadam 1989). Radiographic documentation shows that bones undergoing rapid growth – namely in infants and young children – have the greatest number of changes. In infants, for example, ends of long bones and ribs are most affected and show "generalized bone atrophy and a thickening and increased density" (Stuart-Macadam 1989: 204). In children, rickets can be expressed as thin and porous bone with wide marrow spaces in general undernourishment. Alternatively, in better nourished individuals, bone tissue is more porous because of excessive bone deposition. Children with rickets can oftentimes show pronounced bowing of long bones with respect to both weight-bearing (leg) and non-weight-bearing (arm) bones.

Both scurvy and rickets, however, have been only marginally documented in the archaeological record, and mostly in historical contexts from the medieval period onward (Moller-Christiansen 1958; Maat 1982). Stuart-Macadam (1989) notes that only in the period of industrialization during the nineteenth century in Europe and North America has rickets shown an increase in prevalence.

Anemia is any condition where hemoglobin or red blood cells are reduced below normal levels. Iron-deficiency anemia is by far the most common form in living peoples, affecting more than a half billion of the current world population (Baynes and Bothwell 1990). Iron is an essential mineral, which must be ingested. It plays an important role in many body functions, especially the transport of oxygen to the body tissues (see Stuart-Macadam 1989). The bioavailability of iron from dietary sources results from several factors (see Hallberg 1981; Baynes and Bothwell 1990). With respect to its absorption, the major determinants are the sources of iron contained within foods consumed depending upon the form, heme or nonheme. Heme sources of iron from animal products are efficiently absorbed (Baynes and Bothwell 1990).

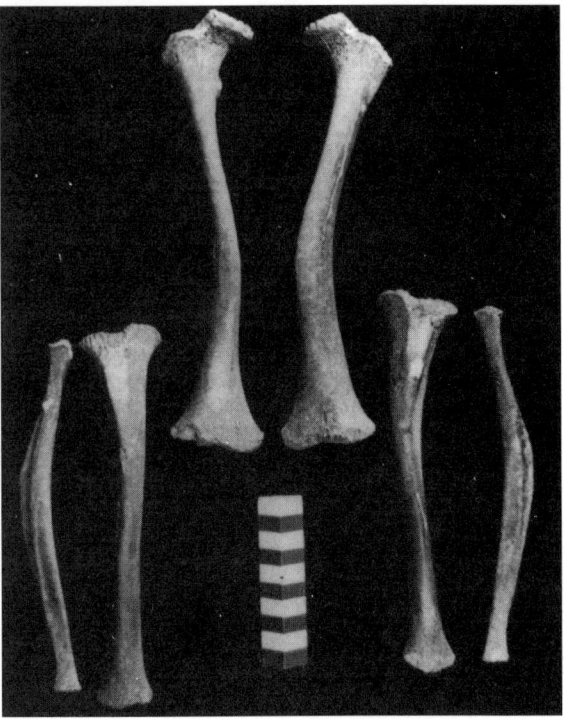

Figure I.1.11. Femora and tibiae of nineteenth-century black American showing limb bone deformation due to rickets. (Photograph by Donald J. Ortner; from Stuart-Macadam 1989, in *Reconstruction of Life from the Skeleton,* ed. Mehmet Yasar Iscan and Kenneth A. R. Kennedy; ©1989; reprinted by permission of the author and Wiley-Liss, a division of John Wiley and Sons, Inc.)

In contrast, nonheme forms of iron from the various vegetable foods have a great deal of variation in their bioavailability. Moreover, a number of substances found in foods actually inhibit iron absorption. Phytates found in many nuts (e.g., almonds, walnuts), cereals (e.g., maize, rice, whole wheat flour), and legumes inhibit dietary iron bioavailability (summarized in Baynes and Bothwell 1990). Moreover, unlike the sources of protein found in meat, plant proteins, such as soybeans, nuts, and lupines, inhibit iron absorption. Thus, populations depending on plants generally experience reduced levels of iron bioavailability. Tannates found in tea and coffee also significantly reduce iron absorption (Hallberg 1981).

There are, however, a number of foods known to enhance iron bioavailability in combination with nonheme sources of iron. For example, ascorbic acid is a very strong promotor of iron absorption (Hallberg 1981; Baynes and Bothwell 1990). Citric acid from various fruits has also been implicated in promoting iron absorption, as has lactic acid from fermented cereal beers (Baynes and Bothwell 1990). In addition, Miguel Layrisse, Carlos Martinez-Torres, and Marcel Roche

(1968; and see follow-up studies cited in Hallberg 1981) have provided experimental evidence from living human subjects that nonheme iron absorption is enhanced considerably by consumption of meat and fish, although the specific mechanism for this enhancement is not clear (Hallberg 1981).

Iron-deficiency anemia can be caused by a variety of other, nondietary factors, including parasitic infection, hemorrhage, blood loss, and diarrhea; infants can be affected by predisposing factors such as low birth weight, gender, and premature clamping of the umbilical cord (Stuart-Macadam 1989, and references cited therein). The skeletal changes observed in the clinical and laboratory settings are primarily found in the cranium, and include the following: increased width of the space between the inner and outer surfaces of the cranial vault and roof areas of the eye orbits; unusual thinning of the outer surface of the cranial vault; and a "hair-on-end" orientation of the trabecular bone between the inner and outer cranial vault (Huss-Ashmore et al. 1982; Larsen 1987; Stuart-Macadam 1989; Hill and Armelagos 1990). Postcranial changes have also been observed (e.g., Angel 1966) but are generally less severe and in reduced frequency relative to genetic anemias (Stuart-Macadam 1989). The skeletal modifications result from the hypertrophy of the blood-forming tissues in order to increase the output of red blood cells in response to the anemia (Steinbock 1976).

Skeletal changes similar to those documented in living populations have been found in archaeological human remains from virtually every region of the globe. In archaeological materials, the bony changes – pitting and/or expansion of cranial bones – have been identified by various terms, most typically *porotic hyperostosis* (Figure I.1.12) or *cribra orbitalia* (Figure I.1.13). These lesions have rarely been observed prior to the adoption of sedentism and agriculture during the Holocene, but J. Lawrence Angel (1978) has noted occasional instances extending into the Middle Pleistocene. Although the skeletal changes have been observed in individuals of all ages and both sexes, Stuart-Macadam (1985) has concluded that iron-deficiency anemia produces them in young children during the time that most of the growth in cranial bones is occurring. By contrast, the presence of porotic hyperostosis and its variants in adults represents largely anemic episodes relating to the early years of growth and development. Thus, it is not possible to evaluate iron status in adults based on this pathology.

Many workers have offered explanations for the presence of porotic hyperostosis since the pathology was first identified more than a century ago (Hill and Armelagos 1990). Recent discussions, however, have emphasized local circumstances, including nutritional deprivation brought about by focus on intensive maize consumption, or various contributing circumstances such as parasitism, diarrheal infection, or a

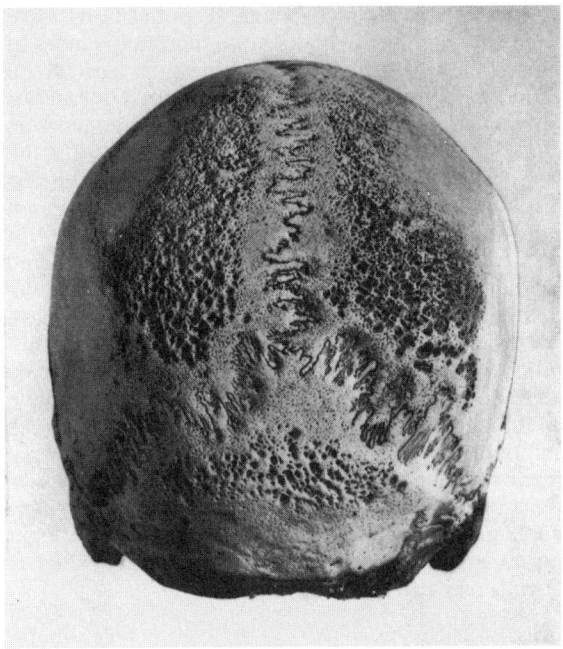

Figure I.1.12. Porotic hyperostosis on prehistoric Peruvian Indian posterior cranium. (Reproduced from Hrdli čka 1914.)

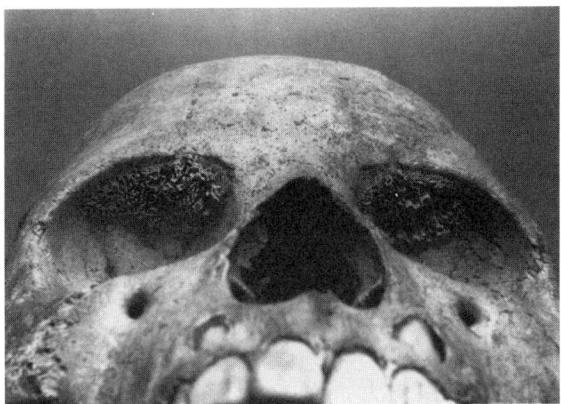

Figure I.1.13. Cribra orbitalia in historic Florida Indian. (Photograph by Mark C. Griffin.)

combination of these factors (e.g., Hengen 1971; Carlson, Armelagos, and Van Gerven 1974; Cybulski 1977; El-Najjar 1977; Mensforth et al. 1978; Kent 1986; Walker 1986; Webb 1989). Angel (1966, 1971) argued that the primary cause for the presence of porotic hyperostosis in the eastern Mediterranean region was the presence of abnormal hemoglobins, especially thalassemia. His hypothesis, however, has remained largely unsubstantiated (Larsen 1987; Hill and Armelagos 1990).

Several human archaeological populations have been shown to have moderate to high frequencies of porotic hyperostosis after establishing agricultural economies. However, this is certainly not a ubiquitous phenomenon. For example, Larsen and co-workers (1992) and Mary L. Powell (1990) have noted that the late prehistoric populations occupying the southeastern U.S. Atlantic coast have a very low prevalence of porotic hyperostosis. These populations depended in part on maize, a foodstuff that has been implicated in reducing iron bioavailability. But a strong dependence on marine resources (especially fish) may have greatly enhanced iron absorption. In the following historic period, these native populations show marked increase in porotic hyperostosis. This probably came about because after the arrival of Europeans, consumption of maize greatly increased and that of marine resources decreased. Moreover, native populations began to use sources of water that were likely contaminated by parasites, which would have brought on an increase in the prevalence of iron-deficiency anemia (see Larsen et al. 1992).

Conclusions

This chapter has reviewed a range of skeletal and dental indicators that anthropologists have used in the reconstruction of diet and assessment of nutrition in past human populations. As noted throughout, such reconstruction and assessment, where we are dealing only with the hard-tissue remains, is especially difficult because each indicator is so often affected by other factors that are not readily controlled. For this reason, anthropologists attempt to examine as many indicators as possible in order to derive the most complete picture of diet and nutrition.

In dealing with archaeological skeletal samples, there are numerous cultural and archaeological biases that oftentimes affect the sample composition. Jane E. Buikstra and James H. Mielke have suggested:

> Human groups have been remarkably creative in developing customs for disposal of the dead. Bodies have been interred, cremated, eviscerated, mummified, turned into amulets, suspended in trees, and floated down watercourses. Special cemetery areas have been reserved for persons of specific status groups or individuals who died in particular ways; for example, suicides. This variety in burial treatments can provide the archaeologist with important information about social organization in the past. On the other hand, it can also severely limit reliability of demographic parameters estimated from an excavated sample. (Buikstra and Mielke 1985: 364)

Various workers have reported instances of cultural biases affecting cemetery composition. In late prehis-

toric societies in the eastern United States, young individuals and sometimes others were excluded from burial in primary cemeteries (e.g., Buikstra 1976; Russell, Choi, and Larsen 1990), although poor preservation of thinner bones of these individuals – particularly infants and young children – along with excavation biases of archaeologists, can potentially contribute to misrepresentation (Buikstra, Konigsberg, and Bullington 1986; Larsen 1987; Walker, Johnson, and Lambert 1988; Milner, Humpf, and Harpending 1989). This is not to say that skeletal samples offer a poor choice for assessing diet and nutrition in past populations. Rather, all potential biases – cultural and noncultural – must be evaluated when considering the entire record of morbidity revealed by the study of bones and teeth.

Representation in skeletal samples is made especially problematical when considering the potential for differential access to foods consumed by past human societies. For example, as revealed by analysis of prevalence of dental caries, women ate more cariogenic carbohydrates than men in many agricultural or partially agricultural societies (reviewed in Larsen 1987; Larsen et al. 1991). Even in contemporary foraging groups where food is supposedly equitably distributed among all members regardless of age or gender, various observers have found that women frequently receive less protein and fats than men, and that their diet is often nutritionally inferior to that of males (reviewed in Speth 1990). In these so-called egalitarian societies, women are regularly subject to food taboos, including a taboo on meat (e.g., Hausman and Wilmsen 1985; see discussions by Spielmann 1989 and Speth 1990). Such taboos can be detrimental especially if they are imposed during critical periods such as pregnancy or lactation (Spielmann 1989; Speth 1990). If nutritional deprivation occurs during either pregnancy or lactation, the health of the fetus or infant can be severely compromised, and delays in growth are likely to occur. Thus, when assessing nutrition in past populations, it is important that contributing factors affecting quality of diet in females or other members of societies (e.g., young children, old adults) and potential for variability in health of these individuals be carefully evaluated.

Of equal importance in the study of skeletal remains is the role of other sources of information regarding diet in archaeological settings, especially plant and animal remains. All available sources should be integrated into a larger picture, including plant and animal food remains recovered from archaeological sites, and corroborative information made available from the study of settlement patterns and ethnographic documentation of subsistence economy. The careful consideration of all these sources of information facilitates a better understanding of diet and nutrition in peoples of the past.

Clark Spencer Larsen

Bibliography

Alvarez, J. O., J. C. Eguren, J. Caceda, and J. M. Navia. 1990. The effect of nutritional status on the age distribution of dental caries in the primary teeth. *Journal of Dental Research* 69: 1564-6.

Alvarez, J. O., Charles A. Lewis, Carlos Saman, et al. 1988. Chronic malnutrition, dental caries, and tooth exfoliation in Peruvians aged 3-9 years. *American Journal of Clinical Nutrition* 48: 368-72.

Alvarez, J. O., and Juan M. Navia. 1989. Nutritional status, tooth eruption, and dental caries: A review. *American Journal of Clinical Nutrition* 49: 417-26.

Ambrose, Stanley H. 1987. Chemical and isotopic techniques of diet reconstruction in eastern North America. In *Emergent horticultural economies of the eastern Woodlands,* ed. William F. Keegan, 87-107. Center for Archaeological Investigations, Southern Illinois University Occasional Paper No. 7. Carbondale, Ill.

Anderson, James E. 1965. Human skeletons of Tehuacan. *Science* 148: 496-7.

1967. The human skeletons. In *The prehistory of the Tehuacan Valley: Vol. 1. Environment and subsistence,* ed. Douglas S. Byers, 91-113. Austin, Texas.

Angel, J. Lawrence. 1966. Porotic hyperostosis, anemias, malarias, and marshes in the prehistoric eastern Mediterranean. *Science* 153: 760-3.

1971. *The people of Lerna.* Washington, D.C.

1978. Porotic hyperostosis in the eastern Mediterranean. *Medical College of Virginia Quarterly* 14: 10-16.

1984. Health as a crucial factor in the changes from hunting to developed farming in the eastern Mediterranean. In *Paleopathology at the origins of agriculture,* ed. Mark Nathan Cohen and George J. Armelagos, 51-73. Orlando, Fla.

Armelagos, George J., David S. Carlson, and Dennis P. Van Gerven. 1982. The theoretical foundations and development of skeletal biology. In *A history of American physical anthropology: 1930-1980,* ed. Frank Spencer, 305-28. New York.

Arnaud, C. D., and S. D. Sanchez. 1990. The role of calcium in osteoporosis. *Annual Review of Nutrition* 10: 397-414.

Atkinson, P. J. 1964. Quantitative analysis of cortical bone. *Nature* 201: 373-5.

Aufderheide, Arthur C. 1989. Chemical analysis of skeletal remains. In *Reconstruction of life from the skeleton,* ed. Mehmet Yasar Iscan and Kenneth A. R. Kennedy, 237-60. New York.

Bada, J. L., M. J. Schoeninger, and A. Schimmelmann. 1989. Isotopic fractionation during peptide bond hydrolysis. *Geochimica et Cosmochimica Acta* 53: 3337-41.

Barrett, M. J., and T. Brown. 1966. Eruption of deciduous teeth in Australian aborigines. *Australian Dental Journal* 11: 43-50.

Baynes, R. D., and T. H. Bothwell. 1990. Iron deficiency. *Annual Review of Nutrition* 10: 133-48.

Benfer, Robert A., and Daniel S. Edwards. 1991. The principal axis method for measuring rate and amount of dental attrition: Estimating juvenile or adult tooth wear from unaged adult teeth. In *Advances in dental anthropology,* ed. Marc A. Kelley and Clark Spencer Larsen, 325-40. New York.

Bennike, Pia. 1985. *Palaeopathology of Danish skeletons.* Copenhagen.

Blakely, Robert L., and David S. Mathews. 1990. Bioarchaeological evidence for a Spanish-Native American conflict in the sixteenth-century Southeast. *American Antiquity* 55: 718-44.

Bogin, Barry. 1988. *Patterns of human growth.* New York.

Boyd, Donna Catherine Markland. 1988. A functional model for masticatory-related mandibular, dental, and craniofacial microevolutionary change derived from a selected Southeastern Indian skeletal temporal series. Ph.D. thesis, University of Tennessee.

Bray, Francesca. 1989. *The rice economies: Technology and development in Asian societies.* Cambridge, Mass.

Brothwell, Don R. 1963. The macroscopic dental pathology of some earlier human populations. In *Dental anthropology,* ed. D. R. Brothwell, 271-88. New York.

Brown, Antoinette B. 1988. Diet and nutritional stress. In *The King site: Continuity and contact in sixteenth century Georgia,* ed. Robert L. Blakely, 73-86. Athens, Ga.

Buikstra, Jane E. 1976. *Hopewell in the lower Illinois River Valley: A regional approach to the study of biological variability and mortuary activity.* Northwestern University Archaeological Program, Scientific Papers No. 2.

Buikstra, Jane E., Lyle W. Konigsberg, and Jill Bullington. 1986. Fertility and the development of agriculture in the prehistoric Midwest. *American Antiquity* 51: 528-46.

Buikstra, Jane E., and James H. Mielke. 1985. Demography, diet, and health. In *The analysis of prehistoric diets,* ed. Robert I. Gilbert, Jr., and James H. Mielke, 359-422. Orlando, Fla.

Bullington, Jill. 1988. Deciduous dental microwear in middle woodland and Mississippian populations from the lower Illinois River Valley. Ph.D. thesis, Northwestern University.

Bumsted, M. Pamela. 1985. Past human behavior from bone chemical analysis: Respects and prospects. *Journal of Human Evolution* 14: 539-51.

Burr, D. B., and R. B. Martin. 1983. The effects of composition, structure and age on the torsional properties of the human radius. *Journal of Biomechanics* 16: 603-8.

Burr, D. B., Christopher B. Ruff, and David D. Thompson. 1990. Patterns of skeletal histologic change through time: Comparison of an archaic Native American population with modern populations. *The Anatomical Record* 226: 307-13.

Burton, J. H., and T. D. Price. 1990. The ratio of barium to strontium as a paleodietary indicator of consumption of marine resources. *Journal of Archaeological Science* 17: 547-57.

Calcagno, James M., and Kathleen R. Gibson. 1991. Selective compromise: Evolutionary trends and mechanisms in hominid tooth size. In *Advances in dental anthropology,* ed. Marc A. Kelley and Clark Spencer Larsen, 59-76. New York.

Carlson, D. S., George J. Armelagos, and Dennis P. Van Gerven. 1974. Factors influencing the etiology of cribra orbitalia in prehistoric Nubia. *Journal of Human Evolution* 3: 405-10.

Carlson, D. S., and Dennis P. Van Gerven. 1977. Masticatory function and post-Pleistocene evolution in Nubia. *American Journal of Physical Anthropology* 46: 495-506.

1979. Diffusion, biological determinism, and biocultural adaptation in the Nubian Corridor. *American Anthropologist* 81: 561-80.

Cassidy, Claire Monod. 1984. Skeletal evidence for prehistoric subsistence adaptation in the central Ohio River Valley. In *Paleopathology at the origins of agriculture,* ed. Mark Nathan Cohen and George J. Armelagos, 307-45. Orlando, Fla.

Cohen, Mark Nathan. 1989. *Health and the rise of civilization.* New Haven, Conn.

Cohen, Mark Nathan, and George J. Armelagos. 1984. Paleopathology at the origins of agriculture: Editors' summation. In *Paleopathology at the origins of agriculture,* ed. Mark Nathan Cohen and George J. Armelagos, 585–601. Orlando, Fla.

Condon, K. W. 1981. The correspondence of developmental enamel defects between the mandibular canine and first premolar. *American Journal of Physical Anthropology* 54: 211.

Cook, Della Collins. 1984. Subsistence and health in the lower Illinois Valley: Osteological evidence. In *Paleopathology at the origins of agriculture,* ed. Mark Nathan Cohen and George J. Armelagos, 237–69. Orlando, Fla.

1990. Epidemiology of circular caries: A perspective from prehistoric skeletons. In *A life in science: Papers in honor of J. Lawrence Angel,* ed. Jane E. Buikstra. Center for American Archeology, Scientific Papers No. 6: 64–86. Kampsville, Ill.

Corruccini, Robert S. 1991. Anthropological aspects of orofacial and occlusal variations and anomalies. In *Advances in dental anthropology,* ed. Marc A. Kelley and Clark Spencer Larsen, 295–324. New York.

Corruccini, Robert S., Jerome S. Handler, and Keith P. Jacobi. 1985. Chronological distribution of enamel hypoplasias and weaning in a Caribbean slave population. *Human Biology* 57: 699–711.

Cutress, T. W., and G. W. Suckling. 1982. The assessment of non-carious defects of the enamel. *International Dental Journal* 32: 119–22.

Cybulski, Jerome S. 1977. Cribra orbitalia, a possible sign of anemia in early historic native populations of the British Columbia coast. *American Journal of Physical Anthropology* 47: 31–40.

Danforth, Marie Elaine. 1989. A comparison of childhood health patterns in the late classic and colonial Maya using enamel microdefects. Ph.D. thesis, Indiana University.

El-Najjar, Mahmoud Y. 1977. Maize, malaria and the anemias in the pre-Columbian New World. *Yearbook of Physical Anthropology* 20: 329–37.

Eveleth, Phyllis B., and James M. Tanner. 1976. *World-wide variation in human growth.* Cambridge.

Evers, Susan E., John W. Orchard, and Richard G. Haddad. 1985. Bone density in postmenopausal North American Indian and Caucasian females. *Human Biology* 57: 719–26.

FAO (Food and Agricultural Organization). 1970. *Amino-acid content of foods and biological data on proteins.* Rome.

Foley, Robert, and Elizabeth Cruwys. 1986. Dental anthropology: Problems and perspectives. In *Teeth and anthropology,* ed. E. Cruwys and R. A. Foley. BAR International Series 291: 1–20. Oxford.

Fomon, S. J., F. Haschke, E. E. Ziegler, and S. E. Nelson. 1982. Body composition of children from birth to age 10 years. *American Journal of Clinical Nutrition* 35: 1169–75.

Frayer, David W. 1988. Caries and oral pathologies at the Mesolithic sites of Muge: Cabeço da Arruda and Moita do Sebastiao. *Trabalhos de Antropologia e Etnologia* (Portugal) 27: 9–25.

Freeman, Leslie G. 1981. The fat of the land: Notes on Paleolithic diet in Iberia. In *Omnivorous primates: Gathering and hunting in human evolution,* ed. Robert S. O. Harding and Geza Teleki, 104–65. New York.

Frisancho, A. Roberto. 1978. Nutritional influences on human growth and maturation. *Yearbook of Physical Anthropology* 21: 174–91.

1979. *Human adaptation: A functional interpretation.* St. Louis, Mo.

Gabr, Mamdouh. 1987. Undernutrition and quality of life. In *Nutrition and the quality of life,* ed. G. H. Bourne. *World Review of Nutrition and Dietetics* 49: 1–21.

Galinat, Walton C. 1985. Domestication and diffusion of maize. In *Prehistoric food production in North America,* ed. Richard I. Ford. University of Michigan, Museum of Anthropology, Anthropological Papers No. 75: 245–78. Ann Arbor.

Garn, Stanley M., and Alponse R. Burdi. 1971. Prenatal ordering and postnatal sequence in dental development. *Journal of Dental Research* 50: 1407–14.

Garn, Stanley M., and D. C. Clark. 1975. Nutrition, growth, development, and maturation: Findings from the Ten-State Nutrition Survey of 1968-1970. *Pediatrics* 56: 300–19.

Garn, Stanley, A. B. Lewis, and D. L. Polacheck. 1960. Interrelations in dental development. I. Interrelationships within the dentition. *Journal of Dental Research* 39: 1040–55.

Garn, Stanley, R. H. Osborne, and K. D. McCabe. 1979. The effect of prenatal factors on crown dimensions. *American Journal of Physical Anthropology* 51: 665–78.

Garn, Stanley, G. M. Owen, and D. C. Clark. 1974. Ascorbic acid: The vitamin of affluence. *Ecology of Food and Nutrition* 3: 151–3.

Garn, Stanley, C. G. Rohmann, M. Behar, et al. 1964. Compact bone deficiency in protein-calorie malnutrition. *Science* 145: 1444–5.

Garn, Stanley, Frederic N. Silverman, Keith P. Hertzog, and Christabel G. Rohmann. 1968. Lines and bands of increased density. *Medical Radiography and Photography* 44: 58–89.

Goodman, Alan H. 1988. The chronology of enamel hypoplasias in an industrial population: A reappraisal of Sarnat and Schour (1941, 1942). *Human Biology* 60: 781–91.

Goodman, Alan H., George J. Armelagos, and Jerome C. Rose. 1980. Enamel hypoplasias as indicators of stress in three prehistoric populations from Illinois. *Human Biology* 52: 512–28.

Goodman, Alan H., and George A. Clark. 1981. Harris lines as indicators of stress in prehistoric Illinois populations. In *Biocultural adaption: Comprehensive approaches to skeletal analysis,* ed. Debra L. Martin and M. Pamela Bumsted. University of Massachusetts, Department of Anthropology, Research Report No. 20: 35–45. Amherst, Mass.

Goodman, Alan H., John Lallo, George J. Armelagos, and Jerome C. Rose. 1984. Health changes at Dickson Mounds, Illinois (A.D. 950-1300). In *Paleopathology at the origins of agriculture,* ed. Mark Nathan Cohen and George J. Armelagos, 271–305. Orlando, Fla.

Goodman, Alan H., Debra L. Martin, George J. Armelagos, and George Clark. 1984. Indications of stress from bones and teeth. In *Paleopathology at the origins of agriculture,* ed. Mark Nathan Cohen and George J. Armelagos, 13–49. Orlando, Fla.

Goodman, Alan H., and Jerome C. Rose. 1990. Assessment of systemic physiological perturbations from dental enamel hypoplasias and associated histological structures. *Yearbook of Physical Anthropology* 33: 59–110.

1991. Dental enamel hypoplasias as indicators of nutritional status. In *Advances in dental anthropology,* ed. Marc A. Kelley and Clark Spencer Larsen, 279–94. New York.

Gordon, Kathleen D. 1987. Evolutionary perspectives on human diet. In *Nutritional anthropology,* ed. Francis E. Johnston, 3–39. New York.

Gracey, Michael. 1987. Normal growth and nutrition. In *Nutrition and the quality of life,* ed. G. H. Bourne. *World Review of Nutrition and Dietetics* 49: 160–210.

Grine, F. E., A. J. Gwinnett, and J. H. Oaks. 1990. Early hominid dental pathology: Interproximal caries in 1.5 million-year-old *Paranthropus robustus* from Swartkrans. *Archives of Oral Biology* 35: 381-6.

Grupe, Gisela, Hermann Piepenbrink, and Margaret J. Schoeninger. 1989. Note on microbial influence on stable carbon and nitrogen isotopes in bone. *Applied Geochemistry* 4: 299.

Guagliardo, Mark F. 1982. Tooth crown size differences between age groups: A possible new indicator of stress in skeletal samples. *American Journal of Physical Anthropology* 58: 383-9.

Hallberg, Leif. 1981. Bioavailability of dietary iron in man. *Annual Review of Nutrition* 1: 123-47.

Harrison, G. A., J. M. Tanner, D. R. Pilbeam, and P. T. Baker. 1988. *Human biology: An introduction to human evolution, variation, growth, and adaptability.* Third edition. New York.

Hartnady, Philip, and Jerome C. Rose. 1991. Abnormal tooth-loss patterns among Archaic-period inhabitants of the lower Pecos region, Texas. In *Advances in dental anthropology,* ed. Marc A. Kelley and Clark Spencer Larsen, 267-78. New York.

Hausman, Alice J., and Edwin N. Wilmsen. 1985. Economic change and secular trends in the growth of San children. *Human Biology* 57: 563-71.

Heaney, Robert P. 1993. Nutritional factors in osteoporosis. *Annual Review of Nutrition* 13: 287-316.

Hengen, O. P. 1971. Cribra orbitalia: Pathogenesis and probable etiology. *Homo* 22: 57-75.

Hill, M. Cassandra, and George J. Armelagos. 1990. Porotic hyperostosis in past and present perspective. In *A life in science: Papers in honor of J. Lawrence Angel,* ed. Jane E. Buikstra. Center for American Archeology, Scientific Papers No. 6: 52-63. Kampville, Ill.

Hillson, Simon. 1986. *Teeth.* Cambridge.

Himes, John H. 1987. Purposeful assessment of nutritional status. In *Nutritional anthropology,* ed. Francis E. Johnston, 85-99. New York.

Himes, John H., R. Martorell, J.-P. Habicht, et al. 1975. Patterns of cortical bone growth in moderately malnourished preschool children. *Human Biology* 47: 337-50.

Hinton, Robert J. 1981. Form and patterning of anterior tooth wear among aboriginal human groups. *American Journal of Physical Anthropology* 54: 555-64.

Hinton, Robert J., Maria Ostendorf Smith, and Fred H. Smith. 1980. Tooth size changes in prehistoric Tennessee Indians. *Human Biology* 52: 229-45.

Howell, F. Clark. 1966. Observations on the earlier phases of the European Lower Paleolithic. *American Anthropologist* 68: 88-201.

1970. *Early Man.* New York.

Howell, F. Clark, and Leslie G. Freeman. 1982. Ambrona: An Early Stone Age site on the Spanish Meseta. *L. S. B. Leakey Foundation News* No. 32: 1, 11-13.

Hrdlička, Aleš. 1914. *Anthropological work in Peru in 1913, with notes on the pathology of the ancient Peruvians.* Smithsonian Miscellaneous Collections 61, No. 18. Washington, D.C.

Hummert, James R., and Dennis P. Van Gerven. 1983. Skeletal growth in a medieval population from Sudanese Nubia. *American Journal of Physical Anthropology* 60: 471-8.

Huss-Ashmore, Rebecca, Alan H. Goodman, and George J. Armelagos. 1982. Nutritional inference from paleopathology. *Advances in Archeological Method and Theory* 5: 395-474.

Hutchinson, Dale L., and Clark Spencer Larsen. 1988. Stress and lifeway change: The evidence from enamel hypoplasias. In *The archaeology of mission Santa Catalina de Guale: 2. Biocultural interpretations of a popula-*

tion in transition, ed. Clark Spencer Larsen. Anthropological Papers of the American Museum of Natural History No. 68: 50-65. New York.

Inoue, N., G. Ito, and T. Kamegai. 1986. Dental pathology of hunter-gatherers and early farmers in prehistoric Japan. In *Prehistoric hunter gatherers in Japan: New research methods,* ed. Takeru Akazawa and C. Melvin Aikens. University of Tokyo, University Museum, Bulletin No. 27: 163-98. Tokyo.

Jantz, Richard L., and Douglas W. Owsley. 1984. Long bone growth variation among Arikara skeletal populations. *American Journal of Physical Anthropology* 63: 13-20.

Johnston, Francis E. 1986. Somatic growth of the infant and preschool child. In *Human growth,* Vol. 2, ed. F. Falkner and J. M. Tanner, 3-24. New York.

Jones, P. R. M., and R. F. A. Dean. 1959. The effects of kwashiorkor on the development of the bones of the knee. *Journal of Pediatrics* 54: 176-84.

Katz, Solomon H. 1987. Food and biocultural evolution: A model for the investigation of modern nutritional problems. In *Nutritional anthropology,* ed. Francis E. Johnston, 41-63. New York.

Katz, Solomon H., M. L. Hediger, and L. A. Valleroy. 1974. Traditional maize processing techniques in the New World. *Science* 184: 765-73.

1975. The anthropological and nutritional significance of traditional maize processing techniques in the New World. In *Biosocial interrelations in population adaption,* ed. Elizabeth S. Watts, Francis E. Johnston, and Gabriel Lasker, 195-231. The Hague.

Keegan, William F. 1989. Stable isotope analysis of prehistoric diet. In *Reconstruction of life from the skeleton,* ed. Mehmet Yasar Iscan and Kenneth A. R. Kennedy, 223-36. New York.

Kelley, Marc A., Dianne R. Levesque, and Eric Weidl. 1991. Contrasting patterns of dental disease in five early northern Chilean groups. In *Advances in dental anthropology,* ed. Marc A. Kelley and Clark Spencer Larsen, 203-13. New York.

Kennedy, Kenneth A. R. 1984. Growth, nutrition, and pathology in changing paleodemographic settings in South Asia. In *Paleopathology at the origins of agriculture,* ed. Mark Nathan Cohen and George J. Armelagos, 169-92. Orlando, Fla.

Kent, Susan. 1986. The influence of sedentism and aggregation on porotic hyperostosis and anaemia: A case study. *Man* 21: 605-36.

Kimura, Kunihiko. 1984. Studies on growth and development in Japan. *Yearbook of Physical Anthropology* 27: 179-213.

Klein, Richard G. 1987. Problems and prospects in understanding how early people exploited animals. In *The evolution of human hunting,* ed. M. H. Netecki and D. V. Netecki, 11-45. New York.

1989. *The human career: Human biological and cultural origins.* Chicago.

Klepinger, Linda L. 1984. Nutritional assessment from bone. *Annual Review of Anthropology* 13: 75-96.

Krouse, R. H. 1987. Sulphur and carbon isotope studies of food chains. In *Diet and subsistence: Current archaeological perspectives,* ed. B. V. Kennedy and G. M. LeMoine. University of Calgary Archaeological Association, Proceedings of the 19th Annual Conference. Calgary, Alberta.

Lallo, John W. 1973. The skeletal biology of three prehistoric American Indian societies from the Dickson mounds. Ph.D. thesis, University of Massachusetts.

Larsen, Clark Spencer. 1982. *The anthropology of St. Catherines Island: 1. Prehistoric human biological adapta-*

tion. Anthropological Papers of the American Museum of Natural History No. 57 (part 3). New York.

1983. Deciduous tooth size and subsistence change in prehistoric Georgia coast populations. *Current Anthropology* 24: 225-6.

1987. Bioarchaeological interpretations of subsistence economy and behavior from human skeletal remains. *Advances in Archaeological Method and Theory* 10: 339-445.

Larsen, Clark Spencer, Christopher B. Ruff, Margaret J. Schoeninger, and Dale L. Hutchinson. 1992. Population decline and extinction in La Florida. In *Disease and demography in the Americas: Changing patterns before and after 1492,* ed. Douglas H. Ubelaker and John W. Verano. Washington, D.C.

Larsen, Clark Spencer, Margaret J. Schoeninger, Dale L. Hutchinson, et al. 1990. Beyond demographic collapse: Biological adaptation and change in native populations of La Florida. In *Columbian consequences, Vol 2: Archaeological and historical perspectives on the Spanish borderlands east,* ed. David Hurst Thomas, 409-28. Washington, D.C.

Larsen, Clark Spencer, Rebecca Shavit, and Mark C. Griffin. 1991. Dental caries evidence for dietary change: An archaeological context. In *Advances in dental anthropology,* ed. Marc A. Kelley and Clark Spencer Larsen, 179-202. New York.

Layrisse, Miguel, Carlos Martinez-Torres, and Marcel Roche. 1968. Effect of interaction of various foods on iron absorption. *American Journal of Clinical Nutrition* 21: 1175-83.

Lindsay, Robert, and Felicia Cosman. 1992. Primary osteoporosis. In *Disorders of bone and primary metabolism,* ed. Frederic L. Coe and Murray J. Favus, 831-88. New York.

Lovejoy, C. Owen, Katherine F. Russell, and Mary L. Harrison. 1990. Long bone growth velocity in the Libben population. *American Journal of Human Biology* 2: 533-41.

Maat, G. J. R. 1982. Scurvy in Dutch whalers buried at Spitsbergen. *Paleopathology Association, Papers on Paleopathology, Fourth European Members Meeting,* ed. Eve Cockburn, 8. Detroit, Mich.

Malina, Robert M. 1987. Nutrition and growth. In *Nutritional anthropology,* ed. Francis E. Johnston, 173-96. New York.

Mann, Alan E. 1981. Diet and human evolution. In *Omnivorous primates: Gathering and hunting in human evolution,* ed. Robert S. O. Harding and Geza Teleki, 10-36. New York.

Martin, Debra L., and George J. Armelagos. 1985. Skeletal remodeling and mineralization as indicators of health: An example from prehistoric Sudanese Nubia. *Journal of Human Evolution* 14: 527-37.

Martin, Debra L., Alan H. Goodman, and George J. Armelagos. 1985. Skeletal pathologies as indicators of quality and quantity of diet. In *The analysis of prehistoric diets,* ed. Robert I. Gilbert, Jr., and James H. Mielke, 227-79. Orlando, Fla.

McElroy, Ann, and Patricia K. Townsend. 1979. *Medical Anthropology.* Belmont, Calif.

McGregor, I. A., A. M. Thomson, and W. Z. Billewicz. 1968. The development of primary teeth in children from a group of Gambian villages and critical examination of its use for estimating age. *British Journal of Nutrition* 22: 307-14.

McHenry, Henry. 1968. Transverse lines in long bones of prehistoric California Indians. *American Journal of Physical Anthropology* 29: 1-18.

McLaren, Donald S. 1976. *Nutrition in the community.* New York.

Meiklejohn, Christopher, Catherine Schentag, Alexandra Venema, and Patrick Key. 1984. Socioeconomic change and patterns of pathology and variation in the Mesolithic and Neolithic of western Europe: Some suggestions. In *Paleopathology at the origins of agriculture,* ed. Mark Nathan Cohen and George J. Armelagos, 75-100. Orlando, Fla.

Mensforth, Robert P., C. Owen Lovejoy, John W. Lallo, and George J. Armelagos. 1978. The role of constitutional factors, diet, and infectious disease in the etiology of porotic hyperostosis and periosteal reactions in prehistoric infants and children. *Medical Anthropology* 2: 1-59.

Merchant, Virginia L., and Douglas H. Ubelaker. 1977. Skeletal growth of the protohistoric Arikara. *American Journal of Physical Anthropology* 46: 61-72.

Milner, George R. 1984. Dental caries in the permanent dentition of a Mississippian period population from the American Midwest. *Collegium Antropologicum* 8: 77-91.

Milner, George R., Dorothy A. Humpf, and Henry C. Harpending. 1989. Pattern matching of age-at-death distributions in paleodemographic analysis. *American Journal of Physical Anthropology* 80: 49-58.

Moller-Christiansen, V. 1958. *Bogen om Aebelholt Kloster.* Copenhagen.

Molnar, Stephen. 1972. Tooth wear and culture: A survey of tooth functions among some prehistoric populations. *Current Anthropology* 13: 511-26.

Molnar, Stephen, and I. M. Molnar. 1985. The incidence of enamel hypoplasia among the Krapina Neanderthals. *American Anthropologist* 87: 536-49.

Moore, K. P., S. Thorp, and D. P. Van Gerven. 1986. Pattern of dental eruption, skeletal maturation and stress in a medieval population from Sudanese Nubia. *Human Evolution* 1: 325-30.

Mottram, R. F. 1979. *Human nutrition.* Third edition. Westport, Conn.

Newbrun, Ernest. 1982. Sugar and dental caries: A review of human studies. *Science* 217: 418-23.

Nordin, B. E. C. 1973. *Metabolic bone and stone disease.* Baltimore, Md.

Ogilvie, Marsha D., Bryan K. Curran, and Erik Trinkaus. 1989. Incidence and patterning of dental enamel hypoplasia among the Neanderthals. *American Journal of Physical Anthropology* 79: 25-41.

Ortner, Donald J., and Walter G. J. Putschar. 1985. *Identification of pathological conditions in the human skeletal remains.* Washington, D.C.

Owsley, Douglas W., and Richard L. Jantz. 1985. Long bone lengths and gestational age distributions of post-contact period Arikara Indian perinatal infant skeletons. *American Journal of Physical Anthropology* 68: 321-8.

Patterson, David Kingsnorth, Jr. 1984. *A diochronic study of dental palaeopathology and attritional status of prehistoric Ontario pre-Iroquois and Iroquois populations.* Archaeological Survey of Canada, Paper No. 122. Ottawa.

Powell, Mary Lucas. 1985. The analysis of dental wear and caries for dietary reconstruction. In *The analysis of prehistoric diets,* ed. Robert I. Gilbert, Jr., and James H. Mielke, 307-38. Orlando, Fla.

1990. On the eve of the conquest: Life and death at Irene Mound, Georgia. In *The archaeology of mission Santa Catalina de Guale: 2. Biocultural interpretations of a population in transition,* ed. Clark Spencer Larsen. Anthropological Papers of the American Museum of Natural History No. 68: 26-35. New York.

Price, T. Douglas. 1985. Late archaic subsistence in the midwestern United States. *Journal of Human Evolution* 14: 449-59.

Roe, Daphne A. 1973. *A plague of corn: The social history of pellagra.* Ithaca, N.Y.

Rose, Jerome C., George J. Armelagos, and John W. Lallo. 1978. Histological enamel indicator of childhood stress in prehistoric skeletal samples. *American Journal of Physical Anthropology* 49: 511-16.

Rose, Jerome C., Barbara A. Burnett, Michael S. Nassaney, and Mark W. Blaeuer. 1984. Paleopathology and the origins of maize agriculture in the lower Mississippi Valley and Caddoan areas. In *Paleopathology at the origins of agriculture,* ed. Mark Nathan Cohen and George J. Armelagos, 393-424. Orlando, Fla.

Rose, Jerome C., Keith W. Condon, and Alan H. Goodman. 1985. Diet and dentition: Developmental disturbances. In *The analysis of prehistoric diets,* ed. Robert I. Gilbert, Jr., and J. H. Mielke, 281-305. Orlando, Fla.

Rose, Jerome C., Murray K. Marks, and Larry L. Tieszen. 1991. Bioarchaeology and subsistence in the central and lower portions of the Mississippi Valley. In *What mean these bones? Integrated studies in southeastern bioarchaeology,* ed. Mary Lucas Powell, Patricia S. Bridges, and Ann Marie Mires, 7-21. Tuscaloosa, Ala.

Ross, Harold M. 1976. Bush fallow farming, diet and nutrition: A Melanesian example of successful adaptation. In *The measures of man: Methodologies in biological anthropology,* ed. Eugene Giles and Jonathan S. Friedlaender, 550-615. Cambridge, Mass.

Ruff, Christopher. 1991. Biomechanical analyses of archaeological human skeletal samples. In *The skeletal biology of past peoples: Advances in research methods,* ed. Shelley R. Saunders and Mary A. Katzenberg. New York.

Ruff, Christopher, and Wilson C. Hayes. 1982. Subperiosteal expansion and cortical remodeling of the human femur and tibia with aging. *Science* 217: 945-8.

Ruff, Christopher, and Clark Spencer Larsen. 1990. Postcranial biomechanical adaptations to subsistence strategy changes on the Georgia coast. In *The archaeology of mission Santa Catalina de Guale: 2. Biocultural interpretations of a population in transition,* ed. Clark Spencer Larsen. Anthropological Papers of the American Museum of Natural History No. 68: 94-120. New York.

Russell, Katherine F., Inui Choi, and Clark Spencer Larsen. 1990. The paleodemography of Santa Catalina de Guale. In *The archaeology of mission Santa Catalina de Guale: 2. Biocultural interpretations of a population in transition,* ed. Clark Spencer Larsen. Anthropological Papers of the American Museum of Natural History No. 68: 36-49. New York.

Sandford, Mary K., ed. 1993. *Investigations of ancient human tissue: Chemical analyses in anthropology.* Langhorne, Pa.

Sarnat, B. G., and I. Schour. 1941. Enamel hypoplasias (chronic enamel aplasia) in relationship to systemic diseases: A chronologic, morphologic, and etiologic classification. *Journal of the American Dental Association* 28: 1989-2000.

Schaafsma, G., E. C. H. van Beresteyn, J. A. Raymakers, and S. A. Duursma. 1987. Nutritional aspects of osteoporosis. In *Nutrition and the quality of life,* ed. G. H. Bourne. *World Review of Nutrition and Dietetics* 49: 121-59.

Schoeninger, Margaret J. 1989. Reconstructing prehistoric human diet. In *Chemistry of prehistoric human bone,* ed. T. Douglas Price, 38-67. New York.

Schoeninger, Margaret J., and Michael J. DeNiro. 1984. Nitrogen and carbon isotopic composition of bone collagen from marine and terrestrial animals. *Geochimica et Cosmochimica Acta* 48: 625-39.

Schoeninger, Margaret J., Katherine M. Moore, Matthew L. Murray, and John D. Kingston. 1989. Detection of bone preservation in archaeological and fossil samples. *Applied Geochemistry* 4: 281-92.

Schoeninger, Margaret J., and C. S. Peebles. 1981. Effects of mollusk eating on human bone strontium levels. *Journal of Archaeological Science* 8: 391-7.

Schoeninger, Margaret J., Nikolaas J. van der Merwe, and Katherine Moore. 1990. Decrease in diet quality between the prehistoric and contact periods. In *The archaeology of mission Santa Catalina de Guale: 2. Biocultural interpretations of a population in transition,* ed. Clark Spencer Larsen. Anthropological Papers of the American Museum of Natural History No. 68: 78-93. New York.

Sciulli, Paul W. 1978. Developmental abnormalities of the permanent dentition in prehistoric Ohio Valley Amerindians. *American Journal of Physical Anthropology* 48: 193-8.

Scott, G. Richard, and Christy G. Turner II. 1988. Dental anthropology. *Annual Review of Anthropology* 17: 99-126.

Scrimshaw, N. S., C. E. Taylor, and J. E. Gordon. 1968. *Interaction of nutrition and infection.* World Health Organization Monograph 57. Geneva.

Sealy, Judith. 1986. *Stable carbon isotopes and prehistoric diets in the south-western Cape Province, South Africa.* Cambridge Monographs in African Archaeology 15, BAR International Series 293. Oxford.

Shipman, Pat. 1986a. Scavenging or hunting in early hominids: Theoretical framework and tests. *American Anthropologist* 88: 27-43.

  1986b. Studies of hominid-faunal interactions at Olduvai Gorge. *Journal of Human Evolution* 15: 691-706.

Shipman, Pat, Wendy Bosler, and Karen Lee Davis. 1981. Butchering of giant geladas at an Acheulian site. *Current Anthropology* 22: 257-68.

Sillen, Andrew, and Maureen Kavanaugh. 1982. Strontium and paleodietary research: A review. *Yearbook of Physical Anthropology* 25: 67-90.

Simpson, Scott W., Dale L. Hutchinson, and Clark Spencer Larsen. 1990. Coping with stress: Tooth size, dental defects, and age-at-death. In *The archaeology of the mission Santa Catalina de Guale: 2. Biocultural interpretations of a population in transition,* ed. Clark Spencer Larsen. Anthropological Papers of the American Museum of Natural History No. 68: 66-77. New York.

Smith, B. Holly. 1984. Patterns of molar wear in hunter-gatherers and agriculturalists. *American Journal of Physical Anthropology* 63: 39-56.

  1985. Development and evolution of the helicoidal plane of dental occlusion. *American Journal of Physical Anthropology* 69: 21-35.

  1991. Standards of human tooth formation and dental age assessment. In *Advances in dental anthropology,* ed. Marc A. Kelley and Clark Spencer Larsen, 143-68. New York.

Smith, Bruce D. 1989. Origins of agriculture in eastern North America. *Science* 246: 1566-72.

Smith, Fred H., Maria Ostendorf Smith, and Robert J. Hinton. 1980. Evolution of tooth size in the prehistoric inhabitants of the Tennessee Valley. In *The skeletal biology of aboriginal populations in the southeastern United States,* ed. P. Willey and F. H. Smith. Tennessee Anthropological Association Miscellaneous Paper No. 5: 81-103. Knoxville, Tenn.

Smith, Patricia, Ofer Bar-Yosef, and Andrew Sillen. 1984. Archaeological and skeletal evidence for dietary change during the late Pleistocene/early Holocene in the Levant. In *Paleopathology at the origins of agriculture,* ed. Mark Nathan Cohen and George J. Armelagos, 101-36. Orlando, Fla.

Speth, John D. 1990. Seasonality, resource stress, and food

sharing in so-called "egalitarian" foraging societies. *Journal of Anthropological Archaeology* 9: 148-88.

Spielmann, Katherine A. 1989. A review: Dietary restrictions on hunter-gatherer women and the implications for fertility and infant mortality. *Human Ecology* 17: 321-45.

Stafford, Thomas W., Klaus Brendel, and Raymond C. Duhamel. 1988. Radiocarbon, ^{13}C and ^{15}N analysis of fossil bone: Removal of humates with XAD-2 resin. *Geochimica et Cosmochimica Acta* 52: 2257-67.

Steinbock, R. Ted. 1976. *Paleopathological diagnosis and interpretation.* Springfield, Ill.

Stewart, R. J. C. 1975. Bone pathology in experimental malnutrition. *World Review of Nutrition and Dietetics* 21: 1-74.

Stewart, R. J. C., and B. S. Platt. 1958. Arrested growth lines in the bones of pigs on low-protein diets. *Proceedings of the Nutrition Society* 17: v-vi.

Stini, William A. 1971. Evolutionary implications of changing nutritional patterns in human populations. *American Anthropologist* 73: 1019-30.

  1990. "Osteoporosis": Etiologies, prevention, and treatment. *Yearbook of Physical Anthropology* 33: 151-94.

Stout, Samuel D. 1978. Histological structure and its preservation in ancient bone. *Current Anthropology* 19: 601-3.

  1983. The application of histomorphometric analysis to ancient skeletal remains. *Anthropos* (Greece) 10: 60-71.

  1989. Histomorphometric analysis of human skeletal remains. In *Reconstruction of life from the skeleton,* ed. Mehmet Yasar Iscan and Kenneth A. R. Kennedy, 41-52. New York.

Stout, Samuel D., and David J. Simmons. 1979. Use of histology in ancient bone research. *Yearbook of Physical Anthropology* 22: 228-49.

Stout, Samuel D., and Steven L. Teitelbaum. 1976. Histological analysis of undercalcified thin sections of archaeological bone. *American Journal of Physical Anthropology* 44: 263-70.

Stuart-Macadam, Patricia. 1985. Porotic hyperostosis: Representative of a childhood condition. *American Journal of Physical Anthropology* 66: 391-8.

  1989. Nutritional deficiency diseases: A survey of scurvy, rickets, and iron-deficiency anemia. In *Reconstruction of life from the skeleton,* ed. Mehmet Yasar Iscan and Kenneth A. R. Kennedy, 201-22. New York.

Sundick, Robert I. 1978. Human skeletal growth and age determination. *Homo* 29: 228-49.

Teaford, Mark F. 1991. Dental microwear: What can it tell us about diet and dental function? In *Advances in dental anthropology,* ed. Marc A. Kelley and Clark Spencer Larsen, 341-56. New York.

Thompson, D. D. 1980. Age changes in bone mineralization, cortical thickness, and Haversian canal area. *Calcified Tissue International* 31: 5-11.

Tobias, P. V. 1967. *The cranium and maxillary dentition of zinjanthropus (australopithecus) boisei.* Cambridge.

Turner, Christy G., II. 1979. Dental anthropological indications of agriculture among the Jomon people of central Japan. *American Journal of Physical Anthropology* 51: 619-36.

Turner, Christy G., II, and Lilia M. Cheuiche Machado. 1983. A new dental wear pattern and evidence for high carbohydrate consumption in a Brazilian Archaic skeletal population. *American Journal of Physical Anthropology* 61: 125-30.

Van der Merwe, Nikolaas J. 1982. Carbon isotopes, photosynthesis and archaeology. *American Scientist* 70: 596-606.

Van Gerven, Dennis P., Rosemary Beck, and James R. Hummert. 1990. Patterns of enamel hypoplasia in two medieval populations from Nubia's Batn El Hajar. *American Journal of Physical Anthropology* 82: 413-20.

Walker, Phillip L. 1978. A quantitative analysis of dental attrition rates in the Santa Barbara Channel area. *American Journal of Physical Anthropology* 48: 101-6.

  1986. Porotic hyperostosis in a marine-dependent California Indian population. *American Journal of Physical Anthropology* 69: 345-54.

Walker, Phillip L., Gregory Dean, and Perry Shapiro. 1991. Estimating age from tooth wear in archaeological populations. In *Advances in dental anthropology,* ed. Marc A. Kelley and Clark Spencer Larsen, 169-78. New York.

Walker, Phillip L., and Jon M. Erlandson. 1986. Dental evidence for prehistoric dietary change on northern Channel Islands, California. *American Antiquity* 51: 375-83.

Walker, Phillip L., John Johnson, and Patricia Lambert. 1988. Age and sex biases in the preservation of human skeletal remains. *American Journal of Physical Anthropology* 76: 183-8.

Wallace, John A. 1974. Approximal grooving of teeth. *American Journal of Physical Anthropology* 40: 385-90.

Webb, Stephen. 1989. *Prehistoric stress in Australian aborigines: A paleopathological study of a hunter-gatherer population.* International Series 490. Oxford.

White, Tim D. 1978. Early hominid enamel hypoplasia. *American Journal of Physical Anthropology* 49: 79-84.

Wing, Elizabeth S., and Antoinette B. Brown. 1979. *Paleonutrition.* New York.

Wolf, George. 1980. Vitamin A. In *Human nutrition,* ed. R. B. Alfin-Slater and D. Kritchevsky, 97-203. New York.

Wu Xinzhi and Zhang Zhenbiao. 1985. *Homo sapien* remains from late palaeolithic and neolithic China. In *Palaeoanthropology and palaeolithic archaeology in the People's Republic of China,* ed. Wu Rukang and John W. Olsen, 107-33. Orlando, Fla.

Yagi, Tamotsu, Yoshihide Takebe, and Minoru Itoh. 1989. Secular trends in physique and physical fitness in Japanese students during the last 20 years. *American Journal of Human Biology* 1: 581-7.

Yarbrough, C., J.-P. Habicht, R. Martorell, and R. E. Klein. 1974. Anthropometry as an index of nutritional status. In *Nutrition and malnutrition: Identification and measurement,* ed. A. F. Roche and F. Falkner, 15-26. New York.

y'Edynak, Gloria. 1989. Yugoslav Mesolithic dental reduction. *American Journal of Physical Anthropology* 78: 17-36.

y'Edynak, Gloria, and Sylvia Fleisch. 1983. Microevolution and biological adaptability in the transition from food-collecting to food-producing in the Iron Gates of Yugoslavia. *Journal of Human Evolution* 12: 279-96.

I.2. ∾ Paleopathological Evidence of Malnutrition

The quantity and nutritional quality of food available to human populations undoubtedly played a major role in the adaptive processes associated with human evolution. This should have been particularly the case in that period of human history from Mesolithic times to the present when epochal changes took place in the subsistence base of many human societies. In the Near East the domestication of plants and animals began toward the end of the Mesolithic period but became fully developed in the Neolithic. This development included agriculture and pastoralism along with cultural changes associated with greater sedentism and urbanism.

Paleopathology, primarily through the study of human skeletal remains, has attempted to interpret the impact such changes have had upon human health. A recent focus has been on the transition from a hunting and gathering way of life to one associated with incipient or fully developed agriculture (e.g., Cohen and Armelagos 1984b; Cohen 1989; Meiklejohn and Zvelebil 1991). One of the questions being asked is whether greater dependence on fewer food sources increased human vulnerability to famine and malnutrition. The later transition into an increasingly sedentary urban existence in the Bronze and Iron Ages has not been as carefully studied. However, analysis of data from skeletal remains in numerous archaeological sites is providing insight into some of the effects upon nutrition that increasing human density and attendant subsistence changes have had.

In the study of prehistoric health, perhaps the least complex nutritional data comes from human remains that have been mummified. Preservation of human soft tissues occurs either naturally, as in the bogs of northern Europe and very arid areas of the world, or through cultural intervention with embalming methods. Some mummies have provided direct evidence of diet from the intestinal contents of their stomachs (e.g., Glob 1971: 42–3; Fischer 1980: 185–9; Brothwell 1986: 92). However, the most ubiquitous source of data comes from human skeletal remains where the impact of dietary factors tends to be indirect, limited, and difficult to interpret.

Generally, only about 10 percent of a typical sample of human archaeological burials will show any significant evidence of skeletal disease. (Clearly the people represented by the normal-appearing burials died of something, but there are no anatomical features that help determine what this might have been.) Of the 10 percent showing pathology, about 90 percent of their disease conditions resulted from trauma, infection, or arthritis – the three predominant pathological skeletal conditions. All other diseases, including those that might be caused by malnutrition, are incorporated in the residual 10 percent, meaning that even in a large sample of archaeological skeletons, one is unlikely to find more than a few examples of conditions that might be attributable to nutritional problems.

Once a pathological condition due to malnutrition is recognized in bone, correct diagnosis is challenging. Identification begins with those nutritional diseases most commonly known today that can affect the skeleton. These are: (1) vitamin D deficiency, (2) vitamin C deficiency, (3) iodine deficiency, (4) iron deficiency, (5) excessive dietary fluorine, (6) protein–calorie deficiency, and (7) trace element deficiencies.

Care needs to be exercised both in establishing a preferred diagnosis for a pathological condition and in interpreting the diagnoses of others. This is particularly the case in interpreting evidence of malnutrition in archaeological remains. Malnutrition is a general state that may cause more than one pathological condition in the same individual, and it may also be accompanied by other disease conditions, making the pathological profile complex and confusing. For example, scurvy and rickets may appear together (Follis, Jackson, and Park 1940), or scurvy may be associated with iron-deficiency anemia (Goldberg 1963).

All of these issues place significant limitations on reconstructing nutritional problems in antiquity. However, emerging research methods, such as stable isotope analysis and bone histology, evidence from related fields, such as dental pathology, and new areas of research concentration, such as infant skeletal studies, may provide additional data. Analysis of stable isotopes of human bone collagen allows us to determine the balance of food sources between terrestrial animal, marine animal, and plant materials (Katzenberg 1992). Isotope analysis of human hair may provide a more refined breakdown of plant materials eaten over a much shorter period than the 25 to 30 years that bone collagen analysis provides (White 1993: 657). C. D. White (1993: 657), working on prehistoric human remains from Nubia, has claimed that isotopic analysis of hair points to a seasonal difference between consumption of plants such as wheat, barley, and most fruits and vegetables and consumption of the less nutritious plants such as sorghum and millet.

Analysis of bone histology by M. Schultz and fellow workers (Schultz 1986, 1990, 1993; Carli-Thiele and Schultz 1994; Schultz and Schmidt-Schultz 1994) has identified features that assist in differential diagnosis in archaeological human skeletal remains. In one study of human remains from an Early Bronze Age (2500 to 2300 B.C.) cemetery in Anatolia, Schultz (1993: 189) detected no anatomical evidence of rickets in an infant sample. However, microscopic examination revealed a rickets prevalence of 4 percent.

Dental paleopathology provides an additional dimension to understanding nutritional problems. For example, caries rate and location may help identify what type of food was eaten (e.g., Littleton and Frohlich 1989, 1993; Meiklejohn and Zvelebil 1991). Enamel hypoplasias, which are observable defects in dental enamel, may provide information about timing and severity of nutritional stress (Goodman, Martin, and Armelagos 1984; Goodman 1991; Meiklejohn and Zvelebil 1991). Patterns of antemortem tooth loss may suggest whether an individual suffered from a nutritional disease, such as scurvy (Maat 1986: 158), or excess calculus or poor dental hygiene (Lukacs 1989).

Thorough analysis of skeletons of infants and children, which until recently has received minimal attention, can also provide valuable information on the health of a population. Indeed, because of a child's rapid growth and consequent need for optimal nutrition, immature skeletons will reflect the nutritional status of a population better than those of adults. This is especially the case with diseases such as scurvy, rickets, and iron-deficiency anemia, whose impact is greatest on children between the ages of 6 months and 2 years (Stuart-Macadam 1989a: 219).

In this chapter, we discuss skeletal abnormalities associated with nutritional diseases for which there is archaeological skeletal evidence in various geographical areas and time periods in the Old World. These diseases are: vitamin D deficiency, vitamin C deficiency, iron deficiency, fluorosis, and protein–calorie deficiency. We will focus on anatomical evidence of nutritional disease but will include other types of evidence as it occurs. For a discussion of the pathogenesis of these diseases we refer the reader to other sources (Ortner and Putschar 1981; Resnick and Niwayama 1988).

Vitamin D Deficiency

Vitamin D deficiency causes rickets in children and osteomalacia in adults. In general, these conditions should be rare in societies where exposure to sunlight is common, as the body can synthesize vitamin D precursors with adequate sunlight. In fact, there has been some speculation that rickets will not occur in areas of abundant sunlight (Angel 1971: 89). Cultural factors, however, may intervene. The use of concealing clothing such as veils, the practice of long-term sequestration of women *(purdah),* or the swaddling of infants (Kuhnke 1993: 461) will hinder the synthesis of vitamin D. Thus, in modern Asia both rickets and osteomalacia have been reported, with the condition attributed to culturally patterned avoidance of sunlight (Fallon 1988: 1994). In the Near East and North Africa cases of rickets have been reported in large towns and sunless slums (Kuhnke 1993: 461).

Vitamin D is critical to the mineralization of bone protein matrix. If the vitamin is not present during bone formation, the protein matrix does not mineralize. Turnover of bone tissue is most rapid during the growth phase, and in rickets much of the newly forming protein matrix may not be mineralized. This compromises biomechanical strength; bone deformity may occur, especially in the weight-bearing limbs, and may be apparent in archaeological human remains.

In the active child, the deformity tends to be in the extremities, and its location may be an indication of when the individual suffered from this disease. Deformities that are restricted to the upper limbs may indicate that the child could not yet walk (Ortner and Putschar 1981: 278), whereas those that show bowing of both the upper and lower limbs may be indicative of chronic or recurring rickets (Stuart-Macadam 1989b: 41). Bowing limited to the long bones of the lower extremities would indicate that rickets had become active only after the child had started walking (Ortner and Putschar 1981: 278).

There is a relatively rare form of rickets that is not caused by a deficiency in dietary vitamin D. Instead, this condition results from the kidneys' failure to retain phosphorus (Fallon 1988: 1994), and as phosphate is the other major component of bone mineral besides calcium, the effect is deficient mineralization as well. This failure may be caused by a congenital defect in the kidneys or by other diseases affecting the kidneys. The importance of nondietary rickets to this chapter is that the anatomical manifestations in the skeleton are indistinguishable from those caused by vitamin D deficiency.

The adult counterpart of rickets in the skeletal record is osteomalacia, whose expression requires an even more severe state of malnutrition (Maat 1986: 157). Women are vulnerable to osteomalacia during pregnancy and lactation because their need for calcium is great. If dietary calcium is deficient, the developing fetus will draw on calcium from the mother's skeleton. If vitamin D is also deficient, replacement of the mineral used during this period will be inhibited even if dietary calcium becomes available. As in rickets, biomechanical strength of bone may be inadequate, leading to deformity. This deformity is commonly expressed in the pelvis as biomechanical forces from the femoral head compress the anteroposterior size of the pelvis and push the acetabula into the pelvic canal.

Undisputed anatomical evidence of rickets or osteomalacia in archaeological remains is uncommon for several reasons. First, criteria for diagnosis of these conditions in dry bone specimens have not been clearly distinguished from some skeletal manifestations of other nutritional diseases such as scurvy or anemia. Second, reports on cases of rickets are often based on fairly subtle changes in the shape of the long bones (Bennike 1985: 210, 213; Grmek 1989: 76), which may not be specific for this condition. Third, cases of rickets that are associated with undernourishment are difficult to recognize because growth may have stopped (Stuart-Macadam 1989b: 41).

A remarkable case from a pre-Dynastic Nubian site illustrates the complexity of diagnosis in archaeological human remains. The case has been described by J. T. Rowling (1967: 277) and by D. J. Ortner and W. G. J. Putschar (1981: 284-7). The specimen exhibits bending of the long bones of the forearm, although the humeri are relatively unaffected. The long bones of the lower extremity also exhibit bending, and the pelvis is flattened in the anteroposterior axis. All these features support a diagnosis of osteomalacia, but the specimen is that of a male, so the problem cannot be associated with nutritional deficiencies that can occur during childbearing. An additional complicating feature is the extensive development of abnormal bone on both femora and in the interosseous areas of the radius/ulna and tibia/fibula. This is not typical of osteomalacia and probably represents a pathological complication in addition to vitamin D deficiency.

Cases of rickets have been reported at several

archaeological sites in Europe for the Mesolithic period (Zivanovic 1975: 174; Nemeskéri and Lengyel 1978: 241; Grimm 1984; Meiklejohn and Zvelebil 1991), and the later Bronze Age (Schultz 1990: 178, 1993; Schultz and Schmidt-Schultz 1994). Reports of possible cases have also been recorded in the Middle East as early as the Mesolithic period (Macchiarelli 1989: 587). There may be additional cases in the Neolithic period (Röhrer-Ertl 1981, as cited in Smith, Bar-Yosef, and Sillen 1984: 121) and at two sites in Dynastic Egypt (Ortner and Putschar 1981: 285; Buikstra, Baker, and Cook 1993: 44–5). In South Asia, there have been reports of rickets from the Mesolithic, Chalcolithic, and Iron Age periods (Lovell and Kennedy 1989: 91). Osteomalacia has been reported for Mesolithic sites in Europe (Nemeskéri and Lengyel 1978: 241) and in the Middle East (Macchiarelli 1989: 587).

Vitamin C Deficiency

Vitamin C (ascorbic acid) deficiency causes scurvy, a condition that is seen in both children and adults. Because humans cannot store vitamin C in the body, regular intake is essential. As vitamin C is abundant in fresh fruits and vegetables and occurs in small quantities in uncooked meat, scurvy is unlikely to occur in societies where such foods are common in the diet year-round. Historically, vitamin C deficiency has been endemic in northern and temperate climates toward the end of winter (Maat 1986: 160). In adults, scurvy is expressed only after four or five months of total deprivation of vitamin C (Stuart-Macadam 1989b: 219–20).

Vitamin C is critical in the formation of connective tissue, including bone protein and the structural proteins of blood vessels. In bone, the lack of vitamin C may lead to diminished bone protein (osteoid) formation by osteoblasts. The failure to form osteoid results in the abnormal retention of calcified cartilage, which has less biomechanical strength than normal bone. Fractures, particularly at the growth plate, are a common feature. In blood vessel formation the vessel walls may be weak, particularly in young children. This defect may result in bleeding from even minimal trauma. Bleeding can elevate the periosteum and lead to the formation of abnormal subperiosteal bone. It can also stimulate an inflammatory response resulting in abnormal bone destruction or formation adjacent to the bleeding.

Reports of scurvy in archaeological human remains are not common for several reasons. First, evidence of scurvy is hard to detect. For example, if scurvy is manifested in the long bones of a population, the frequency will probably represent only half of the actual cases (Maat 1986: 159). Second, many of the anatomical features associated with scurvy are as yet poorly understood, as is illustrated by an unusual type and distribution pattern of lesions being studied by Ortner. The pattern occurs in both Old and New World specimens in a variety of stages of severity

(e.g., Ortner 1984). Essentially, the lesions are inflammatory and exhibit an initial stage that tends to be destructive, with fine porous holes penetrating the outer table of the skull. In later stages the lesions are proliferative but tend to be porous and resemble lesions seen in the anemias. However, the major distinction from the anemias is that the diploë is not involved in the scorbutic lesions and the anatomical distribution in the skull tends to be limited to those areas that lie beneath the major muscles associated with chewing – the temporalis and masseter muscles.

An interesting Old World case of probable scurvy is from the cemetery for the medieval hospital of St. James and St. Mary Magdalene in Chichester, England. Throughout much of the medieval period the hospital was for lepers. As leprosy declined in prevalence toward the end of the period, patients with other ailments were admitted.

The specimen (Chichester burial 215) consists of the partial skeleton of a child about 6 years old, probably from the latter part of the medieval period. The only evidence of skeletal pathology occurs in the skull, where there are two types of lesion. The first type is one in which fine holes penetrate the compact bone with no more than minimal reactive bone formation. This condition is well demonstrated in bone surrounding the infraorbital foramen, which provides a passageway for the infraorbital nerve, artery, and vein. In the Chichester child there are fine holes penetrating the cortical bone on the margin of the foramen (Figure I.2.1) with minimal reactive bone formation. The lesion is indicative of chronic inflammation that could have been caused by blood passing through the walls of defective blood vessels.

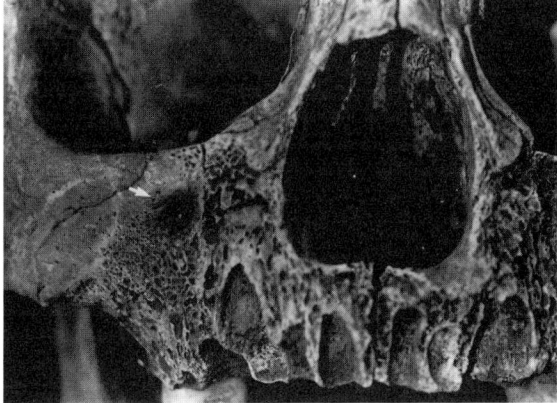

Figure I.2.1. External view of the maxilla of a child about 6 years of age at the time of death. The right infra-orbital foramen exhibits an area of porosity (arrow) with slight evidence of reactive bone formation. Below the foramen is an area of postmortem bone loss that is unrelated to the antemortem porosity. This burial (no. 215) is from the cemetery of the medieval Hospital of St. James and St. Mary Magdalene in Chichester, England.

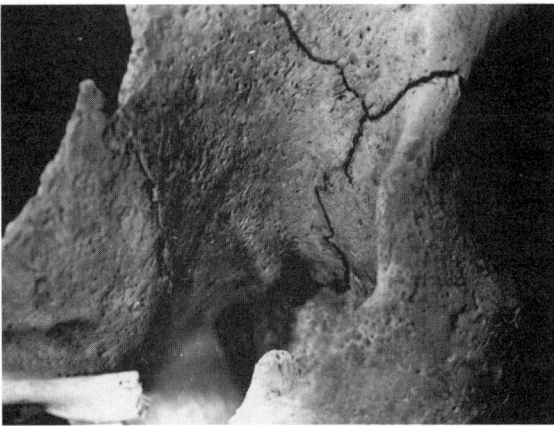

Figure I.2.2. Right sphenoid and adjacent bone surfaces of case seen in Figure I.2.1. Note the abnormal porosity of cortical bone.

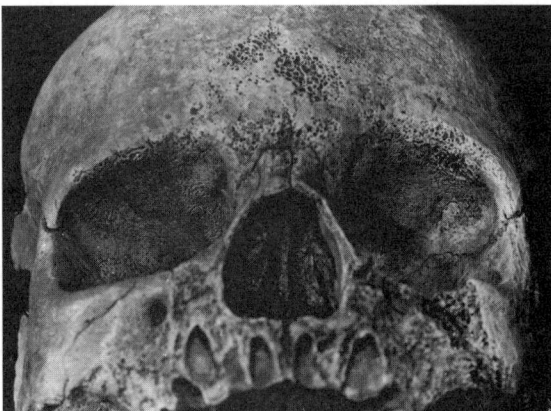

Figure I.2.3. Orbital roof of case seen in Figure I.2.1. Note the enlarged, irregular, and porous surface.

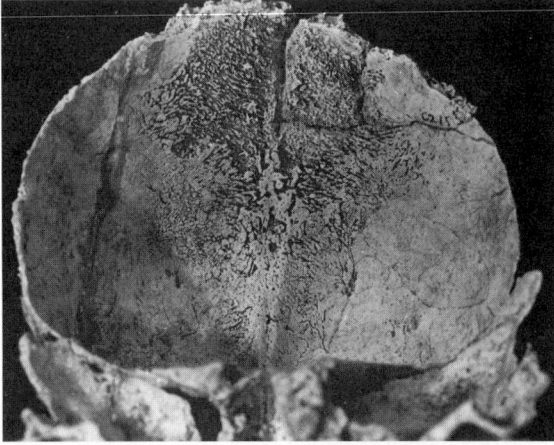

Figure I.2.4. Inner table of the frontal bone of case seen in Figure I.2.1. Note the large area of porous new bone formation.

Another area of porosity is apparent bilaterally on the greater wing of the sphenoid and adjacent bone tissue (Figure I.2.2). This area of porosity underlies the temporalis muscle, which has an unusual vascular supply that is particularly vulnerable to mild trauma and bleeding from defective blood vessels.

The second type of lesion is characterized by porous, proliferative lesions and occurs in two areas. One of these areas is the orbital roof (Figure I.2.3). At this site, bilateral lesions, which are superficial to the normal cortex, are apparent. The surfaces of the pathological bone tissue, particularly in the left orbit, seem to be filling in the porosity, suggesting that recovery from the pathological problem was in progress at the time of death.

The second area of abnormal bone tissue is the internal cortical surface of the skull, with a particular focus in the regions of the sagittal and transverse venous sinuses (Figure I.2.4). Inflammation, perhaps due to chronic bleeding between the dura and the inner table because of trauma to weakened blood vessels, is one possible explanation for this second type of lesion, particularly in the context of lesions apparent in other areas of the skull.

The probable diagnosis for this case is scurvy, which is manifested as a bone reaction to chronic bleeding from defective blood vessels. This diagnosis is particularly likely in view of the anatomical location of the lesions, although there is no evidence of defective bone tissue in the growth plates of the long bones (trümmerfeld zone) as one would expect in active scurvy. However, this may be the result of partial recovery from the disease as indicated by the remodeling in the abnormal bone tissue formed on the orbital roof.

The Chichester case provides probable evidence of scurvy in medieval England. C. A. Roberts (1987) has reported a case of possible scurvy from a late Iron Age or early Roman (100 B.C. to A.D. 43) site in Beckford, Worcestershire, England. She described an infant exhibiting porous proliferative orbital lesions and reactive periostitis of the long bones. Schultz (1990: 178) has discussed the presence of infantile scurvy in Bronze Age sites in Europe (2200 to 1900 B.C.) and in Anatolia (2500 to 2300 B.C.) (Schultz and Schmidt-Schultz 1994: 8). In South Asia pathological cases possibly attributable to infantile scurvy have been reported in Late Chalcolithic/Iron Age material (Lukacs and Walimbe 1984: 123).

Iron Deficiency

Iron deficiency is today a common nutritional problem in many parts of the world. Two-thirds of women and children in developing countries are iron deficient (Scrimshaw 1991: 46). However, physical evidence for this condition in antiquity remains elusive, and detection of trends in space and time remain inconclusive.

There are two general types of anemia that affect the human skeleton. Genetic anemias, such as sickle cell anemia and thalassemia, are caused by defects in red blood cells. Acquired anemias may result from chronic bleeding (such as is caused by internal parasites), or from an infection that will lead to a state of anemia (Stuart-Macadam 1989a; Meiklejohn and Zvelebil 1991: 130), or from an iron-deficient diet. Deficient dietary iron can be the result of either inadequate intake of iron from dietary sources or failure to absorb iron during the digestion of food.

Iron is a critical element in hemoglobin and important in the transfer and storage of oxygen in the red blood cells. Defective formation of hemoglobin may result in an increased turnover of red blood cells; this greatly increases demand for blood-forming marrow. In infants and small children the space available for blood formation is barely adequate for the hematopoietic marrow needed for normal blood formation. Enlargement of hematopoietic marrow space can occur in any of the bones. In long bones, marrow may enlarge at the expense of cortical bone, creating greater marrow volume and thinner cortices. In the skull, anemia produces enlargement of the diploë, which may replace the outer table, creating very porous bone tissue known as porotic hyperostosis. Porotic hyperostosis is a descriptive term first used by J. L. Angel in his research on human remains in the eastern Mediterranean (1966), where it is a well-known condition in archaeological skeletal material. Porotic enlargement of the orbital roof is a specific form of porotic hyperostosis called cribra orbitalia. The presence of both these conditions has been used by paleopathologists to diagnose anemias in archaeological human remains.

Attributing porotic hyperostosis to anemia should be done with caution for several reasons. First, diseases other than anemia (i.e., scurvy, parasitic infection, and rickets) can cause porotic enlargement of the skull. There are differences in pathogenesis that cause somewhat different skeletal manifestations, but overlap in pathological anatomy is considerable. Second, as mentioned previously, some diseases such as scurvy may occur in addition to anemia. Because both diseases cause porotic, hypertrophic lesions of the skull, careful anatomical analysis is critical. Finally, attributing porotic hyperostosis to a specific anemia, such as iron-deficiency anemia, is problematic. On the basis of anatomical features alone, it is very difficult to distinguish the bone changes caused by lack of iron in the diet from bone changes caused by one of the genetic anemias. These cautionary notes are intended to highlight the need for care in interpreting published reports of anemia (and other diseases caused by malnutrition), particularly when a diagnosis of a specific anemia is offered.

Angel (1966, 1972, 1977) was one of the earliest observers to link porotic hyperostosis in archaeological human remains to genetic anemia (thalassemia). He argued that thalassemia was an adaptive mechanism in response to endemic malaria in the eastern Mediterranean. The abnormal hemoglobin of thalassemia, in inhibiting the reproduction of the malarial parasite, protects the individual from severe disease.

As indicated earlier, in malarial regions of the Old World, such as the eastern Mediterranean, it may be difficult to differentiate porotic hyperostosis caused by genetic anemia from dietary anemia. However, in nonmalarial areas of the Old World, such as northern Europe, this condition is more likely to be caused by nongenetic anemia such as iron-deficiency anemia.

Because determining the probable cause of anemia is so complex, few reports have been able to provide a link between porotic hyperostosis and diet. In prehistoric Nubian populations, poor diet may have been one of the factors that led to iron-deficiency anemia (Carlson et al. 1974, as cited in Stuart-Macadam 1989a: 219). At Bronze Age Toppo Daguzzo in Italy (Repetto, Canci, and Borgogni Tarli 1988: 176), the high rate of cribra orbitalia was, possibly, caused by nutritional stress connected with weaning. At Metaponto, a Greek colony (c. 600 to 250 B.C.) in southern Italy noted for its agricultural wealth, the presence of porotic hyperostosis, along with other skeletal stress markers, indicated to researchers that the colony had nutritional problems (Henneberg, Henneberg, and Carter 1992: 452). It has been suggested that specific nutrients may have been lacking in the diet.

Fluorosis

Fluorosis as a pathological condition occurs in geographical regions where excessive fluorine is found in the water supply. It may also occur in hot climates where spring or well water is only marginally high in fluoride, but people tend to drink large amounts of water, thereby increasing their intake of fluoride. In addition, high rates of evaporation may increase the concentration of fluoride in water that has been standing (Littleton and Frohlich 1993: 443). Fluorosis has also been known to occur where water that contains the mineral is used to irrigate crops or to prepare food, thereby increasing the amount ingested (Leverett 1982, as cited in Lukacs, Retief, and Jarrige 1985: 187).

In the Old World, fluorosis has been documented in ancient populations of Hungary (Molnar and Molnar 1985: 55), India (Lukacs et al. 1985: 187), and areas of the Arabian Gulf (Littleton and Frohlich 1993: 443).

Fluorosis is known primarily from abnormalities of the permanent teeth, although the skeleton may also be affected. If excessive fluorine is ingested during dental development, dentition will be affected in several ways, depending upon severity. J. Littleton and B. Frohlich (1989: 64) observed fluorosis in archaeological specimens from Middle Bronze Age and Islamic periods in Bahrain. They categorized their findings into four stages of severity: (1) normal or translucent enamel, (2) white opacities on the enamel, (3) minute pitting with brownish staining, and (4) finally, more severe and marked pitting with widespread brown to black staining of the tooth. They noted that about 50 percent of the individuals in both the Bronze Age and the Islamic periods showed dental fluorosis (1989: 68).

Other cases of dental fluorosis have been reported in the archaeological record. At a site in the Arabian Gulf on the island of Umm an Nar (c. 2500 B.C.), Littleton and Frohlich (1993: 443) found that 21 percent of the teeth excavated showed signs of fluorosis. In Hungary, S. Molnar and I. Molnar (1985) reported that in seven skeletal populations dated from late Neolithic to late Bronze Age (c. 3000 B.C. to c. 1200 B.C.), "mottled" or "chalky" teeth suggestive of fluorosis appeared. The frequencies varied from 30 to 67 percent of individuals (Molnar and Molnar 1985: 60). In South Asia, J. R. Lukacs, D. H. Retief, and J. F. Jarringe (1985: 187) found dental fluorosis at Early Neolithic (c. 7000 to 6000 B.C.) and Chalcolithic (c. 4000 to 3000 B.C.) levels at Mehgarh.

In order for fluoride to affect the skeletal system, the condition must be long-standing and severe (Flemming Møller and Gudjonsson 1932; Sankaran and Gadekar 1964). Skeletal manifestations of fluorosis may involve ossification of ligament and tendon tissue at their origin and insertion (Figure I.2.5). However, other types of connective tissue may also be ossified, such as the tissue at the costal margin of the ribs. Connective tissue within the neural canal is involved in some cases, reducing the space needed for the spinal cord and other neurological pathways. If severe, it can cause nerve damage and paralysis.

Fluorosis may also affect mineralization of osteoid during osteon remodeling in the microscopic structure of bone (Figure I.2.6a). In contrast with the ossification of ligament and tendon tissue, excessive fluorine inhibits mineralization of osteoid at the histological level of tissue organization. It is unclear why, in some situations, fluorosis stimulates abnormal mineralization, yet in other situations, it inhibits mineralization. In microradiographs, inhibited mineralization is seen as a zone of poor mineralization (Figure I.2.6b).

Examples of archaeological fluorosis of bone tissue are rare. However, in Bahrain, excavations from third to second millennium B.C. burial mounds have revealed the full range of this disease (Frohlich, Ortner, and Al-Khalifa 1987/88). In addition to dental problems, skeletons show ossification of ligaments and tendons, and some exhibit ossification of connective tissue within the neural canal. The most severe case is that of a 50-year-old male who had a fused spine in addition to large, bony projections in the ligament attachments of the radius and ulna and tibia and fibula. Chemical analysis indicates almost 10 times the normal levels of fluorine in bone material.

Figure I.2.5. Right lateral view of the ninth through the twelfth thoracic vertebrae from the skeleton of a male about 45 years of age at the time of death. Note the fusion of the vertebral bodies and the ossification of the interspinous ligaments (arrow). Burial (B South 40) is from the Early Bronze Age (c. 2100 B.C.) site of Madinat Hamad in Bahrain.

Protein–Energy Malnutrition

Protein–energy malnutrition (PEM), or protein–calorie deficiency, covers a range of syndromes from malnutrition to starvation. The best-known clinical manifestations are seen in children in the form of kwashiorkor (a chronic form that is caused by lack of protein) and marasmus (an acute form where the child wastes away) (Newman 1993: 950). PEM occurs in areas of poverty, with its highest rates in parts of Asia and Africa (Newman 1993: 954).

PEM has no specific skeletal markers that enable us to identify it in skeletal remains. It affects the human skeleton in different ways, depending on severity and age of occurrence. During growth and development it may affect the size of the individual so that bones and teeth are smaller than normal for that population. There may be other manifestations of PEM during this growth period, such as diminished sexual dimorphism, decreased cortical bone thickness, premature osteoporosis (associated with starvation),

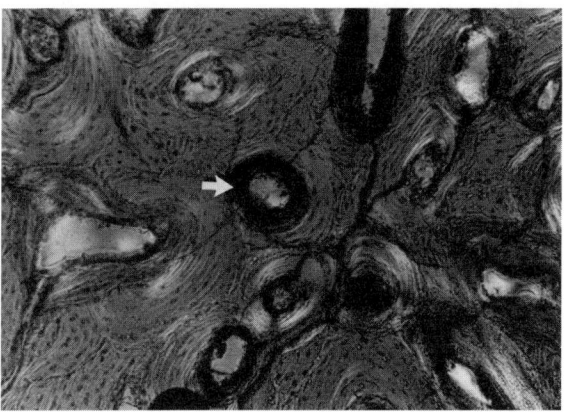

Figure I.2.6a. Photomicrograph of a bone section from the femur of the burial seen in Figure I.2.5. The dark zone (arrow) in several osteons is an area of poor mineralization caused by the toxic effects of excessive fluorine, approximately 125× before reduction.

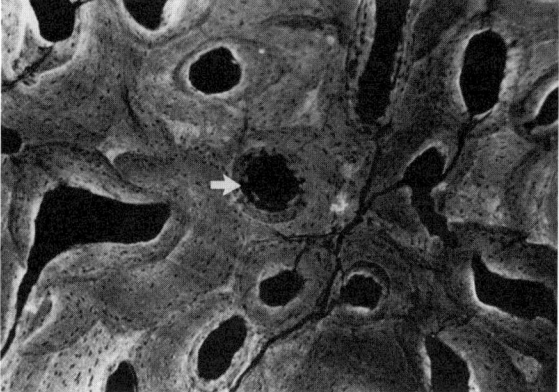

Figure I.2.6b. Photomicrograph of a microradiograph of the bone section seen in Figure I.2.6a. Note the areas of low density (dark to black) that correspond to the dark areas seen in Figure I.2.6a. The arrow indicates one of these areas.

enamel hypoplasias, and Harris lines. Because malnutrition decreases the immune response to infection, a high rate of infection may also indicate nutritional problems. Unfortunately, most of the indicators of growth problems in malnutrition occur in other disease syndromes as well; thus, careful analysis of subtle abnormalities in skeletal samples is needed. Chemical and histological analyses provide supporting evidence of abnormal features apparent anatomically.

PEM is probably as old as humankind (Newman 1993: 953). Written records in the Old World over the past 6,000 years have alluded to frequent famines. Beginning around 4000 B.C. and ending around 500 B.C., the Middle East and northeastern Africa, specifically the Nile and Tigris and Euphrates river valleys, were "extraordinarily famine prone" (Dirks 1993: 162). The skeletal evidence in archaeological remains is based on a number of skeletal abnormalities that, observers have concluded, are the result of nutritional problems.

Several studies suggesting problems with nutrition have been undertaken in northeastern Africa. In reviewing 25 years of work done on prehistoric Nubian skeletal material, G. J. Armelagos and J. O. Mills (1993: 10-11) noted that reduced long bone growth in children and premature bone loss in both children and young women were due to nutritional causes, specifically to impaired calcium metabolism. One of the complications of PEM in modern populations is thought to be interference with the metabolism of calcium (Newman 1993: 953). In Nubia, reliance on cereal grains such as barley, millet, and sorghum, which are poor sources of calcium and iron, may have been a major factor in the dietary deficiency of the population (Armelagos and Mills 1993: 11). In a later Meroitic site (c. 500 B.C. to A.D. 200) in the Sudan, E. Fulcheri and colleagues (1994: 51) found that 90 percent of the children's skeletons (0 to 12 years old) showed signs of growth disturbances or nutritional deficiencies.

There are signs of malnutrition from other areas and time periods as well. In the Arabian Gulf, the Mesolithic necropolis (c. 3700 to 3200 B.C.) of Ra's al Hamra revealed skeletal remains of a population under "strong environmental stress" with numerous pathologies, including rickets, porotic hyperostosis, and cribra orbitalia (Macchiarelli 1989). In addition, indications of growth disturbances in the form of a high rate of enamel hypoplasias and a low rate of sexual dimorphism have led to the conclusion that part of this stress was nutritional (Coppa, Cucina, and Mack 1993: 79). Specifically, the inhabitants may have suffered from protein–calorie malnutrition (Macchiarelli 1989: 587).

At Bronze Age (third millennium B.C.) Jelsovce in Slovakia, M. Schultz and T. H. Schmidt-Schultz (1994: 8) found "strong evidence of malnutrition" for the infant population, but noted that the relatively high frequency of enamel hypoplasia, anemia, rickets, and scurvy, in addition to infection, was not typical for the Bronze Age. Nutritional stress has also been suggested by the presence of premature osteoporosis among the pre-Hispanic inhabitants of the Canary Islands (Reimers et al. 1989; Martin and Mateos 1992) and among the population of Bronze Age Crete (McGeorge and Mavroudis 1987).

Conclusion

A review of the literature combined with our own research and experience leaves no doubt in our minds that humans have had nutritional problems extending at least back into the Mesolithic period. We have seen probable evidence of vitamin C deficiency, vitamin D deficiency, iron-deficiency anemia, fluorosis, and protein–energy malnutrition. However, because the conditions that cause malnutrition may be sporadic or even random, they vary in expression in both time and space. The prevalence of nutritional diseases may be due to food availability that can be affected by local or seasonal environment. For example, crop failure can result from various factors, such as shortage of water or overabundance of pests. Other nutritional problems can be caused by idiosyncratic circumstances such as individual food preferences or specific cultural customs.

Culture affects nutrition in influencing the foods that are hunted, gathered, herded, or cultivated, as well as the ways they are prepared for consumption. Cultural traditions and taboos frequently dictate food choices. All these variables affecting nutrition, combined with differences in observers and the varying methodologies they use in studying ancient human remains, make finding diachronic patterns or trends in human nutrition difficult.

Whether or not humankind benefited from or was harmed by the epochal changes in the quality and quantity of food over the past 10,000 years is, in our opinion, still open to debate. Many studies of skeletal remains conclude that the level of health, as indicated by nutrition, declined with the change from the Mesolithic hunter-gatherer way of life to the later period of developed agriculture. M. N. Cohen and G. J. Armelagos (1984a: 587), in summing up the results of a symposium on the paleopathology of the consequences of agriculture, noted that studies of both the Old and New Worlds provided consistent evidence that farming was accompanied by a decline in the quality of nutrition. Other, more recent studies have indicated agreement with this conclusion. A. Agelarakis and B. Waddell (1994: 9), working in southwestern Asia, stated that skeletal remains from infants and children showed an increase in dietary stress during the agricultural transition. Similarly, N. C. Lovell and K. A. R. Kennedy (1989: 91) observed that signs of nutritional stress increased with farming in South Asia.

By contrast, however, in a thorough review of well-studied skeletal material from Mesolithic and Neolithic Europe, C. Meiklejohn and M. Zvelebil (1991) found unexpected variability in the health status of populations connected with the Mesolithic–Neolithic transition. Part of this variability was related to diet, and they concluded that for Europe, no significant trends in health were visible in the skeletons of those populations that made the transition from hunting and gathering to greater dependence on agriculture, and from mobile to relatively sedentary communities. Although some differences between specific areas (i.e., the western Mediterranean and northern and eastern Europe) seem to exist, deficiencies in sample size mean that neither time- nor space-dependent patterns emerge from their review of the existing data. Clearly, different observers interpret evidence on the history of nutritional diseases in somewhat different ways. This is not surprising given the nature of the data. The questions about the relationship of malnutrition to changes in time and space remain an important scientific problem. Additional studies on skeletal material, particularly those that apply new biochemical and histological methods, offer the promise of a clearer understanding of these issues in the near future.

Donald J. Ortner
Gretchen Theobald

Research support for D. J. Ortner was provided by grants from the Smithsonian Scholarly Studies Program (fund no. 1233S40C). The assistance of Agnes Stix, in preparation of photographic illustrations, and editing, and Janet T. Beck for editing, Department of Anthropology, National Museum of Natural History, is deeply appreciated.

Bibliography

Agelarakis, A., and B. Waddell. 1994. Analysis of non-specific indicators of stress in subadult skeletons during the agricultural transition from southwestern Asia. *Homo* 45 (Supplement): 9.

Angel, J. L. 1966. Porotic hyperostosis, anemias, malarias and marshes in the prehistoric eastern Mediterranean. *Science* 153: 760-3.

　　1971. Early Neolithic skeletons from Catal Huyuk: Demography and pathology. *Anatolian Studies* 21: 77-98.

　　1972. Biological relations of Egyptian and eastern Mediterranean populations during pre-Dynastic and Dynastic times. *Journal of Human Evolution* 1: 307-13.

　　1977. Anemias of antiquity in the eastern Mediterranean. *Paleopathology Association Monograph No. 2:* 1-5.

Armelagos, George J., and James O. Mills. 1993. Paleopathology as science: The contribution of Egyptology. In *Biological anthropology and the study of ancient Egyptians*, ed. W. Vivian Davies and Roxie Walker, 1-18. London.

Bennike, P. 1985. *Palaeopathology of Danish skeletons.* Copenhagen.

Brothwell, Don. 1986. *The Bog Man and the archaeology of people.* London.

Buikstra, Jane E., Brenda J. Baker, and Della C. Cook. 1993. What diseases plagued ancient Egyptians? A century of controversy considered. In *Biological anthropology and the study of ancient Egypt,* ed. W. Vivian Davies and Roxie Walker, 24-53. London.

Carli-Thiele, P., and Michael Schultz. 1994. Cribra orbitalia in the early neolithic child populations from Wandersleben and Aiterhofen (Germany). *Homo* 45 (Supplement): 33.

Cohen, Mark Nathan. 1989. *Health and the rise of civilization.* New Haven, Conn.

Cohen, Mark Nathan, and George J. Armelagos. 1984a. Paleopathology at the origins of agriculture: Editors' summation. In *Paleopathology at the origins of agriculture,* ed. Mark Nathan Cohen and George J. Armelagos, 585-601. New York.

　　eds. 1984b. *Paleopathology at the origins of agriculture.* New York.

Coppa, A., A. Cucina, and M. Mack. 1993. Frequenza e distribuzione cronologica dell' ipoplasia dello smalto in un campione scheletrico di RH5. *Antropologia Contemporanea* 16: 75-80.

Dirks, Robert. 1993. Famine and disease. In *The Cambridge world history of human disease,* ed. K. F. Kiple, 157-63. Cambridge and New York.

Fallon, M. D. 1988. Bone histomorphology. In *Diagnosis of*

bone and joint disorders. Second edition, ed. D. Resnick and G. Niwayama, 1975-97. Philadelphia, Pa.

Fischer, Christian. 1980. Bog bodies of Denmark. In *Mummies, disease, and ancient cultures,* ed. Aidan Cockburn and Eve Cockburn, 177-93. New York.

Flemming Møller, P., and S. V. Gudjonsson. 1932. Massive fluorosis of bones and ligaments. *Acta Radiologica* 13: 269-94.

Follis, R. H., Jr., D. A. Jackson, and E. A. Park. 1940. The problem of the association of rickets and scurvy. *American Journal of Diseases of Children* 60: 745-7.

Frohlich, Bruno, Donald J. Ortner, and Haya Ali Al-Khalifa. 1987/1988. Human disease in the ancient Middle East. *Dilmun: Journal of the Babrain Historical and Archaeological Society* 14: 61-73.

Fulcheri, E., P. Baracchini, A. Coppa, et al. 1994. Paleopathological findings in an infant Meroitic population of El Geili (Sudan). *Homo* 45 (Supplement): 51.

Glob, P. V. 1971. *The bog people.* London.

Goldberg, A. 1963. The anaemia of scurvy. *Quarterly Journal of Medicine* 31: 51-64.

Goodman, A. H. 1991. Stress, adaptation, and enamel developmental defects. In *Human paleopathology: Current syntheses and future options,* ed. D. J. Ortner and A. C. Aufderheide, 280-7. Washington, D.C.

Goodman, A. H., D. L. Martin, and G. J. Armelagos. 1984. Indications of stress from bone and teeth. In *Paleopathology at the origins of agriculture,* ed. Mark Nathan Cohen and George J. Armelagos, 13-49. Orlando, Fla.

Grimm, H. 1984. Neue Hinweise auf ur- und frühgeschichtliches sowie mittelalterliches Vorkommen der Rachitis und ähnlicher Mineralisationsstörungen. *Ärtzliche Jugendkunde* 5: 168-77.

Grmek, M. D. 1989. *Diseases in the ancient Greek world,* trans. Mirelle Muellner and Leonard Muellner. Baltimore, Md.

Hall, Thomas L., and Victor W. Sidel. 1993. Diseases of the modern period in China. In *The Cambridge world history of human disease,* ed. K. F. Kiple, 362-73. Cambridge and New York.

Henneberg, M., R. Henneberg, and J. C. Carter. 1992. Health in colonial Metaponto. *Research and Exploration* 8: 446-59.

Katzenberg, M. Anne. 1992. Advances in stable isotope analysis of prehistoric bones. In *Skeletal biology of past peoples: Research methods,* ed. Shelly R. Saunders and M. Anne Katzenberg, 105-19. New York.

Kuhnke, LaVerne. 1993. Disease ecologies of the Middle East and North Africa. In *The Cambridge world history of human disease,* ed. K. F. Kiple, 453-62. Cambridge and New York.

Littleton, J., and B. Frohlich. 1989. An analysis of dental pathology and diet on historic Bahrain. *Paleorient* 15: 59-75.

1993. Fish-eaters and farmers: Dental pathology in the Arabian Gulf. *American Journal of Physical Anthropology* 92: 427-47.

Lovell, N. C., and K. A. R. Kennedy. 1989. Society and disease in prehistoric South Asia. In *Old problems and new perspectives in the archaeology of South Asia,* ed. M. Kenoyer, 89-92. Madison, Wis.

Lukacs, John R. 1989. Dental paleopathology: Methods of reconstructing dietary patterns. In *Reconstruction of life from the skeleton,* ed. M. Y. Iscan and K. A. R. Kennedy, 261-86. New York.

Lukacs, John R., D. H. Retief, and J. F. Jarrige. 1985. Dental disease in prehistoric Baluchistan. *National Geographic Research* 1: 184-97.

Lukacs, John R., and Subhash R. Walimbe. 1984. Paleodemography at Inamgaon: An early farming village in western India. In *The people of South Asia: The biological anthropology of India, Pakistan, and Nepal,* ed. John R. Lukacs, 105-33. New York.

Maat, George J. R. 1986. Features of malnutrition, their significance and epidemiology in prehistoric anthropology. In *Innovative trends in prehistoric anthropology,* ed. B. Hermann, 157-64. Berlin.

Macchiarelli, R. 1989. Prehistoric "fisheaters" along the eastern Arabian coasts: Dental variation, morphology, and oral health in the Ra's al-Hamra community (Qurum, Sultanate of Oman, 5th-4th millennia B.C.). *American Journal of Physical Anthropology* 78: 575-94.

Martin, C. Rodriguez, and B. Beranger Mateos. 1992. Interpretation of the skeletal remains from Los Auchones (Anaga, Santa Cruz de Tenerife): A case of biocultural isolation. *Papers on paleopathology presented at the 9th European members meeting:* 22-3. Barcelona.

McGeorge, P. J. P., and E. Mavroudis. 1987. The incidence of osteoporosis in Bronze Age Crete. *Journal of Paleopathology* 1: 37.

Meiklejohn, Christopher, and Marek Zvelebil. 1991. Health status of European populations at the agricultural transition and the implications for the adoption of farming. In *Health in past societies: Biocultural interpretations of human skeletal remains in archaeological contexts,* ed. H. Bush and M. Zvelebil, 129-45. Oxford.

Molnar, S., and I. Molnar. 1985. Observations of dental diseases among prehistoric populations in Hungary. *American Journal of Physical Anthropology* 67: 51-63.

Nemeskéri, J., and I. Lengyel. 1978. The results of paleopathological examinations. In *Vlasac: A Mesolithic settlement in the Iron Gates,* Vol. 2, ed. M. Garasanin, 231-60. Belgrade.

Newman, James L. 1993. Protein-energy malnutrition. In *The Cambridge world history of human disease,* ed. K. F. Kiple, 950-5. Cambridge and New York.

Ortner, D. J. 1984. Bone lesions in a probable case of scurvy from Metlatavik, Alaska. *MASCA* 3: 79-81.

Ortner, D. J., and W. G. J. Putschar. 1981. *Identification of pathological conditions in human skeletal remains.* Washington, D.C.

Reimers, C., Emilio Gonzales, Matilde Arnay De La Rosa, et al. 1989. Bone histology of the prehistoric inhabitants of Gran Canaria. *Journal of Paleopathology* 2: 47-59.

Repetto, E., A. Canci, and S. M. Borgogni Tarli. 1988. Skeletal indicators of health conditions in the Bronze Age sample from Toppo Daguzzo (Basilicata, Southern Italy). *Anthropologie* 26: 173-82.

Resnick, D., and G. Niwayama. 1988. *Diagnosis of bone and joint disorders.* Second edition. Philadelphia, Pa.

Roberts, C. A. 1987. Case report no. 9. *Paleopathology Newsletter* 57: 14-15.

Rowling, J. T. 1967. Paraplegia. In *Diseases in antiquity: A survey of the diseases, injuries and surgery of early populations,* ed. D. R. Brothwell and A. T. Sandison, 272-8. Springfield, Ill.

Sankaran, B., and N. Gadekar. 1964. Skeletal fluorosis. In *Proceedings of the first European bone and tooth symposium, Oxford, 1963.* Oxford.

Schultz, Michael. 1986. *Die mikroskopische Untersuchung prähistorischer Skeletfunde.* Liestal, Switzerland.

1990. Causes and frequency of diseases during early childhood in Bronze Age populations. In *Advances in paleopathology,* ed. L. Capasso, 175-9. Chieti, Italy.

1993. Initial stages of systemic bone disease. In *Histology of ancient bone,* ed. G. Grupe and A. N. Garland, 185–203. Berlin.

Schultz, Michael, and T. H. Schmidt-Schultz. 1994. Evidence of malnutrition and infectious diseases in the infant population of the early Bronze Age population from Jelsovce (Slovakia): A contribution to etiology and epidemiology in prehistoric populations. *Papers on paleopathology presented at the 21st Annual Meeting of the Paleopathology Association:* 8. Denver.

Scrimshaw, Nevin S. 1991. Iron deficiency. *Scientific American* 265: 46–52.

Smith, P., O. Bar-Yosef, and A. Sillen. 1984. Archaeological and skeletal evidence for dietary change during the Late Pleistocene/Early Holocene in the Levant. In *Paleopathology at the origins of agriculture,* ed. Mark Nathan Cohen and George J. Armelagos, 101–36. Orlando, Fla.

Stuart-Macadam, P. 1989a. Nutritional deficiency diseases: A survey of scurvy, rickets, and iron-deficiency anemia. In *Reconstruction of life from the skeleton,* ed. M. Y. Iscan and K. A. R. Kennedy, 201–22. New York.

   1989b. Rickets as an interpretive tool. *Journal of Paleopathology* 2: 33–42.

White, Christine D. 1993. Isotopic determination of seasonality in diet and death from Nubian mummy hair. *Journal of Archaeological Science* 20: 657–66.

Zivanovic, S. 1975. A note on the anthropological characteristics of the Padina population. *Zeitschrift für Morfologie und Anthropologie* 66: 161–75.

I.3. ❧ Dietary Reconstruction As Seen in Coprolites

The question of prehistoric dietary practices has become an important one. Coprolites (desiccated or mineralized feces) are a unique resource for analyzing prehistoric diet because their constituents are mainly the undigested or incompletely digested remains of food items that were actually eaten. Thus they contain direct evidence of dietary intake (Bryant 1974b, 1990; Spaulding 1974; Fry 1985; Scott 1987; Sobolik 1991a, 1994a, 1994b). In addition they can reveal important information on the health, nutrition, possible food preparation methods, and overall food economy and subsistence of a group of people (Sobolik 1991b; Reinhard and Bryant 1992).

Coprolites are mainly preserved in dry, arid environments or in the frozen arctic (Carbone and Keel 1985). Caves and enclosed areas are the best places for preserved samples and there are also samples associated with mummies. Unfortunately, conditions that help provide such samples are not observed in all archaeological sites.

Coprolite analysis is important in the determination of prehistoric diets for two significant reasons. First, the constituents of a coprolite are mainly the remains of intentionally eaten food items. This type of precise sample cannot be replicated as accurately from animal or plant debris recovered from archaeological sites. Second, coprolites tend to preserve small, fragile remains, mainly because of their compact nature, which tends to keep the constituents separated from the site matrix. These remains are typically recovered by normal coprolitic processing techniques, which involve screening with micron mesh screens rather than the larger screens used during archaeological excavations.

The limitations of coprolites are also twofold (Sobolik 1994a). First, even though the analysis of coprolites indicates the ingestion of food items, their constituents do not contain the entire diet of an individual or a population. In fact, because the different food items ingested pass through the digestive system at different rates, coprolite contents do not reflect one specific meal. The problem with coprolites is that they contain the indigestible portion of foods. The actual digested portion has been absorbed by the body. Thus, it has been estimated that meat protein may be completely absorbed during the digestion process, often leaving few traces in the coprolite (Fry 1985). However, recent protein residue analyses conducted on coprolites have indicated that some protein may survive (Newman et al. 1993).

A second limitation is that coprolites can reflect seasonal or short-term dietary intake. Individual coprolites often reflect either items a person ate earlier that day or what may have been eaten up to a month before (Williams-Dean 1978; Sobolik 1988). Thus, determining year-round dietary intake using coprolites, even with a large sample, becomes risky and inconclusive.

The History of Coprolite Research

The first observations of coprolites were those from animals of early geologic age; the Cretaceous in England (Mantell 1822; Agassiz 1833–43) and North America (Dekay 1830); the Lower Jurassic in England (Buckland 1829); and the Eocene in France (Robert 1832–33). Later works in North America include coprolites of the ground sloth (Laudermilk and Munz 1934, 1938; Martin, Sabels, and Shutler 1961; Thompson et al. 1980) and other Pleistocene animals (Davis et al. 1984).

The potential of human coprolites as dietary indicators was realized by J. W. Harshberger in 1896. The first analyses, however, were not conducted until after the beginning of the twentieth century. These initial studies were conducted by G. E. Smith and F. W. Jones (1910), who examined the dried fecal remains from Nubian mummies, and by B. H. Young (1910), L. L. Loud and M. R. Harrington (1929), and Volney H. Jones (1936), who studied materials from North American caves. Early coprolite analyses also included samples from Danger Cave (Jennings 1957), sites in Tamaulipas, Mexico (MacNeish 1958), caves in eastern Kentucky (Webb and Baby 1957), and colon contents from a mummy (Wakefield and Dellinger 1936).

The processing techniques for these early analyses

consisted of either cutting open the dry coprolites and observing the large, visible contents, or grinding the samples through screens, in the process breaking much of the material. Improved techniques for analyzing coprolites were later developed by Eric O. Callen and T. W. M. Cameron (1960).

Still used today, these techniques revolutionized the science of coprolite analysis. They involved rehydrating the sample in tri-sodium phosphate, a strong detergent, in order to gently break apart the materials for ease in screening. Processing with tri-sodium phosphate also allowed for the recovery of polleniferous and parasitic materials from the samples, and increased the recovery of smaller, fragile macromaterials. Direct coprolite pollen analyses were soon followed by the first published investigation conducted by Paul S. Martin and F. W. Sharrock (1964) on material from Glen Canyon. Subsequently, there have been other innovative studies (Hill and Hevly 1968; Bryant 1974a; Bryant and Williams-Dean 1975; Hevly et al. 1979).

Coprolite Constituents

Coprolites represent such an unusual data source that their analysis is usually undertaken by specialists, generally by paleoethnobotanists (Ford 1979). A thorough coprolite analysis, however, involves the identification and interpretation of all types of botanical remains (Bryant 1974b, 1986; Fry 1985), such as fiber, seeds, and pollen, as well as nonbotanical remains, such as animal bone and hair, insects, fish and reptile scales, and parasites (to name a few of the many coprolitic constituents). Some recent studies have also identified the presence of wax and lipids through gas chromatography and mass spectrometry analyses and the analysis of phytoliths (Wales, Evans, and Leeds 1991; Danielson 1993). Clearly, then, coprolite analysis covers a myriad of sciences besides paleoethnobotany.

Yet, because coprolite analyses have tended to be conducted by paleoethnobotanists, such studies have tended to focus on the botanical remains. Recently, however, researchers have realized that the botanical portion represents a biased sample of prehistoric diet, and, consequently, studies of the nonbotanical macroremains from coprolites are becoming more prevalent.

A significant early analysis that included the identification and interpretation of a variety of coprolitic constituents was conducted on 50 coprolite samples from Lovelock Cave, Nevada (Napton 1970). As a part of this investigation, Charles L. Douglas (1969) identified eight different animal species through analysis of hair content, and Lewis K. Napton and O. A. Brunetti (1969) identified feathers from a wide variety of birds, most significantly, the mud hen.

A more recent study has focused on small animal remains recovered from coprolites excavated throughout North America (Sobolik 1993). This effort indicates that animals that have been considered noncultural or site-contaminants actually served as human food (Munson, Parmalee, and Yarnell 1971; Parmalee, Paloumpis, and Wilson 1972; Smith 1975; Cordell 1977; Lyman 1982). The large number of coprolites analyzed from North America reveals direct ingestion of small animals, suggesting that small animal remains from sites do, in fact, reflect human dietary patterns, and that reptiles, birds, bats, and a large variety of rodents were an important and prevalent component of the prehistoric diet.

A variety of microremains can be analyzed from coprolites. These constituents include spores and fungi (Reinhard et al. 1989), bacteria (Stiger 1977), viruses (Williams-Dean 1978), and, recently, phytoliths (Bryant 1969; Cummings 1989). The most frequently analyzed microremains from coprolites, however, are pollen and parasites.

Pollen

Pollen is a unique resource in the analysis of coprolites because it can provide information not obtained from the macroremains. If a flower type is frequently ingested, the soft flower parts will most likely be digested. Pollen, depending on size and structure, becomes caught in the intestinal lumen, permitting it to be excreted in fecal samples for up to one month after ingestion. Therefore, the pollen content of coprolites does not reflect one meal, but can reflect numerous meals with a variety of pollen types (Williams-Dean 1978; Sobolik 1988).

Pollen in coprolites can occur through the intentional eating of flowers or seeds, through the unintentional ingestion of pollen in medicinal teas, or by the consumption of plants to which pollen adheres. Pollen, in this context, is considered "economic" because it is actually associated with food or a medicinal item. But it may also become ingested during respiration, with contaminated water supplies, and with food, especially if the food is prepared in an open area (Bryant 1974b, 1987). Such occurrences can be especially prevalent during the pollinating season of a specific plant, such as pine and oak in the spring or ragweed and juniper in the fall. Pollen, in this context, is considered "background" because it was accidentally ingested and was not associated with a particular food or medicinal item.

Pollen types are divided into insect pollinated plants (zoophilous) and wind pollinated plants (anemophilous). Insect pollinated plants produce few pollen grains and are usually insect specific to ensure a high rate of pollination. Indeed, such plants generally produce fewer than 10,000 pollen grains per anther (Faegri and Iversen 1964) and are rarely observed in the pollen record.

Wind pollinated plants, by contrast, produce large amounts of pollen to ensure pollination and are frequently found in the pollen record. The enormous quantity of pollen produced by some plants was highlighted by the study of R. N. Mack and Vaughn M.

Bryant (1974) in which they found over 50 percent *Pinus* pollen in areas where the nearest pine tree is more than 100 miles away. Knut Faegri and J. Iversen (1964) state that an average pine can produce approximately 350 million pollen grains per tree.

In coprolite analyses, this division between pollination types is essential because a high frequency of wind pollinated pollen types in a sample may indicate not diet but rather accidental ingestion from contaminated food or water supplies. A high frequency of insect pollinated pollen types, however, often indicates the intentional ingestion of food containing pollen (economic pollen), since it is unlikely that many grains of this type are accidental contaminants. Bryant (1975) has shown from field experiments that for some of the common insect pollinated types in the lower Pecos region a frequency greater than 2 percent in a coprolite suggests a strong possibility of intentional ingestion of flowers and certain seed types that still have pollen attached, and that a frequency of 10 percent should be interpreted as positive evidence of intentional ingestion.

Parasites and Nutrition

The presence of parasites observed in coprolites can help determine the amount of disease present in populations and indicate much about the subsistence and general quality of life. Examples include studies conducted by Henry J. Hall (1972) and Karl J. Reinhard (1985) in which differences were noted between the prevalence of parasitic disease in hunter-gatherers and in agriculturalists.

Agriculturalists and hunter-gatherers have very different subsistence bases and lifeways, which affect the types of diseases and parasites infecting each group. Hunter-gatherers were (and still are) mobile people who generally lived and moved in small groups and probably had limited contact with outsiders. They lived in temporary dwellings, usually moving in a seasonal pattern, and tended to enjoy a well-balanced diet (Dunn 1968). Subsistence centered on the environment and what it provided, making it the most important aspect of their existence (Nelson 1967; Hayden 1971).

Agriculturalists, by contrast, are generally sedentary and live in larger groups because of the increase in population that an agricultural subsistence base can support. Their dwellings are more permanent structures, and they have extensive contacts with groups because of a more complex society and because of extensive trading networks that link those societies.

Although population increase and sedentary agriculture seem linked, the tendency of sedentary agriculturalists to concentrate their diets largely on a single crop can adversely affect health, even though their numbers increase. Corn, for example, is known to be a poor source of iron and deficient in the essential amino acids lysine and tryptophan. Moreover, the phytic acid present in corn inhibits intestinal absorption of nutrients, all of which can lead to undernourishment and anemia (El-Najjar 1976; Walker 1985). Thus, the adoption of agriculture seems to have been accompanied by a decrease in nutritional status, although such a general proposition demands analysis in local or regional settings (Palkovich 1984; Rose et al. 1984).

Nutritional status, however, can also be affected by parasite infection, which sedentism tends to encourage (Nelson 1967). In the past, as people became more sedentary and population increased, human wastes were increasingly difficult to dispose of, poor sanitation methods increased the chances of food contamination, and water supplies were fouled (Walker 1985). Many parasites thrive in fecal material and create a breeding ground for disease. The problem is exacerbated as feces are used for fertilizer to produce larger crop yields. Irrigation is sometimes used to increase production, which promotes the proliferation of waterborne parasites and also aids the dispersal of bacteria (Cockburn 1967; Dunn 1968; Alland 1969; Fenner 1970; McNeill 1979).

In addition, as animals were domesticated they brought their own suite of parasites to the increasing pool of pathogens (Cockburn 1967; Alland 1969; Fenner 1970; McNeill 1979). And finally, the storage of grains and the disturbance of the local environment, which accompanies agricultural subsistence, can stimulate an increase in rodents and wild animals, respectively, and consequently an increase in their facultative parasites as well (Reinhard 1985).

It seems clear that the quality of the diet declined and parasite load increased as the transition was made to sedentary agriculture. This is not to say that hunter-gatherers were parasite-free. Rather, there was a parallel evolution of some parasites along with humankind's evolution from ancestral nonhuman primates to *Homo sapiens* (Kliks 1983). Then, as human mobility increased, some parasites were lost because of their specific habitat range and because of changes in environment and temperature. But as these latter changes occurred, new parasites were picked up. Probably such changes took place as humans migrated across the cold arctic environment of the Bering Strait into North America. Some parasites would have made the journey with their human hosts, whereas others were left behind (Cockburn 1967; McNeill 1979).

New Approaches to Dietary Reconstruction

Regional Syntheses

As more researchers are analyzing coprolites, regional syntheses of diet are becoming possible. Paul E. Minnis (1989), for example, has condensed a large coprolite data set from Anasazi populations in the Four Corners Region of the southwestern United States, covering a time period from Basketmaker III to Pueblo III (A.D. 500–1300). He observed that for the sample area, local resource structure seemed to be more important for determining diet than chronological differences. For example, domesticated plants, particularly corn, were a consistent dietary item from Basketmaker III to Pueblo III; and there was a "generally stable dietary regime" during the time periods studied, although small-scale changes were also noted (Minnis 1989: 559).

In another example from the Lower Pecos Region of southwestern Texas and northern New Mexico, a total of 359 coprolite samples have been studied (Sobolik 1991a, 1994b). Analysis indicates that the prehistoric populations of the region relied on a wide variety of dietary items for their subsistence. A substantial amount of fiber was provided by the diet, particularly that derived from prickly pear, onion, and the desert succulents (agave, yucca, sotol). A large number of seed and nut types were also ingested, although prickly pear and grass seeds were the most frequent. Animal remains, especially bone and fur, were also observed with a high frequency in the coprolites, indicating that these prehistoric people were eating a variety of animals (e.g., rodents, fish, reptiles, birds, and rabbits). The ingestion of an extremely wide variety of flowers and inflorescences is also indicated by the coprolite pollen data.

Significant differences were also observed in the dietary components of the coprolites. These differences might be attributable to changes in dietary practice, particularly to an increase in the variety of the prehistoric diet. A more plausible explanation, however, is that such differences are a result of the different locations of the archaeological sites from which the coprolite samples were excavated.

These sites are located on a south-north and a west-east gradient. Sites located in the southwestern portion of the region are in a dryer, more desert environment (the Chihuahuan Desert) with little access to water, whereas the sites located in the northeastern portion of the region are closer to the more mesic Edwards Plateau, which contains a diversity of plants and trees and is close to a continuous water supply. Thus, dietary change reflected in the coprolites most likely represents spatial differences rather than temporal fluctuations (Sobolik 1991a).

Nutritional Analyses

Coprolites are extremely useful in providing dietary and nutritional data, although information from botanical, faunal, and human skeletal remains is also needed in any attempt to characterize the nutrition of a prehistoric population (Sobolik 1990, 1994a). A recent study involving the nutritional analysis of 49 coprolites from Nubia was conducted by Linda S. Cummings (1989). This analysis was unique in that the coprolites were taken from skeletal remains buried in cemeteries representing two distinct time periods, including the early Christian period (A.D. 550–750) and the late Christian period (up to A.D. 1450). It is

rare that prehistoric coprolites can actually be attributed to specific people, and the health of individuals can be assessed through both the coprolite remains and the human skeletal material, with one method illuminating the other.

In this case, the human skeletal material suggested that cribra orbitalia indicating anemia was the major indicator of nutritional stress. Coprolite analysis by Cummings (1989) revealed that there was probably a synergistic relationship in the diet of the population between iron-deficiency anemia and deficiencies of other nutrients, mainly folacin, vitamin C, vitamin B_6, and vitamin B_{12}. Cummings also noted differences in the diet and health of the two populations, including differences between males and females and older and younger members.

Pollen Concentration Studies

Although the determination of pollen concentration values has not been attempted in many coprolite studies, such values are important in determining which pollen types were most likely ingested. Studies show that after ingestion, pollen can be excreted for many days as the grains become caught in the intestinal folds. Experiments have also demonstrated that the concentration of intentionally ingested pollen can vary considerably in sequentially produced fecal samples (Kelso 1976; Williams-Dean 1978).

Glenna Williams-Dean (1978) conducted a modern fecal study that analyzed Brassicaceae and *Prosopis* pollen as a small component of pollen ingestion. It was revealed that Brassicaceae pollen was retained in the digestive system for much longer periods of time (up to one month after ingestion) than *Prosopis* pollen. Brassicaceae pollen is an extremely small grain with an average size of 12 micrometers (μm) and has a finely defined outer-wall sculpturing pattern. Both traits would most likely increase the retention of this pollen type in the folds of the intestine, allowing for it to be observed in many fecal samples. *Prosopis* pollen is a spherical, medium-sized grain (average size 30 μm), with a smooth exine sculpturing pattern. The larger size of this grain and the decreased resistance provided by the smooth exine would permit this pollen type to pass more quickly through the intestinal folds without retention.

In light of this study, it can be predicted that larger pollen grains, such as corn *(Zea)* and cactus (Cactaceae), and pollen with little exine sculpturing, such as juniper *(Juniperus),* will move quickly through the human digestive system. Thus, these pollen types would be observed in fewer sequential fecal samples than those of other types. By contrast, smaller pollen grains with significant exine sculpturing, such as sunflower pollen (high-spine Asteraceae), can be predicted to move more slowly through the digestive system, become frequently caught in the intestinal lumen, and thus observed in fecal samples many days after initial ingestion.

Such predictions were subsequently applied in an examination of prehistoric coprolites (Sobolik 1988). This investigation revealed that a high pollen concentration value in coprolite samples should indicate that the economic pollen types observed in the samples were ingested recently. Concentration values of over 100,000 pollen grains/gram of material usually contain recently ingested pollen. But samples that contain less than 100,000 pollen grains/gram of material may contain economic pollen types that were intentionally ingested many days before the sample was deposited (Sobolik 1988). Such samples will also contain a wide variety of unintentionally ingested, background pollen types. Therefore, it is more difficult to recognize intentionally ingested pollen types from samples that contain less than 100,000 pollen grains/gram of material.

Modern fecal studies are, thus, invaluable as guides in the interpretation of prehistoric coprolite pollen content and in indicating the limitations of the data. Many more such investigations are needed to determine both pollen percentage and concentration. The diet of the participants will have to be stringently regulated in order to minimize the influence of outside pollen contaminants, particularly those in bread and canned foods (Williams-Dean 1978). Ideally, such studies will include many people and, thus, as diverse a population of digestive systems as possible over a long period of time. An important addition to such a study would be the observance of the effect of a high-fiber and a high-meat diet on pollen output and fecal output in general.

Medicinal Plant Usage

Documenting prehistoric medicinal plant usage is problematic because it is difficult to distinguish between plants that were consumed for dietary purposes and those consumed for medicinal purposes. Indeed, in many instances plants were probably used both dietarily and medicinally.

Nonetheless, the analysis of plant remains from archaeological sites is often employed to suggest dietary and medicinal intake. Such remains can be deposited through a number of channels, most significantly by contamination from outside sources (i.e., water, wind, matrix shifts, and animals). Plants also were used prehistorically as clothing, shelter, baskets, and twining, and these, when deposited into archaeological contexts, can become mistaken for food or medicinal items. Here, then, is a reason why coprolites, which are a direct indication of diet, can provide new insights into prehistoric medicinal usage (Reinhard, Hamilton, and Hevly 1991).

In an analysis of the pollen content of 32 coprolites recovered from Caldwell Cave, Culberson County, Texas, Kristin D. Sobolik and Deborah J. Gerick (1992) revealed a direct correlation between the presence of plants useful for alleviating diarrhea and coprolites that were severely diarrhetic. This correlation suggests that the prehistoric population of Caldwell Cave was ingesting medicinal plants to help alleviate chronic diarrhea. These plants, identified through analysis of the pollen content of the coprolites, included *Ephedra* (Mormon tea) and *Prosopis (mesquite)*. Interestingly, this investigation confirmed the study conducted by Richard G. Holloway (1983), which indicated that the Caldwell Cave occupants were possibly using *Ephedra* and *Larrea* (creosote bush) in medicinal teas to help cure chronic diarrhea (Holloway 1983).

Mormon tea pollen, leaves, and stems are widely used as a diarrhetic and have been one of the most prevalent medicinal remedies for diarrhea both prehistorically and historically (Burlage 1968; Niethammer 1974; Moore 1979; Moerman 1986). Mesquite leaves are also useful as a medicinal tea for stomach ailments and to cleanse the digestive system (Niethammer 1974). As part of the process of preparing mesquite leaves for a medicinal tea, pollen could also become incorporated into the sample, either intentionally or unintentionally.

In another study, Reinhard and colleagues (1991) also determined medicinal plant usage through analysis of the pollen content in prehistoric coprolites. They found that willow *(Salix)*, Mormon tea *(Ephedra)*, and creosote *(Larrea)* were probably used for medicinal purposes prehistorically and that a large variety of other plants may have been used as well.

Protein Residues

It was previously mentioned that analysis of protein residues in coprolites is a relatively new advance in coprolite studies (Newman et al. 1993). This method attempts to link protein residues with the type of plant or animal that was consumed and involves the immunological analysis of tiny amounts of protein through crossover electrophoresis. The unknown protein residue from the coprolites is placed in agarose gel with known antiserum from different plants and animals. The agarose gel is then placed in an electrophoresis tank with a barbital buffer at pH 8.6, and the electrophoretic action causes the protein antigens to move toward the antibody that is not affected by the electrical action. The solution, which contains the unknown protein residue, and the matching plant or animal species antiserum form a precipitate that is easily identifiable when stained with Coomassie Blue R250 solution (Kooyman, Newman, and Ceri 1992). The samples that form a precipitate indicate that the matching plant or animal was eaten by the person who deposited the coprolite sample.

Two sample sets were selected for an analysis of the protein residues found in coprolites – seven from Lovelock Cave, Nevada, and five from an open site in the Coachella Valley of southern California (Newman et al. 1993). Protein analysis of samples from the open site was not successful. But the samples from Lovelock Cave indicated that human protein residues were found in six of the samples and protein residues from pronghorns were found in four samples. Such an initial study suggests that protein residue analysis can be a successful and important component in the determination of prehistoric diet.

Gender Specificity

A new technique that will distinguish the gender of the coprolite depositor is presently being tested on coprolite samples from Mammoth and Salts Caves, Kentucky, by Patricia Whitten of Emory University. In this technique, which has been successful with primate studies, the gonadal (sex) steroids are removed from each coprolite sample and analyzed according to the content of testosterone, the male hormone, and estradiol, the female hormone. Both steroids can be found in each sample, but their frequencies vary depending upon gender. Modern human samples will first be analyzed to determine the frequencies of each gonadal steroid expected in males and females.

DNA analysis is also being attempted from coprolite samples to determine gender (Mark Q. Sutton 1994, personal communication). This type of research should allow archaeologists to determine dietary differences between males and females in a population and should also help in reconstructing the patterns of differential access to resources.

Conclusions

Reconstructing prehistoric human diets is a vast process requiring a variety of assemblages and disciplines to obtain a complete picture. Coprolite analysis provides a diverse and significant insight into the prehistoric diet. When analyzing the entire diet of a population, researchers must take into consideration information gleaned from other archaeological materials. Past coprolite research has focused on developing new and innovative techniques so that recovery of the diverse data inherent in such samples can be achieved. Such development has allowed researchers not only to observe the macrobotanical and macrofaunal remains from coprolites but also to analyze their pollen, parasite, and phytolith content.

Recent advances have seen the discipline progress toward determining medicinal plant ingestion so as to permit inter- and intraregional dietary comparisons; to determine the protein content of the samples; to analyze the nutritional content of the dietary items; and to determine the gender of the depositor of the sample. Coprolite analysis has definitely advanced out of its infancy, and its contributions to the determination of prehistoric diet, health, and nutrition in the future should prove to be significant indeed.

Kristin D. Sobolik

Bibliography

Agassiz, L. 1833-43. *Recherches sur les poissons fossiles.* 5 vols. Vol. 2. Soleure. Neuchatel, Switzerland.

Alland, A., Jr. 1969. Ecology and adaptation to parasitic diseases. In *Environmental and cultural behavior,* ed. A. P. Vayada, 115-41, Tucson.

Bryant, Vaughn M., Jr. 1969. Late full-glacial and post-glacial pollen analysis of Texas sediments. Ph.D. dissertation, University of Texas.

1974a. Prehistoric diet in southwest Texas: The coprolite evidence. *American Antiquity* 39: 407-20.

1974b. The role of coprolite analysis in archeology. *Bulletin of the Texas Archeological Society* 45: 1-28.

1975. Pollen as an indicator of prehistoric diets in Coahuila, Mexico. *Bulletin of the Texas Archeological Society* 46: 87-106.

1986. Prehistoric diet: A case for coprolite analysis. In *Ancient Texans: Rock art and lifeways along the lower Pecos,* ed. Harry J. Shafer, 132-5. Austin.

1987. Pollen grains: The tiniest clues in archaeology. *Environment Southwest* 519: 10-13.

1990. Pollen: Nature's fingerprints of plants. *Yearbook of science and the future, Encyclopedia Britannica.* Chicago.

Bryant, Vaughn M., Jr., and Glenna Williams-Dean. 1975. The coprolites of man. *Scientific American* 232: 100-9.

Buckland, W. 1829. On the discovery of coprolites, or fossil faeces, in the Lias at Lyme Regis, and in other formations. *Geological Society of London, Transactions* 3: 223-36.

Burlage, Henry M. 1968. *Index of plants of Texas with reputed medicinal and poisonous properties.* Austin, Tex.

Callen, Eric O., and T. W. M. Cameron. 1960. A prehistoric diet revealed in coprolites. *The New Scientist* 8: 35-40.

Carbone, Victor A., and B. C. Keel. 1985. Preservation of plant and animal remains. In *The analysis of prehistoric diets,* ed. R. I. Gilbert and J. H. Mielke, 1-19. New York.

Cockburn, Aidan. 1967. *Infectious diseases: Their evolution and eradication.* Springfield, Ill.

Cordell, Linda S. 1977. Late Anasazi farming and hunting strategies: One example of a problem in congruence. *American Antiquity* 42: 449-61.

Cummings, Linda S. 1989. Coprolites from medieval Christian Nubia: An interpretation of diet and nutritional stress. Ph.D. dissertation, University of Colorado.

Danielson, Dennis R. 1993. The role of phytoliths in prehistoric diet reconstruction and dental attrition. M.A. thesis, University of Nebraska.

Davis, Owen K., Larry Agenbroad, Paul S. Martin, and J. I. Mead. 1984. The Pleistocene dung blanket of Bechan Cave, Utah. In *Contributions in quaternary vertebrate paleontology: A volume in memorial to John E. Guilday,* ed. H. H. Genoways and M. R. Dawson, 267-82. Pittsburgh, Pa.

DeKay, J. E. 1830. On the discovery of coprolites in North America. *Philosophy Magazine* 7: 321-2.

Douglas, Charles L. 1969. Analysis of hairs in Lovelock Cave coprolites. In *Archaeological and paleobiological investigations in Lovelock Cave, Nevada,* ed. L. K. Napton. Kroeber Anthropological Society Special Publication, 2: 1-8.

Dunn, Frederick L. 1968. Epidemiological factors: Health and disease in hunter-gatherers. In *Man the hunter,* ed. R. B. Lee and I. DeVore, 221-8. Chicago.

El-Najjar, M. 1976. Maize, malaria, and anemias in the New World. *Yearbook of Physical Anthropology* 20: 329-37.

Faegri, K., and J. Iversen. 1964. *Textbook of pollen analysis.* New York.

Fenner, Frank. 1970. The effects of changing social organization on the infectious diseases of man. In *The impact of civilization on the biology of man,* ed. S. V. Boyden, 71-82. Canberra, Australia.

Ford, Richard I. 1979. Paleoethnobotany in American archaeology. In *Advances in archaeological method and theory,* Vol. 2, ed. Michael B. Schiffer, 285-336. New York.

Fry, Gary F. 1985. Analysis of fecal material. In *The analysis of prehistoric diets,* ed. R. I. Gilbert and J. H. Mielke, 127-54. New York.

Hall, Henry J. 1972. Diet and disease at Clyde's Cavern, Utah: As revealed via paleoscatology. M.A. thesis, University of Utah.

Harshberger, J. W. 1896. The purpose of ethnobotany. *American Antiquarian* 17: 47-51.

Hayden, Brian. 1971. Subsistence and ecological adaptations of modern hunter/gatherers. In *Omnivorous primates: Gathering and hunting in human evolution,* ed. R. S. O. Harding and G. Teleki, 154-65. New York.

Hevly, Richard H., R. E. Kelley, G. A. Anderson, and S. J. Olsen. 1979. Comparative effects of climate change, cultural impact and volcanism in the paleoecology of Flagstaff, Arizona, A.D. 900-1300. In *Volcanic activity and human history,* ed. Payson D. Sheets and Donald K. Grayson, 120-8. New York.

Hill, J., and Richard H. Hevly. 1968. Pollen at Broken K Pueblo: Some new interpretations. *American Antiquity* 33: 200-10.

Holloway, Richard G. 1983. Diet and medicinal plant usage of a late Archaic population from Culberson County, Texas. *Bulletin of the Texas Archeological Society* 54: 27-49.

Jennings, Jesse D. 1957. *Danger Cave.* University of Utah Anthropological Papers No. 27. Salt Lake City.

Jones, Volney H. 1936. The vegetal remains of Newt Kash Hollow Shelter. *University of Kentucky Reports in Archaeology and Ethnology* 3: 147-65.

Kelso, Gerald. 1976. Absolute pollen frequencies applied to the interpretation of human activities in Northern Arizona. Ph.D. dissertation, University of Arizona.

Kirchoff, Paul. 1971. The hunting-gathering people of North Mexico. In *The north Mexican frontier,* ed. Basil C. Hedrick, J. Charles Kelley, and Carroll L. Riley, 200-9. Carbondale, Ill.

Kliks, Michael. 1983. Paleoparasitology: On the origins and impact of human-helminth relationships. In *Human ecology and infectious diseases,* ed. N. A. Croll and J. H. Cross, 291-313. New York.

Kooyman, B., M. E. Newman, and H. Ceri. 1992. Verifying the reliability of blood residue analysis on archaeological tools. *Journal of Archaeological Sciences* 19: 265-9.

Laudermilk, J. D., and P. A. Munz. 1934. Plants in the dung of *Nothrotherium* from Gypsum Cave, Nevada. *Carnegie Institution of Washington Publication* 453: 29-37.

1938. Plants in the dung of *Nothrotherium* from Rampart and Muav Cave, Arizona. *Carnegie Institution of Washington* Publication 487: 271-81.

Loud, L. L., and M. R. Harrington. 1929. *Lovelock Cave.* University of California Publications in American Archeology and Ethnology.

Lyman, R. Lee. 1982. Archaeofaunas and Subsistence Studies. In *Advances in archaeological method and theory,* Vol. 5, ed. Michael B. Schiffer, 331-93. Tucson, Ariz.

Mack, R. N., and Vaughn M. Bryant, Jr. 1974. Modern pollen spectra from the Columbia Basin, Washington. *Northwest Science* 48: 183-94.

MacNeish, Richard S. 1958. *Preliminary archeological investigations in the Sierra de Tamaulipas, Mexico.* American Philosophical Society Transactions, Vol. 44.

Mantell, G. A. 1822. *The fossils of the South Downs; or illustrations of the geology of Sussex.* London.

Martin, Paul S., B. E. Sables, and D. Shutler, Jr. 1961. Rampart Cave coprolite and ecology of the Shasta Ground Sloth. *American Journal of Science* 259: 102-27.

Martin, Paul S., and F. W. Sharrock. 1964. Pollen analysis of prehistoric human feces: A new approach to ethnobotany. *American Antiquity* 30: 168-80.

McNeill, William H. 1979. *The human condition: An ecological and historical view.* Princeton, N.J.

Minnis, Paul E. 1989. Prehistoric diet in the northern Southwest: Macroplant remains from Four Corners feces. *American Antiquity* 54: 543-63.

Moerman, Daniel E. 1986. *Medicinal plants of native America.* University of Michigan, Museum of Anthropology Technical Reports No. 19. Ann Arbor.

Moore, Michael. 1979. *Medicinal plants of the mountain west.* Santa Fe, N. Mex.

Munson, Patrick J., Paul W. Parmalee, and Richard A. Yarnell. 1971. Subsistence ecology at Scoville, a terminal Middle Woodland village. *American Antiquity* 36: 410-31.

Napton, Lewis K. 1970. Archaeological investigation in Lovelock Cave, Nevada. Ph.D. dissertation, University of California, Berkeley.

Napton, Lewis K., and O. A. Brunetti. 1969. Paleo-ornithology of Lovelock Cave coprolites. In *Archaeological and paleobiological investigations in Lovelock Cave, Nevada,* ed. Lewis K. Napton. Kroeber Anthropological Society Special Publication, 2: 9-18.

Nelson, G. S. 1967. Human behavior in the transmission of parasitic diseases. In *Behavioural aspects of parasite transmission,* ed. E. U. Canning and C. A. Wright, 1-15. London.

Newman, M. E., R. M. Yohe II, H. Ceri, and M. Q. Sutton. 1993. Immunological protein residue analysis of non-lithic archaeological materials. *Journal of Archaeological Science* 20: 93-100.

Niethammer, Carolyn. 1974. *American Indian food and lore.* New York.

Palkovich, A. M. 1984. Agriculture, marginal environments, and nutritional stress in the prehistoric southwest. In *Paleopathology at the origins of agriculture,* ed. M. N. Cohen and G. J. Armelagos, 425-38. New York.

Parmalee, Paul W., Andreas Paloumpis, and Nancy Wilson. 1972. *Animals utilized by Woodland peoples occupying the Apple Creek Site, Illinois.* Illinois State Museum Reports of Investigations. Springfield.

Reinhard, Karl J. 1985. Recovery of helminths from prehistoric feces: The cultural ecology of ancient parasitism. M.S. thesis, Northern Arizona University.

Reinhard, Karl J., R. H. Brooks, S. Brooks, and Floyd B. Largent, Jr. 1989. Diet and environment determined from analysis of prehistoric coprolites from an archaeological site near Zape Chico, Durango, Mexico. *Journal of Paleopathology Monograph* 1: 151-7.

Reinhard, Karl J., and Vaughn M. Bryant, Jr. 1992. Coprolite analysis: A biological perspective on archaeology. In *Advances in archaeological method and theory,* Vol. 4, ed. Michael B. Schiffer, 245-88. Tucson, Ariz.

Reinhard, Karl J., Donny L. Hamilton, and Richard H. Hevly. 1991. Use of pollen concentration in paleopharmacology: Coprolite evidence of medicinal plants. *Journal of Ethnobiology* 11: 117-32.

Robert, E. 1832-33. Sur des coprolithes trouvés à Passy. *Society of Geology France Bulletin* 3: 72-3.

Rose, Jerry C., B. A. Burnett, M. S. Nassaney, and M. W. Blaeuer. 1984. Paleopathology and the origins of maize agriculture in the lower Mississippi Valley and Caddoan culture areas. In *Paleopathology at the origins of agriculture,* ed. M. N. Cohen and G. J. Armelagos, 393-424. New York.

Scott, Linda. 1987. Pollen analysis of hyena coprolites and sediments from Equus Cave, Taung, southern Kalahari

(South Africa). *Quaternary Research, New York* 28: 144–56.

Smith, Bruce D. 1975. *Middle Mississippi exploitation of animal populations.* University of Michigan, Museum of Anthropology Anthropological Papers No. 57. Ann Arbor.

Smith, G. E., and F. W. Jones. 1910. *Archeological survey of Nubia 1907–1908.* Cairo.

Sobolik, Kristin D. 1988. The importance of pollen concentration values from coprolites: An analysis of southwest Texas samples. *Palynology* 12: 201–14.

1990. A nutritional analysis of diet as revealed in prehistoric human coprolites. *Texas Journal of Science* 42: 23–36.

1991a. Paleonutrition of the Lower Pecos region of the Chihuahuan Desert. Ph.D. dissertation, Texas A&M University.

1991b. *The prehistoric diet and subsistence of the Lower Pecos region, as reflected in coprolites from Baker Cave, Val Verde County, Texas.* Studies in Archaeology Series No. 7, Texas Archaeological Research Lab, University of Texas, Austin.

1993. Direct evidence for the importance of small animals to prehistoric diets: A review of coprolite studies. *North American Archaeologist* 14: 227–44.

1994a. Introduction. In *Paleonutrition: The diet and health of prehistoric Americans,* ed. K. D. Sobolik, 1–18. Carbondale, Ill.

1994b. Paleonutrition of the Lower Pecos region of the Chihuahuan Desert. In *Paleonutrition: The diet and health of prehistoric Americans,* ed. K. D. Sobolik. Carbondale, Ill.

Sobolik, Kristin D., and Deborah J. Gerick. 1992. Prehistoric medicinal plant usage: A case study from coprolites. *Journal of Ethnobiology* 12: 203–11.

Spaulding, W. G. 1974. Pollen analysis of fossil dung of *Ovis canadensis* from southern Nevada. M.S. thesis, University of Arizona.

Stiger, Mark A. 1977. Anasazi diet: The coprolite evidence. M.A. thesis, University of Colorado.

Thompson, R. S., Thomas R. Van Devender, Paul S. Martin, et al. 1980. Shasta ground sloth *Nothrotheriops shastense* (Hoffsteter) at Shelter Cave, New Mexico; environment, diet, and extinction. *Quaternary Research, New York* 14: 360–76.

Wakefield, E. F., and S. C. Dellinger. 1936. Diet of the Bluff Dwellers of the Ozark Mountains and its skeletal effects. *Annals of Internal Medicine* 9: 1412–18.

Wales, S., J. Evans, and A. R. Leeds. 1991. The survival of waxes in coprolites: The archaeological potential. In *Archaeological sciences 1989: Proceedings of a conference on the application of scientific techniques to archaeology, Bradford, September 1989,* ed. P. Budd, B. Chapman, C. Jackson, et al. *Oxbow Monograph 9,* 340–4. Bradford, England.

Walker, Phillip. 1985. Anemia among prehistoric Indians of the southwest. In *Health and disease of the prehistoric southwest.* Arizona State University Anthropological Research Papers No. 34, ed. C. F. Merbs and R. J. Miller, 139–64. Tempe.

Webb, W. S., and R. S. Baby. 1957. *The Adena people,* no. 2. Columbus, Ohio.

Williams-Dean, Glenna J. 1978. Ethnobotany and cultural ecology of prehistoric man in southwest Texas. Ph.D. dissertation, Texas A&M University.

Young, B. H. 1910. *The prehistoric men of Kentucky.* Filson Club Publications No. 25. Louisville, Ky.

I.4. ✒ Animals Used for Food in the Past: As Seen by Their Remains Excavated from Archaeological Sites

Animal remains excavated from archaeological sites are, to a large extent, the remnants of animals that were used for food. These remains include the fragmentary bones and teeth of vertebrates, the shells of mollusks, the tests of echinoderms, and the exoskeletal chitin of crustacea and insects. As with all archaeological remains, they represent discarded fragments of a previous way of life.

Organic remains are particularly subject to losses from the archaeological record, through the destructive nature of food preparation and consumption, the scavenging of refuse by other animals, and the deterioration that results from mechanical and chemical forces over time. Other losses come through excavation with inappropriate sieving strategies in which the remains of smaller individuals or species are lost. Nonetheless, despite all of these opportunities for the loss and destruction of organic material, animal remains constitute a major class of the archaeological remains from most sites and in some sites, such as shell mounds, they are the most obvious of the remains. However, even among those remains that are preserved, care must be taken in evaluating the extent to which they may represent a contribution to the prehistoric diet.

One reason for such caution is that all remains recovered are not necessarily those of animals that were consumed. For example, along the Gulf coast of Mexico, dogs were definitely eaten and probably even raised for food (Wing 1978). Their remains were often burned, disarticulated, and associated with those of other food remains. But in the West Indies, complete or nearly complete skeletons of dogs are found in burials and they are rarely associated with midden refuse, suggesting that dogs were not a regular item in the diet (Wing 1991). Dogs probably have played more roles in human culture than any other animal, ranging from food animal to guardian to hunting companion to faithful friend. But other animals, too, such as chickens, cattle, and horses, have likewise played different roles and thus their archaeological remains cannot automatically be assumed to constitute only the remnants of past meals.

Another problem is that some animals that were consumed left few remains. On the one hand, these were small, soft-bodied animals such as insect larvae, and on the other hand, they were very large animals, such as sea mammals or large land mammals that were too heavy to be brought back to the habitation site. In the case of small animals, mandibles of shrimp have recently been identified in some southeastern sites in the United States through the use of fine-gauge sieves (Quitmyer 1985). This find (which was predicted) gives encouragement that other hard parts of otherwise soft-bodied animals can be found if they are carefully searched for. At the other end of the size scale, many very large animals were butchered at the kill site and only the meat was brought back to the home site, leaving little or no skeletal evidence at the latter site of this hunting enterprise.

Such a phenomenon has been termed the "schlepp effect" (Perkins and Daly 1968), which expresses the commonsense but nonetheless laborious practice of stripping the flesh off the carcass of a large animal and carrying it to the home site but leaving most of the heavy supporting tissue, the skeleton, at the kill site. Kill sites of single large prey species such as mammoths *(Mammuthus)* (Agenbroad 1984) and mass kills of bison *(Bison bison)* (Wheat 1972) have been excavated and the strategy of the kill and processing of the carcasses reconstructed. Good evidence points to the selection of prey based on its fatness and carcass use to maximize caloric intakes of the hunters (Speth 1983).

Human Adaptability

Human technology applied to food procurement and preparation is one of the factors responsible for the broad diet that sets humans apart from other animals and has made their worldwide distribution possible. Prehistoric sites with long sequences of occupation are located on every continent except Antarctica, and almost every island (Woodhouse and Woodhouse 1975). Such a wide distribution encompasses a great range of ecosystems with different potentials and limitations for human subsistence exploitation.

By contrasting the animal resources used in sites located in some of the major landforms, both the similarities and differences in the potentials of these ecosystems can be demonstrated. Some of the differences to be examined are between subsistence exploitation in sites located along rivers and on the marine coast. Other comparisons have to do with sites on continents as compared with those on islands, and subsistence in exploiting the arctic as opposed to the humid tropics.

Levels of Extraction

Different levels of extraction of animal foods from the environment obviously can affect the composition of the diet. The hunting, fishing, and gathering of resources are procurement enterprises that result in diverse food composition and variation throughout the year as different resources become available. During the great majority of human history, beginning several million years ago and extending to the time animals were controlled by domestication, the subsistence economy was based upon hunting, fishing, and gathering. Increased control over animals, whether through the maintenance of captive animals or managed hunting, culminated in animal domestication about 10,000 years ago. A comparison of economies dependent on domestic animals with those relying on wild animals for subsistence reveals a range in diversity and dependability of resources.

The Nature of Animal Remains

Nature of Material

As already noted, the remains of animals used for food consist of the supporting tissue such as bone and teeth of vertebrates, shell of mollusks, and chitin of crustaceans. These tissues are composed of inorganic and organic compounds. The relatively rigid structure of the inorganic portions predominate in bone, constituting 65 percent. In tooth enamel the inorganic portion is 99.5 percent by weight. The inorganic portions of these supporting tissues are composed of compounds of calcium.

By their very nature, skeletal remains are attractive to scavengers: Some meat and other soft tissue may have adhered to them and, in addition, bone itself is sought by many animals as a source of calcium.

Other losses of archaeological remains come about through the influence of forces of nature, termed taphonomic factors. Such natural changes include all types of site disturbances such as erosion or stream washing, land movement, alternating freezing and thawing, and acidic soil conditions. The soil conditions are particularly critical for the preservation of bone, which as a calcium compound can be dissolved in acidic conditions. Destruction of bone under acidic conditions is further complicated by the problem of bone loss being greatest in the least well calcified bones of young individuals. In contrast, losses are the smallest in the enamel portion of teeth (Gordon and Buikstra 1981). Alternating freezing and thawing is the other taphonomic factor that is particularly damaging to organic remains. Bones exposed to the sun develop cracks. When these cracks fill with moisture and then freeze, they enlarge and, ultimately, the bone will fragment into pieces that have lost their diagnostic characteristics.

If losses from the archaeological record can complicate reconstruction of the past, so too can additions to the faunal assemblage. Such additions were often animals that lived and died at the habitation site. These are known as commensal animals, the most well known being the black and the Norway rats *(Rattus rattus* and *Rattus norvegicus)* and the house mouse *(Mus musculus)*. Burrowing animals such as moles *(Talpidae)* and pocket gophers *(Geomyidae)* may also dig into a site and become entombed. In addition, middens and habitation sites were occasionally used for burial, and the remains of both people and their animals (i.e., dogs) were thus inserted into earlier deposits.

Other ways in which commensal animals can be incorporated in a midden is by association with the target species. For example, many small creatures, such as mussels, snails, crabs, and barnacles, adhere to clumps of oysters and were often brought to the site on this target species. Occasionally, too, the stomach contents of a target species may contain remains of other animals, which are thus incorporated in the site.

Recovery and Identification

Optimum recovery of faunal material is clearly essential for reconstruction of past diets. In some cases, sieving the archaeological remains with 7-millimeter (mm)-gauge screens will be sufficient to recover the animal remains. But as more and more sieving experiments are conducted and archaeologists gain more and more experience using fine-gauge (2 mm and 4 mm) sieves, it is becoming increasingly obvious that fine-gauge sieves are essential for optimal recovery at most sites. A good example of this importance has to do with what was long thought to be the enigma of the preceramic monumental site of El Paraiso on the Pacific coast of Peru. This site was an enigma because early excavations there uncovered no vertebrate remains, suggesting that the local ancient residents had no animal protein in their diets. It was only when sieving with 2-millimeter-gauge sieves was undertaken that thousands of anchovy *(Engraulidae)* vertebrae were revealed. At last, the part this small schooling fish played in providing fuel for the construction of the monumental architecture was understood (Quilter et al. 1991).

Another methodological problem that needs further consideration at this site and at others is the relative contribution of vertebrates and invertebrates to the prehistoric diet. Mollusk shells are relatively more durable and less likely to be lost to scavengers than are the bones of vertebrates of similar size, which results in a bias favoring mollusks.

In evaluating the potential contribution of vertebrates and mollusks to the prehistoric diet, one must also keep in mind biases in their preservation and recovery. For example, molluskan shells are more massive relative to their edible soft tissues than are the skeletons of vertebrates to their soft tissues. Consequently, shells will be the most visible component of a shell midden even before taking into account the greater durability of shell and the fewer losses to scavengers.

One way some of these problems can be addressed is by making estimations of potential meat weight using allometric relationships between measurable dimensions of the shell or bone and meat weight. Such relationships, of course, can only be developed by using the accurate weights and measurements of modern specimens comparable to the species recovered from archaeological deposits. Knowledge of modern animals and a reference collection are the most important research tools of the faunal analyst.

First, an attempt is made to estimate the minimum weight of the meat represented by the animal remains. Next, this estimate is contrasted with the maximum estimate of the meat weight that could have been provided by the minimum number of individual animals calculated to be represented. If the two estimates are approximately the same, this implies that all of the meat from each animal was consumed at the source of the refuse. Yet if the two estimates differ substantially, it suggests that only portions of some animals were consumed at the site, with other portions distributed within the community.

The Meaning of Animal Remains Assemblages

Animal Exploitation in Different Ecosystems

Riverine versus coastal. Many similarities exist between faunal assemblages from riverine sites and those located along the coast. In each case, both vertebrate and invertebrate aquatic animals were important food sources. Furthermore, these two aquatic situations were subject to influxes of animals, either in breeding congregations or migrations, that augmented the resident fauna. Of course, aquatic species used by riverine fishermen and gatherers were different from those extracted from the sea.

Aquatic organisms, fishes and mollusks, are important in the faunal assemblages of both riverine and coastal sites. Shell mounds are more typically associated with coastal sites, although they do occur along rivers (Weselkov 1987). Riverine shell mounds are accumulations typical of the Archaic time period (about 7000 to 3000 B.P.) in eastern North America, exemplified by those found on the St. Johns River in Florida and the Green River in Kentucky (Claasen 1986). Along coastal shores, shell mounds date from Archaic times to the present.

Gathering mollusks is invariably accompanied by fishing, but the relative contribution of fish and shellfish to the diet follows no pattern. Many shell mounds are visually very impressive and, in fact, are so large that in many places these mounds have been mined for shell material to be used in modern road construction. Less visible components of these archaeological sites are the vertebrate, crustacean, and material cultural remains.

As indicated in the discussion of methods, those for reconstructing the dietary contributions of the two major components of a shell mound are still being perfected. One exciting development has been a greater understanding of the importance (as food) of very small animals in the vertebrate, predominantly fish, components of these mounds.

As already mentioned, the use of fine-gauge screen sieves in the recovery of faunal remains has provided a more accurate understanding of the size range of fishes consumed in the past. Catches of small fishes are being documented in many parts of the world. For example, at four sites in the Darling Region of Australia, otoliths of golden perch *(Maguaria ambigua)* were preserved. These could be used to extrapolate lengths of fishes caught up to 24,000 years ago (Balme 1983). The range in their estimated lengths is

8 to 50 centimeters (cm) and the mean is approximately 20 cm. The range in estimated lengths of sardines *(Sardina pilchardus)* from a fourth-century A.D. Roman amphora is between 11 and 18 cm (Wheeler and Locker 1985). Catfish *(Ariopsis felis)* and pinfish *(Lagodon rhomboides)* from an Archaic site on the southeastern Gulf coast of Florida are estimated to range in length from 4 cm to 25 cm, and the means of the catfish and pinfish are 10 cm and 12 cm, respectively (Russo 1991).

An important question has to do with how these small fishes could be eaten and yet leave skeletal remains behind. Many contemporary diets include small fishes such as sardines and anchovies in which the entire body of the fish is consumed. The answer may lie in the fact that small fishes are used in many parts of the world in the preparation of fish sauces that are made without skeletal tissue. In other words, the well-preserved, intact skeletal remains of small fishes suggest that the fishes might have been employed in sauces.

In addition to mollusks and fishes in the protein portion of a coastal and riverine diet, migratory or breeding congregations would have added significantly to the diet. A well-known example of this phenomenon is the seasonal migration of anadromous fishes such as salmon *(Salmonidae)* and herring *(Clupeidae)* (Rostlund 1952); methods of preserving and storing this seasonal surplus would also have developed.

Other examples of such exploitation include the breeding colonies of sea bird rookeries, sea turtle nesting beaches, and seal and sea lion colonies. Many of these colonies are coastal phenomena and are strictly confined to particular localities. During the breeding cycle, most animals are particularly vulnerable to predation, and people through the ages have taken advantage of this state to capture breeding adults, newborn young, and, in the cases of birds and turtles, eggs.

Unfortunately, only some of the evidence for this exploitation can be demonstrated in the archaeological remains. Egg shells are rarely preserved. Some of the breeding animals in question, like the sea mammals and the sea turtles, are very large and may have been butchered on the beach and the meat distributed throughout the community. Thus, it is difficult to assess the relative importance of these resources within a particular refuse deposit and by extension within the diet of the humans being studied.

Continental versus island. A continental fauna differs from an island fauna in its diversity of species. There is a direct relationship between island size and distance from the mainland and species diversity (MacArthur and Wilson 1967). Human exploitation on a continent can range from catches of very diverse species in regions where different habitats are closely packed, to dependence on one or two species that form herds,

typically in open grasslands. On islands other than very large ones, prehistoric colonists found few species and often augmented what they did find with the introduction of domestic species as well as tame captive animals.

This kind of expansion seems to be a pattern in many parts of the world. For example, several marsupials *(Phalanger orientalis, Spilocuscus maculatus,* and *Thylogale brunii),* in addition to pigs *(Sus scrofa)* and dogs *(Canis familiaris),* were deliberately introduced into the Melanesian Islands between 10,000 and 20,000 years ago (Flannery and White 1991). Similarly, sheep *(Ovis* sp.), goats *(Capra* sp.), pigs *(Sus* sp.), and cats *(Felis* sp.) were all introduced into the Mediterranean Islands at a time when the domestication of animals was still in its initial stages. A variety of wild animals, such as hares *(Lepus europaeus),* dormice *(Glis glis),* foxes *(Vulpes vulpes),* and badgers *(Meles meles),* were also introduced into this area (Groves 1989).

Likewise, in the Caribbean Islands, domestic dogs as well as captive agouti *(Dasyprocta leporina),* opossum *(Didelphis marsupialis),* and armadillo *(Dasypus novemcinctus)* were introduced from the South American mainland, whereas the endemic hystricognath rodent locally called "hutia" *(Isolobodon portoricensis)* and an endemic insectivore *(Nesophontes edithae)* were introduced from large to small islands (Wing 1989).

Although tame animals were doubtless kept by people living on the mainland, they are not easily distinguished from their wild counterparts. But this problem is only part of an increasingly complex picture as human modifications of the environment, either overtly through landscape changes resulting from land clearing or more subtly through hunting pressure, have altered the available species on both islands and continental land masses.

Because of the generally lower species diversity on islands, exploitation of terrestrial species was augmented by marine resources. These were primarily fishes and mollusks. In the Caribbean Islands, West Indian top shell *(Cittarium pica)* and conch *(Strombus gigas),* and a whole array of reef fishes including parrotfishes (Scaridae), surgeonfishes (Acanthuridae), grouper (Serranidae), and jacks (Carangidae), were of particular importance.

Arctic versus humid tropics. The Arctic has long, cold, dark winters but also short summers, with long spans of daylight that stimulate a brief period of extraordinarily high plant productivity. By contrast, the humid tropics have substantially more even temperatures and lengths of daylight throughout a year that in many cases is punctuated by dry and rainy seasons. Needless to say, these very different environmental parameters have a pronounced effect on the animal populations available for human subsistence within them.

Traditional contemporary subsistence activities as

well as evidence from archaeological faunal remains in the Alaskan Arctic indicate that important contributors to the human diet have been caribou *(Rangifer tarandus),* sea mammals – particularly seals *(Callorhinus ursinus* and *Phoca vitulina)* and sea lions *(Eumatopius jubata)* – seabirds, and marine fishes, primarily cod *(Gadus macrocephalus)* (Denniston 1972; Binford 1978; Yesner 1988).

Although the species of animals differ in different parts of the Arctic regions, many characteristics of a northern subsistence pertain. Foremost among these is a marked seasonal aspect to animal exploitation correlated with the migratory and breeding patterns of the Arctic fauna. Moreover, the length of time during which important animal resources, such as the anadromous fishes, are available becomes increasingly circumscribed with increased latitude (Schalk 1977). To take full advantage of this glut of perishable food, people need some means of storage. And fortunately, in a region where temperatures are below freezing for much of the year, nature provides much of the means.

Another characteristic of northern subsistence is the generally low species diversity; but this condition is counteracted by some large aggregations of individuals within the species. Still, the result is that heavy dependence is placed on a few species. At Ashishik Point an analysis of the food contribution of different animals to the prehistoric diet revealed that sea mammals and fishes predominated (Denniston 1972). Of the sea mammals, sea lions are estimated consistently to have provided the greatest number of calories and edible meat. This estimation agrees with the observation by David Yesner (1988) that dietary preference among the prehistoric Aleut hunter-gatherers was for the larger, fattier species.

The fauna of the humid tropics is much more diverse than that of the Arctic, although the tropical animals that people have used for food do not generally form the large aggregations seen in higher latitudes. Exceptions include schools of fishes, some mollusks, bird rookeries, and sea turtle breeding beaches. Many of the animals that have been exploited are relatively small. The largest animals from archaeological sites in the New World tropics are adult sea turtles *(Cheloniidae),* deer *(Mazama americana* and *Odocoileus virginianus),* and peccary *(Tayassu pecari* and *Tayassu tajacu)* (Linares and Ranere 1980). Some of the South American hystricognath rodents, such as the capybara *(Hydrochaeris* sp.), paca *(Agouti paca),* and agouti *(Dasyprocta punctata),* were used and continue to be used widely as food. Fish and shellfish were also very important components of prehistoric diets (Linares and Ranere 1980) and typically augmented those based on terrestrial plants and animals.

The kinds of land mammals that have been most frequently consumed in much of the tropics since the beginning of sedentary agriculture prompted Olga Linares (1976) to hypothesize a strategy for their capture she called "garden hunting." She suggested that many of these animals were attracted to the food available in cultivated fields and gardens and were killed by farmers protecting their crops. Objective ways of evaluating the importance of garden hunting have been proposed, which are based on the composition of the faunal assemblage (Neusius 1996).

Different Levels of Extraction
Hunting, fishing, and gathering. It has been estimated that fully 90 percent of all those who have lived on earth have done so as hunter-gatherers (Davis 1987). The animals that were procured by these individuals varied depending upon the resources available within easy access of the home site or the migratory route. But in addition to these differences in the species that were obtained and consumed, certain constraints governed what was caught, by whom, how the meat was distributed, and how it was prepared. Certainly, technology played an important part in what kinds of animals were caught on a regular basis and how the meat was prepared. Many specialized tools such as water craft, nets, traps, weirs, bows, arrows, and blowguns and darts all permitted the capture of diverse prey.

A limitation imposed on all organisms is that of energy, which meant that food procurement generally took place within what has become known as the "catchment" area (Higgs and Vita-Finzi 1972). This area is considered to be inside the boundaries that would mark a two-hour or so one-way trip to the food source. Theoretically, travel more distant than this would have required more energy than could be procured. Once animal power was harnessed, trips to a food source could be extended. However, another solution to the problem of procurement of distant resources was by adopting a mobile way of life. This might have taken the form of periodic trips from the home site or it might have been a migratory as opposed to a sedentary method of living.

In the past, as today, there was doubtless a division of labor in the food quest. It is generally thought that men did the hunting and fishing (although in many traditional societies today women do the inland, freshwater fishing) whereas the women, children, and older male members of the community did the gathering. Some excellent studies of contemporary hunter-gatherers provide models for these notions about the division of labor. One of the best and most frequently cited is by Betty Meehan (1982) entitled *Shell Bed to Shell Midden,* in which she describes shellfishing practices in detail and the relative importance of shellfish to the diet throughout the year. This is the case at least among the Gidjingali-speaking people of Arnham Land in northern Australia, whose shellfish gathering is a planned enterprise entailing a division of labor for collecting molluscan species.

Food sharing is another phenomenon that probably has great antiquity in the food quest, although admittedly, we know more about the patterns of food sharing from contemporary studies than from archaeological remains. A classic study of sea turtle fishing along the Caribbean coast of Nicaragua (Nietschmann 1973) describes the distribution obligations of meat obtained from the large sea turtle *(Chelonia midas)*. Such patterns make certain that meat does not go to waste in the absence of refrigeration and furthermore assure the maintenance of community members who are less able or unable to procure food for themselves.

That a large carcass was shared can sometimes be detected in an archaeological assemblage of animal remains. As we noted earlier, this observation can occur when estimates of meat yield based on the actual remains recovered are compared with estimates of potential meat obtained from the calculated numbers of individual animals represented in the same sample. Disparity between these two estimates could point to the incomplete deposit of the remains of a carcass, which may indicate sharing, either among the households, or through a distribution network, or even through a market system. Plots of the dispersal of parts of deer carcasses throughout a prehistoric community that was entirely excavated provide a demonstration of food distribution (Zeder and Arter 1996). Perhaps sharing also occurred when many small fishes were caught in a cooperative effort. In this case the catch may have been shared equally with an additional share going to the owner of the fishing equipment.

Communal cooperation was probably also involved in the concept of "garden hunting" (Linares 1976), which can be viewed in the broader perspective of deliberately attracting animals. Food growing in gardens or fields, or stored in granaries, was used as bait to entice animals to come close to a settlement.

Clearly this strategy would have been most successful with animals that ate agricultural products. Some of those so trapped were probably tamed and eventually domesticated, suggesting that it is no accident that many of our domestic and tame animals consume crop plants. Today agriculture and animal husbandry are combined to produce the plant and animal foods consumed throughout most of the world. But the cultivation of crops and the husbandry of animals did not arise simultaneously everywhere. In much of the Western Hemisphere crops were grown in the absence of a domestic animal other than the dog. However, the management, control, and domestication of animals eventually led to a different level of exploitation.

Animal domestication. Domestic animals have skeletal elements and teeth that are morphologically distinct from their wild ancestors. The observable changes are the result of human selection, which is why domestic animals are sometimes referred to as man-made animals. Human selection prior to modern animal husbandry may have been unintentional and more a result of isolation and methods of confinement (e.g., whether animals were tethered, or kept in stalls or corrals).

Animals were, of course, tamed first, and paintings on walls and on pottery sometimes provide evidence of domestication. Selection expressed as changes in the morphology of an animal also indicates domestication, but the state of animal "tameness" is difficult to recognize in the fragmentary remains from archaeological sites and consequently rarely possible to document. Moreover, many animals were held captive and tamed but for some reason never became domesticated, meaning that their skeletal remains do not differ morphologically from their wild counterpart. Collared peccaries *(Tayassu tajacu),* for example, were believed to have been tamed and kept by the Maya for food or ritual purposes (Hamblin 1984), and stone pens found on the island of Cozumel are thought to have been used to keep peccaries for human convenience. At the present time, peccaries are trained by some hunters in Central America to fill the role of watchdogs. Clearly, many motives instigated the taming of animals, but the most important of these undoubtedly was ready access to meat.

Some animals were held in captivity with no effort made to tame them. The captivity of these animals was a means of storing fresh meat. An example of animals still kept this way today are sea turtles maintained in corrals along the shore below low tide. Live animals were also maintained on board ships during long ocean voyages. These practices probably were very old, and animals such as domestic pigs were often released on islands to assure a source of food for the next voyage or for other people who followed.

But control over animals, or even their domestication, did not necessarily mean a sole reliance on them for food. Rather, especially in the early stages of domestication, humans continued to depend on hunted and fished resources. But with the introduction of livestock into new regions, traditional subsistence strategies were modified. An interesting example may be seen in sixteenth-century Spanish Florida, where Spanish colonists, suddenly confronted with wilderness and relative isolation, changed their traditional subsistence in a number of ways. They abandoned many accustomed food resources and substituted wild resources used by the aboriginal people of the region. Moreover, their animal husbandry practices shifted from a traditional set of domesticated animals to just those that flourished in the new environment (Reitz and Scarry 1985). These changes required flexibility. Yet presumably, such changes in subsistence behavior documented for Spanish settlers in Florida were repeated in many places throughout the ages (Reitz and Scarry 1985).

Dependence upon livestock became more complete only after peoples and their agricultural systems were well established. It should be noted, however, that even in industrial societies today, reliance upon domestic animals is not complete. Most contemporary Western diets include fish and other seafood, and wild animal food, such as venison, is viewed as a delicacy and is often the food for a feast.

Accompanying a greater human dependence upon domestic animals for food was an increased human use of the animals' energy and other products. Animals, used for draft, greatly increased the efficiency of agricultural enterprises, and utilizing them for transportation extended the catchment area.

The employment of animals for dairy products was of crucial importance and can be detected in archaeological remains by the kill-off pattern that characteristically shows male individuals killed as young animals and females maintained to old age for their milk (Payne 1973). When such provisions as milk (and eggs) came into use, they provided an edible resource without loss of the animal, and the latter came to be viewed as capital.

Conclusion

The human diet is characterized by the great variety of plants and animals that it includes. The animal protein portion of the diet depends most heavily on vertebrates and mollusks but also includes crustaceans, arthropods, and echinoderms. Historically, this flexibility has been instrumental in the worldwide distribution of human beings.

Despite this flexibility, selection for certain resources was clearly practiced. Usually, certain species were targeted even though a great variety of species were used. When selection was exercised, the determining factors seemed to have been those of a dependable resource and one high in body fat. By resource dependability we mean, for example, the annual salmon run, stable oyster beds, perhaps a captive flock of pigeons or a domestic herd of goats. Selection for animals with the highest body fat has been documented specifically in the preference for sea lions by the prehistoric Aleuts and generally by archaeological remains of the bison, which revealed selection of the fattest individuals. In this connection it should be noted that domestic animals tend to store more fatty tissue than do their wild ancestors, which may have been a further incentive for the maintenance of domesticates (Armitage 1986).

Food distribution and sharing is another characteristic of human subsistence that provided everyone with a degree of security even if personal catches were not successful. Methods of food preparation and storage doubtless varied greatly. Most likely these were salting, smoking, or drying, or a combination, but none of these methods is clearly visible in archaeological remains. It is only when animal remains are found far outside of their normal range (e.g., codfish remains in West Indian historic sites) that one can be sure some method of preservation was employed.

Similarly, cooking methods can be interpreted from archaeological remains only in a general way. It is likely that meat was boiled or stewed when bone was not burned and roasted when it was burned.

Yet such interpretations must be made cautiously because bone can become burned in many ways.

Even though animal remains from archaeological sites are fragmentary and much is often missing from the whole picture, they do provide an important perspective on past human diets.

Elizabeth S. Wing

Bibliography

Agenbroad, L. D. 1984. New World mammoth distribution. In *Quaternary extinctions: A prehistoric revolution,* ed. P. S. Martin and R. G. Klein, 90-108. Tucson, Ariz.

Armitage, Philip L. 1986. Domestication of animals. In *Bio-industrial ecosystems,* ed. D. J. A. Cole and G. C. Brender, 5-30. Amsterdam.

Balme, Jane. 1983. Prehistoric fishing in the lower Darling, western New South Wales. In *Animals and archaeology,* ed. C. Grigson and J. Clutton-Brock, 19-32. Oxford.

Binford, Lewis R. 1978. *Nunamuit ethnoarchaeology.* New York.

Claasen, Cheryl. 1986. Shellfishing seasons in the prehistoric southeastern United States. *American Antiquity* 51: 21-37.

Davis, Simon J. M. 1987. *The archaeology of animals.* New Haven, Conn.

Denniston, Glenda B. 1972. Ashishik point: An economic analysis of a prehistoric Aleutian community. Ph.D. dissertation, University of Wisconsin.

Flannery, T. F., and J. P. White. 1991. Animal translocation. *National Geographic Research and Exploration* 7: 96-113.

Gordon, Claire C., and Jane E. Buikstra. 1981. Soil pH, bone preservation, and sampling bias at mortuary sites. *American Antiquity* 46: 566-71.

Groves, Colin P. 1989. Feral mammals of the Mediterranean islands: Documents of early domestication. In *The walking larder,* ed. J. Clutton-Brock, 46-58. London.

Hamblin, Nancy L. 1984. *Animal use by the Cozumel Maya.* Tucson, Ariz.

Higgs, E. S., and C. Vita-Finzi. 1972. Prehistoric economies: A territorial approach. In *Papers on economic prehistory,* ed. E. S. Higgs, 27-36. London.

Linares, Olga F. 1976. "Garden hunting" in the American tropics. *Human Ecology* 4: 331-49.

Linares, Olga F., and Anthony J. Ranere, eds. 1980. *Adaptive radiations in prehistoric Panama.* Peabody Museum Monographs No. 5. Cambridge, Mass.

MacArthur, Robert H., and Edward O. Wilson. 1967. *The theory of island biogeography.* Princeton, N.J.

Meehan, Betty. 1982. *Shell bed to shell midden.* Canberra, Australia.

Neusius, S. W. 1996. Game procurement among temperate horticulturalists: The case for garden hunting by the Dolores Anasazi. In *Case studies in environmental archaeology,* ed. E. J. Reitz, L. A. Newsom, and S. J. Scudder, 273-88. New York.

Nietschmann, Bernard. 1973. *Between land and water: The subsistence ecology of the Miskito Indians.* New York.

Payne, Sebastian. 1973. Kill-off patterns in sheep and goats: The mandibles from Asvan Kale. *Anatolian Studies* 23: 281-303.

Perkins, Dexter, Jr., and Patricia Daly. 1968. A hunter's village in Neolithic Turkey. *Scientific American* 219: 96-106.

Quilter, Jeffery, Bernardino E. Ojeda, Deborah M. Pearsall, et al. 1991. Subsistence economy of El Paraiso, an early Peruvian site. *Science* 251: 277–83.

Quitmyer, Irvy R. 1985. The environment of the Kings Bay locality. In *Aboriginal subsistence and settlement archaeology of the Kings Bay locality,* Vol. 2, ed. W. H. Adams, 1–32. University of Florida, Reports of Investigations No. 2. Gainesville.

Reitz, Elizabeth J., and C. Margaret Scarry. 1985. *Reconstructing historic subsistence with an example from sixteenth-century Spanish Florida.* Society for Historical Archaeology, Special Publication No. 3. Glassboro, N.J.

Rostlund, Erhard. 1952. *Freshwater fish and fishing in North America.* University of California Publications in Geography, Vol. 9. Berkeley.

Russo, Michael. 1991. Archaic sedentism on the Florida coast: A case study from Horr's Island. Ph.D. dissertation, University of Florida.

Schalk, Randall F. 1977. The structure of an anadromous fish resource. In *For theory building in archaeology,* ed. L. R. Binford, 207–49. New York.

Speth, John D. 1983. *Bison kills and bone count.* Chicago.

Weselkov, Gregory A. 1987. Shellfish gathering and shell midden archaeology. In *Advances in archaeological method and theory,* Vol. 10, ed. M. B. Schiffer, 93–210. San Diego, Calif.

Wheat, Joe Ben. 1972. The Olsen-Chubbuck site: A Paleo-Indian bison kill. *American Antiquity* 27: 1–180.

Wheeler, Alwyne, and Alison Locker. 1985. The estimated size of sardines *(Sardina pilchardus)* from amphorae in a wreck at Randello, Sicily. *Journal of Archaeological Science* 12: 97–100.

Wing, Elizabeth S. 1978. Use of dogs for food: An adaptation to the coastal environment. In *Prehistoric coastal adaptations,* ed. B. L. Stark and B. Voorhies, 29–41. New York.

1989. Human exploitation of animal resources in the Caribbean. In *Biogeography of the West Indies,* ed. C. A. Woods, 137–52. Gainesville, Fla.

1991. Dog remains from the Sorcé Site on Vieques Island, Puerto Rico. In *Beamers, bobwhites, and blue-points,* ed. J. R. Purdue, W. E. Klippel, and B. W. Styles, 389–96. Springfield, Ill.

Woodhouse, David, and Ruth Woodhouse. 1975. *Archaeological atlas of the world.* New York.

Yesner, David R. 1988. Effects of prehistoric human exploitation on Aleutian sea mammal populations. *Arctic Anthropology* 25: 28–43.

Zeder, M. A., and S. R. Arter. 1996. Meat consumption and bone use in a Mississippian village. In *Case studies in environmental archaeology,* ed. E. J. Reitz, L. A. Newsom, and S. J. Scudder, 319–37. New York.

I.5. ❧ Chemical Approaches to Dietary Representation

Dietary reconstruction for past populations holds significant interest as it relates to biological and cultural adaptation, stability, and change. Although archaeological recovery of floral and faunal remains within a prehistoric or historical context provides some direct evidence of the presence (and sometimes quantity) of potential food resources, indirect evidence for the dietary significance of such foodstuffs frequently must be deduced from other bioarchaeological data.

The types of data with dietary significance range from recovered plant and animal remains through evidence of pathology associated with diet, growth disruption patterns, and coprolite contents. Other traditional approaches involving the people themselves – as represented by skeletal remains – include demographic (Buikstra and Mielke 1985) and metabolic (Gilbert 1985) stress patterns.

In addition to bioanthropological analyses, reconstruction of environmental factors and the availability and limits of food species and their distribution for a population with a particular size, technology, and subsistence base are typical components within an archaeological reconstruction. Although these physical aspects are significant, the distribution, or more likely the restriction, of particular foodstuffs from certain segments of the population (because of sex, age, status, food avoidance, or food taboos) may be important cultural system features. The seasonal availability of food and its procurement, preservation, and preparation may also have influenced group dietary patterns and nutritional status (Wing and Brown 1979).

Analysis of skeletal remains may also provide some direct evidence of diet. Type and adequacy of diet have long been of interest to physical anthropologists, especially osteologists and paleopathologists (Gilbert and Mielke 1985; Larsen 1987). More recently, direct chemical analysis of bones and teeth has been attempted in an effort to assess the body's metabolism and storage of nutritive minerals and other elements. L. L. Klepinger (1984) has reviewed the potential application of this approach for nutritional assessment and summarized the early findings reported in the anthropological literature. (In addition, see Volume 14 of the *Journal of Human Evolution* [1985], which contains significant research surveys to that date.)

General Approaches and Assumptions

The pioneering anthropological work in bone chemical analysis and dietary reconstruction can be attributed to A. B. Brown (1973), who examined strontium concentrations in relation to meat and vegetation, and to R. I. Gilbert (1975), who explored the concentrations of five other elements in relation to prehistoric Native American samples in Illinois. The enthusiastic early promise of a relatively easy, straightforward approach to diet reconstruction from elemental concentrations in bone has more recently been tempered by recognition of the biodynamic complexity, methodological problems, and contextual changes occurring through diagenesis of buried bone. Nonetheless, a number of publications in article, dissertation, and book form have appeared in the anthropological literature from the early 1970s to the current time. Although the emphasis, samples, and time frame have varied considerably, the approaches generally share the assumptions that bone is the vital feature for mineral homeostasis and a reservoir for critical elements, and that variations in bone concentrations by individual and group reflect past intakes of dietary concentrations, which in turn reflect local environmental and cultural milieus. A. C. Aufderheide (1989) and M. K. Sandford (1992, 1993a) have provided excellent reviews of the basic premises, biogenic-diagenetic continuum, diversity of methods, and sampling and analytical protocols. Two recent, extremely important, edited volumes (Price 1989; Sandford 1993b) contain the most comprehensive bibliographies currently available and include syntheses of recent findings, remaining problems, and potential research trajectories and protocols.

Initial anthropological bone chemical research focused primarily on the inorganic mineral phase of bone – which typically makes up 75 to 80 percent of the dry weight – and was concerned with the dietary contrasts and trophic levels of early hominids, hunter-gatherers, and agriculturalists. Analysis of the stable isotopes in the organic collagen component (20 to 25 percent) is now frequently undertaken to investigate the relative importance of C3/C4 plants and reliance on maize in the Americas through a consideration of its carbon content (Bumstead 1984). Such analysis is also focused on the equally troublesome problem of the marine/terrestrial protein components of the diet by investigation of nitrogen isotopes. Other isotopes with possible relevance to aspects of dietary reconstruction include those of oxygen, sulfur, and strontium. W. F. Keegan (1989), M. A. Katzenberg (1992), and S. H. Ambrose (1993) provide excellent introductory reviews of the use of isotopes in the analysis of prehistoric diet. H. P. Schwarcz and M. J. Schoeninger (1991) provide a more esoteric review of the theory and technical details of isotopic analysis for reconstructing human nutritional ecology.

Samples, Instrumentation, and Variables

It is probably unrealistic to expect a finely detailed reconstruction of past diets from skeletal chemical data because of the nature of our evidence. A number of factors influence the survival and recovery of human remains. These include mortuary method, climatic conditions, soil chemistry, decomposition rates, and archaeological methods and goals. Although a single individual, may reflect important aspects of the biocultural past, including diet, we should remember that each individual, and the circumstances and context of the recovery of that individual, is unique.

Moreover, because the bone is analyzed not in life, but after death, bone turnover rates must be viewed in relation to age and health status at the time of that death. For aggregate data, especially for statistical comparisons, the representativeness, comparable size, and composition of the samples are also of concern. Chemical analysis should be done only after thorough

and professional osteological analysis is conducted. Useful standardized guides in such analysis are the Paleopathology Association's *Skeletal Database Committee Recommendations* (1991) and the collective recommendations for standard skeletal data collection (Buikstra and Ubelaker 1994).

Accurate demographic profiles are especially important for later considerations of age, sex, health/disease, and perhaps status categories within the population sample. Individual bone samples may be taken for later analysis, especially now that many invaluable skeletal collections are being reburied. Because as little as 1 to 2 grams of bone may be used for chemical analysis, depending upon the instrumentation and method, the removal and laboratory destruction of this amount of bone represents a loss of even less than that of a typical tooth.

Chemical concentrations within bone vary from one bone to another and even in different portions of an individual bone; understandably, earlier comparative studies were difficult before this fact was recognized. Current recommendations are to use cortical bone, preferably from femur midshafts. The particular technique chosen for quantitative elemental analysis will depend upon the number of elements to be analyzed, the cost, and the degree of precision required. Aufderheide (1989) and Sandford (1992) review the theoretical foundations and relative advantage of a number of options. Current laboratory analytical techniques include electroanalysis, light spectrometry, scanning electron microscopy, neutron activation analysis, mass spectrometry, and the widely used inductively coupled plasma (ICP) optical spectrometry for multiple element analysis. Results are typically reported in parts per million of bone or bone ash, the latter preferred (Price et al. 1989).

Although elemental analysis may be conducted directly on bone or in solution, isotopic analysis first requires decalcification, extraction of collagen from bone – approximately 5 milligrams (mg) of collagen is needed – and then analysis through mass spectrometry. Katzenberg (1992) provides a capsular review of the process and cites B. S. Chisholm (1989) and Schoeninger and colleagues (1989) as current basic references. Stringent laboratory conditions and lengthy preparation techniques, frequently with elevated costs, are necessary for isotopic analysis (Ambrose 1990).

Diagenesis appears to be less of a problem with isotopic analysis; however, it must still be considered. Much recent research in elemental analysis has attempted to document and cope with the problems of chemical and physical changes that may occur in buried bone through leaching, contextual contamination, and chemical reactions of bone outside the living body. In addition to the bone, samples of the matrix of soil must be collected and analyzed so that potential contamination may be identified.

Of course, postmortem influences must be detected, but physiological processes may also influence the incorporation and utilization of elements present in a particular diet. Absorption of particular elements ingested may be enhanced or reduced through chemical processes or physiological regulation by competing substances in the diet. Phytates found in some cereals, for example, may bind zinc and iron and reduce the absorption of these elements.

In addition, not all elements are distributed equally through body tissues, and some, such as lead or strontium, may be deposited differentially into bone. Metabolism differences for particular elements may also compound the interpretation. Retention of ingested elements is variable as well in certain tissues as is the rate of bone turnover at different ages and under variable health conditions.

Finally, excretion rates for particular elements depend upon physiological processes and the nature of the element itself. Although there are a great number of variables in the incorporation, retention, and analysis of any particular chemical element in bone, a cautious application of trace element studies with appropriate samples, methods, and situations or research goals continues to hold promise for some aspects of dietary reconstruction. Indeed, despite severe critical evaluation of earlier trace element studies (Radosevich 1993), improved and refined multidisciplinary research and laboratory protocols should prevent the necessity of throwing the baby out with the bathwater.

Anthropological Dietary Chemical Reconstructions

The following sampling of past contributions within anthropological bone chemical research reflects three major thrusts related to diet: trophic level, temporal change in subsistence, and distinctive chemical elements. The general trophic level of past human diets was first investigated by strontium and strontium/calcium ratios. The basic premise was that the relative reliance on meat derived from animals higher on the food chain would be reflected by a lower concentration of strontium in the human bone because of its differential presence and absorption (relative to calcium) along the food chain. For paleoanthropologists concerned with the physical and cultural development of humans and the hunting complex (especially *Australopithecus, Homo habilis,* and *Homo erectus*), it first appeared that the answers could be derived in a relatively straightforward manner (Sillen and Kavanagh 1982). However, the fossilization process itself appears to alter the initial concentration, and other diagenic processes may confound the interpretation (Sillen, Sealy, and van der Merwe 1989).

In the case of more recent human groups, however, an analysis of strontium bone content has proven more fruitful. The anthropological significance of the strontium content of human bone was initially investigated by Brown (1973), and subsequent studies

of strontium content suggest that dietary differences may reflect social stratification. Schoeninger (1979), for example, determined that at a prehistoric Mexican site, higher-ranking individuals – as indicated by interment with more grave goods – had lower levels of strontium and, hence, presumably a greater access to animal protein. Other studies, such as that by A. A. Geidel (1982), appear to confirm the value of strontium analysis in this respect, even though diagenetic change must be evaluated.

Temporal dietary changes and the relative amounts of meat and plants in the diet (perhaps related to population size as well as technological complexity) have been documented in a number of regions. Gilbert (1975, 1977), for Late Woodland Mississippian groups in the Midwest, and T. D. Price and M. Kavanagh (1982), for the same area, document an increasing strontium concentration among groups as they experienced an increasing reliance on cereals and a concomitant decrease in meat availability. Katzenberg (1984) determined similar temporal changes among Canadian groups, as did Schoeninger (1981) for areas of the Middle East.

It should be noted, however, that bone strontium concentrations are strongly influenced by ingestion of marine foods – such as shellfish – and some nuts. J. H. Burton and Price (1990) suggest that low barium/strontium ratios distinguish consumption of marine resources. It should also be noted that soil and water concentrations of strontium and, hence, plant absorption of it, also vary geographically. A final caveat is the documentation of the influences of physiological processes such as weaning (Sillen and Smith 1984) and pregnancy and lactation (Blakely 1989), which elevate bone strontium and depress maternal bone calcium concentrations.

A number of other elements found in food and water (Ca, Na, Sr, Cu, Fe, Mn, Mg, Zn, Al, Fe, Ba) have the potential for assisting in dietary reconstruction. These elements have been analyzed in skeletal samples with varying degrees of success in delineating food categories, temporal changes, and subsample variations related to age, gender, or class. Like strontium, these elements are subject to many of the same modifications and processes from ingestion to deposition into bone, and frequently to the same diagenic processes after death, so the same caveats apply to their analysis and interpretation.

In addition, when these various elements are incorporated together in diets (and later deposited in bone), they may be antagonistic to each other, or enhanced when ingested together or as part of the same diet. In anthropological analysis, although the major elements such as calcium or phosphorous may be significant, the majority of research has been concerned with trace elements in either their total concentration for dietary categories, or as deficiencies related to particular diseases, or at toxic levels, such as lead poisoning.

Although there is a relatively abundant literature on individual trace elements and their role in human metabolism and nutrition in the medical and nutrition literature (Underwood 1977; Prasad 1978; Rennert and Chan 1984), these studies tend to focus on Western diets and modern food standards and samples. The major emphasis within anthropological elemental studies has been with meat and vegetable dietary questions and temporal change, especially in the prehistoric American Southeast and Middle West. Research in other world areas has included Europe (Grupe and Herrmann 1988), Southwest Asia (Sillen and Smith 1984), Sicily (Klepinger, Kuhn, and Williams 1986), Tunisia (Sandford, Repke, and Earle 1988), Australia (Kyle 1986), and Peru (Edward and Benfer 1993).

The theoretical premise behind such investigations is based on the different concentration levels of particular elements in dietary resources that then should vary in the human skeletal concentrations. Meat, for example, is typically associated with increased concentrations of iron, zinc, copper, molybdenum, and selenium. Plants, however, generally have greater amounts of strontium, magnesium, manganese, cobalt, and nickel. Unfortunately, a single plant or animal species rarely possesses a unique chemical signature. Besides the problem of mixed dietary resources, many of the prevailing trace elements overlap (Gilbert 1985), and nuts present special problems (Buikstra et al. 1989). Synthetic critical reviews of relevant literature have been provided by Price (1989), Sandford (1992, 1993a, 1993b), Aufderheide (1989), and J. E. Buikstra and colleagues (1989).

The emerging consensus is that elemental and isotopic studies may indeed be significant in circumstantial dietary reconstructions of past populations. But additional research is necessary to cope with the numerous problems and issues connected with such studies. Among these are diagenesis, laboratory analysis and sample preparation, expansion to skeletal samples of more recent origin, wider geographical representations and inclusions, feeding experiments, and more sophisticated statistical and interpretative techniques.

A number of studies have attempted to deal with the question of diagenesis and the need for adjustments before statistical analysis (Lambert, Szpunar, and Buikstra 1979; Katzenberg 1984; Price 1989; Edward and Benfer 1993; Radosevich 1993). Multiple bone analyses, comparisons with nonhuman animals (herbivores, carnivores, and mixed feeders), more multielement surveys, and careful laboratory evaluation are recommended.

Expansion of multielement or single element studies into more recent historical periods should have the advantage of combining available historic information concerning diet and food habits with the chemical analysis of skeletal samples for a more comprehensive understanding. For example, Aufderheide and colleagues (1981, 1985, 1988) have delineated socioeco-

nomic differences, occupational categories, and probably food storage patterns from the analysis of skeletal lead in the United States colonial period. H. A. Waldron (1981, 1983) and T. Waldron (1982, 1987) have addressed similar problems in the United Kingdom. In like fashion, J. S. Handler, Aufderheide, and R. S. Corruccini (1986) combined nineteenth-century descriptions of "dry bellyache" among Barbados slaves with an analysis of slave remains to demonstrate that "dry bellyache" was actually lead poisoning, the result of contaminated rum from stills with lead fittings. T. A. Rathbun and J. D. Scurry (1991) found regional variation in lead burdens in skeletal samples of whites and blacks from the seventeenth- and eighteenth-century eastern United States. Such variations seem to reflect differences in socioeconomic class, food preparation, and drinking patterns. Whites, who made far greater use of drinking and eating utensils, carried considerably higher lead burdens than blacks, with those of the Middle Atlantic states having slightly higher levels than those of other Southeast samples. Among blacks, females had the highest levels, indicating that they also doubtless had greater access to the whites' lead-contaminated food and drink.

Utilizing techniques of chemical analysis, W. D. Wood, K. R. Burns, and S. R. Lee (1985) and Rathbun (1987) were able to document regional and perhaps cultural differences among rural blacks, plantation slaves, and white elites in the nineteenth-century southeastern United States. Among the findings were that whites apparently had more access to meat than did either enslaved or freed African-Americans.

Similarly, Rathbun (1987) and T. A. J. Crist (1991) found dietary variation by gender, age, and perhaps stress level among a nineteenth-century South Carolina plantation slave sample. Males seem to have relied more heavily on meats, grains, and nuts than females, whose diets consisted more of leafy and leguminous vegetables. The remains of older adults reflected diets of grains, vegetables, and seafood, whereas those of younger adults revealed the consumption of more meats and, perhaps, nuts. Analysis of historical documents concerning food allocations on the plantation suggests that much of this differential was because slaves supplemented plantation rations with food items they collected and cooked themselves. Clearly, in many instances, a combining of historical, anthropological, and chemical information has the potential for providing a richer determination of past dietary contents and the consequences of various dietary regimens.

Summary

In addition to the confounding problems of preservation, diagenesis, data collection, and analysis, if elemental and isotopic chemical analysis of skeletal material is to fulfill its potential in dietary reconstruction, insightful and appropriate avenues of interpretation are necessary. Although descriptive statistics of aggregate data drawn from a sample are useful heuristic devices, selection of appropriate analytical techniques appear to be linked to the nature of the concentration distributions.

Parametric and nonparametric – as well as univariate and multivariate – statistics have been applied to bone chemical quantitative data. The multiple problems and considerations involved have recently been discussed by Buikstra and colleagues (1989), who ultimately recommend principal component analysis. Even though mathematical rigor remains extremely important, insightful interpretations of relationships and findings still seem to require evaluation within a biocultural context.

Schoeninger (1989), for example, attempted to match food component elements and isotopes as well as skeletal analysis for prehistoric Pecos Pueblo and historic Dutch whalers to propose reasonable diets for them. Klepinger (1992) also commented on the importance of reevaluating model hypotheses that are frequently invoked in the light of new data and developing technologies.

Chemical approaches to dietary representation, especially of past groups, can be fascinating, frustrating, and fulfilling. But it seems unlikely that we will soon develop a comprehensive picture of past diets through chemical analysis alone. The complexity of the geochemical, biochemical, biological, physiological, cultural, and social systems involved require collaborative research and multidisciplinary sharing of results. Although each discipline and researcher may contribute various pieces of the puzzle, a clearer image can emerge only through integrative interpretations.The goal appears well worth the effort!

Ted A. Rathbun

Bibliography

Ambrose, S. H. 1990. Preparation and characterization of bone and tooth collagen for isotopic analysis. *Journal of Archaeological Science* 17: 431–51.

1993. Isotopic analysis of paleodiets: Methodological and interpretive considerations. In *Investigations of ancient human tissue: Chemical analyses in anthropology,* ed. M. K. Sandford, 59–130. Langhorne, Pa.

Aufderheide, A. C. 1989. Chemical analysis of skeletal remains. In *Reconstruction of life from the skeleton,* ed. M. Y. Iscan and K. A. R. Kennedy, 237–60. New York.

Aufderheide, A. C., J. L. Angel, J. O. Kelley, et al. 1985. Lead in bone III: Prediction of social content in four Colonial American populations (Catoctin Furnace, College Landing, Governor's Land and Irene Mound). *American Journal of Physical Anthropology* 66: 353–61.

Aufderheide, A. C., F. D. Neiman, L. E. Wittmers, and G. Rapp. 1981. Lead in bone II: Skeletal lead content as an indicator of lifetime lead ingestion and the social correlates in an archaeological population. *American Journal of Physical Anthropology* 55: 285–91.

Aufderheide, A. C., L. E. Wittmers, G. Rapp, and J. Wallgren. 1988. Anthropological applications of skeletal lead analysis. *American Anthropologist* 90: 932–6.

Blakely, R. E. 1989. Bone strontium in pregnant and lactating females from archaeological samples. *American Journal of Physical Anthropology* 80: 173–85.

Brown, A. B. 1973. Bone strontium content as a dietary indicator in human skeletal populations. Ph.D. dissertation, University of Michigan.

Buikstra, J. E., S. Frankenberg, J. Lambert, and L. Xue. 1989. Multiple elements: Multiple expectations. In *The chemistry of prehistoric human bone,* ed. T. D. Price, 155–210. Cambridge.

Buikstra, J. E., and J. H. Mielke. 1985. Demography, diet, and health. In *The analysis of prehistoric diets,* ed. R. I. Gilbert, Jr., and J. H. Mielke, 360–422. Orlando, Fla.

Buikstra, J. E., and D. H. Ubelaker. 1994. *Standards for data collection from human skeletal remains.* Arkansas Archeological Survey, Research Series No. 44. Fayetteville.

Bumstead, M. P. 1984. *Human variation: 13C in adult bone collagen and the relation to diet in an isochronous C4 (Maize) archaeological population.* Los Alamos, N. Mex.

Burton, J. H., and T. D. Price. 1990. Ratio of barium to strontium as a paleodietary indicator of consumption of marine resources. *Journal of Archaeological Science* 17: 547–57.

Chisholm, B. S. 1989. Variation in diet reconstructions based on stable carbon isotopic evidence. In *The chemistry of prehistoric human bone,* ed. T. D. Price, 10–37. Cambridge.

Crist, T. A. J. 1991. *The bone chemical analysis and bioarchaeology of an historic South Carolina African-American cemetery.* Volumes in Historical Archaeology XVIII. Columbia, S.C.

Edward, J. B., and R. A. Benfer. 1993. The effects of diagenesis on the Paloma skeletal material. In *Investigations of ancient human tissue: Chemical analyses in anthropology,* ed. M. K. Sandford, 183–268. Langhorne, Pa.

Geidel, A. A. 1982. Trace element studies from Mississippian skeletal remains: Findings from neutron activation analysis. *MASCA Journal* 2: 13–16.

Gilbert, R. I., Jr. 1975. Trace element analysis of three skeletal Amerindian populations at Dickson Mounds. Ph.D. dissertation, University of Massachusetts.

1977. Applications of trace element research to problems in archaeology. In *Biocultural adaptations to prehistoric America,* ed. R. I. Blakely, 85–100. Athens, Ga.

1985. Stress, paleonutrition, and trace elements. In *The analysis of prehistoric diets,* ed. R. I. Gilbert, Jr., and J. H. Mielke, 339–58. Orlando Fla.

Gilbert, R. I., Jr., and J. H. Mielke, eds. 1985. *The analysis of prehistoric diets.* Orlando, Fla.

Grupe, G., and B. Herrmann. 1988. *Trace elements in environmental history.* Heidelberg.

Handler, J. S., A. C. Aufderheide, and R. S. Corruccini. 1986. Lead content and poisoning in Barbados slaves. *Social Science History* 10: 399–425.

Katzenberg, M. A. 1984. *Chemical analysis of prehistoric human bone from five temporally distinct populations in Southern Ontario.* Ottawa.

1992. Advances in stable isotope analysis of prehistoric bones. In *Skeletal biology of past peoples: Research methods,* ed. S. R. Saunders and M. A. Katzenberg, 105–19. New York.

Keegan, W. F. 1989. Stable isotope analysis of prehistoric diet. In *Reconstruction of life from the skeleton,* ed. M. Y. Iscan and K. A. R. Kennedy, 223–36. New York.

Klepinger, L. L. 1984. Nutritional assessment from bone. *Annual Review of Anthropology* 13: 75–9.

1992. Innovative approaches to the study of past human health and subsistence strategies. In *Skeletal biology of past peoples: Research methods,* ed. S. R. Saunders and M. A. Katzenberg, 121-30. New York.

Klepinger, L. L., J. K. Kuhn, and W. S. Williams. 1986. An elemental analysis of archaeological bone from Sicily as a test of predictability of diagenetic change. *American Journal of Physical Anthropology* 70: 325-31.

Kyle, J. H. 1986. Effect of post-burial contamination on the concentrations of major and minor elements in human bones and teeth. *Journal of Archaeological Science* 13: 403-16.

Lambert, J. B., C. B. Szpunar, and J. E. Buikstra. 1979. Chemical analysis of excavated human bone from middle and late Woodland sites. *Archaeometry* 21: 403-16.

Larsen, C. S. 1987. Bioarchaeological interpretations of subsistence economy and behavior from human skeletal remains. *Advances in Archaeological Method and Theory* 10: 339-445.

Paleopathology Association. 1991. *Skeletal database committee recommendations.* Detroit, Mich.

Prasad, A. S. 1978. *Trace elements and iron in human metabolism.* New York.

Price, T. D., ed. 1989. *The chemistry of prehistoric human bone.* Cambridge.

Price, T. D., G. J. Armelagos, J. E. Buikstra, et al. 1989. The chemistry of prehistoric human bone: Recommendations and directions for future study. In *The chemistry of prehistoric human bone,* ed. T. D. Price, 245-52. Cambridge.

Price, T. D., and M. Kavanagh. 1982. Bone composition and the reconstruction of diet: Examples from the midwestern United States. *Midcontinent Journal of Archaeology* 7: 61-79.

Radosevich, S. C. 1993. The six deadly sins of trace element analysis: A case of wishful thinking in science. In *Investigations of ancient human tissue: Chemical analyses in anthropology,* ed. M. K. Sandford, 269-332. Langhorne, Pa.

Rathbun, T. A. 1987. Health and disease at a South Carolina plantation: 1840-1870. *American Journal of Physical Anthropology* 74: 239-53.

Rathbun, T. A., and J. D. Scurry. 1991. Status and health in colonial South Carolina: Belleview plantation, 1738-1756. In *What mean these bones?: Studies in southeastern bioarchaeology,* ed. J. L. Powell, P. S. Bridges, and A. M. W. Mires, 148-64. Tuscaloosa, Ala.

Rennert, O. M., and W. Chan. 1984. *Metabolism of trace metals in man.* Boca Raton, Fla.

Sandford, M. K. 1992. A reconsideration of trace element analysis in prehistoric bone. In *Skeletal biology of past peoples: Research methods,* ed. S. R. Saunders and M. A. Katzenberg, 79-103. New York.

1993a. Understanding the biogenic-diagenetic continuum: Interpreting elemental concentrations of archaeological bone. In *Investigations of ancient human tissue: Chemical analyses in anthropology,* ed. M. K. Sandford, 3-57. Philadelphia, Pa.

ed. 1993b. *Investigations of ancient human tissue: Chemical analyses in anthropology.* Philadelphia, Pa.

Sandford, M. K., D. B. Repke, and A. L. Earle. 1988. Elemental analysis of human bone from Carthage: A pilot study. In *The circus and a Byzantine cemetery at Carthage,* ed. J. H. Humphrey, 285-96. Ann Arbor, Mich.

Schoeninger, M. J. 1979. Diet and status at Chalcatzingo: Some empirical and technical aspects of strontium analysis. *American Journal of Physical Anthropology* 51: 295-310.

1981. The agricultural "revolution": Its effect on human diet in prehistoric Iran and Israel. *Paleorient* 7: 73-92.

1989. Reconstructing prehistoric human diet. In *The chemistry of prehistoric human bone,* ed. T. D. Price, 38-67. Cambridge.

Schoeninger, M. J., K. M. Moore, M. K. Murray, and J. D. Kingston. 1989. Detection of bone preservation in archaeological and fossil samples. *Applied Geochemistry* 4: 281-92.

Schwarcz, H. P., and M. J. Schoeninger. 1991. Stable isotope analyses in human nutritional ecology. *Yearbook of Physical Anthropology* 34: 283-321.

Sillen, A., and M. Kavanagh. 1982. Strontium and paleodietary research: A review. *Yearbook of Physical Anthropology* 25: 67-90.

Sillen, A., J. C. Sealy, and N. J. van der Merwe. 1989. Chemistry and paleodietary research: No more easy answers. *American Antiquity* 54: 504-12.

Sillen, A., and P. Smith. 1984. Sr/Ca ratios in juvenile skeletons portray weaning practices in a medieval Arab population. *Journal of Archaeological Science* 11: 237-45.

Underwood, E. J. 1977. *Trace elements in human and animal nutrition.* New York.

Waldron, H. A. 1981. Postmortem absorption of lead by the skeleton. *American Journal of Physical Anthropology* 55: 395-8.

1983. On the postmortem accumulation of lead by skeletal tissues. *Journal of Archaeological Science* 10: 35-40.

Waldron, T. 1982. Human bone lead concentrations. In *Romano-British cemeteries at Cirencester,* ed. A. McWhirr, L. Viner, and C. Wells, 203-7. Gloucester, England.

1987. The potential of analysis of chemical constituents of bone. In *Death, decay and reconstructions: Approaches to archaeology and forensic science,* ed. A. Boddington, A. N. Garland, and R. C. Janaway, 149-59. Manchester, England.

Wing, E. S., and A. B. Brown. 1979. *Paleonutrition: Method and theory in prehistoric foodways.* New York.

Wood, W. D., K. R. Burns, and S. R. Lee. 1985. *The Mt. Gilead cemetery study: An example of biocultural analysis from western Georgia.* Athens, Ga.

I.6. ☙ History, Diet, and Hunter-Gatherers

In the years since 1960 there has been a dramatic change in our perception of the diet, nutrition, and health of "hunter-gatherers," who constitute the world's smallest, most "primitive," and presumably oldest-style societies. The Hobbesian perspective (Hobbes 1950, original 1651), which assumes that malnutrition, disease, and hardship characterize primitive life – a view that prevailed among scholars for the nineteenth and the first half of the twentieth centuries – has been challenged during recent decades by a large series of new observations and a new theoretical paradigm.

Contemporary Hunter-Gatherers

Studies of African hunter-gatherers by Richard Lee (1968, see also 1969) and James Woodburn (1968), in the influential anthology *Man the Hunter* (Lee and DeVore 1968), suggested that far from living on the edge of starvation, primitive hunter-gatherers frequently enjoyed not only adequate and well-balanced nutrition but also a relatively light workload.

In his analysis of the diet and workload of the !Kung San hunter-gatherers of the Kalahari Desert in southern Africa, Lee (1968, 1969) noted that the San diet consisted of an eclectic, yet selective, collection of wild foods – mostly (about 80 percent) vegetable, eaten fresh. He found that the San consumed 23 of 85 plant species that they knew to be edible in their environment and 17 of 55 edible animal species.

He calculated that for a relatively small investment of time, San hunter-gatherers obtained an adequate and well-balanced diet. By obtaining chemical analyses of their native foods and estimating the quantity of each food consumed by every individual, he was able to show that theoretically, each individual in the group received sufficient protein, vitamins, and minerals. In contrast to modern diets, what seemed the "limiting" factor – the element in the San diet most likely to be short or lacking – was the number of calories it delivered. Lee estimated the caloric intake at about 2,140 kilocalories (kcal) per person per day during a season of the year that he considered neither the richest nor the poorest.

Similarly, Woodburn (1968), although less precise, was even more sanguine in his description of the diets of the Hadza of Tanzania, who frequented a far richer environment than that of the !Kung San. He described their quest for food as leisurely and richly rewarding.

Medical observations of the San (Truswell and Hansen 1976) confirmed that they showed no signs of qualitative malnutrition, in that they had no visible deficiencies of vitamins, minerals, or protein, although they may have been showing signs of low caloric intake. (Low calorie intake has been cited by various others as responsible for stunting San growth and reducing their fertility.) Also of note was an absence of high blood pressure and elevated serum cholesterol, as well as the scarcity of heart problems. (See also Bronte-Stewart et al. 1960; Wehmeyer, Lee, and Whiting 1969; Metz, Hart, and Harpending 1971). Particularly striking were the observations on both the San and the Hadza suggesting that children did not suffer from the kinds of childhood malnutrition – kwashiorkor, marasmus, and associated weaning diarrhea – that were otherwise so common in African children (Jelliffe et al. 1962; Truswell and Hansen 1976).

At about the same time that these studies were emerging, agricultural economist Ester Boserup (1965) proposed a new model of economic growth in human history. She argued that population growth rather than technological progress had been the main stimulus for economic change. "Primitive" behavior, although usually considered to be a function of ignorance, might, she suggested, be seen as an efficient adjustment to a small population and a small social scale. So-called progress, she argued, might simply be a necessary adjustment to increasing population size,

scale, and density and might be associated with declining rather than improving labor efficiency and declining rather than improving individual welfare.

Based on the work of Boserup, Woodburn, and Lee, a number of archaeologists proposed that the initial adoption of farming by prehistoric hunting and gathering groups, which occurred in various parts of the world beginning about 10,000 years ago (the "Neolithic Revolution"), might also have been a grudging response to ecological stress or population "pressure" on resources. In other words, the Neolithic Revolution might not have been the result of technological progress as had previously been assumed (Binford 1968; Flannery 1969; Cohen 1977).

One of these scholars (Cohen 1977) extended the argument by suggesting that much of what had passed for progress in prehistory might, like the adoption of farming, have been a response to the pressure of growing population, rather than the result of new inventions, since the new "progressive" techniques seemed to represent the input of extra effort for relatively little output. These "improvements" would include the adoption of diets based on small seeds and the development of grindstones to process them; the development of small projectiles for hunting small game; and the increase in shellfish consumption and concomitant development of fishing equipment during the Mesolithic or Archaic stages of prehistoric economic development. It is true that an argument could be mounted that such apparent economic trends may be distorted by problems of archaeological preservation. For example, the scarcity of shellfish remains in earlier prehistory might reflect poor preservation. However, it is difficult to defend a similar argument about the late appearance of grindstones and small projectile points.

Questions and Challenges for the New Perspectives

A number of questions remain about these new perspectives and the data upon which they were originally developed. For example, it is not clear whether the !Kung San are as well nourished and as affluent as Lee presented them (see also Sahlins 1968). Nor is it clear that the !Kung San are typical of modern hunter-gatherers in the quality of their nutrition. And finally, it is not clear that they, or *any* contemporary hunter-gatherers, lead lives that are representative of the historic and prehistoric experience of human hunters.

In the matter of the nutritional state of the !Kung San, G. Silberbauer (1981) has suggested that the groups of San he studied were nutritionally depressed and might have been lacking in B vitamins. Similarly, Edwin Wilmsen (1978) estimated that San caloric intake might fall well below 2,000 kcal per person in the poorest season. Others such as Kristen Hawkes and J. F. O'Connell (1985) and N. Blurton-Jones and P. M. Sibley (1978) have also argued that the San are not as well nourished as they have been described, that their caloric intake may be deficient, and that their "leisure" time may actually be an adjustment to the extreme heat and dryness of the Kalahari, which limits activity for significant portions of the year.

Moreover, Carmel Schrire (1980, 1984) and others have questioned the value of the !Kung San and other contemporary hunter-gatherers as models for prehistory, arguing that they are not remnants of an ancient way of life but, rather, modern societies formed by contemporary political and economic conditions in South Africa and elsewhere. As such, according to Schrire, their experience has little meaning for the study of prehistory.

Some New Evidence

Recent work in several fields has suggested that the broad perspectives introduced by Lee, Woodburn, and Boserup are accurate even though some details of their arguments may be open to challenge (Cohen 1989).

Such work rests, at least in part, on the assumption that despite undeniable pressures and inputs from the larger societies that surround them, contemporary hunter–gatherer societies can (with appropriate caution) be viewed as twentieth-century experiments in the hunting and gathering lifestyle. And as such they can tell us important things about patterns in prehistory even if the groups studied are not pristine remnants of that prehistory. For example, they can presumably tell us about a people's ability to extract balanced diets from wild resources with simple technology lacking any source of energy other than human power. They can tell us about the relative efficiency of different foraging techniques and extraction methods connected with hunting big game, hunting smaller animals, fishing, shellfishing, and gathering and processing various vegetable foods. They can also tell us something about the effect of small group size and mobility on the transmission of infectious disease.

A broader collection of comparative data on twentieth-century hunter–gatherer nutrition from around the world (Cohen 1989) suggests that contemporary hunter-gatherers (with the exception of those in the Arctic, where vegetable foods are scarce) seem routinely to enjoy relatively eclectic and thus well-balanced diets of fresh foods. Moreover, their typical practice of exploiting a relatively wide range of soils tends to minimize the impact of specific nutrient deficiencies (such as iodine) that are associated with particular soils. As a result, these groups are, for the most part, well nourished at least by contemporary developing-world standards; and they are conspicuously well nourished in comparison to the modern world's poor.

Where contemporary hunter-gatherers coexist with farming populations, as is now commonly the case, hunter-gatherers typically operate as specialists who trade protein, vitamins, and variety foods to farmers in exchange for calories (Williams 1974; Peterson

1978; Griffin 1984). It would appear, therefore, that hunting and gathering diets are almost always relatively nutritious in terms of variety and quality but potentially lacking in calories.

Nonetheless, caloric intake by hunter-gatherers appears sufficient when compared to modern developing-world populations. For example, San caloric intake, although considered marginal, is estimated at 2,000 to 2,100 kcal per person per day, although it falls somewhat below 2,000 kcal per person per day in poor seasons (Lee 1969; Wilmsen 1978; Tanaka 1980). Yet this compares favorably with estimated caloric intake in developing-world countries such as India and China, which *averages* only 1,800 to 2,200 kcal (Bunting 1970; Clark and Haswell 1970; Pellet 1983). Moreover, it compares very favorably with estimates for modern urban poor, who may take in as few as 1,100 to 1,500 kcal per person per day (Basta 1977).

Contemporary hunter-gatherers also receive a relatively large part of their diet from animal products. This is in the range of 20 to 40 percent of the diet, which is about the same as that estimated for affluent modern Western people but well above the modern world average. Daily animal protein intake among the San, for example, is estimated by various sources at approximately 30 to 50 grams per person per day (Lee 1968; Wilmsen 1978; Tanaka 1980; Silberbauer 1981), which far exceeds an estimated average of 7 to 10 grams of animal protein per person in modern developing-world countries and among the world's poor (Basta 1977; Peterson 1978).

It should also be noted, in response to the observation that contemporary hunter-gatherers may have low caloric intake, that they live in some of the world's poorest environments and consequently those most difficult to exploit for food. In fact, judging from the nutritional experience of other contemporary hunter-gatherers, it would appear that the !Kung San, although typical in the variety of their diets, are actually somewhat below hunter–gatherer average in their calorie and protein intake (Hawkes and O'Connell 1985; O'Connell, Hawkes, and Blurton-Jones 1988; Cohen 1989). Populations such as the Hadza of Tanzania, who live in a richer foraging area, are estimated to get 3,000 kcal and 50 to 250 grams of meat protein per person per day (O'Connell et al. 1988). Indeed, groups like the Hadza appear to be a better model for prehistory than the San because they live in the same kinds of environments as early human beings. Yet even the Hadza frequent an area now partly depleted of big game (Hawkes, O'Connell, and Blurton-Jones 1992).

Infection and Nutrition

Another important but not always apparent factor that must be considered in assessing the diets of hunter-gatherers is their comparative freedom from parasites, which affect the nutritional value of diets in a variety of ways (Scrimshaw, Taylor, and Gordon

1968; Beisel 1982). Parasites can cause diarrhea, speeding up the flow of nutrients through the intestine, and therefore interfere with nutrient absorption from the intestine into the bloodstream. In some diseases, such as malaria or hookworm, the parasites destroy or consume human tissues (in these cases, red blood cells), which must be replaced. Other parasites, such as tapeworms, simply compete with humans for the vitamins and minerals in our digestive tract. And infection may actually cause the body to deny itself nutrients as a means of destroying the invader, as can be the case with the body withholding iron (Weinberg 1974, 1992).

Parasite load is, to a large degree, a function of habitat. Warmth and moisture generally encourage the survival and transmission of parasites, so that tropical forest hunter-gatherers such as the Pygmies of Zaire have higher parasite loads than those in drier or colder climates (Price et al. 1963; cf. Heinz 1961).

But the parasite load also tends to increase with the size and density of the human population and with permanence of human settlement, regardless of climate, since larger accumulations of filth, of people, and of stored food all facilitate parasite transmission. Diarrhea-causing organisms, for example, are typically transmitted by fecal–oral infection, in which feces contaminate food and water supplies, a problem that is relatively rare among small and mobile groups. Hookworm infection also thrives on human crowding. The worms grow from eggs deposited on the ground in human feces. They then penetrate human skin (usually the soles of feet) and find their way "back" to the intestine, where they live by consuming red blood cells while shedding a new generation of eggs. Obviously, people on the move are less likely to contaminate the soil around them.

Tapeworms, whose life cycles commonly include both people and domestic animals, are also rare in societies that keep no animals but obtain their meat by hunting wild game. Tapeworms typically are passed to domestic animals such as cows and pigs by human feces. The proximity of domestic animals as well as the density of both human and animal populations facilitates transmission.

The !Kung San avoid most such parasites (Heinz 1961). They do suffer from hookworm because even their desert habitat, mobile habits, and small groups do not entirely prohibit transmission; but they suffer only a fairly mild infestation that is not generally sufficient to promote anemia, the main danger of hookworm (see Truswell and Hansen 1976).

In short, increased parasite load diminishes the quality of nutrition, but hunter-gatherers suffer less of a nutritional loss to parasites than other societies in the same environments. The consequence is that hunter-gatherers require smaller dietary intakes than people in those other societies.

Hunting and Gathering
Populations of Prehistory

Reason to believe that the hunting and gathering populations of prehistory were at least as well nourished as their contemporary counterparts can be gleaned from comparing the environments in which prehistoric hunter-gatherers chose to live and those to which their modern counterparts are confined by the pressures of competition with more powerful neighbors. Prehistoric, but biologically modern, human hunter-gatherers seem to have expanded first through relatively game-rich environments, savannas, steppes, and open forests. Occupation of the deserts and jungles in which most hunting and gathering groups now find themselves is a relatively recent phenomenon.

Hunters also seem initially to have focused on medium- to large-sized animal prey plus a relatively narrow spectrum of plant foods. Small game, seeds to grind, fish and shellfish (at least consistently and in quantity) all appear to be relatively recent additions to the human larder. The additions were made in the Mesolithic period of prehistory (Cohen 1977) and were associated with what K. V. Flannery (1973) has called the "broad spectrum revolution," which took place within, approximately, the last 15,000 years. The use of secondary habitats and the adoption of demonstrably inefficient foraging techniques suggest strongly that the diets of hunter-gatherers began to decline under the pressure of their own populations almost from the time that the efficient hunter, *Homo sapiens,* first emerged to spread out around the world.

Actual tests of the relative efficiency of various foraging techniques indicate that prehistoric hunter-gatherers in environments richer in large game than that occupied by contemporary counterparts would have fared well in comparison to contemporary groups. Indeed, numerous investigations point out that when available, large game animals can be taken and converted to food far more efficiently than most other wild resources. Data provided by Stuart Marks (1976) and recalculated by the author (Cohen 1989) suggest, for example, that big game hunters without modern rifles or shotguns in game-rich environments may obtain an *average* of as much as 7,500 to 15,000 kcal for every hour of hunting. Many other studies also suggest that large game, although relatively scarce in the modern world, can be taken with great efficiency once encountered, even if hunters do not use modern firearms (Jones 1980; Blackburn 1982; Rowly Conway 1984; Hawkes and O'Connell 1985).

By contrast, most of the resources taken by contemporary hunters, including small game, fish, shellfish, and small-seeded vegetables, are far less efficient to gather and convert to food. Estimates of shellfish-gathering efficiency, for example, suggest that it produces about 1,000 kcal per hour of work; hunting small game may average no more than 500 to 800 kcal per hour; small seed processing also produces only about 500 to 1,000 kcal per hour (Jones 1980; Winterhalder and Smith 1981; Rowly Conway 1984; Cohen 1989). Collection of nuts may, however, constitute a partial exception. Brazil nuts, for example, can be harvested at rates that provide kcals comparable to hunting. But the nuts must still be cracked and processed into food, both relatively time-consuming activities. Similarly, anadramous (migratory) fish can be harvested very efficiently but only after large weirs have been constructed (Werner 1983; Rowly Conway 1984).

Interestingly, the relative efficiency of hunting large game (when available) appears to hold whether foragers use iron or stone tools. In fact, metal tools apparently add relatively little to hunting efficiency, although they add significantly to the efficiency of gathering vegetable foods, not to mention growing them. In a Stone Age world, therefore, the advantage of being a big game hunter would have been substantially greater than even these modern comparative tests of various economic activities undertaken with metal tools suggest (Colchester 1984; Harris 1988). Hunting large game with spears is also clearly more efficient than hunting smaller game with bows and arrows and small projectile points or nets or probably even primitive muskets – the point being that "improvements" in hunting technology did not offset the loss of efficiency that occurred as prey size became smaller. In addition, hunting large game would have clearly been more efficient than harvesting wild wheat or farming wheat with stone tools such as the sickles and grindstones that appear in human tool kits relatively late in prehistory (Russell 1988). In short, a decline in available big game was apparently more important than any technological innovation in affecting foraging choices and determining the overall efficiency of the economy. The ultimate adoption of farming seems to have been only one in a long series of strategies adopted to offset diminishing returns.

One further point is worth making. Modern hunter-gatherers, such as the !Kung or even the Hadza, who contend with game-depleted environments or those with legal hunting restrictions must clearly be less efficient in putting food on the table than their (and our) prehistoric forebears.

The data also indicate that prehistoric hunters in game-rich environments would have consumed diets containing a larger proportion of meat than most of their contemporary counterparts. Yet as John Speth (1988) has argued, there are limits to the proportion of meat in the diet that a human being can tolerate since meat, without commensurate carbohydrates or fats, is calorically expensive to process. Moreover, meat is a diuretic, so that people like the San, who live in hot deserts where water and calories are both scarcer than protein, may limit meat consumption to conserve water.

The Evidence of Prehistoric Skeletons

There is also a good deal of direct evidence (most of it gathered since 1960) to support the hypothesis that prehistoric hunter-gatherers were relatively well nourished. Their skeletons, often in large numbers, have been analyzed from various regions of the world. In more than 20 areas of the globe (but mostly in North America) it is possible to use these remains to make comparative analyses of the nutrition and health of two or more prehistoric populations representing different stages in the evolution of food technology (Cohen and Armelagos 1984). For example, in specific cases we can compare hunter-gatherers to the farmers who succeeded them in the same region; or compare early hunters to later foragers; or incipient farmers to intensive farmers, and so forth.

Such analyses generally confirm that infection and associated malnutrition become more common as small groups become larger and more sedentary. The skeleton displays nonspecific infections called periostitis when only the outer surface of the bone is affected and osteomyelitis when the infection penetrates deep into the medullary cavity of the bone. Osteomyelitis is rarely found in prehistoric skeletons, but periostitis is routinely found to have been more common in larger and more sedentary groups and can probably be taken as an index of the prevalence of other infectious diseases. In addition, other types of infection can occasionally be glimpsed. For example, a comparison of mummified populations from Peru (Allison 1984) demonstrates an increase in intestinal parasites with sedentism. A comparison of preserved fecal material from different archaeological layers in the American Southwest also demonstrates an increase in parasites with the adoption of sedentism (Reinhard 1988).

Other such evidence can be found in the characteristic lesions on the skeleton left by diseases such as yaws, syphilis, leprosy, and tuberculosis, all of which increase with density or appear only in relatively civilized populations. Tuberculosis appears to be almost entirely a disease of relatively recent, civilized populations in both the Old World and the New (Buikstra 1981; Cohen and Armelagos 1984). Yaws (a nonvenereal disease caused by a spirochete identical to the one that causes syphilis) has been shown to increase with population density among New World Indians (Cohen and Armelagos 1984).

Skeletons also provide fairly specific signs of anemia, or lack of sufficient red blood cell function. The condition is called porotic hyperostosis and cribra orbitalia and appears as a thickening and porosity of the bones of the cranium and eye orbits in response to the enlargement of marrow cavities where red blood cells are formed.

Anemia can result from inadequate dietary intake of iron associated with diets high in maize and other cereals, since the cereals are poor sources of iron and may actually interfere with iron absorption. However, increasingly, anemia is thought to reflect the secondary loss of iron to parasites such as hookworm, and losses in fighting diseases such as tuberculosis, and even the body's own sequestering of iron to fight infection (Weinberg 1974, 1992; Stuart-Macadam 1992). In one particular archaeological sequence from the American Southwest, in which preserved human feces have been examined, anemia was shown to relate to the frequency of parasitic worms in stools rather than to diet (Reinhard 1988, 1992). But whatever the cause, anemia seems to have been primarily a disease of more civilized or sedentary farmers rather than hunter-gatherers everywhere they have been studied, and it *increases* through time in association with group size and sedentism in almost all reported archaeological sequences (Cohen and Armelagos 1984).

One other dietary deficiency disease, rickets in children and osteomalacia in adults, can be diagnosed in the skeleton. Soft or malformed bones resulting from improper calcification can result from lack of calcium or lack of vitamin D in the diet. Most commonly, however, it occurs from lack of exposure to sunlight, because most vitamin D is produced in the skin as the result of exposure to ultraviolet radiation. The archaeological record suggests that rickets is very rare among prehistoric hunter-gatherers but common, as one might predict, among the inhabitants of smog-bound urban ghettos in the last few centuries (Steinbock 1976; Cohen and Armelagos 1984).

Changes in human growth and stature may also reflect a decline in the quality of human nutrition through time. Many authorities consider average stature to be a fairly reliable indicator of nutritional status (see Fogel et al. 1983), and certainly the increase in European and American stature in the last century has been viewed as evidence of improving nutrition. But for centuries prior to the nineteenth century, decline was the predominant trend in human stature.

The first biologically modern human populations of hunter-gatherers throughout Europe and areas of Asia including India seem to have been relatively tall. Unquestionably these Paleolithic hunters were taller than the Mesolithic foragers and Neolithic farmers that came after them (Angel 1984; Kennedy 1984; Meiklejohn et al. 1984; Smith, Bar-Yosef, and Sillen 1984), and the populations of eighteenth-century Europe to which we compare ourselves with considerable pride were among the shortest human groups that ever lived (Fogel 1984).

Retarded growth may also be identified in the skeletons of children whose bones suggest that they were smaller for their age (as determined by the state of tooth formation and eruption at death) than children living at some other time or place. For example, skeletons of children from the Dickson Mounds archaeological site in Illinois suggest that childhood growth was retarded in a farming population when

compared to that of their foraging forebears (Goodman et al. 1984). In addition, malnutrition may show up as premature osteoporosis, the thinning of the outer, solid, cortical portions of bones. This condition seems to be more important in farmers or later populations than in prehistoric hunter-gatherers (e.g., Stout 1978; Smith et al. 1984).

Finally, the adult human skeleton displays scars of biological or nutritional stresses felt in childhood, particularly those associated with weaning malnutrition and weaning diarrhea. Illness while teeth are growing can result in irregularities in tooth enamel that leave a permanent record of stress in the form of visible lines called enamel hypoplasia or microscopic defects called Wilson bands (see Rose, Condon, and Goodman 1985). Prehistoric hunter-gatherers fairly typically show lower rates of these defects than do the farming and civilized populations that followed them, confirming the observation that hunter-gatherer children endured significantly less weaning stress than did farmers or other more "civilized" neighboring populations (Cohen and Armelagos 1984; Cohen 1989).

It is true that some critics object to such conclusions by observing that the use of skeletal indicators of stress in prehistoric populations may be misleading – that, for various reasons and in various ways, skeletons may provide an unrepresentative or biased sample of a once-living population. (For details of the argument see Wood et al. 1992, and Cohen forthcoming). Yet skeletal evidence accords well with ethnographic observations and with predictions of epidemiology. In other words, infection not only increases with sedentism in skeletal populations but also increases in many ethnographic or historically described skeleton groups. Moreover, as already discussed, contemporary hunter-gatherers (and not just prehistoric hunter-gatherers) seem to be well protected against anemia. Put plainly, skeletal data when checked against other results appear to be giving us an accurate and coherent picture of past health and nutrition (Cohen 1989, 1992).

The Texture of the Diet

Although controversies remain about the quality and quantity of food available to both modern and ancient hunter-gatherers, there is little dispute that there have been significant changes in dietary texture throughout history. Contemporary hunter-gatherers as a group (and, presumably, their prehistoric counterparts) eat foods that differ in texture from modern diets in three important ways: Wild foods are comparatively tough to chew; they are high in bulk or fiber; and, with the occasional exception of honey, they lack the high concentrations of calories found in many modern processed foods. These textural differences have several effects on human development and health. First, individuals raised on hunter–gatherer diets develop different occlusion of their teeth in which the upper and lower incisors meet edge to edge. The modern "normal" pattern of slight overbite is actually a consequence of modern soft diets (Brace 1986). Hunter–gatherer diets also generate significantly more tooth wear than do modern diets, so that in contrast to civilized populations, hunter-gatherers are at risk of literally wearing out their teeth.

However, modern diets rich in sweet and sticky substances are far more cariogenic. Significant tooth decay is, for the most part, a relatively recent phenomenon. Historically, rates of caries increased dramatically with the adoption of pottery, grindstones, and farming (which made softer diets possible) and again with the production of refined foods in the last few centuries (Powell 1985). In fact, the difference in caries rates between ancient hunter-gatherers and farmers is so pronounced that many archaeologists use the rate of caries in archaeological skeletons to help distinguish between prehistoric hunters and farmers (see Turner 1979; Rose et al. 1984).

Coarse textured foods have a particularly important effect on two segments of the population, the very old with badly worn teeth and the very young. The problem of feeding the very young may require a mother to delay weaning, and this may help to explain the relatively low fertility of the !Kung – a phenomenon that some, but not all, modern hunter-gatherer populations seem to experience one yet that may have been the experience of hunter-gatherers in prehistory (Cohen 1989; cf. Wood 1990). Without soft foods to wean their children and with "baby food" very difficult to prepare, hunter-gatherers may be forced to nurse both intensively and for a relatively long period. Lactation, especially in combination with low caloric intake and high energy output, is known to exert contraceptive effects (Konner and Worthman 1980; Habicht et al. 1985; Ellison 1990).

But the adoption of cereals and grindstones to prepare gruel by Mesolithic and Neolithic populations would have simplified the problem of feeding the very young whether or not it improved nutrition. And early weaning in turn would help to explain an apparent increase in the growth rate of the human population after the adoption of farming in the Neolithic period, even though no corresponding improvement in health or longevity can be documented (Cohen and Armelagos 1984; Cohen 1989).

The lack of refined foods available to them may also explain the relative immunity of hunting and gathering populations (and many other populations) to diet-related diseases that plague twentieth-century Western populations. For example, the relatively low calorie-for-volume content of hunter-gatherer diets helps to explain the relative scarcity of obesity and obesity-related conditions among such groups. (Even wild animals that must work for a living are relatively lean in comparison to their modern domestic counterparts.) Adult-onset diabetes is very rare in "primitive" societies, although studies in various parts of the world suggest that the same individuals may be diabetes-prone when switched to Western diets (Neel 1962; Cohen 1989). Similarly, high blood pressure is essentially unknown among hunter–gatherer groups who enjoy low sodium (and perhaps also high potassium or calcium) diets, although the same groups develop high blood pressure when "civilized" (Cohen 1989).

High-fiber diets among hunter-gatherers and other "primitive" groups also affect bowel transit time. Members of such groups typically defecate significantly more often than "civilized" people. In consequence, diseases associated with constipation such as appendicitis, diverticulosis, varicose veins, and bowel cancer are all relatively rare among hunter-gatherers (and non-Western populations in general) and are thought to result at least in part from modern, Western low-bulk diets (Burkitt 1982).

In summary, a number of lines of evidence from archaeology, from prehistoric skeletons, and from the study of contemporary populations indicate that small, mobile human groups living on wild foods enjoy relatively well-balanced diets and relatively good health. Indeed, the available evidence suggests that hunter–gatherer diets remain well balanced even when they are low in calories. The data also show that per capita intake of calories and of protein has declined rather than increased in human history for all but the privileged classes. The predominant direction of prehistoric and historic change in human stature has been a decline in size despite the "secular trend" among some Western populations of the last century. Prehistoric remains of more sedentary and larger groups commonly display an increase in general infection and in specific diseases (such as yaws and tuberculosis), combined with an increase in porotic hyperostosis (anemia) and other signs of malnutrition.

Mark Nathan Cohen

Bibliography

Allison, M. J. 1984. Paleopathology in Peruvian and Chilean mummies. In *Paleopathology at the origins of agriculture,* ed. M. N. Cohen and G. J. Armelagos, 515–30. New York.

Angel, J. L. 1984. Health as a crucial factor in changes from hunting to developed farming in the eastern Mediterranean. In *Paleopathology at the origins of agriculture,* ed. M. N. Cohen and G. J. Armelagos, 51–74. New York.

Baker, Brenda, and George J. Armelagos. 1988. The origin and antiquity of syphilis. *Current Anthropology* 29: 703–20.

Basta, S. S. 1977. Nutrition and health in low income urban areas of the Third World. *Ecology of food and nutrition* 6: 113–24.

Beisel, W. R. 1982. Synergisms and antagonisms of parasitic diseases and malnutrition. *Review of Infectious Diseases* 4: 746–55.

Binford, L. R. 1968. Post Pleistocene adaptations. In *New perspectives in archaeology,* ed. S. R. Binford and L. R. Binford, 313–36. Chicago.

Blackburn, R. H. 1982. In the land of milk and honey: Okiek adaptation to their forests and neighbors. In *Politics and history in band societies,* ed. E. Leacock and R. B. Lee, 283–306. Cambridge.

Blurton-Jones, N., and P. M. Sibley. 1978. Testing adaptiveness of culturally determined behavior: Do the Bushmen women maximize their reproductive success? In *Human behavior and adaptation.* Society for the Study of Human Biology, Symposium 18, 135–57. London.

Boserup, Ester. 1965. *The conditions of agricultural growth.* Chicago.

Brace, C. L. 1986. Eggs on the face. . . . *American Anthropologist* 88: 695–7.

Bronte-Stewart, B., O. E. Budtz-Olsen, J. M. Hickey, and J. F. Brock. 1960. The health and nutritional status of the !Kung Bushmen of South West Africa. *South African Journal of Laboratory and Clinical Medicine* 6: 188–216.

Buikstra, J., ed. 1981. *Prehistoric tuberculosis in the Americas.* Evanston, Ill.

Bunting, A. H. 1970. *Change in agriculture.* London.

Burkitt, Denis P. 1982. Dietary fiber as a protection against disease. In *Adverse effects of foods,* ed. E. F. Jelliffe and D. B. Jelliffe, 483–96. New York.

Clark, C., and M. Haswell. 1970. *The economics of subsistence agriculture.* Fourth edition. London.

Cohen, Mark N. 1977. *The food crisis in prehistory.* New Haven, Conn.

1989. *Health and the rise of civilization.* New Haven, Conn.

1992. Comment. In The osteological paradox: Problems of inferring prehistoric health from skeletal samples. *Current Anthropology* 33: 358–9.

forthcoming. The osteological paradox – reconsidered. *Current Anthropology.*

Cohen, Mark N., and G. J. Armelagos, eds. 1984. *Paleopathology at the origins of agriculture.* New York.

Colchester, Marcus. 1984. Rethinking stone age economics: Some speculations concerning the pre-Columbian Yanomama economy. *Human Ecology* 12: 291–314.

Draper, H. H. 1977. The aboriginal Eskimo diet. *American Anthropologist* 79: 309–16.

Ellison, P. 1990. Human ovarian function and reproductive ecology: New hypotheses. *American Anthropologist* 92: 933–52.

Flannery, K. V. 1969. Origins and ecological effects of early domestication in Iran and the Near East. In *The domestication and exploitation of plants and animals,* ed. P. J. Ucko and J. W. Dimbleby, 73–100. London.

1973. The origins of agriculture. *Annual Reviews in Anthropology* 2: 271–310.

Fogel, R. W. 1984. *Nutrition and the decline in mortality since 1700: Some preliminary findings.* National Bureau of Economic Research, Working Paper 1402. Cambridge, Mass.

Fogel, R. W., S. L. Engerman, R. Floud, et al. 1983. Secular changes in American and British stature and nutrition. In *Hunger and history,* ed. R. I. Rotberg and T. K. Rabb, 247–83. Cambridge and New York.

Goodman, A., J. Lallo, G. J. Armelagos, and J. C. Rose. 1984. Health changes at Dickson Mounds, Illinois, A.D. 950–1300. In *Paleopathology at the origins of agriculture,* ed. M. N. Cohen and G. J. Armelagos, 271–306. New York.

Griffin, P. B. 1984. Forager resource and land use in the humid tropics: The Agta of northeastern Luzon, the Philippines. In *Past and present in hunter-gatherer studies,* ed. Carmel Schrire, 99–122. New York.

Habicht, J-P, J. Davanzo, W. P. Buttz, and L. Meyers. 1985. The contraceptive role of breast feeding. *Population Studies* 39: 213–32.

Harris, Marvin. 1988. *Culture, people, nature.* Fifth edition. New York.

Hawkes, Kristen, and J. F. O'Connell. 1985. Optimal foraging models and the case of the !Kung. *American Anthropologist* 87: 401–5.

Hawkes, Kristen, J. F. O'Connell, and N. Blurton-Jones. 1992. Hunting income patterns among the Hadza: Big game, common goods, foraging goals, and the evolution of human diet. In *Foraging strategies and natural diet of monkeys, apes, and humans,* ed. A. Whiten and E. M. Widdowson, 83–91. New York.

Heinz, H. J. 1961. Factors governing the survival of Bushmen worm parasites in the Kalahari. *South African Journal of Science* 8: 207–13.

Hobbes, T. 1950. *Leviathan.* New York.

Jelliffe, D. B., J. Woodburn, F. J. Bennett, and E. P. F. Jelliffe. 1962. The children of the Hadza hunters. *Tropical Paediatrics* 60: 907–13.

Jones, Rhys. 1980. Hunters in the Australian coastal savanna. In *Human ecology in savanna environments,* ed. D. Harris, 107–47. New York.

Kennedy, K. A. R. 1984. Growth, nutrition and pathology in changing paleodemographic settings in South Asia. In *Paleopathology at the origins of agriculture,* ed. M. N. Cohen and G. J. Armelagos, 169–92. New York.

Konner, M., and C. Worthman. 1980. Nursing frequency, gonad function and birth spacing among !Kung hunter gatherers. *Science* 207: 788–91.

Lee, R. B. 1968. What hunters do for a living or how to make out on scarce resources. In *Man the Hunter,* ed. R. B. Lee and I. DeVore, 30–48. Chicago.

1969. !Kung Bushman subsistence: An input-output analysis. In *Ecological studies in cultural anthropology,* ed. A. P. Vayda, 47–79. Garden City, N.Y.

Lee, R. B., and I. DeVore, eds. 1968. *Man the hunter.* Chicago.

Mann, G. V., O. A. Roels, D. L. Price, and J. M. Merrill. 1963. Cardiovascular disease in African Pygmies. *Journal of Chronic Diseases* 14: 341–71.

Marks, Stuart. 1976. *Large mammals and a brave people.* Seattle.

Meiklejohn, C., Catherine Schentag, Alexandra Venema, and Patrick Key. 1984. Socioeconomic changes and patterns of pathology and variation in the Mesolithic and Neolithic of Western Europe. In *Paleopathology at the origins of agriculture,* ed. M. N. Cohen and G. J. Armelagos, 75–100. New York.

Metz, J. D., D. Hart, and H. C. Harpending. 1971. Iron, folate and vitamin B_{12} nutrition in a hunter-gatherer people: A study of !Kung Bushmen. *American Journal of Clinical Nutrition* 24: 229–42.

Neel, J. V. 1962. Diabetes mellitus: A "thrifty" genotype rendered detrimental by progress? *American Journal of Human Genetics* 14: 355–62.

O'Connell, J. F., K. Hawkes, and N. Blurton-Jones. 1988. Hadza scavenging: Implications for Plio/Pleistocene hominid subsistence. *Current Anthropology* 29: 356–63.

Pellet, P. 1983. Commentary: Changing concepts of world malnutrition. *Ecology of Food and Nutrition* 13: 115–25.

Peterson, J. T. 1978. Hunter-gatherer farmer exchange. *American Anthropologist* 80: 335 – 51.

Powell, M. 1985. The analysis of dental wear and caries for dietary reconstruction. In *The analysis of prehistoric diets,* ed. R. I. Gilbert and J. H. Mielke, 307–38. New York.

Price, D. L., G. V. Mann, O. A. Roels, and J. M. Merrill. 1963. Parasitism in Congo Pygmies. *American Journal of Tropical Medicine and Hygiene* 12: 83-7.

Reinhard, Carl. 1988. Cultural ecology of prehistoric parasites on the Colorado Plateau as evidenced by coprology. *American Journal of Physical Anthropology* 77: 355-66.

1992. Patterns of diet, parasites and anemia in prehistoric Western North America. In *Diet, demography and disease,* ed. P. S. Macadam and S. Kent, 219-38. Chicago.

Rose, Jerome C., B. A. Burnett, M. S. Nassaney, and M. W. Blauer. 1984. Paleopathology and the origins of maize agriculture in the lower Mississippi Valley and Caddoan culture areas. In *Paleopathology at the origins of agriculture,* ed. M. N. Cohen and G. J. Armelagos, 393-424. New York.

Rose, Jerome C., K. W. Condon, and A. H. Goodman. 1985. Diet and dentition: Developmental disturbances. In *The analysis of prehistoric diets,* ed. R. I. Gilbert and J. Mielke, 281-306. New York.

Rowly Conway, P. 1984. The laziness of the short distance hunter: The origins of agriculture in western Denmark. *Journal of Anthropological Archaeology* 38: 300-24.

Russell, Kenneth W. 1988. After Eden. *British Archaeological Reports, International Series 391.* Oxford.

Sahlins, M. 1968. Notes on the original affluent society. In *Man the Hunter,* ed. R. B. Lee and I. DeVore, 85-8. Chicago.

Schrire, Carmel. 1980. An inquiry into the evolutionary status and apparent history of the San hunter-gatherers. *Human Ecology* 8: 9-32.

ed. 1984. *Past and present in hunter-gatherer studies.* New York.

Scrimshaw, N., C. Taylor, and J. Gordon. 1968. *Interactions of nutrition and infection.* Geneva.

Silberbauer, George B. 1981. *Hunter and habitat in the central Kalahari.* Cambridge.

Smith, Patricia, O. Bar-Yosef, and A. Sillen. 1984. Archaeological and skeletal evidence of dietary change during the late Pleistocene/early Holocene in the Levant. In *Paleopathology at the origins of agriculture,* ed. M. N. Cohen and G. J. Armelagos, 101-36. New York.

Speth, John. 1988. *Hunter-gatherer diet, resource stress and the origins of agriculture.* Symposium on Population Growth, Disease and the Origins of Agriculture. New Brunswick, N.J. Rutgers University.

Steinbock, R. T. 1976. *Paleopathological diagnosis and interpretation.* Springfield, Ill.

Stout, S. D. 1978. Histological structure and its preservation in ancient bone. *Current Anthropology* 19: 600-4.

Stuart-Macadam, P. 1992. Anemia in past human populations. In *Diet, demography and disease,* ed. P. S. Macadam and S. Kent, 151-76. Chicago.

Stuart-Macadam, P., and S. Kent, eds. 1992. *Diet, demography and disease.* Chicago.

Tanaka, J. 1980. *The San: Hunter gatherers of the Kalahari.* Tokyo.

Truswell, A. S., and J. D. L. Hansen. 1976. Medical Research among the !Kung. In *Kalahari Hunter Gatherers,* ed. R. B. Lee and I. DeVore, 166-95. Cambridge.

Turner, Christie. 1979. Dental anthropological indicators of agriculture among the Jomon People of central Japan. *American Journal of Physical Anthropology* 51: 619-35.

Wehmeyer, A. S., R. B. Lee, and M. Whiting. 1969. The nutrient composition and dietary importance of some vegetable foods eaten by the !Kung Bushmen. *Tydkrif vir Geneeskunde* 95: 1529-30.

Weinberg, E. D. 1974. Iron and susceptibility to infectious disease. *Science* 184: 952-6.

1992. Iron withholding in prevention of disease. In *Diet, demography and disease,* ed. P. Stuart-Macadam and S. Kent, 105-50. Chicago.

Werner, Dennis. 1983. Why do the Mekranoti trek? In *The adaptive responses of Native Americans,* ed. R. B. Hames and W. T. Vickers, 225-38. New York.

Williams, B. J. 1974. *A model of band society.* Memoirs of the Society for American Archaeology No. 39. New York.

Wilmsen, Edwin. 1978. Seasonal effects of dietary intake on the Kalahari San. *Federation Proceedings* 37: 65-72.

Winterhalder, Bruce, and E. A. Smith, eds. 1981. *Hunter gatherer foraging strategies.* Chicago.

Wood, James. 1990. Fertility in anthropological populations. *Annual Review of Anthropology* 19: 211-42.

Wood, James, G. R. Milner, H. C. Harpending, and K. M. Weiss. 1992. The osteological paradox: Problems of inferring prehistoric health from skeletal samples. *Current Anthropology* 33: 343-70.

Woodburn, James. 1968. An introduction to Hadza ecology. In *Man the Hunter,* ed. R. B. Lee and I. DeVore, 49-55. Chicago.

PART II

Staple Foods: Domesticated Plants and Animals

Part II, with its almost 60 chapters that concentrate on staple foods (most of the fruits are treated in Part VIII), constitutes the largest portion of this work. Yet the space devoted to it seems more than justified in light of the immensity of the effort that humans have invested in domesticating the plants of the fields and the animals of the barnyard. In the case of plants, the effort began with the harvesting of wild grains and roots, which probably became a seasonal activity for some hunter-gatherers as the last Ice Age receded and the large mammals - mammoths, mastodons, giant sloths, and the like - were embarking on their journey to extinction. The next leap - a giant one - was from locating wild grains for harvest to planting them in permanent places and then tinkering with them and the soil so they would do a better job of growing.

Wolves were domesticated to become dogs toward the end of the Paleolithic. Like their human companions, they were hunters. But with the beginning of farming, a host of other animals followed them into domestication. In the Old World, goats and sheep, which fed on wild grasses but had no objection to domesticated ones, were probably initially perceived by early farmers as competitors - if not outright thieves - to be fenced out or chased away. But with the precedent of dog domestication to guide them, people began to capture these ruminants and eventually raised them in captivity. In many cases, the purpose seems to have been a supply of animals close at hand for ceremonial sacrifice. But even if meat, milk, hides, hair, and wool were secondary products at first, they were, nonetheless, important ones that quickly rose to primacy. Pigs, cattle, water buffalo, horses, even camels and, later on, chickens may have also been initially sought for sacrifice and then, after

domestication, exploited for their other products, including labor and transportation.

Such a range of large animals that could be domesticated was, however, restricted to the core of the Old World. On its periphery, in Africa south of the Sahara, trypanosomal infection delivered by the tsetse fly often discouraged livestock keeping, and, in the New World, save for dogs, turkeys, and llamas and llama-like creatures, there was relatively little animal domestication carried out. This meant for many an absence of animal fats in the diet, which nature remedied, to some extent, by making the fat in avocados available to many Americans, and palm oil and coconut palms to most in the tropical world.

In the Americas, a shortage of animal protein also meant a heavy reliance on maize, beans, squashes, and potatoes, along with manioc in tropical and subtropical regions; in Africa, yams, millet, sorghum, and a kind of rice sustained life; and in Oceania, taro served as an important staple, along with the sweet potato - an American plant that somehow had diffused throughout that vast area long before the Europeans arrived.

This mystery, along with another occasioned by Old World onions and garlic noted by the expedition of Hernando Cortes in Mexico, may never be solved, and many other such mysteries probably never had a chance to come to light because of the process of food globalization set in motion after 1492. Animals, grains, and vegetables domesticated in the Old World flourished in the New. Beef, pork, and cheese, for example, fitted so naturally into Mexican cuisine that it is difficult to appreciate that they have not been there forever. In similar fashion, the American plants revolutionized the cuisines of the other lands of the globe. Potatoes spread from Ireland to Russia, fields of maize sprang up as far away as China, and manioc combined with maize to cause a population explosion in Africa. Chilli (we stand by our expert's spelling) peppers raced around the globe to add fire to African soups and Indian curries; the tomato was married to pasta in Italy; and, in the other direction, Africa sent varieties of field peas to enliven regional dishes of the Americas and okra to make gumbos.

The continuation of food globalization since 1492 – especially since the 1960s – has caused increasing concern about the atrophy of regional cuisines on the one hand, and the spread of "fast food" on the other. But, as a 1992 Smithsonian exhibition made clear, the "Seeds of Change" discussed in Part II have been broadcast with increasing intensity around the world since the Columbian voyages, and not always with good effect.

II.A

Grains

II.A.1. 🐾 Amaranth

A robust annual herb with seeds as small as mustard seeds, amaranth belongs to the genus *Amaranthus* of the family Amaranthaceae, with 50 to 60 species scattered throughout the world in wild and domesticated forms. Most are weeds, such as pigweed *(A. retroflexus)*, which commonly invades gardens in the United States, whereas others are raised as ornamentals. The genus derives its name from the Greek meaning "unfading," "immortal," or "not withering" because the flowers remain the same after they are dried. Poets have favored the amaranth, therefore, as a symbol of immortality (Sauer 1976; Berberich 1980; Tucker 1986; Amaranthus 1991).

It is as a food, however, that amaranth was and is most important to human populations, either for its leaves or seeds. Two species of amaranth, *A. tricolor* and *A. dubius,* are popular among Chinese-Americans for soup and salad greens. But the most versatile and nutritious are the grain amaranths, because the genus *Amaranthus,* although a non-grass, is capable of producing great amounts of edible grain (Cramer 1987). Three species of amaranth that were domesticated in the Americas and are commonly utilized as grain are *A. hypochondriacus,* known as "prince's feather" in England, from northwestern and central Mexico; *A. cruentus* of southern Mexico and Central America, whose greens are widely utilized in Africa; and *A. caudatus* of the Andes, known as "love-lies-bleeding" in the United States (Sauer 1976; Cole 1979). The first two species are now cultivated in the United States as seed grains, but *A. caudatus* does not do as well in the United States as in the Andes (Tucker 1986).

The amaranth plant grows from 1 to 10 feet tall in an erect or spreading form. It is a broad-leaved plant that bears up to 500,000 black, red, or white seeds on a single large seedhead, made up of thick fingerlike spikes (Cole 1979; Tucker 1986). The leaves are "often variegated with bronze, red, yellow, or purple blotches" (Wister 1985), and the flowers may be orange, red, gold, or purple. Its beautiful colors have led people throughout the world to raise amaranth species as ornamental plants and to cultivate *A. cruentus,* which is a "deep red" form of the plant, as a dye plant (Sauer 1976).

The principal advantage of amaranth is that both the grain and the leaves are sources of high-quality protein. While most grain foods, such as wheat and corn, have 12 to 14 percent protein and lack the essential amino acid lysine, amaranth seeds have 16 to 18 percent protein and are "lysine-rich" (Barrett 1986; Tucker 1986). In areas of the world where animal protein is lacking, the amaranth plant can stave off protein deficiencies. When amaranth flour is mixed with wheat or corn flour in breads or tortillas, the result is a near-perfect protein (eggs which can supply most of the body's protein requirements). Moreover, amaranth has more dietary fiber than any of the major grains (Tucker 1986). Amaranth seeds also contain calcium and phosphorus, whereas amaranth leaves, which can be eaten like spinach, provide dietary calcium and phosphorus as well as potassium, thiamine, riboflavin, niacin, and vitamins A and C. Amaranth is also richer in iron than spinach (Cole 1979; Tucker 1986).

The amaranth grain (which resembles a miniature flying saucer) is covered with a tough coat that the body cannot digest. Therefore, to obtain nutrition from the seeds it must be processed, and by toasting, boiling, or milling transformed into starch, bran, germ, or oil. Milling the grain yields 28 percent germ-bran and 72 percent white flour. Once processed, the tiny seeds have a "nutty flavor" and are used in breakfast cereals and made into flour for breads (Barrett 1986). Amaranth may also be popped like popcorn or made into candies. The Mexicans mix honey or molasses and popped amaranth into a sweet confection they call "alegría" (happiness) (Marx 1977; Cole 1979). Amaranth may even be brewed into a tea (Barrett 1986).

In addition to its nutritional advantages, amaranth "grows like a weed" in many different environments in the Americas, Africa, and Asia. Although it tends to do best in warm, dry climates with bright sunshine, some species flourish in the wet tropical lowlands, and others do well above 10,000 feet in the Andes. They also tolerate adverse soil conditions, such as high salt, acidity, or alkalinity, in which corn will not survive (Brody 1984; Tucker 1986). Besides growing rapidly under bright sunlight, amaranth has the ability to conserve water by partially closing its leaf pores. It can also tolerate dryness up to a point without wilting (Tucker 1986). Thus, it can be cultivated on marginal soils subject to periodic dry spells, which is an important consideration in semiarid regions.

Two disadvantages of amaranth are that the tiny seeds are awkward to work with and should be harvested by hand. In the United States, machine harvesting is possible after the first severe frost, but yields are lower (Tucker 1986). Yet hand-harvesting is not a major obstacle in countries where agricultural labor is plentiful and its cost is low. Another problem is that the domesticated species easily hybridize via wind pollination with the weedy varieties, yielding low-quality seeds (Marx 1977). Like so many plants, amaranth is also attacked by insects and plant diseases (Tucker 1986). These disadvantages may limit amaranth cultivation to gardeners in the United States and small farmers in the developing world.

Origins

According to J. D. Sauer (1976), wild amaranth seeds were gathered by many Native American peoples. As such, they may have contributed significant protein, as well as essential vitamins, to hunting and gathering populations after the big game animals died out in the Americas. Archaeologists can establish a gradual process of domestication with the appearance of pale, white seeds having improved popping quality and flavor. Notably when seed selection is relaxed, the plants return to producing dark seeds. One of the oldest dates for pale-seeded amaranth is 4000 B.C. from Tehuacan, Puebla, in Mexico, where *A. cruentus* has been found. By 2000 B.C., amaranth was part of the basic Mexican diet (Walsh and Sugiura 1991) (Map II.A.1.1). The Andean species of *A. caudatus* was discovered in 2,000-year-old tombs in northwestern Argentina (Sauer 1976). A more recent date of A.D. 500 marks an additional amaranth species, *A. hypochondriacus.* By the fourteenth century A.D., *A. hypochondriacus* was being cultivated in what is now Arizona.

As Sauer's maps (see also Map II.A.1.2) illustrate, the cores of amaranth cultivation in the pre-Columbian period were in Central Mexico, as well as in the Andes from Peru to northwestern Argentina. Additional pockets were in Ecuador close to the equator, Guatemala, southern and northwestern Mexico, and southwest North America. By the time the Spanish arrived at Vera Cruz in 1519, amaranth had evolved into a major crop staple employed to satisfy tribute obligations to the Aztec Empire. Moctezuma II received tribute from 17 provinces each year in ivory-white seeds known as *huauhtli* (Sauer 1950), which permitted the Aztecs to fill 18 imperial granaries. According to W. E. Safford (1916) and Sauer (1950), each granary had a capacity of 9,000 to 10,000 bushels. That so many seeds were collected each year is certainly impressive testimony to the widespread cultivation of amaranth in central Mexico before the Spanish conquest.

In addition, the Aztecs raised amaranth on *chinampas* (floating gardens) and utilized the plant in many ways: as a toasted grain, as green vegetables, and as a drink that the Spanish found "delicious." They also popped it. Since the Aztecs used both the leaves and the seeds, amaranth must have been an important supplement to their diet, especially in times of drought when corn crops died. Why then did the Spanish not adopt such a useful crop? Indeed, not only did the Spanish not adopt amaranth, they actually prohibited it, leaving us to wonder about the extent to which the abolition of such an important source of protein, minerals, and vitamins may have contributed to widespread malnutrition in the sixteenth century.

The Spaniards objected to amaranth because of its ritual uses as a sacred food associated with human sacrifice and "idolatry." In the early sixteenth century, the Aztecs celebrated a May festival in honor of their patron god, Huitzilopochtli, the god of war, at the great pyramid of Tenochtitlan. The ritual centered on an enormous statue of the god made of amaranth dough and included human sacrifices. Placed on a litter, the statue was carried in procession through the city and then returned to the temple where it was broken up by using other chunks of the same dough. The resulting pieces were subsequently consecrated as the flesh and bones of Huitzilopochtli, then distributed among the people, who ate them with a mixture of reverence and fear. The Spanish missionary and ethnographer Bernardino de Sahagún called the ceremonial paste *zoale* or *tzoalli* and noted that it was also fed to those who were to be sacrificed to Huitzilopochtli (Sauer 1950).

Other deities were also represented by *zoale,* such as the fire god Xiuhtecutli or the goddess Chicomecoatl, but the Tepanecs used it to form bird effigies, and the Tarascans made little figures of animals with the bread of *bledos* (the Spanish term for amaranth). On other occasions, such as the new fire ceremony, this celebration of the new 52-year cycle concluded with everyone present eating the bread of *bledos* and honey (Sauer 1950).

Legend:
- ✵ Centers of pre-Conquest ritual use
- ○ Pre-Conquest ⎫
- ⊙ Colonial ⎬ records of cultivation and use
- ● Recent ⎭
- ▲ Herbarium specimens

CHIHUAHUA

⊙ Sahuaripa

▲ Cusihuiriáchic

▲ Guasaremos
▲ Rancho Trigo
⊙ Guéguachic
● Guirocoba

SINALOA

▲ Quebrada de Manzana

▲ Ymaia

● Haiokalita

J A L I S C O

▲ Guadalajara
▲ Tlajomulco ▲ ● Tlaquepaque
Zacoalco ●
Zapotlán
Tuxpan ⊙ Tamazula
●

HIDALGO

MÉXICO
D.F.
TLAXCALA
MORELOS
PUEBLA

MICHOACÁN

⊙ Guauhtla

GUERRERO

▲ Ixtlán de Juárez
▲ Zimatlán

● Atoyac
● Tixtlanzingo

OAXACA

● Suchistepec

0   100   200   300   400   500
Kilometers

Source: Sauer 1950. Map II.A.1.1. Mexico: Localities and regions where grain amaranth cultivation is indicated.

Despite the Spanish prohibition, however, in the more remote parts of Mexico people continued to cultivate the plant and use it for food and ritual. A half century after the conquest amaranth continued to be an important food throughout much of Mexico (1950). As for ritual in 1629 in Guerrero, the priest Ruiz de Alarcón complained that the Indians were still milling amaranth to make dough for the manufacture of little idols of zoale to break up and eat in what appeared to the Spaniards to be a sort of parody of holy communion (Sauer 1950; Early 1992). Even as late as about 1900, a Huichol village of northern Jalisco celebrated one of its major festivals with "cakes" confected to represent animals. Made from amaranth seeds mixed with water, these cakes were usually employed ceremonially (Sauer 1950).

Over time, amaranth was also assimilated into Christian rituals. In the late nineteenth century, a visitor to Mexico described rosaries made of little balls of dough that were called suale (Sauer 1950). Sauer himself met a woman near Guadalajara in 1947 who was growing grain amaranths, making dough of them, and fashioning them into little cakes and rosaries (Sauer 1950). On a field trip to Mexico and Guatemala, Sauer discovered amaranth being cultivated in many patches, often unknown to outsiders. He found it to be most important in the Federal District, State of Mexico, and Morelos. Other states where it was grown were Guerrero, Tlaxcala, Puebla, Michoacán, and Sonora, Chihuahua, and Sinaloa. Thirty years after Sauer, Daniel Early (1977) visited Tulyehualco in Mexico where he observed techniques of amaranth planting on chinampas. In Guatemala, Sauer found that A. cruentus was still being planted by the Maya Indians in association with other crops, as they had done in the pre-Columbian period (Sauer 1950, 1976; Morley and Brainerd 1983).

As in highland Guatemala, Indian farmers in the Andes plant amaranth on "the fringes" of their maize fields. Sauer and others have reported amaranth crops in the highlands of Peru and Bolivia and in northwestern Argentina (Sauer 1950). At that time amaranth plants were known by a variety of names: Achis, achita, ckoito, coyo, or coimi in Peru; and coimi, cuime, millmi, or quinua millmi in Bolivia. As Sauer (1950) notes, the term quinoa was often used for amaranth as well as quinoa.

Amaranth was apparently widely cultivated in the pre-Columbian Andean highlands (Map II.A.1.2). A funerary urn has been found at Pampa Grande in Salta, Argentina, that was full of maize, beans, chenopod seeds, amaranth flowers, and pale seeds identified as A. caudatus (Sauer 1950). In 1971, A. T. Hunziker and A. M. Planchuelo reported finding A. caudatus seeds in tombs at least 2,000 years old located in north-western Argentina (Sauer 1976). But in the Inca period, good descriptions of amaranth are lacking, perhaps because it did not play the same ceremonial role as among the Aztecs. The Incas used maize for their sacred bread rather than amaranth. The first Spanish record that Sauer found (1950) is that of the Jesuit chronicler Bernabé Cobo who reported in 1653 that both red and white bledos were commonly consumed by Native Americans. Cobo also recognized that bledos were different from quinoa (Sauer 1950).

Sometime in the sixteenth century A. caudatus was taken from the Andes to Europe. In his Rariorum Plantarum Historia, Carl Clusius published the first illustration of the species in Antwerp in 1601 (Sauer 1950). He identified it as Quinua, sive Blitum majus Peruanum. Citing Clusius in 1737, Carl von Linné (Linnaeus) named the plant Amaranthus caudatus and indicated that it came from South America (Sauer 1950). A pale-seeded variety of A. hypochondriacus turned up in a sixteenth-century German collection that was found by P. Hanelt in 1968 (Sauer 1976). According to Sauer (1976), all three domesticated species may have been introduced to the Old World via Europe; henceforth, the American varieties of grain amaranth would be grown as ornamental plants in Europe. Other species of European amaranth now grow wild as weeds.

Asia and North America

The global distribution of amaranth before A.D. 1500 suggests that its cultivation is of "great antiquity," and there is no clear picture of the historical diffusion of American amaranths to Asia, or to Africa, for that matter. Amaranth in Asia probably predates 1492, because it is so widely scattered from Iran to China in remote places, such as Manchuria and eastern Siberia; and it is cultivated by isolated populations in high mountain valleys in the Himalayas. It seems to have been a staple in southern India for centuries (Sauer 1950, 1976), and the Indians argue that it was domesticated in India (Cole 1979).

E. D. Merrill (Cole 1979), however, believed that the Portuguese brought amaranth from Brazil to the Malabar coast of India after 1500, where it was widely cultivated by the nineteenth century. Yet Chinese sources may document its antiquity in Asia. According to Sauer (1950), there apparently is a reference to a grain amaranth in a medical tract of A.D. 950, written for the Prince of Shu in modern Sichuan. It lists six kinds of hien, a name that is used for grain amaranths in the same area in modern times.

Most descriptions of cultivated amaranths in Asia are modern, from the nineteenth century on, with a few eighteenth-century references to a European role in diffusing the American plants from Europe to Asia. By the early nineteenth century, amaranth was being cultivated in India, principally in the far south where it was a staple crop in the Nilgiri Hills, and in the north in the foothills of the Himalayas (Sauer 1950, 1976). In the south the people raise it for its seeds, which they convert into flour. Although also grown in the plains regions during the dry winter monsoon, amaranth is especially important in the foothills and mountains of the Himalayas from Afghanistan to Bhutan.

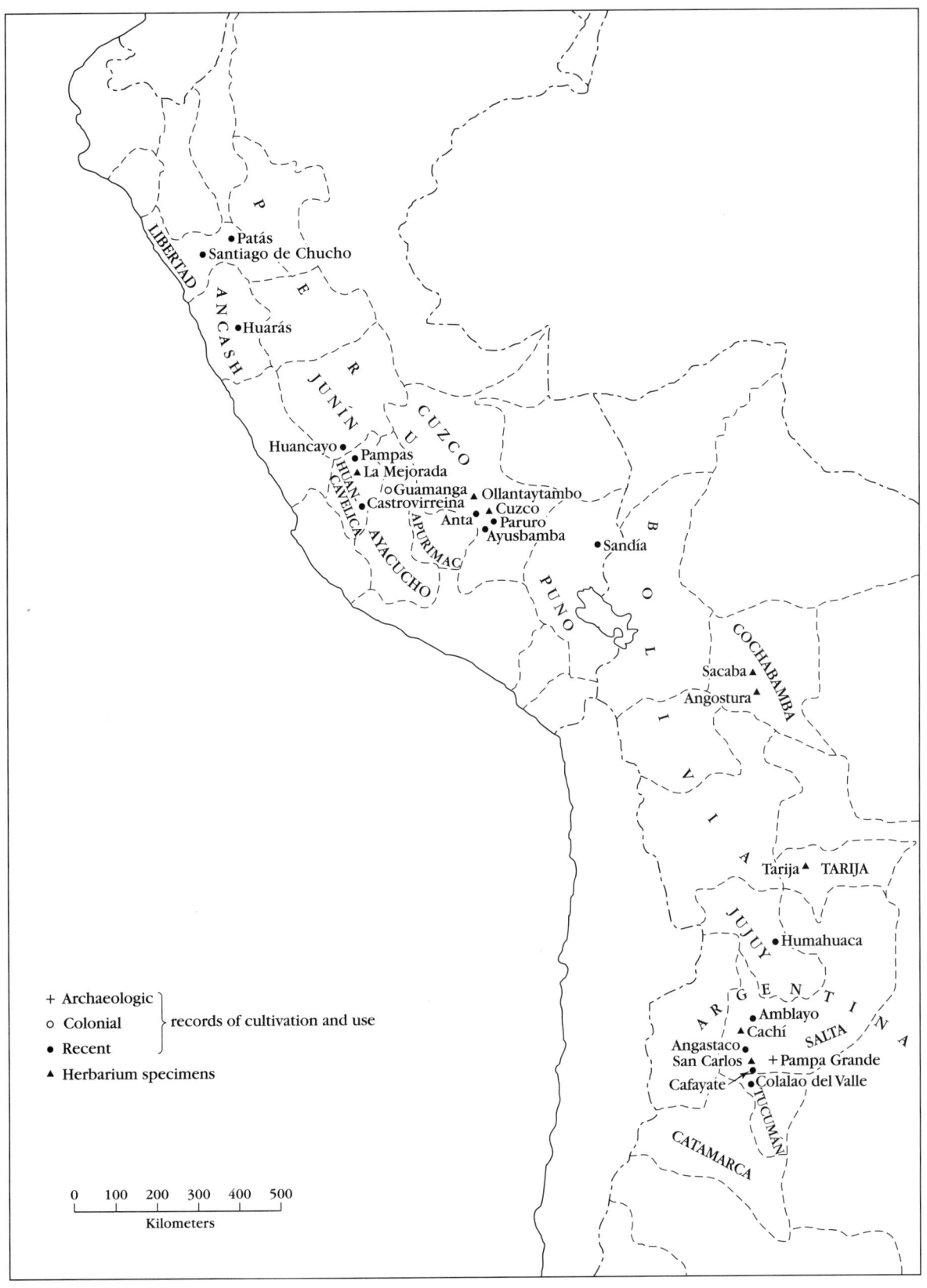

+ Archaeologic
o Colonial   } records of cultivation and use
• Recent
▲ Herbarium specimens

Source: Sauer 1950. Map II.A.1.2. South America: Localities and regions where grain amaranth cultivation is indicated.

Mongoloid nomads on the Tibetan frontier harvest grain at elevations of more than 3,500 meters, while farmers raise *A. caudatus* along with *A. leucocarpus* for grain in Nepal (Sauer 1950). According to Sauer (1950), the Himalayan plants are rich and variable in color with brilliant crimsons and rich yellows (Sauer 1950). Around Tehri in the hills of northern India the grain is popped and made into a dough to form thin cakes. In Nepal the people roast the seeds and eat them in sugar syrup like popcorn balls (Sauer 1950).

Similar popped seeds mixed with a hot sugar syrup are eaten in China, where amaranth seeds are known as *tien-shu-tze,* or millet from heaven. Sauer (1950) received dark-seeded *tien-shu-tze,* grown at elevations of 2,000 to 2,500 meters in northwestern Sichuan and Muping in Sikang. His informant reported that grain amaranths were not grown in Chengtu but in far-off mountain areas. Amaranth was also reportedly grown by the Chinese, who used the seeds to make little cakes (Sauer 1950). In addition, amaranth greens are used for food in China (Zon and Grubben 1976).

In Southeast Asia, amaranth is widely cultivated. In 1747 *A. caudatus* was identified in Indonesia, but the variety widely raised as a vegetable in modern Indonesia and other parts of Asia is *A. tricolor,* as well as species other than *A. caudatus,* such as *A. dubius.* Amaranth is a commercial crop from the Philippines to Taiwan and in Myanmar (Burma), where *A. tricolor* and *A. viridis* are grown (Zon and Grubben 1976).

As A. P. M. van der Zon and G. J. H. Grubben (1976) note, the use of amaranth as a green vegetable is quite extensive in tropical and subtropical regions of Asia and Southeast Asia, where there are many popular names for the plant: *épinard de Chine, amarante de Soudan,* African spinach, Indian spinach, *brède de Malabar,* and Ceylon spinach. Its consumption is nearly always in the form of a cooked spinach.

As of the middle 1970s, pale-seeded *A. hypochondriacus* constituted the bulk of the Asiatic crop; dark-seeded *A. hypochondriacus* and pale-seeded *A. caudatus* were minor components, although their leaves were widely used as a vegetable (Sauer 1976; Zon and Grubben 1976). The third American species, *A. cruentus,* has generally been planted as an ornamental dye plant or herb in Asia. Amaranth cultivation has been spreading in India, and Sauer (1976) believed at that time that India was the one place where amaranth was likely to experience expanded cultivation, perhaps stimulated by plant breeding. This was, of course, before scientists in the United States began extensive research on grain amaranths in the late 1970s and 1980s and American farmers initiated commercial production of amaranth in 1983 (Robinson n.d.).

The Rodale Research Center in Kutztown, Pennsylvania, is one of the leading amaranth research centers in the United States. In part because of amaranth's seed distribution and partly because of promotional efforts, American small farmers are increasingly cultivating the grain. Breads, cereals, cookies, and "Gra-ham" crackers made with amaranth are now available in health-food and grocery stores in the United States.

Africa

How and when amaranth reached Africa is also uncertain. It is widely found as an ornamental plant or weed throughout the continent: from Senegal to Nigeria in West Africa, from Equatorial Africa to Zaire; and to a lesser extent in East Africa. Species have even been identified in Morocco, Ethiopia, and Sudan (Sauer 1950). *A. cruentus* is widespread in Africa, and *A. caudatus* is used as an ornamental and grain amaranth.

According to Zon and Grubben (1976), a variety of *A. cruentus* was introduced "recently" to southern Dahomey (now Benin) from Suriname and has proved to be resistant to drought. Other varieties of *A. cruentus* were widely marketed as a vegetable crop in Dahomey or raised in family gardens. A third American amaranth, *A. hypochondriacus,* was introduced into East Africa in the 1940s as a grain for the Indian population there (Sauer 1976).

That the history of amaranth in Africa remains comparatively unknown may be because of its widespread use in private vegetable gardens. The food preference of many Africans and African-Americans for greens may also mean that amaranth leaves are more important in the diet of Africans than seeds. The problem for the historical record, however, is that the cultivation and consumption of greens usually escapes documentation.

Conclusion

At this stage of research, the historical evolution and diffusion of amaranth remains a research problem for the future. How did amaranth come to be cultivated around the world? Under what conditions and when? As Sauer (1950) notes, amaranth species, cultivation methods, and consumption patterns are remarkably similar in Old and New Worlds. In both areas amaranth tends to be cultivated in the highlands, although the weed species grow well at other altitudes.

Farmers usually cultivate amaranth in conjunction with maize and other crops and consume it themselves in the form of balls of popped seeds, meal, and little cakes, and they use the seeds to make a beverage. It was and is a food crop principally of interest to small farmers and gardeners but one that promises to resolve some problems of world hunger in the twenty-first century. The great advantage of the grain amaranths is that they can be grown on marginal soils where reliable water supplies are problematic and can nourish populations that lack access to animal protein.

Once widely cultivated as a staple crop of the Aztec empire, amaranth has already proven its ability to sustain millions of people in a region lacking in significant sources of animal protein long before the arrival of the

Europeans. If population growth forces small farmers to move to more marginal lands in the next century, amaranth may make an important difference in nutrition levels for people who lack access to good corn or rice lands and cannot afford meat. In short, amaranth may well become an important supplementary food crop in many developing countries in the future.

Mary Karasch

Bibliography

Amaranth. 1989. *Academic American Encyclopedia,* Vol. 1, 321. Danbury, Conn.

Amaranthus. 1991. In *The Encyclopedia Americana International Edition,* Vol. 1, 653. Danbury, Conn.

Barrett, Mariclare. 1986. The new old grains. *Vegetarian Times* 101: 29-31, 51.

Berberich, Steven. 1980. History of amaranth. *Agricultural Research* 29: 14-15.

Brody, Jane E. 1984. Ancient, forgotten plant now "grain of the future." *The New York Times,* Oct. 16.

Cole, John N. 1979. *Amaranth from the past for the future.* Emmaus, Pa.

Cramer, Craig. 1987. The world is discovering amaranth. *The New Farm* 9: 32-5.

Early, Daniel. 1977. Amaranth secrets of the Aztecs. *Organic Gardening and Farming* 24: 69-73.

　　1992. The renaissance of amaranth. In *Chilies to chocolate: Food the Americas gave the world,* ed. Nelson Foster and Linda S. Cordell, 15-33. Tucson, Ariz.

Gates, Jane Potter. 1990. *Amaranths for food or feed January 1979-December 1989. Quick bibliography series: QB 90-29. Updates QB 88-07. 210 Citations from Agricola.* Beltsville, Md.

Hunziker, Armandu T. 1943. Las especies alimenticias de Amaranthus . . . cultivados por los indios de América. *Revista Argentina de Agronomía* 10: 297-354.

Marx, Jean. 1977. Amaranth: A comeback for the food of the Aztecs? *Science* 198: 40.

Morley, Sylvanus G., and George W. Brainerd. 1983. *The ancient Maya.* Fourth edition, rev. Robert J. Sharer. Stanford, Calif.

Robinson, Robert G. n.d. Amaranth, quinoa, ragi, tef, and niger: Tiny seeds of ancient history and modern interest. *Agricultural Experiment Station Bulletin.* St. Paul, Minn.

Safford, W. E. 1916. An economic amaranthus of ancient America. *Science* 44: 870.

Sauer, J. D. 1950. The grain amaranths: A survey of their history and classification. *Annals of the Missouri Botanical Garden* 37: 561-632.

　　1976. Grain amaranths. In *Evolution of crop plants,* ed. N. W. Simmonds, 4-7. London and New York.

Tucker, Jonathan B. 1986. Amaranth: The once and future crop. *BioScience* 36: 9-13.

Walsh, Jane MacLaren, and Yoko Sugiura. 1991. The demise of the fifth sun. In *Seeds of change,* ed. Herman J. Viola and Carolyn Margolis, 16-44. Washington, D.C., and London.

Wister, John C. 1985. Amaranth. In *Collier's Encyclopedia,* Vol. 1: 622. London and New York.

Zon, A. P. M. van der, and G. J. H. Grubben. 1976. *Les légumes-feuilles spontanés et cultivés du Sud-Dahomey.* Amsterdam.

II.A.2. ❧ Barley

That people do not live "by bread alone" is emphatically demonstrated by the domestication of a range of foodstuffs and the cultural diversity of food combinations and preparations. But even though many foods have been brought under human control, it was the domestication of cereals that marked the earliest transition to a food-producing way of life. Barley, one of the cereals to be domesticated, offered a versatile, hardy crop with an (eventual) tolerance for a wide range of climatic and ecological conditions. Once domesticated, barley also offered humans a wide range of valuable products and uses.

The origins of wheat and barley agriculture are to be found some 10,000 years ago in the ancient Near East. Cereal domestication was probably encouraged by significant climatic and environmental changes that occurred at the end of the glaciated Pleistocene period, and intensive harvesting and manipulation of wild cereals resulted in those morphological changes that today identify domesticated plants. Anthropologists and biologists continue to discuss the processes and causes of domestication, as we have done in this book's chapter on wheat, and most of the arguments and issues covered there are not reviewed here. All experts agree, however, on the importance of interdisciplinary research and multiple lines of evidence in reconstructing the story of cereal domestication.

Barley

Readers of this chapter may note some close similarities to the evidence for wheat domestication and an overlap with several important archaeological sites. Nonetheless, barley has a different story to tell. Barley grains and plant fragments are regular components of almost all sites with any plant remains in the Near East, regardless of period or food-producing strategy. Wild barley thrives widely in the Near East today – on slopes, in lightly grazed and fired pastures, in scrub-oak clearings, in fields and field margins, and along roadsides. These circumstances suggest a different set of research questions about barley domestication, such as: What was barley used for? Was its domestication a unique event? And how long did barley domestication take?

In addition, there are subthemes to be considered. Some researchers, for example, have suggested that barley was not domesticated for the same reasons that led to the domestication of other cereals – such as the dwindling of other resources, seasonal shortages, a desire for a sedentary food base, or the need for a surplus for exchange. Instead, barley may have been cultivated for the brewing of ale or beer.

In another view, the very slight differences between the wild and domesticated forms, and the ease with which wild barley can be domesticated, make it difficult to believe that barley domestication did not occur more than once. Geneticists and agricultural historians have generally believed that groups of crops were domesticated in relatively small regions and spread by human migration and trade. If barley was domesticated independently in several different communities, this would indicate that the transition to farming in those areas required little innovation and took place under recurring conditions.

Finally, because of their presence in many excavated sites, ancient barleys provide some of the best archaeological evidence bearing on the general problem of the pace of plant domestication. Whether the process took place over the course of a single human lifetime or evolved over many decades or centuries remains an important issue that may never be resolved with archaeological evidence alone (Hillman and Davies 1990). But the pace of domestication lies at the heart of the debate over the Neolithic – was it revolution or evolution (Childe 1951; Rindos 1984)? Did plant domestication radically transform people's lifestyles, or was it a gradual by-product of long-term behaviors with radical consequences noted only in retrospect? Barley is a crop that may hold answers to such questions.

Archaeological Evidence for the Domestication of Barley

Archaeological evidence points to the domestication of barley in concert with the emergence of Neolithic villages in the Levantine arc of the Fertile Crescent. Pre-Neolithic peoples, notably Natufian foragers (whose cultural remains include relatively large numbers of grinding stones, sickle blades, and storage pits), increasingly depended on plant foods and, perhaps, plant cultivation. Unfortunately, their tools point only to general plant use, and archaeologists continue to discuss which plants were actually processed (e.g., McCorriston 1994; Mason 1995). There is no evidence to suggest that the Natufians domesticated barley or any other plant.

Charred plant remains, the best evidence for domestication of specific plants, have rarely been recovered from pre-Neolithic sites. Preservation is generally poor. In the case of barley, only a few sites prior to the Neolithic contain recognizable fragments, and all examples indicate wild types. A few barley grains from Wadi Kubbaniya, an 18,000-year-old forager site in southern Egypt, were at first thought to be early examples of domesticated barley (Wendorf et al. 1979), but subsequent laboratory tests showed these to be modern grains that had intruded into ancient occupation layers (Stemler and Falk 1980; Wendorf et al. 1984). Other plant remains from Wadi Kubbaniya

included relatively high numbers of wild *Cyperus* tubers and wild fruits and seeds (Hillman 1989).

One of the most extraordinary prefarming archaeological sites to be discovered in recent years is Ohalo II, on the shore of the Sea of Galilee, which yielded quantities of charred plant remains, including hundreds of wild barley grains (Kislev, Nadel, and Carmi 1992). About 19,000 years ago, foragers camped there, and the remains of their hearths and refuse pits came to light during a phase of very pronounced shoreline recession several years ago. Excavators believe that the charred plants found in the site were the remains of foods collected by Ohalo II's Epi-Paleolithic foragers. If so, these foragers exploited wild barley (*Hordeum spontaneum* Koch.), which was ancestral to domesticated barley.

Despite the generally poor preservation of plant remains, there are two Natufian sites with evidence suggesting that foraging peoples there collected some wild barley just prior to the beginnings of agriculture. Wadi Hammeh, a 12,000-year-old Early Natufian hamlet overlooking the Jordan Valley (Edwards 1988), contained charred seeds of wild barley (*Hordeum spontaneum*), wild grasses, small legumes, crucifers, and a range of other plants, as yet unidentified (Colledge, in Edwards et al. 1988). The seeds were scattered among deposits in several round houses, somewhat like the scatter of plant remains at another Natufian site, Hayonim Cave, where Early and Late Natufian dwellers had constructed round houses, possibly seasonal dwellings, within the cave (Hopf and Bar Yosef 1987). To be certain that disturbances had not carried later seeds down into Natufian layers (a problem at Wadi Kubbaniya and at another Natufian site, Nahel Oren), excavators had the charred seeds individually dated. Wild lupines found with wild almonds, wild peas, and wild barley (*Hordeum spontaneum*) suggest that the Natufian inhabitants collected plants that could be stored for later consumption.

Although there is little doubt that some foraging groups collected wild barley, evidence for the beginnings of barley domestication is far more controversial. Until recently, archaeologists were convinced that farmers (as opposed to foragers) had occupied any site containing even a few barley grains or rachis fragments with the morphological characteristics of domestic cereals. Thus, the identification of tough-rachis barley in the Pre-Pottery Neolithic A (PPNA) levels at Jericho (Hopf 1983: 609) implied that the earliest Neolithic occupants domesticated barley in addition to wheats and legumes.[1] A tough rachis inhibits seed dispersal, and wild barleys have brittle rachises that shatter when the seeds mature. Each segment of the rachis supports a cluster of three florets (flowers), from which only one grain develops. If a tough rachis fails to shatter, the seeds remain on the intact stalk, vulnerable to predators and unable to root and grow. Yet a tough-rachis crop is more easily and efficiently harvested by humans. Through human manipulation, the tough-rachis trait, which is maladaptive and scarce in the wild (Hillman and Davies 1990: 166–7), dominates and characterizes domesticated barley. At Jericho, the tough-rachis finds suggested to archaeologists that barley domestication had either preceded or accompanied the evident Neolithic practices of plant cultivation using floodwater manipulation in an oasis habitat.

However, at Netiv Hagdud, a contemporary (PPNA) site to the north of Jericho, Neolithic settlers seem to have practiced barley cultivation (Bar-Yosef et al. 1991), and the recovery there of rich archaeobotanical remains has forced archaeobotanists to rethink the significance of a few barley remains of the domesticated type in Early Neolithic sites throughout the Near East. Built on an alluvial fan in a setting not unlike that of Jericho, Netiv Hagdud proved to contain the foundations of almost a dozen large oval and small round structures. Some of these were probably houses with rock platform hearths and grinding equipment (Bar-Yosef et al. 1991: 408–11). The charred plant remains from the site included thousands of barley grains and rachis fragments, and the opportunity to examine these as an assemblage led to a surprising discovery.

Although a number of fragments clearly displayed a domesticated-type tough rachis (Kislev and Bar-Yosef 1986), archaeobotanists realized that as an assemblage, the Netiv Hagdud barley most closely resembles modern *wild* barley. Even among a stand of wild barley, approximately 12 percent of the spikes have a tough rachis (Zohary and Hopf 1993: 62) because this characteristic regularly appears as the result of mutation and self-fertilization to generate a pair of recessive alleles in a gene (Hillman and Davies 1990: 168). At Netiv Hagdud, the thousands of barley remains (including low numbers of tough-rachis examples) were collected, possibly from cultivated stands, by Early Neolithic people who appear from available evidence to have had no domesticated crops, although some scholars suggest that harvesting timing and techniques might still make it difficult to distinguish between wild and semidomesticated barley (Kislev 1992; Zohary 1992; Bar-Yosef and Meadow 1995). That evidence also implies that occasional domesticated-type barley remains at other Neolithic sites, including Tell Aswad (van Zeist and Bakker-Heeres 1982), may actually belong to an assemblage of purely wild barley.

Other Early Neolithic sites with remains of barley include Gilgal I, a PPNA site with cultural remains similar to those at Netiv Hagdud and Jericho. It is still unclear whether the "large amounts of oat and barley seeds" recovered in the mid-1980s from a silo in one of the Neolithic houses were domesticated or wild types (Noy 1989: 13). Tell Aswad, formerly nearer to Mediterranean oak forests and set beside a marshy lakeshore in the Damascus Basin, has also yielded a mix of rachis fragments, predominantly wild-type but

with some domesticated-type (van Zeist and Bakker-Heeres 1982: 201–4). This same mix of wild and domesticated types was found in early levels at other early sites, including Ganj Dareh on the eastern margins of the Fertile Crescent (van Zeist et al. 1984: 219).

Over time, the percentages of wild-type and domesticated-type barley remains were inverted at sites in the Damascus Basin (van Zeist et al. 1984: 204). Tell Aswad was the earliest occupied of these sites in a 2,000-year sequence of nearly continuous residence there (Contenson 1985), and when it was abandoned, farmers had already settled nearby, at Tell Ghoraifé. Although the barley remains at Ghoraifé included many domesticated-type specimens, it was from evidence of a later occupation at Tell Aswad (8,500 to 8,900 years ago) and the nearby site of Ramad (occupied from 8,200 years ago) that archaeobotanists could unequivocally distinguish between fully domesticated barley and low numbers of wild barley in the same assemblages. The archaeobotanists suggested that the apparent mix of wild and domesticated types in earlier deposits may indicate an intermediate stage in the domestication process (van Zeist and Bakker-Heeres 1982: 184–5, 201–4).

There has never been much doubt that remains of barley from northern Levantine sites indicate plant collection or incipient stages of cultivation without domestication 10,000 years ago. Wild barley (*Hordeum spontaneum* Koch.) is well represented among the plant remains from Mureybit, an Early Neolithic village on the Euphrates River in the Syrian steppe (van Zeist and Bakker-Heeres 1984a: 171). Contemporary levels at Qeremez Dere, also in the steppe, contain abundant remains of fragmented wild grass grains, some of which "seem most probably to be wild barley" (Nesbitt, in Watkins, Baird, and Betts 1989: 21). Plant remains suggest that cereal cultivation was of little importance as one moved further north and east during the first centuries of Neolithic occupation. Cereals were present only as traces in the northern Iraq site of Nemrik 9 along the Tigris River (Nesbitt, in Kozlowski 1989: 30), at M'lefaat (Nesbitt and Watkins 1995: 11), and not at all at Hallan Çemi (Rosenberg et al. 1995) nor at earliest Çayönü (van Zeist 1972).

Available evidence now seems to suggest that domesticated barley appeared in the second phase of the early Neolithic – Pre-Pottery Neolithic B (PPNB) – several hundred years after wheat farming was established.[2] By the PPNB (beginning around 9,200 years ago), several different forms of domesticated barley, two-row and six-row (see the section "Taxonomy"), appeared among plant remains from Neolithic sites. Jericho and Ramad had both forms from about 9,000 years ago (van Zeist and Bakker-Heeres 1982: 183; Hopf 1983: 609). Barley does not seem to have been among the earliest crops in the Taurus Mountains – at PPNB sites such as Çayönü (van Zeist 1972; Stewart

1976) and Çafar Höyük (Moulins 1993). At Neolithic Damishliyya, in northern Syria (from 8,000 years ago), and Ras Shamra on the Mediterranean coast (from 8,500 years ago), domesticated two-row barley was present (van Zeist and Bakker-Heeres 1984b: 151, 159; Akkermans 1989: 128, 1991: 124). In Anatolia, domesticated barley also characterized the first appearance of farming, for example, at Çatal Hüyük (Helbaek 1964b). This is also the case in the eastern Fertile Crescent, where domesticated plants, barley among them, first showed up around 9,000 years ago – at Jarmo (Helbaek 1960: 108-9) and Ali Kosh (Helbaek 1969).

An excellent review of archaeobotanical remains (Zohary and Hopf 1993: 63-4) tracks the subsequent spread of two-row and six-row barley around the Mediterranean coast, across the Balkans, and into temperate Europe. Barley was one of the fundamental components of the Neolithic economic package introduced (and modified) with the spread of Near Eastern farmers across Anatolia and into various environmental zones of Europe (Bogucki 1996), as well as into northern Egypt (Wetterstrom 1993), Central Asia (Charles and Hillman 1992; Harris et al. 1993), and South Asia. By 8,000 years ago, barley agriculture had reached the foothills of the Indus Valley, where it supported farmers at Mehrgarh, one of the earliest settlements in South Asia (Jarrige and Meadow 1980; Costantini 1984).

During these first several thousand years, domesticated barley also spread into the steppes and desert margins of the Near East, expanding farming practices into an ecological niche where risk was high and barley offered what was probably the best chance for crop survival. At Abu Hureyra, in the Syrian steppe near Mureybit, six-row barley appeared earlier than its two-row barley ancestor (Hillman 1975), suggesting that fully domesticated barley crops were introduced to that site (Hillman and Davies 1990: 206), although recent paleoecological models suggest that wild barley grew nearby (Hillman 1996).

By the end of the PPNB, sites with barley were fairly common in very marginal farming zones – including, for example, El Koum 2 (Moulins, in Stordeur 1989: 108), Bouqras (van Zeist and Water-bolk-van Rooijen 1985), and Beidha (Helbaek 1966). At Nahal Hemar cave, in the dry Judean Hills, a single kernel of domesticated barley recovered was presumably imported to the site some 9,000 years ago (Kislev 1988: 77, 80). The spread of barley not only indicates the success of a farming way of life but also offers important archaeological indicators to complement botanical and ecological evidence of the domestication and significance of this vital crop plant.

Botanical Evidence for the Domestication of Barley

Barley grains and barley rachis internodes recovered from archaeological sites show the telling morphological characteristics of wild and domesticated forms, but botanical studies of modern barleys have also provided critical evidence for an interdisciplinary reconstruction of barley domestication. Archaeologists can examine ancient morphology but not ancient plant behavior. It was changes in both characteristics that established barley as a domesticated plant. Not only did the rachis become tough, but the ripening period of barley narrowed, and a single-season seed dormancy became established. Botanical studies have revealed relationships between species and varieties of barley and the precise nature of the changes that must have occurred under domestication.

Taxonomy

As with wheats, taxonomic classification of barleys has changed with expanding scientific knowledge of genetic relationships. Genetic evidence now indicates much closer relationships among what morphologically once appeared to be distinctive species (Briggs 1978: 77). Yet it is the morphological criteria, easily seen, that offer farmers and archaeologists a ready means by which to classify barleys (but see Hillman and Davies 1990, and Hillman et al. 1993, for alternative experimental approaches). Because archaeologists have had to rely largely on morphological criteria to detect the beginnings of domestication, the old species names remain convenient terms for distinguishing between what are now considered barley varieties (new species names in parentheses follow).

Barleys belong in the grass tribe Triticeae, to which wheats and ryes (barley's closest crop relatives) also belong. There are 31 barley species (almost all wild), and nearly three-fourths of them are perennial grasses (Bothmer and Jacobsen 1985; Nilan and Ullrich 1993). Despite the diversity of wild barleys that can be identified today, most botanists and geneticists concur that all domesticated types most probably have a single wild ancestor, *Hordeum spontaneum* Koch. *(H. vulgare* subsp. *spontaneum)* (Harlan and Zohary 1966; Zohary 1969). This plant crosses easily with all domesticated barleys. The major morphological difference between wild and domesticated barley lies in the development of a tough rachis in the domesticate.

Once farmers had acquired a domesticated two-row form of barley, they selectively favored the propagation of a further morphological variant, the six-row form. Barleys have three flowers (florets) on each rachis segment (node). In the wild and domesticated two-row forms, however, only the central floret develops a grain. Thus, one grain develops on each side of a rachis, giving the spike the appearance of two grains per row when viewed from the side. In the six-row form, *Hordeum hexastichum* L. *(H. vulgare* subsp. *vulgare),* the infertility of the lateral florets is overcome: Nodes now bear three grains each, so the spike has three grains on each side. This gives an appearance of six grains per row in side view. A general evolutionary trend in the grass family has been the reduction of reproductive parts; so, for a long time, it was difficult for botanists to accept that one of the consequences of domestication and manipulation of barley has been to restore fertility in lateral spikelets, thereby increasing the grain production of each plant (Harlan 1968: 10).

A final important morphological change was the appearance of naked-grain barleys. In wild cereals, the modified seed leaves (glumes, lemmas, and paleas) typically tightly enclose the grain and form a protective husk. From a human perspective, one of the most attractive changes in domesticated cereals is the development of grains from which the glumes, lemmas, and paleas easily fall away. Because humans cannot digest the cellulose in the husks, such development considerably reduces processing effort. Naked-grain barleys *(Hordeum vulgare* subsp. *distichum* var. *nudum* and *H. vulgare* subsp. *vulgare* var. *nudum)* appeared shortly after the emergence of six-row forms (Zohary and Hopf 1993: 63). Taxonomists have always recognized these as varieties rather than as distinct species of barley.

Genetics

Genetic relationships remain very close among all barleys, and modern taxonomic schemes collapse all cultivated barleys and the wild *Hordeum spontaneum* ancestor into a single species, *Hordeum vulgare* (Harlan and Zohary 1966: 1075; Briggs 1978: 78; Nilan and Ullrich 1993: 3). *H. vulgare* is a diploid with two sets of seven chromosomes ($2n = 14$) and has proved an excellent subject for genetic and cytogenetic analysis (Nilan and Ullrich 1993: 8). Because the plant is self-fertile (that is, male pollen fertilizes its own or adjacent flowers on the same plant), mutations have a good chance of being copied and expressed in the genes of subsequent generations. This attribute was undoubtedly an important feature of barley domestication, for a very few mutations have caused major morphological changes that were easily favored by humans, both consciously and unconsciously (Harlan 1976; Hillman and Davies 1990).

A brittle rachis, for example, is controlled by a pair of tightly linked genes. A mutant recessive allele in either gene (Bt and Bt_1) will produce a tough rachis in homozygous offspring (Harlan 1976: 94; Briggs 1978: 85). This condition will occur rarely in the wild but may be quickly selected for and fixed in a population under cultivation (Hillman and Davies 1990: 166-8). Experimental trials and computer simulations suggest that under specific selective conditions, the homozygous recessive genotype may become predominant in as few as 20 years (Hillman and Davies 1990: 189). Consequently, barley domestication depends on one mutation!

Furthermore, a single recessive mutation also is responsible for fertility in lateral florets and the conversion from two-row to six-row forms (Harlan 1976: 94). Another gene, also affected by a recessive mutant allele, controls the adherence of lemma and palea to the grain. Jack Harlan (1976: 95-6) has postulated a single domestication of wild barley followed by other recessive mutants for six-row and naked forms.

Objections to this parsimonious reconstruction revolve around the many brittle or semibrittle rachis variants of barley, some of which include six-row forms. Barley is rich in natural variants in the wild (Nevo et al. 1979; Nilan and Ullrich 1993: 9), and geneticists have long tried to incorporate six-row brittle forms (e.g., *Hordeum agriocrithon* Åberg) into an evolutionary taxonomy of the barleys. Most now agree that the minor genetic differences, wide genetic diversity, and ease of hybridization and introgression with domesticated forms account for the great number of varieties encountered in the "wild" (Zohary 1964; Nilan and Ullrich 1993: 3).

Ecological Evidence for Barley Domestication

Geographic Distribution

In the tradition of Nikolay Ivanovich Vavilov, geneticists and botanists have documented the distributions of wild and domesticated varieties of barley. The places where wild races ancestral to domesticated crops grow today may indicate the range within which a crop arose, because the earliest cultivators must have encountered the plant in its natural habitat. Patterns of genetic diversity in different areas may also offer clues about the history of a crop plant. Such patterns may suggest, for example, a long and intensive history of manipulation or an isolated strain. Harlan and Daniel Zohary (1966: 1075-7) have summarized the modern distribution of wild barley, *Hordeum spontaneum,* noting many populations outside the core area of the Fertile Crescent where the earliest agricultural villages lay.

Harlan and Zohary distinguish between truly wild barley *(H. spontaneum)* and weedy races – wild-type barleys derived from domesticated barley crops in areas to which barley farming spread after domestication. Modern distribution of truly wild progenitors is closely associated with the geography of semiarid Mediterranean climates and with an ecological relationship with deciduous oak open woodland that covers the lower slopes of the mountain arc of the Fertile Crescent. This landscape was made famous by Robert J. Braidwood's expedition to the "Hilly Flanks," where he and later archaeologists sought to uncover the first farming villages (Braidwood and Howe 1960: 3). A "small, slender, very grassy type" grows wild in steppic environments with somewhat greater temperature extremes and less annual rainfall. Another distinct truly wild race in the southern Levant has extremely large seeds (Harlan and Zohary 1966: 1078).

In areas outside the semiarid Mediterranean woodlands, wild-type barleys survive in a more continental climate (hotter summers, colder winters, year-round rainfall). Because all the collections in such areas have proved to be weedy races (including brittle-rachis, six-row *Hordeum agriocrithon* Åberg from Tibet), their range provides better information on the spread of barley farming than on the original domestication of the plant.

Ecological Factors

Ecologically, wild barley shares some of the preferences of wheat, but wild barley has not only a much more extensive geographical range but also a wider ecological tolerance. Barleys thrive on nitrogen-poor soils, and their initial cultivation must have excluded dump-heap areas enriched by human and animal fertilizers (Hillman and Davies 1990: 159). But the wild barley progenitors do thrive in a variety of disturbed habitats (Zohary 1964). In prime locales, wild barley flourishes on scree slopes of rolling park-woodlands. It likes disturbed ground – in fields and along roadsides – and is a moderately aggressive fire follower (Naveh 1974, 1984).

Ecological and botanical attributes of wild barley have convinced some that it was the first domesticate (Bar-Yosef and Kislev 1989: 640). Archaeological evidence, however, indicates that despite possible cultivation in the PPNA (Hillman and Davies 1990: 200; Bar-Yosef et al. 1991), barley was not domesticated as early as wheat and some legumes. From the perspective of cultivators, wild wheats have several advantages over wild barley, including greater yield for harvesting time (Ladizinsky 1975) and easy detachment of lemma and palea. Modern wild barleys demonstrate a number of features potentially attractive to foraging peoples, including large grain size, ease of mutant fixation, local abundance, and wide soil and climate tolerance (Bar-Yosef and Kislev 1989: 640). Nevertheless, the archaeological record holds earlier evidence of domesticated wheat than of domesticated barley.

Was wheat domestication fast and that of barley slow? Or were these cereals domesticated at the same rate but at different times? Experimental studies offer significant insights into the archaeological record of cereal domestication, including probable causes of ambiguity where wild forms may or may not have been cultivated (Hillman and Davies 1990; Anderson-Gerfaud, Deraprahamian, and Willcox 1991). Although barley domestication can happen very quickly, the rate of domestication would have varied according to planting and harvesting conditions. It would be nearly impossible to discriminate between collection and cultivation (reseeding) of wild barley in the archaeological record; therefore, it is difficult to know whether barley was cultivated for a long time before becoming a recognizable domesticate. The excellent work of Gordon Hillman and Stuart Davies (1990) with mutation rates, cultivation variables, and harvest strategies suggests little inherent difference between wheat and barley plants for their domesticability. Perhaps the very different archaeological record, with a PPNA emergence of domesticated wheat and a later PPNB emergence of domesticated barley, implies that we should look beyond the genetics and ecology of the plants for other variables in the early history of agriculture.

Uses of Barley and Barley Domestication

Today, barley is primarily important for animal feed, secondarily for brewing beer, and only marginally important as a human food. Although researchers typically assume that cereals were first domesticated as foodstuffs, we do not know what prominence, if any, barley had in early agriculturalists' diets. In its earliest, most primitive, hulled form, barley required extra processing to remove lemma and palea. Once naked barleys appeared, one suspects that they were preferred as human food, but one cannot conclude that hulled barleys were domesticated for animal feed. Although the domestication of barley coincided with the appearance of domesticated animals in the Levant, the Natufian and PPNA evidence clearly indicates harvest and, perhaps, cultivation of wild barley before animal domestication. Some quality of barley attracted cultivators before they needed animal feed.

Solomon Katz and Mary Voigt (1986) have hypothesized that barley domestication was a consequence of early beer brewing. They suspect that epi-Paleolithic peoples intensively cultivated wild barley because they had come to understand its use in fermentation and the production of alcohol, and it was this use that prompted the advent of Neolithic farming. Their theory implies that epi-Paleolithic peoples were sedentary, as Natufians apparently were (Tchernov 1991). Beer brewers must also have possessed pottery or other suitable containers, yet the invention of pottery took place long after cereal domestication in the Near East. And if cereal (barley) domestication was brought about by demand for beer, then domestication probably was impelled by social relationships cemented by alcohol rather than by subsistence values of cereal grains. The social context of drinking has been explored recently by a number of anthropologists (e.g., Moore 1989; Dietler 1990) who have emphasized the important roles that alcohol and other costly perishables play in social relationships, especially in matters of reciprocity and obligation.

Perhaps one of the most significant insights into the theory that a fermented beverage (rather than a nutritive grain) impelled domestication lies in the methods by which early beer was made. Recipes on Mesopotamian clay tablets and iconographic documentation clearly indicate that early beer was made from bread (Katz and Maytag 1991) rather than from malt (sprouted grain), as in modern practice. Both bread making and malting produce a fermentation material in which the cereal-grain endosperm has already been partially broken down mechanically and chemically (Hough 1985: 4–5). Archaeologists have detected residues consistent with beer making on ceramics from as early as the late fourth millennium B.C. (Michel, McGovern, and Badler 1992). If this Sumerian beer-making tradition developed from early antiquity, the most parsimonious theory is that beer-making developed from fermented bread.

But even if barley was first cultivated for its food value (perhaps as grits or gruel), it clearly offered an important array of products to farmers. In addition to grain feed, beer, and bread, barley also yielded straw for fodder, thatch, basketry, mudbrick, and pottery temper. Many of these products must have been essential as barley farming spread to arid regions all but devoid of trees, wood, and lush, wild vegetation.

The Spread of Barley Farming

Perhaps the most significant expansion of domesticated barley was into the truly arid steppes and deserts of the Near East, where irrigation was critical to its survival. Hans Helbaek (1964a: 47) has argued that barley was irrigated by the occupants of Tell es Sawwan in the early fifth millennium B.C. Six-row barley was evident among the site's archaeological plant remains, yet with the available rainfall, plants producing even a third as much seed (such as the two-row forms) would have been hard-pressed to survive; the six-row form could have thrived only under irrigation. Six-row barley was one of the principal crops in ancient southern Mesopotamia, and some have even suggested that barley production lay at the heart of the rise of the earliest truly complex societies in a river-watered desert.

Barley farming has also expanded into temperate regions of China, and into the tropics, where dry and cool highland regions (such as in Ethiopia, Yemen, and Peru) offer appropriate locales for cultivation. Christopher Columbus's voyages first brought the crop to the New World (Wiebe 1968), where it spread most successfully in North America (Harlan 1976: 96).

Conclusion

Domesticated barley was an important crop in human prehistory and provided many products to a wide range of settled peoples. Barley has long been considered one of the initial domesticates in the Southwest Asian Neolithic package of cereals and legumes, and in a broad chronological sweep, this conclusion remains true. But recent archaeological and botanical research indicates that domesticated barley did not appear among the very first domesticated plants. With a growing corpus of plant remains, more attention can be paid to regional variation in the Southwest Asian Neolithic, and archaeologists can now develop a more complex understanding of early plant domestication. Just as there seems to be no barley in PPNA agriculture, barley also seems to be absent from early PPNB farming communities in the Taurus Mountains. Archaeologists have long recognized other late domesticates, such as grapes, olives, and other fruits. The progress of barley domestication, along with its origins, offer potentially interesting insights into the development of domestic lifestyles and the expansion and adoption of farming in new ecological zones.

One explanation for different timing of wheat and barley domestication might be found in the possibility that differences in cultivation practices led to differences in cereal domestication. Modern studies suggest that domestication rates should be similar for wheat and barley, but they also demonstrate that different practices – tending cereals on the same or on new plots each year, for example – can affect domestication rates. An archaeological record implying a long period of cultivation for barley prompts us to wonder if cultivators treated wheats and barleys differently. Did they value one cereal more than another? Can we use such evidence from different regions and different crops to understand the significance of different plants in the diets and lives of the earliest cultivators and farmers?

Increasing botanical and ecological knowledge of cereals will help us address such questions. It may be that differences between wheat and barley domestication are related to the ease with which backcrossing between domesticated and wild cereal plants reintroduces wild traits in generations of barley crops. Ongoing experiments in cereal domestication will provide important information.

Ultimately, our reconstruction of barley domestication, and of its prehistoric importance in human diet and nutrition, depends on interdisciplinary research – the combination of archaeological evidence with botanical, ecological, and experimental evidence. There will always be uncertainties. Archaeological sites have been excavated and analyzed by different researchers practicing different methods and taking plant samples of differing quantity and quality. Modern distributions and plant ecology are the result of historical, environmental, and climatic changes, and ecologists and botanists can only guess in what ways these have affected plant geography. Nevertheless, as more archaeological and botanical evidence emerges, some of these uncertainties may be more conclusively addressed and the process of barley domestication more fully understood.

Joy McCorriston

Endnotes

1. Some of the oldest dates from Jericho can be questioned (Burleigh 1983: 760), and as is the case with wheat remains, domesticated-type barley remains from PPNA Jericho may actually be several hundred years younger than the oldest

Neolithic radiocarbon dates (10,300 to 10,500 years ago) suggest.

2. The earliest unequivocal remains of wheat are the relatively large numbers of domesticated emmer in the lowest levels at Tell Aswad (9,800 years ago), from which no wild wheats were recovered (van Zeist and Bakker-Heeres 1982), and at Jericho, outside the range of wild wheats (Harlan and Zohary 1966).

Bibliography

Akkermans, P. M. M. G. 1989. The Neolithic of the Balikh Valley, northern Syria: A first assessment. *Paléorient* 15: 122-34.

    1991. New radiocarbon dates for the later Neolithic of northern Syria. *Paléorient* 17: 121-5.

Anderson-Gerfaud, Patricia, Gérard Deraprahamian, and George Willcox. 1991. Les premières cultures de céréales sauvages et domestiques primitives au Proche-Orient Néolithique: Résultats préliminaires d'expérience à Jalès (Ardèche). *Cahiers de l'Euphrate* 5-6: 191-232.

Bar-Yosef, Ofer, Avi Gopher, Eitan Tchernov, and Mordechai E. Kislev. 1991. Netiv Hagdud: An Early Neolithic village site in the Jordan Valley. *Journal of Field Archaeology* 18: 405-24.

Bar-Yosef, Ofer, and Mordechai Kislev. 1989. Early farming communities in the Jordan Valley. In *Foraging and farming,* ed. David R. Harris and Gordon C. Hillman, 632-42. London.

Bar-Yosef, Ofer, and Richard Meadow. 1995. The origins of agriculture in the Near East. In *Last hunters, first farmers,* ed. T. Douglas Price and Anne Birgitte Gebauer, 39-94. Santa Fe, N.Mex.

Bogucki, Peter. 1996. The spread of early farming in Europe. *American Scientist* 84: 242-53.

Bothmer, R. von, and N. Jacobsen. 1985. Origin, taxonomy, and related species. In *Barley,* ed. D. C. Rasmusson, 19-56. Madison, Wis.

Bottero, Jean. 1985. Cuisine of ancient Mesopotamia. *Biblical Archaeologist* 48: 36-47.

Braidwood, Robert J., and Bruce Howe, eds. 1960. *Prehistoric investigations in Iraqi Kurdistan.* Studies in Ancient Oriental Civilizations, No. 31. Chicago.

Briggs, D. E. 1978. *Barley.* London.

Burleigh, Richard. 1983. Additional radiocarbon dates for Jericho. In *Excavations at Jericho,* ed. K. M. Kenyon and T. A. Holland, Vol. 5, 760-5. London.

Charles, Michael C., and Gordon C. Hillman. 1992. Crop husbandry in a desert environment: Evidence from the charred plant macroremains from Jeitun, 1989-90. In *Jeitun revisited: New archaeological discoveries and paleoenvironmental investigations,* ed. V. M. Masson and David R. Harris (in Russian, manuscript in English). Ashkhabad.

Childe, V. Gordon. 1951. *Man makes himself.* London.

Contenson, Henri de. 1985. La région de Damas au Néolithique. *Les annales archéologiques Arabes Syriennes* 35: 9-29.

Costantini, Lorenzo. 1984. The beginning of agriculture in the Kachi Plain: The evidence of Mehrgarh. In *South Asian archaeology 1981. Proceedings of the 6th international conference of the Association of South Asian Archaeologists in Western Europe,* ed. Bridgit Allchin, 29-33. Cambridge.

Dietler, Michael. 1990. Driven by drink: The role of drinking in the political economy and the case of Early Iron Age France. *Journal of Anthropological Archaeology* 9: 352-406.

Edwards, Phillip C. 1988. Natufian settlement in Wadi al-Hammeh. *Paléorient* 14: 309-15.

Edwards, Phillip C., Stephen J. Bourke, Susan M. Colledge, et al. 1988. Late Pleistocene prehistory in Wadi al-Hammeh, Jordan Valley. In *The prehistory of Jordan: The state of research in 1986,* ed. Andrew N. Garrard and Hans Georg Gebel, 525-65. BAR International Series, No. 396. Oxford.

Harlan, Jack R. 1968. On the origin of barley. In *Barley: Origin, botany, culture, winterhardiness, genetics, utilization, pests.* U. S. Agricultural Research Service, Agriculture Handbook No. 338, 9-82. Washington, D.C.

    1976. Barley. In *Evolution of crop plants,* ed. N. W. Simmonds, 93-8. London.

Harlan, Jack R., and Daniel Zohary. 1966. Distribution of wild wheats and barley. *Science* 153: 1074-80.

Harris, David R., V. M. Masson, Y. E. Brezkin, et al. 1993. Investigating early agriculture in central Asia: New research at Jeitun, Turkmenistan. *Antiquity* 67: 324-38.

Helbaek, Hans. 1960. The paleobotany of the Near East and Europe. In *Prehistoric investigations in Iraqi Kurdistan,* ed. Robert J. Braidwood and Bruce Howe, 99-118. Studies in Ancient Oriental Civilizations, No. 31. Chicago.

Helbaek, Hans. 1964a. Early Hassunan vegetable [*sic*] at Es-Sawwan near Sammara. *Sumer* 20: 45-8.

    1964b. First impressions of the Çatal Hüyük plant husbandry. *Anatolian Studies* 14: 121-3.

    1966. Pre-pottery Neolithic farming at Beidha. *Palestine Exploration Quarterly* 98: 61-6.

    1969. Plant collecting, dry-farming and irrigation agriculture in prehistoric Deh Luran. In *Prehistory and human ecology of the Deh Luran Plain,* ed. Frank Hole, Kent V. Flannery, and James A. Neeley, 383-426. Memoirs of the Museum of Anthropology, No. 1. Ann Arbor, Mich.

Hillman, Gordon C. 1975. The plant remains from Tell Abu Hureyra: A preliminary report. In A. M. T. Moore's The excavation of Tell Abu Hureyra in Syria: A preliminary report. *Proceedings of the Prehistoric Society* 41: 70-3.

    1989. Late Palaeolithic diet at Wadi Kubbaniya, Egypt. In *Foraging and farming,* ed. David R. Harris and Gordon C. Hillman, 207-39. London.

    1996. Late Pleistocene changes in wild plant-foods available to hunter-gatherers of the northern Fertile Crescent: Possible preludes to cereal cultivation. In *The origin and spread of agriculture and pastoralism in Eurasia,* ed. David R. Harris, 159-203. Washington, D.C.

Hillman, Gordon C., and M. Stuart Davies. 1990. Measured domestication rates in wild wheats and barley under primitive cultivation, and their archaeological implications. *Journal of World Prehistory* 4: 157-222.

Hillman, Gordon C., Sue Wales, Frances McClaren, et al. 1993. Identifying problematic remains of ancient plant foods: A comparison of the role of chemical, histological, and morphological criteria. *World Archaeology* 25: 94-121.

Hopf, Maria. 1983. Jericho plant remains. In *Excavations at Jericho,* ed. Kathleen M. Kenyon and Thomas A. Holland, Vol. 5, 576-621. London.

Hopf, Maria, and Ofer Bar-Yosef. 1987. Plant remains from

Hayonim Cave, western Galilee. *Paléorient* 13: 117-20.

Hough, J. S. 1985. *The biotechnology of malting and brewing.* Cambridge.

Jarrige, Jean-François, and Richard Meadow. 1980. The antecedents of civilization in the Indus Valley. *Scientific American* 243: 102-10.

Katz, Solomon, and Fritz Maytag. 1991. Brewing an ancient beer. *Archaeology* 44: 24-33.

Katz, Solomon, and Mary Voigt. 1986. Bread and beer. *Expedition* 28: 23-34.

Kislev, Mordechai E. 1988. Dessicated plant remains: An interim report. *Atiqot* 18: 76-81.

1992. Agriculture in the Near East in the seventh millennium B.C. In *Préhistoire de l'agriculture,* ed. Patricia C. Anderson, 87-93. Paris.

Kislev, Mordechai E., and Ofer Bar-Yosef. 1986. Early Neolithic domesticated and wild barley from Netiv Hagdud region in the Jordan Valley. *Israel Botany Journal* 35: 197-201.

Kislev, Mordechai E., Dani Nadel, and I. Carmi. 1992. Grain and fruit diet 19,000 years old at Ohalo II, Sea of Galilee, Israel. *Review of Paleobotany and Palynology* 73: 161-6.

Kozlowski, Stefan K. 1989. Nemrik 9, a PPN Neolithic site in northern Iraq. *Paléorient* 15: 25-31.

Ladizinsky, Gideon. 1975. Collection of wild cereals in the upper Jordan Valley. *Economic Botany* 29: 264-7.

Mason, Sarah. 1995. Acorn-eating and ethnographic analogies: A reply to McCorriston. *Antiquity* 69: 1025-30.

McCorriston, Joy. 1994. Acorn-eating and agricultural origins: California ethnographies as analogies for the ancient Near East. *Antiquity* 68: 97-107.

Michel, Rudolph H., Patrick E. McGovern, and Virginia R. Badler. 1992. Chemical evidence for ancient beer. *Nature* 360: 24.

Moore, Jerry D. 1989. Pre-Hispanic beer in coastal Peru: Technology and social contexts of prehistoric production. *American Anthropologist* 91: 682-95.

Moulins, Dominique de. 1993. Les restes de plantes carbonisées de Çafer Höyük. *Cahiers de l'Euphrate* 7: 191-234.

Naveh, Zvi. 1974. Effects of fire in the Mediterranean region. In *Fire and ecosystems,* ed. T. T. Kozlowski and C. E. Ahlgren, 401-34. New York.

1984. The vegetation of the Carmel and Sefunim and the evolution of the cultural landscape. In *Sefunim prehistoric sites, Mount Carmel, Israel,* ed. Avraham Ronen, 23-63. BAR International Series, No. 230. Oxford.

Nesbitt, Mark, and Trevor Watkins. 1995. Collaboration at M'lefaat. In *Qeremez Dere, Tell Afar: Interim Report No. 3,* ed. Trevor Watkins, 11-12. Department of Archaeology, The University of Edinburgh.

Nevo, Eviatar, Daniel Zohary, A. D. H. Brown, and Michael Haber. 1979. Genetic diversity and environmental associations of wild barley, *Hordeum spontaneum,* in Israel. *Evolution* 33: 815-33.

Nilan, R. A., and S. E. Ullrich. 1993. Barley: Taxonomy, origin, distribution, production, genetics, and breeding. In *Barley: Chemistry and technology,* ed. Alexander W. MacGregor and Rattan S. Bhatty, 1-29. St. Paul, Minn.

Noy, Tamar. 1989. Gilgal I - a pre-pottery Neolithic site, Israel - the 1985-1987 seasons. *Paléorient* 15: 11-18.

Rindos, David R. 1984. *The origins of agriculture.* New York.

Rosenberg, Michael, R. Mark Nesbitt, Richard W. Redding,

and Thomas F. Strasser. 1995. Hallan Çemi Tepesi: Some preliminary observations concerning early Neolithic subsistence behaviors in Eastern Anatolia. *Anatolica* 21: 1-12.

Stemler, A. B. L., and R. H. Falk. 1980. A scanning electron microscope study of cereal grains from Wadi Kubbaniya. In *Loaves and fishes. The prehistory of Wadi Kubbaniya,* ed. Fred Wendorf and Angela Close, 299-306. Dallas, Tex.

Stewart, Robert B. 1976. Paleoethnobotanical report - Çayönü. *Economic Botany* 30: 219-25.

Stordeur, Danielle. 1989. El Koum 2 Caracol et le PPNB. *Paléorient* 15: 102-10.

Tchernov, Eitan. 1991. Biological evidence for human sedentism in Southwest Asia during the Natufian. In *The Natufian culture in the Levant,* ed. Ofer Bar-Yosef and François Valla, 315-40. Ann Arbor, Mich.

van Zeist, Willem. 1972. Palaeobotanical results in the 1970 season at Çayönü, Turkey. *Helinium* 12: 3-19.

van Zeist, Willem, and Johanna Bakker-Heeres. 1982. Archaeobotanical studies in the Levant. 1. Neolithic sites in the Damascus Basin: Aswad, Ghoraifé, Ramad. *Palaeohistoria* 24: 165-256.

1984a. Archaeobotanical studies in the Levant. 3. Late-Palaeolithic Mureybit. *Palaeohistoria* 26: 171-99.

1984b. Archaeobotanical studies in the Levant. 2. Neolithic and Halaf levels at Ras Shamra. *Palaeohistoria* 26: 151-98.

van Zeist, Willem, Phillip E. Smith, R. M. Palfenier-Vegter, et al. 1984. An archaeobotanical study of Ganj Dareh Tepe, Iran. *Palaeohistoria* 26: 201-24.

van Zeist, Willem, and Willemen Waterbolk-van Rooijen. 1985. The palaeobotany of Tell Bouqras, Eastern Syria. *Paléorient* 11: 131-47.

Watkins, Trevor, Douglas Baird, and Allison Betts. 1989. Qeremez Dere and the Early Aceramic Neolithic of N. Iraq. *Paléorient* 15: 19-24.

Wendorf, Fred R., Angela E. Close, D. J. Donahue, et al. 1984. New radiocarbon dates on the cereals from Wadi Kubbaniya. *Science* 225: 645-6.

Wendorf, Fred R., Romuald Schild, N. El Hadidi, et al. 1979. The use of barley in the Egyptian Late Palaeolithic. *Science* 205: 1341-7.

Wetterstrom, Wilma. 1993. Foraging and farming in Egypt: The transition from hunting and gathering to horticulture in the Nile Valley. In *The archaeology of Africa,* ed. Thurston Shaw, Paul Sinclair, Bassey Andah, and Alex Okpoko, 165-226. London.

Wiebe, G. A. 1968. Introduction of barley into the New World. In *Barley: Origin, botany, culture, winterhardiness, genetics, utilization, pests.* U.S. Department of Agriculture, Agriculture Handbook No. 338, 2-8. Washington, D.C.

Zohary, Daniel. 1964. Spontaneous brittle six-row barleys, their nature and origin. In *Barley genetics I. Proceedings of the first international barley genetics symposium,* 27-31. Wageningen, Netherlands.

1969. The progenitors of wheat and barley in relation to domestication and agriculture dispersal in the Old World. In *The domestication and exploitation of plants and animals,* ed. Peter J. Ucko and Geoffrey W. Dimbleby, 47-66. London.

1992. Domestication of the Neolithic Near Eastern crop assemblage. In *Préhistoire de l'agriculture,* ed. Patricia C. Anderson, 81-6. Paris.

Zohary, Daniel, and Maria Hopf. 1993. *Domestication of plants in the Old World.* Second edition. Oxford.

II.A.3. ✍ Buckwheat

Buckwheat (*Fagopyrum esculentum* Möench) is a crop commonly grown for its black or gray triangular seeds. It can also be grown as a green manure crop, a companion crop, a cover crop, as a source of buckwheat honey (often for the benefit of bees), and as a pharmaceutical plant yielding rutin, which is used in the treatment of capillary fragility. Buckwheat belongs to the *Polygonaceae* family (as do sorrel and rhubarb). Whereas cereals such as wheat, maize, and rice belong to the grass family, buckwheat is not a true cereal. Its grain is a dry fruit.

Buckwheat is believed to be native to Manchuria and Siberia and, reportedly, was cultivated in China by at least 1000 B.C. However, fragments of the grain have been recovered from Japanese sites dating from between 3500 and 5000 B.C., suggesting a much earlier date for the grain's cultivation. It was an important crop in Japan and reached Europe through Turkey and Russia during the fourteenth and fifteenth centuries A.D., although legend would have it entering Europe much earlier with the returning Crusaders. Buckwheat was introduced into North America in the seventeenth century by the Dutch, and it is said that its name derives from the Dutch word *bochweit* (meaning "beech wheat"), because the plant's triangular fruits resemble beechnuts. In German the name for beech is *Buche,* and for buckwheat, *Buchweizen.* Buckwheat has a nutty flavor and, when roasted *(kasha),* a very strong one. It is a hardy plant that grew in Europe where other grains did not and, thus, supplied peasants in such areas with porridge and pancakes.

Buckwheat

Production of buckwheat peaked in the early nineteenth century and has declined since then. During the past decade or so, world production has averaged about 1 million metric tons annually, with the countries of the former Soviet Union accounting for about 90 percent of the total. Other major producing countries are China, Japan, Poland, Canada, Brazil, the United States, South Africa, and Australia. The yield of buckwheat varies considerably by area and by year of production and also with the variety being cultivated. In Canada, the average yield over the past 10 years has been about 800 kilograms per hectare (kg/ha), although yields of 2,000 kg/ha and higher have been produced.

Types and Cultivars

There are three known species of buckwheat: Common buckwheat *(F. esculentum),* tartary buckwheat *(Fagopyrum tataricum),* and perennial buckwheat *(Fagopyrum cymosum).* Common buckwheat is also known as *Fagopyrum sagittatum,* and a form of tartary buckwheat may be called *Fagopyrum kashmirianum.* The cytotaxonomy of buckwheat has not been thoroughly studied, but it is generally believed that perennial buckwheat, particularly the diploid type, is the ancestral form of both tartary buckwheat and common buckwheat.

Tartary buckwheat (also known as rye buckwheat, duck wheat, hull-less, broomless, India wheat, Marino, mountain, Siberian, wild goose, and Calcutta buckwheat) is cultivated in the Himalayan regions of India and China, in eastern Canada, and, occasionally, in mountain areas of the eastern United States. Tartary buckwheat is very frost-resistant. Its seeds – and products made from them – are greenish in color and somewhat bitter in taste. Buckwheat is used primarily as an animal feed or in a mixture of wheat and buckwheat flour. It can also be used as a source of rutin.

Common buckwheat is by far the most economically important species of buckwheat, accounting for over 90 percent of world production. Many types, strains, and cultivars of common buckwheat exist – late-maturing and early-maturing types, Japanese and European types, summer and autumn types. Within a given type there may be strains or varieties with tall or short plants, gray or black seeds, and white or pink flowers. In general, however, common buckwheat varieties from different parts of the world may be divided into two major groups. The first group includes tall, vigorous, late-maturing, photoperiod-sensitive varieties, found in Japan, Korea, southern China, Nepal, and India. Members of the second group are generally insensitive to photoperiod and are small and early-maturing. All of the varieties in Europe and northern China belong to this second group.

Prior to 1950, most producers of buckwheat planted unnamed strains that had been harvested from their own fields or obtained from their neighbors or local stores. Named varieties, developed through plant breeding, were first made available in the 1950s. 'Tokyo', the oldest of the named cultivars introduced into North America, was licensed in 1955 by the Agriculture Canada Research Station in Ottawa. Other cultivars licensed for production in Canada are 'Tempest', 'Mancan', and 'Manor', all developed at the Agriculture Canada Research Station in Morden, Manitoba, since 1965. 'Mancan', which has large, dark-brown seeds, thick stems, and large leaves, is the Canadian cultivar preferred in the Japanese market because of its large seeds, desirable flavor and color, and high yield of groats in the milling process.

Cultivars licensed in the United States are 'Pennquad' (released by the Pennsylvania Agricultural Experimental Station and the U.S. Department of Agriculture [USDA] in 1968) and 'Giant American' (a Japanese-type cultivar, apparently developed by a Minnesota farmer). Cultivars developed in the countries of the former Soviet Union since the 1950s include 'Victoria', 'Galleya', 'Eneida', 'Podolyaka', 'Diadema', 'Aelita', and 'Aestoria'. Representative cultivars from other areas of the world include the following: 'Pulawska', 'Emka', and 'Hruszowska' from Poland; 'Bednja 4n' from Yugoslavia; and 'Botan-Soba', 'Shinano No. 1', 'Kyushu-Akisoba Shinshu', and 'Miyazaki Oosoba' from Japan.

Plant and Seed Morphology

Buckwheat is a broad-leaved, erect, herbaceous plant that grows to a height of 0.7 to 1.5 meters. It has a main stem and several branches and can reach full maturity in 60 to 110 days. The stem is usually grooved, succulent, and hollow, except for the nodes. Before maturity, the stems and branches are green to red in color; after maturity, however, they become brown. The plant has a shallow taproot from which branched, lateral roots arise. Its root system is less extensive than those of cereals and constitutes only 3 to 4 percent of the dry weight of the total plant, which – in conjunction with the large leaf surface – may cause wilting during periods of hot and dry weather.

Buckwheat has an indeterminate flowering habit. The flowers of common buckwheat are perfect but incomplete. They have no petals, but the calyx is composed of five petal-like sepals that are usually white, but may also be pink or red. The flowers are arranged in dense clusters at the ends of the branches or on short pedicels arising from the axils of the leaves. Common buckwheat plants bear one of two types of flowers. The pin-type flower has long styles (or female parts) and short stamens (or male parts), and the thrum-type flower has long styles and short pistils. The pistil consists of a one-celled superior ovary and a three-part style with knoblike stigmas and is surrounded by eight stamens. Nectar-secreting glands are located at the base of the ovary. The plants of common buckwheat are generally self-infertile, as self-fertilization is prevented by self-incompatibility of the dimorphic, sporophitic type. Seed production is usually dependent on cross-pollination between the pin and thrum flowers. Honeybees and leaf-cutter bees are effective pollinators that increase seed set and seed yield.

Plants of tartary buckwheat are significantly different from those of common buckwheat. They have only one flower type and are self-fertile. In addition, they tend to be more husky and more branched and to have narrower, arrow-shaped leaves and smaller, greenish-white flowers. Attempts to transfer the self-compatibility of tartary buckwheat to common buckwheat have proved unsuccessful.

The buckwheat kernel is a triangular, dry fruit (achene), 4 to 9 millimeters (mm) in length, consisting of a hull or pericarp, spermoderm, endosperm, and embryo. Large seeds tend to be concave-sided and small seeds are usually convex-sided. The hull may be glossy, gray, brown, or black and may be solid or mottled. It may be either smooth or rough with lateral furrows. The hulls represent 17 to 26 percent (in tartary buckwheat, 30 to 35 percent) of the kernel weight. Diploid varieties usually have less hull than tetraploids.

Structure of the Kernel

Scanning electron microscopy of the buckwheat kernel has revealed that the hull, spermoderm, endosperm, and embryo are each composed of several layers. For the hull, these are (in order from the outside toward the inside) the epicarp, fiber layers, parenchyma cells, and endocarp. The spermoderm is composed of the outer epiderm, the spongy parenchyma, and the inner epiderm. The endosperm includes an aleurone layer and a subaleurone endosperm, containing starch granules surrounded by a proteinaceous matrix. The embryo, with its two cotyledons, extends through the starchy endosperm. The terminal parts of the cotyledons are often parallel under the kernel surface.

Composition

The gross chemical composition of whole buckwheat grain, the groats, and the hulls is shown in Table II.A.3.1. The mineral and vitamin contents of the whole grains are shown in Table II.A.3.2.

Table II.A.3.1. *Percentage composition of buckwheat seed and its milling products*

Seed or products	Moisture	Ash	Fat	Protein	Fiber	Nitrogen-free extracts
Seed	10.0	1.7	2.4	11.2	10.7	64.0
Groats	10.6	1.8	2.9	11.2	0.9	73.7
Dark flour	11.7	1.2	1.8	8.9	1.0	75.3
Light flour	12.0	1.3	1.6	7.8	0.6	76.7
Very light flour	12.7	0.6	0.5	4.7	0.3	81.1
Hulls	8.0	2.2	0.9	4.5	47.6	36.8
Middlings or shorts	10.7	4.6	7.0	27.2	11.4	39.1

Source: Data from Cole (1931).

Table II.A.3.2. *Average mineral and vitamin contents of buckwheat whole grain*

Minerals (mg/100 g)		Vitamins (mg/kg)	
Calcium	110	Thiamine	3.3
Iron	4	Riboflavin	10.6
Magnesium	390	Pantothenic acid	11.0
Phosphorus	330	Niacin	18.0
Potassium	450	Pyridoxine	1.5
Copper	0.95	Tocopherol	40.9
Manganese	3.37		
Zinc	0.87		

Source: Data from Marshall and Pomeranz (1982).

Carbohydrates

Starch is quantitatively the major component of buckwheat seed, and concentration varies with the method of extraction and between cultivars. In the whole grain of common buckwheat, the starch content ranges from 59 to 70 percent of the dry matter. The chemical composition of starch isolated from buckwheat grains differs from the composition of cereal starches (Table II.A.3.3). The differences are most pronounced in the case of buckwheat and barley. The amylose content in buckwheat granules varies from 15 to 52 percent, and its degree of polymerization varies from 12 to 45 glucose units. Buckwheat starch granules are irregular, with noticeable flat areas due to compact packing in the endosperm.

Buckwheat grains also contain 0.65 to 0.76 percent reducing sugars, 0.79 to 1.16 percent oligosaccharides, and 0.1 to 0.2 percent nonstarchy polysaccharides. Among the low-molecular-weight sugars, the major component is sucrose. There is also a small amount of arabinose, xylose, glucose, and, probably, the disaccharide melibiose.

Table II.A.3.3. *Chemical composition of buckwheat, barley, and corn starch granules smaller than 315 μ*

Constituent	Content (% dry matter)		
	Buckwheat	Barley	Corn
Total nitrogen	0.23	0.19	0.12
Free lipids	2.88	2.42	1.80
Ash	0.27	1.04	1.25
Dietary fiber	31.82	41.12	32.02
Hemicellulose[a]	15.58	14.03	24.13
Cellulose[a]	2.72	4.07	0.91
Lignin[a]	13.52	24.03	6.99

[a]In dietary fiber.

Source: Data from Fornal et al. (1987).

Proteins

Protein content in buckwheat varies from 7 to 21 percent, depending on variety and environmental factors during growth. Most currently grown cultivars yield seeds with 11 to 15 percent protein. The major protein fractions are globulins, which represent almost half of all proteins and consist of 12 to 13 subunits with molecular weights between 17,800 and 57,000. Other known buckwheat protein fractions include albumins and prolamins. Reports of the presence of gluten or glutelin in buckwheat seed have recently been discredited.

Buckwheat proteins are particularly rich in the amino acid lysine. They contain less glutamic acid and proline and more arginine, aspartic acid, and tryptophan than do cereal proteins. Because of the high lysine content, buckwheat proteins have a higher biological value (BV) than cereal proteins such as those of wheat, barley, rye, and maize (Table II.A.3.4). Digestibility of buckwheat protein, however, is rather low; this is probably caused by the high-fiber content (17.8 percent) of buckwheat, which may, however, be desirable in some parts of the world. Buckwheat fiber is free of phytic acid and is partially soluble.

Lipids

Whole buckwheat seeds contain 1.5 to 3.7 percent total lipids. The highest concentration is in the embryo (7 to 14 percent) and the lowest in the hull (0.4 to 0.9 percent). However, because the embryo constitutes only 15 to 20 percent of the seed, and the hull is removed prior to milling, the lipid content of the groats is most meaningful. Groats (or dehulled seeds) of 'Mancan', 'Tokyo', and 'Manor' buckwheat contain 2.1 to 2.6 percent total lipids, of which 81 to 85 percent are neutral lipids, 8 to 11 percent phospholipids, and 3 to 5 percent glycolipids. Free lipids, extracted in petroleum ether, range from 2.0 to 2.7 percent. The major fatty acids of buckwheat lipids are palmitic (16:0), oleic (18:1), linoleic (18:2), stearic (18:0), linolenic (18:3), arachidic (20:0), behenic (22:0), and lignoceric (24:0). Of these, the first five are commonly found in all cereals, but the latter three, which represent, on average, 8 percent of the total acids in buckwheat, are only minor components or are not present in cereals.

Phenolic Compounds

The content of phenolics in hulls and groats of common buckwheat is 0.73 and 0.79 percent (and that of tartary buckwheat, 1.87 and 1.52 percent). The three major classes of phenolics are flavonoids, phenolic acids, and condensed tannins. There are many types of flavonoids, three of which are found in buckwheat. These are flavonols, anthocyanins, and C-glycosylflavones. Rutin (quercetin 3-rutinoside), a well-known flavonol diglucoside,

Table II.A.3.4. *Quality of buckwheat and wheat protein*

Parameter	Buckwheat (g/16gN)	Barley (g/16gN)	Wheat (g/16gN)	Rye (g/16gN)	Maize (g/16gN)
Lysine	5.09	3.69	2.55	3.68	2.76
Methionine	1.89	1.82	1.81	1.74	2.37
Cystine	2.02	2.30	1.79	1.99	2.24
Threonine	3.15	3.60	2.84	3.33	3.88
Valine	4.69	5.33	4.50	4.60	5.00
Isoleucine	3.48	3.68	3.39	3.15	3.78
Leucine	6.11	7.11	6.82	5.96	10.51
Phyenylalanine	4.19	4.91	4.38	4.41	4.53
Histidine	2.20	2.23	2.30	2.33	2.41
Arginine	8.85	5.38	4.62	5.68	4.35
Tryptophan	1.59	1.11	1.03	1.16	0.62
$N \times 625$					
(% in dry matter)	12.25	11.42	12.63	10.61	10.06
TD[a] (%)	79.9	84.3	92.4	82.5	93.2
BV[b] (%)	93.1	76.3	62.5	75.4	64.3
NPU[c] (%)	74.4	64.3	57.8	62.2	59.9
UP[d] (%)	9.07	7.34	7.30	6.54	6.03

[a]TD = true protein digestibility; [b]BV = biological value; [c]NPU = net protein utilization; [d]UP = utilizable protein = protein × NPU/10.

Source: Data from Eggum (1980).

used as a drug for the treatment of vascular disorders caused by abnormally fragile or permeable capillaries, occurs in the leaves, stems, flowers, and fruit of buckwheat.

Grading, Handling, and Storage

Grading

In most countries, buckwheat grain is priced according to its physical condition in terms of size, soundness, and general appearance. In Canada, buckwheat is marketed according to grades established under the Canada Grain Act: Grades are No. 1, No. 2, and No. 3 Canada, and Sample. Grade determinants are a minimum test weight of 58 and 55 kilograms per hectoliter (kg/hL) (for Nos. 1 and 2 Canada), variety (designated by size, large or small), degree of sound-

ness, and content of foreign material (Table II.A.3.5). Grades No. 1 and 2 Canada must be free from objectionable odors; No. 3 Canada may have a ground or grassy odor but may not be musty or sour. Test weight, seed size, and foreign material content are determined on a dockage-free sample. Seed size is determined with a No. 8 slotted sieve (3.18 × 19.05 mm) and becomes part of the grade name (e.g., "buckwheat, No. 1 Canada, large").

"Foreign material" refers to cereal grains (wheat, rye, barley, oats, and triticale), weed seeds, and other grains that are not readily removable by mechanical cleaners, and may include peas, beans, maize, and other domestic or wild weeds. Buckwheat grain containing more than 5 percent foreign material is graded "buckwheat, Sample Canada, (size), account admixture." Damaged seeds include frosted, moldy, distinctly green or otherwise unsound, and dehulled seeds.

Table II.A.3.5. *Primary grade determinants of buckwheat (Canada)*

			Maximum limits of foreign material (%)				
Grade	kg/hL	Degree of soundness	Stones[a]	Ergot	Sclerotinia	Cereal grains	Total foreign material
No. 1	58.0	Well matured, cool and sweet	3	0.0	0.0	1.0%	1.0%
No. 2	55.0	Reasonably well matured, cool and sweet	3	0.05%	0.05%	2.5%	3.0%
No. 3	No min.	May have a ground or grassy odor, but may not be musty or sour	3	0.25%	0.25%	5.0%	5.0%

[a]Number of kernel-size stones in 500 g.

In the United States, buckwheat is not marketed under federally established grades, but some states (for example, Minnesota) have official grain standards that specify the use of Grades 1, 2, 3, and Sample. The grade determinants are similar to those of the Canadian grading system. In Japan, the Buckwheat Millers Association prefers buckwheat that has large, uniform seeds with black hulls and green-colored groats.

Handling

Marketing of buckwheat can be more seriously affected by handling and storage than by other factors such as nutritional quality or processing. The method of handling varies among production areas; nonetheless, in most cases, losses and grain-quality changes occur at postharvest stages. During harvest, in all countries, losses occur, resulting from shattering, germination, depredation by animals, and infection by molds. Threshing is done with combines or by beating the dried plants against stones or wooden bars or by trampling the plants under bullock feet, carts, or tractor wheels.

Transportation of grain from the field to market also results in losses and quality deterioration. Losses during transportation are mainly due to spillage. However, if the grain is exposed to rain or frost during transit, it can subsequently spoil through infection by microorganisms. An efficient system for transportation and distribution of grain must consist of several components, including: (1) collection of grain from farms into consolidated deposits; (2) facilities for short- and long-term storage; (3) loading, unloading, and conveying systems; (4) methods of packaging or bulk handling; (5) roads, railways, and/or waterways; (6) systems for grading the grain and for servicing and maintaining equipment and facilities; (7) systems for recruiting, training, and managing personnel for operation and administration; and (8) systems for research, education, and extension of information to farmers, merchants, and other personnel involved with the overall handling operation.

Storage

Like other grain crops, buckwheat is stored to ensure an even supply over time, to preserve the surplus grain for sale to deficit areas, and for use as seed in the next planting season. Storage of the seeds may be at the farm, trader, market, government, retail, or consumer levels. Storage containers range from sacks to straw huts to bulk storage bins. In developing countries, traditional storage structures include granaries of gunny, cotton, or jute bags as well as those manufactured from reed, bamboo, or wood and plastered with mud and cow dung. In North America, storage structures include metal, concrete, or wooden bins at the farm level,

Table II.A.3.6. *Absorbance of extracted color and tristimulus values of buckwheat samples stored at 25°C and 5 different water activities for 19 months*

Water activity	Moisture content (%)	Absorbance index (A_{420})	Tristimulus values		
			X	Y	Z
0.11	4.1	0.257 b[a]	26.3 c	26.2 c	15.1 b
0.23	6.7	0.233 c	26.7 b	26.5 b	15.1 b
0.31	8.7	0.241 c	27.1 a	27.0 a	15.3 a
0.51	13.0	0.290 a	25.3 d	24.7 d	13.4 d
0.67	13.8	0.238 c	26.4 bc	25.9 c	14.2 c

[a]Means separated by Duncan's multiple range test, 0.01 level of probability.

Source: Data from Mazza (1986).

elevators and annexes at centralized receiving, storage, and shipping points, and concrete silos at grain terminals.

Bagged buckwheat is highly susceptible to attack by insects and rodents. Hence, bulk storage in bins, elevators, and silos is best. Grain bins made of wood are usually square and, by virtue of their construction, possess a multitude of cracks, crevices, and angles that are havens for insects and their eggs and larvae. Concrete bins are usually round, star-shaped, or hexagonal, and star-shaped bins also have crevices that can harbor grain residues, constituting a source of infestation. Moreover, concrete possesses certain sorptive properties and chemical reactivity, and unless coated with an impervious material such as paint, the walls of concrete bins can interfere with fumigation procedures. Metal bins are usually round, possess few crevices, and do not react significantly with protective chemicals.

Neither concrete nor metal allows interchanges between stored grain and the atmosphere; moisture movement resulting from temperature fluctuations, convection, and condensation can result in deterioration and even internal combustion of the grains. A moisture content of 16 percent or less is required for the safe storage of buckwheat. If the seed requires drying, the temperature of the drying air should not exceed 43°C.

During storage at ambient temperature and relative humidity, the color of the aleurone layer changes from a desirable light green to the undesirable reddish brown. This undesirable quality change can be reduced by storing the seed at a lower temperature and at a relative humidity below 45 percent. Table II.A.3.6 gives the absorbance of the extracted color of buckwheat samples stored at 25°C and 0.11 to 0.67 water activity for 19 months. Maximum browning-pigment production occurs at 0.45 to 0.55 water activity, or 45 to 55 percent relative humidity.

Primary Processing

Primary processing of buckwheat includes cleaning, dehulling, and milling. The aim of seed cleaning is to remove other plant parts, soil, stones, weed seeds, chaff, dust, seeds of other crops, metallic particles, and small and immature buckwheat seeds. The extent and sophistication of the cleaning equipment depends largely on the size of the operation and the requirements for the finished product(s). Milling of buckwheat seed can be carried out by virtually any equipment capable of milling cereal grains. Hammer mills, stone mills, pin mills, disk mills, and roller mills have all been used to mill buckwheat. Of these, stone mills and roller mills are probably the most extensively used today.

The milling process may be of two types. In the first and most common type, the whole seeds are first dehulled and then milled. In the second type, the seeds are milled and then screened to remove the hulls. When dehulling and milling are separate operations, the seeds are segregated according to size and may be steamed and dried prior to dehulling. The latter procedure is carried out by impact or abrasion against emery stones or steel, followed by air- or screen-separation of groats and hulls. A widely used buckwheat dehuller is built on the principle of stone-milling, with emery stones set to crack the hull without breaking the groat. The effectiveness of this type of dehuller depends on the clearance between the seed cracking surfaces, and for any seed size there is an optimal setting. The ease of dehulling and the percentage of recovery of undamaged groats depends on variety and moisture content (Table II.A.3.7). From the dehuller, the groats go over sieves of different mesh for sizing into whole groats and two or more sizes of broken groats. Flour is produced by passing the groats through stone and/or roller grinders.

When buckwheat seed is to be processed into flour only, and production of groats is not a requirement, the seeds are ground on break rolls or stone mills and then screened to separate the coarse flour from the hulls. The coarse flour is further reduced by a series of size reduction rolls, each grinding operation followed by a sifting to fractionate the mixture of particles according to their size (Figure II.A.3.1). The flour yield ranges from 50 to 75 percent depending on the size, shape, and condition of the seeds and the efficiency of the dehulling and milling operations.

End Products

Buckwheat flour is generally dark in color because of the presence of hull fragments. In North America, it is used primarily for making buckwheat pancakes and is commonly marketed in the form of prepared mixes. These mixes generally contain buckwheat flour mixed with wheat, maize, rice, oat, or soybean flours and a leavening agent. Buckwheat is also used with vegetables and spices in kasha and soup mixes, and with wheat, maize, or rice in ready-to-eat breakfast products, porridge, bread, and pasta products.

Table II.A.3.7. *Influence of cultivar and moisture content on dehulling characteristics and color of buckwheat seeds stored at 25°C and water activities of 0.23–0.97 for 45 days*

| | | | | Dehulled groat | | Hunter color values[a] | | | | | |
| | | | | | | Whole groat | | Broken groat | | Mixed groat | |
Cultivar	Water activity	Moisture content (%)	Dehulling recovery (%)	Whole (%)	Broken (%)	L	a	L	a	L	a
Mancan	0.23	5.98	69.2	30.1	69.9	52.0	+0.1	68.7	+0.3	63.5	+0.1
	0.52	9.79	67.0	33.3	66.7	53.0	−0.1	60.0	+0.4	58.7	+0.5
	0.75	13.47	65.4	44.5	55.5	52.3	+0.3	56.5	−0.4	57.4	+0.4
	0.97	19.80	65.0	68.5	31.5	51.0	+0.4	57.87	+1.3	53.2	+0.7
Tokyo	0.23	5.84	66.3	28.7	71.3	51.7	+0.7	62.7	+0.5	60.6	+0.3
	0.52	9.77	60.5	33.5	66.5	51.1	+0.7	58.4	+0.1	57.6	+1.3
	0.75	13.30	58.2	45.5	54.5	51.3	+0.7	54.8	+0.3	54.6	+0.8
	0.97	18.74	51.6	75.1	24.9	50.3	+1.8	58.3	+1.1	52.1	+1.0
Manor	0.23	5.93	54.9	37.1	62.9	52.6	+1.4	60.6	+0.8	59.0	+1.0
	0.52	9.90	50.4	35.7	64.3	52.9	+1.9	58.0	+0.7	58.9	−0.7
	0.75	13.50	41.6	48.4	51.6	52.9	+1.5	56.6	+1.4	54.5	+1.2
	0.97	19.13	32.5	61.5	38.5	51.7	+2.1	61.3	+1.7	53.2	+0.4

[a]L = lightness; a = redness when positive and greenness when negative.

Source: Data from Mazza and Campbell (1985).

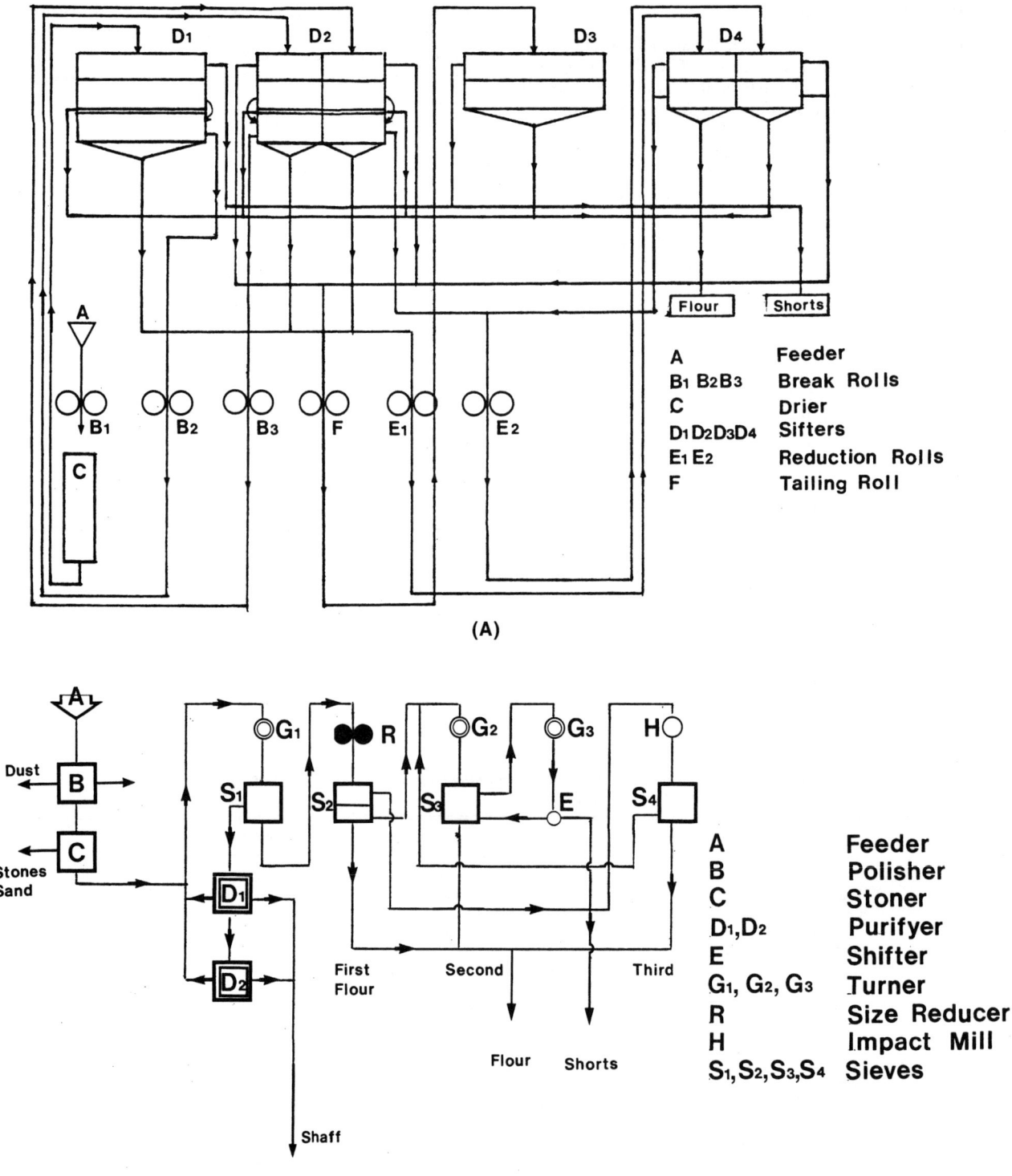

Figure II.A.3.1. Flow diagram of two buckwheat mills: (A) roller mill; (B) stone-roller mill.

In Japan, buckwheat flour is used primarily for making *soba* or *sobakiri* (buckwheat noodles) and *Teuchi Soba* (handmade buckwheat noodles). These products are prepared at *soba* shops or at home from a mixture of buckwheat and wheat flours. The wheat flour is used because of its binding properties and availability. *Soba* is made by hand or mechanically. In both methods, buckwheat and wheat flours are mixed with each other and then with water to form a stiff dough that is kneaded, rolled into a thin sheet (1.4 mm) with a rolling pin or by passing it between sheeting rolls, and cut into long strips. The product may be cooked immediately, sold fresh, or dried. For consumption, the noodles are boiled in hot water, put into bamboo baskets, and then dipped into cold water.

In Europe, most buckwheat is milled into groats that are used in porridge, in meat products (especially hamburger), or consumed with fresh or sour milk. A mixture of buckwheat groats with cottage cheese, sugar, peppermint, and eggs is employed as stuffing in a variety of dumplings. Buckwheat flour is used with wheat or rye flour and yeast to make fried specialty products such as bread, biscuits, and other confectioneries. An extended ready-to-eat breakfast product of high nutritional value, made from maize and buckwheat, is produced and marketed in Western Europe. This product contains over 14 percent protein and 8 percent soluble fiber. Similar products have also been developed in Poland and the former Soviet Union. In most countries, the quality of buckwheat end products is controlled by law.

The pace of development of new food products from buckwheat is expected to increase. This will likely parallel the increasing consumer demand for foods capable of preventing or alleviating disease and promoting health.

G. Mazza

Bibliography

Campbell, C. G., and G. H. Gubbels. 1986. Growing buckwheat. *Agriculture Canada Research Branch Technical Bulletin 1986-7E.* Agriculture Canada Research Station, Morden, Manitoba.

Cole, W. R. 1931. Buckwheat milling and its by-products. United States Department of Agriculture, Circular 190. Washington, D.C.

DeJong, H. 1972. Buckwheat. *Field Crops Abstracts* 25: 389-96.

Eggum, B. O. 1980. The protein quality of buckwheat in comparison with other protein sources of plant or animal origin. Buckwheat Symposium, Ljubljana, Yugoslavia, September 1-3, 115-20.

Fornal, L., M. Soral-Smietana, Z. Smietana, and J. Szpendowski. 1987. Chemical characteristics and physico-chemical properties of the extruded mixtures of cereal starches. *Stärke* 39: 75-8.

Institute of Soil Science and Plant Cultivation, ed. 1986. *Buckwheat research 1986.* Pulawy, Poland.

Kreft, I., B. Javornik, and B. Dolisek, eds. 1980. Buckwheat genetics, plant breeding and utilization. VTOZD za agronomijo Biotech. Ljubljana, Yugoslavia.

Marshall, H. G., and Y. Pomeranz. 1982. Buckwheat: Description, breeding, production and utilization. In *Cereals '78: Better nutrition for the world's millions,* ed. Y. Pomeranz, 201-17. St. Paul, Minn.

Mazza, G. 1986. Buckwheat browning and color assessment. *Cereal Chemistry* 63: 362-6.

Mazza, G., and C. G. Campbell. 1985. Influence of water activity and temperature on dehulling of buckwheat. *Cereal Chemistry* 62: 31-4.

Nagatoma, T., and T. Adachi, eds. 1983. *Buckwheat research 1983.* Miyazaki, Japan.

Oomah, B. D., and G. Mazza. 1996. Flavonoids and antioxidative activities in buckwheat. *Journal of Agricultural and Food Chemistry* 44: 1746-50.

II.A.4. ✍ Maize

Maize (*Zea mays* L.), a member of the grass family Poaceae (synonym Gramineae), is the most important human dietary cereal grain in Latin America and Africa and the second most abundant cultivated cereal worldwide. Originating in varying altitudes and climates in the Americas, where it still exhibits its greatest diversity of types, maize was introduced across temperate Europe and in Asia and Africa during the sixteenth and seventeenth centuries.

Corn

It became a staple food of Central Europe, a cheap means of provisioning the African-American slave trade by the end of the eighteenth century, and the usual ration of workers in British mines in Africa by the end of the nineteenth century. In the twentieth century, major increases in maize production, attributed to developments in maize breeding, associated water management, fertilizer response, pest control, and ever-expanding nutritional and industrial uses, have contributed to its advance as an intercrop (and sometimes as a staple) in parts of Asia and to the doubling and tripling of maize harvests throughout North America and Europe. High-yield varieties and government agricultural support and marketing programs, as well as maize's biological advantages of high energy yields, high extraction rate, and greater adaptability relative to wheat or rice, have all led to maize displacing sorghum and other grains over much of Africa.

On all continents, maize has been fitted into a wide variety of environments and culinary preparations; even more significant, however, it has become a component of mixed maize-livestock economies and diets. Of the three major cereal grains (wheat, rice, and maize), maize is the only one not grown primarily for direct human consumption. Approximately one-fifth of all maize grown worldwide is eaten directly by people; two-thirds is eaten by their animals; and approximately one-tenth is used as a raw material in manufactured goods, including many non-food products.

Maize Literature
Principal sources for understanding the diverse maize cultures and agricultures are P. Weatherwax's (1954) *Indian Corn in Old America,* an account of sixteenth-century maize-based agriculture and household arts; S. Johannessen and C. A. Hastorf's (1994) *Corn and Culture,* essays that capture New World archaeological and ethnographic perspectives; and H. A. Wallace and E. N. Bressman's (1923) *Corn and Corn Growing,* and Wallace and W. L. Brown's (1956) *Corn and Its Early Fathers,* both of which chronicle the early history of maize breeding and agribusiness in the United States. The diffusion of maize in the Old World has been traced in J. Finan's (1950) summary of discussions of maize in fifteenth- and sixteenth-century herbals, in M. Bonafous's (1836) *Natural Agricultural and Economic History of Maize,* in A. de Candolle's (1884) *Origin of Cultivated Plants,* and in D. Roe's (1973) *A Plague of Corn: The Social History of Pellagra.* B. Fussell's (1992) *The Story of Corn* applies the art of storytelling to maize culinary history, with special emphasis on the New World. Quincentenary writings, celebrating America's first cuisines and the cultural and nutritional influence of maize, as well as that of other New World indigenous crops, include works by W. C. Galinat (1992), S. Coe (1994), and J. Long (1996).

More recent regional, cultural, agricultural, and economic perspectives highlight the plight of Mexico's peasant farmers under conditions of technological and economic change (Hewitt de Alcantara 1976, 1992; Montanez and Warman 1985; Austin and Esteva 1987; Barkin, Batt, and DeWalt 1990), the displacement of other crops by maize in Africa (Miracle 1966), and the significance of maize in African "green revolutions" (Eicher 1995; Smale 1995). *The Corn Economy of Indonesia* (Timmer 1987) and C. Dowswell, R. L. Paliwal, and R. P. Cantrell's (1996) *Maize in the Third World* explore maize's growing dietary and economic significance in developing countries. The latter includes detailed country studies of Ghana, Zimbabwe, Thailand, China, Guatemala, and Brazil.

Global developments in maize breeding, agronomy, and extension are chronicled in the publications of Mexico's International Center for the Improvement of Maize and Wheat (CIMMYT), especially in *World Maize Facts and Trends* (CIMMYT 1981, 1984, 1987, 1990, 1992, 1994), and in research reports and proceedings of regional workshops. Maize genetics is summarized by David B. Walden (1978), G. F. Sprague and J. W. Dudley (1988), and the National Corn Growers Association (1992). Molecular biologists who use maize as a model system share techniques in the *Maize Genetics Cooperation Newsletter* and *The Maize Handbook* (Freeling and Walbot 1993). One explanation for the extensive geographic and cultural range of maize lies in its unusually active "promoter," or "jumping," genes and extremely large chromosomes, which have made it a model plant for the study of genetics – the *Drosophila* of the plant world.

Geographic Range
Maize is grown from 50 degrees north latitude in Canada and Russia to almost 50 degrees south latitude in South America, at altitudes from below sea level in the Caspian plain to above 12,000 feet in the Peruvian Andes, in rainfall regions with less than 10 inches in Russia to more than 400 inches on Colombia's Pacific coast, and in growing seasons ranging from 3 to 13 months (FAO 1953). Early-maturing, cold-tolerant varieties allow maize to penetrate the higher latitudes of Europe and China, and aluminum-tolerant varieties increase production in the Brazilian savanna. In the tropics and subtropics of Latin America and Asia, maize is double- or triple-cropped, sometimes planted in rotation or "relay-cropped" with wheat, rice, and occasionally, soybeans, whereas in temperate regions it is monocropped, or multicropped with legumes, cucurbits, and roots or tubers. In North America, it is planted in rotation with soybeans.

Yields average 2.5 tons per hectare in developing countries, where maize is more often a component of less input-intensive multicrop systems, and 6.2

tons per hectare in industrialized countries, where maize tends to be input-intensive and single-cropped. The U.S. Midwest, which produced more than half of the total world supply of maize in the early 1950s, continued to dominate production in the early 1990s, with 210.7 million tons, followed by China (97.2 million tons), and then Brazil (25.2 million tons), Mexico (14.6 million tons), France (12.2 million tons), India (9.2 million tons), and the countries of the former Soviet Union (9.0 million tons). Developing countries overall account for 64 percent of maize area and 43 percent of world harvests (FAO 1993). The United States, China, France, Argentina, Hungary, and Thailand together account for 95 percent of the world maize trade, which fluctuates between 60 and 70 million tons, most of which goes into animal feed.

Cultural Range

Maize serves predominantly as direct human food in its traditional heartlands of Mexico, Central America, the Caribbean, and the South American Andes, as well as in southern and eastern Africa, where the crop has replaced sorghum, millet, and sometimes roots and tuber crops in the twentieth century. The highest annual per capita intakes (close to 100 kilograms per capita per year) are reported for Mexico, Guatemala, and Honduras, where the staple food is tortillas, and for Kenya, Malawi, Zambia, and Zimbabwe, where the staple is a porridge. Maize is also an essential regional and seasonal staple in Indonesia and parts of China.

However, maize is considerably more significant in the human food chain when it first feeds livestock animals that, in turn, convert the grain into meat and dairy products. In the United States, 150 million tons of maize were harvested for feed in 1991; in Germany, three-fourths of the maize crop went for silage. In some developing countries, such as Pakistan, India, and Egypt, the value of maize fodder for bovines may surpass that of the grain for humans and other animals. In Mexico, the "Green Revolution" Puebla Project developed improved, tall (versus short, stiff-strawed) varieties in response to demands for fodder as well as grain.

Since World War II, processing for specialized food and nonfood uses has elevated and diversified maize's economic and nutritional significance. In the United States, for example, maize-based starch and sweeteners account for 20 million tons (15 million tons go to beverages alone), cereal products claim 3 million tons, and distilled products 0.3 million tons. Maize-based ethanol, used as a fuel extender, requires 10 million tons; and plastics and other industrial products also employ maize. The geographic and cultural ranges of maize are tributes to its high mutation rate, genetic diversity and adaptability, and continuing cultural selection for desirable characteristics.

Biology and Biodiversity

More than 300 races of maize, consisting of hundreds of lineages and thousands of cultivars, have been described. But the precise ancestry of maize remains a mystery, and geographical origins and distributions are controversial.

Biological Evolution

Teosinte (*Zea* spp.), a weedy grass that grows in Mexico and Guatemala, and *Tripsacum,* a more distantly related rhizomatous perennial, are maize's closest wild relatives. All three species differ from other grasses in that they bear separate male and female flowers on the same plant. Key morphological traits distinguishing maize from its wild relatives are its many-rowed ear compared to a single-rowed spike, a rigid rather than easily shattered rachis, a pair of kernels in each cupule compared to a single grain per cupule, and an unprotected or naked grain compared to seed enclosed in a hard fruitcase. Unlike the inflorescence structures of other grasses, maize produces a multirowed ear with hundreds of kernels attached to a cob that is enclosed by husks, which makes it amenable for easy harvest, drying, and storage.

Based on interpretations of evidence from cytology, anatomy, morphology, systematics, classical and molecular genetics, experimental breeding, and archaeology, there are three recognized theories about the origins of maize: (1) the ancestor of maize is annual teosinte (Vavilov 1931; Beadle 1939; Iltis 1983; Kato 1984); (2) maize evolved from an as yet undiscovered wild maize or other ancestor (Mangelsdorf 1974); and (3) maize derived from hybridization between teosinte and another wild grass (Harshberger 1896; Eubanks 1995). Although the most popular theory holds that teosinte is the progenitor, present evidence does not clearly resolve its genetic role. Firmer evidence supports the idea that introgression of teosinte germ plasm contributed to the rapid evolution of diverse maize land races in prehistory (Wellhausen et al. 1952). Teosintes–which include two annual subspecies from Mexico (*Z. mays* ssp. *mexicana* and ssp. *parviglumis),* two annual species from Guatemala (*Z. huehuetenangensis* and *Z. luxurians),* and two perennial species from Mexico (*Z. perennis* and *Z. diploperennis*) – have the same base chromosome number (*n* = 10) as maize and can hybridize naturally with it. Like maize, teosintes bear their male flowers in tassels at the summit of their main stems and their female flowers laterally in leaf axils. Although the ears of teosinte and maize are dramatically different, teosinte in architecture closely mimics maize before flowering, and – so far – no one has demonstrated effectively how the female spike might have been transformed into the complex structure of a maize ear.

Tripsacum spp. have a base chromosome number of *n* = 18 and ploidy levels ranging from 2*n* = 36 to

$2n = 108$. *Tripsacum* is distinctive from maize and teosinte because it bears male and female flowers on the same spike, with the staminate (male) flowers directly above the pistillate (female) flowers. This primitive trait is seen in some of the earliest prehistoric maize (on Zapotec urns from the Valley of Oaxaca, Mexico, c. A.D. 500–900, which depict maize with staminate tips) and also in some South American races. *Tripsacum* plants also frequently bear pairs of kernels in a single cupule, another maize trait. The ears of F1 *Tripsacum*-teosinte hybrids have pairs of exposed kernels in fused cupules and resemble the oldest archaeological maize remains from Tehuacan, Mexico (Eubanks 1995). Although the theory that domesticated maize arose from hybridization between an unknown wild maize and *Tripsacum* is no longer accepted, and crosses between *Tripsacum* and maize or annual teosinte are almost always sterile, crosses between *Tripsacum* and perennial teosinte have been shown to produce fully fertile hybrid plants (Eubanks 1995), and *Tripsacum* has potential as a source of beneficial traits for maize improvement.

Molecular evidence for maize evolution includes analyses of isozymes and DNA of nuclear and cytoplasmic genes. Results indicate that isozyme analysis cannot fully characterize genetic variation in *Zea*, and application of this technique to understanding evolutionary history is limited. In addition, certain maize teosintes (*Z. m. parviglumis* and *Z. m. mexicana*), thought to be ancestral to maize, may actually postdate its origin. In sum, the origins of maize remain obscure.

Geographic Origin and Distribution

Most scientists concur that maize appeared 7,000 to 10,000 years ago in Mesoamerica, but controversy surrounds whether maize was domesticated one or more times and in one or more locations. Based on racial diversity and the presence of teosinte in Mexico but not Peru, N. I. Vavilov (1931) considered Mexico to be the primary center of origin. The earliest accepted archaeological evidence comes from cave deposits in Tehuacan, Puebla, in central Mexico. The cobs found there ranged from 19 to 25 millimeters (mm) long and had four to eight rows of kernels surrounded by very long glumes. The remarkably well-preserved specimens provide a complete evolutionary sequence of maize dating from at least as far back as 3600 B.C. up to A.D. 1500. Over this time, tiny eight-rowed ears were transformed into early cultivated maize and then into early tripsacoid maize, ultimately changing into the Nal Tel-Chapalote complex, late tripsacoid, and slender popcorn of later phases (Mangelsdorf 1974). An explosive period of variation, brought about by the hybridization of maize with teosinte, began around 1500 B.C. (Wilkes 1989).

From Mexico, maize is thought to have moved south and north, reaching Peru around 3000 B.C. and

North America sometime later. However, pollen identified as maize was present with phytoliths in preceramic contexts in deposits dated to 4900 B.C. in Panama and in sediments dated to 4000 B.C. in Amazonian Ecuador. Although the identification of maize pollen and phytoliths (as opposed to those of a wild relative) remains uncertain, some investigators (Bonavia and Grobman 1989) have argued that such evidence, combined with maize germ plasm data, indicates the existence of a second center of domestication in the Central Andean region of South America, which generated its own distinct racial complexes of the plant between 6000 and 4000 B.C. Fully developed maize appeared later in the lowlands (Sanoja 1989).

Maize arrived in North America indisputably later. Flint varieties adapted to the shorter nights and frost-free growing seasons of the upper Midwest evolved only around A.D. 1100, although maize had been introduced at least 500 years earlier. Ridged fields later allowed cultivators to expand the growing season by raising soil and air temperatures and controlling moisture. In the Eastern Woodlands, 12-row (from A.D. 200 to 600) and 8-row (from around 800) varieties supplemented the existing starchy-seed food complexes (Gallagher 1989; Watson 1989).

Germ Plasm and Genetic Diversity

Gene banks have collected and now maintain 90 to 95 percent of all known genetic diversity of maize. The largest collections are held by the Vavilov Institute (Russia) and the Maize Research Institute (Yugoslavia), which contain mostly Russian and European accessions. The genetically most diverse New World collections are maintained at the National Seed Storage Laboratory in the United States, CIMMYT and the Instituto Nacional de Investigaciones Forestales y Agropecuarios (INIFAP – the National Institute of Forestry and Agricultural Research) in Mexico, the National Agricultural University in Peru, the National Agricultural Research Institute in Colombia, the Brazilian Corporation of Agricultural Research (EMBRAPA), the Instituto de Nutricion y Tecnologia de los Alimentos (INTA – the Institute of Nutrition and Food Technology) at the University of Chile, Santiago, and the National Agricultural Research Institute (INIA) in Chile. International maize breeding programs operate at CIMMYT and at the International Institute for Tropical Agriculture (IITA), which interface with national maize breeding programs in developing countries (Dowswell, Paliwal, and Cantrell 1996).

The germ plasm collections begun by the Rockefeller Foundation and the Mexican Ministry of Agriculture in 1943 (which classified maize according to productiveness, disease resistance, and other agronomic characteristics) have since been supplemented by the collections of international agricultural research centers that treat additional genetic, cytological, and botanical characteristics (Wellhausen et al. 1952;

Mangelsdorf 1974). All contribute information for the contemporary and future classification and breeding of maize.

Maize Classifications

Maize plants range from 2 to 20 feet in height, with 8 to 48 leaves, 1 to 15 stalks from a single seed, and ears that range from thumb-sized (popcorn) to 2 feet in length. The different varieties have different geographical, climatic, and pest tolerances. The mature kernel consists of the pericarp (thin shell), endosperm (storage organ), and embryo or germ, which contains most of the fat, vitamins, and minerals and varies in chemical composition, shape, and color.

The principal maize classifications are based on grain starch and appearance – these characteristics influence suitability for end uses. In "flints," the starch is hard. In "dents," the kernel is softer, with a larger proportion of floury endosperm and hard starch confined to the side of the kernel. "Floury" varieties have soft and mealy starch; "pop" corns are very hard. "Sweet" corns have more sugar, and "waxy" maizes contain starch composed entirely of amylopectin, without the 22 percent amylose characteristic of dents.

Dents account for 95 percent of all maize. The kernels acquire the characteristic "dent" when the grain is dried and the soft, starchy amylose of the core and the cap contract. Most dent maize is yellow and is fed to livestock; white dents are preferred for human food in Mexico, Central America, the Caribbean, and southern Africa. Flint maize, with its hard outer layer of starch, makes a very good-quality maize meal when dry-milled. It stores more durably than other types because it absorbs less moisture and is more resistant to fungi and insects. Flints germinate better in colder, wetter soils, mature earlier, and tend to perform well at higher latitudes. Popcorns are extremely hard flint varieties; when heated, the water in the starch steampressures the endosperm to explode, and the small kernels swell and burst.

Sweet corns are varieties bred especially for consumption in an immature state. A number of varieties of sweet corn, exhibiting simple mutations, were developed as garden vegetables in the United States beginning around 1800. Sweet varieties known as *sara chulpi* were known much earlier in the Andes, where they were usually parched before eating. Floury maizes are grown in the Andean highlands of South America, where they have been selected for beer making and special food preparations *(kancha)*, and in the U.S. Southwest, where they are preferred for their soft starch, which grinds easily. Waxy varieties are grown for particular dishes in parts of Asia and for use in industrial starches in the United States.

In addition, maize grains are classified by color, which comes mostly from the endosperm but is also influenced by pigments in the outer aleurone cell layer and pericarp. Throughout most of the world, white maize is preferred for human consumption and yellow for animal feed, although Central and Mediterranean Europeans eat yellow maize and indigenous Americans carefully select blue (purple, black), red, and speckled varieties for special regional culinary or ritual uses. Color is probably the most important classification criterion among New World indigenous cultivators, who use color terms to code information on the ecological tolerances, textures, and cooking characteristics of local varieties.

Breeding

The early indigenous cultivators of maize created "one of the most heterogeneous cultivated plants in existence" (Weatherwax 1954: 182). They selected and saved seed based on ear form, row number, and arrangement; kernel size, form, color, taste, texture, and processing characteristics; and plant-growth characteristics such as size, earliness, yield, disease resistance, and drought tolerance. Traditional farmers planted multiple varieties as a hedge against stressors, and Native American populations have continued this practice in the United States (Ford 1994) and Latin America (Brush, Bellon, and Schmidt 1988; Bellon 1991). However, only a small fraction of the biodiversity of traditional maize was transported to North America, to Europe, from Europe to Asia and Africa, and back to North America.

During all but the last hundred years, maize breeding involved open-pollinated varieties – varieties bred true from parent to offspring – so that farmers could select, save, and plant seed of desirable maize types. Hybrid maize, by contrast, involves crossing two inbred varieties to produce an offspring that demonstrates "hybrid vigor," or heterosis (with yields higher than either parent). But the seed from the hybrid plant will not breed true. Instead, new generations of hybrid seed must be produced in each succeeding generation through controlled crosses of the inbred lines. Consequently, save for producing their own crosses, farmers must purchase seed each cultivation season, which has given rise to a large hybrid seed industry, particularly in developed countries.

Hybrid maize had its beginnings in the United States in 1856 with the development by an Illinois farmer of Reid Yellow Dent, a mixture of Southern Dent and Northern Flint types that proved to be high-yielding and resistant to disease. There followed a series of scientific studies demonstrating that increased yields (hybrid vigor) resulted from the crossing of two inbred varieties. W. J. Beal, an agrobotanist at Michigan State University, in 1877 made the first controlled crosses of maize that demonstrated increased yields. Botanist George Shull, of Cold Spring Harbor, New York, developed the technique of inbreeding. He showed that although self-pollinated plants weakened generation after generation, single crosses of inbred lines demonstrated heterosis, or hybrid vigor. Edward East, working at the Connecticut Agricultural Experimental Station during the same period, developed single-cross inbred hybrids with 25 to 30 percent higher yields than the best open-pollinated varieties. A student of East's, D. F. Jones, working with Paul Mangelsdorf, in 1918 developed double-cross hybrids, which used two single-cross hybrids rather than inbred lines as parents and overcame the poor seed-yields and weakness of inbred lines so that hybrid seeds became economically feasible.

By the late 1920s, private seed companies were forming to sell high-yield hybrid lines. Henry A. Wallace, later secretary of agriculture under U.S. president Franklin Roosevelt, established Pioneer Hi-Bred for the production and sale of hybrid seed in 1926, in what he hoped would herald a new era of productivity and private enterprise for American agriculture. From the 1930s through the 1950s, commercial hybrids helped U.S. maize yields to increase, on average, 2.7 percent per year. By the mid-1940s, hybrids covered almost all of the U.S. "Corn Belt," and advances were under way in hybrid seeds that were adapted to European, Latin American, and African growing conditions. Another quantum leap in yields was achieved after World War II through chemical and management techniques. New double- and triple-cross hybrids responsive to applications of nitrogen fertilizers substantially raised yields in the 1960s, and again in the 1970s, with the release of a new generation of fertilizer-responsive single-cross hybrids that were planted in denser stands and protected by increased quantities of pesticides. In the 1980s, however, concerns about cost reduction, improved input efficiency, and natural resource (including biodiversity) conservation supplanted the earlier emphasis on simply increasing yields, with the result that yields remained flat.

Breeders also have been concerned with diversifying the parent stock of inbred hybrids, which are formed by the repeated self-pollination of individual plants and which, over generations, become genetically uniform and different from other lines. To prevent self-pollination when two inbred lines are crossed to produce a hybrid, the tassels are removed from the male parent. Discovery of lines with cytoplasmic male sterility allowed this labor-intensive step to be eliminated, but although it was desirable for the seed industry, the uniform germ plasm carrying this trait (Texas [T] male-sterile cytoplasm) proved very susceptible to Southern Corn Leaf Blight. Indeed, in 1970, virtually all of the U.S. hybrid maize crop incorporated the male sterility factor, and 15 to 20 percent of the entire crop was lost. Researchers and the seed industry responded by returning to the more laborious method of detasseling by hand until new male-sterile varieties could be developed (National Research Council 1972).

Since the 1940s, international agricultural "campaigns against hunger" have been transferring maize-breeding technologies (especially those involving hybrid seed) to developing countries. Henry Wallace, mentioned previously, spearheaded the Rockefeller Foundation's agricultural research programs in Mexico and India, both of which emphasized hybrid maize. Nevertheless, in Mexico the maize agricultural sector remains mostly small-scale, semisubsistent, and traditional, and in much of Latin America, the public seed sector has been unreliable in generating and supplying improved seeds for small farmers working diverse environments; probably no more than 20 percent of Mexico's, 30 percent of Central America's, and 15 percent of Colombia's maize production has resulted from modern improved varieties (Jaffe and Rojas 1994). The Puebla Project of Mexico, which aimed to double the maize yields of small farmers by providing improved seeds, chemical packages, and a guaranteed market and credit, had only spotty participation as maize farming competed unsuccessfully with nonfarming occupations.

Agricultural research programs in British colonial Africa in the 1930s also emphasized the development of hybrid maize seed, an emphasis that was revived in Kenya, Zimbabwe, and Malawi in the 1960s and became very important in the 1980s (Eicher 1995). Zimbabwe released its first hybrid in 1949, and Kenya did the same with domestically produced hybrids in 1964. An advanced agricultural infrastructure in these countries has meant that the rate of adoption of hybrids is extremely high, and in Zimbabwe, the yields achieved by some commercial farmers approach those seen in Europe and the United States. In Ghana, the Global 2000 agricultural project, supported by the Sasakawa Africa Association, has sought to demonstrate that high yields are attainable if farmers can be assured quality seeds, affordable fertilizers, and market access. The success of hybrids in these contexts depends on timely and affordable delivery of seed and other inputs, particularly fertilizers. Tanzania, from the late 1970s through the 1980s, provided a case study of deteriorating maize production associated with erratic seed supply, elimination of fertilizer subsidies, inadequate market transportation, and insufficient improvement of open-pollinated varieties (Friis-Hansen 1994).

Under optimal conditions, hybrids yield 15 to 20 percent more than the improved open-pollinated varieties, and breeders find it easier to introduce particular traits – such as resistance to a specific disease – into inbred hybrid lines. The uniform size and maturation rate of hybrids are advantages for farmers who wish to harvest and process a standard crop as a single unit. From a commercial standpoint, hybrids also carry built-in protection against multiplication because the originator controls the parent lines, and the progeny cannot reproduce the parental type.

Conditions are rarely optimal, however, and a corresponding disadvantage is that the yields of hybrid seeds are unpredictable where soil fertility, moisture, and crop pests are less controlled. Although the introduction of disease-resistant traits may be easier with hybrids, the very uniformity of the inbred parent lines poses the risk of large-scale vulnerability, as illustrated by the case of the Southern Corn Leaf Blight. Rapid response by plant breeders and seed companies to contain the damage is less likely in countries without well-organized research and seed industries. Farmers in such countries may also face shortages of high-quality seed or other inputs, which potentially reduces the yield advantage of hybrid seed. Indeed, in years when cash is short, farmers may be unable to afford the purchase of seed or other inputs, even when available, and in any event, they lack control over the price and quality of these items – all of which means a reduction in farmer self-reliance. Analysts of public and private agricultural research systems further argue that the elevated investment in hybrids reduces the funds available for improving open-pollinated varieties and that some of the yield advantage of hybrids may result from greater research attention rather than from any intrinsic superiority.

Agricultural Research in Developing Countries

In 1943, the Rockefeller Foundation, under the leadership of Norman Borlaug, launched the first of its "campaigns against hunger" in Mexico, with the aim of using U.S. agricultural technology to feed growing populations in this and other developing countries. In 1948, the campaign was extended to Colombia, and in 1954 the Central American Maize Program was established for five countries. In 1957, the program added a maize improvement scheme for India, which became the Inter-Asian Corn Program in 1967. The Ford and Rockefeller Foundations together established the International Center for the Improvement of Maize and Wheat in Mexico in 1963, the International Center for Tropical Agriculture in Colombia in 1967, and the International Institute for Tropical Agriculture in Nigeria in 1967. These centers, with their maize improvement programs, became part of the International Agricultural Research Center Network of the Consultative Group on International Agricultural Research, which was established with coordination among the World Bank, and the Food and Agriculture Organization of the United Nations (FAO) in 1971. The International Plant Genetic Research Institute, also a part of this system, collects and preserves maize germ plasm.

Additional international maize research efforts have included the U.S. Department of Agriculture (USDA)–Kenyan Kitale maize program instituted during the 1960s; the French Institute for Tropical Agricultural Research, which works with scientists in former French colonies in Africa and the Caribbean region; and the Maize Research Institute of Yugoslavia.

The Inter-American Institute of Agricultural Sciences (Costa Rica), Centro de Agricultura Tropical para Investigacíon y Enseñanzas (Costa Rica), Safgrad (Sahelian countries of Africa), Saccar (southern Africa), Prociandino (Andes region), and Consasur (Southern Cone, South America) are all examples of regional institutions for maize improvement (Dowswell et al. 1996).

Cultural History

Middle and South America

In the United States, which is its largest producer, maize is business, but for indigenous Americans maize more often has been considered a divine gift, "Our Mother" (Ford 1994), "Our Blood" (Sandstrom 1991), and what human beings are made of (Asturias 1993). Archaeological evidence and ethnohistorical accounts indicate that ancient American civilizations developed intensive land- and water-management techniques to increase production of maize and thereby provision large populations of craftspeople and administrators in urban centers. Ethnohistory and ethnography depict the maize plant in indigenous thought to be analogous to a "human being," and lexica maintain distinctive vocabularies for the whole plant, the grain, foods prepared from the grain, and the plant's parts and life stages (seedling, leafing, flowering, green ears, ripe ears), which are likened to those of a human. Indigenous terms and usage symbolically identify the maize plant and field (both glossed in the Spanish *milpa*) with well-being and livelihood. In addition, the four principal maize kernel colors constitute the foundation of a four-cornered, four-sided cosmology, coded by color.

An inventive indigenous technique for maize preparation was "nixtamalization" (alkali processing). Soaking the grain with crushed limestone, wood ash, or seashells helped loosen the outer hull, which could then be removed by washing. This made the kernel easier to grind and to form into a nutritious food end product, such as the tortilla in Mexico and Central America or the distinctive blue *piki* bread of the U.S. Southwest. In South America, maize was also consumed as whole-grain *mote*.

Tortillas, eaten along with beans and squash seeds (the "triumvirate" of a Mesoamerican meal), constitute a nutritious and balanced diet. In Mexico and Central America, dough is alternatively wrapped in maize sheaths or banana leaves. These steamed maize-dough *tamales* sometimes include fillings of green herbs, chilli sauce, meat, beans, or sugar. Additional regional preparations include gruels (*atoles,*) prepared by steeping maize in water and then sieving the liquid (a similar dish in East Africa is called *uji*); ceremonial beverages made from various maize doughs (*pozole*, which can also refer to a corn stew with whole grains, or chocolate *atole*); and special seasonal and festival foods prepared from immature maize (including spicy-sweet *atole* and *tamales*). Green corn – a luxury food for those dependent on maize as a staple grain (because each ear consumed in the immature stage limits the mature harvest) – can be either roasted or boiled in its husk.

Andean populations also made maize beers *(chicha)* of varying potency, which involved soaking and sprouting the grain, then leavening it by chewing or salivation (Acosta 1954). Brewed maize comprised a key lubricant of Incan social life (Hastorf and Johannessen 1993). Unfortunately, by the early period of Spanish occupation, indigenous leaders were reported to be having difficulty controlling intoxication, a problem heightened when *chicha* was spiked with cheap grain alcohol – a Spanish introduction.

Other special indigenous preparations included green corn kernels boiled with green lima beans, a dish introduced to the English on the East Coast of North America. The Hopi of the North American Southwest prepared *piki,* or "paper-bread," from a fine cornmeal batter spread on a stone slab lubricated with seed oil (from squash, sunflower, or watermelon seeds). They colored their cornbread a deep blue (or other colors) by adding extra alkalies and other pigments.

All parts of the maize plant were used by indigenous peoples. Tender inner husks, young ears, and flowers were boiled as vegetables, and fresh silks were mixed into tortilla dough. The Navajo prepared a soup and ceremonial breads from maize pollen; sugary juices were sucked out of the pith and stems; and even the bluish-black smut, *Ustilago maydis,* was prepared as a "mushroom" delicacy. Maize ear-sheaths wrapped tamales, purple sheaths colored their contents, and husks served as wrappers for tobacco. Maize vegetation was put into the food chain, first as green manure and, after Spanish livestock introductions, as animal fodder. The dried chaff of the plant was shredded for bedding material, braided into cord and basketry, and used to make dolls and other toys. Corn silks were boiled into a tea to relieve urinary problems, and the cobs served as stoppers for jugs, or as fuel. The stalks provided both a quick-burning fuel and construction material for shelters and fences. These uses continued during the Spaniards' occupation, which added poultry and ruminants as intermediary consumers of maize in the food chain and animal manure as an element in the nitrogen cycle. Indigenous peoples generally ate maize on a daily basis, reserving wheat for festival occasions, whereas those of Spanish descent raised and consumed wheat as their daily bread.

North America

In contrast to the Spaniards, English settlers in North America adopted maize as the crop most suited to survival in their New World environment and learned from their indigenous neighbors how to plant, cultivate, prepare, and store it. Although seventeenth-century Europeans reviled maize as a food fit only for desperate humans or swine (Gerard 1597; Brandes 1992), in North America the first colonials and later immigrants elevated the crop to the status of a staple food. For all Americans, it became a divine gift, a plentiful base for "typical" national and regional dishes, and a crop for great ritual elaboration, annual festivals, husking bees, shows, and later even a "Corn Palace" built of multicolored cobs (in Mitchell, North Dakota). In the process, maize became "corn," originally the generic term for "grain," shortened from the English "Indian corn," a term that distinguished colonial exported maize (also called "Virginia wheat") from European wheat and other grains.

Corn nourished the U.S. livestock industry, the slave economy, and westward expansion. It served as the foundation of the typical U.S. diet – high in meat and dairy products, which are converted corn – and, indeed, of the U.S. agricultural economy. North American populations of European and African ancestry historically turned maize into breads, grits, and gruels. They ate corn in the forms of mush; "spoon bread" (a mush with eggs, butter, and milk); simple breads called "hoecakes" (or "pone"); whole grains in "hominy"; and mixed with beans in "succotash." Coarsely ground "grits" were boiled or larded into "crackling bread," "scrapple," "fritters," and "hush puppies," or were sweetened with molasses and cooked with eggs and milk into "Indian pudding." Culinary elaborations of green corn, for which special varieties of sweet corn were bred, ranged from simple roasted (which caramelizes the sugar) or boiled "corn on the cob" with butter, to chowders and custards. Scottish and Irish immigrants fermented and distilled corn mash into corn whiskey ("white lightning" or "moonshine") or aged and mellowed it into bourbon, a distinctively smooth American liquor named for Bourbon, Kentucky, its place of origin.

Nineteenth-century food industries added corn syrup, oil, and starch to the processed repertoire, and then corn "flakes," the first of a series of breakfast cereals that promoters hoped would improve the healthfulness of the American diet. Popcorn, a simple indigenous food, by the mid-nineteenth century was popped in either a fatted frying pan or a wire gauze basket, and by the end of the century in a steam-driven machine, which added molasses to make Cracker Jacks, a popular new American snack first marketed at the 1893 Columbian Exposition in Chicago. By the late twentieth century, popcorn had become a gourmet food, produced from proprietary hybrid varieties, such as Orville Redenbacher's Gourmet Popping Corn, which boasted lighter, fluffier kernels and fewer "dud" grains and could be popped in a microwave (Fussell 1992). Twentieth-century snack foods also included corn "chips" (tortillas fried in oil). Moreover, North Americans consume large quantities of corn products as food additives and ingredients, such as corn starch, high-fructose syrup, and corn oil, as well as in animal products.

Europe

Maize, introduced by Christopher Columbus into Spain from the Caribbean in 1492–3, was first mentioned as a cultivated species in Seville in 1500, around which time it spread to the rest of the Iberian peninsula. It was called *milho* ("millet" or "grain") by Portuguese traders, who carried it to Africa and Asia (the name survives in South African "mealies," or cornmeal).

Spreading across Europe, maize acquired a series of binomial labels, each roughly translated as "foreign grain": In Lorraine and in the Vosges, maize was "Roman corn"; in Tuscany, "Sicilian corn"; in Sicily, "Indian corn"; in the Pyrenees, "Spanish corn"; in Provence, "Barbary corn" or "Guinea corn"; in Turkey, "Egyptian corn"; in Egypt, "Syrian dourra" (i.e., sorghum); in England, "Turkish wheat" or "Indian corn"; and in Germany, "Welsch corn" or "Bactrian typha." The French *blé de Turquie* ("Turkish wheat") and a reference to a golden-and-white seed of unknown species introduced by Crusaders from Anatolia (in what turned out to be a forged Crusader document) encouraged the error that maize came from western Asia, not the Americas (Bonafous 1836). De Candolle (1884) carefully documented the sources of the misconstruction and also dismissed Asian or African origins of maize on the basis of its absence from other historical texts. But inexplicably, sixteenth- and seventeenth-century herbalists appear to describe and illustrate two distinct types of maize, one "definitely" from tropical America, the other of unknown origin (Finan 1950).

English sources, especially J. Gerard's influential *Herball* (1597: Chapter 14), assessed "Turkie corne" to be unnourishing, difficult to digest, and "a more convenient food for swine than for man." Such disparagement notwithstanding, climate and low-labor requirements for its cultivation favored maize's dispersal. By the end of the sixteenth century, it had spread from southern Spain to the rest of the Iberian peninsula, to German and English gardens, and throughout Italy, where, by the seventeenth century, it constituted a principal element of the Tuscan diet. In both northwestern Iberia and northern Italy, climate favored maize over other cereals and gave rise to cuisines based on maize breads *(broa* and *borona)* and *polenta.* By the eighteenth century, maize had spread across the Pyrenees and into eastern France, where it became a principal peasant food and animal fodder.

A century earlier, maize had penetrated the Balkan Slavonia and Danube regions, and Serbs were reported to be producing *cucurutz* (maize) as a field crop at a time when other grains were scarce. By the mid-eighteenth century, it was a staple of the Hapsburg Empire, especially in Hungary. By the end of the eighteenth century, fields of maize were reported on the route between Istanbul and Nice, and it had likely been an earlier garden and hill crop in Bulgaria. Maize appears to have entered Romania in the beginning of the seventeenth century, where it became established as a field crop by midcentury. T. Stoianovich (1966) traces the complex of Greek-Turkish and Romanian-Transylvanian names for maize across the region and shows how the crop was incorporated into spring planting and autumn harvest rites of local peoples. In these regions, maize, which was more highly productive, replaced millet and, especially in Romania, has been credited with furthering a demographic and agricultural-socioeconomic transition. In the nineteenth century, Hungary was a major producer, along with Romania; by the mid-1920s, the latter country was the second largest exporter of maize (after Argentina) and remained a major producer and exporter through 1939. Romania maintained its own research institute and developed its own hybrids (Ecaterina 1995).

In contrast to the potato – the other major crop from the New World – maize appears to have been introduced across Europe with little resistance or coercion. In Spain, Italy, and southern France, its high seed-to-harvest ratio, relatively low labor requirements, high disease resistance, and adaptability allowed the plant to proceed from botanical exotic to kitchen-garden vegetable to field crop, all within a hundred years (Langer 1975). Throughout Europe, maize was prepared as a gruel or porridge because its flour lacked the gluten to make good leavened bread, although it was sometimes mixed into wheat flour as an extender. Although the custom of alkali processing, or that of consuming maize with legumes, had not accompanied the plant from the New World to the Old, maize provided a healthy addition to the diet so long as consumers were able to eat it with other foods. In the best of circumstances, it became a tasty culinary staple. In the worst, undercooked moldy maize became the food of deprivation, the food of last resort for the poor, as in Spain, where for this reason, maize is despised to this day (Brandes 1992).

Curiously, maize was never accepted in the British realm, where it continued to be "an acquired taste," a sometime famine or ration food, or a grain to feed livestock. During the great Irish famine of 1845, the British government imported maize for food relief – to keep down the prices of other foods and provide emergency rations for the poor. Maize boasted the advantages of being cheap and having no established private "free trade" with which government imports might interfere. Unfortunately, Ireland lacked the milling capacity to dry, cool, sack, and grind it, and in 1846 a scarcity of mills led to the distribution of the whole grain, which was described as irritating rather than nourishing for "half-starving people" (Woodham-Smith 1962). Maize shortly thereafter began to play an important role in British famine relief and as ordinary rations for workers in Africa.

Africa

Portuguese traders carried maize to eastern Africa in the sixteenth century, and Arab traders circulated it around the Mediterranean and North Africa. During the seventeenth century, maize traveled from the West Indies to the Gold Coast, where, by the eighteenth century, it was used as a cheap food for provisioning slaves held in barracoons or on shipboard during the Middle Passage. By the end of the eighteenth century, maize was reported in the interior of Africa (the Lake Chad region of Nigeria), where it appears to have replaced traditional food plants in the western and central regions, especially the Congo, Benin, and western Nigeria, although cassava – because it was less vulnerable to drought and locusts – later replaced maize in the southern parts of Congo (Miracle 1966) and Tanzania (Fleuret and Fleuret 1980).

By the end of the nineteenth century, maize had become established as a major African crop. People accustomed to eating it as the regular fare in mines or work camps, or as emergency rations, now demanded it when conditions returned to normal or when they returned home. Consumption also increased following famine years because people were able to sow earlier-maturing varieties, and even where sorghum remained the principal staple, maize became a significant seasonal food that was consumed at the end of the "hungry season" before other cereals ripened. The British also promoted African maize as a cash crop for their home starch industry.

Today in Africa, ecology, government agricultural and marketing policies, and the cost of maize relative to other staple or nonstaple crops are the factors influencing the proportion of maize in household production and consumption (Anthony 1988). Major shifts toward maize diets occurred in the latter part of the twentieth century, when improved varieties and extension programs, as well as higher standards of living, meant that people could enjoy a more refined staple food – with less fiber – without feeling hungry. Researchers in postcolonial times have developed hybrids adapted to African conditions, but these have met with mixed reactions. In Zimbabwe, where small farmers are well organized and can demand seed and access to markets, most of them plant improved hybrids (Bratton 1986; Eicher 1995). By contrast, in Zambia, smallholders continue to grow traditional varieties for a number of reasons, including the high cost of hybrid seed, shortages of seed and input supplies, inadequate storage facilities, and a culinary preference for varieties that are flintier. The latter are preferred because they have a higher extraction rate when mortar-pounded (superior "mortar yield"), they produce superior porridge, and they are more resistant to weevils. However, even where introduction of improved disease-resistant varieties has been successful, as in northern Nigeria, the gains will be sustainable only if soils do not degrade, the price of fertilizer remains affordable, markets are accessible, and research and extension services can keep ahead of coevolving pests (Smith et al. 1994).

African cuisines favor white maize, which is prepared as a paste or mush and usually eaten as warm chunks dipped in stews or sauces of meat, fish, insects, or vegetables. In eastern and southern Africa, maize is first pounded or ground before being boiled into a thick porridge. But in western Africa, *kenkey* is prepared from kernels that are first soaked and dehulled before being ground, fermented, and heated. *Ogi* is a paste prepared by soaking the kernels, followed by light pounding to remove the pericarp and a second soaking to produce a bit of fermentation. The bran is strained away, and the resulting mass cooked into a paste, mixed with the dough of other starchy staples, and baked into an unleavened bread or cooked in oil. Maize gruels can be soured or sweetened, fermented into a light or a full beer, or distilled. The kernels are also boiled and eaten whole, sometimes with beans, or beaten into a consistency like that of boiled rice. Alternatively, the grains can be parched before boiling, or cooked until they burst. Immature ears are boiled or roasted, and the juice from immature kernels flavored, cooked, and allowed to jell.

Asia

Portuguese introductions of maize to Asia likely occurred in the early 1500s, after which the grain was carried along the western coast of India and into northwestern Pakistan along the Silk Route. By the mid-1500s, maize had reached Honan and Southeast Asia, and by the mid-1600s it was established in Indonesia, the Philippines, and Thailand. In southern and southwestern China during the 1700s, raising maize permitted farming to expand into higher elevations that were unsuitable for rice cultivation, and along with white and sweet potatoes, the new crop contributed to population growth and a consequent growing misery (Anderson 1988). From there, maize spread to northern China, Korea, and Japan.

In the 1990s, maize was a staple food in selected regions of China, India, Indonesia, and the Philippines. Among grains in China, it ranked third in importance (after rice and wheat, but before sorghum, which it has replaced in warmer, wetter areas and in drier areas when new hybrids became available). Maize is consumed as steamed or baked cakes, as mush, in noodles mixed with other grains, and as cracked grain mixed with rice. It is the principal grain in the lower mountains of western and southern China and in much of the central North, and it increasingly serves as a food for the poor. Immature maize is eaten as a vegetable, and baby corn is an important specialty appreciated for its crunchy texture.

In Indonesia, maize is the staple food of some 18 million people (Timmer 1987). Farmers have responded favorably to new technologies and government incentives, such as quick-yielding varieties, subsidized fertilizers, and mechanical tilling and shelling devices. They demand improved seed and subsidized chemicals and carefully match seed varieties to local seasonal conditions in environments that (in places) allow for triple cropping (rice-maize-maize, rice-maize-soy, or rice-maize-cassava sequences). In the 1980s, breeders reportedly could not keep up with the demand for improved white varieties, which cover 35 percent of the area sown in maize and are preferred for human consumption. Humans still consume 75 percent of Indonesia's maize directly, and it is particularly important as a staple in the preharvest "hungry season" before the main rice harvest. Rice remains the preferred staple; the proportion of maize in the diet fluctuates relative to the price of maize versus rice and consumer income.

Summary of Culinary History

Kernels of the earliest forms of maize were probably parched on hot stones or in hot ash or sand. Small hard seeds, in which starch was tightly packed, also lent themselves to popping. Both Mexican and Peruvian indigenous populations grew selected popcorn varieties, which, among the Aztecs, were burst like flowers or hailstones for their water god. Parched maize, sometimes mixed with other seeds, was ground into *pinole,* a favorite lightweight ration for travelers that could be eaten dry or hydrated with water.

Maize grains more commonly were wet-ground – boiled and then ground with a stone quern or pounded with wooden implements (the North American indigenous procedure outside of the Southwest). After soaking the kernels in alkaline and washing to remove the hulls, native peoples either consumed the grains whole (as hominy) or wet-ground them into a dough used to form tortillas (flat cakes), *arepas* (thick cakes), or *tamales* (leaf-wrapped dough with a filling). The arduous process of grinding, which could require up to half of a woman's workday, was later taken over by water- or engine-powered mills; the time-consuming process of shaping tortillas by hand was facilitated by wooden or metal tortilla "presses"; and very recently, the entire process of tortilla manufacture has been mechanized. In 1995, the people of Mexico consumed 10 million tons of tortillas, each ton using 10,000 liters of water to soak and wash the kernels, water that, when dumped, created rivers of calcium hydroxide. An interdisciplinary team has formed a 1995 "Tortilla Project" to create a water-sparing, energy-efficient machine that will turn out a superior nutritional product with no pollutants.

Dry-grinding, characteristic of nonindigenous processing, produces whole maize "meal," "grits," or "flour," which can be "decorticated" (bran removed) or "degerminated" (most bran and germ removed), a separation process also called "bolting," to produce a more refined flour and an end product that stores longer. Hominy is the endosperm product left over after the pericarp is removed and the germ loosened; "pearl" or "polished" hominy has the aleurone layer removed as well. Although separating the bran and germ decreases the vitamin and mineral value, it

makes the oil and residual "germ cake," pericarp, and hulls more easily available for livestock feed.

Simple, boiled maize-meal porridges, which combine whole or degermed meal with water, are the most common forms of maize dishes. In the United States, it is cornmeal mush; in Italy, *polenta;* in Romania, *mamaliga;* and in Africa, *nshima, ugali,* or *foo foo.* In Italy, *polenta* often includes grated cheese and extra fat, and in Yugoslavia, the corn mush contains eggs and dairy products. Maize meal, when mixed with water or milk, can be shaped into simple unleavened flat breads or cakes and baked over an open fire, or in an oven. These were called *hoecakes* in the early United States.

In Asia, maize is "riced"; the cracked kernels are boiled and consumed like the preferred staple of the region. Indeed, improved maize varieties must meet the processing criteria of cracking and cooking to resemble rice. Maize starch, especially in central Java, is processed into flour for porridge, noodles, and snack food. Green maize is also consumed.

Industrial Processing

Industrial processing utilizes either wet or dry milling. Wet milling steeps kernels in water, separates germ from kernel, and then separates germ into oil and meal portions. Each 100 kilograms (kg) of maize yields 2 to 3 kg of oil. Corn oil is popular for its ability to withstand heat, its high level of polyunsaturates, and its flavorlessness. The meal portions of the kernel become starch, gluten, and bran.

The dried starch portion is used in the food, textile, and paper industries. Starch, processed into glucose syrup or powder and high-fructose or dextrose products, sweetens three-fourths of the processed foods in the United States, especially confections and baked goods. In 1991, high-fructose corn syrup, manufactured by an enzyme-isomerization process that was first introduced in the 1960s, accounted for more than half of the U.S. (nondiet) sweetener market (National Corn Growers Association 1992).

Dry milling processes about 2 percent of the U.S. maize crop into animal feeds, beers, breakfast cereals, and other food and industrial products. In a tempering/degerming process the majority of the pericarp and germ are removed, and the remaining bulk of the endosperm is dried and flaked into products such as breakfast cereal. Whole (white) grains are ground into hominy grits and meal. These products, because they still contain the oily germ, have superior flavor but shorter shelf life. Industrialized alkali processing produces a dough that is turned into tortillas, chips, and other "Mexican" snacks.

Special maize varieties are also being bred for "designer" industrial starches. One, high in amylose starch, is used to create edible wrappers for pharmaceuticals, feeds, and foods. Another "super slurper" absorbs up to 2,000 times its weight in moisture and is employed in disposable diapers and bedpads. Still another is being developed into less-polluting road "salt," and other corn starches are being tailored into biodegradable plastic bags, cups, and plates. All told, industrial maize preparations place thousands of different maize-derived items on modern supermarket shelves, including flours and meals for breads and puddings, starch as a thickener, maize ("Karo") syrups or honeys as sweeteners, high-fructose and dextrose syrups as sweetening ingredients in beverages and baked goods, and processed cereals as breakfast or snack foods. Maize-based cooking oils, chips, beers, and whiskeys complete the spectrum. In fact, almost all processed foods (because they contain additives of starch or fat) contain some maize, as do almost all animal products, which are converted maize (Fussell 1992).

Animal Feed Products

Maize is the preferred feedgrain for animals because it is so rich in fat and calories; its high-starch/low-fiber content helps poultry, swine, cattle, and dairy animals convert its dry matter more efficiently than with other grains; it is also lower in cost. Feeds are formulated from whole, cracked, or steam-flaked grains and optimally supplemented with amino acids, vitamins, and minerals to meet the special nutritional requirements of particular domesticated animals. In industrial processing, by-products remaining after the oil and starch have been extracted – maize gluten, bran, germ meal, and condensed fermented steepwater (from soaking the grain), which is a medium for single-cell protein – also go into animal feed.

Silage uses the entire maize plant – which is cut, chopped, and allowed to ferment – to nourish dairy and beef cattle and, increasingly, swine. In developing countries, fresh or dried vegetation and substandard grains are household commodities used to produce animal products. When the entire maize plant (and, in traditional fields, its associated weeds) serves as a feedstuff, it surpasses all other plants in average yield and digestible nutrients per hectare (Dowswell et al. 1996).

Nutrition

Maize provides 70 percent or more of food energy calories in parts of Mexico, Central America, Africa, and Romania. In these regions, adult workers consume some 400 grams of maize daily, a diet marginally sufficient in calories, protein, vitamins, and minerals, depending on how the maize is processed and the supplementary foods with which it is combined. Maize is a better source of energy than other cereal grains because of its higher fat content. Ground maize meal has 3,578 calories per kg, mostly carbohydrate, with about 4.5 percent "good" fat (fat-rich varieties are double this figure), and is high in essential linoleic and oleic fatty acids. It contains about 10 percent protein, roughly half of which is zein that is low in the amino acids lysine and tryptophan. The protein quality is enhanced in traditional Latin American maize diets by alkali processing and consumption with legumes that are high in lysine. Potatoes, if eaten in sufficient quantity, also yield a considerable amount of lysine and consequently often complement maize in highland South America and parts of Europe. Of course, incorporating animal proteins improves the nutritional quality of any diet with grain or tubers as the staple.

Maize is also naturally low in calcium and niacin, but calcium, niacin, and tryptophan content are all enhanced by traditional alkali processing (in which the kernels are cooked and soaked in a calcium hydroxide – lime or ash – solution), which adds calcium and increases the available tryptophan and niacin in the kernels or dough. White maize, usually the favored type for human food, is also low in vitamin A, although this nutrient is higher in properly stored yellow maize. Moreover, in its traditional heartland, maize is combined with chilli peppers, other vegetables, and various kinds of tomatoes and spices, all of which enhance the amount of vitamin A delivered to the consumer, along with other vitamins and minerals. In Africa and Asia, additional vitamins and minerals are added to maize diets when wild or cultivated greens, other vegetables, peanuts, and small bits of animal protein are combined in a sauce. Potash, burned from salt grasses, also enhances the otherwise poor mineral content of the diet (FAO 1953).

Diseases Associated with Maize

Pellagra and protein-deficiency disease (kwashiorkor) are historically associated with maize diets. In addition, as recently as the 1950s, rickets, scurvy, and signs of vitamin A deficiency have all been reported among populations consuming maize diets in Central Europe and eastern and southern Africa. Such deficiency diseases disappear with dietary diversification, expansion of food markets, and technological efforts to improve the micronutrient quality of maize diets.

Pellagra

Pellagra, now understood to be a disease caused in large part by niacin deficiency, was first observed in eighteenth-century Europe among the very poor of Spain, then Italy, France, Romania, Austria, southern Russia, the Ottoman Empire, and outside of Europe in Egypt, South Africa, and the southern United States. It was associated with extreme poverty and usually seen among land-poor peasants, whose diet centered much too heavily on maize. The main symptoms were described as the "three Ds" (diarrhea, dermatitis, and dementia), and four stages were recognized, from malaise, to digestive and skin disorders, to neurological and mental symptoms, and finally, wasting, dementia, and death (Roe 1973).

Although maize was adopted as a garden crop and within 100 years after its appearance was a field crop over much of the European continent, the disease manifested itself only when economic conditions had deteriorated to the point that pellagra victims ("pellagrins") could afford to eat only poorly cooked, often rotten maize. In Spain, this occurred in the 1730s; up to 20 percent of the population may still have been afflicted in the early twentieth century. In Italy, peasants also may have been suffering from the "red disease" as early as the 1730s. Despite efforts to protect the purity of the maize supply and improve diets through public granaries, bakeries, and soup kitchens, the disease persisted until the 1930s, when changes in diet were brought about by improved standards of living and the demise of the tenant-farmer system. In France, where maize had been sown since the sixteenth century and in some areas had expanded into a field crop by the late seventeenth, maize was not widely grown as a staple until the late eighteenth and early nineteenth centuries, when it became the main crop of the southern and eastern regions of the country and was accompanied by pellagra among destitute peasants. The physician Theophile Roussel recommended that the disease be prevented by changing the diet and agriculture so that there was less emphasis on maize. The government responded with legislation encouraging alternative crop and livestock production along with consumption of wheat, and by the early twentieth century, pellagra had largely been eliminated.

In the late nineteenth century, pellagra was reported by a British physician, Fleming Sandwith, in Egypt and South Africa. The disease was also present in the southern United States, although it did not reach epidemic proportions until the first decade of the twentieth century. In epidemiological studies begun in 1914, Joseph Goldberger, a physician working for the Public Health Service, determined that the disease was not contagious but *was* dietary. Furthermore, it was associated not so much with the consumption of maize as with the economic inability to obtain and consume other protective foods along with maize. For prevention and cure, Goldberger prescribed milk, lean meat, powdered yeast, and egg yolks. At the household level, he recommended more diversified farming, including milk cows and more and better gardens.

Goldberger traced the correlation between epidemic pellagra and economic downturns and demonstrated how underlying socioeconomic conditions restricted diets and caused dietary deficiencies among tenant farmers, who ordinarily ate mostly maize and maize products. The number of cases declined in the worst depression years (1932–4) because, when there was no market for cotton, farmers produced diversified food crops and garden vegetables for home consumption. Goldberger also demonstrated that pellagra mimicked "blacktongue" in

dogs and used them as experimental animals to find what foods might prevent pellagra. He conceptualized the "pellagra-preventive" factor to be a water-soluble vitamin but could not identify it (Terris 1964). It was not until 1937 that C. A. Elvehjem and his colleagues demonstrated that nicotinic acid cured blacktongue in dogs, a finding carried over to demonstrate that nicotinic acid prevented pellagra in humans. Lest the public confuse nicotinic acid with nicotine, the Food and Drug Administration adopted the name "niacin" for their vitamin fortification program (Roe 1973: 127), which was designed to eliminate nutrition-deficiency diseases, and in southern states tended to include cornmeal and grits as well as wheat flours. Diversification and improvement of diet associated with World War II production, employment, and high-quality food rations mostly spelled an end to pellagra in the United States.

Since the 1940s, maize diets and pellagra have also been associated with imbalanced protein intake and selected amino acid deficiency. G. A. Goldsmith (1958) demonstrated that dietary tryptophan converts to nicotinic acid in humans at a ratio of 1:45, and anthropologists working with nutritional chemists were able to demonstrate that alkali processing of maize in traditional indigenous diets made more niacin and tryptophan available (Katz, Hediger, and Valleroy 1974). Traditional processing and food combinations also make more isoleucine available relative to leucine, and it has been suggested that excess leucine is another antinutritional factor in maize. Although pellagra has been eliminated in industrialized countries, it remains a plague among poor, maize-eating agriculturalists in southern Africa, where it was reported throughout the 1960s in South Africa, Lesotho, and Tanzania, and in Egypt and India among people who lack access to wheat.

Protein Deficiency

Another nutritional deficiency disease historically associated with diets high in maize is kwashiorkor, conventionally classified as a protein-deficiency disease and associated especially with weanlings and hungry-season diets in Africa (Williams 1933, 1935). Since the 1960s, international maize-breeding programs have sought to overcome lysine deficiency directly, thus giving maize a much better-quality protein. Maize breeders at Purdue University in Indiana, who were screening maize for amino acid contents, isolated the mutant "Opaque-2" gene and developed a variety that had the same protein content as conventional maizes but more lysine and tryptophan.

Although this variety possessed a more favorable amino acid profile, its yields were lower, its ears smaller, its chalky kernels dried more slowly, and it carried unfavorable color (yellow), texture, and taste characteristics. Its softer, more nutritious, and moister starch was more easily attacked by insects and fungi, and its adhesive properties did not make a good tortilla. Mexican researchers at CIMMYT in the 1970s and 1980s eliminated these deficiencies and in the mid-1980s introduced Quality Protein Maize (QPM) with favorable consumer characteristics. The remaining step was to interbreed this superior type with locally adapted varieties. But by the 1980s, nutritionists were questioning the importance of protein or selective amino-acid deficiencies as high-priority problems and focusing instead on improving access to calories. QPM became a technological solution for a nutritional deficiency no longer of interest, and CIMMYT was forced to end its QPM program in 1991. However, national programs in South Africa, Ghana, Brazil, and China are using QPM to develop maize-based weaning foods and healthier snacks, as well as a superior animal feed (Ad Hoc Panel 1988).

Additional Strategies
for Nutritional Improvement

Strategies for improving maize diets focus on new varieties with higher protein quality and essential vitamin contents, better storage, wiser milling and processing, fortification, and dietary diversification. Conventional breeding and genetic engineering have enhanced essential amino acid profiles, especially lysine and methionine contents, although end products so far are principally superior feeds for poultry and pigs. Maize transformation by means of electroporation and regeneration of protoplasts was achieved in 1988, and subsequently by *Agrobacterium* (Rhodes et al. 1988). The first commercial varieties, with added traits of herbicide resistance and superior protein quality, were released in 1996. To improve protein content, maize meals are also fortified with soybean protein meal or dried food yeast *(Tortula utilis)*. Nutritional enhancement through breeding or blending are alternatives to diversifying human (or animal) diets with legumes or animal foods.

Improperly stored maize, with moisture contents above 15 percent, also favor the growth of fungi, the most dangerous being *Aspergillus flavus,* which produces aflatoxin, a mycotoxin that causes illness in humans and animals. Efforts are being taken to eliminate such storage risks and losses.

Future Prospects

Maize has been expanding in geographical and cultural scope to the point where the world now harvests more than 500 million tons on all continents, and the crop is being increasingly directed into a number of nonfood uses, especially in industrialized countries. The supply of maize should continue to increase in response to a growing demand for animal products (which rely on maize feed), for food ingredients industrially processed from maize (such as good-quality cooking oil), and for convenience foods and snack foods (Brenner 1991). The biologi-

cal characteristics of maize that have always favored its expansion support the accuracy of such a prediction: Its adaptability, high yields, high extraction rate, and high energy value deliver higher caloric yields per unit area than wheat or rice, and its high starch and low fiber content give the highest conversion of dry matter to animal product. Technology, especially biotechnology, will influence overall yields as well as nutritive value and processing characteristics. Genetic engineering has already allowed seed companies to market higher protein-quality maize designed to meet the specific nutritional needs of poultry and livestock. Other varieties have been designed to tolerate certain chemicals and permit higher maize yields in reduced-pest environments. The introduction of a male sterility trait, developed by Plant Genetic Systems (Belgium) in collaboration with University of California researchers, is expected to reduce the costs of manual or mechanical detasseling, estimated to be $150 to $200 million annually in the United States and $40 million in Europe (Bijman 1994).

Yet, the favorable agricultural, nutritional, and economic history of maize notwithstanding, the grain presents problems. As we have seen, maize diets have been associated with poverty and illness, especially the niacin-deficiency scourge, pellagra, and childhood (weanling) malnutrition. Moreover, the highly productive inbred hybrids, such as those that contain the trait for cytoplasmic male sterility, have created new genetic and production vulnerabilities (National Research Council 1972). Hybrid seeds also may increase the economic vulnerability of small-scale semisubsistence farmers who cannot afford to take advantage of new agricultural technologies and, consequently, find themselves further disadvantaged in national and international markets. Finally, and paradoxically, maize (like the potato) has been associated with increasing hunger and suffering in Africa (Cohen and Atieno Odhiambo 1989) and Latin America (Asturias 1993).

Ellen Messer

Many thanks to Mary Eubanks, who contributed a substantial text on which the author based the section "Biological Evolution."

Bibliography

Acosta, J. de. 1954. *Historia natural y moral de las Indias.* Madrid.
Ad Hoc Panel of the Advisory Committee on Technology Innovation, Board on Science and Technology for International Development, National Research Council. 1988. *Quality-protein maize.* Washington, D.C.
Allen, W. 1965. *The African husbandman.* Edinburgh.
Anderson, E. N. 1988. *The food of China.* New Haven, Conn.

Anghiera, P. Martíre d' P. 1912. *De Orbe Novo, the eight decades of Peter Martyr d'Anghera,* trans. F. A. Mac-Nutt. New York.

Anthony, C. 1988. *Mechanization and maize. Agriculture and the politics of technology transfer in East Africa.* New York.

Asturias, M. A. 1993. *Men of maize,* trans. G. Martin. Pittsburgh, Pa.

Austin, J., and G. Esteva, eds. 1987. *Food policy in Mexico.* Ithaca, N.Y.

Barkin, D. 1987. SAM and seeds. In *Food policy in Mexico,* ed. J. Austin and G. Esteva, 111-32. Ithaca, N.Y.

Barkin, D., R. L. Batt, and B. R. DeWalt. 1990. *Food crops and feed crops: The global substitution of grains in production.* Boulder, Colo.

Beadle, G. W. 1939. Teosinte and the origin of maize. *Journal of Heredity* 30: 245-7.

Bellon, M. 1991. The ethnoecology of maize variety management: A case study from Mexico. *Human Ecology* 19: 389-418.

Bijman, J. 1994. Plant genetic systems. *Biotechnology and Development Monitor* 19: 19-21.

Bonafous, M. 1836. *Histoire naturelle, agricole et économique du maïs.* Paris.

Bonavia, D., and A. Grobman. 1989. Andean maize: Its origins and domestication. In *Foraging and farming: The evolution of plant exploitation,* ed. D. R. Harris and G. C. Hillman, 456-70. London.

Brandes, S. 1992. Maize as a culinary mystery. *Ethnology* 31: 331-6.

Bratton, M. 1986. Farmer organizations and food production in Zimbabwe. *World Development* 14: 367-84.

Brenner, C. 1991. *Biotechnology for developing countries: The case of maize.* Paris.

Brush, S., M. Bellon, and E. Schmidt. 1988. Agricultural diversity and maize development in Mexico. *Human Ecology* 16: 307-28.

Candolle, A. de. 1884. *Origin of cultivated plants.* London.

CIMMYT (International Center for the Improvement of Maize and Wheat). 1981. *World maize facts and trends. Report 1.* Mexico City.

  1984. *World maize facts and trends. Report 2. An analysis of changes in Third World food and feed uses of maize.* Mexico City.

  1987. *World maize facts and trends. Report 3. An analysis of the economics of commercial maize seed production in developing countries.* Mexico City.

  1990. *World maize facts and trends. Realizing the potential of maize in sub-Saharan Africa.* Mexico City.

  1992. *1991/1992 World maize facts and trends.* Mexico City.

CIMMYT. 1994. *1993/1994 World maize facts and trends.* Mexico City.

Cobo, B. 1890-3. *Historia del nuevo mundo.* Seville.

Coe, S. 1994. *America's first cuisine.* Austin, Tex.

Cohen, D. W., and E. S. Atieno Odhiambo. 1989. The hunger of Obalo. In *Siaya: The historical anthropology of an African landscape,* 61-84. London and Athens, Ohio.

Cohen, J. 1995. Project refines an ancient staple with modern science. *Science* 267: 824-5.

De Janvry, A., E. Sadoulet, and G. Gordillo de Anda. 1995. NAFTA and Mexico's maize producers. *World Development* 23: 1349-62.

del Paso y Troncoso, F. 1905. *Papeles de Nueva Espana, Segunda Serie, geografia y estadistica.* Madrid.

De Walt, K. 1990. Shifts from maize to sorghum production: Nutrition effects in four Mexican communities. *Food Policy* 15: 395-407.

Dowswell, C., R. L. Paliwal, and R. P. Cantrell. 1996. *Maize in the Third World.* Boulder, Colo.

Ecaterina, P. 1995. Corn and the development of agricultural science in Romania. *Agricultural History* 69: 54-78.

Eicher, C. 1995. Zimbabwe's maize-based Green Revolution: Preconditions for replication. *World Development* 23: 805-18.

Eubanks, M. 1995. A cross between two maize relatives: *Tripsacum dactyloides* and *Zea diploperennis* (Poaceae). *Economic Botany* 49: 172-82.

Fernandez de Oviedo y Valdes, G. 1526, 1530. *Historia natural y general de las Indias, islas y tierra firme del mar oceano.* Seville.

Finan, J. 1950. *Maize in the great herbals.* Waltham, Mass.

Fleuret, P., and A. Fleuret. 1980. Nutritional implications of staple food crop successions in Usambara, Tanzania. *Human Ecology* 8: 311-27.

FAO (Food and Agricultural Organization of the United Nations). 1953. *Maize and maize diets.* Rome.

  1993. *Average annual maize area, yield, and production, 1990-1992.* Agrostat/PC Files, Rome.

Ford, R. 1994. Corn is our mother. In *Corn and culture in the prehistoric New World,* ed. S. Johannessen and C. Hastorf, 513-26. Boulder, Colo.

Freeling, M., and V. Walbot, eds. 1993. *The maize handbook.* New York.

Friis-Hansen, E. 1994. Hybrid maize production and food security in Tanzania. *Biotechnology and Development Monitor* 19: 12-13.

Fussell, B. 1992. *The story of corn.* New York.

Galinat, W. C. 1992. Maize: Gift from America's first peoples. In *Chilies to chocolate. Food the Americas gave the world,* ed. N. Foster and L. S. Cordell, 47-60. Tucson, Ariz.

Gallagher, J. P. 1989. Agricultural intensification and ridged-field cultivation in the prehistoric upper Midwest of North America. In *Foraging and farming: The evolution of plant exploitation,* ed. D. R. Harris and G. C. Hillman, 572-84. London.

Gerard, J. 1597. *The herball. Generall historie of plants.* London.

Goldsmith, G. A. 1958. Niacin-tryptophan relationships in man and niacin requirement. *American Journal of Clinical Nutrition* 6: 479-86.

Goodman, M. 1988. U.S. maize germplasm: Origins, limitations, and alternatives. In *Recent advances in the conservation and utilization of genetic resources.* Proceedings of the Global Maize Germplasm Workshop. Mexico.

Harshberger, J. W. 1896. Fertile crosses of teosinte and maize. *Garden and Forest* 9: 522-3.

Hastorf, C. A. 1994. Cultural meanings (Introduction to Part 4). In *Corn and culture in the prehistoric New World,* ed. S. Johannessen and C. A. Hastorf, 395-8. Boulder, Colo.

Hastorf, C., and S. Johannessen. 1993. Pre-Hispanic political change - the role of maize in the central Andes of Peru. *American Anthropologist* 95: 115-38.

Hernandez, F. 1615. *Rerum medicarum Novae Hispaniae, Thesavrus.* Mexico.

Hernandez X., E. 1971. *Exploracion etnobotanica y su metodologia.* Mexico, D.F.

Hewitt de Alcantara, C. 1976. *Modernizing Mexican agriculture: Socioeconomic implications of technological change, 1940-1970.* Geneva.

  1992. *Economic restructuring and rural subsistence in Mexico. Maize and the crisis of the 1980s.* New York.

Hobhouse, W. 1986. *Seeds of change: Five plants which changed the world.* New York.

Iltis, H. 1983. From teosinte to maize: The catastrophic sexual mutation. *Science* 222: 886-93.

Jaffe, W., and M. Rojas. 1994. Maize hybrids in Latin America: Issues and options. *Biotechnology and Development Monitor* 19: 6-8.

Janossy, A. 1970. Value of Hungarian local maize varieties as basic material for breeding. In *Some methodological achievements of the Hungarian hybrid maize breeding,* ed. I. Kovács, 17-22. Budapest.

Jennings, B. 1988. *Foundations of international agricultural research: Science and politics in Mexican agriculture.* Boulder, Colo.

Jimenez de la Espada, M., ed. 1881-97. *Relaciones geograficas de las Indias.* 4 vols. Madrid.

Johannessen, S., and C. A. Hastorf, eds. 1994. *Corn and culture in the prehistoric New World.* Boulder, Colo.

Kato, Y. T. A. 1984. Chromosome morphology and the origin of maize and its races. *Evolutionary Biology* 17: 219-53.

Katz, S. H., M. L. Hediger, and L. A. Valleroy. 1974. Traditional maize processing technologies in the New World. *Science* 184: 765-73.

Kempton, J. H., and W. Popenoe. 1937. *Teosinte in Guatemala.* Contributions to American Anthropology No. 23. Washington, D.C.

Kumar, S., and C. Siandwazi. 1994. Maize in Zambia: Effects of technological change on food consumption and nutrition. In *Agricultural commercialization, economic development, and nutrition,* ed. J. von Braun and E. Kennedy, 295-308. Baltimore, Md.

Langer, W. 1975. American foods and Europe's population growth 1750-1850. *Journal of Social History* 8: 51-66.

Long, J., ed. 1996. *Conquista y comida.* Mexico City.

Mangelsdorf, P. 1974. *Corn: Its origin, evolution, and improvement.* Cambridge, Mass.

Miracle, M. 1966. *Maize in tropical Africa.* Madison, Wis.

Montanez, A., and A. Warman. 1985. *Los productores de maize en Mexico. Restricciones y alternativos.* Mexico City.

National Corn Growers Association. 1992. *Annual report.* St. Louis, Mo.

National Research Council (U.S.) Committee on Genetic Vulnerability of Major Crops, National Academy of Sciences. 1972. *Genetic vulnerability of major crops.* Washington, D.C.

Nutall, Z. 1930. Documentary evidence concerning wild maize in Mexico. *Journal of Heredity* 21: 217-20.

Redclift, M. 1983. Production programs for small farmers: Plan Puebla as myth and reality. *Economic Development and Cultural Change* 31: 551-70.

Rhodes, C. A., D. Pierce, I. Mettler, et al. 1988. Genetically transformed maize plants from protoplasts. *Science* 240: 204-7.

Richards, A. 1939. *Land, labour, and diet in northern Rhodesia: An economic study of the Bemba tribe.* London.

Roe, D. 1973. *A plague of corn: The social history of pellagra.* Ithaca, N.Y.

Root, W., and R. de Rochemont. 1976. *Eating in America: A history.* New York.

Sahagun, B. de. 1950-82. *General history of the things of New Spain.* Florentine Codex. Santa Fe, N. Mex.

Sandstrom, A. R. 1991. *Corn is our blood: Culture and ethnic identity in a contemporary Aztec Indian village.* Norman, Okla.

Sanoja, M. 1989. From foraging to food production in northeastern Venezuela and the Caribbean. In *Foraging and farming: The evolution of plant exploitation,* ed. D. R. Harris and G. C. Hillman, 523-37. London.

Smale, M. 1995. "Maize is life": Malawi's delayed Green Revolution. *World Development* 23: 819-31.

Smith, J., A. D. Barau, A. Goldman, and J. H. Mareck. 1994. The role of technology in agricultural intensification: The evolution of maize production in northern Guinea savannah of Nigeria. *Economic Development and Cultural Change* 42: 537-54.

Sprague, G. F., and J. W. Dudley, eds. 1988. *Corn and corn improvement.* Madison, Wis.

Stoianovich, T. 1966. Le mais dans les Balkans. *Annales* 21: 1026-40.

Taba, S., ed. 1996. *Maize genetic resources.* Mexico.

Terris, M., ed. 1964. *Goldberger on pellagra.* Baton Rouge, La.

Timmer, C. P., ed. 1987. *The corn economy of Indonesia.* Ithaca, N.Y.

Vavilov, N. I. 1931. Mexico and Central America as the principal centre of origin of cultivated plants in the New World. *Bulletin of Applied Botany, Genetics, and Plant Breeding* 26: 135-99.

Walden, David B., ed. 1978. *Maize breeding and genetics.* New York.

Wallace, H. A., and E. N. Bressman. [1923] 1949. *Corn and corn growing.* Fifth revised edition. New York.

Wallace, H. A., and W. L. Brown. [1956] 1988. *Corn and its early fathers.* Revised edition. Ames, Iowa.

Watson, P. J. 1989. Early plant cultivation in the eastern woodlands of North America. In *Foraging and farming: The evolution of plant exploitation,* ed. D. R. Harris and G. C. Hillman, 555-71. London.

Weatherwax, P. 1954. *Indian corn in old America.* New York.

Wellhausen, E. J., L. M. Roberts, E. Hernandez X., and P. Mangelsdorf. 1952. *Races of maize in Mexico.* Cambridge, Mass.

Wilkes, G. 1989. Maize: Domestication, racial evolution, and spread. In *Foraging and farming: The evolution of plant exploitation,* ed. D. R. Harris and G. C. Hillman, 440-55. London.

Wilkes, G., and M. M. Goodman. 1996. Mystery and missing links: The origin of maize. In *Maize genetic resources,* ed. S. Taba, 106. Mexico, D.F.

Woodham-Smith, C. 1962. *The great hunger: Ireland 1845-9.* New York.

II.A.5 ❧ Millets

The caryopses of grasses have been harvested as human food since long before the advent of agriculture. Numerous species are still regularly harvested in Africa and Asia during times of scarcity. Among the many hundreds of species harvested as wild cereals, 33 species belonging to 20 genera were domesticated. Their cultivated cereals are dependent on humans for survival because they have lost the ability of natural seed dispersal and have become adapted to cultivated fields.

Cereals are grown on an estimated 730 million hectares and produce about 1,800 million metric tons of grain annually. Wheat, maize, and rice account for at least 80 percent of the annual world cereal production. Barley, sorghum, oats, rye, and pearl millet represent about 19 percent of cereal grains produced, and the remaining 1 percent of production comes from the other 19 grass species that are still grown as human food. These species are minor in terms of total world cereal production, but some are important components of agriculture in Africa and Asia (de Wet 1989).

Cereals that do not belong to the wheat (*Triticum*), barley *(Hordeum)*, oats *(Avena)*, maize *(Zea)*, or rice *(Oryza)* genera are commonly referred to as millets (de Wet 1989).

American Millets

The first cultivated cereal in the Americas appears to have been a species of *Setaria* (Callen 1965, 1967). Archaeological records indicate that this millet was an important source of food in the Valley of Mexico and in northeastern Mexico before the domestication of maize. E. O. Callen (1967) demonstrated a steady increase in size of caryopses of this millet over 1,500 years of use as a cereal. The species, however, never lost the ability of natural seed dispersal. It was displaced by maize as a cereal during the fifth millennium B.C., but later enjoyed a temporary resurgence in importance when it was probably harvested from weed populations that invaded maize fields.

The archaeological record indicates that another native cereal was cultivated in the southeastern United States before the introduction of maize about 3,000 years ago (Wills 1988). Maygrass (*Phalaris caroliniana* Walt.) was a common component of early agricultural settlements of the region (Chomko and Crawford 1978). It has been proposed that this species was planted by the inhabitants of these early settlements, as they were located well outside the natural range of maygrass (Cowan 1978). Morphological evidence of its domestication, however, is absent.

Two native grass species besides maize, mango (*Bromus mango* Desv.), and sauwi (*Panicum sonorum* Beal) were fully domesticated in the Americas by early farming communities. Mango is the only cereal known to have become extinct in historical times (Cruz 1972). Its cultivation was confined to central Chile. In 1782, it was recorded that the Aracanian Indians of that region grew "el Mango," a kind of rye, and "la Tuca," a kind of barley (Parodi and Hernandez 1964). Claudio Gay, who visited the province of Chiloe in 1837, collected specimens of this cereal that are currently on file at the herbarium of the Natural History Museum in Paris. He was probably the last botanist to see *B. mango* grown as a cereal inasmuch as it was replaced during the eighteenth century by wheat and barley introduced to the New World by European settlers.

Mango was grown as a biannual. In the past, farmers allowed animals to graze on mango fields during the first year and harvested it as a cereal at the end of the next summer (Gay 1865). It is surprising that a biannual species should have been domesticated. However, it may have been the only grass in the region that lent itself to domestication. J. Ball (1884) recorded that the people of northwestern Argentina and adjacent territories harvested a species of *Bromus* as a wild cereal.

Sauwi, another native American, was extensively grown along the flood plains of the Rio Grande until the late nineteenth century (Palmer 1871; Elsasser 1979). It was sown as soon as the water receded (Kelly 1977). Today sauwi is grown only by the Warihios of the southeastern Sonora and adjacent Chihuahua of Mexico (Nabhan and de Wet 1984).

The species *Panicum sonorum* occurs as part of the natural vegetation along the western escarpment of the Sierras from southern Arizona to Honduras. It is an aggressive colonizer and often occurs in large continuous populations. It is relished by grazing animals and harvested as a wild fodder by farmers in the Mexican states of Chihuahua and Sonora. Cultivated sauwi differs conspicuously from wild *P. sonorum* in having larger spikelets that tardily disarticulate from inflorescences at maturity. Sauwi was probably domesticated by farmers who also grew other crops. It is found in an archaeological context associated with beans and cucurbits (Kaemlein 1936). This cereal is a potentially promising fodder crop in semiarid regions of Africa and Asia.

Wild rice of North America (*Zizania aquatica* L.) is the only grass species domesticated as a cereal by present-day plant breeders. Early European explorers were impressed by the extensive use of this wild grass. In 1778, Jonathan Carver reported that wild rice was the most valuable of all the native wild food plants of the country (Carver 1778: 522–5). It had been harvested as a cereal from rivers and lakes in the northern states and adjacent Canada since long before recorded history (Coville and Coves 1894; Jenks 1900; Larsen 1939). Charred remains of wild rice caryopses found in threshing pits date from well before contact with Europeans (Ford and Brose 1975). Wild rice is now harvested from wild populations on a commercial scale, and it is also grown in paddies because such harvests cannot meet demand.

Wild rice was only domesticated very recently (de Wet and Oelke 1979). But the species does not readily lend itself to domestication: Caryopses rapidly lose viability after harvest if not stored underwater or in mud, and the species does not thrive in stagnant water. Therefore, domestication involved a combination of selection for spikelets that persisted on the panicle at maturity and the development of a cropping system that took advantage of natural adaptations of the species.

Wild rice is now successfully grown on a commercial scale. Paddies are constructed so that a minimum water depth of 15 centimeters (cm) can be maintained. These are flooded and seeded in early spring. Germination is rapid, and water level is maintained until the crop matures. Fields are drained, and the crop is mechanically harvested.

African Millets

The Near Eastern cereals, wheat and barley, have been cultivated in North Africa since at least the late fifth millennium B.C. (Clark 1976). However, these temperate cereals are poorly adapted for cultivation in the tropics south of the Sahara, where eight tropical African grass species were locally domesticated.

Sorghum (*Sorghum bicolor* [L.] Moench) is the most important native African cereal. It is grown on some 50 million hectares and produces up to 80 million metric tons of grain annually, primarily for human food or animal feed. Wild sorghum is widely distributed south of the Sahara in the Sudanian climatic zone, which receives 600 to 800 millimeters (mm) of annual rainfall and extends into the wetter Guinean zone. It became a cultivated cereal at least 5,000 years ago (Connah 1967: 25; de Wet 1978; Wendorf et al. 1992).

Pearl millet (*Pennisetum glaucum* [L.] R. Br.), also called bulrush millet, is the second most important native African cereal. It is cultivated across the arid and semiarid tropics of Africa and Asia where no other cereal consistently produces a harvest because of low annual rainfall and high soil temperatures. Pearl millet is grown on about 14 million hectares in Africa and 11 million hectares in India and Pakistan. In areas where annual rainfall exceeds 600 mm in the African and Indian tropics, pearl millet is usually replaced by sorghum as a dry land crop, and in locations where annual rainfall is over 1,200 mm, finger millet or maize becomes the cereal of choice.

The species *Penisetum glaucum* (pearl millet) is morphologically complex. O. Stapf and C. E. Hubbard (1934) recognized 13 cultivated, 15 weed, and 6 wild taxa of this complex species. W. D. Clayton (1972), by contrast, recognized 2 wild species, 2 weed taxa, and 1 cultivated complex. J. N. Brunken (1977), however, demonstrated that these taxa are conspecific. Wild taxa are often difficult to distinguish from weed taxa, which, in turn, grade morphologically into cultivated taxa. Agricultural weeds, known as shibras in West Africa, often resemble cultivated pearl millet, except for their natural seed dispersal. The involucres of cultivated pearl millet do not disarticulate at maturity. Shibras are common in the cultivated pearl millet zone of West Africa and the Sudan. They also occur in southern Angola and Namibia.

Wild pearl millet taxa occur extensively from coastal Senegal and Mauritania to northeastern Ethiopia in the Sahelo-Sudanian (350 to 600 mm annual rainfall) zone. They also extend into the Sudanian (600 to 800 mm) bioclimatic zone and are found along the foothills of mountains in the Central Sahara. Wild taxa are aggressive colonizers of disturbed habitats and are often weedy around villages.

Cultivated pearl millet is genetically and morphologically variable (Brunken 1977; Clement 1985; Marchais and Tostain 1985). Inflorescences range in shape from cylindrical to broadly elliptic and in length from 5 to 200 centimeters. Large inflorescences are commonly produced on plants with single culms, whereas small- to medium-sized inflorescences are produced on plants that tiller.

Four races of pearl millet were recognized by Brunken, J. M. J. de Wet, and J. R. Harlan (1977).

1. Race typhoides is grown across the range of pearl millet cultivation and is characterized by obovate caryopses that are obtuse and terete in cross section. Inflorescences are variable in length, but usually several times longer than wide, and more or less cylindrical in shape.
2. Race nigritarum differs from typhoides, primarily, in having obovate caryopses that are angular in cross section. It is the dominant pearl millet of the eastern Sahel from Sudan to Nigeria.
3. The principal pearl millet in the Sahel west of Nigeria is race globosum. It has large, globose caryopses, and commonly large, candle-shaped inflorescences.
4. Race leonis is the pearl millet common to Sierra Leone, Senegal, and Mauritania. It has oblanceolate caryopses with the apex acute.

Pearl millet could have been domesticated anywhere along the southern fringes of the Sahara (Harlan 1971). Botanical evidence indicates that the *Pennisetum violaceum* complex, as recognized by Clayton (1972), is the progenitor of domesticated pearl millet.

J. D. Clark (1976) suggested that cereal cultivation spread from the Near East to North Africa during the fifth millennium B.C. and subsequently became established across North Africa. With the onset of the present dry phase in North Africa, cultivation of these Mediterranean cereals was eventually confined to the coastal belt, and those farmers forced south by the expanding desert domesticated native grasses as cereals (Clark 1964).

Along the southern fringes of the expanding desert, the most abundant tropical grass species that invites domestication is *P. violaceum*. Its colonizing ability gives rise to large populations that facilitate its harvesting as a wild cereal. Indeed, P. J. Munson (1976) presented archaeological evidence of such harvesting along the southwestern fringes of the Sahara dating as far back as 3,000 years, and O. Davies (1968) reported archaeological remains of cultivated pearl millet in northern Ghana dated at about the same time. Cultivated pearl millet eventually reached India as a cereal some 2,500 years ago (Rao et al. 1963).

Wild pearl millet is a typical desert grass. It produces large numbers of caryopses that can withstand heat and drought and remain dormant in the soil until conditions become favorable for germination. Caryopses germinate rapidly after the first good rains of the season, and seedlings quickly extend roots into the subsurface soil layers. Plants tiller profusely, go dormant under heat or drought stress, and produce new tillers when conditions become favorable for growth and reproduction. The strategy for survival in such a harsh environment is opportunism with respect to moisture availability and tolerance with respect to high temperature.

Cultivated pearl millet retains these adaptations. It grows and develops rapidly under conditions of adequate soil moisture and elevated temperatures, and thus can take advantage of a short growing season, to survive short periods of severe drought, and to resume growth when water becomes available again. Comparisons among genotypes indicate that differences in time of flowering under stress are the major component of yield differences among cultivars (Bidinger, Mahalakshmi, and Rao 1987). This suggests that the high degree of variability in time to flower among landrace populations is the result of natural selection for early flowering and, thus, escape from drought in dry years, and farmer selection for late flowering plants with large inflorescences in wet years (de Wet, Peacock, and Bidinger 1991). These adaptations make pearl millet the dominant cereal in the Sahelo-Sudanian zone of Africa and in semiarid regions of Zambia, Zimbabwe, Namibia, Angola, northwestern India, and adjacent Pakistan.

Finger millet (*Eleusine coracana* [L.] Gaertn.) is another native African cereal that was introduced into India during the first millennium B.C. (Vishnu-Mittre 1968). Finger millet is cultivated in wetter and cooler seasonal rainfall zones of southern Africa on about 1 million hectares and is a major cereal in the Lake Victoria region, particularly in eastern Uganda. In India, finger millet is grown on about 3 million hectares from Uttar Pradesh to Bihar and south to Tamil Nadu and Karnataka, with the states of Andhra Pradesh, Karnataka, and Tamil Nadu the major producers of this cereal. This wide distribution of finger millet has led to considerable controversy over the place of its original domestication and the identity of its wild progenitor (Hilu and de Wet 1976).

Two wild species closely resemble finger millet in gross morphology: *Eleusine indica* [L.] Gaertn., which is widely distributed in both Africa and Asia; and *E. africana* Kennedy-O'Byrne, which is predominantly African. P. J. Greenway (1945) suggested that finger millet had an African origin and that its wild progenitor is *E. africana*. But J. Kennedy-O'Byrne (1957) proposed that *E. indica* gave rise to Indian cultivars and *E. africana* to African cultivars.

More recent cytogenetic and morphological evidence indicates that *E. africana* is the closest wild relative of finger millet. Finger millet is a tetraploid with $2n = 36$ chromosomes, as is *E. africana,* that crosses with the cereal to produce fertile hybrids. Derivatives of such crosses are obnoxious weeds of cultivation in eastern Africa. *Eleusine indica* is a diploid ($2n = 18$) and genetically isolated from the cereal.

In their work, K. W. Hilu and de Wet (1976) taxonomically recognized finger millet as *E. coracana,* subspecies *coracana,* and the wild and weedy African complex as *E. coracana,* subspecies *africana*. Wild finger millet is a common grass along the eastern and southern African highlands and is harvested during times of scarcity.

The antiquity of finger millet cultivation in eastern Africa is not known with certainty (Harlan, de Wet, and Stemler 1976). Impressions of wild, and possibly cultivated, finger millet spikelets occur on potsherds from Neolithic settlements at Kadero in Central Sudan that date back about 5,000 years (Klichowska 1984). Further archaeological evidence presented by Hilu, de Wet, and Harlan (1979) suggests that a highly evolved race of finger millet was grown at Axum, in Ethiopia, by the first century A.D. If these dates are correct, finger millet is the oldest known domesticated tropical African cereal.

This conclusion is not impossible. The concept of agriculture could have been introduced from West Asia into the Highlands of East Africa before the domestication of sorghum and pearl millet along the southern fringes of an expanding Sahara. The Near Eastern cultigens, wheat and barley, are adapted for cultivation on these highlands, and their introduction into eastern Africa could also have led to the domestication of native grasses as cereals.

Finger millet is variable in respect to inflorescence morphology, which is associated with selection and isolation of cultivars by farmers, rather than ecogeographical adaptation. Morphologically similar cultivars are widely grown, and African and Indian cultivars are often difficult to distinguish on the basis of morphology.

Five races of cultivated finger millet were recognized by de Wet and colleagues (1984b). Race coracana is grown across the range of finger millet cultivation in Africa and India. These cultivars resemble subspecies *africana* in having a well-developed central inflorescence branch. Inflorescence branches are 5 to 19 in number, essentially straight, and 6 to 11 cm long. In India, race coracana is often sown as a secondary crop in fields with pearl millet or sorghum.

The most common finger millets in both Africa and India belong to race vulgaris, which is also grown as a cereal in Indonesia. Inflorescence branches are straight, reflexed, or incurved, with all three types frequently occurring in the same field. In India, this race is often planted as a dry-season crop following the harvest of irrigated rice, and in the eastern hills it is often sown in nurseries and transplanted with the first rains of the season to assure an early harvest.

With incurved inflorescence branches, race compacta resembles vulgaris cultivars, but the inflorescences are larger and the lower inflorescence branches are always divided in compacta. These cultivars are commonly known as cockscomb finger millets. Indian cultivars have a branch located some distance below the 4 to 14 main inflorescence branches, but African cultivars usually lack this lower branch. The race is grown in northeastern India, Ethiopia, and Uganda.

Race plana is grown in Ethiopia, Uganda, and the western and eastern ghats of India. Spikelets are large and arranged in two moderately even rows along the rachis, giving young inflorescence branches a ribbon-like appearance. Florets are often so numerous that they almost surround the rachis at maturity.

Race elongata is morphologically the most distinct of the five races of finger millet. Inflorescence branches are long and reflexed at maturity. Cultivars grown in Malawi have inflorescence branches up to 24 cm long. More common are cultivars with inflorescence branches of 10 to 15 cm. Race elongata is grown on the East African highlands and the hills of eastern India.

At least 1 million hectares of finger millet are planted in Africa each year. It is the preferred cereal for brewing beer and is an important food crop in Uganda, Ethiopia, Malawi, Zambia, and Zimbabwe. In India, finger millet is extensively grown by tribal people on the eastern and western ghats and by commercial farmers in Andhra Pradesh and Tamil Nadu. The area under cultivation in India is close to 3 million hectares. H. Doggett (1989) indicates that land planted with finger millet in India increased by about 3 percent annually in the 1980s. Average yield per hectare also increased from 704 kilograms (kg) in the 1950s to over 1,000 kg in the 1990s as a result of breeding African germ plasm into Indian cultivars. In East Africa a breeding program is in progress to develop cytoplasmic-genetic male sterile populations, an effort which could facilitate the production of hybrid cultivars and contribute substantially to yield increases in both Africa and India.

Tef, *Eragrostis tef* (Zucc.) Trotter is an endemic and highly valued cereal of the Ethiopian Highlands (Costanza, de Wet, and Harlan 1979). The grain is used to make *injera,* an unleavened bread that is a staple in Ethiopia, and to brew beer. The wild ancestor of tef has not yet been positively identified, but *Eragrostis pilosa* (L.) P. Beauv., a common grass on the Ethopian highlands, is a strong possibility. T. Kotschy (1862) reported that the grains of this wild species were harvested as a food by the Sudanese while they waited for sorghum to mature. The antiquity of tef cultivation is also not known, but its popularity suggests domesti-

cation before the introduction of wheat and barley to East Africa from the Near East. W. Stiehler (1948) suggested that tef became widely distributed on the Ethiopian highlands only during the rise of the monarchy.

W. C. Harris (1844: 349) noted that 2 races of tef with brown grain and 2 with white grain were sold in Ethiopian markets. A. Trotter (1918) recognized 7 varieties of tef on the basis of spikelet and grain color.

Two species of *Digitaria* are endemic cultivated cereals of the Sahelo-Sudanian climatic zone of West Africa (Chevalier 1950; Porteres 1976). True fonio (*Digitaria exilis* [Kippist] Stapf) is grown from Senegal to Lake Chad, and black fonio (*D. iburua* Stapf) is grown on the Togo highlands and in Nigeria (de Wet 1977). The wild progenitors of these fonios are not known. In West Africa, *Digitaria barbinodis* Henrard, *D. ciliaris* Vanderyst, *D. longiflora,* and *D. ternata* (Hochst.) Stapf (Retz.) Persoon are aggressive wild colonizers and are harvested as cereals during times of scarcity.

Stapf (1915) pointed out morphological similarities between black fonio and *D. ternata,* and between fonio and *D. longiflora.* Fonio is a smaller grass than black fonio. It has 2 to 4 racemes per inflorescence, whereas black fonio has inflorescences with 4 to 10 racemes. Weedy races of fonio occur in Nigeria. Cultivated fonios differ from these weeds only in having lost their natural ability to disperse seeds efficiently.

R. Porteres (1976) recorded that fonio is harvested from some 721,000 acres annually, providing food to more than 3 million people during the most difficult months of the year. Fonios were already important in the fourteenth century when the traveler Ibn Batuta noted that they were extensively available in the markets between Outala in Mauritania and Bamako in Mali (Lewicki 1974: 37–8).

Little research has been done to improve the already impressive yield potential of fonios. Their adaptation to marginal agricultural land, tolerance to drought, and popularity as a food assure their survival as cereals in the arid Sahelian and Sudanian climatic zones of West Africa.

Animal fonio (*Brachiaria deflexa* [Schumach.] C. E. Hubb. ex Robynsis) is a weed that is commonly harvested as a wild cereal across the savanna of Africa. Farmers often encourage animal fonio to invade sorghum and maize fields, where it matures about two months before the major crop is harvested (de Wet 1977). It is sown as a cereal only on the West African Futa Jalon Highlands (Porteres 1951).

Grass weeds differ from their domesticated close relatives primarily in being spontaneous, rather than sown, and in retaining the ability of natural seed dispersal (Harlan, de Wet, and Price 1973). They do not require harvesting or sowing by humans to survive.

Avena abyssinica Hochst. is a weedy, semidomesticate of the Ethiopian highlands (Ladizinsky 1975). It is harvested, threshed, used, and sown with the wheat or barley that it accompanies as a weed. Such cultural practices lead to a loss of natural seed dispersal ability, and as the species is not consciously sown by humans, it has become an obligate weed in cultivated fields.

Indian Millets

Wheat, rice, sorghum, pearl millet, finger millet, foxtail millet, and maize are the most important cereals grown in India. Seven indigenous cereals, mostly grown on marginal agricultural land, were domesticated in India.

Raishan (*Digitaria cruciata* [Nees] A. Camus) and adlay (*Coix lacryma-jobi* L.) are native in the wet tropics of northeastern India. Raishan is grown by the Khasi people of Assam in India and by hill tribes in Vietnam. H. B. Singh and R. K. Arora (1972) reported that this cereal is grown in Assam as a secondary crop in maize or vegetable fields. It is sown in April or May and harvested in September and October. Plants tiller profusely, and culms of individual plants are tied together at time of flowering to facilitate harvesting. Mature inflorescences are rubbed by hand to collect the grains. Dehusked grains are boiled as rice or ground into flour. Raishan is also an important fodder crop in Assam, and it could become a similarly significant fodder in other tropical regions of the world.

Adlay is grown under shifting cultivation from Assam to the Philippines (Arora 1977). It was probably domesticated in tropical eastern India and introduced into Southeast Asia, but it is also possible that adlay was independently domesticated as a cereal in both India and the Philippines. The greatest diversity of cultivated adlay occurs in the Philippines (Wester 1920).

The fruit cases of wild adlay (Job's tears) are used as beads. Fertile female spikelets of all wild *Coix* species are individually enclosed by an involucre that is indurated, glossy, and colored white, gray, or black. The involucres of cultivated adlay are papery, allowing for easy removal of the caryopses from the fruit cases. Adlay grains are cooked as rice or ground into flour to be used in baking bread. Adlay is often grown on banks between rice paddies.

The other five indigenous Indian cereals were probably domesticated in semiarid India where they still form an important part of dryland agriculture.

Sama (*Panicum sumatrense* [Roth.] ex Roem. et Schult.) is grown in India, Nepal, Sikkim, and western Myanmar (de Wet, Prasada Rao, and Brink 1984a). It is an important cereal in the eastern ghats of Andhra Pradesh and adjacent Orissa. Sama is tolerant to drought and produces a crop even in the poorest agricultural soil. It is commonly sown as a mixture with foxtail millet in sorghum or pearl millet fields, where it matures and is harvested first, followed by foxtail millet and sorghum or pearl millet. Mixed planting provides a supply of cereals starting about two

months after planting to the end of the rainy season. A robust race is sometimes planted as a single crop and is an important cereal in the hills of eastern India.

Primitive cultivars of sama resemble the widely distributed *Panicum psilopodium* Trin., except for their persistent spikelets. This wild species crosses naturally with sama to produce fertile hybrids. Derivatives of such hybrids occur as weeds in and around cultivated fields.

Sama has been grown as a cereal in India for at least 4,500 years. S. A. Weber (1991: 107–8) pointed out that carbonized grains of sama are common at the early Harappan agricultural site of Rodji.

Sawa (*Echinochloa colona* [L.] Link) is grown in India, Nepal, and Sikkim (de Wet et al. 1983a). Cultivated kinds of sawa are also known taxonomically as *E. utilis* Ohwi et Yabuno. It is morphologically allied to Japanese millet (*Echinochloa cruss-galli* [L.] P. Beauv.), but sawa is tropical rather than temperate in its distribution. Furthermore, these tropical and temperate domesticated species are genetically isolated from one another (Yabuno 1966). Sawa was probably domesticated in India, whereas Japanese millet seems to have originated in northwestern China. Some Indian cultivars of sawa differ from weedy *E. colona* only in having spikelets that disarticulate tardily rather than readily at maturity, as is common in wild grasses. These weedy sawas frequently occur with cultivated races in the same field, and sawa could have been domesticated originally by an accidental harvest of weed sawas in fields where other cereals were planted.

Four races of sawa are recognized. Races have little geographic distinctiveness but are recognized and maintained by farmers. Race stolonifera resembles wild *E. colona,* except for persistence of spikelets in the cereal and disarticulation of spikelets at maturity in the weed. Race robusta has large inflorescences and is widely grown. It crosses with stolonifera. Derivatives of such hybridization gave rise to the stoloniferous race intermedia. The most distinct race is laxa. It is grown in Sikkim and is characterized by long and slender racemes.

In Africa, *Echinochloa colona* is also an aggressive colonizer of cultivated fields. D. M. Dixon (1969) identified grains of *E. colona* among plant remains from intestines of mummies excavated at Naga ed-Dar in Egypt. The species was probably harvested as a wild cereal in ancient Egypt along the flood plain of the Nile, a practice that remains common today in times of scarcity.

Kodo (*Paspalum scrobiculatum* L.) is an important cereal in Kerala and Tamil Nadu and a minor cereal in India north to Rajasthan, Uttar Pradesh, Bihar, and West Bengal. The species occurs wild across the Old World tropics (Clayton and Renvoize 1982). It is an aggressive colonizer of disturbed habitats and lends itself to domestication. Wild kodo is a perennial, whereas the cultivated cereal is grown as an annual.

Some cultivars of kodo millet root at lower nodes of their decumbent culms to produce new flowering culms after the first harvest. Kodo occurs in the agricultural record of India starting 3,000 years ago (Kajale 1977; Vishnu-Mittre 1977). Little racial evolution has occurred in Kodo millet.

The commonly grown kodo millet resembles spontaneous kinds in having racemes with spikelets arranged in two regular rows on one side of a flattened rachis. Two types of inflorescence aberrations occur occasionally in fields of kodo. In one variant, spikelets are arranged along the rachis in two to four irregular rows, rather than two regular rows. In the other variant, the spikelets are arranged in several irregular rows at the lower part of racemes and become two regular rows near the tip of the racemes. These aberrant plants are more robust and have fewer and better synchronized tillers than common kodo millet. Introgression with weed kodo makes it impossible for farmers to maintain these high-yielding genotypes, although they are carefully selected to provide seed for the next season (de Wet et al. 1983b). Farmers in southern India correctly believe that Kodo millet grains can be poisonous after a rain. The reason for this toxicity is ergot infection.

Korali (*Setaria pumila* [Poir.] Roem. et Schult.) and peda sama (*Brachiaria ramosa* [L.] Stapf) are domesticated Indian weeds that are widely distributed in tropical Africa and Asia. They are often harvested as wild cereals in times of scarcity and are cultivated only by the hill tribes of southern India. Wild and cultivated kinds of both korali and peda sama cross to produce aggressive colonizer populations. Farmers tend to keep the domesticated kinds pure through seed selection.

Eurasian Millets

Four millets – crab grass (*Digitaria sanguinalis* [L.] Scopoli), proso millet (*Panicum milliaceum* L.), foxtail millet (*Setaria italica* [L.] P. Beauv.), and Japanese millet (*Echinochloa crus-galli* [L.] P. Beauv.) – are widely distributed across temperate Europe and Asia.

Crab grass (*D. sanguinalis*) is a cosmopolitan weed. It became semidomesticated in southeastern Europe after having been harvested for millennia. Crab grass never completely lost the ability of natural seed dispersal because it was commonly harvested by swinging a basket to collect the mature grains. The species is an aggressive natural colonizer of disturbed habitats, including cultivated fields. It was a popular cereal in southern Europe during Roman times (Körnicke 1885: 279–84) and was still widely grown as mana or bluthirse in southeastern Europe during the first quarter of the nineteenth century. Crab grass was probably independently domesticated in several parts of its range. It is currently grown as a minor cereal in the Caucasus of Russia and in Kashmir.

Japanese millet (*Echinochloa crus-galli*) is a grass of temperate Eurasia. The barnyard grass found in the American Midwest is an introduced weed race of *E. crus-galli*. *Echinochloa oryzoides* (Ard.) Fritsch, the common weed of rice cultivation, is also distantly related to *E. crus-galli*. Japanese millet is grown as a cereal in China, Korea, and Japan. Cultivated kinds are sometimes, incorrectly, classified as *E. frumentacea* (Roxb.) Link. Little is known about the antiquity of this cereal. H. Helmqvist (1969) suggested that the species was grown in Sweden during the Bronze Age when the climate was milder than it is today. It is no longer grown as a cereal anywhere in Europe.

The genus *Panicum* is widely distributed throughout the warmer parts of the world and is of considerable economic importance. Several species are grown as fodder, others are harvested as wild cereals in times of scarcity, and still others are obnoxious weeds. Proso millet (*Panicum miliaceum*) was once widely cultivated in temperate Europe and Asia but has largely been replaced as a cereal by wheat.

The closest wild relative of proso millet, *Panicum miliaceum* var. *ruderale* Kitagawa is native to central China (Kitagawa 1937). In morphology, it resembles weed races of proso millet that occur across temperate Eurasia but is a less aggressive colonizer than the weed. These weeds represent derivatives of cultivated proso millet that regained the ability of natural seed dispersal through mutation (Scholz 1983).

Proso millet has been grown in central China for at least 5,000 years (Cheng 1973), and it is still grown on about 1.5 million hectares in China. It is also an important cereal in Mongolia, Korea, and northern India. A cultivar of proso millet with glutinous endosperm is favored in China, where its flour is used to make bread. Nonglutinous cultivars are grown in Mongolia and India, and the grains are cooked as rice.

Proso millet has been grown in southern Europe for at least 3,000 years (Neuweiler 1946). It became widely distributed as a cereal in Europe during the Bronze Age. Its popularity declined during the twentieth century, and proso millet is now grown in Europe primarily as a feed for caged birds. It is extensively variable. Five cultivated races are recognized. They are artifacts of selection by farmers and have no ecogeographic validity.

Race miliaceum resembles wild var. *ruderale* in having numerous decumbent culms, each with several racemes. Its inflorescences are large, with spreading branches that commonly lack spikelets at the base. This is the basic race from which the other races were selected under cultivation. It is grown across the range of proso millet cultivation.

Race patentissimum resembles miliaceum in its lax panicles with spreading branches having a sterile zone at the base. Inflorescences, however, become curved at maturity because of the weight of the spikelets. Patentissimum is the common proso millet in India, Bangladesh, Pakistan, and Afghanistan. It is also grown in Turkey, Hungary, Russia, and China. Race patentissimum probably reached India from central Asia during historical times.

Races contractum, compactum, and ovatum are often difficult to distinguish from one another. They represent the highest evolved cultivars of proso millet. Inflorescences are more or less elliptic in shape. Spikelets are crowded along the panicle branches in compactum and ovatum. These branches are erect when young and become curved at maturity. Ovatum cultivars usually have smaller inflorescences than race compactum and are grown in Russia, Turkey, and Afghanistan. Compactum cultivars are grown in Japan, Russia, Iran, and Iraq. In race contractum the lower part of panicle branches are free of spikelets. Race contractum is grown in Europe, Transcaucasian Russia, and China.

Foxtail millet, *Setaria italica*, is grown as a cereal in southern Europe, in temperate Asia, and in tropical India. Its closest wild relative is the cosmopolitan weed, green foxtail (*S. italica viridis* [L.] Thell.). The latter is primarily an urban weed, but as a robust race it is also an obnoxious weed of agriculture (Pohl 1966). This giant green foxtail is derived from introgression between cultivated and wild races.

The antiquity of foxtail millet as a cereal is uncertain. The species could have been domesticated across its range of natural distribution from Europe to Japan (de Wet, Oestry-Stidd, and Cubero 1979). It has been grown as a cereal in China for at least 5,000 years (Cheng 1973) and in Europe for at least 3,000 years (Neuweiler 1946). Foxtail millet was an important cereal during the Yang-shao culture phase in China. Evidence of foxtail millet in storage jars, and the association of farming implements with the Yang-shao culture, suggest that the cereal was cultivated rather than harvested from wild populations (Ho 1975). In Europe foxtail millet commonly occurs in early farming sites in Austria and Switzerland (Neuweiler 1946).

Cultivated foxtail millets are commonly divided into two cultivated complexes. The Chinese-Korean complex with large, pendulous inflorescences is recognized as race maxima, and the European complex with smaller and more erect cultivars is called race moharia (Dekaprelevich and Kasparian 1928). An Indian complex, race indica, was identified by K. E. Prasada Rao and colleagues (1987). The Indian race was derived from moharia through selection for adaptation to the tropics. It is an important cereal among hill tribes of southern India, where it is frequently grown as a mixed crop with sorghum or pearl millet.

F. Körnicke (1885: 238-44) recorded that canary grass (*Phalaris canariensis* L.) was grown as a cereal in southern Europe until the nineteenth century. Flour produced from its grain was mixed with wheat flour for making bread. It is still grown as a feed for birds but no longer used as a human food (Febrel and Carballido 1965). Nothing is known about the antiq-

uity of canary grass as a cereal, and it is probably of recent domestication.

J. M. J. de Wet

Bibliography

Arora, R. K. 1977. Job's tears *(Coix lacryma-jobi)* – a minor food and fodder crop of northeastern India. *Economic Botany* 31: 358-66.
Ball, J. 1884. Contributions to the flora of North Patagonia and the adjacent territory. *Journal of the Linnean Society of Botany, London* 21: 203-40.
Bidinger, F. R., V. Mahalakshmi, and G. D. P. Rao. 1987. Assessment of drought resistance in pearl millet (*Pennisetum Americanum* [L.] Leeke). I. Factors affecting yields under stress. *Australian Journal of Agricultural Research* 38: 37-48.
Brunken, J. N. 1977. A systematic study of *Pennisetum* sect. *Pennisetum* (Gramineae). *American Journal of Botany* 64: 161-7.
Brunken, J. N., J. M. J de Wet, and J. R. Harlan. 1977. The morphology and domestication of pearl millet. *Economic Botany* 31: 163-74.
Callen, E. O. 1965. Food habits of some pre-Columbian Mexican Indians. *Economic Botany* 19: 335-43.
  1967. The first New World cereal. *American Antiquity* 32: 535-8.
Carver, Jonathan. 1778. *Travels through interior parts of North America in the years 1766, 1767 and 1768.* London.
Cheng, Te-Kun. 1973. The beginning of Chinese civilization. *Antiquity* 47: 197-209.
Chevalier, A. 1950. Sur l'origine des *Digitaria* cultives. *Revue International Botanique Appliqué d'Agriculture Tropical* 12: 669-919.
Chomko, S. A., and G. W. Crawford. 1978. Plant husbandry in prehistoric eastern North America: New evidence for its development. *American Antiquity* 43: 405-8.
Clark, J. D. 1964. The prehistoric origins of African culture. *Journal of African History* 5: 161-83.
  1976. Prehistoric populations and pressures favoring plant domestication in Africa. In *Origins of African plant domestication,* ed. J. R. Harlan, J. M. J. de Wet, and A. B. L. Stemler, 67-105. The Hague.
  1984. The domestication process in northeastern Africa: Ecological change and adaptive strategies. In *Origin and early development of food-producing cultures in north-eastern Africa,* ed. L. Krzyzaniak and M. Kobusiewicz, 27-41. Poznan, Poland.
Clayton, W. D. 1972. Gramineae. In *Flora of tropical Africa,* Vol. 3, part 2, ed. F. N. Hepper, 459-69. London.
Clayton, W. D., and S. A. Renvoize. 1982. Gramineae. In *Flora of tropical East Africa,* part 3, ed. R. M. Polhill, 607-12. Rotterdam.
Clement, J. C. 1985. *Les mils pénicillaires de L'Afrique de L'Ouest.* [International Board for Plant Genetic Resources (IBPGR) and Institute Français de Recherche Scientifique pour le Développement en Coopération (ORSTOM),] 1-231. Rome.
Connah, G. 1967. Progress report on archaeological work in Bornu 1964-1966 with particular reference to the excavations at Daima mound. *Northern History Research Scheme, 2nd. Interim Report.* Zaria, Nigeria.

Costanza, S. H., J. M. J. de Wet, and J. R. Harlan. 1979. Literature review and numerical taxonomy of *Eragrostis tef* (t'ef). *Economic Botany* 33: 413-14.

Coville, F. V., and E. Coves. 1894. The wild rice of Minnesota. *Botanical Gazette* 19: 504-6.

Cowan, C. W. 1978. The prehistoric use and distribution of maygrass in eastern North America: Culture and phytogeographical implications. In *The nature and status of ethnobotany*, ed. R. I. Ford, 263-88. Ann Arbor, Mich.

Cruz, A. W. 1972. *Bromus mango*, a disappearing plant. *Indesia* 2: 127-31.

Davies, O. 1968. The origins of agriculture in West Africa. *Current Anthropology* 9: 479-82.

Dekaprelevich, L. L., and A. S. Kasparian. 1928. A contribution to the study of foxtail millet (*Setaria italica* P.B. *maxima* Alf.) cultivated in Georgia (western Transcaucasia). *Bulletin of Applied Botany and Plant Breeding* 19: 533-72.

de Wet, J. M. J. 1977. Domestication of African cereals. *African Economic History* 3: 15-32.

1978. Systematics and evolution of *Sorghum* sect. *Sorghum* (Gramineae). *American Journal of Botany* 65: 477-84.

1981. Species concepts and systematics of domesticated cereals. *Kulturpflanzen* 29: 177-98.

1989. Origin, evolution and systematics of minor cereals. In *Small millets in global agriculture*, ed. A. Seetharama, K. W. Riley, and G. Harinarayana, 19-30. Oxford and New Delhi.

de Wet, J. M. J., and E. A. Oelke. 1979. Domestication of American wild rice (*Zizania aquatica* L., Gramineae). *Journal d'Agriculture Traditionel et Botanique Appliqué.* 30: 159-68.

de Wet, J. M. J., L. L. Oestry-Stidd, and J. I. Cubero. 1979. Origins and evolution of foxtail millets. *Journal d'Agriculture Traditionel et Botanique Appliqué* 26: 159-63.

de Wet, J. M. J., J. M. Peacock, and F. R. Bidinger. 1991. Adaptation of pearl millet to arid lands. In *Desertified grasslands: Their biology and management*, ed. G. F. Chapman, 259-67. London.

de Wet, J. M. J., K. E. Prasada Rao, and D. E. Brink. 1984a. Systematics and domestication of *Panicum sumatrense* (Gramineae). *Journal d'Agriculture Traditionel et Botanique Appliqué* 30: 159-68.

de Wet, J. M. J., K. E. Prasada Rao, D. E. Brink, and M. H. Mengesha. 1984b. Systematics and evolution of *Eleusine coracana* (Gramineae). *American Journal of Botany* 71: 550-7.

de Wet, J. M. J., K. E. Prasada Rao, M. H. Mengesha, and D. E. Brink. 1983a. Domestication of sawa millet (*Echinochloa colona*). *Economic Botany* 37: 283-91.

1983b. Diversity in Kodo millet, *Paspalum scrobiculatum*. *Economic Botany* 37: 159-63.

Dixon, D. M. 1969. A note on cereals in ancient Egypt. In *The domestication and exploitation of plants and animals*, ed. J. P. Ucko and C. W. Dimbleby, 131-42. Chicago.

Doggett, H. 1989. Small millets - a selective overview. In *Small millets in global agriculture*, ed. E. Seetharama, K. W. Riley, and G. Harinarayana, 3-17. Oxford and New Delhi.

Elsasser, A. B. 1979. Explorations of Hernando Alcaron in the lower Colorado River, 1540. *Journal of California Great Basin Anthropology* 1: 8-39.

Febrel, J., and A. Carballido. 1965. Estudio bromatológio del alpiste. *Estudio Bromatológio* 17: 345-60.

Ford, R. I., and D. S. Brose. 1975. Prehistoric wild rice from Dunn farm site, Leelanau Country, Michigan. *The Wisconsin Archaeologist* 56: 9-15.

Gay, C. 1865. *Historia física y política de Chile*, Vol.6. Reprinted in *Agricultura Chilena*, Vol. 2, 1973. Santiago.

Greenway, P. J. 1945. Origin of some East African food plants. *East African Agricultural Journal* 10: 177-80.

Harlan, J. R. 1971. Agricultural origins: Centers and non-centers. *Science* 174: 463-74.

Harlan, J. R., J. M. J. de Wet, and E. G. Price. 1973. Comparative evolution of cereals. *Evolution* 27: 311-25.

Harlan, J. R., J. M. J. de Wet, and A. B. L. Stemler. 1976. Plant domestication and indigenous African agriculture. In *Origins of African plant domestication*, ed. J. R. Harlan, J. M. J. de Wet, and A. B. L. Stemler, 3-19. The Hague.

Harris, W. C. 1844. *The highlands of Aethiopia*. New York.

Helmqvist, H. 1969. Dinkel und Hirse aus der Bronzezeit Südschwedens nebst einigen Bemerkungen über ihre spätere Geschichte in Sweden. *Botanische Notizen* 122: 260-70.

Hilu, K. W., and J. M. J. de Wet. 1976. Domestication of *Eleusine coracana*. *Economic Botany* 306: 199-208.

Hilu, K. W., J. M. J. de Wet, and J. R. Harlan. 1979. Archaeobotanical studies of *Eleusine coracana* ssp. *coracana* (finger millet). *American Journal of Botany* 66: 330-3.

Ho, Ping-Ti. 1975. *The cradle of the east*. Chicago.

Jenks, A. E. 1900. The wild rice gatherers of the upper lakes. *Annual Report of the American Bureau of Ethnology 1989*, part 2, 19: 1013-137.

Kaemlein, W. 1936. A prehistoric twined-woven bag from the Trigo Mountains, Arizona. *Kiva* 28: 1-13.

Kajale, M. P. 1977. Ancient grains from excavations at Nevassa, Maharashtra. *Geophytologia* 7: 98-106.

Kelly, W. H. 1977. Cocopa ethnography. *Anthropological Papers of the University of Arizona* 29: 1-150.

Kennedy-O'Byrne, J. 1957. Notes on African grasses. 24. A new species of *Eleusine* from tropical and South Africa. *Kew Bulletin* 11: 65-72.

Kitagawa, M. 1937. Contributio ad cognitionem Florae Manchuricae. *Botanical Magazine of Tokyo* 51: 150-7.

Klichowska, M. 1984. Plants of the Neolithic Kadero (central Sudan): A palaeobotanical study of the plant impressions on pottery. In *Origins and early development of food-producing cultures in north-eastern Africa*, ed. L. Krzyniak and M. Kobusiewics, 321-6. Poznan, Poland.

Körnicke, F. 1885. Die Arten und Varietäten des Getreides. In *Handbuch des Getreidebaues*, ed. F. Körnicke, and H. Werner, Vol. 1. Berlin.

Kotschy, T. 1862. Reise von Chartum nach Kordafan, 1839. *Petermann's geographische Mittheilungen Ergänzungsheft* 7: 3-17.

Ladizinsky, G. 1975. Oats in Ethiopia. *Economic Botany* 29: 238-41.

Larsen, E. L. 1939. Peter Kalm's short account of the natural use and care of some plants, of which the seeds were recently brought home from North America to the service of those who take pleasure in experimenting with the cultivation of the same in our climate. *Agricultural History* 13 (34): 43-4.

Lewicki, T. 1974. *West African food in the Middle Ages*. London.

Marchais, L., and S. Tostain. 1985. Genetic divergence between wild and cultivated pearl millets (*Pennisetum typhoides*). II. Characters of domestication. *Zeitschrift für Pflanzenzüchtung* 95: 245-61.

Munson, P. J. 1976. Archaeological data on the origins of cultivation in the southwestern Sahara and their implications for West Africa. In *Origins of African plant domestication,* ed. J. R. Harlan, J. M. J. de Wet, and A. B. L. Stemler, 187–209. The Hague.

Nabhan, G., and J. M. J. de Wet. 1984. *Panicum sonorum* in the Sonoran desert agriculture. *Economic Botany* 38: 65–82.

Neuweiler, E. 1946. Nachträge urgeschichtlicher Pflanzen. *Vierteljährliche Naturforschungsgesellschaft Zürich* 91: 122–236.

Palmer, E. 1871. Food products of North American Indians. *United States of America Commerce and Agricultural Report* 1870: 404–28.

Parodi, L. R., and J. C. Hernandez. 1964. El mango, cereal extinguido en cultivo, sobre en estado salvage. *Ciéncia e Invéstia:* 20: 543–9.

Phillips, S. M. 1972. A survey of the genus *Eleusine* Gaertn. (Gramineae) in Africa. *Kew Bulletin* 27: 251–70.

Pohl, R. W. 1966. The grasses of Iowa. *Iowa State Journal of Science* 40: 341–73.

Porteres, R. 1951. Une céréale mineure cultivée dans l'Ouest-Afrique (*Brachiaria deflexa* C.E. Hubbard var. *sativa* var. nov.). *L'Agronomique Tropicale* 6: 38–42.

　　1976. African cereals: Eleusine, fonios, black fonio, teff, brachiaria, paspalum, pennisetum and African rice. In *African plant domestication,* ed. J. R. Harlan, J. M. J. de Wet, and A. B. L. Stemler, 409–52. The Hague.

Prasada Rao, K. E., J. M. J. de Wet, D. E. Brink, and M. H. Mengesha. 1987. Infraspecific variation and systematics of cultivated *Setaria italica,* foxtail millet (Poaceae). *Economic Botany* 41: 108–16.

Rao, S. R., B. B. Lal, B. Nath, et al. 1963. Excavations at Rangpur and other explorations in Gujarat. *Bulletin of the Archaeological Survey of India* 18–19: 5–207.

Scholz, H. 1983. Die Unkraut-Hirse *(Panicum miliaceum* subsp. *ruderale)* – neue Tatsachen und Befunde. *Plant Systematics and Evolution* 143: 233–44.

Singh, H. B., and R. K. Arora. 1972. Raishan (*Digitaria* sp.) – a minor millet of the Khasi Hills, India. *Economic Botany* 26: 376–90.

Stapf, O. 1915. Iburu and fundi, two cereals of Upper Guinea. *Kew Bulletin* 1915: 381–6.

Stapf, O., and C. E. Hubbard. 1934. *Pennisetum.* In *Flora of tropical Africa,* Vol. 9, ed. D. Prain, 954–1070. London.

Stiehler, W. 1948. Studien zur Landwirtschafts und Siedlungsgeographie Äthiopiens. *Erdkunde* 2: 257–82.

Trotter, A. 1918. La *Poa tef* Zuccagni e l'*Eragrostis abyssinica* (Jacq.) Link. *Bolletino della Società Botanica Italiana* 4: 61–2.

Vishnu-Mittre. 1968. Prehistoric records of agriculture in India. *Transactions of the Bose Research Institute* 31: 87–106.

　　1977. Changing economy in ancient India. In *Origins of agriculture,* ed. C. A. Reed, 569–88. The Hague.

Weber, S. A. 1991. *Plants and Harappan subsistence.* Delhi.

Wendorf, F., A. E. Close, R. Schild, et al. 1992. Saharan exploitation of plants 8000 B.P. *Nature* 359: 721–4.

Wester, P. S. 1920. Notes on adlay. *Philippine Agricultural Review* 13: 217–22.

Wills, W. H. 1988. Early agriculture and sedentism in the American Southwest and interpretations. *Journal of World History* 2: 445–88.

Yabuno, T. 1966. Biosystematics of the genus *Echinochloa* (Gramineae). *Japanese Journal of Botany* 19: 277–323.

II.A.6 ❧ Oat

Oat (*Avena* L.) includes 29 to 31 species (depending on the classification scheme) of wild and domesticated annual grasses in the family Gramineae (Poaceae) that comprise a polyploid series, with diploid, hexaploid, and tetraploid forms (Baum 1977; Leggett 1992). The primary cultivated species are hexaploids, *A. sativa* L. and *A. byzantina* C. Koch, although 5 other species have to some extent been cultivated for human consumption. These are the tetraploid *A. abyssinica* Hochst and the diploids *A. strigosa* Schreb., *A. brevis* Roth., *A. hispanica* Ard., and *A. nuda* L. Nevertheless, oat consumed in human diets this century has been almost exclusively hexaploids.

The separation of the two cultivated hexaploids is based on minor, and not always definitive, morphological differences and is of more historical than contemporary relevance. *A. byzantina* (red oat) was the original germ plasm base of most North American fall-sown cultivars, whereas *A. sativa* was the germ plasm base of spring-sown cultivars. Late twentieth-century breeding populations in both ecogeographic regions contain intercrosses of both species. This has led to the almost exclusive use of the term *A. sativa* in describing new cultivar releases.

Oat

Oat is the fifth most economically important cereal in world production after wheat, rice, corn, and barley. It is cultivated in temperate regions worldwide, especially those of North America and Europe, where it is well adapted to climatic conditions of adequate rainfall, relatively cool temperatures, and long days (Sorrells and Simmons 1992).

Oat is used primarily for animal feed, although human consumption has increased in recent years. Human food use is estimated at 16 percent of total world production and, among cereals as foods, oat ranks fourth after wheat, rice, and corn (Burnette et al. 1992). Oat is valued as a nutritious grain; it has a high-quality protein and a high concentration of soluble fiber, and is a good source of minerals, essential fatty acids, B vitamins, and vitamin E (Peterson 1992). Humans generally consume oats as whole-grain foods, which include ready-to-eat breakfast foods, oatmeal, baked goods, infant foods, and granola-type snack bars (Burnette et al. 1992). For human food, the inedible hull (lemma and palea) must be removed, leaving the groat for further processing. A hull-less trait, governed by two or three genes, causes the caryopsis or groat to thresh free of the lemma and palea, as does the wheat caryopsis. There is a renewed interest in hull-less oat in Europe and the Americas, especially for feed use. Several modern hull-less cultivars are available.

Origin and Domestication

The history of oat domestication parallels that of barley (*Hordeum vulgare* L.) and wheat (*Triticum* spp.), the primary domesticated cereals of the Middle East. The primacy of wheat and barley in the Neolithic revolution was due to advantages that their progenitor species had over other local candidates, such as *A. sterilis* L. and *A. longiglumis* Dur.: local abundance, large seed weight and volume, absence of germination inhibitors, and lower ploidy levels (Bar-Yosef and Kislev 1989). In the archaeological record, wild oat appears as weedy admixtures in cultivated cereals prior to, and for several millennia following, the Neolithic revolution. Nondomesticated *Avena* spp. have been identified in archaeological deposits in Greece, Israel, Jordan, Syria, Turkey, and Iran, all dating from between about 10500 and 5000 B.C. (Hopf 1969; Renfrew 1969; Hansen and Renfrew 1978; Hillman, Colledge, and Harris 1989).

Wheat and barley remained predominant as cereal cultivation spread through Europe between the seventh and second millennium B.C. (Zohary and Hopf 1988). The precise time and location of the domestication of oat from the weedy component of these cereals is unknown, but it is believed that oat had an adaptive advantage (over the wheat and barley germ plasm in cultivation at that time) in the cloudier, wetter, and cooler environments of northern Europe.

Support for this theory is provided by Pliny (A.D. 23–79), who noted the aggressive nature of weed oat in cereal mixtures in moist environments (Rackham 1950). Z. V. Yanushevich (1989) reported finding *Avena* spp. in Moldavian and Ukrainian adobe imprints dated as early as 4700 B.C. It is not known if these were cultivated types. However, Z. Tempir, M. Villaret-von Rochow (1971), and U. Willerding (Tempir and the latter are cited in Zohary and Hopf 1988), working in central Europe, found evidence of domesticated oat dating from the second and first millennia B.C. That evidence (which is often a reflection of one of the first steps in the domestication of oat and other cereals) is the elimination of the seed dispersal mechanism. In domesticated oat, the spikelets remain intact on the plant long after ripeness, whereas in the wild species, spikelets abscise and fall from the plant soon after maturity (Ladizinsky 1988).

In China, oat has been cultivated since early in the first millennium A.D. It remains a staple food in north China and Mongolia (Baum 1977), and the hull-less or "naked" oat has been associated with the Chinese production. But despite the cultivation of oat elsewhere, the grain was of minor interest to the Greeks, who considered it a weed; moreover, Egyptian foods are not known to have contained oat and, unlike so many other foods, there is no reference to it in the Bible (Candolle 1886; Darby, Ghalioungui, and Grivetti 1977; Zohary 1982).

During the first century A.D., however, Roman writers began making references to oat (White 1970). Pliny described a fall-sown, nonshattering "Greek-oat" used in forage production and noted that oatmeal porridge was a human staple in Germany. Dioscorides described the medicinal qualities of oat and reported it to be a natural food for horses (Font Quer 1962). Analyses of the gut contents of a mummified body from the same era (recovered from an English bog) revealed that small quantities of *Avena* species, together with wheat and barley, were consumed in the final meal (Holden 1986).

J. R. Harlan (1977) believed that oat domestication occurred separately at each ploidy level, with the diploids domesticated primarily as fodder crops in the Mediterranean area and subsequently widely cultivated throughout northern and eastern Europe, particularly on poor, upland soils. The tetraploid *A. abyssinica,* found exclusively in the highlands of Ethiopia, is an intermediate form between a truly wild and a fully domesticated type. It is a tolerated admixture in cereal production because of the belief that it improves the quality of malt (Harlan 1989). There is, however, disagreement among researchers as to the hexaploid progenitor of cultivated hexaploid oat. Three species – *A. sterilis* L. (Coffman 1946; Baum 1977), *A. hybrida* Petrem. (Baum 1977), and *A. fatua* L. (Ladizinsky 1988) – have been suggested. *A. maroccana* Gdgr. and *A. murphyi* Ladiz. are believed to represent the tetraploid base for cultivated hexaploids (Ladizinsky 1969). These two species have a narrow geographic distribution, confined as they are to southern Spain and Morocco.

From the Roman Era to the Nineteenth Century

Since the Roman era, oat has maintained its dual role as food and feed. In overall European production it has ranked behind wheat, barley, and, in some areas, rye (*Secale cereale* L.). Its prominence in the human diet continued to be greater in northern Europe than in other regions.

During the Middle Ages in northern Europe, a typical three-year crop rotation was fallow followed by wheat followed by oat or barley (Symon 1959). P. D. A. Harvey (1965) provided detailed records from one English village; these most likely reflected usual thirteenth-century production practices. Wheat was planted on half of the total cereal hectarage, with oat planted on one-half to three-quarters of the remaining land. The yield of the oat crop was about five seeds per seed planted, very low by today's standards. Wheat was the cash crop, whereas the oat crop was employed on the farms for feeding horses and cattle; in addition, oat straw was likely an important animal bedding. Lastly, another significant hectarage was planted with barley and oat together, and a small quantity of this mixed crop was used to produce malt. It is interesting to note that Arthur Young (1892) reported similar production practices in Ireland during the mid–eighteenth century.

Oat in the Western Hemisphere

Oat, both wild and cultivated, entered the Americas by two routes (Coffman 1977). *A. byzantina,* as well as the wild-weedy *A. fatua* L. and *A. barbata* Pott ex Link, were all introduced to southern latitudes by the Spaniards. *A. sativa* (and probably *A. fatua*) was transported by the English and other Europeans to the northern colonies. In seventeenth-century colonial agriculture, oat grain was fed to horses and mixed with rye and pea (*Pisum arvense* L.) for cattle feed (Bidwell and Falconer 1925). Where Scottish colonists predominated, it sometimes contributed to the human diet, although oat was not widely grown in the southern colonies of British North America (Grey and Thompson 1933). E. L. Sturtevant (1919) noted that Native Americans in California gathered wild oat and used it in breadmaking.

Oat cultivation moved west with frontier farming. Typical pioneer farmers planted maize (*Zea mays* L.) and some potatoes in the newly turned sod; this was followed the second year with small grains (Bidwell and Falconer 1925). Oat yields of 70 bushels per acre (3,760 kilograms per hectare) were achieved in Indiana by 1838 (Ellsworth 1838). To the north, in Canada, nineteenth-century pioneers relied less on maize and more on wheat and oat.

During the twentieth century, oat production in North America has been concentrated in the north central United States and the prairie provinces of Canada. Spring-sown oat is grown in these areas, whereas fall-sown, or "winter," oat is grown in the southern and southwestern United States (and parts of Europe). Fall sowing permits the crop to grow during mild weather in late autumn and early spring and to mature prior to the onset of high summer temperatures. Fall-sown oat is grazed for winter forage in the southwestern United States. The northern limits of fall-sown production are Kentucky, southern Pennsylvania, and Virginia. Although oat thrives in cooler climates than do wheat and barley, it is more at risk from freezing temperatures than those cereals.

The foundation germ plasm for spring-sown oat in the United States and Canada consists of three Russian cultivars (Kherson, Green Russian, and White Russian), a Swedish cultivar (Victory), and a Greek cultivar (Markton). All five heterogeneous cultivars were introduced into North America during the late nineteenth or early twentieth centuries (Coffman 1977).

The foundation germ plasm for fall-sown oat in the United States comprises two heterogeneous cultivars, Winter Turf and Red Rustproof. Winter Turf was probably introduced from northern Europe, and it may have been cultivated since colonial times (Coffman 1977). Red Rustproof was introduced from Mexico and became very popular after the Civil War. Cultivars resulting from selections within this heterogeneous germ plasm dominated production from Virginia to Texas and California until well into the twentieth century. Fall-sown oat in the United States is used as feed and does not contribute to the human diet. This is not a reflection of its nutritional value; rather, it reflects the proximity of processing mills to the centers of spring oat production in the north central United States and Canada. Oat grain has a relatively low density, which makes transportation expensive.

Progress from Plant Breeding

Oat cultivar improvement through plant selection began in Europe approximately 200 years ago, but, prior to the late nineteenth century, the intensity of the effort remained small by modern standards. In parallel with the development of other cereal grains, oat breeding activity increased worldwide during the early twentieth century. Oat breeding has remained a public sector activity, with a few notable exceptions, but some of these public sector programs in North America are dependent on the financial support of private sector endusers in the food industry. Comprehensive histories of oat breeding have been produced by T. R. Stanton (1936); F. A. Coffman, H. C. Murphy, and W. H. Chapman (1961); and M. S. McMullen and F. L. Patterson (1992).

The progression of methodologies utilized in oat improvement has been similar worldwide. The initial method was the introduction of heterogeneous cultivars from one production region to another for direct cultivation. This was gradually replaced by the development of cultivars from plant selections made within these heterogeneous introductions now growing in a new environment. The third step in the progression was the selection of cultivars from within breeding populations developed by sexual hybridization between parents with complementary arrays of desirable traits. In general, the end product of such a program was a homogeneous pure line cultivar. In the United States, the era of introduction lasted from colonial times to the beginning of the twentieth century. The era of selection within introductions as the predominant source of new cultivars extended from approximately 1900 to 1930. Since that time, the majority of cultivars have resulted from hybridization.

Common themes in oat breeding research during the twentieth century have included field, laboratory, and greenhouse methodologies to improve efficiency of selection for an array of agronomic, disease- and insect resistance, morphologic, and grain-quality traits. In addition, there have been Mendelian and quantitative genetic studies to investigate inheritance and expected progress from selection for these traits; studies of the evolution of species within the genus *Avena;* and, recently, the use of nonconventional techniques centered around biotechnology. This body of work has provided extensive knowledge of the basic biology of oat and has fostered direction and efficiency in applied oat improvement.

Throughout the twentieth century, breeding efforts have been directed at the improvement of grain yield, straw strength, test weight, and resistance to disease and insect pests. Additional efforts have been directed towards groat percentage, kernel weight, and winter hardiness. The cumulative results of these breeding efforts have included notable improvements in all of these areas (Lawes 1977; Rodgers, Murphy, and Frey 1983; Wych and Stuthman 1983; Marshall 1992; Lynch and Frey 1993), as well as the maintenance of disease and insect resistance levels. Yield improvements were not associated with specific phenotypic characteristics (as, for example, with reduced-height genes in wheat) or with germ plasm source, but modern cultivars appeared more adapted, both to high productivity and to heat- and drought-stressed environments, than older cultivars. R. D. Wych and D. D. Stuthman (1983) reported increases in biomass, total N, groat N, and nitrogen harvest index. In general, tillers per plant and kernels per panicle either have remained unchanged or have been reduced. The importance of increased biomass has been emphasized as a route to further yield increases (Moser and Frey 1994). This biomass must result from improved growth rate rather than extended growth duration, and harvest index must be maintained at present levels (Takeda and Frey 1976; Reysack, Stuthman, and Stucker 1993).

Much effort has been directed toward the identification and utilization of novel sources of disease resistance in cultivar development. Crown rust (*Puccinia coronata* Cda. var. *avenae* Fraser and Led.), stem rust (*P. graminis* Pers. f. sp. *avenae* Ericks. and E. Henn.), loose smut (*Ustilago avenae* [Pers.] Rostr.), powdery mildew (*Erysiphe graminis* DC. f. sp. *avenae* Em. Marchal), and barley yellow dwarf virus have received the most attention. For several decades, breeders have been utilizing the wild hexaploid *A. sterilis* as a source of genes for protection against crown rust and other pathogens. Other, more distantly related, species have been utilized to a lesser extent (Sharma and Forsberg 1977; Aung and Thomas 1978). Multiline oat cultivars were developed in the midwestern United States as an alternative strategy for crown rust control (Frey, Browning, and Simons 1985). A multiline cultivar is a mixture of several phenotypically similar genotypes, but each genotype contains a different gene for crown rust resistance. Multilines differ from most late–twentieth-century oat cultivars in that they are not homogeneous pure lines.

Breeding for improved grain composition – that is, groat protein, groat oil, and beta-glucan content – has been emphasized during the past 25 years. Although test weight is the primary quality factor used in purchasing oat, high-yielding cultivars with elevated groat protein levels have been released with regularity during the past 20 years. The range of groat protein in these cultivars is 18 to 21 percent versus 14 to 17 percent in conventional cultivars. The impetus behind this work is the enhancement of the feed value of oat, the maintenance of its standing as a traditional breakfast food, and the increase of its potential for use in the specialty food market (for example, as a protein additive). It is noteworthy that because of the predominance of the globulin fraction in oat storage protein, oat protein quality does not decrease with increases in groat protein percentage (Peterson 1976).

Although an overall negative association between grain yield and groat protein percentage is found in oat, studies consistently report the occurrence of high-protein transgressive segregates with overall agronomic superiority. When breeders have used protein yield (grain yield × groat protein concentration) as the unit of selection, they have been effective in improving both traits simultaneously (Kuenzel and Frey 1985; McFerson and Frey 1991).

Among other findings of importance to the improvement of oat protein are that groat protein is polygenically inherited, but heritability levels are moderate; that gene action is primarily additive; and that genes from *A. sativa* and *A. sterilis* may act in a complementary fashion (Campbell and Frey 1972; Iwig and Ohm 1976; Cox and Frey 1985). Breeders have been directing most of their efforts to the wild *A. sterilis* species as a source of genes with which to increase groat protein percentage and protein yield. Other species, such as *A. fatua* and *A. magna*, have been identified as potentially valuable resources as well (Thomas, Haki, and Arangzeb 1980; Reich and

Brinkman 1984). Oat researchers believe that a further 4 to 5 percent increase in groat protein over that of current high-protein cultivars is a reasonably obtainable breeding objective.

Groat oil content in cultivars typically ranges between 3.8 and 11 percent (Hutchinson and Martin 1955; Brown, Alexander, and Carmer 1966). Approximately 80 percent of the lipid in the groat is free lipid (ether extracted), and triglycerides are the most abundant component of oat oil. Most of the total lipid is found in the bran and starchy endosperm (Youngs, Püskülcü, and Smith 1977). Oat has never been utilized as an oilseed crop, but its mean lipid content is higher than that of other temperate cereal grains. No oat cultivar has been released based solely on elevated oil content, but considerable effort has been expended on studies of this trait, with the goal of alteration through breeding. Initial interest was related to the improvement of the energy value of oat as a livestock feed. Subsequently, V. L. Youngs, M. Püskülcü, and R. R. Smith (1977) indicated that high groat oil concentration could also increase food caloric production, and K. J. Frey and E. G. Hammond (1975) estimated that oat cultivars with 17 percent groat oil (combined with present levels of protein and grain yield) would compete with Iowa soybeans as an oilseed crop for the production of culinary oil.

Inheritance of oil content was studied in crosses of cultivated oat with *A. sterilis* and *A. fatua,* and results indicated that oil content was polygenically inherited, that additive gene effects predominated, that environmental influences were minor, that transgressive segregation was common, and that heritability was high (Baker and McKenzie 1972; Frey, Hammond, and Lawrence 1975; Luby and Stuthman 1983; Thro and Frey 1985; Schipper and Frey 1991a). Thus, when a concerted effort was made to improve groat oil content and oil yield (grain yield × groat oil concentration), the results were impressive (Branson and Frey 1989; Schipper and Frey 1991b). Agronomically desirable lines with up to 15 percent groat oil content were developed rather rapidly. Lower seed and test weights were associated with high groat oil content. Subsequently, lines with oil as high as 18 percent were produced (K. J. Frey, personal communication).

The major fatty acids of oat are palmitic (16:0), stearic (18:0), oleic (18:1), linoleic (18:2), and linolenic (18:3). Of these, palmitic, oleic, and linoleic constitute 95 percent of the fatty acids measured. Oleic and linoleic are comparable in quantity and may be controlled by the same genetic system (Karow and Forsberg 1985). Increased lipid content is correlated with an increase in oleic acid and a decrease in palmitic, linoleic, and linolenic acids (Forsberg, Youngs, and Shands 1974; Frey and Hammond 1975; Youngs and Püskülcü 1976; Roche, Burrows, and McKenzie 1977).

The oil content of advanced breeding lines is monitored routinely by breeders, but fatty acid content is not usually determined. Both simple and polygenic inheritance is involved in the expression of fatty acid content, but heritabilities are moderate to high (Thro, Frey, and Hammond 1983; Karow and Forsberg 1984). Selection for increased oil content should be accompanied by the monitoring of fatty acid composition, with particular attention to palmitic and linoleic acid, if conservation of the fatty acid composition of oat is desired.

Oat genotypes range in beta-glucan concentration from about 2.5 to 8.5 percent (D. M. Peterson and D. M. Wesenberg, unpublished data), but the range in adapted genotypes is narrower (Peterson 1991; Peterson, Wesenberg, and Burrup 1995). Several plant breeders have begun to make crosses with high beta-glucan germ plasm in an attempt to develop cultivars specially suited for human food. High beta-glucan oats are unsuited for certain animal feeds, especially for young poultry (Schrickel, Burrows, and Ingemansen 1992).

World Oat Production

The countries of the Former Soviet Union (FSU), North America, and Europe account for 90 percent of the world's oat production (Table II.A.6.1). Australia produces 4 percent and the People's Republic of China less than 2 percent.

The highest yields are obtained in the United Kingdom, Denmark, Germany, France, the former Czechoslovakia, New Zealand, and Sweden. Cool, moist summers, combined with intensive management practices, are commonplace in these countries. Large-scale producers, such as the United States, Canada, and the FSU, sacrifice high yield per hectare for less intensive management practices. Oat is adapted to cool, moist environments and is sensitive to high temperatures from panicle emergence to physiological maturity. It is more tolerant of acid soils than are other small grains, but less so of sandy or limestone soils. Although oat is adapted to cool temperatures, it is not as winter hardy as wheat or barley. Thus, the bulk of the world's production comes from spring-sown cultivars.

Of the major producers, only the FSU increased production and hectarage over the past three decades. Expanding livestock numbers coupled with the more favorable growing environment in northern regions have made oat more attractive than wheat or barley. The FSU now accounts for 40 percent of world production. All other major producers, including Canada, the United States, Germany, and Poland, have had declining production and hectarage during the same period. Production has declined by 33 percent in Poland and 61 percent in the United States and France. Overall, world production has declined by 23 percent and hectarage by 27 percent, whereas yield per hectare has increased 6 percent over the past 30 years. But production did increase in Australia, New Zealand, South America, Mexico, and Africa during the same period.

The reasons for the generally downward trend in

Table II.A.6.1. *World oat production, area harvested, and yield by continent and country, 1965 through 1994. Continent totals may not sum to world total due to rounding*

	Year and mean production			Year and area harvested			Year and mean yield		
	1965-74	1975-84	1985-94	1965-74	1975-84	1985-94	1965-74	1975-84	1985-94
	1000 t			1000 ha			t ha^{-1}		
North America									
Canada	5203	3542	2968	2878	1782	1280	1.82	1.99	2.31
Mexico	46	78	100	61	84	101	0.78	0.92	1.00
U.S.	11884	8058	4645	6567	4237	2322	1.81	1.91	2.00
Total	17133	11678	7713	9506	6103	3703	-	-	-
South and Central America									
Argentina	491	534	474	380	392	381	1.29	1.36	1.23
Chile	116	138	177	80	84	68	1.45	1.63	2.60
Uruguay	61	40	50	79	49	56	0.76	0.82	0.89
Other	71	149	284	88	154	266	0.81	0.97	1.07
Total	739	861	985	627	679	771	-	-	-
Asia									
P.R. China	819	743	644	1050	710	562	0.78	1.05	1.15
Japan	76	16	6	36	7	3	2.13	2.36	1.88
Turkey	432	355	290	339	208	154	1.29	1.73	1.89
Total	1327	1114	940	1425	925	719	-	-	-
Africa									
Algeria	36	75	68	57	114	110	0.63	0.71	0.64
Morocco	19	31	46	24	39	49	0.85	0.76	0.92
S. Africa	107	78	54	587	456	663	0.18	0.18	0.09
Total	162	184	168	668	609	822	-	-	-
Oceania									
Australia	1233	1363	1576	1343	1205	1103	0.91	1.12	1.41
New Zealand	49	59	72	17	16	18	2.95	3.61	3.80
Total	1282	1422	1648	1360	1221	1121	-	-	-
Former Soviet Union	11088	14404	15221	9447	12167	11042	1.16	1.19	1.38
Western Europe									
Denmark	706	202	131	189	57	30	3.74	3.72	4.54
Finland	1133	1272	1158	502	467	382	2.25	3.00	3.05
France	2414	1812	947	877	550	240	2.80	3.34	3.97
Germany	3590	3781	2356	1060	997	533	3.39	3.79	4.26
Sweden	1468	1403	1355	477	452	380	3.07	3.39	3.59
U.K.	1213	637	525	354	162	107	3.46	4.06	4.93
Other	2523	2449	1968	1497	1238	727	1.69	1.98	2.71
Total	13047	11556	8440	4956	3623	2399	-	-	-
Eastern Europe									
Czechoslovakia	801	458	364	356	160	100	2.30	2.93	3.63
Poland	2981	2541	1993	1350	1084	779	2.22	2.35	2.53
Former Yugoslavia	322	294	233	280	204	129	1.15	1.46	1.80
Other	320	258	473	276	168	268	1.16	1.54	1.76
Total	4424	3551	3063	2262	1616	1276	-	-	-
World Total	49187	44699	38082	30195	27166	22002	1.63	1.65	1.73

Source: USDA, Economic Research Service, Washington, D.C.

oat production have included competition from crops that produce higher levels of energy and protein (such as maize and soybeans), the decline of oat use as a feed grain, changing crop rotation patterns, and government commodity programs that are more favorable to the growing of other crops. Although 79 percent of the crop is used for feed worldwide, changes in production and use in such countries as the United States have resulted in up to 42 percent of the crop going for food and seed in recent years. Over the past decade, the United States has imported an amount equivalent to 14 percent of its annual production.

Oat Milling

The milling of oat for human food typically involves several steps: cleaning, drying, grading, dehulling, steaming, and flaking. In addition, a cutting step may be inserted after dehulling (Deane and Commers 1986). The purpose of oat milling is to clean the grain, remove the inedible hull, and render the groat stable and capable of being cooked in a reasonable time. The history of oat usage for human food is associated with the development of milling technology, which evolved slowly over the millennia and more rapidly over the past two centuries. Most of the early advancements in oat milling were ancillary to improvements in wheat milling.

Primitive peoples prepared oat by crushing the grains between two rocks. As the respective rocks wore into an oval and cup shape, a mortar and pestle were developed. This evolved into the saddlestone, where the grain was ground in a saddlelike depression by the forward and back action of an oval stone. The next development was the quern, which appeared, according to R. Bennett and J. Elton (1898), about 200 B.C.

The quern was a distinct advancement, in that the action involved a rotating stone and a stationary one, rather than an oscillatory movement. The rotating stone typically had a handle for applying the motive force and a hole in the center through which the grain was fed. Further developments included the grooving of the flat surfaces to provide a cutting edge and a channel for the flour, groats, and hulls to be expelled (Thornton 1933). In more sophisticated mills, additional stones were used – one to remove the hull and a second to crush the groat (Lockhart 1983).

Over the next 1,500 years or so, the principal advancements were in the power source, evolving from human-powered to animal-powered, and later to the use of water and wind to turn the stone. In Scotland, the first water-powered mills were in existence by the eleventh century (Lockhart 1983). By the late eighteenth century, the newly developed steam engine was applied to grain mills. Such advances over the centuries allowed the use of larger and larger stones and, thus, increased the capacity of the mills.

Winnowing (separating the hulls from the groats) was originally accomplished by throwing the mixture into the air on a windy hill, the heavier groats falling onto sheets laid on the ground. Later, this step was done in barns situated so that the doors, open at each end, allowed the prevailing breeze to blow away the hulls (Lockhart 1983). A variety of home kilns were also developed to dry oat grains, rendering them easier to mill and imparting a toasty flavor.

The next major advance in oat milling came with the 1875 invention of a groat-cutting machine by Asmus Ehrrichsen in Akron, Ohio. The groats could now be cut into uniform pieces for a higher quality meal. Prior to this development, the crushing of groats had meant a mixture of fine flour and more or less coarse bits of endosperm that made an inferior meal when cooked. Steel-cut oats were also less liable to become rancid than the crushed grain. Steel-cut oats, available today as Scotch oats, were quite popular until superseded by the innovation of oat flakes.

Rollers, known as far back as the 1650s, were used for crushing groats, much as stones had been used. But in the 1870s it was discovered that when partially cooked groats were rolled, they formed flakes. The production and marketing of oat flakes, which began in the 1880s with a pair of small oat processors, was adopted by the (then fledgling) Quaker Oats Company (Thornton 1933: 149–52). Moreover, steel-cut oats as well as whole groats could be flaked, the former producing a faster-cooking product because of its thinner, smaller flakes.

Stones were used to remove oat hulls up until about 1936, when they were replaced with impact hullers. Impact hulling involves introducing the oats to the center of a spinning rotor that propels them outward against a carborundum or rubber ring. The impact removes the hull with minimum groat breakage. This huller has a better groat yield and is more energy efficient than stones (Deane and Commers 1986).

More recent developments in oat products include instant oats, flaked so thin that they cook by the addition of boiling water, and oat bran. Oat bran, the coarse fraction produced by sieving ground groats, contains a higher proportion of soluble fiber (predominantly beta-glucan), useful for lowering high levels of cholesterol (Ripsin et al. 1992).

Current practice in milling oats has been detailed by D. Deane and E. Commers (1986) and by D. Burnette and colleagues (1992) (Figure II.A.6.1). The first steps involve cleaning and grading. Other grains, foreign matter, and weed seeds are removed by a series of separations according to size and density on screens, disc separators, graders, and aspirators. At the same time, oat is separated into milling grade and other grades (light oats, pin oats, slim oats, and double oats), which are used for animal feed. The milling-grade oat is then subjected to drying in ovens to reduce the moisture from about 13 percent to 6 to 7 percent, followed by cooling. Alternatively, the drying may be delayed until after the hulls are removed. Dried oat has tougher groats and is less subject to breakage during the dehulling process.

The huller produces a mixture of groats, hulls, and broken pieces, and these are separated by air aspiration. The groats are separated by size and passed on to the cutting or flaking machinery. Groats that are steel cut into two to four pieces formerly were available as Scotch oats but are now used mostly for other products. The whole and the steel-cut groats are steamed and rolled, producing regular or quick-cooking flakes, respectively. Oat flour is made by grinding oat flakes, steel-cut groats, or middlings. It is used in ready-to-eat breakfast foods and other products. Oat bran is produced by sieving coarsely ground oat flour.

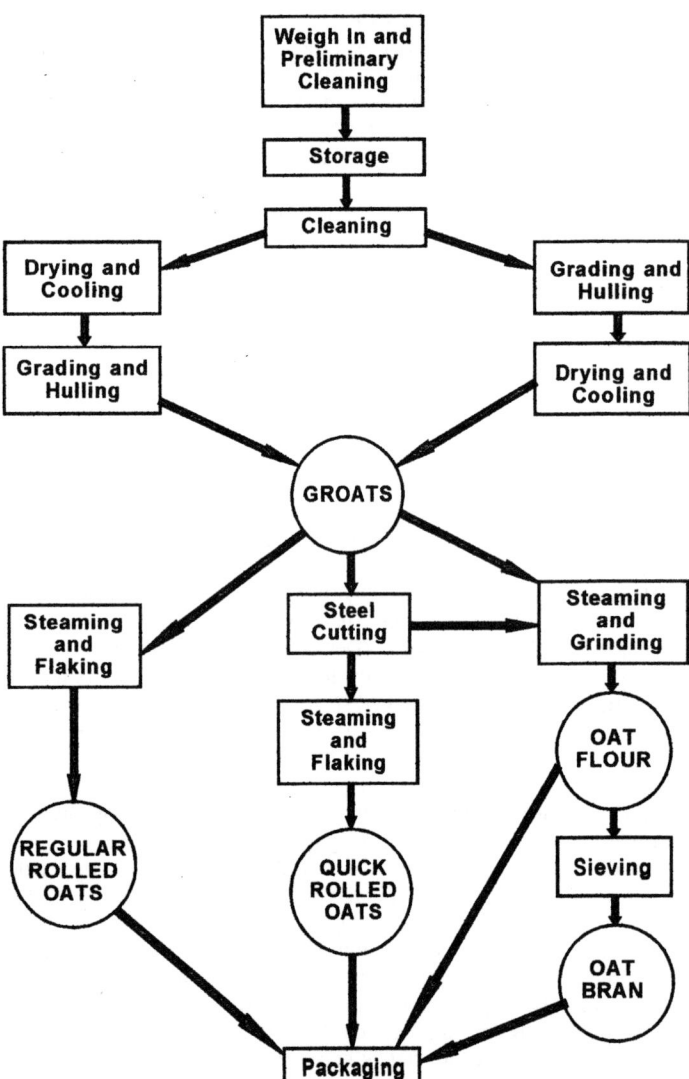

Figure II.A.6.1. Flow diagram of typical oat-milling sequence. (From Deane and Commers 1986.)

Uses of Oat

Although archaeological records indicate that primitive peoples employed oat as a food source, the first written reference to its use was Pliny's observation that the Germans knew oat well and "made their porridge of nothing else" (Rackham 1950). Oatmeal porridge was an acknowledged Scottish staple as early as the fifth century A.D. (Kelly 1975). Porridge was prepared by boiling oatmeal in water, and it was consumed with milk, and sometimes honey, syrup, or treacle (Lockhart 1983). Brose, made by adding boiling water to oatmeal, was of a thicker consistency. In Ireland during the same period, oatmeal porridge was consumed in a mixture with honey and butter or milk (Joyce 1913). Popular in Scotland were oatcakes, prepared by making a dough of oatmeal and water and heating it on a baking stone or griddle, and, in fact, oatcakes are still produced in Scotland by commercial bakeries as well as in the home. In England, a fourteenth-century tale recounted that in times of economic stress, the poor of London ate a gruel of oatmeal and milk (Langland 1968), and in 1597, J. Gerrard indicated that oat was used to make bread and cakes as well as drink in northeast England (Woodward 1931). Because oat flour lacks gluten and produces a flat cake, it must be mixed with wheat flour for bread-making. This was probably a common practice, which extended the quantity of the more valuable, and perhaps less productive, wheat. Gerrard also described medicinal uses of oat to improve the complexion and as a poultice to cure a "stitch" (Woodward 1931).

Young (1892) noted that potatoes (*Solanum tuberosum* L.) and milk were the staple foods of the common people in most of Ireland, but this diet was supplemented occasionally with oatmeal. Following the potato crop failure of 1740, however, oatmeal became the main ingredient in publicly provided emergency foods (Drake 1968).

Both Young and Adam Smith (1776) discussed the diets of the common people of the time. Smith was critical of the heavy dependence on oat in Scotland and believed that potatoes or wheat bread staples produced a healthier population. Young was not critical of oat, but he believed that the relatively healthy rural population in Ireland resulted from consumption of milk in addition to potatoes, rather than the more commonplace ale or tea consumed in England. In mid–nineteenth-century England, the highest-paid factory workers ate meat daily, whereas the poorest ate cheese, bread, oatmeal porridge, and potatoes (Engels 1844). However, oatmeal was a popular breakfast food among the wealthy.

Although oat was produced in the North American colonies from the time of the earliest settlements, it was not considered a human food except in a few predominantly Scottish settlements. A small quantity of oat was imported from Europe and typically sold in drug stores to invalids and convalescents. That oat had medicinal value had been known since Roman times (Woodward 1931; Font Quer 1962), but it was believed, erroneously, that domestically produced oat was not suitable for human consumption. Most nineteenth-century cookbooks in the United States either contained no recipes for oatmeal or suggested it as food for the infirm (Webster 1986). Indeed, the idea of humans consuming oats was a subject of ridicule by humorists and cartoonists in several national publications (Thornton 1933).

The selling of domestically produced oatmeal for human consumption in the United States began in earnest at the end of the nineteenth century, and its increasing popularity with the public can be attributed to the improved technology of producing rolled oat flakes, selling them in packages instead of in bulk, and a marketing strategy of portraying oatmeal as a healthful and nutritious product (Thornton 1933). The story of the marketing of oatmeal to the North American public is notable because it represented the first use of mass marketing techniques that are commonplace today (Marquette 1967).

New food uses for oat continue to be developed and marketed to a generally receptive public. The popularity of ready-to-eat breakfast cereals, many of which are oat based or contain some oat, has contributed to the increased food demand for oat. In the hot cereal market, instant oat products are achieving a greater market share due to consumers' preference for quick breakfast products requiring little, if any, preparation. Research on the effects of oat bran on blood cholesterol levels has also increased demand for oat bran products from health-conscious consumers. Oat is a popular ingredient in breads, cookies, and infant foods.

Nutritional Value

The nutritional value of oat has long been recognized. Although there was no scientific basis for nutritional claims in the Middle Ages, surely it was known that a staple diet of oat supported people accustomed to hard physical labor. Jean Froissart, a historian of the fourteenth century, wrote that Scottish soldiers carried with them, on their horses, bags of oat and metal plates upon which to cook oatcakes (Lockhart 1983). Oat consumption increased markedly in Scotland in the eighteenth century, coincident with a drop in meat consumption (Symon 1959), and much of the Scottish diet during the eighteenth century was oat.

As the science of nutrition developed in the twentieth century, scientists began to measure human needs for vitamins, minerals, essential amino acids and fatty acids, and energy. Foods were analyzed to ascertain their content of these essentials, and cereals, in general, and oat, in particular, were recognized as important contributors to human nutrition. But because of certain deficiencies, grains by themselves could not be considered "complete" foods.

The primary constituent of oat is starch, which constitutes from 45 to 62 percent of the groat by weight (Paton 1977). This percentage is lower than that of other cereals because of the higher levels of protein, fiber, and fat. Oat starch is highly digestible, and oat is a good energy source. Oat protein is higher than that of most other cereals (15 to 20 percent, groat basis) and contains a better balance of essential amino acids (Robbins, Pomeranz, and Briggle 1971). Nevertheless, lysine, threonine, and methionine are contained in less than optimal proportions. The oil content of oat is also higher than that of other cereals, ranging from about 5 to 9 percent for cultivated varieties (Youngs 1986), but genotypes with extreme values have been identified (Brown and Craddock 1972; Schipper and Frey 1991b). Oat oil is nutritionally favorable because of a high proportion of unsaturated fatty acids, including the essential fatty acid, linoleic acid.

The mineral content of oat is typical of that of other cereals (Peterson et al. 1975). Oat provides a significant proportion of manganese, magnesium, and iron and is also a source of zinc, calcium, and copper. Although high in phosphorus, much of this is unavailable as phytic acid. Oat also contains significant amounts of several vitamins – thiamin, folic acid, biotin, pantothenic acid, and vitamin E (Lockhart and Hurt 1986) – but contains little or no vitamins A, C, and D.

In developed countries where food for most people is abundant, the emphasis in nutrition has changed from correcting nutrient deficiencies to avoiding excessive consumption of saturated fats, refined sugar, and cholesterol while consuming foods high in carbohydrate and fiber. Diets containing whole-grain cereals fit well into this prescription for healthful eating. Oat, along with barley, contains a relatively high amount of beta-glucan, a soluble fiber that has been shown in numerous studies to lower the cholesterol levels of hypercholesterolemic subjects (Ripsin et al. 1992).

This knowledge spawned a plethora of products made from oat bran, because it was established that the bran fraction contained a higher concentration of beta-glucan than did whole oat. Although the marketplace has now discarded a number of these products that contained nutritionally insignificant quantities of oat bran, there is a definite place for oat bran in therapy for high blood cholesterol.

David M. Peterson
J. Paul Murphy

Bibliography

Aung, T., and H. Thomas. 1978. The structure and breeding behavior of a translocation involving the transfer of powdery mildew resistance from *Avena barbata* Pott. into the cultivated oat. *Euphytica* 27: 731-9.

Baker, R. J., and R. I. H. McKenzie. 1972. Heritability of oil content in oats, *Avena sativa* L. *Crop Science* 12: 201-2.

Bar-Yosef, O., and M. E. Kislev. 1989. Early farming communities in the Jordan Valley. In *Foraging and farming*, ed. D. R. Harris and G. C. Hillman, 632-42. Winchester, Mass.

Baum, B. R. 1977. *Oats: Wild and cultivated.* Ottawa.

Bennett, R., and J. Elton. 1898. *History of corn milling,* Vol. 1. London and Liverpool.

Bidwell, P. W., and J. I. Falconer. 1925. *History of agriculture in the northern United States, 1620-1860.* Washington, D.C.

Branson, C. V., and K. J. Frey. 1989. Recurrent selection for groat oil content in oat. *Crop Science* 29: 1382-7.

Brown, C. M., D. E. Alexander, and S. G. Carmer. 1966. Variation in oil content and its relation to other characters in oats (*Avena sativa* L.). *Crop Science* 6: 190-1.

Brown, C. M., and J. C. Craddock. 1972. Oil content and groat weight of entries in the world oat collection. *Crop Science* 12: 514-15.

Brownlee, H. J., and F. L. Gunderson. 1938. Oats and oat products. *Cereal Chemistry* 15: 257-72.

Burnette, D., M. Lenz, P. F. Sisson, et al. 1992. Marketing, processing, and uses of oat for food. In *Oat science and technology,* ed. H. G. Marshall and M. E. Sorrells, 247-63. Madison, Wis.

Campbell, A. R., and K. J. Frey. 1972. Inheritance of groat protein in interspecific oat crosses. *Canadian Journal of Plant Science* 52: 735-42.

Candolle, A. de. 1886. *Origin of cultivated plants.* New York.

Coffman, F. A. 1946. Origin of cultivated oats. *Journal of the American Society of Agronomy* 38: 983-1002.

　1977. *Oat history, identification and classification.* Technical Bulletin No. 1516. Washington, D.C.

Coffman, F. A., H. C. Murphy, and W. H. Chapman. 1961. Oat breeding. In *Oats and oat improvement,* ed. F. A. Coffman, 263-329. Madison, Wis.

Cox, T. S., and K. J. Frey. 1985. Complementarity of genes for high groat protein percentage from *Avena sativa* L. and *A. sterilis* L. *Crop Science* 25: 106-9.

Darby, W. J., P. Ghalioungui, and L. Grivetti. 1977. *Food: The gift of Osiris.* New York.

Deane, D., and E. Commers. 1986. Oat cleaning and processing. In *Oats: Chemistry and technology,* ed. F. H. Webster, 371-412. St. Paul, Minn.

Drake, M. 1968. The Irish demographic crisis of 1740-41. In *Historical studies,* ed. T. W. Moody, 101-24. New York.

Ellsworth, H. W. 1838. *Valley of the upper Wabash, Indiana.* New York.

Engels, F. [1844] 1968. *The condition of the working class in England.* Stanford, Calif.

Font Quer, P. 1962. *Plantas medicinales.* Madrid.

Forsberg, R. A., V. L. Youngs, and H. L. Shands. 1974. Correlations among chemical and agronomic characteristics in certain oat cultivars and selections. *Crop Science* 14: 221-4.

Frey, K. J., J. A. Browning, and M. D. Simons. 1985. Registration of 'Multiline E76' and 'Multiline E77' oats. *Crop Science* 25: 1125.

Frey, K. J., and E. G. Hammond. 1975. Genetics, characteristics, and utilization of oil in caryopses of oat species. *Journal of the American Oil Chemists' Society* 52: 358-62.

Frey, K. J., E. G. Hammond, and P. K. Lawrence. 1975. Inheritance of oil percentage in interspecific crosses of hexaploid oats. *Crop Science* 15: 94-5.

Grey, L. C., and E. K. Thompson. 1933. *History of agriculture in the southern United States to 1860.* Washington, D.C.

Hansen, J. R., and J. M. Renfrew. 1978. Palaeolithic-Neolithic seed remains at Franchthi Cave, Greece. *Nature* (London) 271: 349-52.

Harlan, J. R. 1977. The origins of cereal agriculture in the old world. In *Origins of agriculture,* ed. C. A. Reed, 357-83. The Hague.

　1989. Wild-grass seed harvesting in the Sahara and sub-Sahara of Africa. In *Foraging and farming,* ed. D. R. Harris and G. C. Hillman, 79-98. Winchester, Mass.

Harvey, P. D. A. 1965. *A medieval Oxfordshire village: Cuxham 1240 to 1400.* London.

Hillman, G. C., S. M. Colledge, and D. R. Harris. 1989. Plant-food economy during the Epipalaeolithic period at Tell Abu Hureyra, Syria: Dietary diversity, seasonality and modes of exploitation. In *Foraging and farming,* ed. D. R. Harris and G. C. Hillman, 240-68. Winchester, Mass.

Holden, T. G. 1986. Preliminary report of the detailed analyses of the macroscopic remains from the gut of Lindow man. In *Lindow man, the body in the bog,* ed. I. M. Stead, J. B. Bourke, and D. Brothwell, 116-25. Ithaca, N.Y.

Hopf, M. 1969. Plant remains and early farming in Jericho. In *The domestication and exploitation of plants and animals,* ed. P. J. Ucko and G. W. Dimbleby, 355-9. Chicago.

Hutchinson, J. B., and H. F. Martin. 1955. The chemical composition of oats. I. The oil and free fatty acid content of oats and groats. *Journal of Agricultural Science* 45: 411-18.

Iwig, M. M., and H. W. Ohm. 1976. Genetic control of protein from *Avena sterilis* L. *Crop Science* 16: 749-52.

Joyce, P. W. 1913. *A social history of ancient Ireland,* Vol. 2. New York.

Karow, R. S., and R. A. Forsberg. 1984. Oil composition in parental, F$_1$ and F$_2$ populations of two oat crosses. *Crop Science* 24: 629-32.

1985. Selection for linoleic acid concentration among progeny of a high × low linoleic acid oat cross. *Crop Science* 15: 45-7.

Kelly, J. N. D. 1975. *Jerome.* New York.

Kuenzel, K. A., and K. J. Frey. 1985. Protein yield of oats as determined by protein percentage and grain yield. *Euphytica* 34: 21-31.

Ladizinsky, G. 1969. New evidence on the origin of the hexaploid oats. *Evolution* 23: 676-84.

1988. The domestication and history of oats. In *Proceedings of the Third International Oat Conference* (Lund, Sweden, July 4-8, 1988), ed. B. Mattsson and R. Lyhagen, 7-12. Svalöf, Sweden.

Langland, W. 1968. *The vision of Piers ploughman.* New York.

Lawes, D. A. 1977. Yield improvement in spring oats. *Journal of Agricultural Science* 89: 751-7.

Leggett, J. M. 1992. Classification and speciation in *Avena.* In *Oat science and technology,* ed. H. G. Marshall and M. E. Sorrells, 29-52. Madison, Wis.

Lockhart, G. W. 1983. *The Scot and his oats.* Barr, Ayrshire, U.K.

Lockhart, H. B., and H. D. Hurt. 1986. Nutrition of oats. In *Oats chemistry and technology,* ed. Francis H. Webster, 297-308. St. Paul, Minn.

Luby, J. J., and D. D. Stuthman. 1983. Evaluation of *Avena sativa* L./*A. fatua* L. progenies for agronomic and grain quality characters. *Crop Science* 23: 1047-52.

Lynch, P. J., and K. J. Frey. 1993. Genetic improvement in agronomic and physiological traits of oat since 1914. *Crop Science* 33: 984-8.

Marquette, A. F. 1967. *Brands, trademarks and goodwill: The story of the Quaker Oats Company.* New York.

Marshall, H. G. 1992. Breeding oat for resistance to environmental stress. In *Oat science and technology,* ed. H. G. Marshall and M. E. Sorrells, 699-749. Madison, Wis.

McFerson, J. K., and K. J. Frey. 1991. Recurrent selection for protein yield in oat. *Crop Science* 31: 1-8.

McMullen, M. S., and F. L. Patterson. 1992. Oat cultivar development in the USA and Canada. In *Oat science and technology,* ed. H. G. Marshall and M. E. Sorrells, 573-612. Madison, Wis.

Moser, H. S., and K. J. Frey. 1994. Yield component responses associated with increased groat yield after recurrent selection in oat. *Crop Science* 34: 915-22.

Murphy, J. P., and L. A. Hoffman. 1992. The origin, history, and production of oat. In *Oat science and technology,* ed. H. G. Marshall and M. E. Sorrells, 1-28. Madison, Wis.

Paton, D. 1977. Oat starch. Part 1. Extraction, purification and pasting properties. *Stärke* 29: 149-53.

Peterson, D. M. 1976. Protein concentration, concentration of protein fractions and amino acid balance in oats. *Crop Science* 16: 663-6.

1991. Genotype and environmental effects on oat beta-glucan concentration. *Crop Science* 31: 1517-20.

1992. Composition and nutritional characteristics of oat grain and products. In *Oat science and technology,* ed. H. G. Marshall and M. E. Sorrells, 265-92. Madison, Wis.

Peterson, D. M., J. Senturia, V. L. Youngs, and L. E. Schrader. 1975. Elemental composition of oat groats. *Journal of Agricultural and Food Chemistry* 23: 9-13.

Peterson, D. M., D. M. Wesenberg, and D. E. Burrup. 1995. β-glucan content and its relationship to agronomic char-

acteristics in elite oat germplasm. *Crop Science* 35: 965-70.

Rackham, H. 1950. *Pliny natural history,* Vol. 5. Books 17-19. Cambridge, Mass.

Reich, J. M., and M. A. Brinkman. 1984. Inheritance of groat protein percentage in *Avena sativa* L. × *A. fatua* L. crosses. *Euphytica* 33: 907-13.

Renfrew, J. M. 1969. The archaeological evidence for the domestication of plants: Methods and problems. In *The domestication and exploitation of plants and animals,* ed. P. J. Ucko and G. W. Dimbleby, 149-72. Chicago.

Reysack, J. J., D. D. Stuthman, and R. E. Stucker. 1993. Recurrent selection in oat: Stability of yield and changes in unselected traits. *Crop Science* 33: 919-24.

Ripsin, C. M., J. M. Keenan, D. R. Jacobs, Jr., et al. 1992. Oat products and lipid lowering: A meta-analysis. *Journal of the American Medical Association* 267: 3317-25.

Robbins, G. S., Y. Pomeranz, and L. W. Briggle. 1971. Amino acid composition of oat groats. *Journal of Agricultural and Food Chemistry* 19: 536-9.

Roche, I. A. de la, V. D. Burrows, and R. I. H. McKenzie. 1977. Variation in lipid composition among strains of oats. *Crop Science* 17: 145-8.

Rodgers, D. M., J. P. Murphy, and K. J. Frey. 1983. Impact of plant breeding on the grain yield and genetic diversity of spring oats. *Crop Science* 23: 737-40.

Schipper, H., and K. J. Frey. 1991a. Selection for groat-oil content in oat grown in field and greenhouse. *Crop Science* 31: 661-5.

1991b. Observed gains from three recurrent selection regimes for increased groat-oil content of oat. *Crop Science* 31: 1505-10.

Schrickel, D. J., V. D. Burrows, and J. A. Ingemansen. 1992. Harvesting, storing, and feeding of oat. In *Oat science and technology,* ed. H. G. Marshall and M. E. Sorrells, 223-45. Madison, Wis.

Sharma, D. C., and R. A. Forsberg. 1977. Spontaneous and induced interspecific gene transfer for crown rust resistance in oats. *Crop Science* 17: 855-60.

Smith, A. 1776. *The wealth of nations,* Vol. 1. London.

Sorrells, M. E., and S. R. Simmons. 1992. Influence of environment on the development and adaptation of oat. In *Oat science and technology,* ed. H. G. Marshall and M. E. Sorrells, 115-63. Madison, Wis.

Stanton, T. R. 1936. Superior germ plasm in oats. In *USDA yearbook of agriculture,* 347-414. Washington, D.C.

Sturtevant, E. L. 1919. *Sturtevant's notes on edible plants,* ed. U. P. Hendrick. Albany, N.Y.

Symon, J. A. 1959. *Scottish farming.* Edinburgh.

Takeda, K., and K. J. Frey. 1976. Contributions of vegetative growth rate and harvest index to grain yield of progenies from *Avena sativa* × *A. sterilis* crosses. *Crop Science* 16: 817-21.

Thomas, H., J. M. Haki, and S. Arangzeb. 1980. The introgression of characters of the wild oat *Avena magna* (2n = 4 x = 28) into cultivated oat *A. sativa* (2n = 6x = 42). *Euphytica* 29: 391-9.

Thornton, H. J. 1933. *The history of The Quaker Oats Company.* Chicago.

Thro, A. M., and K. J. Frey. 1985. Inheritance of groat oil content and high oil selections in oats (*Avena sativa* L.). *Euphytica* 34: 251-63.

Thro, A. M., K. J. Frey, and E. G. Hammond. 1983. Inheritance of fatty acid composition in oat (*Avena sativa* L.). *Qualitas Plantarum, Plant Foods for Human Nutrition* 32: 29-36.

Villaret-von Rochow, M. 1971. *Avena ludoviciana* Dur. im Schweizer Spätneolithikum, ein Beitrag zur Abstammung des Saathafers. *Berichte der Deutschen Botanischen Gesellschaft* 84: 243-8.

Weaver, S. H. 1988. The history of oat milling. In *Proceedings of the Third International Oat Conference* (Lund, Sweden, July 4-8, 1988), ed. B. Mattsson and R. Lyhagen, 47-50. Svalöf, Sweden.

Webster, F. H. 1986. Oat utilization: Past, present, and future. In *Oats: Chemistry and technology,* ed. F. H. Webster, 413-26. St. Paul, Minn.

White, K. D. 1970. *Roman farming.* Ithaca, N.Y.

Woodward, M. 1931. *Leaves from Gerrard's herbal.* New York.

Wych, R. D., and D. D. Stuthman. 1983. Genetic improvement in Minnesota – Adapted oat cultivars released since 1923. *Crop Science* 23: 879-81.

Yanushevich, Z. V. 1989. Agricultural evolution north of the Black Sea from Neolithic to the Iron Age. In *Foraging and farming,* ed. D. R. Harris and G. C. Hillman, 606-19. Winchester, Mass.

Young, A. 1892. *Arthur Young's tour in Ireland (1776-1779).* London.

Youngs, V. L. 1986. Oat lipids and lipid-related enzymes. In *Oats: Chemistry and technology,* ed. F. H. Webster, 205-26. St. Paul, Minn.

Youngs, V. L., and M. Püskülcü. 1976. Variation in fatty acid composition of oat groats from different cultivars. *Crop Science* 16: 881-3.

Youngs, V. L., M. Püskülcü, and R. R. Smith. 1977. Oat lipids. 1. Composition and distribution of lipid components in two oat cultivars. *Cereal Chemistry* 54: 803-12.

Zohary, D., and M. Hopf. 1988. *Domestication of plants in the old world.* Oxford.

Zohary, M. 1982. *Plants of the Bible.* New York.

II.A.7 ❧ Rice

Economic and Biological Importance of Rice

Rice in Human Life

Among the cereals, rice and wheat share equal importance as leading food sources for humankind. Rice is a staple food for nearly one-half of the world's population. In 1990, the crop was grown on 145.8 million hectares of land, and production amounted to 518.8 million metric tons of grain (paddy, rough rice). Although rice is grown in 112 countries, spanning an area from 53° latitude north to 35° south, about 95 percent of the crop is grown and consumed in Asia. Rice provides fully 60 percent of the food intake in Southeast Asia and about 35 percent in East Asia and South Asia. The highest level of per capita rice consumption (130 to 180 kilograms [kg] per year, 55 to 80 percent of total caloric source) takes place in Bangladesh, Cambodia, Indonesia, Laos, Myanmar (Burma), Thailand, and Vietnam.

Although rice commands a higher price than wheat on the international market, less than five percent of the world's rice enters that market, contrasted with about 16 percent of the wheat. Low-income countries, China and Pakistan, for example, often import wheat at a cheaper price and export their rice.

Biological Value in Human Nutrition

Although rice has a relatively low protein content (about 8 percent in brown rice and 7 percent in milled rice versus 10 percent in wheat), brown rice (caryopsis) ranks higher than wheat in available carbohydrates, digestible energy (kilojoules [kJ] per 100 grams), and net protein utilization. Rice protein is superior in lysine content to wheat, corn, and sorghum. Milled rice has a lower crude fiber content than any other cereal, making rice powder in the boiled form suitable as infant food. For laboring adults, milled rice alone could meet the daily carbohydrate and protein needs for sustenance although it is low in riboflavin and thiamine content. For growing children, rice needs to be supplemented by other protein sources (Hegsted 1969; Juliano 1985b).

The Growing Importance of Rice

On the basis of mean grain yield, rice crops produce more food energy and protein supply per hectare than wheat and maize. Hence, rice can support more people per unit of land than the two other staples (Lu and Chang 1980). It is, therefore, not surprising to find a close relationship in human history between an expansion in rice cultivation and a rapid rise in population growth (Chang 1987).

As a human food, rice continues to gain popularity in many parts of the world where other coarse cereals, such as maize, sorghum and millet, or tubers and roots like potatoes, yams, and cassava have traditionally dominated. For example, of all the world's regions, Africa has had the sharpest rise in rice consumption during the last few decades.

Rice for table use is easy to prepare. Its soft texture pleases the palate and the stomach. The ranking order of food preference in Asia is rice, followed by wheat, maize, and the sweet potato; in Africa it is rice or wheat, followed by maize, yams, and cassava (author's personal observation).

In industrial usage, rice is also gaining importance in the making of infant foods, snack foods, breakfast cereals, beer, fermented products, and rice bran oil, and rice wine remains a major alcoholic beverage in East Asia. The coarse and silica-rich rice hull is finding new use in construction

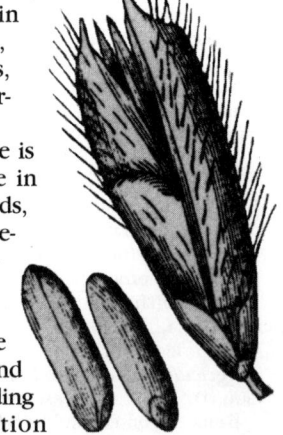

Rice

materials. Rice straw is used less in rope and paper making than before, but except for modern varieties, it still serves as an important cattle feed throughout Asia. Because rice flour is nearly pure starch and free from allergens, it is the main component of face powders and infant formulas. Its low fiber content has led to an increased use of rice powder in polishing camera lenses and expensive jewelry.

Botany, Origin, and Evolution

Botany

Rice is a member of the grass family (Gramineae) and belongs to the genus *Oryza* under tribe Oryzeae. The genus *Oryza* includes 20 wild species and 2 cultivated species (cultigens). The wild species are widely distributed in the humid tropics and subtropics of Africa, Asia, Central and South America, and Australia (Chang 1985). Of the two cultivated species, African rice (*O. glaberrima* Steud.) is confined to West Africa, whereas common or Asian rice (*O. sativa* L.) is now commercially grown in 112 countries, covering all continents (Bertin et al. 1971).

The wild species have both diploid (2n = 2x = 24) and tetraploid (2n = 4x = 48) forms, while the two cultigens are diploid and share a common genome (chromosome group). Incompatibility exists among species having different genomes. Partial sterility also shows up in hybrids when different ecogeographic races of *O. sativa* are hybridized. The cultivated species of *Oryza* may be classified as semiaquatic plants, although extreme variants are grown not only in deep water (up to 5 meters) but also on dry land (Chang 1985).

Among the cereals, rice has the lowest water use efficiency. Therefore, rice cannot compete with dryland cereals in areas of low rainfall unless irrigation water is readily available from reservoirs, bunds, and the like. On the other hand, the highest yields of traditional varieties have been obtained in regions of cloudless skies, such as in Spain, California, and northern Japan (Lu and Chang 1980).

The "wild rice" of North America is *Zizania palustris* (formerly *Z. aquatica* L. [2n = 30]), which belongs to one of the 11 related genera in the same tribe. Traditionally, this species was self-propagating and harvested only by Native Americans in the Great Lakes area. Now it is commercially grown in Minnesota and northern California.

Origin

The origin of rice was long shrouded by disparate postulates because of the pantropical but disjunct distribution of the 20 wild species across four continents, the variations in characterizing and naming plant specimens, and the traditional feud concerning the relative antiquity of rice in India versus China. Among the botanists, R. J. Roschevicz (1931) first postulated that the center of origin of the section *Sativa*

Roschev., to which *O. glaberrima* and *O. sativa* belong, was in Africa and that *O. sativa* had originated from multiple species. A divergent array of wild species was proposed by different workers as the putative ancestor of *O. sativa* (Chang 1976b).

Several workers considered "*O. perennis* Moench" (an ambiguous designation of varying applications) as the common progenitor of both cultigens (Chang 1976b). A large number of scholars had argued that Asian rice originated in the Indian subcontinent (South Asia), although A. de Candolle (1884), while conceding that India was more likely the original home, considered China to have had an earlier history of rice cultivation

On the basis of historical records and the existence of wild rices in China, Chinese scholars maintained that rice cultivation was practiced in north China during the mythological Sheng Nung period (c. 2700 B.C.) and that *O. sativa* of China evolved from wild rices (Ting 1961). The finding of rice glume imprints at Yang-shao site in north China (c. 3200–2500 B.C.) during the 1920s reinforced the popular belief that China was one of the centers of its origin (Chinese Academy of Agricultural Sciences 1986).

Since the 1950s, however, rice researchers have generally agreed that each of the two cultigens originated from a single wild species. But disputes concerning the immediate ancestor of *O. sativa* persist to this day (Chang 1976b, 1985; Oka 1988). A multidisciplinary analysis of the geographic distribution of the wild species and their genomic composition in relation to the "Glossopterid Line" (northern boundary) of the Gondwanaland fragments (Melville 1966) strongly indicated the Gondwanaland origin of the genus *Oryza* (Chang 1976a, 1976b, 1985). This postulate of rice having a common progenitor in the humid zones of the supercontinent Pangaea before it fractured and drifted apart can also explain the parallel evolutionary pattern of the two cultigens in Africa and Asia respectively. It also reconciles the presence of closely related wild species having the same genome in Australia and in Central and South America. Thus, the antiquity of the genus dates back to the early Cretaceous period of more than 130 million years ago.

Evolution

The parallel evolutionary pathway of *O. glaberrima* in Africa and of *O. sativa* in Asia was from perennial wild – → annual wild – → annual cultigen, a pattern common to other grasses and many crop plants. The parallel pathways are:

Africa: *O. longistaminata* - → *O. barthii* - → *O. glaberrima*.
Asia: *O. rufipogon* - → *O. nivara* - → *O. sativa*.

This scheme can resolve much that has characterized past disputes on the putative ancestors of the two cultigens. Wild perennial and annual forms having the same A genome are present in Australia and in Central and South America, but the lack of incipient agriculture in Australia and of wetland agronomy in tropical America in prehistoric times disrupted the final step in producing an annual cultigen.

It needs to be pointed out that the putative ancestors, especially those in tropical Asia, are conceptually wild forms of the distant past, because centuries of habitat disturbance, natural hybridization, and dispersal by humans have altered the genetic structure of the truly wild ancestors. Most of the wild rices found in nature today are hybrid derivatives of various kinds (Chang 1976b; 1985). The continuous arrays of variants in natural populations have impaired definitive studies on the wild progenies (Chang 1976b; Oka 1988).

The differentiation and diversification of annual wild forms into the early prototypes of cultigen in South and mainland Southeast Asia were accelerated by marked climatic changes during the Neothermal age of about 10,000 to 15,000 years ago. Initial selection and cultivation could have occurred independently and nearly concurrently at numerous sites within or bordering a broad belt of primary genetic diversity that extends from the Ganges plains below the eastern foothills of Himalaya, through upper Burma, northern Thailand, Laos, and northern Vietnam, to southwest and southern China.

From this belt, geographic dispersal by various agents, particularly water currents and humans, lent impetus to ecogenetic differentiation and diversification under human cultivation. In areas inside China where winter temperatures fell below freezing, the cultivated forms (cultivars) became true domesticates, depending entirely on human care for their perpetuation and propagation. In a parallel manner, the water buffalo was brought from the swamps of the south into the northern areas and coevolved as another domesticate (Chang 1976a).

In West Africa, *O. glaberrima* was domesticated from the wild annual *O. barthii* (Chevalier 1932); the latter was adapted primarily to water holes in the savanna and secondarily to the forest zone (Harlan 1973). The cultigen has its most important center of diversity in the central Niger delta. Two secondary centers existed near the Guinean coast (Porteres 1956).

Cultivation of the wild prototypes preceded domestication. Rice grains were initially gathered and consumed by prehistoric people of the humid regions where the perennial plants grew on poorly drained sites. These people also hunted, fished, and gathered other edible plant parts as food. Eventually, however, they developed a liking for the easily cooked and tasty rice and searched for plants that bore larger panicles and heavier grains.

The gathering-and-selection process was more imperative for peoples who lived in areas where seasonal variations in temperature and rainfall were more marked. The earlier maturing rices, which also tend to be drought escaping, would have been selected to suit the increasingly arid weather of the belt of primary diversity during the Neothermal period. By contrast, the more primitive rices of longer maturation, and those, thus, more adapted to vegetative propagation, would have survived better in the humid regions to the south (Chang 1976b; 1985). In some areas of tropical Asia, such as the Jeypore tract of Orissa State (India), the Batticoloa district (Sri Lanka), and the forested areas of north Thailand, the gathering of free-shattering grains from wild rice can still be witnessed today (Chang 1976b; Higham 1989).

Antiquity of Rice Cultivation

Although the differentiation of the progenitors of *Oryza* species dates back to the early Cretaceous period, the beginning of rice cultivation was viewed by Western scholars as a relatively recent event until extensive excavations were made after the 1950s in China and to a lesser extent in India. Earlier, R. J. Roschevicz (1931) estimated 2800 B.C. as the beginning of rice cultivation in China, whereas the dawn of agriculture in India was attributed to the Harappan civilization, which began about 2500 B.C. (Hutchinson 1976).

Thus far, the oldest evidence from India comes from Koldihwa, U.P., where rice grains were embedded in earthen potsherds and rice husks discovered in ancient cow dung. The age of the Chalcolithic levels was estimated between 6570 and 4530 B.C. (Vishnu-Mittre 1976; Sharma et al. 1980), but the actual age of the rice remains may be as recent as 1500 B.C. (Chang 1987). Another old grain sample came from Mohenjodaro of Pakistan and dates from about 2500 B.C. (Andrus and Mohammed 1958). Rice cultivation probably began in the upper and middle Ganges between 2000 and 1500 B.C. (Candolle 1884; Watabe 1973). It expanded quickly after irrigation works spread from Orissa State to the adjoining areas of Andhra Pradesh and Tamil Nadu in the Iron Age around 300 B.C. (Randhawa 1980).

In Southeast Asia, recent excavations have yielded a number of rice remains dating from 3500 B.C. at Ban Chiang (Thailand); 1400 B.C. at Solana (Philippines); and A.D. 500 at Ban Na Di (Thailand) and at Ulu Leang (Indonesia). Dates between 4000 and 2000 B.C. have been reported from North Vietnam (Dao 1985) but have not yet been authenticated.

These various reports have been summarized by T. T. Chang (1988, 1989a). The widely scattered findings are insufficient to provide a coherent picture of agricultural development in the region, but rice cultivation in mainland Southeast Asia undoubtedly preceded that in insular Southeast Asia (Chang 1988). The paucity of rice-related remains that were confined to upland sites in northern Thailand could be attributed to the sharp rise in sea level around the Gulf of Thailand during the four millennia between 8000 and 4000 B.C. Floods inundated vast tracts of low-lying land amid which rice chaffs and shell knives for cutting rice stalks were recently found at Khok Phanom Di near the Gulf and dated from 6000 to 4000 B.C. (Higham 1989).

For the Southeast Asian region, several geographers and ethnobotanists had earlier postulated that the cultivation of root crops predated rice culture (Sauer 1952; Spencer 1963; Yen 1977). Yet, this hypothesis falters in view of the apparently rather recent domestication (c. 2000 B.C.) of yams in the region (Alexander and Coursey 1969). In many hilly regions, vegeculture probably preceded dryland rice cultivation, but not in wetland areas. In the cooler regions, rice grains were crucial to early cultivators who could store and consume the harvest during the winter months.

Prior to the 1950s, the belief in the antiquity of rice cultivation in China was based on mythical writings in which "Emperor Shen Nung" (c. 2700 B.C.) was supposed to have taught his people to plant five cereals, with rice among them (Candolle 1884; Roschevicz 1931; Ting 1949; Chatterjee 1951). This view, however, was questioned by many non-Chinese botanists and historians because of the paucity of wild rices in China (or rather the paucity of information on the wild rices) and the semiarid environment in north China (Chang 1979b, 1983). Yet in the 1920s, the discovery of rice glume imprints on broken pottery at the Yang-shao site in Henan (Honan) by J. G. Andersson and co-workers (Andersson 1934) was important in linking Chinese archaeology with agriculture. The excavated materials were considered Neolithic in origin and the precise age was not available, though K. C. Chang later gave this author an estimated age of between 3200 and 2500 B.C.

Extensive diggings in the Yangtze basin after the 1950s yielded many rice remains that pushed back rice culture in China even further into antiquity (Chang 1983). The most exciting event was the finding in 1973–4 of carbonized rice kernels, rice straw, bone spades, hoe blades *(ssu),* and cooking utensils that demonstrated a well-developed culture supported by rice cultivation at the He-mu-du (Ho-mu-tu) site in Zhejiang (Chekiang) Province dated at 5005 B.C. (Chekiang Provincial Cultural Management Commission and Chekiang Provincial Museum 1976; Hsia 1977).

The grains were mostly of the *hsien* (Indica) type but included some *keng* (Sinica or Japonica) and intermediate kernels. The discovery also indicated the existence of an advanced rice-based culture in east China that vied in antiquity and sophistication with the millet-based culture in north China as represented by the Pan-po site in Shenxi (Shensi). Another site at Luo-jia-jiao in Zhejiang Province also yielded carbonized rice of both ecogeographic races of a similar age estimated at 7000 B.P. (Chang 1989a). In a 1988 excavation at Peng-tou-shan site in Hunan Province, abundant rice husks on pottery or red burnt clay as well as skeletal remains of water buffalo were found. The pottery was dated at between 7150 and 6250 B.C. (uncorrected carbon dating). Diggings in neighboring Hubei (Hupei) Province yielded artifacts of similar age, but the grain type could not be ascertained (Pei 1989). Excavations in Shenxi also produced rice glume imprints on red burnt clay dated between 6000 and 5000 B.C. (Yan 1989).

In contrast to all this scholarly effort on the antiquity of rice cultivation in Asia, our understanding of the matter in West Africa rests solely on the writing of R. Porteres (1956), who dates it from 1500 B.C. in the primary Niger center, and from A.D. 1000 to A.D. 1200 in the two Guinean secondary centers.

Chinese history also recorded that rice culture was well established in Honan and Shenxi Provinces of north China during the Chou Dynasty (1122 to 255 B.C.) by Lungshanoid farmers (Ho 1956; Chang 1968). During the Eastern Chou Dynasty (255 to 249 B.C.), rice was already the staple food crop in the middle and lower basins of the Yangtze River (Ting 1961). Wild rices were amply recorded in historical accounts; their northern limit of distribution reached 38° north latitude (Chang 1983).

Based on the above developments, it appears plausible to place the beginning of rice cultivation in India, China, and other tropical Asian countries at nearly 10,000 years ago or even earlier. Since rice was already cultivated in central and east China at 6000 to 5000 B.C., it would have taken a few millennia for rice to move in from the belt to the south of these regions. The missing links in the history of rice culture in China can be attributed to the dearth of archaeological findings from south China and the relatively recent age of rice remains in southwest China (1820 B.C. at Bei-yan in Yunnan) and south China (2000 B.C. at Shih Hsiah in Kwangtung). These areas represent important regions of ecogenetic differentiation or routes of dispersal (Chang 1983).

Linguistic Evidence

A number of scholars have attempted to use etymology as a tool in tracing the origin and dispersal of rice in Asia. The Chinese word for rice in the north, *tao* or *dao* or *dau,* finds its variants in south China and Indochina as *k'au* (for grain), *hao, ho, heu, deu,* and *khaw* (Ting 1961; Chinese Academy of Agricultural Sciences 1986). Indian scholars claimed that the word for rice in Western languages had a Dravidian root and that *ris, riz, arroz,* rice, *oruza,* and *arrazz* all came from *arisi* (Pankar and Gowda 1976). In insular Southeast Asia, the Austronesian terms *padi* and *paray* for rice and *bras* or *beras* for milled rice predominate (Chinese Academy of Agricultural Sciences 1986; Revel 1988).

On the other hand, Japanese scholars have also emphasized the spread of the Chinese words *ni* or *ne* (for wild rice) and *nu* (for glutinous rice) to Southeast Asia (Yanagita et al. 1969). N. Revel and co-workers (1988) have provided a comprehensive compilation of terms related to the rice plant and its parts derived from the linguistic data of China, Indochina, insular Southeast Asia, and Madagascar. Yet among the different disciplinary approaches, linguistic analyses have not been particularly effective in revealing facts about the dispersal of rice by humans. In part, this is because the ethnological aspects of human migration in the Southeast Asian region remain in a state of flux. (For various viewpoints see *Asian Perspectives* 1988: 26, no.1.)

Geographic Dispersal and Ecogenetic Diversification

Early Dispersal

The early dissemination of rice seeds (grains) could have involved a variety of agents: flowing water, wind, large animals, birds, and humans. The latter have undoubtedly been most effective in directed dispersal: Humans carried rice grains from one place to another as food, seed, merchandise, and gifts. The continuous and varied movements of peoples in Asia since prehistoric times have led to a broad distribution of early *O. sativa* forms, which proliferated in ecogenetic diversification after undergoing the mutation-hybridization-recombination-differentiation cycles and being subjected to both natural and human selection forces at the new sites of cultivation. In contrast, *O. glaberrima* cultivars exhibit markedly less diversity than their Asian counterparts, owing to a shorter history of cultivation and narrower dispersal. The contrast is amplified by other factors as shown in Table II.A.7.1.

Initial dispersal of *O. sativa* from numerous sites in its primary belt of diversity involved a combination of early forms of cultivars and associated wild relatives, often grown in a mixture. Biological findings and historical records point to five generalized routes from the Assam-Meghalaya-Burma region. Rice moved: (1) southward to the southern Bengal Bay area and the southern states of India and eventually to Sri Lanka; (2) westward to Pakistan and the west coast of India; (3) eastward to mainland Southeast Asia (Indochina); (4) southeastward to Malaysia and the Indonesian islands; and (5) northeastward to southwest China, mainly the Yunnan-Kweichow area, and further into east, central, and south China. The early routes of travel most likely followed the major rivers, namely, Brahmaputra, Ganges, Indus, Mekong, and Yangtze. Routes of sea travel, which came later, were from Thailand and Vietnam to the southern coastal areas of China, from Indonesia to the Philippines and Taiwan, and from China to Japan, as well as from China to Korea to Japan. These routes are summarized in Map II.A.7.1.

On the basis of ancient samples of rice hulls collected from India and Indochina, covering a span of 10 centuries up to around A.D. 1500, three main groups of cultivars (the Brahmaputra-Gangetic strain, the Bengal strain, and the Mekong strain) have been proposed by T. Watabe (1985). The Mekong strain originating in Yunnan was postulated to have given rise to the Indochina series and the Yangtze River series of cultivars; the latter consisted mainly of the *keng* rices of China. It should be pointed out, however, that the ecogenetic diversification processes following dispersal and the cultivators' preferences could have added complications to the varietal distribution pattern of the present, as later discussions will reveal.

Ecogenetic Differentiation and Diversification

During the early phase of human cultivation and selection, a number of morphological and physiological changes began to emerge. Selection for taller and larger plants resulted in larger leaves, longer and thicker stems, and longer panicles. Subsequent selection for more productive plants and for ease in growing and harvesting led to larger grains. It also resulted in increases in: (1) the rate of seedling growth; (2) tillering capacity; (3) the number of leaves per tiller and the rate of leaf development; (4) the synchronization of tiller development and panicle formation (for uniform maturation); (5) the number of secondary branches on a panicle; and (6) panicle weight (a product of spikelet number and grain weight). Concurrently, there were decreases or losses of the primitive features, such as: (1) rhizome formation; (2) pigmentation of plant parts; (3) awn length; (4) shattering of grains from the panicle; (5) growth duration; (6) intensity of grain dormancy; (7) response to short day length; (8) sensitivity to low temperatures; and (9) ability to survive in flood waters. The frequency of cross pollination also decreased so that the plants became more inbred and increasingly dependent on the cultivators for their propagation (by seed) and perpetuation (by short planting cycles) (Chang 1976b).

Table II.A.7.1 *Contrast in diversification:* Oryza sativa *vs.* glaberrima

Factor	Asia	W. Africa
Latitudinal spread	10° C–53° N	5° N–17° N
Topography	Hilly	Flat
Population density	High	Low
Movement of people	Continuous	Little
Iron tools	Many	None or few
Draft animals	Water buffalo and oxen	?

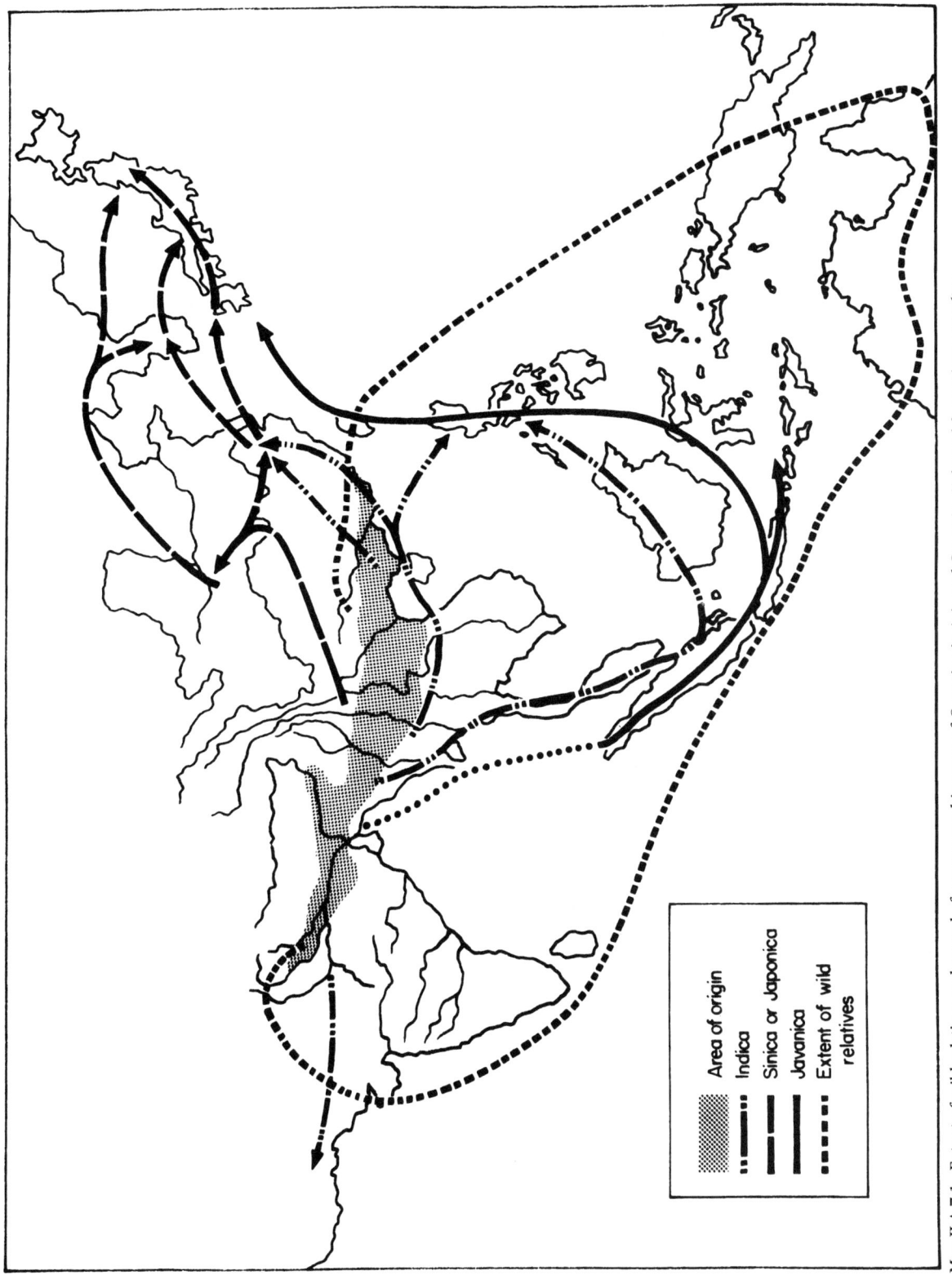

Map II.A.7.1. Extent of wild relatives and spread of ecogeographic races of *O. sativa* in Asia and Oceania. (Adapted from Chang 1976b.)

Legend:
- Area of origin
- Indica
- Sinica or Japonica
- Javanica
- Extent of wild relatives

When rice cultivars were carried up and down along the latitudinal or altitudinal clines or both, the enormous genetic variability in the plants was released, and the resulting variants expressed their new genetic makeup while reacting to changing environmental factors. The major environmental forces are soil properties, water supply, solar radiation intensity, day length, and temperature range, especially the minimum night temperatures. Those plants that could thrive or survive in a new environment would become fixed to form an adapted population – the beginning of a new ecostrain – while the unadapted plants would perish and the poorly adapted plants would dwindle in number and be reduced to a small population in a less adverse ecological niche in the area.

Such a process of differentiation and selection was aided by spontaneous mutations in a population or by chance outcrossing between adjacent plants or both. The process could independently occur at many new sites of cultivation and recur when environmental conditions or cultivation practices changed. Therefore, rich genetic diversity of a secondary nature could be found in areas of undulating terrain where the environmental conditions significantly differed within a small area. The Assam and Madhya Pradesh states and Jeypore tract of India, the island of Sri Lanka, and Yunnan Province of China represent such areas of remarkable varietal diversity (Chang 1985).

Proliferation into Ecogeographic Races and Ecotypes

Continuous cultivation and intense selection in areas outside the conventional wetlands of shallow water depth (the paddies) have resulted in a range of extreme ecotypes: deepwater or floating rices that can cope with gradually rising waters up to 5 meters (m) deep; flood-tolerant rices that can survive days of total submergence under water; and upland or hill rices that are grown under dryland conditions like corn and sorghum. The varying soil-water-temperature regimes in the Bengal Bay states of India and in Bangladesh resulted in four seasonal ecotypes in that area: *boro* (winter), *aus* (summer), transplanted *aman* (fall, shallow water), and broadcast *aman* (fall, deep water). In many double-cropping areas, two main ecotypes follow the respective cropping season: dry (or off) and wet (or main) (Chang 1985).

In broader terms, the wide dispersal of *O. sativa* and subsequent isolation or selection in Asia has led to the formation of three ecogeographic races that differ in morphological and physiological characteristics and are partially incompatible in genetic affinity: Indica race in the tropics and subtropics; javanica race in the tropics; and sinica (or japonica) race in the temperate zone. Of the three races, indica is the oldest and the prototype of the other two races as it retains most of the primitive features: tallness, weak stems, lateness, dormant grains, and shattering panicles.

The sinica race became differentiated in China and has been rigorously selected for tolerance to cool temperatures, high productivity, and adaptiveness to modern cultivation technology: short plant stature, nitrogen responsiveness, earliness, stiff stems, and high grain yield. The javanica race is of more recent origin and appears intermediate between the other two races in genetic affinity, meaning it is more cross-fertile with either indica or sinica. Javanica cultivars are marked by gigas features in plant panicle and grain characters. They include a wetland group of cultivars (*bulu* and *gundil* of Indonesia) and a dryland group (hill rices of Southeast Asia).

The picture of race-forming processes is yet incomplete (Chang 1985). Many studies have relied heavily on grain size and shape as empirical criteria for race classification. Some studies employed crossing experiments and hybrid fertility ratings. Other workers recently used isozyme patterns to indicate origin and affinity. Controversies in past studies stemmed largely from limited samples, oversimplified empirical tests, and reliance on presently grown cultivars to retrace the distant past. The latter involved a lack of appreciation for the relatively short period (approximately 5 to 6 centuries) that it takes for a predominant grain type to be replaced by another (Watabe 1973), which was probably affected by the cultivator's preference. Most of the studies have also overlooked the usefulness of including amylose content and low temperature tolerance in revealing race identity (Chang 1976b, 1985). It should also be recognized that early human contacts greatly predated those given in historical records (Chang 1983), and maximum varietal diversity often showed up in places outside the area of primary genetic diversity (Chang 1976b, 1985).

Parallel to the expansion in production area and dispersal of the cultivars to new lands during the last two centuries was the growth of varietal diversity. In the first half of the twentieth century, before scientifically bred cultivars appeared in large numbers, the total number of unimproved varieties grown by Asian farmers probably exceeded 100,000, though many duplicates of similar or altered names were included in this tally (Chang 1984 and 1992).

The Spread of Asian Rice

Historical records are quite revealing of the spread of Asian rice from South Asia, Southeast Asia, and China to other regions or countries, though exact dates may be lacking. In the northward direction, the Sinica race was introduced from China into the Korean peninsula before 1030 B.C. (Chen 1989). Rice cultivation in Japan began in the late Jomon period (about 1000 B.C., [Akazawa 1983]), while earlier estimates placed the introduction of rice to Japan from China in the third century B.C. (Ando 1951; Morinaga 1968). Several routes could have been involved: (1) from the lower Yangtze basin to Kyushu island, (2) from north China to Honshu Island, or (3) via Korea to northern Kyushu; *hsien* (Indica) may have arrived from China, and the Javanica race traveled from Southeast Asia (Isao 1976; Lu and Chang 1980). The areas that comprised the former Soviet Union obtained rice seeds from China, Korea, Japan, and Persia, and rice was grown around the Caspian Sea beginning in the early 1770s (Lu and Chang 1980).

From the Indian subcontinent and mainland Southeast Asia, the Indica race spread southward into Sri Lanka (before 543 B.C.), the Malay Archipelago (date unknown), the Indonesian islands (between 2000 and 1400 B.C.), and central and coastal China south of the Yangtze River. *Hsien* or Indica-type grains were found at both He-mu-du and Luo-jia-jiao sites in east China around 5000 B.C. (Lu and Chang 1980; Chang 1988). The *keng* or sinica rices were likely to have differentiated in the Yunnan-Kweichow region, and they became fixed in the cooler northern areas (Chang 1976b). On the other hand, several Chinese scholars maintain that *hsien* and *keng* rices were differentiated from wild rices inside China (Ting 1961; Yan 1989). The large-scale introduction and planting of the Champa rices (initially from Vietnam) greatly altered the varietal composition of *hsien* rices in south China and the central Yangtze basin after the eleventh century (Ho 1956; Chang 1987).

The javanica race had its origin on the Asian mainland before it differentiated into the dryland ecotype (related to the aus type of the Bengal Bay area and the hill rices of Southeast Asia) and the wetland ecotype *(bulu* and *gundil)* of Indonesia. From Indonesia, the wetland ecotype spread to the Philippines (mainly in the Ifugao region at about 1000 B.C.), Taiwan (at 2000 B.C. or later), and probably Ryukyus and Japan (Chang 1976b, 1988).

The Middle East acquired rice from South Asia probably as early as 1000 B.C. Persia loomed large as the principal stepping stone from tropical Asia toward points west of the Persian Empire. The Romans learned about rice during the expedition of Alexander the Great to India (c. 327–4 B.C.) but imported rice wine instead of growing the crop. The introduction of rice into Europe could have taken different routes: (1) from Persia to Egypt between the fourth and the first centuries B.C., (2) from Greece or Egypt to Spain and Sicily in the eighth century A.D., and (3) from Persia to Spain in the eighth century and later to Italy between the thirteenth and sixteenth centuries. The Turks brought rice from Southwest Asia into the Balkan Peninsula, and Italy could also have served as a stepping stone for rice growing in that region. Direct imports from various parts of Asia into Europe are also probable (Lu and Chang 1980).

In the spread of rice to Africa, Madagascar received Asian rices probably as early as 1000 B.C. when the early settlers arrived in the southwest region. Indonesian settlers who reached the island after the beginning of the Christian era brought in some Javanica

rices. Madagascar also served as the intermediary for the countries in East Africa, although direct imports from South Asia would have been another source. Countries in West Africa obtained Asian rice through European colonizers between the fifteenth and seventeenth centuries. Rice was also brought into Congo from Mozambique in the nineteenth century (Lu and Chang 1980).

The Caribbean islands obtained their rices from Europe in the late fifteenth and early sixteenth centuries. Central and South America received rice seeds from European countries, particularly Spain, during the sixteenth through the eighteenth centuries. In addition, there was much exchange of cultivars among countries of Central, South, and North America (Lu and Chang 1980).

Rice cultivation in the United States began around 1609 as a trial planting in Virginia. Other plantings soon followed along the south Atlantic coast. Rice production was well established in South Carolina by about 1690. It then spread to the areas comprising Mississippi and southwest Louisiana, to adjoining areas in Texas, and to central Arkansas, which are now the main rice-producing states in the South. California began rice growing in 1909–12 with the predominant cultivar the sinica type, which can tolerate cold water at the seedling stage. Rice was introduced into Hawaii by Chinese immigrants between 1853 and 1862, but it did not thrive as an agro-industry in competition with sugarcane and pineapple (Adair, Miller, and Beachell 1962; Lu and Chang 1980).

Experimental planting of rice in Australia took place in New South Wales in 1892, although other introductions into the warmer areas of Queensland and the Northern Territories could have come earlier. Commercial planting in New South Wales began in 1923 (Grist 1975). The island of New Guinea began growing rice in the nineteenth century (Bertin et al. 1971).

The dissemination of Asian rice from one place to another doubtless also took place for serendipitous reasons. Mexico, for example, received its first lot of rice seed around 1522 in a cargo mixed with wheat. South Carolina's early plantings of rice around 1685–94 allegedly used rice salvaged from a wrecked ship whose last voyage began in Madagascar (Grist 1975; Lu and Chang 1980).

In addition, the deliberate introduction of rice has produced other unexpected benefits. This occurred when the Champa rices of central Vietnam were initially brought to the coastal areas of South China. In 1011–12 the Emperor Chen-Tsung of the Sung Dynasty decreed the shipment of 30,000 bushels of seed from Fukien Province into the lower Yangtze basin because of the grain's early maturing and drought-escaping characteristics. But its subsequent widespread use in China paved the way for the double cropping of rice and the multiple cropping of rice and other crops (Ho 1956; Chang 1987).

As for African rice *(O. glaberrima),* its cultivation remains confined to West Africa under a variety of soil-water regimes: deep water basins, water holes in the savannas, hydromorphic soils in the forest zone, and dryland conditions in hilly areas (Porteres 1956; Harlan 1973). In areas favorable for irrigated rice production, African rice has been rapidly displaced by the Asian introductions, and in such fields the native cultigen has become a weed in commercial plantings.

It is interesting to note that the African cultigen has been found as far afield as Central America, most likely as a result of introduction during the time of the transatlantic slave trade (Bertin et al. 1971).

Cultivation Practices and Cultural Exchanges

Evolution of Cultivation Practices

Rice grains were initially gathered and consumed by prehistoric peoples in the humid tropics and subtropics from self-propagating wild stands. Cultivation began when men or, more likely, women, deliberately dropped rice grains on the soil in low-lying spots near their homesteads, kept out the weeds and animals, and manipulated the water supply. The association between rice and human community was clearly indicated in the exciting excavations at He-mu-du, Luo-jia-jiao, and Pen-tou-shan in China where rice was a principal food plant in the developing human settlements there more than 7,000 years ago.

Rice first entered the diet as a supplement to other food plants as well as to game, fish, and shellfish. As rice cultivation expanded and became more efficient, it replaced other cereals (millets, sorghums, Job's tears, and even wheat), root crops, and forage plants. The continuous expansion of rice cultivation owed much to its unique features as a self-supporting semiaquatic plant. These features include the ability of seed to germinate under both aerobic and anaerobic conditions and the series of air-conducting aerenchymatous tissues in the leafsheaths, stems, and roots that supply air to roots under continuous flooding. Also important are soil microbes in the root zone that fix nitrogen to feed rice growth, and the wide adaptability of rice to both wetland and dryland soil-water regimes. It is for these reasons that rice is the only subsistence crop whose soil is poorly drained and needs no nitrogen fertilizer applied. And these factors, in turn, account for the broad rice-growing belt from the Sino-Russian border along the Amur River (53°N latitude) to central Argentina (35°S).

Forces crucial to the expansion and improvement of rice cultivation were water control, farm implements, draft animals, planting methods, weed and pest control, manuring, seed selection, postharvest facilities, and above all, human innovation. A number of significant events selected from the voluminous historical records on rice are summarized below to illustrate the concurrent progression in its cultivation techniques and the socio-politico-economic changes that accompanied this progression.

Rice was initially grown as a rain-fed crop in low-lying areas where rain water could be retained. Such areas were located in marshy, but flood-free, sites around river bends, as found in Honan and Shenxi Provinces of north China (Ho 1956), and at larger sites between small rivers, as represented by the He-mu-du site in east China (Chang 1968; You 1976). Early community efforts led to irrigation or drainage projects. The earliest of such activities in the historical record were flood-control efforts in the Yellow River area under Emperor Yu at about 2000 B.C. Irrigation works, including dams, canals, conduits, sluices, and ponds, were in operation during the Yin period (c. 1400 B.C.).

A system of irrigation and drainage projects of various sizes were set up during the Chou Dynasty. Large-scale irrigation works were built during the Warring States period (770–21 B.C.). By 400 B.C., "rice *[tao] men*" were appointed to supervise the planting and water management operations. The famous Tu-Cheng-Yen Dam was constructed near Chendu in Sichuan (Szechuan) Province about 250 B.C., which made western Sichuan the new rice granary of China.

Further developments during the Tang and Sung dynasties led to extensive construction of ponds as water reservoirs and of dams in a serial order to impound fresh water in rivers during high tides. Dykes were built around lake shores to make use of the rich alluvial soil (Chou 1986), and the importance of water quality was recognized (Amano 1979).

Among farm implements, tools made from stone (spade, hoe, axe, knife, grinder, pestle, and mortar) preceded those made from wood and large animal bones (hoe, spade); these were followed by bronze and iron tools. Bone spades along with wooden handles were found at the He-mu-du site. Bronze knives and sickles appeared during Shang and Western Chou. Between 770 and 211 B.C. iron tools appeared in many forms. The iron plow pulled by oxen was perfected during the Western Han period. Deep plowing was advocated from the third century B.C. onward. The spike-tooth harrow *(pa)* appeared around the Tang Dynasty (sixth century), and it markedly improved the puddling of wet soil and facilitated the transplanting process. This implement later spread to Southeast Asia to become an essential component in facilitating transplanted rice culture there (Chang 1976a). Other implements, such as the roller and a spiked board, were also developed to improve further the puddling and leveling operations.

Broadcasting rice grains into a low-lying site was the earliest method of planting and can still be seen in the Jeypore tract of India and many parts of Africa. In dry soils, the next development was to break through the soil with implements, mainly the plow, whereas in wetland culture, it was to build levees (short dikes or bunds) around a field in order to impound the water. In the latter case, such an operation also facilitated land leveling and soil preparation by puddling the wet soil in repeated rounds.

The next giant step came in the transplanting (insertion) of young rice seedlings into a well-puddled and leveled wet field. Transplanting requires the raising of seedlings in nursery beds, then pulling them from those beds, bundling them, and transporting them to the field where the seedlings are thrust by hand into the softened wet soil. A well-performed transplanting operation also requires seed selection, the soaking of seeds prior to their initial sowing, careful management of the nursery beds, and proper control of water in the nursery and in the field. The transplanting practice began in the late Han period (A.D. 23–270) and subsequently spread to neighboring countries in Southeast Asia as a package comprised of the water buffalo, plow, and the spike-tooth harrow.

Transplanting is a labor-consuming operation. Depending on the circumstances, between 12 and close to 50 days of an individual's labor is required to transplant one hectare of rice land (Barker, Herdt, and Rose 1985). On the other hand, transplanting provides definite advantages in terms of a fuller use of the available water, especially during dry years, better weed control, more uniform maturation of the plants, higher grain yield under intensive management, and more efficient use of the land for rice and other crops in cropping sequence.

Despite these advantages, however, in South Asia the transplanting method remains second in popularity to direct seeding (broadcasting or drilling) due to operational difficulties having to do with farm implements, water control, and labor supply (Chang 1976a).

Variations of the one-step transplanting method were (1) to interplant an early maturing variety and a late one in alternating rows in two steps (once practiced in central China) and (2) to pull two-week-old seedlings as clumps and set them in a second nursery until they were about one meter tall. At this point, they were divided into smaller bunches and once more transplanted into the main field. This method, called double transplanting, is still practiced in Indochina in anticipation of quickly rising flood waters and a long rain season (Grist 1975).

Weeds in rice fields have undoubtedly been a serious production constraint since ancient times. The importance of removing weeds and wild rice plants was emphasized as early as the Han Dynasty. Widely practiced methods of controlling unwanted plants in the southern regions involved burning weeds prior to plowing and pulling them afterward, complemented by maintaining proper water depth in the field. Fallowing was mentioned as another means of weed control, and midseason drainage and tillage has been practiced since Eastern Chou as an effective means of weed control and of the suppression of late tiller formation by the rice plant.

Different tools, mainly of the hoe and harrow types, were developed for tillage and weed destruction. Otherwise, manual scratching of the soil surface and removal of weeds by hand were practiced by weeders who crawled forward among rows of growing rice plants. Short bamboo tubes tipped with iron claws were placed on the finger tips to help in the tedious operation. More efficient tools, one of which was a canoe-shaped wooden frame with a long handle and rows of spikes beneath it, appeared later (Amano 1979: 403). This was surpassed only by the rotary weeder of the twentieth century (Grist 1975: 157).

Insect pests were mentioned in Chinese documents before plant diseases were recognized. The Odes (c. sixth century B.C.) mentioned stemborers and the granary moth. During the Sung Dynasty, giant bamboo combs were used to remove leaf rollers that infest the upper portions of rice leaves. A mixture of lime and tung oil was used as an insect spray. Kernel smut, blast disease, and cold injury during flowering were recognized at the time of the Ming Dynasty. Seedling rot was mentioned in the Agricultural Manual of Chen Fu during South Sung (Chinese Academy of Agricultural Sciences 1986).

The relationship between manuring and increased rice yield was observed and recorded more than two thousand years ago. The use of compost and plant ash was advocated in writings of the first and third centuries. Boiling of animal bones in water as a means to extract phosphorus was practiced in Eastern Han. Growing a green manuring crop in winter was advised in the third century. The sixth century agricultural encyclopedia Ch'i-Min-Yao-Shu (Ku undated) distinguished between basal and top dressings of manure, preached the use of human and animal excreta on poor soils, and provided crop rotation schemes (Chang 1979b).

Irrigation practices received much attention in China because of the poor or erratic water supply in many rice areas. Therefore, the labor inputs on water management in Wushih County of Jiangsu Province in the 1920s surpassed those of weeding or transplanting by a factor of two (Amano 1979: 410), whereas in monsoonal Java, the inputs in water management were insignificant (Barker et al. 1985: 126).

Because of the cooler weather in north China, irrigation practices were attuned to suitable weather conditions as early as the Western Han: Water inlets and outlets were positioned directly opposite across the field so as to warm the flowing water by sunlight during the early stages of rice growth. Elsewhere, the inlets and outlets were repositioned at different intervals in order to cool the water during hot summer months (Amano 1979: 182). The encyclopedia Ch'i-Min-Yao-Shu devoted much space to irrigation practices: Watering should be attuned to the weather; the fields should be drained after tillage so as to firm the roots and drained again before harvesting.

In order to supplement the unreliable rainfall, many implements were developed to irrigate individual fields. The developments began with the use of urns to carry water from creeks or wells. The urn or bucket was later fastened to the end of a long pole and counterbalanced on the other end by a large chunk of stone. The pole was rested on a stand and could be swung around to facilitate the filling or pouring. A winch was later used to haul a bucket from a well (see Amano 1979 for illustrations).

The square-pallet chain pump came into use during the Eastern Han; it was either manually driven by foot pedaling or driven by a draft animal turning a large wheel and a geared transmission device (Amano 1979: 205, 240). The chain pump was extensively used in China until it was replaced by engine-driven water pumps after the 1930s. The device also spread to Vietnam. During hot and dry summers, the pumping operation required days and nights of continuous input. Other implements, such as the water wheel in various forms, were also used (Amano 1979; Chao 1979).

Although deepwater rice culture in China never approached the scale found in tropical Asia, Chinese farmers used floating rafts made of wooden frames and tied to the shore so as to grow rice in swamps. Such a practice appeared in Late Han, and the rafts were called *feng* (for frames) fields (Amano 1979: 175).

Many rice cultivars are capable of producing new tillers and panicles from the stubble after a harvest. Such regrowth from the cut stalks is called a ratoon crop. Ratooning was practiced in China as early as the Eastern Tsin period (A.D. 317–417), and it is now an important practice in the southern United States. Ratooning gives better returns in the temperate zone than in the tropics because the insects and diseases that persist from crop to crop pose more serious problems in the tropics.

Seed selection has served as a powerful force in cultivar formation and domestication. Continued selection by rice farmers in the field was even more powerful in fixing new forms; they used the desirable gene-combinations showing up in the plantings to suit their farmer's different needs and fancies. The earliest mention of human-directed selection in Chinese records during the first century B.C. was focused on selecting panicles with more grains and fully developed kernels. Soon, varietal differences in awn color and length, maturity, grain size and shape, stickiness of cooked rice, aroma of milled rice, and adaptiveness to dryland farming were recognized. The trend in selection was largely toward an earlier maturity, which reduced cold damage and made multiple cropping more practical in many areas. The encyclopedia *Ch'i-Min-Yao-Shu* advised farmers to grow seeds in a separate plot, rotate the seed plot site in order to eliminate weedy rice, and select pure and uniformly colored panicles. The seeds were to be stored above ground in aerated baskets, not under the ground. Seed selection by winnowing and floatation in water was advised.

Dryland or hill rice was mentioned in writings of the third century B.C. (Ting 1961). During Eastern Tsin, thirteen varieties were mentioned; their names indicated differences in pigmentation of awn, stem and hull, maturity, grain length, and stickiness of cooked rice (Amano 1979). Varieties with outstanding grain quality frequently appeared in later records. Indeed, a total of 3,000 varieties was tallied, and the names were a further indication of the differences in plant stature and morphology, panicle morphology, response to manuring, resistance to pests, tolerance to stress factors (drought, salinity, alkalinity, cool temperatures, and deep water), and ratooning ability (You 1982). The broad genetic spectrum present in the rice varieties of China was clearly indicated.

Harvesting and processing rice is another laborious process. The cutting instruments evolved from knives to sickles to scythe. Community efforts were common in irrigated areas, and such neighborly cooperation can still be seen in China, Indonesia, the Philippines, Thailand, and other countries. Threshing of grains from the panicles had been done in a variety of ways: beating the bundle of cut stalks against a wooden bench or block; trampling by human feet or animal hoofs; beating with a flail; and, more recently, driving the panicles through a spiked drum that is a prototype of the modern grain combine (see Amano 1979: 248–54 for the ancient tools).

Other important postharvest operations are the drying of the grain (mainly by sun drying), winnowing (by natural breeze or a hand-cranked fan inside a drum winnower), dehusking (dehulling), and milling (by pestle and mortar, stone mills, or modern dehulling and milling machines). Grains and milled rice are stored in sacks or in bulk inside bins. In Indonesia and other hilly areas, the long-panicled Javanica rices are tied into bundles prior to storage.

To sum up the evolutionary pathway in wetland rice cultivation on a worldwide scale, cultivation began with broadcasting in rain-fed and unbunded fields under shifting cultivation. As the growers settled down, the cultivation sites became permanent fields. Then, bunds were built to impound the rain water, and the transplanting method followed. As population pressure on the land continued to increase, irrigation and transplanting became more imperative (Chang 1989a).

The entire range of practices can still be seen in the Jeypore Tract and the neighboring areas (author's personal observations). The same process was retraced in Bang Chan (near Bangkok) within a span of one hundred years. In this case, the interrelationships among land availability, types of rice culture, population density, labor inputs, and grain outputs were documented in a fascinating book entitled *Rice and Man* by L. M. Hanks (1972).

In the twentieth century, further advances in agricultural engineering and technology have to do with several variations in seeding practices that have been adopted to replace transplanting. Rice growers in the southern United States drill seed into a dry soil. The field is briefly flushed with water and then drained. The seeds are allowed to germinate, and water is reintroduced when the seedlings are established. In northern California, pregerminated seeds are dropped from airplanes into cool water several inches deep. The locally selected varieties are able to emerge from the harsh environment (Adair et al. 1973).

Recently, many Japanese farmers have turned to drill-plant pregerminated seed on wet mud. An oxidant is applied to the seed before sowing so as to obtain a uniform stand of plants. For the transplanted crop, transplanting machines have been developed not only to facilitate this process but also to make commercial raising of rice seedlings inside seed boxes a profitable venture. As labor costs continue to rise worldwide, direct seeding coupled with chemical weed control will be the main procedures in the future.

For deepwater rice culture, rice seeds are broadcasted on dry soil. The seeds germinate after the monsoon rains arrive. The crop is harvested after the rains stop and the flooding water has receded.

For dryland rice, seeds are either broadcasted, drilled, or dropped (dibbled) into shallow holes dug in the ground. Dibbling is also common in West Africa. Dryland (hill or upland) rice continues to diminish in area because of low and unstable yield. It has receded largely into hilly areas in Asia where tribal minorities and people practicing shifting cultivation grow small patches for subsistence.

Rice Cultivation and Cultural Exchanges

The expansion of rice cultivation in China involved interactions and exchanges in cultural developments, human migration, and progress in agricultural technology. Agricultural technology in north China developed ahead of other regions of China. Areas south of the Yangtze River, especially south China, were generally regarded by Chinese scholars of the north as primitive in agricultural practices. During travel to the far south in the twelfth century, one of these scholars described the local rain-fed rice culture. He regarded it as crude in land preparation: Seed was sown by dibbling, fertilizer was not used, and tillage as a weeding practice was unknown (Ho 1969).

However, the picture has been rather different in the middle and lower Yangtze basins since the Tsin Dynasty (beginning in A.D. 317) when a mass migration of people from the north to southern areas took place. The rapid expansion of rice cultivation in east China was aided by the large-scale production of iron tools used in clearing forests and the widespread adoption of transplanting.

Private land ownership, which began in the Sung (beginning in A.D. 960), followed by reduction of land rent in the eleventh century and reinforced by double cropping and growth in irrigation works, stimulated rice production and technology development. As a result, rice production south of the Yangtze greatly surpassed rice production in the north, and human population growth followed the same trend (Ho 1969; Chang 1987). Thus, the flow of rice germ plasm was from south to north, but much of the cultural and technological developments diffused in the opposite direction.

Culinary Usage and Nutritional Aspects

Rice Foods

Before the rice grain is consumed, the silica-rich husk (hull, chaff) must be removed. The remaining kernel is the caryopsis or brown rice. Rice consumers, however, generally prefer to eat milled rice, which is the product after the bran (embryo and various layers of seed coat) is removed by milling. Milled rice is, invariably, the white, starchy endosperm, despite pigments present in the hull (straw, gold, brown, red, purple or black) and in the seed coat (red or purple).

Parboiled rice is another form of milled rice in which the starch is gelatinized after the grain is precooked by soaking and heating (boiling, steaming, or dry heating), followed by drying and milling. Milled rice may also be ground into a powder (flour), which enters the food industry in the form of cakes, noodles, baked products, pudding, snack foods, infant formula, fermented items, and other industrial products.

Fermentation of milled glutinous rice or overmilled nonglutinous rice produces rice wine (sake). Vinegar is made from milled and broken rice and beer from broken rice and malt. Although brown rice, as well as lightly milled rice retaining a portion of the germ (embryo), are recommended by health-food enthusiasts, their consumption remains light. Brown rice is difficult to digest due to its high fiber content, and it tends to become rancid during extended storage. Cooking of all categories of rice is done by applying heat (boiling or steaming) to soaked rice until the kernels are fully gelatinized and excess water is expelled from the cooked product. Cooked rice can be lightly fried in oil to make fried rice. People of the Middle East prefer to fry the rice lightly before boiling. Americans often add salt and butter or margarine to soaked rice prior to boiling. The peoples of Southeast Asia eat boiled rice three times a day, including breakfast, whereas peoples of China, Japan, and Korea prepare their breakfast by boiling rice with excess water, resulting in porridge (thick gruel) or congee (thin soup).

Different kinds of cooked rice are distinguished by cohesiveness or dryness, tenderness or hardness, whiteness or other colors, flavor or taste, appearance, and aroma (or its absence). Of these features, cohesiveness or dryness is the most important varietal characteristic: High amylose (25 to 30 percent) of the starchy endosperm results in dry and fluffy kernels; intermediate amylose content (15 to 25 percent) produces tender and slightly cohesive rice; low amylose content (10 to 15 percent) leads to soft cohesive (aggregated) rice; and glutinous or waxy endosperm (0.8 to 1.3 percent amylose) produces highly sticky rice. Amylopectin is the other – and the major – fraction of rice starch in the endosperm.

These four classes of amylose content and cooked products largely correspond with the designation of Indica, Javanica, Sinica (Japonica), and glutinous. Other than amylose content, the cooked rice is affected by the rice-water ratio, cooking time, and age of rice. Hardness, flavor, color, aroma, and texture of the cooked rice upon cooling are also varietal characteristics (Chang 1988; Chang and Li 1991).

Consumer preference for cooked rice and other rice products varies greatly from region to region and is largely a matter of personal preference based on upbringing. For instance, most residents of Shanghai prefer the cohesive *keng* (Sinica) rice, whereas people in Nanjing about 270 kilometers away in the same province prefer the drier *hsien* (Indica) type. Tribal people of Burma, Laos, Thailand, and Vietnam eat glutinous rice three times a day – a habit unthinkable to the people on the plains. Indians and Pakistanis pay a higher price for the basmati rices, which elongate markedly upon cooking and have a strong aroma. People of South Asia generally prefer slender-shaped rice, but many Sri Lankans fancy the short, roundish *samba* rices, which also have dark red seed coats. Red rice is also prized by tribal people of Southeast Asia (Eggum et al. 1981; Juliano 1985c) and by numerous Asians during festivities, but its alleged nutritional advantage over ordinary rice remains a myth. It appears that the eye appeal of red or purple rice stems from the symbolic meaning given the color red throughout Asia, which is "good luck."

The pestle and mortar were doubtless the earliest implements used to mill rice grains. The milling machines of more recent origin use rollers that progressed from stone to wood to steel and then to rubber-wrapped steel cylinders. Tubes made of sections of bamboo were most likely an early cooking utensil, especially for travelers. A steamer made of clay was unearthed at the He-mu-du site dating from 5000 B.C., but the ceramic and bronze pots were the main cooking utensils until ironware came into use. Electric rice cookers replaced iron or aluminum pots in Japan and other Asian countries after the 1950s, and today microwave ovens are used to some extent.

Nutritional Considerations

Rice is unquestionably a superior source of energy among the cereals. The protein quality of rice (66 percent) ranks only below that of oats (68 percent) and surpasses that of whole wheat (53 percent) and of corn (49 percent). Milling of brown rice into white rice results in a nearly 50 percent loss of the vitamin B complex and iron, and washing milled rice prior to cooking further reduces the water-soluble vitamin content. However, the amino acids, especially lysine, are less affected by the milling process (Kik 1957; Mickus and Luh 1980; Juliano 1985a; Juliano and Bechtel 1985).

Rice, which is low in sodium and fat and is free of cholesterol, serves as an aid in treating hypertension. It is also free from allergens and now widely used in baby foods (James and McCaskill 1983). Rice starch can also serve as a substitute for glucose in oral rehydration solution for infants suffering from diarrhea (Juliano 1985b).

The development of beriberi by people whose diets have centered too closely on rice led to efforts in the 1950s to enrich polished rice with physiologically active and rinse-free vitamin derivatives. However, widespread application was hampered by increased cost and yellowing of the kernels upon cooking (Mickus and Luh 1980). Certain states in the United States required milled rice to be sold in an enriched form, but the campaign did not gain acceptance in the developing countries. After the 1950s, nutritional intakes of the masses in Asia generally improved and, with dietary diversification, beriberi receded as a serious threat.

Another factor in keeping beriberi at bay has been the technique of parboiling rough rice. This permits the water-soluble vitamins and mineral salts to spread through the endosperm and the proteinaceous material to sink into the compact mass of gelatinized starch. The result is a smaller loss of vitamins, minerals, and amino acids during the milling of parboiled grains (Mickus and Luh 1980), although the mechanism has not been fully understood. Parboiled rice is popular among the low-income people of Bangladesh, India, Nepal, Pakistan, Sri Lanka, and parts of West Africa and amounts to nearly one-fifth of the world's rice consumed (Bhattacharya 1985).

During the 1970s, several institutions attempted to improve brown rice protein content by breeding. Unfortunately, such efforts were not rewarding because the protein content of a variety is highly variable and markedly affected by environment and fertilizers, and protein levels are inversely related to levels of grain yield (Juliano and Bechtel 1985).

Production and Improvement in the Twentieth Century

Production Trends

Prior to the end of World War II, statistical information on global rice production was rather limited in scope. The United States Department of Agriculture (USDA) compiled agricultural statistics in the 1930s, and the Food and Agriculture Organization of the United Nations (FAO) expanded these efforts in the early 1950s (FAO 1965). In recent years, the *World Rice Statistics* published periodically by the International Rice Research Institute (IRRI) provides comprehensive information on production aspects, imports and exports, prices, and other useful information concerning rice (IRRI 1991).

During the first half of the twentieth century, production growth stemmed largely from an increase in wetland rice area and, to a lesser extent, from expansion of irrigated area and from yields increased by the use of nitrogen fertilizer. Then, varietal improvement came in as the vehicle for delivering higher grain yields, especially in the late 1960s when the "Green Revolution" in rice began to gather momentum (Chang 1979a).

Rice production in Asian countries steadily increased from 240 million metric tons during 1964-6 to 474 million tons in 1989-90 (IRRI 1991). Among the factors were expansion in rice area and/or irrigated area; adoption of high-yielding, semidwarf varieties (HYVs); use of nitrogen fertilizers and other chemicals (insecticides, herbicides, and fungicides); improved cultural methods; and intensified land use through multiple cropping (Herdt and Capule 1983; Chang and Luh 1991).

Asian countries produced about 95 percent of the world's rice during the years 1911-40. After 1945, however, Asia's share dropped to about 92 percent in the 1980s, with production growth most notable in North and South America (IRRI 1991; information on changes in grain yield, production, annual growth rates, and prices in different Asian countries is provided in Chang 1993b; Chang and Luh 1991; David 1991; and Chang 1979a).

But despite the phenomenal rise in crop production and (in view of rapidly growing populations) the consequent postponement of massive food shortages in Asia since the middle 1960s, two important problems remain. One of these is food production per capita, which advanced only slightly ahead of population growth (WRI 1986). The other is grain yield, which remained low in adverse rain-fed environments – wetland, dryland, deepwater, and tidal swamps (IRRI 1989). In fact, an apparent plateau has prevailed for two decades in irrigated rice (Chang 1983). Moreover, the cost of fertilizers, other chemicals, labor, and good land continued to rise after the 1970s, whereas the domestic wholesale prices in real terms slumped in most tropical Asian nations and have remained below the 1966-8 level.

This combination of factors brought great concern when adverse weather struck many rice areas in Asia in 1987 and rice stocks became very low. Fortunately, weather conditions improved the following year and rice production rebounded (Chang and Luh 1991; IRRI 1991).

However, the threat to production remains. In East Asia, five years of favorable weather ended in 1994 with a greater-than-usual number of typhoons that brought massive rice shortages to Japan and South Korea. And in view of the "El Niño" phenomenon, a higher incidence of aberrant weather can be expected, which will mean droughts for some and floods for others (Nicholls 1993).

Germ Plasm Loss and the Perils of Varietal Uniformity

Rice is a self-fertilizing plant. Around 1920, however, Japanese and U.S. rice breeders took the lead in using scientific approaches (hybridization selection and testing) to improve rice varieties. Elsewhere, pureline selection among farmers' varieties was the main method of breeding.

After World War II, many Asian countries started to use hybridization as the main breeding approach. Through the sponsorship of the FAO, several countries in South and Southeast Asia joined in the Indica-Japonica Hybridization Project during the 1950s, exchanging rice germ plasm and using diverse parents in hybridization.

These efforts, however, provided very limited improvement in grain yield (Parthasarathy 1972), and the first real breakthrough came during the mid-1950s when Taiwan (first) and mainland China (second) independently succeeded in using their semidwarf rices in developing short-statured, nitrogen-responsive and high-yielding semidwarf varieties (HYVs). These HYVs spread quickly among Chinese rice farmers (Chang 1961; Huang, Chang, and Chang 1972; Shen 1980).

Taiwan's semidwarf "Taichung Native 1" (TN1) was introduced into India through the International Rice Research Institute (IRRI) located in the Philippines. "TNI" and IRRI-bred "IR8" triggered the "Green Revolution" in tropical rices (Chandler 1968; Huang et al. 1972). Subsequent developments in the dramatic spread of the HYVs and an associated rise in area grain yield and production have been documented (Chang 1979a; Dalrymple 1986), and refinements in breeding approaches and international collaboration have been described (Brady 1975; Khush 1984; Chang and Li 1991).

In the early 1970s, China scored another breakthrough in rice yield when a series of hybrid rices (F_1 hybrids) were developed by the use of a cytoplasmic pollen-sterile source found in a self-sterile wild plant ("Wild Abortive") on Hainan Island (Lin and Yuan 1980). The hybrids brought another yield increment (15 to 30 percent) over the widely grown semidwarfs.

Along with the rapid and large-scale adoption of the HYVs and with deforestation and development projects, innumerable farmers' traditional varieties of all three ecogenetic races and their wild relatives have disappeared from their original habitats – an irreversible process of "genetic erosion." The lowland group of the javanic race (bulu, gundill) suffered the heaviest losses on Java and Bali in Indonesia. Sizable plantings of the long-bearded bulus can now be found only in the Ifugao rice terraces of the Philippines.

In parallel developments, by the early 1990s the widespread planting of the semidwarf HYVs and hybrid rices in densely planted areas of Asia amounted to about 72 million hectares. These HYVs share a common semidwarf gene (sd$_1$) and largely the same cytoplasm (either from "Cina" in older HYVs or "Wild Abortive" in the hybrids). This poses a serious threat of production losses due to a much narrowed genetic base if wide-ranging pest epidemics should break out, as was the case with hybrid maize in the United States during 1970–1 (Chang 1984).

Since the early 1970s, poorly educated rice farmers in South and Southeast Asia have planted the same HYV in successive crop seasons and have staggered plantings across two crops. Such a biologically unsound practice has led to the emergence of new and more virulent biotypes of insect pests and disease pathogens that have overcome the resistance genes in the newly bred and widely grown HYVs. The result has been heavy crop losses in several tropical countries in a cyclic pattern (Chang and Li 1991; Chang 1994).

Fortunately for the rice-growing world, the IRRI has, since its inception, assembled a huge germ plasm collection of more than 80,000 varieties and 1,500 wild rices by exchange and field collection. Seeds drawn from the collection not only have sustained the continuation of the "Green Revolution" in rice all over the world but also assure a rich reservoir of genetic material that can reinstate the broad genetic base in Asian rices that in earlier times kept pest damage to manageable levels (Chang 1984, 1989b, 1994).

Outlook for the Future

Since the dawn of civilization, rice has served humans as a life-giving cereal in the humid regions of Asia and, to a lesser extent, in West Africa. Introduction of rice into Europe and the Americas has led to its increased use in human diets. In more recent times, expansion in the rice areas of Asia and Africa has resulted in rice replacing other dryland cereals (including wheat) and root crops as the favorite among the food crops, wherever the masses can afford it. Moreover, a recent overview of food preferences in Africa, Latin America, and north China (Chang 1987, personal observation in China) suggests that it is unlikely that rice eaters will revert to such former staples as coarse grains and root crops. On the other hand, per capita rice consumption has markedly dropped in the affluent societies of Japan and Taiwan.

In the eastern half of Asia, where 90 to 95 percent of the rice produced is locally consumed, the grain is the largest source of total food energy. In the year 2000, about 40 percent of the people on earth, mostly those in the populous, less-developed countries, depended on rice as the major energy source. The question, of course, is whether the rice-producing countries with ongoing technological developments can keep production levels ahead of population growth.

From the preceding section on cultivation practices, it seems obvious that rice will continue to be a labor-intensive crop on numerous small farms. Most of the rice farmers in rain-fed areas (nearly 50 percent of the total planted area) will remain subsistence farmers because of serious ecological and economic constraints and an inability to benefit from the scientific innovations that can upgrade land productivity (Chang 1993b). Production increases will continue to depend on the irrigated areas and the most favorable rain-fed wetlands, which now occupy a little over 50 percent of the harvested rice area but produce more than 70 percent of the crop. The irrigated land area may be expanded somewhat but at a slower rate and higher cost than earlier. Speaking to this point is a recent study that indicates that Southeast Asia and South Asia as well, are rapidly depleting their natural resources (Brookfield 1993).

With rising costs in labor, chemicals, fuel, and water, the farmers in irrigated areas will be squeezed between production costs and market price. The latter, dictated by government pricing policy in most countries, remains lower than the real rice price (David 1991). Meanwhile, urbanization and industrialization will continue to deprive the shrinking farming communities of skilled workers, especially young men. Such changes in rice-farming communities will have serious and widespread socioeconomic implications.

Unless rice farmers receive an equitable return for their efforts, newly developed technology will remain experimental in agricultural stations and colleges. The decision makers in government agencies and the rice-consuming public need to ensure that a decent living will result from the tilling of rice lands. Incentives must also be provided to keep skilled and experienced workers on the farms. Moreover, support for the agricultural research community must be sustained because the challenges of providing still more in productivity-related cultivation innovations for rice are unprecedented in scope.

Although the rice industry faces formidable challenges, there are areas that promise substantial gains in farm productivity with the existing technology of irrigated rice culture. A majority of rice farmers can upgrade their yields if they correctly and efficiently perform the essential cultivation practices of fertilization, weed and pest control, and water management.

On the research front, rewards can be gained by breaking the yield ceiling, making pest resistance more durable, and improving the tolerance to environmental stresses. Biotechnology will serve as a powerful force in broadening the use of exotic germ plasm in *Oryza* and related genera (Chang and Vaughan 1991). We also need the inspired and concerted teamwork of those various sectors of society that, during the 1960s and 1970s, made the "Green Revolution" an unprecedented event in the history of agriculture.

Lastly, control of human population, especially in the less-developed nations, is also crucial to the maintenance of an adequate food supply for all sectors of human society. Scientific breakthroughs alone will not be able to relieve the overwhelming burden placed on the limited resources of the earth by uncontrolled population growth.

Te-Tzu Chang

Bibliography

Adair, C. R., J. G. Atkins, C. N. Bollich, et al. 1973. *Rice in the United States: Varieties and production.* U.S. Department of Agriculture Handbook No. 289. Washington, D.C.

Adair, C. R., M. D. Miller, and H. M. Beachell. 1962. Rice improvement and culture in the United States. *Advances in Agronomy* 14: 61-108.

Akazawa, T. 1983. An outline of Japanese prehistory. In *Recent progress of natural sciences in Japan,* Vol. 8, *Anthropology,* 1-11. Tokyo.

Alexander, J., and D. G. Coursey. 1969. The origins of yam cultivation. In *The domestication and exploitation of plants and animals,* ed. P. J. Ucko and G. W. Dimbleby, 323-9. London.

Amano, M. 1979. *Chinese agricultural history research.* Revised edition (in Japanese). Tokyo.

Andersson, J. G. 1934. *Children of the yellow earth: Studies in prehistoric China.* London.

Ando, H. 1951. *Miscellaneous records on the ancient history of rice crop in Japan* (in Japanese). Tokyo.

Andrus, J. R., and A. F. Mohammed. 1958. *The economy of Pakistan.* Oxford.

Barker, R., R. W. Herdt, and B. Rose. 1985. *The rice economy of Asia.* Washington, D.C.

Bertin, J., J. Hermardinquer, M. Keul, et al. 1971. *Atlas of food crops.* Paris.

Bhattacharya, K. R. 1985. Parboiling of rice. In *Rice: Chemistry and technology,* ed. B. O. Juliano, 289-348. St. Paul, Minn.

Brady, N. C. 1975. Rice responds to science. In *Crop productivity - research imperatives,* ed. A. W. A. Brown et al., 61-96. East Lansing, Mich.

Brookfield, H. 1993. Conclusions and recommendations. In *South-East Asia's environmental future: The search for sustainability,* ed H. Brookfield and Y. Byron, 363-73. Kuala Lumpur and Tokyo.

Candolle, A. de. 1884. *Origin of cultivated plants* (1886 English translation). New York.

Chandler, R. F., Jr. 1968. Dwarf rice - a giant in tropical Asia. In *Science for better living, U.S.D.A. 1968 Yearbook of Agriculture,* 252-5. Washington, D.C.

Chang, K. C. 1968. *The archaeology of ancient China.* Revised edition. New Haven, Conn.

Chang, T. T. 1961. Recent advances in rice breeding. In *Crop and seed improvement in Taiwan, Republic of China,* 33-58. Taipei.

1976a. The rice cultures. In *The early history of agriculture,* ed. J. Hutchinson et al., 143-55. London.

1976b. The origin, evolution, cultivation, dissemination, and divergence of Asian and African rices. *Euphytica* 25: 425-45.

1979a. Genetics and evolution of the Green Revolution. In *Replies from biological research,* ed. R. de Vicente, 187-209. Madrid.

1979b. History of early rice cultivation (in Chinese). In

Chinese agricultural history - collection of essays, ed. T. H. Shen et al. Taipei.

1983. The origins and early cultures of the cereal grains and food legumes. In *The origins of Chinese civilization,* ed. D. N. Keightley, 65-94. Berkeley, Calif.

1984. Conservation of rice genetic resources: Luxury or necessity? *Science* 224: 251-6.

1985. Crop history and genetic conservation in rice - a case study. *Iowa State Journal of Research* 59: 405-55.

1987. The impact of rice in human civilization and population expansion. *Interdisciplinary Science Reviews* 12: 63-9.

1988. The ethnobotany of rice in island Southeast Asia. *Asian Perspectives* 26: 69-76.

1989a. Domestication and spread of the cultivated rices. In *Foraging and farming - the evolution of plant exploitation,* ed. D. R. Harris and G. C. Hillman, 408-17. London.

1989b. The management of rice genetic resources. *Genome* 31: 825-31.

1992. Availability of plant germplasm for use in crop improvement. In *Plant breeding in the 1990s,* ed. H. T. Stalker and J. P. Murphy, 17-35. Cambridge.

1993a. The role of germ plasm and genetics in meeting global rice needs. In *Advances in botany,* ed. Y. I. Hsing and C. H. chou, 25-33. Taipei.

1993b. Sustaining and expanding the "Green Revolution" in rice. In *South-East Asia's environmental future: The search for sustainability,* ed. H. Brookfield and Y. Byron, 201-10. Kuala Lampur and Tokyo.

1994. The biodiversity crisis in Asian crop production and remedial measures. In *Biodiversity and terrestrial ecosystems,* ed C. I. Peng and C. H. Chou, 25-44. Taipei.

Chang, T. T., and C. C. Li. 1991. Genetics and breeding. In *Rice,* Vol. 1, *Production,* ed. B. S. Luh, 23-101. Second edition. New York.

Chang, T. T., and B. S. Luh. 1991. Overview and prospects of rice production. In *Rice,* Vol. 1, *Production,* ed. B. S. Luh, 1-11. Second edition. New York.

Chang, T. T., and D. A. Vaughan. 1991. Conservation and potentials of rice genetic resources. In *Biotechnology in agriculture and forestry,* Vol. 14, *Rice,* ed. Y. P. S. Bajaj, 531-52. Berlin.

Chao, Y. S. 1979. The Chinese water wheel (in Chinese). In *Chinese agricultural history,* ed. T. H. Shen and Y. S. Chao, 69-163, Taipei.

Chatterjee, D. 1951. Note on the origin and distribution of wild and cultivated rices. *Indian Journal of Genetics and Plant Breeding* 11: 18-22.

Chekiang Provincial Cultural Management Commission and Chekiang Provincial Museum. 1976. Ho-mu-tu discovery of important primitive society, an important remain (in Chinese). *Wen Wu* 8: 8-13.

Chen, T. K., ed. 1958. *Rice* (part 1) (in Chinese). Peking.

Chen, T. K. 1960. Lowland rice cultivation in Chinese literature (in Chinese). *Agricultural History Research Series* 2: 64-93.

Chen, W. H. 1989. Several problems concerning the origin of rice growing in China (in Chinese). *Agricultural Archaeology* 2: 84-98.

Chevalier, A. 1932. Nouvelle contribution à l'étude systematique des *Oryza. Review Botanique Applied et Agricultural Tropical* 12: 1014-32.

Chinese Academy of Agricultural Sciences. 1986. *Chinese rice science* (in Chinese). Beijing.

Chou, K. Y. 1986. Farm irrigation of ancient China (in Chinese). *Agricultural Archaeology* 1: 175-83; 2: 168-79.

Dalrymple, D. G. 1986. *Development and spread of high-yielding rice varieties in developing countries.* Washington, D.C.

Dao, T. T. 1985. Types of rice cultivation and its related civilization in Vietnam. *East Asian Cultural Studies* 24: 41-56.

David, C. C. 1991. The world rice economy: Challenges ahead. In *Rice biotechnology,* ed. G. S. Khush and G. Toennissen, 1-18. Cambridge.

Eggum, B. O., E. P. Alabata, and B. O. Juliano. 1981. Protein utilization of pigmented and non-pigmented brown and milled rices by rats. *Quality of Plants, Plant Foods and Human Nutrition* 31: 175-9.

FAO (Food and Agriculture Organization of the United Nations). 1965. *The world rice economy in figures, 1909-1963.* Rome.

Grist, D. H. 1975. *Rice.* Fifth edition. London.

Hanks, L. M. 1972. *Rice and man.* Chicago.

Harlan, J. R. 1973. Genetic resources of some major field crops in Africa. In *Genetic resources in plants - their exploration and conservation,* ed. O. H. Frankel and E. Bennett, 19-32. Philadelphia, Pa.

Hegsted, D. M. 1969. Nutritional value of cereal proteins in relation to human needs. In *Protein-enriched cereal foods for world needs,* ed. M. Milner, 38-48. St. Paul, Minn.

Herdt, R. W., and C. Capule. 1983. *Adoption, spread and production impact of modern rice varieties in Asia.* Los Baños, Philippines.

Higham, C. F. W. 1989. Rice cultivation and the growth of Southeast Asian civilization. *Endeavour* 13: 82-8.

Ho, P. T. 1956. Early ripening rice in Chinese history. *Economic History Review* 9: 200-18.

  1969. The loess and the origin of Chinese agriculture. *American Historical Review* 75: 1-36.

Hsia, N. 1977. Carbon-14 determined dates and prehistoric Chinese archaeological history (in Chinese). *K'ao-ku* 4: 217-32.

Huang, C. H., W. L. Chang, and T. T. Chang. 1972. Ponlai varieties and Taichung Native 1. In *Rice breeding,* 31-46. Los Baños, Philippines.

Hutchinson, J. 1976. India: Local and introduction crops. In *The early history of agriculture,* Philosophical Transactions of the Royal Society of London B275: 129-41.

IRRI (International Rice Research Institute). 1989. *IRRI toward 2000 and beyond.* Los Baños, Philippines.

  1991. *World rice statistics, 1990.* Los Baños, Philippines.

Isao, H. 1976. *History of Japan as revealed by rice cultivation* (in Japanese). Tokyo.

James, C., and D. McCaskill. 1983. Rice in the American diet. *Cereal Foods World* 28: 667-9.

Juliano, B. O. 1985a. Production and utilization of rice. In *Rice: Chemistry and technology,* ed. B. O. Juliano, 1-16. St. Paul, Minn.

  1985b. Polysaccharides, proteins and lipids of rice. In *Rice: Chemistry and technology,* ed. B. O. Juliano, 59-174. St. Paul, Minn.

  1985c. Biochemical properties of rice. In *Rice: Chemistry and technology,* ed. B. O. Juliano, 175-205. St. Paul, Minn.

Juliano, B. O., and D. B. Bechtel. 1985. The rice grain and its gross composition. In *Rice: Chemistry and technology,* ed. B. O. Juliano, 17-57. St. Paul, Minn.

Khush, G. S. 1984. IRRI breeding program and its worldwide impact on increasing rice production. In *Genetic*

manipulation in plant improvement, ed. J. P. Gustafson, 61-94. New York.

Kik, M. C. 1957. The nutritive value of rice and its by-products. *Arkansas Agricultural Experiment Station Bulletin* 589.

Ku, S. H. Undated. *Ch'i min yao shu.* Taipei.

Lin, S. C., and L. P. Yuan. 1980. Hybrid rice breeding in China. In *Innovative approaches to rice breeding,* 35-52. Los Baños, Philippines.

Lu, J. J., and T. T. Chang. 1980. Rice in its temporal and spatial perspectives. In *Rice: Production and utilization,* ed. B. S. Luh, 1-74. Westport, Conn.

Melville, R. 1966. Mesozoic continents and the migration of the angiosperms. *Nature* 220: 116-20.

Mickus, R. R., and B. S. Luh. 1980. Rice enrichment with vitamins and amino acids. In *Rice: Production and utilization,* ed. B. S. Luh, 486-500. Westport, Conn.

Morinaga, T. 1951. *Rice of Japan* (in Japanese). Tokyo.

  1968. Origin and geographical distribution of Japanese rice. *Japan Agricultural Research Quarterly* 3: 1-5.

Nicholls, N. 1993. ENSO, drought, and flooding rain in South-East Asia. In *South-East Asia's environmental future: The search for sustainability,* ed. H. Brookfield and Y. Byron, 154-75. Kuala Lampur and Tokyo.

Oka, H. I. 1988. *Origin of cultivated rice.* Amsterdam and Tokyo.

Pankar, S. N., and M. K. M. Gowda. 1976. On the origins of rice in India. *Science and Culture* 42: 547-50.

Parthasarathy, N. 1972. Rice breeding in tropical Asia up to 1960. In *Rice breeding,* 5-29. Los Baños, Philippines.

Pei, A. P. 1989. Rice remains in Peng-tou-shan culture in Hunan and rice growing in prehistorical China (in Chinese). *Agricultural Archaeology* 2: 102-8.

Porteres, R. 1956. Taxonomie agrobotanique des riz cultives *O. sativa* Linn. et *O. glaberrima* Steud. *Journal Agricultural Tropical Botanique et Applied* 3: 341-84, 541-80, 627-70, 821-56.

Randhawa, M. S. 1980. *A history of agriculture in India,* Vol. 1. New Delhi.

Revel, N., ed. 1988. *Le riz en Asie du Sud-Est: Atlas du vocabulaire de la plante.* Paris.

Roschevicz, R. J. 1931. A contribution to the knowledge of rice (in Russian with English summary). *Bulletin of Applied Botany, Genetics and Plant Breeding* (Leningrad) 27: 1-133.

Sauer, C. O. 1952. *Agricultural origin and dispersals.* New York.

Sharma, G. R., V. D. Misra, D. Mandal, et al. 1980. *Beginnings of agriculture.* Allahabad, India.

Shen, J. H. 1980. Rice breeding in China In *Rice improvement in China and other Asian countries,* 9-36. Los Baños, Philippines.

Spencer, J. E. 1963. The migration of rice from mainland Southeast Asia into Indonesia. In *Plants and the migration of Pacific peoples,* ed. J. Barrau, 83-9. Honolulu.

Ting, Y. 1949. Chronological studies of the cultivation and the distribution of rice varieties *keng* and *sen* (in Chinese with English summary). *Sun Yatsen University Agronomy Bulletin* 6: 1-32.

Ting, Y., ed. 1961. *Chinese culture of lowland rice* (in Chinese). Peking.

Vishnu-Mittre. 1976. Discussion. In *Early history of agriculture,* Philosophical Transactions of Royal Society of London B275: 141.

Watabe, T. 1973. Alteration of cultivated rice in Indochina. *Japan Agricultural Research Quarterly* 7.

1985. Origin and dispersal of rice in Asia. *East Asian Cultural Studies* 24: 33-9.

WRI (World Resources Institute). 1986. *Basic books.* New York.

Yan, W. M. 1989. Further comments on the origin of rice agriculture in China (in Chinese). *Agricultural Archaeology* 2: 72-83.

Yanagita, K., H. Ando, T. Morinaga, et al. 1969. *Japanese history of rice plant* (in Japanese). Tokyo.

Yen, D. E. 1977. Hoabinhian horticulture? The evidence and the questions from northwest Thailand. In *Sunda and Sahul,* ed. J. Allen, J. Golson, and R. Jones, 567-99. London.

You, X. L. 1976. Several views on the rice grains and bone spades excavated from the fourth cultural level of Homo-tu site (in Chinese). *Wen Wu* 8: 20-3.

1982. A historical study of the genetic resources of rice varieties of our country, II (in Chinese). *Agricultural Archaeology* 1: 32-41.

II.A.8 ❧ Rye

Rye As a Grass

Rye (*Secale cereale* L.) is closely related to the genus *Triticum* (which includes bread wheat, durum wheat, spelt, and the like) and has sometimes been included within that genus (Mansfeld 1986: 1447). In fact, it was possible to breed Triticale, a hybrid of *Triticum* and *Secale,* which is cultivated today (Mansfeld 1986: 1449).

Cultivated rye (*Secale cereale*) is also so closely related genetically to the wild rye (*Secale montanum)* that both species would appear to have had the same ancestors. Yet to say that the cultivated rye plant derived from the wild one is an oversimplification because both plants have been changing their genetic makeup since speciation between the wild and cultivated plants first occurred.

The cultigen *Secale cereale* was brought to many parts of the world, but wild rye still grows in the area where cultivated rye originated, which embraces the mountains of Turkey, northwestern Iran, Caucasia, and Transcaucasia (Zohary and Hopf 1988: 64-5; Behre 1992: 142).

The distribution area of wild rye is slightly different from the area of origin of other Near Eastern crops. Wild rye is indigenous to areas north of the range of the wild *Triticum* and *Hordeum* species; these areas have a more continental climate with dry summers and very cold, dry winters. The environmental requirements of cultivated rye reflect these conditions of coldness and dryness: It has a germination temperature of only 1 to 2 degrees Centigrade, which is lower than that of other crops. Indeed, low temperatures are necessary to trigger sprouting (Behre 1992: 145), and the plant grows even in winter if the temperature exceeds 0 degrees Centigrade, although rye can suffer from a long-lasting snow cover. In spring it grows quickly, so that the green plant with unripe grains reaches full height before the summer drought begins (Hegi 1935: 498-9). Obviously, these characteristics make rye a good winter crop. It is sown in autumn, grows in winter and spring, and ripens and is harvested in summer – a growth cycle that is well adapted to continental and even less favorable climatic conditions. There is also another cultigen of rye – summer rye – which is grown as a summer crop. But because of a low yield and unreliability, it is rather uncommon today (Hegi 1935: 497).

Clearly, then, the constitution of the wild grass ancestor of cultivated rye is reflected in the cultivated crop. Rye is predominantly grown as a winter crop, on less favorable soils, and under less favorable climatic conditions than wheat.

The Question of Early Cultivation

There is evidence for the ancient cultivation of rye in the Near East dating back to the Neolithic. Gordon Hillman (1975: 70-3; 1978: 157-74; see also Behre 1992: 142) found cultivated rye in aceramic early Neolithic layers of Tell Abu Hureyra in northern Syria and also at Can Hasan III in central Anatolia. Hillman reports that there were entire rachis internodes at these sites, proof that the selective pressures of cultivation were operating, because only a plant with a nonbrittle rachis can be harvested efficiently. It is not clear, however, if rye was actually cultivated at these Neolithic sites or whether the plant only underwent such morphological adaptations while being sown and harvested as a weedy contaminant of other crops.

To this day, rye remains a vigorous weed in Near Eastern wheat and barley fields, and its nonbrittle rachis internodes resemble a cultivated plant in spite of the fact that it is not intentionally sown. It is harvested together with the more desirable wheat and barley as a "maslin crop" (a crop mixture), and, in climatically unfavorable years, the rye yield is often better than the yield of barley or wheat in these fields. Even an examination of the harvested crop may give the false impression that the rye has been deliberately cultivated. It is interesting to note that such "volunteer" rye is called "wheat of Allah" by Anatolian peasants (Zohary and Hopf 1988: 64) because it is assumed that God "sent" a crop in spite of the bad weather conditions that were unfavorable to the sown wheat.

Possibly this process of unintentionally cultivating rye, while intentionally cultivating wheat and barley, also took place in the early Neolithic fields of Tell Abu Hureyra and Can Hasan III that Hillman investigated. So we do not know if rye was deliberately grown as a crop in its own right or if it was only "wheat of Allah." It is the case that Hillman's evidence for the early cultivation of rye in the Near East contradicts an earlier opinion by Hans Helbaek (1971: 265–78), who assumed that rye derived from central rather than western Asia.

Rye As a Weed

Rye reached Europe at the dawn of the region's Neolithic Revolution, but probably as a weed. Angela M. Kreuz (1990: 64, 163) has discovered rye remains in Bruchenbrücken, near Frankfurt, in central Germany. This site is dated to the earliest phase of the Linearbandkeramik, which is the earliest phase of agriculture in central Europe. Similarly, Ulrike Piening (1982: 241–5) found single rye grains in a Linearbandkeramik settlement at Marbach, near Stuttgart, in southern Germany. But at both sites only single rye grains were found among great amounts of grains of other species. The same is the case with the few other early rye finds in Europe (Piening 1982: 242–4; Behre 1992: 142–3). Thus, the evidence appears to indicate that rye existed during the early phase of agricultural development in Europe as a weed, and an uncommon one at that.

In the Neolithic, however, most grain cultivation took place on fertile loess soils situated in regions where typical winter crop weeds were not present. Such conditions did not favor rye expansion and, consequently, there was little opportunity to compare the durability of rye to that of *Triticum* species, as was the case with the development of the "wheat of Allah" in the maslin crop fields in the Anatolian mountains.

The proportions of rye, however, were greater in some grain assemblages from Bronze Age sites. Many have assumed that rye was cultivated as a Bronze Age crop, especially in eastern central Europe (Körber-Grohne 1987: 44), but the evidence remains scarce and questionable (Behre 1992: 143). Yet spelt *(Triticum spelta),* a grain similar to rye, was commonly grown in this region during the Bronze Age (Körber-Grohne 1987: 74). Because spelt was normally cultivated as a winter crop, spelt grain assemblages from archaeological sites are contaminated with winter crop weed seeds (Küster 1995: 101). Thus, it could be that the beginning of winter crop cultivation favored the expansion of winter rye as a weed in spelt fields. This was probably the case especially in areas less favorable to agriculture that were being cultivated from the Bronze Age forward, as, for example, in some areas of the Carpathians and the Alps, where rye pollen grains have been recorded several times in layers dating to the Bronze Age (Küster 1988: 117). Definitive evidence of an early rye expansion to the Alps, however, awaits more extensive plant macrofossil examination in these marginal agricultural areas high up in the mountains.

Rye As a Secondary Cultivated Crop

Spelt cultivation, possibly as a winter crop, expanded during the Pre-Roman Iron Age to other parts of Europe (Körber-Grohne 1987: 74), as agriculture itself spread to areas with less fertile soils, such as those of sand and gravel in northern central Europe. These soils, as well as the local ecological conditions of humid climate and light snow cover, favor a winter crop plant that grows during mild winter days and in the spring but will not suffer from summer drought on sandy soils.

Pollen (Küster 1988: 117; Behre 1992: 148) and macrofossil evidence (Behre 1992: 143) show that rye became more common during the Pre-Roman Iron Age, perhaps in those winter crop fields on the less favorable soils just described. At this point, rye was still growing as a weed, but because it had the qualities of a cultivated plant under these ecological conditions, rye eventually predominated in fields planted with spelt. This success is typical of secondary plants that are cultivated by chance within stands of other crops.

Karl-Ernst Behre (1992: 143) has compiled a list of the most ancient finds of pure, or possibly pure, rye cultivated during the Iron Age in Europe. This shows concentrations in the eastern Alps, the countries around the Black Sea, and the western and northern marginal areas of Europe.

But rye became more common during the Roman Age, as populations grew, thus increasing the demand for food. During this time, ever greater amounts of lands with less fertile soils were brought under cultivation, and the expansion of winter crop cultivation provided more reliable and greater yields. Abundant *Secale* grains have been discovered on some Roman sites, giving the impression that rye was cultivated as a main crop (Behre 1992: 143–5). It is, however, unlikely that the Romans themselves propagated rye (with which they were unfamiliar) because climate militated against its growth in the Mediterranean region (Behre 1992: 145). Only a few Roman Age sites outside the Roman Imperium have been examined by archaeobotanists so far, but there is clear evidence that rye was grown outside the Empire as a main crop. A detailed study from an area in northern Germany has shown that the shift to rye cultivation took place during the second century A. D. (Behre 1992: 146).

A few hypotheses for the increased importance of rye have been put forward. For one, rye may have been imported from areas outside to sites inside the Imperium (Dickson and Dickson 1988: 121–6), which suggests increased demand, and, in what is not necessarily a contradiction, Behre (1992: 149–50) emphasizes that the expansion of rye during the Roman Age reflects the improvement of harvesting methods beyond the earlier technique of plucking the grain ear by ear. Because all cultivars depend on harvesting for seed dispersal, such a thorough method would not have favored the expansion of rye. But during the Iron Age and Roman times, harvesting methods grew more sophisticated, and the advent of new mowing equipment made rye's dispersal more likely.

Another hypothesis involves climatic deterioration as an explanation for the expansion of rye. To date, however, there is no clear evidence for climatic change during the Roman Age. Most likely then, by way of summary, the major reasons for the increased importance of rye cultivation were the expansion of agriculture to more marginal fields, the growing importance of winter crops, and changing harvesting methods.

Medieval Rye Cultivation

During the Middle Ages, rye became a very important crop in many parts of Europe. As agriculture was introduced to marginal mountainous landscapes, the cultivation of rye was frequently the best alternative. More important, although the acid, sandy soils in northern and north-central Europe became exhausted from overcropping, the custom developed of enriching them with "plaggen," which was heath, cut down and transported from the heathlands to the farmlands (Behre 1992: 152). Although this caused a further impoverishment of the already relatively infertile heathlands, such a practice made it possible to control the fertility of marginal fields and to grow crops near the settlements. On these soils "eternal rye cultivation" (Behre 1992: 152) became possible, allowing cropping every year.

In other regions where rye replaced spelt, as for example in southern Germany, such a replacement resulted from practical reasons (Rösch, Jacomet, and Karg 1992: 193–231). Because spelt is a hulled crop, the grains must be dehusked after threshing. This is not necessary with rye or wheat, but the latter is very sensitive to diseases caused by primitive storage conditions in damp environments. Thus, because it was easier to store rye than wheat, and easier to process rye than spelt, rye replaced spelt in many places during the period between the Roman Age and the Middle Ages (Rösch et al. 1992: 206–13). In other areas, of course, such as the mountains of the Ardennes in Belgium and northern France, and the area around Lake Constance, spelt has been grown until recent times and was never replaced by rye.

The relative importance of a grain crop in the various areas of Germany can be determined from the language of historical documents. This is because the term *Korn* ("corn") signifies the most important crop over the ages. So it is interesting to find that in regions where rye cultivation predominated during the Middle Ages and early modern times, the term *Korn* is connected with rye, but in others it is associated with spelt or wheat.

Rye crossed the Atlantic to the New World with colonists heading to both the south and the north of North America. In the south, Alexander von Humboldt, who visited Mexico at the turn of the nineteenth century, discovered rye growing "at heights where the cultivation of maize would be attended with no success" (Humboldt 1972: 97). In addition, he reported that the plant was seldom attacked by a disease that in Mexico "frequently destroys the finest wheat harvests when the spring and the beginning of the summer have been very warm and when storms are frequent" (Humboldt 1972: 104).

In the north, where rye was also extensively cultivated in colonial New England, symptoms of ergotism (a disease caused by ingestion of the ergot fungus that infects many grains, but especially rye) are believed to have often been manifested by the population. Such symptoms (especially those of nervous dysfunction), are seen to have been present in the Salem witchcraft affair, in the "Great Awakening," and in epidemics of "throat distemper" (Matossian 1989). Certainly ergotism had a long and deadly history in Europe, beginning before the early Middle Ages. Some 132 epidemics were counted between 591 and 1789, the last occurring in France during the time of the "Great Fear," which just preceded the French Revolution and which some have seen as leading to it (Haller 1993).

In conclusion, although rye has been said to be our "oldest crop," and baking company advertisements call rye bread the traditional bread, as we have seen, this is certainly not the case. Only gradually did this crop, which began as a weed among cultigens, grow to prominence. But it has also traveled as far from its origins as the United States and Canada (Körber-Grohne 1987: 40), where the winters are cold enough to stimulate the germination of the grains – the same stimulus rye plants received in the mountains of the Near East before they spread out into eastern, central, northern, and western Europe.

Hansjörg Küster

Bibliography

Behre, Karl-Ernst. 1992. The history of rye cultivation in Europe. *Vegetation History and Archaeobotany* 1: 141–56.

Dickson, C., and J. Dickson. 1988. The diet of the Roman army in deforested central Scotland. *Plants Today* 1: 121–6.

Haller, John S., Jr. 1993. Ergotism. In *The Cambridge world history of human disease*, ed. Kenneth F. Kiple, 718–19. Cambridge and New York.

Hegi, Gustav. 1935. *Illustrierte Flora von Mittel-Europa*, Vol. 1. Second edition. Munich.

Helbaek, Hans. 1971. The origin and migration of rye, *Secale cereale* L.; a palaeo-ethnobotanical study. In *Plant Life* of South-West Asia, ed. P. H. Davis, P. C. Harper, and I. G. Hedge, 265–80. Edinburgh.

Hillman, Gordon. 1975. The plant remains from Tell Abu Hureyra: A preliminary report. In A. M. T. Moore et al., Excavations at Tell Abu Hureyra in Syria: A preliminary report. *Proceedings of the Prehistoric Society* 41: 70–3.

1978. On the origins of domestic rye – Secale cereale: The finds from aceramic Can Hasan III in Turkey. *Anatolian Studies* 28: 157–74.

Humboldt, Alexander von. 1972. *Political essay on the kingdom of New Spain*, ed. Mary M. Dunn. Norman, Okla.

Körber-Grohne, Udelgard. 1987. *Nutzpflanzen in Deutschland*. Stuttgart.

Kreuz, Angela M. 1990. Die ersten Bauern Mitteleuropas. Eine archäobotanische Untersuchung zu Umwelt und Landwirtschaft der ältesten Bandkeramik. *Analecta Praehistorica Leidensia* 23.Leiden.

Küster, Hansjörg. 1988. *Vom Werden einer Kulturlandschaft*. Weinheim.

1995. *Postglaziale Vegetationsgeschichte Südbayerns. Geobotanische Studien zur prähistorischen Landschaftskunde*. Berlin.

Mansfeld, Rudolf. 1986. *Verzeichnis landwirtschaftlicher und gärtnerischer Kulturpflanzen*, ed. Jürgen Schultze-Motel. Second edition. Berlin.

Matossian, Mary Kilbourne. 1989. *Poisons of the past: Molds, epidemics, and history*. New Haven, Conn., and London.

Piening, Ulrike. 1982. Botanische Untersuchungen an verkohlten Pflanzenresten aus Nordwürttemberg. Neolithikum bis Römische Zeit. *Fundberichte aus Baden-Württemberg* 7: 239–71.

Rösch, Manfred, Stefanie Jacomet, and Sabine Karg. 1992. The history of cereals in the region of the former Duchy of Swabia (Herzogtum Schwaben) from the Roman to the post-medieval period: Results of archaeobotanical research. *Vegetation History and Archaeobotany* 1: 193–231.

Zohary, Daniel, and Maria Hopf. 1988. *Domestication of plants in the Old World*. Oxford.

II.A.9 ❧ Sorghum

Grain sorghum (*Sorghum bicolor* [Linn.] Moench) is a native African cereal now also widely grown in India, China, and the Americas. Sorghum ranks fifth in world cereal grain production, and fourth in value (after rice, wheat, and maize) as a cereal crop. It is grown on 40 to 50 million hectares annually, from which up to 60 million metric tons of grain are harvested. In Africa and Asia traditional cultivars are grown, usually with low agricultural inputs, and average yields are below 1 metric ton per hectare. But more than 3 metric tons of grain are harvested per acre in the Americas, where farmers plant modern sorghum hybrids. Sorghum is more tolerant to drought and better adapted for cultivation on saline soils than is maize. It holds tremendous promise as a cereal to feed the rapidly expanding populations of Africa and Asia. In the Americas it is replacing maize as an animal feed.

Morphology and Distribution

The grass genus *Sorghum* Moench is one of immense morphological variation. It is taxonomically subdivided into sections *Chaetosorghum, Heterosorghum, Parasorghum, Stiposorghum*, and *Sorghum* (Garber 1950), and these sections are recognized as separate genera by W. D. Clayton (1972). The genus *Sorghum* is here recognized to include: (1) a complex of tetraploid (2n = 40) rhizomatous taxa (*S. halapense* [Linn.] Pers.) that are widely distributed in the Mediterranean region and extend into tropical India; (2) a rhizomatous diploid (2n = 20) species (*S. propinquum* [Kunth] Hitchc.) that is distributed in Southeast Asia and extends into adjacent Pacific Islands; and (3) a nonrhizomatous tropical African diploid (2n = 20) complex (*S. bicolor* [Linn.] Moench) that includes domesticated grain sorghums and their closest wild and weedy relatives

Sorghum

(de Wet and Harlan 1972). Genetic introgression is common where wild rhizomatous or spontaneous nonrhizomatous taxa become sympatric with grain sorghums, and derivatives of such introgression have become widely distributed as weeds in sorghum-growing regions.

The domesticated sorghum complex is morphologically variable. It includes wild, weed, and domesticated taxa that are divided by J. D. Snowden (1936, 1955) among 28 cultivated species, 13 wild species, and 7 weed species. Following the classification of cultivated plants proposed by Jack R. Harlan and J. M. J. de Wet (1972), the wild taxa are recognized as subspecies *verticilliflorum* (Steud.) de Wet, the weed taxa as subspecies *drummondii* (Steud.) de Wet, and the grain sorghums as subspecies *bicolor* (de Wet and Harlan 1978).

Subspecies *verticilliflorum* includes races verticilliflorum, arundinaceum, virgatum, and aethiopicum. These grade morphologically and ecologically so completely into one another that they do not deserve formal taxonomic rank. This subspecies is indigenous to tropical Africa but has become widely distributed as a weed in tropical Australia (de Wet, Harlan, and Price 1970). It differs from grain sorghum primarily in being spontaneous rather than cultivated and in being capable of natural seed dispersal.

Verticilliflorum is the most widely distributed, and morphologically the most variable, race of the subspecies. It extends naturally across the African savannah, from Senegal to the Sudan and South Africa. It is distinguished from the other races by its large and open inflorescences with long and spreading branches. Verticilliflorum is an aggressive colonizer of naturally disturbed habitats, and it often forms large continuous populations in flood plains. It is commonly harvested as a wild cereal in times of scarcity.

Race arundinaceum is distributed along the margins of tropical forests of the Congo basin. It is sympatric with verticilliflorum along the transition zone between savannah and forest, and the races introgress. Derivatives of such hybridization aggressively colonize areas of forest that are cleared for agriculture. Arundinaceum is typically characterized by large and open inflorescences with long branches that become pendulous at maturity.

Race virgatum occurs along stream banks and irrigation ditches in arid regions of tropical northeastern Africa. Wild populations are harvested as a cereal during times of famine. It is widely sympatric with race verticilliflorum, and gene exchange between them is common. It typically has smaller inflorescences than verticilliflorum.

Race aethiopicum is drought tolerant. It extends across the West African Sahel and into the Sudan. In flood plains, it frequently forms large continuous populations and is harvested as a wild cereal. The distribution and habitat of aethiopicum rarely overlap with the other races. It is characterized by large spikelets that are densely tomentose.

Subspecies *drummondii* is an obligate weed derived through introgression between subspecies *verticilliflorum* and cultivated grain sorghums. It became widely distributed across tropical Africa as part of cereal agriculture. Morphological variation is extensive as a result of hybridization among the different races of grain sorghum and different races of close wild relatives. Stabilized derivatives of such introgression accompanied the cereal to India and the highlands of Ethiopia. Weeds often resemble grain sorghums in spikelet morphology, but they retain the ability of natural seed dispersal.

Grain sorghums also introgress with the Eurasian *S. halepense* to form diploid or tetraploid weedy derivatives. Johnson grass of the American Southwest and some sorghums of Argentina are tetraploid derivatives of such introgression. Diploid derivatives of hybridization between grain sorghum and Johnson grass have recently become obnoxious weeds in the American corn belt.

Subspecies *bicolor* includes all domesticated grain sorghums. The 28 cultivated species recognized by Snowden (1936) are artifacts of sorghum cultivation.

They represent selections by farmers for specific adaptations and food uses, and they do not deserve formal taxonomic rank. Grain sorghums are classified by Harlan and de Wet (1972) into races bicolor, kafir, caudatum, durra, and guinea. Sorghums belonging to different races hybridize where they are grown sympatrically, and cultivars have become established that combine characteristics of two or more of these races. Extensive racial evolution took place in Africa before sorghum was introduced as a cereal into Asia (Harlan and Stemler 1976).

Race bicolor resembles spontaneous weedy sorghums in spikelet morphology, but all cultivars depend on harvesting for seed dispersal. Mississippi chicken corn probably represents a derivative of abandoned cultivated race bicolor that entered America during the slave trade. It is spontaneous and must have regained the ability of natural seed dispersal through mutation. Bicolor sorghums are characterized by open inflorescences, having spikelets with long and clasping glumes that enclose the grain at maturity. Some cultivars of race bicolor are relics of the oldest domesticated sorghums, whereas others are more recent derivatives of introgression between evolutionally advanced cultivars and spontaneous sorghums.

Bicolor sorghums are widely distributed in Africa and Asia but are rarely of major economic importance because of their low yield. Cultivars survive because they were selected for specific uses. They are grown for their sweet stems (chewed as a delicacy), for the high tannin content of the grains (used to flavor sorghum beer), and for use as fodder. Cultivars often tiller profusely, which tends to make their sweet stems desirable as fodder for livestock in Africa.

Race kafir is the most common cultivated sorghum south of the equator in Africa. It never became widely distributed in India and China, probably because of limited trade between southern Africa and India or the Near East before colonial times. Race kafir is characterized by compact inflorescences that are cylindrical in shape. Spikelets have glumes that tightly clasp the usually much longer mature grain. Sorghum has been replaced by maize in areas with high rainfall, but kafir sorghums remain the most important cereal crop of the southern savannahs in areas with between 600 and 900 millimeters (mm) of annual rainfall. At the drier limits of agriculture, sorghum is replaced as a cereal by pearl millet. In the wettest parts, sorghum competes as a food cereal not only with maize but also with finger millet. The grain of kafir sorghums is commonly high in tannin. This provides partial protection against bird damage and confers resistance to grain molds that reduce grain quality. Tannin also, however, reduces the digestibility of porridges produced from kafir sorghums, which today are grown mainly to produce malt for the making of a highly nutritious beer. This beer is commercially produced in Zimbabwe and South Africa.

Race caudatum is distinguished by its asymmetrical grains. The grain is usually exposed between the glumes at maturity, with the embryo side bulging and the opposite side flat or concave. Inflorescences range from very compact to rather open with spreading branches. Caudatum cultivars are highly adaptive and are grown in areas with as low as 350 mm and as high as 1,000 mm of annual rainfall. Selected cultivars are resistant to fungal leaf diseases, to ergot of the grain, and to infestation by insects or the parasitic striga weed. Caudatum sorghums are a major food source of people speaking Chari-Nile languages in the Sudan, Chad, Uganda, northeastern Nigeria, and Cameroon (Stemler, Harlan, and de Wet 1975). Along the flood plains of the Niger River in Chad, caudatum sorghums are grown in nurseries and transplanted to cultivated fields as flood waters recede (Harlan and Pasguereau 1969). The grains are ground into flour from which a fermented porridge is produced. Caudatum sorghums are also commercially grown in Nigeria for the production of malt used in the brewing industry.

Race durra is the most drought tolerant of grain sorghums. Selected cultivars mature in less than three months from planting, allowing escape from terminal drought stress in areas with short rainy seasons. The name *durra* refers to the Arabic word for sorghum, and the distribution of durra sorghums in Africa is closely associated with the spread of Islam across the Sahel. The grain is also extensively grown in the Near East, China, and India. Inflorescences are usually compact. Spikelets are characteristically flattened and ovate in outline, with the lower glume either creased near the middle or having a tip that is distinctly different in texture from the lower two-thirds of the glume. Grains are cooked whole after decortication or are ground into flour to be prepared as porridge or baked into unleavened bread.

Race guinea is distinguished by long glumes that tightly clasp the obliquely twisted grain, which becomes exposed between them at maturity. Inflorescences are large and often open, with branches that become pendulous at maturity. These are adaptations for cultivation in areas with high rainfall, and guinea is the principal sorghum of the West African Guinea zone with more than 800 mm of annual rainfall. Guinea sorghums are also grown along the high-rainfall highlands from Malawi to Swaziland and in the ghats of Central India. It is a principal food grain in West Africa and Malawi. In Senegal, the small and hard grains of an indigenous cultivar are boiled and eaten, similar to the way rice is prepared and consumed in other parts of the world. In Malawi, the sweet grains of a local cultivar are eaten as a snack while still immature. Guinea sorghums are valued for the white flour that is produced from their tannin-free grains.

Intermediate races recognized by Harlan and de Wet (1972) include sorghum cultivars that are not readily classifiable into any one of the five basic races. They combine characteristics of race bicolor with those of the other four basic races, of guinea and caudatum, or of guinea and kafir. Cultivars with intermediate morphologies occur wherever members of basic races are grown sympatrically in Africa. Intermediate cultivars have become widely distributed in India. Modern high-yielding sorghum hybrids combine traits of races kafir, durra, and caudatum in various combinations.

Domestication and Evolutionary History

Cereal domestication is a process, not an event. Domestication is initiated when seeds from planted populations are harvested and sown in human-disturbed habitats (in contrast to naturally disturbed habitats), and it continues as long as the planting and harvesting processes are repeated in successive generations (Harlan, de Wet, and Price 1973). The initial ability to survive in disturbed habitats is inherent in all wild grasses that were adopted as cereals. In fact, as aggressive colonizers, they can form large continuous colonies in naturally disturbed habitats. This weedy characteristic of these plants facilitates harvesting and eventually leads to their domestication. Sowing in cultivated fields reinforces adaptation for survival in disturbed habitats, and harvesting of sown populations selects against mechanisms that facilitate natural seed dispersal. Thus, domesticated cereals have lost the ability to compete successfully for natural habitats with their wild relatives. They depend on farming for suitable habitats and on harvesting and sowing for seed dispersal.

There is little doubt that subspecies *verticilliflorum* gave rise to grain sorghums under domestication. This spontaneous complex of tropical African sorghums is an aggressive colonizer of naturally disturbed habitats, and because it forms large continuous stands, it remains a favorite wild cereal of nomads as well as farmers during times of food scarcity. Snowden (1936) and R. Porteres (1962) have suggested that race arundinaceum (of forest margins) gave rise to guinea sorghums, the desert race aethiopicum to durra sorghums, and the savannah race verticilliflorum to kafir sorghums. Distribution and ethnological isolation certainly suggest three independent domestications of grain sorghum. This, however, is unlikely. Close genetic affinities between specific cultivated races and the spontaneous races with which they are sympatric resulted from introgression. Such introgression continues between grain sorghums and their close, spontaneous relatives. Racial evolution of advanced cultivated races resulted from selection by farmers who grew bicolor sorghums for specific uses, and from natural adaptations to local agro-ecological environments.

The wild progenitor of cultivated sorghums is the widely distributed race verticilliflorum. It could have been domesticated anywhere across the African savanna. Jack Harlan (1971) proposes that sorghum was taken into cultivation along a broad band of the savanna from the Sudan to Nigeria, where verticilliflorum is particularly abundant. H. Dogget (1965) previously had suggested that the initial domestication occurred in the northeastern quadrant of Africa, probably undertaken by early farmers in Ethiopia who learned from the ancient Egyptians how to grow barley and wheat. These two Near Eastern cereals have been grown in Egypt and along the Mediterranean coast of North Africa since at least the fifth century B.C. (Clark 1971).

Tropical agriculture in Africa must have started in the savannah along the southern fringes of the Sahara (Clark 1976, 1984). Archaeological evidence indicates that pearl millet (*Pennisetum glaucum* [Linn.] R. Br.), sorghum, and finger millet (*Eleusine coracana* [Linn.] Gaertn.) were among the earliest native cereals of the savannah to be domesticated.

J. S. Wigboldus (1991) has suggested that there is little evidence to indicate cereal cultivation south of the Sahara before the ninth century of the Christian era. Archaeological evidence, however, indicates that cereal agriculture in the African savanna is much older than this. Inhabitants of the Dhar Tichitt region of Mauritania, extending from the middle of the second to the middle of the first millennium B.C., evidently experimented with the cultivation of native grasses (Munson 1970). During the first phase of settlement, bur grass (*Cenchrus biflorus* Roxb.) seems to have been the most common grass harvested as a wild cereal. It is still extensively harvested in the wild as a source of food during times of scarcity. In the middle phases, *Brachiaria deflexa* (Shumach.) Hubbard, now cultivated on the highlands of Mali (Porteres 1976), and *Pennisetum glaucum,* now grown as pearl millet across the Sahel, became equally common, as shown by their impressions on potsherds. In later phases, starting about 1000 B.C., impressions of what is almost certainly domesticated pearl millet became dominant (Munson 1970). It is not possible, however, to determine whether pearl millet was domesticated at Dhar Tichitt or whether this cereal was introduced to these settlements from other parts of the West African Sahel.

Tropical African grasses were also grown as cereals in eastern Africa before the beginning of the Christian era. Potsherds from a Neolithic settlement at Kadero in the central Sudan, dated to between 5,030 and 5,280 years ago, reveal clear impressions of domesticated sorghum and finger millet spikelets and grains (Klichowska 1984). Both cereals are today extensively grown in eastern and southern Africa. Indirect evidence of early sorghum and finger millet cultivation in Africa comes from the presence of these African cereals in Neolithic settlements of India, dated to about 1000 B.C. (Weber 1991). Other archaeological evidence indicates that sorghum cultivation spread from eastern Africa to reach northeastern Nigeria not later than the tenth century A.D. (Connah 1967) and, together with

pearl millet and finger millet, reached southern Africa not later than the eighth century A.D. (Shaw 1976).

That native grasses were grown as cereals not less than 3,000 years ago along the southern fringes of the Sahara is not surprising. Wheat and barley were grown in Egypt and along the Mediterranean coast of North Africa by the latter part of the fifth millennium B.C. (Shaw 1976), and the knowledge of cereal agriculture reached the highlands of Ethiopia some 5,000 years ago. These Near Eastern cereals cannot be grown successfully as rain-fed crops in lowland tropics. Experimentation with the cultivation of native grasses in the semiarid tropical lowlands seems a logical next step in the development of African plant husbandry. Nor is the absence of domesticated sorghum in West Africa before the tenth century A.D. surprising. Sorghum is poorly adapted to the arid Sahel, where finger millet was domesticated and remains the principal cereal, and an abundance of wild food plants and animals probably made agriculture in the Guinea zone less productive than hunting and gathering during the beginnings of plant husbandry in tropical Africa. Racial evolution gave rise to races guinea, caudatum, durra, and kafir and is associated with adaptation to agro-ecological zones and the isolation of different ethnic groups who adopted sorghum cultivation. Morphological differentiation took place in Africa, except for race durra that may have evolved in Asia after sorghum cultivation became established in southwestern Asia.

Race guinea's open panicles and spikelets with widely gaping glumes are adaptations for successful cultivation in high-rainfall areas. The glumes enclose the immature grain to protect it from infection by grain molds, but they gape widely at maturity to allow the grain to dry rapidly after a rain and thus escape damage. Guinea sorghums, which probably evolved in Ethiopia, are still grown in the Konso region, and from there they may have spread along the mountains south to Swaziland and west to the Guinea coast. Cultivated sorghum belonging to race guinea was already growing in Malawi during the ninth century A.D. (Robbinson 1966). Today, almost half the sorghum production in Nigeria comes from guinea sorghums.

Kafir sorghums evolved south of the equator and never became widely distributed outside the southern African savanna. They are probably relatively recent in origin. Kafir sorghums became associated with Iron Age Bantu settlements only during the eighth century A.D. (Fagan 1967; Phillipson and Fagan 1969). Kafir sorghums are genetically more closely allied to local verticilliflorums than to other spontaneous sorghums. This led Y. Schechter and de Wet (1975) to support Snowden's (1936) conclusion that race kafir was independently domesticated from other sorghums in southern Africa. It is more likely, however, that kafir sorghums were derived from introduced bicolor sorghums that introgressed with local wild sorghum adapted to the arid southern savanna.

As already mentioned, race durra is the most drought-tolerant of all grain sorghums. Their wide distribution in semiarid Asia caused Harlan and A. B. L. Stemler (1976) to propose that durra sorghums evolved in West Asia from earlier introductions of race bicolor. Archaeological remains indicate that bicolor sorghums were grown in India not later than the early first millennium B.C. (Weber 1991). Durras remain the common cultivated sorghums in semiarid Asia. In Africa, they are grown across the Sahel, and their distribution seems to be associated with the expansion of Islam across North Africa.

The cultivation of caudatum sorghums is closely associated in Africa with the distribution of people who speak Chari-Nile languages (Stemler, Harlan, and de Wet 1975). Caudatum sorghums probably represent selections from race bicolor in the eastern savannah during relatively recent times. Bicolor sorghums were important in the Sudan as late as the third century A.D., and archaeological sorghum remains from Qasr Ibrim and Jebel et Tomat in the Sudan belong to race bicolor (Clark and Stemler 1975). The beautifully preserved sorghum inflorescences from Qasr Ibrim date from the second century (Plumley 1970). The only known archaeological remains of caudatum are those from Daima, dated A.D. 900 (Connah 1967). Introgression of caudatum with durra sorghums of the Sahel and with guinea sorghums of West Africa gave rise to a widely adapted complex that is extensively used in modern sorghum breeding.

The spread of sorghum as a cereal to Asia is poorly documented. Carved reliefs from the palace of Sennacherib at Nineveh are often cited as depicting cultivated sorghum (see Hall 1928, plates 30 and 32). But these plants were actually the common reed (*Phragmites communis* Trin.) growing along the edges of a marsh with pigs grazing among them, certainly not a habitat for growing sorghum. Similar plants appear in imperial Sassanian hunting scenes from Iran (for illustrations, see Reed 1965).

In the Near East, sorghum is an important cereal only in Yemen. Sorghum probably reached India directly from East Africa during the latter part of the second century B.C. (Vishnu-Mittre and Savithri 1982), and in India, race durra evolved. From India durra sorghum was introduced to China, probably during the Mongol conquest (Hagerthy 1940), and to the Sahel during the expansion of Islam across northern Africa. Introduction into the New World most likely started with the slave trade between Africa and the Americas. The weedy Mississippi chicken corn may represent an escape from cultivation dating back to colonial times.

Sorghum As a World Cereal

Sorghum is an important rain-fed cereal in the semiarid tropics. Production in recent years has been between 50 and 60 million metric tons of grain harvested from around 45 million hectares. The major production areas are North America (excluding Mexico) with 34 percent of total world production, Asia (32 percent), Africa (26 percent), and South America (6 percent). The Caribbean, Meso America, and South America together account for about 17 percent of world sorghum production, with Mexico producing almost 59 percent of this amount. Potential yield of improved sorghum hybrids under rain-fed agricultural conditions is well over 6 metric tons per hectare. Actual maximum yields are closer to 4 metric tons, and average yields are about 1.5 metric tons per hectare. Sorghum is often grown on marginal agricultural land. In Africa and Asia, where local cultivars are still extensively grown with a minimum of agricultural inputs, average yield is well below 1 metric ton per hectare. Sorghum is grown as a cereal for human consumption in Africa and Asia and as animal feed in the Americas and Australia. Sorghum is also extensively grown as a fodder crop in India.

Sorghum production in Africa extends across the savanna in areas with as little as 300 mm and as much as 1,500 mm of annual rainfall. At the drier limits of its range, sorghum is replaced in Africa by pearl millet, in India by pearl millet or foxtail millet (*Setaria italica* [Linn.] P. Beauv.), and in China by foxtail millet. In areas with more than 900 mm of annual rainfall, maize has replaced sorghum across tropical Africa since its introduction from America during the sixteenth century.

Major factors limiting yield in Africa are infestation of cultivated fields by *Striga* (a parasitic weed) and the abundance of birds that feed on sorghum grain before it is ready for harvest. Some degree of resistance to bird damage is conferred by high tannin content in developing grains. Tannin, unfortunately, reduces the desirability of sorghum as a cereal grain. Digestibility is improved through fermentation, and fermented food products produced from sorghum grain are extensively used where high tannin cultivars are grown.

Striga is parasitic on most cereals and several broad-leaved crops grown in Africa and India. It produces large numbers of seeds and can become so abundant that fields eventually have to be abandoned. Control of *Striga* requires high agricultural inputs, the most important of which is high soil fertility and weeding. Neither is affordable under conditions of subsistence farming. Some local sorghum cultivars are resistant to *Striga,* but these have low grain yield. Attempts to transfer genes for resistance into more desirable genotypes of sorghum are high in priority for breeding projects in West and East Africa, where *Striga* has become a particularly obnoxious weed.

In Asia, the major sorghum-producing countries are China, India, Thailand, Pakistan, and Yemen. In Thailand, sorghum is grown as a dry-season crop, after a rain-fed crop, usually maize, has been harvested. In India, sorghum is grown as a rain-fed crop (kharif) or a dry-season crop (rabi), usually following rice or cotton on soils with good moisture retention. Kharif sorghum is usually mixed with pigeon pea in the field. Sorghum matures and is harvested after 90 to 120 days, allowing the season-long–developing pigeon pea an opportunity to mature without competition.

Kharif sorghums were selected for their ability to mature before the end of the rainy season in order to escape terminal drought stress that severely reduces yield. These cultivars are highly susceptible to infection by grain molds, which greatly reduces the desirability of kharif sorghum as a cereal grain. Market samples have revealed that in central and southern India as much as 70 percent of food sorghum grown during the rainy season is infected with grain molds. Cultivars with high tannin content in developing grains are resistant to infection by grain molds, but their flour yields a poor-quality unleavened bread, the major product of sorghum preparation as a food in India. Long-term breeding programs to produce grain-mold–resistant sorghums with grain acceptable to consumers have consistently failed.

Rabi sorghums escape infection by grain molds as they are grown in the dry season, but yields are low because of terminal drought stress. Prices in the market for these sorghums, however, are sufficiently attractive to make rabi sorghum a major crop in India. Production is well below demand, and attempts to shorten the growing season of rabi sorghums to escape drought and at least maintain yield potential are showing promise. Terminal drought stress commonly leads to lodging of these sorghums because of a combination of infection by stem rot fungi and plant senescence. Lodging makes harvesting difficult and contributes to reduced grain quality. To improve stalk quality and overcome lodging, plant breeders in India introduced genes for delayed senescence into high-yielding cultivars. This allows grain harvest when the stalk is still juicy and the leaves are green. Delayed senescence also greatly improves fodder quality. The stalks of both kharif and rabi sorghums are in demand as animal feed. Around urban areas, the demand by the dairy industry for fodder far exceeds the supply, and farmers often derive a higher income from sorghum stalks than sorghum grain.

Shortage of sorghum grain as a food largely excludes its use as animal feed in Africa and Asia. The grain is eaten in a variety of preparations that vary within and between regions. Grains are ground into flour from which unleavened bread is baked, or the flour is used to produce both fermented and unfermented porridges. The grains are also cracked or decorticated and boiled like rice, or whole grains are popped in heated oil.

Commercial grain sorghum production in Africa and Asia is determined by the availability of reliable supplies of the much-preferred rice, wheat, or maize. Only where these three cereals are not available at competitive prices is sorghum an important commercial crop. In China, sorghum is commercially grown for the production of a popular alcoholic beverage. It is used as a substitute for barley malt in the Nigerian beer industry. In southern Africa, a highly nutritious, low-alcohol beer is commercially produced from sorghum malt and flour, and in Kenya sorghum is used to produce a widely accepted baby food. However, attempts in many countries to replace wheat flour partially with sorghum flour in the baking industry have, so far, met with limited success, even though the quality of the bread is acceptable.

In the Americas, sorghum production is determined by demand for the grain as an animal feed. World feed use of sorghum has reached 40 million metric tons annually, with the United States, Mexico, and Japan the main consumers (Food and Agriculture Organization 1988). These three countries used almost 80 percent of the world's sorghum production in 1993. Although North American demand for sorghum grain has stabilized, in South America, where more than 1 million hectares are under sorghum cultivation, demand exceeds production by about 10 percent annually. This shortfall, predicted to increase throughout the next decade, is now mostly made up by imports from the United States. In the quest for self-sufficiency in animal feed, sorghum cultivation in South America is expanding into areas too dry for successful production of maize and into the seasonally flooded Llanos (with acid soils), where sorghum is more productive than maize.

In Asia, the area under sorghum cultivation is declining to make room for the production of fruits, vegetables, and other foods needed to supply rapidly increasing urban populations. Grain production, however, has remained essentially stable in Asia during the last decade because farmers increasingly grow improved cultivars associated with improved farming practices. This allows production to keep pace with demand, except during drought years when the demand for sorghum as human food far exceeds production.

In several African countries, population increase exceeds annual increase in food production. The Food and Agriculture Organization of the United Nations predicted that 29 countries south of the Sahara would not be able to feed their people as the twenty-first century opened. The concomitant increase in demand for cereals will have to be met by the expansion of production into marginal agricultural land, the growing of improved cultivars, and improved farming practices. Pearl millet is the cereal of necessity in areas with between 300 and 600 mm of annual rainfall, and sorghum is the most successful cereal to grow in areas with between 600 and 900 mm of annual rainfall. Because of that, the future of sorghum as a food cereal in Africa and Asia, and as a feed grain in the Americas and Australia, seems secure.

J. M. J. de Wet

Bibliography

Clark, J. D. 1971. Evidence for agricultural origins in the Nile Valley. *Proceedings of the Prehistory Society* 37: 34-79.

1976. Prehistoric populations and pressures favoring plant domestication in Africa. In *Origins of African plant domestication,* ed. J. R. Harlan, J. M. J. de Wet, and A. B. L. Stemler, 67-105. The Hague.

1984. Epilogue. In *Origins and early development of food-producing cultures in north-eastern Africa,* ed. L. Krzyzaniak and M. Kobusiewicz, 497-503. Poznan, Poland.

Clark, J. D., and A. B. L. Stemler. 1975. Early domesticated sorghum from Sudan. *Nature* 254: 588-91.

Clayton, W. D. 1972. The awned genera of Andropogoneae. *Kew Bulletin* 27: 457-74.

Connah, G. 1967. Progress report on archaeological work in Bornu in 1964-1966. *Northern history research scheme, Second Interim Report, Zaria:* 20-31.

de Wet, J. M. J., and J. R. Harlan. 1972. The origin and domestication of *Sorghum bicolor. Economic Botany* 25: 128-5.

1978. Systematics and evolution of *Sorghum* sect. *Sorghum* (Gramineae). *American Journal of Botany* 65: 477-84.

de Wet, J. M. J., J. R. Harlan, and E. G. Price. 1970. Origin of variability in the spontanea complex of *Sorghum bicolor. American Journal of Botany* 57: 704-7.

Dogget, H. 1965. The development of cultivated sorghums. In *Crop plant evolution,* ed. Joseph Hutchinson, 50-69. London.

Fagan, B. M. 1967. *Iron age cultures in Zambia.* London.

Food and Agriculture Organization of the United Nations. 1988. *Structure and characteristics of the world sorghum economy.* Committee on Commodity Problems, International Group on Grains, Twenty-third Session. Rome.

Garber, E. D. 1950. Cytotaxonomic studies in the genus Sorghum. *University of California Publications in Botany* 23: 283-361.

Hagerthy, M. 1940. Comments on writings concerning Chinese sorghums. *Harvard Journal of Asiatic Studies* 5: 234-60.

Hall, H. R. 1928. *Babylonian and Assyrian sculpture in the British museum.* Paris.

Harlan, J. R. 1971. Agricultural origins: Centers and non-centers. *Science* 174: 468-74.

Harlan, J. R., and J. M. J. de Wet. 1972. A simplified classification of cultivated sorghum. *Crop Sciences* 12: 172-6.

Harlan, J. R., J. M. J. de Wet, and E. G. Price. 1973. Comparative evolution of cereals. *Evolution* 27: 311-25.

Harlan, J. R., and J. Pasguereau. 1969. Decrue agriculture in Mali. *Economic Botany* 23: 70-4.

Harlan, J. R., and A. B. L. Stemler. 1976. Races of sorghum in Africa. In *Origins of African plant domestication,* ed. J. R. Harlan, J. M. J. de Wet, and A. B. L. Stemler, 466-78. The Hague.

Klichowska, M. 1984. Plants of the neolithic Kadero (central Sudan): A palaeoethnobotanical study of the plant impressions on pottery. In *Origin and early development of food-producing cultures in north-eastern Africa,* ed. L. Krzyzaniak and M. Kobusiewicz, 321-6. Poznan, Poland.

Munson, P. J. 1970. Correction and additional comments concerning the "Tichitt Tradition." *West African Archaeological Newsletter* 12: 47-8.

Phillipson, D. W., and B. Fagan. 1969. The date of the Ingombe Ilede burials. *Journal of African History* 10: 199-204.

Plumley, J. M. 1970. Quasr Ibrim 1969. *Journal of Egyptian Archaeology* 56: 12-18.

Porteres, R. 1962. Berceaux agricoles primaires sur le continent africain. *Journal of African History* 3: 195-210.

1976. African cereals: Eleusine, fonio, black fonio, teff, brachiaria, paspalum, pennisetum, and African rice. In *Origins of plant domestication,* ed. J. R. Harlan, J. M. J. de Wet, and A. B. L. Stemler, 409-52. The Hague.

Reed, C. A. 1965. Imperial Sassanian hunting of pig and fallow-deer, and problems of survival of these animals today in Iran. *Postillia* 92: 1-23.

Robbinson, K. R. 1966. The Leopard's kopje culture, its position in the Iron Age of southern Rhodesia. *South African Archaeological Bulletin* 21: 5-51.

Schechter, Y., and J. M. J. de Wet. 1975. Comparative electrophoresis and isozyme analysis of seed proteins from cultivated races of sorghum. *American Journal of Botany* 62: 254-61.

Shaw, T. 1976. Early crops in Africa: A review of the evidence. In *Origins of African plant domestication,* ed. J. R. Harlan, J. M. J. de Wet, and A. B. L. Stemler, 107-53. The Hague.

Snowden, J. D. 1936. *The cultivated races of Sorghum.* London.
1955. The wild fodder sorghums of section *Eu-Sorghum. Journal of the Linnean Society: Section Botany* 55: 191-260.

Stemler, A. B. L., J. R. Harlan, and J. M. J. de Wet. 1975. Caudatum sorghums and speakers of Chari-Nile languages in Africa. *Journal of African History* 16: 161-83.

Vishnu-Mittre and R. Savithri. 1982. Food economy of the Harrapan. In *Harrapan civilization,* ed. G. L. Possehl, 205-22. New Delhi.

Weber, S. A. 1991. *Plants and Harappan subsistence.* New Delhi.

Wigboldus, J. S. 1991. Pearl millet outside northeast Africa, particularly in northern West Africa: Continuously cultivated from c. 1350 only. In *Origins and development of agriculture in East Africa: The ethnosystems approach to the study of early food production in Kenya,* ed. R. E. Leaky and L. J. Slikkerveer, 161-81. Ames, Iowa.

II.A.10 ❧ Wheat

Wheat, a grass that today feeds 35 percent of the earth's population, appeared as a crop among the world's first farmers 10,000 years ago. It increased in importance from its initial role as a major food for Mediterranean peoples in the Old World to become the world's largest cereal crop, feeding more than a billion people in the late twentieth century (Feldman 1976: 121). It spread from the Near East, where it first emerged in the nitrogen-poor soils of a semi-arid Mediterranean climate, to flourish in a wide range of environments – from the short summers of far northern latitudes, to cool uplands, to irrigated regions of the tropics. The real story of its origins

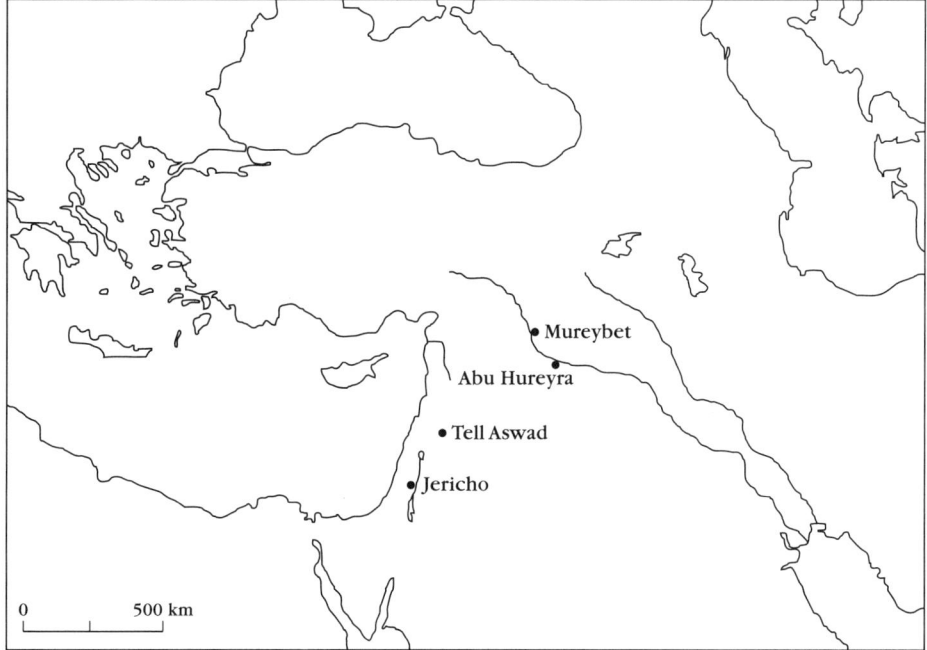

Wheat

disappeared from memory many millennia in the past, although some farming peoples still recount tales of how they received other culti-vated plants from gods, animate spirits, heroic ancestors, or the earth itself. But today we must use botanical and archae-ological evidence to trace the story of wheat's domestication (implying a change in a plant's repro-duction, making it depen-dent on humans) and its spread.

Domesticated wheats belong to at least three separate species (Zohary 1971: 238) and hundreds of distinct varieties, a number that continues to increase because the domestication of wheat continues. All domesticated wheat has lost the physical and genetic characteristics that would allow it aggressively to reseed and sprout by itself – losses which clearly distinguish domesticated wheats from wild relatives. Furthermore, both the remarkable geographic distribution of domesticated wheat and

the species' very survival depend on human beings. If no one collected wheat seeds and planted them in cleared, fertile ground, waving fields of grain soon would support hundreds of weeds, to be replaced by wild plants, and perhaps eventually by saplings and forests. Domesticated wheat and humans help each other in a relationship known as "mutualism" (Rindos 1984: 255).

Although humans domesticated wheat, one may argue that dependence on wheat also domesticated humans. The switch from gathering food to produc-ing food, dubbed the "Neolithic Revolution" by V. Gor-don Childe (1951: 74, orig. 1936), ultimately and fun-damentally altered human development. Both wheat and barley, destined to feed the great civilizations of Mesopotamia, Egypt, Greece, and Rome, originated in the Near East, the earliest cradle of Western civiliza-tion (Map II.A.10.1). And with food production came great social and technological innovations. For exam-ple, because cereals can be stored year-round, early farmers could settle together in larger groups during the seasons when low food availability formerly had forced hunter–gatherers to disperse into small groups. Furthermore, by producing a surplus of cereal food, farmers could support others – people with specialized crafts, administrators, religious castes, and the like. Thousands of years later, cities emerged and empires arose. Clearly, the domestica-tion of a cereal that has fed the Western world (and much of the rest of the world as well) holds a special place in the study of the origins of our foods.

Map II.A.10.1. The Ancient Near East showing sites men-tioned in the text.

The Origins of Wheat and Barley Agriculture

While archaeologists recognize the momentous developments set in motion by food production in the ancient Near East, they continue to debate the essential factors that first caused people to begin farming wheat and barley.[1] How did agriculture begin? Which people first domesticated plants? Why did they do so when they did? And why did farming begin in only a few places? Answers to these questions are significant because with the domestication of wheat, humankind began the shift from hunting and gathering food to producing it. This change in lifestyle set humans on a new evolutionary course, and their society and environment were never the same after farming was established. Because wheat was one of the first crops to be farmed, its role in this fundamental shift has attracted much study, resulting in a variety of models to explain the process of domestication and its causes in the Near East.

The Process of Cereal Domestication

To domesticate wheat, humans must have manipulated wild wheats, either through selective gathering or deliberate cultivation, with the latter implying activities such as preparing ground, sowing, and eliminating competing plants. We owe much of our understanding of the details of this process to the work of several botanists and archaeologists. A Russian botanist, Nikolai Vavilov (1951), for example, discovered that the greatest diversity in the gene pool of wild wheats and barleys is in Southwest Asia. Where diversity is greatest, plants have been growing, fixing mutations, and interbreeding longest. Thus, it can be concluded that Southwest Asia was the ancestral homeland of these plants (Zohary 1970a: 33–5), and subsequent searches for the first farmers have concentrated on this region.

Robert Braidwood, an archaeologist from the University of Chicago, further refined the criteria for the homeland of wild wheats by identifying their modern ecological range, as the semiarid Mediterranean woodland belt known as the "hilly flanks" of the Fertile Crescent (Braidwood 1960: 134) (Map II.A.10.2). He reasoned that prefarming peoples had adapted culturally and ecologically to specific environments over long periods (a process he dubbed "settling in") and that the first wheat farmers had already been living among natural stands of wild wheat.

One of Braidwood's students and a great archaeologist in his own right, Kent V. Flannery, advocated explaining the origins of agriculture in terms of the process of plant domestication. His major contribution to modeling wheat domestication in the Near East stemmed from his recognition that plant domestication may have been the final result in a subtle chain of events that originated with changes in human food procurement occurring much earlier than the actual transition to agriculture (Flannery 1969, 1973: 284). Flannery's "Broad Spectrum Revolution" portrays a shift in human ecology whereby humans began exploiting many previously minor food

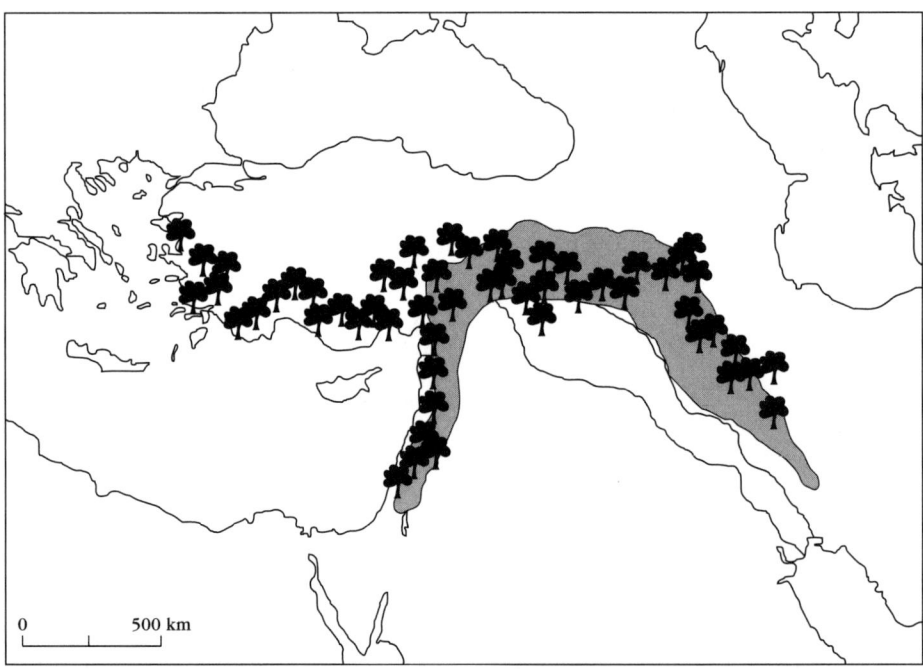

0   500 km

Map II.A.10.2. The Near East with modern "hilly flanks" and Mediterranean woodlands.

sources such as cereals, fish, small game, and water fowl. Ultimately they came to depend on these food sources (1969: 79).

Flannery particularly emphasized the importance of moving cultigens (manipulated but not necessarily domesticated plants) on which humans depended "to niches to which [they were] not adapted" (Flannery 1965: 1251; Wright 1971: 460; Rindos 1984: 26-7). Thus, as people relocated to accommodate shifting population densities (Binford 1968: 332), they attempted to produce rich stands of cereals outside their natural range (Flannery 1969: 80). Such an effort would have helped domesticate wild wheats by preventing relatively rare genetic variants from breeding with the large pool of wild wheat types growing in their natural ranges.

David Rindos (1984) has described the general process of plant domestication from an evolutionary perspective, using the principles of natural selection and mutualistic relationships (coevolution) to describe how cereals, for example, would have lost their wild characteristics. In mutualistic relationships, domesticates and humans enhance each other's fitness, or ability to reproduce. In the case of wheat, women and men began to collect wild seeds in increasing quantities for food, while at the same time inadvertently selecting and replanting seeds from the plants best suited to easy harvesting (Harlan, de Wet, and Price 1973: 311; Kislev 1984: 63). Within a few generations, cultivated wheat plants became dependent on the harvesting process for survival, as wild self-planting mechanisms disappeared from the traits of cultivated wheats (Wilke et al. 1972: 205; Hillman and Davies 1990). The elimination of wild reseeding characteristics from a plant population ultimately accounted for the domestication of wheats.

The Causes of Cereal Domestication

Because the first evidence for agricultural societies occurs at the beginning of the Holocene (our present epoch) after a major climatic change, several archaeologists found a climatic explanation for the origins of agriculture to be plausible. Childe, for example, maintained that agriculture began at the end of the Pleistocene when climate change caused a lush landscape to dry up and become desert. Populations of humans, animals, and plants would have been forced to concentrate at the few remaining sources of water: Their enhanced propinquity would have provided increased opportunity for experimentation and manipulation (Childe 1952: 23, 25). Childe believed that agriculture started in the oases of North Africa and Mesopotamia, and although these locations were probably incorrectly targeted, some of his other hypotheses now seem essentially correct (Byrne 1987; McCorriston and Hole 1991: 60).

Lewis Binford (1968: 332-7) also indicated the importance of climate change when he emphasized the resource stress experienced by permanently set-

tled coastal populations hard-pressed by rising sea levels (also the result of climatic changes at the end of the Pleistocene). He pointed out, however, that population pressure in marginal zones (settled when rising sea levels flooded coastlines and forced populations to concentrate in smaller areas) would "favor the development of more effective means of food production" from lands no longer offering ample resources for scattered hunter-gatherers (1968: 332). Mark Cohen (1977: 23, 40-51) suggested that population growth filled all available land by the end of the Pleistocene; such dense populations eventually would have experienced the population pressure envisioned by Binford.

These ideas, however, only sharpened the question of why agriculture emerged in only a few regions. Accordingly, several archaeologists sought prerequisites – social or technological developments – that may have caused certain "preadapted" groups of hunter-gatherers to adopt farming in the Near East (Hole 1984: 55; Bar-Yosef and Belfer-Cohen 1989: 487; Rosenberg 1990: 409; McCorriston and Hole 1991: 47-9). Robert Braidwood thought that agriculture appeared when "culture was ready to achieve it" (Braidwood in Wright 1971: 457). For example, sedentism, which appeared for the first time just prior to agriculture (Henry 1985: 371-4, 1989: 219), would have profoundly affected the social relations in a group. Sedentary people can store and safeguard larger amounts of food and other goods than can mobile people. Stored goods increase the possibility of prestige being accorded to a relatively few individuals, since more opportunities now exist for redistribution of surplus goods through kinship alliances – the more goods a person distributes to dependents, the greater his prestige (Bender 1978: 213). As we have seen with contemporary sedentary hunter-gatherers, competition between leaders for greater alliance groups arguably stimulates an intensification of productive forces, which in turn provides a "major incentive for the production of surplus" (Godelier 1970: 120; Bender 1978: 213-14, 1981: 154). Perhaps wheat was such a desired surplus.

In parts of Southwest Asia, where sedentism appears to have preceded the development of agriculture (Henry 1981, 1989: 38-9; Bar-Yosef and Belfer-Cohen 1989: 473-4; Moore 1991: 291), it may have been the case that the causes of sedentism also contributed to the shift to food production (Moore 1985: 231; Henry 1989; Watson 1991: 14). On the other hand, Michael Rosenberg (1990: 410-11) argues that increasingly sharper territorial perceptions were the consequences of concentrated resource exploitation in such territories by hunter-gatherer groups already committed to mutualistic exploitation of plant resources.

A combination of factors probably best explains the domestication of cereals and the shift to agriculture in the Near East. Paleoenvironmental evidence indicates that forests widely replaced a drier steppic cover (van Zeist and Bottema 1982). This has prompted Andrew Moore (1985: 232) to suggest that improved resources (resulting from climatic factors) enabled hunter-gatherers to settle; afterward their populations grew in size, so that ultimately they experienced the sort of resource stress that could have led to intensive manipulation of plants. Donald Henry (1985, 1989) also credits climatic change, several thousand years before agriculture emerged, with causing greater availability of wild cereals, which led increasingly to their exploitation. With this came dependence in the form of a sedentary lifestyle near wild cereal stands, and ultimately domestication during an arid spell when resources grew scarce.

Ecological factors play a major role in another combination model, in which the adaptation of wild cereals to a seasonally stressed environment is viewed as an explanation for the rise of agriculture in the Near East. Herbert Wright, Jr. (1977) was the first to recognize an association between the hot, dry summers and mild, wet winters that characterized Mediterranean climates and the expansion of wild, large-seeded, annual cereals. He suggested that these plants were absent from Southwest Asia in the late Pleistocene. Modern climatic models, in conjunction with archaeological evidence and ecological patterns, distinctly point to the southern Levant - modern Israel and Jordan - as the region where wheat farming first began 10,000 years ago (COHMAP 1988; McCorriston and Hole 1991: 49, 58). There, as summers became hotter and drier, plants already adapted to survive seasonal stress (summer drought), including the wild ancestors of wheat and barley, spread rapidly as the continental flora (adapted to cooler, wetter summers) retreated. Some hunter-gatherer groups living in such regions also experienced seasonal shortages of their erstwhile dependable plant resources. One group, the Natufians, named after the Wadi an Natuf in Israel (where archaeologists first found their remains) probably compensated for seasonal stress by increasingly exploiting the large-seeded annual wild wheats and barleys.

These various approaches, spanning nearly 50 years of research in the Near East, have all contributed to an increasingly sophisticated appreciation of the causes and the process of wheat domestication. Based on data that either fit or fail to fit various models, many specific refutations appeared for each model, but these lie beyond the scope of this chapter. In addition, opinions on the process of domestication in the Near East still differ as follows:

1. Was the process fast or slow (Rindos 1984: 138-9; Hillman and Davies 1990: 213)?
2. Did domestication take place once or on many independent occasions (Ladizinsky 1989: 387; Zohary 1989: 369; Blumler 1992: 100-2)?
3. Was domestication primarily the result of biological processes (Binford 1968: 328-34; Flannery 1969: 75-6; Cohen 1977; Hayden 1981: 528-9; Rindos 1984) or the product of social changes (Bender 1978)?
4. Can the domestication process be linked to major changes in the global ecosystem (Childe 1952: 25; Binford 1968: 334; Wright 1977; Byrne 1987)?

Most archaeologists now believe that a complex convergence of multiple factors (climatic changes, plant availability, preadaptive technology, population pressure, and resource stress) accounts for the emergence of agriculture 10,000 years ago in the southern Levant (Hole 1984: 55; Moore 1985; Henry 1989: 40-55, 231-4; McCorriston and Hole 1991: 60; Bar-Yosef and Belfer-Cohen 1992: 39). However, there is still little consensus regarding the rapidity of the shift or the importance to be accorded to any single factor.

Archaeological Evidence for the Domestication of Wheat

The Evidence

The earliest remains of domesticated plants are the charred seeds and plant parts found on archaeological sites that date to the beginning of the Neolithic period. Unfortunately, other evidence for the use of plant foods in the past rarely shows exactly which plants were eaten. For example, grinding stones, sickles, and storage pits all indicate increased plant use and storage during the Early Neolithic period (about 10,000 to 8,000 years ago) (Table II.A.10.1), but they do not indicate which plants were processed (Wright 1994). In fact, such artifacts could have been used to process many kinds of plants and plant tissues, including many grasses, reeds, nuts, and tubers.

Table II.A.10.1. *Prehistoric cultures of the Near East*

Date	Period	Economy	Material culture
12,500–10,200 B.P.	Natufian	Hunting, gathering plants, and perhaps cultivating wild cereals	Grinding stones, storage pits, and sickles
10,200–9600 B.P.	Prepottery Neolithic A (PPNA)	Farming domesticates and hunting	Sickle blades, mudbrick architecture, axes, larger villages
9600–7500 B.P.	Prepottery Neolithic B (PPNA)	Farming domesticates and herding domesticated animals	Lime plaster, polished axes

Following the discovery of Neolithic crop plants (Hopf 1969), archaeologists have employed many analytical techniques to determine (1) whether even earlier peoples also cultivated plants, (2) whether such earlier uses of plant resources would have resulted in domestication, and (3) whether the first farmers originated in the region(s) where domesticated wheat first was found. The ultimate aim of such a quest, of course, has been to resolve the question of whether the earliest charred remains of domesticated wheat actually indicate the first wheat farmers.

In aiming at an answer, one must know the plant resources used by preagrarian hunter-gatherers and how the cultivation practices of the first farmers differed from plant use by their predecessors (Hillman 1989; Hillman, Colledge, and Harris 1989: 240-1). This knowledge, however, has proved elusive, largely because most direct evidence for prehistoric human use of plants has decayed or disappeared. Tools and pits may have been used for processing a wide range of plants. Chemical residues that allow archaeologists to specify *which* plants were eaten during the Early Neolithic period and the preceding Natufian period seldom have been preserved or examined (Hillman et al. 1993). Microscopic studies of the sheen left on flint sickle blades indicate that peoples using these tools reaped cereals (Unger-Hamilton 1989; Anderson 1991: 550), although it is impossible to ascertain which species.

Chemical composition of human bone also provides limited clues to plant consumption. For example, the ratio of strontium to calcium (Sr/Ca) in Natufian and Neolithic skeletons indicates that some early farmers eventually relied more heavily on animal foods than did their immediate Natufian predecessors (Sillen 1984; Smith, Bar-Yosef, and Sillen 1984: 126-8; Sillen and Lee-Thorp 1991: 406, 408). None of these isotopic data, however, have come from the very first farming populations (Pre-pottery Neolithic A); furthermore, such analyses cannot identify the specific plants that the first farmers ate.

The Sites

Neolithic sites with remains of domesticated wheat and other crops are the earliest known farming sites. But practices known to Neolithic farmers surely existed among their Natufian predecessors (Unger-Hamilton 1989) who for the first time in human history used large amounts of cereal processing equipment – grinding stones, sickle blades, storage pits – and lived year-round on one site (Bar-Yosef and Belfer-Cohen 1989: 468-70; Henry 1989: 195, 211-14, 219; Tchernov 1991: 322-9). Yet none of the Natufian sites excavated thus far have revealed domesticated wheat.

Furthermore, the presence of domesticated plants on Neolithic sites, more than any other evidence, has defined our perception of a major economic difference between the first Neolithic farmers and their hunter–gatherer predecessors. Natufians may indeed have cultivated cereals, although they never apparently domesticated them, and traditions of cereal cultivation in conjunction with other gathering and hunting strategies probably persisted long into the Neolithic era when cereal farmers shared the Near East with other groups of people who were not especially committed to cultivation.

A few exceptional excavations have recovered plant remains from pre-Neolithic sites, but most of these have not yet been fully analyzed. The site of Abu Hureyra, along the banks of the Middle Euphrates River in northern Syria, yielded an abundance of charred plant remains reflecting the harvest of many types of wild seeds and fruits: These were gathered primarily in the local environments of the Late Pleistocene – steppe and steppe-forest, wadi banks, and the Euphrates River valley bottom (Hillman et al. 1989: 258-9).

The plant economy of Abu Hureyra's Epipaleolithic hunter-gatherers, however, does not appear to have led directly to farming. The site was abandoned at the time when farming began elsewhere (Moore 1975: 53, 1979: 68), and the evidence for a wide diversity of plants without evidence of intensive use of any particular one (Hillman et al. 1989: 265) is inconsistent with most models of cereal domestication (e.g., Harlan 1967; Rindos 1984; Henry 1989: 55, 216–17, 228; Hillman and Davies 1990: 212).

Instead, most models assume that cereal domestication followed intensive cereal exploitation by hunter-gatherers. At about the time that people abandoned Abu Hureyra, the sedentary inhabitants of nearby Tell Mureybet began to harvest two-seeded wild einkorn wheat and wild rye with unprecedented intensity (van Zeist and Bakker-Heeres 1984: 176-9; Hillman et al. 1993: 106). Although this type of wild wheat never developed into a domesticated plant (Zohary 1971: 239; van Zeist 1988: 58), the pattern of intensive cereal use at Tell Mureybet mirrors the type of economic pattern suggested for the Natufians from the southern Levant, where no plant remains from Epipaleolithic sites have been fully analyzed (Colledge 1991).

The southern Levant is where the earliest domesticated wheat appears. In the period known as the Pre-pottery Neolithic A (approximately 9,000 to 10,000 years ago[2]), the early farming site of Jericho (in the Jordan Valley) has two types of domesticated wheat grains, einkorn and emmer (Hopf 1969: 356, 1983: 581) (Table II.A.10.2). Some of the oldest dates from Jericho can be questioned (Burleigh 1983: 760; Bar-Yosef 1989: 58), and domesticated wheat seeds from Jericho may actually be several hundred years younger than the oldest Neolithic radiocarbon dates (10,500-10,300 years ago) suggest.

Table II.A.10.2. *Principal wheat types*

Wheat *(Triticum)* types					
Botanical name	English name	Ploidy	Rachis	Glumes	Remarks
T. boeoticum var. *aegilopoides*	Wild einkorn	2x[a] AA	Brittle	Tight[b]	Spikelets 1-grained, ancestor of einkorn wheat, modern range in Taurus mts.[c]
T. boeoticum var. *thaoudar*	Wild einkorn	2x AA	Brittle	Tight	Spikelets 2-grained, collected wild in northern Levantine Neolithic,[d] modern range in western Anatolia[e]
T. monococcum	Einkorn	2x AA	Tough	Tight	Domesticated primitive wheat
T. dicoccoides	Wild emmer	4x AABB	Brittle	Tight	Ancestor to emmer, modern range is basalt uplands of Syria, Jordan, Israel, and Taurus[f]
T. dicoccum	Emmer	4x AABB	Tough	Tight	Most favored wheat of the ancient world, widely cultivated, India-Britain
T. durum	Macaroni wheat	4x AABB	Tough	Free	Widely used for pasta, derived from emmer
T. turgidum	Rivet/cone	4x AABB	Tough	Free	Recent (16th C.) species (like *T. polonicum*, 17th C.), derived from macaroni wheat, occasionally branched spikelets
Many other varieties/species		4x AABB	Tough	Free	
T. timopheevii	Timopheevii wheats	4x AAGG	Tough	Free	Group of allotetraploids sharing only 1 genome with emmer and durum wheats; they arose independently in eastern Turkey[g]
T. aestivum	Bread wheat	6x AABBDD	Tough	Free	Major modern cereal crop widely grown; glutin, a sugar, allows yeast to reproduce, thus dough made from this flour rises; must appear after tetraploid wheats (see also *T. spelta*)
T. spelta	Spelt	6x AABBDD	Brittle	Tight	Range in northern Europe, possibly preceded bread wheat,[h] only a relic crop today
No wild hexaploid wheats					
T. speltoides	Goat-faced grasses	2x BB	Brittle	Tight	Probably contributed half the chromosomes of wild emmer
T. tauschii (= *Aegilops squarrosa*)	Goat-faced grasses	2x DD	Brittle	Tight	Contributed glutin and cold-hardiness to crosses with tetraploid wheats, modern distribution Central Asia and Transcaucasia

[a]Ploidy refers to the number of chromosome sets. Diploid plants have 2 sets of chromosomes, whereas tetraploids (4 sets) may arise, as in the case of some wheats, when different diploid plants cross to produce fertile offspring that carry chromosome sets from both parents. Hexaploids (with 6 sets) arise from the crossing of a diploid and tetraploid.

[b]Glumes adhere tightly to grain, protecting it from predators and spoilage. This wild characteristic is not lost until the appearance of free-threshing wheats (with loose glumes easily releasing grains), such as macaroni and bread wheat. Loose glumes apparently were secondarily selected for, since the wheats with this characteristic ultimately derive from glume wheats, such as emmer (Zohary 1971: 240, 243).

[c]Harland and Zohary 1966; Zohary 1971: 239; van Zeist 1988: 54.

[d]van Zeist 1970: 167-72; van Zeist and Bakker-Heeres 1984 (1986): 183-6, 198; Watkins, Baird and Betts 1989: 21.

[e]Harlan and Zohary 1966; Zohary 1971: 239; van Zeist 1988: 54.

[f]Harlan and Zohary 1966; Zohary 1971: 240; Limbrey 1990. One significant advantage of allotetraploidy in plants (chromosome pairs inherited from two ancestor plants) is that the additional genome often increases ecological tolerance in plants so that allotetraploids may occupy the geographic ranges of both parent plants as well as their overlap (Grant 1981).

[g]Lilienfeld 1951: 106, but see Zohary 1971: 241-2.

[h]Zeven (1980: 31) suggests that the expected evolutionary path of wheats would have emmer (a glume wheat) cross with a wild grass (also with tight glumes) to produce spelt wheat: The same wild grass would later cross with durum derived from a mutant emmer strain to produce bread wheat. Mitigating against this scenario is the very early appearance of bread wheat in archaeological sites (Helbaek 1966) and the genetic evidence suggesting that free-threshing characters easily and quickly may become fixed in a population (Zohary and Hopf 1988: 46). Bread wheat probably quickly followed the appearance of hexaploid spelt wheat.

Sources: Kimber and Feldman (1987), Lilienfeld (1951), Percival (1921), Zeven (1980), Zohary (1971), Zohary and Hopf (1988).

Today Jericho lies at the edge of a spring whose outflow creates an oasis in the arid summer landscape of the Jordan Valley. This alluvial fan, created by winter streams flowing from the Judean hills, nourishes palms and summer crops in the midst of a shrubby wasteland, but the area looked different during the Early Neolithic. Most of the sediment accumulated around the site of the early farming village at Jericho has washed downslope since the Neolithic (Bar-Yosef 1986: 161), perhaps because the shady glades of wild trees - pistachio, fig, almond, olive, and pear (Western 1971: 36, 38; 1983) - were stripped from the surrounding hillsides thousands of years ago. The Neolithic inhabitants planted some of the earliest wheat ever farmed, and they depended on the supplemental water provided by the spring and flowing winter streams to ensure their harvests.

The farmers at Jericho necessarily managed water: Floods frequently threatened to damage their habitations and storage areas. They built terrace walls and dug ditches to divert the flow (Bar-Yosef 1986: 161; compare Kenyon 1979: 26-7) from their small round and lozenge-shaped houses with their cobble bases and mud-brick walls (Kenyon 1981: 220-1). Their apparent choice of supplementally watered land to grow wheat was unprecedented, for wild wheats had hitherto thrived on dry slopes at the edge of Mediterranean forest (Limbrey 1990: 46, 48).

The only other site that has yielded domesticated wheat from the same general era as Jericho is the site of Tell Aswad about 25 kilometers southeast of Damascus, Syria (Contenson et al. 1979; Contenson 1985). In the earliest midden layers of this prehistoric settlement, along the margins of a now-dried lake, archaeologists recovered domesticated emmer wheat along with barley and domesticated legumes such as lentils and peas. Any former dwellings had long since been destroyed, perhaps because structures consisted largely of wattle (from reeds) and daub (Contenson et al. 1979: 153-5).

Today Tell Aswad lies outside the green Damascus oasis on a dusty, treeless plain occupied by the modern international airport, but its former setting was quite different. We know from charred seeds of marshy plants, historical accounts of the environment (van Zeist in Contenson et al. 1979: 167-8), and pollen studies (Leroi-Gourhan in Contenson et al. 1979: 170) that the lake once adjacent to the site was much larger; in addition, there were many wild trees adapted to a semiarid Mediterranean forest-steppe (pistachios, figs, and almonds). Pollen of species such as myrtle and buckthorn (*Rhamnus* spp.) may indicate rainfall greater than the annual 200 millimeters today (Leroi-Gourhan in Contenson et al. 1979: 170). Under wetter conditions, farmers were probably able to grow wheat and other crops. When it was drier, they probably used the extra moisture afforded by the lake and autumn flooding to grow wheats beside the lake shores.

Tell Aswad and Jericho are critical sites in the history of wheat agriculture. To be sure, we cannot be certain that the farmers who settled at the edge of Lake Ateibe (Tell Aswad) and near the spring feeding into the Jordan Valley at Jericho were the first people ever to grow domesticated wheat because archaeologists will never know for certain if earlier evidence awaits discovery elsewhere.

It is interesting to note, however, that contemporary evidence in adjacent regions suggests that people had not domesticated plants by 8000 B.C. In the Nile Valley of Egypt, for example, farming appears much later, around 5000 B.C. (Wenke 1989: 136), and in northern Syria on such early settlements as Tell Mureybet, people exploited wild, not domesticated, wheats and rye (van Zeist 1970: 167-72; van Zeist and Bakker-Heeres 1984: 183-6, 198; Hillman et al. 1993: 106). Recent research in the Taurus Mountains of southeastern Turkey has focused on early settled communities that apparently were not intensively exploiting wild or domesticated cereals (Rosenberg et al. 1995). Southern Mesopotamia, where the first cities emerged, saw agricultural settlements only in later times (Adams 1981: 54), and the surrounding mountains continued to support pastoralists and hunter-gatherers long after farming appeared in the southern Levant.

Botanical Evidence

Taxonomy

Botanical and ecological evidence for the domestication of wheat and its differentiation into many species also partially contributes to an understanding of where and when the first domestication occurred. Many different morphological forms of wheat appear in the archaeological record, even as early as the Neolithic deposits at Jericho, Tell Aswad, and Tell Mureybet along the northern Euphrates River (van Zeist 1970: 167-72; van Zeist and Bakker-Heeres 1984: 183-6, 198). The different forms of wild and domesticated wheats are of incalculable value to archaeologist and botanist alike, for these different plants that can be distinguished from archaeological contexts allow botanists and ecologists to identify wild and domesticated species and the conditions under which they must have grown.

The forms recognized archaeologically, moreover, may not always conform to wheat classification schemes used by modern breeders and geneticists. Wheat classification is complex and confusing, for hundreds of varieties have appeared as wheat farming spread around the world. Although many different kinds of wheat can be readily distinguished by their morphological characteristics (such as red or black awns, hairy glume keels, spikelet density), other varieties can cross-fertilize to combine characters in a perplexing array of new plants. The great variability in the visible characteristics of wheats has led to confusion over how to classify different species - a term employed in its strictest sense to describe reproductively isolated organisms (Mayr 1942; Baker 1970: 50-1,

65–6). In the case of wheat, many botanists commonly accept as distinct species morphologically distinct types that can readily cross to form fertile hybrids with other so-called species (Zohary 1971: 238).

Because botanists rely on both morphological and genetic characteristics to identify different wheats, classificatory schemes (of which many exist, for example, Percival 1921; Schiemann 1948; Morris and Sears 1967; Löve 1982) must take both aspects into account (Zohary 1971: 236–7; but compare Baker 1970). Using morphological traits, taxonomists originally split wild and cultivated wheats into at least a dozen different taxa, many of which are highly interfertile. Geneticists, however, maintain that all domesticated wheats belong to four major groups that produce only sterile crosses; furthermore, they include the wild grass genus, *Aegilops,* in the *Triticum* genus, since several taxa of wild *Aegilops* contributed chromosome sets (genomes) to domesticated wheats by crossing with wild wheat plants (Zohary 1971: 236).

Many of the wheats distinguished by taxonomists, however, lose their identifying genetic signatures when charred, abraded, and preserved for thousands of years in archaeological sites. Because fragile genetic material only recently has been demonstrated to have survived this process (Brown et al. 1993), morphological features that can be used to distinguish different wheat types have made traditional taxonomic schemes (based on morphology) of great value to archaeologists. Furthermore, some of the major behavioral characteristics of cultivated and wild wheats do have morphological correlates that endure in the archaeological record. These features also reflect significant events in the domestication of wheat (Figure II.A.10.1).

The most significant of these morphological features is rachis (segmented stem) durability. Wild wheats and wild *Aegilops,* a morphologically distinct grass genus with species capable of crossing with many wheats, have a rachis capable of shattering, once the grains have matured, into pieces bearing one or two grains. These pieces, or spikelets, taper at their bases and carry stiff hairs that act as barbs to facilitate the spikelets' entry into cracks in the soil. In wild wheats, grains are tightly enclosed in tough glumes that protect them from predation.

In domesticated wheats, these features vanish. The rachis fails to shatter when ripe, a feature particularly important to humans who harvest using sickles – the tools introduced by Natufian and early Neolithic groups (Hillman and Davies 1990: 172–7) (Figure II.A.10.2). In the relatively pure stands of wild wheats, at the margins of Mediterranean oak forests where agriculture began, harvesting methods would fundamentally affect the domestication process (Harlan

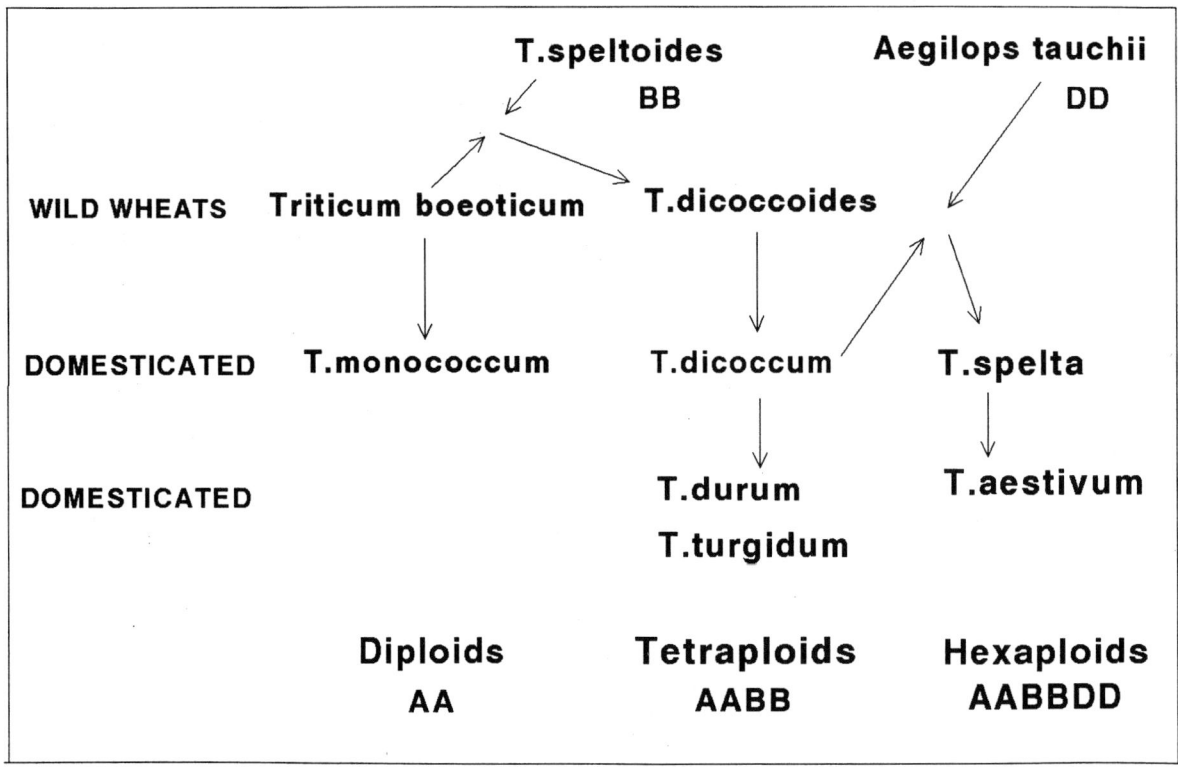

Figure II.A.10.1. Related wheats and goat-faced grasses. (After Zohary 1970b: 241; Hillman, personal communication, 1984).

1967, 1989; Bohrer 1972; Wilke et al. 1972: 205; Hillman and Davies 1990: 172–7). Harvesters use fairly violent motions when equipped with sickles or when uprooting plants to harvest straw and seed. These methods tend to shatter ripe ears, leaving for collection either immature seed (unfit for germination the following year if replanted) or relatively rare genetic mutants with tough rachises. Although these rare plants reproduce poorly in the wild, they are ideal for cultivation, as ripe seed can regenerate if replanted (Helbaek in Braidwood and Howe 1960: 112–13). By unconscious selection (Rindos 1984: 86–9) for a tough rachis gene, harvesters may replace a wild population with a domesticated one in as few as 20 to 30 years (Hillman and Davies 1990: 189).

Wild and domesticated cereals often can be distinguished when examining rachis fragments in archaeological plant remains (for example, Bar-Yosef and Kislev 1986; Kislev, Bar Yosef, and Gopher 1986: 198–9; compare Bar-Yosef and Belfer-Cohen 1992: 37–8). The earliest known domesticated wheats from Tell Aswad exhibit tough rachises (van Zeist and Bakker-Heeres 1982: 192–6). At the same period, the wheats intensively harvested along the Middle Euphrates River at Tell Mureybet (van Zeist 1970: 167–72; van Zeist and Bakker-Heeres 1984: 183–6, 198) and in northern Mesopotamia at the site of Qeremez Dere (Watkins, Baird, and Betts 1989: 21) remained wild, perhaps partly because of a harvesting technique that favored the proliferation of brittle-rachis types in the population. For example, beating wild grass heads over baskets to collect seed was a technique widely employed in many parts of the world where no domestication occurred (Bohrer 1972: 145–7; Wilke et al. 1972: 205–6; Harlan 1989; Nabhan 1989: 112–18). Although baskets and wooden beaters have a low probability of surviving in archaeological sites in the Near East, the remarkable paucity of sickle blades at Tell Mureybet (Cauvin 1974: 59) would support a suggestion that people may have harvested wild cereals by a different method from that used at Jericho and Tell Aswad, where sickle blades are more common.

Cytogenetic Evidence

The results of modern genetic studies have also contributed incomparably to disentangling the history of domesticated wheat. In an effort to improve modern strains of bread wheat and to discover new genetic combinations, biologists have compared the genetic signatures of different varieties, types, and species of wheats. Genetic differences and similarities have allowed specialists to trace relationships among various forms of wild and domesticated wheats and to determine which wild wheats were ancestral to domesticates.

All of the relationships described in Figure II.A.10.1 and Table II.A.10.2 have been confirmed by genetic tests (Zohary 1989: 359). Of particular importance to domestication, the work of H. Kihara has largely defined the cytogenetic relationships between emmer, durum, and hexaploid wheats (Lilienfeld 1951). Domesticated emmer wheat shares close genetic affinities with its wild progenitor *(Triticum dicoccoides = Triticum turgidum* subsp. *dicoccoides)* and is largely a product of unconscious human selection for a tough rachis. Durum wheats and rivet wheats likewise received their 2 chromosome sets from wild emmer (Zohary 1971: 239) and probably are secondarily derived from domesticated emmer through selection for free-threshing characteristics, larger seeds, and various ecological tolerances (for example, Percival 1921: 207, 230–1, 241–3).

Hexaploid wheats, which belong in a single cytogenetic taxon (Zohary 1971: 238; Zohary and Hopf 1993: 24), have no wild hexaploid ancestors: They emerged as a result of a cross between domesticated tetraploid wheats (which may or may not have been free-threshing) and a wild grass native to continental and temperate climates of central Asia (Zohary and Hopf 1988: 46). This implies that hexaploid wheats emerged only when tetraploid wheats spread from the Mediterranean environment to which they were adapted. From archaeological evidence of the spread

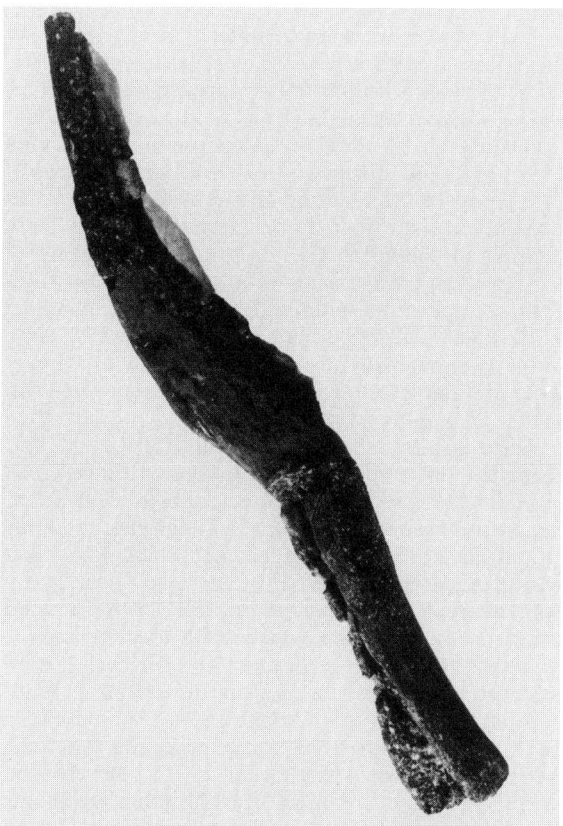

Figure II.A.10.2. Photograph of the Nahal Hemar sickle. (Photo: M. Barazani-Nir, Centre de Recherches Français de Jérusalem, O. Bar-Yosef, and D. Alon.)

of farming, one assumes that hexaploid wheats appeared after 7500 B.C.[3] True bread wheats with loose glumes probably came from spelt ancestors, but only two slight genetic changes produce loose glumes (Zohary and Hopf 1988: 46), implying that the mutations may occur easily and become rapidly fixed in a domesticated population.

Cytogenetic studies also have suggested that domestication occurred in only one population of wild wheats, from which all modern conspecific cultigens (of the same species) are derived. All the varieties and species of tetraploid wheats have the same basic genetic constitution as wild emmer wheat (AABB genomes)[4] rather than timopheevii wheat (AAGG). This indicates that if multiple domestications had occurred, timopheevii wheat, which is morphologically indistinguishable from wild emmer, would have been systematically ignored. A more parsimonious explanation is that of Daniel Zohary (1989: 369), who suggests that emmer wheat was domesticated once and passed from farming community to community (see also Runnels and van Andel 1988). Archaeological evidence on Crete and in Greece (Barker 1985: 63-5) indicates that fully domesticated wheats were introduced to Europe from the Near East (Kislev 1984: 63-5). An alternative hypothesis – that hunter-gatherers in Europe independently domesticated emmer and einkorn from native wild grasses (Dennell 1983: 163) – has little supporting evidence. Botanists using cytogenetic evidence, however, may more easily recognize evidence for single domestication than for multiple events, genetic traces of which can be obscured by other biological and historical processes (Blumler 1992: 99, 105).

Ecology of Wheats

Perhaps it will never be possible to determine unequivocally whether wheat species were domesticated in one place or in several locations. Nevertheless, the ecological constraints limiting the growth of different species, varieties, and forms of wild and domesticated wheats narrow greatly the possibilities of where and under what ecological circumstances wheat may have been domesticated. Ecological constraints have been examined both on a macro and micro scale, and both scales contribute significantly to our understanding of wheat domestication.

On a macro scale, the geographic distributions of discrete species or varieties of wild wheats provide ecological ranges within which, or indeed adjacent to which, researchers locate wheat domestication and the origins of agriculture (Harlan and Zohary 1966) (Maps II.A.10.3-5). Using modern wild wheat distributions, botanists and archaeologists have singled out the southern Levant and Taurus range as the most likely source of domesticated emmer and einkorn (Harlan and Zohary 1966; Zohary 1971: 239-42), although bread wheats may have quickly evolved

from spelt wheat somewhere in the Caspian region (Zohary 1971: 244; Zeven 1980: 32). Timopheevii wheats represent merely a later independent domestication of tetraploids in eastern Anatolia and Georgia. The conclusions of Vavilov, Braidwood, Flannery, Harlan, and D. Zohary depend greatly on modern geographical distributions of wild wheats.

Nevertheless, a serious problem in using the modern ranges of wild wheats is the assumption that these ranges reflect the former natural extent of wild species. In the past 10,000 years in the Near East, climates as well as human land use patterns have fluctuated. Grazing, deforestation, and suppression of natural forest fires have had a profound effect on vegetation (Naveh and Dan 1973; Naveh 1974; Le Houérou 1981; Zohary 1983), altering not only plant distributions but the character of entire vegetation zones (McCorriston 1992).

Water, light, and soil properties determine growth on a local scale within the geographic ranges of wheats. Wheat plants, like many other crops, require land free of competition from established plants that tap water and block light and where the seed may embed itself in the earth before ants or other predators discover it (Hillman and Davies 1990: 164; Limbrey 1990: 46).

Truly wild einkorn and emmer typically thrive on the open slopes at the margins of scrub-oak forests: They are poor competitors in nitrogen-rich soils typical of weedy habitats, such as field margins, habitation sites, and animal pens (Hillman and Davies 1990: 159, 160; Hillman 1991; McCorriston 1992: 217; compare Blumler and Byrne 1991). These latter sites readily support domesticated glume wheats (emmer and einkorn). Their wild relatives prefer clay soils forming on "basalt or other base-rich fine-grained rocks and sediments under warm climates with a marked dry season" (Limbrey 1990: 46). Indeed, some evidence suggests that wild wheats were first harvested from such soils (Unger-Hamilton 1989: 100; Limbrey 1990: 46).

Early farming sites like Jericho, Tell Aswad, and Mureybet, however, were located beside alluvial soils in regions of low rainfall where supplemental watering from seasonal flooding and high water tables would have greatly enhanced the probability that a wheat crop would survive in any given year. If the wild wheats originally were confined to the upland basaltic soils, they must have been deliberately moved to alluvial fields in the first stages of domestication (Sherratt 1980: 314-15; McCorriston 1992: 213-24; compare Hillman and Davies 1990). Removal of a plant from its primary habitat often causes a genetic bottleneck (Lewis 1962; Grant 1981) whereby the newly established population is fairly homogeneous because its genetic ancestry comes from only a few plants. This tends greatly to facilitate domestication (Ladizinsky 1985: 196-7; Hillman and Davies 1990: 177-81).

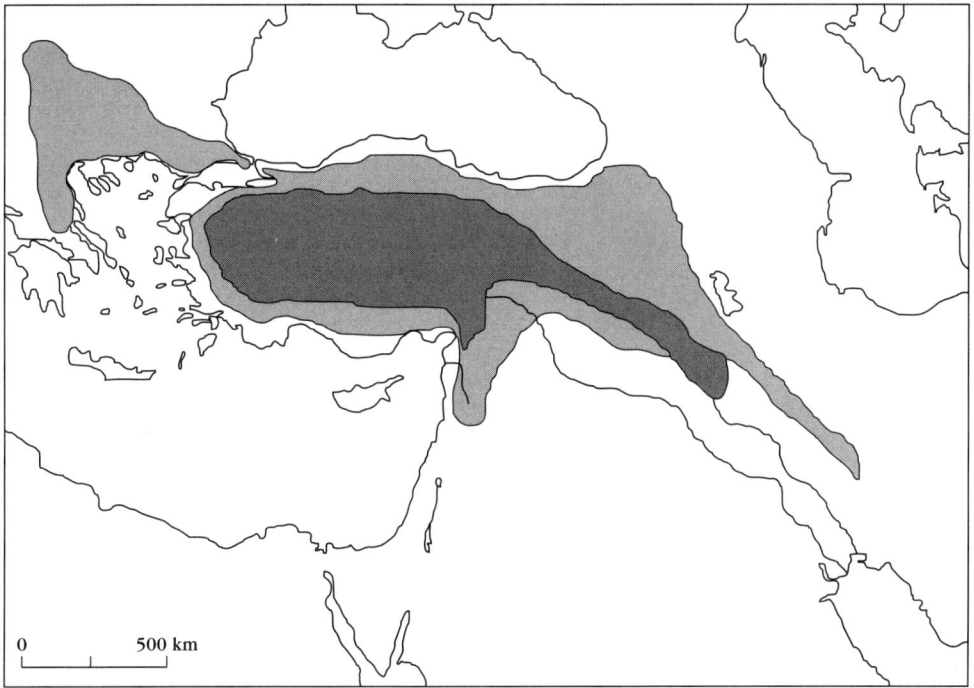

Map II.A.10.3. Geographic distribution of wild einkorn wheat, *Triticum boeoticum.* (After Harlan and Zohary 1966; D. Zohary 1989.) Darker shading indicates nonweedy populations.

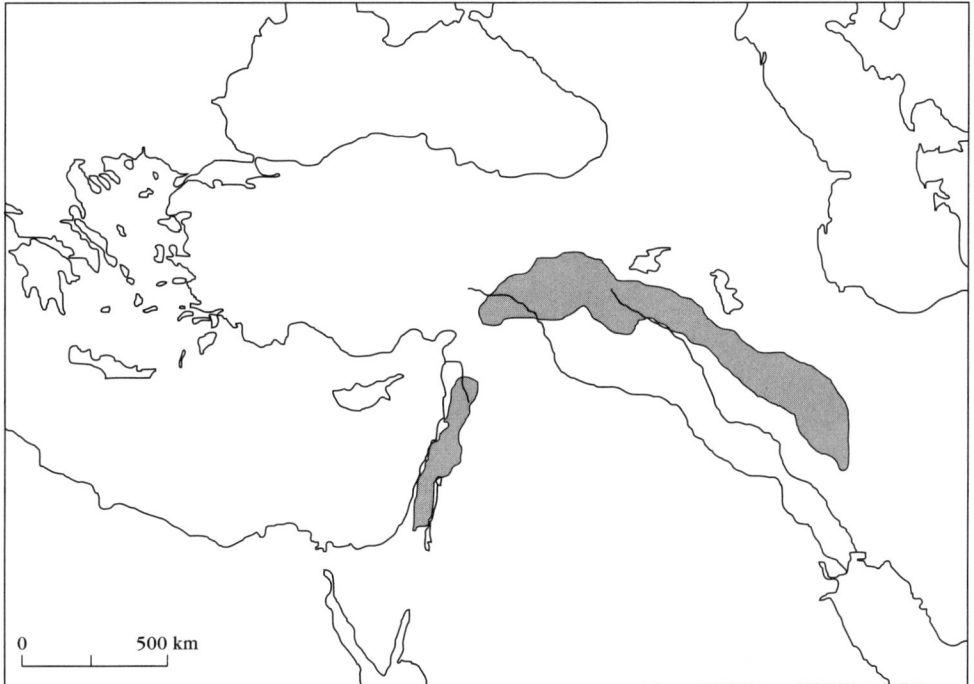

Map II.A.10.4. Geographic distribution of wild emmer wheat, *Triticum dicoccoides.* (After Harlan and Zohary 1966.)

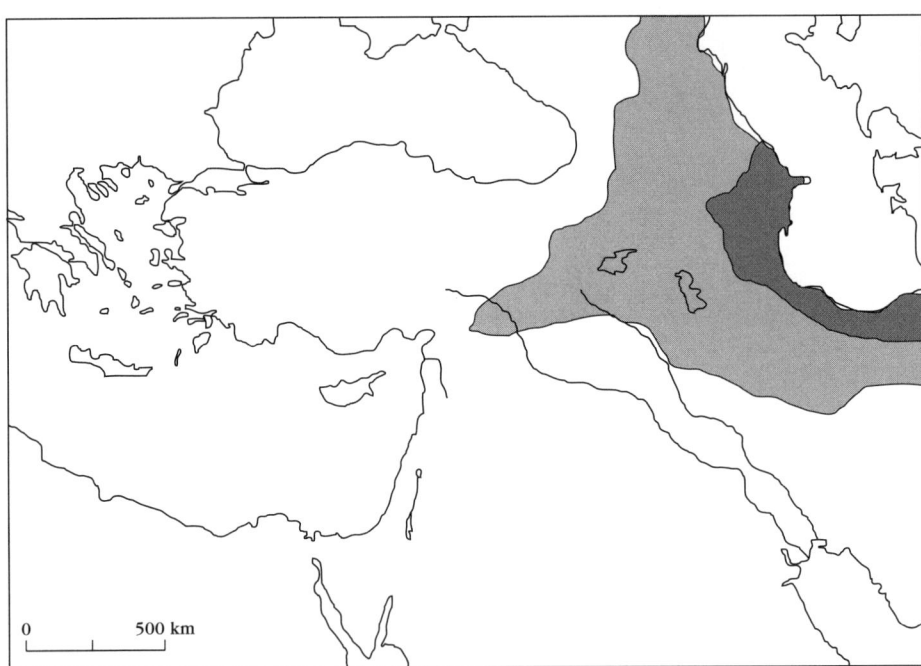

Map II.A.10.5. Geographic distribution of goat-faced grass, *Aegilops tauchii*. (After Harlan and Zohary 1966.)

0   500 km

The Spread of Domesticated Wheats from the Near East

Deliberate planting of wheat in new habitats (supplementally watered alluvial soils) is one of only a few known events in the earliest spread of wheat farming. Archaeologists understand very poorly the processes and constraints that led to the spread of wheat into different environments and regions of the Near East. They understand far better the spread of agriculture in Europe because of research priorities set by Childe and other Western archaeologists who identified the arrival of domesticated wheat in Europe around 6000 B.C. (Barker 1985: 64; Zohary and Hopf 1988: 191) as an event of critical significance in the history of humankind (viewed from a European perspective).

Thus, in contrast with the Near East, in Europe the process of transition from different styles of hunting and gathering to a predominantly agricultural economy and the adaptation of crops such as wheat to new environments has received intense archaeological and theoretical consideration. The progress of Neolithic settlement across the plains of Greece and Italy, up the Balkans and into the river basins of central and eastern Europe, across the forested lands, and into the low countries encompasses many regional archaeologies and localized theoretical explanations. Wheat accompanied the Neolithic nearly everywhere in Europe, although by the time farming took hold in Britain around 3500 B.C., the cultivated varieties of einkorn, emmer, and spelt must have tolerated colder and longer winters, longer daylight during the ripen-

ing season, and greatly different seasonal rainfall than that of the Mediterranean lands from which the crops originated.

Wheat also spread out of the Near East to Africa, where it could be found in northern Egypt after 5000 B.C. (Wenke 1989: 136; Wetterstrom 1993: 203-13). With other introduced crops, wheat fueled the emergence of cultural complexity and replaced any indigenous attempts at agriculture initiated in subtropical arid lands to the south (Close and Wendorf 1992: 69). Because most wheats require cool winters with plentiful rain, the plant never spread widely in tropical climates where excessive moisture during growing and ripening seasons inhibits growth and spurs disease (Lamb 1967: 199; Purseglove 1985: 293). But the grain also spread to South Asia where as early as 4000 B.C. hexaploid wheats were cultivated at the Neolithic site of Mehrgarh (Pakistan) (Costantini 1981). By the third millennium B.C., the Indus Valley civilization, city-states in Mesopotamia, and dynastic Egypt all depended on domesticated wheat and other cereals.

In the sixteenth century, colonists from the Old World brought wheat to the New World. The Spanish introduced it to Argentina, Chile, and California where the cereal flourished in climates and soils that closely resembled the lands where it already had been grown for thousands of years (Crosby 1986; Aschmann 1991: 33-5). The political and social dominance of European imperialists in these new lands and the long history of wheat farming in the Old World - where crop and weeds had adapted to a wide range of temperature, light, and rainfall conditions (Crosby 1986) – largely accounts for the fact that wheat is one of the world's most significant crops today. Its domestication is a continuing process, with yearly genetic improvements of different strains through breeding and new gene-splicing techniques (Heyne and Smith 1967).

Summary

Botanical and archaeological evidence for wheat domestication constitutes one of the most comprehensive case studies in the origins of agriculture. Some of the issues discussed in this chapter remain unresolved. For many of the domesticated wheats, including the primitive first wheats (einkorn and emmer), the integration of botanical and archaeological evidence indicates where and approximately when people entered into the mutualistic relationship that domesticated both humans and their wheats. Less is understood about the origins of hexaploid wheats, largely because the results of archaeological investigations in central Asia have long been inaccessible to Western prehistorians.[5] From botanical studies, however, we can (1) trace the wild ancestors of modern wheats, (2) suggest that isolated events led to the domestication of each species, and (3) reconstruct the environmental constraints within which the first farmers planted and reaped.

Yet, some debate still continues over the question of how wheat was domesticated. Did people in many communities independently select easily harvested plants from weedy wild emmer growing on their dump heaps (Blumler and Byrne 1991)? Or did they, as most believe, deliberately harvest and sow fully wild wheats and in the process domesticate them (Unger-Hamilton 1989; Hillman and Davies 1990; Anderson-Gerfaud, Deraprahamian, and Willcox 1991: 217)? Related questions, of course, follow: Did this latter process happen once or often, and did the first true farmers move these wild plants to seasonally flooded or supplementally watered soils as part of the domestication process?

Scholars also continue to discuss why people began to domesticate wheat in the first place some 10,000 years ago as part of the larger question of the origins of agriculture. Although most agree that many factors were involved in the Near East and that they converged at the end of the Pleistocene, there is no agreement about which factor or combination of factors was most important (for example, Graber 1992; Hole and McCorriston 1992). But because there are no written Neolithic versions of the original crop plants (compare Hodder 1990: 20-1), it is up to us – at the interdisciplinary junction of archaeology and botany – to continue to reconstruct this evolutionary and cultural process in human history.

Joy McCorriston

Endnotes

1. This review is summarily brief; for more thorough treatment, the reader should consult other sources, especially G. Wright 1971, Henry 1989, and Watson 1991. As theoretical explanations for domestication of wheats and barley overlap considerably, both are discussed in this chapter.
2. Neolithic dates are generally quoted as uncorrected radiocarbon dates because exact calendar dates are unknown. The basis for radiocarbon dates is a ratio of carbon isotopes in the earth's atmosphere, but this ratio varies at different times. For later periods, analysts correct for the variation in atmospheric carbon isotope ratios by comparing radiocarbon dates with exact dendrochronological (tree-ring) calendrical dates. Unfortunately, the sequence of old timbers necessary for tree-ring dates does not extend back as far as the Neolithic in the Near East, leaving archaeologists without a dendrochronological calibration scale to correct their radiocarbon dates. Although some progress has been made with isotopically dated coral reefs, there are still problems with variation in atmospheric carbon isotope ratios at different periods. Archaeologists should continue to quote uncalibrated dates.
3. This inference is conservatively based on the dates of proven Neolithic (PPNB) wheat farmers in the Taurus mountains and northeastern Syria and Iraq. Although both areas are poorly known archaeologically in the early Neolithic (Pre-pottery period, they fall within the modern range of the wild goat-faced grass (*Aegilops tauschii*). Since *A. tauschii* contributed genetic tolerance for cold winters (continental and temperate climates) the hexaploid wheats (Zohary, Harlan, and Vardi 1969; Zohary and Hopf 1993: 50), and since hexaploid wheats emerged after the domestication of tetraploids (Zohary and Hopf 1988; 46), the appearance of domesticated emmer in the PPNB (after approximately 7500 B.C.) (van Zeist 1970:10) serves as a *terminus post quem* for the domestication of hexaploid wheats.
4. Kihara defined as a genome "a chromosome set . . . a fundamental genetical [sic] and physiological system whose completeness as to the basic gene content is indispensable for the normal development of gones [the special reproductive cells] in haplo- and zygotes in diplophase" (Lilienfeld 1951: 102). In diploid plants, the genome represents all chromosomes of the plant; in allotetraploids, the genome is derived from the chromosomes of both contributing ancestral plants.
5. A recently initiated research project seeks to clarify agricultural origins in the Caspian region at the site of Jeitun in the Kara Kum desert of Turkmenia (see Harris et al. 1993).

Bibliography

Adams, Robert McC. 1981. *Heartland of cities*. Chicago.
Anderson, Patricia C. 1991. Harvesting of wild cereals during the Natufian as seen from experimental cultivation and harvest of wild einkorn wheat and microwear analysis of stone tools. In *The Natufian culture in the Levant,* ed. Ofer Bar-Yosef and Francois R. Valla 521–56. Ann Arbor, Mich.
Anderson-Gerfand, Patricia, Gérard Deraprahamian, and George Willcox. 1991. Les premières cultures de céréales sauvages et domestiques primitives au Proche-Orient Néolithique: Résultats préliminaires

d'expériences à Jalès (Ardèche). *Cahiers de l'Euphrate* 5-6: 191-232.

Aschmann, Homer. 1991. Human impact on the biota of Mediterranean-climate regions of Chile and California. In *Biogeography of Mediterranean invasions,* ed. F. H. Groves and F. di Castri, 33-41. Cambridge.

Baker, H. G. 1970. Taxonomy and the biological species concept in cultivated plants. In *Genetic resources in plants,* ed. O. H. Frankel and E. Bennett 49-68. Oxford.

Barker, Graeme. 1985. *Prehistoric farming in Europe.* Cambridge.

Bar-Yosef, Ofer. 1986. The walls of Jericho: An alternative interpretation. *Current Anthropology* 27: 157-62.

1989. The PPNA in the Levant - An overview. *Paléorient* 15: 57-63.

Bar-Yosef, Ofer, and Anna Belfer-Cohen. 1989. The origins of sedentism and farming communities in the Levant. *Journal of World Prehistory* 3: 447-97.

1992. From foraging to farming in the Mediterranean Levant. In *Transitions to agriculture in prehistory,* ed. Anne Birgitte Gebauer and T. Douglas Price 21-48. Madison, Wis.

Bar-Yosef, Ofer, and Mordechai E. Kislev. 1986. Earliest domesticated barley in the Jordan Valley. *National Geographic Research* 2: 257.

Bender, Barbara. 1978. Gatherer–hunter to farmer: A social perspective. *World Archaeology* 10: 204-22.

1981. Gatherer–hunter intensification. In *Economic archaeology,* ed. Alison Sheridan and Geoff Bailey. British Archaeological Reports, International Series 96. Oxford.

Binford, Lewis R. 1968. Post-Pleistocene adaptations. In *New perspectives in archaeology,* ed. Sally R. Binford and Lewis R. Binford, 313-41. Chicago.

Blumler, Mark A. 1992. Independent inventionism and recent genetic evidence of plant domestication. *Economic Botany* 46: 98-111.

Blumler, Mark A., and Roger Byrne. 1991. The ecological genetics of domestication and the origins of agriculture. *Current Anthropology* 32: 23-54.

Bohrer, Vorsila L. 1972. On the relation of harvest methods to early agriculture in the Near East. *Economic Botany* 26: 145-55.

Braidwood, Robert J. 1960. The agricultural revolution. *Scientific American* 203: 131-46.

Braidwood, Robert J., and Bruce Howe. 1960. *Prehistoric investigations in Iraqi Kurdistan.* Chicago.

Brown, Terence A., Robin G. Allaby, Keri A. Brown, and Martin K. Jones. 1993. Biomolecular archaeology of wheat: Past, present and future. *World Archaeology* 25: 64-73.

Burleigh, Richard. 1983. Appendix D: Additional radiocarbon dates for Jericho (with an assessment of all the dates obtained). In *Excavations at Jericho,* ed. Kathleen M. Kenyon and Thomas A. Holland, 760-5. London.

Byrne, Roger. 1987. Climatic change and the origins of agriculture. In *Studies in the neolithic and urban revolutions,* ed. L. Manzanilla, 21-34. Oxford.

Cauvin, Marie-Claire. 1974. Note préliminaire sur l'outillage lithique de la phase IV de Tell Mureybet (Syrie). *Annales Archéologiques Arabes Syriennes* 24: 58-63.

Childe, V. Gordon. 1951. *Man makes himself.* 5th edition. New York.

1952. *New light on the most ancient East.* London.

Close, Angela E., and Fred Wendorf. 1992. The beginnings of food production in the eastern Sahara. In *Transitions to agriculture in prehistory,* ed. Anne Birgitte Gebauer and Douglas Price, 63-72. Madison, Wis.

Cohen, Mark N. 1977. *The food crisis in prehistory.* New Haven, Conn.

COHMAP Members. 1988. Climatic changes of the last 18,000 years: Observations and model simulations. *Science* 241: 1043-52.

Colledge, Susan. 1991. Investigations of plant remains preserved in epipalaeolithic sites in the Near East. In *The Natufian culture in the Levant,* ed. Ofer Bar-Yosef and Francois R. Valla, 391-8. Ann Arbor, Mich.

Contenson, Henri de. 1985. La région de damas au néolithique. *Les Annales Archéologiques Arabes Syriennes* 35: 9-29.

Contenson, Henri de, Marie-Claire Cauvin, Willem van Zeist, et al. 1979. Tell Aswad (Damascene). *Paléorient* 5: 153-76.

Costantini, Lorenzo. 1981. The beginning of agriculture in the Kachi Plain: The evidence of Mehrgarh. In *South Asian archaeology 1981, proceedings of the 6th international conference of the Association of South Asian Archaeologists in Western Europe,* ed. Bridgit Allchin, 29-33. Cambridge.

Crosby, Alfred W. 1986. *Ecological imperialism.* Cambridge.

Davis, Simon J. M. 1987. *The archaeology of animals.* New Haven, Conn.

Dennell, Robin W. 1983. *European economic prehistory.* New York.

Feldman, Moche. 1976. Wheats. In *Evolution of crop plants,* ed. N. W. Simmonds, 120-8. London.

Flannery, Kent V. 1965. The ecology of early food production in Mesoamerica. *Science* 147: 1247-56.

1969. Origins and ecological effects of early domestication in Iran and the Near East. In *The domestication and exploitation of plants and animals,* ed. Peter J. Ucko and Geoffrey W. Dimbleby, 73-100. London.

1973. The origins of agriculture. *Annual Review of Anthropology* 2: 271-310.

Godelier, Maurice. 1970. *Sur les sociétés précapitalistes.* Paris.

Graber, Robert Bates. 1992. Population pressure, agricultural origins, and global theory: Comment on McCorriston and Hole. *American Anthropologist* 94: 443-5.

Grant, Verne. 1981. *Plant speciation.* New York.

Harlan, Jack R. 1967. A wild wheat harvest in Turkey. *Archaeology* 20: 197-201.

1989. The tropical African cereals. In *Foraging and farming: The evolution of plant exploitation,* ed. David R. Harris and Gordon C. Hillman, 79-98. London.

Harlan, Jack R., J. M. J. de Wet, and E. G. Price. 1973. Comparative evolution of cereals. *Evolution* 27: 311-25.

Harlan, Jack R., and Daniel Zohary. 1966. Distribution of wild wheats and barley. *Science* 153: 1074-80.

Harris, David R., V. M. Masson, Y. E. Berezkin, et al. 1993. Investigating early agriculture in Central Asia: New research at Jeitun, Turkmenistan. *Antiquity* 67: 324-38.

Hayden, Brian. 1981. Research and development in the Stone Age: Technological transitions among hunter-gatherers. *Current Anthropology* 22: 519-48.

Helbaek, Hans. 1964. Early Hassunan vegetables at es-Sawwan near Samarra. *Sumer* 20: 45-8.

1966. Pre-pottery neolithic farming at Beidha. *Palestine Exploration Quarterly* 98: 61-6.

Henry, Donald O. 1981. An analysis of settlement patterns and adaptive strategies of the Natufian. In *Préhistoire du Levant,* ed. Jacques Cauvin and Paul Sanlaville, 421-32. Paris.

1985. Preagricultural sedentism: The Natufian example. In *Prehistoric hunter-gatherers: The emergence of cultural complexity,* ed. T. Douglas Price and James A. Brown, 365-84. New York.

1989. *From foraging to agriculture: The Levant at the end of the Ice Age.* Philadelphia, Pa.

Heyne, E. G., and G. S. Smith. 1967. Wheat breeding. In *Wheat and wheat improvement,* ed. K. S. Quisenberry and L. P. Reitz, 269-306. Madison, Wis.

Hillman, Gordon C. 1975. The plant remains from Tell Abu Hureyra: A preliminary report. In The excavation of Tell Abu Hureyra in Syria: A preliminary report (A. M. T. Moore). *Proceedings of the Prehistoric Society* 41: 70-3.

1989. Late palaeolithic plant foods from Wadi Kubbaniya in Upper Egypt: Dietary diversity, infant weaning, and seasonality in a riverine environment. In *Foraging and farming: The evolution of plant exploitation,* ed. David R. Harris and Gordon C. Hillman, 207-39. London.

1991. Comment on the ecological genetics of domestication and the origins of agriculture. *Current Anthropology* 32: 39-41.

Hillman, Gordon C., Susan M. Colledge, and David R. Harris. 1989. Plant-food economy during the epi-palaeolithic period at Tell Abu Hureyra, Syria: Dietary diversity, seasonality, and modes of exploitation. In *Foraging and farming: The evolution of plant exploitation,* ed. David R. Harris and Gordon C. Hillman, 240-68. London.

Hillman, Gordon C., and M. S. Davies. 1990. Measured domestication rates in crops of wild type wheats and barley and the archaeological implications. *Journal of World Prehistory* 4: 157-222.

Hillman, Gordon C., Sue Wales, Frances McLaren, et al. 1993. Identifying problematic remains of ancient plant foods: A comparison of the role of chemical, histological and morphological criteria. *World Archaeology* 25: 94-121.

Hodder, Ian. 1990. *The domestication of Europe.* Oxford.

Hole, Frank A. 1984. A reassessment of the neolithic revolution. *Paléorient* 10: 49-60.

Hole, Frank A., and Joy McCorriston. 1992. Reply to Graber. *American Anthropologist* 94: 445-6.

Hopf, Maria. 1969. Plant remains and early farming in Jericho. In *The domestication and exploitation of plants and animals,* ed. Peter J. Ucko and Geoffrey W. Dimbleby, 355-9. London.

1983. Appendix B: Jericho plant remains. In *Excavations at Jericho,* Vol. 5, ed. Kathleen M. Kenyon and Thomas A. Holland, 576-621. London.

Kenyon, Kathleen M. 1979. *Archaeology in the Holy Land.* Fourth edition. New York.

1981. *The architecture and stratigraphy of the Tell. In Excavations at Jericho,* Vol. 3, ed. Thomas A. Holland. London.

Kimber, Gordon, and Moshe Feldman. 1987. *Wild wheat: An introduction.* Special Report No. 353, College of Agriculture, University of Missouri. Columbia.

Kislev, Mordechai E. 1984. Emergence of wheat agriculture. *Paléorient* 10: 61-70.

Kislev, Mordechai E., Ofer Bar-Yosef, and Avi Gopher. 1986. Early neolithic domesticated and wild barley from the Netiv Hagdud Region in the Jordan Valley. *Israel Journal of Botany* 35: 197-201.

Ladizinsky, Gideon. 1985. Founder effect in crop plant evolution. *Economic Botany* 39: 191-9.

1989. Origin and domestication of the southwest Asian grain legumes. In *Foraging and farming: The evolution of plant exploitation,* ed. David R. Harris and Gordon C. Hillman, 374-89. London.

Lamb, C. A. 1967. Physiology. In *Wheat and wheat improvement,* ed. K. S. Quisenberry and L. P. Reitz, 181-223. Madison, Wis.

Le Houérou, Henri Noel. 1981. Impact of man and his animals on Mediterranean vegetation. In *Mediterranean-type shrublands,* ed. F. Di Castri, D. W. Goodall, and R. L. Specht, 479-522. Amsterdam.

Lewis, Harlan. 1962. Catastrophic selection as a factor in speciation. *Evolution* 16: 257-71.

Lilienfeld, F. A. 1951. H. Kihara: Genome-analysis in Triticum and Aegilops. X. Concluding Review. *Cytologia* 16: 101-23.

Limbrey, Susan. 1990. Edaphic opportunism? A discussion of soil factors in relation to the beginnings of plant husbandry in South-West Asia. *World Archaeology* 22: 45-52.

Löve, A. 1982. Generic evolution in the wheatgrasses. *Biologisches Zentralblatt* 101: 199-212.

Mayr, Ernst. 1942. *Systematics and the origin of species.* New York.

McCorriston, Joy. 1992. *The early development of agriculture in the ancient Near East: An ecological and evolutionary study.* Ph.D. dissertation, Yale University.

McCorriston, Joy, and Frank A. Hole. 1991. The ecology of seasonal stress and the origins of agriculture in the Near East. *American Anthropologist* 93: 46-69.

Moore, Andrew M. T. 1975. The excavation of Tell Abu Hureyra in Syria: A preliminary report. *Proceedings of the Prehistoric Society* 41: 50-77.

1979. A pre-neolithic farmer's village on the Euphrates. *Scientific American* 241: 62-70.

1985. The development of neolithic societies in the Near East. *Advances in World Archaeology* 4: 1-69.

1991. Abu Hureyra 1 and the antecedents of agriculture on the Middle Euphrates. In *The Natufian culture in the Levant,* ed. Ofer Bar-Yosef and Francois R. Valla, 277-94. Ann Arbor, Mich.

Morris, R., and E. R. Sears. 1967. The cytogenetics of wheat and its relatives. In *Wheat and wheat improvement,* ed. K. S. Quisenberry and L. P. Reitz, 19-87. Madison, Wis.

Nabhan, Gary P. 1989. *Enduring seeds.* San Francisco, Calif.

Naveh, Zev. 1974. Effects of fire in the Mediterranean region. In *Fire and ecosystems,* ed. T. T. Kozlowski and C. E. Ahlgren, 401-34. New York.

Naveh, Zev, and Joel Dan. 1973. The human degradation of Mediterranean landscapes in Israel. In *Mediterranean type ecosystems: Origin and structure,* ed. Francesco di Castri and Harold A. Mooney, 373-90. New York.

Percival, John. 1921. *The wheat plant.* London.

Purseglove, J. W. 1985. *Tropical crops: Monocotyledons.* Fifth edition. New York.

Rindos, David. 1984. *The origins of agriculture.* New York.

Rosenberg, Michael. 1990. The mother of invention: Evolutionary theory, territoriality, and the origins of agriculture. *American Anthropologist* 92: 399-415.

Rosenberg, Michael, R. Mark Nesbitt, Richard W. Redding, and Thomas F. Strasser. 1995. Hallan Çemi Tepesi: Some preliminary observations concerning early neolithic subsistence behaviors in eastern Anatolia. *Anatolica* 21: 1-12.

Runnels, Curtis, and T. H. van Andel. 1988. Trade and the origins of agriculture in the Eastern Mediterranean. *Journal of Mediterranean Archaeology* 1: 83-109.

Schiemann, E. 1948. *Weizen, Roggen, Gerste. Systematik, Geschichte, und Verwendung.* Jena, Germany.

Sherratt, Andrew. 1980. Water, soil and seasonality in early cereal cultivation. *World Archaeology* 11: 313-30.

Sillen, Andrew. 1984. Dietary variability in the epipalaeolithic of the Levant: The Sr/Ca evidence. *Paléorient* 10: 79-84.

Sillen, Andrew, and Julia A. Lee-Thorp. 1991. Dietary change in the late Natufian. In *The Natufian culture in the Levant,* ed. Ofer Bar-Yosef and François R. Valla, 399-410. Ann Arbor, Mich.

Smith, Patricia, Ofer Bar-Yosef, and Andrew Sillen. 1984. Archeological and skeletal evidence for dietary change during the late Pleistocene/early Holocene in the Levant. In *Paleopathology at the origins of agriculture,* ed. Mark N. Cohen and George J. Armelagos, 101-30. New York.

Tchernov, Eitan. 1991. Biological evidence for human sedentism in Southwest Asia during the Natufian. In *The Natufian culture in the Levant,* ed. Ofer Bar-Yosef and François R. Valla, Ann Arbor, Mich.

Unger-Hamilton, Romana. 1989. The epi-palaeolithic southern Levant and the origins of cultivation. *Current Anthropology* 30: 88-103.

van Zeist, Willem. 1970. The Oriental Institute excavations at Mureybit, Syria: Preliminary report on the 1965 campaign. Part III: The palaeobotany. *Journal of Near Eastern Studies* 29: 167-76.

  1988. Some aspects of early neolithic plant husbandry in the Near East. *Anatolica* 15: 49-67.

van Zeist, Willem, and Johanna Bakker-Heeres. 1982 (1985). Archaeobotanical studies in the Levant. I. Neolithic sites in the Damascus basin: Aswad, Ghoraifé, Ramad. *Palaeohistoria* 24: 165-256.

  1984 (1986). Archaeobotanical studies in the Levant 3. Late-palaeolithic Mureybit. *Palaeohistoria* 26: 171-99.

van Zeist, Willem, and Sytze Bottema. 1982. Vegetation history of the eastern Mediterranean and the Near East during the last 20,000 years. In *Palaeoclimates, palaeoenvironments and human communities in the eastern Mediterranean region in later prehistory,* ed. John L. Bintliff and Willem van Zeist, 277-321. 2 vols. Oxford.

Vavilov, Nikolai I. 1951. The origin, variation, immunity, and breeding of cultivated plants. *Chronica Botanica* 13: 1-6.

Watkins, Trevor, Douglas Baird, and Alison Betts. 1989. Qeremez Dere and the early aceramic neolithic in N. Iraq. *Paléorient* 15: 19-24.

Watson, Patty Jo. 1991. Origins of food production in western Asia and eastern North America: A consideration of interdisciplinary research in anthropology and archaeology. In *Quaternary landscapes,* ed. Linda C. K. Shane and Edward J. Cushing, 1-37. Minneapolis, Minn.

Wenke, Robert J. 1989. Egypt: Origins of complex societies. *Annual Review of Anthropology* 18: 129-55.

Western, A. Cecilia. 1971. The ecological interpretation of ancient charcoals from Jericho. *Levant* 3: 31-40.

  1983. Appendix F: Catalogue of identified charcoal samples. In *Excavations at Jericho,* vol. 5, ed. Kathleen M. Kenyon and Thomas A. Holland, 770-3. London.

Wetterstrom, Wilma. 1993. Foraging and farming in Egypt: The transition from hunting and gathering to horticulture in the Nile Valley. In *The archaeology of Africa,* ed. Thurstan Shaw, Paul Sinclair, Bassey Andah, and Alex Okpoko, 165-225. London.

Wilke, Philip J., Robert Bettinger, Thomas F. King, and James F. O'Connell. 1972. Harvest selection and domestication in seed plants. *Antiquity* 46: 203-9.

Wright, Gary A. 1971. Origins of food production in southwest Asia: A survey of ideas. *Current Anthropology* 12: 447-77.

Wright, Jr., Herbert E. 1977. Environmental change and the origin of agriculture in the Old and New Worlds. In *Origins of agriculture,* ed. C. A. Reed, 281-318. The Hague.

Wright, Katherine I. 1994. Ground stone tools and hunter-gatherer subsistence in southwest Asia: Implications for the transition to farming. *American Antiquity* 59: 238-63.

Zeven, A. C. 1980. The spread of bread wheat over the Old World since the neolithicum as indicated by its genotype for hybrid necrosis. *Journal d'Agriculture Traditionelle et de Botanique Appliquée* 27: 19-53.

Zohary, Daniel. 1970a. Centers of diversity and centers of origin. In *Genetic resources in plants,* ed. O. H. Frankel and E. Bennett, 33-42. Oxford.

  1970b. Wild wheats. In *Genetic resources in plants,* ed. O. H. Frankel and E. Bennett, 239-47. Oxford.

  1971. Origin of south-west Asiatic cereals: Wheats, barley, oats and rye. In *Plant life of southwest-Asia,* ed. Peter H. Davis, Peter C. Harper, and Ian C. Hedge, 235-60. Edinburgh.

  1989. Domestication of the southwest Asia neolithic crop assemblage of cereals, pulses, and flax: The evidence from the living plants. In *Foraging and farming: The evolution of plant exploitation,* ed. David R. Harris and Gordon C. Hillman, 359-73. London.

Zohary, Daniel, Jack R. Harlan, and A. Vardi. 1969. The wild diploid progenitors of wheat and their breeding values. *Euphytica* 18: 58-65.

Zohary, Daniel, and Maria Hopf. [1988] 1993. *Domestication of plants in the Old World.* Second edition. Oxford.

Zohary, Michael. 1983. Man and vegetation in the Middle East. In *Man's impact on vegetation,* ed. W. Holzner, M. J. A. Werger, and I. Ikusima, 163-78. The Hague.

II.B

Roots, Tubers, and Other Starchy Staples

II.B.1   Bananas and Plantains

Bananas represent one of the most important fruit crops, second only to grapes in the volume of world production (Purseglove 1988). J. F. Morton (1987) indicates that bananas are the fourth largest fruit crop after grapes, citrus fruits, and apples. Bananas and plantains are starchy berries produced by hybrids and/or sports of *Musa acuminata* Colla and *Musa balbisiana*. Rare genome contributions from another species may have occurred but are not yet well documented (Simmonds 1986). Additionally, *fe'i* bananas are obtained from *Musa troglodytarum*. Bananas may be differentiated from plantains on the basis of moisture content, with bananas generally averaging 83 percent moisture and plantains 65 percent (but intermediate examples may also be found) (Lessard 1992). Bananas may be eaten raw or cooked. Plantains are usually eaten cooked. Commonly, bananas which are eaten raw are referred to as dessert bananas. Throughout this essay, the term "bananas" is used to refer to both bananas and plantains.

    Bananas, being primarily carbohydrates (22.2 to 31.2 percent), are low in fats, cholesterol, and sodium. Potassium levels are high (400 milligrams to 100 grams of pulp). Bananas are also good sources of ascorbic acid, 100 grams providing 13.3 to 26.7 percent of the U.S. RDA (Stover and Simmonds 1987). During ripening, the starch component is gradually converted to simple sugars (fructose, glucose, and sucrose), while the moisture content of the pulp increases. The time of conversion to simple sugars can also be used to differentiate plantains/cooking bananas (later conversion) from bananas that are eaten raw (earlier conversion).

Banana Plants

Bananas are monocarpic (fruiting once, then dying), perennial, giant herbs that usually are propagated via lateral shoots (suckers). Leaves are produced by a single apical meristem, which typically forms only a low

short stem or pseudobulb. The leaves are tightly rolled around each other, producing a pseudostem with a heart of young, emerging, rolled leaves ending with the terminal production of a huge inflorescence (usually sterile) and, finally, the starchy fruits: bananas or plantains.

Banana plant

Banana suckers emerge from axillary buds on the pseudobulb, thus providing a means of propagation as the fruits are commonly sterile. Suckers are either left in place as a part of a "mat," which includes the parent plant, or they may be removed for planting at new sites. Within a year after a sucker has been planted at a new site, the flowering stem will emerge at the apex of the pseudostem. The flowering stem will gradually bend over, producing a pendulous inflorescence (except in *fe'i* bananas, which have an erect inflorescence).

At the apical end of the stem are sterile male flowers, protected by large, often reddish, bracts (reduced or modified leaves). Higher up the stem are rows of biseriately (in two series) arranged female (or hermaphroditic) flowers (Masefield et al. 1971). The banana fruits developing from the rows of flowers are commonly called "hands," with the individual fruits called "fingers" (Stover and Simmonds 1987). The entire inflorescence, having matured as fruit, may be called a "bunch."

Climate and Soil

Bananas are almost entirely restricted to largely tropical wet zones of the earth. Practically all banana cultivations fall within 30° latitude north and south of the equator (Simmonds 1966), with most of the large growing areas in the tropics between 20° north and south latitude. Bananas are very susceptible to cold temperatures and to drying environments. Their growth is limited by temperature in areas where water is not limited and by water availability in the warmest climates. A mean monthly temperature of 27° C is optimal, with temperatures below 21° C causing delayed growth (Purseglove 1988). Bananas are found growing under optimal conditions in wet or humid tropics when there are at least eight months per year with a minimum of 75 millimeters of rain per month (Stover and Simmonds 1987). Bananas also grow best under intense sunlight, with shading causing delayed growth, although the fruits may be sunburned, turning black, if exposed to excessive radiation.

Bananas will grow, and even produce fruit, under very poor conditions but will not produce an economically viable crop unless planted in relatively deep, well-drained soil (Morton 1987). Bananas can grow on loam, rocky sand, marl, volcanic ash, sandy clay, and even heavy clay, as long as water is not excessively retained in the soil matrix. Well drained, slightly acidic alluvial soils of river valleys offer optimal edaphic conditions.

General Uses

As already mentioned, banana and plantain fruits may be either cooked or eaten raw. The major usage of bananas is as a starch source for local consumption by tropical traditional cultures. Banana starch may be consumed in a variety of products (see the section on *Cultural Uses*), with the bulk of the consumption consisting of very simple sugars mixed with fibers. The fruits represent significant exports from developing countries, particularly in the Neotropics. Bananas are very susceptible to damage during storage and shipping, which has certainly limited their value as foods imported into temperate, industrialized nations.

Where bananas are locally grown, the nonfruit parts of the plants are employed for a variety of purposes. Banana leaves are commonly used in addition to the fruits, with some varieties producing more desirable leaves than fruits. Fresh banana leaves serve as wrapping material for steamed or cooked foods and also as disposable meal platters. Fresh leaves are used medicinally in Rotuma, Samoa, and Fiji for the treatment of a variety of disorders, including headaches, menstrual cramps, and urinary tract infections. Young, unfolded leaves are employed as topical remedies for chest ailments, and the stem juice is used to treat gonorrhea (Uphof 1968).

Juice from fresh banana leaves occasionally serves as a light brown dye or stain. Because of their 30 to 40 percent tannin content, dried banana peels are used to blacken leather (Morton 1987). Dried leaves may be woven as house screens or be a source of fibrous strings for simple weaving or short-term structure construction. Dried leaves may also be employed to absorb salt water for transport to distant locations, where they are burned to produce a salty ash seasoning. Dried green plantains, ground fine and roasted, have reportedly served as a substitute for coffee (Morton 1987), and banana leaves have even been rolled as cigarette wrappers.

Of growing importance is the use of banana plants and fruits in livestock feed (Stover and Simmonds 1987; Purseglove 1988; Babatunde 1992; Cheeke 1992; Fomunyam 1992) and in shading or intercropping with yams, maize, cocoa, coconuts, areca nuts, and coffee (Stover and Simmonds 1987; Swennen 1990). Livestock are fed either dried and crushed fruits or fresh waste fruits and pseudostems with the leaves. Pigs, cattle, and rabbits have all been fed experimentally with mixtures of bananas and banana waste products. When used for intercropping or shading, bananas serve mainly as shade from intense sunlight for the crop of primary interest, but they also provide an intermediate crop while the farmer is waiting for production of his primary crop: cocoa, coconuts, areca nuts, or coffee.

Leaves of the related species *M. textilis* Nee have been used in and exported from the Philippines as a fiber source in the form of abaca. The abaca fiber is applied to the production of ropes, twines, hats, mats, hammocks, and other products requiring hard, strong fibers (Brown 1951; Purseglove 1988).

Biology

More than 500 varieties of bananas are recognized worldwide, although many of these are probably closely related lineages with differing regional names. Extensive research into the genetics, taxonomy, propagation, and distribution of bananas has been carried out by N. W. Simmonds (1957; 1962) and R. H. Stover (Stover and Simmonds 1987).

Taxonomy

Bananas and plantains have been taxonomically referenced by many different scientific names, including *Musa paradisiaca* L., *M. corniculata* Lour., *M. nana* Lour., and *M. sapientum* L. Each of these names is misleading, giving reference to a variety or group of varieties within a hybrid complex of extensively cultivated clones arising from *M. acuminata* Colla and *M. balbisiana* Colla. Simmonds (1962) suggested that the Latin binomials previously mentioned should all be abandoned and replaced by a designation of the clonal lineage represented by the ploidy (chromosome repetition number) and relative contributions of each of the diploid parent species.

The lineages are represented as groups of varieties/clones that share common ploidy levels and relative proportions of ancestral features (*M. acuminata* represented by "A" and *M. balbisiana* by "B"). Simmonds developed a system of scoring each variety on the basis of 15 characters, noting those characters present from the "A" and "B" parents. Additionally, many nonancestral (derived) somatic mutations have been identified, and these can be employed to differentiate the lineages of hybrids/autopolyploids (Stover and Simmonds 1987). It is possible that future systematic studies of bananas will use these ancestral and derived features as plesiomorphic (ancestral) and apomorphic (unique or derived) characters in cladistic and phenetic determinations of the relationships of banana cultivars.

Simmonds's designations are applied as follows for the common bananas with some examples of varieties within each group:

Group AA: Varieties 'Nino', 'Paka', 'Pisang lin', 'Sucrier', and 'Thousand Fingers'. These are primitive diploids found in Malesia, New Guinea, the Philippines, and East Africa.

Group AB: Varieties 'Ney Poovan' and some 'Lady's Fingers'. These diploid hybrids from India are of minor importance.

Group AAA: Varieties 'Cavendish', 'Dwarf Cavendish', 'Gros Michel', 'Highgate', and 'Robusta'. These varieties consist of African and Malesian triploids, which were important in the initial development of the commercial banana trade (mainly 'Gros Michel'), and remain important in much of the present trade ('Dwarf Cavendish').

Group AAB: Varieties 'Ae Ae', 'Apple', 'Brazilian', 'Giant Plantains', 'Hua Moa', 'Red holene', and 'Rhino horn'. These are triploids producing the lower moisture content fruits generally called plantains, which were initially developed in southern India.

Group ABB: Varieties 'ce Cream', 'Kru', 'Orinco', and 'Praying Hands'. These are triploids originating in India, the Philippines, and New Guinea. They are important staples in Southeast Asia, Samoa, and parts of Africa (Purseglove 1988).

Additionally, tetraploid (4 times the base chromosome number) hybrids AAAA, ABBB, AAAB, and AABB have also been produced, but these are presently of little importance. They may, however, become important in the future (Purseglove 1988).

Fe'i bananas (*Musa troglodytarum* L.) differ from other common edible bananas in that they are diploids with erect inflorescences, have red-orange juice, and are not derived from hybrids of sports of *M. acuminata* or *M. balbisiana*. *Fe'i* bananas are prepared as plantains (cooked), having flesh which is rich orange-yellow to reddish in color.

Propagation

The clonal groups are propagated vegetatively with constant selection for desired traits (fruit elegance, flavor, and so forth, and resistance to diseases such as Panama disease, or to nematodes or corm borers). Of the 500 varieties of bananas that are recognized, about half are diploids, with most of the remainder being triploids (Purseglove 1988). Bananas take from 2 to 6 months or more to produce an inflorescence from a new sucker shoot.

Bananas can reproduce by seeds (in the wild primitive varieties) or, as is primarily the case, by suckers (in most cultivated and wild varieties). The suckers may be removed and planted in new locations to expand the range of the variety. Bananas moved from Malesia to Oceania, Africa, and Central America and the Caribbean by means of transplanted suckers.

Diseases

Bananas are afflicted with diseases caused by fungi, bacteria, and viruses. Fungal diseases include Sigatoka leaf spot, crown rot, anthracnose, pitting disease, brown spot, diamond spot, fusarial wilt (Panama disease), freckle disease, and rust. Bacterial infections include Moko, banana finger rot, and rhizome rot. "Bunchy top" is the only widespread virus that attacks bananas. It is transmitted by an aphid vector and can be controlled with insecticides (Stover and Simmonds 1987).

Bananas are also susceptible to damage from nematodes, insect larvae, and adult insects. Caterpillar defoliators are common but do not usually cause sufficient destruction to impact production levels. Boring worms cause some damage to the pseudostems and rhizomes, but nematodes account for most of the damage to those tissues. Thrips and beetles chew and suck on the pseudostems, fruits, and suckers, leaving unsightly scars that reduce the market value of the fruits. Nematodes can cause significant damage, particularly to the commercial 'Cavendish' varieties. The nematodes will commonly attack plants that have been weakened by other pathogens, such as Sigatoka leaf spot, which promotes rotting of the pseudostem, rhizome, and roots.

Of the pathogens listed, fusarial wilt (Panama disease) and Sigatoka leaf spot have had the greatest impact on both the local and commercial production of bananas. Fusarial wilt wrought devastating losses of bananas in the Neotropics between 1910 and 1955, causing commercial banana producers to switch from the 'Gros Michel' variety to 'Cavendish' varieties, which are more resistant to fusarial wilt. Sigatoka leaf spot involves three closely related fungi that destroy the banana leaves and decrease transportability of the fruits (Stover and Simmonds 1987).

History

The wild ancestors of edible bananas (*M. acuminata* Colla and *M. balbisiana* Colla), except for the *fe'i* bananas, are centered in Malesia, a term that refers to the entire region from Thailand to New Guinea – roughly the main trading area of the Malay mariners. Simmonds (1962) has indicated that probably crosses and/or autopolyploidy of these wild ancestors originally took place in Indochina or the Malay Archipelago. Subspecies of *M. acuminata* have also been transported to locations as distant as Pemba, Hawaii, and Samoa, where they may have contributed to the production of new varieties.

The subspecies *malaccensis* produces edible diploid fruits via parthenocarpy and female sterility. These characters would have been fostered by human selection and vegetative propagation, transforming bananas from jungle weeds into a productive crop (Purseglove 1988). According to Simmonds (1962):

Edibility arose in subsp. *malaccensis* near the western edge of the range of *M. acuminata,* and, perhaps, in other subspecies independently; male-fertile edible clones were carried to other areas and intercrossed and outcrossed to local wild forms, generating new phenotypes and new structural chromosome combinations in the process; selection retained the best and the most sterile of these, which, under prolonged clonal propagation, accumulated still more structural changes until, finally, total sterility supervened and clonal propagation became obligatory.

Distribution

A Burmese legend relates that humans first realized bananas could be eaten when they observed birds eating them. The common Burmese generic name for bananas is *hnget pyaw,* meaning "the birds told" (Simmonds 1957; Lessard 1992). Fijians tell a story about a young girl whose lover disappeared while holding her hands in farewell. He was replaced by a banana sucker, which grew "hands" of banana "fingers" that represented the outstretched hands of the lost lover (Reed and Hames 1993).

Bananas are thought to have been distributed from western Melanesia into eastern Melanesia, Polynesia, and Micronesia during the time of aboriginal migrations into these areas. Linguistic evidence indicates a common center of origin of some Polynesian or Micronesian banana varieties in Indo-Malaysia. The movements of these varieties can be traced through two dispersals. The first involved movement into the Philippines, then into Micronesia and, eventually, Polynesia. The second dispersal involved movement into Melanesia first, with a secondary dispersal into parts of Polynesia (Guppy 1906). In the later dispersal, seeded varieties and the *fe'i* bananas constituted the initial wave of introduction, followed by successive waves of nonseeded varieties imported from west to east, penetrating into Oceania such that more varieties may be found in western, and fewer in eastern, Oceania. (This is a general trend for the common banana varieties but not for the *fe'i* bananas, which have the greatest diversity in the extreme east of the distribution.)

Bananas may initially have been introduced into Africa by Arab traders who brought the plants from Malaysia. But they may also have arrived earlier with Indonesians who brought the fruit to Madagascar. Or, of course, they could have been introduced even earlier by unknown individuals from unknown sources. Regardless, the plants subsequently spread across tropical Africa from east to west. Simmonds (1957) indicates that the banana entered the Koran as the "tree of paradise." The generic name *Musa* is derived from the Arabic word *mouz,* meaning banana (Purseglove 1988). Linnaeus applied the name *Musa paradisiaca* as a reference to this ancient terminology.

The name "banana" came from the Guinea coast of West Africa and was introduced along with the plant into the Canary Islands by the Portuguese (Purseglove 1988). At least one clone was taken from the Canary Islands to Hispaniola in 1516. Bananas were carried as food for slaves who originated in areas of traditional banana cultivation, and J. W. Purseglove (1988) surmises that 1516 may mark the first introduction of bananas into the Caribbean and tropical America. Alternatively, bananas may have arrived in the Neotropics via the Spanish trade route from the Philippines. The Spaniards used the name *plátano* for bananas, from which the term "plantain" has been derived (Purseglove 1988).

The Economic Importance of Bananas

The secondary centers of banana distribution in Africa, Central America, and the Caribbean have become the greatest consumers and exporters of bananas. Estimates of the total banana production of the world range from 20 to 40 million tons (Simmonds 1966; Stover and Simmonds 1987), with 4 to 5 million tons per year entering international trade (Morton 1987; Purseglove 1988: 376). Africa is the largest producer of bananas, with some sources saying that half of the world's bananas are produced there. But most African bananas are consumed locally, although some are exported to Europe. Ecuador (the world's largest banana exporter), Colombia, Costa Rica, Honduras, Jamaica, and Panama all export bananas to the United States and Europe, whereas the Philippines and Taiwan export bananas to other Asian countries, particularly Japan.

Three-fourths of internationally traded bananas are grown in Central and South America and the Caribbean, with much of this trade controlled by the United Fruit Company and the Standard Fruit Company. The former has enormous land concessions, regional shipping interests, and distribution networks within the United States (Purseglove 1988). United Fruit developed its economic empire beginning in 1874 in Costa Rica, and subsequently expanded throughout the region. The bananas produced were all of the 'Gros Michel' variety until 1947, when because of increasing losses from Panama disease, the 'Robusta' and other disease-resistant varieties began to replace the 'Gros Michel.' Panama disease (causing leaves to wilt and die) and Sigatoka disease (causing decay spots on leaves and either death of the plant or a greatly reduced crop output) are the two major diseases that have limited the international economic potential of bananas and have also driven the study and introduction of various disease-resistant varieties of the fruit. The economic value of bananas in international trade is, however, a secondary consideration; their major importance is in providing basic local nutrition for many rural populations in tropical, Third World countries.

It is interesting to note that both the *fe'i* bananas and the common bananas have attained their greatest agricultural and human importance in areas far removed from their centers of origin. *Fe'i* bananas originated in Melanesia, spreading and diversifying into the central Pacific, and the common bananas originated in Malesia, spreading and diversifying in Africa, Oceania, India, and, most recently, the Neotropics.

Specific Cultural Usages

Southeast Asia

The origin of bananas was probably within the cultures that developed in Malaysia, Indonesia, Thailand, and Burma. These cultures have long traditions of banana usage. Mature fruits are commonly eaten, but in addition, young fruits are pickled and male buds are consumed as a vegetable in Malaysia and Thailand. Sap from the variety 'Pisang klutum' is mixed with soot and used to give a black color to bamboo basketwork in Java. Also in Java, the fruit stems surrounded by the leaf sheaths of the 'Pisang baia' variety are employed in the preparation of a type of sweetmeat (Uphof 1968). Flowers may be removed from the buds and used in curries in Malaysia. Ashes from burned leaves and pseudostems serve as salt in the seasoning of vegetable curries. Banana plants may be placed in the corners of rice fields as protective charms, and Malay women may bathe with a decoction of banana leaves for 15 days after parturition (Morton 1987).

Although Southeast Asia/Malesia is considered to be the origin of the distribution of bananas, it is important to note that bananas never became as important there as they did in parts of Africa, Oceania, and, more recently, the Neotropics, although production of bananas is increasing in Southeast Asia (Morton 1987; Sadik 1988). Such a relative lack of importance is perhaps connected with the presence of two other competing Southeast Asian starch crops: rice and sago. Rice offers a storable starch source with potentially greater stability of production and yield than bananas. Sago palms of the genus *Metroxylon* are present throughout Malesia in the same areas in which bananas may be found. But as sago production drops off and disappears, there is increased dependence upon bananas and increased diversity in some varieties, including the *fe'i* bananas.

Two areas that certainly must have received some of the earliest diffusions of bananas out of Malesia are the Philippines and India. In these areas, banana cultivation became much more important and variations in usage evolved. Filipinos eat not only the cooked or raw fruits of fresh banana but also the flowers. They employ the leaves and sap medicinally and extract fibers from the leaves. Young inflorescences are eaten both boiled as a vegetable and raw in salads (Brown 1951).

Banana fibers are used in the production of ropes and other products that require durability and resistance to saltwater. Fibers from the sheathing leafstalks are employed in the manufacture of a light, transparent cloth known as "agna" (Brown 1951). Wild banana leaves are used extensively as lining for cooking pots and earthen ovens and for wrapping items that are to be sold in markets. The Filipinos have effectively developed the banana as an export crop with up to a half million tons sent yearly to Japan (Morton 1987).

In India, "the banana plant because of its continuous reproduction is regarded by Hindus as a symbol of fertility and prosperity and the leaves and fruits are deposited on doorsteps of houses where marriages are taking place" (Morton 1987). Virtually the entire above-ground portion of the banana plant is eaten in India. The fruits are cooked or eaten raw, with no clear distinction between plantains and bananas. The young flowers are eaten raw or cooked. The pseudostem may be cooked and eaten as a vegetable or may be candied with citric acid and potassium metabisulphite. India is currently the leading producer of bananas in Asia, with virtually the entire crop employed for domestic purposes (Morton 1987).

Africa

In Africa, bananas reach their greatest importance as a starchy food (Purseglove 1988). Throughout African regions where bananas grow, 60 million people (34 percent of the population) derive more than 25 percent of their calories from plantains and bananas (Wilson 1986). Within Africa, many tropical traditional cultures have come to depend heavily upon bananas as a starch source (Sadik 1988). For example, the Buganda in Uganda typically consume 4 to 4.5 kilograms of bananas per person daily. Tanzanians and Ugandans produce large quantities of beer from bananas ripened evenly in pits. These bananas, after becoming partially fermented, are trampled to extract the juice, which is then mixed with sorghum flour and old beer and allowed to ferment for 12 or more hours. The beer is drunk by people of all ages and has become an important part of the diet (Purseglove 1988).

Sweetmeats, made from dried banana slices, serve as famine foods, preserves, and desserts. Flour can be produced from ripe or unripe fruits, and the flowers are employed as an ingredient in confections. Banana flour is sometimes called Guiana arrowroot, a reference to its importance in West Africa (Uphof 1968). The fruits can be used medicinally for children who are intolerant of more complex carbohydrates and for adults with various intestinal complaints (Purseglove 1988). Additionally, banana pseudostem fibers are used as fishing line in parts of West Africa (Morton 1987).

In West Africa, as in many other parts of the world, bananas are grown in compound gardens and in and around village backyards (Swennen 1990). Proximity to the human population allows for harvesting of the unevenly ripening bananas, a few at a time from each bunch, and the human presence wards off birds and other animals that eat the fruits. In this situation, banana plants typically grow on local refuse dumps, which become rich in nutrients from decaying food products. Banana plants growing in rich soils tend to produce larger bunches, which may become so heavy that the plant falls over. Traditional farmers will place one or more prop poles under the base of growing bunches in order to keep the plants upright.

Oceania

Fried or steamed bananas are staples in many Polynesian cultures. Rotumans serve fried bananas as part of meals containing other dishes; alternatively, an entire meal may consist of fried bananas. Banana fruits are frequently grated or pounded, mixed with coconut cream and fruit juices, and served as a thick beverage. Banana bunches are often found hanging at the edges of cookhouses and ceremonial structures in which a celebration is occurring. Hung in a cookhouse, bananas will slowly ripen over a period of days or weeks, allowing for gradual usage of the bunch. Bananas hung for ceremonial feasts and celebrations will be pit ripened (see below) in advance so that the entire bunch may be eaten ripe on the same day.

Many bananas ripen unevenly, with the more basal (usually higher on a pendulous raceme) fruits ripening first. In these cases, the basal bananas will have ripened and fallen off or been eaten before the apical fingers have even begun to ripen. This natural tendency makes it difficult to cut and use an entire bunch of bananas at one time. A traditional method, which is often used in Polynesia (and elsewhere) to promote even ripening and to increase the rate of ripening, is as follows: A pit (approximately 1 to 2 meters deep) is dug in the ground. It is made sufficiently large to hold several bunches of bananas (up to 10 to 15). The pit is lined with leaves, and fires are built in the edges of the pit. Unripened, but mature, banana bunches are cut from the pseudostems and placed in the pit. The bananas are covered with leaves and the fires are stoked to burn slowly. The pit is covered with soil and left for 3 to 7 days. This process both heats the bananas and extracts oxygen from within the pit. When the pit is opened, the bunches of bananas are found to be entirely and uniformly ripened. Perhaps this ripening process occurs because of increased concentrations of the ethylene produced by the earliest ripening bananas. This in turn would speed the ripening of neighboring fingers, and the exclusion of oxygen and insects would prohibit deterioration of the fruits that ripened first (Stover and Simmonds 1987). The speed of the process is increased by the heat generated by the slowly smoldering fires.

The Neotropics

Neotropical tribes, such as the Waimiri Atroari of Brazilian Amazonia, have incorporated bananas into their diets as both food and beverage. Other neotropical traditional cultures have incorporated bananas not only as food but also as medicinals for stomach ulcers, as antiseptics, and as antidiarrheal remedies (Milliken et al. 1992).

As already mentioned, three-quarters of the worldwide production of bananas for international trade is produced in Central and South America and the Caribbean. This trade is extremely important to the local economies in Colombia, Costa Rica, Honduras, Jamaica, and Panama. The significance of bananas in the United States and Europe has been entirely a function of production in the Neotropics.

The United States

Bananas commonly obtained in the United States may be 'Dwarf Cavendish' or 'Gros Michel' varieties or clones closely related to the 'Dwarf Cavendish' (Simmonds 1986). About 12 percent of the world production of bananas involves these AAA cultivars (Stover and Simmonds 1987). The bananas eaten in temperate countries are typically picked prior to ripening of any of the bananas in a bunch. The bunches are broken down into individual "hands" for shipping from the tropics. Bananas are shipped – usually within 24 hours of harvest – in containers that maintain low storage temperatures from 12° C to –25° C. The unripe bananas may be stored for up to 40 days under controlled conditions of cool temperatures and ethylene-free environments. When ripening is desired, the temperature is raised to 14 to 18° C and ethylene gas is sprayed on the bananas, resulting in rapid, uniform ripening in 4 to 8 days (Stover and Simmonds 1987).

Will C. McClatchey

Bibliography

Babatunde, G. M. 1992. Availability of banana and plantain products for animal feeding. In *Roots, tubers, plantains and bananas in animal feeding,* ed. D. Machin and S. Nyvold, 251-76. Rome. FAO Animal Production and Health Paper No. 95.

Brown, W. H. 1951. *Useful plants of the Philippines,* Vol. 1. Manila.

Cheeke, P. R. 1992. Feeding systems for tropical rabbit production emphasizing roots, tubers and bananas. In *Roots, tubers, plantains and bananas in animal feeding,* ed. D. Machin and S. Nyvold, 235-50. Rome. FAO Animal Production and Health Paper No. 95.

Fomunyam, R. T. 1992. Economic aspects of banana and plantain use in animal feeding: The Cameroon experience. In *Roots, tubers, plantains and bananas in animal feeding, ed. D. Machin and S. Nyvold, 277-89. Rome. FAO Animal Production and Health Paper No. 95.*

Guppy, H. B. 1906. Observations of a naturalist in the Pacific between 1896 and 1899. London.

Lessard, W. O. 1992. *The complete book of bananas.* Homestead, Fla.

Masefield, G. B., M. Wallis, S. G. Harrison, and B. E. Nicholson. 1971. *The Oxford book of food plants.* London.

Milliken, W., R. P. Miller, S. R. Pollard, and E. V. Wandelli. 1992. *The ethnobotany of the Waimiri Atroari Indians of Brazil.* Kew, England.

Morton, J. F. 1987. *Fruits of warm climates.* Greensboro, N.C.

Purseglove, J. W. 1988. *Tropical crops: Monocotyledons.* Essex, England.

Reed, A. W., and I. Hames. 1993. *Myths and legends of Fiji and Rotuma.* Auckland.

Sadik, S. 1988. *Root and tuber crops, plantains and bananas in developing countries.* FAO Plant Production and Protection Paper No. 87. Rome.

Simmonds, N. W. 1957. *Bananas.* London.
  1962. *The evolution of bananas.* London.
  1966. *Bananas.* Second edition. London.
  Bananas, *Musa cvs.* In *Breeding for durable resistance in perennial crops,* ed. N. W. Simmonds, 17-24. Rome. FAO Plant Production and Protection Paper No. 70.

Stover, R. H., and N. W. Simmonds. 1987. *Bananas.* Third edition. London.

Swennen, R. 1990. *Plantain cultivation under West African conditions.* Ibadan, Nigeria.

Uphof, J. C. Th. 1968. *Dictionary of economic plants.* New York.

Wilson, G. F. 1986. Status of bananas and plantains in West Africa. In *Banana and plantain breeding strategies,* ed. G. J. Persley and E. A. DeLanghe, 29-35. Cairns, Australia.

II.B.2 ❦ Manioc

A tropical root crop, manioc is also known as cassava, *mandioca, aipim,* the tapioca plant, and *yuca.* The term cassava comes from the Arawak word *kasabi,* whereas the Caribs called the plant *yuca* (Jones 1959). The word manioc, however, is from *maniot* in the Tupí language of coastal Brazil; *mandioca* derives from *Mani-óca,* or the house of Mani, the Indian woman from whose body grew the manioc plant, according to Indian legends collected in Brazil (Cascudo 1984). Domesticated in Brazil before 1500, *Manihot esculenta* (Crantz), formerly termed *Manihot utilissima,* is a member of the spurge family (Euphorbiaceae), which includes the rubber bean and the castor bean (Cock 1985).

The manioc plant is a perennial woody shrub that reaches 5 to 12 feet in height, with leaves of 5 to 7 lobes that grow toward the end of the branches. The leaves are edible and may be cooked like spinach, but in terms of food, the most significant part of the plant is its starchy roots, which often reach 1 to 2 feet in length and 2 to 6 inches in diameter. Several roots radiate like spokes in a wheel from the stem, and each plant may yield up to 8 kilograms of roots (Jones 1959; Cock 1985; Toussaint-Samat 1992).

There are two principal varieties of manioc – the sweet and the bitter. The sweet varieties have a shorter growing season, can be harvested in 6 to 9 months, and then can simply be peeled and eaten as a vegetable without further processing. If not harvested soon after maturity, however, sweet manioc deteriorates rapidly. The bitter varieties require 12 to 18 months to mature but will not spoil if left unharvested for several months. Thus, people can harvest them at their leisure. The main disadvantage to the bitter varieties is that they may contain high levels of cyanogenic glycosides, which can cause prussic-acid poisoning if the roots are not processed properly (Jones 1959; Johns 1990).

An obvious question is that given the threat of poisoning, why would Amerindians have domesticated such a plant? The answer lies in its many advantages. It is a crop that does well in the lowland tropics where there is a warm, moist climate and no frost, although there are "cold-tolerant varieties" of the plant in the Andes (Cock 1985). In addition, manioc yields good results on soils of low fertility, and it will also tolerate acidic soils more readily than other food staples. One of the most important characteristics of manioc, however, is its ability to survive natural disasters, such as droughts. When other food crops dry up, people survive on manioc roots. Similarly, where storms frequently sweep the land, high winds do not kill the roots, even if they damage the foliage. New shoots soon form, while the roots continue to nourish people and prevent starvation.

Manioc roots are also resistant to locust plagues (an important consideration in Africa) and to destructive predators, such as wild pigs, baboons, and porcupines (Johns 1990). Once processed, manioc can be preserved and stored in a tropical climate as *farinha* (manioc meal) or as a bread (*pan de tierra caliente*, as it was called by late colonial Mexicans [Humboldt 1811]). To produce more manioc plants, farmers do not have to set aside edible roots; instead, they use stem cuttings or seeds to propagate the plant (Cock 1985).

As a food, manioc is very versatile because it can be boiled in a mush, roasted, baked, and even consumed as a pudding (tapioca) or alcoholic beverage (Aguiar 1982). When fresh, the manioc root is primarily a starch, a source of carbohydrates. But the leaf has protein and vitamin A, and the fresh roots may contain calcium, vitamin C, thiamine, riboflavin, and niacin. However, the nutritional value of the roots varies with processing, as vitamins may be leached, and even destroyed, when they are soaked and boiled (Jones 1959). Thus, as a rule, manioc must be supplemented with other foodstuffs in order for a population to avoid malnutrition. In many parts of the world, especially Asia, it also serves as an animal feed.

William Jones (1959: 29) has observed that modern methods for processing manioc roots derive from Indian methods. In order to consume the bitter varieties, they had to detoxify the plant by grating and soaking it to remove the toxic chemicals (Johns 1990). To prepare the coarse meal, known as *farinha de mandioca* (also *farinha de pau*) in Brazil, women, who traditionally process manioc in Amerindian societies, have to wash, peel, and scrape the roots. Some prehistoric populations in South America and the Caribbean even used their upper front teeth in processing manioc.

Using a flat piece of wood studded with small pointed stones as a grater, women convert the roots into a snowy white mass, which is then placed in a *tipiti*, a long cylindrical basket press similar to a Chinese "finger trap." The two ends of the *tipiti* are pulled apart, with one end tied to the ground and the other to the branch of a tree. After the excess liquid has been squeezed out, the pulpy mass is removed, put through a sieve, and then placed on a flat ceramic griddle or metal basin where it is toasted over a low fire. The *farinha* can be kept for months and then eaten dry or mixed with water as a gruel (Jones 1959; de Léry 1990; Toussaint-Samat 1992; and personal observation, Tikuna village, Peru, 1975).

Origins

Although scholars agree that manioc was domesticated in the Americas, there is doubt about the exact location, even though the largest variety of species survive in Brazil. Possible areas of origin include Central America, the Amazon region, and the northeast of Brazil. Milton de Albuquerque (1969), a specialist on manioc in Amazonia, reported that the most primitive form of the plant is found in central Brazil in the state of Goiás, a region subject to prolonged dry seasons, but he believes that the backlands of the state of Bahia are its most probable point of origin. The oldest archaeological records in Brazil, however, come from the Amazon region, where ceramic griddles used in manioc preparation have been found in pre-Columbian sites (Lathrap 1970; Roosevelt 1980).

Of much greater antiquity, however, are remains of the manioc plant that have been discovered in South American excavations in and near the Casma Valley of northern Peru. These have been dated to 1785 B.C. (Langdon 1988). In Mexico, cassava leaves that are 2,500 years old have been found, along with cassava starch in human coprolites that are 2,100 to 2,800 years old (Cock 1985). Preclassic Pacific coast archaeological sites in Mesoamerica have yielded evidence of manioc, which was a staple of the Mayan civilization (Tejada 1979; Morley and Brainerd 1983). The quality of the evidence for manioc in Mesoamerica has led some authors to believe that manioc was first domesticated in Central America rather than Brazil, or that there may have been two regions of origin. Another possibility might be that bitter manioc was domesticated in northern South America, whereas sweet cassava was domesticated in Central America (Cock 1985).

Archaeological evidence for ancient manioc usage also exists in the Caribbean. According to Suzanne Levin (1983: 336), manioc griddles have been found in archaeological excavations in the Lesser Antilles on islands such as St. Kitts, St. Vincent, Antigua, and Martinique. Both the Arawaks and Caribs utilized them, and as they migrated to the islands from South America, they undoubtedly carried with them manioc and the technological knowledge necessary to propagate, cultivate, and process it.

When the Spanish reached the Caribbean and Central America, they discovered the indigenous populations cultivating manioc, a plant they termed *yuca*. Thus, the earliest European description of manioc dates from 1494. In describing the first voyage of

Columbus, Peter Martyr referred to "venomous roots" used in preparing breads (Pynaert 1951). The Portuguese encountered manioc after 1500 on the coast of Brazil. Other sixteenth-century observers, such as the German Hans Staden [1557] (1974) and the Frenchman Jean de Léry [1578] (1990), have left valuable descriptions of what the Brazilians term the most Brazilian of all economic plants because of its close links to the historical evolution of Brazil (Aguiar 1982).

As the Portuguese divided Brazil into captaincies and contested the French for its control, they employed their slaves, both Indian and African, in cultivating food crops, including manioc. Unlike other areas of the Americas, where Europeans refused to adopt Amerindian crops such as amaranth, in sixteenth-century Brazil manioc rapidly became the principal food staple of coastal settlers and their slaves. As the most fertile lands in Pernambuco and the Recôncavo of Bahia were converted to sugar plantations, less prosperous farmers grew manioc on more marginal lands for sale to planters and to people in nearby towns.

When the Dutch invaded Brazil in the seventeenth century, they mastered the Brazilian system of large-scale sugar cultivation, as well as the Brazilian system of food production for plantation slaves, meaning essentially manioc cultivation. After the Dutch were expelled from Brazil in 1654, they carried the Brazilian system to the Caribbean and, henceforth, West Indian planters, such as those on Martinique, "obliged" African slaves to cultivate food crops, including manioc, on their provision grounds (Tomich 1991). Thus, manioc became a part of the slave diet in the Caribbean as in Brazil.

Manioc also enabled fugitive slaves living in maroon communities or in *quilombos* in Brazil to survive on marginal lands in remote or difficult terrain. Although descriptions of manioc cultivation in *quilombos* have usually surfaced in Brazilian records only upon the destruction of *quilombos,* such as Palmares (*Relação das guerras feitas aos Palmares* ... [1675-1678] 1988), Richard Price (1991) has been able to document the cultivation of manioc over two hundred years by the Saramaka maroons of Suriname and their descendants. They raised it in the 1770s as well as in the 1970s (Price 1991).

Manioc, which was closely linked to plantation slavery in the Americas, was also the food staple that enabled the conquest of the tropics. In the pre-Columbian period, a bread made from manioc permitted long-distance trade and exploration in South America as well as lengthy war expeditions. During the European conquest, the Spanish and Portuguese forces in the tropics rapidly adopted manioc bread. Later, rations were doled out to troops fighting the frontier wars of tropical Latin America, and even in twentieth-century Brazil, military forces received "farinha de guerra" (war meal) to sustain them in their

garrisons (Cascudo 1984). The *Bandeirantes* from São Paulo, who explored Brazil's vast interior and discovered gold in the late seventeenth century, were able to do so because of manioc. The Guaraní Indians they pursued and often enslaved in Paraguay also raised manioc (as their ancestors had done for millennia) in the Jesuit missions that gave them refuge (Reff 1998).

In addition to slaves, maroons, soldiers, and explorers, free peasants also subsisted on manioc in Brazil, existing on the margins of plantation society and in the interior. In cultivating manioc for their own subsistence, they frequently produced a surplus, which they sold to planters and to townspeople. Often black and mulatto dependents *(agregados)* of the great sugar planters, these peasants escaped slavery by raising manioc and marketing it (Karasch 1986). Manioc thus supported the emergence of a free peasantry in the shadow of the Latin American plantation societies.

By the end of the colonial period, manioc had emerged as the principal food staple of the enslaved and impoverished in tropical Latin America and, as such, its cultivation, transportation, and commerce contributed greatly to the internal economy of Latin America. Unfortunately for the Latin Americans, however, manioc did not find a niche in global trade because the Portuguese had long before introduced the plant to the rest of the tropical world.

Africa

From Brazil, the Portuguese carried manioc to their stations along the Upper Guinea coast in West Africa and to the Kingdom of Kongo in northern Angola. Although manioc was not readily adopted in sixteenth-century West Africa, it was successfully introduced into the Kingdom of Kongo in what is now the modern country of Angola. Jones (1959) attributes the success of manioc in central Africa to the close ties between the Portuguese and the BaKongo beginning in the 1480s. An oral tradition with reference to the first Portuguese on the Congo-Angola coastline in the 1480s describes the arrival of "white men" who "brought maize and cassava and groundnuts and tobacco" (Hall 1991: 169).

The first documented reference to manioc comes a century later in 1593 in a letter from Sir Richard Hawkins regarding the seizure of a Portuguese ship engaged in the slave trade. Its cargo was, he reported, "meale of cassavi, which the Portingals call *Farina de Paw* [sic]. It serveth for marchandize in Angola, for the Portingals foode in the ship, and to nourish the negroes which they should carry to the River of Plate" (Jones 1959: 62). Thus, by the late sixteenth century, manioc meal was already an item of trade in Angola, as well as a food for the slaves in transit to the Americas. It would serve as a staple of the slave trade until that trade's effective abolition in the mid–nineteenth century.

By the 1660s, manioc was an important food in northern Angola, according to a pair of Europeans who visited Luanda. Oral traditions from nearby areas stress the borrowing of manioc techniques from the Kingdom of Kongo; its use as a vegetable (the sweet variety?) before the people learned more complex processing techniques; and the crop's resistance to locusts. As Jones notes, the Africans who most enthusiastically adopted manioc were those living in the tropical rain forests of the Congo Basin, rather than the people of the grasslands, where maize, millet, or sorghum were cultivated.

In the Americas, the culture of manioc had been perfected by forest peoples, and in Africa, too, it was the forest peoples who welcomed this addition to their food supply. Clearly, it was an important addition, and more than 300 years later, the people of Zaire and Congo continued to consume manioc at an average of about 1 kilogram per person per day, which would have supplied over 1,000 calories. They also utilized cassava leaves as a source of vegetable protein in sauces and soups (Cock 1985: 10).

In West Africa, however, the cultivation of manioc spread more slowly. First introduced from Brazil to Portuguese Guiné and the island of São Tomé, the root had become an important food crop on São Tomé and the islands of Principe and Fernando Pó by 1700, but it found little acceptance on the mainland until the nineteenth century. At the end of the seventeenth century, William Bosman, a Dutch factor at El Mina (now Ghana), identified the foodstuffs of Liberia, Ghana, Dahomey, and Benin as yams and maize. He also listed millet, rice, sweet potatoes, beans, and groundnuts. Apparently, the Africans had accepted the American crops of corn, beans, and groundnuts but not manioc. As Jones (1959) notes, this may have been because farmers could treat corn as another cereal crop, and sweet potatoes were similar to yams. But another reason is that the complex processing methods required by manioc could only have been mastered through close ties to people familiar with them, and the Portuguese did not have the same kind of colonial relationship with the West African states that they did with Angola.

Extensive manioc cultivation did develop in the early nineteenth century, however, as former slaves returned from Brazil to West Africa. In 1910, for example, a Dahoman chief reported the oral tradition that a returned Brazilian (Francisco Felix da Souza) "had taught the Dahomans how to prepare manioc so they could eat it without becoming ill." Returned ex-slaves from Brazil in the 1840s also spread manioc cultivation in western Nigeria (Ohadike 1981: 389). Thus, Africans who had learned to process manioc into *farinha* while enslaved in Brazil played a key role in instructing those in West Africa how to utilize it. There it became known as *gari* or *garri* (Jones 1959).

The further diffusion of manioc in West Africa in the nineteenth and twentieth centuries was linked to European colonialism. As European labor demands disrupted traditional systems of food production, the colonialists sought new food crops to ward off hunger and famine. Migratory workers also dispersed knowledge of manioc cultivation inland from the coast. D. C. Ohadike (1981) argues that the influenza pandemic of 1918 that disrupted traditional agriculture based on yams contributed to the adoption of manioc in the lower Niger because of widespread hunger. Although the Portuguese had introduced manioc to the Niger Delta centuries earlier (Hall 1991), Africans did not choose to use it until the twentieth century because they preferred to cultivate yams (Ohadike 1981). Manioc is now well established as a staple crop in the wetter regions of West Africa (Cock 1985).

Exactly when Europeans imported manioc into East Africa is less certain. It seems improbable that the Portuguese delayed introducing manioc to their colony of Mozambique until 1750, as the historian Justus Strandes claims (Jones 1959). But if Strandes is correct, then the French may have been first to do it when, around 1736, the French governor, Mahé de la Bourdonnais, had manioc brought from Brazil to the island of Mauritius in the Indian Ocean (Pynaert 1951). Two years later, the French Compagnie des Indes introduced manioc to Réunion, an island near the large island of Madagascar across from Mozambique.

The French also sent manioc plants from Brazil to the French islands near Madagascar, where an initial attempt to plant manioc proved a disaster. Africans there were clearly unfamiliar with bitter manioc. When they tried to eat the fruits of their first harvest, they died of poisoning (Hubert and Dupré 1910). After this tragedy, both the French and Africans learned how to process bitter manioc, and they spread the plant and its processing technology to other small islands near Madagascar. At some point, manioc was also transferred from Réunion to Madagascar, where it became a major staple (Fauchère 1914).

During this period while the French were active in the Indian Ocean, the Portuguese, sometime before 1740, may have introduced manioc along with pineapple and corn to the coast of Tanzania and Kenya. Once established on the East African coast, principally the island of Zanzibar and the town of Mozambique, manioc cultivation progressed inland to the great lakes of Tanganyika and Victoria. In the nineteenth century, manioc plants from the east coast met manioc introduced from the Congo Basin. By that time, manioc cultivation had crossed central Africa from west to east, with Africans rather than European colonialists playing the key role in its diffusion (Jones 1959).

The delay in the introduction of manioc to East Africa until the eighteenth century has been attributed by Jones (1959) to the lack of an intensive colonial presence or to a lack of incentive for its introduction because, before 1800, most East African slaves were exported to Arabia, Persia, or India. Moreover, East Africa lacked dense forests, and much of the terrain was covered with wooded savannah so that environmental conditions were not as propitious as in the Congo basin. Even as late as 1850, Jones (1959: 84) concludes, "manioc was either absent or unimportant in most of East Africa . . . except right along the coast and in the vicinity of Lake Tanganyika." Its cultivation spread thereafter, however, because British and German colonial officers required its planting as a famine reserve – a role it has continued to play to the present day.

Manioc is now cultivated throughout Africa, excluding the desert north and the far south, and its range is still extending, as it is often the only crop that farmers can cultivate under conditions of low soil fertility, drought, and locust plagues. In part, the twentieth-century diffusion of manioc in Africa may be closely connected with recent population growth – but as a consequence, rather than a cause. As more and more people have put pressure on the types of fertile lands suitable for yams, millet, and sorghum, the land-poor have had to turn to manioc to ward off hunger. Thus, if population growth continues, manioc may become even more central than it now is to African economies and diets.

Asia

In addition to diffusing manioc to Africa, Europeans also transported the American crop to Asia, although Polynesians may have also introduced it into the Pacific via Easter Island. The first Asian region to receive manioc from the Europeans was the Philippines (Philippines, 1939). Variously termed *balinghoy, Kamoteng-Kahoy,* or *Kamoteng-moro,* manioc was brought to the Philippines by early Spanish settlers. Apparently, manioc plants traveled via Spanish ships across the Pacific from Mexico. As in West Africa, however, its cultivation grew slowly, and it was noted in the late 1930s that manioc in the Philippines "has not been as extensive as in other tropical countries" (Philippines 1939: 3). It had, however, evolved as a major crop in the Mindanao area of the Philippines by the 1980s (Centro Internacional de Agricultura Tropical [CIAT] 1986).

By the seventeenth century, manioc was found in the Moluccas, and by 1653 was being grown on Ambon, one of the outer islands of Indonesia (Pynaert 1951; CIAT 1986). It is likely that the Portuguese brought it to Goa (India) in the early eighteenth century. Additional plants were imported to India from South America in 1794, and from the West Indies in 1840 (Cock 1985). As of 1740, manioc was being raised on Java, and plants taken from there were introduced to Mauritius (CIAT 1986) shortly after the French brought the first manioc plants from Brazil. Thus, Brazilian plants met varieties evolved in Asia on a small island in the Indian ocean.

Mauritius then served as a distribution point for manioc into Sri Lanka (formerly Ceylon), the island at the tip of India, where the Dutch governor, Willem Jacob van de Graaff, introduced it in 1786. Subsequent importations were recorded in 1821 and 1917, and these, too, were from Mauritius. Since then, manioc has been cultivated by peasants, and it is "consumed mainly by the poorest people" (CIAT 1986: 115).

By 1800, manioc cultivation in tropical Asia stretched from Ceylon to the Philippines. It had not, however, replaced Asia's main staple, rice, although it was becoming "the most important" of the American crops "in terms of volume produced" (CIAT 1986: 171). An upland crop in tropical Asia, manioc has served to supplement inadequate supplies of rice, and it was most widely accepted in the land-scarce regions of Java in Indonesia and Kerala in southern India. As in Africa in the nineteenth century, those who convinced or required the inhabitants to accept this famine reserve were the European colonialists, in this case the Dutch in Java and the British in India (CIAT 1986).

European colonialists were especially active in diffusing manioc cultivation and processing techniques in the nineteenth century. They first established a processing and export industry in Malaya in the 1850s and subsequently developed a trade in tapioca with Europe (Cock 1985). In 1886, the Singapore Botanic Gardens introduced new manioc plants to Malaysia (Cock 1985). The Dutch followed by transporting manioc plants from their South American colony of Suriname to Java in 1854. By the early twentieth century, manioc was flourishing (Pynaert 1951), and its cultivation has continued to expand since then.

By the 1980s, at least one-fourth of all manioc grown in Asia was located in Indonesia, with the greatest share on Java (CIAT 1986). Sometime around 1850, manioc was introduced into Thailand, where it has become very popular in the eastern seaboard provinces. Since 1956 it has spread to the northeastern, western, and upper-central provinces of Thailand (CIAT 1986).

The British played a major role in the diffusion of manioc cultivation in southern India, where it was most widely accepted, especially in Kerala. Apparently it was introduced quite late to Calcutta (1794) and Serampur in 1840 (Pynaert 1951). Since then, manioc has evolved in India as a supplementary food staple. It is often consumed as a traditional steam-cooked breakfast dish called *puttu,* or marketed for *sago* (tapioca pearl), starch, and cattle feed (CIAT 1986). It is also a staple food in parts of Myanmar (formerly Burma) (Cock 1985).

Five hundred years after the Europeans discovered manioc, the yield of this American crop abroad has surpassed yields in its homeland. In 1982, the world's manioc production was estimated at 129 million tons, with Asia and Africa accounting for about three-fourths of this production and Latin America contributing only one-fourth.

In tropical Asia, manioc production was nearly 46 million tons in 1982, half of which came from Thailand. The two other major Asian producers were Indonesia and India (CIAT 1986). All this followed upon two decades of rapid growth in manioc production with a doubling of output during the period. The most rapid increases occurred in Thailand, in part due to exports to the European Economic Community. Although manioc is also grown in southern China, mainly on the dryland slopes of Guangdong province and the Guangxi Zhuang autonomous region, accurate statistics for the People's Republic of China are hard to come by. The primary use of manioc in China, however, appears to be as animal feed, especially for hogs (CIAT 1986). It is also grown in Taiwan (Cock 1985).

The Pacific Islands

The final region of manioc production, at present, is the Pacific Islands. In general, scholars have maintained that manioc was not introduced to the Pacific Islands until the mid-nineteenth century. Robert Langdon, however, suggests a different history of diffusion to Oceania. He has recently reported the discovery of a Spanish manuscript recording the presence of *yuca* (a word used in Peru for manioc) on Easter Island in 1770. Captained by Felipe Gonzalez, the expedition sailed from Peru, to reach Easter Island in late 1770. Those who went ashore observed fields of *yuca* under cultivation as well as sweet potatoes, another American crop.

Obviously, the question that this raises is how manioc had reached an island 2,000 miles from South America, unless it had been carried there by Amerindians before Columbus, as Thor Heyerdahl has long argued. Certainly Langdon (1988: 324) observes that the presence of manioc on Easter Island in 1770 "greatly strengthens the case for prehistoric American Indian influence on Easter Island and other islands of eastern Polynesia." In any case, it seems that manioc has now been documented in the Pacific 80 years before Captain Louis A. Bonard took the plant to Tahiti in 1850, from which it spread rapidly to other Pacific islands, where it is now cultivated (CIAT 1986; Langdon 1988).

Conclusion

From a present-day perspective, the contribution of the American crop, manioc, to the world's food supply has largely been unheralded except by Brazilians, by a few historians such as William Jones in his classic *Manioc in Africa,* and by French officials such as Paul Hubert and Emile Dupré in *Le Manioc,* which provides a global view of manioc cultivation as of 1910. Historians have recognized the historical significance of other American crops that played a major role in European history, but it may well be that manioc's historical impact and diffusion have been slighted because it is a tropical, Third World crop.

Nevertheless, manioc has been as significant to the historical evolution of tropical countries, such as Brazil and Zaire, as the potato has been to that of European countries, such as Ireland and Germany. As world population growth continues into the twenty-first century, manioc may assume an even greater role, enabling the rural poor in developing countries to survive hunger and famine. This versatile food crop, which can overcome drought, survive typhoons and locust plagues, and reproduce on marginal soils, may well make a significant difference in population survival in the tropics in the twenty-first century.

Mary Karasch

Bibliography

Aguiar, Pinto de. 1982. *Mandioca - Pão do Brasil.* Rio de Janeiro.

Albuquerque, Milton de. 1969. *A mandioca na Amazônia.* Belém, Brazil.

Brandão Sobrinho, Julio. 1916. *Mandioca.* São Paulo.

Cascudo, Luis da Camara. 1984. *Dicionário do folclore Brasileiro.* Fifth edition. Belo Horizonte.

Centro Internacional de Agricultura Tropical (CIAT) and ESCAP Regional Co-ordination Centre for Research and Development of Coarse Grains, Pulses, Roots and Tuber Crops in the Humid Tropics of Asia and the Pacific. 1986. *Cassava in Asia, its potential and research development needs.* Proceedings of a regional workshop held in Bangkok, Thailand, 5-8 June 1984. Cali, Colombia.

Cock, James H. 1985. *Cassava: New potential for a neglected crop.* Boulder, Colo., and London.

Coe, Sophie D. 1994. *America's first cuisines.* Austin, Tex.

Conceição, Antonio José da. 1979. *A mandioca.* Cruz das Almas, Bahia, Brazil.

Doku, E. V. 1969. *Cassava in Ghana.* Accra, Ghana.

Fauchère, A. 1914. *La culture du manioc à Madagascar.* Paris.

Hall, Robert L. 1991. Savoring Africa in the New World. In *Seeds of change,* ed. Herman J. Viola and Carolyn Margolis, 161-71. Washington, D.C., and London.

Hubert, Paul, and Émile Dupré. 1910. *Le manioc.* Paris.

Humboldt, Alexander von. [1811] 1988. *Political essay on the kingdom of New Spain,* trans. John Black, ed. Mary Maples Dunn. Norman, Okla., and London.

Jennings, D. L. 1976. Cassava. In *Evolution of Crop Plants,* ed. N. W. Simmonds, 81-4. London and New York.

Johns, Timothy. 1990. *With bitter herbs they shall eat it: Chemical ecology and the origins of human diet and medicine.* Tucson, Ariz.

Jones, William O. 1959. *Manioc in Africa.* Stanford, Calif.

Karasch, Mary. 1986. Suppliers, sellers, servants, and slaves. In *Cities and society in colonial Latin America,* ed. Louisa Schell Hoberman and Susan Migden Socolow, 251-83. Albuquerque, N.Mex.

Langdon, Robert. 1988. Manioc, a long concealed key to the

enigma of Easter Island. *The Geographical Journal* 154: 324–36.

Lathrap, Donald W. 1970. *The upper Amazon.* New York and Washington, D.C.

Léry, Jean de. [1578] 1990. *History of a voyage to the land of Brazil, otherwise called America,* trans. Janet Whatley. Berkeley and Los Angeles.

Levin, Suzanne. 1983. Food production and population size in the Lesser Antilles. *Human Ecology* 11: 321–38.

Morley, Sylvanus G., and George W. Brainerd. 1983. *The ancient Maya.* Fourth edition, rev. Robert J. Sharer. Stanford, Calif.

New York World's Fair. 1939. *Manioc.* Brazil: Official Publication. New York.

Ohadike, D. C. 1981. The influenza pandemic of 1918–19 and the spread of cassava cultivation on the lower Niger: A study in historical linkages. *Journal of African History* 22: 379–91.

Onwueme, I. C. 1978. *The tropical tuber crops: Yams, cassava, sweet potato, and cocoyams.* Chichester and New York.

Peckolt, Theodoro. 1878. *Monographia do milho e da mandioca: Sua historia, variedades, cultura, uso, composição chimica, etc. . . . ,* Vol. 3 of *Historia das plantas alimentares e de gozo do Brasil. . . .* Rio de Janeiro.

Philippines, Commonwealth of the. 1939. Department of Agriculture and Commerce. *The cassava industry in the Philippines.* Manila.

Price, Richard. 1991. Subsistence on the plantation periphery: Crops, cooking, and labour among eighteenth-century Suriname maroons. In *The slaves' economy: Independent production by slaves in the Americas,* ed. Ira Berlin and Philip D. Morgan. Special Issue of *Slavery and Abolition: A Journal of Comparative Studies* 12: 107–27.

Pynaert, L. 1951. *Le manioc.* Second edition. Brussels.

Reff, Daniel T. 1998. The Jesuit mission frontier in comparative perspective: The reductions of the Rio de La Plata region and the missions of northwestern Mexico 1588–1700. In *Contested grounds.* ed. Donna J. Guy and Thomas E. Sheridan. 16–31. Tucson, Ariz.

Relação das guerras feitas aos Palmares de Pernambuco no tempo do Governador D. Pedro de Almeida de 1675 a 1678 [and attached documents]. 1988. In *Alguns documentos para a história da Escravidão,* ed. Leonardo Dantas Silva, 27–69. Recife, Brazil.

Rocha Pita, Sebastião da. 1976. *História da América Portuguesa.* São Paulo.

Roosevelt, Anna Curtenius. 1980. *Parmana: Prehistoric maize and manioc subsistence along the Amazon and Orinoco.* New York.

Staden, Hans. [1557] 1974. *Duas viagens ao Brasil,* trans. Guiomar de Carvalho Franco. Belo Horizonte.

Tejada, Carlos. 1979. Nutrition and feeding practices of the Maya in Central America. In *Aspects of the history of medicine in Latin America,* ed. John Z. Bowers and Elizabeth F. Purcell, 54–87. New York.

Tomich, Dale. 1991. Une petite Guinée: Provision ground and plantation in Martinique, 1830–1848. In *The slaves' economy: Independent production by slaves in the Americas,* ed. Ira Berlin and Philip D. Morgan. Special Issue of *Slavery and Abolition: A Journal of Comparative Studies* 12: 68–91.

Toussaint-Samat, Maguelonne. 1992. *History of food,* trans. Anthea Bell. Cambridge, Mass.

Wyman, Donald. 1991. Cassava. *The encyclopedia Americana: International edition,* Vol. 5. Danbury, Conn.

II.B.3 ❧ Potatoes (White)

This chapter presents the paradoxical history of the potato *(Solanum tuberosum)* in human food systems. It is now the fourth most important world food crop, surpassed only by wheat, rice, and maize. In five centuries, this diverse and adaptable tuber has spread from its original South American heartland in the high Andes to all elevation zones in temperate regions of all the continents, and, lately, its production has been increasing most rapidly in the warm, humid, tropical Asian lowlands during the dry season (Vander Zaag 1984).

In the course of its history, the potato adapted, and was adopted, as a highland subsistence crop on all continents. In Europe, it was originally an antifamine food but then became a staple. In Africa and Asia, it has been a vegetable or costaple crop. The potato has been credited with fueling the Industrial Revolution in eighteenth-century Europe but blamed for the mid-nineteenth-century Irish famine. Over three centuries, it also became a central and distinctive element of European regional, and then national, cuisines. Although "late blight" has continued to plague those dependent on potatoes for sustenance (CIP 1994), the potato's popularity has nevertheless grown since the end of World War II, particularly in its forms of standardized industrially produced potato fries, chips, and other frozen and processed "convenience" foods. Acceptance of standard fries (with burgers) and packaged chips symbolizes the "globalization of diet," as McDonald's, Pepsico, and other transnational food firms move potatoes around the world yet another time in their successful creation and marketing of a universal taste for these products.

White potato

In addition, the 1972 creation of an International Potato Center (CIP) in Lima, Peru, with its regional networks, has greatly accelerated the introduction of improved potato varieties and supporting technologies throughout the developing world.

R. N. Salaman's monumental volume charted *The History and Social Influence of the Potato* (1949) – a book that was edited and reprinted in 1985 by J. G. Hawkes, who updated archaeological and agronomic histories and then subsequently issued his own study (Hawkes 1990). The archaeological evidence for the origins of potato domestication is still fragmentary (for example, Hawkes 1990). However, collections, characterizations, and taxonomies of both wild and cultivated forms (Ochoa 1962; Huaman 1983; Hawkes and Hjerting 1989) continue to progress and are generating conclusions about evolutionary relationships that can now be tested with additional cytoplasmic and molecular data from crossability trials (Grun 1990). Such conclusions can also be tested by complementary ethnohistorical, social historical, and culinary historical data (Coe 1994).

Recent biological and cultural histories are recounted in several volumes by CIP (CIP 1984; Horton and Fano 1985; Horton 1987; Woolfe 1987), which also issues an *Annual Report* and a *Potato Atlas.* Key breeding and agronomic advances are also reported in *The Potato Journal, American Potato Journal, European Potato Journal, Potato Research, Proceedings of the Potato Association of America,* and reports by the potato marketing boards of major producing countries. All are contributing to worldwide understanding and utilization of potatoes, which exhibit perhaps the greatest amount of biodiversity of any major food crop (Hawkes and Hjerting 1989: 3), with matching cultural diversity in food and nonfood uses.

The Potato in South America: Origins and Diffusion

Cultivated potatoes all belong to one botanical species, *Solanum tuberosum,* but it includes thousands of varieties that vary by size, shape, color, and other sensory characteristics. The potato originated in the South American Andes, but its heartland of wild genetic diversity reaches from Venezuela, Colombia, Ecuador, Peru, Bolivia, Argentina, and Chile across the Pampa and Chaco regions of Argentina, Uruguay, Paraguay, and southern Brazil and northward into Central America, Mexico, and the southwestern United States. There are more than 200 wild potato species in this wide habitat that extends from high cold mountains and plateaus into warmer valleys and subtropical forests and drier semiarid intermontane basins and coastal valleys.

The greatest diversity in wild potato species occurs in the Lake Titicaca region of Peru and Bolivia, where the potato probably was domesticated between 10,000 and 7,000 years ago. *Solanum*

tuberosum most likely was domesticated from the wild diploid species *S. stenotomum,* which then hybridized with *S. sparsipilum* or other wild species to form the amphidiploid *S. tuberosum* that evolved from the short-day northern Andean subspecies *andigena,* via additional crosses with wild species, into the subspecies *tuberosum,* which had a more southerly, longer-day distribution (Grun 1990; Hawkes 1990). Frost resistance and additional pest and disease resistance were introduced later via hybridizations with additional wild species, which allowed potatoes to be grown at altitudes up to 4,500 meters.

Archaeological Evidence

Fossilized remains of possibly cultivated tubers found on a cave floor in Chilca Canyon suggest that the potato was cultivated at least from about 7,000 years ago, although it is not possible to tell whether these were wild, "dump heap," or already garden acquisitions (Ugent 1970). Potato remains (along with those of sweet potato and manioc) from Ancon-Chillon (to the north of Lima) date from 4,500 years ago; northern coastal remains from the site of Casma date from between 4,000 and 3,500 years ago (Ugent et al. 1982). It is surmised that cultivated varieties were being planted on terraces at intermediate altitudes, extending from the river valleys into the high mountains, by the middle initial period between 4,000 and 3,500 years ago. Coastal remains from the monumental preceramic site of El Paraiso (3,800 to 3,500 years ago) suggest a mixed subsistence strategy, including unspecified *Solanum* plants that might be potatoes (Quilter et al. 1991).

Art provides additional testimony for the potato's centrality and for the antiquity of processed potatoes in pre-Columbian Andean culture. Fresh and freeze-dried potatoes are depicted in ceramics of the Moche people of northern Peru (A.D. 1 to 600), on urns in Huari or Pacheco styles from the Nazca Valley (650 to 700), and later Chimu-Inca pots (Hawkes 1990). Post-contact-period Inca wooden beakers also depict potato plants and tubers.

South American civilizations and states were based on vertically integrated production and consumption systems that included seed crops (especially maize, secondarily quinoa) at lower altitudes, potatoes and other tubers at higher altitudes, and llamas (camelids) to transport goods between zones. Hillside terracing conserved moisture and soils and encouraged the selection of multiple cultivars of a number of species that fit into closely spaced ecological niches. Ridged, raised, or mounded fields (still used for potato cultivation around Lake Titicaca) were a type of specialized field system that saved moisture and also protected against frost. In addition to making use of short-term storage in the ground, Andean peoples stored potatoes in fresh or processed forms. Huanaco Viejo and other Inca sites reveal extensive tuber storage areas, constructed in naturally cool zones, where indigenous farmers (or their rulers) stored whole tubers with carefully managed temperature, moisture, and diffused light to reduce spoilage (Morris 1981). Traditional freeze-drying techniques took advantage of night frosts, sunny days, and running water at high elevation zones and allowed potatoes to provide nourishment over long distances and multiple years, as dehydrated potatoes moved from higher to lower altitudes, where they were traded for grain and cloth.

Biocultural Evolution

As South American cultivators expanded into many closely spaced microenvironmental niches, they selected for thousands of culturally recognized potato varieties of differing sizes, colors, shapes, and textures, with characteristics that provided adequate resistance to pests, frost, and other stressors. At higher altitudes, cultivators selected for bitter varieties of high alkaloid content that were detoxified and rendered edible by freeze-drying (Johns 1990). Culturally directed genetic diversification continues up to the present, as Andean farmers allow wild specimens to grow and hybridize with cultivars, conserving biodiversity while diffusing risk (Ugent 1970; Brush 1992).

The botanical history of the cultivated potato is slowly being assembled by considering together the findings from plant scientists' genetic and taxonomic studies, archaeologists' interpretations of archaeological and paleobotanical remains, and ethnographers' observations and analogies from contemporary farming, food processing, and storage. Plant scientists continue to explore wild and cultivated habitats in the potato's heartland, where they find wild potato species that offer a tantalizing range of useful characteristics to protect against frost; against fungal, viral, and bacterial infections; and against nematodes and insects (for example, Ochoa 1962; Ochoa and Schmiediche 1983). Carnivorous, sticky-haired species, such as *Solanum berthaultii,* devour their prey; others repel them pheromonically by mimicking the scent of insects under stress (Hawkes and Hjerting 1989).

Added into the botanical and archaeological data mix are culinary historians' insights from agricultural, botanical, lexical, and food texts. Guaman Poma de Ayala, shortly after Spanish penetration, depicted and described plow-hoe potato and maize cultivation in his chronicle of the Incas (1583–1613) (Guaman Poma de Ayala 1936). Dictionaries that record concepts of the sixteenth-century Aymara peoples from Peru describe time intervals in terms of the time it took to cook a potato (Coe 1994)!

Indigenous peoples also developed detailed vocabularies to describe and classify potatoes, as well as myths and rituals to celebrate the tubers' importance. Even after conversion to Catholicism, they continued to use potatoes in their religious festivals; for example, garlands of potatoes are used to decorate the image of the Virgin Mary at the festival of the Immacu-

late Conception in Juli, Peru (Heather Lechtman, personal communication).

Indigenous Potato Products

Indigenous use of potatoes has included the development of processing methods to extend their nutritional availability and portability. In high altitude zones, selected varieties undergo freezing, soaking, and drying into a product called *chuño* that is without unhealthful bitter glycoalkaloids, is light and easily transported, and can be stored for several years. To render *chuño* (freeze-dried potato), tubers are frozen at night, then warmed in the sun (but shielded from direct rays). Next, they are trampled to slough off skins and to squeeze out any residual water, and then they are soaked in cold running water.

After soaking for 1 to 3 weeks, the product is removed to fields and sun-dried for 5 to 10 days, depending on the cloud cover and type of potato. As these tubers dry, they form a white crust, for which the product is labelled "white *chuño*" (in contrast to "black *chuño*," which eliminates the soaking step). Another processing method involves soaking the tubers without prior freezing for up to a month, then boiling them in this advanced stage of decay. R. Werge (1979) has commented that the odor of this ripening process is "distinctive and strong" and has noted that, as a rule, this product is consumed where it is produced.

Chuño has a long history of provisioning both highland and lowland Andean populations; it was described by early Spanish chroniclers (for example, José de Acosta 1590) and also mentioned in accounts of sixteenth-century mine rations, in which Spanish mine managers complained about its high price. It is curious that one seventeenth-century source mentioned *chuño* as a source of fine white flour for cakes and other delicacies, although it was usually considered to be a lower-class native food (Cobo 1653). Ordinarily, *chuño* is rehydrated in soups and stews.

Another native product is *papa seca* ("dehydrated potato"), for which tubers are boiled, peeled, cut into chunks, sun-dried, and then ground into a starchy staple that is eaten with pork, tomatoes, and onions. *Papa seca* is consumed more widely than *chuño* in urban and coastal areas and can now be purchased in supermarkets.

In areas of frost, potatoes traditionally were also rendered into starch. Traditional products, however, are in decline, as household labor to produce them is now redirected toward higher-value cash employment or schooling. In addition, such traditional products tend to be thought of as inferior, "poor peasant" foods, so that those with cash income and access to store-bought pasta or rice consume these starches instead.

Biodiversity

Declining potato diversity, a byproduct of the insertion of higher-yielding "improved" varieties into South American field systems, is another reason for the fading of traditional potatoes and potato products. Traditional Andean potato farmers sow together in a single hole as many as 5 small tubers from different varieties and even species, and keep up to 2 dozen named varieties from 3 or 4 species (Quiros et al. 1990; Brush 1992). A particular concern has been whether genetic diversity erodes with the introduction of modern varieties and greater integration of local farmers into regional and national markets. Traditional varieties adapted to lower altitudes (where 75 percent of modern varieties are planted) are at greater risk than those of more mountainous terrains, which are less suited to the cultivation of irrigated, marketable, new varieties. So far, ethnographic investigations do not confirm the conventional wisdom that modern varieties generally compete successfully and eliminate traditional races. Although changes in cropping strategies allocate more land to new, improved varieties, thus reducing the amount of land allocated to traditional varieties, the midaltitude regions that grow modern varieties intensively tend also to devote small areas to older varieties that farmers maintain to meet ritual, symbolic, or preferential local food needs (Rhoades 1984; Brush 1992). In these commercial production zones, the land area allocated to traditional varieties appears to vary with income, with better-off households more likely to maintain larger plots.

Greater production of certain native varieties is actually encouraged by market opportunities. On-farm conservation of potato biodiversity has therefore been favored by the economics of particular native as well as introduced potato varieties, by vertical biogeography, and by persistent cultural customs calling for multiple traditional varieties (Brush, Taylor, and Bellon 1992), and there remains a large amount of as-yet unexploited population variability encoded in folk taxonomies (Quiros et al. 1990). Uniform sowings of improved varieties tend to replace older varieties only in the best-irrigated, midaltitude areas, where farmers harvest and sell an early crop and thus enjoy higher returns for the "new" potatoes. Traditional varietal mixes, however, continue to be grown in higher elevation zones where more extreme and risky environments encourage farmers to propagate a larger variety of them. But unless on-farm conservation programs are encouraged, it may only be a matter of time before erosion occurs.

Andean farmers' ethnotaxonomies ("folk classifications") continue to be studied by anthropologists and plant scientists to learn more about the ways in which traditional peoples recognize and organize plant information. These folk classifications, in most instances, recognize more distinctions than those captured by modern botanical taxonomies, and they also indicate the high value traditional peoples put on maintaining crop species biodiversity as a strategy to reduce risk of total crop failures. The more plant scientists improve their ability to understand the molecular biology, cytology, biochemistry, and genetics of the potato, the more they return to this traditional, natural, and cultural heartland to collect ancient wild and cultivated types and cultural knowledge about how to use potatoes.

In addition, traditional peoples developed ways to store and process potatoes, so that their availability could be extended greatly in time and over space. Agricultural and food scientists, in studying archaeological evidence of cold storage bins (Morris 1981) and contemporary practices (Rhoades 1984), have adopted and disseminated techniques, such as diffused lighting for storage areas and freeze-drying, as ways to increase the potato's food value in other parts of the world. This return to indigenous knowledge at a time of international diffusion of modern molecular technologies is one paradoxical dimension of the potato's history.

The Potato in Europe

Sixteenth-century Spanish explorers, who first observed the potato in Peru, Bolivia, Colombia, and Ecuador, compared the unfamiliar tuber food crop to truffles and adopted the Quechua name, *papa*. The first specimens, arguably short-day *S. tuberosum* ssp. *andigena* forms from Colombia, probably reached Spain around 1570. From there, the potato spread via herbalists and farmers to Italy, the Low Countries, and England, and there was likely a second introduction sometime in the following twenty years. Sir Francis Drake, on his round-the-world voyage (1577 to 1580), recorded an encounter with potatoes off the Chilean coast in 1578, for which British and Irish folklore credits him with having introduced the potato to Great Britain. But this could not have been the case because the tubers would not have survived the additional two years at sea. All European potato varieties in the first 250 years were derived from the original introductions, which constituted a very narrow gene pool that left almost all potatoes vulnerable to devastating viruses and fungal blights by the mid–nineteenth century. *S. tuberosum* ssp. *tuberosum* varieties, introduced from Chile into Europe and North America in the 1800s, represented an ill-fated attempt to widen disease resistance and may actually have introduced the fungus *Phytophthora infestans,* or heightened vulnerability to it. This was the microbe underlying the notorious nineteenth-century Irish crop failures and famine.

Herbal Sources

The potato's initial spread across Europe seems to have involved a combination of Renaissance scientific curiosity and lingering medieval medical superstition. Charles de l'Ecluse or Clusius of Antwerp, who received two tubers and a fruit in 1588 from Philippe de Sivry of Belgium, is credited with introducing the plant to fellow gardeners in Germany,

Austria, France, and the Low Countries (Arber 1938). The Swiss botanist Caspar Bauhin first described the potato in his *Phytopinax* (1596) and named it *Solanum tuberosum* esculentum. He correctly assigned the potato to the nightshade family (Solanum) but otherwise provided a highly stylized, rather than scientific, drawing (1598) and gossiped that potatoes caused wind and leprosy (probably because they looked like leprous organs) and "incited Venus" (that is, aroused sexual desire), a characterization that led to folkloric names such as "Eve's apple" or "earth's testicles." Such unhealthful or undesirable characteristics probably contributed to potatoes being avoided in Burgundy (reported in John Gerard's *The Herball,* 1597) and in other parts of Europe. As a result of such persistent negative folklore, the introduction of the potato, a crop recognized by European leaders to have productive and nutritive capacities superior to those of cereal grains (particularly in cold and dry regions), was stymied for years in Germany and Russia.

Gerard – whose printed illustration in his *Herball* of 1597 provided the first lifelike picture of the potato plant, depicting leaves, flowers, and tubers (the plate was revised with careful observation in the later edition of 1633) – appears to have been fascinated by the plant, even wearing a potato flower as his boutonniere in the book's frontispiece illustration. But he also obscured the true origins of *Solanum tuberosum* by claiming to have received the tubers from "Virginia, otherwise called Norembega," and therefore naming them "potatoes of Virginia." The inaccurate name served to distinguish this potato from the "common potato," *Batata hispanorum* ("Spanish potato") or *Ipomoea batatas* ("sweet potato"). Additionally, "Virginia" at the time served the English as a generic label for plants of New World (as opposed to European) origin. *The Oxford English Dictionary* contains an entry labeling maize as "Virginia wheat," although it makes no reference to Gerard's "potato from Virginia."

Alternatively, Gerard may have confused a tuber truly indigenous to Virginia, *Glycine apios* or *Apios tuberosa,* with the *Solanum* potato after sowing both tubers together and then attributing an English origin to the tuber of greater significance in order to please his sovereign, Queen Elizabeth (Salaman 1985; Coe 1994). In any case, the false designation and folklore persisted into the next century, by which time potatoes had entered the agricultural economy of Ireland. A legend of Ireland credits the potato's introduction to the wreck of the Spanish Armada (1588), which washed some tubers ashore (Davidson 1992). Whatever its origins, William Salmon, in his herbal of 1710, distinguished this "Irish" (or "English") potato from the sweet potato, and "Irish potato" became the name by which "white" (as opposed to "sweet") potatoes were known in British colonies.

Eighteenth- and Nineteenth-Century Diffusions

The original short-day, late-yielding varieties illustrated in Gerard's and other herbals had by the eighteenth century been replaced by farmers' selections for early-maturing varieties that were better suited to the summer day length and climate of the British Isles. The new varieties' superior yield of calories per unit of land made subsistence possible for small farmers who had lost land and gleaning rights with the rise of scientific agriculture and the practice of enclosure. Potatoes also provided a new, cheap food source for industrial workers; Salaman (1949), William McNeill (1974), and Henry Hobhouse (1986) were among the historians who saw the potato as having encouraged the rapid rise of population that brought with it the Industrial Revolution.

Potatoes also spread across Italy and Spain. The Hospital de la Sangre in Seville recorded purchases of potatoes among its provisions as early as 1573 (Hawkes and Francisco-Ortega 1992). By 1650, potatoes were a field crop in Flanders, and they had spread northward to Zeeland by 1697, to Utrecht by 1731, to Overijssel by 1746, and to Friesland by 1765. In some high-altitude areas, they were originally adopted as an antifamine food, but the harsh winter of 1740, which caused damage to other crops, hastened potato planting everywhere. By 1794, the tubers had been accepted as an element of the Dutch national dish, a hot pot of root vegetables (Davidson 1992). Toward the end of the eighteenth century, potatoes had become a field crop in Germany, which saw especially large quantities produced after famine years, such as those from 1770 to 1772 and again in 1816 and 1817. Their popularity was increased not only by natural disasters (especially prolonged periods of cold weather) but also by the disasters of wars, because the tubers could be kept in the ground, where stores were less subject to looting and burning by marauding armies.

Such advantages were not lost on such European leaders as Frederick the Great, who, in 1774, commanded that potatoes be grown as a hedge against famine. Very soon afterward, however, potatoes proved to be not so safe in time of war. The War of the Bavarian Succession (1778 to 1779), nicknamed the *Kartoffelkrieg* ("potato war"), found soldiers living off the land, digging potatoes from the fields as they ravaged the countryside. The war ceased once the tuber supply had been exhausted (Nef 1950).

This war in Germany unintentionally provided the catalyst for popularization of the potato in France. A French pharmacist, A. A. Parmentier, had been a German prisoner of war and forced to subsist on potatoes. He survived and returned to Paris, where he championed the tuber as an antifamine food. His promotional campaign saw Marie Antoinette with potato flowers in her hair and King Louis XVI wearing them as boutonnieres. But widespread potato consumption in France still had to wait another century because, at a time when bread and soup were the French dietary staples, potato starch added to wheat flour produced an unacceptably soggy bread that was too moist to sop up the soup (Wheaton 1983). Widespread utilization of the whole potato in soup or as fries did not occur until well into the following century; even at the time of Jean François Millet's famous "Potato Planters" painting (1861), many French people still considered potatoes unfit for humans or even animals to eat (Murphy 1984).

From the middle eighteenth through nineteenth centuries, potatoes finally spread across central and eastern Europe into Russia. At the end of the seventeenth century, Tsar Peter the Great had sent a sack of potatoes home, where their production and consumption were promoted first by the Free Economic Society and, a century later, by government land grants. But "Old Believers" continued to reject potatoes as "Devil's apples" or "forbidden fruit of Eden," so that as late as 1840, potatoes were still resisted. When, in that year, the government ordered peasants to grow potatoes on common land, they responded with "potato riots" that continued through 1843, when the coercive policy ceased. But, in the next half-century, the potato's obvious superiority to most grain crops and other tubers encouraged its wider growth, first as a garden vegetable and then, as it became a dietary staple, as a field crop (Toomre 1992).

The Social Influence of the Potato

European writers credited the potato with the virtual elimination of famine by the early nineteenth century, without necessarily giving the credit to state political and economic organization and distribution systems (Crossgrove et al. 1990; Coe 1994). Larger-scale potato production subsequently provided surpluses that supported a rise of population in both rural agricultural and urban industrial areas. Potatoes were adopted widely because they grew well in most climates, altitudes, and soils and were more highly productive than grains in both good years and bad. During the seventeenth and eighteenth centuries, selection for earliness and yield gave rise to clones that were better adapted to European temperate, longer-summer-day growing conditions and could be harvested earlier. By the end of the eighteenth century, many varieties were in existence, some specified for human consumption, others as food for animals (Jellis and Richardson 1987). Agricultural workers across Europe increasingly grew potatoes on small allotments to provide food that was cheaper than wheat bread and also inexpensive fodder in the form of substandard tubers. Grains and potatoes, together with the flesh and other products of a few farm animals, provided an economically feasible and nutritionally adequate diet.

No less an authority than Adam Smith, in *An Inquiry into the Nature and Causes of the Wealth of Nations* (1776), estimated that agricultural land allocated to potatoes yielded three times the food/nutrient value of land planted with wheat, so that more people could be maintained on a given quantity of land. Even after workers were fed and the stock replaced, more surplus was left for the landlord. Favorably contrasting the nourishment and healthfulness of potatoes with that of wheat, Smith noted:

> The chairmen, porters, and coalheavers in London, and those unfortunate women who live by prostitution, the strongest men and the most beautiful women perhaps in the British dominions, are said to be, the greatest part of them, from the lowest rank of people in Ireland, who are generally fed with the root.

The single outstanding disadvantage of the potato was that stocks could not be stored or carried over from year to year because the tubers rotted (Smith 1776, Volume 1, Book 1, Chapter 11, Part 1: 161–2).

By this time, potatoes were also providing cheap food for growing industrial populations. Low-cost provisions enabled industrialists to keep wages low (Salaman 1985). Indeed, in both rural and urban areas, more than three centuries of resistance to potatoes was overcome. The tuber had been variously regarded as poisonous, tasteless, hard to digest, and an aphrodisiac; some thought of it as pig food, others as famine food or food for the poor, but such prejudices gradually faded as potatoes became the most affordable food staple. Yet, at the same time, the growth of a potato-dependent population in Ireland elicited dire predictions of calamity (by Thomas Malthus, for one), for potatoes were already proving vulnerable to various diseases. Dependent populations were especially at risk because potatoes could neither be stored for more than a few months nor be easily transported into areas of famine, and because those within such populations tended to be politically powerless and economically exploited. For all these reasons, although Ireland suffered a devastating blight that ruined the potato crop from 1845 to 1848, it might accurately be said that the Irish famine was a man-made disaster that could have been prevented or mitigated by timely British emergency relief and greater noblesse oblige on the part of better-off Irish countrymen.

The Potato and Ireland

The history of the potato in Ireland has been summarized by C. Woodham-Smith (1962), A. Bourke (1993), and C. Kinealy (1995), among others. Such accounts trace the way in which the potato, along with the "conacre" system of land and labor allocation and the "lazy-bed" system of potato cultivation, came to dominate Irish agriculture as British landlords made less and less land and time available for their Irish workers' self-provisioning. The advent of more scientifically based agriculture and the enclosure of common lands had left many landless by the end of the eighteenth century. The "conacre" custom (or economy) allowed landless peasants to rent small plots for 11-month periods in return for agricultural services to the landlord. Peasants managed to feed themselves on such minuscule holdings by setting up raised "lazy" beds in which they placed tubers, then covered them with manure, seaweed, and additional soil to protect them from moisture.

Average yields of potatoes were 6 tons per acre, in contrast with less than 1 ton per acre for wheat or oats. In 1845, the potato crop occupied 2 million acres, and a 13.6 million ton harvest was anticipated, of which slightly less than half would have gone to humans. But grains were higher-value crops, and expansion of roads into the hinterlands during the early decades of the nineteenth century meant that grains could be more easily transported than they previously had been. Thus, values for (grain) export agriculture rose and competed more fiercely with subsistence crops for land. Conacres shrank, and many workers migrated seasonally to Scotland for the harvest, thereby reducing consumption at home and earning additional money for food. This was yet another route by which the potato and its associated social institutions "fed" the industrial economy (Vincent 1995).

"Late blight" *(Phytophthora infestans),* having ravaged potato crops in North America, disrupted this highly vulnerable agroeconomic and social context in the 1840s. The blight first appeared in late July 1845 in the Low Countries, spreading from there to England and finally to Ireland, where the poor farming population had no alternative foods to fall back on. It is ironic that late blight probably was introduced into Europe via new potato varieties that had been imported from the Western Hemisphere to counter epidemics of fungal "dry rot" and viral "curl" that had plagued previous decades. Although some scientists had observed that copper sulfate (as a dip for seed or an application for foliage) offered plants protection against what later came to be understood as fungal diseases, the science of plant pathology and pesticides was not yet far advanced, and no preventive or ameliorative steps were taken. "Bordeaux mixture," an antifungal application suitable for grape vines and potatoes, was not tried until the 1880s.

The blight of 1845 savaged 40 (not 100) percent of the crop, but infected tubers were allowed to rot in the fields, where they incubated the spores of the following years' disasters. In 1846, ideal weather conditions for late blight aided the rapid infection of early tubers, so that barely 10 percent of the crop was salvaged. But in the aftermath of the less-than-total disaster of 1845, the 1846 emergency was largely ignored by the British government, which failed to suspend the Corn Laws and continued both to export Irish grain and to forbid emergency grain imports. Taxes continued to be enforced, evictions soared, and relief measures, which included food-for-work and soup

kitchens, were too few and too late. Bourke (1993), among others, blamed the English as well as the Irish landlords, a well-off greedy few who benefited from the political and economic policies that impoverished the masses.

Sickness accompanied hunger through 1848, with the result that more than a million and a half Irish people either died or emigrated in search of sustenance. Neither the population nor its potato production ever recovered, although to this day, Ireland's per capita potato consumption (143 kilograms [kg] per year) surpasses that of rival high consumers in Europe (the Portuguese consume 107 kg per year and Spaniards 106 kg) (Lysaght 1994).

The potato also remains an enduring "polysemous symbol," celebrated in Irish literature and culinary arts. In the writings of James Joyce, the potato serves as talisman, as signifier of heroic continuity, but also as a symbol of deterioration and decadence (Merritt 1990). Joyce's references to typical Irish national dishes have been collected, with recipes, into a cookbook entitled *The Joyce of Cooking* (Armstrong 1986).

Later European Developments

European descendants of the original *S. tuberosum* ssp. *andigena* clones were virtually wiped out with the arrival of late blight in the mid–nineteenth century. They were replaced by ssp. *tuberosum* varieties that also – like their predecessors – hybridized readily across subspecies. A single clone, named "Chilean Rough Purple Chili," has accounted for a large proportion of subsequent European and North American potatoes, including the "Early Rose" and "Russet Burbank" varieties, the latter of which was introduced into the United States in 1876. In addition to Russet Burbank, several very old varieties still predominate in the United States and Europe, notably "Bintje," introduced into the Netherlands in 1910, and "King Edward," introduced into the United Kingdom in 1902 (Hermsen and Swiezynski 1987). Attempts to broaden the genetic base for breeding accelerated in the 1920s and 1930s, with N. I. Vavilov's Russian expedition that collected frost- and blight-resistant varieties from South America and, subsequently, with the British Empire (later Commonwealth) Potato Collecting Expedition (Hawkes 1990).

Blights and viruses notwithstanding, the potato played an ever-expanding role in European food economies. Epitomized in Vincent Van Gogh's "Potato Eaters" of 1885, but more nobly so in Millet's "Potato Planters" of 1861, potatoes on the European mainland came to symbolize the rugged, honest peasant, wresting life and livelihood from the soil. In England, eastern Europe, and Russia, potatoes played significant nutritional roles during ordinary times and assumed extraordinary nutritional roles in war years (Salaman 1985). Even today they remain the fallback crop in times of turmoil, as was seen in Russia in the severe months of 1992, following glasnost and the reorganization of the economy. An article the same year in the *New Scientist* reported that Russian citizens were planting potatoes everywhere, even illegally in the Losinskii Ostrove National Park, and attempting to steal potatoes from farms!

Europeans were directly responsible for the introduction of potatoes into North America, where they were well established by the eighteenth century. In addition, potatoes accompanied colonists to India, to French Indochina (CIP 1984), to China (Anderson 1988), and to New Zealand where, in the nineteenth century, the Maoris adopted them on the model of other tuber crops (Yen 1961/2). Potatoes also entered Africa with Belgian, British, French, and German colonists, who consumed them as a vegetable rather than as a staple starch. The largest recent expansion of potato cultivation has been in former European colonies, where people in the nineteenth century regarded the tuber as a high-value garden crop and prestigious European vegetable but since then (perhaps in conjunction with the end of colonialism) have come to view it as a staple or costaple garnish and snack (Woolfe 1987).

Potatoes in Developing Countries

In Asia and Africa, the potato has filled a number of production and consumption niches, and its history on these continents has been similar to that in Europe. Once again, despite its advantages as an antifamine, high-elevation alternative to grain, with particular virtues during conflicts, the potato was at first resisted by local farmers, who believed it to be poisonous. In the highest elevation zones, such as the Nepalese Himalayas (Fürer-Haimendorf 1964) and the upper reaches of Rwanda (Scott 1988), potatoes took root as a new staple food crop and contributed to subsistence, surplus, and population expansion. The plants were promoted by savvy rulers, who used demonstration, economic incentives, or coercion to overcome farmers' superstitions and resistance (CIP 1984). In Africa, as in Europe, the popularity of the tubers increased in wartime because they could be stored in the ground.

With the 1972 creation of the International Potato Center (CIP) and its mission to increase potato production and consumption in developing countries while protecting biodiversity, the introduction of improved potato varieties has accelerated around the world. CIP's activities, along with the operation of diverse market forces, have resulted in some African and Asian countries rapidly becoming areas of high potato consumption. Prior to its most recent civil conflict, Rwanda in some localities witnessed per capita consumption as high as 153 to 200 kg per year (Scott 1988) – higher than that in any Western European country, including Ireland. If Rwanda can reattain peace, and agronomic and credit constraints on pro-

duction and infrastructural limits on marketing could be removed, production could expand much farther and faster from the "grassroots," as it has in neighboring Tanzania. There, local farmers in recent years have developed the potato as a cash crop – the result of the introduction of several new varieties brought back by migrant laborers from Uganda, the diffusion of other varieties from Kenya, and the comparative advantage of raising potatoes relative to other cash or subsistence crops (Andersson 1996).

The potato offers excellent advantages as a subsistence crop because of its high yields, low input costs, and favorable response to intensive gardening techniques (for example, Nganga 1984). But potato promotions in Africa ominously echo the terms in which eighteenth- and nineteenth-century British observers praised the tuber. Scientists and political economists should be ever vigilant in ensuring that the potato is not again employed as a stopgap measure in contexts of great social inequality and food/nutritional insecurity, where vulnerability to late blight (or any other stressor) might lead to a repetition of the Great (nineteenth-century Irish) Hunger. Techniques of "clean" seed dissemination and mixed cropping strategies that "clean" the soil are designed to help prevent such calamities now and in the future. But all highlight the need to monitor pests and improve breeding materials so that resistant varieties of the potato are easily available to farmers who have become increasingly reliant on it for food and income.

The same cautions hold for Asia, where production and consumption of potatoes is expanding because of the market as well as international agricultural interests. Since the 1970s, the greatest rate of increase has been in the warm, humid, subtropical lowlands of Asia, where potatoes are planted as a dry-season intercrop with rice or wheat (Vander Zaag 1984), providing income and relief from seasonal hunger (Chakrabarti 1986). The surge in potato production has been spurred in some cases by new seeding materials and techniques. In Vietnam in the 1970s and 1980s, the Vietnamese and CIP introduced superior, blight-resistant clones that could be multiplied by tissue culture and micropropagation methods. Some enterprising farming families then took over the labor-intensive rapid multiplication, so that by 1985, three household "cottage industries" were supplying 600,000 cuttings for some 12,000 farmers (CIP 1984). Production in other Asian nations has also accelerated (for example, in Sri Lanka) as a result of government promotions and policies that have banned imports of all (including seed) potatoes since the 1960s (CIP 1984).

In Central America and the Caribbean, financial incentives and media promotion have been used to increase production and consumption of potatoes in places unaccustomed to them, such as the Dominican Republic, where the state offered credit and guaranteed purchase to potato farmers after the country experienced a rice deficit (CIP 1984). Similarly, during post-hurricane disaster conditions of 1987, Nicaraguans were encouraged to eat more potatoes – these shipped from friendly donors in the Soviet bloc. In South American countries, campaigns are underway to encourage farmers to grow more potatoes for sale as well as for home consumption, as in Bolivia, where economists hope that as part of diversified employment strategies, an increased production and sale of improved potato varieties can have a multiplier effect, reducing unemployment and increasing access to food (Franco and Godoy 1993). But all of these programs highlight the need to reconcile production and income concerns with the protection of biodiversity and reduction of risks.

Maintaining and Utilizing Biodiversity

Modern scientific attempts to broaden the genetic base for potato breeding began with European scientific expeditions in the 1920s and 1930s, including the already-mentioned Russian (Vavilov 1951) and British collections. Today, major gene banks and study collections are maintained at the Potato Introduction Center, Sturgeon Bay, Wisconsin; the Braunschweig-Volkenrode Genetic Resources Center (Joint German-Netherlands Potato Gene Bank); the N. I. Vavilov Institute of Plant Industry in Leningrad; and the International Potato Center (CIP) in Lima. Major potato-producing countries publish annual lists of registered varieties, standardized to report on agronomic characteristics (disease and pest resistances, seasonality, and environmental tolerances) and cooking and processing qualities (industrial-processing suitability for fries, chips, or dehydration; or home-processing aspects, such as requisite cooking times for boiling, baking, roasting, or frying). Additional consumer descriptors include color, texture, flavor, and the extent of any postcooking tendency to blacken or disintegrate.

Acceptably low alkaloid content is the main chemical toxicity concern, especially because glycoalkaloids are often involved in pest-resistance characteristics introduced during plant breeding. In one historical example, U.S. and Canadian agricultural officials were obliged to remove a promising new multiresistant variety (named "Lenape") from production because a scientist discovered its sickeningly high alkaloid content (Woolfe 1987).

Since the 1960s, new varieties have been protected by plant breeders' rights and, internationally, by the *Union Pour la Protection des Obtentions Végétales* (UPOV), which uses a standard set of 107 taxonomic characters to describe individual potato cultivars. UPOV is designed to facilitate exchanges among member countries and so accelerate the breeding process. Collection, conservation, documentation, evaluation, exchange, and use of germ plasm are also regulated by descriptor lists produced in

cooperation with the International Bank for Plant Genetic Resources (IBPGR).

The pace of new varietal introductions is accelerating as more wild species of potential utility for potato improvement are identified and genetically tapped for useful traits that are transferred with the assistance of biotechnology. Wild potatoes with resistance to one pathogen or pest tend to be susceptible to others and may have undesirable growth, tuber, or quality (especially high alkaloid) characteristics. Conventional breeding still requires 12 to 15 years to develop new varieties that include desirable – and exclude undesirable – genes. Protoplast fusion, selection from somaclonal variation, and genetic engineering via *Agrobacterium tumefaciens* are some "unconventional" techniques that promise to widen the scope and quicken the pace of varietal improvement, especially once the genes that control important traits have been characterized. The latter process is facilitated by advances in genetic linkage mapping (Tanksley, Ganal, and Prince 1992) and in practical communication among conventional breeding and agronomic programs (Thomson 1987) that set objectives.

European countries (such as the Netherlands, which has a highly successful seed-potato export business) have been contributing to the development of varieties with superior tolerance for environmental stressors, especially heat and drought, as potato production grows in subtropical countries of Asia and Africa (Levy 1987). Innovative breeding programs also include social components that respond to economic concerns, such as that growing potatoes for market contributes to women's household income. A Dutch-sponsored program in Asia built up a potato network of women social scientists, nutritionists, and marketing experts along these lines. CIP, in consultation with professionals from national programs, coordinates research and varietal development as well as collection and characterization of germ plasm (seed material) from wild resources.

The Significance of CIP

The International Potato Center (CIP) which grew out of the Mexican national potato program funded by the Rockefeller Foundation, is part of the Consultative Group on International Agricultural Research. It provides a major resource and impetus for strategic studies that tap the genetic and phenotypic diversity of the potato and accelerate the introduction of useful characteristics into new cultivars. Since 1972, CIP has built and maintained the World Potato Collection of some 13,000 accessions, characterized as 5,000 cultivars and 1,500 wild types. In addition to South American programs, CIP potato campaigns extend from the plains of India, Pakistan, and Bangladesh to the oases of North Africa and the highlands and valleys of Central Africa.

CIP's major technical activities include an effective

population breeding strategy, "clean" (pest- and disease-free) germ-plasm distribution, virus and viroid detection and elimination, agronomy, integrated pest management, tissue culture and rapid multiplication of seed materials, advancement of true potato seed as an alternative to tubers or microtubers, and improvement of storage practices. In the 1990s, a principal thrust of research has been to generate seed materials resistant to late blight, which has reemerged in a more virulent, sexually reproducing form (Niederhauser 1992; Daly 1996).

Strategies involve breeding for multi-gene ("horizontal") rather than single-gene resistance, development and dissemination of true potato seed (which does not disseminate the fungus), and integrated pest management that relies on cost-effective applications of fungicides (CIP 1994). Training, regional networks, and participatory research with farmers are additional dimensions of CIP programs. Collaborative networks offer courses that allow potato specialists to interact and address common problems. In addition, CIP also pioneered "farmer-back-to-farmer" research, whereby effective techniques developed by farmers in one part of the world are shared with farmers in other geographic areas. For example, as already mentioned, reduction of postharvest losses through diffused-light storage is a technique that CIP researchers learned from Peruvian farmers and then brokered to farmers in Asia and Africa (CIP 1984; Rhoades 1984).

CIP also extends its networking to international food purveyors, such as McDonald's and Pepsico – transnational corporations interested in developing improved, pest-resistant, uniformly shaped, high-solid-content potato varieties to be used in making standardized fries. One goal of such enterprises is to develop local sources of supply of raw potatoes for the firms' international franchises, an accomplishment that would improve potato production and income for developing-country farmers and also reduce transportation costs (Walsh 1990). Although principally engaged in agricultural research and extension, CIP also studies consumption patterns, which can improve the potato's dietary and nutritional contributions while eliminating waste (Woolfe 1987; Bouis and Scott 1996).

Dietary and Nutritional Dimensions

Potatoes – simply boiled, baked, or roasted – are an inexpensive, nutritious, and ordinarily harmless source of carbohydrate calories and good-quality protein, and potato skins are an excellent source of vitamin C. Because a small tuber (100 grams [g]) boiled in its skin provides 16 mg of ascorbic acid – 80 percent of a child's or 50 percent of an adult's daily requirement – the potato is an excellent preventive against scurvy. Potatoes are also a good source of the B vitamins (thiamine, pyridoxine, and niacin) and are rich in potassium, phosphorus, and other trace elements. Nutritive value by weight is low because potatoes are

mostly water, but consumed in sufficient quantity to meet caloric needs, the dry matter (about 20 percent) provides the micronutrients just mentioned, an easily digestible starch, and nitrogen (protein), which is comparable on a dry-weight basis to the protein content of cereals and, on a cooked basis, to that of boiled cereals, such as rice- or grain-based gruels (Woolfe 1987).

Potato protein, like that of legumes, is high in lysine and low in sulfur-containing amino acids, making potatoes a good nutritional staple for adults, especially if consumed with cereals as a protein complement. Prepared in fresh form, however, tubers are too bulky to provide a staple for infants or children without an energy-rich supplement. Food technologists are hopeful that novel processing measures may manage to convert the naturally damp, starchy tuber (which molds easily) into a light, nutritious powder that can be reconstituted as a healthful snack or baby food. They also hope to make use of potato protein concentrate, derived either directly by protein recovery or from single-cell protein grown on potato-processing waste (Woolfe 1987). Both advances would minimize waste as well as deliver new sources of nutrients for humans and animals, rendering potato processing more economical. Containing contaminants in industrial potato processing is still very expensive, but sun-drying, a cottage or village industry in India and other Asian countries, holds promise as an inexpensive way to preserve the potato and smooth out seasonal market gluts.

Preservation looms as a large issue because fungus-infected, improperly stored, and undercooked potatoes are toxic for both humans and livestock. Storage and preparation also can diminish the tuber's sensory and nutritional qualities. Sweetening (enzyme conversion of starch), lipid degradation, and discoloration or blackening are signs of deterioration that reduces palatability and protein value. Storage in direct sunlight raises glycoalkaloid content. Other antinutritional factors, such as proteinase inhibitors and lectins, which play a role in insect resistance in some varieties, are ordinarily destroyed by heat, but undercooking, especially when fuel is limited, can leave potatoes indigestible and even poisonous.

Dietary Roles

Although peeling, boiling, and other handling of potatoes decrease micronutrient values, they remove dirt, roughage, and toxins, as well as render potatoes edible. In their Andean heartland, potatoes have always been consumed fresh (boiled or roasted) or reconstituted in stews from freeze-dried or sun-dried forms. They have been the most important root-crop starchy staple, although other cultivated and wild tubers are consumed along with cereals, both indigenous (maize and quinoa) and nonindigenous (barley and wheat). Despite the importance of the potato, cereals were often preferred. For example, Inca ruling elites, just prior to conquest, were said to have favored maize over potatoes, perhaps because the cereal provided denser carbohydrate-protein-fat calories and also was superior for brewing. For these reasons, the Inca may have moved highland peasant populations to lowland irrigated valley sites, where they produced maize instead of potatoes (Earle et al. 1987; Coe 1994). In South America today, potatoes are consumed as a staple or costaple with noodles, barley, rice, and/or legumes and are not used for the manufacture of alcohol. In Central America and Mexico, they are consumed as a costaple main dish or vegetable, in substitution for beans.

In Europe, potatoes historically were added to stews, much like other root vegetables, or boiled, baked, roasted, or fried with the addition of fat, salt, and spices. Boiled potatoes became the staple for eighteenth- and nineteenth-century Irish adults, who consumed up to 16 pounds per person per day in the absence of oatmeal, bread, milk, or pork. These potatoes were served in forms that included pies and cakes (Armstrong 1986). In eastern Europe and Russia, potatoes were eaten boiled or roasted, or were prepared as a costaple with wheat flour in pasta or pastries. In France, by the nineteenth century, fried potatoes were popular, and potatoes were also consumed in soup. In France, Germany, and northern and eastern Europe, potatoes were used for the manufacture of alcohol, which was drunk as a distinct beverage or was put into fortified wines (Bourke 1993). In Great Britain and North America, there developed "fish and chips" and "meat and potatoes" diets. In both locations, potatoes comprised the major starchy component of meals that usually included meat and additional components of green leafy or yellow vegetables.

In former European colonies of Asia and Africa, potatoes were initially consumed only occasionally, like asparagus or other relatively high-cost vegetables, but increased production made them a staple in certain areas. In central African regions of relatively high production, potatoes are beaten with grains and legumes into a stiff porridge, or boiled or roasted and eaten whole. Alternatively, in many Asian cuisines they provide a small garnish, one of a number of side dishes that go with a main staple, or they serve as a snack food consumed whole or in a flour-based pastry. Woolfe (1987: 207, Figure 6.7) has diagrammed these possible dietary roles and has described a four-part "typology of potato consumption" that ranges from (1) potato as staple or costaple, a main source of food energy eaten almost every day for a total consumption of 60 to 200 kg per year; to (2) potato as a complementary vegetable served one or more times per week; to (3) potato as a luxury or special food consumed with 1 to 12 meals per year; to (4) potato as a nonfood because it is either unknown or tabooed. For each of these culinary ends, cultural consumers recognize and rank multiple varieties of potatoes.

Culinary Classifications

In the United States, potato varieties are sometimes classified, named, and marketed according to their geographical location of production (for example, "Idaho" potatoes for baking). They are also classified by varietal name (for example, Russet Burbank, which comes from Idaho but also from other places and is good for baking) and by color and size (for example, small, red, "White Rose," "Gold Rose," "Yukon Gold," or "Yellow Finn," which are designated tasty and used for boiling or mashing). Varieties are also characterized according to cooking qualities that describe their relative starch and moisture content. High-starch, "floury" potatoes are supposed to be better for baking, frying, and mashing; lower-starch, "waxy" potatoes are better for boiling, roasting, and salads (because they hold their shape); and medium-starch, "all-purpose" potatoes are deemed good for pan-frying, scalloping, and pancakes.

Cookbooks (for example, McGee 1984) suggest that relative starch content and function can be determined by a saltwater test (waxy potatoes float, floury varieties sink) or by observation (oval-shaped, thick-skinned potatoes prove better for baking, whereas large, round, thin-skinned potatoes suit many purposes). Specialized cookbooks devoted entirely to the potato help consumers and home cooks make sense of this great diversity (Marshall 1992; see also O'Neill 1992), offering a wide range of recipes, from simple to elegant, for potato appetizers (crepes, puff pastries, fritters, pies, and tarts); potato ingredients, thickeners, or binders in soups; and potato salads, breads, and main courses. They detail dishes that use potatoes baked, mashed, sauteed, braised, or roasted; as fries and puffs (*pommes soufflés* is folklorically dated to 1837 and King Louis Philippe), and in gratinées (baked with a crust); as well as potato dumplings, gnocchi, pancakes, and even desserts. Potato cookbooks, along with elegant presentations of the tubers in fine restaurants, have helped transform the image of the potato from a fattening and undesirable starch into a desirable and healthful gourmet food item.

Mass production over the years has produced larger but more insipid potatoes that are baked, boiled, and mashed, mixed with fats and spices, fried, or mixed with oil and vinegar in salads. Running counter to this trend, however, has been a demand in the 1990s for "heirloom" (traditional) varieties, which increasingly are protected by patent to ensure greater income for their developers and marketers. In the United States, heirloom varieties are disseminated through fine-food stores, as well as seed catalogues that distribute eyes, cuttings, and mini-tubers for home gardens. There is even a Maine-based "Potato of the Month Club," which markets "old-fashioned" or organically grown varieties (O'Neill 1992) to people unable to grow their own.

Breeders are also scrambling to design new gold or purple varieties that can be sold at a premium. In

1989, Michigan State University breeders completed designing a "perfect" potato ("MICHIGOLD") for Michigan farmers: Distinctive and yellow-fleshed, this variety was tasty, nutritious, high yielding, and disease resistant, and (its breeders joked), it would not grow well outside of Michigan's borders (from the author's interviews with Michigan State University scientists). Also of current importance is a search for exotic potatoes, such as the small, elongated, densely golden-fleshed "La Ratte" or "La Reine," which boasts "a flavor that hints richly of hazelnuts and chestnuts" (Fabricant 1996). These return the modern, North American consumer to what were perhaps the "truffle-like" flavors reported by sixteenth-century Spaniards encountering potatoes for the first time. Such special varieties also may help to counter the trend of ever more industrially processed potato foods that has been underway since the 1940s.

Industrially Processed Potato Foods

Since the end of World War II, processed products have come to dominate 75 percent of the potato market, especially as frozen or snack foods. Seventy percent of Idaho-grown and 80 percent of Washington-grown potatoes are processed, and the proportion is also growing in Europe and Asia (Talburt 1975). Freeze-dried potatoes received a boost during the war years, when U.S. technologists are reported to have visited South America to explore the ancient art of potato freeze-drying and adapt it for military rations (Werge 1979). Since World War II, the development of the frozen food industry and other food-industry processes and packaging, combined with a surging demand for snack and "fast" (convenience) foods, have contributed to the increasing expansion of industrially processed potato products in civilian markets. By the 1970s, 50 percent of potatoes consumed in the United States were dehydrated, fried, canned, or frozen, with close to 50 percent of this amount in the frozen food category. The glossy reports of mammoth food purveyors, such as Heinz, which controls Ore-Ida, proudly boast new and growing markets for processed potatoes (and their standby, ketchup) in the former Soviet Union and Asia.

The other large growth area for fried potatoes and chips has been in the transnational restaurant chains, where fries (with burgers) symbolize modernization or diet globalization. Unfortunately, the "value added" in calories and cost compounds the nutritional problems of consumers struggling to subsist on marginal food budgets, as well as those of people who are otherwise poorly nourished. For less affluent consumers, consumption of fries and other relatively expensive, fat-laden potato products means significant losses (of 50 percent or more) in the nutrients available in freshly prepared potatoes – a result of the many steps involved in storage, processing, and final preparation. Although processed potato foods are not "bad" in themselves, the marginal nutritional contexts in which some people choose to eat them means a diversion of critical monetary and food resources from more nutritious and cost-effective food purchases. The health risks associated with high amounts of fat and obesity are additional factors.

Potato: Present and Future

Potato consumption is on the rise in most parts of the world. In 1994, China led other nations by producing 40,039,000 metric tons, followed by the Russian Federation (33,780,000), Poland (23,058,000), the United States (20,835,000), Ukraine (16,102,000), and India (15,000,000) (FAO 1995). Average annual per capita consumption is reported to be highest in certain highland regions of Rwanda (153 kg), Peru (100 to 200 kg), and highland Asia (no figures available) (Woolfe 1987), with the largest rate of increase in lowland Asia.

Expansion of potato production and consumption has resulted from the inherent plasticity of the crop; the international training, technical programs, and technology transfer offered by CIP and European purveyors; the ecological opportunities fostered by the "Green Revolution" in other kinds of farming, especially Asian cereal-based systems; and overarching political-economic transformations in income and trade that have influenced local potato production and consumption, especially via the fast-food industry. The use of potatoes has grown because of the ease with which they can be genetically manipulated and because of their smooth fit into multivarietal or multispecies agronomic systems, not to mention the expanding number of uses for the potato as a food and as a raw industrial material.

Genetic Engineering

The potato already has a well-developed, high-density molecular linkage map that promises to facilitate marker-assisted breeding (Tanksley 1992). Coupled with its ease of transformation by cellular (protoplast fusion) or molecular (*Agrobacterium*-assisted) methods, and useful somaclone variants, the potato is developing into a model food crop for genetic engineering. By 1995, there was a genetically engineered variety, containing bt-toxin as a defense against the potato beetle, in commercial trials (Holmes 1995). Where the potato is intercropped rather than monocropped, it also encourages scientists to rethink the agricultural engineering enterprise as a multicropping system or cycle, within which agronomists must seek to optimize production with more efficient uses of moisture, fertilizer, and antipest applications (Messer 1996). Resurgent – and more virulent – forms of late blight, as well as coevolving virus and beetle pests, are the targets of integrated pest management that combines new biotechnological tools with more conventional chemical and biological ones.

Potatoes continue to serve as a raw material for starch, alcohol, and livestock fodder (especially in Europe). In addition, they may soon provide a safe and reliable source of genetically engineered pharmaceuticals, such as insulin, or of chemical polymers for plastics and synthetic rubbers. Inserting genes for polymer-making enzymes has been the easy step; regulating production of those enzymes relative to natural processes already in the plant is the next, more difficult, one (Pool 1989). A cartoonist (Pool 1989) captured the irony of saving the family farm – whereby small farmers, on contract, grow raw materials for plastics – by portraying the classic Midwestern "American Gothic" farmer husband and wife standing pitchforks in hand, before a field of plastic bottles!

Potato Philanthropy

With less irony, potatoes have come to serve as a model crop for philanthropy. The Virginia-based Society of St. Andrew, through its potato project, has salvaged more than 200 million pounds of fresh produce, especially potatoes, which has been redirected to feed the hungry. Perhaps the memory of Ireland's potato famine continues to inspire acts of relief and development assistance through such organizations as Irish Concern and Action from Ireland, which, along with Irish political leaders (for example, Robinson 1992), reach out to prevent famine deaths, especially as the people of Ireland mark the 150th anniversary of the Great Hunger.

Concluding Paradoxes

In the foregoing history are at least four paradoxes. The first is the potato's transformation in Europe from an antifamine food crop to a catalyst of famine. Ominously, the principal reliance on this species, which makes possible survival, subsistence, and surplus production in high-elevation zones all over the world, and which yields more calories per unit area than cereals, "caused" the Irish famine of 1845–8 and continues to make other poor rural populations vulnerable to famine.

Paradoxical, too, has been the transformation of this simple, naturally nutritious, inexpensive source of carbohydrate, protein, and vitamins into a relatively expensive processed food and less-healthy carrier of fat in the globalization of french fries and hamburgers.

A third paradox is the enduring or even revitalized importance of Andean source materials for the global proliferation of potatoes. Advances in agronomy and varietal improvement have made the potato an increasingly important and diverse crop for all scales and levels of production and consumption across the globe. But in the face of such geographic and culinary developments, the traditional South American potato cultures continue to present what to some scientists is a surprising wealth of biological, ecological, storage, and processing knowledge (Werge 1979; Rhoades 1984; Brush 1992). The management of biological diversity, ecology of production, and storage and processing methods are three areas in which indigenous agriculture has continued to inform contemporary potato research. Thus, despite dispersal all over the globe, scientists still return to the potato's heartland to learn how to improve and protect the crop.

A fourth paradox is that potatoes may yet experience their greatest contribution to nutrition and help put an end to hunger, not directly as food but as a component of diversified agro-ecosystems and an industrial cash crop. Since their beginnings, potatoes have always formed a component of diversified agro-livestock food systems. Historically, they achieved their most significant dietary role when grown in rotation with cereals (as in Ireland). Today, they are once again being seasonally rotated within cereal-based cropping systems. Because potatoes are intercropped, they stimulate questions about how biotechnology-assisted agriculture can be implemented more sustainably. So far, plant biotechnologists have considered mainly the host-resistance to individual microbes or insects, and never with more than one crop at a time. But adding potatoes to cereal crop rotations encourages scientists, as it does farmers, to look more closely at the efficiency with which cropping systems use moisture and chemicals, and to ask how subsequent crops can utilize effectively the field residues of previous plantings in order to save water and minimize pollution.

Efforts to integrate potatoes into tropical cropping systems, particularly those in the tropical and subtropical lowlands of southern and southeastern Asia, are stimulating such inquiries. Thus, potatoes, perhaps the first crop cultivated in the Western Hemisphere, are now contributing to a revolution of their own in the newest agricultural revolution: the bio- or gene revolution in Asia. In addition, potatoes may also help to save family farms in the United States and Europe by providing income to those growing the crop for plastic.

Ellen Messer

Bibliography

Acosta, José de. [1590] 1880. *Historia natural y moral de las Indias,* trans. E. Grimston, London, 1604. Haklyuyt Society reprint, 1880. Seville.

Anderson, E. N. 1988. *The food of China.* New Haven, Conn.

Andersson, J. A. 1996. Potato cultivation in the Uporoto mountains, Tanzania. *African Affairs* 95: 85–106.

Arber, A. 1938. *Herbals.* Cambridge.

Armstrong, A. 1986. *The Joyce of cooking: Food and drink from James Joyce's Dublin.* Barrytown, N.Y.

Bauhin, C. 1596. *Phytopinax.* Basel.
1598. *Opera Quae Extant Omnia.* Frankfurt.
Bouis, H. E., and G. Scott. 1996. *Demand for high-value secondary crops in developing countries: The case of potatoes in Bangladesh and Pakistan.* International Food Policy Research Institute, Food and Consumption Division Discussion Paper. Washington, D.C.
Bourke, A. 1993. *"The visitation of God"? The potato and the great Irish famine.* Dublin.
Braun, J. von, H. de Haen, and J. Blanken. 1991. *Commercialization of agriculture under population pressure: Effects on production, consumption, and nutrition in Rwanda.* Washington, D.C.
Brush, S. 1992. Reconsidering the Green Revolution: Diversity and stability in cradle areas of crop domestication. *Human Ecology* 20: 145-67.
Brush, S., J. E. Taylor, and M. Bellon. 1992. Technology adoption and biological diversity in Andean potato agriculture. *Journal of Development Economics* 39: 365-87.
Chakrabarti, D. K. 1986. Malnutrition: More should be made of the potato. *World Health Forum* 7: 429-32.
CIP (International Potato Center). 1984. *Potatoes for the developing world: A collaborative experience.* Lima.
1994. *CIP Annual Report 1993.* Lima.
Cobo, B. [1653] 1890-1893. *Historia del nuevo mundo,* ed. M. Jiminez de la Espada. 4 vols. Seville.
Coe, S. 1994. *America's first cuisines.* Austin, Tex.
Crossgrove, W., D. Egilman, P. Heywood, et al. 1990. Colonialism, international trade, and the nation-state. In *Hunger in history,* ed. L. Newman, 215-40. New York.
Daly, D. C. 1996. The leaf that launched a thousand ships. *Natural History* 105: 24, 31.
Davidson, A. 1992. Europeans' wary encounter with tomatoes, potatoes, and other New World foods. In *Chilies to chocolate: Food the Americas gave the world,* ed. Nelson Foster and L. S. Cordell, 1-14. Phoenix, Ariz.
Drake, F. [1628] 1854. *The world encompassed,* ed. W. S. W. Vaux. London.
Earle, T., ed. 1987. *Archaeological field research in the Upper Mantaro, Peru, 1982-83. Investigations of Inca expansion and exchange.* Los Angeles.
Fabricant, F. 1996. French revolution in potatoes comes to America. *New York Times,* 25 September: C6.
Food and Agriculture Organization of the United Nations (FAO). 1995. *FAO Production,* Vol. 48. Rome.
Franco, M. de, and R. Godoy. 1993. Potato-led growth: The macroeconomic effects of technological innovations in Bolivian agriculture. *Journal of Development Studies* 29: 561-87.
Fürer-Haimendorf, C. von. 1964. *The Sherpas of Nepal: Buddhist highlanders.* London.
Gerard, John. 1633. *The herball on general historie of plantes.* London.
Grun, P. 1990. The evolution of cultivated potatoes. *Economic Botany* 44 (3rd supplement): 39-55.
Guaman Poma de Ayala and Felipe Guaman. 1936. Nueva cronica y buen gobierno. In *Traveaux et Mémoires de l'Institut d'Ethnologie* 23, ed. P. Rivet. Paris.
Hawkes, J. G. 1990. *The potato: Evolution, biodiversity, and genetic resources.* Washington, D.C.
Hawkes, J. G., and J. Francisco-Ortega. 1992. The potato during the late 16th century. *Economic Botany* 46: 86-97.
Hawkes, J. G., and P. P. Hjerting. 1989. *The potatoes of Bolivia: Their breeding value and evolutionary relationships.* Oxford.
Hermsen, J. G. Th., and K. M. Swiezynski. 1987. Introduction. In *The production of new potato varieties: Technological advances,* ed. G. J. Jellis and D. E. Richardson, xviii-xx. Cambridge.
Hobhouse, H. 1986. *Seeds of change: Five plants that transformed the world.* New York.
Holmes, B. 1995. Chips are down for killer potato. *New Scientist* 146: 9.
Horton, D. 1987. *Potatoes. production, marketing, and programs for developing countries.* Boulder, Colo.
Horton, D. E., and H. Fano. 1985. *Potato atlas.* International Potato Center. Lima.
Huaman, Z. 1983. *The breeding potential of native Andean cultivars.* Proceedings, International Congress: Research for the potato in the year 2000, 10th anniversary, 1972-82. Lima.
Huaman, Z., J. R. Williams, W. Salhuana, and L. Vincent. 1977. *Descriptors for the cultivated potato.* Rome.
Jellis, G. J., and D. E. Richardson. 1987. The development of potato varieties in Europe. In *The production of new potato varieties: Technological advances,* ed. G. J. Jellis and D. E. Richardson, 1-9. Cambridge.
Johns, T. 1990. *With bitter herbs they shall eat it: Chemical ecology and the origins of human diet and medicine.* Tucson, Ariz.
Kinealy, C. 1995. *The great calamity: The Irish famine 1845-52.* Boulder, Colo.
Levy, D. 1987. Selection and evaluation of potatoes for improved tolerance of environmental stresses. In *The production of new potato varieties: Technological advances,* ed. G. J. Jellis and D. E. Richardson, 105-7. Cambridge.
Lysaght, P. 1994. *Aspects of the social and cultural influence of the potato in Ireland.* Paper presented at the 10th Internationale Konferenz für Ethnologische Nahrungsforschung, Kulturprägung durch Nahrung: Die Kartoffel, 6-10 June 1994.
Marshall, L. 1992. *A passion for potatoes.* New York.
McGee, H. 1984. *On food and cooking.* New York.
McNeill, W. H. 1974. *The shape of European history.* New York.
Merritt, R. 1990. Faith and betrayal, the potato: *Ulysses. James Joyce Quarterly* 28: 269-76.
Messer, E. 1996. Visions of the future: Food, hunger, and nutrition. In *The hunger report: 1996,* ed. E. Messer and P. Uvin, 211-28. Amsterdam.
Morris, C. 1981. Tecnología y organizacion Inca del almacenamiento de víveres en la sierra. In *La Tecnología en el Mundo Andino,* ed. H. Lechtman and A. M. Soldi, 327-75. Mexico.
Moscow's forest falls to hungry potato eaters. 1992. *New Scientist* 134 (April 4): 6.
Murphy, A. 1984. *Millet.* Boston.
Nef, J. U. 1950. *War and human progress.* Cambridge.
Nganga, S. 1984. The role of the potato in food production for countries in Africa. In *Potato development and transfer of technology in tropical Africa,* ed. S. Nganga, 63-9. Nairobi.
Niederhauser, J. S. 1992. The role of the potato in the conquest of hunger and new strategies for international cooperation. *Food Technology* 46: 91-5.
Ochoa, C. M. 1962. *Los Solanum Tuberifoeros silvestres del Peru (Secc. Tuberarium, sub-secc. Hyperbasarthrum).* Lima.
Ochoa, C., and P. Schmiediche. 1983. Systemic exploitation and utilization of wild potato germplasm. In *Research for the potato in the year 2000,* ed. W. J. Hooker, 142-4. Lima.
O'Neill, M. 1989. Potatoes come to power. *New York Times,* 27 September: C1, C10.

1992. Hot potatoes. *New York Times Magazine,* March 29.

Pool, R. 1989. In search of the plastic potato. *Science* 245: 1187-9.

Quilter, J., B. Ojeda E., D. Pearsall, et al. 1991. Subsistence economy of El Paraiso, an early Peruvian site. *Science* 251: 277-83.

Quiros, C. F., S. B. Brush, D. S. Douches, et al. 1990. Biochemical and folk assessment of variability of Andean cultivated potatoes. *Economic Botany* 44: 254-66.

Rhoades, R. E. 1984. *Breaking new ground: Agricultural anthropology.* Lima.

Robinson, Mary. 1992. *A voice for Somalia.* Dublin.

Ross, H. 1979. Wild species and primitive cultivars as ancestors of potato varieties. In *Broadening the genetic base of crops,* ed. A. C. Zeven and A. M. van Harten, 237-45. Wageningen, Netherlands.

Salaman, R. N. [1949] 1985. *The history and social influence of the potato,* ed. J. G. Hawkes. Cambridge.

Salmon, W. 1710. *The English herbal.* London.

Scott, G. J. 1988. *Potatoes in central Africa: A survey of Burundi, Rwanda, and Zaire.* International Potato Center. Lima.

Smith, Adam. [1776] 1904/1950. *An inquiry into the nature and causes of the wealth of nations,* ed. E. Cannon. London.

Talburt, William S. 1975. *Potato processing.* Third edition. Westport, Conn.

Tanksley, S. D., M. W. Ganal, and J. P. Prince. 1992. High density molecular linkage maps of the tomato and potato genomes. *Genetics* 132: 1141-60.

Thomson, A. J. 1987. A practical breeder's view of the current state of potato breeding and evaluation. In *The production of new potato varieties: Technological advances,* ed. D. J. Jellis and D. E. Richardson, 336-46. Cambridge.

Toomre, J. 1992. *Classic Russian cooking: Elena Molokhovets'a gift to young housewives, 1861-1917.* Bloomington, Ind.

Ugent, D. 1970. The potato. *Science* 170: 1161-6.

Ugent, D., Tom Dillehay, and Carlos Ramirez. 1987. Potato remains from a late Pleistocene settlement in south central Chile. *Economic Botany* 41: 17-27.

Ugent, Donald, Sheila Pozorski, and Thomas Pozorski. 1982. Archaeological potato tuber remains from the Cosma Valley of Peru. *Economic Botany* 36: 182-92.

Vander Zaag, P. 1984. One potato, two potato. *Far Eastern Economic Review* n. vol. (August 23): 64-6.

Vavilov, N. I. 1951. The origin, variation, immunity and breeding of cultivated plants, trans. K. Starr Chester. *Chronica Botanica* 13: 1-366.

Vincent, J. 1995. Conacre: A re-evaluation of Irish custom. In *Articulating hidden histories: Exploring the influence of Eric Wolf,* ed. J. Schneider and R. Rapp, 82-93. Berkeley, Calif.

Walsh, J. 1990. In Peru, even potato research is high risk. *Science* 247: 1286-7.

Werge, R. 1979. Potato processing in the central highlands of Peru. *Ecology of Food and Nutrition* 7: 229-34.

Wheaton, B. 1983. *Savoring the past: The French kitchen and tables from 1300 to 1789.* Philadelphia, Pa.

Woodham-Smith, C. 1962. *The great hunger: Ireland 1946-1949.* London.

Woolfe, J. A., with S. V. Poats. 1987. *The potato in the human diet.* New York.

Yen, D. E. 1961/2. The potato in early New Zealand. *The Potato Journal* (Summer): 2-5.

II.B.4 ❧ Sago

Sago is an edible starch derived from the pith of a variety of sago palms, but mostly from two species of the genus *Metroxylon* - *M. sagu* and *M. rumphii.* The sago palms flower only once (hapaxantic) and are found in tropical lowland swamps. Other genera of palms that yield sago starch include *Arecastrum, Arenga, Caryota, Corypha, Eugeissona, Mauritia,* and *Roystonea.* In all, there are about 15 species of sago palms distributed in both the Old World and the New, with the most significant of these, *M. sagu,* located mainly on the islands of the Malay Archipelago and New Guinea. As a staple foodstuff, only the *Metroxylon* genus appears to be in regular use, generally among populations located in coastal, lacustrine, or riverine areas. Worldwide, sago provides only about 1.5 percent of the total production of starch and, consequently, is fairly insignificant as a global food source (Flach 1983). It is processed into flour, meal, and pearl sago, and is often used for thickening soups, puddings, and other desserts.

Prickly Sago palm

Sago starch is extracted in a variety of ways, although the general process is similar from area to area. The trunk of a felled palm is chopped into sections and then split vertically to allow the pith to be removed. The extracted pith is ground and then repeatedly washed and strained. The strained material is allowed to dry, and the result is pellets of sago starch. When processed in this manner, the average yield of one palm (of 27 to 50 feet meters in height) generally ranges between 130 and 185 kilograms (kg) of sago, which can feed a family of between two and four persons for up to three months.

History, Cultivation, and Production

History

The early history of sago palm use as a food is still unclear. Ethnologists and anthropologists have generally relied on native myths and legends to judge when it was introduced into the diets of many groups worldwide. Some, such as E. Schlesier and F. Speiser, have tended to believe that the sago palm has been utilized as a food source in the Pacific islands since prehorticultural days. J. B. Avé (1977), for example, has stated that Neolithic and Mesolithic artifacts found in insular Southeast Asia included tools used in sago preparation. Although this suggests that sago has been cultivated since ancient times, paleohistorians are not so sure. E. Haberland and others, for example, have contended that sago consumption was a postagricultural development (Ruddle et al. 1978).

By most accounts, the sago palm was essential to the early inhabitants of Southeast Asia, and was probably one of the first plants they exploited as part of their subsistence strategy (Avé 1977; Rhoads 1982; Flach 1983). Geographer Carl O. Sauer believed that the plant's domestication took place there, where people in freshwater areas were able to employ native palms in a variety of ways, including the production of starch, drugs, and fish poisons, as well as fishing nets and lines (Isaac 1970). According to the folk history of the Melanau of Sarawak, the tribe has "always eaten sago," even though they claim that rice, not sago, is their staple food (Morris 1974).

Sago, however, has also been an important food source for peoples in other parts of the world. Evidence, although limited, indicates that during the Chinese Tang Dynasty (618 to 907), sago starch from palms grown in southeast China came to rival milled grain for use in making cakes. Additionally, the nutritive value of *Metroxylon* sago was discussed in the *Pen Ts'ao Kang mu* (The Great Herbal), and *Caryota* palms are mentioned in Ki Han's *Nan Fang Ts'ao Mu Chuang* ("Account of the Flora of the Southern Regions") (Ruddle et al. 1978). For the peoples of the Southwest Pacific, sago palms have been important from ancient times to the present; stands of *M. sagu* and *M. rumphii* have provided staple foods over the centuries for many millions of people (McCurrach 1960).

In the Western Hemisphere, the use of sago starch has been less common, although *Arecastrum romanzoffianum, Mauritia flexuosa,* and *Roystonea oleracea* are all varieties that have provided nutritional relief during times of food scarcity. For example, many Paraguayan peasants are said to have survived on sago in the 1870s, following the devastation wrought by the war of the Triple Alliance. And some peoples, such as the Warao Indians of Venezuela, continue to utilize *M. flexuosa* as a dietary staple (Ruddle et al. 1978).

Properties

Sago palms generally reach maturity at about 15 years of age, at which time the tree develops its enormous mass of pith. The pith makes up approximately 68 to 74 percent of the total weight of the tree, whereas the starch content of the pith constitutes about 25 to 30 percent of the pith weight. Raw sago from *Metroxylon* spp. will yield a range of approximately 285 to 355 calories per 100 grams. Nutritionally, about 70 to 90 percent of raw sago is carbohydrate, 0.3 percent is fiber, and 0.2 percent is protein. Although it has a negligible fat content, sago does contain various minerals, including calcium (10 to 30 milligrams [mg]), phosphorus (approximately 12 mg), and iron (0.7 to 1.5 mg) (Peters 1957; Barrau 1960; Platt 1977; Ruddle et al. 1978).

Sago supplies energy needs, but because it is deficient in most other nutrients, its consumption must be complemented with other foods that yield good-quality proteins as well as a range of vitamins. Climate and other environmental factors generally dictate the supplements. In some areas of New Guinea, for example, the inhabitants use leaves and other greens (sometimes grown on platforms raised above water or in limited garden space) along with the products of fishing and hunting. Another source of animal protein is the sago grub, especially for those groups located inland from the wetlands and rivers. Still others have supplemented their diet with coconuts, tubers, roots, and pulses, in addition to greens (Barrau 1960).

Location

The first Western description of sago consumption appears to be that penned by Marco Polo during his travels to Indonesia in the thirteenth century. Polo wrote "Of the Sixth Kingdom, named Fanfur, where Meal is procured from a certain Tree," with the "meal" in question clearly sago starch. A few centuries later, S. Purchas, during his travels in Sumatra, also mentioned sago as a food source (along with rice and millet) (Ruddle et al. 1978). In 1687, W. Dampier noted that sago was one of the more common foods at Mindanao (Tan 1980).

Toward the end of the nineteenth century, sago palms were observed in a number of regions of the world, and Ceram, Borneo, and Sarawak were mentioned as areas of starch production. Today, a survey of sago use would encompass a vast area, ranging over Malaysia and the Pacific Islands (Boulger 1889; Flach 1983).

Sago is fairly common in the western Pacific, where cultivated stands of the palm cover an estimated 10,000 hectares (Firth 1950). It is also present throughout much of the southwestern Pacific area. In Papua New Guinea, for example, there are approximately 1,000,000 hectares of wild sago stands and 20,000 hectares of cultivated stands. Similarly, in Indonesia there are 1 million hectares of wild stands and 128,000 hectares that are cultivated. Rounding out the major areas of sago palm stands are Malaysia with 33,000 hectares of cultivated stands and Thailand and the Philippines with 5,000 hectares each (Flach 1983).

Unlike most plants, the sago palm has not been geographically dispersed, and in experimenting with ways to introduce this crop to new areas, M. Flach (1983) discovered a number of possible reasons for the failure of previous attempts. His own efforts failed in Surinam, probably the result of inadequate care of the plants. An attempt in the south Sudan also failed, most likely because of that region's low humidity. Flach did have success in Vietnam, where a sago palm stand succeeded at Can Tho. But, as he discovered, there are two additional factors that make it difficult to disperse sago palms. One is the problem of obtaining generative material, and the other is the cumbersome size of the vegetative material (Flach 1983).

Moreover, depending on location, the peoples of the different sago palm regions of the world call the palms by a great variety of names. The Papuans, for example, have 23 names for *Metroxylon* and sago. In pidgin English, it is *saksak*. In other areas of New Guinea, the sago palm is known as *abia, aisai, akiri, ambe, api, baiao, balega, barian, da, dou, fi, ipako, na, nafa, ndana, no, poi, pu,* and *wariani*. In the New Hebrides, it is known as *natangora*. In the Fiji Islands, sago is referred to as *ota* or *oat* and as *soqo* or *soqa*, and in the Moluccas it is *lapia*. In Indonesia, sago is known as *rambia, rembia, rembi,* and *rumbia,* along with other similar cognates (Barrau 1960).

Scientific Description

The most important palm trees in sago production are from the genus *Metroxylon,* a term that comes from the Greek words *metra,* meaning "heart of a tree," and *xylon,* meaning "wood" (Whitmore 1973). *Metroxylon sagu* and *Metroxylon rumphii* are economically the most important species in the genus (Flach 1983) and appear to be closely related, as they are found in wild stands mixed together with what appear to be intermediates (Flach 1983).

M. sagu and *M. rumphii* share a great number of characteristics, as well as the common name "sago palm." It is thought that *M. rumphii* originated in Malaysia, New Guinea, and Fiji, whereas *M. sagu* originated in western New Guinea and the Moluccas. The trunks of the two species reach a height of approximately 10 to 15 meters and are generally about 45 centimeters (cm) in diameter (McCurrach 1960; Whitmore 1973). Their leaves grow to 600 or more centimeters in length, and the leaflets are about 60 to 120 cm long and 2.5 to 7.6 cm broad. The flower stalk, which appears above the leaves, is 4 to 5 meters in length. The flower stalk of *M. rumphii* is black and covered with spines, whereas that of *M. sagu* lacks spines. The fruit produced is spherical, dull yellow, and about 5 cm in diameter. The growth cycle of the sago palm ranges from 8 to 17 years (McCurrach 1960; Flach 1983). Although their ideal temperature range has not yet been determined, it is known that sago palms thrive in areas where the temperature only occasionally drops below 15° C.

What is known about the natural habitat of the sago palms has been gleaned largely from observations in environments where they now grow. Indeed, with so little information available, scientists have been forced to study conditions in the natural habitat as well as the centers of cultivation to glean what they can (Flach 1983). Typical of natural habitats are the swamp forests of sago palms in New Guinea, where fresh water is abundant (Barrau 1960).

Outside of swamps, if a climate is too wet, grasses tend to take over and limit propagation. If, on the other hand, the climate is too dry, taller trees will win in competition with the sago palm. It has been suggested that sago palms might survive under drier conditions if well tended. Although sago palms are relatively tolerant of salinity, if the water becomes too brackish, other trees in the vicinity, such as the nipa palm *(Nipa fruiescens),* tend to take over the swamp (Ruddle et al. 1978).

To the conditions of the sago palm's natural habitat, Rhoads (1982) has added the proviso that they are generally "alluvial freshwater swamps" that are frequently located inland from the mouths of large rivers. He has also noted that the mineral soils in which sago palms grow best, especially those high in organic content, need regular flooding for the consistent replacement of nutrients and to discourage the growth of taller trees that keep out sunlight (Rhoads 1982).

Numerous other palms can be sources of sago starch, but they are not so fruitful as *M. sagu* and *M. rumphii.* G. S. Boulger (1889) noted that "inferior" sago could generally be obtained from the Gomuti palm *(Arenga saccharifera),* the Kittool palm *(Caryota urens),* and the Cabbage palm *(Corypha umbraculifera).* In the East Indies, sago could be gotten from *Raphia flabelliformis, Phoenix farinifera,* and *M. filare,* and in South America from *Mauritia flexuosa* and *Guilielma speciosa* (Boulger 1889). There are also a number of *Metroxylon* species in Oceania, including *amicarum, bougainvillense, warburgii, vitiense, upolense, salmonense,* and, presumably, *oxybracteatum* (Ohtsuka 1983).

In South America, additional sago-producing palms have been identified among four different genera: *Syagrus, Copernicia, Mauritia,* and *Manicaria;* moreover, many South American tribes have extracted sago from *Syagrus romanzoffianum* and *Copernicia cerifera* (Wilbert 1976).

Sago Palm Grove Management

Rhoads (1982) determined three general methods of sago palm grove management. The first is simply the process of harvesting sago trees for starch, which (even if only an unintended result) does increase the vitality of the grove: The cutting of palm trunks allows more sunlight to reach nearby shoots, a process that enhances growth and helps to ensure the maturation of at least one sucker, and the damage caused during harvesting by fallen palms and by the construction of work sites in the grove tends to give young sago palm shoots advantages over competitors. Such "unintended management" can be very important to the maintenance and promotion of a sago palm grove (Rhoads 1982).

A second process of sago palm management, termed "horticulture" by Rhoads (1982), involves the planting of suckers or the nurturing and replanting of seedlings. This method, however, is either rare or poorly documented.

A third method of "palm cultivation" involves both the planting of suckers and conscious efforts to change the environment in ways that will promote sago palm growth. One process in which the environment is changed is the creation of artificial swamps by damming streams to flood the groves. Another, observed by Rhoads, is the clearing of the canopy of higher trees to promote sago palm growth. Groves are also sometimes laid out higher up on the slopes of mountains to provide more sunlight for the palms (Rhoads 1982).

Generic Sago Extraction Process

Although sago extraction methods differ somewhat throughout cultures and regions, there are procedures common to all. At the "domestic level," the entire process of sago extraction takes place in the grove itself, thus eliminating the need to transport heavy palm trunks (Flach 1983). Felling the tree occurs when the flowering of the palm indicates that the starch content is at a maximum (Flach 1983). It is also possible to estimate the starch content by taking a small slice from the palm trunk and sampling the starch, either by chewing the pith or by allowing the starch to dry on the axe. If the starch content is too low to merit harvesting the palm, the sample hole is patched with mud (Flach 1983).

If the palm is ready for harvesting, it is felled with an axe, after which the trunk is split lengthwise. (In an alternative method, only the bark is split – and removed.) The pith, when exposed, is "rasped" with a chopper or small hoe (Flach 1983). In the past, choppers were often constructed out of bamboo, but modern choppers are more generally made of metal. The pith is rasped at a straight angle to the fiber while the worker sits on the trunk. The resulting mixture of fiber and rasped pith is next placed on a kind of trough made from palm leaves that has a sieve attached to the lowest end (Flach 1983).

At this point, water is added and kneaded into the mixture to start it flowing, whereupon fibers are caught by the sieve while the starch, suspended in water, flows through the sieve and is collected in a tank, perhaps an old canoe. The starch eventually settles to the bottom, whereas the extra water flows over the side of the tank. The fibrous materials are given to pigs, ducks, and chickens to consume. With this process, it is possible to produce approximately 1 kg of dry starch per hour (Flach 1983).

Larger, although still "small-scale," extraction operations require waterways to transport the sago palm trunks to a processing plant. There they are cut into sections of about 1 to 1.2 meters in length that are easier to work with than entire trunks (Flach 1983). Extraction methods employed at such facilities follow the general model already outlined, although at times different instruments and processes are employed (Flach 1983).

Rasping, for example, is done with a variety of instruments. A board with nails driven through it is sometimes used, but there are also numerous types of engine-powered raspers. At times, a "broad side rasper," which runs parallel to the bark, is employed (Flach 1983).

The kneading and sieving process also varies at the extraction plants. At some, the mixture is trampled, whereas at others a slowly revolving mesh washer constructed of wood or metal is used. Still other plants employ horizontal screen washers or spiral screw washers. It is also possible to combine mechanical stirring with a mesh washer to process the overflow (Flach 1983).

Small ponds are often utilized for the settling process, although another method involves "settling tables." This has the advantage of settling the largest and "cleanest" starch granules – those that bring the highest price on the market – first. The smaller granules, which may contain clay, settle later and yield a grayish, low-quality flour (Flach 1983). Sunlight is often the sole drying agent for the processed starch.

Water quality is a key factor in the entire procedure: Poor water tends to yield sago starch of lesser quality. The refuse created in the production of sago is only of value if domestic animals are nearby. When this is not the case, the refuse is often simply discarded behind plant buildings, creating a stench that is noticeable at quite some distance (Flach 1983).

Extraction Methods in Different Areas

In New Guinea, good use is made of natural stands of sago palms, as well as planted seedlings and suckers. In the swampy lowlands, the semiwild stands require only a minimum of pruning. Those who plant and harvest sago palms throughout the year make periodic visits to the various groves to determine the proper time for harvest (Barrau 1960; Ooman 1971; Ohtsuka 1983).

Sago extraction is usually done by extended family groups in New Guinea. The men fell the palm, making the cut approximately 40 to 70 centimeters above the ground. Next, using axes, they remove half of the surface wood (2 to 4 cm thick) in order to expose the pith. While this is going on, the women construct troughs in which the sago starch will be washed out. Once the men have exposed the pith, the women scrape it out of the trunk and pound it into a mass (Barrau 1960; Ohtsuka 1983).

For starch extraction, the Papuans employ an *abol*, a tool made from two hard sticks and a toughened string of cane that is used much like an adze. (In fact, adze-like tools are common throughout New Guinea.) The actual cutting implement is most often made of stone, wood, or sharpened bamboo, although in areas that have contact with Europe, metal piping is frequently employed (Barrau 1960; Ohtsuka 1983).

In New Guinea, as is typical elsewhere, leaves, a trough, and a sieve are used in the kneading and straining process. The starch-bearing liquid is collected in pans made from leaves or leafstalks, then partly dried and wrapped with palm leaves, usually in the shape of a cylinder or a cone. In one study, it was observed that five women, in about 8.5 hours of extracting, sieving, and drying, were able to produce 54.7 kg of sago (Barrau 1960; Ohtsuka 1983).

In Malaysia, the average yield per sago palm has been estimated at between 113 and 295 kg. The fallen palm tree is cut into logs of 120 to 183 cm in length for rasping. The tools used in rasping have evolved from the *palu*, a sharpened bamboo cylinder with a long wooden handle (which caused many leg injuries), to the *garut*, a wooden board with nails, to mechanized scraping machines, introduced in 1931. One such device consists of a spinning metal disc with serrated edges. Kneading is usually done by trampling, and drying takes place in the sun (Knight 1969; Whitmore 1973).

The extraction process that takes place in a factory is quite similar to the more primitive methods already described. In Singapore, for example, an axe is used to remove the bark, and a two-man nail board is employed in the rasping process. Care is taken to process sago trees in the order in which they arrive at the factory, so as to prevent spoilage. The extracted sago is made into blocks, mixed with water, and then blocked again. They dry in the sun, with occasional turning.

Tikopia provides an example of sago extraction in the western Pacific, where the task proceeds during the rainy season because excess water is readily available. Hoops of iron are used to scrape the trunk after the bark is removed; before iron was introduced, sharp coconut shells were employed. If the work is to be performed in the village instead of in the field, the trunk is cut into sections. Kneading is done in coconut-leaf mesh baskets and the material is then sieved. A trough is filled with the water-and-starch solution and covered with coconut and sago fronds. After the starch has settled, the water is poured off, and the sago is dried and made into flour (Firth 1950).

In South America, where the Warao Indians extract sago from *Manicaria saccifera,* the methods, again, vary only a little from those employed elsewhere. After the tree is felled, the bark is removed, and an adze or hoe *(nahuru)* is utilized to rasp the pith. This hoe typically consists of a blade made of *Mauritia* bark, with a handle constructed of rounded wood and a binding consisting of a two-ply cord made from *Mauritia* bast. The trough employed in the process is made from the trunk of the *temiche* palm. After water has been added to the pith and the mixture kneaded through a strainer, a ball of light brown sago is made.

In South America, sago extraction practices may be part of a disappearing tradition, as the starch is slowly giving way to other agricultural staples, even among the tribes who have used it since prehistoric times (Wilbert 1976).

Sago As Food

It is mainly in New Guinea and neighboring islands that *Metroxylon* has been exploited as a food. A typical swamp grove will have approximately 25 palms per acre per year ready for felling. These will yield a total of about 2,837 to 3,972 kg of crude starch, which will provide from 7 to 10 million calories to its consumers. Sago can be used like any other starch, and peoples familiar with it have developed numerous ways of preserving and consuming it (Boulger 1889; Barrau 1960; Flach 1983).

In the swamp areas of New Guinea, where sago is a staple, the average daily ration per person is a little less than a kilogram, with individual consumption ranging from a bit over 0.5 kg to about 1.5 kg per day. Such quantities of sago deliver from 1,700 to about 4,000 daily calories, which the average family in New Guinea devotes 10 days of each month to acquiring (Ooman 1971).

Preservation

Left dry, sago becomes moldy and spoils. But the starch can be stored by simply placing it in a basket, covering it with leaves, and sprinkling water on it from time to time. With moisture, sago ferments and forms lactic acid, which prevents spoiling. If pottery is available, fresh sago is placed in a jar and covered with water (Barrau 1960; Ooman 1971; Flach 1983).

There are, however, methods of storing sago in a dry state. One is to make sago paste into briquettes by dehydrating it rapidly on a surface above a fire. This method permits the sago to be kept for about one month. Sago can also be dried in the sun, although it is said that this makes it taste "flat" (Barrau 1960; Flach 1983). In general, Papuans tend to think that dried sago loses its flavor.

Supplements

As has been mentioned, nutritional supplements are vital to a diet centering on sago. It must be eaten with some fish or meat (or other whole protein) and with vegetables to provide consumers with a satisfactory intake of the chief nutrients. Thus, in New Guinea, the peoples reliant upon sago, who supplement their diet with fish, hunted game, sago grubs, sago palm heart, leaves, and nuts, probably enjoy a relatively well-balanced diet (Ooman 1971; Dwyer 1985).

Sago Foods

After harvesting, it is common for some of the just-produced sago to be eaten immediately. The women usually prepare it by wrapping a portion in palm leaves or packing it into a section of cane (actually rattan, *Calamus* spp.) and baking it (Ohtsuka 1983). Sometimes, before the sago is baked in a fire, it is mixed with grated coconut or with bean flour (Flach 1983). The remainder of the freshly harvested sago is then wrapped in dry palm fronds to be carried back to the village (Ohtsuka 1983).

The starch is prepared in a number of ways. In areas with pottery, a sago porridge is often served along with condiments, grains, fish, and meat. A biscuit of sago is also made by those who have pottery. In what was Netherlands New Guinea, for example, a sago biscuit was baked in an earthenware mold, which served as the oven.

Areas without pottery will often bake sago paste, rolled in green leaves, in a hot stone oven. This produces a flat cake that often has grated coconut, meat, fish, or greens mixed into it. A cake with grated coconut is called *sago senole*. Sago briquettes, wrapped in sago leaves, are referred to as *sago ega*. *Sago bulu* comes from the cooking of sago paste in green bamboo. A roasted stick of sago paste is called *sago boengkoes*.

In Borneo, sago pellets are used occasionally as a substitute for rice (Barrau 1960). A sago ash may also be produced by burning the wide part of the sago leaf midrib. This can be an important nutritional supplement providing sodium, potassium, calcium, and magnesium.

Pearl sago – another common product from sago starch – is made by pressing wet sago flour through a sieve and then drying it in a pan while stirring continuously. The "pearls" formed are round, and the outer part of the sago pearl gelatinizes to hold them together. Pearl sago is an important ingredient in soups and puddings (Flach 1983). In Sarawak, wet sago flour is mixed with rice polishings and cooked

into pearl form, creating an "artificial rice," certainly a more nutritious food than polished rice. Flach believes that this product has potential as a substitute for rice in Southeast Asia (Flach 1983).

In Tikopia, sago is often made into a flour that is considered a delicacy by those who produce it. On occasion, sago is mixed with other foods to add body, flavor, and softness. Big slabs of sago are also baked for many days in large ovens, and then put aside for times of famine. However, this sago product is considered virtually "unpalatable" by its makers (Firth 1950).

Sago is also employed in foods that are more common in other parts of the world. For example, sago starch can be used in high-fructose syrup as a partial replacement for sucrose (Flach 1983). Sago has also been experimentally added to bread flour. It has been found that adding 10 percent sago to the recipe can improve the quality of the bread produced, although adding more will lower it (Flach 1983).

In addition to the consumption of the palm pith, other parts used as food include the inner shoot of the crown (as fruit or snack), sap from the male inflorescence (boiled into palm sugar, fermented as vinegar or distilled spirit), and the inner kernel (cooked in syrup as a dessert) (Lie 1980). Overall, the uses of sago are as varied as those of other starches.

H. Micheal Tarver
Allan W. Austin

Bibliography

Avé, J. B. 1977. Sago in insular Southeast Asia: Historical aspects and contemporary uses. In *Sago-76: Papers of the first international sago symposium,* ed. Koolin Tan, 21–30. Kuala Lumpur.
Barrau, Jacques. 1960. The sago palms and other food plants of marsh dwellers in the South Pacific islands. *Economic Botany* 13: 151–62.
Boulger, G. S. 1889. *The uses of plants: A manual of economic botany.* London.
Dwyer, Peter D. 1985. Choice and constraint in a Papuan New Guinea food quest. *Human Ecology* 13: 49–70.
Firth, Raymond. 1950. Economics and ritual in sago extraction in Tikopia. *Mankind* 4: 131–43.
Flach, M. 1983. *The sago palm.* Rome.
Isaac, Erich. 1970. *Geography of domestication.* Englewood Cliffs, N.J.
Knight, James Wilfred. 1969. *The starch industry.* Oxford.
Lie, Goan-Hong. 1980. The comparative nutritional roles of sago and cassava in Indonesia. In *Sago: The equatorial swamp as a natural resource,* ed. W. R. Stanton, and M. Flach, 43–55. The Hague.
McCurrach, James C. 1960. *Palms of the world.* New York.
Moore, Harold E., Jr. 1973. Palms in the tropical forest ecosystems of Africa and South America. In *Tropical forest ecosystems in Africa and South America: A comparative review,* ed. Betty J. Meggers, Edward S.

Ayensu, and W. Donald Duckworth, 63–88. Washington, D.C.

Morris, H. S. 1974. In the wake of mechanization: Sago and society in Sarawak. In *Social organization and the applications of anthropology*, ed. Robert J. Smith, 271–301. Ithaca, N.Y.

Murai, Mary, Florence Pen, and Carey D. Miller. 1958. *Some tropical South Pacific island foods: Description, history, use, composition, and nutritive value*. Honolulu.

Ohtsuka, Ryutaro. 1983. *Oriomo Papuans: Ecology of sago-eaters in lowland Papua*. Tokyo.

Ooman, H. A. P. C. 1971. Ecology of human nutrition in New Guinea: Evaluation of subsistence patterns. *Ecology of Food and Nutrition* 1: 1–16.

Peters, F. E. 1957. *Chemical composition of South Pacific foods*. Noumea, New Caledonia.

Platt, B. S. 1977. *Table of representative values of foods commonly used in tropical countries*. London.

Rhoads, James W. 1982. Sago palm management in Melanesia: An alternative perspective. *Archaeology in Oceania* 17: 20–4ff.

Ruddle, Kenneth. 1977. Sago in the new world. In *Sago-76: Papers of the first international sago symposium*, ed. Koonlin Tan, 53–64. Kuala Lumpur.

Ruddle, Kenneth, Dennis Johnson, Patricia K. Townsend, and John D. Rees. 1978. *Palm sago: A tropical starch from marginal lands*. Honolulu.

Stanton, W. R., and M. Flach. 1980. *Sago: The equatorial swamp as a natural resource*. The Hague.

Tan, Koolin. 1977. *Sago-76: Papers on the first international sago symposium*. Kuala Lumpur.

1980. Logging the swamp for food. In *Sago: The equatorial swamp as a national resource*, ed. W. R. Stanton and M. Flach, 13–34. The Hague.

Whitmore, Timothy. C. 1973. *Palms of Malaya*. Kuala Lumpur.

Wilbert, Johannes. 1976. *Manicaria saccifera* and its cultural significance among the Waroa Indians of Venezuela. *Botanical Museum Leaflets* 24: 275–335.

II.B.5 ✎ Sweet Potatoes and Yams

The sweet potato (*Ipomoea batatas,* Lam.) and the yams (genus *Dioscorea*) are root crops that today nurture millions of people within the world's tropics. Moreover, they are plants whose origin and dispersals may help in an understanding of how humans manipulated and changed specific types of plants to bring them under cultivation. Finally, these cultivars are important as case studies in the diffusion of plant species as they moved around the world through contacts between different human populations.

This chapter reviews the questions surrounding the early dispersals of these plants, in the case of the sweet potato from the New World to the Old, and in the case of yams their transfers within the Old World. In so doing, the sweet potato's spread into Polynesia before European contact is documented, and the issue of its penetration into Melanesia (possibly in pre-Columbian times) and introduction into New Guinea is explored. Finally, the post-Columbian spread of the sweet potato into North America, China, Japan, India, Southeast Asia, and Africa is covered. In addition, a discussion of the domestication and antiquity of two groups of yams, West African and Southeast Asian, is presented, and the spread of these plants is examined, especially the transfer of Southeast Asian varieties into Africa.

The evidence presented in this chapter can be viewed fundamentally as *primary* and *secondary*. Primary evidence consists of physical plant remains in the form of charred tubers, seeds, pollen, phytoliths, or chemical residuals. Secondary evidence, which is always significantly weaker, involves the use of historical documents (dependent on the reliability of the observer), historical linguistics (often impossible to date), stylistically dated pictorial representations (subject to ambiguities of abstract representation), remanent terracing, ditches or irrigation systems (we cannot know which plants were grown), tools (not plant specific), and the modern distribution of these plants and their wild relatives (whose antiquity is unknown).

Sweet potato

The Sweet Potato

In general, studies of the origin of domesticated plants have first attempted to establish genetic relationships between these plants and some wild ancestor. In the case of the sweet potato, all evidence employed by previous archaeological, linguistic, and historical investigators establishes its origins in the New World.

The remains of tubers excavated from a number of archaeological sites in Peru provide the most persuasive evidence for this conclusion. The oldest evidence discovered to date is from the central coast region at Chilca Canyon where excavated caves, called Tres

Ventanas, yielded remains of potato (*Solanum* sp.), of jicama *(Achirhizus tuberosus)*, and of sweet potato *(Ipomoea batatas)* (Engel 1970: 56). The tubers were recovered from all levels, including a level in Cave 1 dated to around 8080 B.C.

These plants were identified by Douglas Yen who could not determine if they were wild or cultivated species, although he observed that wild tuber-bearing sweet potatoes today are unknown (Yen 1976: 43). Whether they ever existed is another matter, but at least the findings in these cases suggest the consumption of "wild" sweet potato at 8000 B.C. in Peru, or more radically, a domesticated variety (Hawkes 1989: 488). If the latter is the case, sweet potatoes would be very ancient in the New World, raising the possibility that perhaps sweet potatoes were the earliest major crop plant anywhere in the world.

Sweet potato remains were also present at a Preceramic site, Huaynuma, dating around 2000 B.C., and at an Initial Period site, Pampa de las Llamas-Moxeke in the Casma Valley, dating from around 1800 to 1500 B.C. (Ugent, Pozorski, and Pozorski 1981: 401-15). In addition, remains have been found at the Early Ceramic Tortugas site in the Casma Valley (Ugent and Peterson 1988: 5).

Still other sweet potato remains in Peru were discovered at Ventanilla, dating from around 2000 to 1200 B.C., the Chillon Valley (Patterson and Lanning 1964: 114), the central coast in the third phase of the Ancon sequence dating 1400 to 1300 B.C. (Patterson and Moseley 1968: 120), and the third Colinas phase dating 1300 to 1175 B.C. (Patterson and Mosely 1968: 121).

Thus, archaeological evidence gives a date of *at least* 2000 B.C. for the presence of the domesticated sweet potato in the New World, while suggesting a possible domesticated form as early as 8000 B.C.

The Botanical Data

In the past, a precise identification of the ancestor of the sweet potato was hampered by a lack of taxonomic concordance. However, Daniel Austin's proposal (1978: 114-29) of a Batatas complex with eleven closely related species represents a significant revision. With other species it includes *I. trifida*, which is often identified as the key species for the origin of *Ipomoea batatas* (Orjeda, Freyre, and Iwanaga 1990: 462-7). In fact, an *I. trifida* complex, to include all plants of the section Batatas that could cross with *I. batatas*, has been proposed (Kobayashi 1984: 561-9).

In the early 1960s, a wild Mexican species of *Ipomoea* (No. K-123) that was cross-compatible and easily hybridized in reciprocal crosses was identified (Nishiyama 1961: 138, 1963: 119-28). Though it resembled the sweet potato, it lacked domesticated traits (Nishiyama 1961: 138, 1963: 119-28). Cytological studies showed K-123 had a chromosome number

(n = 45) similar to the sweet potato, and it was identified as *I. trifida* (Nishiyama, Miyazakim, and Sakamoto 1975: 197-208). One concern with K-123 was that it might be a feral sweet potato (Austin 1983: 15-25). But other research proposed that *I. leucantha* was crossed with a tetraploid *I. littoralis* to produce the hexaploid *I. trifida*, with the sweet potato selected from this hexaploid (Martin and Jones 1986: 320).

Critical to the debate is the discovery of the natural production of 2*n* pollen in 1 percent of diploid *I. trifida* (Orjeda, Freyre, and Iwanaga 1990: 462-7). The 2*n* pollen is larger than the *n* pollen, and the diploid populations of *I. trifida* exhibit gene flow between diploids and tetraploids (Orjeda, Freyre, and Iwanaga 1990: 462). Fundamentally, crosses between *n* and 2*n* pollens make various 2×, 3×, 4×, 5×, and 6× combinations of the *I. trifida* complex possible and could result in 6× combinations leading to the sweet potato (Orjeda, Freyre, and Iwanaga 1990: 466). The plants exhibiting this feature come predominantly from Colombia in northwest South America (Orjeda, Freyre, and Iwanaga 1990: 463).

While this new evidence shows how the sweet potato could have arisen from *I. trifida*, the present evidence fails to account for the enlarged storage tuber, nonclimbing vines, red periderm color, and orange roots of the sweet potato (Martin and Jones 1986: 322). It is interesting to note the report of Masashi Kobayashi (1984: 565) that some Colombian varieties of *I. trifida* produce tuberous roots at high elevations. Typically, these plants are found at much lower elevations of between 5 to 20 meters (m) above sea level in Columbia, although some occur at about 1000 m.

Given these observations, it should be mentioned that it is often assumed, after a new species arose through sexual reproduction, that it reached a static stage and that vegetative multiplication has nothing to do with the origin of new forms (Sharma and Sharma 1957: 629). In the various researches into the origin of the sweet potato, investigators have assumed the species arose through sexual reproduction, but karyotypic alterations in somatic cells are common in vegetative reproducing plants, and speciation can occur at those points (Sharma and Sharma 1957: 629). The sweet potato is known to send out roots from the nodes, which will bear small potatoes (Price 1896: 1); therefore, it is possible that karyotypic alterations occurred in the daughter forms, giving rise to new forms, as in some species of *Dioscorea*. This is important because spontaneous mutations occur quite often, and the sweet potato mutates easily using gamma and X rays (Broertjes and van Harten 1978: 70).

In summary, 20 years ago, the singling out of any one species of *Ipomoea* as the ancestral form of the sweet potato represented no more than an educated guess (O'Brien 1972: 343; Yen 1974: 161-70). But today the evidence points strongly to the *I. trifida* complex of plants found in northwestern South America.

Dispersal

Present evidence shows that the sweet potato was introduced into Europe, Asia, Africa, and Australia after Christopher Columbus reached the New World. There is no data to indicate that the plant was known to the ancient civilizations of China, Egypt, Babylon, Persia, Rome, Greece, or India (Cooley 1951: 378), but there is evidence of a pre-Columbian introduction into Oceania. Therefore, in this section, a pre-Columbian and a post-Columbian spread of the sweet potato is outlined, starting with the post-Columbian transfer.

The Post-Columbian Spread

Europe. The sweet potato was introduced into Europe via Spain at the end of the fifteenth century by Christopher Columbus and Gonzolo Fernandez de Oviedo (de Candolle 1959: 55). From this beginning, it spread to the rest of Europe and was called *batata* and *padada* (Cooley 1951: 379).

United States. The sweet potato was brought to Londonderry in New Hampshire by the Scotch-Irish in 1719 (Safford 1925: 223). Yet sweet potatoes are mentioned as growing in Virginia in 1648, and perhaps as early as 1610. Further, they are mentioned in 1781 by Thomas Jefferson (Hedrick 1919: 315). They were also reportedly introduced into New England in 1764, and in 1773 the Indians in the South were reported to be growing them (Hedrick 1919: 315-16).

China. Ping-Ti Ho writes that two theories exist for the introduction of sweet potatoes into China. The first involves an overseas merchant who brought the plants from Luzon, which were given to the governor of Fukien in 1594 to alleviate a famine (Ho 1955: 193). The second claim suggests that sweet potatoes arrived via the southern port of Chang-chou, but no specific date of this alleged introduction is known (Ho 1955: 193). Ping-Ti Ho indicates that whereas the former story may be true, the sweet potato was already in China by 1594, having been observed by 1563 in the western prefecture Ta-li, near Burma (Ho 1955: 193-4). Ho concludes that the introduction could have been either overland or by sea via India and Burma, well before the generally accepted date of 1594.

Japan. An English factory at Hirado was allegedly responsible for first introducing the sweet potato to Japan about 1615. It did not, however, "catch on," and the plant was reintroduced from China in about 1674 to stave off a famine (Simon 1914: 716, 723-4).

India and Southeast Asia. The sweet potato was introduced into India by the Portuguese who brought it to Macão via Brazil (Zavala 1964: 217). Moreover, a Portuguese influence in the spread of the plant to Ambon, Timor, and parts of the northern Moluccas is indicated linguistically, since names for the plant are variations of the word *batata* (Conklin 1963: 132).

In Malaysia the sweet potato is called Spanish tuber (Conklin 1963: 132). In the Philippines it is called *camote* (Merrill 1954: 161-384), whereas in Guam it is called both *camote* and *batat* (Hornell 1946: 41-62; Conklin 1963: 129-36). In the Moluccas and on Cebu it is called *batat* (Merrill 1954: 161-384). The names themselves indicate the source of the plant, since the Portuguese used the Arawak term *(batata)*, whereas the Spanish employed the Nahuatl one *(camote)*.

Africa. Harold Conklin (1963: 129-36) reports that the terms for the sweet potato take the form "*batata, tata, mbatata,* and the like" from much of the African continent south of the Sahara. The other most widespread term is *bombe, bambai, bambaira,* or *bangbe,* with the Indian trade center of Bombay the etymological source of the word and its pronunciation. Names for sweet potato not falling into these categories have a small geographic distribution or are found only in closely related languages, but as lexical entries, they refer to indigenous yams or other root crops. From these data Conklin concludes that the sweet potato was introduced into Africa by the Portuguese from Brazil, probably early in the slave-trade period of the sixteenth century (Conklin 1963: 129-36). In addition, its introduction into West Africa, specifically Angola, probably coincided with Paulo Diasde Novais's charter of colonization in 1571, which included provisions for peasant families from Portugal with "all the seeds and plants which they can take from this kingdom and from the island of São Tomé" (Boxer 1969: 30).

The Portuguese ports of Mozambique probably saw the introduction of the *batata* from India as well, although the presence of the word *batata* cannot always be taken as indicative of a Portuguese association. Their language became the *lingua franca* along the coasts of Africa and Asia (Boxer 1969: 55).

The word *bambai,* by contrast, is obviously linked to the city of Bombay, but that port was not significant in the India trade network until the British acquired it in 1662. Consequently, for the word Bombay to be associated with the sweet potato in Africa suggests either a British connection or possibly Indian clerks and merchants involved with British colonization. Consequently, Bombay's involvement in introducing the sweet potato to Africa could have been as early as the last quarter of the seventeenth century or as late as the nineteenth (O'Brien 1972: 347).

Thus, the evidence seems to suggest that the sweet potato was introduced into Africa by the Portuguese from Brazil and Lisbon in the sixteenth century. A later spread of the plant possibly occurred via British influence in the late seventeenth through nineteenth centuries.

The Pre-Columbian Spread

Polynesia. The traditional view is that the sweet potato was introduced into Polynesia by the Spanish, who brought it to the Philippines in 1521 (Dixon 1932: 41). Moreover, its name in the Philippines, *camote,* is generically related to the Nahuatl *camotl* and *camotili* (Merrill 1954: 317-18). Another point linked to this theory is that the earliest European Pacific explorers, Alvaro de Mendaña and Pedro Fernández de Quiros, did not mention the plant by 1606, although they had visited the Marquesas, Santa Cruz, the Solomons, and New Hebrides (Yen 1973: 32-43).

Yet scholars have also argued that the sweet potato was introduced into Polynesia long before Ferdinand Magellan's 1521 voyage, based on the fact that sweet potatoes were found to be a major part of the economies of the islands located at the points defining the triangle of Polynesia, at the time of their discovery – these being New Zealand in 1769, Hawaii in 1778, and Easter Island in 1722 (Dixon 1932: 45).

Further support for the antiquity of the sweet potato in Polynesia has to do with the very large numbers of varieties found in the South Seas: 48 in New Zealand (Colenso 1880: 31-5), 24 in Hawaii (Handy 1940: 133-5), 16 in the Cook Islands, and 22 in New Guinea (Yen 1961: 368, 371).

Twenty years ago the best evidence to document an early introduction of the sweet potato to Polynesia was historical linguistics that had reconstructed the word for sweet potato in Proto-Polynesian to *kumala* (O'Brien 1972: 349-50). Over the years, other scholars have scrutinized the proposed antiquity of the word for sweet potato, and believe that a Proto-Polynesian origin of the word is plausible (Pawley and Green 1971: 1-35; Biggs 1972: 143-52; Clark 1979: 267-8).

Such linguistic evidence establishes a base line for the antiquity of the sweet potato in Polynesia, and when combined with archaeological information about the peopling of the Pacific, it is possible to hypothesize the approximate time of entry of the plant to the region. Jesse Jennings (1979: 3) suggests a Polynesian presence on Tonga and Samoa around 1100 and 1000 B.C., respectively, with an initial thrust east into the Marquesas by A.D. 300. This early appearance was probably associated with the Lapita penetration of western Polynesia at around 1500 B.C. from Melanesia (Bellwood 1978: 53).

And finally, in the past ten years, another line of secondary evidence has been investigated in New Zealand, where prehistoric storage facilities and manmade soils had been discovered (Leach 1979: 241-8, 1984, 1987: 85-94).

However, much *primary evidence* also exists to indicate a pre-Columbian introduction of the sweet potato into Polynesia.

Hawaiian Islands. Archaeological evidence for antiquity of the sweet potato in Hawaii has been found in the form of a carbonized tuber from a fireplace within a "middle" phase domestic structure at Lapakahi. The fireplace is dated A.D. 1655 ± 90 with a corrected date of A.D. 1635 ± 90 or A.D. 1515 ± 90, giving a range of A.D. 1425 to 1765 (Rosendahl and Yen 1971: 381-3). James Cook visited Hawaii in 1778, and so it would seem that this tuber was incinerated at least 13 years prior to his arrival and potentially as many as 263 years before.

Easter Island. The sweet potato was the major crop plant on Easter Island when it was discovered by Jacob Roggeveen in 1722. Charred remains of the plant were recovered there from a fireplace dating A.D. 1526 ± 100 (Skjolsvold 1961: 297, 303). This gives a range between A.D. 1426 to 1626, making the plant remains pre-European by at least 96 years.

New Zealand. In New Zealand, Maori traditions of reconstructing lineage genealogies back to A.D. 1350 recount the arrival of some mysterious "fleet" with the sweet potato and other domesticated plants and animals aboard (Golson 1959: 29-74). Archaeological evidence for the early presence of the sweet potato may exist in the form of ancient storage pits. Jack Golson, for example, (1959: 45) has argued that pits excavated at the fourteenth-century Sarahs Gully site, may have been storage pits for sweet potatoes (kumara). To R. Garry Law (1969: 245) as well, sites like Kaupokonui, Moturua Island, Skippers Ridge, and Sarahs Gully give evidence of widespread kumara agriculture by A.D. 1300.

Primary archaeological evidence was furnished by Helen Leach (1987: 85) with her discovery of charred sweet potato tubers in a burned pit at a *pa* site from (N15/44) the Bay of Islands. Locally called "Haratua's pa," the site is prehistoric, as are the charred sweet potatoes, a point that seems to confirm that these pits were used to store them (Sutton 1984: 33-5).

In addition to the charred tubers at the Bay of Islands, a single charred tuber was discovered at Waioneke, South Kaipara (Leach 1987: 85), a "classic" Maori site 100 to 300 years old (Rosendahl and Yen 1971: 380). Helen Leach (personal communication, letter dated 13 Feb. 1992) notes that no European artifacts were present, and therefore she considers "these kumara pre-European in origin."

Central Polynesia. The most exciting recent evidence dealing with the antiquity of the sweet potato in Polynesia is the discovery of charred *kumara* tubers at site MAN-44 on Margaia Island in the Cook Island group dated at A.D. 1000 (Hather and Kirch 1991: 887-93). The presence of charred remains this early seems to establish beyond doubt a pre-Columbian introduction into Polynesia.

Micronesia. In the Carolinas, infrared spectroscopy analyses of organic residues found on pottery has documented the presence of the sweet potato (and taro) at the Rungruw site in the southern part of Yap at about A.D. 50 (Hill and Evans 1989: 419-25). The presence of rice and banana at about 200 B.C. at the same site was also established (Hill and Evans 1989: 419-25). Yap and the Carolinas are near the northern fringe of Melanesia.

Melanesia. The spread of the sweet potato into Melanesia appears to be the result of Polynesian and European introduction, with the former probably ancient. When the Solomons were discovered, there was no mention of the plant, although taro and yams were reported (Mendana 1901: 212). Because Polynesians were present in the Solomons, it is possible that they brought the plant, since the word *kumala* is found in Melanesian pidgin on the islands (O'Brien 1972: 356).

The term *kumala* is used in New Caledonia and may be pre-European (Hollyman 1959: 368). The sweet potato was in this area in 1793 (Hollyman 1959: 368), and was grown, in lesser quantities than present, in precontact Fiji (Frazer 1964: 148). Finally, there is evidence of the plant's presence in the New Hebrides at the time of discovery (Dixon 1932: 42-3).

New Guinea. New Guinea is the one region of Oceania where the sweet potato is of profound economic importance today. It is more widely grown in the western part of the island than in the east (Damm 1961: 209) and is of great importance in the highlands of Irian New Guinea (Damm 1961: 209). Among the inhabitants of Wantoat Valley in highland Papua, the sweet potato is the only important cultivated food (Damm 1961: 212-3).

Dating the introduction of the sweet potato into New Guinea, however, is a problem. Some historical data point to a late entry. For example, it was introduced into the Morehead district by missionaries (Damm 1961: 210) and was even more recently introduced to the Frederick-Hendrick Island region (Serpenti 1965: 38). Moreover, a survey of plants and animals in 1825-6 revealed no sweet potatoes on the islands west of New Guinea, on the island of Lakor, on the Arru and Tenimber islands, and the southwest coast of Dutch New Guinea (Kolff 1840). The plant ecologist L. J. Brass has suggested that the sweet potato came from the west some 300 years ago, carried by birds of paradise and by hunters and traders in the Solomons region (Watson 1965: 439), which may point to a European introduction.

Introduction to the South Pacific

The primary evidence available today suggests that the sweet potato had a prehistoric introduction into Polynesia and Micronesia at around the time of Christ, while the linguistic evidence points to its presence during Proto-Polynesian times. If Proto-Polynesian was the language of the Lapita culture populations, then the sweet potato was present in Oceania possibly as early as 1500 B.C. Given these new data, the next question must be about the mechanism that facilitated its transfer into Oceania at this early date, since the plant is definitely a New World species.

In attempting to answer that question, a number of researchers over the years have been struck by the similarity between the Polynesian words for sweet potato *(kumala, kumara)* and the word *cumara* found in some Quechua language dictionaries (Brand 1971: 343-65). This, in turn, has led to the suggestion that the sweet potato came to Polynesia from Peru, with Quechua speakers playing some role.

Alternately, Donald Brand (1971: 343-65) argues that the word was Polynesian and introduced into the Andes by the Spanish. He notes that archaeologists, historians, and philologists consider coastal Ecuador, Peru, and Chile to have been occupied by non-Quechuan and non-Aymaran people until shortly before the arrival of the Spanish. The languages spoken would have been Sek, Yungan, and Chibchan, and their terms for sweet potato were *chapru, open,* and *unt.* The Quechua word is *apichu* and is reported along with the words *batatas, ajes,* and *camotes* in the literature and dictionaries of Peru, whereas the word *cumara* is found only in dictionaries, and *cumar* proper occurs only in the Chichasuyo dialect of Quechua (Brand 1971: 361-2).

If it is true that the Spanish introduced the word, then one need not explain its presence in Polynesia as the result of people going or coming from the New World. And if the word *kumala* is Proto-Polynesia, then the term was created by the Polynesians for a plant in their cosmos.

But this still leaves the question of how it might have entered that cosmos. Since the tuber cannot float at all, let alone the thousands of miles separating Oceania and northwest South America, only two explanations appear possible: Transference was accomplished by either a human or a nonhuman agent.

A human agency might have involved a vessel with sweet potatoes aboard drifting from the New World and being cast upon one of the islands of western Polynesia, like Samoa. If any members of the crew survived, they might well have passed along the South American name for the plant. On the other hand, if an empty vessel reached an inhabited island, it would have been examined along with its cargo, and the sweet potato, looking a great deal like a yam, might have been treated like one until its particular features were known. Finally, during a vessel's long drift, rain water might have accumulated within it, in which case the tubers would have begun to grow, taking hold first in the vessel and then in the soil of some uninhabited island, ultimately becoming feral. Later people finding both the island and the plants would have redomesticated and named them.

An alternative possibility would be transfer by a natural agent. Sweet potato tubers cannot float, but its seeds are more mobile, making birds a likely vehicle. Indeed, Douglas Yen (1960: 373) has suggested the possibility of birds as an agent, and Ralph Bulmer (1966: 178-80) has examined the role of birds in introducing new varieties of sweet potato into gardens in New Guinea by dropping seeds. Bulmer observed that the golden plover, a bird that ranges over Polynesia, is a casual visitor to the west coast of the Americas as far south as Chile. These birds are strong fliers and could have carried the small, hard sweet potato seeds either in their digestive tracts or adhering to mud on their feet.

Another potential nonhuman agent was proposed by J. W. Purseglove (1965: 382-3), who noted that some species of *Ipomoea* are strand plants and are distributed by sea. He points out that dried sweet potato capsules with several seeds can float. Because the Polynesian sweet potatoes are very distinctive, he suggests that this distinctiveness is the predictable result of an introduction by a few seeds. Purseglove also observes that introduced crop plants have a considerable advantage if major pests and diseases have not been transferred.

At present, all of these scenarios are only speculative, but an accidental introduction would explain how the plant reached the area early, and yet account for the absence of other useful New World products (manioc, maize, and so forth), which might have been transferred if any sustained exchange between living people had been involved.

The Yams

Although a number of wild members of *Dioscorea* are edible, there are four domesticated yams that are important to agricultural development: *D. alata* and *D. esculenta* from Southeast Asia, and *D. rotundata* and *D. cayenensis* from West Africa. A fifth domesticated yam, *D. trifida*, is found in the New World (Hawkes 1989: 489), but was not especially significant because of the presence of the sweet potato, manioc (cassava), and potato (Coursey 1975: 194) and, thus, has not been a specific focus of research.

The Southeast Asian varieties are interesting because aspects of their spread into Polynesia can be linked to the spread of the sweet potato, whereas African varieties are significant for the role they played in the development of the kingdoms of West Africa. Like the sweet potato, there is no evidence of the use of yams in classical antiquity, but historical data point to their presence in China in the third century A.D. and in India by A.D. 600 (Coursey 1967: 13-14).

The Botanical Data

The family *Dioscoroeaceae* has hundreds of species, and the *Dioscorea* is its largest genus. In general, the New World members have chromosome numbers that are multiples of nine and the Old World species

multiples of ten (Ayensu and Coursey 1972: 304). The section including the food yams typically has $2n = 40$, but higher degrees of polyploidy do occur (Coursey 1967: 43-4). For example, *D. alata* has $2n = 30$ to 80; *D. esculenta* has $2n = 40, 60, 90, 100$; *D. rotundata* has $2n = 40$; and *D. cayenensis* has $2n = 40, 60$, and 140. *D. trifida*, the New World domesticated yam, has $2n = 54, 72$, and 81 (Coursey 1976a: 71).

The two yams domesticated in Southeast Asia have been major constituents (along with taro, plantains, bananas and breadfruit) of root crop agriculture in the region, and throughout Oceania before European contact. According to D. G. Coursey (1967: 45), *D. alata*, or the "greater yam," is native to Southeast Asia and developed from either *D. hamiltonii* Hook. or *D. persimilis* Prain et Burk. It is unknown in the wild state and today is the major yam grown throughout the world (Coursey 1967: 45-6). *D. esculenta*, or the "lesser yam," is a native of Indochina, has smaller tubers than the "greater yam" (Coursey 1967: 51-2), and occurs in both wild and domesticated forms (Coursey 1976a: 71). The two native African yams, probably ennobled in the yam belt of West Africa, are *D. rotundata* Poir., the white Guinea yam, and *D. cayenensis* Lam., the yellow Guinea yam (Coursey 1967: 11, 48, 58). The most prominent English-speaking scholars to work on the genus *Dioscorea* have been I. H. Burkill and D. G. Coursey (1976b, 1980; see also Coursey 1967: 28 for further discussion). Indeed, Coursey, the preeminent yam ethnobotanist, has developed a detailed theory of their domestication and antiquity in Africa.

Nonetheless, African yams have not received the attention of plant scientists that they need and deserve, especially in terms of cytological research and breeding programs (Broertjes and van Harten 1978: 73-4). This omission is particularly regrettable in light of their ancient importance, but is doubtless the result of yams being displaced by New World cultivars like maize, sweet potato, and manioc in many parts of Africa.

The lack of botanical research, however, allows plenty of room for controversy. For example, some botanists separate West African yams into two species, whereas others argue that there are insufficient criteria (basically, tuber flesh color) to separate them. They suggest the existence of a *D. cayenensis-rotundata* complex under the rubric of one species, *D. cayenensis* (Miege 1982: 377-83).

D. G. Coursey, as mentioned, identifies the two yams as *D. rotundata* Poir., and *D. cayenensis* Lam. (Coursey 1967: 11, 48, 58). He suggests that the former is unknown in the wild, being a true cultigen, and it may have developed from *D. praehensilis* Benth. (Coursey 1967: 59). The latter, however, is found in both a wild and domesticated condition (Coursey 1967: 48), which may indicate that the wild *D. cayenensis* is the ancestor of the domesticated *D. cayenensis*.

J. Miege (1982: 380–1) states that *D. cayenensis* is a complex cultigen most probably made up of several wild species: *D. praehensilis* Benth. for the forest varieties; and *D. sagittifolia* Pax., *D. lecardii* De Wild., *D. liebrechtsiana* De Wild., and *D. abyssinica* Hochst. ex. Kunth for the savanna and preforest types. An implication of the argument that these two domesticated species are but subspecies of *D. cayenensis* is that both the white and yellow Guinea yams could have risen from wild forms of *D. cayenensis*.

Clearly, such uncertainties will only be resolved by concerted research focused not only upon taxonomic issues but especially on cytological ones. A whole series of breeding and cross-breeding studies are essential, and it would be particularly useful to determine whether *Dioscorea* polyploidy is related to $2n$ pollen as it is in *Ipomoea*.

Transformation and Dispersal

As we noted, the four major domesticated yams come from Southeast Asia and West Africa, respectively. This section examines data, primary and secondary, for their antiquity and their movement throughout the world.

Southeast Asia. In the late 1960s, charred and uncharred botanical material was recovered from excavations at Spirit Cave in Thailand. It was associated with the Hoabinhian complex, dated to around 10,000 to 7000 B.C., and was used to argue for the early development of agriculture in Southeast Asia (Gorman 1969, 1970). Later, however, these materials were critically reexamined by Yen (1977: 567–99), who concluded that most of the remains were not domesticates. Yen thought that early yam domestication could not be inferred from these remains, but that it was probably reasonable to suspect that wild yam was being eaten at that time (Yen 1977: 595).

The fundamental evidence for the antiquity of domesticated Southeast Asian yams and other cultivars is linguistic and lies within words for the whole assemblage of plants and animals making up Southeast Asian root crop agriculture. Robert Blust, a linguist, notes (1976: 36) that Proto-Austronesian speakers had pigs, fowl, and dogs and cultivated a variety of root and tree crops including taro, yams, sago, breadfruit, sugarcane, and banana (Blust 1976: Table II.B.6.1). The linguist Ross Clark reports that words for all the crop plants important in Polynesia horticulture – yam, taro, bananas, sugarcane, and sweet potato – reconstruct to Proto-Polynesian (Clark 1979: 267–8). In relation to this, it should be mentioned that a Lapita site on Fiji, dating between 1150 to 600 B.C., has primary evidence for aspects of this economy in the form of bones of dogs, chickens, and pigs (Hunt 1981: 260).

Helen Leach (1984: 20–1) believes that a series of 21 roundish holes about 35 centimeters (cm) in diameter and some 60 cm deep excavated within a 33 square meter area at Mt. Olo in Samoa implies yam cultivation, for she reports that large yams on Fiji and in other parts of Melanesia are planted in individual holes 60 cm in diameter and 45 cm deep. She also argues for the antiquity of root crop agriculture at Palliser Bay in New Zealand through indirect evidence such as storage pits, garden boundaries, old ditches, and "made-soils" (Leach 1984: 35–41). Susan Bulmer (1989: 688–705) makes these same points, but emphasizes the importance of forest clearance, which in New Zealand appears as early as A.D. 400. Indeed, the antiquity of root crop agriculture in New Guinea is documented by this same type of indirect evidence, and Jack Golson outlines a five-phase model of agricultural development and intensification based upon a whole series of field drainage systems that can be dated as early as 7000 B.C (Golson 1977: 601–38).

In sum, the evidence, though more indirect than direct, supports the notion that the domestication of the Southeast Asian yams, *D. alata* and *D. esculenta*, is very ancient, maybe as early as 4500 B.C. This being the case, what of their dispersal?

The first dispersal is clearly associated with its transfer by Proto-Austronesian–speaking peoples throughout the Southeast Asian tropical world. However, the diffusion of these people is in some dispute. For example, Peter Bellwood (1985: 109) argues that the original Pre-Austronesians were located in Taiwan, whence they moved to the Philippines and from there to parts of Indonesia like Borneo, Java, Sumatra, and Malaya, then into the Moluccas, and finally into New Guinea and Oceania (Melanesia, Micronesia, and Polynesia). But Wilhelm Solheim (1988: 80–2) suggests that Pre-Austronesians developed around 5000 B.C. in Mindanao and the northeast Indonesia regions. He argues against Taiwan as a homeland because of the difficulties posed by winds and currents for sailing south to the Philippines. William Meacham (1988: 94–5), however, considers the languages of south China to have been Mon-Khmer, not Austronesian, and argues that these people could not have migrated to Taiwan and from there south into the Philippines. Rather, Meacham suggests, the homeland of the Proto-Austronesians is somewhere in the triangle defined by Taiwan, Sumatra, and Timor, basically encompassing modern Indonesia.

Regardless of which theory of a Proto-Austronesian homeland is correct, once the Proto-Oceanic languages of that family began to differentiate, they also began to provide linguistic evidence for yams and other cultivars. Thus, yams were in Melanesia by 2000 B.C., in Micronesia by 2000 to 1000 B.C., and in eastern Polynesia by 1500 B.C. The bulk of western Polynesia received yam horticulture (depending on when a specific island group was occupied) sometime between A.D. 1 and 1000 (Bellwood 1985: 121).

In addition, the transfer of Southeast Asian yams with Austronesian speakers to regions outside this early core area is documented. They were present in China in the third century A.D. and in India by A.D. 600 (Coursey 1967: 13–14). To the west, yams were introduced (principally *D. alata*) into Madagascar, probably between the eleventh and fifteenth centuries A.D. By the end of the sixteenth century, *D. alata* was grown in West Africa, from whence it was transferred to the New World by a Dutch slaver in 1591 (Coursey 1967: 15–6).

Africa. The student of African yams, D. G. Coursey, argues (1967: 13; 1975: 203; 1976a: 72) that the use of *D. cayenensis* and *D. rotundata* is ancient, and he proposes the following scenario for the process of yam domestication in West Africa (1980: 82–5). He suggests:

1. that hunter-gatherers, before 60,000 B.P. (before the present), utilized many species of wild yam;
2. that the Sangoan and Lupemban Paleolithic stone industries, c. 45,000 to 15,000 B.P., developed hoes or picks to excavate hypogeous plants, including the yams, and at this time started to develop ritual concepts and sanctions to protect these and other plants;
3. that sometime around 11,000 B.P., with the contraction of West Africa forest and savanna environments and appearance of proto-Negro people, microlithic industries developed which point to new human/environment interactions; these interactions involved selection and protection of favored species, particularly nontoxic yams; and this greater control led to population increases, movement into forest environments and a planting of wild plants – a "protoculture" with a final result being the understanding that one could replant stored tubers;
4. that by 5,000 to 4,000 B.P. Neolithic grain-crop people from the Sahara belt, influenced by Middle Eastern agriculturalists, moved south and interacted with yam "protoculturalists" and from this relationship yam-based agriculture developed;
5. and finally, around 2,500 B.P., with the advent of ironworking, West Africa people could expand deeper into the forest which ecologically favored yam over grain crops, and yam growing populations could achieve numerical superiority over grain farmers and create complex culture systems.

Although this model seems reasonable for the most part, the problems of documenting the domestication of West African yams are similar, and in some cases identical, to those associated with Southeast Asia. Here, too, primary evidence is lacking (Shaw 1976: 108–53).

Preliminary research on yam ennoblement, which was begun in 1977 in Nigeria, has led to the discovery that digging wild yams even with modern tools like machetes, shovels, and spades, let alone digging sticks, was arduous work (Chikwendu and Okezie 1989:

345). Wild yams could not be excavated like domesticated ones. They have long, sharp thorns all over their roots, and in addition to cutting through the yam roots, one has to cut through the tangled roots of the forest itself. A pick-like tool would only get caught between the roots. Trenching around a yam patch was the best procedure, but it still took several days just to dig up the first yam (Chikwendu and Okezie 1989: 345). This finding in turn casts some doubt on Coursey's proposal (1967: 13, 1975: 203) that the pick-like stone tools and Lupemban "hoes" of the Sangoan period were used for grubbing yams.

As with research on the Southeast Asian yams, indirect evidence like forest clearance and linguistics is our main avenue of inference. M. A. Sowunmi (1985: 127–9) reports significant changes in pollen counts from a Niger Delta soil core occurring around 850 B.C. He notes a sudden increase in oil-palm pollen and an increase in weed pollens associated with cultivated land, accompanied by a decrease in pollen of rain forest components, such as *Celtis* sp. and *Myrianthus arboreus*. Because there is no evidence of environmental change at that time, he concludes that humans artificially opened the forest for agricultural purposes. Because oil palm and yams are the main cultivars of aboriginal West African agriculture, he believes that these data document their appearance on a large scale.

It should be noted that, on the one hand, iron hoes, axes, and knives appeared in Nigeria (with the Nok complex) only about 300 years later, around 550 B.C. On the other hand, the site of Iwo Eleru has polished groundstone axes, dating as early as 4000 B.C., that could have been used in forest clearance, and Coursey (1967: 197–205, 1976b: 397) argues that yams were grown before the development of an iron technology because many of the peoples of West Africa have strong prohibitions against the use of iron tools in their important New Yam festivals.

Linguistics, as mentioned, is another source of information. Kay Williamson's study (1970: 156–67) of names for food plants within the Kwa Branch of the Niger-Congo family (spoken in the Niger Delta region) isolated "three main layers of names; ancient West African plants, crops of the Malaysian complex introduced long ago, and more recent introductions over the last five hundred years" (Williamson 1970: 163). The oil palm and the yam (*D. cayenensis-rotundata* complex) belong to the oldest layer; the banana, plantain, and water yam (*D. alata*) occurred in the Malaysian layer; and such plants as maize and manioc (cassava) are more recent introductions from the New World some five hundred years ago.

Williamson does not assess the antiquity of the words for yam and oil palm in calendar years, but P. J. Darling (1984: 65) proposes that the Proto-Kwa language dates from between 4,000 and 10,000 years ago. Although he calls these Proto-Kwa speakers Late-Stone-Age hunter-gatherers, it seems clear that as they had words for major domesticated plants, they must already have been farmers. It is interesting that the more recent end of this date range matches Coursey's model for yam "protoculturalists" quite well. Finally, Proto-Niger-Congo not only has the word for yam (and cow and goat) but also the root meaning "to cultivate," and Proto-Niger-Congo may date back to at least 6000 B.C. (Ehret 1984: 29–30).

Thus, the evidence, though indirect, does point to the existence of yam usage and the concept of cultivation at around 6000 B.C. and forest clearance at about 850 B.C., presumably for the purpose of producing oil palms and yams on a wider scale. All of this in turn suggests an antiquity for agriculture in Africa far greater than believed by many scholars, which probably can best be explained in terms of an independent agricultural development in West Africa. Yet the West African yams had no dispersal beyond their region of origin until they were transferred to the tropical New World in association with the slave trade.

Summary

Three main waves of dispersal are associated with the spread of the sweet potato, in what Yen (1982: 20–1) calls the *kumara, kamote,* and *batatas* lines of transfer. The best-known and documented transfer was the post-Columbian spread via Europeans associated with the latter two lines. The Spanish, or *kamote* line, introduced the sweet potato into Europe, the Philippines, Guam, and Malaysia. From the Philippines it was then carried to China and from China ultimately to Japan. English immigrants transmitted it to the United States, English traders brought it to Japan (though it was not accepted), and English missionaries introduced it in parts of Melanesia and Australian New Guinea.

The Portuguese, or *batatas* line, introduced the sweet potato into India and Africa, Ambon, Timor, the northern Moluccas, and Cebu. The African introduction was from the Portuguese into Angola and Mozambique, as well as to Africa via Bombay through English associations with that trade center in India. Apparently the plant was carried from Burma to China after the Indian introduction.

The *kumara* line, the earliest, is associated with the appearance of the sweet potato in Oceania. This transfer has intrigued scholars for years. New primary evidence, combined with linguistic and historical data, point to a pre-Columbian spread somewhere into eastern Polynesia or even into northern Melanesia by the time of Christ. From this region the plant spread to all points of the Polynesia triangle. It then moved to parts of Melanesia via the Polynesians, and traveled from Melanesia into New Guinea. The transfer into New Guinea was probably accomplished by Melanesians, possibly bird of paradise hunters or migrants settling on the southeast coast. Though some specific areas of New Guinea received the plant from

Europeans, in general it was first spread by Melanesians and then by Papuans from the coast into the highlands, probably through the Markham Valley. The way in which early sweet potatoes reached New Guinea cannot presently be determined, but in the light of the Yap data it could be earlier then generally supposed.

The establishment of the sweet potato in many areas of Micronesia, parts of central Polynesia, and sections of Dutch New Guinea, including Lakor and the Arru and Tenimber islands, was prevented by ecological conditions unsuitable to its growth.

Yams also had several waves of dispersal. The Southeast Asian yams moved through the region beginning about 4500 B.C, and on into Oceania by 1500 B.C. They arrived in India and China in the first millennium A.D., and early in the second millennium entered Madagascar. From East Africa they moved to West Africa by the sixteenth century, and at the end of the sixteenth century came to the tropical New World.

General Conclusions

This survey on the problem of the origin and dispersal of the sweet potato and of yams indicates the following. First, the sweet potato originated in northwestern South America around 8000 B.C., in association with the initial development of tropical-forest root crop agriculture. The actual botanical ancestor is probably the result of various n and $2n$ crosses within the *I. trifida* complex.

Primary evidence of the pre-Magellan introduction of the sweet potato into central Polynesia is established at around A.D. 1000, and even earlier, A.D. 50, in Micronesia on Yap. When combined with the archaeology of Oceania, these data suggest, conservatively, that the plant arrived in eastern Polynesia, maybe in the Fiji area, by about 500 B.C. Alternatively, the plant was dispersed by Lapita people sometime between 1500 to 500 B.C. during their movement through Melanesia. From Melanesia it was carried to New Guinea by Melanesians at an unknown date, but this could have taken place prior to the arrival of the Europeans.

The transference between Polynesia and the New World would seem to have been the result of either human accident or natural causes. An introduction by the casting up of a vessel upon some island of eastern Polynesia is possible, but it is equally possible that the plant was spread by natural agents, such as birds carrying seeds or by floating seed capsules. Both these hypotheses need further examination.

The post-European introduction of the sweet potato into Africa, North America, Europe, India, China, Japan, the Philippines, the Moluccas, and other islands in the Indonesian area was the result of Spanish, Portuguese, and English trade, exploration, colonization, and missionization.

The five ennobled yams were domesticated in Southeast Asia, West Africa, and tropical America, respectively, although the last region is not especially important to this study. Southeast Asian yams were probably domesticated before 4500 B.C., whereas the West African yams could be as old as 6000 B.C. but were probably domesticated by the first millennium B.C. The possible botanical ancestors of these yams are a subject of debate, and considerable cytological and taxonomic research is needed before this issue will be resolved. Needless to say, these ancestors will be found to have been native to each respective area.

Patricia J. O'Brien

I wish to thank Dr. Roger Green of the University of Auckland, Dr. Helen Leach of the University of Otago, Dr. Patrick V. Kirch of the University of California at Berkeley, and Dr. Donald Ugent of Southern Illinois University for kindly answering my questions about their research, and also for generously sharing with me reprints of their work.

Bibliography

Austin, Daniel F. 1978. The *Ipomoea batatas* complex - I. Taxonomy. *Bulletin of the Torrey Botanical Club* 105: 114-29.
    1983. Variability in sweet potatoes in America. In *Breeding new sweet potatoes in the tropics,* ed. F. W. Martin, 15-25. Mayaguez, P.R.
Ayensu, Edward S., and D. G. Coursey. 1972. Guinea yams, the botany, ethnobotany, use and possible future of yams in West Africa. *Economic Botany* 26: 301-18.
Bellwood, Peter. 1978. *The Polynesians: Prehistory of an island people.* London.
    1985. *Prehistory of the Indo-Malaysian archipelago.* Sydney.
    1991. The Austronesian dispersal and the origin of languages. *Scientific American* 265: 88-93.
Biggs, Bruce G. 1972. Implications of linguistic subgrouping with special reference to Polynesia. In *Studies in oceanic culture history,* Vol. 3, ed. R. C. Green and M. Kelly, 143-52. Honolulu.
Blust, Robert. 1976. Austronesian culture history: Some linguistic inferences and their relations to the archaeological record. *World Archaeology* 8: 19-43.
Boxer, C. R. 1969. *Four centuries of Portuguese expansion, 1415-1825: A succinct survey.* Berkeley, Calif.
Braidwood, Robert J. 1960. The agricultural revolution. *Scientific American* 203: 130-48.
Brand, Donald D. 1971. The sweet potato: An exercise in methodology. In *Man across the sea,* ed. C. L. Riley, J. C. Kelley, C. W. Pennington, and R. L. Rands, 343-65. Austin, Tex.
Broertjes, C., and A. M. van Harten. 1978. *Application of mutation breeding methods in the improvement of vegetatively propagated crops.* Amsterdam.
Bulmer, Ralph. 1966. Birds as possible agents in the propagation of the sweet potato. *The Emu* 65: 165-82.
Bulmer, Susan. 1989. Gardens in the south: Diversity and change in prehistoric Maori agriculture. In *Foraging and farming: The evolution of plant exploitation,* ed. D. R. Harris and G. C. Hillman, 688-705. London.

Candolle, Alphonse de. 1959. *The origin of cultivated plants.* New York.
Carter, George F. 1977. A hypothesis suggesting a single origin of agriculture. In *Origins of agriculture,* ed. C. A. Reed, 89-133. The Hague.
Chang, K. C. 1981. In search of China's beginnings: New light on an old civilization. *American Scientist* 69: 148-60.
Chikwendu, V. E., and C. E. A. Okezie. 1989. Factors responsible for the ennoblement of African yams: Inferences from experiments in yam domestication. In *Foraging and farming,* ed. D. R. Harris and G. C. Hillman, 418-25. London.
Clark, Ross. 1979. Language. In *The prehistory of Polynesia,* ed. J. D. Jennings, 249-70. Cambridge, Mass.
Colenso, W. 1880. On the vegetable food of the ancient New Zealanders. *Transactions of the New Zealand Institute* 13: 3-38.
Conklin, Harold C. 1963. The Oceanian-African hypotheses and the sweet potato. In *Plants and the migrations of Pacific peoples,* ed. J. Barrau, 129-36. Honolulu.
Cooley, J. S. 1951. The sweet potato - its origin and primitive storage practices. *Economic Botany* 5: 378-86.
Coursey, D. G. 1967. *Yams.* London.
    1975. The origins and domestication of yams in Africa. In *Gastronomy: The anthropology of food and food habits,* ed. M. L. Arnott, 187-212. The Hague.
    1976a. Yams. In *Evolution of crop plants,* ed. N. W. Simmonds, 70-4. London.
    1976b. The origins and domestication of yams in Africa. In *Origins of African plant domestication,* ed. J. R. Harlan, J. M. J. de Wet, and A. B. Stemler, 383-408. The Hague.
    1980. The origins and domestication of yams in Africa. In *West African culture dynamics,* ed. B. K. Swartz, Jr., and R. E. Dumett, 67-90. The Hague.
Damm, Hans. 1961. Die Süsskartoffel (Batate) im Leben der Völker Neuguineas. *Zeitschrift für Ethnologie* 84: 208-23.
Darling, P. J. 1984. *Archaeology and history in southern Nigeria,* Part 1. Oxford.
Dillehay, Tom. 1984. A late ice-age settlement in southern Chile. *Scientific American* 251: 106-17.
Dillehay, Tom, and Michael B. Collins. 1988. Early cultural evidence from Monte Verde in Chile. *Nature* 332: 150-2.
Dixon, Roland B. 1932. The problem of the sweet potato in Polynesia. *American Anthropologist* 34: 40-66.
Early Polynesian migration to New Zealand reported. 1966. *New York Times,* May 12.
Ehret, C. 1984. Historical/linguistic evidence for early African food production. In *From hunters to farmers,* ed. J. D. Clark and S. A. Brandt, 26-39. Berkeley, Calif.
Engel, Frederic. 1970. Exploration of the Chilca canyon, Peru. *Current Anthropology* 11: 55-8.
Frazer, Roger M. 1964. Changing Fiji agriculture. *The Australian Geographer* 9: 148-55.
Golson, Jack. 1959. Culture change in prehistoric New Zealand. In *Anthropology in the South Seas,* ed. J. D. Freeman and W. R Geddes, 29-74. New Plymouth, New Zealand.
    1977. No room at the top: Agricultural intensification in the New Guinea highlands. In *Sunda and Sahul,* ed. J. Allen, J. Golson, and R. Jones, 601-38. London.
    1989. The origins and development of New Guinea agriculture. In *Foraging and farming,* ed. D. R. Harris and G. C. Hillman, 678-87. London.
Gorman, C. F. 1969. Hoabinhian: A pebble-tool complex with early plant associations in southeast Asia. *Science* 163: 671-73.

1970. Excavations at Spirit cave, north Thailand: Some interpretations. *Asian Perspectives* 13: 79–108.

Green, Roger. 1979. Lapita. In *The prehistory of Polynesia,* ed. J. D. Jennings, 27–60. Cambridge, Mass.

Groube, Les. 1989. The taming of the rain forests: A model for late Pleistocene forest exploitation in New Guinea. In *Foraging and farming,* ed. D. R. Harris and G. C. Hillman, 292–304. London.

Hallam, Sylvia J. 1989. Plant usage and management in southwest Australian Aboriginal societies. In *Foraging and farming,* ed. D. R. Harris and G. C. Hillman, 136–51. London.

Handy, E. S. C. 1940. *The Hawaiian planter,* Vol. 1. Honolulu.

Harlan, Jack R. 1977. The origins of cereal agriculture in the old world. In *Origins of agriculture,* ed. C. A. Reed, 357–83. The Hague.

Harris, David R. 1972. The origins of agriculture in the tropics. *American Scientist* 60: 180–93.

Hather, Jon, and Patrick V. Kirch. 1991. Prehistoric sweet potato [*Ipomoea batatas*] from Mangaia Island, central Polynesia. *Antiquity* 65: 887–93.

Hawkes, J. G. 1989. The domestication of roots and tubers in the American tropics. In *Foraging and farming,* ed. D. R. Harris and G. C. Hillman, 481–503. London.

Hedrick, U. P. 1919. *Sturtevant's notes on edible plants.* Albany, N.Y.

Hill, H. Edward, and John Evans. 1989. Crops of the Pacific: New evidence from the chemical analysis of organic residues in pottery. In *Foraging and Farming,* ed. D. R. Harris and G. C. Hillman, 418–25. London.

Ho, Ping-Ti. 1955. The introduction of American food plants into China. *American Anthropologist* 57: 191–201.

Ho, Ping-Ti. 1977. The indigenous origins of Chinese agriculture. In *Origins of agriculture,* ed. C. A. Reed, 413–84. The Hague.

Hollyman, K. J. 1959. Polynesian influence in New Caledonia: The linguistic aspects. *Journal of the Polynesian Society* 68: 357–89.

Hornell, James. 1946. How did the sweet potato reach Oceania? *The Journal of the Linnean Society* 53: 41–62.

Hunt, Terry L. 1981. New evidence for early horticulture in Fiji. *Journal of the Polynesian Society* 90: 259–66.

Jennings, Jesse D. 1979. Introduction. In *The prehistory of Polynesia,* ed. J. D. Jennings, 1–5. Cambridge, Mass.

Kobayashi, Masashi. 1984. The *Ipomoea trifida* complex closely related to the sweet potato. In *Symposium of the International Society of Tropical Root Crops,* ed. F. S. Shideler and H. Rincon, 561–9. Lima.

Kolff, D. H. 1840. *Voyages of the Dutch brig-of-war Dourga,* trans. G. W. Earl. London.

Lathrap, Donald W. 1962. Yarinacocha: Stratigraphic excavations in the Peruvian Montana. Ph.D. dissertation, Harvard University.

1970. *The Upper Amazon.* New York.

1977. Our father the cayman, our mother the gourd: Spinden revisited, or a unitary model for the emergence of agriculture. In *Origins of agriculture,* ed. C. A. Reed, 713–52. The Hague.

Law, R. Garry. 1969. Pits and kumara agriculture in the South Island. *Journal of the Polynesian Society* 78: 223–51.

Lawton, H. W., P. J. Wilke, M. DeDecker, and W. M. Mason. 1976. Agriculture among the Paiute of Owens valley. *The Journal of California Anthropology* 3: 13–50.

Leach, Helen M. 1979. The significance of early horticulture in Palliser Bay for New Zealand prehistory. In *Prehistoric man in Palliser Bay,* ed. B. F. Leach and H. M. Leach, 241–48. Wellington.

1984. *1000 years of gardening in New Zealand.* Wellington.

1987. The land, the provider: Gathering and gardening. In *From the beginning,* ed. J. Wilson, 85–94. Wellington.

MacNeish, Richard S. 1964. Ancient Mesoamerican civilization. *Science* 143: 531–537.

1977. The beginnings of agriculture in central Peru. In *Origins of agriculture,* ed. C. A. Reed, 753–801. The Hague.

Marchant, Alexander. 1941. Colonial Brazil as a way station for Portuguese India fleets. *The Geographical Review* 31: 454–65.

Martin, Franklin W., and Alfred Jones. 1986. Breeding sweet potatoes. *Plant Breeding Reviews* 4: 313–45.

Meacham, William. 1988. On the improbability of Austronesian origins in South China. *Asian Perspectives* 26: 89–106.

Mendana, A. de. 1901. *The discovery of the Solomon Islands.* 2 vols. London.

Merrill, Elmer D. 1954. The botany of Cook's voyages. *Chronica Botanica* 14: 161–384.

Miege, J. 1982. Appendix note on the *Dioscorea cayenensis* Lamk. and *D. rotundata* Poir. species. In *Yams/Ignames,* ed. J. Miege and S. N. Lyonga, 377–83. Oxford.

Nishiyama, Ichizo. 1961. The origin of the sweet potato plant. In *Abstracts of Symposium Papers: Tenth Pacific Science Congress,* 137–8. Honolulu.

1963. The origin of the sweet potato plant. In *Plants and the migrations of Pacific peoples,* ed. J. Barrau, 119–28. Honolulu.

Nishiyama, I., T. Miyazakim, and S. Sakamoto. 1975. Evolutionary autoploidy in the sweet potato (*Ipomoea batatas* [L.] Lam.) and its progenitors. *Euphytica* 24: 197–208.

O'Brien, Patricia J. 1972. The sweet potato: Its origin and dispersal. *American Anthropologist* 74: 342–65.

Orjeda, G., R. Freyre, and M. Iwanaga. 1990. Production of 2*n* pollen in diploid *Ipomoea trifida,* a putative wild ancestor of sweet potato. *Journal of Heredity* 81: 462–7.

Patterson, Thomas C., and Edward P. Lanning. 1964. Changing settlement patterns on the central Peruvian coast. *Nawpa Pacha* 2: 113–23.

Patterson, Thomas C., and M. Edward Moseley. 1968. Late preceramic and early ceramic cultures of the central coast of Peru. *Nawpa Pacha* 6: 115–33.

Pawley, Andrew, and Kaye Green. 1971. Lexical evidence for the proto-Polynesian homeland. *Te Reo* 14: 1–35.

Pickersgill, Barbara, and Charles B. Heiser, Jr. 1977. Origins and distribution of plants domesticated in the New World tropics. In *Origins of agriculture,* ed. C. A. Reed, 803–35. The Hague.

Polynesian settlement of New Zealand. 1966. *New Zealand News* 21: 1–8.

Price, R. H. 1896. *Sweet potato culture for profit.* Dallas, Texas.

Purseglove, J. W. 1965. The spread of tropical crops. In *The genetics of colonizing species,* ed. H. G. Baker and G. L. Stebbins, 375–86. New York.

Reynolds, Robert G. 1986. An adaptive computer model for the evolution of plant collecting and early agriculture in the eastern valley of Oaxaca. In *Guila Naquitz,* ed. K. V. Flannery, 263–89. Orlando, Fla.

Roosevelt, A. C., R. A. Housley, M. Imazio da Silveira, et al. 1991. Eighth millennium pottery from a prehistoric shell midden in the Brazilian Amazon. *Science* 254: 1621–4.

Rosendahl, P., and D. E. Yen. 1971. Fossil sweet potato

remains from Hawaii. *Journal of the Polynesian Society* 80: 379-85.

Safford, William E. 1925. The potato of romance and of reality. *Journal of Heredity* 16: 217-29.

Saggers, Sherry, and Dennis Gray. 1984. The 'Neolithic problem' reconsidered: Human-plant relationships in northern Australia and New Guinea. *Asian Perspectives* 25: 99-125.

Sauer, Carl O. 1952. *Agricultural origins and dispersals.* New York.

Schmitz, Carl A. 1960. *Historische Probleme in nordost New Guinea.* Wiesbaden.

Schoenwetter, James. 1990. Lessons from an alternative view. In *Powers of observation: Alternative views in archeology,* ed. S. M. Nelson and A. B. Kehoe, 103-12. Washington, D.C.

Schoenwetter, James, and Landon Douglas Smith. 1986. Pollen analysis of the Oaxaca archaic. In *Guila Naquitz,* ed. K. V. Flannery, 179-238. Orlando, Fla.

Serpenti, L. M. 1965. *Cultivators in the swamp: Social structure and horticulture in a New Guinea society.* Assen, Netherlands.

Sharma, A. K., and Archana Sharma. 1957. Vegetatively reproducing plants - their means of speciation. *Science and Culture* 22: 628-30.

Shaw, Thurston. 1976. Early crops in Africa: A review of the evidence. In *Origins of African plant domestication,* ed. J. R. Harlan, J. M. J. de Wet, and A. B. L. Stemler, 108-53. The Hague.

1978. *Nigeria: Its archaeology and early history.* London.

Simon, Edmund. 1914. The introduction of the sweet potato into the Far East. *Transactions on the Asiatic Society of Japan* 42: 711-24.

Skjolsvold, Arne. 1961. Site E-2, a circular dwelling, Anakena. In *Archaeology of Easter Island,* Vol. 1., ed. T. Heyerdahl and E. N. Ferdon, Jr., 295-303. Santa Fe, N.Mex.

Solheim, Wilhelm G., II. 1969. Mekong valley flooding. In *Smithsonian Institution Center for Short-Lived Phenomena, "Report on Mekong Valley Flooding"* (no. 58-69). Washington, D.C.

1988. The Nusantao hypothesis: The origin and spread of Austronesian speakers. *Asian Perspectives* 26: 77-88.

Sowunmi, M. A. 1985. The beginnings of agriculture in West Africa: Botanical evidence. *Current Anthropology* 26: 127-9.

Steward, Julian H. 1930. Irrigation without agriculture. *Papers of the Michigan Academy of Sciences, Arts and Letters* 12: 149-56.

Sutton, Douglas 1984. The Pouerua project: Phase II, an interim report. *New Zealand Archaeological Association Newsletter* 27: 30-8.

Turner, C. G. 1989. Teeth and prehistory in Asia. *Scientific American* 260: 88-96.

Ugent, Donald, Tom Dillehay, and Carlos Ramirez. 1987. Potato remains from a late Pleistocene settlement in southcentral Chile. *Economic Botany* 41: 17-27.

Ugent, Donald, and Linda W. Peterson. 1988. Archaeological remains of potato and sweet potato in Peru. *International Potato Center Circular* 16: 1-10.

Ugent, Donald, Sheila Pozorski, and Thomas Pozorski. 1981. Prehistoric remains of the sweet potato from the Casma valley of Peru. *Phytologia* 49: 401-15.

1982. Archaeological potato tuber remains from the Casma valley of Peru. *Economic Botany* 36: 182-92.

Watson, James B. 1965. The significance of a recent ecological change in the central highlands of New Guinea. *Journal of the Polynesian Society* 74: 438-50.

White, J. Peter, and James F. O'Connell. 1982. *The prehistory of Australia, New Guinea and Sahul.* Sydney.

Williamson, Kay. 1970. Some food plant names in the Niger delta. *International Journal of American Linguistics* 36: 156-67.

Yen, Douglas E. 1960. The sweet potato in the Pacific: The propagation of the plant in relation to its distribution. *Journal of the Polynesian Society* 69: 368-75.

1961. The adaption of kumara by the New Zealand Maori. *Journal of the Polynesian Society* 70: 338-48.

1973. Ethnobotany from the voyages of Mendana and Quiros in the Pacific. *World Archaeology* 5: 32-43.

1974. *The sweet potato and Oceania: An essay in ethnobotany.* Honolulu.

1976. Sweet potato. In *Evolution of crop plants,* ed. N. W. Simmonds, 42-5. London.

1977. Hoabinhian horticulture? The evidence and the questions from northeast Thailand. In *Sunda and Sahul,* ed. J. Allen, J. Golson, and R. Jones, 567-99. London.

1982. Sweet potato in historical perspective. In *Sweet potato, proceedings of the first international symposium,* ed. R. L. Villareal and T. D. Griggs, 17-30. Shanhua, Taiwan.

Zavala, Silvio. 1964. New world contacts with Asia. *Asian Studies* 2: 213-22.

II.B.6 ❧ Taro

Taro is the common name of four different root crops that are widely consumed in tropical areas around the world. Taro is especially valued for its starch granules, which are easily digested through the bloodstream, thus making it an ideal food for babies, elderly persons, and those with digestive problems. It is grown by vegetative propagation (asexual reproduction), so its spread around the world has been due to human intervention. But its production is restricted to the humid tropics, and its availability is restricted by its susceptibility to damage in transport.

Taro is most widely consumed in societies throughout the Pacific, where it has been a staple for probably 3,000 to 4,000 years. But it is also used extensively in India, Thailand, the Philippines, and Southeast Asia, as well as in the Caribbean and parts of tropical West Africa and Madagascar (see Murdock 1960; Petterson 1977). Moreover, in the last quarter of the twentieth century taro entered metropolitan areas such as Auckland, Wellington, Sydney, and Los Angeles, where it is purchased by migrants from Samoa and other Pacific Island nations who desire to maintain access to their traditional foods (Pollock 1992).

Although taro is the generic Austronesian term for four different roots, true taro is known botanically as *Colocasia esculenta,* or *Colocasia antiquorum* in

Taro

some of the older literature. We will refer to it here as Colocasia taro. False taro, or giant taro, is the name applied to the plant known botanically as *Alocasia macrorrhiza*. It is less widely used unless other root staples are in short supply. We will refer to it as Alocasia taro.

Giant swamp taro is the name used for the plant known as *Cyrtosperma chamissonis*. This is a staple crop on some atolls, such as Kiribati, and is also grown in low-lying areas of larger islands. We will refer to it as Cyrtosperma taro. The fourth form of taro has been introduced into the Pacific and elsewhere much more recently. It is commonly known as tannia, kongkong, or American taro, but its botanical name is *Xanthosoma sagittifolium*. It has become widely adopted because it thrives in poorer soils and yields an acceptable food supply. We will refer to it as Xanthosoma taro.

The starch-bearing root, termed corm or cormlet, of these four plants makes a major contribution to the human diet, and even the leaves are occasionally used as food, as in the case of young Colocasia leaves. The leaves are also employed as coverings for earth ovens and as wrappings for puddings that are made from the grated starch root and baked in an earth oven. The large leaves of Cyrtosperma taro also provide a good substitute for an umbrella.

Botanical Features

All the taros are aroids of the Araceae family, so we would expect to find close similarities among them. They grow in tropical climates with an adequate year-round rainfall. All taros must be propagated vegetatively, as they do not have viable seeds. Consequently their production for food crops has been engineered by human intervention. Both the corms and the leaves are acrid to some degree, particularly before they are cooked, and cause an unpleasant irritation of the skin and mouth (Tang and Sakai 1983; Bradbury and Holloway 1988).

Colocasia Taro

The Colocasia taro plant consists of an enlarged root or corm, a number of leafstalks, and leaves. The leaves are the main visible feature distinguishing Colocasia from the other taros, particularly Xanthosoma (see Figure II.B.6.1). The Colocasia leaf is peltate, or shield-shaped, with the leafstalk joining the leaf about two-thirds of the way across it. Varieties of Colocasia taro differ in the color of the leafstalk, the shape and color of the leaf and veins, and the number of fully developed leaves. They also differ in the shape, flesh color, and culinary qualities of their tubers. The varieties are recognized by individual names, particularly in those societies in the Pacific where the plant is a major foodstuff. For example, 70 local names were recorded in Hawaii and 67 in Samoa (Massal and Barrau 1956; Lambert 1982). Indeed, fully 722 accessions have been recorded in collections of root crops in South Pacific countries (Bradbury and Holloway 1988).

Colocasia taro can be grown on flooded or irrigated land and on dry land. The planting material consists of the corm plus its leafstalks, minus the leaves. Taros in Fiji are sold this way in the market, so that the purchaser can cut off the root for food and plant the topmost part of the root plus leafstalks, known as a sett, to grow the next crop of taro. Harvesting one taro root therefore yields the planting material for the next crop. The root takes about 7 to 10 months to mature. Once the corm has been cut or damaged, taro rots quickly, making it difficult to ship to distant markets.

Alocasia Taro

Sometimes known as giant taro, or *kape* in Polynesian languages, Alocasia taro is a large-leafed plant that is grown for its edible stem rather than for the root. The fleshy leaves are spear-shaped and can reach more than a meter in length. The stem and central vein of the leaf form a continuous line. The leaves of this taro are not usually eaten.

The edible part is the large and long (a half meter or more), thickened underground stem that may weigh 20 kilograms (kg). It is peeled and cut into pieces to be cooked in an earth oven or boiled.

Cyrtosperma chamissonis   Colocasia esculenta   Xanthosoma sagittifolium   Alocasia macrorrhiza

Figure II.B.6.1. Four types of taros. (Illustration by Tim Galloway).

Alocasia taros are very acrid, as they contain a high concentration of calcium oxalate crystals in the outer layers of the stem. These crystals are set free by chewing and can cause irritation in the mouth and throat if the stem is not thoroughly cooked. The calcium oxalate content increases if the plant is left in the ground too long. For this reason some societies consider Alocasia taro fit for consumption only in emergencies. But in Tonga, Wallis, and Papua New Guinea, varieties with very low oxalate content have been selectively grown to overcome this problem (Holo and Taumoefolau 1982). Twenty-two accessions are held in collections of root crops for the South Pacific (Bradbury and Holloway 1988).

Cyrtosperma Taro

Cyrtosperma taro, called giant swamp taro, also has very large leaves, sometimes reaching 3 meters in height. In fact, a swamp taro patch towers over those working in it. The leaves are spear-shaped and upright, the central vein forming a continuous line with the stem. The edible corm grows to some 5 kg in size, depending on the variety.

This taro prefers a swampy environment and will withstand a high level of water, provided it is not inundated by seawater. It is grown in Kiribati under cultivation techniques that have been carefully developed over several hundred years (Luomala 1974).

Cyrtosperma taro is a highly regarded foodstuff in Kiribati and in Yap, as well as on other atolls in Micronesia and in the Tuamotus. It is also cultivated in the Rewa district of southeast Fiji, and evidence of its former cultivation can be found in northern Fiji, Futuna, and Wallis, where it is employed today as an emergency crop. It is rarely cultivated outside the Pacific.

Xanthosoma Taro

Xanthosoma taro, by contrast, is much more widespread than Cyrtosperma taro and may be found in many tropical areas, including those on the American and African continents, as well as in the Pacific, where several varieties are now being cultivated (Weightman and Moros 1982). Although it is a very recent introduction to the islands relative to the other three taros, it has become widely accepted as a household crop because it is easy to grow, it can be intercropped with other subsistence foods in a shifting cultivation plot, and it tolerates the shade of a partially cleared forest or of a coconut or pawpaw plantation. It cannot stand waterlogging.

The principal tuber of Xanthosoma is seldom ≠harvested because it also contains calcium oxalate crystals. Rather, the small cormlets are dug up, some being ready 7 to 10 months after planting. These are about the size of a large potato, weighing up to half a kilo.

In appearance Xanthosoma taro is often confused with Colocasia taro, the term "eddoe" being used for both. The main difference between them is in the leaf structure; the Xanthosoma leaf is hastate, an arrow or spearhead shape, and not peltate, so that the leafstalk joins the leaf at the edge, giving it a slightly more erect appearance than the Colocasia leaf (see Figure II.B.6.1). The distinctive feature of the Xanthosoma leaf is its marked vein structure together with a marginal vein.

Production

As already noted, all of the taros must be propagated vegetatively as none of them produce viable seeds naturally. They thus require human intervention both for introduction to a new area and for repeated production of a food supply. This factor further strengthens the likelihood of selection of particular varieties that have more desirable attributes as food, such as reduced acridity and suitability to particular growing conditions. The planting material for all the taros is either a sucker or the sett (consisting of the base of the petioles and a 1-centimeter section from the top of the corm).

Dryland or upland cultivation is the most widespread form of cultivation of Colocasia taro, which grows best in a warm, moist environment. It can be grown between sea level and 1,800 meters (m) where daily average temperatures range between 18 and 27 degrees Celsius (C), with rainfall of about 250 centimeters (cm) annually. The setts or suckers are placed in a hole made with a digging stick, with a recommended spacing between plants of 45 cm by 60 cm to produce good-sized corms. Yield will increase with higher planting density (De La Pena 1983).

Irrigated or wetland Colocasia taro is grown in prepared beds in which, to prevent weed seed germination, water is maintained at a level of 5 cm before planting and during the growth of the setts until the first leaves unfurl. The beds may be a few feet across, beside a stream or well-watered area, or they may be in an area some 2 to 3 acres in size, depending on the land and water available. After the first leaves appear, the beds are frequently covered with whole coconut fronds to shade the young plants from the sun.

Irrigated taro planted at a density of 100,000 plants/ha yields 123.9 tons/ha. With 10,000 plants/ha the yield is 41.4 tons/ha (De La Pena 1983: 169-75). Clearly, the more intense techniques developed for wetland cultivation produce a higher yield. But these techniques are suited only to areas where the right conditions pertain, and on the Pacific Islands such areas are limited because of the nature of the terrain. Dryland taro is, thus, more versatile.

Colocasia taro, whether upland or irrigated, may be harvested after a growing period ranging from 9 to 18 months, depending on the variety and the growing conditions. In Fiji some varieties are harvestable at 9 to 11 months after planting, whereas in Hawaii harvest takes place from 12 to 18 months after planting in the commercial fields.

The subsistence farmer, by contrast, harvests only those taros needed for immediate household use. The farmer will cut off the setts and plant them in a newly cleared area of land or in a different part of the irrigated plot. Thus, any one household will have several taro plots at different stages of growth to maintain a year-round supply and to meet communal obligations for feasts and funerals.

Pests and pathogens are a greater problem for Colocasia taro than for the other varieties. Both the leaves and the corm are subject to damage during the growing period from a range of pests and biotic agents (Mitchell and Maddison 1983). In the Pacific, leaf rot and corm rot have been the most serious diseases, spreading rapidly through whole plantations, particularly in Melanesia (Ooka 1983). In fact, these diseases were so severe in the early 1970s that some societies in the Solomons ceased taro consumption and switched to the sweet potato. West Samoa has recently lost its entire crop due to these diseases.

Alocasia is interplanted with yams and sweet potatoes in Tonga and Wallis where it is grown in shifting cultivation plots. The planting material is usually the larger suckers (although cormlets may also be used). These are placed in holes 10 to 25 cm deep, preferably between July and September. If planted with spacing of 1.5 m by 1.5 m Alocasia will yield 31 tons/ha, with an average kape root stem weighing 8 to 10 kg and reaching 1.5 m in length. The plant suffers few pests, is weeded when convenient, and is harvested a year after planting (Holo and Taumoefolau 1982: 84).

Swamp Cyrtosperma production has been culturally elaborated in some Pacific societies so that it is surrounded by myth and secrecy (see Luomala 1974 for Kiribati). The planting material may be a sett or a young sucker, and in Kiribati this is placed in a carefully prepared pit that may be several hundred years old, to which mulch has been constantly added. Each new plant is set in a hole with its upper roots at water level, surrounded by chopped leaves of particular plants chosen by the individual planter and topped with black humic sand. It is encased in a basket of woven palm fronds, to which more compost mixture is added as the plant grows. The larger cultivars are spaced at 90 cm by 90 cm; smaller ones are spaced more closely.

A pit is likely to consist of Cyrtosperma plants at various stages of growth. A corm may be harvested after 18 months – or it may be left for 15 years, by which time it is very fibrous and inedible but still brings prestige to the grower's family when presented at a feast. Yield is uneven due to different cultivation practices but may reach 7.5 to 10 tons/ha. An individual corm may weigh 10 to 12 kg (Vickers and Untaman 1982).

Xanthosoma taro is best grown on deep, well-drained, fertile soils. It tolerates shade and so can be interplanted with other crops such as coconuts, cocoa, coffee, bananas, and rubber, or with subsistence crops such as yams. The planting material is the cormlet or a sett, but the former grows more quickly than the latter. These can be planted at any time of year but grow best if planted just before onset of the rainy season. If they are spaced at 1 m by 1 m, the yield is about 20 tons/ha. The plant, which has few pests or diseases, produces a number of cormlets the size of large potatoes. These can be harvested after six months, but they bruise easily, reducing storage time (Weightman and Moros 1982).

Different planting techniques have been developed over time in order to provide a foodstuff that suits both the palate of those eating it and the local growing conditions. Most taro (dryland Colocasia, Alocasia, and Xanthosoma) is grown under dryland conditions with reasonable rainfall, and it seems likely that the aroids were all originally dryland plants (Barrau 1965). Because the techniques involved in the cultivation of wetland Colcasia and swamp Cyrtosperma taro are more arduous than those of dryland cultivation, one suspects that these plants were encouraged to adapt to wetland conditions, probably to meet specific food tastes.

Origins

Colocasia and Alocasia taro are among the oldest of the world's domesticated food plants. Both apparently have an Asian origin, possibly in India or Burma (Massal and Barrau 1956), but because they consist of vegetal material that has no hard parts, they leave almost no trace in the archaeological record. As a consequence, there has been much room for debate about the early development of the taros.

Some of the debate has centered on the question of whether root crop domestication preceded that of cereals, such as millet and rice, in the Southeast Asia region. Most authorities now agree that root crops came first (e.g., Chang 1977), although C. Gorman (1977) considered rice and taro as sister domesticates. In an overview of the evidence, M. Spriggs (1982) argued that root crops, including taro, were early staples in Southeast Asia, with rice becoming a staple much later.

The time depth is also problematic. It has been suggested that the early agricultural phase of slash-and-burn, dryland cultivation in Southeast Asia took place some 8,000 to 10,000 years ago, with a sequence of dominant cultigens proceeding from root crops to cereals (Hutterer 1983). Dryland taro may have been cultivated for some 7,000 years or more, with wetland (Colocasia) taro forming part of a second stage of development of Southeast Asian food crops (Bellwood 1980).

Prehistorians have given much more attention to

wetland taro irrigation techniques and those used in the production of paddy rice than they have to dryland practices. This is because wetland techniques are said to mark technological innovation and, thus, to be associated with a more complex level of social organization than that required in the production of dryland taro or rice (e.g., Spriggs 1982 for Vanuatu; Kirch 1985 for Hawaii). Yet this does not necessarily mean that foodstuffs produced by irrigation had greater importance in the diet than their dryland counterparts. We need to know the importance of such crops in the food consumption and exchange systems of those people who chose to develop a more complex mode of production. For a food to be considered a staple, the proportion of dietary content is the important aspect, as opposed to the techniques of production or the size of the production units.

Ease of cooking may constitute another reason that taro preceded rice. A hole lined with stones, in which a fire was lit, became an oven with limited tools. The whole taro root could be cooked thoroughly in such an oven, together with fish or pork or other edibles. To cook rice, by contrast, required some form of utensil in which to boil the rice to make it edible, either in the form of cakes, or as a soup.[1]

But if taro, whether Colocasia or Alocasia, had advantages that suggest it was an earlier domesticated foodstuff than rice, its disadvantages lay in its bulk and post-harvest vulnerability. However, advantages outweighed disadvantages, so it is not surprising that these two forms of taro spread as widely as they did across Oceania and into Africa.

Despite its antiquity, however, the origin of Alocasia taro has not attracted as much attention as that of Colocasia taro; similarly, we know more about the origin of Xanthosoma taro than we do about Cyrtosperma taro. This is partly because the Alocasia and Cyrtosperma taros are not as widely used as the other two and partly because, even where they are used as foods (save for Cyrtosperma in Kiribati and Yap), they are not the main foodstuff.

Alocasia taro has its origins either in India (Plucknett 1976) or in Sri Lanka (Bradbury and Holloway 1988) but has been grown since prehistory throughout tropical southeast Asia, as well as in China and Japan (Petterson 1977). Cyrtosperma, by contrast, was said to have been first domesticated either in the Indo-Malaya region (Barrau 1965) or in Indonesia or Papua New Guinea, where it has wild relatives (Bellwood 1980). Both Alocasia and Cyrtosperma taros are abundant in the Philippines, where a number of different varieties of each are known (Petterson 1977). Cyrtosperma remains, discovered there by archaeologists, suggest that it was cultivated at least from A.D. 358 (Spriggs 1982), indicating that there was sufficient time to develop a range of plant types yielding less acridic starch foods.

In their reconstruction of the early forms of the Austronesian language, A. Pawley and R. Green (1974) include words for Alocasia, Colocasia, and Cyrtosperma taros, indicating a time depth in the Pacific of some 3,000 to 4,000 years. Thus, all three plants have probably been domesticated and exchanged for over 5,000 years in tropical Southeast Asia.

Xanthosoma taro differs from the other three aroids in having its homeland in tropical America. Little is known about the Xantharoids before the twentieth century, as J. Petterson (1977) points out in her thesis on the dissemination and use of the edible aroids. But she does offer us one possible reconstruction of the spread of what she calls American taro. It was "a most ancient domesticate of the Western hemisphere," said to have originated in the Caribbean lowlands along the northern coast of South America.

By the time Europeans reached the Americas, Xanthosoma taro had diffused south into northwest South America and north across the Antilles and Central America where several varieties were known.[2] Exactly where Xanthosoma was consumed at this time, and who consumed it, is unclear, although later on taro roots served as an important foodstuff for slaves on sugar plantations.

Geographic Spread

The four aroids have spread around the tropical areas of the world, with Colocasia and Xanthosoma more widely cultivated than Alocasia and Cyrtosperma taros. A range of varieties of each has been developed by human selectivity, and all four are extensively utilized by the island societies of Oceania.

Colocasia taro was carried from its South Asia homeland in both an easterly and a westerly direction, probably some 6,000 years ago (Bellwood 1980). Moving east it became established in Thailand, Malaysia, Indonesia, and the Philippines and from there was carried by canoe into Papua New Guinea, the Marianas, and henceforth into Micronesia and Polynesia (Petterson 1977; Yen 1980; Hutterer 1983; Pollock 1992). The Malay name *tales* is the base of the common term taro as widely used today. In the four areas of Oceania the Colocasia root has gained a reputation as a highly valued foodstuff that also has prestige value (though not as high as Dioscorea yams). Today it is still cultivated as a food in Hawaii, the Marquesas, Tahiti, the Cooks, the Solomons, and Papua New Guinea. It remains a major foodstuff in Samoa, Tonga, Wallis, Futuna, Fiji, and Vanuatu.[3]

The easterly spread of Colocasia taro across the islands of the Pacific is today associated by prehistorians with the development of Lapita culture some 6,000 years ago. Lapita culture is a construct by prehistorians of a period in the settlement of the Pacific, with the spread of a particular form of pottery as its hallmark. Associated with this culture is the cultivation of Colocasia taro in particular, but Alocasia taro as well.

How sophisticated irrigation technology was introduced by these people moving out of Southeast Asia has not been clearly established. It seems likely that dryland taro could have been introduced to a wider range of environments in the Pacific and, thus, was in existence earlier than irrigated or wetland taro.

For our purposes the important consideration is how these production techniques influenced the acceptability of the crop as a foodstuff. Because people in the Pacific today assert that irrigated taro is softer and less acrid, it is likely that the wetland Colocasia taro has undergone more specific selection than the dryland version, depending on how the root was prepared as a food. For the most part it was cooked whole in the earth oven, to be eaten in slices with accompaniments (as discussed in the next section). But in Hawaii, Rapa, and a few small islands it was employed mainly as *poi,* a fermented product made from either upland or wetland taro. The dietary uses of Colocasia taro are thus likely to have influenced which plants were selected for replanting and the techniques (whether wet or dry) of production. Moreover, appropriate cooking techniques had to be developed, as well as methods for overcoming the acidity.

In its westward spread, Colocasia taro was planted in India, where it still forms part of the diets of some societies today. It reached Madagascar where it became widely established between the first and eleventh centuries A.D. It was carried further westward in two branches, one along the Mediterranean and the other across Africa south of the Sahara.

The plant attained significance in West Africa where it has been grown ever since. In the Mediterranean region, it was flourishing in Egypt at the time of Alexander's expedition, where it was known as the Egyptian water lily and Egyptian beans. Virgil and Pliny both referred to the Colocasia plant in their writing, with the latter noting that "when boiled and chewed it breaks up into spidery threads" (quoted in Petterson 1977: 129). Colocasia taro has continued in importance in Egypt and also in Asia Minor and Cyprus until recently when it became too expensive to produce (Petterson 1977).

Colocasia taro reached the Iberian Peninsula probably by about A.D. 714, along with sugar cane. In both West Africa and Portugal the term *enyame* came to be applied to the Colocasia taro and was picked up by other Europeans as a generic name for all unfamiliar root crops. Thus, to English explorers yams meant any number of root crops, including both yams and Colocasia taro (Petterson 1977).

The latter also reached tropical America from the east, and it became a secondary foodstuff for Peruvian, Ecuadorean, and Amazonian peoples, as well as for those of the Caribbean, where it is known as dasheen or eddoe (Petterson 1977: 185). It seems likely that Colocasia taro was carried by the Iberians in their westward explorations and then brought from Africa to feed slaves during the Middle Passage.

By contrast, Alocasia taro has not traveled so widely. It was carried from Southeast Asia mainly into the islands of Oceania where it has been domesticated on some atolls in Micronesia and Polynesia, as well as on some high islands, such as Samoa, Tonga, Wallis, and Fiji. On those islands where it is grown, a number of different varieties of the plant have been developed locally. In all these places the Alocasia taro makes a significant contribution to the diet.

Its westward spread from Indonesia to India was less prolific (Plucknett 1976). Today, Alocasia plants can be found growing as ornamentals in both tropical and subtropical areas, such as Florida (Petterson 1977) and in the northern part of the north island of New Zealand. They do not, however, serve as food.

Cyrtosperma is a small genus that is used as food almost exclusively in the Oceania region.[4] But Xanthosoma taro spread from its homeland along the northern coast of South America out into the northern part of South America and through tropical Central America. It may have been of some importance as a food in Classic Maya civilization (c.A.D. 200-900).[5]

Spanish and Portuguese contacts with America led to the dispersal of Xantharoids into Europe (they were grown in England as a curiosity in 1710) and, probably, into Africa where they may have died out and then been reintroduced. The root was allegedly brought to Sierra Leone in 1792 by former North American slaves who had fled to Nova Scotia after the American Revolution. However, the generally accepted date for the introduction of Xanthosoma taro to sub-Saharan Africa is April 17, 1843, when missionaries carried the American taro from the West Indies to Accra, Ghana.

It subsequently spread from West Africa to Uganda and through the Cameroons and Gabon to attain varying levels of importance. Beyond Africa, it traveled along Portuguese trading lines to India and the East Indies, following a similar route as the sweet potato. But it has not become an important food crop in Asia, except in the Philippines whence it spread to Malaysia (Petterson 1977).

Xanthosoma was introduced to the Pacific only in the last 200 years, probably via Hawaii (Barrau 1961) and Guam in contact with the Philippines (Pollock 1983). Its spread across the Pacific was aided by missionary activity as much as by island exchange, and the names used in Pacific societies today for Xanthosoma taro suggest the routes of transferal.

Taros As Food

Taro is a very important foodstuff in those societies that use it, both in the household and also for feasts and exchanges. But in terms of world food crops, the taros are considered of marginal importance. They rank behind bananas and root crops, such as cassava, sweet potatoes, and yams, in amounts consumed (Norman, Pearson, and Searle 1984: 221). Nonetheless, taros do have potential in promoting diversification of the world food supply and could make a significant contribution if greater agronomic investment was made. The Root Crops program of the Food and Agriculture Organization of the United Nations (FAO) is attempting to address some of these issues, as is the work of the Australian Centre for International Agricultural Research (ACIAR) (Bradbury and Holloway 1988).

In the Pacific, people have a higher regard for taros than any of the other seven common starchy foods (Pollock 1992). Cassava outranks taros in terms of the tons per hectare produced, but that is because it is a good "safety" crop that will grow in poorer soils and can be harvested as needed when the more preferred starches are in short supply. Yet householders in most Pacific societies would not offer cassava to an honored guest or make it their contribution to a celebration; rather they would go to some lengths to procure Colocasia taro or Dioscorea yams or breadfruit for such purposes. In fact, Colocasia taro, yams, and breadfruit are at the very top of the list for everyday consumption in the Pacific and for exchanges and presentation at feasts. They are also the most expensive of the local foods on sale in the urban markets. The other three taros may be maintained as secondary or fallback foods, but the reputation of a rural family still rests in large part on its ability to produce a good supply of Colocasia taro, together with the other desirable crops, for self-maintenance (Pollock et al. 1989).

The taros (and other starch foods) form the major part of the daily diet of Pacific Island people living on their own land today, much as they have in the past. They are the main substance of daily intake, eaten once a day in the past, but now twice a day. Taros, and the other starches, provide the bulk of the food, the "real" food (*kakana dina* in Fijian), but are accompanied by a small portion of another foodstuff such as fish, coconut, or shellfish to form what we call a meal in English. If just one of them is eaten without the other, then people are likely to say that they have not eaten, because the two parts are essential to the mental, as well as physical, satisfaction that food confers (Pollock 1985).

Taro maintains this importance in the minds of contemporary Pacific Islanders living in metropolitan areas such as Wellington. The root may be expensive and hard to find, but these people make a great effort to obtain Colocasia taro for special occasions, such as a community feast, or for a sick Samoan or Tongan who may request a piece of taro to feel better.[6]

According to the accounts left by missionaries and other visitors to the Pacific in the nineteenth century, the amounts of taro (particularly Colocasia taro) consumed by Fijians and Tongans, for example, were prodigious. They especially noted the consumption patterns of chiefs, suggesting that all this taro was a cause of their obesity. We have less information, however, regarding the ordinary people's consumption (see Pollock 1992).

But in Tahiti, and probably elsewhere in the Pacific, food consumption generally varied from day to day and week to week. Europeans were amazed at how Tahitians could cross the very rugged interior of their island, going for four days with only coconut milk to drink, yet when food was available, they consumed very large amounts. Because food habits were irregular, one advantage of taro was that it made the stomach feel full for a long period of time.

Along with notions of routine introduced to the islands by missionaries and administrators came the concept of meals, which usually occur twice daily in rural areas. Taro might be eaten at both the morning and evening meals, and a schoolchild or an adult may carry a couple of slices of taro in a packed lunch. Indeed, schools in Niue are encouraging schoolchildren to bring their lunch in the form of local foods rather than bread and biscuits (Pollock 1983, field notes). Thus, today, an adult may consume a daily total of about 2 kg of Colocasia taro or other starch every day for 365 days of the year.

To a great extent such emphasis on local foodstuffs is the work of local Pacific food and nutrition committees, formed in the early 1980s, that have publicized the benefits of taro and other starches. But in urban areas of the Pacific, taros are scarce, and thus an expensive luxury food. In a Fijian or Samoan marketplace, four Colocasia taros (only enough to feed two adults for one meal) may sell for 5 or 6 dollars, with the other family members having to eat rice or cassava or Xanthosoma taro instead. Those promoting the use of local foods are endeavoring to bring down the price of taros. But to do so requires more agricultural input and other diversifications within the economy.

Colocasia taros are also an essential component of Pacific feasts where they take pride of place, alongside the pigs (used only at feasts), fish, turtle, or (today) beef. Early visitors to the Pacific were amazed at the immense walls of Colocasia taros and yams, topped off with pigs, that formed part of a presentation at a special occasion such as the investiture of a new chief in Fiji or Wallis in the 1860s. These food gifts were contributed by households closely associated with the community hosting the feast and were redistributed to those attending. A great amount of food had to be consumed at these feasts, as there was no means of preserving it (Pollock 1992).

Conversely, there were times when food was very scarce, as after a cyclone or a tidal wave, or during a drought. Such disasters witnessed the Colocasia taro plants damaged and rotted and the Cyrtosperma broken by the wind, so the people had to resort to dryland taro or Alocasia taro or other starches. In very severe cases (such as the devastating cyclone Val in December 1991 on Western Samoa), households had nothing but fallen coconuts and emergency foods, such as Alocasia taro, to rely on.

Exchanges of both planting material and of

harvested taros have constituted a method of adjusting such irregularity in food availability in the Pacific. Before the development of international aid in the 1960s and 1970s, taros and other starches were harvested in Tonga to aid neighbors and relatives in Wallis, Western Samoa, and Fiji. This process of exchange not only enabled families and villages to survive hard times, but it also cemented social relations between whole island nations. In addition, the process of exchange supported the development of a diversified gene pool of the various taros.

Cooking and Processing

All the taros must be cooked very thoroughly because of the oxalic acid crystals in the outer layer of the corm and in the leaves. Thorough cooking reduces the toxicity, and the earth oven allows whole taros to be covered and steamed on hot rocks for two hours or more. In most Pacific societies such an earth oven was made once a day, and in rural areas this is still the case. Boiling on a stove may be quicker, but it is more costly in fuel (Pollock 1992).

Pacific Island people today prefer taro cooked whole and then cut into slices for presentation to the household. Taro must be cooked as quickly as possible after harvesting to retain the best flavor and to avoid decay. Before cooking, each corm or stem of taro is carefully peeled, a process that can produce a skin irritation for those unaccustomed to it, again due to the oxalic acid crystals. The corms or stems are placed either in a coconut leaf basket or on banana leaves around the edge of the earth oven, with the fish (or pig if it is a feast) in the center, and the whole is covered first with leaves, then earth to allow the contents to steam. The oven is opened some two hours later. For special occasions, "puddings" may be made from grated taro mixed with coconut cream and baked in the earth oven.

One of the few societies to develop a processed form of taro was that in Hawaii, where fermented taro was eaten as *poi*. This was made by steaming, peeling, grinding, and straining the corms to yield a thick paste of 30 percent solids, known as "ready-to-mix" *poi,* or if more water was added to yield a thinner paste of 18 percent solids, known as "ready-to-eat" *poi.* Hawaiians refer to the thickness of *poi* as one-finger, two-finger, or three-finger *poi.* Either irrigated or dryland Colocasia taro can be used for making *poi,* but different varieties of Colocasia taro are not mixed.

The thick paste ferments very rapidly due to lactobacilli fermentation, reaching an acidity level of 3.8 by the third day. Hawaiians would wrap the very thick paste, known as *'ai pa'i,* in *ti* leaves until needed. The addition of a little water to the desired portion was all that was required for serving highly esteemed *poi* to accompany fish or pork. The very thin paste, by contrast, lasts only three to four days unrefrigerated, and refrigerated *poi* becomes so rubbery that it is considered inedible (Moy and Nip 1983; Standal 1983; Pollock 1992).

Commercialization

Taros are sold whole and unprocessed in the Pacific. In Fiji, where the petioles are left attached to the corm, Colocasia taros are sold by the bundle of three or four tied together. In Tonga and Western Samoa, Colocasia taros are sold by the corm alone, but again in groups of four or more for a given price. The stems of Alocasia taros are sold by the piece, while the cormlets of Xanthosoma taro are sold by the basket, as are sweet potatoes and other root crops.

More of the crop is sold through middlemen in Fiji and Samoa, although producers themselves use family members as agents.[7] Cyrtosperma taro is seldom sold in these larger markets, except in Tarawa, Kiribati, and Kolonia, Yap.

None of these root crops is very durable, so those marketing taro aim for quick sales. Damaged taros will deteriorate rapidly, hence great care is taken in both the harvesting process for market and in removing the tops in Tonga and Samoa to inflict as little damage to the corm as possible.

As early as 1880, Papeete in the Society Islands became a center for the redistribution of local produce (Pollock 1988). From such small waterside markets have grown the large market centers found around the tropical world today (some covering several acres). In each Pacific Island (and Caribbean Island) there is at least one such market in the urban center, and in larger islands, such as Fiji and Papua New Guinea, there are several markets in the various urban centers. These markets have grown in size and diversity over the last 20 years, as urban populations have increased. Only small amounts of taro are sold through supermarkets (Pollock 1988).

Out-migration of populations from the Pacific Islands (and the Caribbean) to metropolitan centers, such as Auckland, Wellington, Sydney, Honolulu, and Los Angeles, has also stimulated the overseas sale of taros, mainly Colocasia. The Tongan, Samoan, and Cook Islands populations are becoming sizable in those centers where demand for taro, mainly for celebratory occasions, has increased. Taro is available in urban markets, such as Otara in Auckland, and in vegetable shops, especially those where Polynesian communities are located. Prices are high, but families will make sacrifices to present some taro when needed to maintain family honor.

Before these outlets provided a steady supply, the various communities made private arrangements to import boxes of taro from their home islands. As a wider supply has become available and the communities have grown, each community has focused its demand on taro from its own island of origin, claiming that it tastes better. Samoans will track down stores that sell Samoan taro, whereas Tongans and

Rarotongans go in search of taros from their home islands. Island people themselves are acting more and more as the agents and middlemen, with the whole process promoting the production of taro varieties that will endure sea transport.

Taros are also imported in cooked form to New Zealand by returning residents. In Samoa or Niue, puddings are packed either in a chest freezer or a cardboard box and carried as part of the passenger's personal luggage. In New Zealand and Australia the families of the passenger then share in this produce "from home." Such is their social value that several hundred dollars may be spent in overweight luggage in order to transport local foods in this manner.

Another form of commercialization promoted by food and nutrition committees in various Pacific Islands is the use of taro (mainly Colocasia, both corm and leaves) along with other local foods, by hotels, to give tourists a new taste experience. Hawaii has long provided *luau* feasts for its visitors, which included a small portion of *poi* and pork, salmon, and coconut pudding. Now Fiji runs competitions in which chefs from leading hotels create recipes that make use of local foods, including taro. This practice, in turn, is leading to increased cooperation with the agriculture authorities to assist producers in regularizing production to supply the hotels.

In Hawaii, where processed taro has been marketed as *poi* for some 75 years, sales to Hawaiians and to the tourist hotels are supplemented by demand for *poi* in the mainland United States to help individuals suffering from allergies and digestive problems. As a consequence of this activity, Hawaii is the one place in the Pacific where taro plantations have become heavily commercialized and are run by companies rather than by family units.

Taro chips are now being manufactured in various centers around the Pacific. Local companies are selling their product, promoted by food and nutrition committees, in Fiji and Samoa with reasonable success. In Hawaii, entrepreneurial companies, such as Granny Goose Foods, are marketing taro chips alongside the traditional potato chips, thereby drawing taro into the lucrative snack industry.

In other parts of the tropical world, Colocasia taro may be processed into flour or flakes for commercial purposes. A product *Arvi* has been developed by the Central Food Technological Research Institute in Mysore, India, that consists of flour made from Colocasia taro. The corms are washed, peeled, and cut into slices, which are kept immersed in water overnight, then washed again and immersed for another three hours. The slices are blanched in boiling water for five minutes, then sun-dried before being ground into flour. A similar process has been used to make taro flour in Nigeria. The flour can be mixed with wheat flour for baking.

A process for making instant taro flakes has been tried in Taiwan and in Nigeria whereby smoke-dried slices are stored away for later eating. Freezing taro has not been very successful, though a local variety was processed for freezing in Shanghai (Moy and Nip 1983). Taro leaves mixed with coconut cream, known in Samoa as *palusami,* have been canned with reasonable success, but the corm does not can well.

Nutritional Value

The nutritional value of taro has changed over the many years since it was first domesticated. Its users have selected plants that were less toxic, produced larger, less fibrous corms, and better suited their tastes. Such a selection process was facilitated by vegetative propagation, and many different cultivars were developed over time. However, a large proportion of these cultivars have been lost due to lack of interest in root crops by cereal-based colonial powers. Today the FAO and the South Pacific Commission are trying to preserve as many different cultivars in the Pacific as possible so as to increase the diversity of available food crops. Colocasia taro has many more different cultivars than the other three types of taro, indicating its preferred status and its longtime use as a food. The cultivars have different nutritional attributes.

The taro corms of the four different types vary slightly in their composition (see Table II.B.6.1 for details of composition of the four types of taro). All the corms consist mainly of starch and moisture and are high in fiber. They yield between 70 and 133 calories (or 255 and 560 kilojoules) per 100-gram portion, with Alocasia having the lowest range and Xanthosoma taro the highest. The amount of protein varies considerably from 1.12 percent to 2.7 percent depending on the type of taro, its geographical source, and the variety. The corms are also a good source of minerals, particularly calcium, for which Cyrtosperma taro is particularly notable (Standal 1982; Bradbury and Holloway 1988).

Taro leaves consist mainly of moisture and fiber. They are high in protein with a generally higher overall mineral content than the corms. It is only the young leaves of Colocasia taro that are eaten as a rule, although no difference in chemical composition has been found between leaves viewed as edible and those viewed as inedible (Bradbury and Holloway 1988). The use of the leaves as a wrapping in preparations, such as Samoan *palusami,* adds value to the diet on those special occasions when such a dish is served. Food and nutrition committees are trying to encourage the greater use of leaves, but they are not part of the traditional diet.

The fermented form of taro paste developed long ago by Hawaiians has been found to be a highly digestible product suitable for babies, adults with digestive problems, and those with allergies to cereals. The starch granules are small enough to pass readily into the digestive system. This attribute has led to the commercialization of *poi* (Standal 1983).

Table II.B.6.1. *Nutritional value of the four types of taros*

	Energy		Protein (g)	Fat (g)	C.H.O. (g)	Ca (mg)	Iron (mg)	Vit. A (μg)	Thiamine (mg)	Riboflavin (mg)	Niacin (mg)	Vit. C (mg)	Waste A.C. (%)
	(Kcal)	(MJ)											
Taro (Calocasia)	113	0.47	2.0	–	26.0	25	1.0	–	0.100	0.03	1.0	5	20
Taro, giant (Alocasia)	70	0.29	0.6	0.1	16.9	152	0.5	–	0.104	0.02	0.4	–	–
Taro, swamp (Cyrtosperma)	122	0.51	0.8	0.2	29.2	577	1.3	–	0.027	0.11	1.2	–	–
Xanthosoma	133	–	2.0	0.3	31.0	20	1.0	–	1.1	0.03	0.5	10.1	?

Clearly, taro has considerable merits as a food. It is readily cooked in an earth oven with minimal equipment, or it can be boiled or baked on a stove. It provides a high-bulk foodstuff rich in fiber, with acceptable amounts of vegetable protein and calcium. There is enough variety of cultivars to yield different tasting corms (if taste is an important consideration). But these merits have not been recognized widely enough, an issue the FAO Root Crops Program in the South Pacific is attempting to rectify through agricultural development (Sivan 1984; Jackson and Breen 1985). Simultaneously, food and nutrition committees, through their promotion of local foods, are endeavoring to counter the colonial legacy that bread is best.

Summary

Taro has evolved as a food over several thousand years, as people in tropical areas have selected attributes that suit their needs. Those needs included both consumption and production factors, as well as processing techniques. In the Pacific area, where the taros are most widely used, the people have relied heavily on three forms, Colocasia, Alocasia, and Cyrtosperma, along with the other starches such as yams, breadfruit, and bananas as the main elements in their daily diets, eaten together with a small accompanying dish. Xanthosoma taro has been added to this inventory in the last 200 years, as it will grow in poor soils and can be less acrid.

Vegetation propagation allowed a high degree of selectivity. Factors including the taste of the corm and its size, color, moisture, and acridity have determined over time which setts were replanted and which were discarded.

Most taro has been grown in dryland conditions. The selection of varieties of Colocasia taro that would grow in water is a further development, as is the very specialized technique for raising Cyr-

tosperma taro on atolls where the salinity of the water is a problem.

Little development has taken place to diversify the edible product. The corms are peeled and cooked in an earth oven by steaming for a couple of hours and are then served in slices. More recently, boiling has been introduced, but it gives a less acceptable flavor.

Ongoing development of the taros was curtailed, to some extent, by colonial Europeans whose preferred food was bread. Taros and other root crops were considered by these newcomers as a mark of the backward nature of these societies, and the colonists introduced crops of a commercial nature, such as cotton, vanilla, sugar cane, and, more recently, coffee and cocoa. These crops were planted on the best land, and taros were relegated to less desirable areas. The result has been not only a loss of many varieties of taro formerly used but also a scarcity of taros for sale in the markets today over and above those needed for household supply.

Only during the last decade of the twentieth century have the root crops, including taro, merited the attention of agricultural specialists. The worldwide pressure for a more differentiated crop base than just the seven basic food crops has led to programs such as the FAO Root Crops Program and ACIAR's identification of the potential of root crops in the South Pacific. With political independence in the 1960s and 1970s, small nations in the tropics have seen the need to become more self-reliant by reducing their high food import bills. The former importance of the taros has been recognized, and these countries are now taking steps to reestablish them agronomically and economically as a key local crop. The recognition of the importance to health of dietary fiber adds another dimension to taro's desirability. Exports of taro to migrants in metropolitan areas have stimulated the need for particular farming expertise as well as the development of marketing and processing techniques.

Taro has survived a major hiatus in the nineteenth and twentieth centuries that might have seen it eliminated as a crop or dismissed as one of backward, underdeveloped tropical countries. But cereals, even rice, will not grow readily in many of these tropical areas, whereas the taros are a flexible crop that suits shifting cultivation so that farmers can vary the size of their crops from month to month depending on demand. Nutritionally, taro is very good, especially when complemented with fat from fish or pork. Given agronomic support, taro has great potential for further contributions to the world food supply, and finally, it is a crop that has endured thanks to people's strong preference for it as their traditional food.

Nancy J. Pollock

Notes

1. It is ironic that rice has been introduced into modern-day Pacific diets as an emergency foodstuff that is easily transferred from metropolitan countries as a form of food aid to assist cyclone-stricken nations, such as Samoa in 1991. As such, it forms a substitute for locally grown taro, which is badly affected by salt inundation and wind breaking off the leaves, thus causing the corms to rot.
2. See Petterson (1977: 177) for a map of the spread of Xanthosoma taro around central and northern South Africa in contrast with the spread of Colocasia taro in the same area.
3. See Pollock (1992) for a listing of the importance of various starch staples in Pacific societies.
4. See Barrau (1965: 69) for a map showing its origins and distribution in Southeast Asia and the Pacific.
5. Petterson (1977: 178); see also the map on p. 177.
6. See Pollock et al. 1989 for preferences and consumption patterns of taros and other foods by those Samoans living away from their home islands in Wellington, New Zealand.
7. See Chandra (1979) for a detailed discussion of marketing root crops.

Bibliography

Barrau, J. 1961. *Subsistence agriculture in Polynesia and Micronesia.* B.P. Bishop Museum Bulletin No. 223.
1965. L'humide et le sec. *Journal of the Polynesian Society* 74: 329-46.
1975. The Oceanians and their food plants. In *Man and his foods,* ed. C. Earle Smith, Jr., 87-117. Tuscaloosa, Ala.
Bellwood, P. 1980. Plants, climate and people. In *Indonesia, Australia perspectives,* ed. J. J. Fox, 57-74. Canberra, Australia.
Bradbury, H., and W. D. Holloway. 1988. *Chemistry of tropical root crops.* Canberra, Australia.
Chandra, S. 1979. Root crops in Fiji, Part I. *Fiji Agricultural Journal* 41: 73-85.

Chang, K. C. 1977. *Food in Chinese culture.* New Haven, Conn.
de la Pena, R. 1983. Agronomy. In *Taro,* ed. J.-K. Wang, 169-70. Honolulu.
Dignan, C. A., B. A. Burlingame, J. M. Arthur, et al., eds. 1994. *The interim Pacific Islands food composition tables.*
Gorman, C. 1977. A priori models and Thai history. In *The origins of agriculture,* ed. C. A. Reed, 321-56. Mouton, N.S., Canada.
Handy, E. S. C., and Willowdean Handy. 1972. *Native planters in old Hawaii.* Honolulu.
Holo, T. F., and S. Taumoefolau. 1982. The cultivation of *alocasia macrorrhiza* (L.) schott. In *Taro cultivation in the Pacific,* ed. M. Lambert, 84-7. Noumea, New Caledonia.
Hutterer, Karl. 1983. The natural and cultural history of South East Asian agriculture. *Anthropos* 78: 169-201.
Jackson G. V. H., and J. A. Breen. 1985. *Collecting, describing and evaluating root crops.* Noumea, New Caledonia.
Kirch, Patrick V. 1985. *Feathered gods and fishhooks.* Honolulu.
Lambert, Michel. 1982. *Taro cultivation in the South Pacific.* Noumea, New Caledonia.
Luomala, Katharine. 1974. The Cyrtosperma systemic pattern. *Journal of the Polynesian Society* 83: 14-34.
Massal, E., and J. Barrau. 1956. *Food plants of the South Sea Islands.* Noumea, New Caledonia.
Mitchell, W. C., and Peter Maddison. 1983. Pests of taro. In *Taro,* ed. J.-K. Wang, 180-235. Honolulu.
Moy, J. H., and W. Nip. 1983. Processed foods. In *Taro,* ed. J.-K. Wang, 261-8. Honolulu.
Murdock, G. P. 1960. Staple subsistence crops of Africa. *Geographical Review* 50: 523-40.
Norman, M. J. T., C. J. Pearson, and P. G. E. Searle. 1984. *The ecology of tropical food crops.* London.
Ooka, J. J. 1983. Taro diseases. In *Taro,* ed. J.-K. Wang, 236-58. Honolulu.
Pawley, A., and R. Green. 1974. The proto-oceanic language community. *Journal of Pacific History* 19: 123-46.
Petterson, J. 1977. Dissemination and use of the edible aroids with particular reference to Colocasia (Asian Taro) and Xanthosoma (American Taro). Ph.D. thesis, University of Florida.
Plucknett, D. L. 1976. Edible aroids. In *Evolution of crop plants,* ed. N. W. Simmonds, 10-12. London.
1983. Taxonomy of the genus *Colocasia.* In *Taro,* ed. J.-K. Wang, 14-19. Honolulu.
Pollock, Nancy J. 1983. Rice in Guam. *Journal of Polynesian Society* 92: 509-20.
1985. Food concepts in Fiji. *Ecology of Food and Nutrition* 17: 195-203.
1988. The market place as meeting place in Tahiti. In *French Polynesia,* ed. Nancy J. Pollock and R. Crocombe, Suva, Fiji.
1990. Starchy food plants in the Pacific. In *Nga Mahi Maori O te Wao Nui a Tane, Contributions to an international workshop on ethnobotany,* ed. W. Harris and P. Kapoor, 72-81. Canterbury.
1992. *These roots remain.* Honolulu.
Pollock, N. J., A. Ahmu, S. Asomua, and A. Carter. 1989. Food and identity: Food preferences and diet of Samoans in Wellington, New Zealand. In *Migrations et identité, actes du colloque C.O.R.A.I.L.,* Publications de l'Université Française du Pacifique, Vol. 1. Noumea, New Caledonia.
Purseglove, J. W. 1972. Tropical crops. In *Monocotyledons I,* 58-75. New York.
Seeman, B. 1862. *Viti.* London.

Sivan, P. 1984. Review of taro research and production in Fiji. *Fiji Agricultural Journal* 43: 59-68.

Spriggs, M. 1982. Taro cropping systems in the South East Asian Pacific region. *Archeology in Oceania* 17: 7-15.

Standal, B. 1982. Nutritional value of edible aroids (Araceae) grown in the South Pacific. In *Taro cultivation in the South Pacific,* ed. M. Lambert, 123-31. Noumea, New Caledonia.

    1983. Nutritive value. In *Taro,* ed. J.-K. Wang, 141-7. Honolulu.

Tang, C., and W. W. Sakai. 1983. Acridity of taro and related plants in Araceae. In *Taro,* ed. J.-K. Wang, 148-64. Honolulu.

Vickers, M., and V. Untaman. 1982. The cultivation of taro *cyrtosperma chamissonis* schott. In *Taro cultivation in the South Pacific,* ed. M. Lambert, 90-100. Noumea, New Caledonia.

Weightman, B., and I. Moros. 1982. The cultivation of taro *xanthosoma* sp. In *Taro cultivation in the South Pacific,* ed. M. Lambert, 74-83. Noumea, New Caledonia.

Yen, D. E. 1980. The South East Asian foundations of Oceanic agriculture. *Journal de la Societe des Oceanistes* 66-7: 140-7.

⬥

II.C

Important Vegetable Supplements

II.C.1 ⬥ Algae

Algae are eukaryotic photosynthetic micro- and macroorganisms found in marine and fresh waters and in soils. Some are colorless and even phagotrophic or saprophytic. They may be picoplankton, almost too small to be seen in the light microscope, or they could be up to 180 feet long, such as the kelp in the kelp forests in the Pacific Ocean.

Algae are simple, nucleated plants divided into seven taxa: (1) Chlorophyta (green algae), (2) Charophyta (stoneworts), (3) Euglenophyta (euglenas), (4) Chrysophyta (golden-brown, yellow-green algae and diatoms), (5) Phaeophyta (brown algae), (6) Pyrrophyta (dinoflagellates), and (7) Rhodophyta (red algae). A taxon of simple, nonnucleated plants (prokaryotes) called Cyanobacteria (blue-green bacteria) is also included in the following discussion as they have a long history as human food.

Algae are eaten by many freshwater and marine animals as well as by several terrestrial domesticated animals such as sheep, cattle, and two species of primates: *Macaca fuscata* in Japan (Izawa and Nishida 1963) and *Homo sapiens*. The human consumption of algae, or phycophagy, developed thousands of years ago, predominantly among coastal peoples and, less commonly, among some inland peoples. In terms of quantity and variety of species of algae eaten, phycophagy is, and has been, most prevalent among the coastal peoples of Southeast Asia, such as the ancient and modern Chinese, Japanese, Koreans, Filipinos, and Hawaiians.

History and Geography

The earliest archaeological evidence for the consumption of algae found thus far was discovered in ancient middens along the coast of Peru. Kelp was found in middens at Pampa, dated to circa 2500 B.C. (Moseley 1975); at Playa Hermosa (2500–2275 B.C.); at Concha (2275–1900 B.C.); at Gaviota (1900–1750 B.C.); and at Ancon (1400–1300 B.C.) (Patterson and Moseley 1968). T. C. Patterson and M. E. Moseley (1968) believe that these finds indicate that marine algae were employed by the ancient Peruvians to supplement their diets.

Other types of seaweeds were also found in middens at Aspero, Peru, and dated to 2275 to 1850 B.C. by Moseley and G. R. Willey (1973) and at Asia, Peru, and dated to 1314 B.C. (Parsons 1970). Additionally, unidentified algae were found in middens at numerous sites, among them Padre Aban and Alto Salaverry (2500–1800 B.C.); Gramalote, Caballo Muerte (2000–1800 B.C.); Cerro Arena, Moche Huacas (200 B.C. to A.D. 600); and Chan Chan (A.D. 1000–1532) (Pozorski 1979; Raymond 1981).

Furthermore, much evidence exists to indicate a marine algae presence in ancient Peru. The base of the temples at Las Haldas, for example, which date circa 1650 B.C., contained quantities of seaweed and shellfish (Matsuzawa 1978). Small stalks of a seaweed were found in a Paracas mummy bundle (Yacovleff and Muelle 1934: 134), and the giant kelp *Macrocystis humboldtii* was pictured on an ancient Nazca vase (Yacovleff and Herrera 1934–5). In recent times, the native peoples of the Andean highlands have retained the right to come down to the coast, gather and dry seaweed, and transfer it to the mountains, where algae has great value and can be used in place of money. Used as a condiment to flavor soups and stews, dried seaweed minimizes the ravages of hypothyroidism, which is endemic in the Andes (Aaronson 1986). Early visitors reported that dried seaweed was also eaten with vinegar after dinner and sold in the marketplace as a kneaded dry product (Cobo 1956). The cyanobacteria *Nostoc* spp. (called *cushuro, llucllucha,* or *kochayuyo*) grow in Andean lakes and ponds and are also presently used as food (Aldave-Pajares 1965–66; Gade 1975; Browman 1981; and Table II.C.1.1), as they were in early Spanish colonial times (Cobo 1956) and, possibly, in Inca times as well (Guaman Poma de Ayala 1965-6).

Table II.C.1.1. *Algae and blue-green bacteria eaten in contemporary Chile and Peru*

Species	Common name	Eaten as[a]
Cyanobacteria		
Nostoc commune	cushuro[b]	picantes
	elulluchcha[b]	-
	kocha-yuya[b]	-
Nostoc parmeloides	llullcha[b]	-
Nostoc pruniforme	cushuro, cusuro[b]	chupe
	crespito[b]	locro
	unrupa macho[b]	picantes
	macha-masha[b]	mazamorra
Nostoc sphaericum	cashuro[b]	chupe
	cussuro, cusuro[b]	locro
	ururupsha[b]	mazamorro
	rachapa[b]	picantes
Nostoc verrucosum	murmunta[b]	-
Chlorophyta		
Codium fragile	tercioelo[c]	-
Monostroma sp.	yuyo de rio[b]	noodle soup
	lechuga de mar[b]	-
	lechuquita de rio[b]	-
Ulva fasciata costata	lechuquita de rio[b]	picante
Ulva lactuca	luche verde[d]	-
Ulva pappenfussii	cochayuyo[b]	-
Phaeophyta		
Durvillea antarctica	cochayuyo[c,d]	-
Lessonia nigrescens	tinilhue[c]	-
Macrocystis integrifolia	huiro[d]	-
Macrocystis pyrifera	huiro[d]	ceviche
Rhodophyta		
Gigartina chamissoi	cochayuyo[b]	-
	chicorea del mar[c]	-
Gigartina glomerata	cochayuyo[b]	ceviche
	yuyo[b]	picantes
	mococho[b]	soup
Gigartina paitensis	mococho[b]	soup
	cochayuyo[b]	picantes
Gracillaria verrucosa	pelillo[c]	-
Iridaea boryana	luga[c]	-
Porphyra columbina	luche[c]	-
Porphyra leucosticta	cochayuyo[b]	picantes
Prionitis decipiens	piscuchaqui[b]	picantes
Rhodoglossum denticulatum	cochayuyo[b]	ceviche
		picantes
		soup

[a]Common names for Peruvian food from Polo (1977).

[b]Polo (1977).

[c]Dillehay (1989).

[d]Masuda (1985).

Note: Ceviche is a soup with algae, small pieces of fish, lemon, and hot pepper.

Chupe is a soup with milk, algae, eggs, potatoes, and cheese.

Cochayuyo is from the Quecha *cocha* (lagoon or pond) and *yuyo* (herb or vegetable).

Cuchuro is from the Quecha for wavy.

Pachayuo is from the Quechua *pacho* (soil) and *yuyo* (vegetable).

Picantes is a stew made of algae, pieces of fish, potatoes, and hot pepper.

Locro is a maize and meat stew with algae.

Mazamorro is a stew made with pieces of algae and other ingredients.

Moving north in the Americas, *Spirulina maxima,* or *Spirulina geitleriai* (a blue-green bacterium known as *tecuitlatl* [stone excrement] in Nahuatl, the Aztec language), has been eaten in the Valley of Mexico since the beginning of the Spanish colonial period (c. 1524) and was consumed even prior to Aztec times (Furst 1978). Other cyanobacteria, such as *Phormidium tenue* and *Chroococcus turgidus* (called *cocolin* and *Nostoc commune* [*amoxtle* in Nahuatl]), are gathered for consumption from the lakes and ponds of the Valley of Mexico and, very likely, have been since time immemorial (Ortega 1972).

In Africa, another species of cyanobacterium, *Spirulina platensis,* grows abundantly in Lake Chad and is collected, dried, and made into a sauce. It is widely consumed by the Kanembu people of Chad (Leonard and Compère 1967; Delpeuch, Joseph, and Cavelier 1975).

In China, the earliest reference to algae as food occurs in the *Book of Poetry* (800–600 B.C.) (Chase 1941), and Wu's *Materia Medica* indicates that the seaweed *Ecklonia* was utilized as food and medicine as early as 260 to 220 B.C. Another type of seaweed, *Porphyra,* was also used as food according to the *Qiminyaoshu* (A.D. 533–44).

Gloiopeltis furcata has been collected in southern Fujian Province since the Sung Dynasty (A.D. 960–1279) (Tseng 1933), and C.-K. Tseng (1987) states that *Laminaria japonica (haidi)* has been eaten there for about 1,000 years. Several other types of algae were also consumed, according to the *Compendium of Materia Medica (Bencaigangmu)* of the Ming Dynasty (1368–1644), edited by L. Shizhan (1518–93). These included: *Cladophora* spp., *Codium fragile, Ecklonia kurone, Enteromorpha prolifera, Enteromorpha* spp., *Euchema muricatum, Gelidium divaricatum, Gloeopeltis furcata, Gracilaria verrucosa, Laminaria japonica, Monostroma nitidum, Nostoc sphaeroides, Prasiola sinensis, Porphyra* sp., and *Ulva lactuca.*

The cyanobacterium *Nostoc commune* has been eaten in China for the last 400 years (Chu and Tseng 1988), and a related species, *Nostoc coerulum,* was served in this century at a dinner given by a mandarin for a French ambassador (Tilden 1929; Montagne 1946–7). According to Tseng (1990), the large-scale cultivation of the seaweed *Gloiopeltis furcata* began in Fujian Province during the Sung Dynasty.

In Japan, the eating of algae is also an ancient practice. Seaweed was apparently eaten by the early inhabitants of Japan, as it has been found with shells and fish bones at human sites in the Jomon period (10,500–300 B.C.) and the Yayoi period (200 B.C. to A.D. 200) (Nisizawa et al. 1987). In A.D. 701, the emperor established the Law of Taiho in which seaweeds (*Gelidium, Laminaria, Porphyra,* and *Undaria* spp.) were among the marine products paid to the court as a tax (Miyashita 1974).

The blue-green bacterium *Nostoc verrucosum,* currently known as *ashitsuki nori,* was mentioned in *Man Yo Shu* by Yakomichi Otomi in the oldest anthology of 31-syllable odes dating to A.D. 748. Ode number 402 translates: "Girls are standing on the shores of the Wogami-gawa River in order to pick up *ashitsuki nori*." According to the *Wamyosho* (the oldest Chinese–Japanese dictionary in Japan), 21 species of marine algae (brown, green, and red) were eaten by Japanese during the Heiam era (A.D. 794-1185) (Miyashita 1974). In *The Tale of the Genji*, written by Murasake Shikibu (A.D. 978), a marine alga, *Codium fragile,* is mentioned as a food (Hiroe 1969). The Greeks and Romans apparently disliked algae and, seemingly, made no use of them as human food, although they were used as emergency food for livestock. Virgil (70-19 B.C.) called algae *vilior alga* (vile algae), and Horace (65-8 B.C.) seems to have shared his opinion (Newton 1951; Chapman 1970).

The seaweed *Rhodymenia palmata* was eaten in Iceland as early as A.D. 960, according to the *Egil Saga* (Savageau 1920). *Alaria esculenta* (bladder-locks) was (and still is) consumed in Scotland, Ireland, Iceland, Norway, and the Orkney Islands, where it is called alternatively "honey-ware," "mirkles," and "murlins." *Laminaria digitata* ("tangle") is also eaten in Scotland, and *Rhodymenia palmata* ("dulse") is used as food in Iceland, Scotland, and around the Mediterranean, where it is an ingredient in soups and ragouts. Similarly, *Laurencia pinnatifida* ("pepper dulse") is eaten in Scotland, and *Porphyra laciniata* ("purple laver") is used as a condiment in the Hebrides (Johnston 1970).

Algae and Cyanobacteria as Human Food Today

Algae (Chlorophyta, Phaeophyta, and Rhodophyta) and cyanobacteria are now consumed in all countries that possess marine coasts as well as in countries where algae are abundant in lakes, streams, ponds, and rivers. Consumers range from surviving Stone Age peoples to modern hunter-gatherers, to agricultural folk, to industrial peoples.

Algae are used as foods in a wide variety of ways. They are served raw in salads and pickled or fermented into relish. They make a fine addition to soups, stews, and sauces, and are used as condiments. Algae are also roasted, employed as a tea, and served as a dessert, a sweetmeat, a jelly, or a cooked vegetable (see Table II.C.1.2 for countries in which algae are eaten as food and the form of the food).

In industrialized countries, algal products like agar, alginates, and carrageenans are extracted from some seaweeds and used to replace older foods or to create new foods or food combinations.

Table II.C.1.2. *Algae eaten by humans now and in the past*

Species name	Country	Local name	Use	Reference
Cyanophyta				
Aphanothece sacrum	Japan	–	Food	Zaneveld 1950; Watanabe 1970
Brachytrichia quoyi	China	–	Food	Chu and Tseng 1988
	Japan	–	Food	Watanabe 1970
Chroococcus turgidus	Mexico	*Cocol de agua*	Food	Ortega 1972
Nostoc coeruleum	China	–	Food	Montagne 1946–7
Nostoc commune	Peru	*cushuro*	Food	Aldave-Pajares 1969
	Japan	*kamagawa-nori*	Food	Watanabe 1970
	Java	*djamurbatu*	Food	Zaneveld 1950
	Mongolia	–	Food	Elenkin 1931
	Mexico	*amoxtle*	Food	Ortega 1972
	Bolivia	–	Food	Lagerheim 1892
	Ecuador	–	Food	Lagerheim 1892
Nostoc commune var. *flagelliforme*	China	*fa-ts'ai*	Food	Jassley 1988
Nostoc edule = *pruniforme*	China, Mongolia, Soviet Union	–	Soup	Johnston 1970
	Peru	*cushuro*	Food	Aldave-Pajares 1969
Nostoc ellipsosporum	Ecuador	–	Food	Lagerheim 1892
Nostoc parmeloides	Peru	–	Food	Aldave-Pajares 1985
Nostoc sphaericum	Peru	*cushuro*	Food	Aldave-Pajares 1969
Nostoc verrucosum	Peru	*cushuro*	Food	Aldave-Pajares 1969
	Thailand	–	Food	Smith 1933
	Japan	–	Food	Watanabe 1970
Nostoc sp.	Fiji	–	Food	Wood 1965
Nostochopsis lobatus	China	–	Food	Chu and Tseng 1988
Nostochopsis sp.	Thailand	–	Soup, dessert	Lewmanomont 1978
Oscillatoria spp.	Java	*keklap*	Food	Zaneveld 1950
Phormidium tenue	Mexco	*cocol de agua*	Food	Ortega 1972
Phylloderma sacrum	Japan	*suizenji-nori, kotobuki-nori*	Food	Watanabe 1970
Spirulina maxima	Mexico	*tecuitlatl*	Food	Clément, Giddey, and Merzi 1967
Spirulina platensis	Chad	*die*	Sauce	Dangeard 1940

(continued)

Table II.C.1.2. *(Continued)*

Species name	Country	Local name	Use	Reference
Charophyta				
Chara spp.	Peru	–	Food	Browman 1980
Chlorophyta				
Caulerpa sp.	New Caledonia	–	Baked, raw	Barrau 1962
	New Hebrides	–	Salad	Massal and Barrau 1956
	Polynesia	*lum, limu*	Salad	Massal and Barrau 1956
Caulerpa peltata	Malaysia	*lata*	Salad	Zaneveld 1950
	Java	*lata*	Salad	Zaneveld 1955
	Phillippines	–	Salad	Zaneveld 1955
	Indonesia	–	Salad, sweetmeat	Subba Rao 1965
Caulerpa racemosa	Malaysia	*letato*	Dessert	Zaneveld 1955
	Philippines	*ararucip lai-lai*	Salad	Galutira and Velasquez 1963
	Indonesia	–	Raw, sweetmeat	Subba Rao 1965
	Guam	*limu fuafua*	Relish	Subba Rao 1965
	Melanesia	–	–	Massal and Barrau 1956
Caulerpa serrulata	Malaysia	–	Food	Subba Rao 1965
	Celebes	–	Food	Zaneveld 1955
	Singapore	–	Salad	Zaneveld 1955
	Philippines	*gal galacgac*	Food	Zaneveld 1950
Chaetomorpha sp.	Malaysia	*lumut laut*	Food	Zaneveld 1950
Chaetomorpha antennina	Hawaii	*limu hutuito, limu ilic, limumami*	Food	Zaneveld 1959
	Malaysia	*lumut-laut*	Raw	Zaneveld 1950
Chaetomorpha crassa	Philippines	*kauat-kauat*	Sweetmeat	Zaneveld 1950
Chaetomorpha javanica	Indonesia	*lumut laut*	Food	Zaneveld 1950
Chaetomorpha tomentosum	Malaysia	*susu-lopek, laur-laur*	Raw	Zaneveld 1950
Cladophora sp.	Peru	–	Food	Browman 1980
Codium sp.	Philippines	*pocpoclo*	Salad	Galutira and Velasquez 1963
	Samoa	–	Raw, baked	Barrau 1962
Codium fragile	Japan	*miru*	Soup, sauce	Chapman and Chapman 1980
	China	*shulsong*	Food	Tseng 1983
Codium intricatum	Philippines	*pocpoclo*	Salad, cooked vegetable	Velasquez 1972
Codium muelleri	Hawaii	*limu aalaula*	Salad	Zaneveld 1955
	Philippines	*pocpoclo*	Salad	Zaneveld 1955
Codium papillatum	Philippines	*pocpoclo*	Salad, cooked vegetable	Velasquez 1972
Codium tomentosum	Malaysia	*susu-lopek, laur-laur*	Raw	Zaneveld 1950; Subba Rao 1965
Enteromorpha sp.	China	*hu-t'ai*	Condiment	Tseng 1933
	Hawaii	*limu eleele*	Salad	Abbott 1978
	New Caledonia	–	Raw, baked	Barrau 1962
	Philippines	*lumot*	Salad	Galutira and Velasquez 1963
	Northwest North America	–	Food	Madlener 1977
Enteromorpha clathrata	China	taitiao	Food	Tseng 1983
Enteromorpha compressa	Malaysia	–	Food	Zaneveld 1955
	Philippines	*lumot*	Salad	Velasquez 1972
Enteromorpha flexuosa	Hawaii	*limu eleele*	Salad	Chapman and Chapman 1980
Enteromorpha intestinalis	Canada	–	Food	Turner 1974
	Malaysia	–	Food	Zaneveld 1950
	Philippines	*lumot*	Salad	Zaneveld 1955
Enteromorpha plumosa	Philippines	*lumot*	Salad	Galutira and Velasquez 1963
Enteromorpha prolifera	Hawaii, Malaysia, China	*limu eleele*	Salad	Zaneveld 1950
Enteromorpha tubulosa	China	*hu-t'ai*	Food	Tseng 1983
Monostroma sp.	Peru	–	Soup	Polo 1977
	China	*chiao-mo*	Condiment	Tseng 1933
Monostroma nitidum	China	–	Condiment	Xia and Abbott 1987
Monostroma guaternaria	Peru	–	Food	Aldave-Pajares 1985
Oedogonium sp.	India	–	Food	Tiffany 1958
Prasiola japonica	Japan	*kawa-nori, daiyagawa-nori, nikko-nori*	Food	Namikawa 1906; Skvortzov 1919–22; Watanabe 1970
Prasiola yunnanica	China	–	Food	Jao 1947; Jassley 1988
Spirogyra sp.	Burma	–	Food	Biswas 1953
	Canada	–	Food	Turner 1974
	Indochina	–	Food	Léonard and Compère 1967
	Thailand	–	Soup, salad	Lewmanomont 1978

Table II.C.1.2. *(Continued)*

Species name	Country	Local name	Use	Reference
Chlorophyta				
Ulothrix flacca	China	–	Vegetable	Xia and Abbott 1987
Ulva sp.	China	–	Food	Chapman and Chapman 1980
	Japan	*awosa, aosa*	Garnish	Chapman and Chapman 1980
Ulva conlobata	China	–	Tea	Xia and Abbott 1987
Ulva fasciata	Hawaii	*limu pahapaha*	Food	Schönfeld-Leber 1979
	Peru	*cochayuyo*	Food	Masuda 1981
	China	–	Tea	Xia and Abbott 1987
Ulva lactuca	Canada (Bella Coola, Haida, Lillooet Indiands)	–	Food	Turner 1974
	Chile	*luche*	Food	Ohni 1968
	China	*Hai ts'ai*	Soup, salad, vegetable	Tseng 1933
	New Zealand (Maori)		Soup, stew, vegetable	Brooker, Combie, and Cooper 1989
	Peru	*cochayuyo*	Food	Masuda 1981
	Philippines	*gamgamet*	Salad, cooked vegetable	Velasquez 1972
Ulva lactuca	United States, California (Pomo and Kashoya Indians)	*sihtono*	Flavoring	Goodrich, Lawson, and Lawson 1980
	Hawaii	*limu pakcaea*	Soup, salad, garnish	Zaneveld 1955
	Washington (Makah)	*kalkatsup*	Food	Gunther 1945
Phaeophyta				
Alaria crassifolia	Japan	*chigaiso*	Food	Subba Rao 1965
Alaria esculenta	Alaska (Indian)	–	Food	Porsild 1953
	Siberia (Nivkhi)	–	Food	Eidlitz 1969
	Iceland, Ireland, Orkney Islands, Norway, Scotland	–	Food	Johnston 1970
Alaria pylaii	Greenland (Inuit)	*kjpilasat*	Food	Hoygaard 1937
	Greenland (Angmagsalik)	*suvdluitsit*	Food	Ostermann 1938
	Siberia	*me'cgomei*	Food	Eidlitz 1969
Arthrothamnus bifidus	Japan	*mekoashi-kombu chigaiso*	Food	Subba Rao 1965
Arthrothamnus kurilensis	Japan	*chishimanekoashi*	Food	Subba Rao 1965
Ascophyllum nodosum	Greenland	*miserarnat*	Food	Hoygaard 1937
Chnoospora pacifica	Indochina	*rau ngoai*	Salad, relish	Zaneveld 1955
Chorda filum	China	–	Food	Tseng 1983
	Japan	–	Salad	Chapman and Chapman 1980
Dictyopteris plagiogramma	Hawaii	*limu lipoa*	Food	Chapman and Chapman 1980
Dictyopteris repens	Easter Island	*auke*	Food	Ohni 1968
Dictyota sp.	Indonesia	–	Food	Michanek 1975
Dictyota acutiloba	Hawaii	–	Food	Chapman and Chapman 1980
Dictyota apiculata	Hawaii	–	Food	Zaneveld 1955
Durvillea antarctica	Chile	*cochayuyo*	Stew	Ohni 1968
	Peru	*cochayuyo*	Food	Masuda 1981
	New Zealand (Maori)	*rimurapi*	Roasted	Brooker and Cooper 1961
Ecklonia kurome	China	*kunbu, miangichai*	Food	Tseng 1983
Ecklonia stolonifera	Japan	*kizame arame*	Soup, sauce, stew	Chapman and Chapman 1980
Eisenia bicyclis	Japan	*arame*	Soup, stew	Subba Rao 1965
Endorachne binghamiae	China	–	Food	Tseng 1983
Fucus sp.	Alaska (Chugach)	–	Food	Ager and Ager 1980
	Greenland (Inuit)	*mikarkat*	Food	Hoygaard 1937
Heterochordaria abietina	Japan	*matsumo*	Sauce	Subba Rao 1965
Hizikia fusiforme	Japan	*hijiki*	Soup, stew, salad	Subba Rao 1965
Hydroclathrus clathratus	Philippines	*balbalulang*	Salad	Velasquez 1972
Ishige okamurai	China	*tieding cai*	Food	Tseng 1983
Ishige sinicole	China	*hai dai*	Food	Tseng 1983
Kjellmaniella gyrata	Japan	–	Soup	Chapman and Chapman 1980
Laminaria sp.	New Zealand	*rimu roa*	Roasted	Goldie 1904
Laminaria angustata	Japan	*kizami-kombu*	Soup	Chapman and Chapman 1980
			Vegetable	Chapman and Chapman 1980
Laminaria cichorioides	Japan	*chiimi-kombu*	Food	Chapman and Chapman 1980
Laminaria diabolica	Japan	*kuro-tororo kombu*	Food	Chapman and Chapman 1980
Laminaria digitata	Scotland	–	Food	Johnston 1970

(continued)

Table II.C.1.2. *(Continued)*

Species name	Country	Local name	Use	Reference
Phaeophyta				
Laminaria japonica	Japan	*ma-kombu*	Sweetmeat	Subba Rao 1965
	Japan	*ori-kombu*	Food	Subba Rao 1965
	China	*hai'tai*	Food	Simoons 1991
Laminaria digitata	Japan	–	Food	Johnston 1970
Laminaria ochotensis	Japan	*rishiri-kombu*	Food	Chapman and Chapman 1980
Laminaria religiosa	Japan	*hosome-kombu, saimatsu-kombu*	Food	Chapman and Chapman 1980
Laminaria saccharina	France, Great Britain, Ireland	–	Fresh	Chapman and Chapman 1980
Laminaria yezoensis	Japan	–	Food	Chapman and Chapman 1980
Macrocystus integrifolia	British Columbia	–	Food	Turner 1975
Mesogloia crassa	Japan	*futo-mozuku*	Food	Chapman and Chapman 1980
Mesogloia decipiens	Japan	*mozuku*	Food	Chapman and Chapman 1980
Nemacystus decipiens	China	*haida*	Food	Tseng 1983
	Japan	*mozuku*	Food	Chapman and Chapman 1980
Padina australis	Indonesia	*agar-agar, daun-besar*	Sweetmeat	Zaneveld 1951
Pelvetia siliquosa	China	*lujiao cai*	Food	Tseng 1983
Petalonia fascia	Japan	*hondawara*	Soup, sauce	Chapman and Chapman 1980
Postelsia palmaeformis	California (Indian)	*gaye*	Food	Goodrich et al. 1980
Sargassum sp.	China	*hai ts'ai*	Tea, soup	Tseng 1935
	Hawaii	*limu kala*	Food	Schönfeld-Leber 1979
	Malaysia	–	Food	Subba Rao 1965
Sargassum aguifollum	Indonesia, Malaysia	*arien wari*	Raw, cooked	Zaneveld 1965
Sargassum fusiformis	China	*chu-chiau ts'ai*	Soup, vegetable	Tseng 1983
Sargassum granuliferum	Amboina	*arien-wari*	Raw, cooked	Zaneveld 1955
	Indonesia	–	Raw, cooked	Subba Rao 1965
	Malaysia	–	Raw, cooked	Zaneveld 1955
Sargassum hemiphyllum	China	–	Food	Tseng 1983
Sargassum henslowianum	China	–	Food	Tseng 1983
Sargassum horneri	China	–	Food	Tseng 1983
Sargassum pallidum	China	–	Food	Tseng 1983
Sargassum polycystum	Amboina	*arien harulu*	Raw	Zaneveld 1955
	Moluccas	*agar-agar' kupean*		
Sargassum siliquosum	Malaysia	–	Raw, cooked, pickled	Zaneveld 1955
	Philippines	*aragan*	Raw, cooked	Zaneveld 1955
Scytosiphon lomentaria	China	–	Food	Tseng 1983
Turbinaria conoides	Celebes	*labi-labi*	Salad	Zaneveld 1951
	Malaysia		Pickle	Zaneveld 1951
Turbinaria ornata	Malaysia	*agar-agar-ksong*	Pickle	Zaneveld 1955
	Moluccas	*arien essong*	Raw, cooked	Zaneveld 1955
Undaria peterseneeniana	Japan	*wakame*	–	Zaneveld 1955
Undaria pinnatifida	China	–	Food	Simoons 1991
	Japan	*wakame*	Food	Subba Rao 1965
Undaria undarioides	Japan	*wakame*	Food	Chapman and Chapman 1980
Rhodophyta				
Agardhiella sp.	Philippines	*gulaman*	Sweetmeat	Zaneveld 1955
Acanthopeltis japonica	Japan	*yuikiri*	Food	Subba Rao 1965
	Indonesia	–	Vegetable	Subba Rao 1965
Acanthophora spicifera	Philippines	*culot*	Salad, cooked	Velasquez 1972
Ahnfeltia concinna	Hawaii	*limu akiaki*	Salad, baked	Schöenfeld-Leber 1979
Asparagopsis sanfordiana	Hawaii	–	Food	Schöenfeld-Leber 1979
Ahnfeltia taxiformis	China	–	Salad, stew	Montagne 1946-7
	Hawaii	*limu kohu*	Food	Abbott 1987
Bangia fusco-purpurea	China	*hangmaocai*	Salad	Montagne 1946-7
	Hawaii	–	Soup	Xia and Abbott 1987
Caloglossa adnata	Burma	–	Raw, boiled	Zaneveld 1955
Caloglossa leprieurii	Burma	–	Food	Subba Rao 1965
Campylaephora hypnaeides	Japan	*yego-nori*	Food	Subba Rao 1965
Carpopeltis flabellata	Japan	*kome-nori*	Garnish	Subba Rao 1965
Catenella impudica	Burma	–	Salad	Zaneveld 1955
Catenella nipae	Burma	–	Raw, cooked	Boergesen 1938
Chondria tenuissima	Hawaii	*limu oolu*	Food	Schönfeld-Leber 1979
Chondrus elatus	China	–	Food	Johnston 1966
Chondrus ocellatus	China	–	Food	Tseng 1983
	Japan	*makuri-nori*	Food	Subba Rao 1965
Corallopsis salicornia	Indonesia	*bulung-buka*	Vegetable, jelly	Zaneveld 1955; Subba Rao 1965

Table II.C.1.2. *(Continued)*

Species name	Country	Local name	Use	Reference
Rhodophyta				
Dermonema frappieri	China	–	Food	Lee 1965
Dermonema oulvinata	China	–	Food	Tseng 1983
Digenea simplex	Japan	*makuri-nori*	Food	Subba Rao 1965
Eucheuma edule	China	*hai-ts'ai mu*	Food	Tseng 1983
	Indonesia	*agar-agar-besar*	Jelly	Zaneveld 1955
Eucheuma gelatinae	China	–	Food	Tseng 1983
Eucheuma horridum	Malaysia	–	Jelly	Zaneveld 1955
Eucheuma muricatum	Indonesia	–	Jelly	Subba Rao 1965
	Malaysia	–	Agar	Zaneveld 1955
	Philippines	*canot-canot*	Salad, cooked vegetable	Velasquez 1972
Eucheuma serra	Bali	*bulung djukut lelipan*	Agar, vegetable	Zaneveld 1955
Eucheuma speciosa	Tasmania	–	Jelly	Irving 1957
Gelidiella acerosa	Philippines	*culot*	Salad, cooked vegetable	Velasquez 1972
Gelidium sp.	China	*shih-hua-tsh*	Agar	Tseng 1933
	Hawaii	*limu loloa*	Food	Schöfel-Leber 1979
Gelidium amansii	Indonesia	–	Jelly	Subba Rao 1965
Gelidium latifolium	Hawaii	–	Agar	Zaneveld 1955
	Indonesia	*limu loloa*	Jelly	Subba Rao 1965
	Java	–	Agar	Zaneveld 1955
Gelidium rigidum	Indonesia	–	Jelly	Subba Rao 1965
	Malaysia	–	Agar	Zaneveld 1955
Gigartina sp.	Malaysia	–	Food	Subba Rao 1965
	New Zealand	*rehia*	Food	Schöenfeld-Leber 1979
Gigartina chamissoi	Peru	*cochayuyo*	Soup, stew	Polo 1977
Gigartina glomerata	Peru	*cochayuyo*	Soup, stew	Polo 1977
Gigartina intermedia	China	–	Food	Lee 1965
Gigartina teedii	Japan	*cata-nori,shikin-nori*	Food	Subba Rao 1965
Gloiopeltis sp.	China	–	Soup	Tseng 1933
Gloiopeltis coliformis	China	–	Food	Chapman and Chapman 1980
Gloiopeltis furcata	China	–	Food	Chapman and Chapman 1980
	Japan	*funori*	Food	Chapman and Chapman 1980
Gloiopeltis tenax	Taiwan	*funori*	Raw, fried	Chapman and Chapman 1980
Gracilaria sp.	New Zealand	*karengo*	Food	Schönfeld-Leber 1979
Gracilaria conferoides	China	*hai-mein-san*	Food	Tseng 1933
	Philippines	*gulaman*	Salad, cooked vegetable	Wester 1925
Gracilaria coronopifolia	Hawaii	*limu mahauea*	Food	Schönfeld-Leber 1979
	Philippines	*caocooyan*	Dessert	Velasquez 1972
Gracilaria crassa	Philippines	*susueldot-baybay*	–	Zaneveld 1955
Gracilaria eucheumoides	Philippines	*cavot-cavot*	Raw, cooked	Zaneveld 1955
Gracilaria lichenoides	Amboina	*atjar*	Pickled	Zaneveld 1955
	Ceylon	*chan, chow-parsi*	Pudding	Subba Rao 1965
	Hawaii	*limu manauea*	Soup, jelly	Zaneveld 1955
	India	*conji-parsi*	Food	Chapman and Chapman 1980
	Malaysia	–	Pickled	Subba and Rao 1965
Gracilaria salicornia	Philippines	*susueldot-baybay*	Food	Velasquez 1972
Gracilaria taenioides	Malaysia	–	Food	Subba Rao 1965
Gracilaria verrucosa	Philippines	*susueldot-baybay*	Food	Galutira and Velasquez 1963
Grateloupia affinis	Japan	*kome-nori*	Food	Chapman and Chapman 1980
Grateloupia doryphora	Peru	*cochayuyo*	Food	Polo 1977
Grateloupia filicina	China	–	Soup	Xia and Abbott 1987
	Japan	*mukade-nori*	Food	Subba Rao 1965
	Philippines	–	Jelly	Zaneveld 1955
Grateloupia ligulata	China	*hai-ts'ai*	Food	Tseng 1935
Griffithsia sp.	Hawaii	*limu moopuna-kana lipoa*	Food	Schönfeld-Leber 1979
Gymnogongrus disciplinalis	Hawaii	*limu vavaloli*	Food	Subba Rao 1965
Gymnogongrus flabelliformis	Japan	*okitsu-nori*	Food	Subba Rao 1965
Gymnogongrus vermicularis	Hawaii	*limu vavaloli*	Food	Schönfeld-Leber 1979
Halymenia durviliae	Hawaii	*limu lepeahina*	Food	Zaneveld 1955
	Philippines	*gayong-gayong*	Salad, cooked vegetable	Velasquez 1972
Hypnea	Indonesia	–	Dessert	Subba Rao 1965
Hypnea armata	Hawaii	*limu huna*	Food	Schöenfeld-Leber 1979

(continued)

Table II.C.1.2. *(Continued)*

Species name	Country	Local name	Use	Reference
Rhodophyta				
Hypnea cenomyce	Indonesia	–	Food	Zaneveld 1955
Hypnea cernicornis	China	*sa ts'ai*	Food	Tseng 1935
Hypnea charoides	Philippines	*culot tipusa*	Salad	Velasquez 1972
Hypnea divaricata	Amboina	*arien*	Agar, food	Zaneveld 1955
Hypnea nidifica	Hawaii	*limu huna*	Food	Schöenfeld-Leber 1979
Hypnea musciformis	China	*su-wei-tung*	Stew, jelly	Tseng 1935
Iridea edulis	Iceland	–	Food	Chapman and Chapman 1980
	Scotland	*dulse*	Food	Chapman and Chapman 1980
Laurencia sp.	Hawaii	*limu lipeepee*	Salad	Schönfeld-Leber 1979
	Polynesia	*lum, (limu, rimu)*	Cooked	Massal and Barrau 1956
Laurencia botryoides	Hawaii	*tartariptip*	Raw, cooked	Zaneveld 1955
Laurencia okamurai	Philippines	*culot*	Salad, cooked vegetable	Velasquez 1972
Laurencia papillosa	Hawaii	*limu lipeepee*	Cooked salad,	Zaneveld 1955
	Philippines	*culot*	cooked vegetable	Velasquez 1972
Laurencia pinnatifida	Scotland, Western Europe, United States	*pepper dulse*	Seasoning	Chapman and Chapman 1980
Lemanea mamillosa	India	*nungham*	Food	Khan 1973
Liagora decussata	Hawaii	*limu puak*	Food	Scönfeld-Leber 1979
Liagora farinosa	Philippines	*baris-baris*	Food	Zaneveld 1955
Macrocystis integrifolia	British Columbia	giant kelp	Food	Turner 1975
Nemalion helminthoides	Italy, Japan	sea noodles	Food	Chapman and Chapman 1980
Nemalion multifidum	Japan	*tsukomo-nori*	Food	Chapman and Chapman 1980
Nemalion vermiculare	Japan	*umu-somen*	Food	Chapman and Chapman 1980
Porphyra sp.	British Columbia	–	Food	Turner and Bell 1973
	New Zealand	*karengo*	Food	Schönfeld-Leber 1979
Porphyra atropurpurea	Hawaii	*limu luau*	Condiment	Zaneveld 1955
	Philippines	*gamet*	Soup	
Porphyra columbina	Chile	*luche*	Stew	Ohni 1968
	Peru	*cochayuyo*	Stew	Polo 1977
Porphyra crispata	China	*tsu ts'ai*	Condiment, vegetable	Galutira and Velasquez 1963
Porphyra dentata	China	–	Food	Xia and Abbott 1980
Porphyra laciniata	California	–	Baked, raw	Yanovsky 1936
	Hebrides	–	Food	Johnston 1970
Porphyra leucosticta	Hawaii	*limu luau*	Food	Scönfeld-Leber 1979
	Peru	*cochayuyo*	Stew	Polo 1977
Porphyra marginata	China	–	Food	Xia and Abbott 1987
Porphyra perforata	British Columbia	–	Food	Turner 1975
Porphyra suborbiculata	China	*tzu-ts'ai*	Vegetable	Simoons 1991
Porphyra tenera	Japan	*awanori*	Food	Subba Rao 1965
Porphyra vulgaris	California	–	Baked, raw	Yanovsky 1936
Rhodymenia palmata	Canada	*sol*	Nibbled with beer	Chapman and Chapman 1980
	Iceland	*sol*	Cooked, baked	Chapman and Chapman 1980
	Ireland	–	Food	Chapman and Chapman 1980
Rhodoglossum denticulatum	Peru	–	Food	Polo 1977
Sarcodia sp.	Japan	*hosaka-nori, atsuba-nori*	Food	Subba Rao 1965
Sarcodia montagneana	Molluccas	–	Food	Zaneveld 1955
Suhria vittata	South Africa	–	Jelly	Chapman and Chapman 1980

Seaweeds as Fertilizer and Animal Fodder

Seaweeds have been exploited for fertilizer by coastal farmers for centuries (if not millennia) in Europe, North America, the Mediterranean, and Asia (Booth 1965; Waaland 1981). Roman writings from the second century A.D. contain the oldest known evidence of seaweed as a fertilizer (Newton 1951). Seaweed was plowed into fields where it rotted, replenishing the soil with essential minerals. Alternatively, the seaweed was dried and burned, and the ash used as fertilizer, or the fields were "limed" with coralline algae and the sands derived from them (Waaland 1981). Regardless of the method, nitrogen, phosphate, and potassium were delivered to the soil, along with other compounds that may serve as plant growth stimulants, by the use of algae as a fertilizer.

The Gross Chemical Composition of Algae

The gross chemical composition of algae is shown in Table II.C.1.3, where several properties are readily apparent. Although they are relatively poor in carbohydrates (including fiber) and relatively rich in lipids, microalgae are remarkably rich in protein and, thus, a good source of nutrients for humans as well as domestic animals (Aaronson, Berner, and Dubinsky 1980).

Table II.C.1.3. *The gross chemical composition of edible algae (percentage of dry weight)*

Species	Protein	Total carbohydrate plus fiber	Lipids	Total nucleic acids	Ash	HO	Reference no.
Cyanophyta							
Agmenellum guadruplicatum	36	32	13	–	11	–	16
Nostoc commune	21	60	1	–	8	11	14
Nostoc phylloderma	25	59	1	–	12	–	3
Phormidium tenue	11	32	1	–	46	9	3
Spirulina sp.	64–70	–	5–7	4	–	–	13
Spirulina maxima	56–62	16–18	2–3	–	–	–	1
Spirulina maxima	60–71	13–17	6–7	3–5	6–9	–	6
Spirulina platensis	46–50	8–14	4–9	2–5	–	–	8
Spirulina platensis	63	9	3	4	10	9	5
Synechococcus sp.	63	15	11	5	–	–	7
Chlorophyta							
Chlorella vulgaria	52	25	6	–	14	5	4
Chlorella vulgaris	57	32	6	–	8	–	16
Coelastrum proboscideum	49	24	9	–	13	6	4
Enteromorpha sp.	20	58	0.3	–	15	–	9
Enteromorpha compressa	12	–	–	–	10	14	15
Enteromorpha linza	19	–	–	–	19	14	15
Monostroma sp.	20	5	1	–	15	–	9
Ulva sp.	26	46	1	–	23	–	9
Ulva sp.	15	51	–	–	16	19	15
Phaeophyta							
Arthrothamnus bifidus	6	52	0.7	–	17	24	15
Ascophyllum nodosum	5–10	42–59	2–4	–	17–20	12–15	18
Hizikia fusiformis	6	102	1.7	–	19	12	2
Hizikia fusiformis	10	57	0.5	–	–	16	15
Kjellmaniella crassifolia	9	62	0.6	–	28	–	9
Laminaria sp.	2	11	0.6	–	7	–	10
Laminaria sp.	6	49	1	–	21	24	15
Laminaria angustata	9	65	1.7	–	24	–	9
Laminaria angustata	9	66	2.2	–	19	–	9
Laminaria japonica	9	68	1.3	–	22	–	9
Laminaria japonica	9	66	2.2	–	23	–	9
Laminaria japonica	4	88	3	–	18	10	2
Laminaria religiosa	8	67	0.5	–	25	–	9
Sargassum sp.	5	35	1.3	–	25	33	19
Undaria sp.	3	10	0.6	–	7	–	12
Undaria pinnatifida	12	38	0.3	–	31	19	15
Undaria pinnatifida	21	8	1.7	–	31	19	15
Rhodophyta							
Gelidium sp.	13	68	–	–	4	–	15
Gracilaria sp.	4	28	–	–	4	–	15
Gracilaria coronopifolia	8	61	0.1	–	18	13	15
Laurencia sp.	9	62	1	–	19	9	15
Palmaria sp.	20	60	1	–	13	7	17
Porphyra sp.	44	46	2	–	8	–	9
Porphyra laciniata	29	41	2	–	19	9	17
Porphyra tenera	29–36	39–41	0.6	–	–	11–13	11
Porphyra tenera	46	64	0.5	–	12	9	2
Porphyra tenera	28	40	0.8	–	10	17	15
Rhodymenia palmata	8–35	38–74	0.2–4	–	12–37	–	19

Reference Numbers:
1. Clement, Giddey, and Merzi (1967)
2. Kishi et al. (1982)
3. Namikawa (1906)
4. El-Fouly et al. (1985)
5. Becker and Venkataraman (1984)
6. Durand-Chastel (1980)
7. Trubachev et al. (1976)
8. Tipnis and Pratt (1960)
9. Nisizawa et al. (1987)
10. Venkataraman, Becker, and Shamala (1977)
11. Arasaki and Arasaki (1983)
12. Druehl (1988)
13. Clement (1975)
14. Subbulakshmi, Becker, and Venkataraman (1976)
15. Subba Rao (1965)
16. Parsons, Stephens, and Strickland (1961)
17. Drury (1985)
18. Jensen (1972)
19. Morgan, Wright, and Simpsom (1980)

Table II.C.1.4. *Amino acid content of edible algae*

Species	Method of analysis	Ala	Arg	Asp	Cys	Gly	Glu
FAO standard (essential)	1	–	–	–	–	–	–
Prokaryota							
Cyanophyta							
Anabaena cylindrica[a]	1	9.5	6.6	13.9	tr.	6.2	14.0
Calothrix sp.[a]	1	8.7	6.3	12.9	tr.	5.8	14.0
Nostoc commune[a]	1	8.8	7.7	13.2	0.4	6.1	13.8
Spirulina maxima[a]	2	5.0	4.5	6.0	0.6	3.2	8.3
Spirulina platensis[a]	1	8.7	7.0	12.5	0.4	5.8	18.7
Tolypothrix tenuis[a]	1	9.5	8.6	14.2	tr.	5.8	11.8
Eukaryota							
Chlorophyta							
Chlorella pyrenoidosa[a]	1	6.8	5.4	6.6	–	5.5	9.0
Chlorella stigmatophora[a]	1	7.9	8.6	6.5	1.4	5.4	8.5
Chlorella vulgaris[a]	1	9.4	7.2	10.3	1.0	6.8	12.8
Dunaliella teriolecta[a]	1	7.5	7.2	7.5	0.7	5.5	9.5
Ulva lactuca[b]	2	8.2	10.1	7.8	tr.	7.2	6.6
Phaeophyta							
Ascophyllum nodosum[b]	2	5.3	8.0	6.9	tr.	5.0	10.0
Fucus vesiculosus[b]	2	5.4	8.2	9.0	tr.	5.4	11.0
Hizikia fusiforme[b]	1	6.4	5.0	9.9	1.3	5.8	11.8
Undaria pinnatifida[b]	1	4.5	3.0	5.9	0.9	3.7	6.6
Rhodophyta							
Chondrus crispus	2	3.6	28.0	3.7	tr.	3.1	3.4
Porphyra sp.[b]	1	9.9	5.9	8.5	–	6.9	9.3
Rhodymenia palmata[b]	2	7.9	10.8	7.2	tr.	7.5	6.2

[a]Microalgae; [b]macroalgae.

1 = grams/16 grams of nitrogen; 2 = percentage amino acid nitrogen as percentage of total nitrogen.

References:

1. Paoletti et al. (1973)   3. Smith and Young (1955)   5. FAO (1970)
2. Lubitz (1961)   4. Nisizawa et al. (1987)

Algae, especially marine algae, may also contain unusual amino acids not normally found in protein and iodoamino acids (Fattorusso and Piattelli 1980). By contrast, macroalgae are poor in proteins and lipids, but relatively rich in carbohydrates and minerals.

The caloric value of edible algae ranges from 4,405 to 5,410 calories per gram for the Cyanophyta; 4,700 to 4,940 for the Chlorophyta; 4,160 to 5,160 for the Phaeophyta; and 3,290 to 5,400 for the Rhodophyta (Cummins and Wuycheck 1971). The digestibility of seaweeds ranges from 39 to 73 percent, with a net energy availability of 48 to 67 percent (Kishi et al. 1982).

Amino Acid Composition

The amino acid composition of algae and their proteins is shown in Table II.C.1.4. The algae have a full complement of the amino acids found in the animal and plant proteins consumed by humans. The concen-tration of essential amino acids required by humans is very close to the standards set for human foods by the Food and Agriculture Organization of the United Nations (FAO 1970).

Polysaccharides

Algae contain a variety of carbohydrates that serve as energy storage sources or provide structural strength to cell walls and matrices. The storage polysaccharides include mannitol and laminaran or chrysolaminaran in Chrysophyta and Phaeophyta; amylose and amylopectin in Chlorophyta; and Floridean starch in Rhodophyta. The structural polysaccharides include cellulose in the Chlorophyta (or its xylan equivalent in some Chlorophyta and Rhodophyta) and in the mannan of the Phaeophyta. Phaeophyta and Chlorophyta also contain anionic polysaccharides, such as alginic acid, in their cell walls and sulfated glucuronoxylofucans,

His	Ile	Leu	Lys	Met	Phe	Pro	Ser	Thr	Trp	Tyr	Val	Reference
–	4.0	7.0	5.5	3.5	6.0	–	–	4.0	–	–	5.0	–
1.8	6.0	10.4	5.2	2.1	5.7	4.2	6.2	6.9	1.2	6.3	7.1	1
1.7	5.7	8.7	6.8	2.6	5.5	3.4	6.4	7.1	1.1	5.5	6.3	1
1.5	4.4	9.6	5.4	1.3	5.4	4.5	5.4	6.2	1.6	4.7	5.0	1
0.9	4.7	5.6	3.0	1.6	2.8	2.7	3.2	3.2	0.8	–	4.2	2
1.8	6.3	9.8	5.2	2.9	5.3	4.0	5.4	6.1	1.4	5.5	6.6	1
1.4	6.7	8.9	4.7	1.6	5.2	3.3	4.3	4.9	1.7	3.7	7.4	1
1.5	3.6	4.1	7.8	2.0	4.8	3.7	2.7	3.4	1.5	2.9	5.8	2
2.3	3.8	9.3	13.4	1.4	5.5	5.2	4.1	5.0	–	3.7	5.7	3
2.2	4.4	10.4	6.8	2.4	6.1	5.0	5.0	5.1	1.9	4.1	6.6	1
2.5	4.3	10.7	13.9	0.8	6.6	4.1	4.5	2.6	–	4.1	5.3	3
0.2	2.8	5.0	5.8	1.0	3.0	3.4	3.9	4.2	tr.	1.6	4.9	3
1.3	2.8	4.6	4.9	0.7	2.3	2.6	3.0	2.8	tr.	0.9	3.7	3
1.6	3.0	5.0	6.0	0.4	2.6	3.3	3.5	3.3	tr.	1.2	3.9	3
0.9	6.2	0.5	2.9	3.2	5.8	4.8	3.8	3.2	0.8	3.0	10.8	4
0.8	3.7	5.9	1.1	1.8	4.5	5.3	3.2	1.1	1.8	3.7	7.8	4
0.5	2.9	8.5	3.7	2.1	3.7	3.0	2.6	5.4	1.2	1.6	6.9	4
1.1	1.7	2.6	3.3	0.5	1.3	2.1	2.2	2.0	tr.	1.0	2.6	3
1.2	4.0	7.7	2.6	3.4	5.3	4.6	4.8	3.2	1.1	2.4	9.3	4
1.1	3.1	4.6	6.4	0.6	3.1	3.6	4.8	3.9	tr.	1.6	5.1	3

fucoidan, and ascophyllan as storage polysaccharides. Additionally, the Rhodophyta contain galactans (agar and carrageenans) (see Lewin 1974; McCandless 1981). The cyanobacteria have peptidoglycan cell walls and may contain polyglucan granules or polyphosphates as energy storage molecules (Dawes 1991).

Hydrocolloids

Hydrocolloids are water-soluble gums (polysaccharides) commonly obtained from seaweed or other plants that have been employed since antiquity to thicken foods and today are used to thicken, to emulsify, or to gel aqueous solutions in many industries (Spalding 1985). The major hydrocolloids are: (1) agar, which is obtained from species of the red algal genera – *Gelidium, Gracilaria, Pterocladia;* (2) alginates, obtained from species of brown algal genera – *Ascophyllum, Ecklonia, Eisenia, Laminaria, Macrocystis, Nereocystis, Sargassum;* and (3) carrageenans, also obtained from species of the red algal genera – *Abnfeltia, Chondrus, Euchema, Furcellaria, Gigartina, Gymnogongrus, Hypnea, Iridaea, Phyllophora.* Hydrocolloids have great impor-

tance in the food industries, where they are employed in the production of such varied products as glazes, icings, frostings, toppings, frozen foods, cereals, bread, salad dressings, flavors, sausage casings, puddings, desserts, candies, marshmallows, processed meat products, cheese, jams, pie fillings, and sauces (Spalding 1985).

Vitamins and Other Growth Factors

Algae can also be an excellent source of water-soluble and fat-soluble vitamins (Table II.C.1.5). The concentration of specific vitamins in algae varies from species to species and depends on conditions of algal growth, handling, storage, and methods of preparation for eating, as well as on the number of microorganisms found on the surface of macroalgae, which also may be responsible for some of the B vitamins attributed to macroalgae (Kong and Chan 1979).

Tocopherols are a metabolic source of vitamin E, and they are found in most types of algae as alpha-tocopherol. The Fucaceae family of brown algae contains delta-homologues of tocopherol as well as alpha-tocopherol (Jensen 1969), and seaweeds contain 7 to 650 micrograms per gram (Ragan 1981).

Table II.C.1.5. *Vitamin content of edible algae*

Species	A (IU/ 100 g)	D (µg/g)	E (µg/g)	Thiamine (µg/g)	Riboflavin (µg/g)	B_6 (µg/g)	Nicotinate (µg/g)
Prokaryota							
Cyanophyta							
Anabaena cylindrica[a]	–	–	4,000	–	55,000	7,000	78
Spirulina sp.[a]	23,000	–	–	37	46	7	–
Spirulina platensis[a]	–	–	–	28	33	1	–
Eukaryota							
Chlorophyta							
Caulerpa racemosa[b]	–	–	–	1	2	–	21
Chlamydomonas reinhardii[a]	–	–	4	–	–	–	–
Enteromorpha sp.[b]	500	–	–	0.4	5	–	10
Enteromorpha linza[b]	2,900	3	–	2	1	–	28
Monostroma nitidum[b]	–	–	–	1	9	–	10
Ulva sp.[b]	960	–	0.6	0.3	–	–	80
Ulva pertusa[b]	–	–	0.9	3	–	–	8
Phaeophyta							
Ascophyllum nodosum[b]	–	–	–	1-5	5-10	–	10-30
Colpomenia sinuosa[b]	–	–	–	0.3	5	–	5
Dictyota dichotoma[b]	–	–	–	0.8	6	–	15
Dictyopteris prolifera[a]	–	–	–	0.5	4	–	18
Ecklonia cava[b]	–	–	–	1	3	–	19
Eisenia bicyclis[b]	–	–	–	0.2	0.2	–	26
Hizikia fusiforme[b]	450	16	–	0.3	3	–	7
Hydroclathrus clathratus[b]	–	–	–	0.3	3	–	4
Laminaria sp.[b]	440	–	–	0.9	0.2	0.3	30
Padina arboriscenens[b]	–	–	–	0.3	1	–	14
Sargassum fulvellum[b]	–	–	–	0.4	5	–	9
Sargassum nigrifolium[b]	–	–	–	0.4	6	–	17
Sargassum thunbergii[b]	–	–	–	0.4	5	–	5
Spathoglossum pacificum[b]	–	–	–	0.4	0.8	–	25
Undaria pinnatifida[b]	140	–	–	1	1	–	100
Rhodophyta							
Chondrococcus japonicus[b]	–	–	–	1	11	–	8
Chondrus ocellatus[b]	–	–	–	2	15	–	30
Gelidium amansii[b]	–	–	–	7	18	–	20
Gloiopeltis tenax[b]	–	–	–	3	15	–	24
Gracilaria gigas[b]	800	–	–	2	1	–	8
Gracilaria textorii[b]	–	–	–	5	7	–	34
Grateloupia ramosissima[b]	–	–	–	1	6	–	25
Hypnea charoides[b]	–	–	–	1	3	–	22
Laurencia okamura[b]	–	–	–	0.5	10	–	39
Lomentaria catenata[b]	–	–	–	1	3	–	24
Palmaria sp.[b]	–	2	–	0.7	10	–	69
Porphyra laciniata[b]	–	472	–	–	–	–	115
Porphyra tenera[b]	–	44,500	–	2	23	10	68
Porphyra tenera[b]	–	44,500	–	3	12	–	100

[a]Microalgae; [b]macroalgae

References:

1. Kanazawa (1963)
2. Arasaki and Arasaki (1983)
3. Jensen (1972)
4. Drury (1985)
5. Aaronson et al. (1977)
6. Becker and Venkataraman (1984)
7. Jassley (1988)

Pantothenate (µg/g)	Folate (µg/g)	Biotin (µg/g)	Lipoate (µg/g)	B_{12} (µg/g)	Choline (µg/g)	Inositol (µg/g)	Ascorbate (mg/100 g)	Reference
88,000	15,000	–	–	–	–	–	2,000	5
5	510	46	–	1,700	–	–	20	7
–	–	–	–	–	–	–	–	6
6	612	131	295	149	–	581	–	1
–	9,000	260	–	–	–	–	–	5
–	429	–	–	13	–	–	–	2
–	270	198	175	98	358	581	–	1
4	429	115	575	13	79	219	75–80	1
–	118	–	–	63	–	–	–	2
2	118	224	420	63	61	330	27–41	1
–	200–1,000	100–400	–	4	–	–	–	3
3	46	136	540	77	406	146	–	1
0.7	521	187	500	10	77	125	–	1
4	170	163	485	17	242	151	–	1
0.5	–	209	90	3	27	690	–	1
–	–	–	–	–	–	–	–	2
2	218	237	230	6	262	379	–	1
3	857	181	330	66	33	328	0–92	1
–	–	–	–	3	49	405	–	1
2	542	160	230	4	618	1,131	–	1
9	308	282	270	47	95	60	–	1
0.5	249	159	410	21	24	197	–	1
9	308	282	270	47	28	566	–	1
0.3	566	150	655	7	87	144	–	1
–	–	–	–	–	–	–	15	2
1	97	40	250	220	1,337	449	–	1
7	–	69	700	89	856	111	16	1
1	782	61	570	36	4,885	443	–	1
6	676	37	330	15	319	163	–	1
2	304	18	495	212	1,492	324	–	1
10	668	153	985	76	230	668	–	1
2	719	82	530	29	1,119	55	–	1
7	540	95	355	27	636	257	–	1
9	763	95	300	100	1,346	89	4	1
12	220	90	625	25	240	263	–	1
–	–	–	–	–	–	–	5	4
–	–	60	–	–	–	–	17	4
–	88	294	790	290	2,920	62	10–831	1
–	–	–	–	–	–	–	20	2

Algae can also contain vitamin C and beta-carotene, which are among the nutrients presently thought to protect cells against powerful oxidizing agents such as ozone, lipid peroxides, and nitrogen dioxide, and are, consequently, recommended in the diet (Calabrese and Horton 1985; Kennedy and Liebler 1992; Krinsky 1992). Vitamin C is found in all seaweeds in concentrations up to 10 milligrams per gram (Ragan 1981). The fat-soluble vitamin A is synthesized from beta-carotene by humans, and beta-carotene is found in comparatively large amounts in many algae eaten by humans, such as those species in the Chlorophyta, Phaeophyta, Rhodophyta taxa, and blue-green bacteria, as well as other algal taxa (Goodwin 1974).

Table II.C.1.6. *The range of fatty acids found in edible algae*

Fatty acid carbon no.	Percentage range of total fatty acid			
	Cyanophyta 29[a]	Chlorophyta 28[a]	Phaeophyta 11[a]	Rhodophyta 11[a]
14:0	–	1–12	10–12	1–10
16:0	9–54	14–35	15–36	18–53
16:1	4–45	1–29	2–32	2–7
16:2	1–14	1–8	–	0.1–1
16:3	–	1–12	–	–
16:4	–	3–19	–	–
18:0	1–9	1–53	1	1–11
18:1	2–26	2–46	17–19	3–34
18:2	1–37	4–34	2–9	1–21
18:3 (gamma)	5–35	1–6		
18:3 (alpha)	2–18	1–34	7–8	0.4–2
18:4	–	1–29	6–7	0.5–1
20:0	–	0.5–1	–	–
20:1	–	1–17	–	–
20:2	–	1–2	1	–
20:3	–	1–2	1	1–7
20:4	–	1–4	10–11	5–36
20:5	–	2–10	8	17–24
22:0	–	1–3	–	1.5
22:5	–	2–6	–	–
22:6	–	–	–	–

Sources: Adpated from Shaw (1966), Watanabe (1970), and Wood (1974).

[a]Number of species examined for fatty acids in above references.

Ash and Water Content of Algae

As Table II.C.1.3 indicates, seaweeds mostly comprise water and ash. T. Yamamoto and colleagues (1979) examined the ash content of marine algae collected in Japanese waters and found it to vary from 4 to 76 percent. J. H. Ryther, J. A. De Boer, and B. E. Lapointe (1978) found that the wet weight of several seaweeds cultured in Florida consisted of about 10 to 16 percent dry material, 32 to 50 percent of which was minerals. The seaweed ash of *Eisenia bicyclis* includes the following elements (in order of decreasing concentration): potassium, calcium, sodium, phosphorus, magnesium, strontium, zinc, iron, boron, aluminum, copper, titanium, nickel, vanadium, chromium, cobalt, molybdenum, and gallium (Yamamoto et al. 1979). Marine algae can contain up to 5 milligrams of iodine per gram of dried algae, although the amount varies from species to species and from one part of the seaweed to another (Grimm 1952).

Lipids

Algal lipids include the saponifiable lipids: fatty acids (acylglycerols, phosphoglycerides, spingolipids, and waxes) and the nonsaponifiable lipids (terpenes, steroids, prostaglandins, and hydrocarbons). As already noted, microalgae are far richer in lipids than macroalgae (Table II.C.1.3), and algae that grow in colder waters contain more unsaturated fatty acids than do algae that thrive in warm waters. Algae supply nutrients, especially lipids, when they are eaten directly as food, but they can also pass on their nutrients indirectly when they are consumed by zooplankton, which are subsequently eaten by other invertebrates and vertebrates. Algal nutrients are then passed along to humans when they eat invertebrates and vertebrates, such as shellfish and shrimp, and fish or fish-eating birds and mammals, respectively.

Fatty Acids

Algae contain varying amounts of saturated and unsaturated fatty acids (Table II.C.1.6). Algae are rich in alpha- and gamma-linolenic acids and unusually rich in polyunsaturated fatty acids.

Steroids

Steroids are found in all eukaryotic algae, composing between 0.02 to 0.38 percent of their dry weight. Many different steroids, including sterols, are specific to one species of algae. For example, cholesterol is found in large amounts in Rhodophyta, but Phaeophyta and blue-green bacteria contain comparatively smaller amounts (Nes 1977).

Essential Oils

Seaweeds often have a characteristic odor of iodine and bromine when freshly isolated from the sea. Some brown seaweeds, however, may have a unique odor, due to 0.1 to 0.2 percent (wet weight) of essential oils (of which the major hydrocarbons are dictyopterene A and B), which impart a characteristic odor and flavor to the seaweeds belonging to the genus *Dictyopteris* found in Hawaii and known there as *limu lipoa*. *Limu lipoa* is used in Hawaii to season raw fish, meats, and stews. It was one of the only spices known in old Hawaii and was used in Hawaiian recipes much the same as other cultures used pepper and sage (Moore 1976).

Pharmacologically Active Compounds

Algae can possess small amounts of pharmacologically active molecules that affect humans. The polyunsaturated fatty acids of marine seaweeds in the diet may reduce blood pressure in humans; eicosanoids (including prostaglandins) are important biological regulators in humans; and eicosapentaenoic acids may influence the inflammatory process in humans (Beare-Rogers 1988). Algae are known to produce relatively large amounts of polyunsaturated fatty acids (Ackman 1981) and eicosanoids (Jiang and Gerwick 1991). Small amounts of 3-iodo- and 3,5-diiodotyrosine, triiodothyronine, and thyroxine are found in many brown and red seaweeds (Ericson and Carlson 1953; Scott 1954). Betaines have been found in most marine algae and several seaweeds regularly eaten in Japan (Blunden and Gordon 1986). These include the green algae, *Monostroma-nitidum, Ulva pertusa, Enteromorpha compressa,* and *E. prolifera,* and the red alga, *Porphyra tenera,* which, in experiments, have lowered the blood cholesterol of rats (Abe 1974; Abe and Kaneda 1972, 1973, 1975).

Some freshwater and marine cyanobacteria contain protease inhibitors, which can affect protein digestion; about 7 percent of the algal cultures examined by R. J. P. Cannell and colleagues (1987) were positive for protease inhibitors.

Algae contain a large variety of phenols, especially the marine brown and red algae. Some phenols are antimicrobial, and others have been found to be anticancer agents (Higa 1981).

Anthelminthic compounds have been associated with seaweeds for hundreds of years, if not longer. More recently, anthelminthic compounds with neurotoxic properties, such as alpha-kainic acid and domoic acid, were isolated from *Digenea simplex* (Ueyanagi et al. 1957), *Chondria armata* (Daigo 1959), and also from diatoms (Fritz et al. 1992).

H. Noda and colleagues (1990) have reviewed the antitumor activity of the aqueous extracts of several seaweeds, as well as 46 species of marine algae (4 green, 21 brown, and 21 red algae). Certain species of brown algae *(Scytosiphon lomentaria, Lessonia nigrescins, Laminaria japonica, Sargassum ringgolianism),* red algae, *(Porphyra yezoensis* and *Eucheuma gelatinae),* and the green alga *Enteromorpha prolifera* were found to have significant activity against Ehrlich carcinoma in mice. However, the cancer-causing polyaromatic hydrocarbon, 3,4-ben-

zopyrene, has been reported in commercially sold nori (*Porphyra* spp.) (Shirotori 1972; Shiraishi, Shirotori, and Takahata 1973).

Algae, like other plants, contain a variety of compounds, such as amino acids, ascorbic acid, carotenoids, cinnanmic acids, flavonoids, melanoidins, peptides, phosphatides, polyphenols, reductones, tannins, and tocopherols. These molecules may act as reducing agents or free radical interrupters, as singlet oxygen quenchers, and as inactivators of preoxidant metals, thus preventing the formation of powerful oxidizers and mutagens (Tutour 1990).

One seaweed (as yet unidentified), called *limu mualea,* was thought to be highly poisonous in Hawaii (Schönfeld-Leber 1979), and a number of algae and some cyanobacteria produce secondary metabolites that are toxic to humans. Certainly, as with other aquatic organisms, eating algae from polluted waters is hazardous because of potential contamination by microbial pathogens (viruses, bacteria, fungi, or protozoa), toxic metals or ions, pesticides, industrial wastes, or petroleum products (see Jassley 1988 for a review).

Sheldon Aaronson

This work was funded, in part, by PSC/CUNY and Ford Foundation Urban Diversity research awards.

Bibliography

Aaronson, S. 1986. A role for algae as human food in antiquity. *Food and Foodways* 1: 311-15.

Aaronson, S., T. Berner, and Z. Dubinsky. 1980. Microalgae as a source of chemicals and natural products. In *Algae biomass,* ed. G. Shelef and C. J. Soeder, 575-601. Amsterdam.

Aaronson, S., S. W. Dhawale, N. J. Patni, et al. 1977. The cell content and secretion of water-soluble vitamins by several freshwater algae. *Archives of Microbiology* 112: 57-9.

Abbott, I. A. 1978. The uses of seaweed as food in Hawaii. *Economic Botany* 32: 409-12.

Abe, S. 1974. Occurrence of homoserine betaine in the hydrolysate of an unknown base isolated from a green alga. *Japanese Fisheries* 40: 1199.

Abe, S., and T. Kaneda. 1972. The effect of edible seaweeds on cholesterol metabolism in rats. In *Proceedings of the Seventh International Seaweed Symposium,* ed. K. Nisizawa, 562-5. Tokyo.

  1973. Studies on the effects of marine products on cholesterol metabolism in rats. VIII. The isolation of hypocholesterolemic substance from green laver. *Bulletin of the Japanese Society of Scientific Fisheries* 39: 383-9.

  1975. Studies on the effects of marine products on cholesterol metabolism in rats. XI. Isolation of a new betaine, ulvaline, from a green laver *Monosrtoma-nitidum* and its depressing effect on plasma cholesterol levels. *Bulletin of the Japanese Society of Scientific Fisheries* 41: 567-71.

Abe, S., M. Uchiyama, and R. Sato. 1972. Isolation and identification of native auxins in marine algae. *Agricultural Biological Chemistry* 36: 2259-60.

Ackman, R. G. 1981. Algae as sources for edible lipids. In *New sources of fats and oils,* ed. E. H. Pryde, L. H. Princen, and K. D. Malcherjee, 189-219. Champaign, Ill.

Ager, T. A., and L. P. Ager. 1980. Ethnobotany of the Eskimos of Nelson Island [Alaska]. *Arctic Anthropology* 17: 27-49.

Aldave-Pajaras, A. 1969. Cushuro algas azul-verdes utilizados como alimento en la región altoandina Peruana. *Boletín de la Sociedad Botánica de la Libertad* 1: 5-43.

    1985. High Andean algal species as hydrobiological food resources. *Archiv für Hydrobiologie und Beiheft: Ergebnisse der Limnologie* 20: 45-51.

Arasaki, S., and T. Arasaki. 1983. *Vegetables from the sea.* Tokyo.

Baker, J. T., and V. Murphy, eds. 1976. Compounds from marine organisms. In *Handbook of marine science: Marine products,* Vol. 3, Section B, 86. Cleveland, Ohio.

Barrau, J. 1962. *Les plantes alimentaires de l'océanie origine.* Marseille.

Beare-Rogers, J. 1988. Nutritional attributes of fatty acids. *Journal of the Oil Chemists' Society* 65: 91-5.

Becker, E. W., and L. V. Venkataraman. 1984. Production and utilization of the blue-green alga *Spirulina* in India. *Biomass* 4: 105-25.

Birket-Smith, K. 1953. *The Chugach Eskimo.* Copenhagen.

Biswas, K. 1953. The algae as substitute food for human and animal consumption. *Science and Culture* 19: 246-9.

Blunden, G., and S. M. Gordon. 1986. Betaines and their sulphonic analogues in marine algae. *Progress in Phycological Research* 4: 39-80.

Blunden, G., S. M. Gordon, and G. R. Keysell. 1982. Lysine betaine and other quaternary ammonium compounds from British species of Laminariales. *Journal of Natural Products* 45: 449-52.

Boergesen, F. 1938. *Catenella nipae* used as food in Burma. *Journal of Botany* 76: 265-70.

Booth, E. 1965. The manurial value of seaweed. *Botanica Marina* 8: 138-43.

Brooker, S. G., R. C. Combie, and R. C. Cooper. 1989. Economic native plants of New Zealand. *Economic Botany* 43: 79-106.

Brooker, S. G., and R. C. Cooper. 1961. *New Zealand medicinal plants.* Auckland.

Browman, D. L. 1980. El manejo de la tierra árida del altiplano del Perú y Bolivia. *América Indígena* 40: 143-59.

    1981. Prehistoric nutrition and medicine in the Lake Titicaca basin. In *Health in the Andes,* ed. J. W. Bastien and J. M. Donahue, 103-18. Washington, D.C.

Calabrese, E. J., and J. H. M. Horton. 1985. The effects of vitamin E on ozone and nitrogen dioxide toxicity. *World Review of Nutrition and Diet* 46: 124-47.

Cannell, R. J. P., S. J. Kellam, A. M. Owsianka, and J. M. Walker. 1987. Microalgae and cyanobacteria as a source of glucosidase inhibitors. *Journal of General Microbiology* 133: 1701-5.

Chapman, V. J. 1970. *Seaweeds and their uses.* London.

Chapman, V. J., and D. J. Chapman. 1980. *Seaweeds and their uses.* London.

Chase, F. M. 1941. Useful algae. *Smithsonian Institution, annual report of the board of regents,* 401-52.

Chu, H.-J., and C.-K. Tseng. 1988. Research and utilization of cyanophytes in China: A report. *Archives of Hydrobiology, Supplement* 80: 573-84.

Clement, G. 1975. Spirulina. In *Single cell protein II,* ed. S. R. Tannenbaum and D. I. C. Wang, 467-74. Cambridge, Mass.

Clement, G., C. Giddey, and R. Merzi. 1967. Amino acid composition and nutritive value of the alga *Spirulina maxima. Journal of the Science of Food and Agriculture* 18: 497-501.

Cobo, B. 1956. *Obras,* ed. P. Francisco Mateos. 2 vols. Madrid.

Cummins, K. W., and J. C. Wuycheck. 1971. *Caloric equivalents for investigations in ecological energetics.* Internationale Vereinigung für theoretische und angewandte Limnologie. Monograph Series No. 18. Stuttgart.

Daigo, K. 1959. Studies on the constituents of *Chondria armata* III. Constitution of domoic acid. *Journal of the Pharmaceutical Society of Japan* 79: 356-60.

Dangeard, P. 1940. On a blue alga edible for man: *Arthrospira platensis* (Nordst.) Gomont. *Actes de la Société Linnéene de Bordeaux* 91: 39-41.

Dawes, E. A. 1991. Storage polymers in prokaryotes. *Society of General Microbiology Symposium* 47: 81-122.

Delpeuch, F., A. Joseph, and C. Cavelier. 1975. Consommation alimentaire et apport nutritionnel des algues bleues *(Oscillatoria platensis)* chez quelques populations du Kanem (Tchad). *Annales de la Nutrition et de l'Alimentation* 29: 497-516.

Dillehay, T. D. 1989. *Monte Verde.* Washington, D.C.

Druehl, L. D. 1988. Cultivated edible kelp. In *Algae and human affairs,* ed. C. A. Lembi and J. R. Waaland, 119-47. Cambridge.

Drury, H. M. 1985. Nutrients in native foods of southeastern Alaska. *Journal of Ethnobiology* 5: 87-100.

Durand-Chastel, H. 1980. Production and use of *Spirulina* in Mexico. In *Algae biomass,* ed. G. Shelef and C. J. Soeder, 51-64. Amsterdam.

Eidlihtz, M. 1969. *Food and emergency food in the circumpolar area.* Uppsala, Sweden.

Elenkin, A. A. 1931. On some edible freshwater algae. *Priroda* 20: 964-91.

El-Fouly, M., F. E. Abdalla, F. K. El Baz, and F. H. Mohn. 1985. Experience with algae production within the Egypto-German microalgae project. *Archiv für Hydrobiologie Beiheft: Ergebnisse der Limnologie* 20: 9-15.

Ericson, L.-E., and B. Carlson. 1953. Studies on the occurrence of amino acids, niacin and pantothenic acid in marine algae. *Arkiv for Kemi* 6: 511-22.

FAO (Food and Agriculture Organization of the United Nations). 1970. *Amino-acid content of foods and biological data on proteins. FAO Nutritional Studies* No. 24. Rome.

Fattorusso, E., and M. Piattelli. 1980. Amino acids from marine algae. In *Marine natural products,* ed. P. J. Scheuer, 95-140. New York.

Feldheim, W., H. D. Payer, S. Saovakntha, and P. Pongpaew. 1973. The uric acid level in human plasma during a nutrition test with microalgae in Thailand. *Southeast Asian Journal of Tropical Medicine and Public Health* 4: 413-16.

Fritz, L., A. M. Quilliam, J. L. C. Wright, et al. 1992. An outbreak of domoic acid poisoning attributed to the pennate diatom *Pseudonitzschia australis. Journal of Phycology* 28: 439-42.

Furst, P. T. 1978. Spirulina. *Human Nature* (March): 60-5.

Gade, D. W. 1975. *Plants, man and the land in the Vilcanota valley of Peru.* The Hague, the Netherlands.

Gaitan, E. 1990. Goitrogens in food and water. *Annual Review of Nutrition* 10: 21-39.

Galutira, E. C., and C. T. Velasquez. 1963. Taxonomy, distribution and seasonal occurrence of edible marine algae in Ilocos Norte, Philippines. *Philippine Journal of Science* 92: 483-522.

Goldie, W. H. 1904. Maori medical lore. *Transactions of the New Zealand Institute* 37: 1-120.

Goodrich, J., C. Lawson, and V. P. Lawson. 1980. *Kasharya pomo plants.* Los Angeles.

Goodwin, T. W. 1974. Carotenoids and biliproteins. In *Algal physiology and biochemistry,* ed. W. D. P. Stewart, 176-205. Berkeley, Calif.

Grimm, M. R. 1952. Iodine content of some marine algae. *Pacific Science* 6: 318-23.

Guaman Poma de Ayala, F. 1965-6. *La nueva cronica y buen gobierno,* Vol. 3. Lima.

Gunther, E. 1945. *Ethnobotany of western Washington.* Seattle.

Güven, K. C., E. Guler, and A. Yucel. 1976. Vitamin B-12 content of *Gelidium capillaceum* Kutz. *Botanica Marina* 19: 395-6.

Hasimoto, Y. 1979. *Marine toxins and other bioactive marine metabolites.* Tokyo.

Higa, T. 1981. Phenolic substances. In *Marine natural products,* ed. P. Scheuer, 93-145. New York.

Hiroe, M. 1969. *The plants in the Tale of Genji.* Tokyo.

Hoygaard, A. 1937. *Skrofter om Svalbard og Ishavet.* Oslo.

Irving, F. R. 1957. Wild and emergency foods of Australian and Tasmanian aborigines. *Oceania* 28: 113-42.

Izawa, K., and T. Nishida. 1963. Monkeys living in the northern limits of their distribution. *Primates* 4: 67-88.

Jao, C. 1947. *Prasiola Yunnanica* sp. nov. *Botanical Bulletin of the Chinese Academy* 1: 110.

Jassley, A. 1988. *Spirulina:* A model algae as human food. In *Algae and human affairs,* ed. C. A. Lembi and J. R. Waaland, 149-79. Cambridge.

Jensen, A. 1969. Tocopherol content of seaweed and seaweed meal. I. Analytical methods and distribution of tocopherols in benthic algae. *Journal of Scientific Food and Agriculture* 20: 449-53.

1972. The nutritive value of seaweed meal for domestic animals. In *Proceedings of the Seventh International Seaweed Symposium,* ed. K. Nisizawa, 7-14. New York.

Jiang, Z. D., and W. H. Gerwick. 1991. Eicosanoids and the hydroxylated fatty acids from the marine alga *Gracilariopsis lemaneiformis. Phytochemistry* 30: 1187-90.

Johnston, H. W. 1966. The biological and economic importance of algae. Part 2. *Tuatara* 14: 30-63.

1970. The biological and economic importance of algae. Part 3. Edible algae of fresh and brackish water. *Tuatara* 18: 17-35.

Kanazawa, A. 1963. Vitamins in algae. *Bulletin of the Japanese Society for Scientific Fisheries* 29: 713-31.

Kennedy, T. A., and D. C. Liebler. 1992. Peroxyl radical scavenging by B-carotene in lipid bilayers. *Journal of Biological Chemistry* 267: 4658-63.

Khan, M. 1973. On edible Lemanea Bory de St. Vincent - a fresh water red alga from India. *Hydrobiologia* 43: 171-5.

Kishi, K., G. Inoue, A. Yoshida, et al. 1982. Digestibility and energy availability of sea vegetables and fungi in man. *Nutrition Reports International* 26: 183-92.

Kong, M. K., and K. Chan. 1979. Study on the bacterial flora isolated from marine algae. *Botanica Marina* 22: 83-97.

Krinsky, N. I. 1992. Mechanism of action of biological antioxidants. *Proceedings of the Society for Experimental Biology and Medicine* 200: 248-54.

Lagerheim, M. G. de. 1892. La "Yuyucha." *La Nuevo Notarisia* 3: 137-8.

Lee, K.-Y. 1965. Some studies on the marine algae of Hong Kong. II. Rhodophyta. *New Asia College Academic Annual* 7: 63-110.

Léonard, J. 1966. The 1964-65 Belgian Trans-Saharan Expedition. *Nature* 209: 126-7.

Léonard, J., and P. Compère. 1967. *Spirulina platensis,* a blue alga of great nutritive value due to its richness in protein. *Bulletin du Jardin botanique naturelle de l'État à Bruxelles (Supplement)* 37: 1-23.

Lewin, R. A. 1974. Biochemical taxonomy. In *Algal physiology and biochemistry,* ed. W. D. Stewart, 1-39. Berkeley, Calif.

Lewmanomont, K. 1978. Some edible algae of Thailand. Paper presented at the Sixteenth National Conference on Agriculture and Biological Sciences. Bangkok.

Lubitz, J. A. 1961. *The protein quality, digestibility and composition of Chlorella 171105.* Research and Development Department, Chemical Engineering Section. General Dynamics Corporation Biomedical Laboratory Contract No. AF33(616)7373, Project No. 6373, Task No. 63124. Groton, Conn.

Madlener, J. C. 1977. *The sea vegetable book.* New York.

Massal, E., and J. Barrau. 1956. *Food plants of the South Sea Islands.* Noumea, New Caledonia.

Masuda, S. 1981. Cochayuyo, Macha camaron y higos chargueados. In *Estudios etnográficos del Perú meridional,* ed. S. Masuda, 173-92. Tokyo.

1985. Algae. . . . In *Andean ecology and civilization,* ed. S. Masuda, I. Shimada, and C. Morris, 233-50. Tokyo.

Matsuzawa, T. 1978. The formative site of Las Haldas, Peru: Architecture, chronology and economy. *American Antiquity* 43: 652-73.

McCandless, E. L. 1981. Polysaccharides of seaweeds. In *The biology of seaweeds,* ed. C. S. Lobban and M. J. Wynne, 558-88. Berkeley, Calif.

Michanek, G. 1975. *Seaweed resources of the ocean.* FAO Fisheries Technical Paper No. 138. Rome.

Miyashita, A. 1974. *The seaweed. The cultural history of material and human being.* Tokyo.

Montagne, M. C. 1946-7. Un dernier mot sur le *Nostoc edule* de la Chine. *Revue botanique* 2: 363-5.

Moore, R. E. 1976. Chemotaxis and the odor of seaweed. *Lloydia* 39: 181-91.

Morgan, K. C., J. L. C. Wright, and F. J. Simpsom. 1980. Review of chemical constituents of the red alga, *Palmaria palmata* (dulse). *Economic Botany* 34: 27-50.

Moseley, M. E. 1975. *The maritime foundations of Andean civilization.* Menlo Park, Calif.

Moseley, M. E., and G. R. Willey. 1973. Aspero, Peru: A reexamination of the site and its implications. *American Antiquity* 38: 452-68.

Namikawa, S. 1906. Fresh water algae as an article of human food. *Bulletin of the College of Agriculture. Tokyo Imperial University* 7: 123-4.

Nes, W. R. 1977. The biochemistry of plant sterols. *Advances in Lipid Research* 15: 233-324.

Newton, L. 1951. *Seaweed utilisation.* London.

Nisizawa, K., H. Noda, R. Kikuchi, and T. Watanabe. 1987. The main seaweed foods in Japan. *Hydrobiologia* 151/2: 5-29.

Noda, H., H. Amano, K. Arashima, and K. Nisizawa. 1990. Antitumor activity of marine algae. *Hydrobiologia* 204/5: 577-84.

Norton, H. H. 1981. Plant use in Kaigani Haida culture. Correction of an ethnohistorical oversight. *Economic Botany* 35: 434-49.

Oberg, K. 1973. *The social economy of the Tlingit Indians.* Seattle, Wash.

Ohni, H. 1968. Edible seaweeds in Chile. *Japanese Society of Physiology Bulletin* 16: 52-4.

Ortega, M. W. 1972. Study of the edible algae of the Valley of Mexico. *Botanica Marina* 15: 162-6.

Ostermann, H. 1938. Knud Rasmussen's posthumous notes on the life and doings of east Greenlanders in olden times. *Meddelelser Om Grønland,* 109.

Paoletti, C., G. Florenzano, R. Materassi, and G. Caldini. 1973. Ricerche sulla composizione delle proteine di alcuno ceppi cultivati di microalghe verdi e verdi-azzurre. *Scienze e Tecnologia degli alimenti* 3: 171-6.

Parsons, M. H. 1970. Preceramic subsistence on the Peruvian coast. *American Antiquity* 35: 292-304.

Parsons, T. R., K. Stephens, and J. D. H. Strickland. 1961. On the chemical composition of eleven species of marine phytoplankton. *Journal of the Fisheries Research Board of Canada* 18: 1001-16.

Patterson, T. C., and M. E. Moseley. 1968. Preceramic and early ceramic cultures of the central coast of Peru. *Nawpa Pacha* 6: 115-33.

Perl, T. M., L. Bedard, T. Kosatsky, et al. 1990. An outbreak of toxic encephalopathy caused by eating mussels contaminated with domoic acid. *New England Journal of Medicine* 322: 1775-80.

Perl, T. M., R. Remis, T. Kosatsky, et al. 1987. Intoxication following mussel ingestion in Montreal. *Canada Diseases Weekly Report* 13: 224-6.

Petroff, I. 1884. *Alaska: Its population, industries, and resources.* Washington, D.C.

Polo, J. A. 1977. *Nombres vulgares y usos de las algas en el Perú,* Serie de divulgación, Universidad Nacional Mayor de San Marcos, Museo de Historia Natural Javier Prado, Departamento de Botánico, No. 7. Lima.

Porsild, A. E. 1953. Edible plants of the Arctic. *Arctic* 6: 15-34.

Pozorski, S. G. 1979. Prehistoric diet and subsistence of the Moche Valley, Peru. *World Archaeology* 11: 163-84.

Ragan, M. A. 1981. Chemical constituents of seaweeds. In *The biology of seaweeds,* ed. C. S. Lobban and M. J. Wynne, 589-626. Berkeley, Calif.

Raymond, J. S. 1981. The maritime foundation of Andean civilization: A reconsideration of the evidence. *American Antiquity* 46: 806-21.

Reagan, A. B. 1934. Plants used by the Hoh and Quilente Indians. *Transactions of the Kansas Academy of Science* 37: 55-71.

Robbs, P. G., J. A. Rosenberg, and F. A. Costa. 1983. Contento vitamínico de *Scenedesmus quadricauda.* II. Vitamin B-12. *Revista Latinoamericana de Microbiología* 25: 275-80.

Ryther, J. H., J. A. De Boer, and B. E. Lapointe. 1978. Cultivation of seaweed for hydrocolloids, waste treatment and biomass for energy conversion. *Proceedings of the Ninth International Seaweed Symposium,* ed. A. Jensen and R. Stein, 1-16.

Salcedo-Olavarrieta, N., M. M. Ortega, M. E. Marin-Garcia, and C. Zavala-Moreno. 1978. Estudio de las algas comestibles del Valle de México. III. Análisis comparativo de aminoacidos. *Revista Latinoamericana de Microbiología* 20: 215-17.

Savageau, C. 1920. *Utilisation des algues marines.* Paris.

Schönfeld-Leber, B. 1979. Marine algae as human food in Hawaii, with notes on other Polynesian islands. *Ecology of Food and Nutrition* 8: 47-59.

Scott, R. 1954. Observations on the iodo-amino acids of marine algae using iodine-131. *Nature* 173: 1098-9.

Shaw, R. 1966. The polyunsaturated fatty acids of microorganisms. *Advances in Lipid Research* 4: 107-74.

Shiraishi, Y., T. Shirotori, and E. Takahata. 1973. Determination of polycyclic aromatic hydrocarbon in foods. II. 3,4-Benzopyrene in Japanese foods. *Journal of the Food Hygiene Society of Japan* 14: 173-8.

Shirotori, T. 1972. Contents of 3,4-benzopyrene in Japanese foods. *Tokyo Kasei Daigaku Kenkyu Kiyo* No. 12: 47-53.

Simoons, F. J. 1991. *Food in China.* Boca Raton, Fla.

Skvortzov, V. B. 1919-22. The use of Nostoc as food in N. China. *Royal Asiatic Society of Great Britain and Ireland* 13: 67.

Smith, D. G., and E. G. Young. 1955. The combined amino acids in several species of marine algae. *Journal of Biochemistry* 217: 845-53.

Smith, H. M. 1933. An edible mountain-stream alga. *Siam Society of Bangkok. Natural History Supplement* 9: 143.

Spalding, B. J. 1985. The hunt for new polymer properties. *Chemical Weekly* 136: 31-4.

Subba Rao, G. N. 1965. Uses of seaweed directly as human food. *Indo-Pacific Fisheries Council Regional Studies* 2: 1-32.

Subbulakshmi, G., W. E. Becker, and L. V. Venkataraman. 1976. Effect of processing on the nutrient content of the green alga *Scenedesmus acutus. Nutrition Reports International* 14: 581-91.

Tiffany L. H. 1958. *Algae, the grass of many waters.* Springfield, Ill.

Tilden, J. E. 1929. The marine and fresh water algae of China. *Lingnan Science Journal* 7: 349-98.

Tipnis, H. P., and R. Pratt. 1960. Protein and lipid content of *Chlorella vulgaris* in relation to light. *Nature* 188: 1031-2.

Trubachev, N. I., I. I. Gitel'zon, G. S. Kalacheva, et al. 1976. Biochemical composition of several blue-green algae and *Chlorella. Prikladnya Biokhimia Microbiologia* 12: 196-202.

Tseng, C.-K. 1933. *Gloiopeltis* and other economic seaweeds of Amoy, China. *Lingnan Science Journal* 12: 43-63.

  1935. Economic seaweeds of Kwangtung Province, S. China. *Lingnan Science Journal* 14: 93-104.

  1983. *Common seaweeds of China.* Beijing.

  1987. Some remarks on kelp cultivation industry of China. In *Seaweed cultivation for renewable resources,* ed. K. T. Bird and P. H. Benson, 147-53. Amsterdam.

  1990. The theory and practice of phycoculture in China. In *Perspectives in phycology,* ed. V. N. Rajarao, 227-46. New Delhi.

Turner, N. J. 1974. Plant taxonomic systems and ethnobotany of three contemporary Indian groups of the Pacific Northwest (Haida, Bella Coola, and Lillooet). *Syesis* 7: 1-104.

  1975. *Food plants of British Columbia Indians. Part I - Coastal peoples,* Handbook No. 34. Victoria.

Turner, N. J., and M. A. M. Bell. 1973. The ethnobotany of the southern Kwakiutl Indians of British Columbia. *Economic Botany* 27: 257-310.

Tutour, B. le. 1990. Antioxidation activities of algal extracts, synergistic effect with vitamin E. *Phytochemistry* 29: 3757-65.

Ueyanagi, J., R. Nawa, Y. Nakamori, et al. 1957. Studies on the active components of *Digenea simplex* Ag. and related compounds. XLVIII. Synthesis of alpha-kainic acid. *Yakugaku Zasshi* 77: 613.

Velasquez, G. T. 1972. Studies and utilization of the Philippine marine algae. In *Proceedings of the Seventh International Seaweed Symposium,* ed. K. Nisizawa, 62-5. New York.

Venkataraman, L. V., W. E. Becker, and T. R. Shamala. 1977. Studies on the cultivation and utilization of the alga *Scenedesmus acutus* as a single cell protein. *Life Sciences* 20: 223-34.

Waaland, J. R. 1981. Commercial utilization. In *The biology of seaweeds,* ed. C. S. Lobban and M. J. Wynne, 726–41. Berkeley, Calif.

Watanabe, A. 1970. Studies on the application of Cyanophyta in Japan. *Schweizerische Zeitschrift für Hydrologie* 32: 566–9.

Wester, P. J. 1925. *The food plants of the Philippines,* Bulletin No. 39. Manila.

Wood, B. J. B. 1974. Fatty acid and saponifiable lipids. In *Algal physiology and biochemistry,* ed. W. D. P. Stewart, 236–65. Berkeley, Calif.

Wood, E. J. F. 1965. *Marine microbial ecology.* London.

Xia, B., and I. A. Abbott. 1987. Edible seaweeds of China and their place in the Chinese diet. *Economic Botany* 41: 341–53.

Yacovleff, E., and F. L. Herrera. 1934–5. El mundo vegetal de los antiguos peruanos. *Revista Museo Nacional* 3: 241–322, 4: 29–102.

Yacovleff, E., and J. C. Muelle. 1934. Un fardo funerario de Paracas. *Revista Museo Nacional* 3: 63–153.

Yamamoto, T., T. Yamaoka, S. Tuno, et al. 1979. Microconstituents in seaweeds. *Proceedings of the Seaweed Symposium* 9: 445–50.

Yanovsky, E. 1936. *Food plants of the North American Indians.* United States Department of Agriculture Miscellaneous Publication No. 237. Washington, D.C.

Zaneveld, J. S. 1950. The economic marine algae of Malaysia and their applications. *Proceedings of the Indo-Pacific Fisheries Council,* 107–14.

1951. The economic marine algae of Malaysia and their applications. II. The Phaeophyta. *Proceedings of the Indo-Pacific Fisheries Council,* 129–33.

1955. *Economic marine algae of tropical South and East Asia and their utilization.* Indo-Pacific Special Publications, No. 3. Bangkok.

1959. The utilization of marine algae in tropical South and East Asia. *Economic Botany* 13: 90–131.

Zimmermann, U. 1977. Cell turgor pressure regulation and turgor-mediated transport processes. In *Integration of activity in the higher plant,* ed. D. H. Jennings, 117–54. Cambridge and New York.

1978. Physics of turgor and osmoregulation. *Annual Review of Plant Physiology* 29: 121–48.

Zimmermann, U., and E. Steudle. 1977. Action of indoleacetic acid on membrane structure and transport. In *Regulation of cell membrane activities in plants,* ed. C. Marre and O. Cifferi, 231–42. Amsterdam.

Zimmermann, U., E. Steudle, and P. I. Lelkes. 1976. Turgor pressure regulation in *Valonia utricularis:* Effect of cell wall elasticity and auxin. *Plant Physiology* 58: 608–13.

II.C.2 ❧ The *Allium* Species (Onions, Garlic, Leeks, Chives, and Shallots)

The genus *Allium* comprises more than 600 different species, which are found throughout North America, Europe, North Africa, and Asia. Approximately 30 species have been regularly used for edible purposes (although less than half of these are subject to cultivation), with the most important being onions, garlic, leeks, chives, and shallots.

In terms of their common botanical characteristics, alliums are mainly herbaceous plants, incorporating various underground storage structures made up of rhizomes, roots, and bulbs. The foliar leaves alternate, often sheathing at the base to give the superficial impression that they originate from an aboveground stem. As a rule, the flower cluster, or inflorescence, is umbrella-like, with all the flower stalks radiating from the same point (umbel); the flowers are pollinated by insects; the fruits take the form of a capsule or berry; and the seeds are numerous and endospermic.

This genus is placed in the lily family. Most, but not all, of the species possess the pungent odor typical of onion and garlic. In addition to alliums, species of *Ipheion, Adenocalymma, Androstephium, Esperocallis, Talbaghia, Nectarosiordum, Nilula,* and, possibly, *Descurainia* produce pungent odors (Fenwick and Hanley 1985a).

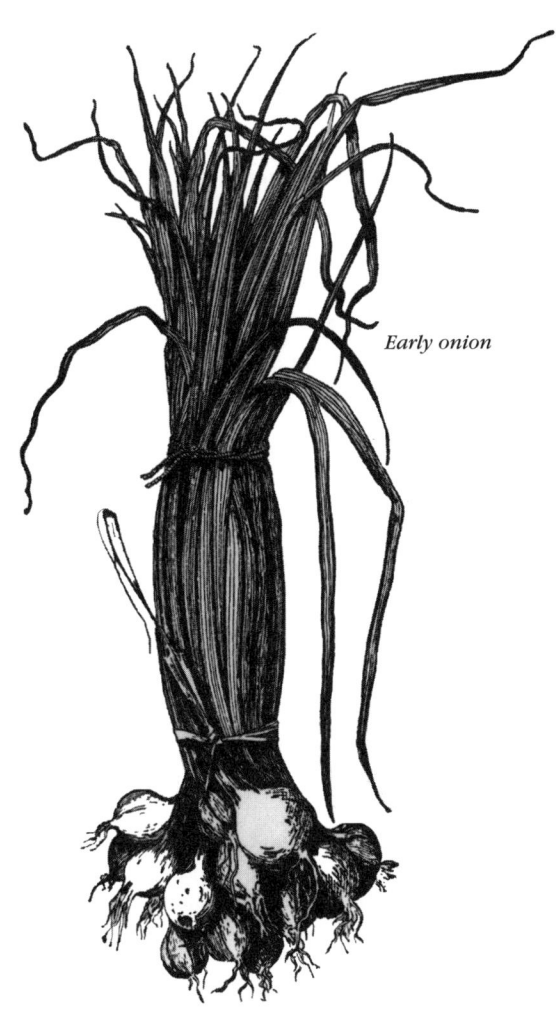

Early onion

Onions

History

Antiquity. The onion *(Allium cepa)* may have originated in Persia (Iran) and Beluchistan (eastern Iran and southwestern Pakistan). But it is also possible that onions were indigenous from Palestine to India. They have been known and cultivated for many thousands of years and no longer grow wild. Their range – virtually worldwide – now includes China, Japan, Europe, northern and southern Africa, and the Americas (Hedrick 1972).

The consumption of onions is depicted in the decoration of Egyptian tombs dating from the Early Dynasty Period, c. 2925–c. 2575 B.C. During the Old Kingdom, c. 2575–c. 2130 B.C., onions were used as religious offerings. They were put on altars and, as is known from mummified remains, were employed in preparing the dead for burial (placed about the thorax and eyes, flattened against the ears, and placed along the legs and feet and near the pelves). Flowering onions have often been found in mummies' chest cavities (Jones and Mann 1963). If Juvenal (Roman poet and satirist, c.A.D. 55–127) is to be believed, a particularly delicious onion was worshiped as a god by certain groups in ancient Egypt (Hyams 1971).

The Greek historian Herodotus reported that onions, along with radishes and garlic, were a part of the staple diet of the laborers who built the Great Pyramid at Giza (2700–2200 B.C.) (Jones and Mann 1963). Egyptian onions were said to be mild and of an excellent flavor, and people of all classes (save for priests, who were prohibited from eating them) consumed them both raw and cooked (Hedrick 1972).

In Sumeria (southern Iraq), onions were grown and widely used for cooking 4,000 years ago (Fenwick and Hanley 1985a), and both garlic and onions have been unearthed at the royal palace at Knossos in Crete (Warren 1970). Minoan voyages from the eastern Mediterranean (2000–1400 B.C.) doubtless helped in dispersing alliums from that region.

The ancient Greek physician Hippocrates (460–375 B.C.) wrote that onions were commonly eaten, and Theophrastus (c. 372–287 B.C.) listed a number of onion varieties, all named after places where they were grown: Sardian (from western Turkey), Cnidian (from southern Turkey), Samothracian (from a Greek island in the northeast Aegean), and Setanian (possibly from Sezze or Setia in central Italy) (Jones and Mann 1963; Warren 1970).

Asia. According to Charaka, a Hindu physician of the second century A.D., the onion (as in ancient Egypt) was thought not to be a suitable food for persons pursuing the spiritual life. Thus, the onion was taboo for orthodox Brahmins, Hindu widows, Buddhists, and Jains (Hyams 1971).

In China, the fifth-century treatise on agriculture, *Ch'i-min-yao-shu* (Essential Arts for the People) by Chia Ssu-hsieh, described the cultivation of *ts'ung,* or spring onion *(Allium fistulosum* L.), along the Red River valley (Li 1969). Infusions of onion have long been used in China as a treatment for dysentery, headache, and fever (Hanley and Fenwick 1985).

In 1886, Kizo Tamari, a Japanese government official, stated that in his country, onions did not have globular bulbs but were grown like celery and had long, white, slender stalks (Hedrick 1972). Interestingly, some modern Japanese communities forbid the cultivation, but not the consumption, of the spring onion (Kuroda 1977).

Europe. Columella (Lucius Junius Moderatus Columella), a Spanish-born Roman agriculturalist of the first century A.D., wrote of the *Marsicam,* which the country people called *unionem* (a term that may be the origin of the English word "onion" and the French *oignon*) (Fenwick and Hanley 1985a). Columella's contemporary, the Roman gourmet Apicius (Marcus Gavius Apicius), created several recipes that employed onions, although he viewed the vegetable as a seasoning rather than a food in its own right (Fenwick and Hanley 1985a).

Writing at about the same time as Apicius, Dioscorides (a Greek military physician) described onions as long or round and yellow or white, and provided detailed discussions of the uses of garlic, onion, and other alliums as medicinal plants (Jones and Mann 1963; Warren 1970).

Still another contemporary, Pliny the Elder, told his readers that the round onion was the best and that red onions were more highly flavored than white. His *Natural History* described six types of onions known to the Greeks: Sardian, Samothracian, Alsidenian, Setanian, the split onion, and the Ascalon onion (shallot). Pliny claimed onions to be effective against 28 different diseases (Fenwick and Hanley 1985a). Then, later on in the first millennium, Palladius (Rutilius Taurus Aemilianus Palladius), a Roman agriculturist in about the fourth century (or later), gave minute directions for culturing onions and comprehensively described their cultivation (Hedrick 1972).

By the beginning of the second millennium, many accounts of foodstuffs were being penned by monks. For example, Peter Damian (1007–72), the founder of a reformed congregation of Benedictines in central Italy, indicated that he permitted a moderate dish of edible roots, vegetables – mostly onions, leeks, and chickpeas – and fruit on days when fasting was not prescribed. These meals were eaten both cooked and uncooked, and sometimes enlivened with oil on special feast days (Lohmer 1988).

The German Dominican monk and scientist Albertus Magnus (1193–1280) did not include onions in his lists of garden plants, but garlic and leeks were represented there, suggesting the esteem in which they were held. Onions, however, were exotic plants understood to have favorable effects on fertility by generating sperm in men and lactation in women (Mauron 1986).

By the sixteenth century, onions were no longer exotic. The Portuguese physician Amatus Lusitanus (1511-68) wrote that they were the commonest of vegetables, occurring in red and white varieties, and had sweet, strong, and intermediate qualities. The German physician and poet Petrus Laurembergius (1585-1639) described some of these qualities, writing of the Spanish onion as oblong, white, large, and excelling all others in sweetness and size; he further reported that at Rome, the Caieta variety brought the highest price, but at Amsterdam the most valued variety was the St. Omer.

A nutritional revolution occurred in the nineteenth century, when food items previously monopolized by the upper classes became available to all. The defeat of scurvy began with the addition to the diet of potatoes and onions, which were progressively supplemented with other legumes and fruits. By the middle of the nineteenth century, deaths from tuberculosis were in decline. Among other things, this was the product of the continuing introduction into the diet of foods containing vitamins A, C, and E, as well as meat and fish, which provide the amino acids vital to the creation of antibodies (Knapp 1989).

The Americas. It is probable that the men of Christopher Columbus's crews sowed onions on Hispaniola as early as 1494, and Hernando Cortés reportedly encountered onions, leeks, and garlic on his march to Tenochtitlan in 1519. Interestingly, native Mexicans apparently had a lengthy acquaintance with this Eurasian plant, because it had a name – *xonacatl* (Hedrick 1972).

Onions were mentioned as cultivated in Massachusetts as early as 1629, in Virginia in 1648, and at Mobile, Alabama, in 1775. By 1806, six varieties of onions were listed as esculents in American gardens. In 1828, the potato onion (multiplier onion) was described as a vegetable of late introduction into the United States, and by 1863, 14 varieties were mentioned (Hedrick 1972; Toma and Curry 1980).

Recent production statistics. The major producers of dry onions (cured but not dehydrated) in 1996 were (in metric tons) China (9,629,895), India (4,300,000), the United States (2,783,650), Turkey (1,900,000), Japan (1,262,000), Iran (1,199,623), Pakistan (1,097,600), and Spain (1,018,100), and total world production was 37,456,390 metric tons. The major producers of spring onions (scallions) were Mexico (702,478), Korea (553,000), Japan (545,600), China (282,329), Turkey (230,000), and Nigeria (200,000), and world production was 3,540,595 metric tons.

The major exporters of onions in 1996 were the Netherlands, India, the United States, Argentina, Spain, Mexico, Turkey, and New Zealand. Major importers were Germany, the Russian Federation, Brazil, Malaysia, Saudi Arabia, and the United Arab Emirates.

Horticulture and Botany

Botany. The common onion is known only in cultivation. Propagation is usually by division, although some strains may also produce seed. Spring onions, used mainly in salads, are always grown from seed and harvested young. Pickling onions are made small by planting them close together (Traub 1968).

Onion leaves are the thickened bases of the normal leaves from the previous season. The bulb is composed of fleshy, enlarged leaf bases; the outermost leaf bases do not swell but become thin, dry, and discolored, forming a covering (Fenwick and Hanley 1985a). The onion usually flowers in the spring. Honeybees prefer the nectar of *A. cepa* to that of *A. fistulosum* (green onions) (Kumar and Gupta 1993).

Cultivation. Two crops of onions are grown each year in the United States. That of the spring is grown in Arizona, California, and Texas. The summer crop, much larger, consists of nonstorage produce, mostly from New Mexico, Texas, and Washington, and storage produce, grown mainly in Colorado, Idaho, Michigan, New York, Oregon, and Washington (Fenwick and Hanley 1985a).

Onions grow best in fine, stone-free, well-irrigated soils. Their comparatively thick, shallow roots require high levels of nitrogen, phosphorous, and potassium for maximum yield. The onion does not compensate for water stress and is sensitive to salinity. Flavor maturation and bulb development are affected by high temperature, high light intensity, soil moisture, and nitrogen deficiency (Brewster 1977a, 1977b). Increased flavor strength is associated with higher levels of applied sulfate (Platenius 1941; Kumar and Sahay 1954). Bulb formation depends upon increased daylength, but the daylength period required varies greatly between cultivars (Austin 1972).

Intercropping and rotation. Onions are the highest-yielding and most profitable inter- or border-crop for finger millet *(Eleusine coracana)* wherever it is grown (Siddeswaran and Ramaswami 1987). With tomatoes, planting four rows of onions (15 centimeters apart) between two rows of tomatoes has provided a 36 percent higher tomato equivalent yield without significantly affecting the number, average weight, and marketable yield of the tomato fruits. The tomato and onion combination also provides the highest net returns and maximum profit (Singh 1991).

Harvesting. Mature onions suffer lower storage losses than those harvested early. As onions reach maturity, the tops soften just above the bulb junction and cause the leaves to fall over. They are usually harvested when most of the plants are in this state

(Kepka and Sypien 1971; Rickard and Wickens 1977). Harvesting methods depend on the size of the crop, the climate, and regional or national practices (Jones and Mann 1963).

After harvesting, unless the crop is immediately sent to market, curing is necessary. The purpose of curing is to dry the skins and the top of the onion, forming an effective barrier against attack by microorganisms and, at the same time, minimizing the weight loss of the bulb. The onion is cured when the neck is tight, the outer scales are dry, and 3 to 5 percent of the original bulb weight is lost (Thompson, Booth, and Proctor 1972).

Curing can be natural or artificial. Windrowing, the traditional method in Britain, leaves the onions in the field, with the leaves of one row protecting the bulbs in the next. Direct exposure of the bulbs to the sun, especially under moist conditions, may lead to fungal damage (Thamizharasi and Narasimham 1993). In many countries, the onions are braided into bunches and hung up to dry (Thompson 1982).

Artificial curing techniques include forced heated air, vacuum cooling, cold storage, and infrared irradiation (Buffington et al. 1981). A small-capacity dryer has been developed in India (Singh 1994).

Storage. In addition to effective harvesting and curing, the critical factors for successful storage are cultivar type, storage conditions, and storage design. Losses from rotting and sprouting are more important than those from desiccation. Onions best suited for long-term storage (up to six months) usually have high amounts of dry matter and soluble solids, a long photoperiod during bulb maturation, and strong pungency. Red onions store better than white ones (Jones and Mann 1963; Thompson et al. 1972).

Temperature and relative humidity are the most important factors in storage conditions. Cold storage produces the best results but is not feasible in the tropics, where high-temperature storage may be effective, because dormancy is longer at 0° C and at 30° C than in between (10–15° C). Humidity should be about 70 to 75 percent (Robinson, Browne, and Burton 1975). Controlled-atmosphere storage losses depends on the quality and condition of the crop prior to storage (Adamicki and Kepka 1974).

In storage design, aeration is important for curing the onions and ventilating the heap. Consequently, slatted floors (or a similar layout, so that air can move through the bulbs from below) are employed. The onions are positioned so that air flows throughout the heap; otherwise, the moist, warm air retained in the middle leads to sprouting or rotting. The heaps should not be more than 8 feet high, and – especially where temperature, aeration, and humidity control are difficult – shallow heaps are recommended (Hall 1980).

Gamma irradiation is an effective inhibitor of sprouting in onion and garlic bulbs. Studies have shown that eating irradiated onions does not harmfully affect animals or their offspring, but irradiation can cause discoloration, may not affect rotting, and may make onions more susceptible to aflatoxin production (Van Petten, Hilliard, and Oliver 1966; Van Petten, Oliver, and Hilliard 1966; Priyadarshini and Tulpule 1976; Curzio and Croci 1983).

Pathogens and Pests
Fungi
DOWNY MILDEW. Downy mildew (*Peronospora destructor* [Berk.] Casp.) was first reported in England in 1841. It is now widespread and particularly prevalent in cool, moist climates such as the coastal regions bordering the North Sea in Britain and those of the northwestern (Washington, Oregon, and California) and northeastern (New York and New England) United States. This fungus attacks onions, garlic, leeks, and chives alike. Early infection may kill young plants, and survivors can be dwarfed, pale, and distorted. Later infection causes chlorosis and yellowing of the leaves and stems. Some plants may be systemically infected and, if used for propagation, can serve as sources of inoculum in the seed crop.

When infected, the bulb tissue tends to soften and shrivel, and the outer fleshy scales become amber-colored, watery, and wrinkled. Underlying scales may appear healthy and yet be heavily infected. The fungus commonly overwinters in young autumn-sown onions whose leaves have been infected by neighboring summer crops.

Downy mildew can be controlled by growing onions on uncontaminated land without adjacent diseased crops. Good-quality, noninfected onions should be used, and planting should be done on open, well-drained land (Fenwick and Hanley 1985a).

WHITE ROT. White rot (*Sclerotium cepivorum* Berk.) was first noted in mid-nineteenth-century England and, like downy mildew, infects all the alliums under scrutiny in this chapter. The fungal attack is favored by dry soil and cool conditions. It develops rapidly between 10° C and 20° C and is inhibited above 24° C, although periods of dry weather can lead to devastating attacks in the field. When young plants are attacked, the disease spreads rapidly. External signs are yellowing and necrosis of leaf tips. Roots and bulbs are also affected. The bulb scales become spongy, are covered with fluffy white mycelium, and develop black sclerotia. The fungus appears to overwinter as sclerotia, and, in fact, the sclerotia may survive 8 to 10 years or more in the absence of host plants. Growing seedlings and sets for transplanting in noninfected soil, and the use of long rotations, are of some benefit in controlling this fungus. Chemical treatment with mercuric chloride, lime, and 2,6-dichloro-4-nitroaniline have also proven effective (Fenwick and Hanley 1985a).

ONION SMUDGE. Common now in Europe and the United States, onion smudge (*Collectotrichum circinans* [Berk.] Vogl.) was first reported in England in 1851. It affects mainly white varieties of onion but has been reported in shallots and leeks. It is confined to the necks and scales, where it causes blemishes, reducing the market value of the crop. Rarely attacking the active growing parts of the plant, it is confined on colored onions to unpigmented areas on the outer scales of the neck. Onion smudge requires warm, moist conditions (10° C to 32° C, optimum 26° C). Conidia, or fungal spores, are produced abundantly and are scattered by spattering rain. With suitable conditions, a conidial spore will germinate within a few hours. Pungent onions resist smudge better than mild ones. Crop rotation, good husbandry, and carbamate sprays can minimize the damage. Drying the onions in hot air may be necessary, and curing under dry, well-ventilated conditions is important (Fenwick and Hanley 1985a).

ONION SMUT. Probably originating in the United States in the late nineteenth century and first reported in Britain in 1918, onion smut (*Urocystis cepulae* Frost) attacks bulb and salad onions as well as leeks, shallots, chives, and garlic. Infection occurs from two to three weeks after sowing, and a high percentage of the infected plants subsequently die. Elongated, leaden streaks discolor the scales and the growing leaves, which can also become thickened and malformed. The streaks develop into smut sori, which rupture and release spores that can survive up to 20 years in soil. Measures to control this fungus include avoiding infected areas, pelleting seed with hexachlorobenzene, dusting with thiram or ferbane, and applying fungicides (Fenwick and Hanley 1985a).

NECK ROT. Caused by three different species of *Botrytis*, neck rot is probably the most widely distributed and most destructive disease of onions in storage. It was first reported in Germany (1876) and then in the United States (1890) and Britain (1894). Infection occurs in the field but is usually not noticed until harvesting occurs. The first signs are a softening of bulb scales and the development of sunken brown lesions; a definite border between fresh and diseased tissue can be seen. The bulb desiccates and collapses. If the onions are stored in moist conditions, a secondary spread may take place. Infection occurs primarily from spores dispersed by wind or water before, during, or after harvest. White onions seem more susceptible than yellow or colored varieties, and pungent onions are less affected than mild-flavored varieties. Practical controls are thin sowing, careful handling during harvest, and providing optimal storage conditions. Zineb and other chemicals, including carbamate sprays, reduce infection, and in recent years, benomyl seed dressings have also been used effectively (Fenwick and Hanley 1985a).

Bacteria

SOFT ROT. The soft rot pathogen (*Erwinia carotovora*) enters onions through wounds that occur during harvest, transportation, and storage, or in the necks of uncured or slow-curing varieties. The infection usually starts at the bulb neck, with external signs of sponginess and a foul-smelling exudate from the neck when the bulb is squeezed. Soft rot occurs most commonly in humid weather and is transported by the onion maggot, which is itself contaminated by the rotting vegetation it consumes and, consequently, lays eggs carrying the bacteria. Control involves avoiding damage to the bulbs during and after harvest, drying them thoroughly and rapidly, using the lowest practicable storing temperature, and eliminating all damaged bulbs (Fenwick and Hanley 1985a; Wright, Hale, and Fullerton 1993). Also important is moving bulbs under cover and drying them if wet weather is expected during field-curing (Wright 1993).

Viruses. "Aster yellows," spread by the six-spotted leafhopper (*Macrosteles facifrons*), is an important viral disease of onion as well as of carrot, barley, celery, endive, lettuce, parsley, potato, and salsify. Yellowing young leaves are followed by the appearance of yellowed shoots; and roots become small and twisted. Control measures consist of reducing or eradicating the leafhopper population where aster yellows is prevalent (Fenwick and Hanley 1985a).

Nematodes. The bulb and stem nematode (*Ditylenchus dipsaci* [Kuhn] Filipjer) is widespread in the Mediterranean region but has also been found on onions and garlic in the United States, on onions in Brazil and England, and on onions and chives in Holland. It causes a condition known as "onion bloat." Dead plant tissue can contain dormant nemas, which are probably an important source of infestation. Chloropicren/steam fumigation and other treatments have proven effective, but bromine-containing nematocides should be avoided. Both onion and garlic are bromine-sensitive and will not produce good crops for up to 12 months if bromine residues are present in the soil.

Ditylenchus dipsaci is widespread in southern Italy, where it reproduces on several wild and cultivated plant species. Among vegetables, the most severely damaged are onion and garlic, but broad bean, pea, and celery also suffer damage. In the Mediterranean area, the nematode mainly infects host plants from September to May, but reproduction is greatest in October, November, March, and April, when soil moisture, relative humidity, and temperatures are optimal. Symptoms of nematode attack are apparent in the field from late February to April and in nurseries during October and November. As a result, early crops are damaged more than late crops. Nematodes survive in the soil and in plant residues. However, seeds from infested plants, except those of broad bean and pea, have rarely been found to harbor nematodes. The use of seeds, bulbs, and seedlings free of nematodes is a prerequisite for successful crop production. Cropping systems, soil treatments with fumigant and nonvolatile nematocides, and soil solarization of infested fields are recommended for effective and economic nematode control (Greco 1993).

Insects. Although many insects can attack onions, the two major culprits are the onion thrip (*Thrips tabaci* Lind.) and the onion maggot, the larval stage in the development of the onion fly (*Hylemya antiqua* Meig.). The onion thrip punctures leaves and sucks the exuding sap, leaving whitish areas on the leaves. Infestation is worse in very dry seasons and can often lead to the destruction of entire crops. Effective chemicals are available to control this pest, and results have shown that a 40 percent bulb-yield reduction occurs on nontreated plots as compared with treated ones (Domiciano, Ota, and Tedardi 1993).

The onion maggot is a pest of considerable economic importance. Both the fly and its eggs are carriers of the soft rot pathogen *E. carotovora* Holland. The adult female lays 30 to 40 eggs in the soil around the onion plant or on the onion itself, especially where plants are damaged, decaying, or already infected with larvae. Good husbandry, the destruction of onion waste, and chemicals such as aphidan, EPBP, fensulfothion, fonofos, malathion, or phoxim are used to control the onion fly and its offspring (Fenwick and Hanley 1985a).

Processing

Dehydrated onion pieces. After grading and curing, onions are peeled using lye or the flame method, whereby the roots and outer shell are burnt off in an oven, and the charred remnants are removed by washing. Next, the onions are sliced by revolving knives and dried by hot air forced upward through holes in the conveyor belt. For good storage and acceptable flavor stability, residual moisture content is about 4 to 5 percent. Moisture content can be reduced to the desired level in one to two hours (Gummery 1977). The onion pieces may then be used as such or converted into granules and flakes (or powder). Dehydrated onion pieces are widely employed in the formulation of sausage and meat products, soups, and sauces (Hanson 1975; Pruthi 1980).

Onion powder. Onion powder is used in cases where onion flavor is required but the appearance and texture of onions are not, as in dehydrated soups, relishes, and sauces. Onion powder is made by grinding dehydrated onion pieces or by spray-drying. For spray-drying, onions are washed free of debris, rinsed, and blended to a puree. Dextrose (30 to 40 percent by weight) is added, and the mixture spray-dried at temperatures below 68° C. It can be dried in four minutes at 65° C to 68° C. The treatment destroys all pathogenic bacteria while reducing the bacterial population, and the end product has excellent keeping properties (Gummery 1977).

Onion oil. Distillation of minced onions that have stood for some hours produces onion-essential oil. The oil is a brownish-amber liquid that contains a complex mixture of sulfur and other volatiles. The oil has 800 to 1,000 times the odor of a fresh onion, and its price may be 1,000 times more expensive as well. It is used for its solubility, lack of color, and strong aroma. However, onion oil cannot be standardized because its composition depends on the onion variety, ecological conditions, season, and processing (Heath 1981).

Onion juice. Onion juice is produced by expressing the bulbs, flash-heating the liquor obtained to a temperature of 140° C to 160° C, and immediately cooling it to 40° C. Next, the juice is carefully evaporated to approximately 72 to 75 percent dry matter to preserve it without chemical additives. The concentrated juice is pale brown in color and possesses a strong, fresh onion odor. Further evaporation to 82 to 85 percent solids darkens the product and gives it a cooked, toasted effect preferred by many. The sensory qualities are sometimes enhanced by returning the aromatic volatile condensate to the juice. The extract is often mixed with propylene glycol, lecithin, and glucose to yield an onion oleoresin that has a flavor 10 times that of onion powder and 100 times that of the original bulb (Heath 1981).

Onion salt. In the United States, onion salt is a mixture of dehydrated onion powder (18 to 20 percent), calcium stearate (an anticaking agent – 1 to 2 percent), and sodium chloride.

Pickled onions. Onions are pickled in a 10 percent salt solution and preserved in vinegar. Generally, silverskin or button onions are used because they give a translucent product with the desired firmness of texture. Lactic acid bacteria are the important fermentation organisms, and care must be taken to keep the solution at 10 percent salinity. Finally, the salt is leached from the onions with warm water, and the bulbs are placed in cold, spiced vinegar and stored in sealed glass jars (Fenwick and Hanley 1985a).

Nutrition

The nutritional content of onions varies by variety, ecological conditions, and climate. According to the Nutrition Data System of the University of Minnesota, 100 grams (g) (3.53 ounces or 0.44 cup) of onion provides 38 kilocalories of energy, 1.16 g of protein, 0.16 g fat, and 8.63 g of carbohydrate.

Using the standard of the *Recommended Dietary Allowances* (tenth edition) for a male between 18 and 25 years of age, approximately 100 g or one-half cup of fresh onion provides 10.7 percent of the Recommended Dietary Allowance (RDA) of vitamin C and 9.5 percent of folacin. Onions are high in potassium (157 milligrams [mg]) and low in sodium (3 mg). They contain small amounts of calcium, copper, iron, magnesium, manganese, molybdenum, phosphorus, selenium, and zinc (Raj, Agrawal, and Patel 1980). Other trace elements in onion are germanium, chromium, and lithium. Onions have no vitamin A and only small amounts of alpha-tocopherol, delta-tocopherol, thiamine, riboflavin, niacin, pantothenic acid, and vitamin B_6.

In addition, 100 g of onions contain only small amounts of three fatty acids: saturated palmitic acid (0.02 g), monounsaturated oleic acid (0.02 g), and polyunsaturated essential linoleic acid (0.06 g). They have 2.1 g of dietary fiber, no starch, and 89.68 g of water. Sucrose (1.3 g), glucose (2.4 g), and fructose (0.9 g) are present. All essential amino acids are present in onions. Arginine (0.16 g), which increases during maturation (Nilsson 1980), and glutamic acid (0.19 g) are the most abundant.

Chemistry

The color of red onions is due to cyanidin glycosides, anthocyanins that contain glucose molecules (Fuleki 1971). With yellow onions, quercetin, a flavonoid, and its glycosides are responsible for the color of the dry scales. The outer scales of onions have been used in Germany for dyeing Easter eggs and household fabrics (Perkin and Hummel 1896; Herrmann 1958). The flavonoid content is usually greatest in the outer leaves and may act as a protection against predators (Tissut 1974; Starke and Herrmann 1976a).

The phenolic compounds catechol and protocatechuic acid are found in greater quantities in colored onions than in white onions. The presence of these compounds in the outer dried scales is a contributing factor to the greater resistance of these types to smudge and neck rot diseases and to fungi-causing wild and soft rots (Walker and Stahman 1955; Farkas and Kiraly 1962).

The most important nonstructural polysaccharide in onion is a group of fructose polymers called fructans. Fructose commonly forms chains of 3 to 10 molecules, with chains of 3 and 4 molecules being the most common. It is thought that these polymers are used for storage carbohydrates and osmoregulation during bulb growth and expansion (Darbyshire and Henry 1978; Goodenough and Atkin 1981).

Onions contain pectins with high methoxyl content and of the rapid-setting kind. Pectin is used in the preparation of jellies and similar food products and is used by veterinarians as an antidiarrheal (Alexander and Sulebele 1973; Khodzhaeva and Kondratenko 1983). Onions also contain several sterols. Beta-sitosterol, cycloartenol, and lophenol are the most common, followed by campesterol. Beta-sitosterol is used as an antihyperlipoproteinemic (Oka, Kiriyama, and Yoshida 1974; Itoh et al. 1977).

Like garlic, onion has exhibited antioxidative activity, which can be increased by microwave heating or boiling. It has been shown that S-alkenyl cysteine sulfoxides are the most active components. Quercetin and other flavone aglycones also contribute to the total antioxidative capacities of onion and garlic extracts (Pratt and Watts 1964; Naito, Yamaguchi, and Yokoo 1981a, 1981b).

Onions produce thiamine propyldisulfide, which corresponds to the allithiamine formed in garlic from thiamine and allicin. Both compounds have been found effective against cyanide poisoning (Carson 1987).

Medicinal Use

Atherosclerotic. Onion is known to have a hypocholesterolemic effect, although not as strong as that of garlic (Bhushan et al. 1976). A study in China compared an onion-growing region to one without local onions. Both regions were similar in living standards, economic level, and dietary habits and customs. But people in the onion-growing region had a death rate from cardiovascular disease of 57 per 100,000 people, as compared with a cardiovascular-disease death rate in the other region of 167 per 100,000. The onion-growing region also had a significantly lower incidence of hypertension, retinal arteriosclerosis, hyperlipemia, and coronary artery disease (Sun et al. 1993).

Hypo- and hyperglycemic effects. A study has revealed that although a water extract of fresh or boiled onion did not affect fasting blood sugar in normal subjects, it did reduce the sugar levels in glucose-tolerance tests in a dose-dependent manner. From this result, it was suggested that onion has an antihyperglycemic effect instead of a hypoglycemic effect (Sharma et al. 1977).

The antihyperglycemic principle in onion has been tentatively identified as 2-propenyl propyl disulfide – a compound that has been found to lower the blood sugar and increase insulin levels but has not been observed to have any effect on free fatty-acid concentrations (Augusti 1974; Augusti and Benaim 1975). Another antihyperglycemic compound causing this effect is diphenylamine, found in onion and tea (Karawya et al. 1984).

Ill-effects of consumption. One problem with the consumption of onions is heartburn, but only among those predisposed to heartburn symptoms (Allen et al. 1990). Onions may also cause discomfort in people with ileostomies and children with Down's syndrome (Bingham, Cummings, and McNeil 1982; Urquhart and Webb 1985).

As early as 1909, cattle deaths were attributed to eating sprouting or decaying onions (Goldsmith 1909; Fenwick and Hanley 1985c). Clinical signs of the condition may include onion odor in breath and urine, tainting of milk, diarrhea, staggering, and collapse. Provided that the illness has not reached an irreversible point, the symptoms (which develop with a week of onion feeding) may decline when the offending ingredient is removed from the diet. Treatment may also include injection of B-complex vitamins with penicillin-streptomycin (Gruhzit 1931; Farkas and Farkas 1974; Kirk and Bulgin 1979).

Garlic

History

Antiquity. Cultivated in the Middle and Far East for at least 5,000 years, garlic *(Allium sativum)* is believed to have originated from a wild ancestor in central Asia and is, possibly, native to western Tartary (Turkestan). At a very early period, garlic was carried throughout the whole of Asia (except Japan), North Africa, and Europe. In ancient China, Egypt, and India, garlic – like onions – was a highly prized foodstuff (Hedrick 1972; Hanley and Fenwick 1985).

In Egypt, the consumption of garlic is shown in tomb art dating from the Early Dynastic Period (c. 2925–2575 B.C.). The Codex Elsers, an Egyptian medical papyrus dating from around 1500 B.C., described 22 garlic preparations employed against a variety of complaints, including headache, bodily weakness, and throat disorders (Fenwick and Hanley 1985a).

The Bible (Num. 11:5) reports that after their Exodus from Egypt (about 1450 B.C.), the Israelites complained to Moses about the lack of garlic, among other things: "We remember the fish which we used to eat free in Egypt, the cucumbers and the melons and the leeks and the onions and the garlic."

The Greeks, along with the Egyptians, regarded garlic as a defense against old age and illness, and athletes participating in the Olympic Games, (which began about 776 B.C.), regularly chewed it to improve stamina (Hanley and Fenwick 1985). Homer, the Greek poet from the eighth century B.C., worked garlic into his tales (Hedrick 1972), including a description of how Odysseus fended off Circe's magic using as antidote a plant "having black root and milk white flower" (Fenwick and Hanley 1985a: 202). Tradition has it that this plant was wild garlic (Fenwick and Hanley 1985a).

Hippocrates (c. 460–370 B.C.) recommended garlic for pneumonia and suppurating wounds, but warned that it "caused flatulence, a feeling of warmth on the chest and a heavy sensation in the head; it excites anxiety and increases any pain which may be present. Nevertheless, it has the good quality that it increases the secretion of urine" (Jones and Mann 1963; Warren 1970; Fenwick and Hanley 1985a: 202).

Asia. Garlic was introduced into China between 140 and 86 B.C. The Chinese word for garlic, *suan,* is written as a single character, which often indicates the

antiquity of a word (Hyams 1971). A fifth-century Chinese treatise on agriculture *(Ch'i-min-yao-shu)* described the cultivation of *suan* along the Red River valley. Chinese leeks, shallots, and spring onions were also discussed, but garlic seems to have been the most important. In addition, *tse suan* – water garlic *(Allium nipponicum* L.) – was mentioned as both a pervasive weed and a cultivated plant (Li 1969). According to Marco Polo (c. A.D. 1254–1324), garlic was used as a complement to raw liver among the Chinese poor (Lucas 1966), and much mention is made of garlic in treatises written in China from the fifteenth to the eighteenth centuries (Hedrick 1972).

In India, an important fifth-century Sanskrit medical manuscript, the *Charaka-Samhita,* based on sources from perhaps five centuries earlier, attributed widespread curative properties to both garlic and onion. It was claimed that they possessed diuretic properties, were beneficial to the digestive tract, were good for the eyes, acted as heart stimulants, and had antirheumatic qualities (Fenwick and Hanley 1985a).

In the Ayurvedic (Sanskrit) and Unani Tibb (Greco-Arabic) systems, garlic has been employed both as a prophylactic and as a cure for a variety of diseases, including arteriosclerosis, cholera, colic, dysentery, dyspepsia, gastric and intestinal catarrh, and typhoid. Duodenal ulcers, laryngeal tuberculosis, and lupus have all been treated with garlic juice, and garlic preparations have been given for bronchiectasis, gangrene of the lung, pulmonary phthisis, and whooping cough (Fenwick and Hanley 1985a).

Today the use of garlic is especially prevalent in Asia, where garlic-based antibiotics are used extensively to replace or complement more sophisticated drugs (Hanley and Fenwick 1985). In addition, in rural villages of Karnataka, in southwestern India, garlic is prescribed for lactating women (Rao 1985).

Europe. Garlic was regularly mentioned in European literature as well, especially for its medicinal benefits. The Roman poet Virgil (79–19 B.C.), for example, in his *Second Idyll* described how Thestylis used the juices of wild thyme and garlic as a prophylactic against snake bites (Warren 1970). A bit later, Pliny the Elder, in his *Natural History,* recommended that garlic be "placed when the moon is below the horizon and gathered when it is in conjunction" (Fenwick and Hanley 1985a: 200) to remove the plant's pungent smell. He devised 61 garlic-based remedies for such conditions as hemorrhoids, loss of appetite, rheumatism, and ulcers (Jones and Mann 1963; Fenwick and Hanley 1985a).

The Romans apparently disliked garlic in general because of its strong scent, but it was fed to laborers to strengthen them and to soldiers to excite courage. The Romans also used garlic as a remedy for diabetes mellitus, and it is probable that it was similarly employed by the Egyptians and Greeks (Hanley and

Fenwick 1985). Carbonized garlic has been found at Pompeii and Herculaneum, which were destroyed in A.D. 79 (Meyer 1980).

The Greek military physician Dioscorides (A.D. 40-90) was clearly impressed with garlic, onion, and other alliums as medicinal plants. He advised garlic for baldness, birthmarks, dog and snake bites, eczema, leprosy, lice, nits, toothache, ulcers, and worms. He also suggested it as a vermifuge and diuretic and as a treatment for rashes and other skin disorders (Warren 1970; Fenwick and Hanley 1985a).

The cultivation of alliums in Western Europe is usually thought to have been stimulated by the Crusaders' contacts with the East in the eleventh, twelfth, and thirteenth centuries. However, much earlier, Charlemagne (742-814) had listed garlic in his *Capitulare de Villis* and mentioned it as of Italian origin (Fenwick and Hanley 1985a). During medieval times, garlic was less appreciated for its taste than for its allegedly favorable effect on sexual potency and performance (Mauron 1986).

Presumably, however, the latter was of little interest to St. Hildegard (1098-1179), a German abbess, mystic, and scientific observer who continued the focus on garlic as medicine by specifically mentioning it in her *Physica* as a remedy against jaundice. The herbal doctors Paracelsus (Philippus Aureolus Paracelsus, 1493-1541) and Lonicerus (Adam Lonitzer, 1528-86) emphasized the antitoxic properties of garlic and its effectiveness against internal worms. At about the same time, Italian physician and botanist Matthiolus (Pietro Andrea Mattioli, 1500-77) was recommending garlic against stomach chills, colics, and flatulence.

The word "garlic" is derived from the old English "gar" (meaning spear) and, presumably, refers to the garlic clove. Geoffrey Chaucer (c. 1342-1400) wrote of "Wel loved garleek, onyons and leekes" (Fenwick and Hanley 1985a: 200), and garlic's pungency was described by William Shakespeare. In *A Midsummer Night's Dream* (Act IV, Scene 1), Bottom tells his fellow actors to eat neither garlic nor onion, "for we are to utter sweet breath," and in *Measure for Measure* (Act III, Scene 2), Lucio criticizes the Duke, who "would mouth a beggar, though she smell brown bread and garlic." A contemporary of Shakespeare described King Henry IV of France as "chewing garlic and having breath that would fell an ox at twenty paces" (Fenwick and Hanley 1985a: 201).

Garlic's medicinal (and supposedly aphrodisiacal) powers were known in England in the sixteenth and seventeenth centuries, and the diarist Samuel Pepys (1633-1703) discovered that the custom in the French navy - to keep the sailors warm and prevent scurvy - was to issue garlic and brandy rations; the British Admiralty followed suit (Fenwick and Hanley 1985a).

At the turn of the nineteenth century, garlic in the form of inhalants, compresses, and ointments was used by the citizens of Dublin against tuberculosis, and the medicinal use of garlic is still common in Bulgaria, Japan, and Russia, among other places (Petkov 1986). In Russia, garlic-based antibiotics are widely employed, and on one occasion, 500 tonnes of garlic were imported to combat an outbreak of influenza (Fenwick and Hanley 1985a).

The Americas. Garlic was introduced to the Americas by the Spaniards. In Mexico, Cortés (1485-1547) apparently grew it, and by 1604, it was said in Peru that "the Indians esteem garlic above all the roots of Europe" (Hedrick 1972). By 1775, the Choctaw Indians of North America (Alabama, Louisiana, and Mississippi) were cultivating garlic in their gardens, and at the turn of the nineteenth century, American writers mentioned garlic as among their garden esculents (Hedrick 1972).

Garlic is widely used today in Latin America as a medicine as well as a food. In Guatemala, for example, it is prescribed for vaginitis by traditional healers, health promoters, and midwives (Giron et al. 1988) and is also employed against helminthic infection, both alone and in conjunction with commercial drugs (Booth, Johns, and Lopez-Palacios 1993). Argentine folk medicine prescribes garlic for antimicrobial use (Anesini and Perez 1993), and in the mountains of Chiapas in southeastern Mexico, Indian sheepherders use garlic and other alliums for veterinary purposes (Perezgrovas Garza 1990).

Production. The major producers of garlic in 1996 were (in metric tons) China (8,574,078), Korea (455,955), India (411,900), the United States (277,820), Egypt (255,500), and Spain (212,400), and world production was 11,633,800 metric tons. Major exporters in 1996 were China, Hong Kong, Singapore, Argentina, Spain, Mexico, and France, and major importers were Malaysia, Brazil, Indonesia, Singapore, the United Arab Emirates, Japan, the United States, and France.

In the United States, garlic production is confined mostly to California. Most of this crop is grown around the town of Gilroy, which calls itself the "garlic capital of the world" (Fenwick and Hanley 1985a).

Horticulture and Botany

Botany. Garlic is known only in its cultivated form but may be related to the wild *Allium longicuspis* of central Asia. Garlic bulbs develop entirely underground, and the plant is either nonflowering or flowers in the spring. Its leaves are flat and rather slender; the stem is smooth and solid. The bulbs are composed of several bulbils (cloves) encased in the white or pink skin of the parent bulb. Each clove is formed from two leaves, the outer cylindrical one being protective and the inner one a storage organ for the bud (Traub 1968).

Cultivation. Although it grows in a wide variety of soils, garlic flourishes best in rich, deep loams with plentiful moisture. Before planting, the bulbs should be dried, treated (e.g., with benomyl) to reduce rotting, and exposed to temperatures between 0° C and 10° C for four to eight weeks to ensure bulbing. Bulbs usually form and enlarge with long days and temperatures above 20° C. Plant spacing affects the size of the bulbs. Italian workers consider a spacing of 40 to 50 per square meter desirable. Doubling this density increases the yield by 50 percent, but then the bulbs are smaller and more suitable for processing than for the fresh market (Tesi and Ricci 1982). When the tops become dry and bend to the ground, harvesting is generally done by hand, although it can be done mechanically. Curing is usually carried out in the ground or in well-ventilated structures, and the dried bulbs can be stored.

Proper curing enables garlic to store well without careful temperature control. The best results are achieved when the bulbs are dried 8 to 10 days at 20° C to 30° C, followed by a reduction of temperature to 0° C with air circulation. Under these conditions, garlic bulbs can be stored from 130 to 220 days, depending on variety and how they were grown (IOS 1983).

Also effective in garlic storage is the application of maleic hydrazide prior to harvest (Omar and Arafa 1979), and gamma irradiation prevents storage losses without an adverse effect on taste, flavor, pungency, or texture (Mathur 1963). For cold storage conditions, it is recommended that garlic be harvested, dried, and packed away from all other crops except onions (Tesi and Ricci 1982).

Pathogens and Pests
The common pests and pathogens of garlic are those discussed in the section about onions.

Processing
Dehydrated garlic. As already mentioned, most of the garlic produced in the United States (90 percent) is grown and processed near the town of Gilroy, California. Gilroy also has the largest dehydration plant in the world, and in this region, more than 60,000 tons annually are processed into 25 different kinds of flakes, salts, and granules.

Dehydrated garlic can contain five times the flavor of the fresh clove, and garlic powder is used extensively in the manufacture of spiced sausages and other foods. To maintain flavor character and prevent lumping and hardening, the powder must be stored free of moisture. Flavor deterioration of stored garlic powder is maximal at 37° C and minimal between 0° C and 2° C. At room temperature, the product is best stored in cans. The packaging of garlic powder (at 6 percent moisture content) in hermetically sealed cans is best of all (Singh, Pruthi, Sankaran, et al. 1959; Singh, Pruthi, Sreenivasamurthy, et al. 1959).

Garlic flavoring. The volatile oil content of garlic is between 0.1 and 0.25 percent. The reddish-brown oil from the distillation of freshly crushed garlic cloves is rich in 2-propenyl sulfides. Often the oil itself is too pungent for efficient manufacturing use, so garlic juice – obtained in a similar manner to onion juice – is employed. Concentrating the juice produces oleoresin garlic, a dark-brown extract with approximately 5 percent garlic oil. The oleoresin has uniformity, good handling, and good processing characteristics.

Nutrition
As with onions, the nutrient content of garlic changes with variety, ecological conditions, and climate. One hundred grams (3.53 ounces, or 0.44 of a cup) of garlic provides about 149 kilocalories of energy, 6.36 g of protein, 0.5 g of fat, and 33.07 g of carbohydrate (Nutrition Coordinating Center 1994).

In light of the RDA standard for males between 18 and 25 years of age, approximately one-half cup of fresh garlic (100 g) would provide them with 10.1 percent of the recommended dietary allowance of protein, 22.6 percent of calcium (181 mg), 17 percent of iron (1.7 mg), 19.1 percent of phosphorus (153 mg), 13.3 percent of copper (0.3 mg), 20.3 percent of selenium (14.2 mg), 52 percent of vitamin C (31.2 mg), 13.3 percent of thiamine (0.2 mg), 10.9 percent of pantothenic acid (0.6 mg), and 61.5 percent of vitamin B_6 (1.23 mg). Garlic is high in potassium (401 mg/100 g), low in sodium (17 mg/100 g), and contains small amounts of magnesium, manganese, molybdenum, and zinc (Pruthi 1980; Raj et al. 1980). Other trace elements in garlic are cobalt, chromium, lithium, nickel, titanium, and vanadium. Garlic contains no vitamin A or E but does have small amounts of riboflavin, niacin, and folacin (National Research Council 1989).

Garlic (100 g) contains only small amounts of four fatty acids: 0.09 g of saturated palmitic acid, 0.01 g of monounsaturated oleic acid, 0.23 g of polyunsaturated essential linoleic acid, and 0.02 g of polyunsaturated essential linolenic acid. It has 4.1 g of dietary fiber, 14.7 g of starch, and 58.58 g of water. Sucrose (0.6 g), glucose (0.4 g), and fructose (0.6 g) are present, as are the essential amino acids – arginine (0.63 g) and glutamic acid (0.8 g) are the most abundant, followed by aspartic acid (0.49 g) and leucine (0.31 g).

Chemistry
Nonflavor compounds. Garlic contains polymers of fructose with up to 51 fructose molecules (Darbyshire and Henry 1981). It also yields pectin. Garlic pectin content includes galactose, arabinose, galacturonic acid, and glucose. It has a much higher viscosity than onion pectin, as well as a lower setting temperature and a longer setting time (Alexander and Sulebele 1973; Khodzhaeva and Kondratenko 1983).

Sterols found in garlic are stigmasterol, B-sitosterol,

and campesterol (Oka et al. 1974; Stoianova-Ivanova, Tzutzulova, and Caputto 1980). Garlic also contains arachidonic and eicosapentaenic acids (Carson 1987).

Garlic has exhibited antioxidant activity in linoleic-acid and minced-pork model systems. This activity can be increased by microwave heating or boiling. It has been shown that S-alkenyl cysteine sulfoxides were the most active. Quercetin and other flavone agly-cones also contribute to the total antioxidant capacities of onion and garlic extracts (Pratt and Watts 1964; Naito et al. 1981a, 1981b).

Allithiamin, discovered in the 1950s by Japanese researchers, is formed in garlic from thiamine and allicin and is absorbed faster in the intestinal tract than thiamine (Fujiwara 1976). Unlike thiamine, allithiamin is not degraded by thiaminase and appears more stable under conditions of heat (Hanley and Fenwick 1985). Allithiamin, which reacts with the amino acid cysteine to regenerate thiamine – yielding 2-propenylthiocysteine – has been found effective against cyanide poisoning (Carson 1987).

Flavor compounds. The first important studies on the composition of garlic oil were carried out by T. Wertheim in 1844 and 1845. While investigating the antibacterial properties of garlic in the 1940s, C. J. Cavallito and others discovered the thiolsulfinate allicin, the most important flavor component of fresh garlic (Carson 1987). This colorless oil is di(2-propenyl)thiolsulfinate. (In this chapter, 2-propenyl is used instead of allyl.) Allicin is probably the first thiolsulfinate isolated from natural sources (Carson 1987).

The compounds responsible for the flavor of alliums are produced from involatile precursors only when tissue maceration occurs. Gamma-glutamyl peptides, containing approximately 90 percent of garlic's soluble, organically bound sulfur, are present in significant amounts and may be the storage form of the flavor precursors (Virtanen 1965; Whitaker 1976). Under these circumstances, alkyl or alkenyl cysteine sulfoxides come into contact with an enzyme, alliinase, and hydrolysis occurs. The initially formed thiolsulfinates can break down to produce a range of organoleptically important sulfur compounds, including disulfides, trisulfides, higher sulfides, and thiols. The flavor properties of the different alliums depend on the types and amounts of these sulfur compounds (Hanley and Fenwick 1985).

Over 90 percent of the flavor-precursor content of garlic is located in the storage leaf (Freeman 1975). Alliin lyase is a major product of the storage bud (clove), accounting for 10 percent of its total protein. Deposits of alliinase are most pronounced around phloem tissue and are concentrated in the bundle sheaths. Little, if any, occurs in storage mesophyll that is not in contact with vascular bundles. This deposition in the clove may reflect the enzyme's role in protecting underground storage buds from decay and predation. Positioning near the phloem suggests that alliin lyase, or compounds related to its activity, may be translocated to and from the clove during development (Ellmore and Feldberg 1994). Alliinase is present in most, if not all, members of the genus *Allium,* and is also found in *Albizzia, Acacia, Parkia,* and *Lentinus* species.

Medicinal Use

Atherosclerotic. Medical claims for the efficacy of garlic against myriad complaints have been made for millennia and are still being made today as science continues to analyze the properties of this tasty vegetable and channel them to medical use.

The second-century Indian physician, Charaka, reported that onion and garlic prevented heart disease and acted as heart tonics (Fenwick and Hanley 1985c). Clots, which can cause strokes and heart attacks, are formed through the aggregation of platelets. Both garlic and onion have a demonstrated ability to inhibit platelet aggregation, possibly by interfering with prostaglandin biosynthesis (Ali et al. 1993).

In a double-blind, placebo-controlled study of 60 volunteers with cerebrovascular risk factors and constantly increased platelet aggregation, it was demonstrated that daily ingestion of 800 mg of powdered garlic (in the form of coated tablets), over four weeks, significantly decreased the ratio of circulating platelet aggregates and inhibited spontaneous platelet aggregation. The ratio of circulating platelet aggregates decreased by 10.3 percent; spontaneous platelet aggregation decreased by 56.3 percent (Kiesewetter et al. 1993).

Some garlic compounds that inhibit platelet aggregation have been identified. These are methyl (2-propenyl)trisulfide (the strongest), methyl (2-propenyl)disulfide, di(2-propenyl)disulfide, and di(2-propenyl)trisulfides. All these compounds are said to be formed from allicin, which is di (2-propenyl)thiosulfinate. There is some evidence that methyl(2-propenyl)trisulfide is more effective on a molar basis than aspirin (Makheja, Vanderhoek, and Bailey 1979; Ariga, Oshiba, and Tamada 1981; Bosia et al. 1983; Apitz-Castro, Badimon, and Badimon 1992; Lawson, Ransom, and Hughes 1992). Recently, a novel amino acid glycoside, (-)-N-(1'-beta-D-fructopyranosyl)-S-2-propenyl-L-cysteine sulfoxide, showed significant inhibition of in vitro platelet aggregation induced by ADP (adenosin diphosphate) and epinephrine (Mutsch-Eckner et al. 1993).

Garlic has also been shown to increase fibrinolytic activity, which inhibits clot formation (Bordia et al. 1978). An excellent epidemiological study of garlic and onion intake in the Jain community in India was done in 1979. Three groups with widely differing allium consumption patterns were chosen: those who had always abstained from onions and garlic; those who consumed only small amounts (<200 g onion, <10 g garlic per week); and those who consumed onions and garlic liberally (>600 g onion, >50 g garlic per week). The three groups were otherwise similar in regard to intake of calories, fat, and carbohydrates. Those who ingested the most alliums had the lowest level of plasma fibrinogen, which is used by the body in forming a blood clot with platelets (Sainani, Desai, Natu et al. 1979).

In a study of dried garlic consumption by 20 patients with hyperlipoproteinemia over a period of four weeks, fibrinogen and fibrinopeptide A significantly decreased by 10 percent. Serum cholesterol levels significantly decreased by 10 percent. Systolic and diastolic blood pressure decreased. ADP- and collagen-induced platelet aggregation were not influenced (Harenberg, Giese, and Zimmermann 1988).

The antithrombotic agents found in garlic that we know about are (E,Z)-ajoene, or (E,Z)4,5,9-trithiadodeca-1,6,11-triene 9-oxide, the major anticoagulant, di(2-propenyl)trisulfide, and 2-vinyl-4H-1,3-dithiene (Apitz-Castro et al. 1983; Block et al. 1984; Block 1992).

It is generally known that both fresh and boiled garlic decrease cholesterol and triglycerides. The Jain epidemiological study, mentioned previously, demonstrated not only that liberal use of onions and garlic decreased total cholesterol, low-density lipoprotein (LDL – the so-called bad cholesterol), and triglycerides, but also that those who consumed even small amounts of alliums were better protected than those who ate no onions or garlic (Sainani, Desai, Gorhe, et al. 1979).

One study, however, found that garlic increased cholesterol in people who had suffered a heart attack. A longer-term trial of garlic's effects on these people was undertaken and lasted 10 months. After 1 month, there was an increase in cholesterol, but thereafter it decreased, and after 8 months, it had declined by 18 percent. The initial increase in serum cholesterol in the heart patients who were fed garlic may have been caused by mobilization of lipid from deposits. Decreases of LDL occurred, and high-density lipoprotein (HDL – the "good" cholesterol) increased (Bordia 1981).

A multicentric, placebo-controlled, randomized study of standardized garlic-powder tablets in the treatment of hyperlipidemia (cholesterol levels over 200 mg/dl) was performed over a 16-week period. The total intake of garlic powder was 800 mg/day, standardized to 1.3 percent of alliin, (+)S-(2-propenyl)-L-cysteine, content (Stoll and Seebeck 1948). Cholesterol levels dropped 12 percent and triglyceride levels dropped 17 percent, with the best lowering effects seen in patients with cholesterol values between 250 to 300 mg/dl (Mader 1990).

To assess the effects of standardized garlic-powder tablets on serum lipids and lipoproteins, 42 healthy adults (19 men and 23 women), with a mean age of 52 (plus or minus 12 years), and with total serum cholesterol levels of 220 mg/dl or above, received, in a randomized, double-blind fashion, 300 mg of standardized garlic powder (in tablet form) three times a day for 12 weeks, or they received a placebo. Diets and physical activities were unchanged. Treatment with standardized garlic at 900 mg/day produced a significantly greater reduction in serum triglycerides and LDL cholesterol than did the placebo. LDL-C (low-density lipoprotein cholesterol) was reduced 11 percent by garlic treatment and 3 percent by placebo ($p < 0.05$), and the baseline total cholesterol level of 262 (plus or minus 34 mg/dl) dropped to 247 (plus or minus 40 mg/dl) ($p < 0.01$). The placebo group showed a change from 276 (plus or minus 34 mg/dl) to 274 (plus or minus 29 mg/dl) (Jain et al. 1993).

Part of the activity of garlic results from an interruption of normal cholesterol biosynthesis (Qureshi et al. 1983). Hepatic cell culture results indicate that the hypocholesterolemic effect of garlic proceeds, in part, from decreased hepatic cholesterogenesis, whereas the triacylglycerol-lowering effect appears to be the result of the inhibition of fatty-acid synthesis (Yeh and Yeh 1994). The garlic compounds di(2-propenyl)thiosulfinate (allicin), S-methyl-L-cysteine sulfoxide, and S-(2-propenyl)-L-cysteine sulfoxide lower cholesterol in animals (Itokawa et al. 1973; Augusti and Matthew 1975). The garlic compounds ajoene, methylajoene, 2-vinyl-4H-1,3-dithiin, di(2-propenyl)disulfide, and allicin inhibit cholesterol synthesis in rat livers by 37 to 72 percent (Sendl et al. 1992). There is some evidence that di(2-propenyl)-disulfide inactivates 3-hydroxy-3-methylglutaryl-CoA (HMG-CoA) reductase (the major cholesterol synthesis enzyme) by forming an internal protein disulfide inaccessible for reduction and making the enzyme inactive (Omkumar et al. 1993). It has also been found that ajoene inactivates human gastric lipase, which causes less absorption of fat to occur in the digestion process and, therefore, lowers triacylglycerol levels (Gargouri et al. 1989).

Meta-analysis of the controlled trials of garlic's role in reducing hypercholesterolemia showed a significant reduction in total cholesterol levels. The best available evidence suggests that garlic, in an amount approximating one-half to one clove per day, decreased total serum cholesterol levels by about 9 percent in the groups of patients studied (Warshafsky, Kamer, and Sivak 1993; Silagy and Neil 1994).

Antimicrobial, antiviral, antihelminthic, and antifungal action. Garlic has been found to be more potent than 13 other spices in inhibiting *Shigella sonnei* (bacillary dysentery), *Staphylococcus aureus* (boils and food poisoning), *Escherichia coli* (indicator of fecal contamination), *Streptococcus faecalis* (indicator of fecal contamination), and *Lactobacillus casei* (found in milk and cheese) (Subrahmanyan, Krishnamarthy, et al. 1957; Subrahmanyan, Sreenivasamurthy, et al. 1957). A mouthwash containing 10 percent garlic extract has been shown to significantly reduce oral bacterial counts (Elnima et al. 1983). However, the antibacterial components of garlic are heat labile. Whole garlic bulbs can lose their antibacterial activity within 20 minutes in boiling water at 100° C (Chen, Chang, and Chang 1985).

Garlic may change the composition of intestinal microflora to favor lactic organisms that are beneficial in the absorption of dietary minerals (Subrahmanyan, Krishnamurthy, et al. 1957; Subrahmanyan, Sreenivasamurthy, et al. 1957). Lactic acid bacteria have been proven to be the least sensitive microorganisms to the inhibitory effects of garlic.

In general, garlic is effective against most gram-positive and gram-negative bacteria. Garlic extracts inhibit the coagulase activity of *S. aureus* (Fletcher, Parker, and Hassett 1974). The *Listeria monocytogenes* population of strain Scott A (a source of food poisoning) was decreased to less than 10 per milliliter in seven days by 1 percent garlic powder (Hefnawy, Moustafa, and Marth 1993). Garlic also inhibits *Vibrio parahemolyticus* (a gastroenteritis-causing pathogen in raw or improperly cooked fish or seafood) (Sato, Terao, and Ishibashi 1993).

Garlic has been found beneficial in cryptococcal meningitis, a frequently fatal disease (Fromtling and Bulmer 1978; Garlic in cryptococcal meningitis 1980; Caporaso, Smith, and Eng 1983). A commercial garlic extract, intravenously infused into two patients, caused their plasma titers of anti-*Cryptococcus neoformans* activity to rise twofold over preinfusion titers (Davis, Shen, and Cai 1990).

Thirty strains of mycobacteria, consisting of 17 species, were inhibited by various concentrations of garlic extract (1.34 to 3.35 mg/ml of agar media). Six strains of *Mycobacterium tuberculosis* required a mean inhibitory concentration of 1.67 mg/ml of media (Delaha and Garagusi 1985).

Garlic has proven effective in leprous neuritis. It is not certain whether this results from the vegetable's topical antibiotic activity or from garlic's ability to improve the thiamin status of the patient (Ramanujam 1962; Sreenivasamurthy et al. 1962).

Allicin, di(2-propenyl)thiosulfinate, the principal fresh-flavor component of garlic, is effective in the range of 1:125,000 against a number of gram-positive and gram-negative organisms. It inhibits the growth of some *Staphylococci, Streptococci, Vibrio* (including *Vibrio cholerae*), and *Bacilli* (including *Bacillus typhosus, Bacillus dysenteriae,* and *Bacillus enteritidis*) but is considerably weaker than penicillin against gram-positive organisms (Carson 1987). Allicin's effect is generally attributed to its interaction with biological -SH (sulfur) containing systems. If -SH-containing systems are necessary components for the growth and development of microorganisms, these processes will be inhibited by allicin. If the toxic compounds are exogenous, then reaction with allicin will lead to detoxification (Cavallito 1946; Wills 1956).

Garlic has exhibited antiviral activity against influenza B virus and herpes simplex type I (nongenital) but not against Coxsaki B1 virus, which, however, usually causes only a mild illness (Carson 1987). Clinical use of garlic preparations in the prevention and treatment of human cytomegalovirus infections is effective (Meng et al. 1993). Because the antiviral effect of garlic extract is strongest when it is applied continuously in tissue culture, it is recommended that the clinical use of garlic extract against cytomegalovirus infection be persistent, and the prophylactic use of garlic extract is preferable in immunocompromised patients (Guo et al. 1993).

The activity of garlic constituents against selected viruses, including herpes simplex virus type 1 (nongenital cold sores), herpes simplex virus type 2 (genital), parainfluenza virus type 3 (bronchitis and pneumonia), vaccinia virus (cowpox, the source of an active vaccine against smallpox), vesicular stomatitis virus (which causes cold sores in humans and animals), and human rhinovirus type 2 (the common cold), has been determined. In general, the virucidal constituents, in descending order, were: ajoene, allicin, 2-propenyl methyl thiosulfinate, and methyl 2-propenyl thiosulfinate (Weber et al. 1992). Ajoene has also shown some activity against human immunodeficiency virus (HIV) (Tatarrintsev et al. 1992).

The effect of serial dilutions of crude garlic extract on adult *Hymenolepis nana* (dwarf tapeworm) was studied to detect the minimal lethal concentration. Garlic was then employed in the treatment of 10 children infected with *H. nana* and 26 children infected with *Giardia lamblia* (giardiasis). Such treatment took the form of either 5 milliliters of crude extract in 100 milliliters of water in two doses per day, or two commercially prepared 0.6 mg capsules twice a day for three days. Garlic was found to be efficient and safe and to shorten the duration of treatment (Soffar and Mokhtar 1991). Garlic appears to affect adversely the development of the eggs of *Necator americanus* (hookworm) but has less effect on the hatched larvae (Bastidas 1969). Rectal garlic preparations may be effective in the treatment of pinworms (Braun 1974).

A single dose of ajoene on the day of malarial infection was found to suppress the development of parasitemia; there were no obvious acute toxic effects from the tested dose. The combination of ajoene and chloroquine, given as a single dose on the day of the infection, completely prevented the subsequent development of malarial parasitemia in treated mice (Perez, de la Rosa, and Apitz 1994).

Ajoene has also been shown to inhibit the proliferation of *Trypanosoma cruzi,* the causative agent of Chagas' disease. An important factor associated with the antiproliferative effects of ajoene against *T. cruzi* may be its specific alteration of the phospholipid composition of these cells (Urbina 1993).

Garlic inhibits the aflatoxin-producing fungi *Aspergillus flavus* and *Aspergillus parasiticus*

(Sharma et al. 1979). Garlic extract inhibits the growth and aflatoxin production of *A. flavus* (Sutabhaha, Suttajt, and Niyomca 1992), and garlic oil completely inhibits sterigmatocystin (a carcinogenic mycotoxin produced by *Aspergillus*) production (Hasan and Mahmoud 1993). Thiopropanal-S-oxide is one of the most active antiaflatoxin components (Sharma et al. 1979).

The ajoene in garlic has been shown to have antifungal activity. *Aspergillus niger* (a frequent cause of fungal ear infections) and *Candida albicans* (yeast) were inhibited by ajoene in concentrations of less than 20 micrograms per milliliter (Yoshida et al. 1987). Ajoene also inhibits the growth of the pathogenic fungus *Paracoccidioides brasiliensis* (South American blastomycosis, which starts in the lungs) (San Blas et al. 1993). Additional studies have shown ajoene to inhibit *Cladosporium carrionii* and *Fonsecaea pedrosoi* (both cause chromoblastomycosis, a fungal disease of the skin) (Sanchez-Mirt, Gil, and Apitz-Castro 1993).

Moreover, extracts of both garlic and onion have been shown to inhibit the growth of many plant-pathogenic fungi and yeasts. Garlic-bulb extracts are more active than onion extracts (Agrawal 1978). Garlic solutions of 1 to 20 percent have been effective against plant pathogens such as downy mildew in cucumbers and radishes, bean rust, bean anthracnose, tomato early blight, brown rot in stone fruits, angular leaf spot in cucumbers, and bacterial blight in beans (Pordesimo and Ilag 1976). Ajoene has been tested in greenhouse experiments, where it completely inhibited powdery mildew in tomatoes and roses (Reimers et al. 1993).

Anticarcinogenic. Some data have suggested an inverse relationship between garlic consumption and gastric cancer. In Shandong Province, China, the death rate from gastric cancer was found to be 3.45/100,000 population in Gangshan County (where garlic consumption is approximately 20 g per person per day), but in nearby Quixia County (where little garlic is eaten), the gastric cancer death rate was much higher, averaging 40/100,000 (Han 1993; Witte et al. 1996). A study of risk factors for colon cancer in Shanghai indicated that garlic was associated with a decreased relative risk (Yang, Ji, and Gao 1993). Some evidence to the same effect has been seen in Italy (Dorant et al. 1993).

Interviews with 564 patients with stomach cancer and 1,131 controls – in an area of China where gastric cancer rates were high – revealed a significant reduction in gastric cancer risk with increasing consumption of allium vegetables. Persons in the highest quartile of intake experienced only 40 percent of the risk of those in the lowest quartile. Protective effects were seen for garlic, onions, and other allium foods. Although additional research is needed before etiologic inferences can be made, the findings were con-

sistent with reports of tumor inhibition following administration of allium compounds in experimental animals (You et al. 1989). Garlic has been shown to reduce cancer promotion and tumor yield by phorbol-myristate-acetate in mice (Belman 1983).

In isolated epidermal cells, at 5 µg per milliliter, garlic oil increased glutathione peroxidase activity and inhibited ornithine decarboxylase induction in the presence of various nonphorbol ester tumor promoters. The same oil treatment inhibited the sharp decline in the intracellular ratio of reduced glutathione to oxidized glutathione caused by the potent tumor promoter, 12-O-tetradecanoylphorbol-13-acetate. It was suggested that some of the inhibitory effects of garlic on skin tumor promotion may have resulted from its enhancement of the natural glutathione-dependent antioxidant protective system of the epidermal cells (Perchellet et al. 1986). The active compound appeared to be di(2-propenyl)trisulfide (Carson 1987).

Other medicinal uses. Garlic has been used to treat hypertension in China and Japan for centuries. Studies in 1921, 1948, and 1969 provided supporting evidence of garlic's antihypertensive ability (Loeper and Debray 1921; Piotrowski 1948; Srinivasan 1969).

In 1990, a study was published in which 47 outpatients with mild hypertension took part in a randomized, placebo-controlled, double-blind trial conducted by 11 general practitioners. The patients who were admitted to the study had diastolic blood pressures between 95 and 104 mm Hg. The patients took either a preparation of garlic powder or a placebo of identical appearance for 12 weeks. Blood pressure and plasma lipids were monitored during treatment at 4, 8, and 12 weeks. Significant differences between the placebo and garlic groups were found during the course of therapy. The supine diastolic blood pressure in the group taking garlic fell from 102 to 91 mm Hg after 8 weeks ($p < 0.05$) and to 89 mm Hg after 12 weeks ($p < 0.01$). Serum cholesterol and triglycerides were also significantly reduced after 8 and 12 weeks of treatment. In the placebo group no significant changes occurred (Auer et al. 1990).

Studies of natural selenium-rich sources have found that high-selenium garlic and onion may have some unique attributes. First, their ingestion does not lead to an exaggerated accumulation of tissue selenium, which both selenomethionine and Brazil nut may cause. Second, unlike selenite, they do not cause any perturbation in glutathione (an antioxidant) homeostasis. Third, they expressed good anticancer activity that was equal to, if not better than, that of selenite (Ip and Lisk 1994).

Garlic odor. Although the problem of onion and garlic breath was first investigated in 1935 (Haggard and Greenberg 1935), many folk remedies – such as strong coffee, honey, yogurt, milk, coffee beans, cloves, and, most commonly, parsley – have long been used (Sokolov 1975). Perhaps, however, there is excessive worry about garlic or onion on the breath. A recent study of male and female shoppers in Helsinki indicated that sweat and alcohol were thought to be the most annoying social odors and those of garlic and perfume or aftershave the least annoying (Rosin, Tuorila, and Uutela 1992).

Studies on the effect of garlic on breast milk have indicated that garlic ingestion significantly and consistently increases the intensity of the milk odor. It was found that infants were attached to the breast for longer periods of time and sucked more when the milk smelled of garlic. There was also a tendency for the infants to ingest more milk. However, if the mother ingested garlic pills regularly, there was no change in the infant's feeding behavior after its initial exposure (Mennella and Beauchamp 1991, 1993).

Leeks

History

As with onions and garlic, leek *(Allium porrum)* consumption is depicted in Egyptian tomb decorations of the Early Dynastic Period (c. 2925 B.C.–c. 2575 B.C.) (Jones and Mann 1963; Fenwick and Hanley 1985a). Leeks were also grown and widely used for cooking in Sumeria (southern Iraq) even earlier (Hanley and Fenwick 1985). In China, the fifth-century treatise on agriculture, *Ch'i-min-yao-shu* (Essential Arts for the People), by Chia Ssu-hsieh described the cultivation of *chiu* (Chinese leek, *Allium ramosum* L.) along the Red River valley, where it has doubtless been cultivated for many centuries (Li 1969).

Leeks were called *prason* in ancient Greece and *porrum* by the Romans. Pliny the Elder, the Roman naturalist, cited Aricia in central Italy as famous for its leeks, and the Emperor Nero (A.D. 37–68) reportedly ate them several days a month to clear his voice, which caused people to call him Porrophagus. The Romans introduced leeks to Britain, where they were widely cultivated by Saxon times (sixth century A.D.), and cottage vegetable plots were often referred to by the name "leac tun" (Hedrick 1972; Fenwick and Hanley 1985a).

Leeks were known in Europe throughout the Middle Ages and were believed – like onions and garlic – to be an erotic stimulant that increased sperm and stimulated desire, especially when prepared with honey, sesame, and almond (Mauron 1986).

In northern England, leek growing remains a serious and highly competitive business, with secrets of cultivation handed down from father to son. In addition, leeks have been the badge of Welshmen from time immemorial. Saint David (c. 495–589) is said to have suggested that the Welsh wear leeks in their hats to enable them to distinguish friend from foe in the heat of battle. Consequently, the leek is worn (and subsequently eaten) in Wales on St. David's Day

(March 1) to celebrate the Welsh defeat of the Saxons in the year 633 (Hedrick 1972; Fenwick and Hanley 1985a).

Horticulture and Botany

The modern leek is not known in the wild. It probably originated in the Near East region around the eastern Mediterranean, where it was much eaten, and was distributed across Europe by the Romans (Traub 1968).

Cultivation. Although leek growing is popular in parts of Britain, commercial production of the plant is centered in France, Belgium, and the Netherlands, with France by far the most important grower (Hanley and Fenwick 1985). Production takes place mainly in Bouches-du-Rhône, Vaucluse, Haute Garonne, Ain, Ille et Vilaine, Manche, and especially in Nord and Loire-Atlantique.

Leeks grow well under most soil conditions but do best in deep loams and peat. Good drainage is essential, and the soil's Ph value should be near 7.0. Leeks can be sowed directly or grown in seedbeds and transplanted. Six varieties of leeks are grown in Britain to ensure year-round cultivation. Harvesting may be mechanical or by hand. A maximum yield of fresh weight and dry matter can be obtained after harvest in October or November (weeks 43 to 45), when nitrate content has decreased to a low and almost stable level (Kaack, Kjeldsen, and Mune 1993). Leeks are then trimmed, either in the field or at a packing station (Fenwick and Hanley 1985a). Leeks store well at 0° C (with 90 to 95 percent relative humidity) for up to 12 weeks (Vandenberg and Lentz 1974).

Nutrition

The Nutrition Data System of the University of Minnesota indicates that 100 g of leeks provides 32 kilocalories of energy, 1.83 g of protein, 0.19 g of fat, and 7.34 g of carbohydrate (Nutrition Coordinating Center 1994).

Approximately one-half cup of fresh leeks would give an 18- to 25-year-old male 9 percent of his RDA of calcium (72 mg), 14.8 percent of iron (1.48 mg), 31.3 percent of vitamin C (18.8 mg), and 32 percent of his folacin (64 mg). Leeks are high in potassium (276 mg/100 g), low in sodium (16 mg/100 g), and contain small amounts of copper, magnesium, phosphorus, selenium, and zinc. They have 38.42 mcg of vitamin A, 230.54 mcg of beta-carotene, and 0.46 mg of vitamin E (alpha-tocopherol 0.37 mg, beta-tocopherol 0.17 mg, gamma-tocopherol 0.17 mg, and delta-tocopherol 0.09 mg), as well as small amounts of thiamine, riboflavin, niacin, pantothenic acid, and vitamin B_6 (National Research Council 1989). All essential amino acids are present in leeks. Aspartic acid (0.17 g) and glutamic acid (0.38 g) are the most abundant, followed by arginine (0.13 g) and proline (0.12 g).

Chemistry

Nonflavor compounds. The flavonoids most often found in leeks have been quercetin, kaempferol, and their derivatives, usually mono- and diglycosides. These are generally found in higher concentrations in the epidermal layer of the leaves and protect the plant from ultraviolet radiation (Starke and Herrmann 1976b).

Leeks contain fructans, polymers of fructose usually having 3 to 12 fructose molecules. Fructose polymers of 12 molecules are the most common (Darbyshire and Henry 1981). Leeks also produce very long chain fatty acids (Agrawal, Lessire, and Stumpf 1984).

Chives

History

Chives *(Allium schoenoprasum)* originated in the north temperate zone. John Gerard (1545–1612), English botanist and barber-surgeon, included chives in his herbal, published in 1597. Described in 1683 as a pleasant sauce and food potherb, and listed as part of seedsmen's supplies in 1726, chives were losing favor in England by 1783. However, botanist E. Louis Sturtevant reported in the nineteenth century that Scottish families were still heavy chive consumers (Hedrick 1972).

Chives are cultivated for use in salads and soups, and many consider them an indispensable ingredient in omelets. They have been much used for flavoring in continental Europe, especially in Catholic countries. Chives were also included in an 1806 list of American esculents (Hedrick 1972).

Horticulture and Botany

Chives are the only one of the allium species native to both the Old World and the New (Simmonds 1976). Indeed, the plant's wild form occurs in Asia as well as in North America and Europe.

Chives flower in spring and summer, and bees are important for their fertilization (Nordestgaard 1983). The plants grow in dense clumps of narrow cylindrical leaves and taller hollow flower stems with globular heads. Their bulbs are elongated and only slightly swollen, but it is the leaves that are usually chopped and used as a garnish for other foods. The plant is mostly homegrown and is also used as an ornamental (Traub 1968).

Pathogens and Pests

As with onions, chives are subject to assault from downy mildew (*P. destructor* [Berk.] Casp.) and onion smut (*U. cepulae* Frost), as well as the bulb and stem nematode (*D. dispaci* [Kuhn] Filipjer).

Food Use and Nutrition

Chives are eaten fresh or dehydrated, the latter being the most common processed form today. The flavor of the chopped leaves remains stable for several months when deep-frozen or freeze-dried (Poulsen and Nielsen 1979).

As with the other alliums, the nutritional content of chives varies by variety, ecological conditions, and climate. One hundred grams of chives will generally provide about 30 kilocalories of energy, 3.27 g of protein, 0.73 g of fat, and 4.35 g of carbohydrate (Nutrition Coordinating Center 1994).

For a male between 18 and 25 years of age, approximately one-half cup of fresh chives delivers 11.5 percent of the RDA of calcium (92 mg), 16 percent of iron (1.6 mg), 12 percent of magnesium (42 mg), 43.4 percent of vitamin A (434.43 mcg RE), 96.8 percent of vitamin C (58.1 mg), and 52.5 percent of folacin (105 mg). Chives are high in potassium (296 mg) and low in sodium (3 mg). They contain small amounts of copper, phosphorus, and zinc. Chives have 2606.59 mcg of beta-carotene and 0.46 mg of vitamin E (alpha-tocopherol 0.37 mg, beta-tocopherol 0.17 mg, gamma-tocopherol 0.17 mg, and delta-tocopherol 0.09 mg) and small amounts of thiamine, riboflavin, niacin, pantothenic acid, and vitamin B_6 (National Research Council 1989).

Medicinal Use

Chives have some antibacterial effects (Huddleson et al. 1944). Extracts of onions and chives possess tuberculostatic activity against human, avian, and bovine strains. In fact, chives show rather more activity than onions and are only slightly less effective than streptomycin (Gupta and Viswanathan 1955). In addition, aqueous extracts of chives have exhibited significant activity against leukemia in mice (Caldes and Prescott 1973).

Shallots

History

Pliny the Elder, in his *Natural History,* mentioned the Ascalon onion (the shallot, *Allium ascalonicum*) as one of six types of onions known to the Greeks (Fenwick and Hanley 1985a). He wrote that it came from Ascalon in Syria, and Joseph Michaud's history of the Crusades affirmed this origin. Shallots were known in Spain, Italy, France, and Germany by 1554, had entered England from France by 1633, and were grown in American gardens by 1806 (Hedrick 1972).

Horticulture and Botany

Shallots were once viewed as a separate species, but botanists now consider them to be a variety of *A. cepa* L. They are cultivated ubiquitously (Hedrick 1972) but not extensively, save in the Netherlands and France (Fenwick and Hanley 1985a).

Food Use and Nutrition

Shallots can be dried in the field, weather permitting. They are employed as a seasoning in stews and soups but can also be used in the raw state, diced in salads, or sprinkled over steaks and chops. Shallots also make excellent pickles (Hedrick 1972).

As with the rest of the alliums, the nutritional content of shallots depends on variety, ecological conditions, and climate. According to the Nutrition Coordinating Center (1994), 100 g (3.53 ounces or 0.44 cup) of shallots yields 32 kilocalories of energy, 1.83 g of protein, 0.19 g of fat, and 7.34 g of carbohydrate.

One-half cup of fresh shallots provides a male between 18 and 25 years of age approximately 9 percent of the RDA of calcium (72 mg), 14.8 percent of iron (1.48 mg), 31.3 percent of vitamin C (18.8 mg), and 32 percent of folacin (64 mg) (National Research Council 1989). Shallots are high in potassium (276 mg) and low in sodium (16 mg). They contain small amounts of copper, magnesium, phosphorus, selenium, and zinc, and also have 38.42 mcg RE of vitamin A (230.54 mcg of beta-carotene) and 0.46 mg of vitamin E (alpha-tocopherol 0.37 mg, beta-tocopherol 0.17 mg, gamma-tocopherol 0.17 mg, and delta-tocopherol 0.09 mg), as well as small amounts of thiamine, riboflavin, niacin, pantothenic acid, and vitamin B_6.

Flavor Compounds

Shallots have the same flavor components as onions but generally contain more methyl, propyl, and (1-propenyl) di- and trisulfides (Dembele and Dubois 1973; Wu et al. 1982).

A study of the volatile oils from raw, baked, and deep-fried shallots identified sulfides, disulfides, trisulfides, thiophene derivatives, and oxygenated compounds. The oils from baked or fried shallots contain decreased amounts of alkyl propenyl disulfides and increased amounts of dimethyl thiophenes (Carson 1987).

Julia Peterson

Bibliography

Adamicki, F., and A. K. Kepka. 1974. Storage of onions in controlled atmospheres. *Acta Horticultura* 38: 53.

Adetumbi, M., G. T. Javor, and B. H. Lau. 1986. *Allium sativum* (garlic) inhibits lipid synthesis by *Candida albicans*. *Antimicrobial Agents and Chemotherapy* 30: 499–501.

Agrawal, P. 1978. Effect of root and bulb extracts of *Allium* spp. on fungal growth. *Transactions of the British Mycological Society* 70: 439.

Agrawal, R. K., H. A. Dewar, D. J. Newell, and B. Das. 1977. Controlled trial of the effect of cycloalliin on the fibrinolytic activity of venous blood. *Atherosclerosis* 27: 347.

Agrawal, V. P., R. Lessire, and P. K. Stumpf. 1984. Biosynthesis of very long chain fatty acids in microsomes from epidermal cells of *Allium porrum* L. *Archives of Biochemistry and Biophysics* 230: 580.

Alexander, M. M., and G. A. Sulebele. 1973. Pectic substances in onion and garlic skins. *Journal of the Science of Food and Agriculture* 24: 611.

Ali, M., M. Angelo Khattar, A. Parid, et al. 1993. Aqueous extracts of garlic *(Allium sativum)* inhibit prosta-

glandin synthesis in the ovine ureter. *Prostaglandins Leukotrienes and Essential Fatty Acids* 49: 855–9.

Allen, M. L., M. H. Mellow, M. G. Robinson, and W. C. Orr. 1990. The effect of raw onions on acid reflux and reflux symptoms. *American Journal of Gastroenterology* 85: 377–80.

Amla, V., S. L. Verma, T. R. Sharma, et al. 1980. Clinical study of *Allium cepa* Linn in patients of bronchial asthma. *Indian Journal of Pharmacology* 13: 63.

Amonkar, S. V., and A. Banerji. 1971. Isolation and characterization of larvicidal principle of garlic. *Science* 174: 1343.

Anesini, C., and C. Perez. 1993. Screening of plants used in Argentine folk medicine for antimicrobial activity. *Journal of Ethnopharmacology* 39: 119–28.

Apitz-Castro, R., J. J. Badimon, and L. Badimon. 1992. Effect of ajoene, the major antiplatelet compound from garlic, on platelet thrombus formation. *Thrombosis Research* 68: 145–55.

Apitz-Castro, R., S. Cabrera, M. R. Cruz, et al. 1983. The effects of garlic extract and of three pure components isolated from it on human platelet aggregation, arachidonate metabolism, release activity and platelet ultrastructure. *Thrombosis Research* 32: 155.

Ariga, T., S. Oshiba, and T. Tamada. 1981. Platelet aggregation inhibitor in garlic. *Lancet* 8212: 150.

Auer, W., A. Eiber, E. Hertkorn, et al. 1990. Hypertension and hyperlipidaemia: Garlic helps in mild cases. *British Journal of Clinical Practice – Symposium Supplement* 69: 3–6.

Augusti, K. T. 1974. Effect on alloxan diabetes of allyl propyl disulphide obtained from onion. *Die Naturwissenschaften* 61: 172.

Augusti, K. T., and M. E. Benaim. 1975. Effect of essential oil of onion (allyl propyl disulphide) on blood glucose, free fatty acid and insulin levels of normal subjects. *Clinica Chimica Acta* 60: 121.

Augusti, K. T., and P. T. Matthew. 1975. Effect of allicin on certain enzymes of liver after a short-term feeding to normal rats. *Experientia* 31: 148.

Auro de Ocampo, A., and E. M. Jimenez. 1993. Plant medicine in the treatment of fish diseases in Mexico. *Veterinaria-Mexico* 24: 291–5.

Austin, R. B. 1972. Bulb formation in onions as affected by photoperiod and spectral quality of light. *Journal of Horticultural Science* 47: 493.

Barone, F. E., and M. R. Tansey. 1977. Isolation, purification, identification, synthesis, and kinetics of activity of the anticandidal component of *Allium sativum*, and a hypothesis for its mode of action. *Mycologia* 69: 793.

Bartzatt, R., D. Blum, and D. Nagel. 1992. Isolation of garlic derived sulfur compounds from urine. *Analytical Letters* 25: 1217–24.

Bastidas, G. J. 1969. Effect of ingested garlic on *Necator americanus* and *Ancylostoma caninum*. *American Journal of Tropical Medicine and Hygiene* 18: 920–3.

Belman, S. 1983. Onion and garlic oils inhibit tumour promotion. *Carcinogenesis* 4: 1063.

Bezanger-Beauquesne, L., and A. Delelis. 1967. Sur les flavonoides du bulbe d'*Allium ascalonicum* (Liliaceae). *Compte Rendu Académie Scientifique Paris Series D* 265: 2118.

Bhatnagar-Thomas, P. L., and A. K. Pal. 1974. Studies on the insecticidal activity of garlic oil. II. Mode of action of the oil as a pesticide in Musca domestico nebulo Fabr and Trogoderma granarium Everts. *Journal of Food Science and Technology (Mysore)* 11: 153.

Bhushan, S., S. Verma, V. M. Bhatnagar, and J. B. Singh. 1976. A study of the hypocholesterolaemic effect of onion *(Allium cepa)* on normal human beings. *Indian Journal of Physiology and Pharmacology* 20: 107.

Bierman, C. J. 1983. Insect repellant. Belgian Patent BE 896,522 (C1.AOIN), August 16. NL Application 82/2, 260, June 4, 1982.

Bingham, S., J. H. Cummings, and N. I. McNeil. 1982. Diet and health of people with an ileostomy. 1. Dietary assessment. *British Journal of Nutrition* 47: 399–406.

Bioelens, M., P. J. deValois, H. J. Wobben, and A. van der Gern. 1971. Volatile flavor compounds from onion. *Journal of Agriculture and Food Chemistry* 19: 984.

Block, E. 1992. The organosulfur chemistry of the genus *Allium:* Implications for the organic chemistry of sulfur. *Angewandte Chemie International Edition in English* 31: 1135–78.

Block, E., S. Ahmad, M. K. Jain, et al. 1984. (E-Z)-ajoene – a potent antithrombic agent from garlic. *Journal of the American Chemical Society* 106: 8295.

Block, E., P. E. Penn, and L. K. Revelle. 1979. Structure and origin of the onion lachrymatory factor. A microwave study. *Journal of the American Chemical Society* 101: 2200.

Booth, S., T. Johns, and C. Y. Lopez-Palacios. 1993. Factors influencing self-diagnosis and treatment of perceived helminthic infection in a rural Guatemalan community. *Social Science and Medicine* 37: 531–9.

Bordia, A. 1981. Effect of garlic on blood lipids in patients with coronary heart disease. *American Journal of Clinical Nutrition* 34: 2100.

Bordia, A. K., S. K. Sanadhya, A. S. Rathore, et al. 1978. Essential oil of garlic on blood lipids and fibrinolytic activity in patients with coronary artery disease. *Journal of the Association of Physicians of India* 26: 327.

Bosia, A., P. Spangenberg, W. Losche, et al. 1983. The role of the GSH-disulphide status in the reversible and irreversible aggregation of human platelets. *Thrombosis Research* 30: 137.

Braun, H. 1974. *Heilpflanzen - Lexikon für Ärzte und Apotheker.* Stuttgart.

Brewster, J. L. 1977a. The physiology of the onion. I. *Horticultural Abstracts* 47: 17.

1977b. The physiology of the onion. II. *Horticultural Abstracts* 47: 103.

Brocklehurst, T. F., C. A. White, and C. Dennis. 1983. The microflora of stored coleslaw and factors affecting the growth of spoilage yeasts in coleslaw. *Journal of Applied Bacteriology* 55: 57.

Brodnitz, M. H., and J. V. Pascale. 1971. Thiopropanal-S-oxide, a lachrymatory factor in onions. *Journal of Agriculture and Food Chemistry* 19: 269.

Brodnitz, M. H., J. V. Pascale, and L. Vanderslice. 1971. Flavour components of garlic extract. *Journal of Agriculture and Food Chemistry* 19: 273.

Brodnitz, M. H., C. L. Pollock, and P. P. Vallon. 1969. Flavour components of onion oil. *Journal of Agriculture and Food Chemistry* 17: 760.

Buffington, D. E., S. K. Sastry, J. C. Gustashaw, Jr., and D. S. Burgis. 1981. Artificial curing and storage of Florida onions. *Transactions of the American Society of Agricultural Engineers* 2: 782.

Caldes, G., and B. Prescott. 1973. A potential antileukemic substance present in *Allium ascalonicum. Planta Medica* 23: 99.

Caporaso, N., S. M. Smith, and R. H. K. Eng. 1983. Antifungal activity in human urine and serum after ingestion of garlic *(Allium sativum). Antimicrobial Agents and Chemotherapy* 23: 700.

Carson, J. F. 1987. Chemistry and biological properties of onions and garlic. *Food Reviews International* 3: 71–103.

Cavallito, C. J. 1946. Relationship of thiol structures to reaction with antibiotics. *Journal of Biological Chemistry* 164: 29.

Chen, H. C., M. D. Chang, and T. J. Chang. 1985. Antibacterial properties of some spice plants before and after heat treatment. *Chinese Journal of Microbiology and Immunology* 18: 190-5.

Curzio, O. A., and C. A. Croci. 1983. Extending onion storage life by gamma-irradiation. *Journal of Food Processing and Preservation* 7: 19.

Darbyshire, B., and R. J. Henry. 1978. The distribution of fructans in onions. *New Phytologist* 81: 29.

1981. Differences in fructan content and synthesis in some *Allium* species. *New Phytologist* 87: 249.

Davis, L. E., J. K. Shen, and Y. Cai. 1990. Antifungal activity in human cerebrospinal fluid and plasma after intravenous administration of *Allium sativum. Antimicrobial Agents and Chemotherapy* 34: 651-3.

Deb-Kirtaniya, S., M. R. Ghosh, N. Adityachaudhury, and A. Chatterjee. 1980. Extracts of garlic as possible source of insecticides. *Indian Journal of Agricultural Science* 50: 507.

Delaha, E. C., and V. F. Garagusi. 1985. Inhibition of mycobacteria by garlic extract *(Allium sativum). Antimicrobial Agents and Chemotherapy* 27: 485-6.

Dembele, S., and P. Dubois. 1973. Composition d'essence shallots *(Allium cepa* L. var. *aggregatum). Annales de Technologie Agricole* 22: 121.

DeWit, J. C., S. Notermans, N. Gorin, and E. H. Kampelmacher. 1979. Effect of garlic oil or onion oil on toxin production by *Clostridium botulinum* in meat slurry. *Journal of Food Protection* 42: 222.

Domiciano, N. L., A. Y. Ota, and C. R. Tedardi. 1993. Proper time for chemical control of thrips-Tabaci Lindeman 1888 on onion allium-cepal. *Anais da Sociedade Entomologica do Brasil* 2: 71-6.

Dorant, E., P. A. van den Brandt, R. A. Goldbohm, et al. 1993. Garlic and its significance for the prevention of cancer in humans: A critical view. *British Journal of Cancer* 67: 424-9.

Dorsch, W., O. Adam, J. Weber, and T. Ziegeltrum. 1985. Antiasthmatic effects of onion extracts – detection of benzyl – and other isothiocyanates (mustard oils) as antiasthmatic compounds of plant origin. *European Journal of Pharmacology* 107: 17.

Ellmore, G. S., and R. S. Feldberg. 1994. Alliin lyase localization in bundle sheaths of the garlic clove *(Allium sativum). American Journal of Botany* 81: 89-94.

Elnima, E. I., S. A. Ahmed, A. G. Mekkawi, and J. S. Mossa. 1983. The antimicrobial activity of garlic and onion extracts. *Pharmazie* 38: 747.

Falleroni, A. E., C. R. Zeiss, and D. Levitz. 1981. Occupational asthma secondary to inhalation of garlic dust. *Journal of Allergy and Clinical Immunology* 68: 156.

Farkas, G. L., and Z. Kiraly. 1962. Role of phenolic compounds on the physiology of plant diseases and disease resistance. *Phytopathologie Zeitschrift* 44: 105.

Farkas, M. C., and J. N. Farkas. 1974. Hemolytic anemia due to ingestion of onions in a dog. *Journal of the American Animal Hospital Association* 10: 65.

Fenwick, G. R., and A. B. Hanley. 1985a. The genus *Allium.*

Part 1. *Critical Reviews in Food Science and Nutrition* 22: 199-271.

  1985b. The genus *Allium*. Part 2. *Critical Reviews in Food Science and Nutrition* 22: 273-377.

  1985c. The genus *Allium*. Part 3. *Critical Reviews in Food Science and Nutrition* 23: 1-73.

Fiskesjo, G. 1988. The *Allium* test – an alternative in environmental studies: The relative toxicity of metal ions. *Mutation Research* 197: 243-60.

Fletcher, R. D., B. Parker, and M. Hassett. 1974. Inhibition of coagulase activity and growth of *Staphylococcus aureus* by garlic extracts. *Folia Microbiologica* 19: 494.

FAO (Food and Agriculture Organization of the United Nations). 1992a. *FAO Yearbook Production* 46: 151-4. 1992b. *FAO Yearbook Trade* 46: 125-7.

Freeman, G. G. 1975. Distribution of flavor components in onion *(Allium cepa* L.), leek *(Allium porrum)* and garlic *(Allium sativum)*. *Journal of the Science of Food and Agriculture* 26: 471.

Fromtling, R. A., and G. A. Bulmer. 1978. In vitro effect of aqueous extract of garlic *(Allium sativum)* on the growth and viability of *Cryptococcus neoformans*. *Mycologia* 70: 397.

Fujiwara, M. 1976. Allithiamine and its properties. *Journal of Nutritional Science and Vitaminology* 22: 57.

Fuleki, T. 1971. Anthocyanins in red onions, *Allium cepa*. *Journal of Food Science* 36: 101.

Gargouri, Y., H. Moreau, M. K. Jain, et al. 1989. Ajoene prevents fat digestion by human gastric lipase in vitro. *Biochimica et Biophysica Acta* 1006: 137-9.

Garlic in cryptococcal meningitis – a preliminary report of 21 cases. 1980. *Chinese Medical Journal* 93: 123.

Giron, L. M., G. A. Aguilar, A. Caceres, et al. 1988. Anticandidal activity of plants used for the treatment of vaginitis in Guatemala and clinical trial of a *Solanum nigrescens* preparation. *Journal of Ethnopharmacology* 22: 307-13.

Goldsmith, W. W. 1909. Onion poisoning in cattle. *Journal of Comparative Pathology and Therapy* 22: 151.

Goodenough, P. W., and R. K. Atkin. 1981. *Quality in stored and processed vegetables and fruit.* New York.

Graham, S., B. Haughey, J. Marshall, et al. 1990. Diet in the epidemiology of gastric cancer. *Nutrition and Cancer* 13: 19-34.

Granroth, B. 1970. Biosynthesis and decomposition of cysteine derivatives in onion and other *Allium* species. *Annales Academiae Scientiarum Fennicae* 154 Series A. II. Chemica: 9.

Granroth, B., and A. I. Virtanen. 1967. S-(2-carboxypropyl) cysteine and its sulphoxide as precursors in the biosynthesis of cycloalliin. *Acta Chemica Scandinavica* 21: 1654.

Greco, N. 1993. Epidemiology and management of *Ditylenchus dipsaci* on vegetable crops in southern Italy. *Nematropica* 23: 247-51.

Gruhzit, O. M. 1931. Anemia in dogs produced by feeding disulphide compounds. Part II. *American Journal of Medical Sciences* 181: 815.

Gummery, C. S. 1977. A review of commercial onion products. *Food Trade Review* 47: 452.

Guo, N. L., D. P. Lu, G. L. Woods, et al. 1993. Demonstration of the anti-viral activity of garlic extract against human cytomegalovirus in vitro. *Chinese Medical Journal* 106: 93-6.

Gupta, K. C., and R. Viswanathan. 1955. In vitro study of anti-tubercular substances from *Allium* species. I. *Allium schoenoprasum*. II. *Allium* cepa. *Antibiotics and Chemotherapy* 5: 18.

Haggard, H. W., and L. A. Greenberg. 1935. Breath odours from alliaceous substances. *Journal of the American Medical Association* 104: 2160.

Hall, C. W. 1980. *Drying and storage of agricultural crops.* Westport, Conn.

Han, J. 1993. Highlights of the cancer chemoprevention studies in China. *Preventive Medicine* 22: 712-22.

Handa, G., J. Singh, and C. K. Atal. 1983. Antiasthmatic principle of *Allium cepa* Linn (onions). *Indian Drugs* 20: 239.

Hanley, A. B., and G. R. Fenwick. 1985. Cultivated alliums. *Journal of Plant Foods* 6: 211-38.

Hanson, L. P. 1975. *Commercial processing of vegetables.* Park Ridge, N.J.

Harenberg, J., C. Giese, and R. Zimmermann. 1988. Effect of dried garlic on blood coagulation, fibrinolysis, platelet aggregation and serum cholesterol levels in patients with hyperlipoproteinemia. *Atherosclerosis* 74: 247-9.

Hasan, H. A., and A. L. Mahmoud. 1993. Inhibitory effect of spice oils on lipase and mycotoxin production. *Zentralblatt für Mikrobiologie* 148: 543-8.

Hashimoto, S., M. Miyazawa, and H. Kameoka. 1983. Volatile flavor components of chive *(Allium schoenoprasum* L.). *Journal of Food Science* 48: 1858.

Heath, H. B. 1981. *Source book on flavors.* Westport, Conn.

Hedrick, U. P. 1972. *Sturtevant's edible plants of the world.* New York.

Hefnawy, Y. A., S. I. Moustafa, and E. H. Marth. 1993. Sensitivity of *Listeria monocytogenes* to selected spices. *Journal of Food Protection* 56: 876-8.

Henson, G. E. 1940. Garlic, an occupational factor in the etiology of bronchial asthma. *Journal of the Florida Medical Association* 27: 86.

Herrmann, K. 1958. Flavonols and phenols of the onion *(Allium cepa)*. *Archive der Pharmazie* 291: 238.

Huddleson, I. F., J. Dufrain, K. C. Barrons, and M. Giefel. 1944. Antibacterial substances in plants. *Journal of the American Veterinary Medical Association* 105: 394.

Hyams, E. 1971. *Plants in the service of man; 10,000 years of domestication.* London.

IOS (International Organization for Standardization). 1983. *Garlic guide to cold storage.* International Standard ISO, New York.

Ip, C., and D. J. Lisk. 1994. Characterization of tissue selenium profiles and anticarcinogenic responses in rats fed natural sources of selenium-rich products. *Carcinogenesis* 15: 573-6.

Itoh, T., T. Tamura, T. Mitsuhashi, and T. Matsumoto. 1977. Sterols of Liliaceae. *Phytochemistry* 16: 140.

Itokawa, Y., K. Inoue, S. Sasagawa, and M. Fujiwara. 1973. Effect of S-methylcysteine sulphoxide, S-allylcysteine sulphoxide and related sulfur-containing amino acids on lipid metabolism of experimental hypercholesterolemic rats. *Journal of Nutrition* 103: 88.

Jain, A. K., R. Vargas, S. Gotzkowsky, and F. G. McMahon. 1993. Can garlic reduce levels of serum lipids? A controlled clinical study. *American Journal of Medicine* 94: 632-5.

Jones, H. A., and L. K. Mann. 1963. *Onions and their allies; Botany, cultivation and utilization.* London.

Kaack, K., G. Kjeldsen, and L. Mune. 1993. Changes in quality attributes during growth of leek *(Allium porrum* L.) for industrial processing. *Acta Agriculturae Scandinavica Section B Soil and Plant Science* 43: 172-5.

Kameoka, H., and S. Hashimoto. 1983. Two sulphur constituents from *Allium schoenoprasum. Phytochemistry* 22: 294.

Karawya, M. S., S. M. Abdel Wahab, M. M. El-Olemy, and N. M. Farrag. 1984. Diphenylamine, an antihyperglycaemic agent from onion and tea. *Journal of Natural Products* 47: 775.

Kepka, A. K., and M. A. Sypien. 1971. The influence of some factors on the keeping quality of onions. *Acta Horticultura* 20: 65.

Khodzhaeva, M. A., and E. S. Kondratenko. 1983. *Allium* carbohydrates. III. Characteristics of *Allium* species polysaccharides. *Khimiia Prirodnukh Soedinenii* 2: 228.

Kiesewetter, H., F. Jung, E. M. Jung, et al. 1993. Effect of garlic on platelet aggregation in patients with increased risk of juvenile ischemic attack. *European Journal of Clinical Pharmacology* 45: 333-6.

Kimura, Y., and K. Yamamoto. 1964. Cytological effects of chemicals on tumours. XXIII. Influence of crude extracts from garlic and some related species on MTK-sarcoma. III. *Gann* 55: 325.

Kirk, J. H., and M. S. Bulgin. 1979. Effects of feeding cull domestic onions *(Allium cepa)* to sheep. *American Journal of Veterinary Research* 40: 397.

Knapp, V. J. 1989. Dietary changes and the decline of scurvy and tuberculosis in 19th century Europe. *New York State Journal of Medicine* 89: 621-4.

Kumar, J., and J. K. Gupta. 1993. Nectar sugar production and honeybee foraging activity in three species of onion (*Allium* species). *Apidologie* 24: 391-6.

Kumar, K., and R. K. Sahay. 1954. Effect of sulfur fertilization on the pungency of onion. *Current Science* 24: 368.

Kuroda, S. 1977. Taboo on breeding cloven-hoofed animals at a community in Mujagi prefecture and its influence on dietary habits. *Journal of the Japanese Society for Food and Nutrition* 30: 249.

Lawson, L. D., D. K. Ransom, and B. G. Hughes. 1992. Inhibition of whole blood platelet aggregation by compounds in garlic clove extracts and commercial garlic products. *Thrombosis Research* 65: 141-56.

Lewis, N. F., B. Y. K. Rao, A. B. Shah, et al. 1977. Antibacterial activity of volatile components of onion *(Allium cepa). Journal of Food Science and Technology (Mysore)* 14: 35.

Li, H.-L. 1969. The vegetables of ancient China. *Economic Botany* 23: 253.

Liakopoulou-Kyriakides, M., and Z. Sinakos. 1992. A low molecular weight peptide from *Allium porrum* with inhibitory activity on platelet aggregation in vitro. *Biochemistry International* 28: 373-8.

Loeper, M., and M. Debray. 1921. Antihypertensive action of garlic extract. *Bulletin of the Society of Medicine* 37: 1032.

Lohmer, C. 1988. Certain aspects of the nutrition of monks in the Middle Ages with the monastic teaching of Peter Damian as example. *Aktuelle Ernährungsmedizin* 13: 179-82.

Lucas, R. 1966. *Nature's medicines - the folklore, romance and value of herbal remedies.* New York.

Lybarger, J. A., J. S. Gallagher, D. W. Pulver, et al. 1982. Occupational asthma induced by inhalation and ingestion of garlic. *Journal of Allergy and Clinical Immunology* 69: 448.

Mader, F. H. 1990. Treatment of hyperlipidaemia with garlic-powder tablets. Evidence from the German Association of General Practitioners' multicentric placebo-controlled double-blind study. *Arzneimittel-Forschung* 40: 1111-16.

Mahajan, V. M. 1981. Antimycotic activity of different chemicals, chaksine iodide, and garlic. *Mykosen* 26: 94.

Makheja, A. N., J. Y. Vanderhoek, and J. M. Bailey. 1979. Properties of an inhibitor of platelet aggregation and thromboxane synthesis isolated from onion and garlic. *Thrombosis and Haemostatis* 42: 74.

Mathur, P. B. 1963. Extension of storage life of garlic bulbs by gamma-irradiation. *International Journal of Applied Radiation and Isotopes* 14: 625.

Mauron, J. 1986. Food, mood and health: the medieval outlook. *International Journal for Vitamin and Nutrition Research* 29S: 9-26.

Mazelis, M., and L. Crews. 1968. Purification of the alliin lyase of garlic, *Allium sativum* L. *Biochemical Journal* 108: 725.

Mazza, G. 1980. Relative volatilities of some onion flavour components. *Journal of Food Technology* 15: 35.

Meng, Y., D. Lu, N. Guo, et al. 1993. Studies on the anti-HCMV effect of garlic components. *Virologica Sinica* 8: 147-50.

Mennella, J. A., and G. K. Beauchamp. 1991. Maternal diet alters the sensory qualities of human milk and the nursling's behavior. *Pediatrics* 88: 737-44.

    1993. The effects of repeated exposure to garlic-flavored milk on the nursling's behavior. *Pediatric Research* 34: 805-8.

Meyer, R. G. 1980. Carbonized feed plants of Pompeii, Herculaneum and the villa at Torre Annunziata. *Economic Botany* 34: 401.

Miller, B. S., Y. Pomeranz, H. H. Converse, and H. R. Brandenburg. 1977. Removing garlic contamination from harvested wheat. *U.S. Department of Agriculture Product Research Report* 173: 1.

Mitchell, J. C. 1980. Contact sensitivity to garlic *(Allium). Contact Dermatitis* 6: 356.

Moore, G. S., and R. D. Atkins. 1977. The fungicidal and fungistatic effects of an aqueous garlic extract on medically important yeast-like fungi. *Mycologia* 69: 341.

Morse, D. L., L. K. Pickard, J. J. Guzewich, et al. 1990. Garlic-in-oil associated botulism: Episode leads to product modification. *American Journal of Public Health* 80: 1372-3.

Munday, R., and E. Manns. 1994. Comparative toxicity of prop(en)yl disulfides derived from Alliaceae: Possible involvement of 1-propenyl disulfides in onion-induced hemolytic anemia. *Journal of Agricultural and Food Chemistry* 42: 959-62.

Mutsch-Eckner, M., C. A. J. Erdelmeier, O. Sticher, and H. D. Reuter. 1993. A novel amino acid glycoside and three amino acids from *Allium sativum. Journal of Natural Products (Lloydia)* 56: 864-9.

Naito, S., N. Yamaguchi, and Y. Yokoo. 1981a. Studies on natural antioxidant. II. Antioxidative activities of vegetables of the *Allium* species. *Journal of the Japanese Society for Food Science and Technology* 28: 291.

    1981b. Studies on natural antioxidant. III. Fractionation of antioxidant extracted from garlic. *Journal of the Japanese Society for Food Science and Technology* 28: 465.

Nasseh, M. O. 1983. Wirkung von Rotextrakten aus *Allium sativum* L. auf Getreideblattläuse Sitobion avenae F. und Rhopalosiphum padi L. sowie die grüne Pfirsich-blattlaus Myzus persicae Sulz Z. *Angewandte Entomologica* 95: 228.

National Research Council. 1989. *Recommended dietary allowances.* Tenth revised edition. Washington, D.C.

Nilsson, T. 1979. Yield, storage ability, quality, and chemical composition of carrot, cabbage and leek at conventional and organic fertilizing. *Acta Horticultura* 93: 209.

1980. The influence of the time of harvest on the chemical composition of onions. *Swedish Journal of Agricultural Research* 10: 77.

Nordestgaard, A. 1983. Growing chives for seed production. *Meddelelse, Statens Planteavlsforsog* 85: 3.

Nutrition Coordinating Center. 1994. *Nutrition Data System Version 2.6/8A/23*. St. Paul, Minn.

Odebiyi, A. I. 1989. Food taboos in maternal and child health: The views of traditional healers in Ile-Ife, Nigeria. *Social Science and Medicine* 28: 985-96.

Oka, Y., S. Kiriyama, and A. Yoshida. 1974. Sterol composition of spices and cholesterol in vegetable food stuffs. *Journal of the Japanese Society for Food and Nutrition* 27: 347.

Omar, F. A., and A. E. Arafa. 1979. Chemical composition of garlic bulbs during storage as affected by MH as a preharvest foliar spray. *Agricultural Research and Development* 57: 203.

Omidiji, O. 1993. Flavonol glycosides in the wet scale of the deep purple onion (*Allium cepa* L. cv. Red Creole). *Discovery and Innovation* 5: 139-41.

Omkumar, R. V., S. M. Kadam, A. Banerji, and T. Ramasarma. 1993. On the involvement of intramolecular protein disulfide in the irreversible inactivation of 3-hydroxy-3-methylglutaryl-CoA reductase by diallyl disulfide. *Biochimica et Biophysica Acta* 1164: 108-12.

Perchellet, J. P., E. M. Perchellet, N. L. Abney, et al. 1986. Effects of garlic and onion oils on glutathione peroxidase activity, the ratio of reduced/oxidized glutathione and ornithine decarboxylase induction in isolated mouse epidermal cells treated with tumor promoters. *Cancer Biochemistry Biophysics* 8: 299-312.

Perez, H. A., M. de la Rosa, and R. Apitz. 1994. In vivo activity of ajoene against rodent malaria. *Antimicrobial Agents and Chemotherapy* 38: 337-9.

Perezgrovas Garza, R. 1990. El uso de la herbolaria como alternativa terapeutica en ovinocultura (The use of medicinal plants as an alternative medicine in sheep farming). *Memoria III Congreso Nacional de Produccion Ovina, Tlaxcala, 25 a 28 de abril 1990*. Universidad Chiapas, Mexico, 242-6.

Perkin, A. G., and J. J. Hummel. 1896. Occurrence of quercetin in the outer skins of the bulb of the onion (*Allium cepa*). *Journal of the Chemical Society* 69: 1295.

Peters, E. J., and R. A. Mckelvey. 1982. Herbicides and dates of application for control and eradication of wild garlic (*Allium vineale*). *Weed Science* 30: 557.

Petkov, V. 1986. Bulgarian traditional medicine: A source of ideas for phytopharmacological investigations. *Journal of Ethnopharmacology* 15: 121-32.

Piotrowski, G. 1948. L'ail en therapeutique. *Praxis* 48: 8.

Platenius, H. 1941. Factors affecting onion pungency. *Journal of Agricultural Research* 62: 371.

Pordesimo, A. N., and L. L. Ilag. 1976. Toxicity of garlic juice to plant pathogenic organisms. *Philippino Journal of Biology* 5: 251.

Poulsen, K. P., and P. Nielsen. 1979. Freeze drying of chives and parsley - optimization attempts. *Bulletin de Institut International du Froid* 59: 1118.

Pratt, D. E., and B. M. Watts. 1964. The antioxidant activity of vegetable extracts. I. Flavone aglycones. *Journal of Food Science* 29: 27.

Priyadarshini, E., and P. G. Tulpule. 1976. Aflatoxin production on irradiated foods. *Food and Cosmetics Toxicology* 14: 293.

Pruthi, J. S. 1980. Spices and condiments. Chemistry, microbiology, and technology. *Advances in Food Research Supplement* 4: 198.

Pruthi, J. S., L. J. Singh, and G. Lal. 1959. Thermal stability of alliinase and enzymatic regeneration of flavour in odourless garlic powder. *Current Science* 28: 403.

Pruthi, J. S., L. J. Singh, S. D. V. Ramu, and G. Lal. 1959. Pilot plant studies on the manufacture of garlic powder. *Food Science* 8: 448-53.

Pushpendran, C. K., T. P. A. Devasagayam, and J. Eapen. 1982. Age related hyperglycaemic effect of diallyl disulphide in rats. *Indian Journal of Experimental Biology* 20: 428.

Qureshi, A. A., Z. Z. Din, N. Abuirmeileh, et al. 1983. Suppression of avian hepatic lipid metabolism by solvent extracts of garlic. Impact on serum lipids. *Journal of Nutrition* 113: 1746.

Raj, K. P. S., Y. K. Agrawal, and M. R. Patel. 1980. Analysis of garlic for its metal contents. *Journal of the Indian Chemical Society* 57: 1121.

Ramanujam, K. 1962. Garlic in the treatment of acute leprosy neuritis. *Leprosy in India* 34: 174.

Rao, M. 1985. Food beliefs of rural women during the reproductive years in Dharwad, India. *Ecology of Food and Nutrition* 6: 93-103.

Reimers, F., S. E. Smolka, S. Werres, et al. 1993. Effect of ajoene, a compound derived from *Allium sativum,* on phytopathogenic and epiphytic micro-organisms. *Zeitschrift für Pflanzenkrankheiten und Pflanzenschutz* 100: 622-33.

Reznik, P. A., and Y. G. Imbs. 1965. Ixodid ticks and phytoncides. *Zoologicheskii Zhurnal* 44: 1861.

Rick, R. C. 1978. The tomato. *Scientific American* 239: 66.

Rickard, P. C., and R. Wickens. 1977. The effect of time of harvesting of spring sown dry bulb onions on their yield, keeping ability and skin quality. *Experimental Horticulture* 29: 45.

Robinson, J. E., K. M. Browne, and W. G. Burton. 1975. Storage characteristics of some vegetables and soft fruits. *Annals of Applied Biology* 81: 399.

Rosin, S., H. Tuorila, and A. Uutela. 1992. Garlic: A sensory pleasure or a social nuisance? *Appetite* 19: 133-43.

Sainani, G. S., D. B. Desai, N. H. Gorhe, et al. 1979. Effect of dietary garlic and onion on serum lipid profile in Jain community. *Indian Journal of Medical Research* 69: 776.

Sainani, G. S., D. B. Desai, S. M. Natu, et al. 1979. Dietary garlic, onion and some coagulation parameters in Jain community. *Journal of the Association of Physicians of India* 27: 707.

San-Blas, G., L. Marino, F. San-Blas, and R. Apitz-Castro. 1993. Effect of ajoene on dimorphism of *Paracoccidioides brasiliensis. Journal of Medical and Veterinary Mycology* 31: 133-41.

Sanchez-Mirt, A., F. Gil, and R. Apitz-Castro. 1993. In vitro inhibitory effect and ultrastructural alterations caused by ajoene on the growth of dematiaceous fungi: *Cladosporium carrionii* and *Fonsecaea pedrosoi. Revista Iberoamericana de Micologia* 10: 74-8.

Sato, A., M. Terao, and M. Ishibashi. 1993. Antibacterial effects of garlic extract on *Vibrio parahaemolyticus* in fish meat. *Journal of the Food Hygienic Society of Japan* 34: 63-7.

Schreyen, L., P. Dirinck, F. Van Wassenhove, and G. Schamp. 1976a. Analysis of leek volatiles by headspace condensation. *Journal of Agricultural and Food Chemistry* 24: 1147.

1976b. Volatile flavor components of leek. *Journal of Agricultural and Food Chemistry* 24: 336.

Schwimmer, S. 1968. Enzymatic conversion of trans(+)-S-(1-propenyl)-L-cysteine-S-oxide to the bitter and odor-bearing components of onion. *Phytochemistry* 7: 401.

Sendl, A., M. Schliack, R. Loser, et al. 1992. Inhibition of cholesterol synthesis in vitro by extracts and isolated compounds prepared from garlic and wild garlic. *Atherosclerosis* 94: 79-85.

Seuri, M., A. Taivanen, P. Ruoppi, and H. Tukiainen. 1993. Three cases of occupational asthma and rhinitis caused by garlic. *Clinical and Experimental Allergy* 23: 1011-14.

Sharma, A., G. M. Tewari, C. Bandyopadhyay, and S. R. Padwal-Desai. 1979. Inhibition of aflatoxin-producing fungi by onion extracts. *Journal of Food Science* 44: 1545.

Sharma, K. K., R. K. Gupta, S. Gupta, and K. C. Samuel. 1977. Antihyperglycaemic effect of onion: Effect of fasting blood sugar and induced hyperglycemia in man. *Indian Journal of Medical Research* 65: 422.

Siddeswaran, K., and C. Ramaswami. 1987. Inter-cropping and border-cropping of compatible crops in finger millet (*Eleusine coracana* Gaertn.) under garden land conditions. *Journal of Agronomy and Crop Science* 158: 246-9.

Silagy, C., and A. Neil. 1994. Garlic as a lipid lowering agent – a meta-analysis. *Journal of the Royal College of Physicians of London* 28: 39-45.

Simmonds, N. W. 1976. *Evolution of crop plants.* London.

Singh, K. K. 1994. Development of a small capacity dryer for vegetables. *Journal of Food Engineering* 21: 19-30.

Singh, L. J., J. S. Pruthi, A. N. Sankaran, et al. 1959. Effect of type of packaging and storage temperature on flavor and colour of garlic powder. *Food Science* 8: 457-60.

Singh, L. J., J. S. Pruthi, V. Sreenivasamurthy, et al. 1959. Effect of type of packaging and storage temperature on ally sulphide, total sulfur, antibacterial activity and volatile reducing substances in garlic powder. *Food Science* 8: 453-6.

Singh, R. V. 1991. Effect of intercrops on performance and production economics of tomato *(Lycopersicon esculentum)*. *Indian Journal of Agricultural Sciences* 61: 247-50.

Smith-Jones, S. 1978. Herbs: Next to his shoes, the runner's best friend may be in the kitchen. *Runner's World* 13: 126-7.

Soffar, S. A., and G. M. Mokhtar. 1991. Evaluation of the antiparasitic effect of aqueous garlic *(Allium sativum)* extract in hymenolepiasis nana and giardiasis. *Journal of the Egyptian Society of Parasitology* 21: 497-502.

Sokolov, R. 1975. A plant of ill repute. *Natural History* 84: 70.

Sreenivasamurthy, V., K. R. Sreekantiah, A. P. Jayaraj, et al. 1962. A preliminary report on the treatment of acute lepromatous neuritis with garlic. *Leprosy in India* 34: 171-3.

Srinivasan, V. 1969. A new antihypertensive agent. *Lancet* 2: 800.

St. Louis, M. E., S. H. Peck, D. Bowering, et al. 1988. Botulism from chopped garlic: Delayed recognition of a major outbreak. *Annals of Internal Medicine* 108: 363-8.

Stallknecht, G. F., J. Garrison, A. J. Walz, et al. 1982. The effect of maleic hydrazide salts on quality and bulb tissue residues of stored "Yellow Sweet Spanish" onions. *Horticultural Science* 17: 926.

Starke, H., and K. Herrmann. 1976a. Flavonols and flavones of vegetables. VI. On the changes of the flavonols of onions. *Zeitschrift für Lebensmittel Untersuchung und Forschung* 161: 137.

1976b. Flavonols and flavones of vegetables. VII. Flavonols of leek, chive, and garlic. *Zeitschrift für Lebensmittel Untersuchung und Forschung* 161: 25-30.

Stoianova-Ivanova, B., A. Tzutzulova, and R. Caputto. 1980. On the hydrocarbon and sterol composition in the scales and fleshy part of *Allium sativum* Linnaeus bulbs. *Rivista Italiana EPPOS* 62: 373.

Stoll, A., and E. Seebeck. 1948. Allium compounds. I. Alliin, the true mother compound of garlic oil. *Helvetica Chimica Acta* 31: 189.

Subrahmanyan, V., K. Krishnamurthy, V. Sreenivasamurthy, and M. Swaminathan. 1957. Effect of garlic in the diet on the intestinal microflora of rats. *Journal of Scientific Indian Research* 160: 173.

Subrahmanyan, V., V. Sreenivasamurthy, K. Krishnamurthy, and M. Swaminathan. 1957. Studies on the antibacterial activity of spices. *Journal of Scientific Indian Research* 160: 240.

Sun, Y., J. Sun, X. Liu, et al. 1993. Investigation and experimental research on the effects of onion on angiocardiopathy. *Acta Nutrimenta Sinica* 14: 409-13.

Sutabhaha, S., M. Suttajit, and P. Niyomca. 1992. Studies of aflatoxins in Chiang Mai, Thailand. *Kitasato Archives of Experimental Medicine* 65: 45-52.

Tatarrintsev, A. V., P. V. Vrzhets, D. E. Ershov, et al. 1992. Ajoene blockade of integrin-dependent processes in the HIV-infected cell system. *Vestnik Rossiiskoi Akademii Meditsinskikh Nauk O* 11/12: 6-10.

Tesi, R., and A. Ricci. 1982. The effect of plant spacing on garlic production. *Annali della Facolta di Scienze Agrarie della Universita dali Studi di Napoli Portici* 16: 6.

Thakur, D. E., S. K. Misra, and P. C. Choudhuri. 1983. Trial of some of the plant extracts and chemicals for their antifungal activity in calves. *Indian Veterinary Journal* 60: 799.

Thamizharasi, V., and P. Narasimham. 1993. Effect of heat treatment on the quality of onions during long-term tropical storage. *International Journal of Food Science and Technology* 28: 397-406.

Thompson, A. K. 1982. *The storage and handling of onions.* Report G160, Tropical Products Institute. London.

Thompson, A. K., R. H. Booth, and F. J. Proctor. 1972. Onion storage in the tropics. *Tropical Research* 14: 19.

Tissut, M. 1974. Étude de la localisation et dosage in vivo des flavones de l'oignon. *Compte Rendu Académie Scientifique* Paris Series D 279: 659.

Tokarska, B., and K. Karwowska. 1983. The role of sulfur compounds in evaluation of flavoring value of some plant raw materials. *Die Nahrung* 27: 443.

Toma, R. B., and M. L. Curry. 1980. North Dakota Indians' traditional foods. *Journal of the American Dietetic Association* 76: 589-90.

Traub, H. L. 1968. The subgenera, sections and subsections of *Allium* L. *Plant Life* 24: 147.

Urbina, J. A., E. Marchan, K. Lazardi, et al. 1993. Inhibition of phosphatidylcholine biosynthesis and cell proliferation in *Trypanosoma cruzi* by ajoene, an antiplatelet compound isolated from garlic. *Biochemical Pharmacology* 45: 2381-7.

Urquhart, R., and Y. Webb. 1985. Adverse reactions to food in Down syndrome children and the nutritional consequences. *Proceedings of the Nutrition Society of Australia* 10: 117.

Usher, G. 1974. *A dictionary of plants used by man.* London.

Vandenberg, L., and C. P. Lentz. 1974. High humidity storage of some vegetables. *Journal of the Institute of Canadian Science and Technology. Alimentation* 7: 260.

Van Dijk, P. 1993. Survey and characterization of potyviruses and their strains of *Allium* species. *Netherlands Journal of Plant Pathology* 99(2S): 1–48.

Van Hecke, E. 1977. Contact allergy to onion. *Contact Dermatitis* 3: 167.

Van Ketal, W. C., and P. de Haan. 1978. Occupational eczema from garlic and onion. *Contact Dermatitis* 4: 53.

Van Petten, G. R., W. G. Hilliard, and W. T. Oliver. 1966. Effect of feeding irradiated onion to consecutive generations of the rat. *Food and Cosmetics Toxicology* 4: 593.

Van Petten, G. R., W. T. Oliver, and W. G. Hilliard. 1966. Effect of feeding irradiated onion to the rat for 1 year. *Food and Cosmetics Toxicology* 4: 585–92.

Virtanen, A. L. 1965. Studies on organic sulphur compounds and other labile substances in plants – a review. *Phytochemistry* 4: 207.

Walker, J. C., and M. A. Stahman. 1955. Chemical nature of disease resistance in plants. *Annual Review of Plant Physiology* 6: 351.

Warren, C. P. W. 1970. Some aspects of medicine in the Greek Bronze Age. *Medical History* 14: 364.

Warshafsky, S., R. S. Kamer, and S. L. Sivak. 1993. Effect of garlic on total serum cholesterol. A meta-analysis. *Annals of Internal Medicine* 119: 599–605.

Weber, N. D., D. O. Andersen, J. A. North, et al. 1992. In vitro virucidal effects of *Allium sativum* (garlic) extract and compounds. *Planta Medica* 58: 417–23.

Wertheim, T. 1845. Investigations of garlic oil. *Annalen der Chemie* 51: 289.

Whitaker, J. R. 1976. Development of flavor, odor, and pungency in onion and garlic. *Advances in Food Research* 22: 73.

Wilkens, W. F. 1964. Isolation and identification of the lachrymogenic compound of onion. *Cornell University, Agricultural Experiment Station Memoir,* 385. New York.

Wills, E. D. 1956. Enzyme inhibition by allicin, the active principle of garlic. *Biochemical Journal* 63: 514.

Witte, J. S., M. P. Longnecker, C. L. Bird, et al. 1996. Relation of vegetable, fruit, and grain consumption to colorectal adenomatous polyps. *American Journal of Epidemiology* 144: 1015.

Wright, P. J. 1993. Effects of nitrogen fertilizer, plant maturity at lifting, and water during field-curing on the incidence of bacterial soft rot of onion in store. *New Zealand Journal of Crop and Horticultural Science* 21: 377–81.

Wright, P. J., C. N. Hale, and R. A. Fullerton. 1993. Effect of husbandry practices and water applications during field curing on the incidence of bacterial soft rot of onions in store. *New Zealand Journal of Crop and Horticultural Science* 21: 161–4.

Wu, J. L., C. C. Chou, M. H. Chen, and C. M. Wu. 1982. Volatile flavor compounds from shallots. *Journal of Food Science* 47: 606.

Yamato, O., T. Yoshihara, A. Ichihara, and Y. Maede. 1994. Novel Heinz body hemolysis factors in onion *(Allium cepa)*. *Bioscience Biotechnology and Biochemistry* 58: 221–2.

Yang, G., B. Ji, and Y. Gao. 1993. Diet and nutrients as risk factors for colon cancer: A population-based case-control study in Shanghai. *Acta Nutrimenta Sinica* 14: 373–9.

Yeh, Y. Y., and S. M. Yeh. 1994. Garlic reduces plasma lipids by inhibiting hepatic cholesterol and triacylglycerol synthesis. *Lipids* 29: 189–93.

Yoshida, S., S. Kasuga, N. Hayashi, et al. 1987. Antifungal activity of ajoene derived from garlic. *Applied and Environmental Microbiology* 53: 615–17.

Yoshikawa, K., K. Hadame, K. Saitoh, and T. Hijikata. 1979. Patch tests with common vegetables in hand dermatitis patients. *Contact Dermatitis* 5: 274.

You, W. C., W. J. Blot, Y. S. Chang, et al. 1989. Allium vegetables and reduced risk of stomach cancer. *Journal of the National Cancer Institute* 81: 162–4.

II.C.3 ⚘ Beans, Peas, and Lentils

The Names

On Sunday, November 4, 1492, three weeks after his first landing in the New World, Christopher Columbus saw lands planted with "*faxones* and *fabas* very diverse and different from ours [those of Spain] and two days afterward, following the north coast of Cuba," he again found "land well cultivated with these *fexoes* and *habas* much unlike ours" (Hedrick 1931: 3).

In a transcription (Dunn and Kelley 1989: 132) from Columbus's diary, the Spanish phrase *faxones y favas* has been translated as "beans and kidney beans" (Morrison and Jane-Vigneras, cited by Dunn and Kelley 1989: 133). But considering what Columbus might have seen in the markets or kitchens of the fifteenth-century Iberian–Mediterranean world, *faxone* probably refers to the African–Asian cowpea *(Vigna unguiculata),* and *fava* surely means the fava (= *faba*), or broad bean *(Vicia faba),* long known in Europe and the Mediterranean–Asian world. Columbus's brief record presaged the long confusion and debate over the names and origins of some important food grain legumes. Had herbalists and botanical authors of the succeeding three centuries taken account of Columbus's recognition that these New World legumes were different from those of Europe, some of the confusion might have been avoided.

The beans, peas, and lentils (pulses, or food grain legumes) discussed in this chapter are legumes, treated in technical botanical literature as members of the very large family Fabaceae (= Leguminosae), subfamily Papilionoideae (having butterflylike flowers), although some taxonomists accord this group family status (Papilionaceae). The names of the species, however, are not changed by the differing positions taken by plant taxonomists on family nomenclature. The flowers of papilionaceous legumes have five petals consisting of one broad standard, two lateral wings, and two keel petals that clasp the 10 stamens and single ovary (which becomes the pod).

Lentil

The Latin and most frequently used English common names of the species of beans, peas, and lentils discussed in this chapter are enumerated in Table II.C.3.1, along with other species having similar names.

The European herbalists of the sixteenth century repeatedly attempted to reconcile their plant world with that of the ancients as represented by the fragmentary remains of the works of Theophrastus and Dioscorides. Their efforts, however, were destined to fail inasmuch as many of their subjects were novel plants newly introduced from the New World and from the reopened contact with Asia and coastal Africa. This nomenclatural dilemma is illustrated by an attempt to reconcile the name of a bean with the appropriate plant. J. P. Tournefort (1656–1708), a notable pre-Linnaean French botanist, sought to clarify the use of *boona* or *baiana* for the broad bean or fava by a well-known sixteenth-century herbalist:

> Dodonaeus [said Tournefort] called this kind of pulse "boona" in Latin, who [Dodonaeus] relying on a Germanism abuses his own language in order to appear learned but our Boona or Bean

seem rather to be derived from the Italian word Baiana which Hermolaus says is the word used by those that sell new BEANS all over the state of Milan and along the Appenine mountains. . . . Garden beans are common and universal in Europe and are a great supply in dearth of Provisions in the spring and whole summer season. . . . The ancients and Dodonaeus believed that beans are windy and the greener the more so. (Tournefort 1730: 386)

Tournefort then disagreed on the suitability of beans in the diet and said that he would leave the hard dry beans to "the laboring men who can better digest them, but [even] those of delicate constitution and sedentary life digest green beans well enough if they eat them with butter and pepper [especially if they will] be at the pain to take off their skins" (Tournefort 1730: 386). Inasmuch as American *Phaseolus* beans had entered Europe by his lifetime, one could wonder whether Tournefort meant *Phaseolus* or *Vicia* "beans." However, his remark concerning the removal of "skins [seed coats]" should end any doubt.

Table II.C.3.1. *Beans, peas, and lentils*

Latin names	English common names
Lens culinaris Meddick.	lentil
Phaseolus acutifolius (A. Gray)	tepary
p. coccineus L.	
(syn. *P. multiflorus* Willd.)	scarlet runner, Windsor bean
P. lunatus L.	lima, butter, sieva bean
P. polyanthus (Greenm.)	polyanthus bean
P. vulgaris L.	common or kidney bean, haricot
Pisum sativum L.	pea, garden pea
Vicia faba L.	broad bean, horse bean, fava, haba

Other taxa mentioned in text

Cicer arietinum L.	chickpea, bengal gram
Lablab purpureus (L.) Sweet	
(syn. *Dolichos lablab* L.)	hyacinth bean
Lathyrus sativus L.	chickling vetch, Khesari dhal
Lens culinaris ssp.	
macrosperma (Baumb)	
Barulina	large-seeded lentil
L. culinaris ssp. *microsperma*	
Barulina	small-seeded lentil
L. ervoides (Brign.) Grande	
L. nigricans (M. Bieb.) Godr.,	
L. orientalis (Bioss.) M. Popov	wild lentil
Vicia ervilia Willd.	erse, French lentil
V. sinensis (L.) Savi ex Hassk.	cowpea, black-eyed pea
Vigna unguiculata (L.) Walp.	
ssp. *unguiculata* (syn.	
V. Sesquipeolis [L.] Fruhw.)	

Sources: Adapted from Aykroyd and Doughty (1964), pp. 15–18, Purseglove (1968), Smartt (1990), Ladizinsky (1993), and other sources.

"Skins" refers to the seed coats. Where the broad bean and American *Phaseolus* beans are concerned, only the broad bean has its skin or testa customarily removed – probably to eliminate substances that are toxic for individuals having an inherited enzyme (glucose-6-phosphate dehydrogenase) deficiency. Even in a contemporary and remote Quechua-speaking community, located in the southern Andes in the vicinity of Cuzco at an altitude of 3,000 to 5,000 meters, which is unfavorable for *Phaseolus* cultivation, cooked *Vicia faba* seeds are always peeled before eating (Franquemont et al. 1990: 83). Because this enzyme-deficiency sensitivity to fava bean components evolved in human populations native to certain malarial regions of Eurasia and Africa (Strickberger 1985: 738), the custom in the Andes was probably introduced along with the fava bean.

Tournefort further assumed the responsibility for ending the quandary of post-Columbian botanists concerning the identity of the fava. He recognized that there was

... much controversy among the botanists as to whether our bean be the bean of the ancients ... that of the ancients was small and round [according to] Theophrastus, Dioscorides and others. But it is strange that a pulse so common should have come close to disuse and been replaced without anybody's knowing anything of this matter. (Tournefort 1730: 386)

The reason for the difference (and confusion), he went on, could be that "their faba was not arrived at the bigness that our Garden Bean now is." But however intriguing the evolutionary explanation, the writers of the classical period, whom he cites, may have been referring to the African–Asian cowpea, *Vigna unguiculata,* rather than one of the small-seeded races of the fava bean.

Contemporary linguistic sources (*Webster's Third New International Dictionary* 1971) derive the familiar English word "bean" from a root common to Old English, Old High German, and Old Norse that apparently once referred to the fava or faba bean, a staple of the Romans. Over the centuries, however, the word has grown to encompass seeds of other plants, including a multitude of legumes besides the fava, most of which belong to other genera – a terminological tangle that botany attempts to avoid through the use of scientific names (Table II.C.3.1).

The distinct identities of these two groups of food crops, favas and *Phaseolus* beans, were being established as seventeenth- and eighteenth-century botany ceased the attempt to reconcile the known species of that period with the fragmentary records of the classical authors. These advances were only the beginning of the solutions to the geographic, temporal, and cultural problems surrounding the origins of these foods.

The Search for Geographic Origins

The origins of most domesticated plants, meaning the time span, the wild relatives, and the conditions (both natural and human-influenced) under which divergences from wild ancestral stock took place, are remote in time and are matters of continued botanical and genetic inquiry.

For Europe and the Mediterranean Basin, sixteenth-century European herbalists turned for information to tradition, the observations of travelers, and the surviving books of classical authors. Linnaeus assimilated the writings of the herbalists and added his contemporary experience with eighteenth-century introductions and collections. Alphonse de Candolle (1964: v) in 1855, and especially in the 1886 edition of his *Origin of Cultivated Plants,* brought to the attention of botanists the utility of archaeological findings for supplementing plant morphology and taxonomy in adducing evidence for the geography of domestication.

In the twentieth century, N. I. Vavilov, following Candolle's pioneering work in geographical botany, embarked on his global, decades-long projects on the origin and genetic variation of cultivated plants. In 1926, Vavilov (1992: 22-7) organized a comparative chart of the morphology of cultivated species of the papilionaceous legumes and presented the rationale for botanical–genetic determination of the centers of origin of these and other crop plants. His geographic centers of origin for crop plants – which have been highly influential and much discussed in the literature of crop plant geography – included eight major and several minor centers (Vavilov 1992: 324-53). The lentil, the pea, and the broad bean were all traced to the Inner-Asiatic Center: northwestern India, Afghanistan, Tadzhikistan, Uzbekistan, and western China. The lentil and pea were also assigned by Vavilov to the Asia Minor Center (the Middle East, Iran, and Turkmenistan). The American common bean and lima bean were both assigned primary centers in the South Mexican–Central American Center, and the lesser-known species, scarlet runner beans and teparies, were also located there. The origin of the little-known polyanthus bean *(Phaseolus polyanthus)* has been documented in the same area (Schmit and Debouck 1991).

New World Beans: *Phaseolus*

The Pathway of Domestication in Phaseolus

The species of domesticated *Phaseolus* beans have shown parallel changes in structure and physiology and share some of these characteristics with the Old World grain legumes. J. Smartt (1990: 111) summarized his own findings and those of others on the nature of evolutionary changes in the *Phaseolus* cultigens. These are gigantism (increased size of seed and other plant parts); suppression of seed dispersal mechanisms (decreased tendency of pods to twist and discharge seeds); changed growth form (especially the loss of rampant vining); loss of seed dormancy; and other physiological and biochemical changes. The genetic bases for seed size, dispersal mechanisms, and growth form are partly understood, and some are even observable in archaeological specimens, in which wild *Phaseolus* beans can be readily distinguished from domesticates by both seed size and nondehiscent pod structure.

The common bean. It is clear in the writings of sixteenth-century herbalists, and later in the works of Linnaeus and Candolle, that the original home of the common bean was unknown to them. It was archaeological excavation on the arid coast of Peru in the last quarter of the nineteenth century that convinced Candolle (1964: 341–2) that *Phaseolus vulgaris* and *Phaseolus lunatus* had been cultivated in the Americas since pre-Columbian times.

At the time of contact with Europeans, varieties of the common bean were grown by Native Americans as far south as Chile and Argentina, and as far north as the valleys of the St. Lawrence and upper Missouri rivers. Edward Lewis Sturtevant (Hedrick 1972: 424) has noted that beans were observed to be in cultivation among Florida Indians by at least three explorers from 1528 to 1562, including Hernando de Soto (in 1539), who said that "the granaries were full of maes and small beans." The Natchez on the lower Mississippi grew beans as a "subsidiary crop" (Spencer et al. 1965: 410), and there is a 1917 description of traditional Hidatsa–Mandan cultivation of beans in hills between the rows of maize or occasionally "planted separately" (Spencer et al. 1965: 343). This observation suggests the planting of erect or semierect beans. Such beans are intermediate between strong climbers and truly dwarf nonclimbing beans. In California, outside of the lower Colorado River drainage where the Mohave grew tepary beans (as did other Yumans, along with maize, cucurbits, and other crops), bean agriculture began with the introduction of Mexican and European crops when the earliest Spanish missions were established. G. W. Hendry (1934) found a bit of seed coat of the common bean cultivar 'Red Mexican', or 'Pink', in a Spanish adobe brick dated 1791 at Soledad.

R. L. Beals (1932) mapped pre-1750 bean cultivation in northern Mexico and the adjacent southwestern and Gulf Coast United States using historical documents and reports by Spanish explorers. Bean distribution coincided with maize cultivation, extending from the Colorado River east to include the Rio Grande Pueblos, Zuni, and Hopi. The area of the eastern Apache in the Pecos River drainage, and of the Comanche, was nonagricultural. Beans were grown from eastern Texas, beginning with the Waco and the Kichai, eastward to the Atlantic.

Southwestern bean horticulture derives from Mexico. P. A. Gepts's (1988: 230) mapping of bean dispersal routes by means of the beans' protein structure corroborates this generally accepted view. Where water is the limiting factor in growth and production, as on the Hopi mesas, varieties having the dwarf or bush habit are planted. Where surface water is available or can be supplied, vining beans are planted with corn or, if planted separately, are provided with poles to climb upon. Except for the pinto or *garapata* group, the common beans collected during the years 1910 to 1912 by G. F. Freeman (1912) among the Papago and Pima do not appear in the archaeology of the southwestern United States. Instead, these beans represent introductions from the Mexican Central Highlands and may well have arrived during the Spanish colonial period.

According to E. F. Castetter and W. H. Bell (1942), the Papago planted teparies in July and harvested in October; the Pima planted twice, when the mesquite leafed out (late March to mid-April) and after the Saguaro harvest (July). The first planting was harvested in June, the second in October. The harvest of teparies and common beans was women's work. The plants were pulled, dried, and threshed on a clean, hard-packed soil floor in the open, in the field, or near the house. Different varieties were planted, harvested, and threshed separately. After threshing they were sealed in baskets or pots for protection from pests. Castetter and Bell (1942) and Freeman (1912) reported only bush beans in which the "vines" (sprawling plants) are grown separately from corn.

Vavilov (1992) and C. B. Heiser (1965) speculated on multiple American origins for the common bean, and substantial evidence has been adduced to show that common beans were domesticated independently in at least two distinct areas: Mesoamerica and Andean America (Kaplan 1981; Delgado Salinas 1988; Gepts 1988).

Lima beans. The lima and sieva beans were recognized by Linnaeus to belong to the same species, which he called *P. lunatus* to describe the "lunar" shape of the seeds of some varieties. The small-seeded or sieva types are natives of Mexico and Central America. These are distinct from the large-seeded South American lima beans, but can be crossed with them, and for this reason are considered to be of the same species. The sievas appear in the archaeological records of Mexico about 1,200 years ago, but do not occur in the known records of Andean archaeology. The large limas of South America, conversely, do not appear in the Mesoamerican or North American record. Seeds of the South American group have been found in Guitarrero Cave, the same Andean cave as the earliest common beans of South America, and have been 14-Carbon dated at the National Science Foundation, University of Arizona Accelerator Facility, to approximately 3,500 years ago (Kaplan 1995). The archaeological evidence of geographic separation coincides with contemporary observations of the distribution of both the wild and cultivated types. It seems clear that the two groups were domesticated independently. Both vining and bush forms are known, but the vining forms predominate in indigenous horticulture.

On the desert north coast of Peru, remains of the large-seeded lima group, dating to about 5,600 years ago (the preceramic period) (Kaplan 1995), were well preserved by the arid conditions and were so abundant that they must have constituted a major part of the diet. Ancient Peruvians even included depictions of beans in their imaginative painted ceramics and woven textiles. Painted pottery from the Mochica culture (A.D. 100–800) depicts running messengers, each carrying a small bag decorated with pictures of lima beans *(pallares)*. Rafael Larco Hoyle (1943) concluded that the lima beans, painted with parallel lines, broken lines, points, and circles, were ideograms. Some of the beans that Larco Hoyle believed to be painted were certainly renderings of naturally variegated seed coats. Other depictions show stick-limbed bean warriors rushing to the attack. Textiles from Paracas, an earlier coastal site, are rich in bean depictions.

Scarlet runner beans. The cultivated scarlet runner bean (*Phaseolus coccineus* L., for the scarlet flowers) is not known in the archaeological record north of Durango, Mexico, where it was grown about 1,300 years ago (Brooks et al. 1962). It has undoubtedly been cultivated for a much longer period in the cool central highlands of Mexico and Guatemala, but in that region, archaeological specimens securely dated and identified as older than a few hundred years are wanting. Runner beans, both purple-seeded and white-seeded, have been collected among the Hopi in historic times, especially by Alfred Whiting during the 1930s.

Tepary beans. The tepary is one of the two cultivated species not to have been named by Linnaeus. The wild type was called *Phaseolus acutifolius* by the nineteenth-century Harvard botanist Asa Gray. However, it was not until the early years of the twentieth century that the cultivated types were recognized by the Arizona botanist, Freeman, to belong to Gray's species rather than simply being varieties of the common bean.

Teparies, now little-known as commercial beans, were cultivated in central Mexico 2,300 years ago (Kaplan 1994), and in Arizona, teparies were being grown 1,000 to 1,200 years ago (Kaplan 1967). Despite their antiquity and ancient distribution, teparies have been absent from village agriculture in historic times, except in the Sonoran Desert biome of northwestern Mexico, Arizona, and New Mexico, and in the area around Tapachula in the Mexican state of Chiapas and in adjacent Guatemala. They are grown and eaten by the Pima, Papago, and peoples of the

lower Colorado River and by some "Anglo" enthusiasts for dryland-adapted crops. Because of their drought tolerance, they have been tested in many arid regions of the world.

Polyanthus beans. A fifth cultivated bean species, *P. polyanthus,* has long been known to be distinct from the other, better-known species, but only recently have its identity and distribution been documented (Schmit and Debouck 1991). To the best of my knowledge this bean of high elevations in Mexico and Central America has never entered into Old World cultivation.

The five *Phaseolus* beans are distinct species. They have different botanical names, applied by plant systematists on the basis of their structural differences. They have the same number of chromosomes ($2n = 22$) but do not freely hybridize. However, the domesticates do hybridize with some wild-growing populations that are regarded as their ancestral relatives.

The Antiquity of Phaseolus Beans: New Evidence

Uncovering the botanical and geographic origins of domesticated crops includes the search for their temporal origins. Candolle (1964), as noted previously, brought to the attention of plant scientists the utility of archaeological evidence in the quest for the temporal as well as the geographic origins of crop plants. The presence of *Phaseolus* beans on the arid coast of Peru in pre-Conquest graves of indigenous peoples did not indicate a specific calendar date for the remains, but it was convincing evidence that *Phaseolus* beans were present in the Americas before contact with European cultures. With the development of radiometric dating by the middle of the twentieth century, it became possible to determine the age of archaeological organic materials with significant precision. However, many of the published dates for the earliest crop plant remains, including beans (Kaplan 1981), are now being questioned because the 14-Carbon determinations of age are "contextual dates," meaning they are based on organic materials in the same strata with the bean remains but not on the beans themselves (Kaplan 1994).

Because of the tendency of small objects, like seeds, to move downward in archaeological contexts, some of the dates now in the literature are too early. The development of 14-Carbon dating by Atomic Mass Spectrometry (AMS), which measures very small samples, has allowed the dating of single bean seeds or pods, and in some instances has produced dates that disagree with the contextual dates. For example, a single bean-pod found in Coxcatlan Cave in the Tehuacan valley, in a content 6,000 to 7,000 years old, was AMS-dated to only 2,285 ±60 years ago (Kaplan 1967, 1994). An early date for beans in South America comes from Guitarrero Cave in the Peruvian Andes, where radiocarbon dates of plant debris are as old as 8,000 years (Kaplan, Lynch, and Smith 1973; Lynch et al. 1985). But the AMS 14-Carbon date for one seed embedded in this debris is 2,430 ±60 years old (Kaplan 1994). Disagreements over the accuracy of AMS dates (unpublished data) versus contextual 14-Carbon dates are being aired, and the debate will continue. However, an AMS date from New England (Bendremer, Kellogg, and Largy 1991) supports a contextual 14-Carbon date, which suggests the entry of common beans into northeastern North America (Ohio) about 1,000 years ago (Kaplan 1970). In the southwestern United States, AMS dates (Wills 1988: 128) of beans from a New Mexico cave agree with contextual dates (Kaplan 1981).

The wild types of all *Phaseolus* bean species are vining types, as the earliest domesticates must also have been; the dwarf-growing types came later. The earliest evidence now available for the presence of the dwarf, or bush, growth habit comes from an accelerator radiocarbon date of 1285 ±55 years ago for bean-plant remains from an archaeological cave site in the northeastern Mexican state of Tamaulipas. The vining or pole beans of each species were planted with corn so that they could depend on the stalks for support. The sprawling and dwarf types could be grown independent of support.

Tracing Bean Migrations

Molecular evidence. Phaseolin is the principal storage protein of *Phaseolus* bean seeds. Gepts (1988) has used the variation in phaseolin structure to trace the dispersal of contemporary common bean cultivars within the Americas and in the Old World. He has shown that the majority of the present-day cultivars of Western Europe, the Iberian Peninsula, Malawian Africa, and the northeastern United States originated in the Andes. The 'C' phaseolin type is found in highest frequency in the Americas in Chile and in the Iberian Peninsula among those Old World regions sampled.

Gepts has applied the phaseolin-structure method to questions of dispersal within the Americas, such as that of the traditional beans of the northeastern United States. There, a majority of the cultivated bean varieties of historic times are of the 'T' phaseolin type, which is the type that is most frequent in Western Europe and in the Andes south of Colombia. 'T' phaseolin is common elsewhere in South America but not in Mesoamerica. Indeed, in Mesoamerica and the adjacent southwestern United States, 'T' types make up only 8 percent and 2 percent, respectively, of the cultivated bean varieties. The archaeological record of crop plants in the northeastern United States is limited because of poor conditions for preservation (humid soils and no sheltered cave deposits), but those beans that have been found, although carbonized, are recognizable as a south-

western United States type (Kaplan 1970). This common bean type, which was dispersed from northwestern Arizona along with eight-rowed corn, must have been of the 'S' phaseolin type, which Gepts has found characteristic of 98 percent of contemporary southwestern common beans. It seems clear that historic-period northeastern bean cultivars are primarily South American, which could have reached the northeastern United States by way of sailing ships, directly from Peruvian and Chilean ports during the late eighteenth and early nineteenth centuries, or from England and France along with immigrants, or through seed importation.

In the foregoing, we see a dispersal pattern that was probably common in much of the New World, and especially in semiarid places in Mesoamerica and the greater Southwest. In dryland prehistoric sites, organic remains are well preserved in the archaeological record, and we see that prehistoric bean cultivars have often been eliminated, or reduced in frequency, by better-adapted (biologically, culturally, economically), introduced cultivars. Such a pattern suggests that Columbus's introduction of beans to Europe from the Caribbean Islands was soon augmented by later introductions from Andean agriculture bearing the 'C' phaseolin type.

Historical evidence. Success in tracing the dispersion of beans from their regions of origin rests to some extent on historical records. But such records are likely to be strongly biased. One of the richest sources of evidence is the body of data available from seed catalogs, magazines, and newspapers devoted to agriculture and horticulture. Such publications, however, are unevenly representative of the larger dispersion picture. The United States, parts of Latin America, and Western Europe may be better represented in this respect than are some other parts of the world. Specialized libraries and archives have preserved some of this published material in the United States for about 200 years. In the United States, the earliest sources for named varieties of garden plants are leaflets or advertisements for seeds newly arrived from England. In Portsmouth, New Hampshire, over a period from 1750 to 1784, 32 varieties of beans, including common beans, both vining and erect types, scarlet runner beans, possibly small-seeded limas, and fava beans, were listed for sale in the *New Hampshire Gazette* (documents courtesy of Strawbery Banke Museum, Portsmouth, N.H.). Earlier still, but less informative, are lists prepared for the guidance of colonists heading for English North America in the seventeenth century, who were advised to supply themselves with peas and (broad) beans, in addition to other vegetable seeds, garden tools, and weapons. We do not begin to detect evidence for the ingress of *Phaseolus* bean cultivars from England and France to the United States until the early nineteenth century.

The Old World: Broad Beans, Peas, and Lentils

As in much of the Americas, the Mediterranean world's combination of cereal grain and food grain legumes has been the foundation for both agriculture and the diet of settled farming communities.

William J. Darby and colleagues (Darby, Ghalioungui, and Grivetti 1977), in tracing food use in Pharaonic Egypt, found papyrus texts and archaeological remains to contain much evidence of food grain legumes in the daily life of the kingdom. Rameses II spoke of barley and beans in immense quantities; Rameses III offered to the Nile god 11,998 jars of "shelled beans." The term " 'bean meal' [medicinal bean meal], so commonly encountered in the medical papyri," could apply to *Vicia faba*, to other legumes, or to the "Egyptian bean" (*Nelumbo nucifera* Gaertner, the sacred lotus), all of which have been found in tombs (Darby et al. 1977: II 683).

Fava beans were avoided by priests and others, but the reasons are not clear. The avoidance of favas by Pythagoras, who was trained by Egyptians, is well known, and it may have been that he shared with them a belief that beans "were produced from the same matter as man" (Darby et al. 1977: II 683). Other ancient writers gave different reasons for the taboo, such as self-denial by priests of a variety of foods, including lentils. And more recently, as already mentioned, favism, a genetically determined sensitivity (red blood cells deficient in glucose-6-phosphate dehydrogenase) to chemical components of fava beans, has suggested still another explanation for the avoidance of this food (Sokolov 1984).

Domestication

Structural change under domestication in fava beans, peas, and lentils is much like that in the *Phaseolus* beans, but there are important differences in what can be determined from archaeological samples. Pods of pulses in Middle Eastern sites are seldom found; hence, the loss of pod dehiscence has not been traced in archaeological materials from that region as it has in the Americas (Kaplan and MacNeish 1960; Kaplan 1986). In an effort to find good characters for distinguishing between wild and domesticated types in Middle East pulses, A. Butler (1989) has studied their seed coat structure but has found that the loss of seed dormancy (the impermeability of seed coats to water, which separates the wild types from the domesticates) cannot readily be detected by examination of the seed coats with scanning electron microscopy, or, at best, there is no single structural change that accounts for the difference between permeability and impermeability. Butler (1989: 402) notes that the surface of testa has been used to distinguish wild from cultivated taxa in Vicieae. With the exception of testa thickness in seeds of *Pisum*, no characters recorded in the seed coat of Vicieae can be associated directly with the presence or absence of hard seed coats. Evidence from seed anatomy of dormancy, and therefore of wildness, is lacking in Vicieae.

The origins and domestication of broad beans, peas, and lentils have been the focus of extensive research by plant geneticists and by archaeologists seeking to understand the foundations of agriculture in the Near East. D. Zohary (1989a: 358–63) has presented both genetic and archaeological evidence (not uncontested) for the simultaneous, or near simultaneous, domestication in the Near East of emmer wheat (*Triticum turgidum* ssp. *dicoccum),* barley (*Hordeum vulgare),* and einkorn wheat (*Triticum monococcum),* "hand in hand with the introduction into cultivation of five companion plants": pea (*Pisum sativum),* lentil (*Lens culinaris),* chickpea (*Cicer arietinum),* bitter vetch (*Vicia ervilia),* and flax (*Linum usitatissimum). V. faba* may also have been among these earliest domesticates (Kislev 1985).

Lentil

Lens culinaris (Lens esculenta), the cultivated lentil, is a widely grown species in a small genus. Archaeological evidence shows that it or its relatives were gathered by 13,000 to 9,500 years ago in Greece (Hansen 1992) and by 10,000 to 9,500 years ago in the Near East (Zohary and Hopf 1988). Candolle (1964) in 1885 wrote of its presence in the Bronze Age sites (the so-called Swiss Lake dwellings) in Switzerland. Lentil cultivation, by historic times, was important and well established in the Near East, North Africa, France, and Spain (Hedrick 1972), and had been introduced into most of the subtropical and warm temperate regions of the known world (Duke 1981: 111). With a production of about 38 percent of the world's lentils and little export (Singh and Singh 1992), the Indian subcontinent – a region in which food grain legumes are an especially important source of protein in the population's largely vegetarian diet – has made this crop one of its most important dietary pulses. Traditionally, two subspecies are recognized on the basis of seed size: *L. culinaris* ssp. *microsperma,* which are small-seeded, and *L. culinaris* ssp. *macrosperma,* which are large-seeded. The large-seeded form is grown in the Mediterranean Basin, in Africa, and in Asia Minor. The small-seeded form is grown in western and southwestern Asia, especially India (Duke 1981: 110–13).

According to G. Ladizinsky (1989: 377, 380) the genus *Lens* comprises *L. culinaris* and four wild species: *Lens nigricans, Lens ervoides, Lens odemensis,* and *Lens orientalis.* The same author, however, notes that the genus may be reclassified to reflect the genetic relationships of the species, thus: *L. culinaris* ssp. *odemensis,* ssp. *orientalis,* ssp. *culinaris; L. nigricans* ssp. *ervoides,* ssp. *nigricans.* Many populations of ssp. *orientalis* and *odemensis* are sufficiently close to ssp. *culinaris* to be used for breeding purposes. However, the chromosome structure within these subspecies indicates that the cultivated lentils evolved from the principal cytogenetic stock of ssp. *orientalis*. Because this cytogenetic stock ranges from Turkey to Uzbekistan (Ladizinsky et al. 1984), there is little evidence of where in this vast region domestication might have first occurred.

Lentil domestication. Ladizinsky (1987) has maintained that the gathering of wild lentils, and perhaps other grain legumes, prior to their cultivation could have resulted in reduced or lost seed dormancy, a factor of primary importance in the domestication of legumes. As an operational definition of cultivation, Ladizinsky accepted the proposal of Jack R. Harlan, who emphasized human activities designed to manage the productivity of crops and gathered plants. As part of the gathering or foraging process, such management could lead to changes in genetic structure and morphology of wild plants.

High rates of seed dormancy observed by Ladizinsky in wild *L. orientalis* populations demonstrated that they are ill-adapted to cultivation. Dormancy, a single-gene recessive trait, is absent from most of the lineages of domesticated *L. culinaris*. Nondormancy is determined by a single dominant allele. A loss of seed dormancy in lentil populations resulting from gathering practices, Ladizinsky (1979, 1987, 1993) has argued, is the result of establishing this mutant dominant allele in small populations where most of the lentil seeds produced are removed by human gathering. A patchy distribution of small populations of annual legume plants, low population density, and intensive gathering would be, under the conditions he defines, advantageous for the increase of the seed-dormancy-free trait. He has concluded that this process would have taken place in wild, noncultivated lentil (and probably in wild pea and chickpea) populations, and would have predisposed these populations to domestication. This, he maintained, was an evolutionary pathway different from that of the cereal grains for which dormancy of seeds is not a barrier to domestication.

Ladizinsky's views have been disputed by Zohary (1989b) and by M. A. Blumler (1991), who both criticized Ladizinsky's assumptions and conclusions. Blumler investigated Ladizinsky's mathematical model for the loss of dormancy in lentils and concluded that fixation of alleles for nondormancy, as a result of intensive human gathering, did not depend upon gathering at all. He further concluded that Ladizinsky's model would predict loss of dormancy under any circumstances and therefore was not tenable as a hypothesis for preagricultural domestication. He went on to propose that lentils, and possibly other legumes that were gathered and brought to camps, might inadvertently have been introduced to campground soils, but that the poorly competitive introductions would have had to be encouraged (cultivated) in order to survive. Blumler thus contested Ladizinsky's proposal

that legumes could have been domesticated prior to actual cultivation and agreed with Zohary that the pathways of domestication in cereals and legumes were similar, and that legume cultivation followed upon the beginning of cereal cultivation.

As noted earlier in this chapter, the virtual absence of grain legume pods from archaeological sites in the Near East contrasts with the record of *Phaseolus* in the Americas. This circumstance makes it difficult to judge the merit of Ladizinsky's view that the forceful dissemination of seeds following pod dehiscence - a process resulting in the loss of much of a valuable food resource - can be circumvented by pulling whole plants. This would be one sort of gathering technique that could be considered predomesticative management. Accordingly, Ladizinsky placed a low value on the loss of pod dehiscence, or shattering in legumes, while agreeing with most of those concerned that the loss of shattering in cereal grains is of high value in the process of domestication.

Zohary, in response (1989b), accorded the suppression of the wild type of seed dispersal in grain legumes equal weight with the parallel process in the cereal grains. In so doing, he reinforced the argument that domestication in the Near Eastern cereal grains and grain legumes were similar processes. These provocative models for the transition of legumes, and other economic plants, from the wild to the domesticated state provide the basis for both field and theoretical tests. As more evidence is gathered, these theories will be revised repeatedly.

Because archaeological legume pods are seldom found among the plant remains of early Near Eastern societies, dehiscence versus nondehiscence of pods cannot be determined as it has been from New World bean remains. The appearance of seed nondormancy as a marker of the domesticated legume has not been made on the basis of archaeological materials for reasons noted previously in connection with Butler's study of seed coat structure. The archaeological record, however, does reveal changes in legume seed size in the Near East, such as small-seeded (diameter 2.5 to 3.0 millimeters) forms of lentil in early (seventh millennium B.C.) aceramic farming villages. By 5500 to 5000 B.C., lentils of 4.2 millimeters in diameter were present in the Deh Luran Valley of Iran, as reported by Hans Helbaeck (cited by Zohary and Hopf 1988: 89). Zohary and M. Hopf regarded the contrast in size between lentils of the early farming villages and those of 1,500 to 2,000 years later as a change under domestication.

Lentils spread into Europe with the extension of agriculture from the Near East in the sixth millennium B.C., where records of this crop and other legumes during the Bronze Age are less abundant than they are in the earlier Neolithic and later Iron Ages (Zohary and Hopf 1988: 87-9). Only their difference in size from the wild types (*L. orientalis* or *L. nigricans*) gives evidence for the development of domesticated lentils, which probably occurred in the Near East (Zohary and Hopf 1988: 91-2). These larger lentils appeared in the Near East as late as the end of the sixth millennium B.C., about 1,500 years after the establishment of wheat and barley cultivation (Zohary and Hopf 1988: 91). Although the archaeological and morphological evidence do not disclose the place of origin of the lentil, it is in the Near East where it occurs early in the large-seeded form and where *L. orientalis* is to be found. The lentil, however, is not mentioned as a food crop by F. J. Simoons (1991) in his comprehensive work on food in China.

Pea

Ever a source of confusion for readers of crop plant history and ethnobotany, common names often serve less to identify than to confound. "Pea" *(P. sativum)*, as well as "bean," illustrates this problem. A name with Latin and Greek origins, "pea," in English, was formed from "pease," which took on the meaning of a plural; the "-se" was dropped by A.D. 1600 and the current form of the word was established (Oxford English Dictionary 1971). Pea is used combined with descriptives to form the names of numerous plants. In the context of this discussion of food grain legume origins, the important distinction is that between *P. sativum* and the grass pea or chickling pea (*Lathyrus sativus* L.), and the cowpea, black-eye pea, or black-eye bean *Vigna unguiculata.*

The grass pea is a minor crop in the Mediterranean Basin, North Africa, the Middle East, and India, and has been documented archaeologically in parts of this broad region since Neolithic times (Zohary and Hopf 1988: 109-10). In India, it is a weedy growth in cereal grain fields and is the cheapest pulse available (Purseglove 1968: 278). During times of famine, it has been consumed in significant amounts even though its consumption has caused a paralysis of the limb joints (Aykroyd and Doughty 1964).

The cowpea, an important crop in the tropics and subtropics, especially in Africa (Purseglove 1968: 322) and Southeast Asia (Herklots 1972: 261), appeared in the Mediterranean Basin in classical times (Zohary and Hopf 1988: 84). A plant mentioned in Sumerian records about 2350 B.C., under the name of *lu-ub-sar* (Arabic *lobia*), may have been a reference to the cowpea (Herklots 1972: 261).

Wild peas include *Pisum fulvum, Pisum elatius (P. sativum* ssp. *elatius),* and *Pisum humile (P. sativum* ssp. *humile, = Pisum syriacum).* Hybrids between *P. sativum* and *P. elatius* or *P. humile* are usually fertile, whereas hybrids between the cultivated pea and *P. fulvum* are fertile only when *P. fulvum* is the pollen parent (Ladizinsky 1989: 374-7). Zohary (1989a: 363-4) reports that similarities in chromosome structure between cultivated peas and *P. humile* populations in Turkey and the Golan Heights point to populations of *humile* having a particular chromosomal

configuration (a reciprocal translocation) as the "direct" ancestral stock of the cultivated peas.

Peas were present in the early Neolithic preceramic farming villages (7500 to 6000 B.C.) of the Near East, and in large amounts with cultivated wheats and barleys by 5850 to 5600 B.C. They appear to have been associated with the spread of Neolithic agriculture into Europe, again together with wheat and barley (Zohary and Hopf 1988: 96-8). In central Germany, carbonized pea seeds with intact seed coats have been found dating from 4400 to 4200 B.C., and these show the smooth surface characteristic of the domestic crop. In Eastern Europe and Switzerland, pea remains have been found in late Neolithic or Bronze Age sites (Zohary and Hopf 1988: 97-8).

The date at which the pea entered China is not known, but along with the broad bean, it was called *hu-tou* or "Persian bean," which suggests an origin by way of the Silk Road in historic times (Simoons 1991: 74-5).

Vicia faba

Ladizinsky (1975) has investigated the genetic relationships among the broad bean and its wild relatives in the section *Faba* of the genus *Vicia.* He concluded that none of the populations of wild species, *Vicia narbonensis, Vicia galilaea,* or *Vicia haeniscyamus,* collected in Israel, can be considered the ancestor of the fava bean. Differences in the crossability, chromosome form, and chromosome number separate the broad bean from these relatives, as do differences in ranges of seed size, presence of tendrils, and epidermal hairs on the pods. Ladizinsky was careful to note that these characters may have evolved under domestication, but given the absence of evidence for derivation of the fava bean from its known relatives, he concluded that the place of origin of the broad bean could not have been in the Middle East.

Ladizinsky further drew attention to what he regarded as a paucity of broad bean remains only "circumstantial[ly]" identified in Neolithic sites of the Middle East and was led by these lines of evidence to conclude that the origin of *V. faba* had to be outside of this region. He further speculated that the occurrence of a self-pollinating wild form of the species in Afghanistan and areas adjacent might be the region in which the now cross-pollinating broad bean originated. Zohary (1977), however, interpreted the archaeological record quite differently, asserting that the distribution pattern of archaeological broad bean remains points to its domestication by the fourth or fifth millennium B.C. in the Mediterranean Basin.

The dates for the introduction of broad beans into China are not secure – perhaps the second century B.C. or later – but it has become an important crop in "many mountainous, remote or rainy parts of China at the present time especially in western China" (E. N. Anderson, cited by Simoons 1991: 75). The earliest introduction of broad beans into North America appears to have taken place in the early seventeenth century when Captain Bartholomew Gosnold, who explored the coast of New England, planted them on the Elizabeth Islands off the south shore of Massachusetts (Hedrick 1972: 594). Less than 30 years later, records of the provisioning and outfitting of the supply ship for New Plymouth list "benes" (and "pease") along with other seeds to be sent to the Massachusetts colony (Pulsifer 1861: 24).

Conclusion

The domestication of food grain legumes in the Americas and in the Mediterranean–West Asian region reveals important parallels. Both groups suppressed, at least in some varieties, the tendency to vine or grow rampantly. The seeds of both have markedly increased in size over their wild counterparts. Both groups have suppressed pod dehiscence, projectile seed dissemination, and seed dormancy, and in both regions, the seeds have functioned primarily as protein sources in predominantly cereal grain diets. Studies in genetics, molecular structure, and archaeology have contributed to an understanding of the origins of species and races within species. Nonetheless, uncertainties over important aspects of the origins and evolution under domestication remain, and are the subject of active multidisciplinary research.

Lawrence Kaplan

Bibliography

Aykroyd, W. R., and J. Doughty. 1964. *Legumes in human nutrition.* FAO. Rome.

Beals, R. L. 1932. The comparative ethnology of northern Mexico before 1750. *Ibero-Americana* 2: 93–225.

Bendremer, J. C. M., E. A. Kellogg, and T. B. Largy. 1991. A grass-lined maize storage pit and early maize horticulture in central Connecticut. *North American Archaeologist* 12: 325–49.

Blumler, M. A. 1991. Modeling the origin of legume domestication and cultivation. *Economic Botany* 45: 243–50.

Brooks, R. H., L. Kaplan, H. C. Cutler, and T. H. Whitaker. 1962. Plant material from a cave on the Rio Zape, Durango, Mexico. *American Antiquity* 27: 356–69.

Butler, A. 1989. Cryptic anatomical characters as evidence of early cultivation in the grain legumes. In *Foraging and farming, the evolution of plant exploitation,* ed. David R. Harris and Gordon C. Hillman, 390–407. London.

Candolle, Alphonse de. [1886] 1964. *Origin of cultivated plants.* Second edition. New York.

Castetter, E. F., and W. H. Bell. 1942. *Pima and Papago Indian agriculture.* Albuquerque, N. Mex.

Darby, William J., Paul Ghalioungui, and Louisa Grivetti. 1977. *Food: The gift of Osiris.* 2 vols. London.

Delgado Salinas, Alfonso. 1988. Otra interpretacíon en torno a la domesticacíon de *Phaseolus.* In *Estudios sobre las revoluciones neolitica y urbana,* ed. L. Manzanilla, 167–74. Mexico.

Duke, J. A. 1981. *Handbook of legumes of world economic importance.* New York.

Dunn, O., and J. E. Kelley, Jr. 1989. *The Diario of Christopher Columbus's first voyage to America 1492–1493.* Norman, Okla.

Franquemont, C., E. Franquemont, W. Davis, et al. 1990. *The ethnobotany of Chinchero, an Andean community of southern Peru.* Field Museum of Natural History, Chicago, *Fieldiana,* Publication No. 1408.

Freeman, G. F. 1912. Southwestern beans and teparies. *Arizona Agricultural Experiment Station Bulletin* 68. Phoenix.

Gepts, P. A. 1988. *Genetic resources of Phaseolus beans.* Dordrecht, Netherlands.

Hansen, J. 1992. Franchthi cave and the beginnings of agriculture in Greece and the Aegean. In *Préhistoire de l'agriculture: Novelles approches expérimentales et ethnographiques.* Paris.

Hedrick, U. P. 1931. *The vegetables of New York,* Vol. 1, Part 2, *Beans of New York.* Albany, N.Y.

  ed. [1919] 1972. *Sturtevant's notes on edible plants.* New York.

Heiser, C. B., Jr. 1965. Cultivated plants and cultural diffusion in nuclear America. *American Anthropologist* 67: 930–49.

Hendry, G. W. 1934. Bean cultivation in California. *California Agricultural Experiment Station Bulletin* 294: 288–321.

Herklots, G. A. C. 1972. Vegetables in Southeast Asia. London.

Kaplan, L. 1967. Archeological *Phaseolus* from Tehuacan. In *The prehistory of the Tehuacan Valley,* ed. Douglas S. Byers, 201–12. Austin, Tex.

  1970. Plant remains from the Blain Site. In *Blain Village and the Fort Ancient tradition in Ohio,* ed. Olaf H. Prufer and Orrin C. Shane, III, 227–31. Kent, Ohio.

  1981. What is the origin of the common bean? *Economic Botany* 35: 240–54.

  1986. Preceramic *Phaseolus* from Guila' Naquitz. In *Guila' Naquitz: Archaic foraging and early agriculture in Oxaca,* ed. Kent Flannery, 281–4. Orlando, Fla.

  1994. Accelerator Mass Spectrometry date and the antiquity of *Phaseolus* cultivation. *Annual Report of the Bean Improvement Cooperative* 37: 131–2.

  1995. Accelerator dates and the prehistory of *Phaseolus.* Paper contributed to the Annual Meeting, Society for American Archaeology, May 5, 1995, Minneapolis, Minn.

Kaplan, L., T. F. Lynch, and C. E. Smith, Jr. 1973. Early cultivated beans *(Phaseolus vulgaris)* from an intermontane Peruvian valley. *Science* 179: 76–7.

Kaplan, L., and R. S. MacNeish. 1960. Prehistoric bean remains from caves in the Ocampo region of Tamaulipas, Mexico. *Botanical Museum Leaflets* (Harvard University) 19: 33–56.

Kislev, M. E. 1985. Early Neolithic horsebean from Yiftah'el, Israel. *Science* 228: 319–20.

Ladizinsky, G. 1975. On the origin of the broad bean, *Vicia faba* L. *Israel Journal of Botany* 24: 80–8.

  1979. Seed dispersal in relation to the domestication of Middle East legumes. *Economic Botany* 33: 284–9.

  1987. Pulse domestication before cultivation. *Economic Botany* 41: 60–5.

  1989. Origin and domestication of the southwest Asian grain legumes. In *Foraging and farming, the evolution of plant exploitation,* ed. David R. Harris and Gordon C. Hillman, 374–89. London.

  1993. Lentil domestication: On the quality of evidence and arguments. *Economic Botany* 47: 60–4.

Ladizinsky, G., D. Braun, D. Goshen, and F. J. Muehlbauer. 1984. The biological species of the genus *Lens. Botanical Gazette* 145: 253–61.

Larco Hoyle, Rafael. 1943. La escritura Mochica sobre pallares. *Revista Geográfica Americana* 20: 1–36.

Lynch, T. F., R. Gillespie, J. A. Gowlette, and R. E. M. Hedges. 1985. Chronology of Guitarrero Cave, Peru. *Science* 229: 864–7.

Oxford English Dictionary. 1971. Compact edition.

Pulsifer, D., ed. 1861. *Records of the Colony of New Plymouth in New England, 1623–1682,* Vol. 1. Boston, Mass.

Purseglove, J. W. 1968. Tropical crops: Dicotyledons. 2 vols. New York.

Schmit, V., and D. G. Debouck. 1991. Observations on the origin of *Phaseolus polyanthus* Greenman. *Economic Botany* 45: 345–64.

Simoons, F. J. 1991. *Food in China, a cultural and historical inquiry.* Boca Raton, Fla.

Singh, U. and B. Singh. 1992. Tropical grain legumes as important human foods. *Economic Botany* 46: 310–21.

Smartt, J. 1990. *Grain legumes, evolution and genetic resources.* Cambridge and New York.

Sokolov, Raymond. 1984. Broad bean universe. *Natural History* 12: 84–7.

Spencer, R. F., J. D. Jennings, et al. 1965. *The Native Americans: Prehistory and ethnology of the North American Indians.* New York.

Strickberger, M. W. 1985. *Genetics.* Third edition. New York.

Tournefort, J. P. 1730. *The compleat herbal, or the botanical institutions of Monsr. Tournefort, Chief Botanist to the late French King. . . .* 2 vols. London.

Vavilov, N. I. 1992. *Origin and geography of cultivated plants,* ed. V. F. Dorofeyev, trans. Doris Löve. Cambridge.

Webster's third new international dictionary of the English language. Unabridged. Springfield, Mass.

Wills, W. H. 1988. *Early prehistoric agriculture in the American Southwest.* Santa Fe, N. Mex.

Zohary, D. 1977. Comments on the origin of cultivated broad bean. *Israel Journal of Botany* 26: 39–40.

  1989a. Domestication of the southwest Asian Neolithic crop assemblage of cereals, pulses, and flax: The evidence from living plants. In *Foraging and farming, the evolution of plant exploitation,* ed. David R. Harris and Gordon C. Hillman, 358–73. London.

  1989b. Pulse domestication and cereal domestication: How different are they? *Economic Botany* 43: 31–4.

Zohary, D., and M. Hopf. 1988. *Domestication of plants in the Old World.* Oxford.

II.C.4 ❧ Chilli Peppers

Chilli peppers are eaten as a spice and as a condiment by more than one-quarter of the earth's inhabitants each day. Many more eat them with varying regularity – and the rate of consumption is growing. Although the chilli pepper is the most used spice and condiment in the world, its monetary value in the spice trade is not indicative of this importance because it is readily cultivated by many of its consumers.

Peppers are the fruit of perennial shrubs belonging to the genus *Capsicum* and were unknown outside the tropical and subtropical regions of the Western Hemisphere before 1492, when Christopher Columbus made his epic voyage in search of a short route to the East Indies. Although he did not reach Asia and its spices, he did return to Spain with examples of a new, pungent spice found during his first visit to the eastern coast of the Caribbean island of Hispaniola

Chilli pepper

(now the Dominican Republic and Republic of Haiti). Today capsicums are not only consumed as a spice, condiment, and vegetable, but are also used in medicines, as coloring agents, for landscape and decorative design, and as ornamental objects.

History

For the peoples of the Old World, the history of capsicums began at the end of the fifteenth century, when Columbus brought some specimens of a red-fruited plant from the New World back to his sovereigns (Morison 1963: 216; Anghiera 1964: 225). However, the fruits were not new to humankind. When nonagricultural Mongoloid peoples, who had begun migrating across the Bering Strait during the last Ice Age, reached the subtropical and tropical zones of their new world, they found capsicums that had already become rather widespread. They had been carried to other regions by natural dispersal agents – principally birds – from their nuclear area south of both the wet forests of Amazonia and the semiarid cerado of central Brazil (Pickersgill 1984: 110). Plant remains and depictions of chillies on artifacts provide archaeological evidence of the use and probable cultivation of these wild capsicums by humans as early as 5000 B.C. By 1492, Native Americans had domesticated (genetically altered) at least four species (MacNeish 1967; Heiser 1976: 266; Pickersgill 1984: 113). No others have subsequently been domesticated.

In the West Indies, Columbus found several different capsicums being cultivated by the Arawak Indians, who had migrated from northeastern South America to the Caribbean Islands during a 1,200 year period beginning about 1000 B.C. (Means 1935; Anghiera 1964; Watts 1987). These migrants traveled by way of Trinidad and the Lesser Antilles, bringing with them a tropical capsicum that had been domesticated in their homeland. They also brought a word similar to *ají* by which the plant was, and still is, known in the West Indies and throughout its native South American habitat (Heiser 1969). Later, a second species reached the West Indies from Mesoamerica along with other food plants, such as maize (corn), beans, and squash (Sauer

1966: 54). It was this, more climatically adaptable pepper species that went forth, bearing the native Nahuatl name *chilli,* to set the cuisines of the Old World tropics afire (Andrews 1993a, 1993b).

The conquest of Mexico and, later, the mastery of Peru also revealed pepper varieties more suited climatically to cultivation in the temperate areas of Europe and the Middle East. And within 50 years after the first capsicum peppers reached the Iberian Peninsula from the West Indies, American chilli peppers were being grown on all coasts of Africa and in India, monsoon Asia, southwestern China, the Middle East, the Balkans, central Europe, and Italy (Andrews 1993a).

The first European depictions of peppers date from 1542, when a German herbal by Leonhart Fuchs described and illustrated several types of pepper plants considered at that time to be native to India. Interestingly, however, it was not the Spanish who were responsible for the early diffusion of New World food plants. Rather, it was the Portuguese, aided by local traders following long-used trade routes, who spread American plants throughout the Old World with almost unbelievable rapidity (Boxer 1969a).

Unfortunately, documentation for the routes that chilli peppers followed from the Americas is not as plentiful as that for other New World economic plants such as maize, tobacco, sweet potatoes, manioc (cassava), beans, and tomatoes. However, it is highly probable that capsicums accompanied the better-documented Mesoamerican food complex of corn, beans, and squash, as peppers have been closely associated with these plants throughout history. The Portuguese, for example, acquired corn at the beginning of the sixteenth century and encouraged its cultivation on the west coast of Africa (Jeffreys 1975: 35). From West Africa the American foods, including capsicums, went to the east coast of Africa and then to India on trading ships traveling between Lisbon and Goa on the Malabar Coast of western India (Boxer 1984).

The fiery new spice was readily accepted by the natives of Africa and India, who were long-accustomed to food highly seasoned with spices, such as the African melegueta pepper (*Aframomum melegueta,* also known as "grains of paradise"), the Indian black pepper *(Piper nigrum),* and ginger *(Zingiber officinale).* In fact, because the plants produced by the abundant, easily stored seeds were much easier to cultivate than the native spices, *Capsicum* became a less expensive addition to the daily diet and was soon widely available to all – rich and poor alike. Thus, within a scant 50 years after 1492, three varieties of capsicums were being grown and exported along the Malabar Coast of India (Purseglove 1968; Watt 1972).

From India, chilli peppers traveled (along with the other spices that were disseminated) not only along the Portuguese route back around Africa to Europe but also over ancient trade routes that led either to Europe via the Middle East or to monsoon Asia (L'obel 1576). In the latter case, if the Portuguese had not carried chilli peppers to Southeast Asia and Japan, the new spice would have been spread by Arabic, Gujurati, Chinese, Malaysian, Vietnamese, and Javanese traders as they traded traditional wares throughout their worlds. And, after Portuguese introduction, both birds and humans carried the peppers inland. Certainly, birds are most adept at carrying pepper seeds from island to island and to inaccessible inland areas (Ridley 1930; Procter 1968).

In the Szechuan and Hunan provinces in China, where many New World foods were established within the lifetime of the Spanish conquistadors, there were no roads leading from the coast. Nonetheless, American foods were known there by the middle of the sixteenth century, having reached these regions via caravan routes from the Ganges River through Burma and across western China (Ho 1955). The cuisines of southwestern Szechuan and Hunan still employ more chilli peppers than any other area in China.

Despite a European "discovery" of the Americas, chilli peppers diffused throughout Europe in circuitous fashion. Following the fall of Granada in 1492, the Spaniards established dominance over the western Mediterranean while the Ottoman Turks succeeded in installing themselves as the controlling power in northern Africa, Egypt, Arabia, the Balkans, the Middle East, and the eastern Mediterranean. The result was that the Mediterranean became, in reality, two separate seas divided by Italy, Malta, and Sicily, with little or no trade or contact between the eastern and western sections (Braudel 1976).

Venice was the center of the spice and Oriental trade of central Europe, and Venice depended on the Ottoman Turks for goods from the fabled Orient. From central Europe the trade went to Antwerp and the rest of Europe, although Antwerp also received Far Eastern goods from the Portuguese via India, Africa, and Lisbon. It was along these avenues that chilli peppers traveled into much of Europe. They were in Italy by 1535 (Oviedo 1950), Germany by 1542 (Fuchs 1543), England before 1538 (Turner 1965), the Balkans before 1569 (Halasz 1963), and Moravia by 1585 (L'Escluse 1611). But except in the Balkans and Turkey, Europeans did not make much use of chilli peppers until the Napoleonic blockade cut off their supply of spices and they turned to Balkan paprika as a substitute. Prior to that, Europeans had mainly grown capsicums in containers as ornamentals.

Well into the nineteenth century, most Europeans continued to believe that peppers were native to India and the Orient until botanist Alphonse de Candolle produced convincing linguistic evidence for the American origin of the genus *Capsicum* (Candolle 1852). In addition, during the 500 years since their discovery, chillies have become an established crop in the Old World tropics and are such a vital part of the cuisines that many in these regions are only now beginning to accept an American origin of the spice that is such an integral part of their daily lives.

It was only after the Portuguese had carried capsicums and other American plants to Africa, Asia, the Middle East, and Europe that the Spaniards played a significant role in the movement of New World crops to places other than Spain, Italy, and, perhaps, Western Europe. This began toward the end of the sixteenth century with the Manila–Acapulco galleon traffic which effected the transfer of numerous plants, as well as goods, between Mexico and the Orient (Schurz 1939).

Moreover, in North America, at approximately the same time that the Manila galleon trade was launched, the Spaniards founded the presidios of Saint Augustine, Florida (1565), and Santa Fe, New Mexico (1598). These settlements initiated Caribbean–Florida and Mexico–American Southwest exchanges of plants long before other Europeans began colonizing the east coast of North America. Interestingly, however, seventeenth-century English colonists introduced peppers from England via Bermuda to their eastern North American possessions (Laufer 1929: 242).

The Names of Chilli Peppers

That Columbus had not reached the Orient did not discourage him from calling the Caribbean Islands the "Indies," the natives "Indians," and the chilli pepper *pimiento* after the completely unrelated black pepper – *pimienta* – that he sought in the East.

The indigenous Arawaks called the fruit *axí,* which was the South American name they brought with them when they migrated north to the Antilles. Although the Spaniards transliterated this to *ají (ajé, agí),* they never adopted the Arawak word, either in the West Indies or in North America.

Nonetheless, in the Dominican Republic and a few other places in the Caribbean, and in much of South America, the pungent varieties are still called *ají. Uchu* and *huayca* are other ancient words used for capsicums by some Amerindian groups in the Andean area. In Spain, American peppers are called *pimiento* or *pimientón* (depending on the size) after *pimienta* (black pepper from India). In Italy, they are called *peperone,* in France, *piment,* and in the Balkans, *paprika.*

In Mexico, however, the Nahuatl-speaking natives called their fiery fruit *chilli.* The Nahuatl stem *chil* refers to the chilli plant. It also means "red." The original Spanish spelling was *chilli,* first used in print by Francisco Hernández (1514–78), the earliest European to collect plants systematically in the New World. But although in his writings (published in 1615) he interpreted the Nahuatl name for capsicums as chilli, that Spanish spelling was later changed to *chile* by Spanish-speaking people in Mexico. To the generic word "chilli" were added the terms that described particular chilli cultivars (two examples are *Tonalchilli,* "chilli of the sun or summer," and *Chiltecpin,* "flea chilli"). In Mexico today, the word *chile* refers to both pungent and sweet types and is used, in the Nahuatl style, combined with a descriptive adjective, such as *chile colorado* ("red chilli"), or with a word that indicates the place of origin, such as *chile poblano* ("chilli from Puebla"). The same Mexican variety can have different names in different geographic regions, in various stages of maturity, and in the dried state.

The Portuguese language uses *pimenta* for capsicums and qualifies the various types – *pimenta-da-caiena* (cayenne pepper), *pimenta-da-malagueta* (red pepper), *pimenta-do-reino* (black pepper), and *pimenta-da-jamaica* (allspice). *Pimentão* can mean pimento, red pepper, or just pepper. *Ají* and *chile* are not found in Portuguese dictionaries, and apparently the Portuguese did not carry those words with them in their travels.

The Dutch and the English were probably responsible for introducing the current capsicum names to the eastern part of the Old World. In Australia, India, Indonesia, and Southeast Asia in general, the term "chilli" ("chillies") or, sometimes, "chilly," is used by English speakers for the pungent types, whereas the mild ones are called capsicums. Each Far Eastern language has its own word for chillies – *prik* in Thai and *mirch* in Hindi, to name but two.

It is in the United States that the greatest confusion exists. Both the Anglicized spelling, "chili" (chilies), and the Spanish *chile (chiles)* are used by some for the fruits of the *Capsicum* plant, but chili is also used as a short form of *chili con carne,* a variously concocted mixture of meat and chillies. The *Oxford English Dictionary* designates "chilli" (after the Nahuatl) as the primary usage, calling the Spanish *chile* and the English chili both variants. *Webster's New International Dictionary,* however, prefers "chili" followed by the Spanish *chile* and the Nahuatl *chilli.* But "chilli" is the term most often used by English-speaking people outside the United States, and it is the spelling preferred by the International Board for Plant Genetic Resources (IBPGR) of the Food and Agriculture Organization of the United Nations (FAO).

Origin

It is difficult to determine exactly where the genus *Capsicum* originated because the nature of that genus is still not fully understood (Eshbaugh 1980). If the genus remains limited to taxa producing the pungent capsaicin, then the center of diversity occurs in an area from Bolivia to southwestern Brazil. But if the genus includes nonpungent taxa, a second center of diversity would center in Mesoamerica. Nonetheless, it is certain that the ancestor of all of the domesticates originated in tropical South America.

There are definite indications that *Capsicum*

annuum originally was domesticated in Mesoamerica and *Capsicum chinense* in tropical northern Amazonia. *Capsicum pubescens* and *C. baccatum* seem to be more commonplace in the Andean and central regions of South America. Thus, the first two species were those encountered by the first Europeans, whereas the other two species were not found until later and are just now becoming known outside their South American home.

Diagnostic Descriptions

The genus *Capsicum* is of the family Solanaceae, which includes such plants as the potato, tomato, eggplant, petunia, and tobacco. The genus was first described in 1700, but that description has become so outdated as to be worthless. The taxonomy of the genus *Capsicum* is in a state of transition, and the taxa finally included may change if the description is expanded to encompass taxa with common traits but nonpungent fruits (Eshbaugh, personal communication).

Currently, the genus consists of at least 20 species, many of which are consumed by humans. Four of the species have been domesticated and two others are extensively cultivated. It is those six species, belonging to three separate genetic lineages, that are of concern to human nutrition.

Capsicum pubescens Ruiz and Pavón
The domesticated *C. pubescens* is the most distinctive species in the genus. The flowers have comparatively large purple or white (infused with purple) corollas that are solitary and erect at each node. Those blossoms, along with the wavy, dark brownish black seeds, are unique among the capsicums. This extremely pungent chilli was domesticated in the Andean region of South America, where it is commonly called *rocoto,* and it is still practically unknown in other parts of the world because it requires cool but frost-free growing conditions and a long growing season at relatively high elevations. Its many varieties include none that are sweet. The fleshy nature of the fruit causes rapid deterioration when mature, and, consequently, it neither travels nor stores well.

Capsicum baccatum var. pendulum (Willdenow) Eshbaugh
Capsicum baccatum var. *pendulum* is recognized by a flower with a cream-colored corolla marked with greenish-gold blotches near the base of each petal and anthers that are whitish-yellow to brown. It is solitary at each node. Although it is quite variable, the typical fruit is elongate with cream-colored seeds. It is indigenous to the lowlands and mid-elevations of Bolivia and neighboring areas. In much of South America, where all pungent peppers are called *ají, C. baccatum* is the "Andean *ají*" (Ruskin 1990: 197). Until recently, it has been little known outside South America. It is only in this species and the common annual

pepper that nonpungent cultivars are known (Ruskin 1990: 198).

Capsicum annuum var. annuum Linné
The flowers of *C.* var. *annuum* are solitary at each node (occasionally two or more). The corolla is milky white and the anthers are purple. The variform fruit usually has firm flesh and straw-colored seeds. The pungent and nonpungent cultivars of this Mesoamerican domesticate now dominate the commercial pepper market throughout the world. A relationship between *C. annuum, C. chinense,* and *Capsicum frutescens* has caused the three to be known as the "*C. annuum* complex." This relationship, however, creates a taxonomic predicament, because some authorities still recognize the first two as distinct but have difficulty determining where *C. frutescens* fits into the picture.

Capsicum annum var. glabrisculum
Capsicum annum var. *glabrisculum* is a semiwild species known as bird pepper. This highly variable, tiny, erect, usually red pepper is cultivated commercially in the area around Sonora, Mexico, and seems to be in the process of domestication. It has a distinct flavor and high pungency and is avidly consumed throughout its natural range, which extends through the southernmost parts of the United States to Colombia. Birds are also keen consumers. These chillies, which have many vernacular names and almost as many synonyms (*Capsicum aviculare* is the most common), sell for 10 times the price of cultivated green bell peppers.

Capsicum chinense Jacquin
There are two or more small, white-to-greenish-white flowers with purple anthers per node of *C. chinense,* often hanging in clusters. The fruit is variform, with cream-colored seeds that tend to require a longer germination period than *C. annuum. C. chinense* was domesticated in the lowland jungle of the western Amazon River basin and was carried to the islands of the Caribbean before 1492. It has diffused throughout the world but to a much lesser degree than *C. annuum,* probably because it does not store or dry well. Nonetheless, it is becoming ever more widely appreciated by cooks and gardeners for its pungency, aroma, and unique flavor, and ever more important in medical, pharmaceutical, and food-industry applications because of its high capsaicin content. Although this morphologically distinct pepper is still considered to be a part of the *C. annuum* complex, there are those who question its position in the genus on genetic grounds.

Capsicum frutescens Linné
Some authors no longer list the semiwild *C. frutescens* as a sustainable species. Although it was once considered to be a member of the *C. annuum* com-

plex, which included three white-flowered species thought to have a mutual ancestor, scholars now have considerable doubt as to the position of the first two in the genus. The small greenish-white flowers of *C. frutescens* have purple anthers. The small fruit with cream-colored seed is always erect, never sweet, and two or more occur at each node. The tabasco pepper is the only variety of this species known to have been cultivated commercially, and this activity has been limited to the Western Hemisphere.

Geographic Distribution

Following the arrival of the Europeans in the Western Hemisphere, the tropical perennial capsicum spread rapidly. It quickly became pantropic and the dominant spice and condiment in the tropical and subtropical areas of the world. In addition, it is an important green vegetable throughout the temperate regions, where it is grown as an annual. Concentrated breeding studies are producing *Capsicum* varieties that can be cultivated in environments quite different from the tropical home of the original.

Biology

Nutritional Considerations

Capsicums have a lot to recommend them nutritionally. By weight, they contain more vitamin A than any other food plant, and they are also a good source of the B vitamins. When eaten raw, capsicums are superior to citrus in providing vitamin C, although their production of vitamin C diminishes with maturity and drying and (as in all plant foods) is destroyed by exposure to oxygen. By contrast, vitamin A increases as peppers mature and dry and is not affected by exposure to oxygen.

Capsicums also contain significant amounts of magnesium and iron. Chillies, of course, are not eaten in large quantities, but even small amounts are important in cases where traditional diets provide only marginal supplies of vitamins and minerals.

The Pungent Principle

A unique group of mouth-warming, amide-type alkaloids, containing a small vanilloid structural component, is responsible for the burning sensation associated with capsicums by acting directly on the pain receptors in the mouth and throat. This vanilloid element is present in other pungent plants used for spices, like ginger and black pepper. Birds and certain other creatures, such as snails and frogs, do not have specific neuroreceptors for pungent vanilloid compounds as do humans and other mammals; consequently, their contact with capsaicinoids has no adverse effects (Nabhan 1985).

The vanillyl amide compounds or capsaicinoids (abbreviated CAPS) in *Capsicum* are predominantly (about 69 percent) capsaicin (C). Dihydrodcapsaicin (DHC) (22 percent), nordihydrocapsaicin (NDHC) (7 percent), homocapsaicin (HC) (1 percent), and homodihydrocapsaicin (HDHC) (1 percent) account for most of the remainder (Masada et al. 1971; Trease and Evans 1983). The primary heat contributors are C and DHC, but the delayed action of HDHC is the most irritating and difficult to quell (Mathew et al. 1971).

Three of these capsaicinoid components cause the sensation of "rapid bite" at the back of the palate and throat, and two others cause a long, low-intensity bite on the tongue and the middle palate. Differences in the proportions of these compounds may account for the characteristic "burns" of the different types of capsicum cultivars (McGee 1984: 12; Govindarajan 1986).

In both sweet and pungent capsicums, the major part of the organs secreting these pungent alkaloids is localized in the placenta, to which the seeds are attached, along with dissepiment (veins or cross walls) (Heiser and Smith 1953). The seeds contain only a low concentration of CAPS. The capsaicin content is influenced by the growing conditions of the plant and the age of the fruit and is possibly variety-specific (Govindarajan 1986: 336–8). Dry, stressful conditions will increase the amount of CAPS. Beginning about the eleventh day of fruit development, the CAPS content increases, becoming detectable when the fruit is about four weeks old. It reaches its peak just before maturity, then drops somewhat in the ripening stage (Govindarajan 1985). Sun-drying generally reduces the CAPS content, whereas the highest retention of CAPS is obtained when the fruits are air-dried with minimum exposure to sunlight.

Capsaicin is hard to detect by chemical tests. It has virtually no odor or flavor, but a drop of a solution containing one part in 100,000 causes a persistent burning on the tongue (Nelson 1910). The original Scoville Organoleptic Test has largely been replaced by the use of high-pressure liquid chromatography (HPLC), a highly reproducible technique for quantifying capsaicinoids in capsicum products. However, the results apply solely to the fruit tested, and therefore they are considered only as a general guide (Todd, Bensinger, and Biftu 1977). Capsaicin is eight times more pungent than the piperine in black pepper. But unlike black pepper, which inhibits all tastes, CAPS obstructs only the perception of sour and bitter; it does not impair the discernment of other gustatory characteristics of food.

Capsaicin activates the defensive and digestive systems by acting as an irritant to the oral and gastrointestinal membranes (Viranuvatti et al. 1972). That irritation increases the flow of saliva and gastric acids and also stimulates the appetite. These functions work together to aid the digestion of food. The increased saliva helps ease the passage of food through the mouth to the stomach, where it is mixed with the activated gastric juice (Solanke 1973). Ingesting CAPS also causes the neck, face, and front of the chest to sweat in a reflexive response to the burning in the mouth (Lee 1954). Very little CAPS is absorbed as it passes through the digestive tract (Diehl and Bauer 1978).

Capsaicin is not water soluble, but the addition of a small amount of chlorine or ammonia will ionize the CAPS compound, changing it into a soluble salt (Andrews 1984: 127) that can be used to rinse CAPS from the skin. Like many organic compounds, CAPS is soluble in alcohol. Oral burning can be relieved by lipoproteins, such as casein, that remove CAPS by breaking the bond it has formed with the pain receptors in the mouth (Henkin 1991). Milk and yoghurt are the most readily available sources of the casein. Because casein, and not fat, removes capsaicin, butter and cheese will not have the same effect as milk.

Studies of CAPS and its relationship to substance P, a neuropeptide that sends the message of pain to our brains, have led investigators to conclude that CAPS has the capacity to deplete nerves of their supply of substance P, thereby preventing the transmission of such messages (Rozin 1990).

Consequently, CAPS is now used to treat the pain associated with shingles, rheumatoid arthritis, and "phantom-limb" pain. It may prove to be a non-addictive alternative to the habit-forming drugs used to control pain from other causes. It does not act on other sensory receptors, such as those for taste and smell, but is specific to pain receptors. Such specificity is becoming a valuable aid to medical research.

Aroma, Flavor, and Color

The flavor compound of capsicums is located in the outer wall of the fruit (pericarp): Very little is found in the placenta and cross wall and essentially none in the seeds (Figure II.C.4.1). Color and flavor go hand in hand because the flavoring principle appears to be associated with the carotenoid pigment: Strong color and strong flavor are linked. *Capsicum pubescens* (*rocoto*) and the varieties of *C. chinense* are more aromatic and have a decidedly different flavor from those of *C. annuum* var. *annuum*. The carotenoid pigments responsible for the color in capsicums make peppers commercially important worldwide as natural dyes in food and drug products. Red capsanthin is the most important pigment. All capsicums will change color from green to other hues – red, brown, yellow, orange, purple, and ripe green – as they mature.

Taste and smell are separate perceptions. Several aroma compounds produce the fragrance. The taste buds on the tongue can discern certain flavors at dilutions up to one part in two million, but odors can be detected at a dilution of one part in one billion. The more delicate flavors of foods are recognized as aromas in the nasal cavity adjacent to the mouth.

Cultivation Requirements

Peppers are best transplanted and not planted directly into the soil outdoors. The seeds should be started in greenhouse benches, flats, or hotbeds at

Figure II.C.4.1. Cross-section of a pepper. (Adapted from Andrews 1995.)

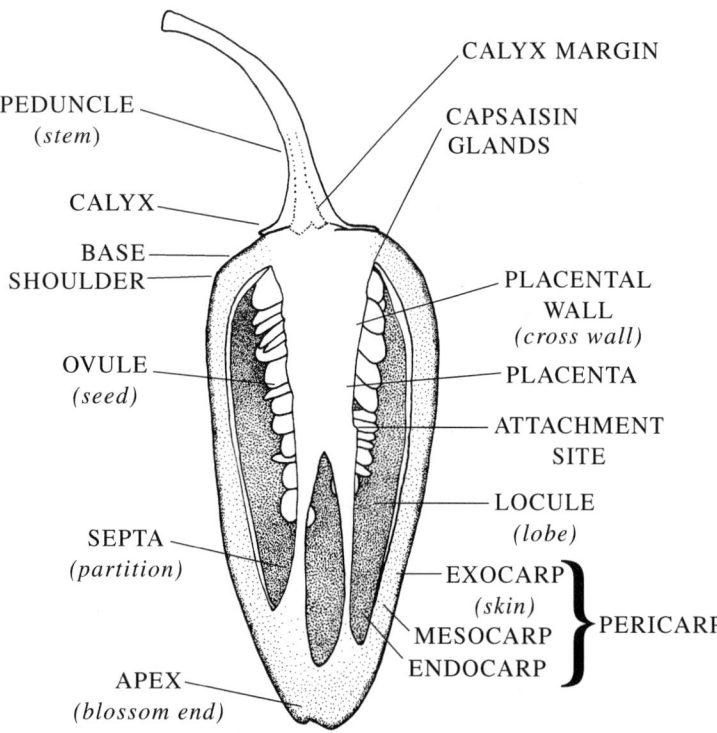

least six weeks before the first frost-free date. They ought to be sown as thinly as possible on a sterile medium and covered no deeper than the thickness of the seed. It is best to water them from the top, with care taken to not dislodge the seed. The seed or seedlings should never be permitted to dry or wilt from the time they are sown until they are transplanted and well started. Germination will require 12 to 21 days at a constant temperature of 21° C for *C. annuum* var. *annuum,* and longer for the other species.

When the true leaves are well formed, one may transplant the seedlings into containers or flats, containing equal parts peat, sand, and loam, and grow them at 21° C. After the plants attain a height of 12 to 15 centimeters (cm), and all danger of frost is past, they can be planted (deeply) in friable soil that is not below 13° C. The plants should be spaced 30 cm apart in rows 38 to 76 cm apart. Peppers require full sun and well-drained soil. They are warm-season plants that do better in a moderate climate, with the optimum temperature for good yields between 18.5° C and 26.5° C during fruit setting (Andrews 1984).

Economic and Other Uses

Perhaps no other cultivated economic plants have fruits with so many shapes, colors, and uses over such a widespread area of the earth as do those belonging to the genus *Capsicum.*

Before World War II, capsicums were eaten daily by one-fourth of the world's population, primarily in the pantropical belt and Korea. Since that time, their consumption as a condiment, spice, and vegetable has continued to increase annually and is no longer limited to the tropical and subtropical areas. Some of the more common food products made with chillies are curry powder, cayenne pepper, crushed red pepper, dried whole peppers, chili powder, paprika, pepper sauce, pickled and processed peppers, pimento, and salsa picante. In 1992, the monetary value of sales of salsa picante, a bottled sauce of Mexican origin made with chillies, onions, and tomatoes, overtook that of tomato catsup in the United States.

However, the use of capsicums goes beyond that of food. The florist and landscape industries have discovered the ornamental qualities of pepper plants to be of considerable value, and designers of tableware, home decorations, fabrics, and paper goods find them to be a popular decorative motif. The medical profession has discovered that certain folk-medicine practices employing chillies, some of which are prehistoric in origin, have merit. Capsaicin, the pungent alkaloid unique to capsicums, is being utilized in modern medicine to treat pain, respiratory disorders, shingles, toothache, and arthritis, and research into the properties of capsaicinoids continues.

Jean Andrews

Bibliography

Andrews, J. 1993a. Diffusion of the Mesoamerican food complex to southeastern Europe. *Geographical Review* 83: 194-204.
  1993b. *Red hot peppers.* New York.
  [1984] 1995. *Peppers: The domesticated capsicums.* Austin, Tex.
Anghiera, P. M. d'. 1964. *Decadas del Nuevo Mundo, por Pedro Martir de Angleria, primer cronista de Indias.* Mexico City.
Boxer, C. R. 1969a. *Four centuries of Portuguese expansion: 1415-1825.* Berkeley, Calif.
  1969b. *The Portuguese seaborne empire, 1415-1825.* London.
  1984. *From Lisbon to Goa 1500-1750. Studies in Portuguese maritime enterprise.* London.
  1985. *Portuguese conquest and commerce in southern Asia 1500-1750.* London.
Braudel, F. 1976. *The Mediterranean and the Mediterranean world in the age of Philip II.* 2 vols. New York.
Candolle, A. P. de. 1852. Essai. *Prodromous* 13: 411-29. Paris.
Columbus, C. 1971. *Journal of first voyage to America by Christopher Columbus.* Freeport, N.Y.
Diehl, A. K., and R. L. Bauer. 1978. Jaloproctitis. *New England Journal of Medicine* 229: 1137-8.
Eshbaugh, W. H. 1968. A nomenclatural note on the genus *Capsicum. Taxon* 17: 51-2.
  1980. The taxonomy of the genus *Capsicum* (Solanaceae). *Phytologia* 47: 153-66.
  1983. The genus *Capsicum* (Solanaceae) in Africa. *Bothalia* 14: 845-8.
  1993. Peppers: History and exploitation of a serendipitous new crop. In *Advances in new crops,* ed. J. J. Janick and J. E. Simon. New York.
Eshbaugh, W. H., S. I. Guttman, and M. J. McLeod. 1983. The origin and evolution of domesticated *Capsicum* species. *Journal of Ethnobiology* 3: 49-54.
Fuchs, L. 1543. *New Kreuterbuch (De historia stirpium in 1542).* Basel.
Govindarajan, V. S. 1985. *Capsicum:* Production, technology, chemistry and quality. History, botany, cultivation and primary processing. *Critical Review of Food Science and Nutrition* 22: 108-75.
  1986. *Capsicum:* Production, technology, chemistry and quality. Chemistry of the color, aroma, and pungency stimuli. *Critical Review of Food Science and Nutrition* 24: 244-355.
Halasz, Z. 1963. *Hungarian paprika through the ages.* Budapest.
Heiser, C. B., Jr. 1969. *Nightshades: The paradoxical plants.* San Francisco, Calif.
  1976. Peppers: *Capsicum* (Solanaceae). In *Evolution of crop plants,* ed. N. W. Simmonds, 265-8. London.
  1985. *Of plants and man.* Norman, Okla.
Heiser, C. B., Jr., and B. Pickersgill. 1975. Names for the bird peppers (*Capsicum* - Solanaceae). *Baileya* 19: 151-6.
Heiser, C. B., Jr., and P. G. Smith. 1953. The cultivated *Capsicum* peppers. *Economic Botany* 7: 214-27.
Henkin, R. 1991. Cooling the burn from hot peppers. *Journal of the American Medical Association* 266: 2766.
Ho, P. T. 1955. The introduction of American food plants into China. *American Anthropologist* 55: 191-201.
Jacquin, N. J. 1776. *Hortus botanicus vindoboncensis.* 3 vols. Vienna.
Jeffreys, M. D. W. 1975. Pre-Columbian maize in the Old

World: An examination of Portuguese sources. In *Gastronomy: The anthropology of food and food habits,* ed. M. L. Arnott, 23–66. The Hague.

Laufer, B. 1929. The American plant migration. *The Scientific Monthly* 28: 235–51.

Lee, T. S. 1954. Physiological gustatory sweating in a warm climate. *Journal of Physiology* 124: 528–42.

L'Escluse, C. 1611. *Curae posteriores post mortem.* Antwerp.

Linnaeus, C. 1753a. *Hortus cliffortianus.* Amsterdam.

1753b. *Species plantarum.* Stockholm.

L'obel, M. 1576. *Plantarum sev stirpium historia.* Antwerp.

MacNeish, R. S. 1967. A summary of the subsistence. In *The prehistory of the Tehuacan Valley.* Vol. 1, *Environment and subsistence,* ed. D. S. Byres, 290–309. Austin, Tex.

Maga, J. A. 1975. *Capsicum.* In *Critical revisions in food science and nutrition,* 177–99. Cleveland.

Masada, Y., K. Hashimoto, T. Inoue, and M. Suzui. 1971. Analysis of the pungent principles of *Capsicum annuum* by combined gas chromatography. *Journal of Food Science* 36: 858.

Mathew, A. G., Y. S. Lewis, N. Kirishnamurthy, and E. S. Nambudiri. 1971. Capsaicin. *The Flavor Industry* 2: 691–5.

McGee, H. 1984. *On food and cooking: The science and lore of the kitchen.* New York.

McLeod, M. J. S., S. I. Guttman, and W. H. Eshbaugh. 1982. Early evolution of chili peppers *(Capsicum). Economic Botany* 36: 361–8.

Means, P. A. 1935. *The Spanish Main: Focus on envy 1492–1700.* New York.

Morison, S. E. 1963. *The journals and other documents of the life of Christopher Columbus.* New York.

Nabhan, G. P. 1985. *Gathering the desert.* Tucson.

Nelson, E. K. 1910. Capsaicin, the pungent principle of *Capsicum,* and the detection of capsaicin. *Journal of Industrial and Engineering Chemistry* 2: 419–21.

Oviedo y Valdés, G. F. de. [1557] 1950. *Sumario de la natural historia de las Indias,* ed. José Miranda. Mexico City.

Pickersgill, B. 1984. Migrations of chili peppers, *Capsicum* spp., in the Americas. In *Pre-Columbian plant migration,* ed. Doris Stone, 106–23. Cambridge, Mass.

Proctor, V. W. 1968. Long-distance dispersal of seeds by retention in digestive tract of birds. *Science* 160: 321–2.

Purseglove, J. W. 1968. Some problems of the origin and distribution of tropical crops. *Genetics Agraria* 17: 105–22.

Ridley, H. N. 1930. *The dispersal of plants through the world.* Ashford, England.

Rozin, P. 1990. Getting to like the burn of chili pepper. In *Chemical senses,* ed B. G. Green, J. R. Mason, and M. R. Kare, 231–69. New York.

Ruskin, F. R., ed. 1990. *Lost crops of the Incas: Little-known plants of the Andes with promise for worldwide cultivation.* Washington, D.C.

Ruiz, H., and J. Pavon. [1797] 1965. *Flora peruviana et chilensis.* 4 vols. Lehrey, N.Y.

Sauer, C. O. 1966. *The early Spanish Main.* Berkeley, Calif.

Schurz, W. L. 1939. *The Manila galleon.* New York.

Smith, P. G., and C. B. Heiser, Jr. 1951. Taxonomic and genetic studies on the cultivated peppers *C. annuum* L. and *C. frutescens* L. *American Journal of Botany* 38: 367–8.

1957. Taxonomy of *Capsicum sinense* Jacq. and the geographic distribution of the cultivated *Capsicum* species. *Bulletin of the Torrey Botanical Club* 84: 413–20.

Solanke, T. F. 1973. The effect of red pepper *(Capsicum frutescens)* on gastric acid secretion. *Journal of Surgical Research* 15: 385–90.

Todd, P. H., Jr., M. C. Bensinger, and T. Biftu. 1977. Determination of pungency due to *Capsicum* by gas-liquid chromatography. *Journal of Food Science* 42: 660–5.

Trease, G. E., and P. W. C. Evans. 1983. Drugs of biological origin. In *Pharmacognosy.* Twelfth edition, ed. G. E. Trease and P. W. C. Evans, 374–6. London.

Turner, W. [1538] 1965. *Libellus de re herbaria.* London.

Viranuvatti, V., C. Kalayasiri, O. Chearani, and U. Plengvanit. 1972. Effects of *Capsicum* solution on human gastric mucosa as observed gastroscopically. *American Journal of Clinical Nutrition* 5: 225–32.

Watt, G. [1889] 1972. *A dictionary of the economic products of India.* Delhi.

Watts, D. 1987. *The West Indies: Patterns of development, culture and environmental change since 1492.* Cambridge and New York.

Willdenow, C. L. 1808. *Enumeratio plantarum horti regii botanici beroliensis.* 2 vols. Germany.

II.C.5 Cruciferous and Green Leafy Vegetables

Cruciferae (Brassicaceae), in the mustard family of the caper order (Capparales), are found on all continents except Antarctica. The cruciferae, so named because of the uniform, four-petaled flowers suggestive of a Greek cross, are an example of a natural family and demonstrate a large amount of diversity. Although most are weeds, the family includes significant food crop plants such as broccoli, cabbage, turnip, and radish. Cruciferae are most abundant in areas north of the equator and exhibit greatest variety in temperate and arid regions. The Mediterranean region is generally considered the site of the family's origination. Nonetheless, many of these cultigens appear to be native to northern Europe, and Reed C. Rollins (1993: 1) contends that the Irano–Turanian region of Eastern Europe and western Asia was the birthplace of at least some members of this plant family. A precise number of species and genera of the cruciferae is undetermined, although estimates range from 340 to 400 genera and 3,000 to 3,500 species (Vaughan, Macleod, and Jones 1976: vii; Rollins 1993: 2).

Taxonomy

The classification of cruciferae presents a challenge because of the large number of members and their unusually homogeneous nature (Hedge and Rechinger 1968: 1). But basic characteristics, both macroscopic and microscopic, mark the family as a whole. Typically the radial flower is characterized by the uniformity of its structure. This already mentioned flower type, four petals in the shape of a Greek cross,

Cabbage

is common to a large majority of this family's species. However, this pattern is altered by deviations, particularly in the structure of the stamen, flowers, and calyx. This is true of genera such as *Romanschulzia, Stanleya,* and *Warea,* and some species of *Streptanthus, Lepidium,* and *Megacarpaea* (Hedge and Rechinger 1968: 1–2; Rollins 1993: 2).

The fruits of the cruciferae, like the floral construction, are fundamentally homogeneous but can demonstrate significant variation in morphology. They play a key role in classification, along with developmental aspects of the plants, such as lifespan, floral maturation, seed germination, and possibly variations in sepal or petal formations (Hedge and Rechinger 1968: 1–2; Rollins 1993: 3).

In addition to a wide variety of macroscopic characteristics, several microscopic features may help identify the cruciferae group, such as the cell shape and configurations, as well as seed mucus (Hedge and Rechinger 1968: 2). A survey of the cruciferae group reveals one of the widest ranges of taxonomic characteristics among plant families, encompassing about 20 usable traits, sometimes existing in six or more states. Because of this high number of features, it is not unusual for authorities to emphasize different characteristics, resulting in, at times, a rather varied system of classification (Hedge and Rechinger 1968: 2).

The focus of this chapter is only on those genera and species associated with food or food products. Most of these species fall within *Brassica,* the best-known genus. Its 35 to 50 species and numerous varieties originated primarily in Europe, the Mediterranean, and Eurasia and include *Brassica oleracea* (cabbage, kale and collards, broccoli, cauliflower, Brussels sprouts, and kohlrabi, also known as *Brassica caulorapa*); *Brassica pekinensis* (Chinese cabbage); *Brassica nigra* (black mustard, also known as *Sinapis nigra*); *Brassica alba* (table mustard, also known as *Sinapis alba*); *Brassica juncea* (leaf mustard, also known as *Sinapis juncea*); *Brassica napobrassica* (rutabaga); and *Brassica rapa* or *Brassica campestris* (turnips). There are, however, other significant food-producing members of this family, such as *Raphanus sativus* (radish) and *Nasturtium officianale* (watercress).

Cruciferae as a Cultivated Food Source

In Europe wild ancestors of the turnip and radish were gathered in prehistoric times, and most of these vegetables have been cultivated and used since the earliest days of recorded history. They are discussed extensively by classical Greek scholars like Theophrastus, and Roman writers, including Marcus Porcius Cato and Lucius Junius Moderatus Columella, as well as in chronicles of food and daily life in medieval and Renaissance Europe, such as *The Four Seasons of the House of Cerruti* (Spencer 1984). This book, compiled in the late 1300s, is based on the manuscript of an eleventh-century Arab physician living in northern Italy. The work describes the foods, drinks, and spices common in that region, along with practices considered good for health. Many cruciferous vegetables were grown during medieval and early modern times in the kitchen gardens of Europe, and particularly Britain, to be eaten in stews and salads.

Brussels sprouts

Then cabbage and its varieties were frequently referred to as "cole" or "coleworts," hence the name "coleslaw" for the popular side dish made with shredded cabbage. In Russia, cabbage, and to a lesser extent, turnips and radishes were important food crops. Along with radishes, a large number of *Brassica* varieties are found in China, where they have been used for centuries. Today, as in earlier periods, the durable and hardy plants of the Cruciferae family continue to play an important part in diets around the globe, and one that seems to increase in importance as more is learned of their nutritional and disease-preventive nature.

Cabbage and Its Varieties

Brassica oleracea includes some of the most significant vegetables used today, such as broccoli, cauliflower, Brussels sprouts, and of course, countless cabbages. With the exception of Brussels sprouts and kohlrabi, cabbage and its varieties have probably been cultivated since before recorded history (Toussaint-Samat 1992: 690). Wild cabbage, the early form of *B. oleracea,* was a small plant also known as "sea cabbage." Its leaves were firm and fleshy, fortified by mineral salts from the seawater it grew near, and even today *B. oleracea* can be found growing wild along the coasts of the English Channel.

Although there are approximately 400 species of cabbage, they can be divided into five groups. The first includes the familiar round, smooth-leafed cabbages that may be white, green, or red, as well as wrinkled-leafed varieties like Savoy. The second group comprises pointed cabbages like European spring and Chinese cabbages. A third category consists of cabbages with abnormally large, budding stems, as for example, Brussels sprouts. Green curly types such as kale represent a fourth group. These are used especially for animal food or for decoration of dishes for presentation, although kale is also featured in some famous soups, and collard greens make frequent appearances on many tables. The last category is made up of flowering cabbages such as cauliflower and broccoli (Toussaint-Samat 1992: 693).

Cabbage. Cabbage is the most durable and successful variety of *B. oleracea*. It is a versatile plant that can be found growing in almost every climate in the world, ranging from subarctic to semitropical. Such an ability to adapt to a wide variety of climatic conditions has enabled the vegetable to survive since prehistoric times. Although initially grown for its oily seeds, cabbage began to be used as a vegetable after people discovered that its green leaves were edible raw or cooked. Its consumption was confined to Asia and to Europe, however, as Neolithic Near Eastern peoples, Hebrews, and Egyptians did not use the plant.

In ancient Greece the writer Theophrastus noted three types of cabbage: curly-leafed, smooth-leafed, and wild. While comparing the curly-leafed and the smooth-leafed varieties he observed that one bore either inferior seeds or none whatsoever. Unfortunately, he did not identify the one to which he referred, but he did say that the curly-leafed kind had better flavor and larger leaves than the smooth-leafed variety. Theophrastus described wild cabbage as having small round leaves with many branches and leaves. The plant had a strong medicinal taste and was used by physicians to ease or cure stomach problems (Theophrastus 1977, 2: 85).

The Roman agronomist Cato the Elder (234-149 B.C.) also noted the medicinal value of cabbage, which, he contended, "surpasses [that of] all other vegetables." Whether eaten cooked or raw, cabbage was believed beneficial to digestion and to be an excellent laxative. Acknowledging the same three types of cabbage identified by Theophrastus, Cato agreed that the wild variety held the best medicinal value and wrote that it could be used as a poultice for all types of wounds, sores, or swellings. In addition, he advised "in case of deafness, macerate cabbage with wine, press out the juice, and instil warm into the ear, and you will soon know that your hearing is improved" (Cato 1954: 151, see also 141, 145). Both the Greeks and Romans believed that eating cabbage during a banquet would prevent drunkenness, and it has been pointed out that "the B vitamins contained in cabbage leaves do seem to have soothing and oxygenating qualities, very welcome when the mind is clouded by the fumes of alcohol. Research at a Texan *[sic]* university extracted a substance from cabbage which is useful in the treatment of alcoholism" (Toussaint-Samat 1992: 691).

In addition, cabbage was apparently inimical to fruits that could provide alcohol. Greek and Roman writers noted that cabbage was "hostile" to grapevines used for making wine. This is thought to be true even today: "Mediterranean farmers never plant it near vineyards in case bees transfer its odour to the bunches of grapes. Nor is it grown near beehives, because it might taint the flavour of the honey" (Toussaint-Samat 1992: 691).

Don Brothwell and Patricia Brothwell (1969) have written that the Romans favored two cabbage varieties known as *cymae* and *cauliculi* and pointed out that some scholars have mistaken *cauliculi* for Brussels sprouts when it was actually cabbage shoots or cabbage asparagus. *Cymae* is usually interpreted as sprouting broccoli and was apparently affordable only by the wealthier elements of Roman society. Moreover, by the time of Julius Caesar (100-44 B.C.), the Romans had enlarged cabbage, lavishing such attention on it and cultivating it to such a size that the poor of Rome could not afford to buy it (Toussaint-Samat 1992: 692). This interest in cabbage by the wealthy was apparently new because the vegetable had seldom been mentioned since the work of Cato, suggesting dietary distinctions between wealthier and poorer Romans that limited the consumption of ordinary cabbage to the latter. According to Brothwell and Brothwell (1969: 118), "this is borne out by Juvenal's satire describing the differences between the food of the patron and that of his poor client – the patron has olives to garnish his excellent fish, the client finds cabbage in his 'nauseous dish.'"

Although the Romans introduced garden varieties of cabbage to northern Europe and Britain, it was not an entirely new food plant in these regions. On the basis of linguistic evidence, Anne C. Wilson (1974: 195) has pointed out that wild cabbage was used as a food source by Iron Age Celts living along the Atlantic coast of Europe prior to their migration to the British Isles. When the Romans did introduce their garden varieties of cabbage, she suggested the Celts favored an open-headed variety because of its similarity to this wild cabbage. However, due to the constant threat of famine during this era, the Celts continued to depend on the hardier wild variety as a safeguard against starvation (Wilson 1974: 196–7).

The fourteenth-century book *The Four Seasons,* mentioned previously, indicates that cabbage continued to enjoy a reputation for medicinal value in Renaissance Italy, although the work mentions some sources that thought cabbage bad for the blood and found its only redeeming quality to be its ability to "clear obstructions," of what kind we are left to wonder. On a less obscure note, cabbage was believed able to "restore a lost voice," and if its juice was cooked with honey and used sparingly as eyedrops it was believed to improve vision (Spencer 1984: 102).

Carroll L. Fenton and Herminie B. Kitchen (1956) divided cultivated cabbage into two main types – the hard-headed and the loose-headed, or Savoy cabbage. It is most likely that loose-headed cabbage evolved directly from wild cabbage found near the Mediterranean and Atlantic coasts of Europe. Its ridged leaves form a head at the top of a very short stalk. By contrast, hard-headed cabbage leaves are wound tightly around each other and around the stalk or "heart." It is believed that hard-headed cabbage developed in northern Europe. Because it does not grow well in warm climates, the Greeks and Romans did not cultivate it. Thus, it was probably developed by the Celts and has been cultivated by the Germans since ancient times. By the 1300s, hard-headed cabbage was common in England, and British soldiers introduced it in Scotland before 1650 (Fenton and Kitchen 1956: 74; Toussaint-Samat 1992: 692).

At first cabbage was an important crop in individual family plots known as kitchen gardens, but by the eighteenth century in England the cultivation of cabbage, along with many other vegetables, had expanded beyond kitchen gardens to the fields (Wilson 1974: 329; Braudel 1981, 1: 170). As early as 1540, Jacques Cartier grew hard-headed cabbages in Canada, and Native Americans used his seeds to plant cabbages along with beans, squash, and corn (Fenton and Kitchen 1956: 74).

In the nineteenth and twentieth centuries the Russians have been among the world's most important consumers of hard-headed cabbage – an item of diet that has been a fundamental part of Russian cuisine for many centuries. It has been especially enjoyed pickled or prepared as cabbage soup called *shchii.* Usually flavored with meat fat or small chunks of meat, this soup consists of chopped cabbage, barley meal, salt, and a touch of *kvass* (Smith and Christian 1984: 252, 275–6).

Collards and kale. Collards (collard greens) and kale are varieties of *B. oleracea* that do not form heads. In fact, kale is very similar to sea cabbage (Fenton and Kitchen 1956: 72), and the primary difference between collard greens, a type of kale, and kale itself is leaf shape. Kale has a short, thick stalk and crinkly blue-green leaves that grow on leaf-stems, whereas collard greens have smooth, broad, yellowish green leaves (Fenton and Kitchen 1956: 72). Although the precise area of origin of collards and kale is unknown, it was most likely in Asia Minor or in the Mediterranean region, where both have been cultivated since prehistoric times. The Greeks and Romans grew several varieties of both kale and collard greens at least 2,200 years ago, followed about 200 years later by Germans and Saxons in northern Europe. They, or quite possibly the Romans, brought these plants to France and Great Britain. For nearly a thousand years kale and collards were the main winter vegetables in England. European colonists carried the seeds to the Americas. Kale and collards were cultivated in western Hispaniola before 1565, and by colonists in Virginia by at least 1669.

Most collards are similar in appearance, but kale has many varieties, some short and some very tall, such as a type of kale grown in England that reaches 8 or 9 feet in height. Today in the United States collards are grown predominantly in the South. An old and popular variety, 'Georgia collards', is characterized by stems 2 to 4 feet high, with leaves growing only at the top. Others include the 'Blue Stem', 'Green Glaze', 'Louisiana', and 'Vates Non-Heading'. Kale's principal types are 'Scotch', 'Blue', and 'Siberian' (Fenton and Kitchen 1956: 72–4; Carcione and Lucas 1972: 63–4).

Broccoli and cauliflower. Although well known today, broccoli and cauliflower are varieties of *B. oleracea* that are rarely mentioned in historical sources, despite being two of the oldest cultivated cabbage varieties. This may be because they were not well differentiated in those sources from the more recognizable cabbage. Jane O'Hara-May (1977: 251) has noted that in Elizabethan England the term "cabbage" referred to "the compact heart or head of the plant," whereas the entire plant was known as cabbage-cole or cole-wort, a term applied to all varieties of cabbage.

Both broccoli and cauliflower, also called varieties of colewort, were cultivated "over 2,500 years ago in Italy or on the island of Cyprus" (Fenton and Kitchen 1956: 76), and broccoli, at least, was a part of Greek and Roman diets more than 2,000 years ago, although apparently it did not reach England until after 1700. When broccoli was introduced, in all likelihood it came from Italy because the English called it "Italian asparagus." In North America, broccoli was referred to in an 1806 book on gardening and grown regularly by Italian immigrants in private plots, but it was largely unknown to the public until the 1920s. It was because of effective marketing on the part of the D'Arrigo Brothers Company, which grew the vegetable, that demand for broccoli skyrocketed in the early 1930s, and it became "an established crop and an accepted part of the American diet" (Fenton and Kitchen 1956: 76; Carcione and Lucas 1972: 23). Today a major variety of broccoli is the 'Italian Green' or 'Calabrese', named after the Italian province of Calabria. Its large central head consists of bluish-green flower buds, called curds. 'De Cicco' is another popular variety that resembles the Calabrese but is lighter green in color. Chinese broccoli, also known as *Gai Lon,* "is more leaf than flower." It is light green in color, with small flower buds and large leaves on a long shank (Carcione and Lucas 1972: 23).

Through selective cultivation of sprouting broccoli, gardeners of long ago were able to produce ever larger clusters that were lighter in color and eventually became cauliflower broccoli and cauliflower. In ancient Greece cauliflower was popular, but after that its popularity declined in the West, where it was little used until the era of Louis XIV (Toussaint-Samat 1992: 691). The vegetable reached England toward the end of the Elizabethan era as part of an influx of new vegetables from Italy and France (Wilson 1974: 362; Braudel 1981, 1: 223), and, in a list of 18 coleworts compiled in 1633, was identified as "Cole Florie" or "Colieflorie" and sold in London markets as "Cyprus coleworts" (O'Hara-May 1977: 251).

Although it is unclear when cauliflower arrived in North America, a number of varieties could be found in seed catalogs by the 1860s (Fenton and Kitchen 1956: 76; Carcione and Lucas 1972: 34). In all European countries, cauliflower is primarily a summer vegetable. It is very popular in Italy – the leading producer in Europe – where it comes in both bright purple and bright green colors. In the United States, typically, one can find only creamy, ivory-white cauliflower. Three of the most widely cultivated varieties in the United States are of the snowball type: 'Early Snowball', 'Super Snowball', and 'Snowdrift'. A larger, more leafy kind is the 'Danish Giant' grown primarily in the American Midwest (Carcione and Lucas 1972: 34; Toussaint-Samat 1992: 694).

Kohlrabi. A variety of *B. oleracea,* kohlrabi is just 400 to 500 years old and thus a relative newcomer to the cabbage genus of *Brassica.* It is one of the few vegetables with an origin in northern Europe. First described in 1554, kohlrabi was known in Germany, England, Italy, and Spain by the end of the sixteenth century. Documentation of its cultivation in the United States dates from 1806. Its common name, kohlrabi, is derived from the German *Kohl,* meaning cabbage, and *Rabi,* meaning turnip. It was developed by planting seeds from thick, juicy-stemmed cabbage, and the plants evolved into a turnip shape, characterized by slender roots at the bottom, a swelling of the stem into a turnip-sized bulb just above the ground, and leaves similar to those of a turnip sprouting on top (Fenton and Kitchen 1956: 77; Carcione and Lucas 1972: 66). Although more delicate, the kohlrabi's taste resembles that of a turnip. Europeans grow frilly-leafed varieties of kohlrabi for ornament, whereas in the United States the two common varieties are both food plants (Carcione and Lucas 1972: 66).

Brussels sprouts. Less than 500 years old and native to northern Europe, Brussels sprouts are also a recent addition to *B. oleracea.* Described as early as 1587, the plant supposedly got its name as the result of its development near the city of Brussels, Belgium. Brussels sprouts were cultivated in England in the seventeenth century and appear to have been introduced into the United States in the nineteenth century, although exactly when, where, and by whom is unclear (Fenton and Kitchen 1956: 76–7; Carcione and Lucas 1972: 25; Wilson 1974: 203).

Mustard

Often found growing in fields and pastures, the mustard varieties *B. nigra* and *B. alba* are characterized by leaves with deep notches and small yellow flowers with four petals forming the shape of a Greek cross, typical of the Cruciferae (Fenton and Kitchen 1956: 66). These mustard varieties evolved from weeds growing wild in central Asia into a food source after humans learned that their pungent seeds improved the taste of meat – a not unimportant discovery in ancient times, when there was no refrigeration and meat was usually a bit tainted (Fenton and Kitchen 1956: 66). Once mustard became recognized as a spice, it was commercially cultivated, and traders carried the seed to China and Japan, Africa, Asia Minor, and Europe.

The Greeks and the Romans first used mustard for medicinal purposes by creating ointments from the crushed seeds and prescribing the leaves as a cure for sore muscles. According to Pliny the Elder, the first-century Roman writer, mustard "cured epilepsy, lethargy, and all deep-seated pains in any part of the body" (1938, I: 64), and also, mustard was an "effective cure for hysterical females" (Carcione and Lucas 1972: 64). In addition to medical applications, the Greeks and Romans came to use the seeds as a spice and the boiled leaves as a vegetable. The Romans also pulverized mustard seeds and added them to grape juice to prevent it from spoiling. This practice later appeared in England, where grape juice was called "must" and both seeds and plants were known as mustseed. Over time, the spelling evolved from "mustseed" to "mustard" (Fenton and Kitchen 1956: 66-7).

By the time of the Middle Ages, mustard was popular as a condiment that seasoned food and stimulated the appetite; it was also used to treat gout and sciatica and as a blood thinner. Caution was advised, however, in smelling mustard powder, although the risk of its rising to the brain could be averted by using almonds and vinegar in its preparation (Spencer 1984: 47).

Of the two varieties of mustard that were cultivated in the United States before 1806, both "ran wild," becoming weeds, as did another type, the Indian mustard, grown for greens (Fenton and Kitchen 1956: 67-8). Today, India, California, and Europe supply most of the world's mustard. Joe Carcione and Bob Lucas noted that wild mustard, also called "Calutzi," colors the California hills a brilliant yellow in springtime. Commercially grown types include 'Elephant Ears', which have large plain leaves, and the curly-leafed varieties, 'Fordhood Fancy' and 'Southern Curled' (Carcione and Lucas 1972: 64). The dry seeds are crushed to produce oil and ground into powder, which is the basis of the condiment.

Chinese Brassica

A large variety of green vegetables are grown in China, and prominent, particularly in the north, are several types of *Brassica* that are native Chinese cultigens. As with cruciferous vegetables in general, their exact classifications are controversial and difficult to sort out. The most common are *B. pekinensis, Brassica chinensis,* and *B. juncea.* The long, cylindrical-headed *B. pekinensis,* known as *Pai ts'ai,* or Chinese cabbage, and by numerous colloquial names in different languages, has white, green-edged leaves wrapped around each other in a tall head reminiscent of celery. The nonheaded *B. chinensis,* identified as *ch'ing ts'ai* in Mandarin and *pak choi* in Cantonese, has dark green, oblong or oval leaves resembling chard, growing on white stalks. Descriptions of *pak choi* and *pai ts'ai* exist in Chinese books written before the year A.D. 500, although both were probably developed even earlier. However, it was not until the early twentieth century that they became commonly known in North America (Fenton and Kitchen 1956: 68; Anderson and Anderson 1977: 327), ironically at a time when Chinese immigration into the United States and Canada was all but nonexistent. It is possible that their expanded use in North America came with the growth of second and third generations of Chinese populations in North America.

Brassica juncea, recognized as *chieh ts'ai* in Mandarin and *kaai choi* in Cantonese, has characteristics similar to *B. chinensis.* Also important in China are *Brassica alboglabra,* named *kaai laan* in Cantonese, which are similar to collard greens; *B. campestris,* the Chinese rapeseed that is a major oil-producing crop (canola oil in the West); and several minor crops including *B. oleracea,* recently introduced from the West. Although quite distinctive, the Cantonese *choi sam* or "vegetable heart" is considered to be a form of *B. chinensis* (Anderson and Anderson 1977: 327).

Along with radishes, these *Brassica* cultigens are the most significant "minor" crops grown in southern China and, combined with rice and soybeans, constitute the diet of millions. Cabbage or mustard greens stir-fried in canola oil and seasoned with chillies or preserved soybean constitutes a nutritionally sound meal without the use of animal products or plants that require large areas of land and are overly labor intensive. Chinese *Brassica* varieties produce large yields and are available throughout the year, particularly in south China (Anderson and Anderson 1977: 328).

Radish

According to Reay Tannahill (1988: 11), radishes, *R. sativus,* were part of the diet of prehistoric hunter–gatherer cultures of Europe and have been grown and eaten, especially pickled, in the Orient for thousands of years. Because of the radish's antiquity and the many varieties that have been cultivated all over the Old World, including the Orient, its precise origin is obscure. Early radishes were probably large enough to be used as a food and not merely as a salad decoration or appetizer. The leaves may also have been eaten as greens (Brothwell and Brothwell 1969: 110).

Cultivated radish varieties were transported across Asia to Egypt about 4,000 years ago, where the Egyptians "ate radish roots as vegetables and made oil from the seeds" (Fenton and Kitchen 1956: 69; see also Darby, Ghalioungui, and Grivetti 1977, II: 664). Two radishes were discovered in the necropolis of Illahoun (Twelfth Dynasty), and the leaves and roots of the specific Egyptian radish variety *aegyptiacus* have been identified (Darby et al. 1977: 664). Fenton and Kitchen claimed that pictures of radishes were chiseled into the walls of a temple at Karnak, on the River Nile (Fenton and Kitchen 1956: 69). According to William J. Darby, Paul Ghalioungui, and Louis Grivetti, however, the evidence of radish use in ancient Egypt is primarily literary, particularly from Pliny's *Natural History.* They pointed out that in all likelihood radishes in Egypt were valued for oil produced from their seeds rather than as a food product. The Egyptians also considered the radish to be of medicinal value in curing a now unknown disease called *Phtheiriasis.* Poorer Egyptians employed radish oil as an inexpensive method of embalming, using it as an enema for emptying the intestines (Darby et al. 1977: 664, 785).

Theophrastus observed that in ancient Greece there existed five varieties of radishes: 'Corinthian', 'Cleonae', 'Leiothasian', 'Amorea', and 'Boeotian'. He noted that those types with smooth leaves had a sweeter and more pleasant taste, and those having rough leaves tasted sharp. Unfortunately, he did not associate varieties with leaf type (Theophrastus 1977, 2: 81-3). Fenton and Kitchen suggested that the Greeks were so fond of radishes that they used golden dishes to offer them to their god Apollo, whereas silver dishes were sufficient for beets, and turnips warranted only bowls of lead (Fenton and Kitchen 1956: 69).

Columella's instructions about the cultivation of radishes establishes their presence in Rome (Columella 1960, 3: 157, 165-9), and Pliny also wrote about the common use of radishes. He indicated that they were grown extensively for their seed oil, but that as a food, he found them a "vulgar article of diet" that "have a remarkable power of causing flatulence and eructation" (Brothwell and Brothwell 1969: 110).

Radishes were introduced to England by the occupying Romans and were known to Anglo-Saxon and Germanic peoples by the early medieval era. Like cabbage, radishes were common in English kitchen gardens by the fifteenth century (Wilson 1974: 196-7, 205), and they reached England's American colonies early in the seventeenth century. Europeans occasionally ate raw radishes with bread, but more common was the use of the roots in a sauce served with meat to stimulate the appetite. So highly did the great Italian composer Gioacchino Rossini regard radishes that they were one of the *Four Hors d'Oeuvres* in his famous opera. For others, however, radishes have inspired mistrust. A *Plague Pamphlet*, printed in London in 1665, noted that the appearance of the dread disease was the result of "eating radishes, a cat catter wouling, . . . immoderate eating of caviare and anchoves, tame pigeons that flew up and down an alley, [and] drinking strong heady beer" (Carcione and Lucas 1972: 104).

Radishes are used today mostly as an appetizer and in salads, and sometimes the young, tender leaves are boiled and served as greens. Radish varieties are numerous, and they come in many sizes (ranging from cherry- to basketball-size), shapes (round, oval, or oblong), and colors (white, red and white, solid red, or black). But their flavors are very similar. Most common in the United States are small, round, red or white varieties, including 'Cherry Belle' and 'Comet'. The 'White Icicle' is a long and narrow white radish. Oriental radishes are the most spectacular, with some, like the Japanese daikon, reaching several feet in length (Fenton and Kitchen 1956: 69; Carcione and Lucas 1972: 104). Europeans grow large, hot-tasting winter radishes, which they store in cool, dark cellars and eat during cold weather. According to an old description, winter radishes could reach a weight of 100 pounds (Fenton and Kitchen 1956: 69). Methods

of serving radishes in the various parts of Asia include pickling them in brine, boiling them like potatoes, eating them raw, and cooking them as fresh vegetables (Fenton and Kitchen 1956: 69-70).

Turnip

Grown since ancient times, the turnip, *B. rapa* or *B. campestris,* has long been prized as a staple winter food, and in some areas it has been the only winter produce available. According to Brothwell and Brothwell, turnip varieties seem to have been indigenous to the region between the Baltic Sea and the Caucasus, later spreading to Europe (Brothwell and Brothwell 1969: 110). Today turnips continue to grow wild in eastern Europe and Siberia. They are almost perfectly round and have white flesh and thin, rough leaves covered by prickly hairs (Fenton and Kitchen 1956: 70). Their cultivation predates recorded history, and excellent storing qualities must have made the vegetable a dependable winter food for livestock as well as people (Brothwell and Brothwell 1969: 110-11).

In antiquity, the name "turnip" also referred to radishes and other root vegetables save leeks and onions (Darby et al. 1977, II: 665). Several varieties of turnips – round, long, and flat – were used by the Romans prior to the Christian Era. Greek and Roman writers indicated that the use was limited largely to "the poorer classes and country folk." Theophrastus wrote that there was disagreement over the number of varieties; he also provided some instructions for their cultivation. He stated that like the radish, the turnip's root grew best and sweetest in wintertime (Theophrastus 1977, 2: 83). Columella pointed out that turnips should not be overlooked as an important crop because they were a filling food for country people and a valuable source of fodder for livestock. In addition, Columella provided his readers with a recipe for pickling turnips in a mustard and vinegar liquid (Columella 1960, 1: 171, 3: 331-3). Apicius recommended mixing them with myrtle berries in vinegar and honey as a preservative. Pliny considered them the third most important agricultural product north of the Po River, and wrote that the leaves were also eaten. Especially interesting was his opinion that turnip tops were even better tasting when they were yellow and half dead (Pliny 1938, 5: 269-71; Brothwell and Brothwell 1969: 111).

The medieval chronicle *The Four Seasons* noted that if soaked in vinegar or brine, turnips could be preserved for up to a year. Sweet-tasting and thin-skinned types were considered the best. Medicinally, the turnip was believed good for the stomach, capable of relieving constipation, and effective as a diuretic. In preparing turnips, the advice was for prolonged cooking, even cooking them twice, to avoid indigestion, flatulence, and swelling. If these problems did occur, however, an emetic of vinegar and salt was recommended as a remedy (Spencer 1984: 109).

Like cabbage and radishes, turnips were a part of

vegetable gardens in Roman Britain. By A.D. 1400, they were common in France, Holland, and Belgium, and at that date were among a quite small number of vegetables that had been known and available in northern Europe for centuries (Fenton and Kitchen 1956: 70; Carcione and Lucas 1972: 123). Explorers and colonists brought turnips to North America in the late sixteenth and early seventeenth centuries, where, because they flourish in cool weather, they became a summer crop in the north and a winter crop in the south. Modern varieties are generally less than 5 inches thick, but a turnip weighing 100 pounds was once grown in California, and during the 1500s, most European turnips weighed 30 to 40 pounds (Fenton and Kitchen 1956: 71). Commercially, there are many varieties grown today, and although shape and skin color may differ, like radishes the taste remains the same. The 'Purple-Top White Globe' and the 'Purple-Top Milan' are grown for their roots, and *'Shogoin',* an Oriental variety, is harvested for its tender greens (Carcione and Lucas 1972: 123-4).

Rutabaga

Rutabagas are occasionally referred to as "Swede turnips" or just "Swedes" because they were developed and grown in Sweden before A.D. 1400. According to Carcione and Lucas (1972: 123), rutabagas appear to be "the result of a meeting of a swinging Swedish turnip and an equally willing cabbage." Although closely related to the turnip, the rutabaga, *B. napobrassica,* is a relatively modern vegetable that is larger and longer than the turnip, with a milder taste and flesh that is yellow-colored rather than white. In addition, its leaves are smooth and thick, whereas turnip leaves are thin, rough, and prickly (Fenton and Kitchen 1956: 70). Cattle and pigs feed on raw rutabagas, but people eat the roots boiled and buttered (Fenton and Kitchen 1956: 71; Drummond and Wilbraham 1991: 180).

Rutabagas spread from Sweden to central Europe and the northern regions of Italy, where in medieval times they were called "Swedes" and housewives were advised to accept only those that were garden-fresh. Although "Swedes" reputedly bloated the stomach, they were delicious when prepared with meat broth. Moreover, they were thought to "activate the bladder," and "if eaten with herbs and abundant pepper, they arouse young men to heights of sexual adventurousness" (Spencer 1984: 58).

Rutabagas were cultivated prior to 1650 in Bohemia, and in 1755 they were introduced to England and Scotland from Holland, where they were initially referred to as "turnip-rooted cabbage," "Swedes," or "Swedish turnips." American gardeners were growing rutabagas by 1806, and today, Canada – along with the states of Washington and Oregon – supplies the United States with rutabagas, which explains their often being called "Canadian turnips" by Americans. Two of the best-known rutabaga types are the 'Laurentian' and the 'Purple-Top Yellow' (Carcione and Lucas 1972: 123-4).

Watercress

Native to Asia Minor and the Mediterranean region, watercress *(Nasturtium officinale)* grows wild wherever shallow moving water is found. It is characterized by long stems and small thick leaves (Carcione and Lucas 1972: 126). According to Brothwell and Brothwell, the Romans consumed watercress with vinegar to help cure unspecified mental problems, and both Xenophon, the ancient Greek general, and the Persian King Xerxes required their soldiers to eat the plant in order to maintain their health (Brothwell and Brothwell 1969: 122; Carcione and Lucas 1972: 126). Ancient cress seeds found in Egypt probably arrived from Greece and Syria, where cress is found among a list of Assyrian plants. Dioscorides maintained that watercress came from Babylon (Brothwell and Brothwell 1969: 122-3).

Stronger-flavored kinds of watercress were preferred in medieval Italy, where they allegedly provided a variety of medicinal benefits. Although watercress was blamed for headaches, it supposedly strengthened the blood, aroused desire, cured children's coughs, whitened scars, and lightened freckles. Additionally, three leaves "picked with the left hand and eaten immediately will cure an overflow of bile" (Spencer 1984: 19).

Cultivation of watercress for sale in markets dates to about 1800 in England, although wild watercress was doubtless gathered by humans for many millennia. Brought to the United States by early settlers, watercress can now be found throughout the country. Soil-cultivated relatives of watercress include peppergrass (also called curly cress), upland cress, lamb's cress, cuckoo flower, lady's smock, mayflower, pennycress, and nasturtiums (Carcione and Lucas 1972: 126).

Nutrition, Disease Prevention, and Cruciferous Vegetables

Cruciferous vegetables have substantial nutritional value. They contain significant amounts of beta-carotene (the precursor of vitamin A), vitamin C (ascorbic acid), and "nonnutritive chemicals" such as indoles, flavones, and isothiocyanates, which contribute to the prevention of diet-related diseases and disorders such as blindness and scurvy. In addition, recent investigations have shown them to be effective in warding off several types of cancer. Studies have linked diets high in vitamin A to cancer prevention, and research also indicates that chemicals like indoles inhibit the effects of carcinogens. Vitamin C is recognized as an effective antioxidant, which is thought to be preventive against the development of some cancers and an inhibitor of the progress of the human immunodeficiency virus (HIV).

Moreover, the substances known as antioxidants are critical in the maintenance of homeostasis, a state of physiological equilibrium among the body's functions and its chemical components. Molecules that form the human body are typically held together by the magnetic attraction between their electrons. Occasionally, however, these molecules exist in an oxidized state, meaning that they have unpaired electrons and are seeking out "molecular partners," often with potentially harmful effects. In this condition, these molecules are known as "free radicals," and because they can react more freely with their surrounding environment, they are capable of disrupting many finely tuned processes essential in maintaining good health. In some cases, free radicals serve no particular function and are simply the waste products of bodily processes, but in others, the body's immune system uses them to fight diseases. Yet even when useful, free radicals can damage nearby tissue and impair bodily functions. To control such damage, the human body uses antioxidants to neutralize the effects of free radicals. Unfortunately, there are often inadequate amounts of antioxidants to eliminate all of the free radicals, and there are also periods or conditions during which the number of free radicals increases along with the damage they inflict. This is particularly true when people are infected with HIV or have developed cancer (Romeyn 1995: 42–3).

In the cases of both HIV and cancer, vitamin C reacts with and neutralizes free radicals. This vitamin also helps increase the overall antioxidant ability of vitamin E by preventing certain functions of vitamin E that can actually inhibit the effects of its antioxidant characteristics. Specifically with regard to cancer prevention, vitamin C, of which cruciferous vegetables have high levels, appears to significantly reduce the risk of contracting stomach or esophageal cancers. Other, less conclusive studies suggest that vitamin C may also inhibit the development of bladder and colon cancer. In addition to its role as an antioxidant, vitamin C acts to inhibit the formation of cancer-causing nitrosamines, which are created by cooking or by digesting nitrites found in food.

In citing over a dozen studies worldwide, Patricia Hausman (1983: 24–5) noted that diets rich in vitamin A provide a surprising amount of protection from cancer in eight different organs. The strongest evidence links vitamin A to the prevention of lung, stomach, and esophageal cancer. Although less conclusive, other studies have recognized the potential of vitamin A to protect against cancer of the mouth, colon, rectum, prostate, and bladder.

The term, "vitamin A", encompasses many substances that can fulfill the body's requirements for this nutrient. Retinol is the form found in foods derived from animal products. Beta-carotene and carotenoids are found in fruits and vegetables; however, carotenoids are only a minor source. For most bodily functions that require vitamin A, any one of these forms will suffice, but it is beta-carotene that is tied most closely to cancer prevention (Hausman 1983: 24–5).

Although it is unclear how beta-carotene aids in the prevention of cancer, some chemists have suggested that it might act as an antioxidant. However, Eileen Jennings has noted that there is little doubt concerning the significance of vitamin A as it relates to gene regulation: "The gene regulator and antiproliferation effects of vitamin A may be the entire explanation for the anticancer effect of vitamin A" (1993: 149). Although the final determination of beta-carotene's antioxidant qualities awaits further study, its ability to act as a cancer preventive has been demonstrated, and thus, it is recommended that the cruciferous vegetables containing high levels of this substance be eaten frequently.

Scientific studies also have demonstrated that cruciferous vegetables further limit cancerous growth because they contain small quantities of indoles, flavones, and isothiocyanates. According to Jennings, these nonnutritive chemicals have been shown "to either stimulate production of enzymes that convert toxic chemicals to less toxic forms or interfere with the reaction of carcinogens with DNA" (1993: 223). Hausman (1983: 82–3) wrote that the enzyme system that produces these cancer inhibitors is recognized as the "mixed function oxidase system." Because the family of cruciferous vegetables contains such high levels of these inhibitors, particularly indoles as well as high levels of beta-carotene and vitamin C, the Committee on Diet, Nutrition, and Cancer of the National Academy of Sciences in 1982 emphasized eating these vegetables often. Broccoli, cauliflower, Brussels sprouts, and cabbage have all been linked to lowering the risk of developing stomach and colon cancer, and some studies indicated a possible connection to a reduced risk of rectal cancer.

The absence of beta-carotene and vitamin C in the diet is also linked to the development of deficiency diseases such as "night blindness" and scurvy. Because of the unavailability of fruits or cruciferous vegetables and other foods containing these nutrients, in many parts of the developing world deficiency diseases remain common. Extended vitamin A deficiency results in a severe defect called xerophthalmia, which affects the cornea of the eye. More often this deficiency causes "night blindness," or nyctalopia, which is the inability to see in a dim light. This problem has been very common in the East for several centuries, and according to Magnus Pyke (1970: 104, 127), at least until the past two or three decades, vitamin A deficiency annually caused thousands of cases of blindness in India.

The earliest prescribed treatment of an eye disorder thought to be night blindness is found in the Ebers Papyrus, an Egyptian medical treatise dating from around 1600 B.C. Rather than prescribing the regular consumption of cruciferous vegetables, however, it suggested using ox liver, itself high in vitamin A, which it claimed was "very effective and quick-acting." Hippocrates and Galen were also familiar with night blindness, the former recommending the consumption of ox liver (in honey) as a remedy. Later Roman medical writings gave similar advice, and Chinese literature contained descriptions of this eye condition by A.D. 610 (Brothwell and Brothwell 1969: 179-80). As already noted, the work on foods in medieval Italy, *The Four Seasons,* contended that the cooked juice of cabbage mixed with honey and used sparingly as an eyedrop improved vision (Spencer 1984: 102).

Like night blindness, scurvy, a disease caused by an insufficient intake of vitamin C, continues to be a serious deficiency disease of the developing world. One of the primary functions of vitamin C is the production of collagen, which helps to build new tissue, in a sense maintaining the very structure of the human body. It can reduce lung tissue damage caused by the activation of the body's immune system and is important to the production of hormones, steroids, and neurotransmitters. It is also required for the "conversion of folate into its active form" and aids in iron absorption (Pyke 1970: 114; Hausman 1983: 43; Romeyn 1995: 44-5). A prolonged lack of vitamin C causes the weakening and breakdown of the body's cell structure and tissue, with scurvy the visible symptom of this phenomenon.

Interestingly, humans are susceptible to scurvy only because of an unfortunate biochemical shortcoming in their genetic makeup. Unlike most animals, humans and four other species are unable to synthesize vitamin C and therefore will suffer from scurvy if the vitamin C intake from their food is insufficient for a long enough period of time (Pyke 1970: 115).

Brothwell and Brothwell suggest that deficiencies in vitamin C were rare prior to the appearance of urban development (beginning in the Neolithic era) because hunter-gatherers had more diversity in their diet. Hippocrates has been credited with the earliest mention of scurvy when he described an unpleasant condition characterized by "frequent haemorrhages" and "repulsive ulceration of the gums" – both features of the disease. Pliny also acknowledged the presence of this condition (which he called *stomacace*) in Roman troops stationed in the Rhine region. Writings from the Middle Ages contain many references to scurvy as well, implying that it was prevalent in the Europe of that era (Brothwell and Brothwell 1969: 181).

Before the introduction of the white potato, the disease was common in the spring in the northern countries of Europe. It has also ravaged sailors during long sea voyages, as well as arctic explorers whose provisions consisted mostly of easily preserved food and lacked fresh fruits and vegetables (Pyke 1970: 113-14). But although the disease is of "considerable antiquity," scurvy occurs infrequently today despite the large numbers of underfed and malnourished people in the world because it is a disease that requires an unusual state of deprivation (Pyke 1970: 112). However, scurvy in children has been reported in recent years in Toronto, Canada, in many communities in India, and in Glasgow, Scotland, and "bachelor scurvy" can occur in instances where older men who live alone fail to consume meals with adequate quantities of vegetables (Pyke 1970: 115).

In order to improve nutritional levels in humans and thus prevent deficiency diseases, as well as improve overall health, Henry M. Munger (1988) has suggested that instead of breeding crops to increase nutrient levels, a more effective, and less expensive, solution is to increase consumption of plants already high in nutritional value. He offered broccoli as an example. Relatively unknown in the United States 50 years ago, broccoli has experienced a dramatic increase in its production, from approximately 200 million pounds in the 1950s to over a billion pounds in 1985. In a 1974 study by M. Allen Stevens on *Nutritional Qualities of Fresh Fruits and Vegetables* that compares the nutritional values of common fruits and vegetables, broccoli was ranked highest in nutritional value because of its substantial content of vitamins A and C, niacin, riboflavin, and nearly every mineral. Additionally, "based on dry weight, broccoli contains protein levels similar to soybean" (Stevens 1974: 89). In an earlier study by Stevens, however, broccoli was ranked twenty-first in contribution to nutrition, based on a formula derived from its production as well as its nutrient content. But by 1981, that ranking had risen to seventh, a direct result of its increased production and consumption levels (Stevens 1974: 89-90; Munger 1988: 179-80).

Munger has maintained that improved nutrition in tropical developing countries can be achieved by adapting nutritious, temperate crops to tropical conditions or by expanding the use of less familiar, highly nutritious tropical vegetables. Two of his primary illustrations involve cruciferous vegetables. In the first case he cited an adaptation of Japanese cabbage hybrids for cultivation in the more tropical lowlands of the Philippines. This move lowered production costs and made cabbage more accessible and affordable to the general population. A second example, *choi-sum* or Flowering White Cabbage, a variety of *B. campestris,* is similar to broccoli and grown near Canton, China. Nearly all parts of this highly nutritious plant are edible. It can be planted and harvested year-round, and its production yield is comparable to that of potatoes and corn in the United States. Because of its efficient production and high nutrient concentration, *choi-sum* also seems to Munger a good candidate for promotion in tropical developing nations (Munger 1988: 180-1, 183).

Summary

The cruciferous family of vegetables includes some of the most nutritionally significant foods produced today. Predominantly European and Asian in origin, these vegetables have a history of cultivation and use that spans many centuries. The ancient Greeks and Romans employed some of them not only as foodstuffs but also for medicinal purposes. They believed that cabbage, for example, could cure a wide range of ailments, from healing wounds to correcting problems with internal organs. In medieval and Renaissance Europe as well as in Russia and China, cruciferous vegetables were found in kitchen gardens and composed an important part of the daily diet. Gradually they were transformed from garden produce into commercial crops and today are abundantly available for sustenance and for good health. Contemporary research suggests a link between cruciferous vegetables and disease prevention. Because of their high levels of vitamin C, beta-carotene, and other disease inhibitors, these food plants help avoid deficiency diseases, prevent some cancers, and retard the development of HIV in the human body. Such findings suggest that the consumption of cruciferous vegetables has a positive effect on health, and consequently they should have a prominent place in the human diet.

Robert C. Field

Bibliography

Anderson, E. N., Jr., and Marja L. Anderson. 1977. Modern China: South. In *Food in Chinese culture: Anthropological and historical perspectives,* ed. K. C. Chang, 319–82. New Haven, Conn.

Baldinger, Kathleen O'Bannon. 1994. *The world's oldest health plan.* Lancaster, Pa.

Braudel, Fernand. 1981. *Civilization and capitalism, 15th–18th century,* trans. Sian Reynolds. 3 vols. New York.

Brothwell, Don, and Patricia Brothwell. 1969. *Food in antiquity: A survey of the diet of early peoples.* New York.

Carcione, Joe, and Bob Lucas. 1972. *The greengrocer: The consumer's guide to fruits and vegetables.* San Francisco, Calif.

Cato, Marcus Porcius. 1954. *On agriculture,* trans. William Davis Hooper, rev. by Harrison Boyd Ash. London.

Columella, Lucius Junius Moderatus. 1960. *On agriculture and trees,* trans. Harrison Boyd Ash, E. S. Forster, and Edward H. Heffner. 3 vols. London.

Darby, William J., Paul Ghalioungui, and Louis Grivetti. 1977. *Food: The gift of Osiris.* 2 vols. London.

Drummond, J. C., and Anne Wilbraham. 1991. *The Englishman's food: A history of five centuries of English diet.* London.

Fenton, Carroll Lane, and Herminie B. Kitchen. 1956. *Plants that feed us: The story of grains and vegetables.* New York.

Hausman, Patricia. 1983. *Foods that fight cancer.* New York.

Hedge, Ian C., and K. H. Rechinger. 1968. *Cruciferae.* Graz.

Jennings, Eileen. 1993. *Apricots and oncogenes: On vegetables and cancer prevention.* Cleveland, Ohio.

McLaren, Donald S., and Michael M. Meguid. 1988. *Nutrition and its disorders.* Fourth edition. Edinburgh.

Munger, Henry M. 1988. Adaptation and breeding of vegetable crops for improved human nutrition. In *Horticulture and human health: Contributions of fruits and vegetables,* ed. Bruno Quebedeaux and Fredrick A. Bliss, 177–84. Englewood Cliffs, N.J.

O'Hara-May, Jane. 1977. *Elizabethan dyetary of health.* Lawrence, Kans.

Pliny the Elder. 1938. *Pliny: Natural history,* trans. H. Rackham. 10 vols. Cambridge, Mass.

Pyke, Magnus. 1970. *Man and food.* New York.

Rollins, Reed C. 1993. *The cruciferae of continental North America: Systematics of the mustard family from the Arctic to Panama.* Stanford, Calif.

Romeyn, Mary. 1995. *Nutrition and HIV: A new model for treatment.* San Francisco, Calif.

Smith, R. E. F., and David Christian. 1984. *Bread and salt: A social and economic history of food and drink in Russia.* Cambridge and New York.

Spencer, Judith, trans. 1984. *The four seasons of the house of Cerruti.* New York.

Stevens, M. Allen. 1974. Varietal influence on nutritional value. In *Nutritional qualities of fresh fruits and vegetables,* ed. Philip L. White and Nancy Selvey, 87–110. Mount Kisco, N.Y.

Tannahill, Reay. 1988. *Food in history.* New York.

Theophrastus. 1977. *Enquiry into plants,* 2 vols., trans. Sir Arthur Hort. Cambridge, Mass.

Toussaint-Samat, Maguelonne. 1992. *A history of food,* trans. Anthea Bell. Cambridge, Mass.

Vaughan, J. G., A. J. Macleod, and B. M. G. Jones, eds. 1976. *The biology and chemistry of the Cruciferae.* London and New York.

Wilson, C. Anne. 1974. *Food and drink in Britain from the Stone Age to recent times.* New York.

Zohary, Daniel, and Maria Hopf. 1993. *Domestication of plants in the Old World.* Oxford.

II.C.6 ❧ Cucumbers, Melons, and Watermelons

Our focus here is on three important cucurbits – cucumber, melon, and watermelon – although cucurbits of less significance such as the citron, bur (or West India gherkin), and some lesser-known melons are also briefly discussed. These plants, together with all the sundry squashes and pumpkins, constitute a taxonomic group of diverse origin and genetic composition with considerable impact on human nutrition. The term "cucurbit" denotes all species within the Cucurbitaceae family.

Cucumber

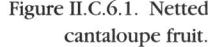
Watermelon

Cucurbits are found throughout the tropics and subtropics of Africa, southeastern Asia, and the Americas. Some are adapted to humid conditions and others are found in arid areas. Most are frost-intolerant so they are grown with protection in temperate areas or to coincide with the warm portion of the annual cycle. Cucurbits are mostly annual, herbaceous, tendril-bearing vines.

The significance of cucurbits in human affairs is illustrated by the abundance of literature devoted to them, albeit much less than that produced on the grains and pulses. Two full-length books have cucurbits as the title (Whitaker and Davis 1962; Robinson and Decker-Walters 1997), and at least four significant publications have been derived from recent conferences on these plants (Thomas 1989; Bates, Robinson and Jeffrey 1990; Lester and Dunlap 1994; Gómez-Guillamón et al. 1996). Moreover, a recent reference book provides an inclusive chapter on cucurbits (Rubatzky and Yamaguchi 1997) and an annual publication is dedicated to their genetics (Ng 1996).

Taxonomy

The Cucurbitaceae family is well defined but taxonomically isolated from other plant families. Two subfamilies – Zanonioideae and Cucurbitoideae – are well characterized: the former by small, striate pollen grains and the latter by having the styles united into a single column. The food plants all fall within the subfamily Cucurbitoideae. Further definition finds cucumber *(Cucumis sativus L.)* and melon *(Cucumis melo L.)* to be within the subtribe Cucumerinae, tribe Melothrieae, and watermelon (*Citrullus lanatus* [Thunb.] Matsum. and Nakai.) is assigned to the tribe Benincaseae, subtribe Benincasinae. The taxonomic sites of West India gherkin (*Cucumis anguria* L.) and citron (*Citrullus lanatus* var. *citroides* [L.H. Bailey] Mansf.) are, as with those just listed, in the same genus. There are about 118 genera and over 800 species in the Cucurbitaceae (Jeffrey 1990a). The melons *(C. melo)* are further subdivided into groups that do not have taxonomic standing but have proved useful horticulturally (Munger and Robinson 1991):

Figure II.C.6.1. Netted cantaloupe fruit.

The Cantalupensis group includes cantaloupe, muskmelon (Figure II.C.6.1), and Persian melon. The fruit are oval or round; sutured or smooth; mostly netted, some slightly netted or nonnetted; and abscise from the peduncle when mature. The flesh is usually salmon or orange colored, but may be green and is aromatic. In the United States, the term "muskmelon" and "cantaloupe" may be used interchangeably, but some horticultural scientists (Maynard and Elmstrom 1991: 229) suggest that they be used to distinguish between types of *C. melo* Cantalupensis group. This group includes the previously recognized Reticulatus group.

The Inodorus group consists of winter melon, casaba (Figure II.C.6.2), crenshaw, honeydew, Juan Canary (Figure II.C.6.3), and Santa Claus (Figure II.C.6.4). The fruit are round or irregular, smooth or wrinkled, but not netted; nor do they abscise from the peduncle at maturity. The flesh is mostly green or white, occasionally orange, and not aromatic.

The Flexuosus group is made up of the snake or serpent melon and the Armenian cucumber. The fruit are quite long, thin, ribbed, and often curled irregularly.

The Conomon group comprises the oriental pickling melon. This fruit is smooth, cylindrical, and may be green, white, or striped. The flesh is white and can taste either sweet or bland.

The Dudaim group includes mango melon, pomegranate melon, and Queen Anne's melon. The fruit are small, round to oval, and light green, yellow, or striped. The flesh is firm and yellowish-white in color.

The Mormordica group is made up of the phoot and snap melon. The fruit are oval or cylindrical with smooth skin that cracks as the fruit matures.

Plant and Fruit Morphology

Cucumber, melon, and watermelon plants share many characteristics but also differ in important ways. As a group they are frost-sensitive annuals with trailing, tendril-bearing vines. The plants are mostly monoecious, the flowers are insect-pollinated, and the fruits are variously shaped, many-seeded berries.

Cucumber

Cucumber plants are annual and may be monoecious, andromonoecious, or gynoecious. They have indeterminate trailing vines with angled, hairy stems bearing triangular-ovate, acute three-lobed leaves. Determinate types with compact plants have been developed for gardens. In monoecious types, staminate flowers appear first and are several times more abundant than pistillate flowers. Flowers occur at the nodes, staminate in clusters or singly close to the plant crown with only one flower of the cluster opening on a single day; pistillate flowers are borne singly on the main stem and lateral branches in monoecious types (Figure II.C.6.5) and singly or in clusters on the main stem and lateral branches on gynoecious types. Pistillate flowers are identified easily by the large inferior ovary that is a miniature cucumber fruit. Both staminate and pistillate flowers are large (2 to 3 centimeters [cm] in diameter) with a yellow, showy five-parted corolla. Fruits of commercial types are

Figure II.C.6.2. Casaba melon.

Figure II.C.6.3. Juan Canary melon.

cylindrical and green when consumed at the imma-ture, edible stage (Figure II.C.6.6). The fruit surface is interrupted with tubercle-bearing white or black spines. White spines are typical of fruit used for fresh consumption that, if allowed to attain maturity, will be yellow, whereas black-spined fruit is often used for processing (pickles) and is orange at maturity.

Seedless or parthenocarpic cucumbers are another distinctive type. The plants are gynoecious with a fruit borne at each axil (Figure II.C.6.7). They are grown on a trellis in protected, screened culture to prevent bees from introducing foreign pollen, which would cause seeds to develop. Fruits are long, straight, smooth, thin-skinned, and medium to dark-green in color. A slightly restricted "neck" at the stem end of the fruit serves to readily identify this unique type. Cucumber fruit destined for fresh markets has a length/diameter ratio of about 4:1; that used for pickle production has a ratio of about 2:5, whereas parthenocarpic fruit have a ratio of about 6:1. Seeds are about 8 millimeters (mm) long, oval, and white (Lower and Edwards 1986: 173–81).

Figure II.C.6.4. Santa Claus melon.

Figure II.C.6.5. Pistillate and staminate cucumber flowers (Courtesy
of National Garden Bureau, Downers Grove, Ill.)

West India Gherkin

These plants are annual, monoecious climbing vines
with flowers, leaves, tendrils, and fruit smaller than
those of cucumber. Fruits, which are spiny, yellow,
oval, and about 5 cm long, are eaten fresh, cooked, or
pickled. The plant may self-seed, escape from cultivation, and become an aggressive weed.

Melon

Melons are mostly andromonoecious and have annual
trailing vines with nearly round stems bearing tendrils
and circular to oval leaves with shallow lobes. Staminate flowers are borne in axillary clusters on the main
stem, and perfect flowers are borne at the first node of
lateral branches. Fruits vary in size, shape, rind characteristics, and flesh color depending on variety. Fruit
quality is related to external appearance, thick, well-
colored interior flesh with high (>10 percent) soluble
solids, and a pleasant aroma and taste (Maynard and
Elmstrom 1991: 229). It is a common misconception
that poor-quality melon fruit results from cross-pollination with cucumber because these species are incompatible. Rather, the poor-quality melon fruit sometimes
encountered is due to unfavorable weather or grow-

Figure II.C.6.6. Cucumbers:
commercial fresh-market
type (right), pickling type
(left), lemon cucumber
(foreground), Armenian
cucumber, which is a
melon, *C. melo* (back-
ground). (Courtesy of
National Garden Bureau,
Downers Grove, Ill.)

ing conditions that restrict photosynthetic activity and, thereby, sugar content of the fruit. Seeds are cream-colored, oval, and on average 10 mm long.

Watermelon

These plants are monoecious, annual, and have trailing thin and angular vines that bear pinnatifide leaves. Flowers are solitary in leaf axils. Staminate flowers appear first and greatly outnumber pistillate flowers. The flowers are pollinated mostly by honeybees. Fruit may range in size from about 1 kilogram (kg) to as much as 100 kg, but ordinary cultivated types are 3 to 13 kg. Shape varies from round to oval to elongated. Coloration of the rind may be light green, often termed gray, to very dark green, appearing to be almost black (Figure II.C.6.8). In addition, the rind may have stripes of various designs that are typical of a variety or type; thus the terms "Jubilee-type stripe" or "Allsweet-type stripe" are used to identify various patterns. Seed color and size is variable. The tendency in varietal development is to strive for seeds that are small (but vigorous enough for germination under unfavorable conditions) and that are dark-colored rather than white – the latter are associated with immaturity. Flesh may be white, green, yellow, orange, pink, or red. Consumers in developed countries demand red- or deep pink–fleshed watermelons, although yellow-fleshed ones are grown in home gardens and, to a limited extent, commercially (Mohr 1986).

Seedless watermelon. Each fruit of standard-seeded watermelon varieties may contain as many as 1,000 seeds (Figure II.C.6.9) and their presence throughout the flesh makes removal difficult.

Figure II.C.6.7. Gynoecious, parthenocarpic greenhouse cucumbers.

Figure II.C.6.8. Variation in watermelon fruit size, shape, and color and flesh color. (Courtesy of National Garden Bureau, Downers Grove, Ill.)

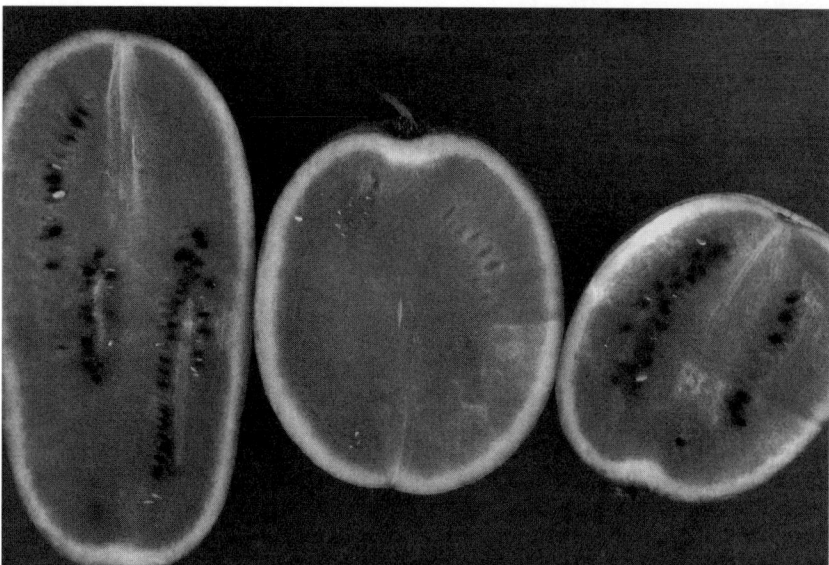

Figure II.C.6.9. Seedless watermelon (center) with seeded watermelon (left and right).

Hybrid seedless (triploid) watermelons have been grown for over 40 years in the United States. However, only recently have improved varieties, aggressive marketing, and increased consumer demand created a rapidly expanding market for them. The seedless condition is actually sterility resulting from a cross between two plants of incompatible chromosome complements. The normal chromosome number in most living organisms is referred to as $2n$. Seedless watermelons are produced on highly sterile triploid ($3n$) plants, which result from crossing a normal diploid ($2n$) plant with a tetraploid ($4n$). The tetraploid is used as the female or seed parent and the diploid is the male or pollen parent. Since the tetraploid seed parent produces only 5 to 10 percent as many seeds as a normal diploid plant, seed cost is 10 to 100 times more than that of standard, open-pollinated varieties and 5 to 10 times that of hybrid diploid watermelon varieties.

Tetraploid lines, usually developed by treating diploid plants with a chemical called colchicine, normally have a light, medium, or dark-green rind without stripes. By contrast, the diploid pollen parent almost always has a fruit with a striped rind. The resulting hybrid triploid seedless melon will inherit the striped pattern, though growers may occasionally find a nonstriped fruit in fields of striped seedless watermelons, the result of accidental self-pollination of the tetraploid seed parent during triploid seed production. The amount of tetraploid contamination depends upon the methods and care employed in triploid seed production. Sterile triploid plants normally do not produce viable seed. However, small, white rudimentary seeds or seed coats, which are eaten along with the fruits as in cucumber, develop within the fruit. The number and size of these rudi-mentary seeds vary with the variety. An occasional dark, hard, viable seed is found in triploid melons. Seedless watermelons can be grown successfully in areas where conventional seeded varieties are produced, although they require some very unique cultural practices for successful production (Maynard 1996: 1–2). With proper care, such watermelons have a longer shelf life than seeded counterparts. This may be due to the fact that flesh breakdown occurs in the vicinity of seeds, which are absent in seedless melons.

Citron

The citron plants resemble those of watermelon except that their leaves are broader and less pinnate. The fruits also resemble watermelon externally, but the rind is quite hard and the flesh is white to light green and may be quite bitter. Because fruit rinds are used to make pickles and are also candied, the citron is also called a "preserving melon." Plants escaped from cultivation may prove to be aggressive weeds in crop fields.

History and Ethnography of Production and Consumption

Relatively little research literature in cultural anthropology, archaeology, or social history focuses specifically on the species of cultivated cucurbits under consideration here. Indeed, some classic as well as recent important texts on the origins of agriculture make no mention of them (Reed 1977; Smith 1995). There are at least four reasons for this lacuna. First, these cultigens are not part of the complex carbohydrate "cores" of the diets found in centers of state formation (see Mintz 1996) and thus have not received the same attention as other staple food crops. Second, the primary centers of domestication for both melon and watermelon are in sub-Saharan Africa, where the exact timing, locations, and processes of domestication are still poorly understood (see Cowan and Watson 1992). Third, some researchers suggest that "cucurbits are usually poorly preserved among archaeological remains. The features considered most indicative of domestication are characteristics of the peduncle (stem), which is rarely preserved. The earliest remains are seed specimens, which often occur in extremely low frequencies because they are likely to have been consumed" (McClung de Tapia 1992: 153). Finally, the ethnographic record contains limited data on the production and consumption of these crops (with a few notable exceptions), reflecting their secondary significance both materially and symbolically in most human societies.

Cucumber

Cucumbers are generally believed to have originated in India, and archaeological and linguistic evidence suggests that they have been cultivated throughout western Asia for at least 3,000 years (Hedrick 1919: 208; Whitaker and Davis 1962: 2–3; Sauer 1993: 45; Robinson and Decker-Walters 1997: 62). From India, the cucumber spread to Greece and Italy – where the crop was significant in the Roman Empire – and slightly later to China and southern Russia. In classical Rome, Pliny reported greenhouse production of cucumbers by the first century, and the Emperor Tiberius was said to have had them at his table throughout the year (Sauer 1993: 46). Cucumbers probably were diffused into the rest of Europe by the Romans and later throughout the New World via colonialism and indigenous trade networks. The earliest records of their cultivation appear in France by the ninth century, Great Britain by the fourteenth century, the Caribbean at the end of the fifteenth century, and North America by the middle of the sixteenth century (Hedrick 1919: 208).

Colonial encounters between Europeans and Native Americans resulted in the rapid diffusion of cucumbers throughout North America. The Spanish began growing them in Hispaniola by 1494, and less than a century later European explorers were noting that a wide range of Native American peoples from Montreal to New York, Virginia, and Florida were cultivating them, along with a large variety of other crops including maize, beans, squash, pumpkins, and gourds. By the seventeenth century, Native American groups on the Great Plains were also cultivating cucumbers – this in a region where the Spanish had been particularly significant in the diffusion of horses and guns, as well as Old World cultigens such as watermelons and cucumbers (see Wolf 1982).

Like other cucurbits, cucumbers have a wide range of consumption uses cross-culturally. They are generally eaten fresh or pickled and are particularly important in the diets of people living in Russia and East, South, and Southeast Asia, where they may also be served as a fresh or cooked vegetable. In India, the fruits are used in the preparation of chutney and curries. Cucumber seeds, young leaves, and cooked stems are also consumed in some parts of Asia.

In addition, since at least the nineteenth century, cucumbers have been used in the production of a large variety of cosmetics, including fragrances, body lotions, shampoos, and soaps (Robinson and Decker-Walters 1997: 63; Rubatzky and Yamaguchi 1997: 585).

Melon

Melon is generally thought to have originated in western Africa (Zeven and Zhukovsky 1975: 30; Bailey 1976: 342; Purseglove 1976: 294; Whitaker and Bemis 1976: 67), with China or India as possible secondary centers of diversity. Wild melons growing in natural habitats have been reported in desert and savanna zones of Africa, Arabia, southwestern Asia, and Australia. As Jonathan Sauer notes, it is unclear where melon was domesticated and "it is conceivable that it was independently domesticated from different wild populations in Africa and southwestern Asia" (Sauer 1993: 44). Melon was an important food crop in ancient China, where archaeological data suggest that it has been cultivated for over 5,000 years (Robinson and Decker-Walters 1997: 23). Archaeological evidence also suggests that melon was cultivated in Iran some 5,000 years ago and in Greece and Egypt about 4,000 years ago (Zohary and Hopf 1988). Given the fruit's probable African origin, this evidence points to a very early date for the first domestication of melon. Tropical forest swidden systems in Africa typically have yams or manioc as dominant staple food crops with melons among the numerous and multiple secondary crops (Harris 1976: 318).

As with cucumbers, melons were cultivated in the Roman Empire and diffused throughout Europe by the Middle Ages where the "variety and quality of melon cultivars were evidently greatly increased by selection in Medieval gardens" (Sauer 1993: 44). As with cucumbers and watermelons, melons were introduced to the New World by Spanish colonial settlers in the late fifteenth and early sixteenth centuries and subsequently spread very rapidly among Native American horticultural groups. Later during the eighteenth century they reached the Pacific Islanders via British explorers.

Ralf Norrman and Jon Haarberg (1980) explore the semiotic role of cucurbits in Western literature and culture and extend this analysis to selected non-Western cultural contexts. Focusing on melons, watermelons, and cucumbers (as well as other domesticated cucurbits), these authors note that cucurbits generally have deep, profound, and complex multivocal symbolic associations with sex and sexuality, fertility, vitality, moisture, abundance, opulence, luxury, gluttony, creative power, rapid growth, and sudden death. More specifically, they note that melons are highly associated with status in colder climate European societies because historically they were "seasonal, expensive and scarce, with all the symbolic development that a commodity with such characteristics usually goes through" (Norrman and Haarberg 1980: 16). Cucurbits also appear frequently in non-Western cosmologies, for example, "in Burmese and Laotian mythology, the creation of man started from a cucurbit" (Norrman and Haarberg 1980: 26). As with other key symbols marked by binary oppositions, symbolic meanings attached to cucurbits can also be employed to convey a broad variety of negative symbolic associations along race, class, and gender lines.

Melon has a large number of different cultivars and a range of cross-cultural consumption uses parallel to the other species of cucurbits discussed in this chapter. Fruits are typically eaten uncooked, although they may also be cooked or pickled in some Asian cuisines. The seeds of some cultivars are roasted and consumed in parts of India. Dried and ground melon seeds are used as food in some African societies. Melon fruits, roots, leaves, and seeds play important roles in the treatment of a wide range of health problems in Chinese traditional medicine (Robinson and Decker-Walters 1997: 69–70).

Watermelon

Watermelons, which were originally domesticated in central and southern Africa (Whitaker and Davis 1962: 2; Robinson and Decker-Walters 1997: 85), are an important part of the "most widespread and characteristic African agricultural complex adapted to savanna zones" in that they are not only a food plant but also a vital source of water in arid regions (Harlan, de Wet, and Stemler 1976; Harlan 1992: 64). Indeed, V. R. Rubatzky and M. Yamaguchi (1997: 603) refer to watermelons as "botanical canteens." In a number of traditional African cuisines, the seeds (rich in edible oils and protein) and flesh are used in cooking. Watermelon emerged as an important cultigen in northern Africa and southwestern Asia prior to 6,000 years ago (Robinson and Decker-Walters 1997: 24). Archaeological data suggest that they were cultivated in ancient Egypt more than 5,000 years ago, where representations of watermelons appeared on wall paintings and watermelon seeds and leaves were deposited in Egyptian tombs (Ficklen 1984: 8).

From their African origins, watermelons spread via trade routes throughout much of the world, reaching India by 800 and China by 1100. In both of these countries, as in Africa, the seeds are eaten and crushed for their edible oils. Watermelons became widely distributed along Mediterranean trade routes and were introduced into southern Europe by the Moorish conquerors of Spain, who left evidence of watermelon cultivation at Cordoba in 961 and Seville in 1158 (Watson 1983). Sauer notes that "watermelons spread slowly into other parts of Europe, perhaps largely because the summers are not generally hot enough for good yields. However,

they began appearing in European herbals before 1600, and by 1625, the species was widely planted in Europe as a minor garden crop" (Sauer 1993: 42). Their first recorded appearance in Great Britain dates to 1597.

Watermelons reached the New World with European colonists and African slaves. Spanish settlers were producing watermelons in Florida by 1576, and by 1650 they were common in Panama, Peru, and Brazil, as well as in British and Dutch colonies throughout the New World (Sauer 1993: 43). The first recorded cultivation in British colonial North America dates to 1629 in Massachusetts (Hedrick 1919: 172).

Like cucumbers and melons, watermelons spread very rapidly among Native American groups. Prior to the beginning of the seventeenth century, they were being grown by tribes in the Ocmulgee region of Georgia, the Conchos nation of the Rio Grande valley, the Zuni and other Pueblo peoples of the Southwest, as well as by the Huron of eastern Canada and groups from the Great Lakes region (Blake 1981). By the mid-seventeenth century, Native Americans were cultivating them in Florida and the Mississippi valley, and in the eighteenth and early nineteenth centuries the western Apache of east-central and southeastern Arizona were producing maize and European-introduced crops including watermelons as they combined small-scale horticulture with hunting and gathering in a low rainfall environment (Minnis 1992: 130–1). This fact is ethnographically significant because other transitional foraging–farming groups, such as the San people of the Kalahari Desert of southern Africa, have parallel subsistence practices involving watermelons. Watermelons and melons were also rapidly adopted by Pacific Islanders in Hawaii and elsewhere as soon as the seeds were introduced by Captain James Cook (1778) and other European explorers (Neal 1965).

In the cultural history of the United States, Thomas Jefferson was an enthusiastic grower of watermelons at his Monticello estate, Henry David Thoreau proudly grew large and juicy watermelons in Concord, Massachusetts, and Mark Twain wrote in *Puddn'head Wilson:* "The true southern watermelon is a boon apart and not to be mentioned with commoner things. It is chief of this world's luxuries, king by the grace of God over all the fruits of the earth. When one has tasted it, he knows what the angels eat." Ellen Ficklen has documented the important role of watermelons in American popular culture in numerous areas including folk art, literature, advertising and merchandising, and the large number of annual summer watermelon festivals throughout the country with "parades, watermelon-eating contests, seed spitting contests, watermelon queens, sports events, and plenty of food and music" (1984: 25).

Growing and exhibiting large watermelons is an

active pastime in some rural areas of the southern United States. Closely guarded family "secrets" for producing large watermelons and seeds from previous large fruit are carefully maintained. According to *The Guinness Book of Records,* the largest recorded watermelon in the United States was grown by B. Carson of Arrington, Tennessee, in 1990 and weighed a phenomenal 119 kg (Young 1997: 413).

African slaves also widely dispersed watermelon seeds in eastern North America, the circum-Caribbean, and Brazil. In the southern United States – where soil and climate conditions were optimal for watermelon cultivation – this crop ultimately became stereotypically, and often negatively, associated with rural African-Americans (see Norrman and Haarberg 1980: 67–70). Watermelons have subsequently figured as key symbols in the iconography of racism in the United States as seen during African-American protest marches in Bensonhurst, Brooklyn, in 1989, where marchers were greeted by Italian-American community residents shouting racial slurs and holding up watermelons.

In the ethnographic record of cultural anthropology, watermelons have perhaps figured most extensively in discussions of foragers and agro-pastoralists of the Kalahari Desert in southern Africa. As early as the 1850s, explorer David Livingstone described vast tracts of watermelons growing in the region. The anthropologist Richard Lee notes that watermelons, in domestic, wild, and feral varieties, constitute one of the most widespread and abundant plant species growing in the central Kalahari Desert. They are easily collected by foraging peoples and "the whole melon is brought back to camp and may be cut into slices for distribution. The melon itself may be halved and used as a cup, while the pulp is pulverized with the blunt end of a digging stick. The seeds may be roasted and eaten as well" (Lee 1979: 488).

Watermelons are among the most popular cultigens for forager-farmers in the Kalahari for the following reasons: "First, they provide a source of water; second, they are relatively drought-resistant, especially when compared to seed crops like sorghum and maize; and third, dried melons are an article of food for both humans and livestock and, after they have been cut into strips and hung on thorn trees to dry, they are easy to store" (Hitchcock and Ebert 1984: 343).

Elizabeth Cashdan emphasizes the point that "normally, when one thinks of agriculture one thinks of food resources, but ... where the dominant factor governing mobility is the availability of moisture, it is appropriate that agriculture should be used to produce a storable form of moisture" (Cashdan 1984: 316). This cultivated water supply allows some Kalahari Desert groups to remain sedentary during both rainy and dry seasons, and watermelons are often stored in large quantities by these societies (Cashdan 1984: 321).

The collection of watermelons by foragers and their incipient domestication by such groups yields insights into probable scenarios for domestication. R. W. Robinson and D. S. Decker-Walters suggest a general process for cucurbits that has a plausible fit with the history and ethnography of watermelons in the Kalahari Desert:

> Aboriginal plant gatherers were probably attracted to some of these products, particularly the relatively large, long-keeping and sometime showy fruits. After fruits were taken back to camp, seeds that were purposely discarded, accidently dropped or partially digested found new life on rubbish heaps, settlement edges or other disturbed areas within the camp. Eventually, recognition of the value of the resident cucurbits led to their tolerance, horticultural care and further exploitation. Finally seeds ... were carried by and exchanged among migrating bands of these incipient cultivators, gradually turning the earliest cultivated cucurbits into domesticated crops. (Robinson and Decker-Walters 1997: 23)

Such a process of domestication is somewhat different from those analyzed for cereal grains, where early transitional forager-farmers exploited densely concentrated stands of the wild ancestors of later domesticated varieties.

Cross-cultural uses of watermelon are quite varied. They are primarily consumed fresh for their sweet and juicy fruits and are often eaten as desserts. In some African cuisines, however, they are served as a cooked vegetable. The rind may be consumed in pickled or candied form. In parts of the former Soviet Union and elsewhere watermelon juice is fermented into an alcoholic beverage. Roasted seeds of this crop are eaten throughout Asia and the Middle East, and watermelon seeds are ground into flour and baked as bread in some parts of India. In addition, watermelons are also sometimes used as feed for livestock (Robinson and Decker-Walters 1997: 24–7, 85; Rubatzky and Yamaguchi 1997: 603).

Variety Improvement

Cucumber

Early cucumber varieties used in the United States were selections of those originally brought from Europe. American-originated varieties such as 'Arlington White Spine', 'Boston Pickling', and 'Chicago Pickling' were developed in the late nineteenth century. Cucumber is prone to a large number of potentially devastating diseases, and its rapid trailing growth makes chemical control of foliar and fruit diseases quite difficult. As a result, interest in the development of genetic disease tolerance has long been the focus of plant breeding efforts and has met with great success:

Tolerance to at least nine diseases has been incorporated into a single genotype. The first monoecious hybrid, 'Burpee Hybrid', was made available in 1945. Although seed costs were higher, multiple advantages of hybrids were soon recognized. Commercial companies built large research staffs to develop hybrids that provided proprietary exclusivity in those species where appropriate. Gynoecious hybrids made their appearance in 1962 when 'Spartan Dawn' was introduced. This all-female characteristic has since been exploited in both pickling and fresh-market types (Wehner and Robinson 1991: 1–3).

Melon

An 1806 catalog lists 13 distinct melon sorts derived from European sources (Tapley, Enzie, and Van Eseltine 1937: 60). Management of plant diseases in melon presents the same difficulties as with cucumbers. Accordingly, incorporation of disease tolerance into commercial types has been a major objective of plant breeders. One type, 'PMR 45', developed by the U.S. Department of Agriculture and the University of California in 1937, represented an enormous contribution because it provided resistance to powdery mildew *(Erisiphe cichoracearum),* which was the most devastating disease of melons in the arid western United States. This variety and its descendants dominated the U.S. market for about 40 years (Whitaker and Davis 1962: 57–9). Hybrids, which now predominate in the Cantalupensis group, began to appear in the mid-1950s with the introduction of 'Burpee Hybrid', 'Harper Hybrid', and others (Minges 1972: 69, 71).

Watermelon

Tolerance to fusarium wilt *(Fusarium oxysporum f. sp. niveum)* and anthracnose *(Colletotrichum orbiculare),* which was a prime objective of watermelon breeding programs, was achieved with the development of three varieties that dominated commercial production for almost four decades. 'Charleston Gray' was developed by C. F. Andrus of the U.S. Department of Agriculture in 1954, 'Crimson Sweet' by C. V. Hall of Kansas State University in 1964, and 'Jubilee' by J. M. Crall at the University of Florida in 1963 (Figure II.C.6.10). These varieties are no longer used to any extent, having been replaced by hybrids of the Allsweet and blocky Crimson Sweet types because of superior quality, high yields, and an attractive rind pattern. In Japan and other parts of Asia, watermelon varieties in use are susceptible to fusarium wilt, so they are grafted (Figure II.C.6.11) onto resistant root stocks (Lee 1994). In addition to diploid hybrids, triploid (seedless) hybrids are expected to dominate the watermelon market in the near future.

Production, Consumption, and Nutritional Composition

Production

Cucumber. As Table II.C.6.1 indicates, well over half of world cucumber and gherkin production occurs in Asia (the term "gherkin" is used here to denote small cucumber, rather than bur or West India gherkin). Though significant production also occurs in Europe and in North and Central

Figure II.C.6.10. 'Jubilee' watermelon developed by J. M. Crall, University of Florida, in 1963.

Figure II.C.6.11. In Japan, watermelon seedlings are grafted by
machine onto Fusarium-resistant
rootstocks.

America, China accounts for about 40 percent of
world production. Other Asian countries with
high cucumber production are Iran, Turkey,
Japan, Uzbekistan, and Iraq. Only the United States,
Ukraine, the Netherlands, and Poland are world
leaders outside of Asia in cucumber production.
Yields in the leading producing countries range
from 8.6 tons per hectare (ha) in Iraq to 500 tons/ha
in the Netherlands. The extraordinary yields in
the Netherlands are because of protected culture
of parthenocarpic types (United Nations 1996:
134–5).

Melon. As with cucumber, Asia produces more than
half of the world's melon crop (Table II.C.6.2). Whereas
Europe, North and Central America, and Africa are
important world production centers, China produces
about 25 percent of the world's crop. Turkey and Iran
are also leading melon-producing countries. Yields in
the leading countries range from 13.0 tons/ha in
Mexico to 26.9 tons/ha in China (United Nations 1996:
122–3). In Japan, melons are usually grown in greenhouses. The very best ones are sold to be used as special gifts. Prices shown (Figure II.C.6.12) are roughly
U.S. $50, $60, and $70 each.

Table II.C.6.1. *World cucumber and gherkin production,
1995*

Location	Area (ha × 10³)	Yield (t × ha⁻¹)	Production (t × 10³)
World	1,200	16.1	19,353
Africa	23	17.0	388
North and Central America	106	13.8	1,462
South America	4	16.8	67
Asia	780	17.1	13,372
Europe	90	27.2	2,434
Oceania	1	15.8	21
Leading countries			
China	468[a]	17.2	8,042[a]
Iran	72[a]	17.4	1,250[a]
Turkey	41[a]	28.0	1,150[a]
United States	71[a]	14.1	992[a]
Japan	19[a]	45.6	866[a]
Ukraine	61	11.0	669
Netherlands	1[a]	500.0	500[a]
Poland	34[a]	10.9	370[a]
Uzbekistan	35[a]	10.0	350[a]
Iraq	40[a]	8.6	346[a]

[a]Estimated.

Source: United Nations (1996), pp. 134–5.

Table II.C.6.2. *World cantaloupe and other melon production, 1995*

Location	Area (ha × 10³)	Yield (t × ha⁻¹)	Production (t × 10³)
World	823	17.0	14,018
Africa	61	16.9	1,024
North and Central America	116	15.6	1,805
South America	41	7.6	309
Asia	460	18.3	8,422
Europe	142	16.8	2,382
Oceania	4	21.1	76
Leading countries			
China	130[a]	26.9	3,492[a]
Turkey	110[a]	16.4	1,800[a]
Iran	88[a]	13.8	1,215[a]
United States	42[a]	20.5	859[a]
Spain	43[a]	19.0	820[a]
Romania	50[a]	13.6	680[a]
Mexico	50[a]	13.0	650[a]
Egypt	25[a]	18.4	480[a]
Morocco	25[a]	16.7	415[a]
Japan	18[a]	22.3	390[a]

[a]Estimated.

Source: United Nations (1996), pp. 122–3.

Figure II.C.6.12. Melons for sale as special gifts in Kyoto, Japan.

Table II.C.6.3. *World watermelon production, 1995*

Location	Area (ha × 10³)	Yield (t × ha⁻¹)	Production (t × 10³)
World	1,823	16.3	29,656
Africa	120	16.3	1,956
North and Central America	134	17.9	2,394
South America	131	8.8	1,153
Asia	905	19.3	17,502
Europe	122	21.8	2,652
Oceania	5	17.0	80
Leading countries			
China	359[a]	18.6	6,696[a]
Turkey	135[a]	28.8	3,600[a]
Iran	145[a]	18.3	2,650[a]
United States	86[a]	21.1	1,808[a]
Korea Republic	38[a]	23.7	900[a]
Georgia	60[a]	13.3	800[a]
Egypt	34[a]	21.2	720[a]
Uzbekistan	62[a]	11.3	700[a]
Japan	22[a]	30.4	655[a]
Moldova Republic	50[a]	13.0	650[a]

[a]Estimated.

Source: United Nations (1996), pp. 146-7.

Watermelon. Asia produces about 60 percent of the world's watermelons with major production in China (23 percent), Turkey (12 percent), Iran (9 percent), Korea Republic (3 percent), Georgia (3 percent), Uzbekistan (2 percent), and Japan (2 percent) (Table II.C.6.3). Yields in the major producing countries range from 11.3 tons/ha in Uzbekistan to 30.4 tons/ha in Japan (Figure II.C.6.13), where much of the production is in protected culture (United Nations 1996: 146-7).

Figure II.C.6.13. Low, supported row covers for watermelon production in Daiei, Japan.

Consumption and Nutritional Composition

Cucurbits, as previously discussed in this chapter, are an important part of the diet in the United States (Table II.C.6.4), where the annual consumption of watermelon, melon, and cucumber amounts to just over 17 kg per person (USDA 1996). Cucurbit fruits are high in moisture and low in fat, which makes them popular with consumers interested in healthy diets (Table II.C.6.5). Those with orange flesh like muskmelon and winter squash are excellent sources of vitamin A. Orange-fleshed cucumbers have been developed recently from crosses between United States pickling cucumber varieties and the orange-fruited "Xishuangbanna" cucumber from the People's Republic of China. The provitamin A carotene content of these cucumbers is equivalent to other orange-fleshed cucurbits (Simon and Navazio 1997). Moderate amounts of essential inorganic elements and other vitamins are provided by the cucurbit fruit. Aside from the low fat content and high vitamin A content of some cucurbit fruits, their principal value in the diet of people living in developed countries is in their unique colors, shapes, flavors, and adaptability to various cuisines.

The internal quality of watermelon fruit is a function of flesh color and texture, freedom from defects, sweetness, and optimum maturity. Unfortunately, these criteria cannot, as a rule, be assessed without cutting the melon. So many watermelons of inferior or marginal quality have been marketed that consumers have increasingly lost confidence in the product. The current supermarket practice of preparing cut and sectioned watermelon provides at least partial assurance of quality to the purchaser, but no indication of sweetness. In Japan, the quality of whole watermelon fruit is assessed by nuclear magnetic resonance (NMR) before marketing. Soluble solids and flesh integrity can be determined nondestructively in seconds (Figure II.C.6.14). As mentioned, because of their exceptional quality, such watermelons can be sold locally for the equivalent of about U.S. $50–$70 (Figure II.C.6.15).

In contrast to the composition of the pulp, watermelon seeds, which are used for food in various parts of the world, are low in moisture and high in carbohydrates, fats, and protein. Varieties with very large seeds have been developed especially for use as food in China, where more than 200,000 tons are produced annually on 140,000 ha land (Zhang 1996).

David Maynard
Donald N. Maynard

Table II.C.6.4. *Per capita consumption of cucumbers, melons, and watermelons in the United States, 1996*

Vegetable	Consumption (kg)
Cucumber – fresh	2.54
Cucumber – processed	2.18
Honeydew melon	1.13
Muskmelon	4.26
Watermelon	7.26
All vegetables – fresh	90.81
All vegetables – processed	106.86

Source: USDA (1996), VGS-269.

Table II.C.6.5 *Nutritional composition of some cucurbits; amounts per 100 g edible portion*

Nutrient	Cucumber (slicing)	Cucumber (pickling)	West India gherkin	Casaba melon	Honeydew melon	Musk-melon	Watermelon (fruit)	Watermelon (seed)	Summer squash	Winter squash
Water (%)	96	96	93	92	90	90	93	5.7	94	89
Energy (kcal)	13	12	17	26	35	35	26	567	20	37
Protein (g)	0.5	0.7	1.4	0.9	0.5	0.9	0.5	25.8	1.2	1.5
Fat (g)	0.1	0.1	0.3	0.1	0.1	0.3	0.2	49.7	0.2	0.2
Carbohydrate (g)	2.9	2.4	2.0	6.2	9.2	8.4	6.4	15.1	4.4	8.8
Fiber (g)	0.6	0.6	0.6	0.5	0.6	0.4	–	4.0	0.6	1.4
Ca (mg)	14	13	26	5	6	11	7	53	20	31
P (mg)	17	24	38	7	10	17	10	–	35	32
Fe (mg)	0.3	0.6	0.6	0.4	0.1	0.2	0.5	–	0.5	0.6
Na (mg)	2	6	6	12	10	9	1	–	2	4
K (mg)	149	190	290	210	271	309	100	–	195	350
Vitamin A (IU)	45	270	270	30	40	3,224	590	–	196	4,060
Thiamine (mg)	0.03	0.04	0.1	0.06	0.08	0.04	0.03	0.1	0.06	0.10
Riboflavin (mg)	0.02	0.2	0.04	0.02	0.02	0.02	0.03	0.12	0.04	0.03
Niacin (mg)	0.30	0.4	0.4	0.40	0.60	0.57	0.20	1.4	0.55	0.80
Ascorbic acid (mg)	4.7	19.0	51.0	16.0	24.8	42.2	7.0	–	14.8	12.3
Vitamin B_6	0.05	0.4	0.4	–	0.06	0.12	–	1.4	0.11	0.08

Sources: Gebhardt, Cutrufelli, and Matthews (1982), Haytowitz and Matthews (1984), and Rubatzky and Yamaguchi (1997).

Figure II.C.6.14. NMR watermelon quality determination in Japan.

Bibliography

Bailey, Liberty Hyde. 1976. *Hortus third.* New York.

Bates, David M., Richard W. Robinson, and Charles Jeffrey, eds. 1990. *Biology and utilization of the cucurbitaceae.* Ithaca, N.Y.

Blake, L. W. 1981. Early acceptance of watermelons by Indians in the United States. *Journal of Ethnobiology* 1: 193–9.

Cashdan, Elizabeth. 1984. The effects of food production on mobility in the Central Kalahari. In *From hunters to farmers: The causes and consequences of food production,* ed. J. Desmond Clark and Steven A. Brandt, 311–27. Berkeley, Calif.

Cowan, C. Wesley, and Patty Jo Watson. 1992. Some concluding remarks. In *The origins of agriculture: An international perspective,* ed. C. Wesley Cowan and Patty Jo Watson, 207–12. Washington, D.C.

Ficklen, Ellen. 1984. *Watermelon.* Washington, D.C.

Gebhardt, S. E., R. Cutrufelli, and R. H. Matthews. 1982. *Composition of foods, fruits and fruit juices - raw, processed, prepared.* U.S. Department of Agriculture Handbook, 8–9.

Gómez-Guillamón, M. L., ed. 1996. *Cucurbits towards 2000.* Malaga, Spain.

Harlan, Jack R. 1992. Indigenous African agriculture. In *The origins of agriculture: An international perspective,* ed. C. Wesley Cowan and Patty Jo Watson, 59–70. Washington, D.C.

Harlan, Jack R., J. M. J. de Wet, and Ann Stemler. 1976. Plant domestication and indigenous African agriculture. In *Origins of African plant domestication,* ed. Jack Harlan, Jan M. J. de Wet, and Ann B. L. Stemler, 3–19. The Hague.

Harris, David R. 1976. Traditional systems of plant food production and the origins of agriculture in West Africa. In *Origins of African plant domestication,* ed. Jack Harlan, Jan M. J. de Wet, and Ann B. L. Stemler, 311–56. The Hague.

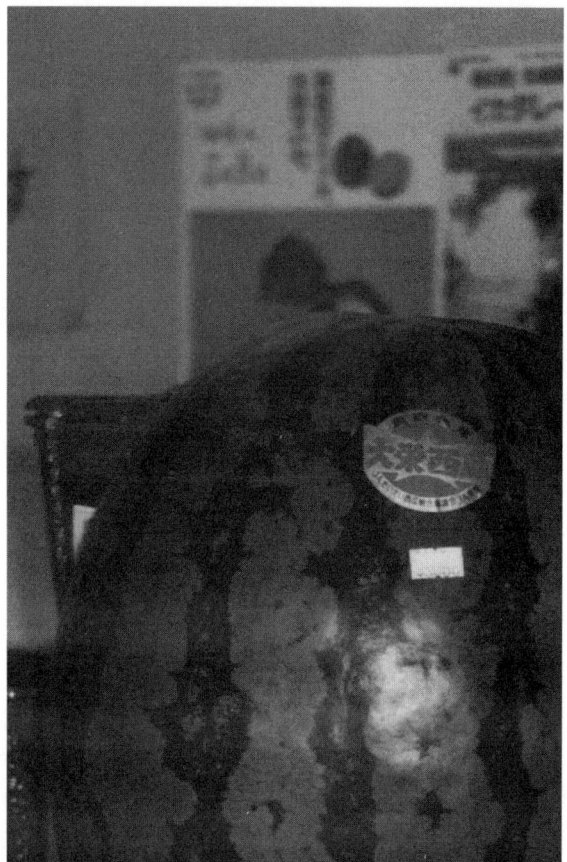

Figure II.C.6.15. Watermelon for sale in Japan at U.S. $50.

Haytowitz, D. B., and R. H. Matthews. 1984. *Composition of foods, vegetables and vegetable products - raw, processed, prepared.* U.S. Department of Agriculture Handbook, 8-11.

Hedrick, U. P. 1919. Sturtevant's notes on cultivated plants. *New York Department of Agriculture Annual Report* 27 (2, II): 1-686. New York.

Hitchcock, Robert K., and James I. Ebert. 1984. Foraging and food production among Kalahari hunter/gatherers. In *From hunters to farmers: The causes and consequences of food production,* ed. J. Desmond Clark and Steven A. Brandt, 328-48. Berkeley, Calif.

Jeffrey, Charles. 1990a. An outline classification of the Cucurbitaceae. In *Biology and utilization of the Cucurbitaceae,* ed. D. M. Bates, R. W. Robinson, and C. Jeffrey, 449-63. Ithaca, N.Y.

1990b. Systematics of the Cucurbitaceae: An overview. In *Biology and utilization of the Cucurbitaceae,* ed. D. M. Bates, R. W. Robinson, and C. Jeffrey, 3-9. Ithaca, N.Y.

Lee, Jung-Myung. 1994. Cultivation of grafted vegetables I. Current status, grafting methods, and benefits. *HortScience* 29: 235-9.

Lee, Richard B. 1979. *The Kung San: Men, women, and work in a foraging society.* New York.

Lester, G. E., and J. R. Dunlap, ed. 1994. *Proceedings of cucurbitaceae 94.* Edinburg, Tex.

Lower, R. L., and M. O. Edwards. 1986. Cucumber breeding. In *Breeding vegetable crops,* ed. M. J. Bassett, 173-207. Westport, Conn.

Maynard, D. N. 1996. *Growing seedless watermelons.* University of Florida, Gainesville.

Maynard, D. N., and G. W. Elmstrom. 1991. Potential for western-type muskmelon production in central and southwest Florida. *Proceedings of the Florida State Horticultural Society* 104: 229-32.

McClung de Tapia, Emily. 1992. The origins of agriculture in Mesoamerica and Central America. In *The origins of agriculture: An international perspective,* ed. C. Wesley Cowan and Patty Jo Watson, 143-72. Washington, D.C.

Minges, P. A., ed. 1972. *Descriptive list of vegetable varieties.* Washington D.C. and St. Joseph, Mich.

Minnis, Paul E. 1992. Earliest plant cultivation in the desert borderlands of North America. In *The origins of agriculture: An international perspective,* ed. C. Wesley Cowan and Patty Jo Watson, 121-41. Washington, D.C.

Mintz, Sidney W. 1996. *Tasting food, tasting freedom: Excursions into eating, culture and the past.* Boston, Mass.

Mohr, H. C. 1986. Watermelon breeding. In *Breeding vegetable crops,* ed. M. J. Bassett, 37-42. Westport, Conn.

Munger, H. M., and R. W. Robinson. 1991. Nomenclature of *Cucumis melo* L. *Cucurbit Genetics Cooperative Report* 14: 43-4.

Neal, M. C. 1965. *In gardens of Hawaii.* Honolulu.

Ng, T. J., ed. 1996. *Cucurbit Genetics Cooperative Report.* College Park, Md.

Norrman, Ralf, and Jon Haarberg. 1980. *Nature and languages: A semiotic study of cucurbits in literature.* London.

Purseglove, J. W. 1976. The origins and migration of crops in tropical Africa. In *Origins of African plant domestication,* ed. Jack Harlan, Jan M. J. de Wet, and Ann B. L. Stemler, 291-309. The Hague.

Reed, Charles A., ed. 1977. *Origins of agriculture.* The Hague.

Robinson, R. W., and D. S. Decker-Walters. 1997. *Cucurbits.* New York.

Rubatzky, V. R., and M. Yamaguchi. 1997. *World vegetables: Principles, production, and nutritive value.* New York.

Sauer, Jonathan D. 1993. *Historical geography of crop plants: A select roster.* Boca Raton, Fla.

Simon, P. W., and J. P. Navazio. 1997. Early orange mass 400, early orange mass 402, and late orange mass 404: High-carotene cucumber germplasm. *HortScience* 32: 144-5.

Smith, Bruce D. 1995. *The emergence of agriculture.* New York.

Tapley, W. T., W. D. Enzie, and G. P. Van Eseltine. 1937. *The vegetables of New York.* Vol. 1, Part IV, *The cucurbits.* New York State Agricultural Experiment Station, Geneva.

Thomas, C. E., ed. 1989. *Proceedings of Cucurbitaceae 89.* Charleston, S.C.

United Nations. 1996. *FAO production yearbook.* Rome.

USDA (U.S. Department of Agriculture). 1996. *Vegetables and specialties: Situation and outlook.* VGS-269. Washington, D.C.

Watson, A. M. 1983. *Agricultural innovation in the early Islamic world: The diffusion of crops and foraging techniques, 700-1100.* New York.

Wehner, T. C., and R. W. Robinson. 1991. A brief history of the development of cucumber cultivars in the United States. *Cucurbit Genetics Cooperative Report* 14: 1-3.

Whitaker, Thomas W., and W. P. Bemis. 1976. Cucurbits. In *Evolution of crop plants,* ed. N. W. Simmonds, 64-9. London.

Whitaker, T. W., and G. N. Davis. 1962. *Cucurbits. Botany, cultivation, and utilization.* New York.

Wolf, Eric R. 1982. *Europe and the people without history.* Berkeley, Calif.

Young, M. C., ed. 1997. *The Guinness book of records.* New York.

Zeven, A. C., and P. M. Zhukovsky. 1975. *Dictionary of cultivated plants and their centers of diversity.* Wageningen, the Netherlands.

Zhang, J. 1996. Breeding and production of watermelon for edible seed in China. *Cucurbit Genetics Cooperative Report* 19: 66-7.

Zohary, Daniel, and Maria Hopf. 1988. *Domestication of plants in the Old World: The origin and spread of cultivated plants in West Asia, Europe, and the Nile Valley.* Oxford.

II.C.7 ⬿ Fungi

Definitions

Fungi are uninucleate or multinucleate, eukaryotic organisms with nuclei scattered in a walled and often septate mycelium (the vegetative part of a fungus). Nutrition is heterotrophic (at least one or more organic molecules required), and fungi usually obtain their nutrients by way of diffusion or active transport.

They lack chlorophyll but may have other pigments such as carotenoids, flavonoids, and so forth.

The true fungi, Eumycota, are grouped into five divisions:

1. Mastigomycotina (aquatic or zoospore-producing fungi) - unicellular or mycelial (coenocytic, no intercellular walls); motile, uni- or biflagellate zoospores during life cycle.
2. Zygomycotina - coenocytic mycelium; sexual state (teleomorph) spores are zygospores which may be absent; asexual state (anamorph) is predominant stage consisting of uni- or multispored sporangia.
3. Ascomycotina - mycelium unicellular to multicellular; regularly septate; asexual state often present; sexual state spores are ascospores formed inside an ascus (sac); no motile state.
4. Basidiomycotina - mycelium unicellular to multicellular, regularly septate; conidial asexual state common; sexual state and motile cells absent.
5. Deuteromycotina - unicellular to multicellular mycelia; regularly septate; conidial asexual state common; no sexual state; no motile cells (O'Donnell and Peterson 1992).

D. L. Hawksworth, B. C. Sutton, and G. A. Ainsworth (1983) have estimated that there are about 250,000 species of fungi, of which Mastigomycotina composes 1.8 percent, Zygomycotina 1.2 percent, Ascomycotina about 45 percent, Basidiomycotina about 25.2 percent, and Deuteromycotina about 26.8 percent.

Most edible fungi belong to divisions 2 to 5, just listed. Yeasts are single-celled fungi that reproduce asexually by budding or fission, or sexually through ascospore formation. The term "mushroom" refers to those macrofungi (visible to the naked eye) with edible fruiting bodies (sporophores), whereas "toadstool" refers to macrofungi with toxic fruiting bodies; both mushrooms and toadstools are found in more than one of the fungal divisions (Hawksworth et al. 1983; Koivikko and Savolainen 1988).

Historical Background

Fungi have been associated with humans since prehistoric times and must have been collected and eaten along with other plants by hunter-gatherers prior to the development of agriculture (Oakley 1962; Monthoux and Lündstrom-Baudois 1979; Pöder, Peintner, and Pümpel 1992). Although their prehistoric use remains uncertain, they may have been employed as food, in the preparation of beverages, and as medicine.

There is, however, no specific evidence for the use of fungi prior to the Neolithic period, when fungi consumption would have been associated with the drinking of mead (yeast-fermented diluted honey) and yeast-fermented beer or wine, and, some-

what later, the eating of yeast-fermented (leavened) bread.

Mesopotamia
Beer was the preferred fermented drink of the Sumerians of the Late Uruk period dating to the late fourth millennium B.C. R. H. Michel, P. E. McGovern, and V. R. Badler (1992) have noted the similarity of the grooves on a Late Uruk jar at Godin Tepe (in the Zagros Mountains of Iran) with the Sumerian sign for beer, *kas*. The grooves contained a pale yellow residue, which the authors thought was an oxalate salt - oxalate salts are the principal molecules in "beerstone," a material found on barley beer fermentation containers. The Sumerians were very fond of beer and brewed at least 19 different kinds. They also used beer in some of their medical prescriptions (Majno 1975). Date and grape wine were known in Babylonia by 2900 B.C. (Saggs 1962).

Egypt
Fungi were eaten or drunk, perhaps unwittingly, in Egypt thousands of years ago, in beer and, later, in wine and bread. Yeasts were discovered in a vase of the Late Predynastic period (3650–3300 B.C.) (Saffirio 1972). J. R. Geller (1992) identified a brewery at Hierakonpolis by examining the chemistry of the black residue found in the brewery vats dating from roughly the same time. Similar beer vat sites have been discovered in Egypt from the Amratian (about 3800–3500 B.C.) through the Early Dynastic period (about 3100–2686 B.C.) (Geller 1989).

A yeast, resembling modern *Saccharomyces* spp. and named *Saccharomyces winlocki,* was found in an undisturbed Theban tomb of the Eleventh Dynasty (2135–2000 B.C.) (Gruss 1928). *S. winlocki* was also found in an amphora containing beer in the tomb of

Field mushroom

Queen Meryet-Amun of the Eighteenth Dynasty (1570-1305 B.C.) at Thebes (Winlock 1973).

The bag press, used to press grapes in the manufacture of wine, is shown on the walls of Egyptian tombs from around 3000 B.C. (Forbes 1967). Wine was drunk by upper-class Egyptians and beer was the beverage of the lower classes. Leavened bread was also a common food, as is illustrated by paintings in the tomb of Ramses III (Goody 1982).

Sudan

According to H. A. Dirar (1993), date wine, beer, bread, and cake may have been made in the Sudanese Kingdom of Yam (2800-2200 B.C.). Two men drinking beer or wine through a bamboo straw are shown in a drawing at Mussawarat es Sufra, a site dating to Meroitic times (from between 1500 and 690 B.C. to A.D. 323). Strabo (7 B.C.) mentioned that the Meroites (Ethiopians) knew how to brew the sorghum beer that is called *merissa* today. Wine, which dated from between 1570 and 1080 B.C., was introduced into the Sudan by Egyptian colonists of the New Kingdom (Dirar 1993).

China

In Chinese folklore, Shen Nung, the "Divine Ploughman," a mythical ruler, taught the people how to use plant medicines and, presumably, taught them about fungi as well. Y. C. Wang (1985) has suggested that the Chinese knew about fungi some 6,000 to 7,000 years ago but offered no specific evidence for their use as food. K. Sakaguchi (1972), who wrote that mold fermentation was traceable to about 1000 B.C. in China, has been supported by T. Yokotsuka (1985).

B. Liu (1958) claimed that in China, mushrooms were first eaten in the Chou Dynasty about 900 B.C. Lui Shi Chuen Zhou, in his *Spring and Autumn of Lui's Family,* recorded the eating of *ling gi (Ganoderma* sp.) about 300 B.C. (Liu 1991). The *Book of Songs,* printed in the Han Dynasty (26 B.C. to A.D. 220), mentioned over 200 useful plants, including a number of common edible mushrooms (Wang 1985). Similarly, the *Book of Rites,* written about A.D. 300, mentions several edible fungi (Wang 1985).

Auricularia auricula and *Auricularia polytricha* ("wood ear") were described by Hsiang Liu (about 300-200 B.C.) and by Hung Wing T'ao (between A.D. 452 and 536). The *T'ang Pen Ts'ao* of the Tang Dynasty (seventh century) described five kinds of *mu-erh,* which grew on various trees. The cultivation of the mushrooms (*Auricularia* spp.) was begun in the Tang Dynasty (A.D. 618-907) (Chang and Miles 1987), although they were probably eaten at least 1,400 years ago (Lou 1982).

The mushroom *Lentinus edodes (shiitake)* was recognized as the "elixir of life" by a famous Chinese physician, Wu Shui, during the Ming Dynasty (1368-1644). This was testimony to a primitive form of *shiitake* cultivation, called *hoang-ko,* that had been developed about 800 years ago (Ito 1978). According to R. Singer (1961), Japanese Emperor Chuai was offered the singular mushroom by the natives of Kyushu in A.D. 199, from which we may infer that they were gathered for consumption much earlier in China.

The Chinese method of producing alcoholic beverages required that *Rhizopus, Mucor,* or *Saccharomyces* spp. be grown spontaneously on compact bricks of wheat flour or other materials called *kyokushi.* This process was said to have been introduced into Japan at the beginning of the fifth century A.D. and, hence, must have been used appreciably earlier in China (Kodama and Yoshizowa 1977).

A pigment from a fungus was mentioned in *Jih Yang Pen Chaio* (Daily Herb), written by Jui Wu in A.D. 1329. The organism producing the pigment was the yeast *Monascus* sp. (Wang 1985), which grows on rice and has been widely used in the Orient. It is the source of a red pigment employed to color such things as wine and soybean cheese (Lin and Iizuka 1982).

The Mongolian conquests introduced another source of fungal foods - cheese - to the Chinese people, who generally shunned dairy products. Su Hui, royal dietician during the reign of Wen Zong (Tuq. Temur) from A.D. 1328 to 1332, wrote *Yenishan Zhengyao* (The True Principles of Eating and Drinking). In it he included dairy products such as fermented mare's milk, butter, and two cheeses (Sabban 1986). Another dietician of the Yuan Dynasty, Jia Ming (A.D. 1268-1374), also discussed the use of cheese over vegetables or pasta and mentioned fungi as food (Sabban 1986).

As previously hinted, cultivation (rather than gathering from the wild) of mushrooms for human food on a large scale may first have begun in China as early as the Han Dynasty (206 B.C. to A.D. 9). In the first century A.D., Wang Chung's *Lun Heng* stated that the cultivation of *chih* (fungus) was as easy as the cultivation of beans. In 1313, procedures for mushroom cultivation were described in Wong Ching's *Book of Agriculture* (Chao Ken 1980).

Fermented protein foods have an ancient history in China (Yokotsuka 1985). According to the *Shu-Ching,* written about 3,000 years ago, *chu* (yeast or fungus) was essential for the manufacture of alcoholic beverages from wheat, barley, millet, and rice as early as the Chou Dynasty, 1121-256 B.C. By the Han Dynasty, *chu* was made in the form of a cake called *ping-chu.* A sixth-century text on agricultural technology, *Chi-Min-Yao Shu,* detailed the preparation of several kinds of *chu* and other fermented foods such as *chiang* (fermented animal, bird, or fish flesh with millet). *Chu* was a common flavoring in the China of the Chou Dynasty (1121-256 B.C.), and *chiang* was mentioned in the *Analects of Confucius,* written some 600 years after that period. S. Yoshida (1985) wrote that fermented soybeans originated in China in the Han Dynasty and were known as *shi*.

Greece and Rome

That the ancient Greeks used fungi as food seems clear, because accidental mushroom poisoning was mentioned in the fifth century B.C. by both Euripides and Hippocrates (Buller 1914-16). Theophrastus (d. 287 B.C.) apparently knew and named truffles, puff-balls, and fungi (Sharples and Minter 1983).

The Romans enjoyed *boleti* (the *Agaricus* of today) and even had special vessels, called *boletari,* to cook the fungi (Grieve 1925). Presumably, a dish of *boleti* concealed the poisonous mushrooms that Agrippina administered to her husband, the Emperor Claudius, so that her son, Nero, could become emperor of Rome (Grieve 1925).

According to J. André (1985), the Romans ate *Amanita caesarea, Boletus purpureus,* and *Boletus suillus,* as well as truffles, puffballs, and morels (Rolfe and Rolfe 1925). Fungi must have been prized by wealthy Romans, for they are mentioned as special delicacies by Horace (65-8 B.C.), Ovid (43 B.C. to A.D. 19), Pliny (A.D. 46-120), Cicero (A.D. 106-143), and Plutarch (A.D. 46-120) (Rolfe and Rolfe 1925; Watling and Seaward 1976). The oldest cookbook presently known was written by Caelius Apicius in the third century A.D. and includes several recipes for cooking fungi (Findlay 1982).

Japan

The earliest reference to mushrooms in Japanese texts is in the *Nihongi* (Book of Chronicles), completed in A.D. 720, which recorded that mushrooms were presented to the Emperor Ojin in A.D. 288 by the local chieftains in Yamato (Wasson 1975). But according to Singer (1961), the earliest consumption of fungi in Japan was in A.D. 199, when the Emperor Chuai was offered *shiitake* by the natives of Kyushu. Mushrooms are rarely mentioned in the early poetry of Japan, but *Manyoshu,* the first anthology of poetry (compiled in the latter half of the eighth century), refers to the pine mushroom, and the *Shui Wakashu* (from about A.D. 1008) mentions it twice. In the *Bun-rui Haiku Zenshu,* written by Masaoka Shiki sometime around the beginning of the sixteenth century, there were 250 verses about mushrooms and mushroom gathering (Blyth 1973).

Mexico

The Spanish conquerors of Mexico reported in the sixteenth century that the Aztecs used a mushroom called *teonanacatl* ("god's flesh"), and sacred mushrooms were pictured in the few Mayan manuscripts that survived the Spanish destruction of "idols and pagan writings." The Mayan *Codex Badianus,* written in 1552 by Martin de la Cruz, an Indian herbalist, mentioned the use of *teonanacatl* for painful ailments.

The *Codex Magliabecchi* (c. 1565) includes an illustration depicting an Aztec eating mushrooms, and Franciscan friar Bernardino de Sahagun (1499-1590) discussed, in his *General History of the Things of New Spain,* the use of *teonanacatl* to induce hallucinations (Guerra 1967). The Aztecs were familiar enough with fungi to give them names: *nanacatl* (mushroom), *teonanacatl* (sacred mushroom), and *quauhtlanamacatl* (wild mushroom). Indeed, the Mazatecs of Oaxaca and the Chinantecs of Mexico still use hallucinogenic mushrooms for divination, medical diagnosis, and religious purposes (Singer 1978).

The Near East

Al-Biruni, an Arab physician of about 1,000 years ago, described the eating of several fungi, including truffles (Said, Elahie, and Hamarneh 1973). *Terfazia urenaria* is the truffle of classical antiquity, and it is prized in the Islamic countries of North Africa and the Near East as *terfaz*. The best truffles were reputed to come from the areas of Damascus in Syria and Olympus in Greece (Maciarello and Tucker 1994).

Europe

Truffles were already a part of Roman cuisine by the first century A.D., when the Roman poet and satirist Decimus Junius Juvenalis wrote: "[T]he Truffles will be handed round if it is Spring, and if the longed-for thunders have produced the precious dainties." At that time, fungi were thought to originate when lightning struck the earth during thunderstorms. Truffles were a part of French cuisine by the time of the Renaissance and were exported to England by the beginning of the eighteenth century (Maciarello and Tucker 1994).

In France, mushrooms were cultivated on manure from horse stables during the reign of Louis XIV (Tounefort 1707), and F. Abercrombie (1779) described an English method of composting such manure for the growth of mushrooms by stacking it, a method still in use today. Mushrooms are still highly prized as food in Europe. Many wild fungi are gathered and eaten, and many more are cultivated or imported (Mau, Beelman, and Ziegler 1994).

Fungi Eaten Now and in the Past by Humans

Fungi have been a prized food of peoples past and present around the world. Many examples of these fungi are listed in Table II.C.7.1, which is meant to be indicative rather than exhaustive.

Fungi are mostly eaten cooked, although some ethnic groups and individuals eat them raw. Today, the people of Asia appear to be the most eclectic consumers of fungi. The Chinese eat perhaps as many as 700 wild and domesticated species. The Japanese use well over 80 species (Imai 1938); the people of India may consume more than 50 species; and the French, not to be outdone, enjoy well over 200 species from one area alone – that of Haute-Savoie (Ramain 1981). Similarly, North Americans eat more than 200 wild and cultivated fungal species (Lincoff 1984).

The reader should be aware that many mushroom genera include both edible and toxic species, and that some mushroom varieties can be edible, whereas others of the same species are not. In the case of some mushrooms, boiling in water before eating will remove toxic or unpleasant secondary metabolites.

Relatively barren areas of the Near East, including parts of Africa and Asia, support thriving populations of truffles, genus *Tirmania*, which are eaten from Morocco and Egypt in North Africa to Israel, Saudi Arabia, and Iraq (Said et al. 1973; Alsheikh, Trappe, and Trappe 1983). Truffles called *fuga* are prized in Kuwait and eaten with rice and meat (Dickson 1971). In some areas of the Arabian Gulf, the truffle crop may be appropriated by the local royal families (Alsheikh et al. 1983).

Today, edible fungi are cultivated or collected in the wild in huge numbers and shipped by air from the source country to consumer countries around the world; fungi may also be canned or dried for long-term storage and later consumption.

Table II.C.7.1. *Fungi eaten by humans around the world now and in the past*

Species by country	People	Local name	Reference
Central Africa			
Boletus sp.			Schnell 1957
Congo			
Auricularia polytricha			"
Boletus sudanicus			"
Cantharellus aurantiaca			"
Clitocybe castanea			"
Lentinus sp.			"
Lepiota sp.			"
Russula sp.			"
Schulzerea sp.			"
Equatorial Africa			
Leucocoprinus molybdites			"
Volvaria diplasia			"
Volvaria esculenta			"
Ivory Coast			
Hygrophoropsis mangenoti			"
Kenya			
Mushrooms		*mbeere*	Scudder 1971
Libya			
Terfazia boudieri		*chatin*	Ahmed, Mohamed, and Hami 1981
Madagascar			
Leucocoprinus molbdites			Schnell 1957
Malawi			
Amanita bingensis	Yao	*nakajongolo*	Morris 1987
Amanita hemibapha	Yao	*katelela*	"
Amanita zambiana	Yao	*utenga*	"
Auricularia auricula		*matwe*	"
Cantharellus congolensis	Chichewa	*riakambuzi*	"
Cantharellus longisporus	Yao	*makungula*	"
Cantharellus tenuis	Chichewa	*ngundasuku*	"
Clavaria albiramea	Yao	*nakambi*	"
Lentinus cladopus	Yao	*nakatasi*	"
Lentinus squarrosus	Yao		"
Psathyrella atroumbonata	Yao	*ujonjo*[a]	"
Psathyrella candolleana	Chichewa	*nyonzive*[a]	"
Russula atropurpura			"

(continued)

Table II.C.7.1. *(Continued)*

Species by country	People	Local name	Reference
Malawi			
Russula delica	Chichewa	*kamathova*	Morris 1987
Russula lepida	Chichewa	*kafidi*[a]	"
Russula schizoderma	Yao	*usuinda*[a]	"
Strobilomyces constatispora	Chichewa	*chipindi*[a]	Pegler and Piearce 1980
Termitomyces clypeatus	Chichewa	*nyonzwe*[a]	"
Termitomyces titanicus			"
North Africa			
Terfazia spp.			Alsheikh, Trappe, and Trappe 1983
Tirmanea nivea			"
Tirmanea pinoyi			"
South Africa			
Terfazia sp.	San Bushmen		Lee 1979
West Africa			
Leucoprenus molybdites			Schnell 1957
Zambia			
Amanita zambiana			Piearce 1981
Cantharellus densifolius			Morris 1987
Cantharellus longisporus			"
Lactarius vellereus			"
Lactarius spp.			Piearce 1981
Lentinus cladopus			"
Macrolepiota spp.			"
Russula spp.			"
Schizophyllum commune			"
Termitomyces spp.			"
Termitomyces titanicus	Chewa		"
Termitomyces clypeatus	Bebba		"
Zimbabwe			
Volvaria volvacea			Irvine 1952
India			
Agaricus arvensis			Purkayastha 1978
Agaricus basianilosus			"
Agaricus bisporus			"
Agaricus campestris			Bose and Bose 1940
Auricularia delicata			Verma and Singh 1981
Bovista crocatus			Purkayastha 1978
Bovista gigantea			Bose and Bose 1940
Calocybe indica			Purkayastha 1978
Cantharellus aurantiacus			"
Cantharellus cibarius			"
Cantharellus minor			"
Calvatia cyathiformis			"
Clavaria aurea			Verma and Singh 1981
Clitocybe sp.			"
Collybia albuminosa			Purkayastha 1978
Coprinus atramentarius			Kaul 1981
Coprinus comatus			"
Coprinus micaceus			"
Elvela crispa			Purkayastha 1978
Elvela metra			"
Enteloma macrocarpum			Bose and Bose 1940
Enteloma microcarpum			"
Geaster sp.			"
Geopora arenicola			Kaul 1981
Lactarius sp.			Verma and Singh 1981
Lentinus edodes			"
Lentinus subnudus			Purkayashta 1978
Lepiota albumunosa			"

Table II.C.7.1. *(Continued)*

Species by country	People	Local name	Reference
India			
Lepiota mastoidea			Purkayashta 1978
Lycoperdon pusillum			"
Lycoperdon pyriformis			Verma and Singh 1981
Macrolepiota mastoidea			Purkayastha 1978
Macrolepiota procera			"
Macrolepiota rachodes			"
Morchella angusticeps			Kaul 1981
Morchella conica			"
Morchella deliciosa			"
Morchella hybrida			"
Pleurotus flabellatus			"
Pleurotus fossulatus			"
Pleurotus membranaceus			"
Pleurotus ostreatus			Bose and Bose 1940
Pleurotus salignus			Kaul and Kachroo 1974
Russula sp.			Verma and Singh 1981
Schizophyllum commune			"
Scleroderma sp.			"
Termitomyces albuminosa			Purkayastha 1978
Termitomyces eurhizus			"
Termitomyces microcarpus			"
Tricholoma gigantium			Verma and Singh 1981
Verpa bohemica			Kaul 1981
Volvariella diplasia			Purkaystha 1978
Volvariella terastius			"
Volvariella volvacea			"
Indonesia			
Lentinus edodes			Hiepko and Schultze-Motel 1981
Lentinus novopommeranus			"
Oudemansiella apalosorca			"
Japan			
Agaricus arvensis			Imai 1938
Agaricus campestris			"
Agaricus hortenisis			"
Agaricus placomyces			"
Agaricus silvaticus			"
Agaricus silvicol			"
Agaricus subrufescens			"
Armillaria caligata			"
Armillaria Matsutake			"
Armillaria mellea			"
Armillaria ventricosa			"
Cantharellus cibarius			"
Cantharellus floccosus			"
Clitocybe extenuata			"
Clitocybe nebularis			"
Clitopilus caespitosus			"
Collybia butyracea			
Collybia nameko			Ito 1917
Collybia velutipes			"
Cortinarius elatus			Imai 1938
Cortinarius fulgens			"
Cortinarius latus			"
Cortinarius multiformis			"
Cortinellus edodes			"
Cortinellus scalpuratus			"
Cortinellus vaccinus			"
Entoloma clypeatum			"
Gomphidus rutilis			"
Gymopilus lentus			"
Gymopilus lubricus			"

(continued)

Table II.C.7.1. *(Continued)*

Species by country	People	Local name	Reference
Japan			
Gomphidus rutilis			Imai 1938
Gymopilus lentus			"
Gymopilus lubricus			"
Hebeloma mesophaeum			"
Hygrophorus chrysodon			"
Hygrophorus erubescens			"
Hygrophorus pudorinus			"
Hypholoma lateritium			"
Lactarius akahatsu			Tanaka 1890
Lactarius deliciosus			Imai 1938
Lactarius flavidulus			"
Lactarius hatsudake			Tanaka 1890
Lactarius luteolus			Imai 1938
Lactarius piperatus			"
Lactarius sanguifluus			"
Lactarius torminosus			"
Lactarius vellereus			"
Lactarius volemus			"
Lepiota naucina			"
Marasmius oreades			"
Pholiota adiposa			"
Pholiota erebia			"
Pholiota Nameko			"
Pholiota praecox			"
Pholiota squarrosa			"
Pholiota squarrosoides			"
Pholiota terrestris			"
Pholiota togularis			"
Pholiota vahlii			"
Pleurotus cornucopiae			"
Pleurotus ostreatus			"
Pleurotus porrigens			"
Pleurotus seriotinus			"
Russula aurata			"
Russula cyanoxantha			"
Russula delica			"
Russula integra			"
Russula lactea			"
Russula virescens			"
Tricholoma albobrunneum			"
Tricholoma cartilagineum			"
Tricholoma conglobatum			"
Tricholoma equestre			"
Tricholoma gambesum			"
Tricholoma humosum			"
Tricholoma nudum			"
Tricholoma personatum			"
Tricholoma pessundatum			"
Tricholoma sejunctum			"
Cortinellus Berkeijana	Ainu		Yokayama 1975
Grifola frondosa			"
Laetiporus sulphureus			"
Lentinus edodes			"
Panellus serotinus			"
Malaysia			
Amanita manginiana			Burkill 1935
Amanita virginea			"
Psalliota campestris			"
Philippines			
Agaricus argyrostectus			Reinking 1921
Agaricus boltoni			"
Agaricus luzonensis			"
Agaricus manilensis			"

Table II.C.7.1. *(Continued)*

Species by country	People	Local name	Reference
Mexico			
Saccharomyces sp.		*chicha bruja*	Singer 1961
Boletus fragrans	Chinantec		Lipp 1991
Schizophyllum commune	Chinantec		"
Ustilago maydis	Chinantec		"
Coriolus sp.	Maya		Alcorn 1984
Lentinus cf. lepideus	Huastec, Maya		"
Schizophyllum commune	Huastec, Maya		"
Ustilago maydis	Huastec, Maya		"
Cantharellus cibarius	Mixe		Lipp 1991
Pleurotus sp.	Mixe		"
Ramaria sp.	Mixe		"
Schizophyllum commune	Mixe		"
Ustilago maydis	Nahua		Martinez et al. 1983
Ustilago maydis	Purepeche		Mapes, Guzman, and Cabellero 1981
Ustilago maydis	Totonacs		Martinez et al. 1983
Ustilago maydis	Teenek		Alcorn 1984
Lentinus lepideus	Teenek		"
Schizophyllum commune	Teenek		"
North America			
Agaricus campestris	Yaki Indians		Mead 1972
Agaricus campestris	Iroquois, Straits Salish		Kuhnlein and Turner 1991
Armillaria mellea	Flathead Indians		Turner 1978
Boletus sp.	Calpella Indians		Chestnut 1902
Bovista plumbea	Omaha Indians		Yanovsky 1936
Calvatia gigantea	Iroquois, Upriver Halkomelem		Kuhnlein and Turner 1991
Calvatia gigantea	Omaha Indians		Yanovsky 1936
Cantharellus cibarius	Nlaka'pamux		Kuhnlein and Turner 1991
Collybia spp.	Flathead Indians		Hart 1979
Fistulina hepatica	Cherokee		Hamil and Chiltoskey 1975
Ganoderma applanatum	Halkomelem		Kuhnlein and Turner 1991
Inonotus obliquus	Woods Cree		"
Lycoperdon giganteum	Iroquois		Yanovsky 1936
Lycoperdon sp.	White Mtn. Apache		Reagan 1929
Lycoperdon sp.	Flathead Indians		Hart 1979
Morchella sp.	Iroquois		Arnason, Hebela, and Johns 1981
Morchella sp.	Lillooet, Halkomelem		Kuhnlein and Turner 1991
Pleurotus ostreatus	Interior Salish		"
Polyporus frondosus	Iroquois		"
Polyporus pinicola	Iroquois		"
Polyporus sulphureum	Iroquois		"
Polystictus versicolor	Dakota Indians		Yanovsky 1936
Russula spp.	Flathead		Hart 1979
Tremelledon spp.	Straits Salish		Kuhnlein and Turner 1991
Tricholoma spp.	Nlaka'pamux		"
Tricholoma magnivelare	Interior Salish		"
Tricholoma populinum	Interior Salish		"
Argentina			
Agaricus campeanus	Onas		Stuart 1977
Cyttaria darwinia	Onas		"
Cyttaria hariotii	Onas		"
Cyttaria hookeri	Onas		"
Fistulina sp.	Onas		"
Polyporus eucalyptorum	Onas		"
Pycnoporus sanguinoreus	Lengua Maskoy		Arenas 1981
Brazil			
Coriolus zonatus	Yanomamo		Prance 1983
Favolus brunneolus	Yanomamo		"
Favolus striatulas	Yanomamo		"
Favolus waikassamo	Yanomamo		"
Gymnopilus hispidellus	Yanomamo		"
Hexagona subcaperata	Yanomamo		"

(continued)

Table II.C.7.1. *(Continued)*

Species by country	People	Local name	Reference
Brazil			
Hydnopolyporus palmatus	Yanomamo		Prance 1983
Lactocollybia aequatorialis	Yanomamo		"
Lentinus crinitis	Yanomamo		"
Lentinus glabratus	Yanomamo		"
Lentinus velutinus	Yanomamo		"
Neoclitocybe bisseda	Yanomamo		Prance 1972
Panus rudis	Yanomamo		"
Pholiota bicolor	Yanomamo		"
Pleurotus concavus	Yanomamo		"
Polyporus sp.	Yanomamo		"
Polyporus aquasus	Yanomamo		"
Polyporus dermoporus	Yanomamo		"
Polyporus stipitarius	Yanomamo		"
Colombia			
Fomes ignarius			Montes 1961
Ecuador			
Auricularia fuscosuccinea	Waorani		Davis and Yost 1983
Peru			
Auricularia nigrescens	Aymara		Herrera 1934
Daedalea repanda			"
Galera sp.			"
Henzites striata			"
Hirneola polytricha			"
Lycoperdon sp.			"
Schizophyllum alneum			"
Schizophyllum commune			"
Ustilago maydis			Gade 1975

[a]*ndiwa* (Chichewa) or *mboga* (Yao) is a relish or side dish of mushrooms fried in oil with onions, tomatoes, and ground nut flour.

Gross Chemical Composition of Fungi

The gross chemistry of edible fungi (Table II.C.7.2) varies with the stage of the life cycle in which they are eaten; for example, the mycelium of *Agaricus campestris,* a common white mushroom, contains 49 percent protein (Humfeld 1948), whereas the sporophore of the same species is 36 percent protein (McConnell and Esselen 1947).

Even the stage in the life cycle of the sporophore may significantly affect the gross chemistry of the fungus (Table II.C.7.3). The sporophore is the fungal part usually eaten, although the mycelium predominates in fermented foods (Purkayastha and Chandra 1976).

Most of the biomass of fungi is water, although there are wide variations in the amount of water in different species (Table II.C.7.2). The dry biomass is mainly carbohydrates, followed by proteins, lipids, and ash, in that order; again, there is wide variation in the amounts of the major components (Table II.C.7.2). In general, dried fungi contain 2 to 46 percent protein, 5 to 83 percent carbohydrates, 1 to 26 percent lipids, 1 to 10 percent RNA, 0.15 to 0.3 percent DNA, and 1 to 29 percent ash (Griffin 1981). Fungal strains with unusually high lipid content have been selected for

this trait and are grown under conditions where lipid synthesis is enhanced. These fungi serve as valuable sources of lipids that are required in large quantities for industrial purposes.

The nutritional value of many edible fungi compares well with other common foods. In essential amino acid content, where meat rates 100 and milk 99, mushrooms are rated at 98. Measuring by amino acid "score," meat scores 100, milk scores 91, and mushrooms score 89, whereas, by nutritional index, meat can score between 59 and 35, soybeans score 31, and mushrooms score 28. Indeed, by any of these criteria, some mushrooms have more nutritional value than all other plants except soybeans; at the same time, however, some edible fungi score much lower by the same criteria (Crisan and Sands 1978). One hundred grams of dried fungal biomass has an energy equivalent of from 268 to 412 kilocalories (Griffin 1981).

Table II.C.7.2 indicates that fungi provide significant amounts of protein. There is, however, some question as to how much of fungal protein is digestible (Crisan and Sands 1978). Fungi also contain sufficient quantities of the essential amino acids required by humans and other animals and have a variety of other nitrogen-containing molecules.

Table II.C.7.2. *Gross chemical composition of fungi as a percentage of fungal dry weight*

Species	No. of samples	Protein	Total carbohydrate plus fiber	Total lipids	Total nucleic acids	Ash	H$_2$O[a]	Ref.
Agaricus bisporus	5	25–33	65–72	2–3	–	8–12	90	1
Agaricus bisporus		30	66	5	–	17	–	4
Agaricus bisporus		30	–	–	–	–	–	5
Agaricus campestris		33	65	2	–	8	90	1
Agaricus merrilli		34	61	2	–	10	89	1
Agaricus perfuscus		35	63	2	–	11	91	1
Armillariella		28	101	6	–	15	–	4
mellea		16	–	–	–	–	–	5
Auricularia polytrica	2	6	97	6	–	5	89	1
Boletus aestivalis		45	35	6	–	15	–	4
Boletus aestivalis		30	–	–	–	–	–	5
Boletus edulis		30	68	3	–	8	87	1
Candida utilis		47	27	5	–	9	6	6
Cantharellus cibarius	2	22	76	5	–	8	92	1
Cantharellus cibarius		18	87	8	–	11	–	4
Clavaria botrytis		9	82	3	–	6	89	1
Clitocybe multiceps		24	69	6	–	12	94	1
Collybia albuminosa		21	76	4	–	7	89	1
Collybia sp.		5	70	4	–	26	95	1
Coprinus atramentarius	2	21	66	4	–	19	93	1
Coprinus comatus		25	66	3	–	13	92	1
Coprinus comatus		23	68	5	–	13	–	4
Flammulina velutipes		18	77	2	–	7	89	1
Hirneola affinis		10	77	14	–	11	98	1
Hypholoma candolleanum		19	77	3	–	14	89	1
Lactarius deliciosus	2	19	68	5	–	6	89	1
Lactarius hatsudake		18	79	3	–	8	93	1
Leccinum scabrum		38	58	8	–	14	–	4
Lentinus edodes	2	16	80	6	–	5	91	1
Lentinus edodes		18	76	2	–	7	90	2
Lentinus exilis		11	83	2	–	4	72	1
Lepiota procera		20	76	4	–	7	84	1
Lepista nebularis		40	51	5	–	13	–	4
Lycoperdon lilacinum		46	51	8	–	8	99	1
Macrolepiota procera		32	52	9	–	16	–	4
Marasmius oreades		36	64	8	–	12	–	4
Morchella crassipes[a]		2	5	1	–	2	90	7
Morchella esculenta	2	23	72	5	1	10	90	1
Morchella esculenta		3	5	0.3	–	2	90	7
Morchella hortensis[a]		3	5	0.3	–	2	90	7
Pholiota nameko		21	73	4	–	8	95	1
Pleurotus eous		18	71	1	–	9	92	2
Pleurotus florida		19	70	2	–	9	92	2
Pleurotus flabellatus		22	69	2	–	11	91	2
Pleurotus limpidus		39	74	9	–	5	93	1
Pleurotus opuntia		9	80	2	–	16	58	1
Pleurotus ostreatus		11	89	2	–	6	74	1
Polyporus sulfureus		14	78	3	–	7	71	1
Russula delica		29	78	9	–	8	–	4
Russula vesca		19	57	6	–	14	–	4
Russula vesca		11	–	–	–	–	–	5
Saccharomyces cerevisiae		37	39	2	8	7	–	9
Suillus granulatus		36	54	7	–	13	–	4
Terfazia boudieri		17	61	6	–	13	78	3
Tricholoma populinum[a]		1	4	1	–	1	94	8
Tricholoma portentosum		26	52	4	–	18	–	4
Tuber melanosporum		23	94	2	–	8	77	3
Volvariella diplasia		29	75	3	–	12	90	1
Volvariella esculenta		34	42	21	–	13	91	1
Volvariella volvacea	3	27	68	7	–	9	8	1
Xerocomus subtomentosus		26	51	8	–	14	–	4

[a]Refers to samples that were analyzed fresh; all others were analyzed when dry.

References:

1. Crisan and Sands (1978)
2. Bano and Rajarathnam (1982)
3. Ahmed, Mohamed, and Hami (1981)
4. Levai (1989)
5. Chang and Hayes (1978)
6. Sinskey and Batt (1987)
7. Litchfield, Vely, and Overbeck (1963)
8. Turner, Kuhnlein, and Egger (1987)
9. Miller (1968).

Table II.C.7.3. *Variations in the gross chemistry of different stages in the development of the* Volvariella volvacea *sporophore*

Chemistry (as % dry weight)	Sporophore stage			
	Button	Egg	Elongation	Mature
Moisture	89	89	89	89
Crude fat	1	2	2	4
N-free carbohydrate	43	51	50	40
Crude fiber	6	5	7	13
Crude protein	31	23	21	21
Ash	9	8	9	10
Energy (Kcal/100 g)	281	287	281	254

Source: Li and Chang (1982).

Soluble carbohydrates in fresh fungi range from 37 to 83 percent of the dry weight. In addition, there are fiber carbohydrates that make up from 4 to 32 percent (Griffin 1981).

The lipid content of fungi ranges from 0.2 percent of the cell or tissue dry weight to as high as 56 percent – more specifically, 0.2 to 47 percent for Basidiomycotina, and 2 to 56 percent for Deuteromycotina (Weete 1974; Wassef 1977). Sporophores' contents of lipids tend to be relatively low, but among them are triglycerides, phospholipids, fatty acids, carotenoids, and steroids, as well as smaller amounts of rarer lipids.

Carotenoids may accumulate in some fungi; in fact, some pigmented fungi have been grown in bulk precisely for carotenoids, which are fed to carp or to chickens to color their eggs and make them more acceptable to the consumer (Klaui 1982). Some of these carotenoids may be converted to vitamin A in humans (Tee 1992).

In addition, some fungi are sufficiently good producers of the B vitamins to make them viable commercial sources of these nutrients. *Saccharomyces* spp., for example, are good sources of B vitamins generally (Umezawa and Kishi 1989), and riboflavin is obtained in goodly amounts from *Ashbya gossppii* fermentations (Kutsal and Ozbas 1989). The water-soluble vitamin content of several fungi are shown in Table II.C.7.4.

Fungal Flavors and Volatiles

The nonvolatile meaty flavors of edible fungi come primarily from the amino acids (glutamic acid is one of the most common), purine bases, nucleotides (such as the shiitake mushroom's guanosine-5'-monophosphate)

Table II.C.7.4. *Vitamin content of edible fungi*

Species	Thiamine (µg/g)	Riboflavin (µg/g)	B$_6$ (µg/g)	Nicotinic acid (µg/g)	Pantothenic acid (µg/g)	Vitamin C (µg/100 g)	Ref.
Agaricus bisporus	10–90	40–50	–	430–570	230	27–82	1
Agaricus bisporus	1	5	22	41	–	4	4
Agaricus bisporus	1,100	5,000	–	55,700	–	–	6
Agaricus bretschneideri	560	110	–	5,100	–	–	6
Agaricus campestris	11	50	–	56	23	82	8
Agaricus campestris	5	21	–	191	–	14	2
Auricularia auricula-judea	120	490	–	5,100	–	–	6
Auricularia polytricha	2	9	–	20	–	–	1
Auricularia polytricha	1	2	–	1	–	1	4
Candida utilis	5	44	33	47	37	–	4
Flammulina velutipes	61	52	–	1065	–	46	1
Lactarius hatsudake	15	–	–	–	–	–	1
Lentinus edodes	78	49	–	549	–	–	1
Morchella sp.	4	25	6	82	9	–	3
Pholiota nameko	188	146	–	729	–	–	1
Pleurotus ostreatus	48	47	–	1,087	–	–	1
Saccharomyces (Brewer's)	44	1,210	–	107	–	–	2
Saccharomyces (Brewer's)	156	43	–	379	–	–	5
Torula sp.	53	450	334	4,173	372	–	10
Torula sp.	140	56	–	444	–	–	5
Tricholoma sp.	6	29	–	885	–	52	1
Volvaria esculenta	90	410	–	4,500	–	3	6
Volvariella volvacea	320	1,630	–	47,600	–	–	7
Volvariella volvacea	12	33	–	919	–	20	1

References

1. Crisan and Sands (1978)
2. Adams (1988)
3. Robinson and Davidson (1959)
4. Haytowitz and Matthews (1984)
5. Bano (1978)
6. Tung, Huang, and Li (1961)
7. Li and Chang (1982)
8. Litchfield (1967)
9. Litchfield, Vely, and Overbeck (1963)

(Nakajima et al. 1961), and the products of the enzymatic breakdown of unsaturated fatty acids. The volatile flavors include C8 compounds, such as benzyl alcohol, benzaldehyde, and other compounds (Mau et al. 1994). Many fungi contain monoterpenes, which produce a variety of flavors and odors; *Trametes odorata, Phellinus* spp., and *Kluyveromyces lactis,* for example, produce linalool (sweet, rose-like), geraniol (rose-like), nerool (sweet, rose-like) and citronellol (bitter, rose-like).

Fungi also produce flavors and odors that are buttery; nutlike; mushroomlike; coconut-like (*Trichoderma* spp.); peachlike (*Fusarium poae, Pityrosporium* spp., *Sporobolomyces odorus, Trichoderma* spp.); flowery and woody (*Lentinus lepideus);* earthy *(Chaetomium globosum);* sweet, aromatic, and vanilla-like *(Bjerkandera adusta);* coconut- and pineapple-like *(Polyporus durus);* sweet and fruity *(Poria aurea);* and passion-fruit-like *(Tyromyces sambuceus)* (Kempler 1983; Schreier 1992).

The flavor of truffles, as in other fungi, is partly caused by nonvolatile organic molecules such as those mentioned previously and by over 40 volatile organic molecules. The aroma of white truffles comes mainly from one of the latter, whereas the Perigord (black) truffle's aroma is the result of a combination of molecules. Species of *Russula,* when dried, have an odor that has been attributed to amines (Romagnesi 1967).

Some fungi produce volatile molecules that attract animals – including humans – or emit distinct flavors (Schreier 1992). Truffles, which are among the most valuable of edible fungi, grow underground on plant roots and produce odors that can only be recognized by dogs, pigs, and a few other mammals. Humans cannot smell them, but those with experience can detect the presence of truffles below the ground by cracks that appear in the soil surface over the plant roots.

The major species of truffles are *Tuber melanosporum* – the black truffle or so-called Perigord truffle – found most frequently in France, Italy, and Spain; *Tuber brumale,* also of Europe; *Tuber indicum* of Asia; and *Tuber aestivum* – the summer truffle or "cook's truffle" – which is the most widespread of all the truffles and the only one found in Britain (Pacioni, Bellina-Agostinone, and D'Antonio 1990).

Fungi and Decay

Along with bacteria, fungi hold primary responsibility for the biological process known as decay, in which complex organic molecules are progressively broken down to smaller molecules by microbial enzymes. The decay process destroys toxic molecules and regenerates small molecules used by microbial or plant life. Examples include carbon as carbon dioxide and nitrogen as amino acids, nitrates, or ammonia. Dead plants and animals are broken down to humus and simpler organic molecules that fertilize the soil and increase its water-holding capacity. These same processes have been used by humans in fermentation and in the production of bacterial and fungal single-cell protein (SCP) from waste or cheap raw materials.

Fungal Fermentation

The process of fermentation or microbial processing of plant or animal foods has served many functions, both now and in the distant past, especially in warm and humid climates where food spoils quickly. Fermentation preserves perishable food at low cost, salvages unusable or waste materials as human or animal food, reduces cooking time and use of fuel, and enhances the nutritional value of food by predigestion into smaller molecules that are more easily assimilated. Sometimes, but not always, fermentation increases the concentration of B vitamins (Goldberg and Thorp 1946) and protein in food (Cravioto et al. 1955; Holter 1988) and destroys toxic, undesirable, or antidigestive components of raw food. Moreover, fermentation can add positive antibiotic compounds that destroy harmful organisms, and the acids and alcohol produced by fermentation protect against microbial reinfection and improve the appearance, texture, consistency, and flavor of food. In addition, fermented foods often stimulate the appetite (Stanton 1985).

In ancient times, preservation of foods (such as milk, cheese, and meat) and beverages (like beer, mead, and wine) by fermentation made it possible for humans to travel long distances on land or water without the need to stop frequently for water or food. As described by Dirar (1993), over 80 fermented foods and beverages are presently used by the people of the Sudan, including 10 different breads, 10 different porridges, 9 special foods, 13 different beers, 5 different wines, 1 mead, 7 dairy sauces, 4 different meat sauces, 5 different fish sauces, 5 flavors and substitutes of animal sauces, and 10 flavors and substitutes of plant origin.

Today a wide variety of mainly carbohydrate-rich substrates, like cereals, are preserved, but protein-rich legumes and fish can also be processed by fungi. The combination of fungi, yeast, and bacteria is often controlled by antibacterials, fatty acids that act as trypsin inhibitory factors, and phytases, which destroy soybean phytates that bind essential metals (Hesseltine 1985). Table II.C.7.5 lists some of the foods that depend on fungal processing before they may be eaten (Beuchat 1983; Reddy, Person, and Salunkhe 1986).

Fungal fermentation of cereals does not lead to a marked increase in the protein content of the grain, but it does contribute to a significant increase in amino acids, especially those considered essential to humans. There is a decrease in carbohydrates during fungal fermentation, and lipids are hydrolyzed to fatty acids. Fungal fermentation may lead to an increase in B-vitamin content, although B_{12} will appear only if bacteria are involved in the fermentation.

Table II.C.7.5. *Foods and beverages that require fungal processing*

Product	Substrate	Geographic area	Fungal species
Alcoholic beverages	Cereals, carbohydrates, fruit	Worldwide	*Saccharomyces* sp.
Ang-kak	Rice	Asia, Syria	*Monascus*
Banku	Maize, cassava	Ghana	Yeast, bacteria
Bonkrek	Coconut press cake	Indonesia	*Rhizopus oligosporus*
Burukutu	Sorghum, cassava	Nigeria	*Candida* spp.
Burung hyphon	Shrimp, fish	Philippines	Yeast
Chee-fan	Soybean whey curd	China	*Mucor* sp., *Aspergillus glaucus*
Cheeses			
Brie	Milk curd	France	*Penicillium camemberti*
Camembert	Milk curd	France	*Penicillium camemberti*
Gorgonzola	Milk curd	France	*Penicillium roqueforti*
Roquefort	Milk curd	France	*Penicillium roqueforti*
Stilton	Milk curd	France	*Penicillium roqueforti*
Chicha	Maize	Peru	Yeast, bacteria
Colonche	Prickly pears	Mexico	*Torulopsis* sp.
Dawadawa	Millet	West Africa	Yeast, bacteria
	African locust bean	Nigeria	Yeast, bacteria
Dhoka	Wheat and/or pulses	India	Yeast, bacteria
Dosai	Black gram	India	Yeast, bacteria
Enjera	Teff	Ethiopia	*Candida guillermondii*
Fermented manioc	Manioc	Zaire	Yeast, fungi, bacteria
Gari	Cassava	West Africa	*Candida* spp.
Hamanatto	Soybean and wheat flour	Japan	*Aspergillus oryzae* and bacteria
Hopper	Rice	Sri Lanka	Yeast, bacteria
Idli	Rice and black gram	India	Yeast, bacteria
Injera	Teff, maize, wheat, barley	Ethiopia	*Candida guilliermundii*
Jalabies	Wheat flour	India, Nepal, Pakistan	?
Jamin-bang	Maize	Brazil	Yeast and bacteria
Kaanga-kopuwai	Maize	New Zealand	Yeast and bacteria
Kanji	Rice, carrots	India	*Hansenuka anomala*
Kaoling liquor	Sweet fruit or juice	China	*Monascus* sp.
Oncom	Peanut press cake	Indonesia	*Neurospor intermedia*, *Rhizopus oligosporus*
Papadam	Black gram	India	*Saccaromyces* spp.
Poi	Taro	Hawaii	Fungi and bacteria
Pozol	Maize	Mexico	Fungi and bacteria
Puto	Rice	Philippines	Fungi and bacteria
Sake	Rice, steamed	Japan	*Aspergillus oryzae* and *Sacchasomyces cerevisiae*
Shoyu	Soy and wheat	Malaysia	*Aspergillus oryzae* and yeast and bacteria
Sierra rice	Unhusked rice	Ecuador	*Aspergillus* spp. and bacteria
Sorghum beer	Sorghum, maize	South Africa	Yeast and bacteria
Soy sauce	Soybeans, wheat	Orient	*Aspergillus* spp., yeast, bacteria
Sufu	Soybean whey curd	China, Taiwan	*Actinomucor elegans*, *Mucor* spp.
Tao-si	Soybeans and wheat flour	Philippines	*Aspergillus oryzae*
Taotjo	Soybeans and wheat or rice	East India	*Aspergillus oryzae*
Taupe	Cassava or rice	Indonesia	Fungi
Tauco	Soybeans, cereal	West Java	*Rhizopus oligosporus*, *Aspergillus oryzae*
Tempeh	Soybeans	Indonesia	*Rhizopus* spp.
Katsuobushi	Fish	Japan	*Aspergillus glaucus*
Kecap	Soybeans, wheat	Indonesia	*Aspergillus* spp., bacteria, yeast
Kenkey	Maize	Africa	Yeast, bacteria, fungi
Khaman	Bengal gram	India	Yeast, bacteria
Kochujang	Hot pepper bean paste	Korea	Yeast, bacteria, fungi
Koji	Rice	China, Japan	*Aspergillus oryzae*
Lao-cho	Rice	Indonesia, China	*Rhizopus* spp., other fungi
Meitanza	Soybean cake	China, Taiwan	*Actinomucor elegans*
Meju	Soybeans	Korea	*Rhizopus* spp., *Aspergillus oryzae*
Merissa	Sorghum	Sudan	*Saccharomyces* spp.
Minchin	Wheat gluten	China	Fungi
Miso	Rice and soybeans, rice and cereals	China, Japan	Fungi
Nan	Wheat	India	Yeast
Nyufu	Fermented dry tofu	East Asia	*Actinomucor repens*
Ogi	Maize	Nigeria, West Africa	Fungi and bacteria
Torani	Rice	India	*Candida* spp., *Hansenula anomale*, other fungi
Waries	Black gram	India	Yeasts
Tuba	Coconut palm sap	Mexico	Yeasts
Kaoliang liquor	Sweet fruit or juice	China	*Monascus* sp.
Manioc, fermented	Manioc	Zaire	Yeast, bacteria, fungi

Sources: Steinkraus (1983); Jay (1986); Paredes-Lopez and Harry (1988); and Chavan and Kadam (1989).

Soybeans constitute a good example. Normally they contain B vitamins, but neither vitamin B_{12} nor significant amounts of proteins. When fermented, however, the B vitamins (except for thiamine) increase, and proteins are completely hydrolyzed to amino acids (Murata 1985). Vitamin B_{12} has been found in all commercial samples of fermented tempe, indicating that bacteria were involved in the fermentation as well (Steinkraus 1985).

In Fiji, carbohydrate-rich crops such as breadfruit *(Artocarpus utilis),* cassava *(Manihot dulcis),* taro *(Colocasia esculenta),* plaintain *(Musa paradisiaca* subsp. *normalis),* banana *(Musa* subsp. *sapientum),* and giant swamp taro *(Alocasia indica)* are preserved for future use by pit-mixed fermentation. This process was probably brought to Tonga during the Lapita period some 2,000 to 3,000 years ago and subsequently spread to Fiji (Aalbersberg, Lovelace Madhaji, and Parekenson 1988).

Single-Cell Protein for Human and Animal Food

Fungi have been employed to produce single-cell protein (SCP) from a variety of waste materials that might otherwise be useless, such as crop straw, bagasse, starchy plant materials, and whey, among others. *Candida* alkane yeasts have been examined for their ability to produce protein-rich biomass and edible calories for pigs and other animals, whereas *Chaetoceros* and *Sporotrichum* spp. have been utilized to enrich the protein content of lignocellulose wastes – like straw – for animal feed. *Rhizopus oligosporus* NRRL 270 has been used to increase the protein content of starchy residues (cassava, potato, and banana), and yeasts have been exploited to produce food and alcohol from whey. Treating manioc with *R. oligosporus* by any of three different fermentation methods has resulted in a marked increase in protein content, seemingly at the expense of the carbohydrate content of the manioc (Ferrante and Fiechter 1983).

Alcoholic Fermentation

In Europe, the Near East, and South and Central America, saccharification of the starch in cereals – such as barley, corn, or wheat – has long been done by malting the grain. This procedure is followed by the production of alcoholic beverages and food through the action of *Saccharomyces* spp. In the Orient, *Aspergillus* spp. and *Rhizopus* spp. remain in use to make alcoholic beverages and foods, and the same two fungal species are also employed to hydrolyze the proteins of fish, meat, beans, pulses, and some cereals.

Other Fungally Fermented Foods

Some cheeses are made flavorful – following the formation of the curd and its processing – through the action of enzymes of the fungi *Penicillium camem-* *bert* (Camembert and Brie) and *Penicillium roqueforti* (Bleu, Gorgonzola, Roquefort, and Stilton). Country-cured hams are produced through fermentation by *Aspergillus* and *Penicillium* spp.; tuna is fermented by *Aspergillus glaucus,* cocoa by *Candida krusei* and *Geotrichum* spp., and peanut presscake by *Neurospora sitophila* (Jay 1986).

Fungal Secondary Metabolites

Fungi produce a large variety of secondary metabolites, but often only when the fungal cells cease active growth. Some of these secondary metabolites are beneficial to humans, whereas others are toxic, and still others may have useful medical effects.

Fungi supply organic acids for industrial uses: citric acid for the food, beverage, pharmaceutical, cosmetic, and detergent industries; itaconic acid for the plastic, paint, and printer's-ink industries; fumaric acid for the paper, resin, fruit juice, and dessert industries (Bigelis and Arora 1992; Zidwick 1992); gluconic acid for the food, beverage, cleaning, and metal-finishing industries; and malic and lactic acids for the food and beverage industries. In addition, several fungi produce rennets for the dairy industry; among these are *Byssochlamys fulva, Candida lipolytica, Chlamydomucor oryzae, Flammulina velutipes, Rhizopus* spp., and *Trametes ostreiformis* (Sternberg 1978).

Certain fungi (especially *Streptomyces* spp.) have proven to be useful as sources of a host of antibiotics that act as inhibitors of bacterial cell-wall synthesis (Oiwa 1992), as antifungal agents (Tanaka 1992), as antiviral agents (Takeshima 1992), and as antiprotozoal and anthelminthic agents (Otoguro and Tanaka 1992). Some also produce antitumor compounds (Komiyama and Funayama 1992), cell-differentiation inducers (Yamada 1992), enzyme inhibitors (Tanaka et al. 1992), immunomodulation agents (Yamada 1992), and vasoactive substances (Nakagawa 1992). In addition, fungi have been used to produce herbicides (Okuda 1992), fungicides, and bactericides of plants (Okuda and Tanaka 1992).

A number of secondary metabolites of fungi, however, are toxic to humans and their domestic animals. Aflatoxins are hepatotoxic and carcinogenic; deoxynivalenol is emetic; ergot alkaloids are vasoconstrictive, gangrenous, hemorrhagic, and neurotoxic; zearalenone causes vulvovaginitis in swine; trichothecenes produce vomiting, oral necrosis, and hemorrhage; ochratoxin causes nephrotoxicity; and macrocyclic trichothecenes cause mucosal necrosis (Marasas and Nelson 1987).

Those species of the fungal genus *Claviceps* that grow on cereals (as for example, *Claviceps purpurea*) produce a variety of pharmacologically active compounds with positive and negative effects on humans. Among these are the alkaloids lysergic acid diethylamide (LSD), ergometrine, ergotrienine, ergotamine, ergosinine, ergocristine, ergocornine, ergocristinene, ergocryptine, and ergocryptinine. Some of these alkaloids are responsible for the disease ergotism, but others are used beneficially – in childbirth, or to treat migraines (Johannsson 1962).

Still other fungi associated with cereals and legumes produce a wide variety of toxins. These have been implicated in aflatoxin and liver cancer in Africa, in esophageal cancer in Africa and Asia, and in endemic nephritis in the Balkans (Stoloff 1987).

A number of fungi (i.e., *Fusarium* and *Gibberella* spp.) produce zearalanol, which exhibits estrogen activity. These estrogen-like compounds are frequent contaminants in cereals and may be responsible for carcinogenesis and precocious sexual development if present in quantity (Schoental 1985).

Aspergillus flavus, which grows on peanuts, soybeans, cereals, and other plants, may produce the hepatocarcinogen aflatoxin and can cause Reye's syndrome in children. *Fusarium* spp., also growing on cereals, can produce trichothecen toxins that cause toxic aleukia (ATA) and *akakabi-byo* ("red mold disease") in Japan.

The commonly cultivated mushroom, *Agaricus bisporus,* may contain phenylhydrazine derivatives that have been found to be weakly mutagenic. Many other edible fungi have shown mutagenic activity (Chauhan et al. 1985); among them is the false morel, *Gyrimitra esculenta,* which has been found to contain 11 hydrazines, including gyromitrin – and 3 of these hydrazines are known mutagens and carcinogens (Toth, Nagel, and Ross 1982; Ames 1983; Meier-Bratschi et al. 1983).

In addition, a number of wild fungi contain poisonous molecules that can cause serious illness or death. The amount of poison varies from species to species and from strain to strain within individual species (Benedict and Brady 1966). Also, humans vary in their tolerance of fungal poisons (Simmons 1971).

Fungal toxins produce a variety of biological effects: Amanitin, phallotoxins, and gyromitrin cause kidney and liver damage; coprine and muscarine affect the autonomic nervous system; ibotenic acid, muscimol, psilocybin, and psilocin affect the central nervous system and cause gastrointestinal irritation; indeed, many of these substances and other unknown compounds found in fungi are gastrointestinal irritants (Diaz 1979; Fuller and McClintock 1986).

Several edible fungi, such as *Coprinus atramentarius, Coprinus quadrifidus, Coprinus variegatus, Coprinus insignis, Boletus luridus, Clitocybe clavipes,* and *Verpa bohemica,* may contain coprine (Hatfield and Schaumburg 1978). Indeed, European *C. atramentarius* may have as much as 160 mg of coprine per kg of fresh fungi. In the human body, coprine is hydrolyzed to l-aminocyclopropanol hydrochloride (ACP), which acts like disulfuram, a synthetic compound known as antabuse and used to treat chronic alcoholics. Antabuse and ACP irre-versibly inhibit acetaldehyde dehydrogenase and prevent the catabolism of ethanol. Thus, coprine plus ethanol leads to severe intoxication when alcoholic beverages are drunk after eating coprine-containing fungi (Hatfield and Schaumberg 1978; Hatfield 1979).

In addition, many mushrooms contain the enzyme thiaminase, which may destroy the vitamin thiamine, leading to thiamine deficiency (Wakita 1976) – especially when the mushrooms are eaten in quantity (Rattanapanone 1979). Several *Russula* spp. may contain indophenolase, which can also be harmful to humans if eaten in large amounts (Romagnesi 1967).

Humans can become allergic to fungi (Koivikko and Savolainen 1988). Moreover, eating fava beans with mushrooms that are rich in tyrosinase may enhance the medical effect of the fava beans – known as favism – because the tyrosinase catalyzes the conversion of L-DOPA to L-DOPA-quinone (Katz and Schall 1986).

Magico-Religious Use of Fungi

As early as the eighteenth century, according to travelers' reports, *Amanita muscaria,* known as the "fly agaric," was eaten by several tribal groups (Chukchi, Koryak, Kamchadal, Ostyak, and Vogul) in eastern Siberia as an intoxicant and for religious purposes. Species of *Panaeolus, Psilocybe,* and *Stropharia* also contain hallucinogens. These fungi were eaten by the Aztecs and the Maya – and are still consumed by *curanderos* in some Mexican tribes – to produce hallucinations for religious purposes, to derive information for medical treatment, and to locate lost objects (Diaz 1979).

Sheldon Aaronson

This work was funded, in part, by research awards from PSC/CUNY and the Ford Foundation.

Bibliography

Aalbersberg, W. G. L., C. E. A. Lovelace Madhaji, and S. V. Parekenson. 1988. Davuke, the traditional Fijian method of pit preservation of staple carbohydrate foods. *Ecology of Food and Nutrition* 21: 173–80.

Abercrombie, J. 1779. *The garden mushroom, its nature and cultivation.* London.

Adams, C. F. 1988. *Nutritive value of American foods.* Agriculture Handbook No. 456. Washington, D.C.

Ahmed, A. A., M. A. Mohamed, and M. A. Hami. 1981. Libyan truffles: Chemical composition and toxicity. *Mushroom Science* 11: 833–42.

Ainsworth, G. C. 1976. *Introduction to the history of mycology.* Cambridge and New York.

Alcorn, J. B. 1984. *Huastec Mayan ethnobotany.* Austin, Tex.

Alsheikh, A., and J. M. Trappe. 1983. Desert truffles: The

genus *Tirmania. Transactions of the British Mycology Society* 81: 83-90.

Ames, B. N. 1983. Dietary carcinogens and anticarcinogens. *Science* 221: 1256-64.

Ames, B. N., J. McCann, and F. Yamaski. 1975. Methods for detecting carcinogens and mutagens with the Salmonella/mammalian microsome mutagenicity test. *Mutation Research* 31: 347-64.

André, J. 1985. *Les noms de plantes dans la Rome Antique.* Paris.

Arenas, P. 1981. *Ethnobotaneca Lengua-maskoy.* Buenos Aires.

Arnason, T., R. J. Hebda, and T. Johns. 1981. Use of plants for food and medicine by native peoples of eastern Canada. *Canadian Journal of Botany* 59: 2189-325.

Atal, C. K., B. K. Bhat, and T. N. Kaul. 1978. *Indian mushroom science I.* Globe, Ariz.

Bano, Z. 1978. The nutritive value of mushrooms. In *Indian mushroom science I,* 473-87. Globe, Ariz.

Bano, Z., and S. Rajarathnam. 1982. *Pleurotus* mushrooms: A nutritious food. In *Tropical mushrooms,* ed. S. T. Chang and T. H. Quimio, 363-80. Hong Kong.

Barrau, J. 1962. Ph.D. thesis, presented to the Faculté des Sciences de Marseille.

Bels, P. J., and S. Pataragetvit. 1982. Edible mushrooms in Thailand, cultivated by termites. In *Tropical mushrooms,* ed. S. T. Chang and T. H. Quimio, 445-61. Hong Kong.

Benedict, R. G., and L. R. Brady. 1966. Occurrence of *Amanita* toxins in American collections of deadly *Amanitas. Journal of Pharmaceutical Science* 55: 590-3.

Beuchat, L. R. 1983. Indigenous fermented foods. In *Biotechnology,* ed. H. J. Rehm, and G. Reed, 8 vols., 5: 477-528. Weinheim, Germany.

Bigelis, R. 1992. Food enzymes. In *Biotechnology of filamentous fungi,* ed. D. B. Finkelstein and C. Ball, 361-415. Boston.

Bigelis, R., and D. K. Arora. 1992. Organic acids of fungi. In *Handbook of applied mycology,* Vol. 4, ed. D. K. Arora, R. P. Elander, and K. G. Mukerji, 357-76. New York.

Blyth, R. H. 1973. Mushrooms in Japanese verse. *Transactions of the Asiatic Society, Japan* 11: 1-14.

Bo, L., and B. Yun-sun. 1980. *Fungi Pharmacopoeia (Sinica).* Oakland, Calif.

Bose, S. R., and A. B. Bose. 1940. An account of edible mushrooms of India. *Science and Culture* 6: 141-9.

Bramley, P. M., and A. Mackenzie. 1992. Carotenoid biosynthesis and its regulation in fungi. *Handbook of applied mycology,* Vol. 4, ed. D. K. Arora, R. P. Elander, and K. G. Mukerji, 401-44. New York.

Buller, A. H. R. 1914-16. The fungus lore of the Greeks and Romans. *Transactions of the British Mycological Society* 5: 21-66.

Burkill, T. H. 1935. *A dictionary of the economic products of the Malay Peninsula.* London.

Cao, J., et al. 1991. A new wild edible fungus - *Wynnella silvicola. Edible Fungi of China* 10: 27.

Casalicchio, G., C. Paoletti, A. Bernicchia, and G. Gooi. 1975. Ricerche sulla composizione aminoacidica di alcuni funghi. *Micologia Italiana* 1: 21-32.

Chang, S. T., and W. A. Hayes. 1978. *The biology and cultivation of edible mushrooms.* London.

Chang, S. T., and P. G. Miles. 1987. Historical record of the early cultivation of *Lentinus* in China. *Mushroom Journal in the Tropics* 7: 31-7.

Chao Ken, N. 1980. The knowledge and usage of fungus in ancient China. *Acta Microbiologica Sinica* 7: 174-5.

Chauhan, Y., D. Nagel, M. Gross, et al. 1985. Isolation of N2-(gamma-[-+-glutamyl]-4carboxyphenyl hydrazine) in the cultivated mushroom *Agaricus bisporus. Journal of Agricultural Food Chemistry* 33: 817-20.

Chavan, J. K., and S. S. Kadam. 1989. Nutritional improvement of cereal by fermentation. *Critical Reviews in Food Science and Nutrition* 28: 349-400.

Chen, G. 1989a. Wild edible and medical fungi resources in Shenyang City. *Edible Fungi of China* 36: 30.

1989b. Wild edible and medical fungi resources in Shenyang City. *Edible Fungi of China* 37: 25-6.

Chestnut, V. K. 1902. Plants used by the Indians of Mendocino County, California. *U.S. National Herbarium:* 294-422.

Colenso, W. 1881. On the vegetable food of the ancient New Zealanders before Cook's visit. *Transactions and Proceedings of the New Zealand Institute* 13: 3-19.

Cravioto, O. R., Y. O. Cravioto, H. G. Massieu, and G. T. Guzman. 1955. El pozol, forma indigena de consumir el maiz en el sureste de Mexico y su aporte de nutrientes a la dieta. *Ciencia Mexicana* 15: 27-30.

Cribb, A. B., and J. W. Cribb. 1975. *Wild foods in Australia.* Sydney.

Crisan, E. V., and A. Sands. 1978. Nutritional value. In *The biology and cultivation of edible mushrooms,* ed. S. T. Chang and W. A. Hayes, 137-81. New York.

Davis, E. W., and J. A. Yost. 1983. The ethnobotany of the Waorani of eastern Ecuador. *Botanical Museum Leaflets Harvard University* 3: 159-217.

Deonna, W., and M. Renard. 1961. *Croyances et superstitions de table dans la Romantique.* Brussels.

Diaz, J. L. 1979. Ethnopharmacology and taxonomy of Mexican psychodysleptic plants. *Journal of Psychedelic Drugs* 11: 71-101.

Dickson, V. 1971. *Forty years in Kuwait.* London.

Dirar, H. A. 1993. *The indigenous fermented foods of the Sudan: A study in African food and nutrition.* Wallingford, England.

FAO (Food and Agriculture Organization of the United Nations). 1970. *Amino acid content of foods.* FAO Nutritional Studies No. 24. Rome.

Ferrante, M. P., and A. Fiechter. 1983. *Production and feeding of single cell protein.* London.

Findlay, W. P. K. 1982. *Fungi, folklore, fiction, and fact.* Eureka, Calif.

Forbes, R. J. 1967. The beginnings of technology and man. *Technology in Western civilization,* ed. M. Kranzberg and C. W. Pursell, Jr., 11-47. New York.

Fuller, T. C., and E. McClintock. 1986. *Poisonous plants of California.* Berkeley, Calif.

Gade, D. W. 1975. *Plants, man and the land in the Vulcanota Valley of Peru.* The Hague.

Gallois, A., B. Gross, D. Langlois, et al. 1990. Flavor compounds produced by lignolytic basidiomycetes. *Mycological Research* 94: 494-504.

Gandhi, S. R., and J. D. Weete. 1991. Production of the polyunsaturated fatty acids arachidonic acid and eicosoentaenoic acid by the fungus *Pythium ultimum. Journal of General Microbiology* 137: 1825-30.

Gardner, W. A., and C. W. McCoy. 1992. Insecticides and herbicides. In *Biotechnology of filamentous fungi,* ed. D. B Finkelstein and C. Ball. 335-59. Boston, Mass.

Geller, J. R. 1989. Recent excavations at Hierakonpolis and their relevance to Predynastic pyrotechnology and settlement. *Cahiers de recherches de l'Institut de papyrologie et d'egyptologie de Lille* 11: 41-52.

1992. From prehistory to history: Beer in Egypt. In *The followers of Horus,* ed. R. Friedman and B. Adams. 19–26. Oxford.

Goldberg, L., and J. M. Thorp. 1946. A survey of vitamins in African foodstuffs. VI. Thiamin, riboflavin and nicotinic acid in sprouted and fermented cereal foods. *South African Journal of Medical Science* 11: 177–85.

Goody, Jack. 1982. *Cooking, cuisine, and class: A study in comparative sociology.* Cambridge and New York.

Grieve, M. 1925. *Fungi as food and in medicine.* Tamworth, England.

Griffin, D. H. 1981. *Fungal physiology.* New York.

Gruss, J. 1928. *Saccharomyces winlocki,* die Hefe aus den Pharaonengräbern. *Allgemeine Brauer und Hopfen Zeitung* 237: 1340–1.

Guerra, F. 1967. Mexican Phantastica - a study of the early ethnobotanical sources on hallucinogenic drugs. *British Journal of Addiction* 62: 171–87.

Guo, W. 1992. Resources of wild edible fungi in Tibet, China. *Edible Fungi of China* 11: 33–4.

Hamil, F. B., and M. U. Chiltoskey. 1975. *Cherokee plants.* Sylva, N.C.

Hart, J. A. 1979. The ethnobotany of the Flathead Indians of western Montana. *Botanical Museum Leaflet* 27: 261–307.

Hatfield, G. M. 1979. Toxic mushrooms. In *Toxic plants,* ed. A. Douglas Kinghorn, 7–58. New York.

Hatfield, G. M., and J. P. Schaumberg. 1978. The disulfuram-like effects of *Coprinus atramentarius* and related mushrooms. In *Mushroom poisoning, diagnosis and treatment,* ed. B. H. Rumack and E. Salzman, 181–6. West Palm Beach, Fla.

Hawksworth, D. L., B. C. Sutton, and G. A. Ainsworth. 1983. *Ainsworth & Bisby's dictionary of the fungi.* Kew, England.

Hayes, W. A. 1987. Edible mushrooms. In *Food and beverage mycology,* ed. L. R. Beuchat, 355–90. New York.

Haytowitz, D. B., and R. H. Matthews. 1984. *Composition of foods.* Washington, D.C.

Herrera, F. L. 1934. Botanica ethnolic. *Revista del Museo Nacional de Lima Peru* 3: 37–62.

Herrero, P. 1984. *La thérapeutique mesopotamienne.* Mémoire No. 48. Paris.

Hesseltine, C. W. 1985. Fungi, people, and soybeans. *Mycologia* 77: 505–25.

Hiepko, P., and W. Schultze-Motel. 1981. *Floristische und ethnobotanische Untersuchungen im Eipomektal. Irian Jaya.* Berlin.

Hohl, H. R. 1987. Cytology and morphogenesis of fungal cells. *Progress in Botany* 49: 13–28.

Holland, H. L. 1992. *Bioconversions,* ed. D. B. Finkelstein and C. Ball, 157–87. Boston.

Holland, H. L., F. M. Brown, J. A. Rao, and P. C. Chenchaiah. 1988. Synthetic approaches to the prostaglandins using microbial biotransformation. *Developments in Industrial Microbiology* 29: 191–5.

Holter, U. 1988. Food consumption of camel nomads in the northwest Sudan. *Ecology of Food and Nutrition* 21: 95–115.

Hu, L., and L. Zeng. 1992. Investigation on wild edible mushroom resources in Wanxian County, Sichuan Province. *Edible Fungi of China* 11: 35–7.

Humfeld, H. 1948. The production of mushroom mycelium (*Agaricus campestris*) in submerged culture. *Science* 107: 373.

Imai, S. 1938. Studies on the Agaricaceae of Hokkaido. *Journal of the Faculty of Agriculture, Hokkaido Imperial University* 43: 359–63.

Irvine, F. R. 1952. Supplementary and emergency food plants of West Africa. *Economic Botany* 6: 23–40.

Irving, F. R. 1957. Wild and emergency foods of Australian and Tasmanian aborigines. *Oceania* 28: 113–42.

Ito, T. 1917. *Collybia nameko* sp. nov. a new edible fungus of Japan. *Japan Academy Proceedings* 5: 145–7.

1978. Cultivation of *Lentinus edodes.* In *The biology and cultivation of edible mushrooms,* ed. S. T. Chang and W. A. Hayes, 461–73. New York.

Jay, J. M. 1986. *Modern food microbiology.* New York.

Johannsson, M. 1962. Studies in alkaloid production by *Claviceps purpurea. Symbolic Botanicae Upsaliensis* 17: 1–47.

Johnson, C. R. 1862. *The useful plants of Great Britain.* London.

Katz, S. H., and J. J. Schall. 1986. Favism and malaria: A model of nutrition and biocultural evolution. In *Plants in indigenous medicine and diet,* ed. N. L. Elkin, 211–28. Bedford Hills, N.Y.

Kaul, T. N. 1981. Common edible mushrooms of Jammu and Kashmir. *Mushroom Science* 11: 79–82.

Kaul, T. N., and J. L. Kachroo. 1974. Common edible mushrooms of Jammu and Kashmir. *Journal of the Bombay Natural History Society* 71: 26–31.

Kempler, G. M. 1983. Production of flavor compounds by microorganisms. *Advances in Applied Microbiology* 29: 29–51.

Kerwin, J. L., and N. D. Duddles. 1989. Reassessment of the roles of phospholipids in sexual reproduction by sterol-auxotrophic fungi. *Journal of Bacteriology* 171: 3829–31.

Klaui, H. 1982. Industrial and commercial use of carotenoids. *Carotenoid biochemistry,* ed. G. Britton and T. W. Goodwin, 309–28. Oxford.

Ko, H. 1966. *Alchemy, medicine, religion in the China of A.D. 320: The Nei Pieu of Ko Hung (Polo-pu-tzu),* Trans. James. R. Ware. Cambridge, Mass.

Kodama, K., and K. Yoshizowa. 1977. Sake. In *Alcoholic beverages,* ed. A. H. Rose, 423–75. London.

Koivikko, A., and J. Savolainen. 1988. Mushroom allergy. *Allergy* 43: 1–10.

Komiyama, K., and S. Funayama. 1992. Antitumor agents. In *The search for bioactive compounds from microorganisms,* ed. S. Omura, 79–103. New York.

Konno, K., K. Hayano, H. Shirakama, et al. 1982. Clitidine, a new toxic pyridine nucleoside from *Clitocybe acromelalga. Tetrahedron* 38: 3281–4.

Konno, K., H. Shirahama, and T. Matsumoto. 1984. Clithioneine, an amino acid betaine from *Clitocybe acromelalga. Phytochemistry* 23: 1003–6.

Kuhnlein, H. V., and N. J. Turner. 1991. *Traditional plant foods of Canadian indigenous peoples.* Philadelphia, Pa.

Kutsal, T., and M. T. Ozbas. 1989. Microbial production of vitamin B_2 (riboflavin). In *Biotechnology of vitamins, pigments and growth factors,* ed. E. T. Vandamme, 149–66. London.

Lee, R. B. 1979. *The !Kung San.* Cambridge and New York.

Levai, J. 1984. Nutritional and utilizable value of some cultivated mushrooms. *Mushroom Science* 12: 295–304.

Lewis, D. H., and D. C. Smith. 1967. Sugar alcohols (polyols) in fungi and green plants. I. Distribution, physiology and metabolism. *New Phytologist* 66: 143–84.

Li, G. S. F., and S. T. Chang. 1982. Nutritive value of *Volvariella volvacea.* In *Tropical mushrooms,* ed. S. T. Chang and T. H. Quimio, 199–219. Hong Kong.

Lin, C.-F., and H. Iizuka. 1982. Production of extracellular pigment by a mutant of *Monascus koalinq* sp. nov. *Applied Environmental Microbiology* 43: 671–6.

Lincoff, G. H. 1984. *Field guide to North American mushrooms*. New York.

Lipp, F. J. 1991. *The Mixe of Oaxaca, religion, ritual and healing*. Austin, Tex.

Litchfield, J. H. 1967. Submerged culture of mushroom mycelium. In *Microbial technology*, ed. H. J. Peppler, 107-44. New York.

Litchfield, J. H., V. G. Vely, and R. C. Overbeck. 1963. Nutrient content of morel mushroom mycelium: Amino acid composition of the protein. *Journal of Food Science* 28: 741-3.

Liu, B. 1958. The primary investigation on utilization of the fungi by ancient Chinese. *Shansi Normal College Journal* 1: 49-67.

    1974. *The gasteromycetes of China*. Vaduz, Liechtenstein.

Liu, P. 1993. Introduction of a valuable edible fungus from Yunnan - *Lyophyllum shimeii* (Kawam.) Hongo. *Edible Fungi of China* 12: 29.

Liu, S. 1991. Discussion on *Ganoderma lucidum* in ancient traditional Chinese medical books. *Edible Fungi of China* 10: 37-8.

Lou, L. H. 1982. Cultivation of *Auricularia* on logs in China. In *Tropical mushrooms*, ed. S. T. Chang and T. H Quimio, 437-41. Hong Kong.

Lowe, D. A. 1992. Fungal enzymes. In *Handbook of applied mycology*, Vol. 4., ed. D. K. Arora, R. P. Elander, and K. G. Mukerji, 681-706. New York.

Maciarello, M. J., and A. O. Tucker. 1994. Truffles and truffle volatiles. In *Spices, herbs and edible fungi*, ed. G. Charalambous, 729-39. Amsterdam.

Majno, G. 1975. *The healing hand: Man and wound in the ancient world*. Cambridge, Mass.

Mao, X. 1991. A trip to Yunnan - edible mushroom kingdom. *Edible Fungi of China* 10: 33-4.

Mapes, C., G. Guzman, and J. Cabellero. 1981. *Ethnomicologia Purephecha*. Lima.

Marasas, W. F. O., and P. E. Nelson. 1987. *Mycotoxicology*. University Park, Pa.

Martinez, A. M. A., E. Perez-Silva, and E. Agurre-Accosta. 1983. Etnomicologia y exploraciones micologicas en la sierra norte de Puebla. *Boletin de la Sociedad Medicina Microbiologica* 18: 51-63.

Martini, A. E. V., M. W. Miller, and A. Martini. 1979. Amino acid composition of whole cells of different yeasts. *Journal of Agriculture and Food Chemistry* 27: 982-4.

Mau, J., R. B. Beelman, and G. R. Ziegler. 1994. Aroma and flavor components of cultivated mushrooms. In *Spices, herbs and edible fungi*, ed. G. Charalambous, 657-83. Amsterdam.

McConnell, J. E. W., and W. B. Esselen. 1947. Carbohydrates in cultivated mushrooms. *Food Research* 12: 118-21.

Mead, G. K. 1972. *Ethnobotany of the California Indians*. Ethnology Series No. 30. Greeley, Colo.

Meier-Bratschi, A., B. M. Carden, J. Luthy, et al. 1983. Methylation of deoxyribonucleic acid in the rat by the mushroom poison, gyromitrin. *Journal of Agriculture and Food Chemistry* 31: 1117-20.

Michel, R. H., P. E. McGovern, and V. R. Badler. 1992. Chemical evidence for ancient beer. *Nature* 360: 24.

Miller, S. A. 1968. Nutritional factors in single-cell protein. In *Single-cell protein*, ed. R. I. Mateles and S. R. Tannenbaum, 79-89. Cambridge, Mass.

Molitoris, H. P., J. L. Van Etten, and D. Gottlieb. 1968. Alterbedingte Änderungen der Zusammensetzung und des Stoffwechsels bei Pilzen. *Mushroom Science* 7: 59-67.

Montes, M. D. 1961. Sobre el uso de hierbas en la medicina popular de Santander (Columbia). *Thesaurus* 16: 719-29.

Monthoux, O., and K. Lündstrom-Baudais. 1979. Polyporacées des sites néolithiques de Clairvaux et Charavines (France). *Candollea* 34: 153-66.

Morris, B. 1987. *Common mushrooms of Malawi*. Oslo.

Murata, K. 1985. Formation of antioxidants and nutrients in tempe. In *Non-salted soybean fermentation*. Asian Symposium, International Committee on Economic and Applied Microbiology. Tsukuba, Japan.

Nakagawa, A. 1992. Vasoactive substances. In *The search for bioactive compounds from microorganisms*, ed. S. Omura, 198-212. New York.

Nakajima, N., K. Ichikawa, M. Kamada, and E. Fujita. 1961. Food chemical studies on 5'-ribonucleotides. Part I. On the 5'-ribonucleotides in various stocks by ion exchange chromatography. *Journal of the Agricultural Chemistry Society, Japan* 9: 797-803.

Needham, J., and L. Gwei-Djin. 1983. Physiological alchemy. In *Science and Civilization in China. Chemistry and Chemical Technology, Spagyrical Discovery and Invention*. Part V: 140. Cambridge.

Nes, W. R. 1977. The biochemistry of plant sterols. *Advances in Lipid Research* 15: 233-324.

Nishitoba, T., H. Sato, and S. Sakamura. 1988. Bitterness and structure relationship of the triterpenoids from *Ganoderma lucidum* (Reishi). *Agricultural Biological Chemistry* 52: 1791-5.

Oakley, K. 1962. On man's use of fire, with comments on tool-making and hunting. In *The social life of early man*, ed. S. Washburn, 176-93. Chicago.

O'Donnell, K., and S. W. Peterson. 1992. Isolation, preservation, and taxonomy. In *Biotechnology of filamentous fungi*, ed. D. B. Finkelstein and C. Ball. 7-33. Boston.

Oiwa, R. 1992. Antibacterial agents. *The search for bioactive compounds from microorganisms*, ed. S. Omura, 1-29. New York.

Okuda, S. 1992. Herbicides. In *The search for bioactive compounds from microorganisms*, ed. S. Omura, 224-36. New York.

Okuda, S., and Y. Tanaka. 1992. Fungicides and antibacterial agents. *The search for bioactive compounds from microorganisms*, ed. S. Omura, 213-23. New York.

Otoguro, K., and H. Tanaka. 1992. Antiparasitic agents. In *The search for bioactive compounds from microorganisms*, ed. S. Omura, 63-78. New York.

Pacioni, G., C. Bellina-Agostinone, and M. D'Antonio. 1990. Odour composition of the *Tuber melanoporum* complex. *Mycological Research* 94: 201-4.

Pan, X. 1993a. Medicinal edible fungi resources in the forest region in Heilongjiang Province. *Edible Fungi of China* 12: 38-9.

    1993b. Medicinal edible fungi resources in Heilongjiang Province. *Edible Fungi of China* 12: 25-7.

Paredes-Lopez, C., and G. I. Harry. 1988. Food biotechnology review: Traditional solid-state fermentations of plant raw materials application, nutritional significance, and future prospects. *Reviews in Food Science and Nutrition* 27: 159-87.

Pegler, D. N., and G. D. Piearce. 1980. The edible mushrooms of Zambia. *Kew Bulletin* 35: 475-92.

Peters, R., and E. M. O'Brien. 1984. On hominid diet before fire. *Current Anthropology* 25: 358-60.

Petrie, W. M., and J. E. Quibell. 1896. *Nagada and Ballas*. London.

Piearce, G. D. 1981. Zambian mushrooms - customs and folklore. *British Mycological Society Bulletin* 139-42.

Pöder, R., U. Peintner, and T. Pümpel. 1992. Mykologische Untersuchungen an den Pilz-Beifunden der Gletschermumie vom Hauslabjoch. *Der Mann im Eis,* ed. F. Hopfel, W. Platzer, and K. Spindler, 313-20. Innsbruck.

Prance, G. T. 1972. An ethnobotanical comparison of four tribes of Amazonian Indians. *Amazonica* 1: 7-27.

1983. The ethnobotany of Amazon Indians: A rapidly disappearing source of botanical knowledge for human welfare. *Bulletin Botanical Survey of India* 25: 148-59.

Purkayastha, R. P. 1978. Indian edible mushrooms - a review. In *Indian mushroom science I,* ed. C. K. Atal, B. K. Bhat, and T. N. Kaul, 351-71. Srinigar, India.

Purkayastha, R. P., and A. Chandra. 1976. Amino acid composition of the protein of some edible mushrooms grown in synthetic medium. *Journal of Food Science and Technology* 13: 86-9.

Radwan, S. S., and A. H. Soliman. 1988. Arachidonic acid from fungi utilizing fatty acids with shorter chains as sole sources of carbon and energy. *Journal of General Microbiology* 134: 387-93.

Ramain, P. 1981. Essai de mycogastronomie. *Revue de Mycologie, Supplement* 12: 4-18, 29-38, 75-82.

Rattanapanone, V. 1979. Antithiamin factor in fruit, mushroom and spices. *Chiang Mai Medical Bulletin* (January): 9-16.

Reagan, A. B. 1929. Plants used by the White Mountain Apache Indians of Arizona. *Wisconsin Archaeologist* 8: 143-61.

Reddy, N. R., M. D. Person, and D. K. Salunkhe. 1986. Idli. In *Legume-based fermented foods,* ed. N. R. Reddy, M. D. Pierson, and D. K. Salunkhe, 145-60. Boca Raton, Fla.

Reinking, 0. A. 1921. Philippine edible fungi. In *Minor products of Philippine forests,* ed. W. H. Brown, 103-47. Manila.

Robinson, R. F., and R. S. Davidson. 1959. The large scale growth of higher fungi. *Advances in Applied Microbiology* 1: 261-78.

Rolfe, R. T., and F. W. Rolfe. 1925. *The romance of the fungus world.* London.

Romagnesi, H. 1967. *Les Russules d'Europe et d'Afrique du Nord.* Paris.

Sabban, F. 1986. Court cuisine in fourteenth-century imperial China: Some culinary aspects of Hu Sihui's Yingshan Zengyao. *Food and Foodways* 1: 161-96.

Saffirio, L. 1972. Food and dietary habits in ancient Egypt. *Journal of Human Evolution* 1: 197-305.

Saggs, H. W. F. 1962. *The greatness that was Babylon.* New York.

Said, H. M., R. E. Elahie, and S. K. Hamarneh. 1973. *Al-Biruini's book on pharmacy and materia medica.* Karachi.

Sakaguchi, K. 1972. Development of industrial microbiology in Japan. *Proceedings of the International Symposium on Conversion and Manufacture of Foodstuffs by Microorganisms,* 7-10. Tokyo.

Schnell, R. 1957. *Plantes alimentaires et vie agricole de l'Afrique Noire.* Paris.

Schoental, R. 1985. Zearalenone, its biological and pathological, including carcinogenic effects in rodents: Implications for humans. *Fifth meeting on mycotoxins in animal and human health,* ed. M. O. Moss and M. Frank, 52-72. Edinburgh.

Schreier, P. 1992. Bioflavours: An overview. In *Bioformation of flavours,* ed. R. L. S. Patterson, B. V. Charlwood, G. MacLeod, and A. A. Williams, 1-20. Cambridge.

Schultes, R. E. 1937. Teonanacatl: The narcotic mushroom of the Aztecs. *American Anthropologist* 42: 424-43.

Schultes, R. E., and A. Hoffmann. 1979. *Plants of the gods.* New York.

Scudder, T. 1971. *Gathering among African woodland savannah cultivators. A case study: The Gwembe Tonga.* Manchester, England.

Semerdzieva, M., M. Wurst, T. Koza, and J. Gartz. 1986. Psilocybin in Fruchtkörpern von *Inocybe aeruginascens. Planta Medica* 2: 83-5.

Sensarma, P. 1989. *Plants in the Indian Puranas.* Calcutta.

Sharples, R. W., and D. W. Minter. 1983. Theophrastus on fungi: Inaccurate citations in Athanaeus. *Journal of Hellenic Studies* 103: 154-6.

Shaw, D. E. 1984. *Microorganisms in Papua New Guinea.* Research Bulletin No. 33. Port Moresby.

Shaw, R. 1966. The polyunsaturated fatty acids of microorganisms. *Advances in Lipid Research* 4: 107-74.

Shinmen, Y., S. Shimazu, K. Akimoto, et al. 1989. Production of arachidonic acid by *Mortierella* fungi. *Applied Microbiology and Biotechnology* 31: 11-16.

Simmons, D. M. 1971. The mushroom toxins. *Delaware Medical Journal* 43: 177-87.

Singer, R. 1961. *Mushrooms and truffles.* London.

1978. Hallucinogenic mushrooms. In *Mushroom poisoning: Diagnosis and treatment,* ed. B. H. Rumack and E. Salzman, 201-14. West Palm Beach, Fla.

Singh, T. B., and K. C. Chunekar. 1972. *Glossary of vegetable drugs in Brhattrayi.* Varanasi, India.

Sinskey, A. J., and C. A. Batt. 1987. Fungi as a source of protein. In *Food and beverage mycology,* ed. L. R. Beuchat, 435-71. New York.

Stanton, W. R. 1985. Food fermentation in the tropics. In *Microbiology of fermented foods,* Vol. 2, ed. B. J. B. Wood, 193-211. London.

Steinkraus, K. H. 1983. Traditional food fermentation as industrial resources. *Acta Biotechnologia* 3: 3-12.

1985. Production of vitamin B-12 in tempe. In *Non-salted soybean fermentation.* Asian Symposium, International Committee on Economic and Applied Microbiology, 68. Tsukuba, Japan.

Sternberg, M. 1978. Microbial rennets. *Advances in Applied Microbiology* 24: 135-57.

Stijve, T., J. Klan, and T. W. Kuyper. 1985. Occurrence of psilocybin and baeocystin in the genus *Inocybe* (Fr:) Fr. *Persoonia* 2: 469-73.

Stoloff, L. 1987. Carcinogenicity of aflatoxin. *Science* 237: 1283.

Strong, F. M. 1974. Toxicants occurring naturally in foods. *Nutrition Reviews* 32: 225-31.

Stuart, D. E. 1977. Seasonal phases in Ona subsistence, territorial distribution and organization. Implications for the archeological record. In *For theory building in archaeology,* ed. L. R. Binford, 251-83. New York.

Takeshima, H. 1992. Antiviral agents. In *The search for bioactive compounds from microorganisms,* ed. S. Omura, 45-62. New York.

Tanaka, H., K. Kawakita, N. Imamura, et al. 1992. General screening of enzyme inhibitors. In *The search for bioactive compounds from microorganisms,* ed. S. Omura, 117-80. New York.

Tanaka, N. 1890. On hatsudake and akahatsu, two species of edible fungi. *Botanical Magazine* 4: 2-7.

Tanaka, Y. 1992. Antifungal agents. In *The search for bioactive compounds from microorganisms,* ed. S. Omura, 30-44. New York.

Tanaka, Y., A. Hasegawa, S. Yamamoto, et al. 1988. Worldwide contamination of cereals by the *Fusarium* mycotoxins nivalenol and zearalenone. I. Surveys of 19 countries. *Journal of Agricultural and Food Chemistry* 36: 979-83.

Tanaka, Y., and S. Okuda. 1992. Insecticides, acaricides and anticoccidial agents. In *The search for bioactive compounds from microorganisms*, ed. S. Omura, 237-62. New York.

Tee, E. S. 1992. Carotenoids and retinoids in human nutrition. *Reviews in Food Science and Nutrition* 31: 103-63.

Terrell, E. E., and L. R. Batra. 1982. *Zizania latifolia* and *Ustilago esculenta*, a grass-fungus association. *Economic Botany* 36: 274-85.

Thrower, L. B., and Y.-S. Chan. 1980. *Gau sun:* A cultivated host parasite combination from China. *Economic Botany* 34: 20-6.

Toth, B. 1983. Carcinogens in edible mushrooms. *Carcinogens and Mutagens in the Environment* 3: 99-108.

Toth, B., D. Nagel, and A. Ross. 1982. Gastric tumorgenesis by a single dose of 4-(hydroxymethyl)benzenediazonium ion of *Agaricus bisporus*. *British Journal of Cancer* 46: 417-22.

Tounefort, J. de. 1707. Observations sur la naissance et sur la culture des champignons. *Mémoires de l'Académie Royale des Sciences,* 58-66.

Tung, T. C., P. C. Huang, and H. O. Li. 1961. Composition of foods used in Taiwan. *Journal of the Formosan Medical Association* 60: 973-1005.

Turner, N. J. 1978. *Food plants of British Columbia Indians. Part II-interior peoples.* Victoria.

Turner, N. J., H. V. Kuhnlein, and K. N. Egger. 1987. The cottonwood mushroom (*Tricholoma populinum* Lange): A food resource of the Interior Salish Indian peoples of British Columbia. *Canadian Journal of Botany* 65: 921-7.

Umezawa, C., and T. Kishi. 1989. Vitamin metabolism. In *Metabolism and physiology of yeasts*, ed. A. H. Rose and J. S. Harrison, 457-88. London.

Usher, G. 1974. *A dictionary of plants used by man.* New York.

Vandamme, E. J. 1989. Vitamins and related compounds via microorganisms; a biotechnological view. In *Biotechnology of vitamins, pigments and growth factors*, ed. E. G. Vandamme, 1-11. London.

Verma, R. N., and T. G. Singh. 1981. Investigation on edible fungi in the north eastern hills of India. *Mushroom Science* 11: 89-99.

Wakita, S. 1976. Thiamine-distribution by mushrooms. *Science Report, Yokohama National University* 2: 39-70.

Wang, Y. C. 1985. Mycology in China with emphasis on review of the ancient literature. *Acta Mycologica Sinica* 4: 133-40.

Wassef, M. K. 1977. Fungal lipids. *Advances in Lipid Research* 15: 159-232.

Wasson, R. G. 1975. Mushrooms and Japanese culture. *Transactions of the Asiatic Society of Japan* (Third Series) 11: 5-25.

Watling, R., and M. R. D. Seaward. 1976. Some observations on puffballs from British archaeological sites. *Journal of Archaeological Science* 3: 165-72.

Weete, J. D. 1974. *Fungal lipid chemistry.* New York.

    1989. Structure and function of sterols in fungi. *Advances in Lipid Research* 23: 115-67.

Weete, J. D., M. S. Fuller, M. Q. Huang, and S. Gandhi. 1989. Fatty acids and sterols of selected hyphochytridomycetes. *Experimental Mycology* 13: 183-95.

Winlock, H. E. 1973. *The tomb of Queen Meryet-Amun at Thebes.* New York.

Wong, H. C., and P. E. Koehler. 1981. Production and isolation of an antibiotic from *Monascus purpureus* and its relationship to pigment production. *Journal of Food Science* 46: 589-92.

Yamada, H. 1992. Immunomodulators. In *The search for bioactive compounds from microorganisms*, ed. S. Omura, 171-97. New York.

Yamada, H., S. Shimizu, and Y. Shinmen. 1987. Production of arachidonic acid by *Mortierella elongata* IS-5. *Agricultural and Biological Chemistry* 51: 785-90.

Yamada, H., S. Shimizu, Y. Shinmen, et al. 1988. Production of arachidonic acid and eicosapentenoic acid by microorganisms. In *Proceedings of the World Conference on the Biotechnology of Fats Oils Industry*. American Oil Chemists' Society, 173-7. Champaign, Ill.

Yanovsky, E. 1936. *Food plants of the North American Indians.* United States Department of Agriculture Misc. Pub. No. 237. Washington, D.C.

Yen, D. E., and H. G. Gutierrez. 1976. The ethnobotany of the Tasaday: I. The useful plants. In *Further studies on the Tasaday*, ed. D. E. Yin and J. Nance, 97-136. Makati, Rizal.

Yokotsuka, T. 1985. Fermented protein foods in the Orient with emphasis on shoyu and miso in Japan. In *Microbiology of fermented foods*, Vol. 1., ed. B. J. B. Wood, 197-247. London.

    1986. Soy sauce biochemistry. *Advances in Food Research* 30: 195-329.

Yokoyama, K. 1975. Ainu names and uses for fungi, lichens and mosses. *Transactions of the Mycological Society, Japan* 16: 183-9.

Yoshida, S. 1985. On the origin of fermented soybeans. In *Non-salted soybean fermentation*. Asian Symposium. International Committee on Economic and Applied Microbiology, 62-3. Tsukuba, Japan.

Zidwick, M. J. 1992. Organic acids. In *Biotechnology of filamentous fungi*, ed. D. B. Finkelstein and C. Ball, 303-34. Boston, Mass.

II.C.8 ❧ Squash

Definition

Wild and domesticated members of the New World genus *Cucurbita* L. (Cucurbitaceae) are typically referred to as "gourds," "pumpkins," and "squashes." The mature fruit of wild plants, technically called a pepo, has gourdlike qualities like a tough rind and dry flesh. These same qualities have led to the term "ornamental gourds" for various cultivars of *Cururbita pepo* L. that are grown for their decorative but inedible fruits. However, the common name for the domesticated *Cucurbita ficifolia* Bouché is "fig-leaf gourd," even though the fleshy fruits are cultivated for human consumption. Because another genus of the Cucurbitaceae, *Lagenaria* L., is considered the true gourd, it is preferable to refer to members of *Cucurbita* differentially, which leads us to the terms "pumpkin" and "squash."

Pumpkin comes from the Old English word "pompion," which is itself derived from the Greek *pepon* and the Latin *pepo* that together mean a large, ripe, round melon or gourd. Traditionally, "pumpkin" has been used to describe those cultivars of *Cururbita argyrosperma* Huber, *Cururbita maxima* Lam., *Cururbita moschata* (Lam.) Poir., and *C. pepo* that produce rotund mature fruits used in baking and for feeding livestock.

"Squash," by contrast, is a term derived from the New England aboriginal word "askutasquash," meaning vegetables eaten green. It was used during the seventeenth century to designate cultivars, usually of *C. pepo,* grown for their edible immature fruits, and by the nineteenth century, called "summer squashes." "Winter squashes," in contrast, are the mature fruits of *C. argyrosperma, C. maxima, C. moschata,* and *C. pepo* that store well and are not usually round; they are prepared as vegetables, baked into pies, or used as forage. Although "winter squashes" are supposed to differ from "pumpkins" in having a milder taste and flesh of a finer grain, the truth is that these culinary categories overlap, adding to the confusion in nomenclature. For the purposes of this discussion, the generic "squash" will refer to all wild and domesticated members of *Cucurbita.*

Squash Growers and Researchers

The story of squash is a story of Native Americans and New World archaeologists, gold-seeking explorers and European colonizers, herbalists and horticulturists, breeders and botanists. Squashes fascinate us all, but none more than the people who have dedicated their careers to squash research. Such research, as we know it, was under way in Europe by the 1800s. Intrigued by the diversity of fruits illustrated in the herbals of the sixteenth and seventeenth centuries (see Whitaker 1947; Eisendrath 1962; Paris 1989), the French horticulturist Charles Naudin (1856) took great pleasure in describing, breeding, and classifying these newcomers to the Old World. By the twentieth century, comprehensive breeding programs were well established in Europe, North America, and Asia. In an attempt to keep pace with the burgeoning of new strains, William Tapley, Walter Enzie, and Glen Van Eseltine (1937) combed the horticultural literature to provide the most detailed descriptions ever of 132 cultivars.

From Russia, organized plant-collecting expeditions were launched to search Middle and South America, eastern Africa, India, and Asia Minor for new landraces. These explorations provided the bases for new classifications (e.g., Bukasov 1930; Pangalo 1930; Zhiteneva 1930; Filov 1966). Other scientists also contributed to the systematics of squash, with Igor Grebenščikov (1955, 1958, 1969) updating an earlier (Alefeld 1866) classification of infraspecific varieties. The Americans E. F. Castetter and A. T. Erwin took a different approach, placing cultivars into horticultural groups as opposed to botanical classes (Castetter 1925; Castetter and Erwin 1927).

During the middle of the twentieth century, archaeological discoveries of ancient squash in the New World (Whitaker and Bird 1949; Whitaker, Cutler, and MacNeish 1957; Cutler and Whitaker 1961; Whitaker and Cutler 1971) provided an added perspective on the history and evolution of these species. In recent decades, some of the most ancient and most accurately dated and identified squash remains (e.g., Kay, King, and Robinson 1980; Conrad et al. 1984; Simmons 1986; Decker and Newsom 1988) have served to highlight the importance of *C. pepo* in the origins and character of North American horticulture (Heiser 1979; Minnis 1992; Smith 1992). Moreover, archaeological studies in South America have also blossomed recently (see Pearsall 1992 and refs. therein), giving us more detailed histories of *C. ficifolia* and *C. maxima.*

Domesticated squashes, with their diversity in fruit characteristics, have long been of interest to horticultural geneticists (e.g., Sinnott 1922; Shifriss 1955; Wall 1961; Robinson et al. 1976). Liberty Hyde Bailey, who explored North America in search of wild species, spent countless hours in his gardens performing breeding and inheritance experiments and making observations on the domesticates (Bailey 1902, 1929, 1937, 1943, 1948).

Thomas Whitaker, a prolific researcher with the United States Department of Agriculture, has been the closest human ally of the cucurbits. He examined relationships among wild and domesticated squashes using all available sources of data, including archaeological remains, hybridization experiments, anatomical

Long white squash

and morphological studies, and various genetic analysis (e.g., Whitaker 1931, 1951, 1956, 1968; Whitaker and Bohn 1950; Cutler and Whitaker 1956; Whitaker and Bemis 1964; Whitaker and Cutler 1965). Other devoted squash enthusiasts of the twentieth century include Hugh Cutler and W. P. Bemis, who often worked and published with Whitaker.

In recent years, individual domesticated squash species have been scrutinized to determine their evolutionary histories from wild progenitor(s) through domestication to diversification and geographic spread. As an additional source of phylogenetic data, isozyme analyses aided Deena Decker-Walters and Hugh Wilson in their examination of *C. pepo* (Decker 1985, 1988; Decker and Wilson 1987), Laura Merrick (1990) in the study of *C. argyrosperma*, and Thomas Andres (1990) in his evaluation of *C. ficifolia*. Similar modern and detailed research is lacking for *C. maxima* and *C. moschata*.

Two very different but nonetheless comprehensive books have been written on members of the Cucurbitaceae. One by Whitaker and Glen Davis (1962) reviews past research to provide the most up-to-date (at that time) coverage on the description, history, genetics, physiology, culture, uses, and chemistry of economically important cucurbits, including squashes. The other, *Biology and Utilization of the Cucurbitaceae*, edited by David Bates, Richard Robinson, and Charles Jeffrey (1990), includes 36 distinct articles written by leading experts of the day and covering the systematics, evolution, morphology, sex expression, utilization, crop breeding, and culture of squashes and other cucurbits.

Plant and Fruit Descriptions

Five domesticated and about 20 wild squash species grow in dry or somewhat humid regions of the tropics, subtropics, and mild temperate zones. Their native turf ranges from the central United States south to central Argentina, with species diversity being greatest in Mexico. The herbaceous vines are not frost-tolerant. However, some of the xerophytic perennials have large storage roots that can survive a snowy winter. Among the mesophytic annuals, which include the domesticates, quick germination, early flowering, and rapid growth have enabled some to adapt to the more extreme latitudes.

Squash plants are monoecious, tendriliferous vines with leaves ranging from entire to lobed and large, yellow to yellow-orange, campanulate flowers. The ephemeral blossoms, opening only once in the morning, are pollinated primarily by specially adapted solitary bees. The inferior ovary of the female flower develops into a gourdlike fruit called a pepo. Pepos of wild plants are usually round with a tough rind and bitter flesh, whereas domesticated fruits generally lack bitterness and are multifarious in their characteristics.

Although primarily outcrossers, individual plants are self-compatible. Hybridization can also occur between some species. In fact, all squash species have 20 pairs of chromosomes and are incompletely isolated from one another by genetic barriers. This ability to cross species boundaries has been important for plant breeders, allowing them to transfer genes controlling favorable qualities from one species to another. In this way, resistance to the cucumber mosaic virus was transferred from a distantly related wild species to cultivated *C. pepo*, using *C. moschata* as the intermediary.

Archaeological remains, hybridization studies, and genetic data suggest that the domesticated species were independently selected from genetically distinct wild progenitors. In spite of their separate origins, *C. argyrosperma* and *C. moschata* are closely related. In fact, *C. argyrosperma* was not recognized as a distinct species until the Russian geneticist K. I. Pangalo (1930) described it as *Cucurbita mixta* Pang. following extensive collecting expeditions to Mexico and Central America. Even so, it can be difficult to correctly identify some plants and fruits. Generally, fruits of *C. argyrosperma* have enlarged corky peduncles, whereas those of *C. moschata* are hard and thin but distinctly flared at the fruit end. Also, the green and/or white fruits of *C. argyrosperma*, which sometimes mature to yellow, rarely display the orange rind coloring that is common among cultivars of *C. moschata*. Foliaceous sepals are largely unique to but not ubiquitous in *C. moschata*. Leaf mottling is more common in *C. moschata* and leaf lobes deeper in *C. argyrosperma*.

Both species have large flowers with long slender androecia, relatively soft pubescence on the foliage, and distinctly colored seed margins. Among the domesticated species, these squashes best survive the hot, humid, low-elevation (usually under 1,500 meters [m] above sea level) climes of the mid-latitudes, often failing to flower when daylengths are too long. But relative to the wide pre-Columbian distribution and diversity in *C. moschata* (Figure II.C.8.1), *C. argyrosperma* has remained limited in its geography and genetic variability.

There are three domesticated varieties of *C. argyrosperma* subspecies (ssp.) *argyrosperma* – variety (var.) *argyrosperma*, var. *callicarpa* Merrick and Bates, var. *stenosperma* (Pang.) Merrick and Bates – and a weedy variety, var. *palmeri* (Bailey) Merrick and Bates (see Table II.C.8.1). Most of the diversity in this squash can still be found in the endemic landraces of the southwestern United States, Mexico, and Central America. The moderately sized, unfurrowed fruits range from globose to pyriform to long-necked; in the latter, the necks may be straight or curved. Rinds are generally decorated with splotchy, irregular green and white stripes, though in var. *callicarpa*, solid white or green fruits are common and the green coloration is often lacy. Commercial cultivars are few, as culinary quality of the pale yellow to orange flesh is relatively poor in this species. Most of the cultivars and landraces in commercial trade today represent var. *callicarpa*.

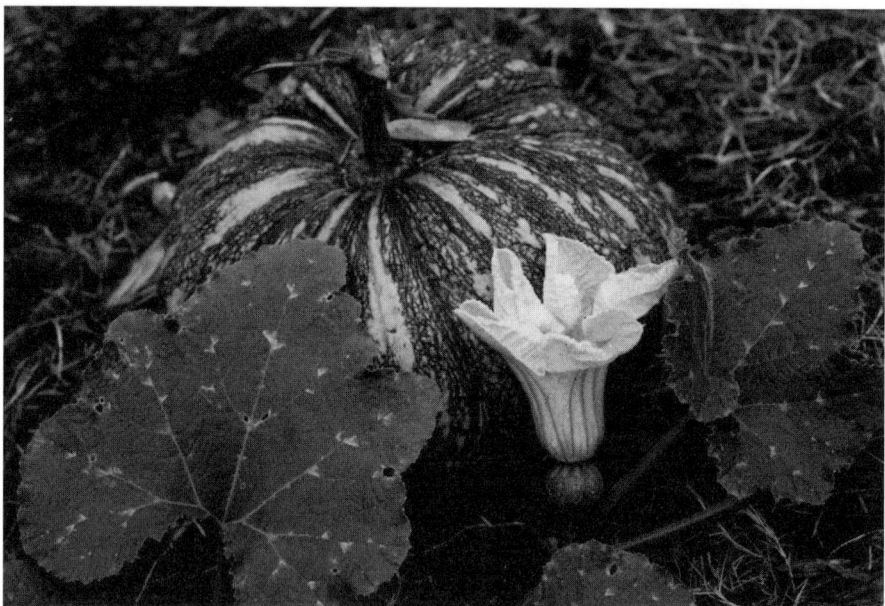

Figure II.C.8.1. The white-splotched leaves, yellow-orange female flower, and immature green-and-white-striped fruit of *Cucurbita moschata*. The swelling of the peduncle where it is attached to the fruit is characteristic of this species.

Fruits of *C. moschata,* weighing up to 15 kilograms (kg) apiece, range from squatty to round to turbinate, pyriform, or oblong to necked. Furrows, sometimes deep, are common and wartiness occasional. The rinds are solid, splotchy, or striped in dark to light greens, whites, creams, yellows, and oranges. Fruit flesh is usually deep yellow or orange.

In North America, cultivars of *C. moschata* have been placed into three horticultural groups – "cheese pumpkins," "crooknecks," and "bell squashes" (see Table II.C.8.2). However, these groups do not satisfactorily accommodate the diversity of landraces that have evolved in tropical regions around the globe. For example, *C. moschata* is widely cultivated in Asia, and several unusual cultivars with names like 'Chirimen', 'Kikuza', 'Saikyo', and 'Yokohama' originated in Japan. Fruit character-

istics resembling those of *C. argyrosperma* ssp. *argyrosperma* indicate that the Japanese cultivars may have arisen from interspecific crossings. Genetic diversity in some northwestern Mexican landraces of *C. moschata* also may be the result of introgression from wild and/or cultivated *C. argyrosperma.*

A. I. Filov (1966) expanded earlier classifications of *C. moschata* to include over 20 varieties in several geographical subspecies. Unfortunately, modern systematic and genetic studies that would confirm the natural relationships among cultivars within and among regions are lacking. Nevertheless, these geographical subspecies do reveal centers of diversification that include Colombia, where the seeds are darker and the plants and fruits small; Mexico, Central America, and the West Indies, where landraces

Table II.C.8.1 *Domesticated varieties of* Cucurbita argyrosperma *ssp.* argyrosperma

Variety	Description	Distribution in North America	Cultivars and comments
var. *argyrosperma*	Fruits mostly striped; peduncle relatively thin; seeds broad, smooth-surfaced, white with gray margins	Eastern and southern Mexico, Central America	'Silverseed Gourd' is grown for its seeds, which are the largest in the genus
var. *callicarpa*	Fruits solid in color, striped or blotchy; peduncle thick; seeds white or golden tan with tan margins, surfaces smooth or etched	Central and northwestern Mexico, southwestern U.S.	'Green Striped Cushaw', 'Japanese Pie', 'Puritan', 'Tennessee Sweet Potato', 'White Cushaw', and various landraces; good-quality fruit flesh
var. *stenosperma*	Fruits mostly striped; dark green tint to the placental tissue; peduncle thick; seeds narrow, smooth-surfaced, white with gray or tan margins	South-central Mexico	'Elfrida Taos'; distribution and characteristics overlap with those of the other varieties; grown mostly for the edible seeds

Table II.C.8.2. *Horticultural groups of* Cucurbita moschata

Horticultural group	Description	Representative cultivars	Comments
Cheese pumpkins	Fruits variable but usually oblate with a buff-colored rind	'Calhoun', 'Kentucky Field', 'Large Cheese', 'Quaker Pie'	Plants are hardy and productive under various growing conditions
Crooknecks	Fruits round at blossom end with long straight or curved necks	'Bugle Gramma', 'Canada Crookneck', 'Golden Cushaw', 'Winter Crookneck'	Very popular in colonial America for pies and stock
Bell squashes	Fruits bell-shaped to almost cylindrical	'African Bell', 'Butternut', 'Carpet Bag', 'Ponca', 'Tahitian'	These cultivars, which are the most popular today, were probably selected from "crookneck" types

are genetically variable and fruits of many shapes and colors can be found in a single field; Florida, which is home to the small-fruited, aboriginal 'Seminole Pumpkin'; Japan with its warty and wrinkled fruits; India, where large soft-skinned fruits abound; and Asia Minor, where fruits again are variable but long barbell-shaped pepos predominate.

Figure II.C.8.2. Seeds of *Cucurbita pepo* (top), *C. moschata* (center), and *C. argyrosperma* (bottom). At the lower right is a seed of 'Silverseed Gourd,' the largest of all squash seeds. Scale equals 1 cm.

Although *C. moschata* is the most widely cultivated squash in underdeveloped tropical countries, as with *C. argyrosperma*, relatively few cultivars have entered the commercial trade of Europe and North America. "Cheese pumpkins" and "crooknecks" were popular in nineteenth-century New England. Today, only various selections from the "bell squashes" are commonly sold by seed suppliers (Figure II.C.8.3).

Cucurbita pepo is characterized by uniformly colored tan seeds, lobed leaves with prickly pubescence, hard roughly angled peduncles, and short, thick, conical androecia (Figures II.C.8.2 and II.C.8.4). Flowers range from small to large, though they are rarely as grand as those of *C. argyrosperma* ssp. *argyrosperma*. Genetic diversity, expressed in the plethora of differing fruit forms, is greatest in this squash. Orange flesh color is not as common in *C. pepo* as it is in *C. maxima* or *C. moschata*.

Cucurbita pepo appears to have shared a Mexican or Central American ancestor with *C. argyrosperma* and *C. moschata*. From those origins, wild populations – ssp. *ovifera* (L.) Decker var. *ozarkana* Decker-Walters, ssp. *ovifera* var. *texana* (Scheele) Decker, ssp. *fraterna* (Bailey) Andres, ssp. *pepo* – spread over North America before at least two domestications of *C. pepo* took place to produce ssp. *ovifera* var. *ovifera* (L.) Decker and cultivars of ssp. *pepo*. Because *C. pepo* can tolerate cooler temperatures than can *C. argyrosperma* and *C. moschata*, this squash flourishes at more extreme latitudes and higher elevations (1,600 to 2,100 m above sea level) to the delight of farmers from southern Canada to the highlands of Central America. Some wild populations and cultivars are well adapted to the northern United States, with seeds that are quick to germinate and early flowering that is responsive to changes in daylength.

Encompassing many hundreds of cultivars, six horticultural groups of *C. pepo* were recognized during the twentieth century (see Table II.C.8.3). "Acorn squashes," "crooknecks," "scallop squashes," and most "ornamental gourds" belong to ssp. *ovifera* var. *ovifera*. Horticulturists have traditionally classified all small, hard-shelled, bitter fruits grown

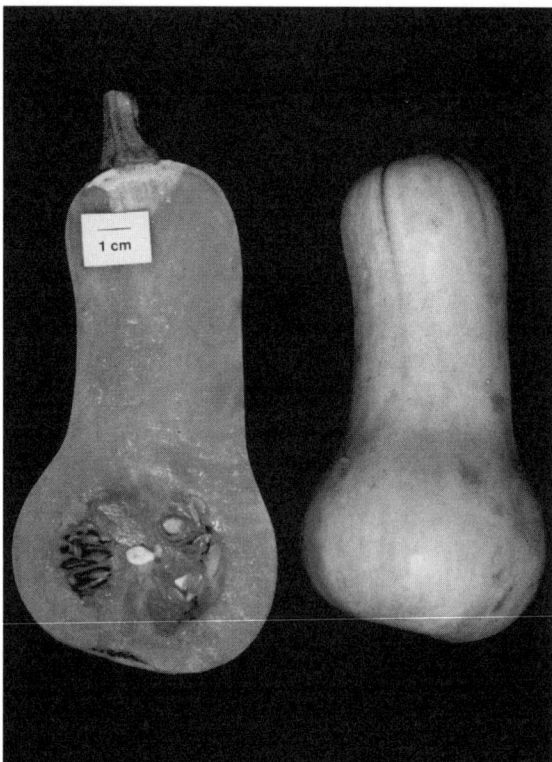

Figure II.C.8.3. 'Butternut', a "bell squash" cultivar of *Cucurbita moschata,* has a cream-colored rind and dark orange flesh rich in carotenes.

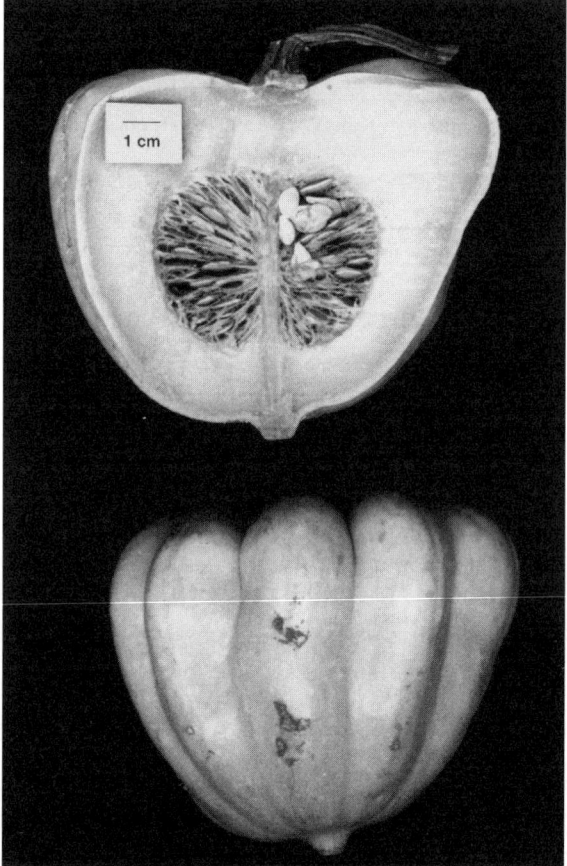

Figure II.C.8.4. An unusual "acorn squash" of *Cucurbita pepo* purchased in Ontario, Canada; cultivar unknown. Flesh and rind are tan colored.

for autumn decorations as ornamental gourds. However, this classification does not reflect the fact that these gourds have various genealogies that include wild populations of ssp. *ovifera,* ssp. *pepo,* and probably ssp. *fraterna.* Pumpkins, such as those grown in temperate to tropical gardens around the globe, and marrows belong to ssp. *pepo.* The former, like acorn squashes, are eaten when mature, whereas the latter, like the crooknecks and scallop squashes, are summer squashes picked during the first week of fruit development. Bushy plants with relatively short internodes have been developed for most of the summer squashes as well as for some of the acorn squashes (Figures II.C.8.5 and II.C.8.6).

Cucurbita maxima is distantly related to the trio just discussed. This squash, whose origins are in South America, exhibits closer genetic affinities to other wild South American species. Like *C. pepo,* some cultivars and landraces of *C. maxima* can tolerate the relatively cool temperatures of the highlands (up to 2,000 m above sea level). Today, this species is grown in tropical to temperate regions around the globe, particularly in South America, southeastern Asia, India, and Africa.

Cucurbita maxima is distinguished by its soft round stems, entire or shallowly lobed unpointed leaves, and spongy, enlarged, terete peduncles. Compared to the other domesticates, the white or brown seeds of this squash are thick, particularly in relationship to their margins. The androecium is short, thick, and columnar. The yellow or orange fruit flesh is fine-grained and of the highest quality (tasty and relatively rich in vitamins) among all squashes. Fruits are quite variable in size, shape, and coloration, with the latter including many shades of gray, green, blue, pink, red, and orange in striped, mottled, or blotchy patterns.

A distinct fruit form characterizes cultivars classified as "turban squashes" (Figures II.C.8.7 and II.C.8.8). The immature ovary protrudes upward from the receptacle, swelling into a turban-shaped fruit with a crown (the part of the fruit not enveloped by the receptacle) upon maturity. Table II.C.8.4 lists some turban squash cultivars and describes five other traditionally recognized horticultural groups – "banana squashes," "delicious squashes," "hubbard squashes" (Figure II.C.8.9) "marrows," and "show pumpkins."

Table II.C.8.3. *Horticultural groups of* Cucurbita pepo

Horticultural group	Description	Representative cultivars	Comments
Acorn squashes	Fruits usually small, of various shapes and colors but always grooved	'Acorn', 'Delicata', 'Fordhook', 'Mandan', 'Sweet Dumpling', 'Table Queen'	A heterogeneous group of uncertain origins but closely related to "scallop squashes"; mature fruits baked as vegetable
Crooknecks	Fruits long, club-shaped with straight or curved neck; rind very hard, yellow to orange, warted	'Giant Crookneck', 'Straightneck', 'Summer Crookneck', 'Yankee Hybrid'	Probably an ancient group of summer squashes although 'Straightneck' cultivars are more recent in origin
Marrows	Fruits long, club-shaped to cylindrical, mildly ridged; rind usually with lacy green pattern	'Cocozelle', 'Moore's Cream', 'Vegetable Marrow', 'Zucchini'	Selected from pumpkins and diversified in Europe; fruits eaten immature
Ornamental gourds	Fruits small of various shapes and colors; rind hard; flesh usually bitter; seeds small	'Crown of Thorns', 'Flat Striped', 'Miniature Ball', 'Nest Egg,' 'Orange Warted', 'Spoon', 'Striped Pear'	A heterogeneous group of multiple origins; some cultivars primitive, others fairly new; fruits not eaten
Pumpkins	Fruits typically large, round or oblong, shallowly to deeply grooved or ribbed; rind relatively soft; seeds large	'Connecticut Field', 'Jack O'Lantern', 'Sandwich Island', 'Small Sugar', 'Vegetable Spaghetti'	Mature fruits used as a vegetable or for pies, jack-o'-lanterns, and forage; grown for edible seeds also
Scallop squashes	Fruits flattened at both ends with edges scalloped around middle; rind hard	'Benning's Green Tint', 'Golden Custard', 'Patty-pan', 'White Bush Scallop'	An ancient group of summer squashes

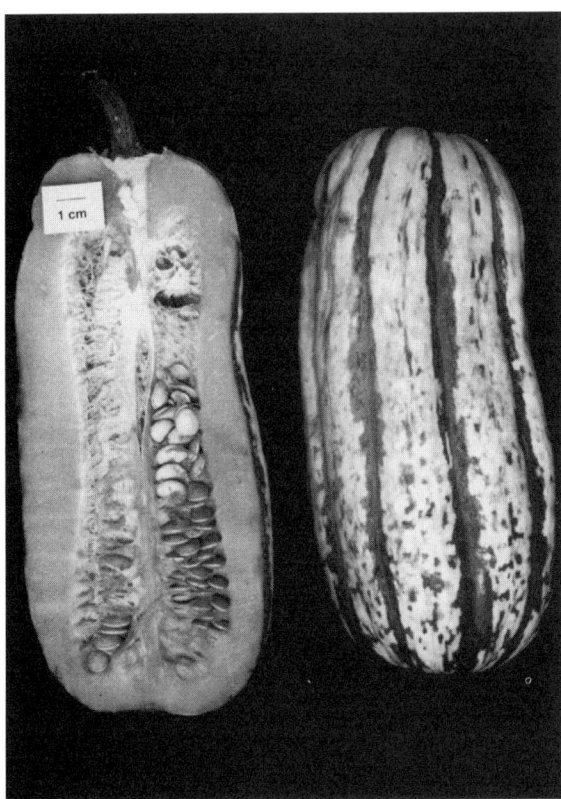

Figure II.C.8.5. 'Delicata' (*Cucurbita pepo*) has a green-and-white-striped rind that turns orange and pale yellow with age. The orange flesh of these long-keeping fruits intensifies in color with storage.

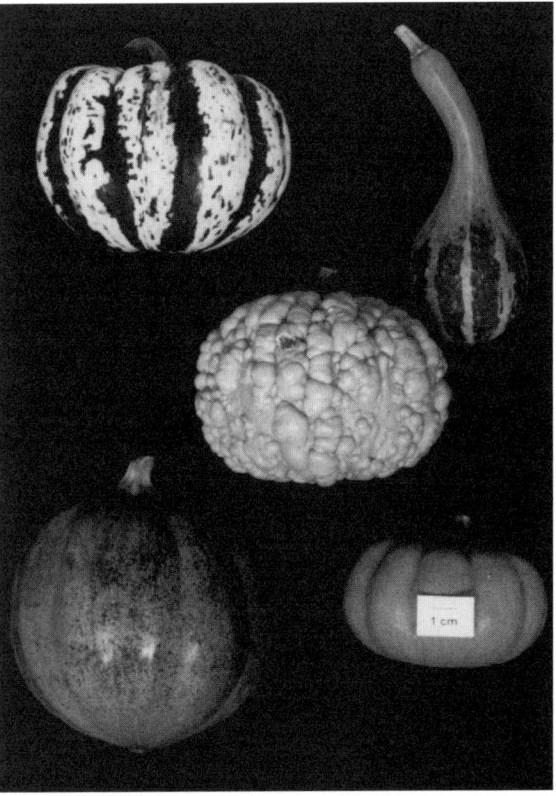

Figure II.C.8.6. Various small-fruited cultivars of *Cucurbita pepo*, including 'Sweet Dumpling' (top left), 'Bicolor Spoon' (top right), 'Orange Warted' (center), 'Table Queen' (bottom left), and 'Jack-Be-Little Pumpkin' (bottom right).

Figure II.C.8.7. 'Turk's Turban' (*Cucurbita maxima*) is often grown as an ornamental because of the deep red rind color. The crown of this fruit has a much paler pattern of green and red splotches.

Over 50 cultivars of *C. maxima* had been commercially traded by the early twentieth century; today, this number has reached over 200. Not all landraces and cultivars can be assigned to the horticultural groups in Table II.C.8.4. Some cultivars, such as the warty 'Victor', were derived from hybridizations between horticultural groups. Local landraces that never entered into, or played only minor roles in, American and European commercial trade often have fruit traits that do not match those characterizing the groups. And although several varieties of *C. maxima* have been proposed over the years, as of yet no one has performed an intensive systematic study of this species to clarify evolutionary relationships among cultivars and groups of cultivars.

Cucurbita ficifolia is not closely related to the other domesticated squashes or to any known wild populations. Distinguishing characteristics include relatively wide, minutely pitted, solid-colored seeds, ranging from tan to black; white, coarsely fibrous flesh; an androecium shaped like that of *C. maxima* but with hairs on the filaments; and rounded lobed leaves. Genetic uniformity in this species is evidenced by the lack of variation in fruit characteristics. The large oblong fruits, measuring 15 to 50 centimeters (cm) long, exhibit only three basic rind coloration patterns: solid white, a reticulated pattern of green on white that may include white stripes, and mostly green with or without white stripes. No distinct landraces or cultivars of *C. ficifolia* have been recognized.

In Latin America today, this cool-tolerant, short-day squash is grown for food in small, high-altitude (1,000 to 2,800 m above sea level) gardens from northern Mexico through Central America and the Andes to central Chile. Usually the mature fruits are candied, but the seeds and immature fruits are eaten as well. *Cucurbita ficifolia* is also cultivated as an ornamental

Table II.C.8.4. *Horticultural groups of* Cucurbita maxima

Horticultural group	Description	Representative cultivars	Comments
Banana squashes	Fruits long, pointed at both ends; rind soft; seeds brown	'Banana', 'Pink Banana', 'Plymouth Rock'	Introduced to the U.S. from Mexico; plants can tolerate high temperatures
Delicious squashes	Fruits turbinate, shallowly ribbed; rind hard; seeds white	'Delicious', 'Faxon', 'Quality'	High-quality flesh; original stock came from Brazil in the late 1800s; similar types occur in Bolivia
Hubbard squashes	Fruits oval, tapering curved necks at both ends; rind very hard; seeds white	'Arikara', 'Blue Hubbard', 'Brighton', 'Hubbard', 'Kitchenette', 'Marblehead'	Inbreeding and hybridization have produced many cultivars
Marrows	Fruits oval to pyriform, tapering quickly at the apex and gradually toward the base; seeds white	'Boston Marrow', 'Golden Bronze', 'Ohio', 'Valparaiso', 'Wilder'	Fruits mature early; original stock probably came from Chile
Show pumpkins	Fruits large, orange; rind soft; seeds white	'Atlantic Giant', 'Big Max', 'Big Moon', 'Etampes', 'Mammoth'	Produces the largest pepos in the genus; grown for show and forage; a lot of diversity in India
Turban squashes	Fruits turban-shaped	'Acorn', 'Buttercup', 'Crown', 'Essex', 'Red China', 'Sweetmeat', 'Turban', 'Warren', 'Sapallito del Tronco'	Many cultivars were selected in Africa, Asia, and Australia from South American stock; some are more bushy than viny

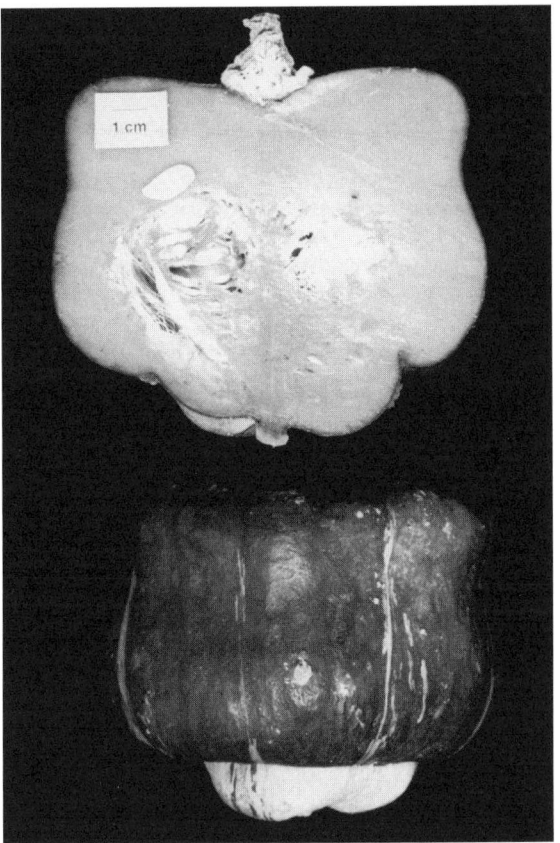

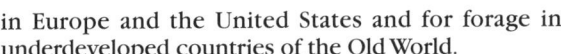

Figure II.C.8.8. 'Buttercup' is a "turban squash" of *Cucurbita maxima*. This fruit has a dark green rind, except for the small crown, which is a pale blue-green. Seeds are white and the flesh dark orange.

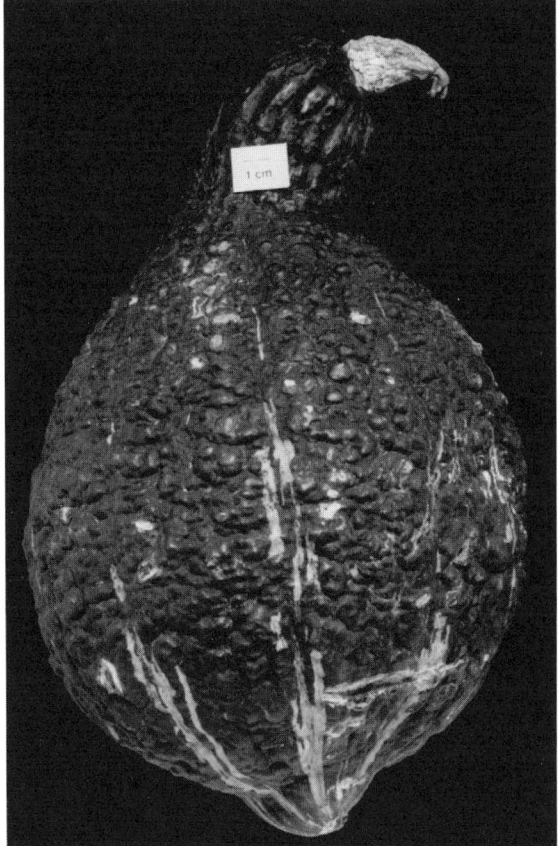

Figure II.C.8.9. This "hubbard squash" of *Cucurbita maxima* has a warted, dark blue-green rind with a few pale stripes. Note the swollen peduncle.

in Europe and the United States and for forage in underdeveloped countries of the Old World.

The Evolution and History of Squashes

The five domesticated squash species were brought under cultivation 5,000 to 15,000 years ago. Native Americans transformed the small green and white gourdlike pepos of wild plants into a cornucopia of colorful and shapely pumpkins and squashes. But long before they were domesticated, wild squash plants made their presence known to human populations. These fast-growing, tenacious vines are prolific opportunists, boldly invading disturbed sites of natural or human origin. Initial human interest in wild squash may have manifested itself in the use of the tough fruit rinds for containers. Additionally, the seeds are a tasty and nutritious source of food. The flesh of wild pepos is too bitter to eat raw. Toxic oxygenated tetracyclic triterpenes, called cucurbitacins, permeate the leaves, roots, and fruits as deterrents to

herbivory. Nevertheless, the frequency of immature peduncles among archaeological remains suggests that the young tender fruits were consumed, probably after leaching out the cucurbitacins through multiple boilings.

The development of nonbitter pepos came about as a result of domestication. Indiscriminate harvesting of fruits from wild or tolerated weedy vines eventually led to the planting of seeds from selected genetic strains. In the process of selecting for larger fruits for containers or larger seeds for consumption, thicker, nonbitter, and less fibrous flesh was discovered and selected for as well. Other changes included the loss of seed dormancy, softer and more colorful fruit rinds, adaptation to shorter growing seasons, and generally larger plant parts. In this way, squash became a major component of diets for the ancient farmers of the New World.

Squash domestication took place at least five times to yield the cultivated members of *C. argyrosperma*, *C. ficifolia*, *C. maxima*, *C. moschata*, and *C. pepo*.

These domestications involved genetically distinct wild populations and at least three different cultural groups inhabiting the eastern United States, Middle America, and South America. A discussion of the evolution of these cultivated squashes along with their history and spread follows.

Cucurbita argyrosperma

Cultivars of *C. argyrosperma* ssp. *argyrosperma* are genetically similar to wild populations of *C. argyrosperma* ssp. *sororia,* a native of low-elevation, mostly coastal habitats in Mexico and Central America. Sufficient evidence exists to support the theory that ssp. *sororia* gave rise to domesticated ssp. *argyrosperma.* Domestication probably took place in southern Mexico, where the earliest remains of ssp. *argyrosperma* date around 5000 B.C. Most of these archaeological specimens belong to var. *stenosperma;* landraces of this variety are still grown in southern Mexico today. With a current distribution ranging from northeastern Mexico south to the Yucatan and into Central America, var. *argyrosperma* is the most widespread variety of ssp. *argyrosperma* (Figure II.C.8.10). Remains of var. *argyrosperma* first appear in the archaeological

Figure II.C.8.10. This mature fruit of *Cucurbita argyrosperma* ssp. *sororia,* measuring about 7 cm. in diameter, was collected from a wild population in Veracruz, Mexico.

record in northeastern Mexico at about A.D. 200. A little later (c. A.D. 400), var. *callicarpa* shows up at archaeological sites in the southwestern United States. The earliest pre-Columbian evidence of *C. argyrosperma* in eastern North America is fifteenth-century remains from northwestern Arkansas. Although the three varieties of ssp. *argyrosperma* could have been selected separately from wild populations of ssp. *sororia,* Merrick's (1990) interpretation of the morphological evidence suggests that var. *stenosperma* and var. *callicarpa* evolved from southern and northern landraces of var. *argyrosperma,* respectively.

The fourth and final variety of spp. *argyrosperma,* var. *palmeri,* is weedy, possessing a mixture of characteristics otherwise representing wild spp. *sororia* and cultivated var. *callicarpa.* It grows unaided in disturbed areas, including cultivated fields, in northwestern Mexico beyond the range of ssp. *sororia. Cucurbita argyrosperma* ssp. *argyrosperma* var. *palmeri* may represent escapes of var. *callicarpa* that have persisted in the wild by gaining through mutation and/or hybridization with ssp. *sororia* those characteristics (such as bitter fruits) that are necessary for independent survival.

Current uses of wild and weedy fruits in Mexico include eating the seeds, using seeds and the bitter flesh medicinally, washing clothes with the saponin-rich flesh, and fashioning containers from the dried rinds. Although the antiquity of these uses is uncertain, selection for edible seeds has remained the dominant theme in cultivation. In southern Mexico and Guatemala, var. *argyrosperma* and var. *stenosperma* are grown for their large edible seeds, with the fruit flesh serving as forage. In southern Central America, indigenous cultures have produced landraces that yield a necked fruit eaten as a vegetable while immature and tender. Selection pressures in northern Mexico have created several landraces of var. *argyrosperma* and var. *callicarpa;* some produce mature pepos with quality flesh for human consumption as well as edible seeds, whereas others are grown for their immature fruits. At twelfth- and thirteenth-century sites in southern Utah, fruits of var. *callicarpa* were employed as containers, a use that persists among some tribes of the Southwest today. The greatest diversity of fruits in the species, represented primarily by var. *callicarpa,* occurs in northwestern Mexico and the southwestern United States

Relative to the post-Columbian changes incurred by other squashes, the spread and further diversification of *C. argyrosperma* cultivars has been limited. A few commercial cultivars such as 'Green Striped Cushaw' were selected from North American stock and grown in New England soon after colonization. A similar type of squash was illustrated in European herbals of the sixteenth century, and additional types were developed in South America and Asia. As a result of the recent trend to identify, save, and distribute native landraces of New World crops, a large number of landraces of *C. argyrosperma* indigenous to North America have entered the U.S. commercial trade under such names as 'Chompa', 'Green Hopi Squash', 'Mayo Arrote', 'Montezuma Giant', and 'Pepinas'.

Cucurbita moschata

The earliest archaeological remains indicative of domestication of *C. moschata* were discovered in southern Mexico (5000 B.C.) and in coastal Peru (3000 B.C.). Ancient Peruvian specimens differ from those of Mexico by having a warty rind and a pronounced fringe along the seed margins. Although Mexico appears to be the more ancient site of domestication, the Peruvian remains and the diversity of Colombian landraces point to South America as a secondary site of early diversification or an independent center of domestication. Unfortunately, wild progenitor populations have not yet been identified for this species. It is possible that they are extinct; however, a few tantalizing finds of wild squash in Bolivia suggest that South American populations of *C. moschata* may be awaiting rediscovery. Among wild squashes known today in Middle America, those of *C. argyrosperma* ssp. *sororia* express the greatest genetic affinity to Mexican landraces of *C. moschata*.

Even though the centers of landrace diversity for *C. moschata* lie in Central America and northern South America, archaeological remains indicate that this species spread to northeastern Mexico by about 1400 B.C. and to the southwestern United States by A.D. 900. The spread of *C. moschata* to the Gulf coastal area and the Caribbean may have been facilitated by early Spanish explorers and missionaries; a distinctive Florida landrace called 'Seminole Pumpkin' (Figure II.C.8.11) is still grown by the Miccusokees of the Everglades.

Among tribes of the Northern Plains, *C. moschata* was definitely a post-Columbian introduction.

The crooknecks and cheese pumpkins, which probably have their origins in North America, were known to colonists and Europeans as early as the 1600s. Variations on the cheese pumpkin theme can be found in the large furrowed pumpkins of India and southeastern Asia. Additional diversification of *C. moschata* took place in Asia Minor, where various fruit types resemble the bell squashes, and in Japan, where selection was for heavily warted rinds. Completing its worldwide travels, this species was well established as a food crop in northern Africa by the nineteenth century.

Cucurbita pepo

The squash represented by the earliest archaeological remains is *C. pepo*. Its seeds and rinds of wild or cultivated material appear in Florida around 10,000 B.C., in southern Mexico around 8000 B.C., and in Illinois at around 5000 B.C. Enlarged seeds and peduncles as well as thicker fruit rinds suggest that this species was definitely under cultivation in southern and northeastern Mexico between 7500 and 5500 B.C. and in the Mississippi Valley between 3000 and 1000 B.C. Cultivation had spread from Mexico to the southwestern United States by around 1000 B.C., and by A.D. 1500, *C. pepo* landraces were being grown throughout the United States and Mexico.

Ancestral North Americans independently domesticated at least two genetically distinct and geographically disjunct subspecies of *C. pepo* to produce the two major lineages of cultivars known today. Although wild populations of ssp. *pepo* (Figures II.C.8.12 and II.C.8.13) are currently unknown

Figure II.C.8.11. Fruit shape in the tan-colored fruits of the 'Seminole Pumpkin' (*Cucurbita moschata*) ranges from round or oblate to oval, oblong, or pear shaped. (Photograph by John Popenoe.)

and possibly extinct, they were probably subjected to the selection pressures of the natives of southern Mexico, giving rise to the majority of Mexican and southwestern U.S. landraces, as well as to "pumpkin" and "marrow" cultivars of this species. As with *C. argyrosperma* and *C. moschata*, human selection with *C. pepo* landraces in southern Mexico focused on producing large seeds within a sturdy round fruit.

Today, wild populations of *C. pepo* range from northeastern Mexico (ssp. *fraterna*) to Texas (ssp. *ovifera* var. *texana*), and north through the Mississippi Valley to southern Illinois (ssp. *ovifera* var. *ozarkana*).

As recently as 250 years ago, wild populations of ssp. *ovifera* may have occurred throughout the Gulf coastal region and certainly in Florida. A whole different lineage of cultivars, classified as ssp. *ovifera* var. *ovifera*, evolved from eastern U.S. populations of var. *ozarkana*. Aborigines of the Mississippi Valley apparently were not as interested as the Mexicans in quickly selecting for large seeds or fleshy fruits. Instead, a variety of small, odd-shaped, hard, and often warty cultivars were used as containers or grown for other nonsubsistence purposes. And although the seeds of early cultivars were probably eaten, in selecting for food, natives of the eastern United States developed several cultivars, such as the precursors of the scallop squashes and crooknecks, that produced tasty immature fruits.

Gilbert Wilson's (1917) treatise on agriculture among the Hidatsa indigenes of the Northern Plains gives us a more detailed account of the aboriginal use of *C. pepo*. These Native Americans cultivated squashes of various shapes, sizes, and colors together, picking them when four days old.

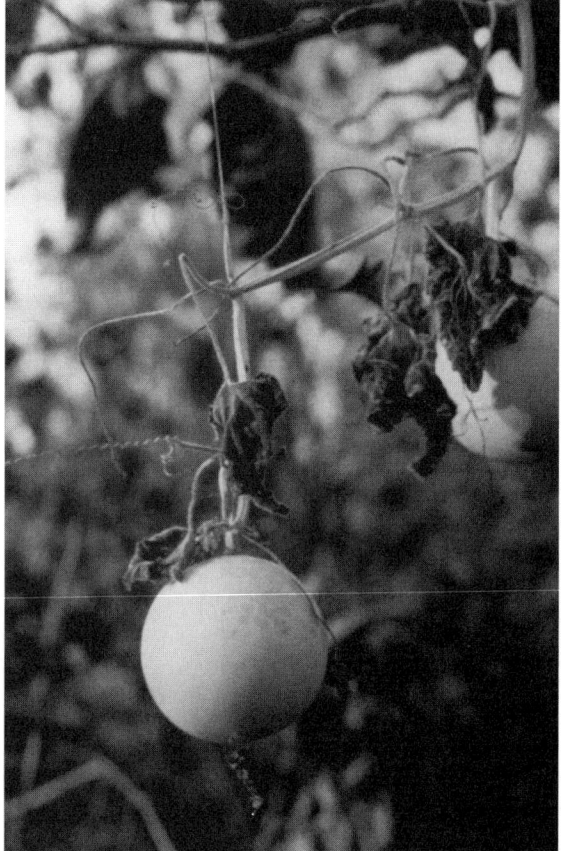

Figure II.C.8.12. The white fruit of this wild *Cucurbita pepo* ssp. *ovifera* var. *ozarkana* plant still clings to the dead vine at a riparian site in the Mississippi Valley. (Photograph by Wes Cowan and Bruce Smith.)

Figure II.C.8.13. From left to right, these green-and-white-striped fruits of *Curcurbita pepo* represent wild spp. *ovifera* var. *texana*, 'Mandan' (a cultivar of var. *ovifera*), and wild ssp. *fraterna*.

The young fruits were eaten fresh or sliced and dried for the winter. The flesh, and sometimes the seeds, of these mature fruits were boiled and eaten. Male squash blossoms did not go to waste either; they were picked when fresh and boiled with fat or dried for later use in mush. One fruit per plant was allowed to mature so as to provide seed for the next planting.

In addition to the two primary centers of domestication of *C. pepo,* a few landraces and cultivars may have been domesticated from wild populations of ssp. *fraterna* in northeastern Mexico. These landraces and those from southern Mexico probably spread to the eastern United States between A.D. 1000 and 1500, if not earlier. The intermingling of cultivars undoubtedly gave rise to new genetic combinations, which accounts for the diversity of fruits encountered by the earliest European visitors. The "acorn squashes," which include the Northern Plains landrace 'Mandan', may have originated in this way when Mexican "pumpkins" met "scallop squashes" in the United States. Similarly, 'Fort Berthold' and 'Omaha' are northern-adapted "pumpkin" landraces that were being grown by Sioux tribes in the early twentieth century.

Fruits representing all of the major horticultural groups are pictured in the herbals of the sixteenth century. More than any other squash, *C. pepo* was enthusiastically embraced by European horticulturists; hundreds of new cultivars, particularly the "marrows," have been developed in Europe and in the United States over the past 400 years. Selection practices emphasized earliness in flowering, compactness or bushiness in growth, and uniformity within a cultivar for fruit characteristics.

Although *C. pepo* was carried to other parts of the globe during the seventeenth century, diversification of landraces was limited primarily to the "pumpkins" of Asia Minor. Nevertheless, unique cultivars did develop elsewhere, such as 'Alexandria' from Egypt, 'Der Wing' from China, 'Nantucket' from the Azores, and 'Pineapple' from South America.

Cucurbita maxima

Numerous landraces of *C. maxima* with differing fruit characteristics can be found throughout South America today. However, archaeological remains are less widespread. Most are from coastal Peru, where the earliest evidence of domestication appears between 2500 and 1500 B.C. Later pre-Columbian remains have been found in Argentina (500 B.C.) and northern Chile (A.D. 600). Early Spaniards noted that landraces of *C. maxima* were being grown by the Guarani indigenes of northeastern Argentina and Paraguay.

The wild progenitor of domesticated *C. maxima* ssp. *maxima* is *C. maxima* ssp. *andreana* (Naud.) Filov, a weedy native of warm temperate regions in northern Argentina, Uruguay, Bolivia, and possibly Paraguay. Hybridization between cultivars and wild populations has contributed to genetic variability in ssp. *andreana,* producing wild fruits that vary from pear-shaped to oblong to round. Some landraces may have been selected from these introgressed populations.

South American aborigines apparently selected for large fruits of ssp. *maxima* with high-quality flesh and good storage capabilities. The largest South American fruits, weighing 20 to 40 kg, are found in landraces from central Chile. Fruits with a woody skin suitable for long storage were noted in Bolivia by Russian explorers in the 1920s. Warty fruits also evolved in South America, and in the twentieth century are found in Bolivia and Peru. Other native landraces yield tasty immature fruits.

Cultivation of *C. maxima* did not spread to northern South America, Central America, and North America until after the European invasion of the sixteenth century. Yankee sailors were supposedly responsible for introducing various cultivars, including 'Acorn', or 'French Turban', 'Cocoa-Nut', and 'Valparaiso', to New England early in the nineteenth century. Although all of the horticultural groups probably have their origins in South America, the spread of *C. maxima* throughout North America yielded some new landraces and cultivars. For example, 'Arikara' and 'Winnebago' are landraces that were grown by aboriginal tribes in North Dakota and Nebraska, respectively, during the beginning of the twentieth century. The "banana squashes" proliferated in Mexico, and "Hubbard squashes," like 'Marblehead', came to the eastern United States from the West Indies during the 1800s.

Visitors took several types of *C. maxima* back to Europe during the sixteenth through nineteenth centuries. Some, like the turban squash called 'Zapallito del Tronco' or 'Tree Squash', came directly from South America. Most cultivars were introduced from colonial North America, but others reached Europe via Asia, Australia, and Africa, where local landraces evolved. For example, 'Red China' is a small turban squash that was brought to Europe from China in 1885. India also became a secondary center of cultivar diversity, particularly for the large "show pumpkin" types. Today, Indian fruits, weighing up to 130 kg, range from spherical to oblong to turban-shaped. Unusually shaped squashes with brown seeds such as 'Crown', 'Triangle', and 'Queensland Blue' are late-maturing Australian cultivars. And in Africa, *C. maxima* was so widespread by the nineteenth century that some botanists mistakenly concluded that Africa was the ancestral home of this squash.

In addition to collecting cultivars from around the globe, the Europeans succeeded in producing their own new strains, particularly in nineteenth-century France. For example, 'Etampes' and 'Gray Boulogne' entered the commercial trade in the 1880s. Selections within the "turban squashes" at this time focused on producing smaller nonprotruding crowns.

Cucurbita ficifolia

Pre-Columbian remnants of domesticated *C. ficifolia* have been found only in Peru, with the earliest seeds, peduncles, and rind fragments dating between 3000 and 6000 B.C. An archaeological seed from southern Mexico that was originally identified as *C. ficifolia* apparently belongs to *C. pepo* instead (cf. Andres 1990). Assuming domestication in northern South America, it is not known when this squash reached Mexico; however, it was being cultivated there in the twelfth century.

No wild species of squash exhibits the type of relationship with *C. ficifolia* that is expected in the pairing of a crop with its wild progenitor. Although definitively wild populations of *C. ficifolia* have not been identified, reports of weedy, self-sustaining plants in Guatemala and Bolivia are intriguing and need to be explored further.

As with the other domesticates, human selection produced relatively large, fleshy, nonbitter fruits with large seeds. However, the overall lack of genetic diversity in *C. ficifolia* relative to the other domesticated squashes suggests that human selection pressures on the former have been limited in their duration, their intensity, their diversity, and their effects.

This cool-tolerant but short-day squash did not reach Europe until the early 1800s, coming by way of southern Asia, where the long-keeping fruits were mainly used to feed livestock, especially during lengthy sea voyages. Although some accessions of *C. ficifolia* have been successfully grown as far north as Norway, the general failure of this species to flower beyond the torrid zone may account in part for its lack of popularity in Europe.

Squash Preparation and Consumption

In rural gardens around the globe, squash is typically planted among other crops, particularly corn, and the vines are allowed to scramble over poles, fences, walls, and other nearby structures. The plants like fertile aerated soil that drains well and lots of space, water, and sunshine. Extremes in temperature or high humidity increase vulnerability to disease. During wet weather, placing a stone or fibrous mat under a fruit lying on the ground prevents the fruit from rotting.

The immature and mature fruits, seeds, flowers, buds, and tender shoot tips and leaves of all of the domesticated squashes can be and have been eaten. Harvest of the one- to seven-day-old fruits of the summer squashes begins seven to eight weeks after planting and continues throughout the growing season. Pumpkin and winter squash fruits take three to four months to mature and are harvested only once, usually along with or later than other field crops. The best seeds are taken from the oldest fruits. Once flowering begins, open male blossoms can be collected almost daily. Leaves and growing tips are picked when needed, but only from healthy, vigorous plants.

Even though immature squashes can be eaten raw, usually they are boiled first and then seasoned to taste. In various cultures, the fresh fruits are sliced, battered, and fried; stuffed with cooked meat and vegetables; boiled and then mashed like potatoes; or added to curries or soups. The Sioux of the Northern Plains sliced fresh four-day-old fruits of *C. pepo,* skewered the slices on willow spits, and placed the spits on open wooden stages for drying. In Mexico and Bolivia, young fruits and seeds of *C. ficifolia* are sometimes blended into a mildly sweetened, alcoholic beverage made from corn mush.

The precursor of the colonial pumpkin pie was a mature pumpkin, probably *C. pepo,* filled with fruit, sugar, spices, and milk. Seeds were removed and ingredients added through a hole cut in the top of the pumpkin. The stuffed fruit was then baked among the coals of an open fire. In a simpler version of this recipe, prepared by aborigines as well as settlers, the fruits were baked first and then sliced and garnished with animal fat and/or honey or syrup. Pumpkin pudding, pancakes, bread, butter, dried chips, and beer have long histories rooted in colonial New England.

In other countries, mature pumpkins and winter squashes are stewed or steamed as vegetables, added to soups, candied, or stored whole or in slices for later use. A presumably ancient aboriginal use of mature fruits of *C. ficifolia* is in making various types of candy. Chunks of flesh are boiled with the seeds in alkali and then saturated with liquid sugar. In Indonesia, the local inhabitants create a delicacy by adding grated coconut to the boiled flesh of *C. moschata.* Of course, the most popular nonfood usage of pumpkin fruits (usually *C. pepo* or *C. maxima*) is for carving jack-o'-lanterns, a nineteenth-century tradition from Ireland and Great Britain.

Although the fruits of all domesticated squashes can be prepared similarly, there are culinary differences among the species with respect to the flavor, consistency, and appearance of the edible flesh. *Cucurbita moschata* and *C. maxima* produce the strongest tasting (mildly sweet and somewhat musky) and deepest colored mature fruits; consequently, these species are favored for canning. Because fruits of *C. maxima* are also the richest in vitamins and finest in texture, they are mashed into baby food. Among the squashes, flesh quality in *C. maxima* generally holds up best when dehydrated and then reconstituted. The elongated fruits of summer squashes make *C. pepo* the foremost producer of easy-to-slice young fruits. Although this species dominates the commercial market, the fuller flavor of the immature pepos of *C. moschata* make *C. moschata* the preferred vegetable in rural China, the Canary Islands, and Central America.

Landraces of *C. argyrosperma* yield the largest edible seeds in a fruit that is otherwise unremarkable. Mature fruits of *C. ficifolia* are the most bland and fibrous of all squashes. However, they store longer than the fruits of the other species (two to three years versus one year) and sweeten with age. The flesh contains a proteolytic enzyme that may be of future commercial value to the food industry. Because of the stringiness of the flesh of *C. ficifolia,* a special Aztec confection called "Angel's Hair" can be prepared from the boiled flesh fibers. Comparable texture in the *C. pepo* cultivar 'Vegetable Spaghetti' allows preparation of the baked or boiled fibrous flesh into a dish resembling the namesake pasta.

For commercial canning, growers have selected high-yielding cultivars like 'Kentucky Field' that have mature fruit flesh of the proper color and consistency. Flavor is less important as it can be controlled with spices. Consistency, which refers to the stiffness or relative viscosity of the processed flesh, is enhanced by using fruits that are barely ripe and by adding the product of a high-consistency cultivar to that of a low-consistency cultivar. Starch, as well as soluble solids, greatly influences consistency. Because fruit storage results in the loss of carbohydrates and in the conversion of starch to sugars, freshly harvested fruits are preferred for the canning process.

Squash seeds, which have a nutty flavor, are eaten worldwide. They are consumed raw, boiled, or roasted, usually with the testa or shell removed. Mexicans grind the roasted shelled seeds into a meal, which is used to make special sauces. In China and India as well as in the New World, rural peoples make pastries from the seeds, often by covering them with syrup and then baking the mass into a type of peanut brittle. Some Chinese cultivars of *C. moschata* and *C. maxima* are grown specifically for their seeds. Similarly, various landraces of *C. argyrosperma* contribute heavily to the commercial production of edible seeds in Mexico.

A "naked seed" cultivar of *C. pepo,* called 'Lady Godiva', produces a seed lacking a testa. These hull-less seeds are popular snacks in the United States. In addition to food, New World aborigines have used squash seeds for a variety of medicinal purposes. A decoction

serves as a diuretic and an antipyretic, the seed oil is applied to persistent ulcers, and the seeds are eaten to expel gastrointestinal parasites. Although rural communities use the seed oil for cooking as well as for medicine, the possibility of commercial extraction of the edible unsaturated oil has yet to be explored.

Aboriginal Americans, including the Aztecs, have a long tradition of eating male squash flowers and floral buds. The large orange blossoms lend seasoning and color to stews, soups, and salads and can be stuffed or battered and fried. Young leaves and shoots, which have relatively low concentrations of the bitter cucurbitacins, are also important potherbs in Mexican cooking. In India, squash leaves and growing tips are eaten as salad greens or added to vegetable curries. Nineteenth-century Indonesians prepared a dish in which fish and young leaves of *C. moschata* were wrapped in banana leaves and roasted under live coals.

Nutritional Content

Sixty to 85 percent of a mature fresh squash fruit is edible, as compared to over 95 percent edibility in immature fruits. The edible portion of a pepo, which is 85 to 95 percent water by weight, is lacking in most nutrients, particularly protein (0.5 to 2.0 percent) and fat (less than 0.5 percent). Carbohydrates are more concentrated in mature fruits (up to 15 percent of the fresh edible portion) than in the tender fruits of the summer squashes (less than 5 percent). Likewise, calories per 100 grams of edible fresh-weight flesh range from 10 to 25 in summer squashes versus 20 to 45 in the mature fruits known as pumpkins and winter squashes.

The most significant dietary contribution of the pepo is the relatively high concentration of carotenes, the precursors of vitamin A, in cultivars with deep yellow to orange flesh (see Table II.C.8.5).

Table II.C.8.5. *Mineral and vitamin content of young fruits (represented by the summer squashes of* Cucurbita pepo*), mature fruits, leaves, and growing tips (including* C. maxima, C. moschata, *and* C. pepo*), and ground seed meal (a mixture of* C. pepo *and* C. maxima*); values are per 100 grams`of dry seed meal or, in the case of the other structures, of the fresh-weight edible portion*

Mineral or vitamin	Immature fruits[a,b,c]	Mature fruits[a,b,c]	Leaves[b,d]	Growing tips[c]	Ground seeds[e]
Potassium (mg)	–	–	–	–	1,111
Magnesium (mg)	–	–	–	–	205
Copper (mg)	–	–	–	–	2.0
Zinc (mg)	–	–	–	–	5.1
Calcium (mg)	14–24	14–50	40,477	–	11.4
Iron (mg)	0.3–0.5	0.4–2.4	0.8, 2.1	31	6.8
Phosphorus (mg)	26–41	21–68	136	–	852
Carotene (mg)	–	0.2–7.8	1.9, 3.6	–	–
Vitamin A (I.U.)	55–450	335–7,810	–	1,000	–
Niacin (mg)	0.4–0.8	0.4–1.0	0.3	1.1	–
Riboflavin (mg)	0.02–0.17	0.01–0.15	0.06	0.21	–
Thiamine (mg)	0.04–0.08	0.05–0.10	–	0.16	–
Ascorbic acid (mg)	5–24	6–45	10, 80	100	–

[a]Whitaker and Davis (1962); [b]Tindall (1983); [c]Martin (1984); [d]Oomen and Grubben (1978); [e]Lazos (1986).

Particularly well studied and rich in these and other nutrients are the 'Butternut' and 'Golden Cushaw' cultivars of *C. moschata* and various "hubbard" and "delicious" squashes of *C. maxima*. As a source of vitamin A, these winter squashes compare with sweet potatoes and apricots. Although the raw flesh is higher in vitamins, a half cup of cooked mashed winter squash provides 91 percent of the U.S. Recommended Dietary Allowance (RDA) of vitamin A, 16 percent of the recommended vitamin C, 12 percent of the recommended potassium, 1.7 grams of dietary fiber, low sodium, and only 40 calories. In addition to the carotenoids, squashes are good sources of other compounds with cancer-fighting potential, including flavonoids, monoterpenes, and sterols.

For some nutrients the best source is not the fruit but other parts of the squash plant (see Table II.C.8.5). Leaves are richer in calcium, growing tips provide more iron as well as higher levels of vitamin C and the B vitamins, and seeds contain various minerals including potassium, magnesium, copper, and zinc. Although the nutritional content of flowers has not been studied, the orange petals are undoubtedly rich in carotenes.

Seeds are the most nutritious part of the plant, containing 35 to 55 percent oil and 30 to 35 percent protein by weight. In fact, the naked seeds of 'Lady Godiva' are very similar in agricultural yield and nutritional content to shelled peanuts.

The edible semidrying oil of squash seeds is dark brown with a green tint and a nutty odor. About 80 percent of the oil consists of unsaturated linoleic (40 to 50 percent) and oleic (30 to 40 percent) acids. The dominant saturated fatty acid, palmitic acid, accounts for about 13 percent of oil composition. As with other oilseeds, proteins in squash seeds are rich in nitrogen-containing amino acids such as arginine but lacking in lysine and sulfur-containing amino acids. These proteins are packaged primarily in globulins called cucurbitins. Whereas the testa is highly fibrous, carbohydrates in the decorticated seeds are limited to cell wall cellulose, phytic acid, and a minimal amount of free sugars; starch is absent. Ground seeds (including the testas) are good sources of minerals, particularly potassium, phosphorus, and magnesium (see Table II.C.8.5).

Deena S. Decker-Walters
Terrence W. Walters

Bibliography

Alefeld, Friedrich. 1866. *Landwirtschaftliche Flora*. Berlin.
Andres, Thomas C. 1990. Biosystematics, theories on the origin, and breeding potential of *Cucurbita ficifolia*. In *Biology and utilization of the Cucurbitaceae*, ed. David M. Bates, Richard W. Robinson, and Charles Jeffrey, 102-19. Ithaca, N.Y.

Bailey, Liberty Hyde. 1902. A medley of pumpkins. *Memoirs of the Horticultural Society of New York* 1: 117-24.
    1929. The domesticated cucurbitas. *Gentes Herbarum* 2: 62-115.
    1937. *The garden of gourds*. New York.
    1943. Species of *Cucurbita*. *Gentes Herbarum* 6: 266-322.
    1948. Jottings in the cucurbitas. *Gentes Herbarum* 7: 448-77.
Bates, David M., Richard W. Robinson, and Charles Jeffrey, eds. 1990. *Biology and utilization of the Cucurbitaceae*. Ithaca, N.Y.
Bukasov, S. M. 1930. The cultivated plants of Mexico, Guatemala, and Colombia. *Trudy po prikladnoj botanike, genetike i selekcii* 47: 1-533.
Castetter, E. F. 1925. Horticultural groups of cucurbits. *Proceedings of the American Society of Horticultural Science* 22: 338-40.
Castetter, E. F., and A. T. Erwin. 1927. A systematic study of squashes and pumpkins. *Bulletin of the Iowa Agricultural Experiment Station* 244: 107-35.
Conrad, N., D. L. Asch, N. B. Asch, et al. 1984. Accelerator radiocarbon dating of evidence for prehistoric horticulture in Illinois. *Nature* 308: 443-6.
Cutler, Hugh C., and Thomas W. Whitaker. 1956. *Cucurbita mixta* Pang. Its classification and relationships. *Bulletin of the Torrey Botanical Club* 83: 253-60.
    1961. History and distribution of the cultivated cucurbits in the Americas. *American Antiquity* 26: 469-85.
Decker, Deena S. 1985. Numerical analysis of allozyme variation in *Cucurbita pepo*. *Economic Botany* 39: 300-9.
    1988. Origins(s), evolution, and systematics of *Cucurbita pepo* (Cucurbitaceae). *Economic Botany* 42: 4-15.
Decker, Deena S., and Lee A. Newsom. 1988. Numerical analysis of archaeological *Cucurbita pepo* seeds from Hontoon Island, Florida. *Journal of Ethnobiology* 8: 35-44.
Decker, Deena S., and Hugh D. Wilson. 1987. Allozyme variation in the *Cucurbita pepo* complex: *C. pepo* var. *ovifera* vs. *C. texana*. *Systematic Botany* 12: 263-73.
Eisendrath, Erna Rice. 1962. Portraits of plants. A study of the "icones." *Annals of the Missouri Botanical Garden* 48: 291-327.
Filov, A. I. 1966. Ekologija i klassifikatzija tykuy. *Bjulleten' Glavnogo botaniceskogo sada* 63: 33-41.
Grebenščikov, Igor. 1955. Notulae cucurbitologicae II. *Kulturpflanze* 3: 50-9.
    1958. Notulae cucurbitologicae III. *Kulturpflanze* 6: 38-59.
    1969. Notulae cucurbitologicae VII. *Kulturpflanze* 17: 109-20.
Heiser, Charles B. 1979. *The gourd book*. Norman, Okla.
Kay, Marvin, Francis B. King, and Christine K. Robinson. 1980. Cucurbits from Phillips Spring: New evidence and interpretations. *American Antiquity* 45: 806-22.
Lazos, Evangelos S. 1986. Nutritional, fatty acid, and oil characteristics of pumpkin and melon seeds. *Journal of Food Science* 51: 1382-3.
Martin, Franklin W. 1984. *Handbook of tropical food crops*. Boca Raton, Fla.
Merrick, Laura C. 1990. Systematics and evolution of a domesticated squash, *Cucurbita argyrosperma*, and its wild and weedy relatives. In *Biology and utilization of the Cucurbitaceae*, ed. David M. Bates, Richard W. Robinson, and Charles Jeffrey, 77-95. Ithaca, N.Y.
Minnis, Paul E. 1992. Earliest plant cultivation in the desert borderlands of North America. In *The origins of agriculture: An international perspective*, ed. C. Wesley Cowan and Patty Jo Watson, 121-41. Washington, D.C.

Naudin, Charles. 1856. Nouvelles recherches sur les caractères spécifiques et les variétés des plantes du genre *Cucurbita. Annales des Sciences Naturelles; Botanique* 6: 5-73.

Oomen, H. A. P. C., and G. J. H. Grubben. 1978. *Tropical leaf vegetables in human nutrition.* Amsterdam.

Pangalo, K. I. 1930. A new species of cultivated pumpkin. *Trudy po prikladnoj botanike, genetike i selekcii* 23: 253-65.

Paris, Harry S. 1989. Historical records, origins, and development of the edible cultivar groups of *Cucurbita pepo* (Cucurbitaceae). *Economic Botany* 43: 423-43.

Pearsall, Deborah M. 1992. The origins of plant cultivation in South America. In *The origins of agriculture: An international perspective,* ed. C. Wesley Cowan and Patty Jo Watson, 173-205. Washington, D.C.

Robinson, R. W., H. M. Munger, T. W. Whitaker, and G. W. Bohn. 1976. Genes of the Cucurbitaceae. *HortScience* 11: 554-68.

Shifriss, Oved. 1955. Genetics and origin of the bicolor gourds. *Journal of Heredity* 36: 47-52.

Simmons, Alan H. 1986. New evidence for the early use of cultigens in the American Southwest. *American Antiquity* 51: 73-89.

Sinnott, Edmund W. 1922. Inheritance of fruit shape in *Cucurbita pepo* L. *Botanical Gazette* 74: 95-103.

Smith, Bruce D. 1992. Prehistoric plant husbandry in eastern North America. In *The origins of agriculture: An international perspective,* ed. C. Wesley Cowan and Patty Jo Watson, 101-19. Washington, D.C.

Tapley, William T., Walter D. Enzie, and Glen P. Van Eseltine. 1937. *The vegetables of New York,* Vol. 1, Part 4. Albany, N.Y.

Tindall, H. D. 1983. *Vegetables in the tropics.* Westport, Conn.

Wall, J. Robert. 1961. Recombination in the genus *Cucurbita. Genetics* 46: 1677-85.

Whitaker, Thomas W. 1931. Sex ratio and sex expression in the cultivated cucurbits. *American Journal of Botany* 18: 359-66.

   1947. American origin of the cultivated cucurbits. *Annals of the Missouri Botanical Garden* 34: 101-11.

   1951. A species cross in *Cucurbita. Journal of Heredity* 42: 65-9.

   1956. Origin of the cultivated *Cucurbita. American Naturalist* 90: 171-6.

   1968. Ecological aspects of the cultivated *Cucurbita. HortScience* 3: 9-11.

Whitaker, Thomas W., and W. P. Bemis. 1964. Evolution in the genus *Cucurbita. Evolution* 18: 553-9.

Whitaker, Thomas W., and Junius B. Bird. 1949. Identification and significance of the cucurbit materials from Huaca Prieta, Peru. *American Museum Novitates* 1426: 1-15.

Whitaker, Thomas W., and G. W. Bohn. 1950. The taxonomy, genetics, production and uses of the cultivated species of *Cucurbita. Economic Botany* 4: 52-81.

Whitaker, Thomas W., and Hugh C. Cutler. 1965. Cucurbits and cultures in the Americas. *Economic Botany* 19: 344-9.

   1971. Prehistoric cucurbits from the valley of Oaxaca. *Economic Botany* 25: 123-7.

Whitaker, Thomas W., Hugh C. Cutler, and Richard S. MacNeish. 1957. Cucurbit materials from the three caves near Ocampo, Tamaulipas. *American Antiquity* 22: 352-8.

Whitaker, Thomas W., and Glen N. Davis. 1962. *Cucurbits.* New York.

Wilson, Gilbert Livingstone. 1917. *Agriculture of the Hidatsa Indians, an Indian interpretation.* Minneapolis, Minn.

Zhiteneva, N. E. 1930. The world's assortment of pumpkins. *Trudy po prikladnoj botanike, genetike i selekcii* 23: 157-207.

II.C.9 ❦ Tomatoes

The tomato is a perennial plant, generally cultivated as an annual crop. It can be grown in open fields, weather permitting, or in protective structures when temperatures are extreme. In commercial operations, tomatoes are usually planted as a row crop and harvested mechanically when they are still in the green stage. They can also be trained on trellises and harvested throughout most of the year by hand. Tomatoes adapt well and easily to a wide diversity of soils and climates, but they produce best in well-drained soil and temperate climate, with at least a few hours of sunlight each day.

The tomato contains significant amounts of the vitamins A and C, although probably less than the general public has been led to believe. Its importance as a provider of these vitamins depends more on the quantity consumed than on the amount of the vitamins in each fruit. Its vivid color, the fact that it can be used as both a raw and cooked vegetable, and its ability to blend easily with other ingredients has made the tomato a popular international food item and one of the most important vegetables on the world market.

Enormous changes have taken place in the use and distribution of the tomato since the time of its prehistoric origins as a wild, weedy plant. A multidisciplinary research strategy, using archaeological, taxonomical, historical, and linguistic sources is employed in this chapter to trace this remarkable transformation. And finally, special attention is given to the tomatoes of Mexico because that region is believed to have been the center of the domestication of the species and because it is there that

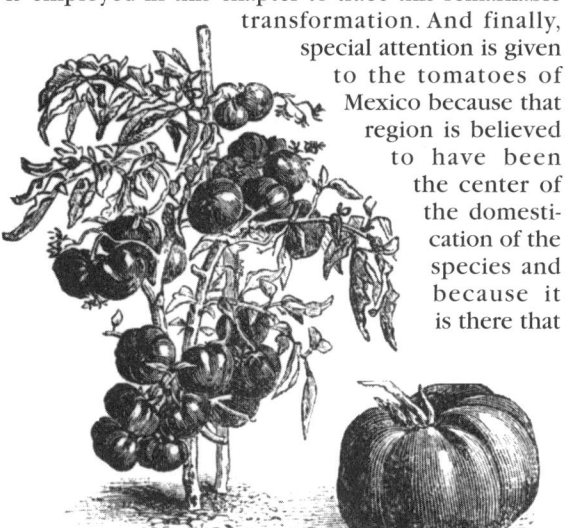

Tomato

tomatoes have the longest history of use, beginning with the indigenous population.

Taxonomy

The commercial tomato belongs to the genus *Lycopersicon.* It is a relatively small genus within the large and diverse family Solanaceae. The genus is currently thought to consist of the cultivated tomato, *Lycopersicon esculentum,* and seven closely related wild *Lycopersicon* species (Rick 1976: 268; Taylor 1991: 2), all of which are native to northwestern South America. The wild relatives of the cultivated tomato are confined to a narrow coastal area extending from Ecuador to northern Chile and the Galapagos Islands. Some of the wild species contain valuable genes for disease and pest resistance that can be useful for plant breeders in developing new types of cultivated tomatoes when crossed with *L. esculentum.* All of the cultivated tomatoes are derived from the species *L. esculentum.*

The cherry tomato, *L. esculentum* var. *cerasiforme,* is believed to be the direct ancestor of modern cultivated tomatoes and is the only wild tomato found outside South America (Rick 1976: 269). It can also be found in Mexico, Central America, and the subtropics of the Old World (Rick 1976: 269). It bears greater genetic resemblance to the cultivated tomato than other wild species, and the two groups can be freely intercrossed (Taylor 1991: 3).

Lycopersicon esculentum and its close relatives are self-pollinating and exclusively inbreeding due to the position of the stigma inside the anther tube. Wild species may have a slightly exserted stigma, which permits outcrossing, usually with the help of bees or the wind. The modification in the position of the stigma is one of the changes brought about by the domestication process. It is easier to produce a homogeneous product from a self-fertilized plant than one that may cross with a related species.

Although the genus *Lycopersicon* is native to the northwestern coast of South America, there is no archaeological evidence that tomatoes were used by ancient Andean cultures. No plant remains have appeared in site excavations, no clay vessels in the shape of tomatoes have been discovered, and there is no word for the tomato in Quechua or other ancient Andean languages. Such a lack of evidence may indicate that although the tomato existed as a wild species in the Andean region, it was never utilized by pre-Hispanic populations. The commercial tomato in use there at the present time is believed to have been a *post-Columbian* introduction from Mexico after the Americas were unified under Spanish rule. In Mexico the tomato is known by the Spanish name *tomate,* derived from the Nahuatl or Aztec *tomatl.*

As Charles Heiser pointed out some years ago, the theory of the origin of the tomato is strikingly parallel in many ways to that of the chilli pepper, *Capsicum*

spp. (1969: 39). The wild species of both are South American in origin. They reached Mesoamerica[1] at an early date, probably by natural means, and there found a favorable ecological niche, were domesticated, and eventually gave rise, respectively, to the cultivated plants *L. esculentum* and *Capsicum annuum.*

Mexican Tomatoes

The most likely region where the tomato was first domesticated is the Puebla–Veracruz area of Mexico, where according to James Jenkins, the greatest varietal diversity of the cultivated form can be found today. It is thought to have reached this area as a weedy cherry tomato, var. *cerasiforme,* and, upon domestication, to have become the larger-fruited *L. esculentum* (1948: 391, 386). The cherry tomato frequently grows wild as a weed in cultivated fields and is better adapted to wet tropical conditions than any of the other species. It is also used as a cultivated plant and is a popular item in the diet of indigenous peoples. Both wild and cultivated tomatoes have a distinct and independent nomenclature in several Indian languages, indicating an ancient introduction.

We will probably never know how the cherry tomato traveled from the Andean region of the hemisphere to Mesoamerica. Winds or water could have transported the seeds, as could birds who consumed the seeds, then eliminated them at some distant point. Perhaps all of these means of transportation were involved in a kind of stepping-stone journey, with stops along the way where the seeds became plants that reproduced, and new seeds were picked up and moved again and again by such vectors.

Alternatively, humans may have had a hand in the diffusion of the wild ancestor of the tomato. Perhaps it was carried by migrating populations who, in spite of the great distance and geographical barriers between Mexico and South America, were able to move from one area to another. Or again, its introduction to Mexico may have resulted from contact between the two areas that some archaeologists believe was established by seafaring traders as early as 1600 B.C. (Green and Lowe 1967: 56–7).

Still other questions have to do with the extent to which indigenous peoples of Mexico came to accept the tomato and incorporate it into their diets. The plant may have caught the attention of food gatherers because of its general similarity to the green husk tomato, *Physalis* (Jenkins 1948: 392). Unlike the plant we just tracked from South America, this plant is native to central Mexico, where it has a significantly longer tradition of dietary usage than the red tomato. Indeed, there is archaeological evidence of its consumption from 900 B.C. in the excavation in the Tehuacan Valley, Puebla, and from 5090 B.C. in the Valley of Mexico (Smith 1967: 248; Flannery 1985: 266). Basalt grater bowls *(molcajetes),* with incised interiors for grinding vegetal matter, appear in the earliest stratigraphic levels of the excavation in Tehuacan, and clay bowls began to appear around 1500 B.C. (MacNeish 1967: 290–309). The word *molcajete* comes from the Nahuatl term *molcaxitl*, composed of *molli* (sauce) and *caxitl* (bowl), or "sauce bowl." One can say with some degree of certainty that they were employed for making salsas of chilli peppers and green (and maybe red) tomatoes, as they are still used in Mexico today.

As in the Andean region, no archaeological evidence of plant remains of the red tomato have been reported from Mesoamerican excavations. In part, this may be because the red tomato is an extremely perishable fruit. However, carbonized seeds are almost indestructible and last indefinitely when they are not mashed or ground up. They can be recuperated from desiccated coprolites (fecal material), which can be reconstituted and returned to their original state in order to be examined. Since coprolites contain the actual materials consumed, analysis of them can provide some important insights into the diet of ancient peoples.

One possible explanation for the absence of tomato seeds in coprolites is that the principal method of preparing tomatoes was by grinding or mashing them in grater bowls or on grinding stones for use in salsas and stews, making the disintegrated seeds impossible to identify in coprolites and other refuse material.

Several changes have taken place in the tomato during the process of domestication. Generally speaking, wild plants have smaller seeds and fruits than the domesticated species. This differentiation can be noted when comparing wild and cultivated tomatoes. Wild tomatoes have two locules, whereas most domesticated fruits are multiloculates, because of an increase in size. Upon domestication, the position of the stigma was established deeper inside the anther tube to insure self-fertilization. Doubt about the extent of such a transformation of the tomato in pre-Columbian times has led some Latin American botanists to view it as a semidomesticated, rather than a fully domesticated plant prior to the arrival of the Europeans. J. León has gone so far as to suggest that it was unimportant as a food crop and considered just another weed in the fields, even though its fruit was the size of some modern varieties (1992: 41–2).

Linguistic evidence is also inconclusive. As previously mentioned, the generic term for the husk tomato in Nahuatl is *tomatl*, with different prefixes or descriptive adjectives used to identify the particular type. The red tomato is known in Mexico by the Spanish term *jitomate* from the Nahuatl *xitomatl*, which may mean "peeled or skinned tomato." The Nahuatl prefix *xi* is possibly derived from the verb *xipehua*, which denotes "to peel, skin, or flay." This could be a reference to the calyx that covers the fruit of the husk tomato and is lacking in the red variety. When ancient Mexicans came across the red-fruited tomato

they may have noted its general similarity to the husk tomato and referred to it by a similar name such as *xitomatl*, or "peeled tomato," to differentiate it from the former fruit.

Unfortunately, sixteenth-century Spanish writers did not distinguish between the *tomatl* and the *xitomatl;* they translated both as *tomate*. Thus, it is impossible to determine which tomato they are referring to unless the Nahuatl text is available. In Bernardino de Sahagún's *The General History of the Things of New Spain,* written in both Nahuatl and Spanish, there are more references to green tomatoes than red, indicating a more frequent use of the former at the time of the European conquest (Sahagún 1951–69).

Nonetheless, all kinds and colors of tomatoes could be bought in the great Tlatelolco market when the Spaniards arrived in Tenochtitlan in 1519. Tomato sellers offered large tomatoes, small tomatoes, green tomatoes, leaf tomatoes, thin tomatoes, sweet tomatoes, large serpent tomatoes, nipple-shaped tomatoes, coyote tomatoes, sand tomatoes, and "those which are yellow, very yellow, quite yellow, red, very red, quite ruddy, bright red, reddish, rosy dawn colored" (Sahagún 1951–69, Book 10: 79). The bad tomato seller was described as one who sold spoiled tomatoes, bruised tomatoes, and those that caused diarrhea (Sahagún 1951–69, Book 10: 68). Clearly, a large variety of tomatoes was for sale in early sixteenth-century Mexico – such a variety that it is impossible to identify some of the types with those on the market today.

Bernal Díaz, who participated in the conquest of Mexico in 1519, related that when the *conquistadors* went through Cholula on their way from Veracruz to Tenochtitlan, the Indians "wanted to kill us and eat our meat" and that "they had their cooking pots ready, prepared with chile peppers, tomatoes and salt . . ." (1980: 148). He also mentioned that the Aztecs ate the arms and legs of their sacrificial victims with a *chimole* sauce, made with chilli peppers, tomatoes, wild onions *(xonacatl),* and salt (1980: 564). The ingredients were nearly the same as that of *salsa mexicana,* in use in most Mexican homes today.

Similarly, stews and salsas, sold on the street or in the markets in sixteenth-century Mexico, were made with red or green tomatoes, chilli peppers, and squash seeds as common ingredients (Sahagún 1951–69, Book 10: 70). Another early visitor to Mexico noted that tomatoes were added to salsas to temper the heat of the chilli peppers (Cervantes de Salazar 1914: 118–11).

The sixteenth-century Jesuit priest José de Acosta, who traveled in Mexico and South America, was no doubt referring to red tomatoes when he described them as fresh and healthy, some being large and juicy, and said they made a tasty sauce and were also good for eating by themselves (1940: 178).

Clearly visitors appreciated the tomato, but it was not until the latter half of the sixteenth century that it became the subject of scientific study. Francisco

Hernandez, the personal physician of Philip II, was commissioned by the king to catalog and describe the medicinal plants being used in New Spain. Hernandez spent the years between 1570 and 1577 traveling throughout the country, preparing a list of the local plants and illustrating them. Unfortunately, his description of the tomato plant gives us little reliable information, because he confused the husk tomato and the red tomato. For example, his chapter on tomatoes is illustrated with a drawing of the former.

Hernandez did note, however, that the tomato was used for medical purposes. The fruit and its juice were used to soothe throat irritations, to treat the discomfort caused by headaches, earaches, and stomachaches, and to ease the pain of mumps (Hernandez 1946, III: 699–715).

There are many references to the production of both species of tomatoes during the colonial period in Mexico. The two were generally planted together, along with chilli peppers, in house gardens, on *chinampas*[2] in small plots, and in open fields.

Tomatoes were probably geographically limited to Mesoamerica, as no mention of them was made by early Spanish chroniclers who visited the Caribbean. Gonzalo Fernandez de Oviedo, for example, who left the most complete description of New World flora, and whose travels took him to the Caribbean and to parts of South America, but not New Spain, did not mention the tomato.

American Plants Reach Europe

The migration of domesticated plants is closely related to human migration because these plants need human intervention and care to survive. Among other things, many lose their dispersal mechanisms after domestication and cannot be diffused without human help. Unfortunately, plant movements have seldom been considered important enough to warrant registration upon arrival in a new country, which can make the study of plant migration an exercise in frustration for the plant historian.

Many American plants arrived in Iberia in the sixteenth and seventeenth centuries, along with the supposedly more precious cargoes of gold and silver. Some seeds were carried on purpose, perhaps by returning Spaniards, who had become accustomed to the taste of New World foods and flavors; others arrived accidentally, hidden in the nooks and crannies of ships.

Not all of the new plants were well received when they first appeared in Europe. This was especially the case with solanaceous ones such as the tomato, the chilli pepper, and the potato, which were regarded with suspicion and fear by Europeans already familiar with other plants of the same family.

Certainly tomatoes were not an easy ingredient to incorporate, even into the Italian diet where they were later to become a mainstay. They neither looked nor tasted like any other vegetable known and used by the Italians, and they had a strange texture and consistency. They were too acid to be eaten while green and looked spoiled when they were soft and ripe. They disintegrated upon cooking and were suspected of being poisonous. Thus, it was only after the passage of some considerable length of time that tomatoes were accepted by the Mediterranean peoples to become as much a part of the local food tradition as are wheat, olives, and wine.

But although culinary acceptance of American foods was delayed, European plant specialists, from the very beginning, displayed great interest in any medicinal qualities they might possess. Old diseases, such as plague, were still affecting parts of Europe in the sixteenth century and had been joined by new diseases, like syphilis, to punish populations. Thus, doctors were in constant search of new remedies to treat these ills. They initially had great hopes for the pharmacologic possibilities of New World organisms but soon realized that the new cultivars offered little relief for European illnesses.

However, the American plants did find a place in botanical gardens, popular among scientists of the time, who also established networks through which they exchanged new and exotic plants as well as information about them. In addition, some became popular as ornamentals and could be found in university gardens and on the estates of the nobility. But the tomato had little to offer as an ornamental. Its flowers are a pale yellowish color, not particularly unusual or attractive, and both its leaves and fruit emit a strong, acrid smell that many plant lovers of the time thought offensive.

Herbals with woodcut engravings became popular in the sixteenth and seventeenth centuries, and scientists used them in an effort to establish some order in the plant world. The New World cultivars were quickly fitted in, and much valuable information about them can be gleaned from these publications. In the case of the tomato, the plants appears as a small, heavily ridged and compressed fruit, but large enough to have gone through the domestication process.

American plants in Europe spread out along two different routes after their arrival in Iberia. One led north via Flanders, the other into the Mediterranean via Italy – with all of the former and significant portions of the latter then under Spanish domination, which facilitated communication between these areas.

The moderate climate and loose soil of the Mediterranean countries proved ideal for the adaptation of the tomato as well as other New World plants. They arrived, not as competition for the local cultigens already in production, but as complementary crops whose planting and harvesting schedules did not coincide nor interfere with those of the traditional Mediterranean crops.

Tomatoes in Spain

Spain was doubtless the first stop for the tomato on its migration throughout Europe because Castile held a monopoly on the transport of its New World products to the Continent. Unfortunately, although officials of the Casa de la Contratación[3] kept a watchful eye on all cargo unloaded in Seville so as to ensure the collection of royal import taxes, they seldom recorded the arrival of new plants. Thus, there is no record of the arrival of the tomato in Seville – the only port for Spanish ships returning from the New World.

In fact, there are few historical references to the use of tomatoes in sixteenth-century Spain. They may have been adopted first by rural people, who ate them fresh with a little salt like their eighteenth-century peasant descendants in southern Spain (McCue 1952: 327). No Spanish cookbooks were published at this time, however, and there is no mention of tomatoes having been a part of the diet in the early years.

Nor were tomatoes included in sixteenth-century Spanish herbals, although several described and illustrated New World plants. The husk tomato, for example, arrived in the sixteenth century and is known to have been cultivated in botanical gardens in southern Spain. It was listed as an exchange plant from the garden of Dr. Juan Castañeda, a physician at the Flamenco Hospital in Seville, to the Belgian botanist Clusius (Charles de l'Ecluse) at the end of the century (Alvarez Lopez 1945: 276). Castañeda appears to have been Clusius's principal supplier of American and Iberian plants. Clusius made several trips to Spain to obtain information and specimens of new plants, but he did not mention having encountered the tomato on his travels.

The first written reference to the cultivation of the tomato in Spain was penned around the turn of the seventeenth century. It appeared in a small book by Gregorio de Rios, a priest who worked in the botanical garden of Aranjuéz, which was supported by the King, Philip II. This book, *Agricultura de jardines, que trata de la manera que se han de criar, governar y conservar las plantas,* mentions several American plants. Rudolf Grewe has translated his comments on the tomato as follows: "Tomatoes [*pomates* in the original]: There are two or three kinds. It is a plant that bears some segmented fruits [*pomas aquarteronadas*] that turn red and do not smell. It is said that they are good for sauces. They have seeds, last for two or three years, and require a lot of water. There is a kind said to be from Cairo" (Grewe 1988: 73). By this time at least some Spaniards had apparently adopted the Aztec method of preparing tomatoes in a sauce.

Tomatoes appeared on the list of purchases of the Hospital de la Sangre in Seville in the early seventeenth century. Four pounds were purchased on July 20, and another 2 pounds on August 17, 1608 (Hamilton 1976: 859). The same account lists the purchase of cucumbers "for making salads," and it is possible that tomatoes were used for the same purpose. This appears to have been the only attempt of the hospital to introduce the tomato into its diet as there seem to have been no further purchases.

In addition to such rather scanty seventeenth-century historical information on the tomato there can be added information from indirect sources. Sixteenth- and seventeenth-century Spanish writers had a fascination with all things from the New World and delighted in borrowing vocabulary from Hispanic Indian languages in their works. Among the words most frequently used were those of fruits and vegetables. Spanish variations of Nahuatl, Quechua, and Caribbean plant names appear in the works of Lope de Vega, Tirso de Molino, Miguel de Cervantes y Saavedra, and Francisco de Quevedo (Morínigo 1946). The new names, including those for the tomato, were used as metaphors, in analogies, or merely for the exotic sounds of the words in poetry and drama.

Painters also found the new fruits and vegetables colorful subjects for still-life paintings that became popular in the sixteenth and seventeenth centuries. Bartolomé Murillo's "The Kitchen of Angels," painted for the Franciscan Convent in Seville, depicts the preparation of a dish using tomatoes and squash, a combination that was to become typically Mediterranean. The seventeenth century witnessed severe economic problems throughout the Mediterranean. In Spain the expulsion of the Moriscos, who had contributed so much to the agriculture of that country, brought a sharp decline in crop production. The resulting famine was joined by the return of the plague, which added to the general misery by considerably reducing the workforce. All of these factors contributed to a severe scarcity of food, which may have encouraged desperate rural peoples to put aside their fear of being poisoned and experiment with tomatoes in their diets.

One suspects this was the case because in the following century it was noted that tomatoes were a common ingredient in the diet of the rich, who ate them because they liked them, and of the poor, who ate them because they had no choice (McCue 1952: 327). Tomatoes were produced in abundance on truck farms and irrigated fields throughout the country, especially in southern Spain, where they could be harvested year-round. Indeed, farmers were eating tomatoes for breakfast, and a plate of fried red tomatoes and peppers constituted the main meal of the day for many (McCue 1952: 327).

Several American plants were fully adopted into the Mediterranean diet in the eighteenth century, and the more abundant and nutritious diet they allowed has been credited by some with bringing about a mid-century increase in the population.

Under the influence of a new and burgeoning merchant class in the eighteenth century, a greater emphasis was placed on simple, regional food and the use of local ingredients by everyone, not just the peasants. American vegetables fit well into this new culinary style and were included in the diet, not as new and exotic dishes, but as ingredients that added new flavors to traditional dishes such as thick soups, stews, ragouts, and goulash. In Spain, for example, tomatoes were incorporated into gazpacho (an ancient bread soup, probably dating from Roman times), the rice dish, paella, and *bacalao* (salted codfish). In the process, such dishes acquired new appearances as well as new flavors. The Spanish food historian Nestor Lujan has written that some would like to believe that Spanish and Italian cuisines only began with the introduction of the tomato, because so many dishes cannot be made without it (Lujan 1989: 126).

Clearly, then, tomatoes were well established in Spain by the nineteenth century. In that century, reports from Spain described an abundant production of tomatoes on truck farms and gardens in that country. It was noted that tomatoes were eaten raw with salt, formed the base of sauces, and were cooked in various other ways (McCue 1952: 328).

Tomatoes in Italy

Italy was probably the first country to receive the tomato after Spain, since, as already mentioned, there was a strong Spanish cultural influence apparent during the sixteenth century in those parts of Italy under Spanish domination.

Italy proved to be an ideal country for the adaptation of American plants. The climate and soil were similar to that of central Mexico, and the new plants adjusted easily to the area. Initially, however, tomatoes were grown only in pots and kitchen gardens because they needed a well-managed water supply during the setting of the fruit in summer, usually a dry season in the Mediterranean.

Unlike other parts of Europe, where fresh vegetables were considered food for the poor, Italians had (and have) a singular appreciation for them. This may have been a heritage of the Roman Empire, when men preferred light, easily digestible foods that could be eaten in a supine position. The pressure of growing populations during the second half of the sixteenth century was probably also an incentive to try the new foods.

The tomato in Italy was first mentioned by Petrus Andreas Matthiolus. In the first edition of his herbal *Della historia e materia medicinale,* published in Venice in 1544, it was not referred to by name, but in his 1554 edition he gave it the name of *pomi d'oro.* Unfortunately, Matthiolus mistakenly referred to the tomato as a member of the mandrake family, which focused suspicion upon the plant for centuries to come, as many botanists and writers repeated his description of the plant time and time again. In the 1544 edition he described the unnamed fruit as seg-

mented, green at first, and then acquiring a golden color upon ripening, and he noted that it was eaten like the eggplant, fried in oil with salt and pepper. From his description, it seems apparent that the first tomatoes to reach Italy were yellow, although in the 1554 edition, he added that they also ripened in tones of red (McCue 1952: 292).

At about the same time as the second edition of Matthiolus appeared, a Flemish botanist, Rembert Dodoens, published his herbal, *Cruydt-Boeck,* in Antwerp. He was apparently the first to assign to the tomato the name *poma amoris* or "love apple," which was adopted in translation by the French and English. This name gave the tomato a certain reputation as an aphrodisiac, which probably did nothing to discourage its use. The engraving that accompanied his work shows the tomato as a small, irregular, flat fruit with prominent segments and the name *Gulden-Appel,* translated from the Italian *pomi d'oro* (McCue 1952: 299).

Interestingly, the name *poma peruviana* was given the tomato by Piero Antonio Michel in his herbal, *I cinque libri di plante,* published in 1575 (Jenkins 1948: 382). This must have been nothing more than a remarkable coincidence because he surely could not have been aware that Peru was, in fact, the center of origin of the tomato. Like other European botanists of the time, he was not well informed about New World geography and may actually have considered it as just one general area.

In 1572, another sixteenth-century Italian herbalist, Guilandini de Padua, called the tomato the "tumatle from Themistitan." It has been pointed out that this designation probably represents a corrupt spelling of Tenochtitlan, the capital city of Mexico, referred to as Temistitan by Hernando Cortés in two of his letters to the Spanish king, written shortly after the Conquest (Jenkins 1948: 382).

We mentioned that in 1554 Matthiolus observed that tomatoes were fried in oil with salt and pepper, like the eggplant. This may be the first recorded description of Italian tomato sauce. However, its first authentic recipe only appeared in 1692 in one of the early Italian cookbooks, *Lo scalco alla moderna,* written by Antonio Latini that was published in Naples (Grewe 1988: 74). Apparently the Spaniards had introduced the Aztec method of preparing the tomato in a sauce into Italy, along with the tomato, because a tomato sauce recipe "in the Spanish style" is included in the book. It called for tomatoes, chilli peppers, onion, salt, oil, and vinegar. However, other recipes for tomato sauce were also published that did not ask for peppers, indicating a separation of these two foods in Europe that were so closely linked in Mesoamerican cooking. The tomato, of course, which combined easily with European ingredients and found multiple uses in the diet, became far more important in Mediterranean cooking than peppers.

The careful hands of Italian gardeners improved

the tomato through selective pressures, turning it into a large, smooth, and thicker-skinned fruit than that which had arrived in the sixteenth century. In addition, they developed a manner of prolonging the use of this perishable vegetable by drying it in the sun, which permitted its reconstitution and use throughout the winter. Much later, tomatoes were canned in southern Italy and became an important item of export. Italian emigrants to the United States and Argentina took their food traditions with them and established a demand for the tomato and tomato sauce in the Americas (Casanova and Bellingeri 1988: 165).

Eastern Mediterranean Tomatoes

The botanist Edgar Anderson has credited the Turks with the diffusion of the tomato into the Levant and the Balkan countries. The Turks probably diffused American plants to eastern Mediterranean countries in the sixteenth century when the Ottoman Empire was dominant in the area. They would have become acquainted with the plants in Italian or Spanish ports and taken them to other countries, much as they did when they took the chilli pepper into Hungary in 1526 (Long-Solis 1988: 62). Peppers and maize also became popular items in the diet of Balkan countries, and Fernand Braudel wrote that it was the Turks who introduced rice, sesame seeds, cotton, and maize into the area in the fifteenth and sixteenth centuries (Braudel 1976, II: 779). In addition, Anderson has noted that there is a wide and apparently coherent area, encompassing the Balkans and Turkey and running along the edge of Iran toward Arabia and Ethiopia, where the tomato has been used for centuries in the everyday diet of common people (Anderson, in McCue 1952: 289–348). The culinary legacy of the Turks is still evident in Mediterranean cuisine from Yugoslavia in the east to Algeria in the west. The popular salads made with tomatoes and peppers, known as *peperonata* in Italy, can be found in the diet of every Mediterranean country, with only slight variations.

Tomatoes in the Far East

Tomatoes became an important part of the Chinese diet only during this century, although they were probably carried to China from the Philippines much earlier. The Spaniards arrived in the Philippines from Mexico in 1564, and after establishing their dominion, introduced many Mesoamerican plants.

From there the tomato reached southern China, perhaps as early as the 1500s, where it was given the name *fan chieh* (barbarian eggplant). The name itself suggests an early introduction. Anderson has pointed out that several crops are known in South China by names that combine the adjective *fan* (southern barbarian) with the name of a long-established Chinese

crop (Anderson 1988: 80). Crops with these names were early introductions; New World crops arriving later are known by the more complimentary adjective *hsi,* meaning Western, or *yang,* meaning ocean (Anderson 1988: 94).

African Tomatoes

Tomatoes are an important food product in Africa today, but the question arises as to how long this has been the case and when they first arrived. The most likely answer is that invaders, explorers, missionaries, and traders all played a role in the tomato's introduction.

The food habits of a region often reflect the influence of such outsiders, and certainly, Portuguese explorers and slave traders would have had an early opportunity to participate in such a cultural transfusion. Probably, Arab traders, active in the ports of Mozambique and Angola, were also instrumental in introducing new crops into Africa.

Another common route for plant diffusion in the early centuries was by way of a well-connected network of monasteries and convents in which seeds and plants were exchanged to help feed the personnel of these institutions. In addition, European botanical gardens had a hand in introducing new plants and crops into English, French, and Dutch colonies of Africa and Asia.

Thus, by at least the seventeenth century, the tomato was in cultivation in North Africa, with an English traveler reporting in 1671 that Spanish *tomates* were grown in the common fields in West Barbary (McCue 1952: 330). Several reports of similar cultivation plots were made in the eighteenth century; by the end of the nineteenth century, tomatoes appear to have been widespread throughout the continent.

Tomatoes in the United States

Despite their being native to the Americas, tomatoes had to be introduced into North America from Europe. Although this introduction occurred in the eighteenth century, tomatoes were slow to gain much of a place in the diet until relatively recently. Today, however, tomatoes rank second only to potatoes as the most important vegetable on the U.S. market. They are also the basic ingredient in that most American of sauces, tomato catsup. In recent years, however, Mexican salsa, composed of tomatoes, chilli peppers, onions, and seasoning has become even more popular on the market than catsup.

The main contribution of the United States to the history of the tomato has been the important role it has played in genetic research programs that have contributed to its improvement. The tomato has many characteristics that make it an ideal subject for plant research. It has an ability to produce and prosper in a diversity of climates and a short life cycle so that it can produce three generations per year under a well-managed program. Tomatoes produce high seed yields. A self-pollinating mechanism practically eliminates outcrossing, although plants can be crossed under controlled conditions. All of these qualities have enabled rapid progress in the improvement of the tomato in the past decades (Rick 1976: 272).

Genetic resources from wild South American species have helped in the development of cultivars that are tolerant to drought, extreme temperatures, and high-salt content in soils and have increased resistance to the diseases and insects that plague tomatoes.

Other improvements are increased crop yields through larger fruit size and an increase in the number of fruits. Improved fruit quality is evident in the shape, texture, color, and flavor of the product. Postharvest handling has been improved and storage durability increased. The restricted growth gene has been exploited, making mechanical harvesting easier because of the uniformity of the height of tomato plants. Harvesters have become more elaborate and larger, allowing them to harvest at a faster rate.

In addition, the tomato has been an ideal subject for research in genetic engineering, where the majority of such research is carried out on plants, such as the tomato, that are important as staple foods in basic diets around the world. Resistance to certain diseases that have proved difficult to treat and an improvement in the control of fruit ripening and color are some of the aspects being investigated. Important changes in the quality of tomatoes can be expected through genetic engineering in coming years.

Janet Long

Notes

1. The term "Mesoamerica" refers approximately to the area between the state of Sinaloa in northwestern Mexico and Costa Rica, which at the time of the Spanish conquest contained peoples sharing a number of cultural traits.
2. *Chinampas* are highly productive farm plots surrounded on at least three sides by water.
3. The Casa de Contratación, or House of Trade, was founded by royal order in 1503 and located in Seville. The Casa served as an administrative focal point for commercial traffic involving Spanish colonies in the New World.

Bibliography

Acosta, J. de. 1940. *Historia natural y moral de las Indias,* ed. Edmundo O'Gorman. Mexico.

Alatorre, A. 1979. *Los 1001 años de la lengua española.* Mexico.

Alvarez Lopez, E. 1945. Las plantas de America en la botanica Europea del siglo XVI. *Revista de Indias* 6: 221-88.

Anderson, E. N. 1988. *The food of China.* New Haven, Conn., and London.

Braudel, F. 1976. *The Mediterranean and the Mediterranean world in the age of Philip II,* Trans. Siân Reynolds. 2 vols. New York.

Casanova, R., and M. Bellingeri. 1988. *Alimentos, remedios, vicios y placeres.* Mexico.

Cervantes de Salazar, F. 1914. *Cronica de la Nueva España.* Madrid.

Díaz del Castillo, B. 1980. *Historia verdadera de la conquista de la Nueva España.* Mexico.

Flannery, K. V. 1985. Los origenes de la agricultura en Mexico: Las teorias y las evidencias. In *Historia de la agricultura: Epoca prehispanica-siglo XVI,* ed. T. R. Rabiela and W. T. Saunders, 237-66. Mexico.

Green, D. F., and G. W. Lowe. 1967. Altamira and Padre Piedra, early preclassic sites in Chiapas, Mexico. *Papers of the New World Archaeological Foundation,* No. 20, Publication No. 15. Provo, Utah.

Grewe, R. 1988. The arrival of the tomato in Spain and Italy: Early recipes. *The Journal of Gastronomy* 3: 67-81.

Hamilton, E. J. 1976. What the New World economy gave the Old. In *First images of America: The impact of the New World on the Old,* ed. F. Chiapelli, 2: 853-84. Los Angeles.

Heiser, C. B., Jr. 1969. Systematics and the origin of cultivated plants. *Taxon* 18: 36-45.

Hernandez, F. 1946. *Historia de las plantas de Nueva España,* ed. I. Ochoterena, 3 vols. Mexico.

Jenkins, J. A. 1948. The origin of the cultivated tomato. *Economic Botany* 2: 379-92.

León, J. 1992. Plantas domesticadas y cultivos marginados en Mesoamerica. In *Cultivos marginados: Otra perspectiva de 1492,* ed. J. E. Hernández Bermejo and J. León, 37-44. Rome.

Long-Solis, J. 1988. *Capsicum y cultura: La historia del chilli.* Mexico.

Lujan, N. 1989. *Historia de la gastronomia.* Spain.

MacNeish, R. S. 1967. A summary of the subsistence. In *The prehistory of the Tehuacan Valley,* ed. Douglas D. Byers, 1: 290-309. Austin, Tex.

McCue, G. A. 1952. The history of the use of the tomato: An annotated bibliography. In *Annals of the Missouri Botanical Garden* 39: 289-348.

Matthiolus, P. A. 1544. *Di pedacio Dioscoride Anazarbeo libri cinque della historia et materia medicinale tradutti in lingua volgare Italiana.* Venice.

Morínigo, M. 1946. *América en el teatro de Lope de Vega.* Buenos Aires.

Rick, C. M. 1976. Tomato (Family Solanaceae). In *Evolution of crop plants,* ed. N. W. Simmonds, 268-72. London.

Sahagún, B. de. 1951-69. *Florentine Codex, the general history of the things of New Spain,* ed. A. J. O. Anderson and C. Dibble. Santa Fe, N. Mex.

Smith, C. E., Jr. 1967. Plant remains. In *The prehistory of the Tehuacan Valley,* ed. Douglas Byers, 1: 220-55. Austin, Tex.

Taylor, I. B. 1991. Biosystematics of the tomato. In *The tomato crop: A scientific basis for improvement,* ed. J. G. Atherton and J. Rudich, 1-22. London.

II.D

Staple Nuts

II.D.1 ☙ Chestnuts

In the mountainous areas of the Mediterranean where cereals would not grow well, if at all, the chestnut *(Castanea sativa)* has been a staple food for thousands of years (Jalut 1976). Ancient Greeks and Romans, such as Dioscorides and Galen, wrote of the flatulence produced by a diet that centered too closely on chestnuts and commented on the nuts' medicinal properties, which supposedly protected against such health hazards as poisons, the bite of a mad dog, and dysentery.

Moving forward in time to the sixteenth century, we discover that "an infinity of people live on nothing else but this fruit [the chestnut]" (Estienne and Liébault 1583), and in the nineteenth century an Italian agronomist, describing Tuscany, wrote that "the fruit of the chestnut tree is practically the sole subsistence of our highlanders" (Targioni-Tozzetti 1802, Vol. 3: 154). A bit later on, Frédéric Le Play (1879, Vol. 1: 310) noted that "chestnuts almost exclusively nourish entire populations for half a year; in the European system they alone are a temporary but complete substitution for cereals." And in the twentieth century, the Italian author of a well-known book of plant-alimentation history mentioned that chestnuts not only were collected to be eaten as nuts

Chestnut

but could also be ground into flour for bread making (Maurizio 1932). He was referring to the "wooden bread" that was consumed daily in Corsica until well into the twentieth century (Bruneton-Governatori 1984). Clearly, then, chestnuts have played an important role in sustaining large numbers of people over the millennia of recorded history (Bourdeau 1894).

The Tree

Geographic location has had much to do historically with those who have found a significant part of their diet at the foot of the chestnut tree. The tree tends to stop bearing fruit north of the fifty-second parallel, and its yield in Eurasia satisfies the growers' wishes only south of a hypothetical line drawn from Brittany to Belgrade and farther east to Trabezon, Turkey – the line ending up somewhere in Iran. In Africa, chestnuts grow only in the Maghreb. In North America, there were many chestnut trees before the first decades of the twentieth century, at which time some three billion were destroyed by a blight. Another species of chestnut exists in China, and Japan is on its way to becoming the world's leading chestnut producer.

Chestnuts grow somewhat haphazardly within these geographic limitations. For example, because they dislike chalky soils, they are rare in Greece, except on some sedimentary or siliceous outcrops, where they can become so abundant that they determine place names, such as "Kastania." In addition, the roots of chestnuts tend to decay in badly drained soils, which helps to explain why the trees thrive on hills and mountainsides. Such exacting requirements also help us pinpoint those regions of Portugal, Spain, France, and Italy where populations were long nourished by chestnuts.

It is true that chestnuts are found beyond the geographic limits just outlined. But these are grown for their wood and not for their fruit (chestnut wood is as strong as oak but significantly lighter) – an entirely different method of cultivation. Fruit-producing chestnut trees must be pruned into low broad shapes, whereas trees for lumber are encouraged to grow tall. In addition, fruit-producing trees require grafting (such as the marrying of hardy to fruit-bearing species) – an activity deemed vital in historical documents (Serre 1600) because the ungrafted tree produces two or three small chestnuts in one prickly pericarp or husk (called a bur) whose only use is for animal feed. Even in our own times, grafting remains necessary as it is practically the only way to avoid the disease enemies of chestnuts that have so menaced the trees since about 1850.

The Nut

After performing the not-so-easy operations of extracting the chestnut from its bur, hard-peel cover, and adhering tannic skin, one has a nourishing nut that is 40 to 60 percent water, 30 to 50 percent glucids, 1 to 3 percent lipids, and 3 to 7 percent protids. In addition, the nut has significant amounts of trace minerals which vary, depending on the soil; and chestnuts are the only nuts to contain a significant amount of vitamin C.

Dried, the chestnut loses most of its water as its caloric value increases. According to the usual conversion table, 100 grams of fresh chestnuts provide 199 calories; dried, they provide almost twice (371 calories) that amount. (For comparative purposes, 100 grams of potatoes = 86 calories; 100 grams of whole grain wheat bread = 240 calories; 100 grams of walnuts = 660 calories.) (Randoin and de Gallic 1976).

When we pause to consider that our sources place the daily consumption of chestnuts by an individual at between 1 and 2 kilograms, we can quickly understand why the chestnut qualifies as a staple food. And like such staples as wheat or potatoes, chestnuts can be prepared in countless ways. Corsican tradition, for example, calls for 22 different types of dishes made from chestnut flour to be served on a wedding day (Robiquet 1835). When fresh, chestnuts can be eaten raw, boiled, baked, and roasted (roasted chestnuts were sold on the streets of Rome in the sixteenth century and are still sold on the streets of European towns in the wintertime).

Chestnuts also become jam and vanilla-chestnut cream, and they are candied. When dried, they can also be eaten raw, but they are usually ground into flour or made into a porridge, soup, or mash (*polenta* in Italy) and mixed with vegetables, meat, and lard. As flour, chestnuts become bread or pancakes and thickeners for stews. Indeed, speaking of the versatility of chestnuts, they very nearly became the raw material for the production of sugar. Antoine Parmentier (that same great apothecary who granted the potato the dignity of human food) extracted sugar from the nuts and sent a chestnut sugarloaf weighing several pounds to the Academy in Lyon (Parmentier 1780). Research on the possibility of placing chestnuts at the center of the French sugar industry was intensified a few years later during the Continental blockade of the early nineteenth century. Napoleon's choice, however, was to make sugar from beets.

A Chestnut Civilization

That the geographical areas favorable to chestnut trees and their fruits were precisely the areas in which populations adopted chestnuts as a staple food seems obvious enough. But in order to make full use of the opportunity, populations had to create what might be called a "chestnut civilization," meaning that they had to fashion their lives around the trees, from planting the trees to processing the fruits.

Planting

Chestnut trees seldom grow spontaneously. Moreover, pollination rarely occurs wherever the trees grow in relative isolation from one another, and fructification is poor when the tree is not regularly attended. For all these reasons, it is generally the case that the presence of a chestnut tree is the result of human activity, in contrast to a random act of nature. This is clearly so in the case of plantations, or trees whose alignment marks the borders of fields and pathways. But it is also the case with the countless clusters of two or three trees that cast their shadows upon the small hilly parcels of poor tenants.

It is important to note, however, that people do not plant chestnut trees for themselves. Rather, they do it for generations to come because the trees do not begin to bear fruit until they are at least 15 years old, and their yield is not optimal until they are 50 years old: "Olive tree of your forefather, chestnut tree of your father, only the mulberry tree is yours," as the saying goes in the Cévennes (Bruneton-Governatori 1984: 116).

Cultivation

Most of the operations connected with chestnut cultivation involve looking after the trees. This means clearing the brush beneath them and, when possible, loosening the soil; giving water when really necessary; fertilizing with fallen leaves; repairing enclosures to keep away stray animals whose presence could be catastrophic and whose taste for chestnuts is well known; and above all, trimming branches so that they will bear a maximum amount of fruit. Yet, tree care is hardly an exacting task, requiring only 3 to 8 days a year per hectare of trees (Bruneton-Governatori 1984). The trees, of course, would survive without even this minimal care, important only for improving the yield of nuts, which prompted some critics in the nineteenth century to compare chestnuts to manna falling directly from heaven into the hands of lazy onlookers (Gasparin 1863, Vol. 4: 742).

Yet, when all of the exacting and repetitive tasks involved in growing and preparing chestnuts are contemplated, with an absence of mechanization the common characteristic, chestnutting suddenly seems like very hard work indeed.

Collecting

Efficient collection required that the area under and around the trees be clean so that few chestnuts would be overlooked. Collecting was a manual job, lasting at least three weeks (chestnuts do not fall all at once), and required the efforts of all members of the family. Perhaps half of the burs – the prickly polycarps – open on the tree or when they hit the soil. The other half had to be shelled, often with the bare and calloused hands of those viewed as tough "chestnut-ters" by fellow workers. Next the fruits were sorted. The very best nuts were sent to market, about 20 percent were judged "throw-outs" for the pigs, and the rest were set aside for domestic consumption.

Chestnut collection was tedious and hard on the back, requiring about 10 hours of labor for an average collection of between 50 and 150 kg per person. An estimate was made that 110 working days were required (100 women-children/days; 10 men/days) to gather the chestnuts from 2 hectares, which would amount to about 5½ tons of fruit (Hombres-Firmas 1838).

Peeling

Fresh chestnuts constituted the bulk of the diet for those who harvested them until about mid-January – about as long as they could safely be kept. But before they could be eaten, the nuts had to be extracted from their rigid shell and stripped of their bitter and astringent skin. This is a relatively easy procedure when chestnuts are roasted, but generally they were boiled. Peeling chestnuts was usually done by men in front of the fire during the long evenings of autumn and winter. To peel 2 kg of raw chestnuts (the average daily consumption per adult in the first part of the nineteenth century) required about 40 minutes. Therefore, some three hours, or more, of chestnut peeling was required for the average rural family of five. The next morning around 6 A.M. the chestnuts, along with some vegetables, were put into a pot to begin boiling for the day's main meal.

Drying

The only way to preserve chestnuts for longer periods was to dry them. The method was to spread out the fruit on wattled hurdles high over the heat and smoke of a permanent fire for about two weeks, often in wooden smoking sheds built specifically for this purpose. Following this step, the dried chestnuts – from 5 to 10 kg at a time – were wrapped in a cloth and rhythmically thrashed against a hard surface to separate the nuts from shells and skins that the drying process had loosened.

Dried chestnuts had the effect of liberating peasants from the irksome chore of daily peeling, and the drying procedure had important social consequences

as well. Diego Moreno and S. de Maestri (1975) have noted that the expanding cultivation of chestnut trees in the sixteenth-century Apennines gave birth to hamlets that sprang up around the smoking sheds.

Grinding and Flour

After the chestnuts were dried, they could be ground into flour that would keep for two or three years, provided it was not subjected to moisture. From this flour pancakes and bread were made, although because chestnut flour does not rise, many commentators refused to call the loaves bread. There were also others who had harsh words for other chestnut products, making fun of "this kind of mortar which is called a soup" (Thouin 1841: 173) or that bread which "gives a sallow complexion" (Buc'hoz 1787: 126).

Chestnut Consumers

Chestnuts were mostly the food of rural peasants in mountainous regions that stretched in a belt from Portugal to Turkey. But they were a well-appreciated food by many accounts, such as those of regionalist connoisseurs who praised the "sweet mucilage" (Roques 1837) and the following 1763 text published in *Calendriers ... du Limousin:*

> All the goods nature and art lavish on the table of the rich do not offer him anything which leaves him as content as our villagers, when they find their helping of chestnuts after attending their rustic occupations. As soon as they set eyes on them, joy breaks out in their cottages. Only mindful of the pleasure they then taste, they are forgetful of the fatigues they endured: they are no more envious of those of the towns, of their abundance and sumptuousness (Calendriers ... du Limousin 1763, reprinted in Bruneton-Governatori 1984: 462).

This is not to say, however, that only peasants ate chestnuts, and, in fact, numerous sources indicate that this foodstuff could be a prized dish at higher levels of society. For example, a French nobleman (Michel de Montaigne 1774) recorded that on October 22, 1580, while on his way to Italy, he ordered raw chestnuts. And, in fact, a Spanish nobleman wrote in his account of a campaign against the Moriscos that the whole company, nobility included, consumed 97.4 tons of bread, 33,582 liters of wine, and 240 tons of chestnuts, as against only 19.3 tons of biscuit and 759 kg of chickpeas (Vincent 1975).

We know that chestnuts were served in Utrecht in 1546 at the royal Golden Fleece banquet, and we have the delightful Marie Marquise de Sévigné (1861, Vol. 2: 133-4) playing the woman farmer who claimed to be "beset with three or four baskets" (of chestnuts): "I put them to boil; I roasted them; I put them in my pocket; they appear in dishes; one steps on them."

This and other quotations tend to obscure the fact that, for the rich in particular, there were chestnuts and then again, there were chestnuts. The French (and the Italians) have two words for chestnut. The ordinary chestnut is called *châtaigne,* whereas the best (and sweetest) chestnut is called a *marron* (which in English is known as the Spanish chestnut). The difference lies in size and form. Usually the husk holds only one *marron* with no dividing skin (the kernel is whole), whereas there may be three or more *châtaignes* in a husk divided by partitions. *Marrons* are the material of commercial candied chestnuts and have historically commanded a price three or four times greater than their common, flawed counterparts. One of the reasons is that the yield of *marrons* is less. Thus, in times past, those who grew them were usually located on a commercial artery and did not depend on chestnuts alone to feed families and pigs.

From the Renaissance on, there were three major commercial roads for chestnuts in Europe. One ran from the Portuguese provinces of Minho and Tras-os-Montes to the harbors of northern Portugal and Galicia where chestnuts were loaded aboard ships, usually bound for Bordeaux. In that port the Iberian chestnuts were combined with chestnuts bought on the Périgueux market and then sent on to Great Britain and the Netherlands. A British author writing of this trade route said that the choicest chestnuts were those grown in Spain or Portugal (Miller 1785).

The French, by contrast, thought the best chestnut was the so-called Lyon chestnut, which was actually an Italian chestnut traveling the second of the three European chestnut arteries. Lyon monopolized the importation of Italian chestnuts, transshipping them to Paris and points farther north. The third route, which also originated in Italy, ran from Milan and Bergamo north to the Germanic countries.

Fresh chestnuts, as we have seen, are perishable, staying fresh for only about three months. And weeks of travel in wagons and the holds of ships did them no good. Thus, transporting chestnuts in bulk was a risky business, and wholesalers fixed their prices accordingly. Only the best chestnuts were shipped, and they went mostly into sweetmeats. In markets they were so costly that only the well-off could purchase them for a tidbit at the table. Consequently, the chestnut trade never did involve large quantities, and most of the chestnuts sold for consumption went through local markets and merchants. In 1872, for example, Paris received barely 6,000 tons of an estimated national crop of 500,000 tons.

The bulk of any chestnut crop, of course, reached no market but was consumed by the peasant families that grew them, along with their poultry and two or three hogs. The British agronomist Arthur Young, who traveled in Limousin, France, during the years 1787–89, calculated that an acre with 70 chestnut trees would feed one man for 420 days or 14 months (Young 1792). This seems a substantial overestimation

of the average number of trees per acre. It was generally the case that between 35 and 100 trees grew on 1 hectare (about 2½ acres). If, however, one assumes that a family living on a hilly and not particularly productive hectare of land could harvest about 2,800 kg of chestnuts, then certainly the chestnuts alone could feed a family for more than half a year. With an average daily consumption of 2 kg per person or 10 kg for a family of five, the 2,800 kg of chestnuts would have fed the family for close to 7 months and a pig or two (350 kg are required to fatten a pig from 100 to 200 kg). The pigs, in turn, might be sold or slaughtered, and one suspects that several pigs on a chestnut farm were a food index of chestnut surpluses.

Chestnuts in Decline

A very good question is why such a useful and valuable foodstuff as chestnuts has today been virtually forgotten. The "golden age" of the chestnut, which seems, in retrospect, to have begun with the Renaissance, had all but vanished by the middle of the nineteenth century (Pitte 1979). It is difficult to quantify the decline because the statistics do not reflect domestic production for self-sufficiency. Nonetheless, a series of events that had a considerable impact on chestnutting can be identified.

One of the first blows dealt to chestnut production (especially in France) was the very hard winter of 1709. According to observers, tree loss was considerable, even to the point of discouraging replanting (*Journal Économique* 1758). The *Intendant* in Limoges reported in 1738 that owners there had not replanted even a twentieth of the trees that had frozen 29 years earlier. And in 1758, a chestnut plantation around the Pau castle was uprooted. Unquestionably, the winter of 1709 caused considerable concern for the future of chestnut cultivation, as did the similarly devastating winters in 1789 and 1870.

A second factor was the substitution of mulberry trees for chestnuts around the Rhone valley, where Lyon and its silk industry exerted considerable influence. Silkworms are fond of mulberry leaves, and the mulberry tree (unlike the chestnut) grows fast and produces quickly. Its cultivation, therefore, encouraged a cash economy as opposed to self-sufficiency.

A third reason for the decline of the chestnut, at least in France, may have been free trade in wheat. In 1664, fear of food shortages had prompted Colbert to take the severe measures of controlling wheat production and prohibiting its exportation. At the same time, the exportation of chestnuts was encouraged. Such regulations lasted about a century before the free traders triumphed over regional monopolists and wheat became a cheap and widely available foodstuff, even competing with chestnuts in regions that had traditionally grown them.

Chestnuts also came under fire beginning in the eighteenth century as a foodstuff deficient in nutrients. A well-off society that tasted a *marron* occasionally pitied the unfortunate peasants who were condemned to gulping down a pigfood – the *châtaigne*. Such a diet represented "The International of Misery and Chestnut," according to Leroy Ladurie (1966).

But this was the time of the Physiocrats, who thought the soil was the only source of wealth and aimed at improving the productivity of farming by questioning all traditional rural economic processes. That chestnuts suffered at their hands is undisputable. In a query sent to provincial learned societies, François Quesnay and Victor Riqueti Mirabeau, both initiators of the Physiocratic school, asked the following questions: "Are there acorns or chestnuts used as foodstuff for pigs? Do chestnuts give a good income? Or are said chestnuts used as food for the peasants, inducing them to laziness?" (Quesnay 1888: 276). And in an agricultural text of a few decades later, the question of laziness was pursued: "To my knowledge, inhabitants of chestnut countries are nowhere friendly with work" (Bosc and Baudrillard 1821: 272). It went on to suggest that they refused to replace their trees with more productive plants because of their fear of taxation and concluded that they were not worthy citizens of the modern state.

Interestingly, the voice of François Arouet Voltaire (1785: 106) was one of the few who defended the chestnut:

> [W]heat surely does not nourish the greatest part of the world. . . . There are in our country, whole provinces where peasants eat chestnut bread only; this bread is more nourishing and tastier than the barley or rye bread which feeds so many people and is much better for sure than the bread ration given to soldiers.

More than two hundred years later we find A. Bruneton-Governatori (1984) agreeing with Voltaire, noting that chestnuts provide a balanced diet and around 4,000 calories of energy. The condemnation the chestnut received in the eighteenth and nineteenth centuries might "raise doubts about the pertinence of contemporary evidence concerning the nutrition of non-elite people."

The half century from 1800 to 1850 was one of slow decline for the European chestnut as fewer and fewer people were interested in cultivating it, eating it, or defending it. One notes 43,000 trees uprooted in the Italian Piedmont between 1823 and 1832, and public surveyors here and there reported that chestnut-planted lands were diminishing. But following the midpoint of the nineteenth century, we have statistics in France that demonstrate vividly the magnitude of the decline. In 1852, there were 578,224 hectares of land given to chestnut cultivation; in 1892, 309,412; in 1929, 167,940; and in 1975, only 32,000 (Bruneton-Governatori 1984).

A final factor in the decline of chestnuts was doubtless the so-called ink disease, which officially began in Italy in 1842, had spread to Portugal by 1853, and reached France by 1860. The disease could kill chestnut trees in two or three years, and entire hectares of dried-up trees discouraged any notions of replanting. And, as mentioned, another disease appeared in North America to kill practically all the chestnuts there.

Thus, chestnuts went the way of so many other foods of the past as, for example, salted codfish. Once popular and cheap foods that fed many, they have now become expensive delicacies for a few.

Antoinette Fauve-Chamoux

Bibliography

Arbuthnot, John. 1732. *Practical rules of diet in the various constitutions and diseases of human bodies.* London.

Bolens, Lucie. 1974. *Les méthodes culturelles du Moyen Age d'après les traités d'économie andalous.* Geneva.

Bosc, Louis, and Jacques Baudrillard. 1821. *Dictionnaire de la culture des arbres et de l'aménagement des forêts.* In Abbé Henri Tessier and André Thouin. *Encyclopédie méthodique, agriculture,* t.VII. Paris.

Bourdeau, Louis. 1894. *Histoire de l'alimentation, substances alimentaires, procédés de conservation, histoire de la cuisine. Études d'histoire générale.* Paris.

Bruneton-Governatori, Ariane. 1984. *Le pain de bois. Ethnohistoire de la châtaigne et du châtaignier.* Toulouse.

Buc'hoz, Pierre-Joseph. 1770. *Dictionnaire universel des plantes, arbres et arbustes de la France.* Paris.

    1787. *L'art de préparer les aliments suivant les différents peuples de la terre.* Paris.

Calendriers Écclésiastiques et civils du Limousin. 1763. *Observations sur le châtaigner et les châtaignes.* Limoges.

Estienne, Charles, and Jean Liébault. 1583. *L'agriculture et maison rustique.* Paris.

Gasparin, Comte Adrien de. 1863. *Cours d'agriculture.* 6 vols. Paris.

Hombres-Firmas, Baron Louis d'. 1838. Mémoire sur le châtaignier et sa culture dans les Cévennes (1819). Published in *Recueil de mémoires et d'observations de physique, de météorologie, d'agriculture et d'histoire naturelle.* Nîmes, France.

Jalut, Guy. 1976. Les débuts de l'agriculture en France: Les défrichements. *La préhistoire française,* Vol. 2: 180–5. Paris.

Journal économique ou mémoires, notes et avis sur les arts, l'agriculture et le commerce . . . 1758. Paris.

Le Play, Frédéric. 1879. *Les ouvriers européens.* 6 vols. Paris.

Le Roy Ladurie, Emmanuel. 1966. *Les paysans du Languedoc.* Paris.

Maurizio, Adam. 1932. *Histoire de l'alimentation végétale depuis la préhistoire jusqu'à nos jours.* Paris.

Miller, Philip. 1785. *Dictionnaire des jardiniers.* Paris.

Montaigne, Michel de. 1774. *Journal de voyage 1580–1581.* Rome and Paris.

Moreno, D., and S. de Maestri. 1975. Casa rurale e cultura materiale nelle colonizzazione dell'Appennino genovese tra XVI e XVII secolo. *I paesagi rurali europei. Deputazione di storia patria per l'Umbria,* Bolletino N° 12, Perugia.

Parmentier, Antoine. 1780. *Traité de la châtaigne.* Bastia, Corsica.

Pitte, Jean-Robert. 1979. L'hommes et le châtaignier en Europe. In *Paysages ruraux européens.* Travaux de la conférence européenne permanente pour l'étude du paysage rural, Rennes-Quimper, 26–30 Sept. 1977.

Quesnay, François. 1888. *Oeuvres économiques et philosophiques,* ed. A. Oncken. Frankfurt and Paris.

Randoin, Lucie, and Pierre de Gallic. 1976. *Tables de composition des aliments.* Paris.

Robiquet, François-Guillaume. 1835. *Recherches historiques et statistiques sur la Corse.* Paris.

Roques, Joseph. 1837. *Nouveau traité des plantes usuelles spécialement appliqué à la médecine domestique et au régime alimentaire de l'homme sain ou malade.* Paris.

Serre, Olivier de. 1600. *Le théâtre d'agriculture et mesnage des champs.* Paris.

Sévigné, Marie Marquise de. 1861. *Lettres.* 11 vols. Paris.

Targioni-Tozzetti, Ottaviano. 1802. *Lezioni di agricoltura, specialmente toscana.* 4 vols. Florence, Italy.

Thouin, André. 1841. *Voyage dans la Belgique, la Hollande et l'Italie (1796–1798).* Paris.

Vincent, Bernard. 1975. Consommation alimentaire en Andalousie orientale (les achats de l'hôpital royal de Guadix). *Annales E.S.C.* 2–3: 445–53.

Voltaire, François Arouet dit. 1785. *Dictionnaire philosophique,* Vol. 48 in *Oeuvres completes.* 92 vols. Paris.

Young, Arthur. 1792. *Travels during the years 1787, 1788 and 1789.* London.

II.D.2 ❧ Peanuts

Peanut or groundnut (*Arachis hypogaea* L.) is a major world crop and member of the Leguminosae family, subfamily Papilionoidae. *Arachis* is Greek for "legume," and *hypogaea* means "below ground." *Arachis,* as a genus of wild plants, is South American in origin, and the domesticated *Arachis hypogaea* was diffused from there to other parts of the world. The origin of *Arachis hypogea* var. *hypogaea* was in Bolivia, possibly as an evolutionary adaptation to drought (Krapovickas 1969). Certainly the archaeological evidence of the South American origins is secure. However, the debate about the pre-Columbian presence of New World plants in Asia (especially India) remains unresolved. The other species of *Arachis* that was domesticated prehistorically by South American Indians was *A. villosulicarpa,* yet the latter has never been cultivated widely.

As the peanut's nutritional and economic importance became recognized, it was widely cultivated in India, China, the United States, Africa, and Europe. Thus, the peanut is another of the New World food crops that are now consumed worldwide. The peanut is popular as a food in Africa and in North America, especially in the United States; peanut-fed pigs produce the famous Smithfield ham of Virginia, and peanut butter is extremely popular. There is also much interest in peanut cultivation in the United States.

Botanically, the varieties of peanuts are distinguished by branching order, growth patterns, and number of seeds per pod. The two main types of peanuts, in terms of plant growth, are "bunch or erect," which grow upright, and "runners or prostrate," which spread out on or near the ground. Commercially, peanuts are grouped into four market varieties: Virginia, Runner, Spanish, and Valencia. The former two include both bunch and runner plants, and the latter two are bunch plants. Details on the life cycle and growth of the peanut and its harvesting are provided later in this chapter (Lapidis 1977). Table II.D.2.1 shows the various characteristics of the four varieties.

Peanuts are also called "groundnuts" because they are not true tree nuts. Peanuts are seeds of tropical legumes with pods that grow underground to protect the plant's seeds from seasonal drought and from being eaten by animals. Peanuts consumed by humans are dried seeds of the Leguminosae family, as are kidney, pinto, lima, and soy beans, as well as peas and lentils. The dried shell of the peanut corresponds to bean and pea pods. The names "peanut" and "ground pea" (as the food was called when it was first eaten in North America) became popular because the dried seed had a nutlike shell and texture, and it looked like a pea. Peanuts are also named "goobers," "earth almonds," "earth nuts," "Manila nuts," "monkey nuts," "pinda," and *pistache de terre.* But these terms sometimes also apply to other plants of similar character, such as *Voandzeia subterranea,* found in West Africa, Madagascar, and South America, and the "hog peanut" *(Amphicarpaea menoica),* found in North America.

Peanut

Table II.D.2.1 *Characteristics of peanut varieties*

Variety	Origin	Season (days)	Nut
Virginia (*Arachis hypogea* var. *hypogaea*)	Probably originated in Amazon	140–160	Large; long; slender; 1–2/pod
Runner	A cross between Virginia and Spanish	140–160	Small to large; stubby; 2–3/pod
Spanish (*Arachis hypogaea* var. *vulgaris*)	Originated in Brazil	90–120	Small; round; 2–3/pod
Valencia (*Arachis hypogaea* var. *fastigiata*)	Originated in Brazil and Paraguay	90–120	Small; 3–6/pod

Source: Adapted from Ockerman (1991), p. 546.

Structure

The peanut plant roots at its nodes and is self-pollinating, with flowers that open and die after fertilization. It is unique in that it flowers above the ground, but after fertilization the fruit develops below ground in the soil.

The peanut consists of the germ (heart), two cotyledons (halves of the peanut), the skin, and the shell. The pod is tough and stays closed as the seeds ripen, but the seeds themselves have soft, digestible coats. They have been eaten by humans ever since South American Indians first domesticated them during prehistoric times.

Origins and History

Evidence exists of peanuts having been grown in Peru as early as 2000 B.C. (Sauer 1993). As mentioned, they are believed to have originated in South America, and many wild species of the genus *Arachis* are found there. Spanish explorers spread the peanut to Europe and the Philippines, and Portuguese explorers took it to East Africa. It reached North America circuitously via the slave trade from Africa, although in pre-Columbian times it probably came to Mexico from South or Central America. The stocks developed in Africa provided the basis for many varieties now grown in the United States. Initially, peanuts were cultivated in the United States for livestock feed to fatten farm animals, especially pigs, turkeys, and chickens. But they gained commercial importance after the Civil War, with much of the credit due to George Washington Carver at the Tuskegee Institute. One of America's most distinguished African Americans of the nineteenth century, Carver spent his life developing various uses for peanut products, and they became important as a food and as an oil source.

In addition, commercial mills that crushed peanuts for oil were developed independently in Asia and Europe. Europe's inability to meet a demand for olive oil led to a market for peanut oil there, with the peanuts coming mainly from West Africa, and then from India after the opening of the Suez canal. Peanuts subsequently were cultivated in all tropical and subtropical parts of the world.

Unique Characteristics

Unlike most legumes, peanuts store oil instead of starch. During the early growth of the cotyledon storage cells (up to about 30 days after the peg or gynophore strikes the soil), starch granules predominate, and lipid and protein bodies are few. After this stage, however, to about 45 days, both lipid and protein bodies increase rapidly, and from 45 to 68 days, protein bodies and especially lipid bodies continue to expand. The plant's protein and fat come from these bodies in the peanut cotyledon. In the final stage, there is little further growth of the cotyledon (Short 1990; Weijian, Shiyao, and Mushon 1991). Most peanuts require 140 to 150 frost-free days to mature, but such factors as growing season, location, and time of fruit set also influence the time required to reach maturity (Cole and Dorner 1992). Table II.D.2.1 gives characteristics of peanut varieties.

Peanut Pathogens and Pests

Approximately a quarter of the peanut fruit and vine crop is lost because of plant disorders wrought by insects, bacteria, fungi, nematodes, and viruses. *Sclerotina minor,* the cause of sclerotina blight, and *Cercospora arachidicola,* the cause of early leaf spot, are two important peanut pathogens. These are controlled by herbicides. Unfortunately, resistance to one is often associated with high susceptibility to the other, and resistance to *S. minor* is also associated with small seed size and an undesirable shade of tan color for the Virginia peanut type (Porter et al. 1992). Bacterial wilt is caused by *Pseudomonas solanacearum.* Fungal species, including *Aspergillus, Rhizopus, Fusarium,* and others, cause various diseases.

The peanut root-knot nematode (*Meloidogyne arenaria* [Neal] Chitwood race 1) is a major pest in the peanut-producing areas in the southern United States. These microscopic worms greatly reduce yields but can be controlled with fumigants and nematicides. Efforts are now moving forward to select *M. arenaria*-resistant species of peanuts, because chemical controls of the pest are becoming more limited (Holbrook and Noe 1992).

Tomato spotted wilt virus (TSWV) decreases seed

number and weight. Other viruses cause such diseases as spotted wilt and chlorotic rosettes. Insects that attack peanuts include the corn rootworm, which causes rot, and the potato leafhopper, which secretes a toxic substance, damaging the leaves.

Staphylococcus aureus brings about microbial degradation of fat in peanuts, but the major pathogen with relevance to human health is a fungal aflatoxin. It is a carcinogenic metabolite of *Aspergillus flavus* and *Aspergillus parasiticus,* which may cause or promote liver cancer in humans, especially when infected nuts are eaten in large quantities.

Although neither pathogen nor pest, drought is another major limiting factor in peanut production, and efforts are now progressing to develop drought resistance in some varieties (Branch and Kvien 1992).

Horticulture

Production

The six leading peanut-producing countries of the world are India, China, the United States, Nigeria, Indonesia, and Senegal. World production of peanuts in the shell for 1992 was 23 million metric tons, with Asia and Africa producing 90 percent of the total (FAO 1993).

In the United States, the state of Georgia leads the nation in peanut production, followed by Texas, Alabama, and North Carolina (United States Department of Agriculture 1992). The most famous peanut producer in the United States is former President Jimmy Carter.

Cultivation

Peanuts need hot climates with alternating wet and dry seasons and sandy soils. Ideally, rainfall or moisture from irrigation should total at least an inch a week during the wet season. Peanuts are planted after the danger of frost is gone, when soil temperatures are above 65° F. The soil is usually treated with herbicides, limed, fertilized, and plowed before planting. Insecticides may then be applied, and herbicides are applied between preemergence and cracking time (postemergence). Postemergence practices involve cultivation, insecticides if needed, and herbicides for weed control. Calcium sulfate is provided to maximize peanut fruit development. This addition of calcium is important in peanut fertilization, because insufficient levels can lead to empty pods with aborted or shriveled fruit (Cole and Dorner 1992). Peanuts are usually rotated with grass crops such as corn, or with small grains, every three years. This rotation reduces disease and soil depletion. Efforts have been made to intercrop peanuts with other plants, such as the pigeon pea or cotton, but these have not been successful.

Harvesting

Only about 15 percent of peanut flowers produce fruit. The harvest includes both mature and immature varieties, as all fruits do not mature at the same time, and about 30 percent is immature at harvesting. Maturity can be estimated in a variety of ways. The "shell-out method" for recognition of maturity has to do with the darkening of the skin (testa) and the inside of the hull. The "hull scrape method" is done by scraping the outer shell layer (exocarp) to reveal the color of the middle shell (mesocarp), which is black in the mature peanut. Peanut harvesting involves removing plants from the soil with the peanuts attached (the upright plant is better suited to mechanical harvesting). A peanut combine is used to remove the pods from the plant.

Storage

After harvesting, the peanuts are cleaned by removing stones, sticks, and other foreign material with a series of screens and blowers. For safe storage the peanuts are dried with forced, heated air to 10 percent moisture.

Cleaned, unshelled peanuts can be stored in silos for up to six months. Shelled peanuts are stored for a lesser time in refrigerated warehouses at 32–36° F and 60 percent relative humidity, which protects against insects. A high fat content makes peanuts susceptible to rancidity, and because fat oxidation is encouraged by light, heat, and metal ions, the fruit is best stored in cool, dry places (McGee 1988). On the whole, however, unshelled peanuts keep better than shelled.

Processing

Peanuts may be processed shelled or unshelled, depending on the desired end product. Those left unshelled are mainly of the Virginia and the Valencia types. They are separated according to pod size by screening; discolored or defective seeds are removed by electronic color sorting, and the stems and immature pods are removed by specific gravity (Cole and Dorner 1992). Peanuts that are to be salted and roasted in the shell are soaked in a brine solution under pressure, and then dried and roasted.

Peanuts to be shelled are passed between a series of rollers, after which the broken shells and any foreign materials are removed by screens and blowers. Next, the shelled peanuts are sorted by size. Any remaining foreign materials and defective or moldy seeds are removed by an electronic eye, which inspects individual seeds. Ultraviolet light is useful for detecting aflatoxin contamination.

Peanuts are frequently blanched to remove the skins and hearts. This can be done by roasting (259–293° F for 5 to 20 minutes), or by boiling, after which they are rubbed to remove the skins. Then the kernels are dried to 7 percent moisture and stored, or converted into various peanut products.

Another method – dry roasting – is popular because it develops a desirable color, texture, and flavor for peanut butter, candies, and bakery products. In this case, unblanched peanuts are heated to 399° F for 20 to 30 minutes, then cooled and blanched.

Shelled peanuts are usually dry roasted in a gas-fired rotary roaster at 399° F, then cooled to 86° F, after which they are cleaned and the skins removed for making peanut butter. Oil-roasted peanuts are placed in coconut oil or partially hydrogenated vegetable oil at 300° F for 15 to 18 minutes until the desired color is achieved, whereupon a fine salt is added. Roasting makes the tissue more crisp by drying and also enhances flavor because of the browning reaction. Relatively low temperatures are used to avoid scorching the outside before the inside is cooked through. The roasting of peanuts also reduces aflatoxin content. For example, roasting for a half hour at 302° F may reduce aflatoxin B_1 content by as much as 80 percent (Scott 1969).

And finally, peanut oil is extracted by one of three different methods: hydraulic pressing, expeller pressing, or solvent extraction.

Food Uses

Traditionally, peanuts were used as a source of oil and, even now, most of the world's peanut production goes into cooking oils, margarines, and shortenings, as well as into the manufacture of soap and other industrial processes. Also called "arachis oil," "nut oil," or "groundnut oil," peanut oil is a colorless, brilliant oil, high in monounsaturates. Virgin oil is mechanically extracted (expeller pressed at low temperature [80–160° F]), and lightly filtered. This method provides the lowest yield but the highest-quality edible oil.

Refined oil is typically produced by solvent extraction. It is made from crushed and cooked peanut pulp, which is then chemically treated in order to deodorize, bleach, and neutralize the flavor of the oil. In the United States, only low-grade nuts are used for oil production. The fatty acid composition is quite variable for a number of reasons, such as genotype, geography, and seasonal weather (Holaday and Pearson 1974). When refined oil is stored at low temperature, a deposit is formed, and hence it cannot be used in salad oils and dressings.

Only peanuts that are free from visible mold and subject to less than 2 percent damage are used for edible purposes. In the United States and Western Europe, most peanuts to be eaten go into the "cleaned and shelled" trade and are consumed as roasted and/or salted nuts, as peanut butter, or as a component of confections.

Because of its high protein and low carbohydrate content, peanut butter was first developed in 1890 as a health food for people who were ill. It is a soft paste made from Virginia, Spanish, or other types of peanuts. The skin and germ are removed, and the kernels are dry roasted and ground. Salt, antioxidants, flavors, and sugars (dextrose or corn syrup) may be added after

grinding. Hydrogenation and/or the addition of emulsifiers prevents separation. "Crunchy style" peanut butter has bits of roasted nuts mixed into it.

Peanut butter is approximately 27 percent protein, 49 percent fat, 17 percent carbohydrate, 2 percent fiber, and 4 percent ash. Its sodium content is approximately 500 mg per 100 g. Peanut butter has good stability even after two years of light-free storage at 80 degrees Fahrenheit (Willich, Morris, and Freeman 1954), and keeps longer if refrigerated. But sooner or later, it becomes stale and rancid.

Peanuts are frequently employed in the cuisines of China, Southeast Asia, and Africa. The residual high-protein cake from oil extraction is used as an ingredient in cooked foods and, in Chinese cooking, is also fermented by microbes.

In recent years, peanuts have been added to a variety of cereal- and legume-based foods to alleviate the problem of malnutrition. Moreover, peanuts in the form of flour, protein isolate, and meal in a mixed product have desirable sensory qualities (Singh and Singh 1991). Peanut flour is made by crushing the shelled, skinned nuts, extracting the oil, and grinding the crushed nuts. In India, the flour is used in supplementary foods, weaning foods, and protein-rich biscuits (Achaya 1980).

In addition, the peanut plant itself has a high nutritional value and can be used for livestock feed or plowed back into the soil to aid in fertilization of future crops (Cole and Dorner 1992). Nonedible nuts are processed into oil, with the cake used for animal feed. Peanut shells, which accumulate in abundance, can be used as fuel for boilers (Woodroof 1966).

Nutritional Value

Protein

Having a higher percentage of protein by weight than animal foods and beans (ranging from 22 to 30 percent), peanuts provide an excellent, inexpensive source of vegetable protein for humans. A 1 ounce serving of oil- or dry-roasted peanuts provides 7 to 8 grams of protein, or 11 to 12 percent of the U. S. Recommended Dietary Allowance (RDA).

The protein quality of the peanut also is high, with liberal amounts of most of the essential and nonessential amino acids (the limiting amino acids in roasted peanuts and peanut butter are lysine, threonine, methionine, and cystine). For this reason, U. S. government nutritional guidelines include peanuts along with other high-quality protein foods, such as meat, poultry, fish, dry beans, and eggs. In the last few decades, cereal- and legume-based plant food mixtures using peanuts have grown in popularity, especially in developing countries, because of the excellent nutritional value of peanut proteins and their low cost. Table II.D.2.2 presents some chemical indices of protein quality for peanuts and other high-protein foods.

New methods for determining free amino acids in whole peanuts are now available (Marshall, Shaffer,

Table II.D.2.2. *Comparison of various indexes of protein quality for peanuts and other protein-rich foods*

Protein source	Essential amino acid index	Observed biological value	PER	NPU
Peanuts	69	57	1.65	42.7
Egg, whole	100	96	3.92	93.5
Beef	84	76	2.30	66.9
Fish	80	85	3.55	79.5
Milk, cow	88	90	3.09	81.6
Beans	80	59	1.48	38.4
Soybeans	83	75	2.32	61.4
Wheat	64	67	1.53	40.3

Note: The essential amino acid index rates protein quality with respect to all of the 11 essential amino acids. The PER (protein efficiency ratio) is an animal bioassay that measures the efficiency of a protein in producing weight gain in rats. The NPU (net protein utilization) is a similar method that adjusts with a control fed no protein whatsoever, and measures the changes in body nitrogen between the two dietary groups and a group of animals sacrificed at the beginning of each feeding period. BV (biological value) uses estimates of retained nitrogen from the difference between ingested nitrogen and that accounted for in urine and feces.

Source: Samonds and Hegsted (1977), pp. 69-71.

and Conkerkin 1989); Table II.D.2.3 shows that peanuts have an amino pattern similar to that of high-quality proteins, and Table II.D.2.4 indicates that peanuts are much higher in protein than other staple plants, save for legumes.

Peanut proteins include the large saline-soluble globulins, arachin and conarachin, and the water-soluble albumins. The relative protein content of peanuts may vary with variety, strain, growing area, and climate. Arachin constitutes about 63 percent, and conarachin 33 percent, of the total protein in peanuts. The remaining 4 percent consists of other proteins, including glycoproteins, peanut lectin (agglutinin), alpha beta amylase inhibitor, protease inhibitors, and phospholipase D.

Fat

Depending on the cultivar, the fat content of peanuts ranges from 44 to 56 percent. Over 85 percent of the fat in peanuts is unsaturated; an ounce of peanuts contains 14 grams of fat, of which about a third is polyunsaturated and over half is monounsaturated. More precisely, peanuts have a polyunsaturated to saturated fat ratio of 2:3; a high proportion of their total fat is monounsaturated (49 to 54 percent), and a low percentage (14 to 15 percent) is saturated (McCarthy and Matthews 1984).

Monounsaturated fats help to lower LDL (low density lipoprotein) cholesterol when they replace saturated fats in the diet, and thus can help reduce risks of coronary artery disease that are associated with hyperlipidemia.

Calories, Carbohydrates, and Cholesterol

Well over three-quarters of the calories in peanuts are from fat, with the remainder from protein and carbohydrate, although the content of the latter varies with

variety and growing conditions. Peanuts usually have about 20 percent carbohydrates, most of which are sucrose (4 to 7 percent) and starch (0.5 to 7 percent). Peanuts have no cholesterol.

Table II.D.2.3. *Comparison of the amino acids in peanuts compared to high-quality proteins*

Amino acid	Mg/g protein	
	Peanuts	High-quality protein pattern
Histidine	27	17
Isoleucine	48	42
Methionine and cystine	27	26
Phenylananine and tyrosine	99	73
Threonine	31	35
Tryptophan	13	11
Valine	58	48
Lysine	41	51

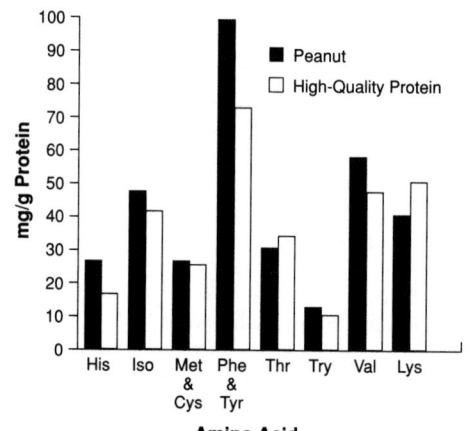

Table II.D.2.4. *Comparison of nutritive value of peanuts with other common cereals and legumes (g/100 g)*

	Water	Protein	Fat	Carbohydrate	Ash	Botanical name
Corn	13.0	8.8	4.0	73.0	1.2	*Zea mays*
Lentils	11.2	25.0	1.0	59.5	3.3	*Lens culinaris*
Peanuts	4.0	26.2	42.8	24.3	2.7	*Arachis hypogaea*
Rice	12.0	7.5	1.7	77.7	1.1	*Oryza sativa*
Soybeans	7.5	34.9	18.1	34.8	4.7	*Glycine soja*
Wheat	12.5	12.3	1.8	71.7	1.7	*Tritian esculentum*

Source: Table based on Spector (1956).

Fiber

The dietary fiber content of peanuts is approximately 7 percent by weight. The percentage of edible fiber is 3.3 (Ockerman 1991a), and of water-soluble fiber 0.77. The latter two percentages were determined by enzymatic figures (Deutsche Forschungsanstalt für Lebensmittelchemie 1991).

Sodium

In their raw state, peanuts are very low in sodium. Unsalted dry-roasted nuts, and "cocktail" nuts, contain no sodium in a 1-ounce serving. However, whole peanuts are usually served salted. A 1-ounce serving of lightly salted peanuts contains less than 140 milligrams of sodium, which is the U. S. Food and Drug Administration's current definition of a low sodium food. But other peanut products, such as "regular salted" nuts, contain higher amounts of sodium.

Vitamins and Minerals

Peanuts are good sources of riboflavin, thiamine, and niacin, and fair sources of vitamins E and K. They are also relatively high in magnesium, phosphorous, sulfur, copper, and potassium.

In the case of niacin, peanuts are rich sources of tryptophan (an essential amino acid that can be converted into niacin) and, in addition, are relatively rich sources of preformed niacin itself, a 1-ounce serving providing 20 percent of the U.S. RDA.

Nutrients and Processing

Under processing conditions in developing countries, dry roasting preserves both the storage stability of peanuts and their nutritional value to a greater extent than oil roasting (DaGrame, Chaven, and Kadam 1990). With roasting, the thiamine content decreases and the color darkens; hence color gives an indication of the extent of thiamine loss. The proteins, vitamins (except thiamine), and minerals are very stable during processing. But blanching or mechanical removal of skin further reduces thiamine content because thiamine is concentrated in the skins (Woodroof 1966). Table II.D.2.5 shows the nutritional composition of *Arachis hypogaea L.*

Table II.D.2.5. *Nutritional value of* Arachis Hypogaea L.

Constituent	Peanuts, plain (/100g)
Water (g)	6.3
Protein (g)	25.6
Fat (g)	46.1
Carbohydrate (g)	12.5
Energy value (kcal)	564
Total nitrogen (g)	4.17
Fatty acids – saturated (g)	8.2
Fatty acids – monounsaturated (g)	21.1
Fatty acids – polyunsaturated (g)	14.3
Cholesterol (mg)	0
Starch (g)	6.3
Total sugars (g)	6.2
Dietary fiber – southgate method (g)	7.3
Dietary fiber – Englyst method (g)	6.2
Na (mg)	2
K (mg)	670
Ca (mg)	60
Mg (mg)	210
P (mg)	430
Fe (mg)	2.5
Cu (mg)	1.02
Zn (mg)	3.5
Cl (mg)	7
Mn (mg)	2.1
Se (µg)	3
I (µg)	3
Vitamin E (mg)	10.09
Thiamin (mg)	1.14
Riboflavin (mg)	0.10
Niacin (mg)	13.8
Trypt/60 (mg)	5.5
Vitamin B$_6$ (mg)	0.59
Folate (µg)	110
Pantothenate (mg)	2.66
Biotin (µg)	72.0
Amino acids (g)	–
Arginine	6.9
Histidine	1.3
Isoleucine	2.6
Leucine	4.1
Lysine	1.9
Methionine	0.6
Phenylalanine	3.1
Threonine	1.6
Tryptophan	0.8
Tyrosine	–
Valine	2.8

Source: Holland et al. (1991) and Ockerman (1991), p. 1331.

Health-Related Issues

Enhancing Protein Quality

Plant proteins, like those in peanuts, which are rich in essential amino acids and nitrogen and low in only a few amino acids, help improve the overall quality of diets, especially diets based on plant proteins. Protein supplementation involves adding to the diet small amounts of a protein that is a rich source of those amino acids that would otherwise be lacking. Protein complementation involves combining protein sources so that they mutually balance each other's excesses or deficiencies (Bressani 1977).

These principles have been used to produce cereal–legume multimixes for humans (Bressani and Elias 1968), and the cuisines of several countries that have traditionally relied on plant protein foods as staples also employ these same principles to good effect, so that protein quality is rarely a problem.

A Weaning Food in Cereal Multimixes

Infants and young children, as weanlings, are growing rapidly and require plenty of high-quality protein. Yet, for cultural and economic reasons, protein–rich animal foods are frequently not readily available in many developing countries. A quarter of a century ago, cereal and cereal–legume multimixes (including peanuts) began to be used to provide a high-protein and high-calorie weaning food for children in this age group. These multimixes can be produced at the local level, are economical, and have excellent results in supporting child growth.

Similarly, many protein-rich cereal- and legume-based foods containing peanuts are now in widespread use in developing countries for alleviating problems associated with protein calorie malnutrition. Peanuts, which are rich in oil and in protein, and are also tasty, are particularly valuable for these purposes (Singh and Singh 1991).

Allergenicity

It is unfortunate that peanuts are not for everyone. The cotyledons, axial germ tissue (hearts), and skin of peanuts contain allergens, and some, but not all, of these are still present after roasting. Because the allergens do not have a characteristic odor or flavor, they cannot easily be detected by peanut-sensitive individuals; thus, labeling of peanut-containing products is essential, save for pure peanut oil, which is not allergenic.

The many different peanut allergens that exist all contain protein. These allergens have been demonstrated by the use of radioallergenabsorbent test (RAST) inhibition, and by immunologic techniques, such as crossed radioimmunoelectrophoresis (CRIE), two-dimensional electrophoresis, and immunoblotting to isolate and characterize the peanut allergens. Then sera from peanut-sensitive individuals is used to determine if specific IgE binding to the various isolated sub-fractions exists. Since the isolation and characterization methods may affect the physical structure of the protein or its subfractions, different techniques may give different results. Nonetheless, at present, it is clear that multiple allergens exist in peanuts.

A well-characterized peanut allergen recently identified in patients with atopic dermatitis and positive peanut challenges is called Ara h I *(Arachis hypogaea I)* in the official nomenclature (Burks et al. 1991). Highly atopic infants and children appear to be particularly likely to form IgE antibodies that respond to peanuts, as well as to other food proteins (Zimmerman, Forsyth, and Gold 1989). Such children begin producing IgE antibodies to respond to inhalant allergens during their first and second years of life; they are defined as highly atopic because their serum IgE levels are 10 times those of normal infants, and their RAST tests are positive on multiple occasions.

Diagnosis. Diagnosis of peanut allergy is difficult because standardized peanut extracts do not yet exist. A RAST can be used on the sera of already sensitive persons for whom a skin test would be dangerous. Double-blind placebo-controlled challenges are definitive but are not often needed. If such double-blind challenges are done, provisions need to be made to cope with emergencies that may arise if an anaphylactic reaction occurs. The allergenicity of hydrolyzed peanut protein must be further studied. It is not clear at what level of hydrolysis allergenicity is lost.

Prevalence of peanut sensitivity. Peanut sensitivity is less prevalent among humans than are, for example, sensitivities to milk and eggs, but peanuts are especially dangerous for a number of reasons. One important reason is that peanuts occur in small amounts in so many different foods and recipes, ranging from satay sauce and "vegeburgers" to main dishes and spreads, making it difficult for those who have the allergy to avoid them (Smith 1990).

The allergy occurs in vegetarians as well as omnivores (Donovan and Peters 1990), and cross-reactivity with other legumes appears to exist. In addition, individuals who are allergic to other foods besides legumes are sometimes allergic to peanuts. Finally, highly atopic individuals, such as asthmatics, and those who suffer from atopic dermatitis or from multiple other food allergies, are likely to be at particular risk.

Signs of peanut allergy. The signs of peanut sensitivity range from urticaria (hives) to angioedema and asthma, and occasionally even to anaphylaxis and death (Lemanske and Taylor 1987; Boyd 1989). Crude extracts of proteins in both raw and roasted peanuts, as well as purified peanut proteins, such as arachin, conarachin, and concanavalin A reactive glycoprotein, are all allergenic in some persons (Barnett, Baldo, and Howden 1983).

Natural history of peanut allergy. Allergic reactions to peanuts usually begin early in life and persist. Studies over a period of several years have now been completed on individuals who exhibited symptoms of peanut allergy in childhood after a double-blind, placebo-controlled challenge, and reacted positively to puncture skin tests at the same time. Most such individuals had avoided peanuts since diagnosis, but those who inadvertently ingested peanuts 2 to 14 years later had reactions. This, coupled with a continued skin reactivity to peanut extract in puncture tests, suggests that peanut-sensitive individuals rarely lose their sensitivity with time (Bock and Atkins 1989). Fatal reactions to peanuts can also occur after many years of abstinence (Fries 1982). Fortunately, peanut oil, at least the usual grade sold in the United States and Europe, which contains no detectable protein, is not allergenic (Taylor et al. 1982). Unfortunately, in other countries the oil may contain enough of the protein to cause allergic reaction.

Allergy treatment. Avoidance of products containing peanut protein is the surest way to avoid peanut allergy. But certain foods may be accidentally contaminated with peanut protein, so that even products supposedly peanut free may be dangerous. Because the prevalence of peanut allergy is high, both labeling and label reading are important. Treatment of peanut sensitivity with immunotherapy has not proved helpful. If a sensitive person does ingest peanuts, self-administered epinephrine may help.

Peanut anaphylaxis is a medical emergency (Sampson 1990). One common cause is consumption of a product containing deflavored and colored peanut protein reformulated to resemble other nuts (Yunginger et al. 1989). In one case, an "almond" icing that was actually made from peanuts led to a fatal reaction (Evans, Skea, and Dolovich 1988). Other possible hidden sources of peanuts are egg rolls, cookies, candy, pastries, and vegetable burgers. Chinese food and dried-food dressings that contain peanuts have also been causes of anaphylactic shock (Assem et al. 1990).

Peanut allergy is probably the major cause of food-related anaphylaxis in the United States. Only a few milligrams will cause reactions in some persons. Those who are at risk of anaphylactic reactions to peanuts should wear medic-alert bracelets and carry preloaded epinephrine syringes and antihistamines. If treatment is needed, repeated doses of epinephrine, antihistamines, corticosteroids, mechanical methods to open airways, oxygen, vasopressors, and intravenous fluids may be necessary to prevent a fatal reaction (Settipane 1989).

Cross-reactivity in allergenicity. Peanuts cross-react in vitro with other members of the Leguminosae family, especially with garden peas, chickpeas, and soybeans, although clinical sensitivity is not always observed (Toorenenbergen and Dieges 1984; Barnett, Bonham, and Howden 1987). Reactions to nonlegume nuts, however, are relatively rare among those allergic to peanuts.

Aflatoxin

Aflatoxins are naturally occurring environmental contaminants that often infest peanuts. These carcinogenic mycotoxins arise from a fungus *(Aspergillus flavus)* that colonizes peanuts under certain environmental conditions or improper storage conditions that permit fungal growth. The aflatoxins B_1 and B_2 are most common in peanuts.

Aflatoxin-contaminated food has been shown to be associated with liver cancer in both humans and several experimental animals. The problem appears to be most severe in Africa and other parts of the world where environmental and storage conditions favor the mold's growth and where processing methods that could identify and eliminate contaminated seeds are still not in place. But it is also a problem in the Orient, where people prefer the flavor of crude peanut oil. This form of the oil is high in aflatoxins.

In highly industrialized countries, aflatoxin contamination generally occurs before the harvest; in developing countries, contamination during storage is an additional and seemingly greater problem. In the former case, insect damage to the pods and roots permits seed contamination by the mold, especially during growing seasons where there is a late-season drought, which increases stress on the plant and also helps to exclude competition by other fungi. In a three-year study it was found that pods are more susceptible to contamination than roots (Sanders et al. 1993). Shriveled peanuts have the highest content of aflatoxin B_1 (Sashidhar 1993).

Under favorable environmental conditions, *Aspergillus flavus* produces millions of spores, which can be carried by the wind for miles (Cleveland and Bhatnagar 1992). Insect damage promotes *Aspergillus flavus* growth when the spores land at a site of insect injury and when the moisture content exceeds 9 percent in peanuts, or 16 percent in peanut meal, and temperatures are 30 to 35° C. Therefore, the only sure method to avoid aflatoxins is to prevent their formation by careful harvesting and quick drying and storage. Food additives, such as sodium bisulfite, sorbate, proprionate, and nitrite, reduce aflatoxin production. Also, certain food components and spices, such as peppers, mustard, cinnamon, and cloves, may inhibit mycotoxin production (Jones 1992).

Visual screening of peanuts will reveal the conidial heads of the *Aspergillus flavus* fungus. Another technique is to screen unshelled nuts for the presence of bright greenish yellow fluorescence (BGYF) under ultraviolet light, using electronic color-sorting techniques. However, neither of these techniques screens out all aflatoxin contamination. For greater precision, chemical tests are used that include thin layer chromatography (TLC) and high performance liquid chromatography (HPLC) (Beaver 1989).

Immunological methods, such as ELISA or affinity column methods, are also useful, although precautions must be taken in performing the analysis since aflatoxins are highly carcinogenic (Wilson 1989). Much research is now in progress on the development of standardized methods for determining aflatoxin in peanut products. Other research concentrates on eliminating the contamination or inactivating it.

Chlorine gas can inactivate one aflatoxin, aflatoxin B_1, and the resulting compounds do not appear to be mutagenic (Samarajeewa et al. 1991). Ammonia and ozone treatments of peanuts also appear to work. As yet, however, these methods are still experimental.

The liver cancer in question is thought to be caused by hepatitis B, with other factors, such as aflatoxin, acting as promoters or as less-potent initiators. In most case-control studies, primary hepatocellular carcinoma is highly associated with antibodies to hepatitis B and C virus; other risk factors, such as peanut consumption (presumably with aflatoxin contamination), smoking, and drinking, are less highly associated (Yu et al. 1991). A recent large study in mainland China showed high correlations of liver cancer with hepatitis B surface antigen (HBsAg+) carrier status, whereas lesser associations were seen with alcohol use and cadmium of plant origin, but none with the measure of aflatoxin exposure that was used (Campbell et al. 1990). However, smaller studies, especially of peanut oils contaminated with aflatoxin, continue to suggest that aflatoxin may be involved in hepatobilliary cancers (Guo 1991).

Aflatoxin: Food safety. In recent years, the European Community has increasingly collaborated on food safety tests, and a great deal of effort has been devoted to developing more sensitive, rapid, and standardized methods for detecting aflatoxin levels in peanut products (Van Egmond and Wagstaffe 1989; Patey, Sherman, and Gilbert 1990; Gilbert et al. 1991). Thanks to this collaboration, standardized methods and materials are now available for assuring valid and reliable food safety testing. Current guidelines are that no more than 20 parts per billion of aflatoxin are permitted.

Developing countries and the aflatoxin problem. As we have mentioned, the problem of aflatoxin contamination is particularly serious in developing countries because of storage and processing problems. Thus, by way of example, aflatoxin levels in Pacific countries such as Fiji and Tonga are high, and so are liver cancer rates. Therefore, in addition to improving inspection methods, techniques must be developed for decreasing the carcinogenicity of aflatoxin-contaminated foods for humans and for animals. One technique that has been helpful in reducing the carcinogenicity of aflatoxin-contaminated groundnut cakes is ammoniation (Frayssinet and Lafarge-Frayssinet 1990). However, more such solutions are needed.

Table II.D.2.6. *Nutritive value of common peanut foods (g/100g)*

	Nut, roasted (Spanish or Virginia, salted)	Peanut butter	Peanut oil
Water, g	1.6	1.7	0
Calories	586	587	884
Protein, g	26	25	0
Carbohydrate, g	19	19	0
Fat	50	51	100

Miscellaneous

Because peanuts are a low-acid food, incorrect commercial canning of peanuts can cause botulism, as a recent case in China showed (Tsai et al. 1990). On a more positive note, peanuts are often used by dentists as foods for masticatory tests for jaw and muscle function (Kapur, Garrett, and Fischer 1990), because they are easy to standardize and familiar to patients (Wang and Stohler 1991). Moreover, roasted peanuts are among the least likely of popular snack foods to cause dental caries (Grenby 1990). Peanuts remain available dry, oil roasted, unsalted, lightly salted, or salted, as well as in a variety of flavors today in the United States (Nabisco Foods Group, Planters Division 1990). And finally, the not fully mature (or green) peanuts can be used as a vegetable that is much appreciated in the southern United States. Green peanuts are boiled in a weak brine solution and usually consumed immediately. If refrigerated, they will last for five days. They can also be frozen or canned.

Table II.D.2.6 shows the nutritive value of various peanut foods.

Johanna T. Dwyer and Ritu Sandhu

Bibliography

Achaya, K. T. 1980. Fat intakes in India. In *Combating undernutrition,* ed. C. Gopalan, 110–12. New Delhi.

Assem, E. S., G. M. Gelder, S. G. Spiro, et al. 1990. Anaphylaxis induced by peanuts. *British Medical Journal* 300: 1377–8.

Barnett, D., B. A. Baldo, and M. E. Howden. 1983. Multiplicity of allergens in peanuts. *Journal of Allergy and Clinical Immunology* 72: 61–8.

Barnett, D., B. Bonham, and M. E. H. Howden. 1987. Allergenic cross reactions among legume foods: An in vitro study. *Journal of Allergy and Clinical Immunology* 79: 433–8.

Basha, S. M. 1991. Accumulation pattern of arachin in maturing peanut seeds. *Peanut Science* 16: 70–3.

Beaver, R. W. 1989. Determination of aflatoxins in corn and peanuts using high performance liquid chromatography. *Archives of Environment Contamination and Toxicology* 18: 315–18.

Bock, S. A., and F. M. Atkins. 1989. The natural history of

peanut allergy. *Journal of Allergy and Clinical Immunology* 83: 900-4.

Boyd, G. K. 1989. Fatal nut anaphylaxis in a 16-year-old male: Case report. *Allergy Proceedings* 10: 255-7.

Branch, W. D., and C. K. Kvien. 1992. Peanut breeding for drought resistance. *Peanut Science* 19: 44-6.

Bressani, R. 1977. Protein supplementation and complementation. In *Evaluation of proteins for humans,* ed. C. E. Bodwell, 204-31. Westport, Conn.

Bressani, R., and L. G. Elias. 1968. Processed vegetable protein mixtures for human consumption in developing countries. In *Advances in food research,* Vol. 16, ed. E. W. Mrak, G. F. Stewart, and C. O. Chichester, 1-78. New York.

Burks, A. W., L. W. Williams, R. M. Helm, et al. 1991. Identification of a major peanut allergen Ara h I in patients with atopic dermatitis and positive peanut challenges. *Journal of Allergy and Clinical Immunology* 88: 172-9.

Burks, A. W., L. W. Williams, S. B. Mallory, et al. 1989. Peanut protein as a major cause of adverse food reactions in patients with atopic dermatitis. *Allergy Proceedings* 10: 265-9.

Bush, R. K., S. L. Taylor, and J. A. Nordlee. 1989. Peanut sensitivity. *Allergy Proceedings* 10: 13-20.

Campbell, T. C., J. S. Chen, C. B. Liu, et al. 1990. Nonassociation of aflatoxin with primary liver cancer in a cross-sectional ecological survey in the People's Republic of China. *Cancer Research* 50: 6882-93.

Castelli, W. P. 1992. Concerning the possibility of a nut. . . . *Archives of Internal Medicine* 152: 1371-2.

Cleveland, T. E., and D. Bhatnagar. 1992. Aflatoxin: Elimination through biotechnology. In *Encyclopedia of food science and technology,* Vol. 1, ed. Y. H. Hui, 6-11. New York.

Cole, R. J., and J. W. Dorner. 1992. Peanuts. In *Encyclopedia of food science and technology,* Vol. 3, ed. Y. H. Hui, 2036-9. New York.

DaGrame, S. V., J. K. Chavan, and S. D. Kadam. 1990. Effects of roasting and storage on proteins and oil in peanut kernels. *Plant Foods for Human Nutrition* 40: 143-8.

Deutsche Forschungsanstalt für Lebensmittelchemie. 1991. *Food composition and nutrition tables 1989-90.* Stuttgart.

Donovan, K. L., and J. Peters. 1990. Vegetable burger allergy: All was nut as it appeared. *British Medical Journal* 300: 1378.

Elin, R. J., and J. M. Hosseini. 1993. Is magnesium content of nuts a factor in coronary heart disease? *Archives of Internal Medicine* 153: 779-80.

Evans, S., D. Skea, and J. Dolovich. 1988. Fatal reaction to peanut antigen in almond icing. *Canadian Medical Association Journal* 193: 231-2.

FAO (Food and Agriculture Organization of the United Nations). 1970. *Amino-acid content of foods.* Rome.

1993. *Food and Agriculture Organization Yearbook: Production, 1992,* Vol. 46. Rome.

Food and Nutrition Board, National Research Council. 1989. *Recommended dietary allowances.* Tenth edition. Washington, D.C.

Fraser, G. E., J. Sabate, W. L. Beeson, and T. M. Strahan. 1992. A possible protective effect of nut consumption on risk of coronary heart disease. *Archives in Internal Medicine* 152: 1416-26.

Frayssinet, C., and C. Lafarge-Frayssinet. 1990. Effect of ammoniation on the carcinogenicity of aflatoxin-contaminated groundnut oil cakes: Long-term feeding study in the rat. *Food Additives and Contaminants* 7: 63-8.

Fries, J. H. 1982. Peanuts: Allergic and other untoward reactions. *Annals of Allergy* 48: 220-6.

Gilbert, J., M. Sharman, G. M. Wood, et al. 1991. The preparation, validation and certification of the aflatoxin content of two peanut butter reference materials. *Food Additives and Contaminants* 8: 305-20.

Greene, K. S., J. M. Johnson, M. Rossi, et al. 1991. Effects of peanut butter on ruminating. *American Journal on Mental Retardation* 95: 631-45.

Grenby, T. H. 1990. Snack foods and dental caries: Investigations using laboratory animals. *British Dental Journal* 168: 353-61.

Guo, H. W. 1991. The study of the relationship between diet and primary liver cancer. *Chinese Medical Journal* 25: 342-4.

Holaday, C. E., and J. L. Pearson. 1974. Effect of genotype and production area on the fatty acid composition, total oil and total protein in peanuts. *Journal of Food Science* 39: 1206-9.

Holbrook, C. C., and J. P. Noe. 1992. Resistance to the peanut root-knot nematode *(Meliodogyne arenaria)* in *Arachis hypogaea. Peanut Science* 19: 35-7.

Holland, B., A. A. Welch, I. D. Unwin, et al. 1991. *McCance and Widdowson's - The composition of foods.* Fifth edition. London.

Jambunathan, G., S. Gurtu, K. Raghunath, et al. 1992. Chemical composition and protein quality of newly released groundnut *(Arachis hypogaea L.)* cultivars. *The Science of Food and Agriculture* 59: 161-7.

Johnson, P., and W. E. F. Naismith. 1953. The physicochemical examination of the conarachin fraction of the groundnut globulins *(Arachis hypogaea). Discussions of the Faraday Society* 13: 98.

Jones, J. 1992. *Food safety.* New York.

Kannon, G., and H. K. Park. 1990. Utility of peanut agglutinin (PNA) in the diagnosis of squamous cell carcinoma and keratoacanthoma. *American Journal of Dermatopathology* 12: 31-6.

Kapur, K. K., N. R. Garrett, and E. Fischer. 1990. Effects of anaesthesia of human oral structures on masticatory performance and food particle size distribution. *Archives of Oral Biology* 35: 397-403.

Klevay, L. M. 1993. Copper in nuts may lower heart disease risk. *Archives of Internal Medicine* 153: 401-2.

Krapovickas, A. 1969. The origin, variability and spread of the groundnut (Arachis hypogea). In *Domestication and exploitation of plants and animals,* ed. P. J. Ucko and G. W. Dimbleby, 427-41. Chicago.

Langkilde, N. S., H. Wolf, H. Clausen, and T. F. Orntoft. 1992. Human urinary bladder carcinoma glycoconjugates expressing T-(Gal-beta [1-3] GalNAc-alpha-I-O-R) and T-like antigens: A comparative study using peanut agglutinin and poly and monoclonal antibodies. *Cancer Research* 52: 5030-6.

Lapidis, D. N., ed. 1977. *Encyclopedia of food agriculture and nutrition.* New York.

Lemanske, R. F., and S. L. Taylor. 1987. Standardized extracts of foods. *Clinical Reviews in Allergy* 5: 23-6.

Marshall, H. F., G. P. Shaffer, and E. J. Conkerkin. 1989. Free amino acid determination in whole peanut seeds. *Analytical Biochemistry* 180: 264-8.

McCarthy, M. A., and R. H. Matthews. 1984. *Composition of foods: Nuts and seed products.* Washington, D.C.

McGee, Harold. 1988. *On food and cooking - The science and lore of the kitchen.* London.

Nabisco Foods Group, Planters Division. 1990. *Why everybody loves a peanut.* Winston-Salem, N.C.

Ockerman, H. W. 1991a. *Food science sourcebook: Food composition, properties and general data,* Vol. 2. New York.

1991b. *Food science sourcebook: Terms and descriptions,* Vol. 1. New York.

Oohira, H. 1992. Morphological and histochemical studies on experimentally immobilized rabbit patellar cartilage. *Medical Journal of Kagoshima University* 44: 183-223.

Oser, B. L. 1959. An integrated essential amino acid index for predicting the biological value of proteins. In *Protein and amino acid nutrition,* ed. A. A. Albanese, 292-5. New York.

Patey, A. L., M. Sherman, and J. Gilbert. 1990. Determination of aflatoxin B1 levels in peanut butter using an immunoaffinity column clean-up procedure: Inter-laboratory study. *Food Additives and Contaminants* 7: 515-20.

Porter, D. M., T. A. Coffelt, F. S. Wright, and R. W. Mozingo. 1992. Resistance to sclerotina blight and early leaf spot in Chinese peanut germplasm. *Peanut Science* 19: 41-3.

Sabate, J., G. E. Fraser, K. Burke, et al. 1993. Effects of walnuts on serum lipid levels and blood pressure in normal men. *New England Journal of Medicine* 328: 603-7.

Sachs, M. I., R. T. Jones, and J. W. Yunginger. 1981. Isolation and partial characterization of a major peanut allergen. *Journal of Allergy and Clinical Immunology* 67: 27-34.

Samarajeewa, U., A. C. Sen, S. Y. Fernando, et al. 1991. Inactivation of aflatoxin B1 in cornmeal, copra meal and peanuts by chlorine gas treatment. *Food and Chemical Toxicology* 29: 41-7.

Samonds, K. W., and D. M. Hegsted. 1977. Animal bioassays: A critical evaluation with specific reference to assessing the nutritive value for the human. In *Evaluation of proteins for humans,* ed. C. E. Bodwell, 69-71. Westport, Conn.

Sampson, H. A. 1990. Peanut anaphylaxis. *Journal of Allergy and Clinical Immunology* 86: 1-3.

Sanders, T. H., R. J. Cole, P. D. Blankenship, and J. W. Dorner. 1993. Aflatoxin contamination of the peanuts from plants drought stressed in the pod or root zones. *Peanut Science* 20: 5-8.

Sauer, J. D. 1993. *Historical geography of crop plants - A select roster.* Boca Raton, Fla.

Scott, P. M. 1969. The analysis of food for aflatoxin and other fungal toxins - A review. *Canadian Institute of Food Science and Technology Journal* 2: 173-7.

Senba, M., K. Watanabe, K. Yoshida, et al. 1992. Endocarditis caused by *Candida parapsilosis. Southeast Asian Journal of Tropical Medicine and Public Health* 23: 138-41.

Settipane, G. A. 1989. Anaphylactic deaths in asthmatic patients. *Allergy Proceedings* 10: 271-4.

Sashidhar, R. B. 1993. Fate of aflatoxin B-1 during the industrial production of edible defatted peanut protein flour from raw peanuts. *Food Chemistry* 48: 349-52.

Short, J. 1990. *Grain legumes: Evolution and genetic resources.* New York.

Singh, B., and H. Singh. 1991. Peanut as a source of protein for human foods. *Plant Foods for Human Nutrition* 41: 165-77.

Smith, T. 1990. Allergy to peanuts. *British Medical Journal* 300: 1354.

Spector, W. S., ed. 1956. *Handbook of biological data.* Bethesda, Md.

Taylor, S. L., W. W. Busse, M. I. Sachs, et al. 1982. Peanut oil is not allergenic in peanut-sensitive individuals. *Journal of Allergy and Clinical Immunology* 68: 372-5.

Toorenenbergen, A. W. van, and P. H. Dieges. 1984. IgE mediated hypersensitivity to taugeh (sprouted small green beans). *Annals of Allergy* 53: 239-42.

Tsai, S. J., Y. C. Chang, J. D. Wong, and J. H. Chon. 1990. Outbreak of type A botulism caused by a commercial food product in Taiwan: Chemical and epidemiological investigations. *Chinese Medical Journal* 46: 43-8.

USDA (United States Department of Agriculture). 1992. *USDA - Agriculture statistics, 1992.* Washington, D.C.

Van Egmond, H. P., and P. J. Wagstaffe. 1989. Aflatoxin B1 in peanut meal reference materials: Intercomparisons of methods. *Food Additives and Contaminants* 6: 307-19.

Wang, J. S., and C. S. Stohler. 1991. Predicting food stuff from jaw dynamics during masticatory crushing in man. *Archives of Oral Biology* 36: 239-44.

Weijian, Z., P. Shiyao, and L. Mushon. 1991. Changes in the morphology and structure of cotyledon storage cells and their relation to the accumulation of oil and protein in the peanut. *Scientia Agricultura Sinica* 24: 8-13.

Willich, R. K., N. J. Morris, and A. F. Freeman. 1954. The effect of processing and storage of peanut butter on the stability of their oils. *Food Technology* 8: 101-4.

Wilson, D. M. 1989. Analytical methods for aflatoxin in corn and peanuts. *Archives of Environmental Contamination and Toxicology* 18: 308-14.

Woodroof, J. G. 1966. *Peanuts: Production, processing, products.* Westport, Conn.

Young, V. R., and N. S. Scrimshaw. 1977. Human protein and amino acid metabolism and requirements in relation to protein quality. In *Evaluation of proteins for humans,* ed. C. E. Bodwell, 11-54. Westport, Conn.

Yu, M. W., S. L. You, A. S. Chang, et al. 1991. Association between hepatitis C virus antibodies and hepatocellular carcinoma in Taiwan. *Cancer Research* 51: 5621-5.

Yunginger, J. W., D. L. Squillace, R. T. Jones, and R. M. Helm. 1989. Fatal anaphylactic reactions induced by peanuts. *Allergy Proceedings* 10: 249-53.

Zimmerman, B., S. Forsyth, and M. Gold. 1989. Highly atopic children: Formation of IgE antibody to food protein, especially peanut. *Journal of Allergy and Clinical Immunology* 83: 764-70.

II.E

Animal, Marine, and Vegetable Oils

II.E.1 ॐ An Overview of Oils and Fats, with a Special Emphasis on Olive Oil

Oils from vegetable sources are playing an increasingly important role in human nutrition, and they, along with foods incorporating them, currently compose 30 percent of the calories in a typical Western diet. In the past, however, vegetable oil utilization was limited, and animal and marine fats were far more important. This chapter discusses the nutritional value of fats and oils widely used in the world today.

Fatty Acid Nomenclature

Most oils consist primarily of triacylglycerols, which are composed of 3 fatty acids esterified to a glycerol molecule. The "essential" fatty acids are a major consideration in assessing the nutritional value of fats and oils. G. O. Burr and M. M. Burr first discovered that fats and oils contained substances that were essential for normal growth and reproduction (Holman 1992), and in the 1970s, convincing evidence was presented to show that the omega-3 fatty acids were also essential in humans. In addition to fatty acids, other components present in fats and oils include fat-soluble vitamins (A, D, and E) and sterols, and as few other compounds in fats and oils are of nutritional importance, only fatty acids, fat-soluble vitamins, and sterols are discussed in this chapter.

The sterols of importance to nutrition include cholesterol and the plant sterols. The structures of common sterols are shown in Figure II.E.1.1. Recently, there has been a great deal of interest in cholesterol oxides, which are formed in cholesterol-containing foods and oils after heating or oxidation and which have been implicated in the development of atherosclerosis (Smith 1987; Nawar et al. 1991).

Fatty acid composition is often presented as an average value representing a middle point in the composition of an oil. There are many factors that affect the fatty acid composition of oilseeds, marine oils, and animal fats. Thus, it is preferable to present a range of fatty acid compositions that are common, rather than to present one value.

World Fat and Oil Production

Current production estimates for important fats and oils are shown in Figure II.E.1.2. Soybean oil is by far the leader, followed by palm, sunflower, and rapeseed oil, with others trailing far behind. The current levels of production of the various vegetable oils reflect relatively recent changes. Palm oil production has increased dramatically in the last few decades, as Malaysia and other Asian countries have promoted it, and in the past half century, soybean oil, once a minor oil, has become the most widely used of all.

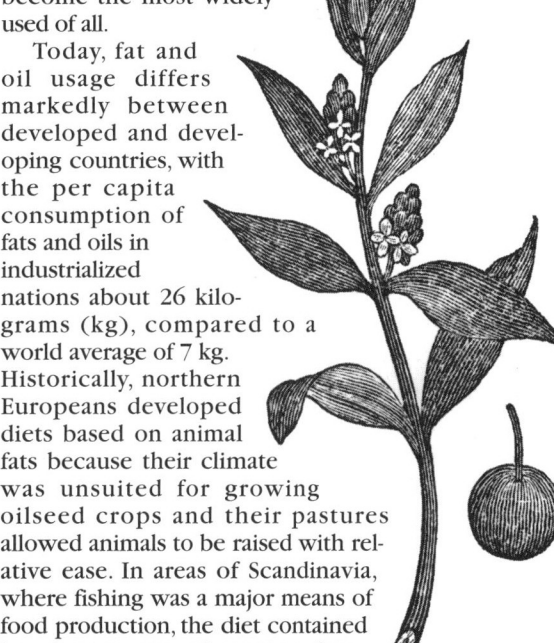

Olive

Today, fat and oil usage differs markedly between developed and developing countries, with the per capita consumption of fats and oils in industrialized nations about 26 kilograms (kg), compared to a world average of 7 kg. Historically, northern Europeans developed diets based on animal fats because their climate was unsuited for growing oilseed crops and their pastures allowed animals to be raised with relative ease. In areas of Scandinavia, where fishing was a major means of food production, the diet contained large amounts of marine fats.

In Africa, Asia, and the Mediterranean, however, because the raising of large numbers of animals was impractical and fish were not dietary mainstays, fats were derived primarily from plants, such as oil palms and olive trees. Thus, historical differences in patterns of fat consumption largely resulted from environmental conditions that fostered the various agricultural practices of the different areas of the world.

Yet, over the past 100 years, there has been a decreased consumption of animal fats and an increase in that of vegetable oils. When vegetable oils were first produced in commercially important quantities, they could not be used to displace animal fats because the latter (for example, butter, lard, and tallow) were solid at room temperature and had specific applications that required solidity. But the process of hydrogenation, developed early in the twentieth century, permitted the manufacture of plastic fats (such as shortening and margarine) based on vegetable oils, and lard and butter were subsequently displaced in the diets of many peoples.

The twentieth-century industrialization of oilseed production, as well as vegetable oil extraction and refining, has been the primary factor leading to large-scale changes in the fat composition of diets around the world, although genetic engineering, breeding, and mutation have also brought significant changes in the fatty acid composition of a number of oilseeds. Moreover, the fatty acid composition of animal fats and aquacultured fish can be altered by dietary manipulation. Such changes complicate discussion of the nutritional benefits obtained from oils.

Oil Extraction and Processing

A knowledge of the ways in which oils are obtained (extracted) and processed is important to an understanding of the nutritional value of the oils. Fats and oils are extracted from animal and vegetable materials by the three main processes of rendering, using the screw press, and solvent extraction.

The first method humans employed to extract oils was undoubtedly rendering, which is still used today to remove fat from animal and fish tissues. In this process, the material to be rendered is heated (either dry or in water), which disrupts the tissues and allows separation of the oil. The quality of the oil yielded by early rendering operations must have been poor, but later developments in processing (such as steam heating) have permitted the rendering of high-quality products. The conventional wet-rendering process includes an initial cooking step, in which the tissue is heated with direct or indirect steam, or is heated as it passes through a conveyer. The cooked material is pressed in continuous or batch presses, and the liquid ("press liquor") is centrifuged to separate the water and oil. The oil obtained may be dried further before storage.

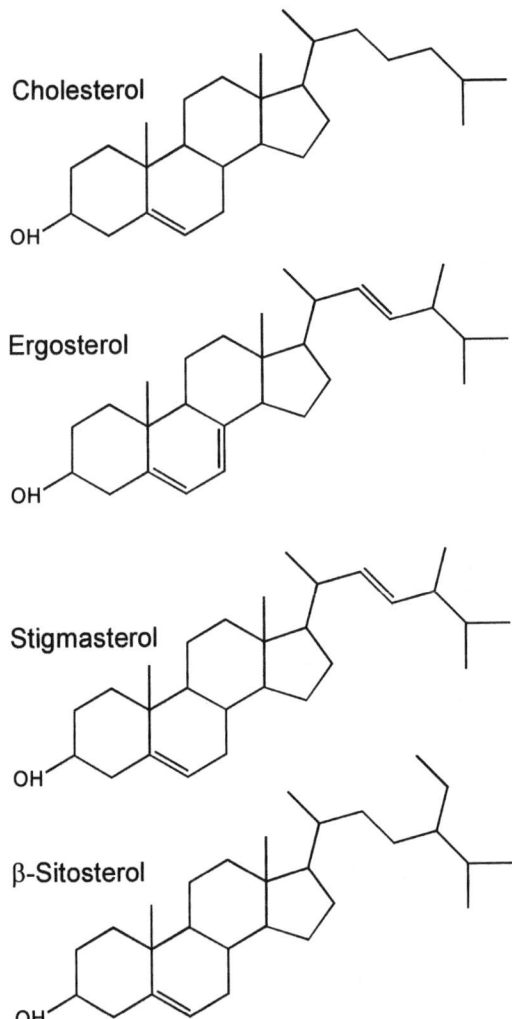

Figure II.E.1.1. The structure of common sterols.

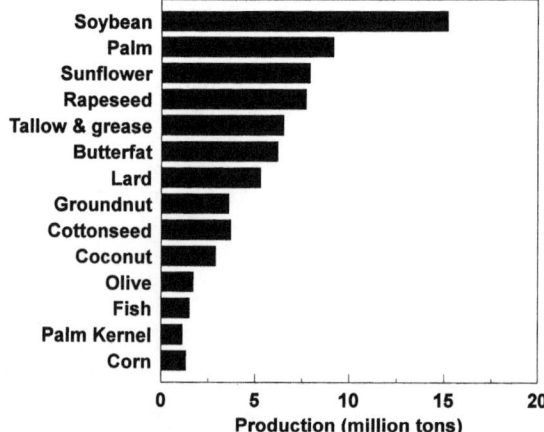

Figure II.E.1.2. Production estimates for important fats and oils.

Table II.E.1.1. *Average oil content of plant sources of oil*

Material	Oil percent
Soy	18–20
Palm fruit	45–50
Sunflower	25–45
Rapeseed (canola)	35–60
Peanut	45–55
Cottonseed	18–20
Coconut (copra)	63–68
Olive	25–30

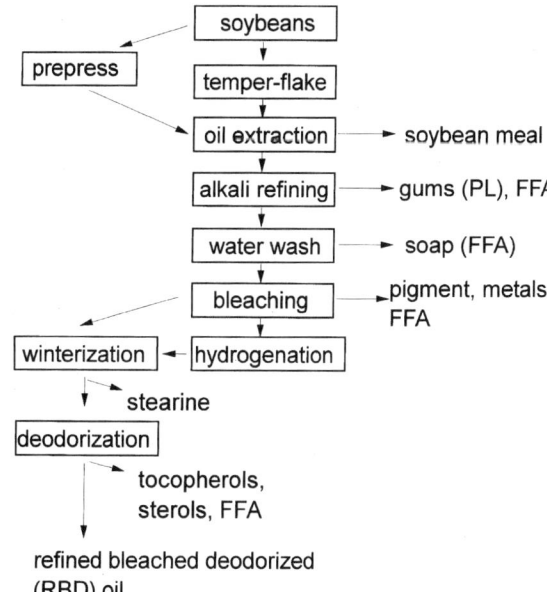

Figure II.E.1.3. Operations in soybean oil extraction and refining.

In the second method, an expeller, or screw press, removes oil from vegetable materials by mechanical pressure. The pressure creates heat, disrupting the tissue and causing the oil to separate, after which it flows out through holes in the press. Such presses have been documented in early Hindu medical texts; the first of these devices, however, doubtless had low output, and the extracted oil was probably used for illumination or for medicine. These were batch presses, which had to be filled with oilseed and then emptied in each extraction step. By contrast, modern screw presses operate continuously and have much greater capabilities than batch presses. Screw-press extraction of oil is most feasible when the oil content of the material to be pressed is high. The oil content of some vegetable sources of oil is shown in Table II.E.1.1 (Sonntag 1979a).

The third method of oil recovery, solvent extraction, was only possible after supplies of solvents with appropriate characteristics became available. The solvent-extraction process for soybeans is outlined in Figure II.E.1.3. The refining steps include alkali neutralization, which results in the removal of phospholipids and free fatty acids; bleaching, which removes pigments, metals, and free fatty acids; and deodorization, which removes odorous compounds, some sterols, and tocopherols.

W. Normann's discovery of liquid phase hydrogenation (which results in loss of polyunsaturated fatty acids and production of monounsaturated "trans" acids) led to the development of plastic fats derived from vegetable sources. Crisco, the first shortening to be sold (1911), was based on hydrogenated cottonseed oil. By the mid-1940s, 65 percent of the cottonseed oil produced in the United States was used to make shortening.

Vegetable Oils

Olive Oil

Olive oil is derived from the fruit of the evergreen tree *Olea europaea,* which grows in temperate climates with warm and dry summers. Around 5,000 or 6,000 years ago, at the eastern end of the Mediterranean, the tough, spiny, wild olive trees dominating the countrysides of Palestine, Syria, and other areas of

the Middle East were first brought under cultivation (Chandler 1950). The trees became gnarled with domestication, and less bushy, and their fruit (green that ripens to brown or to blue-purple-black) was laden with oil. That oil – technically a fruit oil rather than a vegetable oil, as it is classified – doubtless was used to fuel lamps, and it found its way into medicines and cosmetics as well as cooking. The many uses for oil created much demand in the ancient world, which was satisfied by oils made from walnuts, almonds, and the seeds of sesame, flax, and radishes, as well as from olives (Tannahill 1988). The latter, however, were the most productive source of oil from the Bronze Age onward, and their cultivation spread throughout the Mediterranean region, so that the waning centuries of that age found the people of the island of Crete cultivating great numbers of olive trees and growing rich on the export of oil (Trager 1995).

Shortly after the dawn of the Iron Age, the Greek landscape reflected a similar dedication to olive production, spurred in the early sixth century B.C. by the prohibition of Solon (the Greek statesman and legal reformer) of the export of any agricultural produce except olive oil. Greece (like Crete, two millennia earlier) would learn how devastating the effects of monoculture could be when war made trade impossible (Tannahill 1988).

Nevertheless, as a relatively precious product requiring special climate and skills, yet easy to store and ship in jars, olive oil lent itself well to this kind of specialization. Barbarians in contact with the Greeks became good customers, although any possibility of

Greek monopoly ended when Etruscans carried the techniques of olive cultivation into Italy, and Phoenicians did the same for North Africa and the Iberian peninsula.

Because many years are required for olive trees to become productive after planting, olive cultivation in these new areas probably required the passing of a generation or two before its possibilities were appreciated. But certainly one thing worth appreciating was that olive trees seemed to live forever. In Spain, for example, it is said that there are trees some 1,000 years old, which meant that in the absence of some catastrophe, such as disease or fire, the task of planting olive trees and then waiting for them to become productive seldom troubled grove owners more than once, if that (Chandler 1950).

In the first century A.D., Pliny noted a dozen varieties of olives grown as far away from Rome as Gaul (France) and Spain, and certainly it was the case that by the time of the Romans, olive-tree cultivation had caught on in Iberia in a big way. With olive oil a staple in the Roman diet, Spanish oil was a commodity sought throughout the Empire, and henceforth olive oil would be established as the most important dietary oil in southern Europe. In the north – where livestock did well and olive trees did not – cooking was done with butter and lard. Obviously, the cuisines these cooking mediums helped to shape were often strikingly dissimilar.

Within fourteenth-century Spain, olive oil was exported from south to north, and wool and hides from north to south, in a kind of microcosm of greater Europe, and, following the conquest of the New World, American demand continued to stimulate Spain's olive oil industry. As the colonists began to make their own oil, however, the flow of Spanish olive oil across the Atlantic diminished. In North America, Thomas Jefferson tried to grow olives at Monticello, but the cuttings he used would not take root (Trager 1995). At about the same time as this failed experiment in the east of the continent, olive cultivation was successfully launched in California by Spanish missionaries, and by the beginning of the twentieth century, that western state had joined Provence in France and the Lucca district in Italy – in the eyes of at least one American writer – as a producer of some of the world's best olive oils (Ward 1911).

Today, 90 percent of the world's olives go into oil, and only 2 percent of the acreage given over to olive production is outside of the Mediterran-ean region (McGee 1984). In terms of volume, Spain, Italy, Greece, and Portugal are the largest producers, although much of their olive oil is not reflected in production figures because there are many people – with just a few trees – who pick their own olives and take them to local cooperatives to be pressed.

Olives are sometimes picked by hand because they, and the twigs they grow upon, are fragile. However, because the fruit should be all of the same size and degree of ripeness, the same tree might be picked several times, all of which significantly increases the price of the oil (Toussaint-Samat 1992). To avoid picking several times, the fruits are generally treated less elegantly and are knocked off the trees, either from ground level with long poles or with small rakes by harvesters who climb the trees to shower the olives down. The fruits are caught on cloths spread on the ground or (more frequently today) on sheets of plastic.

Olives to be eaten are usually picked green and unripe. But, as Harold McGee (1984: 204) has remarked, anyone who has ever bitten into one knows instantly that something more must be done to render it edible. This something more is generally pickling, which has been practiced since the days of ancient Rome by soaking olives in a solution of lye to remove the bitter glucoside called oleuropein (from *Olea europea*).

Black olives – those that ripen at the time of the first frosts – are the kind made into oil. After they are gathered, they are permitted to stand and get warm, but not to ferment. Then they are washed and crushed. The oldest known technique for extracting oil was that of crushing the fruit underfoot; later, crushing was done by hand, using a pestle, and later still with millstones. In fact, many of the old-style Roman oil mills, with their large millstones operated by donkeys or mules (or by slaves in Roman times) continued in use throughout the Mediterranean area until well into the twentieth century (Toussaint-Samat 1992).

The crushing results in a paste that is pressed to secure the 25 to 30 percent of the olive that is oil. Extra virgin oil, also called "cold-pressed," comes from the first and lightest pressing and is unrefined; moreover, no heat is used to extract further oil. Virgin oil is produced in the same manner but has slightly greater acidity. Cold-pressed olive oil, although it has a wonderful flavor, will not keep as well as refined olive oil and, consequently, must be shielded from the light in cans or dark bottles.

The oil produced by succeeding pressings (usually with heat or hot water added) generally contains substances that give it a bad flavor, whereupon it is refined. Light and extra light oils are olive oils (not virgin) that have been filtered, producing a light scent, color, and taste. Oil labeled "pure" is a combination of virgin oil and that derived from the second pressing. Production of olive pomace oil – the cheapest grade of olive oil – requires hot water, which is added to the residue of olive oil cake, then poured off. This oil, typically not very good, has traditionally been exported to countries where a taste for olive oil has not been highly developed, although it is sometimes consumed by its own producers, who in turn sell their virgin oils for income (Toussaint-Samat 1992).

Table II.E.1.2. *Fatty acid composition ranges (weight percentage) of natural populations of vegetable oils*

	Soybean	Palm	Sunflower	Rapeseed	Peanut	Cottonseed	Coconut	Olive
6:0	0	0	0	0	0	0	<1.2	0
8:0	0	0	0	0	0	0	3.4–15	0
10:0	0	0	0	0	0	0	3.2–15	0
12:0	0	<1.2	0	0	0	0	41–56	0
14:0	<0.5	0.3–5.9	<0.5	<1	<1	0.5–2	13–23	<0.5
16:0	7–12	27–59	4–9	0.5–10	6–14	17–29	4.2–12	7.5–20
16:1	<0.5	<0.6	<0.5	<1	<1	<1.5	0	0.3–3.5
18:0	2–5.5	1.5–14.7	1–6.5	0.5–4	2–6.5	1–4	1–4.7	0.5–3.5
18:1	20–50	27–52	14–70	9–58	40–72	13–44	3.4–12	56–86
18:2ω6	35–60	5–16	20–75	8–27	13–38	33–58	0.9–3.7	3.5–20
18:2ω3	2–13	0.5–5	<0.5	3–21	<0.5	<0.5	0	01.5
20:0	<1	<1	<1	<1.5	1–2	<0.5	<0.2	<0.1
20:1	<1	0	<0.5	5–18	0.5–1.5	<0.5	<0.2	<0.1
22:0	<0.5	0	<1	<1	2–4	0	0	<0.1
22:1	0	0	0	30–60	0	0	0	0
24:0	0	0	<0.2	<2	1–2	0	0	<0.1

A more complicated (and technical) grading system for olive oils is based primarily on the free fatty acid levels: Extra virgin oil, which comes from the first pressing, has an acidity of less than 1 percent and perfect flavor and odor. Virgin oil, from the same pressing, contains less than 3 percent free fatty acids. Extra virgin and virgin olive oils may be processed only by washing, decantation centrifugation, and filtration. Refined olive oils are obtained by refining virgin or extra virgin olive oils, using the same alkali neutralization, bleaching, and deodorization steps employed in refining other oilseeds. Olive pomace oil is produced by solvent extraction from the cake remaining after pressing. It was sometimes called sulfur olive oil in the past, when carbon disulfide was used as an extraction solvent.

To maintain low free fatty acid levels and produce oil of the highest quality, olives must be processed within three days of harvest. This is primarily because ripe olives contain a high amount of water, allowing lipase enzyme activity and a resulting increase in free fatty acid levels. Consequently, in some areas that are not equipped to press olives as fast as they are harvested, either the fruit is left on the trees until it can be processed, or it is stored, which can be a risky procedure.

Olive oil is characterized by a very high oleic acid content averaging around 75 percent (Table II.E.1.2). Palmitic acid is the second most prevalent fatty acid, followed by linoleic and linolenic. There has been a great deal of interest in olive oil as a promoter of human health since the development of the hypothesis that a "Mediterranean diet" is protective against heart disease, perhaps because for centuries, olive oil has been the only oil readily obtainable for human use that has a high oleic characteristic.

Recent developments in oilseed breeding and genetics, however, have produced high-oleic safflower, sunflower, peanut, canola, and soybean oils. Yet, it is unlikely that these will take over the applications of olive oil, which is enjoyed as much for its flavor as for any nutritional advantages it may have. As already noted, because they are not refined, virgin olive oils have a pleasant and characteristic flavor, and of all the major vegetable oils, only olive oil is sold unrefined. The deodorization process undergone by other oils removes compounds that would otherwise produce flavors unsuitable for many applications. In addition, some oils have flavors that can only be characterized as unpleasant.

Olive oil has a moderate amount of tocopherols, primarily alpha-tocopherol. Despite a low level of gamma-tocopherol, olive oil is remarkably stable, which is attributable to its low levels of linoleic and linolenic acids, as well as phenolic compounds that are present. Minor components in olive oil are not removed because the oil is not refined; the levels of some of these compounds are shown in Table II.E.1.3. Finally, it should be noted that olive oil contains very low levels of phospholipids and waxes, which permits the production of a clear oil without refining.

Table II.E.1.3. *Levels of minor components in olive oil*

Component	Mg percentage
Squalene	125–750
Sterols	125–250
Triterpene alcohols	50
Chlorophyll	0.06–0.22
Carotenoids	0.06–0.95

Soybean Oil

The soybean *(Glycine max* L., formerly *Soja max)*, of the family Leguminosae, is grown worldwide for its high-protein content and its oil. There are wild *(Glycine ussuriensis)* and intermediate *(Glycine gracilis)* as well as cultivated *(G. max)* soybean varieties. Although soybeans have been used as food in China for thousands of years, their development as the world's primary oilseed has only taken place since the mid-1940s.

As mentioned (and as shown in Figure II.E.1.2), the production of soybean oil today overshadows all others. The soybean contains 40 to 50 percent protein and an average of 18 to 20 percent lipids (Table II.E.1.1). Its oil is a byproduct of the production of soybean meal, which is primarily used as animal feed. The oil obtained directly from soybeans contains about 88 percent neutral lipid (triacylglycerols and sterols), 10 percent phospholipid, and 2 percent glycolipid. Refined oil contains more than 99 percent triacylglycerols, and it is necessary to remove the phospholipids to produce a stable, clear oil. Like other vegetable oils, save that from olives, soybean oil is usually refined, bleached, and deodorized before use.

Soybeans contain a number of antinutritional compounds, including protease inhibitors, hemagglutinins, saponins, goitrogens, allergens, phytic acid, and oligosaccharides (raffinose, stachyose), as well as isoflavones (phytoesterogens). However, because these compounds are not transferred to the lipid, the oil is essentially devoid of them.

Soybean oil is one of the two common oils that contain appreciable levels of omega-3 fatty acids, and it is ironic that at the same time that some investigators were discovering the important roles played by omega-3 fatty acids in the human diet, other researchers were working to reduce the levels of these fatty acids in soybean oil (Hammond 1992). The reason for the interest in lowering linolenic acid in soybean oil (which ranges from 5.5 to 10 percent) is that it oxidizes at a rate some 2 or more times greater than linoleic acid, which, in turn, oxidizes at a rate about 10 times lower than oleic acid (Hammond 1994). Lowering linolenic acid levels results in a more stable oil; the more unsaturated the oil, the less stable it will be. In the past, soybean oils have been lightly hydrogenated (brush hydrogenation) to reduce the linolenic acid content to less than 3 percent. This is uncommon today because of health interests in oils with no trans acids and also because of problems with cloudiness at refrigeration temperatures.

Recently, there has also been a great deal of interest in reducing the amount of palmitic acid in soybean oil, which is a major dietary source of it. This is because palmitic acid is thought to be one of the three saturated fatty acids most responsible for raising plasma cholesterol in humans (the other two are myristic acid and lauric acid). Varieties of soybeans with modified fatty acid composition have been developed, including low-linolenic, high-stearic, high-oleic, high-palmitic/low-linolenic, high-palmitic, and low-saturate/low-linolenic.

The low-saturate/low-linolenate composition, shown in Table II.E.1.4, has much lower palmitic acid levels than traditional soybean varieties; the other fatty acids are relatively constant. The linolenic and oleic acids are at the high end of the fatty acid ranges in normal soybeans. Lowering the palmitic acid content of soybeans has been a major improvement in terms of nutritional value, and more varieties of oilseeds with tailor-made fatty acid compositions for specific purposes should be seen in the future.

The tocopherol composition of soybean oil is shown in Table II.E.1.5. It should be noted that, in some reported analyses of vitamin E compounds, the beta and gamma isomers are combined, whereas other analyses do not report these isomers. The beta and gamma tocopherols are very similar in structure (Figure II.E.1.4). For most vegetable oils, the alpha and gamma isomers predominate. The alpha isomer is by far the most bioactive of the tocopherol isomers (Table II.E.1.6), but the antioxidant effect appears to be greater for the gamma isomer. Tocopherols are reduced during the refining process at the deodorization stage. Roughly 30 percent of the total tocopherols are removed. The data presented in Table II.E.1.6 are for refined, bleached, and deodorized (RBD) oils.

Table II.E.1.4. *Fatty acid compositions (weight percentage) of modified fatty acid vegetable oils*

	High oleic peanut	Low erucic acid rapeseed (canola)	High oleic sunflower	Low saturate, low linolenate soybean
16:0	5.1	3.9	3.4	3.4
16:1	<0.1	0.2	0	0
18:0	2.3	1.3	4.8	3.4
18:1	80.4	58.2	81.0	32.5
18:2ω6	2.4	21.6	8.1	57.4
18:3ω3	<0.1	12.1	0.49	3.3
20:0	1.3	0.5	0.23	0
20:1	2.1	1.6	0.27	0
22:0	3.0	0.4	1.1	0
22:1	<0.1	<0.1	0	0
24:0	2.1	0	0.36	0
26:0	0.47	0	0	0

Table II.E.1.5. *Tocopherol isomer distribution in dietary fats and oils (µg/g)*

	α	β	γ	δ	α-tocotrienol
Soybean	75–116	34	662–797	266–400	2
Palm	288–360	–	280–360	80	146
Sunflower	110–610	10	30	10	–
Rapeseed	70–190	16	178–430	7.4–40	0.4
Peanut	60–169	5.4	100–200	13	–
Cottonseed	320	–	313	–	5
Coconut	20	–	2.4	–	–
Olive	70–154	–	7.3–25	1–3	–
Cod Liver	220	–	–	–	–
Herring	92	–	–	–	–
Menhaden	75	–	–	–	–
Lard	12	–	–	–	–
Tallow	27	–	–	–	–

Table II.E.1.6. *Approximate biological activity relationships of vitamin E compounds*

Compound	Percentage activity of *d-α*-tocopherol
d-α-tocopherol	100
l-α-tocopherol	26
dl-α-tocopherol	74
dl-α-tocopheryl acetate	68
d-β-tocopherol	50
d-γ-tocopherol	10
d-δ-tocopherol	3
d-β-tocotrienol	30

Tocopherol	R_1	R_2
alpha	CH$_3$	CH$_3$
beta	CH$_3$	H
gamma	H	CH$_3$
delta	H	H

Tocotrienol	R_1	R_2
alpha	CH$_3$	CH$_3$
beta	CH$_3$	H
gamma	H	CH$_3$
delta	H	H

Figure II.E.1.4. Tocopherol composition of soybean oil.

Palm Oil

Although there are many different palms that can provide oil, palm oil of commercial importance is obtained from the African oil palm, *Elaeis guineensis.* The name *Elaeis* is derived from the Greek word for oil. Palm oil is obtained from the fruit, whereas palm kernel oil comes from the seed kernel. Their fatty acid compositions are different, with palm kernel oil having a high content of lauric acid (palm kernel oil is similar to coconut oil in fatty acid composition). Palm oil is currently one of the most common oils worldwide, and oil amounts have increased dramatically since the 1980s.

Palm oil use in human diets can be dated back as far as 3000 B.C. Crude palm oil has a long history of use in western Africa, and in the eighteenth century, trade in the oil began between Africa and Europe. Wild palms are still a significant source of oil in West Africa, but recent increases in oil-palm cultivation have occurred in Latin America and Southeast Asia, with about 70 percent of present-day world palm oil production centered in the latter region.

Palm is the highest yielding of the oil-bearing plants, with an average of between 4 and 10 tons of oil per hectare per annum. Three types of palm have been characterized: *Dura,* with a thin flesh and thick, hard shell; *pisifera,* with thick flesh and little or no shell; and *tenera,* with a thick flesh and intermediate shell. The *tenera* variety is a cross between a *dura* female and pollen-bearing *pisifera.* Because the progeny of *tenera* are not uniform, cloning (asexual reproduction) of this palm has been practiced to improve yield and quality.

Traditional processing of palm to obtain palm oil, as practiced by the local populations, includes separation of the fruit, softening of the fruit, maceration, pressing, and oil purification. The softening process usually takes place by allowing the fruit to ferment in a pile for several days. The fruit may be further softened by boiling and then maceration in a mortar. After placement in a large oil-impermeable container, the oil is separated by kneading the material. Oil is skimmed from the top and may be filtered and then heated to remove the water.

The quantity of recovered oil in older traditional processing was low (less than 40 to 50 percent of total oil), and the quality of this crude oil was poor, compared to oil extracted and refined with more modern methods. If the fruits are not quickly heat treated, the free fatty acid level increases rapidly because of fungal lipases, and indeed, free fatty acid contents as high as 50 percent have been measured in traditionally processed oils. The flavor of oil with a high free fatty acid content is preferred in some areas of West Africa, where palm oils have traditionally been unrefined and have always had a high free fatty acid content. However, for most people, very high free fatty acid levels usually make the oil unsuitable for food use and more amenable to industrial applications, such as soap making. Oils obtained from wild trees by traditional processes are classified as soft (less than 12 percent),

Table II.E.1.7. *Nontriacylglycerol materials in crude palm oil*

Component	Concentration (ppm)
Carotenoids	500–700
Vitamin E compounds	699–1,000
Sterols and sterol esters	360–600
Squalane and aliphatic hydrocarbons	250–550

semisoft (less than 35 percent), or hard (greater than 45 percent), depending on the free fatty acid levels.

Crude palm oil contains a number of nontriacylglycerol components, including carotenoids, tocopherols and tocotrienols, sterols and sterol esters, phospholipids, and hydrocarbons (including squalane). The levels of these compounds in crude palm oil are shown in Table II.E.1.7. Palm oil contains very high levels of tocopherols and alpha tocotrienal (Table II.E.1.5). The carotenoids include lycopene and alpha and beta-carotene and are the cause of the deep red color of the oil. The main carotenoids are alpha- and beta-carotene, which make up over 90 percent of the total. Although there is experimental evidence linking dietary intake of carotene with protection against some types of cancer, the current practice is to remove the carotenes by bleaching to produce light-colored oil. Moreover, removing the carotenoids substantially improves the oxidative stability.

Recently, there has been a campaign virtually condemning the so-called tropical oils (palm, palm kernel, and coconut oils) as bad for human health. The argument has been that because they are high in saturated fats, these oils raise cholesterol levels in the body. Food products have been labeled "we use no tropical oils," their manufacturers and processors employing partially hydrogenated oils instead. Yet the notion that the addition of tropical oils to food products could lead to an increase in cardiovascular deaths ignores the fact that at least in Western diets (and especially in the United States), animal products and soybean oil are the main sources of saturated fats in the diet. It also ignores the cloud of suspicion now enveloping the use of partially hydrogenated oils.

The fatty acid composition of palm oil is quite different from that of coconut or palm kernel oil. The latter are lauric oils with about 80 to 90 percent saturated fat, predominantly lauric acid (41 to 55 percent), myristic acid (13 to 23 percent), and palmitic acid (4 to 12 percent). Palm oil is rich in oleic acid and low in saturates (less than 50 percent), relative to coconut and palm kernel oils. Experimental evidence so far indicates that there is no nutritional danger posed by the inclusion of palm oil in a Western diet, nor, for that matter, is such a danger posed by diets that derive a high percentage of total fat from palm oil (Berger 1994; Ong, Choo, and Ooi 1994). In fact, when palm oil is added to a Western diet, the level of plasma HDL cholesterol typically rises, leading to a better LDL:HDL ratio, and this ratio – rather than the amount of total plasma cholesterol – appears to be the better indicator of the risk of coronary artery disease.

Palm oil can be fractionated to produce olein and stearin fractions; when heated to about 28° C, some 25 percent of the total remains solid (palm stearin). The liquid fraction (palm olein) has a greater unsaturated fatty acid content and can be further fractionated at 20–22° C (facilitated by the addition of a solvent) to yield a more liquid fraction, as well as an intermediate one. The fatty acid compositions of palm olein and palm stearin are shown in Table II.E.1.8. These fractions can be used for particular applications; for example, palm olein is commonly added to infant formulas because of its high oleic acid content. Plastic fats containing zero trans fatty acids are developed by interesterifying palm stearin and a more saturated fat, such as palm kernel oil. Palm olein has been used as a frying medium and has excellent stability because of its low linoleic and linolenic acid content and high levels of tocopherols. Cocoa butter equivalents can also be developed by using intermediate palm oil fractions.

Sunflower Oil

The sunflower *(Helianthus annuus)* is a wildflower that originated in the Americas. It was taken to Spain in 1569 for ornamental use, but later was grown for its oilseeds, especially in Russia. Newer, high-oil strains of sunflower have been developed, with oil contents upwards of 40 percent, as compared with 20 to 32 percent for traditional varieties.

Sunflower oil has a naturally high level of linoleic acid and is low in linolenic acid. The fatty acid composition of sunflower oil is highly variable and depends on climate, temperature, genetic composition, stage of maturity, and even the positions of individual seeds on the head of the flower. As the temperature of a region of sunflower cultivation increases, the oleic acid content increases and that of linoleic acid decreases, although together they always comprise about 90 percent of the fatty acids in sunflower oil.

Table II.E.1.8. *Fatty acid compositions (weight percentage) in palm olein and stearin*

Fatty acid	Olein	Stearin
12:0	0.1–1.1	0.1–0.6
14:0	0.9–1.4	1.1–1.9
16:0	37.9–41.7	7.2–73.8
16:1ω7	0.1–0.4	0.05–0.2
18:0	4.0–4.8	4.4–5.6
18:1ω9	40.7–43.9	15.9–37.0
18:2ω6	10.4–13.4	3.2–9.8
18:3ω3	0.1–0.6	0.1–0.6
20:0	0.2–0.5	0.1–0.6

A typical fatty acid composition in cold environments includes 14 percent oleic acid and 75 percent linoleic acid, whereas in warm environments, it is 50 percent oleic and 43 percent linoleic acid. Because most sunflowers are grown in moderate climates, however, the actual variation in sunflower oil composition is, as a rule, not as marked as it might be.

New varieties of sunflower oil have been developed with modified fatty acid compositions. The fatty acid composition of a sunflower oil high in oleic acid is shown in Table II.E.1.4. High-oleic sunflower oils originated in Russia in the mid–1970s as a result of selective breeding and mutagenesis. The original Russian high-oleic line, "Prevenets," has been developed into sunflower lines that have a stable high–oleic acid composition minimally affected by growing temperature (Morrison, Hamilton, and Kalu 1994). The high-oleic acid and low-linoleic acid composition makes the oil very suitable for frying, and the oxidative stability of products fried in high-oleic sunflower oil is excellent. However, flavor quality has been reported to suffer if the linoleic acid level is too low.

Crude sunflower oil contains a number of non-triglyceride components, including waxes, sterols, hydrocarbons, and tocopherols. Waxes, which create problems because they produce clouding of the oil, are removed in a process whereby the oil is cooled and the solids that develop are filtered off. The tocopherols in sunflower oil consist primarily of alpha-tocopherol, which is good from the viewpoint of human nutrition because this tocopherol is the most biopotent form of vitamin E. However, tocopherols stabilize oils from oxidation, and the gamma and delta forms are much more active antioxidants in vitro than the alpha. In sunflower oil, the low levels of these tocopherols produce a lower-than-expected oxidative stability when compared to other vegetable oils with a higher degree of unsaturation.

Rapeseed (Canola) Oil

Rapeseeds include a number of closely related species in the genus *Brassica*. The three main species *(Brassica nigra, B. oleracea, and B. campestris)* have been manipulated by hybridization and chromosome doubling to produce *B. napus, B. carinata,* and *B. juncea.* The different Brassica species have different seed sizes, colors, oil contents, and proximate compositions. The term "rapeseed" is used for any oil-bearing Brassica seed, including that of mustard. Common names for some rapeseed species are shown in Table II.E.1.9.

The use of rapeseed oil for food and illumination originated in Asia (later spreading to the Mediterranean and Europe), and today, it is the most widely used cooking oil in Canada, Japan, and some other countries. Cultivated in India at least 3,000 years ago, rapeseed was introduced into China and Japan by the time of Christ. By the thirteenth century, rapeseed was cultivated for oil in Europe - especially eastern

Table II.E.1.9. *Common names for rapeseed species*

B. napus	Rape, rapeseed, oil rape, oilseed rape, swede rape
B. campestris	Turnip rape, rapeseed, oil turnip, polish rape
B. juncea	Leaf mustard, Oriental mustard, Indian mustard, rapeseed
B. nigra	Black mustard
B. oleracea	Kale, cabbage

Europe - and recently, it has been grown in Canada and the United States. Its first use was probably as an oil for lamps and lubrication; in addition, the nourishing oil cake residue of rapeseed makes a good feed for cattle.

Research in the 1960s showed that the erucic acid found in rapeseed oil caused fatty infiltration of the heart and changes in the cardiac muscle in experimental animals. The oil was therefore banned in many places, and although subsequent work showed that rapeseed oil presented no threat to human health, there were intensive efforts to develop low–erucic acid cultivars of the plant. In 1985, the U.S. Food and Drug Administration (FDA) conferred a GRAS ("Generally Recognized As Safe") status on rapeseed products; not only was the oil deemed safe, but because of its very low content of saturated fat, it suddenly became viewed as the most healthy of cooking oils. Following the GRAS designation, U.S. production increased greatly, from 27 million pounds in 1987 to almost 420 million by 1994 (Trager 1995). In addition to its own production, the United States imports huge amounts of the oilseeds from Canada, although the end product's name was changed, understandably, from rapeseed to Canola oil.

Recent developments in rapeseed breeding have resulted in seeds that are modified in fatty acid composition, and low–erucic acid rapeseed (LEAR) oils have been produced by Canadian breeding work with *B. napus* and *B. campestris* (Table II.E.1.4). Double-low oils also are low in glucosinolates and include Canola (formerly Canbra) oil. To be considered a Canola or LEAR oil, the erucic acid content must be lower than 3.5 percent, although typically the level is less than 1 percent.

Canola oils are similar to soybean oils in that they contain appreciable levels of linolenic acid. Although some other vegetable oils have higher levels (for example, oils from flax seed or linseed contain about 55 percent linolenic acid), these are not common in the diet and are subject to very rapid rates of oxidation. In no small part because it has the lowest saturated fat content of any major cooking oil, Canola has been called an ideal mixture for health, nutrition, and food use (Ackman 1990). The oil has high amounts of oleic acid, reasonably low linoleic acid, and a moderate omega-6 to omega-3 ratio. The high-oleic level is beneficial nutritionally, as oleic acid tends to lower LDL cholesterol, with no drop – and even a slight increase – in HDL cholesterol, resulting in a net positive change in the HDL:LDL ratio.

Peanut Oil

The peanut or groundnut *(Arachis hypogea)*, like the bean, is a member of the family Leguminosae. It is native to South America, probably originating in or around lowland Bolivia, but as early as 3100 to 2500 B.C., peanuts were common on the coast of Peru, and by the time of the Columbian voyages, they had spread throughout much of the New World (Coe 1994). In the sixteenth century, the peanut was carried to West Africa from Brazil by Portuguese traders, and because it was first brought to the United States from West Africa in slave ships, the misconception arose that the plant was of African origin.

While the Portuguese moved the peanut eastward, the Spaniards carried it west. It was introduced into the Philippines by Ferdinand Magellan and spread thereafter to other parts of Asia. Peanuts can be grouped into four different types: Runner, Spanish, Virginia, and Valencia. Runner peanuts are small and high yielding, Spanish are small seeded, and Virginia are large seeded. Valencia are large seeded and are often found with 3 to 5 seeds per pod.

Normal peanut oil has almost no linolenic acid and about 25 percent linoleic acid. As a rule, it contains about 50 percent oleic acid and is considered a premium oil for food use because of its excellent stability and its pleasant, nutty flavor. As with some other oilseeds, temperature affects the fatty acid composition, with cool climates resulting in greater linoleic and lower oleic acid levels. High-oleic peanuts were developed at the University of Florida during the 1980s and have subsequently become commercially available. A typical fatty acid composition of a high-oleic peanut oil is shown in Table II.E.1.4. Peanut oil, including the high-oleic variety, is characterized by relatively high levels of long-chain saturated fatty acids (up to 6 percent), up to and including 26:0. High-oleic peanut oil is between 7 and 10 times more stable in the face of oxidation than normal peanut oil (O'Keefe, Wright, and Knauft 1993), and roasted high-oleic peanuts have about twice the shelf life of normal peanuts (Mugendi, Braddock, and O'Keefe 1997; Mugendi et al. 1998).

P. J. White (1992) has pointed out that in the past, peanut oil was wrongly reported to contain significant levels of linolenic acid because of the mistaken identification of 20:0 or 20:1ω9 as linolenic acid. Depending on analytical conditions, it is possible to have coelution of linolenic and 20:0 or 20:1ω9. Similarly, reports exist in which arachidonic acid (20:4ω6) has been mistakenly identified in vegetable oils but, in fact, arachidonic acid has never been found in vegetable oils.

Cottonseed Oil

Cotton (any of the various plants of the genus *Gossypium*) has been grown for its fiber – used in the manufacture of rope and textiles – for close to 5,000 years. Doubtless, in the distant past, the oil-rich cotton seeds were also utilized for illumination, as a lubricant, and probably for medicinal purposes. Indeed, most of the vegetable oils seem to have been first utilized for such nonfood applications.

The widespread use of cottonseed oil, however, is a relatively recent phenomenon that began in the United States. Some of the oil is derived from the extra-long staple *G. barbadense,* but the overwhelming bulk of the world's production (90 to 98 percent) comes from the short staple *G. hirsutum,* and short-staple cotton had to await the invention of the cotton gin by Eli Whitney in 1793 to become commercially viable. Thereafter, short-staple cotton spread across the southern United States, and surplus seed was converted into oil. Initial attempts at commercialization, however, were unsuccessful: Unlike long-staple cotton, the short-staple species had a tough seed coat that retained lint.

This problem was resolved in the middle 1850s with the invention of a machine to crack the hulls. High oil prices encouraged cottonseed oil extraction, and in the late 1880s, the Southern Cotton Oil Company was founded in Philadelphia. Its many seed-crushing mills, located throughout the South from the Carolinas to Texas, made it the largest producer of cottonseed oil, as well as the first U.S. manufacturer to make vegetable shortening.

One problem that remained was the odor of cottonseed oil, but this was eliminated at about the turn of the twentieth century with a deodorizing process invented by the company's chemist David Wesson. The procedure involved vacuum and high-temperature processing and led to the production of Wesson Oil, which revolutionized the cooking-oil industry (Trager 1995). Thereafter, cottonseed oil became the first vegetable oil to be used in the United States and then the dominant oil in the world's vegetable oil market until the 1940s.

Cottonseeds contain gossypol, which is produced in the seed glands and must be removed or destroyed in both oil and meal. Gossypol is heavily pigmented and can produce a dark color in the oil, and it is also toxic. Fortunately, it can be almost completely removed during the refining process, and in addition, glandless seeds devoid of gossypol have been developed.

Crude cottonseed oil contains as much as 1 percent of cyclic fatty acids. The main fatty acids are malvalic and sterculic, which are present in the form of glycerides. Cottonseed oil is characterized by a high saturated fat level, which is much higher than that of corn, canola, soybean, sunflower, peanut, and safflower oils.

Coconut Oil

The coconut palm *(Cocos nucifera)* has been enthusiastically described as the "tree of life" or the "tree of heaven" because it provides leaves and fiber for the construction of dwellings and shells for utensils, as well as food, milk, and oil. Although the coconut palm has been exploited by humans for millennia, its origin is subject to debate, with some scholars claiming it to be native to South America and others supporting a Southeast Asian origin. The question is a difficult one because coconuts can still germinate after floating on the ocean for months, a capability which has facilitated their spread throughout the tropical world. Compared with other oilseed crops, coconuts have a high per-acre yield of oil, about half of which is used in nonfood applications (such as soaps and cosmetics), whereas the other half goes into foods.

Coconut oil is extracted from the dried meat of the nuts (copra). Copra has one of the highest fat contents of all the materials used for oil (Table II.E.1.1), making it easy to obtain oil by pressing. Coconut oil contains high levels of the medium chain saturated fatty acids (10:0, 12:0, and 14:0) and is solid at room temperature.

The saturation of coconut oil confers a high degree of stability toward oxidation, but hydrolysis of coconut oil to yield free fatty acids causes soapy off-flavors because of the free lauric acid present. Fatty acids longer than lauric acid, however, produce little or no off-flavor.

Animal Fats and Oils

Milkfat (Butter)

Milkfats are derived from any number of different animals, but most by far is provided by the bovine; consequently, in this chapter, milkfat means that from cows. A lactating cow can produce as much as 30 kg of milk per day with a milkfat level of 2.6 to 6 percent, and thus for many years, butterfat was produced in greater quantity than any other fat or oil.

Milkfat, which has a much more complex composition than any of the other common fats, contains about 97 to 98 percent triglycerides, 0.1 to 0.44 percent free fatty acids, 0.22 to 0.41 percent cholesterol, and 0.2 to 1.0 percent phospholipids. More than 500 different fatty acids have been identified in milk lipids. The fatty acid patterns in milkfat are complicated by mammary synthesis of short-chain fatty acids and extensive involvement of rumen bacteria in lipid synthesis and modification (Jensen 1994). As a rule, butterfat is predominantly composed of palmitic acid, followed by oleic and myristic acids (Table II.E.1.10). About 66 percent of the fatty acids in a typical milkfat are saturated. The trans fatty acid levels in milkfat have reportedly ranged between 4 and 8 percent.

Table II.E.1.10. *Fatty acid composition of butterfat (weight percentage)*

Fatty acid	Range
4:0	2.8–4.0
6:0	1.4–3.0
8:0	0.5–1.7
10:0	1.7–3.2
12:0	2.2–4.5
14:0	5.4–14.6
16:0	26–41
18:0	6.1–11.2
10:1	0.1–0.3
12:1	0.1–0.6
14:1ω5	0.6–1.6
16:1ω7	2.8–5.7
18:1ω9	18.7–33.4
18:2ω6	0.8–3.0

There has been a great deal of interest over the past 30 years in modifying the fatty acid composition of butterfat to decrease the saturated fat content (Sonntag 1979b). Because cows have a rumen, fats that are directly provided in the diet are extensively degraded and hydrogenated. The fat also can have negative effects on the rumen bacteria, causing a lowering of milk and milkfat production. This problem has been solved by providing "protected" fats to the animal.

Methods of protecting fats from rumen metabolism include the polymerizing of protein around fat with formaldehyde and the preparation of calcium soaps, which are mostly insoluble at rumen pH. Dairy fats with high linoleic acid contents have been developed, but they suffer from severe quality problems and are unmarketable (McDonald and Scott 1977).

Recently, dairy fats have been prepared with high oleic and low saturate composition by feeding a calcium salt of high-oleic sunflower oil (Lin et al. 1996a, 1996b). This has provided lower saturated fatty acid composition and higher monoene while maintaining product quality. Oleic acid oxidizes about 10 times more slowly than linoleic acid and provides a better health benefit.

Marine Fats

Marine fats and oils, which are among the oldest exploited by humans for food and other uses, are divided into those from fish (cod, herring, menhaden, sardine, and so forth), from fish livers (cod, shark, halibut), and from marine mammals (whales). Marine oils are characterized by a very complex composition compared to vegetable oils and many animal fats, which poses challenges in the accurate identification and quantification of their fatty acids. Moreover, data derived from old technology may not be accurate.

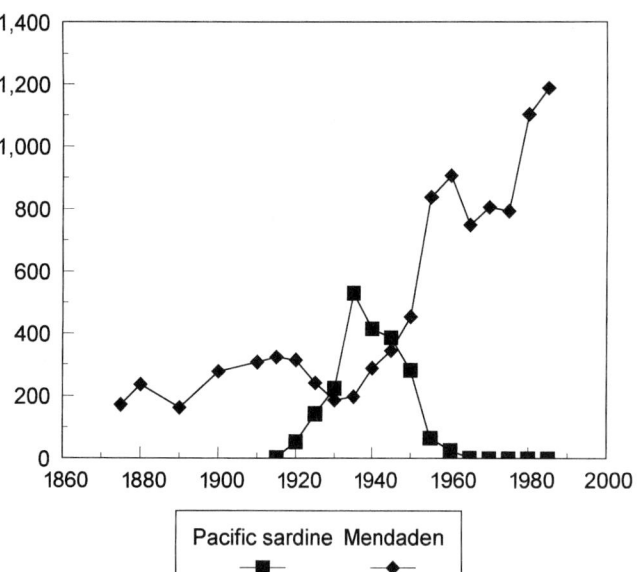

Figure II.E.1.5. Effects of overfishing in Pacific sardine fishery, 1918–60.

Fish oils. Fish oils are obtained from tissues that contain a high fat content, including those of herring, pilchard, menhaden, and anchovy. The production of the various fish oils is dependent on both fishing efforts and overfishing. In Figure II.E.1.5, it can be seen that the Pacific sardine fishery was extremely successful for about 20 years, after which the fish stocks were depleted so that a fishery could no longer be supported. It is sad to note that this is the rule rather than the exception in many fisheries worldwide.

Early production methods consisted of boiling the fish in water, followed by pressing, and then removing the oil by skimming. Improved oil quality and recovery was obtained as steam cooking and screw presses were introduced. Much of the fish oil produced in earlier days went into nonfood uses, such as linoleum, paints, and soaps.

Currently, oils from marine sources constitute some 2 to 4 percent of the world's consumption of fats, and about one-third of the world's fish catch consists of small and bony but high-fat fish that are converted into fish meal and oil. Fish oils for food use are often partially hydrogenated because they oxidize rapidly in comparison with vegetable or animal fats and oils. Partial hydrogenation results in a loss of polyunsaturated fatty acids, monoenes, dienes, and trienes, which obviously has negative effects on the nutritional value of hydrogenated oils. Because of the interest in omega-3 fatty acids found in fish oils, recent work has focused on the incorporation of processed, but not hydrogenated, fish oils in food products.

Fish liver oils. The livers of some fish have a high fat content and are rich in vitamins A and D. Although

many different species of fish (for example, pollock, haddock, shark, halibut) have been exploited for their liver oils, the cod has provided more than 90 percent of the total volume. Cod livers contain from 20 to 70 percent fat; the range is so great because codfish deposit fat prior to spawning and deplete it during spawning. Thus, there is a cyclical fat content in their livers, and this has a dilution effect on the levels of the fat-soluble vitamins.

Cod liver oil was reportedly used for medicinal purposes in the eighteenth century, long before the discovery of vitamins or an understanding of most nutritional diseases. Medical uses included treatment of bone afflictions, rheumatism, tuberculosis, and, later, rickets. There was an intensive search for the active ingredient in cod liver oil that caused such positive therapeutic effects. The hunt was described by F. P. Moller (1895: 69):

> The oldest of these active principles, iodine, was detected as one of the oil's constituents as far back as 1836. . . . When the iodine active principle was exploded another, trimethylamine, took its place, and as a result herring brine, from being a rather neglected commodity, became for a short time the desideratum of the day. After a quick succession of other active principles, too evanescent to be worthy of even an obituary notice, the turn came for the free fatty acids. No theory and no fact then supported the idea that these acids were the active principle. . . . Still, the belief entered some active mind that they were the essential constituents.

Moller concluded incorrectly that there was no specific active principle in cod liver oil. Yet, liver oils provide fat-soluble vitamins. However, when consumed at the levels required to derive significant health benefit from the fatty acids present in fish liver oils, there is a risk of hypervitaminosis A or D.

The levels of fat-soluble vitamins in various fish liver oils are shown in Table II.E.1.11. Excessive levels of both vitamins A and D_3 can be toxic. Although the actual value is not clear, as little as 50 micrograms of vitamin D_3 per day over extended periods appears to produce toxicity symptoms in humans (Groff, Gropper, and Hunt 1995). Daily levels of 250 micrograms for several months have resulted in soft-tissue calcification, hypertension, renal failure, and even death. The recommended daily intake of vitamin D is 5 to 10 micrograms. The vitamin D level in fish oils ranges up to 750 micrograms per gram. Obviously, extended daily use of a high-potency fish oil should be avoided. Cod liver oil, which constitutes the majority of all liver oils sold today, has modest but nutritionally significant levels ranging up to 7.5 micrograms per gram.

The recommended daily intake of vitamin A is 1,000 retinol equivalents. One retinol equivalent is equal to 1 microgram of all-trans retinol. Toxicity is seen at levels around 10 times greater than the RDA, so that a daily intake of 10 mg of all-trans retinol would result in toxic symptoms. Symptoms of toxicity include itchy skin, headache, anorexia, and alopecia. The extremely high vitamin A levels in some liver oils would make it fairly easy to consume toxic amounts of vitamin A.

Whale oils. Whale oils are derived from marine mammals. The worldwide production of whale oils has decreased as populations of whales have been depleted. Oils from the baleen whales (sei, right, blue, humpback, and minke), as well as toothed and sperm whales, have been employed in industrial applications and human food use. Sperm whales *(Physeter macrocephalus),* in particular, were prized in the past for their "spermaceti" oil, which was used in smokeless lamps, as a fine lubricant, in cosmetics, and in automatic transmission oils. One sperm whale could yield 3 to 4 tons of spermaceti.

Whale oils saw food use in some, but not all, countries when whale harvests were high. Europe, Canada, and Japan, for example, utilized hydrogenated whale oil in margarines for almost 50 years. During that time, the production of fish oils was much lower, increasing only as the production of whale oil decreased. Whale oils were also employed in the manufacture of shortenings after hydrogenation, a process which results in the production of many trans fatty acid monoene isomers.

Conclusion

The types and amounts of fats and oils that have been consumed vary greatly worldwide among people and have changed significantly over the past century. Fatty acid intakes will undoubtedly change in the future as oilseeds with altered fatty acid compositions reach new markets.

Sean Francis O'Keefe

Bibliography

Ackman, R. G. 1989. Problems in fish oils and concentrates. In *Fats for the future,* ed. R. C. Cambie, 189-204. Chichester, England.
　1990. Canola fatty acids – An ideal mixture for health, nutrition and food use. In *Canola and rapeseed,* ed. F. Shahidi, 81-98. New York.
　1992. Fatty acids in fish and shellfish. In *Fatty acids in foods and their health implications,* ed. C. K. Chow, 95-135. New York.
Ackman, R. G., S. N. Hooper, and D. L. Hooper. 1974. Linolenic acid artifacts from the deodorization of oils. *Journal of the American Oil Chemists' Society* 51: 42-9.
Ackman, R. G. 1989. Marine mammals. In *Marine biogenic lipids, fats, and oils,* 2 vols. Vol. 2, ed. R. G. Ackman, 179-381. Boca Raton, Fla.
Bailey, B. E. 1952. Marine oils with special reference to those of Canada. *Fisheries Research Board of Canada Bulletin* 89: 1-413.
Berger, K. 1994. Oils from under-utilized palm and forest products. In *Technological advances in improved alternative sources of lipids,* ed. B. S. Kamel and Y. Kakuda, 209-34. New York.
Bimbo, A. P. 1990. Production of fish oil. In *Fish oils in nutrition,* ed. M. E. Stansby, 141-80. New York.
Braddock, J. C., C. A. Sims, and S. F. O'Keefe. 1995. Flavor and oxidative stability of roasted high oleic peanuts. *Journal of Food Science* 60: 489-93.
Chandler, William H. 1950. *Evergreen orchards.* Philadelphia, Pa
Chen, I. C., C. I. Wei, F. A. Chapman, et al. 1995. Differentiation of cultured and wild Gulf of Mexico sturgeon *(Acipenser oxyrinchus desotoi)* based on fatty acid composition. *Journal of Food Science* 60: 631-5.
Coe, Sophia D. 1994. *America's first cuisines.* Austin, Tex.
Formo, M. W. 1979. Fats in the diet. In *Bailey's industrial oil and fat products,* Vol. 1., ed. D. Swern, 233-70. New York.
Groff, J. L., S. S. Gropper, and S. M. Hunt. 1995. *Advanced nutrition and human metabolism.* St. Paul, Minn.

Table II.E.1.11. *Fat-soluble vitamin levels in fish liver oils*

Fish liver oil	Vitamin A, retinol equivalents/g	Vitamin D_3 μg/g
Cod	165-3,000	0.5-7.5
Haddock	45-900	1.3-1.9
Dogfish	60-45,000	0.1-0.7
Halibut	1,200-49,500	13.8-500
Mackerel	900-49,000	19-25
Tuna	15,000-300,000	400-750
Hake	480-960	0.25-3.3
Swordfish	6,000-120,000	50-625

Hammond, E. G. 1992. Genetic alteration of food fats and oils. In *Fatty acids in foods and their health implications,* ed. C. K. Chow, 313–27. New York.

  1994. Edible oils from herbaceous crops. In *Technological advances in improved alternative sources of lipids,* ed. B. S. Kamel and Y. Kakuda, 93–115. New York.

Holman, R. T. 1992. A long scaly tale - The study of essential fatty acid deficiency at the University of Minnesota. In *Essential fatty acids and eicosanoids,* ed. A. Sinclair and R. Gibson, 3–17. Champaign, Ill.

Hunter, J. E. 1992. Safety and health effects of isomeric fatty acids. In *Fatty acids in foods and their health implications,* ed. C. K. Chow, 857–68. New York.

Jensen, R. G. 1992. Fatty acids in milk and dairy products. In *Fatty acids in foods and their health implications,* ed. C. K. Chow, 95–135. New York.

Jones, L. A., and C. C. King, eds. 1993. *Cottonseed oil.* National Cottonseed Products Association. Memphis, Tenn.

Lin, M. P., C. A. Sims, C. R. Staples, and S. F. O'Keefe. 1996a. Flavor quality and texture of modified fatty acid high monoene low saturate butter. *Food Research International* 29: 367–72.

Lin, M. P., C. Staples, C. A. Sims, and S. F. O'Keefe. 1996b. Modification of fatty acids in milk by feeding calcium-protected high oleic sunflower oil. *Journal of Food Science* 61: 24–7.

McDonald, I. W., and T. W. Scott. 1977. Food of ruminant origin with elevated content of polyunsaturated fatty acids. *World Review of Nutrition and Dietetics* 26: 144–207.

McGee, Harold. 1984. *On food and cooking.* New York.

Moller, F. P. 1895. *Cod-liver oil and chemistry.* London.

Morrison, W. H., R. J. Hamilton, and C. Kalu. 1994. Sunflower seed oil. In *Developments in oils and fats,* ed. R. J. Hamilton, 132–52. New York.

Mugendi, J. B., J. C. Braddock, and S. F. O'Keefe. 1997. Flavor quality and stability of high oleic peanuts. In *Chemistry of novel foods,* ed. O. Mills, H. Okai, A. M. Spanier, and M. Tamura, 153–66. Carol Stream, Ill.

Mugendi, J. B., C. A. Sims, D. W. Gorbet, and S. F. O'Keefe. 1998. Flavor stability of high oleic peanuts stored at low humidity. *Journal of the American Oil Chemists' Society* 74: 21–5.

Nawar, W. W., S. K. Kim, Y. J. Li, and M. Vajdi. 1991. Measurement of oxidative interactions of cholesterol. *Journal of the American Oil Chemists' Society* 68: 496–8.

O'Keefe, S. F., D. Wright, and D. A. Knauft. 1993. Comparison of oxidative stability of high- and normal-oleic peanut oils. *Journal of the American Oil Chemists' Society* 70: 489–92.

O'Keefe, S. F., D. Wright, and V. Wiley. 1993. Effect of temperature on linolenic acid loss and 18:3 cct formation in soybean oil. *Journal of the American Oil Chemists' Society* 70: 915–17.

Ong, A. S. H., Y. M. Choo, and C. K. Ooi. 1994. Developments in palm oil. In *Developments in oils and fats,* ed. R. J. Hamilton, 153–91. New York.

Salunkhe, D. K., J. K. Chavan, R. N. Adsule, and S. S. Kadam. 1992. *World oilseeds, chemistry, technology and utilization.* New York.

Smith, L. L. 1987. Cholesterol oxidation. *Chemistry and Physics of Lipids* 44: 87–125.

Sonntag, N. O. V. 1979a. Sources, utilization and classification of oils and fats. In *Bailey's industrial oil and fat products,* Vol. 1, ed. D. Swern, 271–88. New York.

  1979b. Composition and characteristics of individual fats and oils. In *Bailey's industrial oil and fat products,* Vol. 1, ed. D. Swern, 289–478. New York.

Stansby, M. E. 1978. Development of fish oil industry in the United States. *Journal of the American Oil Chemists' Society* 55: 238–43.

Tannahill, Reay. 1988. *Food in history.* New York.

Thomas, L. M., and B. J. Holub. 1992. Nutritional aspects of fats and oils. In *Fatty acids in foods and their health implications,* ed. C. K. Chow, 16–49. New York.

Toussaint-Samat, Maguelonne. 1992. *A history of food,* trans. Anthea Bell. Cambridge, Mass.

Trager, James. 1995. *The food chronology.* New York.

Ward, Artemas. 1911. *The grocer's encyclopedia.* New York.

White, P. J. 1992. Fatty acids in oilseeds (vegetable oils). In *Fatty acids in foods and their health implications,* ed. C. K. Chow, 237–62. New York.

II.E.2 ❧ Coconut

Milk Bottle on the Doorstep of Mankind

In prehistoric times, the water content of the immature coconut fruit was more important as a drink than was any part of the mature nut as a food. In recent history, the emphasis has also been on a nonfood use of coconuts as oil. The oil extracted from the kernel of the ripe coconut is an industrial raw material for products ranging from soap to explosives. From prehistory to the present, coconut has served many human communities around the tropics in a variety of ways. In 1501, King Manuel of Portugal itemized some of its uses at a time when the coconut was first becoming known in Europe: "[F]rom these trees and their fruit are made the following things: sugar, honey, oil, wine, vinegar, charcoal and cordage . . . and matting and it serves them for everything they need. And the aforesaid fruit, in addition to what is thus made of it, is their chief food, particularly at sea" (Harries 1978: 277).

Unfortunately, it is not possible to provide as much information as one might want on the coconut in prehistory. This is because heat and humidity work against the preservation of fossils, and thus there is a dearth of archaeological materials, coprolites, and biological remains on tropical seashores where the coconut palm is native. Coconut residues do not accumulate because the palm grows and fruits the year round. This makes crop storage unnecessary and, in fact, because of their high water content, coconut seednuts cannot be stored; they either grow or rot. And the tender, or jelly, coconut is even less likely to survive in storage.

The sweet liquid in the immature fruit, however, is safe to drink where ground water may be saline or contaminated. It is a very pleasant drink, and coconuts are readily transported by land or sea.

In short, coconut is potable, palatable, and portable! Unlike drinks that are bottled, canned, or otherwise packaged, coconuts are sustainable and recyclable. It has been suggested that as the "milk bottle on the door step of mankind" (Harries 1981), the coconut could have played a significant role in the diets of our human ancestors in the time before agriculture.

Leafy Vegetables, Fruits, and Nuts

Millionaire's Salad

Although not strictly a green leafy vegetable, coconut heart of palm can be compared with blanched leafy vegetables, such as endive, or celery, or globe artichoke. It has been called "millionaire's salad" on the assumption that only the very rich can afford to fell an entire palm and have the leaf stalks cut away to expose the large bud, which is the part that is eaten. Palm hearts are best eaten fresh, but they can be cooked, canned, or pickled (Harries 1993).

Other palms can also be employed in this manner; indeed, with some palm species, harvesting heart of palm is a commercial operation. Certainly palm heart production could easily be commercialized for the coconut palm, especially in tropical coastal areas where tourism has replaced indigenous agriculture. One coconut heart may account for 40 side salads, and over-aged palms, overgrown seedlings from coconut nurseries, and those sprouting like weeds in neglected groves could be used for this purpose. It would even be practical to plant them at high density for sequential harvesting.

Farmers, however, are reluctant to cut down coconut palms, even when these are over-aged. They do not thin out palm stands that are too dense to be productive, and they usually ignore overgrown seedlings. All this may be attributable to a past in which the coconut palm was potentially the sole surviving food plant after a tidal wave or hurricane. Thus, the notion persists among some that to cut down a coconut palm threatens future life support. Moreover, in some communities, coconuts are planted to celebrate a birth, and if the palm dies or is felled, the human life it was planted to commemorate may be jeopardized. A recent example of the extreme reluctance to cut down the trees occurred during Liberia's civil war, when coconut palm hearts were eaten by the starving population only as a last resort.

Apple for the Teacher

Botanically, the coconut fruit is a drupe. Plums, peaches, and cherries, which are also drupes, have edible outer parts to encourage dissemination by animals. Other palms as well, particularly the date, have soft, sweet, and edible fruit, but the coconut is different because the outer covering, the husk, is generally bitter and stringy when young and dry and fibrous when mature. However, some rare individual coconut palms have an edible husk that is less fibrous, spongier, easily cut, and sweet to chew like sugar cane (Harries 1993).

The coconut "apple" is, botanically, the haustorium of the germinating seed. The haustorium begins to develop at the earliest stage of germination, even before the shoot or roots emerge through the husk. Coconuts harvested in this condition are suitable for domestic purposes or for second-grade copra, but generally not for desiccated coconut. Often the apple is put aside to eat. It is slightly sweet, and slightly oily, with a cottony texture. As the endosperm lasts up to 15 months during germination, a large apple is found in well-developed seedlings. In places where coconuts grow, children walking to school may grasp the leaves of a sprouted seednut and uproot it. Still holding it by the leaves, they swing it against the trunk of the nearest mature palm to split the husk and crack open the shell. Then they pick out and eat the apple (Harries 1993).

An unusual form of the mature coconut has a jelly-like endosperm. This can be eaten fresh, scooped with a spoon from the shell of the freshly cracked coconut. It is called *makapuno* in the Philippines, where it is highly esteemed, and *dikiri-pol* or similar names in India and Sri Lanka. It is known in other coconut-growing countries, such as Indonesia, and has been reported in the Solomon Islands. The most interesting fact about it is that the embryo is normal but can only be germinated under the artificial conditions of a tissue culture laboratory.

A coconut with aromatic endosperm, favored in Thailand for drinking and preparing a cooked dessert, is also known in Malaysia and Indonesia.

Lovely Bunch of Coconuts

The coconut has at times been treated as something of a joke by Europeans, and it was popularized in the music hall song, "I've got a luverly bunch of coconuts." Historically, it was first introduced to Europe as *Nux indica,* or the nut from the Indies. This was possibly a generic name applied to the shells of all other palms that survived the long overland journey; and it may have referred to nutmegs as well (Ridley 1912). Such nuts and shells were kept as novelties, and even ornamented (Fritz 1983).

Friar John of Montecorvino (around 1292) described *Nux indica* as "big as melons, and in colour green, like gourds. Their leaves and branches are like those of the date palm" (quoted in Desmond 1992: 9). But it was not until after the Portuguese sailed to the Indian Ocean in 1499, and brought back fresh samples, that the coconut was distinguished from other palm fruits and from the nutmeg (although people in the countries where these plants grow cannot imagine that such a confusion could exist).

After the fibrous husk is removed, the brown, hard-shelled nut can be split to expose the kernel. Unlike an almond, for example, which also has a fibrous outer covering, a shell, and a kernel, the coconut is generally not used as a nut because of its large size, although health food and vegetarian shops often include slices of coconut kernel in packets of mixed nuts. In England, coconuts sold in greengrocers' shops (without husks) are usually split open and hung outside for birds to feed on, especially in winter.

Oils, Fats, and Food

Fish and Chips

Coconut oil is most certainly a part of the diet in the countries where it grows. But equally importantly in those countries, it may be an unguent for the hair, an emollient for the body, a rust inhibitor for iron, and a fuel for lamps. Its first industrial use in Europe was as a lubricant in textile mills, although it subsequently became important to soap makers. Some of the latter are among today's industrial giants, and they still import coconut oil for the excellent lathering properties it imparts. It is interesting to note, however, that when soap manufacturers began using coconut oil, they unintentionally fostered the fish and chip shop.

This famous institution, the forerunner of all fast-food takeaways, became part of the social fabric in Britain (Harries 1988). Fish and chips date from the middle of the nineteenth century. Before then, local "soap-boilers" accumulated animal fat as the major ingredient of laundry soap. But animal fat was chiefly available in the winter months, when animals were slaughtered if they could not be fed, whereas coconut oil was available year-round from overseas colonial possessions that had an abundance both of the crop and of cheap labor.

Whether for soap or for cooking, coconut oil was particularly acceptable because it was convenient to handle. In a cool climate it does not even look like oil; below 20° to 26° C it becomes a greasy, somewhat crystalline, white or yellowish solid fat. In other words, outside the tropics, coconut oil becomes solid and resembles animal fat. It was also a good substitute for animal fat because there was no risk from infectious disease in its production.

The virtues of coconut oil were extolled at the beginning of the twentieth century in an advertisement for "Nut Lard" as:

an absolutely pure vegetable fat, extracted from the coco-nut. It is sweeter than ordinary lard or butter, and cheaper than either. It is white, odourless, does not turn rancid and is infinitely superior to ordinary lard for all culinary purposes. It can be used with the most delicate dishes without altering the natural flavour of the dish.

This advertisement went on to state that "'Nut Lard' contains neither salt nor water ... [and] [i]n cold weather, 'Nut Lard' may become hard – it should then be shredded before using. . . ." The most telling part of the advertisement was that "'Nut Lard' is unequalled

for frying fish, it does not splutter, there is no smell, and it can afterwards be strained and kept for future use" (Anon. 1912: 41–2).

It was in the nineteenth century that such flamboyant advertising became a significant factor in marketing. In particular, industrial soap makers started large-scale advertising of their products, with the prepackaged brand names that still survive today. Such competition put the small, local soap boilers out of business, and when they could no longer sell soap, they looked for something else to do with their existing equipment – deep copper pans over open fires. The coconut oil they had previously used for soap was now put to work frying fish and chips.

Coconut Oil

In coconut-growing countries, coconut oil is prepared in the home by heating coconut milk until a clear oil separates. Commercially, the extraction of oil from copra (dried or smoked coconut meat) is one of the oldest seed-crushing industries in the world. Extraction methods range from simple techniques employed in villages to modern high-pressure expellers and prepress or solvent extraction plants that can process more than 500 tons of copra a day. In Indonesia, some processors cook chopped fresh kernel in previously extracted coconut oil before pressing. Various methods have been developed for "wet" processing of edible grade oil and flour from fresh meat, but none are yet commercially viable (Harries 1993).

Coconut oil is the most important of the small group of commercial fats that contain a high proportion of glycerides of lower fatty acids. The chief fatty acids are lauric (45 percent), myristic (18 percent), palmitic (9 percent), oleic (8 percent), caprylic (7 percent), capric (7 percent), and stearic (5 percent). There is also a minute amount of tocopherol (vitamin E). The natural volatile flavor components of fresh meat and oil are mostly delta-lactones. Lauric oils are characterized by high saponification value and have the lowest iodine value of vegetable oils in common industrial use. Coconut oil, as it is ordinarily prepared in tropical countries, ranges from colorless to pale brownish yellow in hue. In temperate climates, or air conditioning, it appears as a greasy, somewhat white or yellowish, solid fat that has a melting point between 20° and 26° C. Until refined, it has a pronounced odor of coconut. Coconut oil is refined, bleached, and deodorized using standard vegetable oil–processing technology. If coconut oil is cooled until crystallization, part of the oil produces a semi-solid mass, which is then separated under hydraulic pressure.

The solid fraction, coconut stearine, is a harder fat with a higher melting point. It is used as a valuable confectionery fat and as a substitute for cocoa butter because of its brittleness and "snap" fracture. The liquid fraction, coconut oleine, has a correspondingly lower melting point and is used in margarine manufacture. Hydrogenation converts its unsaturated glycerides into stearic glycerides. The resulting product has a melting point higher than coconut stearine and is used as a brittle confectionery fat, which resembles cocoa butter. When refined and deodorized, coconut oil mixed with nonfat milk is often used as a replacement for whole milk. Other uses include the making of imitation dairy products, coffee whiteners, soft-serve desserts, frozen desserts, whipped toppings, milk shake mixes, and chocolate-filled milk.

Coconut oil is used because of its bland flavor, resistance to oxidation, and stability in storage, as well as a unique liquefying property that contributes to the "mouth-feel" of the food of which it is a component. The main nonedible uses are in soaps, detergent foam boosters, lubricating oil additives, mineral flotation agents, shampoo products, and corrosion inhibitors. Lauric oils enhance the lathering quality of soaps, and this quality makes coconut oil particularly useful for hard water or marine soaps. A feature of soapmaking with coconut oil is the higher yield of glycerol (14 percent compared with 10 percent for most oils). Other nonedible uses include illuminating or fuel oil in rural areas and in ceremonial lamps. Coconut stearine is also used to advantage in candle manufacture. Coconut oil will directly fuel unmodified diesel engines.

Copra

When the industrial demand for coconut oil developed in the nineteenth century, sailing schooners, and later tramp steamers, visited Pacific islands where the palm was plentiful. Fresh coconuts are a bulky and perishable cargo because of the husk and high water content. The fruit is made up of about 50 percent husk, 12 percent shell, 10 percent water, and only about 28 percent meat (kernel). The fresh coconut meat itself contains about 47 percent moisture. Thus, it was more convenient to ship copra, which the islanders could prepare in advance by drying the kernels, either in the sun or, if needed quickly, over a fire.

Commercial copra plantations today still use sun drying, direct firing over a barbecue, or indirect hot air in various sorts of kiln. The moisture content is reduced from between 45 and 50 percent to between 6 and 8 percent, and the oil content increases from 35 percent to between 60 and 65 percent. For safe storage, the moisture content of copra should be 6 percent, yet at the first point of sale it often has a much higher level. It dries further during storage, but molds may attack under such conditions. One of these is *Aspergillus flavus,* which produces aflatoxin. The possible presence of this carcinogen should serve as a stimulus for industry to improve copra quality or to bypass making it and process the fresh fruit instead (Harries 1993).

Edible (Ball) Copra

Copra may also form naturally inside the whole ripe nut. As early as the middle of the sixth century, Cosmas Indicopleutes said of the coconut: "If the fruit is gathered ripe and kept, then the water gradually turns solid on the shell, while the water left in the middle remains fluid, until of it also there is nothing left over" (Desmond 1992: 7). Copra formation occurs when nuts are kept in dry environments, and with those varieties that do not germinate quickly. The endosperm (kernel) eventually comes away from the shell and forms a ball of copra that rattles loosely inside the nut. The husk can remain intact so that the shell will not crack, and the whole copra-formation process requires some 8 to 12 months. Fires may be lit to help the drying. The heat and smoke do not contaminate the endosperm, which retains a very high quality (Harries 1993).

Copra Cake and Copra Meal

After the oil is extracted from copra, a good-quality residual cake will contain 6 to 8 percent oil, with a protein content of around 20 percent. Copra meal, the solvent-extracted residue, is 1 to 3 percent oil, depending on the efficiency of the plant. Cattle and poultry feeds incorporate both cake and meal; this combination results in firmer butter and harder body fat in cattle than that induced by other oil cakes. Cake with a high oil content is generally fed to pigs, but a deficiency in certain amino acids, notably tryptophan, lysine, methionine, and histidine, limits the amounts used in animal feeds. If aflatoxin is present in poorly prepared copra, it can pass into the cake or meal (Harries 1993).

Coconut Flour

Coconut flour suitable for human consumption is produced when oil is extracted from fresh coconut kernels rather than from copra. The flour is used in making bread and other foods. But, as just noted, it is not superior to other protein sources in the proportions of the various amino acids (Harries 1993).

Coconut–Confectionery

Sugar and Honey

The coconut palm is also a fine source of nectar. It begins to flower 3 to 5 years after planting, depending on growing conditions, and once started, it opens a new inflorescence regularly at 25- to 30-day intervals throughout the year. The palm goes on flowering for the remainder of its 80-year or longer life span. Every inflorescence includes hundreds of male flowers that open sequentially over a 3-week period, and each contains a drop of nectar when first open, which attracts honey bees and bumblebees in the early morning. Each inflorescence also carries female flowers, sometimes more than a hundred. For about a week each month, female flowers are receptive to pollination for a day or two and produce an almost continuous flow of nectar droplets from three exposed and easily accessible nectaries. The flowers are also visited by birds (honeyeaters), and even by lizards.

The activity of insects draws attention to the nectar, whose sweetness is readily sampled by touching with a finger (easily reached in young palms). These may have been the clues that encouraged early domesticators and cultivators to find a way of increasing the flow of nectar. This method is known as tapping, and it produces toddy, as described in detail in the section "Water into Wine."

Sweet toddy, boiled in shallow pans to its crystallization point, gives a 12 to 15 percent yield of jaggery. This rough sugar is hard, semicrystalline, and golden brown in color. A lesser degree of concentration gives treacle (or syrup) (Harries 1993). Beehives are often kept in coconut groves to enhance fruit set. The year-round flowering in a coconut plantation assures a perpetual supply of nectar, and the hives can also serve as sources of pollen.

Desiccated Coconut

The characteristic taste of coconuts (when mature) and, to a certain extent, their texture (when grated and dried, or desiccated), are among their most important features for spicing and flavoring. In the United Kingdom, television advertisements for a chocolate-covered, coconut-filled confection give an entertaining, but faulty, impression that the coconut falls from the palm already peeled and neatly split in half. In reality, the manual labor involved in making desiccated coconut, including harvesting, peeling, cracking, deshelling, and shredding, is far from amusing and not necessarily rewarding. Australians like their favorite cake covered with desiccated coconut, which makes Australia a large importer of this product. Yet, farmers on neighboring Pacific islands, who cannot grow much else than coconuts, neglect the crop because of low world market prices for their product.

Desiccated coconut was first manufactured in the early 1880s. It is an important product, sensitive to changes in production costs, and easily susceptible to overproduction. Nuts are stored for three or four weeks before being dehusked in the field and carried to the factory. When the shell is chipped off, the kernel comes away easily. Damaged or germinated nuts are rejected to make low-grade copra. The brown testa is removed, usually by hand, though machines are available. The kernels are then washed and sterilized to avoid the risk of salmonella. After sterilization, disintegrators reduce them to a wet meal, or cutters produce fancy cuts, such as threads or chips. Drying is by indirect drier at 75–80° C, or by direct firing at 120° C. The dried product is cooled and graded before being packed. Parings, oil, and drain oil are byproducts.

Desiccated coconut should be pure white, crisp, and have a fresh taste. It should have less than 2.5 percent moisture, 68 to 72 percent oil (on dry weight), less than 0.1 percent free fatty acid (as lauric), and about 6 percent protein. If there is more than 6 to 7 percent sucrose, then sugar has been added. Unavailable carbohydrate is about 18 percent and crude fiber about 4 percent, and there is some mineral content. Desiccated coconut is widely used in sweets, biscuits, cakes, and cake fillings (Harries 1993).

Coconut – Milk, Water, and Wine

The "Cocoa's Milky Bowl"

Dr. Samuel Johnson's *Dictionary* of 1755 contained run-together articles on coco (the nut) and cocoa (the source of chocolate). As a result, spelling became confused, and for some time the word coconut was misspelled as "cocoa-nut." Thus, the poetic allusion to the "cocoa's milky bowl" refers to the "coconut," *Cocos nucifera,* and not to cocoa, *Theobroma cacao* (Child 1974). Yet even explaining this commits a further solecism, because coconut "milk" is a manufactured product. Unfortunately the distinction between coconut milk and coconut water is not always kept clear, even in research publications by coconut scientists. Coconut milk is prepared by squeezing freshly grated endosperm, usually with a little added water, through cloth. On storing, coconut cream forms an upper layer, and when either emulsion is heated, a clear oil separates. This is the basis of the time-honored village method of oil extraction. But coconut cream is also produced industrially in both liquid and spray-dried forms, and the national cuisines of coconut-growing countries use it extensively (Harries 1993).

Water into Wine

Both alcoholic and nonalcoholic beverages that are products of the coconut palm depend on the technique known as toddy tapping. As with other fruit juices, the watery sap that is the toddy can be converted to wine and other products by fermentation and distillation (the sugar content of coconut water from the immature nut also allows it to be fermented, but this is not common). Many types of palms are tapped in Southeast Asia, and the practice dates from at least the seventh century (Burkill 1935).

Unlike maple or rubber trees, which are dicotyledons where the layer of cambium below the bark is tapped, palms are monocotyledons, and the vascular strands are scattered through the tissue. Casual observers sometimes think that it is the coconut leaf stalks that are tapped. In reality, tapping uses the unopened flowering inflorescence. This is a large structure which, when cut in the tapping process and seen from ground level, could, indeed, be mistaken for the cut leaf stalk. There are many flowering stalks within an inflorescence, each able to exude sap. They are packed tightly into an enveloping spathe that would normally split to allow pollination. Binding the spathe tightly prevents it from splitting naturally. It may also be lightly beaten and flexed to stimulate sap flow. Once ready, the end is cut off to allow the sap to drip into a receptacle. The toddy tapper visits the palm, morning and evening, to decant the accumulated sap from the container before fermentation gets too active. Sap flow continues for many days, and each day a sliver is removed to reopen blocked vascular elements and increase flow. This continues until only a stump remains, and the next inflorescence in sequence is prepared.

Obviously, tapped bunches do not flower normally, and the palm ceases to set fruit. If the sap flow decreases, the palm is allowed to rest. The palm may respond with particularly high yields of fruit on the next normal bunches. Excessive tapping followed by high fruit set could shorten the life of the palm. However, the financial return to the farmer would more than compensate for this shorter life (Harries 1993).

Toddy is initially sweet and watery, and the containers used to collect it are rinsed but not sterilized between uses. Because the weather is warm where coconuts grow, and collection is slow because the palms have to be climbed, fermentation to alcohol is practically unavoidable.

Toddy produced overnight and collected first thing in the morning contains about 3 percent alcohol and 10 percent fermentable sugar. Certain additives may slow or stop fermentation. Otherwise, fermentation continuing for 33 hours produces palm wine with an 8 percent alcohol content. Sweet, unfermented toddy contains 16 to 30 milligrams of ascorbic acid per 100 grams, and the content changes little during fermentation. The yeast in fermented toddy adds vitamin B (Harries 1993).

Arrack is the product of the distilling of fermented toddy. Doubly distilled arrack is the basis of local gins, rums, and so forth, with the addition of appropriate flavors.

As with other wine-making substances, coconut toddy can also become vinegar. Fermenting toddy with free access to air produces 45 percent acetic acid in 10 to 14 weeks. This is matured in closed casks for up to 6 months and, perhaps, flavored with spices and colored with caramel.

Coconut Water

The entertainer Harry Belafonte may not have been completely accurate when he sang that coconut water was "good for your daughter" and "full of iron," or that it could "make you strong like a lion." But he was praising the one thing about coconut that makes it different from all other plants – the large amount of water in the immature fruit.

Modern texts on coconut underrate the value of coconut water or overlook the part it played in the domestication of the coconut. Earlier writers had no such reservations. In 1510, Ludovici de Varthema

wrote that "[w]hen the nut begins to grow, water begins to be produced within; and when the nut has arrived at perfection, it is full of water, so that there are some nuts which will contain four and five goblets of water, which water is a most excellent thing to drink . . ." (cited in Harries 1978). As mentioned, coconut water is often wrongly called milk. As early as 1583, by which time the coconut had become well known, Father Thomas Stevens praised the ubiquitous coconut and its refreshing milk [sic], saying "this is so abundant that after drinking the contents of one nut, you scarcely feel the need of another" (Desmond 1992: 29).

The immature fruit, used for drinking, will not fall naturally but must be cut from the palm. Bunches are selected just as they reach maximum size, when a jellylike endosperm begins to line the cavity of the still thin and soft shell. At this stage each nut is full size, full of water with no airspace (it does not splash when shaken), and very heavy. Usually, the harvester cuts one or two entire bunches of nuts and lowers them to the ground on a rope. If they fall, the weight of water cracks or even bursts the soft shell inside the soft husk, whereupon the water drains away and the fruit rots (Harries 1993).

The coconut that is freshly harvested from a bunch that has been in the sun has a natural effervescence and will hiss with released gas when opened. Nevertheless, nature's "packaging" of this "product" leaves it at a disadvantage against internationally trademarked colas and mineral waters, because young coconuts deteriorate over a few days unless kept cool. Cutting away some of the husk reduces their size so they can be more efficiently kept in refrigerated storage, which extends "shelf life" considerably. There are instances when coconuts meant for drinking are transported hundreds of kilometers in refrigerated trucks, but this occurs only when such a vehicle would otherwise travel empty, where the roads are good, and where an affluent urban market has no other access to coconut. Moreover, the use of the coconut as a drink is marginalized by most conventional agricultural treatments. It is seen as reducing the crop of copra from which oil is extracted.

At the proper stage, coconut water contains about 5 percent sugar, and a large nut may have as much as 25 grams of sugar. The water also contains minerals, amino acids, and vitamin C. In addition to fermenting easily, yielding alcohol and vinegar, coconut water has auxinic and growth-promoting properties when used in plant tissue culture. Historically, various medicinal values were attributed to it. There is no doubt that it is a fine oral rehydration fluid for the severe diarrhea of cholera and other diseases. Because coconut water is naturally sterile, it may be injected intravenously to substitute for blood plasma in emergency surgery, and in combination with egg yolk, it finds use as a diluent in artificial insemination.

Coconut – The Tree of Life

Depending on variety, coconut fruit takes from 11 to 15 months to reach maturity, and the palm produces a new inflorescence every 3 to 4 weeks. This means that all the stages of fruit development, from youngest to oldest, are present on any palm at any given time of the year. In the fourteenth century, Jordanus of Séveras, who thought that the coconut was a "marvel," wrote that "both flowers and fruit are produced at the same time, beginning with the first month and going up gradually to the twelfth," so that there are flowers and fruit in eleven stages of growth to be seen together (quoted in Desmond 1992: 9). In this respect it meets the specifications of the biblical Tree of Life, "which bare twelve manner of fruits, and yieldeth her fruit every month" (Revelations 22:2).

According to Peter Martyr (d'Anghiera), writing about 1552, "[s]ome people believe that the germs of these trees were brought by the waves from unknown regions" (Harries 1978: 270). Four hundred years or so later it is now speculated that coconut may have originated on the coasts and islands of Gondwanaland, after which a wild form floated into the Indian and Pacific Oceans, but not the Atlantic. Domestication subsequently occurred in the Malaysian region (Southeast Asia and the western Pacific). The wild and domestic forms were both taken into cultivation, and introgressive hybridization between them produced the wide range of varieties recognized today (Harries 1990).

The original importance of the coconut palm was to coastal communities. With fish and shellfish to eat, coconut provided refreshing, sweet, and uncontaminated drinking water in an otherwise saline environment. No tools were needed to get it, and daily consumption of the water contained in one or two coconuts was enough to ensure good kidney function. The wild type of coconut spread without human interference, but domestication enhanced its drinking qualities in particular. The domestic type depends on human activity for survival and dissemination (Harries 1979).

The coconut preceded the Polynesians in those parts of the Pacific region to which it could float, and the Polynesians took domesticated forms to the islands that they settled (Lepofsky, Harries, and Kellum 1992). Before the development of the copra industry, coconut was a multipurpose plant on small Pacific islands, and its food potential was neither more nor less important than any other use. But another use was in interisland transportation. The islanders in the Indian and Pacific Oceans discovered that coconut husk fibers could be important in building and rigging sailing ships. Moreover, they took young fruit on board, at the start of a voyage, as self-contained, individual servings of uncontaminated drinking water.

The coconut palm was first grown as a plantation crop in the 1840s, because the industrial process for making soap, patented in 1841, required a cheap source of oil, which coconut oil from copra (the dried endosperm of the nut) could provide. And then, between 1846 and 1867, the development of dynamite from nitroglycerine had the remarkable effect of turning glycerine, a once discarded by-product of soap manufacture, into a more profitable item (Harries 1978).

Thus, for industrial and political empire builders, the coconut was a cheap source of raw material and also of war material. The "coconut cult" and "coconut boom" were features of the stock market in the early years of the twentieth century, and coconut plantations were established throughout the tropics.

The strategic importance of the coconut following World War I was clearly demonstrated when the German territories in Africa and the Pacific, with their extensive plantations, were taken away as reparation. As a result, the Japanese administered the Caroline, Mariana, and Marshall islands and, in 1942, they added other important coconut-growing countries to their collection. At the time, Indonesia and the Philippines by themselves accounted for more than 50 percent of the world supply of copra; Indochina, Malaya, Borneo, New Guinea, the Solomons, and the Gilbert Islands provided a further 25 percent.

With the end of the World War II, as nuclear weapons displaced high explosives, the military importance of the coconut gave way to other oil crops. Thus, because of their high palmitic acid content, palm oil and cottonseed oil were preferred over coconut oil for making the new "conventional" weapon, napalm. Similarly, in industry, coconut oil soap, excellent for lathering in hard or saline water, and coconut fiber (coir), valued for resilient, water-resistant rope, were ousted by petroleum-based detergents and synthetic fibers (Harries 1978).

Other animal life forms besides humans have also been associated with the coconut. Two are of cultural interest in relation to coconuts, as well as being foods in their own right: the coconut crab and the palm weevil. The coconut crab, or "robber crab" *(Birgus latro)*, is a massive land-living crab that can climb coconut palm stems and is reputed to cut off nuts before returning to the ground to eat them. Its association with the coconut is not purely fortuitous. The coconut travels long distances over the Indian and Pacific Oceans by interisland floating and can easily carry the small postlarval stages of the crab. This would account for the equally widespread distribution of an otherwise terrestrial crab, which only spends about 30 days of its larval life in coastal waters. Charles Darwin observed that the coconut crab "grows to a monstrous size," and "is very good to eat" (Harries 1983). Unfortunately, on many islands where it was once found, the crab has been eaten to extinction.

Palm weevils *(Rhynchophorus spp.)* are a serious pest in coconut groves, killing palms directly by burrowing in the stem, and indirectly as a vector of the red ring nematode. The palm weevil grubs grow as large as a man's thumb, and subsistence cultivators can collect hundreds of them from fallen or felled palm stems. When fried in their own fat and eaten, the larvae provide a protein- as well as an energy-rich diet.

Another insect activity related to the coconut is the gathering of pollen by honeybees, and today health-food shops sell coconut pollen. As with other pollens, it is collected by incorporating a trap in the hive entrance that removes the pollen pellets as the bees return from foraging. But it could also be collected directly from male flowers. Coconut breeders routinely harvest and process male flowers for kilogram quantities of pollen used in artificial pollination for F_1 hybrid seed production (Harries 1973). Here again, the year-round flowering of the coconut means that regular supplies of pollen are easy to maintain.

When coconut oil was first available in Europe, it was advertised as healthy, whereas animal fats or dairy products were associated with communicable diseases. Now noncommunicable diseases, such as heart diseases and cancer, are of more concern. But the routine use of coconut oil for frying fish or for making margarine had been discontinued in Western societies (mainly as a matter of economic supply and demand) long before the diet conscious became wary of coconut oil, and it continues to be used directly in tropical diets and for vegetable ghee in India.

Coconut oil is easily digested and is absorbed into the system almost as rapidly as butterfat. This is attributed to the low molecular weight of the fatty acids. In common with other vegetable oils, coconut oil contains virtually no cholesterol, but there are objections to its food use because of the high saturation of its fatty acids. In the United States, "tropical oils" have come under attack from pressure groups, whose criticisms overlook the fact that most coconut oil is used for nonedible purposes, and that many of its food uses are to improve the quality of factory-prepared products. Only in coconut-growing countries, where it makes lower quality protein and carbohydrates more acceptable and more digestible, is the coconut still used extensively for cooking. In fact, it may turn out that naturally saturated medium-chain coconut oil is healthier than artificially hydrogenated short-chain vegetable oils.

Finally, what more can be said about the coconut than was said in the "Account of Priest Joseph," circa 1505: "In conclusion, it is the most perfect tree that is found, to our knowledge" (cited in Harries 1978).

Hugh C. Harries

Bibliography

Adair, D., and A. D. Marter. 1982. *The industrial production of coconut cream.* UNIDO Report 10528. Vienna.

Adriano, F. T., and M. Manahan. 1931. The nutritive value of green, ripe and sport coconut (buko, niyog and macapuno). *Philippine Agriculturalist* 20: 3.

Anon. 1912. *The cult of the coconut: A popular exposition of the coconut and oil palm industries.* London.

Balakrishnamurthi, T. S. 1951. Food value of the coconut. *Ceylon Coconut Quarterly* 2: 113-14.

Banzon, J., O. N. Gonzales, S. Y. de Leon, and P. C. Sanchez. 1990. *Coconuts as food.* Quezon City, Philippines.

Behre, A. 1907. The composition of coconut milk. *Pharmazeutische Zeitung* 47: 1046.

Blackburn, G. L., et al. 1989. A re-evaluation of coconut oil's effect on serum cholesterol and athero-genesis. *Asian and Pacific Coconut Community Quarterly Supplement* 18: 1-19.

Blauvelt, K. 1939. The use of non-sterilized coconut milk as an additional nutrient substance in culture media. *Journal of Laboratory and Clinical Medicine* 24: 420-3.

Bodmer, R. 1920. Desiccated coconut. *Analyst* 45: 18.

Burkill, I. H. 1935. *A dictionary of the economic products of the Malay Peninsula,* Vol. 1. London.

Child, R. 1936. Production of sugar from sweet coconut toddy. *Ceylon Trade Journal* 1: 410-15.

　1937. Edible coconut oil. *Tropical Agriculturalist* 89: 270-80.

　1940a. The food value of the coconut. *Journal of the Coconut Industry* (Ceylon) 3: 230-5.

　1940b. A note on coconut flour. *Journal of the Coconut Industry* (Ceylon) 4: 117.

　1941. Coconut toddy and products derived therefrom. *Young Ceylon* 10: 3.

　1974. *Coconuts.* Second edition. London.

Coconut Statistical Yearbook. 1970. Asian and Pacific Coconut Community. Jakarta.

Crawford, M. 1940. Coconut poonac as a food for livestock. *Tropical Agriculturalist* 94: 168-71.

Cruz, A. C., and A. P. West. 1930. Water-white coconut oil and coconut flour. *Philippine Journal of Science* 41: 51-8.

Damoderan, M. 1928. The fermentation of toddy and an account of the micro-organisms producing it. *Journal of the Indian Institute of Science* 11: 63-74.

Date, A. 1965. *Desiccated coconut.* Tropical Products Institute Report No. G12. London.

Dendy, D. A. V. 1975. Protein products from coconut. In *Food protein sources,* ed. N. W. Pirie, 43-6. Cambridge.

Dendy, D. A. V., and B. E. Grimwood. 1973. Coconut processing for the production of coconut oil and coconut protein food and feed products. *Oleagineux* 23: 93-8.

Desiccated coconut. 1886-7. *Tropical Agriculturalist* 6: 34, 771.

Desmond, R. 1992. *The European discovery of the Indian flora.* New York.

Fritz, R. 1983. *Die Gefässe aus Kokosnuss in Mitteleuropa 1250-1800.* Mainz am Rhein.

Gibbs, H. D. 1911. The alcohol industry of the Philippine Islands. *Philippine Journal of Science* 6: 99-206.

Gonzalez, O. N. 1986. State of the art: Coconut for food. *Coconuts Today* 4: 35-54.

Grimwood, B. E., F. Ashman, D. A. V. Dendy, et al. 1975. *Coconut palm products: Their processing in developing countries.* FAO Agricultural Development Paper No. 99. Rome.

Gwee Choon Nghee. 1988. *New technologies open the passage into new usage of coconut milk products.* Presentation at the Association of South East Asian Nations Food Conference '88. Kuala Lumpur.

Hagenmaier, R. 1988. Fresh and preserved coconut milk. *Coconut Research and Development* 4: 40-7.

Harries, H. C. 1973. Pollen collection from coconut flowers by means of a fluid bed dryer. *Euphytica* 22: 164-71.

  1977. The Cape Verde region (1499 to 1549); The key to coconut culture in the Western Hemisphere? *Turrialba* 27: 227-31.

  1978. The evolution, dissemination and classification of *Cocos nucifera. Botanical Review* 44: 265-320.

  1979. Nuts to the Garden of Eden. *Principes* 23: 143-8.

  1981. Milk bottle on the doorstep of mankind. Paper presented at the 13th International Botanical Congress, Sydney.

  1983. The coconut palm, the robber crab and Charles Darwin: April Fool or a curious case of instinct? *Principes* 27: 131-7.

  1988. Cod and chips - coconut and soap: Is there a connection? *Fish Friers Review* (October): 22.

  1989. Coconut as a tropical fruit. In *Aspects of applied biology, Vol. 20: Tropical fruit - technical aspects of marketing,* ed. Association of Applied Biologists, 87-8. Wellesbourne, U.K.

  1990. Malaysian origin for a domestic *Cocos nucifera.* In *The plant diversity of Malesia,* ed. P. Baas, K. Kalkman, and R. Geesink, 351-7. Leyden, Netherlands.

  1991. Wild, domestic and cultivated coconuts. In *Coconut production: Present status and priorities for research.* World Bank Technical Paper No. 136, ed. A. H. Green, 137-46. Washington, D.C.

  1993. Coconut palm. In *Encyclopaedia of food science, food technology & nutrition,* ed. R. Macrae, R. K. Robinson, and M. J. Sadler, Vol. 2: 1098-1104. London.

  1994. Coconut. In *The evolution of crop plants.* Second edition, ed. N. W. Simmonds and J. Smartt, 389-94. London.

Harries, H. C., and E. Almeida. 1993. Coconut as a fresh fruit. Poster Presentation at the November, 1993, International Symposium on Tropical Fruit, Vitória, Brazil.

Hicking, A. 1949. Coconut milk: Substitute for dextrose in normal saline. *Hospital CPS Quarterly* (supplement to *Navy Medical Bulletin*) 22: 1-10.

Jones, S. F. 1979. *The world market for desiccated coconut.* Tropical Products Institute Report No. G129. London.

Leong, P. C. 1953. The nutritive value of coconut toddy. *British Journal of Nutrition* 7: 253-9.

Lepofsky, D., H. C. Harries, and M. Kellum. 1992. Early coconuts in Mo'orea, French Polynesia. *Journal of the Polynesian Society* 101: 299-308.

Levang, P. 1988. Coconut is also a sugar crop. *Oleagineux* 43: 159-64.

Lin, F. M., and W. F. Wilkins. 1970. Volatile flavour components of coconut meat. *Journal of Food Science* 35: 538-9.

Maciel, M. I., S. L. Olivera, and I. P. da Silva. 1992. Effects of different storage conditions on preservation of coconut *(Cocos nucifera)* water. *Journal of Food Processing & Preserving* 16: 13-22.

Menezes, F. G. T., and B. N. Banerjee. 1945. Studies on the digestibility of edible oils and fats. 2. Effects of sterols, carotene and vitamins on pancreatic lipase. *Quarterly Journal of the Indian Institute of Science* 8: 7-30.

Mohanadas, S. 1974. Preservation, bottling and keeping qualities of fresh coconut sap (sweet toddy). *Ceylon Coconut Journal* 25: 109-15.

Monro, J. A., W. R. Harding, and C. E. Russell. 1985. Dietary fibre of coconut from a Pacific atoll: Soluble and insoluble components in relation to maturity. *Journal of the Science of Food & Agriculture* 36: 1013.

Montenegro, H. M. 1985. Coconut oil and its by-products. *Journal of the American Oil Chemists Society* 62: 259.

Moorjani, M. N. 1954. Milk substitute from coconut. *Bulletin of the Central Food Technology Research Institute* (Mysore) 4: 60-1.

Naim, S. H., and A. Husin. 1986. Coconut palm sugar. In *Cocoa and coconut: Progress and outlook,* ed. E. Rajaratnam and Chew Poh Soon, 943-6. Kuala Lumpur.

Nathaniel, W. R. N. 1952. The history of vinegar production and the use of coconut toddy as a raw material. *Ceylon Coconut Quarterly* 3: 83-7.

Nicholls, L., and J. C. Drummond. 1945. Nutritive value of coconut. *Nature* 155: 392.

Norris, K. V., B. Viswenath, and K. C. Nair. 1922. The improvement of the coconut jaggery industry of the West Coast. *Agricultural Journal of India* 17: 353-66.

Northcutt, R. T. 1937. Light, fluffy, substantially non-rancidifiable coconut food product. *Chemistry Abstracts* 31: 4410.

Ohler, J. 1984. *Coconut: Tree of life.* Rome.

Pankajakshan, S. A. S. 1986. Report on the product testing of soft drink prepared from coconut water. *Indian Coconut Journal* 17: 3-10.

Persley, G. J., M. A. Foale, and B. Wright. 1990. *Coconut cuisine.* Melbourne.

Peters, F. E. 1952. The value of coconut meat as a human foodstuff. *Ceylon Coconut Quarterly* 3: 201-5.

  1954. *Bibliography of the nutritional aspects of the coconut.* South Pacific Commission Technical Paper No 58. Noumea, New Caledonia.

Phan, C. B., and R. R. del Rosario. 1983. The preparation of protein hydrolysate from defatted coconut and soybean meals. II. Quality and sensory evaluation of products. *Journal of Food Technology* 18: 163.

Pinto, C. B. 1950. Study of coconut milk and its possible employment in therapeutics. *Revista de Societas Venezolano Quimica* 4: 36-45.

Ridley, H. N. 1912. *Spices.* London.

Scheuring, J. J., and P. H. Tracy. 1942. Substitutes for cocoanut fat in dipping chocolate. *Ice Cream Review* 25: 12, 23, 38, 40.

Som, M. N. M., et al. 1980. Processing of canned coconut milk and coconut butter. In *Cocoa & coconut: Progress and outlook,* ed. E. Pushparajah and Chew Poh Soon, 713-20. Kuala Lumpur.

Subrahmanyan, V., and D. Swaminathan. 1959. Coconut as a food. *Coconut Bulletin* 13: 153-8.

Swetman, A. A., and J. H. Broadbent. 1979. Sugar content variation of coconuts prior to the manufacture of desiccated coconut in Sri Lanka. *Tropical Science* 21: 33-8.

Thampan, P. K. 1975. *The coconut palm and its products.* Cochin, India.

The coconut as a food. 1883-4. *Tropical Agriculturalist* 3: 117.

The milk in the coconut. 1883-4. *Tropical Agriculturalist* 3: 824.

Thieme, J. G. 1968. *Coconut oil processing.* FAO Agricultural Development Paper No. 80. Rome.

Thio, G. L. 1982. Small-scale and home processing of fresh coconut (oil manufacture) and utilization of by-products. *Bulletin of the Department of Agricultural Research* (Royal Tropical Institute, Amsterdam), 309-34.

Timmins, W. H., and E. C. Kramer. 1977. The canning of coconut cream. *Philippine Journal of Coconut Studies* 2: 15–25.

Unson, C. G. 1966. The effect of some food preservatives on coconut toddy. *Ceylon Coconut Planters' Review* 6: 22.

Vanderbelt, J. M. 1945. Vitamin content of coconut milk. *Nature* 156: 174–5.

Verghese, E. J. 1952. Food value of coconut products. *Indian Coconut Journal* 5: 119–29.

Viswanath, B., and K. G. Mayer. 1924. Improvement of coconut jaggery industry. *Agricultural Journal of India* 19: 485–92.

Woodroof, J. G. 1970. *Coconuts: Production, processing & products.* Westport, Conn.

II.E.3 ❧ Palm Oil

The oil palm *(Elaeis guineensis)* is a native of West Africa. It flourishes in the humid tropics in groves of varying density, mainly in the coastal belt between 10 degrees north latitude and 10 degrees south latitude. It is also found up to 20 degrees south latitude in Central and East Africa and Madagascar in isolated localities with a suitable rainfall. It grows on relatively open ground and, therefore, originally spread along the banks of rivers and later on land cleared by humans for long-fallow cultivation (Hartley 1988: 5–7).

The palm fruit develops in dense bunches weighing 10 kilograms (kg) or more and containing more than a thousand individual fruits similar in size to a small plum. Palm oil is obtained from the flesh of the fruit and probably formed part of the food supply of the indigenous populations long before recorded history. It may also have been traded overland, since archaeological evidence indicates that palm oil was most likely available in ancient Egypt. The excavation of an early tomb at Abydos, dated to 3000 B.C., yielded "a mass of several Kilograms still in the shape of the vessel which contained it" (Friedel 1897).

A sample of the tomb material was submitted to careful chemical analysis and found to consist mainly of palmitic acid, glycerol in the combined and free state, and a mixture of azelaic and pimelic acids. The latter compounds are normal oxidation products of fatty acids, and the analyst concluded that the original material was probably palm oil, partly hydrolyzed and oxidized during its long storage. In view of the rather large quantity found, the oil was probably intended for dietary purposes rather than as an unguent.

A few written records of the local food use of a palm oil (presumably from *Elaeis guineensis*) are available in accounts of European travelers to West Africa from the middle of the fifteenth century. Red palm oil later became an important item in the provisioning trade supplying the caravans and ships of the Atlantic slave trade, and it still remains a popular food-stuff among people of African descent in the Bahia region of Brazil (Northrup 1978: 178–86; Hartley 1988: 1–3; R. Lago, personal communication, 1993).

The British Industrial Revolution created a demand for palm oil for candle making and as a lubricant for machinery. In the early nineteenth century, West African farmers began to supply a modest export trade, as well as producing palm oil for their own food needs. After 1900, European-run plantations were established in Central Africa and Southeast Asia, and the world trade in palm oil continued to grow slowly, reaching a level of 250,000 tonnes (metric tons) per annum by 1930 (Empire Marketing Board 1932: 117–23; Hartley 1988: 8–23; Lynn 1989: 227–31).

Meanwhile, the invention of the hydrogenation process for oils and fats in 1902 created the possibility of Western employment of palm products as, for example, in the making of margarine. Yet hydrogenation was more useful for liquid oils like groundnut, palm kernel, and coconut oils than for palm oil. After World War II, further improvements in palm oil refining technology and transport methods made it possible to use largely unhydrogenated palm oil in Western food products (Lim 1967: 130–2; Martin 1988: 45–8).

A rapid expansion of the palm oil export trade followed, accompanied by a marked growth in the plantation sector of production. Between 1962 and 1982, world exports of palm oil rose from about 500,000 to 2,400,000 million tonnes per annum, and Malaysia emerged as the world's largest producer, accounting for 56 percent of world production and 85 percent of world exports of palm oil in 1982. Expanded production in Malaysia was achieved mainly by the privately owned estate sector, which increased its oil palm holdings more than tenfold in the 1960s and 1970s; and by the Federal Land Development Authority (FELDA), whose large-scale schemes organized oil production along plantation lines, although ownership was vested in the workforce of "smallholders" (Khera 1976: 183–5; Moll 1987: 140–62).

By 1990, world production had reached nearly 11,000,000 tonnes per annum, with a worldwide trade of 8,500,000 tonnes (Mielke 1991: 110). Although red palm oil is still used in soups and baked dishes in West Africa, elsewhere in the world, palm oil is eaten mainly in a highly refined form. Its food uses vary from the vanaspati and ghee of India to the margarine, cooking oils, and biscuits of Europe and the United States.

The Oil Palm: Wild and Planted

West Africa

West Africa is the classic region of smallholder production, both of food and export crops. The oil palm, which has been both, flourishes in natural association with yam and cassava cultivation throughout the wetter parts of the region. In eastern Nigeria, which

C. W. S. Hartley (1988: 7, 16) called "the greatest grove area of Africa," densities of 200 palms per hectare (ha) were common in the late 1940s, and densities of more than 300 palms per hectare were not unknown.

These palms were typically self-seeded and tended (to varying degrees) by local farmers. Farther west, in the kingdom of Dahomey and in settlements established by the Krobo people near Accra, some deliberate plantings may have been made as the palm oil export trade developed from the 1830s (Manning 1982; Wilson 1991). However, as J. Reid (1986: 211) has noted, the word *plantation* was often used by contemporary European observers to mean a food farm on which oil palms happened to be growing. Moreover, although in Dahomey descriptions exist of seedlings being transplanted from the bush onto areas cleared for farming by slaves, this does not mean that the practice was universal. In any event, palm oil exports from Dahomey were much smaller than from the Niger Delta, where oil palms were planted deliberately in swampy regions outside their natural habitat, but where the bulk of production was carried out using natural groves. In the 1840s, Dahomey and the Niger Delta exported approximately 1,000 and 13,000 tonnes per annum respectively; by the 1880s these totals had risen to 5,000 and 20,000 (Manning 1982: 352; Reid 1986: 158; Martin 1988: 28-9; Lynn 1989: 241).

Beginning in the late nineteenth century, a number of experimental oil palm plantations were created by Europeans in West and west-central Africa. One of the earliest was founded in Gabon in 1870 by Roman Catholic missionaries (E. J. Mulder, personal communication, 1968). But like many of the other nineteenth-century plantations in West Africa, these ventures were unsuccessful. By comparison with African smallholders, European planters were highly specialized and vulnerable to the marked trading fluctuations of the late nineteenth century. Many also lacked capital but committed themselves to long-term investments of a type that African farmers sensibly rejected.

In the case of palm oil, money was spent paying laborers to produce, plant, and tend seedlings, often on marginal land, in regions where natural groves already contained more palms than local farmers could spare the time to harvest (Hopkins 1973: 212-14; Martin 1988: 46).

Thus, when in 1907 William Lever sought large-scale land concessions in the British West African colonies in order to produce palm oil for his Lancashire soap mills, the Colonial Office was reluctant to help him. In a region characterized by small, fragmented, and often communally owned farms, it was felt that Lever's scheme would be hard to administer, politically risky, and commercially unsound. Lever was left to pursue his dreams in the Belgian Congo, where the existing levels of both trade and population were far lower and where the colonial administration welcomed European enterprise (Hancock 1942: 188-200; Wilson 1954: 159-67).

Following the Lever debate, the West African palm oil industry remained in the smallholders' hands. Few other entrepreneurs came forward to press the case for plantations, although a number of state-run estates were established under French influence in the Ivory Coast after 1960. By 1981 these estates covered a total of 52,000 ha, with a further 33,000 ha planted with oil palms in the surrounding villages (Hartley 1988: 31).

Yet even this development was relatively modest in scale, as shown in unpublished data from Nigeria, West Africa's largest producer of palm oil. The area of wild palm groves, only partly harvested, was estimated at 2,400,000 ha, whereas there were 72,000 ha of estate plantations and another 97,000 ha of smallholder plantations. Estate plantations, which require large consolidated areas, are still difficult to create in Nigeria because the oil palm-growing regions are densely populated and the complex traditional land holding system has been carefully preserved. Elsewhere in West Africa, population densities are lower, but the problems of obtaining labor to sustain plantation developments are correspondingly greater.

Central Africa

In the late nineteenth century, both the German colonizers of Kamerun and the Belgian rulers of the Congo were keenly interested in applying European farming and processing techniques to the palm oil industry (Laurent 1912-13; Rudin 1938; Jewsiewicki 1983). But German botanical and mechanical trials were cut short by World War I, following which the German territories in Africa were divided between the French and the British.

In the Congo, however, Lever's initial land- and produce-buying concessions (granted in 1911) proved to be the foundation for a long process of experimentation, which eventually revolutionized the palm oil industry worldwide. New planting materials led to dramatic increases in yields, thus cutting the cost of production; and improved machinery led to high oil quality at a competitive price. Alongside developments in European and American food-processing techniques, the Congo innovations paved the way for the entry of palm oil into Western diets.

Lever was originally more interested in setting up mills than plantations in the Congo, but his initial investments brought heavy losses (Fieldhouse 1978: 507-9). The fruit supply from wild trees proved hard to control, both in the amount brought to the mill and in its quality upon arrival. Overripe or bruised palm fruit made for highly acidic, low-quality oil, whereas unripe bunches gave low yields. Yet Lever Brothers (and its successor Unilever after 1929) was unwilling to incur the heavy initial costs of planting trees unless planting materials were improved to reduce the running costs. The Germans in Kamerun had identified an exceptionally thin-shelled palm fruit with a high oil content as early as 1902 (Hartley 1988: 50). But their "lisombe" palm, later to become known as the Tenera type, was found only rarely in the wild and failed to breed true.

In a renewed drive to encourage European investment in their colony and, in particular, in oil palm plantations, the Belgians began in 1922 to investigate this German discovery. An experimental plantation of Tenera palms was created at the Yangambi research station in the Congo, and in the 1930s these palms were subjected to a three-year testing program by M. Beirnaert. Meanwhile, private Tenera plantings had been made by Unilever and its subsidiary, the United Africa Company, in the British Cameroons and in the Belgian Congo itself (Courade 1977; Fieldhouse 1978).

Tenera seed also found its way to Sumatra and Malaya in the 1920s, although there, as in Central Africa, it failed to breed true. Beirnaert's painstaking experiments finally showed why: The Tenera palm was actually a hybrid of two other types, the thick-shelled Dura and shell-less Pisifera, and when self-pollinated would produce 50 percent Tenera, 25 percent Dura and 25 percent Pisifera (Beirnaert and Vanderweyen 1941).

Beirnaert's discovery was published at the height of World War II, and it was not until after 1945 that it could be turned to practical use with the establishment of large-scale and long-term Tenera breeding programs. It is ironic that the Congo was not the state that gained the most. Its oil palm plantations did expand from 52,000 ha in 1938 to 93,000 in 1945 and 147,000 in 1958, with a further 98,000 ha under smallholder cultivation by the end of that period (Mulder, personal communication, 1968; Hartley 1988: 30). But political unrest following independence in 1960 led to stagnation and decline in the industry.

Unilever, however, the most important single investor in 1960 with 47,000 ha under oil palms, remained loyal to the newly independent country of Zaire through two decades of intermittent losses and political uncertainty. Thus, Unilever managers remained in place following nationalization in 1975, and the company was allowed to take back full control of the estates two years later (Fieldhouse 1978: 530–45). But at a national level, the research effort was decimated, and new planting was very limited after 1960, in marked contrast to developments at the same time in Southeast Asia.

Southeast Asia

The oil palm was first introduced to Southeast Asia in 1848, when four seedlings, originating from West Africa, were planted in the botanical gardens at Buitenzorg (now Bogor) in Java (Hartley 1988, 21). But this introduction did not lead to a plantation industry for some time, although offspring of the palms were used as ornamentals by tobacco planters.

In 1905 a Belgian agricultural engineer, Adrien Hallet, arrived in Sumatra and noticed that its palms grew more quickly and bore a richer fruit than counterparts in the Congo, where he had previously worked. Just as the oil palms in southeastern Nigeria bore a fruit with more oily pulp and a smaller kernel than their counterparts farther west, so did the Deli Dura palms, descended from the four Buitenzorg seedlings, hold a distinct advantage over the ordinary Duras of West and Central Africa (Leplae 1939: 25–7; Martin 1988: 47).

This superiority probably reflected the optimal soils, rainfall, and sunshine conditions of Southeast Asia, rather than any special genetic quirks of the Buitenzorg palms. However, the fact that all the Deli Duras were descended from so few parents meant that the early planters could expect fairly uniform results (Rosenquist 1986). This lowered the risks associated with plantation cultivation, an effect reinforced by the absence of the palm's usual pests and diseases in its new geographic setting.

The relatively high yields and low risks from planting oil palms in Southeast Asia helped the industry to grow quickly, following the pioneering plantings of Hallet in Sumatra and of his friend Henri Fauconnier in Malaya in the 1910s. By 1919 more than 6,000 ha had been planted in Sumatra, rising to 32,000 in 1925, by which time 3,400 ha had come under cultivation in Malaya. Over the next five years, a further 17,000 ha were planted in Malaya, while the Sumatran area doubled.

This rapid expansion came not only because of growing confidence in the oil palm but also because of the grave postwar problems of the rubber industry. The oil palm was seen as a useful means of diversification to avoid a dangerous dependence on rubber. The pace of new planting slowed during the worldwide slump of the 1930s, but by 1938 Malaya had nearly 30,000 and Sumatra more than 90,000 ha under cultivation (Lim 1967: Appendix 5.2; Creutzberg 1975: Table 11; Hartley 1988: 21).

Developments in Sumatra hung fire for some time after 1945, as shown in Table II.E.3.1. Meanwhile, developments in Malaysia were more rapid, especially after 1960, when the replanting of old rubber estates with oil palms was stimulated by FELDA's smallholder schemes.

Table II.E.3.1. *Indonesia: Oil palm area (thousand hectares)*

Date	Government schemes	Private estates	Small holders	Total
1940	–	–	–	110[a]
1962	–	–	–	under 90[a]
1971	90	50	–	140[b]
1975	120	70	–	190[b]
1980	200	90	10	300[b]
1985	310	150	100	560[b]
1990	–	–	–	1,100[c]

Sources: [a]Hartley (1988), pp. 21–7; [b]Taniputra et al. (1988); [c]Bulletin Perkebunan (1991).

Table II.E.3.2. *Malaysia: Oil palm area (thousand hectares)*

Date	Peninsular Malaysia (Malaya)	Sabah	Sarawak	Total
1938	30	–	–	30[a]
1960	55	–	–	55[a]
1965	80	–	–	80[b]
1970	261	38	1	300[c]
1975	570	60	10	640[c]
1980	910	90	20	1,020[c]
1985	1,290	160	30	1,480[c]
1990	1,660	270	60	1,990[c]
1992	1,760	310	70	2,140[c]

Sources: [a]Hartley (1988) pp. 21–8; [b]Khera (1976) p. 28; [c]Palm Oil Registration and Licensing Authority.

At the same time, the Malaysian government and the estate sector launched several systematic Tenera-breeding efforts, in which high-yielding parents were selected and through which increasingly productive planting materials were generated. The new trees not only yielded more fruit but also produced a type of fruit that was ideally suited to the new screw presses which, having been tried out in the 1950s in the Belgian Congo, became widely used in Malaysia from the mid-1960s. These innovative developments have been described as "one of the world's outstanding agricultural achievements" (Anwar 1981). The land area involved is shown in Table II.E.3.2.

Latin America

A distinct species of the oil palm, *Elaeis oleifera* (also known as *Elaeis melanococca*), is indigenous to Latin America. Since the late 1960s, plant breeders have begun to take an interest in this variety because its oil has a high iodine value and unsaturated fatty acid content, making it especially suitable for food use. However, the fruit is often small, with a thin oil-yielding mesocarp surrounding a large, thick-shelled kernel. Harvested bunches often contain a low proportion of fruit of quite variable quality. Hence, the plant has not been cultivated commercially, although it is frequently found in riverside or swampy areas, and the oil is used locally for cooking, soap boiling, and lamp fuel (Hartley 1988: 85–9, 681–3).

Elaeis guineensis seeds were introduced to Central America by the United Fruit Company, which brought seeds from Sierra Leone to Guatemala in 1920, and from Malaysia to Panama in 1926 and Honduras in 1927. Other introductions from Java and the Belgian Congo followed, but the first commercial planting of 250 ha took place only in Guatemala in 1940. The United Fruit Company's main interest was, traditionally, the production of bananas for export, but large banana-producing areas were destroyed by Fusarium wilt, and in consequence, oil palm and other crops were being tested as replacements.

The oil palm, however, proved vulnerable to disease in its new setting, and difficulties were encountered in identifying suitable growing conditions. Nonetheless, a successful development was founded on the northern coastal plain of Honduras, and in addition to developing plantations on its own land, the United Fruit Company stimulated oil palm cultivation by neighboring smallholders, whose fruit could then be processed in the company mills. Seed was also supplied to other Latin American countries (Hartley 1988: 33–6; D. L. Richardson, personal communication, 1993).

The beginnings of commercial planting in Latin America are summarized in Table II.E.3.3. By 1992 the total area planted to *Elaeis guineensis* in Latin America had grown to 390,000 ha – still a small fraction of the area in Africa or Southeast Asia. The distribution of plantings by country and sector is shown in Table II.E.3.4.

Table II.E.3.3. *Latin America: Earliest oil palm plantings*

Country	Year	Area planted (hectares)
Guatemala	1940	250
Costa Rica	1963	638
Honduras	1964	447
Ecuador	1964	13
Brazil	1967	200
Colombia	1970	4,500
Mexico	1975	200
Venezuela	1976	560
Panama	1976	1,005
Peru	1978	5,500
Dominican Rep.	1981	160
Nicaragua	1984	600

Source: Richardson, personal communication (1993).

Table II.E.3.4. *Latin America: Oil palm area, 1992 (thousand hectares)*

Country	Estates	Smallholders (<100 ha each)	Total
Mexico	1	2	3
Nicaragua	3	–	3
Panama	4	–	4
Dominican Rep.	7	–	7
Guatemala	6	4	10
Peru	6	7	13
Venezuela	21	3	24
Costa Rica	16	9	25
Honduras	7	27	34
Brazil	31	28	59
Ecuador	59	29	88
Colombia	100	20	120
Total	261 (67%)	129 (33%)	390

Source: Richardson, personal communicaton (1993).

Processing Technology

Until the early years of the twentieth century, palm oil was processed only by traditional village methods, by which loose fruits were collected from the ground or a few bunches were cut from the tree. Beginning in the 1920s, however, the United Africa Company and British colonial officials in Nigeria started experimenting with steam cookers and hand presses designed to make production at the village level more efficient in terms of labor use and oil yield. Yet a lack of cash prevented most farmers from trying the new machinery, with the exception of a few lucky recipients of free samples or government subsidies in the 1940s (Martin 1988: 64–6, 127–9).

A separate process of trial and error led to the development of the sophisticated factories required to deal with the volume of fruit produced on modern plantations and to produce oil of the high and standardized quality that would appeal to Western food processors. Such factories handle almost all the palm fruit of Southeast Asia, whereas in West Africa and Latin America, processing is carried out by a wide variety of methods, yielding oil for local consumption and for industrial as well as edible uses in the West.

Whatever the scale and sophistication of the process, the following main steps are required:

1. Separation of individual fruits from the bunch.
2. Softening of the fruit flesh.
3. Pressing out of the oily liquid.
4. Purification of the oil.

Traditional Village Process

Whole, ripe, fresh fruit bunches (FFB) are cut from the palm. With young trees this can be done from ground level. With older trees in West Africa, harvesting is still often accomplished by a man climbing the tree, secured to it by a loop of rope or other locally available materials, such as rattan and raffia fiber (Vanderyst 1920). But on plantations, a curved knife attached to a bamboo is used. After cutting, most of the fruits are still firmly attached to the bunches, which are divided into a few sections, heaped together, moistened, and covered with leaves. Natural fermentation during two to three days loosens the fruits so that they can be picked off the bunch sections by hand.

Following this step, two major variants in the process are used to produce two oils with different characteristics – those of soft oil and those of hard oil. The regions producing each type have changed since Julius Lewkowitsch (1895: 429) identified Salt-pond in present-day Ghana as the cheapest source of hard oil, and Drewin on the Ivory Coast as the best place to buy soft oil. But the basic methods have changed little since they were first described by colonial officials in the 1910s and 1920s (Laurent 1912–13; Gray 1922; Faulkner and Lewis 1923; Martin 1988: 32–3).

For soft oil production, the fruits are separated as soon as they are loose enough and boiled with water for 4 hours to soften the flesh, which is very fibrous. The cooked fruit is emptied into a large container, which may be a pit lined with clay, an iron drum, or a large wooden mortar. It is then reduced to a pulp with pestles or by treading it under foot. The resulting mash may be diluted with water, and the oil is skimmed off or squeezed out of the fibrous mash by hand. In some instances, a sieve made of palm fronds is used to retain the fibers. At this stage the liquid product, which contains oil, water, and fruit fibers, is often boiled up with additional water and skimmed again, although this step is omitted in some cases. Finally, the oil is again heated to boil out the residual water.

Lewkowitsch (1922: 546) also reported on the preparation of small quantities of oil for kitchen use directly from freshly picked fruit, by boiling the fruit and skimming the oil. Such oil had good keeping properties and often a free fatty acid content below 2 percent; but yield was very low, and not available for export.

In the hard-oil process, the fruit is allowed to ferment for 3 or more days longer than in the soft-oil process, until the flesh is soft enough. It is then pulped by treading underfoot in an old canoe or pounding in a mortar. Oil is allowed to drain out for up to 3 days, then water is added, and the mix is trodden again. Further oil rises to the surface and is skimmed. The oil is boiled up with water in another container and finished as described for soft oil.

These two processes differ in some important respects. The prolonged fermentation in the hard-oil process results in a much greater enzymic breakdown of the neutral fat and, therefore, in a much higher free fatty acid content. The yield obtained by this process is also much lower. However, it has a substantial advantage in that the labor and firewood requirements are also much lower. Table II.E.3.5 summarizes these differences.

Table II.E.3.5. *Comparison of village palm oil processes*

	Soft oil	Hard oil
Proportion of oil recovered	40–50%	20–40%
Free fatty acid content	3–12%	20–40%
Elapsed time to produce clean oil (days)	5–7	10–14
Human days' work for one ton oil*	420	133

*Includes harvesting.

Sources: Nwanze (1965), and personal communication, J. H. Maycock of the Palm Oil Research Institute of Malaysia (1991).

The strong characteristic flavors developed during both of these processes, as well as the naturally strong red color of the oil, are appreciated by local cooks and visiting gourmets, but they present severe limitations in the export markets. The high free fatty acid content and solid consistency of hard oil limits its range of uses, making it well suited to soap boiling but not to food processing. The solid consistency of hard oil is not due directly to the free fatty acids formed during the fermentation step but rather to the diglycerides, the other fragments obtained when one fatty acid is split from the neutral triglyceride molecule. M. Loncin and B. Jacobsberg (1965) have demonstrated the formation of a eutectic between triglycerides and diglycerides, resulting in a minimum melting point and maximum softness at a diglyceride content of 7 percent.

Mechanization of the Small-Scale Process

With the rapid twentieth-century growth in West African exports came the introduction of simple machines to reduce labor requirements and increase oil yield from a given quantity of fruit. Early machines, before and after the 1914–18 war, as described by Hartley (1988: 694–703), included a cylinder fitted with manually operated beaters, which was fed with softened fruit and hot water. After "beating," an oil-water mixture was run off through a sieve. Another system used a special cooker and a press as adjuncts to the soft-oil process.

The first device to become widely adopted, however, was a modified wine and cider press: the Duchscher press. This consisted of a cylindrical cage of wooden slats, held in place by iron hoops, and a ram on a screw thread. The screw thread was turned manually by means of long bars (in the manner of a ship's capstan), forcing the ram onto the pulped fruit. The exuding liquid was collected in a trough surrounding the cage.

Similar presses, but using a perforated cylindrical metal cage, are still in use today, giving yields of 55 to 65 percent of the oil present. A recent analysis of the needs for mechanization in the village has concluded that this is still the most practical implement, because it can be made and maintained locally and is inexpensive by comparison with other presses (C. E. Williams, personal communication, 1981). However, farmers in Nigeria (which was once the world's largest exporter of palm oil) have, since the 1950s, been reluctant to invest in this or other improvements because of the low producer prices offered by the state-controlled marketing boards. It is to be hoped that recent reforms of marketing structures in Nigeria and elsewhere in Africa will encourage renewed innovation at the village level (Martin 1988: 126–36).

The next development in pressing was the introduction in 1959 of the hand-operated hydraulic press by Stork of Amsterdam. This was capable of processing 600 to 1,000 pounds of fruit per hour and could recover 80 percent of the oil present. The hydraulic mechanism was later motorized.

A different approach to mechanization brought forth the Colin expeller (first patented in 1904), which in essence is similar to a domestic mincer. It consists of a perforated cylindrical cage, fitted with a spiral screw or "worm," which is turned manually through a gear. Cooked fruit is fed to the worm through a hopper, and the pressure developed as the worm pushes the fruit forward forces oil out through the perforations. Spent fiber and kernels are discharged at the end of the cage. The machine has a capacity of 100 kg cooked fruit per hour, or 250 kg per hour if motorized. The Colin expeller became popular after 1930, mainly in Cameroon. Its limitations were a reduced efficiency with Dura fruit, which forms the bulk of the wild oil palm crop; rapid wear of the screw; and a relatively high cost. The principle of the expeller, however, has been further developed into the screw press found in all modern oil mills (Hartley 1988: 703–5).

The presses described here provided a relatively efficient process for the step of pressing out the oily liquid during oil production and led researchers to seek improvements in the other steps. Several innovations have resulted from a project begun by the Nigerian Institute for Oil Palm Research (NIFOR) during the 1950s in cooperation with the Food and Agriculture Organization of the United Nations (FAO) and the United Nations Development Program (UNDP).

The following unit operations and equipment are involved in palm oil production.

1. Fruit bunch cookers, which are wood-fired cylindrical tanks. They are loaded with cut-up fresh fruit bunches (FFB).
2. A bunch stripper operated by hand, which consists of a cylinder made up of slats and turns on a horizontal axis that tumbles the cooked bunch sections until the individual fruits separate from the bunch and fall between the slats.
3. A digester (to break up the softened fruit and release its oil from its cells), consisting of a horizontal cylinder in which beater arms rotate, driven by a small diesel motor.
4. A hydraulic press, which was introduced in 1959.
5. A clarification unit consisting of two linked tanks, whereby heating with water causes the oil layer in the first tank to overflow at the top into the second tank. There it is dried by the waste heat from the fire under the first tank.

Extraction efficiencies of 87 percent at a free fatty acid (FFA) level of below 4 percent are routinely attainable by this process. Between a quarter and a half ton of fresh fruit bunches per hour can be processed, depending on cooker capacity.

A number of variants of this process are in use:

1. Bunches are allowed to ferment so that only loose fruit is loaded into the cooker. This variant yields oil of higher FFA.
2. The hydraulic presses may be driven by a small diesel engine.
3. Clarification can take place in simple tanks with direct heating.
4. Cooking of bunches may be by steam, whereby whole bunches are loaded into a tank fitted with a perforated plate about 15 centimeters (cm) from the base. Water is boiled under the plate, and the steam penetrates through the bunches.
5. In Ghana, an interesting operating procedure has been developed, in which the mill owner provides mill facilities to the farmers, who are then responsible for the bunch stripping and cooking of the fruit. Mill operatives carry out digesting and pressing procedures, after which the farmers take away the oil from their own fruit for clarification (G. Blaak, personal communication, 1989).

The advantages for the farmers are numerous: They need no capital investment in mill equipment; there are no arguments regarding purchase price of FFB; if farmers produce high-quality Tenera fruit, they retain the full benefit; and farmers pay only a processing charge. Their net profits are higher than those obtained selling FFB, even if they employ labor to carry out their share of the processing.

Larger-Scale Processes

The small-scale processes just described are suitable for the processing of FFB from wild oil palm groves or from smallholdings. The main objective is to produce red palm oil for traditional food use.

The processing of the large quantities of fruit produced by plantations or by large smallholder cooperatives, however, requires a progressively greater degree of mechanization and mechanical handling as the quantity increases. Furthermore, since oil produced on a large scale is usually intended for export or for local refinery processes, the ultimate objective is a neutral oil of bland flavor and nearly white color. To attain this quality, the processes (including the handling of FFB) are designed to minimize the development of free fatty acids and oil oxidation.

A simple factory process of intermediate scale, in which the material is still handled manually between processing stages, is the Pioneer mill, which was developed by the United Africa Company around 1939. It is designed to process about three-quarters of a ton of fruit per hour, which is the equivalent of about 1 ton of fruit bunches, following the removal of the fruit from the bunch stalks. The process consists of the following steps:

1. Autoclaving – 200 kg of fruit is loaded into a vertical batch autoclave mounted on a gantry and cooked under steam pressure of 20 pounds per square inch for 15 minutes.
2. After cooking, the fruit is discharged by gravity into a digester fitted with a stirrer, which breaks it up and releases the oil from the cells.
3. The resulting mash is treated in a basket centrifuge, operating at 1,200 revolutions per minute.
4. The oil flowing from the centrifuge passes through a screen to remove the fiber, and then to a settling tank.
5. The settling tank contains a layer of hot water, and the oil is pumped in below water level. The water is boiled for 15 minutes and then allowed to settle. The oil layer is decanted through a hot-water layer in a second settling tank.
6. The tank is heated to boiling point for 15 minutes and allowed to settle. The clean oil is put into drums.
7. The sludge from the two settling tanks is further treated by boiling and settling, and the residual oil is recovered.

An oil mill of essentially the same design, with a capacity of 2 to 3 tons of fruit per hour, was featured in the Wembley Exhibition of 1924 by Nigerian Products Ltd., Liverpool, and was apparently demonstrated in operation there (Elsdon 1926: 316–22). In 1950 there were 13 Pioneer mills in operation in Nigeria. The numbers increased to 65 in 1953 and more than 200 in 1962, producing about 25,000 tons. But, subsequently, their use has declined (Mulder, personal communication, 1968).

The Pioneer mill cannot meet the needs of well-established plantations generating large volumes of fruit. To keep costs down and output up, it is vital to have a fully mechanized power-operated mill. The development of such mills began in Kamerun and in the Congo before World War I. Mills using centrifuges for oil extraction were in operation in the Congo in 1916, in Sumatra in 1921, and in Malaya in 1925 (Hartley 1988: 703–5). Centrifuges were largely replaced by hydraulic presses in the 1930s, although they were still being operated at Batang Berjuntai, Malaysia, in 1982. Batch-fed hydraulic presses were, in turn, replaced by continuous screw presses, which saved labor and handled much larger volumes of fruit. At this final stage of innovation, the development of agricultural and processing technology went hand in hand. The screw press tended to mangle the fruit of the Dura palm, with its relatively thin layer of oil-bearing mesocarp, but proved ideally suited to the Tenera variety (Maycock, personal communication, 1991).

The principal steps involved in the production of palm oil today are the following:

1. Harvest at optimum ripeness.
2. Transport FFB to an oil mill with minimum bruising.
3. Transfer FFB to sterilizing cages.
4. Sterilize FFB by steam under pressure.
5. Transfer cooked FFB to a bunch stripper.

6. Transfer fruit to a digester.
7. Press in single-screw or twin-screw press.
8. The oily discharge from the press, containing water and fruit debris, is passed through screens and settling tanks.
9. The oil phase from the settling tanks is passed to a clarifying centrifuge. The sludge, or heavy phase, from the settling tanks is centrifuged and the recovered oil returned to the settling tanks.

African Food Uses

In West Africa, palm oil has a wide range of applications. It is employed in soups and sauces, for frying, and as an ingredient in doughs made from the various customary starch foods, such as cassava, rice, plantains, yams, or beans. It is also a condiment or flavoring for bland dishes such as *fufu* (cassava). A basic dish, "palm soup," employs the whole fruit. The following dishes from Ghana are illustrative of the wide range of palm oil use (Wonkyi Appiah, personal communication, 1993).

In the case of palm soup, first wash and boil palm fruits. Next, pound the fruit and mix with water to a paste. Add meat or fish, vegetables, onions, spices, and salt. Boil for 25 minutes and simmer for a further 15. Serve the soup with cooked rice, yam, plantain, *fufu*, or *kpokpoi*. (The latter is a corn dough, steamed and cooked, with okra and palm oil stirred in.)

Palm oil is also used in baked dishes, and one popular dish has different names according to the local language. When *Ofam* in Twi, or *Bodongi* in Fanti, is prepared, ripe plantains are pounded and mixed with spices, some wheat or corn flour, beans, and perhaps eggs. Palm oil is stirred into the mixture and the whole is then baked in the oven. The dish is served with ground nuts. *Apiti* is a similar dish, baked in leaves, without beans or eggs.

The characteristic flavor of palm oil prepared by village methods is an important feature of these dishes. Indeed, it is one of their most "traditional" features. Several of the other key ingredients, such as salt, wheat, or (in popular eastern Nigerian dishes) stockfish, became widely available only in the nineteenth and early twentieth centuries, when they were imported from Europe in exchange for palm oil itself (Martin 1988: 28-9, 50).

Early Western Food Uses

The fully flavored red palm oil produced by West African village methods has not proved suitable for food use in the importing countries of the West, where the consumer requires a bland cooking fat, near white in color, or a margarine, similar in appearance to butter. Today's plantation-produced palm oil can be bleached and neutralized to meet Western requirements, but in the nineteenth and early twentieth centuries, the high FFA content even of "soft"

West African palm oils made them too difficult and uneconomic to neutralize (Andersen 1954: 27). Even before loading aboard ship, they fell far short of the current quality standard of less than 5 percent FFA, 0.5 percent moisture, and 0.5 percent dirt; and a slow ocean voyage did little to improve matters, as the acidity tended to increase en route (Vanneck and Loncin 1951).

Throughout the nineteenth century, exported oil from West Africa was placed in wooden casks usually supplied from Europe in the "knocked down" state and put together before being filled. Sailing ships became much larger in size and were gradually displaced in the second half of the century by steam ships, which were able to call at a greater number of ports and make more regular voyages (Lynn 1989). This development probably improved the overall quality of oil arriving in Europe, but as the oil was still made on a small scale by different methods and carried in casks, there was plenty of variation.

This quality problem could have been resolved in the late 1920s, when bulk storage tanks were installed at some African loading ports, initially in Nigeria and the Belgian Congo. It was then possible for incoming oil to be washed and cleaned before bulking, with an improvement in quality (Iwuchukwu 1965; Mulder, personal communication, 1968). However, hardly any Nigerian palm oil was suitable for the European food industry until the 1940s.

When Sumatran and, later, Malayan plantations started to export oil in the 1920s, their fruit was harvested systematically from the beginning. It was transported with minimal bruising to the factories and processed in a standardized way. Bulk shipment was developed from the outset. The first shore tanks were installed at Belawan in North Sumatra in the 1920s, and oil from Malaya was taken there by steamer from 1931 onward. In 1932 the Malayan planters set up their own Palm Oil Bulking Company with an installation at Singapore (Shipment of palm oil in bulk 1931; United Plantations Berhad, unpublished documents; T. Fleming, personal communication, 1993).

It thus became possible to develop and maintain the quality standards that are now current worldwide. The planters aimed to produce oil of 3.5 percent FFA, which would then fall well within the limit of 5 percent FFA on arrival in Europe or America. Oil arriving at above 5 percent FFA was sold at a discount, depending on the excess acidity (Hartley 1988: 687).

European food manufacturers could now begin to introduce palm oil on a commercial basis, drawing on earlier experiments and fitting it into two long-standing patterns of fat use. In central and northern Europe, indeed in cool weather regions generally, the traditional fats are the products of the farm yard – butter, beef tallow, and lard. In southern Europe, with its dry hot climate, olive oil has been in general use for thousands of years. Thus, consumers have had available either a plastic product of solid appearance or a clear liquid oil, and the cooking and eating habits developed accordingly.

Respect for these traditions led to the invention in 1869 of margarine and its development as a replacement for butter, when the latter was in short supply. Margarine was originally made from beef fat, and the plastic nature of butter was attained by blending in a liquid fraction separated from beef fat by crystallization. Margarine proved so popular that European supplies of beef fat did not suffice. Imports from the New World were important in the nineteenth century, but various imported vegetable oils gradually took the place of beef fat margarine blends as refining techniques developed. The fact that even "soft" palm oil is a solid fat in temperate climates, with a consistency quite similar to butter, made it an obvious candidate for such experiments, and the first recorded trial took place in 1907 (Feron 1969).

The refining and bleaching process required to render suitable palm oil involved a great deal of research and empirical know-how. Illustrative is some unpublished correspondence (copies held by K. G. Berger) between Dr. Julius Lewkowitsch, a consultant chemist in oils and fats, and a Liverpool trading house, the African Association Limited. Dr. Lewkowitsch had invented a process for rendering palm oil into an edible product and had entered into an agreement, dated January 24, 1905, to share the costs of development of the process with the African Association.

Evidently the work proceeded rather slowly, because in September 1907, Lewkowitsch received a letter from the Vice-Chairman of the African Association, saying: "I have sent you under separate cover a sample of refined beef suet. . . . Would it be possible to have the samples of the palm oil products made up to appear like this sample? I am afraid I shall never satisfy my Co-Directors until I can show them a palm oil product they can eat." A successful prototype was probably produced eventually, because in 1910 a small manufacturing concern, V. B. Company, was incorporated and the African Association was paying Lewkowitsch a regular salary as managing director from 1910 to 1912.

The first decade of the twentieth century also saw the introduction of hydrogenation of oils, a process by which liquid oils could be turned into plastic or hard fats to a controlled degree. As a result, vegetable oil–based "shortenings" were produced to replace lard and beef tallow as ingredients for cakes, pastries, and biscuits and as frying fats. Once adequately refined, palm oil was easily introduced in blend formula for these types of products and had the advantage of not requiring hydrogenation. By the mid-1930s, the relatively clean and less acidic plantation-produced palm oil of Malaya and Sumatra was finding a ready market in the United States, where it was used not only in fine toilet soaps but also in the making of compound lard. Over 50,000 tonnes per annum were used in the American compound lard industry between 1935 and 1939 (Lim 1967: 130–2).

Wartime interruptions of supplies from Asia during the 1940s forced American manufacturers to find substitutes for palm oil, and the market was slow to revive afterwards. However, in Britain, wartime shortages of butter encouraged the use of palm oil in both margarine and compound lard, and this market continued to grow in the 1950s (Lim 1967: 131). British manufacturers, through the home Ministry of Food and the West African Produce Control Board, were able to corner the market in British West African palm oil (Meredith 1986). The Produce Control Board and, from 1949, its successor, the Nigerian Oil Palm Produce Marketing Board, played an important role in bringing the quality of this oil up to the standards set in Southeast Asia.

A grading system was set up as follows:

Grade I	under 9 percent FFA
Grade II	9 to 18 percent FFA
Grade III	18 to 27 percent FFA
Grade IV	27 to 36 percent FFA
Grade V	over 36 percent FFA

Higher prices were paid for the better grades, and there was an immediate response from the village producers, which enabled a Special Grade palm oil to be specified in 1950 with maximum 4.5 percent FFA at time of purchase. A significant premium was paid for this oil, with the result that Special Grade oil, which was only 0.2 percent of production in 1950, jumped to over 50 percent by 1954. In 1955, the specification was tightened to 3.5 percent FFA, and by 1965 Iwuchukwu (1965) reported that more than 80 percent of material for export had reached this quality.

Market Developments Since 1950

The development (mainly since the 1950s) of convenience foods and of snack food manufacture on an industrial scale opened up additional uses for palm oil, because of its good resistance to oxidative deterioration and its better ability to withstand the high temperatures used in frying than most alternative oils (Kheiri 1987; Berger 1992). The market developed especially rapidly after 1970, as the trees planted during the 1960s in Malaysia matured and as the Malaysian government and estate sector began to promote their product more actively in the West. Asian markets had also become important by 1980, as Western processing techniques were applied to meet local needs.

Figure II.E.3.1 shows that the world production of palm oil, together with its share in world supplies of oils and fats, increased dramatically from 1970 onward. Yet by this time, in many parts of Africa the industry had declined (Table II.E.3.6). Nigeria, for example, had no exportable surplus of oil after 1970 and, in fact, became a net importer of palm olein in the 1980s. Exports from Zaire became very limited in the 1980s, and the Ivory Coast, with exports of 60,000 to 100,000 tonnes per annum, was left as the only significant African supplier. Meanwhile, as shown in Table II.E.3.6, new Asian producers were emerging, in particular Papua New Guinea and Thailand. By 1990, exportable surpluses of 10,000 to 30,000 tonnes per annum were also reaching the world market from Honduras and Costa Rica (Mielke 1991: 111).

As Malaysian production grew, both the planters and the government realized that it was vital to improve processing methods and to encourage the growth in demand for palm oil. The estate sector took the lead during the 1960s, developing higher grades of crude palm oil to suit European needs. Later, the government joined in the development of refineries and new products to suit Asian, as well as Western, tastes.

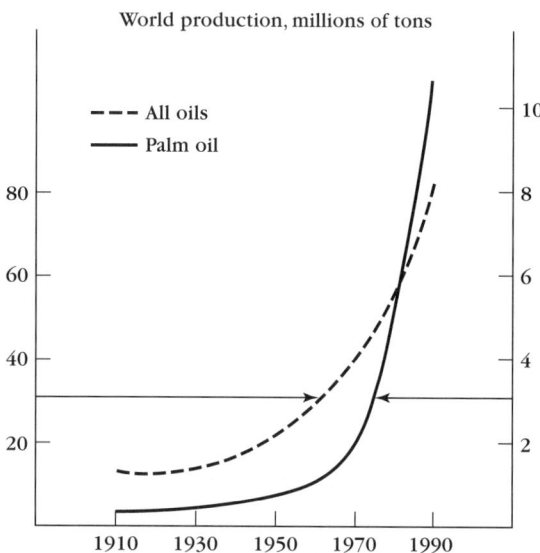

Figure II.E.3.1. World production of palm oil, 1910–90.

Table II.E.3.6. *Palm oil exports from selected countries (thousand tonnes per annum)*

Country	1950–3	1962–5	1970–3	1982–5	1990
Nigeria	180	130	8	–	–
Zaire	140	130	100	8	–
Indonesia	120	120	220	380	1,110
Malaysia	50	120	620	3,000	5,950
Ivory Coast	unknown	1	40	60	140
Papua New Guinea	–	–	–	100	130
Thailand	–	–	–	–	30
World total	520	540	1,000	3,700	8,440

Sources: 1950–85: Hartley (1988) p. 24, and 1990: Mielke (1991), p. 111.

Table II.E.3.7. *Specifications of special grades of crude palm oil*

	SPB	SQ	Lotox
FFA max %	2.0	2.0	2.5
Moisture max %	0.1	0.18	0.18
Impurities max %	0.002	0.02	0.02
Iron max ppm	10.0	4.0	3.0
Copper max ppm	0.5	0.2	0.2
Peroxide value mg/kg max	–	3.0	3.0
Anidine value max	–	–	4.0

Sources: Loncin and Jacobsberg (1965) and Johansson and Pehlergard (1977).

The old standard of 3.5 percent FFA on leaving the factory continued to apply to the bulk of crude Malaysian palm oil. However, in the last 30 years it has been recognized that the production of a stable refined palm oil of good color is also dependent on characteristics other than FFA content, as shown in Table II.E.3.7. In particular, the degrees of oxidation and contamination with catalytic traces of metals are important. But surveys indicate that the peroxide value (a measure of the state of oxidation) of standard palm oil arriving at Malaysian ports or refineries fell from 3.9 milligrams per kilogram to 2.3 milligrams per kilogram between 1974 and 1991 (Jacobsberg 1974; Wong 1981; V. K. Lal, personal communication, 1991).

Planters, both in the Belgian Congo (Zaire) and in Malaysia, also sought to develop a premium product with exceptionally low FFA, obtained through stricter harvesting routines and processing with minimum delay. "Special Prime Bleach" (SPB) grade was developed in the Belgian Congo (Loncin and Jacobsberg 1965), having a maximum of 2 percent FFA and reduced levels of iron and copper contamination, while in Malaysia two special grades became available, namely "SQ" and "Lotox." The SQ and Lotox specifications include limits for oxidation characteristics as well as trace metals and in practice satisfy the most stringent requirements of the European market (Johansson and Pehlergard 1977).

A separate development, which also improved the quality of palm oil arriving in Europe, was the introduction in the 1960s of "parcel tankers." These are specialized ships of up to 30,000 tons. The cargo space is subdivided into a number of separate tanks, generally with a capacity of between 100 and 1,000 tons. Tanks are fitted with separate pumps and pipelines so that different liquid cargoes can be carried without contamination. With the very large export trade from Southeast Asia, parcel tankers are capable of economically carrying palm oil and other oils of different grades to destinations all over the world. Appropriate shore installations have been developed since 1960 in the exporting ports of Southeast Asia and in most receiving ports in Europe, United States, and Japan, and are being developed in countries that have only recently become large importers. Like the development of bulk shipment from Malaya in the 1930s, this innovation was fostered by cooperation among the planters, who marketed their oil through a common Malayan Palm Oil Pool from 1953 to 1974 (Allott and Wong 1977).

By 1974 the volume of Malaysian oil exports and the diversity of markets had grown to the point at which a free marketing system was more appropriate. The range of palm oil products exported was also growing, following the application of the fractionation process first developed for beef tallow in the 1870s. This technique separated crude palm oil into olein and stearin. The olein remains a liquid oil in hot climates and, therefore, readily fitted into the large Indian demand for cooking oil.

From 1970 the Malaysian government encouraged and licensed private enterprises to set up refineries that could both fractionate palm oil and use it in a more traditional manner to produce shortenings for Asian markets. In India, for example, there is a large consumer demand for vanaspati, a shortening developed as a replacement for butterfat ghee. Similar shortening products are traditional in Pakistan, Egypt, and other Middle East countries. Often lacking their own refining facilities, such countries have tended to import palm oil products from Malaysia in fully processed, ready-to-eat form.

The Malaysian government encouraged this trend by offering tax concessions for refineries in their early years and by progressive remission of the export tax on crude palm oil, graded according to the degree of processing of the end product. This development received a mixed reaction in Western Europe, which had ample processing capacity and extensive technical know-how (Berger, personal observation). However, it proved successful in stimulating the growth of new Asian markets, as shown in Table II.E.3.8.

Although private enterprises had an excellent record in developing new processing techniques, they often felt hampered by their distance from major markets, which posed difficulties in designing and introducing new products. In 1979 the Malaysian government set up a specialized Palm Oil Research Institute (PORIM) as a statutory body, financed by a levy on palm oil production. A major part of its mission was the development of application technology for palm oil and the propagation of the information to end users anywhere in the world. By studying consumption patterns of oils and fats, the Institute's staff was able to identify potential new markets and provide the technical input needed for their development (PORIM 1981: 1–5). Their work proved useful to producers worldwide, especially from the late 1980s on when a debate arose over palm oil's nutritional value.

Nutritional Properties of Palm Oil

Briefly, the general nutritional functions of fat are to:

1. Provide energy efficiently.
2. Supply the essential linoleic and linolenic acids.
3. Carry the fat soluble vitamins A, D, and E.
4. Improve the palatability of foods.

The specific nutritional properties of palm oil may be considered in relation to its chemical composition. Typical values are given in Table II.E.3.9.

Table II.E.3.9. *Composition of pam oil*

1. The main fatty acids	Percentage
C14:0	1.0
C16:0	43.7
C18:0	4.4
C18:1	39.9
C18:2	10.3
C18:3	0.4
Others	0.3

2. The main glycerides	Percentage	Major components
Trisaturated	8.5	(PPP)
Mono unsaturated	37.7	(POP, PPO)
Di-unsaturated	11.7	(OOO, PLO)
More unsaturated	11.7	(OOO, PLO)

3. The nonglyceride components

Crude palm oil	Ppm	Main component
Carotenoids	640	beta-carotene, alpha-carotene
Tocopherols	850	gamma-tocotrienol, alpha-tocotrienol, alpha-tocopherol
Sterols	300	beta-sitosterol, campesterol
Triterpene alcohols	800	

Source: Table based on Berger (1983a).

Table II.E.3.8. *Palm oil imports to selected regions (thousand tonnes per annum)*

Region	1960	1970	1980	1990
W. Europe	470	520	830	1,600
United States	20	60	120	130
India	40	–	530	630
Japan	10	40	150	280
Former USSR	1	10	100	210
Pakistan	–	–	270	680
Egypt	–	–	–	330
Iraq	–	–	110	220
S. Korea	–	–	130	220
Turkey	–	–	–	200
Saudi Arabia	–	–	110	130
China	–	–	60	110
World total	620	930	3,682	8,440

Sources: Mielke (1988), pp. 76; (1991), p. 110; and Amiruddin and Ahmad (1984).

Table II.E.3.10. *Tocopherol content of typical refined palm oil*

alpha-tocopherol	180 ppm
alpha-tocotrienol	149 ppm
gamma-tocotrienol	239 ppm
delta-tocotrienol	62 ppm

Source: Gapor and Berger (1983).

The unsaturated acids present are mainly oleic, with a useful level of linoleic and a small amount of linolenic acid. In consequence, palm oil has a high stability to oxidation. Palm oil is readily absorbed and shows a digestibility of 97 percent or greater, similar to that of other common edible oils.

As in other vegetable oils, the middle 2-position is mainly occupied by unsaturated fatty acids. This is different from animal fats, where the 2-position is usually occupied by a saturated fatty acid.

Unrefined, or "virgin," palm oil is one of the richest natural sources of carotenoids. Regrettably, these are removed during the industrial refining process so that their nutritional benefits are lost, except to populations who traditionally use palm oil in the unrefined state.

The tocopherol content (see Table II.E.3.10) is one of the most interesting features in palm oil because it consists mainly of the tocotrienols, with an unsaturated side chain. These are not found in the other common vegetable oils.

Analytical work has shown that an average of 50 to 60 percent of the tocopherol content remains after refining, but the extent of removal depends on the refining conditions used. The tocopherols are important natural antioxidants, although their antioxidant activity is somewhat lower than the synthetic phenolic antioxidants permitted in foods. They are less volatile and, therefore, more persistent in high-temperature conditions, such as in deep-fat frying. The tocopherol content is a major factor in stabilizing palm oil against oxidation. The nutritional benefit of tocopherols in a number of disease conditions in which free radicals or oxidation are implicated has become a very active field of research, although to date little has been done on tocotrienols as such.

The three major component fatty acids of palm oil – palmitic, oleic, and linoleic acids – are also the most common fatty acids found in vegetable oils. Palm oil has been used as a traditional food in West Africa probably for thousands of years, which provides some evidence that it has good nutritional properties.

Research into coronary heart disease in relation to diet led to the general hypothesis of A. Keys, J. T. Anderson, and F. Grande (1957) that saturated fatty acids raised blood cholesterol levels, whereas linoleic acid reduced them. Subsequent refinements of the hypothesis (Hegstedt et al. 1965) indicated that saturated acids did not all have the same effect. In particular, D. M. Hegstedt and colleagues concluded that myristic acid was 3 to 4 times more effective than palmitic acid in raising blood cholesterol levels.

The early work leading to these hypotheses did not use palm oil in the experimental diets. However, between 1985 and 1987, concern was expressed in the media, principally in the United States, that the saturated fatty acid content of palm oil meant that it would raise blood cholesterol levels and was, therefore, an undesirable food component. This assertion was not based on any direct experimental evidence. Instead, a review of the few dietary experiments in which palm oil had been used (as a control, not as the subject of investigation) showed that, in general, a small reduction in blood cholesterol level was experienced (New findings on palm oil 1987).

Subsequently, a study in Nigeria, a principal traditional consumer of palm oil, was published (Kesteloot et al. 1989). Serum lipid levels were measured in 307 men and 235 women, whose ages were 15 to 64 (mean 38.8) for men and 15 to 44 (mean 31.4) for women. Mean values for total serum cholesterol were 156.3 and 170.9, respectively, and for HDL cholesterol 46.0 and 49.0. Subjects consumed their normal diet, with 84 percent of the fat intake from palm oil. These serum lipid levels compared very favorably with black and white populations in the United States, where total fat intake is much higher, and where palm oil comprises only 1 to 2 percent of total fat intake (Park and Yetley 1990).

A number of new dietary studies have addressed the nutritional properties of palm oil, particularly in its effect on blood lipids. T. K. W. Ng and colleagues (1991), for example, found that when palm olein formed 75 percent of fat intake in a normal Malaysian diet, total serum cholesterol was significantly reduced, by 9 percent from the level at entry, and that the reduction was almost entirely in the undesirable LDL cholesterol. The study was carried out on 20 men and 7 women of average age 24.

A. Marzuki and colleagues (1991) used 110 residential high school students of both sexes as subjects (ages 16 to 17). Although the normal menu was provided, palm olein was the sole cooking oil for 5 weeks. This was followed by a "washout" period of 6 weeks on regular cooking oil and a second experimental 5 weeks in which only soya bean oil was used. There was no difference in plasma total LDL or HDL cholesterol between the two trial periods.

K. Sundram and colleagues (1992) carried out a double blind crossover study on 38 men, in which 70 percent of the fat in a normal Dutch diet was replaced by palm oil. There was no effect on total serum cholesterol, but a significant increase of 11 percent in HDL 2 cholesterol, resulting in a beneficial decrease in the LDL/HDL 2+3 ratio. G. Hornstra and co-workers (1991) also measured plasma lipoprotein (a), which is strongly associated with an increased risk of ischemic cardiovascular disease. They found a highly significant 10 percent decrease in this component during the test diet period, and the decrease was greatest in subjects with an initial high level of lipoprotein (a), that is, those with an enhanced risk.

R. Wood and colleagues (1993) examined the effect of six different fats used as components of items of a normal American diet on 30 middle-aged men. When refined palm oil formed 60 percent of the dietary fat intake, there was no significant effect on total cholesterol, but HDL cholesterol was increased compared with the baseline diet.

Ng and colleagues (1992) studied 33 subjects consuming a Malaysian diet containing 34 percent of calories as fat. When palm olein was 23 percent of energy (that is, two-thirds of the fat intake), there was no significant difference in serum total – LDL or HDL cholesterol contents from the levels at entry. The use of olive oil in place of palm olein gave almost identical results, although the ratio of Thromboxane B_2 to Prostacyclin PGFI alpha was significantly lower during the palm olein dietary period.

D. Heber and colleagues (1992) found no increase in the plasma total cholesterol level of 9 subjects, but a small rise in plasma HDL cholesterol when one-half of the dietary fat was palm oil. The diet contained 35 percent energy as fat.

A. S. Truswell and co-workers (1992) conducted 2 trials (21 and 30 subjects, respectively) in which one-half of the dietary fat was palm olein. He found that a 10 percent increase in HDL cholesterol accounted for the 3 percent rise in total cholesterol observed.

The conclusion is that palm oil, used as a dietary fat at a high level – 10 to 20 times that usual in a Western diet – does not raise serum total cholesterol. However, the level of serum HDL cholesterol (popularly described as the "good" cholesterol, because in this form cholesterol is catabolized and removed) was significantly increased in several of the recent studies.

Mention might also be made of two additional studies, by R. C. Cottrell (1991) and C. E. Elson (1992). These authors reviewed 139 and 180 scientific publications, respectively, and both concluded that palm oil was a nutritionally satisfactory component of the diet. Cottrell wrote that "the decision to use palm oil in food products should be based on a rational appraisal of its technical performance value rather than on a misconceived view of the health implications of its use" (Cottrell 1991: 989S–1009S).

Nonetheless, the view still persists in some circles that palm oil is an unhealthy tropical grease, and it is difficult for palm oil producers to counter this perception because the product had little or no public image among Western and Asian consumers before the start of the recent media debate. Processed until it has become an anonymous ingredient, and used in a wide variety of compound fats and such other items as biscuits, its original flavor and feel have been lost to most consumers. But now that the wider nutritional benefits of palm oil's natural carotenoids are becoming more generally recognized, perhaps it is time to rediscover the fully flavored red oil and promote its use, not only in Africa and Latin America but also in Asia and the West.

K. G. Berger
S. M. Martin

Bibliography

Allott, D. H. N., and I. C. H. Wong. 1977. Evolution of palm oil marketing from Malaysia. In *International developments in palm oil,* ed. D. A. Earp and W. Newall, 469-78. Kuala Lumpur.

Amiruddin, M. N., and I. Ahmad. 1984. Prospects for palm oil in the Middle East and selected African countries. In *Proceedings of the international seminar on market development for palm oil products,* ed. Y. Basiron and K. G. Berger, 131-9. Kuala Lumpur.

Andersen, A. J. C. 1954. *Margarine.* London.

Anwar, M. 1981. *Current and prospective situations of the oil palm/palm oil industry.* Palm Oil Research Institute of Malaysia, Occasional Paper No. 1. Kuala Lumpur.

Beirnaert, A., and R. Vanderweyen. 1941. *Contribution à l'étude génétique et biométrique des variétés d'Elaeis guineensis jacquin.* Publications de l'Institut National pour l'Étude Agronomique, Série Scientifique 27. Belgian Congo.

Berger, K. G. 1983a. Palm oil. In *Handbook of tropical foods,* ed. Harvey T. Chan and Marcel Dekker, 447-56. New York.

  1983b. Past, present and future oils and fats supplies. *Proceedings of the Institute of Food Science and Technology* 16: 41-7.

  1992. *Food uses of palm oil.* Kuala Lumpur.

Bulletin Perkebunan. 1991. Vol. 22: 230-1.

Cottrell, R. C. 1991. Introduction: Nutritional aspects of palm oil. *American Journal of Clinical Nutrition* 53: 989S-1009S.

Courade, G. 1977. *Les plantations industrielles d'Unilever au Cameroun.* Yaounde, Cameroon.

Creutzberg, P. 1975. *Changing economy in Indonesia,* Vol. 1. Amsterdam.

Elsdon, G. D. 1926. *Edible oils and fats.* London.

Elson, C. E. 1992. Tropical oils: Nutritional and scientific issues. *Critical Reviews in Food Science and Nutrition* 31: 79-102.

Empire Marketing Board. 1932. No. 54: *Survey of vegetable oilseeds and oils,* Vol. 1: *Oil palm products.* London.

Faulkner, O. T., and C. J. Lewis. 1923. Native methods of preparing palm oil. II. *Nigeria: Second Annual Bulletin of the Agricultural Department,* 3-10.

Feron, R. 1969. Technology and production. In *Margarine: An economic, social and scientific history, 1869-1969,* ed. J. H. Van Stuyvenberg, 83-121. Liverpool.

Fieldhouse, D. K. 1978. *Unilever overseas: The anatomy of a multinational, 1895-1965.* London and Stanford, Calif.

Friedel, M. C. 1897. Sur des matières grasses trouvées dans des tombes égyptiennes d'Abydos. *Comptes Rendu* 24: 648-51.

Gapor, A., and K. G. Berger. 1983. Tocopherols and tocotrienols in palm oil. In *Palm oil product technology in the eighties,* ed. E. Pushparajah and M. Rajadurai, 145-56. Kuala Lumpur.

Gray, J. E. 1922. Native methods of preparing palm oil. *Nigeria: First Annual Bulletin of the Agricultural Department*, 29-50.

Hancock, W. K. 1942. *A survey of British Commonwealth affairs*, Vol. 2, Part 2. London.

Hartley, C. W. S. 1988. *The oil palm (Elaeis guineensis Jacq.).* Third edition. London.

Heber, D., J. M. Ashley, M. E. Solares, et al. 1992. The effects of a palm oil enriched diet on plasma lipids and lipoproteins in healthy young men. *Nutrition Research* 12: S53-S61.

Hegsted, D. M., R. B. McGandy, M. L. Myers, and F. J. Stare. 1965. Quantitative effects of dietary fat on serum cholesterol in man. *American Journal of Clinical Nutrition* 17: 281-95.

Hopkins, A. G. H. 1973. *An economic history of West Africa.* London.

Hornstra, G., A. C. Van Houwelingen, A. D. M. Kester, and K. Sundram. 1991. A palm oil enriched diet lowers serum lipoprotein (a) in normocholesterolemic volunteers. *Atherosclerosis* 90: 91-3.

Iwuchukwu, A. N. 1965. Influence of marketing boards system and preliminary purification on Nigerian palm oil exports. In *Proceedings of oil palm conference at Tropical Products Institute*, 73-7. London.

Jacobsberg, B. 1974. Survey of the palm oil production in 1973. In *Proceedings of the first Malaysian Agricultural Research and Development Institute workshop on palm oil technology*, 72-119. Kuala Lumpur.

Jewsiewicki, B. 1983. Rural society and the Belgian colonial economy. In *History of Central Africa*, Vol. 2, ed. D. Birmingham and P. M. Martin, 95-125. London.

Johansson, G., and P. O. Pehlergard. 1977. Aspects on quality of palm oil. In *International developments in palm oil*, ed. D. A. Earp and W. Newall, 203-23. Kuala Lumpur.

Kesteloot, H., V. O. Oviasu, A. O. Obasohan, et al. 1989. Serum lipid and apolipoprotein levels in a Nigerian population sample. *Atherosclerosis* 78: 33-8.

Keys, A., J. T. Anderson, and F. Grande. 1957. Prediction of serum cholesterol responses of man to changes in fats in the diet. *Lancet* 11: 959-66.

Kheiri, S. A. 1987. End uses of palm oil: Human food. In *Critical reports on applied chemistry*, Vol. 15: *Palm oil*, ed. F. D. Gunstone, 71-83. London.

Khera, H. S. 1976. *The oil palm industry of Malaysia: An economic study.* Kuala Lumpur.

Laurent, M. 1912-13. Notes sur l'Elaeis au Congo Belge. *Bulletin Agricole du Congo Belge*, 3: 938-45; 4: 695-701.

Leplae, E. 1939. *Le palmier à huile en Afrique: Son exploitation au Congo Belge et en Extrême-Orient.* Brussels.

Lewkowitsch, J. 1895. *Chemical technology and analysis of oils, fats and waxes.* London.
    1922. *Chemical technology and analysis of oils, fats and waxes.* Sixth edition. London.

Lim, C.-Y. 1967. *Economic development of modern Malaya.* Kuala Lumpur.

Loncin, M., and B. Jacobsberg. 1965. Research on palm oil in Belgium and the Congo. In *Proceedings of oil palm conference at Tropical Products Institute*, 85-95. London.

Lynn, M. 1989. From sail to steam: The impact of the steamship services on the British palm oil trade with West Africa, 1850-1890. *Journal of African History* 30: 227-45.

Manning, P. 1982. *Slavery, colonialism and economic growth in Dahomey, 1640-1960.* Cambridge.

Martin, S. M. 1988. *Palm oil and protest: An economic history of the Ngwa region, south-eastern Nigeria, 1800-1980.* Cambridge.

Marzuki, A., F. Arshad, T. A. Razak, and K. Jaarin. 1991. Influence of dietary fat on plasma lipid profiles of Malaysia adolescents. *American Journal of Clinical Nutrition* 53: 1010S-14S.

Meredith, D. 1986. State controlled marketing and economic "development": The case of West African produce during the Second World War. *Economic History Review*, 2nd series 39: 77-91.

Mielke, S., ed. 1988. *Oil world.* Hamburg.
    1991. Commodity section. *Oil world annual.* Hamburg.

Moll, H. A. J. 1987. *The economics of the oil palm.* Wageningen, Netherlands.

New findings on palm oil. 1987. *Nutritional Review* 45: 205-7.

Ng, T. K. W., K. Hassan, J. B. Lim, et al. 1991. Non-hypercholesterolemic effects of a palm oil diet in Malaysian volunteers. *American Journal of Clinical Nutrition* 53: 1015S-20S.

Ng, T. K. W., K. C. Hayes, G. DeWitt, et al. 1992. Dietary palmitic acid (16:0) and oleic acid (18:1) exert similar effects on serum cholesterol and lipoprotein profiles in normo cholesterolemic humans. *Journal of the American College of Nutrition* 11: 383-90.

Northrup, D. 1978. *Trade without rulers: Pre-colonial economic development in south-eastern Nigeria.* Oxford.

Nwanze, S. C. 1965. Semi-commercial scale palm oil processing. *Proceedings of oil palm conference at Tropical Products Institute*, 63-6. London.

Palm Oil Registration and Licensing Authority. 1993. *Palm Oil Update: March.* Kuala Lumpur.

Park, Y. K., and E. A. Yetley. 1990. Trend changes in use and current intakes of tropical oils in the United States. *American Journal of Clinical Nutrition* 51: 738-48.

PORIM. 1981. *Palm Oil Research Institute of Malaysia: Annual research report.* Kuala Lumpur.

Reid, J. 1986. Warrior aristocrats in crisis: The political effects of the transition from the slave trade to palm oil commerce in the nineteenth century kingdom of Dahomey. Ph.D. thesis, University of Stirling, Scotland.

Rosenquist, E. 1986. The genetic base of oil palm breeding populations. *Proceedings of international workshop on oil palm germplasm and utilisation, March 1985.* Kuala Lumpur.

Rudin, H. R. 1938. *Germans in the Cameroons, 1884-1914: A case study in modern imperialism.* New Haven, Conn.

Shipment of palm oil in bulk. 1931. *The Planter* 11-12: 353-4.

Sundram, K., G. Hornstra, A. C. Van Houwelingen, and A. D. M. Kester. 1992. Replacement of dietary fat with palm oil: Effect on human serum lipids, lipoproteins and apolipoproteins. *British Journal of Nutrition* 68: 677-92.

Taniputra, B., A. W. Lubis, K. Pamin, and S. Syukur. 1988. Progress of oil palm industry in Indonesia in the last 15 years: 1971-1985. *Proceedings of international oil palm conference, Kuala Lumpur, September 1987*, 27-34. Kuala Lumpur.

Truswell, A. S., N. Choudhury, and D. C. K. Roberts. 1992. Double blind comparison of plasma lipids in healthy subjects, eating potato crisps fried in palm olein or canola oil. *Nutrition Research* 12: S43-S52.

Vanderyst, R. P. H. 1920. La technique indigène de récolte des fruits de l'Elaeis. *Bulletin agricole du Congo Belge* 11: 22-35.

Vanneck, C., and M. Loncin. 1951. Considérations sur l'alteration de l'huile de palme. *Bulletin agricole du Congo Belge* 42: 57–64.

Wilson, C. 1954. *The History of Unilever,* Vol 1. London.

Wilson, L. E. 1991. *The Krobo people of Ghana to 1892: A political and social history.* Athens, Ohio.

Wong, C. Y. 1981. Malaysian crude palm oil quality delivered to refiners. In *Palm oil product technology in the eighties,* ed. E. Pushparajah and M. Rajadurai, 81–7. Kuala Lumpur.

Wood, R., K. Kubena, R. Crook, et al. 1993. Effects of palm oil, margarine, butter, and sunflower oil on the serum lipids and lipoproteins of hormocholesterolemic middle aged men. *Journal of Nutritional Biochemistry* 4: 286–97.

II.E.4 ❧ Sesame

Botanical Description

Sesame (*Sesamum indicum* L.) belongs to the Pedaliaceae, a small family of about 15 genera and 60 species of annual and perennial herbs. These occur mainly in the Old World tropics and subtropics, with the greatest number in Africa (Purseglove 1968). Sesame is a crop of hot, dry climates, grown for its oil- and protein-rich seeds. The oil is valued for its stability, color, nutty flavor, and resistance to rancidity.

A large number of cultivars are known (Bedigian, Smyth, and Harlan 1986). These differ in their maturation time, degree of branching, leaf shape and color, and number of flowers per leaf axil, which may be 1 or 3. The locules in the capsule usually number 4 or 8. The known cultivars also vary in length of capsule, in intensity of flower color, and especially in seed color, which ranges from pure white to black, with intervening shades of ivory, beige, tan, yellow, brown, red, and gray. The seeds are about 3 millimeters long and have a flattened pear shape. The capsules open automatically when dry, causing the seed to scatter.

Production

Sesame is usually grown as a rain-fed crop. It has many agricultural advantages: It sets seed and yields relatively well under high temperatures, it is tolerant of drought, and it does reasonably well on poor soils. It is very sensitive to day length and is intolerant of waterlogging. The major obstacle to the expansion of sesame is its habit of shattering: The absence of non-shattering cultivars, suitable for machine harvest, results in labor-intensive harvest seasons. Because of this obstacle, the crop is not suitable for large-scale commercial production (although breeding for non-shattering traits has been ongoing). Instead, sesame has typically been grown on a small scale for local consumption or in places where labor is cheap. The

major sesame-producing countries, listed in order of decreasing tonnage, are India, China, Myanmar (formerly Burma), Sudan, Nigeria, and Uganda (FAO 1992).

Chemical Composition and Nutritional Value

Oil

The chief constituent of sesame seed is oil, which usually constitutes 40 to 60 percent of seed weight. This is a greater oil content than most other oil crops (Hussein and Noaman 1976; Tinay, Khattab, and Khidir 1976; Salunkhe et al. 1991). Sesame oil content is related to seed color, although this is specific to geographic location. For example, the white-seeded varieties in the Sudan have a lower oil content than the red-seeded varieties (Bedigian and Harlan 1983), but in Ethiopia white or light-colored seeds usually have more oil than dark-colored seeds (Seegeler 1989).

Seed color differences are also economically significant. In West Bengal, white-seeded sesame is sold at a price at least 30 percent higher than that of brown-seeded or black-seeded varieties because of its higher oil content and greater culinary utility (Chakraborty, Maiti, and Chatterjee 1984). But appreciation of sesame by seed color can also be cultural: The Japanese, for example, prefer black-seeded varieties (Y. Kakehashi, personal communication, 1995), whereas the Sudanese prefer white-seeded ones.

Sesame

In a collection of sesame plants from around the world, tested by D. M. Yermanos and colleagues (1972), the mean oil content in 721 samples was 53.1 percent; the oil was clear and colorless in 47.4 percent of the samples and light green in 37.2 percent, with the remaining samples dark green or brown. Short plants tended to have colorless oil, whereas tall plants had light green oil, and early plants had higher seed oil content. Earliness, yellow seed color, and large seed size were associated with a lower iodination value. However, Y. K. Sharma, A. D. Deodhar, and S. K. Gangrade (1975) reported no relationship between oil content and iodination values, free fatty acids, and carbohydrate content.

Fatty acids. Sesame oil contains about 80 percent unsaturated fatty acids, with oleic acid and linoleic acid predominating and present in approximately equal amounts (Lyon 1972). Sesame has more unsaturated fatty acids than many other vegetable oils, and its higher proportion of unsaturated to saturated fatty acids makes it a potentially important dietary source of essential fatty acids. Linoleic acid is required for cell membranes, for transportation of cholesterol in the bloodstream, and for blood clotting (reviewed in Salunkhe et al. 1991).

Antioxidants. Sesame oil is remarkably stable because of its natural antioxidants, sesamin and sesamolin, two compounds not found in any other oil (Bedigian, Seigler, and Harlan 1985). These are phenylpropanoid lignans and serve to protect against rancidity (Weiss 1971; Salih 1993), which may be one reason that sesame is nicknamed the "Queen of Oilseeds." Other unsaponifiable substances in sesame oil include sterols, triterpenes, pigments, and tocopherols.

Protein
The press cake remaining after the oil is expressed is approximately half the initial seed weight and high in protein. C. K. Lyon (1972) reported a protein content range of 17 to 32 percent. Although low in lysine, sesame proteins are especially rich in the essential amino acids methionine and tryptophan, and sesame meal flour is recommended as an excellent source of methionine-rich proteins (Villegas, González, and Calderón 1968). These can be a valuable supplement to pulse proteins, such as those in beans or chickpeas, which contain adequate amounts of lysine but are usually deficient in sulfur-containing amino acids (Fernández de Campoy 1981). S. A. Godfrey, B. J. Frances, and C. S. Kamara (1976) have suggested a combination of cowpea (deficient in methionine) and sesame to overcome the problem of limiting amino acids.

Carbohydrates
The carbohydrate content of sesame seeds (21 to 25 percent) is comparable to that of peanuts and higher than that of soybeans (Joshi 1961). D. J. Wankhede and R. N. Tharanathan (1976) have reported that sesame contains 5 percent sugars – d-glucose, d-galactose, d-fructose, sucrose, raffinose, stachyose, planteose, and sesamose – as well as higher homologues of the planteose series.

Minerals and Vitamins
Sesame seeds are a good source of calcium, phosphorus, and iron. Nearly one-half to two-thirds of the calcium in the seed is present as oxalate, and a major part of it is located in the outer husk of the seed. The seeds are often dehulled for food use; thus, the oxalate does not interfere with the absorption of calcium. Sesame seeds contain high levels of thiamine, riboflavin, and nicotinic acid (Tabekhia and Mohammed 1971). When made into sesame butter, they lose 52.5 percent of their thiamine and 50.2 percent of their nicotinic acid. The oil is rich in vitamin E.

Minor Constituents
Sesame contains among the highest levels of phytate found in nature (Boland, Garner, and O'Dell 1975). In foods, phytate can be detrimental to the absorption of trace elements such as zinc, presumably through formation of a stable insoluble complex that does not release zinc to the absorption sites in the intestinal mucosa. It is conceivable that the indigestible phytate-protein complexes could make zinc and other nutrients even less biologically available. In attempting to isolate and characterize the phytate, B. L. O'Dell and A. de Boland (1976) found that it was not readily extracted by neutral aqueous solvents because it exists as an insoluble magnesium complex.

While studying the natural occurrence of *Fusarium* toxins in feedstuffs, C. J. Mirocha and colleagues (1976) reported, for the first time, the natural occurrence of zearalenone in sesame seed. The presence of aflatoxin B_1 was sought in 292 samples of seeds other than peanuts, and sesame was among the 8 found to contain it, at 0.06 mg per kg (Monacelli et al. 1976).

In addition, unhulled sesame contains 1 to 2 percent oxalic acid (Lyon 1972), which can be removed by decortication.

Changes Effected by Processing
Roasting
Sesame seed is used as a nourishing food as well as a flavoring agent, and its characteristic flavor is developed by dry-roasting the dehulled material. S. N. Chaudhry (1988) investigated the chemical changes in protein quality induced by roasting at various temperatures. He determined that optimal roasting of sesame (with respect to flavor and oil quality) required a temperature of 200° C for a duration of one hour. G.-C. Yen and S.-L. Shyu (1989), however, concluded that sesame oil prepared under optimum processing conditions meant roasting at 200° C for 30 minutes.

Extraction

Sesame oil can be extracted from the whole seeds by several different processes (Johnson and Raymond 1964). Chaudhry (1988), who compared press-extracted to solvent-extracted oil (from roasted sesame seeds), reported that press extraction can release impurities (such as pigments and metal ions) that could react with the oil, resulting in complex formation. Solvent extraction, on the other hand, can cause the loss of desirable flavoring compounds during the evaporation of the solvent. A method of crushing sesame seeds for oil extraction is described in *Law's Grocer's Manual*, published about 1892:

> Sesame is also widely cultivated in Syria, where, in preparing the oil, the grain is soaked in water for 24 hrs, and then placed in an oblong pot, coated with cement, on which two men work a wooden hammer of 20 lb. weight.... Efforts are not made to mash the kernels. The skins are separated in a tub of water, salted to a degree sufficient to float an egg. The bran sinks, while the kernels remain on the surface. The sesame seeds are now broiled in an oven, and sent to the mill to be ground. From the millstone the oil drops into a jar, and is thick, of a dark yellow colour, and sweet (quoted in David 1970: 54).

Toxicity

Sesame seeds are extremely powerful allergens, and sensitized persons may suffer urticaria, Quinke's edema, asthma, and even anaphylaxis (Kägi and Wüthrich 1993). Although such reactions to sesame seeds are rare, the potential danger should be recognized, especially in view of an increasing demand for vegetarian foods.

Origin

Sesame was cultivated in ancient India, Sumer, Egypt, and Anatolia and throughout the Greco-Roman world for its edible seed and for its oil (Bedigian 1985; Bedigian and Harlan 1986). It is often described as the oldest oilseed plant used by humans (Joshi 1961; Weiss 1971). There has been some confusion about its origin, however, that has been discussed by N. M. Nayar and K. L. Mehra (1970), Nayar (1976), and Dorothea Bedigian (1984).

A group of wild and weedy forms native to India and described as *Sesamum orientale* L. var. *malabaricum* Nar. shows close morphological, genetic, and phytochemical affinities to the cultivar. Bedigian (1988) and colleagues (Bedigian, Seigler, and Harlan 1985; Bedigian, Smyth, and Harlan 1986) have provided evidence to support the theory that domesticated sesame arose from this progenitor on the Indian subcontinent. D. Zohary and M. Hopf (1994) concurred with Bedigian and J. R. Harlan (1986) that the botanical evidence supports a relatively late introduc-tion of sesame into the Near East and the Mediterranean region. The genus is restricted to the Indian subcontinent, where there are only a few wild species, and to Africa south of the Sahara, where there are numerous wild species.

The Archaeological Record

The Indian Subcontinent: Harappa

The oldest known remains of sesame seeds were found at the Indus Valley civilization site of Harappa (Vats 1940), in Pakistan, where excavators uncovered "a quantity of lumped and burnt *Sesamum*" specimens. M. S. Vats (1940) dated the sesame to about 3500 to 3050 B.C. but this was before the advent of radiocarbon dating, and the dates are probably much too early (see Bedigian 1985 and Bedigian and Harlan 1986 for reviews of the evidence and its archaeological context). The Indus Valley, however, is probably the area where the plant was first cultivated.

The Preclassical Near East

Mesopotamia. To date, no sesame seeds have been recovered from excavations in Mesopotamia.

Egypt: King Tutankhamen's Tomb. The discovery of sesame seed remains associated with the burial of King Tutankhamen (around 1350 B.C.) pushes back the date of the earliest record for sesame seeds in the Near East (Vartavan 1990). Some 30 boxes of plant remains from his tomb were stored at the Royal Botanical Gardens, Kew, England, where botanist Leonard Boodle worked on cataloging these specimens until his death in the 1930s.

Recently, Christian L. T. de Vartavan, a graduate student, had the good fortune of being allowed to go through these boxes to examine the contents. A letter to Bedigian from Mr. Vartavan, dated July 20, 1988, stated that there were 60 milliliters (ml) of sesame seeds, which were the main ingredients of one of the many containers in the tomb filled with food, drinks, ointments, perfumes, and oils. Vartavan viewed these seeds as "the most striking find" among the remains from the room designated by Howard Carter (who discovered the tomb in 1927) as the "Annexe" to Tutankhamen's tomb. These seeds from the Annexe represent the only find of sesame ever recorded from investigations of ancient Egypt, as well as the earliest sesame from the Near East and from Africa.

Armenia: Karmir Blur. Remains of sesame seeds dated between 900 and 600 B.C. have been found at this early Iron Age Urartian site on the outskirts of Yerevan. Four large jars containing carbonized sesame seed were excavated. Elaborate devices for the extraction of sesame oil indicate that the Urartians processed the seeds for oil (Piotrovskii 1950, 1952;

Kassabian 1957; Bedigian 1985; Bedigian and Harlan 1986).

Jordan: Deir Alla. Some 200 sesame seeds dating from about 800 B.C. were uncovered in Iron Age beds at this site in Jordan, according to R. Neef (1989).

Turkey. Sesame seeds were recovered at the Gordion ruins in Anatolia during the 1989 excavation of the "Destruction Level" (around 700 B.C.). The seeds are from a pure sample (about 250 ml) from within a pot that was found on the floor (along with other pots containing pure wheat, barley, and lentil). Massive burning and the collapse of the roof seems to have effectively sealed the contents on the floor (N. Miller, personal communication, 1990).

Early Literary Records

The Indian Subcontinent
The fact that the Sanskrit words for oil and for sesame seed are the same suggests that sesame may be one of the earliest oil-bearing plants to have been brought under cultivation (Sampson 1936: 221). One of these words, *tíla,* has been employed in religious ceremonies from very early times. It was regarded as holy (Hopkins 1968), and an offering of *tíla* seeds was considered effective in removing sins (Gupta 1971). Offerings of water and sesame were said to free an individual of all debts to his ancestors.

The Near East
Mesopotamia. Early Old Babylonian (OB) documents contain numerous references to sesame oil (Simmons 1978). Texts list the expenditure of sesame oil "for the inner bolt," "for the fire offering," "for the prince," "for the royal purification rite," "for the inner bolt on the day of Akitu," "for the sizkur divine name," "for the Elunum divine name," "for the regular offering," and "for anointing the banner." These are all special cultic applications that employed the oil to lubricate, soap, or fuel someone or something, almost certainly at springtime festivals (W. Doyle, personal communication, 1984).

The article for *ellu* in the *Assyrian Dictionary of the Oriental Institute, Chicago* (better known as the *Chicago Assyrian Dictionary* [CAD], ed. Oppenheim et al. 1958) provides as one definition: "[C]lean, pure in connection with oil, etc. . . . fine oil . . . sweet oil . . . pure sesame oil, sesame oil of the first [pressing]," used for anointing and making perfume. Another definition is: "[H]oly, sacred."

The *šamaššammū* article prepared for the CAD's "Š" volume (Reiner ed. 1989: 301–7) mentions several texts that help to identify *šamaššammū* as sesame. The article itself contains many references to oil pressing, including one text (Keiser 1917) that specifies *šamaššammū pesûtu* (white *šamaššammū.*) The

texts concerning white-seeded *šamaššammū* provide evidence of considerable importance in helping to distinguish flax from sesame because there are no flax cultivars with white seeds (J. Miller, personal communication, 1984).

Egypt. The earliest Egyptian textual reference to sesame seems to have been in the Tebtunis Papyri 3 (Part 2, No. 844) that dates from 256 B.C. (Lucas 1962: 336). H. Deines and H. Grapow (1959) indicated that sesame was used as a medicine. Pliny (1938: 15.7.31) wrote that a large amount of oil in Egypt was obtained from gingelly *(sesamum).*

The difficulty is to identify the ancient words for sesame. There is a striking linguistic resemblance of the Mesopotamian word *šamaššammū* to related Near Eastern terms, such as the Arabic word *simsim* and the name of a plant with edible seeds that is transcribed *smsmt* (Germer 1979). V. Loret (1892) regarded the Coptic name for sesame, *oke,* as Egyptian in origin. Another word from the hieroglyphs, *ake,* referred to a plant that produced oil and had seeds that were used medicinally. *Ake,* then, could be the Egyptian name for sesame (Loret 1892). But whether this later became the highest-quality oil, which was *nhh,* that one encounters from the nineteenth dynasty (1320 to 1200 B.C.) onward, remains a mystery. The assertion by some authors that *nhh* was *Ricinus* oil has been disputed on the grounds that castor oil is unpalatable (Keimer 1924) and also toxic.

Classical Greece
Sesame was cultivated extensively in the Greco-Roman world, but more for its edible seed than for its oil. The writings of Greek travelers and historians make it clear that sesame was well known in Mesopotamia by the time of the Iron Age, which began in about the eighteenth century B.C. About 300 years later, Herodotus (1928) observed that the only oil the Babylonians used was from sesame.

The cultivation of sesame in ancient Armenia was documented in the fifth century B.C. by Xenophon, who wrote: "In (western Armenia) . . . there was a scented unguent in abundance that they used instead of olive oil, made from pork fat, sesame seed, bitter almond and turpentine. There was a sweet oil also to be found, made of the same ingredients." Xenophon also placed sesame in two other parts of Anatolia. One was Cilicia – "[t]his plain produces sesame plentifully, also panic and millet and barley and wheat" (1901: I.ii.22) – and the other was "Calpe Haven in Asiatic Thrace," farther west. "Calpe lies exactly midway between Byzantium and Heracleia," has "good loamy soil . . . produces barley and wheat, pulses of all sorts, millet and sesame, figs in ample supply, numerous vines . . . indeed everything else except olives" (I.ii.22).

Imperial Rome

Cultivation requirements. Columella, in the first century A.D., reported accurately that "it [sesame] usually requires loamy soil, but it thrives no less well in rich sand or in mixed ground.... But I have seen this same seed sown in the months of June and July in districts of Cilicia and Syria, and harvested during autumn, when it was fully ripe" (1941: 2.10.18). He also wrote that "[i]n some districts [of Anatolia] such as Cilicia and Pamphylia, sesame is sown this month [late July to August]; but in the damp regions of Italy it can be done in the last part of the month of June" (11.2.56). This report would seem to indicate that, like the Babylonians, the Cilicians and Pamphylians grew sesame as a second crop after harvesting barley or another earlier crop.

Pliny, also writing in the first century A.D., said that gingelly [*Sesamum*] and Italian millets were summer grains and that gingelly came from India, where it was also used for making oil; and the color of the grain was white. He appears to have known sesame well. His advice for soaking the seeds prior to milling is reminiscent of the practice in Urartu: "Gingelly is to be steeped in warm water and spread out on a stone, and then rolled well and the stone then dipped in cold water so that the chaff may float to the top, and the chaff again spread out in the sun on a linen sheet, before being rolled again" (Pliny 1938: 18.22.98). In addition, E. L. Sturtevant (1972) stated that the Romans ground sesame seeds with cumin to make a pasty spread for bread.

Urartu (Armenia)

Based upon his participation in the excavation of an oil-extraction workshop at the Urartian site of Karmir Blur near Yerevan, Z. Kassabian (1957: 113) reconstructed Urartian techniques for sesame oil production as follows:

> Sesame reserves were brought to the oil press. They were washed in a basin-shaped stone container, 79 cm in diameter, carved from a block of tufa. The basin joined a cylindrical pipe made of the same stone, that allowed waste liquid to drain out beyond the citadel. Sesame seeds were soaked to ease the removal of the tegument. After maceration and thorough pressing, the sesame was moved in a semi-moist condition to the oil press (workroom #2). Here they pounded the sesame using mortars and pestles.

Details about the plant remains and tools uncovered at Karmir Blur have been summarized by Bedigian and Harlan (1986: 146–7). The workrooms were furnished with fireplaces for parching the seed. Other finds included clay storage jars 1.5 meters tall, cakes of pressed sesame (the solid residue that remains after seeds are crushed for oil), and stone mortars, pestles, and graters.

Arabia

Language. Gingelly, a name for sesame that is still often used today in India and Europe, is derived from the Arabic *juljulân* (Dymock et al. 1893; Gove 1967). Spaniards say *ajonjoli,* the French *jugleone,* and present-day Arabic medicinal and botanical works employ both *al-juljulân* and *simsim.* The word *juljulân* was in use by the eighth century, as evidenced in a poem (quoted in *Lisan al-'Arab* [1981]) by Waddâh el Kubani-al Yamani (died 709) (Faroukh 1965): "The people laughed and said: 'The poetry of Waddâh the Kinanite!' My poetry is only salt mixed with *juljulân.*"

Clearly, *juljulân* had the meaning of tiny seeds, and sesame was a plant proverbial for its heavy production of tiny seeds (Charles Perry, personal communication, 1995). But *juljulân* is usually defined as "sesame before the seeds are removed," that is, the capsule. Abu al Gauth said, "*Al-juljulân* is sesame in its hull [or peel], before it is harvested." Charles Perry (personal communication, 1995), a specialist in Near Eastern languages, has discussed the relationships among the various terms. He wrote: "The Hebrew *shumshom* (mentioned in the Mishna but not in the Bible), Aramaic *shushma,* Armenian *shusham,* Turkish *susam,* Arabic *simsim,* Greek *sesamon,* and the rest go back to the word recorded in Sumerian (though whether it's really of Sumerian origin or borrowed from Akkadian, the Semitic language spoken by the Sumerians' neighbors, is a moot question; there were borrowings in both directions). This is the usual Arabic word for sesame. For instance, in the *Arabian Nights,* when Ali Baba says 'open, sesame' he says *iftah, ya simsim.*"

Symbolism in legend. The Sudan Department of Agriculture and Forests and Department of Economics and Trade bulletin on sesame (1938) opens with a concise version of "Ali Baba and the Forty Thieves":

> When the robbers had departed Ali went to the door of the cave and pronounced the magic words he had heard them use, "OPEN SESAME." The door opened and he went inside and the door closed behind him. So astonished was he at the sight of the treasures in the cave and so absorbed in contemplation of them that when at last he desired to leave the cave he had quite forgotten the formula "OPEN SESAME." In vain he cried aloud Open wheat, Open barley, Open maize, Open lentils; none of these availed and the door remained shut.

The significance of sesame in Arab culture is suggested by the fact that it was chosen as "a magical means of commanding access" (Arulrajan 1964). Once, sesame was thought to have mystical powers, and for some it still retains a magical quality. In fact, "open sesame" has become a common cliché that is still used today. But the question "why sesame?" remains, and the answer might be that the high-quality sesame oil could have been thought to act magically to oil locks and open doors; in addition, sesame capsules do dehisce spontaneously (magically?) to release their seeds.

Persia

Symbolism in legend. Another example, this one of sesame employed as an omen, comparable to its usage in the magical incantation "Open Sesame," occurs in the *Iskandarnama* (Book of Alexander), one of the *Sharafnama,* the "Book of Kings," completed A.D. 1010. Accompanied by an illustration of a miniature of Alexander the Great feeding sesame seed to birds (Titley 1979: 8, 10–11), the story

> relates the parleying and battle between Alexander the Great and Darius. The Sultanate *Sharafnama* in the British Library has a rare illustration of an episode in which Darius insulted Alexander by sending him a polo stick and ball and a bowl of sesame seed. Darius was angry because Alexander had not sent him gifts in the traditional manner and despatched a messenger to tell him so. Alexander equally angry replied that Darius had treasure enough already whereupon Darius sent him the polo stick and ball and a bowl of sesame seed saying that as Alexander behaved like a child he should have the playthings of a child. The sesame seed represented the countless soldiers in the great army Darius proposed to send against him. Alexander chose to interpret the gifts in another way and saw them as omens of victory. To him the polo ball represented the world (i.e. Darius' possessions) which Alexander would draw towards himself with the stick (i.e. by means of his army) as in polo. He threw the seed to birds which pecked every grain from the ground and he told Darius that it would be thus that his soldiers would wipe out the army of Darius. He then sent the messenger back to Darius with a bowl of mustard seed as a symbol of his own soldiers. The miniature graphically portrays this incident with a flock of hoopoes, parrots, pigeons, starlings and crows pecking the grain watched by Alexander and his retinue while the polo sticks and bowl of remaining seed are in the background (Titley 1979: 10–11).

China

According to the *Pen Ts'ao Kang Mu* (1596) by Li Shih-Chen, a classic ancient Chinese herbal and medical treatise, sesame was brought from the West by General Chang Ch'ien during the Han dynasty (second century B.C.), probably via the Silk Route. The Chinese name *tzuh-ma* indicates introduction from overseas, and the Han dynasty was marked by expansion that opened China to things foreign, including foreign foods (Yü 1977: 80). Y. S. Yü has written that because sesame appears three times in the text, it seems to have been particularly important. Moreover, he suggests that the "barbarian grain food" *(hu-fan)* enjoyed by Emperor Ling (A.D. 168–88) was most likely grain food cooked with the flavorful sesame.

Yü (1977: 81) quotes another source (Ch'i 1949: 294–5): "Under the Later Han, a great variety of noodle foods were cooked, including boiled noodles, steamed buns (modern *man-t'ou*), and baked cakes with sesame seeds." In T'ang times these were extremely popular foreign cakes, and a steamed variety containing sesame seeds was particularly well liked. In the capital city, these cakes were sold by foreign vendors – seemingly Iranians for the most part – on street corners (Hsiang 1957: 45–6, cited in Schafer 1977: 98). F. W. Mote listed sesame-oil noodles among a group of sacrificial food offerings made to ancestors during the Ming dynasty and suggested: "[W]e can assume that they reveal the tastes and food ideals of the former poor peasant family which now found itself the imperial family, and that the foods offered were also those actually eaten in the imperial household" (Mote 1977: 217).

Record of Modern Usage

India

Sesame is employed extensively in India, especially in the states of Gujarat and Tamil Nadu. Among other things, the seeds, with rice and honey, are used to prepare funeral cakes *(pindas)* that are offered to the ancestors in the Sraddh ceremony by the Sapindas (Dymock et al. 1893). *Tilanna,* sesame-rice balls formed in the shape of cows, are offered to relatives and friends of the deceased after a funeral. This ritual is enacted to say a proper farewell to the departed, and, as mentioned, the offering of sesame seeds is considered effective in removing sins (Gupta 1971). Indeed, *tilanjali* is a derived word meaning "to bid a final good-bye/to leave" (Chaturvedi and Tiwari 1970).

There are also many other uses. According to Dymock et al. (1893: 26–7): "On certain festivals six acts are performed with sesame seeds, as an expiatory ceremony of great efficacy, by which the Hindus hope to obtain delivery from sin, poverty, and other evils, and secure a place in Indra's heaven." These acts are *tilodvarti* ("bathing in water containing the seeds"), *tilasuayi* ("anointing the body with the pounded seeds"), *tilahomi* ("making a burnt offering of the seeds"), *tilaprada* ("offering the seeds to the dead"), *tilabhuj* ("eating the seeds"), and *tilavapi* ("throwing out the seeds"). In proverbial language, a grain of sesame signifies the least quantity of anything. Examples of this usage are *til chor so bajjar chor* ("who steals a grain will steal a sack") and *til til ka hisab* ("to exact the uttermost farthing") (Dymock et al. 1893: 27).

S. M. Vaishampayan (personal communication, 1977) has noted that at the festival of "Makar Sankranti," which takes place on January 14 (when the sun enters the Zodiac sign "Makar," or Capricorn), the Hindus eat a composition of *gur* (brown sugar) and *til,* which they call *tilkut.* Among the Maharashrian Brahmins, elders offer sweetmeats made out of sesame seed and powdered sugar to youngsters, and bless them, saying: "*Tilghya, Gulghua* and *Gode bola,*" which means "have sesame sweets and be sweet with everybody."

Donald Lawrence, Professor Emeritus of Botany at the University of Minnesota, who corresponded with this author about the uses of sesame in India, sent some beads from Pune, India (courtesy of Makarand S. Jawadekar), that are made of sesame seeds encrusted with sugar. Jawadekar, in a letter to Lawrence, dated February 9, 1986, wrote: "Newly wed brides wear, on January 14th, the necklace made out of these sugar-sesame beads – believed to bring good luck."

The Middle East and North Africa

This region shares common foods and similar preparation methods as a result of a historically steady exchange of ideas as well as trade goods. The peoples of Arabia, of the emirates in the Persian Gulf, of Armenia, Egypt, Greece, Iraq, Iran, Israel, Jordan, Lebanon, Somalia, Sudan, and Syria all prepare versions of *hummus* and *baba gannouj,* combining the flavors of chickpea and smoky eggplant with sesame paste, *tahini,* as well as sesame candies and biscuits.

The word for sesame in the Armenian dictionary (Yeran n.d.) is *shushmah,* not unlike the Sumerian word *šamaššammū* (confirmed by Charles Perry, personal communication, 1995). There are two versions of an Armenian coffee cake prepared with sesame. One is *pagharch,* a leavened bread in which the dough is folded with sweetened sesame paste.

Another version is a specialty item prepared just before Armenian Easter. A soft dough is allowed to rise to double its size, and a sesame mixture is brushed upon it. Then the dough is rolled like a slender jelly roll, which is finally coiled into a flat round circle and allowed to rise again before baking. Bread rings topped with sesame seed are sold everywhere in Turkey and take their name, *simit,* from *simsim.* In Morocco, sesame is known as *jinjelan.* It is used in Moroccan bread and desserts and, when toasted, the seeds are a popular garnish for chicken and lamb *tagines.*

In Sudan, sesame used for oil and seed constitutes one of the country's food staples (Bedigian and Harlan 1983). An enormous genetic diversity of traditional sesame cultivars in Sudan seems to correspond with the region's cultural diversity (Bedigian 1991). People are extremely fond of sesame as both a food and a metaphor for something small and precious. Sesame is used in the form of a solid cake blended with sugar, called *tahneeya* in the Sudan; the name for the sesame paste alone is *taheena. Taheena* is employed as a sauce, with fresh tomatoes and cucumbers, or with *tamia,* a fried chickpea patty to which sesame seeds can be added.

Egypt takes 90 percent of Sudan's exported sesame to make *halvah.* Rural growers in Sudan deliver their sesame seeds to oil presses called *assara,* powered by camels or engines (Sudan Department of Agriculture and Forests and Department of Economics and Trade 1938; Bedigian and Harlan 1986).

East Africa

Sesame, *nyim,* is one of the traditional crops of the Luo of western Kenya, and it is very likely that the crop arrived there when the first Luo migrated from the Sudan (Ogot 1967). Yet today, there is substantially less cultivation of sesame than there was at the beginning of the twentieth century. Most of the sesame for sale in western Kenya comes from Uganda, and such a decline in sesame cultivation is not a singular event. Similarly, finger millet, *cal,* which has historical significance for the Luo and was probably brought to Kenya by them during the earliest migrations from the Sudan, is now being replaced by maize, despite the fact that millet is more nutritious. Much of this has to do with British colonialism, which replaced sesame with corn oil or even less healthy hydrogenated shortenings.

When sesame is used in Kenya, it is pounded into a paste to be served with sweet potatoes or with local leafy greens. The paste can be diluted and used as a dip called *dengo;* it may also be added when cooking fish. A *winja,* combining black sesame seeds, finger millet, and dry beef cooked in sesame oil, is a special dish for a new son-in-law before his wedding. The dish is also used to appease spirits and to prevent lightning strikes – in short, to ward off harm.

China and the Far East

The Chinese considered sesame to be the best of the oilseeds, and their name for sesame oil *(hsiang yu)* means "fragrant oil." According to Bray (1984: 524–5): "Not only does it have all the qualities mentioned in the *Thien Kung Khai Wu,* the expressed cake is a protein-rich livestock food (sometimes eaten, fermented, by humans in India and Java), and in China it was recognized as an excellent fertilizer." B. Cost (1989) called sesame seed oil "a contender for the world's most seductively flavored oil, a seasoning fundamental to the cuisines of China and Japan. Like the Chinese sesame paste, the oil is pressed from roasted seeds. Cooking with it is a waste, since it loses its flavor over high heat and is expensive."

Regarding sesame seed paste, Cost (1989) has written that (unlike the Middle Eastern *tahini*) the Chinese paste is made from roasted, rather than raw, sesame seeds. As a flavorful peanut butter–like sauce, it is used mostly in sauces and dressings for cold dishes and salads, but occasionally in marinades. It is also a constituent of *shichimi* ("seven spices"), consisting of the dried orange berry of an indigenous ash (related to the Sichuan peppercorn, and ground dried chillies), flakes of dried orange peel, white poppy seeds, sesame seeds, black hemp seeds, and bits of seaweed. This is a mixture that can be sprinkled over a variety of dishes.

Japanese sesame tools. Y. Kakehashi (personal communication, 1995) has indicated that, in Japan, fresh sesame seeds are toasted prior to adding them to a dish to enhance its flavor. The Japanese use a clay container, designed specifically for this purpose, called *goma iri* (*goma* is sesame). It is glazed inside and is approximately 10 centimeters in diameter and 20 centimeters in length, including the handle. The shape is hollow (like a rubber tire) except for its completely flat bottom; the sides fold inward toward the open center, preventing the seeds from escaping as they pop during the parching. The toasted seeds are collected by pouring them out of the conical funnel-shaped hollow handle. There is also a special ceramic mortar, *suribachi,* for grinding sesame seeds. It has corrugations inside that allow gentle crushing to take place.

Europe

Mary Tolford Wilson (1964) has noted the mercantilistic encouragement the British provided for cultivating sesame in their American colonies. The hope was that sesame oil might replace the olive oil they imported from European rivals, and thus sesame became one of those commodities whose colonial production the British encouraged. By contrast, the use of sesame was discouraged and even prohibited in nineteenth-century France in order to protect local rapeseed-growing interests, a policy that hints at the popularity of sesame at that time.

The United States

If the British contemplated the production of sesame oil in America, it may have been Africans who brought the seed to their attention. One name applied to sesame in the southern United States is *benne*. Lorenzo Turner (1969: 62) has compiled a comprehensive list of Africanisms in the Gullah dialect, in which *bene* is a feminine personal noun that means sesame in Bambara (French West Africa) and Wolof (Senegal and Gambia). Jessica Harris (personal communication, 1995), the culinary historian whose specialty is African-American foods, was astonished to learn this fact. She has not seen many examples of African-American words for foods in which the original language can be so specifically identified.

It is the case, however, that the contributions of African slaves to crop introductions in the Americas have rarely received sufficient recognition. In their free time, slaves tended their own gardens, where they grew vegetables, including greens and "presumably African favorites such as okra, sorghum, black-eye peas, eggplant and benne seed" (Hess 1992: 8). These crops were very likely brought from Africa during the slave trade, along with yams, watermelons, and indigo.

That sesame was in colonial America by 1730 may be seen in a document in the *Records in the British Public Record Office Pertaining to South Carolina.* A letter from one Thomas Lowndes, dated August 26, 1730, reads:

> My Lords, a planter in Carolina sent me some time ago a parcel of seed, desiring I would try it, and see of what use it would be, for if it turn'd to account South Carolina could with ease produce any quantity of it. By an experiment I found twenty one pounds weight of seed produced near nine pounds of good oyl, of which more than six pounds were cold drawn and the rest by fire. The name of the seed is Sesamum it grows in great abundance in Africa and Asia, and the inhabitants of those parts eat it, as well as use it for several other purposes. Pliny and many other good authors ancient and modern treat of this seed. It rejoyces in the Pine Barren Land (which is generally a light sandy soil). . . . This seed will make the Pine Barren Land of equal value with the rice land . . . and is for many purposes even prefereble to oyl olive.

Some decades later, on May 25, 1774, the *Georgia Gazette* printed an early shipping record of sesame (page 2, column 2) aboard the ship *Savannah,* which carried 500 pounds of "benny" along with 20,000 pounds of sago, 200 gallons of soy, 200 pounds of vermicelli, 1,000 pounds of groundnuts, and a 10-gallon keg of sassafras blossom.

The most famous figure of America's early years to be interested in sesame was Thomas Jefferson, who earnestly recommended sesame growing to his friends (Wilson 1964). Jefferson's "Garden Book," which is the richest single source on the crop and records plantings of sesame grown at Monticello as long as the book was kept (to 1824), was edited and published by E. M. Betts in 1944. In it is a letter from William Few of New York to Jefferson, dated January 11, 1808, that was not transcribed by Betts but cited this way: "Tells Jefferson how to extract oil from Beni seeds and the history of its introduction to America." A facsimile of the original manuscript was provided to this author by the Manuscript Division, Library of Congress. Here is the text of the unpublished document:

> When introduced into the southern states? We have no certain account of a tradition of its introduction. The Negroes are well acquainted with it and fond of cultivating it. It was probably introduced from the Slave Coast, but as we

know that it was cultivated up the Mediterranean in very early time, it is possible that we may have received it from that quarter. If the correct orthography of the name could be ascertained it might determine the question. We know that we received our rice from both of these sources and it may have been the same case with the benne. When it was introduced it can be difficult to ascertain as it has never interested us as an object of agriculture or curiosity. We only know that the oldest of our inhabitants remember it from their earliest days.

The Caribbean

Trinidad. Bene (sesame) is included in the lexicon of Wolof contributions to the language in Trinidad (Warner-Lewis 1991). Africans in nineteenth-century Trinidad had a ceremony of thanksgiving and ancestor intercession called the *saraka,* during which animal sacrifice and offerings of unsalted food were made. Ritual plant ingredients for the ceremony included kola nut (sent as a token to guests with their invitations), rum, stout and wine, bene (called *ziziwi*), black-eyed peas and rice, corn cooked with olive oil, and bread. Similarly, a Yoruba wedding in central Trinidad was characterized by a feast that included *bene* made into balls and sugar cake (Warner-Lewis 1991). Rice, black-eyed peas, potato, and grated, dried cassava also formed part of the menu.

Jamaica. That Africa was the source of sesame reaching Jamaica is reflected in a local name, acknowledged in a publication by J. Lunan as early as 1814. Sesame was called *"sesamum Africanum,"* brought to Jamaica under the name of *zezegary,* and Lunan reported that "the first time I saw the plant, it was growing in a negro's plantation, who told me, they ground the seed between two stones, and eat it as they do corn. Their seed-vessels, [are] full of small white seeds, which the negroes call *soonga,* or *wolongo.* The oil that is drawn from it is called *sergilim* oil. The seed is often mixed and ground with coco, to make chocolate" (Lunan 1814: 252). Sesame was prized as a source of oil, with good reason:

[T]here are few which more deserve to be extensively cultivated into general domestic use, [to replace] that abominable rancid butter imported hither from Europe. Nothing but the grossest prejudice, in favor of old habits, can influence the inhabitants to persevere in the importation of that unwholesome, nauseous stuff, and to swallow it every day with their food, when they may supply themselves with so fine, nourishing and wholesome an oil, as the *sesamum,* for an ingredient in their pastry; nor are they less blamable, for continuing to import the olive oil, which is generally rancid before it

arrives and fitter for perukes [wigs] than salads (Long 1774: 809).

Dorothea Bedigian

Bibliography

Anon. 1774. Records of the states of the U.S. *Georgia Gazette,* May 25. Savannah, Ga.

Aristophanes. 1930. *The eleven comedies,* anon. trans. New York.

Arulrajan, R., comp. 1964. *English-Tamil senior dictionary.* Madras.

Bedigian, D. 1984. *Sesamum indicum* L.: Crop origin, diversity, chemistry and ethnobotany. Ph.D. dissertation, University of Illinois.

1985. Is *se-gis-i* sesame or flax? *Bulletin on Sumerian Agriculture* 2: 159–78.

1988. *Sesamum indicum* L. (Pedaliaceae): Ethnobotany in Sudan, crop diversity, lignans, origin, and related taxa. In *Modern systematic studies in African botany,* ed. P. Goldblatt, and P. P. Lowry, 315–21. St. Louis, Mo.

1991. Genetic diversity of traditional sesame cultivars and cultural diversity in Sudan. In *Biodiversity: Culture, conservation and ecodevelopment,* ed. M. L. Oldfield and J. B. Alcorn, 25–36. Boulder, Colo.

Bedigian, D., and J. R. Harlan. 1983. Nuba agriculture and ethnobotany, with particular reference to sesame and sorghum. *Economic Botany* 37: 384–95.

1986. Evidence for cultivation of sesame in the ancient world. *Economic Botany* 40: 137–54.

Bedigian, D., D. S. Seigler, and J. R. Harlan. 1985. Sesamin, sesamolin and the origin of sesame. *Biochemical Systematics and Ecology* 13: 133–9.

Bedigian, D., C. A. Smyth, and J. R. Harlan. 1986. Patterns of morphological variation in sesame. *Economic Botany* 40: 353–65.

Betts, E. M. ed. 1944. *Thomas Jefferson's garden book, 1766-1824.* Philadelphia, Pa.

Boland, A. R. de, G. B. Garner, and B. L. O'Dell. 1975. Identification and properties of phytate in cereal grains and oilseed products. *Journal of Agricultural Food Chemistry* 23: 1186–9.

Bray, F. 1984. *Agriculture,* Vol. 27 of *Science and civilization in China,* ed. J. Needham. Cambridge and New York.

Campbell, J. 1952. *The portable Arabian nights.* New York.

Chakraborty, P. K., S. Maiti, and B. N. Chatterjee. 1984. Growth analysis and agronomic appraisal of sesamum. *Indian Journal of Agricultural Science* 54: 291–5.

Chaturvedi, M., and B. N. Tiwari, eds. 1970. *Hindi-English dictionary.* Delhi.

Chaudhry, S. N. 1988. Characterization and processing of raw and roasted sesame oil. M.S. thesis, Chapman University, Orange, Calif.

Colquitt, H. R. 1933. *The Savannah cook book.* Charleston, S.C.

Columella, L. J. M. 1941. *On agriculture,* trans. H. B. Ash. Cambridge, Mass.

Cost, B. 1989. *Ginger east to west.* Berkeley, Calif.

Crocomo, O. J., and L. C. Basso. 1974. Accumulation of putrescine and related amino acids in K-deficient *Sesamum. Phytochemistry* 13: 2659–965.

Danilevich, A. F. 1977. Changes in content of free amino acids during roasting. *Khlebopekarnaya Konditerskaya Promshlennost* 2: 33–4.

Danilevich, A. F., and A. Aboms. 1973. Changes in amine nitrogen level during fluidized bed searing of sesame seed kernels. *Izvestia Vysshikh Uchebnnykh Zavedenii Pishchevaya Tekhnologiya* 5: 76–9.

David, E. 1970. *Spices, salt and aromatics in the English kitchen.* Harmondsworth, England.

Dawkins, R. M. 1953. *Modern Greek folktales.* Oxford.

Daxin, Z. 1994. The sesame oil mill. *Short Story International* 18: 4–43.

Deines, H., and H. Grapow. 1959. *Wörterbuch der aegyptischen Drogennamen. Grundriss der Medizin der alten Aegypter,* Vol. 6. Berlin.

Donner, H., and W. Roellig. 1964. *Kanaanaische und aramaische Inschriften,* Vol. 2. Wiesbaden.

Dossin, G. 1933. *Lettres de la premiere dynastie Babylonienne,* Vol. 1. Paris.

Dymock, W., C. J. H. Warden, and D. Hooper. 1893. *Pharmacographia Indica,* Vol. 3. London.

Ebeling, E. 1923. Keilschrifttexte aus Assur religiösen Inhalts (KAR 376 r. 19). *Wissenschaftliche Veröffentlichung der Deutschen Orient-Gesellschaft* 34: ii–5.

Ekpenyong, T. E., B. L. Fetuga, and V. A. Oyenuga. 1977. Fortification of maize flour based diets with blends of cashewnut meal, African locust bean meal and sesame oil meal. *Journal of the Science of Food and Agriculture* 28: 710–16.

FAO (Food and Agriculture Organization of the United Nations). 1992. *Production yearbook 1991,* Vol. 45. Rome.

Faroukh, O. 1965. *Tarikh al adab al Arab.* Beirut.

Feigin, S. I. 1979. *Legal and administrative texts of the reign of Samsu-Iluna.* New Haven, Conn.

Fernández de Campoy, M. P. 1981. Development of food products utilizing the complementary protein sources of sesame seed *(Sesamum indicum)* together with either beans *(Phaseolus vulgaris)* or chickpea *(Cicer arietinum).* M.S. thesis, University of Arizona.

Gallant, T. W. 1985. The agronomy, production, and utilization of sesame and linseed in the Graeco-Roman world. *Bulletin on Sumerian Agriculture* 2: 153–8.

Gerhardt. M. I. 1963. *The art of story telling.* Leiden.

Germer, R. 1979. Untersuchung über Arzneimittelpflanzen im alten Ägypten. Ph.D. thesis, University of Hamburg.

Godfrey, S. A., B. J. Frances, and C. S. Kamara. 1976. Protein evaluation of cowpea and benniseed from Sierra Leone. *Tropical Science* 18: 147–54.

Goetze, A. 1956. *Laws of Eshnunna.* New Haven, Conn.

Gove, P. B., ed. 1967. *Webster's third new international dictionary of the English language.* Springfield, Mass.

Gupta, S. M. 1971. *Plant myths and traditions in India.* Leiden.

Herodotus. 1928. *History,* trans. G. Rawlinson, ed. Manuel Komroff. New York.

Hess, K. 1992. *The Carolina rice kitchen: The African connection.* Columbia, S.C.

Hilprecht, H. Unpublished OB tablet 1883: 25 and r. 15. Hilprecht Sammlung, Jena University.

Hopf, M., and U. Willerding. 1989. Pflanzenreste. In *Bastan II,* ed. W. Kleiss, 263–318. Berlin.

Hopkins, E. W. 1968. *Epic mythology.* Delhi.

Hunt, A. S., and C. C. Edgar, eds. and trans. 1932. *Select papyri,* Vols. 1 and 2. Cambridge, Mass.

Hussein, M. A., and M. M. Noaman. 1976. Comparison between white and red sesame seed and oil. *Olaj, Szappan, Kozmetika* 25: 5–7.

Ibn Manzur Muhammed ibn Mukarram. 1981. *Lisan al-Arab.* Cairo.

Ishikawa, S., and H. Tsuji. 1976. Seed coats of sesame removed with cellulase and hemicellulase. *Japan Kokai* 77 90, 647. Patent July 30, 1977. Appl. 76/3, 994. January 19, 1976.

Johnson, L. A., T. M. Suleiman, and E. W. Lusas. 1979. Sesame protein: A review and prospectus. *Journal of the American Oil Chemists' Society* 56: 463–8.

Johnson, R. H., and W. D. Raymond. 1964. Chemical composition of some tropical food plants. III: Sesame seed. *Tropical Science* 6: 173–9.

Joshi, A. B. 1961. *Sesamum.* Hyderabad.

Junior League of Charleston, comp. 1950. *Charleston receipts collected by the Junior League of Charleston.* Charleston, S.C.

Kägi, M. K., and B. Wüthrich. 1993. Falafel burger anaphylaxis due to sesame seed allergy. *Annals of Allergy* 71: 127–9.

Kassabian, Z. 1957. Production of vegetable oil in Urartu. In Armenian. *Izvestia Akademia Nauk Armenia SSR* 4: 107–16.

Keimer, L. 1924. *Die Gartenpflanzen im alten Ägypten,* Vol. 1. Hamburg and Berlin.

Keiser, C. E. 1917. *Letters and contracts from Erech written in the Neo-Babylonian period. Babylonian inscriptions in the collection of James B. Nies. . . .* New Haven, Conn.

Laufer, B. 1919. *Sino-Iranica; Chinese contributions to the history of civilization in ancient Iran,* 288–96. In Field Museum of Natural History Anthropological Series 15. Chicago.

Li Shih-Chen. [1596] 1893. *Pen ts'ao kang mu.* Shanghai.

Little, M. 1991. Colonial policy and subsistence in Tanganyika 1925–1945. *Geographical Review* 81: 375–88.

Long, E. 1774. *History of Jamaica,* Vol 3. London.

Loret, V. 1892. *La flore pharaonique.* Rev. second edition. Paris.

Lowndes, T. 1730. *Records in the British Public Record Office Pertaining to South Carolina* 14: 261–2.

Lucas, A. 1962. *Ancient Egyptian materials and industries.* London.

Lunan, J. 1814. *Hortus Jamaicensis.* Jamaica.

Lyon, C. K. 1972. Sesame: Current knowledge of composition and use. *Journal of the American Oil Chemists' Society* 49: 245–9.

Manley, C. H., P. P. Vallon, and R. E. Erickson. 1974. Some aroma components of roasted sesame seed. *Journal of Food Science* 39: 73–6.

Mehra, K. L. 1967. History of sesame in India and its cultural significance. *Vishveshvaranand Indological Journal* 5: 93–107.

Milne-Redhead, E., and P. Taylor. 1956. Description/label of *Sesamum indicum* specimen No. 9701, collected April 13, 1956, from the Songea district, Tanzania. Located in the East African Herbarium.

Mirocha, C. J., S. V. Pathre, B. Schauerhamer, and C. M. Christensen. 1976. Natural occurrence of *Fusarium* toxins in feedstuff. *Applied Environmental Microbiology* 32: 553–6.

Monacelli, R., E. Aiello, A. di Muccio, et al. 1976. Presence of aflatoxin B$_1$ in oleaginous seeds other than peanuts. *Rivista della Società Italiana di Scienza dell'Alimentazione* 5: 259–61.

Monier-Williams, M. 1964. *Sanskrit-English dictionary.* New Delhi.

Mookerji, R. K. [1912] 1962. *Indian shipping. A history of the sea-borne trade and maritime activity of the Indians from the earliest times.* Allahabad.

Mote, F. W. 1977. Yüan and Ming. In *Food in Chinese culture,* ed. K. C. Chang, 193–258. New Haven, Conn.

National Academy of Sciences. 1973. *Toxicants occurring naturally in foods.* Second edition. Washington, D.C.

Nayar, N. M. 1976. Sesame. In *Evolution of crop plants,* ed. N. W. Simmonds, 231-3. London.

Nayar, N. M., and K. L. Mehra. 1970. Sesame: Its uses, botany, cytogenetics and origin. *Economic Botany* 24: 20-31.

Neef, R. 1989. Plants. In *Picking up the threads: A continuing review of excavations at Deir Allah, Jordan,* ed. G. van der Kooij and M. M. Ibrahim, 30-7. Leiden.

Norman, J. 1995. *The complete book of spices.* New York.

O'Dell, B. L., and A. de Boland. 1976. Complexation of phytate with proteins and cations in corn germ and oil seed meals. *Journal of Agricultural and Food Chemistry* 24: 804-8.

Ogot, B. A. 1967. *History of the southern Luo.* Nairobi.

Oppenheim, A. L., et al., eds. 1958. *The Assyrian dictionary of the Oriental Institute, Chicago,* "E." Chicago.

    1962. *The Assyrian dictionary of the Oriental Institute, Chicago,* "š". Chicago.

Parrot, F. 1845. *Journey to Ararat.* London.

Pinches, T. G. 1899. *Cuneiform texts from Babylonian tablets in the British Museum* 8:8e:10. London.

Piotrovskii, B. B. 1950. *Karmir Blur* I, in Russian. Yerevan.

    1952. *Karmir Blur* II, in Russian. Yerevan.

Pliny. 1938. *Natural history,* trans. H. Rackham. Cambridge, Mass.

Prakash, O. 1961. *Food and drinks in ancient India.* Delhi.

Purseglove, J. W. 1968. *Tropical crops: Dicotyledons,* Vol. 2. New York.

Ratnagar, S. 1981. *Encounters: The westerly trade of the Harappan civilization.* Delhi.

Reiner, E., ed. 1989. *The Assyrian dictionary of the Oriental Institute, Chicago,* Vol. 17, "š". Chicago.

Romans, B. [1775] 1962. *A concise natural history of east and west Florida.* Gainesville, Fla.

Rubenstein, L. 1950. Sensitivity to sesame seed and sesame oil. *New York State Journal of Medicine* 50: 343-4.

Rutledge, S. [1847] 1979. *The Carolina housewife.* Columbia, S.C.

Salih, A. K.-E. M. 1993. Seed oils of *Sesamum indicum* L. and some wild relatives. A compositional study of the fatty acids, acyl lipids, sterols, tocopherols and lignans. Ph.D. thesis, Swedish University of Agricultural Sciences.

Salunkhe, D. K., J. K. Chavan, R. N. Adsule, and S. S. Kadam. 1991. *World oilseeds: Chemistry, technology and utilization.* New York.

Sampson, H.C. 1936. Cultivated crop plants of the British empire and the Anglo-Egyptian Sudan. *Kew Bulletin of Miscellaneous Information,* Additional Series 12: 220-5.

Schafer, E. H. 1977. T'ang. In *Food in Chinese culture,* ed. K. C. Chang, 53-83. New Haven, Conn.

Scheven, A. 1981. *Swahili proverbs: Nia zikiwa moja, kilicho mbali huja.* Washington, D.C.

Schoff, W. H., trans. 1912. *The Periplus of the Erythraean Sea.* London.

Seegeler, C. J. P. 1989. *Sesamum orientale* L. (Pedaliaceae): Sesame's correct name. *Taxon* 38: 656-9.

Sesame culture in the southern states. 1912. *Scientific American* 107: 276.

Sharma, Y. K., A. D. Deodhar, and S. K. Gangrade. 1975. Chemical composition of sesame varieties of Madhya Pradesh, India. *Iran Journal of Agricultural Research* 3: 59-64.

Simmons, S. D. 1978. *Early Old Babylonian documents.* Yale Oriental Series, Vol. 15. New Haven, Conn.

Soden, Wolfram von. 1960. Ellu. *Akkadisches Handwörterbuch,* Vol. 1, 204-5. Wiesbaden.

Soliman, M., S. Kinoshita, and T. Yamanishi. 1975. Aroma of roasted sesame seeds. *Agricultural and Biological Chemistry* 39: 973-7.

Stol, M. 1985. Remarks on the cultivation of sesame and the extraction of its oil. *Bulletin on Sumerian Agriculture* 2: 119-26.

Sturtevant, E. L. [1919] 1972. *Sturtevant's edible plants of the world,* reprint, ed. U. P. Hedrick. New York.

Sudan Department of Agriculture and Forests and Department of Economics and Trade. 1938. *Sesame.* Sudan Government Department of Economics and Trade Bulletin No. 2. Khartoum.

Tabekhia, M. M., and M. S. Mohammed. 1971. Effect of processing and cooking operations on thiamine, riboflavine and nicotinic acid content of some Egyptian national foods. II. Broad beans and sesame products. *Alexandria Journal of Agricultural Research* 19: 285-92.

Theophrastus. 1916. *Enquiry into plants,* trans. A. Hort. Cambridge, Mass.

Tinay, A. H. El, A. H. Khattab, and M. O. Khidir. 1976. Protein and oil components of sesame seed. *Journal of the American Oil Chemists' Society* 53: 648-53.

Titley, N. M. 1979. *Plants and gardens in Persian, Mughal and Turkish art.* London.

Tothill, J. D., ed. 1948. *Agriculture in the Sudan.* London.

Turner, Lorenzo. 1969. *Africanisms in the Gullah dialect.* New York.

Van Beek, G. W. 1969. *Hajar bin Humeid.* Baltimore, Md.

Vartavan, C. de. 1990. Contaminated plant-foods from the tomb of Tutankhamun: A new interpretive system. *Journal of Archaeological Science* 17: 473-94.

Vats, M. S. 1940. *Excavations at Harappa.* Delhi.

Villegas, A. M., A. González, and R. Calderón. 1968. Microbiological and enzymatic evaluation of sesame protein. *Cereal Chemistry* 45: 379-85.

Vishnu-Mittre. 1977. The changing economy in ancient India. In *Origins of agriculture,* ed. C. A. Reed, 569-88. The Hague.

Wankhede, D. J., and R. N. Tharanathan. 1976. Sesame carbohydrates. *Journal of Agricultural and Food Chemistry* 24: 655-9.

Warner-Lewis, M. 1991. *Guinea's other suns: The African dynamic in Trinidad culture.* Dover, Mass.

Weiss, E. A. 1971. *Castor, sesame and safflower.* New York.

Wilson, Mary Tolford. 1964. Peaceful integration: The owner's adoption of his slaves' food. *Journal of Negro History* 49: 116-27.

Wolfert, P. 1973. *Couscous and other good food from Morocco.* New York.

Xenophon. 1901. *March of the ten thousand* (Anabasis), trans. H. G. Dakyns. London.

Yen, G.-C., and S.-L. Shyu. 1989. Oxidative stability of sesame oil prepared from sesame seed with different roasting temperatures. *Food Chemistry* 31: 215-24.

Yeran, E. A. n.d. *English-Armenian pocket dictionary or pocket companion.* Third edition. Boston, Mass.

Yermanos, D. M., S. Hemstreet, W. Saleeb, and C. K. Huszar. 1972. Oil content and composition in the world collection of sesame introductions. *Journal of the American Oil Chemists' Society* 49: 20-3.

Yü, Y. S. 1977. Han. In *Food in Chinese culture,* ed. K. C. Chang, 85-140. New Haven, Conn.

Zohary, D., and M. Hopf. 1994. *Domestication of plants in the Old World.* Second edition. Oxford.

II.E.5 ❧ Soybean

Description

The soybean plant belongs to the legume family *(Leguminosae),* the second largest family of flowering plants, with more than 14,000 species. Identifiable characteristics include a fruit located within a pod that dehisces along a seam from top to bottom. In the case of a soybean, the split takes place when the plant has matured and died to yield 2 to 4 seeds per pod that are easily removed without damage or loss.

The soybean's size, shape, and color is determined by the variety. Soybeans range in size from small (1 centimeter [cm]) to large (3.5 cm), can be flattened or oblong, and are colored yellow, green, brown, or black. They are approximately 8 percent hull, 90 percent cotyledon, and 2 percent hypocotyl (Wolf and Cowan 1971).

Terminology

The terms "soy and "soya" are said to have derived from the Japanese word *shoyu* (or *sho-yu*) that designates a sauce made from salted beans. But the Japanese word may well have been inspired by the ancient Chinese name for the bean, which was *sou.* In Chinese, the word for soy sauce is *jiangyou* (or *chiang-yiu*). C. V. Piper and W. J. Morse (1923) have recorded more than 50 names for the soybean or its sauce in East Asia. In English the bean has been called soya bean, soya, soy, Chinese pea, Japanese pea, and Manchurian bean, to provide just a few of its appellations. For the purposes of this chapter, soya is used synonymously with the soybean and its many products.

Early History

Present-day soybean varieties *(Glycine max),* of which there are more than 20,000, can be traced to the wild soybean plant *Glycine soja* that grew in abundance in northeast China and Manchuria (Hymowitz and Newell 1981). Legends abound concerning the discovery and domestication of this food plant that today is the most widely used in the world (Toussaint-Samat 1993: 51). Around 2700 B.C., the legendary Chinese emperor Shen Nung is said to have ordered plants to be classified in terms of both food and medicinal value, and soybeans were among the five principal and sacred crops (Shih 1959). This dating squares nicely with the judgment of modern authorities on Asian plants that soybeans have been cultivated for at least 4,500 years (Herklots 1972). But there are other sources that indicate that the domesticated soybean (G. *max*) was introduced to China only around 1000 B.C. perhaps from the Jung people who lived in the northeast (Trager 1995).

The court poems of the *Book of Odes,* sixth century B.C., also indicate that the wild soybean came from northern China and that its cultivation began around the fifteenth century B.C. Confucius, who died in 479 B.C., left behind writings that mentioned at least 44 food plants used during Chou times; they included soybeans. But they do not seem to have been very popular in ancient times. Soybeans were said to cause flatulence and were viewed mostly as a food for the poor during years of bad harvests. Nonetheless, soybeans were recorded in the first century B.C. as one of the nine staples upon which the people of China depended, and certainly there were enough people. The first official census conducted in Han China at about that time counted 60 million people, and even if such a number seems implausibly high – especially in light of a census taken in A.D. 280 that showed only 16 million – it still suggests that Chinese agricultural policies were remarkably effective, both in feeding large numbers of people and, one suspects, in encouraging the growth of large numbers of people (Chang 1977: 71). The famine in China in the year A.D. 194 may have been the result of too many mouths to feed and thus responsible, at least partly, for the discrepancy in the two censuses. But in addition, famine forced the price of millet to skyrocket in relation to soybeans, resulting in an increased consumption of the latter – often in the form of bean *conjee* or gruel (Flannery 1969).

Soybean

Early Dissemination

Because the wild soybean was sensitive as to the amount of daylight it required, and because the length of growing seasons varied from region to region, domestication involved much experimental planting and breeding to match different varieties with different areas. That this was done so successfully is a tribute to ancient Chinese farmers who, as noted, were doubtless impelled by an ever-increasing need to feed larger and larger populations of humans and animals. Soybeans ground into meal and then compressed into cakes became food for travelers and soldiers on the move who, in turn, widened knowledge of the plant.

Buddhist priests, however, were perhaps as instrumental as anyone in the domestication of the soybean and absolutely vital to its dissemination (Yong and Wood 1974). As vegetarians, they were always interested in new foods and drinks (such as tea, which they also nurtured to an early success in China). In their monasteries, they experimented with soybean cultivation and usage and found flour, milk, curd, and sauce made from soy all welcome additions to their regimes. As missionaries, they carried the soybean wherever they went, and in the sixth century A.D., they introduced it to Japan from Korea, which they had reached in the first century. Buddhism merged with the native Shinto religion, and the plant quickly became a staple in the Japanese diet.

Not only missionaries but also soldiers, merchants, and travelers helped introduce soybeans to Asian countries. The northern half of Vietnam had soybean food products as early as 200 B.C. During the sixth through the tenth centuries A.D., Thailand received soybeans from southwest China, and India was exposed to them during the twelfth century by traders from Pakistan.

Recent History and Dissemination

The Portuguese began trading in East Asia during the sixteenth century, as did the Spanish and later the Dutch. Yet the soybean was not known in Europe until the end of the seventeenth century when Engelbert Kaempfer published his *Geschichte und Beschreibung von Japan,* an account of his visit to that country during the years 1692–4 as a guest of the Dutch East India Company. He wrote of the bean that the Japanese prized and used in so many different ways, and in 1712, he attempted, not very successfully as it turned out, to introduce this miracle plant to Europe. Its products simply did not fit into the various cuisines of the continent, which, in any event, were only then in the process of fully utilizing the relatively new American plants, such as maize and potatoes.

The botanists, however, were thrilled to have a new plant to study and classify, and Carolus Linnaeus, who described the soybean, gave it the name *Glycine max. Glycine* is the Greek word for "sweet," and "max" presumably refers to the large nodules on the root system, although other sources suggest that the word *max* is actually the result of a Portuguese transcription of the Persian name for the plant (Toussaint-Samat 1992: 52).

Because of scientific interest, the soybean was shuttled about the Continent during the eighteenth century for experimental purposes. In 1765, soybean seeds reached the American colonies with a sailor named Samuel Bowen, who was serving aboard an East India Company ship that had just visited China. Bowen did not return to the sea but instead acquired land in Savannah, Georgia, where he planted soybeans and processed his first crop into Chinese vetch, soy sauce, and a starchy substance incorrectly called sago. In North America as in Europe, however, soybean products did not go well with the various cuisines, and the bean remained little more than a curiosity until the twentieth century, despite efforts to reintroduce it.

By the mid–nineteenth century, the soybean was being rapidly disseminated around the globe as trade, imperialism, clipper ships, and then steamships all joined to knit the world more closely together. The expedition of Commodore Matthew Perry that opened Japan to trade in 1853–4 returned to the United States with the "Japan pea" – actually 2 soybean varieties that were subsequently distributed by the U.S. Commissioner of Patents to farmers for planting. But lacking knowledge of and experience with the plant, the recipients were apparently not successful in its cultivation.

During the American Civil War, when shipping was disrupted, soybeans were frequently substituted for coffee, especially by soldiers of the Union army (Crane 1933: 270). Interest also arose in soybean cultivation as a forage plant, and the Patent Office and the new Department of Agriculture (USDA) encouraged experimental planting. The USDA's role in promoting agricultural research, regulating the industry, and serving as an information generator for farmers proved invaluable to all farmers and certainly to those growing soybeans for the first time (Arntzen and Ritter 1994: 466).

There were 2 stages in processing the soybean plant as a forage crop or hay. The first was to cut the plants just before the leaves turned yellow but after the pods, containing semiripened seeds, had formed, thereby increasing the plants' protein value. In the second stage, the plants were windrowed and left to dry for a day or two, after which the windrows were raked into bunches and dried for another three or four days. Lastly, the bunches were stacked in barns right side up. The average yield of hay using this method was approximately 4 tons an acre, with a protein content of close to 11 percent.

In harvesting the soybean plant for silage, the process called for cutting the plants earlier – when their seedpods contained premature green seeds.

These were made into bundles of about 25 pounds each, then stored in barns until needed. This method traded some protein content for less leaf loss during harvesting.

Soybean plants, processed by either of these methods, lowered the cost of feeding livestock by replacing the more expensive grass hay and corn. Even a combination of soybean hay or silage and traditional feeds resulted in considerably reduced feed costs and supplied more protein than hay or corn alone could deliver.

At the turn of the twentieth century, the population of the United States was swelling with immigrants, and significant technological advances were spinning out of an ever-accelerating industrial process. An increased demand for food spurred soybean cultivation, and processing was facilitated by electric motors to power grinding equipment that made soybean meal more quickly and efficiently than ever before. Mechanized farm implements encouraged the planting of still more land in soybeans, while lowering the costs of harvesting.

The result was that soybeans produced in the United States became competitive with those grown in East Asia, despite the Asian application of very cheap labor. By 1911, the U.S. industry not only processed soybean meal into cakes for livestock feed but also began to press the beans into oil, as China was already doing. Indeed, the high oil content of the soybean (about 20 percent) was arousing substantial commercial interest.

Previously, a shortage of soybeans in the United States and the predominance of cottonseed oil (then called Wesson Oil after David Wesson, who, in 1899, developed a method for clarifying it) had retarded the development of soybean oil. But in 1915, cottonseed oil became scarce because the U.S. cotton was infested with boll weevils, and this in turn led to the processing of soy oil for human consumption. Cottonseed-processing plants quickly became soybean-processing plants, because the presses and other equipment worked equally well with soybeans. Moreover, a new method was discovered for extracting the oil by first grinding the beans, then soaking them in a solution of benzol, naphtha, and ether, which for every bushel (60 lbs.) of soybeans yielded 10.5 pounds of oil and 48 pounds of meal. Thus, soybean oil was efficiently produced at a time when World War I was creating more demand for oils.

None of these lessons in supply and demand were lost on southern farmers, who began to plant soybeans on land barren because of the boll weevil. The USDA also encouraged soybean cultivation in the states of the Midwest. In 1922, a soybean-processing plant was opened in Decatur, Illinois. To ensure a steady soybean supply, the "Peoria Plan" was developed to guarantee Illinois farmers a base price of $1.35 a bushel (Smith and Circle 1972). In addition, farmers throughout the nation were given an induce-

ment to grow soybeans with the passage, in 1923, of the Smoot-Hawley Tariff, which placed import duties of 2 cents per pound on soybeans, 3.5 cents per pound on soybean oil, and $6.00 per ton on soybean meal.

Soybeans became the nation's "Cinderella" crop in the 1920s. Demand was high for soybean cakes, which continued to provide farmers with a high-protein, low-cost animal feed. But it was demand for soybean oil that stimulated still more production; soybeans yielded oil valued at 20 cents per pound, or $400.00 per ton, as opposed to meal worth only $20.00 a ton. Research supported by the processing plants helped plant breeders develop new soybean varieties with higher oil contents.

During the 1920s, this oil went into numerous industrial products, among them soaps, paints and varnishes, linoleum, ink, glycerin, explosives, celluloid, and a substitute for rubber. Moreover, the low cost of soybean production stimulated research to discover still more industrial uses. Yet, soybeans remained an underused food resource because of their relatively high saturated fat content, which made the oil solidify, as well as their high percentage of bad-tasting linolenic acid.

It was during the 1930s that research on soybean oil refinement, flavor reversion, and especially hydrogenation ultimately resolved these problems and opened the way for soybeans to be employed in food products (Toussaint-Samat 1993). Increasingly, the oil found its way into shortenings, margarine, salad dressings, and, of course, cooking oils. In fact, during the Great Depression years, soybean oil was well on its way to becoming the most important food oil in the United States, a status it achieved after World War II and never relinquished.

It is interesting to note that during that war, the only survival rations issued to Japanese soldiers had consisted of bags of soy flour, perhaps illustrative of the fact that despite the growing use of soybeans in the United States, they were still an Asian resource. Following the war, soybeans became the world's most important crop, not because of the Asian influence but because of productivity. Initially, much of the postwar surge of U.S. interest was due to the ability of soybeans to regenerate the soil when planted in rotation with corn (Pepper 1994: 193). During the war, soy margarine had replaced butter on most tables, a use that continued after 1945.

Making a transition to soybeans from a previous concentration on corn, wheat, cotton, or tobacco was scarcely a hardship for farmers because surpluses of these latter crops existed, and because with the passage of the Agriculture Adjustment Act in 1933, restrictions had been placed on the amount of acreage that could be devoted to them. Meanwhile, the government was promoting soybean products by, among other things, organizing the Regional Soybean Industrial Products Laboratory in 1938.

And once again research found industrial applications for soybeans – this time for using soy protein in the paper industry and for making plastics from oil-cake residue in the automobile industry. At the same time, world food requirements in the 1950s increased demand for soy protein for both humans and domesticated animals. During this decade, American farmers responded by producing an annual average of 300 million bushels of soybeans for industrial and food use. In the process, the United States, which prior to World War II had been the world's biggest importer of fats, became its greatest exporter, accounting for fully 75 percent of the world's soybean crop.

Because of plant breeding, the soybean – once a subtropical plant – moved north as far as 52 degrees, and soybean fields became familiar sights from Minnesota to the Deep South. Soybean meal processed in the northern states was carried by rail to barges on the Mississippi River that transported it to New Orleans for shipment to world markets (Forrestal 1982).

In addition to the ease of bulk transportation, soybeans lend themselves to handling in many other ways. They can withstand long storage and shipment over long distances; they are easily harvested in an entirely mechanical procedure; and a growing season of only 15 weeks makes it easy to adjust production to world market demand. In short, as one food author has pointed out, supply can be virtually guaranteed, and if there is overproduction, there is no need to destroy the surplus (Toussaint-Samat 1993).

The people of Far Eastern countries receive, on average, about 12 percent of their protein requirements from soybean products. But despite the high protein content of the soybean and the high quality of that protein, attempts to introduce soya to many poor regions of the world, such as India, Africa, and Latin America, have historically met with little success, with southern South America a notable exception. For example, in Mexico in the 1940s the National Indian Institute handed out soybeans to the impoverished Otomi Indians living in the Mezquital valley. Although the legume flourished in the arid soil, the experiment failed when Otomi women were unable to hand-grind the soybeans to make a decent tortilla (Granberg 1970).

International efforts, however, continue to increase consumption, particularly in the soybean fortification of cereals on which many people rely. All of these cereals – rice, maize, barley, wheat, and rye – yield a protein that is incomplete, meaning that it does not contain all of the essential amino acids. Yet what they lack, soybeans contain, and soybeans are also high in the B vitamins, along with vitamin E, phosphorous, and iron. Thus, in cases where soya is used to supplement other cereals, as in Golden Elbow or Vitalia macaroni, Kupagani biscuits, ProNutro cereal, and Cerealina, the consumer receives a whole protein equal to that provided by meat, fish, and dairy products (Fortified foods 1970).

Processing, Preparation, and Products

The oldest methods of preparing green, immature soybeans for consumption was by roasting or by soaking, grinding, and cooking (Toussaint-Samat 1993). Mature soybeans were processed in much the same manner but with a longer cooking time.

Soybeans, paradoxically, have a very bland taste, which probably inspired the development of flavorful fermented soy products. Such soy processing began in China during the Chou dynasty (1122–246 B.C.) and subsequently spread to other areas of the Far East.

One of the first of these products, and the best known to Westerners, is *shoyu* or soy sauce – a dark brown liquid used extensively in Chinese food preparation – that is obtained by fermenting a combination of soybeans and wheat. The original process entailed first boiling soybeans with *koji (Aspergillus oryzae)* which, in this case, was a mold skimmed from the surface of cooked wheat that had cooled and fermented. Soy sauce has a salty taste and a subtle, but tantalizing, aroma that goes well with rice dishes.

Another product is soy paste, produced in a process similar to that which yields soy sauce, except that the *koji* is derived from barley or rice. Soy paste is also Chinese in origin and evolved from a paste of fish puree called *jiang* that was used before soya became popular. By the time of the Han dynasty in the third century, soy paste had become the important ingredient in *jiang*. Two or three centuries later, the Koreans were producing soy paste and the Japanese got the recipe from them. Today there are numerous such pastes, called *miso*, in everyday use in Japan. The color can vary, depending on the soybean-to-rice or barley ratio. The greater the amount of rice used, the lighter (and sweeter) the product. In the past, soy paste was stored in earthen jars for up to a year, which was said to improve the flavor.

Tempeh kedlee is a third soy product primarily confined to Indonesia, where more than half of the soybeans produced are devoted to it. It has a fine flavor, but not the longevity of other soy products. Also Indonesian in origin is *ontjom*, made by combining the residue of soybean milk with peanuts and allowing the mixture to ferment. The result is a kind of soy sauce with a nutlike flavor.

Still another product that originated in Indonesia (and Thailand as well) is *tao tjo*, made by combining cooked soybeans and roasted rice flour with *koji*. After about four days, a fungus covers the solution, whereupon the mixture is dried in the sun, then soaked in brine. A few days later, sugar and rice yeast are added and the sun, once again, is employed to dry the combined beans and flour. The end product is a sweet soy sauce to accompany vegetable, meat, or fish dishes.

A final Indonesian contribution is *ketjab*, in which bacteria are combined with cooked black beans, fermented, and then placed in salt brine for a week or so. The beans are drained and the residue is cooked several times. The extract that remains is sweetened with sugar and permitted to evaporate further.

A sixth soy product is *natto,* a gray-colored liquid with a strong, musty flavor, produced in Japan by wrapping cooked soybeans in rice straw and allowing the whole to ferment. The taste is something of an acquired one for Westerners and varies depending on locale.

Buddhist monks first developed *hamanatto* in their monasteries. This is still another fermented soy product, obtained in an elaborate procedure employed by the monks that began with soaking whole soybeans for up to 4 hours, then steaming them for 10 hours. Afterward, the beans were covered with *koji* and left to ferment for 20 hours, during which time a green mold developed to cover the beans. Next, they were dried in the sun to lower their moisture content, then placed in wooden buckets with strips of ginger on the bottom. After a year, the soybeans were once more dried in sun – this time until they turned black. The final product was a soybean sauce with a very sweet flavor and a pleasant aroma.

The major Korean contribution to soy products of the world is *kochu chang,* made by mashing boiled soybeans and beginning their fermentation with the addition of a bit of a previous batch, much like starter dough. This mixture was then placed in a sack and hung to dry in the sun for a couple of months, after which time the fermented mash was pulverized and mixed with salt and water. The final step was to put the mixture in an earthen jar to age for three months or so. After chilli peppers reached the East in the sixteenth century, they were added to the mash for additional flavor.

In addition to these sauces, soybeans have been processed by the Chinese and others of the Far East into bean curd, soybean milk, and bean bran. Soybean curd or *tou-fu* is made by wet-grinding the beans into a thin mixture that is strained, then coagulated with gypsum, which causes the proteins to precipitate. The mixture is strained a last time to become bean curd and soy milk, respectively. Bean curd thus provides the Asians with flour and milk, both very important foods in everyday life. The curd itself is often served with rice, meats, vegetables, and fish. It is also added to soups, mashed for making breads and cakes, and deep-fried.

Soybean milk – a vegetable milk – is obviously of considerable importance in a region of the world where little cattle raising takes place and where the human population seems to be uniformly lactose intolerant. In addition to serving as a beverage in its own right, soy milk is processed as a soft drink (Trager 1995).

The sprouts of soybean and mung beans *(Phaseolus aureus)* serve as an instant vegetable high in vitamin C and are also blanched and processed into cellophane noodles. Soybean sprouts are traditionally eaten on the Chinese New Year. Finally, young soybean pods are eaten boiled or roasted as a snack with soy sauce or sesame oil.

Nutrition

East Asians have long been dependent on soybeans for corrections of nutritional deficiencies. Soy sauces and other typical soy products are all concentrates of the B vitamins and contain significant amounts of the minerals calcium, iron, magnesium, phosphorous, and zinc. In addition, as we have already noted, they yield a very high quality protein, as well as important lipids, carbohydrates, and fiber.

Soy protein is also important nutritionally because of the ways in which it is employed in other food products for purposes of emulsion formation, promotion of fat and water absorption, and texture and color control. Foods benefiting from soy protein include bologna, frankfurters, breads, soups, cakes, pasta, gravies, whipped toppings, and simulated meats, vegetables, and fruits (Wolf and Cowan 1971: 52).

Soy flour usage, however, has not lived up to earlier expectations. The flour does have a nutty taste and very fragrant aroma; sweetened with sugar, it is baked into breads, muffins, cakes, cookies, and the like (Piper and Morse 1923). But unfortunately, it has a limited shelf life, which discourages production in large quantities.

It would not do to end this section on the nutritional value of soybeans without noting that they also contain various potentially toxic substances that can inhibit growth, reduce the absorption of fats, enlarge the pancreas, and decrease the energy yield of the diet (Norman 1978: 227). Among these antinutritional agents are trypsin, phytic acid, hemagglutinin, saponin, and phenolic constituents. Fortunately, the process of cooking eliminates the toxicity of soybeans.

Thomas Sorosiak

Bibliography

Adams, Sean. 1996. Sorting look-alike soybeans. *Agricultural Research* 44: 12-13.

Adolph, William H. 1946. Nutrition research in China. *Journal of the American Dietetic Association* 22: 964-70.

Anderson, Eugene N., Jr. 1977. Modern China: South. In *Food in Chinese culture,* ed. K. C. Chang, 70-80. New Haven, Conn.

Arntzen, Charles J., and Ellen M. Ritter, eds. 1994. *Encyclopedia of agricultural sciences.* San Diego, Calif.

Beuchat, Larry R. 1994. Fermented soybean foods. *Food Technology* 38: 64-70.

Beuerlein, Jim, T. T. Van Toai, A. F. Schmitthenner, and S. K. St. Martin. 1987. *The soybean in Ohio.* Ohio Cooperative Extension Service. Ohio State University, Columbus.

Borst, H. L., and L. E. Thatcher. 1931. *Life history and com-*

position of the soybean plant. Ohio Agricultural Experimental Station. Wooster, Ohio.

Carle, Julie. 1996. Research vital to soybean's future. *Sentinel-Tribune* (Bowling Green, Ohio). March 22, Farm edition, p. 11.

Chang, K. C. 1977. *Food in Chinese culture.* New Haven, Conn.

Crane, Helen R. 1933. The story of the soya. *Scientific American* 149: 270-2.

Darwin, Charles. 1868. *The variations of animals and plants under domestication.* London.

Dies, Edward J. 1943. *Soybeans: Gold from the soil.* New York.

Erdman, John W., and E. J. Fordyce. 1989. Soy products and the human diet. *The American Journal of Clinical Nutrition* 49: 725-37.

Flannery, K. V. 1969. Origins and ecological effects of early domestication in Iran and the Near East. In *The domestication and exploitation of plants and animals,* ed. P. J. Ucko and G. W. Dimbleby, 10-112. London.

Forrestal, Dan J. 1982. *The kernel and the bean.* New York.

Fortified foods: The next revolution. 1970. *Chemical Engineering News* 48: 35-43.

Gould, S. J. 1980. *The panda's thumb: More reflections in natural history.* New York.

Granberg, Wilbur J. 1970. *The Otomi Indians of Mexico.* New York.

Hector, J. M. Introduction to the botany of field crops. *Central News Agency Ltd* 2: 697-708.

Herklots, G. A. C. 1972. *Vegetables in Southeast Asia.* London.

Hesseltine, C. W., and H. L. Wang. 1967. Traditional fermented foods. *Biotechnology and Bioengineering* 9: 275-88.

Ho, Ping-ti. 1975. *The cradle of the East: An inquiry into the indigenous origins of techniques and ideas of neolithic and early historic China, 5000-1000 B.C.* Chicago.

Hymowitz, Theodore. 1987. Introduction of the soybean to Illinois. *Economic Botany* 41: 28-32.

Hymowitz, Theodore, and J. R. Harlan. 1983. Introduction of soybean to North America by Samuel Bowen in 1765. *Economic Botany* 37: 371-9.

Hymowitz, Theodore, and C. A. Newell. 1981. Taxonomy of the genus Glycine; domestication and uses of soybeans. *Economic Botany* 35: 272-88.

Liener, Irvine E., and M. L. Kakade. 1980. *Protease inhibitors.* New York.

Mermelstein, Neil H. 1989. Seeds of change. *Food Technology* 46: 86-9.

Norman, Geoffrey A. 1978. *Soybean physiology, agronomy, and utilization.* New York.

Pepper, Gary E. 1994. Soybeans. In *Encyclopedia of agricultural science,* Vol 4: 193-202. New York.

Piper, Charles V., and W. J. Morse. 1923. *The soybean.* New York.

Rindos, David. 1984. *The origin of agriculture.* New York.

Shih, Sheng-Han. 1959. *"Fan Sheng-Chih Shu": An agriculturalist's book of China written by Fan Sheng-Chih in the first century B.C.* Peking.

Shurtleff, William, and A. Aoyagi. 1986. *Thesaurus for soya.* Second edition. Lafayette, Calif.

Simoons, Frederick J. 1990. *Food in China.* Boca Raton, Fla.

Smith, A. K. 1961. *Oriental methods of using soybeans as food, with special attention to fermented products.* U.S. Department of Agriculture. Washington, D.C.

Smith, Allan K., and S. J. Circle. 1972. *Soybeans: Chemistry and technology.* Westport, Conn.

Soskin, Anthony B. 1988. *Non-traditional agriculture and economic development: The Brazilian soybean expansion 1964-1982.* New York.

Tanner, J. W., and D. J. Hume. 1976. *World soybean research.* Danville, Ill.

Toussaint-Samat, Maguelonne. 1992. *A history of food,* trans. Anthea Bell. Cambridge, Mass.

Trager, James. 1995. *The food chronology.* New York.

Van Sanford, D. A. 1993. Selection index based on genetic correlations among environments. *Crop Science* 33: 1244-8.

Wagner, C. K., and M. B. McDonald. 1981. *Identification of soybean cultivars using rapid laboratory techniques.* Ohio Agricultural Research and Development Center. Wooster, Ohio.

Weber, C. R. 1966. Soybeans. *Agronomy Journal* 58: 43-6.

Whigham, D. K. 1976. Expanding the use of soybeans. *Journal of the University of Illinois,* Urbana-Champaign. INTSOY, 10.

Wittwer, Sylvan, et al. 1987. *Feeding a billion: Frontiers of Chinese agriculture.* East Lansing, Mich.

Wolf, W. J., and J. C. Cowan. 1971. *Soybeans as a food source.* Cleveland, Ohio.

Wright, H. E., Jr. 1968. Natural environment and early food production north of Mesopotamia. *Science* 161: 334-9.

Yong, F. M., and B. J. B. Wood. 1974. Microbiology and biochemistry of the soy sauce fermentation. *Advanced Application Microbiology* 17: 157.

II.E.6 ❧ Sunflower

One of the most important of today's oil crops, the sunflower is a unique contribution of temperate North America to the world's major food plants. In addition to its superior oil, the seed of the sunflower is much appreciated as a food. Other parts of the plant were used for a variety of purposes by Native Americans. Today the species is also widely grown as an ornamental for its large showy heads.

Biology

Scientifically, the sunflower crop plant, known as *Helianthus annuus* var. *macrocarpus,* is a member of the family Asteraceae. It is an annual, is unbranched, grows from 1 to 3 meters tall, and bears a single large head up to 76 centimeters (cm) in diameter. Each head contains showy yellow sterile ray flowers and up to 8,000 smaller disk flowers. The latter produce the fruits, technically known as achenes, but commonly called seeds. The fruits, from 6 to 16 millimeters (mm) in length, contain a single seed.

In addition to the cultivated variety, the sunflower also includes branched, smaller-headed varieties *(Helianthus annuus* var. *annuus* and *Helianthus annuus* var. *lenticularis)* that are common as weeds or wild plants in North America from southern Canada to northern Mexico. Forms of the sunflower, particularly those with double flowers or red ray flowers, are cultivated as ornamentals, but more so in Europe than in North America (Heiser 1976).

The genus *Helianthus,* native to North America, comprises 49 species and is divided into four sections (Schilling and Heiser 1981). The sunflower is placed in the section *Helianthus* along with 11 other annual species, all of which are diploid with 17 pairs of chromosomes. The silverleaf sunflower *Helianthus argophyllus* of Texas is the closest relative of the sunflower. The other sections include mostly perennial species, which may be diploid, tetraploid, or hexaploid. One of the perennials, the Jerusalem artichoke, is also cultivated as a food plant for its edible tubers.

Several of the species, both annual and perennial, are occasionally cultivated as ornamentals for their showy flowers (Heiser et al. 1969). *Helianthus* × *laetiflorus* and *Helianthus* × *multiflorus* are particularly widely cultivated for this purpose.

Origin and Early History

In prehistoric times, Native Americans in western North America collected the seeds of wild sunflowers for food, a practice continued by some until early in the twentieth century. In addition to eating the seeds, they also used the plants for pigments. The flowers were employed in ceremonies, the dried stems utilized in construction and for fuel, and various other parts exploited for medicinal purposes.

It has been postulated that the wild sunflower, originally confined to western North America, was a camp-following weed carried to central and eastern North America by the Native Americans, where it became an encouraged weed and, eventually, a deliberately cultivated plant. Mutations occurred, giving rise to monocephalic forms with larger seeds. The archaeological recovery of seeds in eastern North America indicates that the sunflower was domesticated before 1500 B.C. and that it was fairly extensively cultivated before 500 B.C. Some of these prehistoric sunflowers were in no way inferior to modern varieties in size. Early historical records reveal that the sunflower was also cultivated in Mexico and the American Southwest where it is still grown by the Hopi and Havasupai (Heiser 1951).

Along with sumpweed *(Iva annua),* a chenopod *(Chenopodium berlandieri),* and a squash *(Cucurbita pepo),* the sunflower was domesticated in eastern North America before the arrival of maize and other cultivated plants from Mexico (Smith 1989; Gayle 1990). By the time of early historical observations, it seems that maize had become the major crop of Native Americans, although the sunflower was still widely cultivated as a minor crop; sumpweed had disappeared entirely from cultivation.

Sometime after 1492, the sunflower was carried to Europe, the earliest introductions probably being in Spain. The first clear-cut reference to the sunflower is in the herbal of Rembert Dodoens in 1568, where it is illustrated. The plant spread throughout much of Europe, reaching England before the end of the sixteenth century. The sunflower excited curiosity in some places because of its large size, but it was not an early success as a food plant. In fact, it was not until it reached Russia that the seeds became greatly appreciated.

The Holy Orthodox Church of Russia observed very strict dietary regulations during the 40 days of Lent and during Advent. In the early nineteenth century, the list of prohibited foods included nearly all of those rich in oil, but the sunflower, perhaps unknown to the church authorities, was not on the list. The Russian people eagerly adopted the sunflower seed, which could be used while still obeying the letter of the law (Gilmore 1931). The popularity of the sunflower was such that by midcentury or so Russia had become the world's leader in sunflower production.

Oil from sunflower seed was extracted in Russia from the early part of the nineteenth century onward. In addition to the heads, the stems were harvested as an important source of potash, some of which was exported (Putt 1978). Breeding to improve the crop plant commenced early in the twentieth century. Earlier-maturing and higher-yielding varieties were secured, and semidwarf varieties, which could be harvested mechanically, were developed. The oil content of the seeds was increased from 20 to more than 50 percent, and resistance to some pests and diseases was also incorporated into the plant.

Recent History

The two world wars led to great increases in sunflower production, particularly in Romania, Bulgaria, and Hungary. More recently, France and Spain have become major producers, but the former USSR has remained the world's leader and now produces more than half of the world's supply (Table II.E.6.1).

By far the most important sunflower-producing country in the Americas is Argentina, which became an exporter of the seeds early in the twentieth century. For many years, Argentina has been the world's second largest sunflower producer (see Table II.E.6.1).

Only recently, however, has the sunflower again become an important crop in its homeland. In both the United States and Canada, commercial sunflower cultivation was begun in the latter part of the nineteenth century, using varieties from Europe rather than native varieties. Indeed, North American production was, in part, the result of an introduction of improved varieties from the Soviet Union and the later adoption of higher-yielding hybrids (Putt 1978).

The sunflower was initially grown in the United States mostly for silage, but seed production has become increasingly important as people have replaced animal oils with those of plant origin in cooking. A quarter of a century ago, the sunflower, in some years, ranked second only to the soybean as one

Table II.E.6.1. *Sunflower production: Principal sunflower-producing countries in 1990 with 1960 figures for comparison (given in 1,000 metric tons)*

	1960	1990
Argentina	802	3,850
Bulgaria	279	365
Canada	17	115
China	–	1,500
France	3	2,314
Hungary	115	650
India	–	550
Italy	4	301
Morocco	–	160
Romania	529	556
South Africa	87	585
Spain	2	1,314
Turkey	128	900
United States	–	1,032
Former USSR	3,019	6,500
Former Yugoslavia	114	402
World	5,350	22,072

Source: FAO Production Yearbook, Vol. 14 (1961) and Vol. 44 (1991).

of the world's major oil crops. Lately, however, increased production of canola from rapeseed, particularly in Europe and Canada, has allowed this crop to take over the second position in oil production.

Agronomy

The sunflower is primarily a temperate zone crop. It has some tolerance to both high and low temperatures, and temperature may have an effect on oil composition. It is usually grown without irrigation, and although not highly drought tolerant, it often gives satisfactory yields when most other crops are damaged by drought. Sunflowers will grow in a variety of soil types, from clay to somewhat sandy, and respond well to fertilization, which may be done through soil or foliar treatments. Nitrogen is most often the limiting factor in their growth.

The plants may produce toxic residues in the soil so that crop rotation is essential for good growth. Weed control is also necessary, and herbicides are usually employed. In the northern United States, seeds are planted in late April or May. Later plantings affect oil composition adversely. The plants are ready for harvest in four months at which time considerable moisture is still present in the seeds. Thus, drying, usually by forcing air over the seeds, is required before the seeds are stored or transported (Robinson 1978; Schuler et al. 1978).

Pests and Diseases

Like most crops, the sunflower is subject to a number of insect pests, along with fungal and bacterial diseases. All parts of the plant may be attacked by

insects. The most serious pest in the United States is the sunflower moth, which infests the head (Schulz 1978). Downy mildew, a rust, and scherotinia white mold are among the main pathogens that damage the crop (Zimmer and Hoes 1978). Sunflower seeds are a favorite food of many birds, and at times up to 30 percent of the crop is lost to them. The chief culprit in the United States is the blackbird. One method of reducing the loss to birds is to harvest the crop early while the moisture content of the seeds is still high (Besser 1978).

Oil and Protein

The sunflower has excellent nutritional properties. The oil contains high levels of linoleic acid, moderate levels of linolenic acid, and less than 15 percent fatty acids (Dorrell 1978). Extraction of the oil is by solvents after the kernel is crushed or rolled and then cooked. The oil is used for margarine and shortening, as well as for cooking and salad oils. At present, it is little used for industrial purposes but has potential for a number of such applications.

The seed meal left after the extraction of oil serves as animal feed. It has about 28 percent protein and a good balance of amino acids, although it is low in lysine. The hulls, another by-product of the extraction process, are ground and used as filler or roughage in livestock feed in the United States. In other countries, the hulls are also used as fuel (Doty 1978).

Other Uses of the Seed

Although most of the world's sunflower crop goes into oil production, some is used for confectionery food and for feed for birds and pets (Lofgren 1978). The varieties employed for these purposes generally have larger seeds with lower oil content than those grown for oil extraction. The confectionery seeds are used as snack foods, in salads, and in bakery goods. The seeds are frequently shelled, roasted, and salted before reaching the consumer. Large amounts are sold in the shell in the United States for the feeding of wild birds.

Breeding

In the middle of the twentieth century it was realized that utilization of hybrid vigor could produce great increases in the yield of sunflowers. Because of the nature of the flower, the only practical way of making hybrids would be through the employment of cytoplasmic male sterility, and in 1968, Patrice Leclercq of France announced the discovery of cytoplasmic male sterility in crosses of sunflower with *Helianthus petiolaris* (Fick 1978). Fertility restorers were subsequently identified by a number of investigators, and the commercial production of hybrids was soon under way. Yield increases of up to 20 percent resulted, making the sunflower more competitive with a number of other oil crops. Leclercq's cytoplasmic male sterility continues to be used for the creation of hybrids, but other sources of it are now available.

Sunflower breeding through traditional methods is being pursued in France, the United States, Russia, and a few other countries. In addition to increased yields, the principal objectives are to secure resistance to diseases and pests and to improve the oil content and composition. Both intra- and interspecific hybridization are being employed. The wild annual species have proved to be a particularly valuable source of disease resistance. The perennial species have, thus far, been little utilized.

Germ Plasm Reserves

Large seed collections that serve as a valuable reserve of genetic variation are maintained in Russia, the United States, and several other countries. Collections of the wild species are also available, and more than 2,000 accessions have been assembled in the United States (Seiler 1992). Wild *Helianthus annuus* still occurs naturally in large areas of North America, and several other annual species, particularly *Helianthus petiolaris,* have rather extensive distributions. Some of the other annual species occupy more restricted areas, but only one of them, *Helianthus paradoxus,* appears in imminent danger of extinction. Most of the perennial species are still readily available from wild populations in North America.

Charles B. Heiser, Jr.

Bibliography

Besser, Jerome F. 1978. Birds and sunflowers. In *Sunflower science and technology,* ed. Jack F. Carter, 263-78. Madison, Wis.

Dorrell, D. Gordon. 1978. Processing and utilization of oilseed sunflower. In *Sunflower science and technology,* ed. Jack F. Carter, 407-40. Madison, Wis.

Doty, Harry O., Jr. 1978. Future of sunflower as an economic crop in North America and the world. In *Sunflower science and technology,* ed. Jack F. Carter, 457-88. Madison, Wis.

Fick, Gerhardt N. 1978. Breeding and genetics. In *Sunflower science and technology,* ed. Jack F. Carter, 279-338. Madison, Wis.

Gayle, Fritz J. 1990. Multiple pathways to farming in pre-contact eastern North America. *Journal of World Prehistory* 4: 387-435.

Gilmore, Melvin R. 1931. Plant vagrants in America. *Papers of the Michigan Academy of Science, Arts and Letters* 15: 65-78.

Heiser, Charles B. 1951. The sunflower among the North American Indians. *Proceedings of the American Philosophical Society* 98: 432-448.

   1976. *The sunflower.* Norman, Okla.

Heiser, Charles B., Dale M. Smith, Sarah B. Clevenger, and William C. Martin, Jr. 1969. The North American sunflowers *(Helianthus). Memoirs of the Torrey Botanical Club* 22: 1-218.

Lofgren, James R. 1978. Sunflower for confectionery food, birdfood, and pet food. In *Sunflower science and technology,* ed. Jack F. Carter, 441-56. Madison, Wis.

Putt, Eric D. 1978. History and present world status. In *Sunflower science and technology,* ed. Jack F. Carter, 1-29. Madison, Wis.

Robinson, Robert G. 1978. Production and culture. In *Sunflower science and technology,* ed. Jack F. Carter, 89-113. Madison, Wis.

Schilling, Edward E., and Charles B. Heiser. 1981. Infrageneric classification of *Helianthus. Taxon* 30: 293-403.

Schuler, Robert T., H. J. Hiring, V. L. Hofman, and D. R. Lundstrom. 1978. Harvesting, handling, and storage of seed. In *Sunflower science and technology,* ed. Jack F. Carter, 145-67. Madison, Wis.

Schulz, J. T. 1978. Insect pests. In *Sunflower science and technology,* ed. Jack F. Carter, 169-223. Madison, Wis.

Seiler, Gerald. 1992. Utilization of wild sunflower species as sources of genetic diversity for improvement of cultivated sunflower. *Field Crops Research* 30: 195-230.

Smith, Bruce. 1989. Origins of agriculture in eastern North America. *Science* 246: 1566-71.

Zimmer, David E., and J. A. Hoes. 1978. Diseases. In *Sunflower science and technology,* ed. Jack F. Carter, 225-62. Madison, Wis.

II.F

Trading in Tastes

II.F.1 ～ Spices and Flavorings

Plants possess a wealth of different chemical ingredients, ranging from substances with simple structures to very complicated ones, such as terpene or benzoic derivatives. Some are poisonous, others are important raw materials in biochemistry and medicines, while still others are responsible for the appetizing odors we identify with certain foods.

Although the majority of spices are derived from plants, the most important spice is a mineral. Salt has been mined for culinary use (and perhaps, more importantly, as a food preservative) for more than 2,500 years, as well as secured at the seaside by the evaporation of seawater. Saltwater creatures, such as small herrings or other salty-tasting fish, have also been used as spices.

Among the spices of plant origin are such widely used spice plants as pepper and ginger. Other plants are frequently regarded as a flavoring, such as onions, peppers, carrots, and celery. Moreover, there are herbs, such as dandelions and daisies, which in the past were used as spices, as can be seen in old recipes.

Although not normally considered to be spices, certain fruits and nuts, such as rowanberry, cranberry, and hazelnut, are also occasionally recommended in recipes as flavorings. In addition, plant stems, flowers, seeds, fruits, leaves, roots, and even pollen grains have been employed as spices.

Although all spices do not necessarily figure significantly in nutrition, there are other sound reasons for cooking with them, not the least of which are the aromatic ingredients they contain that can influence the taste of food. But spices also have chemical ingredients that aid digestion and play a role in food conservation (as does salt) by inhibiting bacterial growth and rendering the food unpalatable for microbes and insects. Until relatively recently, most spices had been luxury items, and their usage was an indicator of well-established culinary traditions within a relatively long-standing (and presumably highly developed) culture (Stobart 1977; Küster 1987).

The Landscapes of Spices

Spice plants occur in all parts of the world, but some regions, such as the tropics and subtropics, have an abundance of them, reflecting the greater diversity of plant species there. In the subtropics, the number of spice plants was increased by an extensive grazing of grasslands over millennia. Thus, for example, on the steppe landscapes of the Near East, North Africa, and the Mediterranean, cattle, goats, and sheep preferred to graze on mild, nonpoisonous plants without spines and thorns. Such selective pressure on the plant life of a region eventually produced the kind of subtropic grazing areas observed today, one that is characterized by a wealth of spice plants, albeit often spiny ones that are sometimes poisonous if taken in overly large quantities. Thus, the aromas of thyme, lavender, and sage are always present in the Mediterranean air and in the atmosphere of similar landscapes in Asia, as well as in North American areas such as California, Texas, and Florida, where such plants have been introduced by human migrants.

Coriander

Origins of Spices

It is often difficult to reconstruct the origin of certain spices because they have been introduced by humans to many habitations worldwide throughout the ages. In fact, it is sometimes difficult to determine whether a plant is indigenous or introduced to a specific area. The latter may well have occurred before written sources existed, but unfortunately, even in historic times individuals rarely wrote about the introduction of plants.

Some ancient scientists and writers, such as Aristotle, Virgil, and Pliny, mention plants in their manuscripts. But whether they personally knew of those they wrote about or whether they mentioned them only because other scholars in earlier texts had done so is another matter. An added complication is the difficulty of botanically equating the plants referred to by spice names in Greek or Latin texts with their modern equivalents. Put plainly, that a plant was present at a specific time in a specific region often can be determined only by an archaeobotanical analysis of plant materials derived from layers of accurately dated archaeological excavations.

Even when a plant is found among archaeological remains, however, it is often unclear that its use had been as a spice. This question can be definitively answered only with written sources. On the other hand, if pepper grains are found far outside their South Asian area of origin - in a Roman settlement in Europe, for instance - then this strongly suggests the liklihood that there had been a trade in pepper grains. And such a trade of pepper grains makes sense only if one assumes that they were used as spices in ancient Rome.

Having stressed the difficulties of reconstructing the ancient history of spices, we should also emphasize that most of the as-yet unresolved questions surrounding that history are now being addressed in the interdisciplinary work of botanists, archaeologists, and philologists. Such work has already deliniated the most likely areas of the origin of the various spices, as listed in Table II.F.1.1 - a table that also shows that all of the well-known ancient civilizations used a complement of typical spices. Thus, ginger, star anise, and soy were known in early Chinese culture, whereas black pepper was commonly used by ancients in India. In the basins of the Euphrates and Tigris rivers, licorice and coriander have been cultivated since early times; ancient cultures of the Mediterranean used sage and anise. And, of course, vanilla, chocolate, and chilli peppers from the New World have become well-known gifts of the Mesoamerican civilizations.

Table II.F.1.1. *The origin of spices used historically and today*

Spice	Latin name	Area of origin	Time of oldest cultivation/consumption	Parts of plants taken as spice
Ajowan	*Trachyspermum ammi*	NE Africa, S Asia	Unknown	Fruits
Alexanders	*Smyrnium olusatrum*	Mediterranean	Antiquity?	Leaves
Allspice	*Pimenta dioica*	Central America	Pre-Colombian	Fruits
Almond	*Amygdalus communis*	(W) Asia	2d millennium B.C.	Seeds
Angelica	*Angelica archangelica*	N Europe	Medieval	Stems, roots
Anise	*Pimpinella anisum*	S Europe	Bronze Age?	Fruits
Anise-pepper	*Xanthoxylum piperitum*	E Asia	Unknown	Fruits
Asafoetida	*Ferula asafoetida*	Persia, Afghanistan	2,000 B.C.	Dried mill
Avens	*Geum urbanum*	Widespread	Unknown	Roots
Balm	*Melissa officinalis*	E Mediterranean	Antiquity	Leaves
Basil	*Ocimum basilicum*	S Asia (India?)	Antiquity	Leaves
Bay	*Laurus nobilis*	Mediterranean	Antiquity	Leaves
Bergamot	*Monarda didyma*	N America	Unknown	Leaves
Black caraway	*Pimpinella saxifraga*	Europe, W Asia	Unknown	Leaves
Bog myrtle	*Myrica gale*	Northern Hemisphere	Medieval	Leaves
Borage	*Borago officinalis*	(W) Mediterranean	Middle Ages	Leaves, flowers
Burnet	*Sanguisorba* sp.	Europe	Unknown	Leaves
Calamus	*Acorus calamus*	SE Asia, N America	2d millennium B.C.	Roots
Caper	*Capparis spinosa*	Mediterranean, S, W Asia	2d millennium B.C.	Buds
Caraway	*Carum carvi*	Europe	Unknown	Fruits
Cardamom	*Elettaria cardamomum*	Tropical S Asia	3,000 B.C.	Seeds
Cassia	*Cinnamomum aromaticum*	China	3d millennium B.C.	Parts of bark
Cayenne peper	*Capsicum frutescens*	Tropical America	Unknown	Fruits
Celery	*Apium graveolens*	Widespread at seasides	Neolithic	Fruits, leaves
Chervil	*Anthriscus cerefolium*	SE Europe, W Asia	Antiquity	Leaves
Chive	*Allium schoenoprasum*	N hemisphere	Unknown	Leaves
Chocolate	*Theobroma cacao*	Tropical America	Unknown	Seeds
Cinnamon	*Cinnamomum verum*	Ceylon	Antiquity	Parts of bark
Citron	*Citrus medica*	SE Asia	Unknown	Fruit of skin

Table II.F.1.1. *(Continued)*

Spice	Latin name	Area of origin	Time of oldest cultivation/consumption	Parts of plants taken as spice
Clary	*Salvia sclarea*	Mediterranean, W Asia	Antiquity?	Leaves
Clove	*Syzygium aromaticum*	Molukkian Islands	Antiquity	Buds
Coriander	*Coriandrum sativum*	E Mediterranean, W Asia	Neolithic?	Fruits
Costmary	*Chrysanthemum balsamita*	W Asia	Unknown	Leaves
Cowslip	*Primula veris*	Eurasia	Unknown	Leaves, flowers
Cress	*Lepidium sativum*	NE Africa, W Asia	Unknown	Leaves
Cumin	*Cuminum cyminum*	E Mediterranean, W Asia	C. 3,000 B.C.	Fruits
Curry leaf	*Murraya koenigii*	S Himalaya	Unknown	Leaves
Dandelion	*Taraxacum officinale*	Europe	Unknown	Leaves
Dill	*Anethum graveolens*	S Europe? Asia?	3,000 B.C.	Leaves
Elecampane	*Inula helenium*	SE Europe	Antiquity	Roots
Fennel	*Foeniculum vulgare*	Mediterranean	3,000 B.C.	Fruits
Fenugreek	*Trigonella foenum-graecum*	E Mediterranean	3,000 B.C.	Seeds
Galangal	*Alpinia galanga/officinarum*	SE Asia	Unknown	Roots
Garlic	*Allium sativum*	Central Asia	2d millennium B.C.	Bulbs
Garlic mustard	*Alliaria petiolata*	Europe, W Asia, N Africa	Unknown	Leaves
Gentian	*Gentiana lutea*	Europe	Antiquity?	Roots
Geranium	*Pelargonium* sp.	S Africa	Unknown	Oil of leaves
Ginger	*Zingiber officinale*	SE Asia	2d millennium B.C.	Roots
Grains of paradise	*Aframomum melegueta*	W Africa	Unknown	Seeds
Ground ivy	*Glechoma hederacea*	Eurasia	Unknown	Leaves
Hazel nut	*Corylus avellana*	Eurasia	Mesolithic	Seeds
Hop	*Humulus lupulus*	Europe	Medieval	Fruits
Horehound	*Marrubium vulgare*	Asia, S Europe	Antiquity	Leaves
Horseradish	*Armoracia rusticana*	SE Europe, W Asia	Unknown	Roots
Hyssop	*Hyssopus officinalis*	Eurasian mountains	Unknown	Leaves
Indian cress	*Tropaeolum majus*	Tropical S America	Unknown	Leaves
Juniper	*Juniperus communis*	N Hemisphere	Unknown	Fruits
Lady's smock	*Cardamine pratensis*	N Hemisphere	Unknown	Leaves
Lavendar	*Lavandula officinalis*	S Europe	Unknown	Leaves
Lemon	*Citrus limon*	SE Asia	Unknown	Fruit skin
Lemon grass	*Cymbopogon citratus*	SE Asia, Ceylon	Unknown	Leaves
Lime	*Citrus aurantium*	Tropical SE Asia	Unknown	Fruit skin
Liquorice	*Glycyrrhiza glabra*	E Mediterranean, Asia	2,000 B.C.	Roots
Lovage	*Levisticum officinale*	Persia?	Antiquity	Leaves
Mace, nutmeg	*Myristica fragrans*	Mollukkian Islands	2d millennium B.C.	Seeds, seed cover
Marigold	*Calendula officinalis*	Mediterranean?	Unknown	Flowers
Marjoram	*Origanum majorana*	E Mediterranean	Antiquity?	Leaves
Mastic	*Pistacia lentiscus*	Mediterranean, Canary Islands	Antiquity	Resin
Melilot	*Melilotus officinalis*	N Hemisphere	Unknown	Leaves
Milfoil	*Achillea millefolium*	Europe, N Asia	Unknown	Leaves
Mint	*Mentha* sp.	Widespread	Unknown	Leaves
Mugwort	*Artemisia vulgaris*	N Hemisphere	Unknown	Leaves
Mustard	*Brassica* sp., *Sinapis alba*	Eurasia	Antiquity	Seeds
Myrtle	*Myrtus communis*	Mediterranean	Antiquity	Leaves, fruits
Nasturtium	*Tropaeolum majus*	S America	Unknown	Leaves
Nigella	*Nigella sativa*	SE Europe, W Asia	Antiquity	Seeds
Olive	*Olea europaea*	(E) Mediterranean?	Neolithic?	Fruits
Onion	*Allium cepa*	Central Asia	3d millennium B.C.	Bulbs
Orange	*Citrus sinensis*	Tropical SE Asia	Unknown	Fruit skin
Oregano	*Origanum vulgare*	Eurasia	Antiquity	Leaves
Parsley	*Petroselinum crispum*	Mediterranean	3,000 B.C.	Leaves
Parsnip	*Pastinaca sativa*	Europe, W Asia	Antiquity?	Fruits, seeds
Peanut	*Arachis hypogaea*	Brazil	Unknown	Seeds
Pepper	*Piper nigrum*	Tropical SE Asia	Prehistoric India	Seeds
Peppers	*Capsicum annuum*	Tropical America	Unknown	Fruits, seeds
Pine nut	*Pinus pinea*	Mediterranean	Before 2,000 B.C.	Seeds
Pistachio nut	*Pistacia vera*	W Asia	Neolithic	Seeds
Pomegranate	*Punica granatum*	E Mediterranean, W Asia	3d millennium B.C.	Fruits
Poppy	*Papaver somniferum*	(W) Mediterranean	Neolithic	Seeds

(continued)

Table II.F.1.1. *(Continued)*

Spice	Latin name	Area of origin	Time of oldest cultivation/consumption	Parts of plants taken as spice
Purslane	*Portulaca oleracea*	S Asia?	2,000 B.C.	Leaves
Plantain	*Plantago lanceolata*	Eurasia	Unknown	Leaves
Rocket	*Eruca sativa*	Mediterranean, W Asia	Antiquity?	Seeds
Rose	*Rosa* sp.	Widespread	Unknown	Petals, fruits
Roselle	*Hibiscus sabdariffa*	Tropical S Asia	Unknown	Calyx
Rosemary	*Rosmarinus officinalis*	Mediterranean	Antiquity	Leaves
Rowan	*Sorbus aucuparia*	Europe	Unknown	Fruits
Rue	*Ruta graveolens*	Balkans, Italy	Antiquity	Leaves
Safflower	*Carthamus tinctorius*	W Asia	Unknown	Flowers
Saffron	*Crocus sativus*	Greece? Near East?	Unknown	Pollen
Sage	*Salvia officinalis*	Mediterranean	Antiquity	Leaves
Samphire	*Crithmum maritimum*	European coasts, Canary Islands	Antiquity	Leaves
Savory	*Satureja hortensis*	Mediterranean	Roman	Leaves
Screwpine	*Pandanus tectorius*	India, Ceylon	Unknown	Mainly flowers
Sea buckthorn	*Hippophaë rhamnoides*	N Eurasia	Unknown	Fruits
Sesame	*Sesamum indicum*	E Africa? India?	Ancient Orient	Seeds
Silphion	? (extinct)	N Africa?	Antiquity	?
Sorrel	*Rumex* sp.	Widespread	Unknown	Leaves
Southernwood	*Artemisia abrotanum*	SE Europe, W Asia	Antiquity	Leaves
Soy	*Glycine max*	SE Asia	Unknown	Seeds
Star anise	*Illicium verum*	SE Asia	2,000 B.C.	Fruits
Stonecrop	*Sedum reflexum*	Europe	Unknown	Leaves
Sugar beet	*Beta vulgaris*	Europe	18th century	Roots
Sugarcane	*Saccharum officinarum*	SE Asia	Antiquity	Stalks
Sumac	*Rhus coriaria*	Mediterranean, W Asia	Antiquity	Fruits
Sunflower	*Helianthus annuus*	Central America	Unknown	Seeds
Sweet cicely	*Myrrhis odorata*	Europe	Unknown	Fruits
Sweet woodruff	*Asperula odorata*	Europe	Unknown	Leaves
Tamarind	*Tamarindus indica*	Tropical Africa, (India?)	2,000 B.C.	Parts of fruits
Tansy	*Tanacetum vulgare*	Eurasia	Unknown	Leaves
Tarragon	*Artemisia dracunculus*	Asia, N America	2d millennium B.C.	Leaves
Thyme	*Thymus vulgaris*	Mediterranean	Unknown	Leaves
Turmeric	*Curcuma longa*	Tropical SE Asia	Unknown	Roots
Vanilla	*Vanilla planifolia*	Tropical America	Pre-Columbian	Fruits
Violet	*Viola odorata*	Mediterranean, S England	Antiquity?	Flowers
Walnut	*Juglans regia*	E Mediterranean?	Antiquity	Seeds
Watercress	*Nasturtium officinale*	Widespread	Unknown	Leaves
White cinnamon	*Canella alba*	Central America	Unknown	Bark
Wild thyme	*Thymus serpyllum*	Europe, W Asia	Unknown	Leaves
Wood sorrel	*Oxalis acetosella*	N Hemisphere	Unknown	Leaves
Wormwood	*Artemisia absinthium*	Eurasia	Antiquity	Leaves

Spices as Elements of an Urban Lifestyle

It would seem that those emerging from the Old World Neolithic Revolution who pioneered in employing most of the spices were not rural peasants but rather urban dwellers: Historical evidence suggests that it was only in those cultures which gave rise to concentrated settlements that spice use seems to have been known.

In most cases, that use was aimed not so much at making the food more tasty but rather at masking the taste of food that was no longer fresh, or even spoiled. Spoilage was not a major problem with cereal grains and legumes. But it was more of a problem with the less easy-to-conserve oil plant seeds and, of course, a major one with fish, fowl, meat, and animal products such as milk.

Although early humans appear to have been scavengers, it was presumably the ideal among their prehistoric hunter–gatherer successors to consume a hunted animal immediately after it had been killed. This, in turn, would have made the kill of any large animal a social event, with friends and relations joining the hunters in eating the meat while it was still fresh and unspoiled. After everybody had been fed, however, there was probably little interest in the remaining scraps, and because meat conservation technology had not been developed, it was necessary to kill again before meat once more entered the diet.

A similar approach to meat consumption was, doubtless, the case in the first farming communities. But as these early farmers increasingly derived more and more of their nutrients from crops, meat became less important in their diets - much less than it had been among their hunter–gatherer forebears.

Yet the relative dietary importance of various foods shifted again when the first towns or townlike settlements arose. Town dwellers depended for their food on rural settlements, and this demand was more readily met by meat than by grain. Clearly it was far easier for rural producers to drive cattle and sheep, moving under their own power, to a slaughterhouse inside a town than it was to haul bulky, not to mention heavy, containers of grains and legumes to town storage areas from the countryside.

Meat, as a consequence, became an important part of the diet in urban settlements, which led, in turn, to technology that permitted the utilization of the entire carcass. On the one hand, each part of the carcass had food value, and on the other, such utilization avoided the problem of carcass disposal inside or near the settlements, with the attendant difficulties of odors, pests, and even disease associated with the rotting remains.

The first techniques of meat conservation were those of smoking plus salting to preserve meats from insects and microbes that cannot live in a salty environment. However, even salted meat was often spoiled, or at least tasted spoiled, by the time it was consumed, and it was discovered that the spoiled taste could be covered by the addition of pungent spices. Moreover, although people might fall ill from the consumption of spoiled meat, it was learned that other spices could help prevent these consequences by making digestion easier.

Because of such growing knowledge, the people of the towns that demanded meat also demanded spices, and this was especially true of the upper classes. It came to be regarded as sophisticated to mask the taste of spoiled meat and fat in cookery and, thus, spices became a valuable item of exchange.

Elsewhere, and considerably later, other populations that had come to depend heavily on fish learned to preserve them by creating spicy sauces to accompany them. And later in the Americas, spices, especially chilli peppers, enlivened fare that in many cases was essentially vegetarian in nature. Clearly, then, contact with the spice trade that developed in the Eurasian world was not a prerequisite for spice usage. On the other hand, those with money who enjoyed such contact could choose from a variety of seasonings.

The Beginning of the Spice Trade

The spice trade began as early as the trade in precious metals and jewels and dyes and silks - which, along with spices, were ancient items traded over the silk and spice roads in the Near East. Spices first moved between Mesopotamia and Egypt; later, Indian spices were traded to the Levant, and Mesopotamian spices reached the Indus valley (see Table II.F.1.1 for areas of origin). All important trade centers were connected by spice roads, with such trade generally practiced by nomadic peoples, who in later times were the Arabs.

As the spice roads of the Near Eastern deserts were extended to Levantine harbors, spices began traveling by ship to Athens, Rome, Massilia, and other parts of the ancient world. The Greeks and Romans, in turn, added a number of Mediterranean spices to the trade and began to vie for dominance of the trade. In fact, control of the spice trade was one factor in the warfare among the Greeks and Romans and Near Eastern peoples.

Roman consumption of spices from all over the known world was enormous. In fact, the Roman demand for the spice silphion, which was grown in Kyrene in Northern Africa, was so great that it was overexploited until it became extinct. Today silphion is known only through historical documents, and its conventional designation as a member of the Apiaceae plant family can only be a tentative one (Küster 1987). Moreover, because the Romans took spices to all places on the globe where Roman soldiers were garrisoned, Roman cookery became the first cuisine that (at the risk of argument from Chinese historians) might be called "international." In addition, it was the Romans who established the first trade network across the known world to send spices, such as pepper, from Southeast Asia all the way to central Europe (Kucan 1984).

Use of Spices in Medieval Europe

During the European Middle Ages, Roman cookery and its use of spices had come to be well regarded, even in countries far more distant from the pepper-growing areas than ancient Rome had been. Spices, brought to western and northern Europe, were shipped along the western coast of Europe to England, Ireland, France, and the Netherlands. The Rhine river became an important shipping route as well. The Hanseatic merchants traded spices in the North Sea and the Baltic areas, and later, northern Italian and southern German merchants began to trade them overland and via the Alps. Harbor towns like Venice, Genoa, Lisbon, London, Dublin, Amsterdam, and Lübeck became wealthy as a result of the spice trade, as did inland towns like Constance, Augsburg, Nuremberg, and Cracow.

Indeed, at times, medieval European kings and emperors could not reign without the support of the spice merchants, who were very wealthy and exerted considerable political influence. The nickname "Pfeffersack" (pepper sack) was commonly used to refer to a merchant making very high profits from the spice trade. The use of black pepper, which could mask the scent of spoiled meat and fat, came to be regarded as a status symbol. Duke Karl of Bourgogne, regarded in his day as the richest man in Europe, ordered 380 pounds of pepper for his wedding dinner in 1468 (Küster 1987).

Ordinary people, however, could not afford to buy spices from Southeast Asia, which thus remained in short supply despite the trading networks. For this reason, there were often attempts to adulterate spices, which became a serious kind of crime that could result in a sentence of death by burning or decapitation. All of this, in turn, provided a strong motivation for people to discover pungent plants that were available locally and might be substituted for expensive imported spices. Among such finds were juniper, gentian, and caraway - plants that were unpalatable to livestock and, consequently, commonplace in the intensively grazed lands surrounding medieval towns. Gradually their seeds, leaves, fruits, and roots found their way into local cookery.

In Search of New Trading Routes

The Crusades marked the beginning of a crisis in the worldwide spice trade, especially in central Europe, as the significant trade between Arabs and Venetian merchants was disrupted. This development, in turn, produced what might be loosely termed "scientific" research into the origin of spices in central and western Europe. At that time, knowledge of the subject consisted of half-true tales passed down by Greek and Roman writers. But now physicians and others concerned with human health began to think about the active ingredients in herbs and spices, and an argument can be made that a shortage of spices was one of the stimuli that led to the development of Renaissance science.

The spice shortage also contributed to improvements in navigation technology, as several European nations competed to discover sea routes to India. In other words, this early exploration was not so much to bring Western civilization and Christianity to other peoples as to profit from the trade in precious stones, metals, and spices. Similarly, at a later time, ancient civilizations in Africa and Asia were set upon by European colonialists, and one of the precipitating factors for such imperialistic adventures was the competition of spice merchants from western and southern Europe.

The Portuguese found a sea route from Europe to India via the circumnavigation of Africa, which allowed them to bypass Arab intermediaries and bring such spices as pepper and cinnamon directly to Europe. They also discovered new spices, such as the "grains of paradise" (Aframomum melegueta) from western Africa, which they sold instead of pepper by bestowing upon the grains the enticing but misleading name "meleguetta pepper."

Meanwhile, Columbus and others had hypothesized that another possible trading route to India lay to the west, and stimulated in part by the desire to find new sea routes for the spice trade, the Spaniards "discovered" "Western India," or America. However, the Europeans found not pepper but (chilli) peppers, white cinnamon instead of cinnamon, Indian cress instead of cress, as well as chocolate and vanilla. Such American spices became an important part of the wealth of the New World to be exploited by the Old.

By the start of the sixteenth century, western European countries were beginning to assert their control over world trade and politics, largely due to their quest for spices. Thus, the spice trade figured prominently in European colonialism and imperialism and, consequently, in shaping the world political order of today.

The Internationalization of Spices

Since the sixteenth century, and especially since the nineteenth century, many Europeans and Asians have migrated to the Americas, taking with them their culinary traditions, including their knowledge of spices and how to use them. Because such knowledge was subsequently exchanged among different cultural groups, the use of particular spices became increasingly less identified with the cuisines that had originally incorporated them.

First iceboxes and then refrigerators diminished the risk of food spoilage, and thus erased the importance of spices in masking the taste of food going bad - the paramount reason for seeking them in the first place. But if spices were less necessary in cookery for covering up unpleasant tastes, they did provide pleasant flavors of their own, which strongly established them in cookery traditions. And this, coupled with the mass production and marketing that has made them so inexpensive, has ensured their continued widespread usage. Indeed, it is possible today to buy virtually any spice in the supermarkets of the world at an affordable price.

Of course, some national or regional cuisines can still be identified by their traditional spices. Restaurants that specialize in various types of international cuisine have proliferated - especially since the end of colonialism. North Africans who migrated to France established Algerian and Moroccan restaurants in Paris. Many Indonesian restaurants can be found in the Netherlands. Chinese and Indian restaurants have become popular in Great Britain and in the United States - to provide merely a few examples.

Somewhat later, a different development took

place in Germany. During the 1950s and 1960s, a labor shortage in Germany induced many southern Europeans to venture northward seeking employment. And because of this migration, Italian, Balkan, and Greek restaurants with all their accompanying spices are now common in Germany.

Spices are so widely employed today that we scarcely notice their presence. Most understand and would agree that spices improve the taste of food and even aid digestion. But largely forgotten is the fact that the original purpose of spices was to mask bad tastes, rather than provide good ones; and almost completely forgotten is the role that the spice trade played in stimulating scientific thought during the Renaissance and the explorations and the empire building that followed.

Hansjörg Küster

Sugar cane

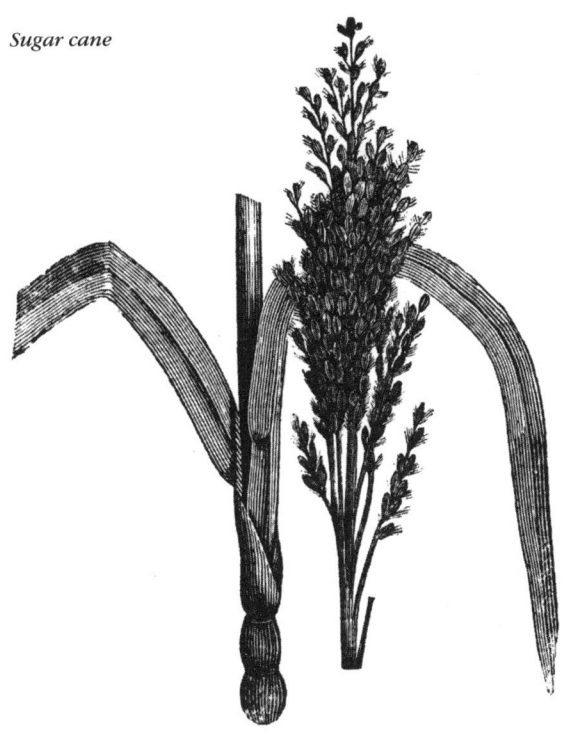

Bibliography

Foster, Nelson, and Linda S. Cordell. 1992. *Chilies to chocolate: Food the Americas gave the world.* Tucson, Ariz.
Kucan, Dusanka. 1984. Der erste römerzeitliche Pfefferfund – nachgewiesen im Legionslager Oberaden (Stadt Bergkamen). *Ausgrabungen und Funde in Westfalen-Lippe* 4: 51–6.
Küster, Hansjörg. 1987. Wo der Pfeffer wächst. *Ein Lexikon zur Kulturgeschichte der Gewürze.* Munich.
Nabhan, Gary Paul. 1985. *Gathering the desert.* Tucson, Ariz.
Stobart, Tom. 1977. *Herbs, spices and flavorings.* Harmondsworth, England.

II.F.2 ❧ Sugar

Sugar is the world's predominant sweetener. It satisfies the human appetite for sweetness and contributes calories to our diet. Sugar is used in cooking, in the preparation of commercially processed foods, and as an additive to drinks; it is also a preservative and fermenting agent. It sweetens without changing the flavor of food and drink. It is cheap to transport, easy to store, and relatively imperishable. These characteristics helped sugar to displace such sweeteners as fruit syrups, honey, and the sap of certain trees, the most famous of which is the North American maple.

Lack of data makes it difficult to establish when sugar became the principal sweetener in any given part of the world, but in every case this has occurred fairly recently. Illustrative are Europe and North America where it was only after 1700 that sugar was transformed from a luxury product into one of everyday use by even the poor. This took place as Brazil and the new West Indies colonies began producing sugar in such large quantities that price was significantly reduced. Lower prices led to increased consumption, which, in turn, fueled demand, with the result that the industry continued to expand in the Americas and later elsewhere in the tropical world.

Since the eighteenth century, the rise in the per capita consumption of sugar has been closely associated with industrialization, increased personal income, the use of processed foods, and the consumption of beverages to which people add sugar, such as tea, coffee, and cocoa. In addition, the relatively recent popularity of soft drinks has also expanded the use of sugar. Annual per capita sugar consumption is now highest in its places of production, such as Brazil, Fiji, and Australia, where it exceeds 50 kilograms (kg). Consumption in Cuba has been exceptionally high, exceeding 80 kg per capita around the beginning of the 1990s. Subsequently, consumption has fallen to a still very high 60 kg per person.

With an annual per capita consumption of between 30 and 40 kg, the countries that were first industrialized in western Europe and North America constitute a second tier of sugar consumers. The poorer countries of the world make up a third group where consumption is low. The figure for China is 6.5 kg, and it is even lower for many countries in tropical Africa. Such a pattern reflects both differences in wealth and the ready availability of sugar to those in the countries of the first group. In the Western industrialized world, concerns about the effects of sugar on health, as well as the use of alternatives to sugar – such as high-fructose corn syrup and high-intensity, low-calorie sweeteners – have stabilized and, in some countries, lowered the use of sugar. Thus, it would seem that further expansion of the industry depends primarily on the poorer countries following the precedent of the richer ones by increasing consumption as standards of living improve. Secondarily, it depends on the ability of the sugar industry to meet competition from alternative sweeteners.

Sugar is the chemical sucrose that occurs naturally in plants. It is most richly concentrated in sugarcane and sugar beet, which are the sources of commercial sugar. Fully refined sugar, whether made from cane or beet, is pure sucrose, and the consumer cannot tell from which of the two plants it derives. But despite the identical end product, the sugarcane and the sugar beet industries differ greatly in methods of production and organization, and each has its own distinctive history and geography.

The Sugarcane Industry

The Raw Material

Sugarcane is a perennial grass of the humid tropics. It requires at least 1,000 millimeters of rain annually, which should fall year-round, although with irrigation the plant can also be grown in dry climates. Temperatures must be above 21° Celsius (C) for satisfactory growth, and the best results are obtained when the temperature exceeds 27° C. Cold temperatures, therefore, impose northern and southern limits on cultivation. Growth ceases when the temperature falls below 11–13° C; light frosts injure the plant, and a prolonged freeze will do serious damage. Sugarcane is tolerant of a wide range of soil conditions and grows well on both hillsides and flat land. With the mechanization of harvesting, a recent development that dates only from the 1950s, the industry has come to prefer flat land where the machines can function most effectively.

The principal parts of sugarcane are the roots and the stem that supports the leaves and the inflorescence. The stem in a mature plant can grow as high as 5 meters (m) and can be thick or thin, depending on the variety. Some stems have soft rinds and are easy to chew on; others have tough rinds, which makes for difficult milling. The color of the stems can range from green through shades of purple, and some varieties are leafy, whereas others are not. Despite these differences, the identification of varieties in the field is usually a matter for experts.

Commercial sugarcane is reproduced vegetatively. Until the late nineteenth century, the commercial varieties were thought to be infertile. Some are, although others set seed under certain climatic and day-length conditions. This discovery has been of basic importance for the breeding of new cane varieties, but commercial sugarcane is still reproduced in the traditional vegetative way. The stems have nodes spaced from 0.15 to 0.25 m apart, each of which contains root primordia and buds. A length of stem with at least one node is known variously as a sett, stem-cutting, or seed-piece. When setts are planted, roots develop from the primordia and a stem grows from the bud. Stems tiller at the root so that the bud in each sett produces several stems.

The first crop, known as plant cane, matures in 12 to 18 months, depending on the climate and variety of cane. The roots, left in the ground after the harvest, produce further crops known as ratoons. Some varieties produce better ratoons than others. As a perennial plant with a deep root system and with good ground coverage provided by the dense mat of stems and leaves, sugarcane protects the soil from erosion. Given adequate fertilizer and water, it can flourish year after year, and there are parts of the world in which sugarcane has been a cash crop for centuries.

All wild and domesticated varieties of sugarcane belong to the genus *Saccharum,* one of the many subdivisions of the large botanical family of *Gramineae.* Because these varieties interbreed, the genus has become a very complex one. Authorities recognize species of *Saccharum: S. robustum* Brandes and Jeswiet ex. Grassl., *S. edule* Hassk., *S. officinarum* L., *S. barberi* Jeswiet, *S. sinense* Roxb. emend. Jeswiet, and *S. spontaneum.* Speciation, however, of the genus is still in dispute.

The status of *S. edule* as a distinct species is problematic, and an argument exists for conflating *S. barberi* and *S. sinense.* There is also discussion as to the places of origin of the species. *S. barberi, S. sinense,* and *S. spontaneum* occur widely in southern Asia and may have originated there. New Guinea is thought by many to have been the place of origin of the other three species, although possibly *S. officinarum* evolved close by in the Halmahera/Celebes region of present-day Indonesia. Four of the species were cultivated for their sugar: *S. barberi* and *S. sinense,* respectively, in India and China; and *S. edule* and *S. officinarum* in New Guinea. *S. robustum* is too low in sucrose to be a useful source of sugar, but its tough fiber makes it valued in New Guinea for fencing and roofing. *S. officinarum* may have been cultivated as an important food for pigs in prehistoric New Guinea (Stevenson 1965: 31–2; Barnes 1974: 40–2; Blackburn 1984: 90–102; Daniels and Daniels 1993: 1–7).

S. officinarum is the species of basic importance to the history of the sugarcane industry. In New Guinea its evolution into an exceptionally sweet cane led to wide diffusion throughout the Pacific islands and eastward through southern Asia to Mediterranean Europe and America. Until the 1920s, nearly all the cane sugar that entered international commerce came from one or another variety of this species.[1] The varieties of *S. officinarum* are known collectively as noble canes, a name the Dutch gave them in the nineteenth century in appreciation of their importance to the sugar industry in Java.

Disease brought the era of the noble canes to an end. In the mid-nineteenth century, Bourbon cane, the standard commercially cultivated variety in the

Americas, had suffered occasional outbreaks of disease, but in the West Indies in the 1880s, disease in Bourbon cane became general and caused a serious reduction in yields. To use the jargon of the sugar trade, this variety "failed."

In the 1880s, disease also devastated the cane fields of Java. The initial response of planters was to replace the diseased cane with other "noble" varieties, but because these too might "fail," this solution was seen at best to be a temporary one. The long-term answer lay in breeding new varieties that would be resistant to disease and rich in sucrose. Cane-breeding research began simultaneously in the 1880s at the East Java Research Station (Proefstation Oost Java) and at Dodds Botanical Station in Barbados. Initially, researchers worked only with *S. officinarum*. Success came slowly, but during the first years of the twentieth century, newly bred varieties began to replace the naturally occurring ones, and substitution was complete in most regions by the 1930s.

In a second phase of research, which benefited from developments in genetics, attractive features from other species of sugarcane were combined with varieties of *S. officinarum*. This process, known as "nobilization," resulted in even further improvements in disease resistance and sucrose content. Nobilized varieties entered cultivation during the 1920s and gradually replaced the first generation of bred varieties (Galloway 1996).

The sugarcane industry has now been dependent on cane breeding for a century, and research remains necessary to the success of the industry. Because varieties "fail," reserve varieties must be on hand to replace them. Some of the aims of breeding programs are long-standing: resistance to disease, insects, and animal pests; suitability to different edaphic and climatic conditions; better ratooning; and high sucrose content. In recent years, additional considerations have come to the fore. Canes have to be able to tolerate herbicides, and in some countries they have to meet the needs of mechanical harvesters.

Cultivation and Harvest

Success in cane breeding gave the sugarcane industry a much improved raw material that enables it to meet more easily a basic requirement of survival in a competitive world, which is the sustainable production of cane rich in sucrose in different climatic and soil conditions. Cane breeding has also added flexibility in dealing with the constant of how best to manage the cane fields with a view to the needs of the mill and factory. A long harvest season is preferable to a short one because it permits the economic use of labor and machinery. Fields of cane, therefore, must mature in succession over a period of months. This can be achieved by staggering the planting of the fields and by cultivating a combination of quick-maturing and slow-maturing varieties. Cane ratoons complicate the operation because they mature more quickly than the plant cane.

Over the years, however, ratoon crops gradually decline in sugar yield, and eventually the roots have to be dug up and the field replanted. Breeding can improve the ratooning qualities of cane. The number of ratoon crops taken before replanting is a matter of judgment, involving the costs of planting and the yield of the crops. Practice over the centuries has ranged from none at all to 15 and even more. Where numerous ratoon crops are the custom, the introduction of new varieties is necessarily a slow process. Planting is still largely done by hand, although planting by machine has increased.

The harvesting of cane presents another set of problems. The cane must be carefully cut close to the ground (the sucrose content is usually highest at the base of the stems) but without damage to the roots. The leaves and inflorescence should not go to the mill where they will absorb sugar from the cane and so reduce the yield. Manual workers can cut carefully and strip the stems, but the work is arduous and expensive. The mechanization of harvesting has been made easier by the breeding of varieties that achieve uniform height and stand erect. The machines can cut and top (remove the inflorescence) with little waste.

Because it is very important to send clean cane to the mill with a minimum of trash, soil, or other debris, preharvest burning of the cane has become a common practice. This removes the living leaves as well as the dead, which lie on the ground and are known as "trash." Burning prepares a field for harvesting and does not damage the stems or reduce the yield of sugar, provided the stems reach the mill within 24 hours. But this last requirement is not new: Breeding has not been able to alter the fact that stems of cane are perishable and, once cut, must be milled quickly to avoid loss of juice and, hence, of sucrose and revenues. The perishable nature of the stems and the expense of transporting them still demand that the mills be located close to the fields where the cane is grown.

Where the owners of the mills also own the fields that supply the cane, coordination of cultivation and harvesting is a relatively easy matter, compared to a situation in which independent cane growers do the supplying. There are mills that rely on hundreds of cane growers, each cultivating a few hectares. In addition to logistical issues, the price the growers are to receive for their cane is a constant source of dispute (Blackburn 1984: 136–288; Fauconnier 1993: 75–132).

From Mill to Refinery

The aim in the mill is to extract the maximum amount of sucrose from the stems; the aim in the factory (usually attached to the mill) is to make maximum use of the sucrose to produce sugar quickly and efficiently. The opaque, dark-green juice that contains the sucrose flows from the mill to the factory where it is first heated and clarified, then condensed by boiling to a thick syrup in which sugar crystals form. This mix, known as a "massecuite," is then separated into sugar crystals and molasses. Early in the history of the industry, both milling and manufacture involved rather simple processes that by modern standards not only were slow and wasteful but also led to rather crude results. Now the milling and manufacture of sugar involve a series of highly sophisticated engineering and chemical operations and take place in what are, in fact, large industrial complexes. The daily grinding capacity of modern mills varies enormously, with the largest exceeding 20,000 metric tons (Chen 1985: 72).

Innovations in processing have never entirely replaced the old methods, and in India, Brazil, and many other countries modern factories coexist with traditional ones. The industry draws a distinction between the products of the two, based on the method of separating the crystals from the molasses. In traditional mills, the massecuite is placed in upright conical pots, and over a period of days, if not weeks, the molasses drains through a hole at the base of the cone, leaving a sugar loaf. In a modern mill, separation is accomplished rapidly in a centrifugal machine that was first employed in sugar factories in the mid-nineteenth century. The terms "centrifugal" and "noncentrifugal" are used in the sugar trade as a shorthand, referring to the products of very different processes of manufacture.

Noncentrifugal sugars are characteristically made for local markets by rural entrepreneurs with simple equipment and little capital. They appear for sale yellowed by molasses, and sometimes still moist, and compete in price with centrifugal sugar. They appeal to people who are especially fond of their taste. The noncentrifugal sugars include the *gur* of India, the *jaggery* of Nigeria, the *rapadura* of Brazil, and the *panela* of Colombia. (Indian *khandsari*

sugar, an interesting anomaly, is produced by traditional methods, except that the crystals are separated in hand-held centrifuges.) The often remote location and modest scale of many noncentrifugal factories means that a proportion of world cane sugar production goes unreported.

Centrifugal sugar, the product of the modern factories, by contrast, enters world trade. The International Sugar Organization, as well as governments and sugar traders, track production; thus, there are detailed, country-by-country, annual statistics on production and consumption (Figure II.F.2.1). Commercial sugars are classified according to their purity, which is measured in degrees of polarization (pol.) with a polarimeter; purity ranges from 0° pol., signifying a total absence of sugar (as in distilled water, for example), to 100° pol., indicating pure sucrose. The basic centrifugal sugar of commerce is known as raw sugar, which, by international agreement, must have a polarization of at least 96°. Raw sugars are not quite pure sucrose and are intended for further processing, meaning that they are to be refined.

Refining is the final stage in the manufacture of sugar. The result is pure sucrose, with a pol. of 100°. The process of refining involves melting the raws, removal of the last impurities, and recrystallization of the sucrose under very careful sanitary conditions. The raws lose a very minor percentage of their weight in the transformation to refined sugar, the amount depending on the pol. of the raws and the technical ability of the refinery (Chen 1985: 634-6). This loss and the expense of refining are built into the selling price of refined sugar.

Refineries are located close to the market where the sugar is to be consumed, rather than the fields where the cane is grown. In the Western world, this

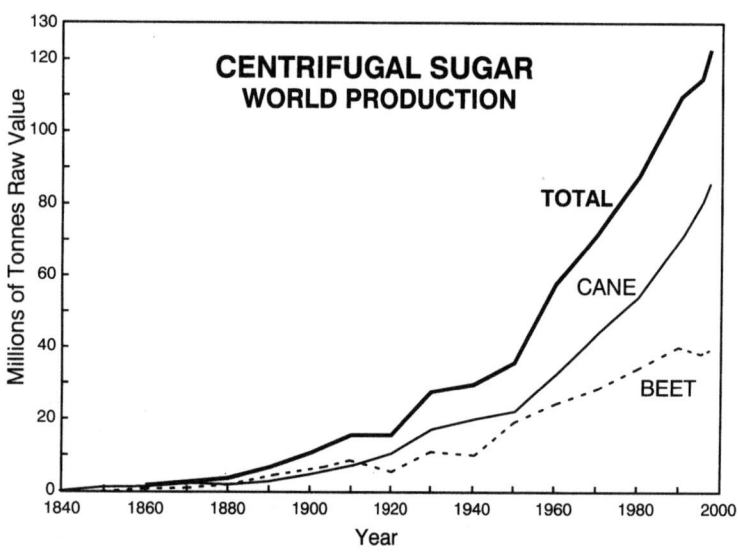

Figure II.F.2.1. Centrifugal sugar; world production. (From Baxa and Bruhns 1967: 302; Blume 1985: 4; International Sugar Organization 1994: 285.)

Figure II.F.2.2. A Caribbean sugar factory. Although simplified, the drawing gives an idea of the activity. (From Pomet 1694: 94.)

pattern was established several hundred years ago (Figure II.F.2.2). Transport in leaky sailing ships meant that sugar inevitably ran the risk of contamination from sea water, and in the hot, humid conditions of a long voyage across tropical seas, sugar crystals coalesced. Thus, there was no point in making a finished product if it was only going to be damaged in transit to the market. In addition, the lack of fuel in the cane-growing regions meant that it was rarely possible to produce the finished product there. The industry does make its own fuel, bagasse, which is the residue of the stems after milling, but during the early centuries of the industry, inefficient furnaces meant that it had to be supplemented with another kind of fuel, usually scarce timber.

In short, the location of refineries in the importing countries reflected the realities of the sugar trade of yesterday. Today, there are clean, rapid, purpose-designed ships, so that long voyages pose little risk of damage to the sugar. And fuel is no longer the problem it once was. A long record of improvements in the design of furnaces and machinery means that an efficiently operated factory produces a surplus of bagasse. Nevertheless, factors continue to favor the location of the refineries in the importing, temperate countries.

Perhaps most importantly, refineries are not limited by harvests but can operate year-round by buying their supplies of raws from producers throughout the world according to season and price. Since the nineteenth century, refineries in some countries have also had the option of adapting to domestic beet sugar. By contrast, a refinery in a cane-growing region, dependent on the local production of raws, can only oper-

ate seasonally, which is not cost-efficient unless it is possible to stockpile or import raws to keep the refinery constantly in operation.

Because of such developments, many sugar factories now skirt the issue of refining by making direct-consumption sugars which, as their name implies, require no further processing. Whites, also known as plantation whites, are the most important of this class of sugar, and have a pol. of up to 99.5°. Whites were intended originally only for local consumption, but they have now entered international commerce to compete with refined sugars (Blackburn 1984: 290-3, 313-14).

Despite what might seem as the diminution of their locational advantages, however, the importing refineries will not yield their role easily. Vested interests continue to be involved, but additional refining is the only value-added part in the sugarcane industry that can be transferred from the producing to the importing countries in order to create jobs. Such refineries also have a trump card – they are close to and know their markets and can create demand as well as deliver what the market wants.

A glance along grocery store shelves reveals the many products of the refineries. There are the standard granular sugars, ranging from coarse to fine, and powdered sugar for icing cakes. The familiar sugar cubes for tea and coffee have been there since as long ago as the mid-1870s (Chalmin 1983: 84). The brown and yellow sugars, whether granular or in lumps, are still called Demerara – named after an administrative division of British Guiana, where, in the mid-nineteenth century, partially modernized factories deliberately produced sugar still colored and flavored by molasses.

It became a recognized trade name that could only be applied to this type of sugar produced in Demerara until 1913, when a court of law in London accepted the argument that the term had become common usage for any brown sugar, whether or not it had been made in Demerara (Barnes 1974: 11). Today, Demeraras are, in general, refined sugars that have been colored and flavored.

Other Products

Sugar is the most important product of the sugarcane industry. But there are also others, one being fuel. Because sucrose can be fermented, as well as crystallized, it is turned into an alcohol that substitutes for gasoline in cars. A substantial portion of Brazil's annual sugarcane crop is used for this purpose. Another use is the creation of fancy molasses (made from clarified, concentrated, very sweet syrup-like juice from which no sucrose has been drawn). This is what is used in cooking, spread on bread and scones, and employed as a topping for pancakes. Fancy molasses was a specialty of Barbados, with North America once the major market, where it sold for less than maple syrup. Barbados still exports fancy molasses, and a similar product is made in several other countries.

In addition, there are by-products of the manufacture of sugar. The most important are molasses, alcoholic beverages, bagasse, and filter mud, each of which has several uses. The molasses that spins from the massecuite in the centrifuges of modern factories is known as final or blackstrap molasses. It contains unextractable sucrose, as well as glucose, fructose, water, and minerals, the composition varying according to the climate and soil in which the cane was grown. Relatively little of this type of molasses enters international trade. One local use is for animal feed (either fed directly to the animals or mixed with other foods). Other derivatives of molasses include industrial alcohol, citric acid, and yeast. But perhaps its best-known use is in the manufacture of alcoholic beverages.

Rum is the sugar industry's best-known drink, flavored and colored with burnt sugar. But there are numerous other cane liquors, such as the *cachaça* of Brazil. Moreover, in cane-growing countries, alcohol is now mixed with imported concentrates to make gin and even whisky. "Choice" molasses, the by-product of noncentrifugal sugar, is also distilled for alcoholic beverages.

Bagasse – the dried cane pulp remaining after the juice is extracted – is a fortuitous by-product of sugar manufacturing that finds important uses. In some countries it is a fuel that generates electricity for the national grid. Ongoing research has also pointed the way to other applications, and it is now employed in the production of compressed fiberboard, various types of paper, and plastics.

Much of the filter mud, the result of clarification of the cane juice, is returned to the cane fields as a fertilizer. But it is also possible to extract a crude wax from it that can be used in the manufacture of polishes. All of these by-products are major contributors to the profitability of the sugarcane industry (Barnes 1974: 446–69; Blackburn 1984: 314, 327–47).

Historical Geography[2]

The manufacture of crystal sugar from sugarcane is one of the world's oldest industries. Its history is markedly episodic, with periods of technological innovation and geographical expansion separating periods of comparatively little change. Sugar became closely linked to major forces in European history when the Portuguese, who, in the fifteenth century, were venturing along the west African coast, discovered that the production and sale of sugar grown on nearby islands, especially Madeira, could be a means of financing the enterprise of reaching the East Indies. In subsequent centuries, sugar became intimately associated with the European colonization of the tropical portions of the New World (Figure II.F.2.3). The demand for labor that it created led to the transatlantic slave trade that carried millions of Africans to the Americas. These were followed by East Indians and other Asians in still more international migrations.

Yet sugar was hardly confined to the Americas, and neither were the historical forces that have shaped the industry from the rise of capitalism through the industrial revolution to twentieth-century advances in science and technology. The first use of sugarcane by humans was doubtless to chew it to obtain the sweet juice, a practice that continues, especially among children. Later, in southern Asia at some unrecorded time, efforts were begun to extract the juice with a simple mill or press and to concentrate it by boiling into a sweet, viscous mass. The first evidence of crystal sugar production appears at about 500 B.C. in Sanskrit texts that indicate it took place in northern India. They describe in rather vague terms the making of several types of sugar for which the principal use seems to have been medicinal. Knowledge of this technique spread from northern India eastward to China and (along with the cultivation of sugarcane) westward into Persia, eventually reaching the east coast of the Mediterranean about A.D. 600.

Sugar making in India and China, however, remained a technologically conservative, small-scale, largely peasant activity until the twentieth century. In China, for reasons that are not entirely clear, sugar joined, rather than displaced, its competitors, becoming one more option in a cuisine that continued to value honey, manna, maltose, and sagwire palm sugar. Clearly, the history of sugar in the East stands in marked contrast to that which unfolded in the West.[3]

The sugar industry entered the Mediterranean basin as part of an agricultural revolution carried out by the Arabs. In the years following the founding of

Figure II.F.2.3. Oxen drawing a cart of cane, with mill in background. (From a bond of the Eastern Cuba Sugar Corp., issued in 1922.)

Islam (Watson 1983), its adherents presided over the introduction of tropical and subtropical crops from Asia to the countries of the Mediterranean, as well as the techniques of irrigation that permitted cultivation throughout hot, dry summers.

To mill sugarcane, the burgeoning industry borrowed existing Mediterranean technology for extracting oil from olives and nuts and, in a second operation, used screw presses to obtain more juice from the bagasse. The juice was then clarified, reduced to the point of crystallization in open pans over furnaces, and the resulting syrup was placed in conical pots from which the molasses drained, leaving a loaf of sugar in each pot. The mills relied on water, animals, and men for power.

The risk of frost in the Mediterranean, together with the need for irrigation water, confined the cultivation of sugarcane to a few favored locations in the Levant, North Africa, Cyprus, Crete, Sicily, and Andalusia. Sugar production on the Atlantic islands of Portuguese Madeira and the Spanish Canaries was also Mediterranean in character. In its Mediterranean phase, however, the industry was labor-intensive, small-scale, and unable to produce large quantities of sugar, which therefore remained a luxury product. In short, there was little change in the technology of the Old World sugar industry between its introduction to the Mediterranean and its decline in the face of competition from the New World nearly 1,000 years later.

This Mediterranean phase did, nevertheless, foreshadow what was to come in the New World: Atlantic sugar was produced by slave labor brought from Africa to plantations in a system like that which would arise in the Americas. Moreover, the manner in which the Venetians and Genoese organized the supply of sugar to continental Europe during the Mediterranean phase also served as something of a blueprint for

things to come. The capital of these Italian city-states established a colonial relationship with the producing regions. They built the first refineries in Bologna and Venice and also drew on slave labor from the coasts of the Black Sea. The Genoese came to concentrate their investments increasingly in the western Mediterranean and were later instrumental in helping to finance the transfer of the industry to the Americas.

The years between 1450 and 1680 mark that transfer, as well as the decline of the Mediterranean industry in the face of American competition. It was a phase not only of technological innovation but also of geographical expansion, with the sugar-producing islands of Madeira, the Canaries, and São Tomé serving as stepping stones across the Atlantic. The Spanish first cultivated sugarcane on Hispaniola in the early 1500s, but the Portuguese, beginning in Brazil during the 1520s, were initially far more successful. The English turned Barbados into a sugar colony during the 1640s, and the sugar industry gradually spread across the Caribbean and to other regions of the New World.

In tropical America, not only did the climatic conditions favor sugarcane cultivation but so did the abundance of land to grow it on and the forests needed to provide fuel for the factories. With these advantages, the American sugar industry assumed an altogether new scale in terms of number of mills, size of land holdings, and quantity of exports. Such an increased scope of activity created a large demand for labor, which the Portuguese, at first, tried to satisfy by employing the indigenous population. But as that population declined in the face of Old World diseases, they turned increasingly to Africa, and the entire American industry soon depended on slave labor from that continent, resulting in the importation of more than 10 million people (Curtin 1969).

Still another development was a technological revolution in the seventeenth century that saw the replacement of the inefficient Mediterranean-style mills used initially in the New World (Galloway 1993: 211–22). Perhaps the most important innovation was a mill which, in its basic design, consisted of three vertically mounted rollers that could be turned by animal, water, or wind power. Such a mill did not require the stems to be chopped into pieces before milling, and the efficiency of its operation made the use of presses redundant. It is interesting to note the strong evidence of the contribution of Chinese technology to this design (Daniels and Daniels 1988). More efficient milling demanded, in turn, more efficient manufacture of sugar, and notable improvements in the design of furnaces allowed a production-line organization for transforming cane juice into crystal sugar.

Sugar colonies with slave-run plantations characterized American industry in the eighteenth century, a period once again of relatively little change in technology, although planters did gradually introduce conservationist measures to preserve the fertility of the soil and supplies of fuel. The sugar colonies exported sugar and rum to Europe and North America and imported slaves and food. Such an economy supported the densest concentrations of population in colonial America.

With the nineteenth century, however, there began another era of innovation in methods of production and of geographical expansion. The successful slave revolt in the French colony of St. Domingue (now Haiti) during the 1790s heralded the beginning of the end of the old regime. Nonetheless, the process of abolition was only completed a century later when the slaves of Cuba and Brazil finally gained their freedom. Many of the former slaves continued to work on sugar plantations, but planters also sought other sources of labor. Between 1838 and 1917, the British recruited workers from their Indian empire and, in so doing, profoundly changed the ethnic composition of many of their colonies. Laborers also came from Madeira, China, Japan, and the Pacific islands to work in the cane fields.

Major nineteenth-century technical innovations included steam power and the replacement of the three-roller mills by horizontally laid iron rollers mounted in sets of three that could be linked with other sets to form a train of six, nine, and even more rollers. With some improvements, this basic design of the mill has continued to the present. Cane-sugar technology also borrowed from the beet industry, especially the use of vacuum pans, in which juice could be boiled at lower temperatures under reduced pressure to save fuel. The centrifuges for separating the crystals from the molasses were also borrowed, and large central factories, which could accommodate the new machinery, gradually replaced traditional mills.

Still another major development was the breeding of new sugarcane varieties. The new technology, coupled with improved varieties of the raw material, helped keep the sugarcane industry competitive with the sugar-beet industry. By the end of the nineteenth century, the manufacture of cane sugar was becoming a capital-intensive agribusiness that relied on continued improvements in technology and methods of cultivation to keep a competitive edge.

During the nineteenth century, the link between the sugar industry and European expansion continued. A rising prosperity among the growing populations of western Europe led to increased demand at a time when European territorial empires extended into Africa, southern Asia, and the Pacific. One result was that sugarcane industries were established in such places as South Africa, Java, Queensland, Fiji, Hawaii, and Taiwan. In southern Asia, the Western, industrial style of sugar production either replaced or operated alongside traditional noncentrifugal producers. By 1900, the sugarcane industry had become one of the major economic activities of the entire tropical world.

The Sugar-Beet Industry

The Raw Material

Sugar beet is a root crop of temperate lands in Eurasia and America that in recent years has also become an important winter crop in North Africa and the Middle East. Obviously, it has adapted to a wide range of climatic and soil conditions, even growing well in the short summers of Finland, the dampness of Ireland, the high altitudes of Iran and Sichua, and the hot, dry Imperial Valley of California. It benefits from irrigation and from long hours of daylight. Differences in temperature, day length, and rainfall do, of course, influence the sugar content of the roots. It is a biennial, storing food in its swollen roots to carry the plants through the first winter and the process of setting seed in the second year. Farmers harvest the roots that contain the sugar at the end of the first year's growing season, thus interrupting the plant's natural cycle. Toward the polar limits of the sugar beet's range, low summer temperatures and extended length of the day encourage some plants to set seed prematurely during the first year, resulting in poor development of the roots. Plants that do this are known as "bolters," which if present in significant numbers, lower the yield of sugar from a field.

Cultivated and wild beets belong to the genus *Beta,* of the family Chenopodiaceae. The species *Beta vulgaris* L. includes the common beet, the mangelwurzel, and the sugar beet. All three have descended from wild sea-beet, *Beta maritima,* by human selection. The Romans used beets, probably *Beta maritima,* as food for both humans and animals and thereby selected for its value as a vegetable. Cultivators in medieval and early modern Europe developed the roots for animal feed, and since the eighteenth century, the capacity of *Beta vulgaris* to store sucrose in its roots has been the focus of breeding. Selection in Germany increased the sugar content of the roots from 7 percent in the eighteenth century to between 11 and 12 percent by the 1850s. The sugar content is now up to 20 percent. In addition to this success, researchers also breed sugar beets to discourage "bolting," to resist disease, and for shape and fibrosity to help in harvesting and milling. Sugar beets provide an example of a rapidly domesticated plant that is still being modified and improved to suit a particular purpose (Bailey 1949: 353; Campbell 1976; Bosemark 1993; Evans 1993: 101–3, 107, 109).

The main stages in the extraction of sucrose from beet have remained basically the same over the last century or so, but there have been improvements in the efficiency of each stage. On arrival at the factory, the beets are washed to remove soil and stones and then sliced into thin, smooth pieces known as "cossettes." The aim is to maximize the surface area of the beet so as to facilitate the diffusion of the sucrose. The cossettes then enter a countercurrent diffuser through which they move against the flow of a hot water extractant. This operation transforms about 98 percent of the sugar from the beet into a raw juice. The juice, in turn, is purified, reduced by evaporation, and crystallized, and the crystals are separated in centrifuges from the mother liquor. Formerly, beet sugar factories produced a raw sugar that was further treated in a refinery; now many factories produce a white sugar that is 99.9 percent pure (Vukov 1977: 13, 421, 426–7; Reinefeld 1979: 131–49; Bichsel 1988).

More than 90 percent of the revenue of the sugar-beet industry comes from sugar. Alcohol production is the best financial alternative to making sugar, but researchers have been unable to generate other by-products that are very lucrative. The lime sludge from the purification process is sold for fertilizer. Citric acid and baker's yeast are produced by fermenting the molasses, and the exhausted cossettes can be used for animal feed (Blackburn 1984: 338–9; Tjebbes 1988: 139–45).

Historical Geography

The sugar-beet industry is only two centuries old. In 1747, a Berlin professor of chemistry, Andreas Marggraf (1709–82), succeeded in extracting a modest quantity of sugar from beet. Although he published the results of his research in French and German, he did not put them to commercial use (Baxa and Bruhns 1967: 95–9). However, his student Franz Carl Achard (1753–1821) was more practical. He improved the raw material by breeding the cultivated fodder beets for sugar content, and he evolved the white Silesian beet, which is the ancestor of all subsequent sugar-beet varieties (Oltmann 1989: 90, 107).

In the years around 1800, Achard was active in promoting the beet industry, and in 1801, with the financial assistance of the King of Prussia, he began to build what may have been the world's first sugar-beet factory (Baxa and Bruhns 1967: 113). Although it was not a financial success, other Prussians followed his initiative, building several small factories in Silesia and around Magdeburg. Russia was the second country to enter the industry: Its first sugar-beet factory opened in either 1801 or 1802 (Baxa and Bruhns 1967: 118; Munting 1984: 22), and the first factory in Austria opened in 1803. In the beginning, the French limited themselves to experiments, as did the Dutch, whose Society for the Encouragement of Agriculture offered a prize for extracting sugar from native plants (Slicher van Bath 1963: 276–7; Baxa and Bruhns 1967: 99–119).

These experimental and very small scale beginnings of the sugar-beet industry were given a considerable boost during the Napoleonic wars. In 1806, Napoleon's ban on the import of British goods and Britain's retaliatory blockade of his empire greatly reduced the supplies of cane sugar that reached continental Europe. Napoleon encouraged the production of beet sugar as a substitute, and landowners in France and the countries north of the Alps tried to respond.

The paucity of seed and unfamiliarity with the requirements of the crop led, however, to a disappointing supply of beet, part of which rotted on the way to the factory because of poor transportation. The number of factories illustrates the extent to which policy overreached reality: In France, in the season that spanned 1812 and 1813, only 158 factories of the 334 for which licenses had been given were actually in working order (Baxa and Bruhns 1967: 139). With the low yields of beet per hectare, low sucrose content, and a disappointing rate of recovery of the sucrose in the factories, beet sugar could not compete with cane once imports from the West Indies resumed after 1815. The beet industry disappeared from Europe except in France where it hung on until better times (Slicher van Bath 1963: 277; Baxa and Bruhns 1967: 134–45).

Those times began in the late 1830s and gathered force throughout the middle of the century, benefiting from improvements in both field and factory. In France, P. L. F. Levèque de Vilmorin (1816–60) was particularly successful in breeding varieties of beet for greater sugar content, with improvements continuing after his death (Baxa and Bruhns 1967: 190–1). In the first generation of sugar-beet factories, the juice was extracted by grinding the beet in animal-powered mills and then placing the pulp in presses (Baxa and Bruhns 1967: 148). In 1821, however, another Frenchman, Mathieu de Dombasle (1777–1843), proposed the procedure of slicing the beets and extracting the sucrose in a bath of water. He called the method maceration, but it is now known as the diffusion process. In 1860, Julius Robert (1826–88) became the first to employ it (Baxa and Bruhns 1967: 150, 176).

Diffusion replaced the mills and presses and remains to this day a standard part of the processing of sugar beet. Vacuum pans were first used in 1835 in a beet factory in Magdeburg, and centrifuges became part of factory equipment during the 1840s (Baxa and Bruhns 1967: 152, 172). An additional development encouraged the revival of the beet industry – the arrival of cheap Russian grain in western Europe where, from the 1820s onward, it caused a fall in grain prices. Western European farmers who had been growing grain now required a substitute crop, and beet was a good candidate. It could fit into the agricultural rotation, growing on land that would previously have been left fallow, and its leaves and roots provided feed for animals. This, in turn, made possible an increase in livestock numbers, which meant more manure. If the roots were sold to a factory, they earned the farmer cash, and the pulp could also be used for feed (Galloway 1989: 131).

Despite the advantages of sugar beet to the agricultural economy and improvements in its raw material as well as factory technology, the beet industry nevertheless was still not competitive with cane. Rather, its revival in the 1830s, and its continued growth, depended on government protection through tariffs on imported cane sugar and incentives of one sort or another, such as subsidized exports. The 1902 Brussels Convention attempted to bring some order to a scene characterized by a protected beet industry and a complaining sugarcane industry, yet protection for beet sugar remains in place (Chalmin 1984: 9–19; Munting 1984: 21–8; Perkins, 1984: 31–45).

The revival of sugar-beet cultivation began in northern France, where it had never entirely died out, and continued in Prussia and the other German states during the 1830s, in Austria-Hungary in the 1840s, and in Russia in the 1850s. By the 1850s, Germany had become the most important producer of beet sugar, responsible by the end of the century for rather more than a third of the European total. By this time, beet cultivation extended from southern Spain in a curve arching north and east through France, the Low Countries, Germany, and eastern Europe, and into the Balkans, Russia, and the Ukraine. It also extended into Denmark and southern Sweden. The industry was particularly important in northern France, in the Low Countries, around Magdeburg in Germany, in Bohemia, and around Kiev in the Ukraine. Great Britain was noticeably absent, refusing to subsidize a beet industry of its own, but rather buying sugar, whether cane or beet, wherever it was cheapest.

Sugar beet remained a predominantly European crop throughout the twentieth century. In the years approaching 1990, Europe accounted for about 80 percent of the world's production of beet sugar, with 40 percent of that production coming from the European Union. Since 1991, production in the countries of the former Soviet Union has lost ground, but this is probably a temporary situation. The geography of the European beet-sugar industry has also remained remarkably constant: Those regions that were important producers at the beginning of the twentieth century remained so at its end. There has been some modest expansion on the periphery into Ireland and Finland, and since the 1920s, Great Britain has finally developed a sugar-beet industry of its own. Two considerations led to the change in Britain's policy towards beet: World War I had revealed the difficulties of relying heavily on continental European producers of sugar and the awkwardness of such dependence. Moreover, sugar beet had the potential of being a useful cash crop for farmers in the agricultural depression that followed the war.

The North American sugar-beet industry dates from the 1880s and has increased steadily, producing nearly 4 million tonnes of sugar a year. The industry is overwhelmingly located in the United States. Beet is grown in the Midwest, but the bulk of the crop grows on irrigated land in the West. In Asia the industry became significant only in the 1920s and has seen rapid expansion since the 1960s (Baxa and Bruhns 1967: 192–201, 221–2, 262–94; International Sugar Organization 1994: 279–85).

Like the cane industry, the sugar-beet industry invests heavily in research. The breeding of new varieties, the methods of harvesting and planting, and improvements in factory technology are all important foci of attention.

The Contemporary Sugar Industry[4]

Production

At the beginning of the twentieth century, beet-sugar production exceeded that of cane sugar, with the total combined production of centrifugal sugar about 12 million metric tonnes raw value (mtrv). However, today cane accounts for most of the sugar produced (about two-thirds). Total combined production reached 100 million mtrv in the mid–1980s and rose to 120 million mtrv by the mid-1990s. This expansion has been fueled by increases in consumption of about 2 percent a year, resulting from a growing world population and improving standards of living in some of the less-developed countries of the world. Noncentrifugal sugar also continues to be an important sweetener: Statistics are almost certainly incomplete but show production in excess of 15 millions tonnes at present.

The sugar industry in some countries is highly protected. The United States, for example, maintains a domestic price for sugar well above the world price and controls the amount of sugar imported. The European Union protects its beet growers, and the industry in India is carefully regulated to control production and domestic prices. Clearly, the interventionist traditions in the industry established long ago remain very much alive.

India is the world's major producer of cane sugar, and its sugar industry continues to grow. Annual centrifugal production has reached 16 million mtrv, which includes nearly 1 million tonnes of khandsari sugar. India is also the world's major producer of noncentrifugal sugar, accounting for perhaps as much as two-thirds of the total. Practically all of this sugar is consumed in India; only rarely, after exceptionally good harvests, are small quantities exported.

Brazil's production has increased rapidly in recent years to reach 13 million mtrv, plus some small-scale production of noncentrifugal sugar known as *rapadura*. The country has the advantages of abundant land and a good climate, and its production is divided between the home sweetener market, fuel alcohol for automobiles, and exports. Brazil has the ability to direct sugar to exports or to fuel alcohol, depending on the world prices. Cuba and Thailand compete for the third and fourth rankings among the world's sugar producers. Cuba's annual production in the late 1980s was around 8 million mtrv, but collapsed to half this amount when the fall of communism in Eastern Europe brought about a loss of its major markets. The Cuban industry's ability to recover remains a major question. Thailand has only recently become an important sugar producer. Its industry is expanding, and production is now in excess of 6 million mtrv, of which two-thirds is exported.

The European Union is responsible for nearly half of the world's beet sugar, about 18 million mtrv annually. Germany and France are the main producers, although Ukraine and Poland produce close to 4 million and 2 million mtrv, respectively. By and large, the beet industry in eastern Europe suffers from poor management and a lack of investment in machinery, and because much land is still publicly owned. The region has enormous potential, however; several western European companies have taken advantage of privatization schemes to buy factories and begin the work of modernization. The United States, China, and Turkey are also major beet-sugar producers. The United States and China are among the relatively small number of countries which, because they extend across a wide range of climatic zones, are able to grow both cane and beet.

Trade

International trade in centrifugal sugar amounts to about 30 million mtrv, or about one-quarter of the total world production, meaning that most sugar is consumed in the country where it is produced. Much of the trade takes place under special arrangements, and only a small portion of the sugar traded internationally sells at the free-market price.

The European Union buys sugar at a preferential price from the former colonies of its member states; the United States allocates import quotas to a large number of countries. Cuba bartered sugar for oil with the former Soviet Union, and now barters with Russia

on a more limited scale. These arrangements have had what might seem curious consequences. The European Union is both a major importer (1.8 million mtrv annually) of sugar from its former colonies and a major exporter (five million mtrv annually) because of its beet production. Some countries (Barbados, Jamaica, Guyana, and the Dominican Republic) export all, or nearly all, of their sugar at a premium price to meet contractual arrangements with the United States and the European Union, and they import at world market price for their own consumption. Refineries also import raw sugar, only to export it again in a practice known to the trade as tolling. This accounts for the presence of the United States on the list of sugar exporters. Quotas limit its imports, but tolling permits the use of otherwise surplus refining capacity and provides employment.

About 75 countries export sugar and about 130 import it – the numbers fluctuate a little from year to year. Most trade in small amounts, and many are minimal participants dealing in less than 10,000 tonnes a year. But the European Union, Ukraine, Cuba, Brazil, Thailand, and Australia all export more than 1 million mtrv annually. Together, these latter countries account for by far the greater part of sugar exports. By way of contrast, the European Union, Russia, Canada, the United States, Japan, and South Korea all import more than 1 million mtrv a year apiece, with Malaysia and Algeria not far behind. Such activities provide certainties, insofar as there can be any, in the sugar trade. The major sources of uncertainty are India and China. They may appear unexpectedly on the market as either importers or exporters if their policies change or if their policy makers misjudge the market situation. Weather is also an uncertainty. Poor or excellent harvests in a number of countries can cause shortages or create surpluses.

In most countries there are stocks of sugar held against sudden shortages and increases in price. The world stocks-to-use ratio in the mid–1990s was considered high, at about 19 percent (USDA 1996: 9). This translates into low free market prices because there are reserves to draw on in case of a sudden shortage. Sugar traders and some governments carefully monitor production, import, export, and consumption data in each country and calculate the buildup and/or drawdown of stocks with a view to predicting demand and prices. There is a very active trade in sugar futures.

Competition

For several hundred years, sucrose in the Western world has been without a serious competitor in the sweetener market, but recently this has changed. The leading caloric competitor is high-fructose corn syrup (HFCS). It is a liquid sweetener made from plants (especially maize) that contain a sufficient amount of starch, although sweeteners are also made from sweet potatoes and tapioca in Asia and from wheat and potatoes in Europe. HFCS appeared in the 1970s, during a period of high sugar prices, but continued in production after sugar prices fell. Sugar usually has a price advantage over HFCS, and HFCS is not always a good substitute for sugar. Bakers and manufacturers of confectionery and cereals prefer sugar because of its "bulking, texture and browning characteristics" (USDA 1995: 18). HFCS is most competitive in the manufacture of soft drinks. The United States is by far the largest producer of HFCS, with the European Union, Canada, Korea, Argentina, and Taiwan making very modest quantities. HFCS has captured rather less than 10 percent of the sweetener market and, in the immediate future, is not expected to expand beyond the liquid sweetener market in a few countries (USDA 1995: 15–20).

Low-calorie, high-intensity sweeteners have gained in significance since the 1980s and claim a small percentage of the sweetener market. Saccharin and aspartame are perhaps the best known. They are attractive to consumers concerned with diet and can compete in price with sugar. Both are used to sweeten coffee, tea, and other beverages ("table-top use"), but aspartame, benefiting from the demand for diet soft drinks, has received approval for a wider range of uses in the European Union, the United States, Canada, and Japan. This branch of the sweetener market is still evolving. Low-calorie sweeteners are used together in some applications, but they also compete with one another and, of course, they compete in the soft drink market with HFCS and sugar (Earley 1989; USDA 1995: 23–4).

The fact that the manufacture of sugar is one of the oldest industries in the world gives the sugar industry a special place in the cultural history of food, but other characteristics also give it a particular interest. It is unique among agro-industries in that it has both tropical and temperate sources of supply of its raw material. It has been responsive throughout its history to developments in science and technology and today continues to invest in research. Government intervention is a long-standing tradition. The importance of sugar to the finances of European imperialism was a great incentive for the colonial powers to attempt to manage the international trade in sugar for their own benefit. Governments continue to intervene to this day with subsidies and protective tariffs to defend vested interests.

The sugarcane industry has had profound economic and social consequences on those parts of the world in which it became a major crop. Indeed, perhaps no other crop has had such a formative influence on societies. The industry has divided societies, along class lines, between the owners of the factories (either local elites or – often nowadays – foreign companies) and the work force. Even where the factories have been nationalized, or are owned by cooperatives, disparities exist in income and prestige between managers and laborers. Because of its great demand for labor – satisfied first by African slavery, then by indentured workers, and finally by free laborers – the industry also produced multiethnic populations that frequently have complex internal politics. Another legacy is economic dependency. Although the empires are gone, many ex-colonies continue to grow sugar as a staple, relying on special arrangements with their former rulers (now members of the European Union), as well as with the United States, that enable them to sell their sugar at a premium above the low price that sugar generally commands on the open market.

The dilemma of dependency has had no easy resolution. Sugarcane producers have little bargaining power, given the oversupply of their product, and alternatives to the cultivation of sugarcane that can provide a better level of employment and income have been difficult to find. Dependency is keenly felt by the populations of the cane-growing countries, and where this sense of frustration is joined with the memory of slavery, as in the Caribbean, sugarcane is a very problematic crop.

J. H. Galloway

Notes

1. This statement requires one reservation. The medieval Mediterranean sugar industry and the early American industry cultivated only one variety of cane, known now in the literature as Creole cane. Opinion differs on the correct botanical identification of this cane. Most authorities accept that it was either a variety of *S. officinarum* (Blackburn 1984: 2, 91) or a hybrid of *S. barberi* and *S. officinarum* (Stevenson 1965: 41). However, Fauconnier (1993: 1) considers it to have been a variety of *S. barberi*.
2. In this section I draw heavily on Galloway 1989.
3. The authoritative discussion of sugar-making in China is that by Christian Daniels (1996).
4. I have used three sources for the statistics in this section: Czarnikow (1997): 55; the International Sugar Organization (1994); and the USDA (1997: 31–6). There are some differences in these data. For a brief discussion of the problems of collecting statistics on the sugar trade, see Ahlfeld and Hagelberg (1989: 59–65).

Bibliography

Ahlfeld, Helmut, and G. B. Hagelberg. 1989. Statistical problems in world sugar balance calculations. In *Sugar. Essays to mark the 125th anniversary of F. O. Licht.* Third edition, ed. Helmut Ahlfeld, 59–65. Ratzeburg, Germany.
Bailey, L. H. 1949. *Manual of cultivated plants.* Rev. edition. New York.
Barnes, A. C. 1974. *The sugar cane.* Second edition. Aylesbury, England.
Baxa, Jacob, and Guntwin Bruhns. 1967. *Zucker im Leben der Völker. Eine Kultur- und Wirtschaftsgeschichte.* Berlin.

Bichsel, S. E. 1988. An overview of the U.S. beet sugar industry. In *Chemistry and processing of sugarbeet and sugarcane,* ed. M. A. Clarke and M. A. Godshall, 1–7. Amsterdam.

Blackburn, F. 1984. *Sugar-cane.* London and New York.

Blume, Helmut. 1985. *Geography of sugar cane.* Berlin.

Bosemark, Nils Olof. 1993. Sugar beet. In *Traditional crop breeding practices: A historical review to serve as a baseline for assessing the role of modern biotechnology,* ed. Organization for Economic Co-operation and Development, 123–36. Paris.

Campbell, G. K. G. 1976. Sugar beet. In *Evolution of crop plants,* ed. N. W. Simons, 25–8. London and New York.

Chalmin, Ph. G. 1984. The important trends in sugar diplomacy before 1914. In *Crisis and change in the international sugar economy 1860–1914,* ed. Bill Albert and Adrian Graves, 9–19. Norwich and Edinburgh, U.K.

Chalmin, Phillippe. 1983. *Tate and Lyle, geants du sucre.* Paris.

Chen, James C. P. 1985. *Meade-Chen cane sugar handbook.* Eleventh edition. New York.

Clark, W. 1823. *Ten views of the island of Antigua.* London.

Curtin, Philip D. 1969. *The Atlantic slave trade. A census.* Madison, Wis.

Czarnikow and Company. 1997 *The Czarnikow sugar review,* No. 1883: 95–6.

Daniels, Christian. 1996. Agro-industries: Sugarcane technology. In *Science and civilization in China,* Vol. 3, ed. Joseph Needham, i–xxvii, 1–539. Cambridge.

Daniels, John, and Christian Daniels. 1988. The origin of the sugarcane roller mill. *Technology and Culture* 29: 493–535.

1993. Sugarcane in prehistory. *Archaeology in Oceania* 28: 1–7.

Earley, Thomas C. 1989. The effect of alternative sweeteners on the structure of the world sugar economy. In *Sugar. Essays to mark the 125th anniversary of F. O. Licht.* Third edition, ed. Helmut Ahlfeld, 191–4. Ratzeburg, Germany.

Evans, L. T. 1993. *Crop evolution, adaption and yield.* Cambridge.

Fauconnier, R. 1993. *Sugar cane.* London.

Galloway, J. H. 1989. *The sugar cane industry. An historical geography from its origins to 1914.* Cambridge.

1993. The technological revolution in the sugar cane industry during the seventeenth century. In *Produc-*
ción y comercio del azúcar de caña en época preindustrial, ed. Antonio Malpica, 211–22. Motril, Spain.

1996. Botany in the service of empire: The Barbados cane-breeding program and the revival of the Caribbean sugar industry, 1880s–1930s. *Annals of the Association of American Geographers* 86: 682–706.

International Sugar Organization. 1994. *Sugar year book.* London.

Munting, Roger. 1984. The state and the beet sugar industry in Russia before 1914. In *Crisis and change in the international sugar economy 1860–1914,* ed. Bill Albert and Adrian Graves, 21–8. Norwich and Edinburgh, U.K.

Oltmann, Wilhelm. 1989. Die Züchtung von Zuckerrüben – Ihr Beitrag zur Verbesserung von Quantität und Qualität. In *Sugar. Essays to mark the 125th anniversary of F. O. Licht.* Third edition, ed. Helmut Ahlfeld, 87–109. Ratzeburg, Germany.

Pack, Christopher, ed. 1996. *The Czarnikow sugar review,* No. 1868.

1997. *The Czarnikow sugar review,* No. 1883.

Perkins, John. 1984. The political economy of sugar beet in imperial Germany. In *Crisis and change in the international sugar economy 1860–1914,* ed. Bill Albert and Adrian Graves, 31–45. Norwich and Edinburgh, U.K.

Pomet, Pierre. 1694. *Histoire générale des drogues.* Paris.

Reinefeld, E. 1979. Progress in the technology of beet-sugar. In *Sugar: science and technology,* ed. G. G. Birch and K. J. Parker, 131–49. London.

Slicher van Bath, B. H. 1963. *The agrarian history of western Europe A.D. 500–1850.* London.

Stevenson, G. C. 1965. *Genetics and breeding of sugar cane.* London.

Tjebbes, Jan. 1988. Utilization of fiber and other non-sugar products from sugarbeet. In *Chemistry and processing of sugarbeet and sugarcane,* ed. M. A. Clarke and M. A. Godshall, 139–45. Amsterdam.

USDA (U.S. Department of Agriculture). 1995. *Sugar and sweetener. Situation and outlook report.* December issue.

1996. *Sugar and sweetener. Situation and outlook report.* June issue.

1997. *Sugar and sweetener. Situation and outlook report.* December issue.

Vukov, Konstantin. 1977. *Physics and chemistry of sugarbeet in sugar manufacture.* Amsterdam.

Watson, Andrew M. 1983. *Agricultural innovation in the early Islamic world.* Cambridge.

II.G

Important Foods from Animal Sources

II.G.1 ❧ American Bison

The American bison *(Bison bison)* is more closely related to cattle than to true buffalo, such as the water buffalo *(Bubalus bubalis)*. Nonetheless, early European settlers called the unfamiliar animal they encountered in North America a "buffelo" *[sic]* and this misnomer has persisted to the present. Because we are so accustomed to thinking of the American bison as a buffalo, the terms are used interchangeably in this chapter.

Long perceived to be an environmental casualty of the conquest of the Great Plains, the American bison has gradually reasserted its presence in North America. Today, there are around 200,000 of the animals alive on the continent, and the danger of species extinction appears to have passed (Callenbach 1996). However, any further expansion of the population is likely to be linked, at least in part, to the animal's economic usefulness, especially as a food source. At present, only a limited number of people are acquainted with the taste of bison. For buffalo meat to become part of the national diet, the advertising and agricultural industries will have to reintroduce a food which, at an earlier time, was essential to many of the continent's inhabitants.

In size and appearance, the bison is imposing and distinctive. A mature male stands from 5 to 6 feet tall at the shoulder and may weigh from 1,800 to 2,400 pounds. Noticeably smaller, females seldom weigh more than 800 pounds. Despite its bulk, the bison is quick and agile and can sprint at speeds of up to 30 miles per hour. Like domestic cattle and sheep, it is cloven hooved; unlike them, both the male and female possess large, curved horns and a prominent hump at the shoulder. Buffalo are usually dark brown in color, although their hue lightens to brownish-yellow during the spring. The animals have two types of hair: a long, coarse, shaggy growth covering the neck, head, and shoulders, and a shorter, woolly growth found on the remainder of the body. During the spring, bison

shed much of this hair, assisting the natural process by rubbing against rocks or trees. Only the head, hump, and forelegs retain hair throughout the year.

In the past, wild bison migrated with the seasons, from north to south and back. Although their diet consisted of various grasses (blue stem, grama, and bunch), it was buffalo grass *(Buchloe dactyloides)* that served as their primary staple. A short, fine plant, buffalo grass requires little water, tolerates extreme temperatures, and is resilient in the face of grazing and trampling. As the bison population declined, this species became scarce as well. Competing plant life that was no longer destroyed by the bison's hooves expanded throughout the plains, and without the wanderings of the bison to spread its seeds (either through manure or by attachment to the animal), buffalo grass was largely replaced by other grasses (Garretson 1938).

The buffalo's mating or "rutting" season commences in early June, reaches a peak in late July and early August, and gradually concludes by the end of September. There is violent competition among the bulls to impregnate the females, followed by a nine-month gestation period and the birth of a single calf (McHugh 1972). In general, the calves mature quickly and are able to mate by their second year, although the animals are not fully grown until the age of six. On the average, the bison's life span is between 20 and 30 years.

History of the Bison

When the European explorers first visited North America, large numbers of bison were present in perhaps 70 percent of the present-day continental United States, as well as in what are now the Canadian provinces of Alberta and Saskatchewan. Indeed, the pre-Columbian buffalo population is often estimated at some 60 million members. As a rule, the animals lived in groups of 20 to 40, gathering into larger herds only for rutting or migration.

Native Americans long utilized the bison as a food

source; archaeological evidence suggests that buffalo hunting was practiced more than 10,000 years ago. However, for the peoples residing in the vast plains stretching from the Rocky Mountains to the Missouri River, the buffalo represented more than simply a source of food and clothing.

In a physical sense, the animal provided the plains inhabitants with many items essential to survival in this environment, in the form of blood, meat, hide, bone, sinew, and manure, that were used for food, rope, weapons, shelter, blankets, clothing, fuel, and medicine (Dary 1974). In a spiritual sense, the buffalo provided the first Americans with still more. Understanding the animal to be one of numerous earthly representatives of a higher power, the Native Americans honored it as a spirit that influenced fecundity, happiness, strength, protection, and healing. Within such tribes as the Assiniboin, Cheyenne, and Kiowa, buffalo skulls served as central totems in ceremonial activities. Particularly revered was the rare albino, or "White Buffalo," believed to be the sacred leader of all herds. Among the Plains Indians, an understanding of the buffalo was perceived as essential for understanding one's own place within the universe (McHugh 1972).

Methods of preparing bison as food were largely determined by the gender of the cooks. When eaten fresh, the meat was often cooked by the hunters, whereas meat curing and preservation were tasks reserved for women. Hunting parties would sometimes use the hide as a cauldron in which to boil the meat. Variations on this practice included lining a hole in the ground with the animal skin or suspending the hide aboveground on sticks over a fire. In addition to boiling, the meat was frequently roasted by rotating it over an open fire.

To cure buffalo meat, Indian women relied on the sun, rather than on salting or smoking – the European methods. Selecting the choicest parts, the women cut the meat into strips, across the grain, in order to maintain alternating layers of lean and fat. These strips were then suspended on elevated racks in full sunlight for several days. The result was a jerky that could be eaten in the dried form or rehydrated by lengthy boiling. When cured, the meat was lightweight and largely imperishable, an ideal staple for a mobile culture (Catlin 1842).

The jerky, however, could be even further condensed when transformed into pemmican, a food whose name is a word from the Cree language – *pimikân,* derived from *pimii,* meaning grease or fat. Pemmican is aptly named. To make it, the Indians placed pulverized jerky into sacks sewn from buffalo hide and then poured hot, liquid marrowfat over it. The fat would both combine with the dried meat and serve to seal the sack. While still molten, pemmican could be formed into shapes convenient for storage or transport. Mostly produced in the form of 90-pound blocks, it was a staple for the Plains Indians, as

well as for the fur trappers and traders who spearheaded the Europeans' advance into the region.

As the Native Americans came to recognize pemmican's value in trade with the whites, additional ingredients were added to appeal to the latter's tastes. Although chokeberries became the most common supplement, some pemmican was flavored with cereals, sugar, and fruits. For trappers, this food was "the bread of the wilderness," a practical staple in terms of availability, stability, and nutrition. Whether the bison population was diminished as a result of such commerce is difficult to establish, although it is certainly probable (Binkerd, Kolari, and Tracy 1977).

Native Americans also incorporated buffalo into their diet in several ways other than as fresh and preserved meat. Various tribes developed methods of preparing blood soups and puddings. Roasted thigh bones were a popular source of tasty marrow, and the tongue was savored. Northern tribes enjoyed boiled fetal calves, and the Hidatsa specialized in grilled buffalo udders filled with milk. The Plains tribes occasionally dined on baked buffalo hides. However, this latter practice was infrequent as hides were generally more valuable for things other than food (McHugh 1972).

The Bison East of the Mississippi

Following the example of the first Americans, early European visitors utilized the buffalo as a source of steaks, stews, and marrow. Throughout the sixteenth century, Spanish explorers, such as Alvar Nuñez Cabeza de Vaca and Vincente de Zaldivar, wrote of consuming buffalo flesh during their adventures. The British, however, who settled east of the buffalo grounds, did not encounter the animal until they began to move inland at the beginning of the seventeenth century. By the end of the colonial era, the buffalo had virtually disappeared from the landscape east of the Appalachians.

The reasons for this disappearance are varied. Although settlers often hunted bison for food, it is doubtful that the human population of the time was numerous enough to eliminate great numbers of the animals. Rather, it seems more likely that as the whites transformed the landscape to meet their needs, the buffalo simply migrated westward away from people. In addition, as farmers began to raise more cattle, their grazing would have reduced the available food supply. Finally, it should be noted that the eastern herd was by no means as large as that of the west.

When European settlement expanded into the area between the Appalachians and the Mississippi, buffalo were once again on hand as a food source. In detailing his travels through Kentucky, Daniel Boone mentioned meals of fresh buffalo, and as other early frontiersmen penetrated the region, they often followed "buffalo roads" – narrow paths formed by herds in search of salt (Rorabacher 1970).

As had happened east of the Appalachians, however, as human settlement continued, buffalo east of the Mississippi became displaced by a changing economy. Initially, settlers relied heavily on bison for food; yet, once farms were established, the animals became nuisances, grazing on land more profitably used to raise cattle or crops. By 1830, the buffalo had disappeared from the East, and the American bison population was compressed into the Great Plains.

The Bison West of the Mississippi

Crowding into the plains created a variety of natural hazards for the buffalo. Food shortages were more common, and fatal diseases (particularly anthrax and bovine tuberculosis) could spread quickly and kill greater numbers as the herds grew more closely together (McHugh 1972).

Such consequences of the bison's westward migration, however, seem insignificant when compared with the destruction wrought by humans during the final third of the nineteenth century. It was then that the forces of economics and politics, as well as human greed, carelessness, and malice, came together in such a manner as almost to remove the American bison from the North American ecosystem. Between 1870 and 1873, the large buffalo herds of Kansas were destroyed. Next to go were the southern herds, and by 1878, the animals were absent from Texas to the edge of the prairie. The vast northern herds of the Dakotas and Montana survived a few years longer, perhaps into 1883. But by 1900, the herds of the Canadian plains were gone, and only about 300 of the animals remained in the United States.

Commercial hunting seems to have been the factor most significant in the buffalo's destruction. The earliest professional hunters in the West sought beavers, not bison, and required the latter only for food. By the early 1820s, however, commercial buffalo hunting had begun in southern Canada, with the primary aim of securing buffalo tongues (a popular delicacy) and hides for shipment to the East and abroad. Often, entrepreneurs recruited Native Americans to do such hunting in exchange for whiskey.

At least at this point, however, the bison's habit of shedding offered a degree of protection against excessive hunting. Because the sale of furry hides (for use as robes) produced the greatest revenue, and because the animals lost their furriness during the summer, hunting them was strictly seasonal. Nevertheless, the desire to trade for the white man's goods resulted in a Native American slaughter of buffalo that has been estimated as 30 percent greater annually than their personal needs required (Dobak 1996).

During the two decades prior to the Civil War, the Great Plains experienced a series of ecological changes that also hastened the disappearance of the bison. Foremost was the proliferation of open-range cattle ranching. Indeed, by 1850, the prairie had become home to more than 50 million cattle that were major competitors for the region's food supply. Moreover, ranchers were unhappy with the seasonal wanderings of the bison, arguing that their grazing rendered the land unfit for beef cattle for as long as two years afterward (Vestal 1952).

At the same time, as human settlement increased and transportation on the prairie improved, the slaughter of the buffalo for industrial purposes escalated. The trade in buffalo robes accelerated as more forts and trading posts dotted the western landscape: In 1850, around 100,000 robes reached the markets of St. Louis, a record total at that time. The increase in civilian and military populations on the plains also meant that still more of the animals were slaughtered for food (Dary 1974).

After 1865, the future of the bison became ever more precarious. With the conclusion of the American Civil War, both the U.S. Army and the railroad corporations sought to consolidate their positions on the plains. Troops were stationed in the West to pacify the Native Americans, and thousands of men migrated to the prairie to lay tracks for the Union Pacific and the Topeka & Santa Fe railroads. Fresh buffalo meat served as the primary fare for both the soldiers and the laborers. Moreover, once the railroads began service through the West, the buffalo again (as they had in the East) became nuisances, routinely wandering onto or across the tracks, blocking trains, and causing long delays. George Bird Grinnell recalled two such delays while traveling on the Kansas Pacific, one of which lasted for around three hours (Grinnell 1892).

In 1870, a refinement in tanning techniques became still another factor in the decrease of the American bison. The animal's summer hide had long been dismissed as economically worthless because there was no known method for transforming the skin into commercial leather. However, once Philadelphia tanners devised such a method, the bison became a year-round target, and the promise of easy money encouraged more and more men to become buffalo hunters (Cronon 1991).

This was especially the case following the financial panic of 1873, when the nation entered a five-year period of severe economic depression. As banks closed and millions of easterners were suddenly unemployed, the seemingly inexhaustible bison herds of the plains offered a chance to earn a living, and perhaps even to acquire wealth. Buffalo hides brought from 2 to 3 dollars each during the 1870s, and a successful hunter might kill more than 250 animals in a single day. In the 1950s, Frank H. Mayer, once a "buffalo runner" himself, recalled:

> The whole Western country went buffalo-wild.
> It was like a gold rush or a uranium rush. Men
> left jobs, businesses, wives, and children and

future prospects to get into buffalo running. There were uncounted millions of the beasts – hundreds of millions, we forced ourselves to believe. And all we had to do was take these hides from their wearers. It was a harvest. We were the harvesters (Mayer and Roth 1958: 21).

Much of the time, hunters worked in gangs, with individuals specifically assigned to shoot or skin the animals. Larger parties would utilize horses to remove the hides quickly: After the buffalo's skin was loosened by making a series of cuts, it was tied to a horse which pulled the hide off the carcass (Wheeler 1923). The skins were awkward and bulky, often weighing more than 100 pounds each. Still, an experienced skinner could have the hide off an animal in about five minutes. Although the financial rewards encouraged efficiency, the animals' abundance more often produced carelessness and waste, and bison slain by commercial hunters were not really "harvested" at all but merely left to rot in the sun.

In general, the bison was easy prey. Seasoned hunters understood its habits and instincts and developed techniques to attack it when confused and vulnerable. Recalling the hunts of the 1870s, one participant stated that "[t]he stupidity of the buffalo was remarkable" (Wheeler 1923: 81). Although there was a modicum of risk in buffalo hunting, accidents were more often the result of human error than of aggressiveness on the part of the hunted. Many retired hunters later wrote about injuries caused by falling off horses or by rifles exploding. Occasionally, too, poor judgment during winter months resulted in death from exposure (Dodge 1959).

In addition to destruction by commercial hunters, the buffalo population was further decimated by increasingly numerous "sport-hunters." As early as the 1830s, such traveling gentlemen as Washington Irving began to test their marksmanship on the buffalo, and during the 1850s, an Irish nobleman, Sir George Goe, indulged in a highly publicized "safari" with 21 wagons and a staff of 40 servants. In a three-year period, his party killed 2,000 bison.

Such "sporting" expeditions became increasingly widespread as the century progressed, especially during the depression that ensued after the "Panic of 1873," when the railroads were determined to increase revenue by increasing the number of passengers going west. Rail executives hit upon the notion of catering to the sportsmen (who seemed to have money and time when most people did not) and advertised special "buffalo trains" that would transport easterners into areas populated by the animals. Upon arrival, the passengers could shoot bison from the comfort (and safety) of the railroad cars. More intrepid hunters might track them on horseback, although in general the procedure was to hire an experienced "scout" to minimize the danger.

The most renowned of such guides was William F. Cody, or "Buffalo Bill," a clever entrepreneur who later prospered as the creator of the traveling "Buffalo Bill's Wild West" show, on the road from 1883 to 1916. Much of Cody's initial fame had resulted from escorting prominent personalities, such as Gordon Bennett II (publisher of the *New York Herald*) and the son of Russian Tsar Alexander II (Aleksandre Nikolayevich), on hunts.

Such expeditions were bloody slaughters. Many hunters recalled ruining expensive rifles because of lengthy periods of continuous and rapid firing that caused them to overheat. If the hunters were successful in making a "stand" – a technique of tricking the buffalo into immobility – the potential for killing was limited only by their ammunition. Numerous parties recorded killing up to 200 animals per hunter per day.

The Final Buffalo Hunts

The impact of such slaughter was not unnoticed at the time. In 1871 and 1872, the territorial legislatures of Wyoming and Montana passed laws intended to reduce buffalo hunting. In the U.S. Senate (also during 1872), Cornelius Cole of California and Henry Wilson of Massachusetts attempted on separate occasions to enact federal protection for the bison. Both, however, were unsuccessful.

Two years later, U.S. Representative Greenburg L. Fort of Illinois sponsored national legislation prohibiting the killing of female bison by anyone not a Native American (Dary 1974). This bill triggered much debate that clearly indicated that its opponents saw in the extermination of the bison the most effective way of subduing the Plains Indians. Indeed, Secretary of the Interior Columbus Delano had endorsed such a position (in his annual report for 1873) by predicting that the disappearance of the bison would eliminate future Native American uprisings by reducing the Native Americans. One of the opponents of Fort's legislation, Samuel S. Cox, bluntly argued that the bill "favored Indians at the expense of white men," whereas only the reverse was desirable (Dary 1974: 127).

Despite strong opposition, the bill passed the House and Senate during the spring of 1874, only to have President Ulysses S. Grant employ a pocket veto that quietly killed it the following year. There seems little doubt that this was a political tactic inspired by the Bureau of Indian Affairs and by General Philip Sheridan.

In fact, Sheridan had clearly laid out a scheme whereby "the extermination of the buffalo herds by meat hunters for the construction gangs of the railroad, by hide-hunters, and finally by tourists shooting from palace-car windows" could hasten the submission of the Native Americans (Slotkin 1992: 426). In a frequently quoted 1875 speech to the Texas Legislature, Sheridan denounced efforts to save the buffalo, explaining that "the hide hunters were doing more to settle the Indian question than the entire Army had done in thirty years, by destroying the Indians' commissary" (Garretson 1938: 128).

If the American bison were not already doomed to near extinction by 1875, the failure of Fort's bill certainly brought it one step closer. Although within a decade a number of western states enacted laws to halt the slaughter, such regulations were rarely enforced, and even had they been, the laws probably appeared too late to reverse the decline of the species. In 1880, the Northern Pacific Railroad extended its lines through North Dakota, thus offering hide hunters ready access to the still-flourishing northern herds. Within three years, almost all of this population was destroyed.

By the end of the century, free-roaming buffalo had disappeared from the Great Plains and could be found only in a few protected situations: national parks, game reserves, and captivity. By 1913, when the "buffalo nickel" 5-cent coin (designed by James Earle Fraser) entered circulation, wild American bison had vanished from the landscape.

The Struggle for Conservation

The capability of the bison to breed in captivity was a critical factor in its escape from extinction. Following the demise of the wild herds at the end of the nineteenth century, a series of conservation measures were undertaken to preserve the species by controlled management of the few survivors. The initial attempt at government-sponsored protection dates from the beginning of the twentieth century and occurred at Yellowstone National Park, which contained the scant remnants of the northern herd. Although Congress had outlawed all buffalo hunting within the park, poaching was widespread and carried no serious penalty before 1894.

Far greater attention was accorded the buffalo following the 1902 appointment of Charles J. Jones as the warden of Yellowstone. Jones increased the size of the bison population by purchasing privately held animals from throughout the United States. Moreover, he segregated the animals into a "wild herd," which functioned with minimal supervision, and a "tame herd," which was closely monitored and given food and protection from deep snow during the winter. Newborn calves were frequently transferred from the wild to the tame herd to ensure their survival.

The publicity given to Jones's efforts subsequently resulted in the formation, in December 1905, of the American Bison Society (ABS). With Theodore Roosevelt serving as honorary president, and its membership composed of both naturalists and sportsmen, the society proved an effective association for the preservation of the buffalo. Working in conjunction with the New York Zoological Society, the ABS advocated the formation of additional federal herds to augment those in Yellowstone. Between 1907 and 1918, the societies assisted in the creation of buffalo reserves in Oklahoma, Montana, Nebraska, and North Dakota (U.S. Department of the Interior 1977).

In addition to such conservation agencies, many Native Americans have made efforts to reestablish the bison in North America. As early as 1873, Walking Coyote, of the Pend d'Oreille, noted the animals' decreasing numbers and attempted to raise a herd of his own from four calves captured in Montana. During the 1930s, both the Crow and Sioux established herds on reservation lands. More recently, in 1990, the Inter-Tribal Bison Cooperative (ITBC) was organized to assist bison-restoration projects undertaken by 31 tribes in 13 states. In viewing the bison as a natural part of the plains ecosystem, the ITBC argued that a return of the animal to its former home would improve the lives of the area's human inhabitants (Garretson 1938; Callenbach 1996).

The conservation strategies of the twentieth century have been remarkably successful. No longer endangered, the bison population has prospered to such a degree that the animal has entered commercial markets as a food item. During the 1970s, breeders created the "beefalo," an animal comprising three-eighths bison and five-eighths bovine parentage. Overall, this hybrid offered little beyond novelty; nutritionally, the meat was inferior to that of the buffalo, and the animal appeared susceptible to an array of diseases. The failure of this experiment suggests that, at least in the near future, the American bison is safe from any further genetic tinkering (National Buffalo Association 1990).

Bison as Food

As livestock, the bison provides a high yield of marketable meat, as well as a nutritious final product in the oven or on the stove. A major disadvantage in raising buffalo, however, is the high start-up cost: Prices of bison calves start at around $1,000, and because buffalo are classified as "exotic animals" by the U.S. Department of Agriculture, aspiring ranchers have less access than cattlemen to government assistance. One considerable advantage is that bison require less food, and far less water, than cattle. Although similar to other bovines in being ruminants capable of digesting other fodder, bison do not depend on succulent grasses. Instead, they prefer short, dry grass, which usually contains a higher percentage of protein. When grazing, bison will consume about 180 pounds less grass per month than cattle of comparable size.

The biggest advantage of the buffalo, however, is its high yield of nutritional meat. With lighter hides, heads, hooves, and tails than Hereford cattle, the buffalo provides a larger percentage of salable meat when dressed (Rorabacher 1970). In addition, when compared to domestic cattle, it is surprisingly disease free (although respiratory ailments, anthrax, and brucellosis appear as occasional illnesses), and as a result, the meat lacks most of the antibiotics and medications contained in commercial beef and is nonallergenic (National Buffalo Association 1990).

Unlike almost all the meat of other types of domesticated livestock, buffalo meat is low in fat (5 grams per half pound of raw bison, compared to more than 18 grams of fat in the same amount of beef). Clearly, in light of concerns for nutritional health, the bison has great potential as a healthful alternative to most other meats. In areas where butchered bison is readily available (primarily in, but not limited to, the American West), the meat is sold in cuts similar to those of beef: steaks, ribs, roasts, and ground meat. Although the per-pound cost of bison for consumers is often 50 percent greater than, or even double, that of beef, the lower ratio of fat means less shrinkage, and consequently, a pound of bison yields substantially more protein than an equal measure of beef or pork.

The nutritional argument notwithstanding, however, there are an assortment of economic and biological factors that will interact in any determination of whether the bison will again become a significant source of food. Currently, the species is raised on small- to medium-sized ranches in herds of 100 to 250 animals for large-scale production. But the buffalo would doubtless have to be fitted into the beef industry model.

Yet feeding, grazing, meat storage, and refrigeration are only a few of the practices within the cattle industry that would probably require modification to accommodate the buffalo. For example, bison are ill suited to feedlots – facilities used by cattlemen for the rapid increase in the size of their animals immediately preceding slaughter. The confinement created by such ranching tends both to increase fighting and to accelerate the spread of disease among bison. Buffalo, then, cannot be harvested with the same efficiency as cattle. Moreover, although proponents of bison exalt the animals' "natural" meat, free of the vitamins and antibiotics common in other foods, it seems possible, at least, that such additives in buffalo meat would be an eventual result of large-scale commercial production.

It is ironic that economic and cultural change, the same forces that nearly destroyed the bison during the nineteenth century, may hasten the ascendancy of the species in the future. For Native Americans, the buffalo was a sacred resource to be utilized according to human need. However, as the original inhabitants of North America were displaced by white settlers, the hunting of bison became an industry that rapidly diminished the animals' numbers.

At present, North Americans are involved in a cultural shift of sorts: Past understandings of what constitutes good nutrition are being rejected, and many people are reluctant to continue to consume the high-fat foods that have traditionally composed their diets. Low-fat red meat from the buffalo appears to be a viable replacement for much of the beef presently produced in America. Consequently, once again, harvesting the animals may offer vast financial rewards to humans. However, it is not difficult to envision large-scale bison ranching resulting in a noticeably different meat product from that presently provided by moderate-sized facilities, perhaps even in an unrecognizable buffalo.

J. Allen Barksdale

Bibliography

Berger, Joel, and Carol Cunningham. 1994. *Bison: Mating and conservation in small populations.* New York.

Binkerd, E. F., O. E. Kolari, and C. Tracy. 1977. Pemmican. *Maricopa Trails* 1: 1–20.

Callenbach, Ernest. 1996. *Bring back the buffalo! A sustainable future for America's great plains.* Washington, D.C.

Catlin, George. 1842. *Letters and notes on the manners, customs, and condition of the North American Indians.* London.

Cronon, William. 1991. *Nature's metropolis: Chicago and the great west.* New York.

Dary, David A. 1974. *The buffalo book: The full saga of the American animal.* New York.

Dobak, William A. 1996. Killing the Canadian buffalo, 1821–1881. *The Western Historical Quarterly* 1: 33–52.

Dodge, Richard I. [1877] 1959. *The plains of the great west and their inhabitants.* New York.

Garretson, Martin S. 1938. *The American bison: The story of its extermination as a wild species and its restoration under federal protection.* New York.

Grinnell, George Bird. 1892. The last of the buffalo. *Scribner's Magazine* 3: 267–86.

Mayer, Frank H., and Charles B. Roth. 1958. *The buffalo harvest.* Denver, Colo.

McHugh, Tom. 1972. *The time of the buffalo.* New York.

National Buffalo Association. 1990. *Buffalo producer's guide to management and marketing.* Chicago.

Rorabacher, J. Albert. 1970. *The American buffalo in transition: A historical and economic survey of the bison in America.* Saint Cloud, Minn.

Schultz, James Willard (Apikuni). 1962. *Blackfeet and buffalo: Memories of life among the Indians.* Norman, Okla.

Slotkin, Richard. 1992. *Gunfighter nation: The myth of the frontier in twentieth-century America.* New York.

Stefansson, Vilhjalmur. 1956. *The fat of the land.* New York.

U.S. Department of the Interior. 1977. *The American buffalo.* Washington, D.C.

Vestal, Stanley. 1952. *Queen of cowtowns: Dodge City.* Lincoln, Neb.

Wallace, Ernest, and E. Adamson Hoebel. 1952. *The Comanches: Lords of the south plains.* Norman, Okla.

Wheeler, Homer W. 1923. *Buffalo days; forty years in the old west: The personal narrative of a cattleman, Indian fighter, and army officer.* Indianapolis, Ind.

II.G.2 ❧ Aquatic Animals

Pre-Christian Origins of Aquatic Husbandry

Primitive Fish Farming in China

Aquatic farming, like many other modern technologies, is credited to early Chinese societies well before 1000 B.C. In its rudest form, some systematic sowing and harvesting of fish in China have been inferred from marks on ancient "oracle bones" that have survived. Simple shapes of fish were perceived to predict favorable times in which to gather fish "seeds," particularly those of the common carp that abound in China's great rivers when the rainy seasons begin, and to sow them in convenient water bodies in floodplains nearer home.

More detailed records of fish husbandry are not found until early classic writings of the Chou Dynasty (1112–221 B.C.). It is not known, however, whether such husbandry was (1) in response to the symbolic cultural and social significance of fish in China, or (2) because of their importance in ornamental ponds built to beautify gardens of the rich, or (3) due to the simple expedient of having fresh food ready at hand each day. In probability, all three reasons are too closely linked to know with any conviction which came first. The common carp has long been a symbol of fortune in China and, therefore, a highly acceptable gift. Indeed, the offering of a live carp (or an image of the fish in jade or ivory rising out of the water to reach the gates of the dragon) recognized the importance of the recipient and bestowed great honor. It is not hard to imagine that both givers and receivers needed a place in which to keep fish alive, and ancient hand-painted scrolls often illustrate scenes from domestic life with tranquil exotic gardens and ornamental fishponds.

The earliest reference in Chinese literature to "aqua-husbandry" as a primitive technology is found in the writings of Fan Li in about 500 B.C. He wrote that culturing carp was one of five ways to make a good living in China, and he described techniques for constructing ponds and for breeding, feeding, and maintaining a healthy fish population. Based on Fan Li's guidelines, simple carp culture for food production flourished for the next thousand years until, quite fortuitously, an event occurred that revolutionized fish culture in China.

In about A.D. 618, during the Tang Dynasty, an emperor whose family name was Li came to the throne. As the name for common carp in Chinese sounded like "lee," the idea of culturing, killing, and eating "lee" was sacrilegious and, thus, banned. The crisis, however, compelled farmers to raise other fish and employ new husbandry practices. Soon four new species were cultured successfully, namely the "silver," "bighead," "mud," and "grass" carps. Furthermore, because of the very different nutritional niches that these fishes occupy in aquatic habitats, the four species could be cultured together in the same pond without competing for food, all of which significantly intensified unit production.

For the husbandry of these new species, farmers soon came to grasp the importance of using organic wastes to increase productivity, and fish culture, as a consequence, became more closely tied to animal and plant husbandry: Manure from pigs and poultry was deposited in fish ponds, and plants and vegetables were grown along their banks. Where ponds could be drained, the enriched sludge was excavated and used as fertilizer for crops. Yields increased dramatically, and polyculture of carp in these integrated farming systems became a key part of rural life in China. Today China annually produces more than 4 million tonnes of freshwater fish almost entirely through the polyculture of eight cyprinids and two or three other species. This figure nearly equals that of all aquatic farm production in the rest of the world.

The spread of fish culture throughout Asia is also credited to the Chinese and to their desire to give tribute, rather than to receive it or to trade. Powerful Chinese naval expeditions moved throughout every inhabited land bordering the China Sea and Indian Ocean for some 500 years before the Great Withdrawal of A.D. 1433, spreading word of the grandeur of each new dynasty, distributing treasures, and teaching skills. Because of their symbolism as valuable gifts, carp, together with simple lessons in fish husbandry, were probably a part of such largesse, especially because the fish are hardy travelers and tolerant of very poor conditions.

The Vivaria of Other Great Cultures

Simple fish husbandry was also practiced in most of the other great cultures. The Egyptians, for example, although not renowned fishermen, built vivaria as adjuncts to their temples and palaces. Their writings indicate that they understood the principles of migration and breeding of fish in the Nile, but there is no evidence of any attempted domestication. Although a staple in the commoners' diet, fish were eschewed by Egyptian kings and priests for symbolic reasons. Some fish were sacred, as they guided the boats that bore the dead to eternity, and others (probably muddy-tasting freshwater species from the waters of the delta) were regarded as unclean.

The Assyrians, on the other hand, including both Sumerians and Babylonians, were greatly addicted to fish and were skilled fishermen. They were known to keep large resources of fish in lakes created by the construction of irrigation dams on the Tigris and Euphrates, and they built vivaria for their temples and in most townships. Records from 422 B.C. describe fishponds belonging to rich merchants and civic prefects, operated for them by individuals under contract for one-half talent of silver and a daily supply of fish.

Vivaria in Sumerian temples can be traced back to 2500 B.C. Each had a keeper, who charged the public to fish these "piscinae" or stew-ponds. Further evidence indicates that piscinae became quite numerous among Assyrian commoners, although it is recorded that ponds built by "poor men" often drew poachers because their owners had no legal redress.

The neighboring Israelites, in spite of their liking for fish and their links with Egyptians and Assyrians, apparently never constructed vivaria. There is no record of such activity in all of their prolific writings until just before Christianity was born, when the Israelites were probably influenced by the practices of the Romans.

Wealthy Greeks and Romans feasted on all the common marine fish and shellfish of the Mediterranean for which, at times, they paid extraordinarily high prices. The Greeks appear to have been satisfied with what they could catch conveniently close at hand, and there is no record of their building vivaria. The Romans, on the other hand, transported seafoods, such as mullet, oysters, and cockles, great distances inland at significant cost and brought back species to Italy from all parts of their empire.

As a consequence, the Romans adopted the Egyptian and Assyrian vivarium, which became a necessary component of all the great estates. Many were constructed indoors, often adjacent to refectories to enable dinner guests to see and choose their own fish, and some were even built on board ships. Although costly to construct and maintain, vivaria proved extremely popular, and what had been intended to keep food fresh in a hot climate became a prestigious showpiece as well, complete with keeper.

The Roman vivaria remained the prerogative of the wealthy. However, the rich brackishwater lagoons and "valli" that surrounded the coast of Italy served the common people in similar fashion. They were especially good sources for mullet, sea bass, sea bream, and eels, which could be trapped inside them.

Whether the practice of keeping fish in vivaria was carried by the Romans throughout their empire is not known. The foundations of excavated Roman houses and fortifications outside Italy reveal pits that held water, but these may have been only for storing drinking water. Probably the defensive moats of larger walled fortifications and cities contained water enriched with human and kitchen wastes, which fell from the walls above and provided good nourishment for certain types of freshwater fish, such as carp. But, on the whole, freshwater fish were not popular with the Romans.

Subsistence Practices of the Middle Ages

Fish Ponds of Tribal Societies

Outside of China, early aquatic farming for food production developed mostly through tribal societies who fished for subsistence and survival. In most such societies, fishermen relied on a variety of fixed traps, in addition to spears and lines with hooks fashioned from bones for traditional fishing. These traps ranged from simple woven and baited baskets suspended in the water, to earthen ponds constructed along the shoreline, to complex labyrinths of fences made from bamboo and covered with reeds that enticed fish into ever-receding spaces from which there was no escape. Doubtless such fishermen also discovered that most fish could be held in captivity in these traps and kept fresh for several days or even longer if some feed was provided. From this discovery it was only a short step to locating places where seasonal resources of fry and fingerlings could be captured in large numbers, impounded in some way, and raised for future harvest.

As exemplified by surviving primitive societies, tribal fishermen have a good understanding of the natural behavior of their quarry and the influence of seasonal and lunar changes and diurnal conditions on their movements. Thus, the trapping and holding of brackishwater fish, such as milkfish and mullet, believed to have started in Indonesia in the fifteenth century, was possible because it was understood that every year, millions of young fish would migrate inshore in early spring to mangroves rich in food. Here they were caught and transferred to shallow ponds crudely fashioned around the estuaries and kept filled with water.

Records show that brackishwater ponds were also an important part of Polynesian societies throughout the Pacific islands at about the same time and that pond practices were quite sophisticated. The earliest recorded date for the construction of fishponds in the Hawaiian Islands is in the middle of the fifteenth century. These tidal ponds, shaped by stone and coral walls on top of reefs, were built around or adjacent to streams so that the fresh water attracted and fed young fish.

Most of the ponds had a system of one-way gates, through which water could be exchanged and small fish moved in (to feed and grow), and by which large fish were trapped at the full moon (as they tried to move out to spawn at sea). Other ponds had no gates, but water was exchanged through the permeable coral walls.

Ancient Polynesian walled fishponds were owned by chiefs and were symbols of importance, built by people drafted for the purpose. By the beginning of the nineteenth century, more than 200 ponds were recorded around the islands of Hawaii. Many were large, with walls from 2,000 to 5,000 feet in length. Each pond had keepers who fed the fish with taro and other vegetation and caught them for the chiefs and their immediate retinue.

Because the common people had no rights to fish in these ponds, they made their own "underwater ponds" in the sea by connecting coral heads with walls, thus trapping fish as the tide receded. They were also allowed to operate fishponds inland in wet areas where taro was grown. The Polynesians were a marine-dependent society, and the large variety of fish abundant around their islands in the Pacific was the principal animal protein in the everyday diet. They were not dependent on fish production in their ponds for subsistence, but used them as a source of food in bad weather and as a ready supply for feasts.

Coastal fishponds were probably built in Asia well before the fifteenth century. The islands of the Hawaiian chain and Tahiti, which lie almost at the limit of Polynesian extension in the Pacific, are known to have been well populated by A.D. 1000 by means of migrations of people descended from the Melanesians of the far western Pacific. Therefore, it is probable that the skills of catching fish and keeping them in captivity were carried from China, through Southeast Asia, into the Melanesian islands, and then on out into the Pacific between the tenth and thirteenth centuries.

The Stew-Ponds of Europe

At the same time that it was extending throughout Asia and the Pacific, the knowledge of fish husbandry also traveled westward into Europe. In the Middle Ages, so-called stew-ponds became increasingly common on large estates. They were a convenient source of fresh protein to alternate with a diet of dried, salted, and pickled foods, and particularly important in times of war and siege.

In similar fashion, coastal beds of common shellfish, such as oysters and mussels, were maintained as reserves of fresh protein. These were protected and conserved by selective harvesting, but there is no evidence of any effort at true domestication.

As with earlier cultures, stew-ponds in western and eastern Europe were associated with priests and nobles. They are evident in the earliest records of many of the religious orders founded in the twelfth century. For example, the original charter of the Kladruby Monastery in Bohemia, dated 1115, describes a fish production pond, and many others are still visible in the ruins of the earliest monasteries.

Stew-ponds were also a common feature of the great estates – most of which were constructed beside fish-laden rivers. In England, the eleventh-century Domesday Book records ownership of "vivariae piscinae" by many large estates and also by smaller landholdings of ordinary country squires and wealthy middle-class merchants. In his prologue to the *Canterbury Tales,* written in 1387–92, Geoffrey Chaucer describes the epicurean Franklin, a "householdere" who "hadde many a breem [bream] and many a luce [pike] in stuwe."

In contrast to such largesse, the feudal system of the European Middle Ages denied landownership and, therefore, stew-ponds, to peasants. All rivers and streams belonged to kings and their barons, who controlled large territories, as well as the game and fish in them. Poaching in rivers as well as in stew-ponds was generally punished by death, and thus fresh fish was a rare commodity for the lower classes and rural peasants. When ancient laws regarding fish and fishing were finally changed (some such statutes remained until the end of the nineteenth century, as in Hungary), the establishment of family stew-ponds was one of the first products of such change.

Toward the end of the Middle Ages, the fish typical of stew-ponds in Europe were native freshwater species, such as bream, perch, carp, barbel, roach, dace, and minnows. Predatory fish, such as pike, tench, eel, and lamprey, were excluded if possible. With the exception of such migratory fish as salmon, those which remained through the winter would probably reproduce in the following spring if the pond was suitable and large enough – thus replenishing the stocks naturally. From this point it was but one more step to the discovery that separate ponds were useful for storing during winter, breeding in spring, and fattening in summer and autumn.

By the middle of the fifteenth century, the construction and management of fishponds was a well-established and integral (but small) part of artisanal life, particularly in eastern Europe. Many towns in Bohemia and Moravia competed with the monasteries and nobles in pond construction, some of which were extraordinarily large. About 20,000 ponds were registered in the archives of this region in the sixteenth century, covering more than 75,000 hectares.

The technology, particularly of carp culture, became quite advanced. Many ponds were managed intensively, with production increasing steadily to between 75 and 100 kilograms per hectare. Techniques were described in books of the period. In 1547 Janus Dubravius, the Bishop of Olomouc, produced his treatise, *Jani Dubravil de Piscinis et Piscium qui in Illis Aluntur Libri Quinquae,* later translated into many languages. It included chapters on economics and diseases and described the work of fish-culture wardens and their organizational guild. Other works by John Taverner (1600) and Gervais Markham (1613) discuss in detail the practices of fish raising, including pond construction, pond fertility, management, feeding, and the best fish to raise. These authors also made observations on the breeding behavior of adults and the care of fry and fingerlings.

The beginning of the Renaissance coincided with the first peak in the early domestication of aquatic animals worldwide. By this time, thanks to the skills of the Chinese, most countries of Asia practiced breeding and propagation of several freshwater fish in captivity and had developed relatively sophisticated production practices. Island communities of the South China Sea and the Pacific Ocean substituted marine fish that could not be bred but that could be gathered in large numbers to stock coastal ponds.

The Europeans had also steadily advanced in management practices for the husbanding of freshwater fish in captivity and relied on natural breeding to supplement their stocks. But the next two hundred years saw stagnation and even decline in aquatic animal domestication. China closed its doors on the world, whereas in Europe there was growing competition for water and for land (Radcliffe 1926; Toussaint-Samat 1992).

The Impact of the Industrial Revolution

The Demise of Inland Fisheries in Europe

At the dawn of the nineteenth century in Europe, the demand for fish and shellfish was met by the traditional and dominant inland fisheries and by some modest estuarine and coastal fisheries. This adequately supplied a population widely dispersed among rural villages or grouped in small agricultural towns and a few principal cities that were trading centers.

Nineteenth-century industrialization, however, which mechanized fishing fleets and opened up large urban markets for iced fresh fish through networks of railways, expanded modest coastal fishing into marine fishery industries at unprecedented speed. Unfortunately, the same industrialization decimated the traditional freshwater fisheries.

The freshwater fisheries of coastal Europe were based mostly on migratory species, predominantly Atlantic salmon, sea trout, and, to a lesser extent, the eel. However, the Industrial Revolution produced an insatiable demand for fresh water, and almost every river and stream was affected. They were dammed to make reservoirs and drained by growing towns, polluted by manufacturing industries built along their banks, and diverted to fill new canals, and their catchments were stripped bare by deforestation.

Furthermore, those fish running the migratory gauntlet were poached with every conceivable trapping device, including explosives and poisons. Although protective fishery laws had been in existence since the fourteenth century, they were largely ignored and not enforced. Finally, adding to this relentless assault on the migratory fisheries, many large lakes and ponds of central Europe – operated since the Middle Ages as inland fisheries for the common carp and other cyprinids – were drained to meet the need for more agricultural land.

In a mere hundred years, and before parliamentarians finally recognized the problem and took action, the Industrial Revolution had polluted all the large and most productive estuaries and rivers in Europe or made them otherwise impassable to fish. Most remain so today. It is fortunate that toward the end of the nineteenth century, public and private organizations were formed to safeguard and monitor inland fisheries and to undertake scientific research to bring about their recovery.

Artificial propagation to replenish falling stocks was one small part of their regulatory response for the management of all fisheries, but this was not the only reason for such development. Another was a growing scientific curiosity in natural history inspired by the voyages of Charles Darwin and Alfred Wallace and also the new field of genetics discovered by the monk, Gregor Mendel.

Fish Propagation and the Hatchery Movement

The breeding of common brown trout was first described by William Yarrell in his *History of the British Fishes,* published in 1841. The book was based on a translation of an original paper written in 1763 by a German naturalist, which had gone largely ignored. The technique was rediscovered in 1844 by two French fishermen, Anton Géhin and Joseph Remy, who not only told of successful fertilization of trout eggs but also of stocking the progeny in the Moselotte River and raising them in a pond. Subsequently, Gottlieb Boccius wrote *A Treatise on the Production and Management of Fish in Freshwater by Artificial Spawning, Breeding, and Rearing,* with the sinister subtitle, *Shewing also the Cause of the Depletion of All Rivers and Streams* (1848).

Other works rapidly followed, notably those of Professor M. Coste in France. Following the publication of his *Instructions Pratiques sur la Pisciculture,* he was invited to lecture on fishery problems throughout Europe. These travels culminated in his publication (1861) of the *Voyage d'Exploration sur le Littoral de la France et de l'Italie,* which described the artificial culture of both fish and oysters. In addition to being generally credited with saving the oyster fisheries of France, he was also responsible for founding the first fish hatchery, built at Huningue, near Basle, in 1852. From this hatchery, eggs were distributed throughout France and other European countries to many rivers before these countries built their own hatcheries.

Coincidentally, there were similar developments in the New World. In Ohio, Theodatus Garlick artificially bred brook trout from eggs that he brought back from Canada in 1853. Within the next 20 years, eggs of a number of common freshwater fish had been reared under primitive laboratory conditions and the young fry put into their natural waters before they would have died in captivity.

The majority of these species were common salmonids, such as brook trout, brown trout, rainbow trout, Arctic char, and members of the large group of Pacific salmon, as well as other popular nonsalmonids, like the shad. All these fish had common attributes. They were readily caught, their eggs were large and visible, and the emergent fry had a plentiful supply of food from the yolk, which avoided the problem of feeding before release.

Many of these early efforts were supported by landowners and gentlemen sportfishermen. With independent financial resources to build hatcheries, these dilettantes started many small programs. In 1868 the first hatchery for Atlantic salmon was built by Samual Wilmot on his own property adjacent to Lake Ontario, Canada. There he released parr into the creek, and in 1867, with money from the government, the Wilmot's Creek hatchery was expanded to produce, in time, about 1 million salmon each year. This was, in all probability, the first actual ranching of salmon raised and released from a hatchery.

Soon fish hatcheries were common throughout North America. The first Pacific salmon hatcheries were built on the McCloud River in northern California in 1872 and in the Columbia Basin on the Clackamas River in Oregon in 1877. By the end of the century, the state of Washington alone had 14 salmon hatcheries, producing more than 58 million fry.

Experiments seemed to know no bounds. Rainbow and brook trout were transplanted from the western United States to trout hatcheries in Europe; and in the mid–1860s fast clippers carried the first shipments of trout and salmon eggs to India, New Zealand, and the new Chitose hatchery in Japan. In the early 1870s, Denmark built a hatchery to raise rainbow trout recently introduced from the United States. However, instead of releasing the young fish to enhance local rivers as others were doing, the Danes continued to keep the fish in captivity. This became the first land-based salmonid farming enterprise and led to Danish domination of the trout industry for the next hundred years.

The great 1883 International Fishery Exhibition in London, which devoted considerable space and attention to the new technology of fish (and shellfish) culture for enhancing declining fisheries, proved to be the springboard for worldwide interest. Many countries, including China, provided wonderfully illustrative and mechanical exhibits, and scientists and public figures alike returned home resolved to implement newly gained ideas.

One such man was Lachlan Maclean, whose successful introduction and acclimatization of trout in South Africa (although achieved only by persistence and endurance) led to other such attempts in all European colonies and overseas territories wherever there were cool mountain streams. Thus, trout were stocked in suitable upland areas throughout East Africa, from South Africa north to Kenya, and transferred to Australia, Tasmania, and New Zealand. They were also shipped to the Andean countries of South America.

In the end, however, most of these essentially private enterprises were not successful. There was still a great lack of understanding about the behavior, reproductive biology, nutrition, and diseases of salmonids; hatcheries were not simple facilities to construct and operate, and fish culture was not cheap. But, fortunately, by this time many governments had established fisheries policies, and fish propagation was an active part of fisheries management. Consequently, by the end of the century almost all private hatcheries had become publicly operated.

The First Propagation of Marine Species

In 1867, following an extensive survey of the oyster fisheries of Europe, the British naturalist Frank Buckland broadened his interest in freshwater perch to include oyster culture. His goal was not directly to produce food, but rather to use artificial culture of aquatic animals to enhance natural fisheries.

Several influential scientists, however, including Thomas Huxley, stated that farming the sea was useless as the sea fisheries were inexhaustible. But, as noted by one of Buckland's proponents, Ernest Holt, this was an overgeneralization. He believed that although the great fisheries for cod and herring and pilchard were beyond the influence of humans (either by overfishing or restocking), there were several smaller but important fisheries in the North Sea, such as that for flatfish, which could be enhanced. Holt showed with statistics the effects of overfishing on the plaice fishery, and in 1897 he proposed four solutions for management – one of which was artificial propagation.

The activity in fish propagation and fisheries research, triggered by the Great Exhibition of 1883, made it clear that temporary facilities for marine culture in fish-processing plants and water mills were totally inadequate. Propagation needed hatcheries, and fishery science needed institutes and laboratories. Consequently, one final contribution of the century to fish culture was the founding of many of today's most famous marine research stations, along with several professional societies.

France was one of the first countries to construct facilities directly in support of marine fish and shellfish culture. Following the successful efforts of Coste in salvaging the French oyster fisheries, coastal centers were built at Concarneau in 1859 and at Arcachon in 1863. In addition, a laboratory was built at Monaco, and in Naples, Italy, the famous Stazione Zooligica was constructed.

In the United States, Spencer Baird was appointed the first Commissioner of Fish and Fisheries in 1871, and fish culture became an official responsibility of the government. The first facility for work on the Atlantic cod was built in Gloucester, Massachusetts, and propagation was successfully achieved in 1878 using the technique developed by the Norwegian G. O. Sars in 1866. The successful propagation and release of other gadoids, and even herring, quickly followed, despite what would be described today as relatively poor conditions. Government funds were provided in 1885 to construct the first commercial marine fish hatchery at Woods Hole, where there was also a small group of scientists carrying out research on marine fish. The results were so good that the government built a second hatchery at Gloucester Harbor.

In the United Kingdom, the Marine Biological Association of England was founded in 1884 by the Royal Society of London, under the presidency of Thomas Huxley. In its first resolution, the society emphasized the necessity of establishing one or more laboratories on the coast of Britain where research could be conducted that would lead to the improvement of zoological and botanical science, and to an increase in knowledge about the resources of the sea.

The first laboratory was opened at Plymouth in 1888 with three professional staff, followed by one in Lowestoft. The new Lancashire and Western Fisheries Committee built laboratories at Port Erin on the Isle of Man and another at Piel Island near Barrow-in-Furness, both under the direction of Professor William Herdman from Liverpool. He began substantial propagation and release work not only with the flatfishes (plaice and flounder) but also with Atlantic cod and haddock.

The first marine hatchery in Scotland was built in 1894 at Dunbar, near Edinburgh, under the direction of James Cossor Ewart. The purpose of the Dunbar hatchery was to raise and release young marine fish to add directly to the fish supply. It began with the propagation of plaice to enhance the coastal fisheries. Ewart was helped by Harald Dannevig who, with his father Gunnar, had built the first commercial hatchery for Atlantic cod in Norway in 1882. Other facilities were built at St. Andrews and Aberdeen, and the newly formed Scottish Marine Biological Association constructed its new laboratory at Millport in the Firth of Clyde.

The fishery science carried out at all these coastal laboratories was well structured, largely because in 1899 and 1901, a gathering of illustrious scientists at Christiana, Sweden, established common methodologies for gathering information and identified specific cooperative programs for biological and hydrographic studies. The "Christiana Programme," as it became known, coordinated some of the first fisheries and marine research over an extensive area of the North Sea, the Northern Atlantic Ocean, and the Baltic Sea.

Early marine laboratories and fish hatcheries had large outdoor ponds or tidal basins for holding broodstock, modeled after those designed by the Dannevigs for cod. But it was soon clear that better control was required for incubation and for subsequent larval rearing, and in the United States initially, the "Chester jar" and then the larger "MacDonald tidal egg-hatching box" were adopted.

In Europe, the "rocking incubator" developed in Norway was more popular. But common to all hatcheries were cumbersome mechanical water systems, all soon blocked by biofouling. Worse still, their metal pipes and valves rapidly corroded, filling the tanks with rust and dangerous toxic ions. New hatcheries were built with dual pipe systems, settling tanks, and sand filters, substantially increasing their costs. Nevertheless, many such problems were not resolved for almost another half century with the advent of inert plastic materials.

Because they were concerned only with the early life stages of aquatic animals, marine hatcheries all over the world had no difficulty in realizing some large production numbers. Three hatcheries in Massachusetts, for example, accounted annually for 3,000 million fry of pollack and flounder. In Australia, under the expert eye of Harald Dannevig (who emigrated there in 1902), the hatchery at Gunnamatta Bay in New South Wales was producing 150 million fry annually; and this was emulated by the new Dunedin hatchery in New Zealand.

Unfortunately, however, despite these massive numbers, the releases had little beneficial effect on the local fisheries. This was because, unlike the eggs of freshwater fish, those of marine species are small and have little in the way of yolk reserves. The eggs hatch out quickly and the emergent larvae must feed almost immediately or die. Culturists knew little of the first feeding requirements of the emergent larvae and consequently, as there was no effort to provide the fry with small live-food organisms, their survival was almost immediately jeopardized.

The First Half of the Twentieth Century

The Influence of the Colonial Empires

In spite of the rapid progress in aquatic husbandry during the final 20 years of the nineteenth century, the first 50 years of the twentieth century were spent marking time. This was a period when efforts, intentional or not, went into building infrastructure, rather than converting scientific and technical advances into commercial production. But it was also a period when colonial and territorial influences in Asia and Africa were at their peak, and these had several useful benefits for the spread of existing technology around the world.

The new field of fisheries, and especially the idea of introducing and stocking familiar sports fish, was of considerable interest to many colonial administrators, who established fisheries departments, appointed fisheries officers, and built research centers and government farms. In many cases, an administrative organization was repeated at the state level. In India, for example, the first government fish farm was established in 1911 in the state of Sunkesula by the Fisheries Department of Madras, and this was followed by stations in Bengal, Punjab, Uttar Pradesh, Baroda, Mysore, and Hyderabad.

In India, not all of this activity was directed at the culture of sports fish, however. Eating meat was forbidden to large parts of the population by religious law, and meat was a scarce and costly commodity for many others. Hence, the possibility of increasing traditional fish production through culture was an attractive option. The gourami (first brought to India in 1841), Chinese carps, and some tilapia species were either introduced or reintroduced and became the basis of considerable practical research.

With its cultural background and strong tradition of fish and shellfish consumption, Japan was one of the earliest countries to establish regional research stations in support of national fisheries. The first was at Aichi, built in 1897, followed in the next 12 years by Shizuoka, Fukuoa, and Kuwana. This program was assisted by one of the earliest pieces of legislation in support of aquaculture, namely the Reclamation Subsidy Act, which designated large areas of land for reclamation for fish culture ponds. New ownership of these lands encouraged the capital investment required to develop them for eel culture, which increased the demand for wild elvers. The situation was further enlivened by a sudden recession in agriculture, which galvanized many farmers to convert their lands to fishponds.

The Japanese occupation of part of China, including Formosa (Taiwan), which was ceded by China in 1895, was accompanied by the transfer of Japanese interest in aquatic culture to the island. The Governor-General of Formosa established and organized an infrastructure for fisheries, much as it existed in Japan, and constructed a fish culture station at Tainan in 1910 under the distinguished scientist Takeo Aoki. Building first on the culture of milkfish (introduced centuries before by Dutch occupiers), the Japanese scientists worked on a variety of species. These included key marine species, such as the yellowtail, sea bream, and abalone, as well as freshwater eels and tilapia introduced from Indonesia. They built several other stations throughout the island, all of which were retroceded to the Republic of China in 1945.

In the colonial countries of Africa, particularly those belonging to Belgium and Great Britain, the priorities were for producing sports fish for recreational fishing and mosquito-eating fish for controlling malaria. The first recorded introductions of sports fish for culture in Africa (in particular, salmonids for cool mountain streams) were mostly confined to the rich agricultural countries with suitable upland areas. These stretched from Kenya down to South Africa and included Uganda, Nyasaland (Malawi), Rhodesia (Zimbabwe), and Swaziland. However, records also reveal the introduction of many other species, such as Chinese carps, and the liberal transfer of many native species, such as the cichlids.

In the north, as part of its continuing irrigation program in the Nile Delta, Egypt built the Barrage Farm in 1919 to receive introductions and produce seed for stocking its coastal lakes. The El Mex Farm was constructed in 1931 at the pumping station near Alexandria, and a number of marine species, such as Dover sole and shrimps, were introduced into inland high-saline waters, such as Lake Qarun.

Conservation and Compensation in the New World

Because of a lack of tangible benefits, North American interest (and investment) in the hatchery propagation of marine species was waning rapidly by the 1920s. But in the United States it was on the increase for freshwater species - especially Pacific salmonids - and, fortunately, the techniques of propagation were now highly reliable. It was fortunate because of the crisis that was beginning to develop in the salmon fisheries of the Pacific Northwest, and nowhere was the crisis more keenly felt than in the vast area of the Columbia River watershed.

The fisheries of the giant Columbia River had supported some 50,000 persons and yielded about 18 million pounds of fish each year. However, a number of factors combined to threaten the salmon resources of the Basin. Among these were the opening of the Pacific Northwest territories at the end of the century, the construction of hydroelectric dams, the diversion of water for irrigation, and poor logging and mining practices.

Fish hatcheries and fish ladders were constructed in the region to mitigate some of the losses, but it was not until the Federal Power Act of 1920 that fishways were required at all private power projects. The Fish and Wildlife Conservation Act of 1934 that followed was the most important legal authority for ensuring both protection and compensation for the salmon fisheries affected by federal water projects. Together, these two acts were responsible for more than 400 million U.S. dollars spent on fish passages and propagation hatcheries constructed in the Columbia Basin.

World War II

During the war, as the North Sea was closed, nearshore fishing was concentrated along the safe west coast in the British Isles. It was proposed that fish production could be supplemented by increasing productivity of some Scottish sea lochs with inorganic fertilizers and by increasing resources of fish through the transplantation of juveniles, particularly flatfish.

Led by Fabius Gross from the University of Edinburgh, a team of scientists began the fertilization of Loch Craiglin with sodium nitrate and commercial superphosphate fertilizers supplied by Imperial Chemical Industries Ltd., the largest national producer. The fertilizers increased productivity in the loch, but most of the nutrients were taken up by the phytoplankton and algae. Food organisms suitable for growing flatfish were also increased, but not with the consistency required to support large populations.

The economics of one of the first true attempts to farm the sea were never tested, however. As fishing vessels began to return to the seas in 1944 and 1945, the group was disbanded, and with the early and untimely death of Gross in 1947, all further technical interest was lost.

Another event concerning aquatic husbandry during the war years occurred in Africa, which was a major resource of raw materials for the allies. Mining in South Africa, and in other countries such as Zambia and Zaire, was greatly expanded, and large pools of labor worked the mines, built railways, and manned ports to maintain the flow of copper and iron ores. This labor force had to be fed and, for a time, meat was secured by large hunting parties and by deliveries of beef from South Africa.

It was not long, however, before local herds of wild game had been depleted and, to make the situation more critical, the beef was being redirected toward armies and to the hungry of Europe. British and Belgian colonial administrators reacted to the crisis by ordering the construction of ponds to produce fish for the miners and their families. Many thousands of small fish ponds were dug and stocked with tilapia and other native species for food. The effort proved successful and, at the end of the war, the Conference Piscicole Anglo-Belge was organized for further postwar development of aquaculture for food production.

A third event involving aquaculture had even more far-reaching importance. Fish farming in what would become Israel had been developed in 1934 by immigrants from central Europe, who brought with them experience in the culture of their traditional (and prized) fish, the common carp. The first kibbutz fish farm was established in 1938 at Nir David, and by the end of the war there were 30 productive kibbutz farms with a water surface of 800 hectares.

Initially, traditional methods were used on the farms, but as land and water became scarcer, new systems and practices were developed that were unique and highly productive for arid lands. In time, these would make Israel self-sufficient in fish production and even an exporter. In addition, the program made the country one of the most progressive in the field of fish culture.

The Birth of Modern Aquaculture

The Postwar Years
The wartime interest in fish farming for food production dimmed with the end of the war. Without extensive harvesting for many years, coastal and oceanic fisheries were ripe for such an effort, and world harvests increased steadily as old fleets of traditional fishery nations were modernized and expanded. In 1950, a world harvest equaling that of 1938 (about 20.5 million tonnes) was realized and this was soon doubled.

The early postwar years, however, were years in which many developing countries were newly independent with swelling populations, and "food self-sufficiency" and "animal protein" became prominent problems. European governments continued to contribute significantly to increasing food resources through production schemes and direct technical assistance. This had a valuable impact on the further development of fish and shellfish farming. Science was taken out of the laboratory and applied in the field.

The pioneers in this effort were trained in basic biological sciences and devoted the greater part of their lives to working overseas on almost every aspect of improving aquatic animal production. C. Fred Hickling, for example, like many of his colleagues from the British Museum, first worked on fisheries in East Africa. He studied the genetics of tilapias and produced the first all-male populations. Later he continued his work at the fish culture station at Malacca in Malaysia, which he expanded with its Latin square of research ponds, and where he contributed to advances in soil and water chemistry.

Similarly, Antoon De Bont and Marcel Huet, from Belgium, spent much of their lives in Central Africa and Indonesia, working on the breeding of tilapias, carps, and general limnology, while Jacques Bard, of France, worked in West Africa and later South America on tilapias and many indigenous species. Other such individuals included W. Schaperclaus from Germany and Elek Woynarovich from Hungary.

In the 1950s, many of these pioneers helped the fish culture staff of the Food and Agriculture Organization of the United Nations (FAO) to spread tilapia species throughout Asia and the Pacific region in an attempt to provide easily produced and readily available protein to the rural poor. Unfortunately, the project was to have long-lasting repercussions, as the fish rapidly replaced indigenous fauna and became pests wherever they were introduced.

After World War II, the pressing priority for food in Japan meant that all forms of agriculture received high priority during the reconstruction, and the old technical infrastructure was rapidly replaced, with emphasis on practical production.

Similarly in Taiwan, following independence in 1949, the old Japanese research stations were used to develop fish and shellfish culture under the Joint Commission on Rural Reconstruction, funded by the Rockefeller Foundation. Under the direction of T. P. Chen, fish culture in Taiwan became an important economic industry, principally for the efficient farming of milkfish and the fattening of eels for the Japanese market. There were also successful research developments, particularly the control of breeding and propagation of silver carp, grass carp, and grey mullet and, for the first time, species of marine shrimp.

In the United Kingdom throughout the late 1950s, the government supported two research projects as part of its general program on marine biological research. One, under James Shelbourne at Lowestoft, was concerned with the breeding and propagation of marine flatfish, whereas the other, under Duncan Waugh at Conway, focused on the propagation of oysters.

In 1961 the British White Fish Authority, a quasi-government organization operated by the fishing industry, instigated projects to carry promising research results from these projects through to commercial implementation. The authority constructed two experimental hatcheries. One, for marine flatfish, was located at Port Erin on the Isle of Man, while the other, for oysters, was situated at Conway. The successful operation of and yields from these hatcheries enabled follow-up efforts to be made at field stations in an attempt to accelerate growth rates. One was constructed in Scotland for the production of flatfish in an enclosed loch at Ardtoe. Another was located at Hunterston in Ayrshire, in the heated effluent from a nuclear electrical generating station.

Shelbourne's successful propagation of marine flatfish in England was possible because of an important earlier discovery made by Gustav Rollefson in 1939. Rollefson had found that the nauplius of the brine shrimp was a useful live-food and small enough for feeding marine fish larvae. Moreover, the eggs of brine shrimp were at times encysted, and they could be stored conveniently for subsequent use.

After the war, the natural production of cysts was first exploited at the Great Salt Lake in Utah for growing tropical fish for the aquarium trade. This was rapidly followed by more controlled production in the solar saltworks of San Francisco Bay. The availability of large and reliable quantities of instant live-food opened the way for marine fish and shellfish production on a hatchery scale, but this time with the potential to produce viable fry instead of fragile, starving larvae.

Uncontrolled Expansion of the 1970s

Throughout the 1960s, work by the White Fish Authority on marine flatfish in England, the growing production of yellowtail in Japan, and the successful farming of eels in Taiwan captured the interest of governments and scientists alike all over the world. The concept of farming the sea, an idea that had lain essentially dormant for more than 50 years, was suddenly reborn, and it was also an idea that reinjected new life into the passive efforts of farming freshwater species.

The 1970s witnessed an explosion of effort by marine biologists the world over. In Norway and England, attention was focused on the production of Atlantic salmon and rainbow trout. In the United States, scientists reinvigorated their work on Pacific salmon and the farming of catfish. Israel, in its continuing search for food self-sufficiency, stepped up its concentration on carp and tilapia production through integrated farming. Hungary produced and bred individual strains of carp and adopted Chinese methods for integrated farming with ducks.

In Japan and Taiwan, work intensified on the production of marine shrimps, followed by efforts in the United States, Panama, Ecuador, Thailand, the Philippines, Indonesia, and England. The Philippines and Indonesia improved their milkfish production. Thailand and the United States pioneered research and development of freshwater prawns. Japan expanded its efforts on abalone, sea bream, mackerels, and edible marine algae. Taiwan improved production of milkfish and bred mullet for the first time. Spain and the Netherlands produced prodigious quantities of mollusks, while France worked on sea bass, flatfish, and oysters, and Italy on sea bass and sea bream. In Europe, Denmark, England, and France revitalized their flagging trout industries, and Germany its eel industry.

Such a decade of intensive effort was assisted in no small way by complementary technologies. Plastics and fiberglass revolutionized hatcheries. Traditional cast-iron and glass piping and large concrete tanks, characteristic of the late nineteenth- and early twentieth-century hatcheries, were replaced by light and easily assembled plastic and fiberglass materials, which were inert and noncorrosive. Floating cages and rafts proved effective substitutes for costly excavated ponds and replaced the need to purchase expensive flat land. And, finally, modern scientific equipment enabled water conditions to be instantly monitored, bypassing lengthy laboratory analyses.

The domestication of aquatic animals was again viewed as a new and promising field of modern agriculture. Governments poured in development funds on promises of a technology to provide cheap protein for rural populations and profits for investors. Professional societies were formed, and the new field was now called "aquaculture," which, unfortunately, would experience still another dip in its progress curve.

The Realities of the 1980s

The optimistic view of the potential of aquaculture generated in the 1970s received a serious setback in the 1980s because when technical achievements in the laboratories were expanded to commercial endeavors, they were not profitable.

The logistics of manufacturing and delivering increasingly large quantities of artificial feed had not been adequately estimated, and such feed often proved to be nutritionally deficient. Thus, large losses of stock were encountered through poor nutrition, which exposed the animals to a variety of new diseases for which there was no treatment.

In addition, there were shortages of skilled labor, and many farms were victims of unforeseen disasters, running the gamut from storms and floods to toxic algal blooms, water pollution, and a general failure of equipment. Consequently, the sporadic quantity and quality of many farmed products were not competitive with those of natural products, and many investments were lost.

The 1980s, therefore, became a period of intensive research. In most cases it amounted to backtracking on matters of nutrition, pathology, and engineering. But research also advanced in new areas, such as induced breeding to improve egg quality and genetics. Work on many species was stopped, and efforts were focused on those species that could be produced reliably and in the quantities to make investments profitable.

Fish and Shellfish as Food

Large resources of protein in the flesh of fish and shellfish contain many readily available amino acids, such as lysine, methionine, and tryptophan, in quantities comparable with those in eggs, meat, and milk. Indeed, with their unsaturated fats, vitamins, minerals, and trace elements, fish and shellfish constitute a near-perfect food for the human body.

Obviously, however, quantitative differences in nutritional composition occur among the many large groups of species, and also within groups at different times of the year. In general, freshwater and brackishwater species contain about 14 to 25 percent protein, whereas marine species contain 9 to 26 percent.

Freshwater species have a low percentage of fat (less than 1 percent), whereas in some marine fish it may be as high as 20 percent. Compared with animal fat, fish oils contain more polyunsaturated fats and, therefore, can be beneficial in reducing the buildup of cholesterol in blood. In addition, fish and shellfish are good sources of calcium and phosphorus, especially when small fish and crustaceans are consumed whole. They also contain iron and traces of copper, as well as B-complex vitamins.

Preservation of Fish

Fish and shellfish offered early cultures a rich source of animal protein. But both were (and are) extremely perishable food commodities, subject to the activity of microorganisms (such as bacteria, molds, and yeasts) and internal chemical deterioration (such as rancidity from breakdown of oils and fats and enzymatic actions), as well as targets of insects and scavengers in storage. Preventive measures to slow down these many processes of deterioration were, therefore, required.

The traditional preservation methods of indigenous cultures around the world today are probably indicative of much trial and error that went on in primitive societies as they perfected their processes and built experience in storing food. Although drying, smoking, salting, boiling, and fermenting have been the five basic traditional methods of preservation or processing, there are many, often subtle, differences in method among and even within cultures. These are due to different preferences for taste, texture, smell, color of the flesh, and social custom. They are also due to the environment of the consumers, the habitation in which they live and store food, and the availability of materials for processing, such as the fish and shellfish themselves, sources of fuel for the fire, and the availability and composition of salt.

Early fishermen must also have learned the hard way that some species, or their body organs, were highly toxic and often lethal, and that such dangers could occur at different times of the year. For example, several mollusks can cause paralytic shellfish poisoning if harvested and consumed during incidences of intensive algal blooms in hot weather, and some individuals within common reef-fish species of the Pacific Ocean may induce ciguatera poisoning. Parts of the fish can also be highly toxic. The puffer fish, for example, which is popular in Japan, must have its poisonous gallbladder carefully removed by licensed handlers before it can be sold.

Food and Fish and Shellfish

The texture, taste, and color of fish and shellfish can be affected by their diet. Farmed fish, particularly those in accelerating temperature regimes, can be fatty. Excess fat, however, can be removed by greatly reducing the diet before harvest, and by increasing water circulation to increase energy utilization.

The direct absorption of geosmin from the water can affect the taste of the flesh. Geosmin is produced by some species of actinomycetes and cyanobacteria, which may bloom under certain chemical and physical conditions. They can produce the earthy-muddy flavors that are common in catfish and other freshwater pond fish and are now reported in some marine shrimps. But such flavors can be avoided if stocks are maintained in high-quality geosmin-free water conditions before harvesting. The color of the flesh is readily changed by additives in the diet. Salmonids, for example, are often fed carotenoid pigments prior to harvest to redden the flesh for increased marketing appeal.

The majority of captive aquatic animals are almost entirely dependent on artificially prepared feeds, although they also consume any natural foods that might be available in their enclosures. Artificial diets are invariably high in animal protein (15 to 40 percent, depending on the age and specific needs of the population), complemented by cereal proteins and carbohydrates, oils, and additives of minerals and vitamins.

In recent years the trend has been to formulate diets for fish containing only oils of polyunsaturated fats, and to include chemical attractants and growth promoters. Fish nutrition remains a primary area of research at present because of its direct influence on the quality of the finished product and because feed is the largest operational cost of farming.

The State of Aquaculture in the Present Day

Aquaculture Products on Today's Markets

The general global prosperity of the 1980s increased market demand for a variety of fish and fisheries products, which made the culture of several new species economically feasible. In addition, such demand stimulated production of those species traditionally associated with farming, such as trout, Chinese and Indian carp, and oysters and mussels.

Investments have also continued in the enterprises of raising aquatic animals for recreational use (sport fishing), for medicines and medical research, for biological assay, and for their many valuable by-products. Moreover, many species are cultured successfully for the ornamental fish trade, and in the last 10 years, some new and unusual species have been cultured.

According to the FAO, there are some 150 individual species or species groups under some form of domestic culture for human consumption worldwide, together with 60 more that are identified only by genera and family names. There are about 90 known species of fish currently farmed, 23 species of crustaceans, 35 species of mollusks, 4 species of algae, and miscellaneous aquatic animals (such as frogs, turtles, sea squirts, pearl oysters, and sponges). Of these, some 34 species may be considered the most important, as they are farmed over a wide geographic area, and their individual total production is more than 20,000 tonnes annually.

In Asia, and to a much lesser extent in Eastern Europe, freshwater fishes are the most popular farmed commodities among consumers. The most important are those that have traditional value and have been in great demand for centuries, particularly silver carp, bighead carp, and common carp.

In western Asia, the indigenous Indian carps remain traditional and important. About 7 million tonnes of Chinese and Indian carps are raised annually. They are relatively cheap because they are easily farmed and require few costly inputs. They are usually sold fresh and uncleaned, or "in the round," and many buyers prefer them still alive. The milkfish remains an important staple fish on traditional markets in the Philippines and Indonesia, but production has decreased as coastal ponds have been converted for raising high-value marine shrimp. Because of the bony nature of milkfish, the flesh is removed and reprocessed, but in recent years there has been an increase in the popularity of small kippered "boneless" fish.

In Africa, and to a lesser extent parts of Asia and Latin America, the tilapias are a cheap and widely available farmed commodity, as they are easily raised by small-scale rural farmers in rain-fed ponds. The Nile tilapia is the most popular species because of its larger size. A domestic hybrid, the red tilapia, is proving to be better for small-scale entrepreneurial farming in these regions and is capturing small but medium-value markets, even in the United States and Europe. Smaller species of tilapia raised in some African countries are used to concoct "relishes," to make leafy energy foods more palatable.

The diverse family of freshwater catfishes all have good medium value. Both local and institutional markets have been developed in the last decade of the twentieth century for these higher-priced species, particularly channel catfish in the United States and South America. Production of channel catfish is so reliable that there is a continuous availability of many product forms for consumers, including "fast foods."

In Europe and North America, the high-value salmonids, which have now been economically important for more than a century, continue to be in great demand. They are raised in both fresh and marine waters. The most popular product for the retail and restaurant trade is pan-size rainbow trout, but by the end of the twentieth century there was intense production of Atlantic salmon, even in Chile and New Zealand. Because of oversupply, prices have dropped considerably, and producers are seeking other markets with a variety of product forms, such as smoked salmon, in a variety of sizes.

The national markets of most developed countries have unmet demands for all farmed marine fish. Compared with freshwater fish, all marine species have medium-to-high value and most are economic to raise. The most popular species currently farmed are mullet, sea bass, bream, grouper, and many marine flatfishes, but progress in raising the volume remains slow.

The most remarkable achievement has been the massive growth in the production of marine shrimp to meet a continuously increasing demand for crustaceans as a whole by markets in Europe, Japan, and the United States. Some 17 of these high-value species are under culture, with the giant tiger prawn and fleshy prawn the most important. Farmed shrimp industries are now economically important to many Asian countries, particularly Indonesia, the Philippines, Thailand, and Taiwan, but they are also important to several countries of Central America and to Ecuador in South America.

Farmed shrimp have advantages in uniformity and, in addition to supplying a range of markets for size, they also satisfy markets for a variety of other product forms. Nonetheless, freshwater crustaceans have not benefited from the popularity of marine shrimps. Farmed species, such as the high-value giant river prawn, freshwater lobsters, and crayfish, are still confined to local markets and usually sold fresh.

Marine mollusks continue to have worldwide consumer appeal. They appear on the luxury markets of developed countries, yet are still farmed for subsistence in some of the poorest countries of Africa. Intensive farm production systems for both oysters and mussels have replaced traditional culture practices in European and Mediterranean countries and also in North America. In Asia, farmed production of the abalone, Japanese or Manila clam, and the blood cockle has been substantially increased by new and rapidly expanding culture fisheries.

Most developed countries have small luxury markets for a number of specialized aquatic groups. These include the meats of certain farmed reptiles, especially crocodilians and turtles (which also have valuable by-products, such as skins and shells), and of amphibians, particularly frogs, which are raised for their legs.

Summary

Aquaculture has proved to be a remarkable sector of economic growth in recent years. The 1992 value of cultured aquatic animals and plants for food was more than 32.5 billion U.S. dollars, almost triple the first estimate of 12 billion U.S. dollars in 1984. This is due mostly to rapid increases in farm production of aquatic animals, as well as rising prices. Since 1984, farm production of aquatic animals alone has increased by 90 percent. Individually, the production of crustaceans has increased by more than 250 percent, finfish by 105 percent, and mollusks by 55 percent.

Domesticated aquatic animal production contributes significantly to meeting an increasing worldwide food demand. Indeed, annual world demand for fishery products by the year 2000 had been predicted to be 110 to 120 million tonnes, of which about 30 percent is for industrial uses, such as oils and animal feeds. Farming of aquatic animals now contributes about 14 million tonnes annually, almost entirely for human consumption. Because most of these products are sold fresh or iced on local markets, such domestic production supplies about half the world's consumption of fresh fishery products.

In terms of quantity and distribution, the traditional species remain the most important. Like agriculture, aquaculture relies on a small number of "crops" for the greater part of its total production. Farming is still dominated by freshwater fish, particularly the cyprinids (which account for half the total aquatic animal production worldwide), followed by the salmonids and tilapines. The penaeids are the most important family of crustaceans, and mytilids and ostreids are the principal mollusks.

The narrow reliance on a few key crops has implications for the future of aquatic farming, particularly with the increasing involvement of bioengineering in the genetics of these species. On the one hand, there is a need to maintain genetic diversity for the viability of major food crops and the conservation of genetic resources. On the other hand, there is a pressing need for the domestication of farmed aquatic animals, similar to that of terrestrial animals and poultry. Most aquatic animals now farmed are still only one or two generations removed from natural (or wild) stocks.

Although there is great optimism for the future domestication of aquatic animals through genetic selection and other technical improvements, there are increasing pressures on the industry. In particular, these are the competition for suitable land and water with urban centers and agriculture activities; the impact of nutrient loading on the environment from intensive production; the spread of farm diseases to wild stocks; and the interbreeding of farmed stocks with wild stocks. Nonetheless, despite these growing issues, and a prolonged and shaky history stretching back over 2,000 years, the domestication of aquatic animals seems here to stay.

Colin E. Nash

Bibliography

Chen, T. P. 1976. *Aquaculture practices in Taiwan.* Oxford.
China Fisheries Society. 1986. *Fan Li on pisciculture.* Peking.
Dobrai, L., and G. Pékh. n.d. *Fisheries in Hungary.* Budapest.
Dunfield, R. W. 1985. *The Atlantic salmon in the history of North America.* Canadian Special Publications of Fisheries and Aquatic Sciences 80. Ottawa.
Dyk, V., and R. Berka. 1988. Major stages of development in Bohemian fish pond management. *Papers of the Research Institute of Fishery and Hydrobiology, Vodňany, Czechoslovakia* 17: 3–44.
Graham, M. 1956. *Sea fisheries.* London.
Hepher, B., and Y. Pruginin. 1981. *Commercial fish farming: With special reference to fish culture in Israel.* New York.
Hickling, C. F. 1962. *Fish culture.* London.
Hora, S. L., and T. V. R. Pillay. 1962. *Handbook on fish culture in the Indo-Pacific region.* Rome.
Matsui, I. 1979. *Theory and practice of eel culture.* Tokyo.
Radcliffe, W. 1926. *Fishing from the earliest times.* London.
Shelbourne, J. E. 1964. The artificial propagation of marine fish. *Advances in Marine Biology* 2: 1–83.
Toussaint-Samat, Maguelonne. 1992. *History of food,* trans. Anthea Bell. Cambridge, Mass.
Vibert, R., and K. F. Lagler. 1961. *Pêches continentales.* Paris.

II.G.3 ❧ Camels

Camels are familiar to most of the English-speaking world only as beasts of burden, as Arab mounts on the silver screen, or as curiosities in the zoo. Camel meat and milk almost never find their way to the local grocer's shelves. In many parts of Africa and Asia, however, camel milk and meat are valuable sources of nutrition for many people. The following is a broad overview of the camel's current role as a food resource and a summary of evidence dealing with the early history of human reliance on camel products.

Camel

latter may be restricted to one or two short seasons, may fail to happen in any given year, or may be localized in a very small geographic area, leaving vast stretches of the environment parched and barren. As a result, the productive potential of these ecosystems varies greatly over time and space, and those inhabiting such areas must be able to adapt quickly to variability in food, forage, and water availability. Camels are often a vital part of the pastoral strategy for coping with such harsh conditions. They cover great distances in search of limited and highly scattered forage and water, which is then efficiently converted into milk and meat for human consumption. In times of prolonged heat or drought, camels may be the only productive livestock and, consequently, are invaluable resources during critical months or seasons of scarcity.

Two Camel Species

There are two extant species of camel: the one-humped dromedary *(Camelus dromedarius)* of the hot deserts of Africa, Arabia, and India; and the two-humped bactrian *(Camelus bactrianus)* of the seasonally cold, higher deserts of the Iranian plateau, central Asia, China, and Mongolia (Figures II.G.3.1 and II.G.3.2). The camel's closest living relatives belong to the once species-rich suborder Tylopoda, which today includes the llama, alpaca, guanaco, and vicuña of South America. In this chapter, the generic term "camel" is used to refer to both species of Old World camels when it is not necessary to distinguish between them. However, it is the case that dromedaries and bactrians are uniquely adapted to the extremes of their native environments, resulting in important differences between them.

The people who keep camels for food are generally nomadic pastoralists, who rely primarily on livestock for their livelihood and move regularly in order to care for their animals, which, in addition to camels, may include other species such as sheep, goats, and cattle. In both Africa and Asia, camel pastoralists inhabit arid environments characterized by extreme, often unpredictable, fluctuations in temperature and rainfall. The

Figure II.G.3.1. *Camelus dromedarius.*

Figure II.G.3.2. *Camelus bactrianus.*

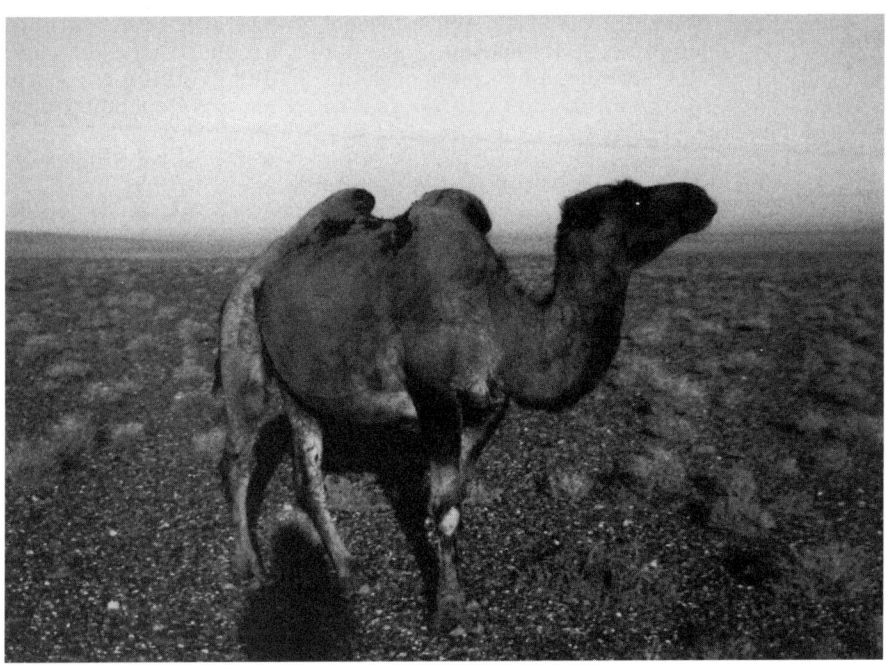

Dromedaries have longer legs, their winter coats are much thinner, and their summer coats are more reflective than those of bactrians. These traits are suited to surviving the intense and prolonged heat of the Arabian and African summers. Bactrians are also adapted to surviving in arid conditions, but their stockier builds and thick winter coats allow them to weather the icy winters of the highland deserts of Asia. In China, bactrians regularly experience temperatures of $-30°$ C ($-22°$ F) in the winter and $42°$ C ($107.6°$ F) in the summer (Wei 1984). Although bactrians can survive in a wide range of temperatures, they are usually not found where the mean annual temperature is above $21°$ C ($69.8°$ F) (Mason 1984).

Dromedaries and bactrians are not perfect biological species because they can (and do) mate. The resulting hybrids are larger than either parent and have one elongated hump. Unlike the hybrid offspring of horses and donkeys, first-generation camel hybrids are fertile (Gray 1954). However, if two first-generation hybrids are mated, the resulting second-generation hybrids display suboptimal qualities and are often infertile (Gray 1954; Bulliet 1975). Hybrid camels can be successfully mated with either a pure-blooded dromedary or a pure-blooded bactrian. The resulting offspring resemble the pure-blooded parent in size and number of humps (Bulliet 1975).

Historically, these first-generation hybrid camels were popular caravan animals due to their larger size and greater stamina than either purebred parent (Bulliet 1975; Toplyn 1995). Hybrid camels were also better able to survive the climatic extremes encountered at either end of the trade routes that connected China and the Iranian plateau with Arabia and Egypt. In order to maintain a constant supply of these large-bodied hybrids for caravan traffic, pastoralists had to continuously breed pure dromedary and bactrian parents so as to obtain viable hybrids. Today, hybrid camels are still being produced in the former Soviet Union, where dromedaries of the Turkmen tribes are bred with Kirghiz bactrian camels (Bulliet 1975).

Geographic Distributions

It is not clear from archaeological and paleontological data whether the natural geographic ranges of dromedaries and bactrians overlap or whether their modern ranges are the result of human intervention. Like horses, camels originated in North America and migrated to Asia around 3 to 4 million years ago (Wilson 1984; Stanley, Kadwell, and Wheeler 1994). During the Pleistocene, many species of camel inhabited the Eurasian and African landmasses. Their bones have been recovered across Asia from Siberia to India, from Eastern Europe, and across North Africa as far south as Olduvai Gorge (Howell, Fichter, and Wolff 1969; Badam 1979; Wilson 1984; Dubrovo and Nigarov 1990; Germonpré and Lbova 1996).

Indeed, camels seem to have been successful animals that enjoyed a wide distribution until the beginning of the Holocene (about 10,000 years ago), after which their remains become extremely rare in the archaeological record of central and southwestern Asia (Bulliet 1975; Zarins 1978; Hoch 1979; Wapnish 1984; Uerpmann 1987; Tchnernov 1989; Germonpré and Lbova 1996). The few pieces of evidence from the early Holocene suggest that wild camels were confined to the southern part of the Arabian Peninsula and the deserts of central Asia, and it was not until about 1500 B.C. that domestic camels began to spread across southwestern and central Asia to occupy their current ranges.

In other words, prior to domestication, wild camels seem to have been close to extinction – inhabiting severely restricted ranges in southern Arabia and in parts of central Asia (Bulliet 1975; Russell 1988). But today, domestic camels inhabit the arid regions of North and East Africa, the Arabian Peninsula, parts of Israel, Jordan, Syria, Turkey, Iraq, Iran, Pakistan, Afghanistan, northwestern India, central Asia, northwestern China, and southern Mongolia (Map II.G.3.1). Dromedaries were also introduced into Australia in the late 1800s, and today 15,000 to 20,000 feral dromedaries roam the central and western parts of that continent (McKnight 1969).

Access to water seems to have played a pivotal role in the decline of wild camel populations and may have been a significant factor in their domestication. Despite the camel's ability to survive without drinking for extended periods (weeks to months depending on the water content of their forage), eventually they do have to replace their water losses. Studies of wild camels in China and Mongolia indicate that severe droughts force them to congregate around the few remaining sources of water, which, among other things, exposes them to increased predation by wolves (Tulgat and Schaller 1992). In fact, recent droughts have caused a sharp decline in the wild camel populations in these areas. Yet domestic camels seem to avoid the problems of drought and predation through their association with humans. In Africa, Arabia, and Mongolia, camels often rely on humans to access water in wells or cisterns, especially when rain-fed waterholes dry up (Yagil 1985). Some camels have been known to wait by a well for weeks in order to secure water.

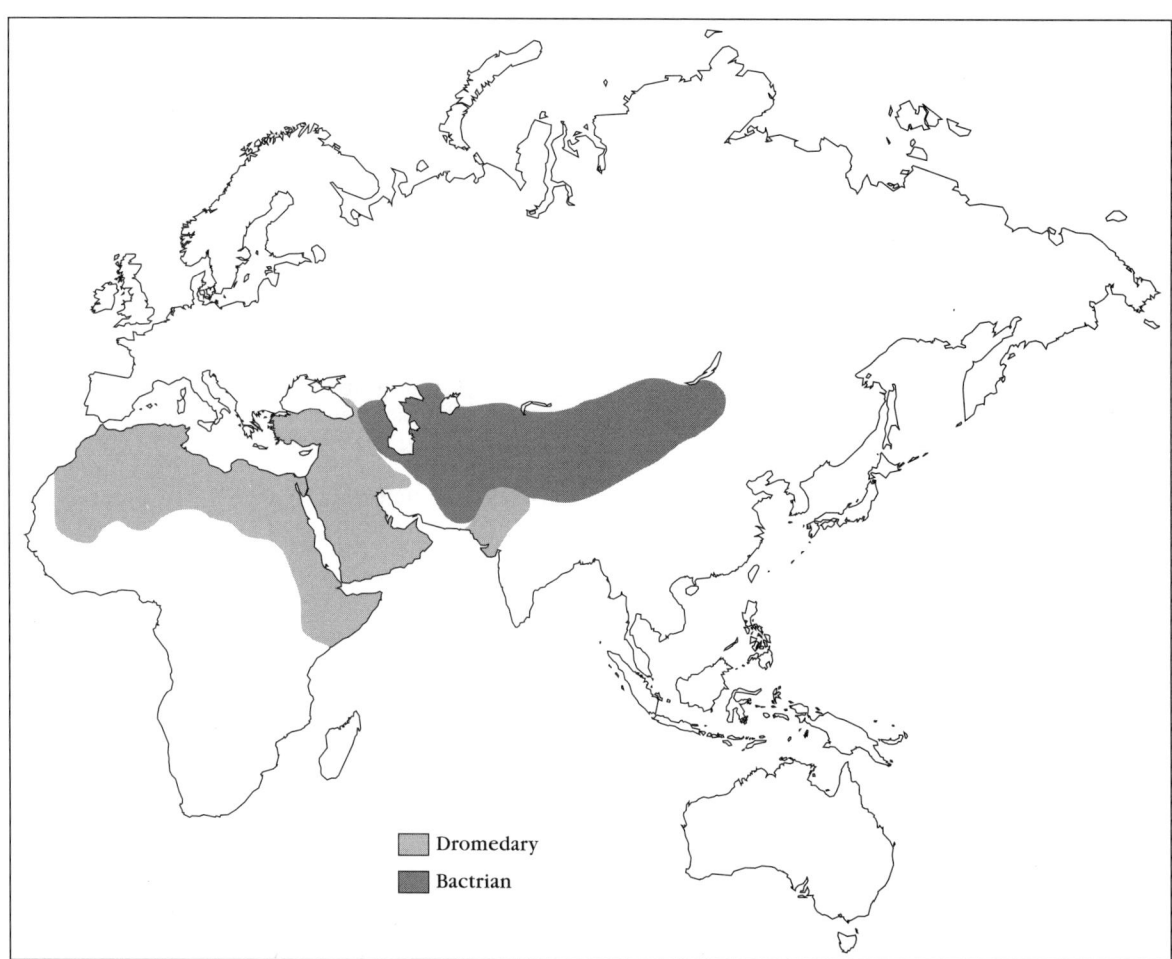

Map II.G.3.1. The approximate modern distribution of camels.

Camels, however, cannot always afford to flee a drought-stricken area for greener pastures and more abundant water because moist environments can also be deadly, especially to dromedaries. Humid environments with standing water are often breeding grounds for tsetse flies that transmit trypanosomiasis and other diseases (Fratkin and Smith 1994), which kill many camels every year and limit the distribution of the dromedary in Africa and India (Wilson 1984; Yagil 1985). Pastoralists are keenly aware that certain swampy areas spread disease and will take their camels there for water only when no other options are available (Fratkin and Smith 1994).

In addition, camels are notoriously maladapted to wet, muddy ground, which, because of their unique physiology of long legs, unilateral gait, and large padded feet, makes them unstable. They often pull muscles, dislocate joints, or break limbs if forced to cross such areas (Russell 1988). Moreover, camels are "front-wheel-drive" animals. Unlike horses, camels use their forelimbs rather than their hind limbs for propulsion. This trait, in combination with padded rather than hoofed feet, leaves them at a severe disadvantage in rocky and mountainous areas (Sato 1980; Russell 1988).

Food and Water Requirements

Compared to other common domestic livestock, such as cattle, sheep, and goats, camels are the most efficient users of water, much of which they can obtain from their herbivorous diet. When necessary, they conserve water by producing a very concentrated urine and dry feces and by reducing water lost through perspiration. In response to solar radiation, dromedaries tolerate core body temperature fluctuations from 34° C to 42° C (93.2° F to 107.6° F) throughout a day (Schmidt-Neilsen 1964), thereby decreasing the need to sweat to regulate body temperature. They can also tolerate a loss of significantly more water relative to their body weight than other livestock, which reach critical limits when they lose 10 percent of their body water (Russell 1988). Dromedaries regularly lose one-third of their body weight in water and survive (Yagil 1985).

The camel's humps are fat deposits that also aid in water conservation. By concentrating fat along the back, the rest of the body is able to cool itself more efficiently. The dorsal fat concentrations not only are insulation against the brunt of solar radiation but also allow the body to radiate heat more efficiently than would be possible if fat were distributed evenly over the whole body. In addition, behavioral mechanisms aid in cooling. During the hottest part of the day, dromedaries tend to lie near each other, facing the sun, which minimizes body surface exposure to direct solar radiation. Calluses on the knees and chest of the camel allow it to rest on hot sands and to elevate its midsection, which enhances airflow beneath the body. Thus, the animal can reach a

greater cooling potential. When water is available, a thirsty camel can replace even extensive water deficits by drinking as much as 200 liters in 3 minutes (Yagil 1985).

The camel's efficient use of water enables it to access seasonally and spatially dispersed high-quality forage that other livestock cannot. Often, forage protein content is inversely related to water availability (Russell 1988). Forage that is abundant after periodic rainfall or in areas around predictable water sources generally contains less protein than plants grown in drier areas. Camels move almost continuously as they graze, enabling them to cover many kilometers (km) each day; in fact, they can graze from 50 to 80 km away from water sources, whereas sheep and goats are limited to 20 to 30 km and cattle to 4 to 13 km (Dahl and Hjort 1976; Sato 1980; Russell 1988). As a result, camels are able to use the more concentrated packages of plant protein that are scattered across the landscape and located far enough away from water sources to be inaccessible to other livestock.

Camels are primarily browsers and are able to eat plant species that other livestock cannot, such as camel thorn, Acacia species, and saltbushes (Yagil 1982). When camels, cattle, sheep, and goats are herded together, they compete for some of the same plants, especially grasses (Sato 1980); consequently, camels are usually herded separately to ensure adequate forage for all livestock.

Although all livestock need salt in their diet, camels need more than sheep, goats, and cattle, and to meet these requirements, they must regularly visit areas with saline water or salt-rich plants (Sato 1980; Bernus 1990; Jabbur 1995). Alternatively, pastoralists may collect salt crystals or salt-rich earth to carry back to their camel herds.

In short, camels are well adapted to living in arid environments because they have evolved many mechanisms to conserve water and are able to consume a wide range of plant species. These adaptations decrease competition with other herbivores that share the same environments. From a husbandry standpoint, however, such adaptations often create extra work for pastoralists. If camels must be watered from a well, the human labor needed to satisfy their thirsts can be substantial, as even a small herd of 10 to 20 animals may need thousands of liters of water (Yagil 1985). This probably explains why, in the biblical story of Rebekah, Abraham's servant was so impressed by Rebekah's offer to water his 10 camels (Gen. 24:29).

Camels' Productive Potential: Labor and Food

Camels are physiologically much better adapted than humans to living in the deserts and semi-deserts of Africa and Asia, yet many people inhabit arid regions of the world. As part of their survival skills, humans have learned to use products from camels and to harness their power. However, not all people utilize camels and camel products the same way.

Labor

Historically, camels were very important for carrying loads over long distances and difficult terrain, and early long-distance trade flourished because of camel caravans. Exotic spices were transported from southern Arabia to the urban centers of Egypt and Mesopotamia during the first millennium B.C. Later, in the early centuries A.D., camels carried trade items along the Silk Route between Persia and China (Bulliet 1975). As mounts and water carriers, camels were also valuable in desert warfare. Some of the earliest literary accounts that mention domestic camels tell of mounted pastoralists from southern Arabia raiding villages to the north, and the animals continued as military mounts until as recently as the early part of the twentieth century in Arabia and India (Bulliet 1975). Camels have also served less dramatic but important roles in the daily lives of nomadic pastoralists, and still today, nomadic pastoralists use the animals to carry dwellings, household belongings, and old or very young people during regular migrations and relocations (Hobbs 1989).

With minimal loads, dromedaries can maintain a pace of 16 km (10 miles) per hour for up to 18 hours (Yagil 1985). Depending on the age, size, and health of the camel, a load of over 300 kilograms (kg) can be carried for several days, and up to 800 kg can be carried for short trips (Gauthier-Pilters and Dagg 1981). Bactrians in China continue to be used primarily as beasts of burden that can easily carry normal loads, averaging 40 percent of their live weight, 35 to 40 km in 24 hours (Wei 1984). Riding camels are also common in China and Mongolia; in fact, in the Chinese deserts, a bactrian camel is considered a more comfortable mount than a horse, and it maintains a pace of 5 to 10 km per hour (Wei 1984).

Today, however, the role of the camel as a transport animal is declining in many parts of the world. Except where automobiles and gasoline are still prohibitively expensive, camels are being replaced by motorized transport.

Milk Quality, Quantity, and Processing

Cross-culturally, milk is the most important edible product obtained from camels. Whether consumed fresh, processed for storage, or mixed with the milk of other livestock, this nutritious product is harvested by almost all pastoralists who keep camels. The absolute quantity and specific qualities of each camel's milk varies with the quantity and quality of available forage and water and the animal's health and age. The nutritional value of camel milk varies because of cultural norms regulating its collection, processing, and distribution within and outside of the pastoral group.

Milk quality. According to J. S. Jabbur (1995), camel milk is higher in vitamin C, fat, protein, and minerals than milk from other livestock raised under the same desert conditions. Certainly, this source of vitamin C is very important to people who inhabit areas where fresh fruits and vegetables are not available year-round. Camel milk contains between 5.7 and 9.8 mg of vitamin C, which is 3 times the amount found in cow's milk and 1.5 times the amount found in human milk (Yagil 1982).

The water content of camel milk varies inversely with the amount of available drinking water. Studies have found that when water was freely accessible, camels produced relatively concentrated milk, consisting of around 86 percent water; when drinking water was restricted, however, the milk became more diluted, with a water content of some 91 percent (Yagil 1982; el Amin 1984; Knoess 1984; Shalash 1984b). Such an adaptation is extremely valuable to both camel calves and people because, in conditions of heat stress and mild dehydration, the diluted milk serves as a source of needed liquid.

The fat content of camel milk also changes in response to the state of hydration of the animal. A hydrated dromedary produces milk with 3.0 percent to 5.38 percent fat, whereas the milk of one that is dehydrated may contain only 1.1 percent fat (Yagil 1982; el Amin 1984; Knoess 1984). Bactrian milkfat has been measured at slightly higher levels – 5.8 percent to 6.6 percent (Shalash 1984b). The various milks produced by other livestock species contain similar amounts of fat. Water buffalo, cows, goats, and sheep produce milk with 7.5, 3.5, 2.8, and 3.7 percent fat, respectively (Knoess 1984). Structurally, camel milkfat is somewhat different from cow, sheep, and goat milkfat in that it is distributed in very small globules (1.2 to 4.2 microns), which are also bound to proteins (Yagil 1982). This structure makes it very difficult to separate the fat from the milk and probably explains claims that butter cannot be made from camel milk. In fact, camel milk can be made into butter and cheese, but with some considerable difficulty, and consequently, when available, sheep, goats, and cattle are generally the preferred sources of milk for these products.

Lactose levels and protein concentrations do not vary with the hydration level of the animal. There are, however, individual and breed differences. Protein may constitute between 2 and 5.5 percent of camel milk, and some camels produce sweeter-tasting milk with lactose levels of 5.8 percent or more. Lower lactose levels are also common and give the milk a slightly sour taste (Yagil 1982). Buffalo, cow, goat, and sheep milk contain similar levels of lactose (Knoess 1984), although those of horse and human milk are higher (6.9 and 7.0 percent, respectively) (Shalash 1984b).

Milk quantity. It is difficult to compare milk yields between dromedaries and bactrians and between different populations of camels from around the world.

Daily milk yields seem to vary a great deal with the season, the age of the calf, and the availability of forage and water. Lactation begins when a camel gives birth, and its duration varies depending on food and water availability. Milk production will normally cease when the camel becomes pregnant again or if the calf dies, but pastoralists have developed ingenious methods of encouraging the camel to continue to produce milk when the latter occurs. For example, the camel is often tricked into thinking that her calf is still alive by the pastoralists' covering another calf with the skin and scent of the dead calf and encouraging it to suckle (Yagil 1982).

As a rule, bactrians lactate continuously for 14 to 16 months (Wei 1984), whereas dromedaries lactate for 12 to 20 months after a calf is born (Sato 1980; Yagil 1982). In parts of Africa, sheep and goats will give milk for only 3 to 4 months, and cattle for about 10 months (Sato 1980). Therefore, if people relied only on cattle or sheep and goats for milk, they would have to do without an important part of their diet for several months at a time.

Various methods of measuring camel milk yields have generated a wide range of daily and annual production estimates. Most of these are not explicit about whether the volume of milk obtained represents only the amount destined for human consumption or whether it also includes the amount normally consumed by the calf. Nevertheless, a survey of the literature indicates that dromedaries produce more milk on average than bactrians and that dromedary milk yields from across Asia, India, and Africa vary between 3.5 and 50 kg per day (Yagil 1982; Knoess 1984). In East Africa, camels produce an average of 3.5 to 4.0 liters of milk per day in the dry season and up to 10 liters per day in the wet season (Fratkin and Smith 1994). This quantity is quite impressive when compared to cattle in the same environment, which were able to produce only 1 liter per day in the wet season and 0 to 0.2 liters in the dry season. In northern Kenya, camels give twice as much milk as cattle and nine times that of sheep and goats (Sato 1980).

A camel's ability to produce milk is also influenced by the number of times it is milked per day, with more frequent milkings increasing a dam's total milk yield by 10 to 12 percent (Shalash 1984b). Milking frequency is a function of the herding practices employed and the household's need for milk. If camels must graze far away from the household, then they are milked less frequently than animals that graze nearby. In Sudan, hydrated camels yield 2.5 to 5 kg of milk at midday, and morning and evening milkings each yield 3.5 to 5 kg, which means a daily milk yield of 8.5 to 15 kg (Hjort and Dahl 1984). Raikas in India can obtain up to 10 liters of milk per day from their camels by milking them three to five times daily (Köhler-Rollefson 1992).

Bactrian camels produce an average of 5 kg of milk per day, although 15 to 20 kg have been obtained from specific animals. In China, most of the milk is left for the calf, and only about 2 kg is milked for human consumption (Yagil 1982).

Milk processing. Cultural practices can have a large effect on the nutritional benefits of camel milk, and many differences exist in milk-processing methods, the percentage of the diet derived from milk and milk products, and the distribution of the milk products within and outside the group. In most instances, camel milk is mixed with the milk of other lactating animals before it is consumed or processed, and if the milk is not to be consumed fresh, it is quickly processed to keep it from spoiling. Such processing usually results in those fermented milk products that are ubiquitous wherever milk is consumed. They are known by a variety of names around the world – such as kefir, *matzoon, dahdi,* yoghurt, and *lebben,* to name a few – but all are produced by the same basic method.

First, the milk is boiled for several minutes, which kills any pathogenic bacteria that may be in it. Once the milk has cooled to 79° F to 86° F, a starter culture from a previous batch of fermented milk is added. The milk is stirred and allowed to ferment overnight at room temperature, after which the resulting product can be safely stored for several days at room temperature (Yagil 1982). The fermentation process generally decreases the lactose content of the milk by converting it to either ethyl alcohol or lactic acid depending on the type of bacteria used. In human populations that do not maintain high lactase (the enzyme needed to digest lactose) levels as adults, soured or fermented milk is the preferred form for consumption (Simoons 1981). However, most human populations that have kept camels for centuries maintain high lactase levels as adults (Yagil 1982).

Another common method of preserving raw milk is to gently boil and evaporate it over a fire. The resulting solids (fats and proteins) are mixed with sugar to form a sweet, buttery, semisolid, cheese-like substance (Yagil 1982). To make butter requires up to 4 hours of churning or the use of a special blender, and the result generally has a greasy consistency. Most often, it is used for cooking, as a cosmetic, and for medicinal purposes. Buttermilk, left over from the butter-making process, often serves as a base for soup (Yagil 1982).

Milk as a Dietary Staple

G. Dahl and A. Hjort (1984) have calculated that 4 kg of camel milk will deliver an individual's daily caloric needs and more than enough protein, which means that a herd of 18 to 20 camels can supply the nutritional needs of a six-person family (two adults and four children). Most camel pastoralists, however, do not live on milk alone; domestic grains, hunted game, and gathered wild plants also contribute significantly to their diets (Hobbs 1989; Fratkin and Smith 1994; Jabbur 1995).

Cultural practices surrounding the use of camel milk vary greatly around the world. In India, for example, its consumption is limited to the camel-breeding caste known as the Raikas (Köhler-Rollefson 1996), and both the sale and the processing of camel milk into curds is taboo, although it may be given away (Köhler-Rollefson 1992). Raikas usually drink camel milk fresh, but on some occasions it is boiled and sweetened or made into rice pudding. Such practices and regulations ensure that most of the milk produced by Indian camels is not consumed by humans and that few Indian people outside of the Raika caste ever taste it.

In Arabia, Africa, and central Asia, however, the camel's milk-producing ability is fully utilized. The Rwala of Arabia claim (apparently correctly) that camel milk, supplemented with wild game, roots, and seeds, constitutes a sufficient diet (Lancaster and Lancaster 1990), although camel milk has recently become less important in the diets of Arabian Bedouins, who are being forced to settle permanently and sell their camel herds (Köhler-Rollefson 1993). For many in Africa, however, milk – including that of camels – is still a major dietary component. It supplies fully 75 percent of the daily calories in Rendille diets, 60 percent in Maasai diets, 60 to 70 percent in Boran diets, and 62 percent in Turkana diets (Fratkin and Roth 1990). In Kazakhstan, milk and milk products can supply up to 90 percent of the daily diet, and although this milk comes from several species of livestock, camels provide 37 percent of the total, sheep another 30 percent, yak 23 percent, and cows 10 percent (Yagil 1982).

Meat

Worldwide, labor and milk are the most important products obtained from camels, and often, camel pastoralists must choose husbandry strategies that optimize the production of milk and labor at the expense of meat yields. Such strategies emphasize the retention of adult females and the culling of young, unnecessary males, with labor supplied by nonpregnant females and/or castrated adult males (Wapnish 1984). The result is to limit the number of mature animals that can be harvested for meat. Generally, only old animals and young males not needed for breeding purposes are slaughtered. In many traditional societies, young camels are slaughtered only for special ceremonies and celebrations, and other unwanted animals are usually sold in commercial markets (Wapnish 1981; el Amin 1984; Köhler-Rollefson 1996).

In modern Sudan, however, pastoralists who raise camels rarely consume their meat but rather sell old animals to international markets for consumption in Egypt, Libya, and Saudi Arabia (el Amin 1984). Meat from old camels is tough and (save for their livers) not highly regarded among urban consumers, whereas meat from camels 5 years old and younger is as tender (and as highly valued) as beef; in fact, camel meat is said to taste like coarse, slightly sweet beef (el Amin 1984; Shalash 1984a).

The slaughter of an adult camel produces a large quantity of meat. Male dromedary carcasses may weigh more than 400 kg, whereas a bactrian may exceed 650 kg (Yagil 1982; Wei 1984). In general, a dressed dromedary carcass yields between 52.6 and 76.6 percent meat (el Amin 1984), and dressed bactrian carcasses have been reported to yield 35.4 to 51.7 percent (Wei 1984). The meat is generally very lean, with the total fat content of a carcass varying between 0 and 4.8 percent, depending on the age and nutritional status of the animal. The fat is concentrated in the hump and around the kidneys; that from the hump is melted and used instead of butter for cooking by some Arabian Bedouins (Jabbur 1995).

In addition to husbandry considerations, cultural and religious proscriptions limit the use of camel meat in many countries. In India, for example, Hindus will not eat camel meat, and it is also avoided by Christian Copts of Egypt, Christian Ethiopians, Zoroastrians of Iran, Mandaeans of Iraq and Iran, Nosaioris of Syria, and many Jews (Yagil 1982).

Blood

Several groups in eastern Africa use the blood of camels (as well as that of cattle) as a food resource that supplies valuable nutrients, including iron, salts, protein, and vitamin D (Yagil 1982). Blood may be drawn from a camel up to twice a month, and the animal can produce between 2 and 5.5 liters with each bleeding (Shalash 1984a; Bollig 1992). Blood is usually processed before consumption by first collecting it in a bowl and stirring it with a stick. Because fibrin, a blood-clotting protein, collects on the stick, it is easily separated from the rest of the blood and generally roasted before it is eaten. The remaining blood is either mixed with milk or boiled and mixed with maize flour (Bollig 1992).

Other Products

Camels provide many other valuable products, including wool, urine, and dung. In Sudan and India, dromedary wool is collected as the animals begin to molt and is used to make jackets, robes, tents, ropes, blankets, and carpets (el Amin 1984; Köhler-Rollefson 1992). In China and Mongolia, bactrian wool is a highly valued product that is often made into cushions, mattresses, bags, and ropes (Wei 1984). Among the Bedouins of Arabia, camel urine is used as a hair tonic (Jabbur 1995). Apparently its high salt content gives hair a reddish tint and prevents vermin infestations. Dung, also a valuable commodity, is often dried and stored for heating and cooking fuel (Jabbur 1995). And finally, if a person is lost in the desert and desperate for water, a camel may be slaughtered for the water contained in its stomach (Jabbur 1995).

Husbandry Considerations

Given the previous discussion of the camel's productive potential, one might wonder why camels are not more widely and intensively herded, or why people bother to herd other livestock with their camels. These questions are best answered by examining the camel's reproductive characteristics and the resulting husbandry strategies employed by camel pastoralists. Pastoralists have developed a variety of strategies that optimize the camel's productive potential in their particular social and ecological environment. Specifically (as already noted), pastoralists must balance the harvesting of camel products today against the need for future herd growth. This is usually calculated in terms of how much milk and meat can be taken for human consumption versus the amount of milk required by calves and the number of animals necessary to meet future production needs and to hedge against future unpredictable calamities.

Life History and Reproductive Characteristics

An animal's ability to reproduce quickly is a valuable trait to pastoralists. Reproductive potential depends on the age of first reproduction, the potential number of offspring per year, and infant mortality. A quick comparison of annual calving rates – 0.4 or less for camels, 0.4 to 0.8 for cattle, and 0.8 to 2.0 for sheep and goats – shows that camels are among the slowest reproducers of any domestic livestock species (Russell 1988; Herren 1992). Their low rate results from a 12- to 13-month gestation period (which is shorter for dromedaries than bactrians) and, typically, a 24- to 36-month span between births. Other factors that lower reproductive potential include the frequent restriction of breeding to rainy seasons and susceptibility to trypanosome, brucellosis, and pasteurellosis infections that trigger abortions.

The interval between births can be narrowed with intensive management practices, but this practice appears to shorten the female's life and limit the total number of offspring (Bollig 1992). Because camel herds increase at a rate of 8 percent or less annually, it takes a minimum of 15 years, and potentially as many as 50 years or more, for one to double in size (Dahl and Hjort 1976; Russell 1988; McCabe 1990). Such slow reproductive rates directly affect how people manage camel herds for food production and how they manage social obligations and their own reproductive rates (Galvin, Coppock, and Leslie 1994). Because camels will lactate only after giving birth and usually stop lactating shortly after becoming pregnant again, pastoralists carefully manage herds to ensure that at least some animals are lactating at any given time. But even with good luck and careful management, only 15 to 22 percent of the females may be lactating at one time. The camel's low calving rate also limits the number of young males that can be slaughtered for meat (Herren 1992). But the trade-off is that

if a calf is slaughtered, all of the dam's milk becomes available for human consumption, providing, of course, that the dam can be tricked into continuing lactation.

Human Labor

Human labor requirements are an important obstacle to the efficient utilization of domestic animals in pastoral societies because the availability of this labor limits the total number of livestock that can be herded by a single household. As we have seen, differing needs for food, water, preferred forage, rates of locomotion, duration of milk production, and breeding cycles prevent sheep, goats, cattle, and camels from being herded in a single group. Labor requirements are not constant throughout the year, but as herds are divided into milking and nonmilking and breeding and nonbreeding groups, more labor is required (Sato 1980; Roth 1990; Fratkin and Smith 1994). Pastoralists also face the constant problem of maintaining that delicate balance between labor requirements necessary to care for livestock and the number of people that can be supported by a given number of livestock (Fratkin and Smith 1994). To achieve and maintain this balance was doubtless at the root of the development of many inheritance, exchange, ritual, and human population control practices among camel pastoralists (Sato 1980; Fratkin and Smith 1994; Galvin et al. 1994).

Differences in livestock water requirements, forage plant species preferences, and grazing speed frequently force pastoral subsistence groups to split up for large portions of the year (Sato 1980; Sperling 1987; Bollig 1992; Fratkin and Smith 1994). This split often takes place along age or gender lines, resulting in dramatically different diets among members of the society (Sato 1980; Galvin et al. 1994). Illustrative are the Rendille of Kenya, who strictly delegate performance of the various herding tasks. Camels may be herded and milked only by young unmarried men; consequently, this segment of the Rendille population spends the longest time away from the main camp and covers the greatest distances during the grazing rounds. While on herding duty, these men subsist solely on camel milk and blood. Unmarried men and women herd small stock (sheep and goats) and consume both maize meal and milk while away from the base camp during the dry season. Adults, children, and the elderly, who remain at the base camp throughout the dry season, must subsist primarily on maize meal because few lactating animals can be supported on the meager forage available near the camp (Sato 1980).

Mixed Herding Strategies

Given that herding several different livestock species requires the division of pastoral societies and more herding labor than "camel-only" strategies, one might ask why so many pastoral societies go to such trouble. The answer is that a mixed pastoral system is an effective hedge against episodes of food scarcity. For example, if a camel herd is wiped out by a disease, it may take a lifetime to rebuild it. Alternatively, sheep and goats, although more likely to die during extended droughts, are able to quickly reproduce their numbers. Moreover, in most pastoral economies, sheep and goats satisfy immediate needs for meat and are often exchanged for grains.

Camels, however, are kept for the products that can be obtained from live animals during times of scarcity. In short, pastoralists use sheep and goats as we would use spending money, whereas camels are a form of stored wealth that might be equated with long-term stock or bond investments. In addition to maintaining diverse livestock herds, many pastoralists further diversify their resource base through trading relationships. They exchange animals and animal products for agricultural and industrial products and may also "loan" animals to relatives and neighbors or "adopt" children if herding requirements exceed the available labor (Russell 1988). These relationships can be used to optimize herd production and labor utilization over a greater geographic area.

Moreover, camels and other livestock can be viewed as a form of stored food for pastoralists. They not only represent food reserves that can be utilized on a regular basis but also serve to concentrate scattered or inedible nutrients into highly nutritious and accessible packages for human consumption (Russell 1988). Additionally, to return to the theme of stored wealth, the ability of camels to survive severe droughts better than other livestock, as well as their 30-year lifespan, makes them desirable "banks." For example, during a series of droughts in northern Africa between 1968 and 1973, the Tuareg lost 63 percent of their cattle and 47 percent of their sheep but only 38 percent of their camels (Bernus 1990). After a severe drought, camels can be sold or exchanged for necessities and to replace lost livestock.

The Camel in Antiquity

Very little is known about the earliest culinary uses of camels because of the nature of the archaeological record and because of the camel's preference for desert environments. The archaeological record is generally best preserved within structures such as buildings, cities, and natural enclosures such as caves. Camels, however, do not, and presumably did not, live in these environments. Not surprisingly, then, very few archaeological sites have produced evidence for the early use of camels. Before they were domesticated, camels were hunted for their meat, hides, and bones, and it is doubtful that they were exploited for their milk until after domestication.

But before humans could hunt wild camels or, later, milk domestic camels, humans first had to come into contact with them, and human–camel interaction

is rarely documented in the archaeological record prior to the third millennium B.C. What little evidence of such contact is available comes from southwestern Asia (the presumed refuge of the wild dromedary) and (for the bactrian camel) from sites on the Iranian plateau, in central Asia, and in China (Map II.G.3.2).

Dromedary Domestication

Camel bones from Paleolithic sites (before 10,000 B.C.) in Egypt, Sudan, Jordan, Syria, and Israel attest to the wide distribution of a camel species – presumably the dromedary – prior to the Holocene. Subsequently, however, camel remains become much more rare, suggesting that they either were not in the vicinity of archaeological sites or, for some unknown reason, were not a regular food source.

Some of the earliest rock art, dated between 6000 and 3500 B.C., shows dromedaries and speared dromedaries (Anati 1970; Zarins 1989), and archaeological evidence confirms the presence of camels in southern Arabia at this time. At Sihi, a shell midden on the Red Sea coast, a camel mandible was recovered and directly radiocarbon-dated to about 7000 B.C. (Grigson 1989). Moreover, camel bones from southern Jordan were found in seventh-millennium-B.C. contexts (Köhler 1984), whereas other camel remains discovered in the United Arab Emirates were likely from the fourth millennium B.C. (Uerpmann 1987).

In southern Arabia, rock art images showing hunting scenes, hunting parties, and the use of bows and arrows provide pictographic evidence that local hunters were responsible for the camel bones found at several of the area's sites and dating from between 3500 and 1900 B.C. (Zarins 1989). Third-millennium-B.C. sites along the Gulf coast of the United Arab Emirates have also yielded numerous such bones (Hoch 1979; Uerpmann 1987), including those from the island site of Umm an-Nar, where, although it is not clear whether the camels were wild or domesticated, they were most certainly introduced by humans (Hoch 1979).

The long history of human–camel interaction in southern Arabia indicates a likely environment for the occurrence of domestication but does not document exactly when such an event might have happened. However, it would seem that we can actually spy early domestic camels to the north of Arabia. In the Sinai and the Levant, camel images are absent from rock art traditions (suggesting that wild camels were unknown), but their bones nonetheless begin to appear in second-millennium-B.C. urban sites (Lernau 1978; Hakker-Orion 1984; Zarins 1989). For an explanation, we return to southern Arabia, where people for millennia had kept sheep, goats, and cattle and lived in permanent structures made of stone. But then, presumably, the ecological changes caused by desiccation and a concomitant expansion of the desert forced the adoption of a more mobile lifestyle. It is believed, in other words, that the bones found on

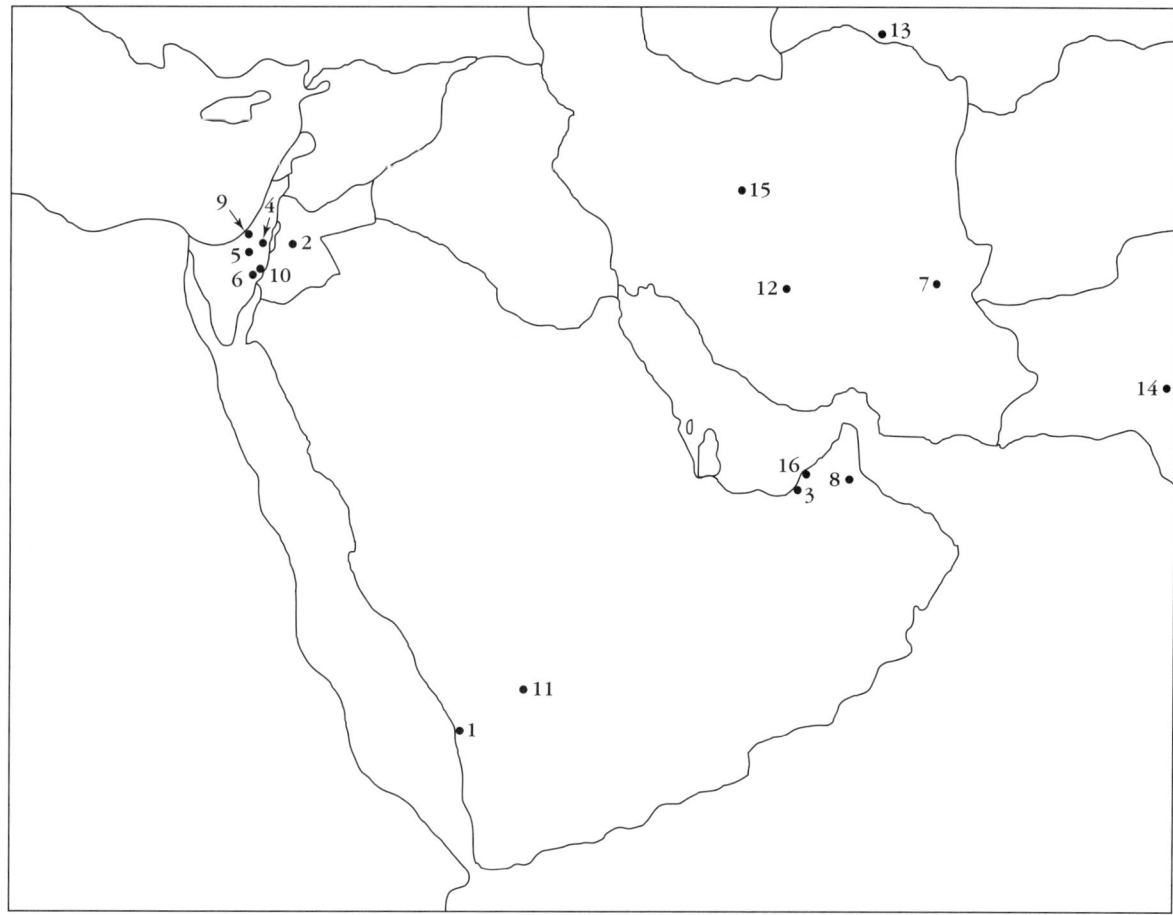

Map II.G.3.2. Archaeological sites mentioned in the text.

1.	Sihi	5.	Bir Resisim	9.	Tell Jemmeh	13.	Anau

1. Sihi
2. Ain al Assad
3. Umm an-Nar
4. Arad

5. Bir Resisim
6. Timna
7. Shar-i Sokhta
8. Hili 8

9. Tell Jemmeh
10. Wadi Arabah site #2
11. Bir Hima region
12. Tal-e Malyan

13. Anau
14. Mohenjo-daro
15. Sialk
16. Ras Ghanada

the northern edge of the desert were those of domes-ticated camels, upon which the now mobile pastoral-ists from southern Arabia had begun to visit the urban centers of the north (Tchnernov 1989; Zarins 1989).

Bactrian Domestication

The early history of human–bactrian interaction is poorly understood at present. This is partly because of a limited amount of archaeological investigation of central Asian sites and partly because of the inaccessi-bility of most Russian and Chinese documents to out-side researchers. Although evidence for the use of bactrian camels in Neolithic China is practically nonexistent (because few animal bones were ever saved or studied), an exception is one camel bone from a site near Lake Burkol in the northeastern part of Xinjiang Province; this bone has been radiocarbon-dated to 3000 B.C. (Olsen 1988). Rock art from north-ern China and Inner Mongolia also attests to the pres-ence of bactrians; however, dates for this art are highly speculative. Not until the Zhou Dynasty (c. 1100–771 B.C.) do Chinese literary sources confirm that bactrian camels were domesticated and employed as beasts of burden (Olsen 1988).

Early evidence for the presence of camels on the Iranian plateau is found at the site of Shar-i Sokhta (Compagnoni and Tosi 1978), where bones, dung (contained in a ceramic jar), and hair (woven into a piece of fabric), dating from roughly 2600 B.C., were found. These discoveries suggest that people were already utilizing several valuable resources from camels that presumably lived near the site. Other finds indicate that camels in the Indus Valley at the site of Mohenjo-daro by 2300 B.C. (Meadow 1984) were bactrians. A pottery shard from a contemporary site on the Iranian plateau depicted a bactrian, and no images of dromedaries have been found from this period (Compagnoni and Tosi 1978). However, there is no consensus on whether the bones from these areas are those of dromedaries or bactrians (Compagnoni and Tosi 1978; Meadow 1984; Wapnish 1984), largely because there is evidence of extensive trading between the Arabian Peninsula and Iran by the first half of the third millennium B.C. (Hoch 1979), and dromedaries could have been introduced to the Iranian sites from Arabia the trading network.

Domestication as Beasts of Burden

The distribution of camel bones at Tell Jemmeh, an urban site in southern Israel, may reveal when and why camels finally became an important domestic animal across southwestern Asia. Their bones are absent from the earliest levels of this site – the Chalcolithic (c. 3200 B.C.) and Middle Bronze II (c. 1650–1550 B.C.) (Wapnish 1981), with the first deposits of camel remains dating from between approximately 1400 and 800 B.C. But over this 600-year period, only 7 camel bones were left behind to be recovered. Eight more showed up for the following century, when the Assyrians began to exert their influence at the site through military campaigns, and 40 bones were deposited between 675 and 600 B.C. – a 75-year period that corresponds to the city's association with the Assyrian invasions of Egypt. Then, from the beginning of the sixth century B.C. until occupation of the site ended at around 200 B.C., over 273 camel bones were left behind. These last four centuries witnessed periods of political instability as first neo-Babylonians, then Persians, and finally Alexander the Great took control of the site.

The question of why camel remains steadily increased in this urban center – if it was well supplied with meat from domestic cattle, donkeys, sheep, goats, pigs, and wild game – may be answered by the fact that camels found increasing economic and political importance as beasts of burden. The long-distance trade in incense and spices from southern Arabia to the Levant and beyond had become lucrative. Empires wanted to control and profit from this trade but needed to be able to supply and move troops in these arid regions. Both enterprises depended on the camel's unique ability to haul heavy loads over long distances while consuming little water, and a whole economy grew up around this ability (Wapnish 1981). Archaeological investigations at two other sites in the region also support this interpretation. Camel bones from Wadi Arabah No. 2 and Timna, two copper-production sites (1350–1150 B.C.), indicate that camels were used to transport this valuable product to urban markets (Rothenberg 1972; Zarins 1989).

At the site of Tal-e Malyan, in present-day Iran, a similar pattern of camel introduction is evident. Although the site was occupied from at least 3400

B.C. and has yielded thousands of animal bones, those of camels do not appear until the Middle Elamite period (1600–1000 B.C.) (Zeder 1984). Regional political instability may have led to the city's decline during these centuries, encouraging people to abandon their urban lifestyles for a more mobile pastoral existence. Camels introduced to the region by caravaneers figured prominently in the new pastoral system.

The Assyrians were instrumental in introducing camels to people across Southwest Asia, although not always peacefully, and their texts and monuments provide us with much of the available evidence about the historical use and distribution of dromedaries and bactrians. Some of the earliest written accounts of dromedaries come from an Assyrian cuneiform text, written between 1074 and 1057 B.C., which mentions that the animals were brought to Nineveh and exhibited with other exotic animals (Zarins 1989). Two bactrian camels are depicted on the Black Obelisk of Shalmaneser III of Assyria, which has been dated to 856 B.C. (Bulliet 1975).

All of the preceding tends to fit rather nicely with a synthetic hypothesis of the origins of dromedary pastoralism proposed by J. Zarins (1989). The camel was probably hunted for its meat in southern Arabia until around 2200 B.C., when dromedaries were domesticated and kept for milking purposes. However, they were not ridden or used as beasts of burden until around 1500 B.C. – about the time when saddles were developed for them. Afterward, camels were increasingly employed for riding and as pack animals for overland trade. After about 1000 B.C., saddle technology was improved, and camels became very important in warfare as mounts for armed soldiers (Bulliet 1975).

The origin of domesticated bactrians is more obscure. Presumably, the process of their domestication followed a similar path, although we do not know if they were domesticated earlier or around the same time as dromedaries. It is clear, however, that by the first millennium B.C., if not earlier, bactrians, too, were being used as pack animals (Bulliet 1975).

The archaeological record also plainly indicates that overland trade and warfare introduced camels to peoples who lived beyond the animals' native deserts. Apparently, these people appreciated the camel's ability to produce copious amounts of milk year-round and to carry large burdens over great distances in environments that were inhospitable to most other livestock. Moreover, the late appearance of indisputably domesticated camels suggests that they were incorporated into already-established pastoral lifestyles with sheep, goats, and cattle.

Our understanding of the origins of the use of camels as a food resource should improve as current efforts in identifying and studying the archaeological traces of early pastoralists are completed and published. In addition, ethnographic studies of modern camel pastoralists that attempt to quantify the costs and benefits of camel husbandry under specified ecological and social conditions would enhance our understanding of the origins of such practices. And finally, an ongoing study of camels' genetic variability may someday help to trace the origins and subsequent dispersal of camels and the pastoral systems associated with camel husbandry.

Elizabeth A. Stephens

A Jacob Javits Fellowship and the Haury Educational Fund for Archaeology generously funded research leading to the production of this chapter. Fieldwork was graciously supported by Dr. John Olsen. I would also like to thank Dr. Mary Stiner, Dr. Carol Kramer, Dr. Stephen Zegura, Dr. Michael Hammer, Jeff Brantingham, Lane Therrell, Dr. Andrew Standeven, and anonymous reviewers for their help, encouragement, and valuable comments on my research.

Bibliography

Anati, E. 1970. Rock engravings of Dahthami wells in central Arabia. *Bollettino del Centro Camuno di Studi Preistorici* 5: 99–158.

Badam, G. L. 1979. *Pleistocene fauna of India: With special reference to Siwaliks.* Deccan College, India.

Bernus, E. 1990. Dates, dromedaries, and drought: Diversification in Tuareg pastoral systems. In *The world of pastoralism: Herding systems in comparative perspective,* ed. J. G. Galaty and D. L. Johnson, 149–76. New York.

Bollig, M. 1992. East Pokot camel husbandry. *Nomadic Peoples* 31: 34–50.

Bulliet, R. W. 1975. *The camel and the wheel.* Cambridge, Mass.

Cashdan, E. A. 1985. Coping with risk: Reciprocity among the Basarwa of northern Botswana. *Man* 20: 454–74.

Compagnoni, B., and M. Tosi. 1978. The distribution and state of domestication in the Middle East during the third millennium B.C. in light of finds from Sharh-I Sokhta. In *Approaches to faunal analysis in the Middle East,* ed. R. H. Meadow and M. A. Zeder, 91–103. Cambridge, Mass.

Dahl, G., and A. Hjort. 1976. *Having herds: Pastoral herd growth and household economy.* Stockholm.

1984. Dromedary pastoralism in Africa and Arabia. In *The camelid: An all-purpose animal,* Vol. 1, ed. W. R. Cockrill, 144–66. Uppsala, Sweden.

Dubrovo, I. A., and A. N. Nigarov. 1990. Plio-Pleistocene fossil vertebrate localities of south-western Turkmenia, U.S.S.R. *Quartarpalaeontologie* 8: 35–45.

el Amin, F. M. 1984. The dromedary of Sudan. In *The camelid: An all-purpose animal,* Vol. 1, ed. W. R. Cockrill, 36–49. Uppsala, Sweden.

Fratkin, E., and E. A. Roth. 1990. Drought and economic differentiation among Ariaal pastoralists of Kenya. *Human Ecology* 18: 385–402.

Fratkin, E., and K. Smith. 1994. Labor, livestock, and land: The organization of pastoral production. In *African pastoralist systems: An integrated approach,* ed. E. Fratkin, K. A. Galvin, and E. A. Roth, 91–112. Boulder, Colo.

Galvin, K. A., D. L. Coppock, and P. W. Leslie. 1994. Diet, nutrition, and the pastoral strategy. In *African pastoralist systems: An integrated approach,* ed. E. Fratkin, K. A. Galvin, and E. A. Roth, 113–204. Boulder, Colo.

Gauthier-Pilters, H., and A. I. Dagg. 1981. *The camel: Its evolution, ecology, behavior, and relationship to man.* Chicago.

Germonpré, M., and L. Lbova. 1996. Mammalian remains from the Upper Palaeolithic site of Kamenka, Buryatia (Siberia). *Journal of Archaeological Science* 23: 35–57.

Gray, A. P. 1954. *Mammalian hybrids: A check-list with bibliography.* Bucks, England.

Grigson, C. 1989. The camel in Arabia – A direct radiocarbon date, calibrated to about 7000 B.C. *Journal of Archaeological Science* 16: 355–62.

Hakker-Orion, D. 1984. The role of the camel in Israel's early history. In *Animals and archaeology,* Vol. 3, *Early herders and their flocks,* ed. J. Clutton-Brock and C. Grigson. 207–12. Oxford.

Hartly, B. J. 1984. The dromedary in the Horn of Africa. In *The camelid: An all-purpose animal,* Vol. 1, ed. W. R. Cockrill, 77–97. Uppsala, Sweden.

Herren, U. J. 1992. Cash from camel milk: The impact of commercial camel milk sales on Garre and Gaaljacel camel pastoralism in southern Somalia. *Nomadic Peoples* 30: 97–113.

Hjort, A., and G. Dahl. 1984. A note on the camels of the Amar'ar Beja. In *The camelid: An all-purpose animal,* Vol. 1, ed. W. R. Cockrill, 50–76. Uppsala, Sweden.

Hobbs, J. J. 1989. *Bedouin life in the Egyptian wilderness.* Austin, Tex.

Hoch, E. 1979. Reflections on prehistoric life at Umm an-Nar (Trucial Oman), based on faunal remains from the third millennium B.C. *South Asian Archaeology* 1977: 589–638.

Howell, F. C., L. S. Fichter, and R. Wolff. 1969. Fossil camels in the Omo Beds, southern Ethiopia. *Nature* 223: 150–2.

Ingold, T. 1983. The significance of storage in hunting societies. *Man* 18: 553–71.

Jabbur, J. S. 1995. *The Bedouins and the desert: Aspects of nomadic life in the Arab East,* trans. L. I. Conrad. Albany, N.Y.

Knoess, K. H. 1984. The milk dromedary. In *The camelid: An all-purpose animal,* Vol. 1, ed. W. R. Cockrill, 176–95. Uppsala, Sweden.

Köhler, I. 1984. The dromedary in modern pastoral societies and implications for its process of domestication. In *Animals and archaeology,* Vol. 3, *Early herders and their flocks,* ed. J. Clutton-Brock and C. Grigson, 201–6. Oxford.

Köhler-Rollefson, I. 1992. The Raika dromedary breeders of Rajasthan: A pastoral system in crisis. *Nomadic Peoples* 30: 74–83.

1993. Camels and camel pastoralism in Arabia. *Biblical Archaeologist* 56: 180–8.

1996. The one-humped camel in Asia: Origin, utilization and mechanisms of dispersal. In *Origins and spread of agriculture and pastoralism in Eurasia,* ed. D. R. Harris, 282–95. Washington, D.C.

Lancaster, W., and F. Lancaster. 1990. Desert devices: The pastoral system of the Rwala Bedu. In *The world of pastoralism: Herding systems in comparative perspective,* ed. J. G. Galaty and D. L. Johnson, 177–94. New York.

Lernau, H. 1978. Faunal remains, strata III-I. In *Early Arad,* ed. R. Amiran, 83–113. Jerusalem.

Mason, I. L. 1984. Origin, evolution, and distribution of domestic camels. In *The camelid: An all-purpose animal,* Vol. 1, ed. W. R. Cockrill, 16–35. Uppsala, Sweden.

McCabe, J. T. 1990. Turkana pastoralism: A case against the tragedy of the commons. *Human Ecology* 18: 81–103.

McKnight, T. L. 1969. *The camel in Australia.* Melbourne.

Meadow, R. H. 1984. Animal domestication in the Middle East: A view from the eastern margin. In *Animals and archaeology,* Vol. 3, *Early herders and their flocks,* ed. J. Clutton-Brock and C. Grigson, 309–27. Oxford.

Newman, D. M. R. 1984. The feeds and feeding habits of Old and New World camels. In *The camelid: An all-purpose animal,* Vol. 1, ed. W. R. Cockrill, 250–92. Uppsala, Sweden.

Olsen, S. J. 1988. The camel in ancient China and an osteology of the camel. *Proceedings of the Academy of Natural Sciences of Philadelphia* 140: 18–58.

Roth, E. A. 1990. Modeling Rendille household herd composition. *Human Ecology* 18: 441–5.

Rothenberg, B. 1972. *Were these King Solomon's mines?* New York.

Russell, K. W. 1988. *After Eden: The behavioral ecology of early food production in the Near East and North Africa.* Oxford.

Sato, S. 1980. Pastoral movements and the subsistence unit of the Rendille of northern Kenya, with special reference to camel ecology. *Senri Ethnological Studies* 6: 1–78.

Schaller, G. 1995. Tracking the Gobi's last wild bears and camels. *International Wildlife* 25: 18–23.

Schmidt-Nielsen, K. 1964. *Desert animals: Physiological problems of heat and water.* Oxford.

Shalash, M. R. 1984a. The production and utilization of camel meat. In *The camelid: An all-purpose animal,* Vol. 1, ed. W. R. Cockrill, 231–49. Uppsala, Sweden.

1984b. The production and utilization of camel milk. In *The camelid: An all-purpose animal,* Vol. 1, ed. W. R. Cockrill, 196–208. Uppsala, Sweden.

Simoons, F. J. 1981. Geographic patterns of primary adult lactose malabsorption. In *Lactose digestion: Clinical and nutritional implications,* ed. D. M. Paige and T. M. Bayles, 23–48. Baltimore, Md.

Sperling, L. 1987. The adoption of camels by Samburu cattle herders. *Nomadic Peoples* 23: 1–18.

Stanley, H. F., M. Kadwell, and J. C. Wheeler. 1994. Molecular evolution of the family Camelidae: A mitochondrial DNA study. *Proceedings of the Royal Society of London* 256: 1–6.

Tchnernov, E. 1989. Faunal turnover and extinction rate in the Levant. In *Quaternary extinctions: A prehistoric revolution,* ed. P. S. Martin and R. G. Klein, 528–52. Tucson, Ariz.

Toplyn, M. R. 1995. Meat for Mars: Livestock, *limitanei,* and pastoral provisioning for the Roman army on the Arabian frontier, A.D. 284–551. Ph.D. thesis, Harvard University.

Tulgat, R., and G. B. Schaller. 1992. Status and distribution of wild bactrian camels: *Camelus bactrianus ferus. Biological Conservation* 62: 11–19.

Uerpmann, H.-P. 1987. *The ancient distribution of ungulate mammals in the Middle East.* Wiesbaden.

Wapnish, P. 1981. Camel caravans and camel pastoralists at Tell Jemmeh. *Journal of the Ancient Near Eastern Society of Columbia University (JANES)* 13: 101–21.

1984. The dromedary and bactrian camel in Levantine historical settings: The evidence from Tell Jemmeh. In *Animals and archaeology,* Vol. 3, *Early herders and their flocks,* ed. J. Clutton-Brock and C. Grigson, 171–200. Oxford.

Wei, D. 1984. The bactrian camel of China. In *The camelid: An all-purpose animal,* Vol. 1, ed. W. R. Cockrill, 98–111. Uppsala, Sweden.

Wilson, R. T. 1984. *The camel.* London.

Yagil, R. 1982. *Camels and camel milk.* Food and Agriculture Organization of the United Nations, Animal Production Paper No. 26. Rome.

1985. *The desert camel.* Basel.

Zarins, J. 1978. The camel in ancient Arabia: A further note. *Antiquity* 52: 44–6.

1989. Pastoralism in Southwest Asia: The second millennium B.C. In *The walking larder,* ed. J. Clutton-Brock, 127–55. London.

Zeder, M. A. 1984. Meat distribution at the highland Iranian urban center of Tal-e Malyan. In *Animals and archaeology,* Vol. 3, *Early herders and their flocks,* ed. J. Clutton-Brock and C. Grigson, 279–307. Oxford.

II.G.4   Caribou and Reindeer

The terms "caribou" and "reindeer" refer to a species of cervid, *Rangifer tarandus,* which has Holarctic distribution. "Reindeer," however, is somewhat ambiguous, as it is used to refer to both the wild and domesticated forms of this species, whereas "caribou" always designates the wild form. Yet "reindeer" is generally preferred in the Old World for both. (The term "wild reindeer" is also sometimes used as a synonym for "caribou," to differentiate from the domesticated animal.) In addition, a separate species of Paleoarctic (Old World) reindeer, *Rangifer arcticus,* was once recognized, but the fact that caribou and reindeer interbreed successfully and produce fertile offspring, particularly in Alaskan herds, led to general unification of the taxon (Banfield 1961).

Reindeer

At least six major modern subspecies of caribou are recognized. Two of these are Paleoarctic in distribution: *Rangifer tarandus tarandus,* the European tundra reindeer, and *Rangifer tarandus fennicus,* the Eurasian forest reindeer. Three are Neoarctic in distribution: *Rangifer tarandus grant* of Arctic Alaska and westernmost Canada, *Rangifer tarandus pearyi* (the "Peary caribou") of eastern Arctic Canada, and *Rangifer tarandus groenlandicus* of Greenland and Baffin Island (Meldgaard 1986). One subspecies, *Rangifer tarandus caribou,* is endemic to the subarctic boreal forest, originally ranging from Alaska to eastern Canada and the northernmost United States but now more limited in distribution. Other varieties are more restricted geographically: *Rangifer tarandus platyrhynchus* lives only on Spitzbergen, and *Rangifer tarandus dawsoni* is confined to the Queen Charlotte Islands.

Prehistory of Caribou/Wild Reindeer Utilization

The genus *Rangifer* exists in the paleontological record throughout the middle to late Pleistocene or Ice Age period and has a probable antiquity of at least 400,000 years. The relative prevalence of caribou remains in paleontological and archaeological sites from this period serves as a sensitive indicator of climatic and vegetational change (Parker 1971; Messier et al. 1988). This is because caribou are tied to arctic tundra or subarctic taiga (open coniferous forest) habitats, which provide their chief foods: lichens, particularly of the genera *Cladonia* and *Alectoria,* and a wide variety of low browse or groundcover plants, including forbs, fungi, willow and birch shoots, and grass and sedge shoots (Kelsall 1968). Thus, the presence of caribou during glacial periods (and their absence during interglacial periods) in central Europe and other parts of northern Eurasia is linked to the expansion and regression of the Scandinavian ice sheet to which these arctic and subarctic environments were tied (Bouchud 1966).

Remains of *R. tarandus* are initially associated with late *Homo erectus* or archaic *Homo sapiens* sites in Europe and, more frequently, with Neanderthal sites. *Rangifer tarandus* existed as a recognizable taxon throughout the Upper Paleolithic period from 40,000 to 10,000 years ago (Banfield 1961). It is a conservative taxon, with little change occurring in caribou throughout the late Ice Age and postglacial periods. During the Upper Paleolithic period, many northern Eurasian hunting populations became specialized in hunting wild reindeer (Sturdy 1975; Mellars 1996; Burke and Pike-Tay 1997). The caribou was probably the most important game animal in western Europe during the Upper Paleolithic, and European cave deposits contain large amounts of caribou bones (Delpech and Heintz 1976; Delpech 1983; Boyle 1990, 1993; Straus 1997; Thacker 1997). Caribou also figure prominently in Ice Age art, as at Lascaux Cave, and

some depictions (as at Trois Frères) suggest that they played an important role in ritual and perhaps shamanistic activities. In the New World, caribou were important to Paleo-Indian hunters throughout North America (Cleland 1965; Funk, Fisher, and Reilly 1970; Spiess, Curran, and Grimes 1985; Peers 1986; Jackson 1988).

After the end of the Ice Age, caribou populations retreated northward to areas offering suitable habitat, such as northern Germany and southern Scandinavia, and many parts of Russia, Alaska, Canada, and Greenland. They were an important focus of Epipaleolithic or Mesolithic hunters throughout this region; their bones are found in archaeological sites, and they were depicted in rock art in each of these areas. With evolving post-Pleistocene climates, caribou became restricted to areas of northern Scandinavia, Siberia, parts of the Russian Far East, and the more northerly areas of Canada and Alaska (Yesner 1995). They have continued to be hunted by various aboriginal populations in all of these regions until the present time (e.g., Birket-Smith 1929; Lips 1947; Chard 1963; Gubser 1965; Nelleman 1970; Simchenko 1976; Irimoto 1981; Hall 1989; Krupnik 1993).

Methods of Caribou/Wild Reindeer Exploitation

Since Upper Paleolithic times, caribou have been a historically important food resource for northern Eurasian hunting peoples for three reasons: the dense aggregation of the animals in bands and herds, their ease of capture, and their nutritional value. Modern caribou tend to congregate in large numbers ranging from dozens (bands) to thousands (herds). Their migratory habits minimize their impact on the relatively delicate plant communities upon which they depend. These migrations may shift groups between forested and open (tundra) environments on a seasonal basis. They frequently involve movement between seasonally important hunting grounds and spring "calving grounds," where females give birth. Contemporary migration distances range from relatively short (for example, on Spitzbergen and islands of the Canadian High Arctic) to very long (in western Canada and Alaska). Factors involved in the distance and location of migration include available forage, protection against predators, and insect infestations (Pruitt 1960; Skoog 1968; Heard 1997).

The nature of caribou migration patterns of the past is unclear. Zooarchaeological data from late Ice Age sites in southwestern France suggest that year-round occupation of some areas was possible by specialized caribou hunters, which may be related to shorter-distance migrations by the animals, as well as to the fact that they existed in significant numbers (Gordon 1988; David and Enloe 1992; Enloe and David 1997; Spiess in press). In comparison with their Arctic habitats of today, southwestern France would have provided a smaller physical area but much greater environmental (particularly altitudinal) diversity, thereby helping to support larger groups of animals. In addition, beginning around 20,000 years ago, caribou were hunted with efficient tools such as spears and atlatls (Bouchud 1966; Delpech 1983; Pike-Tay and Bricker 1993).

In places where they were less available, such as in open forest areas, caribou were a seasonally important resource; their dietary significance seems to have varied in relation to the specificity of the habitat for caribou and the length of local caribou migration routes. Among historically known caribou hunting groups, some maintained a herd-following strategy, whereas others remained in specific areas, usually near annual migration routes, exploiting other resources until the caribou showed up.

The former pattern seems to have been more typical of places where few alternative resources existed, such as the Canadian High Arctic (Gordon 1975), and may also have been true of Scandinavia before the domestication of reindeer (Blehr 1990). The second pattern was more typical of places where alternative resources existed, where annual migration routes were fairly precise, and where caribou could be taken in sufficiently large numbers that their meat could be stored for a considerable time period; such a location was the Brooks Range of northern Alaska (Burch 1972). Situations in which caribou composed the predominant element in the diet yet failed to materialize along a particular migration route in a given year have been well documented; the result was usually starvation for the hunters (Mowat 1952).

Human groups hunting caribou have employed a wide variety of techniques, which Arthur Spiess (1979), Otto Blehr (1990), and Bryan Gordon (1990) have discussed in detail. There are basically two approaches: One involved "mass killing" techniques, in which large numbers of animals were taken from a band or herd at one time, whereas the other saw individual caribou or small numbers of individuals killed. The former tended to be used for hunting large bands or herds (as during seasonal aggregations) when large numbers of humans were available to hunt and where caribou meat was particularly important in the diet. Mass killing techniques involved logistic planning, whereas individual hunting techniques were largely based on opportunistic encounters.

Mass killing techniques were historically used by many groups, including coastal and interior Eskimos, various Athapaskan peoples of interior Alaska and western Canada, some Algonquian groups in the eastern Canadian Subarctic, the Saami peoples of northern Scandinavia, some Siberian groups, and a few of the Rocky Mountain groups of western Canada. Algonquians of northern New England and peoples of the Russian Far East seem to have used individualistic hunting techniques almost entirely. Mass killing techniques were of two types. On land, they involved drives into traps, snares, fences, corrals, or human "surrounds"; in general, this type included any technique in which the caribou were lured into a small area to be killed and butchered (Anell 1969; Morrison 1982). The caribou were also driven into water, with the use of boats, in areas where rivers or lakes lay near migration routes (Arima 1975; Greenman and Stanley 1977; Yesner 1980). Male and female humans of all ages participated in these activities, with which forms of sociopolitical leadership were often associated. These may have ranged from simple task leadership to the involvement of more general leaders or village headmen (for example, the *umialik* or whaling boat captains in North Alaskan villages).

By contrast, individualistic hunting was usually done by men using singly set snares, stalking, and "running down" of game. Killing was done with atlatls, spears, bows and arrows, and the rifles introduced into many indigenous caribou hunting groups during the nineteenth century. For both mass and individualistic hunting various aids were employed, such as decoys (antlers, reindeer skins, calls) and mock caribou made of wood or stone. Some of these approaches may be reflected in the archaeological record; examples might include the caribou headdress from Trois Frères or certain depictions in Scandinavian rock art. Mass killing efforts tended to yield nonselective age and sex groups of caribou, whereas individual hunting techniques were more effective at different times of year to take particular ages or sexes of the animals. The archaeological record indicates that bulls were generally preferred for meat, and today they are larger and have more fat, particularly during the autumn (Yesner 1980). Calves were also sought for their high fat content, and female adults became the preferred prey in early winter, when the bulls were in rut (see Figure II.G.4.1).

Individualistic hunting techniques were also used to take animals at specific times of the year for non-food purposes, such as in late summer and fall, when the quality of reindeer fur was particularly suitable for clothing manufacture. Cows and calves were often sought for their skins. Animals of varying ages and sexes were targeted for the manufacture of specific items of clothing: skin bags, rawhide or "babiche" for snowshoe lacings, as well as covers for dwellings, caches, and sleds (Smith 1978). In addition, antlers were an important resource for tool manufacture. If already shed, antlers could be scavenged, but they could also be taken from animals, particularly males, and generally from adults over 4 years of age, as they produce significantly larger antlers.

Dietary Importance of Caribou/Wild Reindeer

The fact that specialized caribou hunting has been possible among some groups for 40,000 years indicates that the animal is capable of satisfying human subsistence requirements (Burch 1972). However, rarely did historically known groups subsist solely on

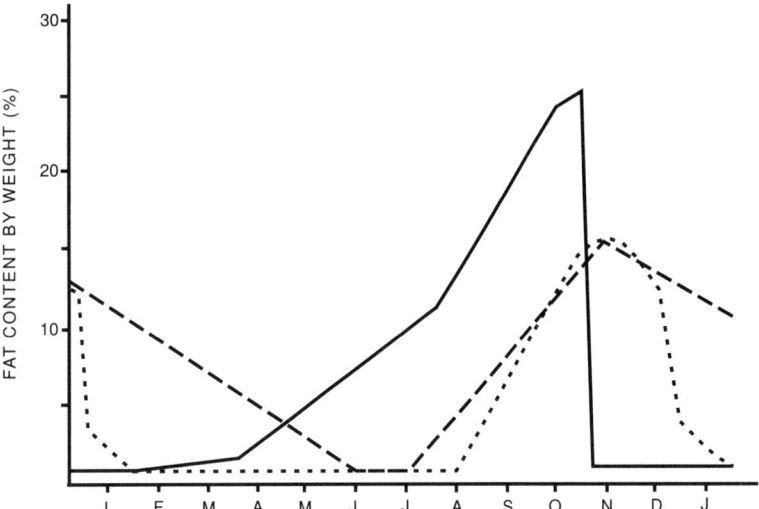

Figure II.G.4.1. Seasonal variation in the fat content of caribou. Mature bulls are represented by a solid line, mature females by a dashed line, and young bulls by a dotted line. (From Spiess 1979: 28; used by permission of Academic Press.)

a caribou meat diet. Past caribou-hunting specialists of the arctic region, such as the Arctic Small Tool peoples (also known as the Denbigh peoples in Alaska and the Dorset peoples in Canada), were historically replaced by more efficient coastal hunters, such as the Thule peoples (ancestral to modern Arctic Eskimos), who combined caribou and sea-mammal hunting. There is also historical and archaeological evidence suggesting that contemporary groups – such as the Nunamiut Eskimos of Alaska, the Caribou Eskimos of Canada, and even the so-called Reindeer Lapps of northern Scandinavia – have developed their specialized lifeways only in the past few hundred years, and that until recently, they migrated between coastal and interior regions, combining caribou hunting with fishing and sea-mammal hunting.

The Caribou Eskimos, living to the west of Hudson Bay in an area where whaling or walrus hunting is less possible today than in other areas (and where shorefast ice requires individual stalking of seals in winter), have been particularly dependent on caribou. They are, however, a group with smaller human populations, simpler technologies, and less complex political structures than other Eskimo peoples. Similarly, among Alaskan Athapaskan groups, those involved primarily with caribou hunting (for example, the Gwich'in) have been more mobile, with a simpler technology, and have been fewer in numbers than other groups that were also involved with salmon fishing and/or seal hunting. Such caribou-dependent groups tends to be very mobile, occupying in the course of a year several different base camps, where they have utilized relatively unsophisticated dwellings such as caribou-hide tents (or even brush lean-tos).

Widespread concern over the availability of caribou was especially characteristic of groups occupying boreal forest regions, where the animals were often scarce (cf. Smith 1978). Such concern took the form of specialized ritual and may have stimulated the development of divination as a technique in caribou hunting. The effect of divination was to randomize the impact of such hunting and therefore minimize the likelihood of overexploitation (Moore 1969). Some authors have even linked the so-called Windigo Psychosis of subarctic Cree peoples to concerns over starvation in the boreal forest.

That caribou-hunting groups occasionally met with starvation is well documented in the ethnographic record. In part, this was a result of the naturally cyclical patterns of caribou abundance in arctic regions. Although it is difficult to establish the antiquity of these patterns, there is some suggestion that they go back hundreds of years in interior Alaska (Yesner 1980), Labrador (Fitzhugh 1972), and Greenland (Gronnow, Meldgaard, and Nielsen 1983; Meldgaard 1983), and they may even have occurred during the Upper Paleolithic in France (David 1973). During caribou population highs, such as in late-nineteenth-century Alaska, intensification of hunting, including widespread construction of "caribou fences," seems to have taken place. At times of population lows, caribou-hunting groups apparently shifted to a more diverse diet that included small game and birds (Yesner 1989). Within the last 150 years, habitat disturbance has led to population expansion of other cervids such as the moose, which subsequently filled the dietary niche formerly occupied by caribou in some parts of interior Alaska.

Because higher metabolic rates are required for human survival under cold conditions, dietary requirements of high-caloric foods are significantly greater in the Arctic region (Draper 1974). Calories are usually provided by fats, which have twice the caloric density of protein or carbohydrates (about 9 calories per gram). However, except for deposits around viscera, under the skin, and in bone marrow, caribou are generally lean, yielding fat at only 10 percent of body weight (Hall 1971). Between 40 and 55 percent of a caribou carcass is meat (White 1953; Hill 1967; Binford 1978). Caribou weights vary from about 35 kilograms (kg) for a juvenile to 150 kg for a large adult male (Kelsall 1968). Such a range provides from 20 to 80 kg of meat but only 3 to 10 kg of fat (Table II.G.4.1).

There is some physical evidence that nutritional deprivation was occasionally associated with those groups that were more caribou-dependent. In the Canadian High Arctic, for example, a greater dependence on caribou may be linked to relatively shorter statures in that region (Laughlin 1966). Although there is evidence for episodic nutritional stress in human skeletons from throughout the Arctic and Subarctic (Yesner 1994), the Caribou Eskimos have shown some of the strongest patterns of development of growth arrest lines, indicative of starvation, of any Eskimo peoples (Buikstra 1976). In addition, studies by the Alaska Dietary Survey (Mann et al. 1962) and by Edward Foulks (1972) have suggested that a caribou diet may be deficient in thiamine and other vitamins.

Caribou/Reindeer Butchery and Consumption

Caribou butchery practices have varied widely among groups. However, common variables in the butchery process have involved transportation requirements and whether immediate or short-term consumption or storage of meat was anticipated. The size of the packages of meat produced would often be related to whether humans, dogs, or sleds (or, today, snowmobiles) were used for transportation. If carcasses were to be used for long-term caching (storage in an underground or rock-lined chamber), they would only be beheaded, eviscerated, and quartered, with further butchery taking place before consumption at a later time. Butchery procedures may also have been affected by whether the animal was being used for purposes other than human consumption (such as clothing manufacture, dog food, or bait for traps).

Arctic peoples compensated for the relative leanness of caribou meat by the way in which the animal was butchered, cooked, and prepared. The final preparation of food sections was strongly related to preference for body parts. These were (and are) fairly constant cross-culturally and were based on the amounts of meat in different parts of the carcass, particularly on fat concentrations and the reliability of those concentrations. In general, because of higher fat content, portions nearer the axial skeleton (ribs and vertebrae), including rib steaks and roasts, were highly desired. Also high on the preference list was the backstrap (backbone musculature), followed by front (brisket, short ribs) and back (pelvis) portions. Rear haunches were generally preferred to front shanks for the same reasons. Kidneys were also prized above other viscera because of higher fat content, followed by the heart and lungs. The most desirable smaller parts included those of the head, particularly the brain, the tongue, and the fat behind the eyes. Intestinal fat was also consumed (Spiess 1979).

If alternative resources were few, a variety of techniques were employed to maximize the nutritional yield from caribou carcasses. One was the smashing or cracking of the articular ends of long bones to obtain marrow, a high-fat, high-protein substance enjoyed by hunting peoples. Afterward, the marrow and bone fragments were sometimes boiled to produce "bone juice." Data from Eskimo informants suggest that marrow was cherished as a source of fat because of high concentrations of low-melting-point fats, particularly oleic acid (Binford 1978). Bones chosen first for marrow extraction were the tibia, the "cannon bones" (metacarpals and metatarsals), the radiocubitis, the femur, and the humerus (Binford 1978: 42). Less desirable as sources of marrow were the pelvis, phalanges, mandible, scapula, and ribs. Thin animals (including nursing females or rut-depleted males) were often avoided because starvation removes fat reserves from the bone marrow.

Both marrow and caribou back-fat have been key ingredients in the traditional dish akutuk, an excellent source of vitamins as well as protein and fat. This dish, colloquially known as "Eskimo ice cream," was prepared in the past by mixing caribou tallow with berries of various types and snow. Depending on the availability of other fats, fish, or sea mammals, oils might also have been added. Today, sugar has become another ingredient in the mix.

A second major nutritional resource obtained by carcass reduction was caribou "bone grease," that is,

Table II.G.4.1. *Weights and edible weights for caribou* (Rangifer tarandus)

Age/Size Group	Weight (kg)	Percentage edible	Meat (kg)	Fat (kg)	Viscera (kg)
Fawn	11	58	3.8	1.1	2.2
Juvenile	34	57	11.8	3.4	6.8
Young adult (female)	57	56	19.8	5.7	11.4
Young adult (male)	81	56	28.1	8.1	16.2
Average adult (female)	72	50	25.5	7.3	14.5
Average adult (male)	110	50	38.2	10.9	21.8
Old adult (female)	84	39	29.2	8.4	16.8
Old adult (male)	153	39	53.1	15.3	30.6

Sources: Hill (1967), Hall (1971), Binford (1978), Spiess (1979), and Yesner (1980).

fats obtained from bone tissue itself (Leechman 1951). These were rendered by first smashing bones into small fragments, then simmering them in a pot of water and skimming off the fat. If not consumed immediately, the fat was generally stored in a cleaned caribou stomach. The best bone grease, referred to as "white" bone grease by Eskimo informants (Binford 1978), was rendered from long bones, whereas the axial skeleton, mandible, sternum, and pelvis were used to produce a less desired "yellow grease." Obtaining both marrow and bone grease could also have been part of the same procedure that employed long bones for tool manufacture (Yesner and Bonnichsen 1979). Carcass reduction for marrow and bone grease most likely took place at times of the year when caribou were scarce and/or stored resources were depleted, particularly in the late winter and early spring.

A final resource that could sometimes be obtained from caribou or reindeer were the stomach contents, that is, fermented plants of various sorts, including lichens. Although these plants cannot be readily digested by humans because of their high cellulose content, they are edible if fermented in the caribou rumen. As such, they can be an excellent source of ascorbic acid (vitamin C), otherwise obtainable only from berries (fresh, frozen, or preserved in fish or sea-mammal oils) or raw meat.

Food Storage and "Social Storage"

Many groups stored their caribou meat. Variables affecting storage included the quantity of meat to be butchered or transported and the ambient temperature at the time of the kill and afterward. There were two basic practices: the caching of unbutchered or roughly butchered meat sections and storage following butchering of the animals. Caching was likely to

occur when large numbers of caribou were killed at one time and the carcasses could not be consumed or transported immediately. This generally took place in late fall or winter, and landmarks were left behind so that the meat could be recovered even if the caches were covered by snow. Meat sections were recovered when the area was revisited during an annual round, whereupon secondary butchering would take place. Unbutchered, cached meat sections were sometimes fed to the dogs, particularly during the winter.

In situations where butchering preceded storage, the hunters employed drying and also (when possible) freezing. Specific butchery methods depended on storage techniques. Drying methods utilized drying racks (Figure II.G.4.2), whereas frozen storage required deep ice cellars, often delved out of the permafrost, that could only be used during winter or spring.

Widespread food sharing was also a technique that helped to maximize both the nutrition obtained from the caribou and the survivability of the caribou-hunting group. In groups using mass killing techniques, the individuals in charge of the hunt often acted as decision makers regarding the division of the meat. Sharing beyond the nuclear family was less likely during periods of relative abundance, but at other times of year (when individual hunting took place) food sharing was ubiquitous. It was widely recognized by various caribou-hunting groups that men differed significantly in their hunting abilities (or luck), and kills were shared with all other members of the group. In such cases, the successful hunter was often in charge of meat distribution.

Finally, trade was a mechanism by which caribou hunters obtained other foods. Among the Nunamiut of northern Alaska and the Tareumiut peoples on the North Alaskan coast, for example, long-distance trading partnerships were developed. During annual ses-

Figure II.G.4.2. A spring drying rack for caribou meat used by the Nunamiut Eskimo of the Brooks Range, northern Alaska. (From Binford 1978: 99; used by permission of Academic Press.)

sions, frequently held during summer months, caribou hides were traded for dried fish, seal meat, and fish and sea-mammal oils. Similar patterns evolved in Scandinavia and Russia.

The Domestication of Reindeer

The domestication of reindeer marked a considerable departure from previous dependence on wild reindeer (caribou). Although human manipulation of caribou populations is thousands of years old, true domestication of reindeer began no more than 400 to 500 years ago in northern Scandinavia and Siberia (Anderson 1958; Vorren and Manker 1962; Levin and Potapov 1964). O. Magnus (1555) is probably the earliest historical source referring to reindeer domestication by Saami (Lapps). However, there is some archaeological evidence from medieval Scandinavia to suggest that this transition may have taken place as early as the beginning of the fifteenth century (Simonsen 1972; Hambleton and Rowly-Conwy 1997). Historical sources suggest that reindeer domestication began with the expansion of peoples from the south into the territory of these northern peoples, including Norse populations in Scandinavia and Evenks (Tungus) in Siberia. These expansions were probably coincident with a climatic optimum in the sixteenth century. The result was removal of reindeer habitat, increased density of northern peoples, and overhunting of reindeer populations, in part resulting from the introduction of firearms. Domestication apparently occurred in order to provide northern groups with a reliable source of food in the face of the decline of reindeer populations. Unlike other northern groups, the Saami regularly milked their reindeer, producing a kind of cheese (Magnus 1555; Utsi 1948). By the seventeenth century, Saami peoples were regularly trading reindeer hides for grain, salt, metal objects, cloth, and alcohol (Schefferus 1674). In part, this trading was to pay for the taxation of reindeer herds imposed by Norse authorities.

Historical sources also indicate that initially the domestication of reindeer (and their herding and use as draft animals) was undertaken as an aid to hunting before it became a sustainable livelihood. Also, in some areas, such as parts of northern Siberia, reindeer herding remained a hunting aid and/or source of reserve food into the twentieth century. Later, more closely supervised and intensive herding took place, beginning no more than 200 years ago. Such herding involved draft reindeer for carrying loads and for riding. As with wild reindeer hunting, domesticated reindeer herding has involved the use of a wide variety of techniques for corralling and killing animals, including, as already mentioned, the use of rifles since the late nineteenth century. At the same time, like cattle herding, it has also involved the use of a wide variety of techniques for breaking animals and for indicating ownership (for example, ear notching).

The necessity for continuous human contact in herding, caring for, and driving reindeer populations created an ever increasing dependence of humans on the animals. This, in turn, necessitated greater reindeer-herding specialization, a more sedentary lifestyle, and, in some cases, a discontinuance of customary transhumant movements into coastal or riverine zones for fishing and/or sea-mammal hunting. The result was the differentiation in Scandinavia between the so-called Mountain Lapps or Reindeer Lapps (focused on reindeer herding), the Forest Lapps, and the Coast Lapps or Fisher Lapps. In Siberia, a similar process can be seen in the evolution of the "Reindeer Chukchi." Development of discrete groups of herders also took place, with differences in reindeer paraphernalia identifying such groups. Problems have also developed in mating or interaction between domesticated reindeer herds and wild reindeer populations, necessitating special efforts to separate these groups.

Reindeer Husbandry in the Twentieth Century

In northwestern Alaska, reindeer herding began in the 1920s with the noted Protestant minister Sheldon Jackson, who introduced the animals into the area (Scheffer 1951; Stern et al. 1980). Jackson believed that reindeer would help to augment the diet of the Bering Strait Inupiat (Northern Eskimo) people, some of whose other resources, especially large baleen whales, had been depleted by the ingress of other populations since the mid-nineteenth century. Jackson brought in Saami (Lapp) herders to help the Alaskan natives learn about reindeer (Vorren 1994). Although the herds depleted some habitats and caused disruption of traditional settlement patterns and lifestyles, reindeer herding continues today in that part of Alaska, where it is a successful enterprise managed by the Northwest Alaska Native Association (NANA).

In the former Soviet Union, large cooperatives, equivalent to communal farms, were established for the marketing and distribution of reindeer meat. Thus, much of the meat was not consumed by local peoples but by others in the region. Payments for reindeer meat were handled by local officials, assisted by Communist Party advisory groups. Such practices have been terminated with the fall of the Soviet Union.

In the latter part of the twentieth century, more extensive and larger-scale reindeer husbandry or ranching has been developed in a number of places, including Alaska, northwestern Canada, western Greenland, and Siberia (Strickon 1965; Sturdy 1972; Ingold 1980). This development has everywhere required the use of modern mechanized equipment, including trucks, airplanes, and particularly snowmobiles (Pelto 1973; Beach 1981; Paine 1994). There have been problems in adapting mechanized systems to reindeer herding because of the traditional skittishness of the animals. Such systems have also continued to transform traditional settlement patterns and lifestyles. The marketing and sale of meat has been initiated in a number of locales, particularly in Scandinavia, Greenland, and Russia. The sale of reindeer meat is more restricted in Canada and Alaska; in the latter region, however, it is a key ingredient in "reindeer sausage," which is widely marketed. The meat is frequently leaner and milder in flavor than that of wild caribou and is preferred by many non-native consumers for that reason. A key reason for the present-day maintenance of reindeer herds in a number of places, including Alaska and Russia, is the strong demand for – and purchase of – reindeer antlers in East Asia. There, the antlers, alleged to possess the properties of a stimulant and an aphrodisiac, are ground to a pharmaceutical powder and retailed to the public.

Survival of a Subsistence Based on Caribou/Reindeer

Both herding and hunting of reindeer have continued to provide meat for indigenous peoples throughout the northern circumpolar region and have proven to be important local sources of human nutrition. To a lesser extent, caribou or wild reindeer are also an important resource for non-native peoples who hunt them and consume their meat. Thus, in Alaska, special permits are required for non-native caribou hunting, and preference is given to those who can demonstrate past reliance on this meat to feed their families. The use of caribou and reindeer is governed by local and national laws. In addition, international treaties, such as that between the United States and Canada, govern the management and exploitation of caribou herds that cross national boundaries. In Scandinavia, such treaties have ensured the movement of traditional Saami herds and herders across the northern part of the region.

Unfortunately, there are a number of threats to the continued use and consumption of caribou and reindeer meat by northern peoples. Habitat disruption has probably had the greatest effect on both wild and domestic reindeer. For example, even in those areas where traditional caribou hunting persists, there is a significant difference between the hunting patterns of the past and those of today. Illustrative is Alaskan archaeological data, which demonstrates that traditional peoples hunted caribou as much as 15 or more years old, but animals of this age are rarely seen in wild populations today (Yesner 1980) (see Table II.G.4.2).

Significant alterations of caribou and reindeer habitats are the result of a number of factors: the increased movement of non-native peoples into arctic regions; the development of oil, mining, and other industries in the Arctic (particularly in Alaska and Russia); and the construction of large hydroelectric projects (particularly in Canada and Scandi-

Table II.G.4.2 *Age distribution of caribou from an Alaskan archaeological site*

Age	Number of individuals
0–12 months (0–1 yr)	14
12–24 months (1–2 yr)	10
24–36 months (2–3 yr)	9
36–48 months (3–4 yr)	27
48–60 months (4–5 yr)	10
60–72 months (5–6 yr)	6
72–96 months (6–8 yr)	8
96–120 months (8–10 yr)	1
120–156 months (10-13 yr)	3
156–180 months (13–15 yr)	5
180–204 months (15–17 yr)	1
204+ months (17+ yr)	1
	$N = 87$

Source: Yesner (1980), p. 31.

navia). The latter has had a particularly strong impact by flooding large areas of the traditional caribou range. In addition, air pollution, particularly that resulting from the Chernobyl reactor accident in the former Soviet Union, has affected the caribou. It is too early to determine the long-term consequences for the subsistence of northern peoples, particularly in Scandinavia and Russia, but reindeer meat will probably continue to be important in these regions for some time. In Alaska and Canada, although some herds have been reduced, others still number in the hundreds of thousands. It is to be hoped that reindeer and caribou will continue to be significant dietary resources well into the twenty-first century.

David R. Yesner

Bibliography

Anderson, R. T. 1958. Dating reindeer pastoralism in Lapland. *Ethnohistory* 5: 361–91.

Anell, Bergt. 1969. Running down and driving of game in North America. *Studia Ethnographica Upsaliensia* 30: 1–300.

Arima, Eugene Y. 1975. *A contextual study of the Caribou Eskimo kayak.* National Museum of Man, Mercury Series No. 5. Ottawa.

Banfield, A. W. F. 1961. *A revision of the reindeer and caribou genus Rangifer.* Ottawa.

Beach, Hugh. 1981. *Reindeer herd management in transition.* Uppsala Studies in Cultural Anthropology No. 3. Uppsala, Sweden.

Binford, Lewis R. 1978. *Nunamiut ethnoarchaeology.* New York.

Birket-Smith, D. 1929. *The Caribou Eskimos.* Report of the Fifth Thule Expedition, Vol. 5, Part 1. Copenhagen.

Blehr, Otto. 1990. Communal hunting as a prerequisite for caribou (wild reindeer) as a human resource. In

Hunters of the recent past, ed. Leslie B. Davis and Brian O. K. Reeves, 304-26. London.

Bouchud, Jean. 1966. *Essai sur le renne et la climatologie du paléolithique moyen et supérieur.* Périgueux, France.

Boyle, Katharine V. 1990. *Upper Palaeolithic faunas from Southwest France: A zoogeographic perspective.* British Archaeological Reports, International Series No. 557. Oxford.

   1993. Upper Paleolithic procurement and processing strategies in Southwest France. In *Hunting and animal exploitation in the Later Paleolithic and Mesolithic of Eurasia,* ed. G. L. Peterkin, Harvey M. Bricker, and Paul Mellars, 1-10. Archaeological Papers of the American Anthropological Association No. 4. Washington, D.C.

Buikstra, Jane E. 1976. The Caribou Eskimo: General and specific disease. *American Journal of Physical Anthropology* 45: 351-68.

Burch, Ernest L., Jr. 1972. The caribou/wild reindeer as a human resource. *American Antiquity* 37: 339-68.

Burke, Ariane, and Anne Pike-Tay. 1997. Reconstructing "l'Age du Renne." In *Caribou and reindeer hunters of the Northern Hemisphere,* ed. Lawrence J. Jackson and Paul T. Thacker, 69-81. Aldershot, England.

Chapdelaine, Claude, ed. 1985. Des éléphants, des caribous, et des hommes: La Période Paléoindienne. *Recherches Amerindiennes au Québec* 15: 1-185.

Chard, Chester S. 1963. The Nganasan: Wild reindeer hunters of the Taimyr Peninsula. *Arctic Anthropology* 1: 105-30.

Cleland, Charles. 1965. Barren ground caribou *(Rangifer arcticus)* from an Early Man site in southeastern Michigan. *American Antiquity* 30: 350-1.

David, François, and J. G. Enloe. 1992. Chasse saisonnière des magdaleniens de Bassin Parisien. *Bulletins et Mémoires Société d'Anthropologie de Paris* 4: 167-74.

David, Nicholas C. 1973. On Upper Paleolithic society, ecology, and technological change: The Noaillian case. In *The explanation of culture change,* ed. Colin Renfrew, 277-303. London.

Delpech, Françoise. 1983. *Les faunes du Paléolithique Supérieur dans le sud-ouest de la France.* Cahiers du Quaternaire No. 6. Bordeaux.

Delpech, Françoise, and E. Heintz. 1976. Les artiodactyles: Cervides. In *La Préhistoire Française,* Vol. 1, ed. Henri de Lumley, 395-404. Paris.

Draper, Harold H. 1974. Aspects of adaptation to the native Eskimo diet: Energy metabolism. *American Journal of Physical Anthropology* 43: 475-85.

Enloe, J. G., and François David. 1997. *Rangifer* herd behavior: Seasonality of hunting in the Magdalenian of the Paris basin. In *Caribou and reindeer hunters of the Northern Hemisphere,* ed. Lawrence J. Jackson and Paul T. Thacker, 52-68. Aldershot, England.

Fitzhugh, William W. 1972. Environmental archaeology and cultural systems in Hamilton Inlet, Labrador. *Smithsonian Contributions to Anthropology* 16: 1-300.

Foulks, Edward F. 1972. *The arctic hysterias of the North Alaskan Eskimo.* American Anthropological Association, Anthropological Studies No. 10. Washington, D.C.

Funk, Robert E., D. W. Fisher, and E. M. Reilly, Jr. 1970. Caribou and Paleo-Indian in New York State: A presumed association. *American Journal of Science* 268: 181-6.

Gordon, Bryan H. C. 1975. *Of men and herds in barrenland prehistory.* National Museum of Man, Mercury Series, Archaeological Papers No. 28. Ottawa.

   1988. *Of men and reindeer herds in French Magdalen-*

ian prehistory. British Archaeological Reports, International Series No. 390. Oxford.

   1990. World *Rangifer* communal hunting. In *Hunters of the recent past,* ed. Leslie B. Davis and Brian O. K. Reeves, 277-303. London.

Greenman, E. F., and George M. Stanley. 1977. Prehistoric Chipewyan harvesting at a Barrenland caribou water crossing. *Western Canadian Journal of Anthropology* 7: 69-83.

Gronnow, Bjarne, Morten Meldgaard, and Jorn Berglund Nielsen. 1983. Aasivissuit – The great summer camp: Archaeological, ethnographic, and zooarchaeological studies of a caribou hunting site in West Greenland. *Meddelelser om Groenland, Man and Society* 5: 1-96.

Gubser, Nicholas J. 1965. *The Nunamiut Eskimos: Hunters of caribou.* New Haven, Conn.

Hall, Edwin S., Jr. 1971. Kangigugsuk: A cultural reconstruction of a sixteenth century Eskimo site in Northern Alaska. *Arctic Anthropology* 8: 1-101.

   ed. 1989. *People and caribou in the Northwest Territories.* Yellowknife, Canada.

Hambleton, Ellen, and Peter Rowly-Conwy. 1997. The medieval reindeer economy in the Varanger Fjord, North Norway. *Norwegian Archaeological Review* 30: 55-70.

Heard, Douglas C. 1997. Causes of barren-ground caribou migrations and implications to hunters. In *Caribou and reindeer hunters of the Northern Hemisphere,* ed. Lawrence J. Jackson and Paul T. Thacker, 27-31. Aldershot, England.

Hill, Richard. 1967. *Mackenzie reindeer operations.* Ottawa.

Ingold, Timothy. 1980. *Hunters, pastoralists, and ranchers.* Cambridge and New York.

Irimoto, Takashi. 1981. *Chipewyan ecology: Group structure and caribou hunting system.* Senri Ethnological Studies No. 8. Osaka.

Jackson, Lawrence J. 1988. Fossil cervids and fluted point hunters. *Ontario Archaeology* 48: 27-41.

Kelsall, John P. 1968. *The migratory barrenground caribou of Canada.* Canadian Wildlife Service Monograph No. 3. Ottawa.

Krupnik, Igor. 1993. *Arctic adaptations: Native whalers and reindeer herders of northern Eurasia.* Hanover, N.H.

Laughlin, William S. 1966. Genetic and anthropological characteristics of arctic populations. In *The biology of human adaptability,* ed. Paul T. Baker and J. S. Weiner, 469-96. Oxford.

Leechman, D. 1951. Bone grease. *American Antiquity* 16: 355-6.

Levin, Michael G., and L. P. Potapov, eds. 1964. *The peoples of Siberia.* Chicago.

Lips, J. 1947. Notes on Montagnais-Naskapi economy (Lake St. John and Lake Mistassinibands). *Ethnos* 12: 1-78.

Loring, Stephen J. 1997. On the trail to the caribou house: Some reflections on Innu caribou hunters in northern Labrador. In *Caribou and reindeer hunters of the Northern Hemisphere,* ed. Lawrence J. Jackson and Paul T. Thacker, 185-220. Aldershot, England.

Magnus, O. 1555. *History of the northern peoples (Historia de gentibus septentrionalibus).* Rome.

Mann, G. V., E. M. Scott, L. M. Hursh, and C. A. Heller. 1962. The health and nutritional status of Alaskan Eskimos. *American Journal of Clinical Nutrition* 11: 31-66.

Meldgaard, Morten. 1983. Resource fluctuations and human subsistence: A zooarchaeological and ethnographic investigation of a West Greenland caribou hunting camp. In *Animals and archaeology: Hunters and their prey,* ed. Juliet Clutton-Brock and Caroline Grigson, 259-72. British Archaeological Reports, International Series No. 163. Oxford.

1986. *The Greenland caribou: Zoogeography, taxonomy, and population dynamics.* Copenhagen.

Mellars, Paul R. 1996. *The Neanderthal legacy: An archaeological perspective from western Europe.* Princeton, N.J.

Messier, F., J. Huot, D. LeHenaff, and S. Luttich. 1988. Demography of the George River caribou herd: Evidence of population regulation by forage exploitation and range expansion. *Arctic* 41: 279-87.

Moore, Omar Khayyam. 1969. Divination: A new perspective. In *Environment and cultural behavior,* ed. Andrew P. Vayda, 121-9. Austin, Tex.

Morrison, David. 1982. Chipewyan drift fences and shooting blinds in the central Barren Grounds. In *Megaliths to medicine wheels: Boulder structures in archaeology,* ed. Michael Wilson, K. L. Road, and K. J. Hardy, 171-85. Calgary.

Mowat, Farley. 1952. *People of the deer.* London.

Nelleman, G. 1970. Caribou hunting in West Greenland. *Folk* 12: 133-53.

Paine, Robert. 1994. *A portrait of Saami reindeer pastoralism.* Washington, D.C.

Parker, G. 1971. *Trends in the population of barren-ground caribou over the last two decades: A re-evaluation of the evidence.* Canadian Wildlife Service, Occasional Paper No. 10. Ottawa.

Peers, Laura. 1986. Ontario Paleo-Indians and caribou predation. *Ontario Archaeology* 43: 31-40.

Pelto, Pertti J. 1973. *The snowmobile revolution: Technology and social change in the Arctic.* Prospect Heights, Ill.

Pike-Tay, Anne, and Harvey M. Bricker. 1993. Hunting in the Gravettian: An examination of evidence from southwestern France. In *Hunting and animal exploitation in the Later Palaeolithic and Mesolithic of Eurasia,* ed. Gail Larsen Peterkin, Harvey M. Bricker, and Paul Mellars, 127-44. Archaeological Papers of the American Anthropological Association No. 4. Washington, D.C.

Pruitt, W. O. 1960. Behavior of the barren-ground caribou. *Biological Papers of the University of Alaska* 3: 1-43.

Scheffer, Victor B. 1951. The rise and fall of a reindeer herd. *Scientific Monthly* 73: 356-61.

Schefferus, J. 1674. *The history of Lapland.* Oxford.

Simchenko, Yri B. 1976. *The culture of reindeer hunters of northern Eurasia.* In Russian. Moscow.

Simonsen, P. 1972. The transition from food-gathering to pastoralism in North Scandinavia and its impact on settlement patterns. In *Man, settlement, and urbanism,* ed. Peter J. Ucko, Ruth Tringham, and Geoffrey W. Dimbleby, 431-9. London.

Skoog, Robert O. 1968. *Ecology of the caribou in Alaska.* Ann Arbor, Mich.

Smith, James G. E. 1978. Economic uncertainty in an "original affluent society": Caribou and caribou-eater Chipewyan adaptive strategies. *Arctic Anthropology* 15: 68-88.

Spiess, Arthur E. 1979. *Reindeer and caribou hunters: An archaeological study.* New York.

In press. Étude de la saison d'habitation au moyen du cement dentaire. In *Les derniers chasseurs du renne le long des Pyrénées,* ed. Lawrence Guy Straus. *Mémoires de la Société Préhistorique Française.* Paris.

Spiess, Arthur E., Mary Lou Curran, and John Grimes. 1985. Caribou *(Rangifer tarandus)* bones from New England Paleo-Indian sites. *North American Archaeologist* 6: 145-59.

Stern, Richard O., Edward L. Arobio, Larry I. Naylor, and Wayne Thomas. 1980. Eskimos, reindeer, and land. *University of Alaska Agricultural Experiment Station Bulletin* 59: 1-205.

Straus, Lawrence G. 1997. Late Glacial reindeer hunters along the French Pyrenees. In *Caribou and reindeer hunters of the Northern Hemisphere,* ed. Lawrence J. Jackson and Paul T. Thacker, 165-84. Aldershot, England.

Strickon, A. 1965. The Euro-American ranching complex. In *Man, culture, and animals,* ed. Anthony Leeds and Andrew Vayda, 229-58. Washington, D.C.

Sturdy, D. A. 1972. The exploitation patterns of a modern reindeer economy in West Greenland. In *Papers in economic prehistory,* ed. Eric S. Higgs, 161-8. Cambridge.

1975. Some reindeer economies in prehistoric Europe. In *Palaeoeconomy,* ed. Eric S. Higgs, 55-96. Cambridge and New York.

Thacker, Paul T. 1997. The significance of *Rangifer* as a human prey species during the central European Upper Paleolithic. In *Caribou and reindeer hunters of the Northern Hemisphere,* ed. Lawrence J. Jackson and Paul T. Thacker, 82-104. Aldershot, England.

Utsi, M. 1948. The reindeer-breeding methods of the northern Lapps. *Man* 48: 97-101.

Vorren, Ornulov. 1994. *Saami, reindeer, and gold in Alaska.* Prospect Heights, Ill.

Vorren, Ornulov, and Ernst Manker. 1962. *Lapp life and customs: A survey.* London.

White, Theodore. 1953. A method of calculating the dietary percentage of various food animals utilized by aboriginal peoples. *American Antiquity* 18: 396-8.

Yesner, David R. 1980. Caribou exploitation in interior Alaska: Paleoecology at Paxson Lake. *Anthropological Papers of the University of Alaska* 19: 15-31.

1989. Moose hunters of the boreal forest? A reconsideration of subsistence patterns in the western Subarctic. *Arctic* 42: 97-108.

1994. Seasonality and resource stress among hunter-gatherers: Archaeological signatures. In *Key issues in hunter-gatherer research,* ed. Ernest L. Burch and Linda J. Ellanna, 99-123. New York.

1995. Subsistence diversity, faunal extinction, and hunter-gatherer strategies in Late Pleistocene/Early Holocene Beringia: Evidence from the Broken Mammoth site, Big Delta, Alaska. *Current Research in the Pleistocene* 11: 154-6.

Yesner, David R., and Robson L. Bonnichsen. 1979. Caribou metapodial shaft splinter technology. *Journal of Archaeological Science* 6: 303-8.

II.G.5 ❧ Cattle

Although cattle have been domesticated for less than 10,000 years, they are the world's most important animals, as judged by their multiple contributions of draft power, meat, milk, hides, and dung. In Asia and Africa, the tie between man and beast is much more than economic (as it is in the West), and domestication itself seems to have occurred for noneconomic reasons. Cattle, like other ruminants, convert cellulose-rich materials

Cattle

– that are otherwise useless to humans as food – into carbohydrates, fats, and proteins. (In industrialized countries, however, cattle are fed grains from cultivated land and consequently can be viewed as competing for foods that could go directly to humans.)

The term "cattle" can have a broad or narrow meaning. One usage subsumes all five domesticated species in the genus *Bos* as cattle. The other restricts the term to only the two main bovines in this genus: European cattle *(Bos taurus)* and zebu cattle *(Bos indicus).* Both animals were derived from the same wild ancestor, the aurochs *(Bos primigenius),* and they can interbreed to produce fertile offspring. Three much more localized Asian species sometimes fall under the rubric of domesticated cattle: mithan *(Bos frontalis,* yak *(Bos grunniens),* and banteng *(Bos javanicus).* The mithan is found in a forested region that encompasses northeast India, northwest Burma, and Bhutan. Its ancestor is the wild gaur *(Bos gaurus).* The yak of Nepal and Tibet was derived from the wild yak *(Bos mutus),* whereas the banteng ("Bali cattle"), found on several islands of the Indonesian archipelago, was domesticated from the wild banteng of the same species. Unless otherwise qualified, the term "cattle" in this chapter refers to the two main species derived from the aurochs.

Domestication

Evidence for the domestication of cattle dates from between 8,000 and 7,000 years ago in southwestern Asia. Such dating suggests that cattle were not domesticated until cereal domestication had taken place, whereas sheep and goats entered the barnyard of humans with the beginning of agriculture. Although the aurochs has been extinct since the seventeenth century, its role as the wild ancestor of cattle has never been seriously disputed. This impressive beast

occurred throughout Eurasia south of the taiga and north of the desert and tropical forest. Paleolithic cave paintings at Lascaux and Altamira in Europe convey a sense of its fierce nobility, which must have awed hunters. At Mesolithic sites in Eurasia, the relative paucity of aurochs bones compared to those of wild sheep – a difficult quarry – and goats suggests a major differential in hunting success.

That humans with primitive technology would have even attempted to tame such a ferocious animal becomes plausible only if one constructs a lure scenario. This setting would have the creation of artificial salt licks to entice the aurochs to a place where the opportunity might present itself to steal a calf from its mother. A young animal, of course, could have been captured and tamed much more easily than an adult.

It is probable that the aurochs underwent transformation into cattle more than once in the prehistory of the Old World. Mitochondrial DNA research indicates that zebu cattle of India were domesticated independently from European cattle and from a different subspecies of the aurochs (Loftus et al. 1994). The clustering of all African zebu within the *B. taurus* lineage is based on the assumption that a zebu ancestor crossbred with earlier *B. taurus* in Africa, and the zebu cattle themselves may have had more than one place of origin. A humped bovid on a Near Eastern figurine dates from the late Bronze Age and corresponds to a similar kind of animal found at Mehrgarh in Pakistan. At that site, both zebu and European cattle are found and together comprise more than 50 percent of the mammalian assemblage (Meadows 1984). Although their origins seem to have been outside the tropics, zebu are well adapted to hot climates, perhaps because much of their early husbandry was in India. Domestication may have enhanced the zebu's characteristic hump, dewlap, generally white color, and alert nature.

Early Neolithic cattle keeping in northern Africa points to a possible separate domestication there as well (Close and Wendorf 1992), and S. Bökönyi (1976) has gone so far as to assert that domestication of cattle from the wild happened repeatedly as late as the classical period of history. Indeed, the first-century-B.C. Roman poet Virgil stated that after a virulent disease had decimated the herds, peasants transformed the aurochs into a domesticated bovine to replace their previous stock. Discrete domestications may have occurred in several places, but the diffusion of domesticated cattle would have been a much more important overall process than repeatedly transforming a ferocious creature over many generations.

As with sheep and goats, the process of domesticating cattle resulted in animals smaller than the wild progenitor. Dated osteological material from Neolithic sites establishes the transition from wild to domesticated, although the sexual dimorphism between the male and female aurochs was not originally appreciated, and the "wild" label was misapplied to the former and "domesticated" to the latter (Grigson 1969). The Fertile Crescent has long been considered the place of initial cattle domestication, but that view tends to reflect the large number of excavations made there. Early signs of Neolithic cattle keeping have also been found in Anatolia (Turkey), where the osteological material at Catal Hüyük provides evidence of the transition from the aurochs of 8,400 years ago to cattle by 7,800 years ago. In short, it is still premature to specify where the first cattle were domesticated.

The extraordinary usefulness of cattle would superficially seem to have been the motivation for their domestication. In other words, given all the benefits that cattle impart, it was logical that the aurochs would come under human control, which is an extension of a deeply rooted Western concept that nature exists to serve the practical needs of people and that necessity has always elicited human ingenuity to provide technical solutions.

However, an alternative to such a materialistic perspective was first proposed by Eduard Hahn (1896), a German geographer-ethnologist. Hahn probed beneath the shallow surface of materialistic motives to see noneconomic forces at work in transforming the animal into what is essentially an artifact of artificial selection. He noted that the curved horns of the aurochs resembled the lunar crescent, which symbolized the Moon Goddess, and suggested that the original reason for domestication was to sacrifice these animals as a reenactment of the goddess's death, with such sacrifices perhaps performed at each waning of the moon.

Such a practice would have required a supply of animals that was initially met by capturing them from the wild. But in the holding pens, some captive bulls and cows (both with long horns) bred, and from these matings, calves occasionally were born that had physical characteristics different from their parents.

Their overall size was smaller, their temperament more docile, and their markings and hide color had unusual variations. Viewed as special, these aurochs born in captivity were also kept as objects of sacrifice but were allowed to breed, and phenotypic distinctiveness enhanced their sacred status.

Some of the next generation to follow may have reinforced the characteristics of the parents, and a gene pool that distinguished these bovines from their wild forebears gradually formed. No longer were they aurochs, but rather cattle, whose sacred roles included pulling ceremonial wagons in religious processions and symbolically plowing the land in fertility rites. Their milk was perceived to be a ritual gift from the goddess, and the most docile cows let themselves be milked by a priest in the presence of their calves. Gradually, the economic usefulness of cattle asserted itself for plowing fields, pulling wagons, and for the meat, milk, and hides, which came to be highly prized. But these were later and secondary benefits of bovine manipulation that initially was prompted by the early mythology of Near Eastern religion. The Eurasian religion of the Upper Paleolithic was supplanted by goddess cults that evolved with the emergence of agriculture and livestock husbandry into fertility cults meant to ensure the prosperity of crops and herds (Isaac 1970).

Evidence for the prehistoric importance of cattle in ritual and the noneconomic motives for domestication comes from Catal Hüyük, a Neolithic archaeological site 50 kilometers south of Konya, Turkey (Mellaart 1967). Many shrines at this reconstructed site, including the earliest one found, have bulls' heads, and an abundance of cattle horn displays suggests that they were venerated as fertility symbols. In another kind of representation, a goddess is shown as having given birth to a bull. Moving to modern times, the previously mentioned mithan (or "Indian bison," as it is sometimes called) is a domesticated animal, but it is not used for draft, meat, or milk. Rather, it is kept as an object of ritual and sacrifice, providing a contemporary example of domestication for noneconomic reasons (Simoons and Simoons 1968). Mithans – periodically killed in ritual sacrifices – occur across a continuum varying from very tame to untamed forest-dwelling animals, and salt, for which they have an insatiable craving, is the enticement that humans employ to attract them.

Early Civilizations

In Mesopotamia, Egypt, and the Indus Valley, cattle served humans as objects of ritual and sources of meat, milk, and draft power, and in all three civilizations, they were the objects of much more intensive human attention than were sheep or goats. Draft animals were indispensable for working irrigated plots in desert and semiarid regions. Cattle required water and grass and needed considerable care. Using cattle for meat seems to have been less important than for draft. During the third Ur dynasty (2112–2004 B.C.), cattle products supplied only 10 percent of total meat needs (Adams 1981). In Mesopotamia, state authority was involved in the organization of cattle keeping, and cattle were called by different terms depending on their function (Zeder 1991).

Ritual use of cattle has been a Eurasian continuity. In ancient Egypt, cattle were regarded as sacred by several cults, particularly that of the goddess Isis, and in Crete, friezes more than 4,000 years old display evidence of bovine importance. At the palace of Minos, for example, the royal couple dressed up as a bull and a cow, and the Minoans also watched specially trained athletes who jousted bulls with acrobatic daring. The Phoenician cult of Baal had a god of fertility represented as a bull – a cult which spread to their colonies as far west as present-day Spain. The early Hebrews worshiped the bull, and in Canaan, the Baal cult was fused with the worship of Yahweh. During King Solomon's reign, the temple housed bulls of bronze and horned sculptures.

In classical antiquity, there is a rich history of bulls offered in ritual sacrifice. Some of these rituals in Greece provided a mechanism to reaffirm the social hierarchy of the polis. Sacred cattle were kept at Eleusis where Demeter was worshiped. In ancient Rome, a white bull was sacrificed at the annual *Feriae Latinae,* and its meat was distributed in proportion to the relative importance of the member cities of the Latin League. In Europe and the Middle East, Judaism, Christianity, and Islam all suppressed such sacred cattle cults as pagan manifestations that competed with their messages, although a lingering remnant is the contemporary Spanish bullfight, which reenacts a sacrifice to symbolize the eternal struggle between humans and nature. In its evolution, bullfighting lost its obvious religious content, which may explain its survival through 2,000 years of Christianity.

Europe

The westward diffusion of cattle throughout Europe was tied to the invention of the wooden plow. The harnessing of a powerful animal to that device made it possible to greatly extend cultivation without a corresponding increase in human population. At the same time, in any one community it freed surplus labor for other activities, which enabled the group to develop greater socioeconomic complexity. Castration of the bull to create an ox was a key element in the spread of the plow. Steady and strong – but docile – the ox made enormous contributions to agriculture. Osteometric evidence shows that oxen were already in use during the fourth millennium B.C., and a figure from Nemea in Greece shows yoked oxen dating from the third millennium B.C. (Pullen 1992).

Farther north in Europe, where wet summers provided abundant forage, cattle had a bigger role to play in livestock husbandry. Following the Middle Ages, an appetite for beef grew, and, in fact, the Europeans' frenetic quest for spices was related to their growing carnivorous tastes. Until the late eighteenth century, cattle were the most important livestock in the uplands of the British Isles, where they grazed mainly on commonly owned natural pastures and secondarily were fed hay cut and stored for winter use. Other animals – sheep, pigs, goats, and horses – were made a part of a land-use system that also favored dairying and the cultivation of grains.

The relative isolation of each region resulted in locally limited gene pools for *B. taurus,* which led to different cattle phenotypes. Three of these, Aberdeen Angus, Shorthorn, and Hereford, have diffused overseas to become modern ranching stock in the Americas; other breeds, such as Devon, Skye, Galloway, Kerry, and Durham, are now rare. Characteristic of British livestock tradition was the close management and selective breeding that imparted a generally docile behavior to the animal. Fat cattle were the aesthetic ideal but also a practical outcome of the high value placed on tallow. Emphasis on pure bloodlines reflected, in part, competition among the landed gentry to produce the best animals, and, in fact, purebred cattle became a symbol of the British ruling class that dominated the world in the nineteenth century. Moreover, that class extended its insistence on purity to its own members as a way of separating the rulers from the ruled in the vast British Empire.

Africa

African bovines kept by humans are usually presumed to have originated as domesticated animals in southwestern Asia, with cattle funneled into Africa through the Sinai Peninsula and, possibly, the Straits of Bab-el Mandeb across the Red Sea, eventually spreading over vast areas of the continent. There is, however, an alternative explanation anchored in the possibility of an independent domestication of cattle in Africa. Evidence that this may have been the case has been found in the northern Sahara, in Algeria, where cave paintings dating from 5,000 to 6,000 years ago indicate a pastoral way of life based on domesticated cattle (Simoons 1971). More recently, an argument has been made for independent cattle domestication in the eastern Sahara as well (Close and Wendorf 1992). Bovid bones found in faunal assemblages have been interpreted to be the remains of domesticated stock kept for milk and blood. Deep wells, dated from the ninth millennium B.C., provided the water without which these cattle could not have survived.

In Africa, more than on any other continent, cattle raising follows a paleotechnic, precapitalistic mode that depends on the natural vegetation of common lands. The transcendental importance of cattle is most apparent in the sub-Saharan eastern half of the continent, where more than 80 million head may be found in an arc across Sudan, Ethiopia, Uganda, Kenya, and Tanzania. Numbers would be much higher than that if nagana disease (spread by tsetse flies) did not make large areas unsuitable for cattle. The ethnographic significance of this geographic concentration was realized only after Melville Herskovits (1926) published his landmark study on the "cattle complex" in East Africa. Subsequent research among different tribal groups – the Karamajong, Nandi, Dodot, Masai, Pakot, and Turkana, among others – validated his contentions of the centrality of cattle in East African life.

Some groups are strongly pastoralist, others may also engage in agriculture. In either case, cattle, whose prestige value surpasses their economic contribution, dominate the pastoral life as well as the social and spiritual activities of each group. Every animal is named and categorized: Among the Masai, for example, each individual animal can be classified according to its matriarchal bovine lineage, a spatial pattern organized by households, and a color/age/sex physical description. A major reason for the naming of cattle in East Africa is that it manifests the affection felt toward bovines as members of the family.

Native religion in East Africa involves cattle sacrifice. Bruce Lincoln (1981) has explained this practice in terms of a "cattle cycle," in which a celestial deity gave cattle to his people. When these animals were stolen by an enemy group (less common today), warriors were enlisted to recover the stolen cattle. The cycle was completed when priests subsequently sacrificed some of the cattle in order to propitiate the celestial deity.

A textbook example of how central cattle can be to the material and social existence of a people can be seen in the Nuer people of the Sudan (Cranstone 1969). Their language is rich in terms that describe and categorize cattle by horn shape, hide color, and age. Milk is a staple food, along with millet, and cattle blood is consumed. Rawhide provides tongs, drums, shields, and bedding, and cattle bones become scrapers, pounders, and beaters. The horns are used to make spoons and spearheads. Cattle dung can be a fuel, but it is also employed in plastering walls, dressing wounds, and, when dried, as a tooth powder. Cow urine is used in washing, cheese making, and dressing skins. The meat and fat of cattle are eaten, but the ritual involved in the slaughter is as important as the food.

Fewer cattle are kept in West Africa than in East Africa, in part because it embraces more desert and forest. The relative importance of cattle varies from tribe to tribe. For example, a dearth of grass and water in the southern Sahara encourages the Tuareg to herd many more goats than cattle, but farther south in the Sahel zone, the Fulani (or Peul) people have become cattle specialists with a spiritual link to their bovines. Each nuclear family owns a herd and knows each animal by name. The Fulani have solved the problem of forage through a symbiosis with their agricultural neighbors to the south. In the dry season, they move their herds south to graze on the stubble of harvested fields. In recompense, the cattle leave manure as fertilizer. Like the tribal peoples of East Africa, the Fulani measure prestige in terms of numbers of animals. They use common pastures, but overstocking has led to range deterioration. One solution for this problem would be the introduction of a commercial system to regularly market young cattle.

India

India has about 200 million head of cattle, more than any other country. Cattle are of great importance as draft animals and as a source of dairy products (milk, curds, ghee), which constitute a significant element of the Indian diet. Cow dung has multiple uses as fuel, fertilizer, and as a ritualistic medium; even cow urine has its sacred applications. The Hindu religion bans the exploitation of cattle for meat and for hides, and to deliberately kill a cow is considered a serious offense in a country whose politicians are committed to protecting the animals. Veneration of cattle is also reflected in the institutions elaborated to protect old cows (Lodrick 1981). At the same time, compliance has its exceptions. Certain tribal groups and some lower-caste Hindus do slaughter cattle and eat their meat.

The cow has elicited much controversy in Hinduism about its origins, for its elevation to sacred status came only after Hinduism was established. One view is that the sacredness of cattle reflects the concept of the sanctity of life *(ahimsa)* that reached Hinduism through Buddhism (Simoons 1994). Opposing this idealistic perspective is the materialist argument that cow protection was ultimately imposed to assure an ongoing pool of plow animals, without which Indian agriculture could not effectively function (Harris 1966).

The New World

Latin America

Cattle began reaching the Western Hemisphere with the second voyage of Christopher Columbus in 1494, when a few head were landed on the island of Hispaniola. They multiplied rapidly – at the same time becoming feral – and eventually were more hunted than herded. Pirates, for example, organized roundups when they wanted fresh meat. From Hispaniola, cattle were taken to other islands and to the mainlands of Central, North, and South America.

In Latin America, cattle raising became an important use of land, especially in the sparsely populated *cerrado* of Brazil, the pampas of Argentina, and the llanos of Venezuela and Colombia. The business was organized in an extensive manner, with fenceless expanses, semiferal animals, mounted cowboys, and low productivity – a system that still prevails over large areas from Mexico to northern Argentina, although the zebu now tends to be more numerous than European cattle. Since the 1970s, cattle ranching has been responsible for most tropical deforestation, especially in Amazonia and Central America, where aggressively spreading grasses of African origin, among them *Panicum, Hyparrhenia,* and *Pennisetum,* have become the forage for millions of cattle. This herbaceous invasion has been termed the "Africanization of the New World tropics," and the expansion of ranching into these areas has been called the "scourge of cows" (Parsons 1970, 1988). Moreover, cattle raising as a "complex" of economic, nutritional, and social factors, and the effects of this complex on the environment and human health, has been denounced as "a new kind of malevolent force in the world" (Rifkin 1992). But from the point of view of their owners, cattle are "walking bank accounts," which become fat on grasses that grow without planting or care.

After the middle of the nineteenth century, cattle ranching moved toward an intensive British style of management on the pampas of Argentina and Uruguay. Throughout the colonial period and beyond, cattle had been raised to make dried and salted beef *(tasajo)* and for hides and tallow. But the nineteenth-century invention of evaporating beef broth to make bouillon cubes provided a new export product to stimulate cattle production, and around 1860, the pampas began to be transformed. The arrival of the Shorthorn, Aberdeen Angus, and Hereford breeds; the introduction of barbed wire fencing; the cultivation of alfalfa; the use of eolian windmills to provide pumped water; and the invention and installation of refrigerated chambers on ships – all set the conditions for the export of high-quality chilled meat to Europe. Since the 1880s, beef exports have underwritten the economies of Uruguay and Argentina.

North America

North American cattle raising has its roots in two very different ranching traditions (Jordan 1993). One came from Andalusia in Spain, specifically from the Guadalquivir marshes, where bovines grazed year-round and were tended by mounted cowboys who used lassos. Transferred from Spain to the Caribbean Islands, this style of ranching was taken to the Carolinas, to the Louisiana coastal plain, and to the Mexican east coast. From Mexico, it diffused northward to southern Texas, with longhorn cattle belonging to the same breed still raised along the Guadalquivir today. Elsewhere in North America, where cold winters intervened, pastoral practices were influenced by those of the British Isles. Thus, the midwestern prairies had a cattle-raising complex that included British breeds of cattle and the use of haying, fencing, barns, and intensive herd management to create docile animals.

Most cattle in North America are "finished off" on grain in feed lots; indeed, more than 70 percent of the grain produced in the United States is fed to cattle and other livestock. A slaughtered steer yields about 60 percent of its weight in beef products, some of which is used as pet food, but most is for human consumption. The remaining 40 percent consists of fat, bones, viscera, and hide that go into a variety of industrial and household products. Cattle tend to be much leaner today than they were a century ago. Demand for low-cholesterol meat, and the use of petroleum-based detergents rather than soaps made from tallow, have greatly reduced the market for both fatty beef and beef fat.

A growing application of animal-raising technologies can be expected to increase the efficiency of cattle raising in the United States and other industrialized countries. Artificial insemination was a common practice by the 1950s, and more recent reproductive techniques include embryo transfer, estrous cycle regulation, embryo splitting, in vitro fertilization, sperm sexing, and cloning. Other techniques promote growth: Anabolic steroids have been used on beef cattle since 1954, and fully 90 percent of feedlot cattle in the United States receive these drugs. In the European Union, steroids are still banned, which has complicated the export of American beef into that large market. For dairy cattle, bovine somatotropin, a protein hormone, increases milk production by about 12 percent. Other technologies relate to processing and marketing. Irradiation of meat kills microorganisms and extends shelf life, and the extraction of water from milk to reduce transportation costs will greatly increase the milkshed range of cities.

Consumption of Bovine Flesh

Except in the few cultures that shun beef as food, bovine flesh has often been regarded as the ultimate measure of a good diet. As Europe regained its prosperity in the three decades after World War II, per capita consumption of beef increased several times. Now, more than 40 percent of all the meat produced in Western Europe is beef. Consumers in some European countries – especially Italy, France, and Austria – are exceptionally fond of veal, which is very young bovine flesh.

In Europe, veal typically comes from calves less than 6 months old that are fed on whole milk or on a formula that includes milk products. Close to half of the bovines slaughtered in France are calves, which yield veal that normally retails for 20 percent more than beef. Veal, tender and subtly flavorful, lends itself to imaginative sauces or accompaniments: Scallopini, osso buco, saltimbocca, and Wiener schnitzel are all well-known veal dishes. In Europe, calves also provide much of the most desirable organ meats: liver, sweetbreads, kidneys, brains, and tongue. In both France and Italy, veal consumption is about one-third that of beef – four times more veal, on a per capita basis, than is eaten in the United States, where beef has been the preferred meat since the nineteenth century.

Today, more than 40 percent of beef consumed in the United States is ground, mostly for hamburgers. The hamburger has become an icon of American popular culture, even though it is said to have originated in Hamburg, Germany. "Hamburger steak" was on Delmonico's menu as early as 1836, and there are numerous claimants for the invention of the hamburger sandwich, including a German immigrant said to have brought the idea to the United States in 1892. Certainly, it was the case that the hamburger began to be nationally known at the 1904 St. Louis World's Fair, where the sandwiches were sold by German immigrants (Trager 1995).

The hamburger – as a snack or a meal – fits into the American quest for efficiency. It cooks thoroughly in less than 8 minutes, and today, fast-food operators normally cook it even before the customer places an order. Hamburger restaurants appeared in American cities beginning in the 1920s, but their organization to maximize efficiency dates from four decades later. Giant franchise corporations with headquarters in the United States have now spread over a major part of the industrialized world. At an international level, these restaurants communicate American values of efficiency, service, and cleanliness, but for many, they also define the failure of the American culinary imagination.

The American middle class is also fond of steak, and well informed about the best cuts. Steak is a favorite restaurant choice, but it is frequently cooked at home as well, often on an outdoor grill. (In 1995, 77 percent of American households owned at least one such grill.) The United States Department of Agriculture (USDA) grading system for beef has its greatest application in steak. "Prime," with the most fat marbling, is the most flavorful, tender, and costly. Only 2 percent of all the beef produced in the country is of prime grade. "Choice" is the most widely sold grade, whereas "select" is leaner, cheaper, and not as tender. Several other countries in the world – notably Argentina – have a much higher per capita consumption of beef than the United States, but this statistic probably includes considerable amounts of organ meats. By contrast, bovine organ meat attracts few consumers in the United States.

In Japan, beef consumption is a relatively recent phenomenon. Meat eating was prohibited until shortly after the Meiji Restoration in 1882. Buddhist beliefs and Shinto influences had banned the killing and eating of four-legged animals, but fish and fowl were consumed, and the Japanese still obtain most of their protein from fish and soybeans. Sukiyaki – thinly sliced, highly marbled sirloin in soy sauce, accompanied by vegetables – has been the preferred beef dish. In the preparation of sukiyaki, the sight of blood, unacceptable in Japanese culture, was avoided. But after World War II, American influences and increasing prosperity introduced hamburger, beef chunks in curry sauce, and skewered beef, and most recently, steak has become accepted in Japan.

Daniel W. Gade

Bibliography

Adams, R. Mc. 1981. *Heartland of cities*. Chicago.

Bökönyi, S. 1976. Development of early stock rearing in the Near East. *Nature* 264: 19-23.

Close, Angela E., and Fred Wendorf. 1992. The beginnings of food production in the eastern Sahara. In *Transitions to agriculture in prehistory*, ed. Anne Birgitte Gebauer and T. Douglas Price, 63-72. Madison, Wis.

Cranstone, B. A. L. 1969. Animal husbandry: The evidence from ethnography. In *The domestication and exploitation of plants and animals*, ed. Peter J. Ucko and G. W. Dimbleby, 247-63. Chicago.

Grigson, Caroline. 1969. The uses and limitations of differences in the absolute size in the distinction between the bones of aurochs *(Bos primigenius)* and domestic cattle *(Bos taurus)*. In *The domestication and exploitation of plants and animals*, ed. Peter J. Ucko and G. W. Dimbleby, 277-94. Chicago.

Hahn, Eduard. 1896. *Die Haustiere und ihre Beziehungen zur Wirtschaft des Menschen*. Leipzig.

Harris, Marvin. 1966. The cultural ecology of India's sacred cattle. *Current Anthropology* 7: 51-66.

Herskovits, Melville J. 1926. The cattle complex in East Africa. *American Anthropologist* 28: 230-72.

Isaac, Erich. 1970. *Geography of domestication*. Englewood Cliffs, N.J.

Jordan, Terry G. 1993. *North American cattle-ranching frontiers*. Albuquerque, N.Mex.

Lincoln, Bruce. 1981. *Priests, warriors and cattle: A study in the ecology of religions*. Berkeley, Calif.

Lodrick, Deryck O. 1981. *Sacred cows, sacred places: Origins and survival of animal homes in India*. Berkeley, Calif.

Loftus, Ronan T., D. E. MacHugh, D. G. Bradley, et al. 1994. Evidence for two independent domestications of cattle. *Proceedings of the National Academy of Sciences* 91: 2757-61.

Meadows, Richard H. 1984. Animal domestication in the Middle East: A view from the eastern margin. In *Animals and archaeology*, Vol. 3, *Early herders and their flocks*, ed. Juliet Clutton-Brock and Caroline Grigson, 309-37. Oxford.

Mellaart, James. 1967. *Catal Hüyük: A Neolithic town in Anatolia*. New York.

Parsons, James J. 1970. The "Africanization" of the New World tropical grasslands. *Tübinger Geographische Studien* 34: 141-53.

  1988. The scourge of cows. *Whole Earth Review* 58: 40-7.

Pullen, D. J. 1992. Ox and plow in the early Bronze Age Aegean. *American Journal of Archaeology* 96: 45-54.

Rifkin, Jeremy. 1992. *Beyond beef: The rise and fall of the cattle culture*. New York.

Simoons, Frederick J. 1971. The antiquity of dairying in Asia and Africa. *Geographical Review* 61: 431-9.

  1994. *Eat not this flesh: Food avoidances from prehistory to the present*. Madison, Wis.

Simoons, Frederick J., and Elizabeth S. Simoons. 1968. *A cere-monial ox of India: The mithan in nature, culture, and history.* Madison, Wis.

Trager, James. 1995. *The food chronology.* New York.

Zeder, Melinda A. 1991. *Feeding cities: Specialized animal economy in the ancient Near East.* Washington, D.C.

II.G.6 ✺ Chickens

Origins

The chicken *(Gallus gallus* or *Gallus domesticus)* is generally considered to have evolved from the jungle fowl *(G. gallus),* which ranges throughout the area between eastern India and Java. Within the nomenclature, *G. domesticus* is normally used by scholars who believe in a polyphyletic origin for the domestic chicken (from *G. gallus, Gallus sonnerati,* and *Gallus lafayettei),* whereas *G. gallus* is used by those who support a unique origin from the various subspecies of wild *G. gallus.* Debates regarding the origin and spread of the domestic chicken focus both on its genetic basis and the "hearth area" of its initial domestication.

The osteological identification of domestic chickens has been made both on a contextual basis (i.e., the occurrence of *Gallus* bones outside of the birds' normal wild range) and on osteometric grounds (i.e., the occurrence of bones that are larger than those of modern wild jungle fowl and therefore would seem to be the result of selective breeding). Recent research of this nature has resulted in a radical revision of the standard view of the domestication of the chicken. The presence of domestic fowl bones in third-millennium-B.C. archaeological excavation contexts at Harappa and Mohenjo-Daro in Pakistan led earlier writers (Zeuner 1963; Crawford 1984)

Chicken

to assume that the chicken was first domesticated in this area. However, in 1988, B. West and B.-X. Zhou presented archaeological data showing domestic chickens to be present at China's Yangshao and Peiligan Neolithic sites, which dated from circa 6000 to 4000 B.C. As a consequence, because wild forms of *Gallus* are entirely absent in China, and as the climate would have been inimical to them in the early Holocene, it seems likely that chickens were domesticated elsewhere at an even earlier date. In the absence of evidence from India, Southeast Asia (i.e., Thailand) has been put forward as a likely hearth area (West and Zhou 1988).

Such a hypothesis seems to square nicely with some recent research on the genetic origins of chickens. In the past, a polyphyletic view often predominated because of the phenotypic diversity of modern chickens (Crawford 1984). But quite recently, A. Fumihito and colleagues (1994) have shown convincingly that all modern chicken genes can be derived from the subspecies of *Gallus* found in northeast Thailand. This demonstration provides a geographical origin for the chicken that harmonizes with the archaeological data and, at least for the moment, disposes of the argument for polygenesis.

Uses

Although chickens are strongly associated with egg production in European and neo-European cultures, elsewhere they have very different associations. In much of Southeast and East Asia they have been bred both for fighting and as decoration; in Japan, for example, there is little evidence for the exploitation of chickens as food until the nineteenth century. On the basis of the present locations of these specialized breeds, I. G. Moiseeva and colleagues (1996) have postulated three centers of breed origin, to which we would add two further categories for highly productive egg layers and meat–egg compromise breeds. Both Aristotle and Pliny referred to distinct fighting and meat breeds at the beginning of the Christian era (Wood-Gush 1959). However, the origin of most of these types (save the intermediate and egg-laying breeds) appears to have been near the zone of their original domestication.

Chickens and Geography

Southeast Asia and Oceania

It is usually conceded that the Austronesians had the chicken – along with the dog and pig – when they began their epic voyages of colonization in the Pacific some 5,000 or more years ago. Chickens have been recovered from Hemudu in Southeast China, dating to 7,000 years ago, and such settlements are usually considered to be ancestral to the main Austronesian expansion (Bellwood 1995). Although direct evidence is lacking for chickens in the Austronesian area until much later, linguistic evidence argues that the fowl traveled with the Austronesians (Zorc 1994).

Central Asia

The chicken has been well documented osteologically from the Harappan civilization of the Indus Valley, where it was introduced by 2500 B.C. (Zeuner 1963). However, in view of both archaeological and linguistic evidence, it appears that chickens did not spread through India but rather around it – heading northeastward from China and through central Asia north of the Himalayas (Nishi 1990; Moiseeva et al. 1996). The fowl was certainly introduced into Iran about this period; Zoroastrian literature makes extensive reference to its crowing at dawn (Wood-Gush 1959).

Linguistics can complement the results of archaeology in tracking the route of the chicken's diffusion. If words for chicken, cock, and chick are compiled for the Old World, some intriguing patterns emerge. There are two extremely widespread roots, ka(C)i and tax(V).[1] The latter is spread from Korea across central Asia to the Near East, North Africa, and south to Lake Chad. This suggests not only that the chicken diffused westward from China as far as central Africa, but that it did so after the principal language phyla were established, as the vernacular terms form a chain of loanwords.

Europe

The discovery of bones – collated by West and Zhou (1988) – in central Asia seems to indicate that the chicken had reached the borders of Europe by 3000 B.C. The earliest finds come from Romania, Turkey, and Greece, where there are at least eight late Neolithic and early Bronze Age sites from which bones have been dated to the third millennium B.C. These finds, contemporary with or slightly earlier than those of the Indus Valley, appear to demonstrate that the initial dispersion of the chicken from Southeast Asia effectively bypassed the Indian subcontinent. This conclusion would seem to be further borne out by "culturally dated" fourth-millennium-B.C. finds in the vicinity of Kiev (Ukraine) that were published in the 1950s, although a great deal of research remains to be done in the area.

The subsequent rate of dispersion of the chicken in Europe appears to have slowed substantially, with most early western and northern European bone discoveries dated to the middle to late first millennium B.C. Indeed, F. Hernandez-Carrasquilla (1992) has sounded a note of caution by refuting all pre–first-millennium-B.C. identifications from Spain as intrusions or errors in attribution and has once again credited the Phoenicians with the domestic fowl's introduction into Iberia.

Chicken domestication became well established in Europe during the Iron Age, and by the time of the Romans, superior breeding or animal husbandry strategies had resulted in substantial size increases in the domestic fowl (Thesing 1977). During the medieval period, the dietary importance of chickens increased relative to that of mammals, with chicken rearing in towns becoming increasingly common (Astill and Grant 1988; Benecke 1993). Unfortunately, chickens were often left to forage amid domestic waste, and less labor-intensive poultry-rearing techniques resulted in a general size reduction for domestic fowl (Thesing 1977), although birds bred in rural areas may have fared better. In Europe, there is little evidence for a great diversity of breeds until the late Middle Ages, or even later; in parts of the Netherlands and Poland, however, there is osteological evidence for both a small and a large breed of chicken in early medieval times (Benecke 1993).

Southwestern Asia and North Africa

In the Levant, there are only a few early chicken identifications, with the earliest finds, from Tell Sweyhat in northern Syria, dating to the late third millennium B.C. (Buitenhuis 1983). The bird does not appear to have been common further south until the first millennium B.C. (West and Zhou 1988). A seal found at Nimrud, dated to 800 B.C., shows a cock (Zeuner 1963). One of the uses of early chickens in this region is indicated by the seventh-century-B.C. representation of fighting cocks on seals and potsherds from Israel/Palestine (Taran 1975).

A much-reproduced painted limestone fragment from the tomb of Tutankhamen clearly illustrates a cock, and several other representations suggest the occasional presence of fowl as exotics in Egypt during the New Kingdom (1425–1123 B.C.) (Carter 1923; Darby, Ghalioungui, and Grivetti 1977, 1: 297 ff.; Crawford 1984). However, they then disappear from the graphic record until about 650 B.C., after which they are represented in abundance (Coltherd 1966). Osteologically, despite several early misattributions, the earliest chicken bones found in Egypt date only to the beginning of the Greco–Roman period (332 B.C. to A.D. 200) (MacDonald and Edwards 1993). It would thus appear likely that the chicken was at first imported into Egypt as an exotic menagerie and fighting bird and gained economic importance only during the late first millennium B.C. – in Ptolemaic times.

Sub-Saharan Africa

Although chickens are central to African culture throughout the continent, the morphology of local fowls remains undescribed, and the routes by which they entered the continent – as well as the dates when that took place – remain poorly known. Archaeologists have tended to favor a rather recent date (MacDonald 1992, 1995; MacDonald and Edwards 1993), whereas linguists have argued for much earlier dates, based on the degree of the embedding of words for chicken (Johnston 1886; Manessy 1972; Blench 1995; Williamson in press).

Osteological evidence of chickens in Africa has become increasingly abundant during the 1990s. The earliest known remains are from the middle of the first millennium A.D., with finds from Mali (MacDonald 1992), Nubia (MacDonald and Edwards 1993), the East African coast (Mudida and Horton 1996), and South Africa (Plug 1996) all dating to this period. No earlier remains are known as yet, and archaeozoologists hypothesize that chickens most likely entered Africa either via the Nile Valley or through an early Greco–Roman east-coast trade between about A.D. 100 and 500. A trans-Saharan introduction (at an earlier date via Phoenician Carthage), however, cannot be excluded.

The linguistic evidence rather strongly suggests multiple introductions: across the Sahara, via the Berbers, on the east coast, and, possibly, a separate introduction to Ethiopia via the Red Sea coast. In addition, early reports of chickens in Mozambique suggest black-feathered types, resembling those in India.

Because, in most cases, African chickens were left to find their own food and were allowed to mate at random, there are no significant African breeds (Kuit, Traore, and Wilson 1986; MacDonald 1992).

The New World

One of the most intriguing controversies in the history of chickens is the question of whether they were present in the New World in pre-European times. Both G. F. Carter (1971) and R. Langdon (1990) have argued strongly that they were, at least in parts of the West Coast. Linguistics (in the sense that chickens do not have names borrowed from European languages), morphology (the distinctive blue eggs of some New World breeds, otherwise known only from China), and the improbable speed of transmission inland that would be required by the assumption of a European introduction all suggest a pre-Columbian introduction from Asia (see also Carpenter 1985). Against this theory, however, is the fact that no undisputed early chicken bones have ever been found in a mainland site. Langdon (1990) has cited reports of blue-egg fowls on Easter Island, which he considers to strengthen evidence of trans-Pacific contact with the South American mainland.

Future Understanding

We know very little about past developments in five geographical areas that are crucial to understanding the domestication and subsequent spread of the domestic fowl: Thailand, Russia/Ukraine, the Indian subcontinent, Southwest Asia, and sub-Saharan Africa. It is crucial that specialized archaeozoologists examine temporally relevant avian skeletal materials from these zones and that they be well apprised of potentially confusing local wild taxa – especially birds such

as guinea fowl, pheasants, and larger francolins – and the criteria for their differentiation (MacDonald 1992).

Complementary results can be obtained from more detailed genetic work on traditional chicken breeds using both DNA and phenotypic characters. Although the chicken is usually considered to be well known, compilations such as those by Ronan Loftus and Beate Scherf (1993) show that there are many poorly described breeds of chicken on the verge of extinction that are kept by traditional societies. A broader view of the origins and distribution of chicken breeds in the world should help us to understand more clearly their role in both subsistence and the interaction of human cultures.

Roger Blench and Kevin C. MacDonald

Note

1. The authors are grateful to Zev Handel and James Matisoff for providing unpublished documentation of chicken names in Sino-Tibetan languages.

Bibliography

Astill, G., and A. Grant. 1988. *The countryside of medieval England.* Oxford.

Bellwood, Peter. 1995. Austronesian prehistory in Southeast Asia: Homeland, expansion and transformation. In *The Austronesians: Historical and comparative perspectives,* ed. Peter Bellwood, James J. Fox, and Darrell Tryon, 96–111. Canberra, Australia.

Benecke, N. 1993. On the utilization of domestic fowl in central Europe from the Iron Age up to the Middle Ages. *Archaeofauna* 2: 21–31.

Blench, R. M. 1995. A history of domestic animals in northeastern Nigeria. *Cahiers des Sciences Humaines* 31: 181–238. Paris.

Brewer, D. J., D. B. Redford, and S. Redford. 1994. *Domestic plants and animals: The Egyptian origins.* Warminster, England.

Buitenhuis, H. 1983. The animal remains from Tell Sweyhat, Syria. *Palaeohistoria* 25: 131–44.

Carpenter, Lawrence K. 1985. How did the "chicken" cross the Andes? *International Journal of American Linguistics* 51: 361–4.

Carter, G. F. 1971. Pre-Columbian chickens in America. In *Man across the sea: Problems of pre-Columbian contacts,* ed. C. L. Riley, J. C. Kelley, C. W. Pennington, and R. L. Rands, 178–218. Austin, Tex.

Carter, H. 1923. An ostracon depicting a red jungle-fowl. *Journal of Egyptian Archaeology* 9: 1–4.

Colherd, J. B. 1966. The domestic fowl in ancient Egypt. *Ibis* 108: 217–23.

Crawford, R. D. 1984. Domestic fowl. In *Evolution of domesticated animals,* ed. I. L. Mason, 298–311. London.

Darby, William J., Paul Ghalioungui, and Louis Grivetti. 1977. *The gift of Osiris.* 2 vols. London.

Dmitriev, N. G., and L. K. Ernst. 1989. *Animal genetic*

resources of the USSR. FAO Animal Production and Health Paper No. 65. Rome.

Fumihito, A., T. Miyake, S.-I. Sumi, et al. 1994. One subspecies of the red junglefowl *(Gallus gallus gallus)* suffices as the matriarchic ancestor of all domestic breeds. *Proceedings of the National Academy of Sciences* 91: 12505-9.

Hernandez-Carrasquilla, F. 1992. Some comments on the introduction of domestic fowl in Iberia. *Archaeofauna* 1: 45-53.

Johnston, H. H. 1886. *The Kili-Manjaro expedition; a record of scientific exploration in eastern equatorial Africa.* London.

Kuit, H. G., A. Traore, and R. T. Wilson. 1986. Livestock production in central Mali: Ownership, management and productivity of poultry in the traditional sector. *Tropical Animal Health and Production* 18: 222-31.

Langdon, R. 1990. When the blue-egg chickens come home to roost. *Journal of Pacific History* 25: 164-92.

Loftus, Ronan, and Beate' Scherf. 1993. *Worldwatch list.* Rome.

MacDonald, K. C. 1992. The domestic chicken *(Gallus gallus)* in sub-Saharan Africa: A background to its introduction and its osteological differentiation from indigenous fowls *(Numidinae* and *Francolinus* sp.). *Journal of Archaeological Science* 19: 303-18.

　　1995. Why chickens?: The centrality of the domestic fowl in West African ritual and magic. In *Animal symbolism and archaeology,* ed. K. Ryan and P. J. Crabtree, 50-6. Philadelphia, Pa.

MacDonald, K. C., and D. N. Edwards. 1993. Chickens in Africa: The importance of Qasr Ibrim. *Antiquity* 67: 584-90.

Manessy, G. 1972. Les noms d'animaux domestiques dans les langues voltaïques. *Langues et techniques, nature et société; approches linguistiques,* Vol. 1, ed. J. M. C. Thomas and L. Bernot, 301-20. Paris.

Moiseeva, I. G., Zhang Yuguo, A. A. Nikiforov, and I. A. Zakharov. 1996. Comparative analysis of morphological traits in the Mediterranean and Chinese chicken breeds: The problem of the origin of the domestic chicken. *Russian Journal of Genetics* 32: 1349-57.

Mudida, N., and M. Horton. 1996. Subsistence at Shanga: The faunal record. In *Shanga: The archaeology of a Muslim trading community on the coast of East Africa,* ed. M. Horton, 378-93. Nairobi.

Nishi, Y. 1990. Can fowls fly hundreds of miles over the Himalayas? In *Asian languages and general linguistics,* ed. T. Sakiyama and A. Sato, 55-77. Tokyo.

Plug, Ina. 1996. Domestic animals during the early Iron Age in southern Africa. In *Aspects of African archaeology: Papers from the 10th Congress of the Pan-African Association for Prehistory and Related Studies,* ed. G. Pwiti and R. Soper, 515-20. Harare, Zimbabwe.

Shmidt, P. 1927. *Domashnyaya ptitsa i ee istoriya* (Poultry and its history). Moscow.

Skinner, N. A. 1977. Domestic animals in Chadic. In *Papers in Chadic linguistics,* ed. P. Newman and R. M. Newman, 175-98. Leiden, The Netherlands.

Taran, M. 1975. Early records of the domestic fowl in Judea. *Ibis* 117: 109-10.

Thesing, R. 1977. *Die Großentwicklung des Haushuhns in vor- und frühgeschichtlicher Zeit.* Ph.D. dissertation, Munich University.

West, B., and B.-X. Zhou. 1988. Did chickens go north? New evidence for domestication. *Journal of Archaeological Science* 15: 515-33.

Williamson, K. In press. Did chickens go west? In *The origins and development of African livestock,* ed. R. M. Blench and K. C. MacDonald. London.

Wood-Gush, D. G. M. 1959. A history of the domestic chicken from antiquity to the 19th century. *Poultry Science* 38: 321-6.

Zeuner, F. E. 1963. *A history of domesticated animals.* London.

Zorc, R. D. P. 1994. Austronesian culture history through reconstructed vocabulary (overview). In *Austronesian terminologies: Continuity and change,* ed. A. K. Pawley and M. D. Ross, 541-94. Canberra, Australia.

II.G.7 ⁓ Chicken Eggs

Hickety Pickety, my black hen
She lays eggs for gentlemen
Gentlemen come here every day
To see what my hen doth lay

Anonymous

History

Eggs from many species of fowl have doubtless been consumed since the very beginning of humankind's stay on earth. In historical times, ancient Romans ate peafowl eggs, and the Chinese were fond of pigeon eggs. Ostrich eggs have been eaten since the days of the Phoenicians, whereas quail eggs, as hard-cooked, shelf-stable, packaged products, are now featured on many gourmet food counters in the United States and Japan. Other eggs consumed by various ethnic groups include those from plovers, partridges, gulls, turkeys, pelicans, ducks, and geese. Turtle eggs have been highly prized, and in starvation situations, any eggs, even those of alligators, have been relied upon.

In this chapter, however, only avian eggs (and these mostly from the chicken) are discussed. Avian eggs in themselves constitute a huge subject: In 1949, A. L. Romanoff and A. J. Romanoff published a book in which they attempted to compile all the facts known, at the time, about the eggs of birds. It contained over 2,400 reference citations.

It is almost obligatory in writing about eggs to first deal with that age-old question: Which came first, the chicken or the egg? Those who believe in creationism rely on holy books, like the Bible, which specify that animals were created. Thus, the chicken came first. But, as Harold McGee has pointed out, the eggs of reptiles preceded by far the evolution of the first birds; consequently, "[e]ggs . . . are millions of years older than birds." He added that *"Gallus domesticus,* the chicken, more or less as we know it, is only 4 to 5 thousand years old, a latecomer even among the domesticated animals" (1984: 55).

McGee placed the ancestors of *Gallus domesticus* (as the Romans named it) in Southeast Asia or India.

Maguelonne Toussaint-Samat was a bit more specific in writing that the chicken is "a descendant of a bird from the Malaysian jungle" (1992: 351). Still others have designated Burma and quite recently Thailand as its homeland, and there has been an argument for multiple origins with as many as four different species of jungle fowl contributing to the modern chicken (Smith and Daniel 1982; Fumihito et al. 1994; Simoons 1994).

The chicken was not only a tardy arrival as a food animal; it may have been domesticated not for food purposes at all but rather because of a perceived need for an on-hand supply of birds for sacrifice and divination. Frederick Simoons (1994) pointed out that these have been traditional uses of the chicken in Southeast Asia and are still roles the bird is called upon to fill by many peoples of the region.

Another early, but nonfood, use for the chicken in Southeast Asia was the sport of cockfighting – a sport that to this day remains immensely popular there, despite thousands of years of opposition by religions such as Hinduism and Buddhism (Simoons 1994).

But cockfighting was not confined to Southeast Asia, and as interest in it spread, so did the chicken. Although there was mention of the bird in Egypt in the early fourteenth century B.C., there seems to be no subsequent mention of it for many centuries thereafter, prompting speculation that it may have disappeared after its initial introduction (Smith and Daniel 1982). The chicken, however, was also in Persia at an early date, and from there it (along with cockfighting) spread out into ancient Greece, where it joined ducks, geese, and guinea fowl in poultry yards around the fifth century B.C. (Toussaint-Samat 1992).

Although a few recipes from the Greeks indicate that eggs were used for baking, and the physicians who compiled the Hippocratic Corpus recommended lightly cooked eggs as the most nourishing way to prepare them, and Aristotle systematically opened eggs at different points in their incubation to describe what he saw, it is doubtful that egg production was, initially at least, a very important reason for maintaining the bird (Smith and Daniel 1982; Toussaint-Samat 1992).

In the Roman period, however, although cockfighting remained a primary reason for keeping chickens, eggs were finally beginning to catch on in the kitchen. The recipes of Apicius (25 B.C.) reveal custards, omelets, and eggs used in a variety of other dishes, as well as by themselves in hard-boiled form (McGee 1984; Touissant-Samat 1994). The Roman physician Galen, however, condemned fried eggs, saying they "have bad juice and corrupt even the foods mixed with them" (cited in Smith and Daniel 1982: 366).

Yet in other parts of the world at about this time, it would appear that egg consumption was avoided more often than not. In part this was because eggs (as well as chickens) were used for divination, in part because eggs were regarded as a filthy food (the product of the semen of a cock), in part because of food taboos (such as those that regulated the diets of pregnant women and their youngsters), and often because it was believed wasteful to eat the egg instead of waiting for the chicken.

China, however, constituted a very large exception to egg avoidance. Both chickens and eggs were important sources of animal protein, and the Chinese are said to have encouraged their use throughout the rest of East Asia. In Southeast Asia and in the Pacific Islands (where the chicken was distributed early on by Asian colonizers), as well as in China, a taste was developed for brooded eggs (with well-developed fetuses). In addition, the Chinese became partial to "100-year-old" eggs that tend to make Westerners gag. But despite the name, the eggs are buried for only a few months in a mixture of saltpeter, clay, tea leaves, and other materials that cause the shells to turn black. The interiors of such eggs take on a "hard-boiled" appearance with green veins running through them (Toussaint-Samat 1992; Simoons 1994).

Moving from the East back to the West after the fall of Rome, darkness descended on both Europe and the chicken, and little is known about the use of eggs on the Continent until the sixteenth century. In the meantime, the Iberians had discovered the New World, triggering many debates for scholars – among them the question of whether chickens were on hand in the Americas when Columbus first arrived in 1492. The answer seems to be no, at least as far as the West Indies (where the Spaniards introduced them) are concerned, but may very possibly be yes, as far as South America is concerned. There, the native people had names of their own for a kind of chicken – and the only one in the world that lays blue and green eggs (Smith and Daniel 1982). Page Smith and Charles Daniel have speculated that this South American *araucana* was not an "indigenous chicken" but instead the product of a union of American grouse with Asian chickens that reached South America with earlier, unrecorded voyagers (1982: 31), most likely Pacific Islanders.

European literature is not completely silent on eggs prior to the Renaissance; we are warned in *Don Quixote de la Mancha* (by Miguel de Cervantes [1547-1616]) not to put them all in one basket, and Francis Bacon (1561-1626) commented on those who would burn their houses down just to roast an egg. Throughout the preceding Middle Ages, however, eggs were mostly mentioned in nursery rhymes. In large part, one suspects that this considerable silence was because eggs were classified as meat by the Church; what with Fridays, Lent, and numerous other days when meat was proscribed, eggs were off the menu about half of the days of the year. As a consequence, most eggs were either used for hatching or were saved to be eaten at Easter. To keep them from spoiling, they were dipped in either liquid fat or wax and then decorated to make them more attractive – hence the custom of "Easter eggs" (Toussaint-Samat 1992).

Although some French and English recipe books from the late fourteenth century contain directions for making custards, omelets, and baked eggs (McGee 1984), Smith and Daniel (1982) suggest that the renaissance of the chicken came only in the sixteenth century with the work of Ulisse Aldrovandi (1522–1605), an Italian who wrote nine volumes on animals, including one on chickens. It was the dawn of a new age of science, and as Aristotle had done some 1,800 years earlier, Aldrovandi systematically examined the egg while at the same time adroitly dodging "that trite and thus otiose . . . question, whether the hen exists before the egg or vice versa" (quoted in Smith and Daniel 1982: 45). It might have been a new age of science, but the Church still had a firm answer for this old riddle.

The egg had made considerable culinary headway by 1651, when Pierre François de la Varenne published *Le cuisinier françois,* a cookbook that provided 60 recipes for eggs (Tannahill 1989). But it is the era embracing the eighteenth and early nineteenth centuries that has been characterized as "The Century of the Chicken" (Smith and Daniel 1982) because of the considerable amount of scientific interest the bird generated. Upon learning about elaborate hatching ovens in Egypt, the French naturalist René de Reaumur wrote a treatise on the subject, and breeding chickens became a preoccupation of European (and North American) country squires with a scientific turn of mind (McGee 1984).

This effort was given considerable impetus in the nineteenth century with the opening of the Chinese port of Canton (in 1834) to foreign traders. One of the first English vessels in the new trade returned with a few chickens of a Chinese breed – "Cochin" fowl, as they were ultimately called – as a present for Queen Victoria. In addition to their startlingly spectacular appearance, the Cochin chickens were superior in meat and egg production to established Mediterranean and European breeds. When they were first exhibited in England, tens of thousands of people showed up to stare, and all breeders had to have one. The same phenomenon took place at the Boston Poultry Show of 1849, where the birds again attracted crowds in the thousands, and even Daniel Webster attended to heap praise on the fowl.

Chickens had suddenly gained a new prominence among barnyard animals, and others of the great Asian breeds followed the Cochin to the West to perpetuate the chicken craze (Smith and Daniel 1982; McGee 1984). Breeding for show – with major emphasis on feather coloring and comb type – continued throughout much of the rest of the nineteenth century, with over 100 different breeds and color variations the result.

The "Century of the Chicken" was also a century of the egg, during which it was incorporated into diets as never before. Boiled eggs for breakfast became a favorite of many, and it was said that entire families of Parisians crowded around every Sunday to admire the dexterity of their sovereign, Louis XIV, who could knock off the small end of an egg with his fork in a single stroke (Toussaint-Samat 1992). The king was also very fond of meringues. Cookbooks provided careful instructions for the preparation of omelets and the poaching of eggs; mayonnaise was invented in the middle of the eighteenth century; the Americans followed the English example of marrying bacon with eggs; and the baking industry boomed (Trager 1995). Consequently, as the end of the nineteenth century approached, eggs were very much in demand in the West, and the emphasis in chicken breeding shifted from show-bird characteristics to productive capacity for eggs, or meat, or both.

Early in the twentieth century, Artemus Ward, in *The Grocer's Encyclopedia,* indicated something of the way that demand was being met. He wrote of "large poultry farms [where] eggs are produced and handled very much as the product of any other factory . . . but," he added, "the greater part of the country's egg supply is still represented by accumulations from thousands of general farmers scattered all over the country" (1911: 223).

This is hardly the case today. Poultry sheds have become meat and egg factories with automated hatcheries (McGee 1984). Major steps in this direction took place in the 1930s and 1940s as John Tyson pioneered the vertical integration of the poultry industry. In 1956, the animal health-products division of Merck Pharmaceutical Company began production of a drug that prevented flock-destroying epidemics of coccidiosis. These events were accompanied by the development of high-protein feeds, after which chicken and egg production became truly automated industries (Trager 1995).

The egg is a fine (and cheap) source of high-quality protein, as well as iron, vitamins E and B_{12}, folacin, riboflavin, and phosphorous, and was long regarded as a near-perfect food. But the egg's yolk is also a source of considerable cholesterol, and with the implication of this substance in blocking heart arteries, demand for fresh eggs fell by almost 25 percent in the decade of the 1980s. In addition, eggs have been blamed of late (with some regularity) for outbreaks of salmonellosis. But although the use of fresh eggs has fallen off, the sale of food products containing eggs has risen significantly (Margen et al. 1992). The industry is hardly a dying one.

The Shell Egg Industry

The egg industry in most of the world is based on chicken eggs. In Southeast Asia there is also a duck egg market. As ethnic populations move, the food products they desire move with them. With the rather large number of Southeast Asian natives now living in other parts of the world, a geographically widespread demand for duck eggs has become a relatively recent phenomenon.

Table II.G.7.1 *Egg production of several countries of the world (in millions of eggs)*

Country	1969	1979	1989
United States	68,700	69,228	67,042
Former Soviet Union	37,000	65,585	84,600
Japan	27,565	33,150	40,383
Germany[a]	15,036	14,962	12,275
United Kingdom	18,450	18,555	17,834
France	11,200	13,840	15,150
Italy	10,281	11,037	11,223
Brazil	7,140	11,035	10,140
Spain	9,670	7,200	12,174
Poland	6,400	8,670	8,200
Mexico	5,657	10,390	14,700
Canada	5,655	5,551	5,500
Netherlands	4,370	8,187	10,711
Belgium, Luxembourg	3,900	3,453	2,724
Czechoslovakia	3,410	4,225	5,628
Romania	3,200	7,085	7,600
Argentina	2,940	3,350	3,350
Hungary	2,600	4,450	4,250
Australia	2,380	3,395	3,286
Republic of South Africa	2,028	3,083	4,012
Turkey	–	–	7,200
China	–	–	140,900
Korea	–	–	6,919

Source: USDA (1970, 1980, 1990).

[a]Production for East and West Germany was combined.

Table II.G.7.1, which includes only the markets for chicken eggs, lists the countries leading in egg production. Data on egg production in China, prior to 1989, are not available, but production there has always been extensive. Prior to 1940, China was the leading nation in the export of dried egg products. In Turkey and Korea, egg production has recently become significant. Figures for Eastern European countries for the 20-year period 1969 to 1989 show an increase in egg production in most of the countries, especially in the former Soviet Union. In countries with production controls, such as Canada, Australia, and the United Kingdom, there was almost no increase. The lower production in the United Kingdom for 1989 was likely influenced significantly by bad publicity relative to the safety of eggs during the mid-1980s. Overall, most countries listed in Table II.G.7.1 had an increase in egg production in excess of population increase.

The concentration of egg production has moved rapidly to larger units in the United States. In 1959, over 49 percent of all eggs in the United States were produced by flocks of less than 1,600 hens. By 1974, only 5.44 percent of all eggs were produced by such small flocks. In 1990, less than 1,000 companies produced over 97 percent of all eggs, with the smallest of these commercial farms having over 30,000 layers.

Egg consumption figures for countries around the world can be approximated by dividing human popu-lation figures for each country into the production figures listed in Table II.G.7.1. There is an international trade for eggs, but in most countries it is a relatively small percentage of total production. The Netherlands might be an exception, as they export many eggs to other European Economic Community (EEC) countries. Shell egg consumption in the United States has been declining since about 1950, when annual consumption was about 400 eggs per person with over 95 percent being in shell egg form. The 1990 consumption of shell eggs had decreased to about 200 per capita, with egg products accounting for over 40 more eggs per person. The use of egg products and eggs in prepared form has been increasing by 1 to 2 percent annually for the last several years. Publicity about potential danger from bacteria in shell eggs will likely result in a continuation of the shift to pasteurized egg products, particularly by institutional feeding establishments.

The egg products industry in the United States is expanding in numbers of companies involved and in volume from each company. The basic products are liquid, frozen, or dried whole egg, egg white, and egg yolk. For reasons of convenience, the shift has been from frozen and dried to liquid products. Developments in pasteurizing procedures and in the aseptic handling of liquids suggest that the shift to liquid will accelerate.

The egg industry is in a growth phase worldwide and will continue to expand because of the wide acceptance of eggs as food of a high nutritional value, especially in terms of protein quality, which makes the egg such a valuable food source for the expanding world population. Research and technology are striving to overcome the problems presented by cholesterol content and microbiological safety.

Egg Formation

At the time of hatching, the female chicken has a rudimentary ovary with over 2,000 ovules or immature egg yolks called oocytes. The egg yolk develops while in a follicle of the ovary. The remainder of the egg, especially the white, or albumen, and the shell, is formed in the oviduct. From these values it is apparent that major changes in the size of the reproductive system take place in relatively short time periods.

It is generally acknowledged that a hen forms an egg in about two weeks. This is true except for the very small core of the yolk. The yolk of the egg is formed in three stages: (1) the part formed during embryonic development of the female chick; (2) the normal slow development of the ovum from the time of hatching to a point in sexual maturity some 10 days prior to ovulation; and (3) the accelerated growth period during the last 10 days before ovulation (release of the ovum or yolk into the oviduct) (Stadelman and Cotterill 1995). The yolk increases in size during the rapid growth stage by the deposition

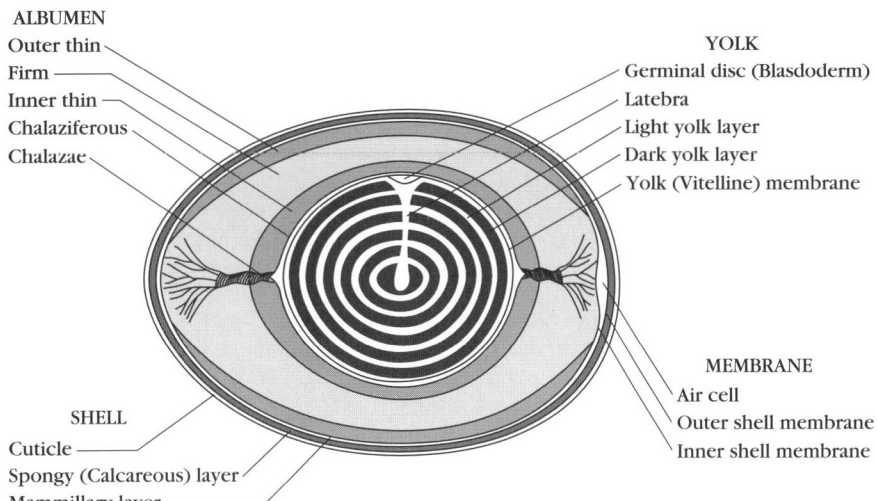

Figure II.G.7.1. Structure of the chicken egg.

ALBUMEN
Outer thin
Firm
Inner thin
Chalaziferous
Chalazae

YOLK
Germinal disc (Blasdoderm)
Latebra
Light yolk layer
Dark yolk layer
Yolk (Vitelline) membrane

MEMBRANE
Air cell
Outer shell membrane
Inner shell membrane

SHELL
Cuticle
Spongy (Calcareous) layer
Mammillary layer

of layers of yolk material. The concentric rings of growth remain intact until the yolk membrane, the vitelline membrane, is broken. The yolk of a normal chicken egg makes up 27 to 33 percent of the total egg weight.

In the oviduct the albumen, or white portion, of the egg, which accounts for about 60 percent of the total egg weight, is deposited around the yolk in about 4.5 hours. The oviduct is made up of five distinct regions. The yolk is released from the ovarian follicle into the infundibulum. A small amount of thick albumen rich in mucin fibers is deposited around the yolk during its 20-minute time of passage, due to peristolic action, into the magnum section of the oviduct. In the magnum section, the yolk collects the rest of the thick albumen and some thin albumen. The developing egg spends about 3 hours in the magnum section prior to entering the isthmus section where the shell membranes and remaining thin white are added during about a 1-hour stay.

The edible portion of the egg is now complete, but about 19 hours is spent in the uterus section where the shell is deposited over the shell membranes. In the posterior section of the uterus the pigments of colored egg shells are deposited on the shell just prior to movement of the intact egg through the vagina.

From the time the first thick albumen is deposited on the yolk until the shell membranes are in place, the yolk spins due to the peristolic movements of the oviduct. The spinning motion causes mucin fibers of the thick albumen to be twisted on opposite sides of the yolk into the chalaza. The chalaza forms a tight mesh over the yolk surface with the loose ends enmeshed in the layers of thick albumen. The chalaza aids in keeping the yolk centered in the albumen.

Another part of the egg often observed is the air cell. This forms between the inner and outer shell membranes after the egg is laid and is usually found in the large end. At the time of lay, the egg is at the body temperature of the hen, about 107° F (42° C), but as it cools, the volume shrinks, which starts the air cell. During the time the egg is held, there is a continual loss of moisture from the egg albumen, which results in an ever increasing air cell size. The rate at which moisture is lost is controlled by atmospheric humidity and porosity of the shell.

Egg Structure

The parts of the egg are shown in Figure II.G.7.1. As discussed in the section on the formation of the egg, the ovum starts development during the embryonic growth of the female chick. The female germ cell is in this structure. During the rapid growth phase of egg formation, the latebra grows to keep the germinal disk on the surface of the yolk. The vitelline membrane expands quickly during the rapid growth phase of yolk development. In a fully developed yolk the vitelline membrane is about 0.024 millimeter (mm) thick (Needham 1931). Depending on the methods used in histological examination of the membrane, there are either two or three layers (Romanoff and Romanoff 1949).

The yolk is deposited in concentric layers during formation. In hard-cooked egg yolks it is possible to differentiate light and dark rings when highly pigmented feedstuffs are fed for a limited period of time each day. The size of the yolk varies directly with egg size. The percentage of the total egg in the yolk varies from 27 to 33 percent. The percentage of the egg as yolk varies with egg size (Marion et al. 1964), with strains laying smaller eggs having a higher percentage of the egg as yolk. According to F. E. Cunningham, O. J. Cotterill, and E. M. Funk (1960), as hens age, the percentage of yolk in the egg increases. Cotterill and

G. S. Geiger (1977) studied yield records from the Missouri Random Sample test and found that the yolk size in eggs decreased from 1965 to 1975. W. W. Marion and others (1964) suggested that all deviations in egg component part percentages are covariates of egg size.

The size of the yolk increases slowly during storage due to a very slow balancing of osmotic pressures between the yolk and albumen. A series of papers by J. Needham and M. Smith (1931), Smith and J. Shepherd (1931), Smith (1931), J. Needham, M. Stephenson, and D. M. Needham (1931), and J. Needham (1931) reported on the relations of yolk to albumen in the hen's egg. The vitelline membrane is a unique entity in its ability to maintain about 50 percent solids in the yolk, with only 13 percent solids in the albumen over many months of storage. At this time, a proven explanation for this phenomenon is not available.

The albumen of the hen's egg consists of four layers that can be identified in the broken-out freshly laid egg. The location of the layers in the intact egg is indicated in Figure II.G.7.1. The inner thick, or chalaziferous, layer is next to the vitelline membrane. This layer of albumen is rich in mucin fibers that are generally lacking in the thin white layers. The outer thick layer is a complex of lysozyme-mucin proteins. This complex disintegrates over time when eggs are in storage.

The shell membranes, inner and outer, are composed of keratin fibers arranged in a web pattern to form a barrier to microbial invasion of the egg contents. The inner membrane is about one-third the thickness of the outer membrane (Romanoff and Romanoff 1949). The combined thickness of the two membranes is about 0.1 mm. Passage of gases or liquids through the membranes occurs largely by osmosis or diffusion.

The egg shell must meet a number of requirements. It must be strong enough and rigid enough to withstand the weight of the adult hen. It must be porous enough to allow respiration for the developing embryo during incubation and still compact enough to prevent microbial invasion or the escape of too much moisture. Additionally, the shell serves as a supply of minerals for the nutrition of the embryo. The outer surface of the egg is the shell, which consists of four layers, all composed primarily of calcium carbonate. The thickness of the egg shell varies among hens. It is normally thickest for hens just starting egg production; thickness decreases as the hens extend their egg-laying cycle. A hot environmental temperature also results in thinner egg shells, as does a low level of calcium in the hen's diet.

Egg Quality Evaluation and Preservation

The basis for quality determination of eggs by nondestructive means in the United States is the *Egg Grading Manual* (U.S. Department of Agriculture 1977). The same characteristics laid out in the manual are used in all countries with various degrees of emphasis on the several quality factors. Quality determinations are divided into external and internal factors. External quality factors are soundness of the shell, cleanliness, and egg shape. The internal factors are air cell size, albumen viscosity, and yolk shadow. The internal factors are judged by passing the egg in front of a bright light source. Other internal factors are freedom from blood spots, bloody albumen, meat spots, or other inclusions. Equipment is currently available that allows for quality evaluation by candling at rates in excess of 72,000 eggs per hour.

In 1981, the quality standards for grades of eggs in the United States were modified (U.S. Department of Agriculture 1981). The grades of eggs that can be offered for sale at retail are AA, A, B, and B*, referred to as B star. The requirements for each grade are detailed for each external and internal quality factor. The application of these standards are discussed by W. J. Stadelman and Cotterill (1995).

Numerous laboratory methods for quality evaluation of eggs have been prepared. Most of these methods are destructive in that the shell is broken and measurements are made on the liquid contents. The most widely accepted method is the Haugh Unit for expressing the albumen condition. This measurement was presented by R. R. Haugh (1937) and modified by A. W. Brant, A. W. Otte, and K. H. Norris (1951). A lesser used system is the United States Department of Agriculture (USDA) score as suggested by Brant and colleagues (1951), which attempts to correlate visual appearance of the broken-out egg, Haugh Units, and candled grade.

Evaluation of shell quality is on the basis of shell strength. The breaking strength has been found to be closely related to shell thickness. On broken-out eggs, measurement of shell thickness is a common method. As the specific gravity of freshly laid eggs is determined primarily by shell thickness, a nondestructive estimation of shell thickness can be made by determining specific gravity of the intact egg.

In terms of quality preservation, the most frequently considered item is albumen condition, which is often expressed as Haugh Units. For a high-quality or grade AA egg, the Haugh Units should be above 78. This value lowers over time as the thick albumen thins. The rate of albumen thinning is a function of temperature. The breakdown or thinning of albumen is relatively rapid at high temperatures, 40° Celsius (C), and slows to almost no change at 1° C. Other than temperature, the carbon dioxide content of the atmosphere surrounding the egg affects the rate of carbon dioxide loss from the egg. With the loss of carbon dioxide, the pH of the albumen rises from about 7.6 in a fresh egg to 9.7 in a stale egg.

Humidity of the atmosphere influences rate of water loss from the egg, which results in increased air cell size. Ideal conditions for long-term storage of eggs are a temperature between 1° C and 3° C and a relative humidity of about 80 percent. For long-term storage, egg shells are usually coated with a colorless, odorless mineral oil that seals the pores of the shell.

A frequently neglected consideration in quality preservation is maintaining cleanliness and soundness of the shells. In summary, egg quality preservation is a function of time, temperature, humidity, and handling.

Egg Sizes

In most parts of the world egg sizes are based on metric weights, with each size up or down being with a 5-gram grouping. Eggs are sold by the dozen in the United States. Egg sizes are based on weight per dozen ranging from pee wee (15 ounces [oz]), small (18 oz), medium (21 oz), large (24 oz), extra large (27 oz), to jumbo (30 oz). For consumer satisfaction it is desirable to pack cartons holding a dozen with uniform-sized eggs of the appropriate weight. Many of the jumbo-sized eggs will contain two yolks.

Egg Chemistry

Shell eggs consist of about 9.5 percent shell, 63 percent albumen, and 27.5 percent yolk, according to Cotterill and Geiger (1977). The total solids of the albumen, yolk, and whole egg are about 12 percent, 52 percent, and 24 percent, respectively. Reviews of the chemistry of egg components were written by R. E. Feeney (1964), T. L. Parkinson (1966), Stadelman (1976), and W. D. Powrie and S. Nakai (1990). Extensive analytical data on the nutrient composition of eggs are given in a publication by the U.S. Department of Agriculture (1989).

The shell membranes are composed of protein fibers, mostly keratin with some mucin, arranged in net fashion to form a semipermeable membrane. The shell membranes provide a significant barrier to bacterial invasion of the albumen.

The egg white consists of a number of proteins, a small amount (less than 1 percent) of carbohydrates and minerals, and no lipids. The composition of the albumen of a freshly laid egg is about 87 percent moisture, 11.5 percent protein, 0.8 percent ash, and 0.7 percent carbohydrates. The carbohydrates are the sugars in glycoproteins. The predominant protein is ovalbumin. The complete amino acid sequence with 385 residues has been determined by A. D. Nisbet and others (1981). The molecular weight of the polypeptide chain is 42,699.

The pH of the albumen in a freshly laid egg is about 7.6, which increases during storage to as high as pH 9.7. The rate of pH change is influenced by temperature, air movement, and shell quality. The pH increase is the result of carbon dioxide loss from the albumen. The pH of the albumen depends on the equilibrium between the dissolved carbon dioxide, bicarbonate ion, carbonate ion, and proteins.

The protein ovotransferrin is referred to as conalbumin in older literature. Its unique characteristic is its ability to bind multivalent metallic ions. With aluminum salts a white precipitate is formed; with copper, the flocculant is yellow; and with ferric iron a red color results. The ovotransferrin is one of the most heat-labile proteins of the albumen. Powrie and Nakai (1990) discuss methods for the isolation of each of the proteins.

Egg yolk might be described as a complex system containing a variety of particles suspended in a protein solution. Another description is that it is an oil-in-water emulsion, with lecithin and the lysoproteins aiding in maintaining a stable emulsion. The yolk consists of a plasma with suspended granules. Fresh egg yolk contains about 52 percent solids and has a pH of 6.0, which rises during storage to 6.9.

Nutritional Value

Eggs are a popular food in all countries of the world and have been since ancient times. Before agriculture developed, eggs were gathered from birds' nests for human food. Although eggs contain about 75 percent water, they are a rich source of high-quality protein and are often used as the protein against which other protein sources are compared. Eggs are also important sources of unsaturated fatty acids, iron, phosphorus, trace minerals, vitamins A, E, and K, and all B vitamins. As a natural source of vitamin D, eggs rank second only to fish oils. Eggs are low in calcium, as the shell is not eaten, and they are devoid of vitamin C (Stadelman and Pratt 1989). The high nutrient density of eggs relative to their caloric content makes them an excellent food for many people with special dietary needs (Stadelman et al. 1988).

Much has been written concerning the relationship of plasma cholesterol level to coronary problems in humans, yet some individuals do not adequately differentiate between plasma, or serum, cholesterol and dietary cholesterol. For most people it would seem that there is only a very slight relationship between the level of cholesterol in their diet and the serum cholesterol level in their blood.

Microbiology

The egg contents at the time of laying are generally free of microbial contamination. During the 1980s it was found that a few eggs, estimated at 1 in 20,000, might contain a bacteria, *Salmonella enteriditis,* in the yolk at the time of production. This bacteria is of great concern to health officials and the egg-producing industry because the organism can cause food poisoning in humans.

The egg has a number of barriers to bacterial invasion. The shell and shell membranes act as physical barriers. In the albumen there are several proteins that influence the ability of organisms to colonize in the egg. Lysozyme will digest cell walls of some bacteria. Avidin removes biotin from the available nutrients for bacteria, and ovotransferrin chelates with ions of iron, making it unavailable. When eggs are cooked, the tying up of biotin or iron is eliminated so these materials are readily available for microorganisms or humans.

Packaging

As egg shells are subject to cracking, packaging has been developed to minimize this loss. In early days eggs were loosely packed in rigid containers using whole grain oats to keep the eggs from contacting the sides of the container or each other. A step forward in innovation was the use of fillers and flats made of cardboard to keep eggs in individual cells in wooden cases. The wooden case was standardized to hold 30 dozen eggs. The next move was to fiberboard cases and a pulp paper filler flat. These cases are now in use for domestic shipments. Most export shipments are still in wooden cases using the filler flat.

For the retailing of eggs, many packages have been and are still being used. The poorest of these, as far as protecting the egg, is a bulk display with paper bags to carry a dozen or more eggs. Pulp paper cartons have been developed to hold from 2 to 18 eggs. These may be coming back into use because of environmental concerns regarding plastic foam cartons.

The Liquid Egg Industry

Shell eggs are converted to liquid products by the removal of the shell. It is required in the United States and some other countries that the shells be removed with no commingling of the shell and liquid portions. The liquid content of the egg is handled as albumen, yolk, whole egg, and various blends of yolk and albumen. Commercial equipment can break and separate yolks from albumen at rates in excess of 36,000 eggs per hour.

Processing Liquid Eggs

The steps of processing liquid eggs include pasteurization, homogenization, packaging, and refrigeration. The liquid products may be converted to frozen, dehydrated, or dried products. An excellent historical review covering early development of the United States egg-products industry was prepared by J. W. Koudele and E. C. Heinsohn (1960).

The pasteurization of eggs is accomplished by heating the liquid to a sufficiently high temperature for a long enough time to kill any pathogenic microorganisms that might be present. As egg proteins coagulate when heated, the pasteurization temperatures and times must be carefully controlled in order to obtain the bacterial reduction with minimal damage to the functional properties of the egg product. Heat damage can be minimized by maintaining a high degree of turbulence in the egg product during the pasteurization process. For whole eggs in the United States, a temperature of 60° C (140° F) for a minimum of 3.5 minutes is required. Higher temperatures for a shorter holding time are accepted. C. R. Murdock and others (1960) compiled information on minimal accepted pasteurization times and temperatures in several countries. In Poland whole egg pasteurization requires 66.1° C to 67.8° C for 3 minutes, in China 63.3° C for 2.5 minutes and in Australia 62.5° C for 2.5 minutes.

Pasteurization temperatures for albumen are sometimes lower than for the whole egg, using longer holding times. The addition of aluminum salts to the albumen results in chelation, with the ovotransferrin allowing the use of higher pasteurization temperatures for albumen (Lineweaver and Cunningham 1966). Ovotransferrin is the most heat-labile of all proteins in the albumen. Egg yolk is rather heat-stable and can be pasteurized by using slightly higher temperatures or longer times than for the whole egg. Cunningham (1990) reported detailed procedures for the pasteurization of different liquid egg products.

A procedure for the ultrapasteurizing of liquid whole eggs was described by H. R. Ball, Jr., and colleagues (1987), and by K. R. Swartzel, Ball, and M. Hamid-Samimi (1989). They utilized temperatures that are higher than the minimum required in the United States with high turbulence in the holding tubes and projected a usable shelf life of the ultrapasteurized whole egg products of up to 24 weeks when stored at 4° C or lower. The commercialization of this procedure will reduce the need for frozen products.

The homogenization of liquid whole egg may be done either before or after pasteurization. It usually follows pasteurization so that any clumping of materials due to the heating would be dispersed in the homogenization operation.

The packaging of egg products is an ever changing operation. The early processors, from the late nineteenth century until the mid-twentieth century, used metal cans, each containing about 30 pounds of product. The next package was a rigid plastic bucket of either 10- or 30-pound capacity. This was followed by the use of waxed cardboard boxes of 4- or 5-pound capacity. Small quantities were packaged in half-pint cardboard containers in a futile attempt at selling the egg products in retail food stores. At present the industry is moving toward the use of flexible film packages with an aseptic packaging technology.

Before the introduction of ultrapasteurization and aseptic packaging, the shelf life of liquid eggs was about 6 days. But now, with a predicted shelf life of up to 24 weeks (Swartzel et al. 1989), it may be possible to sell liquid product at retail. In earlier years much of the liquid product was packaged as indicated and frozen for distribution to food manufacturers.

During World War II there was a great demand for dried egg products for military feeding and to supply civilian populations of countries in the war zones. The usual method of drying was by using a spray drier. Small amounts were pan-dried and freeze-dried. In the drying of eggs it was necessary to remove the reducing sugars normally present in egg albumen to minimize the discoloration that would result from a reaction between such sugars and amino acids abundant in the egg liquid. Desugaring is accomplished by a controlled bacterial or yeast fermentation, by a spontaneous microbial fermentation, or by an enzymatic fermentation using glucose oxidase.

W. M. Hill and M. Sebring (1990) reviewed methods for desugaring liquid eggs. D. H. Bergquist (1990) outlined procedures for the dehydration of liquid eggs and listed seven advantages of the dried products. These are as follows:

1. A low storage cost.
2. A low transportation cost.
3. The ease of sanitary handling.
4. The lack of susceptibility to bacterial growth during storage.
5. An allowance for more precise formulation.
6. The uniformity of product.
7. An allowance for development of new convenience foods.

During the last 20 years a number of additional processed egg products have been introduced in the marketplace, as described by Stadelman and others (1988). The most widely marketed to date have been hard-cooked egg products. They are available as peeled hard-cooked eggs, diced eggs, long eggs, and Scotch eggs. It was estimated that about 1 percent of all eggs sold in the United States in 1990 were in hard-cooked form. Generally, the hard-cooked egg sales are to restaurants rather than at retail.

In summary, eggs have long served as a food for humankind. They have a high-density nutritional value, especially with respect to the protein quality. They contain all nutrients required by humans except vitamin C, but as we do not utilize the shell, the egg is also deficient in calcium. Eggs are usually one of the first solid foods given to infants and frequently constitute a significant portion of the diet of the elderly. Valued for their versatility, they are employed to coagulate, to foam, to emulsify, to color, to flavor, and to control sugar crystallization in some candies. With this wide range of use, eggs remain one of our most economical food staples.

William J. Stadelman

Bibliography

Ball, H. R., Jr., M. Hamid-Samimi, P. M. Foegeding, and K. R. Swartzel. 1987. Functional and microbial stability of ultrapasteurized, aseptically packaged refrigerated whole egg. *Food Science* 52: 1212-18.

Bergquist, D. H. 1990. Egg dehydration. In *Egg science and technology,* ed. W. J. Stadelman and O. J. Cotterill, 285-323. Binghamton, N.Y.

Brant, A. W., A. W. Otte, and K. H. Norris. 1951. Recommended standards for scoring and measuring opened egg quality. *Food Technology* 5: 356-61.

Cotterill, O. J., and G. S. Geiger. 1977. Egg product yield trends from shell eggs. *Poultry Science* 56: 1027-31.

Cunningham, F. E. 1990. Egg product pasteurization. In *Egg science and technology,* ed. W. J. Stadelman and O. J. Cotterill, 243-72. Binghamton, N.Y.

Cunningham, F. E., O. J. Cotterill, and E. M. Funk. 1960. The effect of season and age of bird. 1. On egg size, quality and yield. *Poultry Science* 39: 289-99.

Feeney, R. E. 1964. Egg proteins. In *Symposium on food: Proteins and their reactions,* ed. H. W. Schultz and A. F. Anglinier, 209-24. Westport, Conn.

Fumihito, A., T. Miyake, S-I. Sumi, et al. 1994. One subspecies of the red junglefowl *(Galus galus galus)* suffices as the matriarchic ancestor of all domestic breeds. *Proceedings of the National Academy of Sciences* 91: 12505-9.

Haugh, R. R. 1937. The Haugh Unit for measuring egg quality. *U.S. Egg and Poultry Magazine* 43: 552-5, 572-3.

Hill, W. M., and M. Sebring. 1990. Desugaring egg products. In *Egg science and technology,* ed. W. J. Stadelman and O. J. Cotterill, 273-83. Binghamton, N.Y.

Koudele, J. W., and E. C. Heinsohn. 1960. The egg products industry of the United States. *Kansas State University Agricultural Experimental Station Bulletin No. 423.*

Lineweaver, H., and F. E. Cunningham. 1966. *Process for pasteurizing egg white.* U.S. Patent No. 3,251,697.

Margen, Sheldon, et al., eds. 1992. *The wellness encyclopedia of food and nutrition.* New York.

Marion, W. W., A. W. Nordskog, H. S. Tolman, and R. S. Forsythe. 1964. Egg composition as influenced by breeding, egg size, age and season. *Poultry Science* 43: 255-64.

McGee, Harold. 1984. *On food and cooking.* New York.

Murdock, C. R., E. L. Crossley, J. Robb, et al. 1960. The pasteurization of liquid whole egg. *Ministry of Labor and Health Services Monthly Bulletin* 19: 134-50.

Needham, J. 1931. The relations between yolk and white in the hen's egg. V. The osmotic properties of the isolated vitelline membranes. *Journal of Experimental Biology* 8: 330-44.

Needham, J., and M. Smith. 1931. The relations between yolk and white in the hen's egg. I. Introduction. *Journal of Experimental Biology* 8: 286-92.

Needham, J., M. Stephenson, and D. M. Needham. 1931. The relations between yolk and white in the hen's egg. IV. The formation of lactic acid and alcohol by the yolk. *Journal of Experimental Biology* 8: 319-29.

Nisbet, A. D., R. H. Saundry, A. J. G. Mair, et al. 1981. The complete amino acid sequence of hen ovalbumin. *Environmental Journal of Biochemistry* 115: 335-45.

Parkinson, T. L. 1966. The chemical composition of eggs. *Journal of Science Food Agriculture* 17: 101-11.

Powrie, W. D., and S. Nakai. 1990. The chemistry of eggs and egg products. In *Egg science and technology,* ed. W. J. Stadelman and O. J. Cotterill, 97-139. Binghamton, N.Y.

Romanoff, A. L., and A. J. Romanoff. 1949. *The avian egg.* New York.

Shenstone, F. S. 1968. The gross composition, chemistry and physicochemical basis of organization of the yolk and white. In *Egg quality, a study of the hen's egg,* ed. T. C. Carter, 26-64. Edinburgh.

Simoons, Frederick J. 1994. *Eat not this flesh.* Second edition. Madison, Wis.

Smith, M. 1931. The relations between yolk and white in the hen's egg. III. Gas exchange in infertile eggs. *Journal of Experimental Biology* 8: 312–18.

Smith, M., and J. Shepherd. 1931. The relations between yolk and white in the hen's egg. II. Osmotic equilibration. *Journal of Experimental Biology* 8: 293–311.

Smith, Page, and Charles Daniel. 1982. *The chicken book.* San Francisco.

Stadelman, W. J. 1976. Egg proteins. In *Food colloids,* ed. H. D. Graham, 207–239. Westport, Conn.

Stadelman, W. J., and O. J. Cotterill. 1995. *Egg science and technology.* Fourth edition. Binghamton, N.Y.

Stadelman, W. J., V. M. Olson, G. A. Shemwell, and S. Pasch. 1988. *Egg and poultry-meat processing.* Chichester, England.

Stadelman, W. J., and D. E. Pratt. 1989. Factors influencing composition of the hen's egg. *World's Poultry Science Journal* 45: 247–66.

Swartzel, K. R., H. R. Ball, Jr., and M. Hamid-Samimi. 1989. Method for the ultrapasteurization of liquid whole egg products. U.S. Patent No. 4,808,425.

Tannahill, Reay. 1989. *Food in history.* New York.

Toussaint-Samat, Maguelonne. 1992. *A history of food,* trans. Anthea Bell. Cambridge, Mass.

Trager, James. 1995. *The food chronology.* New York.

U. S. Department of Agriculture. 1970, 1980, 1990. *Agricultural Statistics.* Washington, D.C.

   1977. *Egg Grading Manual, Agricultural Handbook No. 75.* Washington, D.C.

   1981. Revision of shell egg standards and grades. *Federal Register* 46 (149): 39566–73.

   1989. *Composition of foods: Dairy and egg products, raw, processed, prepared.* Agricultural Handbook 8.1. Washington, D.C.

Ward, Artemus. 1911. *The grocer's encyclopedia.* New York.

II.G.8 ❧ Dogs

The Dog as Human Food

The difficulty that confronts one at the very beginning of a study of the dog as human food is the lack of convincing evidence relating to the use of dogs *(Canis familiaris)* as food by early humans. Most of the discussions in published articles are either speculative or employ relatively recent evidence of dog consumption and extrapolate these data to the distant past.

There are some fine published discussions that relate to the eating of dogs in more recent times. One of the best is by Margaret Titcomb (1969), who documents the importance of the dog to human cultures in the ancient Pacific area. Titcomb believes (as do I) that the dog of the Pacific Islands was originally carried by canoe from the Asian mainland along with the pig and chicken for food on the voyage.

It was fed carefully upon vegetables such as taro and breadfruit so that its flesh was palatable to its human owners. Captain James Cook noted in his journal of 1784 that dogs were fed and herded with the hogs. Titcomb (1969) relates that they were fattened on poi and that an informant remembered that relatives penned up puppies to keep them from eating unclean food. They were fed three times a day on poi and broth until fattened. Natives considered baked dog a great delicacy, but they never offered it to foreigners, who held dog meat in great abhorrence, according to the wife of a missionary in 1820.

Preparation of dogs as food is abstracted by Titcomb (1969), who writes: "Like the pig, the dog was killed by strangulation in order not to lose the blood. The blood was poured into a calabash (gourd) used for cooking, and red hot stones were added, causing the blood to coagulate; it was then ready to eat." The meat might be baked or cut up and wrapped in *ti* leaf bundles and cooked in boiling water. An informant stated that the upper part of the backbone was preferred by many diners, although some liked the ribs best, and others preferred the brain. The latter has been attested to by dog skulls, with holes in the crania, found in archaeological excavations.

There is some indication of the numbers of dogs that were used as food from the dance anklets, made of dog teeth, that survive in museum collections. Dog canine teeth were drilled for attachment to fabric bands and worn as dance rattles. One, in the Bishop Museum, has 11,218 teeth; it has been estimated that 2,805 dogs were required to produce the artifact.

Domestic dogs found their way from island to island across the Pacific Ocean. A major reason for their success as immigrants in the region was a total absence of competition from wolves, jackals, and foxes. Pacific Island canids themselves did not become feral, probably due mainly to a lack of adequate food in the wild, which meant they had to rely on their human owners for subsistence.

Today dogs are employed as food for human consumption in many parts of Asia, and China in particular, but the origins and reasons for this practice are not well documented, or if they are, they are probably recorded in one or more of the many Asian sources not yet translated.

Dog Fossils and Their Interpretation

Dog consumption practices in the Pacific and Asia notwithstanding, the dog's main attraction to humans, historically, has been its ability to hunt other animals selected as food by humans rather than serving as a source of food itself.

Over the past 50 years that I have been examining animal bones from archaeological sites, I have yet to see the bones of dogs bearing cut or butcher marks that would indicate that dogs had unquestionably been butchered for food. In the southwestern United States, for example, and particularly in Arizona, there are literally hundreds of articulated prehistoric dog burials and many more isolated postcranial bones. The latter often show evidence of cutting, but it is evident that they were being prepared for bone artifacts. Most represent the shafts of humeri or femora and were scored by flint blades in transverse directions below the proximal articular condyle or the distal articular condyle, resulting in a bone tube when the articular ends were removed. Many of these artifacts, or "tubes," have been recovered from archaeological sites along with the discarded ends of the bones.

Some archaeologists have used the evidence of burned or charred dog bones to indicate meal preparation. However, experiments with fresh material have proven that burned or charred bone is the result of grilling to the point where edible flesh has been completely destroyed. Indeed, it must be destroyed before any change is apparent on the bones.

Generally, the sample size of dog burials is inadequate to determine their value to the associated human population. However, there are several occurrences of multiple dog burials that suggest reasons other than culinary for the buried animals. In Askelon, Persia, 1,238 dog skeletons of all ages, associated with a period dated between 822 and 428 B.C., were excavated and examined by archaeologists (Wapnish and Hesse 1993). There was no evidence of butchering or food preparation associated with these dogs.

Similarly, a site of puppy burials from the first-century-A.D. Roman villa at Lugnano, Italy, was excavated in June 1992. At least some of these dogs were associated with child burials, which may have had some ritual significance. In fact, dogs in association with human burials are not uncommon. Intentional burials of dogs, both separately and with humans, are known from Chinese sites (Figure II.G.8.1). Some of the dogs are in the same coffins with the humans; others have their own separate burial boxes.

Indeed, there is always a danger of misinterpreting dog remains when only bones are present. One of the best examples of this potential for misinterpretation is connected with a 1901 photograph taken on the shore of Penzhina Bay, in eastern Siberia on the Sea of Okhotsk. The photograph shows four large sled dogs hanging by their necks atop long poles that were set into the frozen earth (Perkins 1981). Waldemar Jochelson, the photographer (on what was an American Museum of Natural History expedition), explained:

All along the bank of the Paren River were stakes driven into the snow, with dogs hanging on them, their muzzles pointing upward. In the light of the spring sun, this long row of dog-sacrifices offered a queer and sad sight. I found out that the greater part of the dogs had been killed by the drivers of the sledges in gratitude for their safe return from Gizhiginsk, and to guard their villages from the measles, which a year previous had come to them from that little town. (Perkins 1981)

The dogs were eventually cut down from the poles and buried, and there was no evidence left indicating the circumstances that led to their deaths. It is doubtful that any excavators of the dogs would be able to glean the method of their execution or the reason for their demise. The point is that ritual sacrifices of dogs are not generally recorded. One example is a fenced brick-lined pit, off to one side of the market in Kathmandu in Nepal, whose purpose is for the sacrifice and dismembering of dogs. If it were not for the tourist photographs taken when the rituals are in progress, the small fenced pit might be mistaken for a dry fountain.

At sites in Egypt and prehistoric southwestern North America, dog mummies have been recovered. In the former region, humans did the mummifying, whereas natural causes were responsible in the latter. From these discoveries we can derive information about dog size and color of pelage and can make comparisons with surviving breeds of dogs. Two of the best-preserved animals are a small black-and-white dog and a yellowish-white one (Figure II.G.8.2) from a Basketmaker site at Marsh Pass, Arizona.

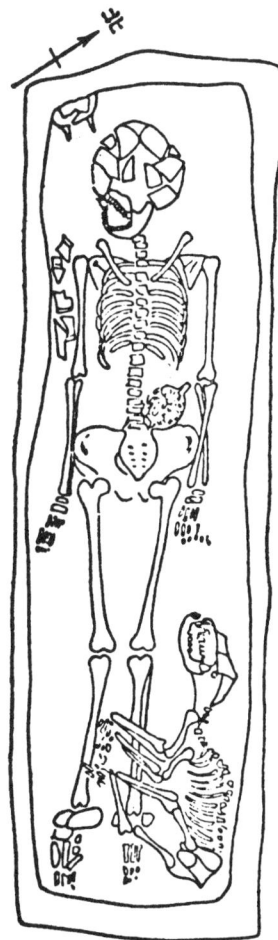

Figure II.G.8.1. Intentional burials of domestic dogs and humans. Neolithic of China; Xiawanggang c. 4000 B.P. (Illustration courtesy of Qi Guo-gin.)

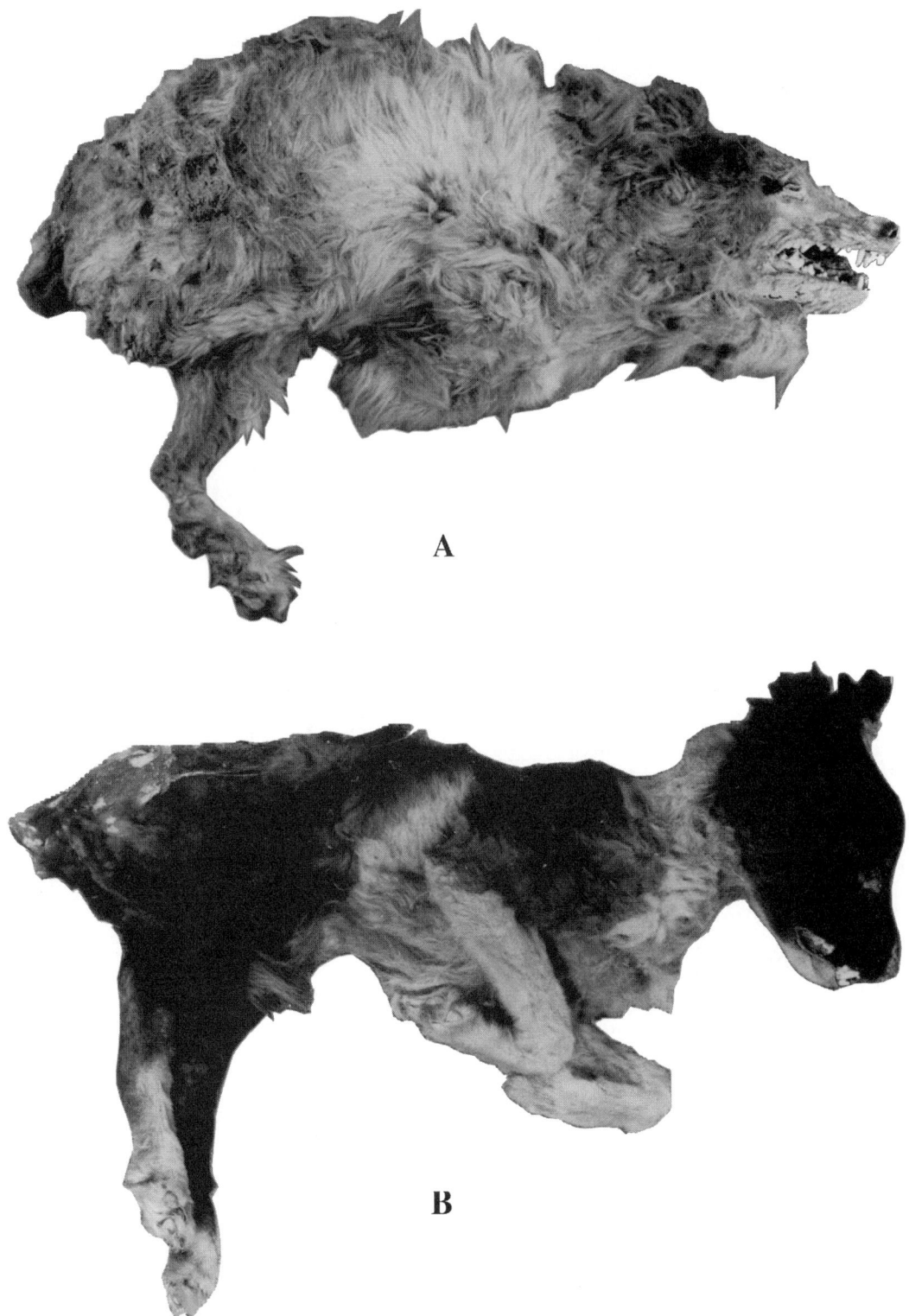

Figure II.G.8.2. Indian dogs, 2,000 years old, early Basketmaker. Natural mummies from White Dog Cave, Marsh Pass, Arizona: (A) yellow-white domestic dog; (B) black-and-white domestic dog. Both are *Canis familiaris*. (Photograph by John W. Olsen.)

Figure II.G.8.3. Typical long-legged Basketmaker domestic dogs, *Canis familiaris,* from vicinity of Marsh Pass, Arizona, 2,000 B.P. (Drawing by Wallace Hughes.)

These dogs were mummified naturally in the hot, dry environment and placed in White Dog Cave with a mummified Pueblo Indian wrapped in a woven shroud. The dogs were a bit longer legged than the mongrels found in the vicinity today, but the color patterning and small size are rather common in the general area of Marsh Pass (Figure II.G.8.3).

Dog Domestication

If the pages of the past are blurred with respect to the use of the dog as food, they are equally hard to read in matters of dog domestication, which constitutes the burden of most of the remainder of this chapter. Much of what has been and is being pub-

lished on the events leading to canid taming and domestication is based more on supposition than on hard evidence. Woven into what follows is my own version of this process (based on Olsen 1985).

Studies relating to the social structures of both humans and wolves shed some light on what *may* have taken place in the initial development and relationship of these two groups of early hunters that eventually culminated in the close relationship between dogs and humans prevailing today throughout much of the world. Foremost among these studies are those by L. D. Mech (1970), M. W. Fox (1971), and B. H. López (1978). Perhaps the best compilation that relates to this relationship is a series of papers edited by R. L. Hall and H. S. Sharp (1978). Several theories dealing with the attitudes of humans toward wolves and of wolves toward humans are discussed in detail in their volume.

Human hunter–gatherer societies and wolf packs were similar in a number of respects. Both comprised social units that were relatively small in number. Both were capable of hunting over open ground or wooded areas, pursuing rather large game and exerting considerable physical effort and energy over prolonged periods to accomplish their goals. Both used hunting methods that required a pack or team effort as opposed to the tactics of a lone hunter.

Faunal evidence from paleoanthropological sites of the late Pleistocene age (c. 10,000 B.C.) indicates that *Homo sapiens,* at this stage of development, depended on a diet that included a sizable portion of game animals. As carnivores, the wolves of this period also depended on wild game, and because hunting game by running it down takes a good deal more time than consuming the kill, one of the characteristics of both these predator groups would have been sharing the spoils of the hunt. Such socialization would have developed independently among both wolves and humans (Hall and Sharp 1978).

Another social feature shared by wolves and humans would have been that gender did not necessarily determine who did the hunting. Rather, such a determination would have depended on the individual's maturity and ability to hunt successfully. The nonhunters of the pack (immature animals), therefore, would gather in rendezvous areas that were selected for regrouping and for the sharing of freshly killed game provided by the active hunting members of the pack (Mech 1970; Hall and Sharp 1978; López 1978). The wolf packs' methods of obtaining game appear to be well organized and planned and should be briefly abstracted here as a possible model of how human hunting societies may have obtained game during the Pleistocene.

As pack hunters, wolves are able to capture and kill animals much larger than themselves. Artiodactyls such as deer, mountain sheep, elk, caribou, and even the moose, a formidable adversary, are all chosen prey. Rabbits, beaver, and (at times) fish in shallow water, as well as other small mammals, are also caught and eaten (Mech 1970). Wolves have been observed to change their hunting tactics more to suit the terrain and weather conditions than to suit the habits of a particular animal that they are pursuing. Their ability to procure food is not always successful; rather, feast or famine may be more the norm for these animals.

The selected prey in an ungulate herd may be an old or weakened animal, but this is not necessarily the case. Healthy, prime adults, as well as immature animals, are also selected and killed by wolves (Mech 1970). The method of bringing down such an animal is for the wolf to run alongside, slashing and tearing at its hindquarters, flanks, and abdomen until it is weak enough from its injuries to be dispatched (López

1978). Wolves may grab an animal, such as the moose or caribou, by the nose, holding on, while other members of the pack close in for the kill (Mech 1970; Hall and Sharp 1978; López 1978).

It is the case, however, that wolves generally choose animals that are easier to procure than healthy, active prey. Animals that are injured, infected by parasites to such a degree that they are weakened, or foundering in deep snow are all known to have been selected by wolf packs for food (López 1978). Animals in this condition, of course, signal their plight to some degree; these signals would not be lost on keen observers, such as wolves (or humans), and the weakened prey would be relatively easy to dispatch.

If a prey animal runs, it is certain to be pursued, especially if it is a lone individual (Mech 1970). To weaken such an animal, particularly if it appears to the wolf to be a strong and healthy adult, the practice of relay hunting may be put into practice, taking advantage of the terrain to wind the pursued. The hunt may end in a rush, terminating the animal's struggles in a few moments, or the dogged pursuit may go on for miles before the pack closes in. Alternatively, a wolf pack of four to six animals may send out two wolves to herd a lone victim into an ambush of the remaining members of the group (Mech 1970).

Wolves that have maintained a territory for a considerable length of time may know the terrain well enough to use shortcuts to intercept running prey. They are also known to hunt into the wind when approaching a feeding herd of artiodactyls.

The similar pack-hunting methods and social structures of early humans and wolves would not, in themselves, have been responsible for the first taming and domestication of the wolf. Perhaps humans observed the wolf's ability to track successfully by scent, or its ability to cover ground swiftly enough to elude human pursuit. It is possible that hungry wolves were enticed (not necessarily by human design) to come close to a campfire, where meat was being cooked and the refuse discarded in the immediate vicinity of the camp. Perhaps wolves that had attached themselves loosely to human habitation areas would consider such camps as their home territory, and their warning growls toward intruders would also warn the human inhabitants of the approach of such outsiders. If such an association occurred, it is not unreasonable to assume that these events would bring about firmer ties between wolves and humans to their mutual advantage. Unfortunately, evidence of the kind needed to prove or disprove this speculation is not the sort that could be preserved in the archaeological record.

If a hunter were to have initiated a closer association with wolves by taking a wolf pup from its den (possibly if a pup's parents were killed), this action would have encouraged imprinting of the substitute human family leader on the young wolf's behavior pattern as it developed and matured in close association with the human hunting group. Thus, J. P. Scott (1950) wrote:

> Behavior studies seem to indicate that the reason for the apparently easy and successful domestication of the wolf lies in the fact that it is a species with highly developed patterns of social behavior and that a large number of these patterns are sufficiently similar to human ones to permit mutual social adjustment between man and wolf. The primary stimuli are so similar in the two species that appropriate and recognizable social behavior is evoked.

But it is also quite possible that there existed a mutual respect between the wolf and human of 10,000 to 15,000 years ago for the hunting prowess of the other. At such a time, humans were themselves probably as rugged and aggressive as the wolves with which they shared a hunting territory.

In order for any animal, including wolves, to be successfully tamed and domesticated, it must be able to suppress its natural or normal living pattern and subjugate it to that which is dictated to it by humans. The wolf (in most instances), and the resulting domestic dog, have been able to do this, as have all of the common domestic animals that are familiar to us. But some animals cannot cross this bridge from wild to domestic. Records extending as far back as early dynastic Egypt indicate that many animals that seemed potential domesticates did not fulfill that potential. Some Egyptians experimented with hyenas, gazelles, and foxes, but they had little success in molding them into household animals. Similarly, the cape hunting dog (not a dog in the true sense of the word), the coyote, the jackal, and all of the large, wild felids were never brought beyond the tame or semi-tame stage. The modern wolf, however, appears to be an animal that will easily and fully accept the companionship of humans in a manner that nearly approaches that of a domesticated dog.

Since we are discussing the possibilities of the first friendly contacts between wolves and humans, it is appropriate to mention at this point the evidence we have for early domestication through osteological changes in the wolf. It is generally known and accepted by workers concerned with early canid domestication that the first observable changes take place in the skulls, jaws, and dentition of these tamed canids. More specifically, these alterations include the foreshortening of the muzzle, or rostrum, and the crowding of the tooth rows, along with a comparative overall reduction in the size of the teeth.

As domestication occurred, the mandibles deepened midway along the horizontal ramus, with a more convex inferior margin than that found in similar-sized wild wolves. These are all characteristics found in most domestic dogs of wolf size. The coronal apex takes a decided backward turn, a condition found in

some Chinese wolves *(Canis lupus chanco)* but generally absent in wolves from other geographic areas (Olsen and Olsen 1977). The foreshortening of the muzzle, or rostral, area of the skull has been observed in the remains of wolves recovered from geographically widely separated paleontological and archaeological sites of late Pleistocene age and later.

One of the earliest documentations of this foreshortening of wolf skulls was made by J. G. Pidoplichko (1969), who described short-faced, and possibly tamed, wolves. Their fossils were collected from excavations conducted in 1954 at a late Paleolithic campsite of mammoth hunters at Mezin in the Chernigov region of the Ukraine. They were found in association with a lithic assemblage amid the remains of 116 individuals of woolly mammoths *(Mammuthus primigenius)*. The remains of wolves with proportions of those living in that area today *(Canis lupus albus)* were also found, along with the three or four short-faced animals.

Pidoplichko coined the taxonomic designation *Canis lupus domesticus* for these short-faced wolves. I, however, would propose to change the taxonomic assignment to *Canis lupus familiaris* for these and other similarly differing wolves and to use the name designated for the domestic dog to identify this Pleistocene race or subspecies, rather than create a new trinomial designation. The use of *familiaris* follows the correct taxonomic progression from a wild wolf, through taming, to the domestic dog. This term seems to be less confusing than the name *domesticus*, which has commonly been used as the scientific name for the domestic cat *(Felis domesticus,* now *Felis cattus)*.

For a number of years, particularly during the 1930s, the Frick Laboratory of the American Museum of Natural History in New York City had field representatives stationed in the Fairbanks area of Alaska. They were there to cooperate with the University of Alaska and the Fairbanks Exploration Company in collecting faunal remains as they were uncovered in muck deposits by hydraulic gold-mining operations. Such placer-mining methods, however, made it impossible to determine the stratigraphic context of a particular bone or artifact, because many had been collected by the gold-dredge crews from the spoil dumps of reworked and discarded matrix.

In fact, there is a general consensus that artifacts from such areas, which may originally have been on the surface, were subsequently relocated several meters below the ground level and mixed with the bones of extinct animals (Rainey 1939). Thus, it might have been possible to find some artifacts in association with the older, extinct animals if different methods of mining had been practiced when the bulk of known Pleistocene vertebrate material was collected in the 1930s.

Between the years 1932 and 1953, 28 more or less complete wolf skulls were obtained from the muck deposits in an area north and west of Fairbanks. The age of the deposits from which these wolf skulls were obtained has been determined as Upper Pleistocene, Wisconsin Age (about 10,000 B.C.). The geologist T. L. Péwé published two reports (1975a, 1975b) on the geology and stratigraphy of this area and the associated recovered fauna. The wolf skulls were collected from dredging operations on Ester Creek, Cripple Creek, Engineer Creek, and Little Eldorado Creek. All of these creeks also yielded Paleolithic artifacts (Rainey 1939). However, the association of these artifacts with the skeletal remains of extinct animals is problematical, because the mechanical mixing of artifacts and bones, just discussed, prevented the collectors from obtaining any evidence that might have existed of a contemporary association of Pleistocene wolves with humans.

T. Galusha, of the Department of Vertebrate Paleontology at the American Museum of Natural History in New York City, worked for many years on the wolf remains from the Fairbanks dredging operations. He noted that a number of the skulls were extremely short-faced for wild wolves and approached modern Eskimo dogs in facial proportions, although they were considerably larger animals overall.

He turned the project over to me shortly before his death, and I continued his studies and compared this collection with a large series of both Pleistocene and Holocene wolves as well as with Eskimo dogs from both Greenland and Siberia. I feel confident at this point in stating that the short-faced wolves from the Fairbanks area appear to be forerunners of the later, domesticated Eskimo dogs.

The proportions of the skulls of these wolves that vary do so in the rostral area. The area of the skull that is anterior to the infraorbital foramen is noticeably foreshortened and constricted laterally in several of the skulls. Two of them (F:AM70933 and F:AM67156) lack anterior premolars. Several others have the full complement of teeth in the abbreviated dental margin. The dentition of F:AM67153 is considerably smaller than the average wolf of that area and approaches the overall tooth size found in the Eskimo dog.

Dishing of the rostrum, when viewed laterally, is evident in all of the short-faced skulls identified as *Canis lupus* from the Fairbanks gold fields. The occipital and supraoccipital crests are noticeably diminished compared to those found in average specimens of *C. lupus*. The occipital overhang of these crests, a wolf characteristic, is about equal in both groups of *C. lupus*. Multivariate analysis of all of the wolves from the Fairbanks collection separated the collection into two groups, based on either their predominant wolf-like or dog-like characteristics. Yet, as has already been noted, it may never be possible to establish if there was a close human association with the Alaskan Pleistocene wolves, because of the types of deposits in which both the wolves and the lithic assemblages

occur and the conditions under which both were collected.

In 1939 and 1940 an Eskimo village site was uncovered that dated from the first millennium B.C. This village, named Ipiutak, is believed to represent an occupation of early Eskimo immigrants from Siberia. The artifacts suggest a Neolithic culture (Larsen and Rainey 1948). The site is located on the tip of Point Hope, Alaska, approximately 125 miles north of the Arctic Circle, and is at the westernmost point of the continent north of the Bering Strait.

At least five more or less complete *Canis* skulls were recovered from the archaeological excavations at Ipiutak. These were studied and reported on by O. J. Murie in an appendix to the site report by H. Larsen and E. Rainey (1948). After comparing these skulls to those of wolves, Eskimo dogs, and other large domestic dogs, Murie decided that they fell into the Siberian class of dogs. Any slight differences between the Ipiutak dog skulls and the Siberian and Alaskan dog skulls with which they were compared were within the size variation considered to be normal for domesticated dogs of this type.

One animal in particular (No. H43) was considered to be a dog–wolf hybrid, as the large size and heavier mandible and teeth approached those of a wolf rather than a dog. Murie concluded that two of the skulls represented the so-called Siberian husky type, three may have been variants of this same type, and the other animal (No. H43) was the hybrid just mentioned. He believed that there was adequate evidence that the Ipiutak dogs were of Asian origin.

Both sides of the Bering Strait have seen numerous explorations and excavations searching for the earliest evidence of habitation sites of the Asian migrants who reached the North American continent. Unfortunately, very little relating to vertebrate remains has been reported. This may be partly because of the poor preservational conditions that characterize this region and that have resulted in an extremely small sample upon which to base our interpretations. However, the subordinate role of organic remains in many early archaeological interpretations has also had a great deal to do with this gap in our knowledge of fossil vertebrates of all taxa from archaeological contexts.

An example of this subordinate role can be seen in the 331-page report on the archaeology of Cape Denbigh (Giddings 1964). The text and 73 plates are devoted to a thorough coverage of nearly all aspects of the excavations on Cape Denbigh, but the recovered faunal remains are listed in a table of only seven lines in one paragraph. No scientific taxonomy is given for these animals, and some remains are classified simply as "bird" or "other." Obviously, it is quite possible to overlook many comparatively small canid fragments if one's interests are funneled in other directions. It is also possible that canids were not collected because it may have been assumed that they represented the common, local wolves, when in actuality they might have represented primitive dogs, as well as wolves or crosses between wolves and dogs.

An intriguing collection of seven large canid skulls that may represent both domestic dogs and wolves or even wolf–dog crosses were found at the Bagnell site, which is a two-component village situated on the edge of a terrace above the Missouri River flood plain just north of Sanger, North Dakota. The dates of the proveniences from which the skulls were collected are from as early as circa A.D. 1590, with the latest occupation from the earliest layer yielding two skulls of domestic dogs of wolf size. Two more of the skulls are definitely those of wolves, but from the later time of occupation; one skull is of a domestic dog, also of wolf size, and the remaining two are of wolves. A most intriguing observation is that one of the domestic dog skulls from the early layer possesses two strong wolf characteristics and seven morphological characteristics that are typical of large, domestic dogs. Admittedly there is a problem of temporal control for these proveniences; however, at this time it does not seem likely that the earliest proveniences contain any intrusive mixtures of dogs that were introduced by Europeans. Large, wolf-sized dogs, particularly those that appear to be wolf–dog hybrids, are so rare in an archaeological context that these Bagnell canids are worthy of considerable note.

Another published account of a large, hybrid cross of a wolf and a dog is that contained in the report of excavations of a bison-kill site in southwestern New Mexico (Speth and Parry 1980). This find, a single canid skull, is illustrated and analyzed in the report, but unfortunately no provenience is given for this specimen. The overall range of dates for all proveniences on the site are from as early as A.D. 1420 ± 125 to A.D. 1845 ± 100. This canid would be of interest in relation to early taming of the wolf and, perhaps, its crossing with smaller Indian dogs, but only if it could be established that it was collected from a provenience that predated the European introduction of large mastiffs or hounds. Since the range of dates is so great, it could easily be the result of a more recent crossing of a European dog and local wolf. (The occurrence is recorded here as a plea to future workers to include all pertinent data and not just that which pertains to comparative zoology.)

To date, the oldest substantiated finds of prehistoric domestic dogs in North America are those from Jaguar Cave, Idaho. Fossil fragments, consisting of incomplete mandibles, a single left mandible, and a small portion of a left maxilla, were all collected from excavations in an early Holocene rock-shelter in the Beaverhead Mountains of Lemhi County, Idaho. The excavations were conducted by a joint expedition of the Peabody Museum of Archaeology and Ethnology at Harvard University and the Idaho State Museum at the Idaho State University in 1961 and 1962. Carbon-14 (14C) dates indicate that the age of the deposits ranges from about 9500 to 8400 B.C. (Lawrence 1967). The site was determined to be a hunting camp (Sadek-Kooros 1972).

An interesting aspect that remains unexplained concerning the canid from this site is its unwolflike appearance (Lawrence 1967), which suggests there may be an even earlier form, as yet undiscovered, that may link these Jaguar Cave dogs with a wild, ancestral form. One would not expect to find these early dogs in a locality so far south as the Jaguar Cave rock-shelter without finding similar remains in sites closer to the Bering Strait. The morphological features that are present in the Jaguar Cave dog fragments are characteristically the same as those that are present in known specimens of *C. familiaris*. For example, critical measurements taken of all fragments indicate that they are too small to be derived from the wolf. They were then compared to the coyote, but they differ from this smaller, wild canid in being more massive, deeper dorsoventrally, and thicker lateromedially. The tooth rows are short when compared to the size of the individual teeth, and this shortening of the jaws is accompanied by crowding of the tooth row. This aspect is particularly noticeable in the area of anterior premolars, where the alveoli do not lie in a straight line; they are, rather, set obliquely. The muzzle, as far as could be projected from the fragments, is more shortened than in the coyote, and this characteristic seems to be well developed, as in later domestic dogs.

Some lower jaws of what are surely coyotes also occurred in the same site. These were determined to be of the local subspecies *Canis latrans lestes*. Canid material from a considerably later site (also in Birch Creek Valley, Idaho), having a 14C date not earlier than 2500 B.C., was also described by B. Lawrence (1967) as belonging to domestic dogs. The specimens included four nearly complete mandibles, a number of mandibular fragments, one broken skull, and two cranial fragments. The specimens from this later site were determined to be very similar in form and size to Eskimo dogs, with which they were compared in the Museum of Comparative Zoology at Harvard University. By inference, the specimens from Jaguar Cave were also from this group of dogs.

There exists a considerable temporal gap between the Jaguar Cave dogs and later prehistoric dogs from other areas in North America. Fossils from areas in the Southwest date from at least the time of Christ (Guernsey and Kidder 1921). From other areas they date perhaps from 8400 B.C. (McMillan 1970). A dog from the Koster site in Illinois (Struever and Holton 1979) has an assigned date of 6500 B.C., and dogs from White's Mound in Richmond County, Georgia, have been given a date of about 500 B.C. (Olsen 1970). F. C. Hill (1972) briefly noted a Middle Archaic dog burial from Illinois with an accompanying date of 5000 B.C.

G. M. Allen (1920) published the first comprehensive discussion of early dogs that were associated with the prehistoric peoples of the Western Hemisphere.

This publication, unfortunately, is now out of date as well as out of print. Most of the critical finds relating to the development of the domestic dog were made subsequent to Allen's work. W. G. Haag (1948) based his evaluations of an osteometric analysis of some eastern prehistoric dogs on Allen's early publication, but Haag's monograph is also out of date.

The monograph by Allen was for many years the standard work that was used to classify domestic dogs found in association with prehistoric human cultures. The author listed these dogs as falling into the following groups, determined by comparative skull measurements and form: "(1) a large, broad-muzzled Eskimo dog, (2) a larger and (3) a smaller Indian dog, from which are probably to be derived several distinct local breeds. Of the larger style of dog, as many as eleven varieties may be distinguished; of the smaller, five" (Allen 1920: 503).

Some years ago I placed southwestern prehistoric dogs into two assemblages, small and large, following, more or less, Allen's classification. The animals in the small group were fox terrier–sized and were further refined or separated into small, short-faced, and small, long-faced dogs. The animals in the large group were long-faced and were comparable in size to the local coyote but a bit heavier in overall proportions. This latter group was referred to by Allen as the large Pueblo Indian dog, or the Plains Indian dog.

However, after examining later published reports and newer finds and reexamining the older finds made during Allen's career, I now conclude that these groupings are, in a sense, artificial – particularly for dogs from the southwestern United States. In fact, the groups actually grade into one another in size, form, and amount of morphological variation, if a large enough collection is examined. The result is a more or less single mongrel group of southwestern Indian dogs, although the entire range of size and form variation is not found in every archaeological site. It is still possible to find representatives of only a part of the spectrum – either small, short-faced or long-faced dogs, or large Pueblo Indian dogs – at specified sites. The overlap is at the extremes of each of these size groups and is quite logical, because the prehistoric Indian dogs were hardly registered American Kennel Club breeds but were, instead, free-breeding, socializing mongrels.

It is, of course, quite simple to pick out representative animals of these differing groups from collections of excavated canids if there are enough individuals assembled from a large number of archaeological sites. The Basketmaker and early Pueblo Indian dogs of the Southwest and those from White's Mound, Georgia, as well as the dogs from the shell heaps of Kentucky or Alabama, all show a close similarity in size and form. But these animals were quite advanced domestic dogs, and most were of a comparatively small size, although – as stated earlier – there are exceptions to this rule (for example, both small and large forms of dogs are found in the same stratigraphic level at the Jaguar Cave site).

Many early and later Pueblo Indian sites have yielded dog remains. In particular, reference is made to immature puppies as well as adults found in levels dating from about A.D. 1125 to 1175 at Antelope House in Canyon de Chelly, Arizona (Kelley 1975). At the Grasshopper Pueblo, built during the fourteenth century in east central Arizona, a number of small domestic dogs were recovered during 16 years of excavation by the University of Arizona Archaeological Field School (Olsen 1980). A unique find of an immature gray wolf, *C. lupus,* consisting of a right premaxilla and deciduous dentition, was also recovered from one of the rooms of this pueblo. This fragment of a wolf pup suggests that it may have been kept as a pet, perhaps with a view toward taming, although this is only speculation.

It is the case, however, that nearly every Pueblo excavation in the southwestern United States has produced some evidence of the domestication of the dog. These sites date from the eleventh through the fourteenth centuries and range in size from Cliff Palace Ruin in Mesa Verde National Park, Colorado (with its multistoried masonry construction of many rooms and great stone towers), to the more modest pueblos at Keetseel and Betatakin in the area of Monument Valley, Arizona. Tree-ring dates for Keetseel range between A.D. 1274 and A.D. 1284; those for Betatakin are between A.D. 1260 and A.D. 1277. By the time of these late dates, the domestic dogs were well advanced and were morphologically the same as present-day dogs.

As of this writing, however, we have yet to recover the ancestral forms of *C. familiaris* that would help to bridge the gap between the small, late Paleolithic wolves and the early Neolithic dogs from Asia and from Jaguar Cave, Idaho, on the one hand, and, on the other hand, the gap between the Jaguar Cave dogs and the well-known series of dogs of the southwestern United States that date from some 2,000 years ago and are still in existence today.

Stanley J. Olsen

Bibliography

Allen, G. M. 1920. Dogs of the American Aborigines. *Bulletin of the Museum of Comparative Zoology, Harvard University* 63: 431–517.

Fox, M. W. 1971. *Behavior of wolves, dogs, and related canids.* New York.

Giddings, J. L. 1964. *The Archaeology of Cape Denbigh.* Providence, R.I.

Guernsey, S. J. and A. V. Kidder. 1921. Basketmaker caves of northeastern Arizona. Monograph in *Papers of the Peabody Museum of Archaeology and Ethnology,* Vol. 8, No. 2. Cambridge, Mass.

Haag, W. G. 1948. An osteometric analysis of some aboriginal dogs. Monograph in *Reports in Anthropology,* Vol. 7, No. 3. Lexington, Ky.

Hall, R. L., and H. S. Sharp. 1978. *Wolf and man.* New York.

Hill, F. C. 1972. *A Middle Archaic dog burial in Illinois.* Evanston, Ill.

Kelley, J. E. 1975. Zooarchaeological analysis at Antelope House: Behavioral inferences from distributional data. *The Kiva* 41: 81-5.

Larsen, H. and F. Rainey. 1948. Ipiutak and Arctic whale hunting culture. Monograph in *Papers of the American Museum of Natural History,* Vol. 41. New York.

Lawrence, B. 1967. Early domestic dogs. *Sonderdruck aus S. F. Säugetierkunde* 32: 44-59.

López, B. H. 1978. *Of wolves and men.* New York.

McMillan, R. B. 1970. Early canid burial from Western Ozark Highland. *Science* 167: 1246-7.

Mech, L. D. 1970. *The wolf.* Garden City, NY.

Olsen, J. W. 1980. A zooarchaelogical analysis of vertebrate faunal remains from Grasshopper Pueblo, Arizona. Ph.D. dissertation, University of Michigan.

Olsen, S. J. 1970. Two pre-Columbian dog burials from Georgia. *Bulletin of the Georgia Academy of Science* 28: 69-72.
    1985. *Origins of the domestic dog.* Tucson, Ariz.

Olsen, S. J., and J. W. Olsen. 1977. The Chinese wolf ancestor of New World dogs. *Science* 197: 533-5.

Perkins, J. 1981. *To the ends of the earth.* New York.

Péwé, T. L. 1975a. *Quaternary geology of Alaska.* Geological Survey Professional Paper 835. Washington, D.C.
    1975b. *Quaternary stratigraphic nomenclature in unglaciated Central Alaska.* Geological Survey Professional Paper 862. Washington, D.C.

Pidoplichko, J. G. 1969. *Late Paleolithic dwellings of mammoth bones in the Ukraine.* Kiev.

Rainey, F. G. 1939. Archaeology in Central Alaska. *Anthropology Papers of the American Museum of Natural History* 36: 351-405.

Sadek-Kooros, H. 1972. Primitive bone fracturing: A method of research. *American Antiquity* 34: 369-80.

Scott, J. P. 1950. The social behavior of dogs and wolves: An illustration of socio-biological sytematics. *Annals of the New York Academy of Sciences* 51: 1001-122.

Speth, J. D., and W. J. Parry. 1980. *Late prehistoric bison procurement in southeastern New Mexico. The 1978 season at the Garnsey Site (LA-18399).* Ann Arbor, Mich.

Struever, S. and F. A. Holton. 1979. *Koster: Americans in search of their prehistoric past.* Garden City, NY.

Titcomb, M. 1969. *Dog and man in the ancient Pacific with special attention to Hawaii.* Honolulu, Hawaii.

Wapnish, P., and B. Hesse. 1993. Pampered pooches or plain Pariahs? The Ashkelon dog burials. *Biblical Archaeologist* 56: 55-79.

II.G.9 ❧ Ducks

The mallard, *Anas platyrhynchos,* is the most ubiquitous taxon in the subfamily *Anatinae* of the family *Anatidae.* It is the ancestor of most domestic ducks, the males of which still sport the ancestral curling feathers of the upper tail (Delacour 1956-64; Gooders 1975; Gooders and Boyer 1986). Because the wild mallard is so widespread in the Northern Hemisphere, it is extremely likely that it was widely utilized by humans and probably domesticated in different areas at different times. The amount of variability in the domestic duck is very small compared with that found in the domestic chicken (Thomson 1964), and it would seem that present-day domestic ducks evolved gradually (Woelfle 1967), in the process becoming larger than the wild type, with much more variety in color, size, and gait (Clayton 1984). Domestic ducks have also lost the ability to fly.

The excellent flavor of duck flesh (as well as the eggs) has been enjoyed from prehistoric times to the present day. An important incentive in breeding ducks for meat has been the fact that they have a fast growth rate and can be killed as young as 6 to 7 weeks of age and still be palatable. A disadvantage, however, is that duck carcasses are very fatty (Clayton 1984).

Ducks are raised in large numbers in many Western countries, such as the Netherlands, Britain, and the United States, although intensive duck production has occurred only in the last 20 years (Clayton 1984). In Britain, most commercial ducks are found in Norfolk (although some are kept in Aberdeen and Dumfries), but these constitute only about 1 percent of all poultry in the country (Urquhart 1983). Ducks are less prone to disease than hens but eat more food. Unfortunately, their eggs are unpopular with British consumers because they are thought to be unclean. Ducks destined for the supermarkets are killed when they are from 7 to 9 weeks old.

It is in the East where fully 75 percent of domestic ducks are found, especially in the Asian countries of Vietnam, Indonesia, Thailand, China, Bangladesh, the Philippines, and Burma. Duck meat contains a high percentage (up to 35 percent) of fat, which is in short supply in many Asian diets, and in China, where less meat is consumed on a regular basis than in the Western world, selection is for ducks with a high fat content (Clayton 1984).

Peking Duck

Present-day domestic ducks range from the small Call, weighing less than 1 kilogram (kg), to the larger strains of Peking and Aylesbury, weighing up to 6 kg. Ducks can be grouped into three categories: meat producers (Rouen and Aylesbury), egg layers (Indian Runner and Khaki Campbell), and ornamental birds (the tiny Call and Crested ducks) (Delacour 1956–64). The Normandy or Rouen duck is quite similar to the wild mallard and, although common worldwide, is of greatest economic importance in Southeast Asia. The bird has a gamy flavor and in France is traditionally killed by strangulation or smothering, thus ensuring that the flesh retains all of its blood and flavor (David 1970).

Most domestic breeds have a characteristic horizontal posture, but some (as, for example, the Indian Runner), are much more erect, which allows them to run very quickly. The selective pressures that encouraged this erectness are not known, nor are the anatomical changes that brought it about, although droving, common for centuries in the Far East, may be a possibility (Clayton 1972, 1984).

Ducks in the Prehistoric Period

The earliest work on bird bones from archaeological sites was carried out in the mid-nineteenth century at shell mounds in Jutland, Denmark (Steenstrup 1855). Little attention, however, was given to the identification of bird bones from archaeological sites in the Northern Hemisphere until the 1980s, and scant research has been undertaken on the taphonomy of bird bones (Ericson 1987; Livingston 1989). Another problem is that morphological differences between similar bones of different taxa of the *Anatidae* are not always distinct and clear-cut. Measurements of bones can help to separate them, but frequently no specific identification can be made, especially if the material is fragmentary. Nevertheless, attempts at distinguishing wild and domestic mallard bones have been made, although there are also zooarchaeological problems in such an undertaking. Anatomical differences that may be associated with domestication have been recognized in several late Saxon faunal collections in Britain, including that of Northampton (Coy 1981, 1989). The flattened facet on the anterior aspect of the *caput femoris,* employed by J. Lepiksaar (1969) for the identification of domestic geese, can also be used for ducks. J. Ekman (1973) applied this technique to remains in seventeenth- or eighteenth-century deposits in Gothenburg, Sweden.

The wild mallard is (and was) highly migratory, with flocks of several thousand birds not unusual (Gooders 1975). Ideally, wild birds are hunted in the late summer and early fall, just after they have grown plump on summer feeding, and prehistoric fowlers generally took the birds at this, their most defenseless period, or while they were molting or nesting in the spring (Clark 1948).

Some Danish Mesolithic wetland sites demonstrate human exploitation aimed almost solely at birds and, in certain cases, seasonal exploitation of just one or a few species. For example, the Mesolithic site of Aggersund on the Limfjord was a specialized camp for the procurement of whooper swans (Grigson 1989).

There are two distinct types of Danish Mesolithic sites. One is the inland bog, associated with the Maglemosian culture of the Boreal age, whereas the other is the coastal midden of the Ertebolle culture of the Atlantic age. The chief Maglemosian sites on Zealand (Mullerup, Svaerdborg, Holmegaard, and Øgaarde) have yielded bird bone assemblages in which the most abundantly represented birds are wild ducks and mute swans. Also represented are grebes, coots, and some sea birds, including cormorants, gulls, and divers of various species (Clark 1948). Marine birds are more strongly represented in the Ertebolle middens. Because of a lack of winter migrants, the Maglemosian sites were probably occupied only during the summer months, but fruitfully so, as evidenced by the presence of cranes and numerous mute swans, as well as young cormorants and sea eagles.

The mute swan and mallard are both resident taxa and remain very common in present-day Denmark (Grigson 1989). Mallards breed all over inland Denmark and molt during the summer in most wetland habitats, usually in small flocks, but occasionally several hundred individuals congregate on large lakes and in densely vegetated marshland.

In addition to the work done in Denmark, we know from efforts in Germany (at Friesack, Landkreis Nauen) that the Mesolithic (9,700 to 7,000 years ago) bird bone assemblage is dominated by the mallard in all phases (Teichert 1993). In Neolithic eastern Europe (western Russia, the northeastern Baltic region, and northern Poland), numerous bird bones have been excavated from wetland settlements. It is thought that some of these may have been specialized waterfowling sites (Zvelebil 1987). Eighty-nine percent of the bone sample at Narva-Riigikula 3 is composed of waterfowl, mainly ducks. The site is situated on a sandy dune separating a lagoon from the open sea and is on the route of the annual migration of waterfowl between their breeding grounds in the Arctic and their winter quarters in southern Scandinavia and northwestern Europe. These wetland sites are of immense importance in preserving bone and plant remains as well as food-processing tool kits – in this case, wooden projectiles with blunted tips – thus making it possible to reconstruct the subsistence strategies of forest-zone hunter-gatherers in a much more comprehensive way than at dry sites.

As was the case in Poland, the wild duck was the chief quarry of the Iron Age inhabitants of Glastonbury Lake Village in Somerset, England. There, the birds were probably dispatched by clay pellets (also excavated from the site) that were well adapted for use with a sling (Andrews 1917).

Ducks in the Historical Period

The Evidence of Domestication

Southeast Asia is claimed to have been a major center of duck domestication (Zeuner 1963; Wood-Gush 1964), especially southern China, where the birds were kept during the Earlier Han Dynasty (206 B.C. to A.D. 220). The first written records of domestic ducks date back to the Warring States period (475–221 B.C.) (Weishu 1989). But according to one authority, the Chinese have had domesticated ducks for at least 3,000 years (Yeh 1980, cited in Clayton 1984), and it is the case that Chinese pottery models of ducks and geese, dating from about 2500 B.C., have been excavated (Watson 1969). However, archaeological evidence of a faunal nature is also needed before any firm conclusions about the antiquity of domestic ducks in China can be reached.

As already noted, Southeast Asia continues today as an important duck-raising area where domestic ducks surpass chickens in economic importance (Zeuner 1963). The duck thrives in watery environments, which promote clean plumage and increased disease resistance. Moreover, in warm, humid climates, with abundant rice paddies and waterways, ducks forage more successfully and produce more eggs than do chickens, which are not fond of this sort of environment (Clayton 1984).

In China, ducks are particularly important in the control of land crabs (which can devastate rice crops); the birds eat the crab nymphs that eat rice seedlings. Ducks are also released into paddy fields to consume locust nymphs, which, unlike adult locusts, are unable to fly. The recognition that ducks are effective instruments in combatting insect pests is probably of great antiquity (Needham 1986).

The main duck taxa winter in southern China and, except during the breeding season, move in large flocks, each consisting of hundreds – or even thousands – of birds. Although many different species of domestic duck have evolved in Jiangsu and other provinces south of the Yangtze River, where duck raising is common, their shapes, colors, and wings still bear much resemblance to those of their ancestors. The well-known Peking duck, for example, evolved through domestication of the mallard. Its feathers have whitened over a long period, but the curling central tail feather shows that the bird is descended from the same ancestor as the domestic ducks in the south (Weishu 1989).

True domestication elsewhere, however, seems to have come much later. Surveying the limited textual evidence (from Aristotle in the fourth century B.C. up to the ninth century A.D.), J. Harper concluded that ducks did not become fully domesticated outside of China until possibly the Middle Ages (Harper 1972).

The pintail *(Anas acuta)* is the most frequently represented taxon of waterfowl in ancient Egyptian art and hieroglyphics (Houlihan 1986), and such illus-trations include depictions of pintails being force-fed. These birds can be tamed easily and remain able to breed (Delacour 1956–64). The widespread marshes of the Nile Delta would have provided excellent wintering grounds for both ducks and geese and, therefore, fowling opportunities for humans. But although geese, chickens, and pigeons are frequently mentioned in Egyptian papyri from the fifth century B.C. onward, ducks are noted only rarely.

Aristotle discussed only chickens and geese in his *Natural History,* and although Theophrastus mentioned tame ducks, he failed to indicate whether they were bred in captivity (Harper 1972). F. E. Zeuner (1963) has asserted that the keeping of domestic ducks in Greek and Roman times was unusual, though not unknown. Duck-shaped vases have been recovered at Rhodes and Cyprus, both centers of the cult of Aphrodite; they were dedicated to the goddess and to her companion, Eros. Ducks may have been on these islands for religious purposes only.

Several species were kept in captivity by the Romans, who maintained aviaries *(nessotrophia)* of wild ducks, probably to fatten them for the table (Toynbee 1973). Varro, writing in 37 B.C., was the first to mention duck raising by the Romans, pointing out that ducks should be enclosed to protect them from eagles as well as to prevent their escape (Hooper and Ash 1935). In the first century A.D., Lucius Junius Moderatus Columella provided advice on keeping ducks (mallard, teal, and pochard) and other waterfowl in captivity, which was considered much more difficult than caring for more traditional domestic fowl (Forster and Heffner 1954).

Columella, along with Marcus Tullius Cicero and Pliny the Elder, recommended that the eggs of wild ducks be gathered and placed under hens to hatch. Columella claimed that ducks raised in this way would breed readily in captivity, whereas birds taken as adults would be slow to commence laying. He also stated that duck keeping was more expensive than the raising of geese, which fed mainly on grass (Forster and Heffner 1954). Marcus Porcius Cato mentioned the fattening of hens, geese, and squabs for the market, but not ducks (Hooper and Ash 1935).

Moving from Rome to other parts of Europe, we find that metrical data from Colchester, England (from the first to the fourth centuries A.D.), indicate that length and breadth measurements of mallard wing and leg bones are within the range of variation for wild mallards (Luff unpublished). Similarly, measurements of mallard remains from the Roman fort of Velsen I in the Netherlands were considered to be of the wild variety; length and width measurements of the mallard bones fit perfectly within the ranges of recent wild mallards studied by H. Reichstein and H. Pieper (1986; also see Prummel 1987).

The Saxons may have had domestic ducks, but as yet the evidence is unclear. Remains unearthed at Saxon Hamwih (Southampton) could have been those of domesticated ducks but could also have been those of wild birds (Bourdillon and Coy 1980). However, J. P. Coy (1989) has suggested that the low proportion of wildfowl at Saxon sites in Britain is indicative of the economic importance of domestic birds such as ducks and chickens.

A bit later, in Carolingian France (the eighth to the tenth centuries A.D.), estate surveys listing payments due feudal lords indicate that chickens and geese served as tender far more frequently than ducks (Harper 1972). Similarly, in Germany, the *Capitularium de Villis* grouped ducks with ornamental birds such as peafowl, pheasants, and partridges, but not with chickens and geese, kept for purely economic reasons (Franz 1967).

The scarcity of wildfowl was most likely significant in hastening domestication. Early medieval England, for example, had apparently witnessed a wholesale slaughter of wildfowl in spite of Acts of Parliament specifically aimed at their conservation, and in 1209, King John, finding insufficient game for his personal falconry, issued a proclamation forbidding the taking of wildfowl by any means (Macpherson 1897). Statutes were also passed by Henry V, and again by Henry VIII, against the destruction of wildfowl. Interestingly, in the price controls of the Poulters' Guild in London, dated to 1370, a distinction was drawn between wild and tame mallards (Jones 1965). Wild mallards were more expensive than tame ones, which suggests that wild birds were more prized than farmyard birds and indicates their general scarcity at that time.

Jean Delacour (1956-64) has suggested that the mallard may have become truly domesticated in Europe only in the medieval period – although, of course, prior to the distinction made by St. Hildegaard (twelfth century) between wild *(silvestris)* and domestic *(domesticus)* ducks (Figure II.G.9.1). Certainly, the latter were being reared in France by the end of the fourteenth century, when the Ménagier de Paris (c. 1390) also distinguished between wild and domesticated ducks (Prummel 1983).

Nonetheless, ducks of domestic origin are uncommon in archaeological contexts of the medieval period (Eastham 1977; Maltby 1979). At early medieval Dorestad (Netherlands), some ducks were larger than others, indicating that they might well have been domesticates (Prummel 1983). However, the majority of remains at that site probably derived from wild specimens, because their measurements fall within the range for modern wild mallards (Woelfle 1967). Many mallard remains from late medieval Amsterdam measured even larger than those from Dorestad, once again suggesting the presence of domestic ducks among the Dutch (Prummel 1983). But by contrast, at Haithabu in northern Germany, duck remains have been firmly identified as deriving from the wild variety (Requate 1960; Reichstein 1974), which was also the case at eleventh- and

twelfth-century Grand-Besle, Buchy, Normandy (Lepiksaar 1966-8).

Although domestic ducks are often identified in archaeological deposits from the sixteenth century onward, they did not increase dramatically in size until the eighteenth and nineteenth centuries, when distinct varieties were recorded. Methods of rearing ducks were modeled on those mentioned by classical authors. G. Markham, for example, in the seventeenth century described ways of keeping wild mallards, teals, widgeons, shellducks, and lapwings that were very similar to those mentioned by Columella (Markham 1614).

In the eighteenth century, breeders began to promote and further develop certain traits for frequent egg laying or rapid growth for meat production, and sometimes breeds were crossed to produce hybrids suitable for both purposes (Batty 1985). Other varieties were used mainly as ornamental birds to decorate gardens and park ponds.

Aspects of Domestication

S. Bökönyi has emphasized the differences between "animal keeping" and "animal breeding," with the former occurring without purposeful selection or the control of feeding, whereas the latter involves the deliberate selecting of specific traits for animal breeding and also control of nutritional intake (Bökönyi 1969).

There are a number of possible reasons why duck domestication in the West lagged so far behind that of the goose and chicken. One is that goslings accept the first living creature that they see as their mother, whereas mallards, who imprint through sound, do not do this. For them it is the call note of the mother that is important in identifying her (Lorenz 1964). Consequently, ducks were much less amenable to domestication, and the Roman idea of placing wild duck eggs under hens to hatch them into domesticity was off the mark because it did not go far enough.

Interestingly, the Comte de Buffon (Georges Louis Leclerc), who authored 32 volumes of *Natural History,* explained how such a procedure did work:

> Eggs taken from the reeds and rushes amidst the water, and set under an adopted mother, first produced, in our farm-yards, wild, shy, fugitive birds, perpetually roving and unsettled, and impatient to regain the abodes of liberty. These however after they had bred and reared their own young in the domestic asylum became attached to the spot and their descendants in process of time grew more and more gentle and tractable, till at last they appear to have relinquished and forgotten the prerogatives of the savage state, although they still retain a strong propensity to wander abroad. (quoted in Bewick 1826)

Figure II.G.9.1. The mallard duck, ancestor of most domestic ducks.

Another reason for what appears to have been tardy domestication in the West has to do with temperature. S. Bottema (1989) has pointed out that domestic fowl in the Near East always have larger numbers of young than those in more temperate regions, which is the result of a higher survival rate connected not with greater clutch size but with higher temperatures.

Temperature, in turn, is linked to diet. If eggs of the teal *(Anas crecca)* are hatched when temperatures are low, the young may not survive, even though teal ducklings in the wild are not affected by cold weather. The reason is that a natural diet in the wild compensates for a lack of body warmth, but in captivity, with a suboptimal diet, a warm temperature becomes a critical factor (Bottema 1989). In fact, it is for this reason that Bottema (1989) has proposed that areas with high spring temperatures (such as much of Asia) would have been the locus for initial duck domestication.

Charles Darwin (1875) was one of the first researchers to deal with morphological changes in domestication. Using a small sample of wild mallard, Aylesbury, Tufted, Penguin, and Call ducks, he found that: (1) In comparison with the wild duck, the domestic duck experienced universal but slight reduction in the length of the bones of the wing relative to those of the legs; and (2) the prominence of the crest of the sternum relative to its length was much reduced in all domestic breeds. In addition, E. Brown (1906: 5), citing Edward Hewitt's breeding of wild ducks in 1862, has commented that "the beautiful carriage of the wild mallard and his mate changes to the easy, well-to-do, comfortable deportment of a small Rouen, for they at each reproduction become much larger."

Yet although most researchers, such as Darwin and Brown, have equated domestication with a size increase, E. P. Allison has suggested that there was a size decrease in mute swans from the Neolithic to the Bronze Age in Cambridgeshire, and that the birds were, on average, significantly larger than recent specimens. This phenomenon is not related to climatic change (Northcote 1981, 1983). But it is related to confinement, which can produce smaller birds that have not been selected for intentionally, such as the shellduck *(Tadorna tadorna)* or the male pintail *(A. acuta)*. It is also related to food conditions in captivity, which can bring about a size decrease (Bottema 1989).

Confinement and food conditions in captivity may also have affected ducks in ways we have yet to understand. Another confounding factor in faunal analysis of mallards from riverine urban sites is that they may have arisen from a number of different populations, including wild, domestic, and scavenging ducks, with the latter most likely to interbreed with the former (O'Connor 1993). Thus, it is debatable just how pure the strains of present-day river mallards are, as they are obviously the product of considerable inbreeding. Ducks can hybridize (doubtless this was responsible for genetic contributions to domestic stock), and, in fact, all breeds of domestic duck can interbreed.

Also bearing on the history of duck domestication has been the birds' fussiness (much greater than that of chickens), which forestalls their development in caged coops because they have large appetites and because their feet are not tolerant of the wire floors. Ducks produce proportionately larger eggs than gallinaceous birds (and their young seem more resistant to starvation) (Marcström 1966), but selection under domestication has been for a larger bird and not for a larger egg. Moreover, duck eggs, as already noted, have never been in high demand in Europe; they are strong in flavor and lack the palatability of hens' eggs (Brown 1930). This is unfortunate, as ducks are naturally prolific layers and the eggs are highly nutritious.

Summary

Current evidence suggests that the origin of duck domestication was in Southeast Asia, and particularly in China. This region is still an important center for duck breeding and consumption, and one where captive, newly hatched ducklings have a greater chance of survival because of relatively higher temperatures.

It is true that more zooarchaeological data – in the form of bones – would be helpful in determining the origins of duck domestication. But because distinctions between the wild and domestic types of ducks are slight, such evidence alone would probably not pinpoint these origins.

Although the Egyptians, Greeks, and Romans kept ducks in captivity, they never truly domesticated them. Compelling evidence for domestication outside of Southeast Asia has only been found for the medieval period and later. In Europe, and particularly in Britain, the widespread pursuit and destruction of waterfowl by the nobility during the early Middle Ages (and probably earlier) may well have provided the impetus for duck domestication.

Because ducks have voracious appetites, feeding them may often have been a problem during winter months, when food shortages were common in non-industrial societies – especially after a poor harvest. Consequently, it is likely that even though tamed, ducks were frequently left to forage as best they could. This inference also suggests that breeding was not controlled, with tame ducks interbreeding with members of the wild population. It was only in the eighteenth and nineteenth centuries that specialized breeds of domestic ducks were reared for meat, eggs, and ornamentation.

Rosemary Luff

Bibliography

Allison, E. P. 1985. Archaeozoological study of bird bones from seven sites in York. Ph.D. thesis, University of York.

Andrews, C. W. 1917. Report on the remains of birds found at the Glastonbury Lake Village. In *The Glastonbury Lake Village*, by A. Bulleid and H. St. George Gray, Vol. 2, 631-7. Glastonbury, England.

Batty, J. 1985. *Domesticated ducks and geese*. Liss, England.

Bewick, T. 1826. *A history of British birds*, Vol. 2. London.

Bökönyi, S. 1969. Archaeological problems and methods of recognizing animal domestication. In *The domestication and exploitation of plants and animals*, ed. P. J. Ucko and G. W. Dimbleby, 219-29. London.

Bottema, S. 1980. Eenden in Nederland. In *Zelzame huisdierrassen*, ed. A. T. Clason, 191-204. Zutphen Thieme, the Netherlands.

1989. Some observations on modern domestication processes. In *The walking larder*, ed. J. Clutton-Brock, 31-45. London.

Bourdillon, J., and J. Coy. 1980. The animal bones. *Excavations at Melbourne St., Southampton, 1971-76. Council for British Archaeology Research Report* 33: 79-121.

Brown, E. 1906. *Races of domestic poultry*. London.

1930. *British poultry husbandry, its evolution and history*. London.

Clark, G. 1948. Fowling in prehistoric Europe. *Antiquity* 22: 116-30.

Clayton, G. A. 1972. Effects of selection on reproduction in avian species. *Journal of Reproduction and Fertility* (Supplement 15): 1-21.

1984. Common duck. In *Evolution of domesticated animals*, ed. I. L. Mason, 334-9. London.

Coy, J. P. 1981. The bird bones. In *Excavations in Chalk Lane, Northampton*, by J. H. Williams and M. Shaw. *Northampton Archaeology* 16: 1-9.

1989. The provision of fowls and fish for towns. In *Diet and crafts in towns*, ed. D. Serjeantson. *British Archaeological Reports* 199: 25-40.

Darwin, Charles R. 1875. *Variation of animals and plants under domestication*. London.

David, E. 1970. *French provincial cooking*. Harmondsworth, England.

Delacour, Jean. 1956-64. *The waterfowl of the world*, Vols. 2, 3, and 4. London.

Eastham, A. 1977. Birds. In *Excavations at Portchester Castle*, ed. B. Cunliffe. Reports of the Research Committee of the Society of Antiquaries of London 34: 233-9.

Ekman, J. 1973. Early medieval Lund, the fauna and the landscape. In *Archaeologica lundensia. Investigationes de antiquitatibus urbis Lundae* 5. Lund, Sweden.

Ericson, P. G. P. 1987. Interpretations of archaeological bird remains: A taphonomic approach. *Journal of Archaeological Science* 14: 65-75.

Forster, E. S., and E. H. Heffner. 1954. *Columella: De re rustica*, Vol 2. London.

Franz, G. 1967. *Capitularium villis. Quellen zur Geschichte des deutschen Bauernstandes im Mittelalter*. Darmstadt, Germany.

Gooders, J. 1975. *Birds, an illustrated survey of the bird families of the world*. London.

Gooders, J., and T. Boyer. 1986. *Ducks of Britain and the Northern Hemisphere*. London.

Grigson, C. 1989. Bird-foraging patterns in the Mesolithic. In *The Mesolithic in Europe*, ed. C. Bonsall, 60-72. Edinburgh.

Harper, J. 1972. The tardy domestication of the duck. *Agricultural History* 46: 385-9.

Hooper, W. D., and H. B. Ash. 1935. *Cato and Varro: On agriculture*. London.

Houlihan, P. F. 1986. The birds of ancient Egypt. In *The natural history of Egypt*, Vol. 1. Warminster, England.

Jones, P. E. 1965. *The worshipful company of poulters of the city of London*. Oxford.

Lepiksaar, J. 1966-8. *Restes d'animaux provenant du Grand Besle, Meddelanden från Lunds Universitets. Historiska Museum*, 85-116.

1969. Nytt om djur från det medeltida Ny Varberg. *Varbergs Museums Arsbok*, 1-32.

Livingston, S. D. 1989. The taphonomic interpretation of avian skeletal part frequencies. *Journal of Archaeological Science* 16: 537-47.

Lorenz, K. 1964. *King Solomon's ring*. London.

Macpherson, H. A. 1897. *A history of fowling*. Edinburgh.

Maltby, M. 1979. The animal bones from Exeter, 1971-75. *Exeter Archaeological Reports* 2: 66-74.

Marcström, V. 1966. Mallard ducklings (*Anas platyrhynchos*) during the first days after hatching. *Viltrevy* 4: 343-70.

Markham, G. 1614. *Cheap and good husbandry*. London.

Mason, I. L. 1984. *Evolution of domesticated animals*. London and New York.

Mead, W. 1931. *The English medieval feast*. London.

Needham, J. 1986. Biology and biological technology. In *Science and civilization in China*, eds. J. Needham and Lu Gwei-djen. Vol. 6, Part 1, Sec. 38. Cambridge.

Northcote, M. 1981. Size differences between limb bones of recent and subfossil mute swans, *Cygnus olor. Journal of Archaeological Science* 8: 89-98.

1983. Morphology of mute swans in relation to domestication. In *Animals and archaeology*, Vol. 2., ed. J. Clutton-Brock and C. Grigson. *British Archaeological Reports, International Series* 183: 173-9.

O'Connor, T. P. 1993. Birds and the scavenger niche. *Archaeofauna* 2: 155-62.

Pichon, J. 1847. *Ménagier de Paris (le), traité de morale et d'économie domestique composé vers 1393 par un bourgeois parisien*. Paris.

Prummel, W. 1983. *Excavations at Dorestad 2. Early medieval Dorestad, an archaeozoological study*. Rijksdienst voor het Oudheidkundig Bodemonderzoek, Amersfoot, the Netherlands.

1987. Poultry and fowling at the Roman castellum Velsen I. *Palaeohistoria* 29: 183-201.

Reichstein, H. 1974. Ergebnisse und Probleme von Untersuchungen an Wildtieren aus Haithabu (Ausgrabung 1963-1964). In *Untersuchungen an Tierknochenfunden (1963-1964)*, ed. H. Reichstein and M. Tiessen. *Berichte über die Ausgrabungen in Haithabu* 7: 103-44. Neumünster, Germany.

Reichstein, H., and H. Pieper. 1986. *Untersuchungen an Skelettresten von Vögeln aus Haithabu. (Ausgrabung 1966-1969)*. Neumünster, Germany.

Requate, H. 1960. Das Hausgeflügel. In *Die Haustiere von Haithabu (Die Ausgrabungen in Haithabu, 3)*, ed. W. Herre, 136-46. Neumünster, Germany.

Seebohm, M. E. 1952. *The evolution of the English farm*. London.

Steenstrup, J. 1855. Et bidrag til Gerrfuglens, Alca impennis Lin., naturhistorie, og saerligt til Kundskaben om dens tidligere Udbredningskreds. *Videnskabelige Med-*

delelser fra den naturhistorisk Forening Kjobenhaun
3: 33-116.

Teichert, L. 1993. Die Vögelknochenfunde von Friesack, Landkreis Nauen, eine paläoökologische und faunen-
geschichtliche Auswertung. In *Festschrift für Hanns-
Hermann Müller. Zeitschrift für Archäeologie* 27:
17-28.

Thomson, A. L. 1964. *A new dictionary of birds*. London.

Toynbee, J. 1973. *Animals in Roman life and art*. London.

Urquhart, J. 1983. *Animals on the farm, their history from the
earliest times to the present day*. London and Sydney.

Watson, W. 1969. Early domestication in China. In *The domestication and exploitation of plants and animals*, ed.
P. J. Ucko and G. W. Dimbleby, 393-5. London.

Weishu, X. U. 1989. *Birds in China*. Beijing.

Willughby, F. 1678. *Ornithology*. London.

Woelfle, E. 1967. Vergleichend morphologische Untersuchun-
gen an Einzelknochen des postcranialen Skelettes in
Mitteleuropa vorkommender Enten, Halbgänse und
Sager. Ph.D. thesis, University of Munich.

Wood-Gush, D. G. M. 1964. Domestication. In *A new dictionary of birds*, ed. A. L. Thomson, 215-18. London.

Yeh, Hsiangkui. 1980. *Fossil ducks and Peking ducks*. China.

Zeuner, F. E. 1963. *A history of domesticated animals*. London.

Zvelebil, M. 1987. Wetland settlements of eastern Europe. In
European wetlands in prehistory, ed. J. M. Coles and
A. J. Lawson, 94-116. Oxford.

II.G.10   Game

Evolutionary Underpinnings

Game (defined here as the meat of wild mammals,
birds, and terrestrial reptiles) has been an important
component of the human diet since earliest times. A
signal difference between the digestive system of
humans and those of their closest primate relatives is
the modification of the guts of the former for the processing of a diet containing substantial quantities of
meat (Chivers 1992). Until the last few thousand
years, all meat-producing animals were wild. The continuing cultural significance of hunting as an activity,
and game as an element of the diet, must be seen in
the light of the age-old importance of game animals in
human biological and cultural evolution.

Although little doubt exists that early hominids
consumed appreciable quantities of game, lively
debate lingers over whether our remote ancestors
were primarily hunters or scavengers (e.g., Shipman
1986; Binford 1988). Nevertheless, there is abundant
evidence that by the time of the appearance of early
modern humans - between 50,000 and 100,000 years
ago - hunting was one of humankind's major activities. It may have been so for uncounted previous
millennia.

A striking sexual division of subsistence labor characterizes most contemporary hunting and gathering
peoples, with men hunting and women gathering (but
see later discussion). Typically, gathered foods more or
less reliably provide the bulk of the calories in the
diet, mainly as carbohydrates, whereas game (and/or
fish) contributes the undependable and sometimes
limiting protein fraction. It has been proposed (Isaac
1978; Isaac and Crader 1981) that this bifurcation in
foraging tasks and products is ancient and is implicated in the coevolution of food sharing, tool use,
paternal investment in offspring, and related features
of the unique human constellation of social behaviors.

Game, particularly large game, is often shared
widely, whereas gathered foods tend to be acquired
and consumed within the family. Meat is usually more
valued than vegetable foods, and hunting is typically a
more prestigious activity than gathering (Kent 1989).
These correlations, too, may be ancient. The ancestral
associations of men with hunting, of hunting with
high social status, and of game with generosity and
display, are an important part of the background of
the presence of game in the human diet.

Subsistence Hunting

Global Trends

Studies of the hunting and gathering societies have
identified geographic regularities in the quantity of
game in the diet of these foraging peoples for whom
wild foods are the foundation of life (Lee 1968;
Jochim 1981). Behind these regularities are climatically determined abundances and availabilities of
game animals relative to other potential human foods.

Close to the North Pole, inedible (for humans) tundra grasses dominate the vegetation, whereas much of
the faunal biomass is in grazing animals (caribou, reindeer) with large herds and highly palatable flesh.
Because much of the circumpolar region is coastal, terrestrial game can often be supplemented by large sea
mammals (seals and whales). Thus, most of the few
high-latitude foraging peoples (Eskimos, native Siberi-
ans) live largely or almost exclusively on game; the
only real alternative food is fish (and that solely for
inhabitants of uncommonly well-favored seaboards).

A good number of cool-temperate hunting and
gathering peoples (40°-60° latitude) have fish as the
primary element in the diet, particularly anadromous
fish (fish that run upriver from the ocean to spawn,
frequently in enormous numbers; see Schalk 1977).
These peoples, however, also consume considerable
game. Well-known ethnographic examples are the
inhabitants of the northwest coast of North America
and the coastal islands of northeast Asia, locations
endowed with rivers supporting reliable and abundant fish runs. Other cool-temperate foraging peoples
(that is, the Cree and Ojibwa of eastern Canada and
several bison-hunting tribes of the North American
Great Plains) make game the basis of their diet and
eat distinctly lesser quantities of fish and vegetable
foods. Cool-temperate regions are mainly forested or
covered with prairie grasses, and wild vegetable foods

are seasonally scarce and often not abundant at the best of times. With the exception of the North American bison, most of the large game tends to be relatively solitary and the availability of fish and game in a locality usually decides the base of the diet.

Hunting and gathering peoples living within 40° of the equator – the majority of all foraging peoples, and the great majority of those for whom we have reliable dietary information – derive most of their diet from gathered vegetable foods. Tubers, nuts, and seeds tend to be abundant and reliable relative to fish and game at these latitudes. Nevertheless, game remains for these peoples the most desirable part of the diet. Its capture attracts more effort and attention than the harvest of vegetable foods, and its procurers are often rewarded with favorable attention ranging from subtle deference to sexual favors (Hawkes 1990).

It is frequently assumed that game's desirability to these lower-latitude foragers derives from its role as the only major source of limiting nutrients, particularly the eight essential amino acids found in animal protein. However, complete inventories and nutritional analyses of these foragers' gathered wild foods remain scarce. That game and fish do supply much (usually most) of their protein is clear; that alternative invertebrate and vegetable protein foods are actually lacking is less clear. Well-documented demonstrations that gathered foods could not supply a protein-adequate diet are still too few to establish the generality of the impression that game is strictly necessary to provide protein for low-latitude hunters and gatherers.

Cultural Evolutionary Trends

Within the last 10,000 years (perhaps a bit earlier in Southeast Asia) plants and animals were domesticated on all continents except Australia. In some regions (e.g., eastern North America, lowland South America), the major edible domesticates were all plants. Here, wild game and fish continued to supply the meat in everyone's diet, not only in early agricultural times but even after domestication had permitted the emergence of stratified societies. In these New World stratified societies, the mighty were differentiated from the lowly in diet as in other aspects of life. However, it was the amount of game, the species of game, and the cuts of meat that distinguished the larders of the haves from those of the have-nots; there was no significant substitution of domestic flesh for wild game.

In other regions (that is, Europe, western Asia), large herd animals were domesticated at around the same time(s) as plants, and livestock became important early in the history of food production. Nevertheless, even though domesticated animals and their products (milk, blood) quickly became major elements in the diet of these mixed farmer-herders, game remained in the diet. The hunt continued in parallel with stock raising throughout most of early village life in the Old World, with wild animals often important in the diet. As food production led eventually to the development of Old World complex societies, hunting survived. At that point, however, the reasons for its persistence – previously a straightforward matter of obtaining food – became divergent.

By the early days of stratified societies, a pattern had been established (e.g., Trigger 1965) that continued through much of history and into the modern world: Hunting, and the presence of game in the diet, was most prominent in the lives of people at the very top and the very bottom of the social hierarchy. Among rulers, hunting lingered as recreation and ostensive display, a demonstration of not needing to rely on the efficient meat production of domesticated animals. Among the peripheral and the poor, hunting persisted because people could not afford domestic animals. The conflict of these classes over access to game lies behind such beloved folklore as the legend of Robin Hood. Among both classes, and into modern times, hunting is pleasurable, and game is a prestige food, although there are higher prestige foods among the impoverished.

Sexual Division of Labor

Although numerous societies have produced the occasional female hunter, and many cultures recognize goddesses of the hunt (the Grecian Artemis or the Indian Chandi), hunting remains predominantly (often exclusively) a male pursuit in almost all societies. Reasons proposed for masculine dominion of the chase range from the advantage in mean strength and speed enjoyed by male hunters to the disadvantages in combining hunting with pregnancy and child care incurred by female hunters. In this connection, the evidence of the tropical forest Agta people of the Philippines is crucial: Among some bands of the hunting, gathering, casually horticultural, and trading Agta, women regularly hunt, and their hunting includes dangerous game – like the wild pig – that they kill close up with machetes and improvised spears.

It is significant, then, that among the Agta, most women's hunting involves dogs; that "during late pregnancy and for the first few months of nursing, a woman will not hunt" (Estioko-Griffin and Griffin 1981: 131); and that "[y]oung mothers . . . are not the major women hunters; mature women with self sufficient children secure most of the game animals considered [of those taken by women] both by number and by weight" (Griffin and Griffin 1992: 310). Although the sexual division of labor appears remarkably weak among the Agta, and the generalization that women are mainly confined to gathering is overthrown by this case, hunting, nonetheless, remains more associated with men than with women.

Optimal Foraging Theory

A body of ecological theory known as Optimal Foraging Theory or OFT (Stephens and Krebs 1986) generates predictions as to the prey species that should be included in the diet of a predator. The general rule is that the predator should choose to pursue individuals of a particular species only when the predator cannot expect to get more or better food for its hunting time by disregarding that species. If there is a statistically reliable expectation that members of more valuable prey species will be taken in the time that would otherwise have been dedicated to the pursuit of members of a less valuable species, then that less valuable species is not in the optimal diet.

For example, if hares in a grassland are difficult to catch, but gazelles are plump and easy to kill, the optimal forager ignores the small and time-costly hares, even when he sees them bounding away, as long as gazelles are plentiful. Time spent chasing a hare is time taken away from searching for gazelles. Hares enter the optimal diet only when gazelles have become so rare that it becomes cost-effective to chase hares. When the mean encounter rate with individuals of each potential game species is known, along with the average time it takes to pursue and kill them and the average amount of meat they provide, then the optimal diet set can be predicted with considerable precision.

Predictions can also be made as to the predator's order of preference for the animals included in the optimal diet set. Predicted choices are easily summarized: Hunters should favor large animals over small and easily killed animals over those that require much time to hunt down and often escape.

Optimal diet set predictions have been tested for a number of subsistence hunters, with observed hunting behavior generally agreeing with the OFT model (Hill and Hawkes 1983; Kuchikura 1988; Kaplan and Hill 1992). Preferred game orderings have also been examined from an OFT perspective. Again, subsistence hunters appear in general to conform to theoretical predictions (Altman 1987; Hawkes, O'Connell, and Blurton-Jones 1991).

Game Allocation

The goal of subsistence hunting is game to eat. However, it is seldom if ever the case that all animals are considered game or that all parts of all game animals are eaten randomly by all members of a society. Rules governing the allocation of game are highly variable cross-culturally. Indeed, the issue of who makes the distribution is far from uniform from one culture to another. In many egalitarian cultures, the game belongs to the man (or woman) who killed it; in others, to the hunter who first wounded it; and in still others, to the person who made the arrow or other weapon with which the kill was accomplished, independent of that person's participation in the hunt. In ranked or stratified societies, the right to distribute the game may belong to the head of the lineage to which the successful hunter belongs, or to a village chief, or to another official.

Among the egalitarian, hunting and gathering !Kung Bushmen of southern Africa, the hunter whose arrow first hit the animal makes the initial distribution of meat, which is to the other hunters in his party. These hunters, in turn, distribute shares to their kin. All the hunters' kin who receive meat have additional kin obligations, and eventually everyone in the camp receives some meat, although portions may be small for individuals genealogically distant from the members of the hunting party (Marshall 1965).

But distribution methods aside, there are often rules of striking salience as to where different parts of animals are directed. Among the egalitarian, horticultural Anggor of New Guinea, when a wild pig is killed, the carcass, once cooked, is parceled out in a detailed way: The extremities are given to local clans; the hunter's clan gets the viscera; old women eat the fetus of a pregnant sow; old men receive cooked blood; and so on (Hurber 1980).

Parts (or all) of particular animals may be reserved for or prohibited to particular people or all people. Among the egalitarian, horticultural Barí of Colombia and Venezuela, the head and tripe of howler monkey are not eaten by anyone, whereas the head of spider monkey is eaten, along with the liver and some other organ meats. Peccary heads are reserved for old men; children are not allowed to consume any part of a bear; and no one eats jaguar.

People in particular statuses may have privileges or prohibitions connected with consumption of designated parts of game animals. Excavations at sites belonging to the late prehistoric Mississippian chiefdom centered at Moundville, Alabama, indicate that preferred cuts of deer meat were sent from outlying areas to elite centers, presumably for consumption by chiefs, their families, and retainers (Welch 1991).

Entire game species may be associated with social statuses. Among contemporary Anglo-Americans, consumption of opossum meat is restricted to rural lower classes, although venison is acceptable at both extremes of the social ladder, and smaller game birds are eaten largely by people of means.

There are a few general principles known for game distribution: (1) Many cultures assign carnivores and scavengers to an "inedible" category; (2) in egalitarian societies, the larger and more unpredictably obtained a game animal is, the more likely it is to be shared widely; (3) in ranked and stratified societies, the largest and most desirable game animals and the best cuts typically go to the most important members of society; and (4) the reproductive parts of otherwise edible animals are often prohibited to some if not all members of a society. Beyond these empirical generalizations, a general theory of food allocations, prescriptions, and proscriptions remains to be constructed.

Game in the Diet

The amount of game in the victuals of subsistence hunting peoples varies from a small fraction, as among many peoples with domestic food animals who also hunt when the opportunity arises (many societies in Oceania are of this type), to virtually the entire diet, as among some Eskimo groups. Some regional trends were mentioned previously. Within subsistence hunting societies, the distribution of game may or may not also be highly variable, with some or all game animals widely distributed and consumed or effectively confined to a minority of the society's members. In general, the higher the proportion of game in the aggregate diet, the weaker the exclusion of classes of individuals within the society from game consumption.

Prestige, Recreational, and Commercial Hunting

Prestige Hunting

Rulers of antiquity were often conspicuous hunters. Near the dawn of recorded history, "the Middle Assyrian king Tiglath-pileser I claimed . . . to have killed 4 wild bulls, 10 elephants and 920 lions – 800 from his chariot and 120 on foot" (Roaf 1990: 154).

Millennia later, in December A.D. 799, on a different continent, Charlemagne and his three sons killed a wolf, 2 European bison, 6 aurochs, 66 boars, and 80 deer in the space of two hours, to the applause of the queen and princesses, at a hunt organized by a count and his foresters. The royal party feasted later that day on the choicest parts of the kill (Halleux 1988).

Marco Polo's description, nearly 500 years later still, of Kublai Khan's yearly round illustrates a number of the features of prestige hunting: its prominence in royal life; its ostensive display; its employment of sumptuary laws; and its ranking of game animals by their suitability as royal prey. For six months of the year, hunting figured large in the life of Kublai Khan's court:

> The three months of December, January, and February, during which the Emperor resides at his Capital City, are assigned for hunting and fowling, to the extent of some 40 days' journey round the city; and it is ordained that the larger game taken be sent to the Court. To be more particular: of all the larger beasts of the chase, such as boars, stags, lions, bears, etc., the greater part of what is taken has to be sent, and feathered game likewise. . . .
>
> After he has stopped at his capital city those three months . . . he starts off on the 1st day of March, and travels eastward towards the Ocean Sea, a journey of two days. He takes with him full 10,000 falconers and some 500 gerfalcons besides peregrines, sakers, and other hawks in great numbers; and goshawks also to fly at the water fowl. . . . The Emperor himself is carried upon four elephants in a fine chamber made of timber, lined inside with plates of beaten gold, and outside with lion' skins. . . . He always keeps beside him a dozen of his choicest gerfalcons,

> and is attended by several of his Barons, who ride on horseback alongside. . . . And when he has travelled till he reaches a place called Katar Modun, there he finds his tents pitched . . . full 10,000 tents in all. . . . The Lord remains encamped there until the spring [May] and all that time he does nothing but go hawking round and among the canebreaks . . . and across fine plains . . . for 20 days journey round the spot nobody is allowed . . . to keep hawks or hounds . . . and furthermore throughout all the emperor's territories, nobody however audacious dares to hunt . . . hare, stag, buck and roe, from . . . March to . . . October. (Polo 1927: 127, 129-33)

Recreational Hunting

Much prestige hunting is clearly recreational, but hunting for enjoyment is not limited to royalty. Indeed, most hunting, even explicitly commercial hunting, has a pleasurable aspect. Although the recreational chase of the upper classes is nowadays often more a matter of public socializing or trophy skins than of table meat (British fox hunting, international big cat hunting), a notable proportion of the recreational hunting of all classes produces edible game such as duck and deer. In modern times, ethical considerations may impel the consumption of this game as a justification for the enjoyment of the hunt, even when the hunter finds it less palatable than the highly processed food to which he is accustomed. Generations of North American boys have learned a version of the "You shoot it, you eat it" hunter's code from their fathers. The pleasures of the hunt may paradoxically cause moderns to eat game they would otherwise omit from their diets.

Commercial Hunting

Hunting in order to sell or barter game has roots more ancient than commonly recognized. There are no contemporary tropical forest hunters and gatherers who do not maintain trading relations – most often game for crops – with agricultural neighbors. It has been proposed that humans did not enter the tropical forest until the invention of agriculture made this interchange possible (Headland 1987; Headland and Bailey 1991). The Pygmies of the Congo Basin have been trading game for crops with their Bantu neighbors for centuries, if not millennia. Similar relations, possibly of comparable antiquity, are maintained with agriculturalists by the hunting and gathering Makú of the Amazon region, the Agta of the Philippines, and a number of Hill Tribes in India. The game-producing hunters and gatherers are typically considered by their agricultural trading partners to be serfs or slaves.

In Western industrial societies commercial meat hunters are also marginal people. Guides and "white hunters" are glamorous figures in fiction and may, in fact, make considerable money, but they provide recreational and prestige hunting for others. They do not make a living by selling the game they hunt themselves. In a sense, contemporary individuals who sell game can be looked at as the cultural descendants of the peripheral individuals who continued to hunt for food while more affluent members of their societies obtained animal protein from domesticated animals.

Game is usually tougher than the meat of domesticated animals, but many consider it to be tastier. Its generally lower fat content has led some to believe that it is healthier as well.

It is indicative of the persistence of social evolutionary trends noted earlier that in the Western world, restaurants habitually serving wild game are of two kinds – the most expensive establishments in major metropolitan centers and small, "mom and pop" places in rural areas. Many people frequenting both kinds of establishments eat game in considerable measure for its status marker value, although of course the prestige of consuming game differs widely in association as well as scope between one type of restaurant and the other. In the former, game is affiliated with wealth and display, whereas in the latter it is primarily linked with recreation and the manly virtues.

Aside from its survival in this and similar commercial contexts, game has largely disappeared from the diet in modern industrial societies. Areas where it is still a notable part of yearly food consumption are uncommon. These include tribal enclaves, a few rural areas where subsistence hunting traditions are strong, and a very few spots where recreational and prestige hunting are major components of the local economy. In prospect, it seems that whatever amount of game remains in the diet of humans in the developed world will be retained for its association with the prestige of the hunt rather than for the nutritional value of the meat itself.

Stephen Beckerman

Bibliography

Altman, J. 1987. *Hunter-gatherers today: An aboriginal economy in north Australia.* Canberra, Australia.

Binford, L. R. 1988. The hunting hypothesis, archaeological methods, and the past. *Yearbook of Physical Anthropology* 30: 1-9.

Chivers, D. J. 1992. Diets and guts. In *The Cambridge encyclopedia of human evolution,* ed. Steve Jones, Robert Martin, and David Pilbeam, 60-4. Cambridge.

Estioko-Griffin, A., and P. B. Griffin. 1981. Woman the hunter: The Agta. In *Woman the gatherer,* ed. Frances Dahlberg, 121-51. New Haven.

Griffin, P. B., and M. B. Griffin. 1992. Fathers and childcare among the Cagayan Agta. In *Father-child relations: Cultural and biosocial relations,* ed. Barry Hewlett, 297-320. Hawthorne, N.Y.

Halleux, G. 1988. Charlemagne à la chasse. *Plaisirs de la chasse* 437: 28-30.

Hawkes, K. 1990. Why do men hunt? Some benefits for risky choices. In *Risk and uncertainty in tribal and peasant economies,* ed. E. Cashdan, 145-66. Boulder, Colo.

Hawkes, K., J. O'Connell, and N. Blurton-Jones. 1991. Hunting income patterns among the Hadza: Big game, common goods, foraging goals and the evolution of the human diet. *Philosophical Transactions of the Royal Society of London* B334: 243-51.

Headland, T. 1987. The wild yam question: How well could independent hunter-gatherers live in a tropical rain forest ecosystem? *Human Ecology* 15: 463-91.

Headland, T., and R. Bailey. 1991. Introduction: Have hunter-gatherers ever lived in tropical rain forest independently of agriculture? *Human Ecology* 19: 115-22.

Hill, K., and K. Hawkes. 1983. Neotropical hunting among the Aché of Eastern Paraguay. In *Adaptive responses of native Amazonians,* ed. Ray Hames and William Vickers, 223-67. New York.

Hurber, P. 1980. The Anggor bowman: Ritual and society in Melanesia. *American Ethnologist* 7: 43-57.

Isaac, G. L. 1978. The food sharing behavior of protohuman hominids. *Scientific American* 238: 90-108.

Isaac, G. L., and D. C. Crader. 1981. To what extent were early hominids carnivorous? An archaeological perspective. In *Omnivorous primates: Gathering and hunting in human evolution,* ed. R. S. O. Harding and G. Teleki, 37-103. New York.

Jochim, M. 1981. *Strategies for survival: Cultural behavior in an ecological context.* New York.

Kaplan, H., and K. Hill. 1992. The evolutionary ecology of food acquisition. In *Evolutionary ecology and human behavior,* ed. Eric Smith and Bruce Winterhalder, 167-201. Hawthorne, N.Y.

Kent, S. 1989. Cross-cultural conceptions of farmers as hunters and the value of meat. In *Farmers as hunters: The implications of sedentism,* ed. S. Kent, 1-17. Cambridge and New York.

Kuchikura, Y. 1988. Efficiency and focus of blowpipe hunting among Semaq Beri hunter-gatherers of peninsular Malaysia. *Human Ecology* 16: 271-305.

Lee, R. B. 1968. What hunters do for a living, or, how to make out on scarce resources. In *Man the hunter,* ed. R. B. Lee and I. DeVore, 30-48. Chicago.

Marshall, L. 1965. The !Kung Bushmen of the Kalahari Desert. In *Peoples of Africa,* ed. J. L. Gibbs, Jr., 241-78. Prospect Heights, Ill.

Polo, M. 1927. *The Book of Ser Marco Polo the Venetian, concerning the kingdoms and marvels of the East,* ed. G. Parks. New York.

Roaf, M. 1990. *Cultural atlas of Mesopotamia and the ancient Near East.* Oxford.

Schalk, R. 1977. The structure of an anadromous fish resource. In *For theory building in archaeology,* ed. L. R. Binford, 207-50. New York.

Shipman, P. 1986. Scavenging or hunting in early hominids: Theoretical framework and tests. *American Anthropologist* 88: 27-43.

Stephens, D. W. and J. R. Krebs. 1986. *Foraging theory.* Princeton, N.J.

Trigger, B. 1965. *History and settlement in lower Nubia.* Yale University Publications in Anthropology, No. 69. New Haven, Conn.

Welch, P. 1991. *Moundville's economy.* Tuscaloosa, Ala.

II.G.11 ❧ Geese

The common domestic geese are derived from two wild species, the greylag, *Anser anser,* and the swan goose, *Anser cygnoides.* The wild greylag is found seasonally throughout most of Eurasia and North Africa, although it is not known to breed south of 45° latitude. The swan goose is confined to East Asia, although the two can freely hybridize at the meeting point of their ranges. It has been argued that the Indian barheaded goose, *Anser indicus,* also played a part in the evolution of domestic geese, because it is interfertile with the aforementioned species (Crawford 1984).

Geese are easily domesticated, and this process probably occurred numerous times. Moreover, the continuing presence of the greylag suggests that there was constant introgression from the wild form, accounting for Charles Darwin's observation that "the amount of variation that it has undergone, as compared with that of most domesticated animals, is singularly small" (cited in Crawford 1984: 345).

Other species of geese have been domesticated on an experimental basis in ancient or modern times. These are:

Canada goose	*Branta canadensis*
White-fronted goose	*Anser albifrons*
Egyptian goose	*Alopochen aegyptiaca*
Spur-winged goose	*Plectopterus gambensis*

However, none of these birds have attained commercial importance.

Despite their distribution, domestic geese are poorly documented across their range, especially the Chinese swan goose, which is virtually absent from all discussions of Chinese animal husbandry. Geese bones, due to their greater size and fragility, are often more comminuted in archaeological deposits than those of chickens and small game birds. Nonetheless, the lack of reports of goose bones from archaeological sites may reflect more the prejudices of archaeology than a real absence.

Geese in Domestication

Not only are geese easily domesticated, but when rendered flightless by their weight, they can be herded long distances. It has been hypothesized that the process of domestication probably began with the capture of wild specimens that were subsequently force-fed to make them too heavy to fly. The fattening of geese for their liver (foie gras) seems to have been known at least from Roman times, when birds were given a mixture of flour, milk, and honey (Zeuner 1963).

Goose eggs, in addition to goose flesh, were eaten in ancient Macedonia and Rome. Like chickens, the birds were also bred for fighting,

especially in Russia (Dmitriev and Ernst 1989). Geese are known in fable for raising the alarm that saved Rome from Gallic invasion in 390 B.C., and they were recorded ethnographically in Europe and South America as guard animals (Zeuner 1963; Crawford 1984). Geese are still reared for their quills, which were once of major importance for writing implements and remain sought after for some musical instruments. Geese are also kept for their down, which is used to stuff pillows, bedclothes, and clothing because of its insulating qualities.

Historical Distribution

Egypt and Southwest Asia
R. D. Crawford (1984) hypothesized that the greylag goose was probably first domesticated in southeastern Europe around 3000 B.C. However, in the absence of any tangible evidence from this region, archaeological findings now indicate Egypt as the first known center of goose domestication. The earliest evidence comes from the Old Kingdom (2723-2300 B.C.), in the form of representations of geese confined in poultry yards, kept in cages, and being herded. The pictures are sufficiently imprecise that it is uncertain whether the greylag goose or the white-fronted goose, *A. albifrons,* is being depicted. Both were trapped and eaten and, on occasion, hand-fed to increase their plumpness for the table (Houlihan and Goodman 1986: 54 ff.).

Arguably domesticated, greylag geese begin to occur osteologically in temple or funerary offerings only during the Middle Kingdom. For instance, they

Geese

have been documented from the queen's burial chambers in the Twelfth Dynasty pyramid of Amenemhat III (1850–1800 B.C.) (Darby, Ghalioungui, and Grivetti 1977; Houlihan and Goodman 1986; Katzmann 1990). Greylag geese were certainly fully domesticated by the Eighteenth Dynasty (1450–1341 B.C.), when tomb paintings showed the distinctive heterogeneous colorings of domesticated *A. anser* flocks (Boessneck 1991). If, however, the white-fronted goose *(A. albifrons)* was domesticated at that time, this practice did not persist, whereas the rearing of the greylag goose spread westward along the North African littoral and into the Near East and Europe. Despite its belligerent nature, the Egyptian goose, *A. aegyptiaca,* was also apparently domesticated for the table in the Old Kingdom, although no trace of this bird remains today (Houlihan and Goodman 1986: 64).

J. Boessneck (1991) has pointed out that the geese remains from Egypt suggest very large animals, exceeding even modern commercial breeds. These "huge domestic geese" are known from the late dynastic periods at Tell el-Maskuta (c. 600 B.C. to A.D. 200), which has yielded close to 1,000 identifiable elements. As with chickens, it may be that domestic geese were originally high-status or cult animals in Egypt and were commonly consumed only in late Dynastic or Ptolemaic times.

Geese are also represented in Mesopotamian art from the early Dynastic period onward, and it appears that in neo-Babylonian times they were farmed out to breeders on a profit-sharing basis (Zeuner 1963: 469).

Europe

The ultimate antiquity of the domestic goose in Europe cannot be effectively determined from the sparse archaeozoological literature. Domestic geese are mentioned in textual sources from the first millennium B.C. onward, as for example in *The Odyssey,* or as depicted on Macedonian coinage (Zeuner 1963: 466–7). These dates are relatively late, however, suggesting that domestic geese may not have been as ancient in Europe as many earlier scholars assumed (e.g., Zeuner 1963; Crawford 1984). Against this interpretation, various authors have noted the antiquity of the term for goose in Indo-European languages (e.g., Hahn 1926). But recent scholarship has shown that Indo-European reconstructions of terms for goose may refer just as easily to wild as to domestic birds (Gamgrelize and Ivanov 1995).

Archaeozoological evidence indicates that the domestic goose did not become widespread in Europe until Roman times. Julius Caesar noted that the Britons did not eat goose because they considered it a sacred bird (Zeuner 1963). After the decline of Rome, the popularity of geese continued to increase and their spread in medieval northern Europe seems to have owed a great deal to the Normans. Geese were of minor importance in the Anglo-Saxon and Viking economies of the British Isles but became almost central after the coming of the Normans in the eleventh to thirteenth centuries (Allison 1985; MacDonald, MacDonald, and Ryan 1993).

The economic importance of geese relative to chickens seems to have depended greatly upon local environment, with high percentages of goose bones showing up in excavations of the medieval fenland cities of East Anglia (e.g., Lincoln and Kings Lynn) (Astill and Grant 1988: 163). Likewise, geese seemed to be the most important small livestock component of the Anglo-Norman economy in parts of Ireland (e.g., Dublin) (MacDonald et al. 1993). Geese had three advantages over chickens: (1) they could be driven rather than carried to market; (2) they could thrive on food of poorer quality than that required by other domestic fowl; and (3) they would have been more significant calorifically under traditional management than chickens. As a consequence of these advantages, evidence suggests that geese made a substantially greater dietary contribution in medieval towns than they did in rural areas (Astill and Grant 1988). However, this once important European food species has been displaced in recent years by the turkey, which is more amenable to modern factory farming techniques (Crawford 1984).

Africa

Sture Lagercrantz (1950: 82–7) reviewed references to geese in Africa and concluded that almost all reports of greylag geese are connected with direct European or Arab contact. It is generally assumed that the domestic goose did not cross the Sahara. It is true that the Songhay people in Mali have geese (Rouch 1954: 21), but this may be the result of relatively recent contacts with Morocco. Al-Umari mentioned that under Mansa Musa, the ruler of Mali in the fourteenth century, the peoples of the "Sudan" kept geese (Levtzion and Hopkins 1981: 267). It is possible, however, these were not *A. anser* but rather another species of goose, domesticated or tamed. The spur-winged goose, *P. gambensis,* has been recorded at San, Bamako, and Segou in Mali, where it is kept as a backyard species, as well as in northeast Nigeria (RIM 1992: 2).

Central and East Asia

The distribution and importance of the domestic form of the Chinese goose appears to be virtually undocumented. No information, either cultural or archaeozoological, is available for the swan goose, though all writers assert that it is embedded in Chinese culture. J. Delacour (1954) stated that goose rearing probably began in China more than 3,000 years ago, and William Watson (1969: 394) referred to pottery models of geese, probably representing domestic individuals, found at Hupei, a Lung Shan site in China.

The most complete documentation of geese in central Asia is in the work of N. G. Dmitriev and L. K. Ernst (1989), describing the livestock of the former Soviet Union. Originally, Chinese geese were widespread in the eastern part of the nation, whereas greylags were in the west with a number of stabilized crosses developing in the center of the country. However, breeding stations have imported numerous European breeds and crossed them with indigenous stock, leading to substantial introgression in local races. Breeds were originally developed specifically for fighting and to resist extremely low temperatures.

Future Research

Information concerning the history of the domestic goose is very sparse. Obviously, an important avenue for the creation of new data on this subject rests with archaeozoology. The greatest difficulty for archaeologists with small and often comminuted assemblages is to sort out wild from domestic geese by means other than inference alone. Fortunately, various criteria have been put forward that seem to reliably differentiate wild and domestic geese in larger bird bone assemblages. These criteria include:

1. A reduction in the length and robusticity in the wing of domestic *A. anser,* coupled with an increase in lower limb robusticity relative to wild taxa (Reichstein and Pieper 1986).
2. A reduction in the wing musculature of flightless, overfed, or clipped *A. anser* with osteological effects, such as the profound reduction of feather attachments on the ulna *(papillae remigales caudales)* (MacDonald et al. 1993).
3. The presence of a flattened facet on the anterior surface of the femoral head, a pathology resulting from an overdependence on the legs for locomotion (MacDonald et al. 1993).

Apart from archaeological inquiry, ethnographic, linguistic, and textual research are also necessary, especially in East Asia. The place of the goose in Chinese culture should be reviewed through examination of iconographic and written sources as well as collation of synchronic descriptions of goose management. Virtually no work has yet been undertaken on the historical genetics of geese, making the task of tracing their diffusion across the Old World extremely problematic. These lacunae probably reflect the lack of current economic significance accorded geese rather than their historical role in human nutrition.

Kevin C. MacDonald
Roger Blench

Bibliography

Allison, E. P. 1985. Archaeozoological study of bird bones from seven sites in York. Unpublished doctoral thesis, University of York.

Astill, G., and A. Grant. 1988. *The countryside of medieval England.* Oxford.

Boessneck, J. 1991. Riesige Hausgänse aus der Spätzeit des alten Ägypten. *Archiv für Geflügelkunde* 55: 105-10.

Crawford, R. D. 1984. Geese. In *Evolution of domesticated animals,* ed. I. L. Mason, 345-9. London.

Darby, William J., Paul Ghalioungui, and Louis Grivetti. 1977. *The gift of Osiris.* 2 vols. London.

Darwin, Charles. 1868. *The variation of animals and plants under domestication.* London.

Delacour, J. 1954. *The waterfowl of the world,* Vol. 1. London.

Dmitriev, N. G., and L. K. Ernst. 1989. *Animal genetic resources of the USSR.* FAO Animal Production and Health Paper, 65. Rome.

Gamgrelize, T. V., and V. V. Ivanov. 1995. *Indo European and the Indo Europeans: A reconstruction and historical analysis of a proto-language and a proto-culture.* Part 1, *The Text.* Trans. Johanna Nichols; ed. Werner Winter. Berlin.

Hahn, E. 1926. Gans. In *Reallexikon der Vorgeschichte,* Vol. 4, ed. M. Ebert, 167. Berlin.

Houlihan, P. F., and S. M. Goodman. 1986. *The birds of ancient Egypt.* Warminster, England.

Hugo, Susanne. 1995. Geese: The underestimated species. *World Animal Review* 83: 64-7.

Ives, P. P. 1951. *Domestic geese and ducks.* New York.

Katzmann, L. 1990. Tierknochenfunde aus Elephantine in Oberägypten (Grabungsjahre 1976 bis 1986/87) Vögel, Reptilien, Fische und Mollusken. Doctoral dissertation, University of Munich.

Lagercrantz, Sture. 1950. *Contributions to the ethnography of Africa,* Studia Ethnographica Upsaliensia, I. Westport, Conn.

Levtzion, N., and J. F. P. Hopkins, eds. 1981. *Corpus of early Arabic sources for West African history.* Cambridge and New York.

MacDonald, R. H., K. C. MacDonald, and K. Ryan. 1993. Domestic geese from medieval Dublin. *Archaeofauna* 2: 205-18.

Reichstein, H., and H. Pieper. 1986. *Untersuchungen an Skelettresten von Vögeln aus Haithabu (Ausgrabung 1966-1969).* Neumünster, Germany.

Resource Inventory and Management (RIM). 1992. *National Livestock Resource Survey.* 6 vols. Abuja: Final report to Federal Department of Livestock and Pest Control Services, Federal Government of Nigeria. Abuja, Nigeria.

Rouch, Jean. 1954. *Les songhay.* Paris.

Schneider, K. H. 1988. *Gänse.* Berlin.

Watson, William. 1969. Early animal domestication in China. In *The domestication and exploitation of plants and animals,* ed. P. J. Ucko, and G. W. Dimbleby, 393-5. London.

Zeuner F. E. 1963. *A history of domesticated animals.* London.

II.G.12 ⁊ Goats

The domesticated goat *(Capra hircus)* is an animal that, although of extraordinary usefulness to humans, experiences sharply different levels of acceptance around the world. Its ruminant ability to digest cellulose is the key to its success as a form of livestock, but its browsing efficiency can often be harmful to marginal environments.

Goat

Origin and Domestication

Goats were domesticated in the Near East from *Capra aegagrus,* known variously as the Persian wild goat, bezoar goat, or *padang.* The males of this ungulate species of the rugged terrain of western Asia have long, scimitar-shaped horns; the females' horns are similarly shaped but shorter. The bezoar goat has been a prey of hunters, in part, at least, because its stomach concretions (also called "bezoars" by physicians) have a widespread but medically unfounded reputation as an antidote for poison. The foothills of the Zagros Mountains is the most plausible area for the origin of goat domestication. Early Neolithic sites contain evidence of goat keeping from as long as 9,000 years ago. Such dating would seem to make the goat a candidate for the world's oldest domesticated herd animal. Brian Hesse (1982) analyzed the abundant goat bones at the site of Ganj Dareh on the cold Iranian plateau and determined that the smaller size of the bones corresponded to domestic goats. Other sites, dated several hundred years later, have yielded further evidence of early goat keeping in the eastern half of the Fertile Crescent. At Jarmo, goats were the most numerous domesticate. At Tepe Ali Kosh, domestic goats preceded domestic sheep. From the east, the domesticated caprine spread westward into the Mediterranean. For example, at Natufian sites in the Levant, the domesticated goat appeared only later as a significant animal in the life of the people. There, and in Egypt, goats have been present for about 7,000 years. In the Nile Valley, goats were integrated into a sedentary agricultural system, but they also could be sustained in the non-irrigated desert beyond.

As with sheep, the domestication process

decreased the average size of goats from that of their ancestors. Although the domestic goat bore a horned resemblance to the bezoar, smaller horns gradually evolved, and a number of polled breeds also emerged. The lop ears and twisted horns of some goat breeds reveal human selection of mutations. As with other domesticated animals, the coat colors and patterns of domestic goats are more diverse than those of their wild ancestors. Unlike sheep, goats have maintained the agility, intelligence, and curiosity of the wild animal. These features enable domestic goats to bond with humans much more strongly than do sheep and, at the same time, to be more willful and combative. As was the case with other animals, domestication increased libido; the adjective "goatish" means "lustful." Although goats and sheep belong to the same family (Bovidae), and even the same tribe (Caprini), these two different genera do not hybridize.

Domestication may not have been for the economic reasons that seem so seductively straightforward today. The need for food was not necessarily a plausible mother of invention, for domestication is a process that occurs over many generations. A quite different motive seems more worthy of consideration. As with sheep and other domesticates, taming and reproduction in captivity may well have begun for the purpose of maintaining a steady supply of sacrificial animals. This theory is suggested by the important role that goats played in religious ritual, often as symbols of fecundity and virility. In Sumer, the deity known as "Enki" had the tail of a fish and the head of a goat. The Israelites sacrificed goats to Yahweh. The well-known figurative concept of the "scapegoat" came from the practice of priests' placing their hands on the heads of goats and recounting the sins of the people.

The importance of sacrifice probably motivated early cult masters to keep a ready supply of animals for this purpose, and controlling reproduction ensured a flow of live animals that the vagaries of hunting could not. Several other religions, such as Zoroastrianism and Hinduism, have sacrificed goats. In the latter case, goats are sacrificed to "Kali," the Hindu goddess of time, who is much revered in the Bengal region of India (Samanta 1994). A healthy male goat, black in color, is prepared for sacrifice through purification rites. Then the animal is decapitated in conjunction with the invocation of Kali, "who thirsts for blood." The blood is ritually drunk; the rest of the goat is then immolated, and sometimes the cooked flesh is eaten.

In the art of ancient Greece, satyrs were the attendants of Dionysus and Pan and had goat-like attributes. They had the legs and hindquarters of a goat, small horns, and goat-like ears. The gods themselves were goat-like: Pan had a man's body and head, but the hooves and horns of a goat; Dionysus, who assumed the form of a goat, was, like Zeus, raised on goat's milk. The cults of Zeus, Apollo, Hera, Hermes, and Artemis all manifested caprine elements. Aphrodite was sometimes depicted as riding a goat. In ancient Rome, goats were sacrificed during the feast of Lupercalia. Goat imagery of the classical period was the source of goat-like demons of the Middle Ages. Witchcraft has used the goat as a symbol of evil. The Biblical metaphor of the sheep (those chosen by God) and the goats (the damned) has doubtless influenced Western thinking about the relative worth of these two animals.

Goat Distribution

The world's pattern of goat keeping is very uneven. The animals play a major role in subsistence economies, where they provide useful products in return for a minimal investment of capital and labor. Thus, nonindustrial countries contain more than 90 percent of the half-billion goats in the world (FAO 1995). Goats adapt well to both dry and wet conditions and to tropical and midlatitude climates, and culture also helps to explain the importance the goat is accorded in the developing world. Islamic societies of the Middle East and North Africa have ennobled the goat as a source of food, and the Arab conquest of North Africa greatly expanded pastoralism as a way of life and the goat's role in it. By contrast, the Romans in North Africa emphasized farming to a much greater extent. Yet the Islamic factor must also be weighed by the ability of the goat to thrive in a subhumid environment. Thus, for example, the rural folk of both Greece and Turkey have paid much attention to goat keeping. The summer drought of the Mediterranean climate has always made it difficult to supply the large amounts of better-quality fodder needed to sustain herds of cattle. Keeping goats as an alternative avoids this constraint.

Though only partly semiarid and Islamic, Nigeria has more goats – about 250 million – than any other country in Africa. No controlled breeding is practiced, and the typical herd comprised several different kinds, including dwarf goats, which stand less than 50 centimeters high (Epstein 1971). Goats constitute about half of the domestic grazing livestock in Nigeria and provide about one-quarter of the meat consumed in that country. Goat meat supplies protein, mostly to rural people, who also sell live animals in markets as a source of income. The animals generally fend for themselves, subsisting largely on browse discovered within a radius of their dwelling compound. Sometimes they are fed vegetable waste from the kitchen, and their owners typically provide water. Night shelter within the compound protects them from preda-

tors and thieves. During the planting season, goats are often tethered to prevent crop destruction. Most of the animals have parasites, and their mortality rate from disease is high.

Goats are also part of the rural tradition in Mexico. Most of the 9 million goats there browse the sparsely vegetated slopes throughout the country. Poor Mexican farmers have long counted on their *cabras* as sources of animal protein and income. The *criollo* breed, which evolved from goats brought from Spain in the sixteenth century, is well adapted to the hot, dry landscape. However, it is low-yielding in edible products and is a carrier of brucellosis, a disease of domestic animals often transmitted to humans. Goat keeping in Mexico today has the reputation of a backward livestock activity, and environmentalists blame free-ranging animals for much of the erosion of the hill lands.

Uses of Goats

Goats provide four major products for human use: meat, milk, fiber, and skins. In nonindustrialized societies, owners typically make use of all four. In Europe, North America, and some other places, goats are normally kept only for their milk.

Meat

Goat meat is a vital addition to the diets of millions of people, although such consumption is not accurately recorded by official market statistics because a goat is often raised and butchered by the same family that consumes it. The small carcass size of a goat allows the animal to be consumed by a household in two or three days, and meat spoilage is consequently less than if a family butchered a cow.

Goat flesh is especially important in rural Africa, the Middle East, and South Asia; in India, members of a number of Hindu castes eat it with equanimity. In several Asian countries, goat and sheep meats are not differentiated, and, in fact, some languages do not distinguish between the two. By contrast, northern Europeans and North Americans generally avoid goat meat, with readily available meat alternatives as well as negative feelings about goats as human food constituting the explanation. In the United States, the flesh has a reputation for being smelly and tough, an opinion based on the cultural prejudices of those who have never eaten it. One major exception, however, is the attitude among people of Latin American origin, who have created a specialized ethnic demand for goat flesh. Superannuated dairy goats are slaughtered for this market, and in southern Texas meat goats are raised for sale (Glimp 1995).

Compared to other forms of livestock, goats have a structural disadvantage in that their higher metabolic rate makes them less efficient meat producers. A 350-kilogram (kg) cow requires the same amount of energy as six goats – each weighing only 25 kg. Moreover, slaughtered goats have a lower percentage of useful parts and, correspondingly, more offal. That same 350-kg cow yields 189 kg of product, whereas the six goats together yield only 81 kg (McDowell and Woodward 1982).

Another problem is that goat meat tends to be dry because the animal has its fat deposited around the viscera rather than in marbled fashion, as do cattle and sheep. Age and sex are also factors. A young doe is palatable, but the tough meat from an old billy goat is not. Adult males have a scent gland that can make the strong flavor of their meat unacceptable to consumers. Kids, however, either as sucklings or when weaned, produce a meat of tender texture and delicate flavor. In France, kid is the only form of goat meat that finds a ready market.

Some goat dealers in the western United States have tried to distribute goat meat commercially under the euphemism of "chevon." Because goat meat is low in fat, producers have sought to capitalize on the national concern about fat in the diet. Sensory experiments have demonstrated that it is possible to use goat meat, alone or in combination with beef, to produce lowfat meat products for consumers who would not ordinarily consume goat meat (James and Berry 1997). More attention to breeding quality meat animals may have a long-term effect in a gradual American acceptance of goats as food. The Boer goat, originally from South Africa, is considered to be the best meat breed.

Milk

Milk is an important product of the goat, and in some areas dairy products constitute the only reason for keeping the animals. Yet from a commercial point of view, goats cannot compete with cows. Milk yields per lactation, duration of lactation, percentage of protein, persistency of milk yield, and the suitability of milking machines are all measures in which cows perform better than goats. Moreover, the need to maintain many more goats than cows for milk production entails more work in milking, more health problems, and more record keeping. However, in the overall perspective of single-family subsistence, the goat's small size fits in better with a family's needs than that of the much larger cow, and goats have a strong home instinct and require less herding than cattle. Compared to sheep, goats have a higher level of milk production, perhaps because the incidence of twinning is high in all breeds.

In Africa and western Asia, milk production is an important aspect of keeping goats. At a country level, India is the world leader in producing goat milk; other producers include Iran, Pakistan, Somalia, and Sudan. The Nubian goat, red or black in color, is an important milking breed of the Old World. It is recognized by its Roman nose, short hair, long legs, and lack of horns.

In zones of Western culture, goat's milk is now less important than in other parts of the world. In Latin America, Mexico and Brazil are the two main producers of goat milk. *Dulce de leche,* a caramelized concoction of sugar and goat's milk, is a much-appreciated sweet in countries settled by Spaniards. In the Mediterranean region, goat's milk is locally available, especially in small villages. In Greece, about one-fourth of the milk supply is still provided by goats.

Moving north, both France and Switzerland produce substantial quantities of goat milk. The Alps have an old caprine tradition, which has given rise to seven dairy-goat breeds, the best known of which are Toggenburg, Saanen, and French-Alpine. Norway is also famous for its high-yielding dairy goats. In Western Europe outside the Mediterranean, however, goat milk is a specialty product. Fresh goat's milk is important for those allergic to cow's milk. In the United States, for example, it has been estimated that about 1 person in 1,000 has a medical need for goat milk (Haenlein 1996). Differences in the protein makeup of goat's and cow's milk make that of the former a nutritious substitute.

The American dairy-goat population of 1.5 million females is divided among six breeds. The Nubian is numerically the leading one but is surpassed in actual milk production by the three long-established Swiss breeds. California is the leading producer of goat's milk in the United States. Total production in the country is estimated at 600,000 tons, and about 300 farms and businesses sell goat's milk or goat-milk products. However, production, processing, and marketing of goat's milk is much less regulated by the states than is cow's milk. "Natural-food" stores often sell goat-milk products, including butter, ice cream, yoghurt, cosmetics, and soaps. In addition, goat milk is used to feed calves for veal production and to nurse zoo animals and pets.

Much of the world's goat milk is converted into yoghurt, butter, and cheese. Middle Eastern countries produce goat cheeses largely unknown outside their borders. Making cheeses has become the main use of goat's milk in Europe, where the relatively high price has encouraged their development as specialties for cheese lovers who enjoy their tangy flavors. When overripe, however, goat cheese can be brittle in texture, acid in smell, and ammoniacal in flavor. France still produces about 20 different kinds of goat cheese. Distinctively shaped and packaged, these cheeses are often sprinkled with a condiment like paprika or black pepper. Other European countries, especially Italy, make some goat cheese, but none of them are recognized for their quality as much as those of France. Until the late 1970s, no goat cheese was made in the United States, but by the 1990s, about 50 percent of American-produced goat milk was used to make cheese. Such cheeses – half imported and half domestic – developed a popular following and a gourmet image conveyed by use of the word "chevre" on the label.

Fleece and Skins

Goats yield other valuable products with their hair and skins. The classic Bedouin tent of southwestern Asia and northern Africa is made of goat hair. Goat fibers have also been used in pastoral societies to make carpets, brushes, and felt. High-quality goat fleece, traded internationally, derives from two specific breeds. One of these is the Angora – almost always white – which came originally from Turkey and has been known since antiquity for its lustrous fleece. Countries of western Asia export this product but do not have a monopoly. Before the Turkish Sultan decreed in 1881 that live Angora goats could not be exported, the breed had already been transported to other parts of the world. They thrive in South Africa, where they were introduced in 1838, but only much later did mohair become the main objective in raising them. At present, some 1.3 million Angora goats around Port Elizabeth in Cape Province yield 6 million kg of mohair annually.

In North America, Angora goats date from 1849 and have become highly concentrated on the Edwards Plateau of southern central Texas. More than 2 million animals are herded there on the open range, primarily to produce mohair for textile, upholstery, and wig-making industries. Mohair is more notable for its strength and luster than for its fineness of fiber. Angora goats in the United States, larger than their Turkish ancestors, are more numerous than those of any other breed.

The cashmere goat's undercoat yields a fine fiber, known in the luxury-fabric trade as cashmere. Cashmere goats live at high elevations in northern India, Tibet, western China, Kirghistan, and parts of Iran. Selection for a cold environment was a factor in evolving the quality of fleece associated with this breed.

Goatskins are a by-product of slaughter for meat. DNA analysis has found that most of the Dead Sea scrolls were written on goatskins preserved in the dry atmosphere of the hills of Palestine. In traditional cultures, goatskins have been used as containers for liquids. Water, wine, and distilled spirits have all been transported and stored in these skins, but the availability of cheap plastic has greatly diminished such usage.

Other Uses

Goat manure is another, usually subsidiary, benefit of raising these animals. At least in one place, the Rif mountain region of northern Morocco, manure has become the raison d'être of goat raising. Large numbers of goats are needed to provide the fertilizer for cannabis production. Marijuana and hashish from this plant enter into the international drug trade, and large quantities of goat manure – without which the soil would soon become exhausted – are needed to maintain production of this profitable crop year after year.

The goat has another use of local importance as a biological control agent: Goats browse undesirable plants that are otherwise expensive and difficult to control. In the western United States, they keep in check aggressive, unwanted plants such as live oak brush, gambel oak, and leafy spurge.

Production Systems

Goats lend themselves well to a pastoral way of life. In the nomadic and seminomadic systems of Africa and Asia, they form a component of the mobile livestock capital, which is moved in constant search of fresh pasture. Goats are not the most appreciated animals in a pastoralist's inventory, but they serve as a better hedge against environmental uncertainty than do cattle or sheep. The Tuareg people of the Sahara keep almost 10 times as many goats as sheep, a rational behavior in their water-scarce environment. In East Africa, goats manifest considerable resistance to the disease trypanosomiasis, which explains part of their importance there.

Goats also fit into a mixed herding and farming economy to provide meat, milk, and other products. Small farms lend themselves to goat keeping. In the tropics, goats can breed year-round; in midlatitudes, breeding occurs seasonally. Goats may be tethered or allowed to range freely on communal grazing areas. They follow a nutrition strategy of choosing grasses of high protein content and digestibility to graze upon, but they will shift to browse if its nutritive value is greater, and unlike cattle, goats can maintain themselves on browse alone.

The Environmental Effects of Goats

Free-ranging goats have a reputation for overgrazing, which happens when their numbers surpass the capacity of the land to support them. Gully erosion results when they destroy the native vegetation and compact the soil with their sharp hooves. Several characteristics of goats favor abuse of the plant cover. A mobile upper lip permits them to graze as close to the ground as sheep at the same time that their browsing capacities exceed those of their fleecy cousins. Thorny plants with small leaves are no hindrance to goats. If browse is in short supply, they will defoliate entire bushes. Goats browse to the height they can reach when standing on their hind legs. They will also forage on leaves by climbing into low trees. With their sharp hooves, they paw away soil to obtain roots and subterranean stems. Allowed to roam, goats can occupy considerable space. On the average, they move 9.7 kilometers (km) per day, compared with 6.1 km for sheep and 5.3 km for cattle (Huston 1978).

It is true that goats have contributed to desertification, but they often get more blame than they deserve. The process begins when first cattle, and then sheep, deteriorate the range, after which the invading brush is suitable only for goats, which can survive and reproduce in such environments. Thus, goats become the last alternative on eroded lands and are often seen as totally responsible for them.

Ultimately, however, destruction of vegetation by goats is a human management failure. An arid hillside combined with excessive numbers of goats will almost always mean harm for that environment. Human unwillingness to control goat density at a desired maximum, or to restrict the animals' mobility, has determined the land-use history of many areas. Humans have frequently introduced goats to islands and then left them to their own devices. Without predators, feral goat populations have exploded and destroyed ecological balances; the histories of many islands, from San Clemente, California, to St. Helena, involve goat stories.

The Mediterranean Plan, funded by the Food and Agriculture Organization of the United Nations (FAO) in the 1950s, was the first concerted international effort to deal with such problems. Impoverishment of the Mediterranean region was attributed to the environmental degradation brought on by overgrazing. We know that some of this process was begun in ancient times because classical authors discussed the goat problem two millennia earlier (Hughes 1994). The Mediterranean localities most heavily dependent on goat products were those with the most serious erosion. In the 1940s, Cyprus, which derived one-third of its milk, two-fifths of its cheese, one-fourth of its meat, and four-fifths of its leather from goats (Thirgood 1987), was deforested because of excessive goat browsing. Vegetation flourishes in the Mediterranean region where goats and sheep are restricted. In northern Morocco, the barren slopes that are grazed by goats contrast with ungrazed enclosures that maintain a luxuriant tree cover.

Daniel W. Gade

Bibliography

Epstein, H. 1971. *The origin of the domestic animals of Africa.* New York.

FAO (Food and Agriculture Organization of the United Nations). 1995. *FAO yearbook.* Rome.

Glimp, Hudson A. 1995. Meat goat production and marketing. *Journal of Animal Science* 73: 291-5.

Haenlein, G. F. W. 1996. Status and prospects of the dairy goat industry in the United States. *Journal of Animal Science* 74: 1173-81.

Hesse, Brian. 1982. Slaughter patterns and domestication: The beginnings of pastoralism in western Iran. *Man* 17: 403-17.

Hughes, J. Donald. 1994. *Pan's travail: Environmental problems of the ancient Greeks and Romans.* Baltimore, Md.

Huston, J. E. 1978. Forage utilization and nutrient requirement of the goat. *Journal of Dairy Science* 61: 988-93.

James, N. A., and B. W. Berry. 1997. Use of chevon in the development of low-fat meat products. *Journal of Animal Science* 75: 571-7.

McDowell, R. E., and A. Woodward. 1982. Concepts in animal adaptation. In *Proceedings of the Third International Conference on Goat Production and Disease,* 387-91. Scottsdale, Ariz.

Samanta, Suchitra. 1994. The "self-animal" and divine digestion: Goat sacrifice to the goddess Kali in Bengal. *Journal of Asian Studies* 53: 779-803.

Thirgood, J. V. 1987. *Cyprus: A chronicle of its forests, land, and people.* Vancouver.

II.G.13 ❧ Hogs (Pigs)

"Pig" is a term used synonymously with "hog" and "swine" for the one domesticated suid species, *Sus scrofa domesticus.* In livestock circles, a pig becomes a hog when it passes the weight threshold of 50 kilograms. The word "swine" transcends age and sex but to many has a pejorative ring. A "gilt" is any immature version of a sow, whereas a "barrow" is a young, castrated male that can never grow up to become a boar. After a piglet has been weaned, it becomes a "shoat." Most of these terms are not used by a general public whose only encounter with this animal is in the supermarket. The meat of this often maligned beast yields some of the world's best-tasting flesh and provides good-quality protein in large amounts.

Domestication

All domesticated pigs originated from the wild boar *(Sus scrofa)* (Epstein 1984). Within that one wild species, more than 20 subspecies are known in different parts of its natural range, which has extended from the British Isles and Morocco in the West to Japan and New Guinea in the East. But where in this vast stretch of territory the first domestication occurred is still uncertain, although the earliest archaeological records (c. 7000-5000 B.C.) have been concentrated in the Middle East and eastern Mediterranean.

Pig

Indeed, the recovery of bones of domesticated pigs has been done at Jericho (Palestine), Jarmo (Iraq), Catal Huyuk (Turkey), and Argissa-Margula (Greece), as well as other sites. But bones older than any of those from these sites were uncovered in 1994 at Hallan Cemi in southeastern Turkey. There, in the foothills of the Taurus Mountains, the pig was apparently kept as early as 8000 B.C., making it the oldest known domesticated creature besides the dog. Moreover, pig keeping at this site was found to predate the cultivation of wheat or barley. Both findings contradict the long-held twin assertions that sheep and goats were the world's earliest domesticated herd animals and that crop growing preceded the raising of herd animals.

An alternative view places the beginning of swine domestication in Southeast Asia. Carl O. Sauer (1952) suggested that the pig under human control diffused from there northward to China. However, Seung Og Kim (1994) has suggested that political elites in northern China established their authority by controlling intensive pig production as early as 4300 B.C. Certainly, archaeology and cultural hubris have combined to convince many Chinese that it was their ancestors who first domesticated the pig. The Chinese ideograph for "home" consists of a character for "swine" beneath another character for "roof" (Simoons 1991).

Certain innate traits of the wild boar make it plausible that multiple domestications have occurred at different times and places in the Old World. This inquisitive, opportunistic artiodactyl may, in part, have domesticated itself by choosing to freely come into association with humans. Garbage at settlement sites provided a regular food supply, and human presence offered protection from large carnivores. Reproduction in captivity could have been initiated when captured wild piglets were tamed. Human control would have been easily accomplished, for it has been observed that the striped piglets of the wild boar behave just like the unstriped piglets of the domesticated species. The next step, unconscious selection, began the long process of evolving regional distinctions in the animal's conformation. However, the emergence of distinctive breeds, as we know them today, dates mostly from the late eighteenth and nineteenth centuries, when artificial selection was implemented on a large scale.

Religion probably lay behind the transformation of the pig from a semidomesticated status to one of greater mutual dependency with humans. In ancient Egypt, followers of Seth sacrificed pigs to that god. On the Iberian Peninsula, the granite sculptures called *verracos,* carved by Celts between the sixth century B.C. and the first century A.D., suggest that pigs might have had a religious role. In ancient Greek and Roman times, pigs were sacrificed to deities. In China, the Manchus believed that a sacrificial pig drove away bad spirits and assured good fortune. In all these groups, the incentive of supplying live animals for cultic purposes could easily have resulted in breeding pigs toward greater dependency on humans.

Advantages of the Pig

From a contemporary utilitarian perspective, the pig is one of the glories of animal domestication. It is prolific. After a gestation period of only 4 months, a sow gives birth to an average of 10 piglets, though litter size may, on occasion, be as large as 30. Growth is rapid. In a 6-month period, piglets of 1.2 kilograms can potentially increase in weight by 5,000 percent. This growth translates into a higher return for energy invested than for other domesticated animals. Another advantage is the omnivory of pigs, which permits a wide range of food options; items that are plentiful and cheap can dominate the intake. For example, surplus crops, such as sweet potatoes in New Guinea, coconuts in Polynesia, maize in the midwestern United States, and barley in Denmark, are frequently enhanced in value because they can be fed to swine. A major disadvantage of pigs is their low ability to digest fibrous plant matter, so that, unlike ruminants, they cannot do well on cellulose alone.

The Range Pig

For most of their domesticated history, swine were kept in one of two ways: free-ranging in forests or sedentary in settlements. In neither case did they compete with humans for food, although pigs have the capacity to eat and thrive on the same nutrients. For the range pig, both plant and animal matter, on and beneath the forest floor, was sought. In Western Europe, where domesticated swine have been known since before 4000 B.C., they ate acorns, chestnuts, beechnuts, hazelnuts, and wild fruits such as berries, apples, pears, and hawthorns. Their powerful mobile snouts and sharp teeth were able to dig mushrooms, tubers, roots, worms, and grubs from the ground. Eggs, snakes, young birds, mice, rabbits, and even fawns were consumed as opportunity arose.

The use of pannage (pasturing in a forest) to feed pigs was recorded from antiquity in Europe and still has not totally disappeared. An abundant iconography suggests the role that swine played in the development of European rural society. The pig is always pictured as an animal with a long flat neck, straight back, narrow snout, small erect ears, and long legs. Nimble and resourceful, it thrived on mast (nuts from the forest floor). In the early Middle Ages, mast rights were a greater source of income from the forest than the sale of wood. But pannage required peasants to enclose their fields with wooden palisades or hedges to prevent pigs from entering and destroying their crops. As concern for forest resources grew, the pannage season was fixed by seigneurial decree. The main feeding period came in the autumn, when nuts, a highly concentrated source of nutrition, fell in large numbers. In many places, it became traditional to begin mast feeding on the feast of Saint Michael (September 29) and to conclude it on the last day of November (Laurans 1976).

Mast feeding has now disappeared from Europe except in a few places. Its best-known survival is in Spain, where the oak woodland still seasonally supports black and red Iberian swine (Parsons 1962). Although by 1990 these rustic mast-feeding breeds made up only 4 percent of the Spanish pig population, the cured pork products derived from them have been prized as especially delectable. Thus, cured hams (*jamon ibérico*) from these swine are very expensive; most famous are those from Jabugo, a meat-packing village in the Sierra Morena north of Huelva.

On his second voyage, Christopher Columbus brought the first pigs to the New World (1493). From an original stock of eight, they multiplied on the Caribbean island of Hispaniola, and many later became feral. Rounded up as needed, pigs were put on board ships bound for Mexico, Panama, Colombia, and all the islands in between. Francisco Pizarro, who had worked with swine in his youth in Extremadura, brought live pigs to the Andean highlands from Panama in 1531. The long-legged, nimble suid was well suited to move along with the expedition parties as a mobile fresh meat supply. Tropical America afforded no acorns or chestnuts, but an abundance of wild fruit, especially from palms, provided nourishment for the pigs. In semiarid zones, seed pods of leguminous trees were the common food of foraging swine.

The first pigs in what is now the United States arrived from Cuba with Hernando de Soto's expedition (1539–42) through the Southeast. Later introductions came from the British Isles, most notably to John Smith's settlement of Jamestown in 1607. A few years later, they had multiplied to several hundred head. In Virginia, and elsewhere in eastern North America, pigs fit well into the forested countryside as foragers. Abundant oak and chestnut mast in the Appalachians offered a good return in meat for almost no investment in feed or care. In late autumn, the semiferal animals were rounded up and slaughtered, and their fatty flesh was made into salt pork, which along with Indian corn was a staple of the early American diet. In the early nineteenth century, these Appalachian pigs were commercialized. The leading national and world position of Cincinnati, Ohio (often jokingly called "Porkopolis"), as a soap manufacturing center owes its origin to pigs brought there on barges for slaughter; their flesh was salted and their fat rendered into soap.

This type of hardy porker and wily beast of folk legend still survives in the Ozarks and elsewhere in the southern United States. In fact, these "razorbacks" could be descendants of those that accompanied the de Soto expedition. The explorer gave gifts of live pigs to the Indians, and when he died in 1542 near what is now Fort Smith, Arkansas, 700 pigs were counted among his property. In addition, Ossabow Island, off the coast of Georgia, still harbors a breed of swine considered to be direct descendants of those brought by the Spaniards.

In addition to the Caribbean Islands, other uninhabited islands around the world became homes of the pig. In many cases, the animals were introduced by explorers and mariners and left to reproduce on their own. Sailors on passing ships often rounded up and slaughtered some of these feral pigs to replenish shipboard larders. Nonetheless, pigs on islands often multiplied to the point where they destroyed native fauna and flora.

In Melanesia, semidomesticated pigs still forage in the forest and are slaughtered primarily for ritual purposes (Baldwin 1983). R. A. Rappaport (1967) has explained the impressive pig feasts among the Tsembaga people of New Guinea as a societal mechanism that fulfills the need to control the size, composition, and rate of growth of the pig population. Without the periodic slaughtering of large numbers, the pigs would seriously damage gardens and crops. Rappaport's effort to understand pigs and ritual as part of a homeostatic balance became one of the landmark works of the developing subfield of cultural ecology. Whether such a pig complex makes economic sense has been debated because, in this case, the animal is not a regular source of human food. But aside from their meat, pigs must be appreciated in manifold ways: as a hedge against uncertainty (e.g., crop failure); as a negotiable store of surplus; as a source of fertilizer; and as disposers of garbage and other wastes.

The Garbage Pig

The garbage pig was essentially "presented" with its food intake, either at a fixed site or within a circumscribed area. In eastern Asia, where centuries-old deforestation and high population densities did not favor mast feeding, pig raising was long ago oriented toward consuming wastes. Important in China and Korea, at one time, was the privy pig, kept to process human excrement into flesh for human consumption. Four young pigs could derive sustenance from the waste of a family of four humans, which provided the animals with approximately 2 kilograms of human excreta and 220 grams of garbage each day (Miller 1990). In Asia, food provided by humans rather than by foraging promoted sedentary habits that, in turn, led to the evolution of several breeds with a swayback and a dishlike face. But even the miniaturized types of Asian pigs have big appetites and large litters.

The garbage pig could also be found in ancient civilizations outside of eastern Asia. Robert L. Miller (1990) has brilliantly reconstructed the scavenging role of the pig in dynastic Egypt. But, thus far, similar

evidence is lacking for ancient Greece and Rome. In
Europe, the garbage pig goes back to the Middle Ages
but seems not to have been common until the fifteenth century, when the so-called Celtic pig, with
white skin and pendant ears, emerged. Families fattened their pigs primarily on food scraps, and when
winter neared, the animals were butchered. Their
meat was cured and their fat rendered to make lard
for cooking and especially for food preservation.
Thus, the human diet was diversified during the cold
months.

This form of pig keeping expanded as forest clearing advanced and the scale of food processing
increased. Grist and oil mills generated large quantities of waste materials that could be consumed by
pigs, as could the garbage from institutions like hospitals and convents. Before proper sewage disposal was
implemented, many cities had swine populations to
serve as ambulatory sanitation services. In medieval
Paris, so many pigs were locally available for slaughter
that pork was the cheapest meat. The monks of Saint
Anthony - the patron saint of swineherds - were
given special rights to keep pigs within the city walls.
In New York City, pigs wandered the alleyways well
into the nineteenth century. Naples was the last large
European city to use pigs for sanitation. Neapolitan
families each had a pig tethered near their dwellings
to consume garbage and excrement.

Certain peasant societies still value the garbage pig
as an element of domestic economy. In much of rural
Latin America, pigs consume what they can find, to be
later slaughtered with minimal investment in feed
(Gade 1987). Lard has been an important product of
pig keeping there. Frying was a cooking innovation
introduced with the European conquest, and native
people learned to depend on this source of animal
fat. Today, however, the meat quality of these haphazardly fed animals no longer meets the health requirements of city dwellers, most of whom get their pork
products through inspected channels.

Unlike sheep, whose wool may be more valuable
than their flesh, or cattle that are kept for their milk
or for use as draft animals, pigs have had no primary
nonmeat uses. A possible minor exception has been
the truffle pig, employed in France - mainly in the
Périgord region - to locate the black truffles synonymous with gourmandise. A trained sow can detect
from 6 meters away the smell of the unseen truffles.

Swine Distribution

World hog distribution is strongly affected by cultural
and ecological factors. More than 40 percent of the
world porcine inventory is in China, where density is
among the highest anywhere: For every three people
in China, there is one pig. Some of this swinish appeal
is cultural preference, though much can be explained
by lack of alternatives. Human population pressure in
China does not permit the extravagance of devoting

large areas of land to grazing herbivores. Swine in
China long had a niche as scavengers, scatovores, and
consumers of surplus food crops.

Europe, including Russia, has about 170 million
pigs, and Denmark is the only country in the world
that has more pigs than people. The United States and
Canada together have about 70 million of the animals,
which means roughly one pig for every four people.
Brazil has about 32 million head. Pigs are more important on many Pacific Islands than their total number
(less than 5 million) would suggest.

The Middle East, however, is one part of the world
that is largely devoid of pigs. Those that are kept generally belong to non-Muslims (such as the Coptic
Christian peasants in Egypt), but some marginalized
Muslims may keep pigs secretly. In humid Southeast
Asia, the Islamic injunction against pigs is somewhat
more nuanced, and in Indonesia, Muslims are among
those who consume the products of the more than 8
million swine in that country.

In India, where the Hindu majority views all flesh
foods as unacceptable elements of the diet, there are
only about 10 million pigs, and in non-Islamic Africa,
pigs number only around 18 million, considerably less
than one might expect. But there African swine fever
has periodically wiped out pig populations.

Elsewhere, the Arctic and Subarctic have historically had few pigs for quite different reasons. Very
short growing seasons do not provide sufficient feed
to maintain them; moreover, piglets cannot survive
extremely cold winters without proper protection.
Thus, in Greenland, the Norse settlements between
A.D. 986 and 1400 had cattle but no pigs.

Pork

Many think that pork is the most savory of all flesh
foods. The abundance and quality of fat keeps the
meat from tasting dry and imparts a characteristically
rich flavor. High pork consumption patterns are
found in both China and Europe. In China, it is more
important than all other meats combined, and use is
made of all parts of the pig, including its liver, kidneys, feet, knuckles, tongue, skin, tail, and blood
(Anderson 1988; Simoons 1991). Most pork cuts are
also fried in lard.

In Europe, more than in China, cured pork products are favored. Germans and Slavs enjoy a range of
sausages such as pork brain sausage *(Gehirnwurst)*,
much appreciated in Germany but unavailable commercially in the United States. In addition, Russians
and Poles are especially fond of suckling pig.

Spaniards also enjoy high pork consumption and
have a special fondness for cured hams and suckling
pigs. *Cochonillo asado,* a strongly traditional Castilian
meal, features a 1-month-old piglet fed only on its
mother's milk and roasted in an earthenware dish.
Spanish enthusiasm for pig meat stems in part from
pork's past importance as a symbol of cultural

identity. Because Moors and Jews did not eat it, Christians saw the meat as more than simple nutrition. In sixteenth-century Spain, pork eating was an acid test faced by Spanish Moriscos and Marranos who publicly claimed conversion to Christianity. Conspicuous pork avoidance could result in an appearance before the tribunals of the Inquisition.

In North America, pork lost its preeminent position to beef in the early twentieth century. Aside from the fact that cattle ranchers were much better organized to promote their product, pork had acquired negative connotations as the main food in the monotonous diet of poor people and pioneers. At one time, pork also had unhealthy associations because of the potential for human infection by the organism *Trichinella spiralis,* carried by pigs, but federal meat inspection to certify trichina-free meat has greatly reduced the incidence of trichinosis. Still, wide knowledge of that old health risk continues to motivate cooks to make sure that pork is served only when fully cooked. Pork is considered done when it reaches an average interior temperature of 75.9° C (170° F).

Spareribs are often used in southern-style barbecue, and bacon, which comes from what the meat trade calls "pork bellies," continues as an important component of the traditional American breakfast. "Chitterlings," made from intestines, are eaten as part of the ethnic cuisine known as "soul food," but they appear in few other cases. In contrast, ham, mostly cured, has wide appeal. Virginia hams, especially those from Smithfield, have had the best reputation among connoisseurs. Fattened on peanuts and corn, Virginia porkers yield a ham that is smoked and then matured for a year.

Avoidance of Pig Meat

Despite the popularity of pork in much of the world, it can also be observed that no other domestic animal has provoked such negative reactions in so many as the pig. In Western countries, swine are commonly seen as a metaphor for filthy, greedy, smelly, lazy, stubborn, and mean. Yet these presumed attributes have not prevented pork consumption. In other cultures, however, strongly negative attitudes toward the pig have historically resulted in its rejection as human food and even, in some cases, as an animal fit to look at.

About one-fifth of the world's population refrains from eating pork as a matter of principle. Muslims, 800 million strong, form the largest block of pork rejecters because the pig is specifically named in the Koran as an object of defilement. A millennium earlier, Jews had also decided that the pig was unacceptable as a source of food. In the Bible (Leviticus), the animal is rejected because it does not meet the arcane requirements of both having a split hoof (which it has) and chewing the cud (which it does not). It is quite possible that the prophet Mohammed acquired his conception of the pig as an unclean animal from the Jewish tradition.

The Jews, in turn, may have gotten their basic and negative idea about the pig from other neighboring peoples (Simoons 1994). Brian Hesse (1990), investigating Iron Age Palestine, found no evidence for a significant cultic role for pigs, which raises the intriguing question of whether Hebrew rules prohibited a food that no one ate in the first place. Although the Hittites of Anatolia kept pigs, they entertained negative notions about them. In dynastic Egypt, swineherds were a caste apart; pigs acquired a reputation for being unclean, and their flesh was not eaten by priests. Marvin Harris (1985) has asserted that because the pig does not fit into the hot and dry conditions of the Middle East, the Israelites banned it as an ecological misfit. Others, however, believe that the history of this fascinating taboo is more complicated than that (Simoons 1994).

Within the Christian tradition, adherents of the Ethiopian Orthodox Church do not consume pork, yet their religiously affiliated Coptic brothers in Egypt do eat it. Many Buddhists and the great majority of Hindus refuse pig meat, although in both cases this avoidance arises more from vegetarian conviction than from any explicit religious taboo toward the animal. The Mongols, those nomadic folk of central Asia whose way of life is ill suited to pig keeping, consider the pig to be a symbol of Chinese culture.

Historic reluctance to keep pigs and consume pork has also been noted in Scotland. Eric B. Ross (1983) has explained the rise of the Scottish aversion to the pig as a response to the ecological cost of keeping pigs after the decline of oak and beech forests. Because sheep raising best suited the subsequent moorland landscape, mutton became a cheaper and socially more acceptable source of animal protein.

Porcine Trends

In most industrialized countries since the 1960s, pig keeping has moved rapidly toward maximizing efficiency of production (Pond 1983). Animals are injected with growth hormones and spend their short lives within buildings in near darkness. Artificially inseminated sows (a technology that appeared in 1932) farrow in narrow steel cages. Piglets are removed early from their mother so that lactation ceases and her sexual receptivity is reactivated. In four months, another litter is produced. Piglets have their incisors removed, tails docked, ears notched, and in the case of males, their testes excised. Most pigs never reach their eighth month, although theoretically the animal can live about 15 years. Modern hog raising seeks to emulate the efficiency levels of the poultry industry. In that quest, its technological center in the United States has shifted from the Midwest to a belt of large corporate farms in eastern North Carolina. In 1994 alone, that latter-day "hog heaven" sent nearly 10 million animals, worth a total of about a billion dollars, to market. The next step, pork processing and trade, is normally quite lucrative, for about 75 percent of a pig's carcass can be made into salable cuts of meat. By-products, such as lard, bristles, gelatin, and cortisone, further enhance profitability.

For almost half a century, a spiced ham product high in fat has been a favorite canned food in the United States and many other countries. Spam, packaged by Geo. A. Hormel and Company of Austin, Minnesota, has a sales volume of close to 100 million cans a year. Since 1937, when it was put on the market, Hormel's Spam has served as an economical source of meat protein for millions of people. In 1991, following a major trend in the American food industry, Spam Lite was introduced; this product, however, barely meets federal requirements for fat content reduction.

Weight- and cholesterol-conscious consumers in Europe and North America have had an impact on the pork industry (Bichard and Bruce 1989). Consumer demand calls for leaner cuts, including substantial fat trimming, in supermarket meat cases. There is also a strong motivation to develop hog breeds with less fat in their muscle tissue, which normally has 5 to 7 percent fat. Pork fat is higher in unsaturated fatty acids than beef, veal, or lamb fat. On the average, one 85-gram serving of pork contains about 79 milligrams of cholesterol.

Lard, as a cooking medium, has ceded its former importance to vegetable oils. In response to this development, a shift in hog breeds toward the Landrace and the Large White has occurred. Of the 15 breeds of swine listed in the 1930 *USDA Agricultural Yearbook,* more than half have now disappeared. Less efficient breeds have also lost ground in Europe, where half of the 66 surviving breeds are now rare, and only 40 of 100 different breeds occurring in China are considered to be economically valuable (Epstein 1969).

International trade in pig meat originates overwhelmingly in Europe. In place for many decades, the single biggest flow of cured and canned pork is from Denmark to the United Kingdom. But even before that trade emerged, bacon had become an integral element of the British breakfast. The word "bacon" is derived from Francis Bacon (1561–1626), whose family crest featured a pig. Japan, although traditionally not a major consumer of pig meat, has become a significant importer of European pork products, and the well-known prosciutto (cured ham), from the Province of Parma in Italy, is now found in upscale shops around the world. Much potential movement of processed pig meat is thwarted because of the prevalence of three diseases, found mainly in underdeveloped countries: foot-and-mouth disease, hog cholera, and African swine fever. In Haiti in the early 1980s, for example, an epidemic of African swine fever killed two-thirds of the country's 1.2 million pigs. The sur-

viving swine constituted a reservoir of the disease and were slaughtered. Then, disease-free swine were imported from the United States and distributed to some of Haiti's 800,000 former pig owners.

Conclusion

The story of the pig in space and time is one of a multifaceted mutualism with humans. Its early roles, as a feeder on garbage or as a free-ranging consumer of mast in the forest, freed the pig from competing with people for the same food. Part of this mutualism was also hygienic because of the animal's capacity for disposing of wastes. Transforming the least noble of materials into succulent protein, however, also engendered enough apparent disgust to ban the animal and its flesh in certain cultures. The pig is now found around the world under vastly different circumstances. In industrialized countries, questions of efficiency and fat control have become of paramount importance, and no other domesticated animal has undergone such major changes in the way it has been kept.

Daniel W. Gade

Bibliography

Anderson, Eugene N., Jr. 1988. *The food of China.* New Haven, Conn.

Baldwin, James A. 1983. Pre-Cookian pigs in Australia? *Journal of Cultural Geography* 4: 17–27.

Bichard, Maurice, and E. Ann Bruce. 1989. Pigmeat production worldwide. *Outlook on Agriculture* 18: 145–51.

Epstein, H. 1969. *Domestic animals of China.* Farnham Royal, England.

1984. Pig. In *Evolution of domesticated animals,* ed. I. L. Mason, 145–62. New York.

Gade, Daniel W. 1987. The Iberian pig in the Central Andes. *Journal of Cultural Geography* 7: 35–50.

Harris, Marvin. 1985. *Good to eat: Riddles of food and culture.* New York.

Hesse, Brian. 1990. Pig lovers and pig haters: Patterns of Palestinian pork production. *Journal of Ethnobiology* 10: 195–226.

Kim, Seung Og. 1994. Burials, pigs, and political prestige in northern China. *Current Anthropology* 35: 119–41.

Laurans, R. 1963. *Le porc dans la société médiévale.* Paris.

1976. Évolution de l'alimentation du porc domestique. I. L'alimentation traditionnelle. In *Le porc domestique* (Ethnozootechnie No. 16), ed. R. Laurans, 22–33. Paris.

Miller, Robert L. 1990. Hogs and hygiene. *Journal of Egyptian Archaeology* 76: 125–40.

Parsons, James J. 1962. The acorn-hog economy of the oak woodlands of southwestern Spain. *Geographical Review* 52: 211–35.

Pond, W. G. 1983. Modern pork production. *Scientific American* 248: 78–87.

Rappaport, R. A. 1967. *Pigs for the ancestors.* New Haven, Conn.

Ross, Eric B. 1983. The riddle of the Scottish pig. *BioScience* 33: 99–106.

Sauer, Carl O. 1952. *Agricultural origins and dispersals.* New York.

Simoons, Frederick J. 1991. *Food in China: A cultural and historical inquiry.* Boca Raton, Fla.

    1994. *Eat not this flesh: Food avoidances from prehistory to the present.* Second edition. Madison, Wis.

II.G.14 ❧ Horses

The horse represents one of the most successful outcomes of animal domestication, but for a variety of reasons it has not been widely used as a source of human food. Very little of the exacting attention given this creature over the past 5,000 years has been directed toward developing its latent meat or milk potential. Artificial selection of this nonruminant herbivore has focused on speed, strength, and configuration.

Domestication

Long before their domestication, wild horses roamed the Eurasian grasslands. They were a favorite subject of the Paleolithic cave art of western Europe, which suggests their status as a major prey species. Certain Upper Pleistocene kill sites, such as that at Solutré, France, have more horse bones than those of any other animal. Human intervention into their breeding came later than with other herd animals. Two wild horses, the tarpan *(Equus ferus gmelini)* and (Nikolai) Przhevalski's horse *(Equus ferus przewalski),* were the ancestors of the domesticated *Equus caballus.* Present knowledge places horse domestication in the grasslands of Ukraine around the fourth millennium before Christ. At Dereivka, a site of the early Kurgan culture, evidence of bit wear recovered archaeologically indicates that people rode horses (Anthony 1986). They also ate them, which is not surprising as the predecessors of these same people were avid consumers of the wild species.

Assuming present-day Ukraine to have been the center of horse domestication, the use of the animal spread westward during the next 500 years to eastern Europe, as well as eastward to the Transcaucasus and southward to Anatolia and the Mediterranean. Horse bones recovered at the site of Malyan (in Iran) that have been ingeniously analyzed reportedly show evidence of horse riding (Anthony and Brown 1989). By 2500 B.C. horses were well established in western Europe. Their main prehistoric role was as pullers of wheeled conveyances and as riding animals, and S. Bökönyi (1984) asserts that horses were used to pull carts before they were ridden. Horses were also eaten; in fact, the flesh of equids was an acceptable food in most societies that adopted them during the first 3,000 years of their domesticated state. Bronze Age sites in eastern Europe have yielded limb bones

broken for the marrow and brain cases cracked open to extract the brain.

The Kurgan people, along with other early Indo-Europeans, also sacrificed horses to honor the dead and propitiate the gods (O'Flaherty 1987; Dexter 1990). This practice was widespread from Europe to South Asia, where the Aryans of India made a strong religious place for the horse. Its role as human food was not very important, although horseflesh was consumed in connection with the *asvamedha,* a sacrifice of horses borrowed from an ancient Indo-European fertility rite (Bhawe 1939). It is especially intriguing to consider that the horse gained ascendancy as a useful and ritually significant animal with the migration of Indo-European people. The Hittites of Anatolia, for example, introduced a higher level of horse keeping than had been there before, and Mediterranean antiquity extended the high prestige of the horse, but with much less ritual killing. The ancient Greeks offered horses in sacrifice to Poseidon, the god of horses, but did not generally consume the flesh. The only Roman horse sacrifice honored Mars.

Horsemeat Avoidance

In the modern world, most people and cultures have rejected the flesh of horses (and its equine relatives, the mule and the donkey) as unfit to eat. But the reasons for avoidance are not necessarily the same everywhere. In some places, the horse is a rare, even absent, animal, so that people have had little opportunity to find out what they were missing. Aside from Iceland, few horses have been kept in the Arctic or Subarctic, primarily because of the large effort needed to store a sufficient amount of fodder to get the animal through long winters. The tropics have not had big horse populations, either. Tropical forests neither suit the horse's food requirements nor favor its physiological well-being. Moreover, in much of Africa, the presence of trypanosomiasis has excluded horses from large areas.

In most parts of the world where the horse is found, neither its meat nor its milk is used. Part of this avoidance can be attributed to religious injunction. Jews, Muslims, Hindus, and, at one time, Christians have all proscribed horsemeat from the diet as a badge of their faith. Orthodox Jews include it as one of the forbidden items in their Levitical list of animals because horses neither chew the cud nor have cloven hooves. Muslims are enjoined in the Koran to eschew this flesh, a prohibition that, perhaps, grew out of the social context of Arab desert oases, where the horse was a luxury animal owned by sheikhs. Horsemeat is not eaten by most Hindus (except for untouchable groups) because it is a flesh food in a primarily vegetarian culture.

Marginalization of horsemeat in Europe had a religious basis. As Christianity spread through Teutonic lands, clerics regarded hippophagy (eating horseflesh) as a pagan residue that was tinged with barbarism. In prehistoric Ireland, horseflesh was eaten in ritual contexts, a practice that survived into the early Middle Ages. A chronicler in the twelfth century described such an occasion in which priestly sexual intercourse with a mare, sacrifice, and consumption of the flesh were involved (Giraldus Cambrensis 1982). Such behavior, outrageous to Christians, explains why horsemeat had such a bad reputation as the continent became more fully Christianized. Boniface, missionary to the Germans, undertook what amounted to a personal lobbying campaign to, successfully as it turned out, persuade the pope to place horseflesh into the forbidden category. Such a ban was certainly not based on health or scripture, but horsemeat, nonetheless, became the only specific food outlawed in the history of Christianity. Today, although most people in the Christian tradition still avoid the flesh of equines, its rejection no longer has much to do with a religious prohibition. Even the *Catholic Encyclopedia* makes no effort to recall this old taboo that had been part of canon law. Rejection can now be attributed mainly to fear of the unfamiliar. The status of the horse as an intelligent companion of humans has surely worked against experimentation with consuming its flesh, except in periods of severe food shortage.

Marvin Harris (1985) has argued that underlying these prohibitions was a stark ecological fact: The horse was an inefficient converter of grass to meat, and when compared to cattle, horses have a higher metabolic rate and a gestation period lasting two months longer. However, as H. B. Barclay (1989) points out, horses also have various advantages over cattle. They enjoy a longer life span and have greater stamina and endurance. In winter pastures, horses, unlike cattle, can paw beneath the snow to graze. Moreover, in central Asia, mare's milk yields are as high as those of cows.

In spite of early religious and later social reprobation, Europe did undergo a hippophagy movement that to some extent changed attitudes toward this meat and, as such, represents a notable case of how a food taboo broke down. Hippophagic experimentation in Europe was widespread around the middle of the nineteenth century, when conscious efforts were made to break with the old prejudice against selling and eating horseflesh. Denmark legalized its sale in 1841, as did the German state of Württemburg; Bavaria followed in 1842, and Prussia in 1843. Other countries (Norway, Sweden, Austria, and Switzerland) also legalized its sale. Russia, where horsemeat has had a historic culinary role, never banned the sale of horsemeat in the first place.

Horsemeat Consumption in Europe

In the European history of horsemeat consumption, France and francophone Belgium stand out. There the cultural barrier to selling and eating horsemeat was more successfully breached than in any other part of Europe. As with so many French attitudes, it began with elite exhortation, but it also occurred in a national culture charmed by culinary diversity and invention. Its beginnings can be traced to governmental decisions that French people should eat more flesh foods. By 1850, the opinion was that the French person's ability to perform industrial work was hindered by insufficient quantities of nitrates in the diet. Ireland was pointed to as a negative case of how dependence on the potato and little or no meat had led to physiological degeneration. In 1853, dietary regulations set a minimum daily intake of 100 grams of meat for a small adult and 140 grams for a large person. In 1889, a government medical commission increased these thresholds to 120 and 200 grams, respectively. In the French Army, the meat ration was increased in 1881 from 250 to 300 grams per day. Regulations about meat also affected institutions. In 1864, hospices and hospitals were directed to provide meat at meals twice a day, preferably roasted, which was judged to be the most nutritious form of preparation.

As meat consumption in France rose, provisioning became an issue. Since horseflesh was then much cheaper, it was judged by the authorities to be especially worthy of adoption among lower-income groups. A group of distinguished French intellectuals and scientists, led by Geoffrey Saint-Hilaire, made a conscious effort to integrate horsemeat into the French diet. Their aim was to show that *chevaline* (as it was called) was nutritious and that the old prejudices had no rational basis. Even the hierarchy of the French Church did not interfere in this conscious rejection of a medieval taboo, and the first specialized horsemeat shop opened in Paris in 1866. Shortly thereafter, dire food shortages associated with the siege of Paris gave many of that city's inhabitants an opportunity to eat horsemeat for the first time.

Two prime factors led to a generalized acceptance of horsemeat in France. First, until the 1920s, horsemeat cost half that of comparable cuts of beef and therefore was within reach of the working class. Second, horsemeat got much publicity as a high-energy food and as ostensibly valuable in physiologically reducing the human temptation to overindulge in alcoholic beverages. In touting horsemeat, the bourgeoisie indicated their conviction that it had an appropriate role to play in the diet of the working class, whose members were the main abusers of alcohol in France.

Two basic kinds of horseflesh later characterized its consumption in France. Red meat, preferred by many for its putative association with high iron content, comes mainly from older horses. A colt (*poulain*) yields light meat, favored for its tenderness and mild flavor approaching that of veal. Patterns of consumption have maintained a certain profile through the decades, with the typical horsemeat consumer in France tending to be young rather than old, working or middle class rather than rich, and urban rather than rural.

Hippophagy in France is highest in the northern part of the country, with southern Belgium an extension of that consumption pattern. Early in the twentieth century, large workhorses were numerous in this part of Europe where the Percheron and the Belgian breeds evolved. Consequently, Paris has had the most avid hippophagists in France, with a per capita consumption three times higher than that of western France and almost seven times higher than that of eastern France. Horsemeat was first promoted in Paris, and it was there that a specialized horse abattoir was set up from which horsemeat was wholesaled elsewhere. The Paris region has also had France's largest concentration of poor people, who became the most enthusiastic consumers of equine products. Paris, Lille, and other northern cities were major markets for red meat from aged animals, whereas hippophagists in Lyon and Grenoble preferred *viande de poulain.*

In spite of considerable commercial activity, horsemeat in France has had a marginal position among meat products. Except during the war years, its consumption has never amounted to more than 5 percent of that of beef. Close to 60 percent of French people do not consume any horsemeat, and of the minority that do, the per capita consumption amounts to only about 5 kilograms per year. One result, but also a cause, of such a pattern is availability. Most French towns have not had a clientele large enough to support a *boucherie chevaline,* and until the 1980s, butchers selling beef could not also sell horsemeat. This prohibition was in the form of a law that had been promulgated to prevent misrepresentation of one meat for another.

Organoleptic perception also affects consumption. Many people, for example, have stated they dislike the flavor of horsemeat. However, disagreement on whether it has a sweetish taste, some other taste, or is simply tasteless suggests differences in the kinds of slaughtered animals or preconceived notions of the meat's characteristics. The appeal of horsemeat may be culturally conditioned. For example, an organoleptic evaluation in the United States of several kinds of lean beef, regular beef, lamb, horse, and horse mixed with beef fat ranked the last two lowest in appearance, smell, and taste (Pintauro, Yuann, and Bergan 1984).

Matters of health and price explain at least part of the drop in per capita consumption of horsemeat from the 1960s to the 1990s. For many years, horsemeat was valued as a particularly healthful food due to an iron content higher and a fat content lower than beef. *Chevaline* reputation suffered, however, in 1967, when a highly publicized salmonella outbreak in a school cafeteria was traced to horsemeat patties. When findings emerged that fresh horsemeat deteriorated more rapidly than beef, the French government banned horsemeat for institutional use. In addition, awareness of *chevaline*'s possible health risk was paralleled by its rising cost. Horsemeat of the first half of the twentieth century was essentially a by-product of animals slaughtered after a useful life of pulling plows or wagons. For that reason, horsemeat was cheap compared to beef. But by the 1970s most horsemeat in France was imported, which influenced its retail price structure.

Thus in the 1990s, the French consumer paid normally as much, if not more, for horsemeat as for beef. This is because sources of horsemeat supply for the French and Belgian markets changed substantially after 1960, when mechanization of agriculture led to a sharp decline in the horse population. To meet the demand in the face of inadequate domestic sources of *chevaline,* live animals or chilled meat had to be imported from Spain, Portugal, and Eastern European countries. Between 1910 and 1980, imports of horses or horse products increased almost three times. European horses were supplemented with those from the Americas, and beginning in the 1970s, the United States became a major supplier for the French market, as did Australia and South America – especially Argentina, with its substantial horse population.

Horses raised specifically for meat production could, in theory, supply the needed tonnages and at the same time ensure quality. Colt meat in France is now mostly produced that way. Fed a controlled diet, horses grow very quickly, although they cannot compare with ruminants as an efficient converter of herbaceous matter. Breeding of the horse as a meat animal has another value of conserving the genetic patrimony of the famous work breeds of horses that are in danger of eventual extinction. In the long run, such activity might also lead to the emergence of a special kind of high-quality meat animal in the way that Hereford or Aberdeen Angus were developed as cattle with distinguishable phenotypes and genotypes.

Horses as Food in Other Countries

Several other European countries, notably Italy, Spain, Germany, and Switzerland, have achieved a small measure of hippophagic acceptance. Search for protein during the war and for some years after that accustomed Europeans to think of alternative possibilities. As recently as 1951, when meat was still scarce, the British consumed 53,000 horses. However, as other meats became abundant, horsemeat faded as a food for people. Moreover, animal rights activists in the United Kingdom have often shown vigilance about protecting the horse from becoming steak on the table.

In Asia, horsemeat is an important food in Mongolia, where the horse has been deeply integrated into a still traditional rural society. In addition, Mongolians consume mare's milk, usually in fermented form (kumiss). Though their religion bars it, Islamic people in Inner Asia have also been known to eat horseflesh.

In Japan, horsemeat is a favorite meat in the preparation of teriyaki, and in the 1980s Japan imported about one-fourth of the tonnage in the world trade of refrigerated or frozen horsemeat. Australia is a major supplier.

In the Western Hemisphere, no national culture has integrated hippophagy into its dietary possibilities, least of all those with a strong orientation toward carnivory. Argentines and Uruguayans, who are mostly of European origin, have rejected it, although some Indians of the pampas ate the meat of horses descended from those brought by the Spaniards. Some North American Indian groups who acquired the horse from the Europeans also ate horseflesh. In the United States, consumption of horsemeat is low; in fact, throughout North America, it is readily available (though not widely consumed) only in the Canadian province of Québec. French immigrants are reported as a major clientele of the 10 horsemeat shops in the city of Montreal in 1992.

The United States is the leading horsemeat-producing country in the world (FAO Production Yearbook 1990). In 1992, nearly 250,000 horses were slaughtered in the country. Thoroughbred race horses, including champions that once got high stud fees, usually end their days at the slaughterhouse. The $500 to $1,000 sale becomes a way to recover something of the high expense of raising them. Commercialization of this product has been both for shipment abroad as human food and for dog food.

In spite of the abundance of horses, equine flesh has never gained acceptance as a human food in the United States. Harris (1985) has concluded that horsemeat did not catch on because beef and pork could be produced more cheaply. More likely, preconceptions about the suitability of horsemeat have stemmed from an earlier bias brought by Europeans. Moreover, a small but vocal minority of Americans are actively opposed to its use as human food. One emotionally based argument is that it demeans such a noble animal to undergo slaughter as human food. Curiously, much less is said about the appropriateness of horsemeat as dog food, suggesting an ethic that requires humans to deal with horses in narrowly defined ways. Horse abuse in the United States receives much more publicity than mistreatment of cattle, sheep, or pigs.

The lack of horsemeat availability in American meat shops says much about the low demand, but proprietors are also afraid of losing business by making it available in the meat case. Episodes over the years of fraudulent labeling of horseflesh as beef have led to the (erroneous) assumption that the former is, by definition, an inferior meat, perhaps even tainted in some way. A slaughterhouse owner in South Carolina, who has long shipped horsemeat to the European market, has made several attempts to introduce horsemeat in his state with no lasting success. As was the case initially in Europe, a lower price for horse-

meat would seem to be the critical mechanism in its acceptance. Yet economics dictate that good-quality horseflesh cannot be sold at a price much below that of beef. An unusually strong American concern for healthful and lowfat foods could possibly give it a niche. But up to now its best-known usage has been at the dining service of the Harvard Faculty Club in Cambridge, Massachusetts. There it has been maintained as a quirky tradition since World War II, when it was difficult to obtain beef.

Daniel W. Gade

Bibliography

Anthony, D. 1986. The "Kurgan culture," Indo-European origins, and the domestication of the horse: A reconsideration. *Current Anthropology* 27: 291–313.
Anthony, D., and D. Brown. 1989. Looking a gift horse in the mouth: Identification of the earliest bitted equids and the microscopic analysis of wear. In *Early animal domestication and its cultural context*, ed. P. Crabtree, D. Campana, and K. Ryan, 99–116. Philadelphia, Pa.
Barclay, H. B. 1989. Professor Harris, horses, and hippophagists. *Anthropos* 84: 213–19.
Bhawe, S. 1939. *Die Yajus des Asvamedha; Versuch einer Rekonstruktion dieses Abschnittes des Yajurveda auf Grund der Überlieferung seiner fünf Schulen.* Bonner orientalistische Studien 25. Stuttgart.
Bökönyi, S. 1984. Horse. In *Evolution of domesticated animals*, ed. I. L. Mason, 162–73. New York.
Dexter, M. R. 1990. The hippomorphic goddess and her offspring. *Journal of Indo-European Studies* 18: 285–307.
FAO production yearbook. 1990. Rome.
Gade, Daniel W. 1976. Horsemeat as human food in France. *Ecology of Food and Nutrition* 5: 1–11.
Giraldus Cambrensis. 1982. *The history and topography of Ireland*, trans. John J. O'Meara. Harmondsworth, England.
Harris, Marvin. 1985. *Good to eat: Riddles of food and culture.* New York.
O'Flaherty, W. D. 1987. Horses. In *The encyclopedia of religion*, ed. M. Eliade, 463–8. New York.
Pintauro, S. J., K. Yuann, and J. G. Bergan. 1984. Nutritional evaluation of horsemeat. In *Protein: Nutritional quality of foods and feeds*, ed. M. Friedman, 187–96. New York.
Robelin, J., B. Boccard, W. Martin-Rosset, et al. 1984. Caractéristiques des carcasses et qualités de la viande de cheval. In *Le cheval: Réproduction, sélection, alimentation, exploitation*, ed. R. Jarrige and W. Martin-Rosset, 601–10. Paris.
Rossier, E. 1984. État actuel de la production et de la consommation de viande chevaline en France. In *Le cheval: Réproduction, sélection, alimentation, exploitation*, ed. R. Jarrige and W. Martin-Rosset, 491–508. Paris.
Simmonds, P. L. 1885. *The animal food resources of different nations.* London.
Simoons, F. J. 1994. *Eat not this flesh: Food avoidances from prehistory to the present.* Second edition. Madison, Wis.
Vigarello, G. 1993. *Le sain et le malsain: Santé et mieux-être depuis le Moyen-Age.* Paris.

II.G.15 ❧ Insects

In the title of a delightful little book published in 1885, Vincent Holt asks, *Why Not Eat Insects?* The "why not" is hard to explain logically, nutritionally, or on the basis of the sheer abundance of these creatures. However, for Europeans and North Americans the eating of insects, or entomophagy, is considered a curiosity at best. And for many the idea is downright repulsive. Insects as food are found only in cartoons, or perhaps on the odd occasion when suitably disguised under a layer of chocolate. Yet for these same people, other invertebrate animals, such as oysters, snails, crayfish, and lobsters, are not only accepted as food but even viewed as delicacies.

In many other parts of the world, however, insects are considered good to eat and are appreciated for their taste as well as nutritional value. Some, like the giant queen ants (*Atta* sp.) of Colombia, are prized as delicacies and supposedly function as aphrodisiacs as well. Others, like the mompani worms of Africa, are frequently included in the diet and much enjoyed. Still others, like the cock chafer grubs of Ireland, although not much esteemed, have been used when more desirable foods were not available.

The purpose of this chapter is to present an overview of the role of insects in the diet in different parts of the world and in different time periods. We first review the use of insects as food within major geographical areas, in the present as well as in the historic and prehistoric past when information is available (a comprehensive list of insect species used as food is provided in Table II.G.15.1). We then summarize general patterns of insect use and provide information on the nutritional value of some commonly consumed insects.

Insects Around the World

The Americas

North America. The use of insects as food is generally frowned upon in North America, notwithstanding the repeated attempts by entomologists to make them more appealing. One of the best known of such attempts is R. L. Taylor's 1975 book, *Butterflies in My Stomach,* and the accompanying recipe guide, *Entertaining with Insects* (1976). The reasons that most North Americans do not include insects in their diets have to do with food preferences rather than nutritional value. The dietary exclusion of insects is sometimes justified by the assumption that many insects carry diseases and therefore eating them is dangerous, but there is little evidence to support such a notion (Gorham 1979).

The prohibition against eating insects among many contemporary North Americans can probably be traced to Europe. European colonists who settled in North America also had strong taboos against consuming insects. In fact, they originally classified the New England lobster as an insect and refused to eat it. But that was in the 1600s. Subsequently, the lobster has, of course, passed from the status of prohibited food to delicacy.

Native Americans, however, did not have the same prejudices against insects as food, and there are a number of ethnographic and historical accounts indicating their importance in the diet. The bulk of these reports are from the western United States, where the most heavily consumed insects were the larvae of the Pandora moth, grasshoppers, and Mormon crickets – insects that occur in great abundance during certain seasons and in certain places in the region.

Pandora moth larvae *(Colorado pandora lindseyi)* are large caterpillars found on a certain pine tree species, *Pinus jeffreyii.* They were reportedly collected in large numbers by Native American peoples, either by hand or by trenching around the bottom of trees when caterpillars descended to pupate in the soil (Fowler and Walter 1985). As recently as 1981, Pandora moth larvae were still being collected (Fowler and Walter 1985).

Grasshoppers were also frequently consumed by early Americans. They occurred in large swarms or "plagues" in drier areas at densities of more than 12,000 insects per square mile in California (Brues 1946). On the beaches of the Great Salt Lake in Utah, grasshoppers washed up by the lake can pile up in long windrows as much as 20 centimeters thick, already salted and sun-dried (Madsen 1989). The return rates for collection in kilocalories (kcal) per hour are greater than for any other known collected resource (Madsen and Kirkman 1988). Grasshoppers are relatively high in some B vitamins and can be stored (dry) for long periods in the form of flour (Sutton 1988).

Crickets are another valuable food resource; they were often collected in large quantities in trenches and stored for use in the winter (Sutton 1988). One of these was the Mormon cricket *(Anabrus simplex),* so named because Mormons tried to kill these crickets off in the late 1800s and in the process caused animosity between themselves and Paiutes (Madsen and Kirkman 1988). There is some indication that insects formed an increasingly substantial part of the Native American diet as the local habitat was modified by European newcomers (Sutton 1988).

Other insects used by the first Americans were shore flies *(Hydropyrus hians),* available in great abundance in some locations, and ants that were made into flour soup (Sutton 1988). Judging by historical accounts, grasshoppers and crickets were usually roasted and ground with pine nuts, grass seeds, or berries to make cakes, which could then be sun-dried and stored. These were called "desert fruitcakes" and (interestingly) were considered a delicacy by European travelers as well as by Native Americans (Madsen 1989).

Table II.G.15.1. *Numbers of species of insects used as food by stage of life cycle and geographic region*

Order/Family	Stage	NA	CA	SA	Afr	PI	Aus	Eur	ME	SEA	EA
Anoplura (sucking lice)											
Pediculidae	a	1	1	1	1	1	1	0	0	0	0
Coleoptera (beetles)											
Bruchidae	l, p, a	2	0	1	0	0	0	0	0	0	0
Buprestidae	l, a	0	0	1	2	0	0	0	0	1	1
Cerambycidae	l	6	7	3	6	5	7	1	1	1	0
Cicindelidae	a	0	2	1	1	1	2	0	0	0	1
Citheroniidae		0	0	0	1	0	0	0	0	0	0
Crysomelidae	l	0	1	0	0	0	0	0	0	0	0
Curculionidae	l	1	3	4	7	5	0	0	0	3	1
Dytiscidae	l, a	1	0	0	1	0	0	0	0	7	8
Elateridae	l	0	0	0	1	0	0	0	0	0	1
Elmidae	a	0	0	2	0	0	0	1	1	1	5
Histeridae	l	0	1	0	0	0	0	0	0	0	0
Hydrophilidae		0	0	0	0	0	0	0	1	1	4
Lucanidae	l	0	1	0	1	0	0	1	1	0	0
Passalidae	l	0	2	2	3	0	0	0	1	0	0
Pentatomidae	a	0	0	0	0	0	0	0	4	0	0
Scarabaeidae	l, a	1	3	2	12	6	2	7	0	10	0
Tenebrionidae	l	0	0	1	1	0	0	1	1	0	1
Diptera (flies)											
Calliphoridae	l	0	0	0	0	0	0	0	0	0	1
Culicidae	a	0	0	0	2	0	0	0	0	0	0
Ephydridae	l, p	2	2	0	0	0	0	0	0	0	0
Leptidae	a, e	1	0	0	0	0	0	0	0	0	0
Muscidae	l	0	1	0	0	0	0	0	0	0	0
Oestridae	l	1	0	0	0	0	0	0	0	0	0
Sarcophagidae		0	0	0	0	0	0	0	0	0	1
Stratomyidae		0	0	1	0	0	0	0	0	0	0
Tipulidae	a, l	1	0	0	0	0	0	0	0	0	0
Ephemeroptera (mayflies)											
Baetidae	a	0	0	0	1	0	0	0	0	0	0
Ephemeridae		0	0	0	0	0	0	0	0	1	1
Hemiptera (bugs)											
Belostomatidae	a, n	0	3	0	0	0	0	0	2	1	1
Coreidae		0	1	0	0	1	0	0	0	0	0
Corixidae	a	0	5	0	3	2	0	0	0	0	0
Lygaeidae	a	0	0	0	0	1	0	0	0	0	0
Naucoridae	a	0	0	0	0	0	0	0	0	2	0
Nepidae	a	0	0	0	1	0	0	0	0	1	0
Notonectidae	e, n, a	0	1	0	0	0	0	0	0	0	0
Pentatomidae	n, a	0	8	0	1	0	0	0	0	0	2
Homoptera (cicadas, hoppers, aphids)											
Cicadidae	a	3	3	1	2	2	1	3	1	4	1
Cicadellidae		0	0	0	0	0	0	0	0	0	2
Coccidae		0	0	0	0	0	0	0	0	0	3
Fulgoridae		0	0	0	1	0	0	0	0	0	0
Membracidae	n, a	0	3	1	0	0	0	0	0	0	0
Psyllidae		0	0	0	0	0	4	0	0	0	0
Hymenoptera (ants, bees, wasps)											
Apidae	e, l, p	0	3	0	2	4	0	0	1	2	2
Cynipidae	a	0	0	0	0	0	0	1	0	0	0
Formicidae	l, p, a	7	9	5	2	1	13	0	1	3	0
Meliponidae	e, l, p	0	6	4	8	3	3	0	0	2	0
Scoliidae	l, p	0	0	0	0	0	0	0	0	0	1
Tiphiidae		0	0	0	0	0	1	0	0	0	0
Vespidae	i, e, l, p	2	13	8	0	0	0	0	0	4	4
Xylocopidae	l, p	1	0	0	0	1	0	0	1	2	0
Isoptera (termites)											
Odontotermitidae		0	0	0	0	0	0	0	0	1	0
Rhinotermitidae	a	1	0	0	0	0	0	0	0	0	1
Termitidae		0	0	5	19	6	2	2	1	0	
Lepidoptera (butterflies and moths)											
Bombycidae	p	0	0	0	5	0	0	0	1	1	1
Citheroniidae	l	0	0	0	1	0	0	0	0	0	0
Cossidae	l	0	2	0	0	0	5	0	0	3	0
Geometridae	l	0	1	0	0	0	0	0	0	0	0

(continued)

Table II.G.15.1. *(Continued)*

Order/Family	Stage	NA	CA	SA	Afr	PI	Aus	Eur	ME	SEA	EA
Lepidoptera (butterflies and moths)											
Hepialidae	1	0	1	0	0	0	2	0	0	0	2
Hesperiidae	1	0	1	1	0	0	0	0	0	0	0
Hyblaeidae	1	0	0	0	0	1	0	0	0	0	0
Lacosomidae		0	0	1	0	0	0	0	0	0	0
Lasiocampidae	l, p	0	0	0	3	0	0	0	0	0	0
Limacodidae	1	0	0	0	1	0	0	0	0	0	1
Megathymidae	1	0	1	0	0	0	0	0	0	0	0
Noctuidae	1	1	4	3	1	0	1	0	0	0	0
Notodontidae	1	0	0	1	9	0	0	0	0	0	0
Pieridae	1	0	1	0	0	0	0	0	0	0	0
Psychidae	l, p	0	0	0	2	0	0	0	0	0	0
Pyralidae	1	0	1	0	0	0	0	0	1	0	0
Saturniidae	l, p	2	3	1	29	0	0	0	1	0	1
Sphingidae	1	1	0	0	1	0	0	0	0	0	0
Unknown	1	1	0	0	1	0	0	0	0	0	0
Neuroptera (alderflies, dobsonflies, lacewings)											
Corydalidae		0	0	1	0	0	0	0	0	0	1
Odonata (dragonflies)											
Aeschnidae	n, l	0	1	0	1	1	0	0	0	1	1
Libellulidae	1	0	0	0	0	1	0	0	0	0	0
Orthoptera (grasshoppers, crickets, mantids, and cockroaches)											
Acrididae	a, n	10	18	8	10	4	1	2	6	3	5
Blattidae		0	0	0	0	0	1	0	0	2	2
Gryllacrididae	a	0	0	0	0	1	0	0	0	0	0
Gryllidae	a	0	0	0	2	2	0	0	1	3	2
Gryllotalpidae	a	0	0	0	1	2	0	0	1	1	1
Mantidae	a	0	0	0	1	1	0	0	0	2	1
Phasmatidae	a	0	0	0	0	2	0	0	0	2	0
Phylliidae	a	0	0	0	0	1	0	0	0	0	0
Pyrogomorphidae	a, l, p	0	0	0	1	0	0	0	0	0	0
Tettiigonidae	a, p	1	0	1	2	1	0	3	1	1	0
Unknown	a	0	0	0	1	0	0	0	0	0	0
Plecoptera (stoneflies)											
Pteronarcidae	a	1	0	0	0	0	0	0	0	0	0
Siphonaptera (fleas)											
Unknown	a	0	0	0	0	1	0	0	0	0	0
Trichoptera (caddisflies)											
Hydropsychidae	1	0	1	1	0	0	0	0	0	0	0
Totals		48	116	56	136	70	120	22	30	67	60

Stage of life cycle: adult (a), egg (e), immature stage (i), larval (l), nymph (n), pupal (p). Geographic regions are North America (NA), Central America and the Caribbean (CA), South America (SA), Africa (Afr), Pacific Islands (PI), Australia and New Zealand (Aust), Europe (Eur), Middle East and South Asia (ME), Southeast Asia (SEA), East Asia (EA). Each named species was counted as one, unnamed species designated simply as spp. were also counted as one species.

References

North America (Aldrich 1912a, b; Bodenheimer 1951; Engelhardt 1924; Fenenga and Fisher 1978; Madsen and Kirkman 1988; Sutton 1985; Sutton 1988; Swezey 1978; Taylor 1975); Central America and Caribbean (Ancona 1933; Bequaert 1921; Bodenheimer 1951; Bristowe 1932; Conconi and Bourges 1977; Conconi et al. 1984; Fladung 1924; Holt 1885; Pierce 1915; Taylor 1975; Yturbide 1986); South America (Bequaert 1921; Bodenheimer 1951; Conconi and Bourges 1977; Dufour 1987; Fladung 1924; Ruddle 1973; Taylor 1975; Wallace 1853); Africa (Bequaert 1921; Bodenheimer 1951; Brickey and Gorham 1989; Chavanduka 1975; Conconi and Bourges 1977; DeFoliart 1990; Fladung 1924; Harris 1971; Hoffman 1947; Oliveira et al. 1976; Quin 1959; Taylor 1975; Turk 1991); Pacific Islands (Bodenheimer 1951; Bristowe 1932; Conconi and Bourges 1977; DeFoliart 1990; Holt 1885; Meyer-Rochow 1973; Taylor 1975); Australia and New Zealand (Bodenheimer 1951; Conconi and Bourges 1977; Fladung 1924; Taylor 1975); Europe (Bodenheimer 1951; Conconi and Bourges 1977; Holt 1885; Pierce 1915); South Asia and the Middle East (Bequaert 1921; Bodenheimer 1951; Conconi and Bourges 1977; Fladung 1924; Hoffman 1947; Pierce 1915); Southeast Asia (Bodenheimer 1951; Brickey and Gorham 1989; Bristowe 1932; Conconi and Bourges 1977; Gope and Prasad 1983; Kevan 1991; Taylor 1975); East Asia (Bodenheimer 1951; Conconi and Bourges 1977; Hoffman 1947; Mitsuhashi 1988; Pierce 1915).

Central America and the Caribbean. In Mexico, J. R. E. de Conconi and collaborators (1984) have documented the consumption of a very wide variety of insects. They found 101 species of insects regularly consumed, fresh, roasted, or fried, at various stages of development. These belong to 31 families in nine orders and include dragonflies, grasshoppers, bugs, lice, treehoppers, cicadas, caddis flies, butterflies, moths, flies, ants, bees, and wasps (Conconi et al. 1984).

Entomophagy has been practiced for a long time in Mexico (Conconi and Bourges 1977), where many insect dishes are considered delicacies. A well-known example is *ahauatle,* a mixture of hemiptera eggs. It was first reported in 1649 by Francisco Hernandez and was still consumed in 1933 (Ancona 1933). The eggs, from four species of aquatic hemiptera (two species of *Krizousacoriza* and two of *Corisella*), were collected on specially prepared bundles of leaves left in the lake water for several days during the principal egg-laying season. This mixture of eggs (said to have a shrimp-like flavor) was then fried with chicken eggs. The insect eggs were also dried and used as a condiment in the preparation of a traditional Christmas Eve dish, *revoltijo.*

The adult insects of both *Krizousacoriza* and *Corisella* were also consumed, usually along with a fifth species, *Notonecta unifasciata.* The adults were gathered in baskets, sun-dried, and sold on the street, as *mosco para los pájaros.* They were also ground and made into small cakes that were grilled. Both the eggs and adults of these species of aquatic insects were sold as fish food in Europe and in the United States (Ancona 1933).

South America. The giant queen ants of the genus *Atta* are prized as a gastronomical delicacy in Colombia. *Atta* are leaf-cutting ants considered to be a major pest in some agricultural areas. The queens of the genus are very large ants that swarm in the early rainy season and can be easily collected as they leave the nest. The gathering and toasting of these ants is a prosperous cottage industry in northeastern Colombia, and they are marketed throughout the country. Ant consumption can be traced to precolonial times: Gonzalo Jimenez de Quesada, founder of the Colombian capital, Santa Fe de Bogotá, described their use by local peoples in the highlands in 1555 (*Nación* 1989).

The consumption of a wide variety of insects (representing 10 orders and more than 50 different species) has been reported among Amerindian groups in South American rain forests. The insects that appear to be most commonly consumed are ants of the genus *Atta,* palm grubs, and caterpillars of various sorts. The consumption of the queen ants occurs throughout the Amazon Basin (Wallace 1853; Bodenheimer 1951; Denevan 1971; Weber 1972; Ruddle 1973; Dufour 1987). The first description of their use was provided by the naturalist Alfred Wallace (1853: 242–3):

> The part eaten is the abdomen, which is very rich and fatty from the mass of undeveloped eggs. They are eaten alive; the insect being held by the head as we hold a strawberry by its stalk, and the abdomen being bitten off, the body, wings and legs are thrown down to the floor, where they continue to crawl along apparently unaware of the loss of their posterior extremities.

Palm grubs, or palm worms, are the large, fatty, legless larvae of wood-boring weevils (genus *Rhynchophorus*) found in the pith of felled palm trees. The weevils are ubiquitous in tropical rain forests, and the utilization of their larvae as a valued food has been widely reported (Bodenheimer 1951; Chagnon 1968; Clastres 1972; Beckerman 1977; Lizot 1977; Milton 1984; Dufour 1987). E. Bancroft, writing in the eighteenth century, claimed they were also highly esteemed by Europeans in Surinam, particularly by the French, who mixed the roasted grubs with bread crumbs, salt, and pepper (Bancroft 1769, cited in DeFoliart 1990). In northwest Amazonia they are eaten both raw and after smoke-drying over a slow fire, as components of normal meals and as snacks. Amerindians "cultivate" palm grubs in the sense that they fell palm trees with the expectation that they will be invaded by weevils and a crop of grubs will be available for harvest in two to three months (Clastres 1972; Beckerman 1977; Dufour 1987).

The consumption of other types of grubs or larvae is frequently mentioned in ethnographic reports. In the northwest Amazon, the larvae of wood-boring beetles are extracted from felled trees (Dufour 1987). One group of Amerindians in the Peruvian montaña region "cultivate," or at least protect, an unidentified grub called *poshori,* found in piles of maize cobs (Denevan 1971).

Caterpillar eating has been reported for a number of Amerindian groups (Lizot 1977; Dufour 1987), but the actual species eaten have been identified for only one group – the Yukpa (Ruddle 1973). In the northwest Amazon region, five different species of caterpillars have been collected, two of them in large amounts (Dufour 1987). Less commonly ingested are soldier ants, termites, wasp and bee brood, and other larvae (grubs) of various sorts. The consumption of adult beetles seems to be even less common, but it has been reported for the Yukpa (Ruddle 1973) and Ache (Hurtado et al. 1985).

Europe

Although entomophagy is no longer common in Europe, insects were eaten throughout the continent at one time. Cock chafer grubs were consumed by peasants and mountain inhabitants until the 1800s and were an important source of protein in Ireland during the famine of 1688 (Bodenheimer 1951). In earlier times, those who could not afford a diet rich in protein and fat relied on insect sources to supplement their predominantly carbohydrate intake (Bodenheimer 1951).

The Greeks and Romans, who heavily influenced European culture, enjoyed insects as a food source (Bequaert 1921). Ancient Greeks apparently considered grasshoppers a delicacy, and even Aristotle reported eating cicadas. He considered them tastiest just before the final instar, but females, laden with eggs, were deemed delicious as well (Bates 1959). The Greeks and Romans also ate a large Melolonthid grub thought to be *Lucanus cervus,* which, according to Pliny, was fattened before consumption (Bequaert 1921).

Africa

The consumption of insects in Africa is still quite widespread (DeFoliart 1989), with caterpillars among the most popular. A recent survey found that 69 percent of Africans interviewed had eaten one or more species of caterpillar or lived in households where at least one species of caterpillar was consumed (Ashiru 1988). The mopanie worm *(Gonimbrasia belina),* the so-called snack that crawls, is one of the best-known edible caterpillars. It is eaten fried, dried, stewed in tomato sauce, and even raw (Brandon 1987). Mompani worms appear to constitute an important source of protein for rural dwellers (Ivbijaro 1990) and were reportedly preferred to meat in some areas when they were in season (Quin 1959).

Caterpillars have become something of a trend on menus around Africa and are currently marketed by a firm in Johannesburg (Brandon 1987; Zimbawe *Herald* 1988). Because they occur in large aggregations, the collection of caterpillars is easier than that of some other insects (Chavanduka 1975). In fact, collection rates of 40 pounds per day have been reported (Brandon 1987).

Locusts also play a significant role in the diet of Africans, particularly *Schistocerca gregaria,* the desert locust (Quin 1959; DeFoliart 1989). Indeed, in the not-so-distance past, the locusts have been so popular that locust swarms were welcomed and their arrival attributed to a mighty spirit (Bequaert 1921). The female locusts loaded with eggs were most commonly eaten, and often a soup was made of the eggs (Berensberg 1907; Bequaert 1921). High in protein and fat, locusts may be an excellent supplement to local diets that consist mainly of carbohydrates (Chavanduka 1975). P. J. Quin (1959) also notes that locusts played a significant role in sustenance and were the most popular meat of all among the Pedi of the Transvaal.

Termites are also utilized as food in Africa, especially during the early rainy season when the reproductive forms fly from the nest in large swarms and can be collected (Brickey and Gorham 1989; Kumar 1990). At one time, termites were such an important addition to the diet that their mounds were fought over as property (Bequaert 1921). Local people knew when these swarms would occur and they would cover mounds for purposes of collection (Curran 1939). Termites can be eaten raw (with care taken to avoid being bitten by the termite first) (Curran 1939) and fried, and they are also roasted. Termites not only are high in fat and protein but also contain a significant amount of lysine, which is not found in maize, a main constituent of the African diet (Chavanduka 1975; Oliveira et al. 1976).

Palm grubs, such as those of the genus *Rynchophorus,* are still consumed in Cameroon, Angola, and other parts of Africa and are occasionally raised specifically for this purpose (Oliveira et al. 1976; DeFoliart 1990). They may be prepared by stewing, frying, or grilling, but one creative recipe suggests boiling them inside coconuts instead (Grimaldi and Bikic 1985, cited in DeFoliart 1990).

Although a recent study indicates that 10 percent of the animal protein in the diet of local people in Zaire comes from insect foods, the general trend in Africa is toward a reduction in entomophagy (DeFoliart 1990; Kumar 1990). This development is, perhaps, due to an increased use of pesticides as well as to exploitation of new habitats in order to accommodate growing populations, both of which have reduced the number of insects to which populations have access (Chavanduka 1975).

Asia

Middle East and South Asia. With the exception of locusts, whose consumption continued into recent times, the Middle East and South Asia have not had a strong history of entomophagy (Bodenheimer 1951). The desert locust, *S. gregaria,* was a major source of food in the Middle East, with up to 9,000 kilograms gathered per day in some areas (DeFoliart 1989). These locusts were prepared by cooking in salt water and then sun-drying, after which they were traded at the market (DeFoliart 1989). During times of famine locusts were frequently ground into flour from which fried cakes were made (Bodenheimer 1951). In 1988, Saudi Arabians were also observed eating locusts, grilled like shrimp, after the worst locust plague in 25 years descended on the west coast (San Francisco *Chronicle* 1988).

Locusts were especially prevalent in the diet of nomadic people such as the Bedouins, who welcomed the periodic swarms (Bodenheimer 1951). The best-known incident in that part of the world involving locust eating, however, concerns John the Baptist's limited fare of locusts (St. John's bread) and honey during his ordeal in the desert. He was observing the decree of Moses found in Leviticus 9:22: "These ye may eat; the locust after his kind and the bald locust after his kind, and the cricket after his kind and the grasshopper after his kind."

A recent study of three tribes in Assam, India, has revealed a surprising number of locusts eaten on a mass scale (Bhattacharjee 1990). No other contemporary insect consumption is documented for South Asia except in Nepal. The Nepalese in the Himalayan foothills are said to prepare a native dish, called *bakuti,* in which the larvae and pupae of giant honeybees are extracted from the wax comb and cooked until they resemble scrambled eggs (Burgett 1990).

Southeast Asia. Entomophagy is still relatively popular in Southeast Asia. In fact, Thailand currently exports frozen steamed ant larvae and pupae to the United States as specialty foodstuffs (Brickey and Gorham 1989). In North Thailand, bee brood is prepared for consumption by steaming entire honeycombs wrapped in banana leaves (Burgett 1990). Such grubs and pupae must be an important food among local people because, as F. S. Bodenheimer (1951) notes, the collection of combs is done at great risk of being stung.

The consumption of beetles has been especially popular throughout Southeast Asia, with 24 species in six families listed by Bodenheimer (1951) alone. He reported that Dytiscid beetles, such as *Cybister* and Hydrophilid beetles, seem to have been the most frequently eaten and those most commonly sold at market (Hoffman 1947). The larvae of longicorn beetles and weevils were also sought by the people of Laos (Bodenheimer 1951). The larvae of *Rhynchophorus schab,* which are found in coconut palms, were roasted, and other *Rhynchophorus* larvae were fattened and sold for a good price at the market.

While in Laos and Siam (now Thailand) in the 1930s, W. S. Bristowe (1932) also noted the popularity of larval as well as adult beetles in this region. Among those he cited as favorites were dung beetles (Scarabaeidae), which were served curried, and the giant water beetle *(Lethocerus indicus),* a great delicacy that was said to taste like Gorgonzola cheese. Bristowe also observed dishes of water, set out with lighted candles in the center, to attract dragonflies and termites. These insects would singe their wings on the candles and fall into the water to be subsequently collected.

Bristowe (1932) claimed that the local people's knowledge of the life history of these food insects was very thorough and that they truly enjoyed eating the insects and were not consuming them strictly out of necessity. Furthermore, he hypothesized that by eating pest insects the people were reducing the amount of damage done to their crops.

The green weaver ant *(Oecophylla smaragdina)* was used throughout South and Southeast Asia in a condiment as well as a drink; both were said to have a rather acidic flavor (Bequaert 1921).

East Asia. Insect consumption is still quite common in some parts of East Asia. Perhaps the most well-known insect eaten in this region is the pupae of the silkworm *Bombyx mori.* These pupae are exported from Korea to the United States (Brickey and Gorham 1989) and are also eaten in China, according to a recent study done by the Institute of Insect Research in Yunnan Province, China (The Research Institute 1990). W. E. Hoffman (1947) observed that the pupae were sold throughout the silk district and often cooked immediately after the silk was unraveled, so as not to waste the valuable resource that accompanied the silk.

The larvae and pupae of Hymenopterans are another food resource currently used in East Asia. Five species of immature bees and wasps utilized as food were identified by the Institute of Insect Research in Yunnan Province. B. Hocking and F. Matsumura noted in 1960 that Japan had been exporting bee pupae in soy to the United States. Interestingly, one of the favorite dishes of Japan's late Emperor Hirohito was wasp pupae and larvae over rice (Mitsuhashi 1988). Bodenheimer (1951) also documented the consumption of the larvae and pupae of *Vespa,* a wasp, in Japan.

Locusts are presently consumed in East Asia, particularly those of the genera *Oxya* and *Locusta* (The Research Institute 1990b). Bodenheimer (1951) described the sale of grasshoppers fried in sesame oil in the local markets in China earlier in this century. Other insects consumed in East Asia included *L. indicus,* the giant water beetle, and caterpillars infected with *Cordyceps,* a fungus. These caterpillars were tied in bundles by the fungus filaments and sold as a delicacy (Hoffman 1947).

Pacific Islands. According to V. B. Meyer-Rochow (1973), insect eating is still a part of the native cultures in Papua New Guinea. Most widely documented are the sago palm grub feasts in which hundreds of pounds of *Rynchophorus bilineatus* larvae are wrapped in banana leaves and roasted. In fact, three species of palm grubs are exploited regularly, along with other larvae and adults of large beetles including many of the family Scarabaeidae (Meyer-Rochow 1973).

New Guineans also consume a great number of Orthopterans, including two species of stick insects, two of mantids, and the female of a species of locust (Meyer-Rochow 1973). Meyer-Rochow hypothesized that insect consumption provided needed dietary protein and fat because the greatest variety and quantity of insects were consumed in areas with the highest population density as well as the lowest amounts of available animal protein.

Termites were also very popular in the Pacific Islands, especially the sexual winged forms, which are higher in fat content. The predominant species eaten, *Macrotermes,* were caught after they flew into fires, burning their wings. In the Philippines, natives were said to eat the locusts that consumed their potato vines – a unique form of pest control (Bodenheimer 1951).

Australia and New Zealand

Despite a general reduction in the use of insects as food worldwide, entrepreneurs in Australia have begun to introduce insects to their commercial food market (Putting Insects on the Australian menu 1990). The insects considered to have the best potential for success include black honey ants, witchetty grubs (the larvae of a Cossid moth), bardi grubs (the larvae of a Cerambycid beetle), and *Trigona* bees. All of these insects have been supplied from around Australia where they are local delicacies. Many restaurants in Australia also now include insects on their menus (Putting Insects on the Australian menu 1990).

The black honey ant *(Camponotus inflatus)* is similar to the honey ant found throughout North and Central America. A modified worker ant with an enlarged body the size of a grape and filled with nectar, the black honey ant was highly sought after by Aboriginal Australians (Bourne 1953) and even considered a totem animal by some clans (Flood 1987; Conway 1990). The digging up of these ants is considered an important traditional practice and is still taught to children (Conway 1990). Other species of ants were also important food resources for Aboriginal Australians (Bodenheimer 1951). Tasmanians had a number of words for the various ants that they identified, and traditional feasts were held during the periods that ant pupae could be obtained (Sutton 1990).

Witchetty grubs were also an important food of Australian Aborigines (Flood 1987). The name "witchetty grub" refers to several types of grubs (Campbell 1926) and probably includes the larvae of the Cossid moth *(Xyleutes leuchomochla),* the giant ghost moth (Hepialidae), and the longicorn beetle (Cerambycidae) (Bodenheimer 1951; Sutton 1990).

Among the most unique and well-documented examples of entomophagy in Australia were the annual Bugong moth feasts that occurred in the Victorian Alps until the 1890s. Moths of *Agrotis infusa* migrate from the plains of New South Wales to aestivate (the summer equivalent of hibernation) every year in the rock crevices and caves of the Bugong Mountains, from which their name was derived (Flood 1987). Enormous numbers of moths have been counted (up to 17,000 per square meter) in some of these crevices and found on the floors of caves to depths of over 1 meter (Flood 1980). Many different tribes of Aboriginal Australians traditionally gathered to feast on the moths, and evidence of these feasts has been carbon dated to about 1,000 years ago (Flood 1980). The moths were smoked out by thrusting a burning bush into the cracks of the rock, then they were thrown into hot ashes or sand to remove the wings and legs (Campbell 1926; Flood 1980). These moths are said to have a nutty flavor and are high in both protein and fat (Campbell 1926; Sutton 1990).

Insects Are Good to Eat

General Patterns of Use
The great number and diversity of insect species (over 600) that have been or are used as food are listed in Table II.G.15.1. The largest variety of species appears to be in the tropics, which probably reflects the greater faunal diversity in these areas and the larger size of individual organisms. But it may also reflect to some extent the amount of research done on the topic in such climates. Comparatively fewer species appear to have been consumed in the more temperate regions of North America, Asia, and Europe. Fewer insect species inhabit these areas, and in general, the size of individual organisms is smaller.

A closer look at the insects listed in Table II.G.15.1 reveals that many of the same types of insects (i.e., in the same orders and families) are consumed in different parts of the world. The most widely consumed are probably the locusts (Acrididae), termites (Termitidae), and palm grubs (Curculionidae) (see Table II.G.15.2). These insects share two characteristics that are significant to their use as human food: (1) Individ-

ual insects are relatively large; and (2) individuals are highly aggregated during at least part of their life cycle. Locusts, for example, are among the largest of insects. They are also gregarious and can form swarms of thousands of individuals. Termites are generally smaller in size but are ubiquitous in tropical ecosystems. The species employed as food can be found in large, easily recognized colonies (for example, *Macrotermes* spp. in Africa), and the reproductive forms of some species can be easily captured during mating flights. Palm grubs, the larvae of weevils, can be as big as sausages. Over 50 percent of the Curculionidae reported are from the genus *Rynchophorus,* a genus found in the Americas, Africa, and Asia, which includes some of the largest of all herbivorous beetles (Crowson 1981). In addition, palm grubs can be harvested in sizable quantities from the pith of felled palm trees.

About 50 percent of the insects listed in Table II.G.15.1 are consumed in immature stages of the life cycle. The advantage to human consumers is that the immature stages are soft-bodied, typically high in fat, usually the largest form of the life cycle, and often in the stage of the life cycle when individual insects can be found in the greatest aggregations. In the order Lepidoptera (butterflies and moths), for example, the larval stage is the stage of the life cycle in which the insect is largest and has the highest energy (caloric) content. Compared to the larvae in the last instar, the adult forms have a lower body mass and a hardened exoskeleton, which reduces their digestibility. The larval stage is also often the stage of the life cycle at which the organisms are the most numerous and highly aggregated, whereas the adults are more mobile and widely dispersed. Furthermore, the larval stage is often long, as opposed to the shorter adult stage (Daly 1985), and therefore offers a greater harvesting opportunity.

Table II.G.15.2. *Number of species of the insects most commonly consumed throughout the world by geographic region (percentage consumed in immature forms in parentheses).*

Geographic region	Number of species[a]			
	Loc	Ter	PG	Total
North America	10	0	1	50 (46%)
Central Amercia, Caribbean	16	0	3	117 (81%)
South America	8	5	4	61 (57%)
Europe	2	0	0	20 (54%)
Africa	10	19	6	155 (63%)
Middle East, South Asia	6	2	0	29 (33%)
Southeast Asia	4	1	3	67 (34%)
East Asia	5	0	1	60 (40%)
Pacific Islands	4	6	4	59 (27%)
Australia, New Zealand	2	2	0	46 (68%)
Total	67	35	22	664

[a]Loc = locusts, Ter = termites; PG = palm grubs.

Table II.G.15.3. *Nutritional value of some insects consumed in tropical South America compared with other animal foods; composition per 100 grams edible portion.*

Food	Moisture (%)	Energy (kcal)	Protein (g)	Fat (g)
Ants, female sexuals (*Atta sexdens*)	6.1	628	39.7	34.7
Ants, female sexuals (*Atta cephalotes*)	6.9	580	48.1	25.8
Termites, soldiers (*Syntermes sp.*)	10.3	467	58.9	4.9
Palm grubs, smoke-dried (*Rhynchophorus sp.*)	13.7	661	24.3	55.0
Caterpillars, smoke-dried (various species)	11.6	425	52.6	15.4
River fish, smoke-dried	10.5	312	43.4	7.0
Tapir, smoke-dried	10.3	516	75.4	11.9

Source: Adapted from Dufour (1987).

Food Value of Insects

In terms of nutrition, insects are comparable to other animal foods. The composition of some insects consumed in tropical South America is shown in Table II.G.15.3, and values for two other common sources of animal protein – dried fish and dried meat – are provided for comparison. The energy value of the insects is high, between 425 and 661 kcal per 100 grams, with the energy values for female alate ants (*Atta* sp.) and *Rhynchophorus* larvae the highest, because both of these are rich in fat. The amount of protein in insects is also relatively high, but its quality appears to be somewhat lower than that of vertebrates (Conconi and Bourges 1977). In relation to more familiar foods, the composition of ants, palm grubs, and caterpillars is comparable to goose liver, pork sausage, and beef liver, respectively. The composition of termite soldiers is roughly comparable to that of non-oily fish, although the latter contain more protein.

Unfortunately, the actual nutritional importance of insects in human diets is not well understood because there is little information on quantities actually consumed.

Summary and Conclusions

Insects are ubiquitous and have been included in human diets in most areas of the world at some time. They are still a component of many current diets. The inclusion of insects in these diets should not be regarded as a mere curiosity, nor should their nutritional importance be overlooked because of their small size. Insects are not only a food prized by many peoples but also a good source of energy, animal protein, and fat. Their dietary importance varies from region to region and group to group, but the wide-spread practice of entomophagy deserves attention in any description or evaluation of human diets.

Darna L. Dufour
Joy B. Sander

Bibliography

Aldrich, J. M. 1912a. Flies of the Leptid genus Atherix used as food by California Indians. *Entomological News* 23: 159-63.

1912b. Larvae of a Saturniid moth used as food by California Indians. *Journal of the New York Entomological Society* 20: 28-31.

Ancona, L. 1932. Los jumiles de Texco. *Anales del Instituto de Biología de Universidad Nacional de México* 3: 149-62.

1933. El ahuautle de Texcoco. *Anales del Instituto de Biología de Universidad Nacional de México* 4: 51-69.

Ashiru, M. O. 1988. The food value of the larvae of *Araphe venata*. *Ecology of Food and Nutrition* 22: 313-20.

Bates, M. 1959. Insects in the diet. *American Scholar* 29: 43-52.

Beckerman, S. 1977. The use of palms by the Bari Indians of the Maracaibo Basin. *Principes* 22: 143-54.

Bequaert, J. 1921. Insects as food. *Natural History* 21: 191-201.

Berensberg, H. P. von. 1907. Uses of insects as food, delicacies, medicines, or in manufactures. *Natal Agricultural Journal* 10: 757-62.

Bhattacharjee, P. C. 1990. Food insect consumption in India. *The Food Insects Newsletter* 3: 8.

Bodenheimer, F. S. 1951. *Insects as human food.* The Hague.

Bourne, G. H. 1953. The food of the Australian Aboriginal. *Nutrition Society Proceeding* 12: 58-65.

Brandon, H. 1987. The snack that crawls. *International Wildlife* 17: 16-21.

Brickey, P. M., and J. R. Gorham. 1989. Preliminary comments on federal regulations pertaining to insects as food. *The Food Insects Newsletter* 2: 1, 7.

Bristowe, W. S. 1932. Insects and other invertebrates for human consumption in Siam. *Transactions of the Entomological Society of London* 80: 387-404.

Brues, C. T. 1946. *Insect dietary; an account of the food habits of insects.* Cambridge, Mass.

Burgett, M. 1990. Bakuti – a Nepalese culinary preparation of giant honey bee brood. *The Food Insects Newsletter* 3: 1.

Campbell, T. G. 1926. Insect foods of the Aborigines. *The Australian Museum Magazine* 2: 407-10.

Chagnon, N. 1968. *The fierce people.* New York.

Chavanduka, D. M. 1975. Insects as a source of protein to the African. *The Rhodesia Science News* 9: 217-20.

Clastres, P. 1972. The Guyaki. In *Hunters and gatherers today,* ed. M. G. Bicchieri, 138-73. New York.

Conconi, J. R. E. de, and H. R. Bourges. 1977. Valor nutritivo de ciertos insectos comestibles de México y lista de algunos insectos comestibles del mundo. *Anales del Instituto de Biología, Seria Zoología* 48: 165-86.

Conconi, J. R. E. de, J. M. P. Moreno, C. M. Mayaudon, and F. R. Valdez. 1984. Protein content of some edible insects in Mexico. *Journal of Ethnobiology* 4: 61-72.

Conway, J. R. 1990. A program profile: Honey ants and the Australian Aborigines. *The Food Insects Newsletter* 3: 2.

Crowson, R. A. 1981. *The biology of coleoptera*. New York.

Curran, C. H. 1939. On eating insects. *Natural History* 43: 84-9.

Daly, H. V. 1985. Insect morphometrics. *Annual Review of Entomology*. 30: 415-38.

DeFoliart, G. 1989. The human use of insects as food and animal feed. *Bulletin of the Entomological Society of America* 35: 22-35.

　　　1990. Hypothesizing about Palm weevil and Palm Rhinoceros beetle larvae as traditional cuisine, tropical waste recycling, and pest and disease control on coconut and other palms – can they be integrated? *The Food Insects Newsletter* 3: 1-6.

　　　1991. Forest management for the protection of edible caterpillars in Africa. *The Food Insects Newsletter* 4: 1-2.

Denevan, W. M. 1971. Campa subsistence in the Gran Pajonal, eastern Peru. *Geographical Review* 61: 496-518.

Dufour, D. L. 1987. Insects as food: A case study from the northwest Amazon. *American Anthropologist* 89: 383-97.

Eerde, E. 1980-1. Butterflies in your stomach? *R&D Mexico* Dec./Jan., 6-8.

Engelhardt, G. P. 1924. The Saturniid moth, *Coloradia Pandora*, a menace to pine forests and a source of food to Indians in eastern Oregon. *Bulletin of the Brooklyn Entomological Society* 19: 35-7.

Fenenga, G. L., and E. M. Fisher. 1978. The Cahuilla use of Piyatem, larvae of the White-Lined Sphinx Moth *(Hyles lineata)*, as food. *The Journal of California Anthropology* 5: 84-90.

Fladung, E. B. 1924. Insects as food. *Maryland Academy of Sciences Bulletin*. October: 5-8.

Flood, J. 1980. *The moth hunters: Aboriginal prehistory of the Australian Alps*. Canberra, Australia.

　　　1987. Moth hunters of the southeastern highland. In *Australians to 1788*, ed. D. J. Mulvaney and J. P. White, 257-91. Sydney.

Fowler, C., and N. Walter. 1985. Harvesting Pandora moth larvae with the Owens Valley Paiute. *Journal of California and Great Basin Anthropology* 7: 155-65.

Gope, B., and B. Prasad. 1983. Preliminary observation on the nutritional value of some edible insects of Manipur. *Journal of Advanced Zoology* 4: 55-61.

Gorham, J. R. 1979. The significance for human health of insects in food. *Annual Review of Entomology* 24: 209-24.

Harris, W. V. 1971. *Termites: Their recognition and control*. London.

Hocking, B., and F. Matsumura. 1960. Bee brood as food. *Bee World* 41: 113-20.

Hoffman, W. E. 1947. Insects as human food. *Proceedings of the Entomological Society of Washington* 49: 233-7.

Holt, V. M. 1885. *Why not eat insects?* London.

Hurtado, A. M., K. Hawkes, K. Hill, and H. Kaplan. 1985. Female subsistence strategies among Ache hunter-gatherers of eastern Paraguay. *Human Ecology* 13: 1-28.

Ivbijaro, M. 1990. Insect consumption in Nigeria. *The Food Insects Newsletter* 3: 4.

Kapoor, V. C. 1985. *Perspectives in insect systematics*. New Delhi.

Kevan, D. K. McE. 1991. The eating of stick insects by humans. *The Food Insects Newsletter* 4: 7.

Kodondi, K. K., M. Leclercq, and F. Gaudin-Harding. 1987. Vitamin estimations of three edible species of Attacidae caterpillars from Zaire. *International Journal for Vitamin and Nutrition Research* 57: 333-4.

Kumar, S. K. 1990. Insect consumption in Zambia. *The Food Insects Newsletter* 3: 4.

Lizot, J. 1977. Population, resources and warfare among the Yanomami. *Man* (n.s.) 12: 497-517.

Madsen, D. B. 1989. A grasshopper in every pot. *Natural History* 7: 22-5.

Madsen, D. B., and J. E. Kirkman. 1988. Hunting hoppers. *American Antiquity* 53: 593-604.

Malaisse, F., and G. Parent. 1980. Les chenilles comestibles du Shaba meridional (Zaire). *Naturalistes Belges* 6: 12-24.

Meyer-Rochow, V. B. 1973. Edible insects in three different ethnic groups of Papua and New Guinea. *The American Journal of Clinical Nutrition* 26: 673-7.

Milton, K. 1984. The protein and carbohydrate resources of the Maku Indians in northwestern Amazonia. *American Anthropologist* 86: 7-27.

Mitsuhashi, J. 1988. Rice with cooked wasps: Emperor Hirohito's favorite dish. *The Food Insects Newsletter* 1: 2.

Nación (Bogota). 1989. June 26.

Oliveira, S., P. de Carvalho, B. de Sousa, and M. Simao. 1976. The nutritional value of four species of insects consumed in Angola. *Ecology of Food and Nutrition* 5: 91-7.

Pierce, W. D. 1915. The uses of certain weevils and weevil products in food and medicine. *Proceedings of the Entomological Society of Washington* 17: 151-5.

Putting insects on the Australian menu. 1990. *The Food Insects Newsletter* 3: 2.

Quin, P. J. 1959. *Food and feeding habits of the Pedi*. Johannesburg.

The Research Institute of Insect Resources in Yunnan Province, China. 1990. *The Food Insects Newsletter* 3: 6.

Ruddle, K. 1973. The human use of insects: Examples from the Yukpa. *Biotropica* 5: 94-101.

San Francisco *Chronicle*. 1988. September 22.

Simmonds, P. L. 1885. *The animal resources of different nations*. London.

Sutton, M. Q. 1985. The California salmon fly Pteronarcys Californica (Plecoptera) as a possible food source in N. E. California. *Journal of California and Great Basin Anthropology* 7: 176-82.

　　　1988. Insects as food: Aboriginal entomophagy in the Great Basin. *Ballena Press Anthropological Papers*. Menlo Park, Calif.

　　　1990. Aboriginal Tasmanian entomophagy. In *Ethnobiology: Implications and applications*, ed. D. A. Posey, W. L. Overal, C. R. Clement, et al. Proceedings of the First International Congress of Ethnobiology, Belém, Brazil.

Swezey, S. L. 1978. Barrett's armyworm: A curious ethnographic problem. *The Journal of California Anthropology* 5: 256-62.

Taylor, R. L. 1975. *Butterflies in my stomach*. Santa Barbara, Calif.

　　　1976. *Entertaining with insects*. Santa Barbara, Calif.

Turk, D. 1991. Book review: Les insectes comme aliments de l'homme. *The Food Insects Newsletter* 4: 5-8.

Wallace, A. R. 1853. On the insects used for food by the Indians of the Amazon. *Transactions of the Royal Entomological Society of London* 2: 241-4.

Weber, N. A. 1972. *Gardening ants: The Attines*. Memoirs of the American Philosophical Society, Vol. 92.

Yturbide, T. C. 1986. *Presencia de la comida prehispanica*. Mexico City.

Zimbabwe *Herald*. 1988. April 12.

II.G.16 ❧ Llamas and Alpacas

The llama *(Lama glama)* and alpaca *(Lama pacos)* are among the few domesticated ungulates whose most important function has not been that of providing food for the people who control them. The llama has been kept primarily as a beast of burden, whereas the more petite alpaca is most valued as a source of an extraordinarily fine fleece. These South American members of the camel family may share a common biological ancestry from the guanaco *(Lama guanicoe)*, for although they have long been designated as separate species, the closeness of the relationship is reflected in fertile offspring when they crossbreed. An alternative point of view now gaining in popularity is that the alpaca descended from the vicuña *(Lama vicugna)*, since both animals are about the same size (44 to 65 kilograms [kg]) and both have the capacity to regenerate their incisor teeth. The distribution of both the llama and the alpaca has been traditionally centered in the Andean Highlands of Peru and Bolivia, with peripheral populations of the former in Chile, Argentina, and Ecuador. In the past three decades growing interest has increased their population on other continents, especially in North America.

Camelid Meat as Human Food

Both animals have been an important source of food in the part of the central Andes where husbandry has been most intensive. In neither case, however, are they raised primarily for their flesh, which is consumed after their most valued functions diminish with age. However, llamas possibly had a more important meat func-

Llamas

tion in the pre-Pizarro Andes before the introduction of European barnyard creatures. The movement of herds from the highlands to the coast could have been a way both to transport goods and to move protein-on-the-hoof to the more densely populated coast, where at the time, meat was much rarer than in the highlands (Cobo 1956). David Browman (1989) suggested that when camelid utilization in the highlands expanded northward, starting around 1000 B.C., and long before the Inca civilization was established, meat production appeared to have been the most important use of these animals. But whether of primary or secondary importance, the protein and fat supplied by this meat have contributed to the health of the animals' Andean keepers, whose diet consists mainly of starch.

Some fresh meat is consumed soon after an animal has been butchered. Recently butchered muscle meat is normally whitish or pinkish. Travelers' reactions to llama flesh have been mixed, although it is not always clear that the opinion is based on actual consumption. J. J. Von Tschudi (1848), for example, described it as "spongy in texture and not agreeable in flavor." It is reportedly as high in protein (more than 20 percent) as other kinds of meat but lower in fat than mutton, pork, or beef (Bustinza Choque 1984). Sausages and a kind of Andean haggis are made from the blood and intestines (Flannery, Marcus, and Reynolds 1989). The soft parts of the animals may also be fried *(chicharrones)*.

Most llama and alpaca meat is dried, which in this region of the world has been the only feasible way to preserve and market it outside the local community. Chunks of the carcass are separated from the bone and cut into thin slices less than 1 centimeter thick. These are usually salted by soaking in a brine solution for several days. Then the meat is exposed for two or three weeks in May and June when night temperatures fall to minus 15° Celsius (C). The alternation of freezing cold at night and intense sunlight in the day dries the meat. Called *charqui* in Spanish (from *ch'arki* in Quechua), the dried meat keeps indefinitely. The term *charqui* has given rise to the English word "jerky," which means strips of dried meat, usually beef. In addition to its transportability, *charqui* is reportedly free of a sarcoporidian parasite that is commonly found in fresh meat (Calle Escobar 1984: 167).

The main consumers of *charqui* are Indians, who barter for it if they do not produce it themselves. *Charqui* continues to be carried in llama trains to lower ecological zones where it is exchanged for maize, fruit, and coca. It is also seen in the periodic markets on the Altiplano of southern Peru and Bolivia and is a staple food in several mining towns. Its main competitor is dried mutton. After sheep were introduced to the Andes in the sixteenth century and Indians subsequently adopted them as their own, the process for making *charqui* was applied to mutton to make *chalona.* Whether fresh or dried, the meat of llamas or alpacas is stigmatized as Indian food, and many mestizos avoid it simply for that reason. Because these animals are not inspected in certified slaughterhouses, questions have arisen about the wholesomeness of the meat.

Llamas and alpacas are led to slaughter typically when their primary functions are deteriorating. However, some other criteria are considered depending on the place or situation. George Miller (1977) pointed out that the most disobedient llamas of the herd are sometimes the ones chosen to be slaughtered. If carried out as a general practice, this kind of culling acts as a selection mechanism for docility. Llamas may also be culled for slaughter if they are unusually small or weak, qualities that inhibit their function as pack animals. Moreover, alpacas may be culled for slaughter if their fleece is multicolored; the international wool trade much prefers white or light fawn-colored fleece and pays higher prices for it. Hybrids (wari or huarizo) between an alpaca and llama have neither of the advantages of the parents and may be preferentially kept as a meat source.

Butchering may also be the result of a need or desire for ritual products from the animal. Bezoar stones, for example, which sometimes occur in the stomach and intestines of llamas and alpacas, were used in native ritual. They were also valued by the Spaniards, who believed them to be an antidote for poison. Fat (pichuwira), especially of llamas, has uses in rites that combine a number of items, including coca leaves, cigarettes, and wine or spirits. Fetuses of pregnant llamas and alpacas are also prized as a ritual item, especially as a substitute for sacrificing live animals in towns and cities. In La Paz, Bolivia, the native herb market sells dried fetuses; typically they are buried under the doorway of a private home to ensure fertility. Formerly, the hides of llamas were used for making sandals, but since the 1950s, Indian footwear in the Central Andes is made with rubber from worn-out truck tires.

No reliable production figures for camelid meat are available; however, the yearly slaughter in Peru and Bolivia may reach 10 percent of the combined llama and alpaca population of more than 6 million animals, which is more or less divided equally between the two (Sumar 1988: 26). Almost 89 percent of alpacas in the world are in Peru; Bolivia has 57 percent of the world's llamas (Bustinza Choque 1984). On a household basis, a poor family may butcher 4 animals a year, whereas a more affluent herder may process up to 12 head a year (Flores Ochoa 1968). Aside from slaughter, llamas may be eaten after they have died of other causes (a newborn killed by diarrhea, for example) (Novoa and Wheeler 1984: 124).

The zone of intensive husbandry today is confined to elevated areas above 3,900 meters (m), all within a 300-kilometer (km) radius of Lake Titicaca. Not surprisingly, Puno produces much more camelid meat than does any other Peruvian department. The paramos (flatlands) of northern Peru, Ecuador, and southern Colombia have rarely contained llamas or alpacas in any sizable numbers, and in much of Colombia and Venezuela there are none at all. In the llama heartland, the colonial period's native beast of burden was displaced to some degree when the llamas' trochas (trails) were widened and mule driving was introduced. When vehicle roads were built in the twentieth century, the displacement was accelerated and the llama population dropped sharply. But that same decline in numbers has not happened with alpacas, which in fact are seen by non-Indians as much more valuable animals.

The Nonmilking Enigma

The nutriments that llamas and alpacas provide do not include milk, and the failure of humans to milk these domesticated herd animals raises some important questions. Unfortunately, written sources have rather frequently contained misinformation, sometimes based on an Old World conceit about the cultural history of the Americas. Examples include assertions that llamas were used as mounts and to pull plows, and that alpacas have been beasts of burden. Encyclopedias, several geography textbooks, articles in Nature and National Geographic, and even a dictionary of zoology contain this error (Gade 1969).

Similarly, milk has been claimed as one of the useful products of the llama and alpaca, yet scholars who have studied Andean camelid domestication, ecology, and economy are silent on the subject.[1] Analyses of the archaeological context by C. Novoa and Jane Wheeler (1984) as well as Elizabeth Wing (1975) and David Browman (1974) contain no hints that Andean people kept any of the camelids for their milk. The Spanish chroniclers who wrote of the Inca say nothing about the native people using milk in any form from either species. Quechua, the language of the Inca and their descendants, differentiates human milk (ñujñu) and animal milk (wilali), but that lexical specificity by itself says nothing about any possible human use pattern of the latter.

If domestication is viewed as a process rather than a sudden occurrence, one might suppose that llamas and alpacas were developed for their milk. If we accept the reports of archaeologists who specialize in camelid bones, then it appears that domestication of the llama and alpaca had occurred by 4000 B.C. (Browman 1989). Thus, one or both of these camelids have been manipulated by humans for some 6,000 years, which (if time were of the essence in domestication) should have turned the animals into abundant milk producers.

If, however, a high level of civilization is critical in explaining the milking phenomenon, then one might expect that the civilization of the Inca (A.D. 1100–1532) would have developed this area of subsistence activity. The Inca knew enough about heredity to breed white llamas for state sacrifice and to have produced a plethora of food surpluses that testified to their skills as sedentary agriculturists and herders. The Inca and the various cultures that preceded them by a millennium were all sufficiently talented to have understood the enormous nutritional benefits of milk from their two camelids.

Milking would also have enabled a more intensive use of the grassy puna (highlands) and *paramo* above the altitudes permitting agriculture. As with cattle in the Old World, the milking (and bloodletting) of llamas might have heightened the value of pastoralism and thus encouraged a nomadic way of life. Indeed, the availability of milk would have given the Indians a sort of nutritional freedom to roam the high country above 4,000 m (3,500 m in Ecuador) at will, in search of good pasture for large herds. Certainly such activity would have been more facultative than the obligate relationship with agriculturalists that evolved in the Andes.

Llamas and alpacas have some habits in common that would theoretically predispose them to being milked by their human keepers. Both have a natural tendency to group in corrals at night. Their parturition occurs during the rainy period from January to March when abundant grass is available and the creamy surpluses of lactating females could have been removed with little deprivation for their nursing young. Finally, their general docility resembles that of sheep much more than cattle.

Why the Milking Void?

The aboriginal absence of milking in the Andes elucidates certain cultural–historical questions about domestication as a process. Least persuasive is the argument that the quantities of milk were too small to make milking a worthwhile effort. The old saying "there is no excess" (e.g., insufficient liquid left over for humans once the young have suckled) could have been originally said of cattle, sheep, goats, or water buffalo. Early in her domestication some 7,000 years ago, a cow must have yielded only small amounts of milk to the person willing to extract it. The large milk volume associated with purebred dairy cows today does not predate the nineteenth century.

Indeed, in the face of a minuscule output, the key question is why peoples in the Old World started to milk in the first place. A German cultural geographer, Eduard Hahn (1896), had perhaps the most compelling insight about the prehistoric origins of milking. He believed that milking originally had a religious, not an economic, motive. Bowls of milk were offered to the lunar mother goddess, a cult that regulated spiritual life in ancient Mesopotamia where cattle were first domesticated. The frothy white substance that sustains early life had considerable symbolic power and thus ritualistic value. The quantity of milk extracted was incidental because it had not yet spread from a ritual use among the priestly castes to become nourishment for common people. Nonetheless, expansion of milk supplies to meet the cultic requirements gave an impetus to select those cows found to have large udder capacity and tractability to human interlopers. Slowly, over many generations of selective breeding, milk quantities increased; one result of this was that the original religious motivation for milking was forgotten, and milk became a common nutriment. In other words, the nutritional benefits of milk became recognized as a sufficient reason to carry on the custom.

Such a process was probably "invented" in one place – the Fertile Crescent of southwestern Asia some 6,000 years ago – and then diffused elsewhere. As this diffusion occurred, milking spread to other domesticated mammals. For example, camels, which replaced cattle in desert environments, were first milked by using the model of bovine milking that had begun two millennia earlier. In fact, Carl Sauer (1952) reasoned that because all the Old World herd animals have been milked, milking may well have been the general motive for domesticating them in the first place.

Quantity of milk aside, another reason put forward for not milking llamas and alpacas has to do with behavioral peculiarities of the species. This line of reasoning posits that a lactating female would not allow people to manipulate the vulnerable underpart of her body, as a defense mechanism to ensure sustenance to the offspring. A related assertion is that llamas and alpacas simply cannot be milked because certain pituitary hormones inhibit the lactating female of these species from releasing her colostrum or milk to any but her own offspring. Although these two characteristics may exist, they nevertheless do not explain the phenomenon of nonmilking, again because of the vast behavioral changes that all dairy mammals have undergone to eliminate their natural refusal strategies. At some point in their domestication, individual animals that did not respond to human intervention were likely to have been culled from the breeding pool. Subsequent generations of the selected species gradually evolved in directions more conducive to human manipulation.

The physiological intolerance of Andean people to milk (lactose intolerance) is still another explanation proposed for the historic nonmilking of llamas and alpacas. As in much of Asia and Africa, most of the native folk of the Americas cannot properly digest fresh milk after they have been weaned due to insufficient amounts of the lactase enzyme in the intestine to break down milk sugars (lactose) (Simoons 1973). When pressed to drink milk, Amerindians often suffer nausea and diarrhea. In Peru, for example, nutritional studies have reported that highland children experience an adverse reaction to milk (Calderón-Viacava, Cazorla-Talleri, and León-Barua 1971; Figueroa et al. 1971).

Yet, as with the arguments already examined, lactose intolerance is still not a convincing explanation for the absence of milking in the Andes. After the Spaniards brought cows, goats, and sheep to them, the Andean peoples followed the European example and began to milk these animals. They used the milk for infant feeding and cheese making. Nursing Indian babies can be fed fresh animal milk with impunity because they still have a high level of the lactase enzyme, whereas cheese is a low-lactose dairy product that many lactose malabsorbers can consume without ill effects. Cheese has another advantage over liquid milk: It is preservable without refrigeration and thus can be transported long distances. Cows' milk predominates in making cheese, but in dry areas goats' milk is also used. Cheese making from ewes' milk has been an activity in the Altiplano of Bolivia south of Oruro since the colonial period.

In summary, then, the failure to have milked llamas or alpacas was probably not due to their low milk production, nor to the innate behavior of this camelid genus, nor can it be attributed to the lactose intolerance of the people who have kept them. This leaves a disarmingly simple reason for not milking llamas and alpacas. It never occurred to the indigenes to do so. For those who appreciate milk, yoghurt, ice cream, butter, and cheese in their diet, this failure to grasp the possibility of milking may seem illogical. Yet the pre-Columbian civilizations of the New World did not employ several other basic traits of material and nonmaterial culture either, including the concept of the wheel, the arch, and any form of real writing. To this lack of invention must be added the failure of diffusion. Isolated by oceans, the Andean people, prior to conquest, had no opportunity to learn about the idea of milking from European, African, or Asian peoples.

Moreover, the use of llama or alpaca milk for ritual purposes never emerged in the Andes as it did in the Fertile Crescent, although Inca state religion manifested many associations with flocks in its spiritual rhetoric and sacrificial practices (Brotherston 1989). The elaborate rituals concerned with fertility, curing, and divination that persist today in the high Andes do not involve milk in any way. It was camelid fat – easier to transport and less perishable than milk – that acquired the symbolic role in human needs to communicate with the supernatural forces.

As noted, Andean peoples first learned about milking cows and ewes from the Spaniards. It is puzzling, however, that after the introduction of milking, the practice was not subsequently extended to llamas and alpacas, particularly in zones above 4,200 m where they had no competition and where a kind of transhumance has prevailed. It is the case that the transfer of the idea of milking from one mammalian species to another has occurred within historic times. In northern Scandinavia, for example, after observing Swedish settlers milk their cows, the Lapps started to milk the domesticated mammal under their control, the reindeer. But although milking a lactating llama or alpaca might well have been tried on occasion over the past half millennium, it was not a practice that emerged as a use pattern or one that disseminated elsewhere. If milking these animals had been anything more than episodic, it would have been recorded in some travelers' accounts and eventually in the ethnographic record.

Llamas and Alpacas as Future Dairy Animals

The milk of the Andean camelids has received little research attention. One study in Peru, which derived 256 milk samples from 71 different lactating alpacas, found that yields in a 12-hour period varied widely from only 15 to 20 cubic centimeters (cc) of milk in some to as much as 500 cc in others, with 300 cc as a rough average (Moro 1954). Butterfat content was found to be between 3 and 4 percent and the pH ranged from 6.4 to 6.8. Porcelain white in color and with no distinctive odor, the alpaca milk examined in this study was somewhat sweeter and more viscous than cows' milk. These organoleptic characteristics contrast with the unusual flavor and salty taste reported for the milk of an Old World camelid, the dromedary, whose milk is nevertheless much appreciated in parts of the Middle East. More detailed biochemical data on camelid milk puts lipid content at 4.716 plus or minus 1.307 percent (Fernandez and Oliver 1988: 301). Development of either the llama or alpaca as a dairy animal would first entail the considerable work of selecting and breeding animals for higher milk yields.

Wider commercialization of the llama or alpaca as a source of food deserves consideration. They have potential as meat animals because their growth is fast: 9 kg at birth, they can weigh 29 kg at 9 months and 54 kg at 3 years (Bustinza Choque 1984). Carcass yield is reportedly higher than that of sheep or cattle. Although they can thrive on forage that extends well beyond the native Andean puna grasses, any serious herd investment would require better data on feeding requirements. Moreover, the prejudice against both meat and milk from these animals would need to be addressed in order to find profitable ways to market them to the public. North America, which had an estimated 23,000 llamas and alpacas in 1990, is now the center for stock improvement and creative thinking on the considerable potential of these animals. However, both Peru and Bolivia, where the diversity of the llama and alpaca gene pool is greatest, have banned the export of live animals beyond their borders.

Daniel W. Gade

Note

1. One dissenter to the otherwise solid generalization that Andean people do not milk camelids was William E. Carter, a trained anthropologist who died in 1983. Carter (1975) affirmed that llamas were milked, which prompted me to correspond with him about it. In his response dated February 28, 1975, Carter wrote, "I have on numerous occasion seen people making cheese out of llama milk and even eaten it. . . . Not much milk is obtained, of course, nor does the milking occur on a regular basis, but milking of the animal is done." Carter, however, did not state the place or places where he purportedly saw this llama cheese, or if he actually watched those llamas being milked. Could these have been accidental cases of

milk fortuitously salvaged from a lactating female that had just lost her young? None of the scholars who has intensively studied llamas or alpacas in their contemporary Andean setting alluded to them as even occasional sources of milk to their human owners (Flores Ochoa 1968; Webster 1973; Orlove 1977; Flannery et al. 1989).

William Walton (1811: 36), one of the earliest serious non-Spanish observers of llamas, stated that "her milk is scanty, and is never used by the Indians for any purpose, they prefer leaving it to the 'llamitos' which are not weaned before the age of six months."

Bibliography

Brotherston, Gordon. 1989. Andean pastoralism and Inca ideology. In *The walking larder,* ed. J. Clutton-Brock, 240-55. Boston.

Browman, David L. 1974. Pastoral nomadism in the Andes. *Current Anthropology* 15: 188-96.

1989. Origins and development of Andean pastoralism: An overview of the past 6,000 years. In *The walking larder,* ed. J. Clutton-Brock, 256-68. Boston.

Bustinza Choque, A. Victor. 1984. The Camelidae of South America. In *The camelid: An all-purpose animal,* 2 vols., ed. W. Ross Cockrill, 112-43. Uppsala, Sweden.

Calderón-Viacava, L., A. Cazorla-Talleri, and R. León-Barua. 1971. Incidencia de malabsorción de lactosa en jovenes Peruanos sanos. *Acta Gastroentereologica Latinamericana* 3: 11.

Calle Escobar, Rigoberto. 1984. *Animal breeding and production of American camelids.* Lima.

Cardozo, G. Armando. 1954. *Los auqenidos.* La Paz.

Carter, William E. 1975. *Bolivia: A profile.* New York.

Cobo, Bernabe. [1890-93] 1956. *Historia del nuevo mundo.* 2 vols. Madrid.

Fernandez, F. M., and G. Oliver. 1988. Proteins present in llama milk. I. Quantitative aspects and general characteristics. *Milchwissenschaft* 43: 299-302.

Figueroa, Rolando B., E. Melgar, N. Jo, and O. L. Garcia. 1971. Intestinal lactase deficiency in an apparently normal Peruvian population. *American Journal of Digestive Diseases* 16: 881-9.

Flannery, Kent V., Joyce Marcus, and Robert G. Reynolds. 1989. *The flocks of the Wamani: A study of llama herders on the punas of Ayacucho, Peru.* San Diego.

Flores Ochoa, Jorge A. 1968. *Los pastores de Paratia.* Mexico City.

Gade, Daniel W. 1969. The llama, alpaca and vicuna: Fact vs. fiction. *Journal of Geography* 68: 339-43.

Hahn, Eduard. 1896. *Die Haustiere und ihre Beziehungen zur Wirtschaft des Menschen.* Leipzig.

Miller, George R. 1977. Sacrificio y benéfico de camelidos en el sur del Peru. In *Pastores de puna: Uywamichiq puna-runakuna,* ed. Jorge Flores Ochoa, 193-210. Lima.

Moro, S. Manuel. 1952-6. Contribución al estudio de la leche de las alpacas. *Revista de la Facultad de Medicina Veterinaria* 7-11: 117-41.

Novoa, C., and Jane C. Wheeler. 1984. Lama and alpaca. In *Evolution of domesticated animals,* ed. Ian L. Mason, 116-28. New York.

Orlove, Benjamin. 1977. *Alpacas, sheep, and men.* New York.

Sauer, Carl O. 1952. *Agricultural origins and dispersals.* New York.

Simoons, Frederick J. 1973. New light on ethnic differences in adult lactose intolerance. *American Journal of Digestive Diseases* 18: 596-611.

Sumar, Julio. 1988. Present and potential role of South American camelids in the high Andes. *Outlook on Agriculture* 17: 23-9.

Von Tschudi, J. J. 1848. *Travels in Peru during the years 1838-1842.* New York.

Walton, William. 1811. *An historical and descriptive account of the four species of Peruvian sheep called "carneros de la tierra."* London.

Webster, Steven. 1973. Pastoralism in the South Andes. *Ethnology* 2: 115-34.

Wing, Elizabeth. 1975. Hunting and herding in the Peruvian Andes. In *Archaeozoological studies,* ed. A. T. Clason, 302-8. Amsterdam.

II.G.17   Muscovy Ducks

Of the two species of domesticated anatines, the Muscovy duck *(Cairina moschata)* is larger, less vocal, and characterized by a fleshy protuberance on the head of the male. It is a duck of tropical American origin, whose wild ancestors nested in trees, whereas the common duck *(Anas platyrhynchos)* was domesticated in the Old World from the ground-dwelling mallard. The two species can mate and produce offspring, but such offspring cannot reproduce.

The Muscovy duck is misnamed, for it never had any special association with Moscow. Most likely the name is the result of a garbled corruption of *canard musqué* ("musk duck"); however, this French term is not an accurate descriptor either. Depending on area, various Spanish names are used for the duck in Latin America. Among these are *pato criollo* ("native duck"), *pato real* ("royal duck"), *pato almisclado* ("musk duck"), *pato machacón* ("insistent duck"), and *pato perulero* ("Peru duck"). In Brazilian Portuguese, it is most commonly called *pato do mato* ("forest duck"). Indigenous names for this bird indicate its New World origin, including *ñuñuma* in Quechua, *sumne* in Chibcha, and *tlalalacatl* in the Nahuatl language of Mexico.

Before the European conquest of the Americas, the bird's apparent distribution extended from north central Mexico to the Rio de la Plata in Argentina (Donkin 1989). It was and still is kept in a wide range of environments, which include the islands of the Caribbean, deserts, humid tropics, temperate plains, and the high elevations of the Andes. Although several colonial chronicles refer to *C. moschata,* such sources do not indicate that these domesticated birds were particularly important to household economies. In Mexico, the turkey has had greater importance in the houseyard. In South America, the Muscovy had no poultry competitors until the Spaniards and Portuguese brought chickens, which – because of their greater egg-laying capacity – were widely adopted.

Precisely how, where, and why the Muscovy duck was domesticated is impossible to say. Two scenarios can be constructed from knowledge of the wild species. One is that the wild duck was trapped – captured alive in fields of crops that it was feeding on. After this it was tamed and began to reproduce in captivity. Alternatively, humans removed fertilized eggs from the nesting holes of wild birds and incubated them until they hatched. The ducklings, which emerge from the egg in 30 days, then imprinted on humans as their surrogate parents. Because the behavioral characteristics of wild Muscovies draw them into ready association with people, their taming and eventual domestication could have been quite common (Nogueira-Neto 1973).

The habitat preference of wild Muscovies, which roost in trees and nest in tree holes, is near rivers and swamps backed by forests. The Caribbean lowlands of Colombia and Panama offer such habitats and today contain wild Muscovies. Yet the just mentioned behavioral characteristics that draw them into association with people make plausible the suggestion that they were domesticated from the wild in several different South and Central American locales as well as the Caribbean lowlands (Nogueira-Neto 1973).

Archaeological evidence charting the past of the Muscovy duck has been derived from bones and from artistic renderings. Osteological material dated as early as 500 B.C. comes from the coastal region of Ecuador. Close by, in northern Peru, potters of the Mochica culture (A.D. 200–700) modeled the Muscovy duck in clay. Abundant zoomorphic evidence of the Muscovy is also found on pottery vessels, gold objects, and stylized masks from pre-Columbian Mexico (Whitley 1973). In view of the latter, a religious role for the bird might be postulated.

Although the domesticated duck has the same species binomial as its wary wild cousin, certain features distinguish *Cairina moschata domestica* from the wild *C. moschata*. Many domesticated Muscovies, for example, have predominantly white plumage – a partial albinism resulting from artificial selection of a sort found in many other domesticated animals. However, feather colors and plumage patterns can vary widely and often resemble those of the wild bird. Truly domesticated birds are unable to fly; artificial selection has reduced their wings to weak appendages. Moreover, the domesticated duck can survive without access to water for swimming or feeding.

Three characteristics of the domesticated drake are his size (more than twice as large as the female), his hisslike vocalization, and his polygamous appetite for constant copulation. In the sixteenth and seventeenth centuries, the odor of musk was also said to characterize this bird, but it is still not clear if such an opinion derived from a distinctive smell of the species, a secondary sexual characteristic of the adult drake, or a dietary element that imparted a peculiar odor to the birds.

In tropical America, Muscovy ducks have been kept for their meat, their fat, and – to a much lesser degree – their eggs. However, they are slaughtered mainly for special occasions, and except where they are kept in large numbers, their role as a food source is peripheral. Indeed, in most parts of tropical America, they do not seem to have a well-defined place in regional cooking, although live birds and their eggs may be sold in some peasant markets. In times of food surpluses, they can be fed and kept alive as a kind of "bank" to be cashed in when they are sold or traded at peasant markets. Normally, it is at lower elevations that farmers raise Muscovies in sizable flocks; in the high Andes, small farmers may keep only two or three.

Raymond Gilmore (1963: 462) has referred to the production of an aromatic powder made from dried duck meat, which counts as another use, as does the large number of insects that Muscovies eat, which extends their usefulness beyond that of a food source. But most of the food Muscovies eat is from plant sources, and thus they are also employed to help keep irrigation ditches clean. On the desert coast of Peru, they are often seen in such ditches – a niche that may have made them initially useful to pre-Columbian irrigation farmers.

In the sixteenth century, the bird was taken to Europe, where its historic pathway of diffusion became confused in the written record, which often did not make the necessary distinction between the imported Muscovy and the common duck already present. In German-speaking Europe, the Muscovy became known as the *Türkische Ente* ("Turkish duck") and, in French, as *canard de Barbarie* (i.e., from the Barbary coast of North Africa). Both these names obviously suggest that the New World origin of the bird was not well understood in Europe at the time. The eighteenth century seems to have marked the high point of popularity of the Muscovy, which, in many cases, was raised by the rural gentry mainly as a curiosity and as an ornament, just as they did with peacocks.

In France, where a restless revision of the culinary imagination has a glorious history, the bird became a meat animal, and it was the French who crossed the Muscovy with the common duck to produce the *mulard* duck. This vigorous duck hybrid has been force-fed grain to produce hypertrophied livers used in making pâté de foie gras. Especially in southwestern France, farms specializing in the production of this delicacy keep both geese and *mulard* ducks.

Elsewhere in the world where they were eventually introduced, Muscovies never acquired much importance in domestic economy. Possible exceptions to this generalization are parts of West Africa, because the tropical origins of Muscovy ducks made them better adapted to hot conditions than other poultry. In Asia, where duck husbandry is important in furnishing sources of animal protein, this relative from the New World has found no real acceptance. Muscovies are an uncommon species in China, which has more ducks than any other country. Failure of the Muscovy to compete is tied in part to its lower productivity, in terms both of egg laying and body size. In addition, it does not fare as well in cold climates as the common duck. In fact, these are the reasons that commercial duck raisers in North America do not use this species. Placed on a world scale, *C. moschata domestica* has been among the less successful domesticated birds.

Daniel W. Gade

Bibliography

Donkin, R. A. 1989. *The Muscovy duck, Cairina moschata domestica: Origins, dispersal and associated aspects of the geography of domestication.* Rotterdam/Brookfield, Vt.

Gilmore, Raymond M. 1963. Fauna and ethnozoology of South America. In *Handbook of South American Indians,* ed. J. H. Steward, 345–464. New York.

Nogueira-Neto, Paulo. 1973. *A criaçao de animais indigenas vertebrados.* São Paulo.

Whitley, G. R. 1973. The Muscovy duck in Mexico. *Anthropological Journal of Canada* 11: 2–8.

II.G.18 ❧ Pigeons

Because humans seem to have had omnivorous ancestors, birds were probably a significant item in the human diet well before historic time. Many kinds of birds can be caught readily, and young adults are generally considered to be superior fare (Cott 1946). Additionally, the eggs of many kinds of birds are highly prized (Cott 1954). In the case of pigeons, the rock pigeon *(Columba livia)* is known to have frequented regions inhabited by our ancestors more than 300,000 years ago (Tchernov 1968).

At present, the domestic chicken *(Gallus domesticus)* and their eggs are extremely important in diets across the globe. Indeed, the husbandry of chickens is economically unequaled by that of any other bird. But the economic and dietary importance of domestic fowl is a relatively recent development and in large part reflects changes brought about by twentieth-century biology.

The domestic fowl, derived from Asian species of the genus *Gallus,* was introduced to the West and became known to people of the Mediterranean Near East only a little more than 2,500 years ago (Wood-Gush 1985). This was perhaps 3,000 years after rock pigeons were domesticated in southwestern Asia (Sossinka 1982) and long after they had become important in human diets. However, because pigeons also figured in early religions of the eastern Mediterranean region, the fact that they were domesticated birds does not explicitly address their use as food. Thus, the dual role pigeons have played in human affairs needs to be distinguished whenever possible.

The family Columbidae is widely distributed (Goodwin 1983). There are some 300 kinds of pigeons known to biologists, and many have been and still are used for food by humans worldwide. The record of dietary use is, however, without detail for most such species, as for example, doves. But it is likely that the flesh of most (although not necessarily their eggs) is suitable for human consumption (Cott 1946, 1954).

Rock Pigeons

The rock pigeon has a history in part coincident with that of humans for at least the past 12,000 years. The earliest information is of two kinds – the organic, subfossil, bony remains of pigeons in midden heaps in caves and the slightly later cultural record of human–pigeon interactions.

Bones from midden heaps, which constitute reasonably direct evidence that humans caught and ate rock pigeons, are present in eastern Mediterranean sites – caves in Israel that were used as dwellings by humans around 11,000 to 12,000 years ago. Because the bones are indistinguishable from those of wild rock pigeons currently living in the Near East (Bar-Yosef and Tchernov 1966), it is possible that immediate post-Pleistocene pigeons might have nested in caves used by humans. And it is also possible that their bones were incorporated into the midden heaps as a result of death by other than human agents. It is considerably more likely, however, that bones in these refuse piles indicate that the pigeons in question served as food for human hunters.

But so long as humans relied on catching wild pigeons – probably squabs from nests – pigeon would have been merely an occasional item of diet. Only after pigeons were domesticated and relegated to a life of confinement in cages did they make a regular appearance on the table. The first such attempts are not recorded, but rock pigeons are readily domesticated (Darwin 1868), and as the following discussion shows, this practice doubtless occurred relatively early.

The earliest evidence of domestication has been found in Sumerian statuary and cuneiform lists; in the remains at a funerary feast in a tomb at Saqqara, Egypt; in Sumerian culture, which includes a version of the Mesopotamian Flood Myth featuring a pigeon; and in small clay religious shrines as well as on sculptures depicting fertility goddesses, Astarte or Ishtar. Slightly later, there are Egyptian bird sacrifices on record and a Babylonian scribal list of bird names in cuneiform. We will briefly explore this evidence, beginning with that which dates from earliest times.

The Sumerian Flood Myth can be dated from a massive flood that occurred about 6,000 years ago (Langdon 1931). In the myth, a "dove" was the first bird released from the still floating Ark, and it returned for the night, signifying no available dry land.

The early Egyptian material includes traces of pigeon bones from a funeral dinner apparently held some 6,000 years ago (Hansell and Hansell 1992). This is the first, and very dim, indication of what may have been domestic pigeons playing a role in human diets.

Sumerian clay shrines, dating from some 4,500 years ago, depict pigeons that were evidently of religious importance. There are also fertility figures from the same period that have pigeons perched on their uplifted arms (Langdon 1931). Quite possibly, the significance of the pigeons in this instance has to do with their unusual reproductive capabilities (the ability of captives to lay eggs and rear young in midwinter).

Around 4,000 years ago it was recorded that the Egyptian King Rameses II offered 58,810 pigeons to the god Ammon, at Thebes (Hansell and Hansell 1992). The large number of birds involved can only mean that Egyptians were practicing pigeon husbandry at that time, for there is no way in which wild rock pigeons could have been rounded up in such numbers.

An Old Babylonian cuneiform tablet dated from 3,830 to 3,813 years ago contains 70 Akkadian bird names in more or less taxonomic groups (Black and Al-Rawi 1987), and no fewer than 3 of the names refer to pigeons, one of which almost certainly applied to the rock pigeon.

A considerable summary of such ancient records treating pigeons as sacred or at least of religious importance may be found in the opening pages of W. Levi (1974). Unfortunately, little of the archaic information provides a positive identity for the early species of domesticated pigeon. Most likely, however, rock pigeons and at least one other species, probably a kind of turtledove, were involved. In addition, of the species of pigeons (and doves) still present in the Near East, the rock pigeon, wood pigeon *(Columba palumbus)*, stock dove *(Columba oenas)*, and turtledove *(Streptopelia turtur)* were surely used as food and may be among the birds represented on the clay shrines and in the lists just discussed.

Rock pigeons have been common, year-round residents in the Near East. They have extremely long breeding seasons, nesting semicolonially in caves and on ledges of coastal and montane cliffs, and are thought to have sometimes become synanthropic in early Near Eastern cities (Glutz and Bauer 1980). Their reproductive capabilities of persistent, serial breeding, beginning early and ending late in the year, when no other kinds of birds are active, would have been readily observed and, thus, part of the knowledge of the time. Such knowledge would have been of considerable importance in fostering efforts aimed at holding pigeons as captives.

Fragmentary evidence as well as outright speculation about human behavior suggests that the domestication of rock pigeons took place between 6,000 and 10,000 years ago. This must have occurred after the development of grain farming (around 10,000 years ago), which was the major human cultural acquisition that permitted animal domestication in the Near East (Harlan and Zohary 1966). But although cereal agriculture and early animal domestication originated in the Near East, the wild rock pigeon has a large geographic distribution (Cramp 1985) overlapping early human agriculture in many regions of Europe and Asia (Piggott 1965; Ammermann and Cavalli-Sforza 1971).

Consequently, rock pigeons could easily have been domesticated at many different places and times in southeastern Europe, North Africa, the Near East, and southwestern and southern Asia. Doubtless, another cultural factor that assisted in the domestication of pigeons was the experience gained by humans in domesticating other creatures. Wolves, for example, were domesticated in the Near East at least 9,000 years ago and even earlier elsewhere (Reed 1969).

Pigeon chicks taken at about 2 weeks of age would have been somewhat less wild than their parents and more likely to have accepted captivity. Wild adult pigeons are nervous captives, do not accept cages, and thus sometimes injure themselves; they also spend less time in reproduction than birds accustomed to confinement. In light of this, one suspects that domestication could have occurred in one of two, somewhat different, ways.

The first would have been for hunters to have captured rock pigeon squabs in nesting caves, with the idea of holding them and feeding them in cages until they grew larger. Gradually, however, humans would have learned to continue such captivity until the birds matured and were able to reproduce. A second scenario would have humans erecting nesting platforms in dove caves. This would have turned them into primordial dovecotes, where the birds could have been harvested and where much could have been learned about their reproductive behavior and ecology.

Concurrent with these scenarios, early cities of the Near East may have been voluntarily colonized by wild rock pigeons. The mud and stone walls of such settlements would have made quite suitable nest sites, with nearby fields of wheat and barley providing nutrition. These synanthropic birds could subsequently have been taken into confinement by either of the two ways just mentioned.

Selection of Pigeons for Food

Captive pigeons probably were unconsciously selected by humans for tameness and reproductive vigor, but they would have been consciously selected for characteristics that increased their utility as high-quality food. The major one of these traits to be modified was size. Wild rock pigeons in the Near East are relatively small and average about 300 grams in undressed weight (Cramp 1985). But today, males of large domestic strains are known to reach more than seven times that size (Levi 1974). Thus, the mating of large individuals would readily have repaid any early pigeon keeper.

We have no documentation for such a selection process, but it is clear that it was practiced. By Roman times, for example, a large-bodied domestic strain (usually identified with today's "runt") was already developed (Levi 1974). The runt is preserved in a variety of substrains by pigeon fanciers and commercial squab producers.

At the time that pigeons were developed for the table, smaller dovecote pigeons were probably also being selected. Dovecote pigeons are domestics that are, for the most part, allowed to fly freely in order to obtain their own food; they are also highly site-specific and return daily to the pigeon house or dovecote in which they were reared. Dovecotes are small buildings, usually raised above the ground and providing quarters for roosting and nesting pigeons as well as access for pigeon keepers to harvest the squabs.

Prior to the time that larger mammals were kept overwinter, pigeons were a reliable source of winter protein for rural people (Murton and Westwood 1966). Indeed, well-fed pigeons with a characteristically high fat content in muscle would have been important to such diets (Barton and Houston 1993). Pigeons have continued to be used for food up to the present time, although recent practice emphasizes the gourmet table rather than the farm kitchen (Levi 1974). As already mentioned, the current dominance of domestic fowl in human diets is a reflection not of its superior quality as a source of animal protein but of its greater adaptability to human poultry husbandry, which guarantees producers large returns on their work or investment.

Pigeon Husbandry in Europe and America

In earlier times, once a pigeon house was constructed, pigeons were easy to keep, at least at low to mid latitudes. The birds of a columbarium fed themselves on wild seeds and waste agricultural grains, and if their food was supplemented in winter, a large number – thousands of pairs – could be maintained throughout the year.

It is not clear at what time pigeon husbandry on such a large scale was found in Europe, but substantial columbariums were in operation in medieval times. Of the ones that are documented, some, such as those set up by thirteenth-century emperor Frederick II, were reasonably elaborate. The emperor's holdings covered southern Italy and eastern Sicily, which were dotted with more than a dozen of his castles.

Frederick moved from one to another of these castles in the course of a year, because the large size of his court regularly required a fresh supply of food. Frequent moves also provided time at any one castle for the satisfactory recycling of wastes in between visits. Each castle had a large dovecote, built within and sharing some of the castle walls, which the court relied on for a significant fraction of its fresh meat (Frederick II 1942). We know these details of the emperor's life because he was an ornithologist as well as a builder of castles. He left behind his writings on birds and the remains of his buildings, which clearly show that the columbarium was an integral part of the castles he designed.

While in Syria, where he was otherwise engaged on a Crusade, Frederick was able to secure novel domestic strains of pigeons. Birds from the Near East may not have been bred for table use, owing to religious practices of the Syrians, but the record is important to us because it suggests widespread pigeon husbandry at that time.

In post-Renaissance Europe, pigeon keeping was, to some extent, restricted to the privileged classes of society – to manor house lords and members of the clergy (Cooke 1920). Many large flocks were maintained, and recent estimates of numbers of dovecote pigeons in England and France in the sixteenth century run to the millions (Cooke 1920; Murton and Westwood 1966). As noted earlier, dovecote birds generally foraged for themselves in the agricultural countryside, going distances of perhaps 20 to 30 kilometers (Ragionieri, Mongini, and Baldaccini 1991).

As a consequence, peasant farmers on the estates and beyond sometimes had serious problems in getting their grains and pulses to sprout because of pigeon depredations. Maturing and ripe grain was also at risk, as was stored grain, for pigeons entered storage sheds if these were not secure. To compound the problem, farmers were prohibited from killing the birds. Indeed, some political historians have suggested that the victimization of farmers by the operation of aristocratic dovecotes contributed to the rebellion against social privilege culminating in the French Revolution of 1789 (Cooke 1920).

Whether true or not, such a sequestering of rights to rear pigeons by the privileged classes of medieval and post-Renaissance Europe speaks loudly of the significance of pigeons in the diet of people of preindustrial Europe and Asia. The birds were especially important in adding fresh protein to wintertime diets for those living at high latitudes or away from seacoasts, or anywhere that cattle could not regularly be overwintered. It is likely that chickens also provided such protein in the cold months (as well as at other times of the year), but chicken reproduction dropped off considerably in winter. Thus, wintertime diets that featured chicken depended on mature birds, in contrast to the use of pigeon squabs, which appeared regularly throughout the year.

Current Pigeon Husbandry

The current architecture of pigeon houses in the Middle East, Mediterranean Europe, and North Africa may be little changed from earlier times, and rural Egyptians still build tall, earthen dovecotes – towers of mud into which clay pots have been placed for pigeons to nest in (Hollander 1959; Hafner 1993). By contrast, rural or small-town Italians use metal screening and planks of wood, usually keeping the birds in a flypen arrangement. But however pigeons are kept, adult birds of less than 7 years of age are employed as breeders, and their squabs are taken for the table at about 30 days of age (Levi 1974). The adults tend to overlap their broods, so that when well fed and fully confined, they may produce 12 to 18 squabs per year (Burley 1980; Johnson and Johnston 1989). Thus, even a small colony of 10 pairs could provide a family with squabs for the table each week.

Dovecote pigeonry in the Americas was introduced by settlers from England, France, and Germany to early seventeenth-century Nova Scotia and Virginia (Schorger 1952). Pigeons for the table (as distinct from racing or show purposes) are kept in much the same fashion today as in earlier times. The major difference is that the pigeon house in America is generally a single-story building that is spread out over a very large area relative to those of historic Europe and Asia, which tended to be columnar (Cooke 1920; Hansell and Hansell 1992).

Because a dovecote or columbarium consists of a large number of boxes, cells, or breeding enclosures in which a pair of birds can build a nest and rear young, a western European columnar columbarium facilitates the work of cleaning up by concentrating the birds' droppings. In contrast, a ranch-style unit of pigeon houses, such as in North America, allows increased time intervals in such housekeeping. The houses are usually of wooden frame construction on a concrete pad; a center aisle allows entry by keepers to the nest boxes for feeding and housekeeping, as well as for keeping track of nests and eggs, marking squabs, and, ultimately, collecting them.

The birds may be confined, which means they live partly in a roofed nest-box enclosure and partly in a screened flypen, open to the elements. The classical dovecote operation was employed until relatively recently, even in commercial establishments (Levi 1974), but it is now found chiefly on single-family farms.

Use as Food

Squabs prepared for the table are about as large as small chickens, but their distribution of edible flesh is different. In contrast to chickens, pigeons are strong-flying birds, and perhaps 30 percent of a squab's overall weight, and 70 percent of the muscular weight, will be in the paired pectorales or flight muscles. Pigeons, although also adept at running and walking, have leg muscles that are proportionally smaller than those of chickens.

Pigeons appear in the world's first cookbook, which is attributed to Apicius, a first-century Roman, but is thought to have originally been a collection of Greek monographs on cookery by several authors (Vehling 1936). If we judge only by the frequency of its pigeon recipes, which number 2 against 18 for chicken, then it would seem that the ascendancy of the latter in human diets was already marked in Mediterranean Europe by the first century. However, since all the chicken recipes could be as readily done with pigeon, it may be that the authors were offering us their own preferences (an author's prerogative) rather than indicating the relative availability of the two sorts of birds. The recipes for pigeon are ones dominated by raisins, honey, and dates, suggesting that perhaps the more pronounced flavor of pigeon is better able than chicken to emerge from such sugary dishes.

In any event, today pigeons are regularly prepared for the table in the same manner as domestic fowls, but because of the more assertive flavor of pigeons, stronger spicing may be used if desired. Pigeon breast muscles are "dark meat," so that a significant fraction of current recipes employ plenty of garlic, and those using wines specify full-bodied reds, or sherries and other fortified wines.

Pigeons Other Than Rock Pigeons

Domesticated rock pigeons are the most important food species of the 300 kinds of pigeons in the world. Only one other, the ringed turtledove *(Streptopelia risoria)*, has been domesticated, but it is smaller than the rock pigeon and not of general significance for human diets. A large number of other kinds of pigeons of variable sizes are also used on occasion for food by humans. Many of these are secured by hunters using guns or nets, such as the North American mourning dove *(Zenaida macroura)*, the European wood pigeon *(C. palumbus)*, and many other Asiatic, African, South American, and Australian species.

Such hunting may be regulated by government restrictions, so that a yearly harvest occurs each autumn when the birds are in fairly dense migratory flocks. But hunting may also be restricted to autumn for economic reasons, as this is frequently the only time in which it is profitable to secure the birds. A notable example is the famous netting operations in the valleys of the Pyrenees between France and Spain – valleys used by a large fraction of European wood pigeons in migration.

Unfortunately, the passenger pigeons *(Ectopistes migratorius)* of North America were hunted at any time of year and became extinct around 1900, although it should be noted that the cutting of the North American hardwood forest, which destroyed a significant food source and was the chief habitat of the birds, was an equally important factor (Bucher 1992). Nonetheless, it is fair to say that pigeons and their relatives comprise a group inordinately disposed toward extinction at the hands of human hunters. No fewer than 15 species have been exterminated in historic time, including such remarkable birds as the dodo *(Raphus cucullatus)* and the solitaire *(Pezophaps solitaria)*, as well as the passenger pigeon. In all instances it is clear that the birds were used for food by humans, but it is a fact that habitat destruction and the introduction of cats, dogs, and rats also contributed to such extinctions, most of which occurred on islands.

Richard F. Johnston

Bibliography

Ammermann, A., and L. Cavalli-Sforza. 1971. Measuring the rate of spread of early farming in Europe. *Man* 6: 674–88.

Barton, N. W. H., and D. C. Houston. 1993. A comparison of digestive efficiency in birds of prey. *Ibis* 135: 363–71.

Bar-Yosef, O., and E. Tchernov. 1966. Archaeological finds and the fossil faunas of the Natufian and Microlithic industries of the Hyonim Cave (Western Galilee, Israel). *Israel Journal of Zoology* 15: 104–40.

Black, J. A., and F. N. H. Al-Rawi. 1987. A contribution to the study of Akkadian bird names. *Zeitschrift für Assyriologie und Vorderasiatische Archäologie* 77: 117–26.

Bucher, E. H. 1992. The causes of extinction of the passenger pigeon. *Current Ornithology* 9: 1–36.

Burley, N. 1980. Clutch overlap and clutch size: Alternative and complementary tactics. *American Naturalist* 115: 223–46.

Cooke, A. 1920. *A book of dovecotes.* London.

Cott, H. B. 1946. The edibility of birds. *Proceedings of the Zoological Society of London* 116: 371–524.

   1954. The palatability of the eggs of birds. *Proceedings of the Zoological Society of London* 124: 335–463.

Cramp, S. 1985, ed. *Handbook of the birds of Europe, the Middle East and North Africa: The birds of the Western Palearc.* Vol. 4. Oxford.

Darwin, C. 1868. *The variation of animals and plants under domestication.* London.

Frederick II. [1250] 1942. *The art of falconry,* trans. C. A. Wood and F. M. Fyfe. Stanford.

Glutz von Blotzheim, U. N., and K. M. Bauer. 1980. *Handbuch der Vögel Mitteleuropas,* Vol. 9. Wiesbaden, Germany.

Goodwin, D. 1983. *Pigeons and doves of the world.* Ithaca, N.Y.

Hafner, D. 1993. *A taste of Africa.* Berkeley, Calif.

Hansell, P., and J. Hansell. 1992. *A dovecote heritage.* Bath, England.

Harlan, J., and D. Zohary. 1966. The distribution of wild wheats and barleys. *Science* 153: 1074–80.

Hollander, W. F. 1959. Pigeons in ancient Egypt. *American Pigeon Journal.* August: 254–5.

Johnson, S., and R. Johnston. 1989. A multifactorial study of variation in interclutch interval and annual reproductive success in the feral pigeon, *Columba livia. Oecologia* 80: 87–92.

Langdon, S. 1931. *The mythology of all races. V. Semitic.* Boston.

Levi, W. 1974. *The pigeon.* Sumter, S.C.

Murton, R., and N. Westwood. 1966. The foods of the rock dove and feral pigeon. *Bird Study* 13: 130–46.

Piggott, S. 1965. *Ancient Europe from the beginnings of agriculture to classical antiquity.* Chicago.

Ragionieri, L., E. Mongini, and E. Baldaccini. 1991. Problemi di conservazione in una popolazione di colombo sylvatico (*Columba livia livia* Gmelin) della Sardegna. In *Atti del convegno genetica e conservazione della fauna,* ed. E. Randi and M. Spagnesi, 35–46. *Supplemento alle Ricerche Biologia della Selvaggina* 18: 1–248.

Reed, C. A. 1969. Patterns of animal domestication in the prehistoric Near East. In *The domestication and exploitation of plants and animals,* ed. P. J. Ucko and G. W. Dimbleby, 361–80. London.

Schorger, A. W. 1952. Introduction of the domestic pigeon. *Auk* 69: 462–3.

Sossinka, R. 1982. Domestication in birds. *Avian Biology* 6: 373–403.

Tchernov, E. 1968. Preliminary investigation of the birds in the Pleistocene deposits of 'Ubeidiya. *Publications of the Israel Academy of Sciences and Humanities,* 1–45.

Vehling, J. D. 1936. *Apicius cookery and dining in imperial Rome.* Chicago.

Wood-Gush, D. G. M. 1985. Domestication. In *A dictionary of birds,* ed. B. Campbell and E. Lack, 152–4. Vermillion, S. Dak.

II.G.19 ❧ Rabbits

Rabbit production is significant in several countries, especially France, Italy, Malta, and Spain, where there is a long tradition of consuming rabbit meat. In the past, great numbers of rabbits were raised by subsistence farmers, who fed them locally collected forages such as weeds, grasses, and vegetable by-products. But with the intensification of agriculture, particularly in the twentieth century, and the decline in "peasant farmers," rabbit production as a cottage industry declined. However, because the tradition of eating rabbit meat endured in western European countries, an intensive, commercial, industrial-scale production of rabbits has developed to meet continuing demand.

Both the origins and the evolution of the domestic rabbit are difficult to trace. Rabbits are in the order Lagomorpha, which dates back about 45 million years in the fossil record to the late Eocene period. Modern lagomorphs (rabbits and hares) belong to two families (Leporidae and Ochotonidae) consisting of 12 genera. They range from the highly successful hares and rabbits of the *Lepus, Oryctolagus,* and *Sylvilagus* genera to several endangered genera and species. Although rabbits and hares appear to have originated in Asia, all breeds of domestic rabbits are descendants of the European wild rabbit *(Oryctolagus cuniculus)* and are Mediterranean in origin. There are more than 100 breeds of domestic rabbits, ranging in size from dwarf breeds with an adult weight of less than 1 kilogram (kg) to giant breeds weighing in excess of 10 kg.

The first recorded rabbit husbandry has been dated to early Roman times, when rabbits were kept in *leporia,* or walled rabbit gardens. They reproduced in these enclosures and were periodically captured and butchered. During the Middle Ages, rabbits were similarly kept in rock enclosures in Britain and western Europe. True domestication, which is believed to have

Rabbit

taken place in the Iberian Peninsula, probably began in the sixteenth century in monasteries. By 1700, several distinct colors had been selected. There are now many different coat colors (for example, agouti, tan, brown, white, blue, black, and red) and coat types (such as angora, normal, rex, satin, and waved), which provide for great diversity in the color and texture of the fur. (The coat-color genetics of rabbits have been reviewed comprehensively by McNitt et al. 1996.)

Domestic rabbits are now raised in virtually all countries, although, in some notable instances, feral rabbits have become major pests. Beginning in the Middle Ages, sailors introduced these animals into islands along various sea lanes – to be used as a source of food – and wherever rabbits were released, they increased greatly in number at the expense of indigenous plants and animals. In 1859, a single pair of European wild rabbits was taken to Australia, and within 30 years, these had given rise to an estimated 20 million rabbits. Feral rabbits also became a serious problem in New Zealand, which (like Australia) offered a favorable environment, abundant feed, and an absence of predators.

Periods of peak interest in rabbit production have coincided with times of economic hardship or food scarcity, both of which have encouraged people to produce some of their own food. In the United States and Europe, such periods during the twentieth century have included the Great Depression of the 1930s and World War II. A few rabbits kept in the backyard and fed weeds, grass, and other vegetation can provide a family with much inexpensive meat, and keeping them is practically trouble-free. Not only do they eat homegrown feeds, rabbits do not make noise and are easily housed in small hutches. When economic times improve, however, the interest in home production of food wanes, and those who ate rabbit meat under conditions of deprivation tend during better times to regard it as a "poor people's food."

Rabbits have a number of biological advantages when raised for meat production (Cheeke 1986, 1987). They experience rapid growth, reaching market weight at 8 to 10 weeks following birth. Their rate of reproduction is high: Theoretically, with immediate postpartum breeding, females (called does) can produce as many as 11 litters per year. And, as already noted, rabbits can be raised on fibrous feedstuffs, forages, and grain-milling by-products (such as wheat bran) and thus do not require high-quality feed grains.

Rabbit meat is a wholesome, tasty product. Compared to other common meats, it is high in protein and low in fat calories, cholesterol, and sodium (Table II.G.19.1) – properties that are related to the animals' low-energy, high-fiber diets. Because they are not fed much in the way of grain, rabbits do not have excess energy (calories) to store as body fat.

Total world production of rabbit meat is estimated to be about 1 million tonnes per annum (Lukefahr and Cheeke 1991). On a per capita basis, the major

Table II.G.19.1. *Nutrient composition of rabbit meat*

Nutrient	Amount of nutrient
Crude protein (%)	18.5[a]
Fat (%)	7.4[a]
Water (%)	71[a]
Ash (%)	0.64[a]
Unsaturated fatty acids (% of total fatty acids)	63
Cholesterol (mg/100 g)	136[b]
Minerals[b]	
Zinc (mg/kg)	54
Sodium (mg/kg)	393
Potassium (g/kg)	2
Calcium (mg/kg)	130
Magnesium (mg/kg)	145
Iron (mg/kg)	29
Vitamins[b]	
Thiamine (mg/100 g)	0.11
Riboflavin (mg/100 g)	0.37
Niacin (mg/kg)	21.2
Pyridoxine (mg/kg)	0.27
Pantothenic acid (mg/kg)	0.10
Vitamin B_{12} (μg/kg)	14.9
Folic acid (μg/kg)	40.6
Biotin (μg/kg)	2.8
Amino acids[c]	
Leucine	8.6
Lysine	8.7
Histidine	2.4
Arginine	4.8
Threonine	5.1
Valine	4.6
Methionine	2.6
Isoleucine	4.0
Phenylalanine	3.2

[a]Wet weight basis.

[b]Dry weight basis.

[c]Amino acids expressed as percentage of protein.

Source: Adapted from McNitt et al. (1996).

rabbit-consuming nations are those already mentioned as leading producing countries – Malta, France, Italy, and Spain – where rabbit has traditionally been an important meat. But in spite of many attempts to develop rabbit production and consumption in other areas, such efforts have largely been unsuccessful, which is especially unfortunate in developing countries, where consumption of good-quality protein is generally low. Moreover, the diet that rabbits consume in no way places them in competition with humans for food. They can be raised in simple structures, and the carcass size is small, so that meat storage with refrigeration is unnecessary.

Nonetheless, despite numerous rabbit development programs in Africa, Asia, and Latin America, there are few if any examples of permanent success following their introduction into local farming systems, with a number of factors accounting for this lack of success. Rabbits are quite susceptible to heat stress, so their performance in tropical countries is poor. Their Mediterranean origin has best suited them for hot, arid climates (for example, northern Africa) rather than hot, humid areas (such as equatorial Africa). In addition, because of the tremendous problems with rabbits following their introduction into Australia, many countries are reluctant to promote rabbit production out of fear that they will encounter similar problems. Concern is also often expressed about zoonoses – diseases that might be transmitted from animals to humans. In the case of rabbits, this fear is especially acute because of the disease tularemia, which humans can acquire when handling wild rabbits. In fact, however, tularemia is not a significant hazard with domestic rabbits. Finally, there is the usual cultural resistance to a new source of meat. Although there are no religious taboos against eating rabbit meat, there is the common perception that the animals are "cute" or "warm and fuzzy," which initiates an aversion in many people to rabbit consumption.

Another problem with disease has to do with myxomatosis. In Britain as well as in Australia, the hunting of wild rabbits and their sale in butcher shops was formerly widespread. But then, in both countries, the need to control the animals led to the introduction of myxomatosis, which is a devastating viral disease causing grotesque facial lesions and swelling, oral bleeding, and a generally distressing appearance. The sight of large numbers of wild rabbits dying with these symptoms hardly whets the appetite for rabbit meat, and needless to say, the traditional marketing and consumption of this meat in countries where myxomatosis was introduced has fallen drastically.

The principal U.S. market for rabbit meat is gourmet restaurants, where it is served as a traditional French specialty. In addition, ethnic markets patronized by European immigrants of French and Italian origin also are significant in large metropolitan areas, especially on the East and West coasts.

By way of conclusion, rabbit production is significant in several Mediterranean countries, where the domestic rabbit originated and was particularly well suited for small-scale production on subsistence or peasant farms. Even in these countries, however, with the introduction of fast-food restaurants and more American-style eating, there is a definite trend of decreasing rabbit consumption, especially among young people, suggesting that the importance of the rabbit as a meat animal will continue to decline. In the United States, strong interest in animal rights and vegetarianism among young people probably means that backyard rabbit production, with home slaughter of the animals, is unlikely to have much appeal. A small rabbit industry, with the production of meat for specialty or gourmet restaurants, is likely the main future of rabbit production in most countries.

Peter R. Cheeke

Bibliography

Cheeke, P. R. 1986. Potentials of rabbit production in tropical and subtropical agricultural systems. *Journal of Animal Science* 63: 1581–6.

1987. *Rabbit feeding and nutrition.* San Diego, Calif.

Lukefahr, S. D., and P. R. Cheeke. 1991. Rabbit project development strategies in subsistence farming systems. *World Review of Animal Production* 68: 60–70.

McNitt, J. I., N. M. Patton, S. D. Lukefahr, and P. R. Cheeke. 1996. *Rabbit production.* Danville, Ill.

II.G.20 ∾ Sea Turtles and Their Eggs

From earliest times the seashore, with its rich and diverse marine fauna, has been a uniquely attractive environment for humans, providing them with accessible, palatable, and protein-rich sustenance (Sauer 1962). Among other foods – at least in warmer seas of tropical latitudes – were giant marine turtles. These could be harvested with relative ease, either on the beaches while nesting or netted or harpooned offshore. Their soft-shell and Ping-Pong-Ball-like eggs, deposited in clutches of 100 or more in the warm sand of favored beaches, provided further nutritious fare.

Among the six or seven species of giant marine reptiles that are recognized, it is the green turtle, the *Chelonia mydas* of turtle-soup fame, that has contributed most to the human diet. Unlike other sea turtles, the greens are exclusively herbivores, thus accounting for the savory quality of their veal-like flesh. Their name derives not from the color of their shell or skin but from the soft, greenish gelatinous material known as calipee, found beneath the plastron (lower shell) and scraped from slaughtered turtles to prepare the thick green soup renowned among gastronomes.

The flesh of other sea turtles, although eaten by some coastal peoples, is generally reputed to have a somewhat uninviting fishy taste. If the animal has ingested toxic algae or crustaceans, it may even be poisonous. The hawksbill (*Eretmochelys imbricata*), prized from antiquity as the source of the beautifully mottled tortoiseshell of commerce, is valued for jewelry and ornamentation, whereas the olive ridley (*Lepidochelys olivacea*) has recently been much sought after for its skin, used to make leather goods. This use has been stimulated by changing styles and a scarcity of crocodile skins. The smaller Kemp's ridley (*Lepidochelys kempii*), the loggerhead (*Caretta caretta*), and the giant leatherback (*Dermochelys coriacea*) have not traditionally been utilized. The eggs of all species are eaten. Egg collection is either an open or a clandestine business on numerous strands throughout the tropical world.

The countless "turtle islands" (such as Islas Tortugas, Iles Tortues, and Schilpad Eilanden) of tropical seas bear witness to the preference of green and other sea turtles for uninhabited offshore islands for nesting as well as to their remarkable fidelity to specific, and sometimes quite small, beaches. They unerringly return to these sites after migrations to feeding areas that may be a thousand or more miles away. Such nesting habits, especially pronounced among the greens and the two ridleys, have made sea turtles particularly vulnerable to human exploitation and lie at the base of their endangered status.

The males spend their entire lives at sea, but the females, once gravid, may make several nocturnal visits to their ancestral beaches during each nesting cycle. These cycles usually come at intervals of four or more years. Scooping out a pit in the sand with their flippers, they bury their one hundred or so eggs before lumbering back to the surf and waiting mates. Two months later, the frenzied hatchlings, not much larger than a silver dollar, emerge to scamper quickly toward the water through a gauntlet of waiting predators. For those that survive, this is the beginning of a long and mysterious migration. As mature adults they will return several years later to the same beach on which they were born. Their imprinting, and the guidance mechanism that allows them, without visible landmarks, to travel the great distances between feeding areas and nesting beaches, remains among nature's grandest enigmas.

Atlantic and Pacific populations, long separated, carry distinctive DNA markers. Moreover, size helps to distinguish the Atlantic turtles from their counterparts on the West Coast of America. The latter constitute the subspecies *Chelonia mydas agassiz,* known locally as *caguama prieta* (black turtle), whose adult members weigh from 65 to 125 kilograms. By contrast, their Atlantic and Indian Ocean counterparts are substantially larger (100 to 200 kilograms), with some from Ascension Island in the past weighing a reported 600 kilograms.

Today, sea turtles are disastrously overexploited by a rapidly expanding world population and are victimized by pollution, coastal development, and new fishing technologies. Worldwide concern for their future has led to the recent imposition of tight controls on sea turtle exploitation by all but traditional fishing folk. In the last few years, all marine turtles save the Australian flatback *(Natator depressus)* have been classified as either "threatened" or "endangered," and traffic in them and products made from them have been largely eliminated through the Convention on International Trade in Endangered Species (CITES), subscribed to by most of the world's nations. With the newly sharpened sensitivity toward conservation, and with trade in turtle products curbed or banned, the days of turtle soup and turtle steaks in the gourmet restaurants of the world's great cities have effectively come to an end.

Old World Cultural Attitudes

Cultural attitudes toward foods, particularly the consumption of animal flesh, may be decisively influenced by religion. Avoidance of sea turtle meat, as with that of the freshwater or land tortoises with which they are often confused, is widespread in South and Southeast Asia (Simoons 1994; Charles Tambiah, personal communication). The eggs are at the same time, much sought after, prized for their presumed health-giving and aphrodisiac properties. Hinduism holds turtles in veneration. Lord Vishnu is said to have taken the form of a sea turtle during one of his reincarnations, raising the world from chaos and conflict. Turtles are thus depicted as bearers of the world and, as such, command respect. Among the devout the meat is not consumed.

In theory, the Islamic faith prohibits eating the meat of reptiles. However, although this is a restriction affecting vast numbers of shore people around the Indian Ocean, it is apparently not operative in North Africa. But, although the Muslim Malay may not eat turtle, the many Chinese living in Singapore and elsewhere in the area have no aversion to it. Turtles offered in urban markets may be taken in nets or harpooned, but turning them over on the beaches is prohibited.

Buddhists, too, avoid turtle flesh, and to gain favor with the deity, they set free turtles that become entangled in their fishing nets. The Burmese are said to consider turtles divine and keep them in tanks on pagoda grounds where they are fed special foods, but this practice may more often involve river turtles. Early Chinese sources refer to freshwater or land tortoises as symbolic of the good and the long life. Only with the conquest of the south in the Han period (206 B.C. to A.D. 220) did sea turtles become generally available. In T'ang times (A.D. 618–907) the green sea turtle and its calipee are recorded as having been a tribute to the royal court paid by the city of Canton (Simoons 1991). In contemporary China, turtles apparently continue to occupy a special niche in folk belief and the apothecary trade. The recent world-record-shattering performances of several female Chinese track-and-field athletes have been attributed to their drinking of turtle blood (*Sports Illustrated,* October 24, 1994).

If there are many cases of abstinence, there are exceptions that test the rule. On Hindu Bali, as among Polynesian and Micronesian groups and converted Christians generally, turtle flesh is especially consumed at festivals and on ceremonial occasions. Pliny long ago wrote of a cave-dwelling people at the entrance to the Red Sea who worshiped the turtle as sacred yet ate its flesh. Among subsistence shore-dwelling communities of the Indian subcontinent and those throughout Southeast Asia on whom religions often rest easily, turtle is still likely to provide a significant and palatable dietary supplement as well as a source of occasional cash income. Pagan coastal peoples in Southeast Asia have generally held sea turtle eggs and flesh in high esteem. Among Australian Aborigines who live close to the sea, the green turtle remains a principal totem.

At the same time, many, and perhaps most, of the turtle beaches of these southern seas support intensive egg-collecting operations under licensing systems controlled by local authorities. These systems are often designed to assure that sufficient quantities of eggs are left to support reproduction of the turtle populations. There were, for example, more than 30 such licensed areas for egg collecting not long ago on the east coast of Malaya. The three Turtle Islands off Sarawak until 1950 consistently yielded harvests of from 1 to 2 million eggs a year, the product of a population of perhaps 10,000 females (Hendrickson 1958). Watchers on each island marked new nests each night with flags, returning in the morning to dig and box the eggs for shipment to Kuching, the Sarawak capital. The proceeds went to charities or the mosques. The killing of sea turtles is prohibited in Sarawak, as in most Southeast Asian countries, but poaching is widespread.

The American Experience

Among Native Americans encountered by the first Europeans in the turtle-rich Caribbean, attention appears to have been focused on the giant reptiles as a source of meat, whereas their eggs were of secondary interest. The green turtle was and still is at the base of the diet of such coastal people as the Miskito of Nicaragua and Honduras, the Baja California tribes, and the Seri of Sonora, all living close to major turtle pasturing grounds. In the West Indies, unfortunately, the large populations of nesting and grazing turtles described by the early chroniclers at Grand Cayman, the Dry Tortugas, and Bermuda were quickly exterminated (Carr 1954). Only at Tortuguero in Costa Rica and on tiny Aves Island off Venezuela do the greens continue to congregate in numbers in the Caribbean.

At least one Carib group in the Lesser Antilles was said not to have eaten sea turtle "for being fearful of taking on the characteristics of that reptile" (Rochefort 1606, 2: 202). Yet eggs were relished. A similar preoccupation with turtle eggs, rather than turtle flesh, was evident for early Indian peoples on the west coast of Mexico and in Brazil. Turtle eggs are smaller than those of poultry but have more fatty yolk. They are often consumed raw. One might speculate, in terms of conservation, whether it is better to take the turtles or their eggs. Had both been subject to unrestrained exploitation, the prospects for the survival of the species would have been bleak much earlier.

The Europeans who first came into contact with the green and hawksbill populations of the Caribbean were not of one accord in their judgment of this fortuitously accessible new resource. The Spanish and Portuguese seemed for the most part uninterested in turtle. Alvise da Cadamosto, the first Portuguese to mention what must have been the green turtle, fed it to his crew in the Cape Verde Islands in 1456 and found it "a good and healthy" food. Fernandez de

Oviedo y Valdez, in his *Historia Natural* of 1526, agreed. But most Spanish and Portuguese chroniclers of the early period ignored the animal or suspected it of being poisonous; it was the later-arriving English who were most outspoken in their praise of the green turtle's virtues (Parsons 1962). Its health-giving qualities were much commented upon by observers of the seventeenth and eighteenth centuries. To John Fryer (1909: 306), writing of East India and Persia in the late seventeenth century, it was "neither fish nor fowl nor good red herring, restoring vigor to the body and giving it a grace and luster as elegant as viper wine does to consumptive persons and worn out prostitutes."

Many an ill-disposed Englishman on Jamaica went to the Cayman Islands during the turtling season to recover his health by feasting on turtle. As a cure for scurvy and relief from the monotony of a hardtack and salt-beef diet, the meat was much prized by explorers, merchantmen, and buccaneers. The great clumsy creatures were abundant, easy to catch, and most important in the tropical heat, able to be kept alive on the decks of ships for weeks. The late Archie Carr (1973) suggested that the green turtle more than any other dietary factor supported the opening up of the Caribbean. It seems to have played a similar role in the Indian Ocean. William Dampier, that rough seaman who, Oliver Goldsmith observed, added more to natural history than half the philosophers who went before him, made repeated and extensive references to sea turtles as a shipboard meat reserve in his *Voyages,* written between 1681 and 1688 (Dampier 1906). In his eyes, the eggs were for natives.

Learning from the Miskito

The coastal Miskito are the world's foremost sea turtle people (Carr 1973; Nietschmann 1973, 1979). The coral cays and shelf off their Nicaraguan home coast are the principal feeding ground for green turtles from the renowned Tortuguero rookery, some 200 miles to the south in Costa Rica. Under subsistence exploitation regulated by local Miskito communities with strong cultural, religious, and economic ties to the species, the population remained stable. But with commercialization, first by Cayman Islanders who had seen the turtles of their own island decimated, and then by other foreign interests, extraction rates became excessive. Yet this coast, between Cape Gracias a Dios and Bluefields, still supports the largest remaining population of greens, and also hawksbills, in the Caribbean. With the recent establishment of the Miskito Coast Protected Area, there is prospect for a return to culturally regulated exploitation after a long period of overuse (Nietschmann 1991).

The Miskito may have taught the English to appreciate turtle. As early as 1633, a trading station had been established among the Miskitos at Cape Gracias a Dios by English adventurers from the Puritan colony at Old Providence Island. From the beginning, relations between natives and traders were amicable, encouraging a sort of symbiotic relationship that was nurtured in part by mutual antagonism toward the Spaniard. The Indians, superb boatmen, had an "eye" for turtles that never ceased to amaze the Europeans. Many an English and Dutch pirate vessel carried at least one Miskito man as a "striker" to harpoon turtle for the mess table. "Their chief employment in their own country," wrote Dampier,

> is to strike fish, turtle, and manatee. . . . for this they are esteemed by all privateers, for one or two of them in a ship will maintain 100 men, so that when we careen our ships we choose commonly places where there is plenty of turtle or manatee for these Miskito men to strike; it is very rare to find privateers without one or more of them. (Dampier 1906, 1: 39)

Caymanian turtlers were working the Miskito shore by at least 1837. From Grand Cayman, turtle boats could reach the cays in three or four days. The turtlers assembled their catch at temporary camps in the cays, carrying them north at the end of the season to be kept in "crawls" until marketed. From 2,000 to 4,000 turtles were taken annually. (A turtle-soup cannery was established in Grand Cayman in 1952 by the Colonial Development Corporation, but it closed after one year.) When, in 1967, this traditional arrangement with the Caymanian turtlers was terminated by the Somoza government and turtling rights were granted to higher bidders, the extraction rate soared to an insupportable 10,000 a year. By 1979, international conservation pressure had forced the Nicaraguan government to shut down the turtle companies and to ban further commercial exploitation (Nietschmann 1993).

Turtle was in as great demand as a slave food in the West Indian colonies in the seventeenth and eighteenth centuries as was salt cod from Newfoundland. But the reptile was also enjoyed by the West Indian white aristocracy. It was considered a special delicacy when eaten fresh. "To eat this animal is the highest perfection," wrote Goldsmith (1825: 164), "instead of bringing the turtle to the epicure, he ought to be transported to the turtle." Janet Schaw, describing her visit to Antigua in the 1770s, wrote:

> I have now seen turtle almost every day, and though I never could eat it at home, am vastly fond of it here, where it is indeed a very different thing. You get nothing but old ones there [London], the "chickens" being unable to stand the voyage; and even these are starved, or at best fed on coarse and improper food. Here they are young, tender, fresh from the water, where they feed as delicately and are as great epicures as those who feed on them. (Schaw 1939: 95)

The special quality of turtle soup was said to be that it did not "cloy." In other words, one could eat almost any quantity without ill effects. Its easily assimilated proteins, without carbohydrate or fat, were pro-claimed to prepare the stomach in superb fashion for what was to come. When banquets started with this soup, the diner was considered best able to enjoy the numerous rich dishes to follow. Goldsmith wrote that turtle "has become a favorite food of those who are desirous of eating a great deal without surfeiting. . . . by the importation of it alone among us, gluttony is freed from one of its greatest restraints" (1825: 674). The soup, flavored with sherry, capsicums, ginger, cloves, and nutmeg, and served piping hot, was considered at its fiery best "when, after having eaten, one is obliged to rest with his mouth wide open, and cool the fevered palate with Madeira or Port" (Simmonds 1883: 366). In 20 years in the West Indies, one doctor professed, he had never heard of an "accident" arising from eating it! It was also held to be an ideal food for convalescents, especially when served in jellied form.

The Dutch, although they partook of it, seem to have been rather indifferent to turtle in the East, perhaps because of their close association with the Malays, who avoided the meat. In the West, the French, while interested, found but a limited supply of green turtle available to them, most of the best turtling grounds being under English control. From the seventeenth-century account of Père Labat, a Dominican monk, it is evident that the animal's merits were not unrecognized. Yet it did not rate so much as a mention in Brillat-Savarin's exhaustive *Physiologie du gout,* written in 1825. For the French, turtle was clearly an English dish.

Spanish Disdain for Turtle

As rivalry between Spain and England intensified, Spanish disdain for what the English considered among the finest of foods heightened. Dampier (1906, 2: 399), describing the turtles found on the Brazilian coast, wrote in 1699:

> neither the Spaniards nor Portuguese lov(e) them; Nay they have a great antipathy against them, and would rather eat a porpoise, tho' our English count the green turtle very extraordinary food. The reason that is commonly given in the West Indies for the Spaniards not caring to eat them is the fear they have lest, being usually foul-bodied, and many of them pox'd (lying as they do so promiscuously with their Negrines and other She-slaves), they should break out loathsomely like lepers; which this sort of food, 'tis said, does much incline men to do, searching the body and driving out any such gross humours.

Richard Walter, writing in 1748 while with Lord George Anson on his voyage around the world, thought it strange, considering the scarcity of provisions on the Pacific coast of Central America,

> that a species of food so very palatable and salubrious as turtle should be proscribed by the Spaniards as unwholesome and little less than

poisonous. Perhaps the strange appearance of this animal may have been the foundation of this ridiculous and superstitious aversion, which is strongly rooted in all of the inhabitants of this coast. (Waltcr 1928: 208)

Of the Indians and Negroes (slaves of the Spaniards) who had been taken as prizes in Peru, Walter noted:

These poor people, being possessed with the prejudices of the country they came from, were astonished at our feeding on turtle and seemed fully persuaded that it would soon destroy us.... it was with great reluctance and very sparingly that they first began to eat it; but the relish improving upon them by degrees, they at last grew extremely fond of it, and preferred it to every other kind of food.... a food more luxurious to the palate than any their haughty Lords and Masters could indulge in. (Walter 1928: 288)

The Spaniards' apparent lack of interest in turtle appears in part a reaction to the close identification of it with the rival and hated English. In his study of Old World food prejudices, Frederick Simoons (1994) has shown the frequency with which particular animals or foods have become identified with particular ethnic, religious, or other groups through the course of history. The tendency to identify peoples with distinctive food habits is only a step from the rejection of foods simply because they are associated with a rival group. Pastoralists' rejection of the pig, an animal closely associated with and symbolic of the settled farmer, is an extreme, but by no means isolated, example of this sort of attitude.

The London Turtle Trade

Although the virtues of turtle had long been familiar to West Indian planters and to men of the sea, its introduction to the tables of London came only in the mid-eighteenth century. The *Gentleman's Magazine* in 1753 and 1754 carried several notices of large sea turtles, brought from Ascension Island and the West Indies, being dressed at public houses in London. One of the turtles was brought by Lord Anson. At the Kings Arms tavern in Pall Mall, the door of the oven had to be taken down to admit the plastron of a 350-pound specimen. "It may be noted," it was observed, "that what is common in the West Indies is a luxury here" (Anon. 1753: 489).

Although these were certainly not the first live green turtles seen in England, they were of sufficient rarity to gain newspaper comment. "Of all the improvements in the modern kitchen," said the *World* in an account of a London banquet at about this time, "there are none that can bear a comparison with the introduction of the turtle" (quoted in *Notes and Queries,* 1884 [6th ser., 9: 114-15]). But Dr. Samuel Johnson, in his *Dictionary* (1775), tersely defined "turtle" as a term "used among sailors and gluttons for a tortoise."

As English demand increased, vessels in the West Indian trade were provided with flat wooden tanks in which live turtles could be deck-loaded. Although they were fed grass and banana leaves on the journey, after arrival at the Leadenhall Street turtle tanks they still had to be fattened before reaching the tables of the well-to-do. The largest, which were not necessarily the best, were often destined for the royal palace. For the less affluent there already were substitutes. As early as 1808, Mrs. Elizabeth Raffald's *The Experienced English Housekeeper* was offering a recipe for "artificial" or mock turtle soup made from a calf's head.

Steamships greatly facilitated the movement of live turtles across the Atlantic. Imports of "preserved turtle" from Jamaica were initiated in 1841. The turtles had been taken by Cayman Islanders and, thus, by British subjects. By 1880 imports of "prepared turtle" were listed as 10,800 pounds. This was apparently the designation applied to the sun-dried meat and calipee that in late years had begun to place turtle soup, by one account, "within the reach of the general consumer." But it was to remain preeminently a prestige food. Mrs. Isabella Beeton called turtle soup "the most expensive soup brought to the table," with 1 guinea the standard price for a quart of it. Her widely read *Mrs. Beeton's Book of Household Management* states:

The price of live turtle ranges from 8d. to 2s. per pound, according to supply and demand. When live turtle is dear, many cooks use the tinned turtle, which is killed when caught, preserved by being put into hermetically sealed canisters, and so sent over to England. (Beeton 1861: 178-80)

The Queen of Soups

"Turtle soup from Painter's Ship & Turtle on Leadenhall Street," wrote one observer at the end of the nineteenth century, "is decidedly the best thing in the shape of soup that can be had in this, or perhaps any other country." Located there, he asserted, was the only "turtle artist" in Europe (Hayward 1899: 24-5). A French visitor described the establishment in 1904. A large pool of water contained upwards of 50 turtles awaiting "sacrifice." Alongside was the slaughter room and next to it the kitchen, where 10 to 12 men were occupied in making this national soup, which was sent out each day to the city, to the provinces, and even to foreign markets. It brought the exorbitant price of 1 guinea per liter for the regular soup and 25 shillings for the clear soup. A bowl of turtle soup served in the restaurant cost 3 shillings, the price including the glass of punch that followed it (Suzanne 1904: 15).

Blending and seasoning were of the greatest importance in soup making and called for much experience and "know-how." Some cooks insisted that the fins and steak or inside red muscle meat of the turtle were chiefly responsible for the flavor, and that genuine "real turtle soup" (the sort that jelled of its own accord on cooling) was properly made only from a broth of turtle meat. To this, diced calipee was added as a relish. Others, especially in London, regarded beef stock as an essential basis of the soup, holding that without it turtle soup tended to lack character. In this they claimed the support of the famous *Maître Chef* Auguste Escoffier.

Tinned turtle products entered midlatitude markets about the middle of the nineteenth century. Some of the first canneries were located within the tropics, close to sources of supply such as one at Pearl Lagoon, Nicaragua. Another in Key West, Florida, employing 10 vessels and 60 men for turtle gathering, was reported in 1880 to be turning out 200,000 cases a year. The "green fat," or calipee, was often tinned separately from the meat and soup. It was once customary to serve it as a side dish, a spoonful being added to the soup if desired. The largest shipments of tinned turtle products were to London, but New York was a substantial secondary market. Although turtle canneries operated from time to time in Jamaica, Nicaragua, Grand Cayman, Mexico, Australia, North Borneo, and Kenya, they were short-lived ventures. In later years, until forced cessation of the trade, the larger share of the green-turtle soup and red meat that went into cans was processed either in the New York area or in London.

The leading London soup maker, John Lusty, Ltd., "By Appointment Purveyors of Real Turtle Soup to the Royal Household since the Reign of Edward VII," had been in business near the London docks and Greenwich Naval Base since at least 1851 (long before the reign of Edward VII). Captains of Royal Navy ships returning from the West Indies or Ascension Island often brought back live green turtles and desired that they be made into soup for presentation to "My Lords of the Admiralty," who prized it as a great delicacy. The West Indies was the principal source of Lusty's supply.

After World War II, however, few live turtles were imported, the animals being slaughtered and refrigerated at the port of shipment. In its last years in business Lusty's supplies (mostly frozen) came from Kenya and the Seychelles. For Bender & Cassel, Ltd., the other major London producer, the Cayman Islands provided the supplies. It was at this time that a substantial demand for green turtle soup developed on the Continent. It became a standard feature on the menus of luxury restaurants, particularly in the larger cities and tourist centers of Germany, the Low Countries, and, to a lesser extent, France. There were canning operations in West Germany, France, Denmark, and Switzerland. For most of these concerns the Indian Ocean seems to have been the principal source of supply.

In the United States, the dominant company in the green-turtle and turtle-soup business was Moore & Company Soups, Inc., of Newark, New Jersey ("Ancora" brand), formerly located in Manhattan. It had begun making turtle soup in 1883. Initially, the turtles arrived at the port of New York deck-loaded on banana boats; later they were trucked, turned on their backs, from Tampa or Key West. In the early 1960s, an average of two truckloads a week arrived at the Newark plant, where they were held in a pond until slaughtered. If frozen, the carcasses were placed in refrigerators.

The End of an Era

In 1962 I hazarded the guess that between 15,000 and 20,000 green turtles a year were finding their way, in one form or another, to the commercial markets of North America and Europe. The guess included those animals slaughtered on the Indian Ocean islands and elsewhere exclusively for their calipee. Although the aristocracy was consuming less turtle soup than in times past, the market had been immensely broadened. What was once reserved for the epicures of London and New York had become available on the shelves of quality grocery stores throughout Europe and America. The implications of such an expanding demand in the midlatitudes, coupled with the growing population of the tropical world, seemed ominous.

But today, with most nations of the world signatory parties to CITES, international commerce in turtles and turtle products has all but ceased, although the animals continue to be exploited on a limited scale by traditional coastal populations, and turtle meat or eggs may be marketed clandestinely. Egg collecting may be permitted under restraining community rules, as at the important olive ridley nesting beach at Ostional on the Pacific coast of Costa Rica or at the Sarawak Turtle Islands. But in Mexico, perhaps most conspicuously in sparsely settled Baja California, illegal poaching for commercial purposes remains widespread. In that country turtle eggs, as well as the penis of the reptile, are prized for their presumed aphrodisiac qualities.

At Mexico's Rancho Nuevo beach (on the Tamaulipas coast), famed for the massive synchronous nesting emergences *(arribadas)* of the rare Kemp's ridleys, eggs for a time were removed to a protected hatchery within hours of being laid to avoid depredation by coyotes, shore birds, and humans. Under a U.S.–Mexico cooperative "head start" program, hatchlings were transferred in large numbers to Texas beaches in the hope of imprinting them and establishing new rookeries (Rancho Nuevo is the lone known Kemp's ridley beach in the world). But the project did not produce the hoped-for results and was finally abandoned as futile (*Marine Turtle Newsletter* 1993: October, 63).

A film made in 1950 of the Tamaulipas *arribada* showed some 40,000 females storming the beach in daylight hours, but the same beach today supports fewer than 1,000 nesters in a season. Apparently the entire world stock of Kemp's ridleys has been severely depleted in the interim, many trapped and damaged in the trawls of commercial shrimpers (Cornelius 1990). Presently large *arribadas* of the vastly more abundant olive ridley turtle occur at one remaining Mexican West Coast beach and at others in Costa Rica and India. The phenomenon, one of the most spectacular examples of mass activity in the animal kingdom, is especially characteristic of the two ridleys. At least three Mexican *arribada* sites had been eliminated by commercial fishermen before government restrictions began to be enforced. An estimated 2 million turtles were slaughtered on the West Coast of Mexico, more to meet demands for leather than for meat, in the five years leading up to 1969, before efforts were made to rationalize the harvest with catch quotas (Cornelius 1990: 54; *Marine Turtle Newsletter* 1991: April, 53). The India site, in Orissa State on the Bay of Bengal, of which the scientific world has only recently become aware, is reported to support *arribadas* of up to 200,000 ridleys, presumably in a single season. Despite the fact that much of the site is within a wildlife reserve, thousands of illegal takings occur offshore annually. The extent to which eggs are collected is unclear. The excessive harvest of eggs has been identified as one of the most important factors causing the decline of sea turtle populations.

In the Caribbean area, turtle deaths have increased with the intensified activities of shrimp trawlers in recent years (National Research Council 1990). Strandings of dead loggerheads on Florida beaches from this cause (13,000 in a recent year, with a small number of greens) have been sharply reduced by the Turtle Exclusionary Devices (TEDs) now required on the U.S. trawler fleet. Extension of their use to other nations is being urged. The ingestion of plastic bags, debris, and toxic substances such as petroleum further contributes to turtle mortality. Tourism and turtles, too, are on a collision course in several places. Coastal resort development and other forms of habitat encroachment deny nesting turtles their habitual nesting localities, as does the increasing artificial lighting along coastlines, to which the greens seem especially sensitive.

Gastronomy or Ecotourism?

Captive breeding programs for the more valued greens and hawksbills have been generally unsuccessful. The Cayman Islands Turtle Farm, established in 1968 as Mariculture, Ltd., for a time raised greens in tanks for export to commercial processors. In the face of CITES restrictions, it has been converted to a successful educational and tourist attraction. Production of meat (and perhaps eggs) continues on a reduced scale for local island consumption. The U.S. market has been closed since 1978, as, increasingly, are those of other countries (Wood 1991; Fosdick and Fosdick 1994). Provision for trade in farmed turtles continues to be sought, but the pressure against any trading in species whose wild populations are endangered or threatened is substantial. Sea turtle research, including the tagging and release of hatchlings and yearlings, has been an additional feature of the farm's activities. In recent years, farms have sought to be self-sustaining, independent of wild stocks of eggs or wild breeding turtles. The animals are fed twice daily with a high-protein, pelletized Purina Turtle Chow. They are slaughtered at 4 years of age, at 20 to 30 kilograms.

If sea turtles have a future it seems likely to be in ecotourism rather than gastronomy. They are featured on the flag, seal, currency, and postage stamps of the Cayman Islands, reflecting their close association with the islands and their presumed emotional appeal to potential visitors. Elsewhere, too, as in Florida, in Costa Rica, on the Great Barrier Reef, and on some islands of the Aegean Sea, "turtle watching" is becoming a featured tourist attraction.

The groundswell of concern for the future of sea turtles that has put all but the Australian flatback on the endangered species lists has led to a surge in scientific research on the animals and on the causes and consequences of their decline (Bjorndal 1981; National Research Council 1990). Representative of this effort are the activities of the Marine Turtle Specialty Group of the International Union for the Conservation of Nature (IUCN) and the *Marine Turtle Newsletter*, a comprehensive quarterly now published in both English and Spanish by the Hubbs–Sea World Research Institute of San Diego, California. So are the symposia on Sea Turtle Biology and Conservation, which are annual workshops devoted to these questions.

Realization of the seriousness of the plight of sea turtles, underscored by the CITES trade restrictions, has led to the effective elimination of turtle steaks, turtle soup, and turtle eggs from the tables of all but a handful of tropical developing countries. We are losing, as a consequence, a palatable and nutritious marine food of unique cultural and historical significance. Turtle meat is remarkably lean, with 5 percent of calories in fat compared to 40 for most meats (James Stewart, M.D., personal communication). The eggs are comparable to chicken or duck eggs in protein content and are rich in vitamin A (Simoons 1991: 366–7). Both the world of gastronomy and the lives of many coastal populations of the tropics are being significantly impoverished as turtle and turtle products, a primary source of red meat and protein, are being forced from menus by the excessive pressures of commercialization as well as by the relentless increase in human numbers.

James J. Parsons

Bibliography

Anon. 1753. *Gentleman's Magazine* 23: 489.
Beeton, Isabella. 1861. *Mrs. Beeton's book of household management: A complete cookery book.* London.
Bjorndal, Karen, ed. 1981. *Biology and conservation of sea turtles.* Washington, D.C.
Carr, Archie. 1952. *The handbook of turtles.* Ithaca, N.Y.
    1954. The passing of the fleet. *Bulletin of the Institute of Biological Science* 4: 17–19.
    1973. *"So excellent a fishe."* New York.

Cornelius, Stephen. 1990. *The sea turtles of Santa Rosa National Park.* San José, Costa Rica.

Dampier, William. 1906. *Dampier's voyages (1679-1701).* 2 vols., ed. John Masefield. New York.

Fosdick, Peggy, and Sam Fosdick. 1994. *Last chance lost? Can and should farming save the green sea turtle? The story of Mariculture Ltd. - Cayman Turtle Farm.* York, Pa.

Fryer, John. 1909. *A new account of East India and Persia 1672-81.* London.

Goldsmith, Oliver. 1825. *A history of the earth and animated nature.* London.

Hayward, Abraham. 1899. *The art of dining.* New York.

Hendrickson, John. 1958. The green turtle (*Chelonia mydas* Linn.) in Malaya and Sarawak. *Proceedings of the Zoological Society of London.* 130 (Series A): 445-535.

Labat, J. B. 1724. *Nouveaux voyages du Père Labat aux Îles de l'Amérique.* 2 vols. The Hague.

Marine Turtle Newsletter. 1991-4. San Diego, Calif.

National Research Council. 1990. *Decline of the sea turtles: Causes and consequences.* Washington, D.C.

Nietschmann, Bernard. 1973. *Between land and water: The subsistence ecology of the Miskito Indians, eastern Nicaragua.* New York.

   1979. *Caribbean edge: The coming of modern times to isolated people and wildlife.* New York.

   1991. Miskito Coast protected area. *National Geographic Research and Exploration* 7: 232-4.

   1993. Nicaragua's new alliance for Indian-Latin America. *Natural Geographic Research and Exploration* 9: 270-1.

Parsons, James. 1962. *The green turtle and man.* Gainesville, Fla.

Raffald, Elizabeth. 1808. *The experienced English housekeeper.* London.

Rochefort, César de. 1606. *The history of the Caribby Islands.* 2 vols. London.

Sauer, Carl. 1962. Seashore - primitive home of man? *Proceedings of the American Philosophical Society* 106: 41-7.

Schaw, Janet. 1939. *Journal of a lady of quality, being a narrative of a journey from Scotland to the West Indies, North Carolina, and Portugal in the years 1774 to 1776.* New Haven, Conn.

Simmonds, Peter. 1883. *Commercial products of the sea.* London.

   1885. *Animal food resources of different nations.* London.

Simoons, Frederick. 1991. *Food in China: A cultural and historical inquiry.* Boca Raton, Fla.

   1994. *Eat not this flesh: Food avoidances in the Old World.* Madison, Wis.

Suzanne, Alfred. 1904. *La cuisine et pâtisserie Anglaise et Américaine.* Paris.

Walter, Richard. [1748] 1928. *Anson's voyage round the world.* London.

Wood, Fern. 1991. Turtle culture. In *Production of aquatic animals,* ed. C. E. Nash, 225-34. Amsterdam.

II.G.21 ❧ Sheep

Probably the earliest domesticated herd animal in the Old World, the sheep *(Ovis aries)* makes an unparalleled contribution of food and fiber. The great advantage of these small ruminants is their ability to digest the cellulose of wild grasses and coarse woody shrubs in their complex stomachs and convert it into usable products.

Origin and Domestication

Sheep were domesticated on the flanks of the Taurus–Zagros Mountains, which run from southern Turkey to southern Iran. Within that arc is found the urial *(Ovis orientalis)*, a wild sheep now generally regarded as the ancestor of the domesticated sheep. Early archaeological evidence of sheep under human control comes from Shanidar Cave and nearby Zaqi Chemi in Kurdistan. Sheep bones recovered in abundance at these two sites have been dated to between 8,000 and 9,000 years ago and contrast with other Neolithic sites close to the Mediterranean, where similar evidence of domesticated sheep is rare. However, accurate species identification has posed problems, for the bones of goats and sheep are often difficult to distinguish from one another. Therefore, some archaeological reports have grouped them together as "sheep/goat" or "caprine."

The domestication process that transformed *O. orientalis* into *O. aries* involved several key changes. The body size of the sheep was reduced from that of the urial. Diminution could have been accomplished over many generations by culling out larger, aggressive males as sires. Selection also occurred for hornlessness, but this process is not complete. Although many breeds of domesticated female (and some male) sheep typically have no horns, in other males the horns have only been reduced in size. Domesticated sheep also have a long tail as compared with the wild ancestor. The most significant physical transformation of the animal was the replacement of the hairy outercoat with wool fibers, which turned the sheep into much more than a food source. As early as 6,000 years ago, woolly sheep had differentiated from hairy sheep, and in ancient Mesopotamia, the raising of wool-bearing animals was a major activity in lowland areas. Selection for white-wooled animals explains the gradual dominance of that color.

Sheep

In spite of the many human uses of sheep, domestication may have been motivated by religion rather than economics. Urials were animals of ritual significance, and to ensure a ready supply for sacrifice, humans may well have sought to tame and then breed them in captivity. At Catal Hüyük in Anatolia, the remains of sanctuaries from between the seventh and sixth millenniums B.C. depict ram heads.

The early use of sheep as sacrificial offerings went hand in hand with a long selection for qualities of fecklessness, timidity, and total dependency. Long after successful domestication, sheep sacrifices continued in religious ritual. The cultic use of sheep was known in ancient Egypt, Greece, Rome, and China. The Hebrew Bible made many allusions to ovine sacrifice, and from this, Christianity developed the idea of the "Lamb of God," a metaphor for Jesus as a sacrificial vessel for the sins of mankind. Unlike Christianity, Islam incorporated sacrifice as a literal requirement of the faith. Each year, during the festival of *Id al-Adha,* every male Muslim is enjoined to slaughter a domesticated animal, in most cases a sheep, as a sign of his submission to the will of God. Sheep accompanied the spread of Islam from its Arabian core, not only because of religious associations but also because the Arabs were, above all, pastoralists.

Ovine Diversity

Through isolation and/or mutation, sheep differentiated into almost 1,000 breeds, most with regional distributions. Some of these have now disappeared as more productive breeds have taken their places. The selection of sheep breeds in Western Europe has been influenced largely by the strong Western bias toward high productivity. During the eighteenth and nineteenth centuries, the breeds of Cheviot, Cotswold, Dorset, Hampshire, Leicester, Oxford, Romney, Shropshire, Suffolk, and Southdown all emerged in the British Isles, bred in some cases for their wool and in others primarily for their meat. The Rambouillet, a smooth-bodied wool breed, originated in France. In the United States, the breeds of Columbia, Debouillet, Montalde, Panama, and Targhee were developed (mostly in the twentieth century) through crossing of different breeds to adapt them to North American environmental conditions.

About 10 percent of classified breeds produce fine wool. Merino sheep are the outstanding source of high-quality wool and, as such, are the most important of all sheep breeds. The long fibers of Merino wool are turned into yarn used for worsted apparel. The history of Merino sheep in Spain is well documented after about A.D. 1500, but their origin is not. It seems most plausible, however, that this breed was brought from North Africa during the Moorish occupation of the Iberian Peninsula.

Genotypic and phenotypic diversity of sheep is greatest in the Near East, where these animals have been part of human livelihoods longer than anywhere else in the world. Breeds of indigenous origin, well adapted to the local environmental conditions, still dominate there. Some breeds, such as the Awassi and Karaman, have fat tails – fat tails being a much-appreciated delicacy in places such as the Middle East; others have semifat tails (e.g., Chios sheep); still others have thin tails, for example, the Karayaka of Turkey. Fat-rumped breeds form yet another category. Near Eastern breeds have several kinds of fleece, or none at all. The good-quality carpet wool yielded by some breeds makes possible the manufacture of Oriental rugs, one of the world's magnificent art forms. Fur-sheep are another category; most famous are lamb pelts from Karakul sheep produced in the Middle East and central Asia, especially in Bokhara, where this breed originated. Many sheep of western Asia also have their variants in Africa (Epstein 1971).

In places where sheep are raised more for their subsistence value, numerous breeds may be represented in a single flock. For example, in northeastern Brazil, an owner may keep hair sheep and those with wool; polled sheep and those carrying horns; sheep with colors ranging from red-brown to white to black-pied; sheep with horizontal ears, but also those with lop ears; sheep with thin tails, but also those with semifat tails. These heterogeneous mixtures are the result of several introductions and free crossings over time. The first sheep were exported to Brazil in the sixteenth century from Portugal and included both the coarse-wooled Churro and the fine-wooled Merino. The Crioulo breed, coarse-wooled and horned, emerged from the Churro. Hair sheep were imported from the Caribbean and elsewhere, and in the twentieth century, sheep were brought from Italy to Brazil.

Keeping of Sheep

Sheep have been kept either as part of pastoral livelihoods or as an element of mixed agropastoralism. In the former, they consume grass and woody shrubs that are part of the natural vegetation. Sheep grazing on the coastal meadows *(prés salés)* of western France has established a standard for high-quality lamb production known throughout the culinary world. When integrated with a farming economy, sheep consume stubble in the fields and, in turn, contribute manure to renew the soil. Sheep are almost never kept in stalls or feedlots as cattle are. Intensive sheep production has lagged far behind that of cattle and pigs.

Where aridity has made agriculture too uncertain or impossible, sheep can survive on sparse wild grasses and woody shrubs. Sheep raising has traditionally been most profitable when natural vegetation on land owned by the community or the state reduced the cost of production. Often, however, the need of such vegetation has involved seasonal movement to find proper forage at all times of the year. In much of the subhumid world, transhumance is the solution to providing livestock with what they need to survive. In the Iberian Peninsula, sheep raising became the most valuable avenue of land use after the introduction of the Merino. The powerful sheepowners' organization, the *Mesta,* obtained priority in deploying their sheep over the countryside. Always in search of more and better pastures, sheep were driven north and south on the Spanish plateau along designated pathways called *cañadas.* The migration of millions of sharp-hoofed animals etched miniature canyons into the land that can still be seen as relict features in the landscape.

Traditional patterns of seasonal sheep movement continue to prevail in the Middle East, North Africa, and central Asia. In Europe, transhumance between high and low pastures is still practiced, but now sheep may be transported by rail and truck rather than on foot. Transhumance is also found in western North America and southern South America, but more in the form of commercial livestock strategy than cultural adaptation. In all forms of sheepherding, shepherds and dogs remain indispensable, for they protect their defenseless charges not only from predators but also from the sheep's own mimetic behavior and innate stupidity.

Sheep Products

Wool

Wool is the main product of commercial sheep raising such as is practiced in Australia, New Zealand, South Africa, Argentina, Uruguay, and North America. Most wool involved in world trade comes from these areas. Wool is also a major product for small farmers throughout the world. Sheep's wool has many advantages: It is resilient, which imparts to fabrics the ability to retain shape and resist wrinkling. Wool traps and retains heat-insulating air, but at the same time its low density permits the manufacture of lightweight fabrics. In addition, wool fiber takes dyestuffs well.

Meat

If all the world's sheep are taken into consideration, meat has been the primary objective of raising them. Fat (tallow) from sheep was once tremendously important for making candles until paraffin replaced it; in the Middle East and Africa, tallow continues to have considerable value as a substitute for cooking oils. Selection for fat tails is ancient. Herodotus mentioned sheep in which the tail constituted one-sixth of the total weight of the butchered animal. In some sheep, the tail is so large and heavy that it is an obstruction to the animal's mobility. Cases are known in which owners have constructed a little wheeled cart to relieve the weight of the tail and keep it from dragging on the ground.

Sheep meat is divided into mutton and lamb, with the latter deriving from an animal of up to 1 year of age and without permanent teeth. Mutton – the meat of a sheep older than 1 year – is the favorite meat of the Middle East and North Africa. Indeed, more than 50 percent of those regions' total meat requirements are satisfied by mutton. The sheep is the prestige animal of Islam, which ecology has encouraged, because the quality and quantity of forage in this part of the world favor it over cattle, which have much larger appetites and more stringent feed requirements in order to thrive. Goats are an alternative to sheep. Pigs are taboo.

Mutton is also culturally important in central Asia as a food, more so than in China, even though that country is the world's leading mutton producer. Australia, with its population of less than 20 million people, nevertheless produces four times as much sheep meat as the United States with 265 million people. Australians eat most of it but also export considerable quantities. The island peoples of Mauritius and Papua New Guinea, for example, derive a major part of their commercial meat supply from imported Australian mutton.

In Europe, sheep meat consumption is only one-eighth that of beef and veal and one-sixteenth that of pork. Among Europeans, the British have been especially fond of mutton, but their consumption of it has declined in recent decades in response to the availability of cheaper sources of protein such as poultry. Nonetheless, the United Kingdom still produces three times more sheep meat than the United States and also relies on mutton imports from Argentina.

The preferred sheep meat in many Western countries is lamb, which is more tender and subtle in flavor than mutton. A century ago, however, lambs were rarely marketed as a source of meat. One specialized variant of lamb is a milk-fed baby, which yields a succulent white flesh. In Mediterranean countries, suckling lamb is a much appreciated Easter delicacy. It is an old specialty *(abbaccho)* of the Roman Campagna, a favorite residential area of Rome in ancient times, and in Greece, milk-fed lamb is considered the height of gourmandise.

As already hinted, Americans eat little sheep meat of any kind. In 1985, less than 1 percent of the red meat consumed in the United States was lamb or mutton (USDA 1987). One explanation for this small amount is that sheep flesh was historically of poor quality because the only sheep slaughtered were those whose wool-bearing days were over. The nineteenth-century rise of the beef-centered meatpacking industry may also have played a role in marginalizing sheep meat. But most persuasive in explaining the weak pattern of sheep meat consumption are protein alternatives. Since 1963, the use of lamb and mutton in the United States has decreased more than 60 percent; during this time, pork, beef, and especially poultry have become relatively cheaper to purchase.

Another contributing factor is meat cuts: Mutton and lamb have a higher ratio of fat and bone than do beef or pork.

Today, what little sheep meat is consumed in the United States is as lamb. Part of that market is composed of immigrant populations, which reduces even more its consumption among mainstream American meat-eaters. The latter group may eat it mainly in restaurants specializing in Greek, Middle Eastern, and French cuisines. However, in some regions of the country, particularly the South and the Midwest, lamb is not even readily available in many supermarkets. Where found, in the meat counters of larger cities, lamb is typically at least as expensive as beef or pork, and usually more so.

Consumers who reject lamb for reasons other than price often state that they do not like its strong taste. The main factors controlling flavor in lamb meat are breed (Rambouillet lambs have a more intense flavor than Columbia lambs); sex (rams have a more intense flavor than wethers or ewes); and age and weight (flavor intensity varies inversely with these) (Crouse 1983).

Milk and Cheese

Milk has been a subsidiary product from sheep for millennia. Today, it is most important in the Middle East, where it is occasionally drunk fresh but is more commonly turned into yoghurt and cheese. Turkey, Iran, and Syria are major producers of dairy products from ewes, but most of these products are not commercialized beyond the local area. In Europe, the human use of sheep's milk is said to have increased when the Hundred Years' War killed off many cattle. Today, however, fresh sheep's milk is no longer consumed by most Europeans. The relative inefficiency of milking sheep, and their low productivity (150 pounds per lactation compared to 20,000 pounds for a cow), has encouraged the conversion of sheep milk into higher-value dairy products. In the Balkans, sheep's milk is made into yoghurt, but elsewhere in Europe, it is almost entirely made into cheese.

Europe's most famous sheep's-milk cheese is Roquefort – made distinctive by its veins of blue-green mold which develops on curd placed to cure in cool limestone caves. "Roquefort" is a controlled appellation (appellation contrôlée), which means that cheeses with this name can come only from a designated territory in the Cévennes region of France with the town of Roquefort as its center. However, the sheep's milk from which the curd is made comes from a much wider area that extends from the Massif Central to the Pyrenees and the island of Corsica. Almost all French sheep's milk produced is now devoted to making Roquefort cheese.

The manufacture of Roquefort is a holdout of tradition; other French cheeses once made with sheep's milk are now made from cow's milk. In Italy, sheep's-milk cheese is called pecorino (pecora is the Italian for ewe); it can be either soft and fresh (ricotta pecorino) or hard (pecorino romano, or simply Romano, used in grated form on pasta). Queijo da serra ("mountain cheese") is a notable cheese from the mountainous interior of Portugal, a country that well into the twentieth century made most of its cheese from sheep's milk. Greece produces large amounts of feta, a sheep's-milk cheese salted and then preserved in a brine of milk, water, and salt.

The lands of the New World produce very little sheep's-milk cheese. About 90 percent of Latin American production comes from the Bolivian Altiplano near Oruro. The native cheese makers of queso de Paria are indigenous people whose ancestors were taught the art of making a soft, unripened cheese by the Spanish conquerors of the Andes. In the United States, sheep's-milk cheese is manufactured on a small scale in the upper Midwest and in California and Vermont. It is considered a gourmet item because sheep's milk commands four to five times the price of cow's milk. One advantage of sheep's milk is that it can be successfully frozen and stored. Hinkley, Minnesota, has a cheese-processing plant that derives its sheep's milk from a wide area.

Environmental Effects of Sheep

Sheepherding has an ecological downside when considered historically over long periods. These ungulates have frequently overgrazed the land and brought about serious erosion, especially in areas where vegetation regenerates slowly. Sheep graze plants much closer to the ground than do cattle, and if uncontrolled, they can even, by consuming tree seedlings, denude an area to the point of preventing regeneration. Sheep contributed to the early formation of eroded landscapes in the Middle East and the Mediterranean region. Even a recently settled land such as Australia shows strong evidence of the sort of damage that intensive sheep raising can do. By 1854, New South Wales had a sheep population of over 12 million. It was an "ungulate irruption" that changed species composition of the vegetation, encouraged the introduction of noxious weeds, and degraded the soil. Sheep introduced into the New World have caused deterioration in the ranges of the western United States, Argentine Patagonia, and the Andean highlands. In Mexico, a case study of the Valle del Mezquital north of Mexico City has documented environmental changes wrought largely by intensive sheep grazing during the colonial period (Melville 1994).

World Production and Trade

More than 1 billion sheep are found in the world today, and they occur on all inhabited continents. Ovines are found in the hottest countries, such as

Somalia and Sudan, but there are also large herds in cold, windswept lands near Antarctica, such as Patagonia in southern Argentina and the Falklands (Malvinas), and on the fringes of the Arctic, as in the Faroe Islands and Iceland. Depending on the area, plains, plateaus, and mountains can all support sheep populations. Tolerance for hot, cold, dry, and wet conditions, along with an absence of any cultural prejudice against the animal and its multifaceted uses, account for its wide distribution.

Asia has about a third of the world's sheep, with especially large populations in China (mainly west and north), Iran, India, Kazakhstan, and Pakistan. Africa's sheep are found in all countries of that continent and, in the northern, western, and eastern parts, are often associated with nomadic, seminomadic, or transhumant groups. As a country (though not as a continent), Australia has, without question, the largest sheep population. Sheep are also the kingpin of agropastoralism in New Zealand, where the sheep–human ratio is among the highest in the world.

Europe (west and east combined) has about as many sheep as Australia. The superhumid United Kingdom and subhumid Spain have the largest ovine populations in the European Union. South America has more than five times as many sheep as North and Middle America taken together. Sheep are the most important domesticated animal in the high Andes of Peru, Bolivia, and Ecuador, where the cold climate and a homespun tradition make wool an especially valuable product. But 5 million sheep are also found in hot northeastern Brazil, where wool has little value. Much farther south, commercial wool production is important in temperate southern Brazil, Uruguay, Argentina, and Chile. The pastoralists of tiny Uruguay, which has about the same number of sheep as the United States, have long grazed sheep and cattle together.

Multispecies grazing in Uruguay contrasts with the conflictive tradition in western North America, where sheepmen and cattlemen pitted themselves against one another in a struggle for domination of the range. Since 1942, the rise of synthetic fibers, a shortage of skilled labor, and the increased cost of land have together forced a decline in the sheep industry in the United States. Nevertheless, entrepreneurial sheep raising on federally owned expanses still constitutes an important use of land in parts of the arid West.

Live sheep also find their way into world trade. Nigeria, Senegal, Kuwait, and especially Saudi Arabia import large numbers of them to be slaughtered in prescribed Islamic fashion. Movements of live sheep from Australia to Saudi Arabia are particularly large, enabling the faithful to satisfy their obligation of dispatching a sacrificial animal during the pilgrimage to Mecca. Normally, more than 1 million sheep are sacrificed each year for this purpose. Much of this slaughter, which wastes the meat, occurs in five abattoirs in Mina, near Mecca (Brooke 1987).

The long-term future of sheep raising in the world appears bright. Ruminant animals possess a keen advantage in being able to make use of arid or steep lands that cannot be cultivated. Sheep are productive, adaptable, and largely noncompetitive with humans. More than any other domesticate, their dual contributions of food and fiber give sheep an economic edge that spreads the risk of keeping them. And, finally, there are no cultural barriers to constrain their use.

Daniel W. Gade

Bibliography

Brooke, Clarke. 1987. Sacred slaughter: The sacrificing of animals at the *hajj* and *Id al-Adha*. *Journal of Cultural Geography* 7: 67–88.

Crouse, John D. 1983. The effects of breed, sex, slaughter weight and age on lamb flavor. *Food Technology* 72: 264–8.

Epstein, H. 1971. *The origin of the domestic animals of Africa.* New York.

FAO (Food and Agriculture Organization of the United Nations). 1995. *FAO yearbook.* Rome.

Mason, I. L. 1980. Sheep and goat production in the drought polygon of northeast Brazil. *World Animal Review* 34: 23–8.

Melville, Elinor E. K. 1994. *A plague of sheep: Environmental consequences of the conquest of Mexico.* New York.

USDA (United States Department of Agriculture). 1987. *Food consumption, prices and expenditures.* Statistical Bulletin No. 749, USDA Economic Research Service. Washington, D.C.

II.G.22   Turkeys

The process of capture, taming, and eventual domestication of most animals is a difficult and lengthy process, often consisting of a trial-and-error approach. One notable exception was the domestication of the North American wild turkey, *Meleagris gallopavo*. The U.S. National Park Service archaeologist Jean Pinkley, while stationed at Mesa Verde National Park, put forth a logical scenario outlining the unique process of taming and domesticating the prehistoric pueblo turkeys of that area. Pinkley (1965) has pointed out that some domesticated animals apparently first exploited humans before becoming another of their agricultural conquests. The turkey is such an example.

The pueblo turkeys had become extinct in the Mesa Verde area by historic times, and the Park Service reintroduced breeding stock in 1944 (Pinkley 1965). This permitted observation of the wild turkeys and their relationship with the employees of the park. The

Turkey

turkeys were timid at first, but as they learned where food could be found – in this case, feeding stations that the government set out for small birds – they took over these sources. They also moved into warm roosting places available in the park's residential areas, and despite efforts to chase them away by tossing Fourth of July cherry bombs and firing guns into the air, the birds continued to congregate in and around park dwellings.

There is little reason to believe that prehistoric humans in Mesa Verde were not tormented by turkeys in much the same manner, and sooner or later, when it dawned on them that the birds could not be driven off or frightened away, the Pueblo Indians would out of despair have begun to corral them to protect crops and foodstores. At this point, recognition of the turkey as a source of food and materials for bone tools would presumably have been a logical next step.

That the turkeys were utilized over a wide area is evidenced by their numerous bones recovered from many archaeological excavations throughout the southwestern United States. All growth and age stages of the turkey – from eggs and poults on through old adults – are represented in these findings. Also of considerable interest are the pens that were constructed long ago in the pueblo region to keep the birds from straying from areas of confinement.

A number of turkey pens have been found associated with early pueblos. I recall walking down the sandy bottom of White Canyon in Utah in 1950 during the uranium boom and spotting a small two-room ruin high on the canyon wall overhead. After a tedious but not particularly dangerous climb, I reached the ledge to find the ruin virtually undisturbed. There were black-on-white bowl fragments lying about, along with stone grinding tools. On one end of the overhanging rock, where it joined with the smooth main cliff face, was a wedge-shaped turkey pen. It was constructed of cottonwood twigs, about the size of a finger in diameter, held together

by plant fibers. The gate had hinges made of leather thongs and had been secured with a tied leather loop. On the floor of the small pen was a thick layer of turkey droppings. As I untied the gate and heard the squeak of the leather thongs as it opened, I thought about the last person who had secured the empty cage, perhaps intending to return with more wild birds.

The determination of whether a turkey was domestic or wild on the basis of skeletal evidence alone is - unlike with many other domesticates – nearly impossible, and when such determinations are advanced they are "shaky" at best. But poultry experts at the Cooperative Extension Service at Clemson University in York, South Carolina, have arrived at an interesting conclusion regarding the color of turkey feathers that may help separate domestic from wild birds.

Color change in feathers is brought about, in part, by the presence of lysine, a biologically important basic amino acid ($C_6H_{14}N_2O_2$) and one of the building blocks of protein. In the case of turkeys, if lysine is not present in the diet in adequate amounts, their feathers lose some of their pigment. Turkeys generally obtain the needed amino acid from natural foods of whole protein, including insects, worms, and grubs. But many vegetable foods are low in lysine, and one of the poorest is corn. Because evidence indicates that corn was one of the major foods given to the Pueblo turkeys, and because confinement would have prevented the birds from foraging for other supplements, this diet may have contributed to the increase in white-tipped feathers that are found with domestic birds.

Two turkeys were and are present in the Americas. These are the ocellated turkey *(Meleagris "Agriocharis" ocellata)* of Central America and southern Mexico, and the turkey that is regarded as the Thanksgiving bird in the United States *(M. gallopavo),* which is found throughout much of North America.

The genus *Meleagris* and, perhaps, the species *gallopavo* are reported from the Pleistocene of North America. The birds are known from a Basketmaker site (see Table II.G.22.1) at Tseahaliso Cave, Canyon Del Muerto, Arizona, having an associated date of 3700 B.C. Turkeys were definitely domesticated by Pueblo I times (A.D. 750–900).

Table II.G.22.1. *Southwestern chronology*

A.D. 1700 to the present	Pueblo V
A.D. 1300–1700	Pueblo IV
A.D. 1100–1300	Pueblo III
A.D. 800/850–1100	Pueblo II
A.D. 750–900	Pueblo I
A.D. 450–750	Basketmaker III
A.D. 1–500	Basketmaker II
Pre-A.D. 1	Basketmaker I

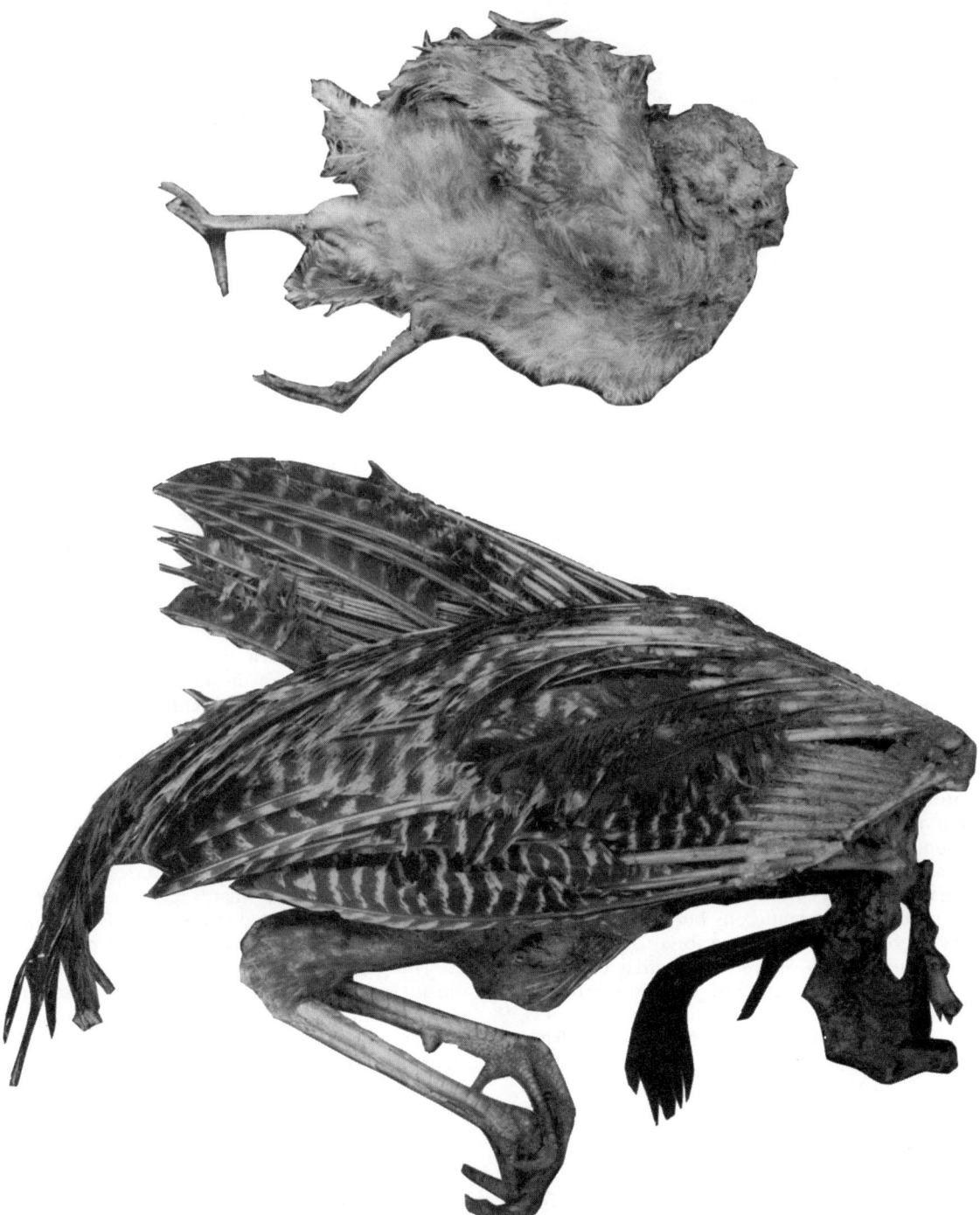

Figure II.G.22.1. Early pueblo domestic turkeys: top, a domestic turkey poult from a pueblo trash slope in Mesa Verde National Park, Colorado; bottom, natural mummy from an archaeological site in Canyon de Chelly National Monument, Arizona. (Photograph by John W. Olsen.)

Most historians agree that Christopher Columbus and his men were probably the first Europeans to see the turkey. During the fourth voyage of Columbus in 1502, his party landed at present-day Honduras, where friendly natives brought them food that included native birds the Spaniards called *gallinas de la tierra,* or "land chickens." Subsequent Spanish visitors to the Mexican mainland also reported the turkey, such as Hernando Cortés, who saw them in the markets of the City of Mexico in 1519.

The ocellated turkey was long familiar to the Maya, and its bones are rather common discoveries in Maya sites in Yucatan and Guatemala. Indeed, the Maya referred to their part of the world as the land of the turkey and the deer. Yet there is little evidence indicating that the ocellated turkey was ever domesticated. Rather, it was probably a captive and not easily induced to breed in captivity.

The first European country to receive the turkey from the New World was Spain; Pedro Alonso Niño took some birds to that country in the early 1500s. The birds were established on Spanish poultry farms by 1530, were in Rome by 1525, were in France by 1538, and then spread rapidly to other parts of the Old World.

Ironically, the travels of the turkey came full circle when English settlers in Virginia brought the bird back to its home continent in 1584. The first turkeys to be brought from Europe to Massachusetts arrived in 1629. But contemporary accounts indicate that the turkey did not achieve its prominent place in the Thanksgiving festival in New England until the late eighteenth century.

This is not, however, to imply that turkeys were scarce in North America. Spanish explorers in the present-day southwestern United States, particularly those with Francisco Vásquez de Coronado from 1540 to 1542, supplemented their food supply with local animals encountered both in the wild and in Indian villages. Indeed, they frequently mentioned foods they encountered in the pueblos of Cibola and Cibuique, and Antonio Castañeda,[1] in his record of the Coronado expedition, noted that at the fortified village of Acoma (atop a large mesa in present-day New Mexico), the villagers gave the Spaniards presents of turkeys.

Coronado himself wrote of seeing domesticated turkeys in the southwestern pueblos. The Indians informed him, however, that the turkeys were not used as food but instead for their feathers that went to make robes (Winship 1896). Coronado, who did not take this statement seriously, claimed that the birds were an excellent source of food. Yet he also wrote that the Hopi pueblos kept both eagles and turkeys for their feathers. Feather-string robes similar to those reported in New Mexico have also been recovered from pre-Columbian Indian burials at several sites in Arizona.

Reports such as this one help explain why for many years archaeologists believed that turkeys were not eaten by the early Basketmakers and Pueblo Indians. But this theory also developed because of a number of complete natural turkey mummies – some buried with offerings of corn – that had been found (Figure II.G.22.1). This discovery was, however, before the thirteenth-century Mug House Ruin at Mesa Verde National Park was excavated (Rohn 1971) and over 1,074 turkey bones were recovered, representing from 183 to 815 individual birds (depending on the method of determining the minimum number of individuals).

Many bones at this site showed signs of butchering, and some were scorched or burned. In fact, turkeys appear to have been the most important source of meat for the Mug House occupants. The turkeys were housed mainly in the ruin's "Room 46," where numerous droppings found in most dry deposits, as well as remains of young birds or poults and some eggshell fragments, indicate that the birds were domesticated to a point at which they were reproducing. However, the limited number of eggshell fragments suggests that eggs were not an important food item (if, indeed, they were used for food at all). Grooved stones at the site may have been used as "anchors" to tether the birds and limit their wandering around the crowded pueblo (Rohn 1971).

Many of the turkey bones from Mug House, and other Pueblo sites, were made into awls, needles, and tubular beads. The bones selected to be "worked" were the humeri, femora, tarsometatarsi, and tibiotarsi. Even though turkey (and eagle) bones appear to be weaker in structure when compared with those of mammals, they are generally quite strong; thus, they could be worked and polished into implements.

A number of turkey humeri indicate that they were intentionally broken, or "captured," and then allowed to grow back, leaving the birds unable to fly again. This method of "wing clipping" is also employed with macaws and is still used by bird collectors in Central America.

Depictions of turkeys are rather common in works of native art. The Hopi kivas at Awatovi Pueblo have identifiable turkeys on the walls. The Mimbres vessels of the Southwest have quite accurate portrayals of turkeys, as well as some other depictions with accurate turkey heads and beards but in combination with anatomical characteristics of reptiles and mammals, such as jackrabbit ears and deer limbs.

One of the more unusual artistic depictions of turkeys found in the southwestern United States is a rather large mural that was painted on the back wall of a cliff dwelling. The dwelling (Classic Pueblo, A.D. 1100–1300), in Arizona's Navajo Tribal Park, is located some 60 to 70 feet above the floor of Little Canyon de Chelly. It is a site that is difficult to reach and, thus, was little known and virtually unvisited until the

1960s. The well-executed mural features three large turkeys roosting in a line.

Assemblages of turkey bones are preserved in many museum collections. Mug House Ruin, already mentioned, and Big Juniper House, also at Mesa Verde, have rather large collections of worked turkey bones. Seventeen bone awls representing the turkey, and one made from a golden eagle, were identified at Big Juniper House.

Worked turkey bones were also encountered in the following sites in prehistoric Arizona: Poncho House (4), Betatakin Pueblo (1), Kiet Siel Pueblo (77), Turkey Cave (3), Awatovi (1), and Wupaki Pueblo (1). Most of these turkey bones are from areas where, historically, the wild turkey is not known. Moreover, Lyndon Hargrave (1939), who did much of the identification of the bones, has pointed out that identifying single bones, particularly incomplete elements, can be less than accurate if turkeys, golden eagles, and sandhill cranes are all represented. Alden Miller (1932) has also reported on bird (including turkey) bones from archaeological sites in Arizona. These bones were from a dwelling site 35 miles north of Flagstaff. They were dated between A.D. 1000 and 1100, their age attested to by pottery types found with the turkey bones.

Clearly, the turkey was prized for much more than just meat, and regardless of the degree to which *M. gallopavo* was considered as a food source in the Southwest, the evidence indicates that it was among the most sought-after animals over a wide area and a considerable span of time.

It is difficult to obtain reliable information on why turkeys were not fully accepted in many areas of the world where they were introduced. A. W. Schorger, in his book *The Wild Turkey; Its History and Domestication* (1966), devoted 36 pages to a discussion of the travels of the North American turkey to England, Norway, Germany, India, Portugal, and Africa, and throughout much of the Western Hemisphere, including Peru and Colombia. Nonetheless, North America seems to be the region where turkeys are most accepted, although no reason has ever been offered for such popularity.

The dog, *Canis familiaris,* and the turkey, *M. gallopavo,* were the only domestic animals present in North America during pre-Columbian times (Figure II.G.22.2). It is true that some workers credit the pre-Columbian Maya with domesticating the Muscovy duck, although my studies of the Maya fauna do not substantiate this hypothesis. In the Caribbean, Columbus observed the Carib Indians with penned (domesticated or merely captive?) muscovies. Obviously we still have much to learn about domesticated fowl in the early Americas.

Stanley J. Olsen

Figure II.G.22.2. Only two domestic animals greeted the first Europeans to visit the southwestern pueblos. They were the dog and the turkey. (Drawing by Wallace Hughes.)

Notes

1. George Parker Winship (1896) presents the narrative of Castañeda in the original Spanish as well as an English translation. He also has compiled a most useful list of original Spanish works on the early Spanish explorers in the New World for the use of scholars who may wish to pursue this subject in greater detail.

Bibliography

Hargrave, Lyndon L. 1939. Bird bones from abandoned Indian dwellings in Arizona and Utah. *The Condor* 41: 206–10.

Jett, Stephen. 1977. *House of three turkeys.* Santa Barbara, Calif.

Miller, Alden. 1932. Bird remains from Indian dwellings in Arizona. *The Condor* 34: 138–9.

Pinkley, Jean M. 1965. The Pueblos and the turkey: Who domesticated whom? In *Memoirs of the Society for American Archaeology Number Nineteen,* ed. T. N. Campbell, *American Antiquity* 31: 70–2.

Rohn, Arthur H. 1971. *Mug House.* U.S. National Park Service Archaeological Research Series No. 7-D. Washington, D.C.

Schorger, A. W. 1966. *The wild turkey; its history and domestication.* Norman, Okla.

Winship, George Parker. 1896. The Coronado expedition, 1540-1542. In *Fourteenth Annual Report of the Bureau of Ethnology, Smithsonian Institution, 1892-1893,* ed. J. W. Powell, 329-598. Washington, D.C.

II.G.23 ❧ Water Buffalo

When the first created man saw the animals that God had made, it is said that he presumptuously, over-rating his powers, asked that he too might be given the creative power to fashion others like them. God granted his request and man tried his prentice hand. But the result was the buffalo, and man seeing that it was not good, asked in disgust that the creative power might be taken back again from him for ever. The buffalo, however, remained as the only living handiwork of man. (Bradley-Birt 1910: 115)

Although of limited value as a clue to the origins of the domesticated water buffalo *(Bubalus bubalis),* this tale from India does reflect the rather low opinion of this bovine held by many, including, it seems, scientists who have shown relatively little interest in it. Considering the large size of its population, its widespread distribution, and its essential role in the economic lives of millions of people, especially in southern and eastern Asia, it is remarkable that so little is known about the water buffalo. Bovine admiration and scholarly attention have been reserved for those more highly regarded distant relatives of the buffalo, the taurine and zebu cattle.

Admittedly, some admirable efforts have been made within the last few decades to remedy this situation. Most of the work that has been done has focused on the present-day conditions and future potential of buffalo husbandry, with breeding, management, and productivity being of central concern.[1] Research on the cultural and historical aspects of the buffalo, however, has been very limited.[2] Certainly, in the discussion of animal domestication, the buffalo has been largely ignored.[3]

This chapter presents the results of a preliminary investigation of the original domestication and history of the water buffalo. A perusal of the available literature reveals a frustrating scarcity of information and very sketchy evidence. Consequently, interpretations must be highly speculative. At this stage in the research definitive answers are well beyond reach, and the best conclusions we can now offer are merely those that might guide future research.

Nomenclature

Although there is general agreement that the domesticated water buffalo represents a single species, its relationship to other bovines[4] has been the subject of much disagreement. It received the name *Bos bubalis* from those naturalists who, beginning with Linnaeus in 1758, believed that bovines were all sufficiently similar to warrant classification under the same genus *(Bos).* Later taxonomists, using elaborate anatomical criteria, argued that bovine differences should be recognized by subgenera or genera status. In the many multiple genera and subgenera schemes that were proposed, a *Bubalus* genus or subgenus was always included for the classification of the water buffalo (and usually the other related "buffalo" – the *anoa, tamarau,* and African buffalo[5]).

The origin of the Latin appellation *bubalus* (or *bubalis*) is unknown. The learned ancients of Greece and Rome used the term, but seemingly in reference to an African antelope, most likely the bubal hartebeest *(Alcelaphus buselaphus).* From Roman through medieval times it was also applied to the European wild bison and the wild auroch (Buffon 1812: 304-8, 316-18; Pliny 1855: 262-3). When a Benedictine monk, Paul the Deacon, recorded the introduction of the domesticated Asian buffalo into Italy during the late sixth century A.D., he used the term *bubali* (Paul the Deacon 1907: 158-9; White 1974: 203-4). Thereafter, the accepted usage for *bubalus* was in reference to the Asian water buffalo.

The word "buffalo" was undoubtedly derived from the Latin *bubalus.* The Old English forms, *buffle* and *buff,* probably evolved through the French form *buffle,* but the present form seems to have entered English from the Portuguese *bufalo.* After some early European travelers in India erroneously used the word "buffalo" to refer to the zebu, the term "water buffalo" came into use to differentiate the true buffalo (Yule and Burnell 1903: 122; Murray et al. 1933: 1157). The confusion continued – as part of what Lynn White, Jr. (1974: 204), has called "the colonial transmission of antique and medieval perversity to North America" – when English speakers mistakenly used the word "buffalo" for the American bison. Use of the term "water buffalo" has been perpetuated as a means of avoiding this further confusion.

Biological and Ecological Characteristics

Appearance

The buffalo has a broad and massive body with short muscular legs ending in large splayed hoofs. Its shoulder height averages about 5 feet, and its length from nose to tail averages about 10 feet. The weight for adult buffalo varies from about 600 to 2,000 pounds. Although their massive bodies do not appear particularly graceful, they do reflect the animals' great strength (Figures II.G.23.1 and II.G.23.2).

Figure II.G.23.1 The domesticated water buffalo. (Photograph by the author.)

Figure II.G.23.2. Wild buffalo in Assam, with typical riparian and tall-grass habitat depicted. (Photo by Philippa Scott, from Pfeffer 1968: 156; courtesy of Chanticleer Press.)

Both sexes carry very distinctive transversely grooved and triangular cross-sectioned horns. These horns normally are crescent-shaped and incline upward, outward, and slightly backward following a single plane extending above and in the same plane as that of the forehead. Many variations in size and shape are found, from the short and tightly curled horns of the Murrah breed of northwestern India to the very long and nearly straight horns of the wild buffalo in Assam.

Shades of slate gray to black are the most common colors for the buffalo's skin and hair. Frequently the animal has light-colored chevrons under the jaw and on the chest and white or gray stockings. Although buffalo are born with a thick coat of long coarse hair, this hair generally becomes sparse as they age. In temperate or high-altitude locations, however, where cold weather is encountered, a heavy coat of hair is retained in the adult stage. Hair whorls are found in all breeds, and their individual distinctiveness has caused them to be used in some countries as a criterion for legal recognition and registration (Cockrill 1974a).

Adaptation and Habitat

Usually described as a denizen of the tropics, the buffalo is not capable of high heat tolerance. Its heat-regulating mechanisms are less efficient than those of European and Asian cattle, and under conditions of exposure to direct solar radiation, the buffalo exhibits a greater rise in body temperature, pulse, and respiration rates, and general discomfort. The buffalo is quicker, however, to show signs of comfort with a lowering of body temperature as a result of shade, artificial showers, or natural rain. As a means of cooling themselves and ridding themselves of insect pests, buffalo, unlike cattle, show a natural inclination to wallow.

The animal's preference for shade and semi-aquatic conditions is at least partially explained by the color and structure of its skin. Like most tropical animals, the buffalo has black skin that absorbs ultraviolet light, thus preventing inflammation and damage to the deeper skin layers. But unlike most tropical mammals that have a coat of light-colored hair that reflects infrared waves, the buffalo has only a sparse coat of dark hair on its dark skin. Although this black surface facilitates the absorption of heat in direct sun, it is also advantageous in shade because of its high heat-radiating powers. The buffalo also suffers from the absence of an efficient perspiring mechanism. The number of sweat glands per unit area of buffalo skin is less than one-sixth that of Western cattle and an even lesser proportion of that of zebu.[6]

Thus, the buffalo is well adapted to a tropical environment provided that environment includes sufficient cooling systems in the form of shade and water. In the wild state these conditions are met with an environment of high rainfall, heavy vegetation cover, and streams, lakes, swamps, or marshes for wallowing. Husbandry practices attempt to duplicate the conditions of the animal's natural habitat as much as possible by providing artificial shade, nearby water bodies for wallowing, and frequent splashing when needed.

The nature of the buffalo's feet, and its dietary habits, further indicates a semiaquatic, humid/tropical adaptation. The exceptional flexibility of its fetlock and pastern joints and its large splayed hoofs enable the animal to move easily in mud and water (Cockrill 1967: 124). Buffalo also reveal the remarkable ability to subsist entirely on those crude fibrous plants that form so much of tropical vegetation (especially around water courses), which other livestock will not touch. Experimentation has shown that compared to the zebu (its major economic rival in South Asia), the buffalo will consume more low-quality roughage, digest it more efficiently, and thereby maintain itself in better condition with greater strength and productivity (Whyte 1968: 218; Whyte and Mathur 1974: 555-6).

The "Swamp" and "River" Buffalo Types

Roderick MacGregor (1941) was probably the first to recognize a significant subdivision within the B. bubalis species. Based initially on his observations of differences in bathing habitat preferences, he distinguished the "Swamp buffalo," which was the native domesticated buffalo of East and Southeast Asia, from the "River buffalo," which was the type generally found in India and farther west.

A number of differences separate these two types. Swamp buffalo prefer mud-bottomed swamps and marshlands in contrast to the River buffalos' preference for rivers with firm bottoms and clear water. Swamp buffalo throughout their range seem to be morphologically very similar, with little specialization having occurred. They appear to be much closer to the wild buffalo than are the River buffalo. The latter, in contrast, show a great deal of regional variation, with many specialized breeds having been developed, especially for improved milk yield. The Swamp buffalo tends to have a shorter body, larger girth, shorter and thinner legs, and a shorter face than the River buffalo. Swamp buffalo horns are fairly uniform in size with the common widespread crescent shape; River buffalo manifest great variety in horn shapes, often with a spiraling curve close to the head.

Population, Distribution, and Uses

Before we venture into the distant past in search of clues to the buffalo's original domestication, it is valuable to view the present-day consequences of that domestication.[7] As the result of many millennia of human–buffalo interaction, the buffalo currently has an extensive geographical range and is involved in a great variety of husbandry contexts. Recent estimates place the total world population of domesticated buffalo at about 142 million (Table II.G.23.1). Although these animals are reported from 31 countries (Map II.G.23.1), a high degree of concentration characterizes this distribution: Ninety-six percent reside in the countries of South, Southeast, and East Asia, with 80 percent in just the three countries of India, Pakistan, and China. India leads all other countries with 54 percent of the world total (about 77 million buffalo). Relatively small numbers are found in Southwest Asia, southern and Eastern Europe, and South America. The only countries within this peripheral zone that possess fairly significant numbers (over 1 million) are Egypt and Brazil.

East and Southeast Asia

In the area east of India, the Swamp buffalo dominates and is essentially a single-purpose animal, contributing primarily to the traction needs of the agricultural system. It is in the wet rice fields of southern China and Southeast Asia that the buffalo distinguishes itself as the preferred draft animal. The humid climate, the mud, and the water suit the animal's constitution and habits. No other domesticated animal can equal the buffalo's ability to carry out the plowing, harrowing, and puddling tasks of wet rice cultivation. Its considerable weight causes it to sink deep in the mud; the flexibility of its fetlock and pastern joints, its large splayed hoofs, coarse limbs, and bulky body allow it to maintain a balanced traction in mud and water; its enormous strength enables it to pull the plow deep into the soil.

In China, the cattle to buffalo ratio is about 4:1, with the buffalo distribution limited almost entirely to the rice-growing area in the southeast. Cattle are preferred in the drier and more temperate northern and western regions (Phillips, Johnson, and Moyer 1945: 62–6; Epstein 1969: 26–32; Cockrill 1976). But in mainland and island Southeast Asia, where wet rice cultivation dominates the agricultural economies, the buffalo becomes more important. The average cattle to buffalo ratio throughout Southeast Asia is about 2:1. Three countries – Laos, Brunei Darus, and the Philippines – actually possess more buffalo than cattle.

Eastern and southeastern Asia is located beyond the traditional limits of milking and milk use in Asia (Simoons 1970). The peoples in this area generally do not include milk or milk products in their diet and exhibit high incidences of primary adult lactose intolerance.[8] A limited market for buffalo milk, however, has been found in some cities and in the small Indian and European communities scattered throughout the region.

Buffalo are rarely raised specifically for meat pro-

Table II.G.23.1. *Population of water buffalo (based on national livestock censuses and FAO estimates for 1991)*

Region/Country	Population	Buffalo per 1,000 people
South Asia		
Bangladesh	810,000[a]	6.8
Bhutan	4,000[a]	2.6
India	77,000,000	88.4
Nepal	3,101,000[a]	158.2
Pakistan	15,031,000	118.7
Sri Lanka	981,000[a]	56.3
Southeast Asia		
Brunei Darus	10,000[a]	36.5
Indonesia	3,500,000[a]	18.6
Kampuchia	760,000[a]	18.7
Laos	1,100,000[a]	257.9
Malaysia	190,000[a]	10.4
Myanmar	2,080,000[a]	48.9
Philippines	2,710,000	42.4
Thailand	4,743,000	84.0
Vietnam	371,000	43.0
East Asia		
China (incl. Taiwan)	21,635,000	18.7
Southwest Asia and Africa		
Egypt	2,550,000[a]	47.6
Iran	300,000	5.4
Iraq	110,000[a]	5.6
Syria	1,000[a]	0.1
Turkey	371,000	6.5
Europe and the former Soviet Union		
Albania	2,000[a]	0.6
Bulgaria	26,000	2.9
Greece	1,000[a]	0.1
Italy	112,000	1.9
Romania	180,000[a]	7.8
Yugoslavia (former)	20,000[a]	0.8
Former Soviet Union	434,000[a]	1.5
South America and the Caribbean		
Brazil	1,490,000	9.7
Trinidad and Tobago	9,000[a]	6.9
Suriname	1,000[a]	2.3
World Total	142,189,000	26.4

[a]FAO estimate.

Source: FAO (1992), pp. 191–3.

duction or for any other purpose. Retired work animals, after having provided 10 to 20 years of service, are either slaughtered or allowed to die a natural death, at which time they contribute meat, horns, and hides to the local economy. While alive, the buffalo produces a very important by-product for the farmer – manure, a valuable alternative or addition to scarce and expensive chemical fertilizers.

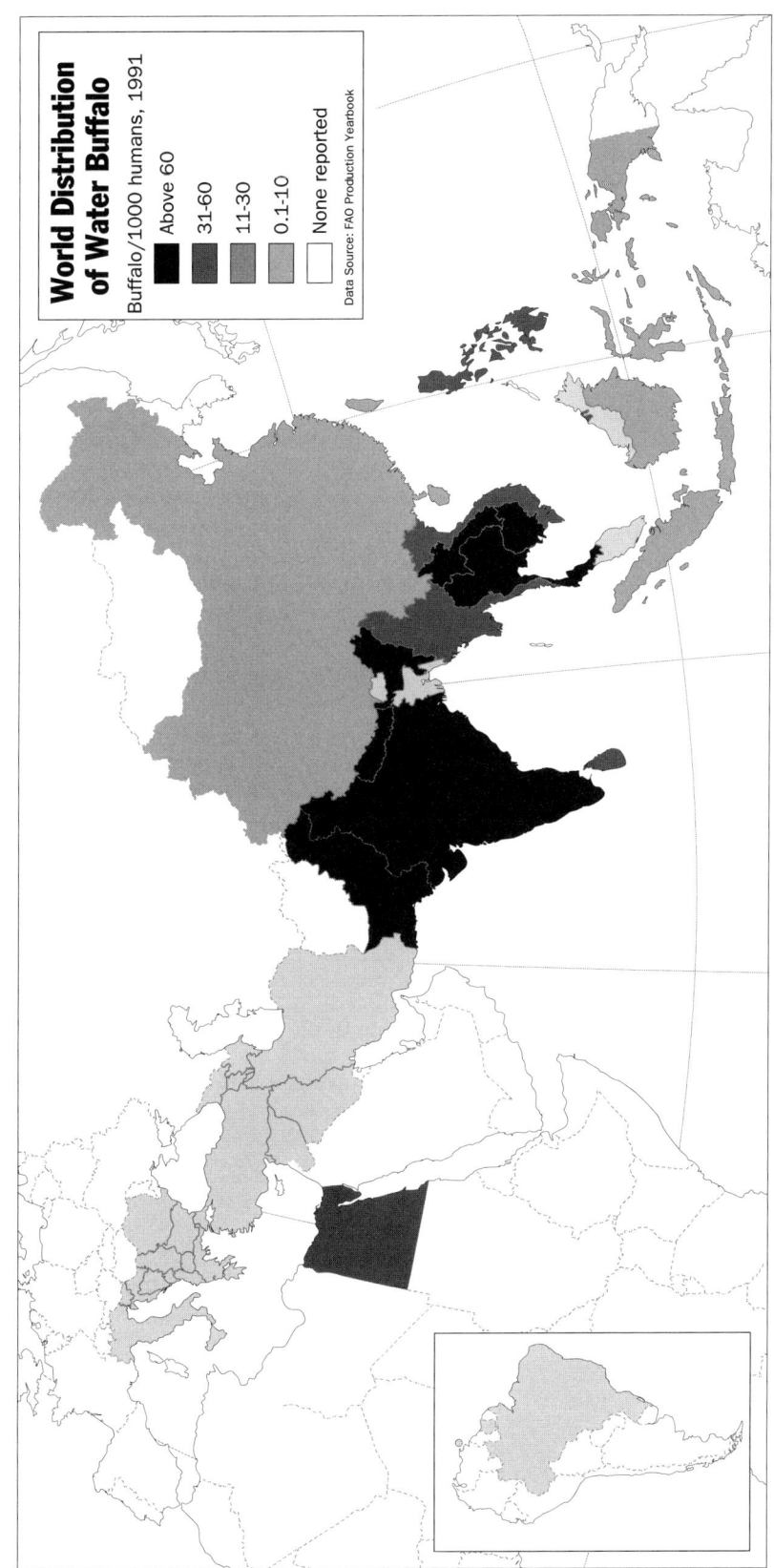

Map II.G.23.1. World distribution of water buffalo.

South Asia

The buffalo is found in its greatest concentration in South Asia and there exhibits its greatest biological diversity and attains its greatest utility as a dairy animal. The distributions of the River and Swamp buffalo meet, and in some places overlap, in South Asia, and, although River buffalo predominate, Swamp buffalo are found in the Assam and Tamil Nadu states of India, and in Bangladesh, Sri Lanka, and Nepal (Porter 1991: 290–1). Selective breeding of River buffalo, primarily in India and Pakistan, has resulted in the formation of several distinct dairy breeds and even a few draft breeds. Probably between 15 and 20 percent of the buffalo in this region can be identified as representatives of defined breeds; the rest are nondescript local varieties (Hoffpauir 1974: 141–51).

As in eastern Asia, the buffalo in South Asia performs an important service as a work animal, especially in the wet rice fields, but this role is subordinate to that of milk production. In India, for example, only about 15 percent of all buffalo are classified as work animals, and they account for only about 10 percent of the total bovine workforce. The more versatile zebu bullock is the generally preferred work animal.

Even though the zebu outnumbers the buffalo in India by about 2.6 to 1, and buffalo account for only about one-third of the bovine population that is milked, over 60 percent of the milk produced comes from buffalo (Hoffpauir 1982: 223). In Pakistan and Nepal, fully two-thirds of the milk produced comes from buffalo (Cockrill 1974b: 605; Khan 1974: 612). Nature (presumably aided by selective breeding) has provided the buffalo with certain milk-producing abilities that are distinctly superior to those of the zebu – namely, the ability to yield more milk (usually between two and three times more), the ability to produce milk with higher butterfat content (between 6.5 and 8.5 percent, compared with 3.0 to 5.0 percent in zebu milk), and the ability to produce this milk while subsisting on poor-quality fodder (Hoffpauir 1977).

In Hindu India the slaughtering of the buffalo and the eating of its flesh is not generally practiced. This is probably explained by the general *ahimsa* (the Hindu/Jain/Buddhist principle of noninjury to living things) and vegetarian proclivities of the Indian culture, rather than by any special status similar to that of the sacred zebu. The Moslems in Pakistan and Bangladesh have no prohibition on the slaughtering of buffalo, but buffalo meat is unpopular because of the poor quality that is marketed. Most Pakistanis and Bangladeshis prefer beef (Cockrill 1974b: 535; Khan 1974: 611).

The population of buffalo in Bangladesh is far less than might be expected, given the predominance of wet rice cultivation throughout this Ganges–Brahmaputra delta area. In fact, it appears that the disasters this country has suffered in recent decades (typhoons, floods, earthquakes, and warfare) have decimated the buffalo population. Most of the buffalo still there are of the Swamp type and are used mainly for work. Small numbers of dairy buffalo have been imported, but milk production remains low (Cockrill 1974b: 533–5).

The adaptability of the buffalo to high altitudes is clearly demonstrated in Nepal, where this tropical animal is maintained in village settings as high as 9,000 feet and is taken for summer pasturage as high as 15,000 feet. In Nepal, the buffalo is truly a multipurpose animal: It provides work power, milk, manure, and meat. In the tropical lowlands of the *terai* (the northern extension of the Indo-Gangetic plain in southern Nepal), it is the preferred draft animal for wet rice cultivation; it is seldom used for work elsewhere. In the lower and middle altitudes, the buffalo is the primary source of milk. Buffalo have been introduced into Nepal from India for the purpose of improving milk production. Whether the native Nepalese buffalo are of the Swamp or River type has yet to be determined. In many mountainous locations, the buffalo is used exclusively for the production of manure, an extremely valuable resource given the low fertility of the mountain soils. Nepalese law permits the killing of male buffalo, and considerable numbers are slaughtered for ritual sacrifice and for the urban meat market (Rouse 1970, 2: 905–6; Cockrill 1974b: 603–9; Epstein 1977: 38–46; Hoffpauir 1978: 238–41).

In many ways Sri Lanka follows the typical Southeast Asian pattern of buffalo use. Its indigenous buffalo is of the Swamp type and serves primarily as a work animal in the rice-growing areas. Some buffalo milk is produced and sold in the form of curd, but generally buffalo owners are not interested in milk production. Frederick Simoons (1970: 561–3) has commented on the survival of a nonmilking attitude among the Sinhalese, the dominant group in Sri Lanka. With a population that is predominantly Buddhist and Hindu, Sri Lanka has a limited demand for meat. Only old, sick, or infertile buffalo are allowed by law to be slaughtered; so the buffalo meat that reaches the markets tends to be tough and without taste (Cockrill 1974b: 629–35; Porter 1991: 291).

Southwest Asia and Egypt

There are few environments in the dry southwestern end of Asia and northern Africa that are suitable for the buffalo. Consequently, those in Iran, Iraq, Syria, Turkey, and Egypt account for only about 2.4 percent of the world's total. The only country in this region where buffalo make a significant economic contribution is Egypt. For the Southwest Asian countries, the cattle to buffalo ratio is 26:1; for Egypt it is 1.4:1.

All of the buffalo in this region appear to be of River buffalo ancestry, having been introduced from South Asia during the first millennium A.D. According to historical records, Sassanians brought domesticated buffalo and their herders from Sind in Pakistan to the marshes of the lower Tigris and Euphrates Delta during the fifth century A.D. Buffalo were established in the Jordan Valley by the eighth century and in Anatolia by the ninth century (White 1974: 204-5). They were not known in ancient Egypt and do not seem to have appeared in the Nile Valley until about the ninth century A.D. (Epstein 1971: 567-8; Cockrill 1984: 57).

The 2.5 million buffalo in the Nile Valley of Egypt today are fully utilized for milk, work, and meat. Egyptians have thoroughly researched their productivity and have developed an efficient husbandry system. Buffalo are highly valued as milk animals and produce far more milk than cattle. Although cattle are more important than buffalo for draft purposes, the latter are used for plowing and harrowing in rice fields, for raising water from wells for irrigation, and for threshing. John E. Rouse (1970: 621-2) reported that only buffalo cows are used for work. The common practice is for male calves to be slaughtered at a very young age for veal, which brings a high market price. Female buffalo are also slaughtered for their meat, but only if they are old, infertile, or injured (Epstein I: 1971: 564; El-Itriby 1974; Porter 1991: 299-300).[9]

Not surprisingly, given the water needs of this bovine, the major concentrations of buffalo in Southwest Asia are in swampy areas and along coasts. The buffalo in Southwest Asia is esteemed only by small numbers of peasant farmers and herders who recognize the animal's unique adaptability to environments that are unable to support other livestock. Throughout this area the buffalo is valued primarily as a milk animal[10] and used very little for work, except in Turkey, where in some areas buffalo are employed in plowing and road haulage. Buffalo meat is merely a by-product from old retired animals (Rouse 1970, 2: 794, 804, 854; Cockrill 1974b: 510-32; Porter 1991: 297, 298).

Europe and Transcaucasia

The existence of the buffalo in the temperate latitudes of Italy, Greece, the Balkan peninsula, and Transcaucasia in the former Soviet Union attests to the animal's ability to tolerate cold winter temperatures. But their numbers are small - the total population being only about 775,000 - and care must be taken to keep these animals warm during the winter; cold winds and sudden drops in temperature can cause fatal illnesses, including pneumonia (National Research Council 1981: 45-6).

All European and Transcaucasian buffalo are of the River type. Historical accounts are sketchy but indicate that domesticated buffalo may have entered Europe by a route north of the Black Sea, from Persia to southern Russia to the Danube Valley and, finally, to Italy by the end of the sixth century A.D. Another likely route could have been from Turkey to Greece, the Balkans, and Italy. They were established in Transylvania by the eleventh century and were numerous in the area around Rome by the twelfth century (Bökönyi 1974: 151; White 1974: 203-6).

The discontinuous and spotty distribution pattern that characterizes the buffalo's existence in Southwest Asia is also found in Europe. In Greece, for example, 90 percent of the buffalo are found in Macedonia and Thrace. In Romania there are two concentrations, one in the central regions near Cluj and Fagaras, and another in the Danube Valley of the south. The Italian buffalo are found mainly in the southern part of the country. The only buffalo in the former Soviet Union are in the Transcaucasus region, where they are most numerous in the Kura Valley and along the Caspian coast in Azerbaijan.

Throughout most of its European and Transcaucasian distribution, the buffalo has served as a triple-purpose animal. Its use as a work animal, originally of primary importance, has declined in recent times with the mechanization of agriculture, especially in Italy, Greece, and Bulgaria. Meat production is growing in importance, although buffalo meat still comes mostly from old animals whose usefulness for work and milk production has been exhausted. The buffalo is highly valued for its rich milk, which is often made into yoghurt and cheese. In Italy, where probably the best buffalo in Europe are found, the emphasis has long been on milk production, with the highly popular mozzarella cheese the major product (Cockrill 1974b: 708, 731-5, 748-54; Polikhronov 1974; Salerno 1974; Porter 1991: 297-9).

Tropical America

Introductions of buffalo into various Caribbean and South American countries during the past 100 years have met with mixed results. Those into Bolivia, Colombia, French Guiana, Guyana, Peru, and Venezuela were apparently unsuccessful, and either the animals have entirely disappeared or their numbers have become too insignificant to be reported in recent censuses. Possibly a thousand buffalo can still be found in Surinam, derived from an 1895 introduction of Swamp buffalo from Southeast Asia, via French Guiana, to work on the sugar plantations. They are used today in logging operations and for meat production. Indian River buffalo were brought into Trinidad and Tobago during the early 1900s, also for the sugar plantations. A sizable population of about 9,000 animals has developed, and they are highly valued for their work power and meat (Cockrill 1974b: 676, 692-7, 705-7; Mahadevan 1974; Porter 1991: 300-2).

The most successful establishment of buffalo husbandry in the Western Hemisphere has been in Brazil. Numerous introductions of both Swamp buffalo (from eastern and southern Asia) and River buffalo (from India and Italy) have occurred over the last century. The nearly 2.5 million Brazilian buffalo today are concentrated in two areas, with about 75 percent in the Amazon Basin and the rest in and around the states of São Paulo and Minas Gerais. The buffalo are used primarily for milk in the latter areas, with meat production secondary although growing in importance. In the Amazon area the buffalo has found a paradise, with ideal environmental conditions. On Marajó Island, large herds of free-ranging buffalo thrive on the tropical grasses and aquatic plants. Buffalo meat and milk command a ready market in the towns of Amazonia, and the animal is also used for road haulage and riding (Gade 1970; Cockrill 1974b: 677–91; Porter 1991: 301).

The Wild Ancestor

Unlike the progenitors of many other domesticated animals, the wild form from which the domesticated buffalo originated is not only known but still survives in a few locations. Wild buffalo differ from the domesticated form chiefly in their greater size, larger horns, and generally more robust and sleek appearance.

The Plio-Pleistocene Buffalo

The evolutionary history of the wild buffalo appears to have begun about 3.5 million years ago in the northwestern corner of the Indian subcontinent. The earliest fossil to show uniquely *Bubalus* characteristics is *Proamphibos* from the upper Dhokpathan Formation (Middle Pliocene) of the Siwalik Hills (Groves 1981: 270, 276).

Within South Asia, when the conditions in the northwest became unfavorable on account of Pleistocene glaciation, the Siwalik fauna, including the buffalo, apparently migrated southward and eastward. The Middle Pleistocene form *Bubalus palaeindicus* has been discovered in the Potwar Plain of northern Pakistan as well as in the Narbada Valley of peninsular India. By the Upper Pleistocene the buffalo was found as far south as Tamil Nadu and as far east as Bihar. As revealed by bone finds and cave paintings[11] over a wide range of the Indian subcontinent, the buffalo was undoubtedly hunted by Paleolithic and Mesolithic peoples throughout the Pleistocene and into the Holocene (Map II.G.23.2 and Table II.G.23.2).

The buffalo appeared in China as early as the Middle Pleistocene (possibly between 1 million and 500,000 years ago), and its remains are often found associated with early hominids/humans in Paleolithic sites. Although most *Bubalus* finds from Chinese sites are reported as being of indeterminate species, some distinct species have been identified. A dozen Pleistocene sites in South China (south of the Qin Ling Mountains) have yielded buffalo remains.

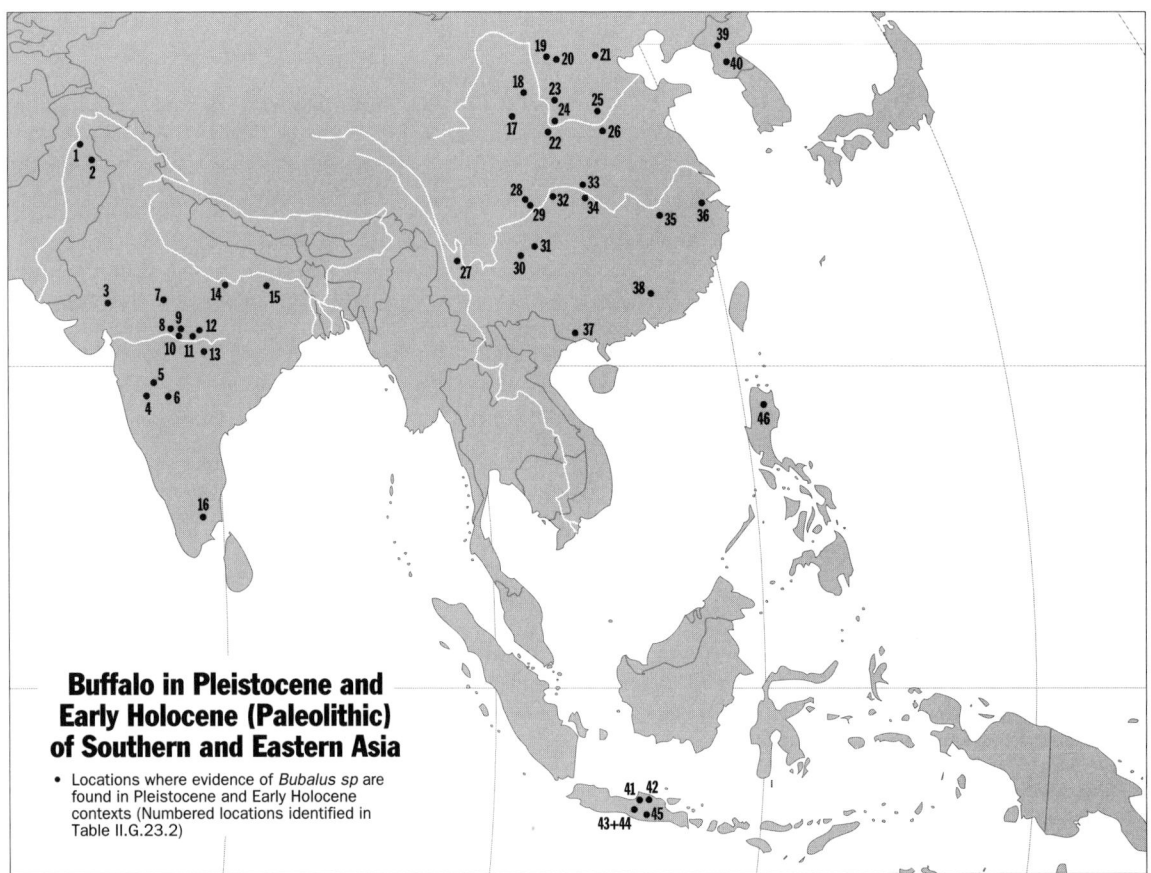

Buffalo in Pleistocene and Early Holocene (Paleolithic) of Southern and Eastern Asia

• Locations where evidence of *Bubalus sp* are found in Pleistocene and Early Holocene contexts (Numbered locations identified in Table II.G.23.2)

Map II.G.23.2. Buffalo in Pleistocene and Early Holocene (Paleolithic) of southern and eastern Asia.

Table II.G.23.2. *Evidence of the existence of* Bubalus *sp. in the Pleistocene and Early Holocene (Paleolithic) of southern and eastern Asia (identification of numbers on Map II.G.23.2)*

Location	Time	Source
India/Pakistan		
1. Campbellpore	Lower/Middle Pleistocene	Terra and Teilhard de Chardin 1936: 796
2. Potwar Plain	Middle Pleistocene	Movius 1944:21
3. Langhnaj	Mesolithic	Sankalia 1946: 148, 314; Fairservis 1971: 95, 100
4. Ghod Valley	Upper Pleistocene	Badam 1985: 413
5. Upper Godavari Valley	Upper Pleistocene	Badam 1984: 756
6. Upper Manjar Valley	Upper Pleistocene	Badam 1984: 757
7. Chibbarnala	(unknown)	Mathpal 1984: 19
8. Itar Pahar	(unknown)	Mathpal 1984: 18
9. Bhopal area	Mesolithic	Mathpal 1984: 16
10. Bhimbetka	Mesolithic	Mathpal 1984: 105-6
11. Adamgarh	Mesolithic	Allchin and Allchin 1968: 83, 256; Sankalia 1978: 87
12. Putli Karar	(unknown)	Mathpal 1984: 17
13. Narbada Valley (near Narsinghpur)	Middle Pleistocene	Terra and Teilhard de Chardin 1936: 820; Wheeler 1959: 43–44
14. Belan and Seoti Valleys	Middle/Upper Pleistocene	Sankalia 1977: 66; Badam 1984: 755
15. Paimar Valley	Upper Pleistocene	Badam 1984: 755
16. Ariyalur region	Upper Pleistocene	Badam 1984: 765
China		
17. Qing-yang	Upper Pleistocene	Aigner 1981: 258
18. Sjara-osso-gol	Upper Pleistocene	Aigner 1981: 83, 84, 248, 303; Defen and Chunhua 1985: 275, 285; Jia and Huang 1985: 212
19. Shuo-hsien	Middle/Upper Pleistocene	Aigner 1981: 225
20. Shiyu	Upper Pleistocene	Pearson 1983: 120; Wu and Wang 1985: 44
21. Zhoukoudian (Localities 1, 7, 9, 13)	Middle Pleistocene	Aigner 1981: 81, 108, 116, 148, 302, 311–14; Defen and Chunhua 1985: 272, 282
22. Dali	Early Upper Pleistocene	Defen and Chunhua 1985: 284; Qiu 1985: 207
23. Dingcun	Early Upper Pleistocene	Aigner 1981: 84, 303; Defen and Chunhua 1985; 284
24. K'o-ho	Middle Pleistocene	Aigner 1981: 82, 178, 302; Chang 1986: 48
25. Hsiao-nan-hai	Upper Pleistocene	Aigner 1981: 89, 303
26. Lingching	Upper Pleistocene	Aigner 1981: 96
27. Lichiang district (Locality 6003)	Upper Pleistocene	Aigner 1981: 59, 295
28. Tungnan	Upper Pleistocene	Aigner 1981: 295
29. Koloshan	Middle Pleistocene	Aigner 1981: 295
30. Chihchin	Middle Pleistocene	Aigner 1981: 295
31. Guanyindong	Middle Pleistocene	Defen and Chunhua 1985: 283
32. Yenchingkou	Middle Pleistocene	Aigner 1981: 295
33. Chihchiang cave	Middle Pleistocene	Aigner 1981: 295
34. Changyang	Middle/Upper Pleistocene	Aigner 1974: 31; Defen and Chunhua 1985: 286
35. Yungshan cave	Middle/Upper Pleistocene	Aigner 1981: 71
36. Jiande	Upper Pleistocene	Defen and Chunhua 1985: 286
37. Ya-p'u-shan and Ma-lang-ch'uan	Early Holocene	Aigner 1981: 64; Chang 1986: 86
38. Northern Kwangtung	Middle Pleistocene	Aigner 1981: 295
Korea		
39. Tokchon cave	Upper Pleistocene	Pokee 1984: 880
40. Sangwon Komunmoru cave	Middle Pleistocene	Pokee 1984: 880, 882
Java		
41. Sampung cave	Early Holocene	Medway 1972: 81; Bellwood 1985: 37, 220
42. Ngandong	Upper Pleistocene	Movius 1944: 86; Koenigswald 1951: 219; Medway 1972: 80; Jacob 1978: 17
43. Djetis	Lower Middle Pleistocene	Medway 1972: 79
44. Trinil (same site as #43, but at higher level)	Middle Pleistocene	Medway 1972: 79; Jacob 1978: 16
45. Patjitan	Late Middle Pleistocene or Early Upper Pleistocene	Movius 1944: 90
Philippines		
46. Cagayan Valley	Middle Pleistocene	Fox 1978: 79; Fox 1979: 230

The Pleistocene buffalo that appear in North China are interpreted as immigrants from the south, and their existence as far north as 40° north latitude attests to their adaptability to cooler and drier environments. The buffalo apparently extended its range eastward from North China into Korea during the Middle Pleistocene. *Bubalus* has been uncovered at two cave sites, Sangwon Komunmoru and Tokchon. As in North China, this presence appears to represent a remarkable adaptation to what must have been a rather harsh Pleistocene environment.

Buffalo ventured out onto the land masses of the Sunda shelf probably as early as they reached China. Although no Pleistocene buffalo have been firmly identified as yet from mainland Southeast Asia, they must have existed there, or at least passed through on their way to Sundaland. A very large form of a now extinct buffalo *Bubalus paleo kerabau* inhabited Java from the early Middle Pleistocene to the early Holocene. The only other indication of the buffalo in island Southeast Asia[12] comes from the discovery of *Bubalus* in association with the Liwanian Flake Tool Tradition in the Cagayan Valley on the Philippine island of Luzon. Robert Fox (1978: 82, 1979: 229–30)

has suggested that Paleolithic hunters, along with the buffalo and other typical Middle Pleistocene mammals, migrated from South China into the Philippines across the then-existing land connections via Taiwan.

A long-distance westward migration of Pleistocene buffalo is evidenced by the finding of *Bubalus* at three sites in Europe (not shown on Map II.G.23.2).[13] A form called *Bubalus murrensis* is known from the two sites at Steinheim and Schönebeck in Germany, both dated from the Mindel-Riss interglacial, about 250,000 years ago, and Riss-Würm interglacial site of possibly 100,000 years ago in the Peneios Valley of Greece. The buffalo seem to have been able to exist in Europe only during the interglacial periods and had disappeared by the beginning of the last (Würm) glaciation (Zeuner 1963: 246; Kurtén 1968: 187; Bökönyi 1974: 149–50).

Holocene Survivals

The wild buffalo probably maintained a broad range throughout southern, eastern, and southeastern Asia well into the Holocene. Evidence of *B. bubalis* has been reported from many archaeological sites in this area, dating from between 10,000 and 2,000 years ago. But whether these findings reflect locations before or

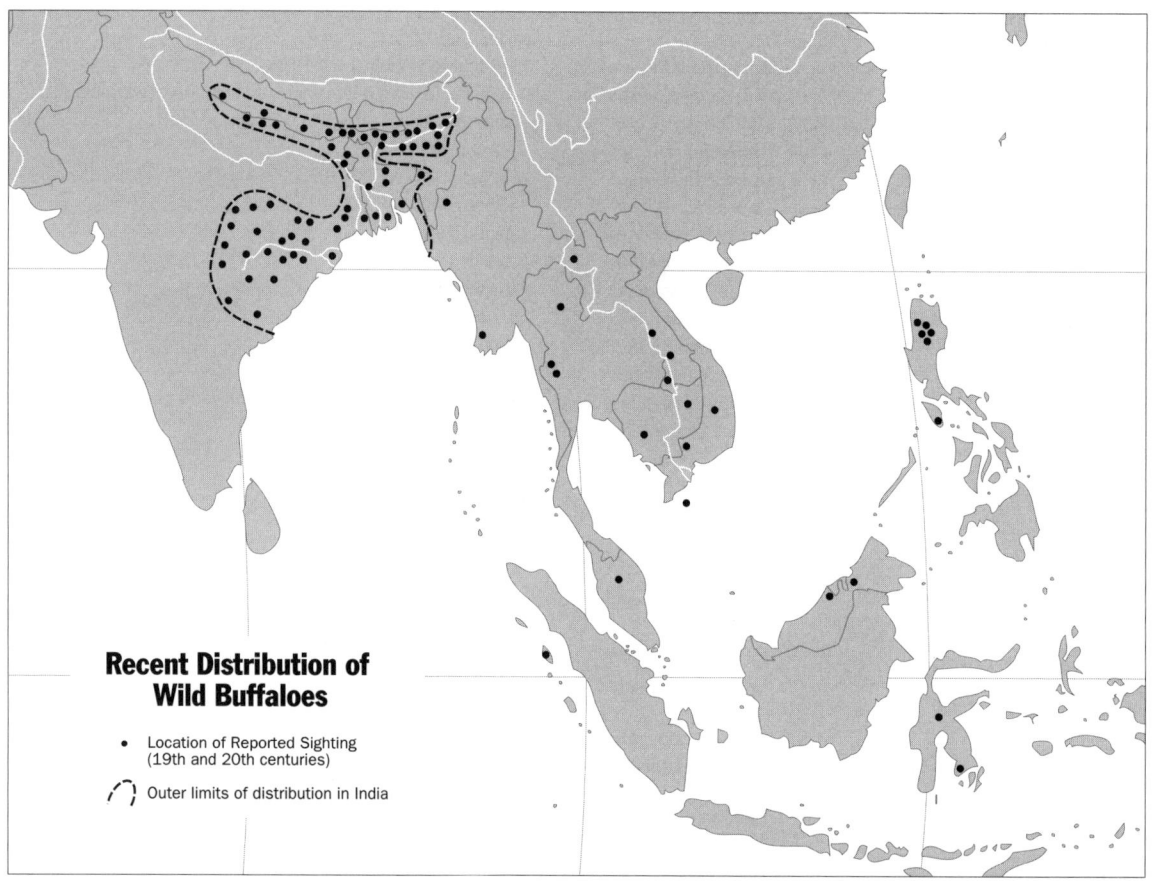

Recent Distribution of Wild Buffaloes

- • Location of Reported Sighting (19th and 20th centuries)

- ⌒ Outer limits of distribution in India

Map II.G.23.3. Recent distribution of wild buffaloes.

after domestication is, in many cases, difficult to say because of the morphological similarity between wild and domesticated buffalo. (The significance of these Neolithic and early Metal Age findings to the question of earliest domestication is discussed later in this chapter.) Consequently, we do not have a clear picture of the distribution of the wild buffalo several thousand years ago when it probably was first domesticated.

Reported sightings during the last two centuries indicate that the wild buffalo's range has generally retreated to east of the 80° meridian in southern and southeastern Asia (Map II.G.23.3). In South Asia, the wild buffalo are known in the *terai* of Nepal, the plains of Bengal and Assam, and lowland areas in Orissa, Madhya Pradesh, and Andhra Pradesh. They are described as generally inhabiting moist lowland riverine tracts where dense and high vegetation cover, usually tall grass jungles, and nearby swamps are available.

The distribution of the wild form of a domesticated species has often proved a valuable indicator of that animal's original place of domestication. This, unfortunately, is not the case with the buffalo. All that can be concluded from the available evidence is that the wild buffalo's distribution has responded to changing environmental circumstances that have occurred during and since the Pleistocene. As conditions under which the buffalo can exist have appeared and disappeared, its range has changed accordingly. Generally, the animal's extremely broad range during the Pleistocene, especially during the interglacial stages, has been shrinking throughout the Holocene. Its recent limited distribution is best seen as merely its last remaining refuge area and not necessarily as indicative of an ancestral hearth of domestication.

Domestication

Archaeological Evidence
The most convincing and satisfying evidence for the place and time of domestication of an animal species would be well-preserved fossilized bones that can be clearly identified as to species and domesticated status. Unfortunately, such evidence is relatively rare for the buffalo because the warm and moist environments in which buffalo usually exist make the chances of good skeletal preservation poor. Even when *B. bubalis* bones can be identified, as they have in many Neolithic and Metal Age sites (Map II.G.23.4 and Table II.G.23.3), the ability to distinguish between wild and domesticated forms is hindered by the absence of clear morphological differences. Consequently, fossil evidence must be very cautiously interpreted.[14]

South Asia. The earliest indication of a possibly domesticated buffalo in South Asia comes from the Indus Valley civilization (about 2300–1750 B.C.). The evidence, collected from the two sites of Mohenjo-daro and Harappa, consists of only a few fossils (teeth, horn cores, and bones[15]), depictions on a small number of seal-amulets

(Figure II.G.23.3), and two small figurines.[16] Many authorities have accepted the notion that the Indus Valley buffalo was domesticated, and some have even suggested that these finds represent the original domestication.[17] Such a conclusion, however, seems to be based solely on the fossils' structural resemblance to the domesticated form and on the fact that a few seals show the buffalo standing in front of an object that has been interpreted as a feeding trough (Figure II.G.23.3).

Evidence that the buffalo existed in the Indus Valley only in the wild state is far more convincing. There are four scenes from seals and prism-amulets that seem to depict the buffalo being hunted. In three scenes (Figure II.G.23.3) a man is shown with a foot on the animal's head, one hand grasping a horn and the other hand holding a spear about to be thrust into the beast. In another scene the buffalo appears to have attacked a number of people who are sprawled around the ground.

When the sex of the animal can be detected, it is always male. As with the depictions of all other bovines, the Indus Valley seals seem to emphasize the power and strength of the bulls rather than the services derived from them or the cows. There are no scenes of the buffalo being milked or pulling a plow or cart, and the so-called food trough also appears on other seals in front of tigers and rhinoceroses. In fact, the troughs are not shown with those animals that were most likely domesticated, such as sheep, goats, elephants, and zebu.[18] Sir John Marshall (1931, 1: 70), the original excavator of Mohenjo-daro, suggested that the troughs represent offerings of food to worshiped animals, both in the wild and in captivity. Others have interpreted the troughs as cult objects or symbols connected to sacrificial ritual (Hiltebeitel 1978: 779).

Interpreting religious content from artifactual remains is, at best, a dangerous endeavor. With the Indus Valley culture in mind, Sir Mortimer Wheeler (1968: 108) has reminded us of "the notorious incapacity of material symbols to represent the true content and affinity of a religion or belief" and of "the indivisibility of religious and secular concepts in ancient times." Much of the attempt to decipher the religion of the Indus Valley people has focused on the interpretation of one particular seal scene, called the "Proto-Siva" scene, in which the buffalo plays a prominent role (Figure II.G.23.3). The significance of the buffalo and other animals shown around the seated godlike figure and the meaning of the buffalo-horn headdress worn by the seated figure are but two of the many concerns scholars have had about this picture. Some writers have assigned an important role to the buffalo in the religious symbolism and ritual life of these people (Sastri 1957: 6–13; Sullivan 1964; Srinivasan 1975-6; Hiltebeitel 1978). If true, the implications could be profound for the question of domestication, suggesting, for example, a ceremonial motivation.

Within the riparian environment of the Indus River and its tributaries, the wild buffalo could have found

Figure II.G.23.3. Depictions of water buffalo on seal-amulets from Mohenjo-daro. (From Mackay 1937–38.)

the marshy and grassy habitats that it prefers. The safest conclusion that can be reached at this point is that the wild buffalo existed in the Indus Valley during the third millennium B.C.; it was possibly hunted for its meat and may even have played some role in the religious life of the people. But the case for the existence of the domesticated buffalo is weak and unconvincing.[19]

The buffalo appears in later archaeological sites in India (see Map II.G.23.4 and Table II.G.23.3), but the domesticated status continues to be indeterminable. Small numbers of buffalo bones have been uncovered in Neolithic and Copper Age sites, dated from the second and first millennia B.C., south and east of the Indus Valley. But the majority of the bones at these sites belong to the domesticated zebu *(Bos indicus)*, and the number of buffalo bones is very small, sometimes no more than a single bone at a site. Some of the bones are charred and have cut marks on them, a clear indication that the animals were cooked and

eaten. An occasional successful hunt of the wild buffalo could easily explain these remains.

The north Indian site of Hastinapura (1100 B.C. to A.D. 300) is said to reflect the expansion of the Indo-Aryan peoples from their original homeland in the Punjab region into the Ganges Valley of Uttar Pradesh. Although the fossil evidence (12 buffalo bones, some charred and with cut marks) is no more convincing than at other sites, it is probably safe to say that these were domesticated buffalo.

We can draw this conclusion because, although archaeological evidence fails us, literary evidence, at least for early historic northern India, throws some light on the question. The oldest literary work, the *Rig Veda,* which is believed to reflect Indo-Aryan culture as early as 1500 B.C., makes reference to "buffaloes yoked in fours," the eating of buffalo flesh by the gods, and the slaughtering of from 100 to 300 buffalo at a time as sacrificial offerings to the god Indra (Griffith 1963, 1: 489, 575, 2: 123, 133, 226).

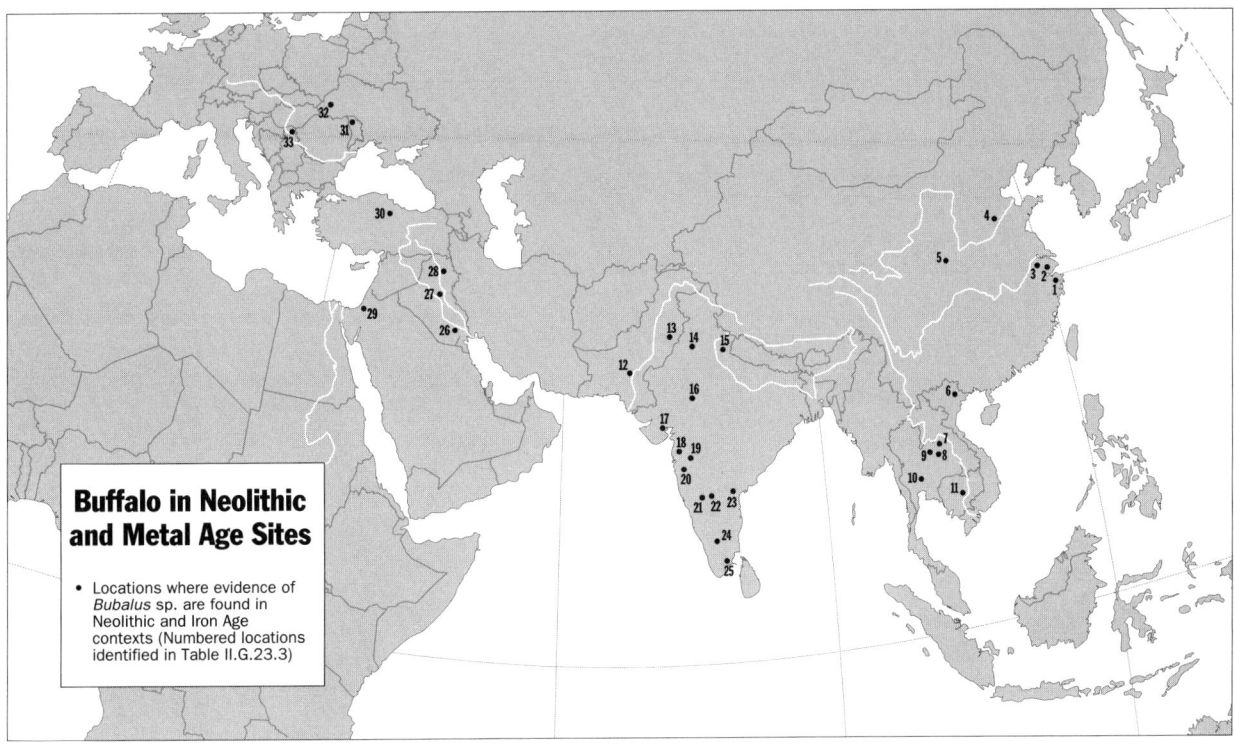

Map II.G.23.4. Buffalo in Neolithic and Metal Age sites.

Table II.G.23.3. *Evidence of the existence of buffalo at Neolithic and Metal Age sites (identification of numbers on Map II.G.23.4)*

Location	Time	Source
China		
1. Ho-mu-tu culture	6500 B.P.	Meacham 1983: 159; Pearson 1983: 124; Bellwood 1985: 219-20; Chang 1986: 211; Zhao and Wu 1986-7: 30-1; Smith 1995: 126, 140
2. Ma-chia-pang culture (aka Lake Ta'i-ha culture and Ch'in-lien-kang culture)	6500 B.P.	Pearson 1983: 131; Chang 1986: 201; Smith 1995: 125
3. Liang-chu culture	6000-4000 B.P.	Chang 1986: 254
4. Anyang	3800-3200 B.P.	Sowerby 1935: 234-7; Creel 1937: 76, 80; Coon 1955: 331; Chang 1980: 31-3, 138-43
5. Shaanxi phase of Lung-shan culture (aka K'o-hsing-chung)	5000-4000 B.P.	Ho 1975: 96; Chang 1986: 279
Southeast Asia		
6. Bo-lum (Bacson culture)	10,000 B.P.	Gorman 1971: 308; Meacham 1977: 423, 437
7. Ban Chiang	3600 B.P.	Higham and Kijngam 1979: 213-16; Higham and Kijngam 1985: 420-2
8. Ban Tong	probably after 4000 B.P.	Higham and Kijngam 1979: 218-19
9. Don Khlang	probably after 4000 B.P.	Higham and Kijngam 1979: 220
10. Chansen	2000 B.P. (Metal Age)	Wetherill 1972: 44, 45; Higham 1977: 404
11. Somron-Seng	possibly 2500 B.P. (Late Neolithic)	Boriskovskii 1970-1: 243
India/Pakistan		
12. Mohenjo-daro	4300-3750 B.P.	Marshall 1931, 1: v, 70-2, 386, 659, 666-8; Prashad 1936: 8-9, 43-6; Mackay 1937-8, 1: 45, 284, 292-3, 298, 311, 330, 336-9, 358-62, 670, 671; Vats 1940: 323; Fairservis 1971: 274, 275, 276, 277
13. Harappa	4300-3750 B.P.	(same as no. 12)
14. Kalibangan	Pre-Harappan/Harappan	Agrawal 1971: 29
15. Hastinapura	3100-1700 B.P.	Lal 1954-5: 107-8, 115-16; Allchin and Allchin 1968: 265
16. Ahar	4000-2500 B.P.	Sankalia 1977: 104
17. Rangpur	4000-2800 B.P.	Rao 1962-3: 155, 157; Allchin and Allchin 1968: 264; Fairservis 1971: 307

(continued)

Table II.G.23.3. (Continued)

Location	Time	Source
India/Pakistan		
18. Nasik	3000–2500 B.P.	George 1955: 142-3; Krishnaswami 1960: 39
19. Nevasa	3250 B.P.	Agrawal 1971: 42
20. Inamgaon	3600–2700 B.P.	Clason 1975: 6; Badam 1985: 414
21. Piklihal	Deccan Neolithic (about 4000–2400 B.P.)	Fairservis 1971: 325
22. Maski	Chalcolithic (about 2600 B.P.)	Thapar 1957: 13, 121-9; Krishnaswami 1960: 41; Agrawal 1971: 43; Fairservis 1971: 328
23. Nagarjunakonda	3000 B.P.	Soundara Rajan 1958: 109-10; Krishnaswami 1960: 42
24. Nilgiri Hills	2000 B.P.	Foote 1901: 22-47; Rea 1915: v, vi; W. A. Noble, personal communication
25. Adichanallur	2000 B.P.	Rea 1915: v, 4
Southwest Asia		
26. Ur	Pre-Akkadian (prior to 4500 B.P.)	Zeuner 1963: 249-50
27. Accad	4500–4100 B.P.	Duerst 1908: 361; Zeuner 1963: 249
28. Grai Resh	Uruk culture period (5500–4900 B.P.)	Lloyd 1947: 6-7
29. Tell el Hesy	3400–3300 B.P.	Bliss 1894: 191
30. Boghazköy	3200–2700 B.P. (Post-Hittite layers)	Bökönyi 1974: 151
Europe		
31. Frumusica	Neolithic	Bökönyi 1974: 150
32. Bukovina	Neolithic	Bökönyi 1974: 150
33. Csoka	Neolithic	Bökönyi 1974: 150

The *Yajur Veda*, dating from the early part of the first millennium B.C., mentions buffalo "reared for purposes of cultivation" (Chand 1959: 234). Although no earlier references exist, it appears that at least by the time of the writing of the Sutras (about 800–300 B.C.), the use of the buffalo for milk was well established (Bühler 1882: 73, 1896: 63; Jolly 1900: 166, 167).

This record probably represents the earliest use of the buffalo as a dairy animal anywhere. Although literal interpretations of this ancient literature are not always possible, it would seem safe at this point to conclude that the buffalo was a domesticated animal in northern India at least 3,000 years ago. For the wetter eastern parts of India, where environmental conditions suit the buffalo particularly well, archaeological and literary evidence is notably scarce. Consequently, the antiquity of the domesticated buffalo in eastern India cannot, as yet, be clearly shown.

Southwest Asia. Mesopotamia presents us with a situation very similar to that of the Indus Valley. The buffalo was undoubtedly well known in ancient Mesopotamia, but its domesticated status is disputed. One site in northern Iraq (Grai Resh), dating from the Uruk culture period (about 3500 B.C.), has yielded a horn core of a buffalo. Most of the remaining evidence is representational, coming from depictions on cylinder seals from the third millennium B.C. Arguments in favor of the buffalo's domesticated status rely mainly on scenes showing the animal in the company of humans (or possibly gods or mythical heroes), in some cases being watered and fed by the human figures (Figure II.G.23.4). Some supporters of this argument propose that the buffalo was actually domesticated by the Sumerians or Akkadians, and others suggest that the animal was imported from the Indus Valley already in a domesticated state.[20] These seal scenes might well reflect, as suggested by Henri Frankfort (1939: 85-94), religious and mythical symbolism, or maybe just artistic imagination or descriptive design. Wild buffalo probably existed at that time in the swamps of the Tigris and Euphrates Delta and could easily have inspired the seal depictions (Duerst 1908: 360-2; Ward 1910: 414-5; Bodenheimer 1960: 50, 102; White 1974: 202).

Whether wild or domesticated, buffalo seem to have disappeared from Mesopotamia possibly by the end of the first millennium B.C., although they may have survived longer in other parts of Southwest Asia. Frederick Bliss (1894) reported that fossil water buffalo teeth, dated between 1700 and 500 B.C., were found at Tell el Hesy, near Gaza in ancient Palestine. Buffalo bones were also found in post-Hittite layers of Boghazköy in north central Turkey, dated between the twelfth and seventh centuries B.C. (Bökönyi 1974: 151). A Sassanian seal depiction of a buffalo (illustrated in Bivar 1969: 83, plate 15 EM1) indicates that the buffalo still existed (or at least was still remembered by artists) in northern Iraq or Iran during the first half of the first millennium A.D.

China. Because of the close association of the domesticated buffalo with wet rice cultivation throughout southern and eastern Asia, some authors have suggested the possibility that the buffalo was originally domesticated as a work animal in the rice-growing area. They usually point to southern China or the

Figure II.G.23.4. Depictions of water buffalo on cylinder seals from Mesopotamia (Akkadian dynasty, about 2300–2100 B.C.). (From Frankfort 1939.)

mainland of southeastern Asia (Zeuner 1963: 251; Bökönyi 1974: 150–1; Clutton-Brock 1981: 140). Until recently there was no archaeological evidence to support this contention. But that has all changed with the astonishing archaeological finds in China during and since the 1970s.

Between about 6,500 and 4,500 years ago, two closely related Neolithic cultures coexisted near the mouth of the Yangtze River; the Ma-chia-pang culture was located north of Hang-chou Bay, and the Ho-mu-tu culture was located to its south. This was a "subtropical, fresh-water wetlands environment of the coastal plain" that was "crisscrossed by rivers and streams and dotted with large and small lakes, ponds, and freshwater marshes" (Smith 1995: 124).

Large quantities of refuse reveal that these people were rice cultivators who probably kept domesticated pigs, dogs, and buffalo. Although the buffalo bones found there are no easier to distinguish as domesticated than at other sites, the unusually large number of bones does indicate a heavily exploited resource. Buffalo shoulder blades were lashed to wooden handles and used as spades, which were the main cultivation tools; no plows were used. Since these people evidently were skilled hunters and fishermen, it could be reasoned that large numbers of wild buffalo existed in the area and were intensively hunted.

If, however, the buffalo was domesticated, which seems to be the unanimous opinion of the excavators and analysts, it undoubtedly was kept for its meat (and shoulder blades); other uses are impossible to determine at this time. It is possible that even without the plow the buffalo might have been used to prepare the rice fields. As is practiced by many rice farmers in South China and Southeast Asia today, the soil can be thoroughly puddled merely by driving one or more buffalo around in the flooded field (Ho 1975: 72).[21] However, the finding of buffalo in association with cultivated rice does not necessarily imply that the animals were actually used in the cultivation process.

Radiocarbon dates place these buffalo in the fifth millennium B.C. Thus, if domesticated, they are the earliest ones known anywhere in the world (Pearson 1983; Chang 1986: 196–201, 208–11; Zhao and Wu 1986–7; Smith 1995: 124–7).[22] Domesticated rice and buffalo have also been found as part of the Liang-chu culture (4000–2000 B.C.), which, although known since the 1930s, is now considered an outgrowth of the Ma-chia-pang culture in the same Yangtze Delta area.

The next appearance of the buffalo in a Neolithic context is in northern China at sites dated from the third millennium B.C. The earlier Neolithic cultures of North China (between 5500 and 2500 B.C.) appear to have been based on the hoe cultivation of millets and the keeping of domesticated pigs, dogs, and chickens. Although a few bovine bones have been found, their identity and domesticated status are uncertain (Ho 1975: 91–5; Smith 1995: 133–40). Bovine remains, claimed as domesticated, are more frequently encountered at later sites, with most identified as *Bos* sp. and only a few as *Bubalus* sp. (from Shaanxi Province).

By early historic times in northern China (second millennium B.C.), the domesticated buffalo seems to have been well established, as the remains from the Shang Dynasty sites near An-yang suggest. Bones identified as belonging to the species *Bubalus mephistopheles* were found in great abundance. Authorities believe that buffalo were able to exist this far north because the climate, as surmised from paleontological and palynological evidence and oracle bone inscriptions, was warmer and wetter than it is today. There seems to be little doubt that these buffalo were fully domesticated, along with cattle, pigs, dogs, sheep, and goats.

Southeast Asia. Archaeology has not been able to offer much support for the rather popular assertion that peninsular Southeast Asia was the place of origin for the domestication of rice and, by association, the buffalo. The oldest presumably domesticated rice in Southeast Asia (from the Non Nok Tha and Ban Chiang sites in Thailand) dates only from the fourth millennium B.C., which makes it at least 1,000 (and possibly 3,000) years younger than the earliest Chinese rice. Demonstration of a great antiquity for the domesticated buffalo has also eluded archaeologists.

One early site in northern Vietnam has yielded buffalo remains dating from about 8000 B.C. Vietnamese archaeologists have suggested that this site, Bo-lum, and the many others belonging to the Bacsonian culture could be associated with the beginnings of agriculture (fruit trees, tubers, leguminous plants, and hill rice) and animal husbandry (dog and buffalo). But this claim appears to be based solely on the assumption that polished stone tools and pottery, which are found at the Bacsonian sites, imply an early Neolithic agricultural society. It is with greater confidence that we can approach the assertion that wet rice cultivation with buffalo-drawn plows existed in northern Vietnam by the time the Bronze/Iron Age Dong Son culture appears (600–400 B.C.). This claim is based on the finding of rice remains and bronze plowshares (Bellwood 1985: 273–5).

The most significant Southeast Asian evidence relating to the buffalo comes from the site of Ban Chiang in the Sakon Nakhon Basin of northeastern Thailand. An analysis of the faunal remains by Charles Higham and Amphan Kijngam (1979, 1985) has shown that the buffalo made its appearance here about 1600 B.C., coinciding with the first appearance of iron metallurgy. Remains of rice have been found throughout the site's occupation period, going back to about 3500 B.C.

Based on the size of the buffalo bones, which are considerably smaller than those of wild buffalo, and on the fact that the buffalo phalanges showed stress areas (indicative of plowing) similar to those found on modern work buffalo, the authors concluded not only that the Ban Chiang buffalo was domesticated but that it was used for plowing. No prehistoric plows have been found at this or any other site in Thailand. Higham and Kijngam reasoned that before 1600 B.C. the people of Ban Chiang were probably collecting wild rice and practicing swidden rice cultivation. With the introduction of the buffalo and iron, the agricultural system changed to an inundation system of wet rice farming. Two other sites in the Sakon Nakhon Basin show similar patterns, with buffalo absent from the earlier levels and appearing only in the later periods, apparently

about the same time (during the second millennium B.C.) as they do in Ban Chiang.

Ethnographic Evidence

When archaeological findings are unsatisfyingly fragmentary, as is certainly the case with the buffalo, we search for any other possible indicators of the prehistoric past. The use of ethnographic evidence is based on the shaky assumption that primitive people living today or in the recent past can provide us with a glimpse, via extrapolation, of ways of life that may have existed long ago.[23] Drawing conclusions from such evidence must be done with great caution. Sometimes several different, yet equally reasonable, scenarios can be postulated.

A cursory investigation of the position of the buffalo among the primitive tribal societies of southern and eastern Asia reveals a surprisingly widespread pattern of use that might suggest an early motive for keeping and domesticating the buffalo. Most of these tribes inhabit hilly regions, practice the plowless shifting cultivation of dry rice, and do not drink milk.[24] Consequently, they usually do not keep domesticated animals for milk production, plowing, or other work.

Yet in spite of the absence of any of these economic uses, many groups do keep domesticated bovines. These animals are slaughtered and their meat eaten, but the motive is not simply the secular dietary desire for meat, which is met by the hunting of wildlife in the nearby forests. The major purpose for keeping these animals is for sacrifice, and their meat is eaten only at ceremonial feasts. Within the southern and eastern Asian realm, the buffalo is the bovine most frequently used for this purpose. Only a few tribal groups prefer other domesticated bovines as sacrificial victims, such as the zebu among a few tribes in India and the mithan among the groups inhabiting the eastern Himalayas and the India–Burma border region. Tribes practicing buffalo sacrifice are scattered throughout the Indian subcontinent, across mainland Southeast Asia, in parts of southern China, and in the hilly interiors of the islands of the Philippines (Map II.G.23.5 and Table II.G.23.4). All of the occasions for buffalo sacrifices are broadly related, in one way or another, to the desire to enhance or maintain the well-being of an individual or community – fertility in its broadest sense.

Economic or Religious Motivation

Given the obviously useful contributions of domesticated bovines to the economic life of humans, it is not surprising that most attempts to explain their origin seek rational and practical motives. Eduard Hahn (1896) was one of the earliest scholars to propose a thesis on cattle domestication that did not conform to the principles of materialistic rationalism. He was the first in a line of speculators who argued that cattle were originally domesticated not for milk, meat, or traction, but to provide sacrificial victims for the worshiped deities.

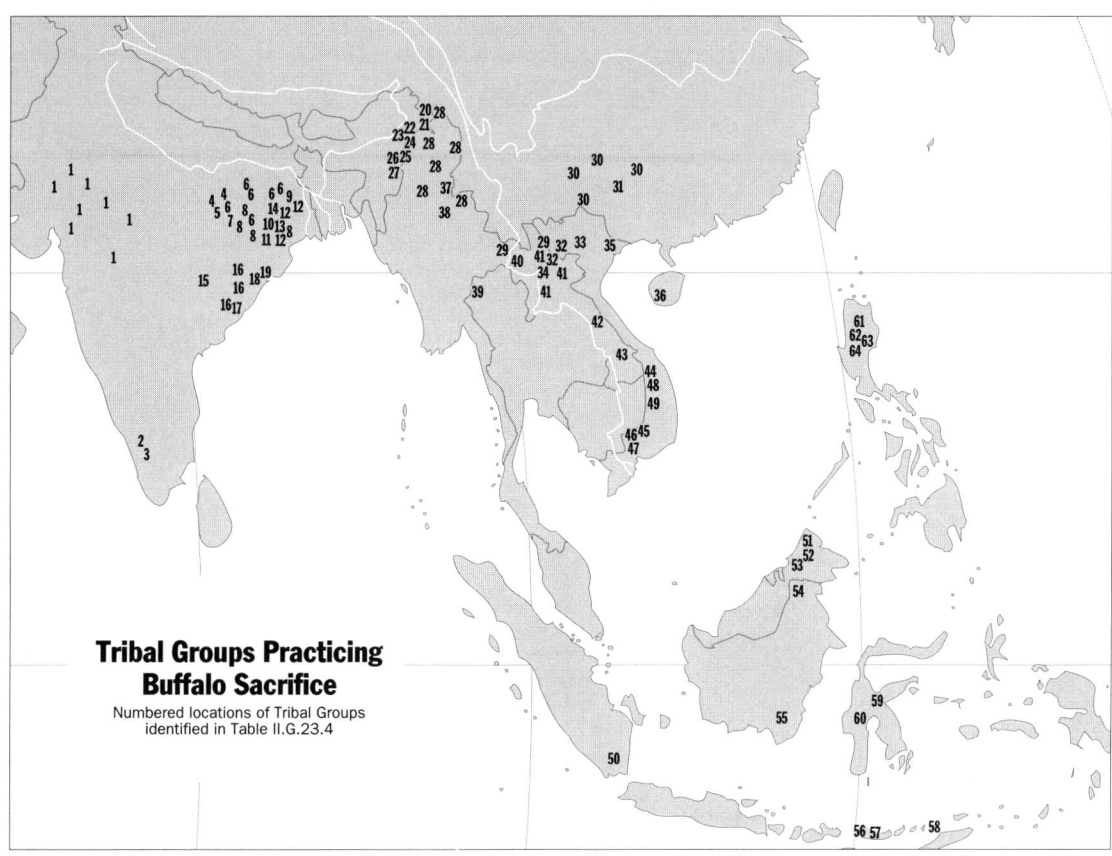

Map II.G.23.5. Tribal groups practicing buffalo sacrifice.

Table II.G.23.4. *Tribal groups practicing buffalo sacrifice (identification of numbers on Map II.G.23.5)*

Tribal name	Language affiliation	Source
India		
1. Bhil	Indo-Aryan (possible Munda origins)	Koppers and Jungblut 1942-5: 647-50; Naik 1956: 194-5; Nath 1960: 49, 209-10
2. Toda	Dravidian	Rivers 1906: 274, 287, 290, 354; Miles 1937: 94; India, Office of the Registrar General 1965: 77
3. Kota	Dravidian	Thurston 1909, 1: 85, 4: 25, 26
4. Korwa	Austroasiatic (Munda)	Dalton 1872: 228; Risley 1892, 1: 513; Majumdar 1944: 33, Das, Chowdhury, and Raha 1966: 130
5. Rautia	Austroasiatic (Munda)	Risley and Gait 1903: 409, 417
6. Oraon	Dravidian	Dalton 1872: 248; Risley 1892, 2: 145; Roy 1915: 191, 1928: 45-56, 68-9; Thakkar 1950: 37
7. Kharwar	Austroasiatic (Munda)	Risley and Gait 1903: 409, 417
8. Munda	Austroasiatic (Munda)	Tickell 1840: 700; Dalton 1872: 186; Risley 1892, 27: 103; Risley and Gait 1903: 144; Bradley-Birt 1910: 34; Crooke 1955: 16
9. Maler	Dravidian	Vidyarthi 1963: vii, 69, 139, 159, 160
10. Kharia	Austroasiatic (Munda)	Dalton 1872: 157; Risley 1892, 1: 468-9; Roy and Roy 1937, 2: 373-6
11. Juang	Austroasiatic (Munda)	Risley 1892, 1:353
12. Santal	Austroasiatic (Munda)	Dalton 1872: 212
13. Ho	Austroasiatic (Munda)	Tickell 1840: 799, 800; Dalton 1872: 186; Risley and Gait 1903: 144; Bradley-Birt 1910: 34, Majumdar 1927: 39, 1950: 256; Crooke 1955: 16
14. Bhumij	Austroasiatic (Munda)	Risley 1892, 1: 124
15. Muria Gond	Dravidian	Grigson 1949: 162-3; Elwin 1947: 66, 197, 657
16. Kond	Dravidian	Risley 1892, 1: 403; Risley and Gait 1903: 408; Imperial Gazetteer of India, 1908: 132; Thurston 1912: 201, 206; Russell 1916, 3: 473-9; Miles 1937: 82, 84, 87; Elwin 1950: 176; Das 1958, 27-30; Bailey 1960: 51

(continued)

Table II.G.23.4. *(Continued)*

Tribal name	Language affiliation	Source
India		
17. Gadaba	Austroasiatic (Munda)	Thurston 1909, 2: 250; Ramadas 1931: 172–3; Elwin 1954: xxv
18. Savara	Austroasiatic (Munda)	Dalton 1872: 147; Thurston 1912: 262–3; Sahu 1942: 82, 84; Bhattacharyya 1952: 9–15; Elwin 1955: 189–91, 229, 267–82, 284–6, 304, 305, 358–75, 378–86
19. Kuttia Kond	Dravidian	Elwin 1954: 352–3; Niggemeyer 1964: 184–211
20. Idu Mishmi	Sino-Tibetan (Tibeto-Burman)	Dalton 1872: 20; Baruah 1960: 22, 37, 80, 87
21. Singpho (Kachin)	Sino-Tibetan (Tibeto-Burman)	Dalton 1872: 16, 17
22. Tangsa	Sino-Tibetan (Tibeto-Burman)	Dutta 1959: 11, 30, 39, 59, 76–9
23. Konyak Naga	Sino-Tibetan (Tibeto-Burman)	Fürer-Haimendorf 1969: 55, 59
24. Chang Naga	Sino-Tibetan (Tibeto-Burman)	Dalton 1872: 16–17; Fürer-Haimendorf 1938: 206, 1946: 85, 127, 174, 176; Hutton 1965: 29, 34, 41
25. Kalyo-Kengyu Naga	Sino-Tibetan (Tibeto-Burman)	Dalton 1872: 16–17; Fürer-Haimendorf 1938: 209, 1946: 85, 127, 174, 176; Hutton 1965: 29, 34, 41
26. Rengma Naga (Eastern)	Sino-Tibetan (Tibeto-Burman)	Mills 1937: 4–11, 91–2
27. Tangkhul Naga	Sino-Tibetan (Tibeto-Burman)	Hodson 1911: 140, 149, 179
Mainland Southeast Asia and South China		
28. Kachin	Sino-Tibetan (Tibeto-Burman)	Enriquez 1923: 29–30; Leach 1964: 118–19, 143–7, 172–3; LeBar, Hickey, and Musgrave 1964: 13, 14, 17
29. Akha	Sino-Tibetan (Tibeto-Burman)	Scott and Hardiman 1900: 593; LeBar et al. 1964: 37
30. Miao of S. China	Miao-Yao	Mickey 1947: 78–80; Beauclair 1956: 29–31; LeBar et al. 1964: 71, 72
31. Chung-Chia	Thai	LeBar et al. 1964: 230
32. Black Thai	Thai	Halpern 1964: 29, 61, Table 19; LeBar et al. 1964: 221, 223
33. White Thai	Thai	Lévy 1959: 164; LeBar et al. 1964: 225
34. Laotian Thai	Thai	Archaimbault 1959: 156–61; Lévy 1959: 162–3; Halpern 1960: 64, 1964: 58, 61, 151, Table 19
35. Tho	Thai	LeBar et al. 1964: 233
36. Li	Kadai	LeBar et al. 1964: 241, 243
37. Wa	Austroasiatic (Mon-Khmer)	Scott 1896: 140, 145, 147: Scott and Hardiman 1900: 497, 505–6, 515; LeBar et al. 1964: 131
38. Palaung (Humai subgroup)	Austroasiatic (Mon-Khmer)	Cameron 1912: xxvii, xxxii, xxxvii
39. Lawa	Austroasiatic (Mon-Khmer)	Young 1962: 53, 54, 55; Kunstadter 1966: 132, 140
40. Lamet	Austroasiatic (Mon-Khmer)	Izikowitz 1951: 66, 67, 100–1, 106, 116, 118, 200–1, 232, 253, 303–5, 309, 316, 322–32, 357–8
41. Khmu	Austroasiatic (Mon-Khmer)	Halpern 1964: 38–9, 64; LeBar et al. 1964: 113–15
42. So	Austroasiatic (Mon-Khmer)	LeBar et al. 1964: 150
43. Alak	Austroasiatic (Mon-Khmer)	LeBar et al. 1964: 135
44. Sedang	Austroasiatic (Mon-Khmer)	Devereux 1937: 4–6; LeBar et al. 1964: 147
45. Mnong	Austroasiatic (Mon-Khmer)	LeBar et al. 1964: 156; Condominas 1966: 10, 11, 13, 1977: 19–20, 25–6, 58–80, 124, 203, 138–41, 1980: 219, 223, 228–40
46. Stieng	Austroasiatic (Mon-Khmer)	Gerber 1951: 230; LeBar et al. 1964: 158
47. Ma	Austroasiatic (Mon-Khmer)	LeBar et al. 1964: 153
48. Djarai	Austronesian (Cham)	Bertrand 1959: 56–7, 62–4, 113, 146, 182
49. Rhadé	Austronesian (Cham)	Bertrand 1959: 56–7, 62–4, 113, 146, 182; LeBar et al. 1964: 254–5
Island Southeast Asia		
50. Abung	Austronesian (Indonesian)	LeBar 1972: 37
51. Dusun	Austronesian (Indonesian)	Rutter 1922: 298; Evans 1923: 40; LeBar 1972: 149
52. Rungus Dusun	Austronesian (Indonesian)	LeBar 1972: 151
53. Idahan Merut	Austronesian (Indonesian)	LeBar 1972: 156
54. Kelabitic Merut	Austronesian (Indonesian)	LeBar 1972: 160, 163
55. Maanyan Dayak	Austronesian (Indonesian)	LeBar 1972: 192
56. Manggarai	Austronesian (Indonesian)	LeBar 1972: 81. 83
57. Endenese	Austronesian (Indonesian)	LeBar 1972: 87, 88
58. Alorese	Austronesian (Indonesian)	LeBar 1972: 97
59. Eastern Toradja	Austronesian (Indonesian)	Downs 1956: 77–91, 100–4; Geertz 1963: 70–6; LeBar 1972: 133
60. Southern Toradja	Austronesian (Indonesian)	Kennedy 1953: 42–3, 128, 136–48; LeBar 1972: 134, 136; Crystal 1974: 125–30, 132–6; Volkman 1980: 40–1, 111–17, 131–55; Nooy-Palm 1986: 5, 10–50, 62–76, 101–3, 116–17, 169–304
61. Kalinga	Austronesian (Indonesian)	Lawless 1975: 191–203; LeBar 1975: 93, 95
62. Bontoc	Austronesian (Indonesian)	Jenks 1905: 76; LeBar 1975: 97
63. Ifugao	Austronesian (Indonesian)	Barton 1946: 100, 194
64. Ibaloi	Austronesian (Indonesian)	Moss 1920: 286, 305–6

Those who followed with sympathetic support, similar premises, and further research included, most notably, Carl Sauer (1952: 88–94), Erich Isaac (1962), and Frederick and Elizabeth Simoons (1968: 234–58). These scholars have pointed out the widespread Eurasian distribution and antiquity of a complex of traits that link bovines, sacrificial practices, and fertility rites. Simoons and Simoons (1968: 261–2) postulated that taurine cattle were the first to be domesticated in this ceremonial context, followed by the buffalo in imitation of cattle, and then by the mithan in imitation of the buffalo.

In the case of the domestication of the water buffalo, we have very little concrete evidence and can offer only speculations that seem to accommodate the fragmented information we have. Nature has provided a massively built and formidable bovine that is ideally suited to tropical and swampy lowland environments. Paleontological evidence places the ancestor of this creature in southern and eastern Asia. Wild buffalo have seemingly adapted to a wide range of habitats as their distribution has expanded and contracted throughout the course of the Pleistocene and Holocene. Until the next discovery, currently available archaeological evidence points to southern China during the fifth millennium B.C. as the most probable place and time for the earliest domestication of the buffalo.

With the invention of the plow, the buffalo's contribution to the wet rice cultivation process was fully realized. Thus far, the earliest indication of the buffalo–plow–wet rice complex comes from northern Thailand about 3,600 years ago at the Ban Chiang site. It is postulated that this complex diffused into the Indo-Malaysian archipelago roughly 1,000 years later (Bellwood 1985: 205, 241–4). This line of thinking, which focuses on the evolving economic benefits accrued from the domesticated buffalo, would fulfill the requirements of materialistic rationalism. If ethnography can be transposed to the Neolithic, an alternative scenario can also be envisioned. Buffalo might have been initially tended for their religious and social value, rather than their economic value. A belief that the sacrificing of buffalo would be repaid with fertility and well-being could have motivated people to begin domestication. To conform with the archaeological evidence, it could be hypothesized that this buffalo sacrificing fertility cult initially developed in South China. Buffalo sacrificing has been reported among the early Thai (Eberhard 1968: 183–93, 216) and the traditional Miao peoples (Mickey 1947: 78–80; Beauclair 1956: 29–31) of that area. This sacrificial complex could have diffused southward into mainland Southeast Asia and from there westward into India.

By historic times, both buffalo systems – the primitive hill farming system with the sacrificial buffalo and the sophisticated lowland rice paddy system with the plow buffalo – were well established and widely distributed in southern and eastern Asia. Archaeology has not, as yet, been able to sort out the chronological relationships between the two systems. The suggestion that the sacrificial buffalo system is antecedent to the plow buffalo system is based primarily on ethnohistorical traditions that commonly identify the hill peoples of southern and eastern Asia as being the indigenous inhabitants and indicate that settlement and cultivation of the lowland plains came later. Without evidence to the contrary, we further assume that the recent cultural practices of these tribal peoples represent survivals from a much earlier time that have been preserved by the groups' relative isolation. Obviously, caution must accompany our speculation.

The popular archetypal image that many Westerners have of the water buffalo is as the lumbering beast of burden patiently pulling a plow and a frail Asian farmer through a flooded rice paddy. Although this may be an accurate depiction of the animal's economic value to humans, it may not reflect the original value conferred upon the water buffalo when it was first brought under domestication. We must consider an additional image of the buffalo as a powerful, virile symbol of fertility that is tied to a sacrificial post and about to be ceremonially slaughtered as an offering to the supernatural.

Biological, archaeological, and ethnographic evidence provides us with only a few fragments with which to construct images. As we try to fit the pieces together, we hope that the images that emerge, as preliminary and speculative as they may be, will be the result of objective, multidimensional analysis that has considered economic, religious, and all other relevant factors.

Robert Hoffpauir

Notes

1. Compilations of available knowledge of the buffalo have appeared from time to time, including Roderick MacGregor (1941), Bradford Knapp (1957), D. C. Rife (1959), W. Ross Cockrill (1967, 1974b, 1976), M. R. de Guzman and A. V. Allo (1975), and National Research Council (1981).

2. The present author's past work on the buffalo has included some cultural and historical considerations in an attempt to understand the current buffalo situation in South Asia (Hoffpauir 1968, 1974, 1977, 1982). Whereas several studies could be cited as examples of the cultural–historical approach to the analysis of domesticated animals, Frederick and Elizabeth Simoons's (1968) masterful study of the mithan *(Bos frontalis)* stands as the model of this approach.

3. Two earlier attempts to address specifically the domestication of the buffalo have revealed how little we know. Frederick Zeuner's often-cited survey, *A History of Domesticated Animals,* devoted only an 8-page portion of one chapter to the buffalo (1963: 245–52), and more recently, Cockrill (1984) contributed a short chapter on the buffalo to Ian L. Mason's anthology, *Evolution of Domesticated Animals.*

4. The term "bovine" refers to those animals that have been classified in the order Artiodactyla, suborder Ruminantia, family Bovidae, subfamily Bovidae. This includes European

domestic cattle,* zebu cattle,* gaur, mithan,* banteng, Bali cattle,* *kouprey,* domestic yak,* wild yak, American bison, European bison, wild Asian buffalo, domesticated water buffalo,* *anoa, tamarau,* and African buffalo. (Asterisks [*] indicate the domesticated forms.)

5. The *anoa* (confined to the island of Sulawesi in Indonesia) and *tamarau* (confined to the island of Mindoro in the Philippines) are still usually classified under the *Bubalus* genus (*Bubalus depressicornis* and *Bubalus mindorensis,* respectively). The mountain *anoa* is sometimes given separate species status under the name *Bubalus quarlesi.* The African buffalo is now regarded as a more distantly related animal requiring a separate genus designation, *Syncerus caffer.*

6. The literature on the environmental physiology of the buffalo is reviewed by Knapp (1957: 37–42) and Mason (1974).

7. This section of the chapter focuses only on the present-day economic contributions of the buffalo. The importance of the buffalo in the socioreligious realm is of great cultural-historical significance, at least in this author's opinion, and is discussed later in the chapter.

8. For comments on those rare situations of milking and milk consumption in this region, the reader is referred to Simoons (1970: 570-7) and Paul Wheatley (1965).

9. Recent experimental introductions of very small numbers of buffalo have occurred in other parts of Africa – specifically in Mozambique, Tunisia, Madagascar, Uganda, Tanzania, Nigeria, Zaire, and Congo – but their current status is unknown (Porter 1991: 300).

10. Esteem for the milk buffalo as an economic resource probably reaches its highest cultural expression in Southwest Asia among the Marsh Arabs (the Ma'dan) of southern Iraq. These "buffalo people" have developed an elaborate cultural system focused on the husbandry of buffalo. The reader is referred to the ethnographic descriptions by Wilfred Thesiger (1954, 1964).

11. For a discussion of the prominent role played by wild buffalo in the cave art of Mesolithic India, see Yashodhar Mathpal (1984, 1985) and V. N. Misra (1985: 119-20).

12. The often-cited identification of two teeth of Upper Pleistocene or early Holocene date found at Niah Cave in northern Borneo as belonging to *Bubalus* (Koenigswald 1958: 624-5) has been disputed by Lord Medway (1965: 162), who believes the teeth could just as well belong to *Bos javanicus,* the Banteng.

13. It was once commonly thought that buffalo named *Bubalus antiquus* roamed over North Africa from the late Pleistocene to the Holocene, as revealed by bone finds and rock paintings and engravings created by Paleolithic and Neolithic hunters (Wulsin 1941). Current opinion, however, identifies these animals as members of the *Syncerus* genus (Zeuner 1963: 245-6). More than 100 years ago, Richard Lydekker (1898: 116) suggested that these buffalo might better be regarded as ancestral to the African buffalo.

14. Unless otherwise mentioned, the sources used for the following discussion of archaeological sites are listed in Table II.G.23.3.

15. For a description of the buffalo remains found at Harappa, see Baini Prashad (1936: 43-6).

16. From Mohenjo-daro, Sir John Marshall (1931, 2: 386) listed only three seals showing buffalo, and E. J. H. Mackay (1937-8, 1: 298, 311, 330, 358-9) recorded one pottery figurine, one bronze figure, eight seals, and two prism-amulets. From Harappa, Madho Sarup Vats (1940: 323) published only two fragmented seals.

17. See, for example, Marshall (1931, 1: v), Prashad (1936: 8-9), M. S. Randhawa (1946: 10), Stuart Piggott (1950: 155-6), V. Gordon Childe (1957: 176), Kaj Birket-Smith (1965: 151),

C. D. Darlington (1970: 55), Henry Hodges (1970: 252), and Cockrill (1984: 55).

18. H. F. Friedrichs (as cited in Mackay 1937-8, 1: 670-1) argued that the presence of the trough before the buffalo, tiger, and rhinoceros indicates that these animals were kept under restraint, that is, that they were not as yet fully domesticated. The symbol was not needed in front of the zebu, sheep, goat, and elephant because these animals were more domesticated and possibly kept in pastures where a feeding trough would be unnecessary.

19. A few authors have indicated their uncertainty about the buffalo's domesticated status in the Indus Valley (Zeuner 1963: 249; Bökönyi 1974: 151; Clason 1977: 268). One writer, D. D. Kosambi (1965: 60), has even expressed the opinion that the buffalo was probably not domesticated in the Indus Valley.

20. Those who have supported the idea of a domesticated buffalo in ancient Mesopotamia include Seton Lloyd (1947: 7), Berthold Klatt (1948: 34), Samuel Noah Kramer (1967: 88), H. Epstein (1971: 569), S. Bökönyi (1974: 151), and Cockrill (1974b: 516, 1984: 56). Zeuner (1963: 249-50), although finding the evidence strongly suggestive of "tame, if not domesticated" buffalo, does admit that the question "remains to be settled." At least one author (Kingdon 1990: 136) has expressed the opinion that Mesopotamia is the place of earliest domestication of the buffalo. Presumably, these authors believe that the buffalo was kept primarily as a meat source, as no evidence has been presented for the buffalo being used for milk or work. Dominique Collon (1987: 187) says that buffalo - she does not specify wild or domesticated - may have been imported from the Indus Valley for the royal zoos during the time of Sargon of Akkad. Epstein (1971: 569) bolsters his argument for the existence of the domesticated buffalo with an ancient Assyrian clay tablet (from about 2000 B.C.) showing the head of a buffalo with "horns curved in a manner that is occasionally encountered in domestic buffaloes but never in the wild beast." Lynn White, Jr. (1974: 202) counters this argument by pointing out that wild African buffalo *(Syncerus)* have such horns.

21. For a long time, the thought has been that the animal-drawn plow was not part of the original technique of wet rice cultivation but was added later (Pelzer 1945: 14). It has been hypothesized that the original form of rice cultivation involved broadcasting the seed onto naturally swampy or seasonally flooded lowland areas. The archaeological findings in the Yangtze Delta appear to be consistent with this hypothesis. The swidden cultivation of dry rice and the irrigation cultivation of wet rice, it is suggested, developed later (Harris 1974: 142; Gorman 1977: 338-40). Initially, no animals may have been used. Buffalo involvement in rice cultivation might have started with the use of the animal for puddling; perhaps only later was it attached to a plow. Wolfram Eberhard (1968: 215) contends that among the Thai of southern China, the practice of plowing, which was adopted very late, was antedated by letting buffalo trample the fields. R. D. Hill (1977: 85, 98, 133, 161, 177) documents this practice during the nineteenth century in Malaya and Siam. It seems to have been widespread among many different groups, such as the Rhadé (LeBar, Hickey, and Musgrave 1964: 252) and Maà' Huang (Condominas 1980: 246) in Vietnam and Cambodia, the Savunese in the Savu Islands of Indonesia (LeBar 1972: 77), the Lampong in south Sumatra (Loeb 1935: 266), the Kalabits in north Borneo (Hose and McDougall 1912: 97-8), and the Kalingas of northern Luzon (Lawless 1975: 82-3).

22. The only evidence of rice cultivation earlier than the Yangtze Delta finds is from the eastern end of the Yangtze

Valley at the site of Peng-tou-shan in the Hupei Basin, dated at between 6400 and 5800 B.C. No evidence of domesticated animals has been uncovered from this site as yet (Smith 1995: 130-1). Rice cultivation cannot be documented before 3600 B.C. in Southeast Asia or before 2500 B.C. in India (Bellwood et al. 1992). Thus far, the oldest evidence of both rice and buffalo domestication comes from the Yangtze Valley of China.

23. The value of this ethnographic approach, when carefully executed, is demonstrated by Simoons and Simoons's (1968) study of the mithan. In the absence of archaeological evidence, a skillful use of ethnographic evidence allowed Simoons and Simoons to develop a very convincing hypothesis for the domestication of this bovine.

24. For the purposes of this discussion, I employ the convention of speaking in the "ethnographic present." Some of the sources used describe conditions as they existed during the late nineteenth and early twentieth centuries. Subsequent acculturation has undoubtedly obliterated many of the (presumably) traditional practices originally observed and described.

Bibliography

Agrawal, D. P. 1971. *The copper Bronze Age in India*. New Delhi.

Aigner, Jean S. 1974. Pleistocene archaeological remains from South China. *Asian Perspectives* 16: 16-38.

1981. *Archaeological remains in Pleistocene China*. Munich.

Allchin, Bridget, and Raymond Allchin. 1968. *The birth of Indian civilization: India and Pakistan before 500 B.C*. Baltimore, Md.

Archaimbault, Charles. 1959. The sacrifice of the buffalo at Vat Ph'u (southern Laos). In *Kingdom of Laos*, ed. René de Berval, 156-61. Saigon.

Badam, G. L. 1984. Pleistocene faunal succession of India. In *The evolution of the East Asian environment*, Vol. 2, ed. Robert Orr Whyte, 746-75. Hong Kong.

1985. The late Quaternary fauna of Inamgaon. In *Recent advances in Indo-Pacific prehistory*, ed. V. N. Misra and Peter Bellwood, 413-15. New Delhi.

Bailey, F. G. 1960. *Tribe, caste, and nation: A study of political activity and political change in highland Orissa*. Manchester, England.

Barton, R. F. 1946. The religion of the Ifugaos. *Memoir Series of the American Anthropological Association* 65: 1-219.

Baruah, Tapan Kumar M. 1960. *The Idu Mishmis*. Shillong, India.

Beauclair, Inez de. 1956. Culture traits of non-Chinese tribes in Kweichow Province, Southwest China. *Sinologica* 5: 20-35.

Bellwood, Peter. 1985. *Prehistory of the Indo-Malaysian archipelago*. New York.

Bellwood, P., R. Gillespie, G. B. Thompson, et al. 1992. New dates for prehistoric Asian rice. *Asian Perspectives* 31: 161-70.

Bertrand, Gabrielle. 1959. *The jungle people: Men, beasts and legends of the Moï country*. London.

Bhattacharyya, Asutosh. 1952. Death rites, funeral ceremonies and idea of life after death among the hill Sora of Orissa. *Bulletin of the Department of Anthropology (Government of India)* 1: 1-16.

Birket-Smith, Kaj. 1965. *The paths of culture*, trans. Karin Fennow. Madison, Wis.

Bivar, A. D. H. 1969. *Catalogue of the western Asiatic seals in the British Museum*, Stamp seals, II: The Sassanian dynasty. London.

Bliss, Frederick Jones. 1894. *A mound of many cities, or Tell el Hesy excavated*. London.

Bodenheimer, F. S. 1960. *Animal and man in Bible lands*. Leiden, the Netherlands.

Bökönyi, S. 1974. *History of domestic mammals in central and eastern Europe*. Budapest.

Boriskovskii, P. I. 1970-1. Vietnam in primeval times, part VII. *Soviet Anthropology and Archeology* 9: 226-64.

Bradley-Birt, F. B. 1910. *Chota Nagpore: A little-known province of the empire*. Second edition. London.

Buffon, George-Louis Leclerc, Comte de. 1812. *Natural history, general and particular*, Vol. 7, trans. William Wood. London.

Bühler, Georg, trans. 1879-82. *The sacred laws of the Aryas, as taught in the schools of Apastamba, Gautama, Vâsishtha, and Baudhâyana*. Vol. 2:14 of *The sacred books of the East*, ed. F. Max Müller. Oxford.

1896. *The sacred laws of the Aryas, as taught in the schools of Apastamba, Gautama, Vâsishtha, and Baudhâyana*. Apastamba and Gautama. Vol. 2:1 of *The sacred books of the East*, ed. F. Max Müller. Oxford.

Cameron, A. A. 1912. A note on the Palaungs of the Kodaung hill tracts of the Momeik State. In *Census of India, 1911*, Vol. 9, Part 1, *Burma*, Appendix A, i-xlii. Delhi.

Chand, Devi, trans. 1959. *The Yajur Veda*. Hoshiarpur, India.

Chang, Kwang-chih. 1980. *Shang civilization*. New Haven, Conn.

1986. *The archaeology of ancient China*. Fourth edition. New Haven, Conn.

Childe, V. Gordon. 1957. *New light on the most ancient east*. New York.

Clason, A. T. 1975. Archaeozoological study in India: Aspects of stock-breeding and hunting in prehistoric and early historic times. *The Eastern Anthropologist* 28: 1-12.

1977. Wild and domestic animals in prehistoric and early historic India. *The Eastern Anthropologist* 30: 241-394.

Clutton-Brock, Juliet. 1981. *Domesticated animals from early times*. Austin, Tex.

Cockrill, W. Ross. 1967. The water buffalo. *Scientific American* 217: 118-25.

1974a. Observations on skin colour and hair patterns. In *The husbandry and health of the domestic buffalo*, ed. W. Ross Cockrill, 48-56. Rome.

ed. 1974b. *The husbandry and health of the domestic buffalo*. Rome.

1976. *The buffaloes of China*. Rome.

1984. Water buffalo. In *Evolution of domesticated animals*, ed. Ian L. Mason, 52-62. New York.

Collon, Dominique. 1987. *First impressions: Cylinder seals in the ancient Near East*. Chicago.

Condominas, George. 1966. The primitive life of Vietnam's mountain people. *Natural History* 75: 8-19.

1977. *We have eaten the forest: The story of a Montagnard village in the central highlands of Vietnam*, trans. Adrienne Foulke. New York.

1980. Agricultural ecology in the Southeast Asian savanna region: The Mnong Gar of Vietnam and their social space. In *Human ecology in savanna environments*, ed. David R. Harris, 209-51. London.

Coon, Carleton S. 1955. *The story of man: From the first human*. New York.

Creel, Herrlee Glessner. 1937. *The birth of China: A study of the formative period of Chinese civilization*. New York.

Crooke, William. 1955. Dravidians (North India). In *Encyclopedia of religion and ethics*, Vol. 5, ed. James Hastings, 1-21. New York.

Crystal, Eric. 1974. Cooking pot politics: A Toraja village study. *Indonesia* 18: 119-51.

Dalton, Edward Tuite. 1872. *Descriptive ethnology of Bengal.* Calcutta.

Darlington, C. D. 1970. The origins of agriculture. *Natural History* 79: 47-56.

Das, Amal Kumar, Bidyut Kumar Roy Chowdhury, and Manis Kumar Raha. 1966. *Handbook on scheduled castes and scheduled tribes of West Bengal.* Calcutta.

Das, Nityananda. 1958. Sukuli puja in a Kondh village. *Vanyajati* 6: 27-30.

Defen, Han, and Xu Chunhua. 1985. Pleistocene mammalian faunas of China. In *Palaeoanthropology and Palaeolithic archaeology in the People's Republic of China,* ed. Wu Rukang and John W. Olsen, 267-89. New York.

Devereux, George. 1937. Functioning units in Ha(rh)ndea(ng) society. *Primitive Man* 10: 1-7.

Downs, Richard Erskine. 1956. *The religion of the Bare'e-speaking Toraja of central Celebes.* The Hague.

Duerst, J. Ulrich. 1908. Animal remains from the excavations at Anau. In *Explorations in Turkestan,* Vol. 2, ed. Raphael Pumpelly, 339-400. Washington, D.C.

Dutta, Parul. 1959. *The Tangsas of the Namchik and Tirap Valleys.* Shillong, India.

Eberhard, Wolfram. 1968. *The local cultures of South and East China,* trans. Alide Eberhard. Leiden, the Netherlands.

El-Itriby, A. A. 1974. The buffalo in the Arab Republic of Egypt. In *The husbandry and health of the domestic buffalo,* ed. W. Ross Cockrill, 651-61. Rome.

Elwin, Verrier. 1947. *The Muria and their ghotul.* London.

    1950. *Bondo highlander.* London.

    1954. *Tribal myths of Orissa.* Bombay.

    1955. *The religion of an Indian tribe.* London.

Enriquez, C. M. 1923. *A Burmese Arcady.* London.

Epstein, H. 1969. *Domestic animals of China.* Farnham Royal, England.

    1971. *The origin of the domestic animals of Africa,* Vol. 1. New York.

    1977. *Domestic animals of Nepal.* New York.

Evans, Ivor H. N. 1923. *Studies in religion, folk-lore, and custom in British North Borneo and the Malay Peninsula.* Cambridge.

Fairservis, Jan. 1971. *The roots of ancient India: The archaeology of early Indian civilization.* New York.

FAO (Food and Agriculture Organization of the United Nations). 1992. *FAO production yearbook, 1991,* Vol. 45. Rome.

Foote, R. Bruce. 1901. *Catalogue of the prehistoric antiquities.* Madras, India.

Fox, Robert B. 1978. The Philippine Paleolithic. In *Early Paleolithic in South and East Asia,* ed. Fumiko Ikawa-Smith, 59-85. The Hague.

    1979. The Philippines during the first millennium B.C. In *Early South East Asia: Essays in archaeology, history and historical geography,* ed. R. B. Smith and W. Watson, 227-41. New York.

Frankfort, Henri. 1939. *Cylinder seals: A documentary essay on the art and religion of the ancient Near East.* London.

Fürer-Haimendorf, Christoph von. 1938. Through the unexplored mountains of the Assam-Burma border. *The Geographical Journal* 91: 201-19.

    1946. *The naked Nagas, head-hunters of Assam in peace and war.* Calcutta.

    1969. *The Konyak Nagas: An Indian frontier tribe.* New York.

Gade, D. W. 1970. Brazil's water buffalo. *Américas* 22: 35-9.

Geertz, Hildred. 1963. Indonesian cultures and communities. In *Indonesia,* ed. Ruth T. McVey, 24-96. New Haven, Conn.

George, J. C. 1955. Appendix II, Identification of bones. In *Report on the excavations at Nasik and Jorwe, 1950-51,* by H. D. Sankalia and S. B. Deo, 142-3. Poona, India.

Gerber, Théophile. 1951. Coutumier Stieng. *Bulletin de l'École Française d'Extrême-Orient* 45: 227-69.

Gorman, Chester. 1971. The Hoabinhian and after: Subsistence patterns in Southeast Asia during the late Pleistocene and early recent periods. *World Archaeology* 2: 300-20.

    1977. A priori models and Thai prehistory: A reconsideration of the beginnings of agriculture in southeastern Asia. In *Origins of agriculture,* ed. Charles A. Reed, 321-55. The Hague.

Griffith, Ralph T. H., trans. 1963. *The hymns of the Rgveda.* 2 vols. Varanasi, India.

Grigson, Wilfrid. 1949. *The Maria Gonds of Bastar.* London.

Groves, C. P. 1981. Systematic relationships in the Bovini (Artiodactyla, Bovidae). *Zeitschrift für Zoologische Systematik und Evolutionsforschung* 19: 264-78.

Guzman, M. R. de, and A. V. Allo. 1975. *The Asiatic water buffalo.* Taipei.

Hahn, Eduard. 1896. *Die Haustiere und ihre Beziehungen zur Wirtschaft des Menschen.* Leipzig.

Halpern, Joel M. 1960. Laos and her tribal problems. *Michigan Alumnus Quarterly Review* 67: 59-67.

    1964. *Economy and society of Laos: A brief survey.* New Haven, Conn.

Harris, David R. 1974. Rice and man in Southeast Asia. *Geographical Review* 64: 140-2.

Higham, Charles F. W. 1977. Economic change in prehistoric Thailand. In *Origins of agriculture,* ed. Charles A. Reed, 385-412. The Hague.

Higham, Charles F. W., and Amphan Kijngam. 1979. Ban Chiang and Northeast Thailand: The palaeoenvironment and economy. *Journal of Archaeological Science* 6: 211-33.

    1985. New evidence for agriculture and stock-raising in monsoonal Southeast Asia. In *Recent advances in Indo-Pacific prehistory,* ed. V. N. Misra and Peter Bellwood, 419-23. New Delhi.

Hill, R. D. 1977. *Rice in Malaya: A study in historical geography.* Kuala Lumpur, Malaysia.

Hiltebeitel, Alf. 1978. The Indus Valley "Proto-Siva," reexamined through reflections on the goddess, the buffalo, and the symbolism of *vahanas. Anthropos* 73: 767-97.

Ho, Ping-ti. 1975. *The cradle of the east: An inquiry into the indigenous origins of techniques and ideas of Neolithic and early historic China, 5000-1000 B.C.* Chicago.

Hodges, Henry. 1970. *Technology in the ancient world.* New York.

Hodson, T. C. 1911. *The Naga tribes of Manipur.* London.

Hoffpauir, Robert. 1968. The domesticated buffalo in India and Pakistan: Its socio-economic distinctiveness as compared with the zebu. M.S. thesis, University of Wisconsin.

    1974. India's other bovine: A cultural geography of the water buffalo. Ph.D. dissertation, University of Wisconsin.

    1977. The Indian milk buffalo: A paradox of high performance and low reputation. *Asian Profile* 5: 111-34.

    1978. Subsistence strategy and its ecological consequences in the Nepal Himalaya. *Anthropos* 73: 215-52.

    1982. The water buffalo: India's other bovine. *Anthropos* 77: 216-38.

Hose, Charles, and William McDougall. 1912. *The pagan tribes of Borneo,* Vol. 1. London.

Hutton, John Henry. 1965. The mixed culture of the Naga tribe. *Journal of the Royal Anthropological Institute of Great Britain and Ireland* 95: 16-43.

Imperial Gazetteer of India, Provincial series. 1908. *Central Provinces.* Calcutta.

India. Office of the Registrar General. 1965. *Census of India, 1961.* Vol. 9, *Madras.* Part 5-C, Todas. Kelhi, India.

Isaac, Erich. 1962. On the domestication of cattle. *Science* 137: 195–204.

Izikowitz, Karl Gustav. 1951. *Lamet: Hill peasants in French Indochina.* Göteborg, Sweden.

Jacob, Teuku. 1978. New finds of Lower and Middle Pleistocene Hominines from Indonesia and an examination of their antiquity. In *Early Paleolithic in South and East Asia,* ed. Fumiko Ikawa-Smith, 13–22. The Hague.

Jenks, Albert Ernest. 1905. *The Bontoc Igorot.* Manila.

Jia, Lanpo, and Weiwen Huang. 1985. The late Palaeolithic of China. In *Palaeoanthropology and Palaeolithic archaeology in the People's Republic of China,* ed. Wu Rukang and John W. Olsen, 211–23. New York.

Jolly, Julius, trans. 1900. *The Institutes of Vishnu.* Vol. 7 of *The sacred books of the East,* ed. F. Max Müller. Oxford.

Kennedy, Raymond. 1953. *Field note on Indonesia: South Celebes, 1949–50.* New Haven, Conn.

Khan, M. Z. 1974. The buffaloes of Pakistan. In *The husbandry and health of the domestic buffalo,* ed. W. Ross Cockrill, 611–15. Rome.

Kingdon, Jonathan. 1990. *Arabian mammals: A natural history.* New York.

Kipling, John Lockwood. 1891. *Beast and man in India: A popular sketch of Indian animals in their relation with the people.* London.

Klatt, Berthold. 1948. *Haustier und Mensch.* Hamburg.

Knapp, Bradford. 1957. *A compilation of available data on the water buffalo.* Washington, D.C.

Koenigswald, G. H. R. von. 1951. Introduction. In *Morphology of Solo man,* by Franz Weidenreich, 211–21. Anthropological papers of the American Museum of Natural History 43. New York.

1958. Remarks on the prehistoric fauna of the great cave at Niah. *The Sarawak Journal* 8: 620–6.

Koppers, Wilhelm, and L. Jungblut. 1942–5. The water-buffalo and the zebu in central India. *Anthropos* 37–40: 647–66.

Kosambi, D. D. 1965. *Ancient India: A history of its culture and civilization.* New York.

Kramer, Samuel Noah. 1967. *Cradle of civilization.* New York.

Krishnaswami, V. D. 1960. The Neolithic pattern of India. *Ancient India* 16: 25–64.

Kunstadter, Peter. 1966. Living with Thailand's gentle Lua. *National Geographic* 130: 122–52.

Kurtén, Björn. 1968. *Pleistocene mammals of Europe.* Chicago.

Lal, B. B. 1954–5. Excavation at Hastinapura and other explorations in the upper Ganga and Sutlej basins 1950–52. *Ancient India* 10–11: 5–151.

Lawless, Robert. 1975. The social ecology of the Kalingas of northern Luzon. Ph.D. dissertation, New School for Social Research.

Leach, E. R. 1964. *Political systems of highland Burma: A study of Kachin social structure.* Reprint of 1954 edition. London.

LeBar, Frank M. 1972. *Ethnic groups of insular Southeast Asia.* Vol. 1, *Indonesia, Andaman Islands, and Madagascar.* New Haven, Conn.

1975. *Ethnic groups of insular Southeast Asia.* Vol. 2, *Philippines and Formosa.* New Haven, Conn.

LeBar, Frank M., Gerald C. Hickey, and John K. Musgrave. 1964. *Ethnic groups of mainland Southeast Asia.* New Haven, Conn.

Lévy, Paul. 1959. The sacrifice of the buffalo and the forecast of the weather in Vientiane. In *Kingdom of Laos,* ed. René de Berval, 162–73. Saigon.

Lloyd, Seton. 1947. *Twin rivers: A brief history of Iraq from the earliest times to the present day.* Bombay.

Loeb, Edwin M. 1935. *Sumatra: Its history and people.* Vienna.

Lydekker, Richard. 1898. *Wild oxen, sheep, and goats of all lands, living and extinct.* London.

MacGregor, Roderick. 1941. The domestic buffalo. *The Veterinary Record* 53: 443–50.

Mackay, E. J. H. 1937-8. *Further excavations at Mohenjo-daro.* 2 vols. Delhi.

Mahadevan, P. 1974. The buffaloes of Trinidad and Tobago. In *The husbandry and health of the domestic buffalo,* ed. W. Ross Cockrill, 698–704. Rome.

Majumdar, D. N. 1927. Death and connected ceremonies amongst the Hos of Kolhan in Singbhum. *Journal and Proceedings of the Asiatic Society of Bengal* (new series) 23: 37–44.

1944. *The fortunes of primitive tribes.* Lucknow, India.

1950. *The affairs of a tribe: A study in tribal dynamics.* Lucknow, India.

Marshall, John. 1931. *Mohenjo-daro and the Indus civilization.* 3 vols. London.

Mason, Ian L. 1974. Environmental physiology. In *The husbandry and health of the domestic buffalo,* ed. W. Ross Cockrill, 88–104. Rome.

Mathpal, Yashodhar. 1984. *Prehistoric rock paintings of Bhimbetka, central India.* New Delhi.

1985. The hunter-gatherer way of life depicted in the Mesolithic rock paintings of central India. In *Recent advances in Indo-Pacific prehistory,* ed. V. N. Misra and Peter Bellwood, 177–83. New Delhi.

Meacham, William. 1977. Continuity and local evolution in the Neolithic of South China: A non-nuclear approach. *Current Anthropology* 18: 419–40.

1983. Origins and development of the Yüeh coastal Neolithic: A microcosm of culture change on the mainland of East Asia. In *The origins of Chinese civilization,* ed. David N. Keightley, 147–75. Berkeley, Calif.

Medway, Lord. 1965. *Mammals of Borneo: Field keys and an annotated checklist.* Singapore.

1972. The Quaternary mammals of Malesia: A review. In *The Quaternary era in Malesia,* ed. P. Ashton and M. Ashton, 63–98. Transactions of the Second Aberdeen–Hull Symposium on Malesian Ecology, Aberdeen 1971. Department of Geography, University of Hull, Miscellaneous Series No. 13. Hull, England.

Mickey, Margaret Portia. 1947. *The Cowrie Shell Miao of Kweichow.* Papers of the Peabody Museum of American Archaeology and Ethnology, Harvard University, 32. Cambridge, Mass.

Miles, Arthur. 1937. *The land of the lingam.* London.

Mills, James Philip. 1937. *The Rengma Nagas.* London.

Misra, V. N. 1985. Microlithic industries in India. In *Recent advances in Indo-Pacific prehistory,* ed. V. N. Misra and Peter Bellwood, 111–22. New Delhi.

Moss, C. R. 1920. Nabaloi law and ritual. *University of California Publications in American Archaeology and Ethnology* 15: 207–342.

Movius, Hallam L., Jr. 1944. *Early man and Pleistocene stratigraphy in southern and eastern Asia.* Papers of the Peabody Museum of American Archaeology and Ethnology, Harvard University, 19. Cambridge, Mass.

Murray, James A. H., Henry Bradley, W. A. Craigie, and C. T. Onions. 1933. *The Oxford English dictionary,* Vol. 1. Oxford.

Naik, T. B. 1956. *The Bhils: A study.* Delhi.

Nath, Y. V. S. 1960. *Bhils of Ratanmal: An analysis of the social structure of a western Indian community.* Baroda, India.

National Research Council, Panel on Water Buffalo (U.S.). 1981. *The water buffalo: New prospects for an underutilized animal.* Washington, D.C.

Niggemeyer, Hermann. 1964. *Kuttia Kond: Dschungel-Bauern in Orissa.* Munich.

Nooy-Palm, Hetty. 1986. *The Sa'dan-Toraja: A study of their social life and religion.* Dordrecht, the Netherlands.

Paul the Deacon. 1907. *History of the Langobards,* trans. William Dudley Foulke. Philadelphia, Pa.

Pearson, Richard. 1983. The Ch'ing-lien-kang culture and the Chinese Neolithic. In *The origins of Chinese civilization,* ed. David N. Keightley, 119–45. Berkeley, Calif.

Pelzer, Karl J. 1945. *Pioneer settlement in the Asiatic tropics: Studies in land utilization and agricultural colonization in southeastern Asia.* New York.

Pfeffer, Pierre. 1968. *Asia: A natural history.* New York.

Phillips, Ralph W., Ray G. Johnson, and Raymond T. Moyer. 1945. *The livestock of China.* Washington, D.C.

Piggott, Stuart. 1950. *Prehistoric India to 1000 B.C.* Harmondsworth, England.

Pliny. 1855. *The natural history of Pliny,* Vol. 2, trans. John Bostock, and H. T. Riley. London.

Pokee, Sohn. 1984. The palaeoenvironment of Middle and Upper Pleistocene Korea. In *The evolution of the East Asian environment,* Vol. 2, ed. Robert Orr Whyte, 877–93. Hong Kong.

Polikhronov, D. St. 1974. The buffaloes of Bulgaria. In *The husbandry and health of the domestic buffalo,* ed. W. Ross Cockrill, 709–30. Rome.

Porter, Valerie. 1991. *Cattle: A handbook to the breeds of the world.* New York.

Prashad, Baini. 1936. *Animal remains from Harappa.* Memoirs of the Archaeological Survey of India, No. 51. Delhi.

Qiu, Zhonglang. 1985. The Middle Palaeolithic of China. In *Palaeoanthropology and Palaeolithic archaeology in the People's Republic of China,* ed. Wu Rukang and John W. Olsen, 187–210. New York.

Ramadas, G. 1931. The Gadabas. *Man in India* 11: 160–73.

Randhawa, M. S. 1946. Role of domesticated animals in Indian history. *Science and Culture* 12: 5–14.

Rao, S. R. 1962–3. Excavation at Rangpur and other explorations in Gujarat. *Ancient India* 18–19: 5–207.

Rea, Alexander. 1915. *Catalogue of the prehistoric antiquities from Adichanallur and Perumbair.* Madras, India.

Rife, D. C. 1959. *The water buffalo of India and Pakistan.* Washington, D.C.

Risley, H. H. 1892. *The tribes and castes of Bengal.* 2 vols. Calcutta.

Risley, H. H., and E. A. Gait. 1903. *Census of India, 1901.* Vol. 1, *India. Part 1, Report.* Calcutta.

Rivers, W. H. R. 1906. *The Todas.* London.

Rouse, John E. 1970. *World cattle.* 2 vols. Norman, Okla.

Roy, Sarat Chandra. 1915. *The Oraons of Chota Nagpur: Their history, economic life, and social organization.* Ranchi, India.

    1928. *Oraon religion and customs.* Calcutta.

Roy, Sarat Chandra, and Ramesh Chandra Roy. 1937. *The Kharias.* 2 vols. Ranchi, India.

Russell, R. V. 1916. *The tribes and castes of the central provinces of India.* 4 vols. London.

Rutter, Owen. 1922. *British North Borneo: An account of its history, resources and native tribes.* London.

Sahu, Lakshminarayana. 1942. *The hill tribes of Jeypore.* Cuttack, India.

Salerno, A. 1974. The buffaloes of Italy. In *The husbandry and health of the domestic buffalo,* ed. W. Ross Cockrill, 737–47. Rome.

Sankalia, H. D. 1946. *Investigations into prehistoric archaeology of Gujarat.* Baroda, India.

    1977. *Prehistory of India.* New Delhi.

    1978. *Pre-historic art in India.* Durham, N.C.

Sastri, K. N. 1957. *New light on the Indus civilization,* Vol. 1. Delhi.

Sauer, Carl O. 1952. *Agricultural origins and dispersals.* New York.

Scott, James George. 1896. The wild Wa: A head-hunting race. *Asiatic Quarterly Review* (third series) 1: 138–52.

Scott, James George, and J. P. Hardiman. 1900. *Gazetteer of upper Burma and the Shan State,* Part 1, Vol. 1. Rangoon.

Simoons, Frederick J. 1970. The traditional limits of milking and milk use in southern Asia. *Anthropos* 65: 547–93.

Simoons, Frederick J., and Elizabeth S. Simoons. 1968. *A ceremonial ox of India: The mithan in nature, culture, and history.* Madison, Wis.

Smith, Bruce D. 1995. *The emergence of agriculture.* New York.

Soundara Rajan, K. V. 1958. Studies in the stone age of Nagarjunakonda and its neighbourhood. *Ancient India* 14: 49–113.

Sowerby, Arthur de Carle. 1935. The domestic animals of China. *The China Journal* 23: 233–43.

Srinivasan, Doris. 1975–6. The so-called Proto-Siva seal from Mohenjo-daro: An iconological assessment. *Archives of Asian Art* 29: 47–58.

Sullivan, Herbert P. 1964. A re-examination of the religion of the Indus civilization. *History of Religions* 4: 115–25.

Terra, H. de, and P. Teilhard de Chardin. 1936. Observations on the upper Siwalik formation and later Pleistocene deposits in India. *Proceedings of the American Philosophical Society* 76: 791–822.

Thakkar, A. V. 1950. *Tribes of India.* Delhi.

Thapar, B. K. 1957. Maski 1954: A Chalcolithic site of the southern Deccan. *Ancient India* 13: 4–142.

Thesiger, Wilfred. 1954. The Ma'dan or marsh dwellers of southern Iraq. *Journal of the Royal Central Asian Society* 41: 4–25.

    1964. *The Marsh Arabs.* London.

Thurston, Edgar. 1909. *Castes and tribes of southern India.* 7 vols. Madras, India.

    1912. *Omens and superstitions of southern India.* London.

Tickell, Lieut. 1840. Memoir on the Hodesum (Improperly called Kolehan). *Journal of the Asiatic Society of Bengal* 9: 694–710.

Vats, Madho Sarup. 1940. *Excavations at Harappa,* Vol. 1. Delhi.

Vidyarthi, L. P. 1963. *The Maler: A study in nature-man-spirit complex of a hill tribe in Bihar.* Calcutta.

Volkman, Toby Alice. 1980. The pig has eaten the vegetables: Ritual and change in Tana Toraja. Ph.D. dissertation, Cornell University.

Ward, William Hayes. 1910. *The seal cylinders of western Asia.* Washington, D.C.

Wetherill, Elkins. 1972. A preliminary report on faunal remains from Chasen. Appendix to Excavations at Chasen, Thailand, 1968 and 1969: A preliminary report, by Bennet Bronson and George F. Dales. *Asian Perspectives* 15: 44–5.

Wheatley, Paul. 1965. A note on the extension of milking

practices into Southeast Asia during the first millennium A.D. *Anthropos* 60: 577-90.

Wheeler, Mortimer. 1959. *Early India and Pakistan, to Ashoka.* New York.

1968. *The Indus civilization.* Third edition. Cambridge.

White, Lynn, Jr. 1974. Indic elements in the iconography of Petrarch's "Trionfo della morte." *Speculum* 49: 201-21.

Whyte, R. O. 1968. *Land, livestock and human nutrition in India.* New York.

Whyte, R. O., and M. A. Mathur. 1974. The buffalo in India. In *The husbandry and health of the domestic buffalo,* ed. W. Ross Cockrill, 548-68. Rome.

Wu, Xinzhi, and Linghong Wang. 1985. Chronology in Chinese palaeoanthropology. In *Palaeoanthropology and palaeolithic archaeology in the People's Republic of China,* ed. Wu Rukang and John W. Olsen, 29-51. New York.

Wulsin, Frederick R. 1941. *The prehistoric archaeology of northwest Africa.* Papers of the Peabody Museum of American Archaeology and Ethnology, Harvard University, 19. Cambridge, Mass.

Young, Gordon. 1962. *The hill tribes of northern Thailand.* Bangkok.

Yule, Henry, and A. C. Burnell. 1903. *Hodson-Jobson: A glossary of colloquial Anglo-Indian words and phrases, and of kindred terms, etymological, historical, geographical and discursive.* London.

Zeuner, Frederick E. 1963. *A history of domesticated animals.* New York.

Zhao, Songqiao, and Wei-Tang Wu. 1986-7. Early Neolithic Hemodu culture along the Hangzhou estuary and the origin of domestic paddy rice in China. *Asian Perspectives* 27: 29-34.

II.G.24 ✎ Yak

Despite recent interest in domesticated animals in general and bovines in particular, there has been little systematic study of yak.[1] Nevertheless, enough is known to warrant a closer consideration of the role these cattle play in the culture, diet, and ecology of the several peoples who exploit them in some of the harshest and most difficult environments of Asia.

Taxonomy, Description, and Habitat

Yak are members of the subfamily of cattle Bovinae.[2] Although the genetic relationships among its members are not precisely understood, Herwart Bohlken (1958: 167-8, 1958-60: 113-202) argues that yak belong to the genus *Bos* and subgenus *Poëphagus.* Moreover, Bohlken draws a further distinction between wild yak, *Bos [Poëphagus] mutus* Przhelval'skii (1883), and domesticated yak, *Bos [Poëphagus] grunniens* Linnaeus (1766). Although wild and domesticated yak are interfertile, domesticated yak can be crossed with a variety of other cattle, including common cattle *(Bos taurus),* and zebu *(Bos indicus)* to produce hybrids of various types.[3]

Yak

Both wild and domesticated yak are massively built, with barrel-shaped bodies carried on legs that are quite short but solid (see Figure II.G.24.1). Although yak have no humps (as zebus do), they do have a dorsal ridgelike prominence that adds to their massive appearance. From this prominence, a short heavy neck slopes downward, ending in a large head with a broad, flat forehead, large eyes, and small ears.

Probably the most conspicuous features of the yak, however, are its horns and hair. The horns are large, dark, and double-curved. That is, they emerge horizontally from either side of the head, curve and extend first upward, then backward. The hair is coarse and shaggy and covers the animal's body almost entirely. The hair is abundant and is generally 4 or more inches in length. Fringing the chest, lower shoulders, sides, flanks, and thighs of the yak is even longer hair, which almost reaches the ground. The tail, too, is entirely covered by long hair, giving it a pronounced bushy appearance.

Wild yak are characteristically black or dark brown, occasionally with lighter colors on the forehead and along the back. Domesticated yak, in contrast, are much more variable in color. They range from black to white, and even piebalds are common.

Large numbers of wild yak once roamed over much of Tibet and the high Himalayas, though they have decreased in numbers and range. Today, only small herds occur, and only in certain restricted and inhospitable places, including small portions of the great mountain ranges of Inner Asia (the Tien Shan, Kunlun Shan, Pamirs, Karakorum) and the most remote areas of the Greater Himalayas. They are also found in small numbers in the dry Changtang, a vast, virtually uninhabited plateau that sweeps across northern Tibet in a great arc, extending from the Tibet–India border in the west to the Koko Nor region in the east.

In the better watered areas of the Changtang, small herds of wild yak give way to the large herds of domesticated yak managed by pastoralists. Domesticated yak also thrive in the more moist regions of Mongolia and central Asia and in the deep river valleys and small plains of southern and eastern Tibet, as well as along the high, south-facing flank of the Himalayas. Here, temperatures are higher, rainfall is much greater and more predictable, and vegetation is more abundant. These are regions occupied by farming folk, who are far more numerous than the pastoral nomads of the plateaus.

Yak in Culture and Diet

Wherever yak are kept, they are a central element in human ecology and adaptation. Farmers, for example, use these animals for a variety of agricultural purposes, including plowing and threshing. Among pastoral nomads, yak are a source of hair for tent-cloth and may be employed in caravan work. For transhumant populations in mountainous regions, who combine certain aspects of pastoral and agricultural economies, yak are employed in these and other ways to wrest a living from often fragile environments. But most important, perhaps, to those who keep yak is the role the animal plays in the direct provision of food for human consumption and nutrition. In this regard, any detailed consideration of the wide variety of useful dietary products supplied by yak must focus on meat, milk, milk products, and blood.

Meat

Although most yak-keeping folk profess Buddhism, a religion that encourages a vegetarian diet by forbidding the slaughter of animals, few abstain from meat eating. Quite the opposite seems to be the case. Flesh foods are relished by most of these people, and every attempt is made to include at least some meat in the main meal each day. This is not always possible, however, because in most regions meat is a seasonal commodity and, in any case, is expensive.

The Buddhist prohibition of slaughter stems from a central concept in Buddha's teachings: *ahimsa*. Slaughter and meat eating compromise Buddhist yak-herders and are a source of guilt, for they contribute to the suffering and death of yak. To escape guilt, people slaughter yak in ways that rationalize and minimize responsibility. For example, calves may be denied the milk of their mothers. Since such animals starve and blood is not shed, death is considered a matter of fate and not the result of human action.

When slaughter by starvation is not practical, other methods are employed. Adult yak, for example, can be suffocated with a cord tied tightly around the animal's mouth and nose. And according to Marion H. Duncan (personal communication), Tibetans of Kham in eastern Tibet fit a leather sack tightly around the animal's muzzle, thereby cutting off air.

Perhaps the most common method of minimizing guilt is to give yak over to a hereditary group of professional butchers for slaughter. Such butchers absolve others of moral responsibility in the affair and are considered damned for their transgressions. Many butchers form a distinct caste in Buddhist societies. Others, such as those of Lhasa, are Moslems, originally from Ladakh or Kansu, who do not adhere to the *ahimsa* concept.

Although the slaughter of yak by butchers takes place throughout the year, especially in larger settlements, slaughtering by farmers and nomads is a seasonal affair. Most are killed in late autumn or early winter when the animals are well fleshed from spring and summer grazing. This is the time of year when winter temperatures facilitate preservation and storage of meat; the timing of the slaughter also reflects an attempt, in regions of limited pasturing opportunities, to minimize overgrazing and herd losses by careful control of herd size.

Figure II.G.24.1. Domesticated yak. (Drawing by Hildreth Burnett.)

Selection of yak to be slaughtered in late autumn or early winter is not random. Rather, each animal is carefully considered, and those deemed least able to survive the harsh winter months are culled out first. To these are added others that are considered poor economic investments. Such yak are usually the male cattle, often yak bulls too old, too sick, or too weak for traction or burden. Female yak are selected if they are dry or past the age of breeding. Selective slaughter, thus, not only provides an abundance of meat but also enhances the ability of the remaining cattle to survive the deprivations of winter. In addition, it results in a more efficient allocation of pasturing and other resources and a more efficient and economical herd.

Meat not eaten immediately after slaughter must be preserved or traded. If fresh meat is traded, distances involved are very limited – within a village, for example, to folk who have little access to meat and who pay cash, barter goods, or provide services in exchange. If properly preserved, however, such meat can be kept for months, even years, and traded over great distances.

Yak meat is preserved in a variety of ways. The lower temperatures of the slaughtering season may be used to freeze it. The meat is also salted and

smoked, but drying is by far the most common method of preservation. Carcasses of slaughtered yak may be simply cut into joints, which are hung outdoors. The joints slowly dry, often shrinking to half their original size.

More commonly, the beef is cut into thin strips, which are set out in the sun to dry, sometimes on cloths spread over the ground, more often on racks erected for this purpose. Beef jerked in this way is very popular in Tibet and the high Nepal Himalaya.

Not only does drying preserve meat, it also reduces its weight, allowing more to be carried on long journeys. In wintertime, dried meat is an important item of barter and sale. This is especially true for pastoral nomads, who use meat and other animal products to trade for the carbohydrate-rich plant foods of farmers and transhumant folk.

Meat also plays a prominent role in the diet of most yak-keeping peoples as a ceremonial or feast food. Among more prosperous families, meat of some kind is eaten nearly every day, but because of the expense involved, poorer families eat meat only occasionally. Whenever possible, however, even the poorest will try to offer a meat dish to visitors and guests. When unable to do so, apologies are given or excuses made.

Not everyone eats yak meat, however, and even those who do often abstain from certain kinds of flesh or from flesh prepared in proscribed ways. Some Tibetans, for example, consume the flesh of yak and female hybrids eagerly but refuse to eat the flesh of male hybrids. When asked why, they reply that male hybrids are sinful animals and their flesh is polluting.

Yak meat that has been roasted, broiled, or fried is considered polluting and impure by virtually all Tibetans and Himalayan Buddhists.[4] Some Tibetan nomads believe that consumption of flesh prepared in these ways will result in sickness or bad luck – the punishment of gods angered by the odor of scorched flesh. Although many farmers and transhumant peoples agree with this pastoral nomadic belief, perhaps in an attempt to emulate this more prestigious group, others strike a compromise. According to them, the indoor roasting, broiling, and frying of meat produces odors that house gods find offensive. If, however, meat is prepared in these ways outside the home, it can be eaten with no harmful effects. In any case, the most common method of cooking yak and hybrid meat is boiling, a method acceptable to all. But flesh is also eaten uncooked, whether fresh or preserved.

In a few areas of Tibet bordering on India, Tibetans have been affected by Hindu views of the sacredness of common cattle. In some cases, Hindus themselves have transferred their views concerning common cattle to yak and hybrids, and in areas under their political influence such flesh has been (at one time or another), difficult or impossible to get. In other cases, Tibetans have taken over Hindu views. Some Tibetans of western Tibet, for example, were reported to view yak as sacred and avoided eating its flesh at all costs. Other Tibetans of the same region, however, who were less affected by Hindu ways, ate yak meat freely (Sherring 1906).

Some inhabitants of the Nepal Himalaya have been similarly influenced by Hindu ideas. The Gurung and Thakali are two such groups. The legends of the Gurungs, a tribal people of west central Nepal, indicate that they once consumed yak flesh freely, but according to Donald Messerschmidt (personal communication), present-day Hinduized Gurung consider this practice abhorrent because they have transferred Hindu ideas concerning common cattle to yak.

The Thakali of the Kali Gandaki Valley gave up eating the flesh of yak in the nineteenth century in an attempt to elevate the social status of their caste and to facilitate establishment of social relations with dominant members of Nepal's Hindu ruling class. Tradition maintains that Harkaman Subba Sherchan (1860–1905), a customs contractor, initiated the banning of yak flesh (Fürer-Haimendorf 1966: 144–5).

Milk

Because of the feelings of guilt associated with the consumption of yak flesh, meat is included in a category of "black" foods, considered unceremonious, harmful, or improper. Milk and milk products, however, are classed as "white" foods, suitable for all occasions and persons. Most yak herders consider milk, in both its fresh and processed states, a tasty food to be consumed eagerly by all ages. But while these views are associated with milk in general, distinctions are made among a variety of milk types, each the product of different mammals. Furthermore, each type of milk occupies a position in a hierarchy of milk preference that varies little, if at all, from place to place.

Among Tibetans and Himalayan folk, for example, there exists a strikingly consistent pattern or hierarchy of milk preference from place to place and group to group. Above all others, milk of yak is preferred, not only for its flavor and richness but also because it is considered especially healthful. Milk of hybrid cows is thought to be less tasty than yak milk but is preferred over that of common cattle (the other component of hybrid parentage).

Distinctions, however, are made by those more familiar with hybrids. The Sherpa of Nepal, for example, distinguish between milk of the two major hybrid types and prefer milk of hybrids (dimdzo) sired by common bulls to that of hybrids (urangdzo) sired by yak bulls. In any case, milk of common cows is not especially liked but is considered superior to the milk of backcross cows and ewes and is consumed when more highly prized milk is not available. Milk of female goats is least preferred and is seldom consumed by Tibetans and Himalayan folk, even the poorest.

This pattern of preference is generally explained in terms of the varying quality of milk types. Quality is defined as "thickness" or "richness." Such terms refer to the fat content of the various milks, for analyses of these milks do indeed show substantial differences in fat content. This content may range widely, however, depending on such factors as the season when the milk was obtained, grazing conditions at the time of milking, and availability and utilization of supplementary feed. Thus, the fat content by volume of yak milk has been assayed by some to be between 4.8 percent and 16 percent (Mittaine 1962: 693; Schley 1967: 45–6, 78). But a study by Peter Schley of experiments on yak, hybrids, and common cattle in the Soviet Union has demonstrated that at any given time, fat content of yak milk is 18 percent to 28 percent greater than that of hybrid cow milk and 39 percent to 97 percent greater than the milk of common cows. Furthermore, the fat content of hybrid cow milk is, according to Schley's figures, 13 percent to 65 percent greater than that of common cows (Schley 1967: 78).

With respect to fat content, the obvious superiority of yak milk to that of hybrids and common cows is somewhat offset by the inability of yak to produce as great a volume of milk as hybrid and common cows. But, as with the fat content of milk, production figures for yak, hybrids, and common cows vary from place to place and season to season. Grazing conditions account for a goodly part of these variations, but milk production also varies with age of milch cows. Yak and hybrid cows, for example, begin lactating at 2 or 3 years of age. As they grow older, and until they reach the age of 10, the lactation period lengthens from approximately 230 days to 300 days. Naturally, this lengthening is reflected in higher production of milk. After this maximum is reached, milk production declines.

Whatever the actual milk production figures are for yak and for hybrids and common cows kept under similar conditions, field observations in the Nepal Himalaya reveal several constants that should be noted. First, hybrid cows produce twice as much milk as yak and 50 percent more than common cows. The latter, however, consistently produce more than yak by about 30 percent.

The second constant reflects the season of milk production. Milk yields for yak, hybrids, and common cows increase as summer waxes and grazing improves, then begin to decline in late summer. In midwinter, lactation nearly ceases, though hybrids tend to be able to lactate during this period somewhat better than yak or common cows. Percentage of fat by volume, however, does not decline with the seasonal decline in milk quantity. Rather, it continues to climb, reaching its maximum when milk yields are lowest. These data confirm the findings of Schley and others but conflict with certain other sources.[5]

Tibetans and others do make some efforts to increase the milk production of their cattle. For example, they use stud that derive from lineages renowned for their milking characteristics. Another technique involves supplemental feeding of lactating yak and hybrids. A number of fodders are used for this purpose, including grasses and leaves collected in pasture and transported to the agricultural village or nomadic camp, where the feed is given to animals in the evening or stored for future use. Also used are fodder crops such as radishes and the straw of harvested grains. And some Tibetan nomads occasionally cultivate fields of planted and volunteer fodder crops for just such use.

Among the more interesting Tibetan customs employed to maximize milk yields is the feeding of salt to lactating cows; more frequent milking, especially as the grazing season progresses; restricting nursing by calves; and stimulating the milk let-down response in stubborn females.[6] In this last, several methods are employed, among them use of calf substitutes, calf dolls, and vaginal insufflation.[7]

Milking of yak and hybrids is done almost exclusively by women and girls; only occasionally will men and boys involve themselves in this work. Whoever does it, the milking procedure seldom varies. The milker always squats beside the cow with her head pressed against the animal's side for balance. The milk pail is set on the ground or held against the milker's thigh by a hook attached to her belt and fitted into a notch in the pail. Robert B. Ekvall, who had extensive experience among the Tibetans of northeastern Tibet, has described the hook as a prized item of female

attire that, when wealth permits, is covered in silver, coral, and turquoise. According to Ekvall, the milking hook has come to symbolize, in nomadic society at least, the female's role in foodgetting (Ekvall 1968: 50).

No distinction is made between milk taken in the morning and that collected in the evening; both are considered equal in all respects. For children, especially, milk is considered a very healthy and nutritious food and may be made more appetizing by the addition of sugar, butter, or some other ingredient. The Mewu Fantzu, a pastoral group of Kansu, are said to consider yak milk better for children than even mother's milk, which they say makes children stupid (Stübel 1958: 8). Although this is probably a radical position, it nonetheless serves as an indicator of the esteem in which yak milk is held.

While some Tibetans allow small children to drink fresh milk, it does not seem to be the practice among adults or children over 4 or 5 years of age. For them, milk must be boiled before it is consumed. When asked to explain why they boil milk before drinking it, many Tibetans insist it is necessary to avoid the diarrhea, flatulence, vomiting, and stomach cramps that would surely follow the drinking of fresh milk. Some, however, maintain that milk is boiled simply to improve its taste and that no medical considerations are involved. Whatever the reason, milk is not boiled very long but rather is heated just until it boils, after which it is quickly removed from the fire.

Milk Products: Butter and Cheese

Most milk is converted into milk products as quickly as possible. There are two reasons for this practice. First, milk processing results in products much less perishable than liquid milk. Second, such products can be transported more easily than liquid milk, even over short distances. Because a great deal of milk is produced and collected in pastures distant from established villages and milk yields vary from season to season, transportability and perishability are important factors that must be dealt with by pastoralists.

Butter is, perhaps, the most important product derived from milk both in amount produced and quantity consumed. Butter derived from the milk of yak has the highest prestige value and is preferred over all others for its taste, richness, and color, which varies from season to season from a golden hue in summer to pale yellow in late winter. No distinction seems to be drawn among butters of various hybrids.

The major instrument of butter making is the churn, and a variety of types are employed, with some made of wood, some of leather, and others of pottery.[8]

Butter making, like milking, is principally a female occupation. However, no universal rule exists on this point. As with milking, the process of butter making varies little. After milk is collected from animals, it is warmed over a fire and stored for about a day perhaps in a churn, or in vessels assigned for that use. In either case, the warmed milk is allowed to curdle. Sometimes, a small amount of starter is added to hasten cur-dling. Once curd is formed, the mass is transferred to a churn and agitated. As soon as butter begins to form, a quantity of warm water is added a little at a time, to encourage the process. As larger clots of butter float to the surface of the buttermilk, they are picked out and squeezed by hand to remove any remaining liquid.

Those who maintain large herds of milch cows produce more butter than is necessary for the normal needs of their families; thus, they store excess butter in a variety of ways for future use, sale, and trade. A common method of storing butter in the Nepal Himalayas nowadays is simply to pack it solidly in 5-gallon kerosene tins. Before tins were commonly available, however, butter was packed in sheep stomachs or wrapped in wet rawhide bags, which, sewn shut and dried, are said to have kept butter from a few months to a year or more. Butter is also stored in wooden boxes and barrels and, according to some Tibetans, pottery containers as well.

Butter, a valuable low-bulk manufacture, is traded widely and is sold by weight. Demand for butter is the result of various factors, not least of which is its prominent role in the diet. Seldom is butter eaten in its raw state. More often it is melted and used in frying or mixed with other foodstuffs. The largest percentage of butter is consumed in the form of *tsocha,* the ubiquitous butter-tea of Tibet and the Himalayan region. *Tsocha* is souplike in consistency and nourishment. And, although the ingredients do not vary at all from place to place, the taste of *tsocha* varies from family to family, perhaps because of the quality or quantity of ingredients used.

Only three ingredients are necessary to make *tsocha:* tea, butter, and salt. Tea, even among the poorest, must be Chinese, imported at great expense in brick or cone form. A quantity of tea is broken off and boiled in water that is then strained and poured into a tea churn. After hot tea is poured into the churn, butter and salt are added. The best *tsocha* is said to be made with yak butter; when this is unavailable, butter of hybrids is used, followed, in order of preference, by the butters of common cows, sheep, and goats. Salt is almost always of Tibetan origin; Indian salt is seldom used because it is thought to cause illness. After being thoroughly churned, the *tsocha* is poured into a kettle for reheating; when hot, it is served in handleless cups or in glasses. *Tsocha* is a dietary staple drunk many times a day by persons of all ages.

Two other factors help explain the high value of butter and the constant demand for this commodity in the marketplaces of Tibet and Nepal. First is the role of butter in discharging social obligations, and second is the multifarious ceremonial role of butter.

With respect to social obligations, in many instances payment in the form of butter is a desirable method of settling accounts. Turning briefly to religious and ceremonial requirements, we find an almost insatiable demand for butter. In lamaseries, for exam-

ple, large quantities are required for making the *tsocha* served to lamas, and enormous amounts are consumed in the many votive lamps kept burning on altars. One scholar has suggested that the larger lamaseries of Tibet required tons of butter each year for just these two purposes (Tucci 1967: 94).

Unlike butter, however, there is no great market for or monetary value attached to the soft and hard cheeses made from yak milk. Nonetheless, cheese, made from buttermilk, is appreciated as a nourishing and tasty addition to meals; as an easily carried, sustaining food for long journeys; and as a treat on festive occasions.

Women, who are solely responsible for cheese making, do not hesitate to mix the buttermilk of yak, hybrids, and common cows in order to produce cheese. The principal concern seems to be the availability of enough buttermilk to warrant the long, tedious process of cheese making and not the composition of the buttermilk.

In any case, after the butter is removed from a churn, the remaining buttermilk is poured into kettles which are set over a fire. The buttermilk is brought to a rolling boil, after which it is removed from the fire to cool. As it cools, the buttermilk separates, forming a thick, spongy, white mass that floats to the surface of a clear liquid.

Solids are skimmed off with a shallow strainer, something like a dipper, and are placed in a cloth bag to allow whey to drain off. What remains in the cloth constitutes soft cheese, which is eaten immediately. On special occasions, sugar is added to make a sweet, tasty mixture. Soft cheese is also fried before eating, mixed with barley flour to form a doughlike food, or boiled with butter, salt, and other spices and served as a soup. More commonly, however, soft cheese is dried to form the second, hard type of cheese.

Hard cheese is produced by drying soft cheese in the sun or by the fire. Sun-drying is much preferred over fire-drying, for the latter darkens the cheese and makes it less tasty. If weather permits, soft cheese is scattered on cloths spread on the ground close to the house. If this is not possible, soft cheese is arranged before an indoor fire, on mats woven of vegetable material. In either case, soft cheese shrinks to about a fourth of its original size, forming a very hard cheese that is said to keep indefinitely.

Hard cheese most commonly is eaten by slowly dissolving pieces in the mouth. But this kind of cheese is also added to stews and soups or dropped into cups of *tsocha.* As an easily carried food, cubes of hard cheese are often taken on journeys to supplement meals purchased on the trail, or they may be the sole sustenance of the traveler.

Blood

Bleeding of live cattle is a widespread and common practice among the peoples of Tibet and Nepal. Bleeding is done for a variety of purposes, principal among them to obtain blood for human consumption.

Unlike milk, butter, and cheese (which are available and eaten throughout the year), blood is a seasonal food. Bleeding of yak for food takes place in late spring and early summer; only if there should be a famine are cattle bled for food in other seasons.

Not all yak are bled for food, however. Yak oxen are the animals most often bled, but occasionally yak cows, if they are not lactating, are bled as well. Hybrid cows seem never to be bled for food, and only persons who have no yak, or insufficient numbers of them, bleed male hybrids. There seems to be no evidence of bleeding common cattle for the sole purpose of procuring blood for food, though they are bled for other reasons. Moreover, no consistent and uniform explanation exists for not bleeding yak dams, female hybrids, and common cattle, but the strong impression is that although bleeding males for food is not quite proper, bleeding females for food is quite offensive.

Perhaps because bleeding cattle for food offends Buddhist sensibilities, Tibetans and Himalayans derive most blood food as a by-product of bleeding for other purposes. One is to prevent disease in cattle and ensure the cattle's survival by encouraging them to gain weight quickly.[9] Such operations, like bloodletting for food, generally take place in late spring and early summer when cattle, after surviving the winter, begin feeding on new grass.

Any animal considered lean or prone to disease is a candidate for bleeding, though more time and consideration is given to the selection of milch cows and dams lest bloodletting cause lactation to cease. Even calves are bled to improve their health and chances for survival. Cattle that are sick or so weak that they are in immediate danger of dying are also bled. But blood drawn from such animals is not considered fit for human consumption.

As previously noted, lactating yak dams and hybrid cows are seldom, if ever, bled to supply their owners with food. And a great deal more care is shown in the selection of females for prophylactic bloodletting operations than is extended to males. Perhaps this more sympathetic treatment of cows is, as some Tibetans suggest, an attempt to reconcile human food needs with the Buddhist view that bloodletting is an improper activity because it involves use of a knife and the spilling of blood.

Or perhaps the explanation of more secular Tibetans is correct. According to them, milch cows and dams are rarely bled because there is always a possibility that the operation will prove fatal or result in cessation of lactation. This thinking suggests that decisions are based purely on selfish and economic grounds and not on higher concerns. In any case, no such consideration is shown to dry cows and to those that have difficulty being impregnated. These animals are bled in spring to improve their chances of pregnancy.[10]

Whatever the purposes of bleeding, the method varies little from place to place and from group to group. Essentially, bleeding begins with the application of a tourniquet, simply a length of rope, around the animal's neck. Often, but not always, a similar tourniquet is tied around the animal's belly or buttocks to force (it is maintained) blood to the neck. Once in place, the neck tourniquet is tightened. If accompanied by another tourniquet, both are tightened. This action causes the blood vessels of the neck to stand out. One of these vessels is chosen, and using a small awl-like instrument or a special handleless chisel-edged tool called a *tsakpu,* the bloodletter makes an incision (not a puncture) of about 1/4-inch to 1/2-inch in length. The blood that spurts from the wound is caught in a container if it is to be prepared as food, or it is allowed to fall directly to the ground if considered inedible.

Varying quantities of blood are taken from cattle, depending primarily upon the sex, size, and condition of the animal. If the animal is male and in good condition, a half gallon of blood may be taken; if it is female and in poor condition, only a pint or so may be removed. If the operation is performed correctly, bleeding stops as soon as the tourniquet is loosened.

Bleeding of cattle is strictly a male task; women never perform the operation under any circumstances. Among nomads, each adult male is an accomplished bloodletter, having learned from his elders during childhood. Among settled folk, some perform the operation on their own cattle, but others, not as skilled, often prefer to have more experienced men bleed their cattle.

If bleeding of cattle is a task assigned to men, preparation of blood for eating is strictly a female occupation. Blood food must undergo some kind of processing because nobody would consume fresh blood. There are a number of methods of preparing blood drawn from live cattle; the particular one employed by a family depends entirely upon personal preference. One of the most common ways of preparing blood food involves simply allowing the blood to coagulate (a process that sometimes is hastened by the addition of salt), after which it is either boiled in water or fried in butter.

Another method of preparation requires that the blood be mixed with water; after a period of time, a thick mass forms that is eaten plain or mixed with salt and/or barley flour. Or barley flour may be mixed with fresh blood to form a dough that is then cooked. Some prefer to put fresh blood into metal containers that are set over a fire to warm. When the blood coagulates into a jellylike substance, it is seasoned with salt and cut into cubes to be eaten plain, fried, or boiled.

Finally, there is a blood food that seems to be peculiar to the Sherpa of Solukhumbu in Nepal. Blood drawn from cattle is allowed to dry out thoroughly and is rubbed between the hands to form a powder. This powder, or "blood flour," is added to various dishes as a seasoning.

However it is prepared, blood is not considered entirely proper as a food. Some Tibetans and Himalayans, more committed to the Buddhist concept of nonviolence, believe that the consumption of blood food is sinful even though the process of blood-letting may benefit cattle. Nevertheless, virtually everyone eats blood food with relish, finding it tasty and nourishing. This religious–dietary dilemma is, perhaps, understandable when it is remembered that blood food is a seasonal commodity, available in large quantities during late spring and early summer. This timing coincides with the period of meat shortage for most Tibetan and Himalayan folk. Meat derived from stocks put up the previous autumn is near depletion at this time, and blood is a welcome addition to the diet, too tempting to forgo.

Richard P. Palmieri

The author is grateful to the National Geographic Society for two research grants that supported fieldwork in the Nepal Himalayas in 1972 and 1973, and to Mary Washington College for financial support that enabled preparation of this manuscript.

Notes

1. Works that focus on yak or at least deal with this animal in a more than cursory fashion include the recent studies of the Sherpa of Khumbu in Nepal by Barbara A. Brower (1991) and Stanley F. Stevens (1993), the collection of essays in the volume edited by Joseph Bonnemaire and Corneille Jest (1976), the several articles by Richard P. Palmieri (1972, 1974, 1980, 1982, and 1987), and three books on Tibetan pastoral nomadism: one by Matthias Hermanns (1948), another by Robert B. Ekvall (1968), and the third by Melvyn C. Goldstein and Cynthia M. Beall (1990).
2. It is, perhaps, useful to clarify the term "yak." It is Tibetan in origin (Tib. *gyag*) and refers specifically to the domesticated male. Females are correctly known as *di* or *dri;* in some regions of the Himalaya, however, females are also called *nak,* although this term more precisely refers to cattle in general.
3. The question of yak hybridization is the focus of several papers, many of them referred to in my study (Palmieri 1987), which deals with the complex nomenclature, animal husbandry practices, and ecology of hybrids among the Sherpa of Nepal.
4. A detailed discussion of the concept of pollution among the Sherpa, for example, can be found in Ortner (1973).
5. The literature on this topic includes a wide range of conflicting figures that are difficult to reconcile. This variability may simply represent data collected in different environments, the contrasting characteristics of dissimilar herds, or the various seasons during which the figures were developed. In any case, the following sources may be consulted: Das (1904: 96-7); King (1926: 75); Kislovsky (1938: 32); Phillips, Johnson, and Moyer (1945: 70); Phillips, Tolstoy, and Johnson (1946: 170); White, Phillips, and Elting (1946: 357); Hermanns (1948: 128); Stübel (1958: 19); Fürer-Haimendorf (1964: 12); and Field and Pandey (1969: 50-2).

6. A discussion of the biological and behavioral bases for the milk let-down reflex can be found in Amoroso and Jewell (1963).
7. In this last, it should be noted that African and European parallels do exist. See, for example, Lagercrantz (1950: 44-50) and Bühler-Oppenheim (1948: 4275-6). With respect to insufflation of yak, see Edgar (1924: 39); Combe (1926: 105-6); Bühler-Oppenheim (1948: 4276); Duncan (1964: 240); and Ekvall (1968: 50).
8. The principal difference between various wooden churns is the apparatus employed to agitate the milk: Some are equipped with dashers, others with paddle-like arrangements. Both the pottery and leather churns are rocked or shaken to produce butter.
9. Some Africans bleed their cattle for similar reasons. See, for example, Kroll (1928: 244) and Lagercrantz (1950: 51-4).
10. Interestingly, farmers in the Bavarian and Austrian Alps also bleed their barren cows just before rutting season in an attempt to increase their chances of becoming gravid. For this information, I am most grateful to Professor Ludwig Erhard of the Tierzucht Forschung e. F. München Institut für Blutgruppenforschung (Munich).

Bibliography

Amoroso, E. C., and P. A. Jewell. 1963. The exploitation of the milk ejection reflex by primitive peoples. In *Man and cattle: Proceedings of a symposium on domestication,* ed. A. E. Mourant and F. E. Zeuner, 126-37. London.

Bohlken, Herwart. 1958. Zur Nomenklatur der Haustiere. *Zoologischer Anzeiger* 160: 167-8.

Bohlken, Herwart. 1958-60. Vergleichende Untersuchungen an Wildrindern (Tribus Bovini Simpson 1945). *Zoologische Jahrbücher* 68: 113-202.

Bonnemaire, Joseph, and Corneille Jest. 1976. *Le yak: Son rôle dans la vie matérielle et culturelle des éleveurs d'Asie centrale.* Paris.

Brower, Barbara A. 1991. *Sherpa of Khumbu: People, livestock, and landscape.* Delhi.

Bühler-Oppenheim, Kristin. 1948. Hilfsmittel zur Erleichterung des Melkens bei Naturvölkern. *Ciba Zeitschrift* 10: 4275-6.

Combe, G. A. 1926. *A Tibetan on Tibet: Being the travels and observations of Mr. Paul Sherap (Dorje Zödba) of Tachienlu.* London.

Das, Sarat Chandra. 1904. *Journey to Lhasa and central Tibet.* New York.

Duncan, Marion H. 1964. *Customs and superstitions of Tibetans.* London.

Edgar, J. Huston. 1924. A strange milking custom. *Man* 24: 39.

Ekvall, Robert B. 1968. *Fields on the hoof: Nexus of Tibetan pastoral nomadism.* New York.

Field, D. I., and K. R. Pandey. 1969. *Pasture, fodder, and livestock development: Trisuli watershed - Nepal.* Kathmandu, Nepal.

Fürer-Haimendorf, Christoph von. 1964. *The Sherpas of Nepal: Buddhist highlanders.* Berkeley, Calif.

1966. Caste concepts and status distinctions in Buddhist communities of western Nepal. In *Caste studies in Hindu-Buddhist contact zones,* ed. Christoph von Fürer-Haimendorf, 140-60. New York.

Goldstein, Melvyn C., and Cynthia M. Beall. 1990. *Nomads of western Tibet: The survival of a way of life.* Berkeley, Calif.

Hermanns, Matthias. 1948. The A Mdo Pa Greater Tibetans: The socio-economic bases of the pastoral cultures of Inner Asia. Ph.D. thesis, Universität Freiberg in der Schweiz, translated for the Human Relations Area Files by Frieda Schutze. New Haven, Conn.

King, Louise (Rin-chen Lha-mo). 1926. *We Tibetans.* London.

Kislovsky, D. 1938. The domesticated animals of Mongolia. *Journal of Heredity* 29: 27-32.

Kroll, Hubert. 1928. Die Haustiere der Bantu. *Zeitschrift für Ethnologie* 60: 177-290.

Lagercrantz, Sture. 1950. *Contribution to the ethnography of Africa.* Lund, Sweden.

Mittaine, Jean. 1962. Milk other than cows' milk. In *Milk hygiene,* ed. M. Abdussalam, et al., 681-94. World Health Organization Monograph Series No. 48. Geneva.

Ortner, Sherry B. 1973. Sherpa purity. *American Anthropologist* 75: 49-63.

Palmieri, Richard P. 1972. The domestication, exploitation, and social functions of the yak in Tibet and adjoining areas. *Proceedings of the Association of American Geographers* 4: 80-3.

  1974. Culture and ecology of Tibetans in the Greater Nepal Himalaya. In *The Conference on Nepal at Claremont,* ed. Merrill R. Goodall, 4-5. Claremont, Calif.

  1980. Preliminary results of field investigations in the Nepal Himalaya. In *National Geographic Society research reports,* ed. Paul H. Oehser, John S. Lea, and Nancy Link Powars, 529-34. Washington, D.C.

  1982. Patterns of Indian pastoralism. In *India: Cultural patterns and processes,* ed. Allen G. Noble and Ashok K. Dutt, 325-36. Boulder, Colo.

  1987. Cattle hybrids among the Sherpa of Nepal. *Journal of Cultural Geography* 7: 89-100.

Phillips, Ralph W., Ray G. Johnson, and Raymond T. Moyer. 1945. *The livestock of China.* Washington, D.C.

Phillips, Ralph W., Ilia A. Tolstoy, and Raymond G. Johnson. 1946. Yaks and yak cattle hybrids in Asia. *Journal of Heredity* 37: 162-70, 206-15.

Schley, Peter. 1967. *Der Yak und seine Kreuzung mit dem Rind in der Sowjetunion.* Wiesbaden.

Sherring, Charles A. 1906. *Western Tibet and the British borderlands.* London.

Stevens, Stanley F. 1993. *Claiming the high ground: Sherpas, subsistence, and environmental change in the highest Himalaya.* Berkeley, Calif.

Stübel, Hans. 1958. *The Mewu Fantzu: A Tibetan tribe of Kansu,* trans. Frieda Schutze. New Haven, Conn.

Tucci, Giuseppe. 1967. *Tibet: Land of snows,* trans. J. E. S. Driver. New York.

White, W. T., Ralph W. Phillips, and E. C. Elting. 1946. Yaks and yak-cattle hybrids in Alaska. *Journal of Heredity* 37: 354-8.

PART III

Dietary Liquids

Drinks, many of which were also globalized in the events following 1492, seem to have produced even more ill effects than foods. Unfortunately, more often than not, they did indigenous peoples unaccustomed to them no good. Along with wine and distilled beverages, beer – which had been brewed since the early stages of the Neolithic – entered all newly discovered corners of the earth as quickly as the Europeans reached them. Superficially more healthful was the spread of tea from China, coffee from Ethiopia, and cocoa from the Americas. But consumers of these beverages also demanded the addition of sugar and the processing of this Asian plant soon became an American enterprise fueled by unwilling African labor, which was also applied to coffee production.

Water that fostered disease was a problem from the very beginning of the Neolithic, and one that grew steadily worse as more and more people crowded together to pollute local sources. Alcoholic beverages were humankind's first line of defense against pathogen-packed water, and later, the procedure of boiling water to make tea, coffee, or cocoa had the same purifying effect. But it was only in the twentieth century that public water supplies were rendered safe to drink in the world's developed countries, and unsafe water remains a problem throughout the developing world.

This means, among other things, that formula feeding of the young continues to cause infant deaths in that world when local water is used, making breast milk by far the best alternative (save of course in the presence of AIDS). Bovine milk, by contrast, is not an especially good food for infants and is positively dangerous for some. In the past, bovine milk imparted bovine tuberculosis (scrofula) to the lactose *tolerant,* and, of course, milk drinking did not even catch on among the bulk of the planet's people (who are lactose *intolerant*), although it is the case that many reduced-lactose products of milk, such as yoghurt and cheeses, have become welcome dietary additions.

Caffeine-carrying kola nuts from Africa helped to launch the soft-drink industry, which became a giant all across the globe during the course of the twentieth century and provided even more stimulation for the sugar industry, not to mention the dental profession.

Khat and kava are among the few beverages of the world that have not been globalized. Khat (more often chewed these days than made into a beverage) remains confined to northeastern Africa, whereas kava is a drink of the Pacific. In the past confined to ceremonial affairs, kava, with its narcoticlike properties, has become a local alternative to alcohol.

III.1   Beer and Ale

Beer and ale are mildly alcoholic beverages made from the action of yeast fermenting a usually grain-based mixture. Throughout their history, they have constituted both a refreshing social drink and an important energy-rich food. The basic ingredients of most beers and ales have included grain, water, yeast, and (more recently) hops, and despite many regional variations, the process of fermenting the grain has changed little over time. To be completely accurate, it must be noted that ale is defined as unhopped beer; in this chapter, however, the terms "beer" and "ale" are employed interchangeably for the period before hops were used.

The Chemical Basis of Fermentation

Before fermentation can take place, yeast, a single-cell fungus occurring naturally in several varieties, must be allowed to act on the sugar present in grain. This releases two crucial by-products, alcohol and carbon dioxide. A grain often used for this purpose is barley – even though, in its natural state, it contains only a trace amount of free sugar – because of its high content of starch, a complex polymer of sugar. Barley also contains substances known collectively as diastases, which convert the barley starches into sugar to be used as food for the growing plant. When barley is crushed and dried carefully, the essential starches and diastases are released and preserved, rendering a substance called "malt."

Until sometime around the ninth century, "beer" was actually "ale," made by a process known as mashing, whereby the barley malt was mixed with hot – but not boiling – water. The effect of the hot water was to induce the diastases to act immediately in breaking down the complex starches into sugar. This process is referred to as conversion and results in "wort," one of its most essential products. The mashing procedure not only produced the brown, sugary wort but also permitted inert elements of the barley, such as the husks, to be drawn off. In the production of pure ale (such as the first human brewers would have made), all that remained was for yeast to act upon the wort so that the sugars could be converted into alcohol and carbon dioxide.

Beginning in approximately the ninth century in central Europe (authorities vary widely and wildly regarding the date but not the place), the procedure began to be modified, and beer came into being with the addition of blossoms from the hop plant. Numerous modern beers are labeled as ale, but as mentioned, technically "ale" means unhopped beer. In order to convert ale into beer, dried hop blossoms are added to the boiling wort mix after the mashing but before the yeast is allowed to act. This releases two resins, lupulon and humulon, that act as excellent natural preservatives, preventing the growth of certain types of bacteria which, although harmless to humans, are detrimental to beer. Before the use of hops, pure ale had a very limited "shelf life" and often spoiled, much as milk does. The diastases in barley also acted against the bacteria in question, but not nearly so effectively as hops. In fact, it can be argued that it was the harnessing of the preservative power of hops that permitted the production, storage, and distribution of beer in large quantities. Moreover, in addition to its antibacterial properties, the hop plant adds flavorful oils that mask the otherwise sweet taste of pure ale (Kloss 1959: 31–2).

Varieties

Today, the use of hops is standard, and very little pure ale has been mass-produced in the twentieth century. Thus, the words *ale* and *beer* have become largely (if wrongly) synonymous. Modern technology and advanced techniques have modified and refined the brewing process considerably. The most commonly mass-produced type of beer is known as a "lager" or a "Pilsner" and is lighter in color and generally milder in taste than other beers. The vast majority of North and South American beers, most European beers, the beers of Australia, and those of nearly all major Asian nations are crafted in the Pilsner style.

Darker beers that are dryer and richer in taste are referred to as porters and stouts, with the latter merely a stronger, drier porter. Several popular German beers make use of large quantities of wheat rather than barley to make *Weizenbier* (wheat beer). Belgium is famous for fruity ales, typically known as "lambic" beers, the production of which involves a complex process of spontaneous fermentation. In addition to the use of fruits to add flavor, as in the case of the lambic beers, one method of increasing taste is "dry-hopping," a process whereby additional hops are added at the end of the process to replace the residue lost when the wort and hop blossoms are first boiled together. Like hops, yeast and sugar are occasionally added to the bottle when it is sealed to further enhance the beer's strength. This is not so much the production of yet another style of beer as it is a method of setting up a secondary fermentation process within the bottle to make stout, porter, and "bitter."

Earliest Origins

No one has yet managed to date the origins of beer with any precision, and it is probably an impossible task. Indeed, there are scholars who have theorized that a taste for ale prompted the beginning of agriculture, in which case humans have been brewing for some 10,000 years (Katz and Voigt 1986). Most archaeological evidence, however, suggests that fermentation was being used in one manner or another by around 4000 to 3500 B.C. Some of this evidence – from an ancient Mesopotamian trading outpost called

Godin Tepe in present-day Iran – indicates that barley was being fermented at that location around 3500 B.C. Additional evidence recovered at Hacinebi Tepe (a similar site in southern Turkey) also suggests that ancient Mesopotamians were fermenting barley at a very early date (Smith 1995).

At present, however, the evidence from both sites is sufficiently sparse to preclude any definitive assertion that the ancient Mesopotamians were the first people to make beer. On the other hand, one can speculate: There is no question that fermentation takes place accidentally (as it must have done countless times before humans learned something about controlling the process), and most investigators believe that barley was first cultivated in the Fertile Crescent region of lower Mesopotamia between the Tigris and Euphrates rivers. Grain is heavy to transport relative to the beer made from it, so it is not surprising that there may be evidence of ale in these outposts and not unreasonable to suspect that accidental fermentation did occur at some point in the ancient Mesopotamian region, leading to beer making (Corran 1975: 15–16).

In any event, we know that not much later the Sumerians were, in fact, making beer. The clay tablets (unearthed from the ancient city of Uruk in Lower Mesopotamia – now Iraq – and dating from the second half of the fourth millennium) that tell the story of Gilgamesh, the fifth king of the second Sumerian dynasty, make it clear that ale was in widespread use (Toussaint-Samat 1992), and Reay Tannahill (1988: 48) has written that "a staggering amount of the Sumerian grain yield went into ale; something like 40 percent of the total."

At approximately the same time, people of the ancient Nubian culture to the south of Egypt were also fermenting a crude, ale-like beverage known as *bousa,* which is still brewed by African farmers and peasants to this day (Smith 1995). Indeed, although many scholars maintain that the Mesopotamian culture was the first to brew beer, others argue that it was the ancient people of East Africa who first produced and consumed a fermented product (Dirar 1993: 20).

In much the same fashion as with grain, the fermentation of fruit and fruit juices probably also occurred by accident at around this same time, leading to the earliest forms of wine. What is more difficult to ascertain, however, is how much knowledge ancient people had of the process. It is also difficult to know with any reasonable certainty how extensive their use of fermented barley was and exactly how much their ale might have resembled what the world now recognizes as beer.

The Importance of Ale in Early Societies

From the beginning of its production, ale (even in its crudest forms) would have been an important addition to an otherwise frequently limited diet. Resem-

bling the chemical makeup of bread in several ways, ale was a convenient package of starches, sugars, and other grain by-products that provided nutritional supplementation. Similarly, for people with few means of storing foods for any length of time and who depended on the vagaries of nature for subsistence, ale could be an excellent (and doubtless at times vital) source of calories.

Moreover, ale (and later beer) afforded an escape from the feces-fouled drinking water that plagued peoples for millennia. Although humans, until very recently, had no knowledge of pathogenic infection, water (and milk) was understood to provoke dangerous illnesses, even death, whereas fermented beverages were considered safe. And because of sterilization by boiling and by the action of yeast, this was generally the case.

Ale was also important because the earliest cultures, particularly those of the Sumerians and Egyptians, attached religious significance to its consumption. And throughout the ages, savants frequently maintained that ale had curative properties. But probably the most important reason for drinking ale and other alcoholic beverages was to achieve a desired level of intoxication. Because invectives against drunkenness can be found in both the Bible and the Koran, we know that people, beset by life's hardships or just seeking relaxation, were reaching that goal a long time ago. Indeed, the ancient Egyptians are credited with celebrating ale consumption by composing some of the world's earliest-known drinking songs.

Brewing in Antiquity

Although the fermenting of barley probably developed independently in several cultures, knowledge of brewing technology doubtless was spread throughout the Middle East by various nomadic peoples. One aspect of brewing technology common to the Egyptians, Sumerians, and Babylonians alike was the use of baked loaves of malted barley and grain that resembled baked bread. There were several variations of this technique, but basically the loaves of barley and wheat, once baked, were covered with water to form a mash, which was then placed in an earthen vessel for a time. In some cases, fermentation probably occurred spontaneously. In others, it was doubtless generated by the presence of yeast cells in the cracks and linings of the earthen vessels that were used over and over again. But in addition, skillful brewers had most likely learned to keep the remains of a previous mix to use as a starter (Smith 1995: 12–13).

The Greeks probably gained most of their understanding of brewing from the Egyptians, although the Babylonians may also have passed along what they knew. The Roman Empire, at its height, had the advantage of being able to borrow brewing techniques eclectically from several cultures. Roman historians, for example, did not credit Rome with spreading information on ale making to the Germanic tribes of Europe. Rather, Tacitus recorded that these peoples were already fermenting a beverage from barley or wheat when they came into contact with Rome. Pliny also wrote of the barbarians and their beer, and it seems likely that the tribes of central and northern Europe gained brewing knowledge not from the Romans but from the Babylonians and other Asian civilizations. Or it could have been a situation such as that of the Celts of the British Isles, who are said to have developed a crude process of fermentation independently, but refined their ale-making skills with technology from other cultures (Corran 1975: 23–4).

Brewing in the Islamic World

By the time of the collapse of the Roman empire in the fifth century, the production of alcoholic beverages had been expanded, and beer was only one of many alcoholic beverages produced in the Arabian peninsula – a list which included a honey-based mead and fermented camel's milk. Their consumption – and especially that of ale – was widespread before the advent of Islam, despite a number of localized religions that had instituted prohibitions against it. Along the caravan and trading routes, houses, taverns, and inns were prosperous businesses that supplied beer and mead to travelers and, in some locations, to townspeople as well (Ghalioungui 1979: 13–15).

The spread of the Islamic religion did not, at first, bring restriction of alcoholic beverages; indeed, the Koran, like the Bible, celebrated the drinking of wine. Rather quickly, however, Islamic teaching began to forbid drinking alcohol, although the degree to which the rule was observed varied from place to place (Ghalioungui 1979: 15).

Egypt was one area in which alcohol continued to be used, although in the years following the entrance of Islam into Egypt, various rulers periodically enforced the Muslim prohibition. But the consumption of fermented beverages was never entirely eradicated (Ghalioungui 1979: 15), and, among the peasant population, *bousa* continued to be produced and consumed as it had been for centuries.

Despite such exceptions, however, Islam had an enormous impact on beer brewing in the Middle East and elsewhere in the Muslim world, with the result that it never was the mass-produced, socially accepted beverage that it became in Europe during the Middle Ages. Europeans, especially monks in the monasteries of the Catholic Church, not only kept the knowledge of brewing alive but also began its refinement into a modern science.

Brewing in Europe

Over the course of the Middle Ages, beer brewing flourished in northern Europe (where foods laden with carbohydrates and fats required much liquid to wash them down) and evolved into a distinct industry (Tannahill 1988). As such, by the end of the Middle Ages, beer had become subject to taxation and also to government regulation (especially in Britain and the German states) aimed at standardizing the brewing process.

In the early Middle Ages, however, monasteries and churches were the principal ale makers in Europe. Because the church was at the center of the lives of the people, monasteries and churches commonly provided the settings for festivals, weddings, and other social gatherings that were lubricated with ale. Indeed, such was the control of the church over access to ale that it became a device for ensuring the participation of parishioners in church rituals. Later, as guilds developed, the church influenced – even controlled – many of their activities with the promise of ale.

In addition, monasteries were much more than just monastic retreats. The growing of food was one of the monks' primary occupations, and as a rule, the land owned by their orders was sufficient enough for the rotation of crops in such a way as to ensure a constant supply of cereals. Much of the cereal produced – including spelt, wheat, oat, and rye, as well as barley – went into ale, the quality as well as quantity of which the monks improved upon, just as they did with their wines and cheeses (Toussaint-Samat 1992). Many monasteries also served as inns that provided room and board for travelers, and some became famous for their ales, their praise carried by church pilgrims, merchants, and others on the move. There is no question that monastery-produced ales, made on a near-industrial scale, brought in a very good income for the various orders.

Later, however, as the Middle Ages progressed, ale production in the towns and countryside began to rival that of the church. And as the craft passed into private hands, it mirrored other early trades with its guilds and specialization. Because of its limited shelf life (prior to the use of hops), ale was usually brewed and distributed on the same site, and consequently, the first brewers outside of the church were generally boardinghouse owners and tavern keepers who provided ale to travelers and guests. Local inns and taverns came to be regarded by townspeople and villagers alike as social gathering places (Corran 1975: 36–7).

Because water is vital to the brewing process, the breweries of taverns and inns had to be located near an abundant water supply. But the type of water was important. If it was hard water with lime, the fermentation process might not work well; if it had iron in it, the beer would always be cloudy.

Women frequently oversaw the breweries while their husbands ran the inns. In fact, women were much involved in the ale business, sometimes owning boardinghouses as well as breweries and holding special licenses to distribute their product.

By the end of the Middle Ages, breweries and drinking establishments of one sort or another had multiplied to the point where they overshadowed the monasteries, both in England and on the Continent. As the church ceased to dominate the brewing industry, states began to take an interest in both taxing and (because of increasing adulteration) regulating it. An example of the former is the 1551 licensing of English and Welsh alehouses for the first time (Trager 1995), although the classic example of regulation had come earlier, in 1516, when William VI, Duke of Bavaria, instituted a *Reinheitsgebot* – an "Edict of Purity" – which decreed that the only ingredients permitted in beer were water, barley, malt, yeast, and hops. The edict is still in effect, now for all of Germany, but it is said that only Bavaria holds to it for exported beers.

Hops, which converted ale into modern beer, were coming into widespread use at about this time. Hop blossoms are derived from the hop plant (a relative of *Cannabis*), and as their use became common, a hop garden was an essential component of a brewery. As noted, the aromatic hop greatly enhanced the taste of ale, as did the addition of other herbs and flavorings. More importantly, however, hops greatly extended the life of ale, which in turn removed the necessity for locating breweries and taverns close to one another. The use of hops was eventually so universal that the brewing of pure ale became nearly extinct, until the modern, twentieth-century "Campaign for Real Ale" movement in Britain sought to revive what was perceived as a dying art.

The revolution that hops worked in the brewing industry, however, was a long time in coming. Since Neolithic times, hops were believed good for one's health and sometimes carried the burden of a reputation as an aphrodisiac. It has been suggested that the utilization of hops in beer can be traced back as far as the ancient Egyptians. But we hear nothing of hops in beer in the Roman world. Pliny tells us only that the Romans ate hop shoots much like asparagus. During the early Middle Ages, hops were grown for medicinal purposes in gardens throughout the central European region from the North Sea and the Baltic to western Austria and northern Italy, but people apparently began putting them in ale only around the eighth or ninth century (Toussaint-Samat 1992).

The hop was only one of many herbs added to ales, but brewers sooner or later noticed that this herb improved the appearance of ale, that it acted as a diuretic, and most importantly, that it was a preservative. Nonetheless, the church successfully fought the widespread adoption of hops for centuries – apparently in part because of the aphrodisiac reputation of the plant, but also because the church, with its virtual monopoly on ale, did not welcome change. Moreover, hops were long viewed as an adulterant added to mask the taste of spoiled beer. Yet, somewhat ironically, it was probably the monks, with their considerable knowledge of medicinal herbs, who had added hops to ale in the first place (Toussaint-Samat 1992).

By the beginning of the sixteenth century, hops had become an essential ingredient for beers made on the Continent, and late in the reign of Henry VIII (died 1547), they were introduced to England. At first, the idea of adding hops to ale was a distressing one for the English, who continued to view them as adulterants and passed laws to prohibit their use. In 1554, however, Flemish hop growers emigrated to England to begin their production in Kent for a wary British brewing industry. Afterward, the use of hops was generally accepted, although many clung to their unhopped ales. Not until around 1700 was ale in England regularly hopped and the terms "ale" and "beer" accepted there as more or less identical (McGee 1984; Trager 1995).

The preservative powers of the hop plant contributed to the development of larger breweries producing beer in ever greater quantities – a trend in both England and Europe throughout the sixteenth and into the seventeenth centuries, especially in Flanders, northern and eastern France, and Bavaria, where the climate best suited the growing of hops. Because hops endowed beer with a greatly extended shelf life, brewers could now locate at a distance from the towns and, consequently, close to less-polluted stretches of streams and rivers, whose waters contributed to better-quality beers. Such moves were also necessitated by the regulatory measures of crowded cities, which sought to minimize the fire hazards arising from kilns burning in brewery buildings constructed of wood. Converting brewhouses into stone or brick structures or, alternatively, moving them out of the cities were both expensive options, and as a result, the sixteenth and seventeenth centuries in Europe also saw a trend toward fewer breweries – but much larger ones that, in many cases, were the forerunners of modern breweries still in operation at the end of the twentieth century.

With the mass production of high-quality beers, brewers cast an eye on the export market, and as exporting beer became a widespread endeavor, states enacted laws to regulate trade. One example of this trend comes from sixteenth-century England, where because of concern that the volume exportation of beer in wood casks and barrels would accelerate the dwindling of the island's supply of timber, brewers were compelled to bring as much wood into the country as they sent away.

Brewing in the New World

Traditional interpretations hold that beer and brewing technology came to the Americas from Europe via the Jamestown settlers and the Pilgrims. However, several indigenous American cultures (outside of North America) had developed fermented products long before the Europeans arrived. In the Andean society of the

Incan empire, the fermentation of beverages was well established – the term *chicha* referring collectively to the numerous indigenous fermented beverages of South America.

The *chicha* of the Incas was elaborated primarily from maize, although there were variants, including beverages made from manioc roots and peanuts, to name just two. It is interesting to note that in the absence of hops, diastases (by-products important for flavoring and increasing alcohol content) were introduced to maize beer from human saliva, as moistened maize powder was rolled into balls and placed in the mouth (Morris 1979: 22).

Evidence from Spanish colonial sources and archaeological finds suggests that the production and consumption of maize beer was fairly widespread in the Andes area. Like the ales of Europe, *chicha* was not only a significant component of religious and economic life but served nutritional needs as well. Its importance was apparent in its large-scale, state-controlled production – revealed by archaeological excavations that have indicated the existence of state-run breweries and distribution centers (Morris 1979: 26-7).

The mass production of *chicha* in the Incan empire was abolished by the Spaniards, but the making of maize beer on a smaller scale remained widespread and continues today in the Andes and elsewhere. The relatively high price of modern beer makes *chicha* an attractive alternative in the rural areas of Central and South America.

Another indigenous American beverage that is still produced is a Brazilian beer known as *kaschiri,* which is fermented from manioc roots. Its manufacture is similar to the Incan maize beer in that the tubers are chewed and moistened by salivation. Maize is also used by Indians in Mexico to make a crude beer called *tesguino.* Far more pervasive, however, was *pulque,* the fermented juice of the *agave,* a plant which later was employed to make tequila. Like other local beverages among impoverished peoples, both *pulque* and *tesguino* still deliver important nutrients to their Mexican Indian consumers.

Since the Spanish conquest in Mexico and South America and the English settlement of North America, none of the indigenous American beverages have been produced on a large scale except for *pulque,* which remained a common drink of poor Mexicans until well into the 1940s. The mass-produced, twentieth-century beers of Central and South America are almost universally hopped Pilsners and employ techniques brought to the New World by Europeans.

Brewing in Early North America

Beer and ale were present from the beginning in the English settlements of North America. Records of both the London Company and the Jamestown colony indicate that beer reached the latter in 1607, its very first year of existence. But in those early years, beer was too bulky (and thus too expensive) to transport efficiently; it also spoiled in the summer heat, and so the colonists soon began brewing their own (Rorabaugh 1979: 108-9). Although barley and hops were not at hand, other basic materials that would ferment, such as persimmons, pumpkins, maize, Jerusalem artichokes, and maple sugar, were abundant in eastern America, and by 1609, the governor of Virginia was advertising for brewers to come to the colony (Baron 1962: 4).

A bit later, in Massachusetts, the Puritans – like other Europeans of the age who justifiably viewed water consumption with intense suspicion – had followed suit and were brewing their own beer. The Puritans also pioneered some of America's first regulatory statutes for the production, distribution, and consumption of the beverage. By 1637, taverns and inns had to be licensed by the General Court, and it was forbidden for them to brew their own product. Rather, beer was to be obtained from a commercial brewer, also licensed by the court, who was enjoined to sell at court-specified prices. By 1629, similar regulations had also been adopted in Virginia (which now had two large brewhouses).

Not that there were all that many taverns in early America, and beer was more often than not brewed and consumed in the home. Those who had access to barley or could afford to import malt from England produced something a European might recognize; other beers continued to be made from local ingredients and from West Indies molasses. In addition, beer was imported on a fairly large scale from England, or from the Netherlands in the case of New Amsterdam, where the Dutch had established beer as a prominent drink back in the 1620s.

Beer production kept pace with the growing population throughout the remainder of the seventeenth century and into the eighteenth, with Philadelphia and Boston becoming major brewing towns. As was the case in Europe, the vast majority of colonial towns had taverns that not only provided places of lodging for travelers but also served as local social centers. These dispensed some beer, but rum and (to a lesser extent) corn whiskey and cider increasingly enjoyed more appeal, and even tea, made available in quantity by British mercantilism, cut into beer consumption. Nonetheless, that consumption grew anyway in the eighteenth century because the population was growing (Baron 1962: 56-8).

Innovations

The eighteenth century also saw numerous innovations in beer production, although as a rule, these were slow to reach America. One illustration has to do with what is typically called porter. During the period, working men in England would often order ale and a few other beers mixed together in a tankard, and tavern keepers came to dread the extra time and effort required to satisfy such a request. Eventually, however, several of these brews were being mixed together in a single cask with extra hops. The resulting dark, strong, beverage was called porter, after the London laborers ("porters") who popularized it. It was during this period as well that many of the familiar English beers, such as Courage, Whitbread, and Guinness, were born.

Another significant technological innovation in beer brewing was glass bottling, which came into widespread use in the eighteenth century. Glass bottles made beer easier to transport and store and, after the advent of sealed bottles, extended its shelf life. But because the Industrial Revolution was first an English and European phenomenon (and because of British mercantile restrictions), glass bottling in America began in earnest only after the Revolution. Glass bottles enabled people to store and consume beer at home with greater ease and, perhaps coupled with the growth of alternative beverages, diminished the role of the tavern in the social life of towns.

By about 1750, coke and coal were providing maltsters with greater control over the roasting of malt, which made possible the brewing of pale and amber beers, and a classification system to differentiate these from the dark stout and porter brews became an important issue. Later in the century, thermometers and hydrometers added more control to the different stages of the brewing process, and in 1817, a "patent malt" was developed that made stout and porter brews lighter than they had previously been – beginning a trend toward less-alcoholic beer that continues to this day (McGee 1984).

Brewing in the Modern World

In the nineteenth century, beer brewing was revolutionized by a process that had originally been discovered back when hops were just beginning to find their way into ale on a regular basis. Until about 1400, "top" fermentation had been the procedure used. However, at about that time in Bavaria, the process of "bottom" fermentation was developed – "top" and "bottom" indicating where yeast collects in the vat. Bottom fermentation permits the manufacture of a lighter beer, but it was not until the 1840s that the technique spread from Bavaria first to Pilsen, Czechoslovakia, and Copenhagen, Denmark, and then to the wider world. "Pilsner lager" became the prototype of modern beers, with only England and Belgium persisting in the use of top fermentation.

Yet even before the spread of the new lager beer, the nineteenth century had begun to witness the rise of large-scale commercial breweries. These were encouraged by the growth of cities, which provided mass markets and rising wages for an ever-growing urban working class. By 1800, brewers in England, such as Whitbread and Barclay Perkins, were producing 100,000 to 200,000 barrels of beer per year. The largest brewer, Arthur Guinness, held a virtual monopoly in Ireland (Hawkins 1979: 14).

At about midcentury, German immigrants set about completely transforming the brewing industry in the United States. It was in 1844 that Frederick Lauer – a second-generation brewer in Reading, Pennsylvania – introduced the new lagering process, and the business of beer exploded. During the 1850s and 1860s, under the direction of other German immigrants, both Milwaukee and St. Louis became the major centers of the lager industry, with Pabst, Schlitz, Miller, and Blatz becoming giants in the former and Anheuser and Busch in the latter. Companies that came into being outside of these centers around this time were Hamm in St. Paul, Heileman in La Crosse, and Stroh in Detroit. Almost overnight, the Pilsner-style beers edged out the darker and richer beers that had first reached America with the English colonists.

More innovations came along to improve them. The development by Copenhagen's Carlsberg brewery of an absolutely pure brewer's yeast - which would end brewing failures - occurred in 1883. With the turn-of-the-century development of airtight kegs and carbonation, America's beers became bubbly, Pilsner-style beers, and in 1935, the Krueger company of New Jersey introduced the first canned beer (Trager 1995).

The Anheuser-Busch company may be said to embody the story of American beer. Formed by German immigrants Eberhard Anheuser and Adolphus Busch in the mid–nineteenth century, it capitalized on improved transportation and aggressive marketing techniques to the extent that, by 1901, the company was producing more than 1 million barrels of beer annually and had become the first to mass-market bottled beer. To provide the freshest beer available, Anheuser-Busch formed its own refrigerated railcar company and was one of the first brewers to employ pasteurization techniques (Smith 1995: 114-15). The company survived Prohibition by producing "near-beer" and malt for home brewers, maintained and even updated its brewing equipment, and emerged aggressively from those difficult times to become the giant it is today.

One reason for the popularity of lager beer in the United States is that hot summer days seem to call for ice-cold beverages, and the heavier beers did (and do) not lend themselves well to chilling. Presumably this explains why the British and many other Europeans drink beer that is at room temperature or perhaps cool but not cold. Another reason, however, is taste. Many believe that chilling removes taste, and in fact, most non-Americans do not particularly care for American beer, which they find to be uniformly bland in taste and lacking in character. European Pilsners contain less in the way of chemicals and generally more in the way of alcohol than American beers. On the other hand, Americans in general – and not just those in the United States – enjoy cold lagers; in fact, Mexico and Brazil are among the world's top beer-producing countries. Mexican breweries in particular make a wide selection of light-tasting lagers, with perhaps Corona, along with Dos Equis (a dark Pilsner), among the best known (Pepper 1996).

It was Americans who introduced Foster's beer to Australia in 1888 and did it "American style" with refrigeration, bottom fermentation, and bottling – in the process creating a product that became Australia's national drink. In Jamaica, by contrast, the famous Red Stripe continued under English influence to be a dark, alelike brew until 1934, after which it finally was transformed into a light-tasting lager (Trager 1995).

Beer was brought to East Africa by the British in 1922 and is brewed there today mainly by East Africa Breweries in both Kenya and Uganda. Kenya Breweries, a subsidiary of East Africa Breweries, produces the Tusker lagers, some of the best-known beers in Africa (Pepper 1996: 135). Nigeria and South Africa, however, are the major beer producers on the African continent. Most of Nigeria's beer is brewed by Guinness and Heineken (both of which have major stakes in Nigeria), along with several indigenous breweries. South Africa's beer is produced by South African Breweries and is almost entirely in the lager style (Pepper 1996: 135).

Lager beer reached Asia in 1904, when German and British entrepreneurs established a Western-style brewery along the coast of northern China, producing a brand known as Tsingtao. The Dai Nippon Beer Company of Japan acquired the Tsingtao Brewery in 1916 and retained it until after World War II. In 1932, Japan continued the spread of lager in East Asia by constructing another brewery in Manchuria and introduced breweries into Korea as well. The Dai Nippon Beer Company, along with Kirin, dominated the Japanese beer market until broken up by American occupation authorities in the aftermath of World War II (Laker 1986: 60, 1987: 25–8).

Throughout the twentieth century, the trend has been toward ever larger commercial brewers. In the United States, for example, the number of large breweries has decreased from more than 200 to less than 50. Today, it is mostly lager beers that are consumed globally, and these are produced by big corporations for large markets – often international ones. Although European and American lagers tend to dominate the world market, one exception to this trend is Singha, a lager from Thailand, which is one of the few Asian beers that enjoy a wide degree of export to the West, especially as Thai restaurants continue to grow in popularity (Pepper 1996: 130).

The exceptions to the dominance of mass-produced, globally marketed beers are the products of some "microbreweries" (but not those connected with the giant brewing companies) that found a ready market in the 1980s and 1990s, when entrepreneurs began distributing innumerable beers that were produced either in a "brew pub" or in a small brewery. Microbrewers offer a uniqueness not found in mass-produced beers, crafting their microbrews in a fashion reminiscent of earlier days, when beer production was confined to monasteries, village breweries, or to the home itself. Generally priced higher than their mass-produced counterparts but with a more refined appeal, microbrews have established a niche among the more affluent consumers in America and Europe.

Phillip A. Cantrell II

Bibliography

Baron, Stanley Wade. 1962. *Brewed in America: A history of beer and ale in the United States.* Boston, Mass.

Bower, Bruce. 1992. Vessel residue taps into early brewing. *Science News* 142: 310.

    1994. Ancient site taps into soldiers' brew. *Science News* 146: 390.

Clark, Peter. 1983. *The English alehouse: A social history, 1200-1830.* New York.

Corran, H. S. 1975. *A history of brewing.* London.

Dirar, Hamid A. 1993. *The indigenous foods of the Sudan: A study in African foods and nutrition.* Cambridge.

Ghalioungui, P. 1979. Fermented beverages in antiquity. In *Fermented food beverages in nutrition,* ed. C. Gastineau, W. Darby, and T. Turner, 3–19. New York.

Hawkins, K. H., and C. L. Pass. 1979. *The brewing industry: A study in industrial organization and public policy.* London.

History with gusto. 1987. *Time,* April 6.

Katz, Solomon H., and Mary M. Voigt. 1986. Bread and beer: The early use of cereals in the human diet. *Expedition* 28: 23–34.

Kloss, C. A. 1959. *The art and science of brewing.* London.

Laker, Joseph. 1986. Suds and substance: The Korean beer industry and Japan's influence on Korean industrialization. *Wheeling Jesuit College Annual:* 56–73.

    1987. Green island beer. *Wheeling Jesuit College Annual:* 25–8.

McGee, Harold. 1984. *On food and cooking.* New York.

Morris, C. 1979. Maize beer in the economics, politics, and religion of the Inca empire. In *Fermented food beverages in nutrition,* ed. C. Gastineau, W. Darby, and T. Turner, 21–34. New York.

Pepper, Barry. 1996. *The international book of beer: A guide to the world's most popular drink.* New York.

Porter, John. 1975. *All about beer.* New York.

Rorabaugh, W. J. 1979. *The alcoholic republic: An American tradition.* New York.

Salem, F. W. 1972. *Beer: Its history and its economic value as a national beverage.* New York.

Schivelbusch, Wolfgang. 1992. *Tastes of paradise: A social history of spices, stimulants, and intoxicants,* trans. David Jacobson. New York.

Smith, Gregg. 1995. *Beer: A history of suds and civilization from Mesopotamia to microbreweries.* New York.

Tannahill, Reay. 1988. *Food in history.* New York.

Toussaint-Samat, Maguelonne. 1992. *History of food,* trans. Anthea Bell. Cambridge, Mass.

Trager, James. 1995. *The food chronology.* New York.

III.2 ❧ Breast Milk and Artificial Infant Feeding

The importance of maternal breast feeding is considerable for infant survival until weaning and beyond. In addition to nutrition, it also provides many of the mother's immunological defenses to a baby whose own defenses are weak at birth. In the past, however, the protective (as well as the nutritive) qualities of maternal milk were unknown, and wet-nursing practices were common for social, cultural, and economic reasons. In the West, maternal breast feeding in the first year of life was most common in rural areas. But animal milks and solid food were given to babies everywhere when breast feeding was not possible, practical, or convenient, or when it was considered insufficient.

Maternal Breast Feeding

During the first year of life, mortality should be independent of the purely nutritional factor. It has been demonstrated that even undernourished mothers, subsisting on around 1,500 calories a day, are able to nourish their babies adequately through breast feeding (Livi-Bacci 1991). Nonetheless, in the past, infant mortality figures (which were usually high) varied enormously with maternal feeding practices. Babies not breast-fed are easily prone to gastrointestinal infections in summer and to respiratory infections in winter. Thus, environmental circumstances and child care were secondary factors of survival when compared with the manner in which infants were nourished.

Mother's milk is in itself complete nourishment for a new infant. However, compared to the milk of a new mother (which comes in response to the direct demand of the suckling child), the milk of a wet nurse has neither the "age" nor the exact composition required for neonates, because usually the nurse has given birth to a child of her own some months earlier. Nevertheless, female milk is preferable to animal milk. Our ancestors were perfectly aware of the age of the milk – its color and consistency – when choosing a wet nurse. Yet before the 1750s, they did not fully appreciate the qualities of human milk and the superiority of a mother's milk for her own child.

The Qualities of Human Milk

The constituents of human milk – water, protein, fat, carbohydrates, minerals, vitamins, lactose, casein, and so forth – have all been examined, and comparisons made with cow's milk and other animal milks (Paul and Palmer 1972; Davidson et al. 1975; Souci, Fachmann, and Kraut 1981). Such studies have demonstrated the advantages of human milk, and they show why cow's milk cannot safely be given to very young children unless it has been processed. This procedure involves dilution with water, to reduce the excessive protein concentration, and also the addition of sugar. Moreover, before pasteurization, cow's milk presented other dangers. Since the milk was not boiled, and bottles and other instruments were not sterilized, artificial feeding could easily produce fatal infections. With direct sucking, however, such consequences were avoided.

The Wasted Colostrum

In European societies, there was a common and widespread belief that a mother's first milk, the colostrum, was not good for the newborn baby, who had to get rid of his or her meconium. Thus, another lactating woman frequently suckled the child for the first four or five days. Unfortunately, delayed lactation for new mothers could result in milk fever, painful milk retention, and unprepared nipples that could discourage her from ever breast-feeding (Fauve-Chamoux 1983).

Nor was such a procedure good for the baby. Although people of many cultures – from ancient Greeks to Mexican Indians (Soranus of Ephesus 1956; Kay 1981) – have shared the belief that the colostrum may be dangerous (indigestible, heavy, and corrupt), it is, although lightly purgative, actually well assimilated and very protective in the antibodies it delivers.

Yet until the middle of the eighteenth century, or even later, medical literature condemned the colostrum. Samuel Tissot, for example, in his bestselling handbook, *Avis au peuple sur sa santé* (1782: 379), wrote:

> The stomach and bowels of the child, when he comes to the world, are full of a thick and sticky substance called *meconium*. This substance must be evacuated before the child is fed with milk, otherwise it would corrupt the milk; it would turn very bitter and produce two kinds of severe problems the child would not survive.
>
> This excrement may be evacuated (1) if no milk is given during the first 24 hours. (2) If water is given during this time, with a little sugar or honey in it; resulting in a dilution of the meconium, a better natural evacuation and perhaps vomiting. (3) To ascertain that all the substance has gone, it is recommended to give, every four or five hours, an ounce of syrup made of *composite chicory,* added with a little water. This diet is of great advantage; it should be common practice, as it is now here [in Switzerland] since the last years; this syrup is better than any others, particularly better than almond's oil.
>
> If the baby is very weak, and if some food is requested during the first day of life, some biscuit, soaked in water, is usually given, or a light *panade* [bread soup].

Most children of preindustrial rural families were fortunate enough to have this treatment succeeded by maternal breast feeding. But for many less-fortunate urban children, it was followed by a regimen of wet nursing and complementary foods.

Control of the Milk Supply

According to the Greek physician Soranus, active in Rome and Alexandria about A.D. 100, a nurse's milk should be regularly tested for consistency and quantity. In order to maintain a good milk supply, any nursing woman had to follow a regimen of diet, rest, and some exercise. Earlier, around A.D. 60, Pliny the Elder in his *Naturalis Historia,* had indicated that some foods helped increase one's milk supply. These included cabbages, fennel, *Agnus castus* seeds, anemone, and the boiled stalk of sow thistle (Pliny 1601; Soranus 1956; Knibiehler and Fouquet 1980).

In late–nineteenth-century literature, it was often recommended that a lactating woman eat good meals, with cereals, lentils, and chocolate. In addition, it was believed that drinking beer, cider, or even coffee would help maintain a "humectant" diet (Delahaye 1990). However, it is interesting to note that, before the 1830s, such literature was astonishingly silent about beverages. From antiquity on, treatises recommending maternal breast feeding seem oblivious to the importance of drinking liquids. Yet 87 percent of human milk is water (Table III.2.1), and so a lactating mother should drink extra liquid to feed the child (Table III.2.2).

Indeed, this may be one of the reasons that so many urban women of the past complained about not being able to produce sufficient milk: They simply did not drink enough liquids. In European urban areas, water pollution was so general that water might have been used for cooking soup but not for drinking, and unboiled water was dangerous to health.

In rural areas, by contrast, peasants knew the respective qualities of various water sources and frequently had easier access to fresh spring water than urban dwellers, although it is true that even in the country, unusual pollution occasionally resulted in serious epidemics. The generally greater access to clean water supplies, however, helped ensure that breast feeding not only remained a predominantly

Table III.2.2. *Daily quantities of milk a healthy child should ordinarily absorb during the first six months of life (averages)*

Age of the child	G/suck	Number of sucklings	Total/day
First days	70	7	420
First weeks	90	7	630
2d month	120	6	720
3d month	140	6	840
4th month	180	5	900
5th month	240	4	960
6th month	120	4	480
	+ extra food		+ 200 water

Sources: Personal observation of a contemporary nurse, France (1981) and Fauve-Chamoux (1983).

rural practice but was also a paying occupation of peasant women, because they were regarded as fit to produce human milk on demand for several years at a time. In addition to earning money, country nurses probably also knew that lengthy lactation might help them avoid another pregnancy.

Delaying Conception: Milk Versus Blood

Acting through a complex hormonal mechanism, lactation can inhibit ovulation under optimal circumstances. However, both ethnographic and demographic data indicate that the relationship between breast feeding and anovulation is not perfect (Corsini 1979). In addition, other data help to disguise the importance of sexual abstinence during the postpartum period. In fact, many historical and/or demographic studies are difficult to interpret because they are mute about breast-feeding habits. When a mother is the sole source of infant nourishment, anovulation is frequent, and many populations have depended on the contraceptive effect of breast feeding for the spacing of births. Yet despite many recent historical studies using family reconstitution methods, the exact role of breast feeding in causing postpartum amenorrhea in past Western societies has eluded quantitative elucidation.

The age of the nurse, her nutrition, body weight, and fatness are all unknown parameters to which sexual behavior should be added (Knodel and Van de Walle 1967; Chamoux 1973b; Corsini 1974; Fauve-Chamoux 1983). Hippocrates and Soranus shared the idea that pregnancy could not occur without menstruation, the resumption of which, they thought, was encouraged by sexual intercourse, with the result that this specific blood altered the milk. Thus, many authorities insisted on the necessity of sexual abstinence during breast feeding (Van de Walle and Van de Walle 1972), but it seems that the great majority of European couples never accepted this taboo.

Soon after birth, part of the mother's blood was said to be transferred to the breasts as milk. "After helping a new life in the maternal uterus, blood goes

Table III.2.1. *Typical analyses of milk from various species*

	Human	Cow	Goat	Ass
Water (g/100ml)	87	87.5	86.5	91
Protein (g/100ml)	1.5	3.5	3.7	1.9
Fat (g/100ml)	4.0	3.5	4.8	1
Carbohydrates (g/100ml)	6.8	5.0	4.5	6.0
Minerals (g/100ml)	0.2	0.7	0.8	0.4
Lactose (g/100ml)	7	4.5	4.1	6.1
Energy (kcal)	68	66	76	41

Sources: Davidson, Passemore, Brock, and Truswell (1975), p. 236; and Souci, Fachmann, and Kraut (1981), pp. 2–20.

up to breasts, following an admirable, natural and economic way, and becomes a sweet and familiar food" (Verdier-Heurtin 1804: 30). Before conception, the female's extra blood was thought to be evacuated every month. Thus, after birth, if the mother did not lactate, her milk might be dangerously "driven back" and could make her sick. If menstruation or pregnancy occurred while wet-nursing, the milk was considered "spoiled" (Chamoux 1973b; Sussman 1982; Fauve-Chamoux 1985; Fildes 1988); in consequence, the milk of a pregnant nurse had a very bad reputation (Kay 1981; Fildes 1988).

Medical literature of the eighteenth century, which is replete with discussions of maternal breast feeding versus mercenary nursing, defended the Hippocratic principle of respect for nature: The free circulation of "humors" should be encouraged, and any impediment to this natural principle might create severe physical and moral troubles. Also common in the literature were references to the dangers of physical and moral contamination: "A child would have been honest if he had suckled his own mother's milk; instead he was a villain, a libertine, a vicious man with a bad temper; from suckling a bad wet-nurse he got all her vices and defaults" (Dionis 1721: 57).

A lascivious or hysterical nurse was believed to transmit her character through her milk, along with various eventual diseases – especially those of a venereal nature. Despite this, however, menstruating wet nurses were numerous, and those who were employed did their best to hide their monthly visitations (as well as any pregnancies) so as to continue nursing.

The Length of the Nursing Period

According to Soranus, the nursing period in his era ranged from 18 to 24 months – until the child could chew. Russian children of the eighteenth century were weaned after some 10 to 15 months of nursing (Chamoux 1973b; Ransel 1988). In Brittany at the beginning of the twentieth century, the weaning limit was 18 months, and "[t]hen my mother definitely closed her shirt and corselet," related Pierre Jakez Hélias (1975). "Then I had to eat my bouillie alone." Another tradition indicated that a child could be weaned when he had grown twenty teeth. In France, children of the rich could be suckled by their wet nurses until age 20 or 22 months.

By contrast, at the end of the ancien régime, the great majority of foundlings who survived were officially weaned when 12 months old. In the Rheims region, however, 54 percent of illegitimate babies were weaned when 12 months old, and 31 percent when 13 months old, for a very simple administrative reason: Wet nurses had a monthly salary, and thus the change took place on the first day of the month. But unfortunately, weaning concerned only the 30 percent of children who survived to secure access to a nurse's breast in the first place. Legitimate city chil-

dren sent to wet nurses in the country were not returned to Paris before 19 or 20 months of age, although they had been weaned some months before. Because treatises of the Enlightenment period did not recommend breast feeding exclusively (Hecquet 1708; Lerebourg 1767; L'Epinoy 1785), semisolid food was also a part of the infant's diet. Thus, some children could be weaned as early as 6 months or even less. The weaning schedule depended on a question of money: A dry nurse was cheaper than a wet nurse, and peasant women could officially sell their milk as soon as their own child reached 7 months (*Code des nourrices de Paris* [1715] cited in Delahaye 1990). It seems, however, that cheating was the norm in Paris as far as this regulation was concerned, and the age of the nurse's milk could be only a guess.

Mercenary Breast Feeding in Europe

Until the middle of the seventeenth century in Europe, the practice of putting a child out to nurse was reserved for the aristocracy. It was standard behavior to hand over an aristocrat's newborn child to a paid nurse, although the nurse was usually strictly supervised by the family. Much later, in the nineteenth century, bourgeois families utilized the system of an "on-the-spot" wet nurse who was given board and lodging and was, like her earlier counterpart, closely supervised. But in between these two periods – during the seventeenth and eighteenth centuries – newborn babies of those who could afford it were often sent to the country, and thus placed out of range of their mothers' control. We do not know how extensive this phenomenon was throughout Europe. In France, it was limited primarily to residents of the main towns (Chamoux 1973a), and in Renaissance Florence, there was a long tradition of urban parents sending infants out to nurse *(a balia)* soon after birth (Klapisch-Zuber 1985).

In preindustrial England, such a practice was never so widespread as in some other parts of Europe, but well-to-do urban families of merchants, lawyers, physicians, and clergymen – especially those residing in London – tended to employ country women a few miles away from the city (Fildes 1988). Similar situations existed in Warsaw, Hamburg, Stockholm, Vienna, and Madrid.

Parental Behavior and Social Norms

In the past, paternal feelings for children who had not yet reached the age of reason were frequently negative. Michel de Montaigne, for example, wrote in his *Essays* (1580), without mentioning his wife's opinion: "I cannot feel that passion necessary to kiss a barely-born child, with neither movement of his soul, nor a recognizable shape to its body, by which it might make itself pleasing to me. Nor have I been inclined to have them fed close by me." He continued that it was "a good school to send them [the small children] to the country, to bring them up in the lowest and commonest way to live under popular and natural law."

Basically, Montaigne's "natural" educational model did not differ very much from that of Jean-Jacques Rousseau. Following the fame he had acquired from the articulation of his philosophy of child care in *Émile* (1762), in 1789 Rousseau wrote in his *Confessions* (1959): "I have neglected my duties as a father, but the desire to do them harm did not enter my heart, and my fatherly entrails could hardly cry out for children who have never been seen." The latter remark was a reference to a wet-nursing arrangement that distanced the mother from her infant. As an earlier observer had lamented:

> I am quite at a loss to account for the general practice of sending infants out of doors, to be suckled, or dry-nursed by another woman, who has not so much understanding, nor can have so much affection for it, as the parents; and how it comes to pass, that the people of good sense and easy circumstances will not give themselves the pains to watch over the health and welfare of their children (Cadogan 1748: 24).

Clearly, a bond between nurse and child frequently replaced that between mother and child, and many medical writers followed Soranus of Ephesus – the most famous gynecological and obstretrical writer of antiquity – who thought that a good wet nurse helped in protecting the mother's health and youth. In the time of Soranus, however, the nurse was present in the family, and her behavior was under strict supervision. In the eighteenth century, this was not the case, and even a mother's quest for elegance and parental desires for tranquillity cannot fully account for putting children out to nurse. Nonetheless, this was a widespread social phenomenon, which resulted in half the babies in Paris being sent outside the capital, no matter what their sex or birth order. The explanation seems to be that it had become common middle-class behavior.

Urban Females and Breast Feeding

Refusing the maternal duty of breast feeding, however, also extended to the lower classes, especially in preindustrial European towns. A French writer in Lyon in the 1860s explained:

> Shopkeepers' wives have, in general, as much importance in their business as their husbands, they cannot nurse for themselves; and besides, they usually live far from their shops, so they have to resort to the wet nursing bureaux. It is the same with female silk workers, who earn almost as much as their husbands and have an interest in putting their children out to nurse in the country (Sussman 1982: 104).

A century before, when women were working hard for the *manufactures,* a police officer in Lyon observed that "[t]heir situation, work, condition do not allow the women any time, any freedom, to feed their own children" (Prost de Royer 1778).

There may, however, have been other reasons, not related to the work of the mothers, for sending children away. To send the newborn child to fresh air, in the belief that the bad urban air spoiled maternal milk, was doubtless one reason. Another may have been the perception that the diet of urban females did not contain enough in the way of appropriate beverages and good-quality proteins. Indeed, in France, consumption of meat in urban areas was very low at the end of the ancien régime (Livi-Bacci 1991). Thus, poor women of the countryside may even have had a better diet than their urban counterparts. Nonetheless, we are forced to wonder again what meaning "motherhood" held for those couples who put their children out to unsupervised country nurses, or what it meant for those mothers, often alone, who abandoned their babies to charity.

Love and Premodern Motherhood

It is doubtful that people of the past did not realize that putting a child out to nurse was risky, and that abandoning a child was to condemn it to death. This makes it difficult to explain how, in those days of enlightened philosophers, the widespread practice of abandonment of newborns (which in pre-Pasteur times usually amounted to infanticide) could coexist with a clear renewal of interest in children (Aries 1962; Shorter 1975; Badinter 1981; Bardet, Corsini, Perez Moreda, et al. 1991).

Indeed, it is morbidly fascinating that Rousseau, the herald of individual morality, seems to have had no difficulty adopting the behavior of contemporary Parisians with regard to bastard children: He abandoned his own children to the Paris foundling hospital. His reasons for this choice are very clear (Rousseau 1959), but the mentality that inspired them remains incomprehensible to us. Rousseau did not belong to any of the social groups regularly acquainted with child abandonment, such as domestic servants, urban workers, or impoverished day laborers, but his children were all bastards, and raising them was apparently not among his priorities. The same held for Thérèse Levasseur, his companion, who seemingly did not fight to keep her children, nor did she try to suckle her succession of babies, boys or girls. In Europe, as many boys were abandoned as girls (Bardet et al. 1991).

An abundant eighteenth-century literature encouraging maternal breast feeding stirred little interest in French, Italian, Russian, Polish, or English urban societies (Hecquet 1708; Lerebourg 1767; L'Epinoy 1785). It was the case that some grand ladies (who could afford to) breast-fed their children and then boasted about it as a way of returning to nature. Similarly, it was fashionable to have one's portrait painted when breast-feeding, like a Madonna (Fauve-Chamoux 1985). All of this was a way to affirm one's modernity and to symbolize an advanced feminism, but it was also the case that men frequently did not wish their wives to breast-feed. Thus, often, aristocratic women who breast-fed their infants only did so during the day; at night, maids or nurses took care of the babies. The day for the child, the night for the husband; the sum was a compromise with God.

Serving the Husband before the Child

Since polygamy is not tolerated in most Christian societies, theologians and confessors have had great difficulty in establishing a hierarchy of sins: A woman was supposed to do everything possible to avoid a too-ardent husband, and, of course, also to avoid adultery. Yet neither could she refuse her wifely duty for too long, even if her aim was to preserve her milk, which helps to explain why confessors finally justified the practice of putting children out to nurse as being the lesser of two evils: "If the husband is in danger of lacking restraint, the woman must, if she is able, put her child out to nurse in order to tend to her husband's infirmity," said the *Abrégé du dictionnaire des cas de conscience* by M. Pontas (1764).

Certainly such a practice preserved the peace of the household by ensuring the father permanent access to his wife's bed. This aristocratic habit was popularized in France and reveals the importance placed by the Catholic Church on conjugal relations. The Church favored the relationship between the parents and relegated the child's interest to second place (Aries 1962; Noonan 1966; Flandrin 1973).

Religious attachment also influenced attitudes with respect to childbearing and nursing. Protestant women generally bore fewer children than their Catholic counterparts and nursed them more often themselves. Infant mortality was, thus, much higher in Catholic than in Protestant families during the seventeenth century (Knodel and Van de Walle 1967). But despite dechristianization and an enormous literature in favor of maternal care, there was no widespread return to maternal feeding at the end of the eighteenth century, and France remained a cornerstone of the nursing industry. Families characteristically had fewer children, but the practices of wet nursing and artificial feeding continued, and until World War I, the custom of putting infants out to nurse remained widespread and infant mortality remained high (Rollet-Echalier 1990). In short, the status of infants did not improve greatly in France (or in western Europe, for that matter) before the first decades of the twentieth century.

Differential Infant Mortality

The consequences of this apparent unconcern for the welfare of the young were of considerable importance. Putting babies out to nurse raised the infant mortality level and, in the absence of contraceptive practice, accelerated the rate of successive pregnancies. France's infant mortality, much higher than that of England, Sweden, or Denmark, was clearly a function of less breast feeding and poor child care (Table III.2.4).

Table III.2.3. *Number of babies, aged less than 1, abandoned in Paris Foundling Hospital, 1773-7, with infant mortality for each group, according to their origin*

	From Hôtel-Dieu	From Paris and the suburbs	From the provinces	Total
Babies abandoned	6,523	14,552	9,039	30,114
Died under 31 days	5,395	10,650	5,854	21,899
Died within 12 months	5,892	12,185	7,180	25,257
Died under 31 days	82.7%	73.1%	64.7%	72.7%
Died within 12 months	90.3%	83.7%	79.4%	83.8%

Sources: Dr. Tenon, Bibliothèque Nationale, Paris, NAF 22746, cited in Chamoux (1973b).

Among Parisian craftsmen who kept their children in the eighteenth century, one baby out of every four died before his or her first birthday. But in Lyon in the 1780s, the "Society for Helping Poor Mothers" paid women 9 pounds a month if they breast-fed their own children during the first year of life. The infant mortality level soon fell to 1 out of 6 babies; the drop was considered a large success. By contrast, however, when infants were systematically put out to nurse, the infant mortality rate at least doubled. Thus, 40 percent of legitimate babies in Rouen died if they were put out to a wet nurse. But when their mothers nursed them, infant mortality dropped to 20 percent, showing the vital importance of maternal breast feeding (Bardet 1973). In Lyon, only one-third came back alive from wet nursing, and in Paris, only between one-half and one-third of legitimate children survived mercenary nursing (Prost de Royer 1778).

From the Refusal of Breast Feeding to Contraception

Rejection of the newborn was accompanied in France by a progressive diminution of family size. In Rheims, at the end of the seventeenth century, women who married before age 20 bore an average of 11 or 12 children. But in the late eighteenth century, on the eve of the French Revolution, women were having only 6 children (Fauve-Chamoux 1985). The conjugal practices of urban elite groups had undoubtedly shown the way with regard to contraception. As early as the 1670s, the leading families of large cities like Rheims or Rouen (Bardet 1973; Fauve-Chamoux 1985) were successfully limiting the number of their children, and social differences in this regard were strongly marked.

During the eighteenth century, behavior that would later be called "Malthusian" took root in the middle class. This was a "family-planning" outlook that implied deep changes in attitude toward the Christian religion, and toward love and procreation. But, for the lower classes, little had changed. Poor mothers, frequently without husbands, often considered that they had no choice but to abandon their children, whether legitimate or not. And this custom continued to confront societies with moral as well as practical questions concerning the care and feeding of the young.

Artificial Infant Feeding

Feeding Foundlings

About one-third of the children abandoned in Paris during the eighteenth century came from the provinces and, thus, were at least a few days old and already sick and underfed. Many of these babies died before reaching the ancient hospital, the Hôtel-Dieu, which also served as a foundling home. Among other things, these deaths tended to skew mortality data and make it appear that, at the Hôtel-Dieu, the mortality of children from the provinces was lower than that of children born and abandoned in Paris (Table III.2.5). In 1772, the king prohibited this transfer of infants to Paris, but the flow continued. The ban was renewed in 1779 but with no better results, and at the end of the *ancien régime*, between 6,000 and 7,000 newborn babies were being abandoned in the capital each year (Table III.2.5).

The mortality of these children was horrifying. More than 80 percent died, with 7 out of 10 deaths occurring during the first month of life and resulting from lack of appropriate food and nursing (Table III.2.3). Three-quarters of those who died were estimated by the authorities to be of illegitimate birth. European urban hospitals of the time, like the Hôtel Dieu, were transformed into depositories for abandoned children.

Paradoxically, however, such institutional efforts may have encouraged the phenomenon of infant abandonment all over Europe (Bardet et al. 1991).

The scarcity of wet nurses for such children was general throughout Europe: Institutions paid low wages and the women they employed were poor, often unfit for proper breast feeding, and frequently without enough maternal milk. Therefore, French hospitals experimented with different methods of nourishing abandoned young children, trying cow's, goat's, and donkey's milk, and often combining the animal milks with water and barley or with "rice water." At the Hôtel-Dieu in Paris, and at similar institutions in Rheims and Milan (where abandoned children were numerous), feeding with animal milks led to the use of feeding bottles and special feeding horns, called *cornets*. These became part of a baby's equipment when leaving the foundling hospital for the wet nurse's home, and they provided a ready means of dry nursing and early weaning.

In Paris at the end of the eighteenth century, there were 208 cradles for foundlings that were permanently occupied. Each saw an ultra-rapid turnover, and each had a personal crystal bottle attached (Chamoux 1973b).

Animal Milk and Baby Food

Cow's milk, mixed with "barley water" in the Paris foundling hospital during the eighteenth century, probably contributed to the death of many children during the first weeks of life. "Wheat water" was also given as a separate drink. A common milk lightener was "lentil water," with a dilution as high as 50 percent for "healthy babies," according to the French physician Dr. J. Tenon,[1] who explained that this liquid was made available "in a porc bladder equipped with a teat or in a feeding-bottle when the children were crying" (Tenon manuscripts, Bibliothèque Nationale, Paris).

Milk from goats was widely known to be lighter, and therefore better, for infants than that of cows. A sixteenth-century observer near Bordeaux, for example, wrote of country women whose breasts did not contain enough milk to feed their infants and consequently called upon goats "to help them" (Montaigne 1580). In 1634, goats were employed by Paris's Hôtel Dieu to feed the foundlings, as had been done successfully in Italy in the previous century (Lallemand 1885).

Table III.2.4. *General infant and child mortality in four European countries during the second half of the eighteenth century*

France 1750–99	England 1750–99	Sweden 1750–99	Denmark 1780–1800
273	165	200	191
215	104	155	156

Source: Livi-Bacci (1991), p. 74.

Table III.2.5. *Number of children abandoned in Paris Foundling Hospital, 1773–7, according to their age and origin*

From Hôtel-Dieu	From Paris and the suburbs		From the provinces		
Newborn	Age less than 1	Age +1	Age less than 1	Age +1	Total
6,523	14,552	462	9,039	1,375	31,951

Source: Dr. Tenon, Bibliothèque Nationale, Paris, NAF 22746, cited in Chamoux (1973b).

Such nourishment was certainly good when the babies were directly suckling the animals. But unfortunately, bottles, with all their attendant germs, were often used as intermediaries, and if another liquid was added – for example, herb tea of *chiendent* ("couch grass") – it made for a dangerous diet. Goats were easier to maintain in an urban institution than donkeys, whose milk had enjoyed a good reputation for its digestibility since Roman times (Table III.2.1). In Paris in the 1880s, donkeys were used for direct suckling at the stable of the *Hospice des Enfants Malades.* But they were troublesome because lactation could not be prolonged unless the animals fed their own foals, and the experiment did not last long. Direct animal suckling, however, was usually a practice in hospitals for syphilitic children, who, because of fear of contagion, were never breast-fed.

Wine was said to be a "tonic" when given in dilution and in small quantity. It was often employed when no milk was available, particularly when the child was being transported without any nurse. For example, it had the effect of keeping abandoned children quiet when they were taken by slow carriage to the Parisian foundling hospital from far away. But alcohol was also believed good for infants when they suffered from gastrointestinal complaints (Fildes 1988). Calvados, champagne, or other spirits may, on occasion, have been ritually added to feeding bottles to celebrate baptisms or like events.

European Bouillies

Solid food for infants consisted of a kind of porridge, called *bouillie* in French. This was a food usually reserved for a weaning diet and for older children. In much of France, wheat was preferred for the porridge (oats were considered a food for animals), but the use of corn was common in southern France after the end of the ancien régime. There, a porridge called *millias,* cooked in a pan, served as a main course for both adults and children. This dish was similar to Romanian *mamaliga* or Italian and Iberian *polenta* (Livi-Bacci 1991).

It is fortunate that such complementary foods were not strictly reserved for weaning or for mercenary nursing but rather were given, along with milk, to very young children in both European and colonial societies. This explains why *marasmus* – the result of a grossly deficient intake of both proteins and calories (Gift, Washbon, and Harrison 1972; Livi-Bacci 1991) – was not a common type of malnutrition in past Western societies. By contrast, many Occidental babies died of too much unaccustomed solid food and too little of their own mothers' milk. One example of such an imbalance was a "biscuit soup" prepared every day in a London foundling hospital. The apothecary complained in 1759 that milk was often forgotten in the mixture: "The biscuit is directed to be boiled in water to a proper consistence and afterward mixed with a proper proportion of milk, but it is now and has been given to the children without any milk at all" (Fildes 1988: 169).

During the 1770s, Tenon collected information from all over France and Europe about artificial baby food. He understood that any artificial food was usually a killer when the very young baby was not or was no longer breast-fed. "Those foods," he wrote, "given as supplements to breast milk, as thick *bouillies* made of ordinary milk, flour, yolk, and wine, sweetened with sugar, destroy the positive effects from the very little milk they happen to suckle; those foods are too thick and too heavy for a delicate baby's stomach" (Chamoux 1973b: 415).

When mother's milk was lacking, Alsatian and German women gave their own children a cream made from rice or bread. In seventeenth-century Brittany, rural mothers often fed their children with a finger, after first warming the bread soup in their own mouths (Lemieux 1985). Certainly, in the past, the easiest food to give a baby, other than milk, was wet and mashed bread.

Such a *panade* figured prominently in the weaning process, which came about when the mother could not, or no longer wanted to, breast-feed her own child. This was often the case when a woman was wet-nursing another child. In Salpétrière Hospital in 1755, for example, children of employed wet nurses were served a portion of *bouillie* in the morning and another in the evening, and given soup at lunch time. A "portion" was half of a big spoonful, and 17 portions were prepared twice a day in a cooking pot called a *bonet.* Most of those children, who rarely received mother's milk, also consumed a daily supplement of a pint of animal milk.

Tenon, who commented so extensively on eighteenth-century baby food, was, for his time, a rare defender of cow's milk, apparently because he was influenced by positive reports of Russian customs. Muscovite children, he wrote, were treated roughly but seemed to become accustomed very early to animal milk and solid food. Indeed, from the very first day of life, Russian babies were fed with salted, mashed bread and cow's milk. "The woman in charge puts the milk in her own mouth to get it warm and spits it in a feeding horn for the baby. When aged ten months, the child is given *cacha,* a sort of gruel from *sarrazin* (buckwheat) – cooked with milk, a much better *bouillie* than the one made in our countries." Three other kinds of traditional Russian baby foods and pastes are mentioned by Tenon. One was made of mashed bread, butter, and beer, another of mashed bread with honey, and still another of mashed bread with premasticated meat. And when the babies cried, they were given, as early as one month of age, a light narcotic made from poppy seeds, commonly used for making traditional pastries (Tenon Manuscripts, Bibliothèque Nationale, Paris).

This diet, Tenon noted with admiration, "never results in *edema*," which is a well-known symptom of malnutrition still observed in twentieth-century developing countries. Sometimes it is called *kwashiorkor* and is the result of a deficiency of protein even when caloric intake is relatively adequate (Gift et al. 1972). In light of Tenon's observation, it seems that Russian children may have enjoyed more good-quality protein in their diet than any dry-nursed babies in western Europe, who were never given meat or fish but only cereals, and who often suffered from edema.

It turns out, however, that Tenon was misled by the French edition of a book concerning the new foundling hospitals of Russia established by Catherine the Great; he believed that Russian women did not usually breast-feed their children (Betzy 1775). Today we know that at the end of the eighteenth century, the feeding of foundlings was as much a problem in Moscow and St. Petersburg as it was elsewhere in Europe. Fully 14,000 babies were registered annually by the Moscow Foundling Hospital (Ransel 1988), and their mortality was estimated to be at least 60 percent, which was roughly comparable to French figures.

During the 1880s, wet nursing became a common female profession in Russia: "The majority of new mothers from our area," wrote a Russian physician, "do not think merely of how it would be best to nurse their baby but how they might best draw advantage from their breast milk; this unfortunate phenomenon is expressed in two forms – either becoming a [private] wet nurse or by taking a foundling, and sometimes not one but several" (Ransel 1988). Such a situation had long been common in most of Europe, but it was one that was in the process of change for the better.

The Swan Song of the Wet Nurse

Many significant changes in baby care occurred during the nineteenth century. Among the middle classes in Europe, in Paris and Lyon as well as in London, Madrid, Vienna, and Moscow, it became expected that the wet nurse would reside in the home of the infant (Fay-Sallois 1980; Sussman 1982; Fildes 1988). In England, however, during early Victorian times, when an unmarried wet nurse left her own baby of six weeks to sell her milk in a London bourgeois family, she condemned him or her to death. Infants of the poor still rarely survived artificial feeding, and the absence of human milk and early weaning sacrificed most illegitimate, as well as many legitimate, children.

In Britain, the Infant Life Protection Bill was passed in 1872, but this failed to stop baby farming and wet nursing. In France, the Roussel Law (1874) had no more immediate effect, but it did oblige families to register all children who were nursed outside the home, to provide the name and address of the wet nurse, and to indicate the fate of the children. This permitted the calculation of regional and national statistics on infant survival and the impact of feeding methods. In Marseille, during 1875, 50 percent of parents employed wet nurses. From the data available, it would seem that 20 percent of wet nurses lived in the homes of the infants and 10 percent lived close to the baby's city. But 70 percent lived far away from the baby's home, sometimes more than 100 miles.

In the 1890s, the importance of pasteurization was understood, and artificial feeding at last became less dangerous. Nevertheless, some baby bottles were impossible to clean properly, especially those with a long tube attached to them.

Conclusion

Information from the World Fertility Survey (*Population Reports* 1986), as well as from recent studies conducted in developing countries where diarrheal diseases are a major problem for infants, shows how important breast feeding can be to infant survival (Carballo and Marin-Lira 1984). In most of western Europe, North America, and Japan, the potential impact of low breast-feeding rates has been attenuated by improved water supply and sanitary systems. But such major changes occurred less than a century ago with the advent of pasteurization techniques in conjunction with cultural, economic, and social changes. In fact, the so-called 3 Ps (Pasteur, Politics, and Progress) worked together to make artificial feeding safer. Therefore, little effort was exerted from the 1940s to the early 1970s to promote breast feeding, and by 1973, the prevalence of maternal breast feeding had fallen to 25 percent in the United States, with a mean duration of three months or less.

However, in the 1980s and 1990s, a return to breast feeding was noticeable in many industrialized countries, and especially among the better-educated mothers (La Leche International 1981). They became aware both of the immunological and antimicrobial properties of their maternal milk and of the "bifidus factor" concerning the intestinal flora of their babies. In addition, mothers understood that breast feeding benefits their infants with less exposure to contaminants, and finally, they realized that their own milk has superior nutritional properties to animal milks.

In the past, mothers had no such knowledge, however, and if babies died in innocence and purity they were supposedly blessed in heaven. Thus, putting children out to nurse remained a common practice during the nineteenth century throughout the Western world and particularly in France. In addition, before the systematic pasteurization of milk and the provision of sterilized bottles, artificial feeding frequently sent babies, especially those abandoned in European institutions, to their graves. Maternal breast feeding remains, as it was in the past, a matter of culture, family norms, and religion.

Antoinette Fauve-Chamoux

Note

1. Dr. J. Tenon's manuscripts, from which I quote, may be found in the collections of the Bibliothèque Nationale, Paris. His project during the 1770s was to reform the French hospital system. His most important opinions about artificial infant feeding habits in late eighteenth-century Europe have been discussed by Chamoux (1973b).

Bibliography

Aries, Philippe. 1962. *Centuries of childhood: A social history of family life.* New York.

Badinter, Elisabeth. 1981. *The myth of motherhood. An historical view of the maternal instinct,* trans. R. DeGaris. London.

Bardet, Jean-Pierre. 1973. Enfants abandonnés et enfants assistés. *Sur la population française du XVIIe et XVIIIe siècles,* 19–48. Paris.

Bardet, J.-P., C. Corsini, V. Perez Moreda, et al. 1991. *Enfance abandonnée et société en Europe, XIVe–XXe siècle.* Rome.

Betzy, M. 1775. *Le plan et les statuts des établissements ordonnés par Catherine II.* Amsterdam.

Cadogan, William. 1748. *An essay upon nursing and the management of children.* London.

Carballo, Manuel, and Angelica Marin-Lira. 1984. *Patterns of breast-feeding, child health and fertility.* Geneva.

Chamoux, Antoinette. 1973a. L'enfance abandonnée à Reims à la fin du XVIIIe siècle. *Annales de Démographie Historique* 1973: 263–301.

    1973b. L'allaitement artificiel. *Annales de Démographie Historique* 1973: 410–18.

Corsini, Carlo. 1974. La fécondité naturelle de la femme mariée: Le cas des nourrices. *Genus* 30: 243–59.

    1979. Is the fertility-reducing effect of lactation really substantial? In *Natural fertility,* ed. Henri Leridon and Jane Menken, 195–215. Liège.

Davidson, Stanley, R. Passemore, J. F. Brock, and A. S. Truswell. 1975. *Human nutrition and dietetics.* Edinburgh.

Delahaye, Marie-Claude. 1990. *Tétons et tétines. Histoire de l'allaitement.* Paris.

Dionis, P. 1721. *Traité général des accouchements.* . . . Paris.

Fauve-Chamoux, Antoinette. 1983. La femme devant l'allaitement. *Annales de Démographie Historique* 1983: 7–22.

    1985. Innovation et comportement parental en milieu urbain XVe–XIXe siècles. *Annales (E.S.C.)* 5: 1023–39.

Fay-Sallois, Fanny. 1980. *Les nourrices à Paris au XIXe siècle.* Paris.

Fildes, Valerie. 1988. *Wet nursing. A history from antiquity to the present.* Oxford.

Flandrin, Jean-Louis. 1973. L'attitude à l'égard du petit enfant et les conduites sexuelles dans la civilisation occidentale. *Annales de Démographie Historique* 1973: 143–210.

Fuchs, Rachel G. 1984. *Abandoned children. Foundlings and child welfare in nineteenth-century France.* Albany, N.Y.

Gift, Helen H., Marjorie B. Washbon, and Gail G. Harrison. 1972. *Nutrition, behavior and change.* Englewood Cliffs, N.J.

Hecquet, Philippe. 1708. *De l'obligation aux mères de nourrir leurs enfants.* Paris.

Hélias, Pierre Jakez. 1975. *Le cheval d'orgueil. Mémoires d'un breton du pays bigouden.* Paris.

Kay, Margarita A. 1981. *Anthropology of human birth.* Philadelphia, Pa.

Klapisch-Zuber, Christiane. 1985. Blood parents and milk parents: Wet nursing in Florence, 1300–1530. In *Women, family, and ritual Renaissance Italy,* trans. L. G. Cochrane, 132–64. Chicago.

Knibiehler, Yvonne, and Catherine Fouquet. 1980. *L'histoire des mères du moyen-âge à nos jours.* Paris.

Knodel, J., and E. Van de Walle. 1967. Breast-feeding, fertility and infant mortality. *Population Studies* 21: 109–31.

La Leche International, ed. 1981. *The womanly art of breast-feeding.* New York.

Lallemand, Leon. 1885. *Histoire des enfants abandonnés et délaissés: Étude sur la protection de l'enfance aux diverses époques de la civilisation.* Paris.

Lemieux, Denise. 1985. *Les petits innocents. L'enfance en Nouvelle-France.* Quebec.

L'Epinoy, Roze de. 1785. *Avis aux mères qui veulent allaiter.* Paris.

Lerebourg, M. 1767. *Avis aux mères qui veulent nourrir leurs enfants.* Utrecht.

Livi-Bacci, Massimo. 1991. *Population and nutrition. An essay on European demographic history.* Cambridge.

Montaigne, Michel de. 1580. *Les essais.* Paris.

Noonan, John T., Jr. 1966. *Contraception: A history of its treatment by the Catholic theologians and canonists.* Cambridge, Mass.

Paré, Ambroise. 1573. *De la génération.* Paris.

Paul, Pauline C., and Helen H. Palmer. 1972. *Food theory and applications.* New York.

Pliny. 1601. *History of the world. Commonly called the natural history of Plinius secundus,* trans. P. Holland. London.

Pontas, M. 1764. *Abrégé du dictionnaire des cas de conscience.* Paris.

Population Reports. 1986. Series M. no. 8 (October): 1–32.

Prost de Royer, Antoine-François. 1778. *Mémoire sur la conservation des enfants.* Lyon.

Ransel, David L. 1988. *Mothers of misery: Child abandonment in Russia.* Princeton, N.J.

Rollet-Echalier, Catherine. 1990. *La politique à l'égard de la petite enfance sous la IIIe République.* Paris.

Rousseau, Jean-Jacques. [1789] 1959. *Les confessions.* In *Oeuvres complètes.* Paris.

Shorter, Edward. 1975. *The making of the modern family.* New York.

Soranus of Ephesus. 1956. *Gynecology,* trans. O. Temkin et al. Baltimore, Md.

Souci, S. W., W. Fachmann, and H. Kraut. 1981. *Food composition and nutrition tables 1981/82.* Stuttgart.

Sussman, G. D. 1982. *Selling mothers' milk. The wet-nursing business in France 1715–1914.* London.

Tissot, Samuel. 1782. *Avis au peuple sur sa santé.* Paris.

Van de Walle, Étienne, and Francine Van de Walle. 1972. Allaitement, stérilité et contraception: Les opinions jusqu'au XIXe siècle. *Population* 4-5: 685-701.

Verdier-Heurtin, J. F. 1804. *Discours sur l'allaitement.* Paris.

III.3 ❧ Cacao

Origins, Varieties, and Cultivation

Cacao *(Theobroma cacao),* "the drink of the gods," and its main by-product, chocolate, are derived from the seeds of a fleshy pod, the fruit of the cacao tree. This tree is a tropical plant, certainly American and probably Amazonian in origin. In the Amazon region it is sometimes still found in its wild state, an understory plant usually well shaded by taller trees with dense foliage.

Today, cacao trees are sometimes grown in direct sunlight, thanks to modern fertilizers and hormonal treatments that help the trees produce a dense upper foliage. Most cacao trees, however, still require shade, and this is often provided by the simultaneous planting of shade trees and cacao saplings. Lemon trees, tall palms, and banana plants are employed, but more common is the aptly named *madre de cacao,* or "mother of the cacao" *(Gliricidia sepium),* another American native now found in all tropical areas. Various acacias and the coral tree have also been used to shade cacao plantations.

There is another species related to cacao, *Theobroma bicolor,* which is now a garden crop, although its pods were collected in the forest from ancient times until late in the Spanish-American colonial period. It does not produce true cacao and is known in Mesoamerica as *pataxte* or *patlaxtli.* Spaniards at first thought *patlaxtli* was harmful, but later they used the pods as a minor food and, in a few places, the tree to shade cacao trees.

There is some disagreement among experts as to cacao types. Many identify two varieties, others three, whereas a few claim that such distinctions evolved within historical times and were brought about by human selection and cultivation. For what it may be worth, most students of the subject agree that there are three types.

The *criollo* or "native" cacaos - that seem to have been grown only in Mesoamerica prior to the arrival of the Europeans - are considered to be the finest. All cacao trees demand considerable care, but *criollos* are the most difficult to cultivate. They are fragile, plagued by many pests, and relatively low in yield, and their cultivation today is limited to Mexico, Central America, Venezuela, and the Caribbean islands. *Criollo* cacao is often used to upgrade the quality of chocolate or

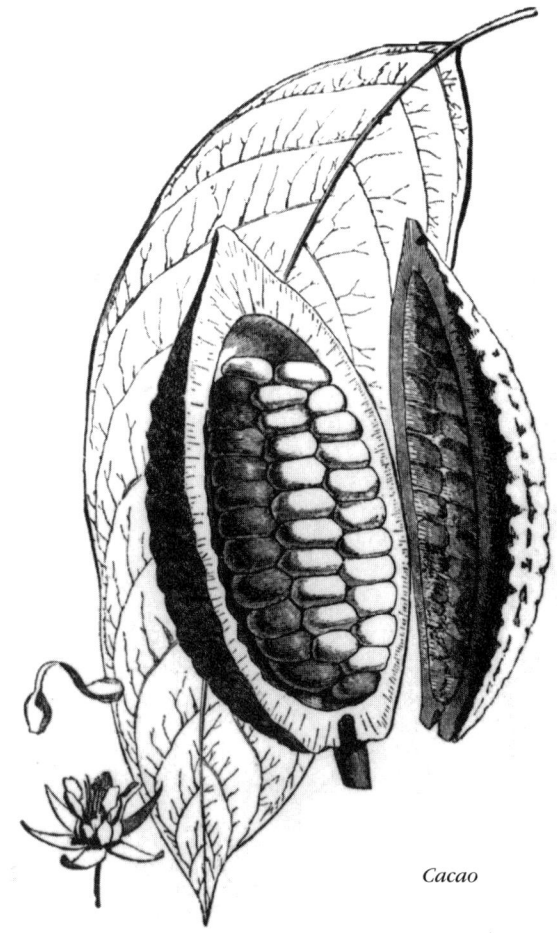

Cacao

chocolate drinks, and connoisseurs place great stock in the percentage of *criollo* cacao in such confections.

Since the Spanish colonial period in America, *forastero* cacaos have been considered hardier and more prolific in yield, although of a lower quality than *criollo* cacaos. The meaning attached to the term *forastero* has varied, although it is always associated with wildness and alien origin. The plant may have spread from Brazil, but by the middle of the seventeenth century, it was thoroughly domesticated and widely cultivated in Ecuador and Venezuela. The Portuguese carried this variety from Brazil to São Tome and other offshore islands of West Africa, from whence it spread to the mainland. Today it is a leading crop in several African countries and in Southeast Asia.

The third variety of cacao, according to several authorities, is a crossbreed between the two original types, and because it was first widely grown on the island of Trinidad, it has acquired the name *trinitario.* This variety is now dispersed and can be found as far from home as Indonesia and other parts of Asia.

Indeed, it may well be that the original Amazonian wild cacaos have become so geographically scattered and modified by human agency that they now appear to be highly distinctive varieties. Experts tend to identify cacaos and their various differences and desired qualities by regions, soils, and kinds of processing, so that Guayaquil cacaos, Brazilian cacaos, and varieties from the Ivory Coast or Malaysia, for example, are all characterized according to aroma, sweetness, the shape and size of the bean, oil or "butter" content, and other attributes.

Domesticated cacao trees are seldom allowed to grow to more than 20 feet in height. They are pruned and topped frequently to keep them accessible and to protect the cacao pods from sunlight and entangled branches. The pods develop from flowers that are fertilized naturally by midges, or artificially, and have the shape and rough size of an American football, although the size can vary greatly. The pod develops on the bark of the trunk or on large branches, not at the end of branches or twigs. The inside of the pod contains the beans or "nibs" and a white pulp, which is consumed by birds, animals, and humans. Cacao trees, although delicate, have a useful life of up to 50 years, but this can vary widely according to care, soil, region, and other circumstances. The trees develop slowly, usually from seedlings, and seldom yield any harvest until the third or fourth year. They are very sensitive to cold and drought and require year-round water from rain or irrigation.

Because cacao trees are too delicate to be climbed, harvesting must be done from the ground. Long poles topped by a cutting implement reach the higher fruit. After the pods are split open, the nibs are separated from the sticky pulp (by machine on modern plantations). The discarded pods are employed as fertilizer or animal fodder. The nibs are then fermented and dried. The workers heap them up in a shaded area and turn them over frequently for several days. Once fermentation is complete – the timing of which requires considerable expertise – the nibs are spread in the sun or dried artificially for a week or more, with workers again often raking and turning them.

The cacao nibs are then graded (nowadays by machine), poured into large sacks, inspected, and shipped to the major markets and consuming countries, where they are transformed and manufactured into hard chocolate, cacao powder, cacao butter, and other products.

A History of American Cacaos

The remote history of cacao is disputed; many deny its Amazonian origin and believe that in its "wild" state, the cacao tree grew in a number of other parts of the Americas, including perhaps the Upper Orinoco flood plain. Because the nibs have a short fertile life, there was difficulty in transporting them elsewhere to plant new seedlings, especially before modern transporta-

tion. Thus, gaps between areas of cultivation and different varieties came into existence.

In any event, it is in Mesoamerica that the first recorded histories of cacao are to be found. The plant and its nibs were part of the most ancient mythologies there. The Olmecs knew cacao, possibly before 1000 B.C., and the word itself, or one like it, may belong to a proto–Mixe-Zoquean language probably spoken by the Olmecs. Cacao was also part of the material and cultural lives of the Maya and their predecessors, as well as the various other societies (including that of the so-called Aztecs) that were destroyed by the Spanish invaders of Mesoamerica.

The Maya were probably the first people to write about cacao via their now-deciphered hieroglyphics. There may have been some link between cacao as a drink and the sacrifice of human blood. Certainly, elite burials and tombs often contained elaborate vessels with cacao drinks in them. Some scholars believe, in fact, that the consumption of cacao was a privilege of the nobility, but to others this practice seems unlikely (or at least not widespread), given the extent of its cultivation in various Mesoamerican tropical lowlands. Probably cacao was drunk (there is, so far, little evidence that it was eaten as a hard substance among Mesoamericans) by people of all classes. The drink was very much a part of public ceremony and ritual.

Cacao beans were an important item in Mesoamerican trade and tribute long before the European invasions. Cacao's climatic requirements, and the sophistication of state systems of trade and tribute, led to regional specialization – perhaps even monoculture – in a few places. In such areas as Guerrero, Colima, Veracruz, Tabasco, and the Gulf of Honduras, cacao was grown in plantation-like settings for export to distant centers. On his fourth voyage in 1502, Christopher Columbus in the Gulf of Honduras came upon a very large seagoing canoe that was transporting a varied cargo that included cacao beans. The most important growing areas, as far as present knowledge goes, were Soconusco (today the Pacific coast of Chiapas, Mexico) and the Pacific coastal plains and piedmonts of present-day Guatemala and El Salvador. From these plantations, large quantities of beans found their way to the highlands as trade and tribute. Soconusco, though distant from Tenochtitlan (now Mexico City), became a prized part of the Aztec conquests and paid tribute to Montezuma. Cacao beans were stored in great warehouses in the capital.

Money, therefore, "grew on trees." Cacao nibs were used as coinage throughout Mesoamerica from ancient times, and at least as far south as Costa Rica during the colonial period, especially when there were shortages of official coinage. Our knowledge of this coinage before the arrival of Europeans, however, is sketchy. In Nicaragua, a distant periphery of Mesoamerica, beans were widely used as petty coins and may have had standard equivalencies, evidence of a formal and official coinage. Additional evidence can be found in a widely used serial system of measures that was based, not on weight, but upon the number of cacao nibs. There is also evidence of a thriving industry in counterfeit cacao beans, another sign of their monetary value. In some regions, however, the beans may have served only as substitute, specialized, or occasional coins.

Mesoamericans had many recipes for cacao drinks. Ground beans were mixed with hot or cold water and with maize, ground chillies, annatto, vanilla, and seeds, roots, and flowers of many kinds. Many of the dishes were soups, and the liquid chocolate, poured into or over many other dishes, was perhaps the ancestor of modern *mole* sauces. These peoples had a preference for chocolate drinks beaten to a froth, and to this end poured chocolate in a stream from one container to another. The upper classes and the *pochteca*, a kind of official merchant class, consumed large quantities of these soups and drinks at festivals and public banquets.

Hernán Cortés and his invading band noticed the many uses of cacao and captured stores of it in Tenochtitlan to use as money. They also saw the flourishing groves in such areas as Soconusco and Izalcos (in present-day El Salvador). In Soconusco, the harvests quickly attracted large numbers of mule trains and merchants. Some of the most lucrative *encomiendas* (grants of the labor and tribute of subject natives) in Central America were in Izalcos where cacao was generally the means of tribute-payment. But Spaniards usually did not try to seize legal ownership of cacao groves, perhaps because cultivation and care of the fragile, valuable trees was both a specialized business and hard work in a humid, tropical climate. Instead, they did their best to monopolize labor in the groves, not to mention the taxes cacao produced, and the cacao trade. Tribute to the crown and to private individuals continued to be paid in cacao long after the Spanish conquests, and large quantities were carried by sea and by land to central Mexico.

Gradually, the new colonial elites made changes in the "cacao economy" – not in the kinds of production or ownership, but rather in the intensity of cultivation and in patterns of distribution and consumption. *Encomenderos* (holders of *encomiendas*) and local royal officials forced native producers to intensify planting and harvesting, which may have been counterproductive for two reasons. First, the Native American population was already in severe decline because of the epidemiological invasion brought on by the arrival of Europeans and Africans. Overwork and other oppressions exacerbated this mortality, and replacements brought in from the highlands died just as quickly. By the late sixteenth century, many of the productive zones were suffering from severe labor shortages. Second, overplanting may also have been self-defeating. Shade trees were cut down, destroying the understory conditions needed by cacao trees. No doubt, labor shortages and changing agricultural conditions were related.

At the same time as production in Mesoamerica declined, consumption rose. If cacao had once been a food limited to the upper classes, itself a doubtful proposition, this soon changed. Shortly after the conquest, it was apparent to some of the enterprising interlopers that cacao consumption was very large indeed; impressionistic accounts describe Indians quaffing massive, almost unbelievable, quantities of chocolate. Trade – often long-distance trade – in the crop became important, and demand was such that suppliers from faraway plantations could pay expensive freight costs and still show a profit.

As Central American production declined, prices in Mexico rose, and even more distant producers entered the market. The fine Central American *criollo* cacaos retained, and still retain, a market niche because of their reputed quality, but the Guayaquil basin of Ecuador and the coastal valleys of Venezuela west of Caracas, along the Tuy River, and south of Maracaibo, replaced Central America, Tabasco, and Guerrero as the largest producing areas. We know little about the origins of this new competition. In both areas, growers used the more hardy and productive *forastero* cacaos.

At first, Venezuelan cacao dominated. From around 1670, as the native populations disappeared, plantations were worked by African slaves. Exports from La Guaira, Maracaibo, and smaller ports were carried on a fleet of small ships to Veracruz, and from there by mule to Puebla and Mexico City. The Venezuelan elite became known as the "grandes cacaos," some of whom owned as many as a quarter of a million trees. In 1728, a clique of Basque entrepreneurs obtained an export monopoly called the Royal Guipuzcoa Company, or, colloquially, the Caracas Company. Between 1730 and 1754, exports nearly doubled to 3,800 tons per year, and a large part of the crop went no longer to Mexico but to Spain. Cacao also became part of a growing contraband trade, with smuggling by the Dutch especially important because of their colony at nearby Curaçao and because of a growing market for cacao in Amsterdam. In fact, Dutch traders dared to establish semipermanent trading depots in Venezuela well upstream on some of the rivers.

Guayaquil cacao plantations came into being at about the same time as those of Venezuela, and soon were shipping to Peru, Central America, and Mexico. Hardy varieties, plentiful water, good soils, and high yields contributed to the production of inexpensive cacaos, and Guayaquil prices, despite long trade routes, were able to undercut those of Central America and even Venezuela. Unlike the plantations in Venezuela, where African slaves were employed, Guayaquil cacao was worked by local laborers, often native migrants from the *sierra*.

Central American growers complained about the flood of inexpensive Guayaquil beans, and the Spanish crown, alarmed that a growing trade between Peru and Mexico would threaten its export trade in European goods to America, prohibited all South American ports – including Guayaquil – from trading with Mexico. Again, contraband and fraud flourished. By 1700, Guayaquil's production rivaled or surpassed that of Venezuela. Later in the century, as free trade grew and faster ships became common, Guayaquil cacao began to reach Spain and other European markets, even though by the late eighteenth century, the region's plentiful exports were satisfying about three-quarters of the Mexican demand.

Amazonian cacao was slow to develop. This area of Brazil was neglected by Portugal and had few settlers. Lisbon was not a large market, and most of the trees, at least at first, were scattered in the forests. By the middle of the eighteenth century, however, Marañón cacao, worked mostly by African slaves, commanded a share of European markets.

Venezuelan cacao plantations spread to Trinidad, where the hybrid *trinitario* developed. Other parts of the circum-Caribbean, such as the coast of Costa Rica, Grenada, Martinique, and Saint-Domingue, also enjoyed ephemeral booms before production sank back, giving them only minor places in the Atlantic markets.

Changing Tastes and New Markets

The first Spaniards to encounter large stocks of cacao quickly realized (and exploited) its lucrative possibilities, especially in Mesoamerica. Their own taste for chocolate, however, developed more slowly. Native peoples sometimes added honey, but most of their recipes were bitter – even biting – to Spanish palates, especially when chilli peppers were added. English pirates, who were even less familiar with chocolate, burned or dumped the cargoes of cacao they captured. Sugar, introduced to the Americas by Spain and Portugal, helped to change minds, as did vanilla and other flavorings, although part of the story of Spanish and Portuguese acceptance of chocolate is also, no doubt, one of acculturation and acquired tastes. By the late sixteenth century, Europeans in the Americas were drinking sweet chocolate with great enthusiasm and had elaborated intricate and expensive containers, cups, and *molineros,* or beating sticks, as frothy chocolate was still favored. So pervasive was the habit of drinking hot chocolate among Creole women that at least one bishop had to forbid it during Mass. An Englishman from Jamaica was amazed at the Spaniards' craving for chocolate drinks, and claimed that they seemed unable to live without them (Hans Sloane manuscript 11.410, folio 321, British Library).

Cacao beans probably reached Europe as early as the 1520s, shortly after the conquest of Mexico, but it was late in the century before regular cargoes were shipped from Veracruz. At first, chocolate was an expensive drink, largely confined to the Spanish court and noble houses. From Spain, it soon spread to Italy and – via a royal marriage – to France, where Ana of Austria, daughter of Philip III, married the young Louis XIII. The next marriage between French and Spanish royalty was that of Louis XIV and the daughter of Philip IV of Spain, Maria Theresa, of whom it was said that her only passions were chocolate and His Majesty – probably in that order.

By the mid–seventeenth century, chocolate houses were common in Paris, although still patronized exclusively by the elite. They had also spread to London, where these establishments soon competed with coffee shops. During the life of Samuel Pepys, the English government official and well-known diarist, chocolate drinks passed from being a novelty to a regular luncheon beverage and a staple of public salons. The Dutch, who had captured Curaçao in 1634, began to send large cargoes of contraband Venezuelan cacao to Amsterdam, which became the great cacao mart of Europe. Ironically, by the late seventeenth century, even Spanish merchants had to buy there.

Chocolate, as a drink, is filling and quite nutritious, and so became popular among all classes in Catholic Europe, especially in the Mediterranean countries. But a problem arose: Was it to be considered a food or a beverage? Did the drinking of chocolate break a religious fast? In the 1660s, the Church decided that because wine – although nutritious – was considered a drink rather than a food, chocolate drinks would be treated the same way. Opinions differed as to chocolate's merits and failings, and these debates continue today. For reasons not yet understood, chocolate became a drink for women and coffee a drink for men in some parts of western Europe.

In the eighteenth century, chocolate was known throughout Europe, and further regional variations developed, as did cultural and fashionable attitudes toward it and its consumption. It was usually sold as a fairly solid paste or block, and already by the early part of the century, these commercial products contained vanilla, sugar, cloves, and other spices. About this time, some drinkers began to add milk or wine. Frothiness was still appreciated, and numerous recipes stipulated the amount of heating needed and the best way of whipping the chocolate to provide the ideal frappé.

The eating of solid chocolate, while still far behind the drink in popularity, also gained acceptance, often in the form of the so-called Spanish sticks. In France, small chocolate pastilles gained favor. Cacao butter, used since the sixteenth century as a cosmetic to improve the complexion, now became of some importance for elite cuisine.

In much of eighteenth-century Europe, chocolate remained an elite and rather expensive drink, sometimes considered a stimulant, or even an aphrodisiac (what exotic substance has not been so imagined?). In England, however, both coffee and chocolate houses lost their upper-class cachet in the second half of the century, and chocolate houses, in particular, came to be associated with raucous behavior, licentiousness, and marginal social groups. But even then, chocolate remained expensive; although American production had increased to supply the growing demand, it had not increased enough to lower the price significantly. Moreover, processing techniques had failed to adapt. In the middle years of the eighteenth century, cacao was grown, harvested, elaborated, and sold much as it had been by Native Americans before Europeans arrived in Mexico.

Some innovations did appear. For example, Joseph S. Fry, who founded a company in England in 1728 (which lasted into the late twentieth century), created factory conditions for the mass production of chocolate products for the English market. Others in England and on the continent followed, but radical transformations in many other areas of the chocolate trade had to wait until the nineteenth and twentieth centuries.

The Industrial, Commercial, and Supply Revolutions

The Dutchman Coenrad Johannes Van Houten was the first in a line of inventors and entrepreneurs who modernized the manufacture of chocolate. He sought a better method for extracting the cacao "butter" or fats from the beans. He had started a factory in Amsterdam in 1815 and was unhappy with the traditional method of boiling the chocolate and then skimming off the fats. By 1828, he had invented and patented a dry press, which left much less butter in the end product. Van Houten then treated this "cocoa" powder with alkaline salts to make it more adaptable to various kinds of mixes, and very quickly, many of the older methods of manufacturing yielded to cocoa. Some twenty years later, an early form of "instant" chocolate had become widely accepted, and about midcentury, Joseph Fry and his sons seized upon this new cocoa powder and began to market the first commercial chocolate bars.

The Van Houten innovation was, historically and gastronomically speaking, just in time. By 1800, chocolate drinks had fallen well behind competing alkaloid beverages. In the West coffee dominated almost everywhere and has remained in the lead to the present day – except in England, where coffee first defeated chocolate and was then, in turn, defeated by tea. Chocolate was to survive and flourish, however, by going its separate way and leaving the field of adult drinks to its competitors. Except in a few of the Mediterranean countries and in parts of Latin America, where chocolate drinks retained popularity, chocolate now became cocoa, heavily sugared and drunk mostly by children and invalids, or chocolate bars and wrapped candy, devoured by all ages and classes.

The early great British rivals of the Fry Company were the Cadburys and Rowntrees. It was the firm of Cadbury, which quickly became the leading British confectioner, that first emphasized the connection between boxes of chocolate and romance. Chocolates and cut flowers became tokens of romantic love and soon were the typical presents given to a woman. Sales of chocolate in boxes and specialty chocolates soared, and increase even more so today, especially on Valentine's Day, at Christmas time, and at Easter – the season for chocolate eggs.

After the breakthroughs of the Dutch and English pioneers, Swiss inventors and businessmen took over. François Louis Cailler and Phillipe Suchard opened modern factories in the 1820s. Henri Nestlé, a chemist who first elaborated powdered milk, and Daniel Peter combined their talents to produce milk-chocolate bars, and Rodolphe Lindt, yet another Swiss, invented a process by which cacao was made smoother to the palate, more homogenized, and of finer aroma. Lindt's "conching" process, which he began in 1879, radically changed the manufacture of chocolate, and his smooth chocolates soon replaced the rougher and grainier ones of the past. Swiss chocolate became the world standard for the chocolate bar, and such companies as Lindt and Nestlé are corporate giants today.

The country that was the scene for Henry Ford's genius now saw the rise of the great entrepreneur of chocolate manufacture and sale. Milton Hershey, like Ford, saw the great possibilities of economies of scale and uniformity in producing and mass marketing for the millions. A confectioner from his youth, Hershey became convinced after a journey to Europe that he should concentrate on chocolate. He built a model workers' town (named after himself) in Pennsylvania, on a much larger scale than those of Cadbury and Rowntree in England. To supply his huge chocolate factory, Hershey also transformed other landscapes: He boasted that the enormous dairy farms surrounding his town supplied 60,000 gallons of milk every working day. In Cuba, vast sugarcane estates were laid out east of Havana, complete with their own railroads and port terminals. (The Hershey empire in Cuba was later nationalized by the Castro government.) The Hershey Company was a model of modern manufacture and merchandising and soon controlled a giant share of the U.S. market.

In spite of mass manufacturers such as Cadbury and Hershey, producers of fine chocolates managed to retain a respectable and profitable share of the market, which has increased in recent years. High-quality chocolates, such as Godiva of Belgium and Valrhona of France, are known worldwide. Chocolate has entered the world of great cuisine, too. Profiteroles, chocolate cakes and pastries, mousses, and humble chocolate ice cream all have fanatical addicts.

Just as Hershey's chocolate for the masses created dairy farms and sugar plantations, it also led to the expansion of cacao production. Cacao has become a world commodity, grown in all tropical regions, and traded and speculated upon in the stock and futures markets of London, New York, Paris, and other financial hubs.

Venezuelan exports, which had seemed so well placed geographically and logistically to supply

European markets during the Spanish colonial years, began to decline around 1800. The wars of independence there were enormously destructive, and Venezuelan producers found themselves less able to hold their own against both old and new competitors. Nonetheless, although coffee replaced cacao as the country's main export after 1830, Venezuela retained a respectable place as a supplier of cacao until about 1900.

It was the Guayaquil plantations of Ecuador, however, that satisfied the largest part of the world's needs in the nineteenth century. The Panama Canal opened, and Ecuador was fortunate (or unfortunate) to have an abundant, inexpensive labor supply from the highlands, where the failure of the textile industry in the face of British competitive imports had sent waves of unemployed workers to the coast. Cacao was promoted by early leaders of the newly independent republic, including its first president, Juan José Flores (1800–64), himself an owner of large plantations. There was a plateau in production – caused by civil war and yellow fever – between 1840 and 1870, but then output again accelerated, reaching more than 20,000 tons per year by 1900. In the first decades of the twentieth century, however, Ecuador's predominance in cacao production finally yielded to two major factors. Witchbroom disease destroyed many of the plantings in the 1920s, and the 1930s saw depressed world prices. As a consequence, new areas in other parts of the world began to compete.

The first threat to Latin American producers and exporters came from islands off the west coast of Africa, where cacao had been introduced to São Tomé and Principe by the Portuguese. Development of the crop's products, however, suffered considerable delay because the islands continued to concentrate on coffee growing with slave labor until that industry suffered a crisis brought on by the abolition of slavery in 1875. Chocolate then took over, although working conditions on the cacao plantations were little better than those of slavery. By 1905, the two islands were the world's leading exporters of cacao beans.

This success aroused interest in the nearby mainland British colonies, although it was often the local people, rather than the colonial government, who developed the crop. By the 1920s, the Gold Coast (now Ghana) led the world in output, and Africa had passed America in cacao exports. The growth in demand during the first 40 years of this century was astonishing. World trade in the commodity went from about 100,000 tons in 1900 to 786,000 tons in 1939, a growth of nearly 800 percent! Nigeria and the Ivory Coast were now rivals of the Gold Coast in cacao production, and other colonies, such as Gabon and the Belgian Congo, were becoming exporters. By the 1990s, the Ivory Coast was the world's leading producer.

Nonetheless, West Africa was losing its dominant position. It produced three-quarters of the world's cacao in 1960, but just over half by the 1990s. Latin American plantings began to revive somewhat, especially on new establishments around Bahia, but the latest rival areas were in Indonesia, and, above all, Malaysia, which by the early 1990s was the world's fourth leading producer of cacao, with annual exports of about 220,000 tons.

The world market in cacao remained impressive at about 2,500,000 tons per year in the 1990s, but that amount was much less than half of the total for coffee and represented just over 2 percent of the world trade in sugar. A constant problem with cacao has been a lack of price stability. Prices have fluctuated widely since World War II, and stabilization agreements have had little success. The United States is by far the leading consumer of cacao, followed by western Europe, Russia, and Japan. Per capita consumption in the United States and western Europe has doubled since 1945. The Swiss eat the most chocolate, followed by the British. The Norwegians and Austrians lead the world as drinkers of chocolate.

To what does chocolate owe its success? It is, for one thing, a well-rounded food, containing glucose, lipids, and proteins. It also provides significant quantities of important minerals, such as potassium and calcium. Of course, such additives as milk and sugar bring other qualities and calories. Cacao contains several stimulants, led by theobromine, then caffeine and serotonin.

Debates based on more impressionistic evidence have raged. Chocolate was long ago accused of being a cause of juvenile acne, but this now appears to be untrue. The argument that chocolate can elevate cholesterol levels has not yet been resolved. Is chocolate addictive? "Chocoholics" would certainly answer in the affirmative. So, we suppose, would the native peoples of sixteenth-century Mesoamerica. Recently, researchers reported that cacao consumption stimulates a mild, marijuanalike effect, reducing stress and encouraging a harmless euphoria. Debates and research continue, and meanwhile, the product's market range expands. Attempts to find substitutes enjoy little success, and the "food of the gods" continues to delight the millions.

Murdo J. MacLeod

Bibliography

Alden, Dauril. 1976. *The significance of cacao production in the Amazon region during the late colonial period: An essay in comparative economic history.* Philadelphia, Pa.

Assoumou, Jean. 1977. *L'économie du cacao.* Paris.

Bergman, James L. 1969. The distribution of cacao cultivation in pre-Columbian America. *Annals of the Association of American Geographers* 59: 85–96.

Chiriboga, Manuel. 1980. *Jornaleros y gran propietarios en 135 años de exportación cacaotera, 1790-1925.* Quito.

Coady, Chantal. 1995. *The chocolate companion: A connoisseur's guide to the world's finest chocolates.* New York.

Coe, Sophie D., and Michael D. Coe. 1996. *The true history of chocolate.* New York.

Fuller, Linda K. 1994. *Chocolate fads, folklore and fantasies: 1000+ chunks of chocolate.* New York.

Harwich, Nikita. 1992. *Histoire du chocolat.* Paris.

Piñero, Eugenio. 1994. *The town of San Felipe and colonial cacao economies.* Philadelphia, Pa.

Young, Allen M. 1994. *The chocolate tree. A natural history of cacao.* Washington, D.C.

III.4 ❧ Coffee

Coffee is a tree or bush that originated in Africa. It was first domesticated in Arabia, and massively consumed in Europe and North America. Later grown in Asia and Latin America, coffee, more than any other crop, has tied together the rich and the poor. Originally a luxury, coffee has become a necessity for consumer and producer alike and, in terms of value, is one of the leading internationally traded commodities today and probably has been the most important internationally traded agricultural product in history.

Coffee, however, has also been one of the most contradictory and controversial of crops. It has linked the religious and the secular, the archaic and the bourgeois, the proletarian and the intellectual, the enslaved and the free, the laborer and the dilettante. It has been accused of destroying societies, of perpetuating vice, and of undermining developing economies.

Origins

The first human consumption of coffee has been obscured by time. But legends abound, such as that of a ninth century A.D. Ethiopian goatherd who tasted the bitter berries that left his flock animated, or about Arab traders, and even Christian monks, who first recognized the virtues of coffee. *Coffea arabica* first appeared natively in Ethiopia, yet the berries went largely ignored before Arabs in Yemen used them to brew a drink. Although some Africans drank coffee made from fresh berries, others roasted it with melted butter, and in a few regions it was chewed without any preparation. However, no extensive local traditions of arabica berry usage developed (see Ukers 1948; Uribe 1954), and consequently, coffee became an exotic crop, growing far from its original home. Indeed, it was only in the twentieth century that African coffee production became substantial.

The mystical Shadhili Sufi, to the east of Ethiopia in Yemen, seem to have been among the first to embrace this wandering crop. They sought elixirs to produce visions granting access to the Godhead, and they also wished to remain awake during their long nighttime chanting rituals, in which they attempted to enter an ecstatic trance. Thus, from the beginning, coffee was employed as both a drug and a social drink. Early accounts, however, speak much more of its physical effects than its taste or efficacy in quenching thirst. A sheikh of the Sufi order who lived in the port town of Mocca in the late fourteenth or early fifteenth century may have been the first to devise a technique for roasting, grinding, and brewing coffee beans.

It was in the mountains of northern Yemen that the arabica was first domesticated, and for two and a half centuries Yemen held a virtual world monopoly on coffee production. But it is interesting to note that in Yemen, many preferred to chew the beans or brew a tea with the husk of *Coffea arabica*, rather than use the beans, and to this day Yemenis do not drink much coffee. They prefer tea or chewing a shrub, *khat*, which not only fills coffee's social role but occupies much of the land suitable for coffee cultivation.

By 1500, the beverage had become widespread on the Arabian peninsula (Hattox 1985; Wenner 1991), with the Sufi probably responsible for spreading coffee drinking to Cairo, Damascus, and Mecca. The drink had been integrated into Sufi rituals, and other Muslims also adopted it into their worship. In Cairo, coffee drinking was concentrated in the square by the mosque. By 1510, we have reports of people drinking coffee in Mecca's Sacred Mosque itself.

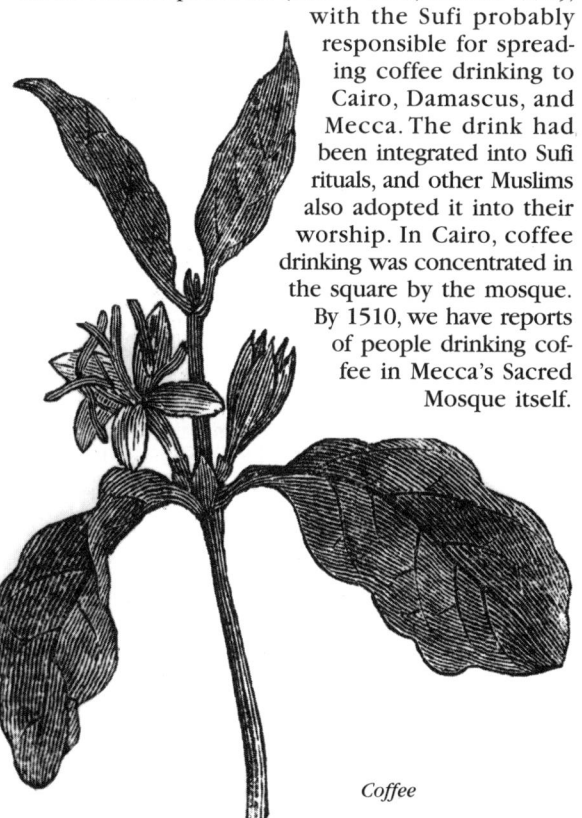

Coffee

The beverage became associated with Mohammed's birthday and was commonly drunk at night during the monthlong fast of Ramadan. Indeed, various legends ascribed coffee's origins to Mohammed, who, through the Archangel Gabriel, gave it to the world to replace the wine that Islam forbade. Certainly, Muslims were instrumental in spreading the beverage throughout the Islamic world as far as India and Indonesia, as the religious brought beans back from their pilgrimages to Mecca (Becker, Hoehfeld, and Kopp 1979).

Coffee was also intimately related to the growth of secular society. The Sufi were not full-time mystics, and as ordinary tradespeople during the day, they spread their taste for the drink to the business world. Its name probably comes from the Arabic *qahwah* – an epithet for "wine" – indicating a replacement of the forbidden alcoholic beverage. Indeed, although coffee grows wild in the region of Ethiopia known as Kaffa, the place is not the origin of its name, just as the coffee "bean" is not a bean but more like a cherry pit. Its name is a corruption of the Arabic for the arabica plant, *bunn.*

As already noted, the thick, dark, hot beverage became popular probably more because of its physical effects and the sociability it encouraged than because of its taste, although its reputed medicinal properties, said to cure mange, may have increased its appeal. But despite the fact that sugar had been grown in the Middle East for hundreds of years before coffee's arrival, it was not added to the brew. Neither was milk, which was blamed for causing leprosy when combined with *qahwah.* In fact, cardamom was the only spice added with any frequency, although in some disreputable quarters, opium and hashish apparently were also stirred in. The fact that coffee grounds must have boiling water poured over them to impart their flavor probably added to the drink's attractiveness. In an era before safe water supplies, boiling was the one sure method of insuring purity.

Probably the technology of coffee making – roasting and grinding the beans and boiling water – caused the beverage, more than almost any other commodity, to be associated with a site. The café was born in the Middle East, and in many cultures that subsequently adopted the beverage, the word for the site and the beverage became the same. R. Hattox (1985) suggests that early merchants, such as two Syrians who introduced coffee from Egypt to Istanbul in 1555, used the coffeehouse as a marketing device. To acquaint new consumers with the beverage, it had to be presented to them hot and correctly brewed. Consequently, these Syrian merchants and many others from the Levant who opened cafés found, in the process, an unoccupied niche in Middle Eastern society. Restaurants were almost unknown, and taverns were forbidden to Muslims. Hence, coffeehouses became one of the few secular public places in Muslim lands where men could congregate with other nonfamily members.

Cafés offered one of the only social possibilities for nightlife. They were an inexpensive place to offer friends entertainment and hospitality, playing an important role in the commodification of what previously had been largely private, domestic functions. Men read, listened to stories and music, watched puppet shows, played backgammon and chess, gambled, and sometimes solicited prostitutes. Such an ambience also led to conversations on forbidden subjects.

The cafés catered to a wide range of clients, sometimes mixing men of various classes. Although some cafés were little more than stalls in the marketplace, others were virtual pleasure palaces. Said the French traveler Philippe Dufour in 1685: "All the cafes of Damascus are beautiful – many fountains, nearby rivers, in tree-shaded spots with roses and other flowers" (Hattox 1985: 81). But because coffeehouses in Cairo, Istanbul, Damascus, and Algiers quickly became centers of political intrigue and fleshly vice (Carlier 1990), government officials soon reacted, and as early as 1511, they burned bags of coffee in the streets of Mecca.

Although some medical authorities claimed that the arabica's cold and dry humors created melancholy and, more seriously, transgressed the laws of Islam by intoxicating its users, these arguments never carried much weight. It was the politically subversive possibilities of the coffeehouse that most worried Middle Eastern rulers. Thus, the Turkish grand vizier was sufficiently concerned about the political effects of the 600 coffeehouses in Istanbul that he decreed that the punishment for operating a coffeehouse was cudgeling; for a second offense, the perpetrator was sewn into a leather bag and thrown into the Bosporus.

Even these draconian measures proved ineffectual, however, and Turkish coffee became famous as the generic name for a certain thick brew in which the grinds were mixed directly into boiling water in small increments, often 10 to 12 times. The Middle East and Southeast Asia were the world's principal coffee drinking areas until roughly the middle of the eighteenth century. But ironically, today the Turks produce and consume virtually no coffee.

European Consumption

The increasing popularity of coffee in seventeenth-century Europe paralleled the emergence of commercial capitalism. The Middle Eastern bean, fostered by the ascetic Sufi to free themselves from worldly matters, evolved into a Western capitalist commodity. Coffee reached Europe via trade, diplomacy, war, and immigration. Venetian traders, with their command of Mediterranean commerce, introduced it into southern Europe. The Dutch, who superseded them in the Orient, were even more important in spreading the arabica.

At first, coffee was regarded in Europe as a medicinal drug that could cure sore eyes, dropsy, gout, and scurvy. Its social role and prestige, however, were considerably enhanced in 1665 and 1666 by the arrival in France of emissaries of the Ottoman sultan who poured the exotic liquor for their aristocratic European guests during extravagant soirees (Leclant 1979; Heise 1987).

According to Austrian lore, coffee first became a drink Europeans found palatable when bags of it were left behind by the Ottoman Turks after their 1683 siege of Vienna failed to break the Austrians' spirit. These spoils of war not only uplifted Viennese spirits but also helped transform coffee from medicine into a leisure drink when the owner of the first Viennese coffeehouse, Georg Kolshitsky, thought to remove the sediment from Turkish coffee and add honey and milk. Elsewhere in Europe, Armenians, Greeks, Lebanese, and other Christian traders from the Levant spread knowledge of the beverage. Southern and central Europeans devised many of the most popular ways of brewing, roasting, and mixing coffee: Espresso, cappuccino, café au lait, and French and Vienna roasts are still familiar terms today.

Yet it was the northern Europeans who became the greatest consumers. In England, coffee was closely tied to the academic community from the beginning: The country's first coffeehouse seems to have been one opened in Oxford in 1637 by a Greek merchant. But soon London merchants were also imbibing the potion in coffeehouses, such as Jonathan's and Garraway's (which served for three-quarters of a century as England's main stock exchanges), the Virginia, the Baltic (which doubled as the mercantile shipping exchange), and Lloyd's Café (which became the world's largest insurance company). In addition to serving as commercial houses and office buildings, coffeehouses became "penny universities" that disseminated the latest news, reading libraries, and the first men's clubs.

Such social areas outside of the home and the court helped stimulate business but also outraged wives. They resented their husbands' addiction to the dark, noisy coffeehouses and the black and nauseous liquid that allegedly caused impotence. Their complaint, which was echoed in other corners of Europe, was in striking contrast to the mullahs' fears that coffee stimulated carnal desires. Charles II, concerned more with café patrons' political discussions than their familial responsibilities, tried unsuccessfully to close down the coffeehouses. It would take the rise of the East India Company, the Indian colonies, and high taxes on coffee to convert Britain to a tea-consuming country (Ellis 1956; Bramah 1972).

On the Continent, cafés symbolized and served the beneficiaries of capitalist prosperity who constituted the new leisure class, although debates continued to rage over the brew's medicinal properties. In the best scientific tradition, Sweden's Gustav III reputedly commuted the death sentences of twin brothers convicted of murder on the condition that one be given only tea to drink and the other coffee. The tea drinker died first – at age 83 – and Sweden became the world's most ardent coffee-consuming nation, with its citizens drinking five cups per person per day by 1975. In 1992, most of the 10 leading coffee-consuming nations on a per capita basis were still in northern Europe: The 10 were (in order) Finland, Sweden, Denmark, Norway, Netherlands, Switzerland, Austria, Germany, France, and Belgium (United States Department of Agriculture 1993).

The eighteenth-century mercantilist policies of tax-hungry kings posed another kind of threat to coffee drinkers. Frederick the Great, for example, was less open-minded than King Gustav and less concerned with his subjects' health than with their political proclivities and the balance of trade. He consequently sought to prevent commoners from drinking the brew by making it a royal monopoly. Although he failed, the high import duties in the seventeenth and eighteenth centuries restricted consumption to the relatively affluent in major cities. The same was true in France and Austria (Heise 1987) and in Switzerland, between 1756 and 1822, there were five different decrees prohibiting coffee importation.

Cafés prospered in the capitals, however. Their great popularity in Paris served to distinguish the elite from their social inferiors, who bought their coffee in the marketplace. The coffeehouse denizens constituted an elite of achievement, a bourgeois elite. Coffee's great virtue, in contradistinction to alcohol, was that it stimulated the body while clearing the mind. Intellectuals now had discussions rather than orgies, and some coffeehouses, such as the Procope in Paris, served as centers of intellectual and artistic life where such men as Voltaire skewered aristocratic foibles.

The Café Heinrichhof in Vienna inspired Johannes Brahms and other great composers, as well as merchants who preferred the sound of money. Other coffeehouses (such as this author's grandmother's Café Mozart in Vienna) hosted cards and billiards and other such less-inspired diversions. The leisure of the coffeehouse was serious business.

Coffeehouses were also intimately involved in the birth of civil society and the democratization of semifeudal aristocracies. Thus, it was in Paris's Café Foy that on July 13, 1789, Camille Desmoulins planned the assault on the Bastille that ushered in a new political age (Oliveira 1984). It is perhaps ironic that his action would also set into motion events that destroyed the coffee plantations of the world's greatest coffee producer, the French colony of St. Domingue (today Haiti).

Coffeehouses continued to be associated with subversion in the nineteenth century. Preparations for the 1848 revolutions were made in the coffeehouses of Berlin, Budapest, and Venice. In France, one of the first responses to threatened revolt was to close down the cafés (Barrows 1991). Ulla Heise (1987) argues, however, that although émigrés continued to plot in cafés after 1850, the coffeehouses lost their revolutionary association. Revolution became more proletarian, and workers tended to frequent taverns, bars, and winehouses. S. Barrows, on the other hand, credits the declining political radicalism of the coffee-houses to the rise of newspapers, music halls, and other places for association.

If coffee in Europe was a part of the middle class's struggle for democracy, coffee itself became increasingly democratized. Although taxes kept the price high, coffee became the breakfast beverage of choice for the Continent's urban working class. To compensate for the high prices, the poor often drank coffee substitutes rather than the arabica (in Germany, *Kaffee* can refer to any number of beverages; the arabica or robusta is called *Bohnenkaffee*).

United States Consumption

As clanging factories gave birth to the industrial age, coffee came to represent labor as well as leisure. North American thirst was instrumental in making coffee a mass consumer product, a drug to prop up the drooping eyelids and awaken the flagging consciousness of an army of laborers. But this could occur only after they had abandoned tea. The citizens of the original 13 British colonies were tea drinkers, in part at least because British taxation and transport policies had made the arabica inaccessible to all but the rich. There were a few coffeehouses, such as Boston's Green Dragon, which Daniel Webster called the "headquarters of the revolution," and The Merchant's Coffeehouse in New York, also associated with the independence movement. But the taverns – which doubled as courtrooms and public meeting halls – were by far the favorite drinking spots in colonial times, although even those were little frequented because of the rural (and in places puritanical) nature of settlements.

United States coffee consumption in 1783 was only one-eighteenth of a pound per capita a year. By the 1830s, however, North Americans had cast aside tea for coffee, and by midcentury they were each drinking more than five pounds a year. Although the 1765 Stamp Act and the Boston Tea Party certainly dampened enthusiasm for tea, commerce and demography were probably more responsible for transforming the United States into the world's greatest coffee market. Resistance to the British East India Company was bolstered by the proximity of the French coffee-producing colonies of St. Domingue (Haiti) and Martinique and, later, Portuguese Brazil.

After independence, Americans were free to trade with these colonies, supplying them with slaves and naval stores in exchange for coffee. Thus, New England merchants introduced coffee into North America in relatively large volume. The price of coffee fell from 18 shillings per pound in 1683 to 9 shillings in 1774 to just 1 shilling in 1783. Such lower prices naturally expanded demand, and government policy further aided the transformation as import taxes on the beans were first lowered and then abolished in 1832. Resumed during the Civil War, they were definitively abolished in 1872.

The absence of a coffeehouse culture in the United States meant that the beverage's popularity was not associated with political subversion as it was in the Middle East and Europe, and its consumption could be encouraged with no political danger. The flood of northern European immigrants from coffee-drinking countries probably also contributed to the shift from tea. Soon coffee drinking became entrenched as a social institution, and annual per capita consumption ballooned from under one pound at independence to nine pounds by 1882.

Nonetheless, it took time for the coffee trade in the United States to become institutionalized. It was originally specialized and artisanal; U.S. importers became involved only after the green beans reached New York. There, they sold them to wholesalers who, in turn, peddled them to thousands of retailers. As in Europe, there was no brand identity early on, with each grocer selling his own blends. But to a much greater extent than Europeans with their cafés, nineteenth-century North Americans bought beans in bulk at the grocers and roasted them at home.

This habit gave the housewife discretion over coffee purchases. Unlike her British sisters, who denounced coffee because of coffeehouses, the North American wife was the one who bought coffee; and brewing a good cup of coffee was often a measure of wifely abilities as a "homemaker." Consequently, in contrast to the customs in the Middle East or Europe, coffee merchandising in the United States became much more oriented to women than men. Arbuckle's 1872 advertisement, the first handbill in color for coffee, shows two women by the kitchen stove, the first complaining "Oh, I have burnt my coffee again," and the second counseling "Buy Arbuckle's Roasted, as I do, and you will have no trouble" (Ukers 1935: 451).

In fact, because so much coffee was purchased at the grocery store, where product differentiation was accentuated (rather than at the café where there was much less variety and brand was not displayed), coffee brand identification first arose in the United States. This was achieved through great efforts to create brand loyalty, although instead of market segmentation and differentiation, there was a tendency toward homogenization.

Today, to attract women to its brands, General Foods, one of the largest coffee merchandisers in the world, brings together hundreds of women in focus groups each year and sends out thousands of questionnaires. The coffee market is still female-oriented in the United States, as is demonstrated by the tendency to employ women in televised coffee advertisements.

Before brand loyalty, however, there came new technology to improve the quality and marketing of coffee. In the nineteenth century, because of fairly primitive transportation and packaging techniques, the quality of coffee once it reached a Cincinnati or an Omaha was fairly poor. Consequently, consumers in such areas had a different idea of how coffee should taste than consumers do today. Some brewed it with an egg to give the drink a rich yellow color. It was also popular to add the uncooked skin of a mild codfish to the pot. In the western states, coffee was put in a saucepan and simmered for two to three hours and reheated as necessary. Mass-consumed coffee was not necessarily good coffee, but the cowboy huddled around the campfire was not a demanding gourmet. Under these conditions, it is not surprising that importers were slow to improve the quality of the coffee they sold. Roasted coffee could not be widely marketed because it lost its taste, and ground roasted beans lost flavor much more quickly. The green bean, on the other hand, could be stored for months or years without harm.

The demand for improved and standardized coffee probably derived in large part from improved transportation, roasting, grinding, and brewing technologies. Although green beans traveled well, they were frequently damaged during long sea voyages aboard sailing ships. Merchant efforts to dye damaged beans with rust, or indigo, or beef blood, or to glaze them with eggs improved their appearance, but not their flavor. Nor did the practice of roasting impaired beans with cinnamon, cloves, cocoa, and onions help much. In addition, coffee grinders did not have sufficiently sharp blades to grind the beans finely, and using mortar and pestle was a laborious business. Consequently, grinds had to remain in contact with water longer to impart their flavor, which had the drawback of creating a bitter brew: Tannin, which causes the bitter taste, begins to be extracted from the grinds about 45 seconds after contact with hot water. And finally, coffeepots were primitive. Before the invention in 1800 of a kind of percolator with a built-in filter, most people simply threw grounds into water, much as with tea.

Many of these difficulties in brewing good coffee were resolved somewhat in the nineteenth century. Railroads sped coffee from the fields to ports where the rapid and relatively large steamships that replaced sailing ships spared the green beans ocean damage. Improved control was achieved over oven temperatures, allowing for more regular roasting by, for example, the spherical roaster invented by an Austrian, Max Bode, in 1851, and the pull-out roaster produced by a New Yorker, Jabez Burns, in 1864. Better grinders, producing finer and more even grounds, were also invented, and a welter of coffeepots were mass-produced. The first predictable pumping percolator, patented in France in 1827, became the most popular North American pot in the first half of the twentieth century. Drip pots were improved with the invention of the disposable filter in 1907 (the prototype, which

was cut from an ink blotter, was a considerable improvement over the previous horsehair filters). These pots were more popular in Europe, as was the espresso pot, first designed in 1837. Such pots were true monuments to the industrial age with its drawbacks and its charms. Espresso pots sometimes exploded. But if they did not, they could do a host of other things (Bersten 1993). One pressure pot also boiled eggs. The Armstong Perc-O-Toaster toasted bread and baked waffles while it perked coffee (Panati 1987).

Improvements in technology led to standardization, and eventually, to a wholesaling oligopoly in the United States. Whereas the French concentrated on devising new pots to improve the quality of brewing for the refined palate, North Americans focused on roasting, packaging, and marketing to reach the mass market. The first packaged roasted coffee was "Osborn's Celebrated Prepared Java Coffee," which appeared in 1860. The first brand to enjoy a national market was "Arbuckle's Ariosa," beginning in 1873. Sales of packaged coffees, however, were slow to replace those of green coffee beans until 1900, when Edwin Norton invented vacuum packing, which allowed roasted, ground coffee to retain its flavor. In 1903, Hills Brothers was the first company to commercially employ the process (Ukers 1935; Uribe 1954).

The ability to preserve roasted coffee in vacuum packages allowed a few national brands to dominate the trade in the United States. (Europeans were much slower to buy canned coffee, preferring beans and cafés). North American firms began to integrate vertically, with the A & P grocery chain in the forefront, even to the extent of stationing buying agents in the interior of Brazil, as well as importing, roasting, packing, and retailing its own brand. Still, many smaller brands and wholesale grocers persisted. In 1923 there were 1,500 roasters and 4,000 wholesale coffee grocers in the United States (Ukers 1930).

The market power of a relatively small number of powerful wholesalers combined with U.S. government policy to create standardization. Since its inception, the wholesale market had been completely unregulated and subject to rampant speculation and fraud. Many traders mixed together a number of coffee qualities, adulterated the mix with chicory and grains, and then called it "Mocca" or "Java." (The name "mocca" derived from Yemen's main port and stood for authentic coffee, not a combination of chocolate and coffee as it does today.) In the 1860s, a typical 122-pound bag of "Java" coffee arrived from Jamaica with about 5 pounds of sticks and stones added to it.

The freewheeling coffee market began to change in 1874 when a submarine cable tied South America to New York and London by telegraph. Information about prices and demand and supply became internationally homogeneous. The establishment, in 1882, of the New York Coffee Exchange, which was instituted to prevent commercial corners from driving up prices (as had happened in 1880), institutionalized access to information, and Le Havre, Hamburg, and London followed with their own major coffee exchanges. Prices and grades thereby became more generalized, and coffee became more purely a commodity as well, in the sense that coffee shipments were now bought and sold on the market floor without the buyer actually seeing the lot in question.

Until the early twentieth century, professionals would judge a sample bean's quality on its color, size, shape, and shine. Later, taste tests were instituted to check aroma, body, bitterness, and richness. Coffees became commodities possessing a bundle of specific, graded attributes. Indeed, with the advent of futures, buyers purchased coffee not yet blossoming on distant trees. By 1880, merchants were already buying an idea, rather than palpable beans: In that year there were 61 million bags bought and sold on the Hamburg futures market when the entire world harvest was less than 7 million bags!

Grinding did not become standardized until 1948 when the National Bureau of Standards of the Department of Commerce issued guidelines for three categories of grind – regular, drip, and fine – which most U.S. producers still follow. Much earlier, however, the Pure Food and Drug Act had decreed in 1907 that imported coffee be marked according to its port of exit. Thus "Santos" became a specific type of coffee, as did "Java" or "Mocca." There were more than a hundred different types of coffee imported into the United States, representing the greatest variety in the world. Importers were now less able to adulterate and defraud buyers.

The buyers, in turn, became more conscious of the quality of their coffee as they were able to buy professionally and uniformly roasted beans. The almost 4 million pamphlets issued by the National Coffee Roasters' Association at the beginning of the twentieth century in a campaign to educate housewives in proper brewing techniques apparently paid dividends. North American per capita consumption almost doubled between 1880 and 1920 to 16 pounds per capita. The growth of cities and factories accelerated the trend. No longer primarily the beverage of spiritual contemplation, commerce, or leisure, coffee became the alarm clock that marked industrial time. North American coffee imports swelled almost ninetyfold in the nineteenth century.

Temperance societies in the United States and Europe began to promote coffee and coffeehouses as the antidote to the alcoholism of the saloon, which was quite an ironic shift from the Islamic mullahs' fear of the brew's intoxicating effects. A sign in one Christian café read: "Coffee-house – God's house; Brandy shop – Devil's drop" (Heise 1987: 227). But there seems to have been no close relationship between coffee and alcohol. Coffee consumption did not suddenly increase in the United States with the onset of Prohibition, nor did consumption sharply drop with the relegalization of alcohol.

In another ironic twist, at the same time that the prohibitionists were singing coffee's praises, makers of cereal-based beverages launched an expensive attack on coffee's harmful properties. Coffee producers responded with an even more expensive defense of their drink. These mass-media campaigns encouraged the oligopolization of the market, and in 1933 just two companies, Standard Brands and General Foods, accounted for half of coffee's $6 million outlay to advertise coffee on the radio.

Despite the "many bugaboos raised by the cereal sinners," coffee became increasingly linked to sociability as ever more was drunk in public places (Ukers 1935: 477). The twentieth century saw the rise of the coffee shop and the cafeteria. Workers, especially white-collar workers needing to pause from their labor and socialize with their colleagues, took coffee breaks. Indeed, the beverage became embedded in popular speech. "Let's have a cup of coffee" came to mean "let's have a conversation."

Restaurants began using coffee to attract customers by keeping the price low and offering unlimited refills. (Iced tea was the only other beverage to be given this privileged status until the recent inclusion of soft drinks). Grocery stores often employed coffee as a loss leader to bring in shoppers, and when in the middle 1970s prices rose steeply, many grocers absorbed the higher price rather than alienate their customers. Because of its strong connection with sociability, its tendency to addict consumers, the medicinal effect of its caffeine, and the small number of substitutes, coffee has come to be viewed as a necessity more than almost any other food or beverage (Lucier 1988; Oldenburg 1989).

The growth of the vast U.S. market for coffee and the beverage's privileged social function led to the expansion both vertically and horizontally of a few companies creating an oligopoly. Today three companies – General Foods, Proctor and Gamble, and Nestlé (which also dominates much of the international market) – are responsible for 80 percent of the U.S. coffee market. They spend hundreds of millions of dollars a year to promote their brands, yet paradoxically, the price and profit levels of coffee remain low, despite the drink's status as a necessity, even a drug, for which the taste is perhaps less important than the effect it produces and the price it commands.

In recent years, however, specialty coffee beans, sold mostly by small companies and cafés, have challenged the conventional wisdom that North American consumers are unwilling to pay a high price for good coffee. Gourmet coffees, offered by creators who stress their national origins, the roast employed, and sometimes the flavorings added, have collectively become the only sector of the U.S. coffee market that is growing. They tend to appeal to younger, more affluent buyers for whom gourmet coffee is more a status symbol or a declaration of one's lifestyle than it is a necessity.

Yet even before the rise in the popularity of gourmet coffee, roasters had sought ways of expanding the mass market. After many attempts, the first commercially successful dried coffee was produced in 1906 by a North American chemist residing in Guatemala. But it attracted few drinkers until World War II when it was included in soldiers' rations, and since that time the market for instant coffee has grown substantially. By the 1960s, as much as one-third of home-prepared coffee was instant soluble. Its ease of preparation helped expand consumption but undermined quality because instant coffee utilizes mostly robusta coffee, which is a faster-growing but more bitter species than the arabica. As with gourmet beans, since the 1980s there has been a trend toward adding other flavorings to soluble coffee to produce specialty drinks that resemble, to name a few, Irish coffee or cappuccino.

Another major innovation has been decaffeinated coffee. It was developed in Germany at the beginning of the twentieth century by Ludwig Roselius, a sworn enemy of caffeine, which he blamed for his father's death. In Roselius's original process, green coffee was steamed and then soaked in a chlorinated organic solvent. Other processes have subsequently been developed, some involving the breeding of coffee trees with low caffeine yields. As coffee has come under attack for contributing to cardiac problems, decaffeinated consumption has soared.

The medical community is divided on the effects of coffee drinking. There are certainly beneficial effects, and the brew is sometimes prescribed in the treatment of barbiturate poisoning, migraines, chronic asthma, and autism in children. That heart ailments may be a negative effect is strongly debated, with each side marshaling impressive evidence. It seems clear that coffee's physical effects vary greatly, depending on the consumer. One study has concluded that for about 14 percent of the population, caffeine dependence produces a physical addiction similar to an addiction to alcohol or cocaine.

Such controversy over the ill effects of coffee helped drive down per capita consumption in the United States from its peak of 3.2 cups per day in the 1960s to 1.8 cups in 1993. Still, health concerns alone cannot explain this retreat because consumption of two other beverages with caffeine – soft drinks and tea – has grown since 1970, with soft drinks more than doubling in per capita consumption to reach almost 40 percent of all beverages consumed. By contrast, milk consumption has declined and that of juices has remained flat (United States Department of Agriculture 1993). No doubt advertising and packaging have had a substantial impact, and it is the case that soft drinks and bottled water (another rapidly growing beverage) require no preparation.

Numerous coffee companies rose to the challenge to compete directly with soft drinks by creating new products, such as prebrewed coffee, bottled iced coffee, and iced cappuccino. This seemed to be the logical terminus of a century-long process in which the activities of roasting, grinding, and brewing, formerly done in the home, became industrialized.

Yet there is a countertrend as well in the growing gourmet market. The swelling army of connoisseurs who want to make American coffee "a national honor," to borrow the words of coffee expert W. Ukers written decades ago (1935; 570), rather than a "national disgrace" are buying a great variety of specialty roasted beans and grinding them at home. Specialty coffeepots and espresso makers also constitute a booming market.

Coffee Drinking in the World

In other parts of the world, the popularity of coffee is at least being sustained or is on the increase. Coffee-producing countries have increased their share of consumption from less than 10 percent of production at the end of the nineteenth century to about one-quarter by the end of the twentieth century. Among coffee growers, Costa Ricans have the greatest taste for their own beans, and Brazilians are second. But even in these nations, per capita consumption is well under one-half that of northern European countries. Africans, except for Ethiopians, consume almost none of the beans they produce. Coffee is still very much a commodity consumed in rich countries and produced by poor ones, and per capita consumption is closely correlated to the wealth of consuming nations. It is also negatively correlated to an ability to grow arabica bushes or to historic ties to the trade (United States Department of Agriculture 1993). Few of the countries earliest involved in coffee's history – Yemen, Turkey, Indonesia, Haiti, or Martinique – are significant consumers, and in Europe, those with the oldest ties to the coffee trade – Greece, Portugal, Italy, and the United Kingdom – are among the lowest consumers. On the other hand, countries in Asia with no historic connection with the arabica – Japan, Korea, and Singapore – are rapidly increasing per capita coffee drinking as incomes climb. In 1992, Japan was the fourth largest coffee importer in the world. In mainland China, the arabica is making inroads not as a proletarian beverage but as a bourgeois one.

Worldwide, the human race drank about 380 billion cups of coffee in 1991[1] or about 76 cups for each man, woman, and child on the planet. Clearly, the exotic drink that Yemenis first tasted nearly 600 years ago has assumed a position of some considerable global importance.

Production in Arabia

Despite the fact that *Coffea arabica* grew wild in Ethiopia and *Coffea robusta* appeared naturally in the Congo, Yemen had a virtual world monopoly on production for about half of coffee's 600 years of lifetime as a commodity. Stern measures were taken to prevent the smuggling out of coffee plants, and although this move was not entirely successful – there are reports of coffee growing on India's Malabar coast and perhaps Ceylon in the sixteenth century – Yemen's grip remained firm until the middle of the eighteenth century. In the early part of that century, Yemen may have been producing some 20 million pounds a year (Raymond 1973–4; Becker et al. 1979).

The beans were grown in small, irrigated mountain gardens in various small, broken areas of northern Yemen, then transported by camel either to port or across the deserts (Daum 1988). The entire crop was consumed in the Middle East and Southwest Asia until the middle of the seventeenth century, and even thereafter, the East remained the main market for another hundred years.

Europeans initially purchased Yemen's coffee through Arabian traders. The Dutch and British East India Companies eventually established factors in Mocca, but they still exercised no control over production and had to make purchases with gold and silver because the Arabs much preferred Asian trade goods to European products. Another drawback was that such wealth attracted pirates, often based in Madagascar. Not satisfied with this precarious trade in a product whose value was growing vertiginously, the Europeans smuggled out coffee plants to begin production elsewhere. This decision ultimately spread the Arabian bean to more than 100 countries on 4 continents. Yemen soon became an inconsequential coffee producer, and the thriving coffee port of Mocca, which probably had more than 30,000 inhabitants at its height, dwindled to 400 stragglers living amidst its ruins in 1901.

Production in Asia

More than any other commodity, coffee was produced in poor colonies and countries for the enjoyment of those in rich countries. But, as we have seen, the Europeans who created coffee colonies (the Dutch, British, French, and Portuguese) were not the ones who consumed the most coffee on a per capita basis. Coffee was not only an export crop but a reexport crop.

In 1690, the Dutch introduced the coffee bush to Java, where their colonial might was soon employed to force peasants to labor on coffee plantations. Others were compelled to grow trees on village lands and give over shares or to sell at fixed low prices to government agents. Although clearly a coercive system, it relied on traditional local power relations and peasant agriculture to extract profit. Technology was primitive and yields low. But costs, for the Dutch, were even lower; so profits were high. The Javanese, however, experienced little capital accumulation or economic development (Kok 1864; Geertz 1971). A different

kind of labor system was employed on the tiny island of Bourbon (renamed Reunion), lying southwest of Madagascar, where French colonists forced African slaves to grow coffee. In the eighteenth century, the island became one of the world's largest coffee producers.

Throughout Asia, coffee growing was a colonial enterprise as it continues to be in Papua New Guinea (Stewart 1992). Dutch and British East Indian colonies were among the world's leading producers until the last part of the nineteenth century when a fungus devastated coffee fields. And disease has plagued coffee growers the world over because "coffee is one of the tropical plants most susceptible to diseases and insect attacks which may destroy whole plantations" (International Institute of Agriculture 1947: 22).

Many East Indian plantations turned to tea or rubber, and where coffee maintained its hold, as in Sumatra, it was mostly the robusta, rather than the disease-plagued arabica, that was grown on peasant plots. Ceylon (Sri Lanka), India, and the Philippines were also major coffee producers into the nineteenth century, but were overwhelmed by Latin American production in the twentieth century.

Production in the Caribbean

The Dutch, who brought some arabica trees to Amsterdam's botanical garden, assisted coffee in its move westward by planting it in Surinam; later some seedlings were transported to Brazil. Another early Dutch contribution to the dissemination of coffee in the Americas was even more circuitous. An arabica tree, given by the mayor of Amsterdam to Louis XIV, was cultivated in Paris's botanical garden. One of its seedlings, however, made its way to the Americas early in the eighteenth century when the Frenchman Gabriel de Clieu carried it across the Atlantic to a New World home in Martinique. From there it spread to St. Domingue (today Haiti) and later the mainland.

On St. Domingue, colonial production was perfected when slaves, already imported to grow sugar on the island, were also employed in the coffee fields. European consumption grew tenfold in the 50 years between 1739 and 1789, with French colonies supplying three-quarters of the total. In fact, relatively inexpensive Caribbean coffee was already displacing Yemeni beans even in the Cairo market, demonstrating, among other things, the competitive advantage of slave labor and plantation agriculture over the garden plots of Yemen and the peasant farms of Java. Nonetheless, the arabica remained a rather exceptional specialty product under mercantilism. In 1800, on the eve of the Industrial Revolution, Europeans consumed on average only about three-quarters of a pound per year.

By the end of that century, however, coffee had become the world's third most important traded commodity in terms of value, thanks to the Industrial Revolution and its transformation of transportation systems and markets. Perhaps fittingly, it was also during the nineteenth century that coffee was grown for the first time on an industrial scale. This occurred in the fields of Latin America where, unfortunately, coffee helped to sustain slavery – even to resurrect it.

The slave revolution in St. Domingue severed the colonial tie with France, abolished slavery, gave birth to modern Haiti, and sent the island's coffee economy into an irreversible decline. But rather than ending slavery, French and Spanish planters made Cuba the next great slave-operated coffee system. Its reign, however, was short-lived because the profitability of sugar overshadowed that of coffee. Meanwhile Brazilians, who were having difficulty competing with Cuban sugar, switched to coffee growing, and Brazil in the 1830s began a domination of world coffee production that has endured to this day. For most of the nineteenth century, Brazil owed that domination to the toil of slaves.

Brazil

The transition from slave-based sugar to coffee growing in Brazil was natural, but not inevitable. An agricultural downturn during the first four decades of the nineteenth century propelled government officials, and even some planters, to reassess the newly independent country's export orientation and reliance on human chattel. But a burst of European and North American demand for coffee redoubled reliance on the export economy and stimulated the craving for slaves; the planter elite, once again, confidently pronounced Brazil an "essentially agricultural country" and, more specifically stated, that Brazil *was* coffee, and coffee meant slaves. The rate at which Africans were landed in Rio de Janeiro and Bahia between 1800 and the abolition of the Atlantic trade in 1850 far surpassed that of any previous place or time. Brazil had been by far the largest importer of African bondsmen and was the last country of the Western world to abolish slavery when emancipation finally arrived in 1888 (Curtin 1969).

Contemporary critics complained that slavery was not only socially dangerous but was also delaying Brazil's social, economic, and political development. Later, in the 1960s, a school of analysis known as "dependency theory" extended this critique. The coffee industry was accused of reinforcing slavery, which, in turn, had impeded the development of a domestic bourgeoisie, restricted commodity and capital markets, skewed wealth distribution, created an unfavorable view of manual labor, and fashioned a liberal oligarchic state that sold national sovereignty and progress in the bags of coffee shipped abroad (Frank 1969; Santos 1974). Indeed dependency theory maintained that not only slavery but also monocultural export economies in general had led to the underdevelopment of neocolonies that were tied to the world economy.

A counter-argument, however, concedes that the *dependistas* were correct in their assessment insofar as the Paraíba Valley (parts of Minas Gerais, Rio de Janeiro state, and São Paulo state) was concerned, but claims that they were wrong in the case of western São Paulo where coffee stimulated capitalist development (Amaral Lapa 1983). There, when emancipation became inevitable, planters turned to immigrant labor. Some 3 million southern Europeans emigrated to Brazil between 1880 and 1930, most of them headed toward São Paulo's coffee fields.

These families of workers helped Paulista planters become agro-industrialists on a scale previously unknown in coffee cultivation. Indeed, Paulistas established some of the largest plantations (*Fazendas*) ever built anywhere, at any time. The Cambuhy Estate, for example, spread out over 250,000 acres on which almost 3 million trees were grown, with the whole tied together by 60 kilometers of private railroad track and 300 kilometers of roads.

These Paulista agro-industrialists directed some of their agricultural capital not only to urban real estate, public works, and government bonds but also to railroads, banks, and even factories. The *fazendeiro* was thus transformed from rentier to capitalist, from coffee baron to entrepreneur. He became the leading partner in what is generally acknowledged to be the most progressive national bourgeoisie in Latin America – indeed, one of the most entrepreneurial in the entire developing world. He industrialized São Paulo, and coffee was transformed from a colonial product to the foundation of the nation-state (Dean 1969; Cano 1977; Silva 1981; Levy 1987).

Albert Hirschman (1981) has argued that coffee had special advantages that encouraged the development of a national bourgeoisie and industrialization. He points out that the relative lack of forward and backward linkages, and the simple technology sufficient to grow and refine coffee without great capital requirements, may have stimulated entrepreneurial initiative by keeping foreigners restricted in their participation to the areas in which their comparative advantages lay, namely commerce and transportation. Thus, unlike petroleum, copper, or even sugar, the production and processing of coffee (except roasting and grinding) was done almost exclusively by nationals. Agricultural production profits remained within Latin America and because coffee did not demand great infusions of capital, planters were free to diversify into other areas.

The economic wealth of planters translated into political power which, when wielded to protect their own interests, led to a fundamental transformation of the liberal state and, ultimately, of the world market for coffee. Beginning with the valorization of coffee in 1906 through the creation of the Institute for the Permanent Defense of Coffee in the 1920s and, finally, the *Departamento Nacional de Café* in 1933, the

Brazilian federal and state governments came to finance most of the world's coffee trade and hold most of its visible stocks. Seven years later, one of the first international commodity cartels was established with the Inter-American Coffee Agreement. And in 1962, the rest of the world's producers were brought under the umbrella in the International Coffee Agreement, which persisted until 1989.

Coffee set the precedent that other raw-material producers would later follow, including those of OPEC. It also transformed the state's role in the domestic economy. By the end of the First Republic in 1930, the Brazilian state was responsible for much of the financing, warehousing, transportation, and sale of coffee and controlled one of the world's largest commodity markets. Coffee, thus, carried Brazil from an archaic slavocratic social formation to state capitalism in half a century (Topik 1987), and the state played a similarly large economic role in most other coffee-producing countries.

Spanish-American Production

In other coffee-producing lands, large-scale plantations like those of Brazil were unusual even during the height of the export boom. In Venezuela, for example, despite a tradition of slave labor and haciendas, smaller-scale production eventually prevailed (Roseberry 1983). In Colombia, the eastern part of the country had a strong colonial tradition of peasants, with no slaves or latifundia, whereas in the west there had been both. The east was the leading growing area until the beginning of the twentieth century when western provinces, such as Cundinamarca and Antioquia, rapidly increased production. But in Cundinamarca, coffee was grown on shares; only in Antioquia were haciendas important social units, and there were also many small growers as well. Nationally, by 1932, 87 percent of all coffee farms had less than 5,000 trees (farmers usually placed 500 to 800 trees per acre), and 74 percent of all production came from farms of less than 20,000 trees, meaning less than 40 acres (Beyer 1947; Nieto Arteta 1971; Palacios 1980).

In Central America, coffee was also grown mostly on small and middle-size farms called *fincas*. Although Costa Rica was far from being a rural democracy (71 percent of the peasantry was landless in 1883) and land ownership was concentrated, even the biggest coffee plantations were often discontinuous and fragmented into a number of small or medium-size lots, sometimes several kilometers apart (Cardoso 1977: 175–6; Seligson 1980). In fact, even the "great estates" in Costa Rica were defined as anything over 76 acres, which in Brazil would scarcely have been considered a middle-sized holding.

Elsewhere in Central America, coffee estates were somewhat larger than in Costa Rica. Nicaragua did have some coffee haciendas, but they were neither numerous nor extensive. El Salvador, the most dependent of all countries on coffee, had a dynamic agrarian bourgeoisie with extremely efficient production techniques and concentrated land holdings. But production was intensive, not extensive as in Brazil. Eugenio Aguilar was considered a large, wealthy planter with two *fincas* that held 230,000 trees on less than 300 acres. But in Guatemala and southern Mexico, with larger frontier areas, there were substantially larger holdings. Many were spread over 5,000 acres in Guatemala, and in Tehuantepec, Mexico, there were several coffee estates with 1.5 million trees on some 20,000 acres (Lindo-Fuentes 1990).

Coffee estates, in general, were smaller in Colombia and Central America than in Brazil because of terrain and transportation problems, along with a shortage of capital and labor, the relative absence of a frontier, and the presence of people with preexisting land claims. To compensate for the higher production costs wrought by such problems, growers had to produce a better coffee that would command a higher price at market.

Higher-quality coffee required more labor-intensive harvesting. Shade trees had to be planted, and the berries were picked individually just as they ripened, in contrast to the procedure of stripping entire branches as was done in Brazil. Workers would sometimes have to pass the same tree six or seven times during the harvest instead of just once. Better quality also demanded the more sophisticated and expensive "wet" method of treating the berry.

While inspecting this method in Costa Rica, the Brazilian planter Jorge Dumont Villares marveled that the preparation of coffee was a "true science" there. The berries were picked, hulled, then left 24 to 40 hours to ferment. Next, they were washed to remove the outer membrane and dried for one or two days. From the drying grounds, the beans were taken to dryers where they were left for 25 to 35 hours to dry. The parchment film was then removed mechanically and the beans sorted by size, quality, and color. Finally, the beans were polished (Villares 1927). Producing high-quality coffee, then, demanded substantial capital and technical expertise, as well as abundant labor. The capital was provided more by mill owners than by growers.

The relationship between coffee and the kind of labor applied to it varied from country to country and changed over time. As noted, coffee reinforced slavery in the Caribbean and in Brazil, but slavery was not common elsewhere in Latin America where other coercive forms of labor were applied. Nonetheless, as we have tried to show, coffee, plantations, and slavery or forced labor were not necessarily linked, and coffee did not always yield a strong landlord class. Rather, in Costa Rica, for example, merchants and millers came to predominate because of the small-holding pattern, and elsewhere merchants also became the dominant class. In Colombia, most of the progressive planters were initially merchants, and only in such areas as Cundinamarca were traditional landlords the coffee growers. Many Nicaraguan *fin-queros* were urban based, and the El Salvador coffee-grower class was largely composed of merchants and other urban-based capitalists who invested in land in the 1880s and 1890s as coffee prices rose. German merchants in Guatemala and Chiapas followed the same path.

In few cases was there much continuity between the colonial landed elite and the coffee bourgeoisie. In fact, many members of the coffee elite were nineteenth-century immigrants. Thus, it is a mistake to refer to the coffee growers of Central America and Colombia as *Junkers* or to discuss "landlord capitalism" as is often done (Winson 1989). Coffee was developed by a new bourgeois group that was not reluctant to invest in other sectors of the economy as well.

This does not mean that there was no resistance to the rule of coffee. In Guatemala, villagers frequently destroyed coffee *fincas* (Cambranes 1985). Peasants in western El Salvador, the center of coffee cultivation, in collaboration with the Communist party, attempted to overthrow the government in 1932. The result was at least 17,000 peasants dead in the grue-some massacre known simply as *La Matanza* (Anderson 1971; North 1985).

The willingness of coffee growers to use violence has often allowed the essence of their rule to con-tinue while changing its appearance. Colombia never had a truly populist ruler; the traditional Liberals and Conservatives still share power. El Salvador and Guatemala have the most ferocious and brutal regimes of Central America, still overseen by descen-dants of the coffee elite. São Paulo was the last state to hold out against the populist leader Getúlio Vargas, even waging civil war against him in 1932.

Yet there has been change. São Paulo, for example, although its economy is now based on the cities and factories that coffee gave birth to rather than on the countryside, has become the home of Latin America's largest socialist party, the *Partido dos Trabalhadores*. In Costa Rica, a revolution in 1949 brought to power a semiautonomous state that has presided over Latin America's most vigorous democracy; and in Nicara-gua, division among growers and a single family's attempt to monopolize wealth led to the creation of the first truly socialist regime on the American main-land. In all of these cases, however, democratic trends began to grow only *after* coffee ceased to be the dominant export.

Socioeconomic Aspects and a Return to Africa

During the years 1850 to 1930, the world coffee mar-ket was fairly homogeneous, with the vast majority of the world's coffee (as much as 95 percent) produced in Latin America. Although there are an estimated 50 different species of the genus *Coffea*, and a much greater number of small species or elementary hybrid-producing forms, over 90 percent of exports before World War II were of the same species, the arabica.

Such apparent uniformity, however, is a bit mislead-ing. Because all coffee is cultivated outside of its nat-ural habitat, under different methods and a wide range of natural conditions, the arabica is different on virtually each plantation (International Institute of Agriculture 1947: 19–20). Beans also differ from year to year. There are 10 generally recognized subspecies.

The international market divided coffee by port of exit and grade of the bean (determined by color, size, and degree of breakage). The main division in the world economy, however, was between "Brazils" and "milds"; the latter, produced in Colombia and Central America, began making inroads into the dominance of the former beginning in the 1920s, when Brazil's cof-fee valorization program propped up the price of the stronger and more bitter "Brazils." Different national crops also varied substantially according to the har-vest season. But the time it took for beans to reach market was not of great consequence because they did not deteriorate over time (as, for example, apples did) and importers maintained large stocks in the consuming countries to smooth the flow to market.

Despite such differences, the producing countries shared many similarities. They exported almost all of their crop to Europe and North America. And all used fairly similar cultivation techniques demanded by the arabica bush or "tree." In order to increase yield and facilitate the harvest (done almost always by hand), the trees were topped in their third year and only allowed to grow to 6 to 16 feet, though in the wild they grow to 35 feet; hence they were often termed bushes rather than trees. The arabica grows best with deep, permeable, well-aerated soil and a minimum rainfall of 50 to 60 inches during germination (coffee lands in Latin America were almost never irrigated as they were in Yemen and Java). It also needs a long, dry season and mild climate, with the optimum tempera-ture between 59 and 77 degrees Fahrenheit.

Coffee-producing countries have also shared a sec-ondary position in the industrialization of coffee. Since the consumers were in the rich countries, the retailing, wholesaling, roasting, grinding, and packag-ing were done in those countries. Growers were, thus, excluded from the most technologically sophisti-cated aspects of the production of coffee, from which the greatest innovations such as packaging, vacuum sealing, and soluble coffee emerged. These, along with roasting and advertising, have also constituted the most lucrative of the forward linkages. Thus the San-tos price was at most half the New York retail price, and if the coffee were sold by the cup rather than the can, the additional labor cost and markup meant that as much as 90 percent of the value added was created in the consuming countries.[2]

Today the supermarket price of standard roasted or ground coffee is 3 to 4 times the New York green price. Restaurants sell coffee by the cup for 6 to 10 times the retail bean price. And the specialty brands are even more expensive. Thus, upwards of three-quarters of the value is added in the consuming countries. The only dent in the consuming countries' market command has been made by the increasing ability of some of the major exporting countries to produce and export soluble coffee.

For most of the coffee-producing Latin American countries, the cultivation of coffee became important toward the end of the nineteenth century or early in the twentieth century, and coffee came to dominate national exports, creating monocultures. In 1929, coffee cultivation was responsible for 71 percent of exports in Brazil, 61 percent in Colombia, 77 percent in Guatemala, 77 percent in Haiti, 54 percent in Nicaragua, 67 percent in Costa Rica, and fully 93 percent in El Salvador (Ukers 1935).

Since World War II, however, coffee cultivation has slowly shifted back to Africa. Although Latin America still produces most of the world's coffee, the crop is no longer responsible for more than half of the exports of any one of its countries. In Africa, however, in the late 1960s, coffee represented more than half the exports of Angola, Burundi, Ethiopia, and Rwanda, and almost half of Uganda's (Barbiroli 1970), and the continent now supplies about 18 percent of total world exports. Africans usually plant the more disease-resistant and faster-maturing robusta bush. It produces a less desirable brew but has been particularly successful in the soluble coffee market.

Coffee has come full circle in Africa. Ethiopians had vast forests of wild arabica trees but did not enter the trade until this century. Indeed, a nineteenth-century Dutch observer wrote that "the plant is not only no object of culture there, but is abandoned to persecution in some parts through the rage of blind fanaticism" (Kok 1864: 210).

European colonial regimes and planters initiated the coffee export economy in Ethiopia, as well as in Kenya, Angola, Uganda, and elsewhere. Africans were sometimes pointedly excluded by law from growing the arabica or robusta, although in Zaire and Ethiopia they were forced to grow or harvest the beans. In the last 40 years, however, decolonization has transformed the situation. Today, the Ivory Coast, Ethiopia, and Uganda are the principal coffee-growing nations of Africa, and African peasants, not European plantation managers, are the overwhelming producers (Clarence-Smith 1994).

Conclusion

Throughout its history, coffee has stimulated ideas, debates, commerce, and development, not to mention numbing people to routine and exposing them to vice and exploitation. And it has helped to subvert cultures, social systems, and governments. In the consuming countries, coffee moved from the mystical and mercantile to become one of the most traded bourgeois products in the world. Coffeehouses operated as centers of a bourgeois lifestyle for literati and businessmen alike, as well as meeting places for those who agitated for democratic politics. Coffee became the fuel of the industrial age.

In the fields of Latin America, however, European and North American demand led first to an intensification of slavery and then, in various places, to the appropriation of village lands, the expulsion of native peoples, and coerced labor. But, although there were large planters, there were also plenty of smallholders.

The story of coffee is clearly one of diversity. Geography, history, and local resistance combined to create a wide variety of social arrangements. To trace the history of coffee is to trace the path of the world economy over the last six centuries. From an Asian monopoly, to a European colonial product, to a global commodity grown on four continents, coffee has linked the different worlds of the producer and the consumer, the underdeveloped and the developed, the free and the enslaved, the rich and the poor, and the bourgeois and the archaic. Sufi Sheikh, sitting in the shade in Mocca, had no idea what a global force he was putting into motion when he sipped the first cup of coffee.

Steven C. Topik

The author would like to thank Gervase Clarence-Smith for his insightful comments.

Notes

1. According to the United States Department of Agriculture (1993), total world consumption in 1991 was 72 million sacks of 60 kilograms each. I multiplied by the recommended 40 cups of coffee to the pound to arrive at the number of cups.
2. This estimate assumes the New York raw material to be 50 percent of the New York wholesale price. It also assumes a 50 percent markup to the Midwest, and a 25 percent profit for the wholesaler and for the retailer. Finally, it reflects the conservative estimate that a retail cup of coffee costs the consumer about twice one made at home. A restaurant cup of coffee costs 7 to 13 times the retail price of coffee.

Bibliography

Amaral Lapa, J. R. do. 1983. *A economia cafeteira*. São Paulo.
Anderson, Thomas P. 1971. *Matanza: El Salvador's communist revolt of 1932*. Lincoln, Nebr.
Barbiroli, G. 1970. *Produzione e commercio internazionale del café*. Bologna.
Barrows, S. 1991. 'Parliaments of the people': The political culture of cafes in the early Third Republic. In *Drinking behavior and belief in modern history*, ed. S. Barrows and R. Room, 87–97. Berkeley, Calif.

Becker, H., Volker Hoehfeld, and Horst Kopp. 1979. *Kaffee aus Arabien: Der Bedeutungswandel eines Welt-Wirtshaftsgutes und seine siedlungsgeographische Konsequenz an der Trockengrenze der Okumere.* Wiesbaden.

Bersten, I. 1993. *Coffee floats, tea sinks: Through history and technology to a complete understanding.* Sydney.

Beyer, R. 1947. *The Colombian coffee industry: Origins and major trends, 1740-1940.* Minneapolis, Minn.

Bramah, E. 1972. *Tea and coffee. A modern view of three hundred years of tradition.* London.

Browning, D. C. 1971. *El Salvador; landscape and society.* Oxford.

Cambranes, J. C. 1985. *Coffee and peasants in Guatemala: The origins of the modern plantation economy in Guatemala, 1853-1897.* Stockholm.

Cano, Wilson. 1977. *Raizes da concentração industrial em São Paulo.* São Paulo.

Cardoso, C. 1977. The formation of the coffee estate in nineteenth-century Costa Rica. In *Land and labour in Latin America,* ed. K. Duncan and I. Rutledge, 165-202. Cambridge.

Carlier, O. 1990. Le café maure. Sociabilité masculine et effervescence citoyenne (Alérie xvii-xx siécle). *Annales E.S.C.* 45: 975-1003.

Clarence-Smith, Gervase. 1994. "Africa and world coffee markets to 1914." Unpublished manuscript.

Curtin, P. 1969. *The Atlantic slave trade: A census.* Madison, Wisc.

Daum, W. ed. 1988. *Yemen: 3000 years of art and civilization in Arabia Feliz.* Innsbruck.

Dean, W. 1969. *The industrialization of São Paulo.* Austin, Tex.

Ellis, A. 1956. *The penny universities.* London.

Frank, A. G. 1969. *Capitalism and underdevelopment in Latin America.* New York.

Geertz, C. 1971. *Agricultural involution.* Berkeley, Calif.

Hattox, R. 1985. *Coffee and coffehouses: The origins of a social beverage in the medieval Near East.* Seattle, Wash.

Heise, Ulla. 1987. *Coffee and coffee-houses,* trans. Paul Roper. West Chester, Pa.

Hirschman, Albert. 1981. A generalized linkage approach to development, with special reference to staples. *Economic Development and Cultural Change* 25, supplement: 67-98.

Holloway, Thomas. 1980. *Immigrants on the land.* Chapel Hill, N.C.

International Institute of Agriculture, Bureau of F.A.O. in Rome. 1947. *The world's coffee.* Rome.

Kok, A. S., ed. 1864. *Colonial essays.* London.

Leclant, Jean. 1979. "Coffee and cafés in Paris, 1644-1693," trans. Patricia M. Ranum. In *Food and drink in history,* ed. Robert Forster and Orest Ranum, 86-97. Baltimore, Md.

Levy, D. 1987. *The Prados of São Paulo, Brazil: An elite family and social change, 1840-1930.* Athens, Ga.

Lindo-Fuentes, H. 1990. *Weak foundations: The economy of El Salvador in the nineteenth century, 1821-1898.* Berkeley, Calif.

Lucier, R. L. 1988. *The international political economy of coffee; from Juan Valdez to Yank's Diner.* New York.

McCreery, M. G., and M. Bynum. 1930. *The coffee industry in Brazil.* Washington, D.C.

Nieto Arteta, L. E. 1971. *El café en la sociedad Colombiana.* Bogotá.

North, L. 1985. *Bitter grounds: Roots of revolt in El Salvador.* Westport, Conn.

Oldenburg, R. 1989. *The great good place.* New York.

Oliveira, J. T. 1984. *História do café no Brasil e no mundo.* Rio de Janeiro.

Palacios, M. 1980. *Coffee in Colombia, 1850-1970; an economic, social and political history.* Cambridge.

Panati, C. 1987. *Extraordinary origins of everyday things.* New York.

Raymond, A. 1973-4. *Artisans et commerçants . . .* Damascuc.

Roseberry, W. 1983. *Coffee and capitalism in the Venezuelan Andes.* Austin, Tex.

  1991. "La falta de brazos: Land and labor in the coffee economies of nineteenth-century Latin America." *Theory and Society* 20: 351-82.

Santos, T. dos. 1974. "Brazil, the origins of a crisis." In *Latin America, the struggle with dependency and beyond,* ed. R. Chilcote and J. Edelstein, 409-90. New York.

Seligson, M. 1980. *Peasants of Costa Rica and the development of agrarian capitalism.* Madison, Wis.

Silva, Sergio. 1981. *Expansão cafeeira e origens da indústria no Brasil.* São Paulo.

Stewart, R. G. 1992. *Coffee: The political economy of an export industry in Papua New Guinea.* Boulder, Colo.

Topik, S. 1987. *The political economy of the Brazilian state, 1889-1930.* Austin, Tex.

Ukers, W. 1930. *Coffee merchandising.* New York.

  1948. *The Romance of coffee: An outline history of coffee and coffee-drinking through a thousand years.* New York.

  1935. *All about coffee.* New York.

United States Department of Agriculture, Foreign Agricultural Service. 1993. *World coffee situation.* Washington D.C.

Uribe, C. A. 1954. *Brown gold: The amazing story of coffee.* New York.

Villares, J. D. 1927. *O café e sua produção e exportação.* São Paulo.

Wenner, M. W. 1991. *The Yemen Arab Republic: Development and change in an ancient land.* Boulder, Colo.

Wickizer, V. D. 1959. *Coffee, tea and cocoa, an economic and political analysis.* Stanford, Calif.

Winson, A. 1989. *Coffee and democracy in modern Costa Rica.* London.

III.5 ❧ Distilled Beverages

Alcoholic beverages have been a part of human culture since at least the Neolithic period. Yet until recently, beverages made from fruits, grains, or honey were considered to be what historian Wolfgang Schivelbusch (1992) has called "organic," meaning that the amount of sugar in the ingredients produced the amount of alcohol in the drinks. Examples of such beverages are beer and wine. Beginning in the period from about A.D. 800 to 1300, however, people in China and the West learned to distill alcoholic liquids. This chapter traces the history of distilled alcohol and discusses the nature of several kinds of liquor.

Distillation and Alcoholic Beverages

Distillation is a method for increasing the alcohol content (and, thus, the potency) of a liquid already containing alcohol – the existing alcohol content usually the result of the fermentation of vegetable sugars. The distillation process separates the alcohol from other parts of the solution by the heating of the liquid to 173° Fahrenheit, a temperature sufficient to boil alcohol but not water. The resulting steam (vaporized alcohol) is collected and condensed, returning it to liquid form – but a liquid with a much higher proportion of alcohol than before. Repeating the process increases the liquor's potency yet further. Because distilled alcohol contains bad-tasting and dangerous chemicals called fusel oils (actually forms of alcohol) and congeners, both by-products of the distilling process, it is often aged in a procedure, originating in the eighteenth century, that rids the beverage of these chemicals. As the liquid ages, its container (preferably made of wood) colors and flavors it to produce a smoother and better-tasting product (Ray 1974).

A constant theme in discussions of distilled liquor is that of fire, which has three different metaphoric meanings. First, beverages are "burnt," or distilled, over the flame of a still. Second, although it is a drinkable liquid, distilled alcohol is capable of combustion. The third meaning is an apt description of the sensation experienced by consumers of distilled spirits. "Firewater," *aguardente, aguardiente* (meaning rough or burning water), and ardent (burning) spirits are all terms referring to such a sensation (Needham 1984).

Stills are the traditional equipment needed to distill alcohol. There are many different types. The earliest known is the *ambix* (plural *ambices*) used by Greek alchemists. *Ambices* were ceramic or metal pots with heads shaped so that liquid would condense inside the head and drain out through a collecting tube. Later, during the Middle Ages, Muslim alchemists, who also employed the *ambix,* added the Arabic article *al-* to its name, hence the term "alembic" for a still (Forbes 1948). When larger amounts of alcohol began to be distilled in the fifteenth and sixteenth centuries, the *ambix* was improved, giving rise to several types of stills.

A common one, the pot still, dates from the sixteenth century. The fermented beverage is boiled in a large pot having a curved top that allows the steam to pass to a coiled cooling pipe called the "worm," in which the vaporized alcohol condenses into a liquid. The distillate then flows from the worm into a receiving vessel. Pot stills, like those used in the sixteenth century, were later carried to the Americas and to other European colonies and remain in use in traditional distilleries. In Europe and the United States, pot stills are employed for the production of such beverages as French brandy, Italian grappa, and Scotch whiskey (Maresca 1992). The liquids produced by a pot still at the beginning (termed "foreshots" by American distillers) and end ("aftershots") of a particular distillation are undrinkable or, at least, foul tasting because of the fusel oils that they contain and are consequently either redistilled or discarded. The liquid produced in the middle of the distillation process is the valuable fraction, and proper separation of the liquor from the by-products requires both experience and skill.

The early nineteenth century saw the invention, by Aeneas Coffey, of a still that permitted more or less continuous distillation (Forbes 1948). This device consisted of two hollow metal columns through which vaporized alcohol rose to condense on metal plates. One column served for distillation and the other for rectification – a process of adjusting the potency of an alcoholic beverage, often by redistillation. But because distillation was continuous, the Coffey still did not permit the separation of the bad-tasting beginning and end by-products from the vital middle of the run. All of it tasted the same, being of uniform but lesser quality. Today, such mechanical stills can process thousands of gallons of liquid at a time, but pot stills are said by many to produce better-quality beverages.

Redistillation is sometimes called "rectification," but this is an ambiguous term, which, legally, can also mean blending one distilled beverage, or "spirit," with other spirits or flavorings. In many cases, tasteless neutral spirit becomes an esteemed beverage with a little help from the rectifying process; examples include some Scandinavian akvavits and Polish vodkas (Grossman 1989). Spirits are also blended with water to make them drinkable.

Alcohol and Distillation – 5500 B.C. to A.D. 1500

Alcoholic beverages were made as long ago as the sixth millennium B.C., as has been documented by the discovery of wine remains in a container at Çatal Hüyük, an archaeological site on the Konya Plain in Turkey (Mellaart 1967). It is probable, however, that wine was produced from dates and figs even earlier (Tannahill 1988). Beer (or, more properly, ale) was in use in ancient Sumer by at least 2500 B.C. and at about that time, or soon afterward, in Egypt (Lichine 1981).

As populations became more crowded, with consequent pollution of water supplies, nearly everyone drank ale or wine. The Romans scorned the ale of the Germanic tribes but made wine a regular part of their own daily regime (Pliny 1940). As a rule, it was mixed with hot water, spices, and perhaps honey (Lichine 1981). People who drank undiluted wine were thought to be depressed or alcoholic (or both), which suggests that the Romans probably would not have been interested in diverting their distillation techniques from alchemy to the production of beverages stronger than wine, even had they thought of it (Tannahill 1988).

Nonetheless, some investigators have sought the origins of distilled beverages in ancient Rome. Pliny the Elder (Gaius Plinius Secundus) mentioned a "wine" that had to be diluted several times before it could (or should) be drunk (Pliny 1940). But this reference is to a wine kept in ceramic vessels and allowed to evaporate over many years, until the result was a thick sludge (Lichine 1981). Pliny also wrote of Falernian wine that could be ignited, that would keep for a decade, and that was strong in flavor. But at that time, wine was often boiled down into a kind of jelly to season foods and make drinks, and it was already known that the vapor from hot wine could be ignited. Thus, in the absence of archaeological evidence of "worm" coils or other kinds of still-head cooling devices, it appears that the manufacture of distilled spirits, at least on any large scale, remained in the future (Needham 1984).

The Greek alchemists, whose stills are portrayed in drawings from the Hellenistic period, may have preceded the Romans in producing small amounts of alcohol. Alchemy, which originated in Egypt and Persia and was then practiced by the Greeks and the Arabs, was a quasi-magical process by which the alchemist sought the "essence" of matter to perfect it in accordance with mystical laws (Needham 1984). Arab alchemists produced a cosmetic eye makeup, the name of which – *kohl* or *kuhl* – conveyed the notion of something fine and subtle emerging from a process of distillation, and it was from *al-kohl* (or *al-kuhl*), and various subsequent renderings like the Portuguese *álcool,* that the English word "alcohol" was derived (Forbes 1948).

Moreover, despite the Islamic prohibition against alcohol consumption, the Arabs are credited, at least in legend, with the spread of liquor to Europe. One well-known account, set in the early fifth century, tells the story of an Irish monk – who later became Saint Patrick – spreading the gospel in the Near East. There, he learned about stills and, on his return to Ireland, brought one with him (McGuire 1993). A more modern version of the tale has the Crusaders learning about alcohol and distillation from the Arabs and bringing home to Europe both taste and technique. Whether there is truth in either story, the historical record of these centuries does not indicate any widespread use of distilled spirits that would also have triggered their widespread misuse – a misuse that certainly would have rated mention in the literature (Schivelbusch 1992).

Distillation, then, continued to remain the property of the alchemists, who in the Middle Ages were distilling water hundreds of times over, reducing it to a residue of mineral salts that was said to be its "essence" (Forbes 1948). About A.D. 800, the Arab scholar Jabir ibn Hayyan invented a much-improved still, and during the centuries from 800 to 1000, Arab alchemists are said to have distilled wine, with its resulting "essence" employed in still further alchemi-

cal experimentation (Toussaint-Samat 1987). This may have been the first time that brandy was made. But with alcohol consumption forbidden by the Islamic religion, there was little incentive to distill such beverages in any quantity (Forbes 1948).

Meanwhile, in China, rice wine – *chiu* (actually an ale) – had long been produced and was as popular there as were grape wines in the West; Chinese ales made from millet also had been brewed for some time (Simoons 1991). However, the fermentation procedure used to make rice wine generally resulted in a stronger beverage than Western ales and beers (Chang 1977).

Like Greece and the Arab world, China also had its alchemists, but Chinese stills were different from those used in the West, having a tube on the side to drain the distillate and allow more of it to be produced. Although the date when this type of still originated is unknown (Needham 1984), fourth-century documents mention a "wine" from the "western regions" that kept for a long time and was extremely strong. This beverage might have been produced by Chinese stills; however, noted sinologist Joseph Needham (1984) has suggested that it came not from Chinese stills but from remote regions of central Asia, where a technique of concentrating alcohol by freezing it had been invented. Although Needham believes that such a technique was a precursor to distillation, he acknowledges that the evidence is confusing and that the references that describe this particular beverage are ambiguous. Moreover, one authority has suggested that, given the paucity of references to distilled spirits in Chinese history (until relatively recently), even if liquor were known, its use could hardly have been common (Simoons 1991).

By the fourteenth century, however, this may no longer have been the case. The *Ying-shih ssu-chi,* a medical work dated to 1368, draws attention to the dangers of overindulgence in distilled alcoholic beverages, and Li Shih Chen (writing in the sixteenth century) stated that liquor had reached China only with the Yuan (Mongol) dynasty of the thirteenth and fourteenth centuries (Chang 1977). Chen mentioned such beverages as "fire wine" and "burnt wine," equating the latter with arrack or distilled palm wine. It is interesting to note that this chronology of alcohol use in China parallels that of brandy, and perhaps even whiskey, in Europe (Simoons 1991).

From about 1000 to 1500, alchemists in Europe repeatedly distilled wine (adding salts to absorb the water portion of the liquid) to produce a distillate that would burn. That the eleventh-century Italian alchemist and scholar Michael Salernus had successfully produced alcohol, for example, is indicated by the following statement: "A mixture of pure and very strong wine with three parts salt distilled in the usual vessel, produces a liquid which will flame up when set on fire but which leaves other substances unburnt" (McCusker 1989: 85). (In Salernus's original manuscript, the words underlined here are written in cipher to prevent others from learning his procedures and formulas.)

Salernus was not alone in reporting such results, and collectively, the alchemists believed that they had extracted the "essence" or "spirit" of wine and that repeated distillations resulted in *aqua vitae* – the "water of life" – which, in this case, was a kind of brandy that until about 1400 was used mostly as a medicine (Braudel 1973). Because the processes of aging and the separation of the different fractions of the distillate were unknown, this liquor would have been harsh, and even harsher if bad wine had been used for the distillation.

Albertus Magnus was another distiller and alchemist who wrote about the virtues of this substance. Its potency seemed to recommend it as a treatment for a variety of illnesses. Indeed, the distillate was acclaimed as the "quintessence," a union of all the elements, even the key to everlasting life (Schivelbusch 1992).

The first real brandy that was not thought of as medicine is said to have been distilled in 1300 by Arnaldus de Villa Nova, a professor at the medical school of Montpelier. He said: "We call it aqua vitae, and this name is really suitable, since it is really a water of immortality" (Christian 1990: 25). On the other hand, both the Irish and the Scots claim to have produced liquor from grain (in contrast to brandy from wine) since the beginning of the last millennium; the Scots called it *uisge beatha* (pronounced wisky-baw), and the Irish called it *uisce beatha*. Both meant "water of life," and the English term "whiskey" derived from them.

The precise dates when Irish and Scotch whiskeys originated may never be known. But we do know that, in the aftermath of Henry II's invasion of Ireland (A.D. 1171), Irish "wine" was taxed. The reference to "wine" could mean honey mead, or ale, but it might also mean whiskey. Indeed, the Old Bushmills brand claims its origin from this date, suggesting that even if the St. Patrick tale is a bit fanciful, whiskey from the Emerald Isle may well have predated brandy in Europe, at least for recreational purposes (McGuire 1993). Certainly the archaeological discovery of a worm cooler and alembic pots in Ulster suggests that at least some distillation had taken place in Ireland by the late Middle Ages (McGuire 1993). However, the size of the vessels indicates domestic distillation on a small scale (E. C. 1859).

In the fifteenth century, better methods of cooling a still's head were developed, and these allowed increased production of distilled beverages (Forbes 1948). The technology spread quickly across Europe, and practically every country developed its own national distilled spirit. Those countries also soon developed laws to tax, restrict, and sometimes even ban such spirits, because by the sixteenth century, drunkenness had become a serious social problem.

People who had previously drunk beer as if it were water were discovering that they could not drink liquor as if it were beer (Schivelbusch 1992).

Centuries earlier, Paracelsus (Philippus Aureolus) had employed the Arabic term *alcool vini* to describe spirits. But it was not until 1730, when the Dutch physician Herman Boerhave used the word alcohol to mean distilled spirits, that it became commonly understood that ale, wine, and distilled beverages all owed their mood-altering capabilities to this chemical (Forbes 1948). Yet because "aqua vitae" and other such appellations continued to be used, it is difficult to discover exactly what kinds of spirits were actually being produced. Indeed, even Scotch whiskey was called aqua vitae (Jackson 1988).

From this point forward, however, the historical picture is sufficiently clear to permit treatment of the individual liquors, and we will attempt to do this in some semblance of chronological order. But before we begin, a word or two is needed about the strength, or "proof," of an alcoholic beverage. The term *proof* originated in connection with the early use of gunpowder in war: "Proof," or good, armor was that which proved resistant to a gunshot. The word entered alcohol terminology as a means of identifying the quality of rum and brandy. "Proof" beverages were of the approved strength – half spirit and half water (McCusker 1989). Their purity could be measured by weighing or by setting the spirit alight. Later, the term came to mean twice the percentage of alcohol in the drink. In the twentieth century, neutral spirit leaving the mechanical still is 180 proof, or 90 percent alcohol (Grossman 1989).

Distilled Spirits in the West

Brandy

First called "brandy wine" (from the Dutch *brandewijn*), brandy means "to burn" or "burnt" in Dutch as well as in other languages, such as the German *Brand* and the Middle English "brand." Brandy is more expensive to make than grain spirits because it must be distilled from fruit and, in the case of cognac, from wine (Ray 1974). As noted, brandy first emerged as a medicine in the eleventh century and only later became popular as a beverage. In Nuremberg, it had apparently become a bit too popular by 1450; in that year, a law was passed to ban the drinking of *aquavit*, which we are told was brandy wine (Forbes 1948). Because in northern Europe beers and ales had long been made by women, during the fifteenth and sixteenth centuries many distilleries were located in private homes. Nonetheless, by 1500, brandy production was subject to taxation in many principalities (Braudel 1973).

Gradually, the French wine country became the center of the brandy industry. Louis XII granted the first license to manufacture brandy in 1514, and the product was employed (among other uses) to fortify wines, which strengthened them at the same time that it stopped fermentation (Braudel 1973). A less expensive brandy for the poor was made from left-over grape skins and seeds. It was and is called *grappa* in Italy, *marc* in France, *aguardente* in Portugal, and *aguardiente* in Spain (Maresca 1992).

A countermovement that pushed up the price was the aging of brandy, a procedure begun about the middle of the eighteenth century (Ray 1974). This process made for a decidedly smoother drink and certainly helped to promote what has been termed the "cult" of brandy, just as the aging of Scotch and Irish whiskeys in oak barrels established a whiskey "cult" (Morrice 1983). Then, as now, the most famous brandies came from the Charente region of France and were named for the town of Cognac. Twice distilled in pot stills from the white wines of the Charente, cognac is blended according to certain formulas and aged for a minimum of three years in oaken barrels. The drink can continue to improve through aging for as many as 50 more years, but that is the effective limit of the process; thus, the legend of fine brandy surviving from the time of Napoleon is a myth. Experts agree that even if such brandy existed, it would be undrinkable (Ray 1974).

Cognac leaves the still at 140 proof, but its potency is reduced by aging because alcohol evaporates through the porous material of the cask, whereas water does not. In addition, sufficient water is added so that cognac is shipped at 80 to 86 proof. The age and quality of a cognac are indicated by a confusing array of letters, stars, and symbols on the label. Armagnac, a well-known brandy from another region of France although much like cognac, is said to retain the flavor of the wine to a greater degree, and its method of distillation is different (Ray 1974).

By the late nineteenth century, the brandy industry was in near ruin because of a vine blight caused by the American vine louse, *Phylloxera,* that destroyed virtually all the vines in Europe (Lichine 1981). A visitor to the Continent at the end of the nineteenth century reported that the "brandy" available was not brandy at all, but rather an ersatz mixture concocted with grain spirits and plums (Spencer 1899). However, the European wine industry, along with the manufacture of brandy, was saved by the introduction of resistant rootstocks of muscadine and scuppernong grapes, native to North America, onto which the famous vines of Europe were grafted (Lichine 1981).

The term, brandy, refers not only to drinks made from grapes and wine but also to a wide variety of beverages made from other fruits and even from honey. Some are true brandies, made entirely from fruit, but many are grain spirits that are merely flavored with fruit. One fruit brandy is kirsch *(Kirschwasser),* a fiery cherry brandy of Switzerland. *Poire* brandy is made from pears, and *framboise* from raspberries. Hungary produces *Barack Palinka,* perhaps the most famous of apricot brandies. Another

important beverage is slivovitz, the plum brandy of the Balkans, sold at 70 and 87 proof. Most of these brandies are bottled as uncolored spirits to preserve the fruit bouquet. In addition, there are countless brandies made from apples in Europe and wherever else apples are grown. Examples are calvados, made in Normandy from hard cider, and applejack, made largely in North America. Calvados is aged, whereas applejack frequently is not, and historically, applejack has been made by freezing as well as by distillation (Grossman 1977; Lichine 1981).

In the Americas, the agave plant contains a juice that is fermented into *pulque,* a beverage that dates from the Aztec period. The brandy *mescal* that is distilled from *pulque* comes in many varieties, with the most famous being tequila (Grimes 1988). In Peru, grape wine has been produced since 1566, with *pisco* the local brandy. Both Mexico and Chile also produce brandy made from grape wines (Lichine 1981).

Moving northward, in colonial New England and in Canada, hard cider was first processed into applejack by freezing, a technique reported much earlier in central Asia (Dabney 1974). In the Appalachian Mountains, whole valleys were planted with fruit trees to make apple and other brandies until the early twentieth century (Marcus and Burner 1992). Although there are references to "British brandy" in seventeenth-century texts, these actually deal with an early grain spirit related to gin; Britain produces virtually no wine or brandy. However, a few British distillers have made brandy from mead, the honey-based wine of the ancient Britons. This beverage, called "honey brandy," has never been common because mead itself is costly, and distilling it yields a very expensive liquor (Gayre 1948).

Spirits from Grain and Cane

The kinds of grain used to make spirits have usually been determined by custom (although sometimes by law, as in the case of licensed distillers) and, perhaps most importantly, by what is available. As a rule, lower-cost and lower-status grains have been employed: To make spirits from wheat would have been a waste of bread grain, and in the sixteenth century, several German states banned the manufacture of grain spirits so as better to control the price of bread (Forbes 1948). Rye has commonly been used in areas with colder climates, such as Canada. In the United States, the abundance of maize has made it the grain of choice (Inglett and Munck 1980), and barley constituted the base of the first whiskeys made in Ireland and Scotland. Many of these grains were ingredients for beers long before whiskeys were made (Jackson 1988).

Irish and Scotch whiskeys. To produce either Irish or Scotch whiskey, soaked barley is permitted to sprout and become malt, as in making beer. However, the mash for whiskey does not include hops. The Scotch malt has traditionally been dried over peat fires that imparted a smoky flavor, whereas Irish malt was dried in ovens. After the grain is made into a mash and allowed to ferment, it is distilled in a pot still -twice to make Scotch and three times to make Irish whiskey (Jackson 1988). The spirits are then permitted to age in oaken casks (from which they acquire their color); then blending takes place. This is a procedure that employs whiskeys that have been aged for different periods of time and that are often made from different ingredients (Morrice 1983). In the case of Scotch, for example, the unblended or "pure" malt can be blended with whiskeys made from other grains, such as oat, rye, and maize.

Modern Scotch seems to date from about the middle of the eighteenth century, its production spurred by a 1745 increase in the tax on ale. Private distillation was banned in the nineteenth century (Morrice 1983). However, the distillation of whiskey was an important source of income for the Highlanders, who raised grain but encountered much difficulty in getting it to market over the rough mountain roads. Consequently, the ban gave rise to a thriving illegal industry that, in distilling the grain, put it into a much more compact (and valuable) form. Doubtless the industry became more profitable after the *Phylloxera* blight that devastated European wine grapes from the 1860s on, made brandy virtually unaffordable, and as a result, increased demand for other alcoholic beverages.

Pot stills were hidden away in the Scottish Highlands and in Ireland, where clans made illegal whiskey, as their kinsmen in America were soon to do as well. The government struck back with raids on the illegal stills; in 1834, there were 692 seizures in Scotland and 8,192 in Ireland. But in 1884 there were only 22 seizures in Scotland, and in Ireland they had fallen off to 829. Clearly, the government was winning the war. Perhaps the greater amount of government activity in Ireland had to do with the fact that in the 1880s, there were only 28 legal distilleries, in contrast to 129 in Scotland (Barnard 1969). Government licensing was profitable: In the 1880s, the government of the United Kingdom derived 40 percent of its revenue from alcohol (Christian 1990).

Scotch whiskey continues to enjoy a certain mystique. But its manufacture has changed considerably, with coal employed to dry the malt instead of peat. The grain spirit most used to blend Scotch is now made from American maize, and Scotland imports all of its maize and much of its barley (Morrice 1983). Somehow, too, much of the romance has disappeared.

Gin. Gin, on the other hand, never had all that much romance attached to it, especially after William Hogarth depicted the excessive drinking of Londoners in his 1751 engraving, "Gin Lane" (Schivelbusch 1992). Less than a century before, the consumption of spirits had been uncommon in England (Austin 1985); most people drank ale or beer, and the wealthy, although

inclined to a little French brandy, mostly prized imported wines, especially those that were fortified, such as port and Madeira from Portugal and its islands and sherry from Spain (Lichine 1981). Indeed, the dramas and diaries of the Restoration period indicate that these wines were preferred by many over even the "great growths" of France.

The individual said to have pushed Britain onto the path toward "Gin Lane" is William of Orange, Stadtholder of Holland, who ascended the English throne in 1689 as joint sovereign with Mary II. William's homeland made gin, and to encourage its importation into England, he discouraged the sale of French brandy and taxed English beer and cider (Watney 1976). The liquor he sponsored with such determination was then called *genever* or *jenever,* the Dutch name for juniper, a medicinal plant whose berries were used to flavor gin, which was itself a distillation of hopped barley mash (Butler 1926). Also named "Hollands gin" by the English, the drink became so popular in the Netherlands that it replaced beer as the beverage of the military (Austin 1985). In fact, by 1787, there were more than 200 distilleries making gin in the Dutch Republic, and only 57 breweries (Schama 1977).

Many of the gin distilleries had doubtless come into existence to supply the English market that William had engineered. In 1700, some half-million gallons were exported to England (George 1965). But it did not take the English long to begin making their own gin, which, they found, was a good way to use up surplus grain. After all, gin could be made from practically any grain, or even from molasses; its distinctiveness lay in the juniper flavoring (Watney 1976). In 1714, 2 million gallons were produced, and by 1737, English distillers were making 5.4 million gallons annually – nearly a gallon for every man, woman, and child in the population (George 1965).

As early as 1725, London alone held 6,187 gin shops, where people unaccustomed to strong spirits were working hard to overcome this handicap (Monckton 1966). It was called a "gin epidemic": Tavern keepers offered to make one "drunk for a penny, dead drunk for two pence, and straw for nothing" (Schivelbusch 1992: 156), meaning that drunkards were thrown into cellars strewn with straw to sleep off their intoxication. In London during a week in 1750, some 56,000 bushels of wheat were used to produce gin, not quite as many as the 72,000 bushels devoted to breadmaking, but close (Monckton 1966).

At this time, however, gin consumption was about to decline. The Gin Act, passed by Parliament in 1736, prohibited the public sale of gin in London and raised taxes on spirits (George 1965). At first, this statute had little effect on gin consumption: Bootleggers, some employing subterfuges such as the labeling of gin as medicine, helped perpetuate the "epidemic" (Watney 1976). Then in 1751, Parliament slapped a very high tax on gin and tightened restrictions on its sale. This effort, coupled with a sudden rise in grain prices, pushed the price of gin beyond the reach of the poor, who switched back to ale and beer, or to coffee and tea, beverages that were becoming increasingly popular (Mintz 1985). By 1782, annual gin production had fallen to 4 million gallons, and a century after that, Britons were consuming annually only about 1.25 gallons per capita of all spirits combined, although per capita beer and ale consumption was 34 gallons (Johnston 1977).

The Beefeaters distillery was established in 1822, and during the nineteenth century, gin was flavored with angelica, cassia, cardamom, coriander, and ginger, as well as juniper berries (Lichine 1981). The martini cocktail is said to have been invented in 1863 by San Francisco bartender Jerry Thomas (who is also credited with inventing the Tom and Jerry). He allegedly named the drink after the town of Martinez upon learning that this was the destination of a departing guest. However, the use of gin in martinis and "gibsons" (the latter garnished with a pearl onion instead of an olive) has chiefly been a twentieth-century phenomenon. In addition, gin is used in many mixed drinks because of its somewhat neutral taste (Lanza 1995). Modern gin is made in industrial stills and is between 80 and 97 proof (Grossman 1977). The most common type of gin is "London dry" made in both Great Britain and the United States. English gins are 94 proof; American versions are between 80 and 94 proof. Dutch gin survives today as a strongly flavored beverage distilled at a lower proof and drunk neat because of its taste (Grossman 1989).

Vodka. Vodka's distillation apparently dates from the sixteenth century, as the Russians followed the example of others in northern Europe and distilled rye – their most abundant grain – into vodka, using the pot still (Pokhlebkin 1992). As with other liquors, the distillation of vodka produced much leftover mash that could be fed to livestock, making it possible to maintain more animals over harsh winters (Christian 1990). Later, in the nineteenth century, potatoes were employed for distillation, but the thick potato mash required special stills. It has been mostly in the twentieth century that maize and wheat have found their way into Russian and Polish stills.

Vodka is thought of by some as a relative of gin, and many of its uses are the same. On the other hand, the Russians and the Poles point out that vodka "is the only beverage that goes with herring, a fish that makes beer taste insipid and wine metallic" (Toussaint-Samat 1987). Vodka means "little water," and the drink has been valued for its colorlessness and purity. It was also much valued by the Russian government for producing revenues (Christian 1990). Prior to the creation of vodka, the bulk of the country's alcohol production was in the form of beers and meads made locally by the peasantry and, thus, not taxable. But vodka was taxable and, in 1861, provided 45 percent

of the revenue of the Russian state. Throughout the nineteenth century, more than 70 percent of expenditures for the Russian army were paid for by vodka taxes (Christian 1990). At the turn of the twentieth century, Russia established its Kristall vodka monopoly (under the control of the ministry of finance), which produced Stolichnaya vodka and some 70 other brands of liquor (Lichine 1981). The monopoly was suspended from 1914 to 1921, as the various Russian governments during World War I, the Bolshevik revolution, and the Russian civil war attempted prohibition (Pokhlebkin 1992), and was finally abandoned following another wave of government-encouraged temperance begun in the 1980s. Vodka is normally between 80 and 100 proof (Grossman 1977).

Grain spirits similar to gin and vodka are common across northern Europe. One example is Scandinavia's akvavit (Lichine 1981) – a name that is variously spelled. This liquor is distilled from a grain or potato base as a neutral spirit, then redistilled with flavoring. Like gin, akvavit is not aged (Grossman 1977). German and Scandinavian schnapps are usually made from fruit or herbs; Dutch *genever* is flavored with sweet-smelling herbs and is also called schnapps in Europe (Lichine 1981).

Rum. In North America, grain and cane spirits were favored over ale, beer, and wine from the beginning of European settlement (Rorabaugh 1979). English ale would not ferment properly in America's climate; cold winters froze it and hot summers caused the top-fermenting yeast to spoil. (Modern American beer is made with German lager yeasts brought by immigrants in the 1840s. These live at the bottom of the vat and can thus withstand extremes of temperature.) Nor did European wine grapes do well on the Eastern seaboard. Some distillation of grain spirits took place and, though never completely abandoned, was put aside as it became evident that the most expedient course was to ship grain to the sugar islands of the West Indies and to make into rum the molasses sent northward in return.

Rum became the favorite American alcoholic beverage until the Revolution. It is produced by distilling the fermented alcohol made from sugarcane juice (sometimes called "dunder" or "burned ale"). The best rums are distilled twice and, in some cases, aged. Rum was made in Barbados in the 1630s and received its name in 1651, when traveler Thomas Ligon remarked that the island's inhabitants were fond of "Rumbullion alias Kill Devil, and this is made of sugar canes distilled, a hot, hellish and terrible liquor" (Ritchie 1981: 116). Both "rumbullion" and "rumbustion," two early dialect names, may have referred to the violence that the drink was said to engender. Rum was shipped to England in the 1660s, but a taste for it there was slow to develop. In 1698, the English imported only 207 gallons. By contrast, the West India colonists drank so much of it that a visitor said they had "bodies like

Egyptian Mummies" (McCusker 1989). Slaves often drank a colorless raw alcohol made from sugarcane juice, called *clairin* in Haiti, *aguardiente* in Mexico, and *cachaça* in Brazil (Lichine 1981). Distilled only once, and devoid of the flavoring and aging that makes a good rum, these harsher beverages actually were rums, although not called by that name; the term "raw rum," however, is sometimes used to refer to *clairin*.

The demand for rum was great in Africa, where it was traded for slaves to be carried to the West Indies to make more sugar. Much rum was also issued to the slaves of the Caribbean, where it subsequently was incorporated into Afro-Caribbean religious and magical rituals (Lichine 1981). The spirit also became part of the medical lore of the region for a few brief decades spanning the end of the seventeenth century and the first half or so of the eighteenth century, when slaves, soldiers, and sailors, who could afford (or were given) only the cheapest rum, came down with the "dry bellyache." The almost unbearable cramps characteristic of this disease were, in fact, symptoms of lead poisoning – the lead having entered the rum from lead fittings in the stills (Handler et al. 1987). Although diminished in frequency, the dry bellyache persisted as late as the Victorian period (Spencer 1899).

Demand for rum in the North American colonies was intense, requiring distilleries in the sugar islands and in New England, South Carolina, Pennsylvania, and the Canadian Maritime Provinces to satisfy it (McCusker 1989). William Penn's thirsty colonists drank rum, and by the 1720s, Marylanders were managing a per capita consumption of at least 2 gallons annually. Rum was relatively cheap: In 1738, rum from any of Boston's 8 distilleries (they numbered 63 by 1750) cost 2 shillings a gallon. In Georgia, a day's wages could keep a laborer drunk for a week. By 1770, the 118 recorded colonial distilleries were producing an annual total of 4,807,000 gallons of rum, an average of 41,000 gallons each (McCusker 1989).

The West Indies sugar industry inexorably became the foundation of British mercantilism that in 1733 led to the passage of the Molasses Act by Parliament. This law heavily taxed molasses and rum shipped to North America from the non-British Caribbean. It drove up the price of inexpensive molasses from French St. Domingue which caused a substantial increase in rum prices. As a consequence the Molasses Act began decades of rum and molasses smuggling that ended only with the American Revolution. In addition to rum being their favorite drink, much of the prosperity of the North American colonists depended on the molasses trade (McCusker 1989).

In 1759, British grain crops failed, leading to an increase in grain prices throughout the following decade, with the result that the English (especially those of the upper classes) began to develop a late appreciation for rum. Indeed, by 1775, England was importing 2 million gallons of rum each year. Much of this was used to make rum punch, although many thought this drink was inferior to Madeira punch, made from the fortified wine of Madeira (Tannahill 1988).

Rum became even more profitable for British planters after the Molasses Act. In 1798 in Jamaica, for example, planters who made £3,000 net profit from sugar could count on an additional £1,300 from rum (Deerr 1950). By this time, the French had been all but removed from the sugar and rum production of the West Indies because of the revolution of St. Domingue and the emergence of an independent Haiti. Yet Britain was about to be more or less eliminated as a major sugar producer as well. In 1807, the British abolished the slave trade and, in 1833, slavery itself. At this point, Brazil and Cuba became the world's most important sources of sugar, with Cuba outdistancing Brazil as the nineteenth century progressed. The Bacardi Rum Company, founded in Cuba in 1862, became the producer, in the twentieth century, of the most popular brand of rum in the world.

Cuban rum tends to be light, as compared with the darker rums from Jamaica and Barbados, the latter often double distilled and aged (Deerr 1950). Haitian rum is midway between these extremes. There is also *arak* rum from Java, made from sugarcane juice fermented with rice and yeast (Grossman 1977). The yeast strains used to ferment sugarcane juice are said to be responsible for the variations in flavor among different kinds of rum (Lichine 1981). However, as sugarcane always ferments within a short time after being cut, it seems clear that wild yeast is adequate to the task of fermenting the cane juice.

Rum has a strong association with the sea and sailors. Those of the United States, Canada, and Britain were huge consumers of rum, and "grog" rations in the latter two navies continued into the 1970s. The term "grog" comes, allegedly, from the eighteenth-century British Admiral Edward Vernon, who wore a grogham (heavy wool) cloak, and to reduce drunkenness among his crews, ordered their rum diluted with water, resulting in the famous rum-based drink named after his outer garment (Tannahill 1988).

Bourbon and other New World whiskeys. Although rum was the drink of colonial Americans, independence from Great Britain severed much of the sugar connection, forcing a greater reliance on local resources. The result was a change to corn whiskey or "bourbon" (as it came to be called), made originally in Bourbon County, Kentucky. By 1800, Americans were drinking some 3.5 gallons of liquor – mostly whiskeys – per capita each year, which seems to represent a substantial increase in consumption over that of rum in previous decades.

Not that Americans had ever relied solely on rum. Grain whiskeys made from rye and corn had been produced on the eastern seaboard practically from the beginning of the colonies, and whiskey was also imported. In fact, each family that arrived with the Winthrop fleet of 1629 was required to carry *aqua vitae* to the Massachusetts Bay Colony, presumably as a medicine (Cressy 1995).

During the eighteenth century, Scottish and Irish settlers brought with them the techniques of whiskey making. Many settled in the southern colonies as farmers, and following the American Revolution, distillation was one way in which farmers might add to their yearly income. Although such activities were pursued virtually everywhere in the new United States, a special enthusiasm for operating stills developed in the back country of the Blue Ridge and Great Smoky Mountains, where (as in Scotland and Ireland) rugged terrain hindered the transportation of grain to market. Although an acre of land might produce 40 to 60 bushels of corn, a horse could carry only four bushels at one time. The same horse, however, could carry 16 gallons of whiskey, which was the equivalent of 24 bushels of grain. Clearly, for the mountain people, distillation represented the most efficient method of preparing corn for sale. In the 1830s, consumption of distilled spirits in America reached a peak of more than 5 gallons per capita annually (Rorabaugh 1979); by this time, whiskey made from corn accounted for most of that amount (Dabney 1974).

Private distillation, though illegal, continued even after roads were constructed through the mountain areas, partly because of tradition, partly because of remoteness (stills were easy to conceal), but mostly because it was increasingly profitable, as taxes on liquor continued to be raised. Thus, although illegal whiskey has been made as far afield as Alaska (where it was called "hooch" after the Hoochinoo, a tribe that made a distilled drink), 60 percent of all arrests for the offense have been made in the mountains of the South (Carr 1972).

Corn, however, was no longer always the primary ingredient in illicit distillation. Sugar was sometimes used to speed up fermentation, resulting in a kind of rum that was, nevertheless, still called whiskey. Sugar whiskey was notorious for the hangovers and headaches it produced. In addition, illegal whiskey was sometimes adulterated with everything from manure to lye (to speed fermentation). It was often distilled in soldered tanks that put lead salts into the liquid, and it was condensed in old automobile radiators. Clearly, illegal whiskey could be dangerous: It killed some people, blinded more, and helped destroy the brains, livers, and stomachs of many others (Dabney 1974).

Today, Kentucky is the center of whiskey production in the United States, although some is made in Tennessee and Virginia (Jackson 1988). Starchy varieties of corn are best for whiskey making. They are wet or dry milled, then fermented before distillation. The two major yeasting processes are sweet and sour mash. Sweet mash whiskey comes from new yeast, whereas yeast from a previous fermentation constitutes one-fourth of the yeast added to grain to produce sour mash whiskey. Sour mash is easier to make, and sweet mash tends to go bad (Grossman 1977). In the United States, a significant portion of the corn crop goes into brewing and distillation (Inglett and Munck 1980). Obviously, bourbon remains an American favorite. It is made from at least 51 percent corn mash distilled at 160 proof, diluted to 80 to 100 proof, and matured for no less than three years (Lichine 1981).

Canada, which produced its share of rum in the Maritime Provinces, turned to whiskey made from rye, now mostly called Canadian whiskey (Jackson 1988; Morrison and Moreira 1988). Straight whiskeys are the products of distillation with nothing added, whereas blended whiskeys are mixtures of whiskey from different distilleries or different years. These two kinds, straight and blended combined, make up about half of the American whiskey market. The remainder is "light" whiskey, which is less flavorful, always blended, and reduced in proof. Like Canadian whiskey, it is often made from rye.

Liqueurs. Liqueurs are grain or cane spirits that have been flavored, are usually sweet, and are normally enjoyed after dinner. Their origin lies in the early years of alcohol distillation, when sugar and flavorings were employed to mask the bad taste of raw alcohol, and until the sixteenth century or so, they were mostly regarded as medicines. Early in that century, however, this began to change. In 1532, Michael Savonarola, a Florentine physician, authored *The Art of Making Waters,* a book of recipes and instructions for producing liqueurs. By the following century, Italy had a flourishing liqueur industry (Austin 1985).

Many of the old liqueur recipes, with "secret" mixtures of flavorings, originated in monasteries. The most famous liqueurs made from such recipes are Chartreuse (from the Chartreuse monastery at Paris) and Benedictine (Grossman 1977). Perhaps the most notorious liqueur is no longer made. This was absinthe, flavored with hallucinogenic wormwood *(Artemisia absinthium)* that caused a variety of physical and mental symptoms, and even death (Conrad 1988). It was produced by Henri-Louis Pernod (Lanier 1995). France finally outlawed absinthe in 1915, and now it is illegal virtually everywhere (Lichine 1981). Liqueurs are flavored with ingredients as mundane as coffee (Kahlua, made in Mexico) and as exotic as the rare green oranges of the Caribbean (Curaçao, from the island of that name). Other famous coffee liqueurs are Tia Maria from Jamaica and Pasha from Turkey (Grossman 1977).

Distilled Spirits in the East

Spirits are not as popular in the East as in the West, despite remarkable historical exceptions, such as the hard-drinking Mongols, who have even been credited with the discovery of distillation. The lukewarm eastern attitude toward liquor has existed in part because of the popularity of tea, in part because opium, betel nut, and other stimulants have historically substituted for strong drink, and in part because of a widespread devotion to beer. Another reason may be that the livers of Asian peoples tend to be low in aldehyde dehydrogenase isozyme (ALDHI), which helps to metabolize alcohol. This condition can cause the face to flush with the ingestion of even very moderate amounts of alcohol – a telltale signal among many who live by Confucian rules of conduct that frown on intoxication. In nineteenth-century imperial China, when strong drink was served, a gentleman not wishing to offend his host might pay someone else to drink it for him (Chang 1977).

Nonetheless, several grain alcohols are produced in the East. In China, *mao tai* – a whiskey made from millet and wheat – is the best known, and has been known to the world since it was served to U.S. President Richard Nixon during his 1972 visit there (Simoons 1991). *San-shao,* meaning "three times burnt," is another Chinese liquor. It is made from sorghum and distilled three times, but is not to be confused with *shao-chiu,* which is distilled from grain ale (Simoons 1991). In Japan, the latter is called *shochu* and competes with local whiskey that is modeled on Scotch (Jackson 1988).

In Mongolia and Siberia, the drink best known from lore and literature is *kumyss* (or *kumiss*), an alcoholic beverage (fermented and sometimes distilled) made from mare's milk. In about the seventh century, the Mongols introduced it in China, where it was popular for a time. Later, however, it acquired a reputation as a drink of barbarians and was so regarded after the Mongols conquered China in the thirteenth century (Chang 1977). A high level of lactose intolerance among the Chinese may also help to explain the disdain for *kumyss,* as well as for other milk products. The distilled form of the drink is sometimes called *arak,* a common Asian name for all kinds of liquor (Lichine 1981).

In Southeast Asia, "toddy," a distilled palm wine made from fermented sap, appears in many varieties that may actually be thought of as brandies. Historically, toddies have been made in primitive stills, although a few are commercially produced (Lichine 1981). However, toddy, and other distilled beverages that exist in Oceania, are poorly documented. The latter have resulted from the distillation by Europeans of local alcoholic beverages; one example is the *okelahao* of Hawaii. This drink, made from *ti* roots fermented in the bilge of a canoe and distilled in a ship's cookpot, has yet to find a market outside the islands (Grossman 1977).

Distilled Spirits and Human Health

Chemically, any distilled beverage consists largely of ethyl alcohol. Other components include esters, fusel oils (isobutyl and amyl alcohols) and, of course, the ingredients added to flavor and color the beverage. Unflavored grain spirit is merely alcohol and water. It is the impurities and additives that largely contribute to hangovers (Dabney 1974). As mentioned, early distilled alcohol was used only as a medicine because distillers did not yet know how to separate the unpleasant beginning and end fractions of the distilled liquid from the middle, and because aging, which mellows the product, was unknown. The effect of the early medicinal wine brandies must have been strong indeed.

Nutritionally, distilled beverages are high in calories but contain little in the way of other nutrients. Because each gram of 86 proof alcohol imparts 7 calories, the average drink bristles with 106 calories, in addition to any calories in the mix (Robertson et al. 1986). Some researchers, however, contend that the calories in alcohol have, in the past, served as an important source of energy for the poor (Braudel 1973). One study suggests that in France during the 1780s, 10 percent of an individual's caloric intake was supplied by alcohol (Austin 1985). The same was probably the case for slaves in the Caribbean: Jamaican rum yields twice the calories of a similar measure of molasses. A counter-argument, of course, is that alcohol was allowed to replace more nutritional foods. John McCusker (1989) has noted that alcohol calories are more quickly absorbed than those from other sources; he credits the ability of early Americans to consume such large amounts of rum and whiskey to this propensity.

Yet, a large amount of any kind of alcohol can be nutritionally disastrous because it destroys vitamin C and the B-complex vitamins. Indeed, about the only remaining cases of frankly nutritional diseases (such as pellagra) found in the developed world are among alcoholics. In addition, although it appears that moderate alcohol consumption can help prevent heart disease, large amounts can help cause it. Alcohol is also suspected of being a factor in the etiology of some cancers and is known to be a culprit in causing much liver damage, including cirrhosis.

Another unfavorable aspect of distilled spirits is the social and physical harm they have historically brought to peoples unaccustomed to them (Mancall 1995). In America, Asia, Africa, and Australia, rum and whiskey became instrumental, in the hands first of European traders and then of European imperialists, in destroying aboriginal life (Miller 1985). It is significant that in Mexico and Peru, where some alcoholic beverages existed at the time of European contact, the aboriginal peoples and their traditions have fared much better than those in places like Australia, where alcohol had been unknown.

Clearly, distilled spirits have had a tremendous impact on human history and health. In a relatively few centuries, their manufacture has moved from the quasi-magical procedure of the alchemists to a global industry that undergirds the economies of entire regions. But from the "gin epidemic" of England to the endemic drunkenness of the Australian aborigines, spirits have also caused such misery that practically every society in the world has laws and customs to regulate their consumption, and many states have tried to outlaw them. That such attempts have been largely unsuccessful demonstrates the existence of a worldwide, collective opinion about the pleasures and profits provided by alcohol, which outweighs the harm it continues to cause.

James Comer

Bibliography

Austin, Gregory. 1985. *Alcohol in Western society from antiquity to 1800: A chronological history.* Santa Barbara, Calif.

Barnard, Alfred. 1969. *The whisky distilleries of the United Kingdom.* Newton Abbot, England.

Barty-King, Hugh, and Anton Massell. 1983. *Rum.* London.

Benes, Peter, ed. 1985. *Foodways in the Northeast.* Boston.

Bergeron, Victor. 1946. *Trader Vic's book of food and drink.* Garden City, N.Y.

Braudel, Fernand. 1973. *Capitalism and material life, 1400-1800.* New York.

Bruce-Mitford, Rupert. 1975. *The Sutton Hoo ship burial.* London.

Butler, Frank. 1926. *Wine and the winelands of the world, with some account of places visited.* London.

Carr, Jess. 1972. *The second oldest profession; an informal history of moonshining in America.* Englewood Cliffs, N.J.

Chang, K. C., ed. 1977. *Food in Chinese culture.* New Haven, Conn.

Christian, David. 1990. *Living water.* Oxford.

Conrad, Barnaby. 1988. *Absinthe: History in a bottle.* San Francisco.

Cressy, David. 1995. *Coming over: Migration and communication between England and New England in the seventeenth century.* New York.

Dabney, Joseph Earl. 1974. *Mountain spirits. A chronicle of corn whiskey from King James' Ulster Plantation to America's Appalachians and the moonshine life.* New York.

Deerr, Noel. 1950. *The history of sugar.* London.

Doxat, John. 1950. *The world of drinks and drinking.* New York.

Driver, Harold. 1961. *Indians of North America.* London.

E. C. (no other name given). 1859. On the antiquity of brewing and distilling in Ireland. *Ulster Journal of Archaeology* 7: 33.

Forbes, R. J. 1948. *Short history of the art of distillation from the beginning up to the death of Cellier Blumenthal.* Leiden, Netherlands.

Gayre, G. R. 1948. *Wassail! In mazers of mead.* London.

George, Mary Dorothy. 1965. *London life in the eighteenth century.* New York.

Grimes, William. 1988. Rio brandy. *Esquire* 110: 18.

Grossman, Harold. 1977. *Grossman's guide to wines, beers, and spirits.* Sixth revised edition. Rev. Harriet Lembeck. New York.

Handler, Jerome S., Arthur C. Aufderheide, and Robert S. Corruccini. 1987. Lead contact and poisoning in Barbados slaves. In *The African exchange,* ed. Kenneth F. Kiple, 140-66. London.

Harrison, Brian. 1971. *Drink and the Victorians.* Oxford.

Holmes, Urban Tignor. 1952. *Daily living in the twelfth century, based on the observations of Alexander Neckam in London and Paris.* Madison, Wis.

Inglett, George, and Lars Munck, eds. 1980. *Cereals for food and beverage.* New York.

Jackson, Michael. 1988. *The world guide to whisky.* Topsfield, Mass.

Johnston, James. 1977. *A hundred years of eating.* Dublin.

Kiple, Kenneth F. 1984. *The Caribbean slave: A biological history.* London.

Kurtz, Ernest. 1979. *Not-God. A history of Alcoholics Anonymous.* Center City, Minn.

Lanier, Doris. 1995. *Absinthe, the cocaine of the nineteenth century: A history of the hallucinogenic drug and its effect on artists and writers in Europe and the United States.* Jefferson, N.C.

Lanza, Joseph. 1995. *The cocktail: The influence of spirits on the American psyche.* New York.

Lichine, Alexis. 1981. *New encyclopedia of wines and spirits.* Third edition. New York.

Mancall, Peter. 1995. *Deadly medicine: Indians and alcohol in early America.* Ithaca, N.Y.

Marcus, Robert D., and David Burner, eds. 1992. *America firsthand: Readings in American history.* Second edition. New York.

Maresca, Tom. 1992. Grappa glorified. *Town & Country Monthly* 146: 40-2.

Maurer, David. 1974. *Kentucky moonshine.* Lexington, Ky.

McCusker, John. 1989. *Rum and the American Revolution: The rum trade and the balance of payments of the thirteen continental colonies.* New York.

McGuire, E. B. 1993. *Irish whiskey: A history of distilling, the spirit trade, and excise controls in Ireland.* New York.

Mellaart, James. 1967. *Çatal Hüyük: A Neolithic town in Anatolia.* New York.

Miller, James. 1985. *Koori.* London.

Miller, Wilbur R. 1991. *Revenuers and moonshiners: Enforcing federal liquor laws in the mountain South, 1865-1900.* Chapel Hill, N.C.

Mintz, Sidney. 1985. *Sweetness and power: The place of sugar in modern history.* London.

Monckton, H. A. 1966. *A history of English ale and beer.* London.

Morrice, Philip. 1983. *The Schweppes guide to Scotch.* Sherborne, England.

Morrison, James H., and James Moreira, eds. 1988. *Tempered by rum: Rum in the history of the Maritime Provinces.* Porters Lake, Nova Scotia.

Needham, Joseph. 1984. Spagyrical discovery and invention. In *Science and civilization in China,* Vol. 5, Part 4. London.

Nelson, Derek. 1995. *Moonshiners, bootleggers, and rum-runners.* Osceola, Wis.

Pliny (Gaius Plinius Secundus) [Venice 1469] 1940. *Natural history,* trans. Harris Rackham, ed. W. Heinemann. London.

Pokhlebkin, William. 1992. *A history of vodka,* trans. Renfrey Clarke. London.

Ray, Cyril. 1974. *Cognac.* New York.

Ritchie, Carson I. A. 1981. *Food in civilization.* New York.

Robertson, Laurel, Carol Flinders, and Brian Ruppenthal. 1986. *The new Laurel's kitchen.* Second edition. Berkeley, Calif.

Roesdahl, Else, and David M. Wilson, eds. 1992. *From Viking to Crusader: The Scandinavians and Europe, 800–1200,* trans. Helen Clarke et al. New York.

Ronnenberg, Herman. 1993. *Beer and brewing in the inland Northwest.* Moscow, Idaho.

Rorabaugh, W. J. 1979. *The alcoholic republic, an American tradition.* New York.

Schama, Simon. 1977. *Patriots and liberators: Revolution in the Netherlands, 1780–1813.* London.

Schivelbusch, Wolfgang. 1992. *Tastes of paradise.* New York.

Simoons, Frederick. 1991. *Food in China: A cultural and historical inquiry.* Boca Raton, Fla.

Smith, Hedrick. 1991. *The new Russians.* New York.

Spencer, Edward. 1899. *The flowing bowl.* Sixth edition. London.

Tannahill, Reay. 1988. *Food in history.* New York.

Toussaint-Samat, Maguelonne. 1987. *Histoire naturelle & morale de la nourriture.* Paris.

Watney, John. 1976. *Mother's ruin: A history of gin.* London.

Watson, Stanley A., and Paul Ramstead, eds. 1987. *Corn: Chemistry and technology.* St. Paul, Minn.

Wigginton, Eliot, ed. 1972. *The Foxfire book: Hog dressing; log cabin building; mountain crafts and foods; planting by the signs; snake lore, hunting tales, faith healing; moonshining; and other affairs of plain living.* Garden City, N.Y.

III.6 ⟋ Kava

Kava is both a plant and a drink made from that plant for ritual occasions. Kava usage is limited mostly to the Pacific basin, where it occurs widely from New Guinea in the west to the Marquesas in the east, and from Hawaii in the north to the southern Cook Islands. Some societies have ceased using it in recent times, whereas others ceased but began again after missionary prohibitions lessened and national independence brought kava to the fore as a mark of national identity (Brunton 1989).

A narcotic effect is commonly thought to be the main reason for kava's consumption, but elaborate rituals have developed with kava as their centerpiece, together with complex rules about who can drink the substance and when. Powerful cultural elements that persisted into the 1990s led to the commercialization of the root; kava is now drunk by overseas island communities in Auckland, Sydney, Honolulu, and Los Angeles. Indeed it seems that kava has evolved as a major force in the maintenance of the identities of Pacific islanders at home and abroad.

"Kava" is the term for the whole plant, which according to Western botanical terminology, is *Piper methysticum,* placing it among the pepper families (Lebot, Merlin, and Lindstrom 1992). But "kava" may also refer to the beverage made from the roots or stem of the plant. Moreover, the term can mean a ritual in which the crushing of the root to make the beverage is a noteworthy activity.

Kava is a reconstructed Proto-Oceanic term within the large Austronesian language family (Biggs, Walsh, and Waqa 1972: 30). It, or a similar word, such as *'ava,* is still widely used throughout the eastern Pacific to refer to the same root. In Pohnpei in Micronesia, the word is *sakau,* a close cognate. In Fiji, kava is referred to as *yaqona,* a term that probably reflects its bitter taste, *qona/kona.* Throughout Vanuatu, which has some 170 vernacular languages and dialects, the terms for kava are quite varied (see Lebot and Cabalion 1988: 54–67 for a list). In northern Vanuatu, kava is known as *maloku,* meaning quiet, subdued (Crowley 1990), while *nikawa,* a close cognate, appears only in Tanna in southern Vanuatu. The local term for kava in Papua New Guinea is also quite varied (see Lebot and Cabalion 1988; Brunton 1989).

Origin and Spread

The origin of the kava plant and the relationships among the many different cultivars found today have both been subjects of detailed study by botanists (Lebot, Aradhya, and Manshardt 1991). Using material collected from throughout the Pacific, they have traced genetic links among the various samples, concentrating particularly on diversity in the Melanesian area.

Vincent Lebot and P. Cabalion (1988) have produced an inventory of the names of local cultivars around the Pacific. From chromosome counts they distinguish the genus *Piper wichmannii* from that of *Piper methysticum. P. wichmannii,* the wild form, has been located only in Melanesia, that is, in parts of New Guinea, the Solomon islands, and northern Vanuatu. In contrast, *P. methysticum,* the cultivated form, has been found throughout the high islands of Polynesia and on the high islands of Pohnpei and Kosrae in eastern Micronesia, and in Melanesia. *P. wichmannii* has been found to have higher isozyme variability than *P. methysticum,* but the two overlap for zymotype 9, leading the authors to suggest that there is no taxonomic distinction between the two plants.

Lebot and Cabalion, along with Vincent Lebot et al. (1991: 181), suggest that what was being selected for was the kavalactones, which have a physiological effect when the product is drunk. They indicate that *P. methysticum* was "domesticated through vegetative propagation from a narrow genetic base in wild fertile progenitor . . . becoming sterile through mutations affecting fertility. . . . Because *P. methysticum* must be cultivated, this plant has resulted from human selection of somatic mutants. . . . That selection process has resulted in variability in both morphological characteristics and the kavalactones" (Lebot et al. 1991: 181). The root of *P. wichmannii,* which according to Vanu-

atu oral tradition was made into a drink, was too powerful in its effect and induced nausea (Weightman
1989: 236). This may be a reason that *P. methysticum*
was developed instead.

Identification of these two closely related species
leads botanists and a historical linguist to suggest that
northern Vanuatu is the center of origin of kava cultivars, which have been domesticated probably in the
last 2,500 to 3,000 years. From Vanuatu, varieties of
kava were introduced to Papua New Guinea, eastern
Micronesia, and Polynesia. This mainly west-east
spread was followed by an east-west spread, from
Tonga and Samoa to East Futuna, from which some
Futunan speakers sailed westward to settle an island
off south Vanuatu that they named West Futuna. From
there it spread to the other Polynesian outliers and
the islands in southern Vanuatu (Crowley 1990).
According to Lebot et al. (1991: 184): "Kava is a relatively late introduction into Polynesia, since there is
no variation in isozymes in that region." Further
details of the genetic history of kava are given in
Lebot, Merlin, and Lindstrom (1992).

Botanical Description

The kava plant is a perennial shrub that reaches one
or two meters in height. It has many stems and bears
a light foliage of heart-shaped leaves. The stems are
notable for being distinctly segmented by a dark
band, similar to bamboo.

The plant is dioecious; that is, it bears male and
female flowers on separate plants. To propagate kava,
a stem bud is taken from a *P. methysticum* male plant,
and from this a root system and shoots develop. Vegetative reproduction, thus, allows a high degree of
selectivity in which plants are selected for propagation. The importance of the plant as a ritual drink has
led to considerable human intervention in its evolution with resulting diversification.

Kava is cultivated along with other root crops,
such as taro and yams, in household gardens and on
shifting agriculture plantations. Preferred locations
vary: In Futuna in the 1960s, the plants were cultivated high on the mountainside because large ants
attacked them nearer the coast (Gaillot 1962); today,
however, kava is cultivated in the plantation area
behind the houses of coastal areas (Pollock 1995a).

To harvest the root in Vanuatu, the plant is dug out
after three to four years of growth when the rootstock and mass of fibrous roots may weigh 5 to 10
kilos. In Futuna and Tonga, the root with its stem still
attached but leaves removed may be offered as a tribute at an important occasion, such as the induction of
a chief. For example, in Tonga for the induction ceremony of the crown prince, some 300 stems and roots
of kava were cultivated and donated by the families
living on lands belonging to the Tongan royal family.
In Samoa the roots may be dried before they are presented at a kava ceremony; each honored guest is pre-

sented with his (or her) stem of kava, so that some
stems may change hands several times before they are
finally pounded to make a kava drink.

Distribution

We surmise that many changes over time have
affected the distribution of the plant, as well as the
beverage and the ritual. Thus, in precontact times, all
three are likely to have been different than those of
today.

There is no reported evidence of the kava plant on
New Caledonia, Easter Island, Belau, Yap, and parts of
Papua New Guinea, nor on the atolls. In the case of
the atolls, the soils are too poor and there is too much
exposure to salt spray. In New Zealand it is likely that
the climate has been too cold for the plant to grow.

Kava, as a drink, also shows no clear patterning.
Records of its employment as a beverage come from
those places that grew kava, which makes sense
because the plant has to be vegetatively propagated
and, consequently, was grown for a reason. But in
places such as Tikopia, the plant continues to grow
even though its usage has disappeared.

In those societies which do employ the plant ritually, a number of variations have developed over time
and space. In some societies, these ritual occasions
are still very formal, as in Futuna, Samoa, and Tonga,
while in others a more secular consumption of kava
has become popular, as in Pohnpei and Vanuatu. In
Fiji, Tonga, Futuna, Pohnpei, and Vanuatu, both ritual
and secular uses are practiced today.

According to missionary accounts, the nineteenth
century saw the customary utilization of kava disappear in Tahiti, the Cook Islands, Hawaii, and Kosrae.
This also happened in southern Vanuatu in the 1920s,
but there kava drinking was revived after independence in 1979 (Brunton 1989). By contrast, on Wallis,
widespread kava ceremonies declined after World War
II and today are held only for very special occasions.
Still another variation is found on the neighboring
islands of Tikopia and Anuta, where in the 1930s kava
was prepared as a drink. But the people did not drink
it; rather, the ritual libation was poured to the gods
(Firth 1970; Feinberg 1981).

Difference may also be found in the ways the root
is prepared for drinking. In some societies it has been
chewed (mainly by young women), while in others it
is pounded or grated. Missionaries exerted a strong
influence to discourage chewing kava because they
considered it to be unhygienic and a way of spreading
disease. In Vanuatu, young men have taken over the
role of preparing the root, but in western Polynesia it
still belongs to women, particularly on very important
occasions.

Some societies process the root when it is green,
whereas others prefer a beverage made from the dry
root. In Fiji, at a highly formal welcoming ceremony, a
whole fresh green plant is presented to the chief

guest. If the fresh green plant is unobtainable, then an appropriate amount of dried, or even powdered, root is presented (Ravuvu 1987: 25).

The patchy nature of kava use has intrigued anthropologists, botanists, and others for a century or more. Edwin Burrows, for example, in his comparison of cultural features of western Polynesian societies (which he saw as distinct from Melanesian and other Polynesian societies), noted that "the western Polynesian kava complex appears as a local elaboration on a widespread Oceanic base. The occurrence of the whole complex in parts of Fiji is probably due to diffusion from western Polynesia. . . . Distinct resemblances to western Polynesian kava customs elsewhere in Melanesia and Micronesia are also probably due to diffusion from western Polynesia" (Burrows 1939: 114-15). In western Polynesia he included Samoa, Tonga, 'Uvea/Wallis, and Futuna along with Fiji.

W. H. Rivers (1914) had earlier attempted to account for this scattered distribution by distinguishing "kava people" from "betel people," suggesting that exploitation of the two forms of the *Piper* plant were mutually exclusive. Betel is a combination of two plant substances, the *Areca catechu* nut and the *Piper betle* leaf, in which the nut is wrapped so that it can be chewed. The leaf contains the narcotic substances.

Ron Brunton (1989), in his society-by-society reexamination of Rivers's thesis, however, indicates that the distribution is not quite so mutually exclusive. His review of the linguistic and archeological evidence suggests to him that the Bismarck Archipelago is the "homeland" of kava, where it was part of an early social complex known as Lapita culture. From there it was traded along a coastal route to southern New Guinea and, later, to Fiji and Polynesia. He hypothesizes that kava moved with the eastward spread of Lapita culture some 3,000 years ago (Brunton 1989: 82). Such a spread was not unidirectional, and kava usage later diffused back westward from Samoa and Tonga. It, thus, reached southern Vanuatu, and Tanna in particular, he argues, several hundred years after it had become a part of the culture of northern Vanuatu. The most likely agents of transmission were the Polynesians of Aniwa and West Futuna, two islands just off the coast of southern Vanuatu (inhabited by Polynesian speakers), who brought kava customs developed in eastern Oceania back to Melanesia (Brunton 1989: 83).

Brunton also considers it likely that kava was once drunk by many peoples in Melanesia who subsequently abandoned it for unknown reasons. Similarly, he argues that betel, too, may have dropped out of use in some societies that may have subsequently exploited kava. Thus, he considers the belief that kava and betel are mutually exclusive to be largely mistaken. Both have been in and out of use over time in various parts of the Pacific (Brunton 1989: 85).

It can be concluded, therefore, that not every island society has employed kava, that the plant does not occur everywhere, and that the ways in which it was employed also differ from place to place. Such fluctuations in occurrence of the plant and the customs associated with it are likely to have marked its long history. This may be because a particular society chose to drop such customs, or was forced to do so after cyclone damage rendered the plant unavailable, as happened in Futuna in 1986 (Pollock field notes 1987). Yet at a later time, the plant could have been reintroduced from a neighboring island along with new ways of employing it. Consequently, today we can see a range of kava usage from very ritual occasions to more secular ones, which may reflect differences in its social importance.

Ritual Uses

Kava rituals have become differentiated in both practice and ideology as societies have dispersed over time and developed their own distinctive cultural characteristics. The rituals took two broad forms: those in which the kava was prepared and drunk, usually in a kava circle, and those in which the whole root was presented to an honored person. But in either case, the root symbolizes the ties between ancestors and present-day peoples, represented by their chiefs and nobles; it, thus, symbolizes both past and present.

The most formal rituals at which kava is drunk begin with the appropriate people seated in an inner circle, with the community assembled around its outer edge. The processing of root to make the beverage is under the direction of the chief officiator for kava ceremonies. The ritual ends when the chief dignitary signals that the circle should break up – often when he himself has moved out of the circle.

Kava rituals take place outdoors as well as in specially designated houses. In Futuna, a house known as *tauasu* is specially set aside for men's nightly kava sessions. For large formal kava ceremonies, at which many communities are present, an outdoor venue is obviously necessary. In Vanuatu, the kava-drinking grounds are outdoor sites, usually under banyan trees.

Processing

The processing of kava, which transforms the whole root into a mass of fibers and pulp, is also highly ritualized. It consists of three steps: pulverizing the root, adding water to the pulp, and serving the liquid. The main person making kava in western Polynesia is usually a young woman, who is aided by several young men.

Processing begins once everyone is seated and the necessary pieces of equipment are in place, including the wooden kava bowl, whole roots, water, the fiber strainer, and serving cups. The kava root, whether green or dried, is cut into small pieces and chewed, pounded, or grated, according to local custom. In the past, chewing the root was the most widespread practice; this task was assigned to several young girls or young men, chosen for their perfect teeth. They washed out their mouths before commencing to chew until all the pulp was macerated, leaving a fibrous ball that each girl took from her mouth and placed in the kava bowl.

The mode of reducing the kava root to pulp has changed over time. As already mentioned missionaries discouraged chewing the root on the grounds that the practice spread disease. Alternative methods call for pounding the root, grinding it between two stones, or grating it. Upon the command of the chief of the kava ceremonies, water is added to the balls of pulp and fiber in the wooden kava bowl. The chief calls out the order as to when the kava should be mixed, how much water is to be added, and when the mixture should be strained. Adding the water is the most significant part of this ceremonial preparation. According to Futunans, it transforms one substance, the root, into another, the beverage. The root, thus, becomes the medium for communication with the gods, a means of both honoring and supplicating them.

The third stage begins once the mixture is ready to be served. Cups are carried to individual participants in the kava circle by young men designated for the task. The chief officiator calls the name of the person to be served. In Samoa these names are exclusively for use in the kava ceremony (known as kava cup names) and are not used in other situations (Williamson 1939).

Upon receipt of the cup, the recipient claps and pours out a small libation to the gods before drinking the remaining liquid in one gulp. In Samoa the first cup, designated for a particular god, used to be poured out by the chief officiator before others were served. The Tikopian practice of pouring out the carefully prepared liquid (Firth 1970) was thus in line with the general ritual procedures, but represented an alternative kind of development in that no living person drank the kava.

Clearly, such rites performed in front of the assembled community are very formalized. All movements and gestures have become stylized, especially in western Polynesia, where those eligible to perform the tasks undergo elaborate training.

Kava Drinking Circle

The seating order at each ceremonial event in western Polynesian societies is established by the kava officiator, who uses his knowledge of the relative status of the participants. The individual with the highest status sits in the center of the arc, with others seated to his left and right according to their relative status. In western Polynesian systems, a *matapule,* or talking chief, sits next to his chief. The circle may consist of between 15 and 40 persons.

The serving of the kava cups according to the order called by the chief officiator, thus, serves to reiterate the community hierarchy in a very visual and visible manner. The status of particular titles relative to one another and the incumbents holding those titles are displayed for community knowledge and affirmation.

Degrees of Formality

The most formal kava circles occur for the investiture of a new supreme chief. Such a ceremony was performed in Tonga in 1976 for the investiture of the crown prince of Tonga, an event that coincided with the Tonga Constitutional Centenary celebrations.

In Futuna and the neighboring island of Rotuma, a number of lesser rituals involving the kava plant were practiced, and some still are. A morning cup of kava was drunk together by chiefs of friendly hamlets to propitiate the spirits for the right outcome of the day's events (Rozier 1963). On 'Uvea/Wallis, by contrast, the range of kava occasions has been reduced to the very formal one for the installation of a new Lavelua (chief) and to some others associated with the Catholic Church's annual first communion celebration.

Although their island is nominally part of western Polynesia, Niueans have had a cultural ideology that differs from that of their neighbors. Edwin Loeb (1926) reported that only the priest was allowed to drink a potion to the gods, doubtless because the island's poor soils make it difficult to grow kava. Hence, its use was limited to priests.

Pohnpei, though in Micronesia, has shared much of the formality of western Polynesian societies, where kava (known as *sakau*) was used to support an elaborate chiefly system. Today, major events that draw the districts together are still marked by a kava ceremony, but much is also drunk informally (Peterson 1995).

In Vanuatu, only the island of Tanna has maintained the ritual use of kava. There, the emphasis is less on the hierarchy of the circle; the focal part of the ritual is when each man spits out the last mouthful of his cup by way of sending messages to the ancestors (Brunton 1989; Lindstrom 1987).

In other parts of Vanuatu, kava is drunk but with considerably less ceremony. The heaviest users have been the healers or controllers of magic, who are said to use the drink to improve their communication with the gods (Young 1995).

In those parts of Polynesia where kava rituals are no longer practiced, we can still glean a notion of their formality from the written accounts by Europeans. In Tahiti, kava was used only by chiefs, but not as part of any religious ritual (Oliver 1987). Similarly, the chiefs in the Marquesas were reported to follow the steps in ritual processing, but no elaborate ceremonials were practiced (Dening 1980). In the Cook Islands, reports indicate only that a bowl of kava was made at an installation ceremony (Gill 1876), but we have no further detail.

In Hawaii, the practice of drinking 'awa died out in the mid–nineteenth century. It was drunk mainly by the ali'i or chiefs, though it was not forbidden to commoners. As E. S. C. Handy summarized the practices: "'Awa's ceremonial uses were simply the expression of the belief that gods like the same good things of life that men did" (1972: 191).

In earlier times, kava usage was also highly ritualized on Tikopia, a small island north of Vanuatu with a Polynesian culture, though geographically among Melanesian peoples. But it differed markedly from western Polynesian practices in one small but important detail. As Raymond Firth (1970: 203) noted, "it was poured out, not drunk." Otherwise its preparation and presentation followed the practices of other Polynesian societies. According to Firth: "the whole ideology of kava concentrated upon its religious significance in ritual. There were no social kava-drinking ceremonies, nor any consumption of kava as a beverage apart from [a very few] casual instances. In such a religious context the material properties of the kava were of less importance than its signalization function" (1970: 204).

Thus, ritual uses of kava across the Pacific vary considerably. Kava drinking almost everywhere has been predominantly the prerogative of chiefs and priests. Where other men are allowed to participate, it linked the more highly ranked senior men with the more lowly ranked. The main function of kava in these rituals is to communicate with the ancestral spirits, thus imbuing kava with an important mediating role. The whole ritual has a social rather than an individual character; it is a group experience.

Exchanges of the Root

Presentations of the kava root to a chief or an honored guest were ritually made to ask for a favor, or to atone for a wrong, or to ask a priest to propitiate the gods for a special service, such as stopping destructive winds (Rozier 1963). Moreover, at ceremonial functions where it was not appropriate to make a kava drink, whole roots might be presented to a visiting dignitary. Such a procedure still occurs in New Zealand within the Samoan community; a visiting dignitary from Samoa or elsewhere is presented with a root as a token of respect.

In Tanna, Vanuatu, kava was at the center of a network of exchanges that linked villages through "paths" or "roads" that connected the various kava-drinking grounds. Social relationships were developed and maintained along these roads, over which knowledge, information, and goodwill also passed (Brunton 1989; Lebot, Merlin, and Lindstrom 1992).

The kava root is also given in exchange for medicine or as a gift between friends. Such exchanges are noteworthy because they demonstrate that the root itself can be more important than the narcotic properties it bears when made into a drink. In other words, it is not necessary for the root to be processed for it to have honorific meaning (Brunton 1989; Lebot, Merlin, and Lindstrom 1992).

Secular Usage

Kava has also been employed informally in Fiji, Futuna, Pohnpei, Tonga, and parts of Vanuatu where ritual preparations were minimized and there were fewer restrictions as to who could drink. Kava was drunk communally at designated meeting places, and kava sessions, lasting all night, were held several times a week. These sessions, although less ritually structured, nevertheless emphasized the symbolic nature of kava drinking and communication with the ancestors.

In Futuna, each village had (and has) its tauasu house for the men. In Tonga, the men may meet in the house of a prominent person. In Vanuatu, kava-drinking grounds were the nightly meeting places in villages, whereas kava clubs are the meeting place in towns. At these nightly sessions in Tonga or Futuna, the root is chewed or crushed by a young man or young woman, who is seated at the kava bowl in order to maintain the supply of the beverage by replenishing the cups of the drinkers and crushing more of the root as needed. The drinkers, all male, sit on mats in an oval around the edge of the house with the kava maker at one end. Such sessions can last until three or four in the morning, but some men quietly drift away as they become sleepy. There is a light buzz of conversation, and the occasional clap as a drinker receives his new cup (Pollock field notes, Tonga 1976).

Such occasions are mainly social, with conversation ranging around political issues and local affairs. In Tonga, Futuna, and Fiji, these sessions enable men to relax in the company of other men of the village and share information. Indeed, a young man is expected to attend if he wants to be viewed as interested in village affairs, and thus a candidate for a leadership position (Sepeliano 1974).

By the 1980s, kava drinking in Vanuatu was also a nightly occasion, though customs varied throughout the islands. The village gathering place, often under a banyan tree, gave way to a kava bar where women and young men also drink. The kava is drunk in one gulp, after which one is expected to spit loudly. Such bars have become very lucrative for their owners.

In Vanuatu certain varieties of the plant have been designated for everyday use, whereas other varieties are drunk only by persons of high rank, and still others are used as traditional medicine. Depending on the varieties available, together with the way they are prepared, kava can precipitate drunkenness, but a bleary-eyed, staggering, and comatose sort, "never hilarious or pugnacious" (Gunn quoted in Weightman 1989: 239). In fact, with the custom of modern kava drinking in Vanuatu, there has arisen a whole range of slang phrases, such as *fowil antap,* "four wheel on top," to describe just one form of drunkenness.

Narcotic Properties

Kava has been labeled a narcotic containing certain pharmacologically active substances long recognized by Western chemists, pharmacists, and others. Certainly missionaries and other outsiders judged drug properties to be the reason for kava usage and took steps to ban its cultivation, processing, and use as a beverage. The main objection seems not to have been to drunkenness but to the soporific effects it produced, which prevented many men from doing a full day's work after a night of drinking kava. Recent ethnographic accounts from Vanuatu have stressed the druglike or narcotic properties of kava (Lindstrom 1987; Lebot and Cabalion 1988; Brunton 1989).

The main chemically active constituents identified by chemists are kawain and the kava lactones. However, despite many years of investigations, mainly in German laboratories (see Lebot and Cabalion 1988) but also in Sydney (Duffield and Jamieson 1991), the precise physiological action of these substances on the human neurological and chemical system is not fully understood.

Kawain is said to be an emotional and muscular relaxant that stabilizes the feelings and stimulates the ability to think and act. It has bactericidal properties and can be used as an antimycotic. It is also a diuretic. Fresh kava has a local anesthetic effect on the chewer's mouth. But its main effect is as a muscle relaxant (Lebot and Cabalion 1988: 35).

The chemical properties of kava and other local plants have long been of interest to visitors to the Pacific. Gilbert Cuzent, a naval pharmacist based in Tahiti from 1858 to 1860, claimed to be the first to identify (in 1858) a substance he called "Kavahine" as a result of experiments carried out on various parts of the kava plant. This claim led to a scientific argument with another French pharmacist, who had also published his analysis of the kava root in April 1857 in the newspaper *Le Messager de Tahiti* and, in 1858, in the *Revue Coloniale.* However, the French Academy of Sciences recognized Cuzent's claim (Cuzent 1860: 189–90).

The major physiological effects are quiescent and numbing, in contrast to the enervating effects of alcohol. The kava drinker may feel a slight numbness around the mouth, but the strongest effect is on the legs; anyone who sits drinking kava for a long period of time finds it hard to stand or walk. There is no loss of consciousness, though the kava drinker may fall asleep after seven or eight cups and be hard to awaken. Some Vanuatu cultivars are more potent than others and so are more favored by drinkers for the quick effect they produce (Crowley 1990).

Kava is also said to lead to loss of appetite and to reduced libido, but such effects are reversible if the person stops drinking it for several weeks (Spencer 1941). Redness around the eyes is also a mark of a heavy drinker, as is a scaly skin.

In his studies of the plant's usage in the eastern Pacific, Edwin Lemert (1967) noted how kava produced a nonaggressive, anaphrodisiac, mildly tranquil and dreamy state. He suggested that it depressed bodily functions such as heart and respiration rates and temperature. He labeled kava drinking "a form of retreatist or avoidance behavior, related to onerous claims which Polynesian social organization periodically makes on individuals" (Lemert 1967: 337). Many authors have noted that the quiescent and soothing effects of kava place it in direct contrast to alcohol. For this reason, kava has been introduced as a counter to heavy alcohol drinking, whether in Vanuatu or among Australian Aborigines (D'Abbs 1995).

It is true that modern writers tend to think that those who drink enough kava become drunk, yet a number of other writers over the past century and a half have either not mentioned any drunkenness, or have said that kava does not lead to such a state and that drinkers only become sleepy and quiescent.

Kava and Alcohol

The relationship between kava and alcohol is one of contrast rather than one of similarity. As W. T. Wawn wrote in 1870: "Kava has a very different effect from alcohol. It is soothing, and a pint of strong kava, or even half that quantity for a beginner, will apparently have no more effect than to make a man desirous of being left alone and allowed to sit quietly and smoke his pipe. . . . Alcohol excites, kava soothes and then stupefies" (quoted in Weightman 1989: 237-8). Other authors have made similar observations. Thus, alcohol and kava satisfy different needs (Lemert 1967: 337).

One major difference between the two substances is that kava is a very social drink (it is almost unheard of for someone to pound a batch of kava for personal drinking), drunk in association with others in ritual settings or in the modern-day kava clubs, where a group of people share a bucketful (or one "brew") of kava.

Nonetheless, as a result of institutionalized drug-classification principles in the West, kava and alcohol have been placed alongside one another. Kava has been a banned substance in the United States since 1958, though there has been a campaign to lift that ban (Lebot and Cabalion 1988: 91). It is also considered a harmful substance in New Zealand, Australia, and Fiji.

Commercial Developments

Kava has been a cash crop for more than 100 years. Since the second half of the nineteenth century, several South Pacific countries have been exporting the dried root to Germany and France for pharmaceutical uses. In the 1880s, a trading house in Wallis sent 30,000 pounds in 18 months at a price of 30 to 35 cents a pound to meet a growing demand in Europe, where it was employed both as a diuretic and for its calming effects (Deschamps 1883).

Today, markets for kava in Germany and France still exist, and processing laboratories import the equivalent of some 200 tons of fresh root from Fiji and Tonga. A study of such demand showed a recognition of the therapeutic properties in kava for antiseptics, expectorants, diuretics, and urogenital stimulants. One product with the brand name Kaviase had been on the market for about 20 years, and in Germany an attempt was made to launch a kava-based soft drink (Weightman 1989: 241).

Certainly, kava has become an important alternative cash crop for several Pacific island societies, and for farmers in parts of Fiji and Vanuatu, it is now their most important cash earner. The crop is widely sold by the bundle of dried roots in the markets throughout Fiji. Purchasers are mainly urban Fijians who have no access to *yaqona* from their own lands. Similarly, in Vanuatu, kava already yields a higher net income per hectare to the farmer than cocoa and coffee (Lebot and Cabalion 1988: 92). It thus provides a form of economic buffer against downturns in tourism due to oil prices and political instability.

Conclusions

The evolution of kava usage over millennia has been marked by a waxing and waning of its popularity, as well as by changes in the plant and its mode of processing. During this time it has been eliminated from some islands by cyclones, salt water inundations, and even warfare when the plants were pulled out by the retreating forces (Gill 1876).

Yet vegetative reproductive properties have enabled varieties to be selected that could be processed into an ever more pleasant beverage, and the range of cultivars has increased markedly in island societies, such as those of Vanuatu where it is of great cultural importance.

The geographical range of kava, however, is more narrow today than it was a hundred years ago. Missionaries sought to eliminate it because it reduced productive work efforts, and other Westerners have included it under the negative rubric of a drug, although there is no medical evidence for long-term harmful effects.

The employment of kava in recent times has been marked by a considerable increase in its secular, as opposed to its ritual, use. In Fiji, Futuna, Pohnpei, Tonga, and Samoa, the Catholic, Methodist, and Congregational churches have taken a less rigid stance against kava drinking, so the rituals have continued and broadened in scope to include welcoming ceremonies for Western visitors and such church activities as first communion. The kava parties now are open to men of all ages and status in the community, although women do not often participate.

Yet the overall development of kava throughout the Pacific during some 3,000 years has been one of ritual usage. Those societies that have maintained kava drinking to present times have done so because it is an important medium in their cultural system. It is steeped in a strong body of local ideology that places the root as central to a communication process, linking the ancestral spirits to the incumbent chiefs and priests, and, thus, the whole living community to those associated with its past.

Nancy J. Pollock

Bibliography

Barrau, Jacques. 1965. L'Humide et le sec. *Journal of Polynesian Society* 74: 329–46.

Biggs, B., D. Walsh, and J. Waqa. 1972. Proto-Polynesian reconstructions with English to Proto-Polynesian finder list. Working papers, Department of Anthropology, University of Auckland.

Bott, Elizabeth. 1972a. Psychoanalysis and ceremony. In *The interpretation of ritual,* ed. J. S. La Fontaine, 205–37. London.

    1972b. The significance of kava in Tongan myth and ritual. In *The interpretation of ritual,* ed. J. S. La Fontaine, 277–82. London.

Brunton, Ron. 1989. *The abandoned narcotic.* Cambridge.

Burrows, Edwin. 1939. *Western Polynesia.* Stockholm.

Crowley, Terry. 1990. Who drank kava. Paper read at Conference on Austronesian Terminologies: Continuity and Change, Australian National University.

Cuzent, Gilbert. [1860] 1983. *Archipel de Tahiti,* ed. J. Florence. Haere Po No, Tahiti.

d'Abbs, Peter. 1995. The power of kava or the power of ideas? Kava use and kava policy in The Northern Territory, Australia. In *The Power of Kava.* Nancy J. Pollock ed. *Canberra Anthropology* 18: no. 1 and 2. Special Volume 166–83.

Dening, Greg. 1980. *Islands and beaches.* Honolulu.

Deschamps, L. 1883. Les Iles Wallis. In *Le tour du monde.* Paris.

Douglas, Mary, ed. 1987. *Constructive drinking.* Cambridge.

Duffield, J., and L. Jamieson. 1991. Development of tolerance to kava in mice. *Clinical and Experimental Pharmacology and Physiology* 18: 571–8.

Feinberg, Richard. 1981. *Anuta: Social structure of a Polynesian island.* Laie, Hawaii.

Feldman, Harry. 1980. Informal kava drinking in Tonga. *Journal of the Polynesian Society* 89: 101–3.

Firth, Raymond. 1970. *Rank and religion in Tikopia.* London.

Gaillot, M. 1962. La rite du kava Futunien. *Études Mélané-siennes* 14-17: 95-105.

Gill, W. W. 1876. *Life in the southern isles.* London.

Handy, E. S. C. 1972. *Native planters in old Hawaii.* Bishop Museum Bulletin No. 233. Honolulu.

Jamieson, Dana, and P. Duffield. 1991. Production of toler-ance to the aqueous extract and lipid soluble extract of kava in mice. Abstract.

Kirch, Patrick, and D. Yen. 1982. Tikopia: The prehistory and ecology of a Polynesian outlier. *Bishop Museum Bul-letin #238.* Honolulu.

Lebot, Vincent, Mallikarjuna Aradhya, and R. Manshardt. 1991. Geographical survey of genetic variation in kava. *Pacific Science* 45: 169-85.

Lebot, Vincent, and P. Cabalion. 1988. *Kavas of Vanuatu.* South Pacific Commission Technical Paper No. 195. Noumea, New Caledonia.

Lebot, V., M. Merlin, and L. Lindstrom. 1992. *Kava: The Pacific drug.* New Haven, Conn.

Lemert, Edwin M. 1967. Secular use of kava in Tonga. *Quar-terly Journal of Studies on Alcohol* 28: 328-41.

Lindstrom, Lamont. 1987. Drunkenness and gender on Tanna, Vanuatu. In *Drugs in Western Pacific Societies; relations of substance,* ed. L. Lindstrom. Lanham, Md.

Loeb, Edwin. 1926. History and traditions of Niue. *Bishop Museum Bulletin #32.* Honolulu.

Marshall, Mac. 1979. *Beliefs, behaviors, and alcoholic bever-ages.* Ann Arbor, Mich.

Newell, W. H. 1947. The kava ceremony in Tonga. *Journal of the Polynesian Society* 56: 364-417.

Oliver, D. 1987. *The Pacific Islands.* Honolulu.

Petersen, Glenn. 1995. The complexity of power, the subtlety of kava: Pohnpei's *sakau.* In *The Power of Kava,* Nancy J. Pollock ed. *Canberra Anthropolgy* 18: special volume nos. 1 and 2, 34-60.

Pollock, Nancy J. 1995a. Introduction: The power of kava. In *The Power of Kava. Nancy J. Pollock, ed.* Can-berra Anthropology 18: special volume nos. 1 and 2, 1-19.

   1995b. The power of kava in Futuna and 'Uvea/Wallis. In *The Power of Kava.* Nancy J. Pollock, ed. *Can-berra Anthropology* 18: Special volume nos. 1 and 2, 136-65.

Quain, Buell. 1948. *Fijian village.* Chicago.

Ravuvu, Asesela. 1987. *The Fijian ethos.* Suva.

Rivers, W. H. 1914. *The history of Melanesian society.* 2 vols. Cambridge.

Rossille, Richard. 1986. *Le kava à Wallis et Futuna.* Collec-tion Iles et Archipels No. 6. Bordeaux, France.

Rozier, Claude, ed. 1963. *Écrits de S. Pierre Channel.* Publica-tion de la Société des Oceanistes no. 9. Paris.

Sepeliano, T. 1974. Enquête sur la reproduction du mode de pro-duction capitaliste dans les iles Wallis et Futuna. Mémoire pour la maîtrise de sociologie, Université de Lyon II.

Spencer, D. 1941. *Disease, religion, and society in the Fiji Islands.* Seattle, Wash.

Weightman, Barry. 1989. *Agriculture in Vanuatu.* Cheam, Surrey.

Williams, Thomas. [1858] 1982. *Fiji and the Fijians.* Suva.

Williamson, R. W. [1939] 1975. *Essays in Polynesian ethnol-ogy,* ed. R. Piddington, 51-112. New York.

Young, Michael. 1995. Kava and Christianity in Central Vanu-atu: with an appendix on the ethnography of kava drinking in Nikaura, epi. In *The power of kava,* Nancy J. Pollock, ed. *Canberra Anthropology* 18: No. 1 and 2 special volume, 61-96.

III.7 Khat

Khat (*Catha edulis* Forsk., Celastracae) is a flowering evergreen tree that grows in parts of eastern Africa and the southwestern highlands of Arabia. Its young leaves and tender stem tips, also called khat, are stimu-lating and produce a mild euphoria when chewed and their juices ingested. Khat has various psycho-stimulant alkaloids, of which the main one, cathinone, is amphetamine related and highly unstable. Khat leaves and shoots contain various alkaloids, of which cathinone and cathine are the primary and secondary active ingredients in stimulating the central nervous system. As with other psychoactive plants, the effects of the active constituents differ from one specimen to another according to the cultivar's size, age, health, and the site conditions of growth, such as exposure, soil, soil moisture, and drainage.

Most of the world's khat is grown in Yemen, Ethiopia, and Kenya, where its use is long established. Khat is a major import of Somalia and Djibouti, and demand in both countries far exceeds domestic pro-duction. During the past half-century, the number of users has increased substantially, and emigrants from the khat-chewing countries have introduced (on a small scale) the use of the drug to some countries in Europe and North America.

International trade in khat is a multimillion-dollar business in the Horn of Africa and southwestern Ara-bia. Daily consumption of the drug is estimated to be about 5 million portions of khat (Kalix 1994: 69), or about 500,000 kilograms of the leaf material chewed. The various estimates of the total number of regular users range from 3 to 6 million. Methcathinone, a syn-thetic, white, chunky powder, known in the United States by the street name "cat," is a substance very dis-similar from khat.

Orthography

"Khat" (pronounced "cot") is an inexact transliteration of the Arabic name of the plant, and is also spelled "qat," "kat," "gat," and "ghat." Philologists consider that the spellings "qāt" or "ḳat" (with diacritical marks) most closely approximate the transliteration of the Arabic in Roman characters.

The Khat Plant

Botanical Description

There are two known species of the genus *Catha: Catha edulis* and *Catha spinosa.* Both were first described by Peter Forsskal in 1775. Only *C. edulis* is cultivated, and in eastern Africa and the southwestern Arabian peninsula it grows at higher, wetter eleva-tions than *C. spinosa,* which occurs wild in northern Yemen.

Khat is a straight, slender tree with a thin bark that varies in color from light gray to dark brown. The trees bear persistent, leathery leaves that are elliptical with finely toothed edges. The leaves are approximately 50 to 100 millimeters (mm) long and 20 to 50 mm broad (Revri 1983: 37). Young leaves are shiny and vary in color from pale green to red, becoming green or yellowish green at full growth. The flowers are small (diameter 4 to 5 mm) and either white or greenish in color. Freshly cut twigs that carry tender new leaves and buds near the end of the branch are most highly appreciated for chewing.

The height of mature trees under cultivation ranges from about 2 to 10 meters (Brooke 1960: 52; Kennedy 1987: 177). The leaves grow rapidly if the plant is well watered, and if heavy harvesting continues throughout the year, the trees retain the form of bushes (Tutwiler and Caprisco 1981: 53). Under very favorable conditions in eastern and eastcentral Africa, wild *C. edulis* grows to a height of about 25 meters (Greenway 1947: 98).

Khat requires a yearly minimum of approximately 400 mm of water from rainfall or irrigation and an average temperature not less than 17 degrees Celsius. Growth is retarded by successive night frosts at high elevations and by rainfall in excess of 800 mm if the soil is not freely drained (Revri 1983: 18–19). Healthy trees may yield for at least 50 years.

C. edulis has been cultivated in greenhouses at various botanical gardens and has been grown in the open for scientific purposes in Egypt, Sri Lanka, Bombay, Algeria, Portugal, southern France, Florida, and southern California.

Cultivation

Khat is reproduced vegetatively from shoots (suckers or sprouts) cut from the basal root or the trunk of the tree. These provide more rapid growth than cuttings from branches. Three or four shoots, 25 to 50 centimeters (cm) long, are planted together in rows of shallow holes at 1 to 2 meter intervals (Revri 1983: 62). Harvesting of leaves usually begins 3 to 4 years after planting. (Brooke 1960: 53; Morghem and Rufat 1983: 215–16).

Kinds of Khat

The total number of the kinds of khat consumed throughout the world, if known, would well exceed 100. There are at least 7 kinds marketed at Dire Dawa, Ethiopia, and more than 40 kinds are recognized in Yemen on the basis of geographical origin (Krikorian 1984: 160). Consumer differentiation among the various kinds is based on the potency of psychostimulation, flavor, and the tenderness of the leaves. These characteristics differ according to growing conditions, husbandry, and farm practice, such as irrigation or lack of it, soil types, and other ecological variables. According to Bob Hill (1965: 16): "It is said that the palates of some chewers are so sensitive that they can distinguish not only in what area the products originate, but the individual field as well."

The health of the plant is also a marketing factor. *C. edulis* is subject to attack by a wide range of insect pests, and a kind of khat called *kuda,* when damaged by a leafhopper (*Empoasca* spp.), is considered to be the best quality in the Alamaya district of Harer. A toxin contained in the saliva that the insect injects into leaf tissue during feeding produces a milky taste that is preferred by connoisseurs of this expensive kind of khat (Hill 1965: 21).

Khat is sold at the retail level in leafy bundles (*rubtah* in Arabic), each bundle wrapped in banana leaves or plastic to preserve freshness. A rubtah contains the minimum quantity of leaves and stem tips that most consumers chew in one day (Weir 1985: 89; Kennedy 1987: 80).

Historical Overview

Uncertain Origin of Domesticated Khat

Neither khat's place of origin nor the manner in which it was diffused has been determined, although most experts accept the view that *C. edulis* was probably first domesticated in the Ethiopian highlands. Based upon his field studies in Ethiopia, Eritrea, and Somalia in 1927, botanist and plant geneticist N. I. Vavilov (1951: 37–8) designated Ethiopia as the center of origin of cultivated khat. According to anthropologist George P. Murdock, khat and coffee are two of some eleven important agricultural plants originally domesticated by the Agau, Cushitic speakers of the central highlands of Ethiopia and "one of the most culturally creative people on the entire continent" (1959: 182–3).

Revri was among the minority of khat specialists who challenged the belief of an Ethiopian genesis of the plant. In his view, Yemen is probably the primary center of origin of khat and Ethiopia the secondary center. On the basis of cytogenetic evidence, Revri concluded that *C. edulis* appears to have evolved from *C. spinosa,* found wild in the Serat Mountains of Yemen. He suggested that *C. edulis,* known to the Arabs as a medicinal plant, may have been taken to Ethiopia in the sixth century A.D. and that it was returned to Yemen as a social stimulant in the fourteenth century (Revri 1983: 4).

Historical Highlights

According to Armin Schopen (1978: 45) and others, the earliest reference to khat is found in *Kitab al-Saidana fi al-Tibb,* a work on pharmacy and materia medica written in A.D. 1065 by the scholar Abu al-Biruni (Abu r-Raihan Muhammad al-Biruni) in collaboration with a physician. The work described khat as "a commodity from Turkestan. It is sour to taste and slenderly made in the manner of *batan-alu.* But qat is reddish with a slight blackish tinge. It is believed that batan alu is red, coolant, relieves biliousness, and is a refrigerant for the stomach and the liver."

Batan-alu is presumably an extract of khat prepared like preserves of fruits and vegetables (Schopen 1978: 45; Krikorian 1984: 136). The fact that al-Biruni, who lived in Ghazni, Afghanistan, identified "Turkestan" (the name loosely applied to the large area of central Asia between Mongolia on the east and the Caspian Sea on the west) as the origin of *batan-alu* is interesting because this and other references to either wild or cultivated *C. edulis* in the region are uncorroborated. It is plausible that khat used in the preparation of *batan alu* were dried leaves grown in Ethiopia and brought to central Asia as one of the myriad trade articles carried along the great caravan routes of the Old World.

The earliest work in which khat was identified as a plant is a book of medicinal remedies written in A.D. 1222 by Nagib ad-Din as-Samarkandi. The author, who resided in the ancient city of Samarkand, a major center of trade in Turkestan during the Middle Ages, recommended khat for its healing properties.

The earliest reliable reference to the general practice of khat consumption is in a chronicle of the wars between the Muslim and Christian states of Ethiopia during the early fourteenth century. The chronicler, a Christian, mentioned that khat was popular and widely consumed among the Muslim population (but shunned by Christians). He also wrote that a Muslim sovereign, Sabr ad-Din, boasted of what he would do when he conquered the Christian realm of King Amda Syon: "'I will take up my residence at Mar'adi, the capital of his kingdom, and I will plant chat there,' because the Muslims love this plant" (Trimingham 1952: 228).

According to John G. Kennedy (1987: 60–78), the popular use of khat in Yemen probably began in the southern part of the western highlands near Ta'izz during the fourteenth or fifteenth century. Customary use of the plant spread slowly northward, and by the end of the eighteenth century, khat was regularly sold in San'a. During the nineteenth century, use of the drug was widespread in the country, and Yemenis began to export khat overland to Aden (the annual trade grew from 1,000 camel loads in 1887 to 2,000 in 1900). Greenway (1947: 99) mentioned that the use of the leaves of *C. edulis* was well known to Ethiopians, Somalis, and Arabs at the time of World War I and that the knowledge of such use was spread to other African tribes through their encounters with the khat-chewing custom during war service in Ethiopia and Kenya.

The earliest concise account of khat in European literature was that of the Swedish physician and botanist Peter Forsskal (1736–63), who was a member of a Danish expedition led by the German geographer Karsten Niebuhr that visited Yemen in 1763. Khat, given the name *Catha edulis*, was among the plants collected in Yemen. Niebuhr, the only survivor of the five members of the expedition, published Forsskal's botanical papers in 1775, and in memory of his friend extended the name *Catha edulis* to "Catha edulis Forsskal" (Revri 1983: 3).

Religious Role of Khat

In most of the legends and early historical accounts of khat, a common theme has been its capacity to enhance wakefulness and, therefore, the ability of the user to carry out religious observance and worship (Trimingham 1952: 228). A frequently heard comment in praise of khat by Muslim users is that it enables them to pray without becoming drowsy even throughout the nights of Ramadan (Brooke 1960: 53). In Ethiopia and in Yemen, stories are told of divine guidance in the discovery of khat and the high regard in which the drug was held by Muslim saints.

A well-known legend tells of Sheikh Ibrahim Abu Zarbay (Zerbin), one of 44 Muslim saints who came from the Hadhramaut (eastern Yemen) to Ethiopia in about A.D. 1430 on a proselytizing mission. He traveled to Harer, converted many to Islam, and is said to have introduced khat to Yemen upon his return (Burton 1910: 66–7).

Khat has long been known in predominantly Christian northern Ethiopia, although it was consumed there almost exclusively by the Muslim minority. Frederick Simoons (1960: 115–16) found that nearly all adult Muslims in the town of Gondar chewed khat, but that among the Wayto of Lake Tana only Muslim holy men did so. In Begemder and Semyen, Christians who are supposedly possessed by Muslim evil spirits use it to appease those spirits and to encourage them to leave (Simoons 1960: 115–16).

In the course of some 400 years (thirteenth to seventeenth centuries) of protracted struggle for territory between Christian and Muslim states in Ethiopia, the Christians came to identify the eating of khat as a distinguishing characteristic of the Muslims and disdained its use. However, in Yemen where Moslems and Jews have regularly used the drug, khat did not become an object of religious identification.

Yemeni Jews have used khat since at least the seventeenth century. Sholem bin Joseph al-Shibezi (1619–86) is the author of a poetic play in which a dialogue between coffee and khat is presented (Krikorian 1984: 151–2, citing J. Kafih 1963: 224–5). The play is still performed in Arabic by Yemeni Jews in Israel (Weir 1985: 75).

Within Islam, khat is at the center of controversy. Richard Burton observed during his visit to Harer, Ethiopia, in 1855 that khat produced "a manner of dreamy enjoyment and the Ulema [authorities in Muslim law and religion] as in Arabia, held the drug to be 'Akl el Salikim,' or the Food of the Pious." Burton also wrote that the literati thought khat had "singular properties of enlivening the imagination, clearing the ideas, cheering the heart, diminishing sleep, and taking the place of food" (1910: 232).

Such an expression of esteem for khat, however, represents a minority view in the Islamic world, and for centuries, its consumption has been the subject of debate by doctors of Islamic law. Khat is not mentioned in the Koran, and the persistent question is:

Does the use of khat contravene the Koran's general injunction against the use of intoxicants? Although not of one mind on the question, Muslim religious leaders in most of the Islamic countries have taken the position that it does.

The following resolution was adopted by the World Islamic Conference for the Campaign against Alcohol and Drugs that met at Medina, Saudi Arabia, in May, 1983:

> After reviewing reports submitted to the Conference on the health, psychological, ethical, behavioral, social and economic damages resulting from khat, the Conference judges khat to be a drug prohibited by religion and accordingly the Conference recommends to Islamic states to apply punishment of the basis of Islamic Shari'ah [canon law] against any person who plants this tree and markets or consumes khat (Al-Hammad 1983: 228).

Earlier, in 1971, the government of Saudi Arabia had banned the importation or use of khat in the kingdom and prescribed severe penalties for violations.

In the Muslim countries where khat is legal, there is an ambivalent attitude toward its use, and opposition to the drug is not necessarily based on religion. Many intellectuals in these countries deprecate the use of khat on the grounds that it is a deterrent to economic and social progress (Weir 1985: 66).

Although, traditionally, khat has appealed more to Muslims than non-Muslims, its use in the Islamic world is and has been minute. As A. D. Krikorian (1984: 163) has pointed out, the Turks in Ottoman-occupied Yemen never adopted the practice, nor did the 60,000 Egyptian soldiers stationed in Yemen from 1962 to 1967. In fact, less than half of one percent of the world's Muslims use the drug.

Geographical Perspective of Khat

Asia

Yemen. Khat is the paramount crop of Yemen, where it is widely consumed and its use is legal. According to The Economist Intelligence Unit Limited (1994–5: 47–8): "It is hard to overestimate the social and economic importance of the stimulant shrub, *qat.* The majority of Yemenis, women less than men, chew the drug most days from early afternoon to evening. The habit is less prevalent in the southern governates and is rare in the eastern regions."

Data on khat are largely unrecorded in Yemen's official statistics, and quantitative assessments are estimates. Some aspects, however, are palpable. According to Tutwiler and Capriso (1981: 52): "Compared to other perishable crops khat has the highest market value, the lowest water requirements, and demands the least output of heavy labor." Beyond all question, khat is the preeminent cash crop of the country.

In fact, a 1992 report of the *Yemen Times* suggested that the value added by the khat sector of Yemen's economy is equivalent to approximately a quarter of the recorded gross national product and about twice the value resulting from cultivation of all other crops (The Economist Intelligence Unit Limited 1994-95: 56). The khat industry of Yemen involves landowners and growers, pickers, packers, transporters, wholesalers, and retailers – some 500,000 people, equivalent to about 20 percent of the working population (The Economist Intelligence Unit Limited 1994-95: 56). A substantial part of government revenue is derived from taxes on khat, although there is little doubt that a large part of the crop escapes levy (The Economist Intelligence Unit Limited 1994-95: 56).

Until the 1970s, khat was too costly to be used frequently by most of the population. But concurrent with the Gulf oil boom that began in 1973-4, an unprecedented number of workers (more than a third of the potential male labor force in North Yemen) migrated for temporary employment to Saudi Arabia and other petroleum-producing countries in the Gulf (Varisco 1986: 2). Remittances sent home by the migrants (annually about 600 to 800 million dollars in the 1980s) created new wealth and a vastly increased demand for khat at home (Varisco 1986).

The early 1980s were exceptionally profitable years for khat farmers. A survey by Shelagh Weir (1983: 67) of a khat-growing community of 4,000 people in Razih Province, North Yemen, near the Saudi Arabian border, found that the market value for land yielding two harvests of khat per year was the equivalent of 90,000 U.S. dollars per hectare. Terraced land, on which two to three harvests of khat per year are common, sold for the equivalent of 200,000 to 600,000 dollars per hectare (Weir 1983: 67). Most holdings range between 0.15 and 0.5 hectares. In 1980, in the district of Rada, a major area of khat production, the estimated net profit of a khat farmer in the second year after the crop matured was the equivalent of about 37,000 dollars per hectare (Varisco 1986: 4).

Critics of the institutionalized use of khat have argued that the transcendent position of *C. edulis* in agriculture has depressed the production of other crops, including the staple grains, and that the large expenditure for khat drains family income that would better be spent on food. Indeed, since the 1970s, importation of foodstuffs has greatly increased in Yemen, and highly processed imported foods have brought changes to the traditional diet (Nyrop 1985: 108). Cereal imports increased 133 percent between 1987 and 1990 and accounted for 16 percent of total imports, compared with 11 percent in 1987 (The Economist Intelligence Unit Limited 1992: 39).

The economy suffered a severe blow, however, when in late 1990, the government of Saudi Arabia expelled all Yemeni migrant workers, terminating Yemen's main source of foreign exchange. The sudden return of some 850,000 Yemenis to their homeland,

and the additional loss of about 1 billion dollars annually in foreign aid from the Arab oil-producing states, had drastic effects on the economy. In mid-1994, unemployment was about 25 percent, and the rate of inflation was about 100 percent annually (The Economist Intelligence Unit Limited 1994-95: 48-9).

Although export of khat from Yemen had ceased in 1974, there are unofficial reports that the depressed economy has prompted efforts in Yemen to increase its export of khat by air to markets in Africa and Europe.

North Yemen (the former Yemen Arab Republic). According to Kennedy, who directed an extensive program of team research on the sociomedical aspects of khat in Yemen during the mid-1970s, "No other society is so influenced by the use of a drug as is North Yemen by the use of qat" (1987: 78). He added that from 80 to 90 percent of adult men and 30 to 60 percent of adult women chew khat more than once each week.

About 70 percent of the country's khat is produced in three areas of the western highlands: the district of San'a; the province of Ibb, Yemen's overall leading agricultural region; and Jabel Sabr (elevation 3,005 meters), the terraced mountain that overlooks the town of Ta'izz and is the oldest and most famous khat-growing area in Arabia (Revri 1983: 16). The greater part of Yemen's khat is consumed in the western interior mountains and plateaus where the majority of the population is located, but freshly harvested leaves are trucked daily from the high elevations, where it is grown, to settlements in the hot, dry coastal plain bordering the Red Sea.

Chewing during the long afternoons in gatherings of friends and acquaintances is a ritual in Yemeni culture that provides a focal point for social contact, informal business dealings, discussion of current events, mediation of disputes, and the free exchange of ideas in a friendly, relaxed milieu. In general, the ubiquitous afternoon "khat party" is a social ritual that underscores the institutionalized role of khat in Yemeni culture and accounts for the major part of the consumption of the drug in the country. Most such parties take place in private residences. They are "open house" affairs, and anyone may participate.

The houses of wealthy urban families have a special room for khat parties called *al Mafraj*, "a place for joyful gatherings" (Weir 1985: 110-11). As a paradigm, it is located with a pleasing overlook on the highest floor of the house, and a large window, extending almost to floor level, provides a good view for the seated guests. Yet, it is the custom that the door and the windows of the mufraj be closed during a khat party. During even ordinary sessions, the room is usually crowded with participants who exult in the oppressive heat and humidity and the smoke from cigarettes and the waterpipe. Users believe that the use of tobacco is essential to the enjoyment of khat

chewing (Kennedy 1987: 86). Because khat inhibits urination and defecation by the constriction of muscular vessels, chewers have the ability to remain seated throughout the session for the customary 4 or 5 hours (Kennedy 1987: 115).

The societies of the khat-chewing countries are segregated by sex, and although men are the main users of the drug, women constitute a significant minority of users. The widespread popularity of khat with women is a fairly recent phenomenon. During the 1970s and 1980s, a period of unprecedented prosperity in Yemen, the domestic chores of both urban and rural women were greatly reduced by technological innovations, such as powered flour mills, piped water supply, and the availability of motor transport. The time available to women for social gatherings was substantially increased, and at a growing proportion of these gatherings, khat was consumed (Weir 1985: 90-1).

South Yemen (the former People's Democratic Republic of Yemen). The strong market for khat in South Yemen is only to a small extent supplied by local production, and (despite some interruptions) for more than a century and a half, the farmed land near Ibb in North Yemen has been the main source of South Yemen's khat. From this major center of production, the drug is transported to markets in the port of Aden (population about 420,000), Yemen's commercial capital.

Until about the time of World War II, khat was transported from Ibb to Lahej by camel caravans, which were subject to pillage en route. Armed raiders pulled the camel loads to pieces in order to "extract a few choice bundles [of khat], with the result that the loads arrived in Aden dried up and unfit for human consumption" (Ingrams 1966: 106).

The government adopted an anti-khat policy, and in 1977, the use and sale of the leaf were limited by law to one day per week (Friday). This restriction, however, ended in 1990 when the two Yemens united.

Saudi Arabia. The small province of Jizan in the southwestern corner of Saudi Arabia is the only part of that country in which consumption of khat is of consequence. The mountain tribespeople in Jizan, settled in rugged highland terrain and in relative isolation, have historically maintained a large measure of autonomy in their internal affairs. The growing and usage of *C. edulis* is centuries old in the uplands of the province, but at present, because of the government's determination to abolish the plant and its use, cultivation of khat exists chiefly, if at all, covertly in the Fayfa area of Jizan. Schopen (1978: 65) identified Jebel Fayfa as the northern limit of khat cultivation in Arabia.

Israel. In the nineteenth century, khat growing was introduced by Yemenite Jews to the region of

Ottoman-ruled Palestine that later became the modern state of Israel (Erich Isaac 1995, personal communication). Large-scale migration of Jews from Yemen began in 1882. By 1948, when Israel was established, about a third of the Jewish population of Yemen had emigrated. The exodus of almost all Jews remaining in Yemen (about 50,000) was accomplished by air transport to Israel, beginning with "Operation on Eagles' Wings" in 1949 (*Jerusalem Post* September 19–25, International Edition 1982: 20).

It was a common practice of Yemeni migrant families to bring shoots of "gat" (*C. edulis*) with them to be planted in home gardens of their new settlements, and in Israel, the cultivation and consumption of khat remain almost exclusively the practices of Yemenite Jews. Immigrant Ethiopian Jews are reported to chew the leaf, as do some young Ashkenazis, who are attracted by the exotic nature of the drug (High on gat 1996: 16). Most khat is consumed by its growers, but the fresh leaves can be found for sale (legally) in some of the open-air "oriental markets" (Arnon Soffer, 1995, personal communication; D. Hemo, 1995, personal communication). A khat-based frozen concentrate, "Pisgat," is made and sold in Israel as a health food. Its maker is reported to claim that the psychotropic effect of two tablespoons of Pisgat (mixed with water or soya milk, or added to ice cream) is equivalent to that achieved by several hours of chewing fresh khat (High on gat 1996: 17). In 1952, the ministry of health reported to the Knesset that although *C. edulis* was a stimulant, there was no reason to ban the leaf; since then, this official view has prevailed.

Afghanistan and Turkestan. In scientific literature, there are a few brief uncorroborated references to the occurrence of the khat plant in Afghanistan and "Turkestan," that is, southcentral Asia. One reference, the most credible, is a two-paragraph communication titled "Catha Edulis," by F. J. Owen, published early this century in a British chemical journal. Owen, an analytical chemist employed by the government of Afghanistan, reported his observations of the use of khat as a beverage by Afghans in Kabul:

> The plant is found in the south of Turkestan and certain parts of Afghanistan to the east of Kabul. . . . After inspecting a specimen brought to me for analysis I recognized it as the *Catha edulis* plant. The natives say that men by its aid can do long marches at night without feeling the least fatigue, also that among the wrestling fraternity here it is used on a large scale, as it greatly increases the muscular powers of the men. . . . It is drunk by many Afghans as a substitute for tea (1910: 1091).

Although more than 80 years have passed since the publication of Owen's communication, however, the existence of khat in Afghanistan (or in any other country in southcentral Asia) is still unconfirmed.

Africa: General Distribution

C. edulis occurs wild and as a cultivated plant in eastern and eastcentral Africa. Wild stands grow sporadically in highlands from the northeastern Horn of Africa to the Sneeuberge Range in the far south of the continent. The plant is reported to be found in Eritrea, Ethiopia, Somalia, Kenya, Uganda, Tanzania, Rwanda, Burundi, Zaire, Zambia, Malawi, Mozambique, Zimbabwe, and the Republic of South Africa.

Ethiopia. Khat is grown in at least 9 (of the 14) administrative areas (provinces) of Ethiopia (Revri 1983: 5). The plant is a prominently cultivated crop in the plow- and grain-farming complex of Harerge and eastern Arsi provinces and is frequently part of the planting complex of the Kefa and the Galla (Oromo) ethnic groups in the Kefa Province where khat ranks second to coffee as a cash crop (Westphal 1975).

The main area of khat cultivation is the Harer Plateau – in the eastern section of Ethiopia's Central Highlands – with commercial centers of production in the administrative subdistricts of Harer, Webera, Garamulata, Chercher, and Dire Dawa (Assefa 1983: 73). All of these are within a radius of 100 kilometers (km) from the city of Harer, where according to local tradition, khat was first domesticated. In any case, its cultivation and use at Harer is older and economically more significant than in other areas in Ethiopia.

Small farm villages are scattered throughout these highlands of Harer, and at elevations between 1,500 and 2,100 meters, climate and soils are favorable for the production of a wide variety of field, garden, and tree crops. Rotation and terracing are practiced, as is irrigation where possible. Durra grain sorghum (*Sorghum vulgare*) is the predominant food crop, and khat is the most valuable cash crop (Brooke 1958: 192) – replacing coffee, which held that position until the middle of the twentieth century. Coffee fell from favor with Hareri farmers after World War II, chiefly because of low prices fixed by the government.

In 1949, Ethiopian Airlines introduced commercial air transportation of freshly cut khat from Ethiopia to Djibouti (French Somaliland) and to the British Crown Colony of Aden (now South Yemen). Transport of the perishable leaves by air was a commercial success from the start. However, the military junta that deposed the Ethiopian emperor, Haile Selassie, and held power during the years 1975 to 1991, sought to suppress its cultivation. Strong measures were employed to achieve that goal (Rushby 1995: 17), but since the end of civil war and the inauguration of a new coalition government in 1991, khat production has resumed without interference.

The export of khat officially earned 16 million U.S. dollars in 1993–4, establishing the drug as Ethiopia's fifth-largest source of revenue (Rushby 1995: 17). Illicit trade in the leaf (smuggling and by other means avoiding excise) probably generates at least as much revenue as the official figures.

Khat is airfreighted twice weekly from Dire Dawa to London and Frankfurt, where it is sold to Ethiopian, Somali, and Yemeni expatriate communities. A small bundle of the leaves, sufficient for two or three hours of chewing, sells in Germany and the United Kingdom for the equivalent of between 6 and 7.50 U.S. dollars (Rusby 1995: 16–17). Ethiopian exports of khat to Europe compete with those from Kenya and Yemen.

Djibouti. The Republic of Djibouti (population about 400,000) is a major consumer of khat. Almost all of the drug is airfreighted from Dire Dawa, Ethiopia, where international cargo flights with freshly cut khat were inaugurated in 1949. The Economist Intelligence Unit Limited (1989: 56) has estimated that as much as 12 tons of khat, valued at about 40 million U.S. dollars, enter Djibouti daily.

Somalia. Indigenous production of *C. edulis* in Somalia is small, and most of the khat consumed in this country is imported from Kenya and Ethiopia. Prior to the creation of the Somali Republic by the merger in 1960 of the (British) Somaliland Protectorate and Italian Somaliland, khat, on a small scale, was mainly used in the city of Hargeysa, the administrative center of the British dependency. After World War II, khat use in the protectorate increased considerably in spite of an official ban on the drug. Severe measures were taken by the colonial government to suppress the khat trade – drivers of trucks used for its transport were jailed and their vehicles destroyed (Elmi 1983: 166). But prohibition proved futile and, in 1957, the protectorate replaced the ban on khat with an import tax on the leaf (Brooke 1960: 57).

After the two Somalilands joined as a republic in 1960, the use of khat rapidly gained popularity in the "Southern Regions" (the former Italian Somaliland), coinciding with increased urbanization and the improvement of surface and air transportation. For two decades the government attempted simply to discourage the practice and finally proscribed it in 1983.

Enforcement efforts, however, were not effective, and as a consequence of the civil war that began in 1991 and the continuing political turmoil, there are no legal restrictions on khat in Somalia at the present time. In fact, it is believed that strife in the capital, Mogadishu, is fueled by the struggle among clan leaders for control of lucrative khat imports and distribution. The value of khat, it is reported, far exceeds that of any other commodity that Somalia imports, including food and weapons (Randall 1993: 15).

In the northern administrative regions of Somalia, the chief market for khat is the city of Hargeysa. A small amount of khat is locally cultivated, but most is imported by trucks from the Harer area in Ethiopia.

Kenya. The preeminent khat-growing area of Kenya is the Nyambeni Hills of the Meru District, extending northeast from the foot of Mt. Kenya for about 120 km. Khat that is cultivated and sold under license by farmers of the Meru ethnic group is the main source of the leaf for consumers in Kenya and for export to Somalia, Uganda, Tanzania, Zaire, and Zambia (Matai 1983: 88).

From local market towns, khat is transported to Nairobi - a fast four-hour drive - or by air from Isiolo to northern market towns. The khat trade is highly seasonal. Shortages and high prices prevail at markets during the months from June to October, when new growth of leaves and shoots is at a minimum (Hjort 1974: 29).

Somalia is the main export market. Every day at dawn, some 15 to 20 airplanes, each with about a ton of khat stuffed in burlap bags, take off for Somalia from Nairobi International Airport. Other flights leave from the town of Meru to smaller markets for khat in Tanzania and Uganda (Lorch 1994: A8). Khat is also flown as cargo from Nairobi to Britain, where it is a legal import. London and Cardiff, where many of the dockworkers are Somalis, are major markets.

The Western Indian Ocean Region

Madagascar. The cultivation, sale, and consumption of khat are legal in Madagascar, where the drug is grown and consumed chiefly by members of the Antakarana ethnic group in the northern extremity of the island. Local names for the plant are "katy" and "gat" (Thomas Herlehy and Daniel Randiriamanalina, 1995, personal communication).

The introduction and early history of khat in Madagascar is obscure. It is possible that *C. edulis* was first brought to the island by Arab traders and immigrants several hundred years ago. Louis Molet (1967: 25) postulated that khat was introduced and spread by Yemeni Arabs and later by Muslims from the Comoro Archipelago. Traders from Kilwa and from Zanzibar may also have played a role in the introduction of khat to Madagascar. In any case, for generations, immigrants from Yemen and the Comoro Islands have settled among the Antakarana and Sakalava ethnic groups in northern Madagascar.

A minority of the population, commonly referred to as "Arabs," are of mixed Yemeni, Comoran, and Malagasy ancestry. They profess Islam, affect Arab (Yemeni) dress, and are said to be foremost in the commercial production of khat (Sharp 1995, personal communication).

It is mostly men that use khat, but the number of women users is said to be increasing. The retail price of a bundle of khat is about 5,000 Malagasy francs (approximately $1.25), which is expensive for most consumers (Sharp 1995, personal communication). As in Yemen, saliva and the juice of the leaves are swallowed, and the residue of chewed leaves is expectorated.

Methods of Khat Consumption

Khat as a Beverage

The practice of drinking water infusions and decoctions of khat is very old but today accounts for a smaller part of khat consumption than in the past. Fresh leaves for chewing, now widely available, provide users with much more psychostimulation than desiccated, boiled leaves. Nevertheless, khat prepared as a beverage is mildly stimulating, and some writers have extolled it as "an excellent beverage plant and worthy of exploitation" (Hill 1952: 481). "The leaf [has] a slightly bitter flavor with a strong, sweet taste of liquorice and has been regarded as nourishing" (Watt and Breyer-Brandwijk 1962: 179).

Catha edulis is one of many plants in Africa used to make "bush tea." In the Cape Province of South Africa, bush teas are popular as tonics and as treatments for urinary and digestive problems. J. M. Watt and M. G. Breyer-Brandwijk (1962: 590) have described two methods of preparing bush tea from young twigs and leaves of the khat tree. In one, flowering shoots are first fermented by being piled in a heap and then allowed to dry. In the other, the leaves are "sweated" in an oven before they are dried in the sun. According to Watt, well-prepared bush tea has a sweet aroma (Watt and Breyer-Brandwijk 1962: 590).

W. Cornwallis Harris, who traveled widely in Ethiopia during the years 1841 and 1842, reported that leaves of khat, well dried in the sun, were either chewed, boiled in milk, or infused in water. "By the addition of honey," wrote Harris, "a pleasant beverage is produced, which being bitter and stimulative, dispels sleep if used to excess" (1844: 423-4). In the region of Ifat (Welo Province), he found that the fresh leaves were chewed as an astringent medicine or taken to dispel sleep, "a decoction in water or milk being drunk as a beverage, which tastes bitter enough" (Harris 1844: 407). According to Simoons (1960: 115), Christians in Debra Tabor (Gondar Province, Ethiopia) use khat leaves to flavor mead *(tedj)*. The addition of *tedj* to a water infusion of khat yields a brown, bitter, mildly intoxicating beverage (Schopen 1978: 85).

Khat as a Masticatory

The chewing of fresh leaves and stem tips is the most common way of using khat as a psychostimulant. Everywhere the technique is much the same. Derek Peters (1952: 36) describes how khat is used as a masticatory in Somaliland. From the user's supply of fresh khat, tender leaves and shoots are carefully selected and stripped from a few branches, compressed into a small mass, placed in the mouth, and chewed. Saliva and plant juices are swallowed. Copious amounts of cold water or other cold beverages are drunk. After 10 to 15 minutes of chewing, most of the juices are extracted from the wad. The process is repeated until - after 3 or 4 hours - the user's supply of khat is exhausted. According to Weir (1985: 97), most consumers chew about 100 to 150 grams of picked leaves in one session; some chew as few as 50 grams, and a minority chew more than 200 grams.

In Yemen, the residue of chewed leaves in the mouth is not swallowed but compressed into a wad and stowed in one cheek (Kennedy 1987: 88). At the end of the chewing session it is expelled into a spittoon. In Ethiopia and East Africa, the chewed parts of the leaves are swallowed with the juice and saliva. Amare Getahun and A. D. Krikorian (1973: 371-2) have suggested that ingested residue may be an important part of the daily intake of food, especially in the case of heavy users of the drug. Other investigators suspect that tannin in the residue may be responsible for the gastrointestinal discomfort that is common among khat chewers.

Khat as a Paste

In Ethiopia, water and honey are added to crushed, dried leaves of khat, and the ingredients are worked into a paste. In Somalia, a paste is made of finely ground dried khat, water, sugar, cardamom, and cloves. Khat paste is commonly eaten by the elderly and by travelers, according to Schopen (1978: 84-5).

Other Modes of Use

Not uncommonly, elderly persons, if unable to chew effectively, pound fresh leaves of khat in a small mortar (which they carry on their person) and drink the juice (Brooke 1960: 53; Kennedy 1987: 88). In eighteenth-century Yemen, travelers and old persons used *madquq,* which is simply khat that is pressed and left to dry in a darkened room for seven days and then pulverized by mortar and pestle. A portion of the dry, granular khat is placed in the mouth, mixed with saliva, and swallowed (Schopen 1978: 86).

There are also brief references in the literature to the practice of smoking khat. For example, "The dried leaves [in Africa] are also sometimes smoked" (Margetts 1967: 358), and "In Arabia the leaves may be dried and smoked like tobacco" (Greenway 1947: 99). Y. Z. Hes mentions that in the towns of Yemen, there are places where one may go in order to make and smoke khat cigarettes (1970: 283-4). But today, with the widespread availability of the freshly cut product, this method of consumption appears to be little used.

Food and Nutritional Characteristics

Karsten Niebuhr, in his book on travels in Arabia published in 1792, ascribed to khat "the virtues of assisting digestion and fortifying the constitution against infectious diseases. Yet its insipid taste gives no indication of its extraordinary virtues" (Niebuhr 1792, Vol. 2: 353-4, cited by Krikorian 1984: 119).

The astringent effect of khat induces intense thirst, and in addition to water, such beverages as tea, coffee, and commercial colas are consumed during the chew. Beer, both commercial and homemade, is a popular thirst quencher with chewers in Kenya and Somalia. Sometimes the host of a khat party in Yemen provides sherbet for the guests during a chewing session.

The nutritional value of khat is important because, to some unknown extent, the leaf is a substitute for conventional foods that would be eaten by the majority of users who chew khat regularly. Solid food is avoided during the chewing session, and for some hours after. Indeed, a well-known effect of khat is the temporary loss of appetite. "The laborers and shop-keepers take khat and regard it as the best substitute for food," write Mulugeta Assefa (1983: 74).

In a 1952 analysis of samples of miscellaneous tropical and subtropical plants and plant products by Margaret Mustard (1952: 31), khat was found to contain "exceptionally large amounts" of ascorbic acid (vitamin C) in leaves and branch tips, and "the ancient custom of qat chewing in Arabia may be inadvertently supplying the people of that country with some of their daily requirement of ascorbic acid" (1952: 34). It is interesting to note that ascorbic acid has been reported to act as an antidote to amphetaminelike substances, such as khat (Krikorian 1984: 154).

The Ethiopian Nutrition Survey (Khat [or chat] 1959: 169), in a nutritional analysis of samples of fresh khat leaves and tender stems, reported that in addition to its vitamin C content, "khat can contribute important amounts of niacin, beta-carotine [sic], calcium and iron to the user's diet" (See Table III.7.1).

According to Weir (1985: 42–3), the diet of khat chewers conforms to traditional Greco-Arab medical doctrine about the functioning of the human body. A healthy body is thought to be one in which an equilibrium is maintained among the four constituent humors – blood, phlegm, yellow bile, and black bile. Each humor has qualities drawn from the categories wet/dry and hot/cold. Blood is moist and hot, phlegm is damp and cold, yellow bile is dry and hot, and black bile is dry and cold. All substances that are taken internally, including khat, food, and medicines, are capable of upsetting the balance among the four humors by causing an excess or a diminution of their qualities when ingested. Khat is cooling and drying:

> In order to achieve the most enjoyable results from an afternoon's qat party, and to offset the "cooling" effects of qat, a man should make himself as hot as possible by eating beforehand a good lunch composed of "hot" foods, and avoiding those classified as "cold." Hot foods are boiled mutton, mutton broth, fenugreek *(bilbah)* broth, chili pepper, white radish, wheat bread and sorghum porridge. . . . The cooling effects of qat are also counteracted during the qat party by closing all the windows of the room and generating a warm and stuffy atmosphere (Weir 1985: 43).

Weir (1985: 172) mentions that fenugreek is, next to mutton, the most important component of the midday meal, which is the main Yemeni meal. In Kennedy's opinion, there is traditional wisdom in the belief that fenugreek soup and a meat sauce gravy are essential components of a "greasy carbohydrate meal [that] nullifies at least some of the potentially negative side effects of the qat" (1987: 82).

Kennedy (1987: 81–2) also points out that it is essential that spicy and well-salted foods be eaten in order to heighten the thirst of the khat user during the chewing session. Pleasure in drinking cool water during the session is an important part of the chewing experience.

Medicinal Uses of Khat

Khat is included in only a few of the many Arab pharmacopoeias and has been very little used in formal medicine. As might be supposed, however, it has a place in folk medicine and traditional remedies. For example, according to Peter Merab, among the dervishes and other Muslim holy orders, chewed khat is spat upon patients as a preliminary step in treatment of the sick. He also mentions that infusions of khat are drunk to treat illness (1921: 176).

In Somalia, khat is believed to have curative properties in treating urinary problems and gonorrhea (Peters 1952: 36). In Tanzania, coughing, asthma, and other respiratory problems are dealt with by drinking khat infusions, and pieces of the tree root are eaten to relieve abdominal pains (Greenway 1947: 99).

In the eighteenth century, Yemenis believed that the use of khat prevented epidemics and that, wherever the khat plant grew, pestilence would not appear (Schopen 1978: 87–8). Khat is used as an analgesic in Madagascar, where "teas" of many different plants are consumed for medicinal purposes. Tea from khat is used by elderly persons to relieve rheumatic ache and by women to ease the pain of menstrual cramps (Sharp 1995, personal communication).

The Psychophysiological Effects of Khat

The psychotropic effects of khat first drew international attention in 1935, when two technical papers on the plant were discussed in the League of Nations' Advisory Committee on the Traffic in Opium and Other Dangerous Drugs (*Bulletin on Narcotics* 1980: 1).

For many years, it was believed that the alkaloid cathine, *d*-norpseudoephedrine, was the main stimulant in khat. But in 1975, a laboratory study – using samples of fresh khat (instead of dried leaves as had been used in previous work) – resulted in the detection and isolation of cathinone, a phenylalkylamine characterized as (-)a-aminopropiophenone (Szendrei 1980: 5). Cathinone, 8 to 10 times stronger than cathine in its effect, is the predominant psychotropic agent in khat (Kalix 1994: 71), which is the only plant known to produce cathinone (LeBelle 1993: 54).

The transformation of cathinone into other less-potent products, such as cathine, begins shortly after the leaves and shoots are removed from the tree (Kalix 1994: 72). With a plasma half-life of only 1.5 hours, cathinone's potency is lost within 48 to 72 hours after harvesting (Kalix 1994: 72), which is the reason khat users prefer to chew only fresh leaves and shoots of the plant. However, deep-freezing prolongs its potency for months (Drake 1988: 532–3).

Alkaloids from khat, used in patent medicines manufactured in Europe during the 1920s and 1930s, were derived only from dried leaf material and, therefore, contained little or no cathinone.

Table III.7.1. *Nutritional components of khat* (Catha edulis)

Vitamins and minerals	Sugars and sugar alcohols	Miscellaneous substances
Ash: 11.59 gm/100 gm dried leaves (includes Mg, Fe, Ca, Cl)	Mannitol	Rubberlike substances
Ascorbic acid: .136 gm/ 100 gm leaves and twigs 0.324 gm/100 gm leaves only	–	–
–	–	Rubberlike substances: volatile oil (traces)
Gm/100 gm plant material Ash 1.6% Ascorbic acid 0.161 Thiamine <0.00005 Niacin 0.0148 Riboflavin <0.00005 β-carotene 0.0018 Iron 0.0185 Calcium 0.290	–	Protein: 5.2% Fiber: 2.7%
–	–	Free amino acids, aspartic acid; threonine; serine; glutamic acid; proline, glycine; alanine; valine; leucine; isoleucine; tyrosine; α-aminobutyric acid; histidine; ornithine; arginine; tryptophan; phenylalanine.
–	Reducing sugars: as hexose: 1.4 gm/100 gm plant material (portion of total sugars may be galactose); dulcitol	Free amino acids: lysine; α-aminobutyric acid; phenylserine; phenylaline choline (0.05%) (dried plant)
–	Glucose, fructose; rhamnose (free); xylose, galactose; dulcitol	–
–	–	Flavonoids; glycosides or carbohydrates; volatile oils
–	–	Steam distillate of dried leaves and young twigs (of Yemen origin) yielded 0.04–0.08% of a yellow essential oil. There were 5 hydrocarbons (α and β-pinens, terpinolene, β-phellandrene, and ocimene); and 6 oxygenated terpenes (α and β-thujone, fenchone, linalool, α-terpineol, and nerol.

Source: After Krikorian and Getahun (1973).

The Khat Experience

A subjective account of khat-induced psychophysiological effects is given by Kennedy. The account is derived from his own experimentation with the drug and from interviews with 803 Yemeni users of khat:

> The first experiential effects of qat are a gradually developing mild euphoria, i.e., alertness, feelings of contentment, confidence, gregariousness, and the flowing of ideas, called the kayf. ["Kayf" is a general term in Arabic for a state of pleasurable well-being]. Under certain variable conditions such as amount of the drug, food intake, personality and physical condition, this kayf phase occasionally develops into confusion. Ordinarily however, the experience gradually transforms into an "introvert phase" of quiet contemplation in which the stimulation of thought processes continues at a rapid pace while physical and vocal activities diminish. Since this is often accompanied by fatigue, previous problems or pessimistic personality characteristics may transform this phase into a mild temporary lowering of mood.
>
> The postsession effects of qat continue for several hours, and, again depending upon the same variable conditions, many of them are rather negative. Sleep is inhibited, hunger is diminished, sexual desire and performance may positively or negatively be affected, and irritability may occur. However, often people experience positive aftermaths, such as feeling closer to Allah, more understanding, and a desire to work. When we look at our interview data pertaining to the experiential aspects of qat-use we find consistent male-female differences, with more males generally reporting the experiences. In the eyes of the average chewer the rewarding experiences associated with qat chewing outweigh the unrewarding ones; they are much more regular and predictable (Kennedy 1987: 130–1).

Adverse Effects of Khat

An apocryphal account of khat's introduction into Yemen from Ethiopia is given by the historian and traveler, Ibn Fadl Allah al'Umari in his work, *Masalik al-Absar,* written between A.D. 1342 and 1349. The king of Yemen, curious about khat, asked an advisor, an Ethiopian familiar with the drug, to describe the effects of chewing the leaf:

> Upon learning that it virtually eliminated the desire to eat, to drink [alcohol?], and to have sexual intercourse, [the king] told him: "And what other pleasures are there in this base world besides those? By God, I will not eat it at all; I only spend my efforts on those three things; how am I going to use such a thing which will deprive me of the pleasures that I get from them?" (Krikorian 1984: 26–7).

Beyond question, a temporary loss of appetite is effected by khat chewing. In laboratory tests, cathinone and cathine markedly inhibit the food intake of rats (*Bulletin on Narcotics* 1980: 84). In addition, nearly all users experience difficulty in sleep following the use of the drug. Only daily heavy chewers reported that their sleep was not inhibited by khat (Kennedy 1987: 128). There is also little doubt that sexual experience is affected by khat, but opinions vary as to whether sexual desire is heightened and ability to perform is enhanced, or whether there is a loss of libido. Examples of both effects are found in the literature: "While sex interest is heightened at first, depressed *libido* and *potentia sexualis* come as the drug effect is maintained, and chronic users may develop impotence" (Margetts 1967: 359; see also Krikorian 1984: 151).

A negative view of the drug, based on its anaphrodisiac properties, is paradoxical, however, because relevant demographic characteristics of the chief khat-using countries suggest that "depressed libido" is hardly a problem. Yemen, for example, has a total fertility rate (the average number of children a woman will have throughout her childbearing years) of 7.7, which is the world's highest, save for Gaza's 8.1 (Population Reference Bureau 1995).

Perhaps the most common ailments related to the level of khat use are gastritis (acute and chronic) and constipation (Kennedy 1987: 218). Tannins in khat (chiefly flavenoids) have long been suspected of adversely affecting the gastric system. At the present time, it is known that tannin content is high, probably between 5 and 15 percent (Kennedy 1987: 185). Many of the most expensive kinds of khat have reddish tints to leaves and shoots, and these kinds are purported to have a lower content of tannins than the others (Drake 1988: 532).

Among women, there is a strong association of the level of khat use with liver and urinary problems. Khat chewing may also be a maternal practice harmful to the fetus. It has been found that healthy full-term infants have a significantly lower average birth weight if the mothers were either occasional or habitual khat chewers (Eriksson, Ghani, and Kristiansson 1991: 106–11).

Legal Considerations

Since the 1950s, khat has been on various agendas of meetings under the auspices of the United Nations Commission on Narcotic Drugs and of the World Health Organization. For many years, the attention of these organizations was directed to the question of agreeing upon a pharmacological definition of *C. edulis.* Eventually, in 1973, it was placed in a group of "dependence-producing drugs," although there is a lack of evidence that khat chewing produces "dependence" in the usual sense of the word.

At the present time, 137 countries are parties to at least one of the three Conventions (1961, 1971, and 1980) of the United Nations International Drug Control Programme. Because khat contains the alkaloids cathinone and cathine, it is a scheduled drug on the 1971 Convention's List of Psychotropic Substances. Parties to the Convention agreed to prohibit the entry of khat without an import permit. However, most parties to the U.N. conventions do not strictly enforce the control measures for khat as required by the treaties.

Europe

The Scandinavian countries are among the minority of European nations that strictly enforce a ban on the import and export of khat. Consumers in the United Kingdom and Germany may purchase khat legally, airborne from Ethiopia, Kenya, and, recently, Yemen (Rushby 1995: 16). In Rome, where use of the drug is popular among Somali expatriates, it is rumored that airport customs inspectors of flights arriving from Ethiopia, Kenya, Yemen, and Israel seldom inquire closely as to the nature of fresh bundles of stems and leaves identified on import declaration forms as "floral stuff" (Nencini et al. 1989: 257).

The United States

Under United States federal law, it is illegal to possess khat for personal use or to import, cultivate, dispense, or distribute it. The alkaloid cathinone is placed in Schedule I, subsection (f) Stimulants, of the Controlled Substances Act (CSA). The CSA defines Schedule I drugs as "highly abusable substances . . . which have no currently accepted medical use in the United States" and which may be used lawfully only in research situations authorized by the Drug Enforcement Administration (U.S. Department of Justice 1988: 4). As provided by the CSA, the penalty for simple possession of khat is imprisonment of not more than one year and a minimum fine of $1,000, or both (Code of Federal Regulations, 21 1994: 1308.12, 841[a], 841[b], 844[a]).

It is believed that most khat enters the United States from Canada in small quantities concealed in luggage aboard aircraft or in private vehicles. Seizures of khat have been made at international airports in Champlain, N.Y., New York City, Newark, Chicago, Dallas, and St. Louis. A total of about 800 kilograms of khat was seized by the U.S. Customs Service between August 1991 and October 1992. In March 1993, the retail price of a kilogram of khat ranged from 30 to 60 dollars (U.S. Department of Justice 1993: 2).

Canada

Khat is currently classified as a "New Drug" in Canada, that is, "new" in the sense that "it has not been sold in Canada for sufficient time to establish the safety and effectiveness of the substance for use as a drug" (Langlois 1995, personal communication). As a New Drug, the sale of khat is prohibited, but not its possession import, export, or consumption. New legislation would place fresh leaves of khat in Schedule II and confine import, export, cultivation, sale, and possession to medical and scientific purposes. Importation would require an official permit. Violations would be subject to fines not to exceed 5,000 dollars and or imprisonment not exceeding three years (Langlois 1995, personal communication).

Clarke Brooke

The author acknowledges the valuable assistance of the following individuals in preparing this paper: P. K. Bailey, Badalkhan Baloch, N. A. Baloch, Richard Halse, W. W. Heiser, Ross Hossie, C. C. Held, Erich Isaac, Fritz Kramer, John Mandeville, Martin Novack, Thomas Poulsen, Jean Pryor, Ziva Razafintsalama, Hiromi L. Sakata, Lesley Sharp, Arnon Soffer, and Frank Wesley.

Bibliography

Al-Hammad, Abed-el-Kader Shiba. 1983. The Shari'ah's position on khat. In *The health and socio-economic aspects of khat use,* ed. B. Shahandeh, R. Geadah, A. Tongue, E. Tongue, et al., 225–30. Lausanne.

Al-Meshal, I. Ibrahim, Shoeb Qureshi, Abdul Rehman, and Mohammed Tariq. 1991. The toxicity of *Catha edulis* (khat) in mice. *Journal of Substance Abuse* 3: 107–15.

Al-Thani, I. M. 1983. Development: The Saudi solution for the problem of khat. In *The health and socio-economic aspects of khat use,* ed. B. Shahandeh et al., 181–94. Lausanne.

Assefa, Mulugeta. 1983. Socio-economic aspects of khat in the Harrarghe administrative region (Ethiopia). In *The health and socio-economic aspects of khat use,* ed. B. Shahandeh et al., 72–7. Lausanne.

Azais, R. P., and R. Chambard. 1931. *Cinq années de recherche archéologiques en Éthiopia. Province du Harar et Éthiopie meridionale.* Paris.

Baird, D. A. 1951. Indian remedies for poor memories. *British Medical Journal* 2: 1522.

Balint, G., H. Ghebrekidan, and E. Balint. 1991. *Catha edulis,* an international socio-medico problem with considerable pharmacological implications. *East African Medical Journal* 68: 555–61.

Bally, P. R. O. 1945. Catha edulis. *East African Medical Journal* 22: 2–3.

Bill C-7. First session, Thirty-fifth Parliament, 42 Elizabeth II, 1994. Ministry of Health, House of Commons, Canada. Ottawa.

Brooke, Clarke. 1958. The durra complex of the Central Highlands of Ethiopia. *Economic Botany* 12: 192–204.

    1960. Khat *(Catha edulis):* Its production and trade in the Middle East. *Geographical Journal* 126: 52–9.

Browne, Dallas. 1990. Qat use in New York City. Research Monograph 105, 1990: 464–5. National Institute on

Drug Abuse. U.S. Department of Health and Human Services. Washington, D.C.

Bulletin on Narcotics. 1980. Special issue devoted to *Catha edulis* (khat), Vol. 32, No. 3.

Burton, Richard F. 1910. *First footsteps in East Africa.* London.

Chevalier, A. 1949. Les cat's d'Abyssinie et d'Afrique Orientale. *Revue de Botanique Appliquée et d'Agriculture Tropicale* 29: 413-17.

Code of Federal Regulations: Food and Drugs. 21. 1994. Part 1300 to End revised as of April 1, 1994. Office of the Federal Register, National Archives and Records Administration. Washington, D.C.

Drake, P. H. 1988. Khat-chewing in the Near East. The Lancet 1 (March 5): 532-3.

Duke, James. 1985. *CRC handbook of medicinal herbs.* Boca Raton, Fla.

Economist Intelligence Unit Limited, The. 1987. *Djibouti EIU Country Report No.4,1987.* London.

1988. *Djibouti EIU Country Report No.1, 1988.* London.

1989. *Djibouti EIU Country Profile 1989-90.* London.

1994. *Ethiopia EIU Country Report No.1, 1994.* London.

1989. *Yemen EIU Country Report 1989:* 56. London.

1992. *Yemen EIU Country Report No. 3, 1992: 21-9.* London.

1994. *Yemen EIU Country Report 1994: 19-27.* London.

1994. *Yemen EIU Country Profile 1994-95.* London.

Elmi, Abdullahi. 1983. The chewing of khat in Somalia. *Journal of Ethnopharmacology* 8: 163-76.

Elmi, A. S., T. H. Ahmed, and M. S. Samatar. 1987. Experience in the control of khat-chewing in Somalia. *Bulletin on Narcotics* 39: 51-7.

Eriksson, M., N. A. Ghani, and B. Kristiansson. 1991. Khat-chewing during pregnancy - effect upon the off-spring and some characteristics of the chewers. *East African Medical Journal:* 106-11.

Geisshusler, S., and R. Breneissen. 1987. The content of psychoactive phenylpropyl and phenylpentenyl khatamines in *Catha edulis* Forsk. of different origin. *Journal of Ethnopharmacology* 19: 269-77.

Getahun, Amare, and A. D. Krikorian. 1973. Chat: Coffee's rival from Harar, Ethiopia. I. Botany, cultivation and use. *Economic Botany* 27: 353-77.

Giannini, A. J., N. S. Miller, and C. E. Turner. 1992. Treatment of khat addiction. *Journal of Substance Abuse Treatment* 9: 379-82.

Gidron, Avner. 1993. Khat or not? *World Press Review* 40: 30.

Great Britain, Naval Intelligence Division. 1946. *Western Arabia and the Red Sea.* Geographical Handbook Series, B.R. 527. Oxford.

Greenway, P. J. 1947. Khat. *East African Agricultural Journal:* 98-102.

Harris, W. Cornwallis. 1844. *The highlands of Aethiopia,* Vol. 3. Second edition. London.

Hes, Y. Z. 1970. Some notes concerning the use of kat *(Catha edulis).* Ha-Refu'ah: 283-4 (in Hebrew). Jerusalem.

Hess, J. J., 1927. Kat. In *The encyclopedia of Islam,* Vol. 2, ed. M. Th. Houtsama, A. J. Wensinck, T. W. Arnold, et al., 808. Leiden.

High on qat. *Jerusalem Post* 1996. International Edition. November 10-16, pp. 16-17.

Hill, A. F. 1952. *Economic botany.* New York

Hill, Bob. 1965. Cat (Catha edulis Forsk). *Journal of Ethiopian Studies* 3: 13-23.

Hill, C. H., and A. Gibson. 1987. The oral and dental effects of q'at chewing. *Oral Surgery, Oral Medicine, Oral Pathology* 63: 433-6.

Hjort, Anders. 1974. Trading miraa: From school-leaver to shop-owner in Kenya. *Ethnos* 39: 27-43.

Ingrams, Harold. 1966. *Arabia and the Isles.* Third edition. London.

Islam, M. W., O. A. Al-Shabanah, M. M. Al-Harbi, and N. M. A. Al-Gharbly. 1994. Evaluation of teratogenic potential of khat *(Catha edulis Forsk).* in rats. *Drug and Chemical Toxicology* 17: 51-68.

Kafih, J. 1963. *Halikhot Teman* (Folkways of Yemen, Jewish life in San'a). Jerusalem.

Kalix, Peter. 1990. Pharmacological properties of the stimulant khat. *Pharmacological Therapy* 48: 397-416.

1994. Khat an amphetamine-like stimulant. *Journal of Psychoactive Drugs* 23: 69-74.

Kalix, Peter, and Olav Braenden. 1985. Pharmacological aspects of the chewing of khat leaves. *Pharmacological Reviews* 37: 149-64.

Karawya M. S., M. A. Elkiey, and M. G. Ghourab. 1968. A study of *Catha edulis* Forsk. growing in Egypt. *Journal of the Pharmaceutical Sciences of the United Arab Republic* 9: 147-57.

Kennedy, John G. 1987. *The flower of paradise.* Dordrecht, Netherlands.

Khat. 1956. *Bulletin on Narcotics* 8: 6-13.

Khat (or chat). 1959. *Ethiopia Nutrition Survey. A Report by the Interdepartmental Committee on Nutrition for National Defense* 30: 166-9. Washington, D.C.

Krikorian, A. D. 1984. Kat and its use: An historical perspective. *Journal of Ethnopharmacology* 12: 115-78.

Krikorian, A. D., and Amare Getahun. 1973. Chat: Coffee's rival from Harar, Ethiopia. II. Chemical composition. *Economic Botany* 27: 378-89.

Langdale-Brown, I., H. A. Ostmasten, and J. G. Wilson. 1964. *The vegetation of Uganda and its bearing on land-use.* New York.

LeBelle, M. J. 1993. Gas chromatographic–mass spectrometric identification of chiral derivatives of khat. *Forensic Science International* 61: 53-64.

Lorch, Donatella. 1994. Despite war, famine and pestilence, the khat trade thrives in East Africa. *New York Times.* December 14, p. A8.

Mack, Ronald. 1995. Khat on a hot tin roof. *North Carolina Medical Journal* 56: 112-14.

Margetts, Edward. 1967. Miraa and myrrh in East Africa - clinical notes about Catha edulis. *Economic Botany* 21: 358-62.

Matai, C. K. 1983. Country report - Kenya. In *The health and socio-economic aspects of khat use,* ed. B. Shahandeh et al., 87-90. Lausanne.

McKee, C. M. 1987. Medical and social aspects of qat in Yemen: A review. *Journal of the Royal Society of Medicine* 80: 762-5.

Merab, Peter. 1921, 1922, 1923. *Impressions d'Éthiopie (L'Abyssinie sous Menelik II.* 3 vols. Paris.

Molet, Louis. 1967. Cadres pour une ethnopsychiatrie de Madagascar. *L'Homme* 7: 5-29.

Morghem, M. M., and M. I. Rufat. 1983. Cultivation and chewing of khat in the Yemen Arab Republic. In *The health and socio-economic aspects of khat use,* ed. B. Shahandeh et al., 215-16.

Murdock, George P. 1959. *Africa: Its peoples and their culture history.* New York.

Mustard, Margaret. 1952. Ascorbic acid content of some miscellaneous tropical and subtropical plants and plant products. *Food Research* 17: 31-5.

Nencini, Paolo, Abdullahi Mohammed Ahmed, and Abdullai Sheik Elmi. 1986. Subjective effects of khat chewing in humans. *Drug and Alcohol Dependence* 18: 97-105.

Nencini, Paolo, Maria Caterina Grassi, Abdikadar Ashkir Botan, et al. 1989. Khat chewing spread to the Somali community in Rome. *Drug and Alcohol Dependence* 23: 255-8.

Nyrop, Richard, ed. 1985. *The Yemens: Country studies.* 2d edition. Washington, D.C.

Ofcansky, Thomas, and LaVerle Berry, eds. 1993. *Ethiopia: A country study.* Fourth edition. Washington, D.C.

Owen, P. J. 1910. Catha edulis. *Journal of the Society of Chemical Industry* 29: 1091.

Pankhurst, Richard. 1961. *An introduction to the economic history of Ethiopia.* London.

Pantelis, Christos, Charles G. Hindler, and John C. Taylor. 1989. Use and abuse of khat *(Catha edulis):* A review of the distribution, pharmacology, side effects, and a description of psychosis attributed to khat chewing. *Psychological Medicine* 19: 657-68.

Paris, R., and H. Moyse. 1958. Abyssinian tea *(Catha edulis* Forsk., *Celastracae).* A study of some samples of varying geographical origin. *Bulletin on Narcotics* 10: 29-34.

Peters, Derek. 1952. Khat: Its history, botany, chemistry and toxicology. *The Pharmaceutical Journal* 169: 17-18, 36-7.

Population Reference Bureau. 1995. *World Population Data Sheet: 1995.* Washington, D.C.

Randall, Teri. 1993. Khat abuse fuels Somali conflict, drains economy. *Journal of the American Medical Society* 269: 12-15.

Revri, Raman. 1983. *Catha edulis Forsk. Geographical dispersal, botanical, ecological and agronomical aspects with special reference to Yemen Arab Republic.* Göttingen.

Rosenzweig, Kurt, and Patricia Smith. 1966. Peridontal health in various ethnic groups in Israel. *Journal of Periodontology* 1: 250-9.

Rushby, Kevin. 1995. The high life. *Geographical* 67: 14-17.

Santagata, Fernando. 1940. *L'Harar. Territorio di pace e di civilta.* Milan.

Sayer, J. A., C. S. Harcourt, and N. M. Collins, eds. 1992. *Conservation of tropical forests.* Africa and London.

Schopen, Armin. 1978. *Das Qat: Geschichte und Gebrauch des Genussmittels Catha Edulis Forsk in der Arabischen Republik Jemen.* Wiesbaden.

Scott, Hugh. 1947. *In High Yemen.* London.

Seyoum, E., Y. Kidane, H. Gebru, and G. Sevenhuysen. 1986. Preliminary study of income and nutritional status indicators in two Ethiopian villages. *Food and Nutrition Bulletin* 8: 37-41.

Shahandeh, B., R. Geadah, A. Tongue, et al, eds. 1983. *The health and socio-economic aspects of khat use.* Lausanne.

Simoons, Frederick. 1960. *Northwest Ethiopia: Peoples and economy.* Madison, Wis.

Sullum, Jacob. 1993. Khat calls. *Reason* 24: 42-3.

Szendrei, K. 1980. The chemistry of khat. *Bulletin on Narcotics.1980. Special issue devoted to Catha edulis (khat)* 3: 5-36.

Trimingham, J. Spencer. 1952. *Islam in Ethiopia.* London.

Tutwiler, Richard, and Sheila Caprisco. 1981. *Yemeni agriculture and economic change: Case studies of two highland regions.* San'a.

Uphof, George. 1974. *A dictionary of economic plants.* Würzburg.

U.S. Department of Justice. 1988. *Drugs of abuse.* Drug Enforcement Administration. Washington D.C.

1993. *Khat Factsheet.* Drug Enforcement Administration. Washington, D.C.

1993. Methcathinone (Cat) Factsheet. Drug Enforcement Administration. Washington, D.C.

Varisco, Daniel. 1986. On the meaning of chewing: The significance of qat *(Catha edulis)* in the Yemen Arab Republic. *International Journal of Middle East Studies* 18: 1-13.

Vavilov, N. I. 1951. *The origin, variation, immunity and breeding of cultivated plants,* trans. K. Starr Chester. New York.

Watt, J. M., and M. G. Breyer-Brandwijk. 1962. *The medicinal and poisonous plants of Southern and Eastern Africa.* Second edition. Livingston, Edinburgh, and London.

Weir, Shelagh. 1983. Economic aspects of the qat industry in North-West Yemen. In *Economy and society in contemporary Yemen,* ed. G. R. Pridham, 64-82. Exeter, England.

1985. *Qat in Yemen: Consumption and social change.* London.

Westphal, E. 1975. *Agricultural systems in Ethiopia.* In collaboration with J. M. C. Westphal-Stevels. Wageningen, Netherlands.

Widler, Peter, Karoline Mathys, Rudolf Brenneisen, et al. 1994. Pharmacodynamics and pharmacokinetics of khat: A controlled study. *Clinical Pharmacology and Therapeutics* 55: 556-62.

Zein, Ahmed Z. 1988. Polydrug abuse among Ethiopian university students with particular reference to khat *(Catha edulis). Journal of Tropical Medicine and Hygiene* 91: 71-5.

III.8 ❧ Kola Nut

Kola nut is an important stimulant and masticatory in Africa. It is about the size of a walnut or a chestnut and varies in color from dark red to creamy white (Chevalier and Perrot 1911; Cohen 1966; Agiri 1972; Lovejoy 1977-8, 1980). This fruit of the kola tree grows in pods that contain from 3 to 15 or more nuts. Pink and white nuts are generally valued highest because they have a sweeter taste and a greater caffeine content than other kola nuts. Kola is richer in caffeine than coffee and most teas and has 3 times as much starch as cacao (Heckel and Schlagdenhauffen 1884; Kraemer 1910; Chevalier and Perrot 1911; Pratt and Youngken 1956; Ramstad 1959). Known by various African names - *goro* or *gourou, ombéné, nangoué, kokkorokou,* and *matrasa* - kola is known as a heart stimulant because it contains kolanin along with caffeine, traces of the alkaloid theobromine (which exists in cacao as well), glucose, and strychnine (Table III.8.1). Both caffeine and theobromine stimulate the nervous system and the skeletal muscles, making kola a psychoactive substance (Kennedy 1987; Jones 1995).

Table III.8.1. *Chemical composition of the pod husk, testa, and nut of kola (dry matter %)*

Composition	Pod husk*	Testa*	Nut*
Crude protein (NS × 6.25)	10.22	14.00	8.06
	(7.69–12.50)	(12.25–17.00)	(7.25–9.81)
Ash	6.05	11.00	2.55
	(5.75–7.58)	(9.23–13.11)	(1.95–3.08)
Crude fiber	16.43	14.36	2.18
	(15.72–18.26)	(13.33–15.77)	(1.83–2.57)
Ether extract	1.0	1.37	0.98
	(0.8–1.4)	(0.94–1.56)	(0.96–1.0)
Nitrogen free extract	66.30	59.00	86.23
	(61.52–70.04)	(52.56–64.25)	(83.54–88.01)
Caffeine	trace	0.44	1.58
		(0.32–0.48)	(0.8–3.0)
Pectin	10.0	5.00	–
	(9.24–11.57)	(4.54–5.50)	
Total Polyphenols	8.80	3.63	6.7
	(8.24–9.8)	(2.50–4.20)	(5.6–8.5)
Total nitrogen	1.63	2.24	1.28
	(1.23–2.0)	(1.96–2.72)	(1.16–1.56)
Nonprotein nitrogen	0.69	0.34	0.88
	(0.5–0.93)	(0.30–0.82)	(0.76–1.16)

*The diagram above shows the chemicals that are contained in kola nuts, which make kola such an important masticatory in Africa.

Source: Ogutuga (1975), pp. 121–5.

Kola

Kola Production

The genus *Cola* is of tropical African origin (Freeman 1893; Irvine 1948; Cohen 1966; Dickson 1969) and belongs to the *Sterculiaceae* family, the species of which are most abundant in tropical Asia (Oliver 1868; Heckel and Schlagdenhauffen 1884). A number of different species grow in the region between Sierra Leone and the Congo (Heckel and Schlagdenhauffen 1884; Kreiger 1954; Kola 1957; Dickson 1969; Morgan and Pugh 1969; Brooks 1980; Anquandah 1982). But of some 40 varieties, only *Cola nitida* and *Cola acuminata* are well known and widely used. The former was the kola of long-distance trade, whereas the latter was grown mainly for local consumption in the forest regions of Africa.

Before the nineteenth century, *C. nitida* was only produced west of the Volta River, and *C. acuminata* grew to the east, especially in Nigeria (Lovejoy 1980; Goodman, Lovejoy, and Sheratt 1995). In the nineteenth century, however, the cultivation of *Cola anomala* and *Cola ballayi* had spread to southern Cameroon, with the nuts exported to the savanna region (Goodman et al. 1995). In Ghana, in addition to *C. nitida* and *C. acuminata*, there are other varieties that include *Cola cardifolia, Cola togoensis*

(Engl & Krause), *Cola johnsonii* (Stapf.), and *Cola verticilata* (Stapf. & Chev.) (Irvine 1969).

Although kola is indigenous to the forest zone of West Africa, the plant has traveled widely. It can be found in East Africa around Lake Nyanza, along the north coast of South America, and in portions of South Asia. In large part, this is because of European colonization. The British, for example, introduced kola into the East Indies, the Seychelles, Ceylon (Sri Lanka), Demerara (Guyana), Dominica, Mauritius, and Zanzibar. Similarly, the French introduced kola into Martinique, Guadeloupe, and Cayenne (Heckel and Schlagdenhauffen 1884).

Cultivation

Kola does well in forest soils and also in savanna areas of forest outliers so long as there is adequate moisture in the rooting zone and the soil has a high content of organic matter. The tree likes low elevations, deep, well-drained soils, and moderate rainfall. Good drainage is essential because the plant cannot withstand flooding (AERLS *Guide* 1982). It grows best in rich, deep soil in forest zones where rainfall does not exceed 50 to 60 inches annually – conditions characteristic of areas where the kola industry has persisted on a commercial scale (Heckel and Schlagdenhauffen 1884; Miles 1931).

The kola tree also flourishes in moist lands either at sea level or a little above. In Labogie in Nupe (Nigeria), kola plantations are situated in sheltered valleys at an elevation of 450 to 550 feet above sea level, where, according to a Royal Botanical Garden bulletin, "[t]he soil is a deep, black, sandy loam and is kept in a continuous state of moisture by streams that are in the valley" (1906: 89). The annual rainfall in this region is about 40 to 50 inches. Similarly, in southwestern Nigeria, kola is generally found in the better-drained areas with light, loamy soils of good depth (Russell 1955; Agiri 1972).

Germination

Polyembryo (in which more than one embryo results from a single ovule) occurs in *C. nitida* (Bodard 1954) and *C. acuminata,* along with multiple shoot/root production and adnation of auxiliary shoots to the main stem axis (Oladokun and Adepipe 1989). In fact, splitting or cutting the nuts brings quicker germination, although this reduces nut size, as well as initial growth after germination is slowed down. In addition, some of the cotyledons produce multiple roots and shoots, whereas others produce roots with no shoots (Oladokun and Adepipe 1989; Brown 1970).

High temperatures and light seem to have no effect on kola germination. Seeds that are freshly harvested take 3 to 9 months to germinate, although seeds stored for about 7 months usually do so within 3 or 4 months of sowing. There is also a pronounced difference between the germination patterns of stored and fresh kola seeds, with seedlings from stored seeds tending to grow faster, larger, and more vigorously than those from fresh seeds (Ashiru 1969; Brown 1970; Karikari 1973).

Propagation

The propagation of kola nuts takes place after the land is prepared at the beginning of the rainy season. The farmer initially clears a portion of the forest and scrapes the soil into "hills" that are "beds" for yam, cassava, and cocoyam. Kola seeds are planted between these beds and spaced about 20 to 27 feet apart so that the food crops will provide shade for the young seedlings (Ashiru 1969; Brown 1970; Karikari 1973).

A kola tree bears fruit after 4 or 5 years and reaches maturity by the tenth year. Because it is a tree of the tropical forest, it is useful to interplant with food crops or with shade trees, such as coffee and cacao. Many of the kola groves or plantations in Ghana are found growing together with cacao (Ossei 1963). Because growth is very slow (about 3 meters in 4 years), the use of seed, rooting of cuttings, grafting of shoots on suitable rootstocks, budding, and aerial layering – or marcottage – are all techniques that have been employed to make seedlings available to farmers who have embraced the crop.

If kola is to be propagated from the seed, the nuts are taken from the pod and wrapped in plantain leaves. Then they are buried in the ground and watered every day until they sprout, after which the young seedlings are transplanted to bear fruit some 4 to 5 years hence (N.A.G. [Kumasi] 1905; Quarcoo 1969; AERLS *Guide* 1982; Szolnoki 1985). Seedlings are also raised in bamboo pots before being transplanted in the field. In some cases, bananas and plantains provide shade for the young plants (Ossei 1963).

Kola is also planted by one or another of four methods of vegetative reproduction (Pyke 1934). In the first, a branch of a healthy kola tree is cut into 2- to 3-foot-long pieces, which are then planted. After germination, these bear fruit in 2 or 3 years (N.A.G. [Kumasi] 1905; AERLS *Guide* 1982). Plant cuttings, one of the most frequently used present-day techniques in cloning fruit trees, is also one of the most ancient methods of vegetative propagation (Archibald 1955; Jones 1968; Ashiru and Quarcoo 1971; Ibikunle 1972; Ashiru 1975). It is very important that cloning be done only from high-yielding kola trees and, more importantly, from trees with a high degree of self- and cross-compatibility.

A second method of vegetative propagation is grafting. Various methods of grafting have been used in the production of kola clones (Ashiru and Quarcoo 1971; Gnanaratum 1972), with wedge grafting, saddle grafting, and the splice and whip-and-tongue grafts said to yield the best results (Jones 1968). In Nigeria, the side-and-wedge grafting technique is widely used.

Budding is a third method of vegetative propagation of kola. Nursery budding ensures the production of vigorous budlings and offers the possibility of virtually all of them continuing to bud in the field. By contrast, *in situ* budding cannot guarantee that 100 percent of the buds will take, although these usually do grow faster than those transferred from the nursery (Archibald 1955; Are 1965; Ashiru and Quarcoo 1971; Ibikunle 1972; Ashiru 1975).

Aerial layering (also known as marcottage) is the fourth method of vegetative propagation by which "an intact branch of a kola tree is induced to produce roots before it is severed from the mother tree" (Ashiru and Quarcoo 1971). After being severed, the cutting may be raised in a nursery or planted directly in the field. Branches that are growing vertically, or nearly so, are the best types to select for marcotting, and such branches should be between 2 and 3 years old. As a method of kola propagation, marcottage is old and well known, but it is also very cumbersome (Toxopeus and Okololo 1967).

Kola is – or at least was – sometimes planted on special occasions. In some cultures of sub-Saharan Africa, for example, it was the custom to bury the umbilical cord of a newborn baby with a kola seed. This indicated a safe delivery, and the kola tree that subsequently grew up became the property of the child. Cultural taboos also play a role in kola planting: In some parts of West Africa, a belief (perhaps spread to limit competition) that "he who plants kola will die as soon as the plant has flowered" militated against its cultivation. Instead, farmers looked for self-sown seedlings and transplanted them (Russell 1955).

The Kola Trade

From time immemorial, the forest and the savanna regions of Africa have been complementary in basic natural products. This complementariness – based on the very different requirements of forest and savanna dwellers – stimulated long-distance exchange between the Volta basin and the Upper Niger (Denham and Clapperton 1826; Lander 1830; Dupuis 1894; Hallet 1965; Bowdich 1966; Arhin 1987). Gold, kola nuts, and salt from the coast constituted the most important items of trade in the Volta Basin of West Africa (Wilks 1962; Fynn 1971).

Evidence from the *Esmeraldo de Situ Orbis* – penned by one of the earliest Portuguese explorers, Duarte Pacheco Pereira – attests to the existence of the West African kola trade as early as the sixteenth century. A materia medica written in 1586 for the Moroccan sultan, Ahmed al-Mansur, mentions that kola was brought from the western Sudan – from "a place called Bitu where there are mines of gold and gold dust" (Wilks 1962: 15).

C. nitida, as an export crop, is reported to have originated in the hinterland of what is now Sierra Leone and Liberia, where it appears to have been commercialized by people who spoke a language of the West Atlantic family of Niger-Congo. People of the Mande branch, who subsequently moved to the forest zone, became the major producers in the fourteenth century. The kola nut trade was then monopolized by Muslim Mande traders who traveled widely throughout the western Sudan (Goodman et al. 1995). By the fifteenth century, the cultivation of *C. nitida* had spread throughout the Ivory Coast region and the Volta basin. It was also being grown in the forests of Sierra Leone, Liberia, and the Ivory Coast, and in the Volta basin of Ghana.

Coastwise trade in kola led to the creation of two diasporic communities – the Bahun commercial network, linking the lower Cacheu River with the Casamance River and the Gambia River, and a parallel Mandinka network to the east, linking the Upper Geba and Upper Casamance with the Middle and Upper Gambia and Upper Niger (Brooks 1980). Although this kola trade antedated the arrival of the Europeans, when Portuguese traders did reach West Africa, they quickly recognized the commercial importance of kola. With the help of African mariners, they began to participate in the kola trade while systematically concealing that participation from royal regulation and sanction (Brooks 1980).

In the eighteenth and nineteenth centuries, the Gold Coast and Sierra Leone supplied kola to northern and, later, southern Nigeria (*Gold Coast Blue Books* 1884–1925; Miles 1931). During the last half of the nineteenth century, however, demand for Gold Coast kola nuts mounted in Britain (Table III.8.2), France, Germany, and the United States, where the nuts were employed in the production of "neo kola," cola-based soft drinks, and pharmaceuticals (*Gold Coast Blue Books* 1884–1925).

The overseas kola trade from the Gold Coast to Europe and the United States developed in three phases. It began with the export of two packages of unknown weight to England in 1867 (Dickson 1969) and continued to grow until, in 1884 and 1885, 400 packages of kola, worth more than £2,000, were sent to Europe and the United States (*Gold Coast Blue Books* 1884, 1885; Freeman 1893; Dickson 1969).

Table III.8.2. *Kola exports to England*

1867	2 pkgs
1884	400 pkgs
1885	400 pkgs
1898	1 ton
1899	9 tons
1900	< 9 tons
1901	< 9 tons
1902	< 9 tons
1903	1 ton
1904	1.5 tons
1906	1.6 tons
1907	2 tons
1908	1.5 tons
1910	< 2 tons
1915	3.5 tons

Source: Gold Coast Blue Books 1884–1925 and Dickson (1969), pp. 151–3.

The second phase of the southern kola trade, which saw the export of kola to Brazil from the 1890s until the 1920s, took the form of exports directly from Ghana, as well as reexports of Ghanaian kola nuts from Nigeria to Brazil (*Gold Coast Blue Books* 1888–1920; Alex 1890).

The third and final phase of the southern kola trade involved exports to Nigeria in the first decades of the twentieth century. The ports of Accra, Winneba, Saltpond, Apam, and Cape Coast became outlets for the these shipments of kola by sea.

The southern axis of the kola trade was also spurred by the purchase of kola by African and European companies trading along the coast of Ghana and by improvements in communication, such as the construction of roads and railways and the introduction of motor transportation, along with mail boats, steamers, and ferries (Danquah 1928; N.A.G. [Accra] 1959; Dickson 1961). The result was a significant increase in kola trade volume.

From the mid-1920s onward, however, the market demand for Ghanaian kola began to decline. One reason was the beginning of large-scale kola cultivation in Nigeria in the 1920s and 1930s (N.A.G. [Accra] 1959; Cohen 1966; Agiri 1977). But another factor was that cacao, now an international crop, had gradually supplanted kola as the backbone of the Gold Coast economy. It is worthy of note, however, that because of interior African markets, the decline in kola exports to Nigeria did not mean a collapse of kola production in Ghana.

Uses of Kola

In the Past

Initially a luxury item, kola later became an item of common usage. Those who grew it, as well as those who used it, often ascribed therapeutic, dietetic, and pharmacological properties to kola. In addition, according to volume 14 of the *American Druggist* (1885), kola was to some extent employed as a substitute for food, in much the same way as coca has been used by residents of the Andes. Indeed, kola is to the African what tobacco or coffee is to the European or betel is to the southeastern Asian – a stimulant and a psychoactive substance (Simmonds 1891; Kumm 1907; Goodman et al. 1995).

The importance of kola as a drug was first recognized outside Africa in the twelfth century by an Arabian physician, who wrote that it was used in the form of a powder for colic and stomachache and had warming properties. A later Portuguese observer testified to the importance of kola nuts thus: "The Black population would scarcely undertake any enterprise without the aid of kola" (Fluckiger 1884: 524), which, among other things, was supposed to protect against the pangs of thirst. However, the first definite mention of kola as a drug came in the work of Odoard Lopez in 1591, and shortly afterward, Andre Alvares de Almada, who had visited Guinea in 1566, wrote his *Tratada Breve dos Rios de Guiné do Cabo Verde* (1594), in which he claimed that kola and betel were used in more or less the same way. At the end of the sixteenth century, James Garet, an apothecary and amateur collector of foreign curios, brought the nuts to the attention of the celebrated Flemish botanist-physician Carolus Clusius (Charles de l'Ecluse) (Fluckiger 1884).

As knowledge of kola reached the outside world, the plant itself began to travel, apparently reaching the Caribbean as early as the seventeenth century. This came about following an urgent request, sent through a Guinean trader by an agent for Jamaican slaveholders, for kola seedlings – urgent, because of kola's well-known property as "a medicinal prophylactic agent or as an ordinary article of food, to avert, as far as practicable, those attacks of constitutional despondency to which . . . Negroes were peculiarly liable" (Attfield 1865: 456–7).

Many accounts of the properties of kola by early writers were borrowed from travelers and were therefore probably exaggerated or distorted to some degree. Since the 1850s, however, research has been carried out by botanists, chemists, and pharmacists on some of the properties ascribed to the kola nut. For example, A. M. F. J. Palisot-Beauvois (1805) asserted that the Negroes of Oware used kola nuts because of the nuts' remarkable ability to impart a pleasant taste to all food or water consumed. Subsequent experiments have confirmed this observation, at least for drinking water, which, even when comparatively stale or impure, becomes quite palatable to the consumer after chewing kola. It is possible that the action of the chemicals in kola on the palatal mucosa creates the "illusion" of sweetness, or perhaps this is the result of kola's high caffeine content.

Another report – this by N. Hudson (1886), a medical inspector in the U.S. Navy – on the results of administering kola paste to a patient suffering from rheumatism, dyspnea, and headache, amply demonstrates some of the pharmaceutical and pharmacological properties of the kola nut. Hudson wrote:

> The patient, a lady of 36, had suffered during childhood from rheumatism. Up to a recent period, however, she had been in good health and able to lead a busy, active life. Eighteen months since, she was attacked with severe endocarditis, from which she recovered slowly, and with a damage to the mitral valves. . . . The action of the heart was feeble and irregular, and there was a good deal of dyspnoea, faintness, and fatigue upon even slight exertion. She had always been subject to occasional headaches, and these now became periodic and severe, occurring at first at intervals of four or five weeks, and lasting two days. Latterly they had increased in frequency and intensity, coming on about twice a month, each

attack causing three days of suffering so severe as to fill the patient's mind with constant dread of a recurrence. The discovery of a ratio of urea much below that of normal urine, with the existence of an occasional granular cast, established the conviction that the headaches were uraemic in character (1885–6: 711).

After about three months of administering kola paste in hot milk at a dosage of about 10 grams once or twice daily, Hudson reported:

> During the first nine weeks of its use there was no recurrence of headache. Then there was a comparatively mild attack, which may fairly be attributable to a suspension of the use of the kola in consequence of the marked improvement. The general condition has materially improved, the heart's action is more regular, and the attacks of dyspnoea and faintness have nearly disappeared. The most characteristic effect seems to have been an immediate relief of a sense of fatigue, a sense of *bien-être* and cheerfulness to which the patient had been long a stranger. The employment of the kola seemed to be satisfying the appetite, for whenever taken, it appeared to serve as a substitute for the following meal. But the nutritive processes were not impaired: on the contrary, the bodily weight increased from ninety-eight to one hundred and five pounds. No marked change in the character of the urea has been observed. The quantity voided has somewhat increased, but the total urea excreted remains at about ten or twelve grammes daily (1885–6: 711).

As Hudson noted, the results of the administration of kola paste were marked and immediate, producing a definite and positive change in the well-being and comfort of the patient (Hudson 1885–6: 712). Thus, as stated by another observer who was a contemporary of Hudson, kola can become a "sustaining and stimulating adjunct in exhaustive and wasting diseases" (Simmonds 1891: 10).

It was also believed that kola "exercises a favourable influence upon the liver, and that white people, living in those regions [where it grows], who chew a small quantity before meals escape constitutional changes due to affections of that organ" (Heckel and Schlagdenhauffen 1884: 585). Finally, kola was said to be advantageous for sportsmen, athletes, and "brain workers" in reducing tension (Uses of kola nut 1890).

Current Ethnopharmacology in Africa

Kola nuts are used for the treatment of certain infections and conditions, such as guinea worm, migraine, and ulcer (Mr. Ansong, Kumasi Cultural Centre, March 5, 1995, personal communication). In the case of guinea worm, the nut is chewed into a paste and applied to the affected portion of the body, and in Ghana, such a paste is used to treat a skin ailment commonly called *ananse*. Fresh kola nuts are also chewed as a stimulant to counteract fatigue (Szolnoki 1985; Burrowes 1986). Kola is used in beverages – such as coffee, tea, and cocoa – to cure indigestion and nervous or bilious headache. It should be pointed out that the medicinal action of kola is not the same as that of an analgesic taken for pain. Kola is not used because of an isolated chemical ingredient; it is used as a complex whole.

Along with the nut, other parts of the kola tree are also employed for their medicinal properties by traditional healers and the peoples of rural Africa (Mr. Anin-Agyei, Dwaben State Oil Palm Plantation, February 28, 1995, personal communication; Mr. Forster, Dwaben State Oil Palm Plantation, February 28, 1995, personal communication; Mr. Ansong, Kumasi Cultural Centre, March 5, 1995, personal communication). The bark is used to treat swellings and fresh wounds, and the roots provide excellent chewing sticks for cleaning the teeth. The pod bark is mixed with other ingredients to become a traditional medicine for reducing labor pains during childbirth (Akhigbe 1988). The latter is very important because traditional birth attendants play a dominant role in rural Africa's health delivery system. Most of the people live outside the cities, and the overwhelming majority of these cannot afford the expense of Western-style medicine. Thus, kola-bark preparations for reducing labor pains are highly prized by traditional birth attendants, even though very little research has been done to determine the properties in kola bark that make childbirth more comfortable for African mothers.

Many people use kola because of its very high caffeine content – one nut contains more caffeine than two large cups of American coffee. It is generally believed that chewing small amounts increases mental activity and reduces the need for sleep (Attfield 1865; Ogutuga 1975; Lovejoy 1980). Consequently, kola is widely used by Ghanaian watchmen (who call it the "watchman's friend") in the course of their vigils, as well as by students who work late into the night. Chewing kola also massages the gums and exercises the teeth.

Yet, that kola can be poisonous to animals raises flags of caution. The chemical composition of kola paste makes it a good bait for trapping mice, who often die when they eat it. Similarly, dogs do not survive when they are given *maasa* (a baked flour meal) mixed with kola paste (Mr. Ansong, Kumasi Cultural Centre, January 30 and March 5, 1995, personal communication). There has, however, been no laboratory analysis to explain the action of the kola paste on either mice or dogs.

Social Uses

Kola provides flavoring for beverages in Africa, Europe, North and South America – indeed, in all parts of the world (Freeman 1893; Irvine 1948; Bovill 1958;

Dickson 1969). In the 1870s, kola was mixed with sugar and vanilla as a tonic for invalids and convalescents and was recommended to travelers as an antidote to fatigue and even hunger (Freeman 1893). In 1886, John S. Pemberton, a druggist in Atlanta, Georgia, invented Coca-Cola when he combined coca and kola extracts as a headache and hangover remedy (Louis and Yazijian 1980). Over time, Coca-Cola (minus the narcotic coca) has become the most popular nonalcoholic beverage in the Western world.

The most common social use of kola in several African countries is as a gift of welcome to friends and guests. Doubtless in part, at least, because of the Islamic prohibition against alcohol consumption, kola is widely used by Muslims (Dalziel 1948; Cohen 1966; Dickson 1969; Morgan and Pugh 1969; Church 1975; Agiri 1977; Lovejoy 1980; Anquandah 1982). A Sokoto tradition not only associates kola with the prophet Muhammed but also asserts that he relished it and gave the nuts as gifts to his favorites. His wealthier followers, in turn, gave kola as alms during high festivals (Tremearne 1913, cited in Ferguson 1972; Russell 1955; Lovejoy 1980).

Dietetic Uses

Kola possesses physiological properties that enable those who eat it to undergo prolonged exertion without fatigue or thirst. Kola has also been said to serve as a preventive of dysentery and other intestinal disorders (Fluckiger 1884), and it has been claimed that kola makes people brave in - even eager for - battle. For all these reasons, kola nuts have historically been dispensed to troops on African battlefields. Askia Mahmoud is reported to have supplied kola to his troops in the sixteenth century, and at the beginning of the nineteenth century, soldiers of the Asante army often chewed kola for days during their campaigns, when there was frequently not enough food to go around (Kreiger 1954; Quarcoo 1971).

In 1852, the German explorer Heinrich Barth thought that soldiers of the Sokoto army were addicted to kola because it was usually distributed to them in the evenings before campaigns (Goodman et al. 1995). Similarly, James Richardson observed that the Emir of Zinder used kola to incite his soldiers before slave raids. In 1890, the German war office ordered 30 tons of kola for the army after conducting experiments with the plant during autumn maneuvers the previous year (Uses of kola nut 1890). At about the same time, troops of the West African Frontier Force stationed in East Africa were given kola rations to enhance their battle readiness (Anyane 1963).

Toward the end of the nineteenth century, a series of interesting experiments on the possible military importance (in dietetic and pharmacological terms) of kola was conducted by R. H. Firth on British soldiers in India. Ordered by the surgeon-general of Her Majesty's forces, these studies indicated that chewing

kola nuts not only seemed to depress the appetite and keep thirst at bay but also increased the individual's energy level and sense of well-being. In addition, the nuts may have proved efficacious in curing hangovers (Firth 1890).

Nearly a century later, studies carried out on the biochemical effects of kola nut extract administered to rats once again demonstrated the stimulating properties of kola in relatively large doses (Ajarem 1990). This is doubtless explicable in part by the caffeine content; however, many more such efforts are required to show why it is that kola has a long-standing reputation as a laxative (but prevents dysentery and other intestinal disorders) and as a heart stimulant (but can also be a sedative). Also demanding explanation are kola's alleged ability to make foul water palatable and its historical fame as an aphrodisiac, a restorer of potency, and an aid to childbirth (Nzekwu 1961; Quarcoo 1969; Goodman et al. 1995).

Certainly kola seems potent as a drug, but save for the research just mentioned, its potentiality remains to be investigated. Given its many current uses in Africa, as well as its role in the soft-drink industry around the world, it is to be hoped that such research will soon be forthcoming.

Edmund Abaka

Bibliography

Adamu, Mahdi. 1978. *The Hausa factor in West African history.* Ibadan, Nigeria.

AERLS (Agricultural Extension and Research Liaison Services). 1982. *Guide to the production of kola.* Extension Guide No. 48 (reprint), Ahmadu Bello University. Zaria, Nigeria.

Agiri, Babatunde. 1972. Kola production in western Nigeria, 1850-1950. A history of the cultivation of Cola nitida in Egba-Owode, Ijebu-Remo, Iwo, and Ota areas. Ph.D. thesis, University of Wisconsin.

1977. The introduction of nitida kola into Nigerian agriculture 1880-1920. *African Economic History* 3: 1-14.

Ajarem, Jamaan S. 1990. Effects of fresh kola-nut extract (cola nitida) on the locomotor activities of male mice. *Acta Physiologica et Pharmacologica Bulgaarica* 16: 10-15.

Akhigbe, F. O. 1988. Kolanut: The characteristics and growth of its literature in Nigeria. *Quarterly Bulletin of the International Association of Agricultural Leadership and Development* 33: 47-52.

Alex, Geo. 1890. To the Marquis of Salisbury, K.G., September 6, 1890. *Royal Botanical Garden, Kew, Bulletin of Miscellaneous Information* 4: 253-60.

Anquandah, James. 1982. *Rediscovering Ghana's past.* Accra and London.

Anthony, K. R. M., Bruce F. Johnston, William O. Jones, and Victor C. Uchendu. 1979. *Agricultural change in tropical Africa.* Ithaca, N.Y., and London.

Anyane, S. La. 1963. *Ghana agriculture. Its economic development from early times to the middle of the twentieth century.* London.

Archibald, J. F. 1955. *The propagation of cacao by cuttings.* West African Cocoa Research Institute, Technical Bulletin No. 3. Nigeria.

Are, L. 1965. Performance of cacao from roughly handled rootstocks grown under different conditions. *Nigerian Agriculture Journal* 2: 61-5.

Arhin, Kwame. 1977. *West African traders in the nineteenth and twentieth centuries.* London.

1987. Savannah contribution to the Asante political economy. In *The golden stool: Studies in the Asante center and the periphery,* ed. Enid Schildkrout, 51-9. New York.

Ashiru, G. A. 1969. Dioxide, light and heat on seed germination and seedling growth of kola (Cola nitida [Ventenant] Schott & Endlicher). *American Society for Horticultural Science Journal* 94: 429-32.

1975. The vegetative propagation of tropical tree crops with emphasis on cacao (Theobroma cacao L.) and kola (Cola Nitida, [Vent.] [Schott & Endlicher]). *Acta Horticulturae* 49: 67-73.

Ashiru, G. A., and T. A. Quarcoo. 1971. Vegetative propagation of kola (Cola nitida [Vent.] [Schott & Endlicher]). *Tropical Agriculture* (Trinidad) 48: 85-92.

Attfield, John. 1865. On the food value of the kola nut - a new source of theine. *Pharmaceutical Journal* (January): 457-60.

Berberich, Charles William. 1974. A locational analysis of the trade routes of the Asante north east frontier network in the 19th century. Ph.D. thesis, Northwestern University.

Boahen, Adu. 1964. *Britain, the Sahara and the western Sudan.* Oxford.

Boaten, Nan Akwasi Abayie I. 1990. Asante: The perception and utilization of the environment before the twentieth century. *Research Review* 6: 19-28.

Bodard, M. 1954. Polyembryo in Cola nitida. In *Proceedings of the 8th International Congress of Botany,* 259-61. Paris.

Bovill, E. W. 1958. *The golden trade of the Moors.* London.

Bowdich, T. E. 1966. *Mission from Cape Coast to Ashantee.* Third edition. London.

Brooks, George. 1980. *Kola trade and state building: Upper Guinea coast and Senegambia 15th to 17th centuries.* Boston University Working Papers, No. 38. Boston, Mass.

Brown, D. A. Li. 1970. A review of germination of kola seed (Cola nitida [Vent.] Schott & Endlicher). *Ghana Journal of Agricultural Science* 3: 179-86.

Burrowes, C. P. 1986. Economic activities of pre-Liberian societies: Production for local use and exchange. *Liberia Forum* 2: 25-44.

Chevalier, Auguste, and Emile Perrot. 1911. *Les kolatiers et les noix de kola.* Paris.

Church, R. J. Harrison. 1975. *West Africa: A study of the environment and man's use of it.* London.

Cohen, Abner. 1966. The politics of the kola trade. *Africa* 36: 18-35.

Curtin, Philip. 1975. *Economic change in precolonial Africa: Senegambia in the era of the slave trade.* Madison, Wis.

Daaku, K. Y. 1970. *Trade and politics on the Gold Coast. 1600-1720.* Oxford.

Dalziel, J. M. 1948. *The useful plants of west tropical Africa.* London.

Danquah, J. B. 1928. *Akyem Abuakwa handbook.* London.

Denham, Dixon and Hugh Clapperton. 1826. *Narrative of travels and discoveries in Northern Central Africa, in the years 1822, 1823 and 1824.* London.

Dickson, K. B. 1961. The development of road transport in southern Ghana and Ashanti since about 1850. *Transactions of the Historical Society of Ghana,* 33-42.

1969. *A historical geography of Ghana.* Cambridge.

Dupuis, Joseph. 1894. *Journal of a resident in Ashantee.* London.

Fage, J. D. 1969. *A history of West Africa.* London.

Ferguson, Phyllis. 1972. Islamization of Dagbon: A study of the Alfanema of Yendi. Ph.D. dissertation, Cambridge University.

Firth, R. H. 1890. The dietetic and therapeutic value of the kola nut. *The Practitioner* 43 (Supplement): 27-35.

Fluckiger, F. 1884. A contribution to the history of kola. *The New Idea* (Detroit) September: 224.

Freeman, Austin. 1893. A journey to Bontuku in the interior of West Africa. *Royal Geographical Society Supplementary Papers* 3: 117-46.

Freeman, Richard Austin. 1967. *Travels and life in Ashanti and Jaman.* London.

Fynn, J. K. 1971. *Asante and its neighbours, 1700-1807.* Evanston, Ill.

Gnanaratum, J. K. 1972. Rooting of cacao cuttings, a new technique. *World Crops* 16: 61-3.

Gold Coast Blue Books. 1884-1925.

Goodman, J., P. E. Lovejoy, and A. Sheratt, eds. 1995. *Consuming habits. Drugs in history and anthropology.* London and New York.

Goody, Jack. 1967. The over-kingdom of Gonja. In *West African kingdoms in the nineteenth century,* ed. Daryll Forde and P. M. Kaberry, 179-205. London.

Hallet, Robin, ed. 1965. *The Niger journal of Richard and John Lander.* London.

Heckel, E., and F. Schlagdenhauffen. 1884. Some African kolas in their botanical chemical and therapeutic aspects. *The Pharmaceutical Journal and Transactions* (January 26): 584-6.

Hudson, N. 1885-6. Kola. *Medical Times and Register* 16: 711-12.

Hunter, Guy. 1973. Agricultural administration and institutions. *Food Research Institute Studies* 12: 233-51.

Ibikunle, B. A. O. 1972. The propagation and growth of nursery stock of *Cola nitida* (Vent.) (Schott & Endlicher). Ph.D. thesis, University of Ibadan, Nigeria.

1975. The germination of *Cola acuminata. Acta Horticulturae* 49: 75-83.

Irvine, F. R. 1948. The indigenous food plants of West Africa. *Journal of the New York Botanical Garden* 49: 225-36.

1969. *West African crops.* London.

Jones, Norman. 1968. Plant breeding: Problems with forest tree species in West Africa. *Ghana Journal of Agricultural Science* 48: 27.

Jones, Stephen Hugh. 1995. Coca, beer, cigars, and yagé: Meals and anti-meals in an Amerindian community. In *Consuming habits. Drugs in history and anthropology,* ed. Jordan Goodman, P. E. Lovejoy, and A. Sheratt, 47-66. London and New York.

Karikari, S. K. 1973. The effect of maturity and storage on the germination of cola nut, (Cola nitida [Ventenant] Schott and Endlicher). *Ghana Journal of Agriculture Science* 49: 225-36.

Kennedy, John G. 1987. *The flower of paradise. The institutionalised use of the drug qat in North Yemen.* Dordrecht, the Netherlands.

Kola. 1957. *The Ghana Farmer* 1: 222.

Kraemer, Henry. 1910. *A text-book of botany and pharmacognosy.* Philadelphia, Pa.

Kreiger, Kurt. 1954. Kola Karawanen. *Mitteilungen des Institutes für Orientforschung, Deutsche Akademie der Wissenschaften zu Berlin* 2: 289-322.

Kumm, H. Kail. 1907. *The Sudan*. London.

Lander, Richard. 1830. *Records of Capt. Clapperton's last expedition to Africa. With the subsequent adventures of the author*. London.

Louis, J. C., and Harvey C. Yazijian. 1980. *The cola wars*. New York.

Lovejoy, Paul E. 1977-8. Kola in West Africa. *Cahiers d'études africaines* 20: 97-134.

1980. *Caravans of kola. The Hausa kola trade 1700-1900*. London and Zaria, Nigeria.

1995. Kola nuts: The "coffee" of the central Sudan. In *Consuming habits. Drugs in history and anthropology*, ed. J. Goodman, P. E. Lovejoy, and A. Sheratt, 103-25. London and New York.

Miles, A. C. 1931. *Report of a cola survey of the eastern Ashanti areas and a general review of the Gold Coast industry, 20 March 1931*. London.

Morgan, W. B., and J. C. Pugh. 1969. *West Africa*. London.

N.A.G. (National Archives of Ghana) (Accra). 1959. *Gold Coast Colony, report of the Department of Agriculture for the year 1930-31*. CSO 8/1/59.

N.A.G. (National Archives of Ghana) (Kumasi). 1905. D.1346, Botanic Gardens, Aburi-Gold Coast, 30/11/1905.

Nzekwu, O. 1961. Kolanut. *Nigeria Magazine* 71: 298-305.

Ogutuga, D. B. A. 1975. Chemical composition and potential commercial uses of kola nut, Cola nitida Vent. (Schott & Endlicher). *Ghana Journal of Agricultural Science* 8: 121-5.

Oladokun, M. A. O., and N. O. Adepipe. 1989. Polyembryony and multiple shoot production in cola acuminata (P. Beauv) Schott and Endlicher. *Nigeria Journal of Botany* 2: 135-42.

Oliver, Daniel. 1868. *Flora of tropical Africa*, Vol. 1. Asford, Kent.

Osim, E. E., and P. M. Udia. 1993. Effects of consuming a kola nut (Cola nitida) diet on mean arterial pressure in rats. *International Journal of Pharmacology* 31: 192-7.

Ossei. 1963. Cola - some aspects of its cultivation and economics in Ghana. *Ghana Farmer* 7: 96-7.

Palisot-Beauvois, A. M. F. J. 1805. *Flore d'Oware et de Benin en Afrique*. Paris.

Pratt, Robertson, and Heber W. Youngken, Jr. 1956. *Pharmacognosy: The study of natural drug substances and certain allied products*. Philadelphia, Pa.

Pyke, E. E. 1934. A note on the vegetative propagation of kola (Cola acuminata) by softwood cuttings. *Tropical Agriculture* (Trinidad) 11: 4.

Quarcoo, T. A. 1969. Development of kola. Its future in Nigeria. *Proceedings of the Agricultural Society of Nigeria* 6: 19-22.

1971. Processing of kola in Nigeria. In *Progress in tree crop research in Nigeria (coca, kola and coffee)*. Cocoa Research Institute. Ibadan, Nigeria.

Ramstad, Egil. 1959. *Modern pharmacognosy*. New York.

Royal Botanical Garden, Kew. 1890. Cola Nut. *Bulletin of Miscellaneous Information* 4: 253-60.

1906. Cola. *Bulletin of Miscellaneous Information* 4: 89-91.

Russell, T. A. 1955. The kola of Nigeria and the Cameroons. *Tropical Agriculture* 32: 210-40.

Simmonds, P. L. 1891. The kola nut of Africa. *American Journal of Pharmacy* 62: 595-7.

Staff of the Division of Agriculture. 1961. Crops other than cocoa and the diseases and pests which affect them. In *Agriculture and land use in Ghana*, ed. J. B. Wills, 360-1. London and New York.

Szolnoki, T. W. 1985. *Fruit and fruit trees of the Gambia*. Hamburg.

The kola nut in western Soudan. 1890. *Pharmaceutical Record* (May): 181.

Toxopeus, H., and G. E. Okoloko. 1967. Cacao marcotting in Nigeria. I. Use, technique and monthly rooting success. *Nigerian Agricultural Journal* 4: 45-8.

Uses of kola nut. 1890. *Pharmaceutical Record* 10 (June): 226.

Wilks, Ivor. 1962. A medieval trade route from the Niger to the Gulf of Guinea. *Journal of African History* 3: 337-41.

III.9 ❧ Milk and Dairy Products

Purity and Danger

Milk occupies a curiously ambiguous place in the history and culture of food. It has been pointed to as an archetypal, almost elementally nourishing food, supremely healthful, reflecting the nurturing relationship of mother and infant. In recent times, its whiteness has come to stand as a symbol of natural goodness and purity. But milk also conceals danger. Its nutritional largesse is equally appealing to hosts of putrefying bacteria, and unless milk is consumed almost immediately, it rapidly deteriorates into a decidedly unwholesome mass. Even in the apparently safe period between lactation and curdling, pathogenic organisms may lurk and multiply with potentially more devastating consequences for a new infant than the more immediately apparent problems of an obviously bad food.

The very processes of corruption, however, also provided the ways by which milk became a more widespread and acceptable food. Some contaminating organisms transform milk toward simple forms of butter, cheese, or yoghurt, and it is in these forms, not as a beverage, that milk has been consumed throughout the greater part of the history of human eating. As a highly ephemeral food then, unless milk is transmitted directly between provider (whether human or animal) and consumer, it is fraught with danger. Preservation has thus been the overriding factor in milk's development as an important food for humans.

Initially, preservation was achieved through manufacture into butter or cheese. Later, briefly, fresh milk was kept safe only by cleanliness of production and speed of transport; in the twentieth century, however, milk has been preserved primarily by means of heat treatment, particularly pasteurization. This preservation of milk, particularly on an industrial scale since the late nineteenth century, highlights another contradictory tension in the nature of its consumption. Milk production is a quintessentially female process, and the resonances of the mothering bond imparted a crucially feminine nature to the whole area of dairying in preindustrial times. Even though milk could only become an important foodstuff by transforming the female milk into a different, harder manufactured solidity, commercial dairies and domestic output remained spheres of women's activity. The femininity of dairy production, however, could not withstand industrial dairying methods, and from the end of the nineteenth century, men began to take over dairying as it became concentrated in bigger, more technically sophisticated industrial plants.

There is a further fundamental dichotomy in the culture and history of milk (one almost unique among foodstuffs) in the very ability of people to digest it. Some people do not have the enzyme - lactase - required to digest lactose, the principal sugar in milk, and the pain and discomfort arising from the inability to absorb milk sugars are reflected in cultural traditions that render even the thought of imbibing milk repulsive. Lactase deficiency affects most of the world's peoples, many of whom regard milk drinking as revolting. Thus, milk has been geographically limited, even though it is universally available. It has been consumed in parts of Asia and Africa, but its consumption has been most significant in Europe and in areas of European colonization, such as Australasia and North America.

These tensions and contradictions in the very nature of milk - a pristine, white, and nutritious beverage, which also harbors and conceals corruption; a whole and complete food which, in principle, demands no preparation but which, in practice for most of its history, has required transformation into something else, and which vast numbers of people literally cannot stomach - are reflected in the history of milk production and consumption. In preindustrial societies, dairy produce had a part to play in peoples' diets, although it was probably not particularly important in terms of overall nutrition. Yet, milk had a cultural resonance, beyond its dietary value, that saw it enshrined in several religious traditions as a signifier of promise and plenty, or as a symbolic link between spiritual and earthly nourishment. From the early eighteenth-century commercialization of agriculture, dairying took on greater economic importance, particularly in provisioning urban centers.

In the nineteenth century, increasing urbanization and the development of rapid transportation and communication systems, particularly railways, began for the first time to create a market for liquid milk on a large scale. Dairying and the production of liquid milk acquired nationalistic significance around the beginning of the twentieth century as a result of growing concern in Western countries about the health of infants. Yet although milk had come to be vitally important, the uncertain hygiene associated with it highlighted the necessity of clean production

and supply. The original dichotomies regulating the consumption of milk remained, however, because the dissemination of liquid milk required enormous mechanical intervention, and its natural purity could be maintained only by industrial processing.

Throughout the twentieth century, as milk eventually became a readily available, clean, and safe commodity, its consumption as a beverage reached a cultural epitome: Its whiteness evoked an image of goodness - a signifier of health and hygiene. Its ascendancy was short-lived, however; in the overfed northern hemisphere, the same nutritional value that had made it so important in the previous decades consigned it to the ranks of dietary sins. At the same time, inappropriate developing-world feeding schemes (based on dried milk) and the recognition of lactase deficiency have undermined the notion of universal goodness and revealed the dangers of a nutritional imperialism.

Milk in Preindustrial Societies

To drink milk is an inherently natural impulse; an infant placed at the breast knows instinctively what to do. As suitable animals (such as mares, asses, ewes, goats, and various kinds of cows) were domesticated, it appears that drinking animal milk became an acceptable practice. Presumably, folk taxonomic associations between humans and other mammals would have indicated that milk was an animal secretion that could be consumed as food, and there are numerous records and legends of infants suckling directly from animals, as well as from a range of artificial devices (Fildes 1986).

As with most other early foods, the origins of dairy products are unclear. Certain natural fermentations give rise to yoghurt or soft, cheeselike substances that are sufficiently different from putrid milk to have encouraged their sampling. There are stories that cheese originated among Near Eastern nomads who may have stored milk in the stomach bags of cows, a common form of container, in which the natural rennet would have given rise to a sort of cheese. Similarly, one might imagine a horseman setting out with a bag of milk, only to find, when he came to drink it, that the agitation of riding had curdled it into a not unpleasant mixture of curds and buttermilk (Tannahill 1973). Whatever the origins, dairy products have had a place in human diets from very early times.

Equally early on in human history, however, a fundamental split occurred in the history and culture of dairy consumption because, as already noted, drinking more than very small quantities of milk causes the majority of the world's adult population to suffer digestive problems. It has been estimated that although more than 96 percent of northern European peoples are able to digest milk, some 50 to 75 percent of Africans, Indians, Near Eastern Asians, eastern Europeans, and virtually all Asian and Native American peoples cannot digest it. Their bodies stop producing lactase – the enzyme that breaks down the milk sugar, lactose – soon after weaning (Tannahill 1973). It has been suggested that an adult ability to break down lactose spread as people moved northward into colder climates. Covering themselves with more clothes, these people experienced shortages of vitamin D previously derived from the action of sunlight. Vitamin D production in the skin, however, is enhanced with a higher intake of calcium, of which milk is a particularly rich source. There would, thus, have been a selective advantage for those people who retained the capacity to digest milk, and over time, the proportion of the population in northern climates with the ability to digest lactose would have increased (Harris 1986).

Such a starkly biological account, however, does not explain the powerful rejection of milk among many Asian peoples and needs to be supplemented with cultural factors. One suggestion is that Chinese agricultural practices worked to exclude milk from the culture; because planting took place year-round, primarily with human labor in areas of high population density, there were few draft animals that could have provided milk. The main flesh animal was the pig, which was impossible to milk; thus, after weaning, Chinese toddlers were not exposed to milk from other sources. By contrast, in subcontinental Asia, draft animals were more prevalent – indeed, were necessary to prepare land for the shorter planting season dictated by a monsoon climate. Because of greater availability of milk, cultural aversion to it did not develop, and dairy products remained an important feature of the diet (Harris 1986). An alternative hypothesis, and one, apparently, traditionally held by Chinese people, is that the aversion to milk arose from the desire to distinguish themselves from the nomads on the northern borders of China, who drank fermented mare's milk (Chang 1977). It does seem that milk products had become a feature of the diet of the northern Chinese aristocracy between the Han and Sung periods, but it appears that, after the ensuing period of Mongolian rule, milk definitely acquired a barbarian reputation (Chang 1977).

In most of the preindustrial world, however, milk (or, more usually, dairy products) had a place in the diet of all those who had domesticated animals and could absorb lactose. Among nomadic pastoralists of the Near East, sheep and goats provided the main source of milk and cheese. On the great open grasslands of central Asia, and extending into eastern Europe, mare's milk, often fermented into the alcoholic liquor *kumiss,* was consumed in large quantities (Tannahill 1973). On subcontinental Asia, the buffalo was the principal source of milk to be made primarily into ghee – a reduced butter in which most of the moisture is removed by heating – for cooking or ceremonial purposes (Mahias 1988). Pastoralists of Africa,

with vast herds of cattle, used a considerable amount of milk in their diets (Pyke 1968). Milk and cheese are also mentioned as foods, medicines, and beauty aids in records of the ancient civilizations of Egypt, Greece, and Rome (Warner 1976).

In Europe, dairy products were a notable part of the peasants' diet wherever they were available. Across the continent, the great majority of people lived on the verge of starvation, particularly during the late winter months and the periodic harvest failures. The basic diet of cereal-based porridge or soup was rarely supplemented with actual meat, and the more prevalent dairy products (or "white meats," as they were called) were welcome sources of animal fat and protein, whether as cheese, butter, beverage, or additions to soup (Mennell 1985). In the early months of the year, however, cheese or butter kept throughout the winter was mostly used up, and cattle not slaughtered the previous autumn struggled to survive until the new grass appeared (Smith and Christian 1984). Thus, though an important source of animal fat and proteins, dairy products (like meat) cannot have been much more than a flavoring for the basically cereal diet of the peasants.

Among the nobility in the late medieval period there was a growing disdain for dairy produce. With upper-class access to often vast quantities of meat, the "white meats" of the peasantry were increasingly scorned, probably especially by the aspiring merchants of the towns. Nonetheless, dairy products did not disappear from the tables of the well-to-do, and in the late sixteenth and early seventeenth centuries, butter became more important in noble larders, although used primarily for cooking and making the elaborate sauces of the new haute cuisine then developing in France and Italy (Mennell 1985).

Perhaps because milk was recognized as a particularly rich and nourishing food, as well as something of a luxury to have in more than small quantities, but also (and one suspects primarily) because of the symbolic importance of the nurturing bond between mother and child, milk has achieved some prominence in myths and religious systems. In the Old Testament, the promised land was one of "milk and honey." The image of a mother goddess suckling her child is a common representation of Earth bringing forth sustenance. The Egyptian mother goddess, Isis, suckled her divine son Horus, while the Greek god Zeus was nurtured by Amalthia (variously depicted as a mortal woman or as a nanny goat). The symbolism of the mother with her infant god passed into Christian representations of the Madonna and Child, which perpetuated the divine linkages between the spiritual and earthly worlds, mediated by the physical nurturing of milk (Warner 1976). Milk and dairy products have a vital role in sacrificial and purifying rituals in Indian religious myths, especially as the life-giving force of the fire god Agni (Mahias 1988).

The place of dairy products in the diet of peoples in nonindustrial societies has remained virtually unchanged over time; they can be an important source of animal protein but remain a minor component of largely cereal or vegetable diets. In northern Europe, however, and particularly in England, the role of milk and dairy products began to change with the wider emergence of commercial agriculture, urbanization, and proto-industrialization, beginning about the end of the sixteenth century and continuing throughout the seventeenth century.

In seventeenth-century England, demand for dairy products increased with the emergence of rural industry and the location of an increasingly higher proportion of the population in towns (Drummond and Wilbraham 1939). Cheese was of growing importance in the diets of urban laborers, particularly in London. It was cheap, nutritious, and also convenient; it could be stored for reasonable lengths of time and could be carried to places of work and eaten easily there. Large quantities of cheese were also required by the navy and by new, large institutions, such as hospitals and workhouses (Fussell 1926-9; Fussell and Goodman 1934-7). This demand was largely met by the commercialized agriculture that had been developing on the larger estates carved out after the Reformation. The numbers of milch cows multiplied, and dairies became necessary and integral parts of English country houses. Dairying was practiced by anyone who had access to a cow, which replaced the sheep as the primary milk provider (Tannahill 1973), and, for the respectable poor in rural areas, could provide an important source of income. The cheese trade also relied on a reasonably efficient transportation system, and London was served by sea as well as by road (Fussell 1966).

Throughout the early phases of expanding commercialization, dairying remained a female domain characterized by an arcane knowledge (Valenze 1991). Although from southern Africa to northern Europe the notion persisted that a woman who handled milk during menstruation might curdle it, the mystery of dairying lay in the special competence of dairymaids (Fussell 1966; Pyke 1968). The dairy in a country house was invariably attached to the kitchen, supervised by the farmer's wife (or the female head of the household in larger concerns), and the production of cheese and butter was a female operation. From the seventeenth century, books of household management included dairying as a routine aspect of the mistress's responsibilities. Hygiene in the dairy was constantly stressed, with detailed instructions provided as to the proper construction and maintenance of the dairy and the duties of the women working in it (Fussell 1966).

By the end of the eighteenth century, wherever dairying continued to be carried out in a preindustrial, subsistence agricultural context, milk products retained their customary position as a minor adjunct to the diet, varying only by degrees among places where dairying was more or less pronounced. But in the industrializing and urbanizing world, large-scale commercial agriculture was beginning to alter the nature of production and consumption of dairy produce and bring about a crucial transformation in the historical culture of milk.

Milk in an Urbanizing World

The tripartite revolution of industrialization, urbanization, and the commercialization and increasing productivity of agriculture had dramatic consequences for food production and consumption. Enough food was produced to fuel enormous population growth, with increasing proportions of that population ceasing to be agriculturally productive. Urban dwellers, as net food consumers, depended on food being brought in from producing areas. Throughout the nineteenth century, this took place not only on a national but an international scale, until most parts of the world became integrated into a global network of food trade, principally geared toward feeding Europe. Thus, surplus dairy producers sent huge quantities of cheese and butter, increasingly manufactured in factories, to northern Europe.

At the same time, there was a growing demand for liquid milk in urban areas, and nearby dairy producers began to concentrate on its supply, partially to offset the competition in manufactured products. Yet, accompanying this expansion of production was an increasing consumer concern about the quality of the milk supply, particularly toward the end of the nineteenth century, when milk was implicated in questions of infant mortality. In the elaboration of a range of measures to control problems of milk adulteration and unhygienic procedures, dairying was completely transformed into a highly mechanized manufacturing and distribution activity, which steadily undermined its traditionally feminine nature. Such a pattern recurred throughout the nineteenth-century developing world – commercial, industrial dairying geared toward a manufactured dairy market, paralleled by the development of liquid milk production in urban areas, which, in turn, gave rise to concern about milk quality.

During the eighteenth century, northern European agriculture became much more productive, with novel crop rotation techniques, new machinery, better land management, and the more intensive methods achieved with enclosure. Dairying benefited from greater attention to fodder crops, which allowed cows to be fed more adequately throughout the winter. Yields still fell during winter months, but more cows survived, and yields quickly recovered with the spring grass (Fussell 1966). Thus, the potential arose for year-round dairying.

By the second half of the eighteenth century, increasing food production was supplying not only a steadily growing rural population but also, in Britain, an explosive increase in urban populations. During the first half of the nineteenth century, the sources of Britain's wealth gradually shifted from agriculture and the landed estates toward manufacturing and industry. This was symbolized by the repeal in 1846 of the Corn Laws, which saw landed and agricultural interests supplanted by the demands of industry for free trade. Yet, as Britain ceased to be agriculturally self-sufficient, free traders had to cater not only to the requirements of industry but also to the need for imported foodstuffs to feed urban industrial workers (Burnett 1989).

Across the globe, producers of agricultural surplus geared up to meet this need (Offer 1989). Australia and New Zealand sent butter and meat to British markets; Ireland and Denmark developed dairying to meet British demand. Danish farmers, recognizing the likely requirements of their rapidly urbanizing neighbor across the North Sea, organized in cooperatives to develop highly efficient methods for producing butter and bacon. In the process, Denmark's national economy became modernized and export driven, yet still based on agriculture (Murray 1977; Keillor 1993).

Ireland had been characterized by very high dairy production and consumption patterns from medieval times, although by the eighteenth century, the continued reliance on dairy foods may be seen as a mark of poverty. As was the case in Denmark, nineteenth-century Irish dairying became more commercialized to supply Ireland's urbanized neighbor, though at the expense of an important source of animal food for its own consumption (O'Grada 1977; Cullen 1992).

In the United States, between the end of the eighteenth century and the middle of the nineteenth, westward expansion had brought new, high-yielding agricultural lands into production. By midcentury, cheese was being shipped down the Erie Canal from upstate New York. But across the vast open spaces of North America, rail transport was the key to the development of dairying. Also crucial was the hand cream separator (Cochrane 1979), which allowed even small farmers to cream off the butterfat that railroads could then take to regional factories to be made into cheese and butter. Industrial methods for manufacturing these products spread across the northeastern and north central states (Lampard 1963; Cochrane 1979). By the second half of the nineteenth century, production and transportation were such that cheese manufactured in the United States or Canada, and butter made in New Zealand, could reach British markets at lower prices than those required by British farmers (Burnett 1989). In addition, an outbreak of rinderpest in England during the 1860s wiped out most of the urban cows, which helped North American dairy products gain a prominent place in British markets (Fussell 1966).

As in the United States, railways in Great Britain were fundamental in enhancing the importance of liquid milk as a beverage. From the 1840s, liquid milk could be brought from the countryside to the towns and sold before it became sour. The perishability of milk had always restricted its scope as a drink. But speed, together with the development of coolers and refrigerated railway cars, increased its viability, and in all areas within reach of an urban center, dairying was increasingly concerned with liquid milk supply. By the second half of the nineteenth century, milk was being carried to London from as far away as Derbyshire, and Lancashire and Cheshire emerged as major dairy counties to supply the conurbations of Liverpool, Manchester, and Stoke (Whetham 1964; Taylor 1974, 1976, 1987). Effectively, the whole of Britain could now be regarded as an urban area, which had an enormous demand for milk.

In North America, the manufacturing of dairy products was concentrated in the lake states of Wisconsin, Minnesota, and Illinois, whereas liquid milk to supply major urban areas was produced in the northeastern and Atlantic seaboard states (Lampard 1963; Cochrane 1979). Thus, better communications and large-scale manufacturing prompted a functional division in dairying. Although manufactured goods, such as cheese, could be carried long distances to urban markets more cheaply than those of a small, local producer, dairying in urban areas enjoyed a protected market for liquid milk that was not susceptible to more distant or foreign competition.

In England, toward the end of the nineteenth century, liquid milk came to be seen almost as an agricultural panacea, and not just for hard-pressed dairy farmers in urban areas. During the great depression of English farming from the mid–1870s to the 1890s, when the full economic impact of imported food began to be felt, farmers increasingly turned to the naturally protected production of liquid milk. More acres reverted to pasture, which was condemned by commentators bemoaning the apparent decline of cereal-based farming, but liquid milk production provided farmers with a welcome respite from foreign competition and helped alleviate the agricultural slump, furnishing a regular cash income throughout the year, helping to clear debts, and bringing some semblance of profitability (Taylor 1974, 1987).

Although few other nations relied so heavily on imports as Britain, by the end of the century, farmers in many countries were feeling the effects of competition in the international food market. In the United States, grain farmers of the mid–nineteenth century found themselves threatened by even higher-yielding lands opening up in the west and sought to diversify, notably into dairying. Delegates were sent from the north central states to study Danish methods, and many Danes forged new careers in the United States, ultimately to the consternation of the Danish government, which feared rivalry for the British market (Keillor 1993). State agricultural colleges and the new experiment stations also sought to improve upon the (popularly perceived) low standards of American dairying. Scientific "book farming," popular with progressives, found an ideal outlet in dairying, with rational and efficient farming methods based on calculated feeding plans, milk recording schemes, and analyses of butterfat content (Johnson 1971; Peagram 1991). Dairying was becoming self-consciously modern.

Some of the grain states, where there has been an overreliance on single crops, saw dairying as a useful means of diversifying. The North Dakota agricultural experiment station, for example, tried in the early twentieth century to offset the state's reliance on spring wheat by promoting dairying. Although for a while North Dakota did become a notable butter producer, it seems that cereal farmers did not adjust happily to the rather different demands of dairy farming (Danbom 1989).

Ultimately, the general pattern of dairying common to urbanizing countries was established in the United States. Liquid milk was the mainstay of farmers with access to urban markets, and the manufacture of other dairy products was concentrated in the north central states (Michigan, Minnesota, and Wisconsin) on the principal rail routes to the East (Haystead and File 1955; Lampard 1963; Cochrane 1979).

The growing industrialization of dairying and the manufacture of dairy products steadily eroded the femininity of dairying. Butter production, especially, had remained an essentially female activity throughout most of the nineteenth century, occupying an important role not only in the domestic economy but also in the wider social relations and status of women in farming communities. Household manufacture of milk products, however, was increasingly replaced by the transportation of milk to railways and factories and by industrial production (all male spheres of activity), and a marked decline occurred in the number of women involved in dairying. In a typically paradoxical process, the more natural, feminine state of liquid milk gained greater prominence, but only through the intervention of mechanical artifacts operated by men. As dairying left the household, an important element of rural female employment, skill, and authority went with it (Cohen 1984; Osternd 1988; Nurnally 1989; Bourke 1990; Valenze 1991).

Also embattled were milk consumers, increasingly concentrated in urban centers, subject to the vagaries of transport systems for their food supply, and suffering the appalling conditions of massive urban expansion. Many people living in towns simply did not have enough to eat; what was available was of indifferent to abominable quality and, frequently, heavily adulterated. Milk and dairy products were part of the diet, but their supply was highly uncertain. The principal sources were urban milk shops, with cowsheds that provoked bitter condemnation from health reformers. Such places were notorious for squalid conditions, with the cows fed on slops and refuse (frequently the

spent grain from distilleries), and disease rife among them (Okun 1986; Burnett 1989). Moreover, milk, whether from urban shops or from roundsmen coming in from the country, was routinely adulterated in the mid–nineteenth century (Atkins 1992). Arthur Hill Hassall, investigating for the *Lancet* in the early 1850s, found that milk was diluted with from 10 to 50 percent water, with that water often from polluted wells and springs (Burnett 1989).

Throughout the second half of the nineteenth century, urban diets in Britain improved noticeably, both in quantity and quality. This was primarily a result of the rise in real wages as general economic prosperity began to percolate down the social strata, but it was also because of an increasing availability of cheap imported food. Food had always been the principal item of expenditure for urban workers, and so any extra real income was invariably spent on food first, both to extend the variety of the diet and to obtain greater quantities. Thus, from the 1890s, more meat, eggs, dairy produce, and fresh vegetables appeared on the tables of the urban working classes (Oddy and Miller 1976, 1985).

The quality of food was also addressed in a more effective fashion. During decades of revelations by such individuals as Frederick Accum about the extent of food adulteration, a series of food purity laws were introduced in Britain. These were initially rather ineffective, but the 1875 Sale of Food and Drugs Act, and the Public Health Act of the same year, began to bring about real improvements in the basic quality of foods (Burnett 1989). This story was a familiar one in most major urban nations during the second half of the nineteenth century. In the United States, for example, reformers (also stimulated by Accum) launched investigations and turned up their own evidence of food adulteration. Effective legislation was introduced by cities and states by the end of the century, culminating in the 1906 Pure Food and Drugs Act (Okun 1986).

Urban populations probably benefited from the volumes of liquid milk brought in by the railways, but fresh milk still became less than fresh very quickly, and although gross adulterants were being eliminated, the problem of the keeping properties of milk remained. Dairy-producing countries had sought means of preserving milk throughout the nineteenth century. During the 1850s, developments in condensing techniques, especially by the American Gail Borden, brought about the formation, in 1865, of the Anglo-Swiss Condensed Milk Company, which soon had factories across Europe. Tinned milk consumption rose rapidly after 1870, and in the early twentieth century, several methods for making dried milk encouraged the emergence of a powdered-milk industry. In New Zealand, a dairy exporter developed the new Just-Hatmaker process of drying milk and this, in turn, gave birth to the giant corporation Glaxo (Davenport-Hines and Slinn 1992). In England, the pharmaceutical company Allen and Hanbury's used a method of oven-drying evaporated milk (Tweedale 1990). Condensed and powdered milk were both popular, as they kept longer than fresh milk; moreover, tinned milk could be diluted more or less heavily according to the vicissitudes of the family economy.

By the beginning of the twentieth century, adult diets had improved (although women remained less fed well into the new century), and the worst excesses of urban squalor, poverty, and deprivation were being addressed. These improvements of diet, sanitation, and housing were reflected in the general falling of mortality rates (McKeown 1969), but infant mortality rates remained stubbornly high. The problem was particularly noticeable in France (which also had a declining birth rate) after 1870 and in Britain during the 1890s. Yet concern for high infant mortality was also expressed in Canada, the United States, Australia, New Zealand, and the Netherlands. The underlying issue was the same: With an increasingly tense international situation brought on by the formation of rival power blocks in Europe and the imperial maneuverings by the United States, greater significance was accorded to the health of a nation's people. Populations began to be seen as national assets, and both their sizes and quality were viewed as of national political, economic, and military importance. Attention was focused on the health of urban populations and, particularly, the health of infants who would be the soldiers, workers, and mothers of the future.

Beginning in France in the 1890s, governments, charities, and local authorities campaigned to promote breast feeding, primarily, but also to provide subsidized milk to mothers with new children (Fildes, Marks, and Marland 1992). There were also increasing demands to improve further the hygiene of the dairy industry and milk supply. Bacteriologists had been studying the flora of milk to investigate its keeping properties and the transmission of infectious disease from animals to humans, with special attention to tuberculosis (TB) and the question of whether bovine TB could be passed to infants in milk. In Britain, the problem was thoroughly examined in a series of royal commissions on TB that effectively created a semipermanent body of bacteriologists investigating questions of milk and meat hygiene. In 1914, the Milk and Dairies Act was passed to prevent the sale of milk from tuberculous cows, while giving local authorities considerable powers of inspection (Bryder 1988; Smith 1988; Atkins 1992).

Similar measures were pursued in many other countries. In Australia, milk institutes were established in Brisbane and Melbourne in 1908 to ensure clean milk supplies (Mein Smith 1992). The same year saw the Canadian Medical Association devise a system of standards for milk hygiene in the dairy industry, which was implemented by local authorities. Toronto and Hamilton established pure milk depots before World War I (Comacchio 1992). Free or subsidized milk was available in the Netherlands from *Gouttes de lait* – modeled closely on the pioneering French milk depots (Marland 1992). In American cities, the emphasis was more on ensuring the quality of milk supplies than on providing subsidized milk, and schemes for regulating standards were devised by many cities, including New York, Philadelphia, and Memphis, and the state of Illinois, with particular emphasis on eradicating TB and promoting the pasteurization of milk (Helper 1986; Shoemaker 1986; Meckel 1990; Peagram 1991).

Such attention given to infant welfare was incorporated into the wider schemes of social welfare developing in the early twentieth century (Lewis 1993). Enthusiasm for the provision of free milk seems to have been relatively short-lived and was replaced with an increasing emphasis on the education of mothers on matters of child care and good housekeeping. But the public-health principles underlying campaigns for clean milk persisted, and the ever-increasing volumes of liquid milk coming into the towns were carefully scrutinized.

Milk in the Twentieth Century

The twentieth century was marked by a massive expansion in the production and consumption of dairy commodities, particularly liquid milk. Rationalized, scientific dairy farming, based on calculated feeding, careful milk recording, and artificial insemination, has produced cows that are virtually milk machines. The production, manufacturing, and distribution of dairy products has become ever more concentrated, yet the continual growth of dairying has required equally prodigious efforts to find markets for the produce.

Around midcentury, milk was viewed as one of humankind's most important foods. Advertisers and scientists alike had convinced the public that milk was a supremely healthy, nourishing, even life-giving substance. Its almost mystical whiteness was, for perhaps the only time in its history, matched by its hygienic purity and popular appeal. Toward the end of the twentieth century, however, health problems connected with milk drinking were uncovered, and inappropriate Western marketing schemes involving milk were exposed as highly detrimental to infants' health in developing countries.

In the early twentieth century, however, dairying appeared to have a glorious future and, with ever-expanding urban populations, more and more farmers turned to liquid milk production. For particularly hard-pressed British farmers, dairying had become the cornerstone of agriculture, outstripping the economic return from cereals (Taylor 1974). In the United States, too, dairying was a fallback for farmers on relatively low-yielding land and a common means of diversifying a narrowly based state agriculture

(Cochrane 1979; Danbom 1989). Such a recourse to dairying, however, carried with it the danger of overproduction. Several strategies were pursued in an effort to deal with dairy surpluses, but by far the favored means was to promote demand. This had expanded on its own in prosperous times as increasing numbers of people with surplus income were able to extend the scope of their diets to include more fresh meat, vegetables, and dairy produce. Beginning in the 1920s and 1930s, a concerted effort was made to encourage consumption of dairy goods and, especially in Britain, the drinking of milk. Such an effort, however, required that the commodity be safe.

Experiments with various types of heat treatment had been conducted to extend the keeping properties of milk (Dwork 1987a). The principle had been established by Louis Pasteur in his studies of beer and wine, and bacteriologists and inventors were not slow to follow up on it. Well into the twentieth century, however, there was significant resistance to the heat treatment of milk (Pyke 1968). It was commonly believed that heating destroyed most of milk's essentially nutritious and health-giving properties, even a vitalist life force (McKee, personal communication). At the same time, there was a school of opinion within the dairy industry that a certain level of natural contamination was necessary to make milk into cheese or butter, and that pasteurized milk was unsuitable for dairy manufacture (Davis 1983). Although the arguments for pasteurization were accepted more readily in the United States than in Britain, debate continued into the 1930s (Meckel 1990). Opponents argued that heat treatment was a technical fix for sloppy procedures and an excuse to produce unclean milk (Davis 1983). Ultimately, however, an increasingly concentrated dairy industry cut through the controversy by routinely pasteurizing all milk it received, which was becoming a necessity because of the large volumes handled and the long distances now covered by milk distributors (Whetham 1976).

A considerable amount of research on nutrition and health was done during the interwar years, particularly in depressed areas of Britain. Experiments by Corry Mann and Boyd Orr on school children showed that groups given milk for a certain period put on more weight, had higher hemoglobin blood counts, and, according to their teachers, demonstrated a greater attentiveness at school; their parents commented that they were also livelier at home (Burnett 1989). In the controversial debates about diet in depressed Britain, milk was an important factor. It was thought that although welfare could not provide a sufficient quantity of food to maintain good health, this goal might be achieved with food supplements, such as milk, needed in fairly small quantities (Webster 1982).

By the 1930s, a culture of dairy consumption was well established in the major dairy manufacturing countries. On the Continent, this primarily involved manufactured butter and, to a lesser extent, cheese; in the United States and in Scandinavia, where liquid milk consumption had a high profile, there was a sound base upon which marketing campaigns could expand demand (Teuteberg 1992). In Britain, although dairying was a major sector of agriculture (and one in which liquid milk was particularly prevalent), people neither ate as much butter as continental Europeans nor drank as much milk as Americans and Scandinavians. Milk was chiefly something to put in tea or give to children, old people, or invalids; indeed, throughout Europe, liquid milk was associated with sickliness or effeminacy (McKee, personal communication).

Thus, one task of the Milk Marketing Boards for England, Scotland, and Northern Ireland, set up after the act of 1933, was to overcome prejudices against milk and stimulate demand for the products of an industry now suffering the consequences of overproduction from the decreasing prices that manufacturers were paying for milk. The Milk Marketing Boards (MMBs), as producer organizations, tried to regulate the dairy market like benign monopolists. Farmers were paid a fixed price for their milk, which was in turn sold to dairy product manufacturers at one price and to liquid milk distributors at a higher one, thus evening out the differences in income that depended on farmers' access (or nonaccess) to a liquid market. As the MMBs undertook to buy all the milk produced by dairy farmers, they had to find markets for it. From the start, a tariff was levied on each gallon to pay for advertising, and a massive campaign was launched, following American models. It stressed the value of milk for health, strength, and beauty, and featured sportsmen and women, manual laborers, and film stars (Jenkins 1970; Whetstone 1970; Baker 1973).

The emphasis on naturalness, whiteness, and purity reflected the contemporary concern for light, space, and healthy living. Milk was marketed to youth through futuristic, American-style milk bars – all chrome, steel, and modernity. The marketing of ice cream was another area in which the British copied from America and the Continent in trying to improve sales (McKee, personal communication). In 1934, drawing on recent discoveries of the vitamin content of milk, the company Cadbury launched a new advertising campaign for its dairy milk chocolate, which was marketed as a food as well as a treat (Othick 1976; Horrocks 1993).

Throughout the 1930s, the virtually unique retail system of doorstep deliveries was established in Britain. Derived from the roundsmen of the eighteenth century who pushed churn-carrying carts through the streets, milk distributors between the wars developed the service of daily deliveries of pint bottles of pasteurized milk to the doorstep (Baker 1973). The MMBs promoted the system and, until recently, the image of the milkman doing his rounds and the bottle on the doorstep were central to the culture of milk in Britain, elevating the milkman to the status of folk hero or comic character. Only with the 1980s or so was there a notable decline in the importance of milkmen, as the greater prevalence of automobiles, refrigerators, and supermarkets have resulted in British consumers joining Americans and other Europeans in buying cartons of milk from stores (Jenkins 1970).

Milk remained important for children during the 1930s, with the Milk Act of 1934 providing subsidized milk for British schoolchildren. The act also continued the practice of baby clinics begun at the turn of the century, which encouraged the habit of drinking milk at an early age (Hurt 1985). Milk for pregnant women and new mothers was also a priority, and the welfare state distributed nourishment for mothers, as well as infants and children, until the program was discontinued in 1972 by the British parliament. The efforts of the MMBs were significant – so much so that as the 1930s came to a close, British people were drinking, on average, a pint of milk more per week than they had in the mid–1920s. Moreover, such a trend continued through the 1950s, when British per capita milk consumption exceeded that of the United States; only Sweden and Ireland had higher levels (Jenkins 1970).

In the last decades of the twentieth century, dairying and dairy products continued to hold an ambiguous status. The market for milk in the major dairy areas of the developed world seemed to be saturated and was even showing signs of diminishing. Consumption peaked sometime during the 1960s and then, depending on place, stabilized or began to shrink (OECD 1976). Nonetheless, dairying has continued to be a significant factor in industrial agriculture throughout the last half of the twentieth century. In Europe, the world's principal dairy-producing region, milk products accounted for between 11 and 35 percent of total farm sales (Butterwick and Rolfe 1968). Such regular cash income is a lifeline for farmers, but the vast sums paid out in subsidies have helped to swell the milk "lakes" and butter "mountains" of surplus production to the absurd point that butter has been used as a feed for the cows that produced the milk to begin with. Since the interwar period, dairy farming has been maintained only by subsidies and tariffs, with overproduction the unhappy outcome (Johnson 1973; Cannon 1987). Developing countries seem to be repeating the experience of the developed West, with liquid milk sectors emerging to supply urban areas (Kurien 1970; Chang 1977; Mahias 1988).

Although dairy farming has been sustained at considerable economic cost, other, more insidious problems have emerged for milk products. The high food value, which made it so important for infants and children until the mid–twentieth century, lead to more or less serious health problems in the overfed late twentieth century. The high-fat content of milk has been implicated in the modern Western illnesses of obesity, coronary artery disease, and a host of digestive and allergic conditions. As a consequence, there has been a marked trend toward skimmed milk and milk powders, and even toward the exclusion of milk from the diet. Similarly, butter has been a victim of concerns about heart disease and body weight and has been steadily replaced by an increasingly more palatable margarine during the twentieth century (Cannon 1987).

To combat health worries, marketers of milk and milk products have focused on their energy-giving properties and high calcium content. Although milk could not realistically be promoted as a slimming aid, as it had been in the 1930s, the industry was still aiming for a pint per person per day, and advertised milk as a provider of instant vitality (Jenkins 1970). Some dairy marketers in recent years have undermined the ground of critics by deliberately proclaiming the richness and luxury of specialized products, such as fresh cream or ice cream. In an ironic reversal of healthy eating advice, cream has been lauded as "naughty – but nice!" and recent advertisements have been aimed at subverting any associations of ice cream with notions of childhood or purity.

A rather more sinister turn of events, however, has also tarnished the pure-white reputation of milk. In the early 1970s, the issue of inappropriate marketing of canned milk and milk powders among developing-world peoples began to receive public attention. In Yemen, for example, a study showed that dried milk and canned milk, provided as part of general food aid, were being fed to babies. This occurred in a country where Western medicine and high-technology goods had high social cachet and where the natural capacities of women were commonly denigrated. The result of the aid was that women neglected to breast-feed their babies and turned instead to proprietary baby foods or artificial milk. Many of these women were unable to read the instructions and had no access to the necessary sterilizing equipment to keep bottles clean, let alone to an adequate supply of fresh, clean water, with the result being an increase in infant mortality. Although resolutions have been made by dairy manufacturers in accordance with World Health Organization (WHO) and United Nations International Children's Emergency Fund (UNICEF) recommendations not to promote goods that might be used as substitutes for breast milk, contraventions continue (Melrose 1981).

Milk remains a singularly, almost uniquely, nutritious foodstuff, invested with elementally significant cultural and nutritional value. Yet milk has a Janus-faced nature – as it nourishes, so can it harm. Its whiteness evokes purity, but may also conceal corruption. Thus, as a commodity made widely available, milk has sometimes attacked the health it was intended to support and killed infants it was meant to nurture.

Keith Vernon

Bibliography

Atkins, P. J. 1980. The retail milk trade in London c. 1790-1914. *Economic History Review* 33: 522-37.

 1991. Sophistication detected: Or the adulteration of the milk supply, 1880-1914. *Social History* 16: 317-39.

 1992. White poison? The social consequences of milk consumption, 1850-1930. *Social History of Medicine* 5: 207-27.

Baker, S. 1973. *Milk to market. Forty years of milk marketing.* London.

Bateman, F. 1990. The marketable surplus in northern dairy farming: New evidence by size of farm in 1860. *Agricultural History* 52: 345-63.

Bourke, J. 1990. Dairywomen and affectionate wives: Women in the Irish dairy industry, 1890-1914. *Agricultural History Review* 38: 149-64.

Bryder, L. 1988. *Below the magic mountain: A social history of tuberculosis in twentieth century Britain.* Oxford.

Burnett, J. 1989. *Plenty and want. A social history of food in England from 1815 to the present day.* Third edition. London.

Butterwick, M., and E. N. Rolfe. 1968. *Food, farming and the common market.* London.

Cannon, G. 1987. *The politics of food.* London.

Cassedy, J. H. 1991. *Medicine in America. A short history.* Baltimore, Md.

Chang, K. C., ed. 1977. *Food in Chinese culture. Anthropological and historical perspectives.* New Haven, Conn.

Cochrane, W. W. 1979. *The development of American agriculture. An historical analysis.* Minneapolis, Minn.

Cohen, M. 1984. The decline of women in Canadian dairying. *Social History [Canada]* 17: 307-34.

Comacchio, C. P. 1992. "The infant soldier": Early child welfare efforts in Ontario. In *Women and children first. International maternal and infant welfare 1870-1945,* ed. V. Fildes, L. Marks, and H. Marland, 97-120. London.

Cullen, L. M. 1992. Comparative aspects of Irish diet, 1550-1850. In *European food history,* ed. H. J. Teuteberg, 45-55. Leicester, England.

Danbom, D. B. 1989. The North Dakota agricultural experiment station and the struggle to create a dairy state. *Agricultural History* 63: 174-86.

Davenport-Hines, R. P. T., and J. Slinn. 1992. *Glaxo: A history to 1962.* Cambridge.

Davis, J. G. 1983. Personal recollections of developments in dairy bacteriology over the last fifty years. *Journal of Applied Bacteriology* 55: 1-12.

Dicksen, P. 1973. *The great American ice-cream book.* New York.

Drummond, J. C., and A. Wilbraham. 1939. *The Englishman's food. A history of five centuries of English diet.* London.

Dupré, R. 1990. Regulating the Quebec dairy industry, 1905-1921: Peeling off the Joseph label. *Journal of Economic History* 50: 339-48.

Dwork, D. 1987a. *War is good for babies and other young children. A history of the infant and child welfare movement in England, 1898-1918.* London.

 1987b. The milk option. An aspect of the history of the infant welfare movement in England 1898-1908. *Medical History* 31: 51-69.

Fildes, V. A. 1986. *Breasts, bottles and babies. A history of infant feeding.* Edinburgh.

Fildes, V., L. Marks, and H. Marland, eds. 1992. *Women and children first. International maternal and infant welfare 1870-1945.* London.

Finlay, M. R. 1990. The industrial utilization of farm products and by-products: The U.S.D.A. regional research laboratories. *Agricultural History* 64: 41-52.

Fussell, G. E. 1926-9. The London cheesemongers of the eighteenth century. *Economic Journal* (Economic History Supplement) 1: 394-8.

 1966. *The English dairy farmer 1500-1900.* London.

Fussell, G. E., and C. Goodman. 1934-7. The eighteenth century traffic in milk products. *Economic Journal* (Historical Supplement) 3: 380-7.

Harris, M. 1986. *Good to eat. Riddles of food and culture.* London.

Haystead, L., and G. C. File. 1955. *The agricultural regions of the United States.* London.

Helper, R. W. 1986. Bovine T.B. and the battle for pure milk in Memphis, 1910-11. *West Tennessee Historical Society Papers* 40: 6-23.

Horrocks, S. 1993. Consuming Science: Science, technology and food in Britain, 1870-1939. Ph.D. thesis, University of Manchester.

Hurt, J. 1985. Feeding the hungry schoolchild in the first half of the twentieth century. In *Diet and health in modern Britain,* ed. D. Oddy and D. Miller, 178-206. London.

Jenkins, A. 1970. *Drinka pinta. The story of milk and the industry that serves it.* London.

Jensen, J. M. 1988. Butter making and economic development in mid-Atlantic America from 1750-1850. *Signs* 13: 813-29.

Johnson, D. G. 1973. *World agriculture in disarray.* London.

Johnson, K. 1971. Iowa dairying at the turn of the century: The new agriculture and progressivism. *Agricultural History* 45: 95-110.

Keillor, S. J. 1993. Agricultural change and crosscultural exchange: Danes, Americans and dairying, 1880-1930. *Agricultural History* 67: 58-79.

Kurien, V. 1970. The Anand and Bombay milk projects. In *Change in agriculture,* ed. A. H. Bunting, 199-206. London.

Lampard, E. E. 1963. *The rise of the dairy industry in Wisconsin.* Madison, Wis.

Lewis, J., ed. 1993. *Women and social policies in Europe.* London.

Mahias, M.-C. 1988. Milk and its transmutations in Indian society. *Food and Foodways* 2: 265-88.

Marland, H. 1992. The medicalisation of motherhood: Doctors and infant welfare in the Netherlands, 1901-1930. In *Women and children first. International maternal and infant welfare 1870-1945,* ed. V. Fildes, L. Marks, and H. Marland, 74-96. London.

McKeown, T. 1969. *The modern rise of population.* London.

Meckel, R. A. 1990. *Save the babies. American public health reform and the prevention of infant mortality 1850-1929.* Baltimore, Md.

Mein Smith, P. 1992. "That welfare warfare": Sectarianism in infant welfare in Australia, 1918-1939. In *Women and children first. International maternal and infant welfare 1870-1945,* ed. V. Fildes, L. Marks, and H. Marland, 230-56. London.

Melrose, D. 1981. *The great health robbery. Baby milk and medicines in Yemen.* Oxford.

Melvin, P. A. 1983. Milk to motherhood: The New York milk committee and the beginning of well-child programs. *Mid-America* 65: 111-34.

Mennell, S. 1985. *All manners of food. Eating and taste in England and France from the Middle Ages to the present.* Oxford.

Murray, J. W. 1977. *Growth and change in Danish agriculture.* London.

Nurnally, P. 1989. From churns to "butter factories." The industrialization of Iowa's dairying, 1860-1900. *Annals of Iowa* 49: 555-69.

Oddy, D., and D. Miller. 1976. *The making of the modern British diet.* London.

1985. *Diet and health in modern Britain.* London.

OECD (Organization for Economic Co-operation and Development). 1976. *Study of trends in world supply and demand of major agricultural commodities.* Paris.

Offer, A. 1989. *The First World War: An agrarian interpretation.* Oxford.

O'Grada, C. 1977. The beginnings of the Irish creamery system 1880-1914. *Economic History Review* 30: 284-305.

Okun, M. 1986. *Fair play in the marketplace. The first battle for pure food and drugs.* DeKalb, Ill.

Osternd, N. G. 1988. The valuation of women's work: Gender and the market in a dairy farming community during the late nineteenth century. *Frontiers* 10: 18-24.

Othick, J. 1976. The cocoa and chocolate industry in the nineteenth century. In *The making of the modern British diet,* ed. D. Oddy and D. Miller, 77-90. London.

Peagram, T. R. 1991. Public health and progressive dairying in Illinois. *Agricultural History* 65: 36-50.

Petty, C. 1989. Primary research and public health: The prioritization of nutrition research in interwar Britain. In *Historical perspectives on the MRC,* ed. J. Austoker and L. Bryder, 83-108. London.

Pyke, M. 1968. *Food and society.* London.

Rosenberg, C. E. 1976. *No other gods. On science and American social thought.* Baltimore, Md.

Shoemaker, S. T. 1986. The Philadelphia pediatric society and its milk commission 1896-1912: An aspect of urban progressive reform. *Pennsylvania History* 53: 273-88.

Smith, F. B. 1988. *The retreat of tuberculosis, 1850-1950.* London.

Smith, R. E. F., and D. Christian. 1984. *Bread and salt. A social and economic history of food and drink in Russia.* Cambridge.

Tannahill, R. 1973. *Food in history.* New York.

Taylor, D. 1971. London's milk supply, 1850-1900: A re-interpretation. *Agricultural History* 45: 33-8.

1974. The English dairy industry, 1860-1930: The need for a reassessment. *Agricultural History Review* 22: 153-9.

1976. The English dairy industry, 1860-1930. *Economic History Review* 29: 585-601.

1987. Growth and structural change in the English dairy industry, c. 1860-1930. *Agricultural History Review* 35: 47-64.

Teuteberg, H. J. 1982. Food consumption in Germany since the beginning of industrialization. A quantitative, longitudinal approach. In *Consumer behaviour and economic growth in the modern economy,* ed. H. Baudet and H. van der Meulin, 233-77. London.

Teuteberg, H. J., ed. 1992. *European food history. A research review.* Leicester, England.

Tweedale, G. 1990. *At the sign of the plough. 275 years of Allen and Hanbury's and the British pharmaceutical industry 1715-1990.* London.

Valenze, D. 1991. The art of women and the business of men: Women's work and the dairy industry c. 1740-1840. *Past and Present* 130: 142-69.

Warner, M. 1976. *Alone of all her sex. The myth and cult of the virgin Mary.* London.

Webster, C. 1982. Healthy or hungry thirties? *History Workshop Journal* 13: 110-29.

Whetham, E. H. 1964. The London milk trade, 1860-1900. *Economic History Review* 17: 369-80.

1976. The London milk trade, 1900-1930. In *The making of the modern British diet,* ed. D. Oddy and D. Miller, 65-76. London.

Whetstone, L. 1970. *The marketing of milk.* London.

Yudkin, J., ed. 1978. *Diet of man: Needs and wants.* London.

III.10 ∾ Soft Drinks

In considering the human body's demand for food and nutrition, the simple need for liquid refreshment is sometimes overlooked. Although this fundamental physiological requirement can be satisfied by drinking an adequate supply of pure water, most people, when given a choice, prefer to achieve the required level of liquid intake with a variety of flavored drinks to stimulate the palate.

Soft drinks are usually defined as nonalcoholic, water-based drinks, although a few may contain alcohol, albeit in quantities too small to warrant their classification as "hard liquor." Soft drinks are usually sweetened – soda water being an obvious exception – and flavored with food acids, essences, and sometimes fruit juices. They are often carbonated – that is, charged with carbon dioxide gas – and, indeed, in North America are referred to as carbonated beverages. In some countries, including the United Kingdom, there is a significant retail market for concentrated soft drinks intended for dilution at home before consumption. Soft drinks in powdered form are similarly marketed for preparation at home. In addition, uncarbonated, ready-to-drink soft drinks are also found.

The flavors of soft drinks may be derived from fruits, nuts, berries, roots, herbs, and other plants. Moreover, fruit (and to some extent vegetable) juices, as such, have grown in popularity in recent years and have come to be included among the soft drinks. In many countries, soft drinks are distinguished from hard liquor by the higher taxation of stronger drinks, for example through excise duties, and the term "nonalcoholic" can sometimes mean merely "non-excisable." However, soft drinks are frequently subject to other taxes, though usually at lower levels than those that are levied on alcoholic drinks. Soft drinks are often distinguished from medicines by legislation. In the past, these distinctions were less precise, and a historical study of soft drinks will include products that began with a mainly medicinal purpose but are regarded today as simple refreshment.

Over the years, the names of various classes of soft drinks have been used very imprecisely. The term "mineral waters," originally and properly confined to spa and spring waters, has subsequently been used for artificial spa waters and even for flavored carbonated drinks. Even today, words like "lemonade" or "pop" may be used colloquially to embrace a wide range of drinks – an imprecision that often prevents our determining the flavor or, indeed, the composition of past drinks. It cannot be assumed, merely because a bygone drink bore the same name as a current one, that it necessarily shared the same compositional standards. Another generic term, "aerated waters," is believed to have been coined by the eighteenth-century French chemist Gabriel Venel, who, in preparing an artificially carbonated water, called it "eau aerée" (aerated water), erroneously believing the carbon dioxide gas to be mere air.

The commercial manufacture of prepacked soft drinks began in the last years of the eighteenth century, and some of its products were known in one form or another well before that. The term "soft drink," however, dates only from the last years of the nineteenth century and seems to have originated in the United States. It is, therefore, strictly anachronistic to refer to such bygone products as soft drinks, although admittedly, an appropriate alternate term is lacking.

Small Beer

Before the mid–seventeenth century, the principal European drinks were what today would be considered alcoholic: beer, ale, mead, cider, perry (fermented pear juice), and wine. Until that time, and beyond, there was – certainly in England – a distinct prejudice against drinking water, as such, unless from sources of proven reputation. Nor was this prejudice wholly unjustified given the contamination of much of the water supply, particularly in populous districts. Nonetheless, cheaper and weaker ales ("small ales") and beers ("small beers"), containing insignificant amounts of alcohol, were produced for those who could afford nothing stronger, and for children. In his fourteenth-century *Piers the Plowman,* William Langland refers to halfpenny ale and penny-ale as beyond the pockets of the poorest laborers. In Leicester, the brewers were especially enjoined to make "good wholesome small drink for the poor people" (Bateson 1901, 2: 288).

An English cookery book of the fifteenth century contains a list of "herbs for the cup." Among those to be grown in the garden were sage, rosemary, hyssop, marjoram, and gillyflower; these were as likely to be used for flavoring mead (made from honey) as for small beers. Nettle beer and heather ale were also found among the small beers. Not surprisingly, small beer was despised by the more hardened drinker. "Doth it not show vilely in me to desire small beer?" asked Shakespeare's Prince Hal before his reformation (*Henry IV, Part II* 2.2.7). And, in mentioning Shakespeare, it is humbling to note that for him, "to chronicle small beer" was to deal in very minor matters indeed!

The strength of church ales is less certain. They were drunk as both a social custom and as a fund-raising exercise. In the seventeenth century, John Aubrey recalled the church ales of his youth as a means of raising funds for the poor before the introduction of a formal system of taxation by local government: "In every parish is, or was, a church house to which belonged spits, crocks etc., utensils for dressing provision. Here the housekeepers met, and were merry and gave their charity: the young people came there too, and had dancing, bowling, shooting at butts, etc., the ancients sitting gravely by, looking on. All things were civil and without scandal" (Barber 1988: 184).

Church ales were numerous but their names distinguished them more by use than by strength. Among them were bride ale, wake ale, and Whitsun ale, all intended for fund-raising of various sorts. Aubrey noted that "the clerk's ale was in the Easter holidays, for his benefit" (Barber 1988: 184). These ales were probably stronger than the small beers; despite Aubrey's assertion of their innocent intent, they certainly attracted clerical and Puritan criticism as giving rise to licentiousness and disorder.

Small beer, however, survived the years. It was to be found in the coffeehouses of late Stuart and Georgian London. In the early nineteenth century, William Cobbett noted that the grass mowers' drink allowance was "two quarts of what they call strong beer, and as much small beer as they can drink" (Jekyll and Jones 1939: 112). An inventory of the cellars of a Berkshire squire at his death in 1822 showed 210 gallons of small beer out of 2,630 gallons of beer and ale of all sorts. Small beer, indeed, but still a measurable quantity.

In his 1833 report *The Poor Laws in London and Berkshire,* Edwin Chadwick noted that every convict on board hulks in England was allowed one pint of small beer a day as part of his diet, and Dr. Jonathan Pereira's *Treatise on Food and Diet* of 1843 included small beer – or, as he called it, table beer – among his dietaries of London hospitals and other institutions. Pereira incidentally noted that whereas a barrel of best Burton ale contained 40 to 43 pounds weight more than an equivalent barrel of water, a barrel of good table beer contained 12 to 14 pounds more, and "common table beer" but 6 pounds more than water. Although in the 1790s Dr. Erasmus Darwin's *Zoonomia* had recommended small beer as part of a diet against "gaol [jail] fever" (typhus), we may suspect that the drink was preferred by these institutions as much for economy as for health.

Other brews were not necessarily so weak. Spruce beer, flavored with leaves of the spruce fir, was known to sailors in the Baltic from at least the sixteenth century, and Canadian Indians taught Jacques Cartier to use it against scurvy at much the same time. In New Zealand in 1773, the explorer Captain James Cook brewed spruce beer and reckoned it a useful defense against the same disease. Unlike most small ales and small beers, which continued to be brewed as and when required rather than being bottled for trading, spruce beer made the transition to the commercial market for prepacked soft drinks, and "spruce beer manufacturer" was to be found as an entry in the London trade directories of the early nineteenth century. And whatever its earlier strength may have been, spruce beer was excluded by the Licensing Act of 1872 from its definition of intoxicating liquor.

Ginger beer and ginger ale are products of the commercial era, but their acceptability, no doubt, owed much to the tradition of small beers and herbal brewing, which continued in the production of hop bitters and the like.

Cordials and Other Domestic Drinks

As small beers derived from the arts of brewing, so cordials owed their origins to the secrets of distillation. Heavily sweetened and highly flavored so that they might even be diluted with water before drinking, cordials would vary in alcohol content according to the recipe of their maker, often a well-to-do country housewife, whose object – partly pleasurable, partly medicinal, but at all times designed to tempt the palate – was summed up in Shakespeare's phrase, "a taste as sweet as any cordial comfort" (*Winter's Tale* 5.3.77).

Homemade cordials survived well into the era of commercial soft drinks, and as late as 1856, George Dodd in *The Food of London* described them as "more frequently the handiwork of some Lady Bountiful, some housewife more than ordinarily clever in domestic economy, than of manufacturers who prepare them for sale" (Dodd 1856: 498). Nonetheless, by then, cordials were also available from commercial manufacturers in both alcoholic and nonalcoholic varieties, the latter being popular as temperance drinks, and they continued in essence-based peppermint, ginger, and clove cordials, the thought of their medicinal origins having for the most part faded.

Among other drinks from the domestic sickroom was barley water, an infusion of pearl barley and water dating from late medieval times, which Thomas Fuller in the seventeenth century described as "an invention which found out itself, with little more than the bare joining the ingredients together" (Fuller 1662: 366). For sixteenth-century invalids there was "water imperial," apparently containing sugar and cream of tartar and flavored with lemons, as well as "manays cryste," a sweetened cordial flavored with rosewater, violets, or cinnamon.

Fruit-Flavored Drinks

In view of the heavy Arab influence on Italian Renaissance cuisine, lemonade may have originated with the Arabs. But in any event, sixteenth-century Italians seem to have been the first Europeans to enjoy this beverage made from freshly squeezed lemons, sweetened with sugar or honey, and diluted with water to make a still, soft drink that could be prepared, sold, and consumed on the premises. Its popularity spread to France and gradually to the rest of Europe, until by the eighteenth century, lemonade of this sort was available from the inns of Scotland to the Turkish baths of Constantinople. In France, lemonade was sold by the itinerant *limonadier,* who stored the drink in a tank carried on his back. In 1676 the *limonadiers* of Paris were formed into a company and granted a patent or monopoly by the government, continuing to sell their drink in this way until at least the end of the following century. During the eighteenth century, lemonade was also valued by the medical profession, and Erasmus Darwin recommended it, among other things, for the relief of kidney stones and gout and in cases of scarlet fever.

Orange juice was first introduced into mid-seventeenth-century England; Samuel Pepys in the 1660s noted with approval this drink that was new to him. A little later, orangeade was also to be found, often containing oranges too bitter to be eaten fresh. Orgeat, a cooling drink flavored with almonds and orange flower water, became a favorite of the patrons of eighteenth-century London refreshment houses and pleasure gardens.

Lemons and Scurvy

In the eighteenth century and earlier, citrus juices were among many articles of diet used in attempts to find a cure for scurvy, a disease which only in the twentieth century was discovered to result from a dietary deficiency of vitamin C. Scurvy particularly affected sailors on extended voyages of discovery with few opportunities for revictualing with fresh foods. Until its cause was known, any cure could only be found by empirical tests. Beer brewed from the spruce fir was considered effacicious. Unsuccessful, however, was malt, although it too had its advocates for a time.

Lemon juice was favored by the early Spanish explorers as an antiscorbutic, and Dutch and English voyagers also included it in their ships' stores, although it was more likely to find a place among the medicines than as a regular article of diet. In the mid–eighteenth century, James Lind conducted and published the results of experiments at sea. His 1753 *A treatise on the scurvy* showed that sailors treated with lemon juice recovered from scurvy, whereas other sailors given other substances did not. But further practical tests were less conclusive, almost certainly because of the loss of vitamin C during the preparation and storage of the juice.

For instance, Captain Cook on his voyages to the Pacific was supplied with lemon juice as a concentrated syrup, with most of the vitamin C unwittingly boiled out in the preparation. Not surprisingly, he was unenthusiastic about the efficacy of citrus juices, even though Joseph Banks, the botanist on the voyage with Cook, successfully dosed himself with lemon juice against what appeared to be the onset of scurvy. It was not until the end of the eighteenth century that the British Admiralty Board introduced lemon juice into the seaman's diet, where it was usually preserved by mixing with rum. In the mid–nineteenth century, lemon juice was largely replaced on British ships with West Indian lime juice. Botanical differences between lemons and limes were little appreciated at that time, and in fact, lime juice, with its lower levels of vitamin C, was less suited to the purpose (Carpenter 1986).

Artificial Mineral Waters

In 1772, Dr. Joseph Priestley's *Directions for Impregnating Water with Fixed Air* (fixed air being his name for carbon dioxide gas) also excited the interest of those seeking a reliable antiscorbutic. Priestley was by no means the first scientist to interest himself in the possibility of artificially reproducing the properties of natural mineral waters. As Sir John Pringle put it when Priestley received the gold medal of the Royal Society in 1773:

> Having learned from Dr. Black that this fixed or mephitic air could in great abundance be procured from chalk by means of diluted spirits of vitriol; from Dr. Macbride that this fluid was of a considerable antiseptic nature; from Mr. Cavendish that it could in a large quantity be absorbed in water; and from Dr. Brownrigg that it was this very air which gave the briskness and chief virtues of the Spa and Pyrmont waters; Dr. Priestley . . . conceived that common water impregnated with this fluid alone, might be useful in medicine, particularly for sailors on long voyages, for curing or preventing the sea scurvy (Pringle 1774: 15).

Intellectual curiosity, rather than commercial advantage, seems to have prompted the early scientists to find ways of extracting and analyzing the salts from natural mineral waters and reconstituting them in their laboratories. Much the same spirit led Priestley to show how water might be artificially carbonated on a commercial scale, and although carbonated water proved no cure for scurvy, Priestley's invention was soon adapted to the commercial production of artificial mineral waters.

Despite the traditional widespread suspicion of water because of its close connection with disease, natural waters were nonetheless valued so long as they either contained mineral salts found in practice to be healthful or were drawn from an exceptionally pure and reliable source. Such waters, however, had to be highly regarded indeed, in light of the high cost of transporting them, usually in heavy glass bottles, over any but short distances. During the reign of George II,

Henry Eyre of London was not only importing from the Low Countries the mineral waters of Spa and dealing in various native waters, but he was also ensuring that all bottles were appropriately sealed to protect his customers from spurious imitations.

Provided the artificial waters carefully replicated the chemical composition of their natural counterparts – which analytical techniques enabled them to do – the economic advantage of manufacture close to the consumer was obvious. As Priestley himself put it: "I can make better than you import; and what cost you five shillings, will not cost me a penny" (Rutt 1831, 1: 177). At much the same time, Torbern Bergman of Uppsala, Sweden, was also experimenting with equipment for the production of artificial mineral waters, and within the next decade, Dr. John Mervyn Nooth was demonstrating to the Royal Society in London a glass apparatus for the production of small quantities of carbonated water.

The first known manufacturer of artificial mineral waters bottled for sale was Thomas Henry, a Manchester apothecary who, by the end of the 1770s, had modified Nooth's apparatus in order to produce artificial Pyrmont and Seltzer waters, as well as to imitate an earlier preparation known as "Bewley's Mephitic Julep," all of which were intended for medicinal purposes rather than for refreshment. Indeed, Henry recommended drinking with the julep "a draught of lemonade, or water acidulated with vinegar or weak spirits of vitriol, by which means the fixed air will be extricated in the stomach" (Henry 1781: 29). This suggestion reflected earlier advice on taking the natural waters; there was no hint, as yet, that flavorings might be added to the waters themselves.

J. H. de Magellan, claiming that Nooth's apparatus took several hours to impregnate water, published (1777) his own method for producing, in a few minutes, artificial versions of "the best Mineral Waters of Pyrmont, Spa, Seltzer, Seydschutz, Aix-la-Chapelle etc." (Magellan 1777: Title), as well as appropriate recipes for doing so. At the same time, he mentioned that he had sent copies of Priestley's pamphlet to different parts of Europe and that a French translation had appeared soon afterward. In 1787, mineral waters were also said to have been manufactured on a commercial scale in Germany.

It was, however, Jacob Schweppe who took up a theoretical suggestion of Priestley's that the use of a "condensing engine" or pressure pump would allow a greater volume of gas to be absorbed in the water than was otherwise possible. Schweppe, German born and a citizen of Geneva by adoption, pioneered the manufacture of artificial mineral waters in that city before setting up business in London in 1792. Producing Seltzer water, Spa water, Pyrmont water, and acidulous Rochelle salt water on something approaching a factory scale, Schweppe also offered a less specific line of aerated alkaline water, soon known as acidulous soda water, which he sold in three strengths – single, double, and triple – according to the amount of soda present, the double being "generally used."

The success of such ventures depended not merely on carbonating the water but on retaining the gas in the liquid until the consumer opened the container, and this in turn depended on the careful corking and sealing of all bottles, which Henry had stressed at the very outset of commercial manufacture. For Schweppe, who was supplying sometimes over long distances, the problem was a real one. As a postscript to a repeat order of 1805: A Birmingham customer complained that many of the bottles from his last order were nearly empty when they arrived because of bad corking.

To prevent the corks from drying out, Schweppe recommended that the bottles be laid on their sides in a cool place or even better kept covered with water – no easy task on a carrier's wagon! Schweppe also made an allowance on empty bottles returned, a custom often retained thereafter in a trade where the bottle represented a significant proportion of the total cost of the product.

Schweppe's partner in Geneva, Nicolas Paul, also made his way to England and operated commercially in London from 1802, having been in business in Paris for a while en route. Like Schweppe, Paul used the process known as the Geneva system or Geneva apparatus, but although he apparently achieved even higher levels of carbonation than Schweppe, the additional gas was, no doubt, largely lost in the pouring out.

By then, soda water had reached Dublin, where it was recommended by Dr. Robert Percival, Professor of Chemistry at Trinity College. Indeed, at one time it was claimed that a Dublin firm had invented soda water, but the product would seem conclusively to have originated with Schweppe. Nonetheless, its early success in Britain, like that of the other artificial waters, was undoubtedly medicinal; in fact, between 1804 and 1833, soda water was subject to stamp duty under the Medicine Tax. The first known manufacturer of soda water in the United States was Benjamin Silliman, operating in New Haven in 1807, and the first United States patent for manufacturing artificial mineral water was issued two years later.

Attempts to match spa waters artificially probably reached their apogee in the 1820s, when Dr. F. A. Struve, of Dresden, opened a range of artificial spas at Leipzig, Hamburg, Berlin, St. Petersburg, and Brighton, supplying careful imitations of the Carlsbad, Ems, Kissingen, Marienbad, Pyrmont, Seltzer, and Spa waters to invalids and a wider public without the necessity of their traveling to the original waters' respective sources.

Elegant and Refreshing Beverages

Gradually, however, the new drinks began to be promoted for refreshment rather than for their specifically medicinal properties. In 1819, an advertisement in the London *Morning Chronicle* described as "elegant and refreshing" the ginger beer and soda water available from one of the new metropolitan makers, and it was by the brewing of ginger beer that the industry expanded from the soda waters, on the one hand, to the sweetened, fruit-flavored drinks of later manufacturers on the other hand.

In Elizabethan times, Arthur Barlowe's "The discovery of Virginia" had referred to the American Indians drinking water "sodden [i.e. boiled] with ginger in it, and black cinnamon, and some times sassafras, and divers other wholesome and medicinable herbs and trees" (Barlowe 1589). A subsequent early American drink was "switchell," a mixture of molasses, vinegar, and ginger. But no reference has been found to ginger beer as such before the first decade of the nineteenth century. After it was first marketed in England, however, its popularity grew swiftly. Perhaps, as Leigh Hunt wrote at the time, because it was found to have "all the pleasantness and usefulness of soda-water without striking cold upon one" (Hunt 1862), ginger beer soon became a staple commodity of even the most modest refreshment stall.

The commercial origins of flavored, sweetened carbonated waters remain more obscure. As early as 1784, Karl Wilhelm Scheele, the Swedish chemist, had produced, from lemon juice, a crystalline substance that he called citric acid. One old trade historian claimed to have seen a manuscript reference to citric acid powder (or concrete acid of lemons, as it was also known) dated 1819, and a recipe for lemonade made with citric acid dated shortly thereafter. Lemonade "syrup" was known at about the same time, and all of these substances may well have been used for making lemonade in the home, employing a variant of Nooth's apparatus later known to the Victorians as the "gazogene" or "seltzogene." Despite such speculation, however, the first positive reference in England to commercially produced effervescent lemonade dates from no earlier than 1833. Such lemonades would have been flavored with citric acid and essential oil of lemon mixed with a sugar syrup, topped up with water, and impregnated with carbon dioxide gas derived in the factory from the action of sulfuric acid on whiting or other forms of chalk. Only at the end of the century did carbon dioxide gas come to be supplied to the soft-drink factory by a specialist manufacturer.

At London's Great Exhibition of 1851, lemonade, ginger beer, spruce beer, seltzer water (by now a generic name), and soda water were among the refreshments available to visitors, alcoholic drinks not being countenanced on the premises. A million bottles of aerated beverages were sold there, according to one contemporary estimate, and the success of the show and of the soft drinks reflected the slowly increasing leisure and spending power of those able to attend, two vital factors in the growth of the industry, not only in Britain but elsewhere in the developed world.

At fairs and race meetings, London costermongers sold lemonade and ginger beer, which they made at home in stone barrels. At the street markets of the mid–nineteenth century, according to Henry Mayhew (1851), soft drinks were available to refresh those shoppers "who have a penny to spare rather than those who have a penny to dine upon." Besides lemonade, raspberryade, and ginger beer, the street markets offered "Persian sherbet, and some highly coloured beverages which have no specific name, but are introduced to the public as 'cooling' drinks; hot elder cordial or wine; peppermint water." Sherbets had been available since at least the seventeenth century as cool fruit drinks originating from Turkey and the East, but later the name became attached to drinks made from effervescent powders containing bicarbonate of soda, tartaric acid or cream of tartar, sugar, and flavorings. As to the drinks with "no specific name," perhaps it is as well that their composition remains a mystery. In the street markets, Mayhew also noted that "some sellers dispensed ginger beer in plain glass bottles which was drank straight from the bottle after the cork obviatry the necessity of a glass."

In France the development of the industry seems to have been slower, with pharmacists holding a monopoly on what remained a localized trade, until their grip was challenged and weakened during the Orleanist years of the 1830s and 1940s. From France, too, at that time, came the soda siphon for dispensing carbonated soft drinks.

The pharmacists of the United States also became adept at producing artificial mineral waters, and as they discovered that the installation of soda fountains brought customers to their retail drugstores, they were encouraged to experiment with an ever wider range of flavored drinks by the mid–nineteenth century. Soda fountains were also taken up in Europe, where, for example, Germany had its *Trinkhallen* and France its *buvettes à eaux gazeuses*. An innovation of the American soda fountains was the addition of sweet cream to many of their products, and the popularity of ice-cream soda, as a vanilla-flavored drink, spread overseas as the century progressed.

Other drinks originating as soda fountain beverages included sarsaparilla, originally a medicinal flavoring derived from plants of the *smilax* species. Curiously, by the time sarsaparilla had become established among the bottled drinks, its flavor had come to be derived from a blend of oil of wintergreen, sassafras, anise, orange, and sometimes licorice. According to Charles Sulz in 1888, sarsaparilla itself was seldom included among the ingredients of what was by then a staple beverage of the American industry, but when it was, the bottler advertised its presence as proof of the superiority of his product over those of his competitors. Root beer was another blend of root, herb, and fruit flavors originating at the American soda fountain but later widely bottled. Sarsaparilla root beer, too, was available in the America of the 1880s. It also contained sassafras, a flavoring derived from the sassafras tree of the eastern seaboard.

Mixer Drinks

Freed from its exclusively medicinal limitations, soda water was found useful in diluting wines and spirits. Lord Byron called for hock and soda water after a drinking bout, and gin and soda water was said to be a favorite tipple of the fast set in the English hunting shires of the 1830s. Brandy and soda later became the drink for gentlemen, and manufactured seltzer and lithia waters were also available as mixers. As soda water became increasingly used as a mixer, many makers gradually reduced its soda content until, eventually, they were applying the name to simple carbonated water. The more scrupulous manufacturer sold such a product as "table water," and if his soda water retained a significant soda content, he was quick to advertise the fact.

Natural spa and spring waters, too, were used as mixers. Even in England, the natural waters of continental Europe were still imported despite local imitations. One London supplier in the 1860s offered not only German, French, and Belgian waters but others from Austro-Hungary and the United States.

The first English soft drink developed specifically as a mixer appears to have been tonic water, which began as a palatable means of ingesting the quinine prescribed for sufferers of malaria contracted in the tropics. In 1858 its inventor, Erasmus Bond, patented it as an "Improved Aerated Liquid," soon known as Indian or quinine tonic water.

Ginger ale seems to have originated a little later, once a method was devised for producing the clear extract of ginger, which distinguished the product from the cloudy ginger beers. A British trade paper of 1876 described the drink as a thing unknown only a few years previously. By then, however, it had become a favorite of the British market and was exported in significant quantities, particularly to America, and principally by the soft-drink firms of Belfast. Indeed, by the turn of the century a trade advertisement was asking: "What go-ahead Mineral Water Maker is there who has not at one time or another longed for the day to come when he would be able to turn out a Ginger Ale equal to the world-famous Belfast Ginger Ales?"

Temperance Drinks

Ginger ale, unadulterated, also took its place among the temperance beverages of Britain and the United States as the powerful social and religious forces moving against the consumption of alcohol gathered momentum on both sides of the Atlantic in the second half of the nineteenth century. Soft-drink manufacturers, serving licensed and temperance outlets alike, generally maintained a diplomatic neutrality in the fierce battles over the drink trade, at the same time expressing occasional ironic amusement at the reformers' description of their nonalcoholic favorites by reference to the names of the very drinks they sought to defeat.

Hop ales, hop beers, dandelion stout: All these and more endeavored to provide alternatives to the workingman's beer, whereas football stout and football punch aimed to attract young men from the sports field. One winter punch was advertised as "the best non-alcoholic substitute for brandy," but in what respect was unspecified. Many such nonalcoholic beverages were fermented, but as one turn-of-the-century writer cryptically noted, "some of them are not fermented and others are not non-alcoholic." Uproar occasionally ensued when analysis revealed that a temperance drink contained as much, if not more, alcohol than the product it sought to supersede.

Further up the market, a full range of nonalcoholic champagnes – sweetened, flavored, carbonated drinks, usually of high quality – resembled champagne in their presentation but not their origins, while nonalcoholic fruit wines, drunk as such or diluted, imitated the syrupy consistency of liqueurs. The American soda fountain, too, flourished under the temperance movement, offering an ever-greater selection of flavors and blends of flavors. This vast increase in choice was the result not only of demand but of the growth of specialist essence houses that supplied the soft-drink industry with flavorings and with careful advice on how best to use them. As a result, essences even came to be used in the manufacture of ginger beer, but the result, although of more uniform consistency, was generally held to lack a certain something of the brewed original.

By then, however, much of the ginger beer available in England was of poor quality, hence this lament from the 1880s: "'Times were' when ginger beer *was* ginger beer, as the name implies; but *now* 'tis generally something quite different" (Good 1880). The writer, Joseph Goold (1880), went on to deplore the widely varying standards by which the drink was being made, in most of which ginger was "conspicuous by its absence," the product having become too often simply another sort of lemonade.

It was also toward the end of the nineteenth century that saccharin became available as an alternative sweetener to sugar in soft drinks. Discovered in 1879, the intensely sweet coal-tar derivative was patented for commercial manufacture in 1885, and early enthusiasts predicted a great future for it in soft-drink manufacture. In practice, although it became a particularly useful sweetener of drinks for diabetics (and later for low-calorie or diet drinks), when it was used in standard products critics considered its no match for the "body" or the palatability given by sugar, which over the years had come to be specially refined for soft-drink manufacture.

Fruit Drinks

The use of lime juice as an antiscorbutic for British seamen has already been noted and the Merchant Shipping Act of 1867 made its provision on shipboard a legal requirement. Until then the method of preserving lime juice had been in a mixture with 15 percent alcohol, but in that year, Lauchlan Rose, a lime and lemon merchant of Leith in Scotland, patented a means of preserving the juice without alcohol. Noting the method of preserving light wines by burning sulfur candles in the casks, Rose prepared a sulfur dioxide solution by passing the gas from burning sulfur through water. When this solution was added to fruit juice, it prevented fermentation and other defects to which unpreserved juices were liable when stored, and Rose marketed the result as lime juice cordial. On shore, the temperance movement and the mixer trade soon found additional uses for the new product.

In the late nineteenth century, squash came onto the market, originally as a still, cloudy, ready-to-drink, juice-based product. In the early twentieth century, John Dixon, an Australian manufacturer, began to put up concentrated fruit drinks, and concentrated lemon squash was introduced into Britain just before World War I. After the war, orange squash followed, then pineapple and grapefruit. Of these, orange and lemon squash proved the most popular.

The origins of barley water as a product of the kitchen have been noted in the section "Cordials and Other Domestic Drinks." The Victorians valued barley water as a drink for the sickroom and also as a temperance beverage, but it was still made at home from commercially available patent barley and, by then, often sweetened and flavored with lemon peel. It was not until the 1930s that bottled lemon barley water was successfully marketed as a concentrated soft drink to which the consumer merely added water. Orange barley water was introduced soon after.

In the 1950s, comminuted citrus drinks were introduced among the concentrates and swiftly rivaled squash in popularity. They were sold as whole fruit drinks, their flavor derived not from the juice alone but also from the natural oils extracted from the peel as the whole fruit was broken down by the process of comminution to provide the base for the drink. Thus, fruit juice became an increasingly important ingredient in soft-drink manufacture. Citrus juices were extensively used: principally orange juice from the United States, Israel, and later Brazil, among other sources, but also lemon juice, traditionally from Italy (or, more specifically, Sicily), and lime and grapefruit juices. Among the temperate fruits, apple juice provided a basis for nonalcoholic ciders.

By the 1890s, an unfermented drink made from cranberry juice was being sold on the streets of St. Petersburg, but this may have been freshly expressed and unpreserved. In England, from the 1930s forward, concentrated black-currant juice drinks exploited the vitamin C available from indigenous sources. Fruit juices, as such, began to be packed for retail sale once ways were found of applying the principles of pasteurization to their preservation. Dr. Thomas B. Welch of New Jersey was said to have set the stage for American fruit-juice processing in this way when, as early as 1869, he began producing an unfermented sacramental wine from grape juice. But it was not until the 1930s that technical advances enabled prepacked fruit juices, including tomato juice, to be retailed on a large scale. Beginning in the 1940s, concentrated and, then, frozen juices also became available.

The citrus juices, especially orange juice, supplied a growing world market during the twentieth century, particularly once the importance of vitamin C in the diet became appreciated. Pineapple from Hawaii, and later from the Philippines, led the rest of the tropical juices in popularity. Apple, pear, and grape were significant among temperate juices consumed as such, and those fruits yielding a more pulpy juice were marketed as fruit nectars. Originally sold in glass bottles or metal cans, fruit juices are now more frequently packed in aseptic cartons, which have also been used for fruit-juice drinks in many countries of the world.

The Coming of the Colas

Amid the plethora of proprietary and patent medicines of the late nineteenth century were tonics of all sorts: These were drinks often containing phosphate and claiming to improve the nervous system and combat lassitude. As soft drinks were themselves taken for refreshment, many of these tonics, designed for a similar purpose, came to be classed under the same heading, and some of the flavors they used were also to be found in drinks designed simply to refresh.

In late Victorian Britain, kola or kaola was a popular soft drink, its essential flavor having been derived from the African kola or cola nut. The nut was known to pharmacists as a source of caffeine, and kola champagne was advertised in London as a tonic and nerve stimulant. Also available was kola tonic, the kola ingredient of which was boldly advertised as "this wonderful food," containing "more nutrient and more capacity for sustaining life than any other natural or prepared article" (Harrod's 1895 *Catalogue* 1972).

Another tonic on the market was coca wine, its stimulant properties derived from the leaves of the coca shrub, which the natives of Peru and Bolivia had long been accustomed to chew as a stimulant, and of which cocaine was a derivative. It was an interest in coca wine that led Dr. J. S. Pemberton of Atlanta, Georgia, in 1886 to combine the coca and the cola in formulating his Coca-Cola, which he, too, marketed as a brain tonic. This is not to say that these were the only flavorings. Like many speciality drinks, then as now, its formulation was a unique blend of flavors closely guarded by successive proprietors.

The word *cola* itself remained generic, and as its popularity increased, so other proprietary cola-based drinks, such as Pepsi-Cola, incorporated it in their brand names. Indeed, it became an objective of the leading brands to distance themselves from their rivals by trademark registration and, if necessary, by litigation. Pemberton and his immediate successors sold their product as a syrup for the soda fountain, which was then still the major outlet for the products of the American soft-drink industry. Only later were the proprietors somewhat grudgingly persuaded to permit others to carbonate and bottle the beverage ready-to-drink.

The licensing of other manufacturers to produce a soft drink from concentrated syrup sold to them by the owner of the brand name set a pattern for the franchising system, which came not only to dominate the twentieth-century American soft-drink industry but, eventually, to promote such brands internationally. Nor was the franchise system confined to colas. The heavy cost of transporting water-based soft drinks in glass bottles was clear from the outset of the commercial industry. There were obvious advantages in carrying a concentrated flavoring rather than the finished product over long distances, provided the proprietor could establish and enforce his standards of quality control on the local bottler so as to maintain the consistency of the consumer's drink and, thus, the product's reputation. Furthermore, a national brand could be advertised much more extensively than a local product, the cost of such advertising being recouped as part of the charge made to the bottler for the concentrate supplied. The franchise system, therefore, offered an attractive option to any owner of a drink or range of drinks, whether in America or elsewhere, looking for a way to expand.

Thus, the Canada Dry Corporation of Toronto established its ginger ale and other products in the United States during the years of prohibition and thereafter in additional markets overseas. Seven-Up, an American lemon-and-lime carbonated drink, was similarly marketed, and the promoters of speciality drinks like Dr. Pepper, a cherry soda that began as a fountain syrup, used the same means to extend their sales of ready-to-drink products at home and abroad.

Franchisers of one brand could also become franchisees of another. In Britain, for example, the old-established firm of Schweppes not only sold its products via associated companies overseas but also linked with the Coca-Cola Corporation to form the production company of Coca-Cola and Schweppes Bottlers in the United Kingdom. But the international success of the franchise system presupposed the existence of a worldwide network of local soft-drink manufacturers available to take it up.

The countries of Europe and North America that had seen the earliest growth of the carbonated soft-drink industry included those nations with the keenest interest in overseas trade. Thus, the techniques of soft-drink manufacture spread overseas along already established trade routes. In an age of imperialism, colonies tended to import from the parent country the machinery, packaging, and many of the ingredients necessary for soft-drink manufacture until such time as they might develop indigenous industries for supplying such essentials. The supply houses of the United States, increasingly important during the nineteenth century, were similarly adept at exporting to local bottlers in countries with which other American merchants were already engaged in general trade.

The success of soft-drink manufacture in different countries depended on a variety of factors: a degree of general sophistication in the country concerned, the competition of other drinks within it, the level of income of its citizens, and their social attitudes to alcoholic and other drinks – even a hot, dry climate was known to encourage soft-drink sales!

The trading nations not only developed existing overseas markets but also fostered new ones. Japan, opened to the world in the second half of the nineteenth century, saw small-scale bottling of carbonated soft drinks by the 1890s, with British techniques, and indeed British equipment, predominating in the early years. After World War II, American franchised soft drinks came onto the Japanese market. Influenced, but by no means dominated, by international trends, Japanese soft-drink manufacturers became adept at introducing new types of drinks and packaging into an increasingly dynamic and sophisticated market.

By the time franchisers began to look overseas, there was – at least in the most promising countries for development – no lack of local bottlers available to take up the franchises. And although international brands competed with local products, they could also stimulate the growth of the local soft-drink market by promoting greater consumption. In some areas where local manufacture was less advanced, the importation of soft drinks could encourage a local industry to develop. For example, many Muslim countries of the Near and Middle East relied initially on a high proportion of imported drinks to meet the demands of a hot climate, a youthful population, and the religious restrictions on – or outright prohibition of – alcoholic drinks. Then, as wealth and demand grew, a sophisticated indigenous industry developed.

Despite the spread of international brands, patterns of soft-drink consumption still varied considerably from country to country, as idiosyncrasies of national palate and social custom determined the way in which a country's total drink market was split among competing beverages. For example, in the Russian states, herbal beverages found a substantial market, with mint, nettle, coriander, and marjoram among the flavorings used. Equally, if not more, popular in Russia was *kvass,* a low-alcohol drink made from stale bread or cereals by the incomplete fermentation of alcohol and lactic acid. It remains to be seen what effect the international brands now being fran-

chised in Russia will have on these traditional flavor preferences.

The Growing Market

Many soft drinks have been seen to owe their origins to notions of a healthy diet current at the time they first appeared, and many continued to remain popular by appealing especially to young people. But in the later twentieth century, other soft drinks were developed that reflected the desire for a healthful diet while also appealing to older people who might hitherto have thought they had outgrown the soft drinks of their youth. Low-calorie soft drinks, designed specifically for weight-conscious adults, arrived in the 1960s. These products used a new artificial sweetener, cyclamate, which blended successfully with saccharin to make a more palatable product. When, later in the decade, cyclamate was banned in many countries, saccharin-only low-calorie drinks proved less acceptable. But with the introduction of new intense sweeteners in the 1980s, the low-calorie market once again expanded.

Natural mineral waters retained their popularity over the years in many countries of continental Europe, but in the final quarter of the twentieth century, vigorous promotion, spearheaded by the Perrier brand, revived dormant markets elsewhere and developed new ones for both carbonated and still waters. Flavored, but still unsweetened, variants of such natural waters further extended their newfound popularity.

A belief in the healthful properties of natural products – and its obverse, a distaste for additives – led to the development of so-called new-age drinks, which are clear and lightly carbonated, with unusual fruit and herbal flavorings, either singly or in combination. They have no added coloring, no salt, no caffeine, and little or no added sugar. For a quite different health market, isotonic or sports drinks were produced, high in sucrose (or sometimes maltose) and designed to quickly replace the body fluids and salts excreted in vigorous exercise.

Alternative refreshment was also increasingly sought in iced tea, a water-based drink, often flavored with soft fruits and, sometimes, with herbs. In these ways the soft-drink industry has continued to innovate and expand in the 200 years of its commercial existence.

Soft Drink Packaging

A history of soft drinks – and certainly of carbonated soft drinks – could scarcely be considered complete without mention of its containers and closures, for if a carbonated soft drink is to be consumed as its manufacturer intended, it must be packed in a container capable of withstanding the pressure of the gas within and sealed with a closure that is not only effective when in place but also readily responsive to the purchaser's efforts to open it. That these several requirements are obvious does not make them necessarily compatible!

The effective sealing of bottles presented problems from the very outset of commercial manufacture. For this purpose, bottles and jars of stoneware or of stout glass were stoppered with corks that needed to be tight or, better still, wired on to the container. Drinks subject to secondary fermentation, such as brewed ginger beer, were especially likely to burst the cork (hence ginger pop) and traditionally came to be packaged in stoneware containers.

Some early glass bottles were oval ended at the base so that they had to be stored on their sides, thus keeping the corks moist and expanded for better sealing. The bottles themselves were usually returnable when empty and were embossed with the bottler's name to promote their safe return. The inconvenience to the customer of the oval-ended bottles – they were sometimes called drunken bottles precisely because they could not stand up – led to their gradual replacement by those with a conventional flat base. These came into use around 1870 but at first were still intended to be stored on their sides.

Early manufacturers despatched their goods in strong wicker baskets, but wooden crates strengthened with wire came to be preferred, particularly once the flat-bottomed bottles arrived. But the modest price of the drinks, relative to their total weight when bottled and crated, made transportation costs an increasingly significant proportion of the whole trading operation. Although the convenience of a flat-base bottle was undoubted, its implications for the drying out of the cork soon led to improvements in bottle sealing.

Beginning in the 1870s, returnable internal screw stoppers became available, made first of hard woods and later of ebonite. Another successful invention of the time was Hiram Codd's bottle with the round glass "marble" stopper in the neck, which the pressure of carbonation kept sealed against the bottle mouth. In the last decade of the century, William Painter's crown cork came to be used for sealing the smaller returnable bottles for mixer drinks. The effectiveness of all the new seals was much improved when fully automatic bottle production superseded hand-blown glass during the first years of the twentieth century.

The internal screw stopper could be opened manually by a sufficiently strong wrist. The Codd's bottle, too, could be opened manually by depressing the marble in the neck, but wooden openers were available to supply any extra force needed. For the crown cork, a bottle opener was necessary and the closure was discarded after use. Returnable bottles and closures had also to be thoroughly washed before reuse, and the inspection of Codd's bottles and stoneware jars after cleaning could cause particular problems for the bottler.

Returnable glass bottles in sizes seldom greater than a quart dominated the industry during the first half of the twentieth century and beyond. They usually bore paper labels, although some had their labeling information permanently embossed or fired onto the container. In the latter half of the century, packaging diversified considerably. Lighter, standardized returnable glass bottles no longer needed to bear their owners' embossed names but consequently became less distinguishable from the throwaway containers of most other bottled goods.

From the 1960s on, often in response to changes in retailing – in particular the growth of supermarkets – carbonated soft drinks were also packed in nonreturnable glass and in steel or, later, aluminum cans. The first cans required special openers, but the ring-pull end was later introduced for manual opening.

In the 1980s, soft-drink bottlers began to make blow-molded plastic containers of polyethylene terephthalate (abbreviated to PET) in sizes larger than the traditional capacities of glass bottles. Even for returnable bottles, the nonreturnable aluminum cap, rolled on to the external screw thread of the bottle neck, gained ground rapidly in the 1960s. Later, resealable closures became commonplace, particularly as bottle capacities increased.

As the second half of the century progressed, draft soft-drink equipment was more frequently introduced into catering establishments. Draft soft drinks were produced either by the premix method, whereby the drinks were carbonated and packed at the manufacturing plant and then taken to the retail outlet to be connected to the dispensing equipment on site, or by the postmix method, whereby the ingredients of the drink were loaded separately into the dispensing equipment, itself designed to mix them with water in preset proportions for dispensing as a finished, ready-to-drink beverage. By midcentury, coin-operated automatic vending machines also sold prepacked soft drinks, and there, too, in the years that followed, new versions were developed that dispensed carbonated drinks into cups by means of either the pre- or postmix method.

Laminated cartons were developed for the packaging of fruit juices and were also used for still soft drinks. This diversification of packaging was also significant in stimulating the growth of the industry in the late twentieth century by ensuring the availability of soft drinks in an ever-increasing number of retail outlets, so that they may now be said to be among the most widely sold manufactured products in the world.

Colin Emmins

Bibliography

Barber, R., ed. 1988. *The worlds of John Aubrey*. London.
Barlowe, Arthur. [1589] 1970. The discovery of Virginia. In *The Tudor venturers: Selected from 'The principal navigations, voyages, traffics and discoveries of the*

English nation made by sea or over land,' by Richard
Hakluyt, ed. J. Hampden. London.

Bateson, M., ed. 1901. *Records of the borough of Leicester.*
4 vols. London.

Carpenter, K. J. 1986. *The history of scurvy and vitamin C.*
New York.

Chadwick, Edwin. 1833. *The Poor Laws of London and Berkshire.* London.

Darwin, Erasmus. 1794. *Zoonomia.* London.

Dodd, George. 1856. *The food of London.* London.

Fuller, T. [1662] 1965. *The history of the worthies of England.* London.

Goold, Joseph. 1880. *Aerated waters and how to make
them.* London.

Harrod's Stores, Ltd. 1972. *Victorian shopping: Harrod's catalogue, 1895. Introduced by Alison Adburgham.* London.

Henry, T. 1781. *A mode of impregnating water in large
quantities with fixed air.* Warrington, England.

Hicks, D., ed. 1990. *The production and packaging of non-
carbonated fruit juices and fruit beverages.* New
York.

Hunt, T., ed. 1862. *Correspondence of Leigh Hunt.* 2 vols.
London.

Jekyll, G., and S. R. Jones. 1939. *Old English household life.*
London.

Kirkby, W. 1902. *The evolution of artificial mineral waters.*
Manchester.

Magellan, J. H. de. 1777. *Description of a glass apparatus for
making . . . the best mineral waters of Pyrmont, Spa,
Seltzer, Seydschutz, Aix-la-Chapelle. . . .* London.

Martin, M. W. 1962. *Twelve full ounces* (Pepsi-Cola). New York.

Mayhew, Henry. 1851. *London labour and the London poor.*
3 vols. London.

Mitchell, A. J., ed. 1990. *Formulation and production of carbonated soft drinks.* New York.

Nichols, S. 1994. *Vimto - the story of a soft drink.* Preston,
England.

Pendergrast, M. 1993. *For God, country and Coca-Cola.* London.

Pereira, Jonathan. 1843. *Treatise on food and diet.* London.

Priestley, J. 1772. *Directions for impregnating water with
fixed air.* London.

Pringle, J. 1774. *A discourse on the different kinds of air.*
London.

Riley, J. J. 1958. *A history of the American soft drink industry.* Washington, D.C.

Rutt, J. T., ed. 1831. *Life and correspondence of Joseph
Priestley.* 2 vols. London.

Simmonds, W. H. 1905. *The practical grocer.* 4 vols. London.

Simmons, D. A. 1983. *Schweppes - the first two hundred
years.* London.

Sulz, Charles H. 1888. *A treatise on beverages or the complete practical bottler.* New York.

Tressler, D. K., and M. A. Joslyn. 1961. *Fruit and vegetable
juice processing technology.* Westport, Conn.

III.11 ❧ Tea

Tea, a drink made from the leaves and buds of
the shrub *Camellia sinensis,* is the most culturally
and economically significant nonalcoholic beverage
in the world. Originating in China, it had spread to
surrounding nations before European contact, after
which it was made a commodity of world importance by the British and Dutch East India Companies. Wars have been waged, nations punished,
and fortunes made and lost because of this beverage. One reason that tea has been a very profitable article of trade is that it is a source of caffeine –
a major factor in its popularity (Willson and Clifford
1992).

Although there are many kinds of herbal beverages
called "teas," in this chapter the term "tea" refers only
to *Camellia sinensis.* Both infusions (pouring hot
water over the leaves) and decoctions (boiling the
leaves in water) have been made from the plant,
which has also been eaten raw, cooked, or pickled
and has even been snuffed.

Botany and Production

Camellia sinensis is native to the mountainous highlands between India and China and, when
untrimmed, can grow to a height of about 10 meters.
One variety, *Camellia sinensis sinensis,* is native to
China, whereas *Camellia sinensis assamica* comes
from India (Harler 1963). A semitropical or tropical
climate is necessary for raising tea; the northernmost
places where it has been grown are South Carolina
(in the United States) and in Asia near the Black Sea.
Bushes grown at high elevations produce the best tea
(Willson and Clifford 1992). Yields range from 700 to
more than 1,800 kilograms (kg) per acre (Harler
1964).

Tea undergoes a long journey from bush to cup.
The leaf buds, which appear in the spring, along with
the leaves directly below them on the stem, are generally hand plucked by skilled workers (Pratt 1982). The
first buds to appear (the "first flush") and the smallest
leaves ("two leaves and a bud" is the ideal) command
the highest price, whereas the larger leaves that can
be cut by machines usually become part of lower-
grade teas.

About 98 percent of the tea that enters the world
market is black tea, and there are four steps required
to ready this tea for Western tastes. The first, "withering," involves drying the leaves to the point at which
they are structurally weak. This is followed by "rolling" the leaves (in the past, between the heels of the
hands), which crushes their cells and blends their
chemical constituents, the characteristic tea polyphenols and the enzyme polyphenol oxidase. Moreover, the twist this imparts to the leaves slows the
rate at which their essence blends with hot water.
"Fermentation" - the third step - actually involves
oxidation by the polyphenol oxidase and is produced by aerating and heating the leaves to between
72° and 82° Fahrenheit for 1 to 2 hours, during
which their flavor develops and they turn a brownish color. The final stage is called "firing" the leaves.
This further heating process stops fermentation (oxidation) by deactivating the enzyme and reduces the

leaves to a moisture content of about 5 percent (McGee 1984). Needless to say, all of these procedures require a highly developed sense of timing on the part of the tea maker.

Although black teas monopolize the international market, the teas drunk in China and Japan are mostly green (Harler 1963). In preparing the latter, the fermentation stage is eliminated, and the enzymes are destroyed by steam or pan heating before the leaves are rolled and fired. In North Africa, too, green tea is common, in this case because the classic word "fermentation," applied to the oxidation process, was misunderstood by Muslim religious and political leaders; they thought the word referred to the formation of alcohol, which their religion prohibited. Thus, this stage of tea preparation was omitted.

The size of the leaves determines the grade of a green tea: The tight, small balls of younger leaves are called "gunpowder"; "imperial" tea comes in larger and looser balls; Hyson varieties are long and looser leaves of mixed ages (McGee 1984). It might be added at this point that Oolong tea stands between green and black teas in that although it is fermented, this is only done briefly for about 30 minutes after rolling.

Grades of black teas, although they may vary, typically conform to guidelines that emerged from the British tea industry in nineteenth-century India and Ceylon (Sri Lanka). Whole leaves, which are generally thought to produce the best flavor, are classified by size and the ways in which they are rolled. For example, Flowery Orange Pekoe leaves are smaller than those of Orange Pekoe, and some of the leaves of Golden Flowery Orange Pekoe have highly prized golden tips (indicating that the tea consists of small, intact leaves), whereas in the case of Tippy Golden Flowery Orange Pekoe, all the tips are golden.

Leaves that have been broken, whether deliberately or not, also make high-quality teas that conform to some of these classifications (for example, Broken Orange Pekoe, Golden Broken Orange Pekoe, or Tippy Golden Broken Orange Pekoe). Small pieces of leaves (debris from the processing of whole and broken leaves) are called "dust," and even smaller ones are called "fannings" (Stella 1992). These go into teabags and brick tea.

Teas are also named for the regions where they grow. For example, black teas from eastern India are known collectively as Darjeeling teas; Oolongs and Lapsang Souchongs come from Taiwan, and Keemun is a black tea from northern China. Teas are sometimes scented: An extreme case is Lapsang Souchong, a large-leafed black tea scented with pinewood smoke (Goodwin 1991). More often, flavoring is done with essential oils before, during, or after firing. This is especially the case with blends – the form in which most teas are generally purchased. Constant Comment, for example, is a blend from Sri Lanka flavored with orange peel; Earl Grey, another blend, is flavored with a citrus oil (McGee 1984).

History

Origins

The true origins of tea are unknown. Wild tea leaves are still used by the tribes of Burma to prepare a beverage and a "tea salad" (made from leaves that have fermented underground for several months and are then mixed with mushrooms, oil, garlic, chilli peppers, and perhaps other ingredients). In that part of the world, tea is also chewed or sniffed as snuff, and many surmise that use of the tea plant originated there and spread to China by the Han dynasty period (206 B.C. to A.D. 221). However, the wild tea plants of nearby Assam, in India, do not produce a palatable brew, and present-day Indian tea culture is wholly the work of the British.

China

The question of whether tea came from elsewhere to Han-dynasty China is obscured by legend. One of the earliest tales would have it that (some 5,000 years ago) a mythical emperor, Shen Nung, drank boiling water into which a wild tea leaf had fallen and, consequently, was the first to taste the beverage. Other legends state that tea bushes first sprang up when a Buddhist monk cut off his eyelids to keep from falling asleep while meditating – this tale, perhaps, was inspired by the Buddhists' heavy use of tea.

Mythology, however, is not as useful to the historian in dating the Chinese use of tea as are the mentions of an herb called *t'u* in the writings of Confucius (551 to 479 B.C.), who remarked "Who can say that *t'u* is bitter? It is as sweet as the shepherd's purse" – which was another herb (Evans 1992: 14). In Chinese, the written character *t'u* later meant tea, so it is at least possible that Confucius knew of the beverage at this early date (Blofeld 1985). At any rate, there seems little question that at least some tea was drunk during the Han dynasty and that the lacquer cups known from this period (the "winged cups") are in fact the earliest teacups (Evans 1992).

Tea was probably used first for medicinal reasons, but the leaf and its lore moved from the medicinal to the artistic during the Tang dynasty (A.D. 618 to 907), a period of increasingly eclectic food and drink choices, which also saw the Chinese enjoying grape wine and butter cakes (Tropp 1982). In about 800, Lu Yu, the first known tea connoisseur, penned the oldest surviving tea manual, the *Cha Ching* or "Scripture of Tea" (Ukers 1935). This book described an elaborate ceremony of tea making, from picking the leaves, to roasting them, to serving the green tea in wide shallow bowls (Lu Yu 1974). All tea at this time was green, which kept rather poorly unless made into cakes (Blofeld 1985), and the Tang-dynasty Chinese also enjoyed spiced tea, made by adding onions, garlic, mint, orange peel, salted black soybeans, or five-spice powder (Blofeld 1985). Although despised by Lu Yu, it was a common drink, and the addition of these flavorings may have either disguised the flavor of poor tea or allowed more bowls to be made from the same amount of leaves. Of course, such beverages also - at least to some extent - prefigured the flower teas, such as "Jasmine" and "Rose Congou" later served in North China, and which subsequently became popular outside China.

Tea ways changed as tea use and tea plantations grew more widespread during the Sung dynasty (960 to 1280). Green tea was powdered, whipped until it was the color of a "river of jade," and served in deeper and wider bowls (Evans 1992). The use of spices and other additives was discontinued. Poets praised tea and referred to *cha tao,* the "Way of Tea" (Blofeld 1985), and the beverage was used in Chan (Zen) Buddhist ceremonies.

Brick tea was employed by the Chinese to buy horses from the central Asian tribes, and in Tibet and Mongolia, it was churned with yak butter and barley or millet into a porridge, the national staple (Kramer 1994). Centuries of Mongol rule in China were followed by the Ming dynasty (1368 to 1644), under which the tea trade widened in scope. To preserve tea for trade, some varieties were fermented into novel black teas that had not previously existed (Evans 1992). Wine pots were employed as teapots for steeping leaf tea, and by 1500, such pots were being made especially for tea (Chow and Kramer 1990). It is entirely possible that the use of a pot, enabling the brew to be poured off the leaves, was connected to the increasing importance of leaf tea, for the brew - especially in the case of black teas - can turn bitter if left in contact with the leaves too long (Chow and Kramer 1990).

Under the Ming, small handleless cups were used with a teapot, and this was the style of tea drinking exported to the West, along with the unglazed earthenware pots of Yixing (favored by tea connoisseurs) and teacups of blue and white porcelain (Chow and Kramer 1990). From the sixteenth through the eighteenth centuries in China, several styles of teapot were in common use, including some with a handle on the side and others with no handle (Kanzaki 1981). These were used for fine green tea, which must be brewed with simmering (rather than boiling) water (Arts 1988). Other types of pots included tiny personal teapots - "personal" because the tea was drunk directly from the spout (Tropp 1982).

Another Chinese development, which never reached the West, was the tea "requiring skill." In this ritual, the finest green tea was packed into a small teapot, boiling water poured over the tea, and the first infusion discarded. The second infusion, however, was drunk as if it were a liqueur, and sometimes even a third infusion was prepared. Such an artistic tea ceremony is still practiced in Taiwan (Blofeld 1985).

Teahouses were social centers in China; they are documented as far back as the Tang dynasty and achieved great prominence from the sixteenth through the eighteenth centuries (Anderson 1994). Patrons bought the "house tea" or had their own brewed for a small fee. Poetry readings, opera singing, or dancers were typical teahouse entertainments. At some establishments, in fact, "singsong girls" (prostitutes) offered the customer other choices in addition to tea (Blofeld 1985). Most teahouses served food: The most common fare was and remains *dimsum,* an array of snacks (Anderson 1994).

In 1644, China was taken over by the central Asian Manchu dynasty, which presided over (among other things) a new fashion of lidded cups called *chung* (Chow and Kramer 1990), in which tea could be both steeped and drunk. *Chung,* however, never became popular in Japan or the West, and even in China, the older types of pots and cups remained in use as well. The origins of many kinds of tea still enjoyed today can be traced to this, China's last imperial dynasty. The Manchu, whose staples on the steppes had been milk and butter, also served milk in black tea, a practice which did become popular in the West (Ukers 1935).

In the early seventeenth century, the Europeans, beginning with the Dutch, sought to trade for tea with China. The Chinese, however, proved to be difficult trading partners. Not only did they claim not to need (and consequently would not accept) anything from the West except the precious metals (silver and gold) and copper but they also kept the secrets of tea growing and processing to themselves - even to the extent of boiling any tea seeds they sold to render them sterile (Goodwin 1991). Indeed, so successful were the Chinese in maintaining European ignorance of matters concerning tea that it was only in the nineteenth century (after some two and a half centuries of tea trading) that their customers learned that black and green tea came from the same plant (Ukers 1935).

The largest of these customers was the British East India Company,[1] which from the 1660s onward carried huge amounts of tea from Canton to Britain but always struggled with the balance-of-payments problem presented by the Chinese insistence on precious metals as the only exchange for tea. One solution for the company was to find products that the Chinese would accept in trade. The other was to grow its own tea, and India became the place where both of these goals were pursued.

In pursuit of the latter solution, Lord Bentinck (William Henry Cavendish), who was appointed governor of India in 1828, created the Tea Committee to foster a tea industry in that land. Several botanists were sent to China to learn about tea cultivation and to recruit Chinese growers to start tea plantations in India. One of these botanists, J. C. Gordon, collected more than 80,000 seeds and sent them to Calcutta, whereupon the British discovered that all varieties of tea came from the same plant (Willson and Clifford 1992).

But it was Robert Fortune - entering China in 1848 as an agent of the Tea Committee and for three years roving about the country's tea regions disguised as a Chinese merchant – who finally unlocked the many mysteries involved in actually producing tea (Beauthéac 1992). Thereafter, Chinese tea was planted in India and, a bit later (after disease had wiped out the island's coffee trees), in Ceylon (Sri Lanka) as well. Tea bushes native to India were subjected to experimentation, hybrids tinkered with, and, ultimately, plants well suited to India's climate were developed. The great tea plantations of British India were born.

Nonetheless, because China continued to supply most of the world's tea, the problem of its insistence on bullion or copper as payment for that tea also continued. Actually, the British had already found one product – cotton from Bengal – that interested the Chinese. Then they hit upon another. Poppies, imported from Turkey, grew well in India, and the British East India Company entered the opium business. No matter that the Chinese government refused to permit the importation of the addictive powder. Intermediaries soon stimulated a lively demand for it across all strata of Chinese society, and as the government continued to object, the British went to war, their gunboats easily overwhelming the Chinese coastal defenses. The Treaty of Nanking (1842) not only forced opium upon the Chinese but also forced open four Chinese ports (in addition to Canton) to European trade. Hong Kong was ceded to the British, and British consuls were admitted to all treaty ports.

The decline of China from its former imperial grandeur continued throughout the remainder of the nineteenth century as foreigners increased their ascendancy, and in the twentieth century, the old China disappeared in the tumult of war and revolution. During these years, a great deal of the ancient art and culture surrounding tea was also destroyed. But it remained (and remains) the national beverage. Throughout the day, people carry with them lidded tea mugs, which, like the *chung,* can be used both for infusion and for drinking (Chow and Kramer 1990). Glass mugs or cups are aesthetically pleasing, because they allow the drinker to view the unfolding of the tea leaves as the tea brews (Chow and Kramer 1990); in fact, there are teas which are specially bred and rolled for this purpose. Teahouses in the new China include opera, television viewing, and even "karaoke" singing as entertainment (Anderson 1994).

Japan

Japan first obtained tea, along with many other cultural practices, from China. Tradition has it that the beverage was carried to Japan by the Buddhist monk Eisai; drinking tea before meditation was for the Buddhists a practical way to keep awake, and early Zen monks drank tea long before it was known elsewhere in the islands. To make it, cakes of tea were powdered, and water was boiled in a kettle and ladled into a bowl. Following this step, the tea was whipped with

a whisk – itself made by splitting bamboo fibers and then bending them with steam into a double cone of curved spines. The early monastic "four-headed tea" was a rite in which a man served tea to guests by whipping individual bowlfuls (Hayashiya 1979).

In Japan, tea service evolved into an elaborate ceremony, continuing the Chinese Sung-dynasty use of whipped green tea, which as employed in the Japanese tea ritual still resembles jade in its deep, clear green color (Chow and Kramer 1990). When the country was unified in the sixteenth century after a long era of war among feudal lords, the cultivation and use of green tea became widespread, and the tea ceremony, which had served as an opportunity for ostentation by the nobility, was remade under the guidance of art collector and tea-master Sen Rikyû, who created the "tea of quiet taste" – a ceremony performed in a small, low hut and passed on to future generations as a tradition. Different kinds of sweets, flowers, incense, stylized conversation, calligraphy, bowls, and other utensils became associated with different "schools" of the tea ceremony, as well as months of the year, places, and so forth. Years of instruction became necessary to master the way of tea; Rikyû's sons and grandsons founded several tea schools, which carry on old traditions to this day (Sen 1979).

During the seventeenth century, leaf tea was introduced from China, and the use of teapots became common. For ordinary tea, a teapot with a spout on the front was used. For fine tea, a hot-water pot *(kyusu)* – more convenient than the older kettle – was employed (Kanzaki 1981). Cups of porcelain in the style of the Chinese Ming dynasty became common alongside the *kyusu.* Although the tea ceremony of Rikyû used powdered tea, another ceremony involving fine-leaf tea also developed, and the *kyusu* employed were often beautiful works of art (Arts 1988).

In 1854, the isolation of Japan came to an end with the Shogun's agreement to allow foreign ships to put into Japanese ports, and in the initial rush to modernize, the Japanese tea ceremony was lost. But at the start of the twentieth century, as Japanese culture underwent a revival, the ceremony became popular once again, a popularity that continues into the present. Tea also figures in popular culture. It is used regularly in homes and restaurants and can even be bought from vending machines. Green tea remains the most popular for daily use, although other kinds, including black tea and herb tea, are also drunk. In 1992, Japan exported a mere 290 tons of tea while importing 160,367 tons (FAO 1993).

India

Although a Dutch seafarer wrote of tea being eaten as well as drunk in India in 1598, accounts of earlier Indian history do not mention the use of tea or its cultivation (Pettigrew 1997). Milk and buttermilk, produced by the country's millions of sacred cattle, were the preferred beverages in India (Tannahill 1988).

The tea cultivation begun there in the nineteenth century by the British, however, has accelerated to the point that today India is listed as the world's leading producer, its 715,000 tons well ahead of China's 540,000 tons, and of course, the teas of Assam, Ceylon (from the island nation known as Sri Lanka), and Darjeeling are world famous. However, because Indians average half a cup daily on a per capita basis, fully 70 percent of India's immense crop is consumed locally (Goodwin 1991; FAO 1993). Tea in India is generally spiced and served with milk, thus incorporating two other prominent Indian products. As a cup of tea with sugar and milk may contain up to 40 calories, this is also a source of quick energy (Harler 1964).

In general, even though India leads the world in tea technology, the methods employed to harvest the crop vary with the type of tea and terrain. Fine-leaf tea is hand plucked, and hand shears are used on mountain slopes and in other areas where tractor-mounted machines cannot go. A skilled worker using hand shears can harvest between 60 and 100 kg of tea per day, whereas machines cut between 1,000 and 2,000 kg. The latter, however, are usually applied to low-grade teas that often go into teabags. The tea "fluff" and waste from processing is used to produce caffeine for soft drinks and medicine (Harler 1963).

Russia

Tea from China reached Tsar Alexis of Russia in 1618, and the Russians quickly adopted the beverage. They adapted the Mongolian "firepot" to their own purposes, creating the charcoal-fueled samovar, which boiled water in its tank and furnished the heat to make tea essence in a small pot atop the device. The essence was diluted with hot water from the tank whenever a cup of tea was desired. Samovars (now electrically heated) are still common, especially in offices and at parties and gatherings where much tea must be made at once. Lump sugar is used for sweetening, and Russians often bite a sugar lump in between sips of tea (Schapira 1982).

Tea is served in glasses with metal holders in public places and in china cups at home. Apples or cranberries (instead of costly lemons) are sometimes added along with sugar, and tea is usually drunk with milk. Pastries and sweets often accompany the beverage. The low price of tea led to its great popularity in Russia, and the tea plantations of Georgia (now a separate nation) are the most northerly in the world. The Russians, however, consider Georgia-grown tea to be inferior (Schapira 1982), and some 325,000 tons of tea were imported by the countries of the former Soviet Union in 1992 (FAO 1993).

Continental Europe

Tea first became popular in the Netherlands in the early seventeenth century. Served in the afternoon – in what would become the British style – it was mixed with sugar and, sometimes, saffron. As the custom of afternoon tea in the home developed, hostesses set aside special rooms, furnished with paintings, tables and chairs (Brochard 1992), and large quantities of tea were reportedly consumed: Montesquieu, for example, saw a Dutch woman drink 30 small cups at one sitting (Brochard 1992). In the Dutch colony of New Amsterdam in North America, water for tea was hawked through the streets, and prior to the dominance of the British East India Company, the Netherlands exported much tea to Britain (Israel 1987).

Tea cultivation in Indonesia, which began under Dutch supervision in the mid–nineteenth century (Ukers 1935), specialized in the production of black teas often used for blends. Tea is still popular in the Netherlands today; in 1992, the United Provinces imported 377,803 tons of tea and reexported 201,306 tons, leaving 176,497 tons for local use (FAO 1993).

Germany and France have historically consumed little tea, although the porcelain works of Meissen in Germany have produced excellent tea services. Some tea is consumed in the Dutch or British fashion in both nations, but most people there prefer coffee.

Britain

Despite the British fondness for tea, it does not have a long history in the islands. The first mention of "chaw" in a sea captain's letter dates from 1597, and not until 1658 was tea first announced for sale at a London coffeehouse (Ukers 1935). From that point forward, however, sugar from British-controlled islands of the Caribbean became plentiful enough to make the new beverage palatable to Englishmen's tastes. But leathern or wooden cups - used for ale - were unsuitable for hot tea, and consequently Ming-style pots and teacups were brought to Britain along with the new beverage.

Expensive at first, tea became more widespread as duties fell. By the 1710s, afternoon tea had become an important convivial occasion for women, who were discouraged from drinking alcohol socially because (according to the new bourgeois code of morals) they could not remain "ladylike" while intoxicated. In addition, eighteenth-century Britain saw the rise of "tea gardens," where tea, snacks, and entertainment could be enjoyed by the bourgeois and upper classes. Sidney Mintz (1985) has commented on the "tea complex" of tea and sugary foods (such as jam and pastries) that came to be popular among the British, doubtless in no small part because of the stimulating effects of caffeine and sugar. According to Benjamin Franklin, eighteenth-century Britons and Anglo-Americans drank 10 pounds of tea per head yearly - which translated into 2,000 cups, or about 5½ cups a day (Pratt 1982).

Such demand invariably led to adulteration in order to color the tea and add weight to shipments. Ash leaves, licorice, iron filings, Prussian blue, sheep dung, and numerous other materials could be found in tea packages, and discarded tea leaves were saved from garbage heaps and washed for resale. Even the tea-loving Chinese happily dyed green tea a brighter green to satisfy British customers who disliked the pale color of the "real thing" (Goodwin 1991). It is interesting to note that some popular scented teas are the products of such adulteration: In the case of Earl Grey, for example, buyers came to demand the scent and flavor produced by the addition of oil of bergamot.

Chinese porcelain was painted with designs made especially for English buyers (such as the famous "willow pattern"), and cups began to be made with handles to enable the drinker to cope with tea hot enough to dissolve sugar – unlike the Chinese green tea, which was brewed at a lower temperature (Pratt 1982). Carried as ballast in sailing ships (one ship might carry as much as 20 tons of porcelain), this "china" was very inexpensive (Atterbury 1982; Hobhouse 1986), but attempts were nonetheless made to copy Chinese porcelain. Such efforts eventually met with success, and by 1742 porcelain was being made in Europe.

British tea tariffs, which played such an important part in bringing about the American Revolution, were repealed the year after American independence was achieved (Goodwin 1991), and the adulteration of tea ceased as it was no longer profitable (Hobhouse 1986). In 1786, the East India Company sold a total of 2.4 million pounds of black tea and 1.15 million of green tea (Ukers 1935). Even in those days, green tea was already losing ground to black, but it was still relatively more popular than it would later become with the massive influx of black teas from India and Africa. Broken grades also sold very well in Britain because of their lower prices (Harler 1963).

The Victorian period found tea perhaps at its zenith, with even the homeless of Whitechapel partaking – a victim of Jack the Ripper was carrying tea on her person, along with sugar and a spoon, at the time of her murder (Tully 1997). The temperance movement was greatly aided by affordable tea, as millions were converted to "tee-totaling," or abstinence from alcohol. The British took tea in the morning, at lunch, at "low tea" (afternoon tea, served in the "low" part of the afternoon), and at "high tea" (or "meat tea"), an early supper served at 6 o'clock (Israel 1987). Strongly scented teas, such as Earl Grey, Jasmine, and Lapsang Souchong, were extremely popular, perhaps because the Victorian regimen of meats and sweets demanded strongly flavored teas to match. The rituals of tea became more complex, and from the drawing rooms (the "withdrawing rooms" to which ladies withdrew while gentlemen remained at the table) of London to the South African bush, the British cherished tea, the "cups that cheer."

In the twentieth century, British workmen continued to break daily for tea, made and served collectively for groups of workers or purchased from nearby shops. In the 1980s and 1990s, the British each consumed some 3 to 4 kg of tea annually. In 1992, the nation as a whole imported 503,350 tons of tea and reexported 122,476 tons, leaving 380,874 tons for local consumption (FAO 1993). The rising popularity of coffee and soft drinks have somewhat diminished tea's popularity, but it remains a staple British beverage, and tearooms flourish throughout much of the English-speaking world, although not in the United States.

The United States

Tea in America has a history going back to the colonial era, when it was used by both Chesapeake planters and Massachusetts merchants and was especially popular in Philadelphia (Roth 1988). As in England during this period, most tea was green and often mixed with sugar, fruits, and liquors to make an alcoholic "punch."

The legendary Boston and Charleston "tea parties" sprang from the British tax on tea, which, unlike other taxes, had not been repealed in the face of colonial protest. The result was a series of civil disorders in which shiploads of tea were destroyed (in Boston) or stolen (in Charleston). In retrospect, these acts were clearly precursors of the Revolution. Contrary to legend, however, tea drinking did not cease because of hostility to Britain, and George Washington continued to breakfast on three bowls of tea. The difference was that this tea no longer reached the United States through British channels, but rather in American ships, the first shipment arriving in 1784 aboard the *Empress of China* (Ukers 1935). But it was the case that, a few decades later, an increase in the availability of cheap, Brazilian, slave-produced coffee brought a gradual decline of tea consumption in favor of coffee.

Two great changes in American tea drinking came about in the early twentieth century. One occurred in 1908, when tea merchant Thomas Sullivan, in order to reduce shipping weight, began to package tea samples in silk bags instead of miniature tins. Some of his customers brewed the tea without taking it out of the bags and requested more tea packaged in this way; Sullivan obliged, and teabags were created. Today, in America, most tea is brewed from teabags (Schapira 1982).

The other innovation was iced tea, supposedly invented at the 1904 World's Fair by Richard Blechynden, an English tea concessionaire who had been sent to the United States to promote black tea. But in the sweltering heat of St. Louis, he was unable to sell hot tea or even give it away. In frustration, he poured the tea over ice and began to serve it cold. Because there is much evidence of iced tea before this event, Blechynden gets more credit for his "invention" than he deserves, but it is probably fair to say that he brought iced tea to the world's attention (Pratt 1982; Israel 1987). Indeed, from this point forward in the United States, the sale of black tea (which makes better iced tea) began to edge out that of green, suggesting that Blechynden gave his employers their money's worth.

Still another development, which many find to be no improvement at all, is the invention of "instant" tea, which is an evaporated powder similar to instant coffee (Willson and Clifford 1992). Instant tea constitutes a significant amount of the tea consumed in the United States, but – as it is not made by brewing – it could be said that it is not really tea at all (Schapira 1982). In the early 1990s, the nation imported 305,017 tons of tea and exported 85,363 tons. Included in the latter was a small amount of tea grown in the United States (FAO 1993).

Until at least very recently, tea cultivation in the United States has never been a profitable enterprise because of climate, although, since the nineteenth century, individual tea bushes have been tended in gardens of the South. Between 1848 and 1852, the operators of a plantation in Greenville, South Carolina, tried to grow tea, and in 1880, John Jackson made an attempt in Summerville, South Carolina. Tea was also grown in several places nearby, but all these efforts were eventually abandoned (Ukers 1935).

In the 1980s, however, Mack Fleming, an engineer for the Lipton Tea Company, purchased the Summerville land and, with the help of Canadian tea taster Bill Hall, began experimentally processing leaves from the tea bushes that still remained. Fleming and Hall transferred tea bushes to Wadmalaw Island near Charleston and invented a machine to shear off the tea buds, literally mowing the tea like a lawn. The resulting product, marketed in both bagged and loose forms as American Classic Tea, is the only tea commercially grown in America. Hawaii, California, and Florida also have climates appropriate for tea growing, but labor costs for harvest are prohibitive.

Other Lands

Brazil and Argentina in South America, and Turkey and Iran in the Near East, produce undistinguished teas – mostly for teabags – as do Tanzania and Malawi in Africa. In Kenya, however, which now ranks fourth among the world's tea-producing nations, some teas are emerging as noteworthy. For the most part, these black teas are grown on plantations on the high plateaus that are understandably similar to those of India, as they were founded by British planters who left that country following independence (Willson and Clifford 1992). In addition, South Africa produces an excellent tea from plants that originated in the Darjeeling area of India; in South Africa, as in Kenya, tea plantations are located on the high plateaus.

Tea and Health

In modern times, tea is one of the world's least expensive beverages, which helps to account for the fact that, after water, it is also the most commonly used beverage. Because it is made with boiled – and therefore sterile – water, tea is safe to consume in areas where water quality may be less than satisfactory.

This is doubtless one of the major reasons that, over the millennia, tea has maintained a reputation for contributing to good health (Weisburger 1997). Buddhist monks in China and Japan, who were physicians as well as tea-masters, used tea to help people through their illnesses. Even today, tea is frequently employed in ancillary therapy for individuals who suffer from various infections, colds, or chronic diseases (Yamanashi 1991). Tea is a diuretic and produces both warmth (if it is served hot) and coolness (because it promotes evaporation of water from the skin) in the body; moreover, the steam of hot tea moisturizes the nose, mouth, and throat. The caffeine in tea is also a "pick-me-up."

Perhaps because tea was first used in China and Japan, historically most research on its health benefits was conducted by Eastern research groups. These groups have held conferences to report on findings that have to do largely with disease prevention and, to a lesser extent, with therapy (Yamanashi 1991). But even though tea became a major beverage in some of Europe and all of the English-speaking world, relatively little research of this nature was done in the West until recently.

Beginning in about 1980, however, a number of laboratories and groups in the United States and Canada – and a few in Europe – have shown an interest in researching relationships between tea and human health. Their findings were summarized at the First International Conference on Tea and Health, held in New York in 1991 (Symposium 1992). Included were reports suggesting that people who drink tea regularly have a lessened risk of coronary heart disease. Moreover, some investigators also noted that tea has a beneficial effect in warding off cancers of the stomach, esophagus, and lung (Katiyar and Mukhtar 1996; Weisburger 1996; Yang et al. 1997), and new research suggests that the caffeine in tea may play a role in such cancer prevention. Black tea and green tea had very similar (if not identical) preventive effects, and a few findings showed delayed growth and even regression of cancers in laboratory animals.

Stimulated by such findings, considerably more research has since been conducted in Europe, North America, and Asia. One interesting area of investigation has to do with the incidence of lung cancer in Japanese men, which is lower than that in their American counterparts, even though the Japanese smoke many more cigarettes on a per capita basis. It has been hypothesized that tea drinking by Japanese men is the key factor.

The chemical basis for the preventive benefits of tea seems to be specific polyphenols in both green and black teas that can act as powerful antioxidants. It is suspected that the risk of heart disease and many types of cancer is lowered by the raised antioxidant level in the bodies of those who drink tea and, conversely, that the conditions promoting these diseases involve abnormally low levels of oxidation. Tea polyphenols also modify intestinal bacterial flora, leading to a decrease in the levels of undesirable bacteria and contributing to the maintenance and increase of desirable bacteria. In fact, tea is the culture medium for the "tea fungus" called *kombucha,* actually a symbiotic bacterial culture used in alternative medicine. Tea can have a specific antibacterial action and, perhaps, a limited but definite effect against specific viruses (Hara 1994). Moreover, recent results suggest that Alzheimer's disease may occur less frequently in aging people who are regular tea drinkers.

One kilogram of tea makes about 440 cups, whereas the same amount of coffee makes about 88 (Harler 1964), which helps to explain both the relative cheapness of tea as a beverage and the higher caffeine content of coffee. The caffeine in tea was once called "theine," but is chemically identical to the caffeine in coffee. Depending on the type of tea, a 150-milliliter cup may contain 30 to 50 milligrams of caffeine, only about one-third of the caffeine found in a cup of coffee (Harler 1963).

Nonetheless, this is sufficient to account for its reportedly pleasant, slightly stimulating effect on mental function, and is doubtless the reason for tea's popularity as a morning beverage. However, the amount of caffeine in tea is low enough that an overdose is unlikely, whereas overdose symptoms ranging from headaches to severe gastrointestinal distress do occur in coffee drinkers (Willson and Clifford 1992). Tea is also available decaffeinated; to achieve this, solid carbon-dioxide extraction is employed to remove caffeine selectively without removing the desirable polyphenols. Thus, decaffeinated tea provides the taste and most of the health benefits of its caffeinated counterpart for caffeine-sensitive tea drinkers and can be consumed in the evening without fear of sleep deprivation.

Ordinary tea, however, can be made as free of caffeine as decaffeinated tea. One way to do this is to brew a first infusion, discard it, and brew a second from the same tea. Caffeine is extracted from tea in 1 to 2 minutes, and so a second infusion will have a weaker taste but no caffeine. Another means is to make "sun tea" by placing cold water with teabags in it in direct sunlight, usually for several hours. The result is a tea virtually free of caffeine, normally served iced. However, it is not known whether the health-promoting antioxidant tea polyphenols remain intact after being subjected to the sun's radiation.

How to Make Tea

Starting with Lu Yu and Sen Rikyû, tea-masters throughout the ages have emphasized both the ease of making good tea and the philosophical significance of the beverage. The following is offered as a basic modern outline of how good tea should be treated.

Start with fine tea, whether whole or bagged, and clean, cold water. Avoid water that has a taste of its own. For green tea, bring the water to a simmer; for black or Oolong, it must be at a rolling boil. Warm the vessel in which the tea will brew by pouring boiling water into and out of it, and add about 3 grams of tea per cup to be brewed. Pour boiling water over the leaves and allow to steep for 3 to 5 minutes, depending on the type of tea. Finally, remove the leaves or teabag from the vessel and pour the tea, adding sugar (or other sweetener), milk, or lemon, as desired. On a cold night, tea with rum, brandy, or bourbon whiskey makes a warming and thus a pleasant beverage.

John H. Weisburger
James Comer

Research in Weisburger's laboratory is supported by grants and contracts from the Tea Trade Health Research Association, Toronto, Canada; the National Cancer Institute, Bethesda, Maryland; the American Cancer Society, Atlanta, Georgia; and gifts from Texaco, Inc., Beacon, New York, and the Friends Against Cancer Team.

Note

1. This company of many names was originally founded as two separate companies: (1) the Governor and Company of Merchants Trading into the East Indies, and (2) the English Company Trading to the East Indies. In 1708, the two merged to become the United Company of Merchants Trading to the East Indies, which was more succinctly called the Honourable East India Company and more familiarly referred to as the John Company (Harler 1964).

Bibliography

Anderson, E. N. 1994. Food. In *Handbook of Chinese popular culture,* ed. Patrick Murphy and Wu Dingbo, 35-54. London.

Anderson, Jennifer. 1991. *An introduction to Japanese tea ritual.* Albany, N.Y.

Arts, P. L. W. 1988. *Tetsubin: A Japanese waterkettle.* Groningen, Netherlands.

Atterbury, Paul, ed. 1982. *The history of porcelain.* New York.

Beauthéac, Nadine. 1992. Tea barons. In *The book of tea,* trans. Deke Dusinberre, 57-99. Paris.

Blofeld, John. 1985. *The Chinese art of tea.* Boston.

Brochard, Gilles. 1992. Time for tea. In *The book of tea,* trans. Deke Dusinberre, 101-95. Paris.

Burwell, Letitia. 1895. *A girl's life in Virginia.* New York.

Castile, Rand. 1971. *The way of tea.* New York.

Chow, Kit, and Ione Kramer. 1990. *All the tea in China.* San Francisco.

Deetz, James. 1977. *In small things forgotten.* Garden City, N.J.

Evans, John C. 1992. *Tea in China: The history of China's national drink.* New York.

FAO (Food and Agriculture Organization of the United Nations). 1993. *FAO trade yearbook, 1992.* Rome.

Farb, Peter, and George Armelagos. 1980. *Consuming passions.* Boston.

Goodwin, Jason. 1991. *The gunpowder gardens.* New York.

Hara, Y. 1994. Prophylactic functions of tea polyphenols. In *Food phytochemicals for cancer prevention.* II. *Teas, spices, and herbs,* ed. C. T. Ho, T. Osawa, M. T. Huange, and T. R. Rosen, 34–50. Washington, D.C.

Harler, Campbell. 1963. *Tea manufacture.* Oxford.

        1964. *The culture and marketing of tea.* London.

Hayashiya, Seizo. 1979. *Chanoyu: Japanese tea ceremony.* New York.

Hobhouse, Henry. 1986. *Seeds of change.* New York.

Hudson, Charles, ed. 1979. *Black drink.* Athens, Ga.

Israel, Andrea. 1987. *Taking tea.* New York.

Kakuzo, Okakura. 1989. *The book of tea.* New York.

Kanzaki, Noritake. 1981. *Japanese teapots.* Tokyo.

Katiyar, S. K., and H. Mukhtar. 1996. Tea consumption and cancer. *World Review of Nutrition and Dietetics* 79: 154–84.

Kramer, Ione. 1994. Tea drinking and its culture. In *Handbook of Chinese popular culture,* ed. Patrick Murphy and Wu Dingbo, 55–76. London.

Lender, Mark Edward. 1987. *Drinking in America.* New York.

Levenstein, Harvey. 1988. *Revolution at the table.* New York.

Lu Yu. 1974. *The classic of tea,* trans. Francis Ross Carpenter. New York.

McGee, Harold. 1984. *On food and cooking.* New York.

Mintz, Sidney. 1985. *Sweetness and power.* New York.

Pettigrew, Jane. 1997. *The tea companion.* New York.

Post, Elizabeth. 1965. *Etiquette.* New York.

Pratt, James Norwood. 1982. *The tea lover's treasury.* San Francisco.

Root, Waverly. 1976. *Eating in America.* New York.

Roth, Rodris. 1988. Tea-drinking in eighteenth-century America: Its etiquette and equipage. In *Material life in America 1600–1860,* ed. Robert Blair St. George, 439–62. Boston.

Schafer, Charles, and Violet Schafer. 1975. *Teacraft: A treasury of romance, rituals, and recipes.* San Francisco.

Schalleck, Jamie. 1971. *Tea.* New York.

Schapira, Joel. 1982. *The book of coffee and tea: A guide to the appreciation of fine coffees, teas, and herbal beverages.* New York.

Schivelbusch, Wolfgang. 1992. *Tastes of paradise.* New York.

Sen, Soshitsu. 1979. *Chado: The Japanese way of tea.* New York.

Smith, Hedrick. 1976. *The Russians.* New York.

Stella, Alain. 1992. Tea gardens. In *The book of tea,* trans. Deke Dusinberre, 21–55. Paris.

Symposium. 1992. Physiological and pharmacological effects of *Camellia sinensis* (tea): First International Symposium. *Prev. Med.* 21: 329–91, 503–53.

Tannahill, Reay. 1988. *Food in history.* New York.

Taylor, Joe Gray. 1982. *Eating, drinking, and visiting in the South.* Baton Rouge, La.

Tropp, Barbara. 1982. *The modern art of Chinese cooking.* New York.

Tully, James. 1997. *Prisoner 1167: The madman who was Jack the Ripper.* New York.

Ukers, W. H. 1935. *All about tea.* New York.

Weisburger, John H. 1996. Tea antioxidants and health. In *Handbook of antioxidants,* ed. E. Cadenas and L. Packer, 469–86. New York.

Weisburger, John H. 1997. Tea and health: A historical perspective. *Cancer Letters* 114: 315–17.

Willson, K. C., and M. N. Clifford, eds. 1992. *Tea: Cultivation to consumption.* London.

Yamanashi, T., ed. 1991. *Proceedings, International Symposium on Tea Science.* Shizuoka, Japan.

Yang, C. S., M. J. Lee, L. Chen, and G. Y. Yang. 1997. Polyphenols as inhibitors of carcinogenesis. *Environmental Health Perspectives* 4: 971–6.

III.12 ～ Water

The ingestion of water in some form is widely recognized as essential for human life. But we usually do not consider water as food because it does not contain any of those substances we regard as nutriments. Yet if its status as a foodstuff remains ambiguous, it is far less so than it has been through much of human history. Water (or more properly "waters," for it is only in the last two centuries that it can really have been viewed as a singular substance) has been considered as food, a solvent for food, a pharmaceutical substance, a lethal substance, a characteristic physiological state, and a spiritual or quasi-spiritual entity.

This chapter raises questions about what sort of substance water has been conceived to be and what nutritional role it has been held to have. Moreover it also explores what we know of the history of the kinds of waters that were viewed as suitable to drink – with regard to their origins, the means used to determine their potability, and their preparation or purification. It also has a little to say about historical knowledge of drinking-water habits (i.e., how much water did people drink at different times and situations?) and water consumption as a means of disease transmission.

What Water Is

Modern notions of water as a compound chemical substance more or less laden with dissolved or suspended minerals, gases, microorganisms, or organic detritus have been held at best for only the last two centuries. Even earlier ideas of water as one of the four (or five) elements will mislead us, for in many such schemes elements were less fundamental substances than dynamic principles (e.g., in the case of water, the dynamic tendency is to wet things, cool them, and dissolve them) or generic labels for regular combinations of qualities. In one strand of Aristotelianism, for example, water can be understood as matter possessing the qualities of being cold and wet; thus whenever one finds those characteristics, one is coming across something more or less watery. It may even be inappropriate to think of water as wholly a natural substance; as we shall see, springs and wells (if not necessarily the water from them) often held sacred status. The primacy of water in the symbolism of many of the world's religions as a medium of dissolution and rebirth invites us to recognize water as numinous in a way that most other foodstuffs are not (Eliade 1958; Bachelard 1983).

At the very least, it is clear that through much of Western history "water" referred to a class of substances. "Waters" varied enormously both in terms of origin (rainfall, snowmelt, dew, and pond, spring, and river water were seen to be significantly different) and from place to place, just as climate and other geographical characteristics – vegetation, soil, topography – vary. Whereas for most of us the modern taxonomy of water quality includes only two classes (pure and impure), in the past subtle and complicated characterizations were nearly universal, especially with regard to water from springs, a matter that fascinated many writers. Indeed, the uniqueness of a water is a key attribute of place, and waters are linked to places in much the same way in which we now associate the characteristics of wines with their places of origin. This idea is evident in the title of the famous Hippocratic treatise "On Airs, Waters, and Places"; it is a central theme in the treatments of post-Hippocratic classical authors like Pliny the Elder and Marcus Pollio Vitruvius, and much the same sensibility seems apparent in Celtic, Teutonic, and Chinese perspectives.

Water varied from place to place in many ways, but one can generalize about the kinds of qualities that interested classical authors. Many did mention taste, and they usually held that the less taste the water had, the better. Taste, in turn, was associated with a host of other qualities that linked the immediate sensory experience of drinking a water with the effects of its continued consumption on health and constitution. Other key factors were coldness, lightness, and heaviness.

Coldness did not necessarily refer to temperature, which in any case could not be measured except subjectively and indirectly. In Chinese cosmology coldness and hotness were part of the universal system of polarities, applied to foodstuffs as well as to many other substances and activities. Water was by definition cool; steeping or cooking things in it (even boiling them) was accordingly a cooling process (Simoons 1991: 24). For the mechanical philosophers of early eighteenth-century Europe, "cold" and "hot" had become terms of chemical composition: Sulfurous water was "hot," that containing niter or alum was "cold" (Chambers 1741).

Lightness appears usually as a subjective quality akin to ease of digestibility. Pliny, in an unusual outburst of skepticism, observed that unfortunately "this lightness of water can be discovered with difficulty except by sensation, as the kinds of water differ practically nothing in weight" (Pliny 1963: book 31, chap. 21). But occasionally lightness was a parameter that could be objectively measured: Equal areas of tissue were wetted in different waters and their weights compared to determine which water was the lighter, and hence the better to drink (Lorcin 1985: 262).

The Classes of Waters

In general, desirable or undesirable properties were associated with the source of the water one obtained, and there was general agreement on the ranking of these sources. Rainwater was usually held to be the best water even though it was also regarded as the quickest to become putrid (though this in itself was not problematic, since the water might still be used after it had finished putrefying). Though some wealthy Romans made much of its virtues, water from melted snow or ice was generally viewed as harmful, possibly because it was associated with goiter, but more likely because, being deaerated, it tasted flat and led to a heaviness in the stomach (Burton 1868: 241; Vitruvius 1960: 239; Pliny 1963: book 31, chap. 21; Diderot and D'Alembert 1969; Soyer 1977: 296; Simoons 1991: 491–2).

Most deemed water from mountain streams (particularly on north-facing slopes) better than water from wells or streams in hot plains because it was held that the heat of the sun was likely to drive off the lighter or best parts of the waters (though Burton, summarizing classical authors, insisted that waters from tropical places were "frequently purer than ours in the north, more subtile [sic], thin, and lighter" [Burton 1868: 241]). Running waters are to be preferred to stagnant waters; waters stored in cisterns were undesirable because they accumulated "slime or disgusting insects" (Pliny 1963: book 31, chap. 21). But none of these generalizations obviated the need to characterize each individual source of water because, as Pliny noted, "the taste of rivers is usually variable, owing to the great difference in river beds. For waters vary with the land over which they flow and with the juices of the plants they wash" (1963: book 31, chap. 32).

Water and Health

Such descriptions clearly indicate that classical authors were much concerned with the effects of waters on health. One can understand their views in terms of a four-part scheme for classifying waters. Some waters are seen as positively beneficial to health, medicaments to be taken to cure various maladies. Others are viewed as good, "sweet" (the term has long been used to describe waters) waters, of acceptable taste and suitable for dietetic use. Still others are regarded as having undesirable qualities as a beverage. Accordingly, they are to be used sparingly, only after treatment, or with compensatory foodstuffs. Finally, authors recognize some waters as pathogenic in some sense, even lethal.

Beyond taste and health effects, waters (particularly spring waters) were characterized in terms of a host of bizarre properties they were believed to have. Pliny tells us (as does Vitruvius) of springs that turn black-wooled sheep into white-wooled sheep, that cause women to conceive, that endow those who drink of them with beautiful singing voices, that petrify whatever is dipped into them, that inebriate those who drink from them or, alternatively, make those who drink of them abstemious (Pliny 1963: book 31, chaps. 3–17). To this one might add the Levitical "bitter waters of jealousy," which possessed the property of identifying adulteresses.

Sometimes authors were explicit in attributing the properties of springs to a concept of chemical admixture: The water had the properties it had owing to what had happened to it, such as the kinds of mineral substances it had encountered underground. Yet the earth was seen as in some sense alive, and we would accordingly be unwarranted in assuming that a modern concept of solution is implied (Eliade 1978). Waters were earth's vital fluids. The Roman architect Vitruvius noted, for example:

> [T]he human body, which consists in part of the earthy, contains many kinds of juices, such as blood, milk, sweat, urine, and tears. If all this variation of flavors is found in a small portion of the earthy, we should not be surprised to find in the great earth itself countless varieties of juices, through the veins of which the water runs, and becomes saturated with them before reaching the outlets of springs. In this way, different varieties of springs or peculiar kinds are produced, on account of diversity of situation, characteristics of country, and dissimilar properties of soils." (Vitruvius 1960: 241–2)

It is probably right to see this linkage of macrocosm and microcosm as something more than analogical; such linkages would remain a part of popular understanding even after the rise of a mechanistic cosmology in the seventeenth century.

The properties of waters might also be understood as manifesting the spirits or resident divinities of springs, because many springs and rivers were thought of as home to (or the embodiment of) a divinity. Such views were held in many premodern cultures, although perhaps best known are the 30,000 nymphs associated by Hesiod with springs in Greece (their brothers were the rivers) (Hesiod 1953: 337–82; Moser 1990; Tölle-Kastenbein 1990). In many, particularly rural, places in France, Britain, Germany, and elsewhere, worship of such divinities persisted well into Christian, and even into modern times. Periodic efforts of the medieval Roman Catholic church to halt such worship usually failed and, in fact, led to the association of wells and springs as sites of miracles linked with particular saints (Hope 1893; Hofmann-Krayer and Bachtold-Stäubli 1927; Vaillat 1932; Guitard 1951; Bord and Bord 1986; Guillerme 1988).

Where water cults were restricted to specific springs, it becomes difficult to deal with questions of why springs were worshiped and what the rituals of worship signified. R. A. Wild has argued that the Nile-worshiping cult of Isis and Sarapis (important and widely distributed during the early Roman empire)

simply understood Nile water as the most perfect water; it was associated with fecundity, for humans as well as for crops, and was known as a fattening water (Wild 1981). One may speculate that in a similar sense the worship of the local water source symbolized and represented the dependence of a community on that water. Mineral springs may also have come to be worshiped for their health-giving properties; equally, a spring's reputation as sacred was an asset to a local economy and made clear to local residents that their locality had a privileged cosmic status (Hamlin 1990a; Harley 1990).

Water as Drink

Water, because it possessed such a broad range of significant and powerful properties, was thus to be used with care in a diet. In the tradition of the Hippocratic writers, authors of medical treatises on regimen had much to say about the conditions of waters and about the circumstances in which water was to be drunk. We should first note that most authors were unenthusiastic about the drinking of water. However much it might seem the natural drink of the animal kingdom, it was also viewed as having a remarkable power to disturb the stability of the human constitution. Summing up the views of classical antiquity on water as beverage, the nineteenth-century chef Alexis Soyer wrote, "water is certainly the most ancient beverage, the most simple, natural, and the most common, which nature has given to mankind. But it is necessary to be really thirsty in order to drink water, and as soon as this craving is satisfied it becomes insipid and nauseous" (Soyer 1977: 299).

The principal later medieval medical text, Avicenna's *Canon of Medicine,* for example, advised one not to drink water with a meal, but only at the meal's end, and then in small quantities. Water taken later, during digestion, would interrupt that process. One was also not to drink water while fasting, or after bathing, sex, or exercise. Nor should one give in to night thirst. To do so would disrupt digestion and would not quench the thirst for long. For Avicenna, a water's temperature was also a crucial determinant of its physiological effect. Too much cold water was harmful, whereas "tepid water evokes nausea." Warm water acted as a purgative; yet too much of it weakened the stomach (Gruner 1930: 228, 401, 407–8; Lorcin 1985). The effects of habitually imbibing certain waters could be cumulative. The Hippocratic text "On Airs, Waters, and Places," for example, held that cold waters had a detrimental effect on women's constitutions: Menstruation was impaired and made painful; breast feeding was inhibited (Hippocrates 1939: 22).

Such a sensitivity to the careful use of water within the diet is also evident in premodern Chinese writings on diet. There, too, one finds recognition of an extraordinary range of properties possessed by different waters (drips from stalactites were seen to enhance longevity) and, accordingly, great interest in classifying sources of water. In China, the preference was for warm (or boiled) water, possibly, though not necessarily, in which vegetable substances had been steeped (i.e., tea). Cold water was deemed to damage the intestines (Mote 1977: 229-30; Simoons 1991: 24, 441, 463).

Although modes of pathological explanation changed over the centuries, concern with the role of waters in regimens remained important up to the mid-nineteenth century and the onset of a medicine more oriented to specific diseases. The Enlightenment authors of the *Encyclopédie* proposed to determine, through a sort of clinical trial, the full physiological effects of water, but they noted that such a project was impossible because one could not do without water (in some form): One could detect only the differential effects of water and other drinks. (They were particularly interested in the claim that water drinking enhanced male sexual performance ["très vigoureux"]; they thought it probable that such tales reflected only the incapacitative effects of alcoholic drink, not the positive effects of water [Diderot and D'Alembert 1969: entry on "eau commune"]). Late-eighteenth-century British medical men were still stressing the emetic and diluent properties of water. Much food with much water could provoke corpulency; too much water with too little food could promote a diet deficient in nutrients, since food would move too quickly through the digestive tract. For some foods, water was not a sufficient solvent; successful digestion of meats, for example, required fermented beverages (though the alcohol in such beverages was seen as a dangerous side effect). Care was to be taken in quenching thirst, which might not simply signal too little internal moisture but instead indicate too much food or the wrong kinds of food (*Encyclopedia Britannica* 1797: entry on "drink"; *Rees Cyclopedia* 1819: entry on "diet").

In antiquity, as in the eighteenth century, the wise physician recognized that general rules like those just mentioned might need modification: One modified them according to a sophisticated explanation of the particular nutritive and other functions of water within the body (further adapted in accord with the constitution and condition of the individual who was to drink it), according to a knowledge of the particular water and the modes of preparation it had undergone. Within the body, water was understood to have a number of effects, both gastronomic and pharmaceutical, but as M. T. Lorcin has noted, in such regimen literature this distinction is inappropriate; health consists of the proper cultivation of the constitution; all ingesta contributed to this (Lorcin 1985: 268).

The chief medical functions of water were as a diluent of food and as a coolant. It acted also as a solvent of food, as an initiator of digestive and other transformations, and as a tonic (a substance that strengthened or gave tone to one's stomach and/or other fibers). It was seen also as a mild purgative (Chambers 1741).

The Treatment of Water

To augment some of the functions just mentioned and retard others, waters might be treated or purified. Some of the harmful qualities of water were understood to be susceptible to neutralization or purification. Avicenna recommended boiling as a good means of purification; he held that the mineral residue left behind contained the congealed "coldness" that was the impurity (Gruner 1930: 223). Water might also be made to pass from a container, by capillary action, along a wick of fleece; the drops falling from the end would be assumed to have been purified. Harmful qualities could also be removed by addition of vinegar or wine or by soaking in the water some substance, such as pearl barley, onions, or wax, which would absorb or counteract injurious matters.

One might also shake a suspect water with sand (a technique remarkably similar to that used by Edward Buchner to obtain bacteria-free water for the experiments that led to the concept of the enzyme). Finally, classical and medieval authors recognized the value of filtration, whether a natural filtration through soil, or an artificial filtration through wool, bread crumbs, or cloth ("in order to make sure there are no leeches or other creatures in it") (Gruner 1930: 222, 454-5; Baker 1948: 1-8; Lorcin 1985: 263). The great potency of water for good and ill, along with its considerable variability from place to place, made it crucial for travelers to be especially careful of the waters they drank: "The traveller is more exposed to illness from the diversity of drinking water than he is from the diversity of foods. . . . it is necessary to be particular about correcting the bad qualities of the drinking water, and expend every effort in purifying it" (Gruner 1930: 454).

Thus, long before there was a clear concept of waterborne disease, there was great deal of appreciation, shared by cultures in many parts of the world, of the various characters of waters and of their manifold effects on health. How assiduously people followed hygienic advice about which waters to drink and how to prepare them, and how far following such advice would have been adequate to prevent waterborne diseases is not clear, but it is clear that in cases where public waterworks existed, such as the aqueducts that supplied Rome, those in charge of their administration were supposed to be concerned, in part, with quality. It seems evident that humans have been subject to waterborne diseases throughout recorded history, and, thus, it is remarkable that there is little mention of epidemics (or even cases) of waterborne diseases prior to the nineteenth century (but see Ackerknecht 1965: 24, 41-2, 47, 134-6; Janssens 1983; Jannetta 1987: 148-9; Grmek 1989: 15-6, 346-50).

One might attribute this lack of waterborne epidemics to relatively low population density or a magnitude of travel that was usually too low to sustain outbreaks of diseases caused by relatively fragile bacteria. In this connection, it is notable that many of the records do deal with diseases that we might now attribute to the hardier parasites. Yet it is surely also the case that a population, aware of the dangers of water and possessing an impressive armamentarium of techniques for improving that water, did much to prevent waterborne disease outbreaks. Even if one does not see the Chinese preference for warmed (ideally boiled) water as representing hygienic consciousness, it surely was beneficial in relatively heavily populated areas where paddy cultivation, with night soil as fertilizer, was customarily practiced (but see Needham: 1970). In other cases, as in the addition of wine to water in early modern France, the action was explicitly a purification, with greater or lesser amounts of wine added according to the estimated degree of impurity of the water (Roche 1984).

The Reclassification of Water

Most clearly for Pliny, but also for many classical, medieval, and early modern authors, "waters" were "marvels," each unique, whether owing to the mix of natural agency to which it had been exposed or to its intrinsically marvelous character (Pliny 1963: book 31, chap. 18). By the seventeenth century, European writers on waters had come to emphasize a binary classification: Water was either common (more or less potable) water or mineral water. "Mineral waters" was the collective term for the remarkable springs Pliny had described. Less and less did they represent the mark of the "hand of providence" on a particular locale; increasingly their properties were understood in terms of the salts or gases dissolved in them (Brockliss 1990; Hamlin 1990a, 1990b; Harley 1990; Palmer 1990).

Far from being unique, any mineral spring could be understood as belonging to one of a few general types. These included chalybeate, or iron-bearing waters, drunk to treat anemia; sulfurous waters, good for skin problems; acidulous waters, full of carbonic and other acids that gave the stomach a lightness; and saline waters, which served usually as purgatives. A good many springs, with a wide variety of constituents (and a few with no unusual chemical constituents at all), were also held to be cures for infertility and other diseases of women (Cayleff 1987).

Springs varied in temperature, which might or might not be significant. That waters in some springs were to be bathed in and that waters from others were to be taken internally was a less formidable distinction than it seems to us now. Bathing was not simply a treatment of the skin; the water (or its essential qualities) was understood to be able to enter the body through the skin or to be able to cause significant internal effect in some other way. Some therapeutic regimens, such as hydropathy, popular among educated Americans and Europeans in the mid-nineteenth century, integrated a wide variety of external and internal applications of water to produce improvements in health, which clients (like Charles Darwin) regarded as dramatic indeed (Donegan 1986; Cayleff 1987; Vigarello 1988; Brockliss 1990; Browne 1990).

The characterization of springs in terms of chemical constituents was not so much a consequence of the maturation of chemical science as one of the sources of that maturation. Such characterizations were necessary for the proprietors of mineral springs to compete in a medical marketplace. People from the rising middle classes, who increasingly patronized mineral waters, were no more willing to trust in miracles in taking the waters than in any other aspect of business. Every spring had its testimonials, miracles, and claims of excellent accommodations and exalted society for its visitors. Thus, the chemical composition of a spring seemed the only reliable means to make a decision on whether one might patronize a lesser-known resort nearby or whether one undertook a lengthy journey (Guitard 1951; Hamlin 1990b; but see Brockliss 1990). Chemistry also provided a means of bringing the spa to the patient through medicinal waters, which could be bottled for widespread distribution (Kirkby 1902; Coley 1984). Following the discovery of the means to manufacture carbonated water by Joseph Priestly and Torbern Bergman, such enterprise gave rise to the soft-drink industry (Boklund 1956).

One effect, of course, of making water part of the domain of chemistry was to reduce "waters" to a mixture of a simple substrate, "water" (whose composition as a compound of hydrogen and oxygen had been recognized by the end of the eighteenth century) with various amounts of other chemical substances. This conceptual transformation was not achieved without resistance, particularly from physicians (often with practices associated with particular springs), who saw their art threatened by the reductionism of chemistry and continued to maintain that each spring had a peculiar "life" that no chemist could imitate and whose benefits could only be obtained if its waters were drunk on-site (Hamlin 1990a, 1990b).

If, in the light of the new chemistry, mineral waters were no more than mixtures of simple substances, common water was even simpler and less interesting. To medical men and to chemists, this *eau commune* was to be evaluated as belonging to one of two mutually exclusive categories: It was either "pure" or "impure." The terms did not refer to the ideal of chemical purity, which was recognized as practically unattainable; they were simply used to indicate whether the water was suitable or unsuitable for general domestic use (including direct consumption).

At the beginning of the nineteenth century, the

chemists' chief conception of impurity in water was hardness, the presence of dissolved mineral earths. Initially, this new focus supplemented, rather than replaced, the sophisticated classical taxonomy of waters (no one championed soft water that was obviously foul), and the quantification of hardness (expressed as degrees of hardness) was simply a valuable service that chemists could (easily) provide. Hardness was an industrially significant distinction; for steam engine boilers and for brewing, tanning, and many textile processes, the hardness of water was the key criterion. It seemed a medically significant criterion, too: Just like the steam boiler, the drinker of hard water could clog up with bladder stones or gout, conditions that attained remarkable prominence in medical practice, at least in eighteenth-century England (*British Cyclopedia* 1835: s.v. "water"; Hamlin 1990b).

Waters in the Industrial World

The nineteenth century saw great changes in views of drinkable water and equally great changes in predominant notions of who was competent to judge water quality. Despite the chemists' infatuation with hardness, traditional senses-based approaches to judging water still prevailed in Europe at the beginning of the century. In choosing waters, ordinary people continued to be guided by tradition, taste, and immediate physiological effects. In many cases the standards they used were those found in the classical literature: Stagnant, "foul" water was to be avoided, clear, light, "bright" water was to be desired.

After midcentury, however, expert definitions prevailed. Often experts would insist that water that looked, smelled, and tasted good, and that had perhaps been long used by a local population, was actually bad. Indeed, in some situations, experts' standards were virtually the opposite of lay standards. Light, sharp water had those qualities because it contained dissolved nitrates, which, in turn, were decomposition products from leaking cesspools. The best-tasting well water might, thus, be the most dangerously contaminated (Hardy 1991: 80–1). Less often, experts would insist that waters that laypeople found objectionable (perhaps because they had a strong taste of peat or iron) were wholly harmless.

No longer were chemists restricting themselves to determinations of hardness. Even though the techniques at their disposal did not change significantly (hardness and other forms of mineral content remained the only characteristics they could determine with reasonable effectiveness), chemists increasingly were claiming that they had defined and had the means to quantify what was objectionable in a water beyond its dissolved minerals. They could, they insisted, measure those qualities that had been the basis of the classical water taxonomy better than these qualities could be detected by the senses.

The key quality that interested them, and which at first supplemented and then displaced concern with hardness or softness, was putridity. "Putridity," while a vague concept, had been the centerpiece of an approach to evaluating water based on one's subjective repugnance to it – owing to its odor, appearance, taste, and associations (the German word *Fäulnis* better embodies such a combination of the visceral and technical). Chemists replaced the senses-based definition of putridity with more arcane indicators of putridity or potential putridity. For much of the nineteenth century, however, they were not in agreement about what precisely these arcane indicators were or the best ways to measure them. Some felt it sufficient to determine the quantity of "organic matter," even though they admitted that this parameter was in some sense an artifact of analytical instrumentation.

Such an approach was contrary to the belief that it was some unknown qualitative factor of organic matter (and not such matter itself) that was associated with putridity and disease. In any case, "foulness" or "putridity" ceased to be a physical state of water and instead became an expert's concept indicating an amount or a presumed condition of "organic" matter. This determination, in turn, was usually believed to correspond to a presumed fecal contamination. Henceforth, the repugnance that "putrid" or "foul" conjured up was to operate through the imagination, rather than directly through the senses.

The champion of this novel perspective was the English chemist Edward Frankland, the leading international authority on water analysis in the 1870s and 1880s. Frankland took the view that it was foolish to try to detect quantities of some unknown disease-generating agency. It was much better simply to try to discover whether water had been subject to contamination in its course through or over the ground. The possibility of dangerous contamination was sufficient reason for public authorities to avoid such supplies of water, and the idea of contamination was to be sufficient to compel ordinary people to avoid its use (Hamlin 1990b).

The shift in approaches to the assessment of water that Frankland exemplifies is a far-reaching one. Associating what might be wrong in water with the presumed commission at some time past of an act of contamination made the religious term "pollution" in its traditional sense of desecration the primary construct for a discussion of water quality, and it came to replace "foul" and "putrid" (Douglas 1966). A presumed act done to the water thus replaced a manifest condition of the water. Although laypersons had known whether water was "foul" at one time, it was up to experts to say whether water had been "polluted." Consequently, water became (and remains) one of very few "foods" whose most important qualities were defined wholly by experts, and whose consumption, accordingly, marked complete trust of the individual in some outside institution: a government, a bottled-water company, or the maker of a filter.

There were, of course, good reasons for such a transformation, and underwriting it was the fear of waterborne (or water-generated) disease. That dense urban environments were dangerous to health was a long-standing medical truth, and water was implicated in this danger: Standing surface water, particularly in marshes, was believed to interact in some way with town filth to generate both fever (particularly malaria) and chronic debilitation. Although consumption of water was not the focus of concern, there was medical consensus that drinking such stuff could not be beneficial to health. Yet at the beginning of the nineteenth century, the doctors were unable to say much about how and in what ways such water was bad, or how it became bad, or how serious a problem bad water might be. Some held that water became harmful by absorbing harmful elements from a filthy urban atmosphere and was simply another means of communicating that state of air. Keeping the water covered would keep it pure, they believed. (Others thought that the putridity was inherent in the water itself and infected the atmosphere.)

Whatever the mechanism, the increasing frequency of epidemic disease was evident in the newly industrialized cities of the nineteenth century. They were swept repeatedly by waves of Asiatic cholera, as well as typhoid fever (only clinically distinguished from other forms of continued fever in the 1840s), and other enteric infections (less clearly identified but no less deadly) (Ackerknecht 1965; Luckin 1984, 1986).

Not until after 1850 were these diseases commonly associated with fecally contaminated water, and even that recognition did not provide unambiguous guidelines for determining water quality because such contaminated water sources only rarely caused severe outbreaks of disease. One might assume that they did so only when contaminated with some specific substance, but as that substance was unknown, it could not be measured, nor was there a clear correlation between the quantity of contamination and the amount of disease. Water that was evidently transmitting cholera was, according to the most sophisticated chemical measures available, substantially purer than water that evidently caused no harm. Some, like Frankland, held that any water that had ever been subject to such contamination should be avoided, but in heavily populated areas, where rivers were essential sources of water, this recommendationn seemed impracticable.

Although these contradictions demonstrated the inadequacy of the lay determinations of water quality, the techniques of the experts were little better prior to the twentieth century. Nonetheless, in the nineteenth century, judging waters became a consummately expert task, so much so that the European colony in Shanghai felt it necessary to send water samples all the way to London to be analyzed by Frankland (MacPherson 1987: 85). And even after the microbes responsible for cholera and typhoid were identified in the 1880s and means were developed for their detection, many experts remained skeptical, unwilling to accept negative findings of their analyses (Hamlin 1990b). But by the early twentieth century, the institution of chlorination, more carefully monitored filtering, and a better understanding of the microbe-removing actions of filters finally led to a widely shared confidence in the safety of urban water supplies (Baker 1948). Such confidence, however, appears to have peaked, and is now in decline.

Town Supplies – Water for All

The fact that cities and towns throughout the world recognize the provision to dwelling houses of piped-in, potable water as an essential component in achieving an acceptable standard of living is remarkable indeed. It involves, in fact, two kinds of public decisions: first, a recognition of a need for a supply of water to be readily available to all settled areas, and second, a recognition of a need for a supply of water to be piped into each dwelling unit.

We usually associate both these features (household water supplies from a public waterworks) as exemplifying the organizational genius of Imperial Rome and lament that it was only in the nineteenth century that authorities, guided by new knowledge of disease transmission and new standards of public decency, again acknowledged water supply as a public duty. Yet a "hydraulic consciousness" was well developed in many medieval and early modern European towns (as well as existing far beyond the Roman empire in the ancient world) (Burton 1868: 241). This consciousness manifested itself in the building of public fountains and pumps, the diversion of brooks for water supply, and even the use of public cisterns and filters, as in Venice. All of these means were used to supply water for industrial purposes, for town cleansing, and for the fighting of fires, as well as for domestic use, but it would appear that the piping of water into individual homes was not felt to be important (Baker 1948: 11–17; Guillerme 1988; Vogel 1988; Dienes and Prutsch 1990; Grewe 1991). High-volume domestic uses of water did not exist; water closets would not become popular until the nineteenth century; bathing was, at least in early modern France, seen to be dangerous to health; and clothing (other than linen) was rarely washed (Vigarello 1988).

By no means was the provision of good drinking water atop this list, but that it was on the list at all is remarkable. How much water people drank, when and where they got it, how public authorities assessed the need for drinkable water and understood their role in supplying it are all questions about which far too little is known. Summarizing pre-nineteenth-century sources, M. N. Baker presented evidence to suggest that urban dwellers did not expect to find raw water drinkable and that knowledge of effective means for treating waters was widespread.

These means ranged from simply allowing sediment in water to settle and then decanting the water to the addition of purifiers (vinegar or wine) or coagulants (alum), or to drinking water only in boiled forms, like tea (Baker 1948: 24–5). The excessive consumption of alcohol was also seen by nineteenth-century temperance advocates as a public response to the unavailability, particularly in poor neighborhoods, of drinkable water (Chadwick 1965: 135–50). It was probably a prudent response: Beer, in particular, was cheap, usually made with a higher-quality water than that readily available, and often more accessible to the poor than water. In Britain it was drunk in hospitals and schools, not just in taverns (Harrison 1971: 37–8, 298–9).

Temperance advocates were often among the champions of public water supplies. But other kinds of reformers became involved, too, sometimes for curious reasons. Those concerned with the morals of the poor worried that a central pump or well was often a locus for the spread of immorality. Children, waiting to fill water containers (sometimes for several hours, if the sources are to be believed), were exposed to bad language, immoral activity, and dangerous ideas. An in-house supply of water could prevent all that. A public drinking fountain movement, begun in Britain in the late 1850s (initially supported by brewers and, surprisingly, not by temperance advocates), received critical support from the Royal Society for the Prevention of Cruelty to Animals, which was concerned about thirsty animals ridden or driven into towns that lacked facilities for watering animals (Davies 1989: 19).

In the century from 1840 to 1940, in almost all of the industrialized world, a public responsibility for providing town dwellers with in-home water was recognized. The timing and circumstances of that recognition varied from society to society (and, significantly, sometimes from town to town), with "public health" considerations usually providing the warrant for that recognition. Adequate sanitary provisions came to include the provision of a water closet in some form and a continuous supply of water that could be drunk without treatment. Whatever its merit on epidemiological grounds, this notion of sanitary adequacy represented the successful promulgation of an ideology of cleanliness and decency that was quite new, and in this transition the status of water changed. No longer was it an aliment whose quality one judged independently for oneself, nor was it something one had to hunt for and sometimes secure only after much labor (Chadwick 1965: 141–2). Instead it was (or was supposed to be) truly a "necessity" of life, something easily and immediately available, nearly as available (and often almost as cheap) as breathable air.

Although the image of water as a public good essential for meeting universal standards of health and decency usually supplied the rationale for undertaking water-supply projects, the ulterior motives of private interests were often more important in actually getting waterworks built. Perhaps the most significant of these private interests were industrial users. Many industries required large quantities of relatively high-quality water, and the capital costs of obtaining such supplies were prohibitive for individual firms. Consequently, they sought to obtain those supplies (sometimes at subsidized prices) through the sanitary betterment of society. In port cities with much warehouse space, the threat of fire was another underlying incentive for a public water supply.

Some towns took early action to secure control of important watersheds, either with the expectation of profitably selling water to their neighbors or of acquiring commercial advantage. Investors found waterworks projects attractive for a number of reasons, among them a steady dividend, or the possibility of selling land or shares at inflated prices. New York's first waterworks project attracted speculators because it functioned as a nonchartered and hence unofficial, bank. Some of the capital raised was used to build a waterworks; the rest went into the general capital market (Blake 1956). It need hardly be said that contractors, plumbers, and lawyers were delighted to support waterworks projects. Water is not usually viewed as an article of commerce in the way that most foods are, yet once it had been defined as a public necessity, there was plenty of money to be made from it (Blake 1956; Hassan 1985; Brown 1988; Goubert 1989).

Although this transformation in the availability of water made water drinking much more convenient, the resultant technologies were by no means regarded as an unmitigated benefit. Networks of water mains (and sewer lines) linked people physically across classes and neighborhoods in ways that they had resisted being linked and sometimes in ways that proved hazardous. A common complaint about sewer systems was that they spread disease rather than prevented it because sewer gas frequently rose through poorly trapped drains into houses. It was believed that one was exposed to any infection that the occupants of any other dwelling on the sewer line permitted to go down the drain. More serious, from the perspective of modern epidemiology, was the potential of water mains to distribute infection – precisely what took place in the 1892 Hamburg cholera epidemic (Luckin 1984, 1986; Evans 1987).

Yet for most of the twentieth century, events like the 1892 outbreak of cholera in Hamburg have been rare in the industrialized world. When properly maintained and supervised, the water networks work well. By the end of the nineteenth century, water engineers, finally possessing the torch of bacteriological analysis to illuminate their work, made the filtering of water a dependable operation, even when the water was heavily contaminated. In the first two decades of the twentieth century, they acquired an even more powerful technique in chlorination. Initially used only when source waters were especially bad or in other unusual circumstances, chlorination quickly became a standard form of water treatment. Even if it was almost always unnecessary, and merely supplementary to other modes of purification, chlorination provided a measure of confidence. That it interfered with (ruined, many might say) the taste of water was no longer of much importance (Baker 1948: 321-56; Hamlin 1990b; O'Toole 1990). Thus, the concept of water as a substance that was necessary to ingest occasionally (even if it was potentially a mode of disease transmission) had, in much of the modern world, very nearly displaced the older concept of "waters" as unique substances, varying from place to place, some of them downright harmful, others with nearly miraculous healthful qualities.

Water in the Present

In recent years, there have been signs that a further transformation of the status and concept of water is under way. In the United States, the authorities responsible for supplying drinkable water are no longer as trusted as they once were (in many parts of the world, of course, such authorities have never known that degree of trust). In some cases that loss of trust reflects a real inability to maintain standards of water quality. But it also reflects public concern about new kinds of contaminants, such as toxic organic chemicals, viruses, and giardia (McCleary 1990; Hurst 1991). In some cases the effects of these contaminants may only be manifest after many years and only through use of the most sophisticated epidemiological techniques (Hand 1988). Nor are customary methods of water analysis or approaches to water purification yet well adapted to such contaminants.

The response of the public has been to revert to a technology, the home water filter (or other water purification devices), that had been popular in the nineteenth century before water authorities were trusted. For some, drinking water has again become a commodity that we think we must go out of our way to secure; something that we haul home in heavy fat bottles from the supermarket. Yet these responses are not adequate to the problem of trustworthiness. The capabilities of domestic water purification devices vary enormously, as does the quality of the product sold by the bottled-water industry and the degree of inspection it receives (Fit to Drink? 1990). Indeed, these responses say less about our need for water we can trust than they do about the institutions we trust.

The rise of the elite bottled mineral waters industry is a reversion too. Pliny tells us that the kings of Persia carried bottled water taken from the River Choaspis with them (Burton 1868: 242); Herodotus and Plutarch referred to an export trade in bottled Nile water – some of it used by devotees of the cult of Isis and Osiris (Wild 1981: 91-4). Such trade was still widespread in the seventeenth and eighteenth centuries. Then, as now, quality control was a problem and customers complained about the excessive price (Kirkby 1902; Boklund 1956; Coley 1984).

The revival of this industry makes it easier for us to appreciate the fine distinctions among waters made by Pliny, Vitruvius, and the medieval and early modern therapists of the regimen. Modern elites have agreed with their predecessors that the taste (can one say bouquet?) of a water really is important, and that through the drinking of fine waters one can cultivate one's health in ways far more delicate than simply keeping one's insides moist and avoiding cholera.

Christopher Hamlin

Bibliography

Ackerknecht, E. 1965. *History and geography of the most important diseases.* New York.

Bachelard, G. 1983. *Water and dreams: An essay on the imagination of matter,* trans. E. Farrell. Dallas, Tex.

Baker, M. N. 1948. *The quest for pure water: The history of water purification from the earliest records to the twentieth century.* New York.

Blake, N. 1956. *Water for the cities: A history of the urban water supply problem in the United States.* Syracuse, N.Y.

Boklund, U. 1956. Tobern Bergman as pioneer in the domain of mineral waters. In *On the Acid of Air,* ed. T. Bergman, 105-28. Stockholm.

Bord, J., and C. Bord. 1986. *Sacred waters: Holy wells and water lore in Britain and Ireland.* London.

Brockliss, L. W. B. 1990. The development of the spa in seventeenth-century France. In *The medical history of waters and spas,* ed. R. Porter, 23-47. Medical History, Supplement, 10. London.

Broughman, J. 1991. The pure truth. *Health* February: 44-6, 57, 102.

Brown, John C. 1988. Coping with crisis? The diffusion of waterworks in late nineteenth-century German towns. *Economic History* 48: 307-18.

Browne, J. 1990. Spas and sensibilities: Darwin at Malvern. In *The medical history of waters and spas,* ed. R. Porter, 102-113. Medical History, Supplement, 10. London.

Burton, R. 1868. *The anatomy of melancholy.* Eighth edition. Philadelphia, Pa.

Cayleff, S. E. 1987. *Wash and be healed: The water-cure movement and women's health.* Philadelphia, Pa.

Chadwick, E. 1965. *Report on the sanitary condition of the labouring population of Great Britain,* edited with an introduction by M. W. Flinn. Edinburgh.

Chambers, E. 1741. *Cyclopedia or universal dictionary of arts and sciences.* Fourth edition. London.

Coley, N. 1984. Preparation and uses of artificial mineral waters (ca. 1680-1825). *Ambix* 31: 32-48.

Davies, P. 1989. *Troughs and drinking fountains: Fountains of life.* London.

Diderot, D., and D. D'Alembert. 1969. *Encyclopédie ou dictionaire raisonné des sciences, des arts, et des métiers par une société des gens des lettres.* Elmsford, N.Y.

Dienes, G. P., and U. Prutsch. 1990. Zur Trinkwasserversorgung von Graz. *Wasser: Ein Versuch,* ed. G. Dienes and F. Leitgeb, 87-90. Graz.

Donegan, J. 1986. *"Hydropathic highway to health": Women and water-cure in antebellum America.* Westport, Conn.

Douglas, M. 1966. *Purity and danger: An analysis of the concepts of pollution and taboo.* London.

Eliade, M. 1958. *Patterns in comparative religion,* trans. Rosemarry Snead. New York.

   1978. *The forge and the crucible: The origins and structures of alchemy.* Second edition. Chicago.

Encyclopedia Britannica. 1797. Edinburgh.

Evans, R. J. 1987. *Death in Hamburg: Society and politics in the cholera years, 1830-1910.* New York.

Fit to drink? 1990. *Consumer Reports,* 27-36.

Goubert, J.-P. 1989. *The conquest of water: The advent of health in the industrial age,* trans. Andrew Wilson. London.

Grabner, E. 1990. Wasser in der Volksmedizin. *Wasser: Ein Versuch,* ed. G. Dienes and F. Leitgeb, 237-41. Graz.

Grewe, K. 1991. Wasserversorgung und -entsorgung im Mittelalter - Ein technikgeschichtlicher Überblick. *Die Wasserversorgung im Mittelalter,* 9-86. Geschichte der Wasserversorgung, 4. Mainz am Rhein.

Grmek, M. 1989. *Diseases in the ancient world.* Baltimore.

Gruner, O. C. 1930. *A treatise on the canon of medicine of Avicenna incorporating a translation of the first book.* London.

Guillerme, A. E. 1988. *The age of water: The urban environment in the north of France, A.D. 300-1800.* College Station, Tex.

Guitard, E. H. 1951. *Le prestigeux passé des eaux minérales.* Paris.

Hamlin, C. 1990a. Chemistry, medicine, and the legitimization of English spas, 1740-1840. In *The medical history of waters and spas,* ed. R. Porter, 67-81. Medical History, Supplement, 10. London.

   1990b. *A science of impurity: Water analysis in nineteenth century Britain.* Berkeley, Calif.

Hand, D. 1988. Poisoned water: The long struggle to be heard. *America's Health* May: 48-53.

Hardy, A. 1991. Parish pump to private pipes: London's water supply in the nineteenth century. In *Living and dying in London,* ed. W. F. Bynum and R. Porter, 76-93. Medical History, Supplement, 11. London.

Harley, D. 1990. A sword in a madman's hand: Professional opposition to popular consumption in the waters literature of southern England and the midlands, 1570-1870. In *The medical history of waters and spas,* ed. R. Porter, 48-55. Medical History, Supplement, 10. London.

Harrison, B. 1971. *Drink and the Victorians: The temperance question in England, 1815-1872.* Pittsburgh, Pa.

Hassan, J. A. 1985. The growth and impact of the British water industry in the nineteenth century. *Economic History Review* 38: 531-47.

Hesiod. 1953. *Hesiod's theogony,* trans. Norman O. Brown. New York. Hippocrates. 1939. On airs, waters, and places. In *The genuine works of Hippocrates,* trans. F. Adams. Baltimore, Md.

Hofmann-Krayer, E., and H. Bachtold-Stäubli, eds. 1927. Brunnen. In *Handwörterbuch des deustchen Aberglaubens.* Berlin.

Hope, R. C. 1893. *The legendary lore of the holy wells of England: Including rivers, lakes, fountains, and springs.* London.

Hurst, C. J. 1991. Presence of enteric viruses in freshwater and their removal by the conventional drinking water treatment process. *Bulletin of the World Health Organization* 69 (1): 113-19.

Jannetta, A. 1987. *Epidemics and mortality in early modern Japan.* Princeton, N.J.

Janssens, P. A. 1983. The *morbus desentericus* in the *historia francorum* of Gregory of Tours (sixth century). *Disease in ancient man: An international symposium,* ed. G. Hart, 263-6. Toronto.

Kirkby, W. 1902. *The evolution of artificial mineral waters.* Manchester, England.

Lorcin, M. T. 1985. Humeurs, bains, et tisaines: L'eau dan médecine médiévale. *L'Eau au Moyen Age,* 259-73. Publications du Cuer Ma, Université de Provence. Marseille.

Luckin, B. 1984. Evaluating the sanitary revolution: Typhus and typhoid in London, 1851-1900. *Urban disease and mortality in nineteenth-century England,* ed. R. Woods and J. Woodward, 102-19. New York.

   1986. *Pollution and control: A social history of the Thames in the nineteenth century.* Bristol, England.

MacPherson, K. 1987. *A wilderness of marshes: The origins of public health in Shanghai, 1843-1893.* Hong Kong.

McCleary, K. 1990. Trouble from your tap. *Health* May: 32-3, 76.

Moser, H. 1990. Brunnen, Bründl und Quellen: Eine volkskundliche Betrachtung. In *Wasser: Ein Versuch,* ed. G. Dienes and F. Leitgeb, 234-6. Graz.

Mote, F. 1977. Yuan and Ming. *Food in Chinese culture: Anthropological and historical perspectives,* ed. K. C. Chang. New Haven, Conn.

Needham, J. and L. 1970. Hygiene and preventive medicine in ancient China. In *Clerks and craftsmen in China and the west,* ed. J. Needham, 340-78. Cambridge.

O'Toole, C. K. 1990. *The search for purity: A retrospective policy analysis of the decision to chlorinate Cincinnati's public water supply, 1890-1920.* New York.

Palmer, R. 1990. "In this our lightye and learned tyme": Italian baths in the era of the Renaissance. In *The medical history of waters and spas,* ed. R. Porter, 14-22. Medical History, Supplement, 10. London.

Partington, Charles, ed. 1835. *British cyclopaedia of the arts and sciences,* 885-95. London.

Paulus Aegineta. 1844. *The seven books of Paulus Aegineta with a commentary,* trans. F. Adams. London.

Pliny. 1963. *Natural history with an English translation in ten volumes,* trans. W. H. S. Jones. Cambridge, Mass.

Rees, Abraham. 1820. *The cyclopedia; or Universal dictionary of arts, sciences, and literature.* London.

Roche, D. 1984. *Le temps de l'eau rare: Du moyen age à l'époque moderne.* Annales E.S.C. 39: 383-99.

Simoons, F. J. 1991. *Food in China: A cultural and historical inquiry.* Boca Raton, Fla.

Soyer, A. 1977. *The pantropheon or a history of food and its preparation in ancient times.* New York.

Taylor, J. G. 1982. *Eating, drinking, and visiting in the south: An informal history.* Baton Rouge, La.

Tölle-Kastenbein, R. 1990. *Antike Wasserkultur.* Munich.

Tuan, Y. F. 1968. *The hydrologic cycle and the wisdom of god: A theme in geoteleology.* Toronto.

Vaillat, C. 1932. *Le culte des sources dans la gaule antique.* Paris.

Vigarello, G. 1988. *Concepts of cleanliness: Changing attitudes in France since the Middle Ages,* trans. J. Birrell. Cambridge, New York, and Paris.

Vitruvius Pollio, Marcus. 1960. *The ten books on architecture,* trans. M. H. Morgan. New York.

Vogel, H. 1988. Brunnen und Pumpereien in der Stadt Bremen. *Wasser. Zur Geschichte der Trinkwasserver-*

sorgung in Bremen. Ausstellungskatalog Bremer Landesmuseum für Kunst – und Kulturgeschichte, 50-67. Bremen.

Wild, R. A. 1981. *Water in the cultic worship of Isis and Sarapis.* Leiden, Netherlands.

III.13 ❧ Wine

Wine is the fermented juice (must) of grapes, and for thousands of years humans have been attempting to perfect a process that occurs naturally. As summer turns into fall, grapes swell in size. Many will eventually burst, allowing the sugars in the juice to come into contact with the yeasts growing on the skins. This interaction produces carbon dioxide, which is dissipated, and a liquid containing alcohol (ethanol) in combination with a plethora of organic compounds related to aroma and taste that have yet to be fully enumerated. Many people have found drinking this liquid so highly desirable that they have been willing to expend enormous effort to find ways of improving its quantity and quality.

In some places both viticulture (grape growing) and viniculture (wine making) emerged as specialized crafts, which today have achieved the status of sciences within the field known as enology. In general, three basic types of wine are produced: (1) still or table wines with alcohol contents in the 7 to 13 percent range; (2) sparkling wines from a secondary fermentation where the carbon dioxide is deliberately trapped in the liquid; and (3) fortified wines whereby spirits are added to still wines in order to boost their alcohol contents into the 20 percent range.

Vine Geography

Grape-bearing vines for making wine belong to the genus *Vitis,* a member of the family Ampelidaceae. Vines ancestral to *Vitis* have been found in Tertiary sediments dating back some 60 million years, and by the beginning of the Pleistocene, evolution had produced two subgenuses – *Euvitis* and *Muscadiniae.* Both were distributed across the midlatitude portions of North America and Eurasia. Glaciation, however, exterminated the Muscadines with the exception of an area extending around the Gulf of Mexico and into the southeastern United States, where one species, *Vitis rotundifolia,* has been used to make sweet wines that go by the regional name of scuppernong.

The distribution of wild *Euvitis* in North America was concentrated east of the Rocky Mountains. In excess of 30 species have been identified, with *Vitis labrusca* being by far the most important in terms of wine making. Its genes are found in all the major grape cultivars such as the Concord, Niagara, Catawba, Dutchess, Delaware, and Elvira. Other species that

have made some significant contributions include *Vitis riparia, Vitis aestivalis,* and *Vitis bourquiniana.*

Across Eurasia, the geography of *Euvitis* reflects the cultural importance of wine. From southwestern Asia through Europe one species, *Vitis vinifera,* dominates, but from central Asia to Japan and Southeast Asia, where drinking wine made from grapes is not a traditional practice, a number of species still can be found. The wine-making superiority of *V. vinifera* undoubtedly led to its replacing competing species. It achieves a balance between sugars and acids that is unmatched by any of the others, and it evolved with human assistance into a self-propagating hermaphrodite capable of producing a virtually unlimited number of cultivars possessed of different colors, aromas, and taste characteristics. Some of the better known of these include Cabernet Sauvignon, Pinot Noir, Chardonnay, Riesling, Syrah, and Nebbiolo, but there are many hundreds of others, most with highly localized distributions.

In the late nineteenth century, French scientists began systematically to hybridize *vinifera* with *labrusca* and other native American vines. Their efforts were aimed at producing varieties that were more disease resistant (ones that could, in particular, resist the two scourges of phylloxera and oidium) and were better able to withstand winter cold. Often called French–American hybrids, they were planted in many parts of Europe during the early twentieth century, but currently most of the vines are being uprooted because of dissatisfaction over their wine-making capabilities. In the eastern United States and Ontario, Canada, however, the hybrids have become increasingly important, and research continues into developing new varieties.

During the last 500 years, humans have carried *Euvitis* to areas outside its natural range. It is now found growing in the tropics, as well as in the midlatitude portions of Chile, Argentina, South Africa, Australia, and New Zealand, where wine making has achieved considerable prominence. Virtually all of the vineyards are planted with *V. vinifera.*

Early History

The earliest archaeological evidence indicating wine that might have been made from domesticated vines comes from a pottery jar, dated to between 7400 and 7000 years ago, which was found at the Neolithic site of Hajji Firuz in the northern Zagros Mountains. Whether this is wine's precise hearth remains for future research to determine. But the general area from the Zagros to the Caucasus Mountains is a reasonable possibility – it lies within the natural range of *V. vinifera* and it is included within the broader Southwest Asian region of plant and animal domestication. From here, wine seems to have diffused in two directions.

One was into Assyria and thence to the Mesopotamian city states of Kish, Ur, and later Babylon, among which it attained the status of a luxury drink meant for priestly and noble classes. The hot, dry, and saline soil conditions of Mesopotamia were not well suited for growing grapes, and thus most of its wines probably were imported from the north.

As with many other facets of culture, wine seems to have entered Egypt from Mesopotamian sources. Vines were established along the Nile by at least 5000 years ago, and during New Kingdom times a highly sophisticated technology of wine growing was in place, including an appreciation of vintages and aging. Wine growing followed the Nile upstream to Nubia, where it persisted until Islam's hegemony over the area was established early in the second millennium A.D.

By 3000 years ago, wine drinking had become widespread in southwestern Asia. It was found among the Canaanites and the closely related Phoenicians, and wine consumption became customary among the Hebrews, who seem to have employed it as a ceremonial drink that was taken in moderation by everyone in the community. Elsewhere, the evidence indicates that wine continued to be restricted to those at the top of the socioeconomic ladder and that it was appreciated largely for the intoxicating effects of its alcohol. Intoxication, indeed, was undoubtedly the reason why almost from its inception wine and religion were bound closely together – wine served as a medium for contacting the gods.

The second route carried wine across Anatolia to the shores and islands of the Aegean. It was adopted by the Minoan civilization on Crete and in Mycenaea, where its production became a specialization of some islands and an important item of commerce. Most significant for later developments, wine became a part of Greek culture, and wherever the Greeks planted their colonies in the Mediterranean, wine drinking, wine growing, and wine commerce followed. Sicily and southern Italy became especially prominent and were given the name Oenotria, the land of vines. Another important site was Massilia (Marseilles), from where the Greek method of wine growing spread inland following the Rhone River valley.

Wine became even more popular because of the cult of the Greek god Dionysus (Bacchus to the Romans). Originating as a minor fertility symbol among the Anatolians, he was transformed into a complex figure representing wine in the context of religious and political protest. These protests often took the form of ecstatic revelries, aided by drunkenness, that were intentionally designed to violate prevailing behavioral norms. The cults spread widely throughout the Mediterranean world and apparently were highly instrumental in creating a greater demand for wine among the populace at large.

The Roman Factor

The Romans are usually credited with having contributed more to the advance of wine than any other people. In fact, they probably were not wine drinkers, or at least not wine growers, when they first embarked on their expansion, but instead acquired the habit from the Etruscans, a people derived either from Minoan or Mycenaean migrants who settled in central Italy. But there is little doubt that wine growing flourished under Roman influence. It was established virtually everywhere on the Italian peninsula, both on large noble-owned estates and as a part of peasant farming systems.

Wine also expanded with the empire. A nearby source of supply was needed for garrisons and administrators, and within Rome itself there was a continuous demand for new wines among the upper classes. Although archaeological evidence indicates that some of the Celtic, Iber, Germanic, and Slavic peoples knew how to make wine, they appear to have been largely beer or mead drinkers. Wherever the Romans imposed their rule, however, fundamental changes in wine's regional significance followed. The Romans not only brought with them a wine-drinking tradition that was copied by others but also set about systematically identifying and developing those areas best suited to vineyards. Key considerations included a nearby market, usually an important town, a riverine or coastal location to facilitate transport, and where possible, slopes for correct exposure to the sun and for facilitating the flow of air and soil moisture drainage.

The greatest amount of Roman wine-growing attention was focused on Gaul and the Rhineland. Today, virtually every important wine region in France and Germany, such as Champagne, Burgundy, Bordeaux, and the Rhineland (and many lesser ones as well) can find prominent Roman influences in its history. Viticulture was a particular specialty of the Romans; they created numerous new grape varieties that were better adapted to more northerly sites and they improved methods of vine cultivation, especially techniques related to pruning and training. Although there is, perhaps, a tendency to credit the Romans with too much in many facets of culture and technology, it is quite clear that the map of wine growing would have been drawn much differently without them.

Decline and Rebirth

The demise of Roman political and military authority led to a reversal of wine's fortunes in Europe. This was not because successors, such as the Franks, Vandals, Goths, Visigoths, and Huns, eschewed wine; rather it resulted from the unsettled conditions that plagued the countryside for several centuries. Vineyards were difficult to maintain in the face of repeated raiding and pillaging, and markets all but disappeared as cities went into decline with the disruption of trade. Wine growing persevered, if on a much reduced scale, and it managed to do so largely because of its role in the Christian liturgy. Wine was needed in order to celebrate the mass, and thus the numerous bishoprics established following Rome's conversion managed to keep small vineyards in production during the difficult times of the middle of the first millennium A.D.

Of longer-term significance, however, were the monasteries, which provided bastions of security amid general insecurity. In terms of wine, the most significant monastic orders were the Benedictines and their offshoot the Cistercians, followed by the Carthusians. Experiments by the monks led to new cultivars and to improvements in numerous aspects of viticulture, especially with regard to site selection. Many of today's most celebrated vineyards in such places as Burgundy, the Reingau, and the Mosel were laid out by monks nearly a thousand years ago.

By contrast, from Persia through western Asia across northern Africa and into Iberia, viticulture was confronted by the advance of Islam and the Koranic injunction against drinking alcohol in any form. Although the spread of Islam was very swift, the elimination of wine growing proceeded much more slowly. Minority Christian and Jewish communities often were allowed to continue to use the beverage largely for the tax revenues wine provided. Thus during the early centuries of Islamic rule, the ban on alcohol varied in terms of how rigorously it was enforced. It never seems to have taken a strong hold in Iberia, and consequently wine growing continued there without serious interruption during the period of Moorish rule. But wine in western Asia and the eastern Mediterranean was under greater pressure, and with the rise to power of the Ottomans, it virtually disappeared over much of the area.

Although Norse raids had slowed the pace of vineyard developments in Europe, expansion was once more under way by the beginning of the twelfth century, even in such northerly locales as the Low Countries and England. The monasteries continued with their plantings and were joined in this endeavor by noble estates, many of which employed wine-growing specialists. Local demand was expanding as wine, at least in Western Christendom, became a more common drink among the populace at large. It was a substitute for unsafe drinking water and widely prescribed as a medication for a variety of ailments. In addition, profits could be gained from exports, particularly to the trading states of the Baltic and North Seas. Much of the wine headed in this direction seems to have come from the Rhineland, including Franconia and Alsace.

Markets and Politics

By the close of the twelfth century, the history of wine growing in Europe was being shaped to an ever increasing extent by a combination of politics and market demands in which England played the most prominent role. Vineyards had been planted in the southern part of that country during Roman times,

and as noted, further developments occurred with the establishment of monasteries.

The Domesday Book recorded in excess of 40 vineyards, and over the course of the next several centuries their numbers multiplied severalfold. Most, however, seem to have been quite small, and the wine they produced never achieved any esteem. It was thin and acidic and used primarily for sacramental purposes. Thus the English had to begin looking elsewhere for the wine they were consuming in ever larger volumes. The future of wine growing in England was further dimmed by the advancing cold of the Little Ice Age. By the seventeenth century, all the English vineyards had fallen into disuse.

Much of the wine the English initially imported came from the Rhineland, but the source of supply shifted to the Loire River Valley and its hinterlands when Aquitaine was joined to England during the middle of the twelfth century. An important commercial center in Aquitaine was Bordeaux, and here a new kind of wine was encountered. Unlike the white to golden-colored wines from the Rhineland and the Loire, the wine here was red, or at least pink. Termed claret, it became the royal favorite and thus the wine in most demand among the upper classes. Yet at this time, only a very small amount of claret actually came from the Bordeaux region itself. Most of it was shipped down the streams converging on the Gironde estuary from the *hauts pays* of the interior, from such places as Bergerac, Gaillac, and Cahors.

In the mid-fifteenth century, following the end of the Hundred Years' War, all of Aquitaine, including Bordeaux, was incorporated within France. This development did not end the flow of claret to England, but the supply became less regular and depended to a great extent on the state of relations between the two countries. English merchants looked for alternatives, which took them southward to Portugal, their political ally against the Spanish and French.

Some red wines were exported from the Minho region of Portugal, but they never developed much of a following. As wars and plans for war grew more frequent toward the close of the seventeenth century, the search for reliable supplies of claret substitutes intensified. Some merchants traveled up the rugged and underdeveloped Duoro Valley from their base at Porto. Only very rough reds were encountered, and their initial reception in England was not very positive.

What caught on eventually, however, was the practice of adding brandy to the still wines. At first this was done at the end of fermentation to increase alcohol content. High-alcohol wines were preferred not only because they were more quickly intoxicating, but also because they did not spoil as rapidly and thin into vinegar. Although not discovered until much later, the wine-spoiling culprits were oxidation and bacterial contamination, and the reactions they produced slowed down at higher alcohol levels.

In the eighteenth century, it was discovered that if brandy was added during fermentation, a sweet wine of much higher quality could be produced, and thus the port of today was born, named for Porto, the place where it was processed and from which it was shipped. It became a highly fashionable drink for English gentlemen, which set off a wave of vineyard plantings that transformed the upper Duoro Valley into a landscape almost totally devoted to wine.

Perhaps the most highly prized wine in England was malmsey. It arrived in Genoese and then Venetian galleys from Cyprus and other Christian-held lands in the eastern Mediterranean, where vineyards had been reestablished by monastic orders in the wake of the Crusades. These sun-drenched lands produced a sweet, golden wine naturally high in alcohol, and thus the malmsey also traveled well. However, the Ottoman advance cut off the source of supply, which once again set in motion a search for alternatives that eventually led to Spain. A wave of vineyard plantings there had accompanied the Reconquest, and the expulsion of the Jews had provided an opportunity for English merchants to set themselves up in business, particularly at the active ports of Cadiz and Sanlúcar. The wine exported from this southern coastal region was initially called sac, and later sherry. The latter was an English corruption of the word Jerez, the town in which most of the wine was made. Like the port wines, sherries were fortified and initially sweet. Later developments led to dry styles gaining preference, with England maintaining an almost exclusive hold on the market. A similar type of wine was produced on the island of Madeira, but because of the papal division of the world, its exports were directed mostly to the Americas.

The other major participant in the wine trade was Holland, where cool growing-season temperatures, poorly drained soils, and high winds virtually precluded the establishment of vineyards. Satisfying most of the Dutch thirst for wine were the vineyards of the Rhineland and the Mosel Valley, but the destruction wrought there by the Thirty Years' War caused the Dutch (like the English) to turn to the Loire Valley and to Bordeaux, where they encouraged the growing of grapes to make white wines.

Dutch tastes, however, were increasingly moving in the direction of spirits, especially brandies. In addition to vineyards, ample timber supplies were required in order to fuel the distilleries, and the Dutch found this combination in two locales, the Charente (Cognac) and Armagnac, two names that have come to define the standards by which brandy is judged.

The Search for Quality

The emergence of noble classes and wealthy merchants in Europe generated a greater concern for wine quality, with those in Burgundy leading the way. There, in the fourteenth century, the combination of the tastes of the dukes and the wine-growing skills of the Cistercians resulted in a purposeful attempt to reduce the quantity of wine produced in order to raise its quality. The monks had determined that the best vineyard sites lay along a faulted escarpment that has since gained the name Côte d'Or, and a Duke, Philippe the Bold, declared the high-yielding Gamay grape banned in favor of the lower-yielding but more aromatic and complexly flavored Pinot Noir (then known as the noirien). At about the same time, quality considerations were singling out the Riesling grape in the Rhineland and the Mosel Valley. Both cases illustrate an important trend in the making – the development of a hierarchy of quality wine regions based in large measure on grape varieties.

Two advances of the seventeenth century were crucial in the quest for wine quality. The first was the discovery of how to make stronger glass bottles, thus providing an inert container in which wine could be stored instead of in wooden barrels, jugs, or, in some instances, leather bags. The bottle then needed a stopper to protect the wine from the deleterious effects of too much oxygen contact. Wood plugs and cloth were tried with limited success, but the solution to the problem proved to be cork. It deterred the passage of air, and cork's pliability meant that it could be made to fill the space between the walls of the bottle's neck. It was now possible to keep new wines fresh longer, and a medium was available to allow wines to age.

One region that profited almost immediately from the use of improved bottles and corks was Champagne. By the fourteenth century, its wines had gained the reputation of being good values. Champagne was close to the Paris market, and reds and whites were made in styles similar to those in Burgundy. Matters began to change, however, in the seventeenth century under the leadership of the Benedictine abbey at Hautvilliers and, most particularly, when the legendary Dom Pérignon assumed the position of cellarmaster. He set meticulous cultivation and vinification standards designed to elevate Champagne's wines to the very top of the quality ranking. Consistency seems to have been what he was seeking most, and to this end he perfected the art of wine blending, something that has been a hallmark of champagne ever since.

One of the problems Dom Pérignon had to deal with was a fizziness that frequently appeared in the wine during the spring following vinification. The cold weather of the late fall sometimes shut down fermentation before it was completed, and it would start up again when the warmer weather of spring arrived. Yet the fizziness produced by the carbon dioxide in the wine was precisely what consumers began to find attractive. It became fashionable to serve this kind of champagne at the court of Louis XIV during festive occasions, and the habit soon spread to other European royal families, setting off a demand that could not be met by relying on an accident of nature. Thus, by the early part of the eighteenth century, secondary fermentation was being purposefully created through the addition of a dose of yeast and sugar to already bottled still wine. Because the carbon dioxide created enormous pressure, strong bottles and a tight seal were both required. During the remainder of the eighteenth century and on through the nineteenth, numerous technological changes continued to improve champagne's quality and thereby its image. It was a different wine than that which Dom Pérignon envisioned, but it achieved the ranking he sought.

No region is more closely associated with the image of wine quality than Bordeaux. As noted, the politics of the seventeenth and eighteenth centuries meant that the supply of claret for the English market was highly unreliable, and often it fell far short of demand. Consequently, claret became a prestigious commodity with attendant high prices. This situation initiated a twofold response from Bordeaux. One was an effort by some producers to make better wines and then to let consumers know with a label which properties or estates had produced them. The wine was thus not just a claret but a claret from this or that estate. The other was to expand markedly the amount of vineyard land. Most of the plantings initially were near the city of Bordeaux, in an area known as the Graves because of its gravelly soils. Because of drainage work carried out by Dutch engineers earlier in the seventeenth century, a considerable amount of land was available in the Médoc promontory to the north of the city, and by the end of the century, most of the best sites, also on gravel, had been planted. Expansion continued during the next century and soon enough wine was being produced in Bordeaux so that supplies were no longer needed from the *hauts pays*. Indeed, these wines were restricted from entering in order to protect local prices.

Wine and wealth in Bordeaux had come to feed on one another. The port was significant in its own right, connecting the southwest of France not only to England but also to the markets of Scotland, Ireland, Holland, and the northern German states. As profits grew, more and more was invested in wine, both by merchants and the landed aristocracy. The latter began to build country estates marked by grand chateaux, which helped to further the elite image of the Bordeaux wines. In terms of prices paid and profits earned, Bordeaux had risen to the top of the wine world.

Imperial Expansion

Wherever possible, wine growing accompanied European imperial expansion. It was introduced into Mexico during the first decades of the sixteenth century and from there spread southward in rapid order to Peru, Chile, and Argentina. Its northward expansion was slower, but eventually by the late eighteenth century it had reached what is now California. Catholic missions had established the first vineyards in both directions. They were small, and the wine produced went mainly to celebrate the mass, but some was also consumed at meals by priests and monks and by nearby Spanish settlers. Wine, however, was not to be given to the local Indians.

Where and when wine was first made in the eastern part of the United States remains in dispute. Some give the credit to French Huguenots at a settlement near Jacksonville, Florida, in the 1560s; others point to the settlers of a contemporaneous Spanish colony on Santa Elena Island off the coast of Georgia; and still others say it was the Jamestown settlers. Whoever they were, they would have used wild native American grapes, including the muscadines. The pungency of wines made from these grapes was not greatly appreciated, and throughout the colonial period attempts were made to grow *vinifera* varieties. Without exception, however, the vineyards died within a few years of planting (we shall see why in the next section). Reconciling themselves to this fact, wine makers turned their attention toward domesticating and improving the indigenous vines, the first of which, known as the Alexander, appeared at the end of the eighteenth century.

Vinifera found a much more hospitable environment at the very southern tip of Africa. Here the Dutch East India Company chose Table Bay as the site for establishing a colony in 1652 to revictual their ships rounding the Cape of Good Hope, and vines were among one of the first crops to be planted. In the late 1680s, a group of French Huguenot refugees arrived; they brought wine-growing expertise with them and extended the area devoted to vineyards. The vines did so well in the mild Mediterranean climatic conditions of the Cape region that not only were the ships resupplied with ample quantities for their crews, but exports were also sent to Europe. One result was a rich dessert-type wine known as Constantia that gained considerable renown in the early 1700s.

Wine growing was attempted by the first Australian settlers who arrived at Sydney Harbor in the 1780s using seeds and cuttings obtained from Europe and the Cape. But the prevailing high heat and humidity militated against success and, in any event, more money could be made raising sheep. It was not until the 1820s that wine growing in Australia finally found a congenial environment in the Hunter Valley. Other areas in Victoria, southern Australia, and western Australia came into production in the 1830s and 1840s when wine-making efforts were also occurring on the North Island of New Zealand.

Disasters in the Making

By the middle of the nineteenth century, wine was entering what many have termed its golden age. It had been an everyday drink among Mediterranean

Europeans for many centuries and was becoming ever more common across the Alps, where a succession of good vintages helped to spur an increase in the areas given over to vineyards. Profits had never been greater, and some areas, notably the Midi of France, became virtual monocultures supplying the demands of the general public. Side by side were other areas catering to the wealthy, now augmented by newly emergent industrial and professional classes. Burgundy, Champagne, and the Rhine/Mosel each had its markets, but no place could challenge the primacy of Bordeaux.

Most of the wine being produced was, in fact, of ordinary quality, but a few properties, mostly located in the Médoc, had managed to distinguish themselves. This led to numerous attempts at classification, the official codification of which was achieved in 1855 for the Paris Universal Exposition. At the top, it divided the wines of the Médoc into first through fifth growths *(crus),* and it then added lower rungs of *crus exceptionneles, crus bourgeois,* and *crus artisans.* The appearance of such a listing, which no other wine region had, created an even greater demand for the top growths, and Bordeaux's image reached new heights.

Nevertheless, disaster was lurking in the background. It started with a powdery mildew, termed oidium, that in the early 1850s was infesting vineyards virtually everywhere in Europe. The fungus retards vine growth by attacking both leaf and stalk, and it also desiccates grapes by breaking their skins. Consequently when it first appeared, yields declined, as was especially the case from 1852 to 1854. Nevertheless, a treatment in the form of sulfur dusts was quickly found, and by the end of the decade oidium, although not eliminated, was being controlled.

But no sooner had oidium come under control than reports of mysterious vine deaths began to emerge. The first came from the lower Rhone Valley, and by 1870, it had become evident that the problem was on the verge of universality. The plague of vine destruction made its way through France (the last region to be visited was Champagne in 1901) and the rest of Europe, and eventually into most of the wine-growing world. Chile was the only major exception, being spared by a combination of distance, desert, and mountains.

In 1868 the culprit was shown to be a minute aphid, *Phylloxera vastratrix,* that destroys vine roots. It is native to North America, and may have entered France on vines that were imported for experiments on ways to better control oidium. With the collapse of the wine industry at hand, numerous, often desperate, attempts were made to rid vineyards of the aphids. Some chemical treatments were moderately effective, but the ultimate solution turned out to be one of grafting European vines onto American roots. Experiments had determined that several species of the latter were tolerant of the aphid's presence and thus

North America, which was the cradle of phylloxera, turned out to be the cradle of the cure.

But the diffusion of phylloxera had drastically altered the wine-growing world. Those regions hit later were able to realize short-term profits. For example, the price of champagne soared, and Italy and Spain filled in the gaps left by the fall of French production in the 1880s and 1890s. In addition, wine growers themselves were on the move. Algeria was a favorite destination for those leaving France, and small numbers also relocated in the Rioja region of Spain, bringing with them new ways of growing vines and making wine with an eye on the larger market. When, at the turn of the century, phylloxera finally hit hard in Italy, Spain, and Portugal, an exodus to Chile, Argentina, and Brazil ensued, leading to the reenergization of these long dormant regions.

Yet a third natural disaster had to be faced, that of downy mildew, which also found its way to Europe on American vines. In a manner similar to oidium, it reduced crop yields and required dusting, this time with a mixture of copper sulfate and lime, to keep it under control.

The labor and cash requirements of grafting and repeated sprayings drove many farmers in Europe out of the wine business, which was no longer something that one could do in a small way. Rather it required new skills and greater financing in order to be competitive, and these were best obtained by specialization. Virtually everywhere, the making of wine was rapidly changing from a craft into a business and a science.

In the United States, oidium, phylloxera, and downy mildew had also taken their toll. Indeed, it was phylloxera that had been responsible for the repeated failure of *vinifera* to survive east of the Rocky Mountains, and in the 1850s an outbreak of oidium had put an end to the country's first wine region of note – the so-called Rhine of America along the Ohio River near Cincinnati. A far more significant disaster, however, was social and political in nature, namely Prohibition. Its origins go back to the temperance crusades of the nineteenth century designed to purify America of all vices, and most especially those thought to be associated with alcoholic beverages. The purification urge culminated in 1919 in passage of the Eighteenth Amendment to the U.S. Constitution (popularly known as the Volstead, or Prohibition, Act), and its 13 years of existence brought nearly total ruin to the country's wine industry. By this time, California had achieved top rank in terms of both quantity and quality, but wineries abounded in many other states. Very few managed to survive Prohibition. Those that did sold sacramental and medicinal wines, as well as grape concentrate for making wine at home, all of which could be done under provisions of the Volstead Act.

Over most of the first half of the twentieth century, the world's wine industry remained in a depressed state. In addition to the ravages wrought by disease and Prohibition in America, the industry had to contend with two world wars, the Russian Revolution (which eliminated an important market for French wines, particularly champagne), and economic depression. In retrospect, the golden age truly glittered.

Recovery and Transformation

Recovery was fueled by the widening base of prosperity of the immediate post–World War II years and by a Europeanization of food habits in many parts of the world. Outside of Europe, wine drinking tended to be relatively uncommon even in those areas settled by Europeans. In general, members of the working and middle classes drank mainly beer and spirits or abstained from alcohol altogether. However, by the 1950s more people could afford wine, and many discovered it as an enjoyable accompaniment with dinner. For others, wine served as a symbol of their upward mobility.

The French were the first to prosper. They had solidified their image as the world's quality leader by developing a legal classification of wines known as *Appellation d'Origine Contrôlée* (AOC). Its outlines were formed early in the twentieth century in order to counter an outbreak of fraud following the wine shortages caused by phylloxera. Fraudulent practices included such things as the marketing of wine from one region under the name of another; placing non-French wines under French labels; and fermenting a range of fruits and other substances in place of grapes.

As the AOC system evolved into its present form, the emphasis was placed on guaranteeing the authenticity, especially the geographic authenticity, of wines. The system defines specific regions, dictates where the grapes that go into the wine of those regions must come from, and also requires adherence to precise viticultural practices that are deemed essential to achieving a wine's particular character. A certain level of quality is implied, but only in a very few instances are taste tests actually performed. The success of the AOC system in heightening the image of French wines meant that other countries began creating their own versions. Each is constructed differently, but the message is basically the same – the government certifies what is in the bottle.

Wineries in California led to other trends. Of special significance was the state's abilities to produce large volumes of consistently good-quality wines at relatively inexpensive prices. Three related factors made this achievement possible. One was the high grape yields attainable in the rich, irrigated central valley of the state; another involved the development of new quality-control technologies, especially ones designed to control fermentation temperatures, permitting bulk manufacturing; and the third was the for-mation of large companies that could afford to adopt these technologies as well as to engage in mass advertising campaigns. Thus, while meeting a demand, the companies were also creating it.

At the same time, other California producers were heading in a somewhat different direction. Following the repeal of the Volstead Act, several smaller-volume wineries in the Napa Valley north of San Francisco had decided to compete with French wines in the prestige market. Their success in the 1950s and early 1960s sparked a wave of winery openings that spread out from the Napa Valley to adjacent Sonoma County and then to other areas of the state. Leading both branches of the industry were researchers at the Davis branch of the University of California. As early as the 1930s they had begun mapping the state into microclimates based on growing-season temperatures, and this work emerged as a guide to what areas should be planted in vineyards. In addition, basic research was initiated into all phases of wine making and the results obtained were quickly disseminated into the vineyards and wineries through various degree-granting and training programs. The application of science to wine began in Europe, but in California it reached new heights that set the standard for the late twentieth century.

During the 1960s and 1970s, wine was in a new golden age, and virtually all predictions made at the time foresaw even better days ahead. Many older wine-producing areas of the globe were modernized so that they could market their products abroad. Suddenly wines were appearing from such places as Hungary, Romania, Yugoslavia, and Algeria. However, the most spectacular change took place in Italy, which quickly went from being a producer of wines meant mostly for local consumption to the world's leading exporter. Wine growing also expanded into many nontraditional areas including China, Japan, Kenya, and American states such as Oregon, Texas, and New Mexico. It even returned to England.

The events of the 1980s and early 1990s, however, did not bear out the optimism of the previous two decades, which to a great extent was built around trends in the U.S. market – a market that seemed to be headed in the direction of making Americans into regular wine drinkers on a par with the Europeans. But the course of upward per capita consumption did not proceed as predicted. The adoption of wine as a meal-time beverage has not spread to the population at large; for most people wine retains its image as something either foreign, elitist, or reserved for special occasions. In addition, a growing neoprohibitionist movement centered around the issues of drunk driving and health has exerted its influence on all alcoholic beverages. Information about wine's contribution to cardiovascular functioning has reversed the decline somewhat, but it is too early to tell if that will turn out to be just another health fad.

In Europe, wine consumption has fallen everywhere, and bottled water and soft drinks are becoming preferred by more and more people. In this instance as well, health and safety issues seem to be major reasons for the change in drinking habits.

The impact of declining demand has, to this point, fallen most heavily on lower-priced, so-called jug or country wines. In areas such as the Midi of France, southern Italy, and the central valley of California, supply is greatly in excess of demand. With no signs of change in the offing, the future portent is one of considerable vineyard abandonment in such areas.

By way of contrast, the demand for prestigious high-priced wines has never been greater. Each year they sell out even as their costs escalate. To some extent, this results from wine drinkers preferring quality to quantity – one or two bottles a week instead of four or five. But wine has also become a collectible for the world's affluent. It is not so much a matter of investing in financial terms, but of investing in status. To hold certain types of wine and then to serve them in the appropriate circumstances is to mark one's social standing. The competition among wine producers for this market is intense, with much of it centering on extolling the geographic features that give a wine its special character. The French, for example, argue for the influence of *terroir,* a term that encompasses all the physical characteristics of the growing site. A variation on this theme is increasingly seen in California, where smaller and smaller wine-producing areas and the individual vineyards are indicated on the label. Very recently, Chile has begun exporting larger volumes of wine, stressing that wine makers there attain a unique quality because in that country they grow ungrafted *vinifera* vines. Oregon and Washington State also employ the same selling technique.

To a large extent, the minutiae of locational differences are emphasized in order to counteract a worldwide trend toward uniformity. Only a small number of grapes are considered suitable for making fine wines. These are dominated by Cabernet Sauvignon and Chardonnay, which along with Riesling, Pinot Noir, and two or three others (depending on who is making the list) constitute the so-called noble family of grapes. The standards are set at numerous wine-tasting competitions and by a small group of wine writers whose opinions are enormously influential in shaping the market. As the preferred grapes spread, they provide an underlying sameness to the wines made from them and pose the likelihood of extinction for many long-standing local varieties.

Uniformity results not only from using similar grapes but from similar ways of doing things in the vineyard and winery. Science and technology have created the means for standardizing wine making around the world, and their application has been facilitated by more and more wine coming under the control of large transnational corporations. The regional distinctions of the past are blurring as wine from places as distant as the Médoc in France, the Maipo Valley in Chile, and the Napa Valley in California all begin to look, smell, and taste alike.

James L. Newman

Bibliography

Adams, L. 1990. *Wines of America.* Third edition. New York.

Amerine, M. A. 1983. *Wines, their sensory evaluation.* New York.

Baxevanis, J. J. 1987a. *The wines of Bordeaux and western France.* Totowa, N.J.

1987b. *The wines of Champagne, Burgundy, and eastern and southern France.* Totowa, N.J.

Blij, H. J. de. 1983. *Wine: A geographic appreciation.* Totowa, N.J.

1985. *Wine regions of the Southern Hemisphere.* Totowa, N.J.

Carter, F. W. 1987. Cracow's wine trade (fourteenth to eighteenth centuries). *Slavonic and East European Review* 65: 537-78.

Catrell, H., and H. L. Stauffer. 1978. *The hybrids.* Lancaster, Pa.

Dickenson, J. 1990. Viticultural geography: An introduction to the literature in English. *Journal of Wine Research* 1: 5-24.

Dion, R. 1959. *Histoire de la vigne et du vin en France.* Paris.

Grace, V. 1979. *Amphoras and the ancient wine trade.* Princeton, N.J.

Hyams, E. S. 1965. *Dionysus: A social history of the wine vine.* New York.

Ilbery, B. W. 1983. The renaissance of viticulture in England and Wales. *Geography* 68: 341-4.

James, M. K. 1971. *Studies in the medieval wine trade.* Oxford.

Johnson, H. 1985. *The world atlas of wine.* Third edition. London.

1989. *Vintage: The story of wine.* New York.

Lachiver, M. 1988. *Vins, vignes et vignerons.* Paris.

Loubère, L. A. 1978. *The red and the white: A history of wine in France and Italy in the nineteenth century.* Albany, N.Y.

1990. *The wine revolution in France.* Princeton, N.J.

Muscatine, D., B. Thompson, and M. A. Amerine. 1984. *Book of California wine.* Berkeley, Calif.

Robinson, J. 1986. *Vines, grapes and wine.* New York.

Seward, D. 1979. *Monks and wine.* London.

Stanislawski, D. 1970. *Landscapes of Bacchus.* Austin, Tex.

1975. Dionysus westward: Early religion and the economic geography of wine. *The Geographical Review* 65: 427-44.

Tehernia, A. 1986. *Le vin de l'Italie romaine: Essai d'histoire économique d'après les amphores.* Rome.

Teiser, R. 1983. *Winemaking in California: The account in words and pictures of the Golden State's two-century-long adventure with wine.* New York.

Unwin, T. 1991. *Wine and the vine: An historical geography of viticulture and the wine trade.* London.

Wagner, P. M. 1956. *American wines and wine-making.* New York.

Webb, A. D. 1984. The science of making wine. *American Scientist* 72: 360-7.

PART IV

The Nutrients – Deficiencies, Surfeits, and Food-Related Disorders

The discovery of the chief nutrients has been essentially a twentieth-century phenomenon. In 1897, Dutch researcher Christian Eijkman, while investigating beriberi in the Dutch East Indies, showed that a diet of polished rice caused the disease and that the addition of the rice polishings to the diet cured it. Fifteen years later, Polish chemist Casimir Funk proposed that not only beriberi but scurvy, pellagra, and rickets were caused by an absence of a dietary substance he called *vitamine;* and the age of vitamins was under way.

This is not to say that much earlier research did not undergird such twentieth-century breakthroughs. The importance to human health of some minerals, such as iron, had long been at least vaguely recognized, and by 1800, it was understood that blood contained iron; since the eighteenth century, some kind of dietary deficiency had been a periodic suspect as the cause of scurvy; and protein was discovered in the nineteenth century. But in addition to both water- and fat-soluble vitamins, the importance and functions of most of the major minerals and the trace minerals, along with amino acids, were all twentieth-century discoveries, as were the essential fatty acids and the nutritional illness now called protein–energy malnutrition (PEM).

One important consequence of the new knowledge was the near-total eradication of the major deficiency diseases. Pellagra, which had ravaged southern Europe and the southern United States, was found to be associated with niacin deficiency; beriberi, the scourge of rice-consuming peoples in the Far East, was linked with thiamine deficiency; and scurvy was finally – and definitively – shown to be the result of vitamin C deficiency.

But as rapidly as these illnesses were conquered, new conditions were identified. There was PEM (mostly in the developing world) and anorexia nervosa (mostly in the developed world). Goiter, the result of iodine deficiency, proved to be a problem in both, and Keshan disease was associated with selenium deficiency and the death of children in China.

In addition, faulty nutrition has been implicated in the chronic diseases that are especially prominent in the countries of the West, such as diabetes, heart-related ailments, and cancer. Much of the problem seems to lie in diets significantly higher in sugar, salt, and fats than those of most other peoples – diets of affluence, which among other things produce obesity that can predispose to heart diseases and diabetes. Yet the link between diet and diseases of a chronic nature has often been sufficiently vague as to result, thus far, in more questions than answers. Consequently, many sensible hypotheses abound, and we have included one of these. Our last chapter in Part IV connects a specific nutriment, milk, and lactose tolerance – an ability to absorb milk after childhood, not shared by most of the world's population – with the high rates of coronary artery disease among the people of northern Europe and those descended from northern Europeans in the United States.

IV.A

Vitamins

IV.A.1 ❧ Vitamin A

Definitions and Nomenclature

Vitamin A is a fat-soluble substance essential to the health, survival, and reproduction of all vertebrates. As with all vitamins, it is needed in only small amounts in the human diet, about 1 to 1.5 milligrams a day. Vitamin A does not occur in the plant kingdom, but plants supply animals with precursors (or provitamins), such as beta-carotene and other carotene-related compounds (carotenoids), that are converted to vitamin A in the intestinal mucosa of animals and humans. Beta-carotene (and other carotenoids) are abundant in all photosynthesizing parts of plants (green leaves), as well as in yellow and red vegetables. Vitamin A, also known as "retinol," is itself a precursor of several substances active in the vertebrate organism; these are collectively termed "retinoids." One retinoid is retinoic acid, an oxidation product of retinol, formed in the liver and other organs and existing in different chemical isomers, such as all-*trans*-retinoic acid and 9-*cis*-retinoic acid, with different functions. Other retinoids are all-*trans*-retinaldehyde and its 11-*cis*-isomer. The latter is active in the retina of the eye, forming the light-sensitive pigment rhodopsin by combination with the protein opsin. In the liver, retinol is stored in the form of its ester (retinyl palmitate).

Retinoids in the animal organism are generally not found in the free state but are bound to specific proteins. Thus, in the blood, retinol is carried by a retinol-binding protein and, within cells, by an intracellular retinol-binding protein. Retinoic acid and retinaldehyde are carried by specific intracellular binding proteins. When carrying out its hormonal function, retinoic acid combines with another set of proteins, called retinoic acid receptors, located in the cell nucleus. The retinoic acid-receptor complex can then interact with specific genes at sites known as retinoic acid response elements, thereby activating these genes and causing them to stimulate (or repress) the expression of specific proteins or enzymes involved in embryonic development, cell differentiation, metabolism, or growth.

Units

At an earlier time, before pure, crystalline retinol and beta-carotene became available through chemical synthesis, the units used to express vitamin A activity were international units (IU). One IU of vitamin A activity was defined as 0.3 microgram (μg) all-*trans*-retinol (Figure IV.A.1.1a). Because of inefficiencies of

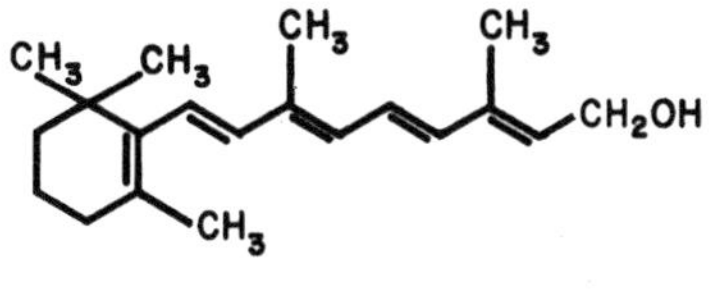

(a)

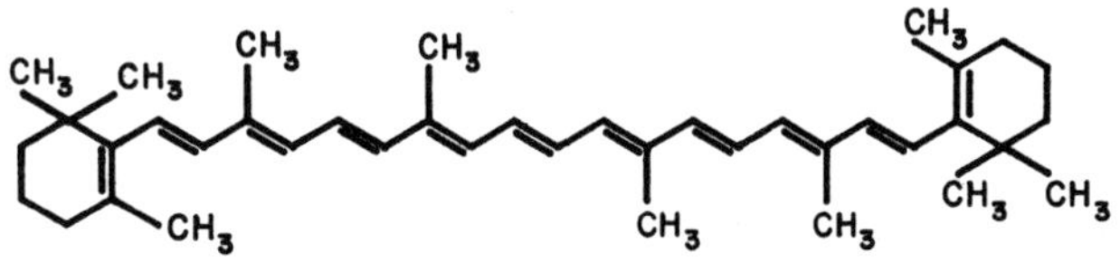

(b)

Figure IV.A.1.1. Chemical structure of all-*trans*-retinol (a) and all-*trans*-beta-carotene (b).

741

absorption and conversion to retinol, 1 IU of beta-carotene was defined as equivalent to 0.6 μg all-*trans*-beta-carotene (Figure IV.A.1.1b). More recently, the accepted unit has become the retinol equivalent (RE), a dietary concept (Underwood 1984). One RE equals 1 μg retinol. Taking into account beta-carotene's average absorbability and conversion to retinol, 1 RE was defined as 6 μg beta-carotene. Of course, it should be noted that absorbability and conversion of dietary beta-carotene can vary greatly with other components of the diet, such as fat or protein.

The Recommended Dietary Intake of vitamin A per day, published by the United States National Research Council, is 500 RE for children, 800 to 1,000 RE for adults, 1,300 RE for pregnant women, and 1,200 RE for lactating women.

History of Vitamin A Deficiency

Night blindness (nyctalopia), meaning defective vision at low illumination, is one of the earliest signs of vitamin A deficiency and was probably the first nutrient-deficiency disease to be clearly recognized. Although the relationship of night blindness to a dietary deficiency of vitamin A was not discovered until the nineteenth century, a cure for an unspecified eye disease, *sharew,* was described in ancient Egyptian texts. Papyrus Ebers (no. 351, c. 1520 B.C.) states: "Another [recipe] for *sharew.* Liver of beef is cooked and squeezed out and placed against it [the eye]. Really excellent." The London Medical Papyrus (no. 35, c. 1300 B.C.) states: "Another recipe [for *sharew*]. Beef liver placed on a fire of straw or emmer or barley and smoked in their [the straw's] smoke; their [the liver's] liquid is squeezed against the eyes" (Wolf 1980: 97).

The word *sharew* apparently refers to a disease of the eyes, and because liver is an especially rich source of vitamin A, and *sharew* was apparently cured by liver, scholars assumed until recently that this disease was caused by vitamin A deficiency and that, therefore, *sharew* meant "night blindness." However, no mention of "night" or "night vision" occurs in any Egyptian source,[1] and we now know that topical application of vitamin A would not be effective in curing night blindness. Much of Egyptian medical practice involved a magic element – the "transfer" of the strength of the ox to the afflicted organ. But the liver would have to be eaten to relieve night blindness. One way that the latter might have occurred has been suggested by A. Sommer, who describes a magical ritual whereby the juice of roasted lamb's liver is applied to the eyes as a cure for night blindness in rural Java today. The liver, however, is not discarded; it is eaten by the patient after the ceremony is finished. Sommer comments that the consumption of the liver is not actually considered part of the ritual. Perhaps the ancient Egyptian ceremony also ended with the patient eating the liver.

The first indisputable recognition of night blind-ness was by the ancient Greeks, who called it nyctalopia (*nyx, nyktos,* "night"; *alaos,* "blind"; *ops, opteos,* "eye") and prescribed the oral administration of liver as a cure. The development of Greek medicine was heavily indebted to Egyptian medical theory and practice, and Egyptian medical ideas had an overriding influence on both the Ionian school of medicine and the school of Cos. However, whereas Egyptian physicians considered disease the result of external, supernatural influences, the Greek physicians observed the patient, thought of disease as a condition of the patient, and designed therapy to fit into a rational system, such as the humoral theory in Hippocratic medicine. Hippocrates and his school produced the collection of writings *Corpus Hippocraticum* (Alexandria, c. 300 B.C.), within which the treatise "Concerning Vision" mentioned nyctalopia as an eye disease that usually afflicts children, along with other ailments such as otitis, sore throat, and fever.

The essay recommends this prescription: "Raw beef liver, as large as possible, soaked in honey [presumably to make it more palatable], to be taken once or twice by mouth" (Hirschberg 1899: 100). This is exactly what modern medicine would prescribe if it was not possible to obtain fish-liver extract or vitamin A pills. Today, it is well known that vitamin A deficiency afflicts principally children, predisposing them to infections because of an impaired immune system. Furthermore, fever coupled with infections is now understood to lead to excessive loss of vitamin A from the body stores, aggravating an incipient deficiency state. Thus, one might marvel at the Hippocratic school's acuity of observation and knowledge of effective therapy.

Galen (A.D. 130–200) provided a precise definition of night blindness, as did Oribasius (born c. A.D. 325), a follower of Galen, who defined night blindness this way: "Vision is good during the day and declines at sundown; one cannot distinguish anything any longer at night" (Guggenheim 1981: 267). Although Galen recommended as a cure the "continuous eating of roasted or boiled liver of goats" (Kühn 1821: 803), he also advised topical treatment: The juice of roasted liver should be painted on the eyes – a residue, perhaps, of the Egyptian influence. Much later, around A.D. 540, Aetius of Amida suggested goat liver, fried with salt but not oil, eaten hot. He also suggested that the "juice that runs out of the liver be applied topically to the afflicted eye" (Guggenheim 1981: 267).

The authors of the Assyrian medical texts (c. 700 B.C.) thought night blindness was caused by the rays of the moon and cured by the application of ass's liver to the eyes. Chinese medicine recognized night blindness, and Sun-szu-mo (seventh century A.D.), in his *1000 Golden Remedies,* described a cure by administration of pig's liver (Lee 1967). Arabic medicine, often derived from the translation of Greek medical texts, leaned toward topical application of liver extract (Hunain Ibn Ishaq, ninth century A.D.). So did a Hebrew treatise from Muslim Spain (Abraham Ibn Ezra, twelfth century), but it added eating liver to the prescription.

The Hippocratic tradition of liver therapy for night blindness survived through the Middle Ages. But with the long sea voyages of discovery that began at the end of the fifteenth century, dietary deficiency diseases, including night blindness, began to appear on board ships. Jacob de Bont (1592–1631), a Dutch physician of the East Indies, described a night blindness that can end in total blindness and prescribed a specific medicament for its cure, namely liver of shark (Lindeboom 1984).

There were many descriptions of night blindness penned by eighteenth- and nineteenth-century Europeans that mentioned that a poor or defective diet was suspected as the cause. In the nineteenth century, for instance, Reginald Heber, Bishop of Calcutta, in *Narrative of a Journey through the Upper Provinces of India: From Calcutta to Bombay* (1824–5), noted:

In our way back through the town a man begged of me, saying that he was blind. On my calling him, however, he came forwards so readily to the torches, and saw, I thought so clearly, that I asked him what he meant by telling me such a lie. He answered that he was night blind ("rat unda"), and I not understanding the phrase, and having been a good deal worried during the day with beggars, for the whole fort is a swarm of nothing else, said peevishly, "darkness is the time for sleep, not for seeing." The people laughed as at a good thing, but I was much mortified afterwards to find that it was an unfeeling retort. The disease of night blindness, that is, of requiring the full light of day to see, is very common, Dr. Smith said, among the lower classes in India, and to some professions of men, such as soldiers, very inconvenient. The Sepoys ascribe it to bad and insufficient food, and it is said to be always most prevalent in scarcity. It seems to be the same disorder to the eyes with which people are afflicted who live on damaged or inferior rice, in itself a food of very little nourishment and probably arises from weakness of the digestive powers. I was grieved to think I had insulted a man who might be in distress, but Dr. Smith comforted me by saying that, even in respect of night blindness, the man was too alert to be much of a sufferer from the cause which he mentioned. (Wolf 1980: 99)

In another nineteenth-century example, during a journey round the globe by an Austrian sailing ship (1857–9), a young ship's doctor, Eduard Schwarz, carried out what appears to have been the first modern rational experiment undertaken to prove or disprove the ancient theory that night blindness could be cured by eating liver. During the long voyage, several cases of night blindness were observed, and Schwarz reported the following:

[A]t dusk, objects appeared to the afflicted darkened, vague, with indistinct contours and as though moved into the far distance; light-absorbing objects could not be perceived, even close by, and the afflicted walked into the ships' walls or railings. Indoors, everything seemed completely dark to them. We experienced the most convincing proof of the efficacy of beef liver against nightblindness on the return journey, when . . . about 20 nightblind sailors were given ox liver to eat, whereupon they were all permanently cured. (Schwarz 1861: 166)

Interestingly, Schwarz also observed that when the night-blind sailors were kept in complete darkness for three days, their night vision recovered, only to be lost again after a few days in daylight. We can conclude from modern knowledge that during dark adaptation, small amounts of vitamin A reserves remaining in the body reached the retina to reform the depleted visual pigment and were lost again upon exposure to light.

It was also in the nineteenth century that the lesion was noted called xerophthalmia (dryness of the conjunctive and cornea), caused by more severe vitamin A deficiency. V. von Hubbenet described night blindness, associated with "silver scales at the cornea" (Guggenheim 1981), that was caused by a faulty diet but could be treated with beef liver. In 1857, David Livingstone, the explorer of Africa, noting corneal lesions in African natives who subsisted on a diet of coffee, manioc, and meal, wrote: "The eyes became affected as in the case of animals fed pure gluten or starch" (Moore 1957: 4).

At the beginning of the twentieth century, an important contribution was made by M. Mori, who in 1904 described widespread xerophthalmia in Japanese children, including large numbers showing keratomalacia, a softening of the cornea ending in corneal ulceration and necropsis and characteristic, as we now know, of severe vitamin A deficiency. Mori reported that the diet of Japanese children consisted of rice, barley, other cereals, "and other vegetables," and he found that liver, and especially cod-liver oil, were curative. He thus connected the disease with a nutritional cause and a cure (the ingestion of a fat or an oil).

Close on the heels of the discovery of vitamin A (described in the next section) were the observations of C. E. Bloch, who, during World War I, studied children in Denmark afflicted with night blindness and keratomalacia (Guggenheim 1981). As a result of the war, the children had subsisted on a diet of fat-free milk, oatmeal, and barley soup. In an important early experiment, Bloch worked with 32 institutionalized children (1 to 4 years old), dividing them into two groups. One group received whole milk instead of the fat-free milk; the other was given vegetable fat (margarine) but not whole milk. The latter showed 8 cases of corneal xerosis, the former remained healthy. All the xerosis cases were cured rapidly with cod-liver oil. Bloch correctly surmised that whole milk, cream, butter, eggs, and cod-liver oil contained lipid substances protecting against corneal and conjunctival xerosis.

History of the Discovery of Vitamin A

The first animal experiments with a vitamin A–deficient diet were those of F. Magendie in 1816 (McCollum 1957). He fed dogs a diet of wheat gluten, or starch, or sugar, or olive oil and described the corneal ulcers that developed (as we now know) because of a lack of vitamin A.

The effects of vitamin A deficiency on growth were first described by G. Lunin in 1881. He found that mice could not survive on a diet of pure casein, fat, sucrose, minerals, and water, but they lived and grew normally with whole dried milk. The outcome of similar experiments led F. G. Hopkins (1906) to postulate "minimal qualitative factors" in the diet necessary for growth and survival (Moore 1957).

An interesting and exciting account of the beginnings of experimental nutrition, which ultimately led to the discovery of vitamin A, was written by E. V. McCollum (1964). At the time McCollum began his research (1907), chemical analysis of foods and animal feed was well advanced. He fed cows rations of hay with wheat, or oats, or yellow maize, of identical composition as far as protein, carbohydrate, fat, and minerals were concerned.

The wheat-fed cows did not thrive but, rather, became blind and gave premature birth to dead calves. The oat-fed cows fared somewhat better, but the maize-fed cows were in excellent condition, produced vigorous calves, and had no miscarriages. McCollum spent four years in trying to determine the reasons for these remarkable results. He addressed questions such as: Did the wheat contain a toxic substance, and what was lacking in wheat that was present in yellow maize? He then conceived the important idea that nutrition experiments could be done much faster and better with small animals, such as mice or rats: They eat much less than larger animals, they can be given purified diets, they reproduce rapidly, and many can be housed at one time (McCollum 1964).

Raising rats, however, was not a popular idea at the Wisconsin College of Agriculture, where McCollum worked, because, as he was told by the dean, "rats were enemies of the farmer." Thus, he surreptitiously started a rat colony in a basement of the Agricultural Hall. In 1915, he found that whereas young rats on a diet of pure protein, pure milk sugar, minerals, and lard (or olive oil) failed to grow, the addition to their diet of butterfat or an ether extract of egg yolk restored their health. Soon after, he determined that adding an ether extract of alfalfa leaves or, even bet-

ter, of liver or kidney, greatly improved the diet's growth-promoting quality. Clearly, he had found a fat-soluble factor that promoted growth in rats.

He saponified butterfat, extracted the unsaponifiable mixture into ether, and added the extract to olive oil: Now the olive oil, with pure protein, sugar, and minerals, supported growth. This experiment, and subsequent ones, proved that butterfat contained a fat-soluble growth factor (other than fat itself) that could be transferred from one fat to another. McCollum ultimately showed that this factor was essential for growth and survival: This was the discovery of vitamin A, then named "fat-soluble factor A" to distinguish it from other accessory dietary factors that were grouped under the term "water-soluble B." Simultaneously, biochemists T. B. Osborne and L. B. Mendel made the same discovery; they published their findings five months later (1915).

In 1919, it was noted by another investigator, H. Steenbock, that active growth-promoting extracts, such as those made from butter, egg yolk, or certain plants (carrots), were yellow, whereas extracts from lard, inactive in growth promotion, were white (Table IV.A.1.1). He realized, however, that active fat-soluble factors existed in white extracts from liver or kidney. Steenbock and P. W. Boutwell thereupon proposed the hypothesis in 1920 (it was not fully confirmed for another 10 years) that fat-soluble factor A was associated with a yellow pigment (now known to be beta-carotene) and suggested that the yellow pigment could be converted to an active colorless form (vitamin A or retinol).

In the meantime, L. S. Palmer (in 1919) threw the subject into confusion by feeding chickens white maize, skimmed milk, and bone meal, a diet free of yellow pigments. When the birds stopped growing and began to fail, he supplemented their diet with a small amount of pork liver, containing no yellow pigment, and found that though the birds had received no yellow pigment, they grew normally and laid eggs. The egg yolks were colorless, but the eggs, when hatched, produced normal chicks.

Table IV.A.1.1. *Association of vitamin A potency with yellow color in food*

Active (yellow) (white)	Inactive, or low potency
Butter	Casein
Egg yolk	Egg white
Cod-liver oil	Lard
Yellow maize	White maize
Carrot	Parsnip
Sweet potato	Ordinary potato
Red palm oil	Palm kernel oil
Outer green leaves of cabbag	Inner white leaves of cabbage
Tomato	Onion
Apricot	Apple

Source: From Moore (1957).

It was not until 1929 that T. Moore resolved the conflict by proving that the yellow pigment extracted from plant sources, butterfat, or egg yolk, and purified as carotene, was converted to the active factor in the animal body. He fed pure, crystalline carotene (yellow) to young rats and observed the accumulation of retinol (colorless) in their livers. He correctly concluded that yellow carotene is the provitamin or precursor of colorless vitamin A (retinol).

Discovery of the Functions of Vitamin A

In the 1930s, the isolation and synthesis of both carotene (now more precisely defined as beta-carotene) and retinol were accomplished, along with an understanding of their chemical structures. The enzymatic conversion of beta-carotene to retinol was later shown to take place in the intestinal mucosa of animals and humans. The requirements and recommended daily allowances of beta-carotene and retinol for animals and humans were also determined.

Early research into the function of retinol was based on physiological and biochemical observations of the responses of experimental animals to diets lacking in beta-carotene or retinol. When weanling rats were fed a vitamin A–deficient diet, their liver stores of retinyl esters became exhausted after about four weeks, and their growth began to decline after five weeks. They then became night blind, and their corneas began to show lesions and to ulcerate after about six weeks on the deficient diet. After this they lost weight precipitously, became sick, and died. This simple feeding experiment highlighted three of the most important physiological functions of vitamin A: It promotes vision, normal differentiation of epithelia (such as the cornea), and growth. Vitamin A deficiency detracts from these functions and, in addition, leads to abnormal bone growth, inhibition of spermatogenesis in male animals, and resorption of the fetus in pregnant females.

The visual function of vitamin A was elucidated in great detail and with exceptional brilliance (culminating in a Nobel Prize) by G. Wald. As we have already noted, night blindness (defective vision at low illumination) was recognized in the eighteenth century as an early symptom of a dietary deficiency; later research indicated that night blindness, and its associated lesions, resulted specifically from a deficiency of vitamin A. It was, therefore, fitting that the function of vitamin A in vision was the first to be defined with a precise mechanism at the molecular level. As Moore (1957: 263) commented: "It may be an inspiring thought . . . that Man's knowledge of the existence of the stars and the vast universe which appears in the heavens each night, comes in the first place from the stimulation by the light rays of delicately poised molecules of vitamin A."

As long ago as 1878, W. Kühne recognized that retinas from dark-adapted frogs, purple in color, changed to yellow when exposed to light. The connection with vitamin A was made in 1925 by L. S. Fridericia and E. Holm, who observed that vitamin A–deficient, light-adapted rats, when put into the dark, formed visual purple at a slower rate than normal rats. Then, in 1929, Holm observed the presence of vitamin A in the retina. However, it was Wald, beginning in 1935, who found that the visual purple of the retina, called rhodopsin, consists of a protein, opsin, combined with "retinene" (later shown by R.A. Morton to be retinaldehyde). Wald and his co-workers (Wald 1968: 230–9) described the visual cycle thus: The 11-*cis*-isomer of retinaldehyde, while attached to opsin in rhodopsin, is isomerized to the all-*trans* form by light; this is the event that triggers the nerve impulse to the brain as perception of light. The all-*trans*-retinaldehyde is released from the opsin and reduced to all-*trans*-retinol. This, in the dark, is isomerized to 11-*cis*-retinol, oxidized to 11-*cis*-retinaldehyde, which recombines with opsin to re-form rhodopsin (dark adaptation), thus completing the cycle.

Elucidation of the metabolic function of vitamin A lagged behind the recognition of its role in vision. The observations of S. B. Wolbach and P. R. Howe (1925) defined the epithelial lesions resulting from vitamin A deficiency, particularly the keratinization of epithelial cells, especially of the cornea, but also of the respiratory, intestinal, and genitourinary tracts. It seemed that vitamin A influenced the differentiation of epithelial cells from the normal simple and pseudostratified phenotype to squamous, metaplastic lesions, starting focally and, ultimately, spreading throughout the epithelium.

Apart from the function of maintaining normal epithelial differentiation, the pathology of vitamin A deficiency also revealed a function of vitamin A in bone growth, shown by the thickened bones in growing, vitamin A–deficient animals. In addition, the deficiency is manifest in reproductive functions; in the male, by cessation of spermatogenesis and atrophy of the testes; in the female, by a defective uterus, placental necrosis, and, ultimately, resorption of the fetus. Indeed, as long ago as 1933, the teratogenic effect of only marginal vitamin A deficiency, which resulted in ocular and genitourinary defects in pig embryos, underlined the necessity of vitamin A to support normal fetal development.

In the 1950s and 1960s, the metabolism of vitamin A was delineated by J. A. Olson and others, and recognition of the importance of its transport proteins followed. This discovery was made by D. S. Goodman with regard to the plasma retinol-binding protein, and by F. Chytil and D. E. Ong with respect to the intracellular-binding proteins. K. R. Norum and R. Blomhoff and others established the basic facts of absorption and liver-storage mechanisms for retinol.

In the 1970s and 1980s, the discovery by U. Saffiotti of an anticarcinogenic action of vitamin A (although still a matter of some controversy) led to an outburst of research effort. In animal experiments, retinol, and particularly its metabolite, retinoic acid, have been demonstrated indisputably to have anticarcinogenic properties. But as applied to human cancer patients, a search for similar activity was disappointing, although a number of isomeric forms and synthetic chemical derivatives of retinoic acid were found to be active against some forms of cancer. For example, acute promyelocytic leukemia has been successfully treated with all-*trans*-retinoic acid; certain skin and head-and-neck cancers have yielded to 13-*cis*-retinoic acid, and retinoic acid and some of its synthetic chemical derivatives have exhibited spectacular cures in a number of skin diseases.

A new era of vitamin A research dawned in 1987, when P. Chambon in Strasbourg, France, and R. M. Evans in San Diego, California, and their respective co-workers, simultaneously discovered the retinoic acid receptors in cell nuclei (Mangelsdorf, Umesono, and Evans 1994). These receptor proteins can bind retinoic acid and, when thus liganded, can activate a number of specific genes to stimulate the cells either to produce specific proteins (enzymes) or to inhibit the activity of other enzymes. In this way, one can arrive at an explanation at the molecular level of the many metabolic functions of vitamin A with regard to embryonic development, differentiation, and growth. This type of action – gene activation – establishes vitamin A (in the form of its metabolite, retinoic acid) as a hormone, similar to the steroid hormones and the thyroid hormone. As was predicted in 1970: "[T]here is no *a priori* reason why a hormone should have to be made by the animal itself. It is quite conceivable that a hormone can be taken in the diet [as vitamin A], stored in the liver, and secreted into the bloodstream when needed. The liver then acts as the endocrine organ" (Wolf and De Luca 1970: 257).

Clinical Manifestations of Vitamin A Deficiency

Vitamin A deficiency diseases appear primarily in the young because, like other mammals, humans are born with low liver reserves. The latter probably results from a placental transport of retinol, which, although generally sufficient for normal development, is not sufficient for building any surplus. After birth, colostrum (and later breast milk) provides the needed vitamin, so long as the mother's intake of vitamin A is adequate. If, after weaning, vitamin A stores have not been built up, and malnutrition plagues the child, deficiency signs will appear. Other causes for vitamin A deficiency are protein malnutrition, when the retinol transport system in blood does not function normally, and chronic malabsorption diseases such as cystic fibrosis.

The first sign of deficiency, as already discussed, is night blindness. With increasing severity of the deficiency, the following ocular signs are exhibited: con-

junctival xerosis; Bitot's spots (white, foamy spots on the conjunctival surface, consisting of sloughed-off cells); corneal xerosis; and corneal ulceration (also called keratomalacia), which often ends in irreversible blindness, a direct consequence of the liquefaction of the corneal stroma. Recently, increased morbidity and mortality, frequently connected with diarrhea and respiratory diseases, has been observed in children with marginal vitamin A intake and no eye lesions (see next section), no doubt caused by a compromised immune system (Underwood 1994). It has also been noted that measles in marginally depleted children can precipitate severe vitamin A deficiency diseases. Figure IV.A.1.2 presents a diagrammatic representation of the deficiency signs.

In adults, vitamin A deficiency gives rise, apart from night blindness, to skin lesions (hyperkeratosis of hair follicles). Moreover, experimentally induced vitamin A deficiency in adult human volunteers caused raised cerebrospinal fluid pressure, loss of the senses of taste and smell, and abnormalities in vestibular function (Wolf 1980: 146–50).

Dangers of Vitamin A Excess

If too little vitamin A is harmful, so also is too much, and emphasis needs to be placed on the dangers of hypervitaminosis A. In technically developed countries, many cases of vitamin A intoxication by ingestion of large doses of retinol or retinyl ester supplements (25,000 IU or more over a prolonged period, i.e., one month or longer) have been reported. It is not difficult to understand the reasoning behind this behavior ("if a little is good for me, a lot must be better"), and such reasoning is encouraged by popular literature, media exaggerations, a vague idea that vitamins generally are beneficial, and incomplete reports of the anticancer effects of vitamin A.

Unfortunately, such reasoning with vitamin A can lead to vitamin A intoxication, with symptoms such as skin rash, desquamation and pruritus of the skin, hair loss, weakness and fatigue, liver damage, bone and joint pain (associated with osteopenia of vertebrae and calcification of spinal ligaments and periosteal tissues in extreme cases), anorexia, and an increase in cerebrospinal fluid pressure, sometimes prompting a misdiagnosis of brain tumor. Hypervitaminosis A is rapidly reversible after the patient stops taking the vitamins. (It should also be emphasized, however, that for metabolic reasons, the provitamin A, beta-carotene, is nontoxic at any dose.)

In addition, recent oral use of an oxidation product of retinol (13-*cis*-retinoic acid) as a drug for the very successful treatment of acne has led to cases of fetal malformations, and there is a risk of abnormalities in the babies if the drug is taken during pregnancy, even at the very earliest stages after conception. Extreme caution is, therefore, indicated to avoid this drug if there is a possibility of pregnancy.

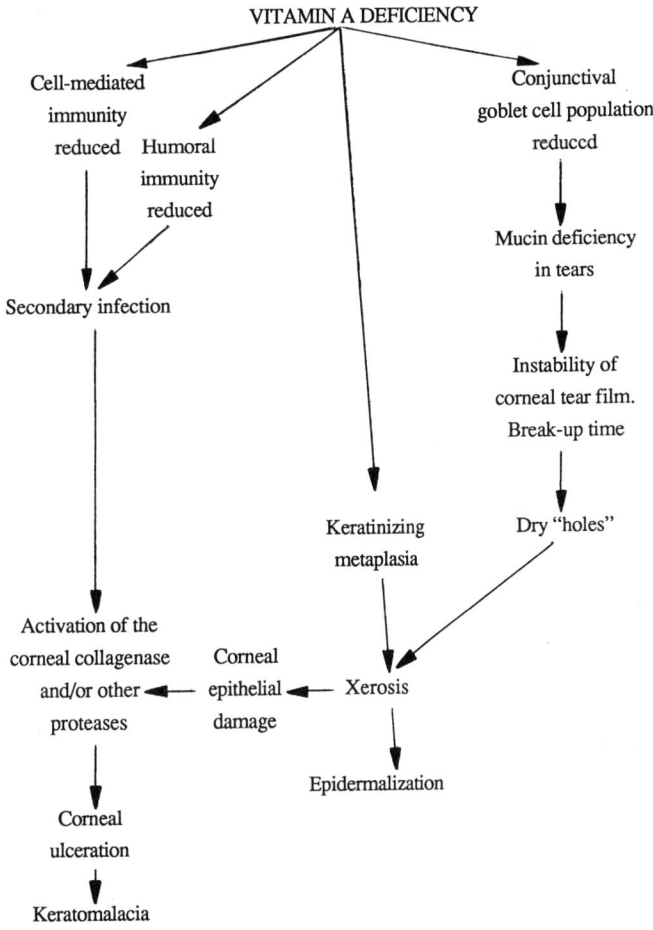

Figure IV.A.1.2. A postulated mechanism for the pathogenesis of keratomalacia in vitamin A deficiency (From unpublished documents, Nutrition Unit, World Health Organization, Geneva, Switzerland, 1994. With permission)

Geographic Distribution and Epidemiology of Vitamin A Deficiency

Vitamin A deficiency clusters in periequatorial areas and is closely associated with areas of poverty and malnutrition. Estimates suggest that about 350,000 preschool children become blind every year because of severe vitamin A deficiency; of these children, 60 percent die within a year (Underwood 1994).

Recent epidemiological surveys have demonstrated that mortality rates of preschool children receiving low or marginal dietary vitamin A, *yet not showing ocular signs of vitamin A deficiency,* could be lowered by 20 to 50 percent through vitamin A supplementation. Meta-analysis revealed a protective effect in lowering mortality by 23 percent in eight different studies done in Indonesia, Ghana, Nepal, India, and Sudan. From these data it is estimated that worldwide, 13 to 14 million children suffer from mild deficiency (no night blindness) with consequent increased risk of childhood infections (measles, respiratory infections, diarrhea). Vitamin A supplementation lowered the risk of death from measles in areas where subclinical vitamin A deficiency was prevalent. The cause of the protective effect of vitamin A is not known, but vitamin A depletion probably compromises the immune system.

Clearly, vitamin A deficiency and depletion are very serious public health problems. The World Health Organization actively monitors and obtains data on the worldwide occurrence of clinical and subclinical vitamin A deficiency and recommends ways to improve the situation. Intervention programs to eliminate the deficiency have been successful in Indonesia and are being implemented in India, Bangladesh, and Tanzania (Underwood 1994). Such programs involve food fortification, distribution of supplements, dietary diversification, and control of infectious diseases. The latter is important because there is a synergistic relationship between infectious diseases and vitamin A deficiency: Subclinical deficiency makes children prone to infectious diseases, and such diseases, in turn, can increase the need for the vitamin and precipitate or worsen a deficiency.

It is ironic and tragic that vitamin A deficiency occurs mostly in periequatorial regions where the

Table IV.A.1.2. *Countries categorized by degree of health; importance of vitamin A deficiency by WHO region (From information available to WHO in May 1994)*

WHO region	Clinical	Subclinical			No data: problem likely
		Severe[a]	Moderate[b]	Mild[c]	
Africa	Benin*	Cape Verde*	Angola*	Liberia*	Botswana
	Murkina Faso	Congo	Guinea*	Madagascar	Algeria
	Cameroon	Gambia	Namibia		Burundi
	Chad	South Africa	Sierra Leone*		Central African Republic
	Ethiopia	Zambia	Zaire*		Côte d'Ivoire
	Ghana		Zimbabwe*		Equatorial Guinea
	Kenya				Gabon
	Malawi				Guinea Bissau
	Mali				Lesotho
	Mauritania				São Tome & Principe
	Mozambique				Swaziland
	Niger				
	Nigeria*				
	Rwanda*				
	Senegal				
	Togo				
	Uganda				
	United Republic of Tanzania				
Americas	Brazil	Mexico	Bolivia	Belize	Cuba
	Dominican Republic	Nicaragua	Ecuador	Colombia	
	El Salvador*	Peru	Honduras*	Panama	
	Guatemala				
	Haiti				
South-End Asia	Bangladesh		Bhutan		Maldives
	India		Indonesia		
	Myanmar		Sri Lanka*		
	Nepal		Thailand		
Eastern Mediterranean	Afghanistan*	Pakistan	Djibouti	Egypt	Iraq
	Somalia		Oman*	Iran	Jordan
	Sudan			Saudi Arabia	Lebanon
	Yemen				Syria
Western Pacific	Cambodia	Papua New Guinea*	China	Malaysia	
	Federal States of Micronesia		Solomon Is.*	N. Mariana Islands*	
	Kiribati				
	Lao People's Dem. Rep.				
	Marshall Is.				
	Philippines				
	Vietnam				

[a]Urgently important public health problem in the whole, or in a substantial part, of the country based on serum retinol levels.

[b]Moderately important public health problem in the whole, or in a substantial part, of the country (subclinical biochemical and/or dietary evidence).

[c]Sporadic occurrence or high risk of a public health problem in part of the country based on dietary and ecological risk factors.

*Insufficient data to be certain of category.

Source: Indicators for assessing vitamin A deficiency and their application in monitoring and evaluating intervention programs and unpublished documents, Nutrition Unit, World Health Organization (Geneva: 1994). With permission.

populations are surrounded by sources of the provitamin, beta-carotene, in the form of green leaves. It is thought that in rice-dependent countries (India, Bangladesh, Indonesia, and the Philippines, for example), vitamin A depletion is caused by the practice of providing weaned children a mostly rice diet, which lacks both vitamin A and beta-carotene. Such ignorance of good nutrition practices could be combated by nutrition education that would lead to the preparation of beta-carotene-rich foods for children.

The principal causes of the deficiency, however, are poverty and infectious diseases. To quote B. A. Underwood: "Rural areas in the affected regions are generally characterized by economic and social underdevelopment, including the quality and distribution of health services, sanitary facilities and potable water. These factors, characteristic of deprivation, are associated with high morbidity and consequently increased nutrition needs." Underwood stresses the ". . . environmental factors that can alter requirements and increase risks of hypovitaminosis A. Such risks are clustered in households and neighborhoods where poverty, poor personal and environmental sanitation, functional illiteracy, social isolation, inadequate access to health and social services prevail" (Underwood 1984: 355).

Vitamin A deficiency is generally found in regions of the globe where protein–energy malnutrition is also prevalent. Animal experiments have shown that a low-protein diet reduces the intestinal enzymes necessary for conversion of beta-carotene to retinol. Thus, a double danger threatens children in such regions: a short supply of beta-carotene *and* protein depletion that may reduce the conversion of available beta-carotene to retinol.

Awareness of this huge problem has finally galvanized governments, and plans were put in motion by the World Health Organization to eliminate vitamin A deficiency by the year 2000.

Vitamin A and Carotenoids in Food

Preformed vitamin A (retinol) is found only in animal foods, with the highest levels in mammalian, fowl, and fish livers, and in fish-liver oil, but with great seasonal variation. The next highest levels are in kidneys and fatty fish (e.g., salmon), whereas a third tier consists of milk, butter, and eggs, again with seasonal variation.

Carotenoids (beta-carotene and related compounds) are precursors of vitamin A that occur in green leaves and yellow and red vegetables and constitute the main source of vitamin A in the human diet. In decreasing order of beta-carotene content, these sources include parsley, sweet potato, broccoli, lettuce, tomato, and cabbage. Smaller, but significant, amounts are in legumes such as chickpeas and green and black grams. Yellow maize also contains beta-carotene. Fowl that eat grains and seeds absorb and accumulate carotenoids in their fat, so that their flesh can also be a source of this provitamin.

A special case as a source of beta-carotene is red palm oil, a vegetable oil used for cooking in several areas of Africa, Southeast Asia, and South America. It contains 0.6 to 1 RE per gram of oil and, in these areas, represents an important source of the provitamin (Underwood 1984: 290). The oil is extracted from the fleshy mesocarp of the palm nut and is prepared by boiling the fruit in water, cooling, and removing the oily layer. Unfortunately, substantial losses of beta-carotene can occur during cooking and storage.

Foods that lack vitamin A or carotenoids are wheat, oats, rice, potatoes, cassava, manioc, onions, nuts, sugar, olive oil, pork, and lard. In light of this lack, it is of interest to consider traditional diets of children in countries where vitamin A deficiency is a widespread public health problem. J. M. May and D. L. McLellan (1970), for example, have described the foods given to children in rural Ethiopia after weaning (at about 18 months of age). These included pancakes (*injera* – made from a local low-protein cereal grain called *toff* [tef], fermented and wet-cooked on a large griddle over an open fire) and a stew (*wot* – made of legumes, barley, onions, and garlic). The *wot* may contain some meat, although two-thirds of rural Ethiopians never eat meat. The children of a family are especially disadvantaged in terms of nutrition because the order of feeding is first the father, then guests, male persons, mother, and, last, children. Often, by the time the children eat, the *wot,* containing small amounts of carotenoids, is gone, and only *injera* is left.

Another example is drawn from Ghana, where the principal diet in rural areas consists of either fermented maize flour *(keuke)* made into a dough and cooked, or a soup or porridge of millet *(tuwonsafe).* In tropical forest regions, sun-dried cassava is ground to a flour *(konkote)* and boiled to a puree. Any oils in the diet are from groundnuts. Once again, fathers eat first, then other males, with women and children last. Moreover, there are taboos against women consuming eggs in some parts of Ghana. Clearly, with such a diet and such cultural habits, vitamin A deficiency is likely to be widespread.

A final example is found in India, where a public health problem exists with respect to vitamin A deficiency: The poor eat principally parboiled rice, or millet or wheat flours mixed with water and cooked as pancakes *(chapattis).* Cooking oil is from seeds; legumes are cooked with spices, and fat and vegetable intake is low (1 percent of the diet). Children are weaned at 2 years, then given boiled milk, diluted with water, along with rice or *chapattis.* No wonder that vitamin A deficiency diseases are prevalent among the poor.

Future Prospects

Basic Biology

Since the discovery, in 1987, of the mechanism of gene activation by retinoic acid, establishing vitamin A as a hormone, progress in the understanding of its basic biology has been breathtakingly rapid. The pleiotropic action of vitamin A (i.e., the multiple physiological functions of this vitamin) in development, growth, and differentiation, and the legion of enzymes affected by it, has been a puzzle since the early work of Wolbach and Howe (1925). This puzzle is now in the process of being solved.

The regulation and control of growth factors, hormones, enzymes, and homeobox genes (i.e., genes controlling embryonic development) by retinoic acid can now be explained on a rational basis because of the discovery of nuclear retinoic acid receptors (RARs), proteins that bind metabolites of retinol (all-*trans*-retinoic acid and 9-*cis*-retinoic acid) and, in a variety of combinations, interact with the DNA in the promoter regions of a large number of genes. These genes are then activated to express specific mRNAs (messenger RNAs) and proteins that can regulate and control development, growth, and differentiation.

Researchers are sequencing the relevant genes and tracing their evolutionary development. They are also in the process of elucidating the genes' interaction with RARs and the functions of the specific proteins expressed (enzymes, hormones, growth factors). Thus, the fields of biochemistry, endocrinology, genetics, embryology, evolution, and oncology will be greatly expanded, all on the basis of our recognition of the nuclear RARs. It has now become clear that the immune system is also influenced by vitamin A, and important advances in research on the action of vitamin A on the immune response can be expected.

Cancer and Other Diseases

Acute promyelocytic leukemia and skin cancer have been successfully treated with vitamin A derivatives. On the basis of experimental work, one can expect other forms of cancer to yield to efforts at treatment by retinoids. Chemoprevention treatment by retinoids of persons at high risk (e.g., recurrent squamous carcinoma of the head and neck) will certainly expand. Skin diseases (acne, psoriasis, and others) have been successfully treated with retinoids, and the possibility exists that rheumatoid arthritis and other inflammatory diseases may ultimately yield to retinoid treatment.

Public Health

Future prospects for the alleviation of the horrendous tragedy of preventable childhood blindness and children's infectious diseases by vitamin A or beta-carotene now lie in the hands of governments, international organizations, and nongovernmental agencies. The problem is not one of science but of economics, education, and, ultimately, politics. The science is merely concerned with methods of determining in which population groups the children are at risk of vitamin A deficiency and the severity of the deficiency. This assessment can be done by blood tests, but simpler methods are being sought. Once the deficient population group has been ascertained, it is necessary to direct efforts for a cure in such a way that the vitamin reaches the children in need. This implementation involves improving the children's overall diet and sanitation, removing parasites, educating the mothers, diversifying the food supply, fortifying foods, and supplementing with vitamins. Considering the millions of children and the multitude of countries affected (see Table IV.A.1.2), each with its own government, bureaucracy, and dietary and cultural traditions, the elimination of vitamin A depletion and deficiency will be a daunting task.

George Wolf

The author thanks Dr. Barbara A. Underwood of the WHO Nutrition Unit, Geneva, Switzerland, for making available and giving permission to use material from unpublished documents from the World Health Organization.

Notes

1. The author is grateful for this information to Dr. John F. Nunn, Northwood, Middlesex, England.

Bibliography

Guggenheim, K. Y. 1981. *Nutrition and nutritional diseases, the evolution of concepts.* Boston, Mass.

Hirschberg, J. 1899. Geschichte der Augenheilkunde. In *Handbuch der gesamten Augenheilkunde.* Second edition, ed. T. Saemische, Vol. 12, Part 2, 98–106. Leipzig.

Kühn, C. G. 1821. *Galeni omnia opera,* Vol. 19, 802–3. Leipzig.

Lee, T. 1967. Nyctalopia. In *Diseases in antiquity,* ed. D. B. Fothwell and A. T. Sandison, 418–19. Springfield, Ill.

Lindeboom, G. A. 1984. Geschichtliche Meilensteine in der Behandlung der Nachtblindheit. *Clio Medica* 19: 40–9.

Mangelsdorf, D. J., K. Umesono, and R. M. Evans. 1994. The retinoid receptors. In *The retinoids,* ed. M. B. Sporn, A. B. Roberts, and D. S. Goodman, 319–50. New York.

May, J. M., and D. L. McLellan. 1970. *The ecology of malnutrition.* New York.

McCollum, E. V. 1957. *A history of nutrition.* Boston, Mass.
    1964. *From Kansas farm boy to scientist.* Lawrence, Kans.

Moore, T. 1957. *Vitamin A.* New York.

Schwarz, E. 1861. *Reise der oesterreichischen Fregatte Novara um die Erde.* Vienna.

Sommer, A. 1978. Cure for nightblindness. *American Journal of Clinical Nutrition* 31: 1489.

Sporn, M. B., A. B. Roberts, and D. S. Goodman, 1994. eds. *The retinoids.* Second edition. New York.

Underwood, B. A. 1984. Vitamin A in animal and human nutrition. In *The retinoids,* Vol. 1, first edition, ed. M. B. Sporn, A. B. Roberts, and D. S. Goodman, 282–392. New York.
    1994. Vitamin A in human nutrition: Public health considerations. In *The retinoids.* Vol. 1, second edition, ed. M. B. Sporn, A. B. Roberts, and D. S. Goodman, 211–28. New York.

Wald, E. 1968. Molecular basis of visual excitation. *Science* 162: 230–9.

Wolbach, S. B., and P. R. Howe. 1925. Tissue changes following deprivation of fat-soluble vitamin A. *Journal of Experimental Medicine* 47: 753–77.

Wolf, G. 1980. Vitamin A. In *Human nutrition, a comprehensive treatise,* ed. R. B. Alfin-Slater and D. Kritchevsky, 96–100. New York.

Wolf, G., and L. M. De Luca. 1970. Recent studies on some metabolic functions of vitamin A. In *Fat-soluble vitamin symposium,* ed. H. F. DeLuca and J. W. Suttie, 257–65. Madison, Wis.

IV.A.2 ☙ Vitamin B Complex: Thiamine, Riboflavin, Niacin, Pantothenic Acid, Pyridoxine, Cobalamin, Folic Acid

The history of the discovery of the B vitamins includes both the recognition that particular diseases can result from dietary inadequacies and the subsequent isolation of specific nutrients from foods that have been found to prevent and to cure those diseases. Most of these dietary deficiencies were first recognized in humans, but in certain instances, the deficiency was produced by feeding restricted diets to experimental animals.

After each of the B vitamins was isolated, extensive biochemical and physiological studies were conducted to define their specific functions. States of B vitamin dependency were also discovered in which the need for a particular vitamin exceeded the physiological level. These vitamin dependencies were found either to have a genetic basis or to be drug-induced.

Moreover, recognition that certain synthetic compounds bearing close chemical resemblance to B vitamins could block the activity of naturally occurring vitamins has led to a better understanding of vitaminic functions and has provided us with certain drugs that are used in cancer chemotherapy and in the treatment of infections and inflammatory diseases.

Vitamin B research, as well as clinical and public health information, is summarized here to emphasize some significant advances in our knowledge of these compounds. But first a note on nomenclature seems appropriate.

B Vitamin Nomenclature

The confusing nomenclature of the B vitamins can only be understood historically. In 1915 E. V. McCollum and M. Davis concluded that young rats needed two unknown "growth factors," one fat-soluble and the other water-soluble, and for convenience they called them "factors A and B," respectively. Casimir Funk had already coined the term "vitamine" in the belief that any unknown factors would prove to have the chemical structure of "amines." J. C. Drummond then suggested that the term be modified to "vitamin," which had no chemical significance, and he called the antiscurvy factor "vitamin C."

Further research showed that "factor B" was made up of at least two components, one heat-labile and the other more stable; these were termed vitamins B_1 and B_2 respectively. Vitamin B_1 was later shown to be the anti-beriberi vitamin, known as thiamine. The B_2 factor was again found to be complex. Among other things, it included riboflavin, which was first named "vitamin G" in honor of Joseph Goldberger, who had made classical studies of pellagra in the United States. The designation vitamin B_3 was given to a compound that seems to have been pantothenic acid but was sometimes incorrectly used to mean niacin. Biotin was first called "vitamin H" by workers in Germany who had shown that its deficiency in rats resulted in abnormalities of the skin (in German *Haut*), and folic acid, at one time, was termed "vitamin M" because it was first shown to be needed by monkeys. Today, however, these three letters, namely, G, H, and M, are no longer used, and the vitamins are known by the names riboflavin, biotin, and folic acid and classified as parts of the vitamin B complex.

Other workers claimed higher numbers in the B series when they believed that they had discovered new growth factors. But many of these assertions seem to have been erroneous claims and only two "B" numberings are still in use: B_6 for pyridoxine and closely related compounds, and B_{12} for cobalamin and its derivatives. The coding is convenient because in each case it covers more than one precise chemical compound.

In recent years, some entrepreneurs engaged in selling materials that have been claimed to cure cancer and other diseases have named their products as vitamins in attempts to portray them as essentially natural materials, and so to escape the strict regulations applying to drugs. An example is B_{17}, or "laetrile," which is not recognized by orthodox nutritionists.

Thiamine

Use of polished rice as a dietary staple has long been known to lead to the development of a disease known as beriberi, which was first described as affecting Japanese sailors as well as prisoners in the Dutch East Indies. Signs of beriberi include paralysis due to polyneuritis and congestive heart failure. Christian Eijkman, a medical officer in Java, was the first to show (1890) that a paralytic illness resembling beriberi could be produced in chickens by feeding them polished rice (Jansen 1950). He, and his successor Gerrit Grijns, also demonstrated that the polyneuritis of beriberi could be cured by feeding rice bran.

In 1912, Funk extracted a substance from rice bran that he believed was the anti-beriberi substance and that he characterized chemically as being an amine. He then coined the term "vitamine" as a contraction of "vital amine." With the discovery of other organic compounds that were "vital" but not amines, the term "vitamin" was used instead. The anti-beriberi vitamin was named thiamine. The biologically active coenzyme form of thiamine is required for the oxidative decarboxylation of pyruvic acid. Thiamine is also required in the metabolism of glucose and many other enzyme-catalyzed reactions.

It has been shown that alcoholics may develop an acute thiamine deficiency if they drink heavily and concurrently go without food. Their condition of acute thiamine deficiency, which is manifested by a confusional state and paralysis of certain eye muscles, is designated as Wernicke's encephalopathy. It responds to high doses of intravenously administered thiamine. If this confusional state is not recognized and treated with thiamine, a chronic organic brain disorder develops, associated with dementia. Those who have this disorder may require institutionalization. Korsakoff's psychosis is believed to be a chronic form of Wernicke's encephalopathy, and the health costs of caring for persons with this disease have led to the fortification of beers with thiamine in an experimental public health intervention in Australia (Yellowlees 1986).

Nicotinic Acid, or Niacin

Pellagra is a disease that we now recognize as being caused by a deficiency in nicotinic acid (niacin). It is characterized by development of a dermatitis, which appears on areas of the body exposed to strong sunlight; by diarrhea, associated with malabsorption of nutrients; and by a severe confusional state. This disease was first described by Gaspar Casal, who wrote of the diet of Spanish peasants with pellagra or *mal de la rosa,* as it was then called (the book was published posthumously in 1762).

Because the Spanish peasants who had this disease subsisted on cornmeal, and because corn, particularly moldy corn, was also the dietary staple of other poverty-stricken populations in southern Europe that developed pellagra, it was believed that the disease was caused by eating a corn-based diet, particularly when the corn had been improperly stored and became moldy. It was also observed that the diet of those with pellagra was especially lacking in animal protein.

It was not until 1914, when pellagra had become a problem in the southern United States, that Goldberger began his studies, which ultimately demonstrated that the nutritional etiology of pellagra produced a comparable condition in dogs called "black tongue" and identified foods that were pellagra-preventing (Roe 1973). Later investigators extracted some of these foods, including liver, and attempted isolation of nutrients lacking in the diets of those with the disease. During this period, independent studies by Otto Heinrich Warburg and Walter Christian identified nicotinic acid as one of the substances forming "coferment," which was thought to be important in normal metabolism. Shortly after this discovery, nicotinic acid was found to be an essential factor for the growth of certain bacteria.

Conrad Elvehjem and his co-workers, who carried out extensive studies at the University of Wisconsin in the 1930s, tested various liver-extract fractions for activity as growth factors in experimental animals. One sample was found to contain a substance that was identified by Wayne Woolley as nicotinic acid. Subsequently, others in Elvehjem's laboratory cured "black tongue" in dogs by feeding them the nicotinic acid obtained from such liver extracts (Kline and Baumann 1971).

Once it was known that nicotinic acid could cure this disease in dogs, Tom Spies gave nicotinic acid to several subjects with pellagra and found that the human disease responded to it as well. The nutrient nicotinic acid was subsequently given the alternate name of niacin in order to avoid lay confusion of the term with nicotine.

Later studies of the metabolism of niacin in experimental animals showed that they could synthesize it from a precursor, which proved to be the amino acid tryptophan. Because animal proteins are particularly rich in tryptophan, this finding helped to explain the old observation that diets of pellagrins were invariably low in meat and milk (Goldsmith 1964).

Nicotinic acid is active biochemically in several coenzyme forms, and it is necessary for the synthesis and breakdown of fatty acids, carbohydrates, and amino acids. In human studies conducted soon after the discovery of its activity as a vitamin, it was found that when large doses of niacin were administered, individuals became flushed. Although this observation was an early indication that niacin might be toxic if given in excessive amounts, it also suggested that high doses might relieve conditions associated with constriction of blood vessels. In fact, the vitamin failed to yield the hoped-for therapeutic advantage, but it was found later that niacin in high doses could reduce blood cholesterol levels (Havel and Kane 1982).

Riboflavin

Riboflavin, another of the B-complex vitamins, was first isolated from the greenish yellow pigment in milk. Its deficiency occurs in populations whose diets are lacking in dairy foods and green vegetables and produces a disease characterized by cracks at the corners of the mouth, sore tongue, dermatitis of the folds of the body, and changes in the eyes that make them sensitive to light exposure. It was realized that some pellagra sufferers in the United States were deficient in riboflavin as well as in niacin. The condition was also described in very low-income, rural populations in India (Sebrell and Butler 1938). In more recent years, this same condition has been identified in alcoholics. Flavins, including two major active forms of the vitamin designated riboflavin, have also been isolated from liver. Furthermore, it has been shown that flavins are necessary for energy utilization and that requirements for riboflavin increase during periods of physical activity (Roe 1991).

Vitamin B$_6$

The term "vitamin B$_6$" embraces a group of closely related compounds: pyridoxine, pyridoxal, and pyridoxamine. Laboratory investigations resulting in the identification of vitamin B$_6$ were launched after it became known that a particular form of dermatitis, which developed in rats fed purified diets, could not be cured with any known nutrient but could be prevented by giving the animals a particular yeast extract.

The early clinical studies of vitamin B$_6$ deficiency were based on observations of infants fed an autoclaved formula diet. Then, during the 1950s, when active research was being conducted on the biochemical functions of vitamin B$_6$, further insight into the clinical manifestations of its deficiency was obtained by putting human volunteers on a diet that lacked the vitamin and giving them a vitamin B_6 antagonist at the same time.

Following this study, vitamin B_6 deficiency was observed in patients who were given the drug isoniazid for the treatment of tuberculosis. It was then realized that the drug was also a vitamin B_6 antagonist. In both the experimentally produced vitamin B_6 deficiency and the drug-induced disease, dermatitis and neurological symptoms developed, and later an anemia surfaced as well, in which iron was improperly utilized. Biochemical studies showed that there were three physiologically active forms of vitamin B_6 and that these forms are interconvertible. They have been found to function in amino acid metabolism, in the synthesis of heme from which hemoglobin is formed, and in neurotransmitter activity (Roe 1985).

Pantothenic Acid

Metabolic pathways that depend on pantothenic acid include those involved with the biosynthesis of cholesterol and steroid hormones. Abnormalities have been described in several different types of experimental animals placed on diets deficient in pantothenic acid. In rats, these changes included slow rate of growth in young animals and graying of the fur in older animals. The fertility of rats has also been shown to decline, and gait disorders have been observed in pigs. In addition, destruction of the adrenal glands, associated with bleeding into these glands, has been found in postmortem examinations of several species in which the deficiency has been induced.

Little is known of human requirements for the vitamin, but because it is widespread in foods, there is little danger of deficiency. Thus, pantothenic acid deficiency has been described only in humans who are very severely malnourished and in volunteers who have been fed both a pantothenic acid–deficient diet and a pantothenic acid antagonist (Fox 1984).

Biotin

Biotin is another B vitamin that is involved in the biosynthesis of fatty acids. Biotin deficiency has been described in infants as a result of an inborn error of metabolism. A biotin deficiency has also been described in infants and in older individuals with intestinal diseases. Both groups were fed formula diets lacking in biotin, and both were concurrently receiving broad-spectrum antibiotics that prevented the intestinal synthesis of this vitamin (Mock et al. 1985).

Folic Acid (Folacin)

In 1929-31, Lucy Wills and her colleagues described a severe anemia among pregnant women living in conditions of purdah (seclusion) in Bombay. Because of cultural taboos, these women ate a monotonous and limited diet in which green vegetables and fruits were lacking (Wills and Mehta 1929-30; Wills and Talpade 1930-1). The anemia was characterized by a severe lowering of the red blood cell count and the appearance of large immature cells in the bone marrow and in the peripheral blood. This so-called macrocytic (large-celled) anemia was cured by giving the women a yeast extract. Subsequent studies showed that certain crude liver extracts could also cure it.

Wills also reported poor pregnancy outcomes for the Indian women who were anemic. She subsequently described the anemia in other populations who lived on diets that lacked fruit and green vegetables. Later investigations led to the isolation of a nutrient, both from liver and from green vegetables, that prevented and cured the same macrocytic anemia. This nutrient was named folic acid, or folacin. Early investigations of folic acid showed that it existed in several different forms that had a number of critical functions in cell maturation.

In other studies, researchers deliberately synthesized chemical analogues of folic acid and demonstrated that these substances not only blocked the normal activity of folic acid but also prevented cell division. Such findings led to the development of specific folic acid antagonists, including aminopterin and methotrexate, which inhibit the division of malignant cells. Methotrexate, which was the less toxic of the two substances, is now employed to control certain forms of cancer and leukemia (Roe 1990). However, it was also found that if aminopterin or methotrexate was taken during the first trimester of pregnancy, birth defects occurred in the offspring. The defects were shown in rat studies to develop if one or another of these drugs was administered during the gestational period of embryogenesis (Nelson 1963).

Another association of folic acid nutriture has been revealed more recently, namely that the risk of women bearing infants with neural tube defects, such as spina bifida, is greatly reduced if they are given supplementary folic acid from the time of conception through the first trimester. Currently, a debate continues about whether or not it would be desirable to fortify cereals with folic acid as a public health measure to prevent neural tube defects (MRC Vitamin Study Research Group 1991).

Vitamin B_{12} (Cobalamin)

Vitamin B_{12} was first isolated as the active factor in liver extracts that, given by injection, maintained subjects suffering from pernicious anemia. This disease was first described by Thomas Addison in the nineteenth century, who observed that it occurred primarily in older men and women and is characterized by the presence of a macrocytic anemia. The changes in the blood picture are identical to those seen in folic acid deficiency. In addition, patients with pernicious anemia may develop an irreversible neurological disorder that leads to sensory loss, including loss of balance. A confusional state may also be present.

Studies of pernicious anemia have revealed that it is an autoimmune disease in which cells in the lining of the stomach are destroyed. As a result, the so-called intrinsic factor found in normal gastric secretion is no longer produced in the stomach and there is a loss of capacity to absorb vitamin B_{12}. Vitamin B_{12} deficiency can also develop when it cannot be absorbed because of surgical loss of the absorption site in the lower part of the small intestine. Aside from these circumstances, a very low intake of vitamin B_{12} can also cause pernicious anemia, although such a low intake is unlikely to occur except with people who are strict vegans, since the vitamin is present only in animal foods. Deficiency signs may, however, take several years to develop because of body stores of the vitamin built up in earlier periods.

Investigations of the cause of the neurological complications of vitamin B_{12} deficiency followed recognition that the same complications may develop in those who are exposed to nitrous oxide (Roe 1985). More recently, more such neurological studies have been carried out on the metabolic defect existing in children with genetic disorders of vitamin B_{12} metabolism (Metz 1993).

Vitamin B_{12} has essential functions in the synthesis of the amino acid methionine and is also required for the interconversion and cellular uptake of different forms of folic acid (Buchanan 1964).

Daphne A. Roe

Bibliography

Bender, D. A. 1992. *Nutritional biochemistry of the vitamins.* Cambridge.

Buchanan, J. M. 1964. The function of vitamin B_{12} and folic acid co-enzymes in mammalian cells. *Medicine* 43: 697–709.

Fox, H. M. 1984. Pantothenic acid. In *Handbook of vitamins: Nutritional, biochemical and clinical aspects,* ed. L. J. Machlin, 437–55. New York and Basel.

Goldsmith, G. A. 1964. The B vitamins: Thiamine, riboflavin, niacin. In *Nutrition: A comprehensive treatise in vitamins, nutrient requirements and food selection,* Vol. 2, ed. G. H. Beaton and E. W. McHenry, 153–4. New York.

Griminger, P. 1972. Casimir Funk: Biographical sketch. *Journal of Nutrition* 102: 1105–14.

Havel, R. J., and J. P. Kane. 1982. Therapy in hyperlipedemic states. *Annual Review of Medicine* 33: 417–33.

Jansen, B. C. P. 1950. Biographical sketch: C. J. Eijkman. *Journal of Nutrition* 42: 1–8.

Kline, O. L., and C. A. Baumann. 1971. Conrad Arnold Elvehjem: Biographical sketch. *Journal of Nutrition* 101: 569–78.

Metz, J. 1993. Pathogenesis of cobalamin neuropathy: Deficiency of nervous system S-Adenosylmethionine? *Nutrition Reviews* 51: 12–15.

Mock, D. M., D. L. Baswell, H. Baker, et al. 1985. Biotin deficiency complicating parenteral alimentation: Diagnosis, metabolic repercussions and treatment. In *Biotin,*

ed. K. Dakshinamurti and H. Bgavagan. *Annals of the New York Academy of Sciences* 447: 314–34.

MRC Vitamin Study Research Group. 1991. Prevention of neural tube defects: Results of the Medical Research Council on vitamin study. *Lancet* 338: 131–7.

Nelson, M. M. 1963. Teratogenic effects of pteroylglutamic acid deficiency in the rat. In *Ciba Foundation symposium on congenital malformations,* ed. G. E. W. Wolstenholme and C. M. O'Connor, 134–51. Boston, Mass.

Roe, D. A. 1973. *A plague of corn: The social history of pellagra.* Ithaca, N.Y.

    1985. *Drug-induced vitamin deficiencies.* Westport, Conn.

    1990. Drug–folate interrelationships: Historical aspects and current concerns. In *Folic acid metabolism in health and disease,* ed. Mary Frances Picciano, E. L. Robert Stokstad, and Jesse F. Gregory III, 277–87. New York.

    1991. Ariboflavinosis. In *Hunter's tropical medicine,* Seventh edition, ed. G. T. Strickland and W. B. Saunders, 934–5. Philadelphia, Pa.

Sebrell, W. H., and R. E. Butler. 1938. Riboflavin deficiency in man: Preliminary note. *Public Health Reports* 53: 2282–4.

Wills, L., and M. M. Mehta. 1929–30. Studies in pernicious anemia of pregnancy: Part I – Preliminary research. *Indian Journal of Medical Research* 17: 777–8.

Wills, L., and S. N. Talpade. 1930–1. Studies in pernicious anemia of pregnancy: Part II – A survey of dietetic and hygienic conditions of women in Bombay. *Indian Journal of Medical Research* 18: 307–10.

Yellowlees, P. M. 1986. Thiamine deficiency and prevention of Wernicke-Korsakoff syndrome. *Medical Journal of Australia* 145: 216–19.

IV.A.3   Vitamin C

In delineating the history of a vitamin, we can often recognize four chronological phases. First, there is the description of a disease of unknown etiology, and second, there is the description of an empirical cure for the disease. Following this step, and often closely associated with it, is the identification of the curative factor – which perforce then becomes known as a vitamin. In the fourth phase the mode of action of the vitamin in preventing the deficiency disease is characterized.

The history of vitamin C (ascorbic acid) conforms to this general pattern. The characterization of the deficiency disease (scurvy) and the empirical discovery of a cure for it are, properly speaking, a part of the history of scurvy and have been dealt with elsewhere in this work. But this chapter is concerned with the subsequent history of the antiscorbutic factor, which conveniently presents itself in three chronological stages: (1) the somewhat ill-defined and open-ended period – from the beginning of the nineteenth century to the 1920s – when the vitamin had the existence of an "unrevealed presence" and was known to exist only because of its preventive influence on the disease scurvy (just as, during the same period, the perturber of Uranus was known to exist long before the "discovery" of the planet Pluto); (2) the 1920s and the 1930s, when vitamin C was named, isolated, and its molecular structure revealed (in that order); and (3) the modern post-1940 period, with its emphasis on the characterization of the biochemical role of vitamin C in preventing scurvy and, more recently, the debatable "extra-antiscorbutic" roles sometimes attributed to it.

The Antiscorbutic Factor

The early history of vitamin C cannot readily be separated from that of the demise of scurvy. By the beginning of the nineteenth century it was generally accepted that it was possible to prevent and cure scurvy by the use of citrus fruits: James Lind's contribution in establishing this belief was of paramount significance. But it was in essence a pharmacological concept rather than a nutritional one; the belief that the citrus fruits were replacing a missing dietary component would have been alien to medical thought at the beginning of the nineteenth century; even Lind himself did not regard fruit and vegetables as obligatory dietary principles in the prevention of scurvy. In other words, not until the end of the nineteenth century was there any general acceptance that scurvy was a deficiency disease resulting from a lack of a specific dietary principle and that the disease could be prevented or cured by appropriate dietary manipulation. Moreover, even this acceptance was complicated by the advent of the germ theory of disease which, some have argued, caused reversion to an infection theory to explain scurvy's etiology.

One of the earliest thinkers to discuss these new ideas was George Budd (1808–82), Professor of Medicine at King's College, London – although as K. C. Carter has indicated, Budd should perhaps be regarded as a developer rather than as an innovator of the "deficiency disease theory" (Hughes 1973; Carter 1977). In 1842, Budd published in the *London Medical Gazette* a series of articles entitled "Disorders Resulting from Defective Nutriment." He described "three different forms of disease which are already traced to defective nutriment" and argued that such conditions resulted from the absence of dietary factor(s) other than carbohydrate, fat, and protein, and that the absence of each of these specific factors would be associated with a specific disease – an idea that lay in abeyance for some 40 years until experimentally proved by N. Lunin. There can be little doubt that the three diseases described by Budd were avitaminoses A, C, and D.

L. J. Harris, himself a significant figure in the later history of vitamin C, aptly described Budd as "the prophet Budd" and referred to an article in which Budd expressed the belief that scurvy was due to the "lack of an essential element which it is hardly too sanguine to state will be discovered by organic chemistry or the experiments of physiologists in a not too distant future" (Budd 1840; Harris 1937: 8).

Little happened, however, to fulfill Budd's prophesy until the beginning of the twentieth century. In 1907, A. Holst and T. Fröhlich of Norway reported experiments in which they had demonstrated that scurvy could be induced in guinea pigs and cured by dietary manipulation (Holst and Fröhlich 1907; Wilson 1975). They used guinea pigs to assess the antiscorbutic value of different foodstuffs and to show the thermolabile nature of the antiscorbutic factor. At the same time there were parallel, but independent, developments in the general theory of vitamin deficiency diseases. F. G. Hopkins, developing earlier work by Lunin, C. A. Pekelharing, W. Stepp, and others, in 1912 published his classic paper in which he demonstrated the presence of growth factors in milk and showed their essential dietary nature (Hopkins 1912); in the same year, Casimir Funk introduced his "vitamin hypothesis," in which he attributed scurvy to the absence of an "anti-scurvy vitamine" (Harris 1937: 1–21).

The use of the guinea pig assay technique for the assessment of the antiscorbutic factor was extended, and in 1917, H. Chick and M. Hume published an important paper in which they reported the factor's distribution in a number of foodstuffs (Chick and Hume 1917). The following year A. Harden and S. S. Zilva published their fractionation studies on lemon juice, in which they demonstrated that the antiscorbutic potency was not attributable (as had been suggested by earlier workers) to the citric acid content (Harden and Zilva 1918). The year after that, J. C. Drummond designated the factor "Water soluble C" (Drummond 1919).

Identification of Vitamin C

Work now began in earnest to identify and isolate the antiscorbutic factor. The Medical Research Council's 1932 publication *Vitamins: A Survey of Present Knowledge* may be referred to for a detailed account of the large number of papers published during the 1920s on what was by then known as "vitamin C." Foremost in these early efforts was Zilva, working at the Lister Institute, London. The essential feature of Zilva's procedure was the precipitation of the factor with basic lead acetate after removal of the bulk of the other organic acids with calcium carbonate. He applied this technique to a variety of sources, such as lemon juice and swede (rutabaga) tissues, and he succeeded in increasing the concentration of the antiscorbutic factor some 200 to 300 times (Hughes 1983).

Other workers were similarly occupied, notably N. Bezssonoff in France and C. G. King in the United States. King has stated that during this period "many investigators had abandoned or failed to publish their work for various reasons." He referred, specifically, to Karl Link of Wisconsin, who had prepared several grams of crude calcium ascorbate during the 1920s but carried his work no further because of lack of financial support (King 1953).

The purest of these early "concentrates" still contained much impurity, and it was not until 1932 that W. A. Waugh and King published their paper "The Isolation and Identification of Vitamin C," which included a photograph of vitamin C crystals (Waugh and King 1932).

These attempts to isolate and characterize vitamin C were paralleled by two separate, but nevertheless highly relevant, developments in related areas. J. Tillmans and P. Hirsch, German government chemists, extensively studied the capacity of lemon juice preparations to reduce the redox dye 2,6-dichlorophenolindophenol, and they claimed that the reducing power of their preparations was always in proportion to their antiscorbutic potency; the indophenol dye technique later became a standard method for the assay of vitamin C. Zilva, however, disagreed with the German findings and appears, at that point, to have been diverted from his main endeavor by an attempt to disprove them (Zilva 1932).

The other significant development at this time was Albert Szent-Györgyi's isolation of hexuronic acid. Szent-Györgyi, a Hungarian biochemist working on plant respiration systems at Groningen in Holland, became interested in a reducing compound present in his preparations. Hopkins invited him to Cambridge to extend his studies, and in 1927, Szent-Györgyi isolated his "Groningen reducing agent" in a crystalline, from oranges, lemons, cabbages, and adrenal glands (Szent-Györgyi 1928).

He proposed to name his crystalline sample "ignose" – thus indicating its apparent relationship to sugars while at the same time underlining his ignorance of its true nature. But Harden, the editor of the *Biochemical Journal* at the time, according to Szent-Györgyi, "did not like jokes and reprimanded me." A second suggestion "godnose" was judged to be equally unacceptable. Szent-Györgyi finally agreed to accept Harden's somewhat more prosaic suggestion "hexuronic acid" – "since it had 6 Cs and was acidic" (Szent-Györgyi 1963: 1–14).

Hexuronic acid was a strongly reducing compound. So, too, according to Tillmans and Hirsch, was the antiscorbutic substance (vitamin C). The suggestion that hexuronic acid and vitamin C were actually one and the same substance appeared in print in 1932 in papers by both J. L. Svirbely and Szent-Györgyi and by Waugh and King, but there can be little doubt that the idea had been mooted some years previously. Who first made the suggestion is, however, unclear, and even the main participants in the drama later appeared uncertain and confused. King (1953) claimed that it was E. C. Kendall in 1929, but according to Hopkins (reported by King) it was Harris in 1928 (King 1953) – and he had, in any case, already attributed the idea to Tillmans and Hirsch (Harris 1937: 95). But E. L. Hirst (a member of the team later involved in chemical studies on the structure of vitamin C) named Waugh and King (Hirst 1953: 413).

Hopkins had already, in 1928, sent a sample of Szent-Györgyi's hexuronic acid to Zilva for comments on its vitamin C potency. According to King, Hopkins was disturbed because Zilva (who, naturally perhaps, was reluctant to admit that his "antiscorbutic preparations" were in reality identical with hexuronic acid) had replied that the sample was not vitamin C, but did so without reporting the evidence of his tests (King 1953).

By 1932, however, evidence in favor of the identity of hexuronic acid as vitamin C was substantial. Waugh and King had shown that their "crystalline vitamin C" cured scurvy in guinea pigs (Waugh and King 1932), and earlier the same year, Svirbely and Szent-Györgyi (now working in his native Hungary) had described the antiscorbutic potency of a sample of "hexuronic acid" isolated from adrenal glands (Svirbely and Szent-Györgyi 1932).

In 1933, in a single-sentence letter in *Nature,* Szent-Györgyi and W. N. Haworth drew attention to the chemical inaptness of the term "hexuronic acid" and suggested the term "ascorbic acid," thus formally acknowledging the antiscorbutic nature of the compound. Harris and his colleagues at Cambridge demonstrated the positive correlation between the hexuronic acid content and the antiscorbutic potency in a wide range of foodstuffs and published a highly convincing "eight-point" proof of the identity of the two substances.

Their three most important points were as follows: (1) Hexuronic acid paralleled antiscorbutic potency; (2) destruction of hexuronic acid by heat or by aeration was accompanied by a corresponding fall in the antiscorbutic activity; and (3) hexuronic acid disappeared from the organs of scorbutic guinea pigs (Birch, Harris, and Ray 1933). There could now be little doubt that hexuronic acid (Tillmans and Hirsch's reducing compound) and vitamin C were one and the same substance.

The situation was not without its human aspects, and even today the question of priority in the discovery of vitamin C still elicits discussion. "The identification of vitamin C is one of the strangest episodes in the history of vitamins," wrote T. H. Jukes in commenting on the appearance in 1987 of a book by R. W. Moss that placed, in Jukes's opinion, too great an emphasis on Szent-Györgyi's contribution (Moss 1987; Jukes 1988: 1290). Moss had implied that King had rushed off his claim for the identity of vitamin C and hexuronic acid after it became clear to him that Szent-Györgyi intended making the same point in a note to *Nature* – a situation curiously reminiscent of the suggestion that Charles Darwin behaved similarly on learning in 1858 that Alfred Russel Wallace was about to publish his theory of evolution.

The emphasis now shifted to the elucidation of the structure of vitamin C. Haworth, a Birmingham (U.K.) chemist, had received from Szent-Györgyi a sample of his "hexuronic acid," and in 1933, in a series of impressive papers, the Birmingham chemist, using both degradative and synthetic procedures, described the structure of the molecule (Hughes 1983). The molecule was synthesized simultaneously, but independently, by T. Reichstein in Switzerland and by Haworth and his colleagues in Birmingham, both groups using essentially the same method.

The synthesis – which, as it later emerged, was quite different from the biosynthetic pathway – was based on the production of xylosone from xylose and its conversion with cyanide to an imino intermediate that, on hydrolysis, gave ascorbic acid. The Swiss group published their results just ahead of the Birmingham workers (Ault et al. 1933, Reichstein, Grussner, and Oppenheimer 1933). The picture was completed the following year when the Birmingham workers joined forces with Zilva to demonstrate that synthetic ascorbic acid produced at Birmingham had exactly the same antiscorbutic potency as a highly purified "natural" sample from the Lister Institute (Haworth, Hirst, and Zilva 1934).

The annual report of the Chemical Society for 1933, with perhaps unnecessary caution, stated that "although it seems extremely probable that ascorbic acid is vitamin C . . . it cannot be said that this is a certainty." Other were less circumspect. A. L. Bacharach and E. L. Smith, addressing the Society of Public Analysts and Other Chemists in November 1933, said that "Vitamin C can now be identified with a sugar acid known as ascorbic acid. . . . Contrary to expectation, it is the first vitamin not merely to have assigned to it a definite molecular formula, but actually to be synthesised by purely chemical means" (Hughes 1983). Budd was correct in his 1840 prophecy that both physiologists and chemists could contribute to the identification of the "antiscorbutic factor." But his "not too distant future" proved to be a period of 93 years!

Biosynthesis and Metabolism of Vitamin C

By the end of the 1930s, serious research had commenced on the biological role of vitamin C. In particular, biochemical reductionists sought to explain the nature of the relationship between the clinical manifestations of scurvy and the biochemical involvements of vitamin C. It was recognized that vitamin C was a powerful biological reductant, and there were early attempts to explain its nutritional significance in terms of its involvement in oxidation-reduction systems – a major theme in prewar biochemistry. But the first clear advance in the biochemistry of vitamin C came from studies of its biosynthesis, and by the early 1950s, the pathway for its formation from simple sugars had been worked out. L. W. Mapson and a colleague at the Low Temperature Research Station at Cambridge (U.K.) fed different possible precursor molecules to cress seedlings and measured the formation of vitamin C. And in the United States, King and co-workers used labeled glucose to chart the biosynthetic pathway in rats (Mapson 1967: 369–80).

The biosynthetic pathway proved to be a comparatively simple one. D-glucuronate (formed from glucose) is converted to L-gluconate and then to L-gulono-gamma-lactone, which in turn is further reduced (via L-xylo-hexulonolactone) to L-ascorbic acid (2-oxo-L-gulono-gamm-lactone). The final enzymatic step is catalyzed by L-gulonolactone oxidase (EC 1.1.3.8.) – in the liver in evolutionarily "advanced" species such as the cow, goat, rat, rabbit, and sheep and in the kidney in other species such as the frog, snake, toad, and tortoise – and it is this enzyme that is lacking in those species unable to synthesize vitamin C.

To date, this biochemical "lesion" has been detected in a small, and disparate, number of species – higher primates (including, of course, humans), guinea pigs, certain bats, birds, insects, and fish (Chatterjee 1973; Sato and Uderfriend 1978). Whether all these species are necessarily scurvy-prone is not quite so clear. A survey of 34 species of New World microchiropteran bats showed that L-gulonolactone oxidase was apparently absent from the livers of all of them (and from the kidneys of at least some of them), but nevertheless, the tissue levels of ascorbic acid (even in species that were fish-eaters or insect-eaters) were similar to those in species that could biosynthesize the vitamin (Birney, Jenness, and Ayaz 1976).

This finding would suggest that the vitamin was being synthesized in organs other than the liver and kidney; or that the metabolic requirement for it was remarkably low; or that there were extremely efficient mechanism(s) for its protection against degradative changes. The whole question of the evolutionary significance of vitamin C – in plants as well as in animals – remains a largely uncharted area.

The rate of endogenous biosynthesis of vitamin C in those species capable of producing the vitamin shows considerable interspecies variation, ranging from 40 milligrams (mg) per kilogram (kg) body weight daily for the dog to 275 for the mouse (Levine and Morita 1985). These values are well in excess of the amounts of the vitamin required to prevent the appearance of scurvy in species unable to synthesize it – a finding that has frequently been used to buttress the claim that vitamin C has a number of "extra-antiscorbutic" roles requiring daily intakes well in excess of the recommended daily amounts.

The total body pool of ascorbic acid in a 70 kg man has been estimated at about 1.5 grams (g) (but according to Emil Ginter it could be three times as great as this [Ginter 1980]), which is attainable in most people by the sustained daily intake of 60 to 100 mg. A daily intake of 10 mg vitamin C results in a body pool of about 350 mg. Scorbutic signs do not appear until the pool falls to below 300 mg (Kallner 1981; "Experimental Scurvy" 1986).

Plasma (and less conveniently, leucocyte) concentrations of ascorbic acid are often taken as an index of the body status of the vitamin. The normal concentration range in the plasma of healthy persons on an adequate plane of nutrition is 30 to 90 micromoles per liter (μmol/L) (0.5–1.6 mg/100 ml). The Nutrition Canada Interpretive Guidelines are often referred to in this respect; these guidelines suggest that values between 11 and 23 μmol/L are indicative of marginal deficiency and that values below 11 μmol/L point to frank severe deficiency – but differences of sex, race, metabolism, smoking habits, and, particularly, of age (factors known to influence plasma ascorbic acid concentrations) reduce the validity of such a generalization (Basu and Schorah 1981; Hughes 1981b).

During a period of vitamin C depletion there is a comparatively rapid loss of vitamin C (a reduction of about 3 percent in the body pool daily) resulting from the continued catabolism of the vitamin and the excretion of its breakdown products in the urine. In humans, the main pathway identified involves the conversion of the ascorbic acid to dehydroascorbic acid, diketogulonic acid, and oxalic acid (in that order), with the two latter compounds accounting for the bulk of the urinary excretion of breakdown products. Smaller amounts of other metabolites, such as ascorbic acid-2-sulphate also occur, and in the guinea pig there is substantial conversion of part of the ascorbic acid to respiratory CO_2. It has sometimes been argued that the excess formation of these catabolites (particularly oxalic acid) should signify caution in the intake of amounts of vitamin C substantially in excess of the amount required to prevent scurvy.

Biochemical Role of Vitamin C

It was noted in the early experiments of Holst and Fröhlich, and confirmed by many subsequent workers, that defective formation of connective tissue was a primary pathological feature of experimental scurvy, and at one time it was believed that this lesion could account for most of the known pathological sequelae of the disease – the petechial hemorrhages, the breakdown of gum tissue, and the impairment of wound repair tissue. Attempts to characterize the biochemical modus operandi of vitamin C in preventing scurvy, therefore, centered initially on the metabolism of collagen – the essential glycoprotein component responsible for imparting strength to connective tissue.

By the 1970s, there was suggestive evidence that the biochemical lesion was located in the hydroxylation of the proline and lysine components of the collagen polypeptide and that vitamin C had an essential role in the process (Barnes and Kodicek 1972). The hydroxylases involved in collagen biosynthesis (prolyl 4-hydroxylase, prolyl 3-hydroxylase, and lysyl hydroxylase) require ferrous iron as a cofactor, and it appears that vitamin C, a powerful biological reductant, has an almost obligatory role in maintaining the ferrous iron in the reduced form. Thus emerged a simplistic and reductionist explanation for the role of vitamin C in

preventing the emergence of the main clinical features of scurvy.

Yet although there can be little doubt that vitamin C plays a critical role in the biosynthesis of collagen, recent studies have suggested that the simple "defective hydroxylation" theory is, perhaps, not the complete story. Studies have indicated that the activity of prolyl hydroxylase and the formation of collagens by fibroblast cultures is not influenced by ascorbic acid; furthermore, ascorbic acid deficiency does not always result in severe underhydroxylation of collagen in scorbutic guinea pigs (Englard and Seifter 1986).

There is increasing evidence that vitamin C may also influence the formation of connective tissue by modifying the nature and formation of the extracellular matrix molecules (Vitamin C Regulation 1990). B. Peterkofsky (1991) has recently suggested that the role of vitamin C in collagen biosynthesis is a dual one – a direct influence on collagen synthesis and an indirect one (mediated perhaps via appetite) on proteoglycan formation.

The complement component Clq, which has a central role in disease resistance, contains a collagen-like segment that is rich in hydroxyproline, and it has been suggested that this segment could offer a link with the putative anti-infective powers widely suggested for vitamin C (Pauling 1976; see also the section on megatherapy). Studies over the last 15 years, however, have failed to demonstrate that the complement system, unlike connective tissue collagen, reflects vitamin C availability (Thomas and Holt 1978; Johnston 1991). Indeed, the belief that vitamin C had anti-infection powers probably stemmed from reports by Harris in 1937 of lowered vitamin C in persons suffering from certain diseases, particularly tuberculosis.

During the 1960s and the 1970s, however, some 25 epidemiological studies were completed in different parts of the world to assess the validity of claims that vitamin C had anti-infection powers, particularly with respect to the common cold. The general conclusion drawn from the results of these studies was that the evidence for a protective/curative role for vitamin C in the common cold was far from convincing (Hughes 1981b: 22–6; Carpenter 1986: 213–16).

There is accumulating evidence, however, that vitamin C may have additional involvements in a range of enzymatic changes unrelated to the formation of collagen. There are three systems of considerable physiological significance in which vitamin C plays an important, and possibly obligatory, role: (1) as the immediate donor for dopamine B-hydroxylase, a key reaction in the conversion of tyrosine to norepinephrine (Englard and Seifter 1986; Fleming and Kent 1991); (2) in the peptidylglycine alpha-amidating monooxygenase system, whereby peptidyl carboxyl-terminal residues are amidated, a process that requires molecular oxygen, copper, and ascorbate and is important in the biosynthesis of a number of neuroendocrine peptides (Englard and Seifter 1986; Eipper and Mains 1991); (3)

in the hydroxylation reactions in the biosynthesis of carnitine from lysine and methionine (Englard and Seifter 1986; Rebouche 1991).

The exact physiological significance of these and other reactions vis-à-vis the clinical manifestations of scurvy is unclear. The first two, having obvious involvements in the endocrine and nervous systems, could well be causally related to various functional derangements of scurvy; and as carnitine has an important role in the transport of fatty acids into the mitochondria, where they may be oxidized to provide energy, it has been suggested that the carnitine involvement could account for the lassitude and fatigue that have been invariably noted as an early feature of scurvy (Hughes 1981a).

Should such involvements require an availability of ascorbic acid greater than that required to prevent the emergence of "classical" scurvy – and there is some evidence that this is so, at least in the case of carnitine biosynthesis – then a revision of the currently accepted Recommended Dietary Allowance/Reference Value would be called for (Hughes 1981a). The current recommended daily intake of vitamin C (60 mg in the United States and recently raised from 30 to 40 in the United Kingdom) is, after all, the amount estimated to prevent the emergence of the classic ("collagen") features of scurvy – and in the United Kingdom, it is based, essentially, on a single experiment completed almost half a century ago on a non-representative population sample.

Source of Vitamin C

Vitamin C is a heat-labile, water-soluble, and readily oxidizable molecule, and its distribution among foodstuffs and the losses resulting from processing and food preparation have been well documented. Studying the losses induced in the vitamin C content of various foodstuffs by simple culinary procedures must be one of the commonest and oft-repeated projects in basic college and university courses, and the amount of unpublished data resulting from these studies must be immense.

The mean daily intake of vitamin C in the United Kingdom (based on noncooked purchases) is about 60 mg daily with potatoes, citrus fruits, and cabbage accounting for 20, 12, and 6 percent, respectively, of the intake. The losses resulting from cooking are substantial, and these are further increased if the cooked food is allowed to stand around before being eaten. Nevertheless, because of the comparatively widespread distribution of the vitamin in plant foodstuffs, and the role of technology in increasing the availability of uncooked plant and vegetable material during the whole year, very few persons today appear to suffer from clinically defined hypovitaminosis C; consequently, frank scurvy is an almost unknown condition.

A recent survey of vitamin C intakes in European countries revealed an interesting, and almost providential, reciprocity between the consumption of two important sources of vitamin C. Of 27 countries studied, Iceland, Switzerland, and France had the lowest annual consumption of cabbage (less than 5 kg per capita) but a high consumption of citrus fruit (over 20 kg); Romania, Poland, and the former Soviet Union, in contrast, had the lowest consumption of citrus fruit (less than 4 kg) but the highest consumption of cabbage (more than 30 kg) (Kohlmeier and Dortschy 1991). Only where a person, for ideological, economic, or supposed "health" reasons subsists on a diet devoid of fruit and vegetables (such as one based on nuts, grain, and/or cooked meat/fish) is scurvy likely to emerge.

The foliage of many flowering plants has an unexpectedly high concentration of vitamin C, with concentrations of up to 1 percent wet weight being attained in some members of the Primulaceae family. The mean concentration for 213 species examined (162 mg per 100 g) was some three times that of those culinary vegetables usually regarded as good sources of the vitamin; and the mean value for the leaves of 41 woody shrubs and trees examined was 293 mg per 100 g – significantly higher than black currants, which are usually cited as the dietary source par excellence of vitamin C (Jones and Hughes 1983, 1984; see also Table IV.A.3.1).

Table IV.A.3.1. *Ascorbic acid content of some plants (mg/100 g fresh weight)*

Culinary vegetables and fruits	
Cabbage	55 (11)
Carrots (roots)	8 (2)
Cauliflower	70 (14)
Peas (seed)	25 (4)
Potatoes (tubers)	28 (4)
Apples (fruit)	10
Black currants (fruit)	180
Oranges (fruit)	55
The antiscorbutics (leaves)	
Cochlearia officinalis (scurvy grass)	63
Nasturtium officinale (watercress)	83
Veronica beccabunga (brooklime)	46
Less widely used antiscorbutics	
Galium aparine (goosegrass)	84
Menyanthes trifoliata (bog bean)	74
Urtica dioica (stinging nettle)	169
Vitamin C–rich leaves	
Primula vulgaris (primrose)	805
Malus domestica (apple tree)	496
Erica tetralix (bog heather)	394
Vicia cracca (tufted vetch)	349

Note: Values in parentheses are for cooked meals taken by elderly patients in hospitals (Jones, Hughes, and Davies 1988 and additional unpublished material).

Source: Based on Jones and Hughes (1983, 1984) and Hughes (1990).

The historically important "antiscorbutic herbs" are among the poorest sources of vitamin C (Hughes 1990). William Perry, who stowed boxes of mustard greens and cress on board his ship in an attempt to fend off scurvy during his Arctic expedition of 1818 (Lloyd and Coulter 1963: 108), would have done better to adorn his stateroom with primrose plants, a single leaf of which, chewed in the mouth daily, would have sufficed to offer complete protection. The exact reason, if any, for these high (and often disparate) concentrations of ascorbic acid in angiosperms is not known; nor is the role of ascorbic acid in plant biochemistry understood. It has been suggested that there is a positive correlation between the concentration of ascorbic acid in plants and corresponding concentrations of phenolic compounds, but the extent to which this reflects a biochemical relationship is a matter of conjecture (E. C. Bate-Smith, personal communication).

Vitamin C Megatherapy

The practice of ingesting daily doses of vitamin C grossly in excess of the amount believed to protect against scurvy and even in excess of the amount known to produce tissue saturation is one of the more controversial aspects of current nutritional thought. The arguments for vitamin C "megatherapy" were initially outlined in the United States by Irwin Stone and later elaborated by Linus Pauling, winner of two Nobel Prizes (Hughes 1981b: 47–53). Stone disputed the adequacy of current recommended daily intakes, basing his case primarily on the rate of biosynthesis of the vitamin by animals producing their own supply and on G. H. Bourne's estimate that the natural diet of the gorilla provides it with a daily intake of some 4.5 g ascorbic acid (Bourne 1949). His arguments for daily intakes of grams rather than milligrams were enthusiastically embraced and extended by Pauling.

Closely interwoven with the megatherapy theory is the claim that vitamin C has a number of extra-antiscorbutic functions (protection against infection and, particularly, the common cold, detoxication, cerebral function, lipid metabolism, longevity, and so forth) that might require significantly raised amounts of the vitamin (Hughes 1981b: 14–34). For example, E. Ginter has for many years carefully presented the thesis that vitamin C plays a part in lipid metabolism, particularly by enhancing the conversion of cholesterol to bile salts, and that it would, therefore, have a hypocholesterogenic function (Ginter and Bobek 1981).

To date, however, there is little evidence that these putative relationships are reflected by a specific and increased demand for vitamin C. And as indicated earlier, some of these supposed secondary roles have now been subsumed in enzymatic terms by the advances of reductionist biochemistry. Secondary (or extra-antiscorbutic) roles for vitamin C could, conceivably, require intakes greater than those necessary for the prevention of classical scurvy, but such increased requirements would, in biochemical terms, scarcely justify the massive intakes recommended by the megatherapists.

Apart from the lack of satisfactory evidence, there are other arguments against vitamin C megatherapy (Jukes 1974; Hughes 1981b: 47–53). Adverse reactions elicited by massive doses of vitamin C and the possibly toxic influence of its breakdown products could well disadvantage the body. Moreover, the ingestion of large amounts of ascorbic acid is a self-defeating exercise as the absorption of large doses is a relatively inefficient process, with less than one-half of a 1 g megadose being absorbed from the gastrointestinal tract and only one-fourth of a 5 g dose (Davies et al. 1984; "Experimental Scurvy" 1986). And, in any case, it is generally accepted that tissue saturation in humans may be satisfactorily attained by a daily intake of 100 to 150 mg or even less. The faith of the megatherapists would have appeared to blind them to the normal canons of scientific assessment.

In the mid-1970s, Pauling espoused perhaps the most controversial of all his vitamin C beliefs. In collaboration with a Scottish surgeon, Ewan Cameron, he began to write extensively on the supposed antitumor activity of vitamin C; more specifically, Cameron and Pauling published the results of a clinical trial in which it was claimed that a megadose (10 g daily) of vitamin C quadrupled the survival time of terminally ill cancer patients (Cameron and Pauling 1976). The methodology of this trial was widely criticized, and a carefully controlled attempt to repeat it at the Mayo Clinic in the United States failed to confirm the Cameron–Pauling claims. For the next 15 years, and in the face of growing reluctance on the part of the scientific press to publish his papers, Pauling continued to present his arguments for the efficacy of vitamin C in the treatment of cancer. An account of this drawn-out battle between Pauling and the American scientific establishment has recently appeared (Richards 1991).

In more general and theoretical terms, it has been suggested that the antioxidant and free-radical scavenger roles of vitamin C support its possible function in the prevention (as contrasted with the cure) of cancer. G. Block has assessed some 90 studies of cancer and vitamin C/fruit intake relationships and has concluded that there is evidence that in the majority of cancers vitamin C may have a significant prophylactic role (Block 1991). In this respect, the possible relationship between vitamin C and nitrosamine-induced cancers has attracted some attention.

It has been speculated that endogenously produced N-nitroso compounds may be important initiators of human cancers. Significant in this respect is the formation of N-nitrosamines and related compounds. Nitrosamines may be formed when nitrate, a suitable "nitrosable" amine, and bacteria coexist – as in the gastrointestinal tract. Nitrate (the main dietary sources of which are fish and root vegetables) is converted by bacterial action to nitrite, which then reacts with amines to produce carcinogenic nitrosamines. Some foods, particularly cured meat products, contain nitrosamines formed during processing.

There is evidence that vitamin C may prevent the formation of carcinogenic nitrosamines from nitrate and may even reduce the carcinogenicity of preformed nitrosamines (Hughes 1981b: 27-9; MAFF 1987). It has been suggested, for example, that a reduction in nitrosamine formation, attributable to citrus fruit vitamin C, may be a contributory factor in determining the comparatively low incidence of large bowel cancer in the "citrus belt" of the United States (Lyko and Hartmann 1980). Sodium nitrite is used in the large-scale preparation of cured meats, bacon, and sausages (primarily to prevent the activity of the highly toxic *Clostridium botulinum*), and these products, consequently, contain a range of preformed nitroso compounds. There may, therefore, be good scientific reasons for regarding orange juice as a useful dietary accompaniment to a fried breakfast!

Vitamin C and Industry

Many tens of thousands of tons of vitamin C are produced synthetically each year from glucose; the initial stages in conversion involve reduction to sorbitol followed by bacterial oxidation to sorbose. Much of this vitamin C finds its way into health-food stores for sale to megatherapy enthusiasts as a putative dietary adjuvant. A substantial proportion is used industrially as a "technological aid"; some is used in meat-curing processes to promote pigment conversion (in this application, it also has an adventitious and unintended role in reducing the formation of volatile N-nitrosamines).

Vitamin C is also widely employed as a permitted antioxidant (sometimes as ascorbyl palmitate) to prevent the formation of rancidity in stored fat products and the phenolic browning of commodities such as dehydrated potatoes. It is used as a flour improver in the Chorleywood Bread Process, where its oxidation product (dehydroascorbic acid) modifies the availability of glutathione in dough development, thereby shortening the period of fermentation.

The use of vitamin C in these technological processes finds general approval on the grounds that one is, after all, adding a beneficial vitamin rather than some untried additive of unknown toxicity. It should be pointed out, though, that little of this additive vitamin C is recoverable from the marketed product, which will, however, contain substantial amounts of vitamin C breakdown products – many of them unidentified and almost all of them of unknown toxicity. Bread is vitamin C–free despite the substantial amounts that may have been added during the Chorleywood process. It has been estimated that the average consumer may ingest up to 200 mg a week of vitamin C breakdown products from additive sources (Thomas and Hughes 1985).

Epilogue

Why vitamin C should have attracted so much attention in nutritional circles – orthodox and otherwise – is difficult to understand. Its almost limitless appeal to health enthusiasts and pseudonutritionists is matched only by the time and attention devoted to it by academic nutritionists. The annual global publication of some 2,000 papers bearing on vitamin C implies an annual research expenditure of some £40,000,000 (about 60 to 70 million U.S. dollars) – a not inconsiderable sum for studying a molecule whose nutritional significance is, at the most, marginal. Vitamin C deficiency is today a rare occurrence, and the evidence for extra-antiscorbutic requirements in excess of the mean daily intake is slender. Perhaps the biochemical versatility of the vitamin C molecule makes it attractive to biochemists who feel that it deserves a much more significant role than that of a somewhat prosaic involvement in the biosynthesis of collagen.

There are some questions that remain unanswered. For example, the apparent negative correlation between blood and tissue concentrations of vitamin C and age is puzzling. Many very elderly subjects – particularly if institutionalized – have virtually no ascorbic acid in their blood, a situation that would almost certainly be associated with the emergence of clinical scurvy in a younger age group. Yet these octogenarians and nonagenarians seem to be in no way disadvantaged by the apparent absence of the vitamin. Is there, then, a negative correlation between aging and dependency upon vitamin C? Such a relationship, if true, would be a remarkably fortuitous one as a substantial proportion of the institutionalized elderly have intakes of vitamin C well below the recommended daily amount. It is a somewhat sobering thought that in these days of scientifically attuned dietetics the mean intake of vitamin C by the institutionalized elderly in the United Kingdom is no greater than it was in hospitals a century and a half ago (Jones, Hughes, and Davies 1988).

In the more rarefied atmosphere of academic biochemistry, however, it is possible to point to real advances in our knowledge of vitamin C over the past 40 years. Today, modern high-performance liquid chromatographic techniques are replacing the classical indophenol dye method for the determination of vitamin C, with an increase in sensitivity and specificity. Our knowledge of possible biochemical involvements of the vitamin has advanced substantially. Sadly, however, one cannot point with equal certainty to any corresponding expansion of our knowledge of the nutritional significance of vitamin C beyond its role in the prevention of classical scurvy.

R. E. Hughes

Bibliography

Ault, R. G., D. K. Baird, H. C. Carrington, et al. 1933. Synthesis of d- and L-ascorbic acid and of analogous substances. *Journal of the Chemical Society* 1: 1419-23.

Barnes, M. J., and E. Kodicek. 1972. Biological hydroxylations and ascorbic acid with special regard to collagen metabolism. *Vitamins and Hormones* 30: 1-43.

Basu, T. K., and C. J. Schorah. 1981. *Vitamin C in health and disease.* London.

Birch, T. W., L. J. Harris, and S. N. Ray. 1933. Hexuronic (ascorbic) acid as the antiscorbutic factor, and its chemical determination. *Nature* 131: 273-4.

Birney, E. C., R. Jenness, and K. M. Ayaz. 1976. Inability of bats to synthesize L-ascorbic acid. *Nature* 260: 626-8.

Block, G. 1991. Epidemiologic evidence regarding vitamin C and cancer. *American Journal of Clinical Nutrition* 54: 1310S-14S.

Bourne, G. H. 1949. Vitamin C and immunity. *British Journal of Nutrition* 2: 346-56.

Budd, G. 1840. Scurvy. In *The library of medicine. Practical medicine,* Vol. 5, ed. A. Tweedie, 58-95. London.

 1842. Disorders resulting from defective nutriment. *London Medical Gazette* 2: 632-6, 712-16, 743-9, 906-15.

Cameron, E., and L. Pauling. 1976. Supplemental ascorbic acid in the supportive treatment of cancer: Prolongation of survival time in terminal human cancer. *Proceedings of the National Academy of Science* 73: 3685-9.

Carpenter, K. J. 1986. *The history of scurvy and vitamin C.* Cambridge and New York.

Carter, K. C. 1977. The germ theory, beriberi, and the deficiency theory of disease. *Medical History* 21: 119-36.

Chatterjee, I. B. 1973. Evolution and biosynthesis of ascorbic acid. *Science* 182: 1271-2.

Chick, H., and M. Hume. 1917. The distribution among foodstuffs . . . of the substances required for the prevention of (a) beriberi and (b) scurvy. *Transactions of the Royal Society for Tropical Medicine and Hygiene* 10: 141-86.

Davies, H. E. F., J. E. W. Davies, R. E. Hughes, and Eleri Jones. 1984. Studies on the absorption of L-xylo ascorbic acid (vitamin C) in young and elderly subjects. *Human Nutrition: Clinical Nutrition* 38: 469-71.

Drummond, J. C. 1919. Note on the role of the anti-scorbutic factor in nutrition. *Biochemical Journal* 13: 77-88.

Eipper, B. A., and R. E. Mains. 1991. The role of ascorbate in the biosynthesis of neuroendocrine peptides. *American Journal of Clinical Nutrition* 54: 1153S-6S.

Englard, S., and S. Seifter. 1986. The biochemical functions of ascorbic acid. *Annual Review of Nutrition* 6: 365-406.

Experimental scurvy in a young man. 1986. *Nutrition Reviews* 44: 13-5.

Fleming, P. J., and U. M. Kent. 1991. Cytochrome b561, ascorbic acid, and transmembrane electron transfer. *American Journal of Clinical Nutrition* 54: 1173S-8S.

Ginter, E. 1980. What is truly the maximum body pool of ascorbic acid in man? *American Journal of Clinical Nutrition* 33: 538-9.

Ginter, E., and P. Bobek. 1981. The influence of vitamin C on lipid metabolism. In *Vitamin C (ascorbic acid),* ed. J. N. Counsell and D. H. Hornig. London.

Harden, A., and S. S. Zilva. 1918. The antiscorbutic factor in lemon juice. *Biochemical Journal* 12: 259-69.

Harris, L. J. 1937. *Vitamins in theory and practice.* New York and Cambridge.

 1953. Chairman's summing-up. *Proceedings of the Nutrition Society* 12: 341-4.

Haworth, W. N., E. L. Hirst, and S. S. Zilva. 1934. Physiological activity of synthetic ascorbic acid. *Journal of the Chemical Society* 2: 1155-6.

Hirst, E. L. 1953. The chemistry of vitamin C. In *Lind's treatise on scurvy,* ed. C. P. Stewart and D. Guthrie, 413-24. Edinburgh.

Holst, A., and T. Fröhlich. 1907. Experimental studies relating to ship beri-beri and scurvy. II. On the etiology of scurvy. *Journal of Hygiene* 7: 634-71.

Hopkins, F. G. 1912. Feeding experiments illustrating the importance of accessory factors in normal dietaries. *Journal of Physiology* 44: 425-60.

Hughes, R. E. 1973. George Budd (1808-1882) and nutritional deficiency diseases. *Medical History* 17: 127-35.

 1981a. Recommended daily amounts and biochemical roles - the vitamin C, carnitine, fatigue relationship. In *Vitamin C (ascorbic acid),* ed. J. N. Counsell and D. H. Hornig. London.

 1981b. *Vitamin C: Some current problems.* London.

 1983. From ignose to hexuronic acid to vitamin C. *Trends in Biochemical Science* 8: 146-7.

 1990. The rise and fall of the "antiscorbutics": Some notes on the traditional cures for "land scurvy." *Medical History* 34: 52-64.

Johnston, C. S. 1991. Complement component C1q unaltered by ascorbate supplementation in healthy men and women. *Nutritional Biochemistry* 2: 499-501.

Jones, E., and R. E. Hughes. 1983. Foliar ascorbic acid in some angiosperms. *Phytochemistry* 22: 2493-9.

 1984. A note on the ascorbic acid content of some trees and woody shrubs. *Phytochemistry* 23: 2366-7.

Jones, E., R. E. Hughes, and H. E. F. Davies. 1988. Intake of vitamin C and other nutrients by elderly patients receiving a hospital diet. *Journal of Human Nutrition and Dietetics* 1: 347-53.

Jukes, T. H. 1974. Are recommended and daily allowances for vitamin C adequate? *Proceedings of the National Academy of Science* 71: 1949-51.

 1988. The identification of vitamin C, an historical summary. *Journal of Nutrition* 118: 1290-3.

Kallner, A. 1981. Vitamin C - man's requirements. In *Vitamin C (ascorbic acid),* ed. J. N. Counsell and D. H. Hornig. London.

King, C. G. 1953. The discovery and chemistry of vitamin C. *Proceedings of the Nutrition Society* 12: 219-27.

Kohlmeier, L., and R. Dortschy. 1991. Diet and disease in East and West Germany. *Proceedings of the Nutrition Society* 50: 719-27.

Levine, M., and K. Morita. 1985. Ascorbic acid in endocrine systems. *Vitamins and Hormones* 42: 1-64.

Lloyd, H. C., and J. L. S. Coulter. 1963. *Medicine and the navy, 1200-1900,* Vol. 4. Edinburgh and London.

Lyko, H. C., and J. X. Hartmann. 1980. Ascorbate, cyclic nucleotides, citrus and a model for preventing large bowel cancer. *Journal of Theoretical Biology* 83: 675-86.

Mapson, L. W. 1967. Biogenesis of L-ascorbic acid in plants and animals. In *The Vitamins,* Vol. 1, ed. W. H. Sebrell and R. S. Harris, 369-83. New York and London.

Ministry of Agriculture, Fisheries, and Food (MAFF). 1987. *Nitrate, nitrite and N-nitroso compounds in food.* London.

Moss, R. W. 1987. *Free radical: Albert Szent-Györgyi and the battle over vitamin C.* New York.

Pauling, L. 1976. *Vitamin C, the common cold and the flu.* San Francisco.

Peterkofsky, B. 1991. Ascorbate requirement for hydroxylation and secretion of procollagen: Relationship to inhibition of collagen synthesis in scurvy. *American Journal of Clinical Nutrition* 54: 1113S-27S.

Rebouche, C. J. 1991. Ascorbic acid and carnitine biosynthesis. *American Journal of Clinical Nutrition* 54: 1147S-52S.

Reichstein, T., A. Grussner, and R. Oppenheimer. 1933. Synthesis of d- and L-ascorbic acid (vitamin C). *Nature* 132: 280.

Richards, E. 1991. *Vitamin C and cancer.* London.

Sato, P., and S. Uderfriend. 1978. Studies on ascorbic acid related to the genetic basis of scurvy. *Vitamins and Hormones* 36: 33-52.

Svirbely, J. L., and A. Szent-Györgyi. 1932. Hexuronic acid as the antiscorbutic factor. *Nature* 129: 576.

Szent-Györgyi, A. 1928. Observations on the function of the peroxidase systems. . . . *Biochemical Journal* 22: 1387-1409.

  1963. Lost in the twentieth century. *Annual Review of Biochemistry* 32: 1-14.

Thomas, M., and R. E. Hughes. 1985. Evaluation of threonic acid toxicity in small animals. *Food Chemistry* 17: 79-83.

Thomas, W. R., and P. G. Holt. 1978. Vitamin C and immunity: An assessment of the evidence. *Clinical and Experimental Immunology* 32: 370-9.

Vitamin C regulation of cartilage modification. *Nutritional Reviews* 48: 260-2.

Waugh, W. A., and C. G. King. 1932. The isolation and identification of vitamin C. *Journal of Biological Chemistry* 97: 325-31.

Wilson, L. G. 1975. The clinical definition of scurvy and the discovery of vitamin C. *Journal of the History of Medicine* 30: 40-60.

Zilva, S. S. 1932. Hexuronic acid as the antiscorbutic factor. *Nature* 129: 690.

IV.A.4 ❧ Vitamin D

Definition and Nomenclature

Vitamin D is a fat-soluble substance required by most vertebrates, including humans, to keep blood calcium and phosphate levels within a narrow normal range and thereby maintain a normal skeleton and optimal cellular function. The term, vitamin D, is a misnomer. Vitamin D is not a vitamin. It is synthesized in the skin, and so, unlike other vitamins, which are essential dietary components, it does not satisfy the criteria for classification as a vitamin. Nor is it a hormone because it is biologically inactive and must be metabolized by the body into a multihydroxylated version, known as calcitriol, which is biologically active and the true hormonal form. Thus vitamin D is more accurately described as a *prohormone*. The natural form of the vitamin, known as vitamin D_3, is a cholesterol-like substance produced in the skin by a nonenzymatic process involving ultraviolet light and heat. An artificial form of the vitamin, with an altered side chain, known as vitamin D_2, is derived from the plant sterol ergosterol and is often used instead of vitamin D_3 as a dietary supplement.

Most of the complexity associated with the nomenclature in the vitamin D field stems from confusion surrounding its discovery during the period 1919 to 1922. Early research showed that the deficiency associated with lack of vitamin D (rickets in children or osteomalacia in adults) was cured by seemingly unrelated treatments: exposure to sunlight or ingestion of a fat-soluble substance. The early nutritional pioneers of that period, including Sir Edward Mellanby and Elmer V. McCollum, realized that several related factors would cure rickets and that one of these substances, vitamin D_3, could be made in the skin. Students often ponder the fate of vitamin D_1. It was a short-lived research entity comprising a mixture of vitamins D_2 and D_3, and the term has no value today. Vitamin D_3 is sometimes referred to as cholecalciferol or, more recently, calciol; vitamin D_2 is known as ergocalciferol or ercalciol. The discovery of the hydroxylated versions of vitamin D by Hector F. DeLuca and Egon Kodicek in the 1967 to 1971 period led to a major expansion of our knowledge of a number of biologically active compounds, but calcitriol is the singularly most important version of these. For purposes of discussing the history of foodstuffs, we shall use the term vitamin D to describe all substances that can be activated to produce biological effects on calcium and phosphate metabolism in humans.

History of Vitamin D Deficiency (Rickets)

Though the nutritional entity vitamin D has been known for only 75 years, the deficiency diseases of vitamin D (rickets and its adult-onset counterpart, osteomalacia) were clearly recognized by Daniel Whistler (1645) in the Netherlands and Francis Glisson (1650) in England as early as the mid-seventeenth century.

In reviewing the history of rickets, we must recognize that rickets and osteomalacia are not the only diseases that affect the skeleton. Others include osteoporosis, which results from loss of total bone (i.e., proteinaceous matrix and minerals), and hormonal imbalances (e.g., hyperparathyroidism). Because diagnostic procedures were primitive until the twentieth century, the term "rickets" may often have been applied to other skeletal abnormalities and conditions not caused by vitamin D deficiency. Nevertheless, in many cases there is sufficient detail in the descriptions provided to recognize the condition.

According to strict medical classification, rickets and osteomalacia encompass a group of skeletal malformations resulting from a spectrum of different causes but having the common feature that *the bone matrix is insufficiently mineralized or calcified.* By far the most common cause of rickets is a lack of vitamin D. This deficiency must be the result of inadequate skin synthesis of vitamin D_3 compounded by low dietary intake of vitamin D. The term "rickets" is thought by most to have its origins in the verb in the Dorset dialect *to rucket*, which means to breathe with difficulty. Yet some claim that the term is derived from the Anglo-Saxon word *wrikken*, meaning to twist.

Rickets is characterized by a deformed and misshaped skeleton, particularly bending or bowing of the long bones and enlargement of the epiphyses of the joints of the rib cage, arms, legs, and neck. Victims have painful movements of the rib cage and hence difficulty breathing. In China, medical texts refer to deformities of the rib cage in severe rickets as "chicken breast." Severe rickets is often accompanied by pneumonia. There is currently much research in progress on a second important function of vitamin D, namely to control the differentiation and development of cells of the bone marrow and immune system. Thus with rickets, the defects of the skeleton may be accompanied by reduced ability to fight infections. Rachitic patients have difficulty holding up their heads, which is sometimes depicted in lithographs from the period circa 1650 to 1700 (e.g., Glisson's "De Rachitide," 1650). A more thorough review of the history of rickets can be found in the extraordinarily detailed book of Alfred Hess (1929) entitled *Rickets Including Osteomalacia and Tetany*. Though rickets is rarely life-threatening, it certainly lowers the quality of life for the afflicted individual and probably leads to secondary problems. One of the best documented of these secondary problems is the development of deformities of the pelvis in young females, which can cause difficulties in childbirth. This topic has been given detailed analysis by the University of Toronto historian Edward Shorter (1982) in *A History of Women's Bodies*. Shorter concludes that before 1920, women who had contracted rickets earlier in life had the risk of a "contracted pelvis" that must have caused numerous deaths during their first delivery.

Discovery of Vitamin D

Around the turn of the twentieth century, several physicians noted a seasonal variation in the incidence of rickets and that the disease was associated with lack of exposure to sunlight. In fact, several researchers also noted a higher incidence of rickets in the industrialized cities of northern Europe (which lay under a pall of smoke caused by burning coal in open fires and factories) than in the rural areas around these centers. The Dickensian character Tiny Tim, of the novel *A Christmas Carol*, clearly represents a child who must have been a common sight in the narrow alleyways of the dark cities of the late nineteenth century. In retrospect, it is easy to see how rickets could be prevalent among the occupants of the sweatshops of such dingy cities when their agrarian cousins on a similar diet, but out in the sun 12 hours a day, had no rickets. Sunbaths were recommended by Edwardian physicians as a cure for this condition, but some believed that the accompanying "fresh-air and exercise," rather than sunlight, were the key ingredients in the cure. In 1912, J. Raczynski (1913; described in Hess 1929) performed a definitive experiment by exposing two rachitic puppies to either sunlight or shade for six weeks and showing that the sunlight-exposed animal had a 1.5-fold higher bone mineral content. Nevertheless, controversy persisted as other researchers claimed to show the importance of "country-air and exercise" in the prevention of rickets and still others showed that the onset of rickets could be accelerated by dietary manipulation. Yet it is now clear that a "rachitogenic diet" (a diet that can lead to rickets) is one that contains adequate amounts of all essential nutrients *except* vitamin D, calcium, and phosphate, the raw materials important in bone mineral formation. Diet alone, however, will not cause rickets. Animals deprived of sunlight and fed a rachitogenic diet grow normally in all respects except that, because they lack bone mineral, they develop severe or "florid" rickets. But animals deprived of sunlight and fed a diet inadequate in many of the chief nutrients grow poorly, and the rickets they develop is difficult to discern against a background of other vitamin deficiencies.

By 1919, it was becoming clear that sunlight was the crucial factor in preventing rickets. Kurt Huldschinsky (1919) cured the disease by exposing patients to a mercury-vapor lamp, thereby showing the importance of the ultraviolet (UV) portion of sunlight. In a stroke of genius, he also showed that irradiation of one arm of a rachitic child cured the skeleton throughout the body, *including the other arm*. He invoked the concept that vitamin D must be "a hormone" because it was a chemical that could heal at a distance. Only much later were Adolf Windaus and colleagues (1936) able to show that vitamin D is made in the skin from a precursor, 7-dehydrocholesterol, thereby completing our understanding of this aspect of vitamin D.

Meanwhile, in the 1920s, nutritional biochemists, including Mellanby and McCollum, were busy isolating several essential nutrients in foodstuffs. They too were able to cure rickets by administration of a fat-soluble substance, termed vitamin D by McCollum to distinguish it from vitamin A, which cured xerophthalmia or night blindness (Mellanby 1919; McCollum et al. 1922). In 1928, Windaus received the Nobel Prize principally for his elucidation of the structure of sterols, including vitamin D. Interestingly, Hess and Harry Steenbock separately had been able to produce vitamin D in food by irradiating it with ultraviolet light (Hess and Weinstock 1924; Steenbock and Black 1924). It became clear that the very process occurring in the skin could be mimicked in the test tube by subjecting certain plant oils or even yeast, containing plant sterols, to UV light. Thus vitamin D_2 was born, and with it, food fortification.

In more recent times, DeLuca, the last graduate student of Steenbock at the University of Wisconsin, showed that vitamin D is converted in the liver to a metabolite, 25-hydroxyvitamin D (Blunt, Schnoes, and DeLuca 1968). This is the main transport form of vitamin D in the body, and its blood level reflects the body's supply of vitamin D. Following this discovery, several groups, most notably those of Kodicek at Cambridge, DeLuca at Wisconsin, and Anthony Norman at the University of California, were able to demonstrate and identify the hormonally active form of vitamin D, calcitriol, for the first time (Fraser and Kodicek 1970; Myrtle, Haussler, and Norman 1970; Holick et al. 1971). Also known as 1,25-dihydroxyvitamin D, this hormone is made in the kidney, but it is important to note that its level in the blood is not simply a reflection of the exposure to sunlight or a measure of dietary intake. The human body can store the fat-soluble vitamin D precursor, make just enough calcitriol hormone for its needs, and save the rest of the vitamin D for "hard times." In the case of our ancestors who lived in the higher latitudes of northern Europe and were exposed to sunlight on a seasonal basis, these stores of vitamin D must have been crucial to help them get through each winter without the development of rickets or osteomalacia.

Foodstuffs and Vitamin D

As already pointed out, diet plays a secondary role in maintaining our supply of vitamin D. Nevertheless, diet can assume a critical importance when exposure to sunlight is compromised. Somewhat surprisingly, most foodstuffs are devoid of vitamin D. The only significant sources are animal liver (vitamin D stores of other vertebrates), egg yolks, and fish oils. Milk, generally thought of as a major source of vitamin D, is not rich in the vitamin, and human milk is an extremely poor source of it. It is a well-established observation in contemporary pediatric medicine that most cases of rickets in infants are found in those who are breast-fed, born in the fall, and kept out of the sun during winter months. Of course, the formula-fed infant of today receives milk fortified with vitamin D.

Most grains, meat, vegetables, and fruits are virtually devoid of measurable amounts of vitamin D, although experts in this field are still perplexed by how such creatures as nocturnal bats surviving on a diet of fruit and insects can avoid rickets! It is possible (although unsubstantiated) that exposure of certain foods (e.g., vegetables or fruits) to sun-drying may generate antirachitic activity, presumably because plant ergosterol would be converted into vitamin D_2. Some cultures (e.g., the Chinese) have a tradition of drying vegetables in the sun, which may increase their vitamin D content.

Recent reports indicate that infants fed a so-called macrobiotic diet, consisting of unpolished rice, pulses, and vegetables with a high fiber content along with small additions of seaweeds, fermented foods, nuts, seeds, and fruits, are particularly susceptible to rickets. In one group of Caucasian children in the Netherlands (Dagnelie et al. 1990), 28 percent had physical symptoms of rickets in late summer, and this statistic rose to 55 percent by the following spring. (One might hope that those who extol this sort of diet will modify their teachings so that small amounts of fatty fish might be included, which would supply much-needed vitamin D.)

The association of vitamin D with fish oils, particularly fish-liver oils, is an interesting one recognized well before the formal discovery of vitamin D and predating even the discovery of the importance of sunlight. In 1789, a Manchester physician named Thomas Percival wrote about the medicinal uses of cod-liver oil at the Manchester Infirmary shortly after it had been introduced into British pharmacopoeia. In fact, one might argue that cod-liver oil is a medicine and not a food, but this is a fine point. There is, however, almost universal agreement that it is not a particularly good-tasting substance and hardly a favorite of children. Hess (1929) wrote that cod-liver oil's chief disadvantages lay in taste and odor. Moreover, it was not always completely prophylactic against rickets.

Hess's last comment is a reference to the variable potency of cod-liver oil because it is a natural product and thus subject to seasonal variation dependent upon the diet of the codfish. A more acceptable but less effective source of vitamin D is fish itself, particularly the fatty saltwater fish: herring, mackerel, tuna, halibut, and salmon. These fish have fat stores in the muscle, and because vitamin D is fat-soluble it is found throughout these fat deposits and is not confined to the liver, as in the cod. Fish roe, like eggs, also contain vitamin D. W. F. Loomis (1970), in a review of rickets, speculated that certain social practices, such as the Christian tradition of serving fish on Friday, might be adaptive responses to rickets. Another was June weddings, which tend to bring the first baby in the spring and permit the rapid growth phase of the first six months of life in summer sunshine. By contrast, the fall baby historically lacked vitamin D because of an infancy during the winter months.

Fortification of Food with Vitamin D

With the discovery that irradiation of ergosterol could produce a molecule (later identified as vitamin D_2) with potent antirachitic activity came the realization that such a preparation could be added to foodstuffs rendering low–vitamin D foods useful in the fight against rickets. As noted earlier, the two problems with foods containing vitamin D are that there are too few of them and that even those foods that contain vitamin D vary widely in potency. Steenbock had the idea to fortify staples of the diet such as breakfast cereals, milk, and margarine with vitamin D in the form of irradiated ergosterol, and because this supplement has a narrower range of variability, the potency of such foods could be assured with some degree of confidence. Some U.S. states and Western countries fortify only milk or margarine; others include breakfast cereals as well. Nonetheless, fortifying even these few foods with vitamin D has virtually eradicated the incidence of rickets in the Western world. The fortification of foods with vitamins including vitamin D is arguably one of the most important medical achievements of the twentieth century and certainly a major achievement of the nutritional sciences.

Nowadays, pure crystalline vitamin D_3 is used in food fortification rather than Steenbock's irradiated ergosterol. Nevertheless, Steenbock's "invention" represents one of the earliest examples of a university (Wisconsin-Madison) patenting the application of fundamental scientific research in the biomedical field. The discovery led to the inception of a new university structure, WARF (Wisconsin Alumni Research Foundation), an institution designed to manage patentable research and recycle profits from such discoveries. Aside from serving as a model for many other similar institutions in the United States and around the world, WARF has spawned a number of other products from its profits on vitamin D fortification, including the rodent poison warfarin and most of the new metabolites of vitamin D itself, including calcitriol, identified and synthesized in the laboratory of DeLuca.

Despite the incredible success of food fortification in the eradication of rickets, over the years the process has met some resistance and even outright opposition amid fears that vitamin D in megadoses could cause hypercalcemia and, consequently, kidney damage. These fears are largely groundless because the doses required to produce renal damage are massive and could not be acquired by ingestion of large amounts of foods, even those fortified with vitamin D (cod-liver oil excepted). Yet one of the most notable examples of resistance came in the Province of Quebec, Canada. Health authorities in this province steadfastly resisted the fortification of dairy products with vitamin D until the early 1970s, when finally they bowed to pressure from a group headed by the notable clinical geneticist Charles Scriver to reduce rickets in the French-Canadian population. Following this decision, statistics from one Montreal hospital (Sainte-Justine pour les Enfants) showed a decline in the annual incidence of rickets from 130 per 1,000 to zero in an eight-year span between 1968 and 1976, which coincided with the introduction of provincial legislation making it mandatory for dairies to fortify milk (Delvin et al. 1978). Today, a similar low incidence of rickets can be documented in every children's hospital in North America. Gone too is the once familiar bowleggedness, the signature of rickets, which often remained with the victim for life and was so common in the Great Depression of the 1930s.

With the end of World War II came mandatory rationing and governmental food fortification in Western Europe. But in 1957 politicians in the United Kingdom bowed to political pressure and drastically reduced vitamin D fortification of cereals and powdered milk following an "outbreak" of infantile hypercalcemia. At the time, the outbreak was believed to be caused by overfortification of food with vitamins D and A, although Donald Fraser, a noted Canadian pediatrician who researched the evidence at that time, now feels that this conclusion was probably incorrect (Fraser et al. 1966). The incidence of infantile hypercalcemia today is now no greater in countries that fortify than those that do not. Furthermore, the disease seems to result from an insult to the fetus in utero rather than a problem of the young child overindulging in fortified food, such as infant formula. Nevertheless, the condition results in mental retardation and heart problems that are largely irreversible and thus must be taken seriously.

To this day, the United Kingdom permits fortification of margarine only, probably at the expense of some increased incidence of rickets and osteomalacia in the population. Certainly, blood plasma levels of vitamin D and its metabolites (except calcitriol) are lower, presumably reflecting reduced stores of vitamin D in Britons when compared to a similar population of Americans and Canadians at the same latitude but given fortified food. In summary, it can be stated that the advantages of food fortification with vitamin D far outweigh any disadvantages. The main value of food fortification with vitamin D is to provide a *constant* year-round supply of the essential nutrient in the diet to augment the seasonal production in the skin.

Geographical Aspects of Vitamin D

Synthesis of vitamin D is both season- and latitude-dependent because vitamin D is made in the skin only by exposure to wavelengths in the UV spectrum of sunlight, and these wavelengths are absorbed by the ozone layer of the atmosphere. Only near the equator does the sunlight remain at an angle high enough for UV rays to penetrate the atmosphere on a year-round basis. Michael Holick of Boston City Hospital conducted experiments in which test tubes containing 7-dehydrocholesterol (the skin precursor to vitamin D) were exposed to light at various times of the day at latitudes from Caracas to Edmonton or Glasgow. He concluded (Webb, Kline, and Holick 1988) that in a city such as Boston, vitamin D is synthesized *only* in the months from April to October. Such a result implies that in most of the northern cities of the world, production of vitamin D_3 is seasonal and rickets might result at such latitudes if vitamin D stores are depleted *and* there is no dietary vitamin D.

Historical records also consistently reveal the geographical segregation of rickets to more northerly latitudes. August Hirsch (1883–6, vol. 3), for example, discussed the paucity of data on the geographical distribution of rickets. Theobald Palm, a Western medical missionary to Japan and China, concluded in a valuable paper in 1890 that sunshine is the main etiological factor in rickets. He compiled anecdotal reports suggesting that rickets was rare in southern China but more common in northern regions of the same country. However, reports in the early 1900s suggested a similar incidence of rickets in New Orleans (30° latitude) and New York (40° latitude). Hess (1929) ascribed this similarity to equivalent average annual sunshine exposure (2,519 versus 2,557 hours). It is interesting to note that of the cities cited by Hess for the year 1923, Phoenix, Arizona, has the highest amount of annual sunshine with 3,752 hours (and no rickets in the population), whereas Glasgow (a hotbed of rickets) has the lowest with 1,086 hours. Since UV light penetration is greater at higher altitudes, we would expect the incidence of rickets to be low in mountain cities, and early studies in cities like Denver (5,000 ft. above sea level) bear this out. Even earlier, in 1844, a Swiss physician had pointed out that rickets was more prevalent in the lowlands than the mountains, again presumably reflecting the relative exposure to UV light (Hess 1929: 50). In more recent times, the pollution of major cities has modified local UV exposure and may have increased our predisposition to rickets by reducing skin synthesis of vitamin D. Thus, geography plays a major role in the distribution of rickets, but the relationship is not a simple one directly dependent on degrees of latitude. It is further modified by climate, altitude, and degree of pollution.

The geography of vitamin D and rickets is also modified by diet. It is important to note that many of the peoples who live in northern latitudes depend upon the sea for their survival (e.g., Eskimos, Haida Indians, Greenlanders, Scandinavians). It is tempting to speculate that the natural incidence of rickets in these cultures has been ameliorated by the higher vitamin D content of their diets (e.g., from fish oils). One anecdotal story relating to the higher fat-soluble vitamin content of Arctic meats is the experience of early Arctic explorers. Several were forced to shoot Arctic animals (such as polar bears) and eat almost all edible organs in order to survive. As a result, some contracted hypervitaminosis A, which causes disorientation and brain swelling, probably from ingestion of polar bear liver containing vast stores of vitamins A and D. Eskimos apparently avoid the liver of the polar bear but still get enough vitamins D and A from the rest of their diet.

Social and Ethnic Aspects of Vitamin D

Because vitamin D is produced in the skin by exposure to UV light, social practices relating to exposure of the skin (such as clothing habits or sunbathing) can be of paramount importance to this production. Primitive humans evolved near the equator and are popularly depicted wearing minimal clothing. These considerations, plus the belief that primitive humans must have spent much of their lives outdoors, suggest that their contraction of rickets was unlikely. But as humans increased in numbers and moved into more and more inhospitable climes, the need for clothing would have become greater and the synthesis of vitamin D in the skin would have been compromised. It is possible that sun worship in early cultures reflects a realization of the importance to health of skin exposure to the sun.

Adaptation to sunlight exposure involved the development of melanin pigment in the skin. People exposed to maximal amounts of sunlight at the equator were the darkest, and those at the highest latitudes of Europe were the lightest. Although the subject is somewhat controversial, modern research indicates that skin melanin not only protects against the harmful effects of sunlight (e.g., skin cancer) but reduces the efficiency of the synthesis of vitamin D. Loomis (1970) suggests that summer bronzing in white populations is a seasonal adaptation to UV light exposure, though there is no evidence that vitamin D synthesis is regulated in an individual by such seasonal pigmentation. However, there is also no evidence that excessive exposure to sunlight can cause hypervitaminosis D and toxicity. The interrelationship of skin pigmentation and migration has some relevance to nutrition. Over the course of the past few centuries there has been considerable migration of certain peoples around the world so that cultural groups exist in climates that "their skin was not designed for."

Much has been written about whites developing skin cancer in Arizona and Australia, and considerable evidence is accumulating that indicates rickets and osteomalacia are common among Asian groups in England and Scotland (Felton and Stone 1966; Ford et al. 1973; Dent and Gupta 1975). There is some possibility that the problems of Asians in Britain are exacerbated by a high-phytate, high-phosphate diet (which tends to chelate calcium in the lumen of the intestine) combined with the avoidance of the typical vitamin D–fortified staples that whites consume.

Black children growing up in southern U.S. cities during the last part of the nineteenth century and the first decades of the twentieth century endured rickets almost as a rite of passage. And Rastafarians living outside of the UV climate of the West Indies may also be at risk for rickets. This is because of strict dietary practices that forbid consumption of artificial infant formulas, coupled with reduced opportunities for UV exposure in inner-city apartment complexes and a skin pigment unsuited to their "new" more northerly homes. There is also speculation (Ward et al. 1982) that the vitamin D–rich fish component of the Jamaican Rastafarian diet has been dropped by those living abroad. With the generation of multicultural societies such as currently exist in the United States, Canada, and many former colonial European countries, this potential problem of widespread rickets needs to be better understood and *dietary* solutions need to be formulated.

Clothing must have been developed for both staying warm in cooler climates and combating the harmful effects of UV light in warmer climates. Some cultures, particularly Moslem and Hindu groups, have very strict traditions of purdah, the practice of keeping the female skin out of the gaze of the public and therefore out of the sun. Though this strict policy does not apply to female children below the age of puberty, Saudi Arabian physicians report a higher female to male ratio in rickets patients that they ascribe to the higher UV exposure of the male children. In most cases, however, the practice of purdah cannot be directly blamed for childhood rickets in Saudi Arabia and North Africa, but it can be held responsible for osteomalacia observed in older females in such populations. And because these women with low reserves of vitamin D bear infants, the low UV exposure might be indirectly responsible for rickets. Detailed studies of the etiology of the rickets observed in Moslem groups (Belton 1986; Underwood and Margetts 1987; Elzouki et al. 1989) suggest the existence of maternal vitamin D deficiency, which results from the extra burden placed upon the mother to provide calcium for the skeleton of the growing fetus. Placental and lactational transfer of vitamin D stores from mother to the neonate are thus minimal, and such deficiencies, coupled with inadequate UV exposure, can result in infantile rickets. It is likely that the strict moral standards that prevailed in past centuries in western Europe leading to limited skin exposure also contributed to the well-documented higher incidence of osteomalacia in women.

Glenville Jones

Bibliography

Belton, N. 1986. Rickets – not only the "English Disease." *Acta Paediatrica Scandinavica* 323 (Suppl): 68–75.

Blunt, J. W., H. K. Schnoes, and H. F. DeLuca. 1968. 25-Hydroxycholecalciferol: A biologically active metabolite of vitamin D. *Biochemistry* 7: 3317–22.

Dagnelie, P., F. Vergote, W. van Staveren, et al. 1990. High prevalence of rickets in infants on macrobiotic diets. *American Journal of Clinical Nutrition* 51: 202–8.

Delvin, E. E., F. H. Glorieux, M. Dussault, et al. 1978. Simultaneous measurement of 25-hydroxycholecalciferol and 25-hydroxyergocalciferol. *Medical Biology* 57: 165–70.

Dent, C., and M. Gupta. 1975. Plasma 25-hydroxyvitamin-D levels during pregnancy in Caucasians and in vegetarian and non-vegetarian Asians. *Lancet* 2: 1057–60.

Elzouki, A., T. Markstead, M. Elgarrah, et al. 1989. Serum concentrations of vitamin D metabolites in rachitic Libyan children. *Pediatric Gastroenterology and Nutrition* 9: 507–12.

Felton, D. J. C., and W. D. Stone. 1966. Osteomalacia in Asian immigrants during pregnancy. *British Medical Journal* 1: 1521–2.

Ford, J. A., D. C. Davidson, W. B. McIntosh, et al. 1973. Neonatal rickets in an Asian immigrant population. *British Medical Journal* 3: 211–12.

Fraser, D., B. S. L. Kidd, S. W. Kooh, et al. 1966. A new look at infantile hypercalcemia. *The Pediatric Clinics of North America* 13: 503–25.

Fraser, D. R., and E. Kodicek. 1970. Unique biosynthesis by kidney of a biologically active vitamin D metabolite. *Nature* 228: 764–6.

Glisson, F. 1650. De Rachitide sive morbo puerili qui vulgo. *The rickets dicitur.* London.

Hess, A. F. 1929. *Rickets including osteomalacia and tetany.* Philadelphia, Pa.

Hess, A. F., and M. Weinstock. 1924. Antirachitic properties imparted to inert fluids and to green vegetables by ultra-violet irradiation. *Journal of Biological Chemistry* 62: 301–13.

Hirsch, A. 1883–6. *Handbook of geographical and historical pathology,* 3 vols., trans. Charles Creighton. London.

Holick, M. F., H. K. Schnoes, H. F. DeLuca, et al. 1971. Isolation and identification of 1,25-dihydroxycholecalciferol. A metabolite of vitamin D active in intestine. *Biochemistry* 10: 2799–804.

Huldschinsky, K. 1919. Heilung von Rachitis durch künstliche Höhensonne. *Deutsche Medizinische Wochenschrift* 45: 712–13.

Loomis, W. F. 1970. Rickets. *Scientific American* 223: 76–91.

McCollum, E. V., N. Simmonds, J. E. Becker, et al. 1922. Studies on experimental rickets. XXI. An experimental demonstration of the existence of a vitamin which promotes calcium deposition. *Journal of Biological Chemistry* 53: 293–312.

Mellanby, E. 1919. An experimental investigation on rickets. *Lancet* l: 407–12.

Myrtle, J. F., M. R. Haussler, and A. W. Norman. 1970. Evidence for the biologically active form of cholecalciferol in the intestine. *Journal of Biological Chemistry* 245: 1190–6.

Palm, T. A. 1890. The geographical distribution and etiology of rickets. *The Practitioner* 45: 270–9.

Percival, T. 1789. *Essays medical, philosophical and experimental on the medical use of cod-liver oil,* Vol. 2. London.

Raczynski, J. 1913. Recherches expérimentales sur le manque d'action du soleil comme cause de rachitisme. *Comptes rendues de l'association internationale de pediatrics* 308. Paris.

Shorter, E. 1982. *A history of women's bodies.* New York.

Steenbock, H., and A. Black. 1924. The induction of growth-promoting and calcifying properties in a ration by exposure to ultraviolet light. *Journal of Biological Chemistry* 61: 408–22.

Underwood, P., and B. Margetts. 1987. High levels of childhood rickets in rural North Yemen. *Society of Scientific Medicine* 24: 37–41.

Ward, P., J. Drakeford, J. Milton, and J. James. 1982. Nutritional rickets in Rastafarian children. *British Medical Journal* 285: 1242–3.

Webb, A. R., L. Kline, and M. F. Holick. 1988. Influence of season and latitude on the cutaneous synthesis of vitamin D_3. *Journal of Clinical Endocrinology and Metabolism* 67: 373–8.

Whistler, Daniel. 1645. De morbo puerili Anglorum, quem patrio idiomate indigenae vocant The Rickets. M.D. thesis, University of Leiden. Leiden, Netherlands.

Windaus, A., F. Schenck, and F. van Werder. 1936. Über das antirachitisch wirksame Bestrahlungsprodukt aus 7-Dehydrocholesteria. *Hoppe Seyler's Zeitschrift für Physiologische Chemie* 241: 100–3.

IV.A.5   Vitamin E

As any nutritional text dated prior to 1970 will indicate, vitamin E has not received much respect from nutritionists. In such texts it is often placed after vitamin K, in the miscellaneous category. This is because it took a good 40 years from its discovery in 1923 (Evans and Bishop 1923) to demonstrate a clear-cut human deficiency disease for vitamin E. Though numerous studies had shown vitamin E to be an essential component of animal diets, deficiency symptoms varied from one species to the next, from reproductive disorders in rats to vascular abnormalities in chickens. Thus, it was not clear that humans had an obligatory requirement for vitamin E. Recent research, however, has shown that this is indeed the case and that vitamin E is just as important to human nutrition as the other vitamins. It is, therefore, pleasing to see that vitamin E is now placed in its proper place in the alphabet of vitamins.

Vitamin E is the nutritional term used to describe two families of four naturally occurring compounds each, the tocopherols and the tocotrienols (Pennock, Hemming, and Kerr 1964). Tocopherols and tocotrienols both contain a chroman ring, which is essential for biological activity, but differ in the degree of saturation of their fatty side chains. They are otherwise interchangeable in their biological role. Each family comprises alpha, beta, gamma, and delta forms, which differ significantly in their potency. Thus, alpha-tocopherol represents the principal source of vitamin E found in the human diet with a small contribution also coming from gamma-tocopherol (Bieri and Evarts 1973). Many texts, including this one, use the terms alpha-tocopherol and vitamin E interchangeably.

Located in the cellular membranes, alpha-tocopherol helps the cell to resist damage from powerful oxidants known as free radicals. These are generated naturally inside the body as by-products of fuel oxidation, and they can be generated artificially by external factors such as radiation, chemotherapy, or pollutants. B. Ames (1983) believes that aerobic respiration using oxygen is the most important of these external factors in generating free radicals and that antioxidants such as vitamin E help to resist free-radical damage. Because of its stabilized chroman ring structure, vitamin E is able to mop up these free radicals and their immediate products, minimizing the damage to the lipids of the membrane and therefore maintaining cell membrane integrity. Simply put, vitamin E stops the fat of the body from turning rancid.

History of the Discovery of Vitamin E

The decade between 1915 and 1925 was one of the most productive in the history of nutrition. The use of semipurified or semisynthetic diets allowed researchers to demonstrate the essential nature of individual components of the diet and, more specifically, to recognize the existence of the vitamins A, B_1, C, and D. Nutritionists (Osbourne and Mendel 1919; Mattill and Conklin 1920) showed that though these diets were able to maintain life, they failed to support reproduction in laboratory animals. Reproductive biologists, thus, realized that the estrous cycle of the female rat or testicular development in the male constituted useful animal models for studying the essential nature of nutritional factors (Long and Evans 1922). Using a basal semipurified diet comprising casein, starch, lard, butter, fats, and brewer's yeast, which would allow rats to grow but not reproduce, groups headed by Herbert M. Evans and L. B. Mendel set about the laborious task of finding a substance that would promote fertility.

Detailed historical accounts of the events surrounding the discovery of vitamin E, its chemistry and biology, have been published by two pioneers in the field, Evans (Evans 1962) and Karl E. Mason, a student of Mendel (Mason 1977). Their recollections are concise, modest accounts of the important milestones in the field, and unlike other accounts of historical events from rival camps, the two actually agree! The reader is referred to the often flowery account of Evans, who describes the identification of a factor in lettuce and wheat germ required for preventing resorption of fetuses in the pregnant rat. He writes:

> Good fairies attended every phase of the advent and early history of vitamin E. We turned our attention at once to the prevention rather than alleviation of these strange resorptions – a prevention which might disclose at once what individual natural foodstuffs carried a missing needed substance. Lettuce, relished by these poor sufferers of our rancid lard diet, was spectacularly successful, and we may have entertained the conviction that vitamin C which was not essential for growth was necessary in pregnancy, had we not quickly shown that not the aqueous, but only the fatty, component of these leaves, the chlorophyll-rich green oil, had worked the good result. Then, to our surprise, wheat was equally remedial, and the concept that vitamin C was involved could not, of course, survive. The good fairies accompanied me to the large Sperry flour mill at a neighboring town, Vallejo, where I found three great streams flowing from the milling of the wheat berry: the first constituted the outer cover or chaff; the second the endosperm, the white so-called flour; and the third which came in flattened flakes, stuck into such units by its oil content – the germ. Night had not fallen that day, before all these components were fed to groups of carefully prepared females – animals which had begun gestation on vitamin E–low diets and were fed both the watery and fatty solutions. Single daily drops of the golden yellow wheat

germ oil were remedial. That an oil might enrich the embryo's dietary needs for vitamin A and vitamin D, the only fat-soluble vitamins then known, was negated at once when we added the well-known rich source of vitamins A and D, cod liver oil, an addition which did not lessen but increased and made invariable our malady. (Evans 1962: 382)

From the words Evans used to describe his rats, we can clearly discern that he cared about the animals he used in those early studies. The factor initially described as "antisterility factor X" was born (Evans and Bishop 1922). Parallel studies by Mason (1925), working with the male rat, showed that the same factor appeared essential to prevent testicular degeneration in the rat. The name, vitamin E, seems to have been suggested by an opportunist, Barnett Sure, in 1924, based upon the vitamin nomenclature of the time, although the endorsement of this title by Evans helped to gain it widespread use (Evans 1925).

Following the discovery of vitamin E, nutritionists spent the next decade describing symptoms of its deficiency in a variety of animals, *except* humans. Research also focused on its chemical nature. Finally in 1936, Evans, working with Gladys and Oliver Emerson, published the identity of vitamin E from wheat germ oil as an alcohol with the chemical formula ($C_{29}H_{50}O_2$). Evans named this substance "alpha-tocopherol." The origin of this name is described in his personal account:

> I well remember their (the Emersons') plea to me to suggest a proper name for their purified substance when success crowned their efforts. I promptly invited George M. Calhoun, our professor of Greek to luncheon in Berkeley in our small Faculty Club. "Most scientists, medical men especially," said Calhoun, "have been guilty of coining Greek-Latin terms, bastards, of course, and we might have to do this." "What does the substance do?" he asked. "It permits an animal to bear offspring," I replied. "Well, childbirth in Greek is *tocos*," he said, "and if it confers or brings childbirth, we will next employ the Greek verb *phero*. You have also said that the term must have an ending consonant with its chemical – 'ol', it being an alcohol; your substance is 'tocopherol,' and the pleasant task assigned me quickly solved and not worth the delightful four-course dinner you have arranged." (Evans 1962: 383)

It is, therefore, evident that vitamin E was renamed alpha-tocopherol for the meager price of a four-course meal.

Erhard Fernholz provided the structural formula for alpha-tocopherol in 1938, and it was first synthesized chemically by the brilliant Swiss chemist Paul Karrer working at Hoffmann-LaRoche laboratories in Basel (Karrer et al. 1938).

Vitamin E Deficiency in Humans

During the period 1925 to 1935 there appeared an ever increasing and confusing series of papers in the nutritional literature showing the importance of vitamin E in the prevention of reproductive defects in rats; prevention of embryonic mortality and encephalomalacia in chicks; and prevention of nutritional muscular dystrophy in guinea pigs and rabbits. How could deficiency of a single nutritional factor cause all these different pathological changes in different laboratory animals but have no apparent parallel condition in humans? Even in avian species like the chick and duck the symptoms were not consistent.

Vitamin E deficiency appeared in different sites: muscular dystrophy in ducklings and vascular changes and encephalopathy in chicks. The common thread tying together all these apparently different defects ascribed to vitamin E deficiency was not immediately evident. Although H. S. Olcott and H. A. Mattill (1931) had pointed out the association of antioxidants and vitamin E in lettuce oil, it was not until 1937 after the discovery of alpha-tocopherol that it became clear that alpha-tocopherol was an antioxidant (Olcott and Emerson 1937). It was still later through the work of researchers such as A. L. Tappel and J. G. Bieri in the late 1950s and early 1960s, that the free-radical theory of lipid peroxidation and the function of vitamin E as an antioxidant developed to the point where the conflicting findings could be rationalized using a single mechanism (Tappel 1962).

According to this free-radical theory, membrane lipids in all membranes of the body should be susceptible to oxidative damage, and the exact location of damage observed in different animal species would depend upon variables such as specific membrane lipid composition, vitamin E content, and cellular metabolic rate. Based upon this theory it became easy to rationalize various patterns of damage due to vitamin E deficiency in different animal species. With this new understanding of the nature of vitamin E action came the realization that vitamin E deficiency in humans might show up in different sites (i.e., different membranes) from those showing vitamin E deficiency in animal tissues. Moreover, the recognition that the common feature of all these deficiency symptoms was damage caused by free radicals began a search for human individuals who might generate or be exposed to higher levels of such destructive factors and who might, therefore, develop vitamin E deficiency. These individuals turned out to be prematurely born infants.

Looking back at the extensive literature on vitamin E in humans, it is clear that clues of vitamin E deficiency in pediatric medicine were emerging even in the late 1940s. The advent of modern neonatal units led to the use of respirators in which newborns were kept in an oxygen-rich environment. Premature infants were particularly favored for this treatment, and two conditions suggesting vitamin E deficiency affecting premature infants came to light: hemolytic anemia, in which erythrocyte membranes have an increased tendency to rupture; and retrolental fibroplasia, in which the blood vessels of the developing retina are damaged, leading to scarring and blindness (Farrell 1980). First observed in the 1940s, these conditions were documented and rationalized for the first time with the advent of the free-radical theory.

Free radicals, generated from the oxygen-rich gaseous mix used in such respirators, attacked cellular membranes, in particular those of red blood cells and the cells of the retina. It should be noted that although premature infants are susceptible to damage resulting from vitamin E deficiency, this is due only in part to an increased "insult" from oxidants; it is also partly the result of reduced vitamin E stores and lower vitamin E levels in their blood. Not surprisingly, the severity of retrolental fibroplasia is markedly decreased by pharmacological doses of vitamin E (Hittner et al. 1981). As the assault on cellular membranes in such fast-growing children is diminished and as vitamin E stores are bolstered in the first weeks of life, the risk of vitamin E deficiency decreases substantially. Consequently, vitamin E deficiency is very difficult to demonstrate in healthy children or in adults eating a standard balanced diet.

Toward the end of the 1950s, the Food and Nutrition Board of the National Research Council of the United States funded a long-term, six-year, dietary study of the relationship between blood vitamin E levels and consumption of polyunsaturated fatty acids (PUFA) in a group of male subjects who were given a diet low in vitamin E. The study became known as the Elgin Project, after the hospital in Illinois where it was carried out (Horwitt 1960). Institutionalized subjects were closely monitored for symptoms of vitamin E deficiency while they underwent the increased stress of a diet with a higher PUFA:vitamin E ratio. Not surprisingly, the subjects failed to develop a clear-cut clinical syndrome except that plasma vitamin E levels dropped and red cells showed an increased tendency to hemolysis, but it took two years for these changes to occur.

If vitamin E deficiency does occur in humans beyond the neonatal period, it is usually secondary to another disease state that results in malabsorption of vitamin E from the diet. Since vitamin E is absorbed with the fat in the diet, conditions that result in fat malabsorption, such as chronic cholestasis (liver disease) or cystic fibrosis where there is pancreatic blockage, will result in vitamin E deficiency. Another rare cause of vitamin E deficiency is the genetic absence of beta-lipoprotein, the transporter of vitamin E in the blood, in a condition known as abetalipoproteinemia (Muller, Lloyd, and Bird 1977).

In such individuals with vitamin E supply or transport problems, there is an increased tendency of red cells to hemolyze and also a shortened red cell survival time. More recently, the medical fraternity has begun to recognize muscle and neurological problems that result from human vitamin E deficiency (Sokol 1988). These abnormalities include loss of reflexes and gait disturbances that are accompanied by pathological changes. Autopsies performed on patients with cystic fibrosis show more advanced axonal degeneration than would be expected of normal age-matched individuals (Sung 1964). It would be surprising if humans were spared all of the neurological and muscular defects observed in animals. However, such human vitamin E deficiency is rarely accompanied by the acute muscle, brain, and blood vessel defects observed in laboratory animals fed semisynthetic diets. We should be thankful that it is not.

Dietary Sources of Vitamin E

The substance alpha-tocopherol is present in the diet in a variety of plant oils, including wheat germ oil and the lettuce oil discovered in pioneering work. Soya bean and other plant oils, which became more common dietary components in the latter half of the twentieth century, contain gamma-tocopherol, a less potent version of vitamin E. It is interesting to note that the unsaturated fatty acids, which are present in plant oils and are so prone to free-radical oxidation in our food, are accompanied by the highest concentrations of vitamin E. It is as if nature realized their sensitivity and put in a natural preservative to protect these oils (Bieri, Corash, and Hubbard 1983). Animal fats contain lower amounts of vitamin E, and fish oils have variable amounts depending upon the diet of the fish and the age of the fish oil. Though cod-liver oil has been shown to contain vitamin E, it also contains a high concentration of polyunsaturated fatty acids that can easily become oxidized by free radicals and, consequently, as noted by Evans (1962), be deleterious rather than protective.

One special food associated with vitamin E is wheat germ bread. Sometimes referred to in Europe as Hovis (from the Latin *hominis vis* meaning "the strength of man"), this bread is made with flour containing five times as much of the fatty germ as wholemeal bread. The procedure by which the wheat germ is stabilized involves separating it from the flour, lightly cooking it in steam, and returning it to the flour. This process was jointly patented in the United Kingdom in 1887 by Richard "Stoney" Smith of Stone, Staffordshire, and Macclesfield Miller and Thomas Fitton of the firm S. Fitton and Son. This was about 35 years before the experiments of Evans, which led to the discovery of vitamin E. Although the health-promoting properties of Hovis were clearly recognized in early advertising campaigns, there is no evidence that Hovis was aimed at special groups of people (i.e., those with muscular, reproductive, or vascular problems). With such rich sources of vitamin E as Hovis bread in our normal diet, it is difficult to consume a diet that will result in vitamin E deficiency.

Other Uses of Vitamin E

The history of vitamin E is much shorter than that of the other vitamins, but the absence for so long of a clear-cut human deficiency syndrome allowed for the development of a number of bogus or exaggerated claims for vitamin E, or at least claims that have never been properly substantiated. Most of these have been built upon deficiency symptoms observed in laboratory animals and not in humans. One, based upon findings in the rat, is that vitamin E is a fertility vitamin. As a result, some physicians used the vitamin to treat a number of conditions that produced spontaneous abortions. In a series of poorly controlled, anecdotal studies, Evan Shute (1939) claimed that vitamin E was particularly effective in countering habitual abortion, which is defined as spontaneous abortion before the sixteenth week of gestation during three successive pregnancies. When others tried to confirm these findings, they failed to do so and were left to conclude, as did C. T. Javert, W. F. Finn, and H. J. Stander:

> There is such a maze of literature the proper cognizance cannot be taken of all the pertinent articles. As the reader reviews them in order to develop his own philosophy let him [all obstetricians were male in those days] be reminded of the following important matters:
>
> i. the high percentage of success irrespective of which vitamin, hormone or method is employed;
> ii. the lack of specific information as to the pathogenesis of human spontaneous abortion. (1949: 887)

This skepticism was found to be well grounded; others who have reviewed three decades of experimentation on abortion have also concluded that vitamin E supplementation is ineffective (Marks 1962).

In addition, there have been numerous claims that large doses of vitamin E are beneficial in cardiovascular conditions such as angina, congestive heart failure, and peripheral vascular disease. Current medical opinion is that these claims are unproven. However, this debate was being revisited in the 1990s with the suggestion that the "oxidized" lipoprotein, LDL, may be the chief villain in atherosclerosis, and that its level in the bloodstream inversely correlates with alpha-tocopherol levels. New clinical studies of vitamin E and the risk of coronary heart disease in both male and female health workers have, again, suggested a protective role for the vitamin (Rim et al. 1993; Stampfer et al. 1993). Consequently, long-term supplementation with vitamin E to prevent heart disease is again being discussed.

The association of vitamin E deficiency with nutritional muscular dystrophy in guinea pigs and rabbits led to trials of its use as a supplement in Duchenne's muscular dystrophy (Berneske et al. 1960). Because this condition is a genetically inherited disease with a different etiology than the nutritional version, it is not surprising that vitamin E was ineffective, but this is not to say that vitamin E supplementation cannot help to alleviate some of the consequences of muscular and neurological disease and, therefore, benefit the patient. The recent elucidation of the molecular defect in Lou Gehrig's disease (ALS) as a lack of the enzyme superoxide dismutase (Rosen et al. 1993) has already led to a reevaluation of dietary antioxidant supplementation in this disease because the enzyme works in concert with vitamin E to reduce free radicals inside the cell. It is hoped that the results will be more positive than those reported recently in another neurological condition, Parkinsonism, where alpha-tocopherol supplementation was unsuccessful as an adjunct therapy to the drug deprenyl (Shoulson et al. 1993).

The old adage that if a little is good, a lot must be better, pervades nutritional science. The association of vitamin E with muscle health has led to the use of vitamin supplements in sports (Cureton 1954). Consequently, vitamin E can be considered one of the earliest performance-enhancing drugs, in use long before anabolic steroids and growth hormones. However, a controlled study of Scottish track-and-field athletes in the early 1970s by I. M. Sharman, M. G. Down, and R. N. Sen dispelled the notion that vitamin E improved performance. Presumably the athletes agreed because they moved on to other treatments.

In the 1970s, megadose vitamin therapy came into vogue in North America, and Senator William Proxmire from Wisconsin, who advocated such self-treatments for improved health, subsequently led opposition to legislation that might have blocked such potentially dangerous megadose vitamin products. Simultaneously in vogue was the free-radical theory of lipid peroxidation, which resulted in the idea that the natural aging process is an inability of the organism to keep up with oxidation (Harman 1956).

A possible solution to the problem came from Ames (1983), who suggested that a battery of dietary and endogenously produced antioxidants, headed by vitamin E and also including glutathione, vitamin C, beta-carotene, and possibly uric acid, might help to slow down this process. Ames concluded that the natural aging process results from an inability to completely prevent the harmful effects of oxidation. As a consequence, megadoses of vitamin E have been consumed by thousands of North Americans in the hope that augmenting the antioxidant supply might help defeat free radicals and prevent aging. Although it is difficult to believe that supplemental dietary vitamin E will prevent aging if alpha-tocopherol levels are already adequate in the blood of the majority of adults, the toxicity symptoms (gastrointestinal disturbances) of vitamin E are minor. Thus there seems not much reason to prevent a little self-experimentation, although it is worth noting that this self-experimentation is ably assisted by the pharmaceutical industry.

As the antioxidant properties of vitamin E have

become more and more evident, the food and cosmetic industry have found wider and wider uses for it. Vitamin E is a poor antioxidant in vitro and is largely replaced by other substances when a preservative is needed in food. However, the vitamin is now added to a broad range of soaps and shampoos and other cosmetic products in the hope of convincing the buyer that it has special properties in skin and hair. The fact that human vitamin E deficiency is not accompanied by skin and hair problems, or that vitamin E might not even enter the hair or skin when applied via this route, does not seem to be a weighty argument for the consumer. Perhaps the most outrageous claim this contributor has come across in recent years is one stating that a cream containing vitamin E might protect against frostbite. It was applied by a Canadian sled-dog racer to the underside of her dogs' testicles to protect them from the harmful effects of the snow and cold (Sokol 1985).

The past two to three decades have, however, also seen some legitimate uses of vitamin E in medical science. The development of total parenteral feeding solutions in the 1970s included a recognition of the essential nature of vitamin E (Bieri et al. 1983). Long-term artificial feeding solutions are, therefore, supplemented with vitamin E. The widespread use of cancer chemotherapeutic agents such as adriamycin, which generates free radicals to kill cancer cells, can be augmented by vitamin E therapy to help protect surviving normal cells. Tissue transplantation normally involves maintenance of donor organs in oxygenated perfusate prior to surgery, a process that leads to free-radical generation. Use of antioxidants and free-radical scavengers helps improve the survival of such organs, presumably by minimizing the damage caused by free radicals. Children with cholestasis and poor vitamin nutriture receiving liver transplants are given water-soluble vitamin E preparations to help the donated organ survive. Vitamin E can also attenuate the damage caused by free radicals released during myocardial infarctions (Massey and Burton 1989). It appears that uses for vitamin E will continue to proliferate well into the new millennium.

Glenville Jones

Bibliography

Ames, B. 1983. Dietary carcinogens and anticarcinogens. *Science* 221: 1256-64.
Berneske, G. M., A. R. C. Butson, E. N. Gould, and D. Levy. 1960. Clinical trial of high dosage vitamin E in human muscular dystrophy. *Canadian Medical Association Journal* 82: 418-21.
Bieri, J. G., L. Corash, and V. S. Hubbard. 1983. Medical uses of vitamin E. *New England Journal of Medicine* 308: 1063-71.
Bieri, J. G., and R. P. Evarts. 1973. Tocopherols and fatty acids in American diets. *Journal of the American Dietetic Association* 62: 147-51.
Cureton, T. K. 1954. Effect of wheat germ oil and vitamin E on normal human subjects in physical training programs. *American Journal of Physiology* 179: 628.
Evans, H. M. 1925. Invariable occurrence of male sterility with dietaries lacking fat soluble vitamin E. *Proceedings from the National Academy of Sciences USA* 11: 373-7.
  1962. The pioneer history of vitamin E. *Vitamins and Hormones* 20: 379-87.
Evans, H. M., and K. S. Bishop. 1922. The existence of a hitherto unrecognized dietary factor essential for reproduction. *Science* 56: 650-1.
  1923. The production of sterility with nutritional regimes adequate for growth and its cure with other foodstuffs. *Journal of Metabolic Research* 3: 233-316.
Evans, H. M., O. H. Emerson, and G. A. Emerson. 1936. The isolation from wheat germ oil of an alcohol, α-tocopherol having the properties of vitamin E. *Journal of Biological Chemistry* 113: 319-32.
Farrell, P. M. 1980. Deficiency states, pharmacological effects and nutrient requirements. In *Vitamin E: A comprehensive treatise*, ed. L. J. Machlin, 520-600. New York.
Fernholz, E. 1938. On the constitution of α-tocopherol. *Journal of the American Chemical Society* 60: 700-5.
Harman, D. 1956. Aging: A theory based upon free-radical and radiation chemistry. *Journal of Gerontology* 11: 298-300.
Hittner, H. M., L. B. Godio, A. J. Rudolph, et al. 1981. Retrolental fibroplasia: Efficacy of vitamin E in a double blind clinical study of preterm infants. *New England Journal of Medicine* 305: 1365-71.
Horwitt, M. K. 1960. Vitamin E and lipid metabolism in man. *American Journal of Clinical Nutrition* 8: 451-61.
Javert, C. T., W. F. Finn, and H. J. Stander. 1949. Primary and secondary spontaneous habitual abortion. *American Journal of Obstetrics and Gynecology* 57: 878-89.
Karrer, P., H. Fritzsche, B. H. Ringier, and A. Salomon. 1938. Synthese des α-tocopherols. *Helvitica Chimica Acta* 21: 820-5.
Long, J. A., and H. M. Evans. 1922. The oestrus cycle in the rat. *Memoirs of the University of California* 6: 1-51.
Marks, J. 1962. Critical appraisal of the therapeutic value of α-tocopherol. *Vitamins and Hormones* 20: 573-98.
Mason, K. E. 1925. A histological study of sterility in the albino rat due to a dietary deficiency. *Proceedings of the National Academy of Sciences USA* 11: 377-82.
  1977. The first two decades of vitamin E. *Federation Proceedings* 36: 1906-10.
Massey, K. D., and K. P. Burton. 1989. α-Tocopherol attenuates myocardial-membrane related alterations resulting from ischemia and reperfusion. *American Journal of Physiology* 256: H1192-9.
Mattill, H. A., and R. E. Conklin. 1920. The nutritive properties of milk; with special reference to reproduction in the albino rat. *Journal of Biological Chemistry* 44: 137-57.
Muller, D. P. R., J. K. Lloyd, and A. C. Bird. 1977. Long-term management of abetalipoproteinemia: Possible role for vitamin E. *Archives of Diseases of Childhood* 52: 209-14.
Olcott, H. S., and O. H. Emerson. 1937. Antioxidants and the autoxidation of fats. IX. The antioxidant properties of the tocopherols. *Journal of the American Chemical Society* 59: 1008-9.
Olcott, H. S., and H. A. Mattill. 1931. The unsaponifiable lipids of lettuce. II. Fractionation. *Journal of Biological Chemistry* 93: 59-64.
Osbourne, J. B., and L. B. Mendel. 1919. The nutritive values of yeast protein. *Journal of Biological Chemistry* 38: 223-7.
Pennock, J. F., F. W. Hemming, and J. D. Kerr. 1964. A reassessment of tocopherol chemistry. *Biochemical and Biophysical Research Communications* 17: 542-8.

Rim, E. B., M. J. Stampfer, A. Ascherio, et al. 1993. Vitamin E consumption and the risk of coronary disease in men. *New England Journal of Medicine* 328: 1450-6.

Rosen, D. R., T. Siddique, D. Patterson, et al. 1993. Mutations in Cu/Zn superoxide dismutase gene are associated with familial amyotrophic lateral sclerosis. *Nature* 362: 59-62.

Sharman, I. M., M. G. Down, and R. N. Sen. 1971. The effects of vitamin E and training on physiological function and athletic performance in adolescent swimmers. *British Journal of Nutrition* 26: 265-76.

Shoulson, I., S. Fahn, D. Oakes, et al. 1993. Effects of toco-pherol and deprenyl on the progression of disability in early Parkinson's disease. *New England Journal of Medicine* 328: 176-83.

Shute, E. V. 1939. The diagnosis and treatment of vitamin E deficiency. In *Vitamin E. A symposium held under the auspices of the Society of Chemical Industry,* ed. A. L. Bacharach and J. C. Drummond, 67-76. Cambridge.

Sokol, A. 1985. Husky hounds are hard to beat in sled racing. *The Toronto Star,* Feb. 28, p. H8.

Sokol, R. J. 1988. Vitamin E deficiency and neurological dis-ease. *Annual Reviews of Nutrition* 8: 351-73.

Stampfer, M. J., C. H. Hennekens, J. E. Manson, et al. 1993. Vitamin E consumption and the risk of coronary dis-ease in women. *New England Journal of Medicine* 328: 1444-9.

Sung, J. H. 1964. Neuroaxonal dystrophy in mucoviscidosis. *Journal of Neuropathology and Experimental Neurol-ogy* 23: 567-83.

Sure, B. 1924. Dietary requirements for reproduction. II. The existence of a specific vitamin for reproduction. *Jour-nal of Biological Chemistry* 58: 693-709.

Tappel, A. L. 1962. Vitamin E as the biological lipid antioxi-dant. *Vitamins and Hormones* 20: 493-510.

IV.A.6 ⚛ Vitamin K and Vitamin K–Dependent Proteins

The term "vitamin K" was first introduced by Henrik Dam in 1935, following discovery of a fat-soluble sub-stance that could prevent bleeding (Dam 1935, 1964). During the years 1928 to 1930, Dam conducted stud-ies on the cholesterol metabolism of chicks at the University of Copenhagen. The chicks were being fed an artificial, practically sterol-free diet to which the then known vitamins A and D were added. He observed hemorrhages (bleeding) in different parts of the body in some of the chicks that had been on the diet for more than two or three weeks. In addition, blood that was examined from some of these chicks showed delayed coagulation or clotting (Dam 1964). The low amounts of cholesterol and fat in the diet were ruled out as the causes of the symptom.

Similar observations were made by W. D. McFar-lane, W. R. Graham, Jr., and G. E. Hall (1931). W. F. Holst and E. R. Halbrook (1933) observed that the symp-toms resembled scurvy, a disease caused by vitamin C deficiency, and could be prevented by addition of fresh cabbage to the diet. These investigators con-cluded that the protective agent in the cabbage was vitamin C. However, when pure vitamin C became available, it was injected into the chicks and failed to prevent the hemorrhagia (Dam 1964).

Large doses of vitamins A and D (fed in the form of fish-liver oils) and commercial carotene also did not prevent the hemorrhagia (Dam 1935). Cereals and seeds did prevent the symptom, and green leaves and hog liver were found to be potent sources of the anti-hemorrhagic factor. Research groups led by Dam and H. J. Almquist worked independently to show that the factor was a new fat-soluble vitamin. Dam's report (Dam 1935) was followed in the same year by that of Almquist and E. L. R. Stokstad (1935). The factor was designated vitamin K (Dam 1935, 1964). According to Dam (1964: 10), "The letter K was the first one in the alphabet which had not, with more or less justification, been used to designate other vitamins, and it also hap-pened to be the first letter in the word 'koagulation' according to the Scandinavian and German spelling."

The elucidation of the structure of vitamin K was achieved in a relatively short time because of the number of large research groups involved. Several reviews are available on the isolation and characteri-zation of vitamin K (Doisy, Binkley, and Thayer 1941; Dam 1942, 1964; Almquist 1979). In 1943, Dam received the Nobel Prize for Physiology or Medicine for his discovery of vitamin K. It is interesting to note that Almquist, who published later but in the same year as Dam, did not share the Nobel Prize. Dam did share the prize with E. A. Doisy, who was honored for the isolation, chemical synthesis, and structural identi-fication of one of the forms of vitamin K.

The Structure of Vitamin K

Many compounds, all closely related, are now recog-nized as having antihemorrhagic activity (Table IV.A.6.1). Common to all is the methylnaphtho-quinone nucleus. This nucleus, known as menadione, has not been isolated from natural sources, but it has been synthesized and does possess biological activity. Attached to the methylnaphthoquinone nucleus are carbon chains that vary both in nature and length. Based on the nature of these carbon side chains, the natural K vitamins are subdivided into two groups: phylloquinone (vitamin K_1) and the menaquinones (MK-*n*). Phylloquinone, the plant product, has a 20-carbon side chain with only one double bond. The menaquinones, synthesized by microorganisms, con-tain side chains with varying numbers of 5-carbon (isoprene) units but always with one double bond per 5-carbon unit. Chain lengths of the known mena-quinones vary from 2 to 13 isoprene units. The *n* in MK-*n* refers to the number of 5-carbon units. A mena-quinone with 4 isoprene units (20 carbons) in its side chain, for example, would be called menaquinone-4, abbreviated MK-4. Humans convert the synthetic menadione nucleus to menaquinone-4.

Table IV.A.6.1. *Vitamin K analogues*

Analogue	Symbol	Source
Menadione	K_3	Synthetic
Phylloquinone	K_1	Plants, animal tissues
Menaquinones	MK-2 to MK-13	Bacteria, animal tissues

Nutritional Aspects of Vitamin K

Since the human body cannot synthesize the naphthoquinone entity, all the K vitamins in humans, at least the quinone nucleus of these compounds, are of extraneous origin. The K vitamins are synthesized by plants as phylloquinone and by bacteria in the intestines as the menaquinones (Table IV.A.6.1).

Phylloquinone, the form of vitamin K synthesized by plants, is the major dietary form of vitamin K (Booth et al. 1993; Booth, Sadowski, and Pennington 1995; Shearer, Bach, and Kohlmeier 1996). It is found in plants and in the tissues of plant-eating animals (Table IV.A.6.2) and is the form of vitamin K that is added to infant formulas and given to infants at birth.

The best sources of phylloquinone are green leafy vegetables and certain oils, such as soybean, rapeseed, and olive oil (Shearer et al. 1996). The values in

Table IV.A.6.2. *Phylloquinone content of common foods*

Phylloquinone concentration ranges in μg of phylloquinone per 100 g (3.5 oz.) food			
0.1–1.0	1–10	10–100	100–1,000
Avocado (1.0)	Apples (6)	Beans, runner (26)	Broccoli tops (179)
Bananas (0.1)	Aubergines (6)	Beans, French (39)	Brussels sprouts (147)
Beef, steak (0.8)	Baked beans (3)	Beans, broad (19)	Cabbage, green (339)
Bread, white (0.4)	Barley (7)	Cabbage, red (19)	Kale (618)
Chicken, thigh (0.1)	Beef, corned (7)	Cauliflower (13)	Lettuce (129)
Coconut oil (0.5)	Beef, minced (2)	Cockpeas (21)	Parsley (548)
Cod, fresh, fillet (0.1)	Bilberries (4)	Cucumber (21)	Rapeseed oil (123)
Corn flakes (<0.1)	Bran, wheat (10)	Greengages (15)	Soybean oil (173)
Flour, white (0.8)	Bread, whole meal (2)	Mustard greens, cress (88)	Spinach (380)
Grapefruit (<0.1)	Butter (7)	Olive oil, extra virgin (80)	Watercress (315)
Ham, tinned (0.1)	Carrots (6)	Peas (34)	
Maize (0.3)	Cheeses, various (2–6)		
Mangoes (0.5)	Chocolate, plain (2)		
Melon, yellow (0.1)	Corn oil (3)		
Melon, water (0.3)	Courgettes (3)		
Milk, cows (0.6)	Cranberries (2)		
Mushrooms (0.3)	Cream, double (6)		
Oranges (<0.1)	Dates, fresh (6)		
Parsnips (<0.1)	Egg yolk (2)		
Peanuts, roast (0.4)	Figs, fresh (3)		
Pilchards, brine (0.6)	Grapes, black (8)		
Pineapple (0.2)	Grapes, green (9)		
Pork, chop, lean (<0.1)	Leeks (10)		
Potatoes (0.9)	Liver, lamb (7)		
Rice, white (0.1)	Liver, ox (4)		
Rice, brown (0.8)	Nectarines (3)		
Salmon, tin, brine (0.1)	Oats (10)		
Sausage, pork/beef (0.2)	Palm oil (8)		
Spaghetti (0.2)	Peaches, fresh (4)		
Tuna, tin, brine (0.1)	Pears (6)		
Turnips (0.2)	Peppers, green (6)		
Yoghurt (0.8)	Peppers, red (2)		
	Plums, red (8)		
	Raisins (4)		
	Rhubarb (4)		
	Safflower oil (3)		
	Sunflower oil (6)		
	Swede (2)		
	Tomatoes (6)		
	Wheat (8)		

Note: Data are for raw foods except where cooked form is indicated. Numbers in parentheses indicate the micrograms of phylloquinone per 100 g (3.5 oz.) food.

Source: Adapted from Shearer, Bach, and Kohlmeier (1996: 1183S). Reprinted with permission.

Table IV.A.6.2 represent analyses of a single sample. Phylloquinone concentrations in plants, however, are affected by the stage of maturation and the geographic location of the plant. Further, different parts of the plant may differ in phylloquinone content. Outer leaves of the cabbage, for example, contain three to six times more phylloquinone than inner leaves (Shearer et al. 1980; Ferland and Sadowski 1992a). Although tea leaves and regular ground coffee contain high concentrations of phylloquinone, the brews are not a dietary source of the vitamin (Booth, Madabushi, et al. 1995). The phylloquinone content of oils declines slightly with heat and rapidly on exposure to daylight and fluorescent light when the oils are stored in transparent containers (Ferland and Sadowski 1992b; Shearer et al. 1996).

Recent evidence indicates that the intestinal absorption of phylloquinone from vegetables is poor and is improved by the simultaneous ingestion of fat (Vermeer et al. 1996). Bile acids, secreted into the intestines in response to fat in a meal, are necessary for the absorption of the fat-soluble K vitamins. There is a need for additional studies on the bioavailability of the K vitamins in foods to complement our knowledge of their vitamin K content (Vermeer et al. 1996).

Less is known about the vitamin K content of menaquinones (synthesized by bacteria) in foods. Livers of ruminant species, such as cows, have been found to have nutritionally significant quantities of menaquinones, but the concentrations of menaquinones in other animal organs were very low (Hirauchi et al. 1989; Shearer et al. 1996). Cheeses contained significant quantities of two different menaquinones, but very low quantities of menaquinones were found in milk and yoghurt (Shearer et al. 1996).

A topic currently in dispute is whether the menaquinones produced by bacterial action in the gut are substantially utilized by humans. Concentrations of various menaquinones have been found to be higher than that of phylloquinone in normal human livers (Usui et al. 1989) and, importantly, antibiotics have been known since the late 1940s and early 1950s to sometimes create a vitamin K deficiency. Nonetheless, the degree of importance of menaquinones in human nutrition has not yet been determined (Suttie 1995), and there are data to suggest that the long-chain menaquinones found in human liver are not as effective a form of the vitamin as phylloquinone. Moreover, elimination of foods high in vitamin K from a normal diet can produce signs of vitamin K insufficiency, suggesting that bacterial synthesis of menaquinones only partially satisfies the human vitamin K requirement (Suttie 1995).

Documented cases of vitamin K deficiency in adults have been uncommon. The National Research Council of the National Academy of Sciences recommends a daily dietary allowance (RDA) of approximately 1 microgram (μg) vitamin K per kilogram (kg) of body weight (National Research Council 1989).

Thus, the requirement for an individual weighing 150 pounds (68 kg) would be 68 μg phylloquinone. The average vitamin K intake of 10 male college students was determined to be 77 μg/day based on analysis of food composites (Suttie et al. 1988) – an average intake that corresponds to 1.04 μg vitamin K/kg body weight. Foods rich in vitamin K, such as spinach, broccoli, and Brussels sprouts, were not usually consumed in significant amounts by these students. This suggests that daily vitamin K intake may vary considerably depending on whether foods rich in vitamin K are consumed (Suttie et al. 1988). Table IV.A.6.2 makes it clear that 100 grams (g) of spinach (380 μg phylloquinone per 100 g) would contribute much to the recommended daily dietary intake of vitamin K, even if phylloquinone is poorly absorbed from this food.

Vitamin K deficiency can result from inadequate intestinal absorption. Because vitamin K is a fat-soluble vitamin, bile acids and pancreatic juice are needed for its absorption. Thus, causes of poor intestinal absorption can be insufficient production of bile acids, inadequate release of bile acids (for example, obstruction of the bile ducts by gallstones), or pancreatic insufficiency (Report of the Committee on Nutrition 1961; Suttie 1991). Levels of all the K vitamins were reduced in patients with chronic hepatitis and liver cirrhosis (Usui et al. 1989). In addition, secondary vitamin K deficiency has been observed in human subjects taking megadoses of vitamin E (Korsan-Bengtsen, Elmfeldt, and Holm 1974). Vitamin E supplementation is currently on the rise because of its role as an antioxidant. However, the effect of large doses of vitamin E on vitamin K status must always be borne in mind.

An upper limit for vitamin K intake has not been set, but 20 μg/100 kilocalories has been suggested by J. W. Suttie and R. E. Olson (Olson 1989). Menadione, which is not a natural form of vitamin K, can cause severe toxic reactions in infants if administered in large doses. Phylloquinone, however, has been given without adverse effects to infants in a single intramuscular dose that is 100 times their RDA. Adult dietary intakes of 10 to 15 times the RDA also cause no adverse effects (Olson 1989).

Function of Vitamin K

Vitamin K is involved in the synthesis of four clotting factors, one procoagulant protein, two anticoagulant proteins, and two bone proteins. The vitamin K–dependent clotting factors are integral to blood coagulation, such that an untreated vitamin K deficiency results in death due to bleeding. There also must be control of coagulation, and the body, therefore, has anticoagulant systems. Two of the known anticoagulant proteins are vitamin K–dependent.

The vitamin K–dependent bone proteins (in contrast to the vitamin K–dependent clotting proteins) have only recently been discovered, and the physiological role of these proteins in bone has not yet been determined.

Figure IV.A.6.1. The vitamin K–dependent carboxylase reaction. The vitamin K–dependent carboxylase converts glutamic acid residues of specific proteins to gamma-carboxyglutamic acid (Gla) residues. Vitamin K hydroquinone is simultaneously converted to vitamin K epoxide. The epoxide is reconverted to vitamin K, which is converted to vitamin K hydroquinone, and the cycle repeats. Warfarin inhibits conversion of the epoxide to vitamin K and conversion of vitamin K to vitamin K hydroquinone.

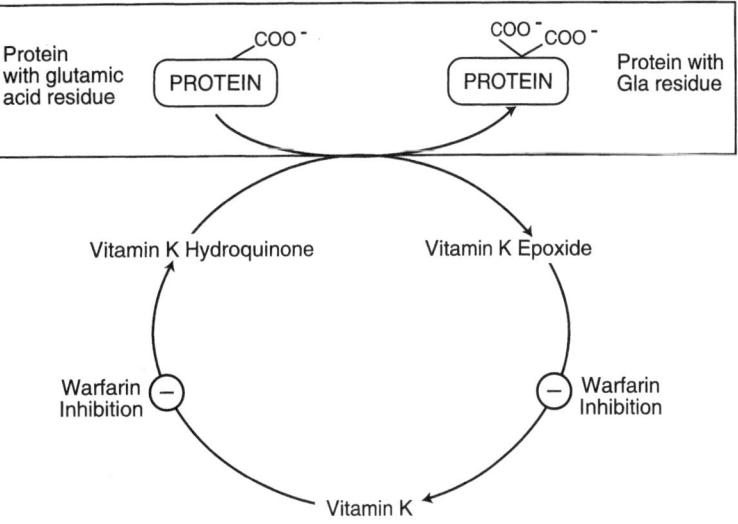

Mechanism of Action of Vitamin K

Vitamin K is a cofactor for an enzyme (vitamin K–dependent carboxylase) that carboxylates specific glutamic acid residues of proteins, converting these amino acid residues to gamma-carboxyglutamic acid residues (Figure IV.A.6.1). This modification occurs after the protein has been synthesized. The gamma-carboxyglutamyl residues are abbreviated Gla.

Although it was established in the early 1950s that vitamin K was necessary for the synthesis of the clotting proteins prothrombin (factor II) and factors VII, IX, and X, the vitamin K–dependent carboxylation reaction was not discovered until 1974. Investigators at that time demonstrated the presence of a new amino acid, gamma-carboxyglutamic acid, in prothrombin (Nelsestuen, Zytkovicz, and Howard 1974; Stenflo et al. 1974). The nature of the carboxylase reaction was soon delineated (Shah and Suttie 1974; Esmon, Sadowski, and Suttie 1975; Suttie 1985). A reduced form of vitamin K (vitamin K hydroquinone) is converted to vitamin K epoxide as the glutamic acid residues of the specific protein are converted to gamma-carboxyglutamic acid residues (Figure IV.A.6.1). At physiological concentrations, vitamin K must be regenerated and reutilized and is recycled. Two reactions take place sequentially to convert vitamin K epoxide to its reduced form (vitamin K hydroquinone) for continued carboxylation (Figure IV.A.6.1). These two reactions are prevented by coumarin anticoagulants, synthetic compounds such as warfarin, which are used medically to counteract excessive clotting.

The vitamin K–dependent (Gla-containing) proteins that have been well characterized include prothrombin and the clotting factors VII, IX, and X (plasma proteins synthesized by the liver); protein Z, a procoagulant plasma protein; protein C and protein S, plasma anticoagulants synthesized by the liver; osteocalcin, also called bone Gla protein; and matrix Gla protein, a bone-matrix protein.

Vitamin K–Dependent Proteins

The clotting proteins. When a cut or injury occurs, platelets (cells in blood) converge on the injury to form a plug, and a clot forms on the platelet plug. This action stops blood loss and prevents the injured person from bleeding to death. A clot is formed by a series of transformations involving more than ten different proteins. In the final stage, fibrinogen, a soluble blood protein, is cleaved by thrombin and converted to fibrin. Fibrin monomers are then cross-linked to form the insoluble or hard clot. A schematic of the clotting cascade is illustrated in Figure IV.A.6.2. Hundreds of papers have been published on the blood clotting cascade; reviews by C. M. Jackson and Y. Nemerson (1980) and by B. Furie and B. C. Furie (1992) provide additional information.

The proteins of the clotting cascade that are vitamin K–dependent are prothrombin (factor II), factor VII, factor IX, and factor X (Figure IV.A.6.2). These proteins, which are central to the blood clotting cascade, are carboxylated after synthesis in a reaction requiring vitamin K (Uotila 1990). The Gla residues make the proteins more negative and endow them with an increased ability to bind positively charged calcium ions. Calcium ions serve as bridges between these proteins and the negatively charged phospholipids of the platelet membrane. The proteins are brought in close proximity to each other on the platelet membrane, augmenting their activation. In the absence of vitamin K, carboxylation of prothrombin and factors VII, IX, and X does not occur. Activation of these factors proceeds so slowly that bleeding may result.

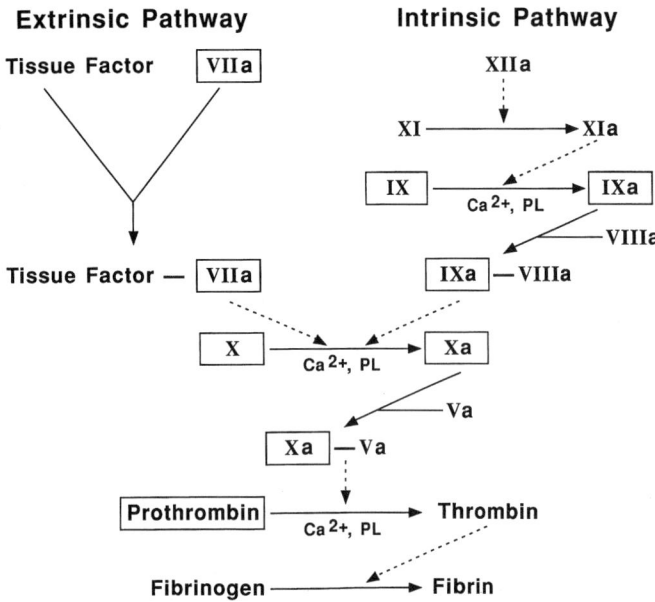

Extrinsic Pathway

Intrinsic Pathway

Figure IV.A.6.2. An outline of the clotting sequence. Dashed lines indicate an enzyme action, and solid lines indicate the activation of a protein, formation of a complex, or conversion of one compound to another. The presence of an "a" indicates that a factor has been activated. Vitamin K–dependent factors are located in rectangles. Calcium ions (Ca^{2+}) and phospholipids (PL), supplied by the platelet membrane, are required in those reactions that involve the vitamin K–dependent cofactors.

In response to a vessel injury, platelets aggregate at the injured site and form a platelet plug. The platelet membrane provides a surface on which a clot will subsequently form. Tissue factor (a protein) is also released at the injured site. It combines with activated factor VII. This complex (tissue factor–factor VIIa) activates factor X, which combines with activated factor V. The factor Xa–factor Va complex is able to activate prothrombin (factor II) to produce thrombin, an active enzyme that cleaves fibrinogen molecules to produce fibrin monomers. The fibrin monomers are cross-linked to produce the hard clot. The tissue factor–factor VIIa pathway for activating factor X is called the extrinsic pathway.

Factor X is also activated by a pathway called the intrinsic pathway. All proteins of the pathway are located in plasma. Factor XII, which is perhaps activated by collagen fibers from the injured blood vessel, activates factor XI. Factor XIa activates factor IX, which then combines with activated factor VIII to produce a factor IXa–factor VIIIa complex, which activates factor X.

At the time of identification of vitamin K as the antihemorrhagic factor, prothrombin and fibrinogen were the only proteins in the clotting cascade characterized as involved in the formation of the fibrin clot. The laboratories of Dam (Dam, Schønheyder, and Tage-Hansen 1936; Dam 1964) and A. J. Quick (Quick 1937) independently demonstrated that the activity of prothrombin was decreased in the plasma of chicks fed hemorrhagic diets. The choice of the chick as the experimental animal in these early studies was fortuitous, since chicks develop the symptoms of vitamin K deficiency more readily than other experimental animals (Suttie 1991). Factors VII, IX, and X, the other vitamin K–dependent clotting factors, were not established as essential plasma proteins and vitamin K–dependent proteins until the 1950s.

Human protein Z, another vitamin K–dependent protein, was purified and first described in 1984 (Broze and Miletich 1984). It is synthesized by the liver and promotes the association of thrombin (activated prothrombin) with phospholipid surfaces, a process necessary for clotting. Protein Z deficiency has recently been described as a new type of bleeding tendency (Kemkes-Matthes and Matthes 1995).

The anticoagulants. For several decades prior to the discovery of protein C (Stenflo 1976), the only known vitamin K–dependent plasma proteins were the clotting proteins II, VII, IX, and X. Protein S was subsequently isolated and purified (Di Scipio et al. 1977). Protein C and protein S are now known to be components of a very important anticoagulant system in plasma (Figure IV.A.6.3). Protein C, when activated and bound to protein S, is able to cleave, and thereby inactivate, two of the activated clotting factors, factors Va and VIIIa (Walker 1980; Stenflo 1984; Esmon 1987). The presence of both coagulant and anticoagulant systems in plasma allows for control of clotting.

Hereditary protein C deficiency and protein S deficiency have been discovered (Griffin et al. 1981; Pabinger 1986; Miletich, Sherman, and Broze 1987; Broekmans and Conrad 1988; Bertina 1989; Preissner 1990; Rick 1990). The clinical manifestation of protein S or protein C deficiency is thrombosis (excessive clotting).

The bone proteins. Until the discovery of osteocalcin (bone Gla protein, BGP) in the 1970s, vitamin K was assumed to function only in coagulation. The Gla residues of osteocalcin, a major protein of bone, pro-

Figure IV.A.6.3. The vitamin K–dependent anticoagulant system. Dashed lines indicate an enzyme action, and solid lines indicate the activation of a protein, formation of a complex, or conversion of one compound to another. The presence of an "a" indicates that a factor has been activated. Vitamin K–dependent factors are located in rectangles.

A complex of activated protein C and protein S cleaves activated factor VIII and activated factor V, rendering them inactive. The inactivation of these two factors causes the cessation of blood coagulation, due to decreases in the rates of the two reactions with the encircled negative signs.

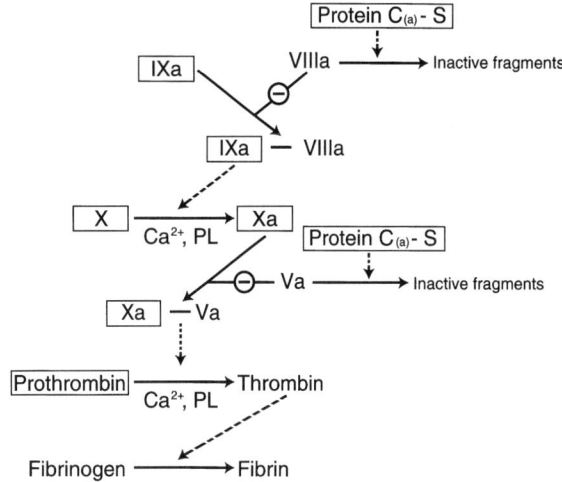

vide a point of interaction between the protein and bone mineral (Hauschka, Lian, and Gallop 1975; Poser and Price 1979). Matrix Gla protein was isolated and identified in 1983 (Price, Urist, and Otawara 1983). The synthesis of osteocalcin and matrix Gla protein is regulated by the hormonal form of vitamin D (1,25-dihydroxyvitamin D) (Price 1988). Two vitamins, vitamins K and D, are thus involved in the synthesis of osteocalcin and matrix Gla protein.

A fetal warfarin syndrome, first reported in 1975, has been found in infants born to mothers on warfarin anticoagulant therapy during pregnancy (Becker et al. 1975; Pettifor and Benson 1975; Shaul, Emery, and Hall 1975). Some of the abnormalities identified have been associated with bone formation. Although the functions of osteocalcin and matrix Gla protein are not yet established, defective carboxylation of these two proteins in the presence of warfarin may be a cause of the bone abnormalities associated with fetal warfarin syndrome (Price et al. 1983; Pauli et al. 1987; Price 1988).

In recent years, several studies have implicated vitamin K insufficiency in the pathogenesis of osteoporosis (Binkley and Suttie 1995; Vermeer, Jie, and Knapen 1995; Shearer et al. 1996; Vermeer et al. 1996). Osteoporosis is an age-related disorder characterized by inadequate skeletal strength due to bone loss (decreased bone density) and a predisposition to bone fractures. Peak bone mass is achieved between ages 25 and 35, and bone loss is a natural process that begins thereafter. The highest rate of bone loss for women, however, occurs within the first three to six years after the onset of menopause. Women are at greater risk for osteoporosis than men because of a lower peak bone density and the rapid postmenopausal loss of bone, related, in part, to reduced estrogen levels.

Low concentrations of vitamin K have been found in the blood of patients with bone fractures. When the vitamin K status is insufficient, vitamin K–dependent proteins tend to be undercarboxylated. Osteocalcin is more sensitive to a low vitamin K intake than the coagulation proteins, and, thus, undercarboxylated osteocalcin is the most sensitive known marker of vitamin K insufficiency. Undercarboxylated osteocalcin has been reported to be increased in postmenopausal women and to be highest in those individuals with the lowest hip bone density and greatest hip fracture risk. Vitamin K supplementation has been shown to decrease bone loss, and clinical trials have been initiated to test the effect of long-term vitamin K supplementation on bone mass. Measurements of undercarboxylated osteocalcin suggest that vitamin K insufficiency, formerly characterized by the status of the coagulation system, may be more common than previously thought (Binkley and Suttie 1995; Vermeer et al. 1996).

Other proteins. Gla-containing proteins have also been purified from kidney (Griep and Friedman 1980), urine (Nakagawa et al. 1983), liver mitochondria (Gardemann and Domagk 1983), and human spermatozoa (Soute et al. 1985). The function of these proteins is not presently known.

Abnormal Carboxylation

Hereditary deficiency of vitamin K–dependent clotting proteins (factors II, VII, IX, and X) can result in a rare bleeding disorder that has so far been diagnosed in only seven patients. The first reports of this disorder were in 1966 (Fischer and Zweymuller 1966; McMillan and Roberts 1966), and data (Brenner et al. 1990) suggest that the defect is abnormal carboxylation (due to a defective liver vitamin K–dependent carboxylase enzyme). Deficiencies in the plasma anticoagulants protein C and protein S have also been observed (Brenner et al. 1990).

Hemorrhagic Diseases of Infants

Although vitamin K deficiency symptoms are not very prevalent in adults, hemorrhagic diseases related to vitamin K deficiency are observed in infants world-wide. Three patterns of vitamin K–deficiency hemorrhage – early hemorrhagic disease of the newborn (HDN), classic hemorrhagic disease of the newborn, and late hemorrhagic disease – have been described. The frequency of these diseases, particularly that of late hemorrhagic disease, has increased during the last decade (Lane and Hathaway 1985; Kries, Shearer, and Göbel 1988; Greer 1995).

Early Hemorrhagic Disease

Early hemorrhagic disease of the newborn is characterized by severe, and sometimes life-threatening, hemorrhage at the time of delivery or during the first 24 hours after birth (Lane and Hathaway 1985; Kries et al. 1988). The bleeding varies from skin bruising, cephalohematoma, or umbilical bleeding to widespread and fatal intracranial, intra-abdominal, intrathoracic, and gastrointestinal bleeding (Lane and Hathaway 1985). The disease is often seen in infants whose mothers have taken drugs during pregnancy that affect vitamin K metabolism, such as therapeutic doses of warfarin. Idiopathic cases (no known cause) have also been reported.

Classic HDN

C. W. Townsend (1894) was the first person to use the term "haemorrhagic disease of the newborn." He described 50 infants who began bleeding on the second or third day of life, most commonly from the gastrointestinal tract, and speculated that the disease was of infectious origin. Dam and colleagues (1952) studied 33,000 infants and concluded that low levels of the clotting factor prothrombin in newborns was secondary to a vitamin K deficiency and occurred primarily in breast-fed infants. The researchers showed that this problem could be prevented by administration of vitamin K to mothers prior to delivery and to the infant shortly after delivery.

Normal full-term infants have reduced blood concentrations of the vitamin K–dependent clotting factors II, VII, IX, and X. Further, the levels of these factors decline during the first few days of life. Hemorrhagic disease of the newborn, often called early vitamin K deficiency, occurs from 1 to 7 days after birth. Breast-fed infants are at risk because of the low vitamin K content of breast milk. Bleeding occurs in the gastrointestinal tract, skin, and nose and at circumcision. The disease is prevented by vitamin K prophylaxis at birth (Lane and Hathaway 1985; Kries et al. 1988; Greer 1995), as indicated in 1952 (Dam et al. 1952).

Late Hemorrhagic Disease

Late hemorrhagic disease (late neonatal vitamin K deficiency) strikes at some infants (1 to 12 months of age) who are predominantly breast-fed and who do not receive vitamin K supplementation (Lane and Hathaway 1985; Hanawa et al. 1988; Kries et al. 1988).

It is characterized by intracranial, skin, and gastrointestinal bleeding.

That late hemorrhagic disease of the neonate has been observed primarily in breast-fed infants may result from the low vitamin K content of human milk (Lane and Hathaway 1985; Kries et al. 1988; Canfield et al. 1990). However, even if administered at birth, vitamin K may not always prevent deficiency in older infants because of their metabolism rates and consequent elimination of the vitamin. In Japan, from January 1981 to June 1985, 543 cases of vitamin K deficiency were reported in infants over 2 weeks of age (Hanawa et al. 1988). Of these, 427 were diagnosed as having idiopathic vitamin K deficiency, and 387 (90 percent) of this group had been entirely breast-fed (Hanawa et al. 1988). The concentrations of phylloquinone in human milk (mean 2.1 µg/liter) have been found to be significantly lower than those found in cows' milk (mean 4.9 µg/liter) and in unsupplemented infant formulas containing only fat from cows' milk (mean 4.2 µg/liter). Supplemented infant formulas, by contrast, had higher levels of phylloquinone than cows' milk; two of those studied had levels of 75.1 µg/liter and 101.8 µg/liter (Harroon et al. 1982; Kries et al. 1987).

It has been proposed that the late neonatal vitamin K deficiency that occurs in predominantly breast-fed infants may not result solely from lower vitamin K intake but from its combination with other factors, including subclinical liver dysfunction (Hanawa et al. 1988; Kries and Göbel 1988; Matsuda et al. 1989). In fact, I. Matsuda and colleagues (1989) have suggested that the higher content of vitamin K in formulas, unlike the lower content of vitamin K in human milk, can actually mask such defects.

In another study, phylloquinone levels and coagulation factors were measured in healthy term newborns until 4 weeks after birth (Pietersma-de Bruyn et al. 1990). Although breast-fed infants had lower serum phylloquinone levels than formula-fed infants, the levels of the vitamin K–dependent clotting factors II and X were comparable in the two groups. Thus, the authors of this study concluded that breast milk contains sufficient vitamin K for optimal carboxylation of the clotting factors. They have also suggested that the vitamin K supplementation of infant formulas results in higher than normal serum levels of vitamin K in infants without a concomitant rise in the levels of the vitamin K–dependent clotting proteins (Pietersma-de Bruyn et al. 1990).

Vitamin K Prophylaxis

Prophylactic use of vitamin K has been recommended for all newborns by the American Academy of Pediatrics since 1961. Vitamin K prophylaxis is standard for all infants in some geographical regions but is, or has been, "selective" (given only to at-risk infants) in others. However, in some regions where the "selective policy" was in effect, there was a resurgence (in the 1980s and 1990s) of hemorrhagic disease (Tulchinsky et al. 1993; Greer 1995).

The mode of administration (oral versus intramuscular) of vitamin K also became an issue of controversy in the 1990s because of reports from one research group (unconfirmed by two other groups) suggesting an association between intramuscular administration of vitamin K to the neonate and the subsequent development of childhood cancers. But in several countries (for example, Sweden, Australia, and Germany) where use of oral vitamin K prophylaxis (compared with intramuscular) has increased, there has been an increased incidence of late hemorrhagic disease. Oral prophylaxis prevents classic hemorrhagic disease but is less effective in preventing late hemorrhagic disease. Prevention of the latter requires repeated oral doses of vitamin K during the first 2 months of life for exclusively breast-fed infants or other infants at risk (for example, infants with liver disease), all of which presents problems with compliance (Greer 1995; Thorp et al. 1995).

The Vitamin K Ad Hoc Task Force of the American Academy of Pediatrics (1993) has recommended that to prevent hemorrhagic disease, phylloquinone be administered at birth to all newborns as a single, intramuscular dose of 0.5 to 1 milligram. The Task Force has also recommended that research be done to judge the efficacy, safety, and bioavailability of oral formulations of vitamin K. Oral supplements of vitamin K to nursing mothers might become an alternative method of prophylaxis to prevent late hemorrhagic disease (Greer 1995). Physicians could also advise pregnant and nursing mothers to increase their intake of green, leafy vegetables.

The Oral Anticoagulants

The discovery of the first coumarin anticoagulant, dicoumarol, has been interestingly described by K. P. Link (1959). During a blizzard on a Saturday afternoon in February 1933, a Wisconsin farmer appeared at the University of Wisconsin Biochemistry Building with a dead cow, a milk can containing blood without clotting capacity, and about 100 pounds of spoiled sweet clover hay. The farmer's cows were suffering from "sweet clover disease," a malady caused by feeding cattle improperly cured hay made from sweet clover. If the type of hay was not changed and if the cows were not transfused, they developed a prothrombin deficit and bled to death. Link and his colleagues began to work on the isolation and identification of the hemorrhagic agent, and in 1939, it was identified as dicoumarol, a coumarin derivative. As a result of the spoilage, coumarin, a natural component of sweet clover, had been converted to dicoumarol (Link 1959).

Since the discovery of dicoumarol, other coumarin derivatives have been synthesized (Link 1959). The most famous of the coumarin derivatives is warfarin, named for the University of Wisconsin Alumni Research Foundation (WARF), which received a patent for the compound. The coumarin compounds interfere with the metabolism of vitamin K, preventing conversion of vitamin K epoxide to vitamin K and also preventing reduction of vitamin K to vitamin K hydroquinone (Figure IV.A.6.1). This interference causes a buildup of vitamin K epoxide, and when physiological levels of vitamin K are present, the inability of the epoxide to be converted to the vitamin creates a relative vitamin K deficiency. The vitamin K–dependent proteins, including the clotting proteins II, VII, IX, and X, are, therefore, not carboxylated – or only partially carboxylated – and remain inactive (Suttie 1990).

The coumarin compounds, particularly warfarin, have been used as oral anticoagulants in the long-term treatment of patients prone to thrombosis (clot formation). The formation of a clot in a coronary artery narrowed by atherosclerosis is a causative factor in the development of acute myocardial infarction (heart attack), and warfarin is used after acute myocardial infarction to prevent further thrombus (clot) formation and reinfarction.

A recent study of the effect of warfarin on mortality and reinfarction after myocardial infarction concluded that "long-term therapy with warfarin has an important beneficial effect after myocardial infarction" (Smith, Arnesen, and Holme 1990: 147). This study involved 607 patients treated with warfarin and 607 patients treated with a placebo. Compared with the placebo group, warfarin therapy reduced the number of deaths by 24 percent, the number of reinfarctions by 34 percent, and the number of cerebrovascular accidents (strokes) by 55 percent.

In anticoagulant therapy, a dose of the anticoagulant is selected that achieves effective anticoagulation and minimizes bleeding complications (Second Report of the Sixty Plus Reinfarction Study Research Group 1982). The advantage of using warfarin for long-term therapy is that an overdosage is corrected by the administration of a large dose of vitamin K. Large doses of vitamin K are converted to vitamin K hydroquinone by enzymes that are not inhibited by warfarin (Link 1959; Suttie 1990). Correspondingly, persons undergoing warfarin anticoagulant therapy should avoid a diet that is high in vitamin K by limiting, among other things, the intake of green, leafy vegetables (Pedersen et al. 1991).

A Note on Hemophilia

Hemophilia is a bleeding disorder caused by a deficiency in one or, more rarely, two of the clotting proteins (De Angelis et al. 1990). The majority (85 percent) of hemophilia patients are deficient in factor VIII (hemophilia A), with 10 to 12 percent deficient in factor IX (hemophilia B). Rarer forms of the disease result from deficiency in other clotting factors. The hemophilia patient must receive injections of the missing protein in order to maintain proper coagulation. Hemophilia is a genetic disease, most commonly transmitted as a sex-linked recessive trait, and is not related to vitamin K status (Furie and Furie 1988).

Myrtle Thierry-Palmer

Bibliography

Almquist, H. J. 1979. Vitamin K: Discovery, identification, synthesis, functions. *Federation Proceedings* 38: 2687-9.

Almquist, H. J., and E. L. R. Stokstad. 1935. Dietary haemorrhagic disease in chicks. *Nature* 136: 31.

Becker, M. H., N. B. Genieser, M. Finegold, et al. 1975. Chondrodysplasia punctata: Is maternal warfarin therapy a factor? *American Journal of Diseases of Children* 129: 356-9.

Bertina, R. M. 1989. The control of hemostasis: Protein C and protein S. *Biomedical Progress* 4: 53-6.

Binkley, N. C., and J. W. Suttie. 1995. Vitamin K nutrition and osteoporosis. *Journal of Nutrition* 125: 1812-21.

Booth, S. L., H. T. Madabushi, K. W. Davidson, and J. A. Sadowski. 1995. Tea and coffee brews are not dietary sources of vitamin K-1 (phylloquinone). *Journal of the American Dietetic Association* 95: 82-3.

Booth, S. L., J. A. Sadowski, and J. A. T. Pennington. 1995. Phylloquinone (vitamin K_1) content of foods in the U.S. Food and Drug Administration's Total Diet Study. *Journal of Agricultural and Food Chemistry* 43: 1574-9.

Booth, S. L., J. A. Sadowski, J. L. Weihrauch, and G. Ferland. 1993. Vitamin K_1 (phylloquinone) content of foods: A provisional table. *Journal of Food Composition and Analysis* 6: 109-20.

Brenner, B., S. Tavori, A. Zivelin, et al. 1990. Hereditary deficiency of all vitamin K-dependent procoagulants and anticoagulants. *British Journal of Haematology* 75: 537-42.

Broekmans, A. W., and J. Conrad. 1988. Hereditary protein C deficiency. In *Protein C and related proteins,* ed. R. M. Bertina, 160-81. New York.

Broze, G. J., Jr., and J. P. Miletich. 1984. Human protein Z. *Journal of Clinical Investigation* 73: 933-8.

Canfield, L. M., J. M. Hopkinson, A. F. Lima, et al. 1990. Quantitation of vitamin K in human milk. *Lipids* 25: 406-11.

Dam, H. 1935. The antihaemorrhagic vitamin of the chick. Occurrence and chemical nature. *Nature* 135: 652-3.

1942. Vitamin K, its chemistry and physiology. *Advances in Enzymology* 2: 285-324.

1964. The discovery of vitamin K, its biological functions and therapeutical application. In *Nobel lectures: Physiology and medicine 1942-1962,* ed. The Nobel Foundation, 8-26. Amsterdam.

Dam, H., H. Dyggve, H. Larsen, and P. Plum. 1952. The relation of vitamin K deficiency to hemorrhagic disease of the newborn. *Advances in Pediatrics* 5: 129-53.

Dam, H., F. Schønheyder, and E. Tage-Hansen. 1936. Studies on the mode of action of vitamin K. *Biochemical Journal* 30: 1075-9.

De Angelis, V., B. M. Orazi, L. Santarossa, and G. Molaro. 1990. Combined factor VIII and factor XI congenital deficiency: A case report. *Haematologica* 75: 272-3.

Di Scipio, R. G., M. A. Hermodson, S. G. Yales, and E. W. Davie. 1977. A comparison of human prothrombin, factor IX (Christmas factor), factor X (Stuart factor), and protein S. *Biochemistry* 16: 698-706.

Doisy, E. A., S. B. Binkley, and S. A. Thayer. 1941. Vitamin K. *Chemical Reviews* 28: 477-517.

Esmon, C. T. 1987. The regulation of natural anticoagulant pathways. *Science* 235: 1348-52.

Esmon, C. T., J. A. Sadowski, and J. W. Suttie. 1975. A new carboxylation reaction. The vitamin K-dependent incorporation of $H^{14}CO_3$ into prothrombin. *Journal of Biological Chemistry* 250: 4744-8.

Ferland, G., and J. A. Sadowski. 1992a. Vitamin K_1 (phylloquinone) content of edible oils: Effects of heating and light exposure. *Journal of Agricultural and Food Chemistry* 40: 1869-73.

1992b. Vitamin K_1 (phylloquinone) content of green vegetables: Effects of plant maturation and geographical growth location. *Journal of Agricultural and Food Chemistry* 40: 1874-7.

Fischer, M., and E. Zweymuller. 1966. Kongenitaler kombinierter Mangel der Factoren II, VII, und X. *Zeitschrift für Kinderheilkunde* 95: 309-23.

Furie, B., and B. C. Furie. 1988. The molecular basis of blood coagulation. *Cell* 53: 505-18.

1992. Molecular and cellular biology of blood coagulation. *The New England Journal of Medicine* 326: 800-6.

Gardemann, A., and G. F. Domagk. 1983. The occurrence of Γ-carboxyglutamate in a protein isolated from ox liver mitochondria. *Archives of Biochemistry and Biophysics* 220: 347-53.

Greer, F. R. 1995. Vitamin K deficiency and hemorrhage in infancy. *Perinatal Hematology* 22: 759-77.

Griep, A. E., and P. A. Friedman. 1980. Purification of a protein containing Γ-carboxyglutamic acid from bovine kidney. In *Vitamin K metabolism and vitamin K-dependent proteins,* ed. J. W. Suttie, 307-10. Baltimore, Md.

Griffin, J. H., B. Evatt, T. S. Zimmerman, et al. 1981. Deficiency of protein C in congenital thrombotic disease. *Journal of Clinical Investigations* 68: 1370-3.

Hanawa, Y., M. Maki, B. Murata, et al. 1988. The second nation-wide survey in Japan of vitamin K deficiency in infancy. *European Journal of Pediatrics* 147: 472-7.

Harroon, Y., M. J. Shearer, S. Rahim, et al. 1982. The content of phylloquinone (vitamin K_1) in human milk, cows' milk and infant formula determined by high-performance liquid chromatography. *Journal of Nutrition* 112: 1105-17.

Hauschka, P. V., J. B. Lian, and P. M. Gallop. 1975. Direct identification of the calcium-binding amino acid Γ-carboxyglutamate in mineralized tissue. *Proceedings of the National Academy of Science* 72: 3925-9.

Hirauchi, K., T. Sakano, S. Notsumoto, et al. 1989. Measurement of K vitamins in animal tissues by high-performance liquid chromatography with fluorimetric detection. *Journal of Chromatography* 497: 131-7.

Holst, W. F., and E. R. Halbrook. 1933. A "scurvy-like" disease in chicks. *Science* 77: 354.

Jackson, C. M., and Y. Nemerson. 1980. Blood coagulation. *Annual Review of Biochemistry* 49: 765-811.

Kemkes-Matthes, B., and K. J. Matthes. 1995. Protein Z deficiency: A new cause of bleeding tendency. *Thrombosis* 79: 49-55.

Korsan-Bengtsen, K., D. Elmfeldt, and T. Holm. 1974. Prolonged plasma clotting time and decreased fibrinolysis after long-term treatment with α-tocopherol. *Thrombosis Diathesis Haemorrhagia* 31: 505-12.

Kries, R. von, and U. Göbel. 1988. Vitamin K prophylaxis:

Oral or parenteral? (Letter). *American Journal of Diseases of Children* 142: 14-15.

Kries, R. von, M. J. Shearer, and U. Göbel. 1988. Vitamin K in infancy. *European Journal of Pediatrics* 147: 106-12.

Kries, R. von, M. J. Shearer, P. T. McCarthy, et al. 1987. Vitamin K content of maternal milk: Influence of the stage of lactation, lipid composition, and vitamin K_1 supplements given to the mother. *Pediatric Research* 22: 513-17.

Lane, P. A., and W. E. Hathaway. 1985. Vitamin K in infancy. *Journal of Pediatrics* 106: 351-9.

Link, K. P. 1959. The discovery of dicoumarol and its sequels. *Circulation* 19: 97-107.

Matsuda, I., S. Nishiyama, K. Motohara, et al. 1989. Late neonatal vitamin K deficiency associated with subclinical liver dysfunction in human milk-fed infants. *Journal of Pediatrics* 114: 602-5.

McFarlane, W. D., W. R. Graham, Jr., and G. E. Hall. 1931. Studies in protein nutrition of the chick. I. The influence of different protein concentrates on the growth of baby chicks, when fed as the source of protein in various simplified diets. *Journal of Nutrition* 4: 331-49.

McMillan, C. W., and H. R. Roberts. 1966. Congenital combined deficiency of coagulation factors II, VII, IX and X. *New England Journal of Medicine* 274: 1313-15.

Miletich, J., L. Sherman, and G. Broze, Jr. 1987. Absence of thrombosis in subjects with heterozygous protein C deficiency. *New England Journal of Medicine* 317: 991-6.

Nakagawa, Y., V. Abram, F. J. Kezdy, et al. 1983. Purification and characterization of the principal inhibitor of calcium oxalate monohydrate crystal growth in human urine. *Journal of Biological Chemistry* 258: 12594-600.

National Research Council (Subcommittee on the Tenth Edition of the RDAs). 1989. *Recommended dietary allowances.* Tenth edition. Washington, D.C.

Nelsestuen, G. L., T. H. Zytkovicz, and J. B. Howard. 1974. The mode of action of vitamin K. Identification of gamma-carboxyglutamic acid as a component of prothrombin. *Journal of Biological Chemistry* 249: 6347-50.

Olson, J. A. 1989. Upper limits of vitamin A in infant formulas, with some comments on vitamin K. *Journal of Nutrition* 119: 1820-4.

Pabinger, I. 1986. Clinical relevance of protein C. *Blut* 53: 63-75.

Pauli, R. M., J. B. Lian, D. F. Mosher, and J. W. Suttie. 1987. Association of congenital deficiency of multiple vitamin K-dependent coagulation factors and the phenotype of the warfarin embryopathy: Clues to the mechanism of teratogenicity of coumarin derivatives. *American Journal of Human Genetics* 41: 566-83.

Pedersen, F. M., O. Hamburg, K. Hess, and L. Ovesen. 1991. The effect of vitamin K on warfarin-induced anticoagulation. *Journal of Internal Medicine* 229: 517-20.

Pettifor, J. M., and R. Benson. 1975. Congenital malformations associated with the administration of oral anticoagulants during pregnancy. *Journal of Pediatrics* 86: 459-62.

Pietersma-de Bruyn, A. L., P. M. van Haard, M. H. Beunis, et al. 1990. Vitamin K_1 levels and coagulation factors in healthy term newborns till 4 weeks after birth. *Haemostasis* 20: 8-14.

Poser, J. W., and P. A. Price. 1979. A method for decarboxylation of γ-carboxyglutamic acid in proteins. Properties of the decarboxylated γ-carboxyglutamic acid from calf bone. *Journal of Biological Chemistry* 254: 431-6.

Preissner, K. T. 1990. Biological relevance of the protein C system and laboratory diagnosis of protein C and protein S deficiencies. *Clinical Sciences* 78: 351-64.

Price, P. A. 1988. Role of vitamin K-dependent proteins in bone metabolism. *Annual Review of Nutrition* 8: 565-83.

Price, P. A., and S. A. Baukol. 1980. 1,25-Dihydroxyvitamin D_3 increases synthesis of the vitamin K-dependent bone protein by osteosarcoma cells. *Journal of Biological Chemistry* 255: 11660-3.

Price, P. A., M. R. Urist, and Y. Otawara. 1983. Matrix Gla protein, a new Γ-carboxyglutamic acid-containing protein which is associated with the organic matrix of bone. *Biochemical and Biophysical Research Communications* 117: 765-71.

Quick, A. J. 1937. Coagulation defect in sweet clover disease and in hemorrhagic chick disease of dietary origin; consideration of the source of prothrombin. *American Journal of Physiology* 118: 260-71.

Report of the Committee on Nutrition. 1961. Vitamin K compounds and the water-soluble analogues. *Pediatrics* 28: 501-7.

Rick, M. E. 1990. Protein C and protein S. Vitamin K-dependent inhibitors of blood coagulation. *Journal of the American Medical Association* 263: 701-3.

Second Report of the Sixty Plus Reinfarction Study Research Group. 1982. Risks of long-term oral anticoagulant therapy in elderly patients after myocardial infarction. *Lancet* 1: 64-8.

Shah, D. V., and J. W. Suttie. 1974. The vitamin K-dependent in vitro production of prothrombin. *Biochemical and Biophysical Research Communications* 60: 1397-1402.

Shaul, W. L., H. Emery, and J. G. Hall. 1975. Chondrodysplasia punctata and maternal warfarin use during pregnancy. *American Journal of Diseases of Children* 129: 360-2.

Shearer, M. J., V. Allan, Y. Haroon, and P. Barkhan. 1980. Nutritional aspects of vitamin K in the human. In *Vitamin K metabolism and vitamin K-dependent proteins,* ed. J. W. Suttie, 317-27. Baltimore, Md.

Shearer, M. J., A. Bach, and M. Kohlmeier. 1996. Chemistry, nutritional sources, tissue distribution and metabolism of vitamin K with special reference to bone health. *Journal of Nutrition* 126 (Supplement 4S): 1181S-6S.

The Sixty Plus Reinfarction Study Research Group. 1980. A double-blind trial to assess long-term oral anticoagulant therapy in elderly patients after myocardial infarction. *Lancet* 2: 989-93.

Smith, P., H. Arnesen, and I. Holme. 1990. The effect of warfarin on mortality and reinfarction after myocardial infarction. *New England Journal of Medicine* 323: 147-52.

Soute, B. A. M., W. Muller-Ester, M. A. G. de Boer-van den Berg, et al. 1985. Discovery of a gamma-carboxyglutamic acid-containing protein in human spermatozoa. *FEBS Letters* 190: 137-41.

Stenflo, J. 1976. A new vitamin K-dependent protein. Purification from bovine plasma and preliminary characterization. *Journal of Biological Chemistry* 251: 355-63.

   1984. Structure and function of protein C. *Seminars in Thrombosis and Hemostasis* 10: 109-21.

Stenflo, J., P. Fernlund, W. Egan, and P. Roepstorff. 1974. Vitamin K-dependent modifications of glutamic acid residues in prothrombin. *Proceedings of the National Academy of Sciences USA* 71: 2730-3.

Suttie, J. W. 1985. Vitamin K-dependent carboxylase. *Annual Review of Biochemistry* 54: 459-77.

   1990. Warfarin and vitamin K. *Clinical Cardiology* 13: VI-16-8.

1991. Vitamin K. In *Handbook of vitamins,* ed. L. J. Machlin, 145–94. New York.

1995. The importance of menaquinones in human nutrition. *Annual Review of Nutrition* 15: 399–417.

Suttie, J. W., L. L. Mummah-Schendel, D. V. Shah, et al. 1988. Vitamin K deficiency from dietary vitamin K restriction in humans. *American Journal of Clinical Nutrition* 47: 475–80.

Thorp, J. A., L. Gaston, D. R. Caspers, and M. L. Pal. 1995. Current concepts and controversies in the use of vitamin K. *Drugs* 49: 376–87.

Townsend, C. W. 1894. The haemorrhagic disease of the newborn. *Archives of Pediatrics* 11: 559–65.

Tulchinsky, T. H., M. M. Patton, L. A. Randolph, et al. 1993. Mandating vitamin K prophylaxis for newborns in New York State. *American Journal of Public Health* 83: 1166–8.

Uotila, L. 1990. The metabolic functions and mechanism of action of vitamin K. *Scandinavian Journal of Clinical Laboratory Investigations* 50 (Supplement 201): 109–17.

Usui, Y., N. Nishimura, N. Kobayashi, et al. 1989. Measurement of vitamin K in human liver by gradient elution high-performance liquid chromatography using platinum-black catalyst reduction and fluorimetric detection. *Journal of Chromatography* 489: 291–301.

Vermeer, C., B. L. M. G. Gijsberg, A. M. Craciun, et al. 1996. Effects of vitamin K on bone mass and bone metabolism. *Journal of Nutrition* 126 (Supplement 4S): 1187S–91S.

Vermeer, C., K.-S. G. Jie, and M. H. Knapen. 1995. Role of vitamin K in bone. *Annual Review of Nutrition* 15: 1–22.

Vitamin K Ad Hoc Task Force, American Academy of Pediatrics. 1993. Controversies concerning vitamin K and the newborn. *Pediatrics* 91: 1001–3.

Walker, F. J. 1980. Regulation of activated protein C by a new protein. A possible function for bovine protein S. *Journal of Biological Chemistry* 255: 5521–4.

Tsai, K. S., H. Heath, R. Kumar, et al. 1984. Impaired vitamin D metabolism with aging in women. Possible role in the pathogenesis of senile osteoporosis. *Journal of Clinical Investigation* 73: 1668–72.

Wachman, A., and D. S. Bernstein. 1968. Diet and osteoporosis. *Lancet* 1: 958–9.

Walker, P. M., and H. M. Linkswiler. 1972. Calcium retention in the adult human male as affected by protein intake. *Journal of Nutrition* 102: 1297–1302.

Warren, J. M., and H. Spencer. 1972. Analysis of stable strontium in biological materials by atomic absorption spectrophotometry. *Clinical Chimica Acta* 38: 435–9.

1976. Metabolic balances of strontium in man. *Clinical Orthopedics and Related Research* 117: 307–20.

Wasserman, R. H., R. A. Corradina, and A. N. Taylor. 1968. Vitamin D-dependent calcium-binding protein. Purification and some properties. *Journal of Biological Chemistry* 243: 3978–86.

Wasserman, R. H., and A. N. Taylor. 1968. Vitamin D-dependent calcium-binding protein. Response to some physiological and nutritional variables. *Journal of Biological Chemistry* 243: 3987–93.

Watts, N. B., S. T. Harris, H. K. Genant, et al. 1990. Intermittent cyclical etidronate treatment of postmenopausal osteoporosis. *New England Journal of Medicine* 323: 73–9.

Whedon, G. D. 1959. Effects of high calcium intake on bone, blood and soft tissue: Relationship of calcium intake to balance in osteoporosis. *Federation Proceedings* 18: 1112–18.

WHO (World Health Organization). 1962. *Calcium requirements.* Technical Report Series, No. 230. Geneva.

Woodhouse, N. J. Y., P. Bordier, M. Fisher, et al. 1971. Human calcitonin in the treatment of Paget's bone disease. *Lancet* 1: 1139–43.

Woodhouse, N. J. Y., F. H. Doyle, and G. F. Joplin. 1971. Vitamin D deficiency and primary hyperparathyroidism. *Lancet* 2: 283–7.

Woodhouse, N. J. Y., S. Tun Chot, P. Bordier, et al. 1973. Vitamin D administration in primary hyperparathyroidism. *Clinical Science* 44: 3P.

Yates, A. J., R. O. C. Oreffo, K. Mayor, et al. 1991. Inhibition of bone resorption by inorganic phosphate is mediated by both reduced osteoclast formation and decreased activity of mature osteoclasts. *Journal of Bone and Mineral Research* 6: 473–8.

Zipkin, I., A. S. Posner, and E. D. Eanes. 1962. The effect of fluoride on the X-ray-diffraction pattern of the apatite of human bone. *Biochimica Biophysica Acta* 59: 255–8.

IV.B

Minerals

IV.B.1 ❧ Calcium

This chapter deals with the history of calcium and its metabolism in adult humans. It should be read in conjunction with Chapter IV.D.4 on osteoporosis, which contains a further discussion of calcium requirements and the effects of a deficiency in adults, and with Chapter IV.A.4 on vitamin D, which deals with the history of rickets, a disease caused in part by a deficiency of calcium resulting from reduced intake or poor absorption.

Historical Aspects

Bone is the main depository of calcium. Fully 99 percent of the body's calcium is in the skeleton, with the rest in extracellular fluid and soft tissues. As early as the sixteenth century, it was recognized by a Dutch physician that the skeleton is not an inactive but a dynamic tissue under hormonal influence and capable of remodeling throughout life (Lutwak, Singer, and Urist 1974). Two specific types of bone cells acted upon in these processes are the osteoblasts (involved in bone formation) and the osteoclasts (involved in bone resorption).

Another important discovery in the history of calcium was made by Sidney Ringer more than 100 years ago. He demonstrated that the contractility of cardiac muscle was stimulated and maintained by the addition of calcium to the perfusion fluid (Ringer 1883). It has also been shown that this important effect of calcium is not limited to cardiac muscle but has a generalized, activating effect in practically all differentiated cells (Opie 1980; Rubin 1982; Campbell 1986). However, in addition to calcium, the presence of specific concentrations of sodium and potassium are needed to achieve this effect (Mines 1911; Lowenstein and Rose 1978).

The state of calcium in the body investigated many decades ago has been subsequently summarized ("The Classic" 1970). The amount of calcium in the body is greater than that of any other positively charged mineral (1,160 grams [g]). Its place of storage is the skeleton, although the small amounts present in the compartments of the extracellular fluid and those of the soft tissues are of great physiological importance because the calcium stored in bone maintains equilibrium with other calcium pools in the body (Rubin 1982).

The interaction and balance of vitamin D, calcitonin, and parathyroid hormone (PTH) are the pillars of normal calcium metabolism, and they play an important role in maintaining a highly controlled calcium homeostasis and normal serum calcium level. This process is based on the direct or indirect action of these substances on the skeleton. Vitamin D is produced by ultraviolet radiation of sunlight on the skin, which yields the vitamin D precursor ergosterol (Hess and Weinstock 1924). The hormones calcitonin and PTH are created, respectively, by the C cells of the thyroid gland and by the parathyroid glands. A deficiency as well as an excessive production and secretion of these three substances can lead to the development of specific disease states.

Vitamin D

Vitamin D, discovered at the beginning of the third decade of the twentieth century, is the substance that acts to prevent rickets. Many of the original reports of the discovery of vitamin D have been republished (Robertson 1969; Pramanik, Gupta, and Agarwal 1971) and are cited here for those who wish to consult them. In addition, the early discovery of the physiological importance of calcium (Ringer 1883) has been redescribed (Fye 1984; Ebashi 1987). The chemical structure of vitamin D was identified by a German chemist, Adolf Windaus, in 1931, and the subsequent commercial production of vitamin D practically eliminated the occurrence of rickets – the vitamin D deficiency disease of children – although treatment with cod-liver oil (rich in vitamin D) also played an important role in the eradication of this disease.

Even though our basic knowledge of vitamin D was obtained between 1919 and 1924, it was not until the 1960s that the vitamin D metabolites were discovered (Lund and DeLuca 1966; Ponchon and DeLuca 1969; Olson, Jr., and DeLuca 1973; DeLuca 1979, 1980, 1988). H. F. DeLuca postulated that vitamin D must be hydroxylated first in the liver and subsequently by 1-alpha-hydroxylation in the kidney to produce the vitamin D hormone 1-alpha-25-dihydroxyvitamin D_3,1,25$(OH)_2D_3$. This is the important vitamin D metabolite that actively affects the absorption of calcium from the intestine. Further studies regarding the mechanism of calcium absorption from the intestine are credited to R. H. Wasserman, who discovered the vitamin D–dependent "calcium binding protein" (CaBP) in the duodenum (Kallfelz, Taylor, and Wasserman 1967; Wasserman, Corradina, and Taylor 1968; Wasserman and Taylor 1968).

Rickets, caused by vitamin D deficiency, was produced experimentally in the 1920s, and much was learned about this illness, which occurs in infancy and childhood at ages of rapid growth (Sherman and Pappenheimer 1921; Steenbock and Black 1924; Pettifor et al. 1978; Pettifor and Ross 1983). Rickets was common in the early part of the twentieth century, and more than 100 years ago it was recognized that a lack of sunlight was responsible, particularly in northern latitudes, where deprivation is most likely to occur. It was also noted that sunlight is curative (Palm 1890; Huldschinsky 1919; Mellanby 1921).

Symptoms of rickets include impaired calcification and excess formation of cartilage in areas of bone growth. The adult form of the disease is called osteomalacia, in which newly formed osteoid does not calcify. This occurs in persons who voluntarily or for other reasons are homebound and therefore not exposed to sunlight.

Several early investigators stated that both rickets and osteomalacia can also be caused by a nutritional deficiency of calcium (McCollum et al. 1921; Theiler 1976; McCollum et al. 1995). Although such a situation would be uncommon, it is possible that the theory was proposed because healing of rickets occurred when a low, insufficient calcium intake of barely more than 100 milligrams (mg)/day was raised to 1,200 mg/day with the simultaneous use of vitamin D. More recent investigators believed it unlikely that vitamin D deficiency alone could produce rickets or osteomalacia but that these diseases occur when there is coexistent calcium deficiency (Pettifor et al. 1981).

Calcitonin

The hormone calcitonin was discovered in 1962 by Harold Copp, who reported that it originates in the parathyroid glands (Copp et al. 1962; Copp 1967, 1969). Calcitonin decreases the calcium level in blood, and this effect was ascribed to decreased bone resorption. The first report of the use of calcitonin in humans came shortly after its discovery (Foster et al. 1966), and further studies revealed that this hormone actually originates in the C cells of the thyroid gland – which, for a while, gave rise to the use of the name "thyrocalcitonin" (Hirsch and Munson 1969). It has been shown experimentally that calcitonin affects not only bone resorption but also bone formation (Baylink, Morey, and Rich 1969).

Because of the ability of calcitonin to cause a decrease in bone resorption, it has been utilized in the treatment of patients with Paget's disease – a deforming and frequently disabling bone disease diagnosed in England more than a century ago (Paget 1877; Bijvoet, Van der Sluys Veer, and Jansen 1968; Shai, Baker, and Wallach 1971; Woodhouse Bordier, et al. 1971). Two available types of calcitonin, primarily salmon calcitonin but also porcine calcitonin, have been joined by human calcitonin. All three types have been (and still are) used in investigative studies of their comparative effectiveness in treating Paget's disease.

Parathyroid Hormone

Parathyroid hormone (PTH), discovered in the early 1920s (Collip 1925), consists of four small pea-sized structures, two of which are located on the upper pole and two at the lower pole of each thyroid lobe. When parathyroid glands, which produce PTH, are functioning normally, the level of secretion depends on the serum calcium level, which in turn depends, in part, on the fraction of the dietary calcium that is absorbed from the intestine and the amount of calcium released from the skeleton by bone resorption. The dietary contribution of calcium to the serum calcium level influences the extent of bone resorption that is induced by PTH to maintain the well-controlled homeostasis of the normal serum calcium level.

The most common clinical aberration of calcium metabolism in hyperparathyroidism is a high level of serum calcium, a low level of serum phosphorus, and frequently, but not invariably, elevated levels of the serum enzyme alkaline phosphatase. There may also be evidence of bone loss on roentgenograms (which can mimic osteopenia) and, more rarely, cystic bone lesions. Kidney stone formation and peptic ulcer of the stomach may also result.

When there is hyperfunction of any of the four parathyroid glands, and excess PTH is secreted, a pathological condition develops that is called primary hyperparathyroidism. This endocrine disorder that affects bone metabolism (primarily the metabolism of calcium and phosphorus) was discovered in the early 1920s in Vienna and discussed in print two years later (Mandl 1926). In 1925, the condition was observed in the United States (Hannon et al. 1930), and shortly after, the first series of patients with hyperparathyroidism in the United States was described (Albright, Aub, and Bauer 1934). A classic study of the parathyroid glands followed in the late 1940s (Albright and Reifenstein 1948).

The symptoms and the treatment of hyperparathyroidism have been extensively discussed in older medical textbooks, which state, as did the classic article by F. Albright, J. C. Aub, and W. Bauer in 1934, that the cause of primary hyperparathyroidism is the enlargement of one or more of the parathyroid glands to form a benign tumor (an adenoma) or a multiple adenomata. However, we now know that the adenoma of a single parathyroid gland or multiple adenomata of the parathyroid glands are the result of hyperfunction of the parathyroid glands – the increased secretion of PTH. The conventional treatment for primary hyperparathyroidism is the surgical removal of the enlarged parathyroid gland or glands.

Reports in the literature also attest to the importance of the role of vitamin D in normal parathyroid function (Mawer et al. 1975). There are also reports of vitamin D deficiency in hyperparathyroidism (Woodhouse, Doyle, and Joplin 1971; Lumb and Stanbury 1974; Mawer et al. 1975; Stanbury 1981), and the use of vitamin D has been recommended for the medical treatment of patients with primary hyperparathyroidism (Woodhouse et al. 1973).

Nutritional Aspects

The nutritional importance of calcium for normal growth and maintenance has been recognized since studies were carried out with experimental animals several decades ago. Those studies that focused on the human calcium requirement, for example, were conducted as early as the 1920s (Sherman 1920), and the importance of calcium in the human metabolism (and its use in therapy) was recognized in the early 1930s (Cantarow 1933). Subsequently, it was shown that a nutritionally high calcium intake resulted in an increased growth rate of children (Stearns, Jeans, and Vandecar 1936; Jeans and Stearns 1938). Textbooks on the importance of calcium began to appear by the late 1930s (Shohl 1939), and the effect of dietary factors on the intestinal absorption of calcium was examined in the early 1940s in a study demonstrating that the presence of dietary protein is necessary for the intestinal absorption of calcium (McCance, Widdowson, and Lehmann 1942).

Early in the 1950s, the interaction in humans of dietary calcium with phosphorus was investigated (Leichsenring et al. 1951), and at about the same time, two studies of the human calcium requirement were carried out in prisons, one in Peru (Hegsted, Moscoso, and Collazos 1952) and one in Scandinavia (Malm 1958). Both of these investigations reported a very low calcium requirement of about 250 mg/day. However, shortly thereafter, it was made clear that a calcium intake of 1,000 mg is necessary to achieve calcium balance (Whedon 1959).

The calcium requirement for skeletal maintenance was investigated at the beginning of the 1970s (Garn 1970), and this study was followed by a determination of the calcium requirement both for middle-aged women (Heaney, Recker, and Saville 1977) and for elderly people (Heaney et al. 1982). In 1984, a strictly controlled metabolic study revealed that 800 mg/day of calcium is insufficient for middle-aged men and that an intake of 1,200 mg is desirable (Spencer, Kramer, Lesniak, et al. 1984). This recommendation was subsequently adopted at a National Institutes of Health Consensus Conference (1995).

As hinted at by the prison studies already mentioned, some investigators believed that humans can adapt to a long-term low calcium intake. Experimentally, however, this was not found to be the case at a calcium intake of 200 mg/day in adults (Spencer and Kramer 1985). It is important to note that bioavailability of calcium for absorption is greatly reduced by substances such as fiber (in large amounts) and phytate in food (Harrison and Mellanby 1934; Mellanby 1949; Ismail-Beigi et al. 1977; Cummings 1978). The negative effect of phytate on calcium has been extensively investigated (Reinhold et al. 1973), but it has also been shown that calcium bioavailability depends on the availability of trace minerals such as copper, iron, and manganese (Strause et al. 1994), and that deficiencies of these trace elements decrease the calcium concentration in bone. The trace element zinc, for example, affects intestinal absorption of calcium in humans (Spencer et al. 1987; Spencer, Norris, and Osis 1992).

The impact of other substances – such as lactose – on the absorption of calcium was reported as early as 1940 (Mills et al. 1940), and 20 years later, a follow-up report was published (Greenwald, Samachson, and Spencer 1963). An extensive review of human calcium requirements was published in the early 1970s (Irwin and Kienholz 1973), and other such surveys have subsequently appeared (Bronner and Peterlik 1995; Bronner and Stein 1995). The suggested recommended dietary allowance (RDA) of calcium in the United States is determined by the Food and Nutrition Board of the National Academy of Science.

Osteoporosis

Osteoporosis is the most common systemic bone disorder in the United States, affecting an estimated 20 million women and perhaps 10 million men. The incidence of osteoporosis is highest for women in the decade after menopause. It occurs much later in men – between the seventh and eighth decades of life. The high incidence of osteoporosis is a major public health problem because of serious complications that may require extensive and costly medical care. The bone loss in women at middle age and older is the result of hormonal deficiency (the loss of estrogen), aging, and other factors that appear to play an important role in causing – or intensifying – the loss of calcium from the skeleton. It has become more and more evident that sufficient calcium intake over the years can play a major role in preventing osteoporosis in later life (Matkovic et al. 1979; Sandler et al. 1985).

The disease develops insidiously over many years, is often asymptomatic, and is frequently discovered accidentally during radiological examination for unrelated medical conditions (Spencer and Kramer 1987). Unfortunately, this means that treatment of osteoporosis is frequently delayed until it is quite advanced, and it may not be detected until complications such as skeletal fractures arise. In the past, physicians assumed that there was no effective treatment available for this disorder. However, in recent years, effective therapeutic modalities have become available for the treatment and even for the prevention of the disease. Among the newer treatment modalities are the biphosphonates (Fogelman et al. 1986; Francis 1995).

When the diagnosis of bone loss is established roentgenographically, osteoporosis is usually advanced, because 30 percent of bone mineral must be lost before the loss will show up on conventional skeletal X rays. The vertebral bodies show poor mineralization and become biconcave; adjacent vertebrae have a "fish-mouth" appearance; and there may be wedging of the involved vertebrae. These changes in bone structure are usually associated with loss of body height, kyphosis, deformity of the chest, and the presence of a "dowager's hump." Routine X rays of the skeleton are not reliable indicators of bone density because of differences in techniques and in subjective interpretations of X-ray findings.

When demineralization of bone is seen on an X ray, this finding does not differentiate between osteoporosis and other demineralizing bone diseases, such as multiple myeloma or hyperparathyroidism. Reliable methods – such as bone density measurements using single and double photon absorptiometry and determining the cortical index – are now available for diagnosing osteoporosis earlier and with more precision than the use of conventional radiographs offers. However, photon absorptiometry (Mazess et al. 1988) is not routinely done because the equipment is not available in all medical centers. Cortical index measurements can be determined by analyzing X rays of the hand and by relating the cortical thickness to the total width of the metacarpal bone.

Another method of determining bone density is radiographic absorptiometry, which utilizes radiographs of the hands and a computer scanner. Newer, sophisticated methods of analyzing bone mass are available in specialized centers. In general, X rays of the thoracic and lumbar spine can indicate the potential existence of postmenopausal osteoporosis. Bone biopsies (needle biopsies) can establish the differential diagnosis of osteoporosis, but this technique is invasive and not acceptable to many patients.

As already noted, a low calcium intake, over prolonged periods of time, results in calcium loss from the skeleton and in a negative calcium balance (Table IV.B.1.1). This condition has an adverse effect on the maintenance of the normal bone structure, and a continued loss of calcium from the skeleton results from bodily efforts to maintain a normal serum calcium level. Moreover, a low calcium intake stimulates the

Table IV.B.1.1. *Calcium balances of males and females during a low calcium intake*

Number of patients	Type of patient	Study days	Calcium, mg/day			
			Intake	Urine	Stool	Balance
10	Male	36	214	104	196	–86
10	Female	30	192	92	174	–74

parathyroid glands to excess secretion of PTH, which in turn leads to increased bone resorption in order to maintain the homeostasis of the normal serum calcium level.

The retention of calcium from a high calcium intake, however, is frequently lower for those with osteoporosis than it is for nonosteoporotic subjects or for patients who suffer from other conditions of bone loss, such as hyperparathyroidism or hyperthyroidism. The absorption of calcium from the intestine is decreased in elderly persons, including osteoporotic females. This appears to be caused in part by a relative vitamin D deficiency that occurs with aging (Tsai et al. 1984) but may also result from generalized functional changes of the intestinal mucosa with age, relating to the absorbability of nutrients in general.

Yet even when calcium is administered by the intravenous route (bypassing the intestine), the retention of calcium is low in osteoporotic patients, indicating the inability of the skeleton to accept the added calcium that has entered the circulation directly (Spencer, Hausinger, and Laszlo 1954). Blood levels of the active vitamin D metabolite $1,25(OH)_2D_3$ have been shown to be low in these patients (Tsai et al. 1984). In the differentiation of calcium loss in conditions other than osteoporosis, the determination of urinary hydroxyproline and of free cortisol levels may be helpful.

Although calcium is the major mineral of the bone structure, other minerals – such as phosphorus, magnesium, zinc, and fluoride – are also important because of the interaction of calcium with these elements and their specific functions in the body. Before these interactions are considered, however, the calcium requirement – the amount of calcium needed to maintain a normal calcium status – requires some attention. The data employed in the following discussion were derived from studies carried out under strictly controlled dietary study conditions in the Metabolic Research Unit at the Veterans Administration (VA) Hospital at Hines, Illinois.

The Calcium Requirement

An adequate intake of calcium throughout life has been shown to play an important role in maintaining the normal bone structure and to contribute to the peak bone mass that is achieved at between 25 and 30 years of age (Heaney 1982; Heaney et al. 1982). The bone mass begins to decline after age 35, and this decrease accelerates in females after the menopause. One can safely assume that the adverse and deleterious effects of aging on the bone mass and on the bone structure would be diminished in advancing age if the skeleton could be more robust at the time when the inevitable and accelerated bone loss begins.

In view of these considerations, the questions arise: What should be the daily calcium intake for the elderly? Is the RDA for calcium adequate for this age group (National Research Council 1989)? For calcium, the RDA for young persons up to the age of 24 years is 1,200 mg, but it is reduced to 800 mg/day for all age groups after age 25, including elderly women (National Research Council 1989). It therefore has seemed important to examine whether the 800 mg calcium intake is adequate to maintain a normal calcium balance at middle age (and to prevent excessive calcium and bone loss) and thereby maintain a normal calcium status and a normal skeletal structure in women with advancing age.

Our studies showed that the calcium balance of middle-aged males was only slightly positive, +30 mg/day with an intake of 800 mg calcium (Table IV.B.1.2) – without considering the dermal loss of calcium, which is usually not determined in metabolic balance studies. The latter is stressed because in calcium balance studies, only the urinary and fecal calcium excretions are determined, and the sum of these excretions is related to the calcium intake. A large percentage of these fully ambulatory middle-aged males (34 percent) were in negative calcium balance at the 800 mg/day intake level. Increasing the calcium intake from 800 to 1,200 mg/day resulted in a significant increase of the calcium balance (Spencer, Kramer, Lesniak, et al. 1984). Yet adding another 800 or even 1,100 mg calcium to the 1,200 mg intake did not significantly improve the calcium balance (Table IV.B.1.2). Such a plateau of the calcium balance at the 1,200 mg calcium intake indicates a threshold for the intestinal absorption of calcium at this level (Spencer and Kramer 1987).

Table IV.B.1.2 also shows that urinary calcium was the same whether the calcium intake was 800, 1,200, or 2,000 mg/day. Only when the calcium intake was increased further – to 2,300 mg/day – did urinary calcium increase. This point is emphasized because of the widespread – and unjustified – concern that increasing the calcium intake beyond the 800 mg level may result in kidney stone formation. Such a concern does become important, however, if there is a history of kidney stone formation or even a family history of renal stones, because a certain percentage of kidney stone formers are hyperabsorbers of calcium.

Although these findings came from studies carried out in an all-male VA hospital, there is no reason to assume that they would not also apply to females of similar age (average 54 years) or older. Indeed, in view of the large percentage of the male subjects with negative calcium balances at the 800 mg calcium intake

Table IV.B.1.2. *Studies of the calcium requirement*

Calcium intake, mg/day	Calcium, mg/day			
	Intake	Urine	Stool	Balance
200	250	85	265	–100
800	820	180	610	+30
1,200	1,250	170	980	+100
2,000	2,060	175	1,750	+135
2,300	2,350	245	1,945	+160

Note: Calcium intake greater than 250 mg was due to the addition of calcium gluconate tablets to the constant low-calcium diet.

level, and in view of the known calcium loss suffered by middle-aged and older women, it seems clear that the calcium intake of older women should be at least as great as that of considerably younger persons – that is, 1,200 mg/day (National Research Council 1989). Thus, some have recommended that the calcium intake of postmenopausal women should be increased to 1,500 mg/day (Heaney 1982).

It is also important to consider that although calcium intake may be adequate, there are certain factors that influence the utilization of calcium. The following subsections describe the effects of various minerals, nutrients, and drugs – phosphorus, magnesium, fluoride, zinc, strontium, protein, alcohol, and medications – on the metabolism of calcium.

Phosphorus

The mineral phosphorus is present in practically all cells of the body and is closely linked to the metabolism of both calcium and protein. The main storehouse of phosphorus is the skeleton, and the bone crystal hydroxyapatite consists of calcium phosphate. But significant amounts of phosphorus are also contained in the soft tissues. Calcium cannot be retained by itself in bone but is retained together with phosphate. In fact, in calcium balance studies, the retention of calcium improved during high phosphorus intakes (Spencer et al. 1965; Spencer, Kramer, Osis, et al. 1978a).

These observations were made during a high phosphorus intake of 2,000 mg/day, compared with a phosphorus intake of 800 mg/day in the control study. But although the phosphorus intake was increased by a factor of approximately 2.5 (from 800 to 2,000 mg/day) in these investigations, no adverse effect of phosphorus on calcium absorption or calcium balance was observed, regardless of whether the high phosphorus intake was given during a very low calcium intake of 200 mg/day or during a high calcium intake of 2,000 mg/day (Spencer et al. 1965; Spencer, Kramer, Osis, et al. 1978a).

With a high phosphorus intake, fecal calcium was slightly but not significantly increased. Therefore, the intestinal absorption of calcium, determined with tracer doses of ^{47}Ca, was also not decreased (Spencer

Kramer, Osis, et al. 1978a). This result is in contrast to the general unjustified belief that a high phosphorus intake decreases humans' intestinal absorption of calcium. Such an assumption is based primarily on animal studies (Draper, Sie, and Bergan 1972; LaFlamme and Jowsey 1972).

The difference in effect, however, points out the difficulty and unreliability of extrapolating animal data to humans. Very few, if any, strictly controlled dietary studies of the effect of phosphorus on calcium absorption have been carried out in humans, and it is possible that amounts of phosphorus greater than 2,000 mg/day may have adverse effects on calcium absorption. The recently reported beneficial effect of biphosphonates in the treatment of osteoporosis (Watts et al. 1990) may result from the action of phosphate in inhibiting bone resorption by decreasing the activity of the osteoclasts (the bone-reabsorbing cells) (Hodsman 1989). Inorganic phosphate has been reported to have this effect (Yates et al. 1991). The usual dietary phosphorus intake is approximately 1,200 mg/day, most of it from proteins in dairy products and meat.

The main impact of added phosphorus on calcium metabolism is a consistent decrease in urinary calcium, regardless of whether the high phosphorus intake occurs during a low or high calcium intake (Goldsmith et al. 1967; Goldsmith et al. 1969; Spencer, Kramer, Osis, et al. 1978a). The decrease in urinary calcium during a high phosphorus intake is usually believed to reflect decreased calcium absorption. However, as already noted, the intestinal absorption of calcium did not decrease during a high phosphorus intake (Spencer, Kramer, Osis, et al. 1978a). Although there was a slight increase in fecal calcium during the high phosphorus intake in our studies (Spencer et al. 1965; Spencer, Kramer, Osis, et al. 1978a), this increase was not significant.

Several factors other than a decrease in calcium absorption can contribute to the decrease in urinary calcium during a high phosphorus intake; these include decreased bone resorption, increased mineralization, and increased bone formation (Pechet et al. 1967; Flanagan and Nichols 1969). As the intestinal absorption of calcium did not decrease during differ-

ent high phosphorus intakes up to 2,000 mg/day, the dietary Ca:P ratio does not appear to play an important role in the intestinal absorption of calcium. This viewpoint was also expressed in 1962 by the World Health Organization.

The importance of phosphorus in human health and in calcium metabolism is indicated by the deleterious effects of phosphorus depletion, which is most commonly induced by the use of medications such as aluminum-containing antacids. Even relatively small doses of such antacids induce a considerable loss of calcium (Spencer, Kramer, Norris, et al. 1982). In addition, small doses – as well as larger therapeutic doses (Lotz, Zisman, and Bartter 1968) – induce phosphorus depletion by the complexation of phosphate through aluminum in the intestine. This is evidenced by a very significant increase in fecal phosphorus, which may be as great as the entire dietary phosphorus intake (Table IV.B.1.3).

The loss of phosphorus via the intestine may lead to its removal from bone in order to maintain the phosphorus level in tissues, enzymes, and plasma. The removal of phosphorus from bone appears to be associated with simultaneous removal of calcium from the skeleton, resulting in an increase in urinary calcium and a negative calcium balance. Thus, significant bone loss has been observed in patients who have taken commonly used aluminum-containing antacids for prolonged periods of time.

The prolonged use of intravenous fluids in the absence of food intake may also result in phosphorus depletion, which is associated with clinical symptoms of weakness and fatigue. To our knowledge, no data are available on the relationship of this type of induced phosphorus depletion and calcium metabolism.

Magnesium

Magnesium is an essential nutrient of great importance in controlling normal cardiac rhythm and cardiovascular function. A low magnesium status has been associated with cardiac arrhythmia as well as with cerebrovascular spasm (Altura and Altura 1981). The RDA for magnesium is 300 mg for women and 400 mg for men (National Research Council 1989). Bone is an important repository for magnesium.

Table IV.B.1.3. *Effect of aluminum-containing antacids on the calcium and phosphorus balance*

Patient	Study	Calcium, mg/day				Phosphorus, mg/day			
		Intake	Urine	Stool	Balance	Intake	Urine	Stool	Balance
1	Control	231	89	229	−87	845	533	323	−11
	Maalox[a]	225	123	264	−132	862	138	673	+51
2	Control	254	86	240	−72	933	482	299	+152
	Maalox[b]	279	421	380	−522	873	18	890	−35

[a]Aluminum-magnesium hydroxide, 30 ml three times daily.

[b]Every hour while awake (15 doses = 450 ml per day).

Magnesium balance studies have shown great variability of the magnesium balance in different individuals, regardless of magnesium intake. During a relatively low magnesium intake of about 220 mg/day, the magnesium balance is usually negative. However, equilibrium or even positive magnesium balances have been observed during a low magnesium intake in our studies on male subjects (Spencer, Lesniak, Kramer, et al. 1980).

The intestinal absorption of dietary magnesium is approximately 50 percent of its intake in persons with normal renal function, regardless of calcium intake (Spencer, Schwartz, and Osis 1988). In contrast, patients with chronic renal failure absorb considerably less magnesium, about one-third that of those with normal renal function (Spencer, Lesniak, Gatza, et al. 1980). It appears that magnesium balance depends on both the present and the past magnesium status of the individual. This was demonstrated by increasing the magnesium intake in adequately nourished subjects from a low of 220 to a relatively high 800 mg/day. Such an increase, however, did not improve magnesium balance when compared with intakes of 220 to 300 mg/day. It would appear, therefore, that the diet of these patients prior to the magnesium absorption studies contained an adequate amount of magnesium.

The interaction of magnesium with calcium warrants discussion because magnesium has been reported to have variable effects on the intestinal absorption of calcium. Reports of some animal studies have suggested that magnesium decreases the intestinal absorption of calcium (O'Dell 1960). But other studies have indicated no change in humans (Schwartz et al. 1973), and still others have reported an increase in calcium absorption. Our investigations under controlled dietary conditions have shown that increasing the magnesium intake more than threefold – from 220 to 860 mg/day – had no effect on the intestinal absorption of calcium (Spencer et al. 1994).

Changing the focus to the effect of calcium on magnesium metabolism, we find reports of the intestinal absorption of magnesium being impaired by calcium in animals (Morris and O'Dell 1961). By contrast, however, our studies on humans – employing both magnesium balance studies and tracer studies using radioactive magnesium (Mg^{28}) – have conclusively shown that both intestinal absorption of magnesium and the magnesium balance did not change when the calcium intake was increased from 200 to 800 and even to 2,000 mg/day (Schwartz et al. 1973).

As phosphorus and calcium are closely linked, the effect of phosphorus on the metabolism of magnesium might warrant brief mention. Whereas phosphorus, like calcium, decreased the absorption of magnesium in animals (O'Dell 1960), increased amounts of phosphorus – up to 2,000 mg/day – had little effect on the magnesium balance of humans (Spencer, Lesniak, Kramer, et al. 1980), regardless of whether these studies were carried out during a low or high calcium intake. How-

ever, a high magnesium intake led to increased fecal phosphorus excretion and to a less positive or even negative phosphorus balance, probably because of the formation of magnesium-phosphate complexes in the intestine. But despite this effect, the calcium balance was not affected (Spencer et al. 1994). Further studies of the effect of magnesium on phosphorus metabolism in humans are needed. Such studies should seek to determine at which level a high magnesium intake has adverse effects on phosphorus metabolism and, potentially therefore, on calcium metabolism.

Fluoride

Fluoride enters the human food chain because of the fluoride content of water and soil. The skeleton is its major repository in the body. Not only is fluoride beneficial in preventing dental caries in children, but there is evidence that it is also important in maintaining the normal bone structure (Zipkin, Posner, and Eanes 1962). Consequently, fluoride affects the metabolism of calcium. Surveys in the United States and in Finland have demonstrated that the prevalence of osteoporosis is lower in places where the water is naturally high in fluoride content than in areas where this condition does not obtain (Bernstein, Sadowsky, and Hegsted 1966).

Because the main storehouse of fluoride is the skeleton, where it is incorporated in the bone crystal hydroxyapatite (leading to its increased strength) (Zipkin et al. 1962), fluoride has been used for the treatment of osteoporosis since the early 1960s (Rich, Ensinck, and Ivanovich 1964; Spencer et al. 1970). As fluoride may interact with various minerals, such as calcium, phosphorus, and magnesium, we investigated the human metabolism of fluoride during the intake of these inorganic elements. During a fluoride intake as high as 45 mg/day (taken as sodium fluoride), the single effect on calcium metabolism was a decrease in urinary calcium, whereas no change occurred in fecal calcium, the intestinal absorption of calcium, and endogenous fecal calcium (the amount of the absorbed calcium excreted into the intestine) (Spencer et al. 1970). There was also little change in the calcium balance, which depended on the decrease in urinary calcium during the high fluoride intake. Increasing phosphorus intake by a factor of 2.5, from 800 to 2,000 mg/day, had no effect on the fluoride balance, regardless of calcium intake (Spencer et al. 1975). Also, increasing magnesium intake approximately threefold during a high fluoride intake had no effect on the fluoride balance (Spencer, Kramer, Wiatrowski, et al. 1978). Several biochemical and therapeutic aspects of the fluoride metabolism in humans have been summarized (Spencer, Osis, and Lender 1981).

Zinc

The importance of the trace element zinc in human health and nutrition has been emphasized in recent decades. The RDA of zinc is 15 mg/day for men and

12 mg/day for women (National Research Council 1989). Zinc and calcium appear to have the same binding sites in the intestine, and, therefore, the absorption and utilization of one may be inhibited by the other. Animal studies have shown that calcium inhibits the intestinal absorption of zinc (Hoekstra et al. 1956; Luecke et al. 1957), but our studies on humans demonstrated that calcium had no effect on the absorption of zinc (Spencer, Kramer, Norris, et al. 1984). Similarly, phosphorus – used in amounts of up to 2,000 mg/day, alone or combined with the same amount of calcium – did not affect the zinc balance nor the net absorption of zinc (Spencer, Kramer, Norris, et al. 1984). These findings contrasted with those obtained in animal studies, with the different results apparently arising from differences in body weights and differences in the amounts of calcium and phosphorus relative to body weight.

Another question was whether zinc affects the intestinal absorption of calcium. Our calcium absorption studies (using ^{47}Ca as the tracer) have conclusively shown that large doses of zinc (140 mg/day of zinc sulfate) significantly decreased the intestinal absorption of calcium when zinc supplements were given during a low calcium intake of 230 mg/day – but not during a calcium intake of 800 mg/day (Spencer et al. 1987). Further investigations have delineated the dose of zinc and the level of calcium intake at which the decrease of calcium absorption would not occur. Decreasing zinc intake from 140 mg to 100 mg during a low calcium intake of 230 mg/day, and decreasing calcium intake from 800 mg to 500 mg during the high zinc intake of 140 mg/day, in both cases had no adverse effect on the intestinal absorption of calcium (Spencer et al. 1992).

Zinc supplements are freely available "over the counter" and are used in unknown dosages by the public with equally unknown intakes of calcium. This practice is of concern for elderly women who may already have a low calcium status and yet may use large doses of zinc during a low calcium intake. Such a combination would decrease the intestinal absorption of calcium and thereby contribute to further deterioration of the state of calcium metabolism in these individuals.

Strontium

Little attention is being paid to strontium, which, like calcium, is primarily deposited in bone. Our studies have shown that the average dietary intake of strontium is low, at 1.5 to 2.5 mg/day (Warren and Spencer 1972, 1976). In 1950, it was suggested that strontium used in conjunction with calcium would be effective in therapy for osteoporosis and that the retention of both calcium and strontium would be additive (Shorr and Carter 1950). About 30 years later, other investigators again demonstrated the beneficial effect of strontium as a therapeutic agent for osteoporosis (Marie et al. 1985). Moreover, our investigations indicated that large amounts of elemental strontium, such as daily doses of

600 to 900 mg (taken as strontium lactate), were well retained and well tolerated. However, it was found that after discontinuation of strontium supplements, a very high percentage of the retained strontium was excreted in three to four weeks (Warren and Spencer 1976).

It may be speculated that this loss of strontium might not have occurred if calcium intake had been high. Some of our preliminary studies show that the intake of added strontium increases the intestinal absorption of calcium, which could be a significant finding. Further examinations of the effect of strontium on the absorption of calcium are needed because very few substances are known to increase the intestinal absorption of calcium.

Protein

Although proteins are not the same sort of nutrients as minerals, the relationship between proteins and the metabolism of calcium is important because proteins play a major role in the formation of the bone matrix and, conversely, have also been reported to bring about an increase in urinary calcium. However, such findings of calcium loss are primarily based on studies using purified proteins (Walker and Linkswiler 1972; Schuette, Zemel, and Linkswiler 1980). Calcium loss does not occur when complex proteins – which are part of the human diet – are used (Spencer, Kramer, Wiatrowski, et al. 1978; Spencer et al. 1983; Spencer, Kramer, and Osis 1988). The widespread belief that "proteins" generally are a cause of calcium loss frequently stems from reports and statements that do not specify or identify the type of protein used. But in considering the calciuric effect of protein in causing calcium loss, it is important to define the source and type of protein: Are the proteins isolated protein fractions, such as specific amino acids, or are they part of complexes of other nutrients, as is usually the case in the human diet?

Our studies, carried out under strictly controlled dietary conditions, have conclusively shown that a high protein intake (using red meat as its source, in large amounts of up to 550 g of meat per day) did not increase urinary calcium excretion (Spencer, Kramer, Osis, et al. 1978b; Spencer et al. 1983). Such a diet was given daily for as long as four months, and an example of the effect of this type of dietary protein on urinary calcium is shown in Table IV.B.1.4.

Moreover, during this high protein intake, there was no change in fecal calcium, nor in calcium balance, nor in the intestinal absorption of calcium, as determined in ^{47}Ca absorption studies. As already discussed, phosphorus decreases urinary calcium excretion. Dietary protein sources such as meat, milk, and cheese have a high phosphate content, which may explain why urinary calcium does not increase during the intake of these complex proteins. Therefore, the high phosphorus content of complex proteins may prevent and/or counteract any increase in urinary calcium – even with the consumption of red meat, an

Table IV.B.1.4. *Effect of a high-protein diet on calcium metabolism*

Patient	Study	Study days	Calcium, mg/day			
			Intake	Urine	Stool	Balance
1	Control	36	824	111	690	+23
	High protein	36	846	118	683	+45
2	Control	60	824	173	661	–10
	High protein	36	875	157	677	+42

Note: High protein given as red meat; high protein = 2 g/kg body weight compared with 1 gm/kg in the control study.

acid-ash food that would be expected to increase the urinary excretion of calcium (Wachman and Bernstein 1968).

Effects of Excessive Alcohol Consumption

Alcohol cannot be classified as a nutrient. However, chronic alcoholism can lead to bone loss (Feitelberg et al. 1987; Laitinen and Valimaki 1991) and to the development of osteoporosis. The etiology of osteoporosis in this case is multifactorial, but a major cause may well be the poor diet – especially low intakes of calcium, proteins, and vitamin D – associated with prolonged excessive alcohol consumption. Studies have suggested abnormalities in vitamin D metabolism (Gascon-Barre 1985) as well as in the adrenal function (Mendelson, Ogata, and Mello 1971), both of which affect the metabolism of calcium.

Changes in the pancreatic function in chronic alcoholism also lead to a loss of calcium – in this case because of the complexation of calcium with fat in the abdominal cavity – and there may be other factors not yet identified. Table IV.B.1.5 shows the prevalence of osteoporosis in our patients with chronic alcoholism (Spencer et al. 1986). Thirty-one percent were less than 45 years old, and 50 percent of these relatively young patients suffering from chronic alcoholism and osteoporosis were less than 40 years old (Spencer et al. 1986).

Table IV.B.1.5. *Patients with chronic alcoholism and osteoporosis*

Number of patients[a]	Age group, in years	Patients with osteoporosis	Percentage of patients with osteoporosis
5	20–30	–	–
33	31–45	14[b]	31
58	46–62	31	69

[a]All male patients.

[b]Fifty percent of these patients were less than 40 years old.

Table IV.B.1.6. *Effect of corticosteroids on the calcium balance*

Patient	Study	Calcium, mg/day			
		Intake	Urine	Stool	Balance
1	Control	240	185	187	–132
	Corticoids[a]	234	287	177	–230
2	Control	1,955	90	1,733	+132
	Corticoids[b]	1,950	209	1,877	–136

[a]Aristocort, 20 mg/day for 24 days.

[b]Aristocort, 40 mg/day for 60 days.

Effect of Medications

Several medications affect the metabolism of calcium, primarily by increasing urinary calcium and thereby causing calcium loss. The effect of glucocorticoids in causing bone loss and osteoporosis, regardless of gender and age, is well known (Lukert and Adams 1976). Table IV.B.1.6 shows two examples of negative calcium balances during treatment with corticosteroids. These medications increase not only urinary but also fecal calcium, resulting in markedly negative calcium balances. This result occurs during both a low calcium intake of approximately 240 mg/day and an approximate tenfold increase of this amount. The data suggested that the loss of calcium induced by glucocorticoids was dose-dependent.

Herta Spencer

Bibliography

Albright, F., J. C. Aub, and W. Bauer. 1934. Hyperparathyroidism. *Journal of the American Medical Association* 102: 1276-87.

Albright, F., and E. C. Reifenstein. 1948. *The parathyroid glands and metabolic bone disease.* Baltimore, Md.

Altura, B. M., and B. T. Altura. 1981. Magnesium ions and contraction of vascular smooth muscles: Relationship to some vascular diseases. *Federation Proceedings* 40: 2672-9.

Avioli, L. V., J. E. McDonald, and S. W. Lee. 1965. The influence of age on the intestinal absorption of ^{47}Ca in women and its relation to ^{47}Ca absorption in postmenopausal osteoporosis. *Journal of Clinical Investigation* 44: 1960-7.

Baylink, D., E. Morey, and C. Rich. 1969. Effect of calcitonin on the rates of bone formation and resorption in the rat. *Endocrinology* 84: 261-9.

Bernstein, D., H. Sadowsky, and D. M. Hegsted. 1966. Prevalence of osteoporosis in high and low-fluoride areas in North Dakota. *Journal of the American Medical Association* 193: 499-504.

Bijvoet, O. L. M., J. Van der Sluys Veer, and A. P. Jansen. 1968. Effects of calcitonin on patients with Paget's disease, thyrotoxicosis, or hypercalcaemia. *Lancet* 1: 876-81.

Bronner, F., and M. Peterlik. 1995. International conference on progress in bone and mineral research. *Journal of Nutrition* 125: 1963S-2038S.

Bronner, F., and W. D. Stein. 1995. Calcium homeostasis - an old problem revisited. *Journal of Nutrition* 125: 1987S-95S.

Campbell, A. K. 1986. Lewis Victor Heilbrunn. Pioneer of calcium as an intracellular regulator. *Cell Calcium* 7: 287-96.

Cantarow, A. 1933. *Calcium metabolism and calcium therapy.* Second edition. Philadelphia, Pa.

The classic: The state of calcium in the fluids of the body. I. The conditions affecting the ionization of calcium. 1970. *Clinical Orthopaedics and Related Research* 69: 4-27.

Collip, J. B. 1925. The extraction of a parathyroid hormone which will prevent or control parathyroid tetany and which regulates the level of blood calcium. *Journal of Biological Chemistry* 63: 395-438.

Copp, D. H. 1967. Hormonal control of hypercalcemia. Historic development of the calcitonin concept. *American Journal of Medicine* 43: 648-55.

1969. Calcitonin and parathyroid hormone. *Annual Review of Pharmacology* 9: 327-44.

Copp, D. H., E. C. Cameron, B. A. Cheney, et al. 1962. Evidence for calcitonin - a new hormone from the parathyroid that lowers blood calcium. *Endocrinology* 70: 638-49.

Cummings, J. H. 1978. Nutritional implications of dietary fiber. *American Journal of Clinical Nutrition* 31: s21-9.

DeLuca, H. F. 1979. W. O. Atwater Lecture: The vitamin D system in the regulation of calcium and phosphorus metabolism. *Nutrition Reviews* 37: 161-93.

1980. The vitamin D hormonal system: Implications for bone diseases. *Hospital Practice* 15: 57-66.

1988. The vitamin D story: A collaborative effort of basic science and clinical medicine. *Federation Proceedings* 2: 224-36.

Draper, H. H., T. Sie, and J. C. Bergan. 1972. Osteoporosis in aging rats induced by high phosphorus diets. *Journal of Nutrition* 102: 1133-42.

Ebashi, S. 1987. Ca2+ in the heart. *Journal of Molecular and Cellular Cardiology* 19: 1-18.

Feitelberg, S., S. Epstein, F. Ismail, et al. 1987. Deranged bone mineral metabolism in chronic alcoholism. *Metabolism* 36: 322-6.

Flanagan, B., and G. Nichols. 1969. Bone matrix turnover and balance in vitro. II. The effect of aging. *Journal of Clinical Investigation* 48: 607-12.

Fogelman, I., L. Smith, R. Mazess, et al. 1986. Absorption of oral diphosphonate in normal subjects. *Clinical Endocrinology* 24: 57-62.

Foster, G. V., G. F. Joplin, I. MacIntyre, et al. 1966. Effect of thyrocalcitonin in man. *Lancet* 1: 107-9.

Francis, R. M. 1995. Oral biphosphonates in the treatment of osteoporosis: A review. *Current Therapeutic Research* 56: 831-51.

Fye, W. B. 1984. Sydney Ringer. Calcium and cardiac function. *Circulation* 69: 849-53.

Garn, S. M. 1970. Calcium requirements for bone building and skeletal maintenance. *American Journal of Clinical Nutrition* 23: 1149-50.

Gascon-Barre, M. 1985. Influence of chronic ethanol consumption on the metabolism and action of vitamin D. *Journal of the American College of Nutrition* 4: 565-74.

Gloth, F. M., and J. D. Tobin. 1995. Vitamin D deficiency in older people. *Journal of American Geriatrics Society* 43: 822-8.

Goldsmith, R. S., P. Killian, S. H. Ingbar, et al. 1969. Effect of phosphate supplementation during immobilization of normal men. *Metabolism* 18: 349-68.

Goldsmith, R. S., C. F. Woodhouse, S. H. Ingbar, et al. 1967. Effect of phosphate supplements in patients with fractures. *Lancet* 1: 687-90.

Greenwald, E., J. Samachson, and H. Spencer. 1963. Effect of lactose on calcium metabolism in man. *Journal of Nutrition* 79: 531-8.

Hannon, R. R., E. Shorr, W. S. McClellan, and E. F. Du Bois. 1930. A case of osteitis fibrosa cystica (osteomalacia?) with evidence of hyperactivity of the parathyroid bodies. Metabolic study I. *Journal of Clinical Investigation* 8: 215-27.

Harrison, D. C., and E. Mellanby. 1934. Phytic acid and the rickets-producing action of cereals. *Biochemistry Journal* 33: 1660-80.

Heaney, R. P. 1982. Calcium intake requirement and bone mass in the elderly. *Journal of Laboratory Clinical Medicine* 100: 309-12.

Heaney, R. P., J. C. Gallagher, C. C. Johnston, et al. 1982. Calcium nutrition and bone health in the elderly. *American Journal of Clinical Nutrition* 36: 986-1013.

Heaney, R. P., R. R. Recker, and P. D. Saville. 1977. Calcium balance and calcium requirements in middle-aged women. *American Journal of Clinical Nutrition* 30: 1603-11.

Hegsted, D. M., I. Moscoso, and C. Collazos. 1952. A study of the minimum calcium requirements of adult men. *Journal of Nutrition* 46: 181-201.

Hess, A. F., and M. Weinstock. 1924. Antirachitic properties imparted to inert fluids by ultraviolet irradiation. *Journal of the American Medical Association* 83: 1845-6.

Hirsch, P. F., and P. L. Munson. 1969. Thyrocalcitonin. *Physiological Reviews* 49: 548-622.

Hodsman, A. B. 1989. Effects of cyclical therapy for osteoporosis using an oral regimen of inorganic phosphate and sodium etidronate: A clinical and bone histomorphometric study. *Bone Mineral* 5: 201-12.

Hoekstra, W., P. K. Lewis, P. H. Phillips, et al. 1956. The relationship of parakeratosis, supplemental calcium and zinc to the zinc content of certain body components of swine. *Journal of Animal Science* 15: 752-64.

Huldschinsky, K. 1919. Heilung von Rachitis durch künstliche Höhensonne. *Deutsche Medizinische Wochenschrift* 45: 712-13.

Irwin, M. I., and E. W. Kienholz. 1973. A conspectus of research on calcium requirements of man. *Journal of Nutrition* 103: 1019-95.

Ismail-Beigi, F., J. G. Reinhold, B. Faraji, et al. 1977. Effects of cellulose added to diets of low and high fiber content upon the metabolism of calcium, magnesium, zinc and phosphorus by man. *Journal of Nutrition* 107: 510-18.

Jeans, P., and G. Stearns. 1938. The effect of vitamin D on linear growth in infancy. II. The effects of intakes above 1800 USP units daily. *Journal of Pediatrics* 13: 730-41.

Kallfelz, F. A., A. N. Taylor, and R. H. Wasserman. 1967. Vitamin D-induced calcium binding factor in rat intestinal mucosa. *Federation Proceedings* 125: 54-8.

LaFlamme, G. H., and J. Jowsey. 1972. Bone and soft tissue changes with oral phosphate supplements. *Journal of Clinical Investigation* 51: 2834-40.

Laitinen, K., and M. Valimaki. 1991. Alcohol and bone. *Calcified Tissue International* 49: s70-3.

Leichsenring, J. M., L. M. Norris, S. A. Lamison, et al. 1951. The effect of level of intake on calcium and phosphorus metabolism in college women. *Journal of Nutrition* 45: 407-18.

Lotz, M., E. Zisman, and F. C. Bartter. 1968. Evidence for a phosphorus-depletion syndrome in man. *New England Journal of Medicine* 278: 409-15.

Lowenstein, W. R., and B. Rose. 1978. Calcium in (junctional) intercellular communication and a thought on its behavior in intracellular communication. *Annals of the New York Academy of Science* 307: 285-307.

Luecke, R. W., J. A. Hoefer, W. S. Brammell, et al. 1957. Calcium and zinc in parakeratosis of swine. *Journal of Animal Science* 16: 3-11.

Lukert, B. P., and J. S. Adams. 1976. Calcium and phosphorus homeostasis in man: Effect of corticosteroids. *Archives of Internal Medicine* 136: 1249-53.

Lumb, G. A., and S. W. Stanbury. 1974. Parathyroid function in human vitamin D deficiency and vitamin D deficiency in primary hyperparathyroidism. *American Journal of Medicine* 56: 833-9.

Lund, J., and H. F. DeLuca. 1966. Biologically active metabolite of vitamin D_3 from bone, liver, and blood serum. *Journal of Lipid Research* 7: 739-44.

Lutwak, L., F. R. Singer, and M. R. Urist. 1974. Current concepts of bone metabolism. *Annals of Internal Medicine* 80: 630-44.

Malm, O. J. 1958. Calcium requirements and adaptation in adult men. *Scandinavian Journal of Clinical Laboratory Investigations* 10 (Supplement 36): 1-290.

Mandl, F. 1926. Klinisches und Experimentelles zur Frage der lokalisierten und generalisierten Osteitis fibrosa. B. Die generalisierte form der Osteitis fibrosa. *Archiv für Klinische Chirurgie* 143: 1-46.

Marie, P. J., S. C. Skoryna, R. J. Pivon, et al. 1985. Histomorphometry of bone changes in stable strontium therapy. In *Trace substances in environmental health,* Vol. 19, ed. D. D. Hemphill, 193-208. Columbia, Mo.

Matkovic, V., K. Kostial, I. Simonovic, et al. 1979. Bone status and fracture rates in two regions of Yugoslavia. *American Journal of Clinical Nutrition* 32: 540-9.

Mawer, B. E., J. Backhouse, L. F. Hill, et al. 1975. Vitamin D metabolism and parathyroid function in man. *Clinical Science of Molecular Medicine* 48: 349-65.

Mazess, R. B., H. S. Barden, M. Ettinger, et al. 1988. Bone density of the radius, spine and proximal femur in osteoporosis. *Journal of Bone and Mineral Research* 3: 13-18.

McCance, R. A., E. M. Widdowson, and H. Lehmann. 1942. The effect of protein intake on the absorption of calcium and magnesium. *Biochemistry Journal* 36: 686-91.

McCollum, E. V., N. Simmonds, M. Kinney, et al. [1921] 1995. Studies on experimental rickets. XVII. The effects of diets deficient in calcium and in fat-soluble A in modifying the histological structure of the bones. *American Journal of Epidemiology* 141: 280-96.

McCollum, E. V., N. Simmonds, P. G. Shipley, and E. A. Park. 1921. VIII. The production of rickets by diets low in phosphorus and fat-soluble vitamin A. *Journal of Biological Chemistry* 47: 507-27.

Mellanby, E. 1921. Experimental rickets. *Medical Research Council Special Report Series* No. 61: 1-78.

⸻ 1949. The rickets-producing and anticalcifying action of phytate. *Journal of Physiology* 109: 488-533.

Mendelson, J. H., M. Ogata, and N. K. Mello. 1971. Adrenal function and alcoholism. I. Serum cortisol. *Psychosomatic Medicine* 33: 145-57.

Mills, R., H. Breiter, E. Kempster, et al. 1940. The influence of lactose on calcium retention in children. *Journal of Nutrition* 20: 467-76.

Mines, G. R. 1911. On the replacement of calcium in certain neuro-muscular mechanisms by allied substances. *Journal of Physiology* 42: 251-66.

Moldawer, M., S. J. Zimmerman, and L. C. Collins. 1965. The incidence of osteoporosis in elderly whites and elderly Negroes. *Journal of the American Medical Association* 194: 859-62.

Morris, E. R., and B. L. O'Dell. 1961. Magnesium deficiency in the guinea pig. Mineral composition of tissues and distribution of acid-soluble phosphorus. *Journal of Nutrition* 75: 77-85.

National Institutes of Health Consensus Conference. 1995. Optimal calcium intake. *Journal of the American Medical Association* 272: 1942-8.

National Research Council. 1989. *Recommended dietary allowances.* Tenth edition. Washington, D.C.

Nordin, B. E. C. 1966. International patterns of osteoporosis. *Clinical Orthopedics and Related Research* 45: 17-30.

Nordin, B. E. C., M. M. Young, L. Bulusu, et al. 1970. Osteoporosis reexamined. In *Osteoporosis,* ed. U. S. Barzel, 47-67. New York.

O'Dell, B. L. 1960. Magnesium requirement and its relation to other dietary constituents. *Federation Proceedings* 19: 648-54.

Olson, E. B., Jr., and H. F. DeLuca. 1973. Vitamin D. Metabolism and mechanism of action. *World Review of Nutrition and Dietetics* 17: 164-88.

Opie, L. H. 1980. Cardiac metabolism: Cetecholamines, calcium, cyclic AMP, and substrates. *Advances in Myocardiology* 1: 3-20.

Osis, D., L. Kramer, E. Wiatrowski, and H. Spencer. 1974. Dietary fluoride intake in man. *Journal of Nutrition* 104: 1313.

Paget, J. 1877. On a form of chronic inflammation of bones (osteitis deformans). *Medical Chirurgical Transactions* 60: 37-64.

Palm, T. A. 1890. Geographical distribution and etiology of rickets. *Practitioner* 45: 270-9.

Pechet, M. M., E. Bobadilla, E. L. Carroll, et al. 1967. Regulation of bone resorption and formation. *American Journal of Medicine* 43: 696-710.

Pettifor, J. M., and F. P. Ross. 1983. Low dietary calcium intake and its role in the pathogenesis of rickets. *South African Medical Journal* 63: 179-84.

Pettifor, J. M., F. P. Ross, R. Travers, et al. 1981. Dietary calcium deficiency: A syndrome associated with bone deformities and elevated 1,25-dihydroxyvitamin D concentrations. *Metabolic Bone Disease and Related Research* 2: 302-95.

Pettifor, J. M., F. P. Ross, J. Wong, et al. 1978. Rickets in rural blacks in South Africa. Is dietary calcium a factor? *Journal of Pediatrics* 92: 320-4.

Ponchon, G., and H. F. DeLuca. 1969. Metabolites of vitamin D_3 and their biologic activity. *Journal of Nutrition* 99: 157-67.

Pramanik, A. K., S. Gupta, and P. S. Agarwal. 1971. Rickets in protein calorie malnutrition. *Indian Pediatrics* 8: 195-9.

Reinhold, J. G., K. Nasr, A. Lahimgarzaden, et al. 1973. Effects of purified phytate and phytate-rich breads upon metabolism of zinc, calcium, phosphorus and nitrogen in man. *Lancet* 1: 283-8.

Rich, C., J. Ensinck, and P. Ivanovich. 1964. The effects of sodium fluoride on calcium metabolism of subjects with metabolic bone diseases. *Journal of Clinical Investigation* 43: 545-56.

Ringer, S. 1883. A further contribution regarding the influence of the different constituents of the blood on the contraction of the heart. *Journal of Physiology* 4: 29-42.

⸻ 1886. Further experiments regarding the influence of small quantities of lime, potassium and other salts on muscular tissue. *Journal of Physiology* 7: 291-308.

Robertson, I. 1969. A survey of clinical rickets in the infant population in Cape Town in 1967 to 1968. *South African Medical Journal* 43: 1072-6.

Rubin, R. P. 1982. *Calcium and cellular secretion.* New York.

Sandler, R. B., C. Slemenda, R. E. LaPorte, et al. 1985. Postmenopausal bone density and milk consumption in childhood and adolescence. *American Journal of Clinical Nutrition* 42: 270-4.

San Fillippo, F. A., and G. C. Battistone. 1971. The fluoride content of a representative diet of the young adult male. *Clinical Chimica Acta* 31: 453-7.

Schuette, S. A., M. B. Zemel, and H. M. Linkswiler. 1980. Studies on the mechanism of protein-induced hypercalciuria in older men and women. *Journal of Nutrition* 110: 305-15.

Schwartz, R., N. A. Woodcock, J. D. Blakely, et al. 1973. Metabolic response of adolescent boys to two levels of dietary magnesium and protein. II. Effect of magnesium and protein level on calcium balance. *American Journal of Clinical Nutrition* 26: 519-23.

Shai, F., R. K. Baker, and S. Wallach. 1971. The clinical and metabolic effects of porcine calcitonin on Paget's disease of bone. *Journal of Clinical Investigation* 50: 1927-40.

Sherman, H. C. 1920. Calcium requirement of maintenance in man. *Journal of Biological Chemistry* 44: 21-7.

Sherman, H. C., and A. M. Pappenheimer. 1921. I. A diet producing rickets in white rats and its prevention by the addition of an inorganic salt. *Journal of Experimental Medicine* 34: 189-98.

Shohl, A. T. 1939. *Mineral metabolism.* American Chemical Society Monograph Series. New York.

Shorr, E., and A. C. Carter. 1950. The value of strontium as an adjuvant to calcium in the mineralization of the skeleton in osteoporosis in man. In *Metabolic interrelations,* ed. E. C. Reifenstein, Jr., and V. Johnson, 144-54. New York.

Spencer, H. 1982. Osteoporosis: Goals of therapy. *Hospital Practice* 17: 131-51.

Spencer, H., H. Fuller, C. Norris, and D. Williams. 1994. Effect of magnesium on the intestinal absorption of calcium in man. *Journal of the American College of Nutrition* 5: 485-92.

Spencer, H., A. Hausinger, and D. Laszlo. 1954. The calcium tolerance test in senile osteoporosis. *Journal of the American Geriatric Society* 2: 19-25.

Spencer, H., and L. B. Kramer. 1985. Factors influencing calcium balance in man. In *Calcium in biological systems,* ed. K. P. Rubin, G. B. Weiss, and J. W. Putney, Jr. New York.

1987. Osteoporosis, calcium requirement and factors causing calcium loss. *Clinics in Geriatric Medicine* 3: 389-402.

Spencer, H., L. Kramer, M. DeBartolo, et al. 1983. Further studies of the effect of a high protein diet as meat on calcium metabolism. *American Journal of Clinical Nutrition* 37: 924-9.

Spencer, H., L. Kramer, M. Lesniak, et al. 1984. Calcium requirements in humans. *Clinical Orthopedics and Related Research* 184: 270-80.

Spencer, H., L. Kramer, C. Norris, et al. 1982. Effect of small doses of aluminum-containing antacids on calcium and phosphorus metabolism. *American Journal of Clinical Nutrition* 36: 32-40.

1984. Effect of calcium and phosphorus on zinc metabolism in man. *American Journal of Clinical Nutrition* 40: 1213-18.

Spencer, H., L. Kramer, and D. Osis. 1982. Factors contributing to calcium loss in aging. *American Journal of Clinical Nutrition* 36: 776-87.

1988. Do protein and phosphorus cause calcium loss? *Journal of Nutrition* 118: 657-60.

Spencer, H., L. Kramer, D. Osis, et al. 1978a. Effect of phosphorus on the absorption of calcium and on the calcium balance in man. *Journal of Nutrition* 108: 447-57.

1978b. Effect of a high protein (meat) intake on calcium

metabolism in man. *American Journal of Clinical Nutrition* 31: 2167-80.

Spencer, H., L. Kramer, E. Wiatrowski, et al. 1978. Magnesium-fluoride interrelationships in man. II. Effect of magnesium on fluoride metabolism. *American Journal of Physiology* 234: E343-6.

Spencer, H., M. Lesniak, C. Gatza, et al. 1980. Magnesium absorption and metabolism in patients with chronic renal failure and in patients with normal renal function. *Gastroenterology* 79: 26-34.

Spencer, H., M. Lesniak, L. Kramer, et al. 1980. Studies of magnesium metabolism in man. In *Magnesium in health and disease,* ed. M. Cantin and M. S. Seelig, 911-19. Jamaica, N.Y.

Spencer, H., I. Lewin, D. Osis, et al. 1970. Studies of fluoride and calcium metabolism in patients with osteoporosis. *American Journal of Medicine* 49: 814-22.

Spencer, H., J. Menczel, and I. Lewin. 1964. Metabolic and radioisotope studies in osteoporosis. *Clinical Orthopedics and Related Research* 35: 202-19.

Spencer, H., J. Menczel, I. Lewin, et al. 1965. Effect of high phosphorus intake on calcium and phosphorus metabolism in man. *Journal of Nutrition* 86: 125-32.

Spencer, H., C. Norris, and D. Osis. 1992. Further studies of the effect of zinc on intestinal absorption of calcium in man. *Journal of the American College of Nutrition* 5: 561-6.

Spencer, H., D. Osis, L. Kramer, et al. 1975. Effect of calcium and phosphorus on fluoride metabolism in man. *Journal of Nutrition* 105: 733-40.

Spencer, H., D. Osis, and M. Lender. 1981. Studies of fluoride metabolism in man. *Science of the Total Environment* 17: 1-12.

Spencer, H., N. Rubio, M. Indreika, et al. 1986. Chronic alcoholism: Frequently overlooked cause of osteoporosis in men. *American Journal of Medicine* 80: 393-7.

Spencer, H., N. Rubio, L. Kramer, et al. 1987. Effect of zinc supplements on the intestinal absorption of calcium. *Journal of the American College of Nutrition* 6: 47-51.

Spencer, H., R. Schwartz, and D. Osis. 1988. Magnesium balances and ^{28}Mg studies in man. In *Trace substances in environmental health,* Vol. 22, ed. D. D. Hemphill, 128-35. Columbia, Mo.

Stanbury, S. W. 1981. Vitamin D and hyperparathyroidism. *Journal of the Royal College of Physicians* 15: 205-16.

Stearns, G., P. C. Jeans, and V. Vandecar. 1936. The effect of vitamin D on linear growth in infancy. *Journal of Pediatrics* 9: 1-19.

Steenbock, H., and A. Black. 1924. XVII. The induction of growth-promoting and calcifying properties in a ration by exposure to ultraviolet light. *Journal of Biological Chemistry* 61: 405-22.

Strause, L., P. Saltman, K. T. Smith, et al. 1994. Spinal bone loss in postmenopausal women supplemented with calcium and trace minerals. *Journal of Nutrition* 124: 1060-4.

Theiler, A. 1976. Rickets and other deficiency diseases of the osseous system (last lecture given by Sir Arnold Theiler Onderstepoort, 1936). *Journal of South African Veterinary Association* 47: 41-2.

Tsai, K. S., H. Heath, R. Kumar, et al. 1984. Impaired vitamin D metabolism with aging in women. Possible role in the pathogenesis of senile osteoporosis. *Journal of Clinical Investigation* 73: 1668-72.

Wachman, A., and D. S. Bernstein. 1968. Diet and osteoporosis. *Lancet* 1: 958-9.

Walker, P. M., and H. M. Linkswiler. 1972. Calcium retention in the adult human male as affected by protein intake. *Journal of Nutrition* 102: 1297-1302.

Warren, J. M., and H. Spencer. 1972. Analysis of stable strontium in biological materials by atomic absorption spectrophotometry. *Clinical Chimica Acta* 38: 435-9.

1976. Metabolic balances of strontium in man. *Clinical Orthopedics and Related Research* 117: 307-20.

Wasserman, R. H., R. A. Corradina, and A. N. Taylor. 1968. Vitamin D-dependent calcium-binding protein. Purification and some properties. *Journal of Biological Chemistry* 243: 3978-86.

Wasserman, R. H., and A. N. Taylor. 1968. Vitamin D-dependent calcium-binding protein. Response to some physiological and nutritional variables. *Journal of Biological Chemistry* 243: 3987-93.

Watts, N. B., S. T. Harris, H. K. Genant, et al. 1990. Intermittent cyclical etidronate treatment of postmenopausal osteoporosis. *New England Journal of Medicine* 323: 73-9.

Whedon, G. D. 1959. Effects of high calcium intake on bone, blood and soft tissue: Relationship of calcium intake to balance in osteoporosis. *Federation Proceedings* 18: 1112-18.

WHO (World Health Organization). 1962. *Calcium requirements.* Technical Report Series, No. 230. Geneva.

Woodhouse, N. J. Y., P. Bordier, M. Fisher, et al. 1971. Human calcitonin in the treatment of Paget's bone disease. *Lancet* 1: 1139-43.

Woodhouse, N. J. Y., F. H. Doyle, and G. F. Joplin. 1971. Vitamin D deficiency and primary hyperparathyroidism. *Lancet* 2: 283-7.

Woodhouse, N. J. Y., S. Tun Chot, P. Bordier, et al. 1973. Vitamin D administration in primary hyperparathyroidism. *Clinical Science* 44: 3P.

Yates, A. J., R. O. C. Oreffo, K. Mayor, et al. 1991. Inhibition of bone resorption by inorganic phosphate is mediated by both reduced osteoclast formation and decreased activity of mature osteoclasts. *Journal of Bone and Mineral Research* 6: 473-8.

Zipkin, I., A. S. Posner, and E. D. Eanes. 1962. The effect of fluoride on the X-ray-diffraction pattern of the apatite of human bone. *Biochimica Biophysica Acta* 59: 255-8.

IV.B.2 ⁊ Iodine and Iodine-Deficiency Disorders

The term "iodine-deficiency disorders" (IDD) is now used to denote all the effects of iodine deficiency on growth and development (Hetzel 1983). In the past, the term "goiter" was used to describe such effects, but IDD has now been generally adopted in the field of international nutrition and health. In the last 10 years, this reconceptualization has helped to focus more attention on the problem of iodine deficiency. For much of our historical treatment, however, we use the terms "goiter" and "IDD" interchangeably.

Extensive reviews of the global geographic prevalence of goiter have been published. One of these, by F. C. Kelly and W. W. Snedden, appeared as a World Health Organization (WHO) monograph in 1960. A second survey was done more recently by J. Stanbury and B. Hetzel (1980), and the reader is referred to these sources for a closer look at the many countries that still have a significant goiter problem. In general, goiter is associated with elevated areas and regions where there has been leaching of iodine from the soil due to glaciation, snow water, high rainfall, or floods. Thus the great mountain chains of the world, the European Alps, the Himalayas, and the Andes, have become well known as goiter areas, and in fact most mountainous regions throughout the world have iodine-deficient areas.

We now know that in addition to mountainous areas, flooded river valleys, such as those of the Ganges, Brahmaputra, and Irawaddy Rivers in Southeast Asia, have their soils leached of iodine and thus are also severely deficient in the mineral. These inescapable geographical facts mean that vast populations are at risk of iodine-deficiency disorders, and unfortunately it is likely that soil erosion in modern times is acting to increase the iodine-deficient areas of the world. It is, of course, axiomatic that populations totally dependent on food grown in such soil, as in systems of subsistence agriculture, will become iodine deficient.

History of Goiter and Cretinism

Descriptions and speculations about goiter and cretinism (the best-known iodine-deficiency disorders) go back to the ancient world. A historical review provides a fascinating succession of cultural concepts culminating in the twentieth century, when the causative role of iodine deficiency was established and the control of the disorders demonstrated. In the waning years of the twentieth century a global action program was organized in order to eliminate this ancient scourge of humankind by the beginning of the new millennium.

The Ancient Civilizations

An old reference to goiter is attributed to a mythical Chinese cultural hero, Shen-Nung. In his book *Shennung pen-ts'ao ching* (the divine husbandman's classic on materia medica), he is said to mention the seaweed sargassa as an effective remedy for goiter. Goiter is also mentioned in the *Shan Hai Ching* (which probably reached its present form about the second century B.C.), which attributes the disease to the poor quality of water. Other references during the Han dynasty (206 B.C. to A.D. 220) and the Wei dynasty (A.D. 200-264) mention deep mental emotions and "certain conditions of life in the mountain regions" as causes of goiter. The treatment of goiter with sargassa weeds is mentioned by the famous early-fourth-century Chinese medical writer Ge Hong. The Chinese also employed animal thyroid in the treatment of goiter – the use of deer thyroid is mentioned in a sixth-century text. Animal thyroid continued to be used in China and is discussed again by an eminent Chinese physician, Li Shih-chen, in his well-known 1596 herbal *Pen-ts'ao kang-mu* (materia medica arranged according to drug descriptions and technical aspects), in which preparations of pig and deer thyroid are mentioned. The continued use of seaweed and animal thyroid over so many hundreds of years in China suggests that there was certainly some benefit derived from these measures in the treatment of goiter.

Elsewhere in the ancient world there is less mention of the disease. In ancient Hindu literature incantations against goiter may be found in the Veda *Atharva* dating from around 2000 B.C. According to the Ebers papyrus, tumors of the neck were also known in ancient Egypt, where they were treated surgically.

In the famous fourth-century B.C. volume *Airs, Waters, and Places,* attributed to Hippocrates, drinking water was regarded as a cause of goiter. At about the beginning of the Christian era, Aulus Celsus described a fleshy tumor of the neck, which he incised to find that it contained honey-like substances and even small bones and hairs (probably a long-standing goiter). It was subsequently deduced by the Roman physician Galen in the second century A.D. that the glands of the neck, including the thyroid, had the function of secreting a fluid into the larynx and the pharynx. Such views continued to be accepted for many centuries and were held by such famous seventeenth- and eighteenth-century physicians as Marcello Malpighi and Herman Boerhaave.

Medieval Europe

It is of interest to note the attention given to goiter in paintings and sculptures of the Middle Ages. The late Professor F. Merke of Berne unearthed a number of fascinating examples from manuscripts and churches. The earliest depiction of goiter and cretinism is in a book in the Austrian National Library in Vienna – the *Reuner Musterbuch* – dating from 1215. The book was originally from the Cistercian Abbey in Reun near the city of Graz in Styria (Austria), where goiter was highly endemic until recent times. The picture (Figure IV.B.2.1) shows a figure with three large goiters and a stupid facial expression, brandishing a fool's staff in one hand while reaching up with the other toward a toad. This was doubtless a goitrous cretin. It was common to depict a fool grasping a cudgel as shown in this figure. The significance of the toad may be related to the popular use of live or dismembered frogs for the treatment of goiter. As Merke points out, this picture of the Reun cretin predates by some 300 years the recognition of the relationship between goiter and cretinism by Paracelsus (Philippus Aureolus Theophrastus Bombastus von Hohenheim).

According to F. de Quervain and C. Wegelin (1936), the term "cretin" most likely comes from the words "Christianus" or "Crestin" in the southeastern French dialect – referring to a *bon chrétien* because of the innocence of these subjects. These sufferers were in fact given special recognition in the medieval world and often regarded as angels or innocents with magical powers (Merke 1984). Clearly the Church did its best to fit them into the prevailing religious culture.

The Renaissance

Felix Plattner of Basel wrote a classic description of goiter and cretinism following a 1562 visit to the Valais:

> In Bremis, a village of the Valais, as I have seen myself, and in the Valley of Carinthia called Binthzgerthal [today the Pinzgau], it is usual that many infants suffer from innate folly [simplemindedness]. Besides, the head is sometimes misshapen: the tongue is huge and swollen; they are dumb; the throat is often goiterous. Thus, they present an ugly sight; and sitting in the streets and looking into the sun, and putting little sticks in between their fingers [a stick resting between their hands], twisting their bodies in various ways, with their mouths agape they provoke passersby to laughter and astonishment. (Langer 1960: 13–14)

Figure IV.B.2.1. "The Reun cretin" from the Reun Model Book, *Reuner Musterbuch,* produced by the Cistercian Abbey at Reun (near Graz), Austria, and dating from 1215. This model book covers everything that an educated "clericus" of the thirteenth century had to know. The cretin has a large trilobed goiter with the third lobe strung over the left shoulder. His right hand clutches at a frog (possibly for healing), and his left hand holds the "fool's scepter" in order to make the mental deficiency clear. (From Merke 1984, with permission.)

Figure IV.B.2.2. Madonna and child by Francesco di Gentili, fifteenth century. The madonna has a goiter and her child looks hypothyroid. (Pinacoteca, Vatican Museums, Rome; photo, Art Resource, New York.)

A study of goiter in sixteenth-century art was made by H. Hunziger (1915); the disease can be readily observed in the Madonnas of the Renaissance. Works by masters such as Jan van Eyck and Lucas Van der Leyden portray it, as do other paintings in the Sienese and Vatican galleries (Figure IV.B.2.2). All this may indicate that the condition was virtually accepted as normal because it was so common. In a later period goiter is also to be seen in the paintings of Peter Paul Rubens, Rogier van der Weyden, and Albrecht Dürer.

During the Renaissance, goiter was believed to be curable by the touch of a king. According to the king's personal physician, Henry IV of France caused 1,500 goiters to regress by touching the patient and using the formula "Le Roi te touche et Dieu te guerit." The "touch" was also practiced by many English kings; Charles II is alleged to have touched 9,200 persons suffering from the "King's Evil" or scrofula (with which goiter was often confused). According to newspaper reports, on March 20, 1710, Queen Anne revived the ancient custom of curing goiter and scrofula by the laying on of hands. As we pointed out, however, in the sixteenth century Paracelsus had recognized the association of goiter and cretinism and attributed the disease to a deficiency of minerals in drinking water. This reasoning rather neatly contrasts the scientific approach with the magic of the King's Touch!

The Seventeenth Century

The study of human anatomy prospered following the sixteenth-century pioneering work of Andreas Vesalius, Matteo Realdo Colombo, Hieronymus Fabricius ab Aquapendente, and Bartolomeo Eustachi. All of these anatomists noted the thyroid gland, which was called the "glandulus laryngis" by Vesalius. Fabricius recognized the connection between the glandulus laryngis and goiter. But the first clear description of the gland was penned in Latin in 1656 by an Englishman, Thomas Wharton (the translated title is *Adenography, or a Description of the Glands of the Entire Body*). Nonetheless, in the seventeenth century the function of the thyroid was not understood. It was usually regarded as secreting a fluid to "humidify" the walls of the larynx, the pharynx, and the trachea. In fact, the function of the thyroid was not understood until the latter part of the nineteenth century, when it was recognized to have an "internal" secretion in the form of the thyroid hormone, and not an external one.

The Eighteenth Century

In the eighteenth century there was a great escalation in scientific observations and the reporting of such observations. Many of these were collected in Denis Diderot's *Encylopédie* (1751–72), in which the term "cretin" appeared in print for the first time in an article by Diderot's co-editor Jean Le Rond d'Alembert. His definition of a cretin was that of "an imbecile who is deaf, dumb with a goiter hanging down to the waist."

The Nineteenth Century

Interest in and concern about the possibility of the control of goiter accelerated in the early nineteenth century when Napoleon Bonaparte ordered a systematic investigation of the disease. He did so because large numbers of young men from certain regions were being rejected as unfit for military duties. Moreover, Napoleon himself had probably seen something of the problem during his march into Italy through the goiter-infested Valais.

Iodine was isolated from the ashes of the seaweed *Fucus vesicularis* by B. Courtois in France in 1811, and in 1820 Jean François Coindet recommended iodine preparations for the treatment of goiter. However, soon afterward marked opposition developed to its employment because of the occurrence of symptoms of toxicity, which we now know was the result of excessive thyroid secretion.

The iodination of salt was first suggested by Jean Baptiste Boussingault, who resided for many years in Colombia in South America. The people among whom he lived obtained their salt from an abandoned mine and felt that this salt conferred special health benefits. In 1825 Boussingault analyzed the salt and found that it contained large quantities of iodine. In 1833 he suggested that iodized salt be used for the prevention of goiter. Unfortunately, an experiment carried out in France once more obscured the importance of iodine in the etiology of the disease. Goitrous families received salt fortified with 0.1 to 0.5 grams (g) of potassium iodide per kilogram (kg) of salt. But the high dosage produced symptoms of an excess thyroid secretion and consequently the treatment again fell into disrepute.

The Twentieth Century

Present-day practice in the prevention and control of goiter is based on the work of David Marine, who in 1915 declared that "endemic goitre is the easiest known disease to prevent." Marine and his colleague, O. Kimball, carried out the first large-scale trials with iodine in Akron, Ohio, from 1916 to 1920. About 4,500 girls between 11 and 18 years of age took part in the experiment. Roughly half of this group had goiter; the other half had normal thyroid activity. Of the group, 2,190 girls were given a daily dose of 0.2 g of sodium iodide in water for 10 days in the spring and 10 days in the autumn, making a total dose of 4.0 g over the year. The remaining 2,305 girls acted as controls. Two facts stand out from the data generated by this experiment: (1) In the group receiving sodium iodide, of 908 girls with a normal thyroid prior to treatment, only 2 (0.2 percent) developed goiter; however, in the control group, of 1,257 girls with previously normal thyroid, goiter appeared in 347 (27.6 percent); (2) in the group treated for goiter, 773 out of 1,282 girls with the disease (60.4 percent) showed a considerable decrease in the size of the thyroid, whereas in the control group, spontaneous regression of the goiter occurred in only 145 out of 1,048 girls (13.8 percent).

Thus both the prophylactic and the therapeutic effects were impressive. Iodism was very rare (only 11 cases) in spite of the extremely large doses of iodine, and the symptoms disappeared within a few days of stopping the administration of sodium iodide.

Mass prophylaxis of goiter with iodized salt was first introduced in 1924 on a community scale in Michigan (Kimball 1937), where it seems probable that the last glaciation had rendered the soil iodine deficient in that state and throughout much of the Great Lakes region. Goiter surveys of schoolchildren and iodine analyses of their drinking water were carried out in four representative counties, where the average goiter rate among 65,537 children was 38.6 percent. Table salt containing 1 part in 5,000 of potassium iodide was then introduced into the children's diet. By 1929 the average goiter rate had fallen to 9 percent. Moreover a follow-up survey conducted by B. Brush and J. Altland (1952) on 53,785 schoolchildren in the same counties showed a goiter rate of only 1.4 percent. It was also reported that in seven large

hospitals in Michigan thyroidectomies accounted for only 1 percent of all operations in 1950 compared with 3.2 percent in 1939. No toxic symptoms of iodide prophylaxis were observed.

The impact of iodized salt on the control of goiter was also vividly demonstrated in Switzerland. As this country is situated in the elevated region of the European Alps, the burden of goiter and cretinism was great throughout the country. In 1923, for example, the Canton of Berne, with a population of about 700,000, had to hospitalize 700 cretins incapable of social life. But with the Cantons' introduction of iodized salt, which proceeded throughout the 1920s, goiter rates fell steeply, and "deaf and dumb institutions" were later closed or used for other purposes.

Observations of Swiss Army recruits revealed definite evidence of this trend of rapid decline throughout the country. Between the years 1925 and 1947, the number of exemptions for military service fell from 31 to less than 1 per thousand. Moreover, following 60 years of the use of iodized salt in Switzerland, a recent review has made clear the benefits it provided in the prevention of all degrees of neurological damage in the Swiss population (Burgi, Supersaxo, and Selz 1990). Indeed, it is now clear that the "spontaneous" disappearance of cretinism throughout Europe was due to a dietary increase in iodine intake. The continued persistence of iodine deficiency and, consequently, goiter and cretinism in Europe is mainly associated with more isolated rural areas that have not undergone the sort of social and economic development that leads to dietary diversification. But even these cases could be completely prevented with the effective distribution of iodized salt.

Goiter and Iodine Deficiency

Iodine deficiency causes depletion of thyroid iodine stores with reduced daily production of the thyroid hormone (T_4). A fall in the blood level of T_4 triggers the secretion of increased amounts of pituitary thyroid stimulating hormone, which increases thyroid activity with hyperplasia of the thyroid. An increased efficiency of the thyroid iodide pump occurs with faster turnover of thyroid iodine, which can be seen in an increased thyroidal uptake of radioactive isotopes ^{131}I and [125]I. These features were first demonstrated in the field in the now classic observations of Stanbury and colleagues (1954) in the Andes of Argentina.

Iodine deficiency is revealed by a determination of urine iodine excretion using either 24-hour samples or, more conveniently, casual samples with determination of iodine content per gram of creatinine. Normal iodine intake is 100 to 150 micrograms per day (μg/day), which corresponds to a urinary iodine excretion in this range (Stanbury and Hetzel 1980). In general, in endemic goiter areas the intake is well below 100 μg/day and goiter is usually seen when the level is below 50 µg/day (Pretell et al. 1972). The rate increases as the iodine excretion falls so that goiter may be almost universal at levels below 10 µg/day. The iodine content of drinking water is also low in areas with endemic goiter (Karmarkar et al. 1974).

Goiter, however, can also arise from causes other than iodine deficiency. Foremost among these are a variety of agents known as goitrogens. Recent research (Ermans et al. 1980; Delange, Iteke, and Ermans 1982) has shown that staple foods from the developing world such as cassava, maize, bamboo shoots, sweet potatoes, lima beans, and millets contain cyanogenic glucosides that are capable of liberating large quantities of cyanide by hydrolysis. Not only is the cyanide toxic but the metabolite in the body is predominantly thiocyanate, which is a goitrogen. Fortunately, these glycosides are usually located in the inedible portions of most plants, or if in the edible portion, in such small quantities that they do not cause a major problem. But such is not the case with cassava, which is cultivated extensively in developing countries and represents an essential source of calories for tropical populations of more than 200 million (Delange et al. 1982).

The role of cassava in the etiology of endemic goiter and endemic cretinism was demonstrated by F. Delange and colleagues (1982) in studies conducted in nonmountainous Zaire, and their observations were confirmed by G. Maberly and colleagues (1981) in Sarawak, Malaysia. One major effect of cassava consumption can be to increase iodine loss from the body by increasing urinary excretion.

It is important to note, however, that chronic consumption of large quantities of cassava does not necessarily result in the development of endemic goiter. Such development depends on the balance between the dietary supply of iodine and the thiocyanate (SCN) generated from the cyanide (hydrocyanic acid [HCN]) content of the cassava. The cyanide content of cassava varies with the linamarin content, and this in turn varies with traditional detoxification processes – including soaking in water before consumption, which greatly reduces the HCN content. However, sun-drying of cassava (as in the Ubangi region of Zaire) is not effective in reducing the HCN content, which can, in turn, produce a high prevalence of goiter and endemic cretinism.

A normal or high iodine intake will protect against the goitrogenic effect of the SCN. In fact, a Belgian group has shown that an iodine to SCN (I:SCN) ratio greater than 7 will achieve this protection. Goiter occurs if the ratio is about 3 and will be of high prevalence when the ratio is below 2. At this low ratio endemic cretinism will also be found in the population.

In summary, four factors will determine the SCN ratio: (1) the level of iodine intake in the diet, (2) the HCN content of fresh cassava roots and leaves, (3) the efficiency of the detoxification process used during the preparation of cassava-based foods, and (4) the frequency and quantity of consumption of these foods.

Cretinism and Iodine Deficiency

The gradual disappearance of cretinism in Europe in the early decades of the twentieth century led to the condition being largely forgotten. But in the 1960s endemic cretinism was virtually rediscovered almost simultaneously in a number of the more remote areas of the world, among them New Guinea, Zaire, India, Indonesia, China, and Brazil.

The clinical manifestations of the condition found in these areas have now been reported in considerable detail (Pharoah et al. 1980), and field studies of thyroid gland function and iodine metabolism have also been made in many countries. Evidence of the association of cretinism with severe iodine deficiency and high goiter rates has been uniformly reported.

One noticeable feature of the condition since its rediscovery has been the occurrence of a wide range of defects in individuals. These range from isolated mental deficiency to deaf-mutism of varying degree to a varying severity of paralysis of the arms and legs. But there are also individuals who appear to be normal apart from some coordination defect, all of which indicates that endemic cretinism is part of a spectrum of defects within an iodine-deficient population. And endemic cretinism is, as we shall see, a community or population disease.

It was R. McCarrison, reporting in 1908 from what was then called the North West Frontier of India (including the Karakoram Mountains, which are now in northern Pakistan), who first clearly distinguished two types of endemic cretins – the "nervous" and the "myxedematous" – from a series of 203 patients whom he had studied. In the nervous type, he recognized mental defect, deaf-mutism, and a spastic diplegia (paralysis) with a spastic rigidity, affecting the legs predominantly, that produced a characteristic walk or gait. Squint was also noted. By contrast, the myxedematous type had all the characteristics of severe hypothyroidism: dry swollen skin and tongue, deep hoarse voice, apathy, and mental deficiency. McCarrison regarded this condition as identical with "sporadic cretinism." He found deaf-mutism present in 87 percent of his 203 cases.

These two types of cretinism are also readily seen in China, where the neurological type is the predominant form. In Hetian district in Xinjiang (only some 300 kilometers east of Gilgit, where McCarrison made his original observations in the first decade of the twentieth century), a similar pattern was observed in 1982 (Figure IV.B.2.3) with neurological, hypothyroid, and mixed types present (Hetzel 1989). Later, these observations in China were confirmed by S. Boyages and colleagues (1988).

Figure IV.B.2.3. A dwarfed cretin from Xingjiang, China, who is also deaf-mute. This condition is completely preventable. Right: the "barefoot doctor" from her village. Both women are about 35 years of age. (Courtesy of Dr. T. Ma, Tianjin, China.)

It is apparent that these two types of cretinism are distinct conditions. As McCarrison recognized, the features of the myxedematous type are essentially the same as those of sporadic cretinism. However, the myxedematous type is associated with the occurrence of hypothyroidism, which causes endemic cretinism, the latter a result of endemic goiter triggered by severe iodine deficiency in an entire community. By contrast, sporadic cretinism occurs all over the world whether or not iodine deficiency is present. It is usually found with evidence of an absent or misplaced thyroid or with a congenital defect in the biosynthesis of the hormone. To prevent confusion, the term "congenital hypothyroidism" is now generally preferred to sporadic cretinism.

It is now established that endemic cretinism, in its fully developed form characterized by severe mental deficiency, deaf-mutism, and spastic diplegia, is epidemiologically associated with high rates of goiter and severe iodine deficiency (levels of 25 μg/day or less compared to a normal intake of 80–150 μg/day), whereas goiter alone is seen at levels below 50 μg/day (Pharoah et al. 1980; Hetzel and Maberly 1986; Hetzel, Potter, and Dulberg 1990). However, as mentioned previously, the apparent spontaneous disappearance of endemic cretinism in southern Europe raised considerable doubt about its relationship to iodine deficiency (Hetzel 1989).

The hypothesis that there was such a relationship was tested for the first time in a controlled trial beginning in the 1960s. Such testing was made possible by the development of a new method for correction of severe iodine deficiency in Papua New Guinea in the form of the injection of iodized oil (McCullagh 1963; Buttfield et al. 1965; Buttfield and Hetzel 1967). Iodized oil or saline injections were given to alternate families in the Jimi River District in the Western Highlands at the time of the first census (1966). Each child born subsequently was examined for evidence of motor retardation, as assessed by the usual measurements involving sitting, standing, or walking, and for evidence of deafness. Examination was carried out without knowledge as to whether the mother had received iodized oil or saline injections (Pharoah, Buttfield, and Hetzel 1971).

Infants presenting with a full syndrome of hearing and speech abnormalities, together with abnormalities of motor development with or without squint, were classified as suffering from endemic cretinism. By these criteria, there were 7 cretins born to women who had received iodized oil out of a total of 687 children. In 6 of these 7 cases, conception had occurred prior to the iodized oil injections (Figure IV.B.2.4). In the untreated group, there were 25 endemic cretins out of a total of 688 children born since the trial began. In 5 of these 25, conception had occurred prior to saline being given.

It was concluded that an injection of iodized oil given prior to a woman's pregnancy could prevent the occurrence of the neurological syndrome of endemic cretinism in the infant. The occurrence of the syndrome in those who were pregnant at the time of oil injection indicated that the damage probably occurred during the first half of pregnancy (Pharoah et al. 1971).

Subsequent studies in Papua New Guinea have revealed a motor coordination defect in apparently normal children subjected to severe iodine deficiency during pregnancy (Connolly, Pharoah, and Hetzel 1979; Pharoah et al. 1981). There is also evidence of an associated intellectual defect (Pharoah et al. 1984; Fierro-Benitez 1986). Thus it is apparent that the effects of severe iodine deficiency in pregnancy go beyond endemic cretinism to affect children in other unpleasant ways. Such observations have been confirmed in Indonesia and Spain (Bleichrodt et al. 1987) and in China (Boyages et al. 1989).

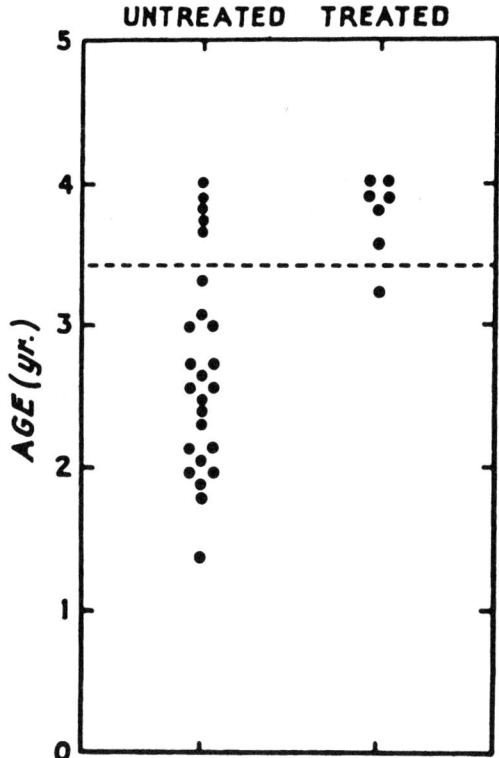

Figure IV.B.2.4. The results of a controlled trial of iodized oil injection in the Jimi River district of the highlands of Papua New Guinea. Alternate mothers were given an injection of iodized oil and saline in September 1966. All newborn children were followed up for the next five years. Each dot represents a cretin child. The figure shows that mothers given iodized oil injections do not have subsequent cretin children, in comparison with the persistence in the untreated group. (From Pharaoh et al. 1971, with permission.)

The importance of the link between iodine deficiency and brain development has led to animal model studies that shed light on the relationship and the mechanisms involved. These studies have revealed reduced brain weight with a reduced number of brain cells during and at the end of pregnancy in iodine-deficient rats, sheep, and marmosets (Hetzel, Chevadev, and Potter 1988). The effect of iodine deficiency is mediated through reduced secretion (by both the maternal and fetal thyroids), which in turn is associated with severe fetal hypothyroidism. To date, the syndrome of neurological cretinism has not been reproduced in an animal species (Hetzel et al. 1988).

The Iodine-Deficiency Disorders

Our concept of the effects of iodine deficiency has undergone a rapid evolution since 1970. Originally

the problem was designated as goiter, which (although a fascinating phenomenon for many thyroidologists) cannot by itself justify a high priority for prevention programs in developing countries. As noted in the introduction, the various effects of iodine deficiency at different stages of life are now included in IDD, which has been generally adopted (Hetzel 1983; *Lancet* 1983). These various disorders (listed in Table IV.B.2.1) occur in populations subjected to iodine deficiency, and all can be prevented by correction of the deficiency. We will now review IDD in detail by reference to the four stages of life in which it occurs.

Iodine Deficiency in the Fetus

In iodine-deficient areas there is an increased rate of abortions and stillbirths, which can be reduced by correction of iodine deficiency (McMichael, Potter, and Hetzel 1980). An increased rate of stillbirths has also been observed in iodine-deficient sheep. In iodine-deficient pastures, lamb losses can be reduced by correction of iodine deficiency, and, it has been suggested, the same is true for goats (Hetzel and Maberly 1986). Pregnancy losses have also been produced experimentally with hypothyroidism. Studies in hypothyroid guinea pigs (produced by surgical removal of the thyroid) reveal a three- to fourfold increase in abortions and stillbirths that can be virtually eliminated by replacement therapy with thyroxine during pregnancy (McMichael et al. 1980).

Table IV.B.2.1. *The spectrum of iodine-deficiency disorders (IDD)*

Fetus	Abortions
	Stillbirths
	Congenital anomalies
	Increased perinatal mortality
	Increased infant mortality
	Neurological cretinism
	mental deficiency
	deaf-mutism
	spastic diplegia
	squint
	Myxedematous cretinism
	dwarfism
	mental deficiency
	psychomotor defects
Neonate	Neonatal goiter
	Neonatal hypothyroidism
Child and adolescent	Goiter
	Juvenile hypothyroidism
	Impaired mental function
	Retarded physical development
Adult	Goiter with its complications
	Hypothyroidism
	Impaired mental function
	Iodine-induced hyperthyroidism

In this same vein, data from Zaire and Papua New Guinea indicate an increased perinatal mortality that reflects an increase in stillbirths. There is also increased infant mortality. In Zaire, the results of a controlled trial of iodized oil injections given in the latter half of pregnancy revealed a substantial fall in perinatal and infant mortality with improved birth weight (Thilly 1981). Low birth weight is generally (whatever the cause) associated with a higher rate of congenital anomalies.

Recent evidence indicates that the various effects of iodine deficiency on the fetus (including abortion, stillbirth, congenital anomalies, and the varying manifestations of cretinism) probably arise from the lowered level of thyroid hormone T_4 in the iodine-deficient mother. The more severe the reduction in the level of maternal T_4, the greater the threat to the integrity of the fetus – a proposition supported by animal data on the causes of abortions and stillbirths (Hetzel et al. 1990).

Iodine Deficiency in the Neonate
In former times neonatal goiter was commonly seen in iodine-deficient areas (Hetzel and Maberly 1986). Neonatal hypothyroidism remains a well-recognized cause of mental defect in the Western world. This is because the development of the brain is dependent on an adequate supply of thyroxine. Only about one-third of normal brain development occurs before delivery of the infant; the other two-thirds is completed in the first two years of life. Hence a normal level of thyroxine is extremely important both during and after pregnancy.

In many countries every newborn child is tested for the level of blood thyroxine (usually taken from a prick in the heel at the fourth and fifth days of life). If, after further investigation, the level is found to be low, and a lowered state of thyroid gland function is indicated, then replacement treatment with daily tablets of thyroxine is begun immediately. The results of such a procedure have been evaluated in several countries and deemed to be generally excellent, provided treatment is given early, meaning within the first month of life. In Western countries, the incidence of such an abnormality runs at 1 per 3,500 live births, and results from (1) the absence of the thyroid; (2) an abnormal position of the thyroid (ectopia); or (3) a defect in the "biochemical machinery" required to produce thyroxine (called a biosynthetic defect) (Burrow 1980).

A much higher incidence, however, is found in iodine-deficient environments. Indeed, observations of blood taken from the umbilical vein (in the umbilical cord), just after birth, have revealed a rate of neonatal hypothyroidism of some 10 percent in Zaire and 5 to 10 percent in northern India and Nepal (Kochupillai and Pandav 1987). In the most severely iodine-deficient environments (more than 50 percent have urinary iodine below 25 µg/gram creatinine, which is 25 percent of normal intake), the incidence

of neonatal hypothyroidism is 75 to 115 per 1,000 births. By contrast in Delhi, where only mild iodine deficiency is present with a low prevalence of goiter and no cretinism, the incidence drops to 6 per 1,000. But in control areas without goiter the level is only 1 per 1,000.

In India chemical observations have been extended to studies of the Intelligence Quotient (IQ) and hearing ability of schoolchildren. It has been shown that there is a marked reduction in IQ scores in villages with a high rate of (chemical) hypothyroidism in comparison with villages without iodine deficiency. Nerve deafness is also much more common, and there is evidence of lowered growth hormone levels in the blood.

The blood level of thyroxine in the neonate is an important indicator of the severity of iodine deficiency. Monitoring of these levels is now being done in India on samples of cord blood taken by birth attendants and subsequently spread on specially prepared filter paper. The samples are then mailed to a biochemistry laboratory where radioimmunoassay is carried out. This arrangement offers a very convenient and inexpensive method for the assessment of the severity of iodine deficiency provided a suitable functioning laboratory is available. The equipment is complex and costly but automated so that large numbers of samples can be processed. Such laboratories are now being gradually established in India, China, and Indonesia, where there are very large iodine-deficient populations. Data from these laboratories indicate a much greater risk of mental defect in severely iodine-deficient populations than is indicated by the presence of cretinism. Unfortunately, because of a gross inadequacy of manpower and money, it is just not possible to diagnose and treat these infants in most developing-world countries as they are treated in the West. This problem, of course, points up the overwhelming importance of prevention.

Iodine Deficiency in Infancy and Childhood
Iodine deficiency in children is characteristically associated with goiter, the classification of which has now been standardized by the World Health Organization (Dunn et al. 1986). Girls have a higher prevalence than boys and the rate increases with age so that it reaches a maximum with adolescence. Thus observations of goiter rates in schoolchildren between the ages of 8 and 14 provide a convenient indication of the presence of iodine deficiency in a community. The congregation of children in schools is a great advantage in providing access to a population and a place where collection of urine samples for detection of urinary iodine can be conveniently carried out.

As already noted, the prevention and control of goiter in schoolchildren was first demonstrated by Marine and Kimball in Akron, Ohio, in 1917. However, Marine and Kimball (1921) recognized that goiter was only part of IDD. They said:

The prevention of goitre means vastly more than cervical (neck) deformities. It means in addition, the prevention of those forms of physical and mental degeneration such as cretinism, mutism and idiocy which are dependent on thyroid insufficiency. Further it would prevent the development of thyroid adenomas which are an integral and essential part of endemic goitre in man and due to the same stimulus. (Marine and Kimball 1921: 1070)

Recent studies of schoolchildren living in iodine-deficient areas in a number of countries indicate impaired school performance and lower IQ scores in comparison with matched groups from non-iodine-deficient areas. In Papua New Guinea, for example, children involved in the controlled trial in the Western Highlands have been tested periodically. Differences in bimanual dexterity were revealed by threading beads and putting pegs into a pegboard – differences that correlated with whether or not the mother was severely iodine deficient (Connolly et al. 1979). Indeed, critical studies using a wide range of psychological tests have shown that the mental development of children from iodine-deficient areas lags behind that of children from non-iodine-deficient areas. But the differences in psychomotor development became apparent only after the age of 2½ years (Bleichrodt et al. 1987; Boyages et al. 1989).

Another question has been whether these differences can be affected by correction of the iodine deficiency. In a pioneering study initiated in Ecuador by R. Fierro-Benitez and colleagues (1986), the long-term effects of iodized oil injections have been assessed by comparison of two highland villages. In one of them (Tocachi) such injections were administered. The other (La Esperanza) was used as a control. Particular attention was paid to 128 children aged 8 to 15 whose mothers had received iodized oil prior to the second trimester of pregnancy and, of course, a matched control group of 293 children of similar age. All children were periodically examined from birth at key stages in their development. Women in Tocachi were injected or reinjected in 1970, 1974, and 1978. Assessments in 1973, 1978, and 1981 revealed the following:

> Scholastic achievement was better in the children of treated mothers when measured in terms of school year reached, for age, school dropout rate, failure rate, years repeated and school marks. There was no difference between the two groups by a certain test (Terman-Merrill, Wechsler scale, or Goodenough). Both groups were impaired in school performance – in reading, writing and mathematics, but more notably the children of untreated mothers. (Fierro-Benitez et al. 1986: 195)

The results indicate the significant role of iodine deficiency, but other factors were also important in the

school performance of these Ecuadorean children, such as social deprivation and other nutritional difficulties.

In 1982 the results were reported of a controlled trial carried out with oral iodized oil in the small Bolivian Highland village of Tiquipaya, 2,645 meters above sea level (Bautista et al. 1982). Each child in the treatment group received an oral dose of 1.0 milliliter (ml) iodized oil (475 mg iodine), whereas children in the second group received 1.0 ml of a mineral oil containing no iodine but of a similar brown color. Subsequent assessment was double-blind so that the group of the child was not known to the examiners. Interestingly, on follow-up 22 months later, the urinary iodine had increased and goiter size had decreased in both groups. This reflected "contamination" of the village environment with iodine, probably the result of fecal excretion by those who had received the iodized oil injections. There were no differences between the two treatment groups in growth rate or in the performance with the tests. However, improvement in IQ could be demonstrated in all those children, regardless of their group, who showed significant reduction of goiter. This was particularly so in girls. It was concluded that correction of iodine deficiency may improve the mental performance of school-age children, but that a bigger dose should be given.

Such studies are now being conducted in a number of countries. More data are required. However, data generated to date point to significant improvement in the mental performance of schoolchildren by the correction of iodine deficiency.

Iodine Deficiency in the Adult

The common effect of iodine deficiency in adults is goiter, although characteristically there is an absence of classical clinical hypothyroidism in adults with endemic goiter. Nonetheless, laboratory evidence of hypothyroidism with reduced T_4 levels is common, associated with apathy, lethargy, and lack of energy.

Iodine administration in the form of iodized salt, iodized bread, or iodized oil have all been demonstrated to be effective in the prevention of goiter in adults (Hetzel 1989). Iodine administration may also reduce existing goiter, particularly in the case of iodized oil injections. The clearly observed benefits of iodine supplementation promote ready acceptance of such measures by people living in iodine-deficient communities.

Such benefits have been well described by J. Li and X. Wang (1987) for the northeast Chinese village of Jixian. In 1978 Jixian had a population of 1,313 people, of whom 65 percent had goiter and 11.4 percent were cretins. The latter included many severe cases and the village was known locally as "the village of idiots." The economic development of the village was retarded; girls from other villages did not want to marry into and live in that village. The intelligence of the student population was known to be low (children aged 10 had a mental development equivalent to those aged 7).

Iodized salt was introduced in 1978, and by 1982 the goiter rate had dropped to 4 percent. No cretins had been born since 1978. The attitude of the people changed greatly, with their approach to life being much more positive than before iodization. Average income increased from 43 yuan per capita in 1981 to 223 yuan in 1982 and 414 yuan by 1984 – the latter higher than the average per capita income of the district.

Before iodization, no family owned a radio in the village. But after iodization 55 families acquired television sets. Some 44 girls have arrived from other villages to marry boys in Jixian, and 7 men have joined the People's Liberation Army, whereas before men from the village had been rejected because of goiter. Such improvements in the level of living were mainly due to the correction of hypothyroidism by iodized salt.

The Demography of IDD

The prevention and control of IDD must be regarded as an urgent problem for the 1 billion of the world's peoples living in an iodine-deficient environment (Table IV.B.2.2). Of these, 350 million live in China and 200 million in India (*World Health Organization Report* 1990) (Map IV.B.2.1).

These populations are at risk of developing one or more of the iodine-deficiency conditions that can retard physical, social, and economic growth and development. Indeed, more than 5 million of the world's people are estimated to be suffering from mental retardation as gross cretins. But in addition,

Table IV.B.2.2. *Estimated prevalence of iodine-deficiency disorders in developing countries, by region and numbers of persons at risk (in millions)*

	At risk	Goiter	Overt cretinism
Africa	227	39	0.5
Latin America	60	30	0.3
Southeast Asia	280	100	4.0
Asia (other countries including China)	400	30	0.9
Eastern Mediterranean	33	12	–
Total	1,000	211	5.7

Source: From *World Health Organization Report* (1990).

three to five times this number suffer from lesser degrees of mental defect because their mothers were iodine-deficient during pregnancy (WHO 1990).

Iodine Technology for Prevention

Iodized Salt
Iodized salt has been the major preventive method used against iodine deficiency since the 1920s. However, there are serious difficulties in the production and quality maintenance of iodized salt for the millions that are iodine deficient. In Asia, the cost of iodized salt production and distribution at present is of the order of 3 to 5 cents per person per year. This

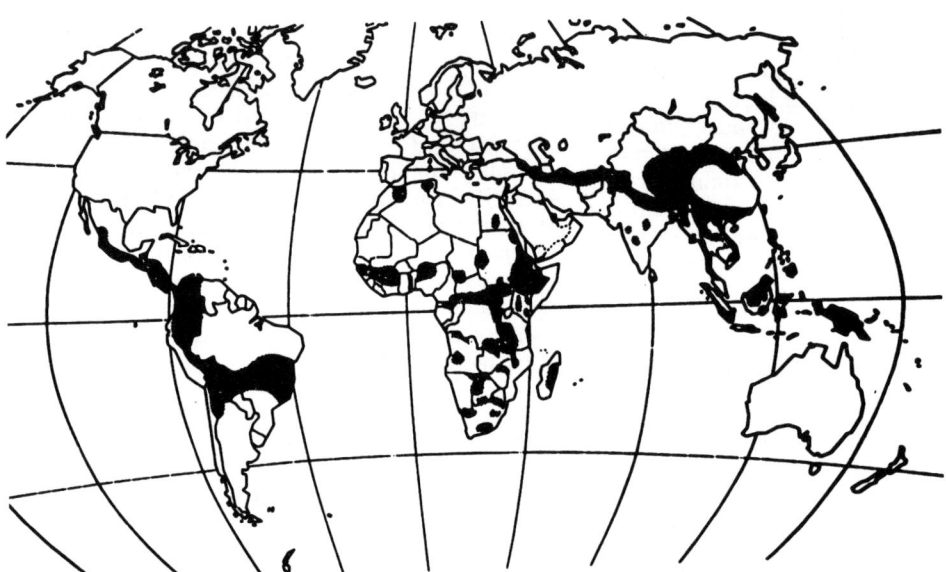

Map IV.B.2.1. The distribution of iodine-deficiency disorders in developing countries. Large populations in Asia provide two-thirds of the one billion at risk due to iodine deficiency of the soil. (From Hetzel 1989 and WHO 1990, with permission.)

must be considered cheap in relation to the benefits produced but there remain logistical problems of getting the salt to the iodine-deficient subjects. In addition, there may be problems with the iodine content – the salt may be left uncovered or exposed to heat, which leads to loss of iodine by volatilization.

Finally, there is the difficulty of getting people to consume the salt. Although the addition of iodine makes no difference to the taste of salt, the introduction of a new variety of the mineral to an area where it has been available, and its source familiar, is likely to be resisted. In the Chinese provinces of Xinjiang and Inner Mongolia, for example, the strong preference of the people for desert salt (of very low iodine content) led to a mass iodized oil injection program to prevent cretinism (Ma et al. 1982).

Iodized Oil by Injection

The value of iodized oil injection in the prevention of endemic goiter and endemic cretinism was first established in New Guinea with trials involving the use of saline injection as a control. Experience in South America and elsewhere has confirmed this value (Hetzel et al. 1980), and, in fact, the quantitative correction of severe iodine deficiency for a period of over four years by a single intramuscular injection (2 to 4 ml) has been demonstrated (Buttfield and Hetzel 1967). Iodized oil can be administered through local health

services, where they exist, or by special teams. In New Guinea, public health teams carried out the injection of a population in excess of 100,000, along with the injection of triple antigen. In Nepal 4 million injections have now been given. In Indonesia some 1 million injections were given between 1974 and 1978, together with the massive distribution of iodized salt (Djokomoeljanto, Tarwotjo, and Maspaitella 1983). A further 4.9 million injections have been given by specially trained paramedical personnel in the period 1979 to 1983. In Xinjiang in China, 707,000 injections were given by "barefoot doctors" between 1978 and 1981, and a further 300,000 to 400,000 injections were being given in 1982 (Ma et al. 1982). Iodized oil is singularly appropriate for the isolated village community so characteristic of mountainous endemic goiter areas. Iodized walnut oil and iodized soybean oil are more recently developed preparations and have been used on a wide scale in China since 1980. As with iodized salt, the striking regression of goiter following iodized oil injection ensures general acceptance of the measure (Figure IV.B.2.5).

In at-risk areas the oil should be administered to all females up to the age of 45 years, and to all males up to the age of 15 years and perhaps beyond. A repeat of the injection would be required in three to five years depending on dose and age. With children the need for a repeat injection is greater than with adults, and

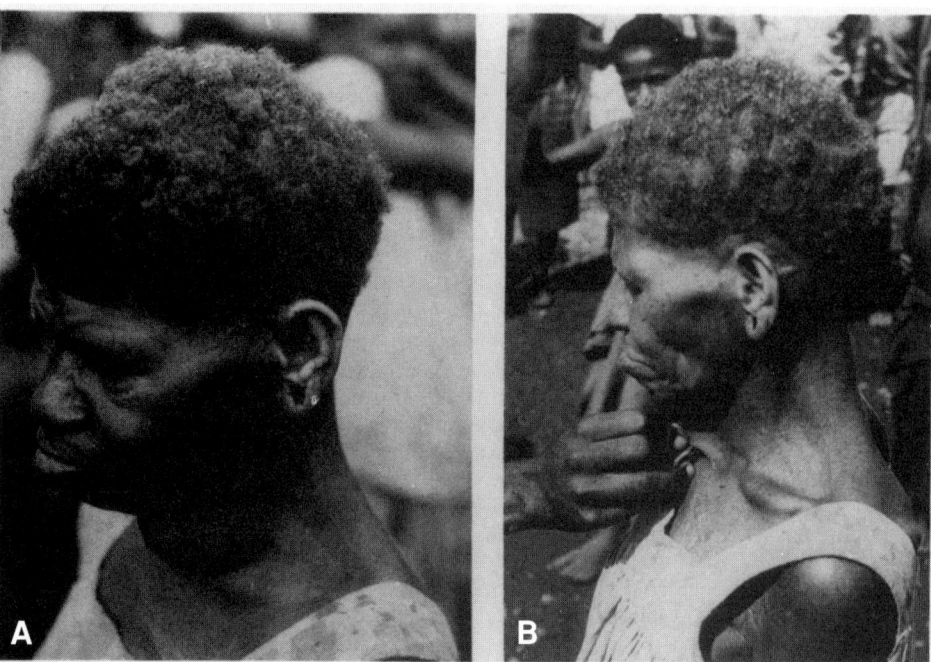

Figure IV.B.2.5. Nodular goiter in a New Guinean (A) before and (B) three months after injection of iodized oil. The photos demonstrate the subsidence of goiter following the injection of iodized oil. (From Butterfield and Hetzel 1967, with permission.)

the dose should be repeated in three years if severe iodine deficiency persists (Stanbury et al. 1974).

Disadvantages of injections are the immediate discomfort produced and the infrequent development of abscesses at the site of injection. Sensitivity phenomena have not been reported (Hetzel et al. 1980), but a potential difficulty is disease transmission through syringes (hepatitis B or HIV infection). A major problem with injections is their cost, although the expense has been reduced with mass packaging to an order of magnitude similar to the costs of iodized salt, especially when the population to be injected is restricted to women of reproductive age and to children, and a primary health-care team is available (Hetzel 1983; SEARO/WHO 1985; Dunn et al. 1986).

Iodized Oil by Mouth

The effectiveness of a single oral administration of iodized oil for one to two years has been demonstrated in South America and in Burma. But recent studies in India and China reveal that oral iodized oil lasts only half as long as a similar dose given by injection (Dunn 1987b). However, oral administration avoids the hazard of transmitting hepatitis B or HIV infection through contaminated syringes. Moreover, oral administration of iodized oil to children could be carried out through baby health centers and schools. A 1 ml dose (480 mg) covers a period of 12 months at present.

Less Common Prevention Technologies

The use of other methods of iodization such as iodized bread and iodized water has not proceeded to the mass population level but may be indicated in special situations.

Iodized Bread

Iodized bread has been used in Holland and in Australia, and detailed observations are available from the Australian island of Tasmania. Since 1949 the Tasmanian population has received iodine dietary supplements in the form of weekly tablets of potassium iodide (10 mg) given to infants, children, and pregnant women through baby health clinics, schools, and antenatal clinics whenever possible. The prevalence of endemic goiter fell progressively during the next 16 years but was not eliminated. The failure to eliminate the disease completely was traced to a lack of cooperation by a number of schools in the distribution of the iodide tablets. The distribution through the child health centers to infants and preschool children was also ineffective because of the children's irregular attendance.

For this reason a decision was made to change the method of prophylaxis from iodide tablets to iodized bread. The use of potassium iodate up to 20 parts per million (ppm) as a bread improver was authorized by the National Health and Medical Research Council of Australia in May 1963, and the necessary legislation was passed by the Tasmanian Parliament in October 1964.

The effects of bread iodization were measured by a series of surveys of palpable goiter rates in schoolchildren. A definite decrease in the visible goiter rate was apparent by 1969. Yet studies of urinary iodide excretion and plasma inorganic iodide in May 1967 revealed no excessive intake of iodide. Correction of iodine deficiency was confirmed by evidence of a fall of 24-hour radioiodine uptake levels in hospital subjects as well as normal plasma inorganic iodine concentration and urine iodine excretion (Stewart et al. 1971).

Thus bread iodization was effective in correcting iodine deficiency in Tasmania in the 1960s. However, today there is a greater diversity of sources for dietary iodine. It is readily available from milk due to the use of iodophors in the dairy industry, and it is also available from ice cream due to the use of alginate as a thickener.

Iodized Water

Reduction in goiter rate from 61 percent to 30 percent with 79 percent of goiters showing visible reduction has been demonstrated following water iodization in Sarawak (Maberly, Eastman, and Corcoran 1981). Similar results have been obtained with preliminary studies in Thailand by Romsai Suwanik and his group at the Siriraj Hospital, Bangkok, and in Sicily (Hetzel 1989). Iodized water may be a more convenient preventive measure than iodized salt and there may be less likelihood of iodine-induced thyrotoxicosis. Certainly this method is appropriate at the village level if a specific source of drinking water can be identified.

The Hazards of Iodization

A mild increase in incidence of thyrotoxicosis has been described following iodized salt programs in Europe and South America and following the introduction of iodized bread in Holland and Tasmania. A few cases have been noted following iodized oil administration in South America. That no cases have yet been described in New Guinea, India, or Zaire is probably due to the scattered nature of the population in small villages and limited opportunities for observation. In Tasmania it was apparent that a rise in incidence of thyrotoxicosis accompanied a rise in iodine intake from below normal to normal levels due to iodized bread, which was finally introduced in April 1966 (Stewart et al. 1971). The condition can be readily controlled with antithyroid drugs or radio-iodine. Nonetheless, in general, iodization should be minimized for those over the age of 40 because of the risk of thyrotoxicosis (Stanbury et al. 1974; Hetzel 1983).

International Action Toward Elimination

Since 1978, there has been increasing concern about a lag in the application of our new knowledge of the iodine-deficiency disorders and their prevention

(Stanbury and Hetzel 1980; Hetzel 1983). A symposium at the Fourth Asian Congress of Nutrition in Bangkok in 1983 brought the problem to the attention of the international nutrition community with the preparation of a comprehensive report on the "Prevention and Control of Iodine Deficiency Disorders for the United Nations System" (*Lancet* 1983).

This report, which was subsequently published (Hetzel 1988b), indicated the need for the establishment of an expert group of scientists and other health professionals committed to bridging the wide gap between research and action. At a WHO/UNICEF Intercountry Meeting in March 1985, in Delhi, a group of 12 such experts agreed to found the International Council for Control of Iodine Deficiency Disorders (ICCIDD). In 1986 an International Board was established and the ICCIDD was formally inaugurated at Kathmandu, Nepal (*Lancet* 1986a).

The ICCIDD has welcomed as members all who have concern for and expertise in IDD and IDD control (*Lancet* 1986a). The main role of the ICCIDD is to make such expertise available to international agencies and national governments who have responsibility for the control of IDD, and so bridge the great gap between available knowledge and its application. At the inaugural meeting in Kathmandu, Nepal, a global review of the IDD problem took place along with an appraisal of current expertise in iodine technology and IDD control programs. This meeting led to the first ICCIDD monograph (*Lancet* 1986b; Hetzel, Dunn, and Stanbury 1987).

The ICCIDD is now a global, multidisciplinary group, consisting of some 300 members from 70 countries, and has a quarterly newsletter and a secretariat in Adelaide, Australia. Support since 1985 has been received from UNICEF (New York) and the Australian government and since 1991 from the Canadian government.

Since 1987, the ICCIDD has become fully active in facilitating interagency cooperation in the prevention and control of IDD by holding a series of interagency meetings and establishing regional interagency working groups (particularly involving WHO and UNICEF, but also some of the bilaterals). A Global Action Plan has now been endorsed by the UN agencies to take account of these developments. The purpose of the Global Action Plan is to provide global and regional support for the establishment and monitoring of effective national IDD control programs. It includes activities at the national, regional, and global levels.

At the national level, such activities include initial assessments, national seminars, communication packages, intersectoral planning with a National IDD Control Commission, evaluation, and monitoring with laboratory services. In Indonesia and China, International Working Groups have now been established by ICCIDD in collaboration with WHO and UNICEF.

At the regional level, the development of a series of regional IDD working groups provides for the necessary close working relationship between ICCIDD, WHO, and UNICEF. The IDD Task Force for Africa has been particularly successful in developing a coordinated strategy involving both multilateral and bilateral agencies.

At the global level, major functions include advocacy and the provision of public information, as well as the maintenance of a global monitoring system.

In view of the progress already achieved and the promising potential of current and planned national prevention and control programs, the goal of eliminating IDD as a major public health problem by the year 2000 was reaffirmed by the 1990 World Health Assembly (*World Health Organization Report* 1990). An escalation of funding now became an essential step in the achievement of this goal.

In September 1990, the World Summit for Children held at the United Nations in New York was attended by 71 heads of state and 80 other government representatives. The World Summit signed a Declaration and approved a Plan of Action that included the elimination of IDD as a public health problem by the year 2000.

This summit was followed in October 1991 by a conference entitled "Ending Hidden Hunger," which was a policy and promotional meeting on micronutrients including iodine, vitamin A, and iron. It was attended by multidisciplinary delegations from 55 countries with major IDD problems. These delegates were nominated by heads of state in response to an invitation by the director general of the World Health Organization, H. Nakajima, and the executive director of UNICEF, James Grant. At this meeting there was a firm commitment to the goal of eliminating IDD and vitamin A deficiency and reducing iron deficiency by one-third of 1990 levels. These various developments encourage the hope that very significant progress would be made toward the elimination of IDD during the last decade of the twentieth century with great benefits to the quality of life of the many millions affected (Hetzel 1989).

Basil S. Hetzel

Bibliography

Bautista, S., P. A. Barker, J. T. Dunn, et al. 1982. The effects of oral iodized oil on intelligence, thyroid status, and somatic growth in school-aged children from an area of endemic goitre. *American Journal of Clinical Nutrition* 35: 127-34.

Bleichrodt, N., I. Garcia, C. Rubio, et al. 1987. Developmental disorders associated with severe iodine deficiency. In *The prevention and control of iodine deficiency disorders,* ed. B. S. Hetzel, J. T. Dunn, and J. B. Stanbury, 65-84. Amsterdam.

Boyages, S. C., J. K. Collins, G. F. Maberly, et al. 1989. Iodine deficiency impairs intellectual and neuromotor development in apparently-normal persons. *Medical Journal of Australia* 150: 676-82.

Boyages, S. C., J.-P. Halpern, G. F. Maberly, et al. 1988. A comparative study of neurological and myxedematous endemic cretinism in western China. *Journal of Clinical Endocrinology and Metabolism* 67: 1262-71.

Brush, B. E., and J. K. Altland. 1952. Goitre prevention with iodised salt: Results of a 30 year study. *Journal of Clinical Endocrinology* 12: 1380-8.

Burgi, H., Z. Supersaxo, and B. Selz. 1990. Iodine deficiency diseases in Switzerland one hundred years after Theodor Kocher's survey: A historical review with some new goitre prevalence data. *Acta Endocrinologica* 123: 577-90.

Burrow, G. N., ed. 1980. *Neonatal thyroid screening.* New York.

Buttfield, I. H., M. L. Black, M. J. Hoffmann, et al. 1965. Correction of iodine deficiency in New Guinea natives by iodised oil injection. *Lancet* 2: 767-9.

Buttfield, I. H., and B. S. Hetzel. 1967. Endemic goitre in eastern New Guinea with special reference to the use of iodised oil in prophylaxis and treatment. *Bulletin of the World Health Organization* 36: 243-62.

Connolly, K. J., P. O. D. Pharoah, and B. S. Hetzel. 1979. Fetal iodine deficiency and motor performance during childhood. *Lancet* 2: 1149-51.

Delange, F., F. B. Iteke, and A. M. Ermans, eds. 1982. *Nutritional factors involved in the goitrogenic action of cassava.* Ottawa.

De Quervain, F., and C. Wegelin. 1936. *Der endemische Kretinismus.* Berlin.

Djokomoeljanto, R., I. Tarwotjo, and F. Maspaitella. 1983. Goitre control program in Indonesia. In *Current problems in thyroid research,* ed. N. Ui, K. Torizuka, S. Nagataki, and K. Miyai, 403-5. Amsterdam.

Dunn, J. T. 1987a. Alternatives to salt and oil for iodine supplementation. In *The prevention and control of iodine deficiency disorders,* ed. B. S. Hetzel, J. T. Dunn, and J. B. Stanbury, 135-40. Amsterdam.

    1987b. Iodised oil in the treatment and prophylaxis of IDD. In *The prevention and control of iodine deficiency disorders,* ed. B. S. Hetzel, J. T. Dunn, and J. B. Stanbury, 127-34. Amsterdam.

Dunn, J. T., E. A. Pretell, C. H. Daza, and F. E. Viteri, eds. 1986. *Towards the eradication of endemic goitre, cretinism, and iodine deficiency.* Washington, D.C.

Ermans, A. M., N. M. Moulameko, F. Delange, and R. Alhuwalia, eds. 1980. *Role of cassava in the aetiology of endemic goitre and cretinism.* Ottawa.

Fierro-Benitez, R., R. Cazar, J. B. Stanbury, et al. 1986. Long-term effect of correction of iodine deficiency on psychomotor and intellectual development. In *Towards the eradication of endemic goitre, cretinism, and iodine deficiency,* ed. J. T. Dunn, E. A. Pretell, C. H. Daza, and F. E. Viteri, 182-200. Washington, D.C.

Follis, R. H., Jr. 1963. A pattern of urinary iodine excretion in goitrous and non-goitrous areas. *American Journal of Clinical Nutrition* 14: 253-68.

Hetzel, B. S. 1983. Iodine deficiency disorders (IDD) and their eradication. *Lancet* 2: 1126-9.

    1988a. Iodine deficiency disorders. *Lancet* 2: 1386.

    1988b. *The prevention and control of iodine deficiency disorders.* Nutrition Policy Discussion Paper No. 3, ACC/SCN, Rome.

    1989. *The story of iodine deficiency: An international challenge in nutrition.* Oxford and Delhi.

Hetzel, B. S., J. Chevadev, and B. J. Potter. 1988. The brain in iodine deficiency. *Neuropathology and Applied Neurobiology* 14: 93-104.

Hetzel, B. S., J. T. Dunn, and J. B. Stanbury, eds. 1987. *The prevention and control of iodine deficiency disorders.* Amsterdam.

Hetzel, B. S., and G. F. Maberly. 1986. Iodine. In *Trace elements in human and animal nutrition.* Fifth edition, ed. W. Mertz, 139-208. New York.

Hetzel, B. S., B. J. Potter, and E. M. Dulberg. 1990. The iodine deficiency disorders: Nature, pathogenesis and epidemiology. *World Review of Nutrition Dietetics* 62: 59-119.

Hetzel, B. S., C. H. Thilly, R. Fierro-Benitez, et al. 1980. Iodised oil in the prevention of endemic goitre and cretinism. In *Endemic goitre and endemic cretinism,* ed. J. B. Stanbury and B. S. Hetzel, 513-32. New York.

Hunziger, H. 1915. *Der Kropf, eine Anpassung an jodarme Nahrung.* Bern.

Karmarker, M. G., M. G. Deo, N. Kochupillai, and V. Ramalingaswami. 1974. Pathophysiology of Himalayan endemic goitre. *American Journal of Clinical Nutrition* 27: 96-103.

Kelly, F. C., and W. W. Snedden. 1960. Prevalence and geographical distribution of endemic goitre. In *Endemic goitre,* ed. World Health Organization, 27-333. Geneva.

Kimball, O. P. 1937. Prevention of goitre in Michigan and Ohio. *Journal of the American Medical Association* 108: 860-3.

Kochupillai, N., and C. S. Pandav. 1987. Neonatal chemical hypothyroidism in iodine deficient environments. In *The prevention and control of iodine deficiency disorders,* ed. B. S. Hetzel, J. T. Dunn, and J. B. Stanbury, 85-93. Amsterdam.

Konig, P. 1981. "Myxedematous" and "nervous cretinism": A historical review. In *Fetal brain disorders,* ed. B. S. Hetzel and R. M. Smith, 229-42. Amsterdam.

Lancet (Editorial). 1983. From endemic goitre to iodine deficiency disorders. *Lancet* 2: 1121-2.

    1986a. Inaugural meeting of the International Council for Control of Iodine Deficiency Disorders. *Lancet* 1: 1164.

    1986b. Prevention and control of iodine deficiency disorders. *Lancet* 2: 433-4.

Langer, P. 1960. History of goitre. In *Endemic goitre,* ed. World Health Organization, 9-25. Geneva.

Li, J.-Q., and X. Wang. 1987. Jixian: A success story in IDD control. *IDD Newsletter* 3: 4-5.

Ma, T., T. Lu, U. Tan, et al. 1982. The present status of endemic goitre and endemic cretinism in China. *Food and Nutrition Bulletin* 4: 13-19.

Maberly, G. F., C. J. Eastman, and J. M. Corcoran. 1981. Effect of iodination of a village water-supply on goitre size and thyroid function. *Lancet* 2: 1270-2.

Marine, D., and O. P. Kimball. 1921. The prevention of simple goitre in man. *Journal of the American Medical Association* 77: 1068-72.

McCarrison, R. 1908. Observations on endemic cretinism in the Chitral and Gilgit Valleys. *Lancet* 2: 1275-80.

McCullagh, S. F. 1963. The Huon Peninsula endemic. The effectiveness of an intramuscular depot of iodised oil in the control of endemic goitre. *Medical Journal of Australia* 1: 769-77.

McMichael, A. J., J. D. Potter, and B. S. Hetzel. 1980. Iodine deficiency, thyroid function, and reproductive failure. In *Endemic goitre and endemic cretinism,* ed. J. B. Stanbury and B. S. Hetzel, 445-60. New York.

Merke, F. 1984. *The history and iconography of endemic goitre and cretinism.* Lancaster. Translated from the German original, 1971, Bern.

Pharoah, P. O. D., I. H. Buttfield, and B. S. Hetzel. 1971. Neurological damage to the fetus resulting from severe iodine deficiency during pregnancy. *Lancet* 1: 308-10.

Pharoah, P. O. D., and K. J. Connolly. 1987. A controlled trial of iodinated oil for the prevention of cretinism: A long-term follow-up. *International Journal of Epidemiology* 16: 68–73.

Pharoah, P. O. D., K. J. Connolly, R. P. Ekins, and A. G. Harding. 1984. Maternal thyroid hormone levels in pregnancy and the subsequent cognitive and motor performance of the children. *Clinical Endocrinology* 12: 265–70.

Pharoah, P. O. D., K. J. Connolly, B. S. Hetzel, et al. 1981. Maternal thyroid function and motor competence in the child. *Developmental Medicine and Child Neurology* 23: 76–82.

Pharoah, P. O. D., F. Delange, R. Fierro-Benitez, and J. B. Stanbury. 1980. Endemic cretinism. In *Endemic goitre and endemic cretinism,* ed. J. B. Stanbury and B. S. Hetzel, 395–421. New York.

Pretell, E. A., T. Torres, V. Zenteno, and M. Comejo. 1972. Prophylaxis of endemic goitre with iodised oil in rural Peru. In *Human development and the thyroid gland – relation to endemic cretinism,* ed. J. B. Stanbury and R. Kroc.

SEARO/WHO. *Iodine deficiency disorders in South East Asia.* 1985. SEARO Regional Papers, No. 10. Delhi.

Stanbury, J. B., G. L. Brownell, D. S. Riggs, et al. 1954. *Endemic goiter: The adaptation of man to iodine deficiency.* Cambridge, Mass.

Stanbury, J. B., A. M. Ermans, B. S. Hetzel, et al. 1974. Endemic goitre and cretinism: Public health significance and prevention. *WHO Chronicle* 28: 220–8.

Stanbury, J. B., and B. S. Hetzel, eds. 1980. *Endemic goitre and endemic cretinism: Iodine nutrition in health and disease.* New York.

Stewart, J. C., G. I. Vidor, I. H. Buttfield, and B. S. Hetzel. 1971. Epidemic thyrotoxicosis in northern Tasmania: Studies of clinical features and iodine nutrition. *Australia and New Zealand Journal of Medicine* 3: 203–11.

Thilly, C. H. 1981. Goitre et cretinisme endémiques: Role étiologique de la consommation de manioc et stratégie d'éradication. *Bulletin of the Belgian Academy of Medicine* 136: 389–412.

Thilly, C. H., F. Delange, and J. B. Stanbury. 1980. Epidemiological surveys in endemic goitre and cretinism. In *Endemic goitre and endemic cretinism,* 157–84. New York.

UNICEF Regional Office Report for South-Central Asia. 1984. Report on iodised salt. Delhi.

Vidor, G. I., J. C. Stewart, J. R. Wall, et al. 1973. Pathogenesis of iodine induced thyrotoxins: Studies in Northern Tasmania. *Journal of Clinical Endocrinology and Metabolism* 37: 901–9.

WHO (World Health Organization). 1960. *Endemic goitre.* Monograph Series No. 44. Geneva.

World Health Organization Report to World Health Assembly. 1990. Geneva.

IV.B.3 ❧ Iron

Iron has played a critical role in the evolution of life. The ancient Greeks, believing iron to be a special gift sent to earth by one of the gods, named it *sideros,* or star (Liebel, Greenfield, and Pollitt 1979). As the second most common metal, iron accounts for 5 percent of the earth's crust; it is also found in both sea- and freshwater (Bernat 1983). Scientists believe that the earth's atmosphere was originally a reducing one with very low oxygen pressure. As a result, large amounts of reduced iron would have been available for living organisms (Bothwell et al. 1979). Iron is an essential element for all organisms, with the possible exception of some *Lactobacillus* (Griffiths 1987; Payne 1988). In animals, the processes of DNA replication, RNA synthesis, and oxygen and electron transport require iron. Today most iron in the environment exists in an oxidized state and is less available to organisms. However, the problems of extracting insoluble iron have been overcome during evolution. A variety of sophisticated mechanisms have evolved that are specific to different kingdoms and/or different species (e.g., mechanisms plants use to be able to live in acidic or iron-poor environments) (Bothwell et al. 1979). Such mechanisms in animals include iron complexing agents, which transport iron and deliver it to cells, and low-molecular-weight compounds, such as fructose and amino acids, that reduce iron into a soluble form (Griffiths 1987; Simmons 1989: 14).

Metabolic processes within humans involve the presence of free radicals, that is, substances that are reactive because of instability in the arrangement of electrons (Wadsworth 1991). Iron may be present as a free radical. Such instability makes iron highly likely to donate or accept electrons. As a result, iron is versatile and able to serve a number of functions within cells. These functions include acting as a catalyst in electron transport processes and serving as a transporter of oxygen. Iron is a key component of hemoglobin, the oxygen carrier found in red blood cells. It is involved in many other extracellular processes as well (Woods, DeMarco, and Friedland 1990). Iron also is required for collagen synthesis, the production of antibodies, removal of fats from the blood, conversion of carotene to vitamin A, detoxification of drugs in the liver, and the conversion of fuel nutrients to energy (Long and Shannon 1983). In addition to its importance in the maintenance of normal metabolic processes, iron involvement in pathological change and initiation of disease is a critical facet of host defense.

Iron occurs in the human body in two states: circulating in blood and in storage. The absolute amount of iron in the body is actually quite small, despite its critical importance in metabolism. A healthy adult has an average of between 4 and 5 grams (g) of iron with a range of 3 to 6 g (Bernat 1983). Approximately 30 percent of all iron in the body is in storage. Most iron utilized in the body is needed by bone marrow to make new red blood cells. After a life span of about 120 days, red blood cells are destroyed and the released hemoglobin is broken down. Liberated iron from the hemoglobin is stored in macrophages in the liver, spleen, and kidney for future use.

Most iron in a healthy person (2.5 to 3 g) is found in red blood cells in the form of hemoglobin (Moore 1973; McLaren, Muir, and Kellermeyer 1983). Small amounts of iron, approximately 0.13 g, occur in myoglobin, a protein in muscle tissues. Only 0.008 g of iron is located in heme tissue enzymes, 0.5 g is in nonheme enzymes, and about 0.004 g is bound to the iron-binding protein transferrin found in blood (Arthur and Isbister 1987).

Between 0.7 and 1.5 g of iron is found in storage (Bezkorovainy 1989). It occurs in either a diffuse soluble form as ferritin, an intracellular protein, or as hemosiderin, an insoluble aggregate form of ferritin (Bezkorovainy 1989). Ferritin is formed when apoferritin (an iron-free protein) combines with freed iron from the breakdown of hemoglobin in senescent red blood cells (Simmons 1989: 14). Basically, ferritin is an apoprotein shell enclosing a core of iron that consists of 24 subunits of either the H or the L type (Worwood 1989). The two types of subunits are of slightly different size and electrical charge. Different organs have various percentages of one or the other type of subunits. For instance, H subunits are predominantly found in ferritin located in the heart and L subunits are predominantly found in ferritin located in the liver. It has been suggested that those organs that have a high iron content, such as the liver and spleen, have a predominance of the L subunits, whereas those with less iron, such as heart, intestine, pancreas, and placenta, have more of the H subunits (Bezkorovainy 1989: 53). Therefore, the L subunit dominated ferritin is thought to be concerned primarily with long-term iron storage whereas the H-dominated ferritin is concerned primarily with preventing iron overload (Bezkorovainy 1989: 53). Although the majority of ferritin is located in the organs that make up the reticuloendothelial system, a small amount exists in plasma. Most ferritin molecules contain only 2,000 atoms of iron (Fairbanks and Beutler 1988). However, up to 4,500 atoms of iron can be incorporated into the ferritin internal cavity. Iron atoms enter the ferritin protein coat through tiny channels or pores, which are formed by the positioning of subunits (Fairbanks and Beutler 1988; Worwood 1980: 204; Worwood 1989). Hemosiderin represents the end point of the intracellular storage iron pathway. Hemosiderin granules are actually denatured, partly degraded, aggregated molecules of ferritin (Bezkorovainy 1989).

Balance is the crucial feature of human iron metabolism. Too much iron is toxic and too little can produce severe anemia (Arthur and Isbister 1987). In fact, much of the toxicity of iron appears to be related to its propensity to form unstable intermediates with unpaired electrons or free radicals (Griffiths 1987). Lethal accumulations of iron can occur in most organs of the body but the liver, spleen, pituitary, and heart are particularly vulnerable to excess iron (Weinberg 1984; Stevens et al. 1988; Cook 1990; Kent, Weinberg, and Stuart-Macadam 1990, 1994). The immune system can also be compromised by excess iron. For this reason it is extremely important that iron be chelated (bound) to prevent uncontrolled free-radical reactions. In normal animals and humans, iron is almost always bound to proteins, leaving only an extremely low concentration of free iron; in fact, in most biological systems iron is bound to complexing agents. Over 99 percent of iron in plasma is chelated to transferrin to prevent uncontrolled free-radical reactions (Griffiths 1987). However, in individuals with hyperferremia (iron overload), as much as 35 percent of iron may not be transferrin-bound, causing iron to accumulate in the liver, spleen, and heart (Weinberg 1989: 10).

By contrast, insufficient iron can produce severe anemia that impairs the quality of life and may eventually lead to cardiac and respiratory failure (Weinberg 1989). The body maintains an equilibrium in part through the transfer of circulating iron to storage, as well as through the conversion of free iron to bound iron. The key to body iron supplies is recycling; only a very small amount is absorbed from food or lost through excretion (sweat, feces, urine, or menstruation). Iron is conserved in a nearly closed system. Each iron atom cycles repeatedly from plasma and extracellular fluid to the bone marrow, where it is incorporated into hemoglobin, and then to the blood, where it circulates for approximately 120 days within erythrocytes (red blood cells). Afterward, iron is released to plasma. This is accomplished by phagocytes (cells that engulf and then consume debris and foreign matter) of the liver or spleen (the reticuloendothelial system[1]) that digest hemoglobin and destroy old erythrocytes. The process releases iron to plasma, which continues the cycle (Fairbanks and Beutler 1988: 195). Within each cycle, small amounts of iron are transferred to storage sites, and small amounts of storage iron are released to plasma. In addition, small amounts are absorbed by the intestinal tract from ingested food containing iron and small amounts are lost through sweat, urine, feces, or blood (Fairbanks and Beutler 1988: 195). Consequently, little dietary iron is needed to replace iron loss.

Iron Requirements in Humans

Because most needed iron is recycled, humans actually require very small quantities to maintain health. For example, healthy 70-kilogram (kg) adult males lose approximately 1 milligram (mg) of iron daily through excretion by the skin and the gastrointestinal and urinary tracts (Bothwell et al. 1989).[2] Required replacements are 1 mg daily. Children lose only about 0.5 mg daily but their required replacement is approximately 1 mg daily to compensate for the needs of growth. Early estimates of iron loss among women of reproductive age were high, an average of 2 to 3 mg per day, resulting in an equal replacement requirement (Hoffbrand and Lewis 1981; Arthur and Isbister 1987). However, more recent and systematic studies call such estimates into question. A Swedish study showed that the average woman loses between

0.6 and 0.7 mg through menstruation; 95 percent of women lose an average of *less* than 1.4 mg per day (Fairbanks and Beutler 1988: 205). Scientists are beginning to recommend that average menstruating women absorb only 1.4 mg iron daily to replace losses (Monsen 1988: 786).

Absorption of iron occurs mainly in the duodenum and jejunum, although all parts of the small intestine and even the colon may be involved. Little is known about the precise mechanisms by which the body's need for iron is communicated to the mucosal cell of the intestine (Cook 1990). But however it is achieved, the body is able to adapt to a wide range of iron requirements and intakes by modifying the rate of gastrointestinal absorption. Absorption of iron varies according to health, physiological status, iron stores, age, and sex. Studies have shown that the absorption of iron from an adequate diet might range from a fraction of a milligram to 3 or 4 mg a day, depending on body iron content. For example, hyperferremia, or iron overload, is associated with decreased iron absorption from dietary sources. Blood loss and true iron deficiency result in increased iron absorption. Absorption also varies according to the iron source. Iron-deficient males absorb 20 percent more nonheme iron and 21 percent more heme iron than iron-replete males (Cook 1990: 304). The same adaptability applies to iron loss. Normal males lose about 0.9 mg of iron per day. In contrast, hypoferremic males lose only about 0.5 mg per day and hyperferremic males lose about 2.0 mg per day (Finch 1989).

According to James Cook (1990), the three major determinants of body iron in healthy individuals are physiological iron demands, dietary supply of available iron, and adaptation. It is the dietary supply of available iron that is most often focused upon by the medical profession and nutritionists. Dietary iron supply is actually determined by three main factors: total iron intake, content of heme iron, and bioavailability of nonheme iron (Cook 1990). However, actual absorption of iron is a function of the adaptability of iron metabolism and an individual's iron status. Dietary iron comes in two forms – heme and nonheme. The largest percentage of dietary iron is inorganic, or nonheme, which is absorbed primarily in the duodenum. Its absorption is influenced by the presence of inhibitors and enhancers found in ingested foods. The most important inhibitors include tannin (found in tea), coffee, phytates in bran, calcium phosphate, egg yolk, polyphenols, and certain forms of dietary fiber. Although bran and phytate in the diet do inhibit iron absorption, there is speculation that high bran and phytate intake may induce changes in the intestines or its microflora over a prolonged period and reduce the inhibitory effect of these substances (Cook 1990). Enhancers include meat and organic acids such as citric acid, lactic acid, alcohol, certain spices and condiments in curry powder, and ascorbic acid (Bothwell et al. 1989).

Unlike nonheme iron, heme iron is absorbed directly into the intestinal cell as an intact porphyrin complex and is unaffected by other components of the diet. Heme iron usually accounts for only 10 to 15 percent of the total daily intake of iron; however, the absorption of heme iron is relatively high and it can account for as much as 25 percent of the iron absorbed from the daily diet (Hallberg 1980: 118).

Most Westerners, who ingest some kind of meat almost daily, easily obtain sufficient amounts of iron to replace daily losses. In fact, in some cases, dietary consumption is four to seven times greater than the amount of iron needed. They also consume iron through fortified foods, such as most wheat products or wine and cider, which can add 2 to 16 mg or more per liter (Fairbanks and Beutler 1988). A study of military personnel showed that 20 to 30 mg of iron per day was ingested, in part because food was cooked in iron containers (Fairbanks and Beutler 1988: 194-5).

Several factors make it difficult to quantify the bioavailability of iron in the body. Uncertainties concerning the nature of the interactions that occur between enhancers and inhibitors make it difficult to determine the true bioavailability of iron from various foods or diets. Compounding the problem are misconceptions that result from not considering a food source within its natural context. Often quoted is the belief that milk is a poor source of iron. Although this is true for humans drinking bovine milk, it is not true for human infants drinking human breast milk. There is a very high bioavailability of iron in human breast milk for human infants. As much as 40 percent of iron in human milk is absorbed by human infants, whereas less than half that amount is absorbed from bovine milk (Pochedly and May 1987). Iron availability of milk is species-specific, and calves absorb significantly more from bovine milk than they would from human milk (Picciano and Guthrie 1976).

Not only is Western dietary intake of iron high; the Recommended Dietary Allowance (RDA) of the United States Food and Nutrition Board is high: 18 mg per day for premenopausal women and 10 mg per day for men and older women (Eaton, Shostak, and Konner 1988). This high RDA leads to perceived high levels of iron deficiency in populations throughout the world. Medical and government policy has traditionally encouraged more iron consumption over less. Accordingly, iron supplements are routinely administered to pregnant women and infants. Iron supplementation on a massive scale has been carried out in the United States since the 1940s when the Food and Nutrition Board of the National Academy of Science endorsed fortification of wheat flour with iron as well as vitamins. It is now standard practice to fortify a broad range of foods, including many of the items available on the shelves of supermarkets around the world. In fact, the only infant formula available to disadvantaged women participating in the American WIC (Women, Infants, and Children) program is one fortified by iron; non-iron-fortified formula is prohibited (Kent et al. 1990). Yet iron is naturally found in almost all foods.

Particularly rich sources of iron include organ meats, red meat, blackstrap molasses, cocoa, oysters, clams, and dried beans (Long and Shannon 1983). Water also can contain iron; that from wells and boreholes can have more than 5 mg of iron per liter (Fairbanks and Beutler 1988: 195). This is in addition to the large amount of iron that can be absorbed by food cooked in iron containers. Even if iron were nonexistent in a person's diet, which is very unlikely, it would take years to produce true dietary iron deficiency without concomitant blood loss that depletes body iron stores: "[I]ron deficiency is almost never due to dietary deficiency in an adult in our community. A diagnosis of dietary iron deficiency in an adult male or postmenopausal female usually means that the site of blood loss has been missed" (Arthur and Isbister 1987: 173). In fact, occult gastrointestinal blood loss has been detected in nearly 50 percent of infants misclassified as dietary-induced iron deficient (Fairbanks and Beutler 1988: 195). In addition, many cases of the anemia of infection/inflammation caused by chronic diseases have been mistaken for iron-deficiency anemia.

Measurement of Iron in Humans

Several blood indices are used to measure iron but only the most common ones are briefly described here (Table IV.B.3.1). One of the most reliable methods is bone marrow aspiration and biopsy, which permits a direct measurement of the body's iron stores as indicated by the amount of ferritin and hemosiderin present. However, because of the discomfort to the subject, the possibility of introducing infection, and the costs involved, the procedure is usually conducted only when other, less invasive measurements indicate a need for a highly accurate assessment.

In past studies hemoglobin and hematocrit (a measurement of the packed cell volume) were employed to ascertain iron sufficiency. The widespread use of automated electronic blood cell counters, such as the Coulter counter, makes hemoglobin/hematocrit values easily obtainable and therefore frequently used

indices to assess iron adequacy. In addition, the relative ease of determining these indices make them popular measurements in situations where automated machines do not exist. Unfortunately, a number of variables interact with and influence these indices, making them poor measures of iron status. Hemoglobin/hematocrit measurements can be unreliable because they are affected by cultural factors, such as smoking, and environmental factors, such as altitude, and the iron content of drinking water and soil (Kent et al. 1990).

Serum iron is also not a very reliable measure of iron status. It, like hemoglobin and hematocrit, is influenced by a number of factors, including a woman's menstrual cycle, the presence of infection, and the time of day blood is drawn (there is a diurnal cycle wherein serum iron values are as much as 30 percent higher in the morning than in late evening [Fairbanks and Beutler 1988: 200]). Transferrin is another component of blood measured to investigate the iron status of a person. Transferrin is a plasma iron-binding protein. One molecule has two iron-binding sites, each of which can bind one atom of ferric iron at each receptor site (Noyes 1985). Although originally thought to be similar, the two iron-binding sites more recently have been recognized as not chemically or physically equivalent for reasons not well understood (Bezkorovainy 1989). The primary function of transferrin is to transport iron from the intestinal tract, spleen, and liver to sites such as the bone marrow for hemoglobin synthesis, to macrophages for storage, to the placenta for fetal needs, or to other cells for iron-containing enzymes (Fairbanks and Beutler 1988: 200).

Most transferrin, between 70 and 90 percent, is transported to bone marrow (Fairbanks and Beutler 1988: 200). Total iron-binding capacity (TIBC) is the capacity of transferrin to bind iron, and it represents the highest amount of iron that the plasma (i.e., serum) can bind (Bezkorovainy 1980: 10; Fielding 1980: 15). In humans, only about one-third of the transferrin iron-binding sites are occupied by iron; the rest are free (Bezkorovainy 1989b). Transferrin saturation, the amount of transferrin that is saturated with iron (calculated by dividing serum iron value by the

Table IV.B.3.1. *Normal hematological values for the more common iron indexes (norms vary slightly according to measurement instrument and source)*

	Hemoglobin (g/dl)	Hematocrit (%)	Transferrin saturation (%)	Serum ferritin (μg/l)	Serum iron (μmol/1)	Transferrin (g/dl)	Red blood cell (μl)	Vitamin B$_{12}$ (pg/l)	Serum folate (ng/ml)	Red cell folate (ng/ml)
Adults										
Males	14-18.2	40-54	16-50	12-250	12.6-27	1.9-4.3	4.4-6.0	200-1,100	3-14	160-600
Females	12-15	38-47	16-50	12-200	12.6-27	1.9-4.3	4.2-5.5	200-1,100	3-14	160-600
Children[a]	11-14.8	33-14.8	16-50	7-140	10.0-27	1.9-4.3	3.4-5.6	200-1,100	3-14	160-600

[a]Values for children are age-dependent.

total iron-binding capacity), is usually considered a better assessment of iron metabolism than is transferrin, serum iron, or total iron-binding capacity alone. Nevertheless, transferrin saturation values are affected by chronic disease and inflammation, in addition to insufficient diet, blood loss, and various types of iron overload. Therefore, by themselves, these measurements are not reliable in determining the etiology of an anemia or iron overload. Furthermore, "transferrin measurements are relatively insensitive, as the degree of change with variation in iron stores is small relative to assay variability. Serum ferritin measurement is a key indicator of iron stores" (Cook and Skikne 1989: 350). In fact, and contrary to conventional practices, physicians are now suggesting different methods to measure iron status: "Traditional tests of serum iron and TIBC may be useful but currently are not recommended for indirect measurement of iron stores [i.e., measurement in the absence of a bone marrow biopsy]" (Beissner and Trowbridge 1986: 88–90). More recently, it has been noted that "a wide range of values for transferrin saturation and total iron-binding capacity is consistent with either iron deficiency anemia or anemia of chronic disease. . . . The two disorders can be distinguished by the serum ferritin level, iron stain of a bone marrow specimen for hemosiderin, or both" (Farley and Foland 1990: 92).

Red blood cell counts are routinely calculated by most automated blood cell counters. Red blood cells are often malformed with reduced life spans in various types of anemia and are associated with ineffective erythropoiesis (or red cell production) (Jacobs and Worwood 1982: 175). However, red blood cells usually have a normal life span in most iron overload disorders without severe liver disease (McLaren et al. 1983). At one time it was thought that red blood cell size might be useful in distinguishing iron deficiency from the anemia of chronic disease. But recent studies have disproved this proposition (e.g., Thompson et al. 1988; Osborne et al. 1989).

Mean corpuscular volume (MCV) reflects the capacity of the cell. A decreased cell size can signify a hemoglobin synthesis disorder, but a smaller size is also associated with both iron-deficiency anemia and anemia of chronic disease/inflammation and other iron disorders, such as thalassemia and sideroblastic anemia. Moreover, elevated MCV can result from a variety of disorders other than infection, including idiopathic ones. Although widely used because it is measured as part of the automated complete blood cell count, the main disadvantage of MCV is that it does "not distinguish true iron deficiency from secondary iron-deficient erythropoiesis due to inflammatory or neoplastic disease" (Cook and Skikne 1989: 351). As a result, a number of researchers contend that MCV can provide only a crude measure of iron status (Labbe and Finch 1980: 52).

Storage iron is held within the ferritin molecule. Experiments show that serum ferritin is the most noninvasive diagnostic indicator of iron status. The reliability of serum ferritin surpasses that of free erythrocyte protoporphyrin, which in the past was thought by some to be more diagnostic in discriminating the etiology of anemia (Zanella et al. 1989). Serum ferritin is a particularly sensitive measurement because it reflects changes in iron stores before they are completely exhausted or, in the case of overload, increased (e.g., Finch and Huebers 1982; Cook and Skikne 1989). There are now numerous studies that show that serum ferritin is a reliable measure of iron stores, second only to actual bone marrow aspirations (e.g., Thompson 1988; Burns et al. 1990; Guyatt et al. 1990).

These hematological measurements together present a reliable view of the iron status of an individual. However, when all are not available, serum ferritin, in conjunction with a measure of the amount of circulating iron, is minimally necessary for reliable interpretations.

Iron and Infection

One of the most exciting frontiers in iron studies concerns the body's efforts to diminish iron content in response to disease. Hypoferremia (or low circulating-iron level) is associated with an array of chronic diseases and inflammatory responses, including neoplasia (cancer), bacterial and parasitic infections, and rheumatoid arthritis (Kent 1992). The associated anemia of chronic disease is characterized by subnormal hemoglobin, subnormal serum iron, subnormal transferrin saturation levels, and normal to elevated serum ferritin levels (Table IV.B.3.2).

Hypoferremia in reaction to chronic diseases and inflammations has been noted in experimental animals as well as in humans. Studies show that within 24 hours after exposure to pathogenic microbes, serum iron levels fall and a resistance to otherwise lethal doses of a variety of pathogens is produced (Payne 1988). There is even a slight drop in

Table IV.B.3.2. *Comparison of laboratory values of anemia of dietary iron deficiency and anemia of chronic disease*

Anemia	Hemoglobin	Serum iron	Transferrin saturation	Serum ferritin	ESR
Iron deficiency	Decreased	Decreased	Decreased	Decreased	Normal
Chronic disease	Decreased	Decreased	Decreased	Normal–Raised	Raised

hemoglobin levels after smallpox revaccination, which is thought to represent a rather innocuous procedure (Reizenstein 1983).

The body reduces iron levels by preventing macrophages from releasing the metal from storage to transferrin and by reducing intestinal iron absorption. Transferrin saturation levels drop concomitantly as iron is sequestered in macrophage storage. Serum ferritin levels increase, serving as an indirect measure of body iron stores. The reduction of available iron affects microorganisms and rapidly multiplying neoplastic (cancer) cells because they require iron for proliferation. However, they either cannot store the element in a nontoxic form, as is the case for a number of pathogens, or they require larger amounts of iron for rapid proliferation than they possess, as is the case for neoplastic cells. Microorganisms requiring host iron include bacteria, fungi, protozoan parasites, and neoplastic cells.

Microinvaders acquire iron from their hosts in several ways. Perhaps most intriguing is acquisition through the production of small iron-binding compounds called siderophores. These iron chelators, or "iron scavengers," seek out iron in the host and donate it to the microorganism that produced them. In addition, some siderophores may serve as iron donors for another strain or species (Bezkorovainy 1980: 305–6). Siderophores compete with the host for the iron-binding proteins. The body responds by producing fever, which reduces the ability of some bacteria to produce siderophores (Lee 1983; Weinberg 1984). That is, fever serves as a countermeasure to microorganism proliferation by inhibiting their ability to extract iron from the host. The resulting hypoferremia prevents pathogens from obtaining sufficient quantities of growth-essential iron; they therefore fail to multiply or multiply with considerable difficulty (Kochan 1973: 22). Studies have documented that "a single episode of fever and/or inflammation in man appears to restrict the release of iron from effete red blood cells by the reticuloendothelial system, leading to a decrease in serum iron concentration and to stimulation of the production of ferritin [to store iron] for a prolonged period" (Elin, Wolff, and Finch 1977: 152).

It has long been recognized that an important deterrent to pathogens in infants is provided by lactoferrin, an iron-binding protein that occurs in breast milk. Lactoferrin binds free iron and thereby deprives microorganisms of necessary iron; it also has a propensity to interact with or complement specific antibodies (Bullen, Rogers, and Griffiths 1974). When iron-binding proteins become saturated with iron there is an increase in the amount of free iron (i.e., nonbound iron that is more accessible to pathogens). Both in vitro and in vivo experiments have shown that the bacteriostatic properties of lactoferrin, for example, are abolished when iron-binding proteins are saturated with iron, making the body more vulner-able to microorganism invasion (Pearson and Robinson 1976).

Understanding hypoferremia as a defense against disease allows us to understand the geographical distribution of anemia. George Wadsworth (1975), for example, noted that levels of hemoglobin in women living in temperate climates usually exceed 10 g per 100 milliliters (ml), whereas usual levels in women living in tropical climates may be only 8 g per 100 ml. The etiology of hypoferremia provides a clue for this otherwise puzzling observation. Parasitic and bacterial infections are endemic in tropical environments (e.g., Goodner 1933). The higher prevalence of infection has been related to the increased total complexity and diversity of the tropical ecological system (Dunn 1968). Hypoferremia is produced by the body in an attempt to ward off the numerous pathogenic insults associated with tropical environments. However, in these cases, and particularly when exacerbated by blood loss and nutrient malabsorption that often accompany protozoan and bacterial infections, hypoferremia might develop to such a severe state that it becomes a problem in and of itself (Stuart-Macadam 1988; Kent and Weinberg 1989; Kent et al. 1990: 67).

The role of hypoferremia as a nonspecific body defense against disease is not completely accepted, although microbiologists in particular have long recognized the role of iron in host defense. As early as 1868 Armand Trousseau noted that iron supplementation reactivated quiescent pulmonary tuberculosis (Weinberg 1984; Keusch and Farthing 1986). Research in 1944 showed that iron-binding proteins in egg whites and serum were involved in the inhibition of Shigella dysentery (Schade and Caroline 1944). Starving humans who are susceptible to some diseases are immune to others in which microorganisms must exact iron from their hosts to obtain the amount needed to proliferate. For example, refeeding programs in Niger reactivated malaria infections (Murray et al. 1976). Similar refeeding programs in Somalia resulted in a recrudescence of a number of different infections, including parasitic and bacillary dysentery, acute infectious hepatitis, brucellosis, tuberculosis, and others (Murray et al. 1976; Murray and Murray 1977). Moreover, a study of two groups of Kenyan Turkana pastoralists indicated lower iron levels enhanced host immunity. One group drank primarily milk; the other group drank milk and consumed over 150 g of fish per day, ingesting almost a third more iron than the non-fish-eating group. Those who ate fish were not anemic but were plagued by malaria, brucellosis, molluscum contagiosum, common warts, diarrhea, and *Entamoeba histolytica*. The non-fish-eating Turkana were slightly anemic but had significantly lower incidences of these diseases (Murray, Murray, and Murray 1980).[3]

There is now a body of literature based on in vivo and in vitro experiments that demonstrates the role of iron in disease (e.g., Weinberg 1966, 1974, 1977, 1984, 1990; Bullen et al. 1974; Masawe, Muindi, and Sway 1974; Strauss 1978; Oppenheimer et al. 1986; Bullen and Griffiths 1987; Crosa 1987; Griffiths and Bullen 1987; Kluger and Bullen 1987; Selby and Friedman 1988; Stevens et al. 1988; Kent et al. 1990, 1994). Even so, a large percentage of the public and even those in the health-care community are not aware that in certain circumstances diminished iron is not a pathological disease state but a physiological defense.[4] They are unaware that the current focus on iron fortification of food and on iron supplementation preparation is misdirected and potentially counterproductive to the body's attempt to ward off illness.

Supplying iron-fortified foods or vitamins to developing countries and disadvantaged minorities in Western nations without ascertaining the prevalence of dietary-induced, versus disease-induced, anemia may be harming the very people the food is intended to help. The practice of indiscriminate food fortification is putting these populations at risk for contracting a variety of diseases, including cancer (Finch 1989). Studies show that the high iron content of most Western diets particularly affects men and postmenopausal women, who, as a result, suffer more from certain types of neoplasia and from myocardial infarction. In fact, recent treatment uses iron chelators to bind iron at the location of inflammation, such as at the joints in rheumatoid arthritis, where it is thought iron causes tissue damage, among other problems (Biemond et al. 1988). In addition, drugs such as aspirin prevent heart attacks, at least in part, by causing chronic intestinal bleeding, which reduces iron levels (Sullivan 1989; also see Arthur and Isbister 1987 for discussion of aspirin and other anti-inflammatory drugs that can cause occult blood loss).

Iron and Heart Disease

Despite extensive epidemiological studies to identify risk factors for coronary disease, many unanswered questions remain. Individuals who have multiple risk factors often never develop cardiac events whereas others who would seem to be low risk experience cardiovascular problems (Sullivan 1989). Therefore, other possible factors, such as iron levels, should be examined for a contributory role in causing heart disease.

Some studies suggest a link between cardiac diseases and iron levels (Sullivan 1989; Salonen et al. 1992). Excess iron, as occurs in beta-thalassemia and chronic iron overload, has been associated with ischemic heart disease and heart attacks (Leon et al. 1979). Men, with more iron than premenopausal women who regularly lose iron through menstruation, also have more heart disease (Weinberg 1983; Sullivan 1989). Postmenopausal women, who have more iron than premenopausal women, have a higher risk of heart disease, although, of course, they constitute an older group. But women taking oral contra-

ceptives, which reduces the amount of menstrual bleeding, are also more prone to heart disease (Sullivan 1983; Frassinelli-Gunderson, Margen, and Brown 1985; Colditz et al. 1987).

Not all cardiologists agree that the association between iron and cardiac disease is causal. However, J. L. Sullivan (1989) and others (Salonen et al. 1992) have suggested that high serum ferritin values, which measure the amount of iron in storage, are a powerful predictor for heart disease. Common iron chelators used clinically to reduce heart attacks, such as deferoxamine and aspirin, cause increased bleeding times and occult blood loss. Moderate to heavy fish consumption causes occult bleeding, thereby reducing iron levels and the risk of heart disease (Kromhout, Bosschieter, and Coulander 1985; Herold and Kinsella 1986; Houwelingen et al. 1987). The consequent reduction in iron levels among consumers of fish and iron chelators or drugs that promote bleeding could be responsible for the reduction of heart disease. This is in contrast to persons who consume large amounts of red meat that contain heme iron, which is more readily absorbed than nonheme iron found in vegetables. Another interesting association between available iron and heart attacks is based on the circadian rhythm of the body. Serum iron levels have diurnal patterns with an increase in the early morning. Heart attacks also occur three times more frequently during this time of day (Sullivan 1989: 1184).

Iron and Parasites

Parasites are a serious threat to the health of rural communities in the tropics; over 90 percent of this population are infected with at least one and often several nematode species, including hookworm, roundworm, and whipworm (Behnke 1987). There are basically three ways in which parasites can cause anemia. One is the anemia of chronic disease discussed earlier. A second way is by competing for the same nutrients as the host, including iron. A third way is by causing actual blood loss. Hookworm (*Necator* sp.), in particular, can cause heavy blood loss and, as a result, anemia. Hookworm infestations have been found in 12 percent to 95 percent of study populations throughout the tropical regions of the world – from the Amazon rain forest to Southeast Asia (Florentino and Guirriec 1984: 65). Malaria parasites are also dependent on iron from their hosts. The distribution of the sickle trait and heterozygous forms of thalassemia, which cause anemia, provide some protection against the malaria parasite.

Iron and Cancer

Another exciting path iron studies are exploring concerns the examination of the role of iron in neoplastic disease. Neoplastic cells require more iron than normal cells because of their rapid proliferation. In an attempt to accommodate their increased need for iron, these cells extract iron from their host. In reaction, the body attempts to prevent their proliferation by producing hypoferremia. Anemia is a commonly associated condition of neoplasia of various types (Miller et al. 1990). The type of anemia that usually occurs with neoplasia is that of chronic disease/inflammation as indicated by elevated serum ferritin levels. For example, patients with acute leukemia, Hodgkin's disease, multiple myeloma, and other malignancies have elevated to highly elevated serum ferritin concentrations that tend to become greater as the disease progresses (Bezkorovainy 1980; Worwood 1980).

Males with higher iron stores than premenopausal women have a significantly increased risk of cancer of the colon, bladder, esophagus, and lung. Women with higher levels of iron because they are postmenopausal or are hyperferremic also have a greater risk of cancer (Selby and Friedman 1988; Stevens et al. 1988). Very high serum ferritin levels are associated with other types of neoplasia, including malignant histiocytosis, primary hepatocellular carcinoma (liver cancer), and multiple malignancies (Hann et al. 1989; Ya-You et al. 1989). Other studies show that serum ferritin levels are significantly different in patients with benign and malignant effusions (abnormal fluid accumulations). Of the patients with benign nonneoplastic effusions, 96 percent had serum ferritin levels below 1,000 nanograms (ng) per ml; very high serum ferritin levels of over 3,000 ng per ml were encountered only in patients with malignancies (Yinnon et al. 1988).

Even more indicative is a study of patients afflicted with malignant histiocytosis and virus-associated hemophagocytic syndrome. At the onset of their disease these patients were anemic while having levels of serum ferritin above 1,000 ng per ml. As the disease progressed, serum ferritin levels increased to greater than 12,000 ng per ml (Esumi et al. 1988). Patients were given either chemotherapy or prednisone, depending on their disease. All patients with consistently high serum ferritin levels died within three months of treatment, whereas all patients with serum ferritin values less than 1,000 ng per ml lived beyond three months and are alive today with normal serum ferritin levels (Esumi et al. 1988). The more severe the disease, the higher the ferritin levels. We interpret these dramatic findings as the body's failed attempt to thwart disease by sequestering as much iron as possible. As the threat of disease decreased, serum ferritin levels began to drop. Noriko Esumi and colleagues (1988: 2071) conclude that "serum ferritin level in histiocytic proliferative disorders is a useful indicator of disease activity in both neoplastic and reactive conditions rather than only a marker of malignant process."

The popular belief that non-Western groups have a lower incidence of cancer because they have healthier diets than Westerners may be correct for reasons other than those usually proposed. As noted earlier, Westerners tend to have high iron levels because of a generally high-iron diet, ubiquitous fortification of cereal products, and the widespread practice of taking vitamins fortified with iron. High iron levels have been implicated in increasing one's vulnerability to neoplasia. It might be that in an attempt to improve our diets to reduce morbidity through the ingestion of excess iron, we actually worsen our diets and encourage high levels of morbidity.

Hyperferremia: Causes and Problems

In addition to high serum ferritin values and high concentrations of iron in the liver and spleen, increased concentrations of iron and ferritin occur in the bile of hyperferremic individuals. Bile iron is increased in patients with idiopathic hemochromatosis to as much as twice that of normal individuals; bile ferritin is increased to as much as five times that of normal individuals (Hultcrantz et al. 1989).

There are basically two types of hyperferremia – acquired and inherited (Table IV.B.3.3). Inherited hyperferremia is usually termed hereditary (or idiopathic) hemochromatosis. This disorder is autosomal (involving a nonsex chromosome) recessive, the responsible gene being located on the short arm of chromosome 6 (Edwards et al. 1988: 1355). Although the full manifestation of the disease occurs only in affected homozygotes, a small proportion of heterozygotes have been found to exhibit minor abnormalities in laboratory tests that measure the body's iron burden (Edwards et al. 1988). The incidence of hemochromatosis in a presumably healthy population of 11,065 European-Americans (with transferrin saturation values of above 62 percent) was 5 people per 1,000; the amount of iron loading in the liver and consequent organ damage varied widely (Edwards et al. 1988). Studies conducted in Scotland and France yielded a lower number of affected individuals, although the incidence was still substantial, ranging from 1 in 400 to 1 in 517 persons (McLaren et al. 1983: 223).

Table IV.B.3.3. *Types of disorders associated with iron overload*

Primary iron overload
Hereditary (idiopathic) hemochromatosis

Secondary iron overload
Hereditary transferrin deficiency
Thalassemia syndromes
African siderosis (African hemosiderosis; also Bantu siderosis)
Kaschin-Beck disease
Transfusional hemosiderosis
Alcoholic cirrhosis with hemosiderosis
Porphyria cutanea tarda
Acquired hemolytic anemia
Ineffective erythropoiesis (red blood cell production)
Pyridoxine-responsive anemia

Source: Adapted from McLaren, Nuir, and Kellermeyer (1983: 206).

Thalassemia syndromes (i.e., thalassemia major, intermedia, minor, and minima) are inherited disorders in which intestinal iron absorption is increased due to the hemolytic anemia and ineffective erythropoiesis (i.e., production of red blood cells). The condition is complicated by transfusion therapy (McLaren et al. 1983: 216). The result is hyperferremia. Occasionally a complete absence of serum transferrin (termed atransferrinemia) occurs in which marrow is without iron but heavy iron deposits are found in the heart, pancreas, liver, and mucous glands (McLaren et al. 1983). The cause is linked to the homozygous expression of an autosomal recessive gene. Heterozygous expression of this recessive gene can also result in anemia.

More unusual is hereditary hypochromic anemia, which is a sex-linked recessive disorder that is variable in its manifestation. A poorly understood disorder, porphyria cutanea tarda, results from a defect in the heme synthetic pathway. This condition is often found in combination with hepatic siderosis (iron storage), possibly from increased dietary iron absorption or heterozygosity for idiopathic hemochromatosis (McLaren et al. 1983: 226).

Acquired hyperferremia results from a number of causes. Three of the most common disorders that produce acquired hyperferremia are transfusional iron overload (also called transfusional hemosiderosis), alcoholism and cirrhosis with hemosiderosis, and African siderosis (or Bantu siderosis). Iron overload can be a by-product of prolonged intravenous iron administration or repetitive transfusions. As a common complication of maintenance dialysis, for example, hyperferremia requires regular phlebotomy (bloodletting) to correct the situation (McCarthy et al. 1989).

Alcohol abuse stimulates absorption of dietary iron and reduces the ability of intestinal epithelial cells to prevent excessive transport of iron into the blood (Mazzanti et al. 1987). Hyperferremia can even occur in individuals who have not yet developed liver damage (Rodriguez et al. 1986).

In most parts of sub-Saharan Africa, African or Bantu siderosis results from brewing beer in iron containers and cooking food in cast-iron pots. Large deposits of iron occur in the liver, spleen, and to a lesser extent, in the macrophages of the bone marrow. One study indicated that the average rural southern African male ingests between 50 and 100 mg of iron daily in beer alone (Bothwell et al. 1965: 893)! In a variety of studies of Africans who died from accidental deaths and other causes in South Africa, between 40 and 89 percent of the subjects exhibited varying degrees of iron overload (Bothwell and Bradlow 1960). The condition is detectable as early as late adolescence and becomes most severe between the ages of 40 and 60 years. In another study 75 percent of the males autopsied manifested siderosis compared with 25 percent of the women (Bothwell and Isaac-

son 1962: 524). The lower incidence of siderosis among women is due to a combination of greater iron loss through menstruation and the cultural practice of women drinking less beer and therefore ingesting less iron.

In the past 25 years the frequency of siderosis has dropped. This decline is particularly notable among urban Africans who do not drink as much of the traditional home-brewed beer as the rural population but still ingest large amounts of alcohol in different forms (MacPhail et al. 1979). A study conducted in the mid-1980s in Zimbabwe revealed that 12 percent of the men tested had an elevated serum ferritin level and a transferrin saturation of over 70 percent (Gordeuk, Boyd, and Brittenham 1986). However, although the frequency of siderosis in various areas of Africa has been declining over the past 25 to 30 years, it remains a serious health problem among a large percentage of rural populations.

Because hyperferremia results in the accumulation of iron in various organs, particularly the liver, spleen, heart, and pancreas, it can lead to severe cirrhosis, heart failure, and diabetes mellitus. Although the precise mechanism(s) involved is not well understood, it appears that tissue damage occurs in the liver and other organs as a result of the toxicity of excess iron. Cirrhosis occurs even in hyperferremic patients who do not drink any alcohol, although the combination of alcohol consumption and hyperferremia exacerbates the cirrhosis (McLaren et al. 1983: 240). In addition, different etiologies of iron overload appear to have slightly different manifestations. For example, the ratio of liver iron to marrow iron was much greater in patients with hereditary hemochromatosis than in those with African siderosis (McLaren et al. 1983: 236).

Hyperferremic individuals are plagued by problems other than those associated with the toxicity of excess iron. For reasons detailed earlier, they also suffer from an increased susceptibility to bacterial and parasitic microorganisms and neoplastic diseases (cancer). For example, one study demonstrated an increased risk of contracting *Yersinia enterocolitica* and *Yersinia pseudotuberculosis* bacteremia in dialysis patients with iron overload (Boelaert et al. 1987). Similar studies revealed an increased risk and virulence from several iron-sensitive microorganisms, including *Listeria monocytogenes, Brucella spp.,* and *Vibrio vulnificus.*

Problems Associated with Insufficient Iron

As in the case of hyperferremia, there are two basic categories of hypoferremia (or low circulating-iron levels) based on their etiology. Most common are the acquired anemias, including iron deficiency, drug-induced anemia, and anemia of chronic disease/inflammation. Less common are hereditary anemias, such as sickle-cell anemia and congenital sideroblastic anemia. Some, such as sickle-cell anemia, are classified in a clinical setting by the morphological shape of the hemoglobin (Table IV.B.3.4).

Macrocytic anemia can be induced by diet, resulting from malabsorption, or it can be caused by an inherited disorder. Because Vitamin B_{12} (cobalamin) and folic acid (folate) are required for normal red blood cell nuclear growth and synthesis, deficiencies of these nutrients can cause anemia (Simmons 1989: 12–14). Vitamin B_{12} deficiency from dietary causes is very rare and occurs only in strict vegetarians who exclude all meat, eggs, and milk. However, this deficiency can also arise from a number of disorders, including impaired absorption of B_{12} or folate such as in pernicious anemia; malabsorption that can result from certain drugs, such as those used to treat sprue and celiac diseases, and gastrectomy; competition from parasites such as the fish tapeworm; hereditary impairment of absorption capabilities; increased requirements of the vitamin due to pregnancy, tumors, and hyperthyroidism; or impaired utilization of the vitamin, as in red cell enzymopathy, abnormal binding proteins, absence of transport protein, or nitrous oxide administration (Simmons 1989: 40).

Folate deficiencies can result from the following: a lack of green vegetables in a diet; alcoholism; impaired absorption due to sprue and celiac diseases; drugs used to treat malignant diseases; malaria and bacterial infections; increased requirements stemming from pregnancy; conditions such as hyperthyroidism; or impaired utilization as occurs with drugs like phenytoin (Simmons 1989: 40–1).

Table IV.B.3.4. *Morphological classification of anemia*

Morphology	Anemia
Macrocytic	Nonmegaloblastic
	Liver disease
	Reticulocytosis
	Megaloblastic
	Vitamin B_{12} deficiency
	Pernicious anemia
	Folate deficiency
	Myelodysplastic syndrome
Hypochromic microcytic	Iron deficiency
	Anemia of chronic disease/inflammation
	Thalassemia
	Hereditary/acquired sideroblastic anemia
	Lead poisoning
Normochromic normocytic	Decreased reticulocytosis
	Renal failure
	Endocrinopathies
	Anemia of chronic disease/inflammation
	Aplasia (idiopathic or secondary)
	Myelophthisis
	Increased reticulocytosis
	Spherocytic (congenital and acquired)
	Nonspherocytic
	Sickle-cell anemia

Two types of hypochromic microcytic anemia are most prevalent. One is caused by blood loss that is not counterbalanced by a sufficient dietary intake. The second, less common cause results from unmet nutritional demands even without blood loss. In men, bleeding from the gastrointestinal tract is the most frequent cause, and although this condition may occur in women as well, menorrhagia (excessive menstrual flow) is more often responsible. The other principal cause of this variety of anemia is chronic disease, in which iron deficiency appears to form a nonspecific defense mechanism against disease.

Less common is sideroblastic anemia, which can be acquired or congenital. Acquired sideroblastic anemia can be drug- or toxin-induced from cancer chemotherapy, antituberculous drugs, and ethanol, or it can be idiopathic, such as preleukemic or dysmyelopoietic syndromes (Beissner and Trowbridge 1986). Patients with sideroblastic anemia tend to accumulate excess iron in the tissues and therefore are vulnerable to many of the problems associated with iron overload. Lead poisoning can also cause hypochromic microcytic anemia.

Some anemias are associated with specific geographical regions. For example, thalassemias are a varied group of inherited disorders characterized by one or more defects in the synthesis of the normal alpha or beta globin chains of hemoglobin. They can occur in homozygous or heterozygous states and include thalassemia major, thalassemia intermedia, thalassemia minor, and thalassemia minima (Simmons 1989: 55). The geographical distribution of thalassemia is primarily in the Mediterranean region, although it is also found in Southeast Asia, the Middle East, and the Orient and among immigrants from those areas. There is much variation in the clinical manifestations of these genetic disorders. The defect in hemoglobin chains causes a reduction in hemoglobin in afflicted individuals. Ironically, and as discussed earlier, thalassemia can also result in iron overload of some organs because intestinal iron absorption is increased due to the hemolytic anemia and ineffective production of red blood cells. In the heterozygous form, however, thalassemia has been postulated to be a deterrent to malaria infections, perhaps by causing a reduction in the amount of circulating iron.

A normocytic normochromic anemia that involves the premature destruction of red blood cells is sickle-cell anemia, an inherited autosomal dominant disorder. Sickle-cell anemia is lethal in the homozygous form, but it can also become symptomatic in heterozygotes in situations of oxygen deprivation such as at high altitudes. Geographically, sickle-cell anemia is most common in equatorial Africa but is also found to a lesser extent in the Mediterranean region and India. This distribution has been attributed to the improved immunity individuals who are heterozygous for the sickle-cell trait have from malaria parasites (e.g., *Plasmodium falciparum*). Approximately 8.5 percent of

American blacks are heterozygous for the sickle-cell trait and are relatively symptom-free; in contrast, homozygous individuals suffer from hemoglobin levels between 5 and 9 g per decaliter (dl), leg ulcers, hematuria, and other afflictions (Simmons 1989: 68–70).

Common autosomal dominant normocytic normochromic anemias that represent a defect in the red cell membrane include hereditary spherocytosis, found primarily in people of northern European descent, and hereditary elliptocytosis, found worldwide (Simmons 1989: 62–4). Spherocytic (congenital and acquired) anemia involves a deficiency in the Glucose-6-phosphate dehydrogenase enzyme (abbreviated G6PD) that is sex-linked with full expression in affected males and partial expression in females (Simmons 1989: 65). Its geographic distribution is worldwide, with the highest frequency in African populations, although it is also found in Italian, Greek, Asian, and Jewish populations.

Congenital nonspherocytic hemolytic anemia results from deficiency in several red cell enzymes, including glucose 6-phosphate dehydrogenase (G6PD). This condition is found in Asian, European, and Mediterranean populations, as well as in other populations to a lesser extent (Simmons 1989). This anemia is also caused by ingestion or contact with the fava bean by Mediterranean peoples (even from just inhaling the pollen of the bean among some sensitive males, usually under the age of 12). It can also be triggered by the use of antimalarial and other drugs in African and Mediterranean populations. A third cause can result from infection with viral or bacterial pathogens worldwide in persons with G6PD deficiency – pathogens include *Escherichia coli, Salmonella, Streptococcus, Rickettsiae,* viral hepatitis, pneumococcal pneumonia, malaria, and rheumatoid arthritis (Simmons 1989: 65).

A variety of anemias are associated with immunological disorders, including transfusion reactions, ABO or Rh blood-group incompatibility between fetus and mother, and autoimmune hemolytic anemia, a condition in which antibodies or lymphocytes attack cells of the person who produced them. The most common type of autoimmune hemolytic anemia is termed warm-antibody because the autoantibody reacts most efficiently with red cells at 37° Celsius (C) and occurs especially in systemic lupus erythematosus and lymphomas. Less common is cold-antibody type, in which the antibodies are optimally reactive at temperatures less than 37° C, including cold hemagglutinin disease and paroxysmal cold hemoglobinuria (Simmons 1989: 78–81).

Conclusions and Future Directions for Research

As we learn more about iron, we learn more of its multifaceted interrelationship with health and disease in a variety of conditions and situations. It is also apparent that this interrelationship is a complex one. For example, lowered iron levels do not necessarily mean higher morbidity, nor is anemia primarily a nutritional disorder. We predict that future studies of iron will concentrate on its role in health, especially during the periods of rapid growth that occur in childhood and pregnancy, and in response to chronic infection, inflammation, and malignancy.

Further elucidation of iron as a cause of, and as a defense against, disease should reduce morbidity levels all over the world. Therefore, we have much to gain through multidisciplinary research that investigates all aspects of iron. Presented here is an overview of the fascinating picture of iron, a picture only now coming into focus.

Susan Kent
Patricia Stuart-Macadam

We are most grateful to Drs. Gene Weinberg, Steven Kent, and Roy Stuart for the valuable comments on a draft of this chapter. Any inadequacies, however, are solely our responsibility.

Notes

1. The reticuloendothelial system is also called the monocyte-macrophage system.
2. This excretion can be broken down into the following: gastrointestinal loss, of which blood comprises 0.35 mg. mucosal 0.10 mg, and biliary 0.20 mg; urinary loss of 0.08 mg; and skin loss of 0.20 mg (Fairbanks and Beutler 1988: 205).
3. Eugene Weinberg (1966, 1974, 1977, 1978, 1981, 1984, 1990) has numerous publications outlining the exact techniques microorganisms use to extract iron from hosts and the techniques hosts have developed to thwart them.
4. For example, most physicians routinely prescribe oral iron for their pregnant patients; others recommend iron supplements to patients with lowered hemoglobin levels without examining serum ferritin levels. We need to reassess the currently popular practice of indiscriminate iron fortification of foods and infant formula.

Bibliography

Arthur, C. K., and J. P. Isbister. 1987. Iron deficiency: Misunderstood, misdiagnosed and mistreated. *Drugs* 33: 171–82.

Behnke, J. M. 1987. Evasion of immunity by nematode parasites causing chronic infections. *Advances in Parasitology* 26: 1–71.

Beissner, Robert, and Arthur Trowbridge. 1986. Clinical assessment of anemia. *Postgraduate Medicine* 80: 83–95.

Bernat, Ivan. 1983. *Iron metabolism.* New York.

Bezkorovainy, Anatoly. 1980. *Biochemistry of nonheme iron in man.* New York.

1989a. Biochemistry of nonheme iron in man. I. Iron proteins and cellular iron metabolism. *Clinical Physiology and Biochemistry* 7: 1–17.

1989b. Biochemistry of nonheme iron in man. II. Absorption of iron. *Clinical Physiology and Biochemistry* 7: 53–69.

Biemond, Peter, Antonius Swaak, Henk van Eijk, and Johan Koster. 1988. Superoxide dependent iron release from ferritin in inflammatory diseases. *Free Radical Biology and Medicine* 4: 185–98.

Boelaert, Johan, Herman van Landuty, Yvan Valcke, et al. 1987. The role of iron overload in *Yersinia enterocolitia* and *Yersinia pseudotuberculosis* bacteremia in hemodialysis patients. *Journal of Infectious Diseases* 156: 384–9.

Bothwell, Thomas, R. D. Baynes, B. J. MacJarlane, A. P. MacPhail. 1989. Nutritional iron requirements and food iron absorption. *Journal of Internal Medicine* 226: 357–65.

Bothwell, Thomas, and Basil Bradlow. 1960. Siderosis in the Bantu. *Archives of Pathology* 70: 279–92.

Bothwell, Thomas, Robert Charlton, James Cook, and Clement Finch. 1965. Oral iron overload. *South African Medical Journal* 30: 892–900.

  1979. *Iron metabolism in man*. Oxford.

Bothwell, Thomas, and C. Isaacson. 1962. Siderosis in the Bantu: A comparison of incidence in males and females. *British Medical Journal* 1: 522–4.

Bullen, J. J., and E. Griffiths. 1987. *Iron and infection*. London.

Bullen, J. J., H. Rogers, and E. Griffiths. 1974. Bacterial iron metabolism in infection and immunity. In *Microbial iron metabolism: A comprehensive treatise*, ed. J. B. Neiland, 383–439. New York.

Burns, Edward, Nahum Goldberg, Christine Lawrence, and Barry Wenz. 1990. Clinical utility of serum tests for iron deficiency in hospitalized patients. *American Journal of Clinical Pathology* 93: 240–5.

Ceriotti, Ferruccio, and Giovanni Ceriotti. 1980. Improved direct specific determination of serum iron and total iron-binding capacity. *Clinical Chemistry* 26: 327–31.

Colditz, G. A., W. C. Willett, M. J. Stampfer, et al. 1987. Menopause and the risk of coronary heart diseases in women. *New England Journal of Medicine* 316: 1105–10.

Cook, James. 1990. Adaptation in iron metabolism. *American Journal of Clinical Nutrition* 51: 301–8.

Cook, James, and Barry Skikne. 1982. Serum ferritin: A possible model for the assessment of nutrient stores. *American Journal of Clinical Nutrition* 35: 1180–5.

  1989. Iron deficiency: Definition and diagnosis. *Journal of Internal Medicine* 226: 349–55.

Crosa, J. H. 1987. Bacterial iron metabolism, plasmids and other virulence factors. In *Iron and infection*, ed. J. J. Bullen and E. Griffiths, 139–70. London.

Dallman, P. R. 1989. Iron deficiency: Does it matter? *Journal of Internal Medicine* 226: 367–72.

Dunn, Frederick. 1968. Epidemiological factors: Health and disease in hunter-gatherers. In *Man the hunter,* ed. Richard Lee and Irven De Vore, 221–8. Chicago.

Eaton, S. B., M. Shostak, and M. Konner. 1988. *The paleolithic prescription*. New York.

Edwards, Corwin, Linda Griffen, David Goldgar, et al. 1988. Prevalence of hemochromatosis among 11,065 presumably healthy blood donors. *New England Journal of Medicine* 318: 1355–62.

Elin, Ronald, Sheldon Wolff, and Clement Finch. 1977. Effect of induced fever on serum iron and ferritin concentrations in man. *Blood* 49: 147–53.

Esumi, Noriko, Satoshi Ikushima, Shigeyoshi Hibi, et al. 1988. High serum ferritin level as a marker of malignant histiocytosis and virus-associated hemophagocytic syndrome. *Cancer* 61: 2071–6.

Fairbanks, Virgil, and Ernest Beutler. 1988. Iron. In *Modern nutrition in health and disease*, ed. Maurice Shils and Vernon Young, 193–226. Philadelphia, Pa.

Farley, Patrick, and Jaime Foland. 1990. Iron deficiency anemia: How to diagnose and correct. *Postgraduate Medicine* 87: 89–101.

Fielding, Jack. 1980. Serum iron and iron binding capacity. In *Iron*, ed. James Cook, 15–43. New York.

Finch, C. A. 1989. Introduction: Knights of the oval table. *Journal of Internal Medicine* 226: 345–8.

Finch, C. A., and H. Huebers. 1982. Perspectives in iron metabolism. *New England Journal of Medicine* 306: 1520–8.

Florentino, Rodolfo, and Romualda Guirriec. 1984. Prevalence of nutritional anemia in infancy and childhood with emphasis on developing countries. In *Iron nutrition in infancy and childhood*, ed. A. Stekel, 61–74. New York.

Frassinelli-Gunderson, E. P., S. Margen, and J. R. Brown. 1985. Iron stores in users of oral contraceptive agents. *American Journal of Clinical Nutrition* 41: 703–12.

Goodner, Kenneth. 1933. Bacteriological and serological studies in Yucatan in 1929. In *The peninsula of Yucatan: Medical, biological, meteorological and sociological studies*, ed. George Shattuck, 201–20. Carnegie Institution of Washington Publication No. 431.

Gordeuk, Victor, R. Devee Boyd, and Gary Brittenham. 1986. Dietary iron overload persists in rural sub-Saharan Africa. *Lancet* 1310–13.

Griffiths, E. 1987. Iron in biological systems. In *Iron and infection*, ed. J. J. Bullen and E. Griffiths, 1–26. London.

Griffiths, E., and J. J. Bullen. 1987. Iron-binding proteins and host defence. In *Iron and infection*, ed. J. J. Bullen and E. Griffiths, 171–210. London.

Guyatt, Gordon, Christopher Patterson, Mahomoud Ali, et al. 1990. Diagnosis of iron-deficiency anemia in the elderly. *American Journal of Medicine* 88: 205–9.

Hallberg, Leif. 1980. Food iron absorption. In *Iron,* ed. James Cook, 117–33. New York.

Hann, Hie-Won, Young Chung, W. Thomas, and Baruch Blumberg. 1989. Increased serum ferritin in chronic liver disease: A risk factor for primary hepatocellular carcinoma. *International Journal of Cancer* 43: 376–9.

Herold, P. M., and J. E. Kinsella. 1986. Fish oil consumption and decreased risk of cardiovascular disease. *American Journal of Clinical Nutrition* 43: 566–98.

Hoffbrand, A. V., and S. M. Lewis. 1981. *Postgraduate haematology*. London.

Houwelingen, R. V., A. Nordoy, E. van der Beek, et al. 1987. Effect of a moderate fish intake on blood pressure, bleeding time, hematology, and clinical chemistry in healthy males. *American Journal of Clinical Nutrition* 46: 424–36.

Hultcrantz, Rolf, Bo Angelin, Erik Björn-Rasmussen, et al. 1989. Eiliary excretion of iron and ferritin in idiopathic hemochromatosis. *Gastroenterology* 96: 1539–45.

Jacobs, A., and M. Worwood. 1982. Iron metabolism, iron deficiency and overload. In *Blood and its disorders*. Second edition, ed. R. M. Hardisty and D. J. Weatherall, 149–97. Oxford.

Kent, Susan. 1986. The influence of sedentism and aggregation on porotic hyperostosis and anaemia: A case study. *Man* 21: 605–36.

  1992. Anemia through the ages. In *Diet, demography and disease: Changing perspectives of anemia,* ed. Patricia Stuart-Macadam and Susan Kent, 1–30. New York.

Kent, Susan, and Eugene Weinberg. 1989. Hypoferremia: Adaption to disease? [letter] *New England Journal of Medicine*: 320, 672.

Kent, Susan, Eugene Weinberg, and Patricia Stuart-Macadam. 1990. Dietary and prophylactic iron supplements: Helpful or harmful? *Human Nature* 1: 53–79.

  1994. The etiology of the anemia of chronic disease. *Journal of Clinical Epidemiology* 47: 23–33.

Keusch G., and M. Farthing. 1986. Nutrition and infection. *Annual Review of Nutrition* 6: 131-54.

Kluger, M. J., and J. J. Bullen. 1987. Clinical and physiological aspects. In *Iron and infection,* ed. J. J. Bullen and E. Griffiths, 243-82. London.

Kochan, I. 1973. The role of iron in bacterial infections, with special consideration of host-tubercle bacillus interaction. *Current Topics in Microbiology and Immunology* 60: 1-30.

Kromhout D., E. B. Bosschieter, and C. de Lezenne Coulander. 1985. The inverse relation between fish consumption and 20-year mortality from coronary heart disease. *New England Journal of Medicine* 312: 1205-9.

Labbe, Robert, and Clement Finch. 1980. Erythrocyte protoporphyrin: Application of the diagnosis of iron deficiency. In *Iron,* ed. James Cook, 44-58. New York.

Lee, G. R. 1983. The anemia of chronic disease. *Seminar in Hematology* 20: 61-80.

Leon, M. B., J. S. Borer, S. L. Bacharach, et al. 1979. Detection of early cardiac dysfunction in patients with severe beta-thalassemia and chronic iron overload. *New England Journal of Medicine* 301: 1143-8.

Liebel, R. L., A. B. Greenfield, and E. Pollitt. 1979. Iron deficiency: Behavior and brain chemistry. In *Nutrition: Pre- and postnatal development,* ed. Myron Winick, 383-439. New York.

Long, P. J., and B. Shannon. 1983. *Focus on nutrition.* Englewood Cliffs, N. J.

MacPhail, A. P., M. O. Simon, J. D. Torrance, et al. 1979. Changing patterns of dietary iron overload in Black South Africans. *American Journal of Clinical Nutrition* 32: 1272-8.

Martinez, J. L., A. Delgado-Irabarren, and F. Baquero. 1990. Mechanisms of iron acquisition and bacterial virulence. *FEMS: Microbiology Reviews* 75: 45-56.

Masawe, A. E., J. M. Muindi, and G. B. Swai. 1974. Infections in iron deficiency and other types of anaemia in the tropics. *Lancet* 2: 314-17.

McCarthy, James, William Johnson, David Nixon, et al. 1989. Transfusional iron overload in patients undergoing dialysis. *Journal of Laboratory and Clinical Medicine* 114: 193-9.

McLaren, Gordon, W. Angus Muir, and Robert Kellermeyer. 1983. Iron overload disorders: Natural history, pathogenesis, diagnosis, and therapy. *Critical Reviews in Clinical Laboratory Sciences* 19: 205-66.

Mazzanti, R., K. S. Srai, E. S. Debnam, et al. 1987. The effect of chronic ethanol consumption on iron absorption in rats. *Alcohol and Alcoholism* 22: 47-52.

Miller, Carole, Richard Jones, Steven Plantadosi, et al. 1990. Decreased erythropoietin response in patients with the anemia of cancer. *New England Journal of Medicine* 322: 1689-92.

Monsen, Elaine. 1988. Iron nutrition and absorption: Dietary factors which impact iron bioavailability. *Journal of the American Dietetic Association* 88: 786-90.

Moore, Carl. 1973. Iron. In *Modern nutrition in health and disease.* Fifth edition, ed. R. S. Goodhart and M. E. Shils. Philadelphia, Pa.

Murray M. J., and A. Murray. 1977. Starvation suppression and refeeding activation of infection: An ecological necessity? *Lancet* 1: 123-5.

Murray M. J., A. Murray, and C. J. Murray. 1980. An ecological interdependence of diet and disease? *American Journal of Clinical Nutrition* 33: 697-701.

Murray, M. J., A. Murray, N. Murray, and M. Murray. 1976. Somali food shelters in the Ogaden famine and their impact on health. *Lancet* 1: 1283-5.

Noyes, Ward. 1985. Anemia as a result of the insufficiency in the production of red cells. In *Hematology and oncology,* ed. Marshall Litchtman, 23-8. New York.

Oppenheimer, S. J., F. D. Gibson, S. B. MacFarlane, et al. 1986. Iron supplementation increases prevalence and effects of malaria: Report on clinical studies in Papua New Guinea. *Transactions of the Royal Society of Tropical Medicine and Hygiene* 80: 603-12.

Osborne, Pamela, Luther Burkett, George Ryan, and Marlene Lane. 1989. An evaluation of red blood cell heterogeneity (increased red blood cell distribution width) in iron deficiency of pregnancy. *American Journal of Obstetrics and Gynecology* 160: 336-9.

Payne, S. 1988. Iron and virulence in the family Enterobacteriaceae. *CRC Critical Reviews in Microbiology* 16(2): 81.

Pearson, H., and J. Robinson. 1976. The role of iron in host resistance. *Advanced Pediatrics* 23: 1-33.

Pochedly, C., and S. L. May. 1987. Iron deficiency anemia in children. *American Family Physician* 35: 195-200.

Picciano, M. F., and H. A. Guthrie. 1976. Copper, iron and zinc contents of mature human milk. *American Journal of Clinical Nutrition* 29: 242-54.

Reizenstein, Peter. 1983. *Hematological stress syndrome: The biological response to disease.* New York.

Rodriguez, M. C., M. S. Henriquez, A. F. Turon, et al. 1986. Trace elements in chronic alcoholism. *Trace Elements in Medicine* 3: 164-7.

Salonen, J. T., K. Nyyssönen, H. Korpela, et al. 1992. High stored iron levels are associated with excess risk of myocardial infarction in Finnish men. *Circulation* 86: 803-11.

Schade, A. L., and L. Caroline. 1944. Raw hen egg white and the role of iron in growth inhibition of *Shigella dysenteriae, Staphylococcus aureus, Escherichia coli,* and *Saccharomyces cerevisiae. Science* 100: 14-15.

Selby, Joseph, and Gary Friedman. 1988. Epidemiologic evidence of an association between body iron stores and risk of cancer. *International Journal of Cancer* 41: 677-82.

Simmons, Arthur. 1989. *Hematology: A combined theoretical and technical approach.* Philadelphia, Pa.

Stevens, R. G., D. Y. Jones, M. S. Micozzi, and P. R. Taylor. 1988. Body iron stores and the risk of cancer. *New England Journal of Medicine* 319: 1047-52.

Strauss, R. 1978. Iron deficiency, infections, and immune function: A reassessment. *American Journal of Clinical Nutrition* 31: 660-6.

Stuart-Macadam, Patricia. 1988. Nutrition and anemia in past human populations. In *Diet and subsistence: Current archaeological perspectives,* ed. B. Kennedy and G. LeMoine, 284-7. Calgary.

Subar, Amy, and Jean Bowering. 1988. The contribution of enrichment and fortification to nutrient intake of women. *Journal of the American Dietetic Association* 88: 1237-45.

Sullivan, J. L. 1983. The sex difference in ischemic heart disease. *Perspectives in Biology and Medicine* 26: 657-71.

　　　1989. The iron paradigm of ischemic heart disease. *American Heart Journal* 117: 1177-88.

Thompson, Warren. 1988. Comparison of tests for diagnosis of iron depletion in pregnancy. *American Journal of Obstetrics and Gynecology* 159: 1132-4.

Thompson, Warren, Thomas Meola, Mack Lipkin, and Michael Freedman. 1988. Red cell distribution width, mean corpuscular volume, and transferrin saturation in the diagnosis of iron deficiency. *Archives of Internal Medicine* 148: 2128-30.

Wadsworth, George. 1975. Nutritional factors in anemia. *World Review of Nutrition and Diet* 21: 75–150.

1991. Iron and anemia. Paper presented at the American Association of Physical Anthropology Conference, Milwaukee, Wis.

Weinberg, Eugene. 1966. Roles of metallic ions in host-parasite interactions. *Microbiological Reviews* 30: 136–51.

1974. Iron and susceptibility to infectious disease. *Science* 184: 952–6.

1977. Infection and iron metabolism. *American Journal of Clinical Nutrition* 30: 1485–90.

1978. Iron and infection. *Microbiological Review* 42: 45–66.

1981. Iron and neoplasia. *Biology and Trace Element Research* 3: 55–80.

1983. Iron in neoplastic disease. *Nutrition and Cancer* 4: 223–33.

1984. Iron withholding: A defense against infection and neoplasia. *Physiological Reviews* 64: 65–102.

1989. Cellular regulation of iron assimilation. *Quarterly Review of Biology* 64: 261–90.

1990. Cellular iron metabolism in health and disease. *Drug and Metabolism Reviews* 22: 531–79.

1992. Iron withholding: A defense against disease. In *Diet, demography, and disease: Changing perspectives of anemia,* ed. Patricia Stuart-Macadam and Susan Kent. New York.

Woods, S., T. DeMarco, and M. Friedland. 1990. Iron metabolism. *American Journal of Gastroenterology* 85: 1–8.

Worwood, M. 1980. Serum ferritin. In *Iron in biochemistry and medicine, II,* ed. A. Jacobs and M. Worwood, 203–44. London.

1989. An overview of iron metabolism at a molecular level. *Journal of Internal Medicine* 226: 381–91.

Ya-You, Ji, Liu Yan-Fang, Wang Bo-Yun, and Yang De-Yun. 1989. An immunocytochemical study on the distribution of ferritin and other markers in 36 cases of malignant histiocytosis. *Cancer* 64: 1281–9.

Yinnon, Amos, Abraham Konijn, Gabriela Link, et al. 1988. Diagnostic value of ferritin in malignant pleural and peritoneal effusions. *Cancer* 62: 2564–8.

Zanella, Alberto, Linda Gridelli, Alessandra Berzuini, et al. 1989. Sensitivity and predictive value of serum ferritin and free erythrocyte protoporphyrin for iron deficiency. *Journal of Laboratory and Clinical Medicine* 113: 73–8.

IV.B.4 ❦ Magnesium

*It's astonishing how much you may see,
in a thicker fog than that, if you only
take the trouble to look for it.*

Charles Dickens, *Christmas Stories*

Magnesium is one of the most plentiful elements in nature and the fourth most abundant metal in living organisms. It is extremely important in both plant and animal metabolism. Photosynthesis does not proceed when the magnesium atom is removed from the chlorophyll molecule. Magnesium also plays a key role in many enzyme reactions that are critical to cellular metabolism and is one of the main determinants of biological excitation (Aikawa 1981).

Despite its ubiquitous distribution and the multiplicity of its actions, magnesium has long been considered as a microelement with a vague physiological role, and not until the early 1930s was it recognized as an essential nutrient. Magnesium deficiency in humans was only described in 1951, and according to several experts, it continues to be diagnosed less frequently than it should be (Whang 1987).

There are many explanations for the reluctance to allow magnesium deficiency a place in medicine; among them are the difficulties in measuring magnesium, which have restrained the accumulation of knowledge. Moreover, the essentially intracellular location of the magnesium ion has discouraged the detection of its deficit. Lastly, because magnesium is so widely distributed in foods, its dietary intake has been assumed to be sufficient to meet the body's requirements.

Actually, pure magnesium deficiency is quite rare. Marginal deficiency of magnesium, however, is believed to occur fairly often in the general population. Moreover, in most diseases causing magnesium deficiency, significant nutritional factors exist.

A Note on Etymology

The word "magnesium" originates from the Greek word *Magnesia.* Magnesia is the eastern peninsular region of Thessaly in central Greece. It was named after the *Magnetes,* a prehistoric Macedonian people, by whom Magnesia was first inhabited in the twelfth century B.C. The *Magnetes* are mentioned by Homer, and the port of Magnesia in the Pagassitic Gulf was the place whence the Argonauts sailed on their way to Colchide. Magnesia was also the name of three different overseas colonies established by the *Magnetes* during the eleventh century B.C.: one in central Crete, and two in the inland of Asia Minor (Map IV.B.4.1).

Magnetes lithos and *Magnesia lithos,* which both mean "stone of Magnesia," were the names given by the ancient Greeks to minerals obtained from the earth of either the metropolitan Magnesia or its Asian colonies. *Magnetes lithos* or *magnetes* (magnet) was the term used for lodestone (native iron oxide that attracts iron). Hippocrates, however, the fifth-century B.C. father of medicine, referred to *Magnesia lithos* as a cathartic (purgative). He recommended (as translated by Paul Potter) that "if the cavity does not have a spontaneous movement, you must clean it out by giving spurge-flax, Cnidian berry, hippopheos, or magnetic stone" (Hippocrates 1988). ("Stone of Magnesia" or "Magnesian stone" would be a more appropriate translation than "magnetic stone.") Presumably, the stone mentioned by Hippocrates was native magnesium carbonate (magnesite), the white and light powder that was later called *magnesia alba* and is still used as an aperient and antacid.

Magnesia alba was prepared from the mother liquors obtained in the manufactures of niter by M. B. Valentini of Giessen, in 1707, but it was confused with "calcareous earth" until 1755, when J. Black of Edin-

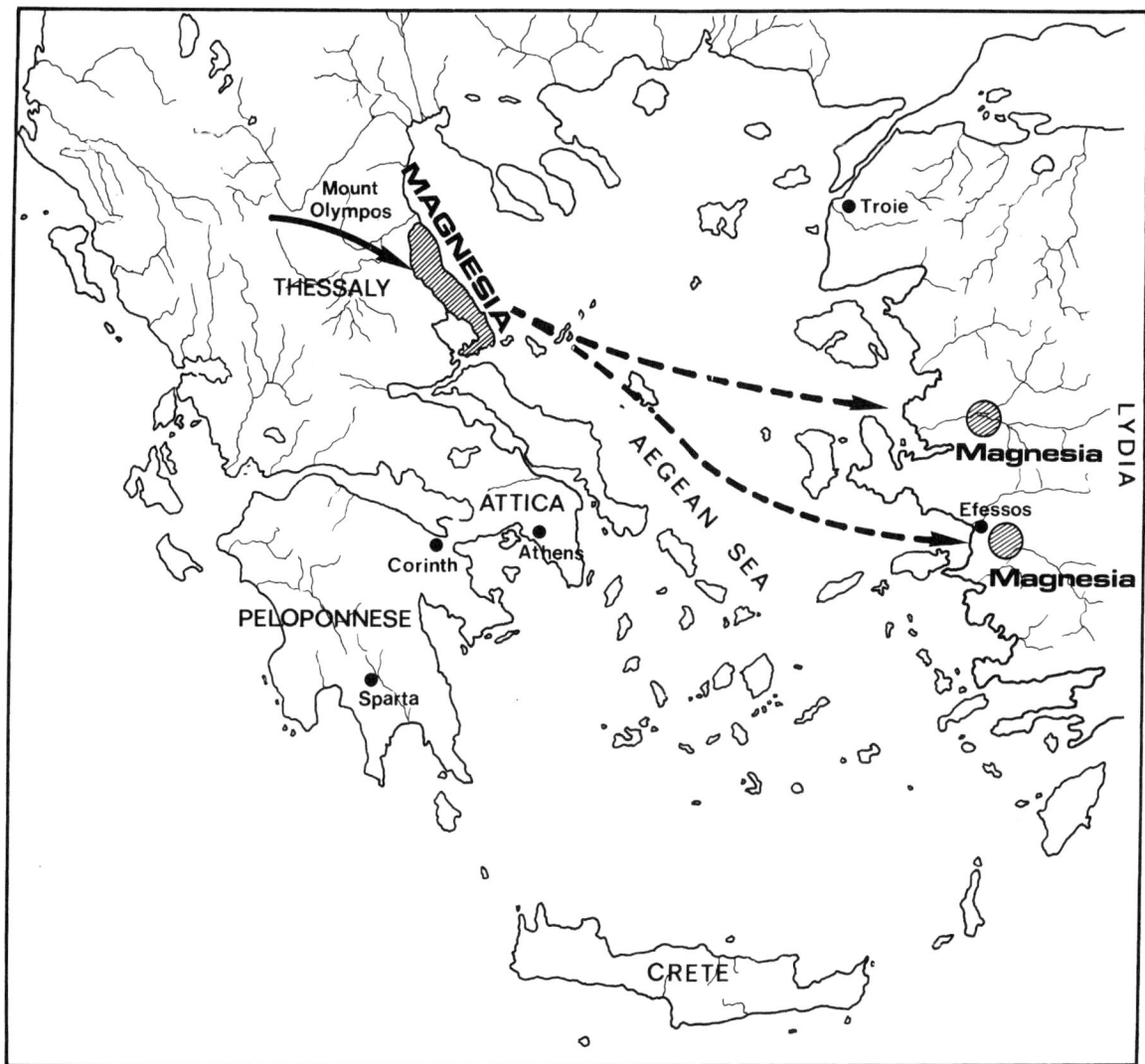

Map IV.B.4.1. Magnesia and its colonies in Asia Minor. The migration of *Magnetes* during the twelfth and eleventh centuries B.C.

burgh distinguished chemical differences between magnesia and lime. In 1807, Sir Humphrey Davy, conducting his studies on earth compounds in London, succeeded in isolating a number of alkali-earth metals that he named barium, strontium, calcium, and magnium after their oxides baryta, strontia, chalk, and magnesia. Before long, "magnesium" replaced magnium as the name of the element derived from magnesia (Durlach 1988b).

Recognition of Magnesium Deficiency

The Early Years

It was near the end of the nineteenth century when the nutritional significance of minerals was first recognized. That not only organic substances but also nonor-

ganic elements contained in food are necessary for life became evident in about 1870, when the German biologist J. Forster demonstrated the lethal effect in dogs of a diet deprived of inorganic salts (Forster 1873). A few years later, J. Gaube du Gers in France reported that mice fed a diet consisting of magnesium-free bread and distilled water were rendered progressively sterile. Impressed by this finding, he hastened to conclude that magnesium is "the metal of vital activity for what is most precious in life: reproduction and sensation" (Gaube 1895).

By 1900, on the American side of the Atlantic, J. Loeb accomplished his original experiments on the physiology of neuromuscular contractions and was able to state that biological excitation "depends upon the various ions, especially the metal ions (sodium, calcium, potassium, and magnesium) existing in definite proportions in the tissue" (Loeb 1900) (Table IV.B.4.1). About the same time, it was discovered that the magnesium atom occupies the central position in the chlorophyll molecule (Willstatter and Stoll 1913). Thus the most fundamental role of magnesium in nature was discovered, for which a 1915 Nobel Prize was awarded.

As postulated by Jerry Aikawa in recent years, life on earth would not be possible without magnesium, since photosynthesis is absolutely dependent on this element and the photosynthetic process is indispensable for the enrichment of the environment with oxygen (Aikawa 1981). An understanding, however, of the myriad roles of magnesium in biology had to await a method suitable for its measurement in biological materials. The first such method was a gravimetric technique involving the precipitation of magnesium ammonium phosphate. It was introduced by L. B. Mendel and S. R. Benedict in 1909 and was subsequently superseded by its modification to a colorimetric procedure (Alcock 1969).

In the following years, a large number of chemical approaches, including adsorption of titan yellow dye by magnesium hydroxide in the presence of a stabilizer, titrimetric, or colorimetric methods measuring various magnesium-dye complexes, and fluorometric techniques (Table IV.B.4.2), were used for the determination of magnesium in plasma or serum, urine, or fecal samples. The multiplicity of methods is indicative of the lack of satisfaction among investigators with any one of them.

An impressive step forward in the understanding of the role of magnesium metabolism in health and disease was made by the availability of atomic absorption spectrophotometry. This simple, precise method permits multiple determinations of minute amounts of magnesium in small samples of biological fluids

Table IV.B.4.2. *Year of first application of different procedures for measuring magnesium in biological materials*

1909	Magnesium ammonium phosphate precipitation
1927	Titan yellow method
1951	EDTA titration
1952	Emission (flame) spectrophotometry
1955	Colorimetric procedures
1959	Fluorometric techniques
1960	Atomic absorption spectrophotometry

and tissues, in a matter of minutes. The theoretical basis of flame spectrophotometry lies in the discovery made by the famous German physicist Gustav Kirchhoff in 1860, that both emission and absorption of light of a specific wavelength are characteristic of a given element. Emission spectrophotometry was first used to measure serum magnesium by V. Kapuscinski and his co-workers in 1952. The quantitative measurement of atomic absorption was conceived by A. Walsh in 1955. J. Alan applied this technique to the measurement of magnesium in plants in 1958, and two years later, atomic absorption spectrophotometry was used for the determination of serum magnesium by J. Willis (Alcock 1969).

Alkaline phosphatase was the first enzyme shown to be activated by magnesium. The discovery was made by H. Erdtmann in 1927. Since then, as many as 300 enzymes have been known to be activated by this cation in vitro, including all those utilizing adenosine triphosphate or catalyzing the transfer of phosphate. Because magnesium is the second most plentiful intracellular cation, it has been postulated that its function also extends to all these enzymes in vivo. By inference, the predominant view has been that magnesium is required for most of the major metabolic pathways in the cell, including membrane transport, protein, nucleic acid, fat and coenzyme synthesis, glucose utilization, and oxidative phosphorylation (Wacker 1969).

Introducing the Concept

The credit for introducing the concept of magnesium deficiency belongs to Jehan Leroy. He showed for the first time that the metal is essential for mammalian metabolisms when he found that white mice fed a diet deficient in magnesium failed to grow (Leroy 1926). However, the most distinctive manifestation of magnesium deficiency was recognized in 1932, when the group led by E. McCollum reported the development of hyperemia and progressive neuromuscular irritability, culminating in generalized and sometimes fatal seizures, in weanling rats fed a diet containing 0.045 millimoles (mmol) per kilogram (kg) of the element (Kruse, Orent, and McCollum 1932).

It should be noted that flaccid paralysis as a pharmacological effect of intravenous magnesium sulfate has been described by French authors since 1869 (Jolyet and Cahours 1869). A distinction, however, should be made between pharmacological properties

Table IV.B.4.1. *Some important dates*

1807	Discovery of magnesium by Sir Humphrey Davy
1900	Experimental evidence that irritability of the nervous system depends upon metal ions, including magnesium (J. Loeb)
1903	Discovery that the magnesium atom occupies the central location in the chlorophyll molecule (R. Willstatter)
1909	Development of a chemical method for the determination of magnesium in biological material (L. Mendel and S. Benedict)
1926	Demonstration that magnesium is essential for growth and life (J. Leroy)
1932	Attribution of grass tetany of ruminants to hypomegnesemia (B. Sjollema)
1934	Description of a clinical syndrome of hypomegnesemia associated with twitching or convulsions (A. Hirschfelder and V. Haury)
1951	Description of clinical magnesium deficiency (E. Flink)
1960	Measurement of serum magnesium by atomic absorption spectrophotometry (J. Willis)

of a substance and manifestations of its metabolic effect. The fact that a generalized convulsion can be controlled by massive parenteral magnesium administration, for instance, does not necessarily mean that the symptom is due to deficiency of this ion.

During the 1950s and 1960s, the early experiments of McCollum and his colleagues were confirmed and extended by many research groups. Experimental magnesium deficiency produced in rats, dogs, cocks, and other animal species was found to be associated with multiple pathological lesions, including nephrocalcinosis, myocardial necrosis, and calcium deposition in the aorta and the coronary and peripheral vessels; and to be accompanied by other metabolic changes, such as hypercalcemia, azotemia, and tissue potassium depletion.

About the time that McCollum published his original findings on experimental magnesium deficiency, a form of spontaneously occurring hypomagnesemic tetany was observed in adult lactating cattle and sheep. The disease, characterized by neuromuscular irritability, tetany, and convulsions, was termed "grass tetany" because the symptoms developed in the affected animals when they were first allowed to graze on fresh green grass in the spring (Sjollema 1932). Grass tetany has since been reported in many parts of the world, including the United States, many European countries, New Zealand, Australia, and Japan. Although there have been numerous investigations, the etiology of the disease is not clear.

Plasma magnesium is usually low in those afflicted, but grass tetany has also been observed in animals with decreased cerebrospinal magnesium levels whose serum magnesium was normal. The diet of the animals, when they are confined indoors during the winter, consists of silage, grains, and grain mash, which are deficient in magnesium, but symptoms of deficiency do not arise until shortly – sometimes within two days – after the animals are turned out on spring grass. It is of interest that the magnesium content of grasses and grazing vegetation in grass tetany–prone areas has been found to be decreased when compared with the vegetation of non-prone areas (Kubota 1981).

In 1959, a second form of hypomagnesemic tetany of ruminants was recognized when R. Smith reported a gradual development of hypomagnesemia in association with progressive irritability and tetany in calves fed for a long time on a pure milk diet. Magnesium supplementation was found to prevent the disease (Smith 1959). It should be noted that cow's milk contains magnesium in fair amounts, but its high phosphate and calcium content can adversely interfere with magnesium absorption.

Magnesium Deficiency in Humans
As early as 1932, B. Sjollema and L. Seekles, by extrapolating data from veterinary medicine, postulated that human cases of tetany may be related to hypomagne-

semia. In 1934, A. B. Hirschfelder and V. G. Haury described seven patients with hypomagnesemia associated with muscular twitching or convulsions and concluded that a clinical syndrome did indeed exist involving low magnesium (hypomagnesemia) accompanied by twitching or by convulsions. One more case of hypomagnesemic tetany was reported by J. F. Miller in 1944. The patient was a 6-year-old boy with associated osteochondrosis of the capital epiphysis of the femurs. Soon after World War II inanition was recognized as a cause of hypomagnesemia, but clinical manifestations were not mentioned (Flink 1980).

The broad spectrum of full-blown manifestations of the magnesium deficiency syndrome was recognized in the early 1950s, when Edmund B. Flink described the amazing case of a woman who, having been on almost continuous intravenous fluid therapy for several months, developed striking neurological symptoms and signs, including almost every form of involuntary movement (Table IV.B.4.3). When first seen by Flink in July 1951 at Minnesota University Hospital, the patient was cachectic, dehydrated, and semicomatose and had severe hyponatremia, hypokalemia, hypophosphatemia, and hypochloremic alkalosis. With the appropriate replacement treatment, serum electrolytes returned to normal within a few days. However, on the sixth day of treatment, the patient began having repeated convulsions associated with gross tremor and myoclonic jerks of extremities, jaw, and tongue, facial

Table IV.B.4.3. *Causes of human magnesium deficiency and year of their first description*

Causes	Year
Inadequate intake	
Starvation	1949
Prolonged fluid therapy without magnesium	1951
Chronic alcoholism	1954
Protein–caloric malnutrition	1960
Defective absorption	
Prolonged diarrhea – any cause	1957
Malabsorption	1960
Increased urinary losses	
Diuretic-induced	1952
Renal diseases	1958
Drug-induced tubular dysfunction	1969
Endocrine and metabolic disorders	
Uncontrolled diabetes with ketoacidosis	1947
Hyperthyroidism	1955
Aldosteronism	1955
Hyperparathyroidism	1956
Other	
Neonatal hypocalcemia, hypomagnesemia	1962
Excessive lactation	1963
Genetic	1965

Source: Data from Wacker and Parisi (1968), Flink (1980), Whang (1987), and Durlach (1988a).

grimacing, choreiform and athetoid movements, and inability to talk or swallow.

These symptoms continued until the eleventh day, when a blood sample was taken for the determination of serum magnesium level. As stated quite emphatically by Flink, "serum magnesium level was obtained for no better reason than that magnesium and phosphate interact and are important intracellular elements" (Flink 1985). Serum magnesium was determined by the titan yellow method and was found to be very low. This finding prompted the intramuscular administration of magnesium sulfate in the daily dose of 2.0 mg. The response was so dramatic that it was characterized by Flink as "unforgettable" (Flink 1985). Tremor decreased after the first dose, and within 24 hours the patient was oriented and able to speak and eat (Fraser and Flink 1951).

One year later, similar symptoms in a patient with alcoholic cirrhosis stimulated the start of clinical and laboratory research on magnesium metabolism in alcoholism by Flink and his colleagues. Much of the knowledge of normal human magnesium metabolism and its alteration in disease originated from these early studies (Wacker and Parisi 1968).

Initially, the discovery of hypomagnesemia in patients with chronic alcoholism and delirium tremens, together with the response of some of these patients to parenteral administration of magnesium, led to the hypothesis that symptoms of alcohol withdrawal were due to magnesium deficiency. However, it was soon realized that many alcoholic patients with near normal serum magnesium levels also had symptoms, whereas others with very low levels did not. It was, therefore, suggested that serum magnesium might not reflect magnesium status, and balance studies were undertaken to elucidate this issue further. It is now quite clear that the main cause of magnesium depletion in alcoholism is inadequate magnesium intake. These early balance studies established the concept of tissue magnesium depletion in the presence of normal serum magnesium levels and revealed increased urinary losses as a possible mechanism of magnesium deficiency. Thus, a significant amount of parenterally administered magnesium was found to be retained by alcoholic patients, indicating tissue magnesium depletion, whereas acute administration of large doses of alcohol was shown to result in increased renal magnesium excretion (Flink et al. 1954). Urinary excretion of magnesium after a load dose has been subsequently established as a feasible test in clinical practice for the evaluation of magnesium status.

That magnesium depletion is likely to occur as a result of drug treatment was first recognized in 1952, when H. E. Martin, J. Mehl, and M. Wertman reported a fall in serum magnesium in association with increased magnesium excretion in 10 patients with congestive heart failure treated with ammonium chloride and mercurial diuretics. Since that time, other diuretics, such as thiazides and loop diuretics; antibiotics, including aminoglucosides, tircacillin, carbenicillin, and amphotericin B; and also cisplatin and cyclosporin have been added to the list of iatrogenic causes of magnesium depletion (Whang 1987).

Intestinal disorders were recognized quite early as a common cause of clinical magnesium deficiency. During the late 1950s and the early 1960s, ulcerative colitis and regional enteritis, along with almost every cause of persistent diarrhea, including chronic laxative abuse, and also intestinal malabsorption due to chronic pancreatitis, short bowel syndrome, gluten enteropathy and tropical sprue, have been reported fairly often in association with symptomatic hypomagnesemia (Table IV.B.4.3).

Data from patients with malabsorption have confirmed previous observations in patients with primary hyperparathyroidism, indicating a relationship between magnesium metabolism and calcium metabolism. Hyperparathyroidism has been recognized as a cause of hypomagnesemia since 1956 (Harman 1956). Although some patients have been found to develop symptoms while hypercalcemic, in most cases hypomagnesemia has accompanied the fall in serum calcium levels after the removal of a parathyroid adenoma and has been attributed to the absorption of magnesium by the "hungry" bones of osteitis fibrosa cystica (Barnes, Krane, and Cope 1957). Since that time, it has been realized that hypercalcemia from any cause, including metastatic osteolysis and multiple myeloma, can be associated with symptomatic hypomagnesemia, because hypercalcemia causes increased excretion of magnesium in the urine (Eliel et al. 1968).

That the two major intracellular cations, potassium and magnesium, behave similarly was originally noted in the course of diabetic ketoacidosis (Martin and Wertman 1947). Similarities between the two ions were further emphasized by the observation that serum potassium and magnesium are both low in cases of primary aldosteronism (Mader and Iseri 1955). Moreover, cardiac arrhythmias, such as ventricular extrasystoles, ventricular tachycardia, and ventricular fibrillation, similar to those induced by hypokalemia, have been described in various clinical disorders known to result in depletion of magnesium. As a matter of fact, the demonstration that in hypertensive patients treated with diuretics, potassium supplementation alone has little effect on ventricular extrasystoles unless magnesium supplementation is added to the regimen has aroused clinical interest in magnesium deficiency significantly over recent years (Hollifield 1984).

Controversial Issues

A Puzzling Syndrome

During the 1960s, human magnesium deficiency was established as a clinical entity beyond any doubt. However, conflicting reports in the literature may have created the view for many that clinical magnesium deficiency is a puzzling syndrome comprising almost every symptom and sign. Such confusion also results partly from the previously mentioned difficulties in assessing magnesium status along with superimposed nonspecific manifestations related to primary illness or other concomitant metabolic abnormalities.

Thus, in addition to the generally accepted signs and symptoms of neuromuscular hyperactivity and disturbance of cardiac rhythm (Table IV.B.4.4), a great variety of manifestations, ranging from difficulty in learning to multiple phlebothromboses, have been proposed as components of the clinical picture of magnesium deficiency (Table IV.B.4.5). Moreover, the observation that even severe magnesium deficiency may have no symptoms or signs has added significantly to the confusion (Martin, Mehl, and Wertman 1952).

The term "spasmophilia" was first introduced by the French physician Nicolas Corvisart in 1852. In 1874, Wilhelm Erb attributed spasmophilia to neuromuscular hyperexcitability, and since then the term has been used to denote "a condition in which the motor nerves show abnormal sensitivity to mechanical or electric stimulations and the patient shows a tendency to spasm, tetany and convulsions" (Dorland 1943).

In 1959, Jean Durlach described a syndrome that he called "hypomagnesemic constitutional spasmophilia." The syndrome, which was considered to be "the nervous form of primary chronic magnesium deficiency in adults," comprised a long list of nonspe-

Table IV.B.4.4. *Generally accepted symptoms and signs of magnesium deficiency*

Neuromuscular manifestations
Muscular twitching and tremor
Myoclonic jerks
Convulsions
Ataxia and nystagmus
Irritability and restlessness
Dysphagia
Dysarthria
Chvostek's sign (and rarely Trousseau's sign)
Tetany (rarely)
Apathy
Coma

Cardiac manifestations
Premature ventricular contractions
Atrial fibrillation
Torsades de pointes
Ventricular fibrillation
Sudden death

Metabolic effects
Refractory hypokalemia
Hypocalcemia

Source: Data from Wacker and Parisi (1968) and Flink (1980).

Table IV.B.4.5. *Additional symptoms and signs attributed to magnesium deficiency by some authors*

Neuromuscular and psychologic manifestations
Anxiety
Depression, hysteria, hypochondria (neurotic triad)
Intellectual and affective retardation
Learning deficiencies
Headaches
Dizziness
Insomnia
Sight weakness
Startle response and noise sensitivity
Neck and back pains
Acroparesthesia
Raynaud's syndrome
"Spasmophilia"

Cardiac manifestations
Coronary artery spasm
Greater size of myocardial infarction

Miscellaneous
Hair and ungueal brittleness
Dysplasia of teeth enamel
Opacification of lens
Ostomalacia
Gastritis, visceral spasm, or dyskinesia ("visceral spasmophilia")
Mitral valve prolapse

Source: Data from Durlach (1988a).

cific neuromuscular, psychological, cardiovascular, and gastrointestinal manifestations, such as anxiety, excessive emotivity, globus hystericus, dyspnea *sine materia,* dizziness, insomnia, headaches, myalgias, cramps, tremors, tetanic attacks, palpitations, Raynaud's syndrome, biliary dyskinesia, epigastric cramps, and syncope. Symptoms were ameliorated by oral administration of magnesium salts. Low erythrocyte magnesium, a positive Chvostek's sign, and abnormal electromyographic, electroencephalographic, and electronystagmographic tracings were reported as characteristic of the syndrome (Durlach and Lebrun 1959).

In the years that followed, the compass of clinical magnesium deficiency was broadened to encompass such divergent manifestations as phlebothrombosis, allergic disorders, intellectual retardation, sight weakness, hepatic dysfunction, cases of dysmenorrhea, spontaneous abortion, and mitral valve prolapse. This broadening of the spectrum of clinical manifestations of magnesium deficiency was based on a great number of cases studied by Durlach and other investigators in continental Europe.

The fact that publication of such cases in English has been rare is indicative of the reluctance of American and British experts to accept the existence of a syndrome such as "idiopathic spasmophilic diathesis" due to magnesium deficiency. However, an incident investigated by the U.S. Food and Drug Administration (FDA) in 1980 and a recent double-blind trial performed in Southampton imply that the idea of the involvement of magnesium deficiency in bizarre clinical syndromes should not be totally rejected.

The incident investigated by the FDA was as follows: 11 high school football players with diet histories suggesting low calcium and magnesium intake were given a phosphate-free, soluble calcium preparation because of leg cramps. They were then subjected to the noise and physical contact of a football game. Over a short period, 8 of them developed serious neuromuscular dysfunction manifested by ataxia, slurred speech, hyperventilation, muscle spasm, and tonicoclonic seizures. All of them recovered without specific treatment, and none developed neurologic sequelae. About 10 years later, W. F. Langley and D. Mann noticed the similarity of this syndrome with grass tetany in animals and postulated that central nervous system magnesium deficiency was responsible for its occurrence. The condition was thought to be brought on by a sudden rise in serum calcium and was termed "reactive symptomatic magnesium deficiency" (Langley and Mann 1991).

The randomized double-blind, placebo-controlled trial in Southampton concerned the effect of intramuscular administration of magnesium sulfate on the symptoms of chronic fatigue syndrome (Cox, Campbell, and Dowson 1991). As stated by the authors, the study was undertaken because many of the symptoms of the chronic fatigue syndrome – anorexia, nausea, learning disability, personality changes, tiredness, and myalgia – are similar to those of magnesium deficiency, and because in a pilot study they found that patients with the syndrome had low red blood cell magnesium concentrations. Within six weeks, red cell magnesium had returned to normal in all patients treated with magnesium. In addition, magnesium administration resulted in improvement in energy, pain perception, emotional reactions, sleep patterns, sense of social isolation, and physical mobility, as scored with the use of the Nottingham health profile. The authors confessed, however, that their trial was small and that there was only 6 weeks of follow-up and, therefore, the results were hardly conclusive (Cox, Campbell, and Dawson 1991).

The "Water Story"

In 1957, J. Kobayashi reported a geographical relationship between stroke-associated mortality and river water acidity in Japan (Kobayashi 1957). This was the beginning of what was later called the "water story." Following the publication of the Japanese data, H. A. Schroeder (1960) investigated the relationship between mortality from different diseases and mineral content of drinking water in the United States, and concluded that the important determinant was water hardness rather than water acidity. Drinking soft water, he suggested, may promote the prevalence of cardiovascular disease, whereas hard water may exert a protective action. Since then, associations between hardness of drinking water and mortality from cardiovascular dis-

ease have been reported in England and Wales, in Sweden, and in Ontario – the softer the water the higher the mortality from cardiovascular disease.

Ten years after the original report of Kobayashi, T. Crawford and M. D. Crawford (1967) compared cardiac lesions found in medicolegal necropsies in cases of sudden death in two areas: Glasgow, a notable soft-water area with a high cardiovascular disease mortality; and London, a city with very hard water and a considerably lower mortality from cardiovascular causes. They realized that despite the large difference in mortality, the incidence of coronary atherosclerosis was similar in both places. This finding was subsequently interpreted to mean that the excess mortality in the soft-water area might correspond to sudden deaths due to fatal ventricular arrhythmias. Moreover, chemical analysis of the coronary arteries revealed very low values for calcium and magnesium in the soft-water area, suggesting that the mineral content of the arteries was related to the mineral content of the drinking water.

On the basis of the evidence just mentioned, a "cardiac water factor" has been postulated to exist. Presumably, such a factor would be either something beneficial in hard water or something harmful in soft water. Since the bulk of water hardness is made up of calcium and magnesium, these two ions have been the more likely candidates for the "cardiac water factor." Magnesium is a much more abundant intracellular ion than calcium. Furthermore, a considerably greater proportion of the daily magnesium intake, as compared with the daily calcium intake, comes from drinking water. Coupled with the arrhythmogenic potential of magnesium depletion, these facts have led to the hypothesis that magnesium is the cardioprotective factor contained in hard water.

In support of this hypothesis, T. W. Anderson and colleagues (1975) found that magnesium concentrations in myocardial samples obtained from accident victims were significantly lower in five soft-water cities of Ontario than in three hard-water cities of the same province. However, a similar report in England at about the same time (Chipperfield et al. 1976) found a significant difference in mean myocardial magnesium concentration between heart muscle samples obtained from noncardiac deaths in two cities with different water hardness, but the difference was "in the wrong direction." This discrepancy led Anderson and colleagues to conclude that if there was any sort of 'water factor' in Britain, it probably involved something beside magnesium (Anderson et al. 1980).

In the meantime, other simple correlation or multivariate statistical studies, including analysis of the data of the World Health Organization myocardial infarction registry network, have failed to discover a causal relationship between water hardness and heart disease mortality. Schroeder's report has been criticized as misleadingly simplistic, because it was based on correlations between just one index of environmental exposure and a set of death rates (Hammer and Heyden 1980). In addition, the demonstration that only a small proportion of the daily mineral element intake comes from drinking water has cast doubt on the possible physiological significance of water hardness.

Advocates of the "water factor," however, have adopted a somewhat different approach that emphasizes not water hardness but the interrelationship of individual elements contained in drinking water, along with the intake of these elements as they are ingested with food (Marier 1981). In this context, of particular interest are the observations of H. Karppanen in Finland, a country with a very high prevalence of cardiovascular disease. Mortality from ischemic heart disease in Finland shows a peculiar geographic distribution: Starting from the eastern areas, where it is extremely high, it decreases continuously toward the western and southwestern part of the country. These regional differences in mortality correlate with differences in the content of exchangeable magnesium in the arable soils: Magnesium concentration in the soil of eastern areas is only about one-third of that of the southwestern areas. Soil is the primary source of magnesium. Low magnesium concentration in soil is, therefore, expected to result in a low magnesium concentration in drinking water, and also in a low magnesium content of the cereal crops, which are a major food source of magnesium.

In addition to these observations, Karppanen has reported a strong positive correlation between the death rate from ischemic heart disease and the estimated average calcium-to-magnesium ratio of the diet in various Organization for Economic Cooperation and Development (OECD) countries. According to Karppanen, this correlation suggests that what really matters in the "water story" is the ratio of calcium-to-magnesium intake rather than the sum or the absolute amount of each of these elements (Karppanen 1981).

Nutrient or Drug?

Magnesium was known as a drug long before it was recognized as a nutrient. Thus, even in the nineteenth century, parenteral magnesium sulfate was used in the management of eclamptic convulsions and also as an ancillary anesthetic agent. In cardiology, magnesium was first introduced in 1935, when L. Zwillinger reported a beneficial effect of intravenous magnesium sulfate on paroxysmal tachycardia and extrasystolic arrhythmia in patients treated with digitalis. Since then, parenteral magnesium salts have been repeatedly used as an antiarrhythmic agent. Intravenous magnesium has also been recognized as a potent vasodilator agent, useful in the treatment of heart failure and angina pectoris.

During the past five years, several randomized clinical trials have examined the effects of intravenous magnesium in acute myocardial infarction. Collectively, these trials strongly suggest that magnesium therapy may result in decreased mortality as well as the frequency of postinfarction arrhythmias. A larger trial with a planned sample size of 2,500 patients was started in 1987 (Woods 1991).

In all these studies and in many of the cases of treatment of cardiac arrhythmias, the beneficial effect of intravenous magnesium has been related to pharmacological action rather than to repletion of a deficit. In fact, when magnesium is given intravenously, serum magnesium levels are usually raised well above normal values. However, hypomagnesemia is an established cause of cardiac arrhythmias, and magnesium deficiency has been shown to be associated with sudden cardiac death and increased mortality in the acute stage of myocardial infarction (Dyckner 1980). Moreover, low levels of magnesium have been found in myocardial tissue obtained at necropsy from patients with acute myocardial infarction. Consequently, under conditions of magnesium deficiency, a supplement of magnesium is expected to have the same favorable effect on cardiac arrhythmias, and possibly the same protective action against myocardial ischemia, as the administration of magnesium salts in pharmacological doses.

On the basis of the evidence just mentioned, it is clear that the characterization of magnesium as a drug or as a nutrient depends on the distinction between pharmacological action and replenishment of deficient stores (Charbon 1989). When there is a proven magnesium deficiency, magnesium acts as a nutrient. The patient is then expected to be completely cured as soon as the deficit is corrected. However, parenteral magnesium salts may be given as a drug. In this case, though, their potency and duration of action will depend on magnesium concentration in plasma, and their effect will be the same in each case of repeated administration.

Adequacy of Intake

Estimates of the daily requirements of magnesium have been largely based on the original calculations published in 1942 by J. Duckworth and G. Warnock, who calculated the magnesium requirements by analyzing the available data from balance determinations done in the 1930s. Currently, the Recommended Dietary Allowance (RDA) proposed by the Food and Nutrition Board of the National Research Institute of the United States is 350 mg per day for men and 300 mg per day for women, providing about 4.5 to 5.0 milligrams (mg) per kilogram of body weight per day (Munro 1980). RDA is increased to 450 mg per day during pregnancy and lactation and to 400 mg per day during adolescence in males. For infants and children the corresponding values are 100 and 200 mg per day.

Magnesium is so plentiful in both plant and animal foods that the recommended daily intake is readily obtained in ordinary diet. Common dietary sources include unprocessed cereal, nuts, legumes, vegetables, seafood, dairy products, meats, and drinking water.

However, Mildred Seelig (1964) in the United States and Durlach (1988a) in France have suggested that magnesium intake in developed countries may be insufficient to meet daily needs. Since then this concern has been shared by many nutritionists.

The shortage of magnesium in contemporary diets has been attributed to the increased reliance of people in most Western countries on highly purified foods, such as sugar, starch, soft drinks, and distilled alcohol, that contain very little magnesium. Agricultural techniques of accelerated growth, resulting in decreased magnesium fixation by plants, and the use of magnesium-poor soil fertilizers, and also of pesticides that inhibit magnesium absorption, are considered as additional causes of decreased magnesium content in food items currently available for civilian consumption in industrialized countries. In fact, analysis of sample meals in the United States, Canada, and several European countries has revealed that the contemporary magnesium intake ranges from minimal adequacy to as low as 50 percent of the RDA (Table IV.B.4.6). This observation seems to hold particularly true for special population groups, such as pregnant women, teenage girls, or elderly people, because of increased needs, limited nutritional intake, or the age-associated decline in intestinal magnesium absorption (Mountokalakis 1987). In view of these considerations, Seelig has suggested that the recommendations for daily magnesium intake should be revised upward to as much as 7 to 10 mg/kg body weight.

Other experts opposed to this view have argued that since the RDA includes a generous margin of safety above the current estimates of the minimal daily requirements, the expression of adequacy of magnesium intake as a proportion of the RDA may be misleading. As a matter of fact, metabolic studies have indicated that a positive magnesium balance can be maintained at intakes as low as 60 percent of the currently proposed RDA. The answer to these arguments has been that because RDA is calculated by analyzing the results of metabolic studies conducted under conditions of relative serenity, it does not take into account possible changes of magnesium requirements related to the stresses of everyday life. The advocates of the "magnesium malnutrition" hypothesis emphasize that although the reported suboptimal intakes do not necessarily lead to overt clinical magnesium deficiency, they may represent a "long-term marginal magnesium insufficiency" with the potential risk of increased vulnerability to several disease processes (Marier 1982). The present uncertainty about evaluating the clinical status of magnesium impedes any attempt to clarify this issue further.

Epilogue

The story of magnesium is a story of discovery and also a story of neglect. Over the past few decades, enthusiasm about magnesium has repeatedly turned

Table IV.B.4.6. *Magnesium intake in the modern-day world*

Locality and special group range)	Year	Population studied	Intake as percentage of RDA (average o
Healthy adults			
United States			
Central states	1961	30 women	54.0–93.0
Boston	1970	955 men	74.9
Canada			
Montreal	1978	15 men	70.6
Montreal	1978	15 women	74.7
Newfoundland	1978	83 men	53.4
Newfoundland	1978	105 women	47.7
United Kingdom	1972	–	76.9
France	1980	–	80.0–100.0
West Germany	1972	1,852 adults	72.3
Special population groups			
Institutionalized people			
United States	1969	men	62.7
Indiana	1977	31 aged men	54.3–71.7
Indiana	1977	34 aged women	54.0–94.3
Belfast	1979	36 aged men	56.6
Belfast	1979	90 aged women	56.3
Pregnant women			
United States	1978	–	45.3
United States	1979	aged 19–29	60.0
Girls			
Indiana	1976	80, aged 12–14	79.3
Indiana	1977	76, aged 12–14	77.0
Tennessee	1980	60, aged 9–11	66.0–100.0

Source: Data from Marier (1982).

to indifference. Since 1971, when the First International Symposium on Magnesium Deficit in Human Pathology was held at Vittel (France), five international congresses and several American and European meetings on magnesium have taken place, and three journals exclusively devoted to magnesium have been published. Yet despite all this worldwide research activity, the practicing physician has relatively little interest in magnesium, and hypomagnesemia is currently the most underdiagnosed electrolyte deficiency (Whang 1987). Moreover, essential data for diagnosis and physiopathology are still lacking.

No doubt magnesium is an important intracellular element with a key role in many metabolic functions. The irony is that this multifaceted role of magnesium in the organism has been the main obstacle in understanding its fundamental function. A characteristic example is the physiological interrelationships of magnesium and hormones. Companion to both calcium and potassium, magnesium has long been assumed to interact with the hormones involved in the homeostasis of these two ions. The evidence, however, now shows that neither parathyroid hormone nor aldosterone exerts an overriding control on magnesium metabolism. Yet the facts that magnesium and calcium are mutually influenced and that hypomagnesemia can cause loss of intracellular potassium, in spite of a normal plasma potassium, are not in question.

Some 30 years ago, magnesium was hardly mentioned in the medical textbooks. Since then, much more information has been acquired. Although most of the current textbooks contain adequate data on the subject, they repeatedly state that magnesium is found in so many foods that, ordinarily, magnesium deficiency is rare in healthy people. It should be noted, however, that although magnesium is well conserved by both the kidneys and the bowel when the supply is limited, it is poorly stored so that a regular intake is needed to avoid deficiency. It is, therefore, natural to assume that a marginal deficiency state may be not uncommon. And once it was realized that magnesium has important cardiovascular effects, emphasis shifted from a focus on overt clinical magnesium deficiency to interest in the concept of marginal magnesium deficiency as a risk factor for cardiovascular disease. The importance of this concept is underscored by the characterization of magnesium as "nature's physiological calcium blocker" (Iseri and French 1984).

Because most of the body's magnesium is intracellular, the challenge for the future is to develop a feasible test in clinical medicine that will give meaningful information on the overall intracellular magnesium status. The question of intracellular magnesium is, without doubt, the most difficult to resolve. It is, however, the clarification of this issue that will enable us to understand better the relationship of magnesium to health and disease and to ascertain the magnitude of the segment of the population that may be deficient in this important nutrient.

Theodore D. Mountokalakis

Bibliography

Aikawa, J. K. 1981. *Magnesium: Its biologic significance.* Boca Raton, Fla.

Alcock, N. W. 1969. Development of methods for the determination of magnesium. *Annals of the New York Academy of Sciences* 162: 707–16.

Anderson, T. W., W. H. Leriche, D. Hewitt, and L. C. Neri. 1980. Magnesium, water hardness, and heart disease. In *Magnesium in health and disease,* ed. M. Cantin and M. S. Seelig, 565–71. New York.

Anderson, T. W., L. C. Neri, G. B. Schreiber, et al. 1975. Ischemic heart disease, water hardness and myocardial magnesium. *Canadian Medical Association Journal* 113: 199–203.

Barnes, B. A., S. M. Krane, and O. Cope. 1957. Magnesium studies in relation to hyperparathyroidism. *Journal of Clinical Endocrinology and Metabolism* 17: 1407–21.

Charbon, G. A. 1989. Magnesium treatment of arrhythmia: Drug or nutritional replenishment? Pitfalls for the experimental design. In *Magnesium in health and disease,* ed. Y. Itokawa and J. Durlach, 223–8. London.

Chipperfield, B., J. R. Chipperfield, G. Behr, and P. Burton. 1976. Magnesium and potassium content of normal heart muscle in areas of hard and soft water. *Lancet* 1: 121–3.

Cox, I. M., M. J. Campbell, and D. Dowson. 1991. Red blood cell magnesium and chronic fatigue syndrome. *Lancet* 337: 757–60.

Crawford, T., and M. D. Crawford. 1967. Prevalence and pathological changes of ischaemic heart disease in a hard-water area and in a soft-water area. *Lancet* 1: 229–32.

Dorland, D. A. N. 1943. *The American illustrated medical dictionary.* Ninth edition. Philadelphia, Pa.

Duckworth, J., and G. Warnock. 1942. The magnesium requirements of man in relation to calcium requirements with observations on the adequacy of diet in common use. *Nutritional Abstracts and Reviews* 12: 167–83.

Durlach, J. 1988a. *Magnesium in clinical practice.* London.
  1988b. Magnesium research: A brief historical account. *Magnesium Research* 1: 91–6.

Durlach, J., and R. Lebrun. 1959. Magnésium et pathogénie de la spasmophilie constitutionelle idiopathique. *Comptes Rendues de la Société de Biologie* 153: 1973–5.

Dyckner, T. 1980. Serum magnesium in acute myocardial infarction. *Acta Medica Scandinavica* 207: 59–66.

Eliel, L. P., W. O. Smith, R. Chanes, and J. Howrylko. 1969. Magnesium metabolism in hyperparathyroidism and osteolytic disease. *Annals of the New York Academy of Sciences* 162: 810–30.

Flink, E. B. 1980. Clinical manifestations of acute magnesium deficiency in man. In *Magnesium in health and disease,* ed. M. Cantin and M. S. Seelig, 865–82. New York.
  1985. Magnesium deficiency in human subjects – a personal historical perspective. *Journal of the American College of Nutrition* 4: 17–31.

Flink, E. B., et al. 1954. Magnesium deficiency after prolonged parenteral fluid administration and after chronic alcoholism complicated by delirium tremens. *Journal of Laboratory and Clinical Medicine* 43: 169–83.

Forster, J. 1873. Beiträge zur Ernährungsfrage. *Zeitschrift für Biologie.*

Fraser, R., and E. B. Flink. 1951. Magnesium, potassium, phosphorus, chloride and vitamin deficiency as a result of prolonged use of parenteral fluids. *Journal of Laboratory and Clinical Medicine* 38: 817–29.

Gaube, J. 1895. *Théorie minérale de l'évolution et de la nutrition de la cellule animale.* Paris.

Hammer, D. I., and S. Heyden. 1980. Water hardness and cardiovascular mortality. An idea that has served its purpose. *Journal of the American Medical Association* 243: 2399–400.

Harman, M. 1956. Parathyroid adenoma in a child. *Journal of Diseases of Children* 91: 313–56.

Hippocrates. 1988. Internal affections. In *Hippocrates,* trans. P. Potter, Vol. 6, 140–1. Cambridge, Mass.

Hirschfelder, A. B., and V. G. Haury. 1934. Clinical manifestations of high and low plasma magnesium. Dangers of Epsom salt purgation in nephritis. *Journal of the American Medical Association* 102: 1138–41.

Hollifield, J. W. 1984. Potassium and magnesium abnormalities: Diuretics and arrhythmias in hypertension. *The American Journal of Medicine* 77: 28–32.

Iseri, L. T., and J. H. French. 1984. Magnesium: Nature's physiological calcium blocker. *American Heart Journal* 108: 188–93.

Jolyet, F., and M. Cahours. 1869. Sur l'action physiologique des sulfates de potasse, de soude et de magnésie en injection dans le sang. *Archives de Physiologie Normale et Pathologique* 2: 113-20.

Karppanen, H. 1981. Epidemiological studies on the relationship between magnesium intake and cardiovascular diseases. *Artery* 9: 190-9.

Kobayashi, J. 1957. Geographical relationship between the chemical nature of river water and death-rate from apoplexy. *Ber Ohara Instituts Landwirschaftliche Biologie* 11: 12-21.

Kruse, H., E. R. Orent, and E. V. McCollum. 1932. Magnesium deficiency in animals. *Journal of Biological Chemistry* 96: 519-32.

Kruse, H., M. Schmidt, and E. McCollum. 1934. Studies on magnesium deficiency in animals. *Journal of Biological Chemistry* 106: 553-72.

Kubota, J. 1981. How soils and climate affect grass tetany. *Crops and Soils Magazine* 33: 15-17.

Langley, W. F., and D. Mann. 1991. Central nervous system magnesium deficiency. *Archives of Internal Medicine* 151: 593-6.

Leroy, J. 1926. Nécessité du magnésium pour la croissance de la souris. *Comptes Rendus de la Société de Biologie* 94: 431-3.

Loeb, B. 1900. On the different effect of ions upon myogenic and neurogenic rhythmical contractions and upon embryonic and muscular tissue. *American Journal of Physiology* 3: 383-96.

Mader, I. J., and L. T. Iseri. 1955. Spontaneous hypopotassemia, hypomagnesemia, alkalosis and tetany due to hypersecretion of orticosterone-like mineralocorticoid. *The American Journal of Medicine* 19: 976-88.

Marier, J. R. 1981. Water hardness and heart disease. *Journal of the American Medical Association* 245: 1316-26.

   1982. Quantitative factors regarding magnesium status in the modern-day world. *Magnesium* 1: 3-15.

Martin, H. E., J. Mehl, and M. Wertman. 1952. Clinical studies of magnesium metabolism. *Medical Clinics of North America* 36: 1157-71.

Martin, H. E., and M. Wertman. 1947. Serum potassium, magnesium and calcium levels in diabetic acidosis. *Journal of Clinical Investigation* 26: 217-28.

Mendel, L. B., and S. R. Benedict. 1909. The paths of excretion for inorganic compounds. IV. The excretion of magnesium. *American Journal of Physiology* 25: 1-7.

Miller, J. F. 1944. Tetany due to deficiency in magnesium. Its occurrence in a child of six years with associated osteochondrosis of capital epiphysis of femurs. *American Journal of Diseases of Children* 67: 117-19.

Mountokalakis, T. 1987. Effects of aging, chronic disease, and multiple supplements on magnesium requirements. *Magnesium* 6: 5-11.

Munro, H. N. 1980. *Recommended dietary allowances*. Ninth edition, 114-36. Washington, D.C.

Schroeder, H. A. 1960. Relations between mortality from cardiovascular disease and treated water supplies. *Journal of the American Medical Association* 117: 1902-8.

Seelig, M. S. 1964. The requirements of magnesium by normal adults. *American Journal of Clinical Nutrition* 14: 342-90.

Sjollema, B. 1932. Nutritional and metabolic disorders in cattle. *Nutrition Abstracts and Reviews* 1: 621-32.

Sjollema, B., and L. Seekles. 1932. Der Magnesiumgehalt des Blutes. Besonders bei Tetanie. *Klinische Wochenschrift* 11: 989-90.

Smith, R. H. 1959. Absorption of magnesium in large intestine of calf. *Nature* 184 (Suppl. 11): 821-6.

Wacker, W. E. C. 1969. The biochemistry of magnesium. *Annals of the New York Academy of Sciences* 162: 717-26.

Wacker, W. E. C., and A. F. Parisi. 1968. Magnesium metabolism. *The New England Journal of Medicine* 278: 712-17.

Whang, R. 1987. Magnesium deficiency: Pathogenesis, prevalence, and clinical implications. *The American Journal of Medicine* 82 (Suppl. 3A): 24-9.

Willstatter, R., and A. Stoll. 1913. *Untersuchungen über Chlorophyll*. Berlin.

Woods, K. L. 1991. Possible pharmacological actions of magnesium in acute myocardial infarction. *British Journal of Pharmacology* 32: 3-10.

Zwillinger, L. 1935. Ueber die Magnesiumwirkung auf das Herz. *Klinische Wochenschrift* 14: 1419-33.

IV.B.5 🐀 Phosphorus

Phosphorus (abbreviated as P) is a highly toxic element, which, when it occurs in the form of a phosphate salt, becomes a nutrient essential for human health. Phosphates are found in practically every type of food and, consequently, are plentiful in the typical diet. Inorganic phosphates (abbreviated as P_i) are absorbed from food as electrically charged salt anions. The organic phosphates (P_o) that exist in cells and extracellular compartments of foods are primarily converted to P_i through digestive processes prior to absorption. A few organic phosphates are apparently absorbed as part of small fat-soluble organic molecules, such as the phosphates of phospholipids. The concentration of P_o molecules, however, is not under homeostatic control, in contrast to the concentration of P_i, which is regulated along with calcium (Ca) in blood and extracellular fluids.

The close association between calcium and P_i in the extracellular body fluids and in bone tissue requires joint consideration of dietary calcium and dietary phosphates for an understanding of their physiological linkages and the important relationship between low calcium intakes and high phosphate intakes. This relationship potentially contributes to altered calcium homeostasis and the loss of bone mass.

Several aspects of P_i are reviewed here in an attempt to place these essential chemical anions in the perspective of their utilization in human health and disease. The physiological functions of P are reviewed first, and a number of general references have also been included in the bibliography for the interested reader.

Physiological Functions of Phosphates

The regulation of P_i in the blood is maintained by a complex homeostatic system that also controls the blood concentration of Ca. P_i ions can follow several potential metabolic pathways after entry into cells.

One immediate use of P_i ions is to phosphorylate glucose through enzymatic steps via kinases. They are also used in the phosphorylation of several other molecules; for example, creatine phosphate serves as an energy reserve in skeletal muscle tissue, and adenosine triphosphate is the primary donor of energy from its high-energy bonds within cells. In addition, several types of phospholipids and nucleic acids incorporate P_i within their molecular structures.

Cellular uses of P in intermediary metabolism are very extensive. Practically all energetic steps utilize high-energy phosphate bonds (adenosine triphosphate, or ATP) for the synthesis of organic molecules: to drive transport systems across cell membranes, to make muscles contract, to allow nerves to conduct impulses and transfer information, to convey genetic information, and to provide skeletal support and protection. In addition, phosphates circulating in blood have buffering activity. Clearly, P_i ions have multiple uses both within and without cells. Mineralized bone serves as an important store of P_i ions that can be retrieved through the action of parathyroid hormone (PTH) on bone cells. Because of the large reservoir of P_i ions, hypophosphatemia and P deficiency are rare events in adults without other major complications.

Phosphates in Foods

In terms of dietary sufficiency, P does not present a problem for human health because of the abundance of molecules containing this element in the food supply. Rather, the potential health problem is dietary Ca insufficiency in relation to excess intake of phosphates over periods of years, or even decades. Phosphorus deficiency, a rare clinical disorder, occurs almost exclusively because of a pathological change in the handling of phosphates, rather than because of a dietary inadequacy. The reason for these encompassing statements is that almost all foods contain phosphate groups in both organic (P_o) and inorganic (P_i) forms, and many of the foods – especially animal products – commonly consumed by all populations of the world are rich in P.

The approximate percentage distribution of foods (by food group) that provide dietary P in the United States is as follows: Milk and dairy products – 30 percent; meat, poultry, and fish – 27 percent; cereal grains and grain products – 20 percent; legumes, nuts, and seeds – 8 percent; vegetables – 7 percent; and other (miscellaneous) foods, including fruits – 8 percent (Figure IV.B.5.1). Although accurate data are lacking, it is presumed that these percentages are similar for the nations of the European Union, along with other Western countries. For populations that consume few dairy foods (or none), the percentage of dietary P contributed by grains, legumes, vegetables, and fruits would be greatly increased, depending on the food traditionally available. Vegetarians of all types, but especially "vegans" (strict vegetarians), have lower P intakes than do omnivores who consume several servings a day of dairy foods and meats. But, even though P intakes by vegans could be insufficient, deficiency symptoms are very unlikely.

As Figure IV.B.5.1 illustrates, P is widely found in foods in their natural unprocessed condition, and available food composition tables report the amounts of P measured in natural foods without any phosphate additives. Unfortunately, no food tables exist for the P content of processed foods. This lack is a serious hindrance to the accurate estimation of total phosphorus consumption from all foods, processed and unprocessed.

Figure IV.B.5.1. Approximate percentage contributions of the major food groups to the consumption of phosphorus. (Note: Phosphate additives are not included in these estimates.) (From USDA, CSFII 1994; adapted from Anderson and Garner 1996.)

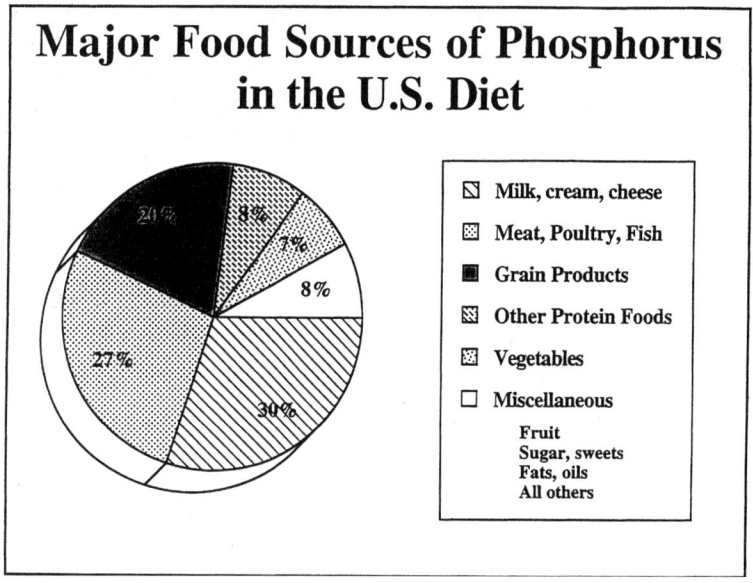

Major Food Sources of Phosphorus in the U.S. Diet

- Milk, cream, cheese
- Meat, Poultry, Fish
- Grain Products
- Other Protein Foods
- Vegetables
- Miscellaneous
  - Fruit
  - Sugar, sweets
  - Fats, oils
  - All others

Plant Foods

Although cereal grains and most vegetables yield good amounts of phosphates, these are nonetheless typically smaller amounts than those provided by animal foods. Moreover, except for highly processed wheat flours and polished rice, cereal grains have much of their P_o bound in phytates that are not completely digested within the gastrointestinal (GI) tract, and therefore, the total amount of P in grains is not available for absorption. Legumes and foods made from them, including soy flour and peanuts, are good sources of P, but this is not the case for most other plant foods, save for nuts such as almonds. Fruits, fruit juices, and vegetable oils contain negligible amounts of P. Table IV.B.5.1 lists the amounts of P (as a combination of both P_i and P_o) and calcium in commonly consumed foods.

Cereal grains contain significant amounts of the polyphosphate phytic acid (inositol hexaphosphate) in the bran and other parts. Each phytate molecule contains 6 P_o groups that become P_i groups when phytates are digested within the lumen of the GI tract by phosphatase enzymes. Food composition tables should be consulted for the phosphorus (combined P_o and P_i) content of specific foods.

Table IV.B.5.1. *Content of phosphorus and calcium in commonly consumed food in mg per serving*

Food Item	Serving size (1)	Phosphorus, mg	Calcium, mg	Calcium: phosphorus ratio
Yoghurt, plain	cup	326	415	1:0.8
Milk, 3.5%	cup	228	291	1:0.8
Milk, skim	cup	247	302	1:0.8
Cheese, Amer.	1 oz	211	174	1:1.2
Mozzarella, skim	1 oz	149	207	1:0.7
Egg, whole	large	86	25	1:3.4
Beef, ground	3 oz	135	8	1:16.9
Pork chop, loin	one	184	8	1:23
Chicken, drumstk	one	81	13	1:6.2
Turkey, white mt	3 oz	186	16	1:11.6
Tuna, water pack	3 oz	103	10	1:10.3
Corn flour	cup	318	8	1:40
Wheat flour	cup	135	19	1:7.1
Oatmeal	0.5 cup	89	9	1:9.9
Bread, whole wheat	slice	74	20	1:3.7
Bread, white	slice	30	35	1:0.9
Potato, white	one	115	21	1:5.5
Potato, sweet	one	63	32	1:2.0
Peas, green	0.5 cup	72	19	1:3.8
Baked beans	0.5 cup	132	64	1:2.1
Broccoli	0.5 cup	50	47	1:1.1
Corn, kernel	0.5 cup	39	2	1:19.5

Source: Hands, FOOD Finder: Food Sources of Vitamins and Minerals (1990).

Animal Foods

Animal foods are rich in P, with eggs, meats, fish, crustaceans, mollusks, poultry, and dairy products containing large amounts of this element. Liver, cheeses, and eggs (yolks) are highest in phosphorus, followed by meats, fish, and poultry, and then by milks (of any fat content). (See Table IV.B.5.1 for a listing of the P content of commonly consumed foods.) Mixed dishes that feature cheese or milk also have large amounts of P.

Food Additives

Phosphates (both P_i and P_o) are increasingly found in the food supplies of economically developed nations because of their widespread use as chemical additives in food applications. The food and beverage industries add a significant amount of phosphates to many foods and to cola-type beverages. Phosphate additives represent a diverse group of molecules, practically all of which are readily solubilized within the stomach or upper small intestine and are thereby highly bioavailable. Processed foods currently consumed by North Americans often have a significantly increased phosphorus content because of the intentional addition of one or more of these phosphate salts (Calvo 1993; Calvo and Park 1996). Phosphate additives have several functions in foods, notably as acids, buffers, anticaking agents, emulsifiers, and sequestrants (Dziezak 1990), and individuals who consume many processed foods (especially those with cheese in them) are estimated to have an increased daily phosphorus intake of 10 to 15 percent.

Supplements

Because practically all foods naturally contain phosphorus, and many processed foods have phosphates added to them, no need for supplementation exists in healthy individuals with normal renal function. Except for very rare clinical cases of renal phosphate wasting condition, or phosphate deficiency in newborns or premature babies, it is difficult to conceive of a situation requiring phosphate supplements.

Phosphate Additives – Recent Changes

The use of phosphate additives in food processing has accelerated since 1950, and in fact, for the first time in history, humankind faces an excess of phosphorus in the food supply because of the intentional addition of an estimated 40 to 50 different phosphate salts (Calvo and Park 1996). This, in turn, has introduced the possibility of an adverse effect of total phosphate consumption (from foods, beverages, and additives) on bone health, much as excess sodium intake from sodium-processed foods has contributed to the high prevalence of hypertension in the United States and other nations.

An interesting aspect of this increased intake of P is that it is not included in national survey estimates of total P consumption, meaning that the true intake of phosphorus in the United States is substantially underestimated (Oenning, Vogel, and Calvo 1988; Calvo and Park 1996). A study by M. S. Calvo and Y. K. Park (1996) shows a trend of increasing availability of phosphate additives in the food supply from specific items, such as frozen pizza, frozen processed poultry, and frozen prepared foods. Particularly worrisome is the increased availability of frozen processed poultry products in the marketplace over the last few years. (Frozen-food manufacturers, especially, utilize phosphate additives because of the phosphates' stability when the foods are thawed or heated.) Fast-food entrees also often contain phosphate additives, but little or none of the phosphate-additive content of these foods is included in estimates of phosphorus consumption (Calvo and Park 1996).

Dietary Intakes of Phosphates

Current dietary patterns in the United States suggest that, on the average, American women are consuming too little Ca in relation to P. In every age category over 11 years, the calcium intakes of females are so low that the median Ca:P ratio falls to 0.6, and approximately 10 percent of the female population has a ratio of 0.4 or less. This low ratio contributes to a persistent elevation (above baseline) of the parathyroid hormone (PTH), the major regulatory hormone affecting Ca and P metabolism.

Figure IV.B.5.2a illustrates the patterns of P and Ca consumption of females in the United States (USDA 1994). These median (50th percentile) intakes are compared to the Recommended Dietary Allowances (RDAs) (National Research Council 1989). Figure IV.B.5.2b shows the Ca:P ratio from the diet of females across the life cycle. The Ca:P ratio of 1:1 is illustrated as a line to demonstrate that this idealized ratio is not met from foods by females (or males) except during the first few months of life when breast milk is consumed.

Requirements and Allowances of Phosphorus

P is an essential nutrient because it is needed for both organic molecules and the mineralized tissues – bones and teeth. Indeed, it has been speculated that calcium-phosphate salts were the substratum for the synthetic steps that resulted in the origin of life in the liquid medium during the early history of the planet Earth.

Phosphorus Requirements

The amounts of P needed in the diet each day depend on several variables, such as stage of development in the life cycle, gender, body size, and physical exertion. Mean requirements of dietary P are not precisely known for either sex during adulthood, but daily U.S.

Median Phosphorus and Calcium Intakes by Females (USDA, 1994)

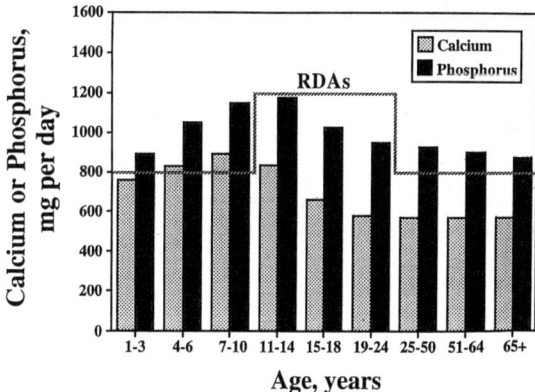

Figure IV.B.5.2a. Median phosphorus and calcium consumption (50th percentile) of females in the United States in comparison to the 1989 Recommended Dietary Allowances (RDAs) for both phosphorus and calcium. (From USDA 1994.)

Calcium to Phosphorus Ratios in the Diets of Females (USDA, 1994)

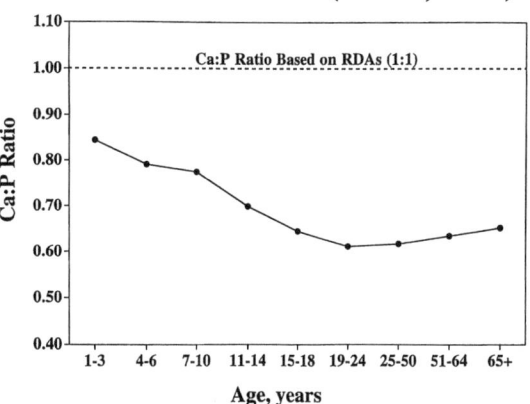

Figure IV.B.5.2b. The dietary calcium to phosphorus (Ca:P) ratio of females across the life cycle, calculated from the data in Figure IV.B.5.2a. The RDAs of calcium and phosphorus generate a 1:1 ratio (dotted line), but this ratio is not achieved except during the first few months of life by infants fed breast milk. (From USDA 1994.)

intakes (roughly between the 10th and 90th percentiles) of P fall in a range of approximately 1,600 to 2,400 milligrams (mg) per day for males and 1,200 to 1,600 mg for females, according to data generated by the U.S. Department of Agriculture's Continuing Survey of Food Intakes by Individuals (CSFII) (USDA 1994; Calvo and Park 1996).

Requirements of P may be as low as 600 to 800 mg a day for females and 800 to 1,000 mg for males, but these are educated guesses only, which assume adequate consumption patterns of calcium. Excess P_i that is absorbed is excreted by individuals with healthy kidneys in practically a 1:1 ratio to intake. In late life and in individuals who have declining renal function, some phosphate ions may be harbored (not truly stored) in mineralized atheromatous deposits within the arteries and in the skin. P balance-assessment methods have been historically helpful in arriving at estimates of P requirements, but they typically have low precision of measurements in feces; therefore, they are not very reliable.

Phosphorus Allowances

Recommended Dietary Allowances have long been established for phosphorus as well as for calcium, and age- and gender-specific recommendations have been kept identical for both of these minerals across the life cycle since the first edition of the RDAs in the early 1940s. These identical values presume a 1:1 ratio of dietary intake of calcium and total phosphorus (P_i and P_o combined), but actual dietary intakes almost never achieve such a ratio except in the early months or years of life. When the typical intake ratio declines to approximately 0.5:1, the homeostatic regulation of serum calcium becomes so significantly challenged that skeletal mass may be lost in order to maintain the blood calcium concentration at a set level.

The Calcium:Phosphorus Ratio and Relationship

The problem with excessive dietary P intakes (or even just adequate intakes) is the imbalance between calcium and phosphorus that can result from typically low dietary calcium consumption patterns (see Figure IV.B.5.2b). Because practically all foods contain phosphates, but only a few have much calcium, eating behaviors that exclude calcium-rich foods (mainly milk and related dairy foods) may contribute to a condition known as nutritional secondary hyperparathyroidism – and one that can be exacerbated in individuals who consume diets rich in phosphate additives and cola drinks with phosphoric acid (Calvo 1993). The high intake of total P is not in itself so much of a problem as are the behaviors that lead to the avoidance of calcium-rich foods. This is because the latter lowers the Ca:P ratio and causes the development of a persistent elevation of PTH (Calvo, Kumar, and Heath 1990). A diet containing adequate amounts of Ca can overcome these adverse effects of P (Barger-Lux and Heaney 1993).

Because long-term prospective human studies of high-P diets have not been published, data from short-term and cross-sectional investigations must be used to assess the adverse effects of persistent low-Ca, high-P intakes on bone status. Unfortunately, only a few researchers have examined this issue of the dietary Ca:P ratio. One four-week investigation of young women consuming a Ca:P ratio of 0.25:1 revealed the undesirable persistent rise in PTH (Calvo

et al. 1990). Another study of cross-sectional data from healthy, young-adult females indicated that too much P relative to calcium in the usual diet has a negative effect on the mineral content and density of bone (Metz, Anderson, and Gallagher 1993).

The mean Ca:P ratio of U.S. adults approximates 0.5:1 (Calvo 1993), and in fact, healthy ratios of intakes of the two elements range from 0.70 to 0.75 when the recommended number of servings from all food groups (based on the Basic Food Guide or Food Pyramid) are consumed each day. In other words, it is very difficult in the United States to achieve a ratio of 1:1, the ratio recommended in the RDAs (National Research Council 1989), without taking Ca supplements. Nonetheless, a healthy eating pattern should include a ratio within the range of 0.7:1 to 1:1. Intake ratios at or below 0.5:1 are of concern because of the likelihood of persistently elevated PTH concentrations and the potential loss of bone mass, which could lead to fragility fractures.

Digestion of Phosphates from Foods

Phosphates in foods exist mainly as organic molecules that must be digested in order to release inorganic phosphate into fluids of the intestinal lumen. P_i anions freed up by digestive enzymes are then ready for absorption; little likelihood exists for their resynthesis or precipitation because of the lower pH level (~6.0 to 7.0) of the upper half of the small intestine.

The common types of enzymes of the gut that break the bonds of phosphate-containing molecules are secreted almost entirely by the exocrine pancreas. These enzymes include phospholipases, phosphatase, and nucleotidase – as these names imply, the enzymes have specific target molecules that contain phosphates. Once these P_i molecules are solubilized in the lumen, all are equal in the sense that the absorbing mechanisms of the small intestine do not discriminate based on the molecule of origin.

Phytates, which occur in large amounts in cereal grains, are rather poorly digested by humans. The reason is that phytase enzymes are not made in the human body, and only the phytase enzymes present in the bran and other parts of the grain can accomplish this chemical digestion.

Intestinal Absorption of Phosphates

Inorganic phosphate anions are efficiently absorbed across the small intestine, primarily in cotransport with cations, in order to maintain the electrical neutrality of cells. The efficiency of absorption (net) of P_i ranges between 60 and 70 percent in adults, almost twice the efficiency (net) of calcium from the diet (that is, 28 to 30 percent) (Anderson 1991). For example, for every 1,000 moles of P_i, approximately 700 are absorbed (net), compared to only 300 (net) from 1,000 of Ca in the diet. Therefore, the excretory mechanisms have to work more efficiently to eliminate the extra P_i absorbed following meals. In children, the net absorption efficiencies may be as high as 90 percent for P_i and 50 percent for Ca. Several factors have adverse effects on P_i absorption, but these typically have little overall influence on P_i utilization, homeostasis, or metabolism. A few factors may enhance P_i absorption, but these, too, have little significance for the overall economy of P_i in the body (Allen and Wood 1994). A high P intake has been reported to have little effect on calcium absorption (Spencer et al. 1978).

The absorption efficiency of P_i declines later in life so that the net absorption of phosphorus from foods is somewhat reduced; probably this occurs in a similar fashion as calcium absorptive efficiency is lowered with age, especially after age 65 in females.

P_i ions are absorbed across all three segments of the small intestine, but the rapid entry into the bloodstream of radioactively labeled phosphates suggests that duodenal absorption occurs both very efficiently and at a high transfer rate. Therefore, the bulk of the absorbed P_i ions are transported across this segment, lesser amounts across the jejunum, and still lesser amounts across the ileum. If the hormonal form of vitamin D – calcitriol or 1,25-dihydroxyvitamin D – is elevated, P_i absorption can be even further enhanced in all segments of the small intestine.

Regulation of Blood Phosphate (P_i) Concentration

The homeostatic regulation of P_i in blood is primarily controlled by PTH, but several other hormones also exert influences on it. The major sites of regulation are the kidneys and the gut. PTH acts on the renal tubules to inhibit P_i reabsorption, while at the same time enhancing Ca reabsorption. The response of the kidneys to the action of PTH is the primary route of loss of P_i from the body. A secondary route is the small intestine, through which intestinal secretions from glands within the serosa of the intestinal lining remove P_i from the bloodstream to the gut lumen. This route of loss of P_i ions is called endogenous fecal excretion, and the quantity of P_i lost by this route may be almost as great as renal losses over a 24-hour period.

Absorption of an excess of P_i tends to lower the blood Ca ion concentration, which then triggers the secretion of PTH from the parathyroid glands. The role of circulating P_i in the secretion of PTH has been investigated in animal models and in human subjects to establish the connection with high dietary phosphorus intake. As mentioned, the absorption of P_i ions is rapid following a meal, much more so than for calcium ions. When an excess of P_i ions exists in the blood, the P_i concentration increases; this change, in turn, drives down the Ca ion concentration through a mechanism involving ionic binding between the two ions.

The net reduction in the concentration of Ca ions then stimulates the secretion of PTH. In turn, PTH enables the transfer of residual circulating Ca and P_i ions into the bone fluid compartment and into other extravascular compartments of the body. (Some investigators suggest that calcitonin, another calcium-regulating hormone, is involved in the movement of these ions into bone and, hence, in the conservation of calcium after a meal.) The persistently elevated PTH, however, tends to undo calcium conservation in the skeleton because this hormone continuously stimulates the reverse transfer of Ca and P_i ions from bone to blood (Calvo et al. 1990). The net result is that the skeleton loses bone mineral when PTH is elevated, even within the normal range of blood concentration, over extended periods of time. (The actual site of loss of this Ca is the gut, which has a poorly regulated secretion of Ca ions through intestinal glands.) PTH also has other roles in the kidney that, in effect, contribute to Ca retention by the body and to the elimination of P_i via urinary excretion.

PTH is considered the major hormone regulating P_i homeostasis because of its powerful roles in enhancing renal and, possibly, intestinal P_i losses while, at the same time, conserving calcium ions. When PTH is elevated, renal P_i reabsorption is largely inhibited, and similarly, the secretion of P_i ions by intestinal mechanisms is enhanced (although an understanding of this route of P_i loss is less established). PTH also acts on bone tissue to increase the transfer of calcium ions from the bone fluid compartment (BFC) and from the resorption of mineralized bone tissue to the blood plasma to restore the calcium ion concentration. By these same actions of PTH, P_i ions are also indirectly transferred from the BFC and bone to the blood.

Phosphate Balance

P balance means that intake of P from foods equals losses in urine and feces (and other sources, such as sweat and skin, which are seldom measured). In effect, P_i ions that are absorbed are accounted for by losses from the body. Under balance conditions, no net gain or loss of P_i ions occurs. This zero-balance state probably only exists during the adult years from roughly 20 to 60. During growth, and during pregnancy and lactation, positive balance states tend to predominate, whereas in late life, phosphate retention may increase and become a major health problem for individuals with declining renal function. Phosphate retention (positive P balance) results from the declining effectiveness of PTH in enhancing renal excretion of P_i ions with decreasing renal function.

A schematic diagram of the P balance of an adult male is shown in Figure IV.B.5.3. An adult male would typically consume 1,200 to 1,400 mg of P a day, whereas an adult female would consume 900 to 1,000 mg per day (USDA 1994; Calvo and Park 1996).

These estimated intakes of P by gender, however, do not include phosphate additives in foods.

Positive P balance (both P_o and P_i), or the net gain of this element by the body, is difficult to measure, but numerous balance studies suggest that P homeostasis (that is, zero balance) is typically maintained even when Ca balance may be significantly negative. Radioisotopic and stable nuclide studies have greatly advanced our knowledge about the fluxes of P_i and Ca ions across the gut and renal tubules in animal models and, to a lesser extent, in human subjects. Balance studies without the use of stable or radioactive nuclides are notoriously fraught with potential errors of collection and measurement, and these difficulties make such studies generally unreliable in the precise quantitative sense.

The uptake of P_i ions by cells requires carrier mechanisms or cotransport systems because of the electrical charge and water-solubility properties of these anions. P_i ions typically cotransport with glucose in postprandial periods, but their charge must be neutralized by cations, typically not calcium ions. Also, after meals, P_i ions enter the bone fluid compartment, but in this case, typically with calcium ions. Calcitonin has been considered primarily responsible for the uptake by bone tissue of these two ionic species following food ingestion and the intestinal absorption of the ions (Talmage, Cooper, and Toverud 1983). After entry into cells, the P_i ions in the cytosol are almost immediately used to phosphorylate glucose or other molecules, and a small fraction of the ions are stored as organic molecules or inorganic salts within cellular organelles.

Some P_i ions that enter bone may enter bone cells, especially osteoblasts or lining cells, whereas other ions bypass the cells and go directly to the BFC, an extension of the blood/extracellular-fluid continuum. In the BFC, P_i ions in solution increase the P_i concentration (activity) that permits these ions to combine with Ca ions in excess of their solubility product constant (Ksp) and form mineral salts (precipitate) in bone extracellular tissue. The formation of hydroxyapatite crystals (mineralization) is essential for structural support and protection of internal organs from environmental trauma. P_i ions are, therefore, essential for the formation of the endoskeletons typical of most vertebrates except cartilaginous fish.

Approximately 60 to 70 percent of P_i ions are cleared by the kidneys in healthy individuals. If PTH is elevated, P_i excretion is enhanced even more, so that P_i losses are further increased. Under the same conditions of elevated PTH, the secretion of P_i by the gut is also increased. The endogenous fecal secretion of phosphates is the second major route of loss that the body uses to maintain P_i ion homeostasis.

Persistently Elevated Parathyroid Hormone

Of the many diseases that have significant alterations in P homeostasis, only two are reviewed in any depth here. The first is persistently elevated PTH in response to a low Ca:P dietary intake pattern, whereas the second is renal secondary hyperparathyroidism resulting from chronic renal failure. Previously, the former was often referred to – perhaps erroneously in the case of humans (in contrast to animals) – as nutritional secondary hyperparathyroidism. In the context of human disease, the term "hyperparathyroidism" is inappropri-

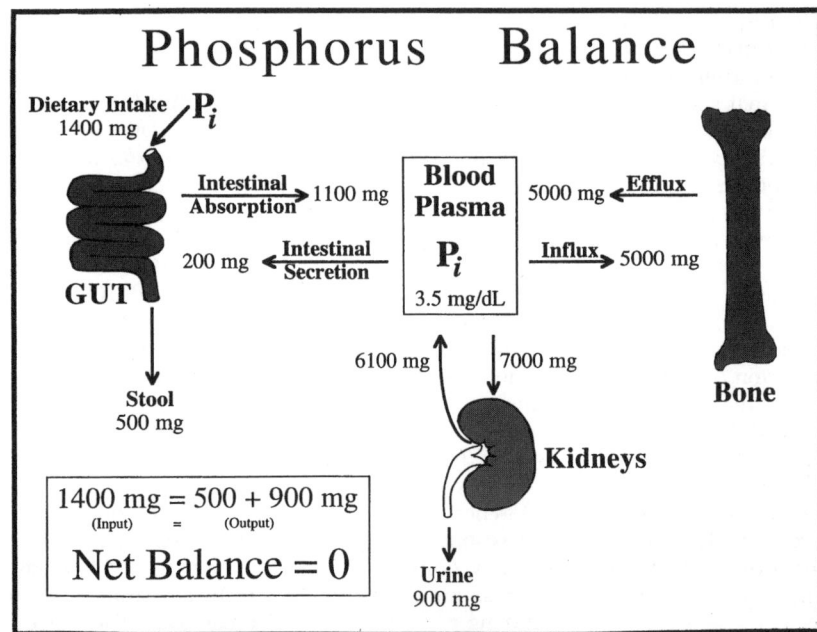

Figure IV.B.5.3. Schematic diagram of phosphorus balance of an adult male. (Adapted from various sources.)

ate because the PTH levels that result from a low Ca:P ratio typically remain within the normal range of blood concentration, although usually at the high end of the range. As mentioned, a persistently elevated PTH, even if it remains within the normal range, contributes to increased bone turnover that can result in a reduction of bone mass and density (Calvo et al. 1990). If this condition continues for a year or longer, it could contribute to fragility fractures because of the thinning of trabecular plates at bone sites, such as the vertebrae, wrist, and proximal femur. On the basis of obtaining a benefit from a PTH value at the lower end of the range, individuals with a low Ca:P ratio would be advised to increase their calcium intake from foods first and from supplements second. An adequate calcium intake is known to reduce serum PTH concentration (Krall and Dawson-Hughes 1994).

Figure IV.B.5.4 diagrams the mechanism through which a low dietary Ca:P ratio contributes to the development of a persistently elevated PTH concen-tration. Figure IV.B.5.5 illustrates the potential changes in bone mass and mineralization of the skeleton in individuals who typically consume diets with low Ca:P ratios compared to those who have normal intake ratios. The persistently elevated PTH is responsible for the limited bone mineralization and the loss of bone mass (Anderson 1996).

Renal Secondary Hyperparathyroidism

Renal secondary hyperparathyroidism results from a severe increase in PTH that occurs because the kidneys can no longer filter and secrete sufficient amounts of P_i ions each day. As the blood concentration of P_i increases, the serum PTH also rises in an attempt to correct the error (increase of serum P_i). The action of PTH on bone tissue then predominates, and the rate of bone turnover continues to increase, unless corrected by renal dialysis or kidney transplantation. Without correction, the net result is a

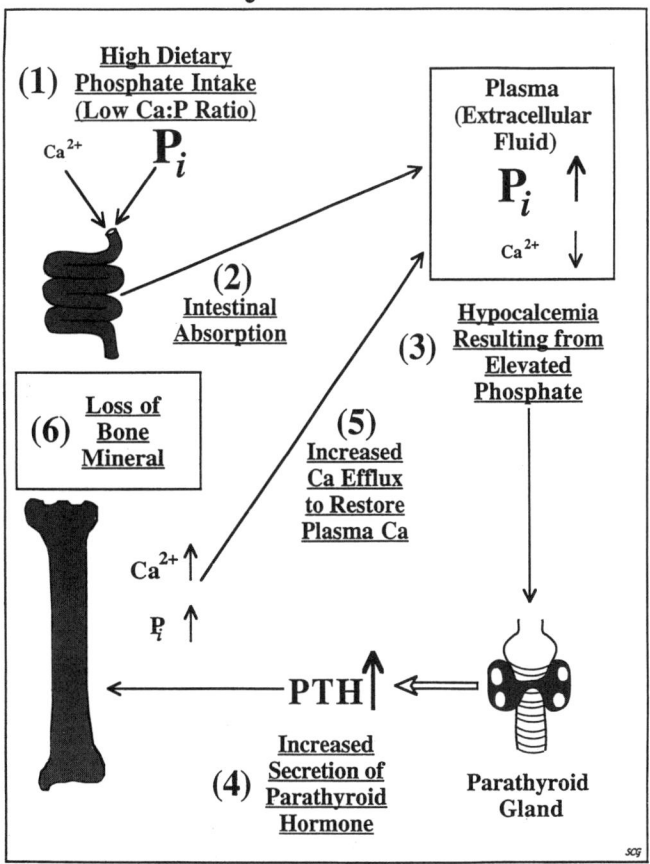

Figure IV.B.5.4. Mechanism through which a low dietary calcium:phosphorus ratio contributes to the development of a persistently elevated parathyroid hormone (PTH) concentration in the blood.

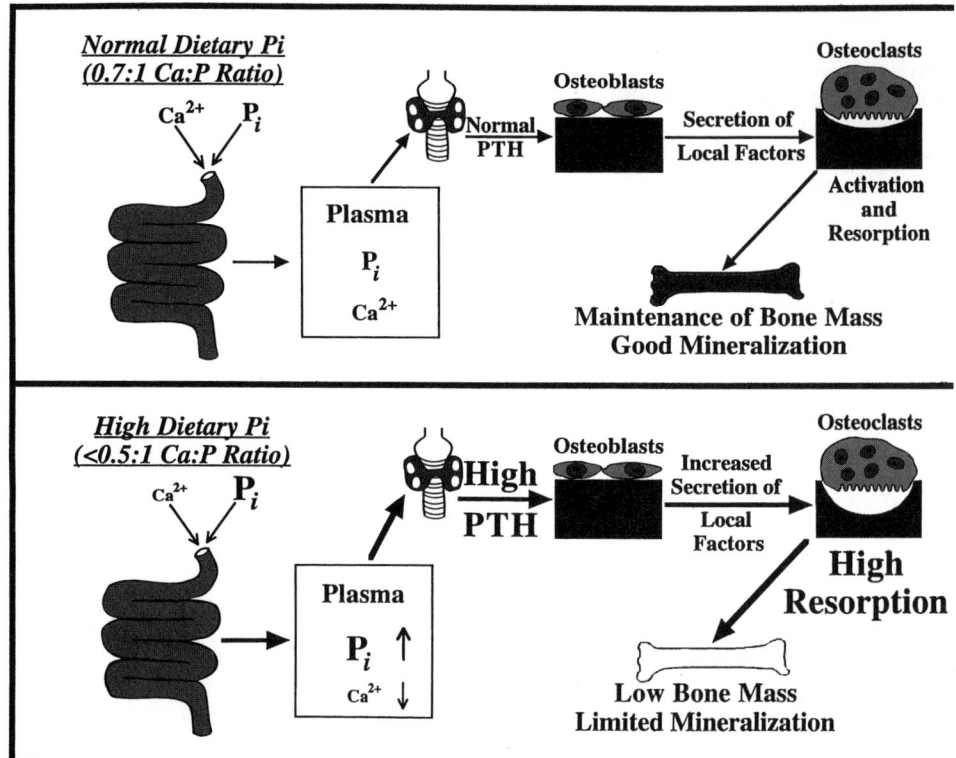

Figure IV.B.5.5. Comparison of parathyroid hormone (PTH) responses of normal and high dietary phosphorus (P_i) and effects of PTH on bone mass.

continuing increase in the serum P_i concentration and a rapid thinning of bone tissue at practically every site in the body. If severe enough, this condition can result in fractures at almost any skeletal location. Oral phosphate binders, such as aluminum or magnesium hydroxides, are usually administered to patients to reduce the amount of P_i absorbed by the small intestine and to enhance calcium absorption, but this strategy typically is not sufficient to stem the gradual increase in serum PTH as the disease progresses.

Potential Adverse Effects

"Over-the-counter" antacids contain mineral salts, which bind phosphate ions that are released from foods or secreted into the gut lumen by glands of the GI tract. If excessive amounts of these antacid drugs (also taken as nutrient supplements when containing calcium and/or magnesium) are ingested, individuals may be at increased risk of lowering their serum phosphate concentration to the point of serious deficiency. It is fortunate that the use of mineral antacids containing calcium, magnesium, aluminum, or some combination has declined greatly of late in the United States because of the availability of more

effective antacid drugs that previously could only be obtained by prescription.

Summary

Phosphorus has important roles in human health. Phosphates participate in diverse functions in the body, both intracellularly and extracellularly as P_i and P_o groups. These anions are especially important in energetic reactions within cells, in nucleic acids, and in other structural molecules and the extracellular tissues of bones and teeth. Dietary deficiency of this element is highly unlikely during practically the entire life cycle.

High intakes of P are common because of the natural widespread availability of phosphates in foods. Moreover, processed foods are likely to contain phosphate additives that contribute to a potentially excessive consumption of phosphorus by individuals in the United States and, most likely, in all economically developed nations throughout the world. When a chronic pattern of low Ca consumption is coupled with high dietary intakes of P (both P_o and P_i), PTH becomes persistently elevated. The potential outcome is low bone mass and an increased risk of skeletal fractures, especially late in life. This adverse relationship between a high dietary P intake and bone loss strongly suggests that the consumption of adequate amounts of Ca are essential for the development and maintenance of bone mass throughout life.

John J. B. Anderson

Bibliography

Allen, L. H., and R. J. Wood. 1994. Calcium and phosphorus. In *Modern nutrition in health and disease.* Eighth edition, ed. M. E. Shils, J. A. Olson, and M. Shike, 144-63. Philadelphia, Pa.

Anderson, J. J. B. 1991. Nutritional biochemistry of calcium and phosphorus. *Journal of Nutritional Biochemistry* 2: 300-9.

1996. Calcium, phosphorus and human bone development. *Journal of Nutrition* 126: 1153S-8S.

Anderson, J. J. B., and C. J. H. Barrett. 1994. Dietary phosphorus: Benefits and problems. *Nutrition Today* 29: 29-34.

Anderson, J. J. B., and S. C. Garner, eds. 1966. *Calcium and phosphorus in health and disease.* Boca Raton, Fla.

Barger-Lux, M. J., and R. P. Heaney. 1993. Effects of calcium restriction on metabolic characteristics of premenopausal women. *Journal of Clinical Endocrinology and Metabolism* 70: 264-70.

Bronner, F., and J. W. Coburn, eds. 1981. *Disorders of mineral metabolism.* 3 vols. New York.

Burckhardt, P., and R. P. Heaney, eds. 1994. *Nutritional aspects of osteoporosis, II.* Serono Symposium. Rome.

Calvo, M. S. 1993. Dietary phosphorus, calcium metabolism, and bone. *Journal of Nutrition* 123: 1627-33.

Calvo, M. S., R. Kumar, and H. Heath III. 1990. Persistently elevated parathyroid hormone secretion and action in young women after four weeks of ingesting high phosphorus, low calcium diets. *Journal of Clinical Endocrinology and Metabolism* 70: 1340-4.

Calvo, M. S., and Y. K. Park. 1996. Changing phosphorus content of the U.S. diet: Potential for adverse effects on bone. *Journal of Nutrition* 126: 1168S-80S.

Dziezak, J. D. 1990. Phosphates improve many foods. *Food Technology* 44: 80-92.

Favus, M. J., ed. 1996. *Primer on the metabolic bone diseases and disorders of mineral metabolism.* Third edition. Philadelphia, Pa.

Hands, E. S. 1990. *FOOD finder: Food sources of vitamins and minerals.* Second edition. Salem, Ore.

Krall, E. A., and B. Dawson-Hughes. 1994. Osteoporosis. In *Modern nutrition in health and disease.* Eighth edition, ed. M. E. Shils, J. A. Olson, and M. Shike, 1559-68. Philadelphia, Pa.

Lobaugh, B. 1996. Blood calcium and phosphorus regulation. In *Calcium and phosphorus in health and disease,* ed. J. J. B. Anderson and S. C. Garner, 27-43. Boca Raton, Fla.

Metz, J., J. J. B. Anderson, and P. N. Gallagher, Jr. 1993. Intakes of calcium, phosphorus, protein and level of physical activity are related to radial bone mass in young adult women. *American Journal of Clinical Nutrition* 58: 537-42.

National Research Council, Subcommittee on the Tenth Edition of the RDAs, Food and Nutrition Board, Commission on Life Sciences. 1989. *Recommended dietary allowances.* Tenth edition. Washington, D.C.

Nordin, B. E. C., ed. 1976. *Calcium, phosphorus and magnesium.* London.

1988. *Calcium.* New York.

Oenning, L. L., J. Vogel, and M. S. Calvo. 1988. Accuracy of methods estimating calcium and phosphorus intake in daily diets. *Journal of the American Dietetic Association* 88: 1076-81.

Spencer, H., L. Kramer, D. Osis, and C. Norris. 1978. Effect of phosphorus on the absorption of calcium and on the calcium balance in man. *Journal of Nutrition* 108: 447-53.

Talmage, R. V., C. W. Cooper, and S. U. Toverud. 1983. The physiologic significance of calcitonin. In *Bone and min-eral research annual,* Vol. 1, ed. W. A. Peck, 74-143. Amsterdam.

USDA (U.S. Department of Agriculture). 1994. *Continuing survey of food intakes of individuals (CSFII): Diet and health knowledge survey 1991.* Springfield, Va.

IV.B.6 ❧ Potassium

Potassium (K) is found in virtually all aerobic cells and is essential to life. It is the third most abundant element in the human body (after calcium and phosphorus) and the eighth most abundant element in the earth's crust, with a mass percent of 1.8, which means that every 100 grams (g) of the earth's crust contains 1.8 g of potassium. Potassium is a very reactive alkali metal with an atomic number of 19 and an atomic weight of 39.098 atomic mass units (amu). Its outer "4s" electron is not bound very tightly to the atom, which is therefore easily ionized to K^+ (Dean 1985), and potassium reacts readily with chlorine to form the salt potassium chloride. Potassium chloride is a white crystalline solid at room temperature with alternating potassium ions and chloride ions on the lattice sites. Potassium is found primarily in seawater and in natural brines in the form of chloride salt. The minerals mica and feldspar also contain significant quantities of potassium (Dean 1985).

The Discovery of Elemental Potassium

Potassium was first isolated in 1807 by Humphry Davy (1778-1829), who electrolyzed "potash" with a newly invented battery designed to contain a series of voltaic cells, with electrodes made out of zinc and copper plates dipped in a solution of nitrous acid and alum. In Davy's time, the term "potash" referred to any number of different compounds, including "vitriol of potash" (potassium sulfate), "caustic potash" (potassium hydroxide), and "muriate of potash" (potassium chloride as well as potassium carbonate), the last of which was formed by leaching ashes from a wood fire and evaporating the solution to near dryness in an iron pot. Today, potash is usually potassium carbonate, although potassium chloride is still called potash by fertilizer manufacturers (Kent 1983: 262). The potash Davy used was potassium hydroxide that he had dried and melted. He wrote of his experiment:

> A small piece of pure potash, which had been exposed for a few seconds to the atmosphere, so as to give conducting power to the surface, was placed upon an insulated disc of platina, connected with the negative side of a battery of the power 250 of 6 and 4, in a state of intense activity; and a platina wire communicating with the positive side, was brought in contact with the upper surface of the alkali. The whole apparatus was in the open atmosphere. Under these circumstances a vivid action was soon observed to take place. The potash began to fuse at both its points of electrization. There was a violent effervescence at the upper surface; at the lower, or negative surface, there was no liberation of elastic fluid; but small globules having a high metallic lustre, and being precisely similar in visible characters to quicksilver formed, and others remained and were merely tarnished, and finally covered with a white film which formed on their surfaces. These globules, numerous experiments soon shewed to be the substance I was in search of, and a peculiar inflammable principle the basis of potash. (Davy 1839–40, 5: 60)

The next day, Davy isolated sodium metal by electrolyzing soda ash (sodium hydroxide) in much the same way. In the history of chemistry, isolating potassium and sodium was no mean accomplishment. It had been suspected by several people, but especially by Antoine Lavoisier (1743–94), that potash was a compound and that the "basis of potash" was, indeed, a metal (Partington 1962, 3: 485). Davy's experiments confirmed this suspicion. Several years earlier, in 1801, Carl Friedrich Kielmeyer, also suspecting that potash was an oxide of some metal, had attempted to electrolyze potash using a voltaic pile but was unsuccessful (Partington 1964, 4: 45). Thus, the credit for discovering the two most important alkali metals clearly goes to Humphry Davy.

Between 1808 and 1809, the French chemists Louis Thenard (1777–1857) and Joseph Gay-Lussac (1778–1850) found that only small quantities of potassium and sodium could be derived by the electrolysis of fused alkali hydroxides and went on to develop a much improved method for producing larger quantities of both (Partington 1964, 4: 94). Thenard and Gay-Lussac reacted the fused alkali with red-hot iron turnings in an iron gun barrel lined with clay and sand and collected the condensed metal vapor in a receiver attached to the gun barrel. An explosion using this dangerous device nearly blinded Gay-Lussac.

A variation that further improved the method for producing potassium used potassium carbonate as the source of potassium and carbon instead of iron as the reducing agent to produce elemental potassium and carbon dioxide as the reaction products. In 1827,

Frederich Wohler (1800–82) first employed potassium produced by this technique to isolate metallic aluminum in more or less pure form. He reacted anhydrous aluminum chloride with potassium metal as the reducing agent and obtained enough aluminum metal to measure its properties (Ihde 1964: 467). Today, metallic potassium is usually produced by reacting molten sodium with molten potassium chloride and condensing the gaseous potassium formed by this reaction. There are very few industrial uses for elemental potassium, although many of its compounds are widely utilized throughout industry and agriculture. For example, potassium nitrate is commonly employed as a fertilizer in the tobacco industry where chloride-containing fertilizers are undesirable.

Potassium in Living Organisms

Despite all of potassium's various functions, its principal function in living organisms is in the transportation of ions across cell membranes. In most animal cells, the internal concentration of potassium ions is between 20 and 30 times higher than the external concentration of potassium ions found in the extracellular fluids. Most cells also have considerably different internal concentrations of sodium ions than are found externally. Neither the reason for the existence of these ionic gradients across the cell membrane nor, for that matter, potassium's principal role in cell metabolism was understood until comparatively recently, and many of potassium's functions in living organisms are still being investigated. It can be said with certainty, however, that moving sodium ions and potassium ions across membranes is an important activity in most organisms, and that if this activity stops, the organism dies.

The Sodium-Potassium-ATPase Pump

The significant step toward understanding potassium's role in animal cells was taken in 1957. In that year, the Danish biochemist Jens Skou, who later won the 1997 Nobel Prize in chemistry, found an enzyme in crab nerve cells that hydrolyzed adenosine triphosphate (ATP) into adenosine diphosphate (ADP) and any one of several phosphorus-containing anions, such as dihydrogen phosphate, in the presence of magnesium ions only if both sodium ions (Na^+) and potassium ions (K^+) were present (Skou 1965: 6). Magnesium ions are always required for enzymes (called ATPases) to catalyze the hydrolysis of ATP.

The unusual property of this enzyme was that neither K^+ nor Na^+ alone had any significant effect on its activity. A short time later, Skou proposed that this Na^+-K^+-ATPase complex was part of a transmembrane pump that pumped Na^+ and K^+ into and out of cells, and that the energy needed for this process was supplied by the hydrolysis of ATP. Many different kinds of animal tissues were soon found to exhibit similar Na^+-K^+-ATPase activity, and it was shown that this enzyme was, indeed, a protein that resided in a cell's membrane, with its sodium ion receptor facing the interior of the cell (or the cytoplasm), and its potassium ion receptor facing the external environment. The Na$^+$-K$^+$-ATPase pumped sodium ions out of the cell and potassium ions into the cell, accompanied by the hydrolysis of ATP. Brain, nerve, and muscle cells – and the electric organ of the electric eel – were discovered to be particularly rich in K$^+$-Na$^+$-ATPase activity (Lehninger 1970: 617).

"Membrane transport" – the pumping of ions across cell membranes – is such an important part of a cell's total activity that it is estimated that more than one-third of the ATP consumed by a resting animal is expended transporting ions across membranes (Stryer 1988: 950). The Na$^+$-K$^+$ pump, in particular, maintains proper electrochemical potentials across cell membranes and maintains the proper concentrations of Na$^+$ and K$^+$, both internally and externally. Because these concentrations are usually far from the equilibrium concentrations, the ions must be pumped against their respective concentration gradients. The sodium-ion and potassium-ion concentration gradients in most animal cells control cell volume, drive the transport of sugars and amino acids across cell membranes, and control the electrical excitability of both nerve and muscle cells.

In the most ubiquitous transport systems in animal cells, the Na$^+$-K$^+$ pump removes 3 sodium ions from the interior of the cell and pumps in 2 potassium ions from the cell's surroundings, using the transmembrane Na$^+$-K$^+$-ATPase to facilitate the transport of the ions. One molecule of ATP is hydrolyzed to supply the necessary free energy. This process is shown schematically in Figure IV.B.6.1. Typically, the internal concentration of potassium ions is approximately 20 times greater than the external concentration of potassium ions. This concentration gradient is maintained also by the free energy supplied by the hydrolysis of ATP and the transmembrane enzyme pump. The ATP supplies

energy to the enzyme by phosphorylating it in the presence of sodium ions and magnesium ions. The phosphorylated enzyme is then dephosphorylated in the presence of potassium ions to regenerate the original enzyme and form a phosphorus-containing ion, such as hydrogen phosphate. The energy stored in the ATP is transferred to the enzyme via the phosphate group bonding to it. The enzyme uses this energy to move ions against their gradients and then gets rid of the phosphate group via hydrolysis.

Potassium in the Nerves and the Nervous System

Potassium ions and sodium ions are found in the nerve cells of virtually all animals and play a vital role in the transmission of nerve impulses. These ions regulate the nerve's transmembrane potential, and it is the transmembrane potential difference between the interior and exterior of a nerve cell that causes the transmission of nerve impulses along the nerve (Atkins 1994: 334). Many K$^+$-Na$^+$ pumps are distributed throughout the nervous system. When a nerve is resting, there is a high internal potassium ion concentration and a high external sodium ion concentration. When the cell experiences a pulse, the nerve cell membrane's structure alters, becoming permeable to sodium ions. Because the membrane is now more permeable to sodium ions, the ions rapidly flow into the interior of the cell and reduce the size of the sodium ion concentration gradient so that it becomes smaller than it was when the nerve was resting. In other words, the Na$^+$ ions and K$^+$ ions exchange places. Because the membrane's potential arises primarily from the difference in concentration on either side of the membrane, the voltage across the membrane drops. This change in voltage triggers the adjacent part of the cell wall to alter its structure. The pulses of collapsing potential pass along the nerve. Behind each pulse, the Na$^+$-K$^+$ pump restores the proper internal sodium ion concentration by pumping out sodium ions and pumping in potassium ions.

Potassium in Muscle Tissue

Generally speaking, muscle tissue can be divided into two classes, smooth and striated. Striated muscle is under voluntary control and has a striated or striped appearance under a light microscope. Striated muscle found in vertebrates contains 2 protein filaments that interact with each other. One of the filaments contains myosin and the other contains 3 proteins – actin, tropomyosin, and troponin. Striated muscle contraction is regulated primarily by calcium ions (Ca^{++}), and the calcium ion concentration is itself regulated by a Ca^{++}-ATPase pump, very similar in kind and function to the Na$^+$-K$^+$-ATPase pumps found in other kinds of cells. In mammalian striated muscle, however, fatigue is associated with a loss of intercellular K$^+$ and a gain in intercellular Cl$^-$, Na$^+$, and H$_2$O, and it may indeed be the case that, in humans, fatigue is related to these changes in the potassium ion concentration

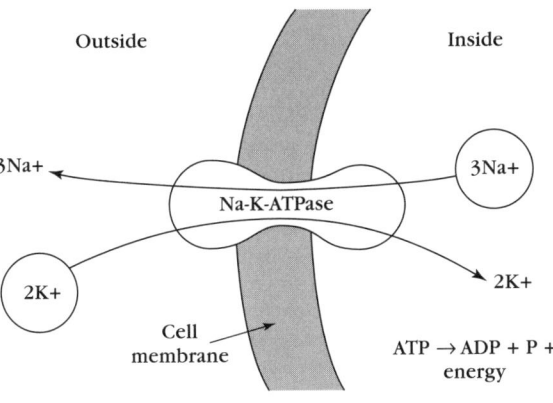

Figure IV.B.6.1. The Na$^+$-K$^+$-ATPase transmembrane pump pumping Na$^+$ ions out of the cell and K$^+$ ions into the cell.

gradient across muscle cells. Lowering the internal potassium ion concentration and raising the external potassium ion concentration depolarizes the cell membrane. The rapid recovery of muscle function following brief rest periods is caused by a reestablishment of the proper potassium ion concentrations and a restoration of the resting potential of the muscle cell's membrane.

Smooth muscle, such as that found in the heart or veins, is not subject to voluntary control. The contraction of smooth muscle is controlled by the degree of phosphorylation of its light chains. Phosphorylation leads to contraction and dephosphorylation leads to relaxation. In smooth muscle, Na^+-K^+ pumps and active transport are directly involved with contraction and relaxation. For example, in vascular smooth muscle, the function of the Na^+-K^+-ATPase pump is to transport 2 potassium ions into the cell for every 3 sodium ions it takes out. The energy for this transport is supplied by phosphorylation. As in striated muscles, extracellular calcium ions also play an important role in cell function, but in smooth muscles this role is primarily to regulate the K^+-Na^+ equilibria extant in the cell (O'Donnell and Owen 1994).

The importance of the Na^+-K^+ pump in smooth muscle function has some intriguing consequences. It is entirely possible – and evidence is mounting that it is more than just possible – that a principal underlying cause of hypertension in humans is an inhibitor of Na^+-K^+-ATPase activity or an impaired Na^+-K^+ pump (Blaustein et al. 1986; O'Donnell and Owen 1994: 687). It is also well known that a certain class of compounds, called cardiotonic steroids, specifically inhibit the Na^+-K^+ pump. These steroids prevent the dephosphorylation of Na^+-K^+-ATPase. As a consequence, these compounds are very important in the treatment of heart disease.

For example, digitalis (an extract from purple foxglove leaves that contains a mixture of cardiac steroids), which is perhaps the best-known remedy for congestive heart failure and has been widely used for centuries, increases the force of heart muscle contraction by inhibiting the Na^+-K^+-ATPase pump (Voet and Voet 1990: 496). This increases the sodium ion concentration inside the cell, thereby causing a reduction in the concentration gradient across the membrane, because the internal sodium ion concentration becomes closer to the external sodium ion concentration. Reducing the sodium ion concentration gradient reduces the extrusion of calcium ions via the Na^+-Ca^{++} exchanger, which increases the internal calcium ion concentration. A high intracellular calcium ion concentration causes the heart muscle to contract (Stryer 1988: 955). Ion exchangers, such as the Na^+-Ca^{++} exchanger, are conduits – or ports – that allow ions to diffuse in and out of a cell via concentration gradients rather than through active transport, and they are not fueled by ATP.

The medicinal effects of digitalis were known long before the compounds themselves were identified

and long before the Na^+-K^+-ATPase pump was discovered. In the 1770s, a woman in Shropshire, England, using extracts from some 20 different herbs, prepared a cocktail that had a remarkable effect on curing congestive heart failure or "dropsy," as it was called. Many people suspected that this woman was a witch because of the curative power of her concoctions. A physician by the name of William Withering heard about the woman's remarkable medicine and, after considerable effort, found that foxglove was the significant herb in the cocktail. He published his findings in 1785 in his classic work, *An Account of the Foxglove and Some of its Medical Properties*. A line from this paper is worth noting: "It [the foxglove] has a power over the motion of the heart to a degree yet unobserved in any other medicine, and this power may be converted to salutary ends" (Estes and White 1965: 110).

Potassium in Protein Synthesis

Protein synthesis on ribosomes requires a high potassium concentration for maximum efficiency. Ribosomes are cellular bodies that serve as the sites for protein synthesis and can be thought of as the cell's protein factories because protein assembly from amino acids, controlled by RNA, takes place on the ribosome's surface (Lehninger 1970: 616).

Potassium in Glycolysis

Potassium is necessary for glycolysis, which is a form of fermentation that ultimately converts glucose ($C_6H_{12}O_6$) into pyruvate (C_3COCOO^-) with the associated production of ATP. Glycolysis can be thought of as a fundamental aspect of the generation of metabolic energy that occurs in virtually all living organisms, including humans. Glycolysis requires potassium ions for maximum activity of one of the enzyme catalysts, pyruvate kinase, which is involved in the process (Stryer 1988: 350). If there is sufficient oxygen present, the pyruvate enters the mitochondria where it is completely oxidized to CO_2 and H_2O. If there is insufficient oxygen present, as is often the case in muscle contraction, pyruvate is converted to lactic acid. In yeast, which is an anaerobic organism, pyruvate is converted to ethanol and carbon dioxide.

In 1897 and 1898, the German chemist Eduard Buchner discovered that when yeast cells were crushed with sand and diatomaceous earth *(kieselguhr)*, the cell-free liquid extract was able to ferment sucrose into alcohol and carbon dioxide. Buchner's results showed, for the first time, that fermentation could occur outside a living cell, and his fermentation experiments contributed greatly to the overthrow of the "vital force" theory then prevalent in the biological sciences, and started the field of modern biochemistry. Even Louis Pasteur thought that fermentation could occur only in living cells. Buchner was awarded the Nobel Prize in chemistry for this work in 1907 (Partington 1964, 4: 309).

Renal Control of Potassium

In humans, the kidneys are responsible for most potassium excretion, although fecal matter does contain about 10 percent of the potassium ingested (Stanton and Giesbisch 1990). However, renal malfunction as a result of disease or trauma often will prevent the proper elimination of potassium from the body. For example, because maintenance of the proper potassium ion balance is vital, the secretion of potassium ions by the distal tubule is one of the kidney's most important functions, and it is the distal tubule that, more or less, regulates the quantity of potassium ions eliminated in the urine. More than 75 percent of the filtered potassium is reabsorbed in the proximal tubule, and this percentage remains nearly constant no matter how much is filtered. About 50 percent of the urinary potassium is secreted into the urine by the distal tubules in normally functioning kidneys. If this secretion is prevented – as, for example, in polycystic kidneys – dangerous levels of potassium ions can accumulate and cause heart failure. Na^+-K^+-ATPase pumps, H^+-K^+-ATPase pumps, and K^+-Cl^--Na^+ cotransport have all been found to control potassium in tissues within the kidneys.

Difficulties with potassium elimination are also encountered if the production of a hormone in the adrenal gland, aldosterone, is inhibited. Aldosterone catalyzes the elimination of potassium ions so that lowering the concentration of this enzyme reduces the rate of potassium ion elimination and can increase potassium ion concentrations in the blood to dangerous levels.

Potassium and Health

Potassium is essential for human life. A normal adult male, weighing 70 kilograms (kg), contains approximately 135 g of the mineral in his body. About 98 percent of this potassium is found in his cells and the other 2 percent in extracellular fluids (Macrae, Robinson, and Sadler 1993, 6: 3668). Potassium deficiency is called hypokalemia and – because potassium is present in most foods – when it occurs, it is often in areas where people exist on subsistence or starvation diets. Severe diarrhea, diabetes, and prolonged use of cortisone can also cause hypokalemia.

For living cells to function properly it is essential they maintain a correct balance between internal potassium ion concentrations and external potassium ion concentrations. There are many factors that influence this balance, in addition to the various pumps and transport systems already described. For example, there must be a normal water balance in the organism, because if the amount of K^+ inside a cell remains fixed and the amount of water increases, the potassium ion concentration will decrease proportionately, or if the amount of water decreases, the potassium ion concentration will increase. A potassium deficiency resulting from urine loss often occurs during the treatment of heart disease because the medication used prevents

sodium and water retention. To reduce this deficiency, foods high in potassium are often prescribed.

Recently, a possible connection between potassium and hypertension has been discovered (Brancati 1996). It was found that African-Americans, a particularly high-risk group for hypertension and acute myocardial infarction, benefited greatly from a diet rich in potassium. Indeed, in a double-blind test, all of the subjects who received potassium supplements reduced their blood pressure – regardless of age, gender, body weight, or alcohol consumption. It was not clear why potassium was especially beneficial for African-Americans. It may be that their diets are particularly low in potassium, but it is more likely the case that, for some reason, African-Americans are especially sensitive to potassium. This finding is certainly also consistent with the mechanism of the Na^+-K^+-ATPase pump discussed earlier.

Potassium and Diet

Potassium is one of the most important elements in the human diet. According to the National Academy of Sciences, a healthy adult should consume between 1,875 milligrams (mg) and 5,625 mg of this mineral daily (National Academy of Sciences 1980: 173). It is probable that the diets of our hunter–gatherer ancestors contained some 2 mg of potassium for every calorie consumed. It is also known that people who consume more than 4 g of potassium each day have a much lower incidence of disease.

Unfortunately, a modern diet typically contains only 0.5 mg of potassium for every calorie consumed, although it is the case that practically all successful dietary weight-loss programs, dietary cholesterol-lowering programs, and dietary blood-pressure–lowering programs contain foods that are high in potassium. Some of these are oranges, tomatoes, peas, spinach, bananas, cantaloupe, and fish (Pennington 1985). Foods that are very high in potassium content, with the exception of potatoes, are relatively low in energy content, which makes them especially healthful for normal adults.

Summary

Potassium is a relatively abundant alkali metal that comprises a significant fraction of the earth's crust. Its salts and oxides are widely used in industry and agriculture. Potassium's role in membrane transport and other metabolic processes make it vital to virtually every living organism. Recently, antibiotics using potassium ions have been discovered, and it is beginning to appear that eating foods rich in potassium or taking potassium supplements can reduce hypertension in humans. Most foods contain some potassium, and the maintenance of good health in normal adults seems to require a diet that contains 4 g of potassium per day.

David S. Newman

Bibliography

Atkins, P. W. 1994. *Physical chemistry*. Fifth edition. New York.

Blaustein, M. P., T. Ashida, W. F. Goldman, et al. 1986. Sodium/calcium exchange in vascular smooth muscle: A link between sodium metabolism and hypertension. *Annals of the New York Academy of Science* 448: 199–216.

Brancati, F. 1996. Effect of potassium supplementation on blood pressure in African Americans consuming a low potassium diet. *Archives of Internal Medicine* 8: 61–7.

Davy, J. 1839–40. *The collected works of Sir Humphry Davy.* 9 vols. London.

Dean, J. A. 1985. *Lange's handbook of chemistry*. Thirteenth edition. New York.

Estes, J. W., and P. D. White. 1965. William Withering and the purple foxglove. *Scientific American* 212: 110–17.

Fitts, R. H. 1994. Cellular mechanism of muscle fatigue. *Physiological Review* 74: 49–94.

Ihde, A. J. 1964. *The development of modern chemistry.* New York.

Kent, J. A. 1983. *Riegel's handbook of industrial chemistry.* New York.

Lehninger, A. L. 1970. *Biochemistry.* New York.

Macrae, R., R. K. Robinson, and M. J. Sadler, eds. 1993. *Encyclopedia of food science, food technology and nutrition.* 8 vols. London and San Diego, Calif.

National Academy of Sciences. 1980. *Recommended dietary allowances.* Ninth edition. Washington, D.C.

O'Donnell, M. E., and N. E. Owen. 1994. Regulation of ion pumps and carriers in vascular smooth muscle. *Physiological Reviews* 74: 683–720.

Partington, J. R. 1962–70. *A history of chemistry.* 4 vols. London.

Pennington, Jean A. 1985. *Bowes and Church's food values of portions commonly used.* New York.

Petrucci, R. H. 1989. *General chemistry.* Fifth edition. New York.

Skou, J. C. 1965. Enzymatic basis for active transport of Na$^+$ and K$^+$ across the cell membrane. *Physiological Reviews* 45: 496–617.

Stanton, B., and G. Giesbisch. 1990. *Handbook of physiology.* Second edition. New York.

Stryer, L. 1988. *Biochemistry.* Third edition. New York.

Voet, D., and J. G. Voet. 1990. *Biochemistry.* New York.

Withering, W. 1785. *An account of the foxglove and some of its medical properties.* London.

IV.B.7 ❧ Sodium and Hypertension

Historically, dietary salt (sodium chloride) has been obtained by numerous methods, including solar evaporation of seawater, the boiling down of water from brine springs, and the mining of "rock" salt (Brisay and Evans 1975). In fact, R. P. Multhauf (1978) has pointed out that "salt-making" in history could be regarded as a quasi-agricultural occupation, as seen in frequent references to the annual production as a "harvest."

Such an occupation was seasonal, beginning with the advent of warm weather or the spring high tide and ceasing with the onset of autumnal rains. Multhauf has argued further that the quest for salt led to the development of major trade routes in the ancient world. The historian Herodotus, for example, described caravans heading for the salt oases of Libya, and great caravan routes also stretched across the Sahara, as salt from the desert was an important commodity exchanged for West African gold and slaves. Similarly huge salt deposits were mined in northern India before the time of Alexander the Great, and in the pre-Columbian Americas, the Maya and Aztecs traded salt that was employed in food, in medicines, and as an accessory in religious rituals. In China, evidence of salt mining dates from as early as 2000 B.C.

Homer termed salt "divine," and Plato referred to it as "a substance dear to the gods." Aristotle wrote that many regarded a brine or salt spring as a gift from the gods. In the Bible (Num. 18:19), it is written: "This is a perpetual covenant of salt before the Lord with you and your descendants also." In the Orient, salt was regarded as the symbol of a bond between parties eating together. In Iran, "unfaithful to salt" referred to ungrateful or disloyal individuals. The English word "salary" is derived from *salarium*, the Latin word for salt, which was the pay of Roman soldiers. Moreover, Roman sausages were called *salsus* because so much salt was used to make them (Abrams 1983).

The preservative properties of salt have maintained the essentiality of the mineral throughout history. It helped meat last over long journeys, including those of marching armies and the migrations of peoples. Salt's power to preserve meat led to the so-called invention of salted herring in fourteenth-century Europe, which has been called "a new era in the history of European salt production" (Multhauf 1978: 9). The technique of pickling preserves food by extracting water from animal tissues, making the dehydrated meat or fish resistant to bacterial attack (Bloch 1976).

During the eighteenth century, other industrial uses began to be found for salt. The invention in 1792 of a way to make sodium carbonate began the carbonated-water industry, and by 1850, 15 percent of the salt of France was going into soda. Since that time, nondietary uses of salt have far outweighed its employment for culinary purposes (Multhauf 1978).

Historically, governments appreciated the importance of salt and have taxed it since ancient times (Multhauf 1978). During the nineteenth century in the United States, a salt tax helped build the Erie Canal, and during the twentieth century in India, Mahatma Gandhi revolted against a salt tax, leading to the famous "March to the Sea." Such has been the importance of salt that one historian has written: "Clearly, anyone who can control the salt supply of a community has powers of life and death. The control of water, being more ubiquitous than salt, is not so simple to put into effect" (Bloch 1976: 337).

Salt and Sodium: Essential to Life

Salt in the Body

In 1684, Robert Boyle became the first to demonstrate scientifically that the "salty taste" in blood, sweat, and tears was actually caused by the presence of salt. After he removed the organic matter from whole blood by ignition, a fixed salt remained, which he found to be virtually identical to marine salt. About a century later (1776), H. M. Rouelle showed that a large proportion of the inorganic materials in blood serum could be isolated in the form of cubic crystals of "sea salt." Later still, in the nineteenth century, J. J. Berzelius and A. J. G. Marcet revealed that sodium chloride was the principal inorganic constituent of other body fluids (both those that occasionally collected in the abdominal cavity, around the lungs or heart, or in a cyst or a blister and those that permanently surrounded the brain and spinal cord) and was present in much the same concentration as in blood serum (Kaufman 1980). In the same century (1807), Sir Humphry Davy discovered both sodium and potassium by passing an electrical current through moist caustic potash or caustic soda. More recently, biomedical researchers have defined sodium as the principal cation of the circulating blood and tissue fluids of animals (Denton 1982).

Sodium is the sixth most common element on earth. Sodium chloride (what we commonly call salt) is the chemical combination of ions of sodium (Na^+, molecular weight 23) and chlorine (Cl^-, molecular weight 35.5) – the latter element, in its pure form, is a deadly greenish-yellow gas that reacts with water to form hydrochloric acid. Forty percent of the weight of common salt is made up of sodium; the remainder is chloride. Pure sodium is never found in nature. When freed from common table salt by electrolysis, sodium is a soft metal, lighter than water, and so reactive with oxygen in the air that it must be specially stored in air-free containers to prevent it from exploding. Sodium also reacts violently with water, as the two together form sodium hydroxide, in the process liberating hydrogen gas, which, in turn, bursts into flame from the heat of the reaction.

Nonetheless, even though a reactive element, sodium is essential to animal and human life. Indeed, life could be defined as the sum of the chemical processes that take place in the solution of salts between and within cells. In humans, the nutrients required to fuel life processes are first chewed and mixed with salt solutions produced by the salivary glands, then dissolved in salt and enzyme solutions from the stomach and pancreas, absorbed as salt solutions from the intestines, and delivered to the cells dissolved in a salt solution that ultimately depends on the ingestion of critical amounts of sodium and water. Excreted body fluids – blood, sweat, and tears – and feces are made up of these salts, and sodium salts are their key ingredient.

The Physical Need for Salt

In the nineteenth century, G. Bunge made the observation that carnivores never sought out salt, but herbivores did. His observation seemed to fit into common knowledge – hunters as well as husbandrymen knew that herbivores came to salt licks – but Bunge suggested something new: that salt was a necessity for life. In his travels he observed in numerous places that carnivores never ate salt but herbivores seemed to have a vital need for a supplement of it. He noted that herbivores excreted 3 to 4 times as much potassium as carnivores and theorized that the much higher potassium content of the vegetarian diet displaced sodium from body salts, causing an increase in the amount excreted in the urine. Therefore he reasoned that continuous consumption of a purely vegetarian diet with large amounts of potassium would make a large intake of sodium necessary for the maintenance of sodium balance (Bunge 1902).

Decades later, anthropologist Alfred Kroeber took issue with this notion of a biologically driven hunger for salt. He observed the Native Americans living along the Pacific coast of the United States and noted that salt was consumed in the south but not in the north. He saw no relationship among such factors as dietary salt use, the relative prevalence of seafood or meat in the diets, and the various climatic conditions, writing: "It must be concluded that whatever underlying urge there may be in physiology as influenced by diet and climate, the specific determinant of salt use or nonuse in most instances is social custom, in other words, culture" (Kroeber 1942: 2). H. Kaunitz found similar situations in areas of Australia, South Africa, and South America and suggested that salt craving might arise from "emotional" rather than innate needs (Kaunitz 1956).

J. Schulkin (1991) has recently noted that among psychologists in the 1930s, it was widely believed that "learning" – not biologically driven physical need – was responsible for the ingestion of minerals. However, C. P. Richter (following American physiologist Walter Cannon's theory of *The Wisdom of the Body* [1932]) took a minority view that "learning" might not be the primary driver, and in 1936, he provided the first experimental evidence for a salt appetite. He removed the adrenal glands from experimental rats, thus depriving them of the sodium-retaining hormone aldosterone – a situation that would prove fatal in the absence of dietary sodium – and the amount of sodium ingested by the adrenalectomized rats increased dramatically. In 1939, he hypothesized that the drive for sodium was innate, and in 1941, he "discovered" that hormonal signals generate sodium hunger. Moreover, in 1956, he showed that during reproduction periods, the ingestion of salt by female rats rose markedly (Schulkin 1991).

One of the key experimental laboratories in the study of sodium metabolism has been the Howard

Florey Institute in Melbourne, Australia, where investigators, under the leadership of Derek Denton (1982), have conducted many experiments. In one of the most notable, researchers trained sheep to press a lever to get salt water to drink. The sheep were then depleted of salt by saliva drainage. When finally given access to the lever for salt water, the sheep within 30 minutes consumed the precise amount of sodium that they had lost. Their "wisdom of the body" was such that, even if the sheep were given salt solutions of varying concentrations, they still consumed the amount required to replace the deficit.

The work of Denton and others strongly supported the view that there is an innate hunger for salt and that the brain controls this behavior (Schulkin 1991). But although there are a number of minerals that are "essential" nutrients, only sodium seems to command a "built-in" hunger; there is no "innate" craving for magnesium or potassium, to choose two examples. On the other hand, it is likely that, in the past, the hunger for sodium abetted the intake of other essential minerals, which would usually have been found in the same "salt-licks" as sodium. Sodium hunger does not *require* "learning," although significant "learning" does interact with innate mechanisms to help guide sodium-hunger behavior (Schulkin 1991). The following is a summary of Schulkin's ideas of the steps involved in the innate sodium-hunger pathway:

1. An animal is "sodium-hungry." (This would result from either a reduction in salt intake or excessive excretion of sodium from nonrenal sources, such as intestines or sweat glands.)
2. A "representation" of salty taste is activated in the brain.
3. The representation serves to guide the animal's behavior in its search for salt – including its location, identification, and ingestion of the mineral.
4. Innate mechanisms are responsible for the sodium-hungry animal:
   a. Ingesting the salt immediately upon its first exposure (no "learning" is required for this), and
   b. Noting the significance of salt when not sodium-hungry.
5. Thus, in terms of b, there is a hedonic shift in the perception of salt that emerges in the salt-hungry animal.
6. The result is a motivated behavior with appetite (physiologic need) and consummatory phases (behavioral want) in search of salt.

Sodium Physiology

Sodium is vital in maintaining the pressure and volume of the blood and the extracellular fluid. A major purpose of the blood is to carry intracellular fluids, bringing nutrients to the cells and removing metabolic products from them. As blood flows through the capillaries, water – containing nutrients – passes from the capillaries into the extracellular spaces to bathe the cells with nutrients and pick up cellular metabolic products (mostly waste), which are then swept by water movement back into the veins and carried to the kidney, liver, and lungs for metabolism or excretion. Sodium is also important in the transmission of nerve impulses, helps to metabolize carbohydrates and proteins, and has independent interactions with other ions – such as those of potassium, calcium, and chlorine – to maintain the "sea within" us. But most importantly, from a medical viewpoint, sodium is a vital factor in the regulation of blood pressure.

Sodium is measured in units of moles or grams. For nutritional purposes, grams are used, usually milligrams (1 gram [g] = 1,000 milligrams [mg]); for clinical purposes (to measure concentration), millimoles per liter are used (1 mole = 1,000 millimoles or mmols). One mole equals the molecular weight of the element. As the atomic weight of sodium is 23, 1 mole of sodium is equal to 23 grams of sodium (23,000 mg), and 2,300 mg of sodium is the same as 100 mmols of sodium.

Until the late 1940s, the measurement of sodium in both biological fluids and diets was a mostly laborious process that required the skills of a quantitative analytical chemist using 13 different steps – including, among others, "ashing," extracting, evaporating, precipitating, washing, and weighing sodium yields on a microbalance – to determine the quantity in a single sample (Butler and Tuthill 1931). But in 1945, a revolution in the analytic accuracy and speed of sodium measurement was begun with the first report of the use of the flame photometric method. In 1945, this technique still required precipitation of plasma before analysis, but by 1947, only dilution of plasma was required (Overman and Davis 1947), and by 1949, instruments were available that could provide very accurate results within 5 minutes using either plasma or urine. By 1953, these devices were in wide use (Barnes et al. 1945; Mosher et al. 1949; Wallace et al. 1951).

The body has built-in "set points" designed to maintain sodium in homeostasis. When it takes in less salt than is lost in the urine, sweat, and stool, the concentration of sodium in the blood falls. When the blood sodium falls below an inherited "set point" (about 140 mmol per liter of serum), an area of the brain that is bathed by blood senses the decreased sodium concentration and activates hormonal defenses to maintain a constant concentration of the mineral. If the concentration of sodium continues to diminish, the kidneys will adjust by accelerating the excretion of water, so that the blood's sodium concentration is maintained at the vital level. If the sodium supply is not replenished, there is a gradual desiccation of the body and, finally, death. In other words, a lack of sufficient sodium causes the organism literally to die of thirst.

By contrast, if blood sodium increases above the set-point level, a secretion of antidiuretic hormone (ADH) is released by the pituitary gland, and thirst mechanisms are activated to find and ingest water until the sodium concentration is reduced. At the same time, ADH causes the kidneys to excrete less water in an attempt to keep the body's sodium at the correct concentration. If, however, the water supply is not replenished, more sodium will be excreted, and eventually, these water losses will lead to death.

The overriding mechanism that regulates total body sodium (and blood pressure) has been termed the "renal-fluid volume mechanism for pressure control" by A. C. Guyton and colleagues (1995). An analysis of the factors controlling blood pressure has shown that it can only be raised by one of two mechanisms: increasing the intake of dietary salt or limiting the kidney's ability to excrete sodium.

Sodium and Human Evolution

The body's need for sodium may also have played a role in genetic variability within the human species. During the 1980s, theories were proposed that suggested such a role in two diseases related to salt metabolism: cystic fibrosis and hypertension.

Cystic fibrosis (CF) is a recessive genetic condition related to sodium metabolism, in which, it was hypothesized, the carrier state had been protective of fluid and electrolyte loss during epidemics of diarrhea in human history. CF carriers, notably children before the age of reproduction, were thought to have protective mechanisms that diminished the loss of water during episodes of infectious diarrhea. Thus, individuals who were genetically enabled to control water and salt losses were more likely to survive to reproductive age. Indeed, the heterozygote carrier has been shown to have less sodium loss in feces than the homozygote noncarrier (Gabrial et al. 1994).

A more controversial evolutionary hypothesis is that one form of hypertension (high blood pressure) – "salt-sensitive" hypertension, which has a high frequency among African-Americans – may result, in part, from genetic adaptation to the African environment and its diseases of the past. More specifically, it has been suggested that – both during the trans-Atlantic slave trade and during the period of slavery itself – individuals able to conserve sodium would have been more likely to survive the dehydrating diseases aboard ship, as well as the debilitation of hard physical labor. If so, then this past experience might be partially responsible for today's prevalence of "salt-sensitive" high blood pressure among black people in the Western Hemisphere (Wilson and Grim 1991; Curtin 1992; Grim and Wilson 1993).

Salt Deficiency

When humans go without salt in the diet, or lose it because of illness, the major symptoms are apathy, weakness, fainting, anorexia, low blood pressure, and, finally, circulatory collapse, shock, and death. Sir William Osler (1978: 121–2), observing dehydrated cholera patients in the late nineteenth century, provided a classic description of the condition:

> [P]rofuse liquid evacuations succeed each other rapidly . . . there is a sense of exhaustion and collapse . . . thirst becomes extreme, the tongue white: cramps of great severity occur in the legs and feet. Within a few hours vomiting sets in and becomes incessant. The patient rapidly sinks into a condition of collapse, the features are shrunken, the skin of an ashy gray hue, the eyeballs sink in the sockets, the nose is pinched, the cheeks are hollow, the voice becomes husky, the extremities are cyanosed, and the skin is shriveled, wrinkled and covered with a clammy perspiration. . . . The pulse becomes extremely feeble and flickering, and the patient gradually passes into a condition of coma.

Many cholera patients in the past could have been saved with rehydration therapy, and it is a central tenet in modern medical treatment that lost body fluids should be replaced with others of the same composition. Replacing a salt loss by giving water or a water loss by giving salt can be fatal. Although a history of the illness and an examination of the patient can provide clues to the type of loss, the best method is to test the blood and urine chemically – a method that only became possible in the 1930s, with the most useful test that which determined the amount of chloride in urine. Accomplished by simply mixing 10 drops of urine with one drop of an indicator and then adding silver nitrate, a drop at a time, until the end point was reached, this was called the "Fantus test" after Dr. Bernard Fantus at the University of Chicago.

This test proved so useful in treating salt- and water-depleted British soldiers in India and Southeast Asia during the mid–1930s that Dr. H. L. Marriott, in his classic text on fluid replacement therapy, stated: "It is my belief that the means of performing this simple test should be available in all ward test rooms and in every doctor's bag" (Marriott 1950: 56).

Most early studies of sodium depletion in humans were prompted by diseases. One was Addison's disease (in which the adrenal gland that makes the sodium-retaining hormone for the body stops working), and another was diabetes (in which a high level of blood glucose forces the excretion of large amounts of water by the kidneys). Such studies were also conducted in cases of extreme depletion brought on by starvation or acute diarrhea. In the 1930s, however, R. A. McCance (1935–6) published his report of a series of experiments that established a baseline on the clinical nature and physiology of sodium depletion in humans.

To induce salt depletion, McCance (1935–6) employed a sodium-free diet combined with sweating. (Because laboratory animals do not sweat, he used humans as his test subjects.) There was no "research-quality" kitchen available, the food was prepared in the McCance home, and the subjects of the experiment – all volunteers – slept and ate there. The diet consisted of sodium-free "casein" bread, synthetic salt-free milk, sodium-free butter, thrice-boiled vegetables, jam, fruit, homemade sodium-free shortbread, and coffee. During recovery periods, the volunteers ate weighed quantities of high-sodium foods (such as anchovies and bacon) and small, weighed amounts of sodium chloride. Sweating was induced by placing the subjects in a full-length radiant heat bath – for two hours with the heat on and then 10 minutes with the heat off. Their sweat was collected in rubber sheets, and a final washing of each subject with distilled water ensured that even small amounts of lost sodium would be accounted for. The subjects' average sweat loss was 2 liters, and they commented that the washing procedure was "not uncomfortable" after 2 hours in the hot bath (McCance 1935–6).

By reducing sodium in the diet, along with inducing sodium losses through sweating, McCance and his colleagues found that only a week was required to make healthy subjects seriously sodium depleted. They maintained 4 volunteers in this condition for an additional 3 to 4 days, so that the total period of deprivation lasted about 11 days.

Detailed measurements of intake (food and water) and output (sweat, urine, and feces) recorded that the subjects lost 22.5 g of sodium and 27.2 g of chloride – or about 50 g of salt. Their body weights dropped by about 1 kilogram (kg) per day, and sodium excretion averaged 3,400 mg of sodium per day for the first 4 days. Weights then stabilized, but sodium loss continued.

As the deficiency progressed, the volunteers all experienced feelings of physical fatigue, anorexia, nausea, difficulty in urinating, and extremely weak pulses. Muscle spasms and cramps – especially cramps in the fingers – were common. The subjects' faces became drawn and "ill-looking," and they slowed mentally, becoming dull and apathetic. McCance was struck by the similarity of a number of these symptoms to those of Addison's disease, but the symptoms and signs all rapidly cleared up when the volunteers resumed consumption of sodium (McCance 1935–6).

Both before and during World War II, as many in the Allied armed forces were severely disabled by heat- and water-related illnesses, there was intense interest in understanding the mechanics of water and salt metabolism and the effects of heat on the human body. Research was even undertaken to see how long a man could survive on a raft in the ocean, or in the desert, so that restrictions could be placed on certain military activities (such as limiting the duration of searches for lost aviators, who, after the specified survival time had passed, might reasonably be presumed dead). Other studies examined the conditions that servicemen could be forced to work under and defined safe limits. For example, after 5 hours of marching in the heat, with full packs and no water, even well-conditioned marines could not continue (Ladell 1949).

During and after World War II, there was also interest in the effects of diarrhea. J. L. Gamble (1945) showed that intestinal secretions contained more sodium than chloride, and D. A. K. Black (1946) reported a series of experiments on 10 men with blood pressures averaging 94 mm Hg SBP/59 mm Hg DBP, who were victims of tropical sprue (a disease characterized by chronic diarrhea). The patients were bedridden, listless, and incapable of exertion. But these symptoms disappeared – and blood pressure rose to normal – with sodium supplementation (Black 1946).

Excess Sodium

Humans, as noted, have evolved complex "redundant systems" to regulate sodium and other essential minerals. For marine animals, deriving sodium from the sea was a relatively easy matter. As evolution progressed, however, satisfaction of sodium needs became a more complicated task. Land dwellers had first to locate sources of sodium, then ingest the mineral, and, further, conserve it within their bodies. To achieve this, physiological and behavioral mechanisms evolved that were designed primarily to protect against a life-threatening deficit of sodium, such as can occur with vomiting, sweating, diarrhea, or kidney malfunction.

But although the body's systems are reasonably effective against sodium deficit, evolution did not do as well in protecting humans against an excessive intake of the mineral. There are two different kinds of excessive sodium intake: (1) acute ingestion of salt without water, or of very salty water (such as seawater or other briny water); and (2) chronic ingestion of toxic levels of sodium in the food supply.

It seems likely that the former was never a major problem in the history of humankind and probably occurred only when people felt forced to drink seawater or the water from salt springs or salt lakes. Chronic ingestion of excess salt in food, however, is both a recent and a very real problem. Until the past few centuries, salt intake was primarily determined by the amount a person chose to add to food ("active intake"). Increasingly, however, as foods were preserved in salt, and especially today with foods processed with salt, the great majority of salt intake has become "passive," meaning that food processors and manufacturers – not consumers – decide the quantity of salt to be included in the foods they produce.

Indeed, it has been estimated that in prehistoric times, the daily human intake of sodium was about 690 mg, with 148 mg derived from vegetables and 542 mg from meat (Eaton and Konner 1985). By contrast, today the U.S. Food and Drug Administration (FDA) recommends keeping dietary intake to

2,400 mg of sodium per day (the amount contained in 6 g – or about 1 teaspoon – of table salt). This is roughly the same amount accepted by an advocacy group that promotes a low-salt diet, Consensus Action on Salt and Hypertension (CASH). Needless to say, even such a "low-salt" diet still delivers 3.5 times the amount of sodium provided by the meat and vegetables of the Paleolithic diet.

Although there is also concern over high salt intake by children, food processors only relatively recently halted their practice of adding sodium to baby food. (Presumably, the mineral was meant to improve the food's flavor for parents.) This change for the better followed the observation by L. K. Dahl, M. Heine, G. Leitl, and L. Tassinari (1970) that young rats with a high sodium intake became hypertensive and remained so for the rest of their lives. But despite this discovery, the average sodium intake by two-year-olds in the United States remains higher than the amount recommended by the FDA and by CASH (Berenson et al. 1981).

Moreover, the average intake throughout much of the industrialized world today is about 10 g of table salt (3,900 mg of sodium) per person per day (James, Ralph, and Sanchez-Castillo 1987; USDA/USDHHS 1995). But only about 10 percent of the sodium consumed occurs naturally in foods; another 15 percent is added by consumers ("active intake"), and the remaining 75 percent is added to food by manufacturers and processors. Therefore, based upon the average industrial diet, only 390 mg of sodium is naturally occurring, 585 mg is added by the consumer, and a substantial 2,925 mg is derived ("passive intake") from sodium added during processing (James et al. 1987).

Obviously, then, a low-salt diet like that of our ancient ancestors seems an impossible goal; increasingly, the population is at the mercy of the food industry. Yet, that industry gains several advantages by using excessive salt in food processing. Salt, added to food, improves flavor and palatability, especially for those who have become addicted to its taste. Salt increases the "shelf-life" of food (although, with today's effective packaging and refrigeration technology, there is little need for the presence of near-toxic levels of sodium in the food supply), and salt adds very inexpensive weight to the final product (by helping to retain water), thereby increasing profit margins. Finally, increased salt consumption stimulates thirst and thus increases consumption of the beverages sold by many of the major food companies (McGregor 1997).

History of Hypertension

"Blood pressure" refers to the force exerted against the walls of the arteries as blood is pumped throughout the body by the heart. This pressure can be measured, and abnormally high levels indicate a condition of "high blood pressure," or hypertension, which is classified into two types. *Secondary* hypertension is that resulting from a known cause, such as a disease of the kidneys, whereas *essential* or *primary* hypertension arises with no evident cause. More than 90 percent of hypertension cases fall into the latter category (Wilson and Grim 1993).

Salt consumption was linked with blood pressure long ago – as early as the second century B.C. in ancient China. In the *Huang-ti nei-ching* ("The Inner Classic of the Yellow Emperor"), it was written that "if too much salt is used for food, the pulse hardens" (Swales 1975: 1).

In 1836, Richard Bright reported on the kidneys and hearts of 100 patients who had died of kidney problems. He noted that, in most instances, when the kidney was small and shrunken, the heart was often markedly enlarged – an indication of high blood pressure (Bright 1836). In the late nineteenth century, R. Tigerstedt and T. G. Bergman (1898) coined the term "renin" in their report that saline extracts from kidney tissue raised blood pressure. A few years later, French researchers L. Ambard and E. Beaujard noted that blood pressure was lowered by the dietary restriction of sodium chloride and raised by its addition or increase; they believed, however, that chloride was the culprit because they were unable to measure sodium content (Ambard and Beaujard 1904).

Many attempts to induce high blood pressure in experimental animals followed but proved inconclusive. In 1934, however, Harry Goldblatt noted that when he placed an adjustable clamp so that it partially blocked the renal artery of a dog, the animal developed a rapid increase in blood pressure that was sustained so long as the clamp remained in place. Research to determine the mechanism causing this high blood pressure began, and by 1940, two teams of investigators (Eduardo Braun-Menendez and colleagues in Buenos Aires and Irving Page and O. M. Helmer in Indianapolis) succeeded in isolating a material that caused vasoconstriction. Both groups reported that there was a substance – coming from the kidneys – that, when mixed with blood, generated a potent vasoconstricting and blood-pressure–raising substance. The South American group called this "hypertensin" and the U.S. group "angiotonin," but eventually the two were determined to be the same chemical, which was named "angiotensin."

Within a few years, W. Kempner (1944) reported that a low-sodium diet decreased blood pressure and heart size even in cases of malignant hypertension. The following year, he described the effects of a low-sodium diet on 65 patients who were hypertensive but showed no evidence of renal disease. After an average of only 48 days on a rice-fruit diet, the average blood-pressure readings decreased from a systolic blood pressure (SBP) of 197 mm Hg and a diastolic blood pressure (DBP) of 115 mm Hg to an SBP of 151 mm Hg and a DBP of 97 mm Hg. In those patients who experienced a decrease in blood pressure, the response was obvious within the first 7 to 10 days on the low-sodium diet, and Kempner observed that the maximum decrease in blood pressure was first attained after only 10 days.

Most early blood-pressure studies were on whites, yet the prevalence of high blood pressure in blacks is much greater and, as mentioned, is thought to result, at least in part, from salt intake. The first report of an association between salt intake and blood pressure in African-Americans was by A. Grollman and colleagues (1945), who studied patients given less than 1 gram (<1,000 mg) of sodium chloride in their daily diets. In the case of two black women, blood pressure declined to normal, promptly rose when salt intake was increased, and then fell again when the low-sodium diet was resumed.

Five years later, V. P. Dole and colleagues (1950) reported the results of a series of studies to evaluate the sodium content of Kempner's rice–fruit diet and its effect on blood pressure and heart size. They confirmed all of Kempner's observations and, further, documented that the effect of the diet was related to its low sodium content and not low chloride (Dole et al. 1950).

The introduction of diuretics, which act to excrete sodium and water via the kidneys, came in the late 1950s, and these were quickly shown to lower blood pressure significantly (Freis et al. 1958). In the 1970s, however, a series of observations made by a research group in Indianapolis (which included Clarence E. Grim, co-author of this chapter) once again focused attention on the relationship between dietary sodium and blood pressure. This culminated in several reports indicating that even a normotensive individual would experience an increase in blood pressure if enough salt was consumed (Murray et al. 1978; Luft et al. 1979). In addition, ethnic differences in sodium metabolism and blood-pressure responses were documented in normotensive subjects; such evidence demonstrated, for the first time, that blacks were more sensitive to salt than whites. These studies also demonstrated the enormous capacity of human kidneys to excrete sodium, which was proof of Guyton's hypothesis that excess salt will always increase blood pressure (Guyton et al. 1995).

Current Thinking on Sodium and Hypertension

Cardiovascular disease is now a major cause of death in all countries of the world, and high blood pressure is the most common (although treatable) precursor of heart disease. Unfortunately, as pointed out in a recent review by J. P. Midgley, A. G. Matthew, C. M. T. Greenwood, and A. G. Logan (1996), most sodium-reduction trials in hypertensive subjects have not yet produced definitive evidence that reducing sodium intake improves long-term health (but see also Staessen et al. 1997). Indeed, some have argued

(based on a single observational study) that reducing salt intake may do more harm than good (Alderman et al. 1995).

Nonetheless, high dietary salt intake has been reported to be associated with other adverse medical outcomes, including death from stroke, enlargement of the heart (a precursor to congestive heart failure), and even asthma mortality (Antonios and McGregor 1995). Moreover, recent population-based studies seem to confirm that the major cause of high blood pressure is an excessive dietary intake of sodium. Using a standardized protocol in a 52-center worldwide study, INTERSALT showed a positive, significant, linear relationship between salt intake and blood pressure. The statistical relationship suggested that each 100 mmol of sodium intake was responsible for a 2 mm Hg increase in systolic blood pressure. In addition, the INTERSALT findings suggest a powerful effect of dietary sodium intake on the rise in blood pressure with age. It has also been argued that a reduction in the average intake of sodium in Britain – from 150 mmol to 100 mmol per day – could reduce strokes and heart attacks in that nation by 22 percent and 16 percent, respectively, and would have a greater impact than that of all of the drugs used to treat high blood pressure (McGregor and Sever 1996).

For the majority of hypertensive persons, it seems well established that lifestyle improvements, such as lowering dietary sodium intake while increasing dietary potassium intake, reducing body weight, and increasing exercise, can lower blood pressure. Although such efforts would likely lower a person's blood pressure by "only" 5 mm Hg, it is important to consider the societal health benefits of such a downward shift across the entire population. From a population-wide perspective, this could dramatically reduce the prevalence of hypertension and cardiovascular disease.

It has been estimated that it costs $1,000 per year to treat each hypertensive person (Elliott 1996). If lifestyle changes could lower the average blood pressure by only 5 mm Hg, then 21.4 million persons would no longer require treatment. This would save the United States about $21 billion a year in the cost of health care for hypertension alone, not to mention the costs saved by the reduction of strokes by about 40 percent and cardiovascular disease by about 25 percent. The potential economic advantage of implementing low-cost lifestyle changes to lower blood pressure across society should be obvious. Indeed, it is clear that most countries of the world will not be able to afford expensive medical therapies to control high blood pressure and should be implementing public-health strategies to lower blood pressure and the devastating consequences of hypertension for a country's workforce.

Thomas W. Wilson
Clarence E. Grim

Bibliography

Abrams, H. L. 1983. Salt and sodium: An anthropological cross-cultural perspective in health and disease. *Journal of Applied Nutrition* 35: 127-58.

Alderman, M. H., S. Madhavan, H. Cohen, et al. 1995. Low urinary sodium is associated with greater risk of myocardial infarction among treated hypertensive men. *Hypertension* 25: 1144-52.

Ambard, L., and E. Beaujard. 1904. Causes de l'hypertension artérielle. *Archives Générales de Médecine* 1: 520-3.

Antonios, T. F., and G. A. McGregor. 1995. Deleterious effects of salt intake other than effects on blood pressure. *Clinical and Experimental Pharmacology and Physiology* 22: 180-4.

Barnes, R. B., D. Richarson, J. W. Berry, and R. L. Hood. 1945. Flame photometry: A rapid analytical procedure. *Industrial Engineering Chemistry, Analytical Edition U.S.* 17: 605-11.

Berenson, G. S., S. R. Srinivasan, G. C. Frank, and L. S. Webber. 1981. Serum lipid and lipoprotein in infants and children and their relationship with diet. *Progress in Clinical & Biological Research* 61: 73-94.

Black, D. A. K. 1946. Salt deficiency in sprue. *Lancet* 2: 671-5.

Bloch, M. R. 1976. Salt in human history. *Interdisciplinary Science Reviews* 1: 336-52.

Bright, R. 1836. Tabular view of the morbid appearances in 100 cases connected with albuminous urine, with observations. *Guy's Hospital Reports* 1: 380-400.

Brisay, K. W. de, and K. A. Evans, eds. 1975. *Salt: The study of an ancient industry.* Colchester, England.

Bunge, G. von 1902. *Text-book of physiological and pathological chemistry.* Second English edition. Translated from the fourth German edition by Florence A. Starling and edited by Ernest H. Starling. Philadelphia, Pa.

Butler, A. M., and E. Tuthill. 1931. An application of the uranyl zinc acetate method for determination of sodium in biological fluids. *Journal of Biological Chemistry* 93: 171-80.

Cannon, Walter Bradford. 1932. *The wisdom of the body.* New York.

Curtin, P. D. 1992. The slavery hypothesis for hypertension among African-Americans: The historical evidence. *American Journal of Public Health* 82: 1681-6.

Dahl, L. K., M. Heine, G. Leitl, and L. Tassinari. 1970. Hypertension and death from consumption of processed baby foods by rats. *Proceedings of the Society of Experimental Biological Medicine* 133: 1405-8.

Denton, D. 1982. *The hunger for salt: An anthropological, physiological, and medical analysis.* Berlin.

Dole, V. P., L. K. Dahl, G. C. Cotzias, et al. 1950. Dietary treatment of hypertension. Clinical and metabolic studies of patients on the rice-fruit diet. *Journal of Clinical Investigation* 29: 1189-1206.

Eaton, B. S., and M. Konner. 1985. Paleolithic nutrition: A consideration of its nature and current implications. *New England Journal of Medicine* 312: 283-9.

Elliott, W. J. 1996. The costs of treating hypertension: What are the long-term realities and pharmacoeconomics? *Postgraduate Medicine* 99: 241-8.

Freis, E. D., A. Wanko, I. M. Wilson, and A. E. Parrish. 1958. Chlorothiazide in hypertensive and normotensive patients. *Annals of the New York Academy of Science* 71: 450.

Gabrial, S. E., K. N. Brigman, B. H. Koller, et al. 1994. Cystic fibrosis heterozygote resistance to cholera toxin in the cystic fibrosis mouse model. *Science* 266: 107-9.

Gamble, J. L. 1945. Congenital alkalosis. *Journal of Pediatrics* 26: 509-18.

Grim, C. E., and T. W. Wilson. 1993. Salt, slavery, and survival: Physiological principles underlying the evolutionary hypothesis of salt-sensitive hypertension in Western Hemisphere blacks. In *The pathophysiology of hypertension in blacks,* ed. J. C. S. Fray and J. G. Douglas, 22-44. New York.

Grollman, A., T. R. Harrison, M. F. Mason, et al. 1945. Sodium restriction in diet for hypertension. *Journal of the American Medical Association* 129: 533-7.

Guyton, A. C., J. E. Hall, T. G. Coleman, et al. 1995. The dominant role of the kidneys in long-term arterial pressure regulation in normal and hypertensive states. In *Hypertension: Pathophysiology, diagnosis, and management.* Second edition, ed. J. H. Laragh and B. M. Brenner, 1311-26. New York.

James, W. P. T., A. Ralph, and C. P. Sanchez-Castillo. 1987. The dominance of salt in manufactured food in the sodium intake of affluent societies. *Lancet* 1: 426-9.

Kaufman, Dale W., ed. 1980. *Sodium chloride: The production and properties of salt and brine.* Washington, D.C.

Kaunitz, H. 1956. Causes and consequences of salt consumption. *Nature* 178: 1141-4.

Kempner, W. 1944. Treatment of kidney disease and hypertensive vascular disease with rice diet. *North Carolina Medical Journal* 5: 125-33.

Korotkoff, N. S. 1905. On methods of studying blood pressure. *IZV Voenno-medakad* 11: 365.

Kroeber, A. L. 1942. Culture element distribution: XV. Salt, dogs, tobacco. *Anthropological Records* 6: 1-20.

Ladell, W. S. S. 1949. The changes in water and chloride distribution during heavy sweating. *Journal of Physiology* 108: 440-50.

Luft, F. C., L. I. Rankin, R. Bloch, et al. 1979. Cardiovascular and humoral responses to extremes of sodium intake in normal white and black men. *Circulation* 60: 697-706.

Marriott, H. L. 1950. *Water and salt depletion.* Springfield, Ill.

McCance, R. A. 1935-6. Experimental sodium chloride deficiency in man. *Proceedings of the Royal Society of London* 119: 245-68.

McGregor, G. A. 1997. President's symposium: Salt, blood pressure, and human health. *American Journal of Hypertension* 10: 220A.

McGregor, G. A., and P. S. Sever. 1996. Salt – overwhelming evidence but still no action: Can a consensus be reached with the food industry? *British Medical Journal* 312: 1287-9.

Midgley, J. P., A. G. Matthew, C. M. T. Greenwood, and A. G. Logan. 1996. Effect of reduced dietary sodium on blood pressure: A meta-analysis of randomized controlled trials. *Journal of the American Medical Association* 275: 1590-7.

Mosher, R. E., A. M. Boyle, E. J. Bird, et al. 1949. The use of flame photometry for the quantitative determination of sodium and potassium in plasma and urine. *American Journal of Clinical Pathology* 49: 461-70.

Multhauf, R. P. 1978. *Neptune's gift: A history of common salt.* Baltimore, Md.

Murray, R., F. C. Luft, R. Bloch, and A. E. Weymen. 1978. Blood pressure response to extremes in sodium intake in normal man. *Proceedings of the Society of Experimental Biology* 159: 432-6.

Osler, W. [1892] 1978. *The principles and practice of medicine.* Birmingham, England.

Overman, R. R., and A. K. Davis. 1947. The application of flame photometry to sodium and potassium determinations in biological fluids. *Journal of Biological Chemistry* 168: 641-9.

Schulkin, J. 1991. *Sodium hunger: The search for a salty taste.* Cambridge.

Staessen, J. A., P. Lijnen, L. Theis, and R. Fagard. 1997. Salt and blood pressure in community-based intervention trials. *American Journal of Clinical Nutrition* 65 (Supplement): 661S-70S.

Swales, J. D. 1975. *Sodium metabolism in disease.* London.

Tigerstedt, R., and T. G. Bergman. 1898. Niere und Kreislauf. *Scandinavian Archives of Physiology* 7-8: 223-71.

USDA/USDHHS (U.S. Department of Agriculture/U.S. Department of Health and Human Services). 1995. *Report of the Dietary Guidelines Advisory Committee on dietary guidelines for Americans.* Washington, D.C.

Wallace, W. M., M. Holliday, M. Cushman, and J. R. Elkinton. 1951. The application of the internal standard flame photometer to the analysis of biologic material. *Journal of Laboratory and Clinical Medicine* 37: 621-9.

Wilson, T. W., and C. E. Grim. 1991. Biohistory of slavery and blood pressure differences in blacks today: A hypothesis. *Hypertension* 17: I122-8.

    1993. Hypertension. In *The Cambridge world history of human disease,* ed. K. F. Kiple, 789-94. Cambridge and New York.

IV.B.8. Other Trace Elements

Beginning early in the twentieth century, scientists were able to qualitatively detect small amounts of several elements in living organisms. In reports, these elements were often described as being present in "traces" or "trace amounts," and within a short time, they became known as the trace elements. Today, trace elements are understood to be those elements of the periodic table that occur in the body in micrograms per gram (μg/g) of body weight or less. They may be essential – that is, they may be indispensable for growth, health, and completion of the life cycle – or they may be nonessential: fortuitous reminders of our geochemical origins or indicators of environmental exposure. Some of the nonessential trace elements can be beneficial to health through pharmacologic action, but all are toxic when consumed in excess.

An essential element is defined by many in the scientific community as an element whose dietary deficiency consistently results in a suboptimal function that is preventable or reversible by physiological amounts of the element. However, other experts accept an element as essential only if it has a defined biochemical function. Thus, there is no universally accepted list of trace elements that are considered essential.

The essential trace elements are usually required by humans in amounts indicated by milligrams per day (mg/d). In 1980, the term "ultratrace element" began to appear in the literature; this was defined as an element with a daily dietary requirement of some 50 nanograms per gram (ng/g) for animals (Nielsen 1980). For

humans, however, the term often is used to indicate elements with an established, estimated, or suspected requirement of less than 1.0 mg/d (generally indicated as micrograms per day, or μg/d) (Nielsen 1994b).

At present, both signs of deficiency and defined biochemical functions in humans are known for only 7 trace and ultratrace elements. The trace elements are copper, iron, and zinc, and the ultratrace elements are cobalt (in the form of cobalamin), iodine, molybdenum, and selenium. Although essential functions have been identified for manganese, unequivocal signs of its deficiency in humans have not been described. Conversely, such signs have been described for chromium and boron, but their specific biochemical functions have not been conclusively defined. Based on animal experiments, and discovery of their essential functions in lower forms of life, 4 other trace or ultratrace elements are probably essential to humans: arsenic, nickel, silicon, and vanadium. In addition, 2 elements with beneficial pharmacological properties are fluorine (anticariogenic) and lithium (antimanic). Since 1970, reports have appeared suggesting that other elements, including aluminum, bromine, cadmium, germanium, lead, rubidium, strontium, and tin, may be essential. However, weak, limited, or controversial data have prevented general acceptance of the essentiality of these elements.

The essential trace elements iron and zinc and the essential ultratrace element iodine are discussed in separate chapters and thus are not addressed here.

Arsenic

History of Oral Intake

Since ancient times, arsenicals have been characterized by actions both benevolent and malevolent. Very early, it was found that some arsenic compounds were convenient scentless and tasteless instruments for homicidal purposes, and until the nineteenth century, arsenic reigned as the king of poisons; indeed even today, the term "arsenic" is primarily thought of as synonymous with poison. Nonetheless, this bad reputation did not prevent it from becoming an important pharmaceutical agent. According to a review by H. A. Schroeder and J. J. Balassa (1966), the medicinal virtues of arsenicals were acclaimed by Hippocrates (460 to 357 B.C.), Aristotle (384 to 322 B.C.), Theophrastus (370 to 288 B.C.), and Pliny the Elder (A.D. 23 to 70).

Beginning in 1905, various arsenicals were developed for pharmacological purposes, and by 1937, they numbered 8,000. Arsenicals were considered at various times to be specific remedies in the treatment of anorexia, other nutritional disturbances, neuralgia, rheumatism, asthma, chorea, malaria, tuberculosis, diabetes, skin diseases, and numerous hematologic abnormalities. Today, however, either the use of arsenic for these disorders has fallen into disrepute or more effective alternatives have taken its place.

Discovery of Nutritional Importance

Reports describing attempts to produce a nutritional arsenic deficiency first appeared in the 1930s. E. Hove, C. A. Elvehjem, and E. B. Hart (1938) found that a milk diet fortified with iron, copper, and manganese, furnishing as little arsenic as 2 µg/day, did not significantly affect growth, hemoglobin concentration, and red blood cell number or fragility in rats. However, an arsenic supplement of 5 µg/day delayed the rate of fall of hemoglobin concentration in rats fed whole milk without mineral supplementation. J. T. Skinner and J. S. McHargue (1946) also found that arsenic supplementation increased hemoglobin concentrations in rats fed a skim milk and sucrose diet adequately supplemented with iron and copper.

H. A. Schroeder and J. J. Balassa (1966) found that rats and mice grew and developed normally when fed diets containing as little arsenic as 0.053 µg/g; additional arsenic in their drinking water improved the appearance of their skin and hair. Perhaps the first findings accepted as evidence for the possible nutritional essentiality of arsenic appeared in 1975 and 1976, when apparent deficiency signs were described for rats, goats, and pigs (Nielsen and Uthus 1984; Anke 1986; Uthus 1994). Subsequently, deficiency signs were reported for chickens and hamsters (Uthus 1994).

Dietary Importance

In goats, pigs, and rats, the most consistent signs of arsenic deprivation were depressed growth and abnormal reproduction characterized by impaired fertility and elevated perinatal mortality (Nielsen and Uthus 1984; Anke 1986). Arsenic deprivation also caused myocardial damage and death during lactation in goats. Some biochemical changes found with arsenic deprivation include depressed plasma triglycerides and taurine concentrations, liver polyamine concentration, liver glutathione S-transferase activity, liver S-adenosylmethionine concentration, and specific activity of S-adenosylmethionine decarboxylase (Uthus 1994). The large number of responses to arsenic deprivation – reported for a variety of animal species by more than one research group – strongly suggests that arsenic is a nutritionally important ultratrace element for higher animals.

Although a biochemical function has not been defined for arsenic, its actions in vitro and the findings from animal deprivation studies indicate a function that affects the formation and utilization of labile methyl groups arising from methionine. Through this effect on methyl group metabolism, arsenic possibly affects the methylation of important molecules, such as DNA. If so, suboptimal methyl metabolism caused by lack of arsenic could be of concern; for example, hypomethylation of DNA can lead to some forms of cancer. It has also been suggested that arsenic plays an important role in human health because of findings that injuries of the central nervous system, vascular diseases, and cancers correlated with markedly depressed serum arsenic concentrations (Mayer et al. 1993). Because arsenic is most likely an essential nutrient, the belief that any form of it is unnecessary, toxic, or carcinogenic must be discarded.

Boron

History of Oral Intake

The recognition that the presence of boron in foods can be both beneficial and detrimental apparently dates from the 1870s. At that time, it was discovered that borax and boric acid could be used to preserve foods, and for the next 50 years or so, borate addition was considered one of the best methods of preserving or extending the palatability of foods such as fish, shellfish, meat, sausage, bacon, ham, cream, butter, and margarine (Gordon 1987). During World War I, the use of boron as a preservative played a vital role in preventing food crises. In other words, in the last decades of the nineteenth century and the first decades of the twentieth century, boron was considered beneficial, and prevailing medical opinion held that boron was innocuous because, despite its widespread use, no deaths had been blamed on it.

As early as 1902, however, some German and American scientists had begun to question this orthodox view. Foremost among the works that changed perceptions about boron was a report by H. W. Wiley (1904), which stated that consumption of boric acid in doses greater than 0.5 g/day for 50 days resulted in disturbances in appetite, digestion, and health in human volunteers. Following this change in perception, the opinion that boron posed a risk to health started to gain momentum, and by the mid–1920s, many countries began legislating against the addition of borates to food. Only during World War II were the new restrictions eased, as shortages made food preservation a major concern in many countries (Gordon 1987). After the war, restrictions were gradually reimposed and by the middle of the 1950s, the use of boron as a food preservative was virtually forbidden throughout the world. At this time, boron also began to receive attention from toxicologists. Because of some accidental poisonings and inappropriate uses in the medical profession, between 1950 and 1980 boric acid and borates were seen as only important to human health from a toxicological point of view.

Discovery of Nutritional Importance

During the 1920s, K. Warington (1923) and A. L. Sommer and C. B. Lipman (1926) showed that boron was an essential nutrient for plants, and in subsequent decades, other investigators attempted – unsuccessfully – to demonstrate that it was essential for higher animals as well (Hove, Elvehjem, and Hart 1939; Orent-Keiles 1941; Teresi et al. 1944). It was reported in 1945 that high dietary boron (100 to 1,000 µg/g) enhanced survival and increased body fat and liver glycogen in potassium-deficient rats (Skinner and McHargue 1945), although further experiments, using a different diet with an unknown basal boron content and with different amounts of boron supplementation, failed to confirm these findings (Follis 1947). The inability in these early studies to produce a boron deficiency in animals apparently resulted in generations of students of biochemistry and nutrition learning that boron was a unique element because it was essential for plants but not for higher animals, including humans.

In the early 1980s, however, this dogma began to change. C. D. Hunt and F. H. Nielsen (1981) reported that boron deprivation depressed the growth of chicks, with the effect seemingly more marked when dietary cholecalciferol was marginally deficient. Moreover, morphological examination of the tibias of chicks indicated that an interaction between boron and cholecalciferol affected bone formation. In the years since this report, circumstantial evidence has accumulated to suggest strongly that boron is an essential nutrient for higher animals and humans.

Dietary Importance

Listing the signs of boron deficiency for animals is difficult because of the large number reported and because most studies of this deficiency in animals have used stressors to enhance the response to changes in dietary boron. However, although the nature and severity of the changes varied with dietary composition, many of the findings indicated that boron deprivation impairs calcium metabolism, brain function, and energy metabolism (Hunt 1994; Nielsen 1994a; Nielsen 1997). They also suggest that boron deprivation impairs immune function and exacerbates adjuvant-induced arthritis in rats.

Humans as well as animals respond to changes in dietary intake of boron (Nielsen 1994a; Penland 1994; Nielsen 1997). Among the effects of boron deprivation in men over the age of 45, postmenopausal women, and postmenopausal women on estrogen therapy were the following: an effect on macromineral and electrolyte metabolism evidenced by decreased serum 25-hydroxycholecalciferol and increased calcitonin (when dietary magnesium and copper were low); an effect on energy substrate metabolism suggested by increased serum glucose and decreased serum triglycerides; an effect on nitrogen metabolism indicated by increased blood urea nitrogen and serum creatinine and decreased urinary hydroxyproline excretion; an effect on oxidative metabolism indicated by decreased erythrocyte superoxide dismutase and serum ceruloplasmin; and an effect on erythropoiesis and hematopoiesis suggested by decreased blood hemoglobin and mean corpuscular hemoglobin content combined with increased hematocrit, platelet number, and erythrocyte number.

Boron depletion also depressed the elevation in serum 17-beta-estradiol and plasma copper caused by estrogen ingestion, altered electroencephalograms so that they suggested diminished behavioral activation (for example, more drowsiness) and mental alertness, and impaired psychomotor skills and the cognitive processes of attention and memory.

Although a defined biochemical function is not yet known for boron, accumulated knowledge about its nutritional effects and metabolism has resulted in the recognition that boron may be of practical nutritional importance. However, no clinical disorder can be conclusively attributed to suboptimal boron nutriture. Because boron affects the macromineral metabolism, it seems likely that an inadequate boron intake may contribute to some disorders associated with suboptimal calcium metabolism, such as osteoporosis.

Chromium

Discovery of Nutritional Importance

By 1948, chromium had been recognized as a consistent component of plant and animal tissue. The first suggestion that chromium might have biologic activity appeared in 1954 (Curran 1954), when it was found that chromium enhanced the synthesis of cholesterol and fatty acids from acetate by rat liver. In 1959, trivalent chromium was identified as the active component of the "glucose tolerance factor," which alleviated the impaired glucose tolerance in rats fed certain diets apparently inadequate in chromium (Schwarz and Mertz 1959). Between 1964 and 1968, the first reports appeared indicating that chromium could affect glucose tolerance in humans (Mertz 1993).

Subsequently, it was found that chromium supplementation also decreased serum cholesterol concentrations and normalized exaggerated insulin responses to glucose loads. Despite these suggestive findings, chromium did not receive much attention as a possible essential element for humans until 1977, when apparent chromium deficiency signs were found in a patient receiving total parenteral nutrition (Jeejeebhoy et al. 1977). Shortly thereafter, other patients receiving total parenteral nutrition were found to exhibit abnormalities of glucose metabolism that were responsive to chromium supplementation.

Dietary Importance

In 1959, it was reported that chromium-deficient rats exhibited a glucose intolerance similar to that of clinical diabetes mellitus (Schwarz and Mertz 1959). Since that time, several other deficiency signs have been described for animals, including impaired growth, elevated serum cholesterol and triglyceride concentrations, increased incidence of aortic plaques, corneal lesions, and decreased fertility and sperm count (Anderson 1988). Many of these signs were made more evident by using nutritional, metabolic, physiological, or hormonal stressors.

Signs of apparent chromium deficiency have been found in three women receiving long-term total parenteral nutrition containing low amounts of chromium. One subject, who had received total parenteral nutrition for 3.5 years, exhibited impaired glucose tolerance and glucose use, weight loss, neuropathy, elevated free fatty acid concentrations, depressed respiratory exchange ratio, and abnormalities in nitrogen metabolism (Jeejeebhoy et al. 1977). These abnormalities were alleviated by chromium supplementation. Another subject, who had received total parenteral nutrition for 5 months, developed severe glucose intolerance, weight loss, and a metabolic encephalopathy-like confusional state. All of these abnormalities were reversed by chromium supplementation (Freund, Atamian, and Fischer 1979). Chromium supplementation also reversed the development of unexplained high blood and urine glucose in a third patient who had followed a total parenteral nutrition regimen of several months' duration (Brown et al. 1986).

Although these three descriptions of human chromium deficiency are somewhat dissimilar, in all cases the apparently chromium-deficient subjects exhibited impaired glucose tolerance, or high blood glucose with glucose spilling into the urine, and a refractoriness to insulin. In addition, since 1966, a large number of reports from numerous research groups have described beneficial effects from chromium supplements in subjects with degrees of glucose intolerance ranging from low blood sugar to insulin-dependent diabetes. Most recent are reports that relatively high chromium supplementation (200 to 1000 μg/day of chromium picolinate) decreased blood glucose and glycated hemoglobin in 162 Beijing, China, residents with high blood glucose (Anderson et al. 1997); such supplementation also decreased blood glucose, C-peptide, and insulin concentrations in gestational diabetic women undergoing a glucose tolerance test (Jovanovic-Peterson, Gutierrez, and Peterson 1996). Thus, there is a growing body of evidence suggesting that chromium supplements may be a viable treatment option for some people with diabetes resulting from inadequate synthesis of insulin or insulin resistance. In other words, chromium is potentiating the action of low amounts of insulin or improving its efficiency so that the need for exogenous sources is reduced or eliminated. Beneficial effects of chromium supplementation on blood lipid profiles also have been reported.

Even though a biochemical function has not been defined for chromium, it most likely is an essential element. Even the skeptics of chromium essentiality agree that chromium can be beneficial because of its positive effects on glucose and lipid metabolism in some individuals. This is apparently the reason that in 1980 an Estimated Safe and Adequate Daily Dietary Intake (ESADDI) was established for chromium (National Research Council 1980). For children over age 7 and adults, this amount is 50 to 200 μg/day.

There is some evidence that an intake of chromium of less than 20 μg/day is inadequate, and dietary surveys indicate that a significant number of people consume less than this amount. Thus, it seems possible that inadequate chromium status may be partially responsible for some cases of impaired glucose tolerance, high blood glucose, low blood glucose, refractoriness to insulin, and, ultimately, diabetes. Furthermore, because impaired tissue responsiveness to insulin is a possible risk factor for cardiovascular disease, and because chromium deprivation has unfavorable effects on cholesterol and lipid metabolism, inadequate chromium status may increase susceptibility to ischemic heart disease.

Copper

Discovery of Nutritional Importance

The presence of copper in plant and animal tissues was recognized early in the nineteenth century, but this was thought to be the result of accidental contamination. The first indication that the mineral was associated with specific biochemical substances occurred when it was found in blood proteins in snails (Harless 1847). Copper was also found in the tail-feather pigment of the turaco (Church 1869) and was shown to be a constituent of octopus hemocyanin (Fredericq 1878). The discovery of reproducible amounts of copper in the human brain (Bodansky 1921) stimulated acceptance of the fact that it was definitely a physiological constituent of biological material.

Its universal distribution in plants prompted the hypothesis that copper was a catalyst participating in life processes (Fleurent and Lévi 1920; Guérithault and Maquenne 1920), and soon afterward, McHargue (1925, 1926) produced evidence suggesting that the element was beneficial in the diet of rats. Conclusive evidence that copper is an essential nutrient, however, came from studies of hemoglobin regeneration in anemic rats. In 1928, it was demonstrated that copper supplementation prevented both anemia and growth-stunting in young rats on milk-only diets (Hart et al. 1928), and subsequently, anemia caused by copper deprivation was shown to occur in chickens, cows, dogs, goats, pigs, sheep, rabbits, and humans.

Shortly after the initial discovery that rats required the mineral, certain naturally occurring copper-deficiency disorders were identified in cattle (salt-sickness in Florida and *lecksucht* in the Netherlands) and sheep (enzootic neonatal ataxia in Western Australia) (Neal, Becker, and Shealy 1931; Sjollema 1933; Bennetts and Chapman 1937). In addition to poor growth and anemia, copper deficiency was characterized by defects in pigmentation, keratinization of wool, bone formation, reproduction, myelination of the spinal cord, cardiac function, and connective tissue formation.

During the 1960s and 1970s, the first descriptions of copper deficiency in humans began to appear.

Deficiency symptoms were described for premature babies (Al-Rashid and Spangler 1971; Ashkenazi et al. 1973) and for young Peruvian and Chilean children with severe malnutrition and chronic diarrhea (Cordano, Baertl, and Graham 1964; Graham and Cordano 1969). Anemia, neutropenia, and osteoporosis were the main characteristics of the deficiency. The discovery of a genetic disease (Menkes disease) with characteristics of copper deficiency also showed that low copper status could adversely affect humans (Danks et al. 1972a, 1972b). Since 1984, reports have appeared describing signs of copper deficiency in adults brought on by depletion–repletion experiments (Klevay and Medeiros 1996).

Dietary Importance

Recent studies, mostly with rodents, have shown that copper deficiency results in a large number of defects associated with the cardiovascular system, including abnormal electrocardiograms, connective tissue abnormalities in blood vessels, enlarged hearts, altered fatty acid profiles, glucose intolerance, abnormal blood pressure, elevated blood cholesterol, pleural effusion, and ventricular aneurysms (Klevay and Medeiros 1996).

The importance of copper for malnourished children and premature infants has been described. Subsequent to its discovery, an ESADDI of 2 to 3 mg for adults was established (National Research Council 1980); some years later, this was changed to 1.5 to 3.0 mg (National Research Council 1989). Human depletion–repletion studies in adults have indicated that copper intakes of 0.65 to 1.02 mg/day are insufficient. Some subjects fed diets containing this amount exhibited changes in serum cholesterol, heart rhythm, and oxidative metabolism – measured by erythrocyte superoxide dismutase activity, serum ceruloplasmin, and mononucleated white cell cytochrome c oxidase (Klevay and Medeiros 1996). Such changes suggest that a low copper status can increase the risk for ischemic heart disease (Klevay 1990), a suggestion in urgent need of confirmation because pooled data from surveys in Belgium, Canada, the United Kingdom, and the United States have revealed that approximately one-third of 849 diets supplied copper in quantities of less than 1.0 mg/day (Klevay et al. 1993).

Fluorine

Discovery of Nutritional Importance

Fluorine first attracted nutritional attention in the 1930s, when unsuccessful attempts were made to show that low fluoride intakes produced any kind of pathology in rats and when fluoride was identified as the factor causing a mottled condition of tooth enamel known as "Colorado brown stain" and other such descriptive names (Whitford 1990). It was also noted at that time that fewer dental caries occurred in those individuals with mottled enamel, and subse-

quently it was discovered that fluoride intakes could be achieved that brought about caries reduction without mottling. As a consequence, water fluoridation was begun as a public health measure in 1945.

In the 1960s, an association was made between high fluoride intake and a reduced incidence of osteoporosis (Messer 1984). However, although the use of pharmacologic amounts of fluoride to prevent bone loss is still being investigated, its usefulness in this regard seems limited. Another round of fluoride confusion came in the early 1970s, when scientists suggested that fluoride was necessary for hematopoiesis, fertility, and growth in mice and rats (Messer 1984). It turned out, however, that this assertion was based on experiments in which animals were not fed optimal diets, and it was later concluded that the effects of fluoride were only achieved through pharmacologic mechanisms.

Dietary Importance

At present, there is no substantive evidence that fluoride is an essential nutrient. The major known biological action of fluoride is its ability to protect against pathological demineralization of calcified tissues, which is not an essential function in the true sense, but a beneficial action delivered through pharmacological mechanisms. Nonetheless, because fluoride was recognized as having beneficial properties through oral intake, ESADDIs for various times in the life cycle were established; for adults, this amount is 1.5 to 4.0 mg (National Research Council 1989).

Manganese

Discovery of Nutritional Importance

Between 1913 and 1921, manganese was found to be a constant component of plant and animal tissues, and in 1923, it was shown to be required by plants and microorganisms (McHargue 1923). Attempts to demonstrate that manganese was required by laboratory animals were unsuccessful, however, because the purified diets employed were so deficient in other essential nutrients that even the addition of manganese did not result in normal growth and survival. In 1931, it was found that manganese was essential for the growth of mice and also for normal ovarian activity in both mice and rats; it was vital to preventing testicular degeneration in rats as well (Kemmerer, Elvehjem, and Hart 1931; Orent and McCollum 1931; Waddell, Steenbock, and Hart 1931). Five years later, researchers learned that perosis ("slipped tendon") and nutritional chondrodystrophy in poultry were caused by inadequate manganese intake (Wilgus, Norris, and Heuser 1936, 1937; Lyons and Insko 1937). The identification of a specific biochemical function for manganese remained elusive for many years, but finally, in 1962, the mineral was found to have a specific role in the synthesis of the mucopolysaccharides of cartilage (Leach and Muenster 1962). The first report of a possible case of human manganese deficiency appeared in 1972 (Doisy 1972).

Dietary Importance

Manganese deficiency symptoms have been induced in many species of animals. They include impaired growth, skeletal abnormalities, disturbed or depressed reproductive function, ataxia of the newborn, and defects in lipid and carbohydrate metabolism (Freeland-Graves and Llanes 1994; Finley and Johnson 1996). Establishing the signs of manganese deficiency in humans, however, has been difficult.

The first possible description of manganese deficiency in humans was that of a man who had been fed a semipurified diet for an extended period of time (Doisy 1972). He developed weight loss, depressed growth of hair and nails, dermatitis, and low blood cholesterol. Moreover, his black hair developed a reddish tinge, and his clotting protein response to vitamin K supplementation was abnormal. Subsequent to the appearance of these signs, it was realized that manganese had been left out of his diet, and the subject responded to a mixed hospital diet containing manganese. Unfortunately, no supplementation with manganese alone was tried, and thus, although this case is often cited as an example of human manganese deficiency, the experimental design does not permit this to be stated conclusively.

Another report indicated that men fed only 0.11 mg/day of manganese for 35 days exhibited decreased cholesterol concentrations in serum, a fleeting dermatitis, and increased calcium, phosphorus, and alkaline phosphatase in blood (Friedman et al. 1987). Short-term manganese supplementation for 10 days, however, failed to reverse these changes, and consequently, whether the observed changes were caused by manganese deprivation can be questioned. Probably the most convincing report of a human manganese deficiency is that concerning a girl, age 4 years, who had been maintained on total parenteral nutrition that was low in manganese since she was 9 days old. She developed short stature, brittle bones, and low serum manganese; manganese supplementation improved bone density and longitudinal growth (Norose 1992). In addition to the symptoms just discussed, a low manganese status has been associated with osteoporosis and epilepsy; that is, patients with these conditions often have low serum or plasma manganese concentrations (Freeland-Graves and Turnlund 1996). Although such limited findings have made it difficult to establish the nutritional importance of manganese, most scientists do not doubt that it is essential for humans.

Molybdenum

Discovery of Nutritional Importance

From the toxicological point of view, molybdenum became important when it was discovered that the drastic scouring disease of cattle, "teart," was caused by ingestion of excessive molybdenum, high amounts of which were present in herbage growing in the affected areas (Ferguson, Lewis, and Watson 1938). From a nutritional viewpoint, in 1930 molybdenum was reported to be essential for the growth of *Azotobacter*, a nonpathogenic bacterium found in soil and water (Bortels 1930).

Subsequently, it was discovered that molybdenum was needed by nearly all nitrogen-fixing organisms, and by 1939, the mineral was known to be both required by higher plants (independent of its role in nitrogen fixation) and consistently present in animal tissues (ter Meulen 1932; Arnon and Stout 1939). However, an early attempt to show that molybdenum was required by laboratory animals was unsuccessful (Teresi, Elvehjem, and Hart 1942), and later attempts to produce symptomatic molybdenum deficiency in rats and chicks were only successful when the diets contained massive amounts of tungsten, an antagonist of molybdenum metabolism (Higgins, Richert, and Westerfeld 1956). In 1981, the first report appeared of a human molybdenum deficiency caused by a dietary lack (Abumrad et al. 1981).

Dietary Importance

There are very few descriptions of molybdenum deficiency signs in humans (Rajagopalan 1988). In one study, four young men exhibited no clinical signs after consuming a diet with a molybdenum content of only 22 µg/day for 102 days (Turnlund et al. 1995). However, the low amount of the mineral resulted in decreased urinary excretion of uric acid and an increased urinary xanthine excretion after the administration of a load of adenosine monophosphate. These findings indicated that xanthine oxidase (a molydoenzyme) activity was decreased.

The most convincing case of molybdenum deficiency was found in a patient receiving prolonged parenteral nutrition therapy (Abumrad et al. 1981). The patient's symptoms (which were exacerbated by methionine administration) included high blood methionine and oxypurine concentrations, low blood uric acid concentration, and low urinary excretion of uric acid and sulfate. The patient suffered mental disturbances that progressed to coma, but supplementation with ammonium molybdate improved the clinical condition, reversed the sulfur-handling defect, and normalized uric acid production.

A human genetic disorder caused by a lack of functioning molybdenum as part of the enzyme sulfite oxidase has been identified (Rajagopalan 1988). This genetic disease is characterized by severe brain damage, mental retardation, and dislocation of ocular lenses, and results in increased urinary output of sulfite, S-sulfocysteine, and thiosulfate, and a marked decrease in sulfate output.

Although molybdenum deficiency has not been recognized as a nutritional problem, it cannot be ignored because there may be unrecognized situations in which molybdenum nutriture plays an important role. For example, the molybdenum hydroxylases apparently are as important as the microsomal monooxygenase system in the metabolism of drugs and compounds foreign to the body (Beedham 1985). Perhaps low molybdenum hydroxylase activity (caused by molybdenum deficiency) would have undesirable consequences when a person is stressed by high intakes of xenobiotics. An ESADDI has been established for molybdenum; for adults it is 75 to 250 μg (National Research Council 1989).

Nickel

Discovery of Nutritional Importance

The earliest study of the biologic action of nickel appeared in 1826, when signs of oral nickel toxicity were described in rabbits and dogs (Nriagu 1980). The first reports on the presence of the mineral in plant and animal tissues appeared in 1925 (Berg 1925; Bertrand and Mâcheboeuf 1925), and although it was suggested that nickel was nutritionally essential in 1936 (Bertrand and Nakamura 1936), the first direct evidence for its essentiality for higher animals appeared in 1970 (Nielsen and Sauberlich 1970). By 1984, extensive signs of nickel deprivation had been reported for 6 animal species – chickens, cattle, goats, pigs, rats, and sheep (Nielsen 1984). Unfortunately, many of these symptoms may have been manifestations of pharmacologic actions of nickel; that is, high dietary nickel used in some experiments may have alleviated an abnormality caused by something other than a nutritional deficiency of nickel (for example, many diets used in the experiments were apparently low in iron) (Nielsen 1985).

Studies of nickel since 1984 probably give a more accurate picture of its nutritional role in higher animals. Support for the essentiality of the mineral has come from the identification of nickel enzymes in lower forms of life; the first to be identified was jackbean urease in 1975 (Dixon et al. 1975). Since then, nickel has been found to be an essential component of urease from bacteria, mycoplasma, fungi, yeast, algae, higher plants, and invertebrates (Mobley, Island, and Hausinger 1995). Nickel also has been identified as an essential component of three redox enzymes in bacteria involved in hydrogen oxidation, methane biogenesis, and acetate formation; these enzymes are hydrogenase, methylcoenzyme M reductase, and carbon monoxide dehydrogenase (Lancaster 1988). A nickel deficiency in humans has not been reported.

Dietary Importance

Recent studies (Nielsen 1995) suggest that nickel deprivation in goats and rats results in depressed growth, reproductive performance, and plasma glucose and alters the distribution of other elements in the body, including calcium, iron, and zinc. As with other ultratrace elements, the nature and severity of the signs of nickel deprivation are affected by the composition of the diet. For example, both vitamin B_{12} (Nielsen et al. 1989) and folic acid (Uthus and Poellot 1996) affect the response to nickel deprivation. This correlation, in turn, has resulted in the hypotheses that vitamin B_{12} is necessary for the optimal expression of the biological role of nickel and that nickel has an essential function closely related to vitamin B_{12} metabolism.

The recent discoveries of nickel essentiality and its defined biochemical functions in various microorganisms, plants, and animals indicate that it is also an essential nutrient for humans. Nonetheless, until more is known about its physiological function, it is inappropriate to specify that certain disorders might be wholly, or even partially, attributable to abnormal nickel nutrition or metabolism. But because the nickel content in some human diets can be lower than that which induces changes in animals, it may well turn out that nickel will be found to be an element of concern in human nutrition.

Selenium

Discovery of Nutritional Importance

From the biological point of view, the early history of selenium focused on its toxicological properties. The first report appeared about 1295 in the writings of Marco Polo (Trelease and Beath 1949). He described a poisonous plant (most likely seleniferous) growing in the mountains of western China, which, when eaten by beasts of burden, caused their hoofs to drop off – a phenomenon known to occur in cattle and horses that consume plants containing toxic amounts of selenium. The first scientific description of selenium toxicity, however, appeared only in 1842 (Moxon and Rhian 1943), and the element received little further attention until 1935. At that time, selenium poisoning (caused by the consumption of grains and forages high in this element) was found responsible for two diseases of livestock – known as "blind staggers" and "alkali disease" – that occurred in the northern plains of the United States (Franke and Painter 1935). This discovery stimulated investigation of the distribution of selenium in rocks, soils, plants, and animals.

In 1957, selenium came under consideration as an essential nutrient when it was found that it prevented liver necrosis in vitamin E deficient rats (Schwarz and Foltz 1957) and exudative diathesis in vitamin E deficient chicks (Patterson, Milstrey, and Stokstad 1957; Schwarz et al. 1957). The following year it was reported that muscular dystrophy, which occurred in lambs and calves in certain areas of the world, was caused by selenium deficiency (Muth et al. 1958; Proctor, Hogue, and Warner 1958). Subsequently, researchers identified areas of the world that were home to naturally occurring selenium deficiency, which impaired the growth, health, and fertility of animals living in them. Identification of a biochemical function for selenium in mammals came in 1973, when the element was shown to be a constituent of the enzyme glutathione peroxidase (Rotruck et al. 1973). Reports first appeared in 1979 indicating that a naturally occurring clinical condition – Keshan disease – was partially attributable to low selenium intake (Keshan Disease Research Group 1979).

Dietary Importance

All known pathologies of selenium deficiency in animals can be alleviated by luxuriant intakes of vitamin E. Thus, the nutritional importance of selenium is most evident in vitamin E deficient animals. A variety of pathological changes attributable to combined deficiencies of selenium and vitamin E have been described for several animal species. These changes result in dysfunctions of the brain, the cardiovascular system, the liver, the muscles, and the fetus. Many of the pathological conditions caused by the combined deficiencies can be modified by other dietary factors, including the intake of polyunsaturated fatty acids, sulfur amino acids, and synthetic antioxidants (Combs and Combs 1984).

Evidence that selenium can be of practical nutritional importance came from studies of the relationship between selenium and Keshan disease, an endemic cardiomyopathy affecting children and young women that occurs in an area running from northeastern to southwestern China (Levander and Burk 1994). The primary pathological changes in Keshan disease include heart enlargement with multiple focal degenerative necrosis and fibrous replacement of the myocardium. Selenium supplementation was found effective in preventing Keshan disease, the incidence of which varied with several other factors, and it has been suggested that low vitamin E status or oxidant stress caused by viral or bacterial infection may be contributory factors. Other reports of selenium deficiency came from studies of patients on long-term total parenteral nutrition. The signs of deficiency in these patients included bilateral muscular discomfort and a dilated cardiomyopathy that histopathologically resembled Keshan disease (Levander and Burk 1994).

Finally, it was found that a luxuriant intake of selenium achieved by supplementation (200 µg/day) was effective in preventing the occurrence of some forms of cancer (Clark et al. 1996). Because the preceding discovery indicated that those individuals who are selenium deficient can be considered at risk for developing pathology, people should achieve an intake meeting the Recommended Dietary Allowance of 70 and 55 µg/day for adult men and women, respectively (National Research Council 1989).

Silicon

Discovery of Nutritional Importance

Silicon has long been thought important in maintaining health in humans. Before much was known about it in biology, one of the luminaries of medical science,

Louis Pasteur, predicted that silicon would prove to be an important therapeutic substance for many diseases (Becker et al. 1983), and at the beginning of the twentieth century, numerous French and German reports suggested that the prediction of Pasteur would become fact. These reports described therapeutic successes in treating numerous diseases – including atherosclerosis, hypertension, and dermatitis – with sodium silicate, with simple organic silicon compounds, and with tea made from the silicon-rich horsetail plant. However, by 1930, these "therapeutic successes" had come to be viewed as failures, and in the face of inadequate evidence for silicon's biological activity, the mineral faded into medical obscurity.

During the next four decades, silicon – as consumed in the diet – was generally considered a biologically inert, harmless, nonessential element for living organisms, except for some lower forms of life (diatoms, radiolarians, and sponges) in which silica meets a structural need (Carlisle 1984). But then, in 1972, it was reported that silicon was essential for bone formation (Carlisle 1972), and at about the same time, other studies appeared suggesting, as had those of the early twentieth century, that inadequate dietary silicon may contribute to some cases of atherosclerosis, hypertension, some bone disorders, and the aging process. However, these studies have generally been ignored because a specific biochemical role for silicon, which could explain the mechanism behind such occurrences, has not been identified.

Dietary Importance

Most of the signs of silicon deficiency in animals indicate aberrant metabolism of connective tissue and bone. Illustrative are chicks on a silicon-deficient diet that exhibit structural abnormalities of the skull, depressed collagen content in bone, and long-bone abnormalities characterized by small, poorly formed joints and defective endochondral bone growth (Carlisle 1984). Silicon deprivation can also affect the response to other dietary manipulations. Thus, although rats fed a diet low in calcium and high in aluminum accumulated high amounts of aluminum in the brain, it was found that relatively high silicon supplements prevented such accumulation (Carlisle and Curran 1987).

Similarly, whereas high dietary aluminum depressed brain zinc concentrations in thyroidectomized rats fed low dietary silicon, relatively high silicon supplements prevented the depression (Carlisle, Curran, and Duong 1991). This effect, however, was not seen in nonthyroidectomized rats. Other biochemical actions indicating that silicon is an essential element include its consistent presence in collagen; and in bone tissue culture it is needed for maximal bone prolylhydroxylase activity (Carlisle, Berger, and Alpenfels 1981). Silicon deficiency decreases ornithine aminotransferase (an enzyme in the collagen formation pathway) in rats (Seaborn and Nielsen 1996). Thus, ample evidence exists to suggest that silicon is an essential nutrient for higher animals, including humans.

Findings from animals indicating that silicon nutriture affects macromolecules – such as glycosaminoglycans, collagen, and elastin – suggest that silicon is needed for healthy bones, brains, and blood vessels (Seaborn and Nielsen 1993). Although more needs to be known about the physiological or biochemical function and requirement for silicon, speculation has materialized on the possible involvement of silicon deprivation in the occurrence of several human disorders, including atherosclerosis, osteoarthritis, osteoporosis, hypertension, and Alzheimer's disease. Such speculation indicates the need for more work to clarify the consequences of silicon deficiency in humans.

Vanadium

Discovery of Nutritional Importance

A report on the toxicity of vanadium was published in 1876 (Priestley and Gamgee 1876) but apparently failed to stimulate interest in the mineral's biological actions. Consequently, the subject lay dormant until the turn of the twentieth century, when various French physicians used vanadium as a panacea for a number of human disorders. Shortly thereafter, a classic paper on the pharmacological and toxicological actions of vanadium appeared (Jackson 1912) – at about the time that extremely high vanadium concentrations were found in the blood of ascidian worms (Henze 1911, 1912). The hypothesis that vanadium has a physiological role in higher animals has had a long, yet muddled, history. In 1949, O. Rygh reported that vanadium might be needed by animals because it markedly stimulated the mineralization of bones and teeth and prevented caries formation in rats and guinea pigs. In 1950, D. Bertrand wrote that "we are completely ignorant of the physiological role of vanadium in animals, where its presence is constant." In 1963, H. A. Schroeder, J. J. Balassa, and I. H. Tipton indicated that although vanadium behaves like an essential trace metal, final proof of its essentiality for mammals was still lacking. But in 1974, L. L. Hopkins, Jr., and H. E. Mohr stated: "[W]e are secure in the concept that vanadium is an essential nutrient." Subsequent reviews, however, have presented a convincing argument that the evidence for the nutritional essentiality of vanadium was inconclusive (Nielsen 1984, 1985). That is, much of the evidence for essentiality may have been the result of high vanadium supplements (10 to 100 times the amount normally found in natural diets) inducing pharmacologic changes in animals fed imbalanced diets. The most substantive evidence for vanadium essentiality has appeared only since 1987.

Dietary Importance

Signs of apparent vanadium deprivation have been described in goats (Anke et al. 1989) and rats (Uthus and Nielsen 1990; Nielsen, Poellot, and Uthus 1997).

For goats, such signs include depressed milk production and skeletal deformations of the forelegs, including thickening of the forefoot tarsal joints. Vanadium-deprived rats exhibit altered thyroid hormone metabolism, especially if stressed with high or low iodine intakes. Supporting the suggestion that vanadium is an essential element for higher animals are the findings of functional roles for vanadium in lower forms of life. Algae, lichens, fungi, and bacteria all have enzymes that require vanadium for activity. These enzymes include haloperoxidases, which catalyze the oxidation of halide ions by hydrogen peroxide, thus facilitating the formation of a carbon-hydrogen bond (Vilter 1995).

Numerous biochemical and physiological functions for vanadium have been suggested on the basis of its in-vitro actions on cells and pharmacologic actions in animals; these actions (Willsky 1990) include insulin-mimetic properties, numerous stimulatory effects on cell proliferation and differentiation, effects of cell phosphorylation-dephosphorylation, effects on glucose and ion transport across the plasma membrane, and effects on oxidation-reduction processes.

Based on circumstantial evidence from animal deprivation studies and the functional roles of vanadium in lower forms of life, it seems quite possible that the mineral may be found essential for some enzyme reaction important to human health, perhaps one that is involved in thyroid metabolism. However, until a biochemical function is definitively identified for vanadium, its nutritional importance will be uncertain. Knowledge of a biochemical function is also needed in order to disentangle the element's pharmacologic actions from its nutritional actions. Yet, because vanadium is so pharmacologically active, a beneficial pharmaceutical role for this element may be found.

Summary

Trace elements were known to be present in biological materials more than 100 years ago, and several were found to be essential for plant and animal life more than 60 years ago. Studies of the pharmacological and beneficial properties of various trace elements, which were being done in the nineteenth century, continue today. However, except for iron, iodine, and cobalt (as cobalamin), the possibility that some trace elements are of practical nutritional importance did not receive much attention until about 30 years ago. At that time, excitement abounded about trace elements, and the new knowledge of them was considered a breakthrough toward better health.

One trace element after another was identified as essential, or at least suggested to be essential, and new functions were being found for those already established as essential. As these new essential elements or new functions were identified, hopes were raised that trace element nutriture would help to unravel the causes of some diseases, especially those that are chronic and associated with aging. Unfortunately, this has not occurred, but research does continue to show that some trace elements are more important than is currently acknowledged. The history of investigations into the trace elements iron, iodine, zinc, and selenium indicates a likelihood that several more elements - especially boron, copper, and chromium - will be found to be of nutritional (and clinical) importance for human health and longevity.

Forrest H. Nielsen

Bibliography

Abumrad, N. N., A. J. Schneider, D. Steel, and L. S. Rogers. 1981. Amino acid intolerance during prolonged total parenteral nutrition reversed by molybdate therapy. *American Journal of Clinical Nutrition* 34: 2551-9.

Al-Rashid, R. A., and J. Spangler. 1971. Neonatal copper deficiency. *New England Journal of Medicine* 285: 841-3.

Anderson, R. A. 1988. Chromium. In *Trace minerals in foods*, ed. K. T. Smith, 231-47. New York.

Anderson, R. A., N. Cheng, N. Bryden, et al. 1997. Elevated intakes of supplemental chromium improve glucose and insulin variables with type II diabetes. *Diabetes* 46: 1786-91.

Anke, M. 1986. Arsenic. In *Trace elements in human and animal nutrition*, Vol. 2, ed. W. Mertz, 347-72. Orlando, Fla.

Anke, M., B. Groppel, K. Gruhn, et al. 1989. The essentiality of vanadium for animals. In *6th International Trace Element Symposium*, ed. M. Anke, W. Baumann, H. Bräunlich, et al., 17-27. Jena, Germany.

Arnon, D. I., and P. R. Stout. 1939. Molybdenum as an essential element for higher plants. *Plant Physiology* 14: 599-602.

Ashkenazi, A., S. Levin, M. Djaldetti, et al. 1973. The syndrome of neonatal copper deficiency. *Pediatrics* 52: 525-33.

Becker, C.-H., D. Matthias, H. Wossmann, et al. 1983. Investigations on a possible medical importance of silicon. In *4. Spurenelement Symposium Jena*, ed. M. Anke, W. Baumann, H. Bräunlich, and C. Brückner, 142-8. Jena, Germany.

Beedham C. 1985. Molybdenum hydroxylases as drug-metabolizing enzymes. *Drug Metabolism Reviews* 16: 119-56.

Bennetts, H. W., and F. E. Chapman. 1937. Copper deficiency in sheep in Western Australia: A preliminary account of the etiology of enzoötic ataxia of lambs and an anemia of ewes. *Australian Veterinary Journal* 13: 138-49.

Berg, R. 1925. Das Vorkommen seltener Elemente in den Nahrungsmitteln und menschlichen Ausscheidungen. *Biochemische Zeitschrift* 165: 461-2.

Bertrand, D. 1950. Survey of contemporary knowledge of biogeochemistry. 2. The biogeochemistry of vanadium. *Bulletin of the American Museum of National History* 94: 403-56.

Bertrand, G., and M. Mâcheboeuf. 1925. Sur la présence du nickel et du cobalt chez les animaux. *Comptes Rendus de l'Académie des Sciences* 180: 1380-3.

Bertrand, G., and H. Nakamura. 1936. Recherches sur l'importance physiologique du nickel et du cobalt. *Bulletin de la Société Scientifique d'Hygiène Alimentaire et d'Alimentation Rationnelle* 24: 338-43.

Bodansky, M. 1921. The zinc and copper content of the human brain. *Journal of Biological Chemistry* 48: 361-4.

Bortels, H. 1930. Molybdenum as a catalyst in the biological fixation of nitrogen. *Archiv für Mikrobiologie* 1: 333-42.

Brown, R. O., S. Forloines-Lynn, R. E. Cross, and W. D. Heizer. 1986. Chromium deficiency after long-term total parenteral nutrition. *Digestive Diseases and Sciences* 31: 661-4.

Carlisle, E. M. 1972. Silicon: An essential element for the chick. *Science* 178: 619-21.

1984. Silicon. In *Biochemistry of the essential ultratrace elements,* ed. E. Frieden, 257-91, New York.

Carlisle, E. M., J. W. Berger, and W. F. Alpenfels. 1981. A silicon requirement for prolylhydroxylase activity. *Federation Proceedings* 40: 886.

Carlisle, E. M., and M. J. Curran. 1987. Effect of dietary silicon and aluminum on silicon and aluminum levels in rat brain. *Alzheimer Disease and Associated Disorders* 1: 83-9.

Carlisle, E. M., M. J. Curran, and T. Duong. 1991. The effect of interrelationships between silicon, aluminum and the thyroid on zinc content in the brain. In *Trace elements in man and animals - 7,* ed. B. Momčilović, 12.16-17. Zagreb, Croatia.

Church, A. H. 1869. Researches on turacin, an animal pigment containing copper. *Philosophical Transactions of the Royal Society of London* 159: 627.

Clark, L. C., G. F. Combs, Jr., B. W. Turnbull, et al. 1996. Effects of selenium supplementation for cancer prevention in patients with carcinoma of the skin: A randomized controlled trial. *Journal of the American Medical Association* 276: 1957-63.

Combs, G. F., Jr., and S. B. Combs. 1984. The nutritional biochemistry of selenium. *Annual Review of Nutrition* 4: 257-80.

Cordano, A., J. M. Baertl, and G. G. Graham. 1964. Copper deficiency in infancy. *Pediatrics* 34: 324-6.

Curran, G. L. 1954. Effect of certain transition group elements on hepatic synthesis of cholesterol in the rat. *Journal of Biological Chemistry* 210: 765-70.

Danks, D. M., P. E. Campbell, B. J. Stevens, et al. 1972a. Menkes' kinky hair syndrome. An inherited defect in copper absorption with widespread effects. *Pediatrics* 50: 188-201.

Danks, D. M., B. J. Stevens, P. E. Campbell, et al. 1972b. Menkes' kinky-hair syndrome. *Lancet* 1: 1100-3.

De Renzo, E. C., E. Kaleita, P. G. Heytler, et al. 1953. Identification of the xanthine oxidase factor as molybdenum. *Archives of Biochemistry and Biophysics* 45: 247-53.

Dixon, N. E., C. Gazzola, R. L. Blakeley, and B. Zerner. 1975. Jack bean urease (EC 3.5.1.5). A metalloenzyme. A simple biological role for nickel? *Journal of the American Chemical Society* 97: 4131-3.

Doisy, E. A., Jr. 1972. Micronutrient controls on biosynthesis of clotting proteins and cholesterol. In *Trace substances in environmental health,* ed. D. D. Hemphill, 193-9. Columbia, Mo.

Ferguson, W. S., A. H. Lewis, and S. J. Watson. 1938. Action of molybdenum in nutrition of milking cattle. *Nature* 141: 553.

Finley, J. W., and P. E. Johnson. 1996. Manganese deficiency and excess in rodents. In *Trace elements in laboratory rodents,* ed. R. R. Watson, 85-106. Boca Raton, Fla.

Fleurent, E., and L. Lévi. 1920. Sur la présence du cuivre dans l'organisme végétal et animal. *Bulletin de la Société Chimique France* 27: 441-2.

Follis, R. H., Jr. 1947. The effect of adding boron to a potassium-deficient diet in the rat. *American Journal of Physiology* 150: 520-2.

Franke, K. W., and E. P. Painter. 1935. Selenium in proteins from toxic foodstuffs. IV. The effect of feeding toxic proteins, toxic protein hydrolysates, and toxic protein hydrolysates from which the selenium has been removed. *Journal of Nutrition* 10: 599-611.

Fredericq, L. 1878. Recherches sur la physiologie du poulpe commun (Octopus vulgaris). *Archives de Zoologie Expérimentale et Générale* 7: 535.

Freeland-Graves, J., and C. Llanes. 1994. Models to study manganese deficiency. In *Manganese in health and disease,* ed. D. J. Klimis-Tavantzis, 59-86. Boca Raton, Fla.

Freeland-Graves, J. H., and J. R. Turnlund. 1996. Deliberations and evaluations of the approaches, endpoints and paradigms for manganese and molybdenum dietary recommendations. *Journal of Nutrition* 126: 2435S-40S.

Freund, H., S. Atamian, and J. E. Fischer. 1979. Chromium deficiency during total parenteral nutrition. *Journal of the American Medical Association* 241: 496-8.

Friedman, B. J., J. Freeland-Graves, C. Bales, et al. 1987. Manganese balance and clinical observations in young men fed a manganese-deficient diet. *Journal of Nutrition* 117: 133-43.

Gordon, V., ed. 1987. The case of the toxic life-preserver. *Borax Review* 2: 10-12.

Graham, G. G., and A. Cordano. 1969. Copper depletion and deficiency in the malnourished infant. *Johns Hopkins Medical Journal* 124: 139-50.

Guérithault, B., and M. L. Maquenne. 1920. Sur la présence du cuivre dans les plantes et particulièrement dans les matières alimentaires d'origine végétal. *Comptes Rendus des Sciences Société de Biologie et de ses Filiales et Associées* 171: 196-8.

Harless, E. 1847. Über das blaue Blut einiger wirbellosen Thiere und dessen Kupfergehalt. *Müller's Archiv für Anatomie und Physiologie,* 148-56.

Hart, E. B., H. Steenbock, J. Waddell, and C. A. Elvehjem. 1928. Iron in nutrition. VII. Copper as a supplement to iron for hemoglobin building in the rat. *Journal of Biological Chemistry* 77: 797-812.

Henze, M. 1911. Untersuchungen über das Blut der Ascidien. I. Mitteilung. Die Vanadiumverbindung der Blutkörperchen. *Hoppe-Seyler's Zeitschrift Physiological Chemistry* 72: 494-501.

　　1912. Untersuchungen über das Blut der Ascidien. *Hoppe-Seyler's Zeitschrift Physiological Chemistry* 79: 215-28.

Higgins, E. S., D. A. Richert, and W. W. Westerfeld. 1956. Molybdenum deficiency and tungstate inhibition studies. *Journal of Nutrition* 59: 539-59.

Hopkins, L. L., Jr., and H. E. Mohr. 1974. Vanadium as an essential nutrient. *Federation Proceedings* 33: 1773-5.

Hove, E., C. A. Elvehjem, and E. B. Hart. 1938. Arsenic in the nutrition of the rat. *American Journal of Physiology* 124: 205-12.

　　1939. Boron in animal nutrition. *American Journal of Physiology* 127: 689-701.

Hunt, C. D. 1994. The biochemical effects of physiologic amounts of dietary boron in animal nutrition models. *Environmental Health Perspectives* 102 (Supplement 7): 35-43.

Hunt, C. D., and F. H. Nielsen. 1981. Interaction between boron and cholecalciferol in the chick. In *Trace elements in man and animals (TEMA-4),* ed. J. McC. Howell, J. M. Gawthorne, and C. L. White, 597-600. Canberra, Australia.

Jackson, D. E. 1912. The pharmacological action of vanadium. *Journal de Pharmacologie* 3: 477-514.

Jeejeebhoy, K. N., R. C. Chu, E. B. Marliss, et al. 1977. Chromium deficiency, glucose intolerance, and neuropathy reversed by chromium supplementation, in a patient receiving long-term total parenteral nutrition. *American Journal of Clinical Nutrition* 30: 531-8.

Jovanovic-Peterson, L., M. Gutierrez, and C. M. Peterson. 1996. Chromium supplementation for gestational diabetic women (GDM) improves glucose tolerance and decreases hyperinsulinemia. *Diabetes* 45: Abs 1263.

Kemmerer, A. R., C. A. Elvehjem, and E. B. Hart. 1931. Studies on the relation of manganese to the nutrition of the mouse. *Journal of Biological Chemistry* 92: 623-30.

Keshan Disease Research Group. 1979. Observation on the effect of sodium selenite in prevention of Keshan disease. *Chinese Medical Journal* 92: 471-82.

Klevay, L. M. 1990. Ischemic heart disease: Toward a unified theory. In *Role of copper in lipid metabolism,* ed. K. Y. Lei and T. P. Carr, 233-67. Boca Raton, Fla.

Klevay, L. M., J. P. Buchet, V. W. Bunker, et al. 1993. Copper in the western diet (Belgium, Canada, U.K., and USA). In *Trace elements in man and animals - TEMA-8,* ed. M. Anke, D. Meissner, and C. F. Mills, 207-10. Gersdorf, Germany.

Klevay, L. M., and D. M. Medeiros. 1996. Deliberations and evaluations of the approaches, endpoints and paradigms for dietary recommendations about copper. *Journal of Nutrition* 126: 2419S-26S.

Lancaster, J. R., Jr., ed. 1988. *The bioinorganic chemistry of nickel.* New York.

Leach, R. M., Jr., and A.-M. Muenster. 1962. Studies on the role of manganese in bone formation. I. Effect upon the mucopolysaccharide content of chick bone. *Journal of Nutrition* 78: 51-6.

Levander, O. A., and R. F. Burk. 1994. Selenium. In *Modern nutrition in health and disease.* Eighth edition, Vol. 1, ed. M. E. Shils, J. A. Olson, and M. Shike, 242-51. Philadelphia, Pa.

Lyons, M., and W. M. Insko, Jr. 1937. Chondrodystrophy in the chick embryo produced by manganese deficiency in the diet of the hen. *Kentucky Agricultural Experimental Station Bulletin* 371: 61-75.

Mayer, D. R., W. Kosmus, H. Pogglitsch, et al. 1993. Essential trace elements in humans. Serum arsenic concentrations in hemodialysis patients in comparison to healthy controls. *Biological Trace Element Research* 37: 27-38.

McHargue, J. S. 1923. Effect of different concentrations of manganese sulfate on the growth of plants in acid and neutral soils and the necessity of manganese as a plant nutrient. *Journal of Agricultural Research* 24: 781-93.

　　1925. The association of copper with substances containing the fat-soluble A vitamin. *American Journal of Physiology* 72: 583-94.

　　1926. Further evidence that small quantities of copper, manganese and zinc are factors in the metabolism of animals. *American Journal of Physiology* 77: 245-55.

Mertz, W. 1993. Chromium in human nutrition: A review. *Journal of Nutrition* 123: 626-33.

Messer, H. H. 1984. Fluorine. In *Biochemistry of the essential ultratrace elements,* ed. E. Frieden, 55-87. New York.

Mobley, H. L., M. D. Island, and R. P. Hausinger. 1995. Molecular biology of microbiological ureases. *Microbiological Reviews* 59: 451-80.

Moxon, A. L., and M. Rhian. 1943. Se poisoning. *Physiological Reviews* 23: 305-37.

Muth, O. H., J. E. Oldfield, L. F. Remmert, and J. R. Schubert.

1958. Effects of selenium and vitamin E on white muscle disease. *Science* 128: 1090.

National Research Council. 1980. *Recommended dietary allowances.* Ninth edition. Washington, D.C.

1989. *Recommended dietary allowances.* Tenth edition. Washington, D.C.

Neal, W. M., R. B. Becker, and A. L. Shealy. 1931. A natural copper deficiency in cattle rations. *Science* 74: 418-19.

Nielsen, F. H. 1980. Interactions between essential trace and ultratrace elements. *Annals of the New York Academy of Sciences* 355: 152-64.

1984. Ultratrace elements in nutrition. *Annual Review of Nutrition* 4: 21-41.

1985. The importance of diet composition in ultratrace element research. *Journal of Nutrition* 115: 1239-47.

1994a. Biochemical and physiologic consequences of boron deprivation in humans. *Environmental Health Perspectives* 102 (Supplement 7): 59-63.

1994b. Ultratrace minerals. In *Modern nutrition in health and disease.* Eighth edition, ed. M. E. Shils, J. A. Olson, and M. Shike, 269-86. Philadelphia, Pa.

1995. Individual functional roles of metal ions *in vivo.* Beneficial metal ions. Nickel. In *Handbook of metal-ligand interactions in biological fluids. Bioinorganic medicine,* Vol. 1, 257-60. New York.

1997. Boron in human and animal nutrition. *Plant and Soil* 193: 199-208.

Nielsen, F. H., R. A. Poellot, and E. O. Uthus. 1997. Vanadium deprivation alters the changes in plasma thyroid hormone concentrations, pancreatic amylase activity, and serum lactate dehydrogenase activity in the BB rat caused by increasing dietary iodine. *FASEB Journal* 11: A148.

Nielsen, F. H., and H. E. Sauberlich. 1970. Evidence of a possible requirement for nickel by the chick. *Proceedings of the Society for Experimental Biology and Medicine* 134: 845-9.

Nielsen, F. H., and E. O. Uthus. 1984. Arsenic. In *Biochemistry of the essential ultratrace elements,* ed. E. Frieden, 319-40. New York.

Nielsen, F. H., T. J. Zimmerman, T. R. Shuler, et al. 1989. Evidence for a cooperative metabolic relationship between nickel and vitamin B$_{12}$ in rats. *Journal of Trace Elements in Experimental Medicine* 2: 21-9.

Norose, N. 1992. Manganese defiency in a child with very short bowel syndrome receiving long-term parenteral nutrition. *Journal of Trace Elements in Experimental Medicine* 5: 100-1.

Nriagu, Jerome O. ed. 1980. *Nickel in the environment.* New York.

Orent, E. R., and E. V. McCollum. 1931. Effects of deprivation of manganese in the rat. *Journal of Biological Chemistry* 92: 651-78.

Orent-Keiles, E. 1941. The role of boron in the diet of the rat. *Proceedings of the Society for Experimental Biology and Medicine* 44: 199-202.

Patterson, E. L., R. Milstrey, and E. L. R. Stokstad. 1957. Effect of selenium in preventing exudative diathesis in chicks. *Proceedings of the Society for Experimental Biology and Medicine* 95: 617-20.

Penland, J. G. 1994. Dietary boron, brain function, and cognitive performance. *Environmental Health Perspectives* 102 (Supplement 7): 65-72.

Priestley, J., and A. Gamgee. 1876. On the physiological action of vanadium. *Philosophical Transactions of the Royal Society of London. Series B: Biological Sciences* 166: 495-556.

Proctor, J. F., D. E. Hogue, and R. G. Warner. 1958. Selenium, vitamin E and linseed oil meal as preventatives of mus-cular dystrophy in lambs. *Journal of Animal Science* 17: 1183-4.

Rajagopalan, K. V. 1988. Molybdenum: An essential trace element in human nutrition. *Annual Review of Nutrition* 8: 401-27.

Richert, D. A., and W. W. Westerfeld. 1953. Isolation and identification of the xanthine oxidase factor as molybdenum. *Journal of Biological Chemistry* 203: 915-23.

Rotruck, J. T., A. L. Pope, H. E. Ganther, et al. 1973. Selenium: Biochemical role as a component of glutathione peroxidase. *Science* 179: 588-90.

Rygh, O. 1949. Recherches sur les oligo-éléments. II. De l'importance du thallium et du vanadium, du silicium et du fluor. *Bulletin de la Société Chimie Biologique* 31: 1403-7.

Schroeder, H. A., and J. J. Balassa. 1966. Abnormal trace metals in men: Arsenic. *Journal of Chronic Diseases* 19: 85-106.

Schroeder, H. A., J. J. Balassa, and I. H. Tipton. 1963. Abnormal trace metals in man - vanadium. *Journal of Chronic Diseases* 16: 1047-71.

Schwarz, K., J. G. Bieri, G. M. Briggs, and M. L. Scott. 1957. Prevention of exudative diathesis in chicks by factor 3 and selenium. *Proceedings of the Society for Experimental Biology and Medicine* 95: 621-5.

Schwarz, K., and C. M. Foltz. 1957. Selenium as an integral part of factor 3 against dietary necrotic liver degeneration. *Journal of the American Chemical Society* 79: 3292-3.

Schwarz, K., and W. Mertz. 1959. Chromium (III) and the glucose tolerance factor. *Archives of Biochemistry and Biophysics* 85: 292-5.

Seaborn, C. D., and F. H. Nielsen. 1993. Silicon: A nutritional beneficence for bones, brains and blood vessels? *Nutrition Today* 28: 13-18.

1996. Dietary silicon affects some collagen synthesizing enzymes in rats. *FASEB Journal* 10: A784.

Sjollema, B. 1933. Kupfermangel als Ursache von Krankheiten bei Pflanzen und Tieren. *Biochemische Zeitschrift* 267: 151-6.

Skinner, J. T., and J. S. McHargue. 1945. Response of rats to boron supplements when fed rations low in potassium. *American Journal of Physiology* 143: 385-90.

1946. Supplementary effects of arsenic and manganese on copper in the synthesis of hemoglobin. *American Journal of Physiology* 145: 500-6.

Sommer, A. L., and C. B. Lipman. 1926. Evidence of the indispensable nature of zinc and boron for higher green plants. *Plant Physiology* 1: 231-49.

Teresi, J. D., C. A. Elvehjem, and E. B. Hart. 1942. Molybdenum in the nutrition of the rat. *American Journal of Physiology* 137: 504-8.

Teresi, J. D., E. Hove, C. A. Elvehjem, and E. B. Hart. 1944. Further study of boron in the nutrition of rats. *American Journal of Physiology* 140: 513-18.

ter Meulen, H. 1932. Distribution of molybdenum. *Nature* 130: 966.

Trelease, S. F., and O. A. Beath. [1892] 1949. *Selenium. Its geological occurrence and its biological effects in relation to botany, chemistry, agriculture, nutrition, and medicine by Sam F. Trelease and Orville A. Beath.* New York and Laramie, Wyo.

Turnlund, J. R., W. R. Keyes, G. L. Peiffer, and G. Chiang. 1995. Molybdenum absorption, excretion and retention studied with stable isotopes in young men during depletion and repletion. *American Journal of Clinical Nutrition* 61: 1102-9.

Uthus, E. O. 1994. Arsenic essentiality and factors affecting its importance. In *Arsenic. Exposure and health,* ed. W. R. Chappell, C. O. Abernathy, and C. R. Cothern, 199-208. Northwood, England.

Uthus, E. O., and F. H. Nielsen. 1990. Effect of vanadium, iodine and their interaction on growth, blood variables, liver trace elements and thyroid status indices in rats. *Magnesium and Trace Elements* 9: 219–26.

Uthus, E. O., and R. A. Poellot. 1996. Dietary folate affects the response of rats to nickel deprivation. *Biological Trace Element Research* 52: 23–35.

Vilter, H. 1995. Vanadium-dependent haloperoxidases. In *Metal ions in biological systems, Vol. 31: Vanadium and its role in life*, ed. H. Sigel and A. Sigel, 325–62. New York.

Waddell, J., H. Steenbock, and E. B. Hart. 1931. Growth and reproduction on milk diets. *Journal of Nutrition* 4: 53–65.

Warington, K. 1923. The effect of boric acid and borax on the broad bean and certain other plants. *Annals of Botany* 37: 629–72.

Whitford, G. M. 1990. The physiological and toxicological characteristics of fluoride. *Journal of Dental Research* 69: 539–49.

Wiley, H. W. 1904. Influence of food preservatives and artificial colors on digestion and health. I. Boric acid and borax. *U.S. Department of Agriculture Bulletin No. 84.* Washington, D.C.

Wilgus, H. S., Jr., L. C. Norris, and G. F. Heuser. 1936. The role of certain inorganic elements in the cause and prevention of perosis. *Science* 84: 252–3.

  1937. The role of manganese and certain other trace elements in the prevention of perosis. *Journal of Nutrition* 14: 155–67.

Willsky, G. R. 1990. Vanadium in the biosphere. In *Vanadium in biological systems. Physiology and biochemistry*, ed. N. D. Chasteen, 1–24. Dordrecht, the Netherlands.

IV.B.9   Zinc

In 1869, J. Raulin showed for the first time that zinc is a growth factor for *Aspergilus niger.* Then, in 1926, it was discovered that zinc is essential for higher plants (Sommer and Lipman 1926). The importance of zinc in the growth and development of rats was demonstrated in 1934 (Todd, Elvehjem, and Hart 1934), and in 1955, H. F. Tucker and W. D. Salmon related a disease in swine called parakeratosis to a deficiency of zinc. Shortly thereafter, zinc was shown to be a growth factor for chickens (O'Dell, Newberne, and Savage 1958).

The manifestations of zinc deficiency in animals include growth failure, loss of hair, thickening and hyperkeratinization of the epidermis, and testicular atrophy. Zinc deficiency in breeding hens results in decreased hatchability and gross anomalies in embryonic skeletal development.

Although the importance of zinc for animals was established 60 years ago, it has only been during the past 30 years that zinc deficiency in humans has been recognized. In 1974, the Food and Nutrition Board of the National Research Council of the National Academy of Sciences made a landmark decision in establishing a recommended dietary allowance (RDA) for zinc.

Discovery of Zinc Deficiency in Humans

Studies in Iran

In 1958, this author joined the staff of Dr. Hobart A. Reimann, Chief of Medicine at the Nemazee Hospital of Pahlevi University in Shiraz, Iran. In the fall of that year, Dr. James A. Halsted of the Saadi Hospital of Pahlevi University invited me to discuss a patient who had severe anemia.

The patient was a 21-year-old male, who appeared to be only a 10-year-old boy. In addition to severe growth retardation and anemia, he had hypogonadism, hepatosplenomegaly, rough and dry skin, mental lethargy, and geophagia. His intake of animal protein had been negligible. He ate only wheat flour and unleavened bread and consumed nearly 0.5 kilograms (kg) of clay daily (the habit of geophagia in the villages around Shiraz is fairly common). Ten more cases that were similar arrived at the hospital for my care within a short period of time.

We documented the existence of iron-deficiency anemia in the patients, but there was no evidence of blood loss. We considered three possible mechanisms of iron deficiency: (1) The availability of iron in the high-cereal, protein-containing diet was most probably very low due to high phytate levels in the bread, which bind iron; (2) that geophagia further decreased iron absorption (as Minnich and colleagues [1968] observed later); and (3) that an excessive loss of iron by sweating in the hot summers of Iran may have contributed significantly to negative iron balance.

After administration of ferrous sulfate (1 gram per day) orally and a nutritious hospital diet containing adequate animal protein, the anemia was corrected, hepatosplenomegaly improved, subjects grew pubic hair, and genitalia size increased (Prasad, Halsted, and Nadimi 1961). Liver function tests were unremarkable except for the serum alkaline phosphatase activity, which increased after treatment. Retrospectively, two explanations seem plausible: (1) Ordinary pharmaceutical preparations of iron might have contained appreciable quantities of zinc as a contaminant, and (2) animal protein in the diet most likely supplied available zinc, thus inducing the activity of alkaline phosphatase, a known zinc metalloenzyme.

It was difficult to account for all of the clinical features solely by tissue iron deficiency because growth retardation and testicular atrophy are not normally found in iron-deficient experimental animals. Moreover, since this syndrome was fairly prevalent in the villages near Shiraz, the rare syndrome of hypopituitarism as an explanation for growth retardation and hypogonadism was considered to be very unlikely.

We explored the possibility that zinc deficiency may have been present concomitantly with iron deficiency in these patients (Prasad et al. 1961). Because heavy metals may form insoluble complexes with phosphate, we speculated that some factors responsible for decreased availability of iron in these patients with geophagia may also have decreased the availability of zinc. B. L. O'Dell and J. E. Savage (1960) observed that the phytate (inositol hexaphosphate) present in cereal grains markedly impaired the absorption of zinc. Changes in the activity of alkaline phosphatase as observed in our patients had also been noticed after the zinc supplementation of deficient animals. Thus, it seemed that the dwarfism, testicular atrophy, retardation of skeletal maturation, and changes in serum alkaline phosphatase activity of our subjects might be explained by zinc deficiency.

I. I. Lemann (1910) had previously reported a similar clinical syndrome in patients who had hookworm infection in the United States, but this was not related to a nutritional deficiency. Similar cases from Turkey were reported by F. Reimann (1955), but without detailed descriptions. He considered a genetic defect to be a possible explanation for certain aspects of the clinical syndrome.

Studies in Egypt

In October 1960, Dr. William J. Darby invited me to meet with him at the U.S. Naval Medical Research Unit in Cairo, Egypt, where I shared with him my speculation that zinc deficiency in the Middle East was prevalent and was responsible for widespread growth retardation and male hypogonadism. The next day, Professor Darby and I went to nearby villages to assess if, indeed, growth-retarded adolescents were clinically recognizable. We were accompanied by an Egyptian male nurse who spoke both English and Arabic.

Because of the striking clinical similarities between Iranian and Egyptian dwarfs, I was able to recognize several subjects who looked like 8- or 10-year-old boys, but whose chronological ages, on questioning, appeared to be 18 to 20 years. This assured me that, indeed, growth retardation and male hypogonadism were also prevalent in Egyptian villages. Following this experience, Professor Darby approved plans to investigate zinc metabolism in growth-retarded subjects.

The clinical features of Egyptian growth-retarded subjects were remarkably similar to those of the Iranians, except that the Iranian dwarfs had more pronounced hepatosplenomegaly, a history of geophagia, and no hookworm infection. The Egyptian subjects, by contrast, had both schistosomiasis and hookworm infestations but no history of geophagia.

A detailed investigation of the Egyptian cases was carried out with associates A. Miale, Z. Farid, H. H. Sandstead, and A. Schulert. The dietary history of the Egyptian subjects was similar to that of the Iranians. The consumption of animal protein was negligible, with the diet consisting mainly of bread and beans (*Vicia fava*).

Zinc concentrations in plasma, hair, and red cells were decreased, and ^{65}Zn studies showed that the plasma zinc turnover was greater, the 24 h exchange-able pool was smaller, and the excretion of ^{65}Zn in stool and urine was less in the growth-retarded subjects in comparison to controls (Prasad, Miale, and Farid 1963). These studies established for the first time that zinc deficiency occurs in humans, without advanced cirrhosis. Liver function tests and biopsies revealed no evidence of cirrhosis in our subjects (Prasad et al. 1963b). Furthermore, in contrast to cirrhosis patients, who excreted abnormally high quantities of zinc in the urine, our patients excreted less zinc in urine than did control subjects. We also ruled out other chronic diseases that might have affected the serum zinc concentrations.

Serum iron was decreased, unsaturated iron binding capacity was increased, serum copper was slightly increased, and serum magnesium was normal in our subjects. Hair analysis for manganese, cobalt, molybdenum, and other elements revealed no difference when compared to the normal subjects. We found no evidence for deficiency of serum B_{12}, ascorbic acid, vitamin A, carotene, or folic acid.

Iranian physicians had commonly believed that growth retardation and sexual hypofunction were the results of visceral leishmaniasis and geophagia. We, however, found no evidence of leishmaniasis in Iran. The role of geophagia was unclear, although we suspected that excess phosphate in the clay prevented absorption of both iron and zinc. The predominantly wheat diet in the Middle East, now known to contain high quantities of phytate and fiber, most probably reduced the availability of zinc.

In Egypt the cause of dwarfism was commonly considered to be schistosomiasis, and in China investigators had also implicated schistosomiasis as a causative factor for growth retardation. Yet, because the Iranian subjects exhibited dwarfism but did not have schistosomiasis or hookworm infections, the question arose as to whether schistosomiasis was the fundamental cause of dwarfism in Egypt. We initiated an investigation to find the answer (Prasad, Schulert, and Miale 1963; Prasad 1966).

It was known that schistosomiasis or hookworm infection was nonexistent in the oasis villages of Kharga, located 500 kilometers (km) southwest of Cairo, although the people of Kharga are culturally and nutritionally similar to those in the delta region. Hence, we conducted a field study in Kharga on 16 patients with hypogonadism and dwarfism. Their anemia was mild, and none had either schistosomiasis or hookworm disease. Concentrations of iron and zinc in the serum were subnormal.

Because red blood cells are rich in both iron and zinc, blood loss due to hookworm and schistosomiasis in the delta villages contributed significantly to both iron and zinc deficiencies. But in Kharga, parasitic infections were not present, and the artesian spring, the principal source of water for the Kharga villages, revealed iron and zinc concentrations of 3,170 and 18 micrograms per liter (μg/l), respectively.

In Cairo, by contrast, the iron and zinc concentrations of drinking water were 70 and 400 µg/l, respectively. Thus, although the foods consumed by the subjects in both the delta region and the oasis villages were similar, those in the latter probably derived a significant amount of iron but no zinc from their water source. Consequently, a better iron status for individuals in Kharga villages, in comparison to those in delta villages, was due to higher iron intake from water and lack of blood loss due to parasites.

Although dwarfism and hypogonadism had previously been attributed to schistosomiasis in Egypt and China, our demonstration of the existence of such patients in Iran and Kharga, where schistosomiasis was absent, showed that this parasitic infection was not necessarily responsible for these clinical features.

We were, however, unable to account for the hepatosplenomegaly on the basis of liver disease. This left three possibilities: anemia, zinc deficiency, or a combination of the two. In each case, the size of the liver and spleen decreased significantly after zinc supplementation, suggesting that zinc deficiency may have played an as-yet undefined role in hepatosplenomegaly.

In the Middle East, we examined only male subjects, as females refused to participate. But later studies from Iran by J. A. Halsted and co-workers (1972) demonstrated that zinc deficiency was probably prevalent in females manifesting growth retardation.

Our further investigations in Egypt showed that the rate of growth was greater in patients who received supplemental zinc as compared with those given iron, or those with only an adequate animal protein diet (Prasad 1966; Sandstead et al. 1967). Pubic hair appeared in all subjects within 7 to 12 weeks after zinc supplementation was initiated. Genital size became normal, and secondary sexual characteristics developed within 12 to 24 weeks in all zinc supplemented patients. No such changes were observed in a comparable length of time in the iron-supplemented group or in the group on an animal protein diet alone. Thus, our studies demonstrated that both growth retardation and gonadal hypofunction in these subjects were related to zinc deficiency. The anemia was due to iron deficiency and responded to oral iron treatment.

Chronology of Other Observations

By using the dithizone technique, R. E. Lutz (1926) assayed zinc in various tissues and concluded that the body of a 70 kg man contained 2.2 grams (g) of zinc, a figure remarkably close to that which is accepted today. R. A. McCance and E. M. Widdowson (1942) were the first to report on the absorption and excretion of zinc, and showed that the principal route of zinc excretion was in the feces, with only a small amount lost in urine.

I. Vikbladh (1950) measured serum zinc concentration by dithizone technique and reported that the level was 19.7 ± 0.24 micromoles per liter (µmol/l), a value in general agreement with those reported by using modern methods. Vikbladh (1951) also observed that the serum zinc concentration was decreased in many chronic diseases, including liver disease. B. L. Vallee and colleagues (1956) reported that the serum zinc concentration decreased in patients with cirrhosis and suggested that the hypozincemia of these subjects was conditioned by hyperzincuria.

Our studies in the early 1960s demonstrated for the first time the effects of zinc deficiency on human growth and gonadal development (Prasad, Miale, Farid et al. 1963a, 1963b; Prasad, Schulert, Miale et al. 1963; Sandstead et al. 1967), and that this deficiency may have various causes in different populations. It is now evident that nutritional, as well as conditioned, zinc deficiency may complicate many disease states in human subjects.

In 1968, R. A. MacMahon, M. L. Parker, and M. McKinnon (1968) first observed zinc deficiency in a patient who had steatorrhea. Subsequently, zinc deficiency was discovered to be common in patients with malabsorption syndromes (McClain, Adams, and Shedlofsky 1988).

V. Caggiano and co-workers (1969) were the first to report a case of zinc deficiency in the United States. The patient was Puerto Rican with dwarfism, hypogonadism, hypogammaglobulinemia, giardiasis, strongyloidiasis, and schistosomiasis. Zinc supplementation resulted in improved growth and development.

In 1972, a number of Denver children from middle-class families were reported to exhibit evidence of symptomatic nutritional zinc deficiency (Hambidge et al. 1972). They consumed a predominantly cereal protein diet low in available zinc. Growth retardation, poor appetite, and impaired taste acuity were all related to a deficiency of zinc in the children, and they were corrected with supplementation. Symptomatic zinc deficiency in United States infants was also reported later by K. M. Hambidge, C. E. Casey, and N. J. Krebs (1983). In addition, our own recent studies in the United States have shown that zinc deficiency in the well-to-do elderly may be fairly prevalent (Prasad et al. 1993). Clearly, then, a substantial portion of the U.S. population may be at risk of zinc deficiency.

Meanwhile, Halsted and colleagues (1972) published a study involving a group of 15 men who were rejected at the Iranian army induction center because of "malnutrition." Two women were also included in their study. All were 19 or 20 years old, with clinical features similar to those reported earlier by A. S. Prasad and colleagues (Prasad et al. 1961, 1963a, 1963b). They were studied for 6 to 12 months. One group was given a well-balanced diet, containing ample animal protein plus a placebo capsule. A second group was given the same diet, plus a capsule of zinc sulfate containing 27 mg zinc. A third group received the diet for a year, with zinc supplementation during the last six months.

The zinc-supplemented subjects grew considerably faster and showed evidence of earlier onset of sexual function (as defined by nocturnal emission in males and menarche in females) than those receiving the well-balanced diet alone (Halsted et al. 1972).

A clinical picture, similar to those reported by our studies involving zinc-deficient dwarfs, has been observed in many developing countries. Therefore, it must be the case that various levels of zinc deficiency prevail in countries where diets depend too heavily on cereals.

P. M. Barnes and E. J. Moynahan (1973) studied a 2-year-old girl with severe acrodermatitis enteropathica, who was receiving diiodohydroxyquinoline and a lactose-deficient synthetic diet. The response to this therapy was not satisfactory. It was noted that the concentration of zinc in the patient's serum was profoundly decreased, and oral zinc sulfate was administered. The skin lesions and gastrointestinal symptoms cleared completely, and the girl was discharged from the hospital. When zinc was inadvertently omitted from the child's regimen, she suffered a relapse; however, she promptly responded to oral zinc again.

In the original report, the authors attributed the girl's zinc deficiency to the synthetic diet, but it soon became clear that zinc was fundamental in the pathogenesis of acrodermatitis enteropathica – a rare inherited disorder – and the clinical improvement reflected improvement in zinc status. This interesting observation was quickly confirmed in other patients throughout the world. The underlying pathogenesis of zinc deficiency in these patients is most likely dietary malabsorption of zinc, the mechanism of which remains to be determined.

R. G. Kay and C. Tasman-Jones (1975) reported the occurrence of severe zinc deficiency in subjects receiving total parenteral nutrition for prolonged periods without zinc. T. Arakawa, T. Tamura, and Y. Igarashi (1976) and A. Okada and co-workers (1976) announced similar findings in this circumstance. These observations have been documented by several investigators, and in the United States, zinc is routinely included in total parenteral fluids for subjects who are likely to receive such therapy for extended periods.

W. G. Klingberg, Prasad, and D. Oberleas (1976) were the first to report severe parakeratosis, alopecia, and retardation of growth and gonadal development in an adolescent with Wilson's disease who received penicillamine therapy. Zinc supplementation completely reversed these clinical manifestations.

Recent literature suggests that several findings in patients with sickle cell anemia, such as growth retardation, male hypogonadism, abnormal dark adaptation, and abnormal cell-mediated immunity, are related to a deficiency of zinc (Prasad et al. 1975, 1981; Warth et al. 1981; Prasad and Cossack 1984; Prasad et al. 1988). Hyperzincuria due to renal tubular dysfunction has been noted in such subjects, and this may be a contributing factor in the pathogenesis of zinc deficiency. Hypogeusia, decreased serum testosterone level, and hyperprolactinemia due to zinc deficiency have been observed in male patients with chronic renal disease (Mahajan et al. 1979, 1980, 1982, 1985). Zinc supplementation has corrected the abnormalities that have been associated with these disparate circumstances.

During the past three decades, a spectrum of clinical deficiency of zinc in human subjects has been recognized. If the deficiency is severe, it may be life-threatening. The symptoms developed by severely zinc-deficient subjects include bullous-pustular dermatitis, diarrhea, alopecia, mental disturbances, and intercurrent infections due to cell-mediated immune disorders. These manifestations are seen in patients with acrodermatitis enteropathica, following total parenteral nutrition (without zinc), and after penicillamine therapy.

Growth retardation, male hypogonadism, skin changes, poor appetite, mental lethargy, abnormal adaptation to darkness, and delayed wound healing are some of the indicators of moderate zinc deficiency in human subjects. Causes of moderate zinc deficiency that have been well documented include nutritional factors, malabsorption, sickle cell disease, chronic renal disease, and other debilitating conditions.

The beneficial effect of zinc in healing wounds of patients with zinc deficiency was first reported by W. J. Pories and W. H. Strain (1966). The symptom of abnormalities of taste was first related to a deficiency of zinc in humans by R. I. Henkin and D. F. Bradley (1969), and such abnormalities, which are reversible by zinc supplementation, have been observed in patients with chronic renal disease (Mahajan et al. 1980).

Marginal Deficiency of Zinc

Although the importance of zinc to human health has now been elucidated and its deficiency recognized in several clinical conditions, it was only recently that an experimental human model was established to permit a study of the specific effects of a mild zinc deficiency (Prasad, Rabbani, and Abbasi 1978; Abbasi et al. 1980; Rabbani et al. 1987; Prasad et al. 1988).

We did this by developing a semisynthetic soy-protein-based diet that supplies 3 to 5 milligrams of zinc per day (mg zinc/d) (Rabbani et al. 1987). All other nutrients in the diet are consistent with the RDA (1974, 1989). Male volunteers, ages 20 to 45 years, were first given a hospital diet containing animal protein for 4 to 8 weeks, which averaged 12 mg zinc/d. After that, the subjects received the experimental diet containing 3 to 5 mg zinc/d, which continued for 28 weeks. Following this period, the volunteers received a daily 27 mg zinc supplement for 12 weeks while still consuming the experimental diet. Throughout the study, all nutrients, including protein, amino acids, vitamins, and minerals (both macro- and microelements), were kept constant, except zinc, which was varied as outlined above. By this technique, we were able to induce a specific zinc deficiency in men.

Our dietary manipulation created a negative zinc balance of approximately 1 mg per day, and we calculated that in a six-month period a total of about 180 mg of negative zinc balance was achieved. A 70 kg adult male contains approximately 2,300 mg of zinc, and, therefore, a loss of 180 mg of zinc would seem to be only 8 percent of the total body zinc. But this is not necessarily the case. Approximately 28 percent of the zinc in the human body resides in bone, 62 percent in muscle, 1.8 percent in the liver, and 0.1 percent in the plasma pool. Only 10 percent of the total body zinc pool exchanges with an isotopic dose within a week's time (Prasad et al. 1963a; Foster et al. 1979).

In an adult animal model, zinc concentrations in muscle and bone do not change as a result of mild or marginal zinc deficiency. In cases of mild or marginal zinc deficiency, one cannot expect a uniform distribution of the deficit over the entire body pool, and most likely the compartments with high turnover rates (liver and peripheral blood cells, such as lymphocytes, granulocytes, and platelets) suffer a disproportionate deficit. Thus, if one were to consider that only 200 to 400 mg zinc, which is represented by liver zinc and the mobile exchangeable pool, is the critical pool, a negative balance of 180 mg from this pool may be a considerable fraction.

Our studies in this model have indicated that a mild or marginal deficiency of zinc in humans is characterized by neurosensory changes, oligospermia, decreased serum testosterone concentration, hyperammonemia, decreased lean body mass, decreased serum thymulin activity, decreased IL-2 production by peripheral blood mononuclear cells, decreased NK cell activity, and alterations in T-cell subpopulations. All of these manifestations can be corrected by zinc supplementation.

When zinc deficiency was very mild (5.0 mg zinc intake during the 20- to 24-week zinc-restricted period), the plasma zinc concentration remained more or less within the normal range, whereas the zinc concentration of lymphocytes and granulocytes declined (Meftah et al. 1991). Within 8 weeks of zinc restriction, the activity of lymphocyte ecto 5'nucleotidase (5'NT), serum thymulin activity, and IL-2 production by peripheral blood mononuclear cells decreased, and the intestinal absorption of ^{70}Zn increased significantly, suggesting that lymphocytes, thymus, and intestinal cells are very sensitive to zinc restriction (Meftah et al. 1991; Lee et al. 1993; Prasad et al. unpublished observation).

Biochemical Advances in Zinc Metabolism

D. Keilin and J. Mann (1940) were the first to demonstrate that carbonic anhydrase was a zinc metalloenzyme. Over the next 20 years, only five additional zinc metalloenzymes were identified, but in the last 30 years the total number has greatly increased. If related enzymes for different species are included, more than 200 zinc metalloenzymes are now known to exist (Chesters 1982; Galdes and Vallee 1983).

I. Lieberman and co-workers (1963) have shown that several enzymes necessary for nucleic acid synthesis in microorganisms require zinc. It is now well known that zinc is needed for DNA polymerase 1 (in *Escherichia coli*), bacterial RNApolymerase (in *E. coli*), and reverse transcriptase (in avian myeloblastosis virus) (Wu and Wu 1983).

Until 1965, there was no evidence that zinc-dependent enzymes were adversely affected as a result of zinc deficiency. Our investigations then demonstrated that the activity of various zinc-dependent enzymes was reduced in the testes, bones, esophagus, and kidneys of zinc-deficient rats in contrast to their pair-fed controls, and that this reduction of activity correlated with the decreased zinc content of the tissues (Prasad, Oberleas, Wolf et al. 1967).

Several studies have shown that zinc deficiency in animals impairs the incorporation of labeled thymidine into DNA. This effect has been detected within a few days of the institution of a zinc deficient diet in experimental animals, suggesting that dietary zinc deficiency may result in an immediate impairment of DNA synthesis. Prasad and Oberleas (1974) provided evidence that this early reduction in DNA synthesis was due to an adverse effect of zinc restriction on the activity of deoxythymidine kinase. These results were confirmed by I. E. Dreosti and L. S. Hurley (1975), who showed that the activity of deoxythymidine kinase in 12-day-old fetuses taken from females exposed to a dietary zinc deficiency during pregnancy was significantly lower than in ad-libitum-fed and restricted-fed controls.

Zinc and Immunity

P. J. Fraker, S. Hass, and R. W. Luecke (1977) revealed that severely and marginally zinc-deficient young adult-A/Jax mice have abnormal T-helper cell function. In addition, it is now known that other T-lymphocyte-mediated functions are found to be adversely affected by zinc deficiency. By using the young adult mouse as a model, it was demonstrated that a moderate period of suboptimal zinc administration causes thymic atrophy, lymphopenia, and alterations in the proportions of the various subsets of lymphocytes and mononuclear phagocytes (Fraker et al. 1986). As a result, antibody-mediated responses to both T-cell-dependent and T-cell-independent antigens are significantly reduced. Cytolytic T-cell responses, NK-cell activity, and delayed-type-hypersensitivity (DTH) reactions are also depressed.

In humans, patients with acrodermatitis enteropathica (a genetic disorder of zinc absorption) exhibit atrophic thymus, lymphopenia, anergic DTH responses, and reduced NK-cell activity (Fraker et al. 1986). Impaired DTH responses, correctable with zinc supplementation, were reported in zinc-deficient sickle cell anemia patients (Ballester and Prasad 1983), as were decreased NK-cell activity, decreased IL-2 activity, decreased serum thymulin activity, and alterations in lymphocyte subpopulations (Prasad et al. 1988).

Metallothionein

Metallothionein (MT) was discovered in 1957. M. Margoshes and Vallee (1957) identified a cadmium-binding protein in equine kidney cortex responsible for the natural accumulation of cadmium in the tissues. Metal and sulfur content are extremely high in MTs. In human cells, expression of the ISO-MT genes appears to be regulated differentially by cadmium, zinc, and glucocorticoids, and ISO-MT genes are indications for tissue-specific expression (Kagi and Schaffer 1988). A number of studies have led to the identification of various DNA segments serving as promoter sites in the 5'region of various MT genes in induction by metal ions and hormones. In the mouse MT-1 gene, the functional metal responsive promoter is composed of a set of four closely related metal-regulatory elements, each made up of eight nucleotides and localized near the TATA box.

Zinc may be the regulator of the mRNA strands responsible for de novo synthesis of MT in intestinal cells (Cousins 1979). It has been suggested that MT programs the fluctuating levels of zinc in and out of intestinal cells and plays an important role in regulating the absorption and/or excretion of not only zinc but also cadmium and copper.

Zinc and Gene Expression

The importance of zinc in DNA-binding proteins as regulators of gene expression has been recently recognized (Brown, Sander, and Argos 1985; Miller, Mclachlan, and Klug 1985; Klug and Rhodes 1987). The first zinc-finger protein to be recognized was transcription factor-IIIA of xenopus Laevis, which contained tandem repeats of segments with 30 amino acid residues, including pairs of histidines and cysteines (Miller et al. 1985). The presence of zinc in these proteins is essential for site-specific binding to DNA and gene expression. The zinc ion apparently serves as a strut that stabilizes folding of the domain into a finger-loop, which is then capable of site-specific binding to double-stranded DNA. The zinc-finger loop proteins provide one of the fundamental mechanisms for regulating gene expression of many proteins. In humans, the steroid hormones (and related compounds, such as thyroid hormones, cholecalciferol, and retinoic acid) enter cells by facilitated diffusion and combine with respective receptors (which contain the DNA-binding domain of the zinc-finger loops) either before or after entering the nucleus. Complexing of a hormone by its specific receptor evidently initiates a conformation change that exposes the zinc-finger loops, so that they bind to high-affinity sites on DNA and regulate gene expression (Hollenberg et al. 1985; Hughes et al. 1988; Sunderman and Barber 1988).

Interaction of Zinc with Other Elements

Zinc blocks the absorption of dietary copper, and also copper in the endogenous secretions (Brewer et al. 1988). Earlier, Prasad, Brewer, Schoomaker et al. (1978) observed that when subjects with sickle cell anemia were treated with 150 mg zinc/d in divided doses in order to reduce the number of irreversible sickle cells in the peripheral blood, they showed a decrease in the concentration of serum copper and ceruloplasmin. This observation led us to consider treatment of Wilson's disease patients with zinc. Our studies showed that zinc therapy in Wilson's disease patients leads to a negative copper balance, most likely by induction of MT synthesis in the intestines, whereby copper is sequestered and ultimately excreted in the feces (Brewer et al. 1983, 1987). According to our experience, zinc is an effective copper removal agent, is well tolerated, and prevents accumulation of copper in the liver (Brewer et al. 1983, 1987, 1988).

Ananda S. Prasad

This work was supported in part by grants from NIH/NIDDK (No. DK31401); NIH/NCI (No. CA 43838); the Food and Drug Administration (No. FDA-U-000457); Labcatal Laboratories, Paris, France; and the Veterans Administration Medical Research Service.

Bibliography

Abbasi, A. A., A. S. Prasad, P. Rabbani, and E. DuMouchelle. 1980. Experimental zinc deficiency in man: Effect on testicular function. *Journal of Laboratory and Clinical Medicine* 96: 544–50.

Arakawa, T., T. Tamura, and Y. Igarashi. 1976. Zinc deficiency in two infants during parenteral alimentation for diarrhea. *American Journal of Clinical Nutrition* 29: 197–204.

Ballester, O. F., and A. S. Prasad. 1983. Anergy, zinc deficiency and decreased nucleoside phosphorylase activity in patients with sickle cell anemia. *Annals of Internal Medicine* 98: 180–2.

Barnes, P. M., and E. J. Moynahan. 1973. Zinc deficiency in acrodermatitis enteropathica: Multiple dietary intolerance treated with synthetic zinc. *Proceedings of the Royal Society of Medicine* 66: 327–9.

Brewer, G. J., G. M. Hill, R. D. Dick, et al. 1987. Treatment of Wilson's disease with zinc. III. Prevention of reaccumulation of hepatic copper. *Journal of Laboratory and Clinical Medicine* 109: 526–31.

Brewer, G. J., G. M. Hill, A. S. Prasad, et al. 1983. Oral zinc therapy for Wilson's disease. *Annals of Internal Medicine* 99: 314–20.

Brewer, G. J., V. A. Yuzbasiyan, V. Iyengar, et al. 1988. Regulation of copper balance and its failure in humans. In *Essential and toxic trace elements in human health and disease,* ed. A. S. Prasad, 95–103. New York.

Brown, R. S., C. Sander, and P. Argos. 1985. The primary structure of transcription factor TF-III A has 12 consecutive repeats. *FEBS Letter* 186: 271-4.

Caggiano, V., R. Schnitzler, W. Strauss, et al. 1969. Zinc deficiency in a patient with retarded growth, hypogonadism, hypogammaglobulinemia, and chronic infection. *American Journal of Medical Science* 257: 305-19.

Chesters, J. K. 1982. Metabolism and biochemistry of zinc. In *Clinical, biochemical and nutritional aspects of trace elements,* ed. A. S. Prasad, 221-38. New York.

Cousins, R. J. 1979. Regulatory aspects of zinc metabolism in liver and intestine. *Nutrition Review* 34: 97-103.

Dreosti, I. E., and L. S. Hurley. 1975. Depressed thymidine kinase activity in zinc deficient rat embryos. *Proceedings of the Society of Experimental and Biological Medicine* 150: 161-5.

Foster, D. M., R. L. Aamodt, R. I. Henkin, and M. Berman. 1979. Zinc metabolism in humans. A kinetic model. *American Journal of Physiology* 237: R340-9.

Fraker, P. J., M. E. Gershwin, R. A. Good, and A. S. Prasad. 1986. Interrelationship between zinc and immune function. *Federation Proceedings,* 45: 1474-9.

Fraker, P. J., S. Hass, and R. W. Luecke. 1977. Effect of zinc deficiency on the immune response of the young adult A/Jax mouse. *Journal of Nutrition* 107: 1889-95.

Galdes, A., and B. L. Vallee. 1983. Categories of zinc metalloenzymes. In *Metal ions in biological systems,* ed. H. Sigel, 1-54. New York.

Halsted, J. A., H. A. Ronaghy, P. Abadi, et al. 1972. Zinc deficiency in man: The Shiraz experiment. *American Journal of Medicine* 53: 277-84.

Hambidge, K. M., C. E. Casey, and N. J. Krebs. 1983. Zinc. In *Trace elements in human and animal nutrition,* Vol 2, ed. M. Mertz, 1-137. New York.

Hambidge, K. M., C. Hambidge, M. Jacobs, and J. D. Baum. 1972. Low levels of zinc in hair, anorexia, poor growth, and hypogeusia in children. *Pediatric Research* 6: 868-74.

Henkin, R. I., and D. F. Bradley. 1969. Regulation of taste acuity by thiols and metal ions. *Proceedings of the National Academy of Science USA* 62: 30-7.

Hollenberg, S. M., C. Weinberger, E. S. Ong, et al. 1985. Primary structure and expression of a functional human glucocorticoid receptor cDNA. *Nature* 318: 635-41.

Hughes, M. R., P. J. Malloy, D. G. Kieback, et al. 1988. Point mutations in the human vitamin D receptor gene associated with hypocalcemia rickets. *Science* 242: 1702-5.

Kagi, J. H. R., and A. Schaffer. 1988. Biochemistry of metallothionein. *Biochemistry* 27: 8509-15.

Kay, R. G., and C. Tasman-Jones. 1975. Zinc deficiency and intravenous feeding. *Lancet* 2: 605-6.

Keilin, D., and J. Mann. 1940. Carbonic anhydrase. Purification and nature of the enzyme. *Biochemistry Journal* 34: 1163-76.

Klingberg, W. G., A. S. Prasad, and D. Oberleas. 1976. Zinc deficiency following penicillamine therapy. In *Trace elements in human health and disease,* Vol. 1, ed. A. S. Prasad, 51-65. New York.

Klug, A., and A. Rhodes. 1987. "Zinc-fingers." A novel protein motif for nucleic acid recognition. *Trends in Biochemical Science* 12: 461-9.

Lee, D.-Y., A. S. Prasad, H. Constance, et al. 1993. Homeostasis of zinc in marginal human zinc deficiency: Role of absorption and endogenous excretion of zinc. *Journal of Laboratory and Clinical Medicine.* 122: 549-56.

Lemann, I. I. 1910. A study of the type of infantilism in hookworm disease. *Archives of Internal Medicine* 6: 139-46.

Lieberman, I., R. Abrams, N. Hunt, and P. Ove. 1963. Levels of enzyme activity and deoxyribonucleic acid synthesis in mammalian cells cultured from the animal. *Journal of Biology and Chemistry* 238: 3955-62.

Lutz, R. E. 1926. The normal occurrence of zinc in biological materials: A review of the literature, and a study of the normal distribution of zinc in the rat, cat and man. *Biochemistry Journal* 34: 991-7.

MacMahon, R. A., M. L. Parker, and M. McKinnon. 1968. Zinc treatment in malabsorption. *Medical Journal of Australia* 2: 210-12.

Mahajan, S. K., R. J. Hamburger, W. Flamenbaum, et al. 1985. Effect of zinc supplementation on hyperprolactinemia in uremic men. *Lancet* 2: 750-1.

Mahajan, S. K., A. S. Prasad, W. A. Briggs, and F. D. McDonald. 1982. Correction of taste abnormalities and sexual dysfunction by zinc (Zn) in uremia. A double-blind study. *Annals of Internal Medicine* 97: 357-71.

Mahajan, S. K., A. S. Prasad, J. Lambujon, et al. 1980. Improvement of uremic hypogeusia by zinc: A double-blind study. *American Journal of Clinical Nutrition* 33: 1517-21.

Mahajan, S. K., A. S. Prasad, P. Rabbani, et al. 1979. Zinc metabolism in uremia. *Journal of Laboratory and Clinical Medicine* 94: 693-8.

Margoshes, M., and B. L. Vallee. 1957. A cadmium protein from equine kidney cortex. *American Journal of the Chemical Society* 79: 4813-14.

McCance, R. A., and E. M. Widdowson. 1942. The absorption and excretion of zinc. *Biochemistry Journal* 36: 692-6.

McClain, C. J., L. Adams, and S. Shedlofsky. 1988. Zinc and the gastrointestinal system. In *Essential and toxic trace elements in human health and disease,* ed. A. S. Prasad, 55-73. New York.

Meftah, S., A. S. Prasad, D.-Y. Lee, and G. J. Brewer. 1991. Ecto 5′nucleotidase (5′NT) as a sensitive indicator of human zinc deficiency. *Journal of Laboratory and Clinical Medicine* 118: 309-16.

Miller, J., A. D. Mclachlan, and A. Klug. 1985. Repetitive zinc-binding domains in the protein transcription factor III-A for xenopus oocytes. *EMBO Journal* 4: 1609-14.

Minnich, V., A. Okevogla, Y. Tarcon, et al. 1968. The effect of clay on iron absorption as a possible cause for anemia in Turkish subjects with pica. *American Journal of Clinical Nutrition* 21: 78-86.

National Research Council. 1974. *Recommended dietary allowances.* Eighth edition. Washington, D.C.

    1989. *Recommended dietary allowances.* Tenth edition. Washington, D.C.

O'Dell, B. L., P. O. Newberne, and J. E. Savage. 1958. Significance of dietary zinc for the growing chicken. *Journal of Nutrition* 65: 503-18.

O'Dell, B. L., and J. E. Savage. 1960. Effect of phytic acid on zinc availability. *Proceedings of the Society of Experimental and Biological Medicine* 103: 304-6.

Okada, A., Y. Takagi, T. Itakura, et al. 1976. Skin lesions during intravenous hyperalimentation: Zinc deficiency. *Surgery* 80: 629-35.

Pories, W. J., and W. H. Strain. 1966. Zinc and wound healing. In *Zinc metabolism,* ed. A. S. Prasad, 378-94. Springfield, Ill.

Prasad, A. S. 1966. Metabolism of zinc and its deficiency in human subjects. In *Zinc metabolism,* ed. A. S. Prasad, 250-302. Springfield, Ill.

    1988. Clinical spectrum and diagnostic aspects of human zinc deficiency. In *Essential and toxic trace elements in human health and disease,* ed. A. S. Prasad, 3-53. New York.

Prasad, A. S., A. A. Abbasi, P. Rabbani, and E. DuMouchelle. 1981. Effect of zinc supplementation on serum testosterone level in adult male sickle cell anemia subjects. *American Journal of Hematology* 19: 119-27.

Prasad, A. S., G. J. Brewer, E. B. Schoomaker, and P. Rabbani. 1978. Hypocupremia induced by zinc therapy in adults. *Journal of the American Medical Association* 240: 2166-8.

Prasad, A. S., and Z. T. Cossack. 1984. Zinc supplementation and growth in sickle cell disease. *Annals of Internal Medicine* 100: 367-71.

Prasad, A. S., J. T. Fitzgerald, J. W. Hess, et al. 1993. Zinc deficiency in the elderly. *Nutrition* 9: 218-24.

Prasad, A. S., J. A. Halsted, and M. Nadimi. 1961. Syndrome of iron deficiency anemia, hepatosplenomegaly, hypogonadism, dwarfism and geophagia. *American Journal of Medicine* 31: 532-46.

Prasad, A. S., S. Meftah, J. Abdallah, et al. 1988. Serum thymulin in human zinc deficiency. *Journal of Clinical Investigation* 82: 1202-10.

Prasad, A. S., A. Miale, Jr., Z. Farid, et al. 1963. Zinc metabolism in patients with the syndrome of iron deficiency anemia, hypogonadism, and dwarfism. *Journal of Laboratory and Clinical Medicine* 61: 537-49.

1963b. Biochemical studies on dwarfism, hypogonadism, and anemia. *Archives of Internal Medicine* 111: 407-28.

Prasad, A. S., and D. Oberleas. 1974. Thymidine kinase activity and incorporation of thymidine into DNA in zinc-deficient tissue. *Journal of Laboratory and Clinical Medicine* 83: 634-9.

Prasad, A. S., D. Oberleas, P. Wolf, et al. 1967. Studies on zinc deficiency: Changes in trace elements and enzyme activities in tissues of zinc-deficient rats. *Journal of Clinical Investigation* 46: 549-57.

Prasad, A. S., P. Rabbani, A. Abbasi, et al. 1978. Experimental zinc deficiency in humans. *Annals of Internal Medicine* 89: 483-90.

Prasad, A. S., E. B. Schoomaker, J. Ortega, et al. 1975. Zinc deficiency in sickle cell disease. *Clinical Chemistry* 21: 582-7.

Prasad, A. S., A. R. Schulert, A. Miale Jr., et al. 1963. Zinc and iron deficiencies in male subjects with dwarfism and hypogonadism but without ancylostomiasis and schistosomiasis or severe anemia. *American Journal of Clinical Nutrition* 12: 437-44.

Rabbani, P. I., A. S. Prasad, R. Tsai, et al. 1987. Dietary model for production of experimental zinc deficiency in man. *American Journal of Clinical Nutrition* 45: 1514-25.

Raulin, J. 1869. Chemical studies on vegetation. *Annals of Science Nature* 11 (in French): 93-9.

Reimann, F. 1955. Growth anomalies and malformations in iron-deficient states. *Proceedings of the 5th Kongr Eur Gesellschaft Haematology*, Freiburg, FRG: HM Keller, (in German) 546-50.

Sandstead, H. H., A. S. Prasad, A. S. Schulert, et al. 1967. Human zinc deficiency, endocrine manifestations and response to treatment. *American Journal of Clinical Nutrition* 20: 422-42.

Sommer, A. L., and C. B. Lipman. 1926. Evidence of indispensable nature of zinc and boron for higher green plants. *Plant Physiology* 1: 231-49.

Sunderman, F. W., Jr., and A. M. Barber. 1988. Finger loops, oncogenes, and metals. *Annals of Clinical and Laboratory Science* 18: 267-88.

Todd, W. R., C. A. Elvehjem, and E. B. Hart. 1934. Zinc in the nutrition of the rat. *American Journal of Physiology* 107: 146-56.

Tucker, H. F., and W. D. Salmon. 1955. Parakeratosis or zinc deficiency disease in pigs. *Proceedings of the Society of Experimental Biological Medicine* 88: 613-16.

Vallee, B. L., W. E. C. Wacker, A. F. Bartholomay, et al. 1956. Zinc metabolism in hepatic dysfunction. I. Serum zinc concentrations in Laennec's cirrhosis and their validation by sequential analysis. *New England Journal of Medicine* 255: 403-8.

Vikbladh, I. 1950. Studies on zinc in blood. *Scandinavian Journal of Clinical Laboratory Investigation* 2: 143-8.

1951. Studies on zinc in blood. *Scandinavian Journal of Clinical Laboratory Investigation* (Suppl) 3: 1-74.

Warth, J. A., A. S. Prasad, F. Zwas, et al. 1981. Abnormal dark adaptation in sickle cell anemia. *Journal of Laboratory and Clinical Medicine* 98: 189-94.

Wu, F. Y., and C. Wu. 1983. The role of zinc in DNA and RNA polymerases. In *Metal ions in biological systems,* ed. H. Sigel, 157-92. New York.

IV.C

Proteins, Fats, and Essential Fatty Acids

IV.C.1 ❧ Essential Fatty Acids

The history of the scientific documentation of the need for fat in the diet began with the early nineteenth-century work of Michel Eugene Chevreul (Mayer and Hanson 1960). He showed that lard contained a solid fat, which he termed stearine, and a liquid fat he called elaine (later shown to be the isomer of oleine), and in 1823, this work was published in a treatise, *Chemical Investigations of Fats of Animal Origin*. Chevreul also crystallized potassium stearate, naming it "mother-of-pearl" and calling its acidified product "margarine" (from the Greek word for mother-of-pearl). In addition, Chevreul isolated various acids from fats and distinguished them on the basis of their melting points.

Meanwhile in 1822, Edmund Davy had reported that iodine would react with fats, and by the end of the century, work by L. H. Mills and Baron Hubl led to the procedure devised by J. J. A. Wijs in 1898 for determining a fat's "iodine value" or "iodine number" – a measure of the extent to which a fat is unsaturated, based on its uptake of iodine. Highly saturated coconut oil, for example, has an iodine number of 8 to 10, whereas that of highly unsaturated linseed oil ranges from 170 to 202.

Phospholipids were described in 1846 by N. T. Gobley, who found that egg yolk had a substance that contained nitrogen and phosphorus in addition to glycerol and fatty acids. He named it lecithin. The nitrogenous base was shown to be choline by A. Strecker in 1868, and J. W. L. Thudichem described kephalin in 1884 (Mayer and Hanson 1960).

These early advances in chemistry and methodology were necessary before the major leap to studying the fats in nutrition could be taken. Indeed, advances in chemistry and technology have preceded key discoveries in the study of essential fatty acids and their functions throughout its history.

The Concept of Essential Fatty Acids

During the late 1920s, several groups of investigators explored questions of the nutritional value of fat that went beyond the knowledge that dietary fats provided energy and contained vitamins A and D. Among them were Herbert M. Evans and George O. Burr, who experimented with diets that were sufficiently purified to exclude fat. In three published papers (1927a; 1927b; 1928), they described a previously unknown deficiency disease that resulted from an absence of dietary fats and suggested the existence of a new vitamin, "vitamine F." Shortly after this, at Yale University, Ava Josephine McAmis, William E. Anderson, and Lafayette B. Mendel determined that a nonsaponifiable fraction of cod liver oil delivered vitamin A – but no fat – to experimental rats, and that slightly better growth was achieved when about 20 milligrams (mg) of peanut oil was fed to the rats along with the cod liver oil fraction. Animals receiving the most peanut oil grew best. The researchers wrote, with exemplary caution, that "whether this apparent beneficial effect of a small amount of fat is due to its content of vitamin A or other vitamins, or to its acting as a vehicle for the fat-soluble vitamins, or whether fat per se is essential, is not conclusively demonstrated" (McAmis, Anderson, and Mendel 1929: 262).

At the same time, George and Mildred Burr, at the University of Minnesota, published their results from feeding a very low fat diet to rats (1929). They concluded that there was, indeed, a requirement for fat in the diet and also believed that they had discovered a new deficiency disease curable by the feeding of small amounts of unsaturated fats or pure "linolic [sic]" acid. The following year, they coined the term "essential fatty acids" (1930).

The symptoms observed in rats that were considered indicative of dietary insufficiency included late failure of growth, kidney lesions, abnormal water consumption (because of excessive extradermal water loss), scaly skin, and necrotic tails. However, the concept of the essentiality of fatty acids was not immediately accepted. Critics pointed out that the skin lesions of rats, for example, were also seen with some B-vitamin deficiencies and thus not specific to fat deficiency. In addition, there was confusion surrounding the nature of the "fat-free" diets fed to rats because those consuming cornstarch managed some growth, whereas those on sucrose did not.

These questions were explained by the studies of Evans and Samuel Lepkovsky (at the University of California, Berkeley), who, first of all, showed that there was enough fat in cornstarch to support some growth in rats (1932a). They determined further that, if saturated fat (in this case, coconut oil) rather than carbohydrate was fed to the rats, deficiency symptoms became evident even more rapidly (1932b). In still another experiment (1932c), they isolated the fatty acid methyl esters from carcasses of rats that had been on either the fat-free or the supplemented diets, fed the esters to other rats, and discovered that the iodine numbers of fatty acids from fat-free–fed animals were higher than those from rats fed supplemented diets, thus showing that the degree of unsaturation is not a criterion of fatty acid essentiality.

The fat from the rats fed fat-free diets contained more unsaturated fatty acids than that from other rats at weaning, but the unsaturated fatty acids present did not relieve the deficiency symptoms, which was the first indication of the biosynthesis of eicosatrienoic acid. This phenomenon was later observed by Raymond Reiser and colleagues (1951) and finally explained by A. J. Fulco and J. F. Mead (1959). In the meantime, Evans, Lepkovsky, and E. A. Murphy had added both failure of reproduction and lactation in female rats (1934a, 1934b) and sterility in male rats (1934c) to the list of deficiency symptoms.

Requirement for Essential Fatty Acids

The reports of skin lesions in rats fed fat-free diets caused pediatrician Arild E. Hansen (1933) to suspect that infants suffering from eczema had an unsatisfied fat requirement. Hansen treated the condition with various oils, and shortly thereafter, Theodore Cornbleet reported the highly successful treatment of eczema by dietary supplementation with corn oil (1935). He also noted that this supplementation brought relief to his patients with asthma.

Later, in collaboration with Hilda F. Wiese and others at the University of Texas School of Medicine in Galveston, Hansen studied essential fatty acid requirements using dogs as the experimental model (Hansen and Wiese 1951). As their methods for quantifying fatty acids progressed from fractionation of methyl esters to spectrophotometric analysis of the alkali-conjugated fatty acids (Wiese and Hansen 1953), Hansen and Wiese were able to determine serum levels of unsaturated fatty acids in both poorly nourished (Hansen and Wiese 1954) and healthy (Wiese, Gibbs, and Hansen 1954) children. This work resulted in hard evidence of a deficiency of essential fatty acids that could occur in infants; it also resulted in recommendations for dietary intake of linoleic acid based upon the serum levels of di-, tri-, and tetraenoic acids of infants fed formulas containing different sources of fat (Wiese, Hansen, and Adams 1958). The researchers concluded that the dietary linoleate needed to provide optimum serum concentrations of polyunsaturated fatty acids was about 4 percent of the total calories. This advance in understanding the biochemistry of fatty acids in serum led to the use of biochemical criteria for defining nutrient deficiency.

Interrelationships among Fatty Acids

The alkaline isomerization method for analyzing specific fatty acids had led to the deduction that arachidonic (tetraenoic) acid was formed from dietary linoleic acid and that pentaenoic and hexaenoic acids were formed from dietary linolenic acid (Rieckehoff, Holman, and Burr 1949; Widmer and Holman 1950). Moreover, studies by Ralph Holman and his group at the Hormel Institute, University of Minnesota, also determined that linoleic and linolenic acids were not interconvertible. These findings were confirmed by the use of radioisotopically labeled fatty acids (Steinberg et al. 1956), and radioisotope tracer methods were used to define the source of Evans and Lepkovsky's (1932c) noncurative polyunsaturated fatty acid. A trienoic acid was identified by Fulco and Mead (1959) as 5,8,11-eicosatrienoic acid, which they found was derived from oleic acid.

During the 1960s, gas-liquid chromatography became the method of choice for the identification and quantification of fatty acids. A series of dose-response studies using single pure unsaturated fatty acids was conducted by Holman and his associates (Holman 1964), who developed interaction relationships which showed that the ratio of triene (eicosatrienoic acid) to tetraene (arachidonic acid) was proportional to the linoleate concentration in the diet of rats. They also determined that the diene and triene fatty acids were competitive with each other in conversions to longer-chain metabolites. For instance, 0.1 percent of energy as linolenate inhibited metabolism of linoleate by 50 percent, whereas it required 3.2 percent of linoleate to inhibit linolenate conversion by 50 percent. Interpretation of their many experiments led to the presentation of the sequence of chain elongation and desaturation of linoleic acid as 18:2 to 18:3 or 20:3; 18:3 to 20:3 to 20:4 or 22:3; 20:4 to 22:4 to 24:4 or 22:5. In the absence of linoleate and linolenate, the conversion of endogenous oleate (18:1) to 20:3 and 22:3 becomes dominant.

Nomenclature for Essential Fatty Acids

In studies prior to those of Holman and others in the 1960s, the original common names of the fatty acids were used. However, as the complexities of their double-bond configurations began to define their places in metabolism, it became necessary to establish simple and clear nomenclature. Diene, triene, monoene, and saturated, along with chain length, were no longer sufficient to describe physiologically important activities of the compounds. The locations of the double bonds were clarified, but the delta notation for the position of the double bonds was confusing when applied to chain elongation and desaturation. Holman (1964) used nomenclature based on the position of the double bond in relation to the nth (or omega) carbon. The linoleic acid family began with a double bond at the n minus 6 position; therefore, it was called the omega 6 family. The naturally occurring polyunsaturated fatty acids have methyl interrupted, rather than conjugated spacing; so linoleate is 18:2 omega 6,9. In the same pattern, linolenic acid is 18:3 omega 3,6,9. The importance of the specificity of desaturases was yet to be explained.

Importance of Human Requirements

Even though it had become accepted that linoleate was an essential nutrient, recommendations for dietary consumption were considered only for infants. Hansen, the pediatrician, agreed with Holman, the biochemist, that 0.5 to 1 percent of energy was enough, based upon keeping the triene–tetraene ratio below 0.4 (Holman 1973). By this time, the feeding of a fat-deficient diet to human subjects was not acceptable, so human studies were conducted using supplements; and, of course, diagnosis of malnourished infants also yielded findings.

The definitive proof of essential fatty acid requirement, however, came with the advent of intravenous feeding and its ability to provide total nutritional support (made possible by the method of implantation of a catheter in the superior vena cava, allowing infusion of hyperosmolar fluid) for long periods of time (Dudrick et al. 1968). Early formulas used glucose-protein hydrolysate fluid with electrolytes, minerals, and vitamins added, and reports of essential fatty acid deficiency symptoms in infants began to appear (Hallberg, Schuberth, and Wretlind 1966). Fatty acid analyses were made when a case came to the attention of the Hormel Institute group, which reported that after 100 days of total parenteral nutrition, the infant had a triene–tetraene ratio of 18 and extreme scaliness of skin (Paulsrud et al. 1972).

The first efforts to add lipids to intravenous formulas were unsuccessful. An emulsion containing cottonseed oil proved unacceptable because of toxic reactions, and that experience delayed general use of lipid emulsions (Alexander and Ziene 1961). Indeed, as late as 1973, the U.S. Food and Drug Administration had

not approved the addition of fat preparations to parenteral formulas, and reports continued of essential fatty acid deficiency in infants (White et al. 1973). A 10 percent soybean oil emulsion, which employed a nontoxic emulsifying agent, egg phospholipid, and a smaller fat particle (0.5 microns in diameter), finally proved to be acceptable (Bivins et al. 1980).

Infants were not the only ones at risk for essential fatty acid deficiency from total parenteral nutrition. Adults with lesions of the gastrointestinal tract were reported to have biochemically defined linoleate deficiency (Wapnick, Norden, and Venturas 1974). Fourteen patients had triene–tetraene ratios with an average of greater than 2. Adults who had sufficient stores of adipose tissue fat were not believed to be at risk of essential fatty acid deficiency until the use of total parenteral nutrition (TPN) showed that this was not necessarily the case. When glucose and amino acids were infused continuously, lipolysis of adipose tissue fat was suppressed, and biochemical evidence of deficiency was present even if some fat was provided by oral nutrition in combination with parenteral feeding (Stein et al. 1980). By the mid–1970s, however, intravenous fat emulsions had become generally available, and it was accepted that a sufficient supply of linoleic acid was one of the important factors to be considered in every case of parenteral nutrition (Wolfram et al. 1978).

The Essentiality of Linolenic Acid

The earliest studies of unsaturated fatty acids (in common and chemical names; see Table IV.C.1.1) showed that both linoleic and linolenic acids had beneficial effects upon the clinical signs of deficiency in rats. Linoleic and arachidonic acids cured the deficiency's symptoms of growth retardation, skin lesions, and excessive water consumption, whereas linolenic acid only cured growth retardation (Burr 1942). Attempts were subsequently made by a group of investigators at Berkeley to produce linolenic acid deficiency by maintaining rats for 3 generations on a diet lacking n-3 fatty acids. Levels of n-3 in tissues became very low, but small amounts remained and the rats showed no abnormality in growth, reproduction, or appearance (Tinoco et al. 1971). The Berkeley investigators then used radioactive carbon-labeled linolenic acid to trace the impact on dietary fat sources when linolenic acid was converted to docosahexaenoic acid (Poovaiah, Tinoco, and Lyman 1976). Measured in liver phospholipids, the radioactivity was recovered as 20:5n-3 and 22:6n-3. The dietary fat supplements containing n-6 fatty acids (linoleic and arachidonic acids) reduced the conversion of 20:4n-3 to 20:5n-3 (desaturation), whereas the n-3 supplements (18:3n-3 and 22:6n-3) reduced the conversion of 20:5n-3 to 22:5n-3 (elongation) (Figure IV.C.1.1). The researchers concluded that 22:6n-3 may control its own formation by regulating elongation.

Table IV.C.1.1. *Unsaturated fatty acids*

Chemical description	Chemical name	Common name
18:1n-9	9-octadecenoic	Oleic, 18:1ω9
18:2n-6	9,12-octadecadienoic	Linoleic, 18:2ω6
18:3n-6	6,9,12-octadecatrienoic	Gamma-linolenic, 18:3ω6
18:3n-3	9,12,15-octadecatrienoic	Alpha-linolenic, 18:3ω3
20:3n-6	8,11,14-eicosatrienoic	Dihomogamma-linolenic, 20:3ω6
20:4n-6	5,8,11,14-eicosatetraenoic	Arachidonic, 20:4ω6
20:5n-3	5,8,11,14,17-eicosapentaenoic	Timnodonic EPA, 20:5ω3
22:4n-6	7,10,13,16-docosatetraenoic	Adrenic, 22:4ω6
22:5n-6	4,7,10,13,16-docosapentaenoic	22:5ω6
22:5n-3	7,10,13,16,19-docosahexaenoic	Cervonic DHA, 22:5ω3

Evidence, though inconclusive, that linolenic acid is essential was gathered by examining tissues of rats depleted of the n-3 family. Brain and retinal tissue retained docosahexaenoic acid tenaciously through two generations of rat growth (Tinoco, Miljanich, and Medwadowski 1977; Tinoco et al. 1978), but prolonged deprivation of n-3 fatty acids resulted in reduced visual acuity in infant monkeys and defective electroretinographic responses in monkeys and rats (Neuringer, Anderson, and Connor 1988). As was the case with linoleic acid, patients requiring intravenous feeding have been important in proving that linolenic acid is essential in humans. Patients on TPN, observed by K. S. Bjerve (1989) from 1987 to 1989, experienced scaly and hemorrhagic dermatitis, hemorrhagic folliculitis of the scalp, growth retardation, and impaired wound healing. But the addition of different oils showed that 1.0 to 1.2 percent of energy as linolenate was necessary to obtain a normal concentration of n-3 fatty acids and relieve the symptoms.

The Discovery of Prostaglandins

Meanwhile, in Sweden, Sune Bergstrom and his colleagues (1962) had determined the structure of a new class of compounds that had been isolated from the vesicular glands of sheep and were named prostaglandins. The subsequent discovery that essential fatty acids were the natural precursors of the prostaglandins was made simultaneously by Bergstrom's team, by a group in Holland, and by another at the Upjohn Company in the United States (Bergstrom 1972). That essential fatty acid deficiency could affect prostaglandin functions was shown by Bergstrom and L. A. Carlson (1965).

The first international conference on prostaglandins was held in 1972, and Bergstrom, who opened the meeting, commented on the difficulty of evaluating analytical methods for prostaglandins. At that time, bioassay and gas chromatography–mass spectrometry (GC-MS) were being used. Radioimmunoassay was quite new and considered unreliable, as were bioassays. Bergstrom (1973) called for intensive discussion of the analytical questions. Daniel H. Hwang, at the time a doctoral student in nutrition, proposed that in order to study dietary effects on prostaglandin status, a reliable radioimmunoassay should be developed. GC-MS was not sensitive enough and was too time-consuming and expensive to be used for analysis of large numbers of biological samples.

Very little was known then about the metabolism of prostaglandins. The short half-life, explosive synthe-

OLEIC ACID

$$\text{N-9} \quad 16{:}0 \xrightarrow{\text{E}} 18{:}0 \xrightarrow{\Delta 9} 18{:}1 \xrightarrow{\Delta 6} 18{:}2 \xrightarrow{\text{E}} 20{:}2 \xrightarrow{\Delta 5} 20{:}3$$

(diet and *de novo* synthesis)

LINOLEIC ACID

$$\text{N-6} \quad 18{:}2 \xrightarrow{\Delta 6} 18{:}3 \xrightarrow{\text{E}} 20{:}3 \xrightarrow{\Delta 5} 20{:}4 \xrightarrow{\text{E}} 22{:}4 \xrightarrow{\text{E}} 24{:}4 \xrightarrow{\Delta 6} 24{:}5 \xrightarrow{\beta\text{-ox}} 22{:}5$$

(dietary essential fatty acid)

LINOLENIC ACID

$$\text{N-3} \quad 18{:}3 \xrightarrow{\Delta 6} 18{:}4 \xrightarrow{\text{E}} 20{:}4 \xrightarrow{\Delta 5} 20{:}5 \xrightarrow{\text{E}} 22{:}5 \xrightarrow{\text{E}} 24{:}5 \xrightarrow{\Delta 6} 24{:}6 \xrightarrow{\beta\text{-ox}} 22{:}6$$

(dietary essential fatty acid)

Figure IV.C.1.1. Desaturation (Δ), elongation (E), and chain shortening (ß-ox, beta oxidation) of families of unsaturated fatty acids.

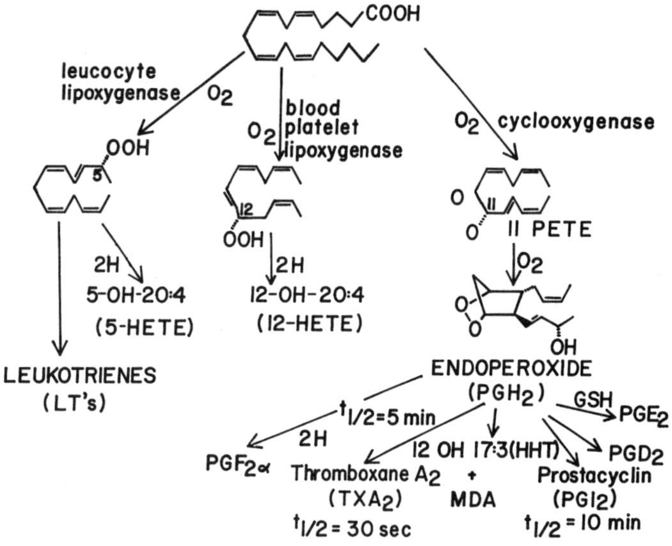

Figure IV.C.1.2. Conversion of arachidonic acid (eicosatetraenoic acid) into eicosanoids. Lipoxygenases convert 20:4n-6 to hydroxyperoxyeicosatrienoic acid (HETE) that is converted to leukotrienes. Cyclooxygenases convert 20:4n-6 to peroxyeicosatrienoic acid (PETE) that converts to endoperoxide (PGH$_2$) that is converted to prostaglandins (PG), thromboxane (TX), or prostacyclin (PGI$_2$). The half-life ($t_{1/2}$) of thromboxane in vivo is 30 seconds and that of prostacyclin is about 10 minutes.

sis in response to trauma, and tissue specificity were yet to be discovered. Serendipitously, Hwang and colleagues (1975) chose to analyze blood serum from rats that had been anesthetized, and these experiments were the first to apply the discovery of prostaglandins to the understanding of essential fatty acid functions and requirements. Rats were fed diets containing corn oil or beef tallow as the source of fat, which showed that there was a positive effect of corn oil (containing linoleic acid) on the synthesis of PGE$_1$ and PGF$_{2\alpha}$.

Subsequently, the laboratory of Melvin M. Mathias and Jacqueline Dupont (1985) demonstrated a biphasic response of prostaglandin synthesis to the dietary content of linoleic acid. The response to 0 to 2 percent of energy from linoleate was an increase in prostaglandin synthesis; with 2 to 5 percent of energy there was a decrease; and above 5 percent of energy there was a gradual increase up to the maximum content of linoleic acid fed (27 percent of energy). The 0 to 2 percent energy response to linoleate was associated with a disappearance of eicosatrienoic acid. Responses to a higher consumption of linoleate were not correlated with arachidonic acid concentration in serum (Fig. IV.C.1.2).

The importance of the relation of dietary linoleate to eicosanoid synthesis meant the addition of a functional measurement to the earlier indications of essential fatty acid deficiency, both clinical and biochemical. This functional indicator of essential fatty acid requirement suggested that 5 to 10 percent of linoleate is desirable (Dupont and Dowd 1990).

Modern History

Excessive extradermal water loss, one of the first symptoms described of essential fatty acid deficiency, has been explained. A major specific function of linoleate is in skin ceramides, where the linoleate is incorporated into acylglucosylceramides and acylceramides (Hansen and Jensen 1985). Linoleate is the only fatty acid substantially incorporated into these sphingolipids. On another front, the details of control of elongation and desaturation and interrelationships among the families of fatty acids are still being investigated (Cook et al. 1991; Cunnane et al. 1995; Sprecher et al. 1995).

Since the 1970s, an enormous literature about prostaglandin metabolism has accumulated. The term "eicosanoids" was introduced in 1980 to describe the class of substances having 20 carbon atoms derived from n-6 and n-3 fatty acids. Because eicosanoids are regulators of a large array of physiological functions, there are many possible manifestations of deficiency of their precursors. The attention given to the very long-chain fatty acids from marine animals (fish oils) has created another large body of literature about the interplay between metabolism of omega-3 (n-3) and omega-6 (n-6) families of fatty acids. The competition between the two families for enzymes of chain elongation, desaturation, and conversion to active metabolites first demonstrated by Holman (1964) has introduced additional complexity into the attempt to define the dietary requirements for the two families. We know that a source of 18 carbon n-3 and n-6 fatty acids is a dietary necessity, but whether there may be health benefits from consumption of the longer chain products – 20:4n-6, 22:5n-3, and 22:6n-3 – is a current topic of intensive research. Infant requirements for brain development are important considerations for assuring appropriate recommendations for infant formulas and supplements (Carlson et al. 1993).

A broad range of ongoing research is aimed at defining the functions of n-3 fatty acids, and a deficiency has been associated with the function of rhodopsin (Bush et al. 1994). Many aspects of brain and behavioral development are linked to the availability of linolenic acid and its products (Neuringer, Reisbick, and Janowsky 1994). The effects of the ratio of dietary linoleic to linolenic acids is the subject of current research (Jensen et al. 1996), and immune functions and cell signaling are also current topics of study of fatty acid functions and metabolism (Hayek et al. 1997; Hwang in press).

Summary

The evolution of an understanding of essential fatty acids has progressed through several scientific developmental phases. The earliest was the ability to prepare diets of sufficient purity to exclude lipids, which led to the conclusion that some fat was essential. The substantive proof of a human requirement – that is, that the fatty acids were essential to the diet – had to await the advent of total parenteral feeding. In about the same era, eicosanoids were discovered, which opened a new world for understanding the functions of essential fatty acids. With the tools of science today, the profound participation of fatty acids in all aspects of cellular life and function should provide great excitement as well as great challenges to all scientists interested in the expansion of the science of nutrition.

Jacqueline L. Dupont

Bibliography

Alexander, C. S., and L. Ziene. 1961. Fat infusions. Toxic effects and alterations in fasting serum lipids following prolonged use. *Archives of Internal Medicine* 107: 514.

Bergstrom, S. 1972. Introduction, International Conference on Prostaglandins, 1972. In *Advances in the Biosciences* 9: 1-5.

Bergstrom, S., and L. A. Carlson. 1965. Lipid mobilization in essential fatty acid deficient rats. *Acta Physiologica Scandinavica* 64: 479-80.

Bergstrom, S., F. Dressler, R. Ryhage, et al. 1962. Prostaglandin and related factors. VIII. The isolation of two further prostaglandins from sheep prostate glands. *Arkiv Kemi* 19: 563-7.

Bivins, B. A., R. P. Rapp, K. Record, et al. 1980. Parenteral safflower oil emulsion (Liposyn 10%). Safety and effectiveness in treating or preventing essential fatty acid deficiency in surgical patients. *Annals of Surgery* 203: 307-15.

Bjerve, K. S. 1989. N-3 fatty acid deficiency in man. *Journal of Internal Medicine* 225 (Supplement 1): 171-5.

Burr, G. O. 1942. Significance of the essential fatty acids. *Federation Proceedings* 1: 224-33.

Burr, G. O., and M. M. Burr. 1929. A new deficiency disease produced by the rigid exclusion of fat from the diet. *The Journal of Biological Chemistry* 82: 345-67.

1930. On the nature and the role of fatty acids essential in nutrition. *The Journal of Biological Chemistry* 86: 587-621.

Bush, R. A., A. Malnoe, C. E. Reme, and T. P. Williams. 1994. Dietary deficiency of N-3 fatty acids alters rhodopsin content and function in rat retina. *Investigative Ophthalmology and Visual Science* 35: 91-100.

Carlson, S. E., S. H. Werkman, P. G. Rhodes, and E. A. Tolley. 1993. Visual acuity development in healthy preterm infants: Effect of marine-oil supplementation. *American Journal of Clinical Nutrition* 58: 35-42.

Cook, H. W., D. M. Byers, F. B. St. C. Palmer, et al. 1991. Alternate pathways in the desaturation and chain elongation of linolenic acid, 18:3(n-3), in cultured glioma cells. *Journal of Lipid Research* 32: 1265-73.

Cornbleet, T. 1935. Use of maize oil (unsaturated fatty acids) in the treatment of eczema. *Archives of Dermatology and Syphilology* 31: 224-6.

Cunnane, S. C., M. A. Ryan, K. S. Craig, et al. 1995. Synthesis of linoleate and alpha-linolenate by chain elongation in the rat. *Lipids* 30: 781-3.

Dudrick, S. J., D. W. Wilmore, H. M. Vars, and J. E. Rhoads. 1968. Long-term total parenteral nutrition with growth, development, and positive nitrogen balance. *Surgery* 64: 134-42.

Dupont, J., and M. K. Dowd. 1990. Icosanoid synthesis as a functional measurement of essential fatty acid requirement. *Journal of the American College of Nutrition* 9: 272-6.

Evans, H. M., and G. O. Burr. 1927a. A new dietary deficiency with highly purified diets. *Proceedings of the Society for Experimental Biology and Medicine* 24: 740-3.

1927b. A new dietary deficiency with highly purified diets. II. Supplementary requirement of diet of pure casein, sucrose, and salt. *Proceedings of the Society for Experimental Biology and Medicine* 25: 41-8.

1928. A new dietary deficiency with highly purified diets. III. The beneficial effect of fat in diet. *Proceedings of the Society for Experimental Biology and Medicine* 25: 390-7.

Evans, H. M., and S. Lepkovsky. 1932a. Vital need of the body for certain unsaturated fatty acids. I. Experiments with fat-free diets in which sucrose furnishes the sole source of energy. *The Journal of Biological Chemistry* 96: 143-56.

1932b. Vital need of the body for certain unsaturated fatty acids. II. Experiments with high fat diets in which saturated fatty acids furnish the sole source of energy. *The Journal of Biological Chemistry* 96: 157-64.

1932c. Vital need of the body for certain unsaturated fatty acids. III. Inability of the rat organism to synthesize the essential unsaturated fatty acids. *The Journal of Biological Chemistry* 99: 231-4.

Evans, H. M., S. Lepkovsky, and E. A. Murphy. 1934a. Vital need of the body for certain unsaturated fatty acids. IV. Reproduction and lactation upon fat-free diets. *The Journal of Biological Chemistry* 106: 431-40.

1934b. Vital need of the body for certain unsaturated fatty acids. V. Reproduction and lactation upon diets containing saturated fatty acids as their sole source of energy. *The Journal of Biological Chemistry* 106: 441-4.

1934c. Vital need of the body for certain unsaturated fatty acids. VI. Male sterility on fat-free diets. *The Journal of Biological Chemistry* 106: 445-50.

Fulco, A. J., and J. F. Mead. 1959. Metabolism of essential fatty acids. VIII. Origin of 5,8,11-eicosatrienic acid in the fat-deficient rat. *The Journal of Biological Chemistry* 234: 1411-16.

Hallberg, D., O. Schuberth, and A. Wretlind. 1966. Experimental and clinical studies with fat emulsion for intravenous nutrition. *Nutra Dieta* 8: 245.

Hansen, A. E. 1933. Serum lipid changes and therapeutic effect of various oils in infantile eczema. *Proceedings of the Society for Experimental Biology and Medicine* 31: 160-1.

Hansen, A. E., D. J. D. Adam, A. N. Boelsche, et al. 1957. Manifestations of fat deficiency in infants. *Federation Proceedings* 16: 387.

Hansen, A. E., and H. F. Wiese. 1951. Fat in the diet in relation to nutrition of the dog: I. Characteristic appearance and gross changes of animals fed diets with and without fat. *Texas Reports on Biology and Medicine* 9: 491-515.

1954. Essential fatty acids and human nutrition: II. Serum level for unsaturated fatty acids in poorly-nourished infants and children. *Journal of Nutrition* 52: 367-74.

Hansen, H. S., and B. Jensen. 1985. Essential function of linoleic acid esterified in acylglucosylceramide and acylceramide in maintaining the epidermal water permeability barrier. Evidence from feeding studies with oleate, linoleate, arachidonate, columbinate and a-linolenate. *Biochimica and Biophysica Acta* 834: 357-63.

Hayek, M. G., C. Mura, D. Wu, et al. 1997. Enhanced expression of inducible cyclooxygenase with age in murine macrophages. *Journal of Immunology* 159: 2445-51.

Holman, R. T. 1964. Nutritional and metabolic interrelationships between fatty acids. *Federation Proceedings* 23: 1062-7.

1973. Essential fatty acid deficiency in humans. In *Dietary lipids and postnatal development*, ed. C. Galli, 127-43. New York.

Hwang, D. H., and S. H. Rhee. 1999. Receptor-mediated signaling pathways: Potential targets of modulation by dietary fatty acids. *American Journal of Clinical Nutrition* 70: 545-56.

Hwang, D. H., M. M. Mathias, J. Dupont, and D. L. Meyer. 1975. Linoleate enrichment of diet and prostaglandin and prostaglandin metabolism in rats. *Journal of Nutrition* 105: 995-1002.

Jensen, C. L., H. Chen, J. K. Fraley, et al. 1996. Biochemical effects of dietary linoleic/α-linolenic acid ratio in term infants. *Lipids* 31: 107-13.

Mathias, M. M., and J. Dupont. 1985. Quantitative relationship between dietary linoleate and prostaglandin (icosanoid) biosynthesis. *Lipids* 20: 791-801.

Mayer, J., and S. D. Hanson. 1960. Michel Eugene Chevreul – A biographical sketch. *Journal of Nutrition* 72: 3-7.

McAmis, A. J., W. E. Anderson, and L. B. Mendel. 1929. Growth of rats on "fat-free" diets. *The Journal of Biological Chemistry* 82: 247-62.

Neuringer, M., G. J. Anderson, and W. E. Connor. 1988. The essentiality of n-3 fatty acids for the development and function of the retina and brain. *Annual Review of Nutrition* 8: 517-41.

Neuringer, M., S. Reisbick, and J. Janowsky. 1994. The role of n-3 fatty acids in visual and cognitive development: Current evidence and methods of assessment. *Journal of Pediatrics* 125: S39-47.

Niswender, G. D., A. M. Akbar, and T. M. Nett. 1975. Use of specific antibodies for quantification of steroid hormones. *Methods in Enzymology* 36, Part A: 16-34.

Paulsrud, J. R., L. Pensler, C. F. Whitten, et al. 1972. Essential fatty acid deficiency in infants by fat-free intravenous feeding. *American Journal of Clinical Nutrition* 25: 897-904.

Poovaiah, B. P., J. Tinoco, and R. L. Lyman. 1976. Influence of diet on conversion of $^{14}C_1$-linolenic acid to docosahexaenoic acid in the rat. *Lipids* 11: 194-202.

Reiser, R., B. Gibson, M. J. Carr, and B. G. Lamp. 1951. The synthesis and interconversions of polyunsaturated fatty acids by the laying hen. *The Journal of Nutrition* 44: 159-76.

Rieckehoff, I. G., R. T. Holman, and G. O. Burr. 1949. Polyethenoid fatty acid metabolism. Effect of dietary fat on polyethenoid fatty acids in rat tissues. *Archives of Biochemistry* 20: 331-40.

Sprecher, H., D. L. Luthria, B. S. Mohammed, and S. P. Baykousheva. 1995. Reevaluation of the pathways for the biosynthesis of polyunsaturated fatty acids. *Journal of Lipid Research* 36: 2471-7.

Stein, T. P., G. P. Buzby, W. C. Hargrove, III, et al. 1980. Essential fatty acid deficiency in patients receiving simultaneous parenteral and oral nutrition. *Journal of Parenteral and Enteral Nutrition* 4: 343-5.

Steinberg, G., W. H. Slaton, D. R. Howton, and J. F. Mead. 1956. Metabolism of essential fatty acids. IV. Incorporation of linoleate into arachidonic acid. *The Journal of Biological Chemistry* 220: 257-64.

Tinoco, J., R. Babcock, R. Hincenbergs, et al. 1978. Linolenic acid deficiency: Changes in fatty acid patterns in female and male rats raised on a linolenic acid-deficient diet for two generations. *Lipids* 13: 6-17.

Tinoco, J., P. Miljanich, and B. Medwadowski. 1977. Depletion of docosahexaenoic acid in retinal lipids of rats fed a linolenic acid-deficient, linoleic-acid containing diet. *Biochimica and Biophysica Acta* 486: 575-8.

Tinoco, J., M. A. Williams, I. Hincenbergs, and R. L. Lyman. 1971. Evidence for nonessentiality of linolenic acid in the diet of the rat. *Journal of Nutrition* 101: 937-46.

Wapnick, S., D. A. Norden, and D. J. Venturas. 1974. Essential fatty acid deficiency in patients with lesions of the gastrointestinal tract. *Gut* 15: 367-70.

White, H. B., M. D. Turner, A. C. Turner, and R. C. Miller. 1973. Blood lipid alterations in infants receiving intravenous fat-free alimentation. *The Journal of Pediatrics* 83: 305-13.

Widmer, C., and R. T. Holman. 1950. Polyethenoid fatty acid metabolism. II. Deposition of polyunsaturated fatty acids in fat-deficient rats upon single fatty acid supplementation. *Archives of Biochemistry* 25: 1-12.

Wiese, H. F., R. H. Gibbs, and A. E. Hansen. 1954. Essential fatty acids and human nutrition: I. Serum level for unsaturated fatty acids in healthy children. *Journal of Nutrition* 52: 355-65.

Wiese, H. F., and A. E. Hansen. 1953. Semimicromethod for unsaturated fatty acids of blood serum. *Journal of Biological Chemistry* 202: 417.

Wiese, H. F., A. E. Hansen, and D. J. D. Adams. 1958. Essential fatty acids in infant nutrition. I. Linoleic acid requirement in terms of serum di-, tri- and tetraenoic acid levels. *Journal of Nutrition* 66: 345-60.

Wolfram, G., J. Eckart, B. Walther, N. Zollner. 1978. Factors influencing essential fatty acid requirement in total parenteral nutrition (TPN). *The Journal of Parenteral and Enteral Nutrition* 2: 634-9.

IV.C.2 ❧ Proteins

The word "protein" was coined by Jöns Jakob Berzelius in 1838. For the previous 150 years, however, there had been the concept of an "animal substance," slight variants of which were thought to make up muscles, skin, and blood. In each form the substance was initially believed to be gluey. But it turned into hard, hornlike material when heated and became foul-smelling when kept under moist, warm conditions, giving off an alkaline vapor. This contrasted with the properties of starch and sugar and most whole plants that went to acid during damp, warm storage.

For people interested in nutrition, the obvious question was: "How does the animal kingdom, which as a whole lives on the plant kingdom, convert what it eats into the apparently very different animal substance?" Humans were, of course, included in the animal kingdom and assumed to have essentially the same nutritional system as animals. Some eighteenth-century discoveries threw light on the problem.

In 1728, the Italian scholar Jacopo Beccari announced that he had discovered the presence of a material with all the characteristics of "animal substance" in white wheat flour. When he wetted the flour to make a ball of dough, then washed and kneaded it in water, the fine, white starchy particles washed out. What remained was a sticky pellet of gluten, which, if its origin were unknown, would be judged animal in nature. Beccari concluded that the presence of this portion of preformed "animal substance" made wheat particularly nutritive. Wheat flour, as a whole, did not show animal properties because the greater quantity of starch overwhelmed the reactions of the gluten.

Nitrogen in Nutrition

Later in the eighteenth century, with the development of the new chemistry, the main elements were identified, and ammonia, the "volatile alkali," was shown to be a compound of nitrogen and hydrogen. Gluten was also found to contain nitrogen, in common with animal tissues, whereas starches, fat, and sugars did not.

At first it was thought that the process of animal digestion and nutrition must consist of the combining of nutrients in plant foods with atmospheric nitrogen in order to "animalize" them. In particular, it seemed that this theory might explain the slow digestion process and large storage stomachs in ruminant animals. However, further work in France made this appear less likely.

First, François Magendie reported in 1816 that dogs failed to survive for more than a few weeks on foods like fats and sugars that contained no nitrogen. Then, in the 1830s, Jean Boussingault showed that the nitrogen present in the hay and potatoes eaten by a cow was enough to balance the quantities present in the milk it secreted together with its regular daily nitrogen losses. There was, therefore, no need to suppose that atmospheric nitrogen was involved in animal nutrition. But because of the importance of nitrogen in nutrition, Boussingault concluded that plant foods should be valued in terms of their relative nitrogen contents. Thus, he believed that dry beans, with

roughly twice the nitrogen content of grains, had twice their nutritional value.

By this time, further work on the composition of plants had shown that although they all contained nitrogenous compounds, most of them, unlike wheat gluten, were soluble in water, yet could be precipitated by heat or acid. In 1838, Gerritt Mulder, a Dutch physician who had taught himself chemical analysis, published a claim that all the important "animal substances" he had analyzed had the same basic formula, corresponding to 40 atoms of carbon, 62 of hydrogen, 10 of nitrogen and 12 of oxygen, which can be expressed more simply as $C_{40}H_{62}N_{10}O_{12}$. They differed in their properties only because they had different numbers of atoms of sulfur and/or phosphorus adhering to them. He sent his paper to the Swedish chemical authority, Jacob Berzelius, who replied that this was a most important discovery of the "fundamental or primary substance of animal nutrition" and that this substance deserved to be called "protein" after the Greek god Proteus.

The leading German organic chemist, Justus Liebig, confirmed Mulder's finding and went on to argue that, from a chemical point of view, it was the plant kingdom alone that had the power of making protein. Animal digestion only loosened the association between their molecules to make them soluble and absorbable into the bloodstream and immediately ready for deposit into the animal system. The leading French scientists accepted this view but added that vegetable oils and carbohydrates were also required. Their combustion was needed within the animal body to maintain animal heat.

Protein as a Muscle Fuel

Liebig, although he had himself done no physiological work, developed a whole series of dogmatic statements as to the functions of nutrients in the body. He believed that the energy needed for the contraction of muscles came solely from the breakdown of some of their own protein, which was then immediately decomposed further, with the nitrogenous portion appearing as urea in the urine. A subject's requirement for protein was, therefore, proportional to his or her performance of physical work. The role of fats and sugars was merely to protect living tissues (which reacted with oxygen that penetrated them) from the danger of oxygen damage. Consequently, protein was the only true nutrient.

Liebig's views were accorded great weight, although there were many grounds on which they could be criticized. For example, in 1862, Edward Smith, a physician and physiologist who had been studying the health and diet of the inmates of London prisons, reported a study of factors influencing the daily output of urea. Prisoners who ate the same rations each day and engaged in hard labor three days per week were found to excrete almost the same quantity of urea on the day (and following night) of the labor as on the days when not laboring. However, the labor caused greatly elevated carbon dioxide output in the breath. The main factor influencing urea production appeared to be the amount of protein eaten in the previous 24 hours.

In 1865, Adolf Fick and Johannes Wislicenus, on the faculty of a Swiss university, followed up these findings. They put themselves on a protein-free diet for 24 hours and ascended almost 2,000 meters on a path to the summit of a convenient mountain. They calculated the amount of work done during the ascent and measured the amount of nitrogen in the urine they excreted. From this they calculated that they had each metabolized approximately 37 grams (g) of protein. Their friend in England, Edward Frankland, now calculated that the metabolism of protein yielded 4.37 kilocalories per gram.

By this time the principle of the "conservation of energy" had been accepted, and James Joules had estimated that 1 kilocalorie was equivalent to 423 kilogram-meters (kg-m) of mechanical work against the force of gravity. The energy released from the protein was, therefore, equivalent to some 68,000 kg-m. However, the net work required to lift each scientist up the mountain was approximately 140,000 kg-m, about twice as much. And further work has shown that muscles operate at something like 25 percent efficiency, so that four times the minimal theoretical amount of fuel is required. The conclusion was, therefore, that the energy required for muscular effort does not come primarily from protein but from dietary fats and carbohydrates.

Although Liebig's grand scheme had been discredited, German workers, in particular, continued to maintain that a high-protein intake was desirable to maintain both physical and nervous energy. They argued this on the grounds that people from countries where the diet was largely vegetarian and low in protein lacked "get-up-and-go," and that wherever people were unrestrained by poverty and could eat what they wished, they chose a high-meat, high-protein diet. The first U.S. government standards, issued at the end of the 1800s by Wilbur Atwater, the Department of Agriculture's nutrition specialist, followed the same line in recommending that physically active men should eat 125 g of protein per day.

Such a notion did not go unchallenged, however. From 1840 on, there had been a vegetarian "school" in the United States, which argued that eating meat was overstimulating and conducive first to debauchery and then to exhaustion of the irritated tissues. John Harvey Kellogg (cofounder of the family's breakfast-food enterprise) believed that meat and other sources of excessive protein in the diet could putrefy in the large intestine, resulting in autointoxication. These ideas were regarded by the scientific establishment as unscientific and not meriting attention. However, in 1902 a serious challenge to the "high-protein" school was mounted by Russell Chittenden, professor of physiological chemistry at Yale.

Chittenden had six of his colleagues, a dozen army corpsmen, and a group of Yale's athletes spend approximately six months on diets containing no more than one-half of the Atwater standard for protein. These men all remained healthy and vigorous in mind and body. Chittenden concluded, in his account published in 1904, that such diets were not only adequate but preferable because they put less strain on the kidney to cope with the excretion of both urea and the less soluble uric acid.

His findings stimulated an active debate among medical men. Most believed that Chittenden's findings were still too limited to recommend wholesale dietary changes. For example, the subjects in his study had not been subjected to sudden stresses or to periods of inadequate feeding in which they had to rely on reserves. Moreover, experiments with dogs kept on low-protein diets had revealed that although they remained healthy and in nitrogen balance for a time, they eventually weakened and died. Chittenden, however, followed up this line of work with dogs in his own laboratory and concluded that it was not lack of protein that was responsible for long-term problems with some diets but a lack of one or more unknown trace nutrients. This conclusion constituted one of the stimuli for the work that dominated nutritional studies for the next 40 years and revealed the existence of the vitamins.

Amino Acids in Nutrition

By 1905, another question gaining prominence was whether the proteins that had now been isolated from many foods could all be considered equivalent in nutritional value. It had long been known that gelatin, obtained by autoclaving bones, would not support growth in dogs, even though it had the same nitrogen content as ordinary tissue proteins. But because it displayed some physical differences, such as remaining soluble in boiling water, it had been set aside from the "protein" classification.

Advances in the study of proteins required a better knowledge of their composition. That they did not diffuse through fine-pored membranes showed them to be large molecules. But during digestion, their physical properties changed dramatically. With the isolation of the digestive agent "pepsin" from the stomach walls of slaughtered animals, and then of "trypsin" from pancreatic juice, the process could be studied in more detail.

As early as the 1860s, workers had been surprised to discover the presence of "leucine" and "tyrosine" in digests of protein with pancreatic juice. These two compounds were already well known. They were recoverable from the product of boiling proteins with sulfuric acid and had been shown to be "amino acids" – meaning that they contained both an acid group and a basic one and were relatively small molecules, each with less than 25 atoms. However, the procedure yielding them seemed so severe as to have no relation to the mild conditions of the digestive system, and it was thought that the compounds might well have been produced by the hot and strong acid conditions.

Gradually, by in vitro digestion, and milder acid or alkali refluxing of proteins, a whole range of amino acids were recovered, and crude methods were developed to analyze the quantities of each that were present. Also, evidence accumulated that the compounds actually absorbed through the gut wall after digestion were simple amino acids. Early investigators had felt it unlikely that nature would employ such a system because it seemed extremely wasteful to break proteins down, only to rebuild the same compounds within the animal. Or were they the same compounds?

Some of the first experiments comparing the nutritional values of different proteins were carried out by Lafayette Mendel (from Chittenden's group) and the plant chemist Thomas Osborne. They found that young rats would grow if given a diet of fat, carbohydrates, minerals, crude vitamin concentrates, and purified casein (a milk protein). However, with zein (a protein from corn) as the protein source, the rats did not grow unless the diet was fortified with *both* lysine and tryptophan. Chemical analysis had already indicated that zein lacked these two amino acids, and thus these two were characterized as "essential amino acids," meaning that they were essential or indispensable in the diet of growing rats. The results also indicated that animals used amino acids to build their own body proteins.

After 20 years of further experiments of this kind, W. C. Rose and his colleagues were able to obtain good growth in rats with diets containing *no* protein, but just a mixture of amino acids in its place. Table IV.C.2.1 summarizes their findings about the 20 amino acids present in animal proteins, some of which were indispensable ("essential") and some of which the rat could make for itself ("nonessential") if they were not supplied in its diet. Further work led to the development of values for the quantity of each indispensable amino acid that rats required for optimal growth.

Another group of studies compared the relative values of different protein sources (or of mixtures) for the support of growth in rats. The mixed proteins from individual vegetable foods (grains, beans, and so forth) all supported some growth, but not to quite the same extent as the mixed proteins in milk, meat, or eggs. The first limiting amino acid (meaning that this was the amino acid that increased growth when added as a single supplement) in most grains was lysine. This was to be expected in view of the growing rat's known requirement for lysine and the low analytical value of lysine in grains. The corresponding first limiting amino acid in most beans and peas was found to be methionine. Because the two classes of materials had different deficiencies, one would expect a mixture of grains and legumes to support better growth in rats, and this has been confirmed.

Table IV.C.2.1. *Reproduction of the final summary of the rat's requirements for amino acids, as determined by Rose and his colleagues in 1948*

Classification of amino acids with respect to their growth effects in the rat	
Essential	Nonessential
Lysine	Glycine
Tryptophan	Alanine
Histidine	Serine
Phenylalanine	Cystine*
Leucine	Tyrosine[†]
Isoleucine	Aspartic acid
Threonine	Glutamic acid[‡]
Methionine	Proline[‡]
Valine	Hydroxyproline
Arginine[§]	Citrulline

*Cystine can replace about one-sixth of the methionine requirement, but has no growth effect in the *absence* of methionine.

[†]Tyrosine can replace about one-half of the phenylalanine requirement, but has no growth effect in the *absence* of phenylalanine.

[‡]Glutamic acid and proline can serve individually as rather ineffective substitutes for arginine in the diet. This property is not shared by hydroxyproline.

[§]Arginine can be synthesized by the rat, but not at a sufficiently rapid rate to meet the demands of *maximum* growth. Its classification, therefore, as essential or nonessential is purely a matter of definition.

Source: Rose, Oesterling, and Womack (1948). Reprinted in Carpenter 1994, p. 133.

Human Requirements

Rats, however, although useful as models, differ from humans (even in this context) in important ways. Humans spend most of their lives as adults, not growing at all but needing protein just for "maintenance." And in childhood, human growth is extremely slow compared to the growth of rats. Thus, we take something like six months to double our birth weight, which a young rat does in a few days. And at six months, the rat is fully matured, yet the child is still only one-tenth of its mature size. Moreover, although the tissue proteins of rats and humans are similar, hair protein is very different, and the rat has to synthesize proportionally more.

It was necessary, therefore, to discover whether humans needed to be supplied with the same essential amino acids as those needed by rats. But because it was neither practical (nor ethical) to keep young children on what might be inadequate experimental diets for long periods in order to compare their growth rates, the normal method of experimentation was to feed adult volunteers for periods of two weeks or so on diets in which there were mixtures of amino acids in place of protein.

If an essential amino acid were missing, the subject would, within a very few days, show a negative nitrogen balance, meaning that the amount of combined nitrogen found in urine and feces, plus the smaller estimated quantity rubbed off in skin and hair losses, had exceeded the daily nitrogen intake. Fortunately, no harm seems to come to humans in negative balance for a short period, and bodily reserves refill rapidly on resumption of a complete diet.

The first major finding from this work was that essential and nonessential amino acid needs are the same for humans as for the young rat. However, researchers were surprised to discover how low the quantitative need for each essential amino acid appeared to be in order to maintain nitrogen balance. In fact, the combined total of essential amino acids came to only 16 percent of the total protein requirement, even though they make up about 45 percent of our body proteins. Thus, it seemed that almost any mixture of foods that provided at least the minimum amount of total protein needed would automatically meet adult needs for each essential amino acid. For young children, however, it was felt safer to set a higher standard for amino acids, corresponding more or less to the composition of the proteins in breast milk. For older children, a compromise was adopted in official recommendations, with a pattern midway between that found to be needed for nitrogen balance in adults and that in human milk. These standards are summarized in Table IV.C.2.2.

There have been recent criticisms of the practice of basing standards solely on short-term nitrogen balance experiments, with V. R. Young (1986) and colleagues (1988, 1989) at the Massachusetts Institute of Technology (M.I.T.) arguing that the method itself has sources of error. These researchers have carried out sophisticated studies using diets based on amino acids, with a single essential amino acid labeled with an isotope so that its metabolism can be followed. They concluded that the levels at which the essential amino acids are required, in relation to total protein needs, are quite similar to the levels in which they occur in the body. Even after subjects have had time to adjust to lower intakes, the rate of renewal of body tissues is reduced, which may have adverse effects in a time of stress.

As Atwater suggested over a century ago, it is possible that intakes higher than those needed for nitrogen balance could confer some more subtle long-term benefits. However, there are as yet no studies of peoples living for long periods on diets borderline in protein but well served with all other nutrients that would clarify the situation. And in any event, it seems clear that even the higher amino acid levels proposed by the M.I.T. group are being fulfilled by the diets of most people, at least in the developed countries.

The Protein Contribution of Different Foods

The obvious way to express the level of protein in a food is as a percentage of the weight, like "g per 100g." But such a measurement can be deceptive. For example, it would show ordinary white bread to have nearly 3 times the protein content of cow's milk because milk is 90 percent water, whereas bread is only about 34 percent water. Alternatively, one could compare the amounts of protein in equal weights of dry matter, but the common nutritional value of the great majority of the dry matter is its contribution of usable energy, whether from carbohydrate, fat, or protein. Thus, nutritionists have found it useful to compare the protein concentration of different foods in relation to their total calorie values. This could be expressed as "g per 100 kcalories," but it is easier (as protein itself has an average energy value of 4kcal/g) to express the concentration as "protein calories as a percent of total calories" (PCals%).

Although most of the time people have an instinct to eat enough food to meet their energy needs, there is a question of whether this quantity will also include enough protein.

Returning to the comparison of bread and milk, we can make the following comparisons:

	Protein (g)	Energy (kcal)	PCals%
1 slice white bread (32 g)	3	96	12.5
1 cup whole milk (244 g)	8	150	21.3
1 cup skim milk (245 g)	8	86	37.2

In terms of PCals%, milk is richer in protein than bread, meaning that to get the same quantity of protein from bread as from a cup of milk, one would have to consume more total calories. Similarly, it can also be seen that although a cup of whole milk and one of skim milk (with the cream removed) have the same protein content, the PCals% values are very different, with the value for the skim milk being higher. There are equally large differences between different meat preparations, as can be seen in the comparison of a pork chop and a chicken breast:

Table IV.C.2.2. *The World Health Organization (1985) estimates of human requirements for protein and selected amino acids, by age*

	Protein (g/kg body weight)	Lysine (mg/g protein)	Methionine + cystine (mg/g protein)
Infant			
(3–4 months)	1.47	103	58
Child (2 years)	1.15	64	27
School child			
(10–12 years)	1.00	44–60	27
Adult	0.88	12	22

Table IV.C.2.3. *The typical protein concentrations of a variety of foods (edible portions only) expressed as "protein calories as a percentage of total calories" (PCals%)*

Animal foods		Grain products	
Poached cod	86	Oatmeal	14.5
Roast chicken breast		Whole wheat bread	13.5
without skin	72	White bread	12.5
Stewed rabbit	68	Sweet corn	12
Broiled salmon	50	Brown rice	11
Skim milk	37	Cornmeal	10
Boiled egg	32	White rice	9
Cheddar cheese	25	Sorghum flour	8.5
Fried pork chop	25	Corn flakes, packaged	7.5
Salami (beef and pork)	22		
Whole milk	21	**Roots, fruits, etc.**	
Liver sausage	17	Baked potato	10
		French fries	5
Legumes		Banana	5
Tofu (from soy)	43	Sweet potato	4
Green peas	27	Plantain	3
Black beans	26	Cassava flour	1
Kidney beans	25	Fats and sugars	0
Chickpeas	21		

	Protein (g)	Energy (kcal)	PCals%
Pan-fried pork chop (89 g)	21	334	25
Roasted chicken breast			
without skin (86 g)	27	142	72

What this shows is that in a fried pork chop, for every 1 g protein (that is, 4 kcal) there are, in addition, 12 kcal from fat, whereas in the roasted chicken breast, 1 g protein is accompanied by only 1.6 kcal from fat. The PCals percentage values for a range of foods are set out in Table IV.C.2.3. These are "average" or "typical" values. Some animal carcasses are fatter than others, and the composition of plant foods can change significantly according to the environment in which the plants are grown, as well as the stage of harvesting. Wheats also differ significantly, with some strains being selected for high or low protein content according to the use for which the flour is marketed.

It is true that animal-product foods are generally higher in protein than plant products and also that people in the more affluent "Westernized" countries eat higher levels of animal products. However, the total protein intake in affluent cultures is not that much larger. The offsetting factor in these cultures is the higher consumption of sugars, fats, and alcoholic beverages, all of which contribute calories but no protein. Moreover, in many developing countries, some kind of beans forms a regular part of the day's food, and they are a rich source of protein. Thus, calculations commonly indicate that diets in both rich and poor countries have mostly between 10.5 and 12.5 percent of their total calories in the form of protein.

The Food and Agriculture Organization of the United Nations (FAO) publishes estimates of the daily food supplies per head that are available in different countries. Here are three examples:

	Total kcal	Protein (g)		% of protein from animals	PCals%	Fat (g)	Sugars (g)
		Veg.	Animal				
U.S.A.	3640	37	72	66	12.0	164	579
Romania	3330	58	44	43	12.3	95	295
Ghana	2200	33	13	28	8.4	43	64

In this comparison, based on recent data, we see that in Romania, a relatively poor European country, the average individual took in only about 60 percent as much animal protein as a counterpart in the United States, but the total protein supply was almost identical. This was because the Romanians ate much less fat and sugar and received correspondingly more calories from grains, which generally have 10 to 13 PCals%. This offsetting, however, breaks down when the staple energy food is not a grain but a starchy root with only 1–3 PCals%, as in West Africa, where cassava is a common staple. The data for Ghana illustrate this. Despite the low fat and sugar intakes, there is still only an overall 8.4 PCals% in the food supply estimated to be available for the average person. Of course, the first "red light" that we see upon looking at the data is the low total calorie intake, which is only 60 percent of the corresponding U.S. value. Not all the U.S. foods are actually consumed of course: There is a great deal of waste, with fat trimmed off meat and stale food thrown out. Conversely, there may be some unrecorded food sources in Ghana. But it is a general finding that, even if there is a good supply of starchy roots, their sheer bulkiness makes it difficult to consume enough to meet energy requirements, particularly for young children, so that neither energy nor protein needs are fully met.

Not surprisingly, West Africa is also the part of the world where the disease kwashiorkor was first studied. It strikes children 1 to 3 years old who appear bloated, though their muscles actually are shrunken. They often have ulcerated and peeling skin and are utterly miserable. Unless treated, they are likely to die. The condition is now thought to be due to a combination of undernutrition (in both protein and energy) with the stress of infections. Recovery can be rapid if the victims are given concentrated food, by stomach tube at first, if necessary. The food mix does not need to be high in protein; mixes with as little as 5 PCals% have proven successful.

Except for children subsisting on bulky and very low protein staples, there seems to be no problem of protein deficiency for people in any culture who can afford to satisfy their calorie needs, unless they are consuming extremely atypical diets. The Recommended Dietary Allowances (RDAs) for protein in the United States are summarized here for three groups, together with the estimated energy needs of individuals in those groups if moderately active:

Population group	Assumed bodyweight (kg)	Protein RDA (g)	Energy needs (kcal)	PCals% required
Children, ages 1–3	13	16	1,300	4.9
Women, ages 25–50	63	50	2,200	9.1
Men, ages 25–50	79	63	2,900	8.7

It is interesting to note that when one calculates the proportions of protein required (PCals%) for each class, the results are unexpected. Traditionally, wives have thought that men, as the "breadwinners" of the family, needed most of the meat, and children at least some extra dairy protein, but as can be seen, it is actually women who are estimated to need the highest proportion of protein in their diet. And for people involved in greater levels of physical activity, all the evidence indicates that their calorie needs increase greatly but not their protein needs, so that the resulting PCals% of their needs is decreased. Put another way, the extra food they need to meet their needs can be of quite low protein content. Similarly, although the protein needs per kg body weight of a 1- to 3-year-old child are 50 percent greater than for an adult, its energy requirement per kg is nearly 200 percent higher so that, once again, the PCals% of its needs are lower.

Returning to the estimated average food supplies in Ghana, it can be seen that the mix is just about at the lower limit for protein. However, the RDA for protein, as for all other nutrients except energy, does include a margin of safety, and the level of physical activity is always higher in developing countries where there is less mechanical transport.

For countries like the United States or Romania, the protein supplies are clearly well above the standard requirement levels. Thus, it follows that a high intake of meat cannot be justified because of the protein that it contributes. In fact, a major concern of late has been that the protein intake of affluent individuals may be undesirably high. Some have problems because their kidneys are inefficient in excreting the urea resulting from protein metabolism. And, even in healthy people, high-protein diets cause increasing urinary losses of calcium. Certainly, this effect is undesirable in a society whose growing percentages of older people contain more and more individuals whose bones have been weakened because of the loss of a considerable proportion of their mineral substance (mostly calcium phosphate). It is now recommended that we not consume more than twice our RDA for protein. This would mean an upper level of 100 g protein for a woman weighing 63 kg (139 lb.).

Kenneth J. Carpenter

Bibliography

Carpenter, K. J. 1994. *Protein and energy: A study of changing ideas in nutrition.* New York.

National Research Council. 1989. *Recommended Dietary Allowances,* Tenth edition. Washington, D.C.

Porter, J. G. W. and B. A. Rolls, eds. 1973. *Proteins in human nutrition.* London.

Rose, W. C., M. J. Oesterling, and M. Womack. 1948. Comparative growth on diets containing ten and nineteen amino acids, with further observations upon the role of glutonic and aspartic acid. *Journal of Biological Chemistry* 176: 753–62.

Young, V. R. 1986. Nutritional balance studies: Indicators of human requirement or of adaptive mechanisms. *Journal of Nutrition* 116: 700–3.

Young, V. R., D. M. Bier, and P. L. Pellet. 1989. A theoretical basis for increasing current estimates of the amino acid requirements in adult man, with experimental support. *American Journal of Clinical Nutrition* 50: 80–92.

Young, V. R., and P. L. Pellet. 1988. How to evaluate dietary protein. In *Milk proteins: Nutritional, clinical, functional, and technological aspects,* ed. C. A. Barth and E. Sehlimmer, 7–36. New York.

World Health Organization. 1985 *Energy and protein requirements.* Technical Report Series no. 724. Geneva.

IV.C.3 ❧ Energy and Protein Metabolism

In conventional scientific usage, when the word metabolism is joined with energy, it takes on a somewhat different meaning than when it is joined with protein. The latter - protein metabolism - usually includes consideration of the biochemical pathways of amino acids, the building blocks of protein, whereas energy metabolism is frequently assumed to include only the specific role of energy without consideration, in any detailed way, of the pathways involved in the breakdown and synthesis of the various carbohydrates and lipids that supply food energy.

In this chapter, the major thrust concerned with energy is an emphasis on historical considerations of understanding and meeting human food energy needs. In the case of protein, the role of amino acids in generating energy, protein quality (including digestibility), and human protein requirements will be given emphasis. Finally, there is some discussion of protein–energy relationships, the problems connected with an excess and a deficit of food energy in the diet, and protein–energy malnutrition.

Food Energy

The most pressing problem for humans throughout their history has been the basic one of securing food to satisfy hunger and food-energy needs. But the fact that the human population in different parts of the world (despite subsisting on different diets), seemed before about 1900 to experience approximately the same level of health had led some physiologists to believe that all foods were rather similar (McCollum 1957). In fact, this view was rooted in the ancient "many foods–single aliment" concept of Hippocrates and Galen. By the turn of the twentieth century, however, views were rapidly changing, and although knowledge of the specialized roles of amino acids, vitamins, and minerals was hazy and often contradictory, proteins, fats, and carbohydrates (starches and sugars) could be distinguished and analyzed in foods and diets. Thus, with the advances in food analysis and refinements of nutritional needs the "many foods–single aliment" concept was no longer tenable.

Heat and Life

Because the human body became cold after death, it was not surprising that some mechanism of heat production came to be considered synonymous with life at an early stage in human history. Hippocrates (born 460 B.C.) noted in one of his aphorisms:

> Growing bodies have the most innate heat; they therefore require the most food for otherwise their bodies are wasted. In old people the heat is feeble and they require little fuel, as it were, to the flame, for it would be extinguished by much. (Lusk 1933: 8)

The Greeks explained the mechanisms of health and illness in terms of the four "humors" in the body. When the body was in health, these humors were in balance, whereas excess or deficiency caused illness. Special foods or drugs could restore the proper balance and, hence, health. It was also observed from the earliest times that when an adult partook of a great deal of food, he or she did not necessarily gain in weight. Hippocrates believed this was due to a constant loss of insensible perspiration and the elimination of heat, which he conceived to be a fine form of matter.

Half a millennium later, Galen (130-200 A.D.) was more specific than Hippocrates in drawing a direct analogy between flame and innate heat, writing that "[t]he blood is like the oil [of a lamp], the heart is like the wick and the breathing lungs an instrument which conveys external motion" (Lusk 1933: 12).

The Middle Ages saw few developments in the area of nutrition, but during the Renaissance, Leonardo da Vinci (1452-1519) again took up the analogy of a flame to refer to life by stating that "where there is life there is heat" and "where flame cannot live no animal can sustain its existence" (Lusk 1933: 18). This remark was later echoed by Robert Boyle in 1660, who wrote that "neither a flame nor an animal can live in a vacuum" (Lusk 1933: 25). A contemporary of Boyle, John Mayow (born 1643), who died at the age of 36, appeared to have an understanding of respiration and the role of blood (that was only rediscovered a century later) when he wrote:

> Respiration consists furthermore in the separation of the air by the lungs, and the intermixture with the blood mass of certain particles absolutely necessary to animal life, and the loss by the inspired air of some of its elasticity. The particles of the air absorbed during respiration are designed to convert the black or venous blood into the red or arterial. (Lusk 1933: 35)

Development of Scientific Concepts

Fuel was long understood as burning to produce heat or power, but an understanding of the importance of air in supporting combustion and respiration had to await identification of the gases. Later, when burning was recognized as the combining of fuel with oxygen and the giving off of carbon dioxide and heat, the respiration of animals and humans was accepted as a special case of combustion. Although many still believed that a "vital" or God-given force controlled all life processes, quantitative relationships began to be developed between individual foods and their use in the body to produce predictable amounts of heat.

The concept of heat remained central to the explanatory framework of traditional physiology. Every part of the body had its own innate heat, and the heat in the extremities was continuously being dissipated into the surrounding environment. This heat had to be replenished from some source in the body, which was identified as the heart, and the heat, together with the beating of the heart, generated the "vital spirit" out of air and blood. The vital spirit was, in turn, carried by activated arterial blood.

This view was replaced following the discovery of circulation by William Harvey in 1628. In the process of searching for the origin of body heat, later investigators tried to decide whether the heartbeat was involved with producing it or whether the motion of the blood created friction, and therefore heat, as it passed through the vessels of the body. The lungs were considered by Harvey to represent an important heat-dissipating mechanism that prevented the cardiac generation of heat from exceeding the body's tolerance.

The Discovery of the Gases

Physiology prospered in the early years of the eighteenth century but during its latter part lost prominence to chemistry. By then, chemists had developed analytical methods to at least begin to determine the ultimate constituents of body fluids and tissues (Kinney 1988).

With the work of Joseph Priestley (1733-1804) oxygen was discovered (1774).

Antoine Laurent Lavoisier, in turn, recognized that carbon dioxide was a compound of carbon and oxygen and further demonstrated that the respiration of animals involved CO_2. A table from the 1790 English translation of his text *Traité élémentaire de chimie* indicates that the names oxygen, hydrogen and azote (nitrogen) were replacing several older terms for the gases. By use of an ice calorimeter (a device whereby heat produced from a living animal could be estimated from the amount of ice that was melted), Lavoisier was able to demonstrate that respiration was very slow combustion and that predicted heat agreed well with that which was measured.

Nutritional Experimentation

In the overlapping areas of protein and energy metabolism, French physiologist Jean-Baptiste Boussingault (1802–87), in 1844, performed a series of experiments using a cow fed only foods relatively low in protein (potatoes and beets) to prove that the manufacture of tissue protein did not require the incorporation of nitrogen from the air. A few years later, Carl von Voit and T. L. Bischoff (1860) in Germany confirmed that all the nitrogen in the body could come from the foods eaten and that the condition of nitrogen equilibrium or nitrogen balance could be established when the level of nitrogen intake was held constant. A major controversy developed during this period over the production of animal fat. Justus von Liebig maintained that the formation of fat from sugar was possible in the animal body, whereas other chemists, following the lead of Jean-Baptiste Dumas, maintained that fat in food was the only source of body fat. Boussingault, however, in 1845 proved conclusively that animals could produce fat from carbohydrates (McCollum 1957).

A series of studies that significantly linked protein and energy metabolism were those undertaken by Edward Smith in England in 1857. They demonstrated the effects of different conditions of life on the magnitude of energy requirements of human subjects. His major observation was that there was comparatively little change in the amount of urea (the major protein metabolite) voided during wide variations in the amount of labor performed, whereas the carbon dioxide produced increased in proportion to the amount of exercise. He devised a treadmill experiment with human subjects that provided strong evidence that the energy for muscular work could not have been derived from muscle degradation and almost conclusive evidence that the muscles were deriving energy from nonnitrogenous food. Unfortunately, the high authority of Liebig, who thought energy was derived from muscle degradation, prevented Smith's studies from securing the attention they deserved.

In 1866, however, Adolf Fick and Johannes Wislicenus reported their famous mountain-climbing experiment of the previous year, using themselves as subjects, to confirm Smith's tread-mill studies and also to put Liebig's theory of muscular work to a crucial test. They abstained from protein food for some 17 hours before beginning the ascent of the Faulhorn, a peak in Switzerland with an altitude of 1,656 meters

(5,433 feet). The climb to the summit required 6 hours, and during this time and for another 7 hours afterward, they consumed only carbohydrates and fats. Throughout they collected their urine, which was later analyzed for nitrogen content. During the 13-hour period, Fick produced 5.74 grams of urinary nitrogen and Wislicenus 5.54 grams. They reported:

> We can assert from our own experience in the mountain ascent, that in spite of the amount of work and abstinence for 31 hours from albuminous food, neither of us felt the least exhausted. This could hardly have been the case if our muscular force had not been sustained by the non-nitrogenous food in which we partook. (McCollum 1957: 126)

In the same year, E. Frankland (1866) pointed out that these results could be interpreted only by taking into account the amount of energy evolved in the combustion of a unit of muscle substance and by considering the work equivalent of this energy. In addition, he showed that the energy that the body derived from protein was equal to the difference between the total heat of combustion less the heat of combustion of urea, the major substance whereby the nitrogen in protein foods was eliminated. Frankland thus confirmed the conclusions already reached by Smith and by Fick and Wislicenus that muscles work at the expense of energy derived from the oxidation of the nonnitrogenous fats and carbohydrates (McCollum 1957).

The development of the concepts of intermediary metabolism of foodstuffs – that is, the step-by-step conversion of materials to the ultimate products, water and carbon dioxide (CO_2), with the liberation of energy – was a slow intellectual process and had to await the accretion of knowledge of organic chemistry and, above all, the realization of the catalytic nature of the enzymes and their infinite variety (Levine 1978).

Respiration Chambers and Calorimetry

Voit and M. Pettenkofer were leaders in the new studies of respiration and energy balance, at first using small chambers for animals. A much larger apparatus was then constructed in which both the total carbon excretion (breath, urine, and feces) could be measured and the quantity of individual foods actually burned in the human body could be determined. This was a remarkable technological achievement and a significant scientific advance. On the death of Pettenkofer in 1901, Voit (quoted in Kinney 1988) wrote:

> Imagine our sensations as the picture of the remarkable process of the metabolism unrolled before our eyes and the mass of new facts became known to us. We found that in starvation protein and fat alone were burned, that during work more fat was burned and that less

fat was consumed during rest, especially during sleep; that the carnivorous dog could maintain himself upon an exclusive protein diet, and if to such a protein diet fat were added, the fat was almost always entirely deposited in the body; that carbohydrates, on the contrary, were burned no matter how much was given and that they, like the fat of the food, protected the body from fat loss, although more carbohydrates than fat had to be given to effect this purpose; that the metabolism in the body was not proportional to the combustibility of the substances outside the body, but the protein which burns with difficulty outside, metabolizes with the greatest ease, then carbohydrates, while fat, which readily burns outside, is the most difficult to combust in the organism (Kinney 1988: 524).

Max Rubner (1854–1932), who was trained in the laboratories of Voit, determined standard food energy (caloric) values for the major foodstuffs. He continued to demonstrate, until well into the twentieth century, that the animal body followed the law of the conservation of energy.

W. O. Atwater (1844–1907), an American who had studied under Voit in Germany, returned to the United States to work with a physicist at Wesleyan University in developing a large calorimeter capable of measuring precisely the amount of heat given off by a person living in it.[1] This calorimeter confirmed the earlier experimentation of Voit, Pettenkofer, and Rubner and demonstrated that the energy expended by a person in doing any work, such as static bicycle riding, was equal to the heat released by the metabolism of food in the body. The physiologist F. G. Benedict extended Atwater's work by constructing special equipment at the Carnegie Institute in Boston for the simultaneous measurement of gaseous metabolism and heat production. An example from one of their studies is shown in Table IV.C.3.1. On a daily basis, the difference between heat determined and heat estimated was only –1.6 percent. The precision obtained in these experiments was remarkable and was obtained without computer assistance!

The finding from the calorimeter work that received the most attention in Atwater's lifetime concerned alcohol. In 1899 he reported that if a subject drank alcohol in small portions over the course of the day, it was almost fully oxidized and replaced the food energy equivalent of either fat or carbohydrate. At this level, therefore, it acted as a food (Atwater and Benedict 1899). This finding was advertised by the liquor trade, and Atwater was subsequently attacked by temperance advocates as a disgrace to his church and to his profession (Pauly 1990). He defended himself vigorously and, while agreeing that abstinence was certainly the safest way to avoid addiction, argued nevertheless that for most people,

Table IV.C.3.1. *Energy exchange in humans: An example from Atwater and Benedict*

		Total: 4 days	Daily average
a.	Heat of combustion of food eaten	9848	2462
b.	Heat of combustion of feces	304	76
c.	Heat of combustion of urine	538	135
m.	Heat of combustion of alcohol eliminated	84	21
d.	Estimated heat of combustion of protein gained (+) or lost (–)	–277	–69
e.	Estimated heat of combustion of fat gained (+) or lost (–)	–539	–135
f.	Estimated energy of material oxidized in the body a – (b + c + m + d + e)	9738	2434
g.	Heat determined	9576	2394
h.	Heat determined greater (+) or less (–) than estimated (f – g)	–162	–40
i.	Heat determined greater (+) or less (–) than estimated (h + f) (percent)	–	–1.6

Source: Atwater and Benedict (1899).

moderate consumption was possible and seemed to improve their well-being rather than damage it (Carpenter 1994b). (We have heard recent echoes of this debate following recommendations in the Dietary Guidelines for the United States concerning alcohol consumption.)

Further related studies undertaken by Atwater (1899) and his associates (Atwater and Bryant 1900), which overlapped those of Rubner, made determinations of the fuel value of foods by the use of a bomb calorimeter and by comparing those determinations with the heat produced in the body. A bomb calorimeter permits the complete combustion of the sample in the presence of oxygen under pressure, with the direct determination of the heat produced by measurement of the temperature rise in the surrounding water. A diagram of Atwater's bomb calorimeter is shown in Figure IV.C.3.1.

It was found that the total (gross) energy produced by combustion of food with oxygen in a bomb calorimeter was greater than the metabolizable energy of the same food when utilized in the body. However, when account was taken of digestibility (that is, not all the food consumed was absorbed into the body) and of the energy lost in the urine (that is, the urea produced from protein), then there was essential agreement. Fuel values of foods were compared with their analytical composition, and thus were born the 4:9:4 Atwater factors, where the metabolizable energy of foods, in kilocalories per gram, could be readily calculated from the contents of carbohydrate, fat, and protein. These concepts were reported, essentially in their present form, in the texts of R. Hutchison (1903) and H. C. Sherman (1914).

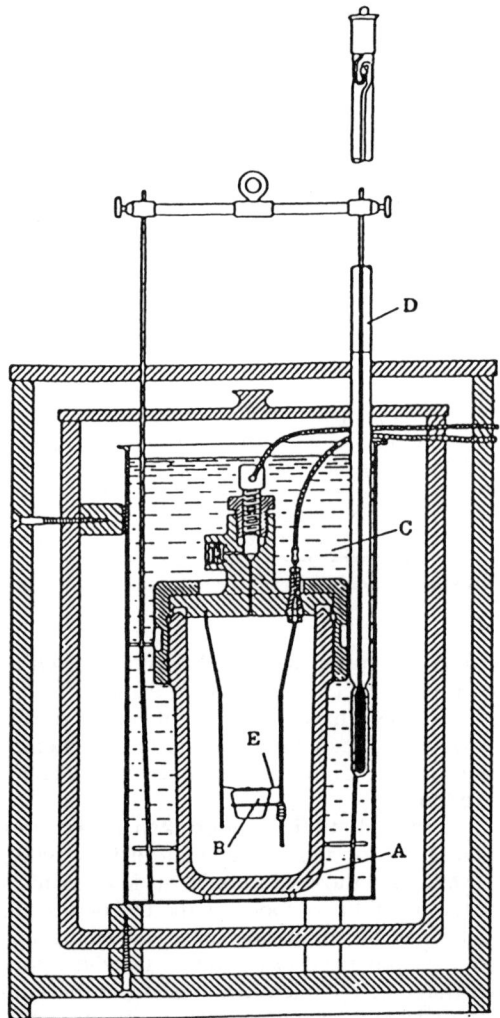

Figure IV.C.3.1. The Atwater bomb calorimeter: (A) heavy steel bomb filled with oxygen under pressure; (B) capsule inside bomb containing weighted sample; (C) weighed amount of water at known initial temperature; (D) thermometer of high accuracy; (E) electric ignition wire. (From Sherman 1952.)

The unit used today for food energy, deriving from these and other basic physical studies, is the kilocalorie (kcal). This is the amount of heat necessary to raise 1 kilogram of water from 15° to 16° Celsius. The international unit of energy is the more scientifically fundamental joule (J). Although not greatly used in the United States in a nutritional context, the joule is widely employed in Europe. To convert from kilocalories to kilojoules (kJ), the rounded value 4.2 may be used (1 kcal = 4.184 kJ). The classical Atwater metabolizable energy conversion factors of 4 kcal/gram (g) of food protein and carbohydrate and 9 kcal/g of food fat have been verified and are adequate for computa-

tion of the energy content of customary diets (Miles, Webb, and Bodwell 1986). Alcohol (ethanol) has a computed food energy value of 7 kcal/g or 5,600 kcal/liter (L). It should be noted that in the original Atwater calculations, carbohydrate was measured by difference (that is, only protein, fat, and minerals were determined in the food, and the residue after allowing for water content was considered to be mainly carbohydrate). This, therefore, included fiber.

The Development of Modern Nutritional Science

Although the complex details of intermediary metabolism remained to be discovered as the twentieth century began, the basic framework of the modern science of nutrition had been laid down. Free sugars and their polymers furnished glucose for bodily functions, including muscular work: Excess carbohydrate could be stored as glycogen and fats, thus providing a fuel reserve that could furnish energy during periods of fasting. The views of Liebig concerning heat and work were recognized as mistaken by Hutchison in his text of 1903:

> We now know that bodily heat is not a thing apart and requiring to be provided for by itself, but that it is an inevitable accompaniment of cell life. Life and heat are inseparable, and in fulfilling its other function in the body a cell cannot help producing heat also (Hutchison 1903: 3).

Hutchison went on to indicate that as far as the cells of the body were concerned, it was a matter of indifference whether carbohydrate, protein, or fat were the original sources of the food energy. In strict energy terms this remains true, although the specific role of the energy sources, especially fat, in relation to chronic disease risk is now central to dietary guidance.

Lusk, author of several monographs and texts on nutrition (Lusk 1914, 1928, and 1933), and yet another who trained with Voit in Germany, dedicated the first edition of his monograph *The Elements of the Science of Nutrition* to his mentor in 1906. That an essentially modern view of nutrition had developed by this time can be seen from Lusk's writing (1914: 4):

> The workshops of life require fuel to maintain them and a necessary function of nutrition is to furnish fuel to the organism so that the motions of life continue. Furthermore the workshops of life are in a constant state of partial breaking down and materials must be furnished to repair worn out parts. In the fuel factor and the repair factor lie the essence of the science of nutrition.

Lusk (1914) also held modern views on the social aspects of nutrition, as is indicated in his lecture to the New York Academy of Medicine, which advocated nutritious school meals, family nutrition education, and national nutritional labeling of foods.

Another major activity in the early years of the twentieth century became the determination of the basal metabolic rate (BMR) in many subjects together with the development of prediction procedures for estimating BMR from body weight or from body surface area (Harris and Benedict 1919). The BMR is the rate of heat production, measured directly or indirectly, when the subject is at rest and has not eaten for several hours. The normal range for large populations was thought to be relatively narrow. Variations in the BMR of supposedly normal individuals were often attributed to carelessness in experimental procedure, rather than to the existence of real differences. The field of calorimetry became devoted mainly to examining abnormalities in BMR associated with various diseases, in particular, thyroid disease, diabetes, and the more common fevers.

Equipment for determining BMR was standard in hospital laboratories until about 1950, at which time new chemical methods for measuring materials in the urine and blood related to thyroid metabolism caused hospitals to abandon the measurement and, consequently, to terminate the last remaining quantitative approach to energy metabolism in patients. In the hospital environment, research on energy expenditure in surgical patients returned under the leadership of Kinney (1988), who utilized a head canopy system that was acceptable to acutely ill patients and still permitted medical care as required.

There has been an enormous resurgence of interest in energy balance studies in recent years as a result of the growing concern over the hazards of obesity and the realization that we still have much to learn about energy metabolism and the control of energy balance.

World Supply of Food Energy

The energy, fat, and protein supply in rich and poor countries is shown in Table IV.C.3.2. Carbohydrate is the major source of food energy in both industrialized (52 percent) and developing (70 percent) countries. For the rich industrialized countries, the fat proportion (35 percent) is next in importance, but this proportion is much lower (20 percent) in developing countries. Whereas the proportion of the food energy as protein (PCal percent) is similar (12 percent to 10 percent) in both sets of countries, the proportion of that protein originating from animal sources differs greatly and is very much lower in developing countries, whose people receive considerably more of their protein from cereals.

The main dietary carbohydrates are shown in Table IV.C.3.3. Carbohydrates produce energy for metabolism through their initial conversion to acetyl coenzyme A (acetyl CoA), which is also the central point in the metabolism of protein and lipids for energy (Figure IV.C.3.2). Because storage fats can be synthesized from acetyl CoA, there is some degree of interconversion of the macronutrients, and we have the biochemical explanation of the fat synthesis controversy that taxed the early physiological chemists. The reverse conversion cannot occur to any significant degree, and fat is not a source of carbohydrate and protein.

Table IV.C.3.2. *Food availability data for industrialized and developing countries. Data for 1994*

	Industrialized countries	Developing countries
Food energy kcal/day	3356	2573
Total protein g/day	103.4	64.4
Animal protein g/day	62.2	17.1
Fat g/day	131.9	56.1
Derived data		
PCal%[1]	12.3	10.0
FCal%[2]	35.4	19.6
Animal protein % total protein	60.2	26.6
Cereal protein % total protein	24.3	53.3
Sugar as % total calories	9.5	5.9
Carbohydrates as % total calories	52.3	70.4

[1]Protein calories as percentage of total calories.

[2]Fat calories as percentage of total calories.

Source: FAOSTAT (1996).

Table IV.C.3.3. *The principal dietary carbohydrates*

Source	Maize, rice, wheat, potato	Cane and beet sugar	Milk
Polysaccharide	Starch	–	–
Disaccharide	Maltose	Sucrose	Lactose
Monosaccharide	Glucose	Fructose + Glucose	Galactose + Glucose

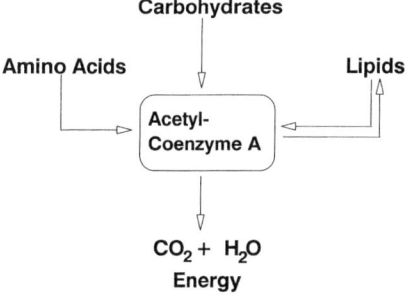

Figure IV.C.3.2. An overview of the combustion of fuels for energy. Acetyl coenzyme A is formed from carbohydrates, fats, and amino acids. Whatever the source, a large fraction of it is oxidized to CO_2 and H_2O, although any excess may be used to form lipids as an energy reserve.

Lipid is the overall chemical term used to describe the fats and oils; of these, the triglycerides (glycerol esterified with 3 fatty acid molecules) are the most abundant form in the diet. Although lipids differ widely in their compositions, the major pathways for their synthesis and breakdown begin and end with acetyl coenzyme A. Proteins are converted to acetyl CoA through a number of other intermediaries common mainly to the metabolism of carbohydrates. An outline of these latter pathways is shown in the section "Amino Acid Metabolism."

Thus, the energy of food is liberated by chemical changes, mostly oxidations, and is converted into mechanical work and heat. It is used to power the organic syntheses necessary for tissue maintenance and for growth in the young, and energy is also needed for the internal work of the body, the beating of the heart, the movements of the respiratory muscles, and the maintenance of the differences in the chemical contents of the cell fluids and the body fluids. Present descriptions of these processes include such terms as "biochemical energetics" and "free energy," but these modern explanations still conform to the broad descriptive strokes used in the early years of the century. The concept of burning fuels, not only for the energy with which to move but also for the energy necessary to build tissues and the like, is our rationalization of these processes (McGilvery 1979). Examples of the more important energy-producing and energy-consuming reactions in plants and animals include the following:

Energy-producing (exergonic)	Energy-consuming (endergonic)
Oxidation of fuels (carbohydrates, fats, and proteins)	Mechanical movement
Photosynthesis	Synthesis of cellular constituents
Fermentations	Creation of concentration gradients
	Storage of fuels

The sequence of reactions in the cell by which acetyl groups are oxidized is the "citric acid cycle" (or "Krebs cycle"), and for this discovery made in the 1930s, Hans Krebs (1900–81) shared the Nobel Prize in 1953. The reactions of the cycle function in sequence and as a unit to remove electrons from acetyl groups within the mitochondria and to feed the electrons into the oxidative phosphorylation pathway with the ultimate transfer to molecular oxygen. The overall result is the production of energy-rich adenosine triphosphate (ATP) from the oxidation of acetyl groups. A simple overview of energy production from the macronutrients is illustrated in Figure IV.C.3.2.

Human Energy Expenditure and Its Components

The main factors that influence daily energy need are basal metabolic rate (BMR) or resting energy expenditure (REE), physical activity, and thermogenesis. The last term may produce confusion for nonspecialists because the word means the generation of heat, and all energy expenditure generates heat. Thermogenesis is additional heat generation above that of REE and physical activity. All factors are affected directly or indirectly by individual variables, such as age, sex, body size, and, to a lesser degree, climate.

Resting Energy Expenditure

Unless the activity level is high, the most important single component of overall energy requirement is the energy expended at rest (REE). Customarily, basal metabolism, or basal metabolic rate (BMR), has been included as one of the factors affecting overall energy requirement. In practice, however, the chief interest is in resting energy expenditure (REE), namely, the energy expended by a person in a normal life situation while at rest and under conditions of thermal neutrality. The REE includes the thermic effect of meals and is an average minimal expenditure for the periods of the day and night when there is no exercise and no exposure to cold. REE is influenced by, among other things, age, height, weight, and sex. Although no equation for predicting REE can be completely accurate, several include age, sex, weight, and height and can predict REE with sufficient accuracy to serve as a first step in determining group or individual requirements.

An animal loses heat through the surface of the body, and the capacity for heat production is related to the volume of the body. It was therefore reasoned in the early 1800s that the larger the animal, the greater the heat production relative to the heat loss. Rubner later proposed that when metabolic rate was expressed in relation to the body surface area, the effect of body size disappeared. More elaborate studies were undertaken in the 1930s by Kleiber (see Kleiber 1961), who presented strong evidence against surface area being the determining factor of basal metabolism. Rather, he suggested that metabolism should be considered as a power function of body weight. Lacking a better definition of metabolic size, he proposed a three-fourths power of body weight as the best correlation between body size and resting metabolism. Later relationships were proposed with fat-free body mass, rather than with body weight alone. Lean body mass is a more recent term, and the concept has been further extended to the metabolizing body-cell mass by measuring total exchangeable potassium (Kinney 1988). Nevertheless, for humans, weight is the major variable and may, together with age and sex, be sufficient for predictive purposes.

The Food and Agriculture Organization of the United Nations (FAO) equations (FAO/WHO/UNU 1985) are shown in Table IV.C.3.4. The Harris-Benedict equations, which also include height, have been widely used in the United States for predicting the energy requirements of hospitalized patients; they are also shown in Table IV.C.3.4. In relation to the Harris-

Benedict equations, Sherman (1952) referred to their empirical nature and remarked that they "may be somewhat disconcerting at first glance. On working through the two formulas, however, it will be seen that there is . . . [no] great difference in the basal metabolisms of the sexes" (Sherman 1952: 161).

Thermogenesis

The thermic responses to food and to cold were formerly thought to be independent. N. J. Rothwell and M. J. Stock (1983) proposed that brown adipose tissue may perform a regulatory function in response to overfeeding. Rats could become obese on a palatable snack-food diet but maintained normal body weights when given less palatable rat chow. The brown adipose tissue of the rats with abnormal weight gain was markedly increased, suggesting that the overfeeding may have led to a substantial increase in dietary induced thermogenesis.

Diet-induced thermogenesis (DIT) is any change in energy expenditure induced by diet. This can be divided into obligatory and adaptive components. DIT reaches a maximum about 1 hour after the meal is consumed and virtually disappears 4 hours afterward. There have been reports of subjects who have apparently eaten excessively for long periods but who have gained much less weight than would have been predicted had they stored this excess as adipose tissue. The efficiency with which energy intake is utilized may vary greatly within the same individual and may explain the large variations noted in many experiments. Variations in thermogenesis have been an important research area in explaining some of the discrepancies between theory and actual observations of energy balance. Some researchers, however, now claim that the energy intake data in these observations may have been underestimated and that there may be no significant discrepancies (Heymsfield et al. 1995; Seale 1995).

Physical Activity

A dominant factor influencing overall energy needs is the proportion of time an individual devotes to moderate and heavy activities, in contrast to those that are light or sedentary. Little is known, however, about why apparently similar individuals differ in their selected

Table IV.C.3.4. *Equations for predicting basal metabolic rate from body weight (W) and age*

Equations from FAO				
Age range (years)	kcal/day	Correlation coefficient	MJ/day	Correlation coefficient
Males				
0–3	60.9 W – 54	0.97	0.255 W – 0.226	0.97
3–10	22.7 W + 495	0.86	0.0949 W + 2.07	0.86
10–18	17.5 W + 651	0.90	0.0732 W + 2.72	0.90
18–30	15.3 W + 679	0.65	0.0640 W + 2.84	0.65
30–60	11.6 W + 879	0.60	0.0584 W + 3.67	0.60
>60	13.5 W + 487	0.79	0.0565 W + 2.04	0.79
Females				
0–3	61.0 W – 51	0.97	0.255 W – 0.214	0.97
3–10	22.5 W + 499	0.85	0.0941 W + 2.09	0.85
10–18	12.2 W + 746	0.75	0.0510 W + 3.12	0.75
18–30	14.7 W + 496	0.72	0.0615 W + 2.08	0.72
30–60	8.7 W + 829	0.70	0.0364 W + 3.47	0.70
>60	10.5 W + 596	0.74	0.0439 W + 2.49	0.74

W = weight in kilograms.

Source: FAO/WHO/UNU (1985).

Harris-Benedict equations

For males: $H = 66.473 + 13.752\,W + 5.003\,S - 6.755\,A$
For women: $H = 65.501 + 9.563\,W + 1.850\,S - 4.676\,A$

H = Total heat production in 24 hours

W = Weight in kilograms

S = Stature in centimeters

A = Age in years

Source: Harris and Benedict (1919).

level of physical activity (Hill et al. 1995). Average physical activity in Western society is now considered to be undesirably low. Estimates of energy needs were originally based on physical activity associated with different occupations, but occupational needs have declined significantly in recent years with the introduction of labor-saving machinery and devices. Simultaneously, there has been an increase in many discretionary activities, resulting in great variability among individuals. The widespread adoption of jogging and other forms of fitness activities are obvious examples. Thus, the traditional specification of energy needs based on occupation is no longer adequate.

Three categories of discretionary activity that affect energy needs have been recognized (FAO/ WHO/UNU 1985): optional household activities, which include working in the garden or repairing and improving the home; socially desirable activities, which are especially important contributors to the energy needs of children, who require additional energy to explore their surroundings, to learn, and to adjust their behavior in order to relate to other children; and physical fitness activities, which contribute to the well-being of sedentary workers through leisure-time exercise. It is now considered more important in weight control to recommend increased physical activity, rather than reduced energy intake, because there is a range of benefits to health beyond the maintenance of energy balance (Conway 1995). This is in sharp contrast to the recommendations made by the American Medical Association in 1951 whereby it was stated that "it is seldom wise to attempt the alteration of calorie balance by changing the energy output; it is far easier and surer to adjust the intake" (AMA 1951: 274).

Other Factors Affecting Energy Requirements

Age. REE varies with the amount of metabolically active tissue in the body, with the relative proportion of each tissue in the body, and with the contribution of each tissue to total metabolism. These all vary with age. Changes in the body composition of children, adults, and elderly people are taken into account when energy requirements of a particular population group are calculated by use of the empirical equations that link REE with age. Activity patterns also change with age. Children become progressively more active once they are able to walk, and the physical activity patterns of adults are dependent not only upon their occupation but also upon their own leisure activity. When adults retire from work, their change in habits must be recognized when estimating energy requirements.

Sex. Although there are differences in the body weight and body composition of boys and girls beginning during the first few months of life, such differences are relatively small until children reach 9 to 10 years of age. Changes then accelerate throughout adolescence. After maturity, men have greater muscle mass, whereas women's bodies generally contain a greater proportion of fat. In practice, REE per unit of total body weight is not greatly different in men and in women. The energy requirement for physical activity has often been related to different occupational needs. In recent years, however, occupational and discretionary activity requirements of both sexes have become increasingly similar.

Body size. Persons with large (or small) bodies require proportionately more (or less) total energy per unit of time for activities such as walking, which involve moving mass over distance. Their hourly rates of REE will also be slightly higher or lower than the average. Energy allowances must be adjusted for the variations in requirements that result from such differences in body size. Weight may be used as a basis for adjusting allowances for different body sizes within a given age and sex category, provided the individuals are not appreciably over or under their desirable weights. Persons who are overweight often compensate for the increased energy cost of carrying their extra weight by decreasing daily activity.

Climate. In industrialized societies, most persons are protected against cold by warm clothes and heated environments. Many also live and work in air-conditioned buildings, so the effects of high temperatures are reduced. Yet, everyone is not insulated from environmental exposure, and when there is prolonged exposure to cold or heat, energy allowances may need adjustment.

Food Energy Requirements

The energy requirement of an individual has been defined as

> [t]hat level of energy intake from food which will balance energy expenditure when the individual has a body size and composition, and level of physical activity, consistent with long-term good health; and which will allow for the maintenance of economically necessary and socially desirable physical activity. In children and pregnant or lactating women the energy requirement includes the energy needs associated with the deposition of tissues or the secretion of milk at rates consistent with good health (FAO/WHO/UNU 1985: 12).

As the definition suggests, energy expenditure can often be the basis for estimating energy requirements. The most frequently used procedure for determining energy expenditure consists of a combination of a timed activity record (that is, the total duration of each of the important activities throughout the whole 24 hours of the day) and an energy value in kcal or kJ per minute for each of these activities. These energy values may be derived from either published data or from actual measurement of oxygen consumption. Time spent at BMR or REE (sleep or rest) can often be a major component of the day's need.

A modified procedure for estimating average daily expenditure is to multiply the basal metabolic rate (BMR) or resting energy expenditure (REE) by an appropriate daily *average* activity factor, which is dependent on the degree and duration of physical activity. The latter is often termed the PAL (physical activity level). Thus: Daily Energy Expenditure = BMR × PAL. The PAL may vary from about 1.2 to 1.4 for relatively inactive people but up to 2.0 or more in the case of people who are physically very active. The value of the daily PAL may be obtained from questionnaires on habitual physical activity. Estimated values (FAO/WHO/UNU 1985; IDECG 1996) for PALs at various levels of habitual activity at different ages are shown in Table IV.C.3.5.

The doubly labeled water (DLW) method (Lifson, Gordon, and McLintock 1955) for the measurement of energy expenditure makes use of the stable isotopes ^{18}O and ^2H. The rates of disappearance from body water are determined following the oral administration of a known amount of doubly labeled water. Both energy expenditure and water output over several days can subsequently be calculated. Although the theoretical advantages of the DLW procedure, such as the ability to provide data on free-living individuals in almost any context, are considerable, there are counterbalancing drawbacks (Durnin 1996): The technicalities of the analysis of CO_2 output are such that expensive equipment and technical expertise are highly necessary. In addition, the isotope ^{18}O is expensive. Lastly, the calculations only provide information on CO_2 output for a period of several days. Nevertheless, the procedure is now widely used (Conway 1995), and many of the requirement data for various population groups – as well as estimates of PALs in the IDECG (1996) "Energy and Protein Requirements" report – are

from DLW determinations. Comparisons between DLW and other procedures, demonstrating a close agreement in findings, have been reported by Seale (1995).

Respiration chambers or whole-body calorimeters can have a role in assessing requirements but are highly expensive and technically complex. Few of these chambers exist, and their usefulness is restricted to specific basic problems that do not require a natural, free-living environment. But such devices can still play a research role in studying the relationship between energy metabolism and heart rate, diet-induced thermogenesis, DLW validation, and the influence of varying proportions of energy-supplying nutrients on energy metabolism. Extrapolation from heart rate to energy expenditure is useful for certain population groups, such as young children, the elderly, and those who are ill.

Energy expenditure has sometimes been indirectly estimated from energy intake, although the potential for error can be enormous, especially when intake is estimated from an interview based on a remembered food consumption for one day (24-hour recall). Self-recording of energy intake also frequently underestimates intakes when compared with measurements made by more direct procedures (Heymsfield et al. 1995; Seale 1995). However, when the procedure for measuring energy intake has been performed in an acceptable fashion by experienced observers, the results may be essentially the same as energy expenditure simultaneously measured (Durnin 1996).

Despite a much greater understanding of energy balance, many discrepancies still exist between self-reported food energy intakes and weight gain. Comparisons have been made by S. B. Heymsfield and colleagues (1995) between actual (DLW and indirect calorimetry) and estimated (self-reported) energy intakes. The studies revealed a considerable degree of underestimation of energy intake when using self-reporting procedures. In consequence, many of the cited discrepancies between food energy intake and weight gain may not really exist, and thermogenesis may not need to be invoked to explain the differences.

Table IV.C.3.6 presents energy intakes and requirements for various population groups in the early 1900s. The high requirement values it reveals were reasonable and acceptable when much manual labor was essential. However, the more recent international recommendations shown in Table IV.C.3.7 are much lower for all age groups. In Table IV.C.3.8, data on food energy and protein availability for a number of world regions are presented for the year 1994. These data are population averages, indicating that many people in the least developed countries are likely to be at risk of food energy inadequacy, whereas many of those in developed regions may be suffering from surfeit. The differences in protein availability, especially that from animal sources, are also noteworthy.

Table IV.C.3.5. *Physical activity levels suggested to estimate total daily energy expenditure from the mean basal metabolic rate of children, adolescents, and adults*

		Habitual physical activity		
Age (y)	Sex	Light	Moderate	Heavy
1–5	M, F	1.45	1.60	–
6–13	M	1.55	1.75	1.95
14–18	M	1.60	1.80	2.05
6–13	F	1.50	1.70	1.90
14–18	F	1.45	1.65	1.85
Adult	M	1.55	1.80	2.10
	F	1.55	1.65	1.80

Source: Child and adolescent data IDECG (1996). Adult data FAO/WHO/UNU (1985).

Table IV.C.3.6. *Early protein and energy intakes from Europe and America with requirement estimates*

Intake and requirement groups	Protein gm/day	Fat gm/day	kcal	PCal%	FCal%
Europe					
Blacksmith U.K.	176	71	4117	17.1	15.5
Brickmaker Germany	167	117	4641	14.4	22.7
Carpenter Germany	131	68	3194	16.4	19.2
Tailor U.K.	131	39	3053	17.2	11.5
Workman Russia	132	80	3675	14.4	19.6
Workman Sweden	134	79	3436	15.6	20.7
North America					
Factory worker Canada	109	109	3622	12.0	27.1
Glassblower Massachusetts	95	132	3590	10.6	33.1
Mechanic Massachusetts	127	186	4428	11.5	37.8
U.S. Army ration	120	161	3851	12.5	37.6
U.S. Navy ration	143	184	4998	11.4	33.1
U.S. average 53 students	103	138	3500	11.8	35.5
Requirements for hard work					
Voit	145	100	3370	17.2	26.7
Rubner	165	70	3644	18.1	17.3
Playfair	185	71	3750	19.7	17.0
Atwater	150	150	4060	14.8	33.3
Diets for normal work					
Atwater	112	148	2992	15.0	44.5
Chittenden	58	140	2729	8.5	46.2
Chittenden low intake	41	79	1584	10.4	45.1

PCal%: Protein calories as percentage of total calories.

FCal%: Fat calories as percentage of total calories.

Source: Hutchinson (1903). Normal work requirements data for Atwater and Chittenden from Sherman (1914).

Table IV.C.3.7. *International food energy requirements 1950–96*

	Weight kg	FAO 1950	FAO/WHO/UNU 1985 kcal/kg/d	IDECG 1996
0–6 mo.	3.6–7.6	–	118	90
6–12 mo.	8.0–9.7	110	94	88
Children and adolescents			kcal/d	
1–3 yr.	12.2	1200	1380	922
4–6	18.2	1600	1750	1323
7–9	25.3	2000	2030	1587
10–12	36.3	2500	2068	1894
13–15 F	49.9	2600	2140	2007
13–15 M	50.9	3200	2515	2457
16–20 F	56.3	2400	2135	2098[1]
16–20 M	65.5	3800	2835	2908[1]
Adult F	55.0	2300	2100	2100
Adult M	65.0	3200	2700	2700
Pregnancy	–	+ 450	+ 285	+ 225
Lactation	–	+ 1000	+ 500	+ 685

[1]16–18 years.

Note: Adult requirements are for light-to-moderate activity levels:

Some international recommendations for requirements of food energy, together with discussions of the issues involved, have been provided by FAO (1950), FAO/WHO/UNU (1985), and IDECG (1996), whereas recommendations for the United States are discussed by Pellett (1990a). Food-energy requirements specifically for adults are dealt with by Shetty and colleagues (1996), and pregnancy and lactation are considered by Prentice and colleagues (1996).

Protein

Historical Background

Proteins are associated with all forms of life, an observation that dates back at least to the original identification of proteins as a class by G. J. Mulder (1802–80), who wrote in 1840:

> In both plants and animals a substance is contained, which is produced within the former, and imparted through their food to the latter. It is unquestionably the most important of all known substances in the organic kingdom. Without it no life appears possible on this

Table IV.C.3.8. *Distribution of food energy, fat, and protein in the various world regions*

Data for 1994	Food energy kcal/d	Total protein g/d	Animal protein g/d	Plant protein %	Animal protein %	Cereal protein %	FCal%
World	2718	72.1	25.8	64.2	35.8	45.9	23.1
Developed countries	3206	98.0	55.2	43.7	56.3	29.6	32.5
Industrialized countries	3356	103.4	62.2	39.8	60.2	24.3	35.4
North America, developed	3591	112.6	72.1	35.9	64.0	21.9	35.3
Oceania, developed	3123	102.2	70.7	30.8	69.2	18.7	35.3
Western Europe	3398	102.5	61.5	40.0	60.0	24.3	39.5
Developing countries	2573	64.4	17.1	73.6	26.6	53.3	19.6
Africa, developing	2336	58.3	11.4	80.4	19.6	53.9	18.1
Asia, developing	2600	64.8	16.0	75.3	24.7	56.0	19.0
Latin America, developing	2732	70.4	31.9	54.7	45.3	35.7	25.4
Least developed	2013	49.9	9.0	82.0	18.0	58.9	14.8

FCal% = Fat calories as percentage of total calories.

Source: Derived from FAOSTAT (1996).

planet. Through its means the chief phenomena of life are produced. (Block and Bolling 1951: v)

We now recognize that the major importance of protein in the diet is to act as a source of amino acids, some of which are essential (indispensable) dietary constituents. This is because their carbon skeletons are not synthesized in the bodies of animals. Others are nonessential (dispensable) because they can be made within the animal from readily available carbon and nitrogen precursors. All animal species need some preformed amino acids in their diets (Munro and Crim 1988). The essential amino acids (EAAs) for humans include histidine, isoleucine, leucine, lysine, methionine, phenylalanine, threonine, tryptophan, and valine; moreover, cysteine and tyrosine are synthesized in the body from methionine and phenylalanine, respectively.

An additional 9 amino acids (alanine, arginine, aspartic acid, asparagine, glutamic acid, glutamine, glycine, proline, and serine) are also present in proteins but are not necessary in the diet because the body can usually manufacture them as needed, provided there is an adequate source of nitrogen and glucose. Sufficient synthesis may not take place in some circumstances, and some nonessential amino acids may become conditionally essential. This can occur, for example, in preterm infants (Tsang et al. 1993), following liver damage in the adult, and in the presence of certain potentially toxic materials.

The proteins of living matter act, among other things, as enzymes, as structural features of the cell, as messengers (peptide hormones), and as antibodies. The accumulation of proteins during growth and development, and the maintenance of tissue proteins in the adult, represent important objectives in ensuring nutritional well-being. A knowledge of the way in which dietary protein is optimally utilized by the body allows determination of protein needs for health and for the restoration of body tissue following disease (Munro and Crim 1988).

Amino Acids and the Quality of Protein

Before the first decade or so of the twentieth century, it was thought that proteins were all of generally similar nutritional value, despite recognition of very obvious differences in their chemical and physical properties.

Rubner, however, in the late 1890s, observed that proteins of varying origins were not of the same value in nutrition, and the earlier work of the Magendie Commission on Gelatin had demonstrated that gelatin could not support life (McCollum 1957). But these efforts and numerous nitrogen balance studies performed after the 1850s were essentially disregarded until the beginning of the next century (see Munro 1964a) when work reported from England confirmed that the different values resulted from lack of amino acids (Willcock and Hopkins 1906–7).

Sherman (1914), in the first edition of his textbook (the eighth edition appeared in 1952), defined protein in basically modern terms: "The word protein should designate that group of substances, which consist, as far as at present is known, essentially of combinations of alpha-amino acids and their derivatives" (1914: 26). By 1914, Lusk, in a lecture to the New York Academy of Sciences on the importance of proteins, could provide an almost complete list of those amino acids recognized today as constituents of proteins, with methionine and threonine the most notable absentees.

Within a decade of Lusk's lecture, Thomas B. Osborne and Lafayette B. Mendel at Yale University had convincingly demonstrated that there were major differences in the quality of proteins and had established the basis of our present evaluation techniques. Mendel suspected that the concentration of protein in a diet was not a completely satisfactory indicator of its ability to support growth, whereas Osborne had isolated a number of pure proteins. Thus began a most fruitful collaboration whereby Mendel studied the growth response of rats that were fed the proteins isolated by Osborne.

They found, quite early in their studies, that the various isolated proteins differed in their potential to support growth because the weight gain (of rats) per unit of protein consumed varied significantly. Hence was born the PER or protein efficiency ratio (Osborne, Mendel, and Ferry 1919), which remained the official method for the evaluation of protein in the United States (Pellett 1963) until the protein quality evaluation report by the FAO/WHO in 1991. From these collaborative studies came the early conclusions that rats grew better on animal proteins than on plant proteins, but that adding some of the then newly isolated and chemically identified amino acids to plant proteins could make them equal to animal proteins in their growth-promoting ability. The broad principles of protein nutrition that we accept today were well known by the second decade of the twentieth century (Mendel 1923).

Whether, however, there were fundamental differences between animal and vegetable proteins remained an important issue. It was a debate in which agreement was reached much earlier in scientific circles than in the public arena, where it remained an issue at least until the 1950s (Block and Bolling 1951). By that time it was agreed that an essential amino acid from a plant was the same as one from an animal but that the proportions present in plant and animal foods could differ and that mixing proteins in the diet (complementation) could confer nutritional benefits.

Nitrogen balance techniques had been in use at least since Boussingault in 1839, but the determination of the biological values of proteins from nitrogen balance data is generally attributed to K. Thomas (1909). The ability to scale the nutritional differences in proteins numerically arose in the first and second decades of the twentieth century with the introduction of the PER by Osborne, Mendel and E. L. Ferry (1919) and the refinement of Thomas's nitrogen balance techniques by H. H. Mitchell in 1924.

Protein and Amino Acid Analysis

Before nitrogen balance and other biological methods for the evaluation of protein quality could be used in any routine manner, improvements in procedures for the analysis of protein were required. Although the Dumas procedure (which converted the nitrogen of protein to gaseous nitrogen that could then be measured) had been available since 1835, it was not until 1883 that J. Kjeldahl described a convenient procedure for converting the nitrogen of most organic materials into ammonia. The procedure involved boiling the material in the presence of concentrated sulfuric acid and a catalyst. After release with a strong base, the ammonia could be determined by acid–base titration. Numerous modifications of the method have

been proposed, but it remains remarkably similar in its essentials to the original procedure and is still widely used.

Nitrogen in foods comes not only from the amino acids in protein but also from additional forms that may, or may not, be used as part of the total nitrogen economy in humans and animals. The nitrogen content of proteins in foods can vary from between about 15 to 18 percent, depending on the amino acids in these proteins. In addition, purines, pyrimidines, free amino acids, vitamins, creatine, creatinine, and amino sugars all contribute to the total nitrogen present. Urea is also a major contributor in foods as important as human milk.

Because the average content of nitrogen (N) in protein is 16 percent, the nitrogen content multiplied by 6.25 is frequently used to convert N to protein. This should then be termed "crude protein." It is not always appreciated that the amino acids themselves show a very large range in their content of nitrogen. Whereas tyrosine has less than 8 percent N, lysine has 19 percent and arginine contains 32 percent. The presence of an amide group in an amino acid can double the N content; aspartic acid contains 10 percent N, but asparagine contains 21 percent. For other N-containing compounds, values can even be higher, with 47 percent N in urea and some 80 percent in ammonia. In practice, most protein evaluation techniques are actually evaluating the nitrogen present but are calling it protein (N × 6.25). Because a number of other factors from 5.3 to 6.38 (Jones 1941) may be used to convert food nitrogen to protein in different foods, considerable potential for confusion exists (Pellett and Young 1980).

Early in the twentieth century as the ability developed to detect and identify amino acids, it was realized that they were present in living materials, not only as components of their proteins but also as free amino acids. It also became clear that there were many more amino acids in living systems than the 20 or so known to be present in proteins. Because all amino acids behave in a rather similar chemical manner, additional techniques, often of a physicochemical nature, such as column chromatography, became necessary to solve the complex problems of separating and determining their presence in foods (Moore and Stein 1954; Moore, Spackman, and Stein 1958).

A major milestone was the description (Spackman, Stein, and Moore 1958) of an automatic analyzer allowing separation and quantitative analysis of amino acids based on ion-exchange column chromatography. As a result, modern dedicated amino acid analyzers quantitatively separate protein hydrolysates into their constituent amino acids in 1 hour or less and physiological fluids in about 2 hours.

In the introduction to the first edition of their major work on the amino acid composition of food proteins, R. J. Block and D. Bolling wrote:

It has been our experience that a food protein may be a good source of those nutritionally valuable amino acids which are most commonly estimated (i.e., cystine, methionine, arginine, histidine, lysine, tyrosine and tryptophan) and yet be deficient in one or more of the other essentials for which analytical methods are more difficult and often less accurate (1951: xiv).

Threonine was not listed, but the other essential amino acids considered at the time to be difficult to analyze (leucine, isoleucine, valine, and phenylalanine) have rarely proved to be in deficit in normal foods or diets. Analytical techniques for amino acids at the time were chemical and followed in a direct manner from those developed by Fischer (1901). Large quantities of protein were required before amino acid composition could be undertaken, and accuracy was poor.

Even today, when techniques such as ion-exchange chromatography are in use, the accuracy and reproducibility of analyses for cystine, methionine, and tryptophan are problematic, not least because of destruction of amino acids during the hydrolysis stage of analysis (see FAO/WHO 1991). Current views are that although the supply of any of the essential amino acids and of total nitrogen may theoretically limit protein utilization, only lysine, threonine, tryptophan, and the sulfur-containing amino acids are likely to be limiting in normal foods or diets. Even further, we now believe that in diets based on predominantly cereal protein sources, lysine may be the only amino acid that conditions overall protein quality (Pellett and Young 1988, 1990; Pellett 1996; Young, Scrimshaw, and Pellett 1997).

Digestibility of Protein

Although one would have expected the concept of digestibility to have developed early in the history of nutrition, a view of digestion and digestibility that we would recognize today did not arise until the middle of the nineteenth century. Following Hippocrates, the common view was that although there were many kinds of foods, there was but a single aliment. The belief of a single aliment prevailed throughout many centuries because little knowledge of the chemical nature of the various foodstuffs existed. Even in the early days of scientific nutrition research, William Beaumont (famous for his studies on digestion using a subject with a fistulous opening in his stomach caused by a gunshot wound), still held to this belief despite the then-developing opinions on the role of proteins, fats, and carbohydrates as chemically present in foods (McCollum 1957). In his own words, "the ultimate principles of aliment are always the same, from whatever food they may be obtained" (Beaumont 1833: 275) and "no other fluid produces the same

effect on food that gastric juice does; and it is the only solvent of aliment" (Beaumont 1833: 278).

Although the dictionary definition of digestibility – "capable of being digested" – embraces both the scientific and the popular conception of the term, scientifically the term should suggest a numerical proportion of the nutrient capable of being digested (absorbed). In contrast, popular usage of the word "digestibility" merely seems to imply that indigestion is being avoided. The concept of being absorbed applies to any nutrient, but in practice, the term digestibility is mainly employed for food energy and for protein, whereas "bioavailability" is used to describe the degree of absorption and/or utilization of other nutrients.

Digestibility considerations were recognized as important in studies published by Boussingault from the 1840s onward. He made a number of quantitative experiments to determine the rate at which different constituents of food disappeared from the digestive tract and at the same time tabulated the theoretical amounts of vegetable feeds that would produce equal effects on the growth of animal muscle. As an example, if a standard 10 pounds (lbs.) of hay were needed to produce a certain amount of muscle, only 2 lbs. of linseed oil cake and 5 lbs. of oats, respectively, were required to do the same. Or, again to produce the same growth, 52 lbs. of wheat straw and 61 lbs. of turnips were needed. These values were, in effect, comparative protein nutritional values of feeds and, as with the majority of our current biological techniques of protein evaluation, implicitly included digestibility as a component.

Boussingault (1850) was also the first to distinguish between nitrogen as ammonium salts and nitrogen as urea in urine and was instrumental in initiating nitrogen balance experiments in farm animals. His studies (see McCollum 1957) were followed at Rothamsted in England by the work of J. B. Lawes and J. H. Gilbert in 1859. They fed two pigs that were closely similar in weight, one with lentil meal containing 4 percent nitrogen and the other barley meal containing 2 percent nitrogen. The pig fed lentil meal excreted more than twice as much urea nitrogen as did the other fed barley meal. It was evident that the pigs on these two sources of protein retained very different percentages of their food protein for conversion into body protein.

Under the impetus of the naval blockades during World War I, Rubner, in Germany, took up investigations on the nutritive value of bread. His general conclusion, following a number of digestibility studies, was that flour milled at a rate above 70 percent was poorly used by humans. The nitrogen in bran was, however, an excellent food for cattle, and the high-fiber milling residue was therefore recommended for animal feed.

Although digestibility considerations were known to be important, and it was recognized that digestibility was inclusive in most biologically determined protein quality values, the concept suffered relative neglect for a long period, with amino acid composition data given far greater attention. Only recently has the relevance of digestibility as perhaps the more important component of protein quality (that is, compared to amino acid composition) again been emphasized (FAO/WHO 1991).

Amino Acid Metabolism

The development of the concepts of intermediary metabolism of protein and amino acids – that is, the stepwise conversion of these materials to the end products, urea, water, and CO_2, with the liberation of energy – has been a continuously evolving process since the early years of the twentieth century. Hopkins in 1913 emphasized that "in the study of the intermediate processes of metabolism we have to deal, not with complex substances which elude ordinary chemical methods, but with simple substances undergoing comprehensible reactions" (Hopkins 1913: 653). Probably the major event in this progression of knowledge was the discovery of the Krebs-Henseleit cycle (Krebs and Henseleit 1932; Cohen 1981). The concept of the "cycle" became fundamental, not only for understanding the excretion of urea but also to the whole future of biochemistry. As Krebs remarked (see Estabrook and Srere 1981) at his 80th birthday symposium:

> Perhaps the most novel and fundamental contribution was the discovery of the urea cycle. It preceded the tricarboxylic cycle for the Nobel Prize. It was very important to have the concept of "the cycle.". . . And we know, of course, by now that there are many dozens, if

not hundreds, of cyclic processes (Estabrook and Srere 1981: xvii).

Dietary proteins are subjected in the body to a series of metabolic reactions, which are outlined in Figure IV.C.3.3. Following ingestion, protein foods undergo digestion, whereupon the amino acids are liberated by the digestive enzymes. Amino acids are then absorbed as free amino acids and as two and three amino acid compounds (di- and tripeptides). Nonabsorbed protein and/or nitrogen compounds appear in the fecal material but may have been subjected to further bacterial reactions in the large intestine. For most protein foods, nitrogen absorption is in excess of 90 percent. Following the distribution of the free amino acids between the extra- and intracellular amino acid pools, subsequent reactions can be considered in four categories:

1. Part of the free amino acid pool is incorporated into tissue proteins. Because of subsequent protein breakdown, these amino acids return to the free pool after a variable length of time and thus become available for reutilization for protein synthesis or for catabolism.
2. Part of the intracellular amino acid pool undergoes catabolic reactions, mainly in the liver. This process leads to loss of the carbon skeleton as CO_2 or its deposition as glycogen and fat, whereas the nitrogen is eliminated as urea via the Krebs-Henseleit cycle.
3. Nonessential amino acids are made in the body using amino groups derived from other amino acids (including the EAAs if they are in excess of requirement) and from carbon skeletons formed by reactions common to the intermediary metabolism of carbohydrate (Table IV.C.3.9).

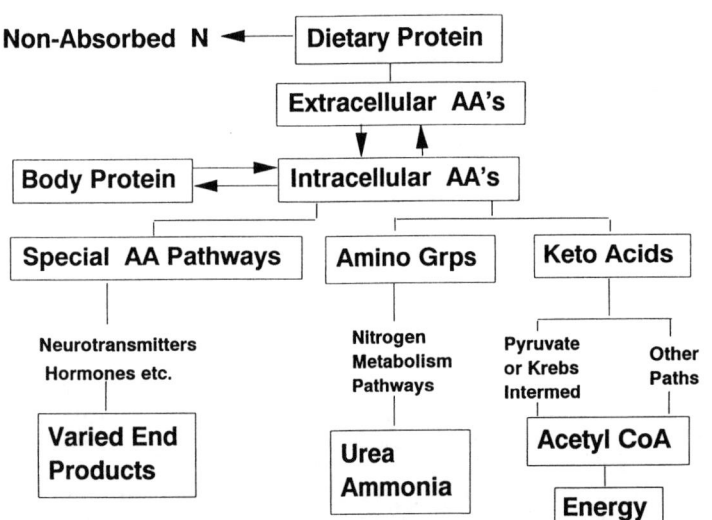

Figure IV.C.3.3. Metabolism of dietary protein. After the absorption of amino acids they are either incorporated into protein or are metabolized into α ketoacids and amino groups. Acetyl coenzyme A may either be used for energy or stored as fat. Pyruvate or Krebs cycle intermediaries may be used for the synthesis of glucose. Additional pathways involve the special role of amino acids for other uses as described in Table IV.C.3.10.

Table IV.C.3.9. *Summary of nonessential amino acid biosynthesis in mammals*

Amino acid	Precursor	Pathway
Alanine	Pyruvate	Transamination
Glutamate	αKG	Transamination
	αKG	GDH (+NH$_4$)
Glutamine (ATP/Mg)	Glutamate	+ NH$_4$
Aspartate	OAA	Transamination
Asparagine	Aspartate	+ NH$_4$
Serine	3-P glycerate	Phosphoserine HO-pyruvate
Glycine	Serine	THF needed
Methionine	Homocysteine	Betaine needed
Cyst(e)ine	Serine + homocysteine	Cystathionine
Tyrosine	Phenylalanine	Bioptherin need
Proline	Glutamate	Semialdehyde
Arginine	Glutamate	Ornithine

Abbreviations: GDH glutamic dehydrogenase.

αKG alpha ketoglutaric acid

OAA oxaloacetic acid

THF tetrahydrofolate

Note: Methionine is an essential amino acid but can be synthesized from homocysteine, which, however, is not a normal dietary constituent.

4. Some free amino acids are used for synthesis of a number of new and important N-containing compounds. Examples are shown in Table IV.C.3.10 and include purine bases, creatine, gamma amino butyric acid, serotonin, and catecholamines. However, the portion of the total amino acid requirement devoted to this important function is small in absolute terms in comparison with the amount of amino acids needed for protein synthesis.

A summary listing of the end products formed from both the nitrogen and the carbons of the major amino acids as they are degraded is shown in Table IV.C.3.11, and a diagrammatic overview of the breakdown of the amino acids for energy and for other purposes is also illustrated in Figure IV.C.3.4.

Amino Acid Scoring Systems

Overlapping the development of animal assays for evaluating protein quality were significant advances in organic chemistry that allowed purification and isolation of both proteins and the amino acids. The next major advances in studies of protein metabolism were made by W. C. Rose and his associates at the University of Illinois. Their investigations, which began in the 1920s and extended until the 1950s, were able to distinguish, as unequivocally as is possible in the biological sciences, between the essential (indispensable) and the nonessential (dispensable) amino acids (Rose 1957).

Table IV.C.3.10. *Other functions of some amino acids*

Amino acid	Precursor of	Role
Alanine	Pyruvate	Amino transport Gluconeogenesis
Arginine	Creatine	Energy metabolism
	Ornithine	Urea formation
	Polyamines	Cell division?
	Oxaloacetic acid	Gluconeogenesis
Aspartic acid	Aparagine	Ammonia transport
	Purine, pyrimidines	Nucleic acids
Cysteine	Glutathione	Oxidation/reduction Amino acid transport
	Taurocholic acid	Fat absorption
Glutamic acid	α-ketoglutarate	Gluconeogenesis, transamination
	Glutamine	Ammonia transport
	Glutathione	Oxidation/reduction
	γ-amino butyric acid	Neurotransmitter
Glutamine	Purines, pyrimidines	Nucleic acids
	Amino sugars	Glycoproteins
	Citrulline	Ammonia transport
Histidine	Histamine	Biological amine
Lysine	Carnitine	Lipid transport
Methionine	S-adenosylmethionine	Methylation reactions
Phenylalanine	Tyrosine	Hormone synthesis
Serine	Ethanolamine, phosphoserine	Phospholipid synthesis
	4-sphingenine	Cerebroside synthesis
Tryptophan	Serotonin	Neurotransmitter
	Niacin	Vitamin
Tyrosine	Melanin	Pigment
	Catecholamines	Hormones
	Thyroxin	

Note: These functions are additional to the roles as constituents of proteins and as energy sources.

The early studies were on rats fed rations containing mixtures of the then-known amino acids in place of protein. The rats did not grow, despite the fact that the concentrations of amino acids were similar to those in milk protein (casein). They did grow, however, when a small amount of intact casein was added. This suggested the presence of an unknown substance in casein, which was later identified as threonine, the last of the essential amino acids in proteins to be recognized.

By the omission of amino acids one at a time, the 10 essential amino acids required by the rat were identified, and their daily needs could be estimated. Similar techniques were subsequently extended to humans, with the help of graduate students who not only isolated or synthesized the amino acids but also served as experimental subjects for nitrogen balance studies.

As human amino acid requirements became known, comparisons were made with the amino acid composition of foods and diets. Subsequently, the capacity of various proteins to meet human protein and amino acid requirements was compared and evaluated, and the results were called protein or amino

Table IV.C.3.11. *Fate of the nitrogen and the carbon atoms in the degradation of the amino acids for energy*

Amino acid	Nitrogen path	Carbon path
Aspartate	Used for argine or appears as NH_4 in purine nucleotide cycle	Fumarate formed from both pathways. Oxaloacetate can also be formed through transamination
Glutamate and precursors		
Glutamate	As ammonia (GDH) or as aspartate (AAT)	As alpha-ketoglutarate
Glutamine	Amide N as NH_4	As glutamate
Proline	As Glutamate	As glutamate
Arginine	Two appear in urea, one in glutamate	One appears in urea and five C in glutamate
Ornithine (if excess is produced)	Terminal N transferred to α-KG to give glutamate	Glutamate semi-aldehyde to glutamate
Pyruvate and precursors		
Alanine	In glutamate by transamination	As pyruvate
Serine	Direct to NH_4 by SDH	As pyruvate
Cysteine	In glutamate by transamination	As pyruvate (sulfur as sulfate)
Threonine	Direct to NH_4 by SDH	Succinyl CoA (a homologue of pyruvate) via propionyl CoA
Branched chain amino acids		
Leucine	In glutamate by transamination	As acetoacetate via 3-hydroxy-3-methylglutaryl CoA
Isoleucine	In glutamate by transamination	CoA (via propionyl CoA) and acetyl CoA
Valine	In glutamate by transamination	As succinyl CoA via propionyl CoA
Aromatic amino acids		
Phenylalanine	In glutamate by transamination	As acetoacetate and fumarate
Tyrosine (formed from phenylalanine by hydroxylase)	In glutamate by transamination	As acetoacetate and fumarate
Tryptophan	One N appears as alanine, one as NH_4	Three C appear as alanine, four as crotonyl CoA, and one as formate and three as CO_2
Other amino acids		
Lysine	Both Ns transferred to glutamate	Two appear as CO_2 and four as crotonyl CoA
Glycine bon	As NH_4	As CO_2 and pyruvate. Originate from two glycine via one-carbon pathways
Histidine	One N and five C as glutamate, two N as NH_4	As glutamate and as methylidine-H_4 folate
Methionine	Released as NH_4 via homocysteine	Four carbons as succinyl CoA via cystathionine and propionyl CoA. Sulfur from homocysteine appears in cysteine

acid scores (Block and Mitchell 1946). The amino acid composition of egg protein was the first reference pattern proposed because it was known to be of high quality in animal-feeding studies. It did not, however, prove to be a suitable pattern, and many proteins scored poorly in relation to egg. This was because the levels of indispensable amino acids contained in egg were well above estimated human needs.

Direct comparison with human amino acid requirements soon followed as these data became available (FAO 1957; FAO/WHO 1973; FAO/WHO/UNU 1985; FAO/WHO 1991). The general expectation developed that not only should the score be able to predict the potential nutritional value of a food (or diet) for humans but that such a score should also correlate directly with the results of animal assays, such as net protein utilization (NPU). This did not always follow, and we now consider that the appropriate standard for dietary assessment for humans should be the human amino acid requirement pattern. Some amino acid scoring patterns recommended for protein evaluation purposes in recent years are shown in Table IV.C.3.12.

Protein Requirements

The earliest estimates of protein requirements, made by L. Playfair (1853), Voit (1881), and Atwater (1891), were derived from observations of protein consumption, whereas the later studies, including those of R. H. Chittenden (1904), Sherman (1920) and E. F. Terroine (1936) were based on a more physiological approach in that estimates were made of the minimum amount of protein required to support body nitrogen equilibrium.

Actual protein requirement data have been debated for many years; even as early as 1919, Osborne noted that the amount of protein that should be included in

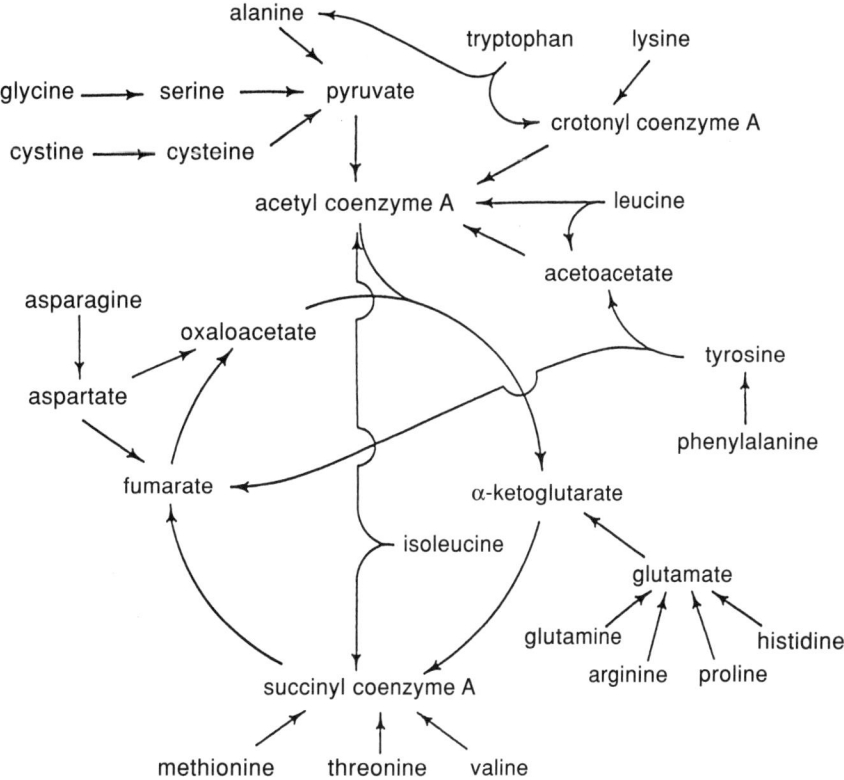

Figure IV.C.3.4. Metabolic pathways for the amino acids.

the human diet had long been a matter of debate among physiologists and nutrition experts, yet no agreement seemed to be in sight. Starting with a Health Committee of the League of Nations in 1936 and continuing to the present (IDECG 1996), estimates of human protein requirements and dietary protein allowances have been proposed by various national and international working groups. The major committees concerned with protein are shown in Table IV.C.3.13. These estimates, or "standards," have been the basis for food and agricultural policies and programs, and for the planning and evaluation of diets for groups of individuals. The strengths and weaknesses of such international committee efforts to establish protein requirements have been examined by N. S. Scrimshaw (1976), who recognized that the recommendations reached by a committee are often less rigorous than those that would be proposed by an individual.

Table IV.C.3.12. *Recommended scoring patterns, 1950-91 (mg/g protein)*

	EGG	FAO (1957)	FAO/WHO (1973)	NAS–NRC (1974)	FAO/WHO/UNU (1985)			FAO/WHO (1991)		
					Infant	Child	School-age children	Adult	Infant	All other ages
Iso	54	42	40	42	46	28	28	13	46	28
Leu	86	48	70	70	93	66	44	19	93	66
Lys	70	42	54	51	66	58	44	16	66	58
Saa	57	42	35	26	42	25	22	17	42	25
Aaa	93	56	61	73	72	63	22	19	72	63
Thr	47	28	40	35	43	34	28	9	43	34
Trp	17	14	10	11	17	11	9	5	17	11
Val	66	42	50	48	55	35	25	13	55	35
TOTAL	490	314	360	356	434	320	222	111	434	320

Source: FAO/WHO (1991).

Table IV.C.3.13. *International protein recommendations (1936–96)*

1936	League of Nations: Health
1957	FAO: Protein
1965	FAO/WHO: Protein
1973	FAO/WHO: Protein/Energy
1985	FAO/WHO/UNU: Protein/Energy
1991	FAO/WHO: Protein Quality
1996	IDECG: Energy/Protein

Today, one might echo the sentiments Osborne penned in 1919, as each expert committee reports its findings. Nevertheless, agreement is now much closer, especially when we compare present recommendations (Table IV.C.3.14) with some of the high values for intakes and, hence, requirement recommendations proposed in the early 1900s (Table IV.C.3.6). These earlier data, especially those from the United States, are also remarkable for the very high levels of both fat and food energy recommended. In contrast, the recommendations from Chittenden (1907) are also shown in Table IV.C.3.6. Using himself as a subject, he consumed much lower levels of protein and maintained health. He did, however, eventually lose some weight. From his reported body weight his protein intake was 0.71 g/protein/kg/day, a little below the adult safe levels of 0.75 g/kg recommended by FAO/WHO/UNU (1985). In contrast, the Atwater (1891) recommendations for a man weighing 70 kg represented 1.6 g/kg/day.

Different committees have made different recommendations, sometimes based on the same original data (Irwin and Hegsted 1971). As an example, in a 1957 FAO report, the recommendations for adults were reduced significantly from the Sherman (1920) recommendations by applying different assumptions to the same data. These data extended back to the work of Atwater and others in the 1890s. At times, new recommendations have been generated based on data not available to earlier committees as, for example, with the young child data, originating from Guatemala, in a 1985 FAO/WHO/UNU report.

Revisions in the standards have had a profound effect on the interpretation of the possible protein nutritional status of a population. When, in the 1940s and 1950s, young child protein allowances were placed as high as 4.5 g/kg, a world protein problem was postulated. By revision of the protein requirement values downwards to about one-third of the previous allowances, total food energy rather than protein became the limiting factor, and the global "protein gap" disappeared at a stroke of a pen. These and other problems were discussed in scathing fashion by D. S. McLaren (1974) in an essay on "The Great Protein Fiasco." A more recent example that influenced international agricultural policy was the recommendation from the FAO/WHO/UNU (1985) group concerning adult needs for essential amino acids. The implications from the recommendations (subsequently replaced) were that EAA needs could be fully met in the adult by a cereal protein such as wheat, and that the consumption of complementary proteins was no longer necessary.

The requirement for dietary protein consists of two major components: (1) total nitrogen to serve the needs for synthesis of the nutritionally dispensable (nonessential) and conditionally indispensable amino acids, as well as for other physiologically important nitrogen-containing compounds, and (2) the nutritionally indispensable (essential) amino acids that cannot be made by human tissues and so must be supplied from the diet. The most recent recommendations by a UN committee (FAO/WHO/UNU 1985) for all age groups are shown in Table IV.C.3.15. Comparative recommendations by various groups for selected ages over a number of years have already been shown in Table IV.C.3.14.

Protein requirements can be estimated in several ways (Pellett 1990b). One is to measure all losses of nitrogenous compounds from the body when the diet is devoid of protein and then assume that sufficient nitrogen from high-quality dietary protein to replace these obligatory nitrogen losses will provide the adult human subjects with their requirements. For the child, the needs for growth must also be considered. This is called the factorial method because it is based on

Table IV.C.3.14. *Summary of some recent committee recommendations for practical protein allowances in various age groups*

		Committee					
Age group	League of Nations 1936	FAO 1957	U.K.[1] 1969	FAO/WHO 1973	NAS–NRC 1974	FAO/WHO/UNU 1985	IDECG 1996
		g protein per kg per day					
Infants (1–2 years)	3.50	1.65	1.20	1.20	1.35	1.20	0.97
Teenage (15 years, boys)	1.50	0.69	0.57	0.72	0.67	0.87	0.84
Adults (35 years, men)	1.00	0.53	0.46	0.57	0.60	0.75	0.53

League of Nations (1936) allowances are expressed in terms of mixed dietary protein. All other allowances are in terms of high-quality, highly digestible protein.

[1]United Kingdom Department of Health and Social Security

Table IV.C.3.15. *FAO/WHO/UNU (1985) safe levels of protein intake**

Age group	Males		Females
	g protein/kg body weight[†]		
3–6 months	–	1.85	–
6–9 months	–	1.65	–
9–12 months	–	1.50	–
1–2 years	–	1.20	–
2–3 years	–	1.15	–
3–5 years	–	1.10	–
5–7 years	–	1.00	–
7–10 years	–	1.00	–
10–12 years	1.00	–	1.00
12–14 years	1.00	–	0.95
14–16 years	0.95	–	0.90
16–18 years	0.90	–	0.80
Adults	0.75	–	0.75
Pregnancy	–	–	+ 6[‡]
Lactation 0–6 months	–	–	+ 17.5[‡]
6 months +	–	–	+ 13[‡]

*Assembled from FAO/WHO/UNU (1985) report.

[†]Uncorrected for biologic values (amino acid scores) of mixed dietary proteins for infants and children and for digestibility for all groups.

[‡]Additional protein per day (grams).

adding up a series of factors or fractions of total need, which represents maintenance requirements (obligatory nitrogen losses) as well as specific needs, such as those for growth in the child or milk production in the lactating female. The factorial approach as used by FAO/WHO (1973) is illustrated in Table IV.C.3.16. Enough protein to replace these losses and needs should meet requirements (Munro and Crim 1988).

A second procedure for estimating protein requirements is to determine directly the minimum amount of dietary protein needed to keep the subject in nitrogen equilibrium (balance). Ideally, the two methods should arrive at similar estimates of protein requirements. For infants and children, optimal growth, and not zero nitrogen balance, is the criterion used; similarly, the additional needs of pregnancy and lactation must be fulfilled. For the infant in the first months of life, however, human milk intake may be taken as equivalent to need. In an FAO/WHO/UNU (1985: 98) report, the basic assumption was that "protein needs of an infant will be met if the energy needs are met and the food contains protein in quantity and quality equivalent to breast milk."

The requirements for the nutritionally indispensable (essential) amino acids are currently a matter of considerable debate. This is largely because of the ^{13}C-tracer studies reported by Young, D. M. Bier, and Pellett at MIT in 1989. The term "pattern of requirements" means the amount of a specific amino acid required per unit of protein need. Some amino acid requirement patterns have been shown in Table IV.C.3.12.

Such estimates have been criticized, in part because of the high food energy levels that were present in these diets (Young et al. 1989; FAO/WHO 1991) and have now been replaced by use of the FAO/WHO/UNU (1985) young child requirement pattern for all ages above infancy (FAO/WHO 1991).

Some average data on the amino acid composition of foods from the Massachusetts Nutrient Data Bank are shown in Table IV.C.3.17. Lysine is at a much lower concentration in cereals when compared with animal proteins. The sulfur-containing amino acids are distinctly lower in legumes and fruits, whereas threonine is lower in cereals and in fruits/vegetables. For the other indispensable amino acids, concentrations do not vary greatly, and these amino acids are also rarely in deficit in real diets. The nutritional significance of these data for humans is dependent on the choice of the reference amino acid requirement pattern used (Table IV.C.3.12). Clearly, if the FAO/WHO/UNU (1985) amino acid requirement pattern for the adult were to be used, it would indicate that no food protein, even from cereals, would show limitation and that complementation was no longer necessary to meet protein needs. Most cereal-based diets, however, would be lysine limited when compared to the FAO/WHO (1991) pattern. Because of these problems, use of the adult pattern from FAO/WHO/UNU (1985) has now been abandoned.

Table IV.C.3.16. *Factorial approach for human protein requirements: Adapted from FAO/WHO (1973)*

A. Estimate obligatory N losses (O_N): from the sum of urinary, fecal, skin, and miscellaneous losses. These data are obtained from measurements made when subjects are consuming nonprotein diets.

B. Estimate N requirements for growth (G_N), pregnancy (P_N), and lactation (L_N) from N content and amount of new tissue in growth, and in fetal and maternal tissues in pregnancy. For lactation, N content of milk is multiplied by average milk volume.

C. Thus minimum nitrogen requirement for growth = O_N + G_N. *Note:* G_N will be zero for an adult and will vary with age for a child.

D. Adjust for efficiency of N utilization: add 30% (not to be confused with protein quality; see G. below).
   Requirement = $(O_N + G_N) \times 1.3$

E. Adjust for individual variability (an additional 30%)
   Safe Practical Allowance (SPA) + $[(O_N + G_N) \times 1.3] \times 1.3$

F. Additional allowance for pregnancy (A_P) or lactation (A_L)
   $A_P = (P_N \times 1.3) \times 1.3$ or $A_L = (L_N \times 1.3) \times 1.3$

   Adjustments made both for efficiency of nitrogen utilization (+30%) and for individual variability (+30%).

G. Values for nitrogen as computed above are converted to protein ($N \times 6.25$). These values are in terms of proteins of high quality, such as egg or milk proteins, and further adjustments are necessary to increase allowances when average protein quality value is less than 100%.

Thus: $$\frac{\text{Recommended Protein Allowance (Adjusted for quality)}}{} = \frac{\text{SPA}}{\text{Protein Quality}}$$

Table IV.C.3.17. *Amino acid composition of major food groups from the Massachusetts Nutrient Data Bank*

	Food group								
	Animal Mean ± SD		Cereals Mean ± SD		Legumes Mean ± SD		Nut/Seeds Mean ± SD		Fruit/Veg Mean ± SD
Amino acid									
N	1726		170		153		153		572
Iso	46.7	(4.7)	39.8	(4.6)	45.3	(4.2)	42.8	(6.1)	38.5 (10.8)
Leu	79.6	(6.0)	86.3	(26.3)	78.9	(4.2)	73.5	(9.0)	59.1 (19.6)
Lys	84.3	(7.1)	30.5	(9.8)	67.1	(3.8)	43.5	(12.7)	49.2 (13.3)
Saa	37.7	(3.3)	41.1	(4.3)	25.3	(2.8)	37.7	(11.7)	23.6 (7.2)
Aaa	74.9	(8.2)	83.0	(9.2)	84.9	(6.3)	88.0	(16.9)	64.0 (18.4)
Thr	43.4	(2.6)	33.6	(5.4)	40.0	(3.3)	37.9	(5.4)	35.1 (8.7)
Trp	11.4	(1.5)	12.1	(3.3)	12.3	(2.4)	15.4	(4.6)	10.8 (3.9)
Val	51.2	(5.6)	51.1	(6.9)	50.5	(4.0)	55.6	(10.3)	45.9 (12.6)

Note: SDs are calculated from the observations recorded in the data bank but not all are truly independent variables.

Major differences exist between the lysine supply in developing and developed countries (Pellett 1996), as is illustrated in Table IV.C.3.18. Because of these differences, Young, Scrimshaw, and Pellett (1997) have speculated that in some regions of the world, lysine fortification of wheat flour may offer potential for overcoming limitations in protein quality in the available dietaries. Lysine fortification of cereal-based animal feeds is common practice.

Protein-Energy Ratios

Human nitrogen metabolism is highly sensitive to altered dietary intakes of both protein and energy caused by substrate availability, as well as by hormone mediation, which can influence the status of body nitrogen and energy metabolism. Other areas of concern relate to protein–energy malnutrition (PEM). Severe deficiencies of protein and/or food energy, especially in association with infections, can lead to PEM. However, imbalance between protein and energy levels, as for example with excess food energy

together with low protein diets, can also produce metabolic abnormalities, such as the kwashiorkor form of PEM. The role of infection in the pathogenesis of PEM is mediated, at least in part, by hormonal changes, which can directly affect both protein and energy metabolism in previously well nourished individuals. The protein–energy ratio in formulas is of special importance in catch-up growth following infection (Dewey et al. 1996) and also for the needs of preterm infants (Tsang et al. 1993).

Body protein or nitrogen balance in the healthy mature human is maintained within relatively narrow limits, indicating a regulation that is achieved by varying the rate of N excretion in relation to changes in N intake and the individual's metabolic state. H. N. Munro (1951, 1964b), D. H. Calloway and H. Spector (1954) and Calloway (1975) have demonstrated that nitrogen balance is influenced by the intake of both protein and energy, even when that of energy is more than adequate; in consequence, estimates of protein requirements, based on nitrogen balance, can be affected by the level of energy available. Changes in

Table IV.C.3.18. *Mean values per capita for the availability of specific indispensable amino acids in developed and developing regions. Data for 1994*

	Amino acid							
	Per day (mg)				Per g protein (mg/g)			
Region	Lys	Saa	Try	Thr	Lys	Saa	Try	Thr
Developing[1]	2947 (841)	2160 (583)	693 (205)	2204 (509)	49 (7)	36 (2)	11 (1)	37 (2)
Developed and transitional[2]	6149 (1172)	3619 (561)	1177 (195)	3799 (604)	64 (5)	38 (0.6)	12 (0.4)	40 (1)

[1]Data for 61 countries.

[2]Data for 29 countries.

( ) = SD

Calculated from food balance sheet data (FAOSTAT 1996).

food energy intake, below or above energy needs, affect nitrogen balance. The improvement in nitrogen balance caused by an increase in energy intake, however, can be attenuated if protein is inadequate; conversely, the beneficial effects of an increase in protein can be inhibited by an inadequate energy intake. Published nitrogen balance studies relating the influences of protein on energy and energy on protein requirements have been reevaluated by Pellett and Young (1992), who postulate that the effects on N balance are continuous when either protein or energy are increased and dispute the proposals of Munro and Calloway that the relationships exist as a series of plateaus. In summary, therefore, nitrogen balance must be seen as a result of both protein and energy intakes, and each must be defined before use can be made of the data for establishing protein requirements.

Metabolic Regulation of Food Intake

The initiation and termination of feeding are complex processes that involve a large number of signals to the central nervous system. In humans, cultural and social conventions are significant modifiers of the impact of metabolic and physiological signals. Historically, the focus of research on the regulation of energy intake has been motivated by observation on the physiological constancy of adult body weight and concern with deviations that occur in obesity and starvation. Maintenance of energy balance appears to be a primary goal of the mechanism controlling feeding behavior (Anderson 1988). Because metabolic energy is ultimately derived from the three macronutrients – carbohydrates, fat, and protein – each has been investigated for its role in control mechanisms (Mayer 1955). The presence of breakdown products in the gastrointestinal tract may directly or indirectly provide signals to the brain. Nutrients and hormones passing the liver result in changes in plasma concentrations, which, in turn, may signal the brain either directly or indirectly through a complex system of neurotransmitters. M. I. Friedman (1995) has proposed that eating behavior is triggered by a signal that is tied to ATP concentrations in the liver and is carried to the brain via afferents in the vagus nerve. The brain organizes the information arising from the metabolism of food and directs feeding so that the intake of energy and macronutrients is quantitatively regulated.

Problems of Excess and Deficit

Classification of body size by use of the Body Mass Index (BMI), a version of weight-for-height (W/H^2: weight in kg, height in meters), to assess for overweight and obesity has been in use since it was originally proposed by A. Quetelet in the latter part of the nineteenth century. More recently, it has been extended as a means of classifying undernutrition in adults (FAO 1994; James and Ralph 1994). Full agreement on the exact cut-off points to be used has not

Table IV.C.3.19. *A proposed classification using BMI (WT/HT^2)*

CED Grade III	<16.0
CED Grade II	16.0–16.9
CED Grade I	17.0–18.4
Normal	18.5–24.9
Overweight	25.0–29.9
Obese	30.0–40.0
Morbid obese	<40.0

Note: BMI (WT/HT^2) is defined using weight in kilograms and height in meters.

Source: Adapted from USDHHS (1988) and FAO (1994).

yet been reached, but a provisional classification that ranges from severe undernutrition to severe overnutrition is shown in Table IV.C.3.19.

Obesity

That obesity could be a life-threatening condition was recognized by Hippocrates, who observed in one of his aphorisms that "[p]ersons who are naturally very fat are apt to die earlier than those who are slender" (Lusk 1933: 8). Because of the significant public health implications of obesity (see Pi-Sunyer 1988 and USDHHS 1988), much research activity has centered on its causation and prevention, but disagreements remain on most major issues. Nevertheless, it is generally agreed that obesity must represent the end result of a cumulative positive error in energy balance and, hence, a failure in whatever mechanism is supposed to maintain the situation. The nature of the mechanism is not agreed upon, although many hypotheses have been advanced. On one extreme is the view presented by L. S. P. Davidson and R. Passmore (1969), who wrote that "since the immediate causes of obesity are overeating and under-exercising the remedies are available to all, but many patients require much help in using them" (Garrow 1974: 4). Conversely, the opposite end of the spectrum is typified by E. B. Astwood, who suggested that "obesity is an inherited disorder and due to a genetically determined defect in an enzyme; in other words that people who are fat are born fat and nothing much can be done about it" (Garrow 1974: 4).

Malnutrition and Wasting

Associations between wasting, illness, and food were made early in the history of medicine but moved from being solely descriptive to the experimental with the studies of Lavoisier in the late 1700s. Release of heat from organic fuels metabolized in the living body was demonstrated to follow the same pattern of combustion as was observed in vitro. Loss of tissue mass during starvation was shown to involve oxidation of endogenous fuel stores in order to generate the energy required for life in sustaining metabolic activities. By the mid–nineteenth century there was a general consensus that the diet must contain a source of energy in order to maintain health, which was expanded later to the periodic, if not daily, need for some 40 essential nutrients. Health is characterized by a range of body compositions, tissue functions, and metabolic activities, and the fundamental aim of nutritional assessment is to gather information on these areas so as to compare with the healthy reference population (Heymsfield and Williams 1988). Such comparisons can allow for formal definitions of the undernourished.

Malnutrition and starvation are extreme conditions, and the terms were originally used in a rather synonymous sense. Lusk (1928) placed the study of starvation as fundamental to the study of nutrition and defined both terms:

> Nutrition may be defined as the sum of the processes concerned in the growth, maintenance, and repair of the living body as a whole or of its constituent organs. An intelligent basis for the understanding of these processes is best acquired by a study of the organism when it is living at the expense of materials stored within itself, as it does in starvation. Starvation or hunger is the deprivation of an organism of any or all the elements necessary to its nutrition. Thus when carbohydrates and fats only are eaten, protein hunger ensues. Complete starvation occurs when all the required elements are inadequate. (Lusk 1928: 75)

We no longer use "starvation" for the absence of a single nutrient, and the word now usually refers to a chronic, inadequate intake of dietary energy. Clinical starvation is, however, typically accompanied by multiple nutrient deficiencies. Quite divorced from the realities of the developing world, most scientific studies of starvation have used normal-weight or otherwise healthy subjects. Such investigations permit the clearest description of the metabolic response to starvation. One particular study (Keys, Brozek, Henschel et al. 1950), in which volunteer subjects, starting at normal weight, received about half of their normal intake over a 6-month period, is an acknowledged classic of physiological research. L. J. Hoffer (1988) noted that modern studies of starvation at the cellular level may not be directly applicable to the physiological situation. Whole-body studies thus remain essential but cannot always be ethically performed. Therefore, experimental data, including observations on "professional fasters" reported from the earlier years of the twentieth century (e.g. Lusk 1928), continue to be relevant.

How long a human can survive without food depends largely on the size of the individual's energy stores. Provided that water is supplied, there are many reliable records of healthy people who have survived 4 to 8 weeks with no food at all, and several of these were described by Lusk (1928). J. V. G. A. Durnin and Passmore (1967) have indicated that a healthy man or woman can fast completely for 2 weeks and suffer no permanent ill effects. Most well-nourished persons can afford to lose 25 percent of their body weight

without danger to life. This is about the level achieved by the volunteers in the Keys study (1950). Very few have survived a loss of 50 percent of their body weight, although a dog recovered completely following weight reduction from 26.3 to 9.7 kg (Lusk 1928).

The essential features of the metabolic response to starvation are altered rates and patterns of fuel utilization and protein metabolism aimed at minimizing fuel needs and limiting lean tissue loss. The nature of the starvation diet determines the pattern of hormone levels and fuel consumption. In total fasting (and in other states of carbohydrate deprivation), fat oxidation dominates in a metabolic setting of low insulin levels and ketosis. Fuel utilization by the brain, kidney, and muscle is markedly altered in total fasting. The brain switches from exclusively glucose to predominantly ketone body oxidation. The fuel of resting muscle switches from predominantly fatty acids to ketone bodies, finally returning, after weeks of total fasting, to fatty acid oxidation again (Hoffer 1988). Other changes involve a rapid loss of labile body protein, followed by a prolonged period during which further protein losses are minimized in association with a slowed rate of synthesis and breakdown of body protein.

Unlike experimental starvation, the clinical diseases of protein–energy malnutrition are greatly influenced by associated environmental and health variables. Such conditions are commonly accompanied by many dietary deficiencies in addition to protein or energy, and the evolution of the syndrome is critically influenced by the effects of physiological stress. Severe undernutrition, now termed chronic energy deficiency (CED), is of major consequence worldwide and can be assessed by the use of Body Mass Index (see Table IV.C.3.19). Among the consequences to populations so affected are more sickness, lower work capacity and, hence, lower incomes, reduced social activity, and an increased risk of low-birth-weight (LBW) babies (FAO 1994; James and Ralph 1994).

Nutritional marasmus and kwashiorkor are considered to be the extreme forms of protein–energy malnutrition (PEM). The causes of PEM are complex and involve factors other than food insufficiency (Latham 1990). It is still unclear why some children develop nutritional marasmus, whereas others manifest features of kwashiorkor, including edema (Waterlow 1984). There is no doubt, however, that the major cause of nutritional marasmus is inadequate food intake, especially energy to meet the requirements for both metabolism and normal growth (Latham 1990).

Kwashiorkor was originally described and explained by Cicely Williams (1933) as a nutritional disease of childhood associated with a maize diet. Subsequently, protein deficiency in the presence of relatively adequate energy intake was identified as the main cause (Waterlow 1955). This hypothesis was supported by animal experiments in which kwashiorkor-like features were produced using a protein deficient diet with excess food energy. However, following publication of "The Great Protein Fiasco"

(McLaren 1974), it became widely accepted that energy deficiency was a much greater public health problem than was protein deficiency.

More recently, aflatoxin poisoning (Hendrickse 1984) was proposed as the cause of kwashiorkor; few, however, would agree that it is the sole cause, but it may be a contributing factor. The etiology of the disease remains under debate, but most scientists and physicians consider that although other factors play a role, kwashiorkor is usually due to a deficiency of protein relative to food energy (calories), with the disproportion exacerbated by infection. Even if the dietary intake itself is balanced, infection and infestation may cause anorexia, reduce food intake and nutrient absorption and utilization, or result in nutrient losses (Latham 1990). Kwashiorkor is not confined to children. Previously well-nourished adults have been found to develop the disease (termed famine edema) during food shortages (Latham 1990) or when food is withheld during a period of catabolic stress.

Peter L. Pellett

Notes

1. Atwater was such an important figure in the history of nutrition in the United States that it would be remiss not to expand on his role as the essential founder of the present-day, widespread, and important United States Department of Agriculture (USDA) nutrition activities. A Centennial Celebration Symposium was held in Washington in 1993 and is reported in a special issue of the *Journal of Nutrition* (Vol. 124, No. 9S). The abstract of the Centenary Lecture by Kenneth Carpenter (1994b) on the life and times of W. O. Atwater is quoted directly:

> Wilbur Atwater, the son of a Methodist minister, grew up in New England and was an undergraduate during the Civil War. He obtained his Ph.D. in agricultural chemistry at Yale in 1869, and spent the next two years in post-graduate study in Germany. In 1874 he was appointed to the Faculty of Wesleyan University, and was their first Professor of Chemistry. For two years (1875-77) he directed the first agricultural experiment station in the U.S. at Wesleyan. When it was transferred to Yale he gradually changed his interest to human nutrition, and how the poor could make more economical food choices, though he believed that they needed to maintain high-protein intakes if they were to remain productive. In 1887, with the passage of the Hatch Act, a second experiment station was established in Connecticut with Atwater as director. He also served for nearly 3 years as the first director of the Office of Experiment Stations in Washington, D.C. His next ambition was to have the first human calorimeter in the U.S. This was operating at Wesleyan by 1893, and his team was able to compare the net energy values of carbohydrates, fats and alcohol in sparing body tissues. He compiled data from many sources for the composition and digestibility of foods, and also organized the setting up of cooperative programs of nutritional studies, funded by the U.S. Department of Agriculture, in many States. His active life ended with a stroke in 1904 (Carpenter 1994b; 1707S)

Bibliography

AMA (American Medical Association). 1951. *Handbook of nutrition.* Second edition. New York and Philadelphia, Pa.

Anderson, G. H. 1988. Metabolic regulation of food intake. In *Modern nutrition in health and disease.* Seventh edition, ed. M. E. Shils and V. R. Young, 557-69. Philadelphia, Pa.

Astwood, E. B. 1962. The heritage of corpulence. *Endocrinology* 71: 337-41.

Atwater, W. O. 1891. American and European dietaries and dietary standards. *Storrs Agricultural Experimental Station 4th annual report,* 106-71. Middletown, Conn.

          1899. Discussion of the terms digestibility, availability, and fuel value. *Storrs Agricultural Experimental Station 12th annual report,* 69-110. Middletown, Conn.

Atwater, W. O., and F. G. Benedict. 1899. *Experiments on the metabolism of matter and energy in the human body.* Bulletin no. 69, U.S. Department of Agriculture. Washington, D.C.

Atwater, W. O., and A. P. Bryant. 1900. Availability and fuel value of food materials. *Storrs Agricultural Experimental Station 12th annual report for 1899,* 73-110. Middletown, Conn.

Barclay, A. 1937. *Pure chemistry: A brief outline of its history and development, Part 1 - historical review.* London.

Beaumont, W. 1833. Experiments and observations on the gastric juice, and the physiology of digestion. Plattsburg, N.Y. Facsimile of the original edition reprinted on the occasion of the XIIIth International Physiological Congress, Boston, Massachusetts, 1929.

Block, R. J., and D. Bolling. 1951. *The amino acid composition of proteins and foods.* Second edition, ed. Charles C. Thomas. Springfield, Ill.

Block, R. J., and H. H. Mitchell. 1946. The correlation of the amino-acid composition of proteins with their nutritive value. *Nutrition Abstracts and Reviews* 16: 249-76.

Calloway, D. H. 1975. Nitrogen balance of men with marginal intakes of protein and energy. *The Journal of Nutrition* 105: 914-23.

Calloway, D. H., and H. Spector. 1954. Nitrogen balance as related to caloric and protein intake in active young men. *American Journal of Clinical Nutrition* 2: 405-11.

Carpenter, K. J. 1994a. *Protein and energy: A study of changing ideas in nutrition.* Cambridge and New York.

          1994b. The life and times of W. O. Atwater (1844-1907). *The Journal of Nutrition* 124: 1707S-14S.

Chittenden, R. H. 1904. *Physiological economy in nutrition.* New York.

          1907. *The nutrition of man.* New York.

Cohen, P. P. 1981. The ornithine-urea cycle: Biosynthesis and regulation of carbamyl phosphate synthetase I and ornithine transcarbamoylase. In *Biological cycles. Current topics in cellular regulation,* Vol. 18, ed. R. W. Estabrook and P. Srere, 1-19. New York and London.

Conway, J. M., ed. 1995. Advances in human energy metabolism: Balancing energy requirements and energy intake. *American Journal of Clinical Nutrition.* 62 (5S): 1033S-179S.

Davidson, L. S. P., and R. Passmore. 1969. *Human nutrition and dietetics.* Fourth edition. Baltimore, Md.

Dewey, K. G., G. Beaton, C. Fjeld, et al. 1996. Protein requirements of infants and children. Supplement, ed. N. S. Scrimshaw, J. C. Waterlow, and B. Schürch. *Energy and Protein Requirements, European Journal of Clinical Nutrition* 50 (Supplement 1): S119-50.

Durnin, J. V. G. A. 1996. Energy requirements: General principles. Supplement, ed. N. S. Scrimshaw, J. C. Waterlow, and B. Schürch. *Energy and Protein Requirements, European Journal of Clinical Nutrition* 50 (Supplement 1): S2-10.

Durnin, J. V. G. A., and R. Passmore. 1967. *Energy, work and leisure*. London.

Estabrook, R. W., and P. Srere, eds. 1981. *Biological cycles. Current topics in cellular regulation*, Vol. 18. New York and London.

FAO (Food and Agricultural Organization of the United Nations). 1950. Calorie requirements. *FAO Nutrition Studies No. 5.* Washington, D.C.

    1957. Protein requirements. *FAO Nutrition Studies No. 16.* Rome.

    1994. Body mass index: A measure of chronic energy deficiency in adults. *FAO Food and Nutrition paper No. 56,* P. S. Shetty, W. P. T. James et al., Rome.

FAO/WHO (Food and Agricultural Organization of the United Nations/World Health Organization). 1965. Protein requirements. Report of a joint FAO/WHO expert committee. *FAO Nutritional Studies No. 37.* Rome.

    1973. Energy and protein requirements. Report of a joint FAO/WHO ad hoc expert committee. *WHO Technical Report Series No 522.* Geneva.

    1991. Protein quality evaluation. Report of a joint FAO/WHO expert consultation. *FAO Food and Nutrition Paper No. 51.* Rome.

FAO/WHO/UNU (Food and Agricultural Organization of the United Nations/World Health Organization/United Nations University). 1985. Energy and protein requirements. Report of a joint FAO/WHO/UNU expert consultation. *Technical Report Series No 724.* Geneva.

FAOSTAT. 1996. Computerized information series. *Food Balance Sheets 1961-1994,* Food and Agriculture Organization. Rome.

Fischer, E. 1901. Ueber die Hydrolyse des Caseins durch Salzsäure. *Zeitschrift für Physiologische Chemie* 33: 151-76.

Friedman, M. I. 1995. Control of energy intake by energy metabolism. *American Journal of Clinical Nutrition* 62 (Supplement): 1096S-100S.

Garrow, J. S. 1974. *Energy balance and obesity in man.* New York.

Harris, J. A., and F. G. Benedict. 1919. *A biometric study of basal metabolism in man.* Carnegie Institute of Washington Publication 279. Washington, D.C.

Hegsted, D. M. 1976. Energy needs and energy utilization. In *Present knowledge of nutrition.* Fourth edition, ed. D. M. Hegsted. Washington, D.C.

Hendrickse, R. G. 1984. The influence of aflatoxins on child health in the tropics with particular reference to kwashiorkor. *Transactions of the Royal Society of Tropical Medicine and Hygiene* 78: 427-35.

Heymsfield, S. B., P. C. Darby, L. S. Muhlheim, et al. 1995. The calorie: Myth, measurement and reality. *American Journal of Clinical Nutrition* 62 (Supplement): 1034S-41S.

Heymsfield, S. B., and P. J. Williams. 1988. Nutritional assessment by clinical and biochemical methods. In *Modern nutrition in health and disease.* Seventh edition, ed. M. E. Shils and V. R. Young, 817-60. Philadelphia, Pa.

Hill, J. O., C. Melby, S. L. Johnson, and J. C. Peters. 1995. Physical activity and energy requirements. *American Journal of Clinical Nutrition* 62 (Supplement): 1059S-66S.

Hoffer, L. J. 1988. Starvation. In *Modern nutrition in health and disease.* Seventh edition, ed. M. D. Shils, and V. R. Young, 774-94. Philadelphia, Pa.

Hutchison, R. 1903. *Food and the principles of dietetics.* New York.

IDECG (International Dietary Energy Consultancy Group).

1996. International dietary energy consultancy group, Energy and protein requirements. Supplement, ed. N. S. Scrimshaw, J. C. Waterlow, and B. Schürch. *European Journal of Clinical Nutrition* 50 (Supplement 1).

Irwin, M. I., and D. M. Hegsted. 1971. A conspectus of research on protein requirements of man. *Journal of Nutrition* 101: 385-430.

James, W. P. T., and A. Ralph. 1994. The functional significance of low body mass index. *European Journal of Clinical Nutrition* 48 (Supplement 3): 51-202.

Jones, D. B. 1941. Factors for converting percentages of nitrogen in foods and feeds into percentages of protein. *U.S. Department of Agriculture Circular No. 183.* Washington, D.C.

Keys, A., J. Brozek, A. Henschel, et al. 1950. *The biology of human starvation.* Minneapolis, Minn.

Kinney, J. M. 1988. Food as fuel: The development of concepts. In *Modern nutrition in health and disease.* Seventh edition, ed. M. E. Shils and V. R. Young, 516-32. Philadelphia, Pa.

Kleiber, M. 1961. *The fire of life: An introduction to animal energetics.* New York.

Krebs, H. A., and K. Henseleit. 1932. Untersuchungen über die Harnstoffbildung im Tierkörper. *Zeitschrift für Physiologische Chemie* 210: 33-66.

Latham, M. C. 1990. Protein energy malnutrition. In *Present knowledge of nutrition.* Sixth edition, ed. M. L. Brown, International Life Sciences Institute, 39-46. Washington, D.C.

League of Nations, Technical Commission of the Health Committee. 1936. *The problem of nutrition. Report on the physiological bases of nutrition,* Vol. 2. Geneva.

Levine, R. 1978. Introduction: Modern development of the principles of nutrition. In *Diabetes, obesity and vascular disease: Metabolic and molecular interrelationships,* Part 1, ed. H. M. Katzen and R. J. Mahler, 1-5. New York and London.

Lifson, N., G. B. Gordon, and McLintock. 1955. Measurement of total carbon dioxide production by means of D_2O^{18}. *Journal of Applied Physiology* 7: 704-10.

Lusk, G. 1914. *The fundamental basis of nutrition.* New Haven, Conn.

    1928. *The elements of the science of nutrition.* Fourth edition. Philadelphia, Pa., and London.

    1933. *Nutrition.* New York.

Mayer, J. 1955. Regulation of energy intake and the body weight: The glucostatic theory and the lipostatic hypothesis. *Annals New York Academy of Sciences.* 63: 15-42.

McCollum, E. V. 1957. *A history of nutrition.* Boston, Mass.

McGilvery, R. W. 1979. *Biochemistry: A functional approach.* Philadelphia, Pa., and London.

McLaren, D. S. 1974. The great protein fiasco. *The Lancet* 2: 93-6.

Mendel, L. B. 1923. *Nutrition: The chemistry of life.* New Haven, Conn.

Miles, C. W., P. Webb, and C. E. Bodwell. 1986. Metabolizable energy of human mixed diets. *Human Nutrition Applied Nutrition* 40A: 333-46.

Mitchell, H. H. 1924. A method of determining the biological value of protein. *Journal of Biological Chemistry.* 58: 873-903.

Moore, S., D. H. Spackman, and W. H. Stein. 1958. Chromatography of amino acids on sulfonated polystyrene resins. *Analytical Chemistry* 30: 1185-90.

Moore, S., and W. H. Stein. 1954. Procedures for the chromatographic determination of amino acids on four percent cross-linked sulfonated polystyrene resins. *Journal of Biological Chemistry* 211: 893-907.

Munro, H. N. 1951. Carbohydrate and fat as factors in protein utilization and metabolism. *Physiological Reviews* 31: 449-88.

1964a. Historical introduction: The origin and growth of our present concepts of protein metabolism. In *Mammalian protein metabolism*, Vol. 1., ed. H. N. Munro, 1-29. New York and London.

1964b. An introduction to nutritional aspects of protein metabolism. In *Mammalian protein metabolism*, Vol. 2, ed. H. N. Munro, 3-39. New York and London.

Munro, H. N., and M. C. Crim. 1988. The proteins and amino acids. In *Modern nutrition in health and disease*. Seventh edition, ed. M. E. Shils and V. R. Young, 1-37. Philadelphia, Pa.

National Academy of Sciences - National Research Council (NAS-NRC). 1974. *Improvement of protein nutriture: Food and nutrition board*. Washington, D.C.

Needham, J., and E. Baldwin. 1949. *Hopkins and biochemistry, 1861-1947*. Cambridge.

Osborne, T. B. 1919. What and how much should we eat. *Atlantic Monthly* 122: 332-41.

Osborne, T. B., L. B. Mendel, and E. L. Ferry. 1919. A method of expressing numerically the growth promoting value of proteins. *Journal of Biological Chemistry* 37: 233-99.

Pauly, P. J. 1990. The struggle for ignorance about alcohol: American physiologists, Wilbur Olin Atwater and the Woman's Christian Temperance Union. *Bulletin of Medicine* 64: 366-92.

Pellett, P. L. 1990a. Food energy requirements in humans. *American Journal of Clinical Nutrition* 51: 711-22.

1990b. Protein requirements in humans. *American Journal of Clinical Nutrition* 51: 723-37.

1996. World essential amino acid supply with special attention to South-east Asia. *Food Nutrition Bulletin* 17: 204-34.

Pellett, P. L., ed. 1963. Evaluation of protein quality. Publication 1100, National Academy of Sciences - National Research Council. Washington, D.C.

Pellett, P. L., and V. R. Young. 1988. The contribution of livestock products to human dietary needs with special reference to West Asia and North Africa. Workshop on Small Ruminants in Mediterranean Areas, International Centre for Agricultural Research in Dry Areas (ICARDA), December 1987. Aleppo, Syria.

1990. Role of meat as a source of protein and essential amino acids in human protein nutrition. In *Meat and health*, ed. A. M. Pearson and C. E. Dutson, 329-70. London and New York.

1992. The effects of different levels of energy intake on protein metabolism and of different levels of protein intake on energy metabolism: A statistical evaluation from the published literature. In *Protein-energy interrelationships*, ed. N. S. Scrimshaw and Beat Schürch. International Dietary Energy Consultancy Group, Nestlé Foundation, 81-121. Lausanne, Switzerland.

Pellett, P. L., and V. R. Young, eds. 1980. Nutritional evaluation of protein foods. *UNU/WHP Food and Nutrition Bulletin Supplement No. 4*, United Nations University. Tokyo.

Pi-Sunyer, F. X. 1988. Obesity. In *Modern nutrition in health and disease*. Seventh edition, ed. M. E. Shils and V. R. Young, 795-816. Philadelphia, Pa.

Prentice, A. M., C. J. K. Spaaij, G. R. Golgberg, et al. 1996. Energy requirements of pregnant and lactating women. Supplement, ed. N. S. Scrimshaw, J. C. Waterlow, and B. Schürch. *Energy and Protein Requirements, European Journal of Clinical Nutrition* 50 (Supplement 1): S82-111.

Rose, W. C. 1957. The amino acid requirements of adult man. *Nutritional Abstracts and Reviews* 27: 631-47.

Rothwell, N. J., and M. J. Stock. 1983. Diet-induced thermogenesis. In *Mammalian thermogenesis*, ed. L. Giardier and M. J. Stock, 50-63. London.

Scrimshaw, N. S. 1976. Strengths and weaknesses of the committee approach: An analysis of past and present recommendations for protein in health and disease. *New England Journal of Medicine* 294: 136-42, 198-203.

Seale, J. L. 1995. Energy expenditure measurements in relation to energy requirements. *American Journal of Clinical Nutrition* 62 (Supplement): 1042S-6S.

Sherman, H. C. 1914. *Chemistry of food and nutrition*. New York.

1920. Protein requirement of maintenance in man and the nutritive efficiency of bread protein. *Journal of Biological Chemistry* 41: 97-110.

1952. *Chemistry of food and nutrition*. Eighth edition. New York.

Shetty, P. S., C. J. K. Henry, A. E. Black, and A. M. Prentice. 1996. Energy requirements of adults: An update on basal metabolic rates (BMR's) and physical activity levels (PAL's). Supplement, ed. N. S. Scrimshaw, J. C. Waterlow, and B. Schürch. *Energy and Protein Requirements, European Journal of Clinical Nutrition* 50 (Supplement 1): S11-23.

Spackman, D. H., W. H. Stein, and S. Moore, S. 1958. Automatic recording apparatus for use in the chromatography of amino acids. *Analytical Chemistry* 30: 1190-205.

Terroine, E. F. 1936. The protein component of the human diet. *Quarterly Bulletin Health Organization, League of Nations* 5: 427-92. Geneva.

Thomas, K. 1909. Über die biologische Wertigkeit der Stickstoffsubstanzen in verschiedenen Nahrungsmitteln. Beiträge zur Frage des physiologischen Stickstoffminimums. *Archiv für Anatomie und Physiologie, Physiologische Abteilung*, 219-302.

Tsang, R. C., A. Lucas, R. Uauy, and S. Zlotkin. 1993. *Nutritional needs of the preterm infant*. Baltimore, Md., and London.

USDHHS (U.S. Department of Health and Human Services). 1988. The surgeon general's report on nutrition and health. DHHS(PHS) Publication No. 88-50210. Washington, D.C.

Van Slyke, D. D. 1911. The analysis of proteins by determination of the chemical groups characteristic of the different amino acids. *Journal of Biological Chemistry* 10: 15-55.

Waterlow, J. C. 1955. Protein malnutrition. Proceedings of a conference in Jamaica 1953. Cambridge.

1984. Kwashiorkor revisited: The pathogenesis of oedema in kwashiorkor and its significance. *Transactions of the Royal Society of Tropical Medicine and Hygiene* 78: 436-41.

Willcock, E. G., and F. G. Hopkins. 1906-7. The importance of individual amino acids in metabolism. *Journal of Physiology* 35: 88-102.

Williams, C. D. 1933. A nutritional disease of childhood associated with a maize diet. *Archives Diseases of Children* 8: 423-33.

Young, V. R., D. M. Bier, and P. L. Pellett. 1989. A theoretical basis for increasing current estimates of the amino acid requirements in adult man with experimental support. *American Journal of Clinical Nutrition* 50: 80-92.

Young, V. R., N. S. Scrimshaw, and P. L. Pellett. 1998. Significance of dietary protein source in human nutrition: Animal and/or plant proteins. In *Feeding a world population of more than eight billion people: A challange to science*, ed. J. C. Waterlow, 205-22. New York.

IV.D

Deficiency Diseases

IV.D.1 ᐤ Beriberi

The complex of clinical disturbances long known as beriberi has been recognized since early in the twentieth century as arising because of a deficiency of thiamine. Like others in the group of B vitamins, thiamine has essential coenzyme functions in intermediary metabolism. The principal role of this water-soluble molecule is that of precursor of thiamine pyrophosphate (thiamine diphosphate), a coenzyme (often referred to as cocarboxylase) in energy generation through oxidative decarboxylation of alpha-ketoacids, such as pyruvic acid and alpha-ketoglutaric acid. Thiamine pyrophosphate serves also as the coenzyme for transketolase, a catalyst in the pentose phosphate pathway of glucose metabolism. Measurement of transketolase activity in erythrocytes and stimulation of activity by added thiamine pyrophosphate is the most convenient and sensitive method for detecting human thiamine deficiency. As the pyrophosphate and/or the triphosphate, thiamine appears also to have a role in facilitating conduction in peripheral nerves.

Like most vitamins, thiamine cannot be synthesized in the body and must be acquired in the diet. It is found in many foods and is most abundant in grains, legumes, nuts, and yeast. All meats and most dairy products contain some thiamine, but the richest sources are pork and eggs. Milk, however, is not a rich source. As a water-soluble vitamin, thiamine is easily lost in cooking water. Fish can supply good amounts, but with fermentation of raw fish, the enzyme thiaminase may alter the thiamine molecule, blocking its biological activity. Dietary thiamine is actively absorbed, mainly in the small intestine. The recommended daily dietary allowance is 1.2 to 1.5 milligrams for adult males and 1.0 to 1.1 milligrams for adult females, depending upon age, with a 50 percent increase in requirements during pregnancy and lactation. Up to about 25 milligrams can be stored by a healthy person, especially in heart muscle, brain, liver, kidney, and skeletal muscle.

With a deficient diet, skeletal muscle soon begins to lose thiamine, followed by the liver, nervous system, and heart. Some intestinal bacteria are known to synthesize thiamine (Altschule 1978: 96), but this action probably contributes little, if at all, to human thiamine stores. Most thiamine excreted in urine is free, but some is also released as the pyrophosphate. Some thiamine may be lost in sweat, but the significance of this loss for workers in hot conditions remains to be clarified. Thiamine is low in toxicity, although very large doses may have some side effects. Large doses, however, are rapidly excreted, and so persistent toxic effects are rare.

The clinical consequences of advanced thiamine deficiency reflect, especially, the involvement of the cardiovascular system and the nervous system, both peripheral and central. The consequences of severe deficiency will certainly be disabling and may be fatal.

In the sections that follow, thiamine deficiency is first considered in the past, then in the present, with due attention to its distribution, to groups and populations at special risk, and to the range of clinical features. Cultural, socioeconomic, and behavioral factors, which influence risk, clinical responses, and outcomes, are noted. The final sections examine the history of research on etiology and of work leading to control and prevention.

Beriberi in the Past

Thiamine deficiency does not appear to leave behind any of the kinds of distinctive pathological evidence that permit paleopathologists to recognize diseases of the past. A comprehensive survey of pathological conditions in human skeletal remains (Ortner and Putschar 1985) includes no conditions assignable to deficiency of any of the B vitamins, and it seems unlikely that future studies of soft tissue remains will reveal any such evidence. Nevertheless, it is likely that thiamine deficiencies occurred in ancient populations, sporadically at least, even long before the beginnings of grain cultivation.

It has been shown that antithiamine factors occur in a variety of foods. Thermolabile thiaminases have been identified in the viscera of fresh fish, in shellfish, and in certain bacteria. Thermostable thiaminases exist in some animal tissues and in plants associated with caffeic and tannic acids (Paige 1988: 558). Some studies have shown an association of these factors with thiamine deficiency, and thus beriberi. S. L. Vimokesant and colleagues (1975), for example, have described thiamine deficiency in Thailand associated with the consumption of fermented raw fish, the chewing of fermented tea leaves, and the use of betel nuts. They suggest that the antithiamine activity of betel nuts and fermented tea may be induced by their high content of tannic acid. Ingestion of raw clams, which contain thiaminase, has also been shown to destroy thiamine in the human gastrointestinal tract. Some of these kinds of dietary preferences and practices have, no doubt, ancient origins in the human diet.

Early grain cultivation provided important new sources of dietary thiamine, and it is unlikely that simple milling procedures, even in rice-growing regions, led to severe thiamine deficiency, although diets based on rice stripped by steam milling and polishing of its thiamine-rich husks were later widely responsible for the disease. Ancient beriberi, as described in China, may more often have been due to thiaminase or other antithiamine activity than to the absence of the vitamin in the diet because of milling practices or dependence on thiamine-poor foods.

August Hirsch (1885: 572–3) records that beriberi, known as *kak-ke* ("disease of the legs"), can be traced back more than 2,000 years in China:

> Inquiries . . . have succeeded in proving that the word "kak-ke" occurs in a Chinese work dating from about 200 B.C., and that there is an unambiguous description of the disease in another work of some one hundred and thirty years later date. Other references to beriberi in China occur in writings of the third, seventh, and eighth centuries of the present era; and in a medicine book belonging to the end of the tenth century, there is already a distinction drawn between a "dry" or paralytic kak-ke and a "wet" or dropsical [one]. Of the disease in Japan the earliest record is in a medical treatise of the ninth century of our era. . . . For the East Indies the first notice of it occurs in the medico-topographical treatise of Bontius [De Medicina Indorum by Jacob Bontius (1592–1631), a Dutch physician], who was acquainted with the disease there in the seventeenth century under its colloquial name "beriberi."

B. C. P. Jansen (1956: 2) provides a slightly earlier Dutch record: "Already in the year 1611 the first Governor-General of the Dutch East India Company wrote that in the Dutch East Indies there was a disease named beriberi which caused paralysis in the hands and feet."

Beriberi is commonly recorded in dictionaries, encyclopedias, and other modern sources as a term derived from a word in Sinhala (Sinhalese), meaning weakness. Hugh M. Sinclair (1982), however, refers to Bontius's "excellent account of beriberi, the name meaning 'sheep,' since the partial paralysis of the disease caused patients to walk like sheep" – this, indeed, is the correct derivation of the word, as any comprehensive Malay–Indonesian dictionary will show. In Kamus Pelajar Federal (1973), for example, the Malay word *biri-biri* is assigned two meanings: (1) sheep, and (2) beri-beri (the disease). Hirsch (1885: 569), writing as early as the 1860s, casts doubt on alternative suggestions that the word beriberi derived from "Cingalese" or "Hindustani" words. Hirsch leaned toward a Malay origin, citing Bontius (who offered a mistaken transliteration of *biri-biri* – "bharyee" – a word said to mean "sheep"). Hirsch also noted another early Dutch author's suggestion that a Malay language word, "biribi" (obviously biri-biri, pronounced rapidly), meaning an "abrupt and tripping gait," was the origin of the term beriberi.

Thiamine deficiency remained an endemic problem until the second half of the nineteenth century. Although present in many parts of the world, beriberi usually appeared as a sporadic disease in individuals, groups, or populations at special risk because of "restricted," thiamine-poor diets. However, with the introduction of the steam-powered rice mill (about 1870), the disease became widespread and at times epidemic in some populations, especially in eastern and southeastern Asia. As a product of industrial and technological expansion, rice – commercially milled and relatively inexpensive – became generally available in a time of maritime competition and increasing establishment, in many societies, of prisons, asylums, military installations, and other institutions that offered only restricted diets.

In the closing decades of the nineteenth century in Japan, for example, beriberi (usually known as *kakke*) was present throughout the country, but was especially prevalent in military garrisons and on warships and naval training ships (Williams 1961). In Malaya, too, at the turn of the century, beriberi was widely distributed but especially conspicuous in closed institutions, such as jails and asylums for the mentally ill (Byron 1951).

It may be noted, however, that most populations in the Indian subcontinent, and Indian immigrant groups generally, remained almost free of beriberi during this period of technological, military, and institutional expansion – as they still do today. This is understandable because, throughout this region, rice has long been parboiled before milling. The unhusked rice, after preliminary soaking, is boiled in domestic vessels or steamed under pressure in the larger mills. The B vitamins are fixed in the grain so that they are not removed with the bran, and remain behind in the milled rice. The parboiling process has long been preferred because the woody outer husk is split, rendering its removal easier during milling (Davidson and Passmore 1966: 261). Beriberi has been endemic in only one Indian state, along the coast of Andhra Pradesh north from above Madras to Vishakhapatnam, and this, according to Sir Stanley Davidson and R. Passmore (1966: 412), is the only area in India where raw-milled rice is the principal cereal.

The vast literature on beriberi reflects its profound impact on morbidity and mortality during the late nineteenth and early twentieth centuries. But this literature also reveals the confusion that existed about the disease, its identity, its causation, and its clinical effects. Beriberi had acquired many other names – regional, local, and culturally specific – in previous centuries, but cosmopolitan medical practitioners and researchers added a considerable variety of their own terms (for example, endemic multiple neuritis, panneuritis epidemica, polyneuritis endemica, ship beriberi, infantile beriberi). These reflected the notion that beriberi might be several quite different diseases, an idea created by the diverse clinical effects of thiamine deficiency and by the common occurrence of several or multiple nutritional deficiencies in the same thiamine-deficient patient.

Beriberi Today

Thiamine deficiency disease persists in the modern world, but its epidemiology is very different from that of a century ago. Epidemic classical beriberi is rarely seen today. Although signs and symptoms of famine-related thiamine deficiency occur all too often, they are likely to be accompanied by clinical evidence of multiple deficiencies of vitamins and other nutrients. War, disaster, and drought-induced famines will continue into the future as contributors to deficiencies of thiamine, but beriberi as a distinct clinical entity will probably seldom occur in those circumstances.

As an endemic disease, however, beriberi has not disappeared. Some beriberi still occurs where rice is the staple cereal, polished rice is preferred, parboiling is not practiced, and few other sources of thiamine exist in the diet. In other areas, where rice is not the staple, beriberi may occur occasionally when refined carbohydrate foods are dominant in the diet. Davidson and Passmore (1966: 412), for example, mention the common occurrence of beriberi early in this century in the fishing communities of Newfoundland and Labrador. Often cut off during the long winter from outside provisions, people in these areas depended upon winter stores consisting mainly of flour made from highly milled wheat. Beriberi probably continues to appear today in similar circumstances of prolonged and extreme isolation.

In some countries, beriberi is so intimately associated with culturally maintained dietary preferences and practices that it is likely to persist well into the future. In northern Thailand, as noted, consumption of fermented raw fish has been reported to be an important cause of beriberi. Vimokesant and colleagues (1975) also concluded that antithiamine activity of fer-

mented tea and betel nuts must contribute to persistent thiamine deficiency in that region. However, to what extent these effects may result from destruction of thiamine, or from loose binding and partial blocking of activity, remains unclear. Further evaluation of these findings is warranted because of the wide use of these substances not only in Thailand but elsewhere in Asia. If the extensive use of betel nut in some regions of India interferes with thiamine activity or retention, it appears, nevertheless, that the thiamine-preserving effect of rice parboiling can maintain a sufficient thiamine balance to minimize the appearance of signs and symptoms of deficiency. This too is, however, a topic in need of further study, particularly in relation to the occurrence and significance of subclinical or borderline thiamine deficiency.

In addition to the problem of endemic beriberi, thiamine deficiency occurs sporadically in many countries, especially as a result of chronic alcoholism, but also in association with some chronic illnesses and with long-term parenteral nutrition (Altschule 1978: 98). As Richard S. Rivlin (1988) reports, thiamine absorption is exquisitely sensitive to ingested ethanol, which can significantly interfere with absorption. Alcoholics may fail to absorb most of their dietary thiamine – thiamine which is likely to be limited, in any case, as the diet is increasingly impaired and restricted. Rivlin notes that about 25 percent of alcoholics admitted to general hospitals in the United States have evidence of thiamine deficiency by either clinical or biochemical criteria. He cites evidence as well that alcohol can adversely affect the intermediary metabolism of thiamine, and that chronic liver disease, resulting from alcoholism, may impair the conversion of thiamine to thiamine pyrophosphate.

Clinical Features

The clinical distinction between wet and dry forms of beriberi can be traced back at least to the ninth century in Japan (Henschen 1966: 170) and to the tenth century in China (Hirsch 1885). The wet–dry differentiation has continued to appear in clinical classifications of thiamine deficiency disorders to the present day, with infantile beriberi accorded separate status in most breakdowns. Some have chosen to describe the disease in terms of three clinical clusters characterized by edema, nervous system signs and symptoms, and symptoms of disorder in the cardiovascular system (Meade 1993). Sinclair (1982) offers the classification adopted here. He sees severe thiamine deficiency giving rise to the following forms of beriberi:

1. Acute beriberi – including acute cardiac beriberi and infantile beriberi, along with Wernicke's encephalopathy (as the acute or subacute component of the Wernicke-Korsakoff syndrome).
2. Chronic beriberi – including dry beriberi, wet beriberi, and chronic beriberi heart (and here

Korsakoff's psychosis may be added as the other, more chronic component of the Wernicke-Korsakoff syndrome).

Acute Cardiac Beriberi

The picture of acute cardiac beriberi is that of congestive failure and cardiac overactivity manifested by dyspnea, orthopnea, precordial pain, palpitations, tachycardia, and edema. In its most fulminant form it has been known in East Asia as *Shoshin* beriberi. These acute forms of cardiac beriberi, uncommon today, were well known to clinicians in Asia a century ago; many patients died of heart failure. With intravenous thiamine, acute cardiac beriberi can readily be treated, with dramatic results.

Infantile beriberi, a condition in infants who are breast-fed by thiamine-deficient mothers, is, as Sinclair (1982) notes, very similar to acute cardiac beriberi in adults. Once common in eastern Asia, the condition usually occurs very early in life, with sudden onset and rapid progression to death. The anorexic, restless infant shows signs of developing cardiac failure, including tachycardia, dyspnea, edema, and aphonia, responsible for a characteristic grunt (the beriberi cry). Although less often recognized today, infantile beriberi, like cardiac beriberi in the adult, will respond well to intravenous or intramuscular thiamine. Improvement of the nursing mother's thiamine nutrition is also essential.

Wernicke's Encephalopathy

First described by Carl Wernicke in 1881, Wernicke's encephalopathy is an acute or subacute cerebral form of beriberi, only recognized as a consequence of thiamine deficiency during and just after World War II, in prisoner-of-war camps. Today it is a disorder associated principally with chronic alcoholism. The pathological changes are characteristically localized, involving the optic nerve, the gray matter around the third and fourth ventricles, and the aqueduct of Sylvius. Clinical features include nystagmus, diplopia, ophthalmoplegia, anorexia, vomiting, insomnia, mental apathy and disorientation, hallucinations, and variable loss of memory. Ataxia appears occasionally. In many cases, signs of peripheral neuropathy are also evident. The condition responds well to treatment with thiamine injections.

Dry Beriberi

In this once common clinical variety of beriberi, it is primarily the peripheral nervous system that is disordered. Dry beriberi is an ascending symmetrical bilateral peripheral neuritis. Early in the course, the complaints may be vague, beginning with stiffness, leg cramps, and numbness in the feet and ankles. Knee and ankle reflexes are first increased, then diminished, and finally lost as the disease advances. Muscle weakness spreads upward in the lower extremities. Affected muscles become tender, painful, numb, and eventually atrophic, sometimes with hyperextension of the knee joints. Ataxia follows, with a characteristic gait (which led to the coining of the name "beriberi," meaning sheep). Hands and arms may also be affected, but not usually until signs and symptoms in the legs are pronounced. Thiamine therapy will arrest the progression and relieve the patient of most symptoms, but all of the damage in advanced disease may not be fully reversible.

Wet Beriberi

This chronic form of beriberi is primarily an edematous condition accompanied, in varying degree, by signs and symptoms of cardiac malfunction. Renal function generally remains intact. Early in the course, edema usually begins in the feet and legs, then extends upwards to the abdomen (producing ascites), thorax, pericardium, and face. Muscle wasting, if present, may be masked by edema. With pulmonary congestion, the chambers of the right heart dilate and the heart begins to fail. Anorexia is invariable, vomiting and diarrhea may occur, and thus the body begins to starve. The patient with wet beriberi is always at risk of a sudden increase in edema, circulatory failure, severe dyspnea, and death.

Chronic Beriberi Heart

Cardiac damage can occur as a result of thiamine deficiency without other signs and symptoms of beriberi. This chronic condition, now referred to as "beriberi heart," is most often associated with chronic alcoholism and/or a history of marked nutritional deficiency. When these causal factors are present, the diagnosis can be suspected when unexplained tachycardia, palpitations, venous congestion, characteristic electrocardiographic changes, and right heart enlargement are noted. Edema may also appear, but not with the same prominence as in cases of wet beriberi.

Causal Research

As beriberi extended its geographical range, incidence, and prevalence in the second half of the nineteenth century, it attracted increasing attention from medical investigators, who began the long process of causal research that extended into the first decades of the twentieth century. Hirsch, in his great *Handbook of Geographical and Historical Pathology*, first published between 1860 and 1864, gave many pages to a description of the disease and to a review and analysis of etiologic possibilities. He found it necessary to discard as principal causes climate, soil, lifestyle, and occupation, among other factors. He could only conclude that beriberi must arise as a result of some intoxication, that is, exposure to a poison. Later the idea emerged that beriberi might appear because of infection, and, until late in the century, theorizing was directed principally to these two causal possibilities.

The search for an infectious agent or a chemical poison, probably in food, continued throughout the remainder of the nineteenth century, but no one interested in beriberi and diet in this period considered the possibility of a deficiency of some specific substance (Williams 1961: 16). Two naval officers (the Dutch naval doctor, F. S. van Leent, and the chief of the Japanese naval medical service, K. Takaki) were successful in reducing the incidence of beriberi on shipboard by broadening diets previously limited largely to rice (Jansen 1956; Williams 1961). These achievements, pointing clearly to some dietary factor in beriberi, were not widely known or acknowledged at the time.

The first step toward the recognition of the role of thiamine deficiency in beriberi came in 1890 with the publication of a report by Christiaan Eijkman, a Dutch military surgeon in Java, of his studies of polyneuritis in domestic fowl. His experiments were initiated to uncover a presumed infectious cause of the disease by inoculating laboratory chickens with supposedly infectious material from beriberi patients. These birds, fed on crude rice, remained healthy, but when they were later switched to a diet of boiled and polished white rice, left over from the hospital, they began to show signs of polyneuritis not unlike that in human beriberi.

Still later, the chickens were returned to a crude rice diet, after the hospital chief forbade the use of the polished luxury rice for laboratory animals. The neuritis soon disappeared. Intrigued by this change, Eijkman fed two groups of fowl, one with crude rice, the other with polished rice. The latter group developed the same beriberi-like neuritis. The result of this simple experiment was decisive, not only in the history of beriberi but also as the beginning of the much wider field of research on vitamins and specific nutritional deficiencies. Eijkman expanded his investigations in Java until 1896, when he returned to Holland, eventually to a professorial appointment and to the award in 1929 (one year before his death) of a Nobel Prize in Physiology and Medicine, "for his discovery of the antineuritic vitamin."

Eijkman's experimental work with fowl in Java was continued by another Dutch scientist, Gerrit Grijns, who soon became the first to express the theory "that in food there occur in small quantities unknown organic substances essential for health" (Jansen 1956). Grijns called them protective substances. He was able to extract such a substance, soluble in water, from rice bran and to employ it in the treatment of human beriberi. Later Casimir Funk coined the name "vitamine" (later shortened to "vitamin") for a protective substance, an amine that he had isolated and assumed (wrongly as it turned out) to be the same as that studied by Eijkman and Grijns (Byron 1951; Jansen 1956).

The studies in Java were confirmed and extended in Malaya early in the new century (Byron 1951). W. L.

Braddon, who published much evidence to show that the cause of beriberi was connected intimately with the consumption of polished white rice, could only explain his findings as due to a poison in the rice. His work provided a foundation for three scientists, H. Fraser, A. T. Stanton, and W. Fletcher, at the Institute for Medical Research in Kuala Lumpur. During the decade following 1905, in their studies of road workers (and in Fletcher's study of patients at an asylum), these investigators further demonstrated the significance of rice polishing in the causation of beriberi. Fraser and Stanton also failed in all attempts to isolate a poison from rice, and they concluded, as Grijns had earlier, that the answer to the problem of beriberi must lie in a nutritional defect, that is, in the absence of an essential protective substance. Fraser and Stanton were never able to isolate the substance, but their studies led them to call for, and advocate, practical measures to cure and prevent beriberi – measures that were to prove very successful. After 1911, the use of polished white rice was prohibited in all Malayan government institutions, the danger of polished rice consumption was widely publicized, and government rice mills began to produce undermilled rice for use in hospitals and public institutions, including prisons and asylums. These actions served to lower dramatically the incidence of beriberi in Malaya within just a few years.

After 1910, as the results of the Malayan studies and preventive actions became known, E. B. Vedder and others in the Philippines started similar programs for the prevention and treatment of the disease. Vedder also encouraged Robert Williams, a scientist at the Bureau of Science in Manila, to begin studies that were to lead, in 1933, to the isolation and final chemical characterization of the protective substance. Some years earlier, in Java, Jansen and W. F. Donath had succeeded in isolating crystals of the antiberiberi factor, but their chemical analysis, limited by the apparatus then at hand, was incomplete, missing the presence of sulfur in the molecule (Jansen 1956). After the final synthesis, in 1936, Williams named the chemical "thiamin." The spelling was later changed to thiamine, but Williams's original spelling is still often used.

Prevention

Southeast and East Asian countries pioneered in developing strategies for the prevention of beriberi. As we have seen, prevention of shipboard beriberi through dietary change was initiated by Japanese and Dutch naval medical officers late in the nineteenth century, long before the recognition of thiamine's role. The section "Causal Research" also took note of the development, early in the twentieth century, of countrywide preventive programs and policies, begun in Malaya and the Philippines many years before thiamine was isolated, characterized, and synthesized.

These programs stressed changes in rice milling to preserve bran, together with public education about the risks associated with dependence upon a diet based on polished white rice.

After 1936 the pace quickened as production of inexpensive synthetic thiamine made food enrichment possible. By 1941 the first standards for the enrichment of bread were established in the United States, and enrichment requirements soon followed, during World War II. Enrichment of whole-grain rice presented more problems than flour enrichment for bread, but even these difficulties were overcome so that today thiamine enrichment is available in rice-based diets, as well as in those for which bread is a staple.

For people throughout the world who consume many other kinds of processed foods, including corn and macaroni products, thiamine is also commonly available, as it is in many varieties of vitamin preparations. In the United States today, many individuals are consuming vitamins, often including thiamine, far in excess of the recommended dietary allowances, and it is estimated that one-third of individuals 65 years of age and older in this country are taking some kind of nutritional supplement (Rivlin 1988).

Williams concluded his 1961 book, *Toward the Conquest of Beriberi,* with a chapter on the prospects for eradication of the disease, as advocated by a joint United Nations committee (World Health Organization 1958). This committee, meeting under the sponsorship of the Food and Agriculture Organization and the World Health Organization, recommended six preventive measures that, taken together, could be expected largely to eliminate, if not actually eradicate, beriberi in countries where rice is a staple food:

1. General improvement of the diet to increase its thiamine content.
2. Encouragement of the use of undermilled rice.
3. Encouragement of the use of parboiled rice.
4. Promotion of methods of preparing and cooking rice to preserve its thiamine content to the greatest extent possible.
5. Enrichment of rice.
6. Increased use of synthetic thiamine in various ways other than rice enrichment.

Each of these measures continues today to have its role in beriberi prevention. It should be noted, however, that the committee was not aware, in the 1950s, of the possible extent of the problem of interference with thiamine activity and availability through the actions of thiaminase and other antithiamine agents. Even now this problem remains largely undefined, although in some countries, certainly in northern Thailand and, probably, in areas of Myanmar (Burma), dietary preferences, especially for fermented raw fish, are considered to be the most important causes of endemic beriberi.

Sporadic and subclinical or marginal thiamine deficiency persists today and will continue to do so. Eradication of this deficiency is not in prospect, but neither is recurrent epidemic beriberi.

Frederick L. Dunn

Bibliography

Altschule, Mark D. 1978. *Nutritional factors in general medicine. Effects of stress and distorted diets.* Springfield, Ill.

Byron, F. E. 1951. Beri-beri. In *Fifty years of medical research in Malaya.* Studies from the Institute for Medical Research, Federation of Malaya, No. 25: 98–118. Kuala Lumpur.

Davidson, Stanley, Sir, and R. Passmore. 1966. *Human nutrition and dietetics.* Third edition. Edinburgh and London.

Henschen, Folke. 1966. *The history of diseases,* trans. Joan Tate. London.

Hirsch, August. 1885. *Handbook of geographical and historical pathology,* Vol. 2, trans. Charles Creighton. London.

Jansen, B. C. P. 1956. Early nutritional researches on beriberi leading to the discovery of vitamin B1. *Nutrition Abstracts and Reviews* 26: 1–14.

Kamus Pelajar Federal. 1973. *Learner's Dictionary.* Kuala Lumpur and Singapore.

Meade, Melinda S. 1993. Beriberi. In *The Cambridge world history of human disease,* ed. K. F. Kiple, 606–12. Cambridge and New York.

Ortner, Donald J., and Walter G. J. Putschar. 1985. *Identification of pathological conditions in human skeletal remains.* Smithsonian Contributions to Anthropology No. 28. Washington, D.C.

Paige, David M. 1988. *Clinical nutrition.* Second edition. St. Louis, Mo.

Rivlin, Richard S. 1988. Vitamin B1 (thiamin) structure and biochemical function. In *Cecil textbook of medicine.* Eighteenth edition, 1229–30. Philadelphia, Pa.

Sinclair, Hugh M. 1982. Thiamin. In *Vitamins in medicine,* Vol. 2. Fourth edition, ed. Brian M. Barker and David A. Bender, 114–67. London.

Vimokesant, S. L., D. M. Hilker, S. Nakornchai, et al. 1975. Effects of betel nut and fermented fish on the thiamin status of northeastern Thais. *American Journal of Clinical Nutrition* 28: 1458–63.

Williams, Robert R. 1961. *Toward the conquest of beriberi.* Cambridge, Mass.

World Health Organization. 1958. *Fifth report of the Joint FAO/WHO Expert Committee on Nutrition.* Geneva.

IV.D.2 ❧ Iron Deficiency and Anemia of Chronic Disease

Until the nineteenth century, unspecified chronic anemia was known as chlorosis, or the "green sickness," referring to the extreme pallor that characterized severe cases. For centuries, "chlorosis, or green sickness, was attributed to unrequited passion. Medieval Dutch painters portrayed the pale olive complexion of chlorosis in portraits of young women" (Farley and Foland 1990: 89). Although such extreme cases are not common in Western societies today, less severe acquired anemia is quite common. In fact, acquired anemia is one of the most prevalent health conditions in modern populations.

Technically, anemia is defined as a subnormal number of red blood cells per cubic millimeter (cu mm), subnormal amount of hemoglobin in 100 milliliter (ml) of blood, or subnormal volume of packed red blood cells per 100 ml of blood, although other indices are usually also used. Rather than imputing anemia to unrequited love, modern medicine generally imputes it to poor diets that fail to replenish iron loss resulting from rapid growth during childhood, from menstruation, from pregnancy, from injury, or from hemolysis. One of today's solutions to the frequency of acquired anemia is to increase dietary intake of iron. This is accomplished by indiscriminate and massive iron fortification of many cereal products, as well as the use of prescription and nonprescription iron supplements, often incorporated in vitamin pills. However, a nutritional etiology of anemia as dietary has, in the past, been assumed more often than proven. Determining such an etiology is complicated by the fact that the hematological presentation of dietary-induced iron deficiency anemia resembles the anemia of chronic disease. Of the many types and causes of acquired anemia, only those associated with diet and chronic disease are discussed here (for an overview of others, see Kent and Stuart-Macadam this volume).

Anemia Due to Diet or Chronic Disease?

Although causes differ, patients with either iron-deficiency anemia or the anemia of chronic disease/inflammation have subnormal circulating iron levels called hypoferremia. Below-normal levels of circulating iron are manifested in low hemoglobin/hematocrit, serum iron, and transferrin saturation levels. Because serum ferritin is an indirect measure of iron stores, it provides a sensitive index to distinguish these two anemias (Cook and Skikne 1982; Zanella et al. 1989). When the body does not have enough iron as a result of diet, bleeding, or other causes, serum ferritin values are subnormal and reflect the subnormal amount of iron in the bone marrow. In the anemia of chronic disease/inflammation, however, serum ferritin levels are normal to elevated because circulating iron is transferred to storage, as reflected by the combination of subnormal circulating iron levels with normal or elevated serum ferritin values.

Removing iron from circulation reduces its availability to pathogens that require it for proliferation (Weinberg 1974, 1984, 1990, 1992). When compared with bone marrow aspirations, serum ferritin values

correctly detected iron deficiency in 90 percent of patients; serum iron in 41 percent; total iron binding capacity in 84 percent; and transferrin saturation in 50 percent (Burns et al. 1990). Erythrocyte sedimentation rate (ESR) is a nonspecific measure of the presence of infection or inflammation. If used in combination with serum ferritin, ESR can be useful in distinguishing anemia of chronic disease from iron deficiency anemia (Beganovic 1987; Charache et al. 1987; Witte et al. 1988).

Although diet is most often attributed as the cause of iron-deficiency anemia, in the absence of blood loss or parasites, even the most frugal diets rarely result in iron-deficiency anemia. According to C. K. Arthur and J. P. Isbister (1987: 173), "iron deficiency is almost never due to dietary deficiency in an adult in our community [i.e., Western society]." The average person requires very little iron intake to replace that lost through perspiration, menstruation, and urination because as much as 90 percent of the iron needed for the formation of new blood cells is derived from recycling senescent red blood cells (Hoffbrand 1981). In addition, individuals suffering from iron deficiency absorb significantly more iron from the same diet and excrete significantly less iron than nondeficient individuals. In other words, "the intestine can adjust its avidity to match the body's requirement" (O'Neil-Cutting and Crosby 1987: 491). Nonetheless, it has been estimated that approximately 30 percent of a world population of nearly 4.5 billion are anemic, with at least half of this 30 percent (500 to 600 million people) thought to have iron-deficiency anemia (Cook and Lynch 1986). Even in affluent Western societies, 20 percent of menstruating females have been reported to be iron deficient (Arthur and Isbister 1987: 172). Recent surveys in the United States, however, indicate that these figures are much too high (Cook et al. 1986).

Elsewhere, researchers have discovered, to their surprise, that diet is not always responsible for the acknowledged high morbidity of a particular region. According to P. Aaby (1988: 290–1), "We started out by assuming that malnutrition was the major determinant of high child mortality and that changing this pattern would have a beneficial effect on mortality. Much to our distress, we found very little evidence that nutritional status [as measured by the presence of anemia] was strongly related to the variation in nutritional practices."

Failure to distinguish anemia etiology correctly can be seen in several studies. For example, Arthur and Isbister report that "of 29 patients 'diagnosed' as having iron deficiency anaemia, only 11 patients in fact had true iron deficiency when reviewed by the authors. Most patients had the anaemia of chronic disease that was misdiagnosed as iron deficiency. There is a strong clinical impression amongst hematologists that this problem of misdiagnosis is not unique to hospital based specialists but also applies more widely" (Arthur and Isbister 1987: 172). Almost 50 percent of infants diagnosed as iron deficient were found to have occult gastrointestinal blood loss without anatomic lesions, which was the source of their anemia (Fairbanks and Beutler 1988: 208). Although the following discussions are hampered somewhat by the fact that not all studies include serum ferritin tests needed to distinguish dietary iron-deficiency anemia from the anemia of chronic disease, an attempt is made to differentiate when possible and to indicate when this is not possible.

Diet and Iron-Deficiency Anemia

When iron-deficiency anemia is caused by severely deficient diets, it appears to be a straightforward problem: Not enough iron is ingested to replace losses. In reality, many cases of iron-deficiency anemia involve unidentified blood loss that causes, accentuates, and/or perpetuates dietary-induced iron-deficiency anemia. (Note that throughout this paper, we are specifically discussing iron and diet, not protein, vitamins, and other nutrients that are also integral parts of a diet).

Anemia is rarely caused by diet alone. This is partly because healthy humans lose only 1 to 3 milligrams (mg) iron per day and partly because almost all food and, in many areas, drinking water contain some iron. Women in a Swedish study lost between 0.6 and 0.7 mg of iron through menstruation and 95 percent lost on average *less* than 1.4 mg per day (Fairbanks and Beutler 1988: 205).

Most individuals are able to replenish these losses with a normal diet. For example, Westerners ingest meat almost daily and consume additional iron in fortified foods (such as that contained in many wheat products). Wine and cider can provide 2 to 16 mg or more iron per liter (Fairbanks and Beutler 1988). Moreover, depending on the quantity of the body's iron stores, between 15 and 35 percent of heme iron, which is found in red meat, poultry, and fish, and between 2 and 20 percent of nonheme iron in plants is absorbed (Monsen 1988: 787). Higher amounts of nonheme iron in vegetables are absorbed when consumed with heme iron in meat or in combination with iron absorption enhancers, such as ascorbic acid (Hallberg, Brune, and Rossander 1989). Several studies of the amount of iron ingested by North Americans indicate that normal individuals who are not suffering from unnatural blood loss consume sufficient iron to prevent deficiency. For example, a study of 51 women found that those who consumed only poultry or fish or who were vegetarians had a mean iron intake of 12 mg, whereas those who regularly ate red meat had a mean iron intake of 13 mg (Monsen 1988: 789). The mean iron intake of 162 women in another study was 11.1 mg (Subar and Bowering 1988). Female long-distance runners ingested between 11.5 mg and 14 mg per day (Manore et al. 1989).

Blood loss and true iron deficiency also result in increased iron absorption. Research shows that iron-replete men with sufficient iron stores absorb 2.5 percent of nonheme iron ingested, as compared to 26 percent of the heme iron consumed (Cook 1990). These percentages can be contrasted with iron-deficient males who absorb 22 percent more nonheme iron than normal males and 47 percent more heme iron (Cook 1990: 304). The same flexibility applies to iron loss. Normal males lose about 0.9 mg of iron per day. In contrast, hypoferremic males lose only about 0.5 mg per day, and hyperferremic males lose about 2.0 mg per day (Finch 1989).

Although 82 percent of women studied in New York State recorded an average consumption of only 75 percent of the United States Recommended Dietary Allowance (RDA) of iron, the amount ingested was a mean of 11.1 mg, which exceeds the amount of iron loss through normal physiological processes (Subar and Bowering 1988; also see Brennan et al. 1983 for similar conclusions based on a study of low-income pregnant women). Thus, if we arbitrarily assume an absorption rate of 18 percent of all iron consumed, the mean iron available is well above the 1.4 mg required by menstruating women. This suggests that previously recommended replacement needs of average menstruating women may have been set too high. More scientists today recommend that average menstruating women need to absorb only 1.4 mg iron daily to replace losses (Monsen 1988: 786). In fact, the RDA is higher than the average iron loss for all groups. As a result, many people take in less than the RDA levels of iron without suffering dietary iron deficiency.

Albeit rare, severely iron-deficient diets do exist, though not necessarily because of low iron intake. Adult East Indian vegetarians ingest large quantities of iron, as much as 30 mg per day (Bindra and Gibson 1986). At the same time, they consume such large amounts of inhibitory substances that some suffer from iron-deficiency anemia (Bindra and Gibson 1986). These items include tannin (especially from tea); dietary fiber; coffee; calcium phosphate; soy protein; and phytates in bran and nuts, such as walnuts, almonds, peanuts, hazelnuts, and Brazil nuts (Macfarlane et al. 1988; Monsen 1988; Muñoz et al. 1988). The larger the amount of phytate consumed, the less iron is absorbed (Hallberg, Brune, and Rossander 1989). What appears to occur is that although the diet contains sufficient iron for replacement of normal physiological losses, inhibitory factors limit the absorption of that iron.

In addition to malabsorption of iron, moderate-to-heavy consumption of fish has been associated with a significantly increased bleeding time test in both males and females (Herold and Kinsella 1986; Houwelingen et al. 1987; Sullivan 1989). The prolonged bleeding time presumably results in significantly more blood loss and lower iron stores. This may explain why young women who habitually eat fish as their major source of protein have levels of serum ferritin and anemia similar to those of strict vegetarians who consume iron inhibitory substances (Worthington-Roberts, Breskin, and Monsen 1988). Here again, we see that the amount of iron ingested is not directly related to levels of anemia. Occult blood loss and iron absorption are more important as relevant factors fostering iron-deficiency anemia than is the actual amount of dietary iron ingested.

Illness and the Anemia of Chronic Disease

The anemia of chronic disease/inflammation has the same hematological presentation as dietary iron deficiency anemia, with the exception of normal to elevated serum ferritin levels. As stated earlier, both normal-to-elevated serum ferritin (reflecting adequate or above-normal iron stores) and elevated ESR indicate the presence of infection and/or the inflammatory process. In fact, such conditions, created by the body's generalized nonspecific defense against invading pathogens or neoplasia (cancer), reduce the availability of circulating iron. This denies to many bacteria, parasites, and neoplastic cells the iron they need to proliferate. These hematological changes are caused by the production of interleukin-1, interleukin-6, and tumor necrosis factor alpha (Weinberg 1992).

There is abundant research to support the conclusion that anemia is one of the body's defenses against disease (fever and the manufacture of various cytokines are other defenses [Kent, Weinberg and Stuart-Macadam 1994]). A broad spectrum of illnesses is associated with the anemia of chronic disease (Cash and Sears 1989). The role of iron in enhancing infections and anemia as a defense have been detailed in a number of publications by Eugene Weinberg (1974, 1984, 1986, 1990, 1992). Most bacteria and parasites require iron but cannot store it. They survive and thrive by extracting needed iron from their host. As a consequence, increased available iron can be detrimental to health, as can be seen in modern populations receiving iron supplements or consuming large amounts of dietary iron. For example, the incidence of serious bacterial infections increased significantly when infants were given intramuscular iron-dextran (Barry and Reeve 1977: 376):[1] "When the iron administration was stopped the incidence of disease in Polynesians decreased from 17 per 1,000 to 2.7 per 1,000 total births." Other research substantiated the association between an increased incidence of bacterial infections, such as *Escherichia coli* sepsis, and the administration of intramuscular iron-dextran in neonates (Becroft, Dix, and Farmer 1977).

A number of health problems are connected with increased iron intake. In New Guinea, infants with respiratory infections given iron-dextran had longer hospital stays and higher morbidity than those not given iron supplements (Oppenheimer et al. 1986a). Malarial infection was greatly increased in infants with

higher transferrin saturation levels, leading the investigators to conclude that hypoferremia has a protective role against malaria (Oppenheimer et al. 1986b). Furthermore, in a study of 110 patients in Africa, those with anemia had fewer malarial attacks than those with higher iron levels (Masawe, Muindi, and Swai 1974). Anemic patients who did not exhibit signs of malaria developed malaria *after* iron therapy was initiated. In contrast to nonanemic Turkana from Kenya, mildly anemic Turkana who consume little meat, poultry, or other heme iron have a lower incidence of infectious diseases, including such various infections as malaria, brucellosis, and amebiasis (Murray, Murray, and Murray 1980a). Among the Maasai, anemic individuals had a significantly lower incidence of amebic dysentery. Examination of the cow's milk consumed by Maasai "showed that it not only had a concentration of iron below the minimum necessary for the growth of *E. histolytica* [an amoeba] but also contained partly saturated lactoferrin and transferrin, which may actively compete with the parasite in the colon for ambient iron" (Murray, Murray, and Murray 1980b: 1351).

When associated with malaria and other infections, serum ferritin levels are generally increased in anemic children (Adelekan and Thurnham 1990). This indicates that iron stores are present in these children, despite the lowered serum iron, transferrin saturation, and hemoglobin levels, all of which suggests strongly that the anemia is not the result of dietary inadequacies. The body removes circulating iron to storage in an attempt to reduce its availability to invading malaria parasites or bacteria. Food taboos that restrict young children's intake of iron by prohibiting the consumption of meat are found in many areas where malaria is endemic, from Africa to India to Malaysia and New Guinea (Lepowsky 1985). These taboos may be partially explained as an attempt to aid the body's hypoferremic defense against malaria (Lepowsky 1985: 120).

Some diseases result in highly elevated transferrin saturation levels that make iron much more accessible to pathogens. In diseases such as leukemia, patients have been observed with sera that were 96 to 100 percent saturated (normal is 16 to 50 percent). As a consequence, leukemia patients are unusually susceptible to infection (Kluger and Bullen 1987). Thus in one study of 161 leukemia patients who died, 78 percent of the deaths were attributed to infection and not to leukemia directly (Kluger and Bullen 1987: 258).

Another investigation provides an excellent demonstration of the direct relationship between anemia of chronic disease and infection/inflammations. Over a period of 30 days, researchers analyzed the blood of healthy, well-nourished, and nonanemic infants before and after they were immunized with live measles virus (Olivares et al. 1989). After immunization, the hemoglobin, serum iron, and transferrin saturation levels fell significantly, whereas serum ferritin levels rose significantly as the body shifted circulating iron to storage. These levels persisted for 14 to 30 days, while the body produced hypoferremia, or low levels of circulating iron, in an attempt to make iron less available. Even "in those infants with prior evidence of normal iron status, the viral process induced changes indistinguishable from iron deficiency" (Olivares et al. 1989: 855). The authors noted that changes in the white blood cells mimicked a bacterial infection, as did changes in iron levels; in both cases, rapid proliferation of the virus imitated the rapid proliferation of bacteria (Olivares et al. 1989: 855). The body was unable to differentiate between the proliferation of bacteria and the proliferation of the virus and responded in the same manner by producing hypoferremia.

Anemia in Prehistory

In prehistoric populations, the distribution of anemia equaled or surpassed that found in today's world. There was a general increase in anemia through time, ranging from a few, extremely rare occurrences in the Paleolithic (Anderson 1968) to the Mesolithic (Janssens 1970), to more common occurrence in the Neolithic (Angel 1967), and the Bronze Age (Cule and Evans 1968). Anemia was even more frequent in recent groups, such as the prehistoric American southwestern Pueblos (El-Najjar 1977).

Prehistoric study is possible because anemia is identifiable in skeletal material by a cranial deformation called porotic hyperostosis (also known as cribia orbitalia when the orbits are affected). Physical effects include cranial lesions that are characterized by a sievelike porosity involving parts of the outer skull, often causing a thinning of the outer table, textual changes, and sometimes a "hair on end" appearance (Moseley 1965; Stuart-Macadam 1987). Porotic hyperostosis was originally thought to result from hereditary anemias, such as thalassemia or sickle cell anemia. More recently, chronic acquired anemia has been identified from roentgenograms (X rays) as a cause of porotic hyperostosis visible in living young anemic children (Shahidi and Diamond 1960; Powell, Weens, and Wenger 1965). More recent and conclusive studies confirm the link between porotic hyperostosis and acquired anemia (Stuart-Macadam 1987).

Whereas it is not difficult to identify anemia in skeletal populations, it is most difficult to differentiate dietary iron-deficiency anemia from the anemia of chronic disease. At first it was thought that the chemical makeup of bones was an indirect measure of the amount of meat consumed (Bumsted 1980, 1985). However, problems of chemical contamination through mineral loss and contact with minerals in soil have yet to be resolved. A study specifically designed to test the reliability of current bone chemical analyses concluded that their "results suggest that post-

mortem alteration of dietary tracers in the inorganic phases of bone may be a problem at all archaeological sites and must be evaluated in each case" (Nelson et al. 1986: 1941) Other problems associated with stable isotope and trace element analyses of bone are numerous, and interpretations utilizing current techniques are not conclusive (Klepinger 1984; Aufderheide 1989; Keegan 1989; Sillen, Sealy, and van der Merwe 1989). However, indirect measures of dietary iron and disease, which rely on a basic understanding of iron, anemia, diet, and disease, are possible. The presence of porotic hyperostosis in nonhuman primates, such as chimpanzees, gorillas, orangutans, and various species of Old World monkeys, including baboons (Hengen 1971), reinforce the unlikelihood that an impoverished diet is frequently the cause.

Anemia in the New World

Poor diet, sometimes in combination with infectious diseases, has served as the usual explanation for skeletal evidence of anemia among prehistoric Native Americans from the eastern United States to South America. However, faunal remains, mobility patterns, new medical information, and other nontraditional lines of evidence indicate that disease, rather than diet, may often be a better interpretation.

Eastern United States. Although some investigators still claim a maize-dependent diet as the sole or primary cause of porotic hyperostosis in prehistoric southeastern skeletal populations (Robbins 1986), more recent reevaluations suggest that diet may *not* have been a major cause. During the Mississippian period, an increase in porotic hyperostosis in children, particularly those under the age of six, occurred in the lower Illinois Valley. Nutritional anemia alone was probably rare in this age group, especially among breast-fed children. However, the condition coincides with a general increase in destructive bone lesions indicative of chronic inflammations in skeletal populations (Cook 1984: 257–9). During the period of these burials (between A.D. 1100 and 1300), Cahokia grew to be the largest pre-Columbian city in North America, with a population of 25,000 to 43,000 (Cook 1984). Non-Western sedentary, aggregated communities often have heavy pathogen loads, as discussed in the section "Anemia of Sedentism." The skeletal populations exhibit a concomitant increase in anemia and inflammation. This combination illustrates the link between increased population density and increased health problems. Diet cannot be implicated in anemia because during this time the:

> Mississippian diet based on archaeological data and ethnohistoric documentation . . . seems remarkably abundant in the essential elements: protein from both animal and vegetable sources, carbohydrates from cultivated and collected plant foods, and oils from seeds, nuts,

and animal fat, all of these rich in minerals and vitamins from undepleted soils. . . . This ecological diversity, coupled with the sophisticated systems of multiple cropping, surplus food storage, and redistribution described by early European observers, offered protection against nutritional stress from local fluctuations in weather and resource populations. (Powell 1988: 58)

Also during the Mississippian period at Dickson Mounds, Illinois, the incidence of porotic hyperostosis rose from 13.6 percent to 51.5 percent, which coincided with dramatic increases in infectious bone lesions (Goodman et al. 1984: 289). According to investigators, samples from earlier periods had infection rates of 25 percent of the tibiae examined, but then rose to 77 to 84 percent during the later Mississippian period (Goodman et al. 1984). Although the authors attributed the rise in infectious lesions to nutritional stress brought on by an intensification of agriculture in the later period, a change in demography and, particularly, in aggregation may well be responsible. Studies indicate that the earlier Late Woodland sites in the area had population estimates of 50 to 75 individuals; later Mississippian sites had 440 to 1170 individuals (Goodman et al. 1984). Such an important and dramatic demographic change must have had serious health consequences. These Illinois examples are not isolated cases for the eastern United States. In fact, similar rates of increased infection and porotic hyperostosis through time are reported for the Ohio River Valley (Perzigian, Tench, and Braun 1984) and Georgia (Larsen 1984).

Southwestern United States. A maize-dependent diet has also been implicated in the increase through time of porotic hyperostosis in skeletal material from the southwestern part of the United States. Mahmoud Y. El-Najjar and colleagues were among the first and certainly the most prolific to detail the association between frequency of porotic hyperostosis over time and increasing horticultural activities (El-Najjar et al. 1976; El-Najjar 1977). However, as in the eastern United States, the archaeological data from the Southwest do not seem to support a view of diets sufficiently impoverished as to account for the spectacular increase in porotic hyperostosis through time in Anasazi skeletal populations. Instead, archaeological, ethnographic, and ethnohistorical sources all indicate a varied diet, including meat from both wild and domesticated animals, with the latter including turkeys and dogs (Kent and Lee 1992). In addition, wild plants were consumed in combination with maize, beans, and squash, all of which constituted an adequate diet in terms of iron (Kent 1986).

What, then, caused the increase in porotic hyperostosis? As the Anasazi began to adopt horticulture in general, and maize cultivation in particular, they became more sedentary and aggregated, living in communities called pueblos. Although this was not a linear progression that occurred everywhere, neither was the rise in porotic hyperostosis linear. Higher frequencies of porotic hyperostosis occur in skeletal populations from large, sedentary, aggregated pueblos in which disease was more common than in skeletal populations from smaller, more dispersed settlements where it would have been more difficult for disease vectors to infect populations (Kent 1986). Coprolite data (preserved fecal material) support this interpretation by documenting a lower parasite load for the upland populations in contrast to the valley groups. Coprolites containing parasites from various Anasazi sites are significantly correlated with porotic hyperostosis, whereas those containing different portions of either maize or animal residue are not (Reinhard 1992). In other words, dietary evidence of reliance on meat or maize was not correlated with skeletal evidence of anemia, but parasitism was correlated with porotic hyperostosis.

Elsewhere in the United States. Anemia, apparently caused by chronic diseases and inflammations, produced relatively high levels of porotic hyperostosis throughout the prehistoric United States. It can be seen in coastal California Native American skeletal populations who had a heavy dietary dependence on marine resources (Walker 1986). Eskimo skeletal populations also reveal relatively high percentages of porotic hyperostosis, some of which are even higher than those of southwestern and eastern prehistoric populations (Nathan 1966). Certainly the Eskimo example of porotic hyperostosis was not the result of an insufficient intake of meat. Instead, it was probably the result of seasonally sedentary aggregations and associated disease common to the winter villages. Prehistoric skeletons from all parts of Texas exhibit much lower incidences of porotic hyperostosis; less than 5 percent of 348 adult crania and 15.1 percent of 73 juvenile crania had any evidence of porotic hyperostosis (Goldstein 1957). Although precise locations of the various skeletal material were not cited, it is probable that the populations examined represent the nomadic groups that inhabited much of Texas; if so, this would explain the low incidence of infectious disease and porotic hyperostosis.

Central and South America. High frequencies of porotic hyperostosis were found on the crania of prehistoric Maya from Central America. For example, 21 skulls of Mayan children 6 to 12 years old were found in the Sacred Cenote of Chichén Itzá in the Yucatan; 67 percent had porotic hyperostosis. A number of the adult crania from the cenote also had healed examples of the pathology (Hooton 1940). Prehistoric Maya living in Guatemala suffered from both a high rate of infectious diseases, as evidenced by lesions thought to be related to yaws or syphilis, and to dietary inadequacies, such as vitamin C deficiency, as evidenced by bone lesions (Saul 1973). As a consequence, it is difficult to determine whether the porotic hyperostosis was caused by true dietary deficiency, by infectious diseases, or by a combination of the two.

In contrast, a study of Ecuadoran skeletal populations clearly demonstrates the influence of disease in promoting porotic hyperostosis. Although coastal populations ate iron-rich seafood, in addition to meat and cultivated products, skeletal populations reveal increasingly higher frequencies of porotic hyperostosis over time as they became more sedentary and aggregated (Ubelaker 1992). Coastal peoples suffered from conditions aggravated by large-village life, such as probable parasitic infestations, including hookworm, which causes gastrointestinal bleeding.[2] An examination of mummies from coastal Peru and Chile indicates that the most common cause of death was acute respiratory disease in adults and children (Allison 1984). Approximately half of the mummified individuals died from their first attack of pneumonia (Allison 1984). In contrast, porotic hyperostosis is not common in skeletons of maize farmers who occupied more dispersed habitations in the highlands of Ecuador, where parasites cannot survive because of the altitude and cold climate (Ubelaker 1992).

Although prehistoric cases of dietary-induced porotic hyperostosis may occur, they probably are not representative of entire populations. Iron-deficiency anemia caused by extremely inadequate diets is thought to result from factors not common until the twentieth century. Although not all paleopathologists (particularly those who are more diet-oriented and are less hematologically oriented), agree with the emphasis placed here on the anemia of chronic disease, many recent studies and reinterpretations agree that this is a better explanation than iron deficiency.

Anemia in the Old World

The Old World represents a vast area occupied by humans for a long time period, and thus only a few examples of prehistoric incidences of anemia are presented here.

Hereditary (for example, thalassemia) and acquired cases of anemia from the Mediterranean area cannot be differentiated, although porotic hyperostosis is found in skeletal populations from the area (Angel 1984). In the Levant, Mesolithic Natufians apparently had good health, as did the Paleolithic hunter-gatherers who preceded them, although sample size is very small (Smith et al. 1984). They remained a relatively healthy population during the early Neolithic. Deterioration began in later periods when population aggregations grew larger and more permanent and infectious diseases became endemic. According to P. Smith, O. Bar-Yosef, and A. Sillen, "This deterioration . . . seems to be related to chronic disease rather than to periodic

bouts of food shortages, as indicated by the distribution of developmental lesions in the teeth and bones and the poor condition of all individuals examined" (Smith et al. 1984: 129).

In South Asia, there was a similar trend toward increasing porotic hyperostosis and infection, which has been attributed to nutritional deficiencies and disease (Kennedy 1984) but may also have been caused by demographic factors. Skeletons from the Harappan civilization city of Mohenjo-Daro on the Indus River, Pakistan, have a relatively high incidence of porotic hyperostosis; this led one anthropologist to suggest the possible presence of thalassemia and malaria in the area 4,000 years ago (Kennedy 1984: 183). However, the occurrence of malaria is difficult to evaluate, particularly in light of the high population density of Mohenjo-Daro, which could have promoted a number of infectious diseases common to such sedentary aggregations.

Porotic hyperostosis is found at varying frequencies throughout European prehistory (Hengen 1971), but as no systematic temporal study has been done to date, it is not possible to delineate and interpret trends. However, an interesting geographical pattern has been discerned that suggests that populations located closer to the equator have higher levels of porotic hyperostosis. This might be the result of generally higher pathogen loads in these areas (Stuart-Macadam 1992). However, porotic hyperostosis was well represented, particularly in children, in a large Roman-British cemetery (Stuart-Macadam 1982). This is interesting because it has been suggested that lead poisoning, which can cause severe anemia, was one of the factors that contributed to the ultimate collapse of the Roman Empire (Gilfillan 1965).

According to some research, prehistoric Nubian populations experienced nutritional deficiencies after they became agriculturalists (Armelagos et al. 1984). This interpretation is based on the occurrence of porotic hyperostosis, long-bone growth patterns compared to North Americans, dentition abnormalities, and premature osteoporosis. Moreover, bone growth patterns of skeletons from a medieval Nubian Christian cemetery, (A.D. 550 to 1450) have been used to interpret nutritional stress (Hummert 1983). Nonetheless, it is usually recognized that such stress can be caused by a number of nutritional deficiencies not necessarily related to iron. More recent coprolite data have been employed in support of the hypothesis that an impoverished diet caused the high frequency of porotic hyperostosis in Christian Nubian populations (Cummings 1989). However, it is possible to interpret the data quite differently. For example, it should be noted that meat does not usually preserve in coprolites, and humans do not usually ingest large bones that would be indicative of meat consumption. Therefore, the amount of meat consumed may be substantially underrepresented when interpreting coprolite data. Bearing this in mind, it is impressive that

33.3 percent of the 48 coprolites analyzed contained evidence of fish bones or scales, as well as one pig bone and an unidentifiable mammal bone (Cummings 1989: 86–92). Such evidence contradicts the contention that a diet poor in iron produced the high incidence of porotic hyperostosis in this population.

Anemia in Australia

Frequencies of both infection and anemia (porotic hyperostosis) are low in the desert region of Australia, particularly when compared to other parts of the continent, such as the Murray River area (Webb 1989). Murray River skeletons display a pronounced increase in porotic hyperostosis and infections coinciding with archaeological evidence of restricted mobility, aggregation, and possible overcrowding (Webb 1989: 145–8). Such evidence again suggests that the anemia in question is the result of chronic disease and not diet. Though lower than in the Murray River area, the relative high incidence of anemia and infection that occurred among prehistoric Aborigines occupying the tropical portions of Australia can be attributed to parasitism, such as hookworm (Webb 1989: 155–6).

Acquired Anemia in Today's World

The perspective of dietary deficiency and the anemia of chronic disease presented here permits new insights into a variety of issues facing contemporary populations. Because iron-deficiency anemia and the anemia of chronic disease have not always been distinguished, particularly in earlier studies, the two are discussed together and are differentiated whenever possible.

Anemia of Sedentism

As noted, heavy pathogen loads are characteristic of non-Western sedentary aggregations. In such settings, high morbidity rates are visible, not only hematologically but also in the frequency of parasitic infections. For example, studies indicate that nomadic Amazonians had a lower frequency of parasitic infection than seminomadic horticulturalists and sedentary villagers. In these latter populations, 100 percent of some age groups were infected with parasites (Lawrence et al. 1980). As a whole, the sedentary populations had many more multiple parasitic infections, ranging from 4.2 to 6.8 species per person (Lawrence et al. 1980). Sedentary and aggregated Brazilian Amazonian villages had roundworm (*Ascaris*) infections, ranging from 65 to 100 percent of the population, and heavy worm burdens, including hookworm and whipworm (*Necator americanus, Trichuris trichura*) (Chernela and Thatcher 1989). This situation contrasts with the inhabitants of more nomadic and dispersed villages that had half that rate of roundworm infection (34 percent) and light worm burdens that were asymptomatic (Chernela and Thatcher 1989).

From 60 to 100 percent of the residents of two Colombian villages were found to be infested with parasites (Schwaner and Dixon 1974). In one that lacked sanitation of any kind and in which shoes were rarely worn, 100 percent of the population had either double or triple infections (roundworm, whipworm, and hookworm). Of the 60 percent of those infected in the other village (that had outdoor latrines and where shoes were worn), 70 percent were infected by more than one species (Schwaner and Dixon 1974: 34). Sedentism, aggregation, and the lack of adequate sanitation are all implicated in creating breeding grounds for parasitic and other types of infections. Such conditions lead to high morbidity and chronic hypoferremia as the body attempts to defend itself against the heavy pathogen load. Furthermore, heavy infestations of hookworm and other parasites cause blood loss that even good diets cannot replenish.

The relationship between sedentism and anemia can be more easily seen by comparing nomadic and sedentary people who consume similar diets, thereby factoring out diet as a causal variable of anemia. Hematological research among recently sedentary and still nomadic Basarwa ("Bushmen" or San, as they have been referred to in the literature) illustrates hypoferremia operating in a modern population. The 1969 population of the !Kung Basarwa (who live in the northwestern part of the Kalahari Desert) contained a few ill individuals, as do most populations, but was judged as mostly healthy (Metz, Hart, and Harpending 1971). Their meat intake did not change dramatically between the dry seasons of 1969 and 1987 (Kent and Lee 1992). There were, however, significant changes in mobility patterns, from a relatively nomadic to a relatively sedentary pattern. Concomitant higher morbidity rates ensued. Also, the number of individuals with below-normal serum iron and transferrin saturation levels rose significantly between 1969 and 1987 (Kent and Lee 1992). It is significant that the 1987 Dobe !Kung population, with a roughly adequate meat intake, had more individuals with subnormal serum iron and transferrin saturation values than did the Chum!kwe !Kung population, with an acknowledged deficient diet (Fernandes-Costa et al. 1984; Kent and Lee 1992). It is furthermore significant that no individuals had low serum ferritin values among the Dobe !Kung, which would indicate a dietary deficiency.

To evaluate the role of sedentism in promoting the anemia of chronic disease, a hematological study was conducted in 1988 among a different group of recently sedentary Basarwa living near the Kutse Game Reserve in the eastern half of the Kalahari (Kent and Dunn 1993). Their diet was repetitive but adequate; meat was consumed several times a week (Kent and Dunn 1993). The Kutse Basarwa often complained of illness; respiratory problems were common. Both serum iron and transferrin saturation means were significantly lower for the 1988 Kutse Basarwa than those obtained in 1969 or 1987 among the Dobe Basarwa (Kent and Dunn 1993). At the same time, serum ferritin levels were higher in the adult Kutse population than in the 1987 adult !Kung. This is consistent with the view that the anemia of chronic disease is more prevalent in situations of high morbidity where the body attempts to protect itself from continuous cycles of insult. The children's mean ferritin remained approximately the same (Kent and Dunn 1993).

If hypoferremia operates in response to heavy and chronic pathogen loads, then it should be visible in more than just the hematological profile of a population. Ethnographic observations and informant interviews indicate that there is a high level of morbidity at Kutse but not a deficient diet (Kent and Dunn 1993). Both the 1987 !Kung and 1988 Kutse Basarwa hematological studies indicate that the anemia of chronic disease is common in these populations and is activated in situations of high morbidity. A 1989 follow-up hematological study of the Kutse community reinforces the interpretation of an adequate diet but high morbidity as a result of aggregation (Kent and Dunn n.d.). As pointed out, anemia is not a body defect or disease but is actually a defense against a heavy pathogen load, which operates by reducing circulating levels of iron required by organisms to proliferate.

Anemia of Development and Modernization

Development and modernization projects are often promoted both by local governments and by international businesses and foreign governments as a means to westernize a developing country. Generally, nontraditional subsistence activities are encouraged because the government or politically dominant group believes the change to be beneficial. Extremely deficient diets documented by Susan Stonich (1991), Benjamin Orlove (1987), and others are the consequence of governmental pressure to grow export crops for a world market, which is a relatively recent phenomenon. This type of severe dietary deprivation has usually been correlated with colonialism (Franke 1987; Ross 1987).

Nomadic peoples have been targets of development and modernization schemes. For example, sedentarization at Chum!kwe, located in Namibia on the western edge of the Kalahari Desert, began in 1960. At that time the South African administration of the Namibia Territory decided to move all the !Kung Basarwa of Nyae Nyae into a single settlement (Kent and Lee 1992). For the next 20 years the waterhole at Chum!kwe (augmented by boreholes) supported a standing population of 800 to 1,000 people. These conditions of high aggregation, with its attendant social, nutritional, and alcohol-related stresses, were prevailing when a 1981 study was made (Fernandes-Costa et al. 1984).

At Chum!kwe in 1981, hunting and gathering had fallen to very low levels due to the high level of aggregation and reduced mobility of the population (Fernandes-Costa et al. 1984). Store-bought foods and government rations, high in refined carbohydrates, formed the mainstay of the diet; some milk and grain from home-grown sources supplemented the diet. Meat was eaten infrequently. By the 1980s alcohol abuse had become a major social problem, with Saturday night brawls often resulting in injury and death (Volkman 1982). Young children as well as adults drank beer, which sometimes provided the only calories consumed all day (Marshall and Ritchie 1984: 58). The health of the Chum!kwe population was portrayed as poor.

The investigators attributed the incidence of anemia primarily to nutritional causes. However, 35.9 percent of all adults had a serum ferritin value above 100 nanograms per milliliter (ng/mL), indicating the presence of the anemia of chronic disease. No men and only 6 percent of women had subnormal serum ferritin levels (Fernandes-Costa et al. 1984). Diet was also thought to be responsible for the 33 percent of children who had subnormal serum ferritin levels (less than 12 ng/mL), although bleeding from parasitic infections could be another explanation. In fact, 3 of 40 stool samples contained *Giardia lamblia* and 8 of 40 samples had hookworm *(Necator americanus)* (Fernandes-Costa et al. 1984: 1302). Both parasites can cause lowered serum ferritin and other iron indices through blood loss and competition with the host for nutrients. Unfortunately, the age and sex of the afflicted are not mentioned; however, children tend to become infected from parasites more often than adults and tend to have a heavier parasite load than adults. Thus, parasites might explain the number of children with subnormal serum ferritin values.

A very similar situation occurred among the Australian Aborigines. They were encouraged to live at settlements where they subsisted on government subsidies of flour and sugar (Taylor 1977). The consequence of this planned social change implemented by the government was malnutrition and frequent infections:

After weaning from breast milk, the children graduated to the staple and nutritionally deficient diet of the settlement and entered its unhygienic, usually overcrowded, and certainly highly pathogenic environment. Here they acquired repeated respiratory and gastrointestinal infections which, if they did not prove fatal, may have impaired the children's ability to absorb nutrients from the diet [through malabsorption caused by the anemia of chronic disease and by numerous types of infections]. Thus the problem was compounded and a vicious cycle seemed to be set up in which the survivors of the process proceeded to adulthood to rear more children under the same circumstances. (Taylor 1977: 147–8)

Anemia around the World

In the United States the frequency of anemia is fairly low, approximately 6 percent or less for children under 17 years of age; more girls than boys have subnormal levels (Dallman 1987). The number of children with subnormal hemoglobin values declined from 7.8 percent in 1975 to 2.9 percent in 1985 (Centers for Disease Control 1986). A similar decline occurred in adults as indicated in the Second National Health and Nutrition Examination Survey (NHANES II, 1976–80). In this study of 15,093 subjects, anemia was found in 5.7 percent of infants, 5.9 percent of teenage girls, 5.8 percent of young women, and 4.4 percent of elderly men (Dallman, Yip, and Johnson 1984). The later surveys included serum ferritin measurements and differentiated between iron-deficiency anemia and anemia of chronic disease (Expert Scientific Working Group 1985). Therefore, the decline may be more illusory than real in that the more recent surveys separated the two anemias, which made the overall frequency of each appear to be less. Although based on a small sample size, anemia of chronic disease accounted for 10 percent of anemic females between 10 to 44 years of age, 34 percent of anemic females between 45 and 74 years of age, and 50 percent of anemic males (Expert Scientific Working Group 1985: 1326).[3]

There are a few populations with a lower rate of anemia than that in the United States. One example is the Waorani Indian horticulturalist–hunters of eastern Ecuador. In 1976, none of the 114 individuals studied, including males and females of all ages, had subnormal hemoglobins or hematocrits, despite a few light helminth infestations and four children with presumed bacterial-induced diarrhea (Larrick et al. 1979: 155–7). Once again, the low frequency of anemia was probably the result of a seminomadic, dispersed settlement pattern.

Anemia frequency is much higher in other parts of the world. During the 1970s, studies conducted of nonwhite children in South Africa showed a higher prevalence of iron-deficiency anemia (38.8 percent) and anemia of chronic disease (18.8 percent) than figures reported for the same time period in the United States (Derman et al. 1978).

In regions such as southeast Asia, a high incidence of hookworm infections cause bleeding. Surveys in these areas show that the frequency of anemia is correspondingly high, ranging from 25 to 29 percent in males and from 7 to 45 percent in nonpregnant women and children (Charoenlarp et al. 1988). Approximately 20 percent of the subjects given oral iron for three months as part of a study in Thailand remained anemic, and some of the individuals ended up with serum ferritin levels above 100 µg/L

(Charoenlarp 1988: 284–5). Both the lack of response to oral iron supplementation and the serum ferritin levels above 100 are common indications of the anemia of chronic disease; the other incidences of anemia can be attributed to various amounts of hookworm and other parasitic infections. Between 5 to 15 percent of women, 3 to 27 percent of children, and 1 to 5 percent of men in Burma were anemic, but no serum ferritin values were measured; hookworm infection rates varied from 0 to 70 percent, depending upon locality (Aung-Than-Batu et al. 1972).

Anemia was found in 22 percent of pregnant women, 12 percent of nonpregnant women, and 3 percent of men in seven Latin American countries (Cook et al. 1971). Unfortunately, serum ferritin was not measured, and so it is not possible to distinguish the percentage of individuals with iron deficiency or with anemia of chronic disease.

Anemia and parasites. Parasite load is an influential factor in the frequency of anemia around the world. Parasites both compete with the host for nutrients and can cause bleeding resulting in substantial iron losses. The body responds to parasitic infections with hypoferremia to deprive the parasites of needed iron. Most common in the tropical regions of the world, parasitic distribution is related to the ecological complexity and diversity that characterize such habitations (Dunn 1968; Stuart-Macadam 1992). Hookworms can cause as much as 0.21 ml of blood loss per worm per day in infected individuals (Ubelaker 1992).

In Bangladesh, where over 90 percent of children have helminth infections, between 74 percent and 82 percent of the children tested had subnormal hemoglobin levels (Florentino and Guirriec 1984). Serum ferritin studies were not included. However, because of the blood loss associated with helminth infections, individuals were probably suffering from iron-deficiency anemia, albeit not diet induced. Of 1,110 children tested in India, 33.8 to 69.4 percent were anemic; 26.7 to 65.3 percent suffered from roundworm *(Ascaris)* and *Giardia* infections, both of which cause anemia (Florentino and Guirriec 1984). Although the link with parasites is a little more tenuous among Nepal villagers, 67.6 percent of nonpregnant women had subnormal hemoglobin levels; the high consumption of dietary iron absorption inhibitors may also be a factor in causing anemia in this population (Malville 1987).

In Indonesia, 37.8 to 73 percent of children studied were anemic, and 22 to 93 percent were infested with hookworm, probably causing their anemia (Florentino and Guirriec 1984: 85). This study also reported that in Malaysia and Singapore, 83 percent of 30 children were anemic; in the Philippines, 21.1 to 47.2 percent of 2,509 children, depending on their age group, were anemic; and in China, 23 percent of 1,148 children were anemic.

Among various Pygmy hunter–gatherer groups, parasite levels are extremely high because of fecal contamination and the high level of parasites characteristic of tropical environments (Pampiglione and Ricciardi 1986). Various types of malaria *(Plasmodium falciparum, Plasmodium malariae,* and *Plasmodium ovale)* were found in 18.1 to 59.4 percent of 1,188 people from four different groups of Pygmies living in the Central African Republic, Cameroon, and Zaire (Pampiglione and Ricciardi 1986). Numerous other parasites were also present: hookworms (41.3 to 85.8 percent); roundworms (16.7 to 64.9 percent); amoebas *(Entamoeba,* 6.4 to 35.8 percent); *Giardia* (5.3 to 11.4 percent); whipworm *(Trichuris,* 77.9 to 91.9 percent); and others (Pampiglione and Ricciardi 1986). Many individuals suffered from several parasitic infections, in addition to yaws (10 percent with active symptoms), scabies, chiggers, and other afflictions (Pampiglione and Ricciardi 1986: 160–1). Neighboring Bantu-speaking farming peoples, despite more access to Western medical care and medicine, also have a high incidence of parasitism. Malaria *(P. falciparum)* was found in 91.2 percent of 321 persons; 26.8 percent suffered from amoebas; 53 percent from roundworms; 80.3 percent from hookworms; 69.8 percent from whipworm; and 16.5 percent from *Giardia* (Pampiglione and Ricciardi 1986: 163–4).

In Liberia, pregnant women in one study also had high rates of parasitism: 38 percent had hookworm; 74 percent had roundworm; and 80 percent had whipworm (Jackson and Jackson 1987). Multiple infections were also common; between 24 and 51 percent of the women had two infections and 12.5 percent had three infections (Jackson and Jackson 1987).

In Bolivia, 11.2 to 44 percent of children tested were anemic (Florentino and Guirriec 1984). Of these, 79 percent suffered from roundworm and 12 percent had hookworm infections (Florentino and Guirriec 1984).

The intention here is not to provide a detailed overview of anemia throughout the world, which would require an entire book. Rather, it is to show that anemia is a widespread condition in non-Western societies due to endemic chronic infections and parasitic diseases. In some of the cases mentioned in this section, poor health in general resulted from ill-planned development schemes or encouragement of cash or export crops at the expense of subsistence farming, creating contaminated water supplies and poor sanitation. This should present a challenge to Western societies to eradicate disease aggressively in developing countries. Development agencies need to become more aware of the underlying causes of anemia and high morbidity in many of these countries. Attempts to change agricultural patterns to produce more food per acre or the provision of iron supplements may not achieve the goal of eliminating anemia on a worldwide basis.

Anemia in infants and children. The decline in the number of children with acquired anemia in Western nations is as impressive as the decline in the number of adults with anemia. One study in the United States showed that in 1971, 23 percent of 258 children were anemic, whereas in 1984, only 1 percent of 324 children were anemic (Dallman and Yip 1989). More recent surveys show that of those few children who are anemic, the majority have the anemia of chronic disease rather than dietary iron deficiency, as evidenced by normal-to-elevated serum ferritin levels (Reeves et al. 1984; Jansson, Kling, and Dallman 1986).

There is a vast literature on anemia in infants and children (for example, Pochedly and May 1987). Most relate the anemia to the rapid growth of children and the low iron content of diets, although many do not distinguish between iron-deficiency anemia and anemia of chronic disease (Ritchey 1987). For example, a study of 148 British toddlers claims that lower hemoglobin levels are associated with diet: (1) prolonged lactation and (2) early introduction of whole cow's milk (Mills 1990). Consumption of cow's milk before 12 months of age has been shown to cause gastrointestinal bleeding in 39.5 percent of infants fed cow's milk versus 9.3 percent of infants fed formula (Fomon et al. 1981).

We cannot assume, however, that all of these cases of childhood anemia were the result of dietary factors because serum ferritin was not measured. In fact, there are more compelling reasons to suggest that at least some of the anemia was the anemia of chronic disease. Women who breast-feed their children the longest (a year or more) in Western societies tend to be the underprivileged, who are also subjected to higher rates of infection or inflammation due to crowding, inadequate housing, and the stress of minority status (see the section "Anemia and Sociopolitical Class and Race"). Such children may be at higher risk from pathogens and have greater incidence of the anemia of chronic disease. Clearly, serum ferritin must be measured in order to make reliable conclusions from any study of anemia. It is interesting to note that a study of 9 hospitalized children (6 fed formula and 3 fed cow's milk) indicated that those with lower hemoglobin levels, attributed to starting cow's milk at 6 months of age, were less likely to be hospitalized for infections than infants fed formula who had higher hemoglobin levels (Tunnessen and Oski 1987). This could be interpreted as the effect of lower hemoglobin levels, which provides protection against infections both in the contracting of diseases and in their virulence. Subnormal serum ferritin values revealed in the 17.4 percent of infants fed cow's milk versus only 1 percent of infants fed enriched formula could be the result of increased diarrhea and gastrointestinal bleeding associated with cow's milk feeding, as well as to allergies to cow's milk found in 0.3 to 7.5 percent of children (Foucard 1985; Tunnessen and Oski 1987).

Further difficulty in interpreting the etiology of anemia in children is caused by the fact that most minor illnesses that commonly afflict children, as well as immunization, can significantly depress hemoglobin levels (Dallman and Yip 1989). Iron-deficiency anemia is simulated in these cases because hemoglobin levels drop, but the anemia of chronic disease is the actual cause, as evidenced by normal serum ferritin levels. Moreover, serum iron levels drop significantly during the first year of life and are lower than adult levels as a normal physiological developmental change (Saarimen and Siimes 1977; Dallman and Reeves 1984).

In an attempt to combat anemia, most health-care workers routinely recommend iron-fortified infant formula without first ascertaining if an infant is anemic and if so, why. For example, the Women, Infant, and Children (WIC) program requires disadvantaged women to use iron-fortified formulas; nonfortified formulas are not provided (Kent, Weinberg, and Stuart-Macadam 1990). Fortified infant formulas were routinely prescribed by all but 16 percent of 251 physicians in Washington State (Taylor and Bergman 1989). It is hoped that the information presented here demonstrates the potential deleteriousness of this practice. Fortified formulas should be used only in cases where infants have anemia due to bleeding or other conditions known to create insufficient levels of iron to maintain health.

Anemia and Pregnancy

Pregnancy is often associated with a mild iron deficiency that has been linked to the nutritional needs associated with the rapid growth of a fetus. However, a few researchers have suggested that slight hypoferremia may help defend mother and fetus from invading pathogens (Weinberg 1987; Stuart-Macadam 1987). Such a defense may be particularly valuable during the latter phases of gestation when cell-mediated immunity lessens to prevent immunological rejection of the fetus (Weinberg 1987). That lower iron levels are a normal physiological part of pregnancy is supported by a number of studies that have failed to demonstrate any benefit derived from routinely prescribed prophylactic iron (Hemminki 1978; Bentley 1985). Nonetheless, many physicians continue to recommend that pregnant women take oral iron supplements.

There are anemic pregnant women with serum ferritin values below the normal 12 ng/mL. Premature labor was recorded in 48 percent of pregnant women with serum ferritin values below 10 ng/mL, in contrast to 11 percent who had normal serum ferritin levels (Goepel, Ulmer, and Neth 1988; Lieberman et al. 1988). However, a very large study of 35,423 pregnant women reported no reliable association between anemia and problem pregnancies:

When the hematocrits of women in term labor were compared with those of women in preterm labor, a spurious dose-response effect for anemia was created. We conclude that anemia is not a strong factor in the pathogenesis of preterm birth and that comparison of hematocrits from women who are in preterm and term labor produces biased results (Klebanoff et al 1989: 511).

Furthermore, and importantly, "we do not believe that there is sufficient evidence to justify a randomized clinical trial of treatment of borderline anemia during pregnancy" (Klebanoff et al. 1989: 515).

Anemia and the Elderly

Elderly men and postmenopausal women have the highest incidence of the anemia of chronic disease among all North Americans surveyed (Cook et al. 1986). Although some physicians have regarded anemia as a "normal" part of aging, a number of studies have shown that it often is the anemia of chronic disease resulting from increased vulnerability to pathogens and neoplasia, perhaps because of lowered immune defense (Zauber and Zauber 1987; Daly and Sobal 1989; Thomas et al. 1989). Serum ferritin levels rise with age, probably because the elderly have increased susceptibility to systemic insults (Zauber and Zauber 1987; Baldwin 1989; Daly 1989; Stander 1989). Whereas only 13 percent of 259 elderly persons had anemia, 77 percent had the anemia of chronic infections (Guyatt et al. 1990: 206). The frequency of infectious diseases may not be primarily the result of age alone but, instead, of social factors involved with aging in Western society, such as depression, poor care, and crowding in nursing homes. That is, the anemia of chronic disease may be more common among the elderly than the population in general because of social variables unique to this group.

Anemia and Sociopolitical Class and Race

Whatever the cause of anemia, dietary or chronic diseases, it is still the poor person's disease. While the prevalence of anemia has dropped for African-Americans as it has for all Americans, the frequency of anemia is still higher than among other groups. Anemia among African-Americans dropped from 21 percent between 1975 and 1977 to 19.2 percent between 1983 and 1985 (Yip et al. 1987). Unfortunately, serum ferritin was not measured in earlier surveys, making conclusions based on improved iron and general dietary nutrition problematic. However, later studies that include ESR (sedimentation rate, an indication of infection) show that the anemia of chronic disease is more prevalent among lower socioeconomic classes, including African-Americans (Yip and Dallman 1988).

It was once proposed that a racial characteristic of blacks is a significantly lower hemoglobin level than that of whites, and as a result, some researchers suggested using separate hemoglobin standards based on race (Garn, Smith, and Clark 1975; Garn and Clark 1976; Garn, Shaw, and McCabe 1976). However, only hemoglobin and hematocrit were analyzed in these studies. Genetics, paleontology, physiology, anatomy, and other sciences all suggest that there are neither absolute races of humans nor corresponding genes that are restricted solely to one segment of the human population; that is, there are no "black" genes that all blacks share.[4] So-called racial groups are based on continuous traits that are arbitrarily divided into supposedly discrete groups. This is particularly true in Western society where so much gene flow (that is, interracial matings) has occurred.

What, then, accounts for the lower hemoglobin levels among African-Americans? There are a number of sociological reasons that cause one subgroup to be subjected to more bodily insults than another, particularly in a society where racism is, unfortunately, all too common (Kent 1992). There are hematological data to support this contention. Later studies that performed serum ferritin measurements show that whereas African-Americans have lower hemoglobin levels, they concomitantly have higher serum ferritin levels, ranging from 271.7 ng/mL in black men to 111 ng/ml in black women; this contrasts to 93.63 in white men and 37.9 ng/ml in white women (Blumenfeld et al. 1988). Even though sedimentation rates (or ESR) were not elevated among a sample of African-Americans in one study, there was a higher incidence of chronic diseases as indicated by the number of serum ferritin levels above 100 ng/ml, which, in combination with low hemoglobin levels, defines the anemia of chronic disease/inflammation. Other investigations corroborate these findings. Of 78 African-Americans studied, 17.6 percent had elevated serum ferritin levels, leading the investigators to conclude that in addition to the anemia of chronic disease, there also were a number of individuals with iron overload who also suffered from occult inflammatory conditions (Haddy et al. 1986: 1084). The reason that more blacks than whites have the anemia of chronic disease is probably related to poverty. Many suffer from overcrowding, inadequate shelter, poor medical care, and the stress of minority status.

Black and white economic levels were matched in the studies mentioned. However, blacks within the same level of income as whites may suffer more stresses and infectious diseases because of their minority position and associated problems, such as prejudice and alcoholism, which were not taken into account in these studies. Other research indicates that whereas blacks have a lower hematocrit, it is only 0.7 percent lower than that of whites; R. Yip, S. Schwartz, and A. Deinard report the the "lower value in blacks may be accounted for by mild thalassemias, which are associated with lower hematocrit values. The use of the same diagnostic criteria for anemia among all races will permit uniform detection of nutritional anemia" (Yip, Schwartz, and Deinard 1984: 824). The higher incidence of thalassemias associated with blacks in the United States is a geographical, not a racial, trait since whites indigenous to Mediterranean regions cursed in the past with endemic malaria also have a higher rate of thalassemias.

Various other minorities in North America are impoverished and suffer from prejudice, which is reflected in their hematology. The prevalence of anemia among Chinese-Canadians is similar to that of black Americans but dissimilar to that of white Americans (Chan-Yip and Gray-Donald 1987). Hispanic females between the ages of 20 and 44 had statistically higher levels of anemia than whites or blacks, although it is unfortunate that the etiology of the anemia was not determined (Looker et al. 1989). Thus, lower hemoglobin levels are not specifically a black-associated trait but do appear to be a minority-associated trait.

Native Americans are similarly affected with significantly higher incidences of anemia. Between 22 and 28 percent of Alaskan Native Americans were found to be anemic: Of these, 65 percent had iron deficiency and 35 percent had the anemia of chronic disease (Centers for Disease Control 1988). Parasites were not investigated in these studies, but earlier studies of this group indicate that they are common and a potential reason for the reported high frequency of iron deficiency (Rausch 1951; Schiller 1951). Pneumococcal disease also is endemic among Alaskan natives (Davidson et al. 1989). Poverty and poor nontraditional diets, combined with overcrowding in semisedentary and sedentary villages, contribute to this unfortunate situation. As discussed in the section "Elsewhere in the United States," skeletal material reveals that anemia was common in this population in the past as well, even though large quantities of heme iron in the form of meat were routinely consumed. Such anemia was the result of endemic health problems associated with winter village life and infection with parasites from contact with infected dogs, seals, polar bears, and other animals with which native Alaskans were in contact (Kent 1986).

By contrast, Native American children in Arizona were reported to have lower rates of anemia (Yip et al. 1987). This is difficult to assess because information was not provided as to which group of Native Americans was involved in the study. The frequency of anemia could be related to the dispersed settlement patterns of some groups, such as the Navajos, or to the season when the study was conducted, because many Native American children attend boarding schools during the winter but spend the summer at home. The frequency might also be attributed to the length of time children are breast-fed, which, at least in the past, was of longer duration than among Euroamerican children. In other studies,

Native Americans had the same relatively low rate of anemia as Euroamerican children (Yip, Schwartz, and Deinard 1984). Whatever the cause, the lower incidence of anemia among Arizona Native Americans in contrast to Alaskan Native Americans again demonstrates that anemia is not related to genetic or racial factors but is related to environmental and sociopolitical factors, such as poverty and its associated diseases, like alcoholism.

Anemia and Alcoholism, AIDS, Drugs

Anemia, primarily of chronic diseases, is correlated with a number of health problems currently affecting all countries to various degrees. Although alcohol enhances iron absorption and can cause overload and consequent pathologies (Rodriguez et al. 1986), alcoholics may also suffer from anemia. Between 13 to 62 percent of chronic alcoholics are anemic, primarily as a result of acute blood loss and illness, including liver disease (Savage and Lindenbaum 1986).

AIDS, or acquired immunodeficiency syndrome, is associated with anemia, but its interpretation is difficult. Anemia may be the result of the body's defense against the virus or its defense against the many secondary infections associated with AIDS. Anemia in AIDS patients can also be partly related to malnourishment from malabsorption associated with the condition. The latter is the least likely explanation, however, because the anemia is associated with normal or increased serum ferritin levels (Beutler 1988).

Secondary infections are more likely to cause anemia in this group. Many AIDS patients suffer from neoplasia of various types (especially Kaposi sarcoma and non-Hodgkin's lymphoma) and from a wide range of bacterial infections that are particularly virulent because of the host's weakened resistance (Brasitus and Sitrin 1990). As a result of their compromised immunological systems, AIDS patients are often afflicted with atypical mycobacterial infections as well (Ries, White, and Murdock 1990). Whatever the ultimate cause of the anemia, it appears that the hypoferremia associated with AIDS is primarily the anemia of chronic disease and occurs as the body attempts to defend itself against very formidable infections.

Anemia and Performance

It has long been suggested that iron-deficiency anemia adversely affects performance, as measured by a battery of tests designed to evaluate activity, ability, and endurance (Dallman 1989). In fact, many studies claim to demonstrate a relationship between poor mental or physical performance and low hemoglobin level. However, a number of these studies indicate that changes noted were not statistically significant, did not include a control group, or were ambiguous in what prompted the improvements noted (Lozoff and Brittenham 1987; also see Lozoff, Jimenez, and Wolf 1991, who indicate the difficulties in determining cause and effect). The problem encountered here,

as throughout this discussion of anemia, is the separation of cause and consequence: physiological problem or defense.[5]

Furthermore, serious questions exist in almost every study that interprets behavioral, mental, or other functional limitations associated with dietary iron-deficiency anemia. For instance, no one denies that someone severely iron deficient as a result of blood loss will perform poorly compared to a healthy person. However, when anemia is reversed, other health problems are also corrected. Intake of calories, protein, and vitamins is improved in most of the studies designed to investigate performance and anemia. In the case of anemia of chronic disease, disease and/or parasite loads were reduced as the result of medication. Is it the increase in iron that is causing the improvement in skills, or is it the improvement in overall health and nutrition? Ingestion of oral iron can stimulate appetite, and there is often a weight gain associated with higher hemoglobin levels (Kent et al. 1990). It is this overall improvement in nutrition that has been suggested as the cause of the improved mental faculties (Wadsworth 1992).

Iron is necessary to catalyze various facets of the humoral and cell-mediated immune systems (Weinberg 1984). However, severely deficient individuals are not usually part of the performance test groups reported in the literature. Although iron-deficient individuals have a lower maximum work capability and endurance (Gardner et al. 1977; Lozoff and Brittenham 1987), we again are left with questions. How much of poor performance is related to iron deficiency and how much is related to poor calorie, vitamin, and protein intake and to parasitic or other disease?

Other research cannot be assessed. For example, one study compared anemic and nonanemic Chilean infants by conducting various mental and psychomotor tests that included talking and walking. Anemic infants performed more poorly than nonanemic ones (Walter et al. 1989). The difficulty in interpreting this finding is that the mental and psychomotor skills were calculated for each group according to their iron status and not according to gender. Female infants, in general, maturate more rapidly than males; therefore, the gender composition of each group is vital for determining if the nonanemic group performed better than the anemic one simply because it was composed of more female infants, regardless of the presence or absence of anemia. After three months of iron supplementation, which reversed the anemia, "no significant improvement was detected between the scores at 12 and 15 months of age" (Walter et al. 1989: 12). This suggests either that the gender composition of the groups may have affected initial performance rates or that the anemia itself did not significantly affect the infants' ability on the tests.

Many studies, particularly earlier ones, also do not measure serum ferritin levels but simply define all anemia as iron deficiency from poor diets and ignore improvements in health during the study (Soemantri, Pollitt, and Kim 1985; Chwang, Soemantri, and Pollitt 1988). In one study, anemic and nonanemic Thai fifth-grade students received either an iron supplement or a placebo concurrently with an anthelminthic drug to kill parasites (Pollitt et al. 1989). In addition, all other infections were treated on the first day of the study. Consequently, the end results are not comparable to the initial test results; that is, the cause of changes could be attributed to improved general health as much as to improved iron status.

As noted by Moussa Youdim (1989), test results often implicate factors other than iron, such as social and economic status, as the causes of differences in anemic and iron-replete students' performance before treatment. Even without taking this into account, studies indicate no difference in performance between treated and untreated children, and research "provides no support for an assumption of causality [between test scores and iron supplementation]" (Pollitt et al. 1989: 695).

Iron-deficient infants in Costa Rica who were weaned early (average 4.9 months) or never breast-fed (16 percent) were given cow's milk, known to cause gastrointestinal bleeding in a high percentage of infants (Lozoff et al. 1987). These children performed less well on a series of mental and motor tests than did nonanemic infants (Lozoff et al. 1987). Later, after their anemia was corrected with iron supplements, their performances improved (Lozoff et al. 1987). It is suggested that rectifying blood losses, rather than diet, made the difference.

Nondietary causes of anemia are prevalent in many of the populations studied, as in New Guinea, where both malaria (and anemia of chronic disease) and thalassemia are common. A series of tests to measure attention span were given to New Guinea infants: malaria-positive and negative and iron-dextran supplementation with malaria and without (Heywood et al. 1989). The only significant difference recorded was that malaria-positive infants, regardless of iron supplementation, had longer fixation times than did infants with no evidence of malaria, regardless of iron supplementation (Heywood et al. 1989). As Horowitz (1989) points out, the precise meaning of longer fixation times is not known; differences may not reflect mental development but the opposite, or may simply be a reflection of age, maternal education, or general health status.

The results of another study of iron-deficient children in Indonesia was also ambiguous. After receiving iron supplementation, neither anemic nor iron-replete children significantly improved performance on some tests, but both groups improved on other tasks (Soewondo, Husaini, and Pollitt 1989). Factors not investigated, such as increases in caloric intake, changes in psychological state, or normal physiological maturation, may improve scores, regardless of anemia. If such

is the case, it creates problems with many of the studies that attempt to measure anemia and performance. An insightful commentary by Betsy Lozoff on this study concludes that "at this stage in the research on the behavioral effects of ID [iron-deficiency anemia], it seems reasonable to keep asking whether alterations in affect, motivation, or fatigue might underlie cognitive-test-score findings" (Lozoff 1989: 675).

Anemia and Sports

An interesting correlation exists between marathon runners and subnormal serum ferritin levels. Although a high cutoff of less than 20 ng/mL was used to determine iron deficiency among 30 female high school long-distance runners, 45 percent were classified as anemic; among 10 other female runners, 50 to 60 percent were classified as anemic (Rowland et al. 1988; Manore et al. 1989). Several studies indicate that regardless of dietary iron intake, individuals who ran the most miles per week had the lowest ferritin levels; if injury that prevented further running occurred, iron indexes rose (Manore et al. 1989).

Lowered serum ferritin levels in athletes have been attributed to many factors: increased iron loss through heavy sweating; trauma; slightly increased destruction of red blood cells in stressed tissues, such as muscles and the soles of the feet; common use of analgesics, such as aspirin and aspirinlike drugs, which cause blood loss; and gastrointestinal blood loss (Robertson, Maughan, and Davidson 1987). A significant, though clinically unimportant, increase in fecal blood loss occurred in male marathon runners who had not taken any drugs prior to running. The 28 percent who had taken an analgesic known to promote bleeding had blood losses that could eventually result in anemia (Robertson et al. 1987). Most physicians consider the blood loss and its cause inconsequential in healthy athletes and do not recommend routine hematological monitoring or iron supplementation (Wardrop 1987).

Conclusions and Direction of Future Studies

Despite many studies supporting the view that iron fortification and supplementation might be harmful for infants, pregnant women, and others (for example, Hibbard 1988), some physicians continue to advocate indiscriminate iron fortification (Arthur and Isbister 1987; Taylor and Bergman 1989). However, a growing number of studies concerning the anemia of chronic disease conclude that "[o]ur data . . . do not support the routine prescription of iron . . . in patients on CAPD [continuous, ambulatory peritoneal dialysis]" (Salahudeen et al. 1988). In fact, even though the use of iron chelators that bind iron to reduce chronic diseases is still experimental, initial studies look promising (Vreugdenhil et al. 1989). That is, less iron rather than more may reduce morbidity.

Treating all anemia as dietary iron-deficiency anemia can have potentially deleterious effects on populations most needing health-care assistance. Iron-deficiency anemia occurs in areas where war, export or cash cropping, and other extreme situations deny people their basic requirements of calories, vitamins, and nutrients to sustain life. Dietary improvements are sorely needed in those situations. Anemia from blood loss primarily from parasites, and also from the premature introduction of cow's milk to infants, is an acute health-maintenance problem. Rectification through medication and improved sanitation and education is needed. Anemia of chronic disease is a positive defense against infections and inflammation and, as such, should not be interfered with; however, the underlying diseases that cause the anemia need to be eradicated.

Iron supplementation is a relatively easy, inexpensive counter to dietary anemia. Perhaps that partially explains why so many people cling to the idea that iron taken orally or through injections will reduce morbidity. However, the complexity of iron and its relationship to anemia are emphasized here to show that simple solutions cannot solve complex problems.

Susan Kent

This chapter is dedicated to Dr. Eugene Weinberg and his work. I greatly value the comments and suggestions made by Drs. Steven Kent and Weinberg. I thank Dr. Kenneth Kiple for giving me the opportunity to write this paper and for editorial advice. Marian Blue also provided editorial suggestions.

Notes

1. One study (Baltimore, Shedd, and Pearson 1982) contends that studies in vivo do not support the conclusions from studies in vitro of excess iron predisposing individuals to infections. One explanation for their finding that increased iron does not increase *E. coli* growth is that a few bacteria, including *E. coli* possessing K_1 antigen, are virulent even without iron supplementation (Payne and Finkelstein 1978). This group of pathogens "appeared to produce greater quantities of compounds (siderophores) which stimulated microbial growth in low-iron media than did the nondisseminating pathogens" (Payne and Finkelstein 1978: 1428). Unfortunately, the Baltimore, Shedd, and Pearson (1982) study does not specify whether the *E. coli* they investigated contained the K_1 antigen, but it is possible that other mutants of a bacterium may be able to proliferate in low-iron media. The vast majority of other studies contradict these authors.

2. Although at one time it was thought that hookworm was not indigenous to the Americas, hookworm was found in a 1,100-year-old Peruvian mummy and in a 3,500-year-old Brazilian mummy (Allison 1974; Ferreira, de Araujo, and Confalonieri 1980, 1983).

3. The same hematological surveys detected iron overload in 1.3 percent of 157 healthy urban adults, a figure similar to the percentage of anemic individuals for males (Haddy et al., 1986). However, in a larger study that involved 11,065 subjects, iron overload as measured by elevated transferring saturation levels was detected in only 0.8 percent of men and 0.3 percent of women (Edwards et al. 1988). The problem with interpreting this study is that the subject population

was drawn from blood donors, a practice that tends to lower transferrin saturation levels. The actual prevalence of iron overload appears to be roughly similar to anemia in males under the age of 45.

4. There are a few specific genes associated with particular populations within black or other racial categories but not genes that only blacks share to the exclusion of all other groups.

5. A similar problem of distinguishing cause and effect can be seen with the immunological system and anemia. Some investigators claim their studies illustrate that anemia causes an impairment in the immunological system, which affects the body's ability to ward off disease (e.g., Vyas and Chandra 1984). Others claim their studies illustrate that anemia improves immunity from disease (Murray and Murray 1977). For instance, despite in vitro studies that show experimentally that there is a decrease in bactericidal capabilities in neutrophils, in vivo studies of human infections show that "no noticeable increase was observed in respiratory, gastrointestinal, or in morbidity, either in the few days before the initiation of iron therapy, or in the subsequent 15 days of close clinical and laboratory follow-up, confirming previous observations that iron-deficiency anemia, even when severe, does not appear to compromise immune mechanisms to the extent of allowing ominous clinical manifestations" (Walter et al. 1986).

Bibliography

Aaby, Peter. 1988. Observing the unexpected: Nutrition and child mortality in Guinea-Bissau. In *Micro-approaches to demographic research,* ed. John Caldwell, Allen Hill, and Valerie Hull, 278–96. London.

Adelekan, Delana, and David Thurnham. 1990. Plasma ferritin concentrations in anemic children: Relative importance of malaria, riboflavin deficiency, and other infections. *American Journal of Clinical Nutrition* 51: 453–6.

Allison, Marvin J. 1984. Paleopathology in Peruvian and Chilean populations. In *Paleopathology at the origins of agriculture,* ed. Mark Cohen and George Armelagos, 515–29. Orlando, Fla.

Allison, Marvin J., Alejandro Pezzia, Ichiro Hasegawa, et al. 1974. A case of hookworm infestation in a pre-columbian American. *American Journal of Physical Anthropology* 41: 103–6.

Anderson, James. 1968. Late Paleolithic skeletal remains from Nubia. In *The prehistory of Nubia,* ed. Fred Wendorf, 996–1040. Dallas, Tex.

Angel, J. Lawrence. 1967. Porotic hyperostosis or osteoporosis. In *Diseases in antiquity,* ed. Don Brothwell and A. T. Sandison, 378–89. Springfield, Ill.

1984. Health as a crucial factor in the changes from hunting to developed farming in the eastern Mediterranean. In *Paleopathology at the origins of agriculture,* ed. Mark Cohen and George Armelagos, 51–74. Orlando, Fla.

Armelagos, George, Dennis van Gerven, Debra Martin, and Rebecca Huss-Ashmore. 1984. Effects of nutritional change on the skeletal biology of northeast African (Sudanese Nubian) populations. In *From hunters to farmers: The causes and consequences of food production in Africa,* ed. J. Desmond Clark and Steven Brandt, 132–46. Berkeley, Calif.

Arthur, C. K., and J. P. Isbister. 1987. Iron deficiency: Misunderstood, misdiagnosed and mistreated. *Drugs* 33: 171–82.

Aufderheide, Arthur. 1989. Chemical analysis of skeletal remains. In *Reconstruction of life from the skeleton,* ed. Mehmet Iscan and Kenneth Kennedy, 237–60. New York.

Aung-Than-Batu, M. B., U. Hla-Pe, M. Thein-Than, and M. B. Khin-Kyi-Nyunt. 1972. Iron deficiency in Burmese population groups. *American Journal of Clinical Nutrition* 25: 210-18.

Baldwin, J. Gilbert. 1989. True anemia: Incidence and significance in the elderly. *Geriatrics* 44: 33-6.

Baltimore, R., D. Shedd, and H. Pearson. 1982. Effect of iron saturation on the bacteriostasis of human serum: In vivo does not correlate with in vitro saturation. *Journal of Pediatrics* 101: 519-23.

Barry, D. M., and A. W. Reeve. 1977. Increased incidence of gram-negative neonatal sepsis with intramuscular iron administration. *Pediatrics* 60: 908-12.

Bates, C. J., H. J. Powers, and D. I. Thurnham. 1989. Vitamins, iron, and physical work. *Lancet* 2: 313-14.

Becroft, D. M., M. R. Dix, and K. Farmer. 1977. Intramuscular iron-dextran and susceptibility of neonates to bacterial infections. *Archives of Diseases of Childhood* 52: 778-81.

Beganovic, Sead. 1987. The erythrocyte sedimentation rate. *Annals of Internal Medicine* 107: 425-6.

Bentley, D. P. 1985. Iron metabolism and anaemia in pregnancy. *Clinics in Haematology* 14: 613-28.

Beutler, Ernest. 1988. The common anemias. *Journal of the American Medical Association* 259: 2433-7.

Bindra, Gursh, and Rosalind Gibson. 1986. Iron status of predominantly lacto-ovo vegetarian East Indian immigrants to Canada: A model approach. *American Journal of Clinical Nutrition* 44: 643-52.

Blumenfeld, Nadia, Mary Fabry, Benjamin Thysen, and Ronald Nagel. 1988. Red cell density is sex and race dependent in the adult. *Journal of Laboratory and Clinical Medicine* 112: 333-8.

Brasitus, Thomas A., and Michael D. Sitrin. 1990. Intestinal malabsorption syndromes. *Annual Review of Medicine* 41: 339-47.

Brennan, Ruth, Mary Kohrs, James Nordstrom, et al. 1983. Nutrient intake of low-income pregnant women: Laboratory analysis of foods consumed. *Journal of the American Dietetic Association* 83: 546-50.

Bumsted, M. Pamela. 1980. VT-CH-94: Vermont's earliest known agricultural experiment station. *Man in the Northeast* 19: 73-82.

　1985. Past human behavior from bone chemical analysis – Respects and prospects. *Journal of Human Evolution* 14: 539-51.

Burns, Edward, S. N. Goldberg, Christine Lawrence, and Barry Weinz. 1990. Clinical utility of serum tests for iron deficiency in hospitalized patients. *American Journal of Clinical Pathology* 93: 240-5.

Cash, Joseph, and David Sears. 1989. The anemia of chronic disease: Spectrum of associated diseases in a series of unselected hospitalized patients. *American Journal of Medicine* 87: 638-44.

Centers for Disease Control and Prevention U.S. 1986. Declining anemia prevalence among children enrolled in public nutrition and health programs: Selected states, 1975-1985. *Morbidity and Mortality Weekly Report* 35: 565-7.

　1988. High prevalence of iron deficiency anemia among Alaskan native Children. *Morbidity and Mortality Weekly Report* 37: 200-2.

Chan-Yip, Alice, and Katherine Gray-Donald. 1987. Prevalence of iron deficiency among Chinese children aged 6 to 36 months in Montreal. *Canadian Medical Association Journal* 136: 373-8.

Charache, Samuel, et al. 1987. Noninvasive assessment of tissue iron stores. *American Journal of Clinical Pathology* 88: 333-7.

Charoenlarp, P., S. Dhanamitta, R. Kaewvichit, et al. 1988. A WHO collaborative study on iron supplementation in Burma and in Thailand. *American Journal of Clinical Nutrition* 47: 280-97.

Chernela, Janet, and Vernon Thatcher. 1989. Comparison of parasite burdens in two native Amazonian populations. *Medical Anthropology* 10: 279-85.

Chwang, Leh-chii, A. G. Soemantri, and Ernesto Pollitt. 1988. Iron supplementation and physical growth of rural Indonesian children. *American Journal of Clinical Nutrition* 47: 496-501.

Clydesdale, Fergus. 1983. Physicochemical determinants of iron bioavailability. *Food Technology* 133-44.

Cohen, Mark and George Armelagos, eds. 1984. *Paleopathology at the origins of agriculture.* Orlando, Fla.

Cook, Della. 1984. Subsistence and health in the lower Illinois Valley: Osteological evidence. In *Paleopathology at the origins of agriculture,* ed. Mark Cohen and George Armelagos, 235-69. Orlando, Fla.

Cook, James. 1990. Adaption in iron metabolism. *American Journal of Clinical Nutrition* 51: 301-8.

Cook, James, et al. 1971. Nutritional deficiency and anemia in Latin America: A collaborative study. *Blood* 38: 591-603.

Cook, James, and Sean Lynch. 1986. The liabilities of iron deficiency. *Blood* 68: 803-9.

Cook, James, and Barry Skikne. 1982. Serum ferritin: A possible model for the assessment of nutrient stores. *American Journal of Clinical Nutrition* 35: 1180-5.

Cook, James, Barry Skikne, Sean Lynch, and Molly Reusser. 1986. Estimates of iron sufficiency in the U.S. population. *Blood* 68: 726-31.

Corwin, Edwards, Linda Griffin, David Goldgar, et al. 1988. Prevalence of hemochromatosis among 11,065 presumably healthy blood donors. *New England Journal of Medicine* 318: 1355-62.

Cule, John, and I. Lynn Evans. 1968. Porotic hyperostosis and the Gelligaer skull. *Journal of Clinical Pathology* 21: 753-8.

Cummings, Linda. 1989. Coprolites from medieval Christian Nubia: An interpretation of diet and nutritional stress. Ph.D. dissertation, Department of Anthropology, University of Colorado, Boulder.

Dallman, Peter. 1987. Has routine screening of infants for anemia become obsolete in the United States? *Pediatrics* 80: 439-41.

　1989. Iron deficiency: Does it matter? *Journal of Internal Medicine* 226: 367-72.

Dallman, Peter, and Jerry Reeves. 1984. Laboratory diagnosis of iron deficiency. In *Iron nutrition in infancy and childhood,* ed. A. Stekel, 11-43. New York.

Dallman, Peter, and Ray Yip. 1989. Changing characteristics of childhood anemia. *The Journal of Pediatrics* 114: 161-4.

Dallman, Peter, Ray Yip, and Clifford Johnson. 1984. Prevalence and causes of anemia in the United States, 1976 to 1980. *American Journal of Clinical Nutrition* 39: 437-45.

Daly, Mel. 1989. Anemia in the elderly. *American Family Physician* 39: 129-36.

Daly, Mel, and Jeffery Sobal. 1989. Anemia in the elderly: A survey of physicians' approaches to diagnosis and workup. *Journal of Family Practice* 28: 524-8.

Davidson, Michael, Cynthia Schraer, Alan Parkinson, et al. 1989. Invasive pneumococcal disease in an Alaskan native population, 1980 through 1986. *Journal of the American Medical Association* 261: 715-18.

Derman, D. P., et al. 1978. Serum ferritin as an index of iron nutrition in rural and urban South African children. *British Journal of Nutrition* 39: 383-9.

Dunn, Frederick. 1968. Epidemiological factors: Health and disease in hunter-gatherers. In *Man the hunter,* ed. Richard Lee and Irven DeVore, 221–8. Chicago.

Edwards, Corwin, et al. 1988. Prevalence of hemochromatosis among 11,065 presumably healthy blood donors. *New England Journal of Medicine* 318: 1355–62.

El-Najjar, Mahmoud Y. 1976. Maize, malaria and the anemias in the pre-Columbian New World. *Yearbook of Physical Anthropology* 20: 329–37.

Expert Scientific Working Group. 1985. Summary of a report on assessment of the iron nutritional status of the United States population. *American Journal of Clinical Nutrition* 42: 1318–30.

Fairbanks, Virgil, and Ernest Beutler. 1988. Iron. In *Modern nutrition in health and disease,* ed. Maurice Shils and Vernon Young, 193–226. Philadelphia, Pa.

Farley, Patrick, and Jaime Foland. 1990. Iron deficiency anemia: How to diagnose and correct. *Postgraduate Medicine* 87: 89–101.

Fernandes-Costa, F. J., John Marshall, Clair Ritchie, et al. 1984. Transition from a hunter-gatherer to a settled lifestyle in the !Kung San: Effect on iron, folate, and vitamin B12 nutrition. *The American Journal of Clinical Nutrition* 40: 1295–1303.

Ferreira, L. F., A. J. de Araujo, and U. Confalonieri. 1980. The finding of eggs and larvae of parasitic helminths in archaeological material from Unai, Minas Gerais, Brazil. *Transcripts of the Royal Society for Tropical and Medical Hygiene* 74: 780–800.

   1983. The finding of helminth eggs in a Brazilian mummy. *Transcripts of the Royal Society for Tropical and Medical Hygiene* 77: 65–7.

Finch, C. A. 1989. Introduction: Knights of the oval table. *Journal of Internal Medicine* 226: 345–8.

Florentino, Rodolfo, and Romualda Guirriec. 1984. Prevalence of nutritional anemia in infancy and childhood with emphasis on developing countries. In *Iron nutrition in infancy and childhood,* ed. A. Stekel, 61–74. New York.

Fomon, S. J., E. E. Ziegler, S. E. Nelson, and B. B. Edwards. 1981. Cow milk feeding in infancy: Gastrointestinal blood loss and iron nutritional status. *Journal of Pediatrics* 98: 540–5.

Foucard, T. 1985. Development of food allergies with special reference to cow's milk allergy. *Pediatrics* 75: 177–81.

Franke, Richard. 1987. The effects of colonialism and neocolonialism on the gastronomic patterns of the Third World. In *The evolution of food,* ed. Marvin Harris and Eric Ross, 455–79. Philadelphia, Pa.

Garby, L., L. Irnell, and I. Werner. 1969. Iron deficiency in women of fertile age in a Swedish communities, III: Estimation of prevalence based on response to iron supplementation. *Acta Medica Scandinavica* 185: 113–30.

Gardner, Gerald, V. Reggie Edgerton, Brian Senewiratne, et al. 1977. Physical work capacity and metabolic stress in subjects with iron deficiency anemia. *American Journal of Clinical Nutrition* 30: 910–17.

Garn, Stanley, and Diane Clark. 1976. Problems in the nutritional assessment of black individuals. *American Journal of Public Health* 66: 262–7.

Garn, Stanley, Helen Shaw, and Kinne McCabe. 1976. Black-white hemoglobin differences during pregnancy. *Ecology of Food and Nutrition* 5: 99–100.

Garn, Stanley, Nathan Smith, and Diane Clark. 1975. Lifelong differences in hemoglobin levels between blacks and whites. *Journal of the National Medical Association* 67: 91–6.

Gilfillan, S. C. 1965. Lead poisoning and the fall of Rome. *Journal of Occupational Medicine* 7: 53–60.

Goepel, E., H. U. Ulmer, and R. D. Neth. 1988. Premature labor contractions and the value of serum ferritin during pregnancy. *Gynecologic and Obstetric Investigation* 26: 265–73.

Goldberg, A., and A. Reshef. 1972. Vitamin A and iron in infants' diets in Israel. *Journal of the American Dietetic Association* 60: 127–30.

Goldstein, Marcus. 1957. Skeletal pathology of early Indians in Texas. *American Journal of Physical Anthropology* 15: 299–307.

Goodman, Alan, John Lallo, George Armelagos, and Jeremy Rose. 1984. Health changes at Dickson Mounds, Illinois (A.D. 950–1300). In *Paleopathology at the origins of agriculture,* ed. Mark Cohen and George Armelagos, 271–305. Orlando, Fla.

Guyatt, Gordon, Christopher Patterson, Mahmoud Ali, et al. 1990. Diagnosis of iron-deficiency anemia in the elderly. *American Journal of Medicine* 88: 205–9.

Haddy, Theresa, Oswaldo Castro, Sohail Rana, and Roland Scott. 1986. Iron status and liver function in healthy adults: A multiracial pilot study. *Southern Medical Journal* 79: 1082–5.

Hallberg, Leif, Mats Brune, and Lena Rossander. 1989. Iron absorption in man: Ascorbic acid and dose-dependent inhibition by phytate. *American Journal of Clinical Nutrition* 49: 140–4.

Hemminki, Elina. 1978. Routine administration of iron and vitamins during pregnancy: Review of controlled clinical trials. *British Journal of Obstetrics and Gynecology* 85: 404–10.

Hengen, O. P. 1971. Cribra orbitalia: Pathogenesis and probable etiology. *Homo* 22: 57.

Herbert, Victor. 1988. Recommended dietary intakes (RDI) of iron in humans. *American Journal of Clinical Nutrition* 45: 679–86.

Herold, P. M., and J. E. Kinsella. 1986. Fish oil consumption and decreased risk of cardiovascular disease. *American Journal of Clinical Nutrition* 43: 566–98.

Heywood, Alison, Stephen Oppenheimer, Peter Heywood, and Damien Jolley. 1989. Behavorial effects of iron supplementation in infants in Madang, Papua New Guinea. *American Journal of Clinical Nutrition* 50: 630–40.

Hibbard, Bryan. 1988. Iron and folate supplements during pregnancy: Supplementation is valuable only in selected patients. *British Medical Journal* 297: 1324–7.

Hoffbrand, A. V. 1981. Iron. In *Postgraduate hematology,* ed. A. V. Hoffbrand and S. M. Lewis, 35–42. New York.

Hooton, Ernest. 1940. Skeletons from the Cenote of Sacrifice at Chichén Itzá. In *The Maya and their neighbors,* ed. Clarence Hay, 272–80. New York.

Hornabrook, R. W. 1977. Human adaptability in Papua New Guinea. In *Population structure and human variation,* ed. G. A. Harrison, 285–309. Cambridge.

Horowitz, Frances. 1989. Comments on Heywood et al. *American Journal of Clinical Nutrition* 50: 630–40.

Houwelingen, R. V., A. Nordoy, E. van de Beek, et al. 1987. Effect of a moderate fish intake on blood pressure, bleeding time, hematology, and clinical chemistry in healthy males. *American Journal of Clinical Nutrition* 46: 424–36.

Hummert, J. R. 1983. Cortical bone growth and dietary stress among subadults from Nubia's Batn el Hajar. *American Journal of Physical Anthropology* 62: 167–76.

Jackson, Robert, and Linda Jackson. 1987. Biological and

behavioral contributors to anemia during pregnancy in Liberia, West Africa. *Human Biology* 59: 585-97.

Janssens, Paul. 1970. *Palaeopathology: Diseases and injuries of prehistoric man.* London.

Jansson, L. T., S. Kling, and P. R. Dallman. 1986. Anemia in children with acute infections seen in a primary care pediatric outpatient clinic. *Pediatric Infectious Diseases* 5: 424-7.

Keegan, William. 1989. Stable isotope analysis of prehistoric diet. In *Reconstruction of life from the skeleton,* ed. Mehmet Iscan and Kenneth Kennedy, 223-36. New York.

Kennedy, Kenneth. 1984. Growth, nutrition and pathology in changing paleodemographic settings in South Asia. In *Paleopathology at the origins of agriculture,* ed. Mark Cohen and George Armelagos, 169-92. Orlando, Fla.

Kent, Susan. 1986. The influence of sedentism and aggregation on porotic hyperostosis and anaemia: A case study. *Man* 21: 605-3.

1992. Anemia through the ages: Changing perspectives and their implications. In *Diet, demography, and disease: Changing views of anemia,* ed. Patricia Stuart-Macadam and Susan Kent, 1-32. New York.

1992. Excavations at a small Mesa Verde Pueblo II Anasazi site in southwestern Colorado. *The Kiva* 57.

Kent, Susan, and David Dunn. 1991. A hematological study of a recently sedentary Kalahari village: Implications for the past and the future. [Manuscript submitted for publication].

1993. Etiology of hypoferremia in a recently sedentary Kalahari village. *American Journal of Tropical Medicine and Hygiene* 48: 554-67.

1996. Anemia and the transition of nomadic hunter-gathers to a sedentary life-style: Follow-up study of a Kalahari community. *American Journal of Physical Anthropology* 99: 455-72.

Kent, Susan, and Richard Lee. 1992. A hematological study of !Kung Kalahari foragers: An eighteen year comparison. In *Diet, demography, and disease: Changing views of anemia,* ed. Patricia Stuart-Macadam and Susan Kent, 173-200. New York.

Kent, Susan, Eugene Weinberg, and Patricia Stuart-Macadam. 1990. Dietary and Prophylactic iron supplements: Helpful or harmful? *Human Nature* 1: 55-81.

1994. The etiology of the anemia of chronic disease and infection. *Journal of Clinical Epidemiology* 47: 23-33.

Klebanoff, M., et al. 1989. Facts and artifacts about anemia and preterm delivery. *Journal of American Medical Association* 262: 511-15.

Klepinger, Linda. 1984. Nutritional assessment from bone. *Annual Review of Anthropology* 13: 75-96.

Kluger, M. J., and J. J. Bullen. 1987. Clinical and physiological aspects. In *Iron and Infection,* ed. J. J. Bullen and E. Griffiths, 243-82. London.

Larrick, James, James Yost, Jon Kaplan, et al. 1979. Patterns of health and disease among the Waorami Indians of eastern Ecuador. *Medical Anthropology* 19: 147-89.

Larson, Clark. 1984. Health and disease in prehistoric Georgia: The transition to agriculture. In *Paleopathology at the origins of agriculture,* ed. Mark Cohen and George Armelagos, 367-92. Orlando, Fla.

Lawrence, Dale, James Neel, Stanley Abadie, et al. 1980. Epidemiological studies among Amerindian populations of Amazonia: Intestinal parasitosis in newly contacted and acculturating villages. *American Journal of Tropical Medicine and Hygiene* 29: 530-7.

Lepowsky, M. 1985. Food taboos, malaria and dietary change: Infant feeding and cultural adaption on a Papua New Guinea Island. *Ecology of Food Nutrition* 16: 117.

Lieberman, Ellice, Kenneth Ryan, Richard Monson, and Stephen Schoenbaum. 1988. Association of maternal hematocrit with premature labor. *American Journal of Obstetrics and Gynecology* 159: 107-14.

Looker, Anne, Clifford Johnson, Margaret McDowell, and Elizabeth Yetley. 1989. Iron status: Prevalence of impairment in three Hispanic groups in the United States. *American Journal of Clinical Nutrition* 49: 553-8.

Lozoff, Betsy. 1989. Comment on Soewondo, Husaini, and Pollitt. *American Journal of Clinical Nutrition* 50: 673-4.

Lozoff, Betsy, and Gary Brittenham. 1987. Behavioral alterations in iron deficiency. *Hematology/Oncology Clinics of North America* 1: 449-64.

Lozoff, Betsy, Gary Brittenham, Abraham Wolf, et al. 1987. Iron deficiency anemia and iron therapy effects on infant developmental test performance. *Pediatrics* 79: 981-95.

Lozoff, B., E. Jimez, and A. W. Wolf. 1991. Long-term developmental outcome of infants with iron deficiency. *New England Journal of Medicine* 325: 687-94.

Macfarlane, Bruce, et al. 1988. Inhibitory effect of nuts on iron absorption. *American Journal of Clinical Nutrition* 47: 270-4.

Malville, Nancy. 1987. Iron deficiency anemia among village women of the Middle Hills of Nepal. Ph.D. dissertation, University of Colorado, Boulder.

Manore, Melinda M., Phyllis D. Besenfelder, Christine L. Wells, et al. 1989. Nutrient intakes and iron status in female long-distance runners during training. *Journal of the American Dietetic Association* 89: 257-9.

Marshall, John, and Claire Ritchie. 1984. Where are the Ju/wasi of Nyae Nyae? Changes in a Bushman Society: 1958-1981. *University of Cape Town Centre for African Studies* 9: 1-187.

Masawe, A. E., J. M. Muindi, and G. B. Swai 1974. Infections in iron deficiency and other types of anaemia in the tropics. *Lancet* 2: 314-17.

Metz, J., D. Hart, and H. C. Harpending. 1971. Iron, folate, and vitamin B_{12} nutrition in a hunter-gatherer people: A study of the !Kung Bushmen. *The American Journal of Clinical Nutrition* 24: 229-42.

Mills, A. F. 1990. Surveillance for anaemia: Risk factors in patterns of milk intake. *Archives of Disease in Childhood* 65: 428-31.

Monsen, Elaine. 1988. Iron nutrition and absorption: Dietary factors which impact iron bioavailability. *Journal of the American Dietetic Association* 88: 786-90.

Moseley, John. 1965. The paleopathologic riddle of "symmetrical osteoporosis." *American Journal of Roentgenology, Radium Therapy and Nuclear Medicine* 95: 135-42.

Muñoz, Leda, Bo Lönnerdal, Carl Keen, and Kathryn Dewey. 1988. Coffee consumption as a factor in iron deficiency anemia among pregnant women and their infants in Costa Rica. *American Journal of Clinical Nutrition* 48: 645-51.

Murray, M. J., and A. Murray. 1977. Starvation suppression and refeeding activation of infection: An ecological necessity? *Lancet* 1: 123-5.

Murray, M. J., Anne Murray, and C. J. Murray. 1980a. The salutary effect of milk on amoebiasis and its reversal by iron. *British Medical Journal* 280: 1351-2.

1980b. An ecological interdependence of diet and disease? *American Journal of Clinical Nutrition* 33: 697-701.

Murray, M. J., A. Murray, N. Murray, and M. Murray. 1976. Somali food shelters in the Ogaden famine and their impact on health. *Lancet* 1: 1283-5.

Nathan, Hilel. 1966. Cribra orbitalia: A bone condition of the orbit of unknown nature: Anatomical study with etiological considerations. *Israel Journal of Medical Science* 2: 171–91.

Nelson, Brue, et al. 1986. Effects of digenesis on strontium, carbon, nitrogen and oxygen concentration and isotopic composition of bone. *Geochimica et Cosmochimica Acta* 50: 1941–9.

Olivares, Manuel, et al. 1989. Anemia of a mild viral infection: The measles vaccine as a model. *Pediatrics* 84: 851–5.

O'Neil-Cutting, Mary, and William Crosby. 1987. Blocking of iron absorption by a preliminary oral dose of iron. *Archives of Internal Medicine* 147: 489–91.

Oppenheimer, S. J., F. D. Gibson, S.B. MacFarlane, et al. 1986a Iron supplementation increases prevalence and effects of malaria: Report on clinical studies in Papua New Guinea. *Transactions of the Royal Society of Tropical Medicine and Hygiene* 80: 603–12.

Oppenheimer, S. J., S. B. MacFarlane, J.B. Moody, et al. 1986b. Effect of iron prophylaxis on morbidity due to infectious disease: Report on clinical studies in Papua New Guinea. *Transactions of the Royal Society of Tropical Medicine and Hygiene* 80: 596–602.

Orlove, Benjamin. 1987. Stability and change in highland Andean dietary patterns. In *The evolution of food,* ed. Marvin Harris and Eric Ross, 481–515. Philadelphia, Pa.

Pampiglione, Silvio, and Maria Ricciardi. 1986. Parasitological surveys of Pygmy groups. In *African Pygmies,* ed. Luigi Cavalli-Sforza, 153–165. Orlando, Fla.

Payne, S., and R. Finkelstein. 1978. The critical role of iron in host-bacterial interactions. *Journal of Clinical Investigations* 61: 1428–40.

Perzigian, Anthony, Patricia Tench, and Donna Braun. 1984. Prehistoric health in the Ohio River Valley. In *Paleopathology at the origins of agriculture,* ed. Mark Cohen and George Armelagos, 347–66. Orlando, Fla.

Pochedly, Carl, and Steven May. 1987. Iron deficiency anemia in children. *American Family Physician* 35: 195–200.

Pollitt, Ernesto, Phongjan Hathirat, Nittaya Kotchabhakdi, et al. 1989. Iron deficiency and educational achievement in Thailand. *American Journal of Clinical Nutrition* 50: 687–97.

Powell, James, Stephen Weens and Nanette Wenger. 1965. The skull roentgenogram in iron deficiency anemia and in secondary polycythemia. *American Journal of Roentgenology, Radium Therapy, and Nuclear Medicine* 95: 143–7.

Powell, Mary. 1988. *Status and health in prehistory: A case study of the Moundville chiefdom.* Washington, D.C.

Rausch, Robert. 1951. Biotic interrelationships of helminth parasitism in Alaska. *Bulletin of the National Research Council* no. 122: 113–14.

Reeves, J. D., R. Yip, V. Kiley, et al. 1984. Iron deficiency in infants: The influence of antecedent infection. *Journal of Pediatrics* 105: 874–9.

Reinhard, Karl. 1992. Diet, demography, and disease: The coprolite evidence. In *Diet, demography, and disease: Changing perspectives of anemia.* ed. P. Stuart-Macadam and S. Kent, 219–58. New York.

Ries, Kristen, George White, and Richard Murdock. 1990. Atypical mycobacterial infection caused by *Mycobacterium marinum. New England Journal of Medicine* 322: 633–4.

Ritchey, A. Kim. 1987. Iron deficiency in children: Update on an old problem. *Postgraduate Medicine* 32: 59–69.

Robbins, Louise. 1986. Biosocial maladaptation among prehistoric maize agriculturalists: The role of trace elements. In *Skeletal analysis in southeastern archaeology,* ed.

Janet Levy, 97–102. North Carolina Archaeological Council Publication 24. Chapel Hill.

Robertson, J. D., R. J. Maughan, and R. J. Davidson. 1987. Faecal blood loss in response to exercise. *British Medical Journal* 295: 303–4.

Rodolfo, Florentino, and Romualda Guirriec. 1984. Prevalence of nutritional anemia in infancy and childhood with emphasis on developing countries. In *Iron nutrition in infancy and childhood,* ed. A. Stekel, 61–74. New York.

Rodriguez, M. C., M.S. Henriquez, A.F. Turon, et al. 1986. Trace elements in chronic alcoholism. *Trace Elements in Medicine* 3: 164–7.

Ross, Eric. 1987. Overview of trends in dietary variation from hunter-gatherer to modern capitalist society. In *The evolution of food,* ed. Marvin Harris and Eric Ross, 7–55. Philadelphia, Pa.

Rowland, Thomas, Molly Deisroth, Gerald Green, and John Kelleher. 1988. The effect of iron therapy on the exercise capacity of nonanemic iron-deficient adolescent runners. *American Journal of Childhood* 142: 165–9.

Saarinen, Ulla, and Martti Siimes. 1977. Developmental changes in serum iron, total iron-binding capacity, and transferrin saturation in infancy. *Journal of Pediatrics* 91: 875–7.

Salahudeen, A. K., S.R. Varma, T. Karim, et al. 1988. Anaemia, ferritin, and vitamins in continuous ambulatory peritoneal dialysis. *Lancet* 1: 1049.

Saul, Frank. 1973. Disease in the Mayan era: The pre-Columbian evidence. In *The classic Maya collapse.* ed. Patrick Culbert, 301–24. Albuquerque, NM.

Savage, David, and John Lindenbaum. 1986. Anemia in alcoholics. *Medicine* 65: 322–38.

Schiller, Everett. 1951. Observations on arctic parasitology with special reference to the status of Echinococcosis and Diphyllobothriasis in Alaska. *Bulletin of the National Research Council* 122: 91–2.

Schwaner, Terry, and Carl Dixon. 1974. Helminthiasis as a measure of cultural change in the Amazon Basin. *Biotropica* 6: 32–7.

Shahidi, Nasollah, and Louis Diamond. 1960. Skull changes in infants with chronic iron-deficiency anemia. *New England Journal of Medicine* 262: 137–9.

Sillen, Andrew, Judith Sealy, and Nikolaas van der Merwe. 1989. Chemistry and paleodietary research: No more easy answers. *American Antiquity* 54: 504–12.

Smith, Patricia, Ofer Bar-Yosef, and Andrew Sillen. 1984. Archaeological and skeletal evidence for dietary change during the Late Pleistocene/Early Holocene in the Levant. In *Paleopathology at the origins of agriculture,* ed. Mark Cohen and George Armelagos, 101–36. Orlando, Fla.

Soemantri, A. G., Ernesto Pollitt, and Insum Kim. 1985. Iron deficiency anemia and educational achievement. *American Journal of Clinical Nutrition* 42: 1221–8.

Soewondo, Soesmalijah, M. Husaini, and Eernesto Pollitt. 1989. Effects of iron deficiency on attention and learning processes in preschool children: Bandung, Indonesia. *American Journal of Clinical Nutrition* 50: 667–74.

Stander, Paul. 1989. Anemia in the elderly: Symptoms, causes, and therapies. *Postgraduate Medicine* 85: 85–96.

Stonich, Susan. 1988. Integrated socioeconomic, remote sensing, and information management procedures for rural development and agricultural policy design. Paper presented at the 1988 Annual Meeting of the Society for Applied Anthropology, Tampa, Fla.

1991. The political economy of environmental destruction: Food security in Honduras. In *Harvest of want: Food* security in Mexico and Central America. ed. Scott Whiteford and Anne Ferguson, 35–55. Boulder, Colo.

Stuart-Macadam, Patricia. 1982. A correlative study of a paleaeopathology of the skull. Ph.D. dissertation, Cambridge University.

1987. Porotic hyperostosis: New evidence to support the anemia theory. *American Journal of Physical Anthropology* 74: 521–6.

Stuart-Macadam, Patty. 1992. Porotic hyperostosis: A new perspective. *Journal of Physical Anthropology* 87: 39–47.

Subar, Amy, and Jean Bowering. 1988. The contribution of enrichment and fortification to nutrient intake of women. *Journal of the American Dietetic Association* 88: 1237–45.

Sullivan, Jerome. 1989. The iron paradigm of ischemic heart disease. *American Heart Journal* 117: 1177–88.

Taylor, James, and Abraham Bergman. 1989. Iron-fortified formulas: Pediatricians' prescribing practices. *Clinical Pediatrics* 28: 73–5.

Taylor, John. 1977. Diet, health and economy: Some consequences of planned social change in an aboriginal community. In *Aborigines and change: Australia in the '70s*, ed. R. M. Berndt, 147–58. Canberra.

Thiele, M., M. Geddes, E. Nobmann, and K. Petersen. 1988. High prevalence of iron deficiency anemia among Alaskan native children. *Journal of the American Medical Association* 259: 2532.

Thomas, Anita, Valda Bunker, Maureen Stansfield, et al. 1989. Iron status of hospitalized and housebound elderly people: Dietary intake, metabolic balances, hematological and biochemical indices. *Quarterly Journal of Medicine* 70: 175–84.

Tunnessen, Walter, and Frank Oski. 1987. Consequences of starting whole cow milk at 6 months of age. *Journal of Pediatrics* 111: 813–16.

Ubelaker, Douglas. 1992. Porotic hyperostosis in prehistoric Ecuador. In *Diet, demography, and disease: Changing perspectives on anemia,* ed. Patricia Stuart-Macadam and Susan Kent, 201–18. New York.

Volkman, Toby Alice. 1982. The San in transition, Vol I. *Cultural Survival* 9: 1–56.

Vreugdenhil, G., A. J. Swaak, G. J. Kontoghorghes, and H. G. van Eijk. 1989. Efficacy and safety of oral iron chelator L in anaemic rheumatoid arthritis patients. *Lancet* 2: 1398–9.

Vyas, Devhuti, and R. K. Chandra. 1984. Functional implications of iron deficiency. In *Iron nutrition in infancy and childhood,* ed. A. Stekel, 45–59. New York.

Wadsworth, George R. 1992. Physiological, pathological an dietary influences on the hemoglobin level in circulating blood and the influence of iron in the diet. In *Diet, demography, and disease: Changing views of anemia,* ed. Patricia Stuart-Macadam and Susan Kent, 63–104. New York.

Walker, Phillip. 1986. Porotic hyperostosis in a marine-dependent California Indian population. *American Journal of Physical Anthropology* 69: 345–54.

Walter, Tomas, Sonia Arredondo, Marianela Arevalo, and Abraham Stekel. 1986. Effect of iron therapy on phagocytosis and bactericidal activity in neutrophils of iron-deficient infants. *American Journal of Clinical Nutrition* 44: 877–82.

Walter, Tomas, Isidora de Andraca, Patricia Chadud, and Carmen Perales. 1989. Iron deficiency anemia: Adverse effects on infant psychomotor development. *Pediatrics* 84: 7–17.

Wardrop, C. A. 1987. Runners' anaemia: A paper tiger. *British Medical Journal* 295: 455–6.

Webb, Stephan. 1989. *Prehistoric stress in Australian aborig-ines: A paleopathological study of hunter-gatherer population.* BAR International Series 490: 1–197.

Weinberg, Eugene. 1974. Iron and susceptibility to infectious disease. *Science* 184: 952–6.

1978. Iron and infection. *Microbiological Review* 42: 45–66.

1983. Iron in neoplastic disease. *Nutrition and Cancer* 4: 223–3.

1984. Iron withholding: A defense against infection and neoplasia. *Physiological Reviews* 64: 65–102.

1986. Microorganism. *McGraw-Hill Yearbook of Science and Technology,* 282–3.

1987. Pregnancy-associated immune suppression: Risks and mechanisms. *Microbial Pathogenesis* 3: 393–7.

1989. Cellular regulation of iron assimilation. *Quarterly Review of Biology* 64: 261–90.

1990. Cellular iron metabolism in health and disease. *Drug Metabolism Reviews* 22: 531–79.

1992. Iron withholding in prevention of disease. In *Diet, demography, and disease: Changing perspectives of anemia,* ed. Patricia Stuart-Macadam and Susan Kent, 105–150.

Witte, David L., Debbie S. Angstadt, Sue H. Davis, and Robert D. Schrantz. 1988. Predicting bone marrow iron stores in anemic patients in a community hospital using ferritin and erythrocyte sedimentation rate. *American Journal of Clinical Pathology* 90: 85–7.

Woods, S., T. DeMarco, and M. Friedland. 1990. Iron metabolism. *American Journal of Gastroenterology* 85: 1–8.

Worthington-Roberts, Bonnie, Maryann Breskin, and Elaine Monsen. 1988. Iron status of premenopausal women in a university community and its relationship to habitual dietary sources of protein. *American Journal of Clinical Nutrition* 47: 275–9.

Yip, Ray, Nancy Binkin, Lee Fleshood, Frederick Trowbridge. 1987. Declining prevalence of anemia among low-income children in the United States. *Journal of American Medical Association* 258: 1619–23.

Yip, Ray, and Peter Dallman. 1988. The roles of inflammation and iron deficiency as causes of anemia. *American Journal of Clinical Nutrition* 48: 1295–1300.

Yip, Ray, Samuel Schwartz, and Amos Deinard. 1984. Hematocrit values in white, black, and American Indian children with comparable iron status. *American Journal of Diseases in Childhood* 138: 824–7.

Youdim, Moussa. 1989. Comment on Pollitt et al. *American Journal of Clinical Nutrition* 50: 687–97.

Zanella, Alberto, Linda Gridelli, Alessandra Berzuini, et al. 1989. Sensitivity and predictive value of serum ferritin and free erythrocyte protoporphyrin for iron deficiency. *Journal of Laboratory and Clinical Medicine* 113: 73–8.

Zauber, N. Peter and Ann Zauber. 1987. Hematologic data of healthy very old people. *Journal of American Medical Association* 257: 2181–4.

IV.D.3 ❧ Keshan Disease

Discovery and Characteristics of the Disease

Keshan disease (KD) is a unique endemic cardio-myopathy in China with high incidence and mortality. Its etiology and pathogenesis are not as yet completely clear.

In the winter of 1935, an outbreak of an unknown disease with sudden onset of precardial oppression, pain, nausea, vomiting (yellowish fluid), and fatal termination in severe cases occurred in Keshan County, in Heilongjiang Province of northern China. Because its cause was not known, it was named after the place of outbreak by a Japanese military surgeon (Apei 1937).

Later, Keshan disease was also reported from other parts of China and, in fact, research now indicates that the condition has been prevalent in that country for close to 200 years. The earliest-known account of the disease was found in an inscription on a stone pillar at Jinling Temple, Xiaosi village, Huanglong County, Shaanxi Province, in 1812 (Shan and Xue 1987).

Epidemiological Characteristics

There are three major epidemiological characteristics of Keshan disease. The first is its regional distribution. Keshan disease areas are focally distributed in a belt extending from northeast to southwest China and usually located in hilly land. There are isolated spots known as "safety islands" surrounded by affected areas. The second is population susceptibility. Children below 15 years of age and women of childbearing age in northern China, and children below 10 years of age in southern China, constitute the most susceptible populations. They all live in rural areas and in farm families. The third characteristic is seasonal prevalence. The peak season of Keshan disease in northern China is in winter, but in the south it is in summer. There is also a natural fluctuation of prevalence from year to year.

The annual incidence, mortality, and case fatality of Keshan disease in China are shown in Figure IV.D.3.1. The peak years of 1959, 1964, and 1970 had incidences of 6.02, 4.17, and 4.04 per 10,000, respectively, and the mortality was 1.996, 0.978, and 0.676 per 10,000 (Sun et al. 1982; Sun 1987; The Ministry of Public Health of China 1987–95).

Clinical Manifestations

There are no specific symptoms and signs that clearly identify Keshan disease. But according to the degree of heart function insufficiency and of compensative status, Keshan disease is classified into four clinical types: acute, subacute, chronic, and latent (Ge et al. 1983).

Acute cases usually occur suddenly, with acute heart function insufficiency such as cardiogenic shock, severe arrhythmia, and pulmonary edema. The prominent characteristic of the chronic type is chronic congestive heart failure, which is the consequence of acute or subacute types or a result of a long-standing cardiac disorder of an insidious onset. Moderate or severe heart enlargement is always seen in chronic cases.

Subacute cases occur primarily in children. The onset is less sudden and the insidious period is about one or two weeks. The clinical manifestations of the subacute type are mainly cardiogenic shock and/or chronic congestive heart failure, and most patients have facial edema and galloping rhythm of the heart. Latent cases may be discovered as only an incidental finding upon routine physical examination. They usually show a mildly enlarged heart with normal heart function, abnormal electrocardiogram changes of the right bundle branch block, and infrequent premature ventricular contractions.

Pathological Observations

A large number of autopsies have been carried out since the recognition of Keshan disease in 1935. More than 3,600 autopsy cases were collected in the 1950s,

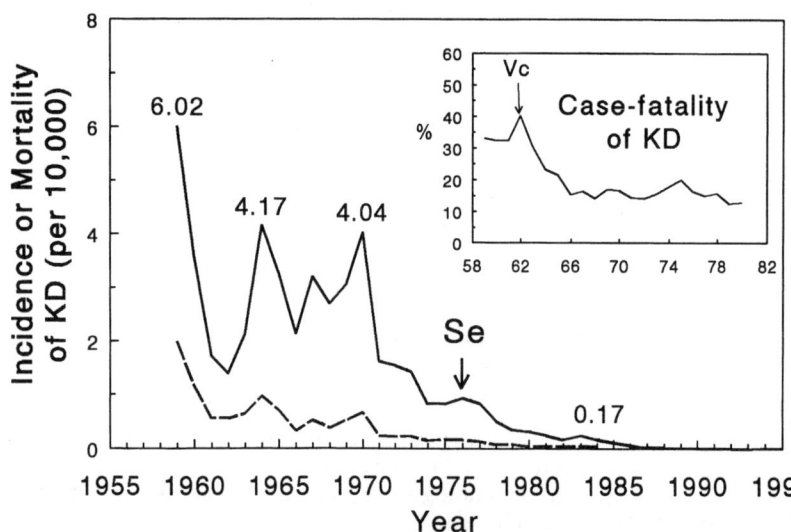

Figure IV.D.3.1. The incidence, mortality, and case-fatality of Keshan disease in China. Solid line (—) is the incidence of Keshan disease (1/10,000). Dashed line (---) is the mortality of Keshan disease (1/10,000).

when there was a heavy prevalence of the disease in northern China. Later, an endemic cardiomyopathy that was prevalent in children in southern China was studied and in 1965 identified as Keshan disease. Since then, large amounts of epidemiological, clinical, and pathological data have been accumulated in the south.

Multifocal necrosis and fibrous replacement of the myocardium are the principal pathological features of Keshan disease (Ge et al. 1983). Two patterns of myocardial necrosis are distinguishable by light microscopy. One is myocytolysis; the other is contraction band necrosis. Myocytolysis exists in the majority of cases and is regarded as a representative lesion of Keshan disease. It seems to be initiated by mitochondrial disorganization and results in the final disappearance of the myofibers. Contraction band necrosis is characterized by myofibril segmentation and has been considered to be the consequence of the severe circulatory disorders predominantly observed in acute cases.

Treatment

There is no specific therapy for Keshan disease. However, the method of administering a megadose of ascorbic acid (vitamin C) in cases of acute and subacute Keshan disease was discovered by Xian Medical College in 1961 (Research Laboratory of Keshan Disease of Xian Medical College 1961). It was a breakthrough in the treatment of Keshan disease and particularly effective in patients with cardiogenic shock. Since then, the case fatality of the acute type of Keshan disease has decreased significantly from 80 percent to less than 20 percent (Figure IV.D.3.1). Patients with congestive heart failure require prompt and optimal digitalization, although the response in some cases is poor. Other treatments (antibiotics, oral diuretics, and moderate restriction of salt) are used for the control of congestive heart failure (Yang et al. 1984).

The Relation between Selenium and Keshan Disease

In the 1960s, it was found that white muscle disease (WMD) in young ruminants caused by selenium (Se) deficiency often occurred in areas affected by Keshan disease, and some similarities in clinical symptoms and pathological features between Keshan disease and white muscle disease were found. The scientists in the Institute of Shaanxi Veterinary Medicine suggested that both Keshan disease and white muscle disease could be responsive to selenium. Small-scale human intervention studies were carried out by several research groups, and some encouraging results were obtained; however, the effectiveness of Se supplementation was demonstrated only by a large-scale selenium intervention study in Mianning County, Sichuan Province, in southwestern China. This study was carried out from 1974 to 1976 by the Keshan Disease Research Group, Chinese Academy of Medical Sciences (Keshan Disease Research Group, Chinese Academy of Medical Sciences 1979).

Sodium Selenite Intervention

In 1974, 119 production teams observed children of susceptible age (1 to 9 years) in three villages of Mianning County. In 1975, the study was extended to include 169 teams in four villages. One-half of the children were given sodium selenite tablets and the other half a placebo. The assignment to one of these groups was made randomly and remained unchanged during the two years of the investigation. The subjects took sodium selenite once a week, with a dosage of 0.5 milligrams (mg) for those aged 1 to 5 years and a dose of 1.0 mg for those 6 to 9 years old. Because of the convincing results obtained in 1974 and 1975 (to be discussed shortly), the control groups were abandoned and all subjects were given sodium selenite in 1976 and 1977.

A Keshan disease hospital was established in the area under investigation; there, diagnosis and subtyping of the disease were carried out according to the criteria set up in 1974 by the National Seminar of the Etiology of Keshan Disease. Electrocardiograms, heart roentgenograms, and physical examinations were performed on patients admitted to the hospital for observation. In some cases, blood Se content, glutathione peroxidase (GPX), serum glutamic oxalacetic transaminase (GOT), and glutamic pyruvic transaminase (GPT) activity were determined. Patients receiving treatment at other medical units were transferred to the hospital after the improvement of their general condition. Follow-up examinations were carried out each year to study the progress of individual patients.

The incidence and prognosis of the subjects investigated are shown in Table IV.D.3.1. In 1974, among the 3,985 children in the control group, there were 54 cases of Keshan disease (13.55 per 1,000), whereas only 10 of the 4,510 Se-supplemented subjects fell ill (2.22 per 1,000). The difference between the incidence of the two groups was highly significant ($P < 0.01$). A similar difference was found in 1975. In 1976, when all subjects were given selenite, only 4 cases out of 12,579 subjects occurred, which further lowered the incidence to 0.32 per 1,000. There was 1 case of the typical subacute type among 212 children who failed to take selenite. In 1977, there were no new cases among the 12,747 supplemented subjects. These results indicated that sodium selenite intervention had a significant effect in reducing incidence of Keshan disease. The Se-supplemented subjects had not only a lower incidence but also lower mortality and better prognosis.

In 1976 and 1977, liver function tests and general physical examinations were given to 100 subjects who had taken Se tablets weekly for three to four years. The results were not significantly different from

Table IV.D.3.1. *Keshan disease incidence and prognosis of selenium-supplemented and control children (1-9 years old) in Mianning County, Sichuan Province, China, during 1974-7[a]*

Groups	Year	Subjects	New cases	Incidence (‰)	Prognosis			
					Turned chronic	Turned latent	Improved	Death
Se-supplemented	1974	4,510	10	2.22	1	9	0	0
	1975	6,767	7	1.03	0	6	0	1
	1976	12,579	4	0.32	0	2	0	2
	1977	12,747	0	0	0	0	0	0
(Total)		36,603	21	0.57	1	17	0	3
Control	1974	3,985	54	13.55	2	16	9	27
	1975	5,445	52	9.55	3	13	10	26
	1976	212	1	4.72	1	0	0	0
(Total)		9,642	107	11.10	6	29	19	53

[a]There are significant differences of incidence between the two groups in each year and in total (P < 0.01).

those for the unsupplemented children and indicated that selenium-supplementation produced no untoward side effects.

In 1976, observations on the effects of sodium selenite were extended beyond Mianning County to include Dechang, Xichang, Yuexi, and Puge Counties. All children (1 to 12 years old) in some of the most severely affected areas were supplemented with selenite as just described, whereas the children in the nearby areas served as unsupplemented controls. The results, summarized in Table IV.D.3.2, show that in each year the incidence of Keshan disease among the Se-supplemented children of the five counties was significantly lower than that among the unsupplemented children. Similar results were obtained by Xian Medical College in a study in Huanglong County, Shaanxi Province, from 1975 to 1977 (Research Laboratory of Keshan Disease of Xian Medical College 1979).

Because of the convincing evidence of the efficacy of sodium selenite in preventing Keshan disease, it has been widely used since 1976 in tablet form, as an addition to table salt, and as a fertilizer. Concomitantly, the incidence and mortality of Keshan disease decreased to 0.17 and 0.04 per 10,000, respectively (Figure IV.D.3.1).

Occurrence in Selenium-Deficient Areas

Since regional distribution is the first epidemiological characteristic of Keshan disease, the discovery of environmental differences between areas that are affected by Keshan disease and those that are not has been an important goal in the study of its etiology.

A fluorometric method for determining Se content and another method for determining glutathione peroxidase (GPX) activity were adapted and set up by the Keshan Disease Research Group of the Chinese Academy of Medical Sciences in 1972 and 1975. Sampling techniques indicated that blood and hair Se content and blood GPX activity of residents in Keshan disease–affected areas were lower than those of people in nonaffected areas (see Table IV.D.3.3). However, after the oral administration of sodium selenite for 1 year, the blood GPX activity of children in Keshan disease–affected areas had increased to levels comparable to those of children in nonaffected areas (see Table IV.D.3.4).

It was assumed that the low-selenium status of people living in Keshan disease–affected areas was caused by a low dietary selenium intake. Therefore, large samples of cereals, soil, water, and human blood, hair, and urine from Keshan disease–affected areas (11 provinces, 42 counties, 77 spots) and nonaffected

Table IV.D.3.2. *Keshan disease incidence in selenium-supplemented and control children (1-12 years old) in five counties of Sichuan Province, China, during 1976-80[a]*

Year	Se-supplemented			Control		
	Subjects	New cases	Incidence (‰)	Subjects	New cases	Incidence (‰)
1976	45,515	8	0.17	243,649	488	2.00
1977	67,754	15	0.22	222,944	350	1.57
1978	65,953	10	0.15	220,599	373	1.69
1979	69,910	33	0.47	223,280	300	1.34
1980	74,740	22	0.29	197,096	202	1.02
Total	323,872	88	0.27	1,107,568	1,713	1.55

[a]There are significant differences of incidence between the two groups in each year and in total (P < 0.01).

Table IV.D.3.3. *Selenium levels in human blood and hair from residents in Keshan disease-affected and nonaffected areas in 1972-3*

Subjects[a]	Blood Se (ng/g)[b]	Hair Se (ng/g)[b]
KD-affected areas		
KD patients	18 ± 9 (42)[a]	107 ± 53 (21)[f]
Farmers	21 ± 7 (24)[a]	
Nonaffected areas (near KD areas)		
Farmers	32 ± 4 (20)[b]	187 ± 51 (20)[g]
Staff members in town	41 ± 21 (10)[c]	
Nonaffected areas (far from KD areas)		
Staff members (A) in city	173 ± 44 (16)[d]	712 ± 97 (13)[h]
Staff members (B) in city	255 ± 38 (17)[e]	834 ± 156 (11)[k]

[a]Staff members (A) were the members of a KD research group of the Chinese Academy of Medical Sciences and had been in KD areas for less than one year; staff members (B) had never been in KD areas.

[b]Values are means ± SD; number of samples is in parentheses; values not sharing a common superscript in a vertical column are significantly different ($P < 0.05$) by the t-test.

areas (20 provinces, 86 counties, 110 spots) were collected. The data indicated that the samples containing less than 20 nanograms/gram (ng/g) of Se in blood or 120 ng/g in hair or 10 ng/g in cereals were almost exclusively from Keshan disease–affected areas, whereas samples with Se content of more than 50 ng/g in blood or 200 ng/g in hair or 20 ng/g in cereals were all from nonaffected areas (Yang et al. 1982). These data could be considered the threshold of Se content in assessing the risk of Keshan disease, especially for those who live on a rather simple diet composed mainly of locally grown cereals (Table IV.D.3.5).

Similar results from more than 10,000 samples were reported by the Institute of Geography, Chinese Academy of Sciences (Group of Environmental and Endemic Disease 1982; Xu et al. 1982). Based on a large amount of data, a map of selenium distribution in China was published in *The Atlas of Endemic Diseases and Their Environments in the People's*

Table IV.D.3.4. *Blood gluthathione peroxidase (GPX) activities of children from Keshan disease-affected and nonaffected areas in 1975*

Subjects	Blood GPX (units)
KD-affected areas	
KD child patients	57.1 ± 6.1 (22)[a]
Healthy children	60.5 ± 5.6 (63)[a]
Se-supplemented children	76.1 ± 8.4 (58)[b]
Nonaffected areas (near KD areas)	
Children in farmer's family	73.6 ± 13.8 (20)[b]
Nonaffected areas (far from KD areas)	
Children in farmer's family	77.5 ± 9.8 (22)[b]

Note: Values are means ± SD; number of samples is in parentheses; values not sharing a common superscript are significantly different ($P < 0.01$) by the t-test.

Table IV.D.3.5. *Selenium contents of blood, hair, and grains in Keshan disease-affected and nonaffected areas*

Samples	KD areas (ng/g)	Overlapping areas (ng/g)	Non-KD areas (ng/g)
Human blood	< 20	20–50	> 50
Human hair	<120	120–200	>200
Staple grain	< 10	10–20	> 20

Republic of China (1989). It shows that low-selenium areas are distributed in a belt extending from northeast to southwest China, which is consistent with the geographical distribution of Keshan disease.

The results obtained by medical, veterinary, and geographical scientists all indicated that Keshan disease occurs only in selenium-deficient areas, which explains the epidemiological characteristic of its regional distribution. The fact that the blood and hair Se levels and GPX activity of farming residents are lower than those of nonfarming residents in the same Keshan disease–affected areas at least partially explains the characteristic of population susceptibility. In view of the results just described, it was concluded that selenium deficiency is the basic cause of Keshan disease occurrence.

Biochemical Changes

There were no significant differences in Se status and GPX activity between Keshan disease patients and other residents of the same areas (Zhu, Xia, and Yang 1982). There were also no changes in hair Se content to accompany the seasonal or yearly fluctuation of Keshan disease prevalence (Sun et al. 1980). These facts suggest that the etiology of Keshan disease cannot be explained by selenium deficiency alone and that there is a need to understand the ways in which selenium prevents Keshan disease.

A Study on Keshan Disease Patients

A comprehensive scientific survey of Keshan disease in Chuxiong prefecture, Yunnan Province, southwestern China, was conducted from 1984 to 1986 by 293 workers from 16 laboratories in seven provinces. The objective was to examine 3,648 children from 56 villages in Keshan disease-affected and nonaffected areas and compare the two groups. One hundred and sixty-seven children who were Keshan disease patients were treated, and 27 autopsies were carried out on patients who had died of subacute Keshan disease. Autopsy controls consisted of those who died from other diseases in both affected and nonaffected areas. The results of this survey were published in the *Collected Work of Comprehensive Scientific Survey on Keshan Disease in Chuxiong Prefecture (1984-1986)* (Yu 1988).

Table IV.D.3.6 *Selenium contents and glutathione peroxidase (GPX) activities in tissues from patients with subacute Keshan disease (Sub-KD) and controls in affected (Control-A) or nonaffected areas (Control-NA)*

		Sub-KD	Control-A	Control-NA
Selenium (ng/g fresh)	Heart	25 ± 10 (6)[a]	55 ± 32 (4)[a]	134 ± 32 (3)[b]
	Liver	52 ± 30 (6)[a]	89 ± 50 (4)[a]	256 (1)
GPX (U/mg protein)	Heart (H_2O_2)	10 ± 5 (11)[a]	26 ± 21 (7)[b]	73 ± 12 (20)[c]
	(t-BOOH)	10 ± 5 (11)[a]	29 ± 25 (7)[b]	80 ± 12 (2)[c]
	Liver (H_2O_2)	7 ± 4 (4)[a]	38 ± 11 (3)[b]	
	(t-BOOH)	23 ± 5 (4)[a]	47 ± 25 (3)[b]	
	Kidney (H_2O_2)	20 ± 7 (4)[a]	78 ± 39 (3)[b]	
	(t-BOOH)	32 ± 2 (4)[a]	85 ± 36 (3)[b]	

Note: Values are means ± SD: number of samples is in parentheses; values not sharing a common superscript in a horizontal row are significantly different ($P < 0.01$) by the t-test.

The comparison of Se content and GPX activity in the tissues of patients with subacute Keshan disease (Sub-KD) and those of the controls in affected (Control-A) and nonaffected areas (Control-NA) is shown in Table IV.D.3.6. There was a tendency for Keshan disease patients to have lower heart and liver Se levels than the controls, and their GPX activity was significantly lower than that of the controls. Other results supported the hypothesis that the heart is the organ most susceptible to selenium deficiency.

Other oxidant defense indices in the myocardium of child patients with Sub-KD were measured. The results showed that the activity of superoxide dismutase (SOD) in the myocardia of Sub-KD patients was significantly lower than that of Control-NA subjects, but malondialdehyde (MDA) and free radicals were higher than those of Control-NA. These results indicated that there was an accumulation of lipid peroxides and free radicals in Keshan disease patients. However, there were no differences between Sub-KD patients and controls in glutathione reductase (GR) and glutathione-S-transferase (GST) activity.

Ultrastructural observations showed that mitochondria in the myocardia of Sub-KD patients appeared to be most commonly and conspicuously affected and were involved early. In general, the changes in biochemical functions occurred before the structural damage. The results indicated that the activity of succinate dehydrogenase (SDH), cytochrome C oxidase (CCO), and H+-ATPase, and content of Co Q in the myocardial mitochondria of Sub-KD patients were lower than those of Control-NA. These findings implied that the lesions of the mitochondria affect mostly the respiratory chain of the inner membrane. Changes in membrane potential and decreased fluidity of membrane lipid were observed in the myocardial mitochondria of Sub-KD patients. The content of Se in the mitochondria was one-eighth that of Control-NA (Yu 1988). It is likely that the structural and functional abnormalities of the myocardial mitochondria of patients with Keshan disease may result from selenium deficiency. In addition, the mitochondria constitute one of the calcium pools and play an important role in regulating the calcium concentration in cells.

The increased calcium content in the myocardial mitochondria of Sub-KD patients may have an intrinsic relationship with the functional abnormalities.

From this comprehensive survey, it was concluded that relatively weak oxidant defenses, mainly low GPX activity, and insufficient vitamin E (less than 8 μg/ml plasma in people living in Keshan disease–affected areas) created a selenium-deficient population susceptible to oxidant stresses that resulted in damage to myocardial structures and functions and finally in the occurrence of Keshan disease.

Effects of Se Deficiency

It was not clear whether differences in dietary patterns (aside from selenium intake) between people in Keshan disease–affected and nonaffected areas were involved in the etiology of Keshan disease. Three studies were carried out in 1987, 1989, and 1991 in Mianning and Dechang Counties, Sichuan Province, where there was a very high incidence of Keshan disease there was during the 1970s. These two counties are only 150 kilometers (km) apart and have the same dietary patterns. According to the results from a nutrition survey in 1985, conducted by the Anti-Epidemic Station of Liangshan Autonomous Prefecture, the dietary selenium intake was 11 μg per day for both counties. The only difference was a supplementation of selenized salt (15 μg selenium per g salt, as sodium selenite) in Mianning County from 1983 onward, so the people of Mianning had 69 μg of extra selenium per day, giving them a total selenium intake of 80 μg per day. Table IV.D.3.7 shows the results of a study conducted in 1987 (Xia, Hill, and Burk 1989; Hill et al. 1996) following selenized salt supplementation for 4 years. Not only were the blood Se levels of children in Mianning County higher than those in Dechang County, but the GPX activity of their plasma was three times as high, and plasma selenoprotein P concentrations were also much higher. Linear regression analysis of plasma showed that selenium concentration, GPX activity, and selenoprotein P concentration correlated well with each other. There were no differences in other indices for oxidant defense capability between the residents of the two counties.

Table IV.D.3.7. *Indexes for oxidant defense capability in the blood of children from Dechang and Mianning Counties in 1987*

		Dechang (–Se)		Mianning (Se-salt)	
Selenium	Blood (ng/g)	18 ± 10	(22)[a]	47 ± 9	(18)[b]
	Plasma (ng/g)	13 ± 55	(22)[a]	40 ± 11	(18)[b]
	RBC (ng/g)	26 ± 9	(22)[a]	47 ± 9	(19)[b]
GPX	Plasma (U/L)	29 ± 15	(21)[a]	87 ± 15	(15)[b]
	RBC (U/gHb)	2.8 ± 1.7	(21)[a]	8.4 ± 3.3	(19)[b]
Selenoprotein P	Plasma (U/L)	0.10 ± 0.04	(22)[a]	0.39 ± 0.17	(17)[b]
SOD	RBC (U/mgHb)	17 ± 7	(22)	17 ± 3	(19)
Catalase	RBC (U/gHb)	238 ± 48	(22)	231 ± 29	(19)
Glutathione reductase	RBC (U/gHb)	3.3 ± 1.0	(22)	4.2 ± 1.3	(19)
GSH	Plasma (μM)	4.7 ± 0.6	(21)	4.4 ± 1.0	(16)
	RBC (mM)	2.5 ± 0.4	(19)	2.1 ± 0.7	(19)
Vitamin E	Plasma (μg/ml)	4.0 ± 1.2	(22)	3.8 ± 1.2	(19)
MDA	Plasma (nmol/ml)	6.7 ± 2.2	(22)	6.0 ± 2.6	(19)

Note: Values are means ± SD: number of samples is in parentheses; values not sharing a common superscript in a horizontal row are significantly different ($P < 0.001$) by the t-test.

Effects of age and sex. In the 1989 study, blood samples were taken from 401 healthy subjects (half male and half female) in Dechang County. The lowest levels of selenium and GPX activity were found in the youngest (2 to 5 years old) and oldest (more than 60 years old), and no significant sex difference was found. These data were consistent with the occurrence of Keshan disease in children, the susceptible population group (Xia et al. 1994).

Changes in selenium intake. It was found that the selenium status and GPX activity of residents of Dechang County increased gradually year after year to reach the levels of persons in nonaffected areas in 1991. Coincidentally, there was no occurrence of Keshan disease in this year. Therefore, it was necessary to check the selenium intake of the local residents. In the 1991 study, the selenium contents of rice, table salt, and the mixed diet were measured. The data showed that selenium in rice was 16.6 ± 4.3 μg/kg (n = 10), which was in the same range as that of KD-affected areas (<20 ng/g in grain, see Table IV.D.3.5), but selenium intake from the diet was estimated to be 38 ± 28 μg/day (n = 30), which reached the minimum requirement of 20 μg/day (Yang et al. 1985; Yang and Xia 1995). This change probably resulted from the inadvertent distribution of selenized salt in Dechang County and, with the improvement of the local economy, the increased consumption of food from selenium-adequate areas. It was confirmed that the decrease of Keshan disease incidence in Dechang County correlated with an improved selenium status because of an increase in dietary selenium intake.

Marginal vitamin E status. Vitamin E (VE), an important constituent of the oxidant defense system, protects biological membrane tissue as a free-radical scavenger and has a synergistic effect with selenium.

Animal studies have indicated that cardiac injury can be developed in animals fed a diet deficient in both selenium and vitamin E but that neither deficiency by itself causes cardiac injury (Van Vleet, Ferrans, and Ruth 1977; Konz et al. 1991). Other animal studies have indicated that myocardial injury can occur in animals fed a diet of foods from Keshan disease–affected areas and that this condition can be alleviated by the supplementation of selenium or vitamin E or both (Wang et al. 1991). Plasma vitamin E of residents of Keshan disease–affected areas ranged from 2 to 8 μg/ml, which is a low marginal status (Keshan Disease Research Group, Chinese Academy of Medical Sciences 1977a; Li et al. 1988; Xia et al. 1989; Zhu et al. 1991). This low marginal vitamin-E status could act as a promoting cofactor in the occurrence of Keshan disease. If so, vitamin E supplementation might be helpful in improving the low selenium status of residents of Keshan disease areas.

The Etiology of Keshan Disease

Although the overall incidence of Keshan disease has steadily declined since the 1980s, there was a question of whether there was a corresponding change in the selenium status of local populations at risk. Geographic scientists collected 4,600 samples (rock, soil, water, cereals, animal fur, and human hair) from 217 sampling spots and monitored the incidence of Keshan disease for three years in the 1980s (Tang et al. 1991). The results (see Table IV.D.3.8) indicated that the environmental selenium status was still as low as that in the 1970s, but the selenium level in hair had increased to a normal level (see Table IV.D.3.5). It is believed that in addition to deliberate selenium supplementation, there has been inadvertent supplementation as a previously self-sufficient lifestyle gave way to a commodity economy, in which foods with higher selenium content were imported into the affected

Table IV.D.3.8. *Comparison of selenium contents in cereals and human hair between the 1970s and 1980s*

	1970s		1980s	
Corn (µg/kg)	13 ± 6	(157)[a]	10 ± 9	(90)[b]
Rice (µg/kg)	14 ± 8	(47)	15 ± 11	(31)
Wheat (µg/kg)	14 ± 7	(115)	13 ± 9	(96)
Hair (µg/kg)	85 ± 32	(815)[a]	192 ± 96	(44)[b]

Note: Values are means ± SD; number of samples is in parentheses; values not sharing a common superscript in a horizontal row are significantly different (P < 0.001) by the t-test.

areas. In addition there has been an increase in the consumption of animal products in recent years. All of this would seem to confirm that an adequate selenium status is necessary for the prevention of Keshan disease.

Although selenium deficiency can explain the epidemiological characteristic of the regional distribution of Keshan disease, it only partially explains the susceptibility of populations. Because the selenium status of residents in Keshan disease–affected areas does not change with seasonal fluctuation of the incidence of the disease, another potential cofactor (or cofactors) must be involved in its occurrence. Such cofactors would act as promoters or stimulators during selenium deficiency.

The potential cofactors in the etiology of Keshan disease can be classified into four categories:

1. An insufficiency of nutrients that have relative biological function with selenium, such as VE, methionine, and iodine.
2. An excess of elements that have antagonistic interaction with selenium, leading to poor availability of selenium.
3. The prevalence of mycotoxins that contaminate foods and damage the myocardium.
4. A virus infection in which the target organ is the heart (Su 1979; Bai et al. 1984).

Present information does not permit ruling out any one of these as a cofactor in selenium deficiency and in the etiology of Keshan disease.

Clearly, much work remains to be done, even though studying the etiology of Keshan disease presents some difficulties. One problem is that there are no ideal animal models for Keshan disease; another is that almost no new Keshan disease patients can be found (only 57 new patients were reported in the whole country in 1995). However, it is believed that the pathogenic factors in Keshan disease areas are still active because, according to the Annual Report from the Ministry of Public Health of China there are about 50,000 latent Keshan disease patients in the country. Therefore, work will continue.

Yiming Xia

Bibliography

Apei, H. 1937. Report of etiological survey on Keshan disease. *Research Reports of Continental Academy* 1: 1–10.

Arthur, J. R., F. Nicol, and G. J. Beckett. 1990. Hepatic iodothyronine deiodinase: The role of selenium. *Biochemical Journal* 272: 537–40.

Bai, J., S. Wu, K. Ge, et al. 1984. The combined effect of selenium deficiency and viral infection on the myocardium of mice. *Acta Academiae Medicinae Sinica* 2: 29–31.

Beck, M. A., P. C. Kolbeck, L. H. Rohr, et al. 1994a. Amyocarditic coxsackievirus becomes myocarditic in selenium deficient mice. *Journal of Medical Virology* 43: 166–70.

1994b. Vitamin E deficiency intensifies the myocardial injury of coxsackievirus B3 infection of mice. *Journal of Nutrition* 124: 345–58.

Beck, M. A., P. C. Kolbeck, Q. Shi, et al. 1994. Increased virulence of a human enterovirus (coxsackievirus B3) in selenium deficient mice. *The Journal of Infectious Diseases* 170: 351–7.

Beck, M. A., Q. Shi, V. C. Virginia, and O. A. Levander. 1995. Rapid genomic evolution of non-virulent coxsackievirus B3 in selenium-deficient mice results in selection of identical virulent isolates. *Nature Medicine* 1: 433–6.

Becker, K. B., M. J. Schneider, J. C. Davey, and V. A. Galton. 1995. The type III 5-deiodinase in *Rana catesbeiana* tadpoles is encoded by a thyroid hormone-responsive gene. *Endocrinology* 136: 4424–6.

Behne, D., A. Kyriakopoulos, H. Meinhold, and J. Köhrle. 1990. Identification of type I iodothyronine 5'-deiodinase as a selenoenzyme. *Biochemical and Biophysical Research Communications* 173: 1143–9.

Davey, J. C., K. B. Becker, M. J. Schneider, et al. 1995. Cloning of a cDNA for the type II iodothyronine deiodinase. *Journal of Biological Chemistry* 270: 26786–9.

Editorial Board of *The Atlas of Endemic Diseases and Their Environments in the People's Republic of China.* 1989. *The atlas of endemic diseases and their environments in the People's Republic of China.* Beijing.

Ge, K., A. Xue, J. Bai, and S. Wang. 1983. Keshan disease – an endemic cardiomyopathy in China. *Virchows Archive of Pathological Anatomy and Histopathology* 401: 1–15.

Ge, K., A. Xue, and S. Wang. 1980. Ultrastructural changes of myocardial necrosis of Keshan disease. Light and electron microscope comparative study with a cytolocalization technique. *Chinese Journal of Medicine* 60: 407–9.

Group of Environmental and Endemic Disease. 1982. The relation of Keshan disease to the natural environment and the background of selenium nutrition. *Acta Nutrimenta Sinica* 4: 175–82.

Hill, K. E., and R. F. Burk. 1982. Effect of selenium deficiency and vitamin E deficiency on glutathione metabolism in isolated rat hepatocytes. *Journal of Biological Chemistry* 257: 10668–72.

Hill, K. E., and R. F. Burk. 1994. Selenoprotein P – an extracellular protein containing multiple selenocysteines. In *Selenium in biology and human health,* ed. R. F. Burk, 119–31. New York.

Hill, K. E., Y. Xia, B. Kesson, et al. 1996. Selenoprotein P concentration in plasma is an index of selenium status in selenium-deficient and selenium-supplemented Chinese subjects. *Journal of Nutrition* 126: 138–45.

Keshan Disease Research Group, Chinese Academy of Medical Sciences. 1974. A study on the relationship between selenium and Keshan occurrence. In *The Proceedings of the National Symposium on the Etiology of Keshan Disease,* 181-200. Shenyang.

1977a. Comparison of vitamin E contents of serum from residents living in Keshan disease affected and non-affected areas. *Collected papers on Keshan disease* 1: 71-7. Beijing.

1977b. Glutathione peroxidase activities in blood of residents in Keshan disease areas. *Collected papers on Keshan disease* 1: 67-70.

1979. Observation on the effect of sodium selenite in prevention of Keshan disease. *Chinese Medical Journal* 92: 471-6.

Konz, K. H., R. A. Walsh, K. E. Hill, et al. 1991. Cardiac injury caused by selenium and vitamin E deficiency in the minipig: Biochemical and hemodynamic studies. *Journal of Trace Elements in Experimental Medicine* 4: 61-7.

Li, G., J. Yang, Y. Ren, et al. 1988. Distribution of lipid metabolism in children in endemic areas of Keshan disease. In *Collected work of comprehensive scientific survey on Keshan Disease in Chuxiong Prefecture 1984-1986,* ed. W. Yu, 247-9. Beijing.

Ministry of Public Health of China. 1987-95. Annual reports on national healthy statistics. Beijing.

Research Laboratory of Keshan Disease, Xian Medical College. 1961. Study on clinical effect and mechanism in treatment of acute Keshan disease with large dosage of vitamin C. *Chinese Journal of Internal Medicine* 6: 346-50.

1979. Observations on the efficacy of sodium selenite in the prevention of acute onset of Keshan disease. *Chinese Journal of Internal Medicine* 59: 457-9.

Shan, S., and A. Xue. 1987. The information of Keshan disease and its prevention and treatment in Shaanxi Province. In *The study on prevention and treatment of Keshan disease in China,* ed. W. Yu, 61-8. Beijing.

Su, C. 1979. Preliminary results of viral etiology of Keshan disease. *Chinese Medical Journal* 59: 466-72.

Sun, J. 1987. The policy of "the prevention first" is most important in the prevention and treatment of Keshan disease - review on the history of preventing and treating Keshan disease in China. In *The study on prevention and treatment of Keshan disease in China,* ed. W. Yu, 1-24. Beijing.

Sun, J., Y. Lu, G. Wu, and R. Teng. 1982. A survey of the epidemic of Keshan disease in the north of China. *Chinese Journal of Endemiology* 1: 2-5.

Sun, S., T. Yin, G. Wang, et al. 1980. The relationship between seasonal prevalence of Keshan disease and hair selenium of inhabitants. *Chinese Journal of Preventive Medicine* 14: 17-9.

Tang, J., W. Zhu, R. Li, and W. Wang. 1991. The relationship between Keshan disease and environment selenium, some vital elements. *Chinese Journal of Endemiology* 10: 269-74.

Ursini, F., M. Maiorino, and C. Gregolin. 1985. The selenoenzyme phospholipid hydroperoxide glutathione peroxidase. *Chinese Journal of Biochemistry and Biophysics* 839: 62-70.

Van Vleet, J. F., V. J. Ferrans, and G. R. Ruth. 1977. Ultrastructural alterations in nutritional cardiomyopathy of selenium-vitamin E deficient swine. I. Fiber lesions. *Laboratory Investigations* 37: 188-96.

Wang, F., D. Kang, S. Liu, et al. 1991. The relation of both selenium and vitamin E deficiency to etiology of Keshan disease. *Chinese Journal of Control of Endemic Disease* 6: 306-7.

Xia, Y., K. E. Hill, and R. F. Burk. 1989. Biochemical studies of a selenium-deficient population in China: Measurement of selenium, glutathione peroxidase and other oxidant defense indices in blood. *Journal of Nutrition* 119: 1318-26.

Xia, Y., J. Piao, K. E. Hill, and R. F. Burk. 1994. Keshan disease and selenium status of populations in China. In *Selenium in biology and human health,* ed. R. F. Burk, 181-96. New York.

Xu, G., W. Xue, P. Zhang, et al. 1982. Selenium status and dietary selenium content of populations in the endemic and non-endemic areas of Keshan disease. *Acta Nutrimenta Sinica* 4: 183-90.

Yang, G., J. Chen, Z. Wen, et al. 1984. The role of selenium in Keshan disease. In *Advances in nutrition research,* Vol. 6, ed. H. H. Draper, 203-31. New York.

Yang, G., G. Wang, T. Yin, et al. 1982. Relationship between the distribution of Keshan disease and selenium status. *Acta Nutrimenta Sinica* 4: 191-200.

Yang, G., and Y. Xia. 1995. Studies on human dietary requirements and safe range of dietary intakes of selenium in China and their application in the prevention of related endemic diseases. *Biomedical and Environmental Sciences* 8: 187-201.

Yang, G., R. Zhou, S. Yin, et al. 1985. Investigation on selenium requirements of Chinese people. I. Physiological, minimal requirements and minimum dietary allowance. *Hygiene Investigation* 14: 24-8.

Yu, W. 1988. *Collected work of comprehensive scientific survey on Keshan disease in Chuxiong prefecture (1984-1986).* Beijing.

Zhu, L., Y. Cheng, J. Piao, et al. 1991. The antioxidative ability and oxidative factors of children in Keshan disease affected areas of Sichuan Province. *Chinese Journal of Endemiology* 10: 7-11.

Zhu, L., Y. Xia, and G. Yang. 1982. Blood glutathione peroxidase activities of populations in Keshan disease affected and non-affected areas. *Acta Nutrimenta Sinica* 4: 229-33.

IV.D.4 ❧ Osteoporosis

Calcium and Life

Calcium is the fifth most abundant element in the biosphere, after oxygen, silicon, aluminum, and iron. It is present in high concentration in seawater and in all fresh waters that support an abundant biota. Fortuitously, the calcium ion has just the right radius to fit neatly within the folds of various peptide chains. Calcium thereby stabilizes and activates a large number of structural and catalytic proteins essential for life. In this capacity calcium serves as a ubiquitous second messenger within cells, mediating such diverse processes as mitosis, muscle contraction, glandular secretion, blood coagulation, and interneuronal signal transmission. Controlling these activities requires careful regulation of the concentration of calcium in critical fluid compartments. This regulation is accomplished in two basic ways.

At a cellular level, calcium is ordinarily sequestered

within intracellular storage compartments. It is released into the cell sap when needed to trigger various cellular activities, and then quickly pumped back into its storage reservoirs when the activity needs to be terminated. This control mode is exemplified by the accumulation and release of calcium by the sarcoplasmic reticulum of striated muscle. The second type of control, utilized by many tissues in higher organisms, is the tight regulation of the calcium level in the blood and extracellular fluids that bathe all the tissues. Individual cells, needing a pulse of calcium, simply open membrane channels and let calcium pour in from the bathing fluid; they then pump it back out when the particular activity needs to cease.

Bone and the Regulation of Calcium Levels

Each mode of control requires both a reserve supply of calcium and a place to put an excess of calcium: In the first mode, the source and sink are within the cell; and in the second, they are outside the cell but still within the organism. The extracellular calcium reserve (and sink) in the higher vertebrates has, over the course of evolution, become the organ system we call bone. Along the way, building on the hardness of calcium deposits, bone acquired the mechanical and structural functions that have become its most prominent features.

The fossil record shows that bone evolved independently many times over the course of vertebrate evolution, usually in a marine environment where bone probably functioned primarily as a sink for calcium (since the fluid in contact with the gill surfaces represented an essentially inexhaustible source). The hardness of bone served many useful, but secondary purposes, ranging from dermal armor, to teeth, to internal stiffening. As mechanisms of controlling concentration of minerals in the internal environment evolved to higher levels of refinement and an internal sink became less necessary, the internal skeleton dropped out of many fish genera, which retained only the structural portions that were vital – teeth and dermal armor.

But in amphibians and terrestrial vertebrates, living outside of a buoyant medium, the internal stiffening could not be dropped. It provided structural support and mechanical strength, and it permitted movement against gravity. Also, deprived of constant contact with a bathing medium high in calcium, the organism now became more dependent upon internal reserves of calcium to ensure maintenance of constant calcium concentrations in the extracellular fluids.

While this need for a calcium reserve in terrestrial vertebrates is virtually self-evident, it is useful to note that the sink function, sequestering of excess calcium, remains important on dry land as well. (If calcium were constantly in short supply, of course, then a reserve sufficient to serve a structural function could never be accumulated in the first place.) Typically, in the life of a terrestrial vertebrate, the reserve function

of the skeleton is called upon only intermittently. At other times the skeleton stores excesses of calcium made available from the environment. This process, as already noted, is constantly needed in a marine habitat but occurs mainly on feeding for most terrestrial vertebrates.

Once vertebrates came out onto dry land, two sometimes competing objectives had to be managed: maintaining the extracellular fluid calcium level and maintaining the size of the skeletal reserve. Whereas the former could be managed in a marine environment by adjusting fluxes of ions across the gill membranes, on dry land it had to be done by adjusting the net flow of calcium into and out of bone. In this process bone mass itself actually changes as the skeleton functions to support the body fluid calcium levels, and skeletal structural strength necessarily changes in parallel. The size of the reserve, which is the basis for bone strength, is ultimately limited by forces acting outside the skeleton, that is, by adjusting inflow from ingested foods and outflow through the kidney, as well as by a mechanical feedback system within the skeleton (see following discussion). It must be noted, however, that the extraskeletal portion of that regulatory system works adequately only when ingested food contains sufficient calcium.

Calcium Abundance in the Diets of Terrestrial Vertebrates

Calcium is so abundant in even the terrestrial environment that most wild foods contain relatively large quantities of it. In fact, much of the calcium content of several leafy plants, notably the halophytes (for example, spinach), represents a plant tissue analogue of the bony sink of marine vertebrates. In other words, the plant creates calcium deposits as a means of keeping calcium levels from rising too high in plant tissue fluids. However, that sequestered calcium remains a part of the plant and hence becomes available to the animal eating it.

By the time they eat sufficient food to meet total energy needs, most mammals have inevitably ingested a great deal of calcium. This calcium load is generally so great that higher vertebrates have evolved mechanisms to prevent being swamped by an excess of calcium. One of these has been the development of a relative absorptive barrier at the intestine, and the second has been the ability to damp out any elevations in extracellular fluid calcium by promptly transferring an excess of absorbed calcium into bone.

But there are some delicate trade-offs involved here, particularly in terrestrial vertebrates, where the structural significance of the skeleton is crucial (even if a secondary function, from an evolutionary standpoint). The absorptive barrier can only be partial, or it would not be possible to accumulate adequate skeletal mass to serve a structural function, nor to repay temporary withdrawals from the reserve. Urinary excretion might take care of an absorbed surplus, and in fact certainly does so in most vertebrates, but calcium is relatively insoluble, and renal capacity for handling large excesses of calcium is limited by the propensity of the kidney tissue to calcify. Thus, organisms evolved mechanisms for temporarily putting excess calcium into the skeleton during the absorptive phase after feeding and then withdrawing it from the skeleton, as needed, during periods of fasting or starvation.

The need for a reserve during fasting is not because calcium is consumed in the various metabolic processes that it activates (as would be the case, for example, with ascorbic acid or the B vitamins) but because calcium is lost every day through skin and excreta. Further, during childbearing, calcium is transferred from the mother to the progeny, both in utero and through lactation. Hence, there is an obligatory calcium need throughout life, first to accumulate skeletal mass during growth and then to offset daily losses at all ages.

Bone Remodeling and Bone Mass

Bone has no capacity simply to soak up or release calcium ions on need. Rather, these functions are served by forming and destroying actual packets of bony tissue. Collectively these processes of formation and resorption are termed "bone remodeling." Remodeling occurs throughout life and serves several essential functions.

In the adult skeleton, the first step in remodeling is almost always bone resorption; the old material has to be cleared away before new bone can be deposited. In reabsorbing bone, osteoclasts attach to a bony surface and secrete acid to dissolve the mineral and proteolytic enzymes to digest the matrix. They thereby physically remove a volume of bone. The calcium content of that volume is released into the bloodstream and becomes available both to support the level of calcium in the extracellular fluids of the body against the various drains to which it may be subject and to meet the calcium demands of bony sites elsewhere in the body that happen currently to be in their mineralization phase.

Bone is formed by osteoblasts, which first deposit a protein matrix on an excavated surface and then act on it to create crystal nuclei of calcium phosphate. Thereafter, these nuclei grow by accretion, without further cell work, spontaneously adding calcium and phosphate ions drawn out of the blood that flows past the mineralizing site. Once deposited at any given site, calcium is permanently trapped and can be removed only by the process of bone resorption at that site.

Remodeling fluxes into and out of bone, in the mature adult, are typically in the range of 300 to 500 milligrams of calcium (mg Ca) per day, or about two to four times as large as the aggregate of the external calcium fluxes (absorption and excretion).

Calcium Homeostasis

The balance between bone formation and resorption is adjusted so as to keep the calcium concentration of the extracellular fluid constant. The process is mediated mainly through the action of what are termed "calciotrophic hormones" – principally parathyroid hormone, calcitonin, and calcitriol – with parathyroid hormone being the most important in mature adults, and calcitonin and calcitriol notably more important in infancy.

Parathyroid hormone secretion is evoked by a fall in extracellular fluid calcium level, and calcitonin secretion by a rise. Parathyroid hormone acts to raise falling calcium levels by activating bone remodeling, by reducing renal calcium losses, and by increasing renal synthesis of calcitriol, the active hormonal form of vitamin D (which enhances intestinal absorption efficiency). Activation of remodeling helps raise a falling calcium level because resorption precedes formation, and thus in its early phases, remodeling provides a temporary surplus of calcium. Calcitonin, in contrast, lowers elevated calcium levels by temporarily suppressing bone resorption, thus stopping the release of calcium from bone.

The activity of maintaining the constancy of extracellular fluid calcium concentration is termed "calcium homeostasis." The body's ability to adjust bone remodeling balance is an important physiological defense of the calcium levels in the extracellular fluids of the body, providing needed calcium when the level would otherwise drop and soaking up surplus calcium when it would otherwise rise.

Given the calcium abundance in the diets of virtually all mammals, the reserve function in subhuman species operates mainly during periods of excessive skeletal demand or transient environmental scarcity. Such episodic withdrawal from the reserves is illustrated most clearly in what happens during antler formation in several species of deer each spring. Antlers consist of bone; their growth is usually so rapid that absorbed food calcium cannot keep up with demand, particularly given the relatively poor nutritional quality of early spring food sources. Accordingly, parathyroid hormone secretion increases sharply when antler formation begins, and a burst of bone remodeling is initiated throughout the skeleton. Because the initial phase of remodeling is resorptive, a temporary surplus of calcium is made available for antler mineralization. Later, antler growth slows or stops, and the remodeling loci throughout the skeleton enter their own phase of bone formation (which proceeds at a somewhat slower pace than for the antlers). Those sites then get the calcium they need from a diet that now contains calcium-rich summer grasses and foliage.

Averaged over the year, environmental calcium is usually quite sufficient to permit deer to build and to discard all that accumulated antler calcium annually, and then to start the process all over again. Remodeling is adjusted in this case to help with a temporary calcium "cash-flow" problem.

So long as the microscopic scaffolding of bone from which calcium is borrowed remains intact, as in the deer, there is always the potential for restoration of most or all of the bone lost through remodeling imbalances. But this is only true if adequate exogenous calcium becomes available in time. This borrowing mechanism creates a structural problem for the skeleton when absorbed dietary calcium remains chronically below the demand created by daily losses. Since, under those circumstances, the calcium borrowed from bone cannot be repaid, the remodeling imbalance continues and bone mass continues to be eroded. If this process reaches the point where structural elements are lost (for example, trabecular plates are perforated or trabecular spicules disconnected), much of the loss becomes effectively irreversible, and the deficiency can no longer be corrected, at least by restoring the missing nutrient.

Intrinsic Control of Skeletal Mass

While the ability of the skeleton to release calcium for homeostatic purposes (by tearing down its own bony substance) is effectively limitless, the ability to store excess calcium is much more limited. This is because, as has already been noted, calcium can be stored only by forming new bone in excess of the amount resorbed. But there has to be some ceiling here. Otherwise, in a typically calcium-rich environment, higher vertebrates, storing continuing surpluses of calcium, would become all bone.

How much bone an organism possesses when calcium intake is not the limiting factor depends mainly upon the degree of mechanical strain each bone experiences. Throughout the terrestrial vertebrates each bone adjusts its density (through balancing resorption and formation) so that it experiences in the range of 1,000 to 1,500 microstrain in ordinary use. (Strain is the bending any structure undergoes when it is loaded; 1,000 microstrain is a dimensional deformation of 0.1 percent.) So far as is now known, no surplus of nutrients will lead to more bone accumulation than what is required to produce and maintain that degree of stiffness. Thus, homeostatically, bone mass is adjusted to support body fluid calcium levels; and structurally, bone mass is regulated to produce an optimal stiffness (not too massive, not too flimsy).

The control system regulating this structural aspect of bone mass is not fully understood, but it is known to be site-specific and to be intrinsic to bone (rather than extrinsic as with calcium homeostasis). What this system amounts to is that local bone formation exceeds local bone resorption when bone deforms excessively, making it stiffer, and the opposite occurs when local bone deformation is minimal. Thus, like muscle, bone hypertrophies with use and atrophies with disuse.

Both the intraosseous stiffness-optimizing system and the extraosseous calcium homeostatic system alter bone mass by regulating the balance between bone formation and bone resorption, that is, they both use the remodeling apparatus to alter bone density. In certain circumstances they reciprocally influence one another. For example, when the homeostatic system acts to reduce density, it thereby leads to increased strain on routine loading of the skeletal region involved. This, in turn, creates a signal to restore lost bone as soon as environmental calcium becomes available once again.

This departure from optimal mass levels is always downward – borrowing and then paying back. There is only limited capacity to store calcium above current structural needs for bone. Although the homeostatic surplus is literally vast, relative to metabolic functions of calcium, there is virtually no bodily ability to build a structural surplus, at least relative to current levels of mechanical usage. Instead, the structural reserve of the skeleton lies in the fact that normal bone can withstand greater deformation than the 1,000 to 1,500 microstrain of everyday use. The limit is closer to 7,000 microstrain, but its actual value depends upon how rapidly and how often a load is experienced. This margin of safety is what protects us from fracture when we experience low-level falls and bumps.

Osteoporosis

Definition and Expression

Osteoporosis is a disorder of bone characterized by excessive fragility due either to a decrease in bone mass or to microarchitectural deterioration of bone tissue (or both). It is a structural weakness in an organ system that, as has already been noted, serves as a source and a sink for calcium in its primary evolutionary function.

The bony fragility that constitutes osteoporosis is expressed in a propensity to develop fractures on minor injury. This fragility may involve virtually any bone in the skeleton. Stereotypical fracture syndromes involve such regions as the spine, the upper end of the femur (hip fracture), and various extremity sites, for example, wrist and shoulder. But ribs, pelvis, hands, and feet are also common fracture sites in patients with osteoporosis.

Bases for Bony Fragility

Osteoporosis is not a unitary disorder and does not have a single pathogenesis. Basic engineering considerations make it clear that the strength and stiffness of bone, as is true for any structure, derive from four main sources: the intrinsic physical properties of its component material; the mass density of that material; the spatial arrangement of the material; and the loading history of a given member (which expresses itself in an accumulation of ultramicroscopic defects called "fatigue damage"). When any structure fails under load, it is because of relative weakness due to insufficiency of one or more of these strength determinants.

In most of the osteoporotic fracture syndromes there is, currently, no recognized abnormality of the bony material itself. The bony substance in the skeleton of patients with osteoporosis is qualitatively much like the bony substance in normal individuals. Instead, the principal bases for weakness in osteoporotic bone are to be found in (1) a decreased amount of bony material, or mass density (to which the term "osteoporosis" literally refers); (2) accumulated fatigue damage in that bone which is present; or (3) architectural defects in the latticework of trabecular (or cancellous) bone. These latticework defects, in turn, are of two types, microfractures of trabecular elements, which have previously occurred under loading but have not yet fully healed (and which thereby render the latticework weak), and preferential severance (and loss) of the horizontal bracing trabecular elements that give the lattice much of its stiffness.

Interactions of several of the more important contributing factors are illustrated in Figure IV.D.4.1. Where nutrition, and specifically calcium, come into this complex interplay of fragility factors is predominantly through their effect on bone mass density, that is, through the size of the calcium reserve. Thus, although important, calcium intake is only one of several interacting factors that can lead to osteoporosis. Some individuals will develop fragility fractures because bone mass is reduced, but others will develop them because of failure to repair fatigue damage or because of defective trabecular architecture. Even in regard to decreased bone mass, calcium shares the stage with other important factors such as gonadal hormone deficiency, physical inactivity, and a variety of lifestyle factors such as alcohol abuse and smoking. These factors also reduce bone mass, but their action on bone is largely independent of nutrition. (High blood alcohol levels poison bone cells, just as they do cells of other tissues. Hence, it is not surprising that bone tissue fails variously in habitual alcohol abusers. The mechanism of the effects of tobacco is unknown. Smoking women have earlier menopause and lower postmenopausal estrogen levels than nonsmokers, but this is probably only part of the explanation.)

Until the multifactorial character of osteoporosis causation was fully understood, there had been confusion about the importance of calcium, mainly because published studies did not always show a protective effect of an adequate calcium intake. Figure IV.D.4.1 forcefully emphasizes why a universal protective effect is an unrealistic expectation. All that an adequate calcium intake can do is to help the organism build the largest possible skeleton during growth and to protect the skeleton against one-sided calcium withdrawals during maturity. But a high calcium intake will not counteract, for example, effects of alcohol abuse or physical inactivity.

Nevertheless, available evidence suggests that if a fully adequate calcium intake could be assured for every member of the population, as much as 50 percent of the osteoporosis burden of the developed nations would be alleviated. Even so, there would still be 50 percent that persists. These cases would have bases other than nutritional inadequacy.

Osteoporosis: A Disorder of a Nutrient Reserve

Although osteoporosis, when caused by inadequate calcium intake (either during growth or during the adult years), can be said to represent a nutritional disorder, it is important to recognize that the primary metabolic function of calcium is never even remotely compromised. Thus, those forms of osteoporosis that result from inadequate calcium intake can be said to be disorders of a nutritional reserve, and not nutritional deficiency in the usual sense (as might occur with vitamin C and scurvy, or with vitamin D and rickets). Fat may be the only analogue of this unique nutritional situation, serving not only as an energy reserve but as insulation for warm-blooded organisms living in a cold environment.

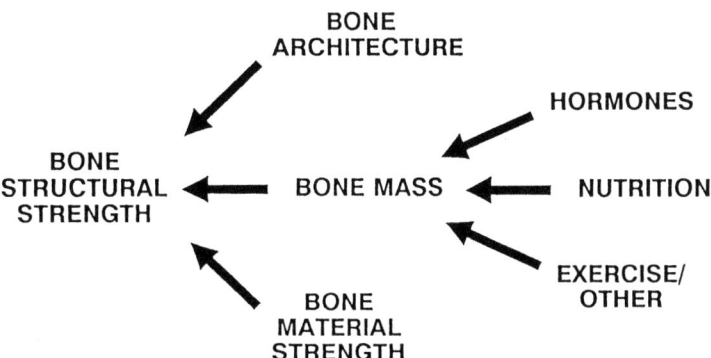

Figure IV.D.4.1. Causal connections of some of the major factors influencing bone strength. Nutrition is only one of the factors that influence bone mass, and bone mass, in turn, is only one of the factors influencing bone strength. Bone material strength, in this diagram, includes the effect of fatigue damage discussed in the text. (© Robert P. Heaney 1991; reproduced with permission.)

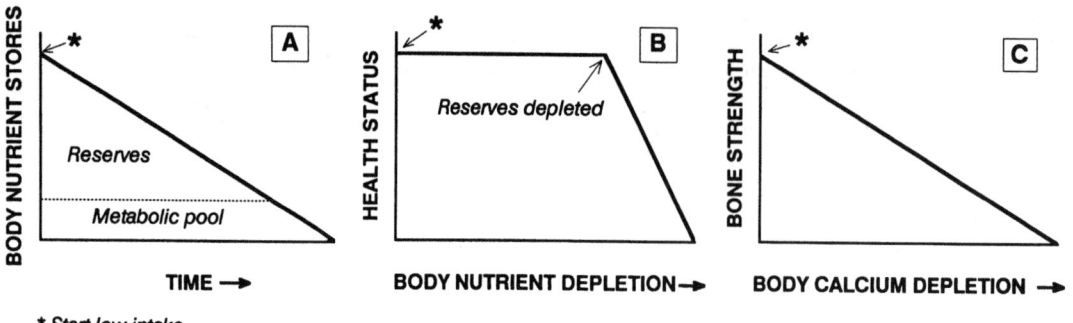

* Start low intake

Figure IV.D.4.2. Schematic illustration of the relationship between body depletion of a nutrient and health status: (A) the depletion of body stores of a nutrient after placing the organism on a deficient intake; (B) the pattern common to
most vitamins, in which health is maintained unchanged until the reserve is
exhausted; (C) the pattern exhibited by calcium, in which health, as reflected in
skeletal strength, declines steadily as the reserve itself is depleted. (© Robert P.
Heany 1992; reproduced with permission.)

The difference between these two types of nutritional deficiency is illustrated schematically in Figure
IV.D.4.2, which contrasts the effects produced by
depletion of the body content of a nutrient such as
vitamin C with the effects of calcium depletion. In the
former case, where the reserves are only that, and
serve no other function, health is maintained until the
entire reserve is depleted. Then, as the active metabolic pool declines, dysfunction develops. With calcium, by contrast, any depletion of the reserve produces a corresponding decrease in skeletal strength.
The skeleton would be rendered totally useless as a
structure long before the metabolic pool of calcium
would be compromised.

One of the problems this arrangement creates
for the nutritional scientist is that a deficiency of
calcium sufficient to compromise the structural
dimension of the reserves will have no impact upon
the basic metabolic function of calcium. Thus, a
calcium deficiency sufficient to produce osteoporosis will not be reflected in appreciable decreases in
calcium concentration in the circulating fluids, nor
in the critical cell compartments where calcium
functions as a second messenger, nor even in the
ready availability of calcium ions for that crucial
function. For this reason there are no blood or urine
tests that, alone or in combination, are diagnostic
either for this phase of calcium deficiency or for
osteoporosis.

Calcium Requirement

Definition
A requirement for a specific nutrient has traditionally been defined as the intake necessary to prevent
the expression of the disease or disability associated
with deficiency of that nutrient. In recent years

there has been a tendency to broaden that definition
to read: the intake required to promote optimal
health. In the case of calcium, neither approach is
particularly apt, as the foregoing discussion has
emphasized, inasmuch as health in this instance is
not a matter of the basic metabolic function of calcium but of the size of the calcium reserve. Hence a
calcium requirement relative to bone health needs
to be defined as the intake necessary (1) for building
the largest bone mass possible within the genetic
program of the individual, and (2) for maintaining
that reserve against unbalanced withdrawals after
growth has ceased. Any unrepaired decrease in the
size of the reserve, other things being equal, reduces
bone strength.

The Bases for a Calcium Requirement
Because providing during times of need is precisely
what a reserve is for, this process cannot properly be
considered harmful in itself. A problem develops only
when the process is one-sided, with reserves drawn
down but not replenished. In this connection, it will
be useful to review here both certain quantitative
aspects of how the body maintains constant calcium
levels in its blood and extracellular fluids, and how
and why an unbalanced situation develops.

As mentioned previously, foods available to high
primates and hunter–gatherer humans in their natural
states are rich in calcium. In fact, nutrient densities of
such foods average in the range of 70 to 100 mg
Ca/100 kilocalories (kcal). When calculated for an
energy intake sufficient to sustain a hunter–gatherer
of typical body size, this density range translates to a
daily calcium intake of 2,000 to 3,000 mg, substantially in excess of what most modern humans get, and
four to six times what an adult female in the United
States typically ingests.

Figure IV.D.4.3. Relationship of calcium intake, absorption efficiency, and net absorption. All the points along a single curve represent the same net absorption value and thus define, for that value, what the intake would have to be to achieve that level of net absorption for any given absorption fraction. (© Robert P. Heaney 1991; reproduced with permission.)

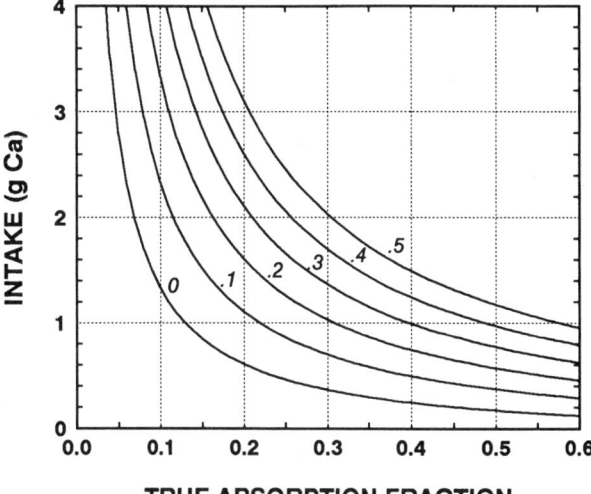

Only after the advent of cultivated cereal grains at the agricultural revolution did humans shift from a diet with a high calcium density to one with a low calcium density.

Intestinal absorption. As already noted, calcium absorption is inefficient, averaging in the range of 30 percent of ingested intake in healthy adults at intakes in the range of the current Recommended Dietary Allowance (RDA) (800 mg for adults). Absorption efficiency varies inversely as roughly the square root of ingested intake, which means that although efficiency rises as intake falls, the evoked rise in absorption fraction will not be sufficient to offset the actual drop in intake.

Furthermore, digestive secretions themselves contain calcium (typically in the range of 150 mg/day in a healthy adult). Because this calcium is secreted along the length of the gut, it is reabsorbed at only about 85 percent the efficiency of ingested calcium (which is itself absorbed inefficiently). This secreted calcium constitutes a cost of digestion, and most of it will be lost in the feces.

This two-directional traffic means that net absorption will always be less than gross absorption. For example, at an intake of 600 mg/day and an absorption efficiency of 30 percent, net absorption will be only about 63 mg, or barely 10 percent of intake. In fact, at low intakes, net absorption will commonly be negative, that is, there will be more calcium going out in the feces than is coming in by way of the mouth. This does not represent intestinal pathology but is an inevitable consequence of the combination of low absorption efficiency and calcium secretion with the digestive juices.

The quantitative character of this relationship is depicted schematically in Figure IV.D.4.3, which shows various iso-absorption contours relating intake and absorption efficiency to various values for net absorption (from 0 to 500 mg Ca/day). For example,

to achieve a net absorption of 200 mg/day (close to the figure required to offset extraintestinal losses in healthy adults), intake must be 1,030 mg at an absorption efficiency of 30 percent, and 1,605 mg at an absorptive efficiency of 20 percent.

The fact of low, and even negative, net absorption might be construed to indicate that the organism does not need much calcium after all, but that would be a misreading of the evidence. With the naturally high calcium intake of the hunter–gatherer diet, the customary exposure of the gut is to a calcium-rich ingestate, and even with low absorption efficiency, net absorption would always be positive. But in fact, the low absorptive performance of the gut in mammals is an evolutionary adaptation to this environmental surfeit. Unfortunately, a low absorption fraction is maladaptive for modern diets. Our bodies have adapted to a high-calcium diet, and the time span from the agricultural revolution to the present has been much too short to have allowed evolution toward greater absorptive efficiency.

Some nutrient factors interfere with calcium absorption and thereby raise the calcium requirement. Certain kinds of fiber bind calcium and thereby reduce its absorption. Wheat bran does this, for example. However, this is not true for all fiber: The fiber of green leafy vegetables does not interfere at all with absorption. Overall, the effect of fiber in our diets is relatively small, and even widely ranging fiber intakes would not be expected to exert very large effects on calcium absorption. A second factor reducing calcium absorption is caffeine, a substance widely considered among the lay and the scientific communities to be a risk factor for osteoporosis. It turns out, however, that the caffeine effect is also small and, except for very high daily coffee intakes, would not pose much of a problem. For example, the negative effect on calcium absorption of a single brewed cup of coffee is such that calcium balance deteriorates by about 3 mg. This quantity is so small that its impact can be easily offset by as little as an ounce of milk.

Renal and dermal losses. Urinary and dermal calcium losses are also important determinants of nutrient requirement. Dermal losses occur through sweat and also through shed epithelial structures (dry skin, nails, and hair – all of which contain calcium). For the most part dermal losses are unregulated and thus constitute an irreducible daily drain that must be offset from the diet or, failing that, from the bony reserves.

Urine calcium in humans is determined predominantly by body size and by intake of protein and sodium and only to a lesser degree by calcium intake itself. Protein intake increases urinary calcium loss largely through the catabolism of sulfur-containing amino acids and the excretion of the consequent sulfate load (an endogenous equivalent, as it were, of the acid rain problem produced by burning sulfur-containing fossil fuels). High sodium intake also tends to wash calcium out through the kidneys. High sodium intake is another major dietary change that has occurred for the most part only very recently. Hunter-gatherers and high primates typically have sodium intakes nearly two orders of magnitude (something on the order of 100 times) lower than modern-day humans. In Switzerland, where careful records of salt imports have been kept, per capita salt consumption has increased by a factor of 10 since 1850 alone.

Urine calcium rises with body weight from infancy to adolescence. Infants can reduce urinary calcium losses to near zero when calcium intake drops. Children have an intermediate ability to conserve calcium at the kidney, and adolescents, strikingly, maintain high urinary calcium values irrespective of their calcium intake. This makes them, at a time when calcium requirements for bone growth are at their absolute maximum, particularly vulnerable to environmental scarcity. A partial explanation for the change with age may lie in the fact that infants and small children have relatively low salt intakes, and instead of burning ingested protein as fuel, they build at least some of it into new tissue. Thus neither of the factors driving the higher urine calcium values of older persons are prominent early in life.

The combination of unrecovered digestive juice calcium, minimal urinary calcium loss, and dermal loss, which occur under conditions of calcium restriction, constitutes what is called "obligatory loss." In normal adults consuming typical Western diets, this loss amounts to something in the range of 150 to 250 mg/day, probably more often on the higher side of the range than on the lower. Whenever the absorbed intake is insufficient to compensate for this obligatory loss, bone remodeling will be adjusted so that resorption exceeds formation and thus bone mass will decrease. In other words, the organism calls upon its calcium reserves.

Recommended Dietary Allowances

A Recommended Dietary Allowance (RDA) is a population-level estimate of the daily intake that would be sufficient to meet the actual requirement for a given nutrient for virtually every member of the population. RDAs are deliberately set above the average requirement so as to assure meeting the needs of those with above-average needs.

The RDAs for calcium in the United States are 800 mg/day for children up to age 11, 1,200 mg/day from ages 12 to 24, and 800 mg/day thereafter. (During pregnancy and lactation, the RDA rises to 1,200 mg/day.) There is growing evidence that these requirements are low, and what follows will summarize the best current information about what the true requirement may be. In this connection it is worth recalling once again that wild plant foods are rich in calcium. As a result, the human calcium intake for foragers was almost certainly substantially above not only current intakes but even the RDAs. While there has been a bias in the scientific community in favor of current dietary practices, there should be no surprise when evidence indicates that intakes closer to (though still on the low side of) what our foraging forebears apparently got, may in fact better meet our needs.

Requirements during Growth

Threshold intake. One aspect of the relationship of calcium to bone health, relevant to a consideration of requirement, is the fact that calcium is a threshold nutrient. This means that calcium intake will limit the amount of bone a growing organism can acquire, at least up to some threshold value, and that above that intake further increases will no longer have any effect on bone mass accumulation. This concept is illustrated in Figure IV.D.4.4, which shows, first in Panel A, what the idealized relationship between intake and bone mass accumulation during growth would look like, and then, in Panel B, what experiments studying the effect of calcium intake on bone accumulation during growth have actually found in laboratory animals.

As far as bone is concerned, the optimal intake during growth would be an intake at or above the threshold, and the RDA would be a value sufficiently above the *average* threshold value to allow for the fact that different individuals will have differing values at which the threshold occurs. This interindividual variation reflects differences in absorption efficiency and in ability to restrict urinary loss.

It is important to recognize, in this regard, that calcium intakes below the threshold value will not necessarily limit growth in stature. It takes very serious depletion for that effect to occur, and even then it is hard to be certain that a low intake of calcium is the responsible factor, since intake of other essential nutrients is commonly reduced under such circumstances, as well.

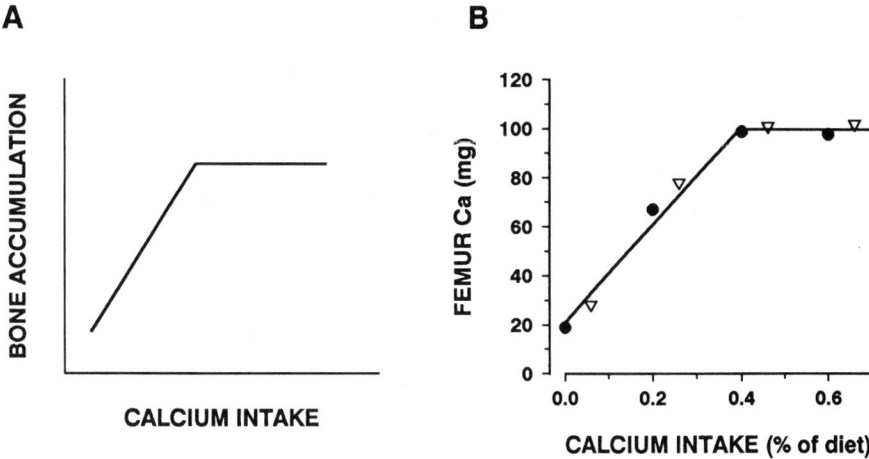

Figure IV.D.4.4. Threshold behavior of calcium intake: (A) Theoretical relationship of bone accumulation to intake. Below a certain value – the "threshold" – bone accumulation is a linear function of intake; in other words, the amount of bone that can be accumulated is limited by the amount of calcium ingested. Above the threshold, bone accumulation is limited by other factors and is no longer related to changes in calcium intake. (B) Actual data from two experiments in growing rats, showing how bone accumulation does, in fact, exhibit a threshold pattern. (Redrawn from data in Forbes, Weingartner, Parker, et al. 1979, in *Journal of Nutrition* 109: 1652–60; © Robert P. Heany 1992; reproduced with permission.)

What happens during growth under conditions of suboptimal calcium intake is, instead, simply that the skeleton achieves its genetically programmed external size and shape but is internally flimsier, meaning the bone cortices are thinner and more porous, and the trabeculae thinner and more widely spaced. Less mass is spread over a growing volume and the structure is thus intrinsically weaker.

While it is relatively easy to do threshold experiments in laboratory animals (as in Figure IV.D.4.4), it is much harder to do (or to justify) such experiments in growing children. Instead of the threshold approach, much of the judgment in regard to calcium requirement and RDAs during growth has been based upon actual food practices in populations that seem to be developing "normally." There is an obvious circularity in that reasoning, because if current bone mass values are normative, then current intakes are manifestly sufficient to support "normal" bone development. Thus current intakes conform with the requirement, the average child is getting what he or she needs, and all is right in this best of all possible worlds.

However, osteoporosis has now reached epidemic proportions in the developed nations, and failure to develop the peak bone mass genetically programmed has to be considered a partial explanation. Thus current intakes, although "normal" in the sense of being usual, are not necessarily optimal.

Estimating the threshold intake. A traditional approach to the determination of nutrient requirements has been to perform what is technically referred to as a metabolic balance study – a study in which human subjects live in a laboratory environment and in which intake and output of the nutrient under study are carefully measured. The balance between intake and output is computed, and for nutrients that are not altered by their metabolism, such as minerals like calcium, that balance is a surrogate for body retention or loss, that is, skeleton building or destruction.

One of the problems with the metabolic balance technique is that although theoretically ideal, the result that it produces is inherently imprecise. That problem can be minimized by doing a large number of such studies, because the uncertainty range about the average estimate of balance declines as the square root of the number of studies. But balance studies are so difficult and expensive to perform that few investigators can accumulate a large enough experience to give the required precision at the several levels of intake that must be studied in order to determine the requirement.

Velimir Matkovic of Ohio State University has attempted to solve this problem by assembling all of the published balance studies performed on growing humans, spanning a 70-year period from 1922 to 1991. After excluding those that did not meet certain a priori criteria, he was able to assemble over 500 published studies, a number large enough to give some reasonable certainty to the estimates and also to ascertain whether the threshold behavior observed in animals (Figure IV.D.4.4) is also found in growing humans.

He and I, working together on this project, found that the threshold behavior did, in fact, apply to growing humans, one example of which is shown in Figure IV.D.4.5. This work also allowed us to estimate the average threshold intake at various stages during growth. These threshold values are presented in Table IV.D.4.1, by age group from infancy through age 30. Equivalently, these values are average requirements for the population of growing humans. As already noted, the corresponding values for RDAs would be higher still. It can be seen that all of the threshold values in Table IV.D.4.1 are above the current RDAs in the United States. Nevertheless, intakes at or above these threshold values would have been common in human hunter-gatherers living in equilibrium with their environment, and hence, although such intakes would be atypical by modern standards, they can hardly be considered unnaturally high.

Corroborating evidence. This means of estimating requirements during growth is probably the best available approach to the problem, and although it produces values above the current RDAs, it is important to recognize that its estimates are not, in fact, at variance with other recent data, which tend to show that, other things being equal, more calcium intake during growth leads to more bone mass accumulation. Thus, very recently C. C. Johnston, Jr., and his colleagues from Indiana University reported results of a double-blind, placebo-controlled study in identical twin children. Calcium supplementation given to one member of a twin pair produced more bone mass accumulation than in the unsupplemented twin.

A striking feature of that study was the fact that the unsupplemented members of each twin pair averaged an intake that was already above the official RDA for calcium for the age concerned. This behavior suggests that the official RDA value is below the threshold (see Figure IV.D.4.4).

Similarly, R. R. Recker and his colleagues from Creighton University have recently reported results from a longitudinal study of bone mass accumulation in women aged 20 to 30. They showed both that bone mass continues to accumulate at a rate of about 1 percent per year to age 30, and that calcium intake (specifically the calcium-to-protein ratio of the diet) was the single most important determinant of how much bone was added during that decade.

Requirement during Maturity

From age 30 until menopause in women, and from age 30 until the beginning of senescence in men, the requirement for calcium can be defined as the intake necessary to offset obligatory losses, or, put another way, the intake needed simply to keep the body in equilibrium, neither gaining nor losing calcium. Current estimates indicate that the mean requirement is in the range of 800 to 1,200 mg/day for typical Western diets for both men and women. It would probably be substantially less in individuals who have low protein or low sodium intakes (or both). This is because, as already noted, both high protein and high sodium intakes increase urinary calcium loss and hence decrease the ability of the body to conserve calcium when calcium intake is reduced.

Incidentally, this observation is not to suggest that calcium is somehow a "good" nutrient and that protein and sodium are somehow "bad." Rather, it simply emphasizes that requirements are not abstract absolute values but are reflections both of metabolic activity of the organism and of other constituents in the diet.

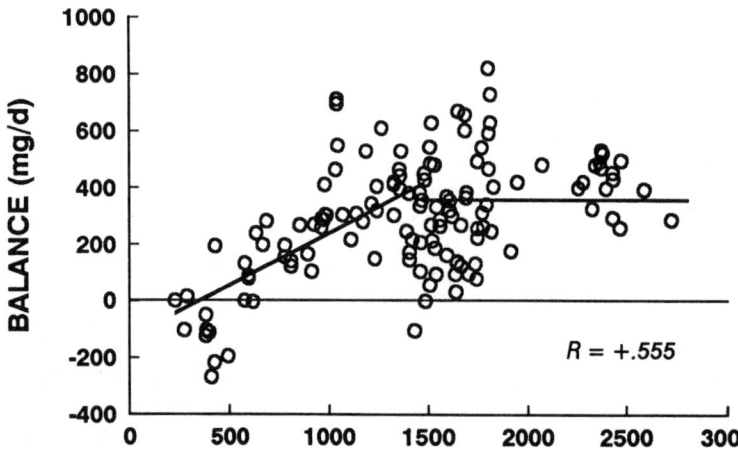

Figure IV.D.4.5. Relationship of calcium intake to calcium balance in adolescents. Above the threshold intake value (1,480 mg/day), balance no longer changes with intake, whereas below the threshold, balance and intake are directly correlated. (© Robert P. Heaney 1991; reproduced with permission.)

Table IV.D.4.1. *Threshold calcium intakes during growth*

Age (in years)	Threshold intake (mg/day)
0–1	1,090
2–9	1,390
9–17	1,480
18–30	957

If one can judge from the food habits of contemporary hunter-gatherers, they would not have had much experience with sodium; however, high-protein diets would have been common. Meat is a very efficient food source, rich in many essential nutrients, and some studies have suggested that for human foragers, protein intake might have accounted for as much as 35 percent of total calories – a higher intake than even that achieved by typical citizens of developed nations. But the diet of hunter-gatherers, as has already been noted, was also very high in calcium, and so a high protein intake would not have created an effective calcium deficiency as it does when calcium intake is as low as is commonly found in U.S. diets.

Requirements during Postmenopause and Senescence

During the declining years, the calcium requirement can no longer be defined as the intake required to offset obligatory losses. This is because bone loss occurs now for intrinsic reasons as well as for homeostatic ones. Even the richest of diets cannot totally prevent this kind of bone loss.

Menopausal bone loss. The first example is the bone loss that occurs in women during the early postmenopause (from cessation of menses to 5–10 years later). To the extent that there has been any controversy or apparent disagreement about the importance of an adequate calcium intake in adults, that controversy has centered around what occurs during this brief period in a woman's life. This is a time when typical women lose something approaching 15 percent of the bone mass they possessed immediately before cessation of ovarian function. Virtually without exception, studies of calcium intake or calcium supplementation during this time have shown that calcium has little or no effect on this bone loss.

There is now general agreement that bone loss at this time is due almost exclusively to loss of gonadal hormones. (The same type of loss follows castration in males.) While many of the details of the mechanism remain uncertain, it can be said that this loss reflects a downward adjustment of bone mass to a new steady state, just as occurs with immobilization. During that approach to a new postmenopausal equilibrium value, nonhormonal forces, such as calcium or exercise, are without effect – simply because the change in bone mass is due specifically to the diminution of

gonadal hormones and not to low calcium intake or inadequate exercise. In fact, during the few years after menopause, so much calcium may be made available from bone that there may be no external calcium requirement at all. However, when the new steady state is approached and bone loss slows, all the old interactions reappear.

This conceptual framework was not available to investigators until recently, which may explain why so many previously published studies of the effect of calcium chose to address the early postmenopausal period. Those years are, of course, the time when bone loss is the most rapid and the value of successful intervention is most evident, so it is not surprising that it has been extensively studied. But loss at that life stage is caused by estrogen lack and is best prevented by estrogen replacement.

Senescence. Bone loss during senescence in both men and women is a complex process and has many determinants. This is to some extent true earlier in life as well, but nonnutritional factors loom larger during the declining years of life. As a general rule, mechanical loading on the skeleton decreases with age, in part because older people do less strenuous work and in part, also, because with maturity they become more graceful and efficient in what they do. Thus, some downward adjustment in bone mass simply reflects a decline in mechanical need. Inevitably that decreases the effective strength reserve, which is useful to resist the impact of falls. As already noted, the mechanical adjustment system responds to current usage, not to potential injury. This type of decline in skeletal mass is not nutritionally related and, in the practical order, cannot be appreciably altered by assuring a high calcium intake.

However, a number of changes also occur in the calcium economy of the aging person. There is a decline in absorption efficiency at the intestine, a partial resistance to vitamin D action on the intestine, and a decrease in the ability to synthesize calcitriol, the active hormonal form of vitamin D. Additionally, in women who are deprived of estrogen after menopause, there is deterioration in the ability to conserve calcium at the kidney. For all of these reasons, older persons absorb calcium less well from the diet and retain less of what they do absorb.

This means that calcium intake requirement rises in the elderly. Unfortunately, actual intake tends to go in the wrong direction. With a decline in physical activity, there is a tendency for food intake itself to go down, and that almost always reduces the intake of all nutrients, calcium among them. This combination of increased need and decreased intake in the elderly sets the stage for intake-related bone loss.

The majority of investigations of the relationship of calcium intake to bone status in the elderly – particularly the double-blind, placebo-controlled trials of B. Dawson-Hughes and her colleagues at Tufts University and of Petra Elders and her colleagues at the Free University of Amsterdam – show that additional calcium intake will reduce, to a substantial extent, the degree of bone loss that is otherwise occurring in ostensibly normal, healthy individuals. Total intakes shown to be adequate for this purpose have generally been in the range of 1,000 to 2,000 mg of Ca/day. As already noted, although such intakes are higher than current practice, they cannot be considered high when compared with the typical intakes of our foraging ancestors.

The fact that published studies show such a dramatic reduction in what had otherwise been considered an inevitable, age-related loss of bone indicates that a substantial fraction of that loss was not inevitable after all but was diet-related. This conclusion is even more forcefully emphasized by the findings of three important European studies. One, performed in France, randomized more than 3,200 elderly women (average age 84) to receive either a placebo or 1,200 mg calcium plus 800 IU vitamin D. Not only did the supplemented women stop losing bone, but fractures also declined dramatically within 18 months of starting treatment. The other studies, one undertaken in Finland and the other in Switzerland, although differing somewhat in design from the French study, nevertheless also clearly showed fracture reduction in elderly individuals given calcium or vitamin D supplements.

Miscellaneous Considerations

Calcium Intake and Bone Remodeling

We have already noted that one of the causes of bone fragility is the accumulation of unrepaired microscopic fatigue damage, something that occurs inevitably in all structural materials when they are loaded, but which, given the living character of bone in most vertebrates, is susceptible of repair. That repair is accomplished by bone remodeling, which has been visited, so far in this chapter, mainly as a means of altering bone mass. In fact, bone remodeling has the dual function of both adjusting mass and replacing damaged bone. Failure to effect that replacement in a timely fashion permits fatigue damage to accumulate to the point where serious structural failure can occur on application of relatively small forces.

Effecting this repair depends first upon the body's ability to sense the presence of microscopic damage. Available evidence suggests that the threshold of bone sensitivity to such damage is determined to a substantial extent by the circulating level of parathyroid hormone (PTH). But PTH secretion, in turn, is influenced predominantly by calcium need, and ultimately, therefore, by calcium intake. Thus, a constant high-calcium diet, particularly with the intake spread out over the course of the day, leads to low PTH levels, and therefore to a low sensitivity of the apparatus that detects fatigue damage. The practical import of these considerations is not known for certain, but several investigators have expressed concern about the possible dangers of a constant suppression of the remodeling process.

How could this be a problem if, as already noted, human hunter-gatherers had calcium intakes substantially higher than we now experience? Presumably, their PTH levels would have been substantially below ours. However, there is no fossil evidence that hunter-gatherers suffered an undue fracture burden. Thus either the PTH levels in human foragers were not, in fact, constantly low, or the threshold for detection of fatigue damage is below even the low PTH levels produced by a chronic high calcium intake. The former seems to be the more likely explanation.

Although *average* calcium intakes would have been high for the hunter-gatherers, it becomes clear on reflection that under field conditions, food intake, and thus calcium intake, could not have been a constant affair. There would have been inevitable periods of fasting and of environmental scarcity. In fact, the PTH mechanism evolved precisely to handle such times of calcium need, and its very presence in mammals may be taken as presumptive evidence of at least periodic calcium deprivation.

In addition to seasonal variation in food availability, females were subject to the regular predictable calcium drain of pregnancy and lactation. Another example of periodic need, already cited, is antler formation in deer. At the beginning of antler formation, there is a burst of PTH-mediated remodeling throughout the skeleton. This causes, as it were, a flurry of "spring housecleaning," which, if it had not occurred earlier, serves to remodel areas of fatigue damage that had accumulated in the skeleton over the preceding year. In this way, antler formation in male deer produces a drain analogous to that produced by pregnancy and lactation in female mammals generally.

Thus, even superficial reflection serves to make clear that the "natural" situation would have been one in which PTH is periodically evoked, and therefore one in which conditions would periodically be right for resorption and replacement of damaged bone.

That, however, is not the situation that obtains in civilized, adult, affluent humans who have few children, who lactate even less often, and who rarely experience prolonged periods of fasting or deprivation – in other words, typical adults in developed nations. Is a constant high intake of calcium optimal for these individuals? One cannot say with any assurance one way or the other. Possibly a periodic calcium "vacation" might be salutary. Possibly the once common Christian practice of fasting during Lent and four times a year at the Ember Days, and the still prevalent practice among observant Muslims of fasting during Ramadan, may evoke effects that are as salutary for the body as for the soul.

Recovery after Illness, Injury, and Disability

One common, if not quite universal, feature of even an affluent, protected, developed-world life is the fact of injury, illness, and disability, events that, however temporary and repairable, nevertheless enter the lives of most humans. Generally, these events are periods of reduced nutrient intake, sometimes of enhanced excretory loss of critical nutrients, and often periods of reduced mobility and physical activity as well. Reduced physical activity always leads to a reduction in bone mass, even in well individuals; such disuse loss is aggravated in the presence of illness.

What happens during recovery from such episodes? Usually, as far as a sense of well-being, health, and vigor are concerned, we return to our former status. But if our regular calcium intake is just sufficient to maintain equilibrium, that is, to offset daily losses, then, ipso facto, that intake will not be sufficient to permit replacement of the bone lost during the preceding illness or disability. We have no consciousness of our bone mass, so we are unaware that this part of our bodies has not fully recovered.

Periodic episodes of this sort over a person's adult life, and particularly during the declining years, can contribute significantly to age-related bone loss. Such loss, however, is not necessarily irreversible until, as already noted, it proceeds to the point where some of the bony scaffolding is lost. (Then there is no chance of rebuilding what was once there.) It would seem important, therefore, to ensure, during recovery from periodic episodes of illness or disability, that our calcium intake is augmented, for the simple and obvious reason that the intake must be sufficient, at that time, not only to offset obligatory losses but also to replace bone mass lost during the preceding weeks.

Calcium in the Treatment of Osteoporosis

Although calcium is a necessary component of most treatment regimens for established osteoporosis, it is rarely sufficient by itself. Calcium is *necessary* because it is not possible to restore lost bone without providing adequate quantities of the building blocks of bone. That means a high calcium intake. But calcium alone is rarely sufficient because a high calcium intake suppresses bone remodeling. Although this suppression helps to stabilize bone mass and slow bone loss, at the same time it impedes substantial gain in bone mass. Bone gain requires additional stimulation by osteogenic factors or medications (such as growth hormone or sodium fluoride). Then, with that kind of bone-building stimulus, an adequate calcium intake helps to assure that the weakened bone can be rebuilt without having to shift calcium from other skeletal regions – robbing Peter to pay Paul, as it were.

One might wonder why a high calcium intake is compatible with bone gain during growth yet does not act the same way in older persons with established osteoporosis. The answer is simply that during growth, the body produces large quantities of tissue-building factors such as growth hormone. These factors are nearly absent in older persons with osteoporosis. Furthermore, the violent mechanical loading of the skeleton typical of childhood and adolescence creates a powerful local stimulus to strengthen the skeleton. By contrast, a partially disabled, hurting, elderly person with one or more osteoporotic fractures generally decreases his or her physical activity – a situation that leads to bone loss irrespective of calcium intake.

Because of lowered calcium absorptive efficiency both with age and with decreased physical activity, generally large quantities of calcium are required as part of an osteoporosis treatment regimen. The exact quantities are uncertain, but they probably fall in the range of 1,500 to 2,500 mg/day. This is more than most persons with restricted activity can get from readily available foods, and some resort will usually have to be made to calcium-fortified foods or to calcium supplement tablets.

Ethnicity

Although bony fragility is not confined to Caucasians, it is much more common among whites than among blacks or Asians, and among Caucasians it is more common among those of northern European ancestry. Partly for these reasons, most of the research relating calcium to osteoporosis has been done in Caucasians. Despite a generally lower calcium intake than their white counterparts, blacks in the United States have heavier bone mass at all ages, from infancy onward. Moreover blacks, both in Africa and in the United States, have lower fracture rates than whites, even after correcting for differences in bone mass. Asians have bone mass values at least as low as Caucasians and seem to lose bone with age much as do whites, but available data suggest that fragility fractures, particularly hip fractures, are less common among them. These ethnic differences in fracture rate probably reflect the fact, noted earlier, that fragility has many bases, and that it takes more than just bone loss to result in a fracture. For example, the angled upper segment of the femur is shorter in Asians than in Caucasians. Engineering analysis has shown that long upper segments are structurally weaker than short ones. This difference, based ultimately in genetics, has a mechanical, structural basis, rather than a nutritional one.

American blacks have been studied somewhat more intensively than other non-Caucasian groups, and thus more is known about their calcium economy. Norman Bell and his colleagues at the Medical University of South Carolina have shown that at least a part of the explanation for their greater bone mass is a generally higher resistance of their bones to serve as a calcium reservoir. Thus, in maintaining extracellular fluid calcium levels, blacks require a higher level of PTH to release calcium from bone than do whites.

As noted earlier, PTH also enhances both intestinal absorption and renal conservation of calcium. Thus the higher PTH levels of blacks result in better utilization of dietary calcium, with a consequent skeletal-sparing effect.

Conclusion

Calcium is a nutrient, not a drug. The only disorder it can be expected to prevent or alleviate is calcium deficiency. The skeleton serves both as structural support for our bodies and as a reserve of calcium needed to maintain the constancy of body fluid calcium levels. Calcium deficiency, as it affects us, is a reduction in the size of the reserve and thus in its structural strength. An adequate intake will ensure that calcium deficiency will neither cause skeletal weakness in its own right nor aggravate the weakness produced by other causal factors. But calcium will not prevent or reverse the bone loss and fragility due to other factors. The evidence indicates that calcium deficiency is prevalent in the adult populations of Europe and North America and that it contributes in an important way to their osteoporotic fracture burdens.

Robert P. Heaney

Bibliography

Christiansen, C., ed. 1991. Proceedings of a symposium: Consensus development conference on osteoporosis. *American Journal of Medicine* 91: S5B.

Dawson-Hughes, B., G. E. Dallal, E. A. Kralli, et al. 1990. A controlled trial of the effect of calcium supplementation on bone density in postmenopausal women. *New England Journal of Medicine* 323: 878-83.

Eaton, S. B., and D. A. Nelson. 1991. Calcium in evolutionary perspective. *American Journal of Clinical Nutrition* 54: 281-7.

Elders, P. J. M., J. C. Netelenbos, P. Lips, et al. 1991. Calcium supplementation reduces vertebral bone loss in perimenopausal women: A controlled trial in 248 women between 46 and 55 years of age. *Journal of Clinical Endocrinology and Metabolism* 73: 533-40.

Forbes, R. M., K. E. Weingartner, H. M. Parker, et al. 1979. Bioavailability to rats of zinc, magnesium, and calcium in casein-, egg-, and soy protein-containing diets. *Journal of Nutrition* 109: 1652-60.

Heaney, R. P. 1989. Osteoporotic fracture space: An hypothesis. *Bone and Mineral* 6: 1-13.
  1990. Estrogen-calcium interactions in the postmenopause: A quantitative description. *Bone and Mineral* 11: 67-84.
  1992. Calcium intake and bone health in the adult. In *Clinics in applied nutrition*, ed. R. Chernoff and R. P. Heaney, 10-29. Reading, Mass.

Holbrook, T. L., E. Barrett-Connor, and D. L. Wingard. 1988. Dietary calcium and risk of hip fracture: 14-year prospective population study. *Lancet* 2: 1046-9.

Johnston, C. C., Jr., J. Z. Miller, C. W. Slemenda, et al. 1992. Calcium supplementation and increases in bone mineral density in children. *New England Journal of Medicine* 327: 87.

Matkovic, V., and R. P. Heaney. 1992. Calcium balance during human growth. Evidence for threshold behavior. *American Journal of Clinical Nutrition* 55: 992-6.

Matkovic, V., K. Kostial, I. Simonovic, et al. 1979. Bone status and fracture rates in two regions of Yugoslavia. *American Journal of Clinical Nutrition* 32: 540-9.

McCarron, D. A., M. Lipkin, R. S. Rivlin, and R. P. Heaney. 1990. Dietary calcium and chronic diseases. *Medical Hypotheses* 31: 265-73.

Recker, R. R., K. M. Davies, S. M. Hinders, et al. 1992. Bone gain in young adult women. *Journal of the American Medical Association* 268: 2403-8.

Recommended Dietary Allowances. 1989. Tenth edition. Washington, D.C.

IV.D.5 ❧ Pellagra

Pellagra is a chronic disease that can affect men, women, and – very rarely – children. The onset is insidious. At first, the afflicted experience malaise but have no definite symptoms. This is followed by the occurrence of a dermatitis on parts of the body exposed to sunlight. A diagnosis of pellagra is strongly indicated when the dermatitis appears around the neck and progresses from redness at the onset to a later thickening and hyperpigmentation of the skin in affected areas. The dermatitis appears during periods of the year when sun exposure is greatest. Other symptoms, including soreness of the mouth, nausea, and diarrhea, begin either concurrently with the skin changes or shortly thereafter. Diarrhea is associated with impaired nutrient absorption, and as a result of both dietary inadequacies and malabsorption, pellagrins frequently show clinical signs of multiple nutritional deficiencies.

Late signs of pellagra include mental confusion, delusions of sin, depression, and a suicidal tendency. Occasionally, these psychiatric signs are accompanied by a partial paralysis of the lower limbs. In the final stages of the disease, wasting becomes extreme as a result of both a refusal to eat (because of nausea) and pain on swallowing (because of fat malabsorption). Death is from extreme protein–energy malnutrition, or from a secondary infection such as tuberculosis, or from suicide (Roe 1991).

Pellagra as a Deficiency Disease

Since 1937, it has been known that pellagra is the result of a deficiency of the B vitamin niacin (Sydenstricker et al. 1938), and that the deficiency usually arises as a consequence of long-term subsistence on a diet lacking in animal protein or other foods that would meet the body's requirement for niacin (Carpenter and Lewin 1985). However, a sufficient quantity in the diet of the amino acid tryptophan – identified as a "precursor" of niacin (meaning that the body can convert tryptophan into niacin) – has also been found to cure or prevent the disease (Goldsmith et al. 1952). This explains why milk, for example, helps combat pellagra: Milk contains relatively little niacin but is a good source of tryptophan. Pellagra is most strongly associated with diets based on staple cereals, especially maize. This grain has historically been the daily fare of those who develop the disease: Maize is high in niacin content, but much of this niacin is in a chemically bound form that prevents absorption of the vitamin by the body (Goldsmith 1956).

History

Early Observations in Europe

Pellagra was initially described during the first third of the eighteenth century, when Gaspar Casal, a Spanish physician, wrote of an illness that had arisen among the peasants of the town of Oviedo, who subsisted largely on maize. The disease was termed *mal de la rosa* because of a peculiar sunburn-like dermatitis – its telltale mark. Casal's book, published posthumously (1762), includes a frontispiece showing a classical figure with a "rose" on the top of each hand and foot and a chain of "roses" around the neck. The "roses" appear as if branded on the skin, suggesting that their appearance betokened a stigmatized condition (Roe 1973).

Casal studied the multisymptom disease that appeared to affect only the poorest laborers in this sharecropping region. He described how the afflicted lived on a diet of maize flour made into flat, baked cakes. The only other items of their diet were a few turnips, chestnuts, cabbages, beans, and apples. Casal found that the disease could be treated by providing milk, cheese, and other foods of animal origin to those afflicted.

Shortly after pellagra made its appearance in northern Spain, it was seen in Italy, where there was extreme poverty among the peasants of Tuscany, as well as those living in the area of Venice. A diet of polenta, or corn mush – and very little else – was the usual fare of those who earned their living under the Italian system of *mezzadria,* or sharecropping. Their poverty meant little access to animal foods, and by the turn of the nineteenth century, pellagra had reached epidemic proportions in parts of Italy, especially in Lombardy, where it was estimated that from 5 to 20 percent of the population were its victims.

It was in northern Italy, where the peasants called the disease "the Rose," that another new but lasting name, "pellagra" (*pelle* plus *agra,* or "rough skin"), was given to the illness by Italian physicians and other educated observers, who also developed new theories to explain its etiology and epidemiology. Some suggested that pellagra was caused by "insolation" or excessive exposure to the sun. Most, however, suspected that pellagra was caused by eating moldy

maize meal, and indeed, this belief persisted until the time of World War I.

Maize was a grain of the New World, unknown in Europe before the voyages of Christopher Columbus. At first, its food value was of little interest to Europeans, although one seventeenth-century herbalist, Caspar Bauhinus, cautioned against consuming too great a quantity of the new grain, as it produced an "itch." But maize proved superior to other food crops, not only because of its higher yield of grain per acre but also because – as a new crop – it was not immediately subject to taxes, tithes, and feudal dues. By the end of the eighteenth century, it was grown in much of southern and eastern Europe, especially in Italy, Romania, and Spain.

It seems likely that by the time of Casal, pellagra was already endemic in parts of Europe. Political and economic trends had made peasants in both Italy and Spain even poorer, which forced an extremely limited diet on them. Interestingly, however, French peasants at that time, although equally poor, neither raised nor consumed as much maize as their southern neighbors. Consequently, it was only later, during the first third of the nineteenth century, that pellagra struck in France – at just about the time that that country's expanding maize crop was becoming a more significant part of the diet.

Casal recognized that pellagra had some relation to diet: He was aware of its close association with maize consumption and knew that it could be cured by improving and varying what people ate. François Thièry, a French physician who studied Casal's still unpublished manuscript, announced these conclusions when he wrote the first published account of the disease, which appeared in 1755. Following the 1762 publication of Casal's work, little was heard of pellagra in Spain until the 1840s. In that decade, however, a second French physician, Théophile Roussel, conducted an investigation and concluded that a number of differently named illnesses then plaguing Spain were all, in fact, pellagra. Soon afterward, Roussel began to work for the adoption of effective pellagra-preventing policies in his own country.

Africa

Throughout the rest of the nineteenth century, it became clear that pellagra was rampant in other parts of the world as well. During the 1890s, British epidemiologist Fleming Sandwith, working in Cairo, realized that endemic pellagra was all around him and began a systematic study of the disease. Like his predecessors, he found that pellagra was associated with a maize-based diet and extreme poverty (he added that residence in rural areas and exposure to the sun also seemed to be factors) and voiced agreement with the view that consumption of spoiled maize was the primary cause.

With his findings on endemic pellagra in Egypt, and a similar study he conducted of pellagra among the Bantu people of South Africa during the Boer War, Sandwith had shown that the illness was by no means confined to Europe; in fact, at the end of the nineteenth century, it seemed obvious that pellagra had established far greater footholds elsewhere. His discovery was a significant accomplishment, but perhaps an even greater one was that through his reports and publications on pellagra (the first important ones to be written in English), he helped create awareness of the condition among physicians in the United States, who were unwittingly facing a pellagra epidemic of their own and would soon take the lead in fighting the disease.

The Americas

American Indians. It is generally accepted that at the time of Columbus's first voyage to the New World, maize cultivation was already widespread among the various American Indian groups (especially those of Central America and Mexico) and exerted a profound influence on their cultures. So important was this crop that a number of traditions described the origins of maize in miracle stories and creation myths (Roe 1973). Many such legends suggested "that man was formed from maize"; all saw maize as the "basic sustenance for the body and the soul" (Roe 1973: 10–11).

But despite the importance of maize in pre-Columbian culture and diet, the peoples of Mesoamerica seem not to have been troubled by pellagra. Indeed, their reliance on maize, while they apparently remained immune to the disease, posed a problem for early investigators advocating a link between maize-based diets and pellagra incidence (Roe 1973). But unlike European pellagrins, who consumed cornmeal mostly as mush, the Indians made their corn into tortillas – a process that involved soaking the maize grains in a lime solution, or perhaps liming them through treatment with campfire ashes. According to sixteenth- and seventeenth-century Spanish reports, such techniques were already in use at the time of European contact, and, in fact, archaeological evidence suggests that the process, virtually unchanged today, was first developed many centuries earlier (Roe 1973).

Many modern specialists in nutrition have suggested that the lime treatment of maize grain released its chemically bound niacin and made the vitamin available to the Indians, and some evidence indicates "that the amount of niacin so freed can be just sufficient to prevent pellagra" (Roe 1973: 15). But this explanation has not seemed sufficient to others, who have pointed to additional factors that operated (and still operate) to prevent the disease. Chief among these are the other niacin-containing vegetable foods that were eaten as well as maize, including squashes, chillies, and especially beans (both grown with maize and eaten with maize products). In addition, some sources of animal protein (usually rich in niacin), such as corn grubs and locusts, were consumed more or less regularly (Roe 1973).

Slaves, sharecroppers, and millworkers. Although the American Indians had historically not suffered from pellagra, other groups were not so fortunate. Even though physicians in the United States lacked knowledge of the disease, medical records permit the identification of a number of cases as far back as the early nineteenth century; in fact, it now seems clear that by the end of that century, pellagra was virtually epidemic, especially in the American South, and had been for some time. Southern agriculture, too long geared toward the production of cotton, had failed to diversify, with the result that the diet of the poorest classes of society lacked much in the way of variety (Etheridge 1972, 1993; Roe 1973; Beardsley 1987). Pellagra seems to have been a periodic visitor to slave cabins during antebellum decades and, later, plagued the southern poor generally; however, it was frequently ignored or – because of its protean symptoms – confused with other diseases (Kiple and Kiple 1977).

In the early years of the twentieth century, however, a pellagra epidemic occurred among mental patients at the Alabama Institution for Negroes, and unlike previous incidents, this outbreak received a measure of publicity. Moreover, it appears that this was not the first time physicians at the institution had seen the disease, and two of them, George H. Searcy and Emit L. McCafferty, produced a report on 88 pellagra patients, 57 of whom had died. Published in the *Journal of the American Medical Association* in 1907, this study provided the kind of information that helped other physicians to recognize the disease (Roe 1973). In the months that followed, thousands of cases were diagnosed, most of them in southern states.

Miracle "cures" for pellagra began to appear, and physicians, despite the debatable effectiveness of such "medicines" and the danger posed to their patients, made liberal use of "Fowler's solution," "Atoxyl," "Salvarsan," and other arsenical preparations. They also employed purges, antiseptic injections, various tonics, blood transfusions from recovered pellagrins, and, in one case, "treatment" with static electricity. A U.S. congressman referred to the latter "cure" as "simply marvelous" (Roe 1973: 95).

Also much in evidence were patent medicines such as "Ez-X-Ba River, The Stream of Life," which was sold for 5 dollars a bottle by the Dedmond Remedy Company, founded in 1911 by Ezxba Dedmond. This product was reputed to cure pellagra within weeks, and early in its history the company claimed hundreds of cures. Another such was "Pellagracide," made by the National Pellagra Remedy Company. Both of these firms, based in South Carolina, were challenged in 1912 by that state's Board of Health, and their products were attacked as fraudulent by the American Medical Association. Analysis of the concoctions revealed no active elements at all, but the companies remained in business. In 1913, "Doctor" Baughn's

American Compounding Company followed much the same course with its "Baughn's Pellagra Remedy" in Alabama. The quack medicines enjoyed much more popularity and confidence among the general public than did the treatments offered by legitimate physicians; indeed, the first encounter many poor pellagra victims had with a medical doctor was when they were near death and committed to a mental hospital (Roe 1973).

Except for institutionalized people (frequently victims of nutritional deficiency diseases because of a restricted diet), southerners suffering from pellagra were generally to be found among the rural poor, many of whom eked out a living by sharecropping, or among the workers in textile mills and their families. It could be said that the millworkers themselves "were in a way institutionalized" in areas where much of the housing, employment, food sources, and medical care were controlled by the firms operating the mills. Indeed, the millworkers' situation was perhaps fractionally worse than that of their rural counterparts, who sometimes had greater access to what little fresh food was produced (Beardsley 1987: 56-7).

Following the epidemic at the mental home in Alabama, the U.S. Public Health Service entered the battle against pellagra, and beginning in 1914, epidemiologist Joseph Goldberger succeeded in curing institutionalized pellagrins by altering their diets. His next trial, also successful, was to induce the disease in prison inmates who volunteered to subsist on a restricted diet. In addition, he proved through experiments on himself and his colleagues that pellagra was neither transmittable nor infective.

Moreover, Goldberger initiated a multiyear study of the disease which revealed that poverty and lack of dietary variety were consistently associated with pellagra in the American South. This study, which later attained renown as a classic model of epidemiology, showed conclusively that pellagrous millworkers and agricultural laborers were on the lowest rung of the economic ladder, and that the traditional diet of the southern poor – cornmeal bread, "fatback" pork, and molasses – was all the food that most such people had access to, or could afford. Thus, poverty, manifesting itself through bad nutrition, had resulted in pellagra attaining epidemic proportions among the lowest-paid classes in the society.

Goldberger had proved that the cause of pellagra was a dietary deficiency and, furthermore, had demonstrated that the deficiency – and therefore the disease – resulted from the prevailing social and economic conditions. Further dietary tests indicated that the diet of pellagrins lacked some crucial element, which was referred to as the pellagra-preventing factor (the "P-P factor" for short), and that this substance, though yet unidentified, was present in meat and dairy foods and some vegetables.

A Disease of an Inferior Social Group

Class inequalities have been used from early times to account for variances in the prevalence of endemic diseases among social groups. Yet the reasons advanced to explain why the poor are more susceptible to certain diseases have changed over the years. In the past, their disease vulnerability was blamed on "bad blood," unclean habits, angry gods, and – somewhat more correctly – the fact that they lived in close proximity to their animals. Today, the blame is placed on an unwillingness to seek preventive health care or to eat the type of diet known to reduce disease risks.

In the case of pellagra, almost all major contributors to the literature of the past subscribed to the view that it was found only among indigent people. Indeed, "the Rose" was considered to be a "brand" of extreme poverty. However, as with other diseases, explanations of why the poor contracted pellagra – and more affluent people did not – have varied.

Hereditary Weakness and Susceptibility

From the time that pellagra was first described until the end of World War I, the occurrence of multiple cases of pellagra in a single family was explained as a hereditary weakness within that family. That pellagra was a manifestation of "bad blood" was a common extrapolation of the beliefs of the Eugenists. At the height of the Eugenics movement, it was believed that children with "bad" traits were born of marital unions between parents who carried these predispositions. Such a theory might be considered a forerunner of human genetics. However, Eugenists believed that "bad blood" was a function of moral traits as well as of traits relating to physiognomy and disease susceptibility. Clearly underpinning the Eugenists' apparently scientific explanation of the pellagra trait was the traditional association of moral weakness and disease. The origin of the concept of "bad blood" lies in the idea that evil is inherited (Ricoeur 1967).

G. K. Chesterton wrote in his book *Eugenics and Other Evils* (1922) that H. G. Wells should be given a medal as the Eugenist who destroyed Eugenics. Wells's argument (1903) was that we cannot be certain of the inheritance of health because health is not a quality but rather a comparative term. Yet despite Chesterton's assertion that Wells put the Eugenists' theories to rest, the idea of "bad blood" persisted and has been frequently used to refer to the taint of syphilis as well as that of pellagra. Moreover, disease vulnerability was somehow supposed to be related to inferior social position. Curiously, physicians who viewed pellagra as the result of inferior parentage could also think in terms of traits that were risk factors for the disease – these same traits also being risk factors for criminal behavior and alcohol abuse.

Diathesis and Biotype

Jean-Marie Gustave Hameau (1853) wrote that "[*l*]*a pellagre est une diathèse particulière,*" a statement that reflects the viewpoint of many observers of the disease from the late eighteenth through the nineteenth century. The people considered susceptible to pellagra were indigent peasants whose vulnerability was somehow linked to their lifestyle.

A corollary idea was that specific "biotypes" were susceptible to pellagra. Dr. Charles Davenport, for example, believed that pellagra was a communicable disease, but only among people of particular biotypes. In a paper published in 1916, he wrote of the risk of acquiring pellagra: "It appears that certain races or blood lines react in the pellagra families in a special and differential fashion." He also believed that the type of constitution a person possessed determined the progress of the disease (Davenport 1916).

Criminality and Hereditary Pellagra

Pellagra was also thought to occur more frequently among the criminal classes, or at least among those with the potential for wrongdoing. Thus, particularly in the nineteenth century, the social environment of pellagrins was believed to play a definitive role in explaining their disease.

Cesare Lombroso, who became professor of psychiatry at Pavia in 1862, centered his research on relationships between mental and physical disorders. He thought that criminals could be identified by certain physical characteristics. He was also convinced that there were intrinsic physical and moral characteristics that explained an individual's susceptibility to toxins in moldy maize grain, which (he believed) caused pellagra (Lombroso 1869, 1893).

Lombroso thought in terms of a hereditary pellagra that existed in both a mild and a severe form. Hereditary pellagra, he wrote, could be recognized in the second year of life when it was manifested by pain, indigestion, a voracious appetite, diarrhea, and cachexia. Moreover, those afflicted with hereditary pellagra also suffered physical anomalies such as faulty development of the skull with brachycephaly or dolichocephaly, a receding forehead, badly set ears, asymmetry of the face, and abnormalities of the external genitalia (Lombroso 1893).

Pellagra and Alcohol Abuse

Once pellagra had been noted as endemic in the United States, it was observed to be common among those who drank to excess, and the term "pseudopellagra" was sometimes used to describe the disease when it occurred in alcoholics. Such a term implied only that these patients had a pellagra-like disease, but eventually it was recognized that genuine pellagra was particularly common among alcoholics, although the reasons for their vulnerability were not understood.

In 1928, J. V. Klauder and N. W. Winkleman reported their studies of pellagra among alcoholics and stressed that the disease was most likely to occur in chronically heavy drinkers who had been on binges lasting several weeks. The researchers also made the observation that during these "debauches," the alcoholics ate very little food, and usually only food of one type – soup. The soup in question was, no doubt, frequently a handout of soup kitchens and not likely to be laden with nutrients. Thus, in the case of some alcoholics, pellagra vulnerability was to some extent linked to a dependence of the have-not group on donated food provided as charity.

N. Jolliffe (1940) was the first nutritionist to observe that there were different reasons why alcoholics so often developed pellagra. He suggested that there were four causal relationships between the disease and alcohol abuse. First, the gastritis associated with heavy alcohol consumption could lead to poor food intake. Second, alcohol-related changes in the gastrointestinal tract could interfere with vitamin absorption. Third, alcohol might be substituted for foods containing vitamins. And last, there was probably an increased vitamin requirement in alcoholics, which resulted from alcohol ingestion.

But despite the possibility of a scientific explanation for the prevalence of pellagra among alcohol abusers, both physicians and the lay public were – and often still are – of the opinion that pellagra strikes alcoholics because of their bad health habits in general (and, perhaps, because of their "immoral ways" in particular). In a 1911 review of cases of pellagra, Dr. Beverley Tucker of Richmond, Virginia, discussed the "pernicious habits" of 15 of her 55 patients with the disease. The habits she considered "pernicious" included the abuse of alcohol, tobacco, and opium.

Revelation of the Social Causes of Pellagra

In the United States, support for the concept that endemic pellagra was a result of extreme poverty came from the studies carried out by Goldberger and his colleagues, G. A. Wheeler and the economist Edgar Sydenstricker. These individuals comprised the first American team to employ epidemiological methods and economic analysis to explain the prevalence and distribution of pellagra in the South. In their 1916 study of cotton-mill villages in South Carolina, the investigators found that the proportion of families with pellagra declined as income increased. Those families with more than one case were always within the lowest income group.

Poor hygiene and sanitation, as well as differences in age and gender distribution – all of which had been considered significant factors – were only gradually eliminated as causes. It became clear that, in general, households with higher incomes and access to food sources outside the factory commissaries, including the produce of home-owned cows, pigs, and poultry, enjoyed a much lower incidence of pellagra. Thus, buying power and access to pellagra-protective foods conferred disease "immunity" (Goldberger, Wheeler, and Sydenstricker 1918, 1974). Sydenstricker also showed in a later study that family income had to be very low before the standard of living forced consumption of a pellagra-producing diet (Sydenstricker 1933; Roe 1973).

Eradication Policies in France and the United States

Soon after its discovery (by the mid–eighteenth century), pellagra was also explained as either an outcome of exposure to extreme climates or a product of contagion. In the mid–nineteenth century, Daniel Drake (1850) grouped causes of disease into three classifications. These included telluric or geological, climatic or meteorological, and social or physiological influences. Later in the century, diseases were also found to be caused by agents such as light, food toxins, and pathogens. As each of these agents of disease was recognized, it became a suggested cause of pellagra. Infection, for example, was popular as a causative agent because it seemed plausible that poor sharecroppers, living in fly-infested dwellings, might acquire the supposed "germ" from their surroundings.

Yet the applicability of the germ theory to pellagra could not be demonstrated, and – especially as nutrient deficiencies had been implicated in other diseases, like scurvy – the interest of researchers returned to the diet of the afflicted. But partly because of deliberate attempts to downplay the poverty of workers, and partly because of the reluctance of medical practitioners to agree on a nutritional explanation, it took a long time for the etiology of pellagra to be understood.

In an interesting observation, S. J. Kunitz (1988), in a paper dealing with hookworm infestation and pellagra, remarked that past explanations of these diseases were influenced by investigators' ideologies and values rather than being derived from analyses of the intrinsic nature of the illnesses. Kunitz further suggested that such biases also conditioned approaches to disease prevention and cure.

Perhaps such influences can be seen in the totally different public-health approaches to pellagra eradication adopted in France in the 1840s and in the United States in the 1940s. In France, Roussel, without any knowledge of the biological cause of pellagra but with a keen observer's eye for the social environment, urged the French government to drain the salt marshes in southwestern France, where the disease was most prevalent, so that a diversity of food crops could be grown and animals raised. More generally, he was also remarkably successful in getting the French government to change the country's agricultural system in ways that contributed to the health of the inhabitants of the rural regions (Roussel 1845, 1866).

In the United States, Conrad A. Elvehjem of the University of Wisconsin discovered the pellagra-preventing factor, first called nicotinic acid and later named niacin. This "breakthrough" occurred in 1937 as a result of his study of blacktongue, the canine equivalent of pellagra (Elvehjem et al. 1938), and Elvehjem was subsequently influential in promoting the enrichment of bread and cereal grains with niacin in an effort to bring the career of pellagra to a close. The mandatory enrichment program was instituted in 1943, following the recommendation of the Food and Nutrition Board, of which Elvehjem was a member (Wilder and Williams 1944).

Yet, as T. H. Jukes (1989) has pointed out, however successful the bread- and cereal-enrichment program was in preventing endemic pellagra, it was already generally accepted by the 1940s that pellagra could be prevented – and also cured – by what he termed a "good" diet; in this context, a "good" diet was one that included milk and meat. The government, however, chose not to concentrate on changing the living conditions of the disadvantaged, such as sharecroppers and millworkers, but rather adopted a policy of providing them with cheap, niacin-containing staple foods.

Thus, neither the sharecropping system nor pellagra were ended by enlightened public policy. Although the beginning of the end of pellagra in the United States lay in the expedient of food fortification, its ultimate demise can only be found in the economic events of the 1930s and 1940s, which, by bringing greater affluence to the South, both eliminated pellagra as a major health concern and spurred the end of sharecropping (Roe 1974).

Endemic Pellagra in Refugee Camps

Pellagra, however, is far from dead in the developing world and is often seen in the midst of chaotic situations. For example, the disease surfaced a few years ago in Malawi, when thousands of Mozambicans fled the civil conflict in their own country to seek refuge there. Once in Malawi, they lived in refugee camps or nearby villages, where – between July and October 1989 – 1,169 cases of pellagra were diagnosed among refugees living in 11 sites. From February 1 through October 30, 1990, another 17,878 cases were reported among a population of 285,942 refugees; in other words, over 6 percent were afflicted. But the rate of affliction varied from one location to another, ranging from 0.5 percent to 13.2 percent. Moreover, females were more than seven times as likely to be afflicted as males; young children, however, were substantially less affected than adults, as has generally been the case during outbreaks of pellagra. The disease was also less common among those who lived in integrated villages rather than in camps (Editorial 1991).

French epidemiologists working for *Médecins*

Sans Frontiéres, who investigated the epidemic, found that those refugees who escaped pellagra were more likely to have gardens, have a daily supply of peanuts (an important niacin-containing staple of the region), or have the ability to mill maize. At the time of the epidemic, peanut distribution had been disrupted, and the maize sent in by donor nations was neither vitamin-enriched nor even ground into meal. Thus, those who developed pellagra were totally dependent on the maize ration, and the greater vulnerability of women was explained by the tendency of males to appropriate nuts, meats, and fish (foods high in niacin as well as tryptophan, its precursor) for themselves.

Clearly, the appearance of a major epidemic of pellagra toward the end of the twentieth century – when the means of preventing the disease have been known for more than 50 years – suggests a substantial error in judgment by supposedly compassionate nations.

Lessons to Be Learned

At the risk of belaboring points that have already been made, by way of conclusion it seems worthwhile briefly to revisit some past notions about pellagra. The first of these is that pellagra was the fault of the afflicted, rather than of those who maintained the existing inequalities of the social system. The second (not all that different from the first) was that the eating habits of pellagrins were the consequence of an unwillingness to change their lifestyles.

Some social critics of the past did better than the scientists in understanding pellagra. French novelist Edmond About (1858), for example, clearly indicated his grasp of the social causes of the disease when he had one of his characters remark that pellagra would continue to exist in the marshy southwestern area of his country (the Landes region) until the nature of the environment changed. His succinct prediction,

> *Tant que Lande sera lande,*
> *La pellagre te demande*

(As long as the Landes remains a moor,
There pellagra will claim the poor),

suggests that pellagra was the fault of the society in which it raged rather than that of the peasant who suffered the deprivations of such a society.

In rural areas of the southern United States, the sharecroppers' "bad habit" of eating an unvaried diet of cornmeal with occasional fatback and molasses – the "three Ms": maize, molasses, and meat (but only the fatback type of meat) – was understood to increase their nutritional risk of pellagra. In urban environments, the "bad" food habits of alcoholics were thought to explain their pellagra susceptibility. Lost in this tendency to blame the victim was the fact that sharecroppers ate a deficient diet because they had little or no access to food other than the "three

Ms." Similarly, pellagra susceptibility in "down-and-out" alcoholics can be explained by society's inability to accept alcoholism as a disease and the consequent belief that alcoholics should not receive adequate nutritional assistance because this would only encourage them to continue in their lifestyle.

In the case of refugee camps, not only were the refugees viewed as an inferior social group, but (as with the alcoholics who were the urban pellagrins of the 1920s and 1930s) they were fed with indifference by donor nations without any effort to improve their health and quality of life. Even today, nations that send food to those living in such camps assume little responsibility for providing an adequate diet for the recipients. Rather, they continue to ship food – like maize – that is unfamiliar to the consumers and is grossly deficient in nutrients.

Certainly, past – often elitist – views of pellagra as the fault of the pellagrin are no longer acceptable today. Moreover, instead of claiming the conquest of endemic pellagra as a scientific triumph, we might ask why pellagra came about in the first place and why it persisted for so long. Finally, we should ask why, even after the means of pellagra prevention are fully understood, there are still serious outbreaks of the disease in various parts of the world.

Daphne A. Roe
Stephen V. Beck

Thanks to Dr. Charles C. Dickinson, III, for his help with the quotation from the work of Edmond About.

Bibliography

About, E. 1858. *Maître Pierre.* Second edition. Paris.

Albera, G. M. 1784. *Trattato teorico pratico delle malattie dell' insolato di primavera volgarmente dette della pellagra.* Varese, Italy.

Bateman, T. 1813. *A practical synopsis of cutaneous diseases.* London.

Beardsley, Edward H. 1987. *A history of neglect: Health care for blacks and mill workers in the twentieth-century South.* Knoxville, Tenn.

Black Report. 1982, 1988. In *Inequalities of health,* 33–42. London.

Carpenter, K. J., and W. J. Lewin. 1985. A reexamination of the composition of diets associated with pellagra. *Journal of Nutrition* 115: 543–52.

Casal, G. 1762. De affectione quae vulgo in hac regione "mal de la rosa" nuncupatur. In *Historia natural y medica de el Principado de Asturias: Obra posthuma,* Vol. 3, 327–60. Madrid.

Chesterton, G. K. 1922. *Eugenics and other evils.* London.

Davenport, C. B. 1916. The hereditary factor in pellagra. *Archives of Internal Medicine* 18: 32–75.

Drake, D. 1850. *A systematic treatise, historical, etiological and practical on the principal diseases of the interior valley of North America.* Cincinnati, Ohio.

Editorial. 1991. Outbreak of pellagra among Mozambican refugees – Malawi, 1990. *Monthly Morbidity and Mortality Report* 40: 209–13.

Elvehjem, C. A., R. J. Madden, F. M. Strong, and D. W. Woolley. 1938. The isolation and identification of the anti-black-tongue factor. *Journal of Biological Chemistry* 123: 137–49.

Etheridge, Elizabeth W. 1972. *The butterfly caste: A social history of pellagra in the South*. Westport, Conn.

1993. Pellagra. In *The Cambridge world history of human disease*, ed. Kenneth F. Kiple, 918–24. Cambridge and New York.

Frapolli, F. 1771. *Animadversiones in morbum vulgo pelagram*. Milan.

Frye, N. 1981. *The great code*. New York.

Goldberger, J., G. A. Wheeler, and E. Sydenstricker. 1918. A study of the diet of non-pellagrous and pellagrous households. *Journal of the American Medical Association* 71: 944–9.

1920. A study of the relation of diet to pellagra incidence in seven textile-mill communities of South Carolina in 1916. *Public Health Report* 35: 648–713.

1974. A study of the relation of family income and other economic factors to pellagra incidence in seven cotton mill villages in South Carolina in 1916. In *The challenge of facts: Selected public health papers of Edgar Sydenstricker*, ed. R. V. Kasius, 263–313. New York.

Goldsmith, G. A. 1956. Studies on niacin requirements in man. II: Comparative effects of diets containing lime-treated and untreated corn in the production of experimental pellagra. *American Journal of Clinical Nutrition* 4: 151–60.

Goldsmith, G. A., H. P. Sarett, U. D. Register, and J. Gibbens. 1952. Studies of niacin requirement of man. I. Experimental pellagra in subjects on diets low in niacin and tryptophan. *Journal of Clinical Investigation* 31: 533–42.

Guthrie, D. 1945. *A history of medicine*. London.

Hameau, J.-M. G. 1853. *De la pellagre*. Paris.

Hauerwas, S. 1975. *Character and the Christian life*. San Antonio, Tex.

Jolliffe, N. 1940. The influence of alcohol on the adequacy of the B vitamins in the American diet. *Quarterly Journal of Studies on Alcohol* 1: 74–84.

Jukes, T. H. 1989. The prevention and conquest of scurvy, beriberi and pellagra. *Preventative Medicine* 18: 877–83.

Kiple, Kenneth F., and Virginia Himmelsteib King. 1981. *Another dimension to the black diaspora: Diet, disease, and racism*. Cambridge.

Kiple, Kenneth F., and Virginia H. Kiple. 1977. Black tongue and black men: Pellagra and slavery in the antebellum South. *The Journal of Southern History* 43: 411–28.

Klauder, J. V., and N. W. Winkleman. 1928. Pellagra among chronic alcoholic addicts. *Journal of the American Medical Association* 90: 364–71.

Kunitz, S. J. 1988. Hookworm and pellagra: Exemplary diseases in the New South. *Journal of Health and Social Behavior* 29: 139–48.

Lombroso, C. 1869. *Studii clinici ed experimentali sulla natura causa e terapia della pellagra*. Bologna.

1893. Sull'etiologia e sulla cura della pellagra (1892). *Lavori di Congresso di Medicina*, 160–86. Milan.

Marie, A. 1908. *La pellagre*. Paris.

Parsons, T. 1972. Definitions of health and illness in the light of American values and social structure. In *Patients, physicians and illness*, ed. E. G. Jaco, 97–117. New York.

Ricoeur, P. 1967. *The symbolism of evil*. Trans. Emerson Buchanan. Boston, Mass.

Roe, D. A. 1973. *A plague of corn: The social history of pellagra*. Ithaca, N.Y.

1974. The sharecroppers' plague. *Natural History* 83: 52–63.

1991. Pellagra. In *Hunter's tropical medicine*. Seventh edition, ed. G. T. Strickland, 932–4. Philadelphia, Pa.

Roussel, T. 1845. *De la pellagre*. Paris.

1866. *Traité de la pellagre et de la pseudopellagre*. Paris.

Samuel, Viscount. 1949. *Creative man and other addresses*. London.

Strambio, G. 1785–9. *De pellagra observationes in regio pellagrosorum nosocomio factae a calendis junii anni 1784, usque adfinem anni 1785*. 3 vols. Milan.

Sydenstricker, E. 1933. *Health and environment*. New York.

Sydenstricker, V. P., H. L. Schmidt, M. C. Fulton, et al. 1938. Treatment of pellagra with nicotinic acid and observations in fifty-five cases. *Southern Medical Journal* 31: 1155–63.

Tucker, B. R. 1911. Pellagra, with the analytical study of 55 non-institutional or sporadic cases. *Journal of the American Medical Association* 56: 246–51.

Underhill, F. P. 1932. Clinical aspects of vitamin G deficiency. *Journal of the American Medical Association* 99: 120–4.

Wells, H. G. 1903. *Mankind in the making*. Leipzig.

Wilder, R. M., and R. R. Williams. 1944. *Enrichment of flour and bread: A history of the movement*. Washington, D.C.

IV.D.6 ❧ Pica

Broadly stated, pica is the term given to the compulsive consumption of substances not generally considered food. However, a precise definition of pica is somewhat elusive because understandings of what constitutes "food," what symptoms signify pica, and explanations of what causes the condition vary with historical and cultural context. A more specific definition of pica is "the chronic, compulsive eating of nonfoods such as earth, ashes, chalk, and lead-paint chips . . ." (Hunter 1973: 171), but it may also include a "false or craving appetite" or "deliberate ingestion of a bizarre selection of food," as well as the compulsive ingestion of nonnutritive or nonfood items such as ice and ice water (Parry-Jones and Parry-Jones 1994: 290).

Pica, in various forms, has been widely noted historically and geographically, primarily in medical texts and anthropological writings (see, for example, Laufer 1930; Cooper 1957; Anell and Lagercrantz 1958). Its practice, although not considered a disease, is of medical concern because ingestion of some substances may result in disease. Additionally, there are types of pica that have been linked by medical researchers to the correction of mineral deficiencies (see, for example, Coltman 1969; Crosby 1971; Hunter 1973). Pica is classified by the DSM-III-R (American Psychiatric Association 1987) and the ICD-10 of the World Health Organization (1992) as an eating disorder, along with anorexia nervosa, bulimia, and infant rumination. Various forms of pica have also been associated with mental retardation.

The incidence of pica in any particular population is difficult to determine because of a tendency to conceal eating behavior that may be considered abnormal or deviant within the cultural context. In addition, the varying definitions of pica we have taken note of also contribute to difficulty in documenting the scope of the behavior. Thus, although pica has been widely observed (both historically and geographically) and has been the subject of much research in many disciplines, it remains poorly understood.

Classifications

Pica is generally classified according to the type of substance consumed. Names for subclassifications of pica are comprised of the Greek word for the ingested substance and the suffix from the Greek word "phagein," meaning "to eat" (Moore and Sears 1994). Cross-culturally, the most commonly noted and explored type of pica is geophagy or geophagia, the consumption of earth and especially clay. Other types include ingestion of ice or ice water (pagophagia); laundry starch (amylophagia); hair (trichophagia); gravel, stones, or pebbles (lithophagia); leaves, grass, or other plants (foliophagia); feces (coprophagia); and unusual amounts of lettuce (lectophagia), peanuts (gooberphagia), and raw potatoes (geomelophagia). Paint, plaster, coal, chalk, cloth, pepper, coffee grounds, paper, cigarette butts, and other household items are also commonly consumed by those engaged in pica (Feldman 1986: 521).

There is some agreement historically and cross-culturally that the populations most prone to pica are young children, pregnant women, persons with mental illness, and the mentally retarded. There is also similarity cross-culturally in the types of items most frequently consumed. These include coal, ice, chalk, plaster, and various types of earth, in particular clay.

As a rule, children who engage in pica are under the age of 6 (Castiglia 1993). The things they consume are restricted by proximity to their grasp and normally tend to be relatively harmless items such as cloth, dirt, leaves, sand, and small rocks or pebbles (Parry-Jones and Parry-Jones 1992). Children who chew furniture or eat paint or plaster can be harmed, and plumbophagia, the ingestion of lead paint, is an important cause of lead poisoning. In fact, the practice of plumbophagia has led to the banning of lead-based paints for interior use in homes.

Trichophagia refers to the ingestion of hair and is one of the types of pica found most often among children. It is especially associated with the habit of girls chewing on long hair and is believed to be related to other, somewhat common, behaviors such as chewing one's fingernails and chewing pencils (Higgins 1993). Trichophagia is of medical concern when substantial amounts of hair result in the formation of "hair balls" within the intestinal tract.

History

The term "pica" was first coined by the French physician Ambroise Paré in the sixteenth century, although references to the syndrome predated him by centuries. Aristotle and Socrates both wrote about "earth eating," and during the classical periods of Greece and Rome, red clay lozenges from Lemnos were believed by physicians such as Galen to be antidotes for poison and cures for illnesses. They were also believed to facilitate childbirth. The lozenges were called *terra sigillata* (sealed earth) and stamped with the seals of the goddesses Artemis and Diana. As Christianity spread, these seals were replaced with Christian symbols and the lozenges, blessed by monks, were traded throughout western Europe and the Mediterranean region with the approval of the Roman Catholic Church (Hunter and De Kleine 1984).

The word "pica," and its older variant, *cissa,* come from the Latin word for "magpie," a bird thought to have a not very discriminatory appetite where edible and nonedible substances were concerned. Nineteenth-century medical texts describe both the eating behavior of magpies and that of humans with pica as consisting of an appetite for unusual edible and nonedible items (see, for example, Hooper 1811). The misconception that the magpie consumed earth and clay was likely based on observations of magpies collecting clay to build nests.

Pica was classified in Greek and Roman medical texts as a form of morbid or depraved appetite. In 1638, M. H. Boezo distinguished pica, the consumption of nonfoods, from "malacia," a voracious appetite for "normal" foods. He attributed malacia in pregnant women to mental changes thought to occur in pregnancy. (As early as the sixth century A.D., pica was thought to result from the cessation of menstruation during pregnancy [Cooper 1957]). Today, malacia, or the craving and binge eating of specific foods, is considered a form of pica (Castiglia 1993). (For the early literature on pica, see Cooper 1957 and Halsted 1968.)

In mid-sixteenth-century England, pica was associated with coal eating among pregnant women and children. But within western Europe and the United States from the sixteenth century through the late nineteenth century, pica was commonly understood as the consumption by young women of substances such as lime, coal, vinegar, and chalk so as to achieve a pale complexion and otherwise improve on appearance (Parry-Jones and Parry-Jones 1994: 290). Historically, this condition was said to be accompanied by "chlorosis" or "green sickness" in prepubescent girls and young women. Chlorosis, a disease recognized from the sixteenth century through the late nineteenth century, was characterized by a loss of menses or irregular menstruation and was accompanied by symptoms such as listlessness, pallid skin, loss of appetite, and weight loss.

It is interesting to note that the debate in early medical literature about the causes of chlorosis prefigures the current debate about pica and iron deficiency in terms of cause and effect. For example, the consumption of nonfoods by young women in order to achieve a pale complexion could easily have resulted in iron-deficiency anemia or chlorosis. However, iron-deficiency anemia can cause cravings for nonfoods, and chlorotic females ingested large amounts of unusual foods such as pepper, nutmeg, and raw corn, as well as nonfoods such as plaster. In addition, psychological reasons such as sexual frustration and nervous conditions were considered possible causes of both chlorosis and pica (Loudon 1980). In the twentieth century, pica among young women has been manifested by excessive consumption of real foods such as fruit and vegetables and nonfood substances like ice (Parry-Jones and Parry-Jones 1992). (For an extensive historical account of pica within Western industrialized cultural contexts, see Parry-Jones and Parry-Jones 1994).

In various regions of the world, especially in tropical zones, pica most often takes the form of geophagy. Harry D. Eastwell has noted that geophagy is associated with the "world's poor or more tribally oriented people" (1979: 264). Other investigators have characterized such groups as constituting "subsistence" societies (Hunter 1973), although in this chapter, the term "nonindustrialized" societies is used. In these societies, geophagy has been observed for many centuries and variously attributed to religious, cultural, and physiological causes (Hunter 1973; Hunter and De Kleine 1984; Parry-Jones and Parry-Jones 1992). Geophagy, or "dirt eating," was also thought to be a peculiar affliction of enslaved Africans and, later, lower-income African-Americans and whites in the southern United States, who were characterized as "dirt eaters" (Forsyth and Benoit 1989).

Etiology

Explanations of pica are numerous, reflecting the diversity of items consumed and the geographical regions within which the compulsive consumption occurs. In addition to the historical and cultural practices just mentioned, explanations also include psychiatric disorders and psychological and physiological needs, satisfaction of oral needs, behavioral disorders, responses to physiological or psychological stress, and the use of nonfoods for medicinal or pharmacological purposes (see, for example, Talkington et al. 1970; Hunter 1973; Crosby 1976; Eastwell 1979; Hunter and De Kleine 1984; Prince 1989; Horst 1990; Reid 1992). In fact, the practice of pica is so widespread both geographically and historically that one might be tempted to question its characterization as an abnormal practice.

Nonetheless, at least in the West, pica is considered an aberrant behavior warranting medical or psycho-logical treatment. Within the medical literature, pica is discussed in terms of possible biological causes and their negative consequences. The psychological literature characterizes pica as a pathological behavior linked to other eating disorders or found among populations of children and the mentally retarded.

However, this tendency to view pica as a pathological eating practice, an idiosyncrasy of "primitive" peoples, or an affliction primarily of the rural and impoverished has resulted in a failure to recognize the nutritional, medicinal, and cultural importance of geophagy in nonindustrialized cultural contexts.

Geophagy (Geophagia)

Geophagy, or the consumption of earth substances, is the most widely observed and researched type of pica. The term "geophagy" was first coined by Aristotle and means "dirt eating." Geophagia has also been termed *allotriophagia* by Sophocles, *erdessen* in medieval Germany, *mal d'estomac* in French, *citta* in Latin, and *cachexia africana* – literally meaning a "wasting away of Africans" – a phrase employed by slave owners and physicians in the West Indies and southern United States.

Despite the historical evidence for various forms of pica throughout the world, geophagy is the only type to be discussed extensively from a cross-cultural perspective, especially in ethnographic anthropological and geographical literature. In transcultural perspective, both anthropologists and geographers have described it as a socially acceptable custom, with specific cultural meanings and functions. Such literature reports geophagy to be most frequently practiced in tropical areas of Africa, Latin America, and the Caribbean, as well as in the southern United States. It is also practiced widely in parts of Iran, India, and China, and in tropical areas of Indonesia and Oceania (Anell and Lagercrantz 1958; Hunter 1973).

In the Andes Mountains of Peru and Bolivia, two dozen comestible or edible earth substances have been found listed in pre-Columbian Incan sources, and about six different comestible earths have been discovered archaeologically in pre-Incan contexts. In fact, evidence that the practice of eating earth is at least some 2,500 years old in the Andean region was discovered when a specimen of comestible earth was recovered from a Bolivian site dating from 400 B.C. (Browman and Gundersen 1993). Although cultural explanations have been popular, physiological explanations of geophagy as an adaptive human behavior are also important (Hunter 1973; Hunter and De Kleine 1984; Johns and Duquette 1991; Browman and Gundersen 1993).

Some of the first domesticated plants contained substances toxic to humans and were treated in processes involving earth substances to make them less toxic. The absorptive properties of clay were well known to ancient physicians who included *terra sig-*

illata and *terra silesiaca* in their pharmacopoeias for the treatment of poison (Dannenfeldt 1984). Several authors note the example of a condemned man, during the sixteenth century, who elected to swallow a lethal dose of mercury if he were first allowed to ingest clay. He reportedly survived an amount of mercury three times the normal lethal dose and was granted a pardon for having contributed to the medical knowledge of the time (Halsted 1968; Dannenfeldt 1984). In our times, kaolinite is the common type of clay used in medicines and the primary ingredient in commercially marketed Kaopectate.

Clay is also used medicinally in nonindustrialized societies where hookworm is a common ailment. This intestinal parasite causes gastric distress that is frequently alleviated with clay. Clay is also employed as a treatment for diarrhea, heartburn, and intestinal gas and has been used to relieve nausea and vomiting in pregnant women (Anell and Lagercrantz 1958; Hunter 1973). But authorities caution that the practice of geophagy can also introduce intestinal parasites into the body (Castiglia 1993) as well as cause intestinal blockage and excessive wear of dental enamel.

John M. Hunter (1973) hypothesized that a connection exists between mineral deficiencies (particularly those resulting from increased nutritional requirements during pregnancy) and the cultural practice of geophagy in Africa. Moreover, along with Renate De Kleine, he suggested that clay eating in Central America may be a "behavioral response to a physiological need" created by various mineral deficiencies, particularly during pregnancy (Hunter and De Kleine 1984: 157). Similarly, Donald E. Vermeer investigated geophagy among the Tiv of Nigeria and the Ewe of Ghana and discovered that clays were consumed during pregnancy as a treatment for diarrhea as well as for the minerals that they contain (Vermeer 1966; Vermeer and Frate 1975).

Hunter, who described geophagy in Africa as "common among children and adults" (1973: 171), acknowledged that the practice also has a cultural basis. For example, earth, taken from a shrine or holy burial site, is eaten for religious purposes or to swear oaths. However, earth eating is most commonly viewed as a remedy. Syphilis, diarrhea, and gastrointestinal discomfort caused by parasitic diseases (such as hookworm) are all conditions treated with geophagy by the general population, but in Africa, the practice of consuming clay is most frequently found among pregnant women. In a field study conducted in the Kailahun District of Sierra Leone, Hunter (1984) found that 50 percent of pregnant women ate clay from termite mounds and 7 percent ate vespid mud or clay from mud-daubing wasps' nests. In both cases, the mud was cooked over a fire until dried and blackened. An analysis of the clay to determine mineral content and availability for humans led Hunter to conclude that the practice of geophagy was "sensible and appropriate behavior" – as the clays made a significant contribution to the calcium, manganese, iron, and other mineral requirements of pregnant women (1984: 11).

In other parts of Africa, well-known and highly regarded clays are "extracted, processed, and passed from producers through middlemen to retailers and reach a wide consumer public through a network of periodic markets" (Hunter 1973: 173). Analysis of the nutritional content of a sample of such clays from Ghana revealed that clays of distinctive shapes (indicating a sort of brand) provided mineral supplementation in distinctive, varying proportions. For example, Hunter wrote:

> a distinctive end-to-end, truncated cone-shaped clay (sample six), is richest in two macronutrients, potassium and magnesium, but is poor in calcium. Another distinctive clay, sample 12, the slim, fingerlike bar, is richest in two micronutrients, zinc and manganese, but is weak in iron and copper. (1973: 177)

Hunter concluded that in view of the deficiencies inherent in the diets of many Africans, clays supplement those diets with a wide range of minerals important for pregnant women.

Moving to the other side of the world, Hunter and De Kleine (1984) also evaluated the nutritional properties of clay used to make tablets sold at religious shrines in Belize. Samples were tested for 13 minerals, and the conditions of digestion were simulated to determine the bioavailability of those minerals. Although the tests showed great variation in the amount of minerals available, in all cases the mineral content (and mineral availability) was sufficiently strong to suggest that the clay did indeed provide nutritional supplementation. A daily dose of from 1 to 6 tablets delivered 11 minerals in varying degrees, depending on the clay sampled. For example, 1 tablet yielded 73 milligrams of calcium and 68 micrograms of copper, among other minerals. A sample dose of 6 tablets provided 10 milligrams of iron, more than 200 micrograms each of nickel and manganese, and 12 micrograms of cobalt. When compared with U.S. Recommended Dietary Allowances and recommended supplements during pregnancy, a single tablet provided about 9 percent of the recommended iron and calcium.

Yet some types of clay are suspected of having properties that inhibit the absorption of minerals from the gastrointestinal tract, and there is no consistent agreement that iron from clay is useful in correcting anemia. Still, Hunter (1973), De Kleine (Hunter and De Kleine 1984), and David L. Browman and James N. Gundersen (1993) have asserted that clays can serve as a culturally acceptable and nutritionally functional source of mineral supplementation within some nonindustrialized societies.

In addition, there is an economic factor. Vermeer (1966, 1971) and Hunter (1973) have both documented how clay is incorporated into trade practices and how its processing has been the basis for local cottage industries.

Cultural Diffusion: Case Studies

Perhaps the best approach to understanding the phenomenon of geophagy involves the merging of nutritional, cultural, and economic explanations. In other words, from an African standpoint it might be viewed as a physiologically based adaptive behavior supported by religious and other cultural beliefs and institutionalized within the local economy.

Moreover, many have noted the diffusion of geophagy via the slave trade with the result that the practice was frequently observed among enslaved Africans in the West Indies, South America, and the southern United States. In addition, forms of geophagy continue to be documented among African-Americans in the southern United States and among those who migrated to northern cities and took the practice with them. It was common to have dirt or clay from a particular site in the South sent north by relatives. However, more recently, amylophagia (consumption of laundry starch) seems to have replaced clay eating, and geophagy generally seems to have declined significantly in recent decades.

During the last century, *cachexia africana* was of concern to physicians and plantation owners, who viewed it as an important cause of death among enslaved Africans. The condition they described seems similar to the syndrome of chlorosis we have already described. Both chlorosis and *cachexia africana* were characterized by a seemingly uncontrollable desire for the substances that are eaten. Although the reasons advanced for the aberrant appetites of young white women and African slaves are different, in both cases questions of cause and effect arise. David Mason (1833) was one of the first to suggest that obsessive dirt eating or *atrophia a ventriculo* (stomach atrophy), as he termed it, was actually a consequence of disease, and not its cause. He wrote:

> The train of symptoms that progressively arise from atrophy of the stomach and dirt-eating are indigestion and emaciation; a bloated countenance; a dirty-yellow tinge in the cellular tissue of the eyelids; paleness of the lips and ends of the fingers; whiteness of the tongue; great indolence, with an utter aversion to the most ordinary exertion; palpitation of the heart; difficult, or rather frequent and oppressed, respiration, even during moderate exercise, which never fails to induce a rapid pulse; habitual coldness of the skin; and occasional giddiness of the head, attended with a disposition to faint, sometimes causing a state of stupor. (1833: 292)

In addition, he noted a change in the color and density of blood, the appearance of skin ulcers, polypi in

the heart, and pathologies of the liver and gallbladder. Mason also reported that the obsession with nonfood items extended to eating "cloth, both linen and woolen..." (1833: 291).

Mason and later authors (Laufer 1930; Anell and Lagercrantz 1958) discussed a variety of conflicting explanations for the disease. Plantation owners often considered it either a kind of addiction or a means of escaping work, or both, and punished geophagy with confinement, beatings, and the use of metal mouthlocks. But others believed that homesickness and depression or abusive conditions led to the consumption of dirt; Berthold Laufer (1930) and Bengt Anell and Sture Lagercrantz (1958) mention the conviction, held by some, that geophagy was a deliberate, slow form of suicide among the enslaved Africans. Mason, by contrast, foreshadowed the current general debate about iron deficiency and pica in his belief that dirt eating was "rather a consequence than a cause of the disease" and suggested that the earth eaten contained "useful ingredients mixed up with much hurtful matter" and that "iron and alkalis are of great efficacy in this disease" (1833: 289, 292). He recommended exercise, proper diet, cleanliness, and proper clothing, as well as purely medical treatment with emetics, purgatives, and tonics. Unlike geophagy more generally, *cachexia africana* appeared to afflict both men and women in large numbers.

Hunter (1973) has noted similarities between geophagy in Africa and that practiced more recently by African-Americans in the United States, leading him along with others (see, for example, Vermeer and Frate 1975) to the view that geophagy arrived in the United States with enslaved Africans in a process of cultural diffusion. In both geographical locations the practice is found most often among women (especially pregnant women), and clays are gathered from special sites such as anthills, termitariums, or river banks and often referred to by the location (Forsyth and Benoit 1989). In Africa and in the southern United States, clays are shaped, baked, or sun-dried before eating and are claimed to have health-giving properties, as well as providing satisfaction. Reasons cited by southern women (black and white) reflect folk beliefs about the medicinal qualities of earth eating, while also indicating its character as an addiction:

> I craves it. I eat dirt just the same way you would smoke a cigarette. I crave something sour like the taste of clay. It seems to settle my stomach. I know I shouldn't eat it. When I go up in Jasper County I get it, but can't find any good dirt here. This Biloxi dirt ain't no good, so I gets my sister in Birmingham to send it to me. I never heard of a man eating dirt. They not got the same taste a woman has. My mother eats it because she be's in the change and they say it will help her. When I was a child I was coming home from Sunday School and it had rained. I

could smell the dirt on the bank and started to eat it then. Have kept it up. I would eat more dirt than I do, but I have a hard time getting it. (quoted in Ferguson and Keaton 1950: 463)

In moving to non-Western case studies of pica, we can encounter one of the few of a psychological nature. This one concerns an "epidemic" of pica (geophagy) that took place in Aboriginal coastal towns of northern Australia during 1958 and 1959 (Eastwell 1979). As diarrhea was presumed to be the cause of the earth eating, white nurses in the area treated patients with placebo tablets and with Kaopectate. The "epidemic" was ended, but the cessation of geophagy produced a community-wide disorder of hypochondriasis, and another outbreak of geophagy occurred among Aboriginal women who were past the years of childbearing.

Eastwell (1979), who discussed the epidemic, believed that the hypochondriasis and the earth eating of postmenopausal women had deep sociocultural causes. He argued that within the aboriginal hunting-and-gathering mode of subsistence, geophagy was originally practiced for medicinal purposes, but this function disappeared after these small-scale societies were colonized by the British. As the traditional hunting and gathering came to an end, the practice of geophagy was transformed into an indigenous cultural statement of Aboriginal status. Thus, bereft of its traditional medicinal function, the practice of pica among Aboriginal women became not only a type of protest, reflecting gender status, but also constituted a psychological adjustment strategy for women, whose economic importance diminished during the shift from a nomadic to a sedentary existence.

In a separate example, involving cultural diffusion and social change, Hunter and De Kleine (1984) provided a case study demonstrating the interaction of cultural and nutritional aspects of geophagia in Belize, where the indigenous population was resettled by the Spaniards in Santiago de Esquipulas, a pre-Columbian town of economic and religious importance to the Maya. "Esquipulas was noted for its shrine, health-giving earth, and sulfurous springs; thus it served as a place of spiritual significance and healing activity" (Hunter and De Kleine 1984: 157). The Spaniards built a chapel at the site to house a crucifix carved of balsam and orangewood. The crucifix darkened over time with the burning of incense and candles and became known as *Nuestro Senor de Esquipulas, el Cristo Negro,* or "the Black Christ." The Black Christ was worshiped by the Indians and symbolized a cultural fusion of Christian and Mayan beliefs by bringing an "Indian saint" into what was a new religion for the Mayas. The Black Christ also became known for its miraculous cures, which focused attention on the healing properties of the spring and mud at the site.

In the 1700s, the site was formally recognized by the Catholic Church, and a sanctuary for the Black Christ was constructed. The shrine continues to be of religious importance; pilgrims visit it, particularly on January 15, the Day of Esquipulas, and during Lent. Prior to the institution of border regulations requiring passports and visas, an estimated 100,000 pilgrims annually visited the shrine to be cured of ailments including "leprosy, blindness, muteness, insanity, paralysis, rabies, yellow fever, malaria, tetanus, and hemorrhages" (Hunter and De Kleine 1984: 158).

Many of the alleged cures were credited to the *tierra santa* (holy clay) at the site, which is believed to have health-giving properties and is blessed by the Roman Catholic Church. *Tierra santa* was (and is) sold at the shrine in the form of clay pressed into small cakes, stamped with images of the Virgin Mary, the Black Christ, and other saints. The clay tablets or *benditos* (blessed ones) (either eaten or dissolved in water and drunk) are believed to alleviate diseases of the stomach, heart, and eyes, to ease menstrual difficulties, and to facilitate pregnancy and childbirth.

As the cult of the Black Christ and the reputation for cures spread throughout Central America, new shrines were built that also became associated with curative, blessed earth. Indeed, by the end of the eighteenth century there were shrines in at least 40 towns where supposedly curative earths were available for consumption.

Pagophagia and Amylophagia

Within Western industrialized societies, recent medical literature on pica is dominated not so much by geophagy as by pagophagia and amylophagia. The term "pagophagia," first used in 1969 by Charles Coltman, a U.S. Air Force physician, refers to the compulsive consumption of ice and other frozen substances. Some, however, do not view pagophagia as a form of pica because ice (and ice water) consumption can be a positive measure in controlling body weight and addictions such as the use of tobacco. In addition, of course, chewing ice is more socially acceptable within industrialized countries than eating dirt. Like geophagy, pagophagia is strongly associated by many researchers with iron and other mineral deficiencies.

Amylophagia, by contrast, is the eating of laundry starch, which is associated almost exclusively with women. It was first observed in rural areas of the southeastern United States, where it was thought by some to have replaced dirt eating. As we have already noted, Hunter described a process of cultural diffusion and change occurring as geophagy from Africa was brought first to the southern United States:

Next came the northward migration of blacks to the urban ghettos of Cleveland, Chicago, New York, and Detroit. Such migrants ask their southern relatives to mail them boxes of clay for consumption during pregnancy. At this state, however, the forces of culture conflict come to the fore: lack of local clay in the concrete jungles of the North, pressures of poverty, and stress on kinship ties with the South lead to the consumption of laundry starch replacing traditional geophagy. But micronutrient minerals are totally lacking in the starch. Calories apart, nutritional inputs are zero; gastric irritation is caused. A cultural practice is now divorced from nutritional empiricism; cultural adjustment to socioenvironmental change has broken down, and atrophy and decay are the result. (1973:193)

Perhaps significantly, a similarity between dirt and laundry starch in texture (although not in taste) has been noted by investigators. The reasons cited by women for consuming laundry starch include the alleviation of nausea and vomiting associated with pregnancy and various folk beliefs, found largely among African-Americans, that consuming starch during pregnancy helps the baby "slide out" during delivery, promotes a healthy baby, or a whiter (or darker) baby (O'Rourke et al. 1967).

Like pagophagia and geophagia, as well as other forms of pica, amylophagia has also been associated with iron deficiency. Deleterious consequences include impacted bowels and intestinal obstructions.

Pica during Pregnancy

Pica has been associated since classical times with pregnant women. Until the twentieth century, pregnancy was commonly believed to cause mental instability – manifested, for example, in unusual food cravings. More recent studies of food preferences during pregnancy, however, report that changes in these, as well as the onset of specific cravings, are not universal phenomena.

Much of the research on pica among pregnant women in the United States has focused on those living in rural areas. The prevalence of pica among women considered at risk seems to have declined by about half between 1950 and 1970, but it has remained fairly constant from 1970 to the present. Nonetheless, it was estimated that pica is practiced by about one-fifth of pregnant women in the United States who are considered at "high risk" for this behavior. "High-risk" factors include being African-American, living in a rural area, having a family history of pica, and having practiced pica during childhood (Horner et al. 1991). Pregnant black women are over four times more likely than their white counterparts to engage in pica behavior. Additionally, pregnant women living in rural areas are more than twice as prone to pica as those living in urban areas.

Although some investigators have found no significant association between age and pica among pregnant women (Dunston 1961; Butler 1982), others have observed that pregnant women who practice pica tend to be relatively older than those who do not. It is interesting to note that women who report consuming clay tend to be older than those who report consuming starch (Vermeer and Frate 1979). One study, reanalyzing data from previous research, indicated that pregnant women who did practice pica were six times as likely to have a history of childhood pica than pregnant women who did not. Women who practice pica during pregnancy are also more likely to report pica behavior among family members, particularly their mothers and grandmothers (Lackey 1978). Little evidence of pica among white and upper-income women may reflect a lack of research among these populations (Keith, Brown, and Rosenberg 1970; Horner et al. 1991).

Among pregnant women in the United States, the three forms of pica that occur most frequently are geophagia, amylophagia, and pagophagia (Horner et al. 1991). Although, as we have noted, some researchers believe that as African-American women migrated to northern urban areas, laundry starch became a substitute for the more traditional clay eaten in the South (Keith et al. 1970), other research indicates that consumption preferences themselves might be changing, with younger women preferring starch over clay. In one study of rural women in North Carolina, participants indicated a preference for starch, even though their mothers had consumed both clay and starch (Mansfield 1977). Explanations of pica during pregnancy, like those of pica in general, range from the psychological through the cultural, to the nutritional (Horner et al. 1991; Edwards et al. 1994).

A recent study of eating habits and disorders during pregnancy mentions the case of a woman who, at 32 weeks of pregnancy, developed a craving for coal, reporting she found it "irresistibly inviting" (Fairburn, Stein, and Jones 1992: 668). Two other participants in the study developed a taste for eating vegetables while still frozen, which indicates something of the difficulty involved in determining pica incidence. The consumption of frozen vegetables, although not defined as pica by these researchers, would surely be considered a type of pagophagia by others.

In terms of medical consequences, pica has been related to anemia and toxemia among pregnant women and newborn infants (Horner et al. 1991). In some cases, pica reportedly contributed to dysfunctional labor (through impacted bowels) and maternal death (Horner et al. 1991). Pica during pregnancy has also been associated with a "poor" functional status of fetuses and infants, perinatal mortality, and low birth weight.

The authors of a report on pica in the form of baking-powder consumption that caused toxemia during pregnancy have pointed out that previous investigators discovered a significant correlation between toxemia and geophagia, but not between toxemia and amylophagia (Barton, Riely, and Sibai 1992). The case involved a 23-year-old black woman with anemia and hypokalemia who admitted to a one-and-a-half-year history of consuming up to 7 ounces of Calumet baking powder daily. The baking powder was considered a family remedy for gas discomfort. Ingestion of baking powder, comprised of 30 percent sodium bicarbonate with cornstarch, sodium aluminum sulfate, calcium acid phosphate, and calcium sulfate, is known to increase blood pressure. In this case, liver dysfunction and hypokalemia also resulted.

The psychological aspects of pica among pregnant women are similar to those of other pica practitioners. In addition to reporting a craving for the ingested substance, pregnant women exhibiting pica commonly say that they feel anxious when the substance is unavailable yet experience a sense of considerable satisfaction during and after eating the substance (Horner et al. 1991).

Pica and Iron Deficiency

Although no definitive connection has been established between pica and nutritional deficiencies, many have consistently linked pica with iron deficiency and its consequent anemia. Indeed, some have estimated that upward of 50 percent of patients with iron-deficiency anemia practice pica (Coltman 1969; Crosby 1976). It is interesting to note that the correlation of pica with anemia dates back to medieval times, and that iron therapy was prescribed as a cure even then (Keith et al. 1970).

As pointed out previously, pica behavior during pregnancy has also been strongly associated with iron-deficiency and iron deficient anemia. What remains unresolved is a problem of cause and effect. As Dennis F. Moore and David A. Sears wrote: "Some authors have suggested that the habit may induce iron deficiency by replacing dietary iron sources or inhibiting the absorption of iron. However, considerable evidence suggests that iron deficiency is usually the primary event and pica a consequence" (1994: 390). Although some insist that ingested starch inhibits iron absorption, Kenneth Talkington and colleagues (1970) have reported that this is not the case. These authors concluded that iron deficiency and anemia result from amylophagia only when laundry starch replaces nutritional substances in the diet.

Turning to clay ingestion, studies have found that its effect on iron absorption varies and depends upon the type of clay ingested. Some clays impair iron absorption, whereas others contain large amounts of iron. However, as already mentioned, there is no consistent agreement that iron from clay is useful in correcting anemia (Coltman 1969; Keith et al. 1970; Crosby 1976).

Coltman (1969), who first used the term pagophagia, was also one of the first to link the practice with iron deficiency. Indeed, he reported that the compulsive consumption of ice could be stopped within one or two weeks with iron treatment, even in instances where iron supplementation was not sufficient to correct iron-deficiency anemia. This dovetails with the work of William H. Crosby (1976), who has noted that although ice neither displaces other dietary calories nor impairs iron absorption, it is still the case that pagophagia is diminished when treated with iron supplements. Moreover, other cases of pica involving unusual ingested substances (e.g., toothpicks, dust from venetian blinds, and cigarette ashes) also respond positively to iron supplements (Moore and Sears 1994).

Perhaps even more powerful support for iron deficiency as a cause of pica comes from findings that intramuscular injections of iron diminish the habit of pica in children. But there is also evidence that intramuscular injections of a saline solution have the same effect, suggesting that the additional attention paid to children with pica behavior may help to reverse the condition (Keith et al. 1970).

Countering this theory, however, are two cases of childhood pica in which parental attention was apparently not a factor. One involved a 6-year-old boy with a 2-year history of ingesting large amounts of foam rubber, whereas the second case was that of a 2-year-old boy with a 6-month history of eating plastic and rubber items. Both of these cases of pica behavior were resolved through the administration of iron supplements, even though there was no increase in parental attentiveness (Arbiter and Black 1991).

In 1970, Louis Keith, E. R. Brown, and L. Rosenberg summarized the medical questions surrounding pica that required further investigation and clarification. These were:

1. Is iron-deficiency anemia a direct adverse consequence of pica?
2. Is iron-deficiency anemia an indirect result of nutritional replacement by unnatural substances, allaying the appetite for nutritional foods by filling?
3. Are so-called cures of the habit of pica among children the result of increased attention or of injections of iron or saline solution?
4. If those "cures" among children are the result of therapy, should the therapy consist of iron injections, saline injections, or an adequate diet high in iron content?
5. Is the mechanism of pica among children different from that among adults, especially pregnant women? Would injections of iron reverse the habit in pregnant women?
6. Does the coexistence of amylophagia and anemia adversely affect the pregnant woman, or are these two separate and distinct unrelated concomitant adverse conditions? (1970: 630)

As we have seen, although almost three decades have elapsed, there is still no consensus within the medical community regarding the answers to these questions. Instead, they are still being asked.

The physiological mechanism linking iron deficiency and pica behavior is not known. As Crosby noted, "Somewhere in our emotional circuits iron deficiency can sometimes cross the wires" (1976: 342). Somewhat more scientifically, it has been suggested that pica cravings are generated by a functional disorder of the hypothalamus, which is sensitive to changes in iron levels (Castiglia 1993).

As for pagophagia, Mary Elks (1994) has made two observations. She noted that even in industrialized nations, both geography and culture play a role in determining how pagophagia is viewed. For example, in England and other European countries compulsive ice eating is considered pathological behavior, perhaps indicative of disease. However, in the warmer climate of the southern United States, ice eating may be regarded as normal. In addition, she reported a case involving an entire family practicing pagophagia, including a 14-month-old girl for whom, Elks believed, ice consumption should not be assumed to be a learned behavior. She suggested that in some cases, familial or heritable factors cause pagophagia that is independent of other types of pica and probably not correlated with iron deficiency.

Psychological Explanations of Pica

Pica, as we have observed, is included as an eating disorder (along with anorexia nervosa, bulimia, and rumination in infancy) in the classification systems of the DSM-III-R of the American Psychiatric Association (APA) (1987) and the ICD-10 of the World Health Organization (1992). Pica is defined by the APA as the repeated consumption of nonnutritive substances for a period of at least one month, when the behavior is not attributable to another mental disorder.

It is interesting to note that psychological literature on eating disorders discusses pica in early childhood as a risk factor for bulimia in adolescence (Marchi and Cohen 1990). Moreover, some aspects of pica, such as excessive consumption of ice, ice water, lemon juice, and vinegar, are linked with anorexia nervosa (Parry-Jones 1992; Parry-Jones and Parry-Jones 1994). Pica has also been associated with rumination in children and persons with mental retardation; in such cases, the behavior may be interpreted as a regressive behavior reflecting oral needs that have not been met (Feldman 1986). Poor feeding and weaning practices are more frequently observed in children with pica than in those without (Singhi, Singhi, and Adwani 1981). In addition, comparisons of children who have iron-deficiency anemia and who practice pica and children with anemia who do not practice pica show that the former score higher on measures of stress, including that caused by maternal deprivation, child abuse, and parental separation (Singhi et al. 1981).

It is important to understand that psychological explanations themselves tend to reflect cultural beliefs in the Western industrialized world, in contrast to religious and spiritual beliefs of cultures in other areas. To view all types of pica behavior as pathology risks a failure to recognize other important issues, such as cultural variation in food preference, indigenous medicinal and nutritional knowledge, and the very real question of the effects of nutritional deficiencies.

Discussion

Although explanations of pica vary with the type of substance consumed and with the cultural context, there are several consistent themes in the literature. One is that whereas men do practice pica, the behavior is most frequently associated with women and children. Second, regardless of cultural context and whether pica is considered acceptable among adults, there seems to be a uniform concern about the practice of pica by children.

A third has to do with similarities shared by the substances most frequently consumed. They tend to be brittle, dry, and crunchy. Moreover, the smell of the clay and soil is cited as important in a variety of cultural contexts, as is the location from which the clay or earth is obtained. These sites are frequently the homes of living things such as termites or crayfish. There is also a pattern, historically and geographically, of consumption of earth or clay from sites of special significance. Such sites may be religious, as in Latin America and Africa, locally distinctive, as in the southern United States, or they may be places of burial, as in Asia, Africa, and Europe. Finally, there is a cross-cultural consistency in the debate concerning the relationship of pica to iron and other mineral deficiencies, and in the debate over whether the practice is psychologically or physiologically based.

One question that remains unexplored (in fact, it is barely mentioned in the literature) is why the definitions and syndromes associated with pica are not extended to the many practices in which men rather than women more typically engage, such as chewing tobacco and cigars or pipe stems, using snuff, and chewing toothpicks, betel nut, and chewing gum. While these habits may not generally involve consumption, they are not so dissimilar from the practices of pagophagia. Certainly, it appears that the relationship between the forms of pica we have discussed and other cravings and sources of oral satisfaction is an area in need of further investigation.

Margaret J. Weinberger

Bibliography

American Psychiatric Association. 1987. *Diagnostic and statistical manual of mental disorders (DSM-III-R)*. Washington, D.C.

Anell, Bengt, and Sture Lagercrantz. 1958. *Geophagical customs.* Studia ethnographica Upsaliensia 17, Uppsala, Sweden.

Arbiter, E. A., and Dora Black. 1991. Pica and iron-deficiencyanaemia. *Child: Care, Health, and Development* 17: 231-4.

Barton, John R., Caroline A. Riely, and Baha M. Sibai. 1992. Baking powder pica mimicking preeclampsia. *American Journal of Obstetrics and Gynecology* 167: 98-9.

Bell, Kenneth E., and David M. Stein. 1992. Behavioral treatments for pica: A review of empirical studies. *International Journal of Eating Disorders* 11: 377-89.

Browman, David L., and James N. Gundersen. 1993. Altiplano comestible earths: Prehistoric and historic geophagy of highland Peru and Bolivia. *Geoarchaeology* 8: 413-25.

Butler, P. M. 1982. Pica practices as an influence on iron deficiency anemia. Ph.D. thesis, East Carolina University, Greenville, N.C.

Castiglia, Patricia T. 1993. Pica. *Journal of Pediatric Health-Care* 7: 174-5.

Coltman, Charles A. 1969. Pagophagia and iron lack. *Journal of the American Medical Association* 207: 513-14.

Cooper, Marcia C. 1957. *Pica.* Springfield, Ill.

Crosby, William H. 1971. Food pica and iron deficiency. *Archives of Internal Medicine* 127: 960-1.

   1976. Pica: A compulsion caused by iron deficiency. *British Journal of Haematology* 34: 341-2.

Danford, D. E. 1982. Pica and nutrition. *Annual Review of Nutrition* 2: 303-22.

Dannenfeldt, K. H. 1984. The introduction of a new sixteenth-century drug: *terra silesiaca. Medical History* 28: 174-88.

Dunston, B. N. 1961. Pica, hemoglobin and prematurity and perinatal mortality. Ph.D. dissertation, New York University School of Education, New York.

Eastwell, Harry D. 1979. A pica epidemic: A price for sedentarism among Australian ex-hunter-gatherers. *Psychiatry* 42: 264-73.

Edwards, C. H., A. A. Johnson, E. M. Knight, et al. 1994. Pica in an urban environment. *Journal of Nutrition* 124 (Supplement): 954S-62S.

Elks, Mary. 1994. Familial pagophagia. *Southern Medical Journal* 87: 963-4.

Fairburn, Christopher G., Alan Stein, and Rosemary Jones. 1992. Eating habits and eating disorders during pregnancy. *Psychosomatic Medicine* 54: 665-72.

Feldman, Marc D. 1986. Pica: Current perspectives. *Psychosomatics* 27: 519-23.

Ferguson, James H., and Alice Glenn Keaton. 1950. Studies of the diets of pregnant women in Mississippi: The ingestion of clay and laundry starch. *Louisiana State Medical Society Journal* 102: 460-3.

Forsyth, Craig J., and Genevieve M. Benoit. 1989. Rare, ole, dirty snacks: Some research notes on dirt eating. *Deviant Behavior* 10: 61-8.

Halsted, J. A. 1968. Geophagia in man: Its nature and nutritional effects. *American Journal of Clinical Nutrition* 21: 1384-93.

Higgins, Brian. 1993. Pica. In *The Cambridge world history of human disease,* ed. Kenneth F. Kiple, 297-332. Cambridge and New York.

Hooper, R. 1811. *Quincy's lexicon-medicum. A new medical dictionary.* London.

Horner, R. D., C. J. Lackey, K. Kolasa, and K. Warren. 1991. Pica practices of pregnant women. *Journal of the American Dietetic Association* 91: 34-8.

Horst, Oscar H. 1990. Arcilla geofagica en America. *Meso-america-antigua* 19: 169-76.

Hunter, John M. 1973. Geophagy in Africa and the United States: A culture-nutrition hypothesis. *Geographical Review* 63: 170-95.

   1984. Insect clay geophagy in Sierra Leone. *Journal of Cultural Geography* 4: 2-13.

Hunter, John M., and Renate De Kleine. 1984. Geophagy in Central America. *Geographical Review* 74: 157-69.

Johns, Timothy, and Martin Duquette. 1991. Detoxification and mineral supplementation as functions of geophagy. *American Journal of Clinical Nutrition* 53: 448-56.

Karp, Joyce Gerdis, Laura Whitman, and Antonio Convit. 1991. Intentional ingestion of foreign objects by male prison inmates. *Hospital and Community Psychiatry* 42: 533-5.

Keith, L., E. R. Brown, and C. Rosenberg. 1970. Pica: The unfinished story; background; correlations with anemia and pregnancy. *Perspectives in Biology and Medicine* 13: 626-32.

Kiple, Kenneth. 1984. *The Caribbean slave: A biological history.* Cambridge.

   1988. ed. *The African exchange: Toward a biological history of black people.* Durham, N.C.

Kiple, Kenneth, and V. Himmelsteib King. 1981. *Another dimension to the black diaspora: Diet, disease and racism.* Cambridge.

Lackey, C. J. 1978. Pica - a nutritional anthropology concern. In *The anthropology of health,* ed. E. E. Bauwens, 121-9. St. Louis.

Laufer, Berthold. 1930. Geophagy. In *Anthropological series,* Field Museum of Natural History, Vol. 18 (2): 99-198, Chicago.

Loudon, I. S. L. 1980. Chlorosis, anaemia and anorexia nervosa. *British Medical Journal* 281: 1669-75.

Mansfield, C. 1977. *Investigation of pica in Pitt County, North Carolina.* Greenville, N.C.

Marchi, M., and P. Cohen. 1990. Early childhood eating behaviours and adolescent eating disorders. *Journal of the American Academy of Child and Adolescent Psychiatry* 29: 112-17.

Mason, David. 1833. On atrophia a ventriculo (mal d'estomac), or dirt eating. *Edinburgh Medical and Surgical Journal* 39: 289-96.

Melville, Bendley, and Valery Francis. 1992. Dietary habits and superstitions of rural Jamaican women during pregnancy. *European Journal of Clinical Nutrition* 46: 373-4.

Moore, Dennis F., and David A. Sears. 1994. Pica, iron deficiency, and the medical history. *The American Journal of Medicine* 97: 390-3.

O'Brien, Robert. 1985. *The encyclopedia of the South.* New York.

O'Rourke, D. E., J. G. Quinn, J. O. Nicholson, and H. H. Gibson. 1967. Geophagia during pregnancy. *Obstetrics and Gynecology* 29: 581-4.

Parry-Jones, Brenda. 1992. Pagophagia or compulsive ice consumption: A historical perspective. *Psychological Medicine* 22: 561-71.

Parry-Jones, Brenda, and William L. Parry-Jones. 1992. Pica: Symptom or eating disorder? A historical assessment. *British Journal of Psychiatry* 160: 341-54.

Parry-Jones, William L., and Brenda Parry-Jones. 1994. Implications of historical evidence for the classification of eating disorders: A dimension overlooked in DSM-III-R and ICD-10. *British Journal of Psychiatry* 165: 287-92.

Pope, Janet F., Jean D. Skinner, and Betty R. Carruth. 1992. Cravings and aversions of pregnant adolescents. *Journal of the American Dietetic Association* 92: 1479-82.

Prince, Isolde. 1989. Pica and geophagia in cross-cultural perspective. *Transcultural Psychiatric Research Review* 26: 167-97.

Rehm, M. D., and Philip A. DeSimone. 1991. A proposed mechanism for cardboard-induced iron-deficiency anemia. *The American Journal of Medicine* 90: 768-9.

Reid, Russell M. 1992. Cultural and medical perspectives on geophagia. *Medical Anthropology* 13: 337-51.

Singhi, S., P. Singhi, and G. B. Adwani. 1981. Role of psychosocial stress in the cause of pica. *Clinical Pediatrics* 20: 783-5.

Talkington, Kenneth, Norman F. Gant, Daniel E. Scott, and Jack A. Pritchard. 1970. Effects of ingestion of starch and some clays on iron absorption. *American Journal of Obstetrics and Gynecology* 108: 262-7.

Vermeer, Donald E. 1966. Geophagy among the Tiv of Nigeria. *Association of American Geographers* 56: 197-204.

   1971. Geophagy among the Ewe of Ghana. *Ethnology* 10: 56-72.

Vermeer, Donald E., and Dennis A. Frate. 1975. Geophagy in a Mississippi county. *Annals of the Association of American Geographers* 65: 414-24.

   1979. Geophagia in rural Mississippi: Environmental and cultural contexts and nutritional implications. *American Journal of Clinical Nutrition* 32: 2129-35.

World Health Organization. 1992. *The ICD-10 classification of mental and behavioural disorders.* Geneva.

IV.D.7 ❧ Protein–Energy Malnutrition

Protein–energy malnutrition (PEM) is the current term for a group of nutritional diseases related to dietary protein and energy (calorie) intake. These diseases are most frequently seen in infants and young children in developing countries but may be a feature of famine or the result of illness for people of all ages throughout the world. Research during the twentieth century has considerably clarified the causes and manifestations of what are now known as dietary-related effects on the growing or mature individual. PEM includes conditions known in the medical world as kwashiorkor, marasmus, and growth retardation in children. Related to PEM are pellagra, starvation, and protein malnutrition. Infection, debilitating disease, and surgical procedures are frequently complicated by PEM. It is, therefore, a factor of importance in determining morbidity and mortality and has to be taken into account by health-care personnel at all levels.

Historical Concepts of Protein and Energy

Early reports of what may have been PEM lack the clinical, pathological, and biochemical details that make identification certain. The history of PEM is thus confined to the nineteenth and twentieth centuries, and it is only in the last 50 years that clarification of the various forms that PEM can manifest has emerged.

In his book *Protein and Energy,* Kenneth J. Carpenter has provided a detailed survey of nutritional science as it was known in the period from 1614 to 1893 (Carpenter 1994: 1-99). Of particular interest in relation to later discoveries is that the first "balance studies" were carried out by Italian scientist S. Santorio in 1614. He weighed his food and drink as well as his excreta (urine and feces) and measured changes in his own weight. There was an unexplained daily disappearance of 5 pounds of material that he attributed to a breakdown of body tissue that was then secreted through the skin as insensible perspiration; the losses were made good by the nourishment ingested. This was only a more quantitative restatement of Galen's view in the second century that "[o]ur bodies are dissipated by the transpiration that takes place through the pores in our skins that are invisible to us; therefore we need food in a quantity proportionate to the quantity transpired" (Carpenter 1994: 1).

Anton Lavoisier's work in the late eighteenth century (1770 to 1790) made him the "Father of Nutritional Science." His first contribution was the recognition of the distinction between compounds that could change their character and simple substances or elements (e.g., carbon, hydrogen, nitrogen, oxygen, and others). His second contribution was an understanding that combustion and respiration involved similar processes of oxidation that could explain the phenomenon of "animal heat."

Among those who followed Lavoisier was Jean-Baptiste Boussingault, who published the first table of the nitrogen content of foods in 1836. The protein radical was discovered just two years later by Gerrit Mulder and was considered to be the essential ingredient for both body building and physical activity. By the end of the nineteenth century, however, it was realized that protein was not the main or obligatory source of energy and that it is the oxidation of carbohydrates and fatty acids on which we rely for continued physical work.

Definition and Nomenclature

Description of the various syndromes that we now include in PEM began around 1850, and in the subsequent hundred years, much confusion in terminology arose. However, E. Kerpel-Fronius, a well-known Hungarian pediatric investigator who bridged both the pre- and post-1950 eras, clarified the old and new nomenclature, which has made it possible to identify references in early case reports (Kerpel-Fronius 1983: 30–4). He showed that the contradictions in terminology were rooted in regional differences, age of weaning, local foods, and prevalence of infections, and he classified the various types of malnutrition we now call PEM in the following way:

1. Hypoalbuminemic forms (low serum proteins)
   i. Edematous
      a. Kwashiorkor
      b. Mehlnährschaden
   ii. Hypoalbuminemic forms without edema
2. Dry forms without hypoalbuminemia
   i. Underweight (dystrophic infants)
      a. Stationary stage
      b. Repairing stage with retardation in height (stunted infants)
   ii. Marasmus (atrophy)
      a. Moderately severe
      b. Severe forms
   iii. Severest form in young infants (athrepsia or decomposition in the classic texts of pediatrics)

Reference to this classification assists considerably in identifying in older literature the various forms of what is now known as PEM. A current definition of PEM is the Wellcome classification shown in Table IV.D.7.1, which refers to children (Wellcome Trust Working Party 1970), whereas a broad current understanding of the nutritional basis of PEM is as follows:

1. Protein quantity and/or quality (amino acid pattern of the protein) intake that is below the minimal requirements for growth and health, with or without an energy intake that is less than energy expenditure on muscle activity, heat production, growth, and other energy requirements.
2. Excessive loss of protein and energy in diarrhea and acute and chronic diseases. (Waterlow 1992: 152–8)

PEM can, of course, be complicated by mineral deficiencies (e.g., of sodium, potassium, calcium, phosphorus, or iron), by deficiencies of trace elements (e.g., zinc or chromium), and by vitamin deficiencies (e.g., of vitamins A, D, C, or K). Much of this understanding has come about through intensive worldwide research during the last 50 years, which is discussed in the remainder of this chapter. We begin with marasmus.

Marasmus 1850 to 1950

"Marasmus" means "wasting away of the body" (from the Greek *marasmos*) and is a term applied mainly to infants and children (the term "wasting" is employed for similarly afflicted adults) (Figure IV.D.7.1). It occurs when the diet is grossly deficient in energy. Such a diet also necessarily fails to meet protein requirements. Marasmus may become manifest in wholly breast-fed infants when the milk is quantitatively insufficient, but more frequently it occurs after

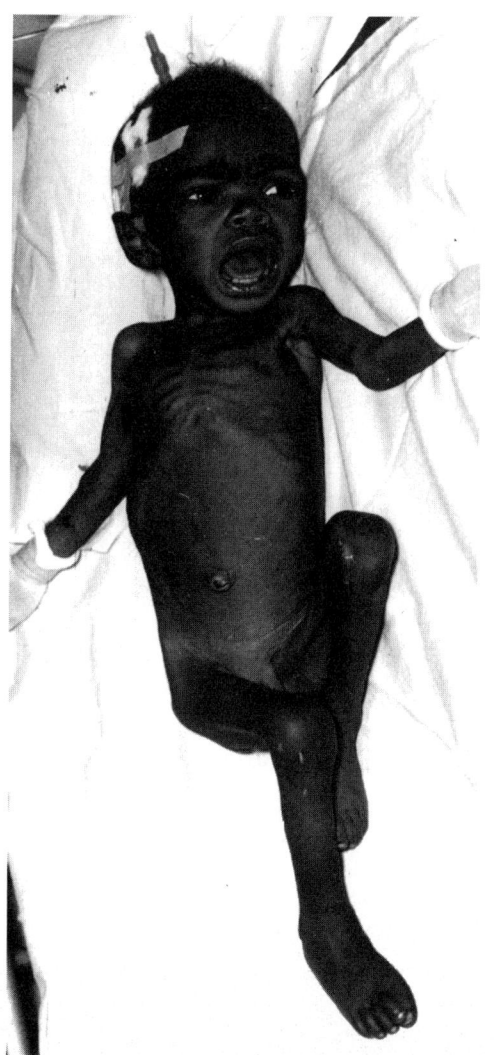

Figure IV.D.7.1. Marasmus. Age about 7 months grossly underweight. No skin lesions and no edema. (Photograph courtesy of Groote Schuur Hospital, Cape Town, South Africa.)

Table IV.D.7.1. *The Wellcome classification of PEM*

Weight (percentage of standard)	Edema Present	Edema Absent
60–80	Kwashiorkor	Underweight
60 or less	Marasmic Kwashiorkor	Marasmus

Source: Wellcome Trust Working Party: 1970.

early weaning to diluted or low-energy bottle feeds or cereal paps. In the age group from 1 to 5 years, marasmus occurs when food of any kind is in short supply, as in conditions of war, civil unrest, famine, extreme poverty, or just lack of care for the child. Often, it is produced by starvation that occurs during treatment of diarrhea or other infections, but it can also stem from severe weight loss brought on by chronic pyogenic disease, tuberculosis, syphilis, AIDS, and tropical infestations.

The presenting symptoms are failure to thrive, irritable crying, or apathy. Diarrhea is frequent, and the child has a shrunken or wizened appearance, even though it is ravenously hungry. The degree of underweight for age is extreme, and the muscles are weak and atrophic. Currently, marasmus is diagnosed when the weight is 60 percent or less of the 50th percentile of the National Center for Health Statistics (NCHS) standards (Table IV.D.7.1). However, based on prewar literature, Kerpel-Fronius wrote that if the degree of wasting reaches 35 to 40 percent of the average body weight, recovery is impossible (Kerpel-Fronius 1947).

An interesting description of the clinical signs of marasmus was given in a speech by Charles Dickens at a fund-raising dinner for the Hospital for Sick Children on February 9, 1858. After discussing the tens of thousands of children who were dying because of poverty and sickness, he described a tour of the old town of Edinburgh, where lived some of the city's worst-lodged inhabitants. In one of the most wretched dwellings, "there lay, in an old egg box, which the mother had begged from a shop, a little feeble, wasted, wan, sick child. With his little wasted face and his little hot, worn hands folded over on his breast, and his little bright, attentive eyes looking steadily at us" (Dickens 1956: 607).

Prevalence

Exact figures of the prevalence of marasmus are difficult to obtain because of the confusion of nomenclature and diagnosis. But marasmus must have been a leading cause of morbidity and mortality among infants and preschool children during the latter half of the nineteenth century and the early part of the twentieth century – and in Europe and North America as well as the rest of the world. A large percentage of the victims were illegitimate foundlings, who represented from 15 to 45 percent of all newborn infants in most European capitals. In the poor hygienic conditions of the "foundlings' homes," death claimed between 30 and 90 percent during the first year of life.

Similar rates of mortality occurred in North American institutions. H. D. Chapin (1915), examining 11 foundling institutions in New York, discovered a death rate of 422 per 1,000 for children under 2 years of age – compared with a community-wide figure of only 87 per 1,000. In 1921, Oscar M. Schloss,

the author of the annual report of the Infants' Hospital in Boston, called attention to "the frequent relationships of both malnutrition and acute infections to infant deaths" and stressed their importance as fields of research (Smith 1983: 138). Marasmus and atrophy do not appear as diagnoses in lists of patient admissions from the period 1883 to 1913, but figures for debility, dysentery, and diarrhea are high. In 1882, more than one-third of admissions were for "debility."

With the two world wars, marasmus was especially prevalent in besieged cities of Europe, such as Warsaw, Leningrad, and Budapest. But by 1950, and since then, marasmus resulting from poverty and sickness has become very rare in the so-called developed world. It remains, however, a nutritional problem in the developing countries of Africa, the Middle East, South and Central America, and Southeast Asia (Bellamy 1996: 98).

Research

From 1850 to 1950, numerous medical research reports on marasmus appeared, and many of these have been outlined, at least in part, in recent publications (Kerpel-Fronius 1983; Hansen 1991). Early in the twentieth century, German and French pediatricians stressed that the fate of undernourished infants depended on whether they escaped infection: It was thought that a rapid decline in the weight curve, ending in severe marasmus, could seldom be caused just by semistarvation (Kerpel-Fronius 1983: 64–8).

In a 1905 analysis of the bodies of marasmus victims and normal infants, a striking difference was discovered in fat content. Fat content in marasmic infants was only 1.7 percent of body weight, compared with 13.1 percent in normal babies. In 1920, body water in marasmic infants was found to be increased from 70 to 80 percent, and it was noted that the brain, kidneys, and skeleton were relatively preserved in marasmus.

Ten years earlier dextrose saline had been used for collapsed and dehydrated cases – including those of infantile atrophy, as recorded in an article about the activities of the Boston Floating Hospital (Beaven 1957). Losses of potassium, sodium, and chloride in diarrhea had been demonstrated by K. Schmidt in 1850, L. F. Meyer in 1910, L. Tobler in 1911, and I. Jundell in 1913 (Darrow 1946). In 1915, it was confirmed that increased water, fat, chloride, sodium, and potassium losses occurred in loose stools of infants, including those with marasmus (Holt, Courtney, and Fales 1915). The authors of this study pointed out that in therapy, potassium and magnesium were needed in addition to water and sodium, but it was not until 1946 (when it was proved that potassium could safely be added to intravenous fluids) that this advice was followed. This addition cut mortality from 32 to 6 percent (Darrow 1946; Govan and Darrow 1946).

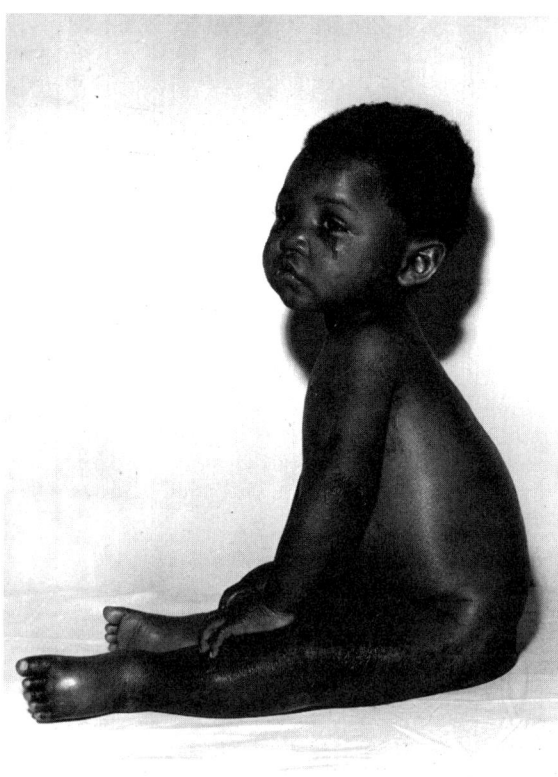

Figure IV.D.7.2. Kwashiorkor. Age 10 months. Skin lesions and edema. (Photograph courtesy of Groote Schuur Hospital, Capetown, South Africa.)

Kwashiorkor to 1954

Marasmus was the first syndrome of what we now know as PEM to become the focus of wide interest, concern, and research, especially between 1850 and 1950. But from 1935 onward, kwashiorkor became another intensively studied and important nutritional disease. The term "kwashiorkor" was introduced by Cicely Williams, who wrote: "The name kwashiorkor indicates the disease the deposed baby gets when the next one is born, and is the local name in the Gold Coast for a nutritional disease of children, associated with a maize diet" (1935: 1151-2) (Figure IV.D.7.2). Williams explained (1973) that the word comes from the Ga language of Accra, Ghana, and J. C. Waterlow (1991) has identified at least 31 distinct vernacular names in tropical Africa. Other regions also have words that doubtless frequently mean kwashiorkor. Among the common names in English, for example, are nutritional dystrophy, infantile pellagra, nutritional edema, and wet marasmus. In Spanish-speaking countries, kwashiorkor was referred to as a multiple deficiency state – *distrofia pluricarencial.*

Before naming the disease, Williams had published a paper giving its clinical description (Williams 1933). Afflicted infants were of preschool age (1 to 4), and their diet generally involved breast feeding with supplementary feeds of maize paps low in protein content. On examination, there was edema, wasting diarrhea, sores of mucous membranes, desquamation of the skin on the legs and forearms, and a fatty liver. The disease was uniformly fatal unless treated. This description provided by Williams fits perfectly with our current clinical definition of kwashiorkor, except that since 1933, retardation of growth has been more emphasized and there is now detailed knowledge of the changes in function of various systems and organs (Hansen and Pettifor 1991).

In a 1952 World Health Organization (WHO) report, the name kwashiorkor was applied to the syndrome in Africa, and the relationship of the disease to a low-protein diet was firmly established (Brock and Autret 1952). This study and report had been initiated by the Joint FAO (Food and Agriculture Organization)/WHO Expert Committee on Nutrition at its first session in Geneva in October 1949. The committee had found that one of the most widespread nutritional disorders in tropical and subtropical areas was an ill-defined syndrome known by various names such as kwashiorkor, malignant malnutrition, polydeficiency disease, and so forth. It was resolved that WHO conduct an inquiry into the various features of kwashiorkor, and, subsequently, the FAO was asked to cooperate. J. F. Brock (WHO) and M. Autret (FAO) traveled extensively throughout Africa over a period of two months in 1950, after which they concluded "that kwashiorkor is the most serious and widespread nutritional disorder known to medical and nutritional science" (Brock and Autret 1952: 72).

In subsequent years, FAO and WHO sponsored other studies in Central America, Brazil, and southern India, and research units in various parts of the world began to concentrate their efforts on determining the etiology, pathogenesis, treatment, and prevention of kwashiorkor.

The similarities and differences between marasmus and kwashiorkor soon became evident and gave rise to intensive debate. D. B. Jelliffe proposed the term "protein calorie (energy) malnutrition" (PEM) to cover the spectrum of syndromes that range from marasmus to kwashiorkor (Jelliffe 1959). This concept was a major contribution in understanding the variations of this group of nutritional diseases.

A history of kwashiorkor appeared in 1954 (Trowell, Davies, and Dean 1954). It discussed an early description of the disease, written by J. P. Correa in 1908 in the Yucatan. Waterlow, in his recent article on the history of kwashiorkor, found an even earlier description from Mexico by F. Hinojosa in 1865 (Waterlow 1991: 236). H. C. Trowell and his colleagues (1954) made it apparent that up to 1954, kwashiorkor had a worldwide distribution. They supported their contention by listing approximately 250 publications from Africa, Asia, Europe, North and Central America, and South America that contained details on established or probable cases of the disease (Trowell 1954). Most of these dated from between 1920 and 1950, and some early reports from German workers on *Mehlnährschaden* are of especial interest (Czerny and Keller 1925–8). This term, which is best translated as "damaged by cereal flours," was used to indicate infant malnutrition resulting from imbalanced (excess starch) feeding habits, and the researchers described a clinical picture similar to that of kwashiorkor. In Germany at the time, it had become popular to use cereal gruels instead of milk when a child had gastrointestinal difficulties. The gruels were usually made without milk, and the return of loose stools when milk was once again added to the diet was too often regarded as an indication of sensitivity to milk. The many similarities between *Mehlnährschaden* and kwashiorkor in terms of etiology, pathology, and treatment suggest that these German researchers – in a developed country – may well have been describing kwashiorkor in the early part of the century.

In their book on kwashiorkor, Trowell and colleagues (1954) present a fascinating historical description of the puzzling features of the disease that had confounded investigators and triggered controversies. Among these were the similarities of kwashiorkor to pellagra, the fact that many cases did not have skin rashes, that fatty livers were found in nearly all cases, the role intestinal parasites might play in the disease, and the various forms of treatment. However, what emerged clearly was that lack of protein in the diet was an important cause – a lack caused by dependency on foods that supply adequate carbohydrate but little protein, such as cassava and cereal foods like rice, corn, millet, and sorghum. A distinction between kwashiorkor and infantile pellagra was based on a difference in the distribution of dermatosis (in kwashiorkor the diaper area; in pellagra on exposed areas such as the face, hands, and feet) and a failure of kwashiorkor victims to respond to nicotinic acid unless a high-protein diet was simultaneously given (Trowell et al. 1954: 118–19).

The treatment recommended for kwashiorkor in 1954 was cow's milk, given in a concentrated form with little lactose and less fat. However, the exact nature of the factor(s) responsible for bringing about improvement in the children's condition had not been determined. Serum biochemistry showed that treatment increased serum albumin, cholesterol, nonspecific esterase, and cholinesterase. But the completeness of recovery and the ultimate prognosis could not at that time be assessed. Moreover, the authors felt that many children suffered from a mild form of kwashiorkor that could not be accurately defined and needed much further investigation (Trowell et al. 1954).

Earlier, the distinction between marasmus and kwashiorkor in tropical countries had been made in an important monograph, in which children with fatty liver disease (kwashiorkor) were distinguished from those who were undernourished but had no evidence of liver damage (Waterlow 1948). The clinical manifestations of the second group were retarded growth and loss of body fat and resembled the condition known in Europe as infantile atrophy or marasmus. Cases of marasmus were mostly below 60 percent of expected weight for age – the current criterion for a marasmus diagnosis.

Kwashiorkor Since 1954

Following the authoritative reports of Brock and Autret (1952) and Trowell and colleagues (1954), there was intense research into PEM on a worldwide basis. This research was funded by international and national agencies now aware of the high infant and child morbidity and mortality occurring in developing or underdeveloped areas. In addition, academic institutions and individual researchers alike were stimulated to look into such questions. The results have been summarized in recent authoritative publications that have brought our knowledge of PEM up to date (Waterlow 1992; Carpenter 1994).

Dietary Treatment of Kwashiorkor

By 1954, it was clear that milk – as a source of protein – induced recovery, although mortality was still high in seriously ill cases. Brock (personal communication) posed the questions: What was it in milk that brought about recovery? Was it the protein in milk, and if so, what factors or amino acids of that protein initiated it? Were the other constituents of milk, such as the fat, carbohydrate, minerals, trace elements, vitamins, or as yet unknown factors, important for recovery?

A series of clinical trials and balance studies, conducted at Cape Town, South Africa (a nontropical area), from 1953 to 1956, concentrated on what exactly brought about the cure for kwashiorkor and established that a vitamin-free synthetic diet of 11 mostly essential amino acids, glucose, and a mineral mixture could cure the skin rashes, regenerate serum albumin concentration, improve appetite, and eliminate the edema suffered by kwashiorkor victims (Hansen, Howe, and Brock 1956). It was further shown that potassium deficiency as a result of diarrhea and poor intake of potassium-containing foods was an important cause of edema. In fact, edema could resolve without change in serum albumin concentration if potassium depletion was corrected (Hansen 1956).

These studies ended the mystery of what milk contained that initiated recovery from the disease by establishing that protein (amino acid) deficiency was an essential feature of kwashiorkor and that there was no unknown factor involved. Nonetheless, energy deficit was subsequently emphasized by many authors, but often children with kwashiorkor had enjoyed adequate energy intake and, as with all nutritional deficiency disorders, concurrent vitamin, mineral, and trace-element deficiencies can cause added complications. Milk contains all of these elements except for iron and was thus shown to be an ideal food with which to treat children suffering from kwashiorkor.

Because milk is not universally available, however, there was much interest during the 1950s in the question of whether plant proteins could provide a satisfactory substitute. Nitrogen balance studies during recovery from kwashiorkor (Hansen et al. 1960) revealed that nitrogen (protein) retention was very strong with a milk diet. On a maize (corn) diet, nitrogen retention was much less, but it was greatly improved by the addition of the amino acids missing in maize (lysine and tryptophan), or a legume (pea flour), fish flour, or milk (Hansen 1961). The Institute for Nutrition in Central America and Panama (INCAP) successfully developed a mixture of corn, sorghum, cottonseed flour, and yeast that had good results. It was commercially produced as "Incaparina" in Guatemala and other Central American countries, but it became too expensive for the people who needed it most (Carpenter 1994: 173–5). The extensive study and work with "Incaparina" did, however, prove that commercial vegetable mixtures could be used as a weaning food to promote growth and prevent kwashiorkor.

Between 1955 and 1975 there were numerous other efforts to find substitutes for milk (Carpenter 1994: 161–79). A Protein Advisory Group (PAG) was established by WHO in 1955 and subsequently supported by FAO and the United Nations International Children's Emergency Fund (UNICEF) to stimulate worldwide research into high-protein foods that might close the so-called protein gap between developed and underdeveloped countries. However, in 1974, a challenging article by D. S. McLaren called into question the importance of protein in the prevention of PEM and stressed that energy depletion was at least as important as lack of protein, if not more so. He argued that marasmus was a more widespread disease than kwashiorkor and that too much emphasis had been placed on – and too much money invested in – the production of protein-rich food mixtures, ". . . whilst children were lost in the unchecked scourge of malnutrition" (McLaren 1974: 95). Although much controversy followed this article (Carpenter 1994: 180–203), the emphasis on the production of high-protein foods waned, and interest became focused on improving food quantity rather than quality (Waterlow and Payne 1975).

Unfortunately, the debate that continues to the present day on the relative importance of protein and energy has often lost sight of the earlier concepts of kwashiorkor and marasmus. Marasmus implied wasting from overall energy lack or starvation, whereas kwashiorkor was characterized by a low-protein diet

that frequently had an adequate energy component. In between the two extremes is marasmic kwashiorkor, which has features of both. Milder cases that manifest only growth retardation (Table IV.D.7.1) can result from a lack of either protein or energy or a combination of the two. A current explanation of the dietary background of PEM is that variations in energy intake, total protein intake, and "quality" of protein (the amino acid pattern) are responsible for the individual clinical forms of PEM.

A protein intake of less than the minimal requirements will result in low serum proteins (hypoalbuminemia) and failure of growth, even in the presence of adequate energy intake (Hansen 1990). Unfortunately, in many parts of the world, most of the dietary protein comes from a single source, often a cereal. Cereals have the disadvantage of being low in total protein content and lacking in essential amino acids, such as lysine (in the case of wheat) or both lysine and tryptophan (in the case of maize). Populations subsisting solely on these foods are thus at risk of energy and protein depletion, and children in particular are at risk of PEM in one form or another. Inevitably, vitamin, mineral, and trace-element deficiencies can complicate PEM in varying degrees, as does infection.

In a review of much new work on protein and energy requirements, Waterlow (1992: 229–59) has concluded that contrary to much that has been published in recent years, some weaning diets in developing countries contain marginal amounts of protein, even when consumed in quantities that satisfy children's energy needs. Such a marginal diet may satisfy the protein needs of many – perhaps most – children, but not all. Any group of children, as of adults, appears to have a range of protein (and energy) requirements. On marginal intakes, children at the upper end of the range will be at risk. This does not conflict with a controversial finding (Gopalan 1968) that there was no difference, quantitative or qualitative, between the diets of children who developed kwashiorkor or marasmus.

The Liver and Kwashiorkor

A well-described characteristic of kwashiorkor is a fatty infiltration of the liver (Williams 1933). As already mentioned, Waterlow even described kwashiorkor as "fatty liver disease" and distinguished it from cases of undernourishment (marasmus) that showed no evidence of fatty infiltration (Waterlow 1948). In 1945, the Gillman brothers in South Africa published a paper on the successful treatment of fatty liver with a powdered stomach extract, "Ventriculan" (Gillman and Gillman 1945). They referred to their patients as cases of infantile pellagra and, using the liver biopsy technique, observed that such infants had greater or lesser amounts of fat in the liver (without infection) and that the fat accumulation resolved with successful treatment. The Gillmans felt that

"Ventriculan" supplied an essential substance, but other investigators could not confirm their findings and speculated that it was the protein in the diet that was producing the cure.

At that time, there was a high prevalence of cirrhosis of the liver in Africa, and it was thought that suffering PEM early in life might be an underlying cause. This suggestion was refuted, however, by a five-year follow-up study of kwashiorkor cases in a nontropical environment, which demonstrated that there was complete recovery of the liver with no residual cirrhosis (Suckling and Campbell 1957). In 1969, it was found that there was a connection between fatty liver and serum lipoprotein concentrations (Truswell et al. 1969), and it was hypothesized that fat accumulates in the liver because of the failure of fat transport out of the liver – a failure resulting from the impaired synthesis of apolipoprotein B, which, in turn, is a consequence of protein deficiency. This remains the current view (Waterlow 1992: 61–5).

PEM and Infection

A classic work on the synergistic association of malnutrition and infection was published in 1968 (Scrimshaw, Taylor, and Gordon 1968). In the case of PEM, the condition predisposes to other diseases, but diseases can also bring on the condition. For example, children with PEM are particularly susceptible to respiratory and gastrointestinal infections, whereas measles frequently precipitates severe PEM. An intriguing question is whether PEM interferes specifically with the protective immune responses or whether the generally poor environmental conditions associated with PEM (which implies frequent exposure to infection) means the child with PEM has less metabolic reserve to resist infection. For example, although exposure to measles will infect a well-nourished child and a child with PEM equally, the well-nourished child will survive with some weight loss, whereas the child with PEM, already underweight, becomes severely ill and frequently dies.

The various and complex ways in which immunity to infection can be impaired by PEM has been recently reviewed (Waterlow 1992: 290–324). Although in some communities the relationship between PEM and infection is linear, in others there is a much weaker association. But what is clear is that a child with severe PEM is seriously at risk of infection in any community. An early observer of reduction of cell-mediated immunity in PEM (Smythe et al. 1971) also noted reduction in the weight of the thymus gland as well as a reduced size of the spleen, lymph nodes, tonsils, appendix, and Peyer's patches.

Much interest has also been shown recently in the role of vitamin A deficiency in the susceptibility of PEM victims to infection, especially respiratory disease and diarrhea (Sommer, Katz, and Tarwotjo 1984). Earlier, it was demonstrated that some patients with kwashiorkor had dangerously low levels of plasma vitamin A (Konno et al. 1968), and treatment of measles with large doses of vitamin A has given good results (Hussey and Klein 1990), which, in conjunction with widespread immunization, means that measles is no longer the threat to the life of PEM victims that it was in 1969 (Morley 1969).

Diarrhea has always been a clinical characteristic of kwashiorkor and marasmus, both as a precipitating factor in a marginally malnourished child and as a continuing recovery-retarding drain of electrolytes, energy, and protein. The organisms and viruses responsible have been well defined (Waterlow 1992: 297), but in the case of PEM victims, frequently no pathogens are isolated. Balance studies on patients recovering from kwashiorkor have revealed a remarkably high daily fecal loss (500 to 1,000 grams [g] per day compared with a normal figure of 100–150 g/day), part of which was found to have been caused by lactose intolerance as a result of secondary lactase deficiency in the duodenum (Bowie, Brinkman, and Hansen 1965; Bowie, Barbezat, and Hansen 1967).

At the time, this discovery was thought to be a breakthrough in the cause of the diarrhea in PEM; further experience, however, revealed that lactose intolerance is not universal in PEM, although it can explain the severe diarrhea that frequently occurs when PEM cases are treated with milk. Diarrhea also occurs in PEM because the gastrointestinal tract atrophies and becomes paper-thin and almost transparent. The mucosa of the intestine has a reduced absorptive surface, and electron microscopy reveals considerable disorganization of the intracellular architecture (Shiner, Redmond, and Hansen 1973). Marked improvement occurs within a few days of treatment.

Looking back on the last 50 years of research on diarrhea in PEM, it is apparent that infection, intestinal atrophy, lactose intolerance, and immunological deficiencies all play their part. Recently, the advent of AIDS has particularly affected the immunological defenses in infected children, resulting in diarrhea, severe wasting, and marasmus or kwashiorkor. In a summing up of all the recent evidence, it can be said that there is a causal relationship between a state of malnutrition (PEM) and diarrhea morbidity and mortality (Waterlow 1992: 313, 339). The same may be said for respiratory disease (pneumonia) and measles, but not for malaria, which has little or no relation to the state of nutrition (Waterlow 1992: 333). Confounding factors in morbidity and mortality are vitamin A deficiency, breast feeding, sanitary facilities, and the mother's education, caring capacity, and availability.

PEM and Body Composition

The profound physical changes in marasmus (wasting) and kwashiorkor (edema) stimulated research into body composition when new techniques became available after 1950. In Waterlow's (1992) extensive review of the subject, he shows the inconsistencies between different studies and points out that there is still no agreed-upon understanding of the mechanisms of fluid-retention edema. There is a considerable loss of muscle mass and of fat, particularly in marasmus, and as a result, there is an increase of total body water as a percentage of body weight both in kwashiorkor with edema and in marasmus without edema.

Based on evidence available so far, the difference between the two could be that children with edema have more extracellular fluid, which is probably related to the extent of potassium depletion (Mann, Bowie, and Hansen 1972). Kwashiorkor children with edema have lower total body potassium than marasmus cases without edema. It is of interest that the increase of total body water – and of extracellular water as a percentage of body weight – represents a reversion to an earlier stage of development. This means that the weanling child with PEM has the composition and size of a younger child (Hansen, Brinkman, and Bowie 1965). Total body protein is severely depleted in PEM victims, and compared with normal children of the same height, there is a greater deficit of total protein than of body weight. Cellular protein is greatly depleted, but collagen (structural protein) is little affected (Picou, Halliday, and Garrow 1966). The brain is relatively well preserved when compared with other organs in PEM. However, computed tomography has recently shown there is some reversible shrinkage of brain mass (Househam and De Villiers 1987).

PEM in General

Growth Retardation and PEM

A constant feature of kwashiorkor has been growth retardation, occurring in children even before the disease is recognized. Weight, height, and bone development are all affected. In the second half of the twentieth century, anthropometric indices – weight, height, weight-for-height, arm circumference, and skinfold thickness – have been greatly refined and used extensively in the assessment of health and disease. In the Wellcome classification of PEM (Table IV.D.7.1), weight is used as a basis of defining differences between the various syndromes, which has proved most valuable in comparing PEM in different communities and countries.

F. Gomez, R. Ramos-Galvan, S. Frenk, and their colleagues in Mexico were the first to divide deficits in weight-for-age into three categories of severity, based on Harvard growth standards (Gomez et al. 1956). This classification had the drawback that it combined in one number the figures for height-for-age and weight-for-height (Waterlow 1992: 189) and was not widely adopted. The Harvard growth charts for height and weight of children in the United States proved

valuable as a standard against which to compare the growth of children with PEM. They were used in the initial Wellcome classification of PEM (Table IV.D.7.1), although later they were superseded by charts from the U.S. National Center for Health Statistics (NCHS), which – though similar – were more thoroughly worked out in terms of statistics. These charts were accepted and published by WHO as international standards (WHO 1983).

There have, however, been controversies concerning the use of these standards, ranging from questions about possible ethnic and environmental influences on growth to debates over the desirability of using national growth charts. Yet environmental and income differences have enormous effects in local surveys (Wittmann et al. 1967), which makes the use of local standards impractical, especially as there is often a secular trend toward improvement in disadvantaged groups. Currently, for the community and individual assessment of children with PEM, cutoff points on the international charts are employed; for example, children who are below the third percentile, or 2 standard deviations below the mean figures for height, weight, or weight-for-height indices, are suspect for PEM (Waterlow 1992: 212–28).

In clinic and field assessments, the "Road to Health" weight charts have revolutionized preschool health assessment even among the most unsophisticated populations. These charts are issued to mothers at the birth of their children and updated at each visit to a primary care center, physician, or hospital. D. Morley (1973) had demonstrated the value of continuously monitoring weight gain and of making the mother responsible for keeping the record. This is an interesting example of the practical procedures that grew out of the early observations of the growth of African children with kwashiorkor (Trowell et al. 1954: 70–3).

The retardation of growth caused by kwashiorkor immediately raised questions about its reversibility. Provided there were improvements in nutrition and environment, could a preschool child regain his or her genetic potential for growth? An early prospective study, started in 1959, monitored children admitted to hospitals with kwashiorkor for a subsequent period of 15 years (Bowie et al. 1980). This study showed that growth retardation resulting from severe PEM is reversible if environment and food intake are reasonably adequate during the prepubertal years. In similar studies, the increment in height was very much the same as that achieved by children in the United States, regardless of the degree of stunting at 5 years (Waterlow 1992: 195–211). As Waterlow has discussed, however, where catch-up has not occurred, stunting caused by long-continued protein and energy lack can lead to functional consequences, for example, a reduction in absolute capacity for physical work. For a given workload, people who are small, even though fit, are at a disadvantage. Thus, research on body growth in PEM has gone on to stimulate investigation into many interesting aspects of human development and function.

PEM and Intellectual Development

In 1963, a pioneering follow-up study of marasmic infants in South Africa focused on the possible effects of PEM on brain size and intellectual development (Stoch and Smythe 1963). This sparked ongoing worldwide research and intense political interest. Decreased brain weight in a state of malnutrition was reported from East Africa in 1965 (Brown 1965), and, as mentioned earlier, computed tomography has demonstrated that there is a reversible shrinkage of brain mass in kwashiorkor (Househam and De Villiers 1987). The more difficult assessment of the effect of PEM on intellectual development is confused by the interaction of nutrition per se and other environmental factors such as poor social conditions, nurturing, education, and environmental stimulation. In addition to protein and energy, other nutrients – iron, potassium, trace elements, or vitamins, to name a few – may be deficient, and this, too, may affect mental development (Grantham-McGregor 1992).

There is, however, some evidence that PEM does not necessarily cause permanent damage to the intellect. Follow-up studies have failed to demonstrate differences in intellectual development between ex-kwashiorkor patients, their nonaffected siblings, and other children from the same environment (Evans, Moodie, and Hansen 1971). Planned stimulation in hospital has produced recovery of cognitive development (to a normal level) in kwashiorkor children (Cravioto and Arrieta 1979: 899), and a recent study in Jamaica showed that a nutritional supplement provided significant benefits to stunted children between 9 and 24 months of age, as did stimulation alone – but the two together had the best result (Grantham-McGregor 1992).

A WHO symposium in 1974 concluded that in spite of the widely held opinion that PEM in early life permanently jeopardizes mental development, the evidence to support this contention was scanty. Twenty-three years later, this still appears to be the case, but it does seem probable that there is an interaction between malnutrition and other environmental factors, especially social stimulation, and that a child's intellectual status is the result of this interaction. However, good nutrition in the first two years of life enables an underprivileged child to make better use of what stimulus there is in the environment. This kind of beginning has a long-lasting effect on intelligence even if nutrition after this period is less than optimal (Evans et al. 1980).

The Social Background of PEM

Trowell and colleagues (1954: 49–51) pointed out that PEM has always been associated with poor communities and occurs among the most depressed social classes. These researchers also mentioned social customs at the time of weaning, and of course Williams interpreted the word kwashiorkor to mean the "disease of the displaced child" – displaced by the next baby (Williams 1935). In addition to these basic factors, overpopulation and the movement of rural people to urban areas were considered important. A. Moodie (1982), a social worker who devoted her working life to the study of the background of PEM, as seen in a nontropical area of Africa, has reviewed the literature, including some of her own studies. She noted the following as constituting the essential background of PEM:

1. Economic inadequacy or poverty – rural or urban.
2. Lack of sophistication and knowledge loosely termed ignorance and the cultural factors underlying this state.
3. Problems of overpopulation and too large families. (Here the mother suffers and it is through the mother that child nutrition is mediated. In all programs for prevention the well-being of the mother should be a priority.)
4. Social disorganization, especially illegitimacy and alcohol abuse.
5. High incidence of infection and diarrhea.
6. Early weaning and decline of breast feeding.

In an urban study funded by WHO, low income was found to be critical (Wittmann et al. 1967). In another investigation, sociological and cultural factors such as the working mother appeared to be more important (Shuenyane et al. 1977). There have been many studies throughout the world showing what Waterlow has termed the multiplicity of causes. He grouped them under three headings: lack of food, infection, and psychosocial deprivation (Waterlow 1992: 9–11). It has been pointed out that economists and other planners are now recognizing that nutritional indicators (for example, growth retardation or the clinical features of PEM) provide a more sensitive, objective, and easily collected measure of socioeconomic development than conventional indicators such as per capita income (Church, Burgess, and Burgess 1991: 569–70).

Prevention of PEM

With the high prevalence of PEM in some areas of developing countries (marasmus afflicts 5 to 10 percent and stunting 30 to 60 percent of the under-5 population), prevention has received much attention from international and government agencies. These organizations have been aided by economists and social scientists as well as by nutritionists and health scientists, and the literature has grown enormously (Waterlow 1992: 361–92).

The basic strategy for achieving "health for all" by the year 2000 is Primary Health Care (PHC). This plan includes growth monitoring, health education, maternal and child health care, family planning, immunization against major infantile diseases, and appropriate treatment of common diseases, like oral rehydration treatment for diarrhea. There is no doubt that these measures, implemented by PHC teams, have had an overall effect on preventing PEM, which has shown a decline in prevalence in many countries (Bellamy 1996: 54). The details of nutrition inputs in primary care are well described in a recent publication (Church et al. 1991). The problem of PEM needs a *holistic* approach. Health teams and public-health authorities can reduce mortality and morbidity with active programs of clinical care, rehabilitation, and food supplementation, but they cannot affect the prevalence of PEM resulting from underlying socioeconomic and cultural realities. Physicians must have the active, integrated, and effective cooperation and assistance of economists, agriculturalists, and governments to eradicate PEM.

Treatment of PEM

In a remarkable but little-quoted paper, published in an obscure journal, skimmed lactic acid milk was shown to reduce the 40 to 60 percent mortality of severe kwashiorkor to 20 percent (Altmann 1948). The author stressed the importance of small feeds initially until appetite returned. He also stressed the danger of severe dehydration that causes 5 out of 6 of the deaths. A colleague at the same hospital later found that the use of intravenous fluids in dehydrated cases cut mortality by half (Kahn 1959: 161–5). The same principles of feeding and rehydration are followed today (Waterlow 1992: 164–86), with perhaps more emphasis on oral rehydration. Refinements include supplements of potassium, magnesium, zinc, vitamin A, folic acid, and iron. Blood transfusion is used only for very severely anemic children. Because of the frequency of infections, antibiotics are routinely given and, in tropical areas, malaria and other infestations have to be dealt with, using appropriate therapy and prophylaxis. Mortality of severe PEM cases should now be less than 10 percent. Less severe cases of PEM respond well – with negligible mortality – to diets providing adequate energy and protein.

History of the Cause of PEM

Waterlow (1992) has concluded that there is no reason to abandon the concepts put forward many years ago, namely, that kwashiorkor develops when the diet has a low protein–energy (P/E) ratio and that when energy is limiting, the end result is marasmus. To this it should be added that individual children vary in their requirements of nutrients. If the P/E ratio is marginal, protein or energy may be a limiting factor for some children but not for others. Research has shown that total protein intake and the quality of the protein (the amino acid pattern) are also important. In areas where PEM occurs, vitamin, mineral, and trace-element deficiencies can complicate the basic syndrome to varying degrees, as does infection.

Recently, it has been hypothesized that all the serious features of kwashiorkor – edema, fatty liver, infection, and mortality – can be explained by an excess of free radicals (Golden and Ramdath 1987). This theory has not yet been firmly established, and in any case, children still have to be short of protein or energy before they become susceptible to free-radical excess. Another theory is that kwashiorkor results from aflatoxin poisoning (Hendrickse 1984). Aflatoxins come from fungi growing on improperly dried nuts. However, aflatoxins cannot be blamed for kwashiorkor and marasmus that occur where there is no aflatoxin contamination of the diet.

PEM in Perspective

In the nineteenth and twentieth centuries, PEM, as a particularly important nutritional deficiency in infants and children, has become recognized and better understood. This has come about through extensive worldwide observation and research, and recent emphasis has been on the effect of PEM on health, growth, and intellectual development.

As we enter the twenty-first century, we have the knowledge, if not always the means, to limit the prevalence of PEM in individuals and communities at risk. A looming danger is the "demographic trap," the situation that arises when population growth exceeds growth in food production or availability (King and Elliot 1994: 528). Signs of the trap are already present in several countries, particularly in Africa (Bonneux 1994). If this situation is not addressed by fertility control, PEM is likely to remain with us for the foreseeable future.

J. D. L. Hansen

Bibliography

Altmann, A. 1948. The syndrome of malignant malnutrition (kwashiorkor, infantile pellagra). Its conception as a protein deficiency and its treatment with skimmed lactic acid milk. *Clinical Proceedings (Cape Town)* 7: 32–53.

Beaven, P. 1957. A history of the Boston Floating Hospital. *Pediatrics* 19: 629–38.

Bellamy, C. 1996. *The state of the world's children.* Oxford.

Bonneux, L. 1994. Rwanda: A case of demographic entrapment. *Lancet* 344: 1689–90.

Bowie, M. D., G. O. Barbezat, and J. D. L. Hansen. 1967. Carbohydrate absorption in malnourished children. *American Journal of Clinical Nutrition* 20: 89–97.

Bowie, M. D., G. L. Brinkman, and J. D. L. Hansen. 1965. Acquired disaccharide intolerance in malnutrition. *Journal of Pediatrics* 66: 1083–91.

Bowie, M. D., A. D. Moodie, M. D. Mann, and J. D. L. Hansen. 1980. A prospective 15-year follow-up study of kwashiorkor patients. Part I. Physical growth and development. *South African Medical Journal* 58: 671–6.

Brock, J. F., and M. Autret. 1952. *Kwashiorkor in Africa.* Geneva.

Brown, R. E. 1965. Decreased brain weight in malnutrition and its implications. *East African Medical Journal* 42: 584–95.

Carpenter, K. J. 1994. *Protein and energy: A study of changing ideas in nutrition.* Cambridge.

Chapin, H. D. 1915. A plea for accurate statistics in infants' institutions. *Archives of Pediatrics* 32: 724–6.

Church, M. A., A. Burgess, and L. Burgess. 1991. Nutrition in primary care in developed and developing countries. In *Textbook of pediatric nutrition,* Third edition, ed. D. S. McLaren, D. Burman, M. R. Belton, and A. F. Williams, 557–91. Edinburgh.

Cravioto, J., and R. Arietta. 1979. Stimulation and mental development of malnourished infants. *Lancet* 2: 899.

Cullen, W. 1789. *A treatise of the materia medica.* 2 vols. Edinburgh.

Czerny, A., and A. Keller. 1925–8. *Des Kindes Ernährung, Ernährungs Störungen Ernährungs Therapie.* Second edition. Leipzig.

Darrow, D. C. 1946. The retention of electrolytes during recovery from severe dehydration due to diarrhoea. *Journal of Pediatrics* 28: 515–40.

Dickens, C. [1858] 1956. Speech on behalf of the Hospital for Sick Children. *Journal of Pediatrics* 49: 607.

Evans, D., M. D. Bowie, J. D. L. Hansen, et al. 1980. Intellectual development and nutrition. *Journal of Pediatrics* 97: 358–63.

Evans, D., A. D. Moodie, and J. D. L. Hansen. 1971. Kwashiorkor and intellectual development. *South African Medical Journal* 45: 1413–26.

Gillman, T., and J. Gillman. 1945. Powdered stomach in the treatment of fatty liver and other manifestations of infantile pellagra. *Archives of Internal Medicine* 76: 63–75.

Golden, M. H. M., and D. Ramdath. 1987. Free radicals in the pathogenesis of kwashiorkor. *Proceedings of the Nutrition Society* 46: 53–68.

Gomez, F., R. Ramos-Galvan, S. Frenk, et al. 1956. Mortality in second and third degree malnutrition. *Journal of Tropical Pediatrics* 2: 77–83.

Gopalan, C. 1968. Kwashiorkor and marasmus: Evolution and distinguishing features. In *Calorie deficiencies and protein deficiencies,* ed. R. W. McCance and E. M. Widdowson, 49–58. London.

Govan, C. D., and D. C. Darrow. 1946. The use of potassium chloride in the treatment of the dehydration of diarrhoea in infants. *Journal of Pediatrics* 28: 541–9.

Grantham-McGregor, S. M. 1992. The effect of malnutrition on mental development. In *Protein energy malnutrition,* ed. J. C. Waterlow, 344–60. London.

Habicht, J. P., R. Martorell, C. Yarbrough, et al. 1974. Height and weight standards for pre-school children. How relevant are ethnic differences in growth potential? *Lancet* 1: 611–15.

Hansen, J. D. L. 1956. Electrolyte and nitrogen metabolism in kwashiorkor. *South African Journal of Laboratory and Clinical Medicine* 2: 206–31.

  1961. The effects of various forms of supplementation on the nutritive value of maize for children. In *Meeting protein needs of infants and children.* National Academy of Sciences, National Research Council, Pub. No. 843, 89–102. Washington, D.C.

  1990. Malnutrition review. *Pediatric Reviews and Communications* 4: 201–12.

  1991. Marasmus. In *History of pediatrics, 1850–1950,* ed B. L. Nichols, A. Ballabriga, and N. Kretchmer, 219–31. New York.

Hansen, J. D. L., G. L. Brinkman, and M. D. Bowie. 1965. Body composition in protein calorie malnutrition. *South African Medical Journal* 39: 491–5.

Hansen, J. D. L., E. Howe, and J. F. Brock. 1956. Amino acids and kwashiorkor. *Lancet* 2: 911–13.

Hansen, J. D. L., and J. M. Pettifor. 1991. Protein energy malnutrition (PEM). In *Textbook of pediatric nutrition.* Third edition, ed. D. S. McLaren, D. Burman, N. R. Belton, and A. F. Williams, 357–90. Edinburgh.

Hansen, J. D. L., H. E. Schendel, J. A. Wilkins, and J. F. Brock. 1960. Nitrogen metabolism in children with kwashiorkor receiving milk and vegetable diets. *Pediatrics* 25: 258–82.

Hendrickse, R. G. 1984. The influence of aflatoxins on child health in the tropics with particular reference to kwashiorkor. *Transactions of the Royal Society of Tropical Medicine and Hygiene* 78: 427–35.

Holt, L. E., A. M. Courtney, and H. E. Fales. 1915. The chemical composition of diarrhea as compared with normal stools in infants. *American Journal of Diseases of Childhood* 9: 213–24.

Househam, K. C., and F. J. K. De Villiers. 1987. Computed tomography in severe PEM. *Archives of Disease in Childhood* 62: 589–642.

Hussey, G. D., and M. Klein. 1990. A randomized controlled trial of vitamin A in children with severe measles. *New England Journal of Medicine* 323: 160–4.

Jelliffe, D. B. 1959. Protein-calorie malnutrition in tropical preschool children: A review of recent knowledge. *Journal of Pediatrics* 54: 227–56.

Kahn, E. 1959. Prognostic criteria of severe protein malnutrition. *American Journal of Clinical Nutrition* 7: 161–5.

Kerpel-Fronius, E. 1947. Infantile mortality in Budapest in the year 1945. *Journal of Pediatrics* 3: 244–9.

  1983. *The pathophysiology of infantile malnutrition.* Budapest.

King, M., and C. Elliot. 1994. Cairo: Damp squibs or Roman candle? *Lancet* 344: 528.

Konno, T., J. D. L. Hansen, A. S. Truswell, et al. 1968. Vitamin A deficiency and protein calorie malnutrition in Cape Town. *South African Medical Journal* 48: 950–5.

Mann, M. D., M. D. Bowie, and J. D. L. Hansen. 1972. Potassium in protein calorie malnutrition. *South African Medical Journal* 46: 2062–4.

Martorell, R. 1985. Child growth retardation: A discussion of its causes and its relationship to health. In *Nutrition adaption in man,* ed. K. Blaxter and J. Waterlow, 13–30. London.

McLaren, D. S. 1974. The protein fiasco. *Lancet* 2: 93–6.

Moodie, A. 1982. Social background of child nutrition. In *Textbook of pediatric nutrition.* Second edition, ed. D. S. McLaren and D. Burman, 349–63. New York.

Morley, D. 1969. Severe measles in the tropics. *British Medical Journal* 1: 297–300, 363–5.

  1973. *Pediatric priorities in the developing world.* London.

Picou, D., J. Halliday, and J. S. Garrow. 1966. Total body protein, collagen and non-collagen protein in infantile protein malnutrition. *Clinical Science* 30: 346–51.

Scrimshaw, N. S., C. E. Taylor, and J. E. Gordon. 1968. *Interactions of nutrition and infection.* WHO Monograph Series, No. 57. Geneva.

Shiner, M., A. O. B. Redmond, and J. D. L. Hansen. 1973. The jejunal mucosa in protein energy malnutrition. A clinical, histological and ultrastructural study. *Experimental and Molecular Pathology* 19: 61–78.

Shuenyane, E., S. Mashigo, C. Eyberg, et al. 1977. A socioeconomic, health and cultural survey in Soweto. *South African Medical Journal* 51: 495–500.

Smith, C. A. 1983. *The Children's Hospital of Boston.* Boston, Mass.

Smythe, P. M., M. Schonland, G. G. Brereton-Stiles, et al. 1971. Thymolymphatic deficiency and depression of cell-mediated immunity in protein-calorie malnutrition. *Lancet* 2: 939–44.

Sommer, A., J. Katz, and I. Tarwotjo. 1984. Increased risk of respiratory disease and diarrhea in children with preexisting mild vitamin A deficiency. *American Journal of Clinical Nutrition* 40: 1090–5.

Stoch, M. B., and P. M. Smyth. 1963. Does undernutrition during infancy inhibit brain growth and subsequent intellectual development? *Archives of Disease in Childhood* 38: 546–52.

Suckling, P. V., and J. A. H. Campbell. 1957. A five-year follow-up of coloured children with kwashiorkor in Cape Town. *Journal of Tropical Pediatrics* 2: 173–80.

Trowell, H. C., J. M. P. Davies, and R. F. A. Dean. 1954. *Kwashiorkor.* London.

Truswell, A. S., J. D. L. Hansen, C. E. Watson, et al. 1969. Relation of serum lipids and lipoproteins to fatty liver in kwashiorkor. *American Journal of Clinical Nutrition* 22: 568–76.

Waterlow, J. C. 1948. *Fatty liver disease in the British West Indies.* Medical Research Council Special Report Series, No. 263. London.

   1991. Kwashiorkor. In *History of pediatrics, 1850–1950,* ed. B. L. Nichols, A. Ballabriga, and N. Kretchmer, 233–46. New York.

   1992. *Protein energy malnutrition.* London.

Waterlow, J. C., and P. R. Payne. 1975. The protein gap. *Nature* 258: 113–17.

Wellcome Trust Working Party. 1970. Classification of infantile malnutrition. *Lancet* 2: 302–3.

Williams, C. D. 1933. A nutritional disease of childhood associated with a maize diet. *Archives of Disease in Childhood* 8: 423–33.

   1935. Kwashiorkor: A nutritional disease of children associated with a maize diet. *Lancet* 2: 1151–2.

   [1963] 1973. The story of kwashiorkor. *Nutrition Reviews* 31: 334–40.

Wittmann, W., A. D. Moodie, S. Fellingham, and J. D. L. Hansen. 1967. An evaluation of the relationship between nutritional status and infection by means of a field study. *South African Medical Journal* 41: 664–82.

World Health Organization (WHO). 1974. Malnutrition and mental development. *WHO Chronicle* 28: 95–102.

   1983. *Measuring change in nutritional status. Guidelines for assessing the nutritional impact of supplementary feeding programmes for vulnerable groups.* Geneva.

IV.D.8 ❧ Scurvy

The human body requires an adequate supply of ascorbic acid (L-xyloascorbic acid or vitamin C) to enable it to function normally, and a lack of the vitamin results in the emergence of the condition known as scurvy (scorbutus or avitaminosis C). Unlike plants, and the majority of animals thus far studied, humans are unable to produce ascorbic acid endogenously and, thus, are dependent upon dietary sources – mainly fruit and vegetables – for a supply of the vitamin. In the absence of vitamin C, formation of collagen, an essential glycoprotein component of connective tissue, is impaired, which is believed to be the main underlying biochemical lesion in scurvy (Counsell and Hornig 1981; Englard and Seifter 1986).

The earliest signs of scurvy (fatigue and lassitude) may emerge in humans some 12 weeks after removal of dietary vitamin C, and the more overt traditional signs (hemorrhagic spots under the skin *[petechiae],* softening of the gums, and defective wound healing) after some 17 to 26 weeks of deprivation.

In 1753, James Lind concluded his pioneer study of scurvy with a chronological *Bibliotheca Scorbutica,* which imparted a mild historical flavor to his text (Stewart and Guthrie 1953). But more than a century was to pass before the first sustained efforts to produce a history of the disease emerged. One of these was J. Maré's 200-page article in the *Dictionnaire Encyclopédique des Sciences Médicales* in 1880, and the second was August Hirsch's 60-page article in his *Handbook of Geographical and Historical Pathology* (1883–6). Both of these pioneer works are now completely eclipsed by K. J. Carpenter's comprehensive *History of Scurvy and Vitamin C* (1986), to which the reader is referred for a more extended treatment.

Simple logic dictates that scurvy became a clinical possibility when evolving hominoids (unlike most other animals) lost the ability to biosynthesize vitamin C from carbohydrate precursors. This loss would, presumably, only have occurred in an environment that provided early humans with an adequate intake of dietary vitamin C. By the same token, scurvy itself would not have emerged until a change in food consumption patterns or in the seasonal availability of the vitamin resulted in a deprivation of vitamin C.

The main dietary sources of vitamin C are fruit and vegetables, particularly when eaten raw, and to a much lesser extent, fresh meat (salting or drying meat results in a loss of its vitamin C content). Grains, nuts, eggs, and dairy products (with the exception of fresh milk, which contains small amounts) provide little or no vitamin C.

There can be little doubt that the unstable and fluctuating environmental conditions of primitive humans must have, from time to time, produced highly scorbutigenic situations, but the precise frequency of the disease in prehistoric and early historic times is obscure. Some commentators have claimed to discern descriptions of scurvy in the writings of early classical writers such as Pliny and Paulus Aeginita, but this must remain a matter of considerable conjecture.

There is some evidence that scurvy afflicted the armies of the Crusaders in the thirteenth century, and the writings of Jacques de Vitry (c. 1220) and Jean Sire de Joinville (1224–1319) have been quoted in this respect (Major 1978: 585–6). Indeed, de Joinville's description of the "army sickness" reveals a situation at least as fearful as the depredations of the attacking Turks:

... our legs shrivelled up and became covered with black spots, and spots of the colour of earth, like an old boot: and in such of us as fell sick the gums became putrid with sores, and nor man recovered of that sickness, but all had to die.... The proud flesh in our men's mouth grew to such excess that the barbour-surgeons were obliged to cut it off, to give them a chance of chewing their food or swallowing anything. It was piteous to hear through the camp the shrieks of the people who were being operated for proud flesh, for they shrieked like women in childbirth. (Major 1978: 586)

Scurvy as an Occupational Disease

Curiously enough, the change that most clearly and finally precipitated the emergence of scurvy as a recognizable disease was not so much dietary as technological. Scurvy first established itself as a discrete and clearly definable feature of early medicine because of those technological advances that enabled the building of ships capable of prolonged sea voyages.

By the end of the fifteenth century the ship had acquired the structure that was to characterize it for the next three centuries, and the newer naval technology meant that humans could now remain at sea for months at a time – long enough to deprive themselves of an adequate supply of the fresh fruit and vegetables that are the main dietary source of vitamin C. Consequently, it was during the early voyages of exploration in the fifteenth century that the first clear pictures of scurvy emerged. In this sense scurvy (or scorbutus as it was described in the Latin texts of the day) may truly be regarded as one of the earliest occupational diseases.

Perhaps the most widely quoted example of explorer's scurvy is that described by Jacques Cartier, the Breton explorer, who during his discovery of the Saint Lawrence River in 1536 lost 25 of his crew to a "strange and cruell disease." Certainly his description of their condition – the loss of strength and "their skins spotted with spots of blood of a purple colour ... [and] their gummes so rotten, that all the flesh did fall off, even to the rootes of the teeth, which did also almost all fall out" is consistent with the petechiae and connective tissue defects now accepted as cardinal features of scurvy (Major 1978: 586).

But a similar condition prevailed among the crew of Vasco da Gama during his return voyage from Africa in 1498; and almost a hundred years later Richard Hawkins could assert that during his 20 years at sea he had witnessed some 10,000 cases of scurvy (Carpenter 1986: 1–26).

A century and a half after that, George Anson lost three-fourths of his men and officers, mostly to scurvy, in his 1740–4 voyage around the world. In fact, it has been estimated that during the critical period between 1600 (when long sea voyages had become more common) and 1800 (when the prophylactic effect of lemon juice rations had proved effective), scurvy was responsible for over 1 million deaths among seamen – almost certainly more than the sum total lost during the same period in naval battles, shipwrecks, and to diseases other than scurvy (Roddis 1951: 48, 72).

In the seventeenth century scurvy was considered primarily a scourge of sailors and soldiers. "In Navies and Camps, Scorbutick Feavers are very frequent, and arrive to a great height of malignity, sweeping them away like the Plague sometimes" wrote Everard Maynwaringe in 1664, adding "And I remember, in a hard and long voyage at sea, most of our people were very Scorbutick ... who at our first setting out were sound and healthy" (Maynwaringe 1679: 57).

Much was written about the possible causes of scurvy among sailors. Bad (i.e., cold and wet) air, poor diet, idleness, and a melancholy outlook were viewed as major predisposing causes. Overindulgence in salted meat was held to be a main dietary cause – particularly as this could explain the peculiar prevalence of the condition among sailors. And some commentators introduced their own specific dietary causes. Thomas Willis, for example, blamed sugar, whereas Maynwaringe accused tobacco, although neither explanation gained general acceptance.

"Land Scurvy"

George Budd, one of the more competent writers on scurvy in the early nineteenth century, wrote, "Scurvy has, unquestionably, existed in the north of Europe from the most remote antiquity. That we have no mention of it in the early history of the northern nations must be imputed to the extreme ignorance of the people, especially as regards medicine" (Budd 1840: 58).

It is the case that medieval medical texts and herbals contain no clearly identifiable references to scurvy, although the numerous remedies for loose or "wagging" teeth have sometimes been thought to indicate unrecognized scurvy (e.g., Henslow 1899: 112). Nor does scurvy appear to have been included among the main diseases responsible for hospitalization in medieval England (Clay 1909). Thus, as already suggested, the general consensus would appear to relate the recognition and acceptance of scurvy as a specific clinical lesion to its occurrence among sailors during the fifteenth and sixteenth centuries.

Certainly it was in the sixteenth century that sporadic references to scurvy began to appear in the medical texts and herbals. Thus, although there are no recognizable references to scurvy in the herbals of Leonhard Fuchs (1542), Hieronymus Bock (1552), and Pietro Andrea Mattioli (1565), William Turner's *Herbal* (1568) comments on its appearance on the Continent. And Henry Lyte's translation of R. Dodoens' *Cruÿdeboeck* (1578) refers to:

Spoonewote [*Cochlearia* sp., scurvy grass] ... a singular remedie against the disease of the mouth ... called by the Hollanders and Frise-landers Scuerbuyck, against whiche evill it hath bene lately proved to be very good and is in great estimation and much used of the Hollan-ders and Friseans. (Dodoens 1578: 117–18)

Similarly, J. C. von Kraftheim's *Consiliorum et Episto-larum Medicinalium* (1591: 285) gave dietary pre-cepts to be followed in scurvy. But surprisingly, Philip Barrough's comprehensive *The Method of Physick* (third edition, 1596) contained no reference to scurvy, nor did Felix Plater's *Observationum in Homines Affectibus Plerisque, Corpori & Animo ...* (1651). However, William Clowes, in his *A Profitable and Necessary Booke of Observations ...* (1596) described treating two sailors who were "sicke at the sea of the Scorby."

One of the earliest descriptions of scurvy in Eng-lish can be found in Thomas Johnson's version of J. Gerarde's *Herbal* (1633) as part of the entry for scurvy grass *(Cochlearia officinalis)*, the most favored of the antiscorbutic herbs (see following). It related scurvy to its supposed classical "precursors" and is worth quoting in some detail:

The juice of Spoonewort given to drinke in Ale or Beere ... perfectly cureth the disease called of *Hippocrates, Voluulus Hematites:* of *Pliny, Stomacace;* of *Marcellus, Oscedo* and of the later writers, *Scorbutum* of the Hollanders and Frisians, *Scuerbuyck:* in English, the Scurvie ... this filthy, lothsome, heavy, and dull disease, which is very troublesome and of long continu-ance. The gums are loosed, swolne, and exulcer-ate, the mouth greevously stinking; the thighes and legs are withall very often full of blew spots, not much unlike those that come of bruises; the face and the rest of the body is oftentimes of a pale colour: and the feet are swolne, as in a dropsie ... a disease haunting the campes, which vexe them that are besieged and pinned up and it seemeth to come by eating of salt meates, which is increased and cherished with the cold vapors of the stone walls ... Hip-pocrates has written: their gums (saith he) are infected, and their mouthes stinke that have great spleenes or milts and ... can hardly be cured of this malladie, especially of the ulcers in the legs and blacke spots. The same is affirmed by Paulus Aegineta in this third booke, 49 chap-ter, where you may easily see the difference between this disease and the black jaunders, which many times are so confounded together that the difference or distinction is hard to be known but by the expert chirurgions who offentimes serving in the ships, as wel her Majesties as merchants, are greatly pestered with the curing thereof.... (Gerarde 1633: 402)

By the early seventeenth century references to cases of scurvy among land dwellers were beginning to appear; initially, it was believed that there were two forms of the disease, and references were made to "sea scurvy" and to "land scurvy." This dichotomy continued until it was finally dispelled by Lind in 1753. Such an apparent sudden increase in the inci-dence of scurvy among land dwellers in Britain dur-ing the seventeenth century was commented on by a number of writers. Marchmont Nedham in his *Medela Medicinae* (1665) supported his claim that scurvy was on the increase in England by referring to the Bills of Mortality, which recorded an increase in the deaths from scurvy from 5 in 1630 to over 100 in 1656. Similarly, Gideon Harvey commented in 1675:

Many years it [scurvy] remained on that Coast [i.e., Holland] before we were sensible of it here in England: for there are many Physicians yet living who in the former part of their Prac-tice had so much as heard of the Name of this Disease, whereas within the last 20 or 30 years past it's grown very familiar among us. (Harvey 1675: 211)

There is confirmatory evidence that in Wales, too, scurvy was regarded as a new disease at the begin-ning of the seventeenth century. Sir Thomas Wiliems of Trefriw, a priest and practicing physician, compiled the manuscript for his projected *Thesaurus Linguae Latinae et Cambrobritannicae* during the period 1604–7; under the entry for the plant "Britanica" he refers to scurvy as "a new disease in our land, Wales" ("clevyt newydh yn ein gwlad ni Cymru") (Hughes 1990).

William Vaughan (1575–1641), also writing from Wales, reflected the growing importance of scurvy in seventeenth-century medicine in his *The Newlanders Cure* (1630). He recommended the tops and leaves of turnips as antiscorbutics; more significant, perhaps, he used contemporary thought on scurvy to illustrate his anti-papist sentiments in his verses "Description of the Catholicke Scurvy ingendered by the Mystery of Iniquity ...":

..As doth the former scurvy beate
For want of Sunne and Motions heate
Upon the Spleene, the Breathe and Skinne
So doth that Old and Scurvy sinne
Withe Purple Spots go on to Stayne
Both Soule and Body, all for Gaine ...
(Vaughan 1630: 112)

Whether these writings reflected a true increase in the incidence of scurvy among land dwellers, or merely indicated a greater awareness of its presence, is not known. According to John Floyer (better known for his introduction of a minute watch to measure pulse rate), "Scurvy was a new Name for an old Disease" – and there were others who regarded scurvy merely as an older disease that had changed its nature (Floyer 1722: 3; King 1970: 149).

Diet and Scurvy

A true increase in the incidence of scurvy would have required a fairly substantial change in the dietary pattern (or in the dietary availability of vitamin C), and there is little evidence that any such substantial and sudden change occurred in Britain at the time. Rather, such knowledge as is available would appear to suggest that the consumption of turnips, cabbage, and other vegetables by the "husbandman" sector of the population of Britain in the seventeenth century would have provided them with adequate amounts of the vitamin (Powicke 1926).

Yet with diets of the poorer classes of the day, one is less certain. And of earlier centuries little is known, although if one accepts the general view that the pre-sixteenth-century working-class diet was predominantly grain-based with supplements of salted and/or dried meat or fish but with very little fresh fruit and vegetables, then scurvy must have been of frequent occurrence (Prentice 1939: 118–36).

Of the fifteenth-century peasant diet, it has been written:

> . . . it seems likely that the winter diet of salt bacon, bread and peas gave little protection against scurvy, so that by the end of the winter most of the poor country people must have been in at least a pre-scorbutic condition. (Drummond and Wilbraham 1964: 77)

However, the comparative absence of any clearly recognizable references to scorbutic afflictions among a population that during the winter period presumably subsisted on a scorbutigenic diet is somewhat puzzling.

It was not until the enthusiasm of the Dutch market gardeners spilled over into seventeenth-century Britain that a general, albeit small, reduction in the scorbutigenic potential of the British diet occurred. Yet this, for some unaccountable reason, would seem to be the period that witnessed an apparent increase in the incidence of scurvy. However, a much more significant change in the British diet was yet to occur. The end of the seventeenth century witnessed the introduction of the potato on a large scale – a crop that was subsequently to become, for a very substantial proportion of the population, the main dietary source of vitamin C and, hence, the prime protector against widespread scurvy.

Potatoes and Scurvy

In 1662 a Committee of the Royal Society considered a proposition "to plant Potatoes through all ye parts of England," and in 1664 Forster pressed the case for widespread cultivation of the potato in his *England's Happiness Increased.* It is not known to what extent Forster's advice was acted upon, although Thomas Moffet claimed in 1665 that "pottato-roots are now so common and known amongst us, that even the Husbandman buys them to please his Wife" (Moffet 1746: 324). In 1691 Richard Baxter, the religious writer, in his last literary composition *(The Poor Husbandman's Advocate)* suggested that all smallholders should plant a quarter of an acre of potatoes to provide themselves with "a half year's wholesome food" (Powicke 1926).

Nevertheless, it is unlikely that these statements reflected any widespread use of the potato, and it is probable that until the end of the seventeenth century it remained primarily a horticultural curiosity cultivated by that sector of the populace least likely to suffer from dietary inadequacies, a situation reflected by the somewhat esoteric recipes for its use in the cookery books of the period (e.g., Salmon 1696: 263).

In the eighteenth century, however, potatoes were much more widely grown. According to *The Complete Farmer* (1777):

> the culture of this plant has, within these last thirty years, been extended to almost every part of England. . . . It is esteemed, and now very generally used at the tables of persons of all ranks; and inestimable for the poor being a cheap and very wholesome food . . . in Ireland, particularly in the province of Munster, they are the principal, and almost the only food of the poor there for almost eight months in the year. (Society of Gentlemen 1777)

The importance of the potato in the social etiology of scurvy has not always been fully appreciated, although Carpenter has clearly underlined the significant role that it played in the history of scurvy, particularly in Britain and in Ireland. Its significance stems from two facts. First, although comparatively low in vitamin C (10 to 20 milligrams [mg] per 100 grams [g]), potatoes were eaten in such large amounts that they frequently accounted for a very high proportion of the vitamin, and for many they represented its sole source. In Ireland, during the nineteenth century, daily consumptions of up to 4.5 to 6.5 kilograms (kg) per person were recorded (Letheby 1870: 26; Salaman 1970: 331), which would have provided an estimated daily intake of about 400 to 600 milligrams of vitamin C – some 40 to 60 times the quantity required to prevent scurvy. In the 1840s, scurvy was, therefore, a natural consequence of the failure of the potato crop. As suggested earlier, unlike potatoes, cereal grains contain no vitamin C, and thus the maize imported to alleviate the famine had no effect at all against scurvy.

It is also important to note that potatoes can be stored for many months with very little loss of fluid (and consequently with a retention of ascorbic acid), thereby providing a source of the vitamin well into the winter when fresh sources are absent. Even today a substantial sector of the population of Britain obtains the bulk of its vitamin C from potatoes, particularly in the winter months.

By the same token, many of the outbreaks of scurvy in the nineteenth century (as in the Irish Famine of 1845-8 and in the Exeter hospital epidemic in 1846) were directly traceable to a reduced supply of potatoes (Carpenter 1986: 101; Shapter 1847: 945-8). In charting the history of scurvy, a role of paramount significance must be accorded to the potato; its establishment in Italy and Spain some centuries before it attained popularity in Britain was possibly a factor in determining the higher frequency of scurvy in northern Europe in the sixteenth and seventeenth centuries (Salaman 1970: 142-6). During the last three centuries the potato has doubtless protected millions of people from the ravages of the disease.

Early Writers and Theories

Many of the reports of scurvy in Europe in the sixteenth century emphasized its essential prevalence in the colder northeastern areas. "The Scurvy is properly said to be endemical in most of our Northern Countrys, that border upon the Baltick Sea, or adjacent to the German Ocean: As Denmark, Swedland, Norway, Ffrisland, Holland, England etc. But in High Germany, France, Spain and Italy, the Scurvy is accounted sporadical . . . but here and there one" (Maynwaringe 1679: 16). Such was the comparative rarity of scurvy in southern France that Lazarus Riverius, writing "from my study in Montpelier on the 8th of July 1653," dismissed the condition, commenting, "The scurvy is usual in the North [of France?] but almost unknown in the South . . . (Riverius 1655: 357-61). The non sequitur that a cold and damp atmosphere conduced to scurvy prevailed in Europe until well into the eighteenth century.

A. S. Hess, however, in commenting on the apparent absence of references to scurvy in the classical medical writings, offered a truer explanation: "Greek, Roman and Arabic writers do not seem to have been acquainted with scurvy. This is as we should expect, for fruits and vegetables grew in such plenty in these southern countries that scurvy must have been a disorder of rare occurrence" (Hess 1920: 1). This (together with the comparatively early adoption of the potato in southwestern Europe) is presumably also the explanation of the differential distribution pattern of scurvy reported for Europe in the sixteenth and seventeenth centuries.

A parallel development to this apparent increase in scurvy (or the recognition of it) among land dwellers in parts of northern Europe in the seventeenth century was the appearance of the first medical texts devoted entirely to the condition. Unfortunately, however, it is impossible to determine whether the appearance of the texts resulted in an increased awareness of the condition, and hence an apparent increase in its incidence, or whether the texts were produced in response to a genuine increase in the frequency of the disease.

In any event, these medical texts first appeared on the Continent, and J. Ecthius's De Scorbuto (1541) is usually regarded as the pioneer study; the ensuing two centuries saw a substantial proliferation of "scorbutic" texts – Lind in 1753 referred to some 40 of them in his Treatise; but few of these early compilations showed any great originality of thought or interpretation. Probably the two most influential were John Wier's De Scorbuto published in Basel as a part of his Medicarum Observationum . . . in 1567 and Severinus Eugalenus's De Morbo Scorbuto Liber . . . first published in 1604 and then again in much changed forms under the hands of subsequent editors up to 1658.

John Wier [Wierus] – better known perhaps for his De Praestigiis Daemonum (1563) (a treatise opposing the persecution of witches) – was probably the more scientific of the two. His treatise on scurvy was reprinted in its entirety by Daniel Sennert in 1624 as one of the six component works in his De Scorbuto (1624). In the prefatory remarks to an English translation that appeared in 1622, the translator indicated that he had translated Wierus rather than Ronsseus or Langius or Ecthius because of a tendency on their part to "wade into deep difficulties" and because they "paynteth out the signes, and poynteth to the cure, but affordeth not the pith and marrow of speciall medicines . . ." (Wier 1622: ii).

Wier's De Scorbuto was also the basis of the Traetice of the Scorbut written in 1676 by Gwilym Pue [Puw], a Welsh Catholic recusant priest and physician. Pue's treatise, incidentally, contained a case history of a supposedly scorbutic patient – probably Pue himself (Hughes In press). S. Eugalenus exerted a similar influence during a slightly later period, and he was freely quoted until well into the eighteenth century, but his work, even in the later "improved" editions, was less well presented and much more anecdotal than that of Wier. Lind was highly critical of Eugalenus and of Willis, the English physician who uncritically represented Eugalenus in his Tractatus de Scorbuto (1667).

Despite the considerable attention that it attracted, very little, in reality, was known about scurvy in the seventeenth and eighteenth centuries. There was fairly general agreement about its main clinical features but little was known of its cure and still less of its cause. The traditional belief that it was essentially a disease of the spleen persisted until well into the eighteenth century. The situation was further complicated by a tendency to assume that there were different types of scurvy. As indicated earlier, it was believed that "sea scurvy" was a different condition from "land scurvy"; there were references too to "hot scurvy" and to "cold scurvy," to "acid scurvy" and to "alkaline scurvy," and the situation was further confused by the belief that these categories were not mutually exclusive.

Furthermore, there were probably different "grades" of scurvy, corresponding to different degrees of vitamin C deprivation. Scurvy, when it occurred among land dwellers, was presumably often a case of chronic partial vitamin C deficiency (hypovitaminosis C) rather than the "full" scurvy (avitaminosis C) that afflicted sailors after their much longer periods of complete deprivation of the vitamin. Hence the confusion between the clear-cut symptoms of complete deficiency among sailors and the chronic (and often seasonal) hypovitaminosis C that could befall land dwellers.

The "Antiscorbutic" Plants

The classical interpretation that diseases and ill health reflected a change in the humoral balance of the body was a powerful element in seventeenth- and eighteenth-century medical thought. Dietary and pharmacological treatments advocated for diseases were frequently devised primarily to counteract or correct the supposed deviant humoral patterns. Edward Strother, in introducing his influential *An Essay on Sickness and Health* in 1725, was quite categorical on this point: "It is therefore a standing Rule that our Meats and Drinks ought to consist, as nearly as can be, of Particles contrary to the Cause of the Disease reigning . . ." (1725: 30).

Correspondingly, eighteenth-century texts on diet and nutrition attached considerable importance to a categorization of foods in terms of their supposed humoral properties so that physicians could select appropriate foods to counteract specific diseases. "The best way of curing the Gout," wrote W. Stephens (1732: 60) "is to hinder the Generation of this gouty Humour in the Body; this is to be effected no other way, that I know of, but by Diet."

The same was to hold true in the case of scurvy. For "hot," "alkaline," "sea," scurvy, cooling acidic foods, such as oranges and lemons, were advocated; "cold," "acid," "land," scurvy, in contrast, could be treated by the "hot" antiscorbutic plants such as scurvy grass, brooklime, and the cresses. Thus there developed a tradition, reinforced by empirical observations, that "sea-scurvy" could be treated by oranges and lemons, whereas the methods of choice for scurvy among land dwellers centered on the antiscorbutic herbs. When John Woodall extolled the virtues of lemon juice as a cure for scurvy among sailors he carefully contrasted its value with that of the traditional antiscorbutics "namely Scurvy-grasse, Horse reddish roots, Nasturtia Aquatica . . . and many other good meanes" whose virtues extended, however, "only to the Cure of those which live at home . . ." (Woodall 1639: 61).

Turner, in describing the virtues of brooklime in his *Herbal* of 1568, penned what must be one of the earliest references to scurvy in an English herbal:

". . . I have proved it my selfe by experience that brooklyme is very good for a decease that reigneth much in Freseland called the Scourbuch. I sod the herbe in butter milke, the cheese and butter taken away, and gave the patientes it so" (128). Clearly, this statement lends further support to the belief that scurvy was either comparatively rare or unrecognized in sixteenth-century Britain.

As it happens, the concentration of foliar ascorbic acid in the three antiscorbutic herbs (*Cochlearia officinalis* [scurvy grass], *Veronica beccabunga* [brooklime], and *Nasturtium officinale* [watercress]) – and particularly in scurvy grass – is low when compared with other angiosperms. Although fresh preparations of the "antiscorbutics" would, in sufficient amounts, certainly have cured scurvy, it seems likely that their entry into, and retention by, sixteenth-century medical literature probably reflected a priori thoughts on the humoral nature of "land scurvy" more than any observed genuine therapeutic value.

James Cook provided his crew with a wide range of vegetables and fruit and scurvy grass collected whenever available, and this, no doubt, protected them from the disease. Had Cook, however, relied on fresh scurvy grass alone, a weekly supply of some 100 pounds of scurvy grass leaf would have been required for a ship with a complement of 100, to provide the Dietary Reference Value of vitamin C (40 mg daily) for the prevention of scurvy.

Nevertheless, the antiscorbutic triumvirate retained a position of importance in the herbals of the sixteenth, seventeenth, and eighteenth centuries, although, as has recently been shown, almost all of the original ascorbic acid would have been lost because of the form in which the preparations were ultimately administered – a finding that must cast considerable doubt on their overall effectiveness (Hughes 1990).

A Nosological Safety Net

The picture was further confused in the eighteenth century by a readiness of physicians to describe a whole range of unrelated conditions as "scurvy"; and the term became a convenient nosological safety net for the not inconsiderable number of diagnostic failures of the century. In the words of one physician: "It is yet a suficient Answer to Patients when they enquire into their ailments to give this Return to a troublesome Enquirer, that their Disease is the Scurvy, they rest satisfied that they are devoured with a Complication of bad Symptoms . . ." (Strother 1725: 150). At the end of the century the maverick Sir John Hill declared on the title page of his *The Power of the Water Dock against the Scurvy* (1777) that "If any one is ill, and knows not his Disease, Let him suspect the Scurvy."[1]

With such confusion surrounding scurvy, one cannot with any certitude delineate the true importance of the ailment among land dwellers in the seventeenth and eighteenth centuries, and in the absence of details of dietary patterns (and particularly of the consumption of vegetables by the population in general), there must remain considerable doubts about its true incidence. About all that is clear is that the use of the term "scurvy" was almost certainly more common than the disease itself.[2]

Nevertheless, epidemics did occur; Hirsch lists some 30 such outbreaks during the eighteenth century in such diverse areas as Canada, Denmark, and Russia (1885: 521-3). Among the seafaring population, however, the picture was much more clearly delineated, and right through the seventeenth and eighteenth centuries scurvy was the most feared of all the hazards associated with long sea voyages, and with good cause. As we have already noted, it has been estimated that between 1600 and 1800 scurvy accounted for some million deaths at sea and that in almost every naval campaign of any length during this period scurvy played an important role (Roddis 1951: 72).

James Lind

The name of James Lind is deservedly associated with a substantial advance in the understanding of scurvy. A ship's surgeon, he soon came face-to-face with the ravages of the disease among sailors. Others before him had successfully used empirically discovered remedies in the cure of scurvy, and their use of citrus fruits as the antiscorbutic remedy par excellence was well established (see, for example, Zulueta and Higueras 1981). This was presumably known to Lind, who himself quoted J. G. H. Kramer's observation ". . . if you have oranges, lemons or citrons . . . you will, without other assistance cure this dreadful disease" (Stewart and Guthrie 1953: 154).

John Woodall in his *The Surgions Mate* (1617) quite clearly drew attention to the prophylactic value of lemon juice – which had, in any case, already been successfully used by James Lancaster in his East Indian voyage at the beginning of the century. In 1696 William Cockburn underlined the importance of fresh fruit and vegetables to sailors in his *Sea Disease, or Treatise of their Nature, Cause and Cure* and in his *Essay on Sickness and Health* (1725). Edward Strother also had pointed out that "eating Lemons and Oranges" would cure scurvy in sailors.

But Lind's achievement was that he subjected these empirically derived claims, and others, to the test of scientific experimentation in what has been claimed to be the first controlled clinical study in the history of medicine. Here is a description of it in Lind's own words:

On the 20th of May, 1747, I took twelve patients in the scurvy, on board the *Salisbury* at sea. Their cases were as similar as I could have

them. They all in general had putrid gums, the spots and lassitude, with weakness of the knees. They lay together in one place, being a proper appartment for the sick in the fore-hold; and had one diet common to all, viz. water-gruel sweetened with sugar in the morning; fresh mutton-broth often times for dinner; at other times puddings, boiled biscuit with sugar etc. and for supper, barley and raison, rice and currants, sago and wine, or the like. Two of these were ordered each a quart of cyder a day. Two others took twenty-five gutts [drops] of *elixir vitriol* three times a day, upon an empty stomach; using a garble strongly acidulated with it for their mouths. Two others took two spoonsfuls of vinegar three times a day upon an empty stomach having their gruels and other food well acidulated with it, as also the gargle for the mouth. Two of the worst patients, with the tendons in the L arm rigid (a symptom none of the rest had) were put under a course of sea water. Of this they drank half a pint every day, and sometimes more or less as it operated, by way of gentle physic. Two others had each two oranges and one lemon given them each day. These they [ate] with greediness at different times, upon an empty stomach. They continued but six days under this course, having consumed the quantity that could be spared. The two remaining patients took the bigness of a nutmeg three times a day, of an electuary recommended by an hospital-surgeon, made of garlic, mustard seed, *rad. raphan.*, Balsam of Peru, and gum myrrh; using for common drink, barley water well acidulated with tamarinds; by a decoction of which with the addition of *cremor tartar,* they were gently purged three or four times during the course.

The consequence was that the most sudden and visible good effects were perceived from the use of the oranges and lemons; one of those who had taken them, being at the end of six days fit for duty. The spots were not indeed at that time quite off his body, nor his gums sound; but without any other medicine, than a gargarism of *elixir vitriol* he became quite healthy before we came into Plymouth which was on the 16th of June. The other was the best recovered of any in his condition; and being now deemed pretty well, was appointed nurse to the rest of the sick. Next to the oranges, I thought the cyder had the best effects. . . . (Stewart and Guthrie 1953: 145-7)

Lind's note on the partial efficacy of cider has been quoted in support of the thesis that cider, as prepared traditionally in the eighteenth century, would have contained significant amounts of vitamin C and that it could have played a significant role in the prevention of scurvy (French 1982: 59-66). Although this may have been the case, such evidence as is available would suggest that in general, very little of the original vitamin C would survive a fermentation procedure (Hughes 1975, 1990).

Lind's book *A Treatise of the Scurvy* appeared in 1753; a second edition was published in 1757 and a third and "updated" version in 1772 (a bicentenary reprint of the first edition was published in 1953 [Stewart and Guthrie 1953]). A French translation appeared in 1756 with subsequent reprints, and an Italian translation was published in 1766.

Not all of Lind's conclusions, however, were characterized by the same degree of scientific acumen that he displayed in his famous "scurvy trial," and it is clear that he claimed "antiscorbutic" properties for preparations that modern analysis would suggest are quite devoid of vitamin C (Hughes 1975). Nevertheless, his *experimental* demonstration that oranges and lemons could cure scurvy, his critical assessment of the literature of scurvy, his demonstration that the distinction between "land scurvy" and "sea scurvy" was a spurious one, and his advocacy of the use of various prophylactic foods by ships' crews must place him among the most significant figures in the history of nutrition.

Unfortunately, although subsequent commentators advocated the official adoption of lemon juice by the naval authorities as a prophylactic measure, they met with little success for many decades (Carpenter 1986: 73, 87). The purchase of vegetables by ship captains was sanctioned but the practice soon lapsed, and scurvy among sailors continued unabated. Indeed, when the Channel Fleet returned to port in 1780 after a cruise of only six weeks, there were 2,400 cases of scurvy present (Lloyd 1981: 12).

But in 1795, largely as a result of the advocacy of Gilbert Blane, himself a prominent and influential naval surgeon (actually "physician to the fleet"), the official issue of lemon juice to naval personnel in Britain was sanctioned (the practice was not, however, officially extended to the merchant service until 1844). Within two years, cases of scurvy in naval hospitals were rare occurrences, and there were clinicians who complained that they had never seen a true case of scurvy – a situation that would have been unthinkable a few years previously. J. Turnbull's almost monotonously successful treatment of the few scorbutic sailors arriving at Liverpool in 1848, merely providing them each with two lemons daily, was, perhaps, the final elegant vindication of Lind's pioneer study (Turnbull 1848).

Limes and Scurvy

A minor setback in keeping scurvy at a distance occurred in the 1850s when, for economic reasons, the British Admiralty contracts were changed so that the West Indian lime *(Citrus aurantiifolia)* was sub-stituted for the lemon *(Citrus limon)*. The superficial similarity between the two fruits had already led to the use of the terms "lime juicer" and "limey" by Americans in referring to British ships and sailors. Furthermore, the terms "lemon juice" and "lime juice" were used carelessly and often without distinction in referring to the two species. In fact, at the beginning of the century the lime was sometimes referred to as the "sour lemon" (Green 1824: 316).

An unfortunate consequence of this change was the reported failure of stored lime juice to offer protection against scurvy – as in the ill-fated "Nares" expedition to the Arctic in 1875. The apparent failure of lime to prevent scurvy led to the rejection by some observers of the thesis that lack of fresh fruit and vegetables was the only cause of scurvy. A. H. Smith, in a comprehensive article stimulated by outbreaks of scurvy among troops issued lime juice during the First World War, concluded that lime juice (as contrasted with lemon juice) as an antiscorbutic agent was "worthless" (Smith 1919).

The reason for this apparent lack of antiscorbutic potency on the part of lime juice preparations is still incompletely understood. It is true that lime juice has a lower vitamin C content than lemon juice, but it is still high enough to be regarded as a moderately good source of the vitamin. It is possible that the vitamin C molecule is much less stable in lime juice than in lemon juice – a belief that was apparently confirmed by Harriette Chick in 1918 using the guinea pig as an assay system. This observation would suggest that the protective and stabilizing factors present in lemon juice (high acidity, tannins, anthocyanins, etc.) are less potent in lime juice preparations. However, in a recent study, Carpenter found no essential difference between the rate of loss of ascorbic acid in lime and lemon juices (Carpenter 1991, personal communication). Whatever the true explanation, the apparent discrepant protective capacities of the two forms was an important feature in the history of scurvy, introducing a puzzling diversionary element into an otherwise fairly smooth development.

Scurvy in the Nineteenth Century

In general, the importance of scurvy diminished during the nineteenth century. It no longer posed a problem to mariners (the greater rapidity of sea vessels was a contributory factor in this respect), and it no longer occupied a position of importance in the medical texts. The eighteenth-century tendency to use the term "scorbutic" indiscriminately with reference to almost any unidentifiable or challenging condition seemed also to be dying. And an increase in the intake of vegetables (and to a lesser extent, fruit) reduced the possibility of scurvy occurring among the general population.

Nevertheless, sporadic outbreaks of scurvy occurred from time to time, and a number of these led to detailed reports in the medical press – some of them substantial ones, such as that by J. O. Curran in 1847 of cases of scurvy following the potato famine in Ireland (Curran 1847) and that of R. Christison describing a similar outbreak in Scotland in 1846 (Christison 1847).

Scurvy outbreaks occurred most frequently in "closed" communities subjected to the same (inadequate) dietary pattern – hospitals, prisons, and workhouses. The numerous reports presented to Parliament in the nineteenth century on conditions in the prisons and workhouses provide useful information on the adequacy of the diets in these institutions (Johnston 1985). The availability of potatoes – and to a lesser extent, vegetables – was of paramount importance in this respect; fruit was almost totally absent from the normal prison and workhouse diet. Thus, the outbreaks of scurvy among convicts at Millbank in 1822 and in Pentonville in 1847 were a direct result of a lack of vegetables.

W. Baly, in 1843, in a simple type of controlled experiment, was able to show that outbreaks of scurvy at Pentonville Prison could be eliminated by including adequate amounts of potatoes in the diet (Baly 1843). In 1851, R. Boyd described two cases of scurvy (a female aged 38 and a male aged 59) in the Somerset County Pauper Lunatic Asylum resulting from "a continued diet of one meal of bread and cheese daily for three months." Of particular significance to Boyd was the observation that this occurred "despite a plentiful allowance of cider (nearly 3 pints daily), which is supposed to be antiscorbutic" (Boyd 1851: 520; see also French 1982).

In the second half of the century potatoes were a regular feature of such institutional diets and outbreaks of scurvy diminished, although some cases still occurred among sailors despite the official adoption of lemon juice as a prophylactic. "It is very rare for London physicians to see cases of scurvy such as they are presented at our seaports," wrote P. Black in 1876 (12), confirming Boyd's earlier statement that "Scurvy is now seldom seen in ordinary hospital practice in this country except in the [naval] hospital ship *Dreadnought*" (Boyd 1851: 520). Nevertheless, there were still isolated epidemics in communities deprived of fresh food supplies for long periods – as among British soldiers in the Crimean War and among some of the persons on Arctic expeditions.

"Explaining" Scurvy in the Nineteenth Century

Attempts to "explain" the nature of scurvy continued. In particular, efforts were made to relate it to the absence of fresh fruit and vegetables in the diet, and by the middle of the nineteenth century there was a fair consensus that this was the main cause of the disease. Just as in the eighteenth century, when there had been attempts to accommodate scurvy within the then popular humoral theory of disease, so in the

nineteenth century there were efforts to explain it by drawing on concepts borrowed from the embryonic nutritional science of the period. This explanation involved an interesting conceptual shift from the conviction that there were positive causes of scurvy (such as coldness or too much dietary salt) to the belief that it resulted from a dietary deficiency – albeit an undefined one.

Two writers were particularly vocal in developing this theme. One was George Budd, a pioneer thinker in the development of the concept that there were clearly definable "Disorders Resulting from Defective Nutriment" (to use the title of his series of articles in the *London Medical Gazette* in 1842 [Budd 1840, 1842]). The second was Robert Barnes, who in 1864 produced his less widely available *On the Occurrence of Sea Scurvy in the Mercantile Navy. . . .* Budd, in a frequently referenced article in Tweedie's *Library of Medicine,* stated quite unambiguously that scurvy was the result of a lack of a single essential dietary principle and of that alone; he furthermore described this antiscorbutic principle as a thermolabile one, present in fresh fruit and vegetables and with uncanny foresight prophesied that it would "be discovered by organic chemistry or the experiments of physiologists in the not too distant future" (Budd 1840: 77; Hughes 1973).

Twenty years later Barnes reaffirmed the essential dietary nature of scurvy in a 10,000-word official report. Basing his arguments on "experiments and facts" he stated, "There is no fact so well attested by the history of mankind as the dependence of scurvy upon the negation of fresh vegetable food . . . the abolition of scurvy is entirely a question of diet, and a very simple question of diet." Barnes, basing his calculations on returns obtained from the Dreadnought (Naval) Hospital, attempted to arrive at a figure for the depletion period necessary for the emergence of scurvy and concluded that "symptoms such as . . . blotches like bruises, swelling of the gums, lassitude and emaciation . . . have generally been manifest in from 60 to 80 days." He acknowledged, however, that there was a strong factor of individual variation (Barnes 1864: 330).

But what was the nature of this deficient element that was absent from scorbutigenic diets yet present in vegetables and fruits? E. A. Parkes, an eminent clinician, presented the problem in four simple sentences, logically and within the currently accepted framework of dietary knowledge in 1869:

The peculiar state of malnutrition we call scurvy is now known not to be the consequence of general starvation, though it is doubtless aided by this. Men have been fed with an amount of nitrogenous and fatty food sufficient not only to keep them in condition, but to cause them to gain weight, and yet have got scurvy. The starches also have been given in quite sufficient amount without preventing it. It seems, indeed clear that it is to the absence of some of the constituents of the fourth dietetic group, the salts, that we must look for the cause. (1869: 492)

And the missing components in Parkes's opinion were the salts of organic acids, such as citric, malic, and tartaric – compounds known to be of vegetable origin. Parkes's advice, included in his army manual *Practical Hygiene,* was that, "In time of war every vegetable should be used which is safe to use, and, when made into soups, almost all are tolerably pleasant to eat.... Good lemon juice should be issued daily (1 oz.) and it should be seen that the men take it" (1869: 494).

Parkes's theory of the nature of scurvy was by no means the only one in the field during the nineteenth century. There were many others, and as late as 1908, J. M. Cowan, writing in the standard Oxford manual *A System of Diet and Dietetics,* while admitting "the undisputed fact that a plentiful diet of fresh vegetables cures the disease" went on to state, "The exact nature of the fault is, however, undetermined" (1908: 645). Cowan referred to a number of theories of scurvy then in vogue. These were a deficiency of potash salts; a deficiency of dietary bases (alkali); ptomaine poisoning; and a specific infection (Cowan 1908: 645). Cowan's uncertainty about the cause of scurvy was echoed in 1911 by the *Encyclopedia Britannica,* which stated, "... the modern tendency is to suspect an unknown micro-organism ... even among the more chemical school of pathologists it is disputed whether the cause is the absence of certain constituents in the food or the presence of some actual poison ..." (517).

Had Cowan been aware of it, these alternative theories had already been rendered redundant by an experiment reported the previous year from Oslo – in Carpenter's opinion "the most important single paper in the whole history of this subject" (Carpenter 1986: 173). This was the classic study by A. Holst, in which he produced scurvy in guinea pigs by feeding them a grain diet – in an experiment originally designed to study the nature of beriberi.

Holst had fortuitously chosen one of the few species unable to produce vitamin C endogenously and had fed them a diet completely lacking in vitamin C. The guinea pigs died after a month on the diet, and it was noted that the tissues showed degenerative changes similar to those known to occur in human scurvy (Holst and Frohlich 1907). Until the characterization of the "antiscorbutic factor" and the development of chemical methods of assessing it in the 1930s, the prevention of scurvy in guinea pigs was the standard technique for measuring the antiscorbutic potency of a preparation.

The last quarter of the nineteenth century also witnessed a proliferation of interest, both in America and in Europe, in "infantile scurvy" – a form of avitaminosis C occurring in very young children and characterized primarily by defective bone development. It was later referred to as "Barlow's disease," after Thomas Barlow, a London physician, who described its true nature and distinguished it from rickets, with which it was frequently associated and often confused (Evans 1983).

It is interesting to note that the emergence of infantile scurvy, like that of "sailors' scurvy" three centuries previously, was probably a consequence of developments in technology, namely, too great a dependence on processed foodstuffs from which the vitamin C had been destroyed and, in particular, evaporated and condensed milks, the use of which increased significantly during the second half of the nineteenth century (Carpenter 1986: 158-72). The subsequent introduction of orange juice supplements for babies ensured the sudden eradication of "Barlow's disease," although isolated reports from Germany, as late as the 1980s, described its occurrence in babies fed only on oat gruel.

Experimental Scurvy in Humans

Following the identification of ascorbic acid as the "antiscorbutic factor," human volunteers attempted to induce scurvy in themselves by subsisting on a vitamin C–free diet. J. Menshing, in Germany, ate a virtually vitamin C–free diet for 100 days; his blood vitamin C fell to zero but there were no discernible signs of scurvy. H. Rietschel and H. Schick repeated the experiment, extending the period of deprivation to 160 days but again without the appearance of any overt signs of scurvy (Rietschel and Mensching 1939). J. H. Crandon, in the United States, deprived himself of vitamin C and noted the appearance of the first recognizable signs of scurvy after some 5 months (Crandon, Lund, and Dill 1940).

However, the first controlled study designed to produce scurvy in humans was undertaken at Sheffield in England during the latter stages of the Second World War and published in 1953 (eight years after the conclusion of the work) as Medical Research Council Special Report (Medical Research Council 1953). Twenty young volunteers (aged 21 to 34) took part in the experiment; anecdotal reports indicate that they were conscientious objectors to military service, although, understandably perhaps, this information was not included in the official report of the study.

All participants were placed on a vitamin C–free diet. Ten received no supplements; seven were given 10 mg ascorbic acid daily; and three received 70 mg ascorbic acid daily. The general picture to emerge was that the classical signs of scurvy (hyperkeratotic follicles, gum lesions, impaired wound healing – in that order) were experienced by those in the deficient group but not by either of the supplemented groups.

The hair follicle changes occurred after 17 weeks of deprivation and the gum changes after 26 weeks – somewhat later than the corresponding period calculated by Barnes in 1864. The difference presumably reflected differences in the subjects' vitamin C status at the beginning of the deprivation period. Furthermore, a supplement of 10 mg ascorbic acid was sufficient to restore the scorbutic subjects to normal health.

The report recommended that "in order to arrive at a figure for a daily allowance which covers individual variations and includes a safety margin, it is suggested that the minimum protective dose of 10 mg be trebled" (Medical Research Council 1953: 145). For 40 years the United Kingdom Recommended Daily Allowance for vitamin C remained at 30 mg, and the experimental evidence for this amount was the single "Sheffield Study" of 1944 – a study that, in terms of sex and age alone, it may be argued, was based on a completely unrepresentative population group.

A similar investigation, but with fewer participants, was reported from the United States in 1969. The subjects in this instance were prisoners who "bought" remission periods by subjecting themselves to scurvy. The signs of deficiency appeared somewhat earlier than in the "Sheffield Study" – skin lesions in 8 to 13 weeks and gum changes in 11 to 19 weeks (Hodges et al. 1971). Both the Sheffield and the U.S. projects included wide-ranging physiological and pathological examinations, and further projects of this nature are unlikely to add very much to our clinical knowledge of the condition.

There remain, of course, peripheral problems that are of some academic interest but of little practical significance, such as the identification of further species unable to synthesize ascorbic acid and, therefore, susceptible to scurvy – and the mirror image of this, the search for a mutant form of guinea pigs resistant to scurvy. One of the more interesting current problems centers on the apparent refractiveness of the elderly to scurvy; it has been shown that persons over 80 years of age may have extremely low blood levels of ascorbic acid without the emergence of any of the expected clinical features (Hughes 1981: 60).

Scurvy Today

Our current knowledge of the vitamin C requirement of the body allows us, in a perverse way, to assess the validity of some historical claims of dietary interest. L. Cornaro, who reputedly attained a century of life by prudent living, recommended for the poorer and older members of the community a diet of bread, panada, and eggs. A diet so structured, however, would be almost completely lacking in vitamin C and almost certain to produce scurvy in a matter of months (Cornaro 1768: 98). Similarly, the numerous accounts of survival for considerable periods on diets, which simple inspection indicates to be completely

vitamin C–free (such as that of John Ferguson, who in the eighteenth century lived, allegedly for 18 years, only on water, whey, and barley water [Umfreville 1743]), must now be regarded as largely apocryphal.

The life, and untimely death, of William Stark was more in keeping with what we now know of scurvy and vitamin C. Stark, perhaps the best known of all dietary masochists, achieved historical immortality by experimenting on his own body. He may be regarded as the founder of the now firmly rooted "Death by Diet" brigade. A 29-year-old unmarried physician living in London, he decided to test whether very simple diets would support health. From July 1769 to February 1770 he subsisted on diets such as meat, bread, and water; or bread and cheese; or honey and bread; or sugar and water. This highly scorbutigenic regime was relieved only by a small amount of fruit on one occasion in December 1769. Stark died on February 23, 1770, almost certainly from scurvy, judging by the entries in his detailed diary of the study. It is interesting to note, despite his general lassitude and fatigue, entries such as "had strong desires," "Venus semel," and "Venus bias," which appeared at least weekly in his diary up to within a fortnight of his death, suggesting little impairment of the procreative capacity even in severe scurvy (Smyth 1788; Drummond and Wilbraham 1935).

Scurvy is today a rare condition – so rare that individual cases usually merit a short note in the medical press. Persons on a mixed, balanced diet would normally be expected to daily ingest more than the amount of ascorbic acid required to protect them against the disease. Thus, in the United Kingdom the mean ascorbic acid intake is some 60 mg daily – 50 percent above the current U.K. Reference Daily Intake of 40 mg. The only persons likely to fall into a scurvy-risk category are those who, for economic or dietary reasons, subsist on a diet deficient in fruit, vegetables, and fresh meat – such as a diet based primarily on nuts and grain and dairy products or the proverbial American scorbutigenic diet of doughnuts and black coffee.

Indeed, even the ingestion of large amounts of fresh meat (particularly liver) will provide sufficient amounts of vitamin C to prevent scurvy in the comparative absence of fruit and vegetables. This explains why Eskimos (the name of which, apparently, means "raw flesh eaters") remain scurvy-free even though their intake of plant sources is minimal. A turn-of-the-century account underlines this fact:

In 1893, at Kharborova, a Samoyad settlement on the Yugor Straits . . . six Russian priests, whose religion forbade them to eat reindeer or other such meats, but allowed salted fish, were left in a hut by a wealthy mine-owner to pass the winter. . . . A small Russian peasant boy was left to wait on them. The priests lived almost exclusively on tea, bread and salted fish; the boy lived upon similar food, except that instead of the salted fish he ate fresh reindeer meat. None of them had any vegetables. In the following May, when the Samoyads and peasant traders returned, they found that all the six priests had died of scurvy, whereas the little boy, who had lived upon fresh meat and had not eaten salted fish was alive and well, and had buried all his late masters in the snow. . . . (Jackson and Harley 1900: 252-3)

Recently reported cases of scurvy include that of a 9-year-old American girl who consumed nothing but tuna sandwiches and iced tea (without lemon) (Ellis, Vanderveen, and Rasmussen 1984), and that of a 24-year-old British male whose main form of sustenance was peanut butter sandwiches (Pozniak and Tomson 1983).

Epidemics of scurvy have been equally rare in the twentieth century. They occurred on a limited scale among soldiers in World War I (Smith 1919) and, particularly, among Indian personnel fighting in Iraq, where some 11,000 cases were reported (Willcox 1920). J. D. Comrie stated that he had personally examined 600 cases of scurvy in 1919 in North Russia (Comrie 1920).

Even today, however, we have the occasional reminder that the history of scurvy is not as completely closed a book as modern science would perhaps lead us to believe. Recently it has been reported that scurvy remains a serious public-health problem for Ethiopian refugees in Sudan and Somalia, where the incidence of scurvy in six camps ranged from 14 percent to 44 percent. It was found that the standard relief food (mainly cereals, legumes, and oil) distributed to the refugees was almost completely deficient in vitamin C (Desenclos et al. 1989).

The condition sometimes described as "chronic scurvy" or hypovitaminosis C (in which a person subsists on a suboptimal intake of vitamin C but without the emergence of the clinical features of overt scurvy) may affect substantial sectors of a population and, in particular, the institutionalized elderly; but its clinical significance, if any, is a matter of continuing dispute that need not concern us here.

R. E. Hughes

Notes

1. The water dock was not the only plant to have been the subject of a monograph devoted to its supposed antiscorbutic properties; Andreas Moellenbrok's *Cochlearia Curiosa* was translated into English in 1676, and a century later John Edwards published his . . . *Goose Grass or Clivers and its Efficacy in the Cure of the most inveterate Scurvy.*

2. Ironically, the situation is today completely reversed. In a recent paper it was pointed out that "Scurvy is a disease which can mimic other more serious disorders such as deep vein thrombosis and systemic bleeding disorders . . . [and] because the clinical features of scurvy are no longer well appreciated scorbutic patients are often extensively evaluated for other disorders" (Reuler, Brondy, and Cooney 1985).

Bibliography

Baly, W. 1843. On the prevention of scurvy in prisoners, pauper [and] lunatic asylums etc. *London Medical Gazette* 1: 699-703.

Barnes, R. 1864. Report on the occurrence of sea scurvy . . . *Public Records (Commissioners Reports)* 28.

Black, P. 1876. *Scurvy in high latitudes.* London.

Boyd, R. 1851. Two cases of scurvy. *Lancet* 1: 519-20.

Budd, George. 1840. Scurvy. In *The library of medicine*, Vol. 5, ed. A. Tweedie, 58-95. London.

1842. Disorders resulting from defective nutriment. *London Medical Gazette* 2: 632-6, 712-16, 743-9, 906-15.

Carpenter, K. J. 1986. *The history of scurvy and vitamin C.* Cambridge.

Christison, R. 1847. Account of scurvy as it has lately appeared in Edinburgh . . . *Monthly Journal of Medical Science* 8: 1-22.

Clay, R. M. 1909. *The medieval hospitals of England.* London.

Comrie, J. D. 1920. Scurvy in North Russia. *Edinburgh Medical Journal* 24: 207-15.

Cornaro, L. 1768. *Discourses on a sober and temperate life.* London.

Counsell, J. N., and D. H. Hornig, eds. 1981. *Vitamin C (ascorbic acid).* London and Englewood Cliffs, N.J.

Cowan, J. M. 1908. Diet in diseases of the blood. In *A system of diet and dietetics,* ed. G. A. Sutherland, 625-52. London.

Crandon, J. H., C. C. Lund, and D. B. Dill. 1940. Human experimental scurvy. *New England Journal of Medicine* 223: 353-69.

Curran, J. O. 1847. Observations on scurvy as it has lately appeared throughout Ireland and in several parts of Great Britain. *Dublin Quarterly Journal of Medical Science* 4: 83-134.

Desenclos, J. C., A. M. Berry, R. Padt, et al. 1989. Epidemiological patterns of scurvy among Ethiopian refugees. *Bulletin of the World Health Organization* 66: 309-16.

Dodoens, R. 1578. *A niewe herball or historie of plantes . . .* translated by Henry Lyte. London.

Drummond, J. C., and A. Wilbraham. 1935. William Stark, M.D. *Lancet* 2: 459-62.

1964. *The Englishman's food.* Revised edition. London.

Ellis, C. N., E. E. Vanderveen, and J. E. Rasmussen. 1984. Scurvy. A case caused by peculiar dietary habits. *Archives of Dermatology* 120: 1212-14.

The Encyclopaedia Britannica. 1911. Vol. 24, 517. Cambridge.

Englard, S., and S. Seifter. 1986. The biochemical functions of ascorbic acid. *Annual Review of Nutrition* 6: 365-406.

Evans, P. D. 1983. Infantile scurvy: The centenary of Barlow's disease. *British Medical Journal* 287: 1862-3.

Floyer, John. 1722. *History of cold-bathing.* Fifth edition. London.

French, R. K. 1982. *The history and virtues of cyder.* New York and London.

Gerarde, J. 1633. *The herball or generall historie of plantes . . . amended by Thomas Johnson.* London.

Green, T. [1824]. *The universal herbal.* London.

Harvey, G. 1675. *The disease of London or a new discovery of the scorvey.* London.

Henslow, G. 1899. *Medical works of the fourteenth century.* London.

Hess, A. S. 1920. *Scurvy past and present.* London.

Hirsch, A. 1883-6. *Handbook of geographical and historical pathology,* Vol. 2, trans. C. Creighton. London.

Hodges, R. E., J. Hood, J. E. Canham, et al. 1971. Clinical manifestations of ascorbic acid deficiency in man. *American Journal of Clinical Nutrition* 24: 432-43.

Holst, A., and T. Frohlich. 1907. Experimental studies relating to ship beri-beri and scurvy. II. On the etiology of scurvy *Journal of Hygiene* 7: 634-71.

Hughes, R. E. 1973. George Budd (1808-1882) and nutritional deficiency diseases. *Medical History* 17: 127-35.

    1975. James Lind and the cure of scurvy. *Medical History* 19: 342-51.

    1981. *Vitamin C.* London.

    1990. The rise and fall of the "antiscorbutics"; some notes on the traditional cures for "land scurvy." *Medical History* 34: 52-64.

    In press. De Sceletyrrbe . . . or a Traetise of the Scorbut. *The Journal of Welsh Ecclesiastical History.*

Jackson, F. G., and V. Harley. 1900. An experimental inquiry into scurvy. *Proceedings of the Royal Society* 66: 250-64.

Johnston, V. J. 1985. *Diet in workhouses and prisons 1835-1895.* New York and London.

King, L. S. 1970. *The road to medical enlightenment.* London and New York.

Letheby, H. 1870. *Lectures on food.* London.

Lind, J. 1753. (See Stewart and Guthrie 1953.)

Lloyd, C. C. 1981. In *Starving sailors: The influence of nutrition upon naval and maritime history,* ed. J. Watt, E. J. Freeman, and W. F. Bynum, 9-15. Bristol, England.

Major, R. H. 1978. *Classic descriptions of disease.* Third edition. Springfield, Ill.

Maynwaringe, Everard. 1672. *Marbus Polyrhizos and Polymorphaeus: A treatise of the scurvy. . . .* London.

Medical Research Council. 1953. *Vitamin C requirements of human adults.* Special Report Series, No. 280. London.

Moffet, T. 1746. *Health's improvement.* London.

Parkes, E. A. 1869. *A manual of practical hygiene.* London.

Powicke, F., ed. 1926. Richard Baxter, The poor husbandman's advocate. *Bulletin of the John Rylands Library* 10: 464.

Pozniak, A. L., and C. R. Tomson. 1983. Clinical Curio: Scurvy in a 24-year-old. *British Medical Journal* 286: 881.

Prentice, E. P. 1939. *Hunger and history.* New York and London.

Reuler, J. B., V. C. Brondy, and T. G. Cooney. 1985. Adult scurvy. *Journal of the American Medical Association* 253: 805-7.

Rietschel, H., and J. Mensching. 1939. Experimenteller C-Vitaminhunger am Menschen, ein Betrag zur Frage des C-Vitaminbedarfs *Klinische Wochenschrift* 18: 273.

Riverius, Lazarus. (Rivièr, Lazare) 1655. *The practice of physick in several books . . . by Nicholas Culpeper . . . Abdiah Cole . . . William Rowland being chief of translation of the works of . . . Lazarus Riverius.* London.

Roddis, L. S. 1951. *James Lind.* London.

Salaman, R. 1970. *The history and social influence of the potato.* Cambridge.

Salmon, William. 1696. *The family-dictionary.* Second edition. London.

Shapter, Thomas. 1847. "On the recent occurrence of Scurvy in zar and the neighbourhood." *Medical Gazette* May 21: 945-8.

Smith, A. H. 1919. A historical inquiry into the efficacy of lime-juice for the prevention and cure of scurvy. *Journal of the Royal Army Medical Corps* 32: 93-116, 188-208.

Smyth, J. C. 1788. *The works of the late William Stark, M.D. with experiments dietetical and statical, revised and published by James Carmichael Smyth, M.D., F.R.S.* London.

Society of Gentlemen. 1777. Potatoes. *The complete farmer.* Third edition. London.

Stephens, W. 1732. *Dolaeus upon the cure of the gout by milk-diet.* London.

Stewart, C. P., and D. Guthrie, eds. 1953. *Lind's treatise on scurvy.* Edinburgh.

Strother, Edward. 1725. *An essay on sickness and health.* London.

Sutherland, G. A., ed. 1908. *A system of diet and dietetics.* London.

Turnbull, J. 1848. Observations on the scurvy. *Lancet* 1: 601-4.

Turner, W. 1568. *The first and second parts of the herbal . . .* London.

Umfreville, T. 1743. *The case of Mr. John Ferguson . . .* London.

Vaughan, William. 1630. *The newlanders cure . . .* London.

[Wier, J.] 1622. *Discourse of the scorby, translated out of Wyers' observations.* London.

Willcox, W. H. 1920. The treatment and management of diseases due to deficiency of diet: Scurvy and beri-beri. *British Medical Journal* 1: 73-7.

Woodall, J. 1617. *The surgions mate or military and domestique surgery.* London.

Young, Arthur. 1780. *A tour in Ireland,* Vol. 2, Second edition. London.

Zulueta, J. de. and L. Higueras. 1981. Health and navigation in the South Seas: The Spanish experience. In *Starving sailors: The influence of nutrition upon naval and maritime history,* ed. J. Watt, E. J. Freeman, and W. F. Bynum, 85-99. Bristol, England.

IV.E

Food-Related Disorders

IV.E.1 ☙ Anorexia Nervosa

Definition

Anorexia nervosa is a psychophysiological disorder – usually of young females – characterized by a prolonged refusal to eat or maintain normal body weight, an intense fear of becoming obese, a disturbed body image in which the emaciated patient feels overweight, and the absence of any physical illness that would account for extreme weight loss. The term "anorexia" is actually a misnomer, because genuine loss of appetite is rare and usually does not occur until late in the illness. In reality, most anorectics are obsessed with food and constantly struggle to deny natural hunger.

In anorexia nervosa, normal dieting escalates into a preoccupation with being thin, profound changes in eating patterns, and a loss of at least 25 percent of the original body weight. Weight loss is usually accomplished by a severe restriction of caloric intake, with patients subsisting on fewer than 600 calories per day. Contemporary anorectics may couple fasting with self-induced vomiting, use of laxatives and diuretics, and strenuous exercise.

The most consistent medical consequences of anorexia nervosa are amenorrhea (ceasing or irregularity of menstruation) and estrogen deficiency. In most cases amenorrhea follows weight loss, but it is not unusual for amenorrhea to appear before noticeable weight loss has occurred. The decrease in estrogen causes many anorectics to develop osteoporosis, a loss of bone density that is usually seen only in postmenopausal women (Garfinkel and Garner 1982).

By the time the anorectic is profoundly underweight, other physical complications resulting from severe malnutrition begin to appear. These include bradycardia (slowing of the heartbeat), hypotension (loss of normal blood pressure), lethargy, hypothermia, constipation, the appearance of "lanugo" or fine silky hair covering the body, and a variety of other metabolic and systemic changes.

In addition to the physical symptoms associated with chronic starvation, anorectics also display a relatively consistent cluster of emotional and behavioral characteristics, the most prominent of which grows out of the anorectic's deviation from normal eating habits. Severe restriction of food intake is sometimes alternated with bulimic phases, in which the anorectic engages in uncontrolled or excessive eating followed by self-induced vomiting and laxative abuse. Other unusual eating habits may include monotonous or eccentric diets, hoarding or hiding of food, and obsessive preoccupation with food and cooking for others.

Emotionally, anorexic patients are often described as being perfectionist, dependent, introverted, and overly compliant. Although studies have failed to find a consistent psychiatric symptom pattern for the disorder, frequently reported neurotic traits include obsessive-compulsive, hysterical, hypochondriacal, and depressive symptoms. A decrease in or disappearance of sexual interest is also a frequent concomitant of anorexia nervosa.

A distorted body image is an almost universal characteristic of anorectics, with many patients insisting they are overweight even when their bodies are extremely emaciated. As a result, most individuals with anorexia nervosa deny or minimize the severity of their illness and are usually highly resistant to therapy. The anorectic's refusal to acknowledge her nutritional needs, and her steadfast insistence that nothing is wrong, make anorexia nervosa one of the most recalcitrant disorders in contemporary medicine.

Distribution and Incidence

Once considered to be extremely rare, the reported incidence of anorexia nervosa has more than doubled during the past 20 years (Herzog and Copeland 1985). The disorder is especially prevalent among adolescent and young adult women. Ninety to 95 percent of anorectics are young and female, and as many as 1 in 250 females between 12 and 18 years of age may develop the disorder. The exact incidence of anorexia and other eating disorders is difficult to determine, however, because of problems in conducting reliable epidemiological studies and the small samples on which many such studies are based (Crisp, Palmer, and Kalucy 1976).

The onset of anorexia nervosa occurs most often during adolescence, although some patients have become anorexic as early as age 11 and as late as the sixth decade of life. Patients are typically high achievers, with normal or above average intelligence. They also tend to come from middle- or upper-class families, although evidence of anorexia nervosa among working-class and poverty-class women is growing (Bulik 1987; Gowers and McMahon 1989; Dolan 1991).

Anorexia nervosa is comparatively rare in men: Approximately 5 to 10 percent of anorectics are male. The clinical picture for male anorexic patients is also much different from that for women. In general, male anorectics tend to display a greater degree of psychopathology, are often massively obese before acquiring the disorder, are less likely to be affluent, and are even more resistant to therapy than their female counterparts (Garfinkel and Garner 1982). There is growing evidence, however, that anorexia nervosa and bulimia are more common among men than previously believed. This is particularly true among homosexual men, who tend to experience more dissatisfaction with body image than do heterosexual men (Yager et al. 1988; Silberstein et al. 1989; Striegel-Moore, Tucker, and Hsu 1990).

Anorexia nervosa was also once thought to be comparatively rare among American blacks, Hispanics, Native Americans, lesbians, first- and second-generation ethnic immigrants, and individuals from disadvantaged socioeconomic backgrounds (Herzog and Copeland 1985). Recent research in this area, however, has indicated that the incidence of anorexia and other eating disorders among these groups is much higher than previously thought (see the section "Geographic and Demographic Features").

Etiology and Epidemiology

Although the etiology of anorexia nervosa is an area of intense investigation, researchers have yet to reach a consensus about the origin of the disorder. The most sophisticated thinking on the subject regards anorexia nervosa as a multidetermined disorder that involves an interplay of biological, psychological, and cultural factors. Advocates of this model view these three etiological factors as reciprocal and interactive and believe it is simplistic to isolate one component as the single underlying cause of the disorder (Garfinkel and Garner 1982; Brumberg 1988).

Joan Brumberg (1988) has developed a multideter-mined etiological model based on a two-staged conceptualization of anorexia nervosa that delineates the relative impact of sociocultural influences and individual biological and psychological variables in precipitating the disorder. In the first stage – the "recruitment" phase of the illness – sociocultural factors play the dominant role. During this period, cultural assumptions that associate thinness with female beauty lead certain women into a pattern of chronic dieting. Indeed, research on the sociocultural causes of anorexia nervosa has linked the increased incidence of anorexia nervosa and other eating disorders with the tremendous cultural attention given to dieting and food, increasingly thinner standards of beauty, and the fitness movement (Schwartz, Thompson, and Johnson 1982; Chernin 1985; Orbach 1986; Bordo 1993). Yet sociocultural variables alone cannot explain why some women but not others move from chronic dieting to anorexia nervosa. Therefore, other individual factors must be implicated in the final development of the illness.

Brumberg's model of anorexia nervosa relies on a second stage – career or acclimation – to correct the shortcomings of sociocultural explanations of the disorder. During the career phase, specific biological and psychological features determine which individuals develop the full-blown psychopathology of anorexia nervosa. In order to explain the transition between the recruitment and career phases of anorexia nervosa, Brumberg relies on recent research in the biological and social sciences, which has sought to uncover the unique physiological and psychological characteristics of anorexic patients.

Since the early 1900s, a number of different endocrinological and neurological abnormalities have been postulated as underlying biological causes of anorexia nervosa: hormonal imbalance, dysfunction in the satiety center of the hypothalamus, lesions in the limbic system of the brain, and irregular output of vasopressin and gonadotropin (Herzog and Copeland 1985). The search for a biomedical cause of anorexia nervosa is made difficult, however, by the fact that chronic starvation itself produces extensive changes in hypothalamic and metabolic function. Researchers in this area have yet to find a common biological characteristic of the anorexic population that is unmistakably a cause rather than a consequence of extreme weight loss and malnutrition (Brumberg 1988).

A more satisfactory explanation of the biological factors that contribute to the "career" phase of anorexia nervosa is the "addiction to starvation" model proffered by the British psychiatrists George I. Szmukler and Digby Tantum (1984). According to Szmukler and Tantum, patients with fully developed anorexia nervosa are physically and psychologically dependent on the state of starvation. Much like alcoholics and other substance abusers, anorectics find something gratifying or tension-relieving about the state of starvation and possess a specific physiological substrate that makes them more susceptible to starvation dependence than individuals who merely engage in chronic dieting. Szmukler and Tantum add, however, that starvation dependence is not the total explanation of anorexia nervosa. Rather, they believe that starvation dependence acts in conjunction with a range of sociocultural, psychological, and familial factors that encourage certain individuals to use anorexic behavior as a means of expressing personal anguish.

Current psychological models of anorexia nervosa fall into three basic categories: psychoanalytic, family systems, and social psychology. In both the psychoanalytic and family systems models, anorexia nervosa is seen as a pathological response to the developmental crisis of adolescence. Orthodox psychoanalysts, drawing on the work of Sigmund Freud, view the anorectic as a girl who fears adult womanhood and who associates eating with oral impregnation (Brumberg 1988). Family systems theory, however, offers a more complex explanation of the relationship between adolescence and anorexia nervosa. On the basis of clinical work with anorectics and their families, family systems therapists have found that the majority of anorexic patients are "enmeshed," meaning that the normal process of individuation is blocked by extreme parental overprotectiveness, control, and rigidity. Anorexia nervosa is therefore seen as a form of adolescent rebellion against parental authority (Minuchin, Rosman, and Baker 1978; Bruch 1988).

Research in social psychology and the field of personality has devised several psychological tests to distinguish the psychological characteristics of anorectics from others in their age-group. One study has shown that although many of the psychological traits of anorectics and other women are indistinguishable, anorectics display a markedly higher degree of ineffectiveness and lower amount of self-esteem. Other studies have proposed that anorectics have actual cognitive problems with body imaging; still others suggest a relationship between anorexia nervosa and sex-role socialization (Garfinkel and Garner 1982).

Some researchers have attempted to fit anorexia nervosa within other established psychiatric categories such as affective disorders and obsessional neurosis. Many anorectics, in fact, display behavior patterns associated with obsessive-compulsive disorders: perfectionism, excessive orderliness and cleanliness, meticulous attention to detail, and self-righteousness. This correlation has led a number of researchers to suggest that anorexia nervosa is itself a form of obsessive-compulsive behavior (Rothenberg 1986). Depressive symptoms are also commonly seen in many patients with anorexia nervosa. Various family, genetic, and endocrine studies have found a correlation between eating disorders and depression. However, the association between anorexia nervosa and other psychiatric disorders remains controversial (Garfinkel and Garner 1982; Herzog and Copeland 1985).

History

The extent to which people suffered from anorexia nervosa in the past has been a subject of much historical debate. Some clinicians and medical historians have suggested that anorexia nervosa was first identified in 1689 by the British doctor Richard Morton, physician to James II (Bliss and Branch 1960; Silverman 1983). The medieval historian Rudolph Bell (1985) has dated the origins of anorexia nervosa even earlier, claiming that the medieval female saints, who were reputed to live without eating anything except the Eucharist, actually suffered from anorexia nervosa.

Other historians, however, have argued that attempts to label all historical instances of food refusal and appetite loss as anorexia nervosa are simplistic and maintain that the historical record is insufficient to make conclusive diagnoses of individual cases (Bynum 1987; Brumberg 1988). Although these historians agree that the final physiological stage of acute starvation may be the same in contemporary anorectics and medieval ascetics, the cultural and psychological reasons behind the refusal to eat are quite different. Thus, to reduce both to a single biomedical cause is to overlook the variety of social and cultural contexts in which certain individuals have chosen to refuse food.

The modern disease classification of anorexia nervosa emerged during the 1860s and 1870s, when the work of public asylum keepers, elite British physicians, and early French neurologists partially distinguished anorexia nervosa from other diseases involving loss of appetite (Brumberg 1988). In 1859, the American asylum physician William Stout Chipley published the first American description of sitomania, a type of insanity characterized by an intense dread or loathing of food (Chipley 1859). Although Chipley found sitophobia in patients from a broad range of social groups and age-groups, he identified a special form of the disease that afflicted adolescent girls.

Chipley's work was ignored by his contemporaries, however, and it was not until the 1870s, when two influential case studies by the British physician William Withey Gull and the French alienist Charles Lasègue (Lasègue 1873; Gull 1874) were published, that physicians began to pay significant attention to anorexia in girlhood. Gull's primary accomplishment was to name and establish anorexia nervosa as a coherent disease entity, distinct from mental illnesses in which appetite loss was a secondary feature and from physical "wasting" diseases such as tuberculosis, diabetes, or cancer. Despite widespread acclaim for Gull's work with anorexic patients, however, late-nineteenth-century clinicians generally rejected the conception of anorexia nervosa as an independent disease. Instead, they viewed it either as a variant of hysteria that affected the gastrointestinal system or as a juvenile form of neurasthenia (Brumberg 1988).

Nineteenth-century physicians also tended to

focus on the physical symptom of not eating and ignored the anorexic patient's psychological reasons for refusing food. An important exception was Lasègue, who was the first to suggest the significance of family dynamics in the genesis and perpetuation of anorexia nervosa. Because of the somatic emphasis of nineteenth-century medicine, however, most medical practitioners of that time disregarded Lasègue's therapeutic perspective. Instead, they directed medical intervention toward restoring the anorectic to a reasonable weight and pattern of eating rather than exploring the underlying emotional causes of the patient's alleged lack of appetite (Brumberg 1988).

In the twentieth century, the treatment of anorexia nervosa changed to incorporate new developments within medical and psychiatric practice. Before the Second World War, two distinct and isolated models dominated medical thinking on anorexia nervosa. The first approach was rooted in late-nineteenth-century research in organotherapy, a form of treatment based on the principle that disease resulted from the removal or dysfunction of secreting organs and glands (Brumberg 1988). Between 1900 and 1940, a variety of different endocrinologic deficiencies were proposed as the cause of anorexia nervosa. In 1914, Morris Simmonds, a pathologist at the University of Hamburg, published a clinical description of an extreme cachexia due to destruction of the anterior lobe of the pituitary. Because patients with anorexia nervosa and those with Simmonds's disease shared a set of common symptoms, many clinicians assumed that a deficiency in pituitary hormone was the cause of both conditions (Brumberg 1988).

Other researchers implicated thyroid insufficiency as the cause of anorexia nervosa. Research conducted at the Mayo Clinic in Rochester, Minnesota, during the period between the two world wars established the relationship between thyroid function and body weight and led many physicians to regard anorexia nervosa as a metabolic disorder caused by a deficiency in thyroid hormone. Throughout the 1920s and 1930s, insulin, antuitrin, estrogen, and a host of other hormones were also employed in the treatment of anorexia nervosa (Brumberg 1988).

The second major approach to anorexia nervosa in the early twentieth century grew out of the field of dynamic psychiatry, which emerged during the 1890s and early 1900s. Beginning in the last decade of the nineteenth century, practitioners in dynamic psychiatry increasingly focused on the life history of individual patients and the emotional sources of nervous disease. Two of the leading pioneers in this new field – Sigmund Freud and Pierre Janet – were the first to suggestively link the etiology of anorexia nervosa with the issue of psychosexual development. According to Freud, all appetites were expressions of libido or sexual drive. Thus, not eating represented a repression of normal sexual appetite (Freud 1959). Similarly, Janet asserted that anorexic girls refused food in order to retard normal sexual development and forestall adult sexuality (Janet 1903).

Because of the enormous popularity of endocrinologic explanations, the idea of anorexia nervosa as a psychosexual disturbance was generally overlooked for more than 30 years. By the 1930s, however, the failure of endocrinologic models to establish either a predictable cure or a definitive cause of anorexia nervosa, the growing reputation of the Freudian psychoanalytic movement, and increased attention to the role of emotions in disease led a number of practitioners to assert the value and importance of psychotherapy in the treatment of anorexia nervosa. Although biomedical treatment of the disorder continued, most clinicians argued that successful, permanent recovery depended on uncovering the psychological basis for the anorectic's behavior. Following up on the work of Freud and Janet, orthodox psychiatrists during this time postulated that refusal to eat was related to suppression of the sexual appetite and claimed that anorexic women regarded eating as oral impregnation and obesity as pregnancy (Brumberg 1988).

After World War II, a new psychiatric view of eating disorders, shaped largely by the work of Hilde Bruch, encouraged a more complex interpretation of the psychological underpinnings of anorexia nervosa. Although Bruch agreed that the anorectic was unprepared to cope with the psychological and social consequences of adulthood and sexuality, she also stressed the importance of individual personality formation and factors within the family that contributed to the psychogenesis of anorexia nervosa. Here, Bruch revived Lasègue's work on the role of family dynamics in anorexia nervosa. According to Bruch, the families of most anorexic patients were engaged in a dysfunctional style of familial interaction known as "enmeshment": Such families are characterized by extreme parental overprotectiveness, lack of privacy of individual members, and reluctance or inability to confront intrafamilial conflicts. Although superficially these families appeared to be congenial, Bruch wrote, this harmony was achieved through excessive conformity on the part of the child, which undermined the child's development of an autonomous self. Anorexia nervosa, according to Bruch, was therefore a young woman's attempt to exert control and self-direction within a family environment in which she otherwise felt powerless (Bruch 1973, 1988).

Bruch was also primarily responsible for the tremendous growth in the popular awareness of anorexia nervosa and other eating disorders in the 1970s and 1980s. Through her book, *The Golden Cage: The Enigma of Anorexia Nervosa* (1978), which sold over 150,000 copies, and numerous articles in *Family Circle* and other popular magazines, Bruch brought anorexia nervosa into common American parlance.

At the same time that the American public was becoming increasingly aware of anorexia nervosa, the number of reported cases of the disorder grew tremendously. This phenomenon has led some clinicians and social commentators to suggest that the popularization process itself may promote a "sympathetic host environment" for the disorder (Striegel-Moore, Silberstein, and Rodin 1986). As Bruch herself observed: "Once the discovery of isolated tormented women, it [anorexia nervosa] has now acquired a fashionable reputation, of being something to be competitive about. . . . This is a far cry from the twenty-years-ago anorexic whose goal was to be unique and suggests that social factors may impact the prevalence of the disorder" (Bruch 1988: 3–4).

Geographic and Demographic Features

Until recently, anorexia nervosa was believed to be a disorder largely confined to the United States, Canada, and Western Europe. Researchers also thought that the disease was virtually nonexistent in people of color and/or those from disadvantaged socioeconomic backgrounds. As early as 1880, S. Fenwick observed that anorexia nervosa "is much more common in the wealthier class of society than amongst those who have to procure their bread by daily labor" (Fenwick 1880: 11). This image of anorexia nervosa as a disease of abundance has persisted into the present day. Many researchers suggest that individuals from non-Western societies, minority groups, and impoverished backgrounds are "protected" from eating disorders because thinness is not highly valued in these communities, and fatness is often viewed as a sign of health and prosperity (Andersen and Hay 1985; Gray, Ford, and Kelly 1987; Gowers and McMahon 1989). The apparent absence of the disorder in developing nations and its high incidence among affluent social groups in Westernized countries led many clinicians to classify anorexia nervosa as a "culture bound" syndrome, meaning a disorder that is restricted to certain cultures primarily because of their distinctive psychosocial features (Prince 1985).

As a result of these views, none of the early literature on anorexia nervosa mentioned individuals from minority groups, non-Western countries, or lower socioeconomic classes (Bruch 1966; Kendall et al. 1973; Garfinkel and Garner 1980). The first cases of nonwhite anorectics appeared in a paper by M. P. Warren and R. L. Vande Wiele (1973), which noted 1 Chinese and 1 black person out of 42 patients seen at their New York clinic between 1960 and 1971. Other articles from the late 1970s and early 1980s mentioned one or two cases of nonwhite anorectics but did not offer any explanations of this phenomenon (Jones et al. 1980; Hedblom, Hubbard, and Andersen 1981; Garfinkel and Garner 1982; Roy-Byrne, Lee-Benner, and Yager 1984).

More recently, research on nonwhite and non-Western anorectics has grown significantly: Investigators have identified cases of the disorder in Malaysia (Buhrich 1981), Greece (Fichter, Elton, and Sourdi

1988), Nigeria (Nwaefuna 1981), Zimbabwe (Buchan and Gregory 1984), and Ethiopia (Fahy et al. 1988). The non-Western country to receive the most attention from researchers has been Japan, probably because it is one of the most Westernized East Asian countries. In Japan, anorexia nervosa and a binge-eating syndrome called *Kirbarashi-gui* have been well documented by researchers for a number of years (Nogami and Yabana 1977; Azuma and Henmi 1982; Nogami et al. 1984; Suematsu et al. 1985).

Within the United States and Great Britain, there has been a growing body of research on the incidence of anorexia nervosa in blacks (Pumariega, Edwards, and Mitchell 1984; Andersen and Hay 1985; Nevo 1985; Robinson and Andersen 1985; White, Hudson, and Campbell 1985; Silber 1986; Gray et al. 1987; Hsu 1987; Thomas and James 1988), Hispanics (Silber 1986; Hiebert et al. 1988; Smith and Krejci 1991), Asian-Americans and British-Asians (Nevo 1985; Root 1990), and Native Americans (Rosen et al. 1988; Whitehouse and Mumford 1988; Smith and Krejci 1991), as well as recent immigrants from Eastern Europe (Bulik 1987), the Middle East (Garfinkel and Garner 1982), and the Caribbean (Thomas and Szmukler 1985; Holden and Robinson 1988). Researchers have also challenged the notion that lesbians are "protected" from eating disorders because lesbian ideology challenges culturally prescribed beauty ideals (Striegel-Moore et al. 1990; Thompson 1994).

Although all of this recent research indicates that the number of reported cases of anorexia nervosa and other eating disorders is substantially lower in non-whites, lesbians, and individuals from non-Western countries, there is a difference of opinion on what this implies about the actual incidence of eating disorders in these groups. Some researchers who have investigated anorexia nervosa in racial minorities have suggested that the disorder is linked more to socioeconomic class than to race and argue that the growing incidence of nonwhite anorectics reflects the growing economic prosperity of certain minority group members. These researchers argue that as non-whites become more prosperous, their exposure to white, middle-class beauty standards increases, thereby making nonwhites more vulnerable to anorexia and other eating disorders. Because fewer nonwhites than whites belong to the middle and upper economic classes, fewer nonwhites become anorexic (Pumariega et al. 1984; Andersen and Hay 1985; Robinson and Andersen 1985; White et al. 1985; Gray et al. 1987; Hsu 1987; Thomas and James 1988).

Other investigators, however, have exposed methodological and philosophical flaws behind this kind of argument. Some have suggested that the reason there are so relatively few nonwhite anorectics is because people of color do not have the same access to health-care facilities as whites. Because most of the studies of anorexia nervosa record only those sufferers who come to the attention of medical and psychiatric facilities, nonwhites who lack access to these facilities will not be acknowledged by health-care researchers. Moreover, even those minorities who do have access to medical care may feel threatened by a white-dominated medical profession and/or may be embarrassed to seek help for a mental health problem. Thus, the actual number of nonwhites with anorexia nervosa in the general population may be greater than indicated by case reports (Rosen et al. 1988; Root 1990; Dolan 1991; Smith and Krejci 1991; Thompson 1994).

In addition, some have argued that racial stereotypes about who is most vulnerable to anorexia nervosa can explain the apparent rarity of the disorder in minority groups. Anorexia nervosa is frequently referred to in medical and popular literature as a "Golden Girl's Disease" that afflicts only young girls from white, Western European, privileged backgrounds (Root 1990). Consequently, this ethnocentric bias may lead medical personnel to misdiagnose or underdiagnose eating disorders in persons of color (Silber 1986; Hiebert et al. 1988; Rosen et al. 1988; Dolan 1991; Thompson 1994).

Even those who agree that minority group status may "protect" nonwhites from eating disorders also argue that this status does not necessarily protect specific individuals within these groups. As Maria Root (1990: 534) notes in a recent article on eating disorders in women of color: "Individuals within each racial/ethnic group are subject to the standards of the dominant culture, particularly when the culture-of-origin is devalued by the dominant culture." Because thinness in Western and Westernized societies is associated with higher social class, and the attendant social power, resources, and opportunities, some individuals of color may see the pursuit of a slim body-type as a ticket to upward social mobility and acceptance by the dominant culture (Root 1990; see also Silber 1986 and Thompson 1994).

Whatever the explanation, the standard image of anorexia nervosa as a privileged white girl's disease is increasingly being called into question. The disorder has been detected in a variety of racial, ethnic, and socioeconomic groups and in both Western and non-Western societies, although at the moment the number of cases among these groups appears to be relatively rare. Clearly, more research is needed before any definitive statements on the incidence and form of eating disorders in nonwhite and non-Western groups can be made.

Heather Munro Prescott

Bibliography

Anderson, Arnold, and Andy Hay. 1985. Racial and socioeconomic influences in anorexia nervosa and bulimia. *International Journal of Eating Disorders* 4: 479-87.

Azuma, Y., and M. Henmi. 1982. A study of the incidence of anorexia nervosa in schoolgirls. *Annual report of research group in eating disorders:* 30-4.

Bell, Rudolph. 1985. *Holy anorexia.* Chicago.

Bliss, Eugene L., and C. H. Hardin Branch. 1960. *Anorexia nervosa: Its history, psychology, and biology.* New York.

Bordo, Susan. 1993. *Unbearable weight: Feminism, western culture, and the body.* Berkeley, Calif.

Brown, L. 1987. Lesbians, weight, and eating: New analyses and perspectives. In *Lesbian psychologies,* ed. Boston Lesbian Psychologies Collective, 294-310. Chicago.

Bruch, Hilde. 1966. Anorexia nervosa and its differential diagnosis. *Journal of Nervous and Mental Disease* 141: 555-66.

  1973. *Eating disorders: Obesity, anorexia nervosa, and the person within.* New York.

  1978. *The golden cage: The enigma of anorexia nervosa.* New York.

  1988. *Conversations with anorexics,* ed. Danita Czyzewski and Melanie A. Suhr. New York.

Brumberg, Joan Jacobs. 1988. *Fasting girls: The emergence of anorexia nervosa as a modern disease.* Cambridge, Mass.

Buchan, T., and L. D. Gregory. 1984. Anorexia nervosa in a black Zimbabwean. *British Journal of Psychiatry* 145: 326-30.

Buhrich, N. 1981. Frequency and presentation of anorexia in Malaysia. *Australian and New Zealand Journal of Psychiatry* 15: 153-5.

Bulik, Cynthia. 1987. Eating disorders in immigrants. *International Journal of Eating Disorders* 6: 133-41.

Bynum, Caroline Walker. 1987. *Holy feast and holy fast: The religious significance of food and medieval women.* Berkeley, Calif.

Chernin, Kim. 1985. *The hungry self: Women, eating, and identity.* New York.

Chipley, William S. 1859. Sitomania: Its causes and treatment. *American Journal of Insanity* 26: 1-42.

Crisp, A. H., R. L. Palmer, and R. S. Kalucy. 1976. How common is anorexia nervosa? A prevalence study. *British Journal of Psychiatry* 128: 549-54.

Dolan, Bridget. 1991. Cross-cultural aspects of anorexia nervosa and bulimia. *International Journal of Eating Disorders* 10: 67-78.

Fahy, T. A., P. H. Robinson, G. F. M. Russell, and B. Sheinman. 1988. Anorexia nervosa following torture in a young African woman. *British Journal of Psychiatry* 153: 385-7.

Fenwick, S. 1880. *On atrophy of the stomach and on the nervous affections of the digestive organs.* London.

Fichter, M. M., M. Elton, and L. Sourdi. 1988. Anorexia nervosa in Greek and Turkish adolescents. *European Archives of Psychiatric and Neurological Science* 237: 200-8.

Freud, Sigmund. [1918] 1959. From the history of an infantile neurosis. In *Collected papers,* Vol. 3. Trans. Alix and James Strachey. New York.

Furnham, A., and N. Alibhai. 1983. Cross-cultural differences in the perception of female body shapes. *Psychological Medicine* 13: 829-37.

Garfinkel, Paul E., and David M. Garner. 1980. Sociocultural factors in the development of anorexia nervosa. *Psychosomatic Medicine* 10: 647-56.

  1982. *Anorexia nervosa: A multidimensional perspective.* New York.

Garner, David M., Marion Olmstead, and J. Polivy. 1983. Development and validation of a multi-dimensional eating disorder inventory of anorexia and bulimia. *International Journal of Eating Disorders* 2: 15-34.

Gowers, Simon, and John McMahon. 1989. Social class and prognosis in anorexia nervosa. *International Journal of Eating Disorders* 8: 105-9.

Gray, James, Kathryn Ford, and Lily Kelly. 1987. The prevalence of bulimia in a black college population. *International Journal of Eating Disorders* 6: 733-40.

Gull, William. 1874. Anorexia nervosa (apepsia hysterica, anorexia hysterica). *Transactions of the Clinical Society of London* 7: 22-8.

Hedblom, J., F. A. Hubbard, and A. E. Andersen. 1981. A multidisciplinary treatment program for patient and family. *Journal of Social Work in Health Care* 7: 67-86.

Herzog, David B., and Paul M. Copeland. 1985. Eating disorders. *New England Journal of Medicine* 313: 295-303.

Hiebert, K. A., M. A. Felice, D. L. Wingard, et al. 1988. Comparison of outcome in Hispanic and Caucasian patients with anorexia nervosa. *International Journal of Eating Disorders* 7: 693-6.

Holden, N. L., and P. H. Robinson. 1988. Anorexia nervosa and bulimia nervosa in British blacks. *British Journal of Psychiatry* 152: 544-9.

Hsu, George. 1987. Are eating disorders becoming more prevalent among blacks? *International Journal of Eating Disorders* 6: 113-24.

Janet, Pierre. 1903. *Les obsessions et la psychasthénie.* New York.

Jones, D. J., M. M. Fox, H. M. Babigian, and H. E. Hutton. 1980. Epidemiology of anorexia nervosa in Monroe County, New York, 1960-1976. *Psychosomatic Medicine* 42: 551-8.

Kaye, W. H., H. Gwirtsman, T. George, et al. 1986. Caloric consumption and activity levels after weight recovery in anorexia nervosa: A prolonged delay in normalization. *International Journal of Eating Disorders* 5: 489-502.

Kendall, R. E., D. J. Hall, A. Hailey, and H. M. Babigian. 1973. The epidemiology of anorexia nervosa. *Psychological Medicine* 3: 200-3.

Lacey, J. H., and B. M. Dolan. 1988. Bulimia in British black and Asians: A catchment area study. *British Journal of Psychiatry* 152: 73-7.

Lasègue, Charles. 1873. De l'anorexie hystérique. *Archives générales de médecine* 1: 385-7.

Lawlor, B. A. 1987. An atypical eating disorder in a black man. *Journal of the National Medical Association* 79: 984-6.

Lawlor, B. A., R. C. Burket, and J. A. Hodgin. 1987. Eating disorders in American black men. *Journal of the National Medical Association* 79: 984-6.

Lawlor, B. A., and C. S. W. Rand. 1985. Bulimia nervosa in a black woman. *American Journal of Psychiatry* 142: 1514.

Minuchin, Salvador, Bernice L. Rosman, and Lesley Baker. 1978. *Psychosomatic families: Anorexia nervosa in context.* Cambridge, Mass.

Morton, Richard. 1689. *Phthisiologia, seu exercitationes de phthisi.* London.

Nasser, M. 1986. Comparative study of the prevalence of abnormal eating attitudes among Arab female students of both London and Cairo Universities. *Psychological Medicine* 16: 621-5.

Nevo, Shoshana. 1985. Bulimic symptoms: Prevalence and ethnic differences among college women. *International Journal of Eating Disorders* 4: 151-68.

Nogami, Y., and F. Yabana. 1977. On Kibarashi-gui. *The Japanese Journal of Psychiatry and Neurology* 31: 159-66.

Nogami, Y., T. Yamaguchi, H. Ishiwata, et al. 1984. The prevalence of binge eating among the Japanese university population. *Journal of Nihon University Medical Association* 43: 749-52.

Nwaefuna, A. 1981. Anorexia nervosa in a developing country. *British Journal of Psychiatry* 138: 270.

Orbach, Susie. 1986. *Hunger strike: The anorectic's struggle as a metaphor for our age.* New York.

Prince, Raymond. 1985. The concept of culture-bound syndrome: Anorexia nervosa and brain-fag. *Social Science and Medicine* 21: 197-203.

Pumariega, Andres, Palmer Edwards, and Carol Mitchell. 1984. Anorexia nervosa in black adolescents. *American Academy of Child Psychiatry* 23: 111-14.

Pyle, R. L., J. E. Mitchell, and E. D. Echert. 1981. Bulimia: A report of 34 cases. *Journal of Clinical Psychiatry* 42: 60-4.

Robinson, Paul, and Arnold Andersen. 1985. Anorexia nervosa in American blacks. *Journal of Psychiatric Research* 19: 183-8.

Root, Maria P. 1990. Disordered eating in women of color. *Sex Roles* 22: 525-36.

Rosen, Lionel, Christine Shafer, Gail Dummer, et al. 1988. Prevalence of pathogenic weight-control behaviors among Native American women and girls. *International Journal of Eating Disorders* 7: 807-11.

Rothenberg, Albert. 1986. Eating disorder as a modern obsessive-compulsive syndrome. *Psychiatry* 49: 45-53.

Roy-Byrne, P., K. Lee-Brenner, and J. Yager. 1984. Group therapy for bulimia. *International Journal of Eating Disorders* 3: 97-116.

Schwartz, Donald M., Michael G. Thompson, and Craig L. Johnson. 1982. Anorexia nervosa and bulimia: The socio-cultural context. *International Journal of Eating Disorders* 1: 20-36.

Silber, Tomas. 1986. Anorexia nervosa in blacks and Hispanics. *International Journal of Eating Disorders* 5: 121-8.

Silberstein, L. R., M. Mishkind, R. H. Striegel-Moore, et al. 1988. Behavioral and psychological implications of body dissatisfaction: Do men and women differ? *Sex Roles* 19: 219-32.

1989. Men and their bodies: A comparison of homosexual and heterosexual men. *Psychosomatic Medicine* 51: 337-46.

Silverman, Joseph. 1977. Anorexia nervosa: Clinical and metabolic observations in a successful treatment plan. In *Anorexia nervosa,* ed. Robert A. Vigersky, 331-9. New York.

1983. Richard Morton, 1637-1698: Limner of anorexia nervosa: His life and times. *Journal of the American Medical Association* 250: 2830-2.

Smith, Jane, and Jonathon Krejci. 1991. Minorities join the majority: Eating disturbances among Hispanic and Native American youth. *International Journal of Eating Disorders* 10: 179-86.

Stein, A. 1989. All dressed up, but no place to go? Style wars and the new lesbianism. *Outlook* 2: 34-42.

Striegel-Moore, Ruth, Lisa R. Silberstein, and Judith Rodin. 1986. Toward an understanding of risk factors in bulimia. *American Psychologist* 41: 246-63.

Striegel-Moore, Ruth, Naomi Tucker, and Jeanette Hsu. 1990. Body image dissatisfaction and disordered eating. *International Journal of Eating Disorders* 9: 493-500.

Suematsu, H., H. Ishikawa, T. Kuboki, and T. Ito. 1985. Statistical studies on anorexia nervosa in Japan: Detailed clinical data on 1,011 patients. *Psychotherapy and Psychosomatics* 43: 96-103.

Szmukler, George I., and Digby Tantum. 1984. Anorexia nervosa: Starvation dependence. *British Journal of Medical Psychology* 57: 303-10.

Thomas, J. P., and G. S. Szmukler. 1985. Anorexia nervosa in patients of Afro-Caribbean extraction. *British Journal of Psychiatry* 146: 653–6.

Thomas, Veronica, and Michelle James. 1988. Body image, dieting tendencies, and sex role traits in urban black women. *Sex Roles* 18: 523–9.

Thompson, Becky W. 1994. *A hunger so wide and so deep: American women speak out on eating problems.* Minneapolis, Minn.

Warren, M. P., and R. L. Vande Wiele. 1973. Clinical and metabolic features of anorexia nervosa. *American Journal of Obstetrics and Gynecology* 117: 435–49.

White, William C., Lisa Hudson, and Stephen J. Campbell. 1985. Bulimarexia and black women: A brief report. *Psychotherapy* 22: 449–50.

Whitehouse, A. M., and D. B. Mumford. 1988. Increased prevalence of bulimia nervosa amongst Asian schoolgirls. *British Medical Journal* 297: 718.

Willi, J., and S. Grossmann. 1983. Epidemiology of anorexia nervosa in a defined region of Switzerland. *American Journal of Psychiatry* 140: 564–7.

Yager, J., F. Kurtzman, J. Landsverk, and E. Weismeier. 1988. Behaviors and attitudes related to eating disorders in homosexual male college students. *American Journal of Psychiatry* 145: 495–7.

IV.E.2 ❧ Celiac Disease

Historical Perspective

Celiac disease has been recognized for centuries (Dowd and Walker-Smith 1974) by physicians aware of its major symptoms of diarrhea and gastrointestinal distress accompanied by a wasting away in adults and a failure to grow in children. The Greek physician Aretaeus (first century A.D.) called the condition *coeliac diathesis* – coeliac deriving from the Greek word *koeliakos,* or abdominal cavity. The British physician Samuel Gee provided what is generally considered the first modern, detailed description of the condition, which he termed the *coeliac affection* in deference to Aretaeus, in a lecture presented at St. Bartholomew's Hospital in London (Gee 1888). At present, celiac disease (or, especially in Britain, coeliac disease) is the most commonly used term for the condition, although various others may be encountered, including celiac syndrome, celiac sprue, nontropical sprue, and gluten-sensitive enteropathy.

There were perceptions, certainly since Gee's time, that celiac disease was a consequence of, or at least affected by, diet. Gee (1888: 20) noted that "[a] child, who was fed upon a quart of the best Dutch mussels daily, throve wonderfully, but relapsed when the season for mussels was over." Such associations with diet led to wide-ranging dietary prescriptions and proscriptions (Haas 1924; Sheldon 1955; Weijers, Van de Kamer, and Dicke 1957; Anderson 1992). Some physicians recommended exclusion of fats – others, exclusion of complex carbohydrates. At times, so many restrictions were applied simultaneously that it became impossible to maintain a satisfactory intake of calories.

Because dietary treatments of celiac disease were of limited effectiveness, the food connection remained a puzzle until the end of the 1940s when a Dutch physician, W. K. Dicke, observed that removal of wheat from the diet of celiac patients led to dramatic improvement (Dicke 1950). It eventually became clear that the efficacy of the various diets recommended prior to Dicke's discovery was in proportion to the extent that wheat was excluded from them. Initial fractionation studies pointed to the gliadin protein fraction as being most harmful to celiac patients (Van de Kamer, Weijers, and Dicke 1953).

Soon after Dicke (1950) reported the harmful effects of wheat on celiac patients, a series of investigations indicated that rye, barley, and oats were also harmful, whereas rice and maize (corn) were not (Dicke, Weijers, and Van de Kamer 1953; Van de Kamer et al. 1953; Weijers et al. 1957). With children, and most adults, the exclusion of wheat, rye, barley, and oats from the diet usually brought about a complete, or largely complete, recovery.

During the 1950s, the development of intestinal biopsy techniques (Shiner 1956; Crosby and Kugler 1957; Brandborg, Rubin, and Quinton 1959) enabled pieces of tissue to be recovered from the intestine for examination and testing, and it was recognized that ingestion of wheat and related grains often resulted in damage to the intestinal mucosa, including the absorptive cells, or enterocytes, lining the interior surface of the intestine. The enterocytes are responsible for the absorption of almost all nutrients; the damage to them provided a basis for the gastrointestinal symptoms and malabsorption.

Familial associations, as well as its rarity among the Chinese, the Japanese, and blacks in sub-Saharan Africa (McNeish et al. 1974), indicated a likely genetic basis for celiac disease. Subsequent findings of strong associations with particular histocompatibility antigens supported this possibility (Kagnoff 1992) and, along with the presence of circulating antibodies to wheat gliadin proteins in patients on a gluten-containing diet, suggested that an abnormal immune response initiated intestinal damage in susceptible individuals.

A detailed understanding of the basis for celiac disease remains to be achieved. Neither the initiating event triggered by wheat gliadin proteins or products derived from them by digestion, nor the mechanisms leading to tissue damage in the small intestine following ingestion of wheat are completely understood. On the basis of current knowledge, it appears that celiac disease has resulted from the convergence of various evolutionary developments: These include human evolution (especially evolution of the immune system), the evolution of wheat and related grasses, the evolution of the protein structures apparently unique to wheat and closely related species, and the evolution of culture – specifically the development of agriculture and the spread of wheat farming (Figure IV.E.2.1).

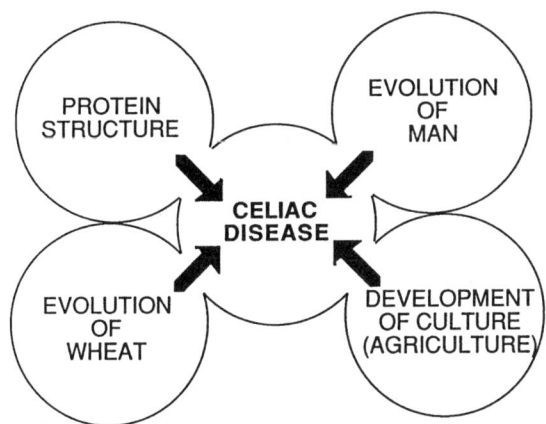

Figure IV.E.2.1. Evolutionary factors combine to produce celiac disease.

Geographical Distribution of Celiac Disease

Celiac disease is commonly thought of as largely afflicting people of European ancestry, and reports of cases among the Chinese, the Japanese (Kihara, Kukida, and Ichikawa 1977), and black Africans are sufficiently rare as to make it unlikely that this assumption is incorrect (also see McNeish et al. 1974; Simoons 1981). However, studies throughout much of the world either are inadequate or have yet to be done.

There are some parts of Asia where rice, a harmless grain (see ahead for definitions of harmful grains), is the predominant cereal grain in the diet, and in some parts of Africa, teff and millet – likely to be harmless cereal grains – predominate. To what extent a low intake of wheat, rye, barley, and oats in Asia and Africa contributes to the apparently low incidence of celiac disease is unknown. Furthermore, in some parts of the world – the United States, for example – medical personnel may have only minimal knowledge of celiac disease and fail to recognize it, whereas in Britain and much of Western Europe, physicians are much more attuned to its signs, which may be highly varied. The likelihood of failure to recognize celiac disease is doubtless substantially greater in some Asian and African countries and may contribute to the perception that it is rare in these places. The difficulties in diagnosing celiac disease and in developing statistical information about its incidence and prevalence have been discussed by R. F. A. Logan (1992a, 1992b).

The incidence of celiac disease varies throughout Europe and with time. For example, crude incidence rates (number of cases per 1,000 births) in various parts of Sweden currently range from about 2.2 to 3.5 per 1,000, whereas in neighboring Denmark, the rate is about 0.1 per 1,000 (Greco et al. 1992). Furthermore, the incidence varies with time, possibly indicat-ing the contribution of some environmental factor. Prior to 1983, incidence of the disease in Sweden was much lower, but it began to increase at about that time, and it has been speculated that an increase in the amount of gluten in infant formulas was responsi-ble for the rise (Maki et al. 1992). The suggestion has also been made (on the basis of screening of blood donors for antigliadin antibodies) that the incidence of celiac disease in Denmark may be similar to that of Sweden although largely undiagnosed (E. Grodzinsky, personal communication, cited by Ascher and Kris-tiansson 1994).

Ireland was reported to have a high incidence of celiac disease – about 4 per 1,000 births during an 11-year period prior to 1973, particularly in the west near Galway (Mylotte et al. 1973). Since that time, however, the incidence among children under the age of 12 has fallen by 62 percent (Stevens, Egan-Mitchell, et al. 1988), in contrast to the rise experienced in Sweden. The reasons for the decline in Ireland are unclear; they perhaps involve dietary changes such as an increase in the frequency of breast feeding or a decrease in the early introduction of grains to the diet of infants. Or some other undefined factor, perhaps a change in the type of viral infections prevalent in the population, may be involved.

The incidence in the United States has not been established, but a recent study of a Minnesota popula-tion (Talley et al. 1994) estimated the incidence as 0.01 per 1,000 person-years and the prevalence at 1 per 5,000. Because of the diversity of the U.S. popula-tion, which includes significant numbers of people having African, Chinese, or Southeast Asian ancestry, it might be expected that prevalence would be less than that of Europe as a whole, which is about 1 per 1,000. Whether the prevalence among U.S. residents of European extraction approximates that of Euro-pean populations remains to be established, but it would be surprising to find that it is different.

Most studies of incidence and prevalence have focused on clearly recognizable disease resulting from significant damage to the absorptive epithelium of the intestine, often diagnosed by intestinal biopsy to show loss of villous structure and followed by removal of wheat and other harmful grains from the diet to demonstrate recovery of mucosal structure and function. It is becoming obvious, however, that there are many people who have subclinical celiac disease (Marsh 1992a), so that the true incidence of celiac disease may be at least two to three times greater than that represented by those with signifi-cant damage to the epithelium.

Origins of Agriculture and Wheat Farming

A diploid wheat and barley were likely to have been among the first crops cultivated by humans who were spearheading the Neolithic Revolution about 10,000 years ago. Wild diploid species of wheat, probably *Triticum boeoticum* and *Triticum urartu,* or possibly the wild tetraploid species *Triticum dicoccoides,* had most likely been harvested by hunter-gatherers for some considerable time. These species of *Triticum* were probably extant for perhaps 16 million years (Shewry et al. 1980) before domestication occurred (Harlan 1977) and thus those who pioneered in cultivating it probably had a reasonably good understanding of the plant's life cycle. The origin of wheat cultivation is likely to have been somewhere in the Fertile Crescent area of the Middle East, perhaps near Jericho.

Frederick Simoons (1981) has discussed the possible effects of the spread of wheat farming (from likely centers of origin in the Middle East) on populations with members genetically susceptible to celiac disease. He used a genetic marker for celiac disease and compared the incidence of this marker in populations throughout the world with the incidence of celiac disease. The marker selected was a human leukocyte antigen, HLA-B8 (a class I major histocompatibility complex [MHC] protein). HLA-B8 had been demonstrated to have approximately threefold greater occurrence in celiac patients (Falchuk, Rogentine, and Strober 1972; Stokes et al. 1972) than in normal individuals of the same populations, although it is now known that certain class II MHC proteins show even better correlations and are more likely to play a direct role in the processes of celiac disease (Kagnoff, Morzycka-Wroblewska, and Harwood 1994). The data available to Simoons were, however, limited to HLA-B8.

Simoons reasoned that the greater rate of occurrence of celiac disease among people with the HLA-B8 antigen gave researchers a tool to use in their study of the illness. By determining the distribution of the antigen among human populations, researchers could predict which people were more at risk of developing the disease. Although there are exceptions, such that populations without HLA-B8 may yet have high levels of celiac disease (Logan 1992a), the assumption appears to have general validity.

It turned out that there were two geographic centers in Old World populations with noticeably higher frequencies of HLA-B8, one in western Europe, centered about the British Isles, and one in northwestern India, centered about the Punjab region. These regions also fell within the major areas of wheat cultivation, and in both there had been reports of relatively high incidences of celiac disease. They also represented, to a considerable degree, the boundaries of the spread of wheat farming throughout its geographical range up to relatively recent times (in this analysis, about 1000 B.C.) from its point of origin.

There appeared to be a gradient in the incidence of HLA-B8 throughout the range of wheat cultivation, such that low levels of the antigen were found at the likely origin of wheat cultivation and higher levels at the periphery. Simoons (1981) assumed that high levels of HLA-B8 were once typical of peoples at the ori-

gin and suggested that the gradient observed from the center to the periphery might well reflect the effects of a selective genetic disadvantage to members of the population carrying HLA-B8 – along with other genes for susceptibility to celiac disease. Thus, the high levels of HLA-B8 in populations that took up wheat farming late (in the west of Ireland, for example) in its spread from the center of origin, along with high incidences of celiac disease, would reflect the lesser time available for the selective disadvantage to have diminished marker levels.

One obvious discrepancy was northwestern China, where wheat farming was introduced quite late through trade. This major wheat-growing area, although somewhat beyond the contiguous area of the earlier spread of wheat farming, might reasonably be considered its periphery.

There was, however, neither evidence of celiac disease nor high levels of HLA-B8 in the wheat-growing regions of China. A possible explanation for this was the likelihood that immune systems evolved differently in different populations to protect against relatively specific infectious diseases. Geographically distant populations would have been exposed to different stresses, thereby resulting in different complements of histocompatibility antigens. Furthermore, histocompatibility antigens that provided resistance to one disease might, quite coincidentally, enhance susceptibility to another, and this may well be true of genes for susceptibility to celiac disease (Strober 1992). Thus, the absence of celiac disease in the wheat-growing areas of China may well reflect the absence of the susceptibility genes in the Chinese population. Although hampered by a lack of adequate information, the analysis by Simoons (1981) is at least a highly interesting attempt to deal with what must have been selective pressures on populations containing the genes for susceptibility to celiac disease as wheat farming spread from the Middle East throughout Western Europe.

Definition of Harmful Cereal Grains and Components

Wheat, Rye, Barley, and Oats

Early conclusions regarding the toxicity of cereal grains and their constituents were based mainly on the ability of a grain to produce malabsorption of fats in celiac patients. Despite the lack of the more sophisticated approaches available today, early test results generally seem convincing. Currently, examination of mucosal biopsy specimens has become fairly common. When a flattened mucosa is found, with loss of villous structure, wheat and other harmful grains are removed from the diet to see if improvement follows. If it does, a subsequent challenge and biopsy to test for relapse may follow, although subsequent challenge has come to be reserved for special circumstances (Walker-Smith et al. 1990) because supporting antibody tests (tests for circulating antigliadin and antiendomysium antibodies) have lessened the likelihood of misdiagnosis (McMillan et al. 1991). In recent years, however, the situation has become more complicated through recognition that a flattened mucosa may actually be an extreme response and that there are many gluten-sensitive people who show less obvious evidence of the disease (Marsh 1992a). Circulating antigliadin antibodies may be indicative of celiac disease or at least a related gluten-sensitive condition in the absence of any evidence of mucosal changes, particularly when symptoms are present (O'Farrelly 1994).

Relatively few subjects were used in the testing of some grains or grain fractions in early work. This has been a continuing problem, resulting largely from the difficulties inherent in the requirement for human subjects in celiac disease research. It has become fairly clear that response to challenge may vary greatly from one patient to another and for a single patient over time. Furthermore, a considerably delayed response to challenge is not unusual, even when the challenge is with wheat, presumably the most toxic of the cereal grains (Egan-Mitchell, Fottrell, and McNicholl 1978; Walker-Smith, Kilby, and France 1978).

The variations in response known to occur might explain the opposing conclusions arrived at by various investigators regarding the harmful effects of oats. For example, Dicke, H. A. Weijers, and J. H. Van de Kamer (1953) asserted that oats are toxic, whereas W. Sheldon (1955) concluded that they are not. Part of the problem apparently arises from the relatively small proportion of avenins, the likely toxic fraction, in oat grain proteins (Peterson and Brinegar 1986): Avenins may make up only about 10 percent of the total protein in oats. Furthermore, when small numbers of subjects are involved, the average response of one group can be quite different from that of another. Because a negative response in one or a few patients might indicate only that the feeding time was too short, a clear positive response, as in the studies of oat protein toxicity by P. G. Baker and A. E. Read (1976), should perhaps be given more weight than a negative response, as in the study by A. S. Dissanayake, S. C. Truelove, and R. Whitehead (1974). The latter effort, however, included testing by intestinal biopsy – the more rigorous test – whereas the former did not.

A recent feeding trial using oats with 10 confirmed celiac patients produced no harmful effects as indicated by changes in mucosal architecture, endomysial antibody development, and infiltration of intraepithelial lymphocytes (Srinivasan et al. 1996). The relatively low percentage of avenins in oats may complicate this study in that a daily dosage of 50 grams (g) of oats was fed for 3 months. This would correspond to about 5 g of avenins per day. If 50 g of wheat had been fed instead, the patients would be eating at least 40 g of gliadins per day. Nevertheless, subsequent challenge of two of the patients with only 0.5 g of gluten per day produced evidence of intestinal damage. Thus, the toxicity of oats must be considered questionable on the basis of this latest study, as there are now two careful studies that showed no evidence of toxicity and only one study that was positive. It should also be emphasized that the supposedly positive study did not include biopsies.

In other cases, the test materials may not have been well defined. It is possible that the maize (corn) flour used in early testing was actually maize starch and relatively free of protein (Simoons 1981); the conclusion that maize proteins are not harmful may not have as rigorous a scientific base as is generally thought. There is, however, no obvious reason to question the apparent safety of maize.

A lack of sensitivity of the available testing methods, combined with inadequate test length, may have been responsible for the early conclusions that wheat starch is safe for celiac patients (Dicke et al. 1953). These conclusions, however, were challenged in later work (Ciclitira, Ellis, and Flagg 1984; Freedman et al. 1987a, 1987b; Skerritt and Hill 1990, 1991) as a consequence of the development of sensitive monoclonal antibody tests for gliadins (but also see Booth et al. 1991). Such tests have demonstrated the presence of small amounts of gliadins in wheat starch preparations, although the question of how harmful these small amounts may be to celiac patients is controversial (Ejderhamn, Veress, and Strandvik 1988; Hekkens and van Twist-de Graaf 1990; Campbell 1992).

It may be that rigorous scientific studies have proved toxicity in celiac disease only for wheat (and wheat proteins). To a considerable extent, conclusions regarding the toxicity of rye and barley – and, conversely, the lack of toxicity for rice and maize – are not based on an adequate amount of rigorous scientific testing. (Rigorous studies of oats are beginning to appear, and these support an absence of toxicity for this grain.)

Wheat Evolution

Wheat is a member of the grass family (Gramineae), as are the other grains – rye, barley, and oats – that are suspected of harming people with celiac disease. Of course, triticale, a cross between wheat and rye, is toxic, as would be expected for any other similar crosses that included genetic material from one or more of the toxic grains.

The grasses are a relatively recent evolutionary development. They are angiosperms, flowering plants, that developed somewhere between 100 and 200 million years ago (Cronquist 1968). Fossil evidence for grasses goes back only about 65 million years. They became widespread during the Oligocene epoch about 25 to 40 million years ago (Thomasson 1980), which, when it is considered that life has been evolving on earth for about 4 billion years, is a relatively short time. Cereal grains presumably evolved more recently within the time frame of grass evolution.

The ancestors of wheat, barley, and rye were

diploid species with 7 chromosomes in the haploid state, or 14 chromosomes in vegetative cells. Barley first diverged from the common ancestral line, followed by rye. The line eventually gave rise to a series of diploid species that may be classed as *Triticum* species (Morris and Sears 1967). A natural cross occurred at some unknown time between two slightly diverged *Triticum* species, presumably *Triticum urartu* and *Triticum speltoides,* that gave rise to a new species through a process of polyploid formation in which chromosomes become doubled.

Without chromosome doubling, a cross between related species, such as those of *Triticum,* can take place, but the offspring is infertile because of a failure by the chromosomes to pair during meiosis. Polyploid formation occurs naturally, albeit rarely, perhaps through a process involving unreduced gametes (Harlan and de Wet 1975). This process can also be achieved in the laboratory through the use of chemicals (such as colchicine) that interfere with spindle formation to block chromosomal separation at anaphase. Either way, the result is a doubled set of chromosomes, a condition that allows for each original chromosome set to pair with its identical replicated set, thus avoiding the chromosome pairing problems that occur in crosses between species. The result of allopolyploid formation between *T. urartu* and *T. speltoides* was a new fertile species, called a tetraploid because it incorporated four sets of chromosomes in vegetative cells (designated AABB). Durum wheats (*Triticum turgidum* var. *durum*), used for pasta making, belong to one of the varietal groups of the AABB tetraploids.

Some time after wheat cultivation began, a tetraploid wheat crossed accidentally with a weed growing in the same field (*Triticum tauschii* var. *strangulata*), followed by chromosome doubling to give rise to a hexaploid species, which, because the genome of *T. tauschii* was designated D, had the composition AABBDD. Bread wheats (*Triticum aestivum* var. *aestivum*) produce a more elastic dough than durum wheats and have properties that lend themselves to the retention of gases produced during yeast fermentation (leavening) of doughs. It was in the context of the evolution of wheat and closely related species that proteins arose with amino acid sequences capable of initiating damage in persons with celiac disease.

Gluten Protein Evolution

The gluten proteins of wheat (a monocotyledonous plant) and certain closely related species – including rye, barley, and, with qualifications, oats – are unique among plant storage proteins in having exceptionally high proportions of the amino acids glutamine and proline. It was suggested (Kasarda 1980, 1981) that because of their unique composition, the extensive occurrence of repeating sequences based largely on glutamine and proline, and their occurrence only in recently evolved grass species, wheat prolamins are a late evolutionary development. Subsequently, with the development of molecular biological techniques, gene sequencing provided evidence of short amino acid sequences in most wheat prolamins, homologous to sequences found in storage globulins of more distantly related dicotyledonous plant species (Kreis et al. 1985). This discovery pushes the possible age of the ancestral genes back to within the period during which the flowering plants have existed – perhaps 100 million years.

However, repetitive sequences make up major parts of all gluten proteins, whereas the homologous sequences just mentioned occurred only in nonrepetitive regions. These repetitive sequences, having major proportions of glutamine and proline, apparently do not have counterparts in proteins of species outside the grass family. Accordingly, it seems likely that at least the repetitive domains of gluten proteins, which have slightly differing repeat motifs according to type, are of more recent (<~65 million years) origin. All of the various repeating sequences include glutamine and proline residues, and although the repeats are often imperfect, comparison allows a consensus repeating sequence to be recognized. It is at least possible that the most active (in celiac disease) peptides may result from variations on the themes represented by the consensus sequences, as a consequence of these imperfections, rather than from the consensus sequences themselves, but that remains to be established.

There is reasonably strong evidence that the peptides with sequences found in the repeat domain of alpha-gliadin are capable of triggering the intestinal damage characteristic of celiac disease. Furthermore, significant sequence similarities between gluten proteins and other proteins are rare. The first important similarity found was between alpha-gliadin and the E1b protein (Kagnoff et al. 1984), produced in conjunction with infection by adenovirus 12, which infects the human gastrointestinal tract. Recently, similarities have been found for peptides produced in conjunction with infection by other types of adenovirus (Lähdeaho et al. 1993).

The recent evolution of repeating sequence domains in gluten proteins through extensive duplication of the DNA codons (for glutamine and proline, along with a few other amino acids) corresponding to the repeat motifs may be the basis for the lack of homologies or similarities with other proteins. Most proteins do not have large amounts of glutamine and proline. Hence, the sequences active in celiac disease are likely to be confined to the grass family.

Fractionation of Wheat

Gluten

The wheat kernel is made up largely of the endosperm, the interior part of the grain, which constitutes about 85 percent of the kernel. In the milling process, the crushed kernels are fractionated by siev-ing. The crushed endosperm is the source of white flour, and the outer layers of the kernel yield the bran and germ fractions. Endosperm cells are largely made up of starch granules (about 75 percent) surrounded by a proteinaceous matrix. The proteins of this sur-rounding matrix are mainly storage proteins; upon germination of the seed, they are broken down to provide a source of nitrogen for use by the new plant. The storage proteins are to a large extent the same as the proteins of gluten, which contribute elasticity, yet at the same time extensibility, to flour–water doughs.

Gluten (Beccari 1745), prepared by washing away the starch granules from dough, constitutes the result-ing cohesive, elastic mass of protein. It usually retains about 15 percent albumins and globulins, which are water- and salt-soluble proteins, respectively, accord-ing to the classification system of T. B. Osborne (1907). The remainder of the protein may be consid-ered to constitute true gluten proteins, notable for their high percentages of two amino acids, glutamine and proline, which provided the basis for the name prolamins (Osborne 1907). Glutamine usually makes up 30 to 55 percent, and proline 15 to 30 percent, of the amino acids in gluten proteins. These two amino acids seem fairly certain to be included in the amino acid sequences of gluten proteins that are active in celiac disease.

The Meaning of "Gluten-Free"

Celiac patients, the physicians who treat them, and the various organizations that represent celiac patients usually indicate that a food safe for someone with celiac disease is "gluten-free." This use of the term "gluten" is sometimes confusing. Traditionally, gluten, as just mentioned, is the cohesive, elastic pro-tein obtained when a wheat flour dough is kneaded in excess water to wash away the starch granules (Beccari 1745). The resultant gluten ball can only be obtained readily from wheat-flour doughs, with diffi-culty from rye, and probably not at all from barley or oats. Cereal chemists would not ordinarily refer to "rye gluten" or "barley gluten," let alone "oat gluten," but would refer specifically to the equivalent storage proteins in these grains (for example, the proteins equivalent to the gliadin proteins of wheat are called hordeins in barley, secalins in rye, and avenins in oats). The term gluten has become corrupted in recent times, however, occasionally being used in industry to refer to the protein residues from other grains. For example, when maize is separated into starch and protein fractions, the protein fraction is often referred to as "corn gluten."

What celiac patients wish to know about a food when they ask if it contains gluten is: Does it contain wheat, rye, barley, or oat proteins or any of the harm-ful peptides that are derived from the storage pro-teins of these grains during food processing or through the action of the digestive enzymes? Use of the term gluten-free is particularly awkward when applied to seeds of rather distantly related plants, such as the dicots amaranth and quinoa. These plants are not known to have proteins at all similar to gluten proteins. However, because quite small peptides of specific amino acid sequence may be active in celiac disease, it is not beyond possibility that equivalent sequences might occur in generally quite different proteins of distantly related species. Despite its ambi-guities, the term gluten-free in relation to foods for celiac patients is already well established, and finding a satisfactory and short alternative may be difficult.

Digestion and Nutrient Absorption

Digestion of proteins commences in the stomach with partial denaturation (unfolding) of the large pro-tein polypeptide chains by hydrochloric acid, which enhances their breakdown into smaller polypeptide chains by the proteolytic enzyme pepsin. In the highly acidic conditions of the stomach, pepsin is very active, cleaving a number of different peptide bonds. Breakdown of food proteins in the stomach is incomplete (Gray 1991), and relatively large peptides pass from the stomach into the duodenal part of the small intestine. Enzymes secreted by the pancreas – trypsin and carboxypeptidases – enter the interior (lumen) of the small intestine to continue digestion of proteins until they are broken down into amino acids or small peptides. Peptides this small are unlikely to be active in celiac disease.

Breakdown of proteins to amino acids or short peptides, both of which can be absorbed, is probably complete in the distal small bowel, even in celiac patients, as evidenced by a gradient of intestinal dam-age from the duodenum through the jejunum in active celiac disease. The ileum may remain free of tis-sue damage (Rubin et al. 1962). Instillation of wheat proteins into the ileum (Rubin et al. 1962) or the rec-tum (Dobbins and Rubin 1964; Loft, Marsh, and Crowe 1990) produces similar damage to that seen in the small intestine, indicating that the entire epithelial surface is susceptible to the damaging effects of wheat proteins or peptides. The final breakdown of food particles to relatively small molecules, and their active or passive absorption for use by the body, takes place at the membranes of cells lining the surface of the small intestine.

Almost all nutrients, ranging through amino acids, sugars, fatty acids, vitamins, and minerals are absorbed from the small intestine so that damage to this absorptive surface may have many manifestations in celiac disease. Obviously, a deficiency of calories from carbohydrates and fats and a deficiency of amino acids needed for protein synthesis can be responsible for a loss of weight or a failure to thrive, but the effects of malabsorption are often more diverse, rang-ing from osteoporosis in later life as a consequence of a failure to absorb calcium adequately to nerve degeneration as a consequence of a failure to absorb vitamins. The large intestine, or colon, extracts water and electrolytes from the food residues while bacterial action on these residues reduces the bulk of indigestible materials, such as cellulose. Relatively little absorption of nutrients occurs in the colon.

When intestinal biopsy was introduced in the 1950s, it was demonstrated that the surface of the intestinal mucosa in patients with active celiac disease appeared flattened as a consequence of the loss of villous structure and enhanced proliferation of immature cells in the crypts. Subsequently it was recognized that the microvilli of mature enterocytes were often damaged as well. Together, these losses significantly diminish the absorptive surface area and give rise to an increased crypt layer with an immature population of enterocytes having incompletely developed enzyme and transport activities. The net result is a diminished capability to absorb nutrients, although it should be noted that malabsorption may occur even in patients with little or no obvious damage to the epithelium.

It has been noted that initial responses to gluten challenge included infiltration by lymphocytes of the epithelium and lamina propria and thickening of the basement membrane and that these changes preceded major changes in mucosal structure (Shmerling and Shiner 1970; Marsh 1992a), providing strong support for the involvement of immunological processes in the destruction of the absorptive epithelium. A highly significant association of celiac disease with certain proteins of the major histocompatibility complex (histocompatibility antigens) also provides evidence for involvement of the immune system and a genetic predisposition to the disease. The inheritance of celiac disease appears to be complex, however, involving two or more genes (Strober 1992), and an environmental contribution, such as a viral infection or stress, may be necessary before the genetic predisposition comes into play (Kagnoff et al. 1984). What remains to be clarified is how these immune processes are triggered by gliadin peptides and how they ultimately result in the loss of epithelial absorptive cells.

Mechanisms of Tissue Damage

The way in which ingested gluten protein triggers events in the body that may ultimately bring about damage to the absorptive epithelium of the small intestine is unknown. The first important hypothesis put forward postulated that a key enzyme, a protease that could degrade proteins, was absent in celiac patients. As a consequence, certain harmful gliadin peptides that would, in the normal person, have been broken down and rendered harmless, continued to exist with a consequence of either direct toxicity on the absorptive epithelial cells or initiation of immune responses that secondarily damaged the epithelium

(Cornell 1988). Although it is difficult to disprove this hypothesis beyond any reasonable doubt, no missing enzyme has ever been found despite considerable research effort to locate it. Furthermore, the likelihood that limited digestion of proteins in the stomach results in exposure of at least the proximal small intestine (duodenum) to fairly large peptides raises the question of why most people do not suffer some damage from such peptides.

The missing enzyme hypothesis was largely supplanted by the proposal that binding of gluten proteins or peptides to the enterocytes targeted them specifically for destruction and that enhanced proliferation of crypt cells, in response to destruction of the villous enterocytes, resulted in flattening of the mucosal surface, one of the major characteristics of advanced disease. Unfortunately, no evidence for the binding of gluten proteins or peptides to enterocytes in vivo has been found. The finding that enterocytes were capable of expressing MHC class II antigens that might be capable of presenting small gluten peptides of perhaps 10 to 20 amino acid residues to T cells raises the question of how effective the search for the binding of peptides to enterocytes has been, insofar as the methods used (often based on antibody probes produced in response to stimulation with intact proteins) were unlikely to recognize such small gluten peptides.

The strong correlation of celiac disease with particular class II histocompatibility antigens, which present peptides to T cells (lymphocytes), thereby activating them, has resulted in a currently favored hypothesis in which this presentation to T cells and binding of gliadin/gluten peptides to T cells is the initiating process that results in damage to the mucosal tissues, especially those underlying the epithelial cells (enterocytes). Binding of peptides by T cells may, however, activate a number of pathways, and beyond the activation step, the details of the hypothesis become rather vague.

Genes and Proteins of the Major Histocompatibility Complex

It is clear that there is an increased incidence of celiac disease in certain families, providing support for the hypothesis that there is a genetic predisposition to the disease. We continue to stress, however, that this predisposition may be insufficient for development of the disease without the intervention of some environmental factor – other than gluten proteins.

Celiac disease occurs in about 14 percent of siblings, 8 percent of parents, and 15 percent of children of celiac patients (Strober 1992). Although dizygotic (fraternal) twins do not show major differences from normal siblings in their tendency to develop celiac disease, monozygotic (identical) twins are about 70 percent concordant for the disease. The fact that 30 percent of the identical twins are discordant, with one having the disease and the other being free of it, is strong support for the necessary role of an environmental factor, such as viral infection (Kagnoff et al. 1984) or some other stressful event.

It was recognized in conjunction with attempts to transplant tissues from one individual to another, that certain protein antigens (human leukocyte antigens, or HLA molecules) had to be matched to avoid rejection of the foreign tissue. These proteins, now often called the proteins of the major histocompatibility complex (MHC proteins, MHC antigens), are coded by a cluster of genes on human chromosome 6. MHC proteins are cell-surface receptors, proteins that bind peptides at specific binding sites for presentation to a receptor site on T cells. The T-cell receptor must interact simultaneously with both the MHC molecule and the peptide presented by the MHC molecule before the presentation is recognized as a signal for the T cell to carry out some other function. An activated T cell might go on, for example, to activate B lymphocytes to produce antibodies, or it must suppress the normal immune response to antigens encountered as part of our food intake (development of oral tolerance). The latter function may be especially important because, presumably, in most people the immune response to gluten peptides has been suppressed, whereas in celiac patients, certain gluten peptides trigger an immune response capable of damaging the small intestine.

The MHC proteins of concern to us here are divided into class I and class II on the basis of a number of distinguishing characteristics, one of which is the type of cell on which they are expressed. Class I antigens appear on most cells, whereas class II antigens are found mainly on cells of the immune system, although class II antigens are expressed on the surfaces of enterocytes as well. The first demonstrations of associations between MHC proteins and celiac disease indicated that a class I antigen, designated HLA-B8, was found in nearly 90 percent of celiac patients but in only about 20 percent of controls (Falchuk, Rogentine, and Strober 1972). This antigen, HLA-8, was the genetic marker that, as was discussed earlier by Simoons, was thought to determine the incidence of celiac disease throughout the world.

However, subsequently it became clear that associations of celiac disease with class II antigens were even stronger than those of the class I antigen HLA-B8. Particularly strong associations have been found for the HLA class II alleles DR3 and DQ2. The association with HLA-B8 apparently resulted from linkage disequilibrium in which certain closely linked genes tend to remain associated during genetic recombinations to a greater extent than would be expected.

The associations of celiac disease with various MHC proteins observed throughout the world are quite complex (see reviews of Kagnoff 1992; Tighe and Ciclitira 1993), but they are sufficiently strong to make it seem likely that class II antigens are directly involved in the mechanisms responsible for tissue damage in celiac disease – possibly by presenting peptides derived from gluten proteins to T cells.

In support of the possibility that gliadin peptide binding by T cells is involved in celiac disease, K. E. A. Lundin and colleagues (1993) have found that T-cell lines derived from intestinal biopsies recognized gliadin peptides, and the cell lines were mainly stimulated by antigen presentation in the context of the DQ heterodimer. In addition, H. A. Gjertson, Lundin, and colleagues (1994) found that a peripheral blood lymphocyte clone from a celiac patient specifically recognized a synthetic peptide corresponding to alpha-gliadin residues 31-47. Further interest in the role of class II MHC proteins derives from studies showing that HLA-DR molecules, which are expressed by enterocytes of normal individuals or of celiac patients on a wheat-free diet (Arnaud-Battandier et al. 1986; Ciclitira et al. 1986), became differentially expressed in the crypt cells of celiac patients (but not in those of normal controls). This occurred when gluten proteins or peptides were added to biopsied tissues in culture that had been obtained from treated patients on a wheat-free diet (Fais et al. 1992).

W. Strober (1992) has pointed out that because discordance for celiac disease is much less common in identical twins than in siblings who have apparently identical complements of histocompatibility antigens (MHC proteins), it seems likely that the difference cannot be explained by an environmental factor because the contribution of environmental effects should have been about the same for the sets of twins and siblings. Strober considers this as strong evidence for a contribution by some non-MHC-defined disease gene. Whether or not this gene turns out to lie outside the MHC complex, celiac disease is likely to have a two-locus basis. D. A. Greenberg, S. E. Hodge, and J. I. Rotter (1982) considered that the available data fit best with a recessive-recessive two-gene model, but studies in the west of Ireland (Hernandez et al. 1991) favored dominance for the gene associated with the HLA locus. Conclusions may be somewhat dependent on the population studied, as many diseases show variation in their genetic basis.

Associated Diseases

Many different diseases have been reported to occur concurrently with celiac disease, including dermatitis herpetiformis, insulin-dependent diabetes, Down syndrome, IgA nephropathy, and epilepsy associated with cerebral calcifications (Bayless, Yardley, and Hendrix 1974; Gobbi et al. 1992; Collin and Maki 1994). In only a few diseases are statistically significant data available for the establishment of an association with celiac disease.

Dermatitis herpetiformis is a disease manifested by a rash with small blisters and IgA deposits even in uninvolved skin (Fry 1992). It is quite strongly associated with celiac disease. Intestinal lesions similar to those encountered in celiac disease are found upon biopsy of about two-thirds of patients with dermatitis herpetiformis, and a gluten-free diet usually improves both the skin rash and the intestinal lesions. Furthermore, even those patients without significant damage to the intestinal epithelium usually have an increased number of intraepithelial lymphocytes, and patients without obvious mucosal damage have developed such damage when their intake of gluten was increased. Nevertheless, malabsorption is much less common in dermatitis herpetiformis than in celiac disease (Kumar 1994). Indeed, the incidence is rather less than that of celiac disease, with dermatitis herpetiformis occurring about half as frequently as celiac disease in Sweden and perhaps one-fifth as frequently in Scotland (Edinburgh).

Insulin-dependent diabetes mellitus also shows a definite association with celiac disease. Between 5 and 10 percent of children with celiac disease have diabetes mellitus, whereas about 1 to 3 percent of children with diabetes mellitus have celiac disease (Visakorpi 1969; Strober 1992). Both celiac disease and insulin-dependent diabetes mellitus share an association with the histocompatibility antigen HLA-DR3 (Maki et al. 1984), and the common MHC gene(s) may predispose individuals carrying them to both conditions.

Down syndrome may be weakly associated with celiac disease. J. Dias and J. Walker-Smith (1988) found an increased incidence of Down syndrome in celiac patients compared with the incidence in the general population. They considered this as supporting evidence for earlier findings (Nowak, Ghisham, and Schulze-Delrieu 1983). M. Castro and colleagues (1993) have confirmed a significant increase in celiac disease among Down syndrome patients and found that antigliadin antibodies provide a useful screening tool to look for celiac disease among these patients. In addition, there are reports that patients with schizophrenia, autism, and IgA nephropathy have apparently benefited by removing wheat (and related harmful grains) from their diets, although such reports are not universally accepted as valid.

There have been extensive attempts to show a correlation between schizophrenia and celiac disease (Dohan 1966, 1988; Lorenz 1990), but the results have not been convincing. Evidence for intestinal damage in the group of schizophrenics studied by F. M. Stevens and colleagues (1977) was no greater than that for controls, and there was no significant increase in serum antireticulin antibodies. Both intestinal damage and antireticulin antibodies are usually present in celiac patients taking a normal (wheat-containing) diet. Nevertheless, published reports from physicians indicating that removal of wheat from the diet can produce a marked reduction in psychotic symptoms for some schizophrenics were considered sufficiently convincing by K. Lorenz (1990) to indicate that in at

least a subset of schizophrenics, wheat has an adverse effect on the disease. Even in studies where no positive correlation was found, investigators noted that some patients did apparently show considerable improvement on a wheat-free ("gluten-free") diet (Rice, Ham, and Gore 1978).

Some celiac patients on a gluten-free diet, perhaps about 25 percent (Ansaldi et al. 1988), have indicated that they feel temporary psychological disturbance upon eating wheat, including symptoms such as irritability, hostility, depression, or a general feeling of mental unease. Although such symptoms may be "normal" in the face of physiological changes produced by eating wheat, investigation of a connection between such responses in celiac patients and the effects of wheat in the diet of carefully selected schizophrenics might be worthwhile. Again, even if wheat in the diet does adversely affect the course of schizophrenia, the mechanisms involved may be quite different from those involved in producing intestinal damage in celiac disease.

The role of wheat in autism is also controversial, but development of the hypothesis that wheat and casein exacerbate the symptoms of autistic patients parallels that for schizophrenia. The hypothesis is based so far on studies that indicate value for a wheat-free diet in improving behavior of patients with autism (Reichelt et al. 1991), although these studies are not well controlled because of the difficulties in carrying them out with patients who may not be able to supply informed consent. It has been discovered that amino acid sequences found in the primary structures of wheat gliadin proteins and casein proteins are similar to those of endorphins and other neuroactive peptides termed exorphins (Zioudrou, Streaty, and Klee 1979). It has been proposed that these, along with other neuroactive peptides from wheat, are responsible for the exacerbation of symptoms claimed for schizophrenic patients on a normal, wheat-containing diet (Zioudrou et al. 1979; Dohan 1988). This working hypothesis is also favored by some researchers investigating the possibility that wheat and casein proteins in the diet exacerbate symptoms in autistic patients (Reichelt et al. 1991). According to the hypothesis, food-protein-derived neuroactive peptides pass through the wall of the intestine and also pass the blood-brain barrier to affect brain function. This results in a variety of abnormal behaviors.

Abnormal peptide patterns appear in the urine of autistic subjects and schizophrenics (Cade et al. 1990; Shattock et al. 1990; Reichelt et al. 1991), and the hypothesis has been put forward that these abnormal patterns reflect to some extent the abnormal absorption and then excretion of exorphin peptides derived from wheat or milk proteins in the diet. This implies either excessive passage through the intestinal wall and/or a failure in some other way to process these peptides into harmless forms. However, that these abnormal urine peptide patterns truly represent excretion of peptides of dietary origin does not seem to have been proved.

IgA nephropathy is a kidney disease characterized by protein and blood in the urine and IgA deposits in the kidney (Stevens, Lavelle, et al. 1988). Although the severity is variable, the disease can lead to chronic renal failure. Reports of concurrence with celiac disease, the presence of circulating IgA antibodies to gluten proteins, and patient improvement (even with nonceliac patients) on a gluten-free diet have led to speculation that there may be a connection between the two diseases (Coppo et al. 1986; Sategna-Guidetti et al. 1992). It has been suggested that IgA nephropathy might be similar to dermatitis herpetiformis, with the main difference being that IgA deposits form in the kidney rather than in the skin. However, the evidence indicates that epithelial damage is uncommon in IgA nephropathy, although the activities of marker enzymes in the brush border were significantly lower (Stevens, Lavelle, 1988). Gliadin proteins or peptides have been found in complex with the IgA deposits in IgA nephropathy (Russel et al. 1986), and similar associations should be sought in dermatitis herpetiformis.

Celiac patients have been found to be at increased risk of developing certain types of cancer (Holmes et al. 1989; Logan et al. 1989; Holmes and Thompson 1992), especially small intestinal lymphoma. Nonetheless, the absolute risk of a celiac patient dying from this cancer is small because the incidence in the normal population is quite low.

G. K. T. Holmes and colleagues (1989) found in a study of 210 patients that those who had been on a strict gluten-free diet for more than 5 years did not have significantly increased risk of developing lymphoma. But the risk of developing lymphoma was reported to be high (1 in 10) for celiac patients who were diagnosed late in life (over the age of 50). The investigators did not discuss what constituted a "strict gluten-free diet," and J.A. Campbell (1992) has pointed out that it would not have been unusual for patients who thought themselves to be on a strict gluten-free diet to be using products containing wheat starch, which has a small amount of gluten in it. It seems prudent for celiac patients to follow a strict gluten-free diet as recommended by Holmes and colleagues (1989), but whether traces of gluten in the diet, such as might result from use of wheat-starch products, contribute to the development of malignancies late in life does not appear to have been established.

Conclusion

Human evolution has produced a complex immune system designed to protect us from harmful parasites, bacteria, viruses, and foreign substances. Human cultural development has led to a dependence on agriculture, and in a large part of the world, a heavy dependence on wheat and related grain crops as part of that agriculture. The proteins of these grain crops have evolved in a somewhat isolated manner (in part because they are recently evolved) such that particular amino acid sequences have appeared in these proteins that can induce the immune system in a susceptible subset of people into damaging the absorptive layer of cells lining the small intestine. The mechanisms are not very well understood, but they seem to involve a failure of the suppression mechanisms by which oral tolerance to food-protein antigens is developed in normal individuals.

Donald D. Kasarda

Part of this chapter is excerpted from the author's "Toxic Cereal Grains in Coeliac Disease" (1994), pp. 203-20, in *Gastrointestinal Immunology and Gluten-Sensitive Disease*, ed. C. Feighery and C. O'Farrelly. The author thanks Professor Conleth Feighery, of Trinity College in the University of Dublin, Ireland, for permission to refer to unpublished results achieved by him and his colleagues, and for his comments on the manuscript.

Bibliography

Altschul, S. F., W. Gish, W. Miller, et al. 1990. Basic local alignment search tool. *Journal of Molecular Biology* 215: 403-10.

Ammerman, A. J., and L. L. Cavalli-Sforza. 1971. Measuring the rate of spread of early farming in Europe. *Man* 6: 674-88.

Anderson, C. M. 1992. The evolution of a successful treatment for coeliac disease. In *Coeliac disease,* ed. M. N. Marsh, 1-16. London.

Anderson, C. M., A. C. Frazer, J. M. French, et al. 1952. Coeliac disease: Gastrointestinal studies and the effect of dietary wheat flour. *Lancet* 1: 836-42.

Ansaldi, N., K. Tavassoli, D. Faussone, et al. 1988. Clinical and histological behaviour of previously diagnosed children with coeliac disease when rechallenged with gluten. In *Coeliac disease: 100 years,* ed. P. J. Kumar and J. Walker-Smith, 237-9. Leeds, England.

Arnaud-Battandier, N. Cerf-Bensussan, R. Amsellem, and J. Schmitz. 1986. Increased HLA-DR expression by enterocytes in children with celiac disease. *Gastroenterology* 91: 1206-12.

Ascher, H., and B. Kristiansson. 1994. Childhood coeliac disease in Sweden. *Lancet* 344: 340-1.

Auricchio, S., G. De Ritis, M. De Vincenzi, et al. 1984. Agglutinating activity of gliadin-derived peptides from bread wheat: Implications for coeliac disease pathogenesis. *Biochemical and Biophysical Research Communications* 121: 428-33.

Baker, P. G., and A. E. Read. 1976. Oats and barley toxicity in coeliac patients. *Postgraduate Medical Journal* 52: 264-8.

Bayless, T. M., J. H. Yardley, and T. R. Hendrix. 1974. Coeliac disease and possible disease relationships. In *Coeliac disease: Proceedings of the Second International Coeliac Symposium,* ed. W. Th. J. M. Hekkens and A. S. Peña, 351-9. Leiden, the Netherlands.

Beccari, J. B. 1745. De frumento. *De Bononiensi Scientiarum et Artium Instituto atque Academia Commentarii,* 7 vols. II, Part 1, 122-7. Bologna.

Bernardin, J. E., R. M. Saunders, and D. D. Kasarda. 1976.

Absence of carbohydrate in celiac-toxic A-gliadin. *Cereal Chemistry* 53: 612-14.

Bietz, J. A. 1982. Cereal prolamin evolution revealed by sequence analysis. *Biochemical Genetics* 20: 1039-53.

Blanco, A., P. Resta, R. Simeone, et al. 1991. Chromosomal location of seed storage protein genes in the genome of *Daspyrum villosum* (L.) Candargy. *Theoretical and Applied Genetics* 82: 358-62.

Booth, C. C., M. S. Losowsky, J. A. Walker-Smith, and J. D. W. Whitney. 1991. Inter-laboratory variation in gluten detection by ELISA kit. *Lancet* 337: 1094.

Brandborg, L. L., C. E. Rubin, and W. E. Quinton. 1959. A multipurpose instrument for suction biopsy of the esophagus, stomach, small bowel, and colon. *Gastroenterology* 37: 1-16.

Bronstein, H. D., L. J. Haeffner, and O. D. Kowlessar. 1966. Enzymatic digestion of gliadin: The effect of the resultant peptides in adult celiac disease. *Clinica Chimica Acta* 14: 141-55.

Bruce, G., J. F. Woodley, and C. J. H. Swan. 1984. Breakdown of gliadin peptides by intestinal brush borders from coeliac patients. *Gut* 25: 919-24.

Cade, R., H. Wagemaker, R. M. Privette, et al. 1990. The effect of dialysis and diet on schizophrenia. In *Psychiatry: A World Perspective,* Vol. 3, ed. C. N. Stefanis, A. D. Rabavilas, and C. R. Soldatos, 494-500. New York.

Campbell, J. A. 1992. Dietary management of celiac disease: Variations in the gluten-free diet. *Journal of the Canadian Dietetic Association* 53: 15-18.

Castro, M., A. Crino, B. Papadatou, et al. 1993. Down's syndrome and celiac disease: The prevalence of high IgA-antigliadin antibodies and HLA-DR and DQ antigens in trisomy 21. *Journal of Pediatric Gastroenterology and Nutrition* 16: 265-8.

Chicz, R. M., R. G. Urban, W. S. Lane, et al. 1992. Predominant naturally processed peptides bound to HLA-DR1 are derived from MHC-related molecules and are heterogeneous in size. *Nature* 358: 764-8.

Ciclitira, P. J., H. J. Ellis, and N. L. K. Fagg. 1984. Evaluation of a gluten free product containing wheat gliadin in patients with coeliac disease. *British Medical Journal* 289: 83.

Ciclitira, P. J., D. J. Evans, N. L. K. Fagg, et al. 1984. Clinical testing of gliadin fractions in coeliac disease. *Clinical Science* 66: 357-64.

Ciclitira, P. J., J. M. Nelufer, H. J. Ellis, and D. J. Evans. 1986. The effect of gluten on HLA-DR in the small intestinal epithelium of patients with coeliac disease. *Clinical and Experimental Immunology* 63: 101-4.

Collin, P., and M. Maki. 1994. Associated disorders in coeliac disease: Clinical aspects. *Scandinavian Journal of Gastroenterology* 29: 769-75.

Coppo, R., B. Bassolo, C. Rollino, et al. 1986. Dietary gluten and primary IgA nephropathy. *New England Journal of Medicine* 315: 1167-8.

Cornell, H. J. 1974. Gliadin degradation and fractionation. In *Coeliac disease: Proceedings of the Second International Coeliac Symposium,* ed. W. Th. J. M. Hekkens and A. S. Peña, 74-5. Leiden, the Netherlands.

 1988. Wheat proteins and celiac disease. *Comments in Agricultural and Food Chemistry* 1: 289-313.

Cronquist, A. 1968. *The evolution of flowering plants.* Boston.

Crosby, W. H., and H. W. Kugler. 1957. Intraluminal biopsy of the small intestine: The intestinal biopsy capsule. *American Journal of Digestive Diseases* 2: 236-41.

Cuadro, C., G. Ayet, C. Burbano, et al. 1995. Occurrence of saponins and sapogenols in Andean crops. *Journal of the Science of Food and Agriculture* 67: 169-72.

De Ritis, G., S. Auricchio, H. W. Jones, et al. 1988. In vitro (organ culture) studies of the toxicity of specific A-gliadin peptides in celiac disease. *Gastroenterology* 94: 41-9.

De Ritis, G., P. Occorsio, S. Auricchio, et al. 1979. Toxicity of wheat flour proteins and protein-derived peptides for in vitro developing intestine from rat fetus. *Pediatric Research* 13: 1255-61.

Dias, J., and J. Walker-Smith. 1988. Down's syndrome and coeliac disease. In *Coeliac disease: 100 years,* ed. P. J. Kumar and J. A. Walker-Smith, 277-9. Leeds, England.

Dicke, W. K. 1950. Coeliiakie: Een ondersoek naar de nadelige invloed van sommige graansoorten op de lijder aan coeliakie. M.D. thesis, University of Utrecht, Utrecht, the Netherlands.

Dicke, W. K., H. A. Weijers, and J. H. Van de Kamer. 1953. Coeliac disease. II. The presence in wheat of a factor having a deleterious effect in cases of celiac disease. *Acta Paediatrica* (Stockholm) 42: 34-42.

Dissanayake, A. S., S. C. Truelove, and R. Whitehead. 1974. Lack of harmful effects of oats on small-intestinal mucosa in coeliac disease. *British Medical Journal* 4: 189-91.

Dobbins, W. O., and C. E. Rubin. 1964. Studies of the rectal mucosa in celiac sprue. *Gastroenterology* 47: 471-9.

Dohan, F. C. 1966. Cereals and schizophrenia: Data and hypothesis. *Acta Psychiatrica Scandinavica* 42: 125-32.

 1988. Genetic hypothesis of idiopathic schizophrenia: Its exorphin connection. *Schizophrenia Bulletin* 14: 489-94.

Dowd, B., and J. Walker-Smith. 1974. Samuel Gee, Aretaeus, and the coeliac affection. *British Medical Journal* 2: 45-7.

Dvorak, J., D. D. Kasarda, M. D. Dietler, et al. 1986. Chromosomal location of seed storage protein genes in the genome of *Elytrigia elongata. Canadian Journal of Genetics and Cytology* 28: 818-30.

Egan-Mitchell, B., P. F. Fottrell, and B. McNicholl. 1978. Prolonged gluten tolerance in treated coeliac disease. In *Perspectives in coeliac disease,* ed. B. McNicholl, C. F. McCarthy, and P. F. Fottrell, 251-7. Baltimore, Md.

Ejderhamn, J., B. Veress, and B. Strandvik. 1988. The long-term effect of continual ingestion of wheat starch–containing gluten-free products in coeliac patients. In *Coeliac disease: 100 years,* ed. P. J. Kumar and J. Walker-Smith, 294-7. Leeds, England.

Engler, J. A., M. S. Hoppe, and M. P. van Bree. 1983. The nucleotide sequence of the genes encoded in early region 2b of human adenovirus type 7. *Gene* 21: 145-59.

Fais, S., L. Maiuri, F. Pallone, et al. 1992. Gliadin induces changes in the expression of MHC-class II antigens by human small intestinal epithelium. Organ culture studies with coeliac mucosa. *Gut* 33: 472-5.

Falchuk, G. M., R. L. Gebhard, C. Sessoms, and W. Strober. 1974. An in vitro model of gluten-sensitive enteropathy. *Journal of Clinical Investigation* 53: 487-500.

Falchuk, Z. M., D. L. Nelson, A. J. Katz, et al. 1980. Gluten-sensitive enteropathy: Influence of histocompatibility type on gluten sensitivity in vitro. *Journal of Clinical Investigation* 66: 227-33.

Falchuk, Z. M., F. N. Rogentine, and W. Strober. 1972. Predominance of histocompatibility antigen HL-A8 in patients with gluten-sensitive enteropathy. *Journal of Clinical Investigation* 51: 1602-5.

Fluge, Ø., K. Sletten, G. Fluge, et al. 1994. In vitro toxicity of purified gluten peptides tested by organ culture. *Journal of Pediatric Gastroenterology and Nutrition* 18: 186-92.

Forssell, F., and H. Wieser. 1994. Dinkelweizen und Zöliakie. *Bericht 1994, Deutsche Forschungsanstalt für Lebensmittelchemie.* Garching, Germany.

Frazer, A. C. 1956. Discussion on some problems of steator-rhea and reduced stature. *Proceedings of the Royal Society of Medicine* 49: 1009-13.

Frazer, A. C., M. B. Fletcher, C. A. C. Ross, et al. 1959. Gluten-induced enteropathy: The effect of partially-digested gluten. *Lancet* 2: 252-5.

Freedman, A. R., G. Galfre, E. Gal, et al. 1987a. Detection of wheat gliadin contamination of gluten-free foods by a monoclonal antibody dot immunobinding assay. *Clinica Chimica Acta* 166: 323-8.

1987b. Monoclonal antibody ELISA to quantitate wheat gliadin contamination of gluten-free foods. *Journal of Immunological Methods* 98: 123-7.

Fry, L. 1992. Dermatitis herpetiformis. In *Coeliac disease,* ed. M. N. Marsh, 81-104. London.

Gautam, A. M., C. B. Lock, D. E. Smilek, et al. 1994. Minimum structural requirements for peptide presentation by major histocompatibility complex class II molecules: Implications in induction of immunity. *Proceedings of the National Academy of Sciences* (U.S.) 91: 767-71.

Gee, Samuel. 1888. On the coeliac affection. *St. Bartholomew's Hospital Reports* 24: 17-20.

Gjertsen, H. A., K. E. A. Lundin, L. M. Sollid, et al. 1994. T cells recognize a peptide derived from alpha-gliadin presented by the celiac disease associated HLA-DQ (alpha 1*0501, beta 1*0201) heterodimer. *Human Immunology* 39: 243-52.

Gjertsen, H. A., L. M. Sollid, J. Ek, et al. 1994. T cells from the peripheral blood of coeliac disease patients recognize gluten antigens when presented by HLA-DR, -DQ, or -DP molecules. *Scandinavian Journal of Immunology* 39: 567-74.

Gobbi, G., F. Bouquet, L. Greco, et al. 1992. Coeliac disease, epilepsy, and cerebral calcifications. *Lancet* 340: 439-43.

Gray, G. 1991. Dietary protein processing: Intraluminal and enterocyte surface effects. In *Handbook of physiology: The gastrointestinal system IV,* 411-20. New York.

1992. Starch digestion and absorption in nonruminants. *Journal of Nutrition* 122: 172-7.

Greco, L., M. Maki, F. Di Donato, and J. K. Visakorpi. 1992. Epidemiology of coeliac disease in Europe and the Mediterranean area. A summary report on the multi-centre study by the European Society of Pediatric Gastroenterology and Nutrition. In *Common food intolerances 1: Epidemiology of coeliac disease,* ed. S. Auricchio and J. K. Visakorpi, 25-44. Basel.

Greenberg, D. A., S. E. Hodge, and J. I. Rotter. 1982. Evidence for recessive and against dominant inheritance at the HLA-"linked" locus in celiac disease. *American Journal of Human Genetics* 34: 263-77.

Haas, S. V. 1924. Value of banana treatment of celiac disease. *American Journal of Diseases of Children* 28: 420-1.

Harlan, J. R. 1977. The origins of cereal agriculture in the Old World. In *Origins of agriculture,* ed. C. A. Reed, 357-83. The Hague.

Harlan, J. R., and J. M. J. de Wet. 1975. On Ö. Winge and a prayer: The origins of polyploidy. *Botanical Review* 41: 361-90.

Hekkens, W. Th. J. M. 1978. The toxicity of gliadin: A review. In *Perspectives in coeliac disease,* ed. B. McNicholl, C. F. McCarthy, and P. E. Fottrell, 3-14. Baltimore, Md.

Hekkens, W. Th. J. M., A. J. Ch. Haex, and R. G. J. Willighagen. 1970. Some aspects of gliadin fractionation and testing by a histochemical method. In *Coeliac disease,* ed. C. C. Booth and R. H. Dowling, 11-19. London.

Hekkens, W. Th. J. M., C. J. Van den Aarsen, J. P. Gilliams, Ph. Lems-Van Kan, and G. Bouma-Frölich. 1974. Alpha-gliadin structure and degradation. In *Coeliac disease: Proceedings of the Second International Coeliac Symposium,* ed. W. Th. J. M. Hekkens and A. S. Peña, 39-45. Leiden, Netherlands.

Hekkens, W. Th. J. M., and M. van Twist-de Graaf. 1990. What is gluten-free – levels and tolerances in the gluten-free diet. *Die Nahrung* 34: 483-7.

Hernandez, J. L., J. P. Michalski, C. C. McCombs, et al. 1991. Evidence for a dominant gene mechanism underlying celiac disease in the west of Ireland. *Genetic Epidemiology* 8: 13-28.

Hitchcock, A. S. 1950. *Manual of the grasses of the United States.* Second edition, rev. A. Chase. USDA Miscellaneous Publication No. 200. Washington, D.C.

Holmes, G. K. T., P. Prior, M. R. Lane, et al. 1989. Malignancy in coeliac disease – effect of a gluten free diet. *Gut* 30: 333-8.

Holmes, G. K. T., and H. Thompson. 1992. Malignancy as a complication of coeliac disease. In *Coeliac disease,* ed. M. N. Marsh, 105-35. London.

Jos, J., L. Charbonnier, J. Mossé, et al. 1982. The toxic fraction of gliadin digests in coeliac disease. Isolation by chromatography on Biogel P-10. *Clinica Chimica Acta* 119: 263-74.

Jos, J., L. Charbonnier, J. F. Mougenot, et al. 1978. Isolation and characterization of the toxic fraction of wheat gliadin in coeliac disease. In *Perspectives in coeliac disease,* ed. B. McNicholl, C. F. McCarthy, and P. E. Fottrell, 75-89. Baltimore, Md.

Jos, J., M. F. de Tand, F. Arnaud-Battandier, et al. 1983. Separation of pure toxic peptides from a beta-gliadin subfraction using high-performance liquid chromatography. *Clinica Chimica Acta* 134: 189-98.

Kagnoff, M. F. 1992. Genetic basis of coeliac disease: Role of HLA genes. In *Coeliac disease,* ed. M. N. Marsh, 215-38. London.

Kagnoff, M. F., R. F. Austin, J. J. Hubert, et al. 1984. Possible role for a human adenovirus in the pathogenesis of celiac disease. *Journal of Experimental Medicine* 160: 1544-7.

Kagnoff, M. F., J. I. Harwood, T. L. Bugawan, and H. A. Erlich. 1989. Structural analysis of the HLA-DR, -DQ, and -DP alleles on the celiac disease–associated HLA-DR3 (DRw17) haplotype. *Proceedings of the National Academy of Sciences* (U.S.) 86: 6274-7.

Kagnoff, M. F., E. Morzycka-Wroblewska, and J. I. Harwood. 1994. Genetic susceptibility to coeliac disease. In *Gastrointestinal immunology and gluten-sensitive disease,* ed. C. Feighery and C. O'Farrelly, 131-44. Dublin.

Karagiannis, J. A., J. D. Priddle, and D. P. Jewell. 1987. Cell-mediated immunity to a synthetic gliadin peptide resembling a sequence from adenovirus 12. *Lancet* 1: 884-6.

Kasarda, D. D. 1980. Structure and properties of alpha-gliadins. *Annales de Technologie Agricole* (Paris) 29: 151-73.

1981. Toxic proteins and peptides in celiac disease: Relations to cereal genetics. In *Food, nutrition, and evolution: Food as an environmental factor in the genesis of human variability,* ed. D. W. Walcher and N. Kretchmer, 201-16. New York.

Kasarda, D. D., T. W. Okita, J. E. Bernardin, et al. 1984. Nucleic acid (cDNA) and amino acid sequences of alpha-type gliadins from wheat (*Triticum aestivum*). *Proceedings of the National Academy of Sciences of the United States of America* 81: 4712-16.

Katz, S. I., Z. M. Falchuk, M. V. Dahl, et al. 1972. HL-A8: A genetic link between dermatitis herpetiformis and gluten-sensitive enteropathy. *Journal of Clinical Investigation* 51: 2977-80.

Kendall, M. J., P. S. Cox, R. Schneider, and C. F. Hawkins. 1972. Gluten subfractions in coeliac disease. *Lancet* 2: 1065–7.

Kihara, T., S. Kukida, and Y. Ichikawa. 1977. Ultrastructural studies of the duodenal epithelium of Japanese celiac sprue. *Journal of Clinical Electron Microscopy* 10: 5–6.

Krainick, H. G., and G. Mohn. 1959. Weitere Untersuchungen über den schädlichen Weizenmehle-effekt bei der Coliakie. 2. Die Wirkung der enzymatischen Abbauprodukte des Gliadin. *Helvetica Paediatrica Acta* 14: 124–40.

Kreft, I., and B. Javornik. 1979. Buckwheat as a potential source of high quality protein. In *Seed protein improvement in cereals and grain legumes,* Vol. 2, 377–83. International Atomic Energy Agency. Vienna.

Kreis, M., P. R. Shewry, B. G. Forde, et al. 1985. Structure and evolution of seed storage proteins and their genes with particular reference to those of wheat, rye, and barley. *Oxford Surveys of Plant Molecular and Cell Biology* 2: 253–317.

Kumar, P. 1994. Dermatitis herpetiformis. In *Gastrointestinal immunology and gluten-sensitive disease,* ed. C. Feighery and C. O'Farrelly, 158–68. Dublin.

Kumar, P. J., T. S. Sinclair, M. J. G. Farthing, et al. 1984. Clinical testing of pure gliadins in coeliac disease. *Gastroenterology* 86: 1147–52.

Lafiandra, D., S. Benedettelli, B. Mariotta, and E. Porceddu. 1989. Chromosomal location of gliadin coding genes in *T. aestivum* ssp. *spelta* and evidence on the lack of components controlled by Gli-2 loci in wheat aneuploids. *Theoretical and Applied Genetics* 78: 177–83.

Lähdeaho, M.-L., P. Parkonnen, T. Reunala, et al. 1993. Antibodies to adenovirus E1b protein derived peptides of enteric adenovirus type 40 are associated with coeliac disease and dermatitis herpetiformis. *Clinical Immunology and Immunopathology* 69: 300–5.

Lajolo, F. M., U. M. Lanfer Marquez, T. M. C. C. Filesetti-Cozzi, and D. Ian McGregor. 1991. Chemical composition and toxic compounds in rapeseed (*Brassica napus* L.) cultivars grown in Brazil. *Journal of Agricultural and Food Chemistry* 39: 1933–7.

Lew, E. J.-L., D. D. Kuzmicky, and D. D. Kasarda. 1992. Characterization of LMW-glutenin subunits by RP-HPLC, SDS-PAGE, and N-terminal amino acid sequencing. *Cereal Chemistry* 69: 508–15.

Loft, D. E., M. N. Marsh, and P. Crowe. 1990. Rectal gluten challenge and the diagnosis of coeliac disease. *Lancet* 335: 1293–5.

Logan, R. F. A. 1992a. Epidemiology of celiac disease. In *Coeliac disease,* ed. M. N. Marsh, 192–214. London.
  1992b. Problems and pitfalls in the epidemiology of coeliac disease. In *Common food intolerances 1: Epidemiology of coeliac disease,* ed. S. Auricchio and J. K. Visakorpi, 14–24. Basel.

Logan, R. F. A., E. A. Rifkind, I. D. Turner, and A. Ferguson. 1989. Mortality in celiac disease. *Gastroenterology* 97: 265–71.

Lorenz, K. 1990. Cereals and schizophrenia. In *Advances in cereal science and technology,* Vol. 10, ed. Y. Pomeranz, 435–69. St. Paul, Minn.

Lundin, K. E. A., H. Scott, T. Hansen, et al. 1993. Gliadin-specific, HLA-DQ (a1*0501, b1*0201) restricted T cells isolated from the small intestinal mucosa of celiac disease patients. *Journal of Experimental Medicine* 178: 187–96.

Maki, M., O. Hällstrom, T. Huupponen, et al. 1984. Increased prevalence of coeliac disease in diabetes. *Archives of Disease in Childhood* 59: 739–42.

Maki, M., K. Holm, H. Ascher, and L. Greco. 1992. Factors affecting clinical presentation of coeliac disease: Role of type and amount of gluten-containing cereals. In *Common food intolerances 1: Epidemiology of coeliac disease,* ed. S. Auricchio and J. K. Visakorpi, 76–82. Basel.

Maki, M., S. Koskimies, and J. K. Visakorpi. 1988. Latent coeliac disease. In *Coeliac disease: 100 years,* ed. P. J. Kumar and J. A. Walker-Smith, 245. Leeds, England.

Mantzaris, G., and D. P. Jewell. 1991. In vivo toxicity of a synthetic dodecapeptide from A gliadin in patients with coeliac disease. *Scandinavian Journal of Gastroenterology* 26: 392–8.

Marsh, M. N. 1992a. Gluten, major histocompatibility complex, and the small intestine. *Gastroenterology* 102: 330–54.
  1992b. Mucosal pathology in gluten sensitivity. In *Coeliac disease,* ed. M. N. Marsh, 136–91. London.

McMillan, S. A., D. J. Haughton, J. D. Biggart, et al. 1991. Predictive value for coeliac disease of antibodies to gliadin, endomysium, and jejunum in patients attending for biopsy. *British Medical Journal* 303: 1163–5.

McNeish, A. S., C. J. Rolles, R. Nelson, et al. 1974. Factors affecting the differing racial incidence of coeliac disease. In *Coeliac disease: Proceedings of the Second International Conference,* ed. W. Th. J. M. Hekkens and A. S. Peña, 330–6. Leiden, the Netherlands.

Messer, M., C. M. Anderson, and L. Hubbard. 1964. Studies on the mechanism of destruction of the toxic action of wheat gluten in coeliac disease by crude papain. *Gut* 5: 295–303.

Morris, R., and E. R. Sears. 1967. The cytogenetics of wheat and its relatives. In *Wheat and wheat improvement,* ed. K. S. Quisenberry and L. P. Reitz, 19–87. Madison, Wis.

Mylotte, M., B. Egan-Mitchell, C. F. McCarthy, and B. McNicholl. 1973. Incidence of coeliac disease in the west of Ireland. *British Medical Journal* 24: 703–5.

Nowak, T. V., F. K. Ghisham, and K. Schulze-Delrieu. 1983. Celiac sprue in Down's syndrome: Considerations on a pathogenic link. *American Journal of Gastroenterology* 78: 280–3.

O'Farrelly, C. 1994. Wheat protein sensitive disease may be independent of intestinal structural changes. In *Gastrointestinal immunology and gluten-sensitive disease,* ed. C. Feighery and C. O'Farrelly, 169–80. Dublin.

Offord, R. E., B. S. Anand, J. Piris, and S. C. Truelove. 1978. Further fractionation of digests of gluten. In *Perspectives in coeliac disease,* ed. B. McNicholl, C. F. McCarthy, and P. F. Fottrell, 25–9. Baltimore, Md.

Osborne, T. B. 1907. *The proteins of the wheat kernel.* Washington, D.C.

Peterson, D., and A. C. Brinegar. 1986. Oat storage proteins. In *Oats: Chemistry and technology,* ed. F. H. Webster, 153–203. St. Paul, Minn.

Rahnotra, G. S., J. A. Gelroth, B. K. Glaser, and K. J. Lorenz. 1995. Baking and nutritional qualities of a spelt wheat sample. *Lebensmittel-Wissenschaft und -Technologie* 28: 118–22.

Reichelt, K. L., A. M. Knivsberg, G. Lind, and M. Nødland. 1991. Probable etiology and possible treatment of childhood autism. *Brain Dysfunction* 4: 308–19.

Rice, J. R., C. H. Ham, and W. E. Gore. 1978. Another look at gluten in schizophrenia. *American Journal of Psychiatry* 135: 1417–18.

Rubenstein, I., and D. E. Geraghty. 1986. The genetic organization of zein. In *Advances in cereal science and technology VIII,* 297–315. St. Paul, Minn.

Rubin, C. E., L. H. Brandborg, A. M. Flick, et al. 1962. Studies of celiac sprue. III. The effect of repeated wheat instillation into the proximal ileum of patients on a gluten-free diet. *Gastroenterology* 43: 621–41.

Russel, M. W., J. Mestecky, B. A. Julian, and J. H. Galla. 1986. IgA-associated renal diseases: Antibodies to environmental antigens in sera and deposition of immunoglobulins and antigens in glomeruli. *Journal of Clinical Immunology* 6: 74–9.

Satcgna-Guidetti, C., G. Ferfoglia, M. Bruno, et al. 1992. Do IgA antigliadin and IgA antiendomysial antibodies show there is latent celiac disease in primary IgA nephropathy? *Gut* 33: 476–8.

Shattock, P., A. Kennedy, F. Rowell, and T. Berney. 1990. Role of neuropeptides in autism and their relationships with classical neurotransmitters. *Brain Dysfunction* 3: 328–45.

Sheldon, W. 1955. Coeliac disease. *Lancet* 2: 1097–1103.

Shewry, P. R., J.-C. Autran, C. C. Nimmo, et al. 1980. N-terminal amino acid sequence homology of storage protein components from barley and a diploid wheat. *Nature* 286: 520–2.

Shewry, P. R., S. Parmar, and D. J. C. Pappin. 1987. Characterization and genetic control of the prolamins of *Haynaldia villosa*: Relationship to cultivated species of the Triticeae (rye, wheat, and barley). *Biochemical Genetics* 25: 309–25.

Shewry, P. R., P. A. Sabelli, S. Parmar, and D. Lafiandra. 1991. Alpha-type prolamins are encoded by genes on chromosomes 4Ha and 6Ha of *Haynaldia villosa* Schur (syn. *Daspyrum villosum* L.). *Biochemical Genetics* 29: 207–11.

Shewry, P. R., S. J. Smith, E. J.-L. Lew, and D. D. Kasarda. 1986. Characterization of prolamins from meadow grasses: Homology with those of wheat, barley, and rye. *Journal of Experimental Botany* 37: 633–9.

Shewry, P. R., A. S. Tatham, and D. D. Kasarda. 1992. Cereal proteins and celiac disease. In *Coeliac disease*, ed. M. N. Marsh, 305–48. London.

Shiner, M. 1956. Duodenal biopsy. *Lancet* 1: 17–19.

Shmerling, D. H., and M. Shiner. 1970. The response of the intestinal mucosa to the intraduodenal instillation of gluten in patients with coeliac disease in remission. In *Coeliac disease*, ed. C. C. Booth and R. H. Dowling, 64–74. Edinburgh.

Shorrosh, B. S., L. Wen, K. C. Sen, et al. 1992. A novel cereal storage protein: Molecular genetics of the 19kDa globulin of rice. *Plant Molecular Biology* 18: 151–4.

Simoons, F. J. 1981. Celiac disease as a geographic problem. In *Food, nutrition, and evolution: Food as an environmental factor in the genesis of human variability*, ed. D. N. Walcher and N. Kretschmer, 179–99. New York.

Sjøstrom, H., S. U. Friis, O. Norén, and D. Anthonsen. 1992. Purification and characterization of antigenic gliadins in coeliac disease. *Clinica Chemica Acta* 207: 227–37.

Skerritt, J. H., and A. S. Hill. 1990. Monoclonal antibody sandwich enzyme-immunoassays for determination of gluten in foods. *Journal of Agricultural and Food Chemistry* 38: 1771–8.

  1991. Self-management of dietary compliance in coeliac disease by means of ELISA "home test" to detect gluten. *Lancet* 337: 379–82.

  1992. How "free" is "gluten-free"? Relationship between Kjeldahl nitrogen values and gluten protein content for wheat starches. *Cereal Chemistry* 69: 110–12.

Sollid, L., G. Markussen, J. Ek, et al. 1989. Evidence for a primary association of coeliac disease to a particular HLA-DQ a/b heterodimer. *Journal of Experimental Medicine* 169: 345–50.

Srinivasan, U., N. Leonard, E. Jones, et al. 1996. Absence of oats toxicity in adult coeliac disease. *British Medical Journal* 313: 1300–1.

Sterchi, E. E., and J. F. Woodley. 1977. Peptidases of the human intestinal brush border membrane. In *Perspectives in coeliac disease*, ed. B. McNicholl, C. F. McCarthy, and P. F. Fottrell, 437–49. Baltimore, Md.

Stern, M., A. Stallmach, B. Gellerman, and H. Wieser. 1988. In vitro testing of gliadin peptides. In *Coeliac disease: 100 years*, ed. P. J. Kumar and J. A. Walker-Smith, 148–51. Leeds, England.

Stevens, F. M., B. Egan-Mitchell, E. Cryan, et al. 1988. Decreasing incidence of coeliac disease. In *Coeliac disease: 100 years*, ed. P. J. Kumar and J. A. Walker-Smith, 306. Leeds, England.

Stevens, F. M., E. Lavelle, M. Kearns, et al. 1988. Is IgA nephropathy (Berger's disease) dermatitis herpetiformis of the kidney? In *Coeliac disease: 100 years*, ed. P. J. Kumar and J. A. Walker-Smith, 280–3. Leeds, England.

Stevens, F. M., R. S. Lloyd, S. M. J. Geraghty, et al. 1977. Schizophrenia and coeliac disease – the nature of the relationship. *Psychological Medicine* 7: 259–63.

Stokes, P. L., P. Asquith, G. K. T. Holmes, et al. 1972. Histocompatibility antigens associated with adult coeliac disease. *Lancet* 1: 162–4.

Strober, W. 1992. The genetic basis of gluten-sensitive enteropathy. In *The genetic basis of common diseases*, ed. R. A. King, J. I. Rotter, and A. Motulsky, 279–304. New York.

Sturgess, R., P. Day, H. J. Ellis, et al. 1994. Wheat peptide challenge in coeliac disease. *Lancet* 343: 758–61.

Talley, N. J., M. Valdovinos, T. M. Petterson, et al. 1994. Epidemiology of celiac sprue: A community-based study. *American Journal of Gastroenterology* 89: 843–6.

Tao, H. P., and D. D. Kasarda. 1989. Two-dimensional gel mapping and N-terminal sequencing of LMW-glutenin subunits. *Journal of Experimental Botany* 40: 1015–20.

Thomasson, J. R. 1980. Paleoagrostology: A historical review. *Iowa State Journal of Research* 54: 301–17.

Tighe, M. R., and P. J. Ciclitira. 1993. The implications of recent advances in coeliac disease. *Acta Paediatrica* 82: 805–10.

Van de Kamer, J. H., and H. A. Weijers. 1955. Coeliac disease. V. Some experiments on the cause of the harmful effect of wheat gliadin. *Acta Paediatrica* 44: 465–9.

Van de Kamer, J. H., H. A. Weijers, and W. K. Dicke. 1953. Coeliac disease. IV. An investigation into the injurious constituents of wheat in connection with their action on patients with coeliac disease. *Acta Paediatrica* (Stockholm) 42: 223–31.

Van der Hulst, R. R. W. J., B. K. van Kreel, M. F. von Meyenfeldt, et al. 1993. Glutamine and the preservation of gut integrity. *Lancet* 341: 1363–5.

Van Roon, J. H., A. J. Ch. Haex, W. A. Seeder, and J. de Jong. 1960. Chemical and biochemical analysis of gluten toxicity. No. II. *Gastroenterologia* 94: 227–35.

Visakorpi, J. K. 1969. Diabetes and coeliac disease. *Lancet* 2: 650.

Walker-Smith, J. A., S. Guandalini, J. Schmitz, et al. 1990. Revised criteria for diagnosis of coeliac disease. *Archives of the Diseases of Childhood* 65: 909–11.

Walker-Smith, J. A., A. Kilby, and N. E. France. 1978. Reinvestigation of children previously diagnosed as coeliac disease. In *Perspectives in coeliac disease*, ed. B. MacNicholl, C. F. McCarthy, and P. F. Fottrell, 267–76. Baltimore, Md.

Wang, S.-Z., and A. Esen. 1986. Primary structure of a proline-rich zein and its cDNA. *Plant Physiology* 81: 70–4.

Weijers, H. A., J. H. Van de Kamer, and W. K. Dicke. 1957. Celiac disease. In *Advances in pediatrics*, Vol. 9, ed. S. Z. Levine, 277–318. Chicago.

Wieser, H., and H.-D. Belitz. 1992. Isolation and fragmentation of the coeliac-active gliadin peptide CT-1. *Zeitschrift für Lebensmittel-Untersuchung und -Forschung* 194: 229–34.

Wieser, H., H.-D. Belitz, and A. Ashkenazi. 1984. Amino acid sequence of the coeliac active peptide B 3142. *Zeitschrift für Lebensmittel-Untersuchung und -Forschung* 179: 371–6.

Wieser, H., H.-D. Belitz, A. Ashkenazi, and D. Idar. 1983. Isolation of coeliac active peptide fractions from gliadin. *Zeitschrift für Lebensmittel-Untersuchung und -Forschung* 176: 85–94.

Wieser, H., H.-D. Belitz, D. Idar, and A. Ashkenazi. 1986. Coeliac activity of the gliadin peptides CT-1 and CT-2. *Zeitschrift für Lebensmittel-Untersuchung und -Forschung* 182: 115–17.

Wieser, H., G. Springer, H.-D. Belitz, et al. 1982. Toxicity of different wheat gliadins in coeliac disease. *Zeitschrift für Lebensmittel-Untersuchung und -Forschung* 175: 321–6.

Woodley, J. F. 1972. Pyrrolidonecarboxyl peptidase activity in normal intestinal biopsies and those from coeliac patients. *Clinica Chimica Acta* 42: 211–13.

Zhai, C. K., X. L. Jiang, Y. S. Xu, and K. J. Lorenz. 1994. Protein and amino acid composition of Chinese and North American wild rice. *Lebensmittel-Wissenschaft und -Technologie* 27: 380–3.

Zioudrou, C., R. A. Streaty, and W. A. Klee. 1979. Opioid peptides derived from food proteins: The exorphins. *The Journal of Biological Chemistry* 254: 2446–9.

Zubillaga, P., J. C. Vitoria, A. Arrieta, et al. 1993. Down's syndrome and celiac disease. *Journal of Pediatric Gastroenterology and Nutrition* 16: 168–71.

IV.E.3 ❧ Food Allergies

Adverse Food Reactions and Allergies

An adverse food reaction is defined as any untoward reaction following the ingestion of food (Lifshitz 1988). These reactions generally fall into two categories: food intolerance and food hypersensitivity. Intolerances are nonimmunologic (Sampson and Cooke 1990) and are responsible for most adverse food reactions. They may be idiosyncratic, due to metabolic disorders, or caused by pharmacological substances such as toxins or drugs present in food. Food additives can also be a cause of food intolerance or hypersensitivity and can produce respiratory and gastrointestinal complaints (Lifshitz 1988).

True food hypersensitivity, or allergy, is an adverse food reaction involving immunologic mechanisms. It is initiated by production of specific antibodies, otherwise known as immunoglobulins, in reaction to food constituents. The body manufactures antibodies as part of its regular defense system against foreign invaders such as viruses and bacteria. In certain individuals, the immune system is triggered to elicit a specific antibody, called immunoglobulin E (IgE), against various environmental substances like pollens, pet dander, insect venoms, and foods. The common immunologic mechanisms involved can cause food-allergic reactions to resemble allergic reactions to honeybee stings or penicillin.

Mechanism

In food-allergic individuals, IgE antibodies are produced against food components and circulate in the blood. Upon reaching certain cells, known as mast cells and basophils, the IgE becomes fixed to the cell surface and remains there. These cells contain high quantities of special receptors for IgE; rat mast cells have been found to contain $2\text{-}5 \times 10^5$ receptors per cell (Mendoza and Metzger 1976). A large portion of the IgE in the body is fixed to these cells, and when they become armed with IgE, they are said to be "sensitized."

Mast cells are present in many tissues of the body, and basophils are present in the blood. When certain food components, or allergens, are ingested and circulate in the blood, they come in contact with the IgE bound to the mast cell or basophil surface. This contact causes a chain of events to occur in the cells, leading to the release of granules containing certain mediators that are responsible for the clinical manifestations of the allergic reaction. This immediate allergic reaction is classified as a Type I hypersensitivity reaction according to the Gell and Coombs classification (Coombs and Gell 1975). Most food-allergic reactions are of this type (Moneret-Vautrin 1986), although other mechanisms have been shown to be responsible in some cases (Chandra and Shah 1984).

The substances released from the cells include histamine and serotonin, but many other mediators are also released (Barrett and Metcalfe 1988). The major influences of these mediators are vasodilation, smooth muscle contraction, and a general increase in vascular permeability.

A small amount of any food protein remains undigested and passes through the gut wall and into the circulatory system (Steinmann, Wottge, and Muller-Ruchholz 1990). During the neonatal period the gastrointestinal barrier to protein uptake and transport is immature. Therefore, excessive amounts of food proteins may be transported into the circulatory system. In addition, it is possible that a large quantity of protein is not broken down intracellularly due to immature cell function. During this period, infants may become sensitized to ingested allergens; and later, when the mucosal barrier is mature, small amounts of allergen absorbed by the gut can cause a reaction.

It has been suggested that food-allergic reactions are caused by pathologically increased gut permeability (Sampson 1990a); this claim has been refuted by studies with cow's milk–allergic children in which the gut was not shown to be more permeable than in control children (Walker 1984; Powell et al. 1989). However, the permeability of the gastrointestinal barrier does increase following mast cell activation, thereby allowing more allergen through the barrier and, perhaps, increasing the allergic response (Barrett and Metcalfe 1988).

Mast cells located on the mucous surfaces of the gastrointestinal tract are thought to play a major role in IgE-mediated food hypersensitivity reactions (Barrett and Metcalfe 1988). The gastrointestinal tract contains comparatively large numbers of mast cells – for example, the human duodenum contains 20,000 per cubic millimeter (Norris, Zamchek, and Gottlieb 1962), whereas human skin contains 7,000 per cubic millimeter (Mikhail and Miller-Milinska 1964).

Food allergy can develop only if the allergen crosses the gastrointestinal barrier. The clinical manifestations of food allergy depend on the transport of allergens across the barrier, giving rise either to local allergic reactions or, from the systemic circulation, to systemic responses. Penetration of the gut depends on the size and structure of the allergen, changes occurring as a result of digestion, gut permeability (depending on age and preexisting disease), and interaction with other antibodies located in the gut. More factors to be considered are individual responses to various amounts of allergen, sufficient IgE binding at the mast cell or basophil, and the susceptibility of the affected organs to the mediators that are released.

Symptoms

Clinical manifestations of mediator release depend on the part of the body that is affected. Table IV.E.3.1 lists symptoms associated with food-allergic reactions. The most common manifestations are gastrointestinal, dermal, and respiratory (Sampson and Cooke 1990), and they represent contact of allergen with populations of sensitized mast cells present in the affected tissues.

Gastrointestinal symptoms, including nausea and vomiting, cramping, abdominal distension, flatulence, and diarrhea, are especially frequent in infants and young children (Barrett and Metcalfe 1988). Chronic ingestion of offending foods by sensitive people may cause fecal blood loss, malabsorption, and other long-term manifestations (Buckley and Metcalfe 1982). Skin reactions to food allergens in such individuals can include pruritus, edema of the lips, tongue, gums, oral mucosa, and pharynx. Urticaria (hives) is the most common skin manifestation and can be diffuse or localized.

Table IV.E.3.1. *Symptoms of food allergy*

Gastrointestinal	Respiratory	Cutaneous
Abdominal cramps	Asthma	Urticaria
Diarrhea	Laryngeal edema	Angioedema
Nausea	Rhinitis	Atopic dermatitis
Vomiting	Wheezing	

The reactions are very individualistic and diverse (Collins-Williams and Levy 1984). Initially, some individuals may experience immediate contact reactions on their lips and tongue, whereas others do not experience a reaction until the offending food has moved farther down the gastrointestinal tract.

Respiratory symptoms can be divided into two categories: upper airway distress, which in food-allergic reactions is usually caused by laryngeal edema, and middle airway distress, produced as a consequence of bronchoconstriction, with resulting edema and pulmonary mucus production (Collins-Williams and Levy 1984). Respiratory symptoms are infrequent with food allergies, although asthma has been associated with allergies to cow's milk, soybeans, and peanuts (Minford, MacDonald, and Littlewood 1982; Chiaramonte and Rao 1988).

Atopic dermatitis, a chronic inflammatory skin disease, is characterized by dry, easily irritated, intensely pruritic skin. The role of food hypersensitivity in atopic dermatitis has been debated for decades (Burks et al. 1988). IgE-mediated reactions to foods may contribute to the pathogenesis of atopic dermatitis (Sampson and McCaskill 1985); A. W. Burks and co-workers (1988) reported that 96 percent of atopic dermatitis subjects examined in their study developed skin reactions after food challenge.

Anaphylactic shock is a rare, acute, and potentially fatal form of food-allergic response. It is a generalized vasodilation triggered by significant mast cell degranulation and can involve a number of organ systems. If the cardiovascular system is affected, shock and low cardiac output result, and involvement of the respiratory tract can induce bronchospasm, pulmonary edema, and laryngeal edema. In food-induced anaphylactic shock, the gastrointestinal tract can respond with abdominal cramping and vomiting. Anaphylactic reactions may advance rapidly, beginning with mild symptoms that can progress to cardiorespiratory arrest and shock over a one- to three-hour period.

For example, an individual experiencing an anaphylactic food-allergic reaction may notice tongue itching and swelling, or palatal itching at first, then throat tightening, perhaps followed by wheezing and cyanosis. Chest pain and urticaria may be noted, and the individual may have gastrointestinal symptoms such as abdominal pain, vomiting, or diarrhea. A progression of symptoms can lead to potentially life-threatening hypotension and shock.

As there are no official means of reporting anaphylactic episodes, the actual frequency of these reactions is unknown, although J. W. Yunginger and colleagues at the Mayo Clinic (1988) documented 8 cases of fatal food-induced anaphylaxis in a period of 16 months. Exercise-induced food anaphylaxis is a type of reaction that develops during or shortly after exercise following the ingestion of certain foods. In documented cases, exercise most often occurred within 2 hours of ingestion. The foods implicated have included celery, lentils, peaches, shellfish, and wheat. Neither exercise alone nor food alone were sufficient to induce anaphylaxis (Maulitz, Pratt, and Schocket, 1979; Buchbinder et al. 1983; Kushimoto and Aoki 1985; Silverstein et al. 1986).

Symptoms of food-induced anaphylaxis may include cutaneous erythema, itching, and urticaria, which can progress to vascular collapse or upper respiratory obstruction (Schocket 1991). The pathophysiological mechanism of these reactions has not been elucidated, but heightened mast cell responsiveness to physical stimuli may be involved (Sheffer et al. 1983). It has been shown that avoidance of the offending food 8 to 12 hours prior to exercise usually eliminates difficulties.

Incidence and Natural History

The incidence of true food allergy is probably less than the general population perceives. Although studies have shown that at least one in four adults with allergies believe that they have experienced adverse reactions following ingestion or handling of foods (Sampson and Metcalfe 1992), it is estimated that just 2 to 3 percent (Bock 1987; Sampson and Cooke 1990) of the pediatric population and 1 to 2 percent of the adult population suffer from allergic reactions to food (Sampson and Cooke 1990). The true prevalence is unknown, however, and other estimates range from 0.3 to 10 percent of the total population (Taylor 1980; Johnstone 1981; Taylor 1985; Barrett and Metcalfe 1988; Schreiber and Walker 1989).

Food allergy is also influenced by culture and eating habits. For example, allergies to fish are more common in Japan and Norway than elsewhere because consumption of fish is higher in those countries (Aas 1966). The frequency of food hypersensitivity varies by ethnic group and socioeconomic class (Lieberman and Barnes 1990). Its etiology includes many factors, but genetics seem to play a large role. Studies with children have shown that the risk for allergy with one allergic parent is approximately 50 percent and for bilateral parental allergy 67 to 100 percent (Schatz et al. 1983).

Frequency of food allergy is highest in infancy and early childhood and diminishes with increasing age (Collins-Williams and Levy 1984). It is most prevalent between 1.5 and 3 years of age (Kjellman 1991). Although young children appear more likely to outgrow their food allergies, older children and adults may also lose their sensitivity if the offending food is removed from the diet. Investigations have shown that one-third of children and adults lose their clinical reactivity after one to two years of allergen avoidance (Sampson and Scanlon 1989).

Differences in disappearance rates depend on the allergen and the individual; for example, many children with allergy to cow's milk can tolerate small amounts of milk by the time they are 3 years old, and

egg allergy tends to decline before age 7. But allergies to nuts, legumes, fish, and shellfish tend to remain a problem for a much longer time (Bock 1982; Collins-Williams and Levy 1984).

Although exposure to food allergens can occur in utero through placental passage, most studies have shown that prenatal sensitization to food is infrequent (Halpern et al. 1973; Croner et al. 1982; Hamburger et al. 1983; Kjellman and Croner 1984). However, the case of an infant with strong skin-test reactivity to wheat and milk at the age of 5 hours has been reported (Kaufman 1971). Some fully breast-fed infants have been observed to have allergies to egg and cow's milk (Warner et al. 1980), and significant amounts of cow's milk casein have been detected in breast milk for up to 12 hours after maternal ingestion (Stuart et al. 1984).

There have been a number of studies on breast feeding to determine what benefit it might have in preventing food sensitization (Halpern et al. 1973; Saarinen et al. 1979; Juto and Bjorkstein 1980; Hide and Guyer 1981; Buscino et al. 1983). The results are conflicting, and the only consistent observation is that prolonged breast feeding (greater than four months and preferably six) and delayed introduction of solid food seem to be beneficial in the prevention of food allergy (Zeiger 1988). Breast feeding and maternal avoidance of common allergenic foods is suggested if there is a family history of allergy and a high serum IgE level at birth (Michel et al. 1980).

Causative Agents

Traditional Foods

The most commonly implicated foods in food allergy are listed in Table IV.E.3.2. The allergenic substances are usually proteins (Aas 1978b). Adults tend to be allergic to shellfish, legumes (especially peanuts), crustacea, tree nuts, and wheat (Bock and Atkins 1990; Sampson 1990a; Sampson and Cooke 1990). Children tend to be allergic to milk and eggs more frequently. Any food, however, has the potential to cause an IgE-mediated reaction. Very severe reactions are most often seen with peanuts, eggs, fish, and nuts (Collins-Williams and Levy 1984). In fact, peanuts are the most common cause of life-threatening reactions (Sampson 1990b). In a period of 16 months, a

Table IV.E.3.2. *Common allergenic foods*

Cow's milk
Crustacea – shrimp, crab, lobster
Eggs
Fish
Legumes – peanuts and soybeans
Shellfish – clams, oysters, scallops
Tree nuts
Wheat

research team at the Mayo Clinic reported 4 cases of death due to peanut-induced anaphylactic shock (Yunginger et al. 1988).

With the widespread introduction of new and "exotic" foods into our diets, it is anticipated that newly described allergic reactions will be reported. D. A. Moneret-Vautrin (1986), for example, has noted that with the relatively recent introduction of soybeans to the diet in France, the incidence of observed soybean allergy has increased to the point where it has become the third most common food allergy. Another example is kiwi fruit, which is not indigenous to the United States and became available as a result of importation in the 1980s. Following its introduction, allergic reactions to kiwi fruit were suddenly reported (Fine 1981; Fallier 1983).

Genetically Engineered Foods

Some concerns are being raised regarding nontraditional foods produced using genetic engineering techniques. These techniques allow for the fast and easy transfer of proteins from one food into another and for increased nutritional or other benefits, such as viral resistance. But there also is the potential for allergenic proteins from some foods to be transferred into other foods; how or whether these foods should be labeled is still being debated. Another compelling issue is whether genetic engineering techniques could potentially change the protein structure so that it could become allergenic once transferred and reproduced in the engineered food. The United States Food and Drug Administration has been and will continue to be working on policies governing the regulation of bioengineered foods, with allergenicity a key issue (Kessler et al. 1992).

Food Allergens

Most allergenic foods contain multiple allergens. For example, egg white is a complex mixture of at least 20 proteins, of which 5 or 6 are allergenic (Langeland 1982). The existence of multiple allergens in cow's milk (Goldman 1963; Bleumink and Young 1968) and peanuts (Barnett, Baldo, and Howden 1983) is well known. Most major food allergens range from 14 to 70 kilodaltons (1,000 atomic mass units) in molecular weight (Aas 1976; King 1976; Chiaramonte and Rao 1988). The upper molecular size observed for these allergens may be due to the permeability limits involved in the gastrointestinal barrier of the host. The allergen must be of adequate molecular intricacy to interact with the elements of the immune system, but quite low limits of molecular size exist; for example, small fragments of the codfish allergen, 6,500 and 8,500 daltons in size, possess pronounced allergenic activity (Elsayad et al. 1972). T. Ishizaka and K. Ishizaka (1984) have shown that the release of mast cell mediators depends on the bridging of two cell-fixed IgE molecules by the allergen. If such bridging is critical, the allergic response should, in fact, depend on the

number of allergenic determinants and their distribution on the surface of the allergen and not necessarily their size.

Common food allergens that have been fully or partially purified or characterized include codfish (Elsayad and Aas 1971), cow's milk (Goldman et al. 1963; Bleumink and Young 1968), eggs (Anet et al. 1985), peanuts (Barnett and Howden 1986; Burks et al. 1991; Burks et al. 1992), soybeans (Shibaski et al. 1980; Herian, Taylor, and Bush 1990), and shrimp (Hoffman, Day, and Miller 1981; Daul et al. 1992).

Most common allergenic food proteins appear to be heat-stable and resistant to proteolytic processes, such as peanut, shrimp, and codfish allergens, although many lose their allergenic activity during digestion or cooking (Aas 1984). Therefore, the allergenicity of a food may be influenced by the way in which the food is prepared, processed, or stored. For example, ovalbumin, the third most important allergen of eggs, is moderately heat-labile and is found only in small amounts in cooked egg (Hoffman 1979). Similarly, heating denatures some cow's milk allergens and makes them less allergenic (Bahna and Gandhi 1983). Individuals allergic to fresh fruits and vegetables can often tolerate these foods after they are cooked, canned, or frozen (Hannuksela and Lahti 1977; Eriksson 1978).

Cross-Reactivity

When a sensitive individual produces IgE antibodies directed against a certain food component and then encounters another food with similar components, an allergic response may occur. Structural allergenic similarities may exist within families of biologically related foods. Since dietary elimination of the offending food is the only "tried-and-true" method of preventing an allergic reaction, cross-allergenicity among related foods is of concern to allergists and patients. Food-allergic individuals often report cross-reactivity among other foods in the same families and are cautioned to avoid eating other closely related foods.

The most common food families associated with cross-reactions are fish, citrus fruits, legumes, shellfish, mollusks, and crustaceans (Chiaramonte and Rao 1988). Certain allergens are also apparently common to both foods and pollens. Common allergens have been reported in melon, banana, and ragweed pollen (Anderson et al. 1970), celery and mugwort pollen (Pauli et al. 1985), and apple and birch pollen (Lahti, Bjorkstein, and Hannuksela 1980).

"True" clinical cross-reactivity, however, is often difficult to establish without performing oral challenge studies. Reports in the literature seem to indicate that the occurrence of clinical cross-reaction is infrequent (Bock 1991). Extensive in vitro "allergenic cross-reactivity" (binding of IgE antibody that is specific for a different food allergen) has been documented. For example, D. Barnett, B. Bonham, and M. E. H. Howden

(1987) found that 25 percent of sera from legume-sensitive patients reacted strongly with peanut, garden pea, soybean, and chickpea extracts. Another research team also found extensive in vitro cross-allergenicity with peanuts, soybeans, peas, and lima beans in patients with legume sensitivity (Bernhisel-Broadbent, Taylor, and Sampson 1989).

However, an earlier study by the same researchers indicated that clinical results and in vitro results did not correlate well in evaluating allergenic cross-reactivity in the legume family (Bernhisel-Broadbent and Sampson 1989). Fifty-nine percent of skin-test-positive patients reacted to oral challenge, but only (approximately) 3 percent reacted in oral challenges to more than one legume. These studies show that although IgE antibodies can cross-react with related foods and cause positive skin tests in some cases, clinical manifestations are rare, and being allergic to one food does not necessarily rule out the consumption of biologically related foods.

Occupational Food Allergy

Development of allergic disease can be associated with occupational exposure to food proteins, and most occupational sensitizing agents are food-derived protein allergens (O'Neil and Lehrer 1991). Exposure is facilitated through inhalation and contact, and syndromes include occupational asthma, hypersensitivity pneumonitis, and skin reactions, including contact dermatitis and contact urticaria.

But although allergen levels in the workplace can be very high, only a small percentage of exposed workers develop occupational responses, suggesting that host factors play an influential role. For example, a history of allergy seems to influence development of sensitivity in some instances of occupational allergic disease, such as occupational asthma caused by exposure to green coffee beans (Jones et al. 1982). By contrast, however, family or individual history of allergy has not been shown to be a factor in the development of occupational asthma due to exposure to snow crab (Cartier et al. 1984).

Although the pathophysiology of many occupational food reactions has not been ascertained, the role of IgE in occupational asthma in bakers is well known (Hendrick, Davies, and Pepys 1976; Block et al. 1983). Most occupational allergens that are also foods have not been shown to induce symptoms following ingestion by workers sensitized via inhalation. Occupational asthma related to food products has been most often associated with seafood, eggs, grains, spices, herbs, coffee, tea, and mushrooms, whereas hypersensitivity pneumonitis, although low in occurrence, has been associated with molds used in cheese production, poultry proteins, fish meal, and mushroom spores. Dermatological reactions precipitated by food have been most often linked with fish, seafood, mustard, garlic, onion, cashews, and lettuce.

Diagnosis of Food Allergy

The diagnosis of food allergy is complicated. As we have seen, adverse food reactions can be caused by immunologic, nonimmunologic, and unknown factors (Hawrylko and Murali 1988). Substantiation of food allergy involves meticulous medical evaluation, since self-diagnosis is often unreliable. Elimination diets are frequently the initial approach to diagnosis of food allergy. The suspected offending food is first eliminated for two to four weeks, then reintroduced in small quantities and the patient's response is recorded (Cummings and Bock 1988).

Skin Testing

Skin testing is the most popular diagnostic tool for evaluating food allergy. It was first used in 1966 to identify children allergic to codfish (Aas 1966). The techniques for skin tests are varied and include puncture, prick, scratch, and intradermal methods. A positive response results in a skin reaction forming a "wheal-and-flare." Results are recorded by measuring the wheal-and-flare diameter and comparing them to negative (saline solution) and positive (histamine) controls. Clinically significant wheals are 3 millimeters or more in diameter (Cummings and Bock 1988). But the use of skin testing is precluded in the face of anaphylactic or other severe reactions, as well as generalized dermatitis, and positive skin tests may be inhibited by the use of some medications, especially certain antihistamines and drugs with antihistamine effects (Chodirker 1985).

A major problem with skin testing is that food allergen extracts have not been standardized. Food skin-test extracts are usually crude preparations of unknown composition, and accurate diagnosis of food allergy has, in part, been impeded by the lack of standardized extracts. This may ultimately be responsible for the variability in the predictive accuracy of food skin tests. H. A. Sampson (1988), for example, compared extracts from three commercial firms for their positive predictive accuracy against oral-food-challenge results and discovered that they ranged from 0 to 79 percent. Negative predictive accuracies were much better, ranging from 85 to 100 percent. C. Ortolani and co-workers (1989) found that skin-test extracts prepared with fresh foods produced more sensitive results when compared to commercial extracts. As an increasing number of food allergens are isolated and fully characterized, the potential for use of standardized food extracts increases.

Double-Blind, Placebo-Controlled Food Challenge

The double-blind, placebo-controlled food challenge (DBPCFC), in which a suspected offending food or placebo is administered in capsules or masked in other food, has been called the "gold standard" for the diagnosis of food allergy (Collins-Williams and Levy

1984; Cummings and Bock 1988; Sampson 1988; Bock 1991). This method was initially used in the investigation of immediate hypersensitivity reactions to foods in asthmatic children (May 1976). But S. A. Bock and F. M. Atkins (1990) recently reported a study of a group of food-allergic children over a period of 16 years. Fully 39 percent had positive DBPCFC results. Other investigators have reported good correlation of DBPCFC results with other laboratory methods for diagnosing food allergy (Bernstein, Day, and Welsh 1982; Sampson 1988; Parker et al. 1990).

Although controversy exists regarding the use of skin tests alone for diagnosis (Bernstein, Day, and Welsh 1982; Bock and Atkins 1990), some investigators have found good correlation between food-challenge studies and skin-test results. For example, one such study, which focused on a group of adults with histories of immediate adverse reactions to foods, discovered that 90 percent of those in the group who were food-challenge-positive were also skin-test-positive (Atkins, Steinberg, and Metcalfe 1985). Similarly, Bock and Atkins (1990) noted that 98 percent of positive food reactions to oral challenge were accompanied by a positive skin test in children past their third birthday. But in younger children the correlation dropped to 83 percent.

Nonetheless, other investigators have found false-positive skin tests in patients who were food-challenge-negative (Bernstein et al. 1982; Sampson and Albergo 1984). In general, a negative skin-test result is a good indicator of absence of IgE-mediated hypersensitivity (Sampson 1988; Parker et al. 1990).

Radioallergosorbent Assay

The first assay developed for measuring IgE blood levels was the radioallergosorbent assay (RAST), which was initially described in 1967 (Wide, Bennich, and Johansson 1967). RAST is specific and reproducible (Hawrylko and Murali 1988); however, it measures only circulating, and not tissue-bound, IgE. For this reason, it is less sensitive than skin tests for the detection of specific IgE. In addition, a RAST test is not necessary if the skin test is negative, as circulating IgE will not be present if there is no tissue-bound IgE (May 1976; Sampson and Albergo 1984; Chodirker 1985; Bock and Atkins 1990). Generally, sensitivity of RAST for food allergens varies from 50 percent to more than 90 percent (May 1976). RAST is still widely used in the allergy field to augment skin testing in diagnosis. Sensitivity of RAST for food allergens could be improved, as could skin-test reliability, if there were technical advances in the purification of food allergens.

Basophil Histamine Release

In this technique, blood basophils are obtained from an allergic patient. They are incubated with an allergen for a specified time, and the release of mediating histamine, caused by the presence of the allergen, is measured (May et al. 1970; Hirsch and Zastrow 1972).

In one study employing purified cow's milk proteins, wheat, soybean, and ovalbumin extracts, release of histamine from cells was found in 25 to 50 percent of pediatric subjects who also had positive skin tests, and no histamine was released in skin-test-negative patients (May and Alberto 1972).

In another study, however, food extracts did not induce release of histamine in patients with food allergy (Dockhorn 1969). H. Nolte and colleagues (1989), using gut mast cells obtained during biopsies of food-allergic patients, found that histamine release from intestinal mast cells could not be correlated with histamine release by blood basophils. Therefore, there are differences in the ability of food extracts to elicit a response in mast cells from different organs.

As with other diagnostic allergy assays, the sensitivity of the basophil histamine release assay could probably be improved by the use of purified food-allergen preparations. In addition, the technique is neither convenient nor easy to perform and, therefore, is not used widely for diagnosis.

Treatment and Prevention of Food Allergy

Elimination Diets

Elimination diets are the only proven effective therapy for food allergy, once the offending food is identified (Chodirker 1985; Schreiber and Walker 1989). In patients with severe reactions to foods, strict avoidance is indicated, which may include cross-reacting foods, prepared foods (unless one is absolutely certain of all ingredients), and the inhalation of aerosols of the implicated food (Rao and Bahna 1988).

Despite the apparent low incidence of clinical cross-reactivity, food-allergic persons are encouraged to use caution when eating a biologically related food for the first time. The recommendation is usually to avoid the offending food for a number of years, if not for the remainder of the patient's life. However, this advice may be adjusted for children, as they tend to outgrow certain food allergies, such as those to eggs and milk.

Avoidance

Food-allergic individuals must read food labels and ingredient listings diligently, as these usually reveal the presence of the offending ingredient. This task can be difficult, and a certain amount of "education" in reading labels is necessary, because particular terms used by food processors can camouflage the presence of allergenic proteins. "Natural flavorings" may include soybean and/or milk proteins, and "caramel flavoring" may contain milk proteins. "Hydrogenated vegetable protein" commonly contains soybean proteins but can be comprised of other types of vegetable protein. In addition, it can be difficult to identify and avoid some types of allergenic foods. An example is peanuts, which after pressing and deflavoring, are then reflavored and sold as other types of nuts, such as almonds. Though they smell, taste, and look like tree nuts, these deflavored peanuts have been found to retain their allergenic qualities (Nordlee et al. 1981) and can pose a serious threat to unsuspecting peanut-allergic people.

Sensitive individuals may also be inadvertently exposed to foods contaminated with allergenic proteins during processing. In one documented case, for example, the inadequate cleaning of common equipment caused sunflower butter to become contaminated with peanut butter and elicited an allergic reaction in a peanut-sensitive patient (Yunginger et al. 1983).

Antihistamines

Antihistamines have been suggested for use in children with mild food allergies before mealtime (Bahna and Furukawa 1983). However, since antihistamines work by competitive inhibition (Furukawa 1988), they cannot completely prevent allergic reactions, and individuals with severe reactions should not rely on them.

Perspective on the Development of Allergy

Allergic disease is difficult to trace in archaeological or historical records. Evidence of foods or medicines used in the past is very limited (Lieberman and Barnes 1990), and the symptoms of allergy can mimic those of other diseases, thereby concealing accounts of allergic reactions in records and notes.

It has been theorized that allergy is a fairly recent development in the history of the human race. A prominent characteristic of parasitic infections in humans is an elevated level of IgE (Johansson, Bennich, and Berg 1972). But because parasitic infections and allergic disease seem to be mutually exclusive (Merrett, Merrett, and Cookson 1976), allergy could be the result of an ecological transition from endemic parasitosis to improved sanitary conditions that eliminate or reduce parasitic exposure (Lieberman and Barnes 1990). An interesting discovery is a higher frequency of allergies among urban than rural residents in developing countries, but higher IgE levels in rural people than among urban asthmatics and individuals with allergies (Godfrey 1975; Merrett et al. 1976). The advent of modern, hygienic conditions and the elimination of parasitic infection could, therefore, be responsible for spawning production of IgE against other substances in our environment.

Susan L. Hefle

Bibliography

Aas, K. 1966. Studies of hypersensitivity to fish. *International Archives of Allergy* 29: 346-63.

   1976. Common characteristics of major allergens. In *Molecular and biological aspects of the acute allergic reaction,* ed. S. G. O. Johansson, K. Strandberg, and B. Ovnas, 3-19. New York.

   1978a. Studies of hypersensitivity to fish – a clinical study. *International Archives of Allergy* 8: 39-50.

   1978b. What makes an allergen an allergen. *Allergy* 33: 3-14.

   1984. Antigens in food. *Nutrition Reviews* 42: 85-91.

Anderson, L. B., Jr., E. M. Dreyfuss, J. Logan, et al. 1970. Melon and banana sensitivity coincident with ragweed pollenosis. *Journal of Allergy* 45: 310-19.

Anet, J., J. F. Back, R. S. Baker, et al. 1985. Allergens in the white and yolk of hen's egg. A study of the IgE binding by egg proteins. *International Archives of Allergy and Applied Immunology* 77: 364-71.

Atkins, F. M., S. S. Steinberg, and D. D. Metcalfe. 1985. Evaluation of immediate adverse reactions to foods in adult patients. I. Correlation of demographic, laboratory, and prick skin test data with response to controlled oral food challenge. *Journal of Allergy and Clinical Immunology* 75: 348-55.

Bahna, S. L., and C. T. Furukawa. 1983. Food allergy: Diagnosis and treatment. *Annals of Allergy* 51: 574-80.

Bahna, S. L., and M. D. Gandhi. 1983. Milk hypersensitivity. I. Pathogenesis and symptomatology. *Annals of Allergy* 50: 218-23.

Barnett, D., B. A. Baldo, and M. E. H. Howden. 1983. Multiplicity of allergens in peanuts. *Journal of Allergy and Clinical Immunology* 72: 61-8.

Barnett, D., B. Bonham, and M. E. H. Howden. 1987. Allergenic cross-reactions among legume foods – an in vitro study. *Journal of Allergy and Clinical Immunology* 79: 433-8.

Barnett, D., and M. E. H. Howden. 1986. Partial characterization of an allergenic glycoprotein from peanut (*Arachis hypogaea* L.). *Biochimica et Biophysica Acta* 882: 97-105.

Barrett, K. E., and D. D. Metcalfe. 1988. Immunologic mechanisms in food allergy. In *Food allergy,* ed. L. T. Chiaramonte, A. T. Schneider, and F. Lifshitz, 23-43. New York.

Bernhisel-Broadbent, J., and H. A. Sampson. 1989. Cross-allergenicity in the legume botanical family in children with food hypersensitivity. *Journal of Allergy and Clinical Immunology* 83: 435-40.

Bernhisel-Broadbent, J., S. L. Taylor, and H. A. Sampson. 1989. Cross-allergenicity in the legume botanical family in children with food hypersensitivity. II. Laboratory correlates. *Journal of Allergy and Clinical Immunology* 84: 701-9.

Bernstein, M., J. H. Day, and A. Welsh. 1982. Double-blind food challenge in the diagnosis of food sensitivity in the adult. *Journal of Allergy and Clinical Immunology* 70: 205-10.

Bleumink, E., and E. Young. 1968. Identification of the atopic allergen in cow's milk. *International Archives of Allergy* 34: 521-43.

Block, G., K. S. Tse, K. Kijek, et al. 1983. Baker's asthma; clinical and immunologic studies. *Clinical Allergy* 13: 359-70.

Bock, S. A. 1982. Natural history of food sensitivity. *Journal of Allergy and Clinical Immunology* 69: 173-7.

   1987. Prospective appraisal of complaints of adverse reaction to foods in children during the first three years of life. *Pediatrics* 79: 683-8.

   1991. Oral challenge procedures. In *Food allergy: Adverse reactions to foods and food additives,* ed. D. D. Metcalfe, H. A. Sampson, and R. A. Simon, 81-95. Boston, Mass.

Bock, S. A., and F. M. Atkins. 1990. Patterns of food hypersensitivity during sixteen years of double-blind, placebo-controlled food challenges. *Journal of Pediatrics* 117: 561-7.

Buchbinder, E. M., K. J. Bloch, J. Moss, and T. E. Guiney. 1983. Food-dependent exercise-induced anaphylaxis. *Journal of the American Medical Association* 250: 2973-4.

Buckley, R. H., and D. D. Metcalfe. 1982. Food allergy. *Journal of the American Medical Association* 20: 2627-31.

Burks, A. W., S. A. Mallory, L. W. Williams, and M. A. Shirrell. 1988. Atopic dermatitis: Clinical relevance of food hypersensitivity reactions. *Journal of Pediatrics* 113: 447-51.

Burks, A. W., L. W. Williams, C. Connaughton, et al. 1992. Identification and characterization of a second major peanut allergen, Ara h II, with use of the sera of patients with atopic dermatitis and positive peanut challenge. *Journal of Allergy and Clinical Immunology* 900: 962-9.

Burks, A. W., L. W. Williams, R. M. Helm, et al. 1991. Identification of a major peanut allergen, Ara h I, in patients with atopic dermatitis and positive peanut challenges. *Journal of Allergy and Clinical Immunology* 88: 172-9.

Buscino, L., F. Marchetti, G. Pellegrini, and R. Berlini. 1983. Predictive value of cord blood IgE levels in "at-risk" newborn babies and influence of type of feeding. *Clinical Allergy* 13: 503-8.

Cartier, A., J.-L. Malo, F. Forest, et al. 1984. Occupational asthma in snow-crab processing workers. *Journal of Allergy and Clinical Immunology* 74: 261-9.

Chandra, R. K., and A. Shah. 1984. Immunologic mechanisms. In *Food intolerance,* ed. R. K. Chandra, 55-66. New York.

Chiaramonte, L. T., and Y. A. Rao. 1988. Common food allergens. In *Food allergy,* ed. L. T. Chiaramonte, A. T. Schneider, and F. Lifshitz, 89-106. New York.

Chodirker, W. B. 1985. Diagnostic methods for assay of specific IgE antibodies in patients with suspected allergic disease. *Canadian Medical Association Journal* 132: 1370-1.

Collins-Williams, C., and L. D. Levy. 1984. Allergy to food other than milk. In *Food intolerance,* ed. R. K. Chandra, 137-86. New York.

Coombs, R. R. A., and P. G. H. Gell. 1975. Classification of allergic reactions responsible for clinical hypersensitivity and disease. In *Clinical aspects of immunology,* ed. P. G. H. Gell, R. R. A. Coombs, and P. J. Lachmann, 761-81. Oxford.

Croner, S., N. M. Kjellman, B. Ericksson, and A. Roth. 1982. IgE screening in 1701 newborn infants and the development of atopic disease during infancy. *Archives of Disease in Childhood* 57: 364-8.

Cummings, N. P., and S. A. Bock. 1988. Clinical methods for diagnosis. In *Food allergy,* ed. L. T. Chiaramonte, A. T. Schneider, and F. Lifshitz, 289-99. New York.

Daul, C. B., M. Slattery, J. E. Morgan, and S. B. Lehrer. 1992. Identification of a common major crustacea allergen. *Journal of Allergy and Clinical Immunology* 89: 194.

Dockhorn, R. J. 1969. Histamine release from the leukocytes of food-allergic individuals using whole food extract antigens. *Annals of Allergy* 27: 409-16.

Elsayad, S., and K. Aas. 1971. Characterization of a major allergen (cod): Observations on effect of denaturation on the allergenic activity. *Journal of Allergy and Clinical Immunology* 47: 283-91.

Elsayad, S., K. Aas, K. Sletten, and S. G. O. Johansson. 1972. Tryptic cleavage of a homogenous cod fish allergen and isolation of two active polypeptide fragments. *Immunochemistry* 9: 647-61.

Eriksson, N. E. 1978. Food sensitivity reported by patients with asthma and hay fever. *Allergy* 33: 189-96.

Fallier, C. J. 1983. Anaphylaxis to kiwi fruit and related "exotic" items. *Journal of Asthma* 20: 193-6.

Fine, A. J. 1981. Hypersensitivity reaction to kiwi fruit (Chinese gooseberry, *Actinidia chinensis*). *Journal of Allergy and Clinical Immunology* 68: 235-7.

Furukawa, C. T. 1988. Nondietary management of food allergy. In *Food allergy,* ed. L. T. Chiaramonte, A. T. Schneider, and F. Lifshitz, 365-75. New York.

Godfrey, R. C. 1975. Asthma and IgE levels in rural and urban communities of the Gambia. *Clinical Allergy* 5: 201-7.

Goldman, A. S., D. W. Anderson, W. A. Sellers, et al. 1963. Milk allergy. I. Oral challenge with milk and isolated milk proteins in allergic children. *Pediatrics* 32: 425-43.

Halpern, S. R., W. A. Sellars, R. B. Johnson, et al. 1973. Development of childhood allergy in infants fed breast, soy, or cow milk. *Journal of Allergy and Clinical Immunology* 51: 139-51.

Hamburger, R. N., S. Heller, M. Mellin, et al. 1983. Current status of the clinical and immunologic consequences of a prototype allergic disease program. *Annals of Allergy* 51: 281-90.

Hannuksela, M., and A. Lahti. 1977. Immediate reaction to fruits and vegetables. *Contact Dermatitis* 3: 79-84.

Hawrylko, E., and M. R. Murali. 1988. Immunologic tests for food allergy. In *Food allergy,* ed. L. T. Chiaramonte, A. T. Schneider, and F. Lifshitz, 301-20. New York.

Hendrick, D. J., R. J. Davies, and J. Pepys. 1976. Baker's asthma. *Clinical Allergy* 6: 241-50.

Herian, A., S. L. Taylor, and R. K. Bush. 1990. Identification of soybean allergens by immunoblotting with sera from soy-allergic adults. *International Archives of Allergy and Applied Immunology* 92: 192-8.

Hide, D. W., and C. M. Guyer. 1981. Clinical manifestations of allergy related to breast and cow's milk feeding. *Archives of Disease in Childhood* 56: 172-5.

Hirsch, S. R., and J. E. Zastrow. 1972. Basophil degranulation: A new method of observation and its correlation with skin testing. *Journal of Allergy and Clinical Immunology* 50: 338-47.

Hoffman, D. 1979. Immunochemical identification of allergens in egg white. *Journal of Allergy and Clinical Immunology* 64: 159-63.

Hoffman, D. R., E. D. Day, and J. S. Miller. 1981. The major heat stable allergen of shrimp. *Annals of Allergy* 47: 17-22.

Ishizaka, T., and K. Ishizaka. 1984. Activation of mast cells for mediator release through IgE receptors. *Progress in Allergy* 34: 188-235.

Johansson, S. G. O., H. Bennich, and T. Berg. 1972. The clinical significance of IgE. *Progress in Clinical Immunology* 1: 157.

Johnstone, D. E. 1981. Current concepts in the natural history of allergic disease in children. *Respiration* 42: 34-41.

Jones, R. N., J. M. Hughes, S. B. Lehrer, et al. 1982. Lung function consequences of exposure and hypersensitivity in workers who process green coffee beans. *American Review of Respiratory Disease* 125: 199-202.

Juto, P., and B. Bjorkstein. 1980. Serum IgE in infants and influence of type of feeding. *Clinical Allergy* 10: 593-600.

Kaufman, H. S. 1971. Allergy in the newborn: Skin test reactions confirmed by the Prausnitz-Kustner test at birth. *Clinical Allergy* 1: 363-7.

Kessler, D. A., M. R. Taylor, J. H. Maryanski, et al. 1992. The safety of foods developed by biotechnology. *Science* 258: 1561-2.

King, T. P. 1976. Chemical and biological properties of some atopic allergens. *Advances in Immunology* 23: 77-105.

Kjellman, N. M. 1991. Natural history and prevention of food hypersensitivity. In *Food allergy: Adverse reactions to foods and food additives,* ed. D. D. Metcalfe, H. A. Sampson, and R. A. Simon, 319-31. Boston, Mass.

Kjellman, N. M., and S. Croner. 1984. Cord blood IgE determination for allergy prediction – a follow-up to seven years of age in 1,651 children. *Annals of Allergy* 53: 167–71.

Kushimoto, H., and T. Aoki. 1985. Masked type I wheat allergy. *Archives of Dermatology* 121: 355–60.

Lahti, A., F. Bjorksten, and M. Hannuksela. 1980. Allergy to birch pollen and apple, and cross-reactivity of the allergens studies with the RAST. *Allergy* 35: 297–300.

Langeland, T. 1982. A clinical and immunological study of allergy to hen's egg white. III. Allergens in hen's egg white studied by crossed radioelectrophoresis (CRIE). *Allergy* 37: 521–30.

Lieberman, L. S., and K. C. Barnes. 1990. Food allergies and adverse food reactions: An anthropological perspective. In *Food allergies and adverse reactions,* ed. J. E. Perkin, 207–232. Gaithersburg, Md.

Lifshitz, F. 1988. Food intolerance. In *Food allergy,* ed. L. T. Chiaramonte, A. T. Schneider, and F. Lifshitz, 3–21. New York.

Maulitz, R. M., D. S. Pratt, and A. L. Schocket. 1979. Exercise-induced anaphylactic reaction to shellfish. *Journal of Allergy and Clinical Immunology* 63: 433–4.

May, C. D. 1976. Objective clinical and laboratory studies of immediate hypersensitivity reactions to foods in asthmatic children. *Journal of Allergy and Clinical Immunology* 58: 500–15.

May, C. D., and R. Alberto. 1972. In-vitro responses of leucocytes to food proteins in allergic and normal children: Lympocyte stimulation and histamine release. *Clinical Allergy* 2: 335–44.

May, C. D., M. Lyman, R. Alberto, and J. Cheng. 1970. Procedures for immunochemical study of histamine release from leukocytes with a small volume of blood. *Journal of Allergy* 46: 12–20.

Mendoza, G., and H. Metzger. 1976. Distribution and valency of receptor for IgE on rodent mast cells and related tumor cells. *Nature* 264: 548–50.

Merrett, T. G., J. Merrett, and J. B. Cookson. 1976. Allergy and parasites: The measurement of total and specific IgE levels in urban and rural communities in Rhodesia. *Clinical Allergy* 6: 131–4.

Michel, F. B., J. Bousquet, P. Greillier, et al. 1980. Comparison of cord blood immunoglobulin E concentrations and maternal allergy for the prediction of atopic diseases in infancy. *Journal of Allergy and Clinical Immunology* 65: 422–30.

Mikhail, G. R., and A. Miller-Milinska. 1964. Mast cell population in human skin. *Journal of Investigative Dermatology* 43: 249–54.

Minford, A. M. B., A. MacDonald, and J. M. Littlewood. 1982. Food intolerance and food allergy in children: A review of 68 cases. *Archives of Disease in Childhood* 57: 742–7.

Moneret-Vautrin, D. A. 1986. Food antigens and additives. *Journal of Allergy and Clinical Immunology* 78: 1039–45.

Nolte, H., P. S. Skok, A. Kruse, and P. O. Schiotz. 1989. Histamine release from dispersed human intestinal mast cells. *Allergy* 44: 543–53.

Nordlee, J. A., S. L. Taylor, R. T. Jones, and J. W. Yunginger. 1981. Allergenicity of various peanut products as determined by RAST inhibition. *Journal of Allergy and Clinical Immunology* 68: 376–82.

Norris, H. T., N. Zamcheck, and L. Gottlieb. 1962. The presence and distribution of mast cells in the human GI tract at autopsy. *Gastroenterology* 44: 448–55.

O'Neil, C. E., and S. B. Lehrer. 1991. Occupational reactions to food allergens. In *Food allergy: Adverse reactions to foods and food additives,* ed. D. D. Metcalfe, H. A. Sampson, and R. A. Simon, 207–36. Boston, Mass.

Ortolani, C., M. Ispano, E. A. Pastroello, et al. 1989. Comparison of results of skin prick tests (with fresh foods and commercial food extracts) and RAST in 100 patients with oral allergy syndrome. *Journal of Allergy and Clinical Immunology* 83: 683–90.

Parker, S. L., A. Leznoff, G. L. Sussman, et al. 1990. Characteristics of patients with food-related complaints. *Journal of Allergy and Clinical Immunology* 86: 503–11.

Pauli, G., J. C. Bessot, A. Dietemann-Molard, et al. 1985. Celery sensitivity: Clinical and immunological correlations with pollen allergy. *Clinical Allergy* 15: 273–9.

Powell, G. K., P. J. McDonald, G. J. Van Sickle, and R. M. Goldblum. 1989. Absorption of food protein antigen in infants with food protein-induced enterocolitis. *Digestive Diseases and Sciences* 34: 781–8.

Rao, Y. A., and S. L. Bahna. 1988. Dietary management of food allergies. In *Food allergy,* ed. L. T. Chiaramonte, A. T. Schneider, and F. Lifshitz, 351–64. New York.

Saarinen, U. M., A. Backman, M. Kajossari, and M. Simes. 1979. Prolonged breast-feeding as prophylaxis for atopic disease. *Lancet* 2: 163–72.

Sampson, H. A. 1988. Comparative study of commercial food antigen extracts for the diagnosis of food hypersensitivity. *Journal of Allergy and Clinical Immunology* 82: 718–26.

1990a. Food allergy. *Current Opinion in Immunology* 2: 542–7.

1990b. Peanut anaphylaxis. *Journal of Allergy and Clinical Immunology* 86: 1–3.

Sampson, H. A., and R. Albergo. 1984. Comparison of results of skin-tests, RAST, and double-blind placebo-controlled food challenges in children with atopic dermatitis. *Journal of Allergy and Clinical Immunology* 74: 26–33.

Sampson, H. A., and S. K. Cooke. 1990. Food allergy and the potential allergenicity-antigenicity of microparticulated egg and cow's milk proteins. *Journal of the American College of Nutrition* 9: 410–17.

Sampson, H. A., and C. C. McCaskill. 1985. Food hypersensitivity and atopic dermatitis: Evaluation of 113 patients. *Journal of Pediatrics* 107: 669–75.

Sampson, H. A., and D. D. Metcalfe. 1992. Food allergies. *Journal of the American Medical Association* 268: 2840–4.

Sampson, H. A., and S. M. Scanlon. Natural history of food hypersensitivity in children with atopic dermatitis. *Journal of Pediatrics* 115: 23–7.

Schatz, M., R. S. Zeiger, M. Mellon, and R. Porreco. 1983. Asthma and allergic diseases during pregnancy: Management of the mother and prevention in the child. In *Allergy: Principles and practice,* ed. E. Middleton, Jr., C. E. Reed, and E. F. Ellis, 935–86. St. Louis, Mo.

Schocket, A. L. 1991. Exercise- and pressure-induced syndromes. In *Food allergy: Adverse reactions to foods and food additives,* ed. D. D. Metcalfe, H. A. Sampson, and R. A. Simon, 199–206. Boston, Mass.

Schreiber, R. A., and W. A. Walker. 1989. Food allergy: Facts and fiction. *Mayo Clinic Proceedings* 64: 1381–91.

Sheffer, A. L., N. A. Soter, E. R. McFadden, Jr., and K. F. Austen. 1983. Exercise-induced anaphylaxis: A distinct form of physical allergy. *Journal of Allergy and Clinical Immunology* 71: 311–16.

Shibaski, M., S. Suzuki, H. Nemob, and T. Kurome. 1980. Allergenicity of major component protein of soybean. *International Archives of Allergy and Applied Immunology* 61: 441–8.

Silverstein, S. R., D. A. Frommer, B. Dobozin, and P. Rosen.

1986. Celery-dependent exercise-induced anaphylaxis. *Journal of Emergency Medicine* 4: 195–9.

Steinmann, J., H. U. Wottge, and W. Muller-Ruchholz. 1990. Immunogenicity testing of food proteins: In vitro and in vivo trials in rats. *International Archives of Allergy and Applied Immunology* 91: 62–5.

Stuart, C. A., R. Twiselton, M. K. Nicholas, and D. W. Hide. 1984. Passage of cows' milk protein in breast milk. *Clinical Allergy* 14: 533–5.

Taylor, S. L. 1980. Food allergy. *Journal of Food Protection* 43: 300–6.

1985. Food allergies. *Food Technology* 39: 98–105.

Walker, W. A. 1984. Absorption of antigens and haptens. In *Food intolerance,* ed. R. K. Chandra, 17–54. New York.

Warner, J. O. 1980. Food allergy in fully breast-fed infants. *Clinical Allergy* 10: 133–6.

Wide, L., H. Bennich, and S. G. O. Johansson. 1967. Diagnosis of allergy by an in vitro test for allergen antibodies. *Lancet* 2: 1105–7.

Yunginger, J. W., M. B. Gaurerke, R. T. Jones, et al. 1983. Use of radioimmunoassay to determine the nature, quantity, and source of allergenic contamination of sunflower butter. *Journal of Food Protection* 46: 625–9.

Yunginger, J. W., K. G. Sweeney, W. Q. Sturner, et al. 1988. Fatal food-induced anaphylaxis. *Journal of the American Medical Association* 260: 1450–2.

Zeiger, R. S. 1988. Prevention of food allergy. In *Food allergy,* ed. L. T. Chiaramonte, A. T. Schneider, and F. Lifshitz, 329–50. New York.

IV.E.4 ❧ Food-Borne Infection

Numerous infectious diseases are acquired by the ingestion of contaminated food, milk, or water. Such illnesses have a worldwide distribution, although, predictably, the incidence is greatest in those countries where deficiencies exist in the provision of adequate sanitation and hygiene.

Yet outbreaks of food poisoning and other food-borne infections occur with frequency even in the most developed countries of the world. Here increasing demand for vast quantities of readily available food has been met by increased reliance on intensive farming techniques, industrialization of food production, introduction of various methods for preservation, and expanding networks for transport, storage, and distribution.

Many of the stages involved in the commercial processing and production of food provide ideal opportunities for the entry, maintenance, and multiplication of microbes. Consequently, several outbreaks of food-borne infection occur each year in developed nations, with the size of the outbreak reflecting the extent of the distribution of the product. Containment measures rely heavily upon early diagnosis and close cooperation between clinicians, medical microbiologists, and officials of public-health departments and are aimed at rapid detection of the source of infection and prompt action to curtail the outbreak. The mea-

sures taken must include immediate withdrawal of the incriminated article of food from sale to the public, dissemination of clearly worded information to consumers defining the source and mode of spread of the infection, and – where appropriate – guidelines on methods of preventing cross-infection between individuals.

Outbreaks of food-borne diseases occurring in Britain in recent years have included (1) salmonellosis spread via infected poultry meat, powdered baby milk, hens' eggs, imported chocolates, and spaghetti; (2) *Escherichia coli* infection transmitted through hamburger meat; (3) botulism from yoghurt that was flavored with contaminated hazelnut puree; and (4) listeriosis from soft cheeses. Recognition of the phenomenal cost entailed in the investigation and control of such outbreaks has led to a heightened awareness of the need for effective measures to curtail the incidence of food-borne diseases. Accordingly, recommendations have been formulated for improving the microbiological quality of food. However, the subject is a complex one and problems continue to arise.

Natural History of Infection

Food and water may transmit infectious diseases when they contain critical numbers of live pathogenic microorganisms that are adapted to invade and colonize the body of the victim through the gastrointestinal tract (see Table IV.E.4.1). Typhoid fever and viral hepatitis are typical examples of such diseases. In some cases the mere presence in food of products of microbial growth, such as toxins, is sufficient to induce disease even though the microbes themselves may have been destroyed. These microbial toxins are relatively heat-stable, retaining their activity even after the food has been heated before consumption, as, for example, staphylococcal enterotoxin and botulinum toxin. Strictly speaking, these are examples of food-borne intoxications in contrast to infections, but it is customary among microbiologists to include them under the rubric of infections.

A characteristic feature of food-borne infection is that, in general, the food concerned looks and tastes appetizing, with no obvious signs of spoilage. This is because the large numbers of bacteria required to cause symptoms in humans would also cause visible signs of spoilage in the food. And that food is unlikely to be consumed.

Thus, in most cases of food-borne infection, the causative agent does not come from spoiled food but from contaminated food and water that have been infected by traveling from host to host via the fecal–oral route. That is to say, the microbes discharged in the feces of an infected human or animal find their way via food, water, or unwashed hands into the mouth of a new host. The organisms are swallowed and proceed to establish themselves on, or in, the mucus membrane lining the gut, or they may pen-

Table IV.E.4.1. *Organisms causing food-borne disease*

Cestodes (Tapeworms)	*Taenia saginata, Taenia solium* *Diphyllobothrium latum* *Echinococcus granulosus* *Hymenolepis nana*
Nematodes (Roundworms)	*Trichinella spiralis* *Ascaris lumbricoides* *Enterobius vermicularis* *Trichuris trichiura* *Angiostrongylus* species *Gnathostoma spinigerum*
Trematodes (Flukes)	*Fasciola hepatica* *Fasciolopsis buski* *Opisthorchis* species *Heterophyes heterophyes* *Metagonimus yokogawai* *Gastrodiscoides hominis* *Paragonimus westermani*
Protozoa	*Cryptosporidium parvum* *Giardia lamblia/intestinalis* *Microsporidium* *Toxoplasma gondii* *Sarcocystis* species *Entamoeba histolytica* *Balantidium coli*
Fungus	*Aspergillus* and *Fusaria* species
Bacteria	*Campylobacter coli, Campylobacter jejuni* Salmonella enteric fever group: *Salmonella typhi,* *Salmonella paratyphi* A, *Salmonella* *paratyphi* B, *Salmonella paratyphi* C gastroenteritis group: *Salmonella enter-* *itidis, Salmonella typhimurium,* and others *Shigella dysenteriae, Shigella flexneri,* *Shigella boydi, Shigella sonnei* *Escherichia coli:* enteropathogenic (EPEC), enterotoxigenic (ETEC), enteroinvasive (EIEC), enterohaemorrhagic (EHEC) *Yersinia enterocolitica, Yersinia pseudotuberculosis* *Vibrio cholerae, Vibrio eltor, Vibrio parahaemolyticus, Vibria vulnificus* *Clostridium welchi, Clostridium botulinum* *Bacillus cereus, Bacillus licheniformis, Bacillus subtilis, Baeillus anthracis* *Staphylococcus aureus* *Aeromonas hydrophila* *Plesiomonas shigelloides* Brucella: *Brucella abortus, Brucella melitensis, Brucella suis* *Mycobacterium bovis* *Coxiella burnetti*
Virus	Hepatitis A virus and hepatitus E virus Poliomyelitis virus Rotavirus Small round structured viruses (Norwalk and Norwalk-like agents) Astrovirus Calicivirus
Prion (?)	Agent causing bovine spongiform encephalopathy, which may infect humans who eat diseased meat (not proven but suspected)

etrate the gut wall to invade other parts of the body, traveling in the bloodstream and lymphatic channels.

Multiplication of the organisms in their chosen sites is often followed by symptoms of the disease, although symptomless or subclinical infection may also occur. In either case, large numbers of the organism leave the patient (voided in feces, vomit, urine) ready to repeat the cycle in a new and susceptible host. Such diseases may belong to one of two categories: (1) diseases of the gastrointestinal tract, in which the symptoms may include diarrhea, vomiting, and abdominal pain, such as cholera, dysentery, or bacterial and viral gastroenteritis; and (2) diseases with symptoms not necessarily related to the gastrointestinal tract, such as toxoplasmosis, poliomyelitis, brucellosis, and typhoid fever.

Source of Infection

Infection at the Source

The meat of an animal infected with the parasite causing toxoplasmosis, sarcocystis, or tapeworm is infective when eaten undercooked or raw. Eggs laid by hens that are infected with *Salmonella enteritidis* often transmit infection when the egg is eaten raw or undercooked. The question of whether bovine spongiform encephalopathy may be readily transmitted to people eating beef from infected cattle is still hotly debated, but it is becoming more widely accepted that this transmission can occur. Milk from infected animals, when consumed without prior heat treatment, transmits diseases like tuberculosis, brucellosis, and Q fever.

Infected fish may also transmit infection (fish tapeworm) when eaten raw or undercooked. Shellfish contaminated with the organism *Vibrio parahaemolyticus,* which normally grows in the salty water of warm seas, cause food poisoning when ingested. Some fish and mollusks acquire powerful heat-stable toxins through their food and are then able to transmit diseases like ciguatera fish poisoning and paralytic or neurotoxigenic shellfish poisoning to people eating them. These animals feed on toxin-containing dinoflagellates and concentrate the toxins in their flesh. The fish, however, appear to be unharmed by the toxin. In contrast, scombroid fish poisoning is acquired by eating a preparation of the scombroid group of fish, like smoked mackerel, that has been subjected to substandard processing and/or improper storage conditions prior to smoking. Here, bacteria that are commonly present – such as species of *Proteus* and *Klebsiella* – act on, and break down, the histidine present in the musculature to yield histamine and other substances (scombrotoxin). The symptoms produced on ingestion mimic those of histamine poisoning.

Contamination in the Slaughterhouse

Meat is often contaminated with organisms that normally inhabit only the lumen of the gut of animals but escape when the intestinal wall is damaged during slaughter and evisceration. This occurrence seems to be the most common route of transmission of such infections in Britain. Typical of this group of pathogens are *Clostridium perfringens* and species of *Salmonella, Campylobacter,* and *Yersinia.* Some species of *Salmonella* are able to cause a disseminated septicemic illness in their hosts, as, for example, *S. enteritidis* in poultry, which spreads to the heart and other organs that are used as giblets.

Food that is contaminated in this way may then contaminate other clean food by direct contact, as happens when raw meat comes into contact with cooked food, either directly as in refrigerators, or indirectly through use of the same preparation surface or knife.

Fecal Contamination of Food and Water

Both human and animal feces, which contaminate food and water, are major causes of diarrheal diseases. These diseases are especially prevalent in countries lacking adequate facilities for the safe disposal of sewage or protected water supplies. The role of flies, rodents, and birds in the transfer of pathogens from infected feces to food is well documented. Moreover, the washing of salad vegetables or fruit in water contaminated with human or animal sewage results in the transfer of diseases like typhoid, cholera, and bacillary or amoebic dysentery, as well as gastroenteritis caused by *E. coli,* Campylobacter, and Salmonella infections.

Bivalve shellfish (oysters, clams, and mussels) that are harvested from shallow inshore coastal waters adjacent to an outflow of sewage often contain large numbers of fecal pathogens. These animals are filter feeders, filtering large amounts of water each day to extract their food. The microbes present in fecal particles are concentrated in the flesh of the mollusk, which – when eaten raw or undercooked – may transmit diseases like typhoid fever, hepatitis A and E, and viral gastroenteritis. In addition, whereas the process of depuration (leaving the shellfish in tanks of purified water for over 24 hours prior to sale) removes most of the bacteria from the mollusks, viruses remain intact. Heat treatment is therefore required to inactivate them.

Waterborne infections commonly occur in areas lacking chlorinated water supplies. They are also associated with wars and other causes of sudden, uncontrolled movement of populations that disrupt normal services. Waterborne infections occur from time to time in developed countries, resulting in explosive outbreaks in the area of distribution of the water supply concerned.

Generally, such outbreaks follow a sudden or unforeseen breakdown of chlorination or filtration in the water purification plant, but they are also seen in institutions that are situated in remote areas and maintain their own water supply. It is notable that the cysts of some gastrointestinal protozoan parasites, such as species of *Giardia,* along with *Entamoeba histolytica,* are resistant to the standard chlorination process used for drinking water. Improperly filtered but adequately chlorinated tap water has resulted in several recent outbreaks of cryptosporidiosis in Britain and the United States.

In developing countries, where infective diarrheal diseases are common, debility arising from the illness compounds the effects of malnutrition, and childhood mortality rates are excessive. Up to 15 out of every 1,000 children in some areas die before the age of 5 from diarrheal disease transmitted by water.

Food Handlers

Food may be contaminated due to poor standards of hygiene among those who handle and prepare it. These food handlers may be: (1) "carriers" who harbor and continue to excrete pathogenic microorganisms and are thereby able to transmit them to others, even if they themselves no longer suffer from symptoms of the disease or have never had any symptoms; (2) people who are not yet symptom-free following gastrointestinal illness; and (3) those who are caring for patients with such diseases. The danger lies in the transmission of microorganisms to food via unwashed hands and poor toilet hygiene, or by aerosols caused by sick food handlers vomiting in preparation areas. Food handlers typically cause outbreaks of staphylococcal food poisoning, viral gastroenteritis, and enteric fever, which is particularly significant in the commercial or bulk preparation of food. Staphylococcal food poisoning is especially relevant here since the toxin produced can resist heat treatment.

Contamination from the Environment

Microorganisms found in the environment may contaminate food and water. The spores (resistant forms) of *Clostridium botulinum* survive for long periods of time in the soil and mud of lakes and rivers. They may contaminate vegetables and fish and secrete a powerful neurotoxin into the food. *Listeria monocytogenes,* found in the gut of cattle, sheep, and other animals and in soil and grass, may contaminate foods such as unpasteurized milk products. Moreover, the ability of listeriae to grow and multiply at temperatures prevailing in most domestic refrigerators contributes to the problem of preventing infection.

Canned food has often been found contaminated with organisms that have gained entry through tiny undetected faults in the seal. During manufacture, cans of food are first heat-sterilized, then cooled by immersion in water before the labels are attached. When the cans undergo sudden cooling, material from the outside gets sucked into the interior, and infective agents gaining entry at this stage may then multiply freely in the food. If the food is to be eaten uncooked or only lightly cooked, it presents a hazard. A can of imported corned beef was implicated as the source of the outbreak of enteric fever in Aberdeen in 1964. At the canning factory in South America, the cans were cooled in untreated water taken from a river close to the factory. Further investigation revealed that raw sewage from a neighboring settlement was discharged directly into the river upstream from the factory. Enteric fever was endemic in this community.

Back in Aberdeen, the infected corned beef was sliced and sold to the public through a retail outlet, resulting in the outbreak. The causative agent was identified and traced back to the retail premises, revealing the corned beef as the source of the outbreak. All cans belonging to the same batch as that causing the outbreak were withdrawn from sale. However, in spite of this action, the outbreak was observed to continue, with the diagnosis of more new cases in the area. It later became apparent that other items of precooked food sold in the shop, like ham, had been cross-contaminated when they were sliced on the same machine as the contaminated meat. Following this observation, the outbreak was brought under control by enforcing measures for (1) preventing further sale of contaminated food and (2) thorough cleaning and decontamination of all equipment and work surfaces involved. Canned food has also been implicated in outbreaks of botulism, staphylococcal food poisoning, and other diseases. In Great Britain, the most common food-borne infections today are campylobacter and salmonella gastroenteritis acquired from poultry and meat. Among the salmonellae, the incidence of *S. enteritidis* phage type 4 is now increasing steadily in England and many other countries.

Bacterial Food Poisoning

The food-poisoning group of organisms include *Staphylococcus aureus, Salmonella* species, *Clostridium perfringens, Bacillus cereus, Clostridium botulinum,* and *Vibrio parahaemolyticus.*

The term "food poisoning" is generally used in a restricted way to exclude clinical entities like typhoid and cholera, but it includes those conditions in which intestinal disturbances commonly occur, resulting in diarrhea and vomiting (with or without other symptoms). It is caused by ingesting either live bacteria or products of bacterial growth – the latter arising after the microbes have multiplied in the food for some hours before it is eaten.

This vital initial period of bacterial multiplication in food is an essential feature in the natural history of all bacterial food poisoning, as it ensures that a vastly increased number of bacteria are present in the food. The "challenge dose" of bacteria (the number that have to be ingested in order to cause disease) is much higher in the food-poisoning group than it is with other diseases, like typhoid and shigellosis, where food merely acts as a vehicle for transmission of the infection. *C. botulinum* is included in the food-poisoning

group, although the symptoms produced here are neurological rather than gastrointestinal, because this pathogen from the soil must grow and multiply for several hours in food before it is able to cause disease.

Crucial factors in the evolution of an outbreak of food poisoning include the type of food involved, the way in which it has been prepared, and the duration and temperature of storage prior to eating. As with most other food-borne infections, the food looks and tastes normal.

Bacterial food poisoning may belong to three different types, depending on the mechanism of pathogenesis observed:

1. In the *infective type,* as caused by *Salmonella,* large numbers of live organisms must be consumed. They then invade the cells lining the small intestine, where further multiplication occurs, causing inflammation, diarrhea, and vomiting. The time interval between ingesting the food and developing symptoms (the incubation period) is between 14 and 36 hours.
2. In the *toxic type,* caused by *S. aureus, B. cereus,* and *C. botulinum,* the phase of multiplication in food results in the release of toxins. When ingested, these toxins (preformed in the food) are responsible for producing the symptoms. It is not necessary to ingest the live organisms. Rapid heating of the food may destroy the bacteria but allow heat-stable toxins to remain active. In contrast to the previous type, the incubation period here is fairly short – a few hours – because the preformed toxin is able to act immediately on the gut.
3. The *intermediate type,* caused by *C. perfringens,* has an incubation period of 8 to 20 hours. The toxin is released not in the food but in the gut of the host, following ingestion. The release of toxins here coincides with the formation of spores (a resistant form of the bacterium). Prolonged low-temperature cooking or inadequate reheating of infected, leftover meat stews and casseroles increases the occurrence of this disease, because it stimulates sporulation of the *C. perfringens* in the gut of the host.

It is apparent that three important criteria have to be satisfied for the successful development of food poisoning. These are as follows:

1. Introduction of organisms into the food at some stage during its preparation.
2. Inadequate cooking. Most microbial agents in food are destroyed by cooking at high temperatures for the prescribed length of time. When frozen food, like meat, is cooked before it is completely thawed out, the temperature reached in the center of the meat may not be sufficient to kill the bacteria even when the outside looks well done.
3. Leaving food standing at an ambient temperature for several hours, enabling the bacteria to multiply

and attain the infective dose. Refrigeration of food stops multiplication of most of the harmful pathogens, with the exception of species like *Yersinia enterocolitica* and *L. monocytogenes,* which are particularly adapted for growth at temperatures of 0 to 4 degrees Celsius (°C). Freezing suspends replication of all pathogens but fails to kill them. After frozen food is allowed to thaw, bacteria may start to multiply again if kept standing at room temperature. Hence, careful attention is important at all stages of food preparation to ensure adequate cooking and prevent contamination. Furthermore, if food is not to be eaten without delay, it should be rapidly chilled before freezing for storage.

Clearly, even contaminated food is not harmful if properly cooked and eaten right away. But when eaten raw, inadequately cooked, or after remaining for a long time in a warm environment, contamined food may transmit disease. Bacteria in food replicate rapidly by binary fission, doubling their numbers progressively at intervals of less than 20 minutes by a simple process of division in which each cell gives rise to two daughter cells. Food provides the ideal nutrient for bacteria, which continue to multiply, so that in just over 3 hours a starting population of 1,000 organisms (which is too low a dose to cause food poisoning) may reach the level of millions and constitute an effective challenge dose. In most outbreaks, food has been left for longer than 3 hours and the starting population may be higher than 1,000. Organisms like *Campylobacter, Shigella,* and the typhoid bacillus are infective at a much smaller dose level than the food-poisoning group, and in this case it is not necessary for the infected food to remain at room temperature for several hours in order to be able to transmit infection. Indeed, organisms like *Campylobacter* and viruses do not multiply in food. As already mentioned, in this case, food merely acts as a vehicle for transmission of these agents.

Most pathogenic bacteria are unable to grow in acidic food (pH less than 4.5) or in food with a low moisture content. Similarly, high salt or sugar concentration in preserved food inhibits many bacteria. However, they may survive for long periods of time in dried food products.

Staphylococcal Food Poisoning

The food-poisoning strains of *S. aureus* are usually harbored by human food handlers, either in septic skin lesions (boils and whitlows) or as a part of the normal resident microbial flora of the nose or skin. Transfer of such organisms to food may be restricted by the use of a no-touch technique in its preparation. This is especially relevant for large-scale processing of food. Food poisoning does not occur if the contaminated food is either eaten before the bacteria have a

chance to multiply, heated before the bacteria multiply and produce toxins (*S. aureus* are readily killed by heat), or refrigerated promptly and served chilled, to prevent multiplication of surviving bacteria.

If contaminated food is first refrigerated and then left standing for a considerable length of time in a warm room, the bacteria are able to multiply again. *S. aureus* multiplies rapidly over a wide range of temperatures, liberating its heat-stable enterotoxin. The type of food involved here is usually that which requires little or no cooking and has a high fat content, like cream cakes, trifles, and ham sandwiches. When eaten, the toxin acts on the host, causing symptoms of nausea, vomiting, and abdominal pain (but rarely with diarrhea) within 1 to 6 hours of ingestion. The toxin appears to act on nerve endings in the gut, transmitting its message to the center in the brain that controls vomiting.

Most cases are self-limiting. Recovery occurs rapidly, usually within 12 hours, and no treatment is required. If the infected food is heated to 70° C before serving, the *S. aureus* will be killed, but the toxin is still active, and even boiling for 30 to 60 minutes may not inactivate it. Moreover, *S. aureus* is not inhibited by a high concentration of salt. Therefore, foods like ham and other semipreserved meat with a high salt and high fat content make an ideal medium for staphylococcal growth and multiplication. Prevention involves stringent measures for personal and environmental hygiene in the food preparation area, the covering of skin lesions with waterproof dressings, rapid refrigeration of prepared food that is not to be eaten right away, and thorough cooking of soups and meats before eating. Control of food handlers and use of the no-touch technique are important in the food manufacturing industry.

Salmonella Food Poisoning

Salmonellosis is a disease affecting both humans and animals and may be transmitted between them (a zoonosis). There are over 200 species of salmonellae, and they are widely distributed in nature, inhabiting the intestines of wild as well as domestic animals and household pets. They frequently contaminate meats, especially chicken, along with eggs, milk, and other products. Intensive farming techniques have resulted in widespread infection in the food chain, and mechanized mass processing of poultry carcasses ensures the cross-contamination of most poultry sold in shops.

Chickens infected with *S. enteritidis* are able to pass the infection on in their eggs. Infected humans acting as food handlers may also transmit infection unless scrupulous attention to hygiene is observed with regard to hand-washing after using the toilet and before handling food. Milk that is not heat-treated may also transmit salmonellae. The organism is readily killed by boiling for half an hour, so poor culinary practices are largely to blame for outbreaks of salmonellosis in humans. Examples of such practices include cooking inadequately thawed large frozen joints of meat, low-temperature cooking, allowing cooked food to come in contact with uncooked meat or its juices, and prolonged storage at room temperature after inadequate cooking.

This last factor is the most important one because it enables an effective infective dose of salmonellae to develop in the food. Normal gastric acidity is sufficient to kill many ingested pathogens, but this defense may be breached when the microbe is taken in large numbers along with food that temporarily neutralizes the protective mechanism. Frequent outbreaks of salmonella food poisoning continue to occur in many developed nations because of (1) infected manufactured food; (2) the practice of adding raw egg to food that is to be eaten uncooked; and (3) importation of food products from areas with a high disease prevalence.

The strain of *Salmonella* responsible for an outbreak of gastroenteritis often points to the species of animal from which the food derived, as many strains have preferred hosts. *S. enteritidis* and *Salmonella typhimurium* are commonly found in poultry and cattle, *Salmonella dublin* in cattle, and *Salmonella hadar* in turkeys. However, at times, certain strains appear to sweep through an entire population of livestock, probably because of contaminated feed and intensive farming techniques involving overcrowding and animal stress. The infection is often asymptomatic in humans and other animals, but continued excretion of the pathogen in feces enables transmission to occur.

This excretion is especially marked when animals are maintained in overcrowded situations and is reflected in the high incidence of infection in flocks of poultry and in beef cattle. During slaughter and evisceration, gut contents often contaminate the meat. Cross-contamination of other carcasses then occurs either through direct contact with the meat or by contact with contaminated surfaces and equipment. Thus, all retailed meat may be regarded as potentially contaminated.

Consumption of an infecting dose of 10^5 to 10^6 organisms is required in order to establish infection. This amount is readily achieved if improperly cooked meat is left to cool at room temperature for 3 or more hours. Fewer cells (10 to 100) may cause illness in very young children or in the elderly, especially if the pathogens are carried in high-fat foods such as cheese, cheesecake, salami, or hamburgers. Low numbers may also be infective when waterborne. A high fat content in food is believed to protect the salmonellae to some extent during cooking. This may be relevant to the survival of *S. enteritidis* phage type 4 in eggs and meat.

Since 1985, this particular strain has appeared with increasing frequency among the poultry population and has now spread to epidemic levels among them. In birds, the infection is not confined to the gut but passes into the bloodstream to give a severe septicemia, and the eggs are infected before they are laid. Thorough cooking of the eggs or pasteurization of bulked eggs would destroy the pathogen. Pasteurization entails heating the product to a temperature of either 63 to 66° C for a period of 30 minutes or 71° C for 15 seconds. This form of heat treatment kills all vegetative pathogens like salmonellae in milk and eggs.

Human infection follows the ingestion of approximately 1 million organisms, which then invade the intestinal mucosal cells and cause local inflammation. The incubation period lasts for 14 to 36 hours and is followed by diarrhea and vomiting, with or without abdominal pain. Most infections are self-limiting and do not require any treatment, but in more severe cases, supportive therapy with rehydration is implemented. In very young babies or in elderly or debilitated patients, for instance, the disease may follow a septicemic course, giving rise to a serious life-threatening condition that necessitates the administration of appropriate antibiotics as well as rehydration. Following recovery, a small proportion of people may retain organisms in the gut for a varying period of time and continue to excrete them intermittently in the feces. If these "carriers" are employed as food handlers, they may transmit the organism to foods unless scrupulous attention to hygiene is observed.

Salmonella organisms may be introduced into manufactured food products at various stages in the production line. For example, they may enter after the heating stage and cause widespread outbreaks. Intercontinental outbreaks have been traced to chocolates and cheeses. Critical monitoring of production procedures to detect and control the possibility of microbiological contamination at every stage is of vital importance. Although it would be ideal to reduce salmonellosis in the livestock by measures like heat treatment of all animal feed and improvement of farming techniques, this aim is not readily achievable.

Legislation to enforce heat treatment of all milk sold from retail outlets has helped reduce milk-borne outbreaks in humans. However, the occasional undetected breakdown of a pasteurization unit has resulted in the sale of contaminated milk that has caused outbreaks. Countries lacking basic sanitation and hygiene tend to have a higher prevalence and transmission rate of salmonellosis. Foodstuffs imported from such areas (for example, spices like pepper) may require more than the usual decontamination. Alternatively, spices and the like can be added to food before it is cooked rather than afterward; this, too, prevents the problem.

Clostridium Perfringens Food Poisoning

This food poisoning is associated with reheated leftover meat dishes, like stews. The causative organism is a normal commensal of the gut of humans and other animals. It is a strict anaerobe able to grow and multiply only in an environment devoid of oxygen. Clostridia are able to produce tough, resistant spores that survive in adverse environments, and these spores germinate into vegetative cells. Multiplication can occur only in the vegetative state and not in spore form.

Inadequate cooking of meat enables the spores to survive. *C. perfringens* type A has particularly heat-resistant spores that can survive prolonged boiling, and these strains are associated with outbreaks of food poisoning, usually in institutions such as nursing homes. The type of food involved is, generally, meat dishes such as large joints cooked at a low temperature, or stews and broth when there is insufficient heat penetration to kill off all the spores.

Furthermore, the spores are protected by the protein-rich food. If the cooked food is eaten right away, it is generally safe, but when such food is left for between 3 and 5 hours at room temperature, it provides the ideal anaerobic conditions for the spores to germinate and the vegetative cells to multiply. Multiplication is rapid, with a mean doubling time of only 7 minutes at 41° C. The infecting dose of 10^8 organisms per gram of food is soon attained. If, at this stage, the food is thoroughly reheated (to over 70° C), the vegetative cells are killed and the food is rendered safe.

If the food is only partially reheated (up to or below 60° C), though, the cells survive, and when ingested, they sporulate in the gut and shed the vegetative fragment, which releases a heat-labile enterotoxin. This acts on the small intestinal mucosa, damaging the brush border of epithelial cells at the tip of the villous processes. There is an outpouring of fluid and electrolytes resulting in violent, watery diarrhea and abdominal colic, occurring 8 to 20 hours after ingestion of the food. Vomiting and fever are uncommon, but nausea may be present. Recovery occurs within 24 hours in most cases, and no specific treatment is required. However, in elderly, debilitated individuals, severe dehydration may result, necessitating supportive therapy with rehydration.

Prevention involves the high-temperature cooking of meat in small amounts, rapid refrigeration if it is not eaten immediately, and reheating of all leftover meat dishes to a temperature higher than 70° C to destroy the vegetative cells. Cooking methods like frying and grilling have an advantage in that they deliver very high temperatures directly to contaminated meat surfaces.

Bacillus Cereus Food Poisoning

B. cereus produces spores that help it to survive in adverse conditions such as drying and heat. Unlike the clostridia, this organism is an aerobe (growing in the presence of oxygen). It is found widely distributed as a saprophyte in the environment and on cereals like rice. In fact, outbreaks of *B. cereus* food poisoning are frequently associated with reheated rice dishes such as fried rice and take-out fast food from Chinese restaurants. Bacterial spores survive the short cooking period involved, and if the rice is left at an ambient temperature for several hours to dry, germination of the spores occurs. The bacterial cells then multiply rapidly in the rice and liberate various enterotoxins. When the precooked rice is stir-fried to make fried rice, the heat-stable toxin is not destroyed by the short exposure to heat and may cause symptoms shortly after ingestion. When boiled rice is stored in a refrigerator, it goes lumpy, and when subsequently stir-fried, it fails to present the aesthetically acceptable appearance of well-separated grains of rice. This probably accounts for the tendency, especially in fast-food outlets, to leave precooked rice at room temperature for several hours and reheat it as required.

Two distinct types of disease symptoms are observed with *B. cereus* infection, depending on the type of toxin formed:

1. In the emetic type, vomiting is common. The incubation period here is 1 to 5 hours, and symptoms include nausea, vomiting, malaise, and, sometimes, diarrhea, lasting for 6 to 24 hours. This type is caused by a heat-stable toxin and is associated with cereals, especially the cooked rice just mentioned. The condition may, of course, be prevented by eating freshly cooked rice while it is hot; but if this is not possible, then the food should be maintained at over 60° C or stored at temperatures of about 8° C.
2. The diarrheal type is the rarer of the two and is due to the production of a heat-labile enterotoxin associated with lightly reheated meat sauces, puddings, and vegetables. Symptoms include profuse watery diarrhea, abdominal cramps, and, sometimes, vomiting occurring 8 to 16 hours after eating the food. Recovery is generally complete in 12 to 24 hours.

Botulism

Botulism is a neuroparalytic disease caused by the ingestion of very small amounts of botulinum toxin. An oral dose of 0.005 μg may be lethal for humans. *C. botulinum* is a spore-producing organism that can grow only in the absence of oxygen. The tough spores are found worldwide in the soil and in the mud of lakes and rivers. When food like fish, vegetables, and meat is contaminated with soil containing the spores and is then left at room temperature, the spores germinate and multiplication of the organism occurs.

Some strains grow in temperatures as low as 3.3° C. During the growth process, a powerful neurotoxin is produced, which, when ingested, results in symptoms of botulism, following an incubation period of 18 to 36 hours. The preformed toxin causes a muscular paralysis with hoarseness, visual disturbances, headache, nausea, vomiting, and difficulty in swallowing and speaking. If left untreated, death from respiratory or cardiac arrest is a real danger. Symptoms may last from several weeks to many months.

A less severe disease is caused in infants ingesting spores of *C. botulinum.* These spores germinate in the infant's gut, releasing toxin in the intestine. Symptoms of flaccidity and weakness, with difficulty in feeding, are the presenting symptoms of infantile botulism. Treatment includes administration of antitoxin antibodies to attempt to neutralize the toxins.

Prevention relies on the destruction of spores by thorough heating of all preserved food. This is especially relevant to home-preserved food – the cause of many outbreaks. The high acid content of certain foods prevents the growth of this organism, but preformed toxin retains its activity when added to acid food. As mentioned previously, in an outbreak in England in 1989, the source was contaminated hazelnut puree used to flavor yoghurt. The toxin in food may be destroyed by heating at 85° C for 5 minutes.

Vibrio Parahaemolyticus Food Poisoning

This form of food poisoning is related to the ingestion of undercooked or raw shellfish or fish. *V. parahaemolyticus* has a predilection for high salinity and grows well in the warmer seas. The shellfish and fish taken from such sites may be contaminated with the organism. When undercooked shellfish are eaten, symptoms of diarrhea and vomiting, fever, and abdominal cramps appear within 16 to 48 hours, resolving in 2 to 7 days. Other halophilic (salt-loving) bacteria, like *Vibrio vulnificus,* may cause a septicemic infection in people eating raw oysters. Prevention depends on the adequate cooking of seafood.

Other Bacterial Food-Borne Infections

Apart from the food-poisoning group of organisms, many other bacteria transmitted in food may also cause infection.

Campylobacteriosis

Campylobacteriosis occurs throughout the world and is the most common cause of acute infective diarrhea in most developed countries. The organisms *Campylobacter coli* and *Campylobacter jejuni* are widely distributed in nature, infecting the gut of domestic and wild animals, poultry and wild birds, and also humans. Poultry and cattle are important sources of human infection, because in addition to developing acute infection, they may become symptomless excreters of the organism with long-term carrier status. This is a classic example of a zoonosis (a disease transmitted between animals and humans) and, therefore, as is the case with nontyphoid salmonella, cannot easily be eradicated.

The curved, spiral-shaped organism is found in large numbers in the gut contents of infected animals and is commonly transferred to poultry and animal meat during slaughter and evisceration. Most poultry carcasses sold in shops are consequently contaminated with the organisms. They may also be transferred from the feces of infected animals, wild birds, or humans to unprotected drinking water supplies or to food. Outbreaks occur most frequently after the consumption of improperly cooked poultry but have also taken place after the drinking of milk that was not heat-treated and unchlorinated water.

The infective dose is small (a few hundred bacteria), and the incubation period is approximately 3 days. The disease produced is an acute enterocolitis, and lesions are seen in the intestinal mucosa similar to those produced by shigellae or salmonellae. A characteristic feature of campylobacter is that the incubation period is followed by a period of a few days when the patient feels ill with headache, malaise, fever, and abdominal pain (the prodromal period). This is followed by a dysentery-like illness with frequent stools, sometimes containing blood and mucus. The prodromal symptoms help differentiate this illness from that caused by salmonellae or shigellae. Furthermore, the symptoms of abdominal pain and diarrhea seen here may be more prolonged. In fact, the pain may be so severe as to lead to a misdiagnosis of acute appendicitis and to the patient undergoing unnecessary abdominal surgery.

In most cases, recovery occurs within a week, and there is no need for antibiotic therapy. However, in debilitated or immunodeficient patients the organism may spread through the blood to cause a severe systemic infection, requiring appropriate antibiotic therapy.

Prevention of infection is achieved by measures that break the routes of transmission, such as the following:

1. Thorough cooking of all meat.
2. Observance of good principles of kitchen hygiene, like preventing contact between cooked food and raw meat, including contact with surfaces on which the raw food was placed first.
3. Heat treatment of milk by pasteurization or sterilization.
4. Adequate chlorination of the water supply or boiling of untreated drinking water.

Because the campylobacter organisms are so widespread in the animal kingdom, it would be unrealistic to hope to eradicate them entirely. It would, however, be useful to reduce the incidence of campylobacteriosis in poultry stocks and farm animals by good principles of farming and processing, while preventing human infection by observance of the simple measures recommended. This is also true of nontyphoid salmonellosis. Unlike salmonellae however, the campylobacter do not appear to multiply in food that is kept warm. The infective dose is low, and heavy contamination of food ensures transmission. Any food may be contaminated by direct or indirect contact with the feces of infected domestic pets, other animals, birds, or humans.

Shigellosis (Bacillary Dysentery)

Shigellosis is a common disease seen throughout the world, but unlike nontyphoid salmonellae and campylobacter, shigellae infect only humans – there is no known animal host. The species involved are *Shigella dysenteriae, Shigella flexneri, Shigella boydi* and *Shigella sonnei,* and the severity of the diseases they produce decreases in this order.

Shigella sonnei, the mildest of the four forms, causes outbreaks mainly among young children in institutions like daycare centers and elementary schools. Poor toilet hygiene is the main cause of transmission in such cases. Outbreaks also occur in military barracks, institutions for the mentally handicapped, and in populations subjected to major social upheavals with a breakdown in the normal pattern of life.

Shigella dysenteriae, which causes the most severe of the four infections, is commonly seen in Asia. A high level of transmission is maintained in those countries with unprotected water supplies, a lack of facilities for the safe disposal of sewage and poor environmental conditions and personal hygiene practices.

The infective dose is small, and the disease is readily transmitted from person to person. There is no need for the organism to multiply in food in order to cause disease, as is the case with salmonella food poisoning. Following ingestion, the organism invades superficial layers of the cells lining the intestinal lumen, causing ulceration and inflammation that results in bleeding, secretion of mucus, and exudation of pus. The symptoms are diarrhea with loose stools containing blood, mucus, and pus. The severity of the illness varies with the species involved. The infection is localized to the intestine and does not invade deep tissues or the bloodstream except in very severe forms.

Antibiotic therapy is restricted to the serious forms of illness, like *S. dysenteriae,* or any severe form of dysentery occurring in the very young or debilitated patient. In most cases antibiotics are contraindicated as they may prolong symptoms and excretion of shigellae in the feces.

Prevention in the developed countries involves improving toilet hygiene, especially among children in institutions and schools. In developing countries lacking environmental hygiene and safe water supplies, travelers are well advised to drink only bottled or boiled water and to avoid uncooked or salad vegetables and fruit that is to be eaten unpeeled.

Typhoid Fever (Enteric Fever)

Tyhoid fever is a severe febrile septicemic illness that is endemic in countries with poor sanitation and affects only human hosts – animals are not involved.

The causative organism, *Salmonella typhi,* is transmitted from one host to the next, usually through water supplies contaminated with human sewage. Food handlers also play an important role in the transmission. Recovery from this fever may be associated with the carrier state, which may last for a lifetime, with intermittent excretion of *S. typhi* in feces and urine. Such a state occurs when the organism continues to live in the gallbladder or kidneys of the host but no longer causes adverse symptoms. However, it is excreted from time to time in the feces of the carrier and may, therefore, be transmitted to other hosts. It is important to identify such carriers, educate them on food hygiene, and exclude them from following a career in the food industry.

Food may act as a vehicle for the transmission of this disease, which is by the fecal–oral route. Symptoms appear after an incubation period of about 10 to 14 days, with fever, headache, malaise, and, sometimes, diarrhea or constipation. Such symptoms are severe, and fatal complications may occur if untreated. Treatment with an appropriate antibiotic is important in all cases of enteric fever. Prevention requires the provision of protected, chlorinated water supplies and safe sewage disposal. In endemic areas it is wise to boil all drinking water or to treat it with chlorine tablets. Travelers to endemic zones are advised to drink only bottled water and not to eat salad vegetables, uncooked food, or unpeeled fruit. A vaccine containing heat-killed *S. typhi* is available but gives only partial protection, so the prevention of infection remains the main aim.

Paratyphoid fever caused by *Salmonella paratyphi* A, B, or C is a milder form of the infection just discussed. *Salmonella paratyphi* B is the strain transmitted in Europe, whereas *S. paratyphi* A and C are endemic in other areas.

Escherichia coli Gastroenteritis

This form of infection is possibly the most common cause of diarrhea in the world. Specific strains of this large family of organisms are involved in causing human gastroenteritis. Their natural habitat is the gut of humans and animals, and transmission is from person to person or by the intake of contaminated water or food. The infective dose is small, and there is no need for the organism to multiply in food for several hours before becoming infective.

The disease is prevalent in areas with poor environmental hygiene and frequently causes diarrhea in travelers to these areas (appropriately termed Aztec two-step, Rangoon runs, Delhi belly, Tokyo trots, and gippy tummy). In developed countries, outbreaks of infantile gastroenteritis have occurred in hospitals, and more recently, outbreaks of hemorrhagic colitis and hemolytic uremic syndrome have been reported where the causative organism was *E. coli* serotype 0157, transmitted in undercooked hamburgers. It is possible that some strains cause zoonotic infection, whereas with others, human hosts are the sole source of infection.

The organisms have been classified according to the way in which disease is produced: Hence there is enteropathogenic *E. coli* (EPEC), enterotoxigenic *E. coli* (ETEC), enteroinvasive *E. coli* (EIEC), and vero-toxin-producing or enterohemorrhagic *E. coli* (VTEC or EHEC).

In developing countries, diarrhea and dehydration brought on by such infection is a major cause of infant mortality. Adults are also affected from time to time, but they appear to develop a measure of immunity from constant exposure to all the different strains in the community. Travelers to infected areas, however, are unprotected and extremely susceptible to all the new organisms in the environment.

EPEC strains belong to certain known serogroups and, in the past, have caused outbreaks of gastroenteritis in infants and young children. Symptoms include diarrhea and vomiting, and severe dehydration may occur. Thus, unless supportive treatment is initiated rapidly, mortality rates can be high. Adults may also be occasionally infected. The mechanism of pathogenesis of EPEC strains is not clearly understood, but the organisms remain within the lumen of the gut and produce changes in the appearance of the cells lining the small intestine. Antibiotic therapy is restricted to the severely ill and debilitated cases.

All ETEC strains secrete enterotoxins, of which there are two types: heat-labile toxin (LT) and heat-stable toxin (ST). These toxins act locally on the cells of the intestinal mucosa, stimulating them in such a way as to result in a net outpouring of fluid and electrolytes from the bowel wall into the lumen.

The disease rarely occurs in temperate climates. In developing countries, however, it is common in children and is an important cause of travelers' diarrhea. Sewage contamination of water supplies is important in transmission. ETEC strains do not invade the body but remain in the gut lumen closely attached to the surface of the mucosal cells by means of short fibrillar processes (colonization factors). The toxin is secreted in the gut lumen and is internalized by the mucosal cells. Recovery occurs in a few days when the cells of the small intestine are replaced by fresh ones. Cells in the small intestinal mucosa are normally shed and replaced very rapidly. Because there is no inflammation in the gut wall, the stools contain no inflammatory cells. This is in sharp contrast to shigellosis and salmonellosis. Treatment is strictly supportive, with rapid correction of dehydration a lifesaving remedy.

EIEC strains (like *E. coli* serotype 0124) cause invasive disease similar to shigella dysentery, with ulceration of the intestinal mucosa that results in diarrhea with blood, mucus, and pus in stools. Food-borne infection is common, and cross-infection can occur.

EHEC (VTEC) strains have caused outbreaks of bloody diarrhea in people eating undercooked hamburgers. When meat is ground, it enables the organisms to grow better and cause greater contamination. The hemorrhagic colitis may be followed by hemolytic uremic syndrome (kidney failure and anemia due to the destruction of the red blood cells and destruction of thrombocytes). Many patients suffer only mild diarrhea, whereas others are seriously ill. *Escherichia coli* serotype 0157 is particularly associated with such outbreaks. The incubation period is 2 to 9 days. A contagious spread of the disease may also occur and is important in hospital outbreaks. Prevention is similar to the prevention of shigellosis with the added incentive to ensure that hamburgers are properly cooked.

Cholera

Cholera is a purely human, intestinal form of disease, characterized by profuse watery diarrhea (rice-water stools), that frequently leads to dehydration and death in untreated cases. It spreads along the fecal–oral route, with waterborne transmission most responsible for explosive outbreaks. Transmission from person to person also occurs. Flies can spread it, and the disease may also be food-borne. Fecal pollution of seawater can contaminate seafood which, if eaten raw or undercooked, may transmit the disease. No animal host has been detected for the cholera vibrio. Normal levels of gastric acid provide some defense against such infections in humans. The disease is more likely to occur in those with no or low levels of gastric acid.

Vibrio cholerae remains in the lumen of the gut attached to the surface of mucosal cells. The pathogenesis is mediated by a toxin that is secreted into the gut by the organism. This toxin is internalized by the cells and stimulates an outpouring of fluid and electrolytes, resulting in profuse diarrhea with the potential of causing death from dehydration (up to 20 liters per day of fluid loss). The mode of action of the cholera toxin is similar to that of *E. coli* LT. Indeed, the two toxins are similar in structure. There is no damage to the mucosa, and with modern medical treatment, recovery occurs in a week's time in most cases.

That treatment involves rapid rehydration. Oral rehydration with frequent small drinks of an electrolyte and glucose solution is usually used. In severe cases intravenous fluid infusion is necessary. Orally administered tetracycline is useful in reducing the period of excretion of the vibrio and also the severity of symptoms.

The latest cholera pandemic is due to the El Tor variant of *V. cholerae,* which causes a milder form of cholera than that seen in the nineteenth-century pandemics that swept the globe. It began in the 1960s in Southeast Asia and was spread by travelers, first to the Middle East and Africa and then to South America. Outbreaks, common where water supplies and environmental sanitation are poor or nonexistent, are especially likely in camps for refugees from wars or natural disasters.

Cholera prevention. Careful disposal of human sewage is essential, along with the provision of safe chlorinated water supplies or, failing that, boiled or bottled water. *Vibrio eltor* is more difficult to control because it causes a milder disease, meaning there are more ambulant cases to disseminate it more widely. A vaccine is available, but its protection is of short duration, and there is considerable doubt as to its efficacy.

Yersiniosis

Yersiniae are part of the normal gut flora of domestic and wild animals. Human infection is acquired by the ingestion of inadequately cooked meat containing sufficient numbers of the organism. *Y. enterocolitica* induces a typical food-poisoning-type syndrome with mild or moderate diarrhea, fever, and abdominal pain. Nausea and vomiting are rare, but mesenteric adenitis (inflammation of the abdominal lymph nodes) may occur and lead to misdiagnosis as acute appendicitis. Symptoms appear within 16 to 48 hours after the meal and may last for a period ranging from 24 hours to 4 weeks. Reactive arthritis is a complication that may occur following this infection, especially in people of HLA type B27. A heat-stable enterotoxin is produced by the organism that may contribute to the pathogenesis in the gut. However, the infection is not confined to the gut, as the organism invades the body to cause inflammation in the mesenteric lymph nodes.

A characteristic feature of this organism is its ability to grow and multiply in the cold at 0° C; consequently, refrigeration of contaminated food does not prevent the development of an infective dose. The bacteria, however, are readily inactivated by adequate cooking. Another strain, *Yersinia pseudotuberculosis,* is also found in the gut of animals and infects humans eating contaminated meat. It often causes a febrile illness with mesenteric adenitis, and sometimes a fulminant typhoid-like condition ensues. The yersiniae are associated with outbreaks of apparent acute appendicitis among young schoolchildren.

Listeriosis

The listeriae are pathogens of humans and animals that have the unusual property of being able to grow well at refrigerator temperatures as low as 4° C. They are widely distributed in the environment as well as in the guts of animals and humans. Contamination of food is therefore likely unless particular care is taken at all stages of food preparation and production to prevent contamination. The types of food associated with recent large outbreaks include unpasteurized milk products (like soft cheeses), cook-chilled chicken from supermarkets, and coleslaw made with cabbage that was fertilized by sheep manure. The organism frequently contaminates animal feeds, increasing its prevalence in the environment, but it does not grow at a low pH in the presence of organic acids.

When ingested by humans, listeriae may bring on a mild form of influenza-like illness, but in neonates, the elderly, and debilitated persons they may cause severe septicemia or meningitis. In pregnant women a mild influenza-like illness, followed by abortion or still-birth, is often reported. Newborn babies may acquire the organism from the maternal birth passage and develop a fulminating septicemia or meningitis.

The organism is destroyed by the pasteurization of milk or the thorough cooking of food. Prevention of the contamination of food with environmental organisms is an important consideration.

Plesiomonas Shigelloides

This organism is another environmental bacterium that is widely distributed in nature and has been occasionally implicated in sporadic cases and outbreaks of diarrhea in many countries. It is found in freshwater (rivers and ponds), mud, fish, dogs, cats, and other animals. Adequate cooking of food destroys the organism.

Brucellosis (Undulant Fever)

Brucellosis is also called undulant fever because the disease often presents with bouts of fever alternating with afebrile periods. It is a zoonosis and is primarily a pathogen of goats, cattle, pigs, and camels. Humans acquire the infection by ingesting live brucellae in unpasteurized milk from infected animals, as well as through infective secretions from animals. Veterinary surgeons, farmers, and abattoir workers are especially at risk.

The main species of importance to humans are *Brucella abortus* from cattle, *Brucella melitensis* from goats, and *Brucella suis* from pigs. *Brucella melitensis* causes a more severe infection (Malta fever) than the other two species. The symptoms follow the ingestion of infected goats' milk or goats' cheese, and the condition is endemic in Europe, Africa, and the Far East. *Brucella suis* causes infection in America. In cattle, *B. abortus* causes abortion because of the organism's predilection for the placenta due to the high concentration of erythritol in bovine placenta and in the fetal fluids. Vigorous multiplication, therefore, occurs at this site, and the cow's milk will contain live brucellae, making it highly infectious, as are products made from it like butter, cheese, and cream.

In humans, the infection causes a protracted systemic illness. The organism is distributed in the bloodstream to various tissues, causing joint and muscle pains, headache, malaise, and depression. In many cases the disease runs a mild course, but in others a prolonged and disabling form of presentation is seen, especially when untreated.

Routine pasteurization of milk stops this mode of transmission so that only those in direct contact with infected animals remain at risk because the bacillus lives inside the cells of the host. Treatment with antibiotics must be continued over a long period and repeated to ensure recovery.

Tuberculosis

Tuberculosis is generally transmitted by a respiratory route, but it can also be acquired by drinking unpasteurized cows' milk. The organism *Mycobacterium bovis* infects cows and passes in the milk to humans. It usually causes enlargement of lymph nodes in the neck or abdomen; fever, loss of weight, and can cause pulmonary symptoms. Treatment with several antibiotics is required. The infection may also spread in the bloodstream to involve other sites like meninges, bone, joints, and other organs.

Tuberculosis prevention. Pasteurization, boiling, or heat sterilization of milk renders it safe for use. Infected animals may be identified by tuberculin skin testing. They are then slaughtered to prevent spread to other herds. In humans, the BCG vaccine may be used to confer protection against this disease.

Q Fever

Q fever is an influenza-like febrile illness associated with patchy pneumonic consolidation of the lungs that humans acquire from animals by drinking untreated milk or by inhaling their infective secretions. The causative organism *Coxiella burnetti* has a worldwide distribution, affecting various domestic and wild animals and birds.

This organism is particularly resistant to desiccation and can survive heat-treatment temperatures only slightly less than those recommended for pasteurization of milk. The infection in humans may occasionally be severe, with complications like osteomyelitis, endocarditis, meningoencephalitis, and hepatitis. Treatment requires antibiotics, and prevention involves adequate pasteurization or heat treatment of all milk.

Food-Borne Viruses

Any virus transmitted by the fecal–oral route may be transmitted in food. Viruses can contaminate food at its source or during preparation. Mollusks and shellfish growing in coastal waters that are polluted with fecal material often contain human intestinal viruses. Oysters, clams, and mussels, eaten raw or incompletely cooked, can result in outbreaks of infection by the hepatitis A virus and small round structured viruses (SRSVs) such as those seen recently around the Gulf of Mexico. Outbreaks of virus infection acquired by drinking unchlorinated water have also been reported in other countries (poliomyelitis and hepatitis A and E). Chlorination of water prevents waterborne virus infection. Depuration of oysters and bivalve mollusks in clean water does not remove viruses as easily as it removes bacteria. Therefore, adequate cooking, by raising the temperature to 85 to 90° C and maintaining it there for between 1 and 5 minutes, is recommended.

Viral infections may also be transmitted to food by food handlers who are excreting the virus. A characteristic feature of these viral food-borne infections is the frequent occurrence of secondary cases following the outbreak. Here, person-to-person transmission occurs after the initial food-borne outbreak.

Viral Gastroenteritis

The viral agent most frequently found to cause food-borne outbreaks of gastroenteritis in Great Britain belongs to the group of SRSVs also known as Norwalk and Norwalk-like agents. SRSVs cause an acute short-lived attack in which vomiting is a prominent feature. The disease usually affects adults and is associated with outbreaks of gastroenteritis in restaurants, canteens, and institutions like hospitals. Food handlers are implicated in the transmission, especially when they have had a bout of projectile vomiting in the food preparation area. But any kind of food may also be involved in this form of transmission; raw oysters, for example, have been the source of outbreaks in recent years. Secondary cases usually follow the primary cases and are a result of transmission by airborne aerosols. The clinical picture presented is of a flulike illness with nausea, vomiting, diarrhea, and abdominal pain, following an incubation period of 1 to 2 days. Symptoms resolve within a further 1 to 2 days.

Control measures include scrupulous personal and environmental hygiene, the use of chlorine-based compounds to disinfect contaminated surfaces, and adequate cooking of shellfish.

Rotavirus

Rotavirus infection affects mainly schoolchildren, though adults may also be infected. It has a worldwide distribution, causing enteritis following a fecal–oral or airborne spread – usually in winter months. The incubation period is 48 to 72 hours. The symptoms presented are diarrhea and vomiting. The disease is acute and self-limiting, but moderate dehydration may result. Malnourished and debilitated children in developing countries may be severely affected. Treatment is mainly supportive (rehydration), and recovery is seen in a few days.

Viral Hepatitis

Hepatitis A virus. Hepatitis A affects mainly children and young adults in schools, colleges, and military camps. The virus is excreted in feces 7 to 10 days before the onset of symptoms and for a few days after that. Transmission occurs by the fecal–oral route during this period. Food handlers are important in this transmission since they are infectious before they become ill. Transmission also occurs by water, from flies, and in food, especially shellfish. The incubation period is from 3 to 6 weeks and is followed by symptoms of anorexia, fever, nausea, vomiting, and abdominal pain. Jaundice appears 3 to 10 days later, and the patient then starts to feel better. Prevention includes standard measures of hygiene and well-cooked food. A vaccine is now available to protect against hepatitis A infection. Normal human immunoglobulin, to provide passive protection over a period of 4 to 6 months, has been given to those traveling to endemic areas.

Hepatitis E virus. Waterborne outbreaks of hepatitis E virus infection (a recently recognized entity) have been reported from many countries. It is transmitted by the oral–fecal route, and food-borne infection (especially by shellfish) is a distinct possibility. Preventive measures include the provision of safe water supplies and protection of food from fecal contamination.

Poliomyelitis

Poliomyelitis is a disease affecting only the human host and is transmitted by the fecal–oral route, mainly through contaminated drinking water, although food may also act as a vehicle of infection. The infection usually causes only mild intestinal or systemic disturbances. Occasionally, however, a serious form of the illness is seen with involvement of the meninges, severe paralysis, and even death. In these cases recovery may leave permanent disabilities. A good vaccine is available to prevent the disease, which, it is hoped, will mean its eradication all over the world through a mass vaccination campaign. Meanwhile, improvement in environmental and personal hygiene reduces its transmission.

Bovine Spongiform Encephalopathy (BSE)

BSE is a recently recognized disease of cattle caused by a transmissible agent (prion) that resembles the agent of scrapie in sheep. Cattle develop spongelike areas in the brain, with vacuoles appearing in the gray matter. The infectious agent is extremely resistant to heating and standard sterilizing temperatures, and its incubation period is very long, ranging from 2 to 8 years. It is thought that the scrapie agent from infected sheep may have adapted itself to a new host (cattle), possibly as a result of the practice of feeding sheep protein to cattle. Whether BSE can be transmitted to humans eating infected meat has been a topic of debate for some time, but recent concern over outbreaks of "mad-cow disease" in Britain has prompted a wide belief that this is so. Although as yet unproven, BSE infection from food is suspected to be the cause of a number of human cases of a new type of the rare, deadly brain malady known as Creutzfeldt-Jakob disease.

BSE prevention. Precautions to be taken include the destruction of all BSE-infected animals and their milk, banning the feeding of ruminant-derived protein to cattle, and prohibiting the sale of bovine offal from organs like the brain, intestine, and spinal cord, where the agent may replicate. In recent years, the British beef industry has been badly hurt by these and other efforts to control the disease.

Protozoal Infections

Amebiasis

Amebiasis is a disease with a worldwide distribution that occurs mainly where sanitation and hygiene are lacking. Transmission is mediated by the viable cysts of *Entamoeba histolytica,* which are tough-coated, rounded forms of the parasite, excreted in the feces of infected humans. The incubation period is between 2 and 6 weeks. Following ingestion of the cysts in contaminated water or food, excystation occurs in the intestines, and the liberated vegetative cells or trophozoites establish themselves in the large bowel. Ulcers are produced in the bowel wall, resulting in symptoms of amebic dysentery, namely diarrhea with blood and mucus in the stools. Infection may spread in the blood to cause abscesses in other organs like the liver, lung, and brain.

In many cases, noninvasive, symptomless infection continues for years, making carriers of people who excrete cysts in their feces and who are, thus, a potential threat to others, but these cases may convert to the symptomatic state when conditions are appropriate – as, for example, in the immunocompromised patient. The vegetative form, called trophozoite (feeding stage), is only occasionally seen in the feces (in diarrheal stool), is noninfective, and is rapidly destroyed in the environment. But the presence of a tough wall around the cyst (resting stage) renders it highly resistant to adverse environmental conditions. Cysts can survive for 2 to 4 weeks outside the host. They develop from trophozoites in the lumen of the gut and are passed out in the feces. Nuclear division and further development occurs within the cyst, even after it has been voided from the body.

Travelers often develop symptoms following ingestion of contaminated food or drink in countries where transmission is high. Oral or anal sex is also a possible route of transmission of this disease (for example, the "gay bowel syndrome" occurring among homosexual people). Prevention is achieved by the provision of good-quality water supplies or by boiling all drinking water (cysts are not killed by chlorine), safe disposal of sewage, screening food handlers to exclude cyst passers, and treatment of already infected individuals.

Cryptosporidiosis

Occurring in both humans and animals, infection by *Cryptosporidium parvum* is transmitted to the former mostly in rural areas, following contact with animals or consumption of contaminated milk, water, or food that has not been heat-treated. Explosive outbreaks in urban areas (Milwaukee, for example, where in 1993 more than 400,000 people became infected) are usually the result of waterborne spread. The cysts are not destroyed by chlorination but may be removed from drinking water by filtration. Indeed, a malfunction in the filtration of water in sand beds is believed to have caused several outbreaks of this disease in Great Britain. Outbreaks have also arisen from consumption of unpasteurized milk. The pasteurization process destroys this pathogen.

The incubation period is between 3 and 11 days. Following ingestion, the organism emerges from the cyst and penetrates the epithelial cells lining the intestinal lumen, coming to lie just beneath the membrane within a vacuole. Here, organisms multiply to form the oocysts that are released in the feces. The symptoms include impaired digestion, malabsorption, profuse watery diarrhea, vomiting, and weight loss. In the immunocompetent host, recovery occurs within 7 days. Immunosuppressed patients, however, develop severe and protracted diarrhea with dehydration and prostration, as is seen when AIDS patients are infected.

There is no effective treatment for this infection apart from supportive measures like rehydration. Prevention of infection involves preventing oocysts from coming in contact with food or water, provision of safe drinking water, and proper cooking of all food.

Giardiasis

Giardiasis is an infection principally of the small bowel, with symptoms of diarrhea, passage of bulky, pale, offensive stools, abdominal cramps and distension, malabsorption, weight loss, and fatigue. The malabsorption involves mainly fats and fat-soluble vitamins. The disease is characteristically seen as severe bloodless diarrhea in children. The trophozoite form of *Giardia lamblia/intestinalis* inhabits the duodenum and upper ileum, closely attached to the mucosa. Transmission is by the cyst forms, which are passed in stools that contaminate water and, sometimes, food. Cysts are destroyed by boiling but not by the routine chlorination of drinking water. Hence, the importance, as with cryptosporidium, of providing efficient preliminary sand filtration. The infective dose is said to be as low as 10 cysts. Following ingestion, excystation occurs, and the trophozoites are responsible for the intestinal pathology. Heavy infestation damages the mucosa and atrophies the villous processes, but there is no penetration into intestinal cells. The disease has a worldwide distribution and is found in relation to poor hygiene and the substandard quality of drinking water. The incubation period is between 1 and 3 weeks, and the disease, if untreated, lasts for 4 to 6 weeks. Symptomless carriage is a common feature. Prevention involves the use of boiled or filtered water and protection of food from contamination.

Other Intestinal Protozoa

Balantidium coli. This is a normal inhabitant (commensal organism) of the pig bowel. It has a worldwide distribution but rarely causes disease in humans. Those ingesting the cysts may develop a symptomless carrier status, or invasion of the colonic mucosa may lead to symptoms of colitis.

Isospora belli. This infection is particularly found in association with diarrhea in patients with acquired immunodeficiency disease (AIDS). In normal individuals it is possibly a cause of symptom-free infection or of mild transient diarrhea. Little is known about the life cycle. The organism inhabits the small bowel, cysts are passed in the stools, and transmission is believed to be by direct person-to-person transfer or via food or water.

Microsporidium. This group of organisms is found in a range of host species. The organisms have also occasionally been isolated from patients with AIDS and are now believed to be opportunistic pathogens. They are possibly transmitted during the spore stage, voided in the stools of an infected host, and they contaminate food or water. When swallowed by the new host, the organisms enter the gut mucosal cells and multiply there, producing symptoms of intractable diarrhea.

Toxoplasma gondii

Toxoplasmosis is a food-borne systemic infection with a wide geographical distribution. Serological tests indicate that a large proportion of the human population has been infected at some stage in life.

Toxoplasma gondii has a complex life cycle, with its definitive or final host (in which a sexual stage of development occurs) being the domestic cat and some of its wild relatives. The sexual stage takes place in the intestine of the cat, which then excretes oocysts in its feces, although the cat is rarely ill with the infection. Indeed, this relationship typifies a successful parasitization, where neither the host nor the parasite appears to suffer. The intermediate host, in which the asexual life cycle occurs, may belong to a wide range of species, including *Homo sapiens,* who is infected by ingesting the oocysts from cat feces. The parasites then travel via the bloodstream to infect cells in diverse parts of the body, where they multiply asexually (by fission), producing infective cysts. The incubation period may range from 5 to 20 days.

In the healthy individual, the infection is controlled by the immune response, although the parasite may evade immune surveillance by encysting in various tissue cells, surrounding itself with a tough coat, and continuing to multiply at a slow rate within the cyst. Damage to tissues may occur at these sites in immunocompromised individuals like AIDS patients. Pregnant women acquiring the acute infection may transfer the infection transplacentally to the fetus, which may be seriously damaged as a consequence. As in the immunocompromised patient, lesions may occur in the fetal brain, lung, liver, and other tissues with a fatal outcome.

The majority of people infected (often in childhood) develop no symptoms, but some develop a glandular fever-like syndrome, with fever and generalized enlargement of lymph glands. The disease may sometimes present with inflammatory lesions of the eye (choroidoretinitis). Avoidance of infection involves rigorous attention to hygiene, prevention of contamination of food with cat feces, the cooking of all meat before consumption, and advice to pregnant women to avoid contact with cat litter and feces.

Sacrocysts

Sarcocystis hominis causes a disease in humans (the definitive host), with mild symptoms like nausea, diarrhea, and malaise appearing a few hours after the ingestion of raw, infected meat from animals like cattle, sheep, and pigs (intermediate hosts) that contain the encysted infective forms. It is a common infection in animals but rare in humans. This is perhaps because of low transmissibility, inactivation by cooking or freezing, or the frequent occurrence of subclinical infection. The oocysts are passed in the feces of infected humans, and animals ingesting these oocysts develop the tissue cysts.

Trematodes (Flukes)

Adult trematode worms may inhabit either the intestinal tract, the bile ducts, or the lungs. Trematodes are flat, leaflike organisms having an alternating sexual cycle in the final (definitive) host and an asexual multiplication cycle in the intermediate host. Many trematodes have, in addition, a second intermediate host.

Fascioliasis

The liver fluke, *Fasciola hepatica,* is a common parasite of sheep and cattle kept in damp pastures in many parts of the world, and it is only occasionally found in humans. The adults live in the bile duct of the host and produce eggs that are passed in the feces of sheep and cattle. The developing form (miracidium) leaves the eggs and enters a suitable snail host. Here it multiplies asexually, and in 4 to 5 weeks the infective form leaves the snail and encysts on vegetation such as grass, watercress, or radishes growing at the site. Humans acquire the infection by eating the raw, infected vegetables. The young fluke then excysts and penetrates through the duodenum, goes to the liver, and settles in the bile ducts.

Symptoms of dyspepsia, nausea, fever, and abdominal pain occur in the acute stage. In the chronic stage, pain, enlargement of the liver and obstructive jaundice, and anemia may occur. Prevention involves protecting vegetation to be eaten raw from cattle or

sheep feces and eliminating snails by draining pastures or using molluscicides.

Fasciolopsis

Fasciolopsis is the intestinal infection involving snails that occurs in China and some other parts of Asia. The large-sized fluke *Fasciolopsis buski* attaches itself to the wall of the small intestine of its host and passes its eggs in the feces. When the eggs find themselves in freshwater ponds, they hatch, and the larvae infect freshwater snails, in which they develop further. On leaving the snails, they encyst on the fruit and roots of water plants, like the water calthrop, water chestnut, and lotus. Pigs and humans are common hosts of the infection, which they acquire by eating the infective encysted forms on raw aquatic vegetation. Children in endemic areas often peel this material with their teeth, thus enabling entry of the parasite. Following ingestion, the parasite emerges from the cyst, attaches itself to the wall of the intestine, and develops into an adult.

In most cases the infection is asymptomatic, but where there is heavy infestation, symptoms include diarrhea, vomiting, and gripping pain. Diagnosis is confirmed by finding the eggs in the feces. Prevention involves careful peeling or cooking of water-grown vegetables before consumption in endemic areas. The cysts are killed by the drying of water plants or by a few minutes of boiling. It is necessary to keep human or pig feces away from ponds.

Heterophyiasis and Metagonimiasis

Heterophyes and *Metagonimus* species are small flukes that attach themselves to the wall of the small intestine between the villi. Eggs are passed in the feces into water, and larvae emerge to enter freshwater snails. The larvae emerge from the snails in due course to infect freshwater fish. Human infection follows ingestion of infective cysts in raw fish. The larvae excyst and establish themselves in the gut where they grow to adults, causing nausea, diarrhea, and abdominal colic. Adequate cooking of fish and prevention of fecal pollution of freshwater are important preventive measures.

Clonorchiasis and Opisthorchiasis

Infection with *Clonorchis* species occurs mainly in the Far East. Infection with *Opisthorchis* species occurs in the Far East, in Poland, in the Ukraine, and in Siberia. Adults are small flukes that live in the bile duct. Eggs, passed in the feces, infect snails in slow-flowing streams.

After a stage of development, larvae leave the snail and encyst themselves beneath the scales of freshwater fish. When raw or undercooked fish is eaten, the flukes excyst in the intestine and migrate up to the bile duct. Light infection may cause only vague symptoms related to the biliary tract. However, signs of biliary obstruction, portal hypertension, and enlargement of liver and spleen may occur in heavy infection. Dogs can also be infected and act as reservoirs of infection. Prevention involves the cooking of fish and treatment of feces before their use as fertilizers.

Gastrodisciasis

Human infection occurs in India (Assam), Bangladesh, Vietnam, China, and Russia, where adult *Gastrodiscoides hominis* attach themselves to the large intestine (colon or caecum), and eggs pass out in the feces to enter and develop in pond snails. The infective form then leaves to encyst on vegetation, like water calthrop. Eating infected raw vegetables leads to human infection and superficial inflammation of the intestinal mucosa. The presenting symptoms are diarrhea and passage of mucus in stools. Pigs act as a reservoir of infection. Prevention includes the careful peeling and washing of all water vegetables and keeping pig feces away from the water. Dried waterplants can be fed to pigs because drying inactivates the parasite.

Paragonimiasis

Paragonimiasis is seen in Asia, Africa, and America. The lung fluke - *Paragonimus westermani* - infects humans and animals that eat crustaceans like freshwater crabs and crayfish. The fleshy adults live in pairs in the lungs, resembling large coffee beans in size and shape. Eggs may be coughed up in sputum or swallowed and passed in feces. When they reach fresh water, the larvae emerge and penetrate snails. After a stage of development, the larvae leave the snails to penetrate and encyst in crabs and other crustaceans. When these are eaten uncooked, they can transmit the infection. Pickling processes that fail to kill the larvae are also often involved in transmission of the infection. Excystation in the small intestine enables the young fluke to emerge, penetrate the gut wall, and migrate across the diaphragm and into the lungs. Granulomatous changes occur in the lung surrounding the fluke, and symptoms include dry cough, pain in the chest, difficulty in breathing, and the coughing up of blood. Prevention involves the proper cooking of crustaceans and care in handling and washing them so as not to cause cross-contamination with other food.

Cestodes (Tapeworms)

Adult tapeworms all have flat, tape-like bodies and live in the intestinal tract. The body is segmented and the eggs are contained in the terminal segments, which are passed out in the feces. These eggs are infective.

Taeniasis

Taenia saginata (beef tapeworm). Human infection with this tapeworm occurs when raw or slightly cooked beef is eaten. Cattle are infected by eating infective eggs and develop cysticercosis, whereby infective larvae are found encysted in the muscles. When beef is eaten raw by humans, the larvae emerge and attach themselves to the walls of the small intestines and grow into adults of 5 to 20 meters in length. The terminal segments containing eggs drop off, emerging with feces to remain infective on grass and vegetation contaminated by human feces. The eggs are eaten by cattle and hatch out in the duodenum. The parasites then penetrate through the intestinal wall to reach the bloodstream and are carried to the muscles, where they form fluid-filled cysts (cysticerci). Each of these contains an infective larva that, when ingested raw by humans, can grow into an adult tapeworm in the gut. Cysts are killed by cooking at over 56° C.

The symptoms involved are vague abdominal complaints, with segments of worm occasionally wriggling out of the anus. Prevention includes cooking beef adequately, inspecting all meat intended for sale, and the condemnation of any "measly" meat containing tiny pinhead-sized cysts.

Taenia solium (pork tapeworm). People are at risk of contracting this tapeworm in countries where much pork is eaten, including Eastern Europe, China, Indonesia, South Africa, Mexico, and Chile. The infection is carried in pigs as infective cysticerci in the muscles. People acquire the infection by ingesting undercooked or raw pork. The infective form then leaves the cyst and attaches itself to the mucosa of the small intestine, where it proceeds to grow over the next 10 weeks to its full length of between 2 and 10 meters. The terminal segments containing the eggs are passed out in the feces. Pigs eat the infective eggs in soil or feces, and the larvae hatch out, penetrate the gut wall, and travel by the bloodstream to encyst in the musculature, causing cysticerci. As in cysticercus bovis, each cyst contains the infective cephalic end of the worm, which, when ingested by the definitive host (human), excysts and attaches itself to the small intestine, where the worm develops to the adult form. Symptoms are abdominal pain, diarrhea, and passage of segments through the anus.

Humans may also develop cysticercosis when they ingest the eggs of *Taenia solium* along with raw vegetables or drinking water. The larval forms migrate to and encyst in muscles, brain, and other tissues. Autoinfection may possibly cause cysticercosis in humans when reverse peristalsis carries eggs up to the stomach and duodenum, enabling hatching and migration of larval forms. The larvae in the cysticerci die off within a year and become calcified. Symptoms produced are related to the site of the lesion; for example, Jacksonian epilepsy can occur when the cysts form in the brain.

Prevention of transmission is achieved by (1) eating only well-cooked pork; (2) inspection of pig carcasses in the slaughterhouse to eliminate any that show signs of cysticercosis infection; and (3) safe disposal of human feces to interrupt the transmission to pigs.

Hymenolepiasis

Hymenolepiasis is cosmopolitan in distribution. Children in institutions and the immunodeficient or malnourished are particularly prone to it. The dwarf tapeworms of *Hymenolepis* species do not require an intermediate host. The adult worm lives in the small intestine, passing its eggs in the feces. When these eggs are ingested by other humans along with contaminated food or water, infection occurs. Autoinfection also takes place when eggs hatch out in a patient's gut; they develop into adults in 2 weeks.

Hydatidosis (Echinococcosis)

Hydatid disease occurs in the sheep- and cattle-rearing areas of the world, mainly those in South America, Kenya, Vietnam, and China. The adult *Echinococcus granulosus* is small, less than 1 centimeter in length, and inhabits the small intestine of carnivorous animals like dogs – the definitive hosts. The terminal segments of the worm, which contains the eggs, are passed in the dog's feces and can survive for months on pastures. When eaten by the intermediate host (humans, cattle, sheep, goats), the eggs hatch and the larval form penetrates the intestinal wall to be carried by the bloodstream to various parts of the body where hydatid cysts develop. The sites affected are often the liver, lung, brain, or bone, with the slow-growing cyst consisting of a laminated cyst wall filled with fluid and containing many infective forms (hydatid sand). When the tissue form is eaten raw, as happens when dogs are fed infected offal in farming regions, adult worms develop in the dog to repeat the cycle.

Symptoms of a slow-growing, space-occupying cyst are related to the site of the lesion. Treatment often requires careful surgical removal of the cyst. Prevention involves personal hygiene to avoid the ingestion of eggs from dogs, with regular worming of dogs to eliminate the tapeworm, and sanitary disposal of infected offal and viscera of slaughtered animals.

Diphyllobothriasis

Diphyllobothriasis occurs in temperate and subarctic countries where fish is eaten raw, as in Finland, the former Soviet Union, Japan, Canada, the United States, and Chile. The adult *Diphyllobothrium latum* (fish tapeworm) measures 3 to 10 meters long and remains attached by the head end to the mucosa of the small intestine. Eggs are discharged on their own (not within the segments as in taeniasis), pass out in feces, and hatch when they reach fresh water. The parasite now waits to be ingested by a freshwater microcrustacean (cyclops), in which it develops further. If this tiny freshwater cyclops is ingested by a freshwater fish, the larva emerges and penetrates the intestinal wall, developing into its infective form in the muscles of the fish. People ingesting infected raw fish acquire the disease, the symptoms of which include diarrhea, vomiting, fatigue, abdominal pain, dizziness, and megaloblastic anemia. Diagnosis is based on looking for eggs in stools. Prevention means avoiding raw fish, for the infective larvae can be killed by cooking, freezing, or thorough pickling procedures. Human sewage should be treated before discharge into water.

Nematodes (Roundworms)

Ascariasis

Ascariasis is a common disease in areas with poor sanitation, especially in the tropics. Infection with *Ascaris lumbricoides* (roundworms) is achieved by ingesting embryonated eggs on food, like salad vegetables. The larvae hatch, penetrate the wall of the duodenum, and travel in the bloodstream to the lungs, where they develop further. They then penetrate the alveoli and come up the trachea to be swallowed down into the intestines, where they settle in to mature in the ileum. Adults live in the lumen of the gut for up to 2 years, and their eggs are passed in the feces. The eggs are thick-walled and able to resist drying and the standard procedure for sewage treatment. They are, however, killed by heat over 60° C. These eggs require a further period of 10 to 50 days to develop in warm moist soil before they become infective. They may be consumed on raw salad vegetables or unpeeled fruit.

The majority of cases remain symptomless although respiratory symptoms occur when the larvae are traversing the lungs (cough, chest pain, pneumonitis with eosinophilia). When a heavy worm load is present in the intestine or when allergic reactions to the worm occur, symptoms of digestive disorder or intestinal obstruction may be observed. Diagnosis may be made by demonstrating eggs in feces. Prevention is accomplished by thorough washing of all salad vegetables, improvement of sanitation, safe disposal of sewage, and treatment of existing cases.

Trichuriasis

The adult nematode *Trichuris trichiura* (whipworm or thenoworm) has a narrow anterior whiplike portion and a broader posterior end. The whole worm is 40 centimeters long and lives in the colon with the anterior whiplike end embedded in the mucosa. Eggs are passed in feces, develop in warm moist soil, and are ingested by another human host. Larvae hatch to penetrate the wall of the large intestine where they develop into the adult form. They then return to the lumen of the colon, embed their whiplike ends by tunneling through mucosa, and repeat the cycle.

In children, following heavy infestation, the disease may present as retarded growth and malnutrition. Sometimes a prolapsed rectum may occur. Prevention measures are the same as those for ascariasis.

Enterobiasis

Enterobiasis is a common disease in most parts of the world, including temperate countries. The adult *Enterobius vermicularis* (pinworm) is about 11 millimeters long and lives in the lumen of the large bowel. Females lay their eggs on the skin around the anus, which causes intense itching. When scratched, the eggs are transferred on fingers or through dust to food. After they are ingested, larvae emerge to develop into adults in the bowel. The disease is common among children, can affect whole families, and is seen in institutions.

Diagnosis involves the demonstration of eggs in skin around the anus, whereas prevention involves hand washing and treatment of whole families or institutions. The cleaning of bedclothes and rooms to remove eggs is also essential.

Trichinosis

Infection with *Trichinella spiralis* in animals is worldwide, but human infection is mainly seen in Eastern Europe, the Arctic regions, South America, Asia, and East Africa. The domestic pig is the main source of infection, and the infective larval form is found encysted in the muscles. When eaten in raw or undercooked pork, it develops into the adult worm, which lives embedded in the mucosa of the small intestine. The adult is viviparous, producing many live larvae, which penetrate the intestinal wall to be carried in the blood to muscles, where they coil up forming cysts.

Symptoms include diarrhea, abdominal pain, and pain in the muscles. Heavy infection causes severe illness and may be fatal due to the involvement of the nervous or cardiac systems.

Diagnosis is confirmed by looking for larvae in muscle biopsies, and prevention is accomplished by cooking meat at over 60° C or deep freezing it to kill the larva. In addition, improving their feed prevents pigs from contracting the disease.

Sujatha Panikker

Bibliography

Adak, G. K., E. O. Caul, and J. M. Cowden. 1991. Infection with small round structured viruses, England and Wales 1981-1990. *Communicable Disease Report of Central Public Health Laboratory Services* 1: 13, 141-4.

Dunbar, E. M. 1990. Botulism. *Journal of Infection* 20: 1-3.

Hughes, J. M. 1985. Food poisoning. In *Principles and practice of infectious diseases*. Second edition, ed. G. L. Mandel, R. G. Douglas, and J. E. Bennett, 680-91. New York.

Muller, R., and J. R. Baker. 1990. *Medical parasitology*. London.

Parker, M. T., and L. H. Collier. 1990. *Topley and Wilson's principles of bacteriology, virology and immunity*. 5 vols, 1: 243-308; 3: 49-54, 315-29, 423-572; 4: 323-413. London.

Waites, W. M., and J. P. Arbuthnott. 1990. Foodborne illness: An overview. *Lancet* 336: 722-5.

IV.E.5   Food Sensitivities: Allergies and Intolerances

Foods and beverages contain nutrients that are essential to human life, but they also contain elements that, for some individuals, may be harmful to health or even life-threatening. Foods and beverages may cause adverse reactions when ingested, but humans also can have adverse reactions to foods through inhalation (Edwards, McConnochie, and Davies 1985; Kemp, Van Asperen, and Douglas 1988), skin contact (Mathias 1983), or injection (Flu Shots and Egg Allergy 1992; Schwartz 1992).

Sensitivity to foods may be caused by immunologic abnormalities or by other mechanisms, such as host enzyme deficiency. Food sensitivities caused by immunologic abnormalities are commonly referred to as food allergies, whereas food sensitivities caused by nonimmunologic mechanisms are referred to as food intolerances (Anderson 1990; Beaudette 1991). This chapter reviews major considerations with regard to both classifications of food sensitivities. It should also be noted that a disorder called "pseudo-food allergy syndrome" exists. This syndrome is a psychological disorder in which the sufferer believes in the existence of a food allergy that cannot be confirmed by clinical testing (Pearson and Rix 1983, Pearson 1988).

Food Allergies

Allergic, or immunologically based, reactions to food most commonly involve a Type I or IgE mediated reaction (Anderson, 1990) as classified by R. R. A. Coombs and P. G. H. Gell (1975). The stages of the Type I reaction are illustrated in Table IV.E.5.1. It has been theorized that IgE mediated reactions to food may be related to a reduction in the need to produce IgE in response to intestinal parasitic infection. This theory, known as the "mast cell saturation hypothesis," speculates that when the majority of IgE antibodies are bound to intestinal parasites, fewer antibodies are available to bind with food antigens. Production of high levels of IgE to fight parasitism would be protective, whereas production of high levels of IgE specific for food antigens is counterproductive to health (Godfrey 1975; Merrett, Merrett, and Cookson 1976; Lieberman and Barnes 1990).

In food allergy, the Type I reaction involves production of IgE antibodies that are tailored to food allergens. Food allergens are most commonly proteins but also may be glycoproteins or glycolipids (Bindels and Verwimp 1990). In order for a food allergen to stimulate IgE production, it must be absorbed and be of the appropriate size and shape to bridge IgE antibodies on the mast cell surface (Perkin 1990; Taylor 1990). Although most individuals are able to digest food proteins without eliciting an allergic response, individu-

Table IV.E.5.1. *The Type I allergic reaction*

Stage	Description
1st	Familial predisposition: To make IgE allergen-specific antibodies–Atopy.
2d	Sensitization and fixation: Specific allergen exposure, sensitization to form IgE allergen-specific antibodies followed by mast cell (or basophil effector cells) fixation.
3d	An-Ab interaction, mediator release/formation: reexposure to specific allergen, allergen +IgE antibody interaction followed by both preformed chemical mediator release from mast cells (or basophils) or activation of other mediator pathways outside the effector cells.
4th	Immune inflammation: Influx of leukocytes and monocytes. Release of other chemical mediators from all types of cells, plus tissue reactive substances from eosinophils. Release of cytokine histamine releasing factor (HRF) to promote nonspecific reactivity.
5th	Clinical reactions: (1) Early phase–within minutes to hours an allergic reaction occurs, including vasodilation, smooth muscle contraction, and hyperglandulin secretion. (2) Late phase – in one-third to one-half of all cases, in 6 to 12 hours a late inflammatory reaction occurs that is characterized by eosinophil (and other leukocytes and monocytes) infiltration – tissue damage and other mediator release (from all cells). (3) Prolonged phase – clinical hyperreactivity induced by nonspecific chemical mediator release, following nonallergic stimuli and modified by HRF.

Source: Perkin 1990: 4.

als who are atopic seem to absorb food antigens in a form that causes their cells to produce IgE. When food allergens are of the appropriate size, they are capable of binding with IgE and triggering the release of chemicals that cause the clinical manifestations of food allergy. Chemicals commonly implicated in the allergic process include histamine, leukotriences and cytokines (Metcalfe, 1991).

In some individuals, exercise may play a role in stimulating the food allergy response (Sheffer et al. 1983). Food-dependent anaphylaxis related to exercise is thought to be associated with chemical mediator release from mast cells in conjunction with an abnormal functioning autonomic nervous system, specifically increased parasympathetic activity and decreased sympathetic activity (Fukutomi et al. 1992). Abnormalities of IgE synthesis associated with other disorders may result in the secondary appearance of food allergy. D. S. Mazza, M. O'Sullivan, and M. H. Grieco (1991) have published a case report of food allergy that developed secondary to infection with the human immunodeficiency virus.

There are types of food-related immunologic reactions that are not believed to be Type I. Heiner's syndrome (a bovine milk-associated respiratory disorder) and celiac sprue are two examples of adverse food reactions believed to be associated with other types of immunologic reactions (Anderson 1990).

Food allergy is more common in children than adults although food allergy can develop at any age. One study that surveyed physicians estimated that allergy prevalence was 7 percent for adults and 13 percent for children (Anderson 1991). Another often-cited study estimates the prevalence of allergy in children to be from 0.3 to 7.5 percent, with adults having a lower prevalence (Buckley and Metcalfe 1982). One theory used to explain the relatively higher level of allergy prevalence in children relates to infancy-associated intestinal immaturity, which, some believe, results in greater passage of larger proteins across the gut with resultant stimulation of IgE production (Walker 1975; Udall et al. 1981). But the primacy of a more permeable intestine in terms of allergy causation has recently been questioned by T. Jalonen (1991), who has postulated that greater intestinal permeability is a secondary phenomena for food allergy rather than an initiating event.

Infants may become sensitized to food allergens in utero since IgE can be synthesized before birth and large food proteins can cross the placenta. It should be noted, however, that although prenatal sensitization occurs, it is a relatively rare event (Strimas and Chi 1988). P. G. Calkhoven, M. Aalbers, V. L. Koshte, and colleagues (1991) have postulated the existence of a "high food responder phenotype" based on their findings that certain children seem to demonstrate allergic responses to a wide variety of foods. High cord IgE levels or high levels of serum IgE measured seven days after birth are considered to be predictive of subsequent food allergy development in an infant (Chandra, Puri, and Cheema 1985; Strimas and Chi 1988; Ruiz et al. 1991). A low level of CD8+ suppressor cells in the neonatal period is also predictive of the potential for allergy development (Chandra and Prasad 1991).

Breast feeding is often cited as being allergy protective, but this is an extremely controversial subject (Kramer 1988; Perkin 1990). Certainly there are physiological reasons to suggest that breast feeding may be protective against food allergies or at least may delay food allergy development. These reasons include (1) the relative lack of exposure to food antigens associated with breast feeding; (2) the presence of secretory IgA in breast milk, which is believed to aid in reducing the intestinal entry of large food protein molecules; (3) the stimulation of infantile IgA production by breast milk; (4) the opportunity for less intestinal antigen uptake because of the decreased incidence of gastrointestinal infections associated with breast feeding; (5) the presence in breast milk of anti-inflammatory properties, such as histaminase and arylsulfatase, and (6) the provision of IgG antibodies in breast milk that are targeted at food antigens (Pittard and Bill 1979; Atherton 1983; Businco et al. 1983 ; Ogra et al. 1984; Goldman et al. 1986; Michael et al. 1986). Low breast milk IgA levels have been associated with an increased likelihood of developing infantile cow's milk allergy (Savilahti et al. 1991).

Clinical studies that have examined breast feeding in relation to food allergy have not demonstrated a clear-cut protective or delaying effect (Kramer 1988; Perkin 1990), perhaps because of numerous methodological problems involved in this type of research. If breast feeding is protective, it is generally believed that exclusive breast feeding (no solid foods and no formula) should be practiced for at least six months (Bahna 1991; Kajosaari 1991). Since this is seldom done in the United States, the measurement of any allergy-prevention benefits of breast feeding is difficult.

Food allergies may disappear over time. Young age at food allergy onset coupled with a mild clinical reaction may mean that an individual will ultimately develop tolerance for an offending food. A more severe clinical reaction profile and older age of food allergy onset are associated with greater likelihood of allergy persistence. Allergies to certain foods, such as peanuts or crustacea, also tend to be allergies that persist through time (Anderson 1991). Food allergy developing in adulthood may be related to occupational exposure to food antigens (Anderson 1991; Metcalfe 1991). Baker's asthma, caused by allergic reactions to several wheat proteins, is one of the most studied occupational allergies (Prichard et al. 1985; Anderson 1991).

Certain foods have been commonly identified as implicated in the causation of food allergies. Among these are cow's milk, soybeans, wheat, eggs, nuts, and seeds (including cottonseed, which can be highly allergenic), crustacea (shrimp, lobster, crawfish), and fish. Also implicated are noncitrus fruits and vegetables (for example, tomato, celery, watermelon, pear, cherry, apple), citrus fruits, and spices (Perkin 1990). Table IV.E.5.2 outlines currently identified food allergens in some of the major food categories linked to allergy (Perkin 1990). Food types linked to allergy reflect cultural dietary patterns (Esteban 1992; Walker 1992).

The literature continues to identify new food categories that may cause allergic reactions in some individuals. Foods recently identified include squid (Carrillo et al. 1992), grand keyhole limpet and abalone (Morikawa et al. 1990), annatto dye (Nish et al. 1991), jícama (Fine 1991), and Swiss chard (de la Hoz et al. 1991). Progress has also been made in terms of identifying other factors, such as mites, that may be related to food allergies. For example, A. Armentia, J. Tapias, D. Barber, and colleagues (1992) have demonstrated that an allergic reaction may be precipitated by exposure to the wheat flour storage mite *Lepidoglyphus destructor.* Foods or beverages used as folk remedies may also elicit allergic reactions. J. Subiza, J. L. Subiza, M. Alonzo, and co-workers (1990) have described allergic responses that were initiated by washing the eyes with chamomile tea. Even human breast milk may contain allergenic food proteins (Gerrard and Shenassa 1983; Kilshaw and Cant 1984; Gerrard and Perelmutter 1986).

Table IV.E.5.2. *Major food allergens*

Food	Identified allergens
Cow's milk	Beta-lactoglobulin, alpha-lactalbumin, casein
Soybeans	Globulin 2S, Globulin 7S, Globulin 11S, hemagglutinin
Shrimp	Sa-I, Sa-II, antigen I, antigen II
Fish	Allergen M, protamine sulfate
Egg white	Ovalbumin, ovotransferrin, ovomucoid
Egg yolk	Apovitellenin I, Apovitellenin VI

The determination of the extent to which foods related to one another in botanically defined plant families trigger allergies has long been of interest. When such a reaction occurs, it is called cross-reactivity. Legumes (Barnett, Bonham, and Howden 1987) and crustacea (Sachs and O'Connell 1988) are often studied in this regard. Cross-reaction between environmental and food allergens has also been reported. Birch pollen has been noted to be cross-reactive with the carrot and apple (Ortolani et al. 1988), and banana and latex have recently been reported as cross-reactive (M'Raihi et al. 1991). The phenomenon of cross-reactivity is one that is currently ill defined and is a subject of debate in terms of its clinical relevance.

Clinical signs and symptoms of food allergy are numerous, and diagnosis of food allergy is a complex process. Clinical manifestations may occur in selected body systems, such as the respiratory system or the skin, or may be a more generalized phenomenon, such as anaphylaxis. There are also specific syndrome symptom complexes that have been linked to food allergy.

Skin symptoms of food allergy may include hives, angioedema, eczema, and itching and/or redness (Anderson 1991). Eczema is particularly common in children and usually occurs on the elbows, knees, and perhaps the face (Burks 1992). Respiratory symptoms may include rhinitis, wheezing, and asthma.

Certain food allergies also produce gastrointestinal symptoms, such as nausea, vomiting, and diarrhea (Anderson 1991; Beaudette 1991; Metcalfe 1991). Cow's milk allergy is particularly noted for its association with gastrointestinal symptoms. It may also be associated with low-grade gastrointestinal bleeding and, thus, may be a cause of anemia (Wilson and Hamburger 1988).

Anaphylaxis is a systemic manifestation of food allergy. It is also potentially deadly, although it may be mild and simply characterized by simultaneous allergic manifestations in several organ systems. But the term is commonly used to refer to the more serious form of multiorgan system reaction that includes the development of cardiovascular shock, severe respiratory distress, and even death (Anderson 1990). Symptoms of classic food allergy generally appear within one to two hours after ingestion of the offending food, although in some cases, symptoms can appear as much as 12 hours following consumption (Anderson 1990).

Several clinical syndromes have also been associated with food allergy. These include oral allergy syndrome, eosinophilic gastroenteritis, food protein-induced enterocolitis syndromes, and hypersensitive furrowed mouth (Anderson 1991; Metcalfe 1991).

Oral allergy syndrome, as described by C. Ortolani, M. Ispano, E. Pastorello, and colleagues (1988), is initially manifested by irritation and swelling of the lips, which is then followed by hives, respiratory problems, and, in some cases, the development of anaphylactic shock. The oral allergy syndrome is associated with allergies to certain fruits and vegetables, notably celery (Ortolani et al. 1988; Pauli et al. 1988). J. A. Anderson (1991) has estimated that 0.1 to 0.2 percent of the general population may experience oral allergy syndrome. The syndrome is more frequently seen in persons who are sensitive to ragweed pollen.

Eosinophilic gastroenteritis associated with food allergy is characterized clinically by gastrointestinal disturbance, elevated levels of eosinophils, the presence of eosinophils in the stomach and intestine, and elevated levels of IgE (Anderson 1991; Metcalfe 1991). The syndrome of food protein-induced enterocolitis is seen in infants and is characterized by diarrhea, malabsorption, and high levels of eosinophils (Metcalfe 1991).

Hypersensitive furrowed mouth syndrome is characterized by mouth swelling and the development of cracks and furrows in the mouth. Anderson (1991), who described this problem, has associated it with consumption of large amounts of foods rich in protein.

Diagnosis of food allergy can be complex. It involves analysis of the clinical history, epicutaneous skin testing, and/or the use of in vitro assays, such as the radioallergosorbent test (RAST) or the enzyme-linked immunosorbent assay (ELISA) (Anderson 1990).

Elimination diets and the analysis of diet-symptom diaries may also be used in the diagnostic effort (Olejer 1990; Burks and Sampson 1992). The "gold" standard for diagnosis of food allergy is the double blind placebo-controlled food challenge (Olejer 1990). In children under the age of three years, skin testing is not a reliable indicator of food allergy, and single blind food challenge is more commonly employed to determine foods to which a child has an adverse reaction (Olejer 1990; Beaudette 1991). Diagnostic procedures used for research purposes are being studied for potential clinical application. These include basophil histamine release assay and assay of intestinal mast cell histamine release (Burks and Sampson 1992).

Once a food allergy is diagnosed, treatment primarily involves instructing the patient to eliminate the offending substance from the diet. This requires that the allergic individual pay careful attention to food preparation techniques and food labeling. Unfortunately, food labels are not always helpful and can even be misleading. A label of kosher-parve, for example, generally denotes a milk-free product, but a recent report indicated that a dessert labeled as kosher-parve was found to contain milk protein (Jones, Squillace, and Yunginger 1992). In this instance, the milk proteins were present in the product as the result of a faulty production process that permitted milk contamination from previous use of the equipment.

In some cases, individuals may not understand the wording on food labels. R. N. Hamburger (1992) noted that one of his patients did not recognize that the term "calcium caseinate" meant the presence of milk protein. Eating outside of the home also presents special problems. The National Restaurant Association has recently launched an allergy awareness program and is attempting to make restaurant owners more aware of the needs of patrons with food allergies (Restaurant Food Allergy Awareness 1992).

Special attention must be paid to the nutritional adequacy of diets when foods are eliminated. Nutritional deficits, such as insufficiencies of calories, protein, and calcium, have been noted in children following restricted diets for food allergies (Lloyd-Still 1979; Sinatra and Merritt 1981; David, Waddington, and Stanton 1984).

For limited periods of time, elemental diet formulas may be useful for managing food allergies. These formulas contain protein that has been extensively hydrolyzed. However, the relatively poor taste and high cost of these products generally make them a poor long-term solution for food allergies. They can, however, help symptoms resolve and can bring relief prior to the development of a restricted dietary program of traditional foods.

Formula-fed infants who are allergic to cow's milk protein are placed on alternative formulas. These may include a soy-based formula or one of casein hydrolysate (Olejer 1990). The use of soy formulas, however, to treat infants with cow's milk allergy is controversial, and whey hydrolysate formulas are currently not recommended as treatment for such infants (American Academy of Pediatrics 1983; Businco et al. 1992).

Hypoallergenic formulas are defined as those that can be tolerated by children with cow's milk allergy, such that 90 percent will experience no symptoms at a 95 percent level of confidence (Sampson 1992). Casein hydrolysate formulas are currently regarded as hypoallergenic (Oldaeus et al. 1992; Rugo, Wahl, and Wahn 1992). Breast-fed infants who are allergic to food proteins transferred through breast milk may be treated by the mother's restriction of the offending foods from her diet (Perkin 1990).

Traditionally, pharmacological approaches have had limited application in the treatment of food allergies. Epinephrine is used as an antianaphylactic agent, and antihistamines and corticosteroids are employed to alleviate allergy symptoms (Doering 1990). Oral cromolyn is effective in some cases for treating food allergy or other food-related problems, such as migraine (Doering 1990; Knottnerus and Pelikan 1993). Injection treatment with peanut extract is currently being investigated (Oppenheimer et al. 1992), as are such drugs as loratadine (Molkhou and Czarlewski 1993) and pancreatic enzyme supplements (Bahna and McCann 1993).

Research efforts are attempting to find ways that food allergies can be prevented or delayed. One thrust of the research is to examine infant formulas for those types that can delay or prevent allergies. Although not currently recommended for cow's milk allergy treatment, whey hydrolysates have been demonstrated by some studies to be protective (Chandra and Prasad 1991; Vandenplas et al. 1992); other studies have found that casein hydrolysate formula can decrease the occurrence of atopic dermatitis (Bahna 1991) and eczema (Mallet and Henocq 1992).

The majority of food allergy prevention focuses on alterations of both maternal and infant diet. As early as 1983, Hamburger, S. Heller, M. H. Mellon, and colleagues began testing the efficacy of a maternal elimination diet (no eggs, peanuts, and milk during the last trimester of pregnancy and during lactation) in conjunction with modifications in the infant's diet, such as delayed introduction of solids and breast feeding supplemented only by casein hydrolysate formula. But this type of regimen has yet to prove successful even though it may help to delay allergy appearance (Zeiger et al. 1986; Zeiger et al. 1989). Preventive strategies, such as the restrictive regimen just described, are used with infants who are considered at high allergy risk as determined by cord blood IgE levels (greater than 2 micrograms per liter) and a positive family history of allergy (Beaudette 1991). M. Kajosaari (1991) has demonstrated that delay of solid feeding until the age of six months can help prevent food allergy, and such a delay is currently standard dietary advice.

Food Intolerances

Some individuals experience adverse reactions to foods that cannot be explained by an immunologic mechanism. Several substances seem to elicit clinical problems through these alternative pathways that include enzyme deficiencies and pharmacological mechanisms (Schwartz 1992). Examples of food components associated with intolerance include lactose, histamine, gliadin, aspartame, sulfites, tartrazine, and monosodium glutamate. Some of these components are naturally present in foods, whereas others occur as food additives.

Lactose (or milk sugar) consumption causes problems because of inadequate amounts of intestinal lactase activity (MacDonald 1988). Symptoms of lactose intolerance include diarrhea, pain, and abdominal bloating (Scrimshaw and Murray 1988). The most common type of lactose intolerance is termed primary lactase deficiency. It occurs sometime following weaning and is found in varying degrees from mild to severe. It is a common condition among the majority of the world's populations (Savaiano and Kotz 1988). Lactose intolerance can also occur as a secondary event subsequent to intestinal damage (Penny and Brown 1992).

Histamine, a preformed chemical mediator for allergic reactions, is naturally present in some foods and wines (Malone and Metcalfe 1986; Anderson 1990). Most of the time, histamine in foods does not cause problems because it is quickly broken down by enzymes in the digestive process. Some individuals do experience symptoms of histamine sensitivity, which include headache and reddening of various body parts, such as the eyes, face, and hands. Histamine sensitivity problems may also be seen when histidine is degraded to become histamine in fish and cheeses (Burnett 1990). Scombroid fish poisoning is the name given to the clinical complex (headache, flushing, and neck pain) caused by eating dark fish meat in which histidine has broken down to histamine because of improper storage and high temperatures. This syndrome can be treated with histamine antagonist drugs (Morrow et al. 1991).

Gliadin, a component of gluten, is a natural food substance that can cause adverse reactions in some individuals. It occurs in grain products such as wheat, rye, and barley. Celiac sprue, an intestinal disorder, and dermatitis herpetiformis, a skin disorder, are the clinical manifestations of intolerance to gliadin. A transient, rare form of gluten hypersensitivity, similar to celiac sprue, has also been reported in very young children (Iacono et al. 1991).

Celiac sprue, the intestinal form of gliadin intolerance, is characterized by iron deficiency, weight loss, diarrhea, malabsorption, abdominal distension, and altered mental capabilities. Persons suffering chronically from celiac sprue appear to be at increased risk for the development of cancer (Holmes et al. 1989) and osteoporosis later in life (Mora et al. 1993). Recent work has focused on identifying and describing peptides of gliadin that cause the damage in celiac sprue (Cornell, Weiser, and Belitz 1992). The disease may have an immunologic basis, but this has not been fully described; and for the moment at least, celiac sprue is classified as a food intolerance rather than a food allergy.

Dermatitis herpetiformis, the skin form of gliadin intolerance, is characterized by a rash with itching and blistering. Granular deposits of the immunoglobulin IgA between skin layers are also characteristic of dermatitis herpetiformis (Beaudette 1991).

Aspartame is a nutritive artificial sweetener added to a variety of foods. It was introduced into the marketplace in 1981 (Tollefson and Barnard 1992). Adverse reactions reported in conjunction with aspartame ingestion include headache, memory loss, depression, dizziness, changes in vision, and seizures (Bradstock et al. 1986; Roberts 1990). L. Tollefson and R. J. Barnard (1992) have indicated, however, that an analysis by the United States Food and Drug Administration does not support the assertion that aspartame causes seizures. The postulated mechanism for aspartame's link to headache is via increasing serum tyrosine levels (Schiffman et al. 1987). One study has cited an immune basis for aspartame sensitivity manifested by hives (Kulczycki 1986). Aspartame, however, has not been shown to degranulate basophils or mast cells (Garriga and Metcalfe 1988). Therefore, in general, adverse reactions in conjunction with aspartame tend to be reported under food intolerance because of an unknown mechanism or mechanisms. After failing to reproduce hypersensitivity reactions to aspartame, M. M. Garriga, C. Berkebile, and D. D. Metcalfe (1991) noted that aspartame should not induce an IgE mediated response because it is easily broken down in the brush border of the intestine.

Sulfites are another category of food additive associated with adverse reactions in selected individuals. About one percent of the general United States population is estimated to be sulfite sensitive (Folkenberg 1988); this figure rises to about 5 percent of the asthmatic population (Nagy et al. 1993). As in the case of aspartame, most sulfite-associated adverse reactions cannot be linked to an immune mechanism, although an immune abnormality may be responsible for a reaction in a small number of individuals. W. N. Sokol and I. B. Hydick (1990) demonstrated basophil histamine release and obtained a positive skin test in a patient who had symptoms of angioedema, nasal congestion, and hives. Examples of clinical problems seen in conjunction with sulfite sensitivity include low blood pressure, hives, angioedema, intestinal cramping and chest tightness (Perkin 1990).

Sulfite sensitivity seems to have different clinical manifestations with asthmatics, where it is manifested by bronchial dysfunction (spasm or constriction), dizziness, flushing, wheezing, and perhaps anaphylaxis (Perkin 1990). Recently, sodium bisulfite has also been linked to genetic damage in lymphocytes (Meng and Zhang 1992). One postulated mechanism for sulfite sensitivity is the initiation of a cholinergic reflex by sulfur dioxide's action upon tracheobronchial receptors (Anibarro et al. 1992). With some individuals, it is believed that a deficiency of sulfate oxidase may be responsible (Simon 1987; Perkin 1990). Deaths and severe reactions related to sulfite sensitivity have resulted in strict labeling regulations when sulfites are present in foods in excess of 10 parts per million (ppm) (Schultz 1986). Experimentation is also under way to determine if the use of cyanocobalamin can prevent sulfite-induced respiratory distress (Anibarro et al. 1992).

Tartrazine, or FD&C Yellow 5, is another food additive cited as causing adverse reactions in susceptible individuals. Tartrazine is used to produce various food colors including yellow, green, and maroon (Dong 1984; Schneider and Codispoti 1988), and more than half of the daily food dye consumption in the United States is in the form of tartrazine (Beaudette 1991). Clinical symptoms indicating an adverse reaction to this food additive include hives, asthma, angiocdema, photosensitivity, eczema, purpura, and anaphylaxis (Michaelsson, Petterson, and Juhlin 1974; Desmond and Trautlein 1981; Pereyo 1987; Perkin 1990; Devlin and David 1992). J. Devlin and T. J. David (1992) recently indicated that they could confirm tartrazine intolerance in only 1 of 12 children whose parents reported that tartrazine consumption worsened their child's eczema. Although the mechanism of tartrazine sensitivity is unknown, the cause has been postulated as an excess of bradykinin production (Neuman et al. 1978). There is a link between aspirin sensitivity and tartrazine sensitivity with a cross-reactivity of 5 to 25 percent reported (Settipane and Pudupakkam 1975; Condemi 1981).

Monosodium glutamate (MSG) as the cause of adverse food reaction has been a source of great controversy. It is used as a food additive because of its ability to enhance flavors (Beaudette 1991). The most often cited potential adverse reaction to MSG is Chinese Restaurant Syndrome characterized by such symptoms as development of tears in the eyes, facial flushing, tightness and burning, nausea, sweating, headache, and vascular abnormalities (Ghadimi and Kumar 1972; Gann 1977; Goldberg 1982; Zautcke, Schwartz, and Mueller 1986).

Symptoms of this syndrome usually occur shortly after consumption of an MSG-containing food, and problems generally resolve in less than one hour (Beaudette 1991). Some scientists suggest that the role of MSG as the causative agent of the Chinese Restaurant Syndrome remains unproven because of a lack of a demonstrated dose-response effect (Beaudette 1991), and histamine has been proposed as an alternative culprit (Chin, Garriga, and Metcalfe 1989). In addition to Chinese Restaurant Syndrome, other potential adverse reactions to MSG consumption have been reported. These include headache, angioedema, and asthma (Diamond, Prager, and Freitag 1986; Allen, Delohery, and Baker 1987; Squire 1987). It has also been suggested that there may be a subset of the population for whom the potential excitotoxicity of glutamate could be a problem (Barinaga 1990).

Prevention and treatment of food intolerance involves avoidance of the foods and beverages that contain the offending substances. Careful reading of food labels is critical. In the case of lactose intolerance, some individuals can consume small amounts of milk or dairy products, such as yogurt or cheese, which have a low lactose content. In addition, some find it beneficial to employ special dairy products in which the lactose has been partially hydrolyzed or broken down or to use tablets that serve to break down lactose in foods and beverages. Celiac sprue and dermatitis herpetiformis are treated with a gluten-restricted, gliadin-free diet (Beaudette 1991), sometimes referred to as a gluten-free diet. The gluten-free diet has recently been shown to relieve the primary symptoms of these conditions, and also to aid in protecting against bone loss (Mora et al. 1993) and cancer (Holmes et al 1989). Some have advocated the use of a low gluten diet for the treatment of celiac sprue (Kumar et al. 1985; Montgomery et al. 1988), but at present this is in the exploration stage as a potential treatment alternative.

Summary

Foods and beverages may cause clinical problems through immunologic or physiological mechanisms. When immunologic mechanisms are confirmed, the condition is called a food allergy. The term food intolerance is used to denote clinical problems associated with food when an immunologic mechanism cannot be confirmed.

Common food allergens in the United States include cow's milk, soybeans, wheat, eggs, nuts, seeds, and crustacea. Food allergies are more common in children than adults. Most food allergies are of the Type I IgE mediated variety. Avoidance of the foods that cause problems is the mainstay of current prevention and treatment efforts.

Food intolerance may be associated with natural food components or with food additives. Natural food components that cause clinical problems include lactose (milk sugar), histamine, and gliadin. Food additives linked to intolerance include aspartame, sulfites, monosodium glutamate, and tartrazine. Here again, dietary avoidance is the key to preventing and treating food intolerances, although pharmacological agents may be useful in treating symptoms associated with food allergies or intolerances. Several new pharmacological approaches are now being investigated.

Research in the area of food intolerances continues to look at immune mechanisms (particularly those in addition to Type I) and other physiological mechanisms that cause clinical problems related to exposure to foods and beverages. Research efforts are also underway to characterize the specific components that cause food allergies and to find new ways of treating them. In addition, testing of potential preventive or delaying approaches will continue to be a research focus in future years.

Judy Perkin

Bibliography

Allen, D. H., J. Delohery, and G. Baker. 1987. Monosodium-L-glutamate-induced asthma. *Journal of Allergy and Clinical Immunology* 80: 530-7.

American Academy of Pediatrics Committee on Nutrition.
1983. Soy protein formulas: Recommendations for use in infant feeding. *Pediatrics* 72: 359.

Anderson, J. A. 1990. Food allergy or sensitivity terminology, physiologic bases and scope of the clinical problem. In *Food allergies and adverse reactions,* ed. J. E. Perkin, 1-13. Gaithersburg, Md.

1991. The clinical spectrum of food allergy in adults. *Clinical and Experimental Allergy* 21 (Suppl. 1): 305-15.

Anibarro, B., T. Caballero, C. Garcia-Ara, et al. 1992. Asthma with sulfite intolerance in children: A blocking study with cyanocobalamin. *Journal of Allergy and Clinical Immunology* 90: 103-9.

Armentia, A., J. Tapias, D. Barber, et al. 1992. Sensitization to the storage mite *Lepidoglyphus destructor* in wheat flour allergy. *Annals of Allergy* 68: 398-403.

Atherton, D. J. 1983. Breastfeeding and atopic eczema. *British Medical Journal* 287: 775-6.

Bahna, S. L. 1991. Breast milk and special formulas in prevention of milk allergy. *Advances in Experimental Medicine and Biology* 310: 445-51.

Bahna, S. L., and M. L. McCann. 1993. Tolerance to multiple food allergens by pancreatic enzyme supplement. *Journal of Allergy and Clinical Immunology* 91: 151.

Barinaga, M. 1990. MSG: Amino acids: How much excitement is too much? *Science* 247: 20-2.

Barnett, D., B. Bonham, and M. E. H. Howden. 1987. Allergenic cross-reactions among legume foods – an *in vitro* study. *Journal of Allergy and Clinical Immunology* 79: 433-8.

Beaudette, T. 1991. *Adverse Reactions to Food.* Chicago.

Bindels, J. G., and J. Verwimp. 1990. *Allergenic aspects of infant feeding – Nutricia Research Communications 2.* Zoetermeer, the Netherlands.

Bradstock, M. K., M. K. Serdula, J. S. Marks, et al. 1986. Evaluation of reactions to food additives: The aspartame experience. *American Journal of Clinical Nutrition* 43: 464-9.

Buckley, R. H., and D. Metcalfe. 1982. Food allergy. *Journal of the American Medical Association* 1248: 2627-31.

Burks, A. W. 1992. Food allergies and eczema. *Food Allergy News* 2: 1, 6.

Burks, A. W., and H. A. Sampson. 1992. Diagnostic approaches to the patient with suspected food allergies. *Journal of Pediatrics* 121: S64-71.

Burnett, J. W. 1990. Histamine poisoning. *Cutis* 46: 388.

Businco, L., G. Bruno, P. G. Giampietro, and A. Cantani. 1992. Allergenicity and nutritional adequacy of soy protein formulas. *Journal of Pediatrics* 121: S21-8.

Businco, L., F. Marchetti, G. Pellegrini, et al. 1983. Prevention of atopic disease in "at risk newborns" by prolonged breastfeeding. *Annals of Allergy* 51: 296-9.

Calkhoven, P. G., M. Aalbers, V. L. Koshte, et al. 1991. Relationship between IgG 1 and IgG 4 antibodies to foods and the development of IgE antibodies to inhalant allergens. I. Establishment of a scoring system for the overall food responsiveness and its application to 213 unselected children. *Clinical and Experimental Allergy* 2: 91-8.

Carrillo, T., R. Castillo, J. Caminero, et al. 1992. Squid hypersensitivity: A clinical and immunologic study. *Annals of Allergy* 68: 483-7.

Chandra, R. K., and C. Prasad. 1991. Strategies for the prevention of food allergic associated atopic disease. *Advances in Experimental Medicine and Biology* 310: 391-6.

Chandra, R. K., S. Puri, and P. S. Cheema. 1985. Predictive value of cord blood IgE in the development of atopic disease and role of breast-feeding in its prevention. *Clinical Allergy* 15: 517–22.

Chin, K. W., M. M. Garriga, and D. D. Metcalfe. 1989. The histamine content of oriental foods. *Food Chemistry and Toxicology* 27: 283–7.

Condemi, J. J. 1981. Aspirin and food dye reactions. *Bulletin of the New York Academy of Medicine* 57: 600–7.

Coombs, R. R. A., and P. G. H. Gell. 1975. Classification of allergic reactions responsible for clinical hypersensitivity and disease. In *Clinical aspects of immunology*, ed. R. R. A. Coombs and P. G. H. Gell, 761–81. Oxford.

Cornell, H., H. Weiser, and H-D. Belitz. 1992. Characterization of the gliadin-derived peptides which are biologically active in coeliac disease. *Clinica Chimica Acta* 213: 37–50.

David, T. J., E. Waddington, and R. H. J. Stanton. 1984. Nutritional hazards of elimination diets in children with atopic eczema. *Archives of Diseases of Childhood* 59: 323–5.

de la Hoz, B., M. Fernandez-Rivas, S. Quirce, et al. 1991. Swiss chard hypersensitivity: Clinical and immunologic study. *Annals of Allergy* 67: 487–92.

Desmond, R. E., and J. J. Trautlein. 1981. Tartrazine (FD&C yellow #5) anaphylaxis: A case report. *Annals of Allergy* 46: 81–2.

Devlin, J., and T. J. David. 1992. Tartrazine in atopic eczema. *Archives of Diseases of Childhood* 67: 709–11.

Diamond, S., J. Prager, and F. G. Freitag. 1986. Diet and headache - is there a link? *Postgraduate Medicine 1986* 79: 279–86.

Doering, P. 1990. Drug therapy of food allergies. In *Food allergies and adverse reactions*, ed. J. E. Perkin, 69–79. Gaithersburg, Md.

Dong, F. M. 1984. *All about food allergy*. Philadelphia, Pa.

Edwards, J. H., K. McConnochie, and B. H. Davies. 1985. Skin-test reactivity to egg protein - exposure by inhalation compared to ingestion. *Clinical Allergy* 15: 147–50.

Esteban, M. M. 1992. Adverse food reactions in childhood: Concept, importance, and present problems. *Journal of Pediatrics* 121: S1–3.

Fine, A. J. 1991. Hypersensitivity reaction to jícama (Pachyrhizus, yam bean). *Annals of Allergy* 66: 173–4.

Flu Shots and Egg Allergy. 1992. *Food Allergy News* 2: 7.

Folkenberg, J. 1988. Reporting reaction to additives. In *Safety first: Protecting America's food supply*, FDA Consumer Special Report 88-2224. Rockville, Md.

Fukutomi, O., N. Kondo, H. Agata, et al. 1992. Abnormal responses of the autonomic nervous system in food-dependent exercise–induced anaphylaxis. *Annals of Allergy* 68: 438–45.

Gann, D. 1977. Ventricular tachycardia in a patient with "Chinese restaurant syndrome." *Southern Medical Journal* 70: 879–81.

Garriga, M. M., C. Berkebile, and D. D. Metcalfe. 1991. A combined single-blind, double-blind, placebo-controlled study to determine the reproducibility of hypersensitivity reactions to aspartame. *Journal of Allergy and Clinical Immunology* 87: 821–7.

Garriga, M. M., and D. D. Metcalfe. 1988. Aspartame intolerance. *Annals of Allergy* 61 (Part II): 63–9.

Gerrard, J. W., and L. Perelmutter. 1986. IgE-mediated allergy to peanut, cow's milk, and egg in children with special reference to maternal diet. *Annals of Allergy* 56: 351–4.

Gerrard, J. W., and M. Shenassa. 1983. Sensitization to substance in breast milk: Recognition, management, and significance. *Annals of Allergy* 51: 300–2.

Ghadimi, H., and S. Kumar. 1972. Current status of monosodium glutamate. *American Journal of Clinical Nutrition* 25: 643–6.

Godfrey, R. C. 1975. Asthma and IgE levels in rural and urban communities of the Gambia. *Clinical Allergy* 5: 201–7.

Goldberg, L. 1982. Supraventricular tachyarrhythmia in association with the Chinese restaurant syndrome. *Annals of Emergency Medicine* 11: 333.

Goldman, A. S., L. W. Thorpe, R. M. Goldblum, and L. A. Hanson. 1986. Anti-inflammatory properties of human milk. *Acta Paediatrica Scandinavica* 75: 689–95.

Hamburger, R. N. 1992. Misleading hazardous food labels. *Annals of Allergy* 68: 200–1.

Hamburger, R. N., S. Heller, M. H. Mellon, et al. 1983. Current status of the clinical and immunological consequences of a prototype allergic disease prevention. *Annals of Allergy* 51: 281–90.

Holmes, G. K. T., P. Prior, M. R. Lane, et al. 1989. Malignancy in celiac disease: Effect of a gluten-free diet. *Gut* 30: 333–8.

Iacono, G., A. Nocerino, S. Guadalini, et al. 1991. Transient gluten hypersensitivity. *Journal of Pediatric Gastroenterology and Nutrition* 12: 400–3.

Jalonen, T. 1991. Identical intestinal permeability changes in children with different clinical manifestations of cow's milk allergy. *Journal of Allergy and Clinical Immunology* 88: 737–42.

Jones, R. T., D. L. Squillace, and J. W. Yuninger. 1992. Anaphylaxis in a milk-allergic child after ingestion of milk-contaminated kosher-pareve-labeled "dairy-free" dessert. *Annals of Allergy* 68: 223–7.

Kajosaari, M. 1991. Atopy prophylaxis in high risk infants. *Advances in Experimental Medicine and Biology* 310: 453–8.

Kemp, A. S., P. P. Van Asperen, and J. Douglas. 1988. Anaphylaxis caused by inhaled pavlova mix in egg-sensitive children. *Medical Journal of Australia* 149: 712–3.

Kilshaw, P. J., and A. J. Cant. 1984. The passage of maternal dietary proteins into human breast milk. *International Archives of Allergy and Applied Immunology* 75: 8–15.

Knottnerus, I., and Z. Pelikan. 1993. Protective effects of oral cromolyn (OSCG) on migraine due to the adverse reactions to foods. *Journal of Allergy and Clinical Immunology* 91: 150.

Kramer, M. S. 1988. Does breastfeeding help protect against atopic disease? Biology, methodology, and a golden jubilee of controversy. *Journal of Pediatrics* 112: 181–90.

Kulczycki, A., Jr. 1986. Aspartame-induced urticaria. *Annals of Internal Medicine* 104: 207–8.

Kumar, P. J., G. Harris, J. Colyer, et al. 1985. Is a gluten-free diet necessary for the treatment of celiac disease? *Gastroenterology* 88: 1459.

Lieberman, L. S., and K. C. Barnes. 1990. Food allergies and adverse food reactions: An anthropological perspective. In *Food allergies and adverse reactions*, ed. J. E. Perkin, 207–32. Gaithersburg, Md.

Lloyd-Still, J. D. 1979. Chronic diarrhea of childhood and the misuse of elimination diets. *Journal of Pediatrics* 95: 10–13.

MacDonald, I. 1988. Carbohydrates. In *Modern nutrition in health and disease*, ed. M. E. Shils and V. R. Young, 38–51. Philadelphia, Pa.

Mallet, E., and A. Henocq. 1992. Long term prevention of allergic diseases by using a protein hydrolysate formula in at-risk infants. *Journal of Pediatrics* 121: S95–100.

Malone, M. H., and D. D. Metcalfe. 1986. Histamine in foods: Its possible role in nonallergic adverse reactions to ingestants. *New England Regional Allergy Proceedings* 7: 241–5.

Mathias, C. G. T. 1983. Contact urticaria from peanut butter. *Contact Dermatitis* 9: 66–8.

Mazza, D. S., M. O'Sullivan, and M. H. Grieco. 1991. HIV-1 infection complicated by food allergy and allergic gastroenteritis: A case report. *Annals of Allergy* 66: 436–40.

Meng, Z., and L. Zhang. 1992. Cytogenetic damage induced in human lymphocytes by sodium bisulfite. *Mutation Research* 298: 63–9.

Merrett, T. G., J. Merrett, and J. B. Cookson. 1976. Allergy and parasites: The measurement of total and specific IgE levels in urban and rural communities in Rhodesia. *Clinical Allergy* 6: 131–4.

Metcalfe, D. D. 1991. Immune mechanisms in food allergy. *Clinical and Experimental Allergy* 21 (Suppl. 1): 321–4.

Michael, F. B., J. Bousquet, A. Dannaeus, et al. 1986. Preventive measures in early childhood allergy. *Journal of Allergy and Clinical Immunology* 78: 1022–7.

Michaelsson, G., F. Petterson, and L. Juhlin. 1974. Purpura caused by food and drug additives. *Archives of Dermatology* 109: 49–52.

Molkhou, P., and W. Czarlewski. 1993. Effect of loratadine on increased intestinal permeability in children with atopic dermatitis related to food allergy. *Journal of Allergy and Clinical Immunology* 91: 150.

Montgomery, A. M. P., A. K. J. Goka, P. H. Kumar, et al. 1988. Low gluten diet in the treatment of adult celiac disease: Effect on jejunal morphology and serum antigliadin antibodies. *Gut* 29: 1564–8.

Mora, S., G. Weber, G. Barera, et al. 1993. Effect of gluten-free diet on bone mineral content in growing patients with celiac disease. *American Journal of Clinical Nutrition* 57: 224–8.

Morikawa, A., M. Kato, K. Tokuyama, et al. 1990. Anaphylaxis to grand keyhole limpet (abalone-like shellfish) and abalone. *Annals of Allergy* 65: 415–7.

Morrow, J. D., G. R. Margolies, J. Rowland, and L. J. Roberts. 1991. Evidence that histamine is the causative toxin of scombroid-fish poisoning. *New England Journal of Medicine* 324: 716–20.

M'Raihi, L., D. Charpin, A. Pons, et al. 1991. Cross-reactivity between latex and banana. *Journal of Allergy and Clinical Immunology* 87: 129–30.

Nagy, S. M., S. S. Teuber, P. Murphy, and S. M. Loscutoff. 1993. Adverse reactions to a salsa containing high levels of sulfites. *Journal of Allergy and Clinical Immunology* 91: 150.

Neuman, I., R. Elian, H. Nahum, et al. 1978. The danger of 'yellow dyes' (tartrazine) to allergic subjects. *Clinical Allergy* 8: 65–8.

Nish, W. A., B. A. Whisman, D. W. Goetz, and D. A. Ramirez. 1991. Anaphylaxis to annatto dye: A case report. *Annals of Allergy* 66: 129–31.

Ogra, P. L., R. C. Welliver, M. Riepenhoff-Talty, and H. S. Foden. 1984. Interaction of mucosal immune system and infections in infancy: Implications in allergy. *Annals of Allergy* 53: 523–34.

Oldaeus, G., C. K. Bradley, B. Bjorksten, and N. I. Kjellman. 1992. Allergenicity screening of "hypoallergenic" milk-based formulas. *Journal of Allergy and Clinical Immunology* 90: 133–5.

Olejer, V. 1990: Diagnosis of food allergy. Part II. The dietitian's perspective. In *Food allergies and adverse food reactions,* ed. J. E. Perkin, 30–49. Gaithersburg, Md.

Oppenheimer, J. J., H. S. Nelson, S. A. Bock, et al. 1992. Treatment of peanut allergy with rush immunotherapy. *Journal of Allergy and Clinical Immunology* 90: 256–62.

Ortolani, C., M. Ispano, E. Pastorello, et al. 1988. The oral allergy syndrome. *Annals of Allergy* 61: 47–52.

Pauli, G., J. C. Bessot, P. A. Braun et al. 1988. Celery allergy: Clinical and biological study of 20 cases. *Annals of Allergy* 60: 243–6.

Pearson, D. J. 1988. Psychologic and somatic interrelationships in allergy and pseudoallergy. *Journal of Allergy and Clinical Immunology* 81: 351–60.

Pearson, D. J., and K. J. B. Rix. 1983. Food allergy: How much is in the mind? A clinical and psychiatric study of suspected food hypersensitivity. *Lancet* 1: 259–61.

Penny, M. E., and K. H. Brown. 1992. Lactose feeding during persistent diarrhoea. *Acta Pediatrica* Suppl. 381: 133–8.

Pereyo, N. 1987. Tartrazine, the complement system and photosensitivity. *Journal of the American Academy of Dermatology* 17: 143.

Perkin, J. E. 1990. Major food allergens and principles of dietary management. In *Food allergies and adverse reactions,* ed. J. E. Perkin, Gaithersburg, Md.

Pittard, W. B., and K. Bill. 1979. Immunoregulation by breast milk cells. *Cellular Immunology* 42: 437–41.

Prichard, M. G., G. Ryan, B. J. Walsh, and A. W. Musk. 1985. Skin test and RAST responses to wheat and common allergens and respiratory disease in bakers. *Clinical Allergy* 15: 203–10.

Restaurant food allergy awareness program. 1992. *Food Allergy News* 2: 2.

Roberts, H. J. 1990. Obstacles confronting consumer advocates: An overview of health-related issues. *Journal of the Florida Medical Association* 77: 761–5.

Rugo, E., R. Wahl, and U. Wahn. 1992. How allergenic are hypoallergenic infant formulae? *Clinical and Experimental Allergy* 22: 635–9.

Ruiz, R. G., D. Richards, D. M. Kemeny, and J. F. Price. 1991: Neonatal IgE: A poor screen for atopic disease. *Clinical and Experimental Allergy* 21: 467–72.

Sachs, M. I., and E. J. O'Connell. 1988. Cross-reactivity of foods – mechanisms and clinical significance. *Annals of Allergy* 61: 36–40.

Sampson, H. A. 1992. Adverse food reactions. *Journal of Pediatric Gastroenterology and Nutrition* 15: 319–20.

Savaiano, D. A., and C. Kotz. 1988. Recent advances in the management of lactose intolerance. *Contemporary Nutrition* 13 (General Mills Nutrition Department Newsletter): 9, 10.

Savilahti, E., V-M. Tainio, L. Salmenpera, et al. 1991. Levels of IgA and cow's milk antibodies in breast milk vs. the development of atopy in children. Low colostral IgA associated with cow's milk allergy. *Advances in Experimental Medicine and Biology* 30: 417–25.

Schiffman, S. S., C. E. Buckley, H. A. Sampson, et al. 1987. Aspartame and susceptibility to headache. *New England Journal of Medicine* 317: 1181–5.

Schneider, A. T., and A. J. Codispoti. 1988. Allergic reactions to food additives. In *Food allergy, a practical approach to diagnosis and management,* ed. L. T. Chiaramonte, A. T. Schneider, and F. Lifshitz, 117–51. New York.

Schultz, C. M. 1986. Sulfite sensitivity. *American Journal of Nursing* 86: 914.

Schwartz, R. H. 1992. Allergy, intolerance, and other adverse reactions to foods. *Pediatric Annals* 21: 654–62, 665–74.

Scrimshaw, N. S., and E. B. Murray. 1988. The acceptability of milk and milk products in populations with a high prevalence of lactose intolerance. *American Journal of Clinical Nutrition* 48 (Suppl): 1083–159.

Settipane, G. A., and R. K. Pudupakkam. 1975. Aspirin intolerance, III. subtypes, familial occurrence and cross-reactivity with tartrazine. *Journal of Allergy and Clinical Immunology* 56: 215–21.

Sheffer, A. L., N. A. Soter, E. R. McFadden, Jr., and K. F. Austen. 1983. Exercise-induced anaphylaxis: A distinct form of physical allergy. *Journal of Allergy and Clinical Immunology* 71: 311–16.

Simon, R. A. 1987. Sulfite sensitivity. *Annals of Allergy* 59: 100-5.

Sinatra, F. R., and R. J. Merritt. 1981. Iatrogenic kwashiorkor in infants. *American Journal of Diseases of Childhood* 135: 21-3.

Sokol, W. N., and I. B. Hydick. 1990. Nasal congestion, urticaria, and angioedema caused by an Ig-E mediated reaction to sodium metabisulfite. *Annals of Allergy* 65: 233-7.

Squire, E. N. 1987. Angio-oedema and monosodium glutamate. *Lancet* 1: 988.

Strimas, J. H., and D. S. Chi. 1988. Significance of IgE level in amniotic fluid and cord blood for the prediction of allergy. *Annals of Allergy* 61: 133-6.

Subiza, J., J. L. Subiza, M. Alonso, et al. 1990. Allergic conjunctivitis to chamomile tea. *Annals of Allergy* 65: 127-32.

Taylor, S. L. 1990. Food allergies and related adverse reactions to foods: A food science perspective. In *Food allergies and adverse reactions,* ed. J. E. Perkin, 189-206. Gaithersburg, Md.

Tollefson, L., and R. J. Barnard. 1992. An analysis of FDA passive surveillance reports of seizures associated with consumption of aspartame. *Journal of the American Dietetic Association* 92: 598-601.

Udall, J. N., P. Colony, L. Fritze, et al. 1981. Development of gastrointestinal mucosal barrier, II. the effect of natural versus artificial feeding on intestinal permeability to macromolecules. *Pediatric Research* 15: 245-9.

Uragoda, C. G. 1980. Histamine poisoning in tuberculosis patients after ingestion of tuna fish. *American Review of Respiratory Diseases* 121: 157-9.

Vandenplas, Y., B. Hauser, C. Van den Borre, et al. 1992. Effect of a whey hydrolysate prophylaxis on atopic disease. *Annals of Allergy* 68: 419-24.

Walker, W. A. 1975. Antigen absorption from the small intestine and gastrointestinal disease. *Pediatric Clinics of North America* 22: 731-46.

   1992. Summary and future directions. *Journal of Pediatrics* 121: S4-6.

Wilson, N. W., and R. N. Hamburger. 1988. Allergy to cow's milk in the first year of life and its prevention. *Annals of Allergy* 61: 323-7.

Zautcke, J. L., J. A. Schwartz, and E. Mueller. 1986. Chinese restaurant syndrome: A review. *Annals of Emergency Medicine* 15: 1210-13.

Zeiger, R. S., S. Heller, M. H. Mellon, et al. 1986. Effectiveness of dietary manipulation in the prevention of food allergy in infants. *Journal of Allergy and Clinical Immunology* 78: 224-38.

   1989. Effect of combined maternal and infant food-allergen avoidance on development of atopy in early infancy: A randomized study. *Journal of Allergy and Clinical Immunology* 84: 72-89.

IV.E.6 ❧ Lactose Intolerance

Lactose is a disaccharide composed of linked molecules of the simple sugars glucose and galactose. Dietary lactose is obtained almost exclusively from milk. Infants and young children digest lactose with an enzyme, lactase, which splits the molecule into the two readily absorbable simple sugars. The majority of adults, however, have lost this ability and are lactose malabsorbers. Those malabsorbers who display clinical symptoms after milk consumption are described as lactose intolerant.

Lactose is a major constituent of the milk of all mammals except sea lions (Kretchmer 1993). Human milk contains the highest lactose concentration, about 7 percent; lactose levels in commonly milked animals, such as camels, goats, sheep, and cows, run between 4 and 5 percent. Adult animals, like most humans, lose the ability to digest lactose. This suggests that adult loss of lactase is a normal mammalian trait and that adult ability to split lactose is an "abnormal" evolutionary innovation.

Definition and History

Lactose malabsorption and intolerance must be distinguished clinically from allergy to milk proteins, which is a rare but serious genetic problem in infants. This essay focuses on primary adult onset lactase deficiency, but two other forms of the syndrome must be noted. Lactase deficiency may be secondary due to damage to the small intestine from heavy parasitic infections (especially the protozoan *Giardia lamblia*); to other severe intestinal infections; to AIDS; and to ionizing radiation, some drugs, and gastric surgery (Castiglia 1994; Tamm 1994). Total inability to synthesize lactase is another rare genetic disorder that was obviously lethal until modern times. If diagnosed promptly, such cases can now be managed with soy-based infant formulas.

Gastrointestinal distress in adults after milk consumption was described in ancient Greek and Roman texts, and there were isolated clinical reports in the late nineteenth and early twentieth centuries, but the problem was not widely studied until the development (in the 1960s) of new techniques to study enzymatic action in the intestine. Consequently, the high prevalence of diminished lactase activity in healthy adults was described only in the early 1960s, with especially important work done by A. Dahlqvist and his associates (Dahlqvist 1977). Worldwide surveys in the 1960s and 1970s showed that loss of lactase activity in adulthood is the common condition in humans and that terms like "lactase deficient" incorrectly imply that this is somehow abnormal (Flatz 1987).

Biology and Clinical Manifestations

Lactase (technically lactase-phlorizin hydrolase), is a protein produced in the cells of the epithelium of the small intestine. It is most concentrated in the mucosal cells of the brush border of the jejunum (Buller and Grand 1990). Production of lactase begins to decline in most children between the ages of 2 to 5, around the time of weaning. Most adults retain only about 10 percent of infant-level lactase activity. But Finnish children who become lactase deficient often do so as teenagers; the reasons for this late onset are unknown (Arola and Tamm 1994).

If lactose-intolerant people consume significant quantities of milk or other dairy products, unmetabolized lactose passes through the small intestine to the large intestine, where it is acted upon by the resident facultative bacterial flora. These bacteria split lactose into acetic, butyric, propionic, and other short-chain fatty acids, which can be absorbed by intestinal cells and used as metabolites. Among the by-products are carbon dioxide, hydrogen, and methane, which can cause a gassy, bloated, and/or nauseous feeling.

It is generally thought that the abundance of short-chain molecules increases osmotic pressure within the intestinal lumen, causing water to pass into the lumen, sometimes in amounts that produce diarrhea (Castiglia 1994), but this has recently been questioned by H. Arola and A. Tamm (1994). They suggest that bacteria that produce larger amounts of iso-fatty acids – those with branched carbon chains in contrast to the normal straight chain forms – may provide protection against diarrhea. Although the intestinal flora of an individual tend to remain relatively stable over time, commensal bacterial populations vary considerably among people. Those persons with large colonies of the types of bacteria that efficiently metabolize lactose and produce significant quantities of iso-fatty acids (for example, members of the genus *Bacteriodes*) would be less likely to display symptoms (Arola and Tamm 1994). They would be lactose malabsorbers but not necessarily lactose intolerant.

Genetics

The mechanisms controlling lactase production were disputed for many years. Some researchers, drawing on studies of gene regulation in bacteria, argued in the 1960s that lactase was a substrate-inducible enzyme; that is, that lactase production was believed to be stimulated by the presence of its substrate, lactose. In this view, populations that did not use milk as adults lost the ability to produce lactase, whereas groups that did consume milk and milk products retained lactase capability.

Biochemical studies cast doubt on this theory, and family studies have demonstrated that lactase production is controlled by an autosomal gene, recently located on chromosome 2. Persistence of lactase production is a dominant trait (Buller and Grand 1990; Arola and Tamm 1994). Following the terminology suggested by Gebhard Flatz (1987), the two alleles are designated LAC*P for lactase persistence and LAC*R for normal adult lactase restriction. The LAC locus appears to be a regulatory gene that reduces lactase synthesis by reducing the transcription of messenger RNA (Arola and Tamm 1994). Persons inheriting LAC*P from both parents would have lactase persistence into adulthood; those getting LAC*R alleles from both parents would display lactase restriction as adults. Heterozygotes would get different alleles and be LAC*P/LAC*R, but since LAC*P is dominant, lactase activity and ability to digest milk would persist beyond childhood.

Nutritional Implications

As milk and milk products are such rich sources of protein, calcium, carbohydrates, and other nutrients, the nutritional consequences of lactose intolerance in infants and children can be devastating, even lethal, unless other dietary sources are used. Formulas based on soybeans help many youngsters. Adults can get protein from other animal and vegetable sources or from fermented milk products. Yoghurt with live bacterial cultures may be tolerated well. Calcium can be obtained from dark green vegetables or from the bones of small sardines or anchovies consumed whole (Kretchmer 1993). It has been suggested that low milk consumption in elderly lactose intolerance adults might contribute to osteoporosis (Wheadon et al. 1991), but this has not been demonstrated. Lactose-free dairy products and oral lactase preparations are commercially available and help many people enjoy and gain the nutritional benefits of ice cream and other milk-based foods (Ramirez, Lee, and Graham 1994).

Lactase persistence is uncommon in Africans, Asians, southern Europeans, and the indigenous populations of the Americas and the Pacific. Questions have arisen concerning the use of milk as food for children. The American Academy of Pediatrics (AAP), noting the high nutritional value of milk for growing children, has determined that almost all U. S. children under 10, regardless of family background, can digest reasonable quantities of milk. The AAP recommends that the school-lunch half pint (about 240 milliliters [ml]) of milk be supplied to children up to this age, and notes that intolerance to 240 ml is rare even among older teens (American Academy of Pediatrics 1978). Similar results have been reported for African children in South African orphanages (Wittenberg and Moosa 1991). Malnourished African children, such as famine victims, also tolerate up to 350 ml of milk well, which allows the use of this valuable source of nutrients in emergency situations (O'Keefe, Young, and Rund 1990).

Testing for Lactase Persistence

Clinical diagnosis and population surveys for lactose digestion capabilities present several challenges. Clinical symptoms are discovered by self-reporting; thus, double-blind studies, in which neither the experimenter nor the subject knows if a challenge dose contains lactose or a placebo, are most useful. Direct lactase assay using biopsy specimens of intestinal mucosa is obviously an expensive and invasive method, practical only in particular clinical cases. Indirect assays require subjects to fast for several hours before being given doses of lactose in solution.

Then various tests are used to measure the splitting and subsequent metabolism of the disaccharide. Many of the older methods are cumbersome and imprecise. Blood samples may be tested for glucose before lactose challenge and at intervals afterward. High blood glucose levels after lactose ingestion indicate that lactose is being split in the intestine. A variant of this method is to measure blood galactose. Since the liver metabolizes galactose, a dose of ethanol is given shortly before the experimental lactose to inhibit liver action. Another approach is to measure hydrogen gas excreted through the lungs. Subjects who cannot digest lactose will have hydrogen produced by colonic bacteria. Respiratory hydrogen can be conveniently and efficiently measured by gas chromatography. The ethanol-galactose and hydrogen methods are considered the most reliable; the hydrogen technique is cheaper, easier, and noninvasive (Flatz 1987).

Not only must the population studies of lactase activity be methodologically correct, the subjects must also be truly representative of their populations. Studies done on very small numbers of subjects or on hospital patients or other special groups may be unrepresentative. Indeed, some older studies may be unreliable due to poor techniques or sampling problems. Intermarriage and genetic interchange also complicate analysis of the distribution of lactase persistence. Nonetheless, there has been great interest in the geographical and ethnic distribution of adult lactase persistence and the evolution of this unusual phenotype.

Distribution of Lactase Persistence

Several authors have compiled the results of regional studies (Flatz 1987; Kretchmer 1993; Sahi 1994). Some of the major findings are summarized here in Table IV.E.6.1.

It should be noted that data for northern India and Pakistan are suspect and that figures for Finno-Ugrian groups in northern Russia and western Siberia (Khanty, Mansi, Mari, Mordva, Nentsy) are based on small, possibly unrepresentative, samples and older methods (Valenkevich and Yakhontova 1991; Kozlov, Sheremeteva, and Kondik 1992). There is little hard information for the Balkan or Iberian peninsulas, Slavic territories east of Poland, Siberia, central Asia, or the Indian subcontinent. It would also be interesting to have more data on East African pastoralists, such as the Maasai, and on Baggara Arab and other cattle-keeping groups of the West African Sahel.

A high proportion of lactase persisters was noted in northwestern Europe in the early 1970s, and there were similar reports from northern India, from Bedouin and other pastoral populations in the Middle East and northern Africa, and from the Tutsi pastoralists of the Uganda-Rwanda region of East Africa. Very low rates were found among eastern, and most southern, Asians, most Africans, and native populations of the Americas and the Pacific, and only modest rates were found in southern and eastern Europe. In North and South America, Australia, and New Zealand, adult lactase ability is closely linked to place of origin; for example, white Australians resemble their European counterparts in lactase persistence, whereas Aborigines are almost entirely lactose intolerant. Varying degrees of Spanish and Indian

ancestry may explain regional differences in Mexico (Rosado et al. 1994). Similarly, a higher than expected prevalence of lactase persistence among Buryat Mongols of Russia's Lake Baikal region may be due to gene flow from European Russians (Kozlov et al. 1992).

Adult lactase capability appears to have evolved in two, and possibly three, geographic areas. The case is clearest and best documented for northern Europe, where there are very high percentages around the Baltic and North Seas. High levels of lactase persistence seem closely linked to Germanic and Finnic groups. Scandinavia, northern Germany, and Britain have high levels, as do the Finns and Estonians, the Finnic Izhorians west of St. Petersburg, the Mari of the middle Volga basin, and, to a lesser extent, their more distant relations, the Hungarians.

There is a general north–south gradient in Europe, which is evident within Germany, France, Italy, and perhaps Greece. As noted, more information is needed for Spain, Portugal, and eastern Europe, but there may be something of a west–east gradient in the Slavic lands. Varying frequencies of the LAC*P allele among Lapp groups may be related to differing lengths of historical use of reindeer and cow's milk and to admixture with other Scandinavians (Sahi 1994).

The second center of adult lactase persistence lies in the arid lands of Arabia, the Sahara, and eastern Sudan. There, lactase persistence characterizes only nomadic populations heavily dependent on camels and cattle, such as the Bedouin Arabs, the Tuareg of the Sahara, the Fulani of the West African Sahel, and the Beja and Kabbabish of Sudan. Lower rates among Nigerian Fulani may indicate a higher degree of genetic mixing with other peoples than among the Fulani of Senegal. In contrast, surrounding urban and agricultural populations, whether Arab, Turkish, Iranian, or African, have very low rates. It is interesting to note that the Somali sample also had a low frequency of the LAC*P allele. Possibly, pastoral Somali have higher prevalences than their urban compatriots.

A third center of adult lactase persistence has been suggested among the Tutsi population of the Uganda-Rwanda area of the East African interior. The Tutsi are an aristocratic cattle-herding caste of Nilotic descent who have traditionally ruled over agricultural Bantu-speakers. Table IV.E.6.1 shows that only 7 percent of a sample of 65 Tutsi adults were lactase deficient, but the data are old, there certainly has been some mixture with Bantu-speakers, and the study should be replicated. The Nilotic peoples of the southern Sudan, whence the Tutsi originated a few centuries ago, do not display this trait. Unless the Tutsi result can be confirmed, and the Maasai and other East African Nilotic groups can be tested, this third center of the LAC*P allele must be considered doubtful. If it does exist, it probably arose as a fairly recent mutation, as there are no obvious historical mechanisms to account for gene flow between the Tutsi and desert dwellers farther north.

Table IV.E.6.1. *Distribution of lactose phenotypes*

Country	Group	# High LDC	# Low LDC	% Low LDC	Frequency LAC*P allele[a]
Europe					
Sweden	Swedes	396	4	1	.90
Finland	Swedish-speakers	84	7	8	.72
Finland	Finnish-speakers	371	78	17	.58
Finland	Fisher Lapps	82	28	25	.50
Finland	Mountain Lapps	235	110	32	.43
Finland	Skolt Lapps	70	106	60	.23
Denmark	Danes	743	19	3	.83
Netherlands	Dutch	14	0	0	1.00
Britain	British	90	6	6	.76
Ireland	Irish	48	2	4	.80
France	Northern French	48	14	23	.52
France	Southern French	40	31	44	.34
Spain	Spaniards	226	39	15	.61
Germany	Germans	548	98	15	.61
Germany	Northwest Germans	405	36	8	.72
Germany	Northeast Germans	191	55	22	.53
Germany	Western Germans	157	25	14	.63
Germany	Bavarians	191	30	14	.63
Germany	Southwest Germans	104	32	23	.52
Austria	Austrians	422	106	20	.55
Czech Republic	Czechs	175	25	13	.64
Poland	Poles	172	103	37	.39
Hungary	Magyars	337	198	37	.39
Slovenia	Slovenes	99	54	35	.41
Italy	Northern Italians	191	192	50	.29
Italy	Southern Italians	31	78	72	.15
Italy	Sicilians	29	71	71	.16
Greece	Greeks	452	520	53	.27
Greece	Peloponesian Greeks	?	?	75	.13
Cyprus	Greeks	19	48	72	.15
Russia	Russians-St. Petersburg	210	38	15	.61
Russia	Russians	?	?	12.5–16.3	.60–.65
Russia	Izhorians	78	54	41	.36
Russia	Mordvinians	?	?	11.1	.67
Russia	Mari	?	?	81	.10
Russia	Mansi	3	9	75	.13
Russia	Khanty	3	7	70	.16
Russia	Nentsy	1	4	80	.11
Russia	Buryat Mongols	11	9	45	.17
Estonia	Estonians	467	183	28	.47
Latvia	Latvians	?	?	32	.43
Asia and Pacific					
Turkey	Turks	135	335	71	.16
Israel	Sephardic Jews	22	46	68	.18
Israel	Oriental Jews	29	65	69	.17
Israel	Ashkenazi Jews	11	42	79	.11
Jordan	Bedouin	123	39	24	.51
Jordan	Jordanians	43	161	79	.11
Syria	Syrians	7	68	91	.05
Saudi Arabia	Bedouin	12	2	13	.64
Egypt	Northern Egyptians	106	282	73	.15
Egypt	Central Egyptians	17	94	85	.08
Iran	Iranians	7	33	83	.09
Afghanistan	Pashtoons	15	56	79	.11
Afghanistan	Other Afghans	10	50	83	.08
Pakistan	Punjabi	132	190	59	.23
India	Northern Indians	194	70	27	.48
India	Central Indians	46	79	63	.21
India	Southern Indians	20	40	67	.18
Sri Lanka	Singhalese	55	145	73	.15
Thailand	Thais	0	149	100	0.00
China	Han	19	229	92	.04
China	Mongols	24	174	88	.06
China	Kazakhs	46	149	76	.13
China	Uighurs	26	16	38	.38
Taiwan	Chinese	0	71	100	0.00
Japan	Japanese	10	56	85	.08
Indonesia	Javanese	5	48	91	.05
Fiji	Fijians	0	12	100	0.00
Papua New Guinea	Various tribes	12	111	90	.05
Australia	Aborigines	48	97	67	.18
Africa					
Nigeria	Ibo, Yoruba	12	101	89	.06
Nigeria	Fulani	7	2	22	.53
Niger	Tuareg	103	15	13	.64
Senegal	Fulani	29	0	0	1.00
Somalia	Somali	58	186	76	.13
Kenya	Bantu-speakers	19	52	73	.15
Uganda, Rwanda	Bantu-speakers	14	100	88	.06
Uganda, Rwanda	Tutsi	65	5	7	.74
South Africa	Bantu-speakers	28	144	84	.08
South Africa	San (Bushmen)	3	62	95	.03
Sudan	Kabbabish nomads	39	12	24	.51
Sudan	Beja nomads	252	51	17	.59
Sudan	"Blacks"–farmers	20	64	76	.13
Sudan	Nilotics	72	210	75	.13
Americas					
Greenland	Eskimos	18	101	85	.08
Greenland	Mixed European-Eskimo	67	41	38	.38
United States	Native Americans	11	210	95	.03
United States	Blacks	138	252	65	.19
United States	Mexican-Americans	147	158	52	.28
Mexico	"Mexicans"	69	332	83	.09
Colombia	Mestizos	30	15	33	.43
Colombia	Chami Indians	0	24	100	0.00
Bolivia	Ayamara Indians	7	24	77	.12
Peru	Mestizos	26	68	72	.15

[a]Assuming genetic equilibrium and calculated from the Hardy-Weinberg law.

Sources: Flatz (1987), Zheng et al. (1988), Valenkevich and Yakhontova (1991), Koslov, Sheremeteva, and Kondik (1992), and Kretchmer (1993).

Evolution of Lactase Persistence

Frederick J. Simoons (1969, 1970) has advanced the thesis that lactase persistence is closely linked to dairying. His culture-evolution hypothesis is that groups that kept cattle and other milk animals would gain a selective advantage if adults retained the ability to use milk and milk products as food. A mutation like LAC*P would be nutritionally beneficial, and the growing number of milk-using adults would then be encouraged to devote more effort toward livestock raising. In general, the distribution of adult lactase persistence and dairying shows a positive relationship. In areas with no dairying tradition, such as China, Oceania, Pre-Columbian America, or tropical Africa, few adults can digest lactose.

Northern Europe presents the opposite case. More data around the periphery of the two postulated centers would be highly desirable, and we know little about most of the stock-raising societies of central Asia. Still, although the correspondence is not perfect, and gene flow through population mixing complicates the picture, the association seems strong. Given the origins of cattle keeping about 4000 to 3500 B.C. in northern Europe, and even earlier in the Middle East, there probably has been enough time for modest selective pressures to have produced observed LAC*P rates (Sahi 1994).

Other selective forces may also have been at work. Flatz (1987) has suggested that calcium absorption was such a factor in northern Europe. Lactose is known to facilitate calcium absorption in the intestine. The cold, cloudy climate frequently discouraged skin exposure to sunlight, thereby reducing the body's production of vitamin D. Relatively little dietary vitamin D was available, and so in its absence, calcium was poorly absorbed. Northern populations were thus vulnerable to rickets and osteomalacia. Pelvic deformities made births more difficult. The gradual extinction of the Greenland Viking colony is an example; skeletal evidence shows that such bone diseases were common among this moribund population. A mutant LAC*P allele would not only allow adults to use an excellent source of calcium, but the lactose would also facilitate its absorption. While not proven, this hypothesis has attracted much attention. It would complement the theory that the pale skin of northern Europeans is a genetic trait maximizing the utility of sunlight in vitamin D production and, hence, calcium absorption.

Similarly, other selective pressures facilitating the survival of mutant LAC*P alleles have been postulated for the Sahara–Arabian Peninsula desert region. There is a high degree of dependency on milk among many groups of desert pastoralists, and so a positive link between lactase persistence and milking seems very plausible. In addition, it has been argued (Cook 1978) that the simple fact that milk is a liquid would give adults who could consume it in large quantities a powerful selective advantage. The theory, while unproven, certainly seems plausible. G. C. Cook's suggestion that lactase persistence conveyed some resistance to gastrointestinal diseases has attracted much less support. At least for cholera, his claim must be rejected, based on what we know of the historical geography of the disease. Cholera seems to have been restricted to the Indian subcontinent until very recent times.

Finally, it seems most likely that the European and Arabia-Sahara centers of LAC*P prevalence, and the Uganda-Rwanda center (if it in fact exists), arose independently. Population movement and gene flow can be very extensive and, no doubt, have played a substantial role around the centers. Despite the efforts of some authors to find a common origin in the ancient Middle East, it is simpler to suggest independent origins than to postulate gene flow from the Middle East to Scandinavia and to the interior of East Africa. The problem might be resolved in the future if gene sequencing could show that the LAC*P alleles in Sweden and Saudi Arabia are, in fact, the same or are distinct forms of the gene with a similar function.

Conclusions

Lactose malabsorption is the normal condition of most adults. Many suffer the clinical symptoms of lactose intolerance if they consume milk, especially in large amounts. In two, or possibly three, places, genetic mutations have arisen that allow adults to gain the nutritional and culinary benefits of milk and many other dairy products. This ability has evolved along with cultural developments with profound implications for livelihood, including, in the northern European case, the development of mixed farming. East Asian, African, Oceanic, and Amerindian peoples, of course, thrived without this genetic trait and its cultural consequences. Their infants and young children enjoyed the nutritional advantages of milk; adults ate other things, including fermented milk products. Milk can be consumed by most lactose-intolerant older children in moderate amounts, and so milk can be a valuable nutrient for the undernourished or famine stricken. Modern commercial lactase products allow most lactose-intolerant adults to consume dairy products; thus, pizza and ice cream need not be forbidden foods.

Finally, the LAC*P and LAC*R genes are interesting far beyond their biomedical significance. Along with linguistics, archaeology, and physical anthropology, further research on lactase genes and other genetic markers will provide clues to the prehistory of peoples, their migrations and interminglings, and the origins and development of major language families.

K. David Patterson

Bibliography

American Academy of Pediatrics, Committee on Nutrition. 1978. The practical significance of lactose intolerance in children. *Pediatrics* 62, no. 2: 240-5.

Arola, H., and A. Tamm. 1994. Metabolism of lactose in the human body. *Scandinavian Journal of Gastroenterology* 202 (Supplement): 21-5.

Buller, Hans A., and Richard J. Grand. 1990. Lactose intolerance. *Annual Review of Medicine* 41: 141-8.

Castiglia, Patricia T. 1994. Lactose intolerance. *Journal of Pediatric Health Care* 8: 36-8.

Cook, G. C. 1978. Did persistence of intestinal lactase into adult life originate on the Arabian Peninsula? *Man* 13: 418-27.

Dahlqvist, A. 1977. The basic aspects of the chemical background of lactase deficiency. *Postgraduate Medical Journal* 53: 57-64.

Flatz, Gebhard. 1987. Genetics of lactose digestion in humans. *Advances in Human Genetics* 16: 1-77.

Kozlov, A. I., V. A. Sheremeteva, and V. M. Kondik. 1992. Issledovanie lactaznogo polimorfiza u predstavitelei razlichnykh etnoterritorialnykh grupp. *Biologicheskie Nauki* 1: 64-8.

Kretchmer, Norman. 1993. Lactose intolerance and malabsorption. In *The Cambridge world history of human disease*, ed. Kenneth F. Kiple, 813-17. Cambridge and New York.

O'Keefe, S. J., G. O. Young, and J. Rund. 1990. Milk tolerance and the malnourished African. *European Journal of Clinical Nutrition* 44: 499-504.

Ramirez, F. C., K. Lee, and D. Y. Graham. 1994. All lactase preparations are not the same: Results of a prospective, randomized, placebo-controlled trial. *American Journal of Gastroenterology* 89: 566-70.

Rosado, J. L., C. Gonzalez, M. E. Valencia, et al. 1994. Lactose maldigestion and milk intolerance: A study in rural and urban Mexico using physiological doses of milk. *Journal of Nutrition* 124: 1052-9.

Sahi, T. 1994. Genetics and epidemiology of adult-type hypolactasia. *Scandinavian Journal of Gastroenterology* 202 (Supplement): 7-20.

Simoons, F. J. 1969. Primary adult lactose intolerance and the milking habit: A problem in biological and cultural interrelations. I. Review of the medical research. *American Journal of Digestive Diseases* 14: 819-36.

  1970. Primary adult lactose intolerance and the milking habit: A problem in biological and cultural interrelations. II. A culture historical hypothesis. *American Journal of Digestive Diseases* 15: 695-710.

Tamm, A. 1994. Management of lactose intolerance. *Scandinavian Journal of Gastroenterology* 202 (Supplement): 55-63.

Valenkevich, L. I., and O. I. Yakhontova. 1991. Rasprostrannennost' defitsita laktazy sredi narodov SSSR. *Voprosy Pitaniya* 4: 10-13.

Wheadon, M., A. Goulding, G. O. Barbezat, et al. 1991. Lactose malabsorption and calcium intake as risk factors for osteoporosis in elderly New Zealand women. *New Zealand Medical Journal* 104: 417-19.

Wittenberg, D. F., and A. Moosa. 1991. The practical significance of lactose maldigestion in institutionalised black children. *South African Medical Journal* 79: 70-2.

Zheng, Jia-ju, Gong Zeng-liang, Xue Lian-sheng, et al. 1988. Lactose malabsorption and its ethnic differences in Hans and Uygurs. *Chinese Medical Journal* 101: 284-6.

IV.E.7 ✑ Obesity

Obesity is a dimension of body image based on a society's consideration of acceptable body size and, as such, is the focus of anthropological, sociological, and psychological study (de Garine and Pollock 1995). However, most of the research on obesity in Western societies has focused on medical issues ranging from genetic etiology to therapeutic interventions. Overfatness or obesity is a major health problem in countries that are affluent and is increasing in prevalence among the socioeconomic elite of those that are modernizing. An estimated 90 million Americans - one-third of the population - are substantially above their range of desirable body weight; in some other populations more than half of their members fit into this category.

Of course, some fat or adipose tissue is essential for life and serves a number of functions. It provides metabolic fuel; thermal insulation; a reservoir for vitamins, hormones, and other chemicals; and protection for the viscera and dermal constituents, such as blood vessels, nerves, and glands (Beller 1977). However, an excessive accumulation of fat is associated with an increased risk for diabetes, hypertension, cardiovascular and musculoskeletal problems, and in general, a reduced life expectancy. Moreover, in many societies, fatness elicits a psychosocial stigma.

Definitions and Diagnosis

Body weight is the most widely used anthropometric indicator of nutritional reserves, and weight relative to height is an acceptable measure of body size for growth monitoring and for most epidemiological surveys. Overweight and obesity, though often used synonymously, are not the same. S. Abraham and co-workers (1983) clearly made the distinction in analyzing data from the first U.S. National Health and Nutrition Examination (NHANES) survey. Overweight was defined as an excess in body weight relative to a range of weights for height. In this report, individuals over the 85th percentile of weight for height standards are considered overweight. Obesity was defined as an excess of body fat based on the sum of the triceps (upper arm) skinfold and subscapular (back) skinfold. Skinfold measurements using calipers that pinch a fold of skin and subcutaneous fat at specific sites (for example, waist, abdomen, thighs, upper arm, and back) are used in equations to estimate body fat stores and are compared with reference percentile tables (Himes 1991).

Many recent studies have used the Body Mass Index (BMI), which is the weight in kilograms divided by height in meters squared, to categorize body size. This index was devised by the Belgian mathematician Adolphe Quetelet (1796-1874) and is also referred to as the Quetelet index. (The Ponderal Index, which is the quotient of the height in inches divided by the cube root of the weight in pounds, has been similarly used.)

Overweight is defined as a BMI above 27.3 for women and 27.8 for men. These BMIs represent approximately 124 percent of desirable weight for men and 120 percent of desirable weight for women, defined as the midpoint of the range of weight for a medium-size skeletal frame from the 1983 Metropolitan Insurance Company Height and Weight Tables. The World Health Organization uses a similar range of BMIs: below 20 (lean), 20 to 25 (acceptable), 25 to 29.9 (moderately overweight), 30 to 39.9 (severely obese), and greater than 40 (morbidly obese). Epidemiological studies frequently use a BMI of 30 as the delimiter for obesity for both sexes.

Other anthropometric measurements have been used as alternatives to body weight in assessment of obesity. Body girth measurements or circumferences at specific anatomical locations have a high correlation with body mass. A commonly used measure is the circumference of the upper arm. This measurement, in conjunction with the triceps skinfold, has been used to compare the fat and lean components of the arm and thus to provide a measurement of energy and protein stores. More sophisticated, expensive, and time-consuming techniques assess the lean and fat components of the body. These techniques have included densitometry, magnetic resonance imaging (MRI), basic X rays, computerized tomography (CAT) scans, ultrasound, bioelectrical impedance, total body water, and body potassium levels (Lukaski 1987).

Skinfolds, circumferences, and imaging techniques assess the regional distribution of fat deposits. A central distribution of fat is referred to as an apple shape. A lower torso distribution of fat on the hips is referred to as a pear shape. The apple shape, often measured as a high waist-to-hip ratio of circumferences, is associated with internal deposits of abdominal fat and increased risk for coronary artery disease and adult onset diabetes. By contrast, the pear shape is not associated with increased disease risk (Bouchard and Johnston 1988).

Epidemiology

Current estimates of the prevalence of obesity indicate that it has reached epidemic proportions in some populations (Table IV.E.7.1). The most widely cited statistics on weight are those from NHANES III and are based on a random sample of the U.S. population between 1988 and 1991 in which 31 percent of males and 35 percent of females ages 20 to 74 years were considered overweight (Table IV.E.7.1). Table IV.E.7.2 presents the percentages of adults defined as obese with BMIs ≥30. More alarming are the recent estimates of the percent overweight and obese done by the Institute of Medicine of the National Academy of Science (1995). Viewed in light of BMIs that are 25 or greater, 59 percent of American males and 49 percent of females are overweight or obese. Two percent of males and 4 percent of females are considered morbidly obese with BMIs over 40. A 5-foot 4-inch woman with a BMI of 40 weighs 230 pounds.

Table IV.E.7.1 *Prevalence of overweight (1980s–90s), based on Body Mass Index (kg/m²) or weight for height references*

Population	Ages	Males (%)*	Females (%)*
North America			
United States population	20–74	31	35
Non-Hispanic white	20–74	32	34
African-American	20–74	31	49
Mexican-American	20–74	36	47
Seminole Native American	Adult	>50	>50
Pima	Adult	>50	>50
Zuni	Adult	29–35	55–66
Canadian population	25–64	9	8
Canadian Cree & Ojibwa	Adult	45–54	>90
South Pacific			
Micronesian	Adult	85	93
Polynesian	Adult	48	79
Melanesian	Adult	31	65
Asian	Adult	12	36
Native Hawaiian	Adult	85	52
Europe			
English	18–84	13	15
Italian	45–64	10	11
Finnish	50–9	12	30
Dutch	50–64	5	10
Australia	25–64	7	9
South Africa	15–84	15	18
South America			
Costa Rican	40–5	8	14
Salvadoran	40–5	0	2
Guatemalan	40–5	0	6
Nicaraguan	40–5	3	16
Panamanian	40–5	2	2
Honduran	40–5	3	6

*Rounded to the nearest percentage point.

Sources: Data are from many sources.

A survey of Micronesian Islanders indicates that 85 percent of males and 93 percent of females are overweight, whereas among native Hawaiians, a Polynesian group, 85 percent of males and 62 percent of females are overweight. Obesity is also prevalent in a number of native North American groups. A survey of Seminoles and Pimas has revealed that more than 50 percent of the adults are obese, whereas among the Canadian Cree and Ojibwa more than 90 percent of females and between 45 and 54 percent of males were so categorized. Among other ethnic groups within the United States there also are high levels of adult obesity: In Texas, fully 66 percent of male Mexican-Americans and 60 percent of females are obese, as were almost 50 percent of female African-Americans and 31 percent of males nationwide. Table IV.E.7.1 and Table IV.E.7.2 present the proportion of obese or overweight adults in a number of countries.

Table IV.E.7.2. *Prevalence of obesity**
(Body Mass Index ≥ 30 kg/m²)

Country/region	Age	Percentage males	Percentage females
United States			
White	40–9	14.8	16.4
Black	40–9	23.1	33.0
Hispanic	40–9	18.5	38.7
Pima Indian	35–44	64.0	75.0
Canada	35–44	12.0	16.0
France	16–84	7.0	8.0
Sweden	15–44	4.8	3.9
Italy	45–64	9.9	11.1
Netherlands	35–49	4.2	5.0
United Kingdom	35–49	7.9	8.6
Germany	25–69	16.0	16.0
Costa Rica	40–5	5.7	14.4
El Salvador	40–5	0.0	1.5
Guatemala	40–5	0.0	5.6
Honduras	40–5	2.8	6.0
Australia	25–64	8.6	13.3
South Africa			
Cape Peninsula	35–44	14.3	15.6
Solomon Islands			
Urban	35–54	19.0	43.0
Samoans (Hawaii)	45–54	45.0	55.0
India (Bombay)	15–76	6.2	10.7
Thailand	over 30	11.1	11.1

*Data are from 1980s.

Source: Bouchard (1994), pp. 27–30.

Obesity can begin in early life. Eleven percent of U.S. children (ages 6 to 11 years), 13 percent of adolescent males (ages 10 to 17), and 9 percent of adolescent females are overweight. Outside of the United States, M. Gurney and J. Gorstein (1988), who surveyed the preschool populations of 34 countries, found ranges of obesity from 1 to 11 percent. By way of a few examples, in Jordan and Tahiti 2 percent of the preschoolers were obese, in the United Kingdom 3 percent, in Canada 6 percent, and in Jamaica the figure was 10 percent. There are no comparable multinational studies for school-age children.

Obesity in childhood and adolescence is a good predictor of obesity in adulthood. In one study, a third of the obese adults examined were already overweight or obese at 7 years of age, and two-thirds were overweight or obese by age 14. Studies in the United States and Britain found that between 40 and 74 percent of obese 11- to 14-year-old youngsters became obese young adults.

Secular Trends in Overweight

Since 1960, surveys in the United States have tracked changes in the proportion of those overweight and obese in the population. In general, adult average weight and the proportion of individuals who are overweight have grown larger. Overweight preva-

lence for adults increased 8 percent between the recording periods of NHANES II (1976–80) and NHANES III (1988–91), as shown in Table IV.E.7.3. The mean BMI jumped from 25.3 to 26.3 and the mean body weight increased by 3.6 kg. The proportion of overweight children and adolescents, in particular, has been augmented, although a countertrend can be seen among the older (over 70 years) segment of the population. Thus for women 60 to 74 years of age, there was a decrease in the percent overweight from 45.6 percent to 41.3 percent. However, among African-American females, corresponding figures for the younger cohort (50 to 59 years) showed an increase from 35 to 52 percent overweight. By contrast, African-American males age 60 to more than 80 years had the lowest percent of overweight individuals in comparison with white and Hispanic Americans. It is notable that during the two decades from 1960 to 1980, no consistent secular trends were found for whites or blacks ages 12 to 17 years and 18 to 34 years. However, this changed significantly with the NHANES III data, which revealed increasing obesity in both of these groups.

Based on self-reports in a Harris Poll, 74 percent of Americans ages 28 and older stated in 1996 that they were overweight. This was an increase from 71 percent in 1995, 69 percent in 1994, and 59 percent in 1986. In the United Kingdom during the decade 1980 to 1990, the percentage of adult males classified as overweight grew from 39 to 48 percent and those who were obese from 6 percent to 8 percent. The proportion of women classified as overweight increased from 32 percent to 40 percent and obese from 8 percent to 13 percent. Overweight percentages were highest for males and females 50 to 64 years of age.

Gender

Childbearing and menopause are associated with weight gain, obesity, and an increasing waist-to-hip ratio. Maternal body fat is gained during pregnancy in response to the hormonal milieu, with a third of women gaining more than 5 kilograms of adipose tissue. In the United States, the mean net weight gain

Table IV.E.7.3. *Age-adjusted and age-specific prevalence of overweight (1960–91)*

Population groups	NHES 1 (1960–2)	NHANES I (1971–4)	NHANES II (1976–80)	NHANES III (1988–91)
White males	23.0	23.8	24.2	32.0
White females	23.6	24.0	24.4	33.5
Black males	22.1	23.9	26.2	31.8
Black females	41.6	43.1	44.5	49.2

Note: NHES = National Health Examination Survey

NHANES = National Health and Nutrition Examination Survey

Source: Kuczmarski et al. (1994), pp. 205–11.

with each childbearing cycle is 1 kilogram above that normally gained with aging. Americans put on approximately 20 pounds from age 25 to 55. Lactation mobilizes fat, but selectively from the femoral region, and, therefore, there is still an increase in the waist-to-hip ratio. Menopause has also been reported to increase the waist-to-hip ratio and add an average 20 percent body fat mass, compared to the premenopausal state. Both subcutaneous and internal visceral abdominal fat increase in postmenopausal women.

Obesity is approximately twice as prevalent among women as men in the United States, although this disparity is the most striking in certain populations, such as African-Americans, Mexican-Americans, Puerto Ricans, and Western Samoans (Tables IV.E.7.1 and IV.E.7.2). By contrast, Hawaiians, Nauruans, Native Americans, Alaskan natives, and Mexican-Americans have the highest obesity prevalence among males. Obesity is only slightly more prevalent among black, Puerto Rican, and Cuban-American men than among non-Hispanic white men. Asian-Americans (of Chinese, Japanese, Filipino, and Indochinese origin) have a lower obesity prevalence than other minority groups in the United States, although this may be changing. Some groups, such as the California Japanese, have recently developed moderately high BMIs.

P. Brown and M. Konner (1987) have noted that females appear to become obese with modernization. They suggested that the sex ratio of obesity is a marker for a population on a trajectory of economic development and westernization. That is, an excess of female versus male obesity is more likely to be observed in poorer populations in the developing world and less so in affluent Western populations. The data are generally consistent with this interpretation.

Brown's (1991) cross-cultural survey using the Human Relation Area File data found that 81 percent of societies for which there was sufficient data rated "plumpness" or being "filled out" as an attribute of beauty in females. This was particularly true of fat deposits on the hips and legs. Bigness for women in some groups is a sign of power, beauty, and maternity. Indeed, anthropologists have described the practices of populations in Polynesia (Pollock 1995) and West Africa (Brink 1995), where young women are secluded for a year or more in "fattening huts" prior to marriage. Such plumpness is not only considered desirable in a woman but also reflects positively on the socioeconomic status of her family and its ability to feed a daughter without having to rely on her labor.

Modernization

The construct of modernization encompasses a wide variety of lifestyle changes, including physical activity patterns, diet, and psychosocial stress. Many "diseases of civilization" (Trowell and Burkitt 1981) have been associated with westernization or modernization.

For example, the Pimas of Arizona have the highest rate of diabetes of any known population – a condition that is accompanied by a high prevalence of obesity among individuals of all ages. However, this is not the case with a small group of Pima whose ancestors migrated to Mexico some 700 to 1,000 years ago and who live today in a remote, mountainous location with a traditional lifestyle that is in marked contrast to the Arizona Pima. These Mexican Pima are lighter in weight and shorter and have lower BMIs, plasma cholesterol levels, and rates of diabetes. Consequently, it would seem that much of the problem with the Arizona Pima lies in lifestyle. Suggestive as well was a study conducted by K. O'Dea (1984), who took a group of diabetic Australian Aborigines away from an urban lifestyle to live as hunters and gatherers for seven weeks in northwestern Australia. The subjects lost an average of 8 kilograms and experienced improved carbohydrate metabolism.

In another study, the situation was reversed, whereby 13 Tarahumaras living a traditional lifestyle in northern Mexico were fed a diet typical of affluent societies for five weeks. On average, these subjects gained 3.8 kilograms (or 7 percent of their initial body weight) and had dramatic increases in plasma lipids and lipoprotein levels. Clearly, such investigations indicate that aspects of modern lifestyle can significantly contribute to obesity as well as other deleterious metabolic changes. They point to the benefits of a diet low in animal fat and high in complex carbohydrates, as well as the importance of high levels of physical activity (McMurphy et al. 1991).

In addition, migration studies have shown that populations moving from traditional to westernized environments experience large increases in body weight, along with rising rates of diabetes and other metabolic changes (Bindon and Baker 1985; Bindon 1995).

Geography

Derek Roberts's study (1953) of the geography and climate of 220 societies revealed that height and weight ratios are related to mean annual temperatures and that people are fatter the farther away they live from the equator. In other words, populations are fattest where summers are the coldest and leanest where summers are the hottest (Beller 1977). Put another way, if height is held constant, heavier people are found in the world's colder climates. Roberts hypothesized that cold stimulates the adrenal glands which, in turn, increase fat deposits.

In the United States, obesity is most common in the Northeast and Midwest, and rates are significantly higher in metropolitan regions than in rural areas. However, cutting across geographic distinctions are ethnic group concentrations and socioeconomic classes. In modernizing countries, the more affluent segments of populations exhibit a higher prevalence of obesity regardless of rural or urban location. But in industrialized countries, the lower socioeconomic classes have the higher prevalence, and in addition, immigrant populations show increases in body weight compared to their sedentary counterparts or populations of origin. Finally, within a country, migration from rural to urban areas also leads to obesity.

Lifestyle Factors

Physical Activity

Physical inactivity has been related to increases in body weight and to obesity in both children and adults. Research by William Dietz and S. L. Gortmaker (1985) has demonstrated a linear relationship between the number of hours of television watching and body weight among Americans. Moreover, cross-sectional studies indicate that there is a negative relationship between energy expended for physical activity and body fat content. However, these associations do not prove that low levels of physical activity promote high levels of body fat because the association can also mean that individuals with existing high levels of body fat are rendered unable to exercise vigorously or for extended durations.

Both aerobic exercise and resistance training result in decreases in body fat by increasing energy expenditure during the actual period of exercise and subsequent periods of rest. Thus, exercise can promote a negative energy balance provided that there is not compensatory energy intake for those calories expended during and after exercise. Exercise has been found to be moderately successful in promoting and maintaining weight loss, and in some studies, weight loss was sustained with moderate exercise after the cessation of dieting.

Diet

M. Suzuki and N. Hosoya (1988) have succinctly modeled the relationship between obesity in adulthood and dietary changes, by arguing that modernized diets and food habits tend to accelerate the storage of body fat, regardless of the amount of energy that is ingested. Involved are (1) decreased carbohydrate and increased fat proportions in daily energy intake; (2) gorging just before resting; (3) increase of simultaneous intake of fats and sugars; (4) increased consumption of cereals in refined forms, such as flour, rather than unrefined, unprocessed grains; (5) increased consumption of soft, digestible foods rather than hard and more difficult to digest (for example, fibrous) foods; and (6) increased consumption of alcohol.

Although the primary focus has been on caloric intake, data also indicate that the composition of the diet is important in terms of metabolic rate, energy storage, and the production of obesity. Both the amount and the composition of food influence body-weight regulation. In a clinical study by T. Horton and colleagues (1995), carbohydrate overfeeding produced progressive increases in oxidation and total energy expenditure, resulting in 75 to 80 percent of excess energy being stored. Fat overfeeding had a minimal effect on oxidation and total energy expenditure, leading to storage of 90 to 95 percent of excess energy. Excess dietary fat led to a greater fat accumulation than did excess dietary carbohydrates. Other investigations have demonstrated that individuals with a family history of obesity are more likely to suffer the obesity-promoting effects of high-fat diets than individuals without such a family history (Bouchard and Bray 1996).

Epidemiologic data from both the United States and Great Britain have shown that sugar intake is inversely related to obesity prevalence but that BMI and the percent of calories from fat are positively correlated. Indeed, a number of studies indicate that it is dietary fat, rather than sugar intake, that promotes obesity. However, a high-carbohydrate intake may cause hyperinsulinemia that, in turn, promotes fat storage. Excess intake of any macronutrient can contribute to weight gain, especially when associated with low energy expenditure.

The nutritional epidemiological transitions that promote obesity are, in part, fueled by multinational food corporations, which have introduced calorically dense foods that are advertised widely. The U.S. Department of Agriculture estimates that in the United States alone, the food and restaurant industry spends approximately 36 billion dollars annually on advertising, and some campaigns for single items (for example, a new soft drink or a new hamburger) exceeded 50 million dollars in 1996 and 1997. The trend in the United States is to increase the size of fast-food items (for example, "supersize," or "giant size"), which are generally high in fat, carbohydrates, sodium, and calories to begin with. The larger portions tend to be eaten as quickly and completely as the regular ones. Thus, McDonald's "supersize" serving of fries, which contains 540 calories, represents a 20 percent increase in calories over their "regular" serving. A "king size" candy bar may be as much as 80 percent larger than the regular size bar, and a large popcorn in a movie theater is 50 percent bigger than a medium size. In the United States, a mean of 3,700 kilocalories are available each day for every man, woman, and child, representing a third more than the recommended dietary allowance for men and twice that for adult women.

The explosion of "light" and "low fat" and "fat free" foods has led consumers to believe that these items are also calorie reduced or even calorie free, although their caloric content may be equal (or nearly so) to the nonspecialized product. (One venerable exception is the diet soft drink, and the new calorie-free fat substitutes now entering the market may constitute others.) Salad bars, also popular in the United States, can be equally deceptive. Consumers put high-calorie salad dressings on low-calorie salads to the extent that the caloric content of the salad exceeds that of a meal containing animal protein and fat. American women 19 to 50 years of age get more fat from salad dressings than from any other food (Hurley and Collins 1997).

Obesity is promoted not only by the consumption of fat but also by the overconsumption of carbohydrates and protein. Americans, in particular, are consuming too many of these macronutrients while maintaining or insufficiently reducing their intake of fats. Data from NHANES I (1970s) and NHANES II (1976–80) indicated that Americans only reduced their fat intake from 42 percent to 38 percent of calories – still far above the recommended fat intake of 30 percent of total daily calories (Bray 1993b).

Smoking

Smokers weigh consistently less than nonsmokers, and when individuals stop smoking they generally gain weight. Ex-smokers reach body weights similar to those of age- and sex-matched nonsmokers, although gross obesity appears to be more frequent in ex-smokers than in those who have never smoked. The increases in body weight of ex-smokers stem from a number of causes, including increased food consumption and decreased metabolic rate. In one study, it was found that young adults who smoked 24 cigarettes per day had a 200 kilocalorie greater daily expenditure of energy than when not smoking, and this increased energy expenditure was independent of energy intake and physical activity (Hofstetter et al. 1986). Another study revealed that middle-age and older male smokers had higher waist-to-hip ratios than nonsmokers, after controlling for BMI, dietary and alcohol intake, and activity levels (Troisi et al. 1991).

Socioeconomic Factors

Many studies have demonstrated a striking inverse relationship between socioeconomic status and the prevalence of obesity, particularly among women in developed countries. This relationship is true regardless of whether socioeconomic status (SES) is based on family income, educational level, or occupation. Fully 30 percent of women of lower SES in the United States are obese compared with less than 5 percent of those of the upper status groups. Some investigations have demonstrated that upwardly mobile women are less obese than women who remain in a low SES. The prevalence of obesity for men in lower SES is 32 percent compared with 16 percent among upper-class men.

Obesity is a socioeconomic disability in Western cultures. In general, the theory is that socioeconomic status influences obesity by education, income, and occupation, causing variations in behavior that change energy consumption and expenditure. However, obesity influences socioeconomic status by the stigmatization and discrimination it elicits, which, in turn, limits access to higher SES roles. There are ample data showing discrimination against obese individuals in terms of access to education, hiring for a variety of occupations, salary, and advancement (Allon 1982; Cassell 1995).

In a pioneering study, J. Sobal and A. J. Stunkard (1989) looked at the relationship between socioeconomic status and obesity in both developed and developing societies. They found that there was an inverse relationship between SES and obesity in industrialized societies, even stronger for women than for men, but a direct relationship in developing societies. The data pertaining to children are less clear. For boys in industrialized societies, the relationship between SES and obesity was either inverse or absent, but in developing countries it was clearly direct. For girls in industrialized countries, the relationship was inverse, as it was for women, whereas no relationship was found in developing countries.

Income is related to obesity mostly through access to resources. Individuals and families with higher incomes have more options in terms of access to food and food choices, although actual caloric intake may not vary by income. Occupation is related to obesity primarily through lifestyle factors in terms of energy expenditure on the job and during leisure activities. And finally, educational levels have been related to the prevalence of obesity, as lower educational levels are associated with lower income.

History of Obesity

Anthropological constructions have indicated a hunter–gatherer lifestyle during most of human history that was marked by much physical activity to secure adequate food, interspersed seasonally with decreased food intake. This variation selected genetically for individuals who were able to store energy as fat to carry them through lean times. Both contemporary foraging populations and those engaged in the incipient domestication of plants and animals show seasonal changes in weight that reflect variations in the availability of foods.

Studies of traditional hunting and gathering populations report no obesity. In contrast, many examinations of traditional societies undergoing processes of modernization that include production of generally high-carbohydrate food crops demonstrate a rapid increase in the prevalence of obesity. In fact, H. C. Trowell and D. P. Burkitt (1981) have noted that obesity in modernizing societies is the first "disease of civilization" to appear. The rapidity with which obesity becomes a health problem in the modernization process highlights the critical role of behavioral factors in its causation, as well as the evolutionary genetic propensities that were adaptive for traditional, calorically expensive lifeways.

Given the rarity of obesity in preindustrial societies, it is not surprising that there is a lack of ethnomedical terms for the obese state (Brown 1991). In fact, thinness has often been seen as a symptom of starvation or as a sign of disease, whereas plumpness has been viewed as a marker of health. For example, the Tiv of Nigeria distinguish between the very positive category of "too big" and the unpleasant condition of "to grow too fat." In some societies, for women in particular, fatness has been and remains a symbol of maternity and nurturing. The concepts that fat babies and children are healthy and that food is a symbol of love and nurture are nearly universal (Brown and Konner 1987). Moreover, from an evolutionary perspective, there are many biological advantages to the maintenance of energy stores as fat. These include an ability to survive longer during a fast, a greater ability to fight infectious diseases, fewer gastrointestinal tract problems, less anemia, healthier and higher birth-weight babies, and earlier age of menarche (Cassidy 1991).

The ethnographic data concerning body preferences in males is relatively weak, although it does suggest a preference for a more muscular physique, moderately tall stature, and general largeness. Traditionally, big, but not necessarily obese, men have been seen as successful. However, historical trends show variations in positive and negative associations with obesity.

Historical Medical Concepts

George Bray (1992) has outlined the scientific and medical history of ideas concerning obesity. In the Hippocratic texts, obesity was associated with infertility in women, a laxity of muscle, a red complexion, and sudden death. To lose weight meant strenuous physical activity before consuming meals prepared with sesame seasoning and fat because these satiated appetite. Dieters were to eat just once a day, take no baths, sleep on a hard bed, and walk naked as long as possible. Galen (130–215), who followed in the Hippocratic tradition, identified types of obesity and prescribed bulky foods with low nutrient content, baths before eating, and vigorous exercise.

The first monographs in which obesity was the primary subject were published in the seventeenth century. A mechanistic model of the body was popularly invoked, although there were other theories about fatness based on fermentation and putrefaction as the basis for an iatrochemical model.

The medical history of the eighteenth century was dominated by Hermann Boerhaave (1688–1738), who has been called the "most successful clinician and medical teacher of the century" (Ackerknecht 1982: 130), although his influence was exercised mostly through the students he trained. During the first part of the century, the earliest English language monograph on obesity and 34 doctoral dissertations dealing with the subject were published. A common theme was the imbalance of various systems resulting in disease. For example, the essay by Thomas Short (1690–1772) – a pioneer in vital statistics – on the origin of corpulence attributed it to blood stored in the oily parts of the body and not sufficiently discharged by perspiration. Short thought that fat was stored in little bags. He noted that corpulence was more common in countries with "wet air," which he believed decreased perspiration. Foods that were soft, smooth, sweet, and oily, as well as slothfulness, led to obesity. Thus, exercise was viewed as important, as were diets light in foods of a "detergent kind." Less nutritious kinds of food, such as fish, were to be consumed sparingly. Also recommended was less sleep, a reduction in passions, gentle evacuations, and tobacco smoking to stimulate the nerves of the mouth (Bray 1992).

During the second half of the eighteenth century, Boerhaave's students dispersed from Leyden to found new centers of clinical medicine at Edinburgh and Vienna, and during these years obesity, corpulence, and polysarcia became "species" following a Linnaean system of classification.

In the aftermath of the French Revolution, a new vitality emerged in clinical medicine, stimulated by the Paris Clinical School, as well as in basic sciences. The concept of energy balance developed, following the work of Antoine L. Lavoisier (1743–94) and the elaboration of the law of thermodynamics by Hermann L. F. von Helmholtz (1821–94). T. K. Chambers wrote extensively on obesity using theoretical models derived from thermodynamics.

English clinical medicine in the nineteenth century is notable for a work by W. Wardd entitled *Comments on Corpulency, Liniments and Leanness* (1829), which describes a number of clinical cases of massively obese individuals. In 1863 William Banting (1779–1878) penned the first popular diet pamphlet. Banting, a London undertaker, who had personally lost considerable weight to regain his health, advocated a diet of lean meat, dry toast, soft-boiled eggs, green vegetables, and liquids (Bray 1992).

The adipocyte (fat cell) was identified in German laboratories, and advances in neurology led to the description of several hypothalamic-pituitary causes of obesity, such as the Fröhlich syndrome (1901) and the Prader-Willi hyperphagia syndrome (1956); the Pickwickian hypoventilation syndrome (1956) is a nonneurologic type of obesity-associated ailment (Burwell et al. 1956; Butler 1990).

In the twentieth century we have seen an evergrowing understanding of the psychological, social, and neurophysiological mechanisms that control food intake. We have also just begun to develop important pharmaceutical interventions targeted at pathologies within these mechanisms.

Obesity in America

Hillel Schwartz (1986) and Jo Anne Cassell (1995) have both reviewed the history of obesity in the United States. Although many Americans currently associate body weight and size with moral weakness, such negative perspectives do not have a long history, and in fact, attitudes toward overweight people have changed many times throughout history. In general, when food was scarce, such individuals were viewed as prosperous and envied by their neighbors. By contrast, in times and societies with ample food, fashion usually favored slim and lean figures. In many instances, however, no moral judgments were attached to either overweight or lean status.

Beginning in the medieval period and continuing in America throughout the eighteenth century, morality plays were popular entertainment. Gluttony, one of the cardinal sins, frequently appeared as a theme involving excess or greed – and certainly a lack of self-restraint with regard to food and drink. The sin, however, was in consuming more than one needed and leaving others with less than their share. Body size or shape were not factors in gluttony, and being overweight carried no implication of sin.

In the early part of the nineteenth century, medicine focused on appetite and not thinness, and most physicians believed that fat represented a reserve that could be called upon in the event of disease, trauma, or emergency. Beginning at about mid-century, however, attitudes began to change under the influence of such individuals as Sylvester Graham (1794–1851) and the Kellogg brothers, who advocated a vegetarian regimen, coarsely milled flour, the consumption of cereal grains, and moderation in diet. They declared gluttony an evil, and obesity became a moral issue. During the Victorian period, however, in a counter-movement, fashion again began favoring a rounded body shape and seven-course family dinners. Diamond Jim Brady and his companion, Lillian Russell, were widely admired for their insatiable appetites and came to symbolize the exuberant excesses of the era (Cassell 1995).

By the turn of the twentieth century, scientists had come to believe that body fat had its origin in the fat of foods consumed and that dietary fat passed unchanged through the digestive tract to be absorbed and deposited. Fat was again out of fashion. Cartoons and jokes about overweight persons began to appear in newspapers and magazines. Stout, once a perfectly good word, became uncomplimentary, and a person who was fat was considered ugly. William Howard Taft, at 6 feet 2 inches tall, weighed 355 pounds when he was President of the United States (1909–13). Newspaper cartoons showed his rotund size, and when he got stuck in the White House bathtub, the event was well publicized. A variety of products to help in weight loss suddenly became available, including appetite suppressants, diuretics, stimulants, and purgatives. Special teas, bath salts, and mechanical devices were also employed (Schwartz 1986).

A 1912 study by actuaries of insurance policy holders provided height, weight, and mortality figures that became the data base for actuarial tables used to determine, for the first time, that there was a relationship between body weight, health, and mortality. According to these statistics, moderate weight gain was appropri-ate before age 35 but became increasingly harmful in later life. Excess body fat had become a serious health liability, and during World War I, the entire nation went on a diet. Rationing and conservation efforts designed to ensure adequate rations for the soldiers also con-veyed the notion that it was patriotic to be thin; to carry excess weight was un-American.

Obesity researchers in the 1920s and 1930s were divided as to whether obesity was due to exogenous or endogenous causes. "Exogenous" people overate but had firm muscles and were basically in good health. They were cheerful and happy. "Endogenous" people had a deficient metabolism, flaccid muscles, and poor health and were sad or sour in nature. Not surprisingly, men were generally placed in the former group and women in the latter. For some researchers, weight was a genetic matter, with fatness a dominant trait and slenderness a recessive trait.

As early as 1911, thyroid supplements had become available and were regularly prescribed for "glandu-lar" disorders. Indeed, for a brief period in the postwar years, American physicians thought that many obese patients were suffering from inadequate amounts of thyroid hormones. So long as it seemed that there were endocrinologic and genetic causes for obesity, there was once again an abatement of moral judg-ment. But in the 1930s, medicine concluded that few people had true thyroid deficiencies after all, and nutritional scientists had reached the position that people were overweight simply because they ate too much. Moral judgments returned, and obesity was recast as the outcome of psychological problems lead-ing to overeating.

The introduction of motion pictures with their fre-quently svelte movie stars led, among other things, to the popularity of weight-loss diets, particularly those originating in California. Perhaps the most famous was the "Hollywood 18-Day Diet." Another was the "banana diet" – the product of bananas and skim milk in a blender – and a forerunner of today's liquid diets.

Research emphasis changed once again in the 1940s as scientists defined obesity as "over-fatness." People learned that they might be overweight, but not overfat, and dieticians began to measure body fat with skinfold calipers. Psychological theories focused on such issues as depression, lack of self-esteem, bore-dom, and inner emptiness as precursors to overeat-ing, which also acted as popular explanations. Fatness as a signal of psychological distress continues to be influential in many weight-loss programs that employ support groups.

In the 1950s, changes in American society brought more attitudinal changes about dieting and weight control. Supermarkets began to offer a number of low-calorie and diet products. Among these were 900-kilocalorie-per-day liquid-diet formulas that were an instant success and continue to be widely available in the United States. Surveys reported that 40 percent of all families were regularly using low-calorie or diet products by 1962 and 70 percent by 1970 (Cassell 1995).

In today's marketplace, novel fat substitutes are occupying shelves along with earlier sugar substitutes. New products from cookies to ice cream are both fat and sugar free. Books on dieting have also been popular, and in the 1960s, those on weight loss were best-sellers, especially if the authors promised that loss without the need to give up one's favorite foods. Five million copies of *The Doctor's Quick Weight Loss Diet* (Stillman and Baker 1967) were sold in 1967 alone, and books on dieting continued to lead book sales in the 1990s. In addition, in 1972 psychological therapy started to employ behavioral therapy, which has continued as a popular approach both for diet groups and commercial weight-loss centers. How, why, and where persons ate became as important as what they ate.

In the 1980s, Americans began to focus on physical fitness and exercise as a way to promote good health. A plethora of articles on dieting appeared in newspapers and popular magazines, along with information on increased activity levels. The message was to lose weight with exercise and diet, so as to be happier, healthier, and more attractive. A diet industry mushroomed to assist Americans in losing weight. The number trying to do so was estimated to be one-fourth of men and one-half of women, and annual sales of diet products had exceeded 30 billion dollars by the end of the 1980s.

Nonetheless, the incidence of obesity in America continued to increase and, predictably, there has been something of a backlash. In today's environment some overweight individuals have used the courts to press cases of discrimination based on body size, and there is a growing antidiet movement, with fashion houses, magazines, and psychological and educational support groups that champion the obese. These groups, such as the National Association to Advance Fat Acceptance (California), Ample Opportunity (Oregon), and the Diet/Weight Liberation Project (New York), promote positive images of obese individuals, arrange for social gatherings with singles groups, and work toward equity at places of employment and other venues where there is discrimination against obese individuals.

Many groups have newsletters; there are a number of national magazines, such as *Radiance: The Magazine for Large Women* (Oakland, Calif.), and some presses specialize in publications about obesity, food, eating disorders, and related psychosocial, political, and medical issues, as, for example, Fat Liberation Publications (Cambridge, Mass.). Other inroads are being made in the media and on educational and economic fronts to reduce the stigma of obesity in the United States. Given the high percentage of overweight Americans, the tide may once again be turning.

Nonetheless, Cassell (1995) suggests that weight watching and concern for body image have become an integral part of American culture as we enter the twenty-first century, and there is still great pressure to be thin. The health risks of excessive body fat are well documented scientifically, and articles on the subject appear daily in the popular literature. At the same time, a person's overweight status does not automatically imply ill health, and more effort on the part of health professionals is being directed toward evaluating an individual's overall health status before a recommendation for weight loss is made.

Causes of Obesity

Obesity has a multifactorial etiology, which includes genetic factors, metabolic and behavioral phenotypes, and environmental agents. Because it is a condition of excessive storage of energy, an understanding of energy balance is fundamental to understanding obesity. Energy balance is equal to energy intake minus energy expenditure, and, consequently, obesity becomes the result of a positive energy balance. Yet, energy balance is exquisitely sensitive. The average nonobese American male consumes approximately 1 million kilocalories per year, but his body fat stores remain unchanged if he expends an equal number of calories. However, a change of only 10 percent either in intake or output can lead to a 30-pound weight change in a single year (Bray 1987). More subtly, a gain of 11 kilograms (24 pounds) of weight during a 40-year time span can come about with a mean daily discrepancy between intake and expenditure of only 5 kilocalories.

Energy Intake

Individual differences in metabolic mechanisms are not well understood. Cross-sectional studies reporting energy intake for individuals with different body compositions have found that obese individuals may have high, normal, or even low energy intakes relative to normal-weight subjects (Lachance 1994) and that there is a poor correlation between daily energy intakes and expenditures (Edholm 1973). For most adults, the sensitivity of the energy balance system for change is less than 1 percent per year. The "normal" adult contains 140,000 kilocalories of energy in body fat, 24,000 kilocalories in protein, and only about 800 kilocalories in carbohydrate. Consequently, although an individual consuming 2,000 kilocalories per day of which 40 percent is carbohydrate will ingest an amount of carbohydrate comparable to body stores, protein intake will average only about 1 percent of total stores and fat intake considerably less than 1 percent (Bray 1987, 1993a, 1993b).

Energy balance with regard to the macronutrients has been illuminated in recent years by the discovery of specific enzymes and neurotransmitters with receptors in the central nervous system. The brain is sensitive to changes in circulating glucose levels, and a glucostatic mechanism may regulate the intake of fat and carbohydrates – the primary energy substrates. Carbohydrate stores have a high turnover rate and can be depleted quickly and frequently so that signals exist to monitor and correct for carbohydrate imbalances. Fat stores, on the other hand, are nearly limitless, and turnover is slow and infrequent. Thus, as a rule, increased energy intake results in increased fatness (Bray 1993a; Horton et al. 1995).

Energy Expenditure

Energy expenditure has a number of components, the most important of which is basal metabolic rate (BMR). The total energy cost of any given activity is equal to the BMR plus the work done and the heat produced. For sedentary populations, the BMR may comprise 50 percent to 70 percent of the daily energy expenditure. Wide variations in BMR are not accounted for by food intake, meaning that those people with the highest calculated BMRs are not those who eat the most food. However, BMR is depressed in starvation, in individuals with a restricted caloric intake, and in many obese individuals (Bouchard 1994).

Consistent with these findings are studies of energy expenditure involving both involuntary (for example, fidgeting) and voluntary movement that indicate that physical activity is reduced in obese individuals. However, even though physical activity is reduced, there is a higher cost for activity in overweight individuals, resulting in a tendency toward normal or even high levels of energy expenditure for a particular physical activity. In these instances much of the energy is lost as heat, rather than in muscular work. One problem of cross-sectional data is that finding an average level of energy intake for an individual who is already obese tells us little about previous levels of energy intake and energy expenditure that may have contributed to the development of obesity in the first place.

It is likely that genetic predisposition to obesity lies not only in a lower BMR but also in the reduction of heat production that occurs following a meal, that is, in lower diet-induced thermogenesis. A subnormal thermogenic response to food has been reported in clinical experiments among obese individuals and those who have been obese in the past (the postobese), as well as among subjects maintaining a desirable weight on relatively low food intake. In sum, obese individuals are metabolically more efficient than lean individuals.

Taste Preference and Obesity

Taste preferences represent a major determinant of food intake and have been linked to obesity and weight gain. Genetic differences in taste preferences are heritable (Perusse and Bouchard 1994). For example, sensitivity to phenylthiocarbamide (PTC) is controlled by a major single gene. Individuals who can taste PTC, a bitter synthetic compound, avoid or reduce intake of foods containing chemically similar, but naturally occurring, compounds, such as cabbage, broccoli, and Brussels sprouts. Research indicates that some obese individuals may have an elevated preference for foods high in carbohydrates and fats, such as ice cream, chocolate, or pastries (Drewnowski 1988). In contrast, anorectic subjects show a preference for sweet but not for fatty foods. Food preferences may be regulated, in part, by peptides that stimulate the central nervous system, increasing neurotransmitters, such as beta endorphins, and, consequently, feelings of well-being. Finally, simply tasting (not swallowing) fat, either in cream cheese or peanut butter, increases insulin production and serum triglycerides. Such findings suggest that sensory receptors in the mouth initiate digestive responses not triggered directly by the nutrient and that the sensory qualities of fat may promote preference for fatty foods (Radloff 1996).

Psychological Factors

In recent years there has been a major change in discussions concerning the psychological aspects of obesity. In earlier psychogenic theories, obese persons were assumed to suffer from emotional disturbances and failures of impulse control. However, systematic assessment of the nature and extent of psychological problems of obese individuals have changed the psychogenic views of obesity to a somatogenic one. The psychosocial problems in question arise primarily from the stigma attached to obesity in contemporary societies.

Genetic Factors

Investigations of the genetic factors in human obesity have developed rapidly. Traditional family studies of parent, offspring, and sibling data identify the extent to which obesity is familial, but they pose the problem of separating the shared environment of families from genetic factors. Adoption studies overcome some of the difficulties encountered in family studies because individuals have a shared environment but not a biological relationship. Moreover, identical and fraternal twin studies can shed light on genetic as well as environmental contributions (Bouchard et al. 1988, 1990; Bouchard 1994).

Inheritable features include metabolic rates, hormone and enzyme levels, and the amount and patterning of subcutaneous fat. Data from a number of studies indicate that Body Mass Index has a heritability (range 0 to 1) from 0.4 to 0.6, suggesting that genes may be responsible for approximately one-half of the total phenotypic variation in obesity. Adoption studies found that BMIs correlated more strongly with biological than adoptive parents. Investigations in Denmark and Iowa of adult twins showed a high heritability of 0.8. Additive and nonadditive genetic components point to many obesity-promoting genes (Bouchard 1994).

A number of important genes that control eating and

weight gain have been discovered in mice. These have human analogs, but obesity-promoting mutations of these genes have not been located in humans. Recently, mutations in the leptin receptor gene have been found among the Pimas of Arizona, the Finns, and the French (Bouchard and Bray 1996; Gibbs 1996). The obese gene encodes for leptin, a hormone produced by fat cells. Mice with a mutation in this gene produce either no leptin or a malformed version and are obese with weights up to three times those of normal mice. The diabetes gene codes for a receptor protein that responds to leptin by reducing appetite and increasing metabolism. Mice with a mutation of this gene do not receive the leptin signal and get very fat from infancy. Other genes are "fat" and "tubby." Mice with mutations in either gene put on weight gradually, more like the human pattern. Recent work on leptin and leptin receptors has focused on developing appropriate pharmacological interventions. Leptin causes obese and normal mice to lose weight by signaling the brain that the body has enough fat, which in turn suppresses appetite.

The search for genes and their products that control appetite led to the discovery in 1996 of the hormone urocortin, which is a powerful appetite suppressant in rats. Other promising research has concentrated on a neuropeptide that stimulates appetite and on lipoprotein lipase, an enzyme involved in fat deposition (Gibbs 1996).

Consequences of Obesity

Mortality

A number of studies have focused on mortality and morbidity associated with overweight and obesity. Those done in Norway, Canada, and the United States indicate that BMIs associated with lowest mortality lie in the range of 15 percent below to 5 percent above ideal weight, although recently, some physicians have argued that failure to control for the effects of smoking produces an artificially high mortality in leaner subjects. All studies with more than 20,000 participants have shown a positive relationship between overweight and mortality. But the Build Study of 1979 indicated that above-average weights are associated with optimal life expectancy. Moreover, 40 percent of all smaller employee, community, and random population studies have failed to demonstrate a relationship between body weight and mortality (Sjostrom 1993).

Similarly, the First National Health and Nutrition Examination Survey 9-year follow-up found that there was no additional risk associated with overweight among women and a statistically significant but moderate additional risk (relative risk 1.1 to 1.2) for men ages 55 to 74 years. Low body weight, however, was associated with increased mortality (relative risk 1.3 to 1.6), except for women age 55 to 64 years. These results suggest a need for clinically specific definitions of obesity and overweight, especially among the elderly (Tayback, Kumanyika, and Chee 1990).

A change in weight has also been associated with mortality in adulthood. The Nurses' Study, using age 18 as the standard, showed that increases in weight up to 9.9 kg either reduced or left unchanged the relative risk of mortality. However, weight increases of 10 to 19.9 kg and 20 to 34.9 kg resulted in relative risks of 1.7 and 2.5, respectively. In the Framingham Study, an estimated 10 percent loss in body weight corresponded with a 20 percent reduction in the risk of developing coronary artery disease (Committee on Diet and Health 1989). Independent of weight or BMI, a high waist-to-hip ratio or large deposits of fat in the center of the body (related to internal stores of visceral fat) are associated with increases in mortality and morbidity.

Data also suggest that obesity as assessed by BMI or other measures may mean different mortality and morbidity risks for different populations. For example, overall mortality was not associated with obesity among the Pima except for the most obese men (Knowler et al. 1991). Among Japanese-American men in the Honolulu Heart Program, the BMI, subscapular skinfold thickness and central obesity predicted coronary artery disease, but only subscapular skinfold thickness predicted stroke (Curb and Marcus 1991b).

Morbidity

A wide variety of disorders and problems are caused or exacerbated by obesity (National Institutes of Health 1985; Bouchard and Johnston 1988), and T. Van Itallie (1985) has listed these by organ system. For the cardiovascular system they are premature coronary artery disease, ventricular arrhythmia and congestive heart failure, hypertension, stroke, and varicose veins. Obesity can affect the respiratory system in terms of alveolar hypoventilation or the Pickwickian syndrome, obstructive sleep apnea, and ventricular hypertrophy. Under the digestive system rubric there may be an increase in gall bladder and liver diseases. For the hormonal and metabolic systems, diabetes mellitus, gout, and hyperlipidemia are the most common results of obesity. Kidneys may be affected, resulting in proteinuria and renal vein thrombosis. The skin may develop striae and plantar callus, and osteoarthritis of the knee and spine are exacerbated by obesity. Obesity increases the risk of endometriosis and breast cancer in women and can impair reproductive and sexual functions. Obesity also enhances the risk of surgical and anesthetic procedures and reduces physical agility, which can lead to accident proneness. Finally, obesity may interfere with the diagnosis of other disorders by physically obscuring their presence.

Social Stigma of Obesity

Obese individuals in the United States suffer from social and psychological prejudice. Even children hold these prejudices. When a group of 6-year-olds were shown a fat person's silhouette and asked to describe the person's characteristics, they said "lazy, cheating and lying" (Czajka-Narins and Parham 1990). In another study where children were shown drawings of an obese child, a child in a wheelchair, a child on crutches, a facially disfigured child, and a child amputee, they disliked only the latter more than the overweight child. Furthermore, children prefer to play with thin rather than fat rag dolls, and parents prefer to have thin rather than obese children photographed.

Obese adolescent females have reported fewer dates and less participation in school organizations than nonobese adolescents. College students, when asked whom they were least likely to marry, ranked obese individuals fifth lowest in desirability, following an embezzler, a cocaine user, an ex-mental patient, and a shoplifter. Adults rate nonobese figures as happier, having more friends, smarter, more attractive, less lonely, and less mean than obese persons. College students in another study stated that obese individuals were warm and friendly but also unhappy, without self-confidence, self-indulgent, undisciplined, lazy, and unattractive. It is interesting, however, that psychological profiles of obese individuals show personality characteristics and achievement levels that belie these prejudicial views (Probart and Lieberman 1992).

Health professionals in the United States also hold negative views of obese individuals. They consider obese individuals to be hypochondriacal, possessing impaired judgment, having inadequate hygiene, and indulging in inappropriate and self-injurious behavior. Additionally, they find obesity to be aesthetically displeasing. As mentioned, there is an active segment of the U.S. population working to counter such widespread prejudices (Price et al. 1987).

Treatment for Obesity

Dieting

Dieting is a routine aspect of life for many Americans, even among some who are not obese. Studies indicate that in the United States, 33 to 44 percent of adult women and 22 to 34 percent of adult men are actively dieting at any given time and that Americans spend an estimated 30 to 50 billion dollars a year on weight-loss programs. The incidence of dieting varies little by ethnicity for women, but among men, Hispanic Americans have the highest proportion of dieting and African-Americans the lowest. Dieting is most common among well-educated and higher socioeconomic classes (Kopelman et al. 1994; Elmer-Dewitt 1995).

Reports of dieting by high-school-age students are common. The National Adolescent Student Health Survey of eighth and tenth graders revealed that 61 percent of girls and 28 percent of boys reported dieting to lose weight. However, a longitudinal study of Arizona adolescents by the Nichters (1991) found extensive discourse about dieting but little modification of food behaviors or weight loss. Very few girls in this study reported using vomiting, diet pills, laxatives, or diuretics as weight-control methods. Many girls responded that they did not "diet to lose weight" but rather "watched what they ate continually" and avoided "fattening foods." Eighty-five percent rarely or never counted calories, nor did they know how many calories they consumed.

Although caloric restriction (usually 1,200 to 1,000 kcal/day) should be the only method of treatment for obesity, long-term analyses of results show that 95 percent of those who are successful at weight loss regain it within one to two years. Very low calorie diets (400 to 800 kcal/day) lead to rapid weight loss, but there is little evidence that long-term weight maintenance is improved. Repeated weight gain and loss cycles are called weight cycling or yo-yo dieting. Although there are questions about altered metabolism with weight cycling, lean tissue mass does not appear to be lost at an increased rate with each cycle (Garner and Wooley 1991).

Many weight-loss programs provide special foods low in calories and high in fiber as part of a comprehensive program. Weight-reduction clinics and lay support groups use a combination of diet with behavioral and exercise intervention. These approaches have costs associated with them, ranging from expensive diet clinics that provide specialized care with a multidisciplinary team of psychologists, dieticians, physicians, and exercise specialists to inexpensive lay support groups, such as Weight Watchers, Take Off Pounds Sensibly (TOPS), and Overeaters Anonymous. Recently, work-site and school weight-control groups have also been formed, emphasizing both weight loss and relapse prevention.

Behavioral therapy as an adjunct to dietary treatment improves compliance and may improve long-term results. Elements of behavioral therapy include self-monitoring of dietary intake; control of external eating stimuli; analyses and changes in eating behavior, including speed, time of day, and locus of activity; rewards for weight loss and weight maintenance; nutritional education; physical activity to improve both weight loss and overall well-being; and cognitive restructuring, concentrating on positive goals to counter negative, self-defeating thoughts (Kanarek et al. 1984).

Exercise

A number of mechanisms have been proposed to explain the association between exercise and weight control. The most frequently advanced benefits are an increase in lean body mass, resulting in a higher basal metabolic rate; increases in metabolic rate produced by the exercise and enduring beyond specific bouts of exercise; the energy expenditure of the activity itself; and the psychological benefits, including self-esteem, modulation of mood, and improved body image. The current recommendation is for regular low-level exercises (a heart rate below 60 or 70 percent of the maximum) that are beneficial and easy to maintain over a long duration.

A number of techniques can be employed to improve adherence to an exercise plan. These include setting goals, a program of relapse prevention, and behavior changes involving stimulus control and reinforcement in a social environment, perhaps including one's spouse. When they begin to exercise, many overweight individuals face a combination of physical and psychosocial burdens related to negative feelings associated with past experience. Some studies indicate that exercise alone can produce a modest gain in lean body mass and a loss in fat in weight-stable individuals. However, both animal and human experiments show that exercise does not conserve lean weight in the face of significant energy deficit (Stunkard and Wadden 1992; Bouchard and Bray 1996).

Drugs

In cases of extreme obesity or when there is fear of comorbidities associated with a central distribution of fat, drug therapy may be warranted. These drugs include agents that act on the noradrenergic and serotonergic systems, opioid receptors, and peptide agonists or antagonists. The most popular drugs – fenfluramine, fluoxetine, or dexfenfluramine and phentermine – increase serotonin levels. Other classes of drugs include thermogenic drugs, growth hormone agonists, and drugs that act directly on the gastrointestinal system, including enzyme inhibitors and inhibitors of absorption. These drugs are not without risk (heart valve abnormalities and pulmonary hypertension, for example, have been linked to a phentermine–fenfluramine pill) and, in fact, have not been used with substantially large populations long enough to assess long-term benefits or risks. This is partly because there was a hiatus of about 20 years in the United States when drugs were not developed specifically to treat obesity. Now, however, there are a number of pharmaceutical companies in the process of developing such new drugs (Gibbs 1996).

Surgery

A surgical procedure may be warranted for morbidly obese individuals. This may be in the form of liposuction or surgical reduction of fat deposits, usually from the abdominal apron. But food ingestion can be restricted by temporarily wiring the jaws, or its absorption can be reduced either through the reduction of stomach capacity by stapling or by creating a small intestinal bypass. Surgical intervention, however, is not without risk and sequelae, such as severe diarrhea.

Summary

Overweight and overfatness (that is, obesity) are conditions of epidemic proportions related to food consumption and activity patterns. The human ability to store fat and selectively mobilize it evolved as a defense against food shortages, cold climates, demanding physical labor, disease, and the physiological requirements of pregnancy and lactation. Our understanding of the physiological and genetic basis for obesity has increased considerably in the last decade.

Obesity has been linked to increased mortality and morbidity in nearly all organ systems. Moreover, psychosocial stigmatizing of the obese, at least in affluent countries, has an adverse impact on their education, occupation, social interaction, and self-esteem.

In the United States, a multibillion-dollar "diet industry" has developed that includes new diet products, medications, clinics, health clubs, support groups, and obesity specialists. With all of these efforts, including the increasing availability of fat- and sugar-free foods, we continue to get fatter – in the United States and around the world.

Leslie Sue Lieberman

Bibliography

Abraham, S., M. D. Carroll, M. F. Najjar, and R. Fulwood. 1983. *Obese and overweight adults in the United States.* Hyattsville, Md.

Abraham, S., and C. L. Johnson. 1980. Prevalence of severe obesity in adults in the United States. *American Journal of Clinical Nutrition* 33: 364-9.

Abraham, S., C. L. Johnson, and M. F. Najjar 1979. *Weight and height of adults 18-74 years of age: United States 1971-7: Age, sex, and race distribution for weight and height.* Hyattsville, Md.

Ackerknecht, Erwin H. 1982. *A short history of medicine.* Rev. edition. Baltimore, Md.

Allon, N. 1982. The stigma of obesity in everyday life. In *Psychological aspects of obesity: A handbook,* ed. B. Wolman, 130-74. New York.

Aluli, Non E. 1991. Prevalence of obesity in a native Hawaiian population. *American Journal of Clinical Nutrition* 53: 1556S-60S.

Ashwell, M. 1994. Obesity in men and women. *International Journal of Obesity* 18 (Supplement 1): 51-7.

Associated Press. 1996. Many Americans are overweight poll finds. *Gainesville Sun* (Fla.), February 5, p. 3A.

Atkinson, R. L., and V. S. Hubbard. 1994. Report on the National Institute of Health workshop on pharmacologic treatment of obesity. *American Journal of Clinical Nutrition* 60: 153-6.

Baba, S., and P. Zimmet, eds. 1990. *World data book on obesity.* New York.

Banting, W. 1864. *Letter on corpulence addressed to the public.* Third edition. London.

Beller, A. S. 1977. *Fat and thin: A natural history of obesity.* New York.

Bindon, J. R. 1995. Polynesian responses to modernization: Overweight and obesity in the South Pacific. In *Social aspects of obesity,* ed. I. de Garine and N. J. Pollock, 227-51. Amsterdam.

Bindon, J. R., and P. T. Baker. 1985. Modernisation, migration and obesity among Samoan adults. *Annals of Human Biology* 12: 67-76.

Bolton-Smith, C., and M. Woodward. 1994. Dietary composition and fat to sugar ratios in relation to obesity. *International Journal of Obesity* 18: 820-8.

Bouchard, C. 1994. *The genetics of obesity.* Boca Raton, Fla.

Bouchard, C., and G. A. Bray. 1996. *Regulation of body weight: Biological and behavioral mechanisms.* New York.

Bouchard, C., and F. E. Johnston. 1988. *Fat distribution during growth and later health outcomes.* New York.

Bouchard, C., A. Tremblay, J. P. Despres, et al. 1988. Sensitivity to overfeeding: The Quebec experiment with identical twins. *Progress in Food and Nutrition Science* 12: 45-72.

1990. The response to long-term overfeeding in twins. *New England Journal of Medicine* 322: 1477-90.

Bradden, F. E. M., B. Rogers, M. E. J. Wadsworth, and J. M. C. Davis. 1988. Onset of obesity in a 36 year birth cohort study. *British Medical Journal* 273: 297-303.

Bray, G. A. 1987. Obesity – A disease of nutrient or energy balance? *Nutrition Review* 45: 33-43.

1988. Perspective: Future research in obesity. In *Diet and obesity,* eds. G. A. Bray, J. LeBlanc, S. Inoue, and M. Suzuki, 229-43. Tokyo.

1992. Obesity: Historical development of scientific and cultural ideas. In *Obesity,* ed. P. Björntorp and B. N. Brodoff, 281-94. Philadelphia, Pa.

1993a. The nutrient balance approach to obesity. *Nutrition Today* 28: 13-18.

1993b. *Obesity: Comparative methods of weight control.* Westport, Conn.

Bray, G. A., ed. 1979. *Obesity in America.* HEW (PHS) National Institute of Health Publication No. 79-359. Washington, D.C.

Brink, P. J. 1995. Fertility and fat: The Annang fattening room. In *Social aspects of obesity,* ed. I. de Garine and N. J. Pollock, 71-85. Amsterdam.

Broussard, B. A., A. Johnson, J. Himes, et al. 1991. Prevalence of obesity in American Indians and Alaskan natives. *American Journal of Clinical Nutrition* 53: 1535S-1542S.

Brown, P. J. 1991. Culture and the evolution of obesity. *Human Nature* 2: 31-57.

1993. Cultural perspectives in the etiology and treatment of obesity. In *Obesity: Theory and therapy.* Second edition, ed. J. J. Stunkard and T. A. Wadden, 179-93. New York.

Brown, P. J., and M. Konner. 1987. An anthropological perspective on obesity. *Annals of the New York Academy of Science* 499: 29-46.

Brownell, K. D. 1995. Exercise in the treatment of obesity. In *Eating disorders and obesity: A comprehensive handbook,* ed. K. D. Brownell and C. G. Fairburn, 473-8. New York.

Burch, H. 1973. *Eating disorders: Obesity, anoxeria, and the person within.* New York.

Burwell, C. S. 1956. Extreme obesity associated with alveolar hypoventilation - a Pickwickian syndrome. *American Journal of Medicine* 21: 811-18.

Butler, M. G. 1990. Prader-Willi syndrome: Current understanding of cause and diagnosis. *American Journal of Human Genetics* 35: 319-32.

Cassell, J. A. 1995. Social anthropology and nutrition: A different look at obesity in America. *Journal of the American Diabetic Association* 95: 424-7.

Cassidy, C. 1991. The good body: When big is better. *Medical Anthropology* 13: 181-213.

Cavalli-Sforza, L. L. 1981. Human evolution and nutrition. In *Food, nutrition and evolution: Food as an environmental factor in the genesis of human variability,* ed. D. N. Walcher and N. Kretchmer, 1-7. New York.

Committee on Diet and Health, National Research Council. 1989. *Diet and health: Implications for reducing chronic disease risk.* Washington, D.C.

Conway, J. 1995. Ethnicity and energy stores. *American Journal of Clinical Nutrition* 52: 1067S-71S.

Crawford, M., and D. Marsh. 1989. *The driving force: Food, evolution and the future.* London.

Curb, J. D., and E. B. Marcus. 1991a. Body fat in Japanese Americans. *American Journal of Clinical Nutrition* 53: 1552S-5S.

1991b. Body fat, coronary heart disease and stroke in Japanese men. *American Journal of Clinical Nutrition* 53: 1612S-15S.

Czajka-Narins, D. M., and E. S. Parham. 1990. Fear of fat: Attitudes toward obesity. *Nutrition Today* 25: 26-32.

Dawson, D. 1988. Ethnic differences in female overweight: Data from the 1985 National Health Interview Study. *American Journal of Public Health* 78: 1326-9.

de Garine, I., and N. J. Pollock, eds. 1995. *Social aspects of obesity.* Amsterdam.

Dietz, W. H., and S. L. Gortmaker. 1985. Do we fatten our children at the television set? Obesity and television viewing in children and adolescents. *Pediatrics* 75: 807-12.

Drewnowski, A. 1988. Obesity and taste preferences for sweetness and fat. In *Diet and obesity,* ed. G. A. Bray, J. LeBlanc, S. Inoue, and M. Suzuki, 101-12. Tokyo.

Dullo, A. G., and D. S. Miller. 1987. Obesity: A disorder of the sympathetic nervous system. *World Review of Nutrition and Diet* 50: 1-56.

Eaton, S. B., M. Shostak, and M. Konner. 1988. *The paleolithic prescription: A program of diet and exercise and a design for living.* New York.

Edholm, O. G. 1973. Energy expenditure and food intake. In *Energy balance in man,* ed. M. Apfelbaum, 51-60. Paris.

Elmer-Dewitt, P. 1995. Fat times. *Time,* January 16, pp. 58-65.

Epstein, F. H., and M. Higgins. 1952. Epidemiology of obesity. In *Obesity,* ed. P. Björntrop and B. Brodoff, 330-42. Philadelphia, Pa.

Folsom, A. R., G. L. Burke, C. L. Byers, et al. 1991. Implications of obesity for cardiovascular disease in blacks: The CARDIA and ARIC studies. *American Journal of Clinical Nutrition* 53: 1604S-11S.

Forbes, G. B. 1992. Exercise and lean weight: The influence of body weight. *Nutrition Reviews* 50: 157-61.

Garfinkel, L. 1985. Overweight and cancer. *Annals of Internal Medicine* 103: 1034-6.

Garn, S. M., P. E. Cole, and S. M. Bailey. 1979. Living together as a factor in family-line resemblances. *Human Biology* 51: 565-87.

Garner, D. M., and S. C. Wooley. 1991. Confronting the failure of behavioral and dietary treatment for obesity. *Clinical Psychological Review* 11: 729-80.

Gibbs, W. W. 1996. Gaining on fat. *Scientific American* 275: 88-94.

Goldblatt, P. B., M. E. Moore, and A. J. Stunkard. 1965. Social factors in obesity. *Journal of the American Medical Association* 192: 1039-44.

Goodman, N., S. A. Richardson, S. M. Dombusch, and A. H. Hastorf. 1963. Variant reactions to physical disabilities. *American Sociological Review* 28: 429-35.

Gotmaker, S. L., A. Must, and J. M. Perrin. 1993. Social and economic consequences of overweight in adolescence and young adulthood. *New England Journal of Medicine* 329: 1008-19.

Gurney, M., and J. Gorstein. 1988. The global relevance of obesity: An initial overview of available data. *World Health Statistical Quarterly* 41: 251-4.

Harlan, W. R., J. R. Landis, K. M. Flegal, et al. 1988. Secular trends in body mass in the United States 1960-1980. *American Journal of Epidemiology* 128: 1065-74.

Harris, M. B., and S. D. Smith. 1983. The relationships of age, sex, ethnicity and weight to stereotypes of obesity and self-perception. *International Journal of Obesity* 7: 361-71.

Hazuda, H. P., B. Mitchell, S. Hoffner, and M. Stern. 1991. Obesity in Mexican American subgroup: Findings from the San Antonio Heart Study. *American Journal of Clinical Nutrition* 53: 1529S-34S.

Himes, J. H. 1991. *Anthropometric assessment of nutritional status.* New York.

Hippocrates. 1849. *The genuine works of Hippocrates translated from the Greek with a preliminary discourse and annotations,* trans. F. Adams. London.

Hofstetter, A., Y. Schutz, E. Jeqvier, and J. Wahren. 1986. Increased 24-hour energy expenditure in cigarette smokers. *New England Journal of Medicine* 314: 79-82.

Horton, T., H. Drougas, A. Brachey, et al. 1995. Fat and carbohydrate overfeeding in humans: Different effects on energy storage. *American Journal of Clinical Nutrition* 62: 19-29.

Hurley, J., and G. Collins. 1997. Let use be your guide. *Nutrition Action Health Letter* 24: 8-9.

Institute of Medicine. 1995. *Weighing the options: Criteria for evaluating weight management programs.* Washington, D.C.

Kahn, H., and D. Williamson. 1991. Is race associated with weight change in U.S. adults after adjustment for income, education and marital factors? *American Journal of Clinical Nutrition* 53: 1566S-70S.

Kanarek, R. B., N. Orthen-Gambill, R. Marks-Kaufman, and J. Mayer. 1984. Obesity: Possible psychological and metabolic determinants. In *Human Nutrition: A Comprehensive Treatise. No. 5 Nutrition and Behavior,* ed. J. R. Geller, 339-96. New York.

Knowler, W. C., D. J. Pettitt, M. Soad, et al. 1991. Obesity in the Pima Indians: Its magnitude and relationship with diabetes. *American Journal of Clinical Nutrition* 53: 1543S-51S.

Kopelman, P. G., N. Finer, K. R. Fox, et al. 1994. Association for the Study of Obesity (ASO) consensus statement on obesity. *International Journal on Obesity* 18: 189-91.

Kuczmarski, R. J., K. M. Flegal, S. M. Campbell, and C. L. Johnson. 1994. Increasing prevalence of overweight among U.S. adults. The National Health and Nutrition Examination Surveys, 1960-1991, *Journal of American Medical Association* 272: 205-11.

Kumanyika, S. 1993. Special issues regarding obesity in minority populations. *Annual of Internal Medicine* 119: 550-4.

  1994. Obesity in minority populations: An epidemiological assessment. *Obesity Research* 2: 166-82.

Lachance, P. A. 1994. Scientific status summary: Human obesity. *Food Technology* (February): 127-36.

Leibel, R. L., N. K. Edens, and S. K. Fried. 1989. Physiologic basis for the control of body fat distribution in humans. *Annual Review of Nutrition* 9: 417-43.

Leigh, J. P., J. Fries, and H. B. Hubert. 1992. Gender and race differences in correlation between body mass and education. *Journal of Epidemiology and Community Health* 46: 191-6.

Levitsky, D. A., and R. Troiano. 1992. Metabolic consequences of fenfluramine for the control of body weight. *American Journal of Clinical Nutrition* 55: 167S-72S.

Lieberman, L. S., and C. K. Probart. 1992. Body weight: The ideal, the normal and the desirable. *Collegium Antropologicum* 16: 279-95.

Lohman, T. G. 1992. *Advances in body composition assessment.* Champaign, Ill.

Low-cals are booming all over the market. *Progressive Grocer* 49: 1169.

Lukaski, H. C. 1987. Methods for the assessment of human body composition: traditional and new. *American Journal of Clinical Nutrition* 46: 537-58.

Martin, R. J., B. D. White, and M. G. Hulsey. 1991. The regulation of body weight. *American Scientist* 79: 528-41.

Massara, E. B. 1989. *Que gordita! A study of weight among women in a Puerto Rican community.* New York.

Mayer, J. 1969 *Overweight: Causes, costs and controls.* Englewood Cliffs, N.J.

McGarvey, S. 1991. Obesity in Samoans and a perspective on its etiology in Polynesians. *American Journal of Clinical Nutrition* 53: 1586S-94S.

McMurphy, M. P., M. T. Sesqueria, S. L.Conner, and W. E. Conner. 1991. Changes in lipid and lipoprotein levels and body weight in Tarahumara Indians after consumption of an affluent diet. *New England Journal of Medicine* 325: 1704-8.

Melnyk, M. G., and E. Weinstein. 1994. Preventing obesity in black women by targeting adolescents: A literature review. *Journal of the American Dietetic Association* 94: 536-40.

Metropolitan Life Insurance Company. 1983. Metropolitan height and weight tables. *Statistical Bulletin of the Metropolitan Insurance Company* 64: 2-9.

Meyer, J., and A. J. Stunkard. 1993. Genetics and human obesity. In *Obesity: Theory and therapy.* Second edition, ed. A. J. Stunkard and T. A. Wadden. New York.

Najjar, M. F., and M. Rowland. 1987. *Anthropometric reference data and prevalence of overweight: United States 1976-1980.* Washington, D.C.

National Institutes of Health. 1985. Health implications of obesity: National Institute of Health consensus development conference statement. *Annals of Internal Medicine* 103: 1073-7.

  1992. *Weight loss and obesity.* Bethesda, Md.

Nichter, N., and M. Nichter. 1991. Hype and weight. *Medical Anthropology* 13: 249-84.

O'Dea, K. 1984. Marked improvement in carbohydrate and lipid metabolism in diabetic Australian Aborigines after temporary reversion to traditional lifestyle. *Diabetes* 33: 596-603.

Perri, M. C., S. F. Sears, and J. E. Clark. 1993. Strategies for improving maintenance of weight loss: Toward a continuous care model of obesity management. *Diabetes Care* 16: 200-9.

Perusse, L., and C. Bouchard. 1994. Genetics of energy intake and food preferences. In *The genetics of obesity,* ed. C. Bourhard. Boca Raton, Fla.

Pollock, N. J. 1995. Social fattening patterns in the Pacific: The positive side of obesity. In *Social aspects of obesity,* ed. I. de Garine and N. J. Pollock, 87-109. Amsterdam.

Price, J. H., S. M. Desmond, R. A. Krol, et al. 1987. Family practice physicians' beliefs, attitudes and practices regarding obesity. *American Journal of Preventive Medicine* 3: 339-45.

Probart, C. K., and L. S. Lieberman. 1992. Cultural influences on normal and idealized female body size. *Collegium Antropologicum* 16: 297-301.

Radloff, J. 1996. The taste of fat may pose a heart risk. *Science News* 149: 373.

Ravelli, G. P., Z. A. Stein, and M. W. Susser. 1976. Obesity in young men after famine exposure in utero and early infancy. *New England Journal of Medicine* 295: 347-53.

Ravussin, E., M. Valencia, J. Esparza, et al. 1994. Effects of a traditional lifestyle on obesity in Pima Indians. *Diabetes Care* 17: 1067-74.

Ritenbaugh, C. 1982. Obesity as culture-bound syndrome. *Cultural, Medicine and Psychiatry* 6: 347-61.

  1991. Body size and shape: A dialogue of culture and biology. *Medical Anthropology* 13: 173-80.

Roberts, D. F. 1953. Body weight, race and climate. *American Journal of Physical Anthropology* 11: 533-58.

Rodin, J. 1981. Current status of the internal-external hypothesis for obesity. *American Psychologist* 36: 361-92.

Rolls, B. J. 1991. Effects of artificial sweeteners on hunger, food intake and body weight: A review. *American Journal of Clinical Nutrition* 53: 872-8.

Schacter, S., and J. Rodin. 1974. *Obese humans and rats.* Potomac, Md.

Schlundt, O. G., D. Taylor, J. O. Hill, et al. 1991. A behavioral taxonomy of obese female participants in a weight loss program. *American Journal of Clinical Nutrition* 53: 1151-8.

Schwartz, H. 1986. *Never satisfied: A cultural history of diet, fantasies and fat.* New York.

Silverstone, J. T. 1993. Appetite-suppressant drugs. In *Obesity: Theory and therapy.* Second edition, ed. A. J. Stunkard and T.A. Wadden, 275-85. New York.

Sims, E. A. H., and E. S. Horton. 1968. Endocrine and metabolic adaptation to obesity and starvation. *American Journal of Clinical Nutrition* 21: 1455-70.

Sjostrom, L. 1993. Impacts of body weight, body composition and adipose tissue distribution on morbidity and mortality. *Obesity: Theory and therapy.* Second edition, ed. A. J. Stunkard and T. A. Wadden, 13-41. New York.

Sobal, J., and A. J. Stunkard. 1989. Socioeconomic status and obesity: A review of the literature. *Psychological Bulletin* 105: 260-75.

Society of Actuaries. 1959. *Build and blood pressure study.* Washington, D.C.

Society of Actuaries and Association of Life Insurance Medical Directors of America. 1979. *Build Study.* Chicago.

Stern, M. P., C. Gonzales, D. B. Mitchell, et al. 1992. Genetics and environmental determinants of type II diabetes in Mexico City and San Antonio. *Diabetes* 41: 484-92.

Stevens, J., J. E. Keil, P. F. Rust, et al. 1992. Body mass index and body girths as predictors of mortality in black and white women. *Archives of Internal Medicine* 153: 1257-62.

Stillman, I. M., and S. J. Baker. 1967. *The doctor's quick weight loss diet.* Englewood Cliffs, N.J.

Stunkard, A. J. 1979. Obesity and social environment: Current status, future prospects. In *Obesity in America.* HEW (PHS) NIH Publication No. 79-359, ed. G. A. Bray. Washington, D.C.

Stunkard, A. J., A. Y. Cohen, and M. R. Felix,. 1989. Weight loss competitors and the worksite: How they work and how well. *Preventive Medicine* 18: 460-74.

Stunkard, A. J., J. R. Harris, N. L. Pederson, and G. E. McClearn. 1990. The body mass index of twins who have been reared apart. *New England Journal of Medicine* 298: 1483-99.

Stunkard, A. J. and T. I. A. Sorensen. 1992. Obesity and socioeconomic status - A complex relationship. *New England Journal of Medicine.* 239: 1036-7.

Stunkard, A., and T. Wadden. 1992. Psychological aspect of human obesity. In *Obesity,* ed. P. Björntorp and B. N. Brodoff, 352-60. Philadelphia, Pa.

Styles, M. H. 1980. Soul, black women and food. In *A woman's conflict: The special relationship between women and food,* ed. J. R. Kaplan. 161-76. Englewood Cliffs, N.J.

Sugar consumption and health: Summary of a critical review of the literature. 1995. *Nutrition Update* (Summer): 2-4.

Suzuki, M., and N. Hosoya. 1988. Obesity and alteration of food habits with westernization. In *Diet and obesity,* eds. G. A. Bray, J. LeBlanc, S. Inoue, and M. Suzuki, 1-8. Tokyo.

Tayback, M., S. Kumanyika, and E. Chee. 1990. Body weight as a risk factor in the elderly. *Archives of Internal Medicine* 150: 1065-72.

Troisi, R. J., J. W. Heinold, P. S. Vokonas, and S. T. Weiss. 1991. Cigarette smoking, dietary intake and physical activity: Effects on body fat distribution - The Normative Aging Study. *American Journal of Clinical Nutrition* 53: 1104-11.

Trowell, H. C., and D. P. Burkitt. 1981. *Western diseases and their emergence and prevention.* Cambridge, Mass.

Tucker, L., and M. Bagwell. 1991. Television viewing and obesity. *American Journal of Public Health* 81: 908-11.

Van Itallie, T. B. 1985. Health implications of overweight and obesity in the United States. *Annals of Internal Medicine* 103: 983-8.

  1992. Body weight, morbidity and longevity. In *Obesity,* ed. P. Björntorp and B. N. Brodoff, 361-9. Philadelphia, Pa.

Wadden, T. A. 1993. The treatment of obesity. In *Obesity: Theory and therapy.* Second edition, ed. A. J. Stunkard and T. A. Wadden, 197-217. New York.

Wadden, T. A., and A. J. Stunkard. 1987. Psychopathology and obesity. *Annals of the New York Academy of Science* 499: 55-65.

Wardd, W. 1829. *Comments on corpulency, liniments and leanness.* London.

Weigley, E. S. 1984. Average? Ideal? Desirable? A brief overview of height-weight tables in the United States. *Journal of the American Dietetic Association* 84: 417-23.

Welty, T. K. 1991. Health implications of obesity in American Indians and Alaskan natives. *American Journal of Clinical Nutrition* 53: 1616S-20S.

  1994. Fitness through the ages: Stay in shape in your 20s, 30s, 40s and beyond. *American Health* 13: 74.

White, A., G. Nicolas, K. Foster, et al. 1993. *Health survey for England 1991.* London.

Wilmsen, E. 1978. Seasonal effects of dietary intake in the Kalahari San. *Federation Proceedings* 37: 65-71.

World Health Organization (WHO). 1988. *Measuring obesity: Classification and description of anthropometric data.* Report on a WHO consultation on the epidemiology of obesity. Copenhagen.

Wu, C. 1996. No-cal powder may sub for food's fat. *Science News* 150: 132.

IV.F

Diet and Chronic Disease

IV.F.1 ~ Diabetes

Diabetes mellitus (DM) is a heterogeneous group of endocrine disorders characterized by hyperglycemia (high blood sugar levels) during fasting or following a meal. Other characteristic symptoms of diabetes include excessive urination, urine containing sugar, hunger, thirst, fatigue, and weight loss. The disorder is caused by a resistance to the action of insulin, or a lack or insufficient production of insulin to transport glucose from the blood into cells where it is used as the primary energy source for cellular metabolism. Although diabetes has been a recognized disease for at least two millennia, only since the mid–1970s has there been a consensus on the classification and diagnosis of DM.

Insulin-dependent diabetes mellitus, also called juvenile diabetes or Type I diabetes, is an autoimmune disease that generally affects individuals under the age of 20 and has an acute onset. Noninsulin-dependent diabetes mellitus, Type II, or maturity onset diabetes mellitus, has a complex etiology often associated with obesity and most frequently occurs among individuals over 40 years of age. Ninety to 95 percent of diabetes worldwide is of the latter type. Gestational diabetes appears to be a subset of Type II diabetes, and there are rare genetic syndromes, such as hemochromatosis, drugs, and infections, associated with pancreatic diseases that can cause diabetes. The underlying pathophysiology of Type II diabetes involves the increasing resistance of cells, particularly muscle and adipose (fat) cells, to the transport of glucose across the cell membrane. This resistance or impaired glucose tolerance leads to the classic diagnostic criterion of abnormally high blood sugar concentrations. Glucose also appears in other bodily fluids, particularly urine. The presence of sugar in urine is called glycosuria. This was one of the first signs used in the diagnosis of diabetes. The urine of diabetics tastes sweet and, hence, may attract insects. Such observations were made by early Greek physicians.

This chapter focuses on the relationship of diet and diabetes in historical and cross-cultural perspectives. Three areas are addressed: (1) diet and etiology or causation of diabetes; (2) diet and the pathogenesis of diabetes; and (3) diabetes and diet therapy.

Ancient History through the Middle Ages

Physicians in ancient China, Egypt, Greece, and India wrote accurate clinical descriptions of diabetes. As early as the sixth century B.C., Hindu physicians recognized the clinical symptoms of diabetes and attributed them to dietary indiscretion. The Indian physician Susruta, for example, described the disease as the result of overindulgence in rice, flour, and sugar, which caused the urine to be like an elephant's in quantity. To counter excessive intake, Indian physicians in the *Caraka-Samttita* (c. 123) recommended moderate diets high in carbohydrates and fiber.

Diabetes in Indian Ayurvedic medicine has a complex etiology and pathogenesis. In Ayurveda, the human body is composed of three fundamental elements - *doshas, dhatus,* and *malas.* Health is maintained by a balance of these elements, and, consequently, a disturbance of equilibrium causes disease. There are three *doshas* that control various aspects of physiology. Each *dosha* has five divisions, and a disturbance in any one of these can cause diabetes. In addition, the body contains 13 categories of *srotas* (channels of circulation through which pass basic tissue elements), *doshas,* and waste products. Lack of exercise, sleeping during the day (thereby suppressing digestive functions), and excessive fatty food and alcohol consumption can disturb the *srota* involved in carrying the vital substances that comprise fat tissue resulting in diabetes.

More specifically, the etiology of diabetes can be attributed to the excessive consumption of yoghurt, the flesh of animals living in water and marshes, and rice or wheat and starch, especially in refined foods. Excessive worry also plays a role in consumption, sleep, and activity patterns. The treatment for diabetes in traditional Ayurvedic medicine involves reducing the body fat and inadvertently but effectively regulating the function of the pancreas with the use of *kerela* (bitter gourd). It is recommended in a dose of 30 milliliters twice a day, preferably on an empty stomach. Other botanicals are also used, including the long pepper *(Piper longum),* amalaki *(Emblica officinalis),* turmeric *(Curcuma longa),* Indian pennywort *(Hydrocotyle asiatica),* aconite, "Monk's Hood," "Blue Rocket," "Friar's Cap" (genus *Aconitum*), caltrops, ground burra-nut, puncture vine *(Tribulus terrestris),* and pure honey with hot water. Most vegetables are recommended for individuals with diabetes, but any forms of sugar, rice, potato, banana, cereals, and fruit are to be avoided. Fat is to be ingested in limited quantity.

In Chinese medicine, diabetes is a disease characterized by excessive, sweet urine and described in terms of *chi. Chi* is an energy force, or power, existing as a balance between "yin" and "yang." Yin is the force that is feminine, negative, cold, and dark, whereas yang is the force that is masculine, positive, warm, and bright. All substances of heaven and earth are divided into five elements: metal, wood, water, fire, and the earth. The body is a microcosm of these elements with a balance of yin and yang. Balance results in the maintenance of health, whereas a disturbance in this equilibrium produces ill health or disease. The excessive intake of sweets can cause obesity that, in turn, leads to excessive *chi* pushing up in the body and trapping yang in the stomach and large intestine, causing diabetes mellitus.

Although these organs are specifically involved, DM is seen as a whole-body malfunction. Diabetes is divided into three kinds of "thirst" based on location. Upper thirst involves the lung and heart, middle thirst the stomach and spleen, and lower thirst the liver and kidneys. People with a greater yin (female) body composition are the most susceptible to these three types of thirst. Traditional treatment modalities include diets low in carbohydrates and fat, light exercise, herbal medicinals, relaxation, and acupuncture.

Because diabetes mellitus had been relatively rare in Asian countries until the 1990s, current recommendations and treatment modalities often follow the Western biomedical models of etiology, pathogenesis, and therapy. G-Hyon Gang, investigating polytherapeutic approaches to diabetes in contemporary Korea, found that a majority of diabetics employ biomedical treatment plans with insulin or oral hypoglycemic agents and diet regulation. Salts and herbal preparations are used as adjuvants.

The Ebers Papyrus (c. 1550 B.C.) contains a prescription for an antidiabetic diet of wheat germ and okra. Both have been shown to lower blood glucose in animals. Early Arabic physicians described abnormal appetites and the loss of sexual function, but they did not note the sweetness of diabetic urine.

Aretaeus the Cappadocian (A.D. 81-138?) is credited with coining the word "diabetes." In Greek this means "to run through" or "to siphon." Having observed patients with extreme thirst and frequent and copious urination, he reasoned that their bodies acted like siphons sucking in water at one end and discharging it at the other. In his medical textbook, *The Causes and Signs of Acute and Chronic Disease,* he described diabetic patients as tormented by a burning thirst and thought diabetes was the sequela of an acute disease that attacks the bladder and kidneys. Aretaeus did not note that the urine of diabetics is sweet. He prescribed purgation; a mild diet consisting of sweet wine, cereals, and fruit; and steam baths. He advised a diet high in complex carbohydrates, including cereals, groats, and gruels, but one that also included simple sugars, such as those in fruit juices, dates, and raw quinces. The Greek physician Galen (A.D. 130-210?) also considered DM to be a disease of the kidneys and bladder. For Galen, treatment consisted of overcoming the acidity of the humors, slowing the movement of blood, and cooling overheated kidneys.

From the Renaissance to the 1920s

Diabetes was accorded little attention during the Middle Ages, but starting in the fifteenth century, urine became the focus for experimentation, and the amount and sweetness of urine was used to judge the efficacy of various therapies. Paracelsus (A.D. 1493-1541) evaporated the urine of diabetics and referred to the crystalline residue as "salt." He deduced that this "salt" causes the thirst and the production of excessive urine. He believed this was an imbalance of the humors resulting from a combination of "sulfur" and "salts" in the blood that overflowed into the kidneys, causing inflammation and excessive urinary excretion. He recommended steam baths and "julsip."

In the seventeenth century, Thomas Willis (1621-1675) noted the sweet taste of urine and may have been the first European to describe this classic symptom of DM. He prescribed tincture of antimony, as well as water of quicklime with shavings of sassafras. He also recommended anise, licorice, and raisins. Like others before him, Willis considered diabetes a disease of the blood. He thought the etiology related to particles of flesh that were dissolved in the blood, releasing the sweetness, and, therefore, recommended thickening the blood with starch and salt. A contemporary, Thomas Sydenham, proposed that diabetes was caused by the incomplete digestion of what he referred to as chyle of the blood. Other contemporaries proposed the treatment of sugar sickness with the use of bleeding, undernutrition, milk diets, opium therapy, and drinking lime water to neutralize acids.

In 1776, Matthew Dobson of Manchester was able to demonstrate and assay the amount of sugar in urine by evaporating it and weighing the dried residue. Dobson remarked that this residue looked and tasted like "ground sugar," and, hence, glycosuria became an important diagnostic tool that continues in use today. In fact, measuring the amount of sugar in the urine permits an assessment of the effectiveness of therapeutic interventions. In 1815, Michel E. Chevreul identified sugar (that is, glucose) in blood and, since the 1980s, blood glucose monitoring has been considered preferable to testing the urine for glucose.

Dobson had proposed a therapeutically rational diet high in meat and fat and low in grains and breads for diabetics. John Rollo, working in the late 1790s, prescribed rancid meat (preferably pork) and milk with the objective of restricting sugar intake and reducing glycosuria. He believed that diabetes was the result of a stomach disorder, which, by causing the improper digestion of food, prevented the proper assimilation of sugar. He noted that the amount of urine depended on the type of food that was eaten: Urinary production increased after the ingestion of vegetables and decreased when diets were high in animal fats and proteins. He advised his patients to consume breakfast and bedtime snacks of 24 ounces of milk, 8 ounces of lime water, and bread and butter. A noontime meal featured pudding made from blood and suet, and the evening meal included old, as opposed to fresh, meat from game. John Rollo's work was based on extensive metabolic studies of obese diabetic patients in the Greenwich Naval Hospital. His findings shifted the focus from the kidneys to the gastrointestinal tract and provided a scientific basis for therapeutic diets high in fat and protein and low in carbohydrates.

Gross autopsies performed in the 1850s and 1860s revealed no pancreatic abnormalities of diabetics. In 1855, the French physiologist Claude Bernard discovered that the liver secretes glucose from the animal starch or glycogen stored in it, whereas Bernard and Moritz Schiff found that the "destruction" of the pancreas in experimental animals did not result in the onset of diabetes. These findings supported the belief that a liver disease was the source of diabetes, but attention was redirected to the pancreas in 1889, when Joseph von Mering and Oscar Minkowski demonstrated that the complete removal of the pancreas did cause diabetes in dogs.

In the second half of the nineteenth century, work proceeded on two fronts: the anatomical and physiological elucidation of the pancreas and dietary interventions to control diabetes. In 1869, Paul Langerhans, in his M.D. thesis, described previously unrecognized cells in the rabbit pancreas, without suggesting any function for them. In 1893, Gustave Laguesse named these cells the "islets of Langerhans." Meanwhile, Minkowski, Laguesse, Eugene Opie, and others demonstrated that these cells produced an internal secretion that controlled glycosuria.

Observations by Apollinaire Bouchardat, culminating in a book on glycosuria in 1875, distinguished between insulin-dependent and noninsulin-dependent diabetics. Bouchardat imposed a very low carbohydrate diet to control glycosuria. Since then, recommendations for the inclusion of carbohydrates in the diet have varied enormously, depending on the prevailing ideas concerning pathophysiology and observations of patients' success (Table IV.F.1.1). Based on the earlier work of Rollo, meat-based diets were very popular in the middle and late 1800s. Some diets included nonsucrose sugars, such as the sugar alcohols (for example, sorbitol), and milk sugar or lactose. Low-starch vegetables, such as celery and Jerusalem artichokes, were also included.

Von Mering proposed a meal plan of 250 grams (g) of meat, 80 to 120 g of rice, semolina, or buckwheat grits, and an unlimited amount of stale bread. When carbohydrates were advocated as part of dietary control, they were generally high fiber, complex, starchy carbohydrates, such as oats. The starvation regimen often found in the late 1800s and prior to the discovery of insulin in 1921 was, in part, based on Bouchardat's observation that during the siege of Paris in 1871, the imposed starvation regimens or undernutrition led to better control of diabetic symptoms. This and later observations served as the basis for the "star-

Table IV.F.1.1. *A historical perspective on dietary recommendations for people with diabetes*

Years	Comments	Carbohydrate	Protein	Fat
Pre–1921	Starvation diets before insulin therapy	Very low	Very low	Very low
1920–1940	Advent of insulin therapy; diets based on food weights, high fat	20%*	10%	70%
1940–1970	First American Diabetes Association (ADA)/American Dietetic Association (ADA) exchange lists (1950)	40%	20%	40%
1971	Revised ADA/ADA dietary recommendations	45%	20%	35%
1986	New ADA/ADA dietary recommendations and exchange lists	≤60%	12–20%	<30%
1994	Individualized diets, less restriction, emphasis on low-fat and high-carbohydrate diet	Variable – but high ≤60%	10–20%	Variable – but <30% with <10% from saturated fat

*Percentage of daily calories.

vation diet." It is interesting to note that investigators at the Institute for Diabetes, Endocrinology and Metabolic Research in Zagreb recently observed an improvement in glucose control, primarily through weight loss, in populations in the war-torn former Yugoslavia.

Diets in the Age of Insulin Therapy

In 1921, Charles Best and Frederick Banting isolated pancreatic secretions and named them "insulin." They realized that insulin was responsible for the control of blood glucose levels and the appearance of the clinical symptoms of diabetes. During the 1920s, other endocrinologists characterized the hormones of the pituitary and adrenal glands and indicated that these were also involved in metabolism. However, insulin alone constitutes the antidiabetic hormone therapy in use today for all Type I diabetics and for some Type II diabetics who do not respond to oral hypoglycemic tablets (developed in the 1950s) or diet or exercise. Although it was first used therapeutically in 1922, it was not until the 1950s that appropriate bioassays of insulin were developed.

During the 1920s, Carl Petren advocated a diet high in fat because he was dissatisfied with the starvation and high-protein and high-carbohydrate diets. He deduced that an increase in nitrogen from protein metabolism aggravated acidosis, although we now know that ketoacidosis results from excessive use of fatty acids for energy. He also noted that a high fat intake had a protein-sparing effect that promoted increased carbohydrate use without increases in hyperglycemia and glycosuria. In addition, high-fat diets helped patients maintain their body weight. In the high-fat diet, 70 to 80 percent of the calories were consumed as fat, 10 to 20 percent were consumed as carbohydrates, and 10 percent, or less, as protein.

In the 1930s, H. P. Himsworth exonerated carbohydrates as a cause of worsening metabolic control, which led to a wider acceptance of increased carbohydrate use in diabetic diets. Diets in contemporary times have become increasingly liberal, with a current emphasis on those that are high in carbohydrates and fiber, but contain only moderate amounts of protein, and are low in fats, especially saturated fats (Table IV.F.1.1).

In the 1940s, the American Dietetic Association (ADA), the American Diabetes Association (ADA), and the U.S. Public Health Service sponsored a committee to develop a meal plan or diet that could be easily employed by diabetics. During this time period and well into the 1950s, meal plans were calculated on a daily basis with calories from macronutrients divided into percentages of carbohydrate (40 percent), protein (20 percent), and fat (40 percent).

In the 1950s, the exchange system was developed with its six categories of starches and bread, meat and meat substitutes, vegetables, fruits, milk, and fat.

The exchange lists included foods by weight or volume that contained a specific quantity of calories, carbohydrate, protein, and fat. For example, one exchange from the starch–bread group equaled 80 kilocalories, 15 g of carbohydrate, 3 g of protein, and a trace of fat, whereas one exchange in the meat and meat substitute group for the lean meat category would be the equivalent of 55 kilocalories, 7 g of protein, and 3 g of fat.

Diabetics were taught to adhere rigidly to these exchanges, which were computed on the basis of the total number of calories appropriate for the individual to maintain, lose, or gain weight. Therefore, the number of exchanges in each group would be predicated on the total number of calories prescribed for the patient (for example, a 1,200 or 1,800 calorie diet). Table IV.F.1.1 illustrates the changes in the ADA/ADA recommendations for these proportions. In general, over the years, there has been a decline in the recommended proportion of fats, particularly saturated fats, an increase in carbohydrates, and a moderate decrease in protein. The exchange system did offer flexibility in devising diets that had both variety and palatability. A patient could have, for example, 8 ounces of milk or 8 ounces of yoghurt or 8 ounces of buttermilk, all the equivalent of one milk exchange with approximately the same amount of carbohydrate, protein, and fat content in all three. For a bread-starch exchange, one could have a slice of bread, six saltine crackers, or half a cup of rice, potato, oatmeal, or peas.

Diabetics using insulin therapy are required to eat at regular intervals during the day and to take one or more injections corresponding to food ingestion. The use of both regular and lente, or delayed-action, insulin helps maintain insulin levels to utilize the glucose from food. Various schemes have been proposed for the division of calorie intake throughout the day to correspond to periods of exercise and rest. In general, individuals using insulin therapy often have a snack before retiring. Children are frequently given snacks during late morning and late afternoon, as well as at bedtime. For insulin-dependent diabetics, snacking is especially important before exercise because exercise has an insulinlike effect that can lead to hypoglycemia – a potentially dangerous, even fatal, condition. Nutritionally preferred snacks normally have included a combination of protein, fat, and carbohydrate and explicitly excluded refined sugar. Until very recently, nonnutritive sugar substitutes provided the main sweeteners for "treats" for both children and adults with diabetes.

Dietary recommendations for diabetics in the 1980s, and continuing into the 1990s, have emphasized a decrease in fat intake, primarily because coronary heart disease is more frequent among diabetics, especially those who are obese when compared to age- and sex-matched peers without DM. A few studies that controlled for dietary components have demonstrated that increases in fat in the diet may be responsible for the movement of people from impaired glucose tolerance to frank diabetes. Recommendations are for diets low in saturated fat, cholesterol, and, more recently, polyunsaturated fats in favor of monounsaturated fats, such as those found in olive oil. There continues to be a renewed "heart-healthy" focus in diabetic diets. Limiting dietary fat decreases the frequently observed hyperlipidemias and enhances weight control in noninsulin-dependent diabetic adults. The World Health Organization (WHO) and various European professional societies recommend a total fat intake equal to or less than 30 percent of total energy intake, saturated fat equal to or less than 10 percent, and the maintenance of serum cholesterol equal to or less than 200 milligrams per deciliter. Because hypertension and vascular diseases, including strokes, are more frequent among diabetics, the recommended salt intake has also been decreased.

Over the last decade, careful attention has been paid to the types of dietary fats, although lowering plasma cholesterol levels has been the primary concern of "heart-healthy" diets. Lipid levels are only partially a reflection of dietary cholesterol and, in fact, are much more responsive to saturated fat intake and to the polyunsaturated–saturated fat ratio. Dairy products (milk, cheese, and yoghurt) contain both cholesterol and saturated fat, which has led to recommendations for lowfat dairy products and fat substitutes in bakery products. Fat substitutes, particularly for weight control, are now common in prepared foods in the United States. Like sugar substitutes, they will most likely become widely distributed and available for home food preparation. Among the different types of dietary fats, stearic acid appears to be a saturated fat that does not raise plasma cholesterol levels. It is common in beef and chocolate.

Polyunsaturated fats play an important role in lipid-lowering diets, particularly the omega-3 fatty acid series in fish oil. Monounsaturated fatty acids, like those in olive oil, have been associated with diets in the Mediterranean region where rates of coronary artery disease are low, yet fat intake is often relatively high. Olive oil is rich in one of the monounsaturated fatty acids, oleic acid, which can lower plasma cholesterol levels. Dietary recommendations may continue to become more specific as we understand the different roles of fats in the body and their contribution to diabetes, coronary heart disease, and obesity. At the moment, the ADA/ADA are recommending 30 percent or less of the total calories from fat and, of this, 10 percent or less from saturated fat, 10 to 15 percent from monounsaturated fat, and the rest from polyunsaturated fatty acids. This may be difficult to achieve for most among the general public, but with proper dietary education for diabetics, such recommendations, it is hoped, will help diminish both the morbidity and mortality associated with heart and vascular diseases.

Diet and Diabetes: Issues in the 1990s

Two nutrition policy and nutrition education initiatives for the U.S. population have had an impact on dietary recommendations for diabetics. These are the Food Guide Pyramid and the new food nutrition labels. For many decades in the twentieth century, the United States focused on the four food groups: bread and starches, meat and meat substitutes, dairy products, and fruits and vegetables. But in 1992, the U.S. Department of Agriculture (USDA) adopted a Food Guide Pyramid, putting foods into five groups plus a high-fat, high-sugar group. In the bread, cereal, rice, and pasta group, individuals are to eat 6 to 11 servings a day. Translated into the exchange system, this is approximately 80 calories per exchange with 15 g of carbohydrate, 3 g of protein, and a trace of fat. From the fruit and vegetable group, individuals are to eat daily 3 to 5 servings of vegetables (at approximately 25 calories a serving with 5 g of carbohydrate and 2 g of protein) and 2 to 4 servings of fruit (at 60 calories a serving with 50 g of carbohydrate). For the milk group, including milk, yoghurt, and cheese, 2 to 3 servings are recommended with an exchange value of 90 calories per serving, 12 g of carbohydrate, 8 g of protein, and 1 g of fat. For the meat, beans, eggs, and nut group, 2 to 3 servings a day are recommended at 55 to 100 calories per serving, 7 g of protein, and 3 to 8 g of fat. At the top of the pyramid, foods from the fats and sweets group are to be used sparingly with approximately 45 calories and 5 grams of fat for each fat exchange. The base of the pyramid is comprised of foods high in carbohydrates and has become the focus of nutrition recommendations for the U.S. population as a whole. The emphasis in the 1990s is to normalize the diet of individuals with diabetes by emphasizing wise choices from the same range of foods recommended to the general population. Thus, the ADA/ADA Exchange lists have been translated into the new Food Guide Pyramid scheme.

Recognizing the need to address ethnic food diversity and in keeping with the goal of individualizing diets, the ADA/ADA has produced a series of ethnic and regional food guides that feature specialty food items, for example, matzo, potato pancakes, and gefilte fish, among traditional and festive Jewish food items, and the tortillas, frijoles, and menudo of Mexican-American diets. Such foods are listed by exchange group and portion size, with a complete accounting of the calories and macronutrients for a portion. In addition, they include amounts of sodium, potassium, and fiber and a division of the fatty acids into saturated, monounsaturated, and polyunsaturated. These food guides are available for both professionals and patients.

After years of debate and deliberation by many interested parties, Americans, beginning in 1993, finally started to see the fruits of that controversy in the form of new food labels on most products carried by American supermarkets. The new food labels entitled "Nutrition Facts" provide serving size, the number of servings per container, the percent of calories in a serving, and the percent of calories from fat, as well as the total amount of fat and saturated fat, cholesterol, sodium, carbohydrate, dietary fiber, sugar, and protein. These nutrients are also presented as the percent of daily calories for 2,000 and 2,500 kilocalorie diets. In addition, listings on the labels include the percent of the daily requirement for vitamins A and C, along with calcium and iron contained in one serving of the food. The new food labels have been touted as an important point-of-purchase tool for diabetics, enhancing appropriate food choices with a balance of macronutrients, micronutrients, and calories.

Nancy Cooper (1988) summarized the important diet and nutrition goals for individuals with diabetes in the 1990s. These goals were as follows:

1. To restore normal blood glucose and lipid levels, thereby preventing hyperglycemia and/or hypoglycemia and delay the development of long-term cardiovascular, renal, retinal, and neurological complications.
2. To insure normal growth rates for children and adolescents with diabetes and to attain and/or maintain a reasonable body weight for adults.
3. To promote weight loss in obese individuals with changes in food intake and eating behaviors and an increase in physical activity.
4. To develop an individualized meal plan based on diet history, medication protocols, and activity levels that will benefit overall health and control diabetes.

New approaches to reach these goals are based on research that defines the physiological roles of food and the behaviors that involve food consumption. Work beginning in the 1970s by Phyllis Crapo and colleagues and D. J. A. Jenkins and colleagues radically changed ideas about carbohydrates based on the glycemic index of foods. The glycemic index is the area under a blood glucose response curve for a test food, divided by the area under the blood glucose response curve for a standard glucose load × 100. The response curve is developed from blood glucose measurements made both before food ingestion and at 30-minute intervals after, for a duration of 180 minutes. In testing a number of foods, these researchers discovered that the glycemic index for "refined carbohydrates" or sugars was very similar to those of many complex carbohydrates. For example, potatoes and sucrose both have very high glycemic indices, whereas pasta has a much lower glycemic index than either potatoes or bread. Numerous factors affect the glycemic response, such as the fiber and fat in food, cooking and processing of food, and the rate of food ingestion. There are many low glycemic foods such as peanuts, lentils, legumes, pasta, and dairy products. High glycemic foods include refined cereals, breads, and many root vegetables. Fat in a food will decrease the glycemic index. In the 1980s, researchers began to test meals rather than individual food items and discovered that there was a balance of glycemic indices among foods. Therefore, a food with a high glycemic index can be balanced by foods that have low glycemic indices in meal planning. The other consequence of glycemic index research has been the realization and scientific rationale that it is appropriate to include refined carbohydrates (that is, sugars) in meals because glycemic response studies have shown that equal grams of carbohydrate from sucrose and different types of starches produce similar glucose responses. Sugar, in moderation, is no longer prohibited.

The decade of the 1990s also saw a resurgence of interest in non-Western medical treatments and dietary prescriptions for diabetes. Although American physicians and dietitians have been particularly wary of claims made for dietary supplements, a 1992 issue of the *Journal of the American Diabetes Association,* Florida Affiliate, noted the finding of Richard Anderson that cinnamon increases by ninefold the ability of insulin to metabolize blood glucose. British researchers, particularly S. Swanston-Flatt, P. Flatt, C. Day, and C. Bailey have produced a number of publications evaluating traditional medicines prepared from herbs, spices, and plants. They now have a compendium of more than 700 different species of plants that have been advocated for diabetes treatment.

The efforts of these researchers are particularly noteworthy because they have completed a number of animal experiments, testing individual plants. One notable effect has been the reduction of intestinal glucose absorption because of the high fiber content of many of the plants advocated for diabetes control. Their article in *Proceedings of the Nutrition Society* (1991) is a particularly good summary of their experiments. Some of the herbs and spices they have tested include goat's rue, Java plum, nettle, and sumac. For vegetables they have looked at members of the brassica or cabbage family, lettuce, onion, and potato. They found, for example, that an extract of onion bulb improved glucose tolerance without altering plasma insulin response in normal mice. They also discovered that it exerted a hypoglycemic effect on noninsulin-dependent diabetics. They have tested a number of mushrooms and have found that, in diabetic mice, some of these stimulate insulin release and reduce the severity of hyperphagia, polydipsia, and weight loss.

Many teas made from extracts or infusions of fruits have been tested as well. The fruits have included apple, lime, lemon, raspberry, and blackberry, although most of these have failed to show a significant effect in diabetic animals. Yeast has also been viewed as an important source of chromium and B vitamins that may be deficient among some diabetics. Brewer's yeast has long been held to contain a factor that improves glucose tolerance, but no effect on glycemic control was evident in their testing of diabetic mice. The British researchers also found that the use of bitter melon or kerela *(Momordica charantia)*, which is consumed as a vegetable in Asian diets, improves oral glucose tolerance without altering insulin response. West Indian cerasee and mistletoe both show some glucose-lowering effect. Infusions of alfalfa or lucerne *(Medicago sativa)*, used to treat diabetes in South Africa, and eucalyptus leaves have proven somewhat effective in reducing hyperglycemia in mice. The British investigators advocate the use of these hypoglycemic agents as an adjunct to traditional therapy.

Starting with the oat bran craze of the late 1980s in the United States, an increased focus on fiber in the diet of diabetics has also occurred. But prior to that time, J. W. Anderson's research in the 1970s indicated an important hypoglycemic and hypolipidemic effect of fiber in the diet of diabetics. Recent work has focused on elucidating the different types of fiber, particularly digestible and nondigestible fiber, and their impact on glycemic control, cholesterol levels, weight reduction, and gastrointestinal disorders. Contemporary researchers advocate a diet yielding approximately 40 grams of fiber per day, which is about twice the usual intake of the U.S. population. Although the efficacy of such as a regimen has been shown in clinical studies, it may be difficult for individuals to modify their food intake sufficiently to obtain this amount of fiber and still eat a palatable meal.

Most research has not found a causal link between the onset of diabetes and diet (for example, sugar intake). However, several recent studies have indicated a link between cow's milk ingestion, the production of antibodies against casein (cow's milk protein), and the onset of Type I diabetes. Investigators suggest that this immune response can trigger an autoimmune response against the insulin-producing cells of the pancreas, destroying them and causing insulin-dependent diabetes mellitus. Although other researchers have not found such a link, cow's milk allergy is common among children.

Research on the role of breast feeding in the etiology of Type I diabetes has produced evidence both confirming and refuting the relationship. The arguments focus on the immunity conferred upon the infant by mother's milk, as well as the protection from immunological responses that could be catalyzed by cow's milk or cow's milk–based infant-feeding formulas, especially in very young infants.

Finally, we should note that Gerald Reaven (1992) has proposed that prenatal and early postnatal undernutrition, followed by overnutrition later in life, can also pose a risk for the onset of diabetes. He suggests that this disruption of normal embryogenesis produces an underlying mechanism of insulin insufficiency and/or glucose intolerance that can have a contributory effect on micro- and macrovascular disease and hypertension, as well as diabetes. He calls this Syndrome X.

Obesity has been a focus for the 1990s. Approximately 70 to 90 percent of adults are obese at the time diabetes is diagnosed. Weight reduction and/or weight control have been a primary goal of nutritional intervention. Unfortunately, the success rates of such nonpharmacological therapies have been very low. Most of the interventions have focused on behavior modification to reduce caloric intake and increase caloric expenditure. Special prescription diets are recommended for individuals who are showing the sequela or complications of diabetes, particularly low-sodium diets for those with hypertension and lower-protein diets for those with renal disease. The fourth population for which there are extensive dietary prescriptions are Type I diabetics and gestational diabetics who need special dietary control during pregnancy to insure healthy outcomes for their infants and themselves. During the 1990s, a greater emphasis has been placed on prophylactic diets to prevent obesity and the complications of diabetes.

In summary, the 1994 ADA/ADA recommendations set dietary goals for people with diabetes that are, generally, the same as those for the general population. The aim is to maintain a normal weight, reduce fat, increase fiber, reduce salt, and limit alcohol intake. The use of nonnutritive sweeteners and fats has been recommended. The new emphasis on the liberalization of diets, the availability of new foods, nonnutritive sweeteners, and fats will help to change the therapeutic diet from one that is only moderately palatable to one that is both desirable and efficacious in achieving the dietary goals for people with diabetes.

Leslie Sue Lieberman

The author wishes to thank Sarah Gross, M.S., R.D., and G-Hyon Gang, M.A., Ph.D., for their contributions to this chapter.

Bibliography

American Diabetes Association. 1987. Nutritional recommendations and principles for individuals with diabetes mellitus. *Diabetes Care* 10: 126-32.

    1991a. Position statement: Nutritional recommendations and principles for individuals with diabetes mellitus. *Diabetes Care* 14: 20-7.

    1991b. Position statement: Use of noncaloric sweeteners. *Diabetes Care* 14: 28-9.

    1994. Position statement: Nutritional recommendations and principles for people with diabetes mellitus. *Diabetes Care* 17: 519-22.

American Diabetes Association and American Dietetic Association. 1987. *Exchange lists for meal planning.* Alexandria, Va.

Anderson, J. W., and A. O. Akanji. 1991. Dietary fiber – an overview. *Diabetes Care* 14: 1126-31.

Anderson, J. W., and K. Ward. 1979. High carbohydrate, high fiber diets for insulin treated men with diabetes. *American Journal of Clinical Nutrition* 21: 2312-21.

Aretaeus. 1856. *The extant works of Aretaeus, the Cappadocian,* ed. and trans. Francis Adams. London.

Baker, D. J. P. 1994. *Mothers, babies, and disease in later life.* London.

Bennion, M. 1979. *Clinical nutrition.* New York.

Bernard, Claude. 1855. Sur le mécanisme de la formation du sucre dans le foie. *Centre de la Recherche de l'Académie de Science* 41: 46-9.

Bliss, Michael. 1982. *The discovery of insulin.* Chicago.

Boyd, Eaton. 1988. *The paleolithic prescription: A program of diet and exercise and a design for living.* New York.

British Diabetic Association. n.d. Dietary recommendations for the 1980s (manuscript). London.

    1992. Dietary recommendations for people with diabetes: An update for the 1990s. *Diabetic Medicine* 9: 189-202.

Campbell, Donald. 1973. *Arabian medicine and its influence on the middle ages.* New York.

Chevreul, M. E. Eugène. 1815. Note sur le sucre de diabète. *Annuaire de la Chimie* 95: 319-20.

Committee on Diet and Health, Food and Nutrition Board, Commission on Life Sciences, National Research Council. 1989. *Diet and health: Implications for reducing chronic disease risk.* Washington, D.C.

Cooper, Nancy A. 1988. Nutrition and diabetes: A review of current recommendations. *The Diabetes Educator* 14: 428-32.

Dash, Bhagwan. 1989. *Ayurvedic cures for common diseases.* New Delhi.

Dash, Bhagwan, and Manfred M. Junius. 1983. *A hand book of Ayurveda.* New Delhi.

Day, C. 1990. Hypoglycaemic compounds from plants. In *New antidiabetic drugs,* ed. C. J. Bailey and P. R. Flatt. London.

Diabetes Care and Education Dietetic Practice Group, American Diabetic Association. 1989a. *Jewish food practices, customs, and holidays. Ethnic and regional food practices: A series.* Alexandria, Va.

    1989b. *Mexican American food practices, customs, and holidays. Ethnic and regional food practices: A series.* Alexandria, Va.

Diabetes Control and Complications Trial (DCCT) Research Group, The. 1993. Nutrition interventions for intensive therapy in the diabetes control and complications trial. *Journal of the American Dietetic Association* 93: 765-72.

Dobson, Matthew. 1776. Experiments and observations on the urine in diabetes. *Medical Observations and Inquiries* 5: 298-316.

Ebstein, E. 1989. Diabetes, sugar consumption and luxury throughout the ages. In *Diabetes - its medical and cultural history,* ed. D. Von Engelhardt, 101-6. New York.

Estes, J. Worth. 1989. *The medical skills of ancient Egypt.* Canton, Mass.

Franz, J. J., E. S. Horton, J. P. Bantle, et al. 1994. Nutrition principles for the management of diabetes and related complications. *Diabetes Care* 17: 490-518.

Gerstein, H. C. 1994. Cow's milk exposure and type I diabetes mellitus. A critical review of the clinical literature. *Diabetes Care* 17: 13-19.

Grandjean, Ann C., and Carol J. Bennett. 1980. *Eat less food.* Omaha, Neb.

Grundy, Scott M. 1991. Dietary therapy in diabetes mellitus. Is there a single best diet? *Diabetes Care* 14: 796-801.

Hazlett, Lucille. 1992. From raw quinces to gruel to insulin: A brief history of diabetes discovery and treatment. *Diabetes Interview* 2: 9.

Himsworth, H. P. 1935. The dietetic factor determining the glu-cose tolerance and sensitivity to insulin of healthy men. *Clinical Science* 2: 67-94.

    1935-6. Diet and the incidence of diabetes mellitus. *Clinical Science and Molecular Medicine* 2: 117-48.

Hippocrates. 1949. *Ancient medicine and other treatises,* ed. and trans. Francis Adams. Chicago.

Hollenbeck, Claire B., and Ann M. Coulston. 1991. Effects of dietary carbohydrate and fat intake on glucose and lipoprotein metabolism in individuals with diabetes mellitus. *Diabetes Care* 14: 774-85.

Huh, Joon. 1596. TongUiPoKam [collection of classified medical prescriptions], translated into current Korean language in 1966 by YoungHoo Kim, Kilgu Shin, Jaesung Kim, and Wonshic Bae. Seoul.

Jenkins, D. J. A. 1982. Lente carbohydrate: A new approach to dietary management of diabetes. *Diabetic Care* 5: 634-41.

Jenkins, D. J. A., T. M. S. Wolever, S. Bacon, et al. 1980. Diabetic diets: High carbohydrate combined with high fiber. *American Journal of Clinical Nutrition* 33: 1729-33.

Joslin, Elliott Proctor. 1916. *Treatment of diabetes mellitus.* Philadelphia, Pa.

    1921. The prevention of diabetes mellitus. *Journal of the American Medical Association* 76: 79-84.

    1994. *Joslin's diabetes mellitus.* Thirteenth edition, ed. G. Ronald Kahn and Gordon C. Weir. Philadelphia, Pa.

Journal of the American Diabetes Association/Florida Affiliate. 1992. Cinnamon, a health benefit. *Diabetes Journal* 2: 3.

Krause, M. V., and L. K. Mahan. 1979. *Food, nutrition and diet therapy.* Sixth edition. Philadelphia, Pa.

Leeds, A. R. 1979. The dietary management of diabetes in adults. *Proceedings of the Nutrition Society* 38: 365-71.

Lepine, R. 1909. *Le diabète sucre,* ed. F. Alcan. Paris.

Levine, R. 1986. Historical view of the classification of diabetes. *Clinical Chemistry* 32 (Suppl.): 84-6.

Lieberman, Leslie Sue. 1993. Diabetes. In *The Cambridge world history of human disease,* ed. K. Kiple, 665-76. New York and Cambridge.

Lu, Gwei-Djen, and Joseph Needham. 1980. *Celestial lancets: A history and rationale of acupuncture and moxa.* Cambridge.

Marble, A. 1989. John Rollo. In *Diabetes - its medical and cultural history,* ed. D. Von Engelhardt, 230-4. New York.

Marshall, J. A., S. Hoag, S. Hetterly, et al. 1994. Dietary fat predicts conversion from impaired glucose tolerance to NIDDM: The San Luis Valley diabetes study. *Diabetes Care* 17: 50-6.

Maryniuk, Melinda D. 1989. Hyperlipidemia and diabetes: The role of dietary fats. *The Diabetes Educator* 15: 258-64.

McQuillan, J. E., and M. S. McQuillan. 1982. Discovery of insulin and control of diabetes mellitus. *Janus* 69: 97-118.

Medvei, Victor C. 1982. *A history of endocrinology.* Lancaster, England.

Nathan, David M. 1987. The glycemic index: Meat and potatoes or just gravy. *Diabetes Care* 10: 524-5.

National Diabetes Data Group. 1979. Classification and diagnosis of diabetes mellitus and other categories of glucose intolerance. *Diabetes* 28: 1039-57.

National Institutes of Health. 1987. Consensus development conference on diet and exercise in non-insulin-dependent diabetes mellitus. *Diabetes Care* 10: 639-44.

Nuttall, F. 1993. Dietary fiber in the management of diabetes. *Diabetes* 42: 503-8.

Pan, David A., A. J. Hulbert, and L. H. Storlien. 1994. Dietary fats, membrane phospholipids, and obesity. *Journal of Nutrition* 124: 1555-65.

Powers, M. A. 1988. *Nutrition guide for professionals - diabetes education and meal planning.* Alexandria, Va.

Rabinowitch, J. M. 1935. Effects of the high carbohydrate - low calorie diet upon carbohydrate tolerance in diabetes mellitus. *Canadian Medical Association Journal* 26: 136-44.

Rapp, Stephen, Patricia Dubbert, and Paul Burkett. 1986. Food portion size estimation by men with Type II diabetes. *Journal of the American Dietetic Association* 86: 249-51.

Reaven, Gerald M. 1992. Syndrome X. *Blood Pressure Supplement* 4: 13-16.

Saundby, R. 1908. Diabetes mellitus. In *A system of medicine by many writers,* ed. C. Allbutt and H. D. Rolleston, 167-212. London.

Schadewaldt, H. 1989. History of diabetes mellitus. In *Diabetes - its medical and cultural history,* ed. D. Von Engelhardt, 405-7. New York.

Schumacher, H., and J. Schumacher. 1989. Then and now: 100 years of diabetes mellitus. In *Diabetes - its medical and cultural history,* ed. D. Von Engelhardt, 246-7. New York.

Shin, Jae Yong. 1989. *DangRyoByong gua sogal* (Diabetes, and the disease of exhaustion and thirst). Seoul.

Shuman, C. R., and I. L. Spratt. 1981. Office guide to diagnosis and classification of diabetes mellitus and other categories of glucose intolerance. *Diabetes Care* 4: 335.

Striker, Cecil. 1961. *Famous faces in diabetes.* Boston.

Swanston-Flatt, S., P. R. Flatt, C. Day, and C. J. Bailey. 1991. Traditional dietary adjuncts for the treatment of diabetes mellitus. *Proceedings of the Nutrition Society* 50: 641-51.

Taylor, R., and P. Zimmet. 1983. Migrant studies and diabetes epidemiology. In *Diabetes in epidemiological perspective,* ed. J. I. Mann, K. Pyorala, and A. Teuscher, 58-77. Edinburgh.

The Papyrus Ebers. 1937. *The Papyrus Ebers: The greatest Egyptian medical document.* Copenhagen.

Tinker, Lesley Fels, Joan M. Heins, and Harold S. Holler. 1994. Commentary and translation: 1994 nutrition recommendations for diabetes. *Journal of the American Dietetic Association* 94: 507-11.

Trowell, H., D. P. Burkitt, and K. Heaton. 1985. *Dietary fiber, fiber-depleted foods and disease.* London.

U.S. Department of Agriculture. 1990 (rev. 1995). *Dietary guidelines for Americans.* Hyattsville, Md.

Von Engelhardt, D. 1989. Outlines of historical development. In *Diabetes - its medical and cultural history,* ed. D. Von Engelhardt, 3-10. New York.

Von Mering, J., and O. Minkowski. 1889. Diabetes mellitus nach Pankrease Stirpation. *Zentralblatt für klinische Medizin* 10: 393-4.

Welch, Robert W. 1991. Diet components in the management of diabetes. *Proceedings of the Nutrition Society* 50: 631-9.

West, K. M. 1978. *Epidemiology of diabetes and its vascular lesions.* New York.

Wilder, R. M. 1989. Karl Petren. A leader in pre-insulin dietary therapy of diabetes. In *Diabetes - its medical and cultural history,* ed. D. Von Engelhardt, 405-7. New York.

Willis, Thomas. 1684. On excessive pissing and the remedy for it particularly of the diabetes (or pissing disease) into the theory and cure for which we here inquire. In *Pharmaceutics rationalis,* 71-6. London.

Wrenshall, Gerald Alfred. 1962. *The story of insulin: Forty years of success against diabetes.* London.

Wylie-Rosett, J., and H. Rifkin. 1985. The history of nutrition and diabetes. In *Nutrition and diabetes,* ed. L. Jovanovic and C. M. Peterson, 1-13. New York.

Zeman, F. J. 1983. *Clinical Nutrition and Dietetics.* Lexington, Mass.

IV.F.2 ❧ Nutrition and Cancer

As early as the 1930s, experiments on laboratory animals revealed that diet can considerably influence the process of cancer causation and development (carcinogenesis) (Tannenbaum 1942a, 1942b; Tannenbaum and Silverstone 1953). It was several decades later, however, that the first epidemiological studies appeared to indicate that diet could play a role in human cancer. A key conference held in 1975, entitled "Nutrition in the Causation of Cancer," summarized the existing knowledge and hypotheses (Wynder, Peters, and Vivona 1975). From that moment, research in experimental systems, including animal models and epidemiological studies, increased rapidly, providing extensive information on the impact of nutritional traditions and specific macro- and micronutrients on several types of cancer. Considerable progress had already been made in several underlying sciences. For example, advances had been achieved in understanding the mechanisms of action of nutrients, the process of carcinogenesis, and the classification of carcinogens according to their mode of action (Kroes 1979; Weisburger and Williams 1991).

In particular, epidemiological studies on the international variations in incidence rates for certain cancers pointed to the existence of one or more exogenous factors that could be controlled. Observational studies had been conducted with migrants from countries with lower incidence rates to countries with higher incidence rates. A rapid increase from the lower to the higher incidence in those migrants supported the suggestion that environmental causes, and especially prevailing dietary habits, may influence the development of a number of neoplasms.

For example, in the Western world, high incidences of cancers in the lung, colon and rectum, breast, prostate, pancreas, endometrium, and ovary were observed. But these diseases were, until recently, quite rare in Japan and other Asian countries, where cancers of the stomach, esophagus, and liver were the major diseases. Yet, in migrant populations the risk of cancer shifted from the risk prevalent in their native country to that seen in the new host country, sometimes within the same generation (colon), sometimes in the next generation (breast) (Parkin 1993).

The results of experimental and epidemiological studies have led to hypotheses concerning factors involved in cancer causation. In fact, E. L. Wynder and G. B. Gori (1977) and R. Doll and R. Peto (1981) estimated that 35 percent of cancer mortality may be attributable to diet, thereby placing diet at the same "risk factor" level as smoking, which was calculated to cause about 30 percent of cancer mortality. In fact, current views suggest that dietary habits may account for 55 to 60 percent of cancer mortality. The interpretation of such multidisciplinary investigations has shed light on underlying mechanisms of cancer causation and has provided an understanding of the role of specific dietary risk factors.

In this chapter, the focus is the role of diet in cancer causation. First, attention is drawn to aspects of mechanisms in carcinogenesis. The major strengths and weaknesses of experiments in animal models and epidemiological studies are discussed, and then the major diet-related causes are examined and their suggested mechanisms and possible preventive measures described. The safest (but in the public's perception the most dangerous) intentional additives in food are evaluated for their cancer risk, as are nonintentional contaminants, along with substances that occur naturally in food. Finally, the key role that diet may play in an integrated approach to (chronic) disease prevention is presented. Health promotion through research-based nutrition not only is important for the individual but, on a global level, may also appreciably lower the cost of medical care. A research-based healthy lifestyle is designed to allow people to "die young, as late in life as possible," as Dr. Ernst L. Wynder, president of the American Health Foundation, has said.

Tumor Models: Strengths and Weaknesses

Animal tumor models are often used in experimental designs to study the mechanisms of cancer causation, to examine the effects of modulating factors on the genesis and development of cancer, to assess therapeutic modalities, and to explore possible adverse effects.

Tumor models are specifically used to investigate etiologic and physiopathological properties or processes, especially those which, for obvious practical and ethical reasons, cannot be studied in humans. The ideal animal tumor is histologically similar to the human neoplasm of concern, and latency period, growth, and tendency to metastasize should both be predictable and resemble those of the human neoplasm. The animals should be cost effective, be easily available, and have a genetic uniformity. Variables should be controllable, thereby making it possible to investigate the influence of isolated factors (Davidson, Davis, and Lindsey 1987; Galloway 1989; Weisburger and Kroes 1994).

For research into matters of nutrition and cancer, chemically induced tumors in animals, predominantly those in rats and mice, are the most important models because they usually best mimic existing types of human cancer (Kroes et al. 1986). For most, if not all, nutrition-related human cancers, tumor model systems are available. They provide an ideal research tool for investigating the influence of individual factors, either in the initiation phase or in the promotion–progression phase of tumor development, or in the overall process.

Possible leads from epidemiological studies can be further investigated in models, thus providing more detailed information, especially regarding risk factors and mechanisms that can be the basis for new epidemiological studies to test a presumed hypothesis. However, animal tumors are only approximations that are rarely identical to human disease. For example, relatively high dosages of genotoxic carcinogens are used to induce the tumor, which tends to distort circumstances when modulating factors are investigated.

Tumor metabolism, growth, potential for and pattern of metastasis, and clinical features can also differ from the human disease. Multiple tumors often occur in models, but seldom in humans. Moreover, the nutrition patterns of experimental animals can be quite distinct from those of humans. Nonetheless, diets can be designed in terms of macro- and micronutrient intake that mimic specific human nutritional traditions.

Animal studies are best understood as providing support for epidemiological studies. It is the integration of results from epidemiological and animal studies that provides the best insight into the etiology and growth of cancer, as well as its treatment, and brings us nearer to the ultimate goal of such research, cancer prevention.

Epidemiological Studies Concerning Nutrition and Cancer

Epidemiological research on cancer and diet seeks to associate exposure to certain dietary factors with the occurrence of cancer in selected population groups. Studies can be descriptive, reporting the occurrence of cancers in populations, in subgroups of a given population, or in a certain population over time. Observed patterns may be related to particular variables, such as diet, but although the results of such investigations are suggestive, they are certainly not definitive. Their use is especially valuable, however, in identifying populations at risk.

Correlation studies investigate the possible relationships between more-or-less crude exposure data and cancer incidence data in different populations or nations in order to generate new hypotheses. But they are generally of limited value, because national per-capita food intake and cancer incidence data are only approximations and differ from place to place in terminological definition and accuracy. Results should be used mainly as an indication of trends or relationships.

Another type of investigation is the case control

study, in which the investigator is able to collect data from individuals instead of groups, and confounding variables can be controlled to a certain extent. In studies of a specific type of cancer, food intake data are collected and are compared to data similarly obtained in matched controls. When known biases and chance can be excluded, associations can be made between exposure and disease. Case control studies are relatively cheap and are of short duration but never prove causal relationships.

Much more expensive, time consuming, and elaborate are prospective cohort studies that focus on individuals in a given (large) population and establish exposure or nutrition data before the occurrence of the disease. Thus, at the time of disease occurrence, exposure data of the patients are compared to data from people not having the disease, thereby providing evidence for a possible causal relationship. Drawbacks in such studies are that the exposure assessment at any given time may not be representative of the individual's whole life, and this is especially likely in the case of diet.

Finally, intervention studies provide the investigator with the possibility of a random assignment of subjects of a given (often high-risk) population into groups that are treated or fed differently under controlled conditions. In this type of trial, causal relationships can be established.

In investigations focused on the relationship between nutritional factors and cancer, the methods used for determining dietary intake are crucial and difficult. All dietary intake measures share certain limitations, because people vary in their abilities to estimate the amount of something they have eaten. Indeed, sometimes they may even fail to notice or report consumption of certain foods, and they usually possess insufficient knowledge about the ingredients in the foods they consume. A further handicap is that accuracy in dietary recall deteriorates over time. Finally, in the case of cancer, it is very difficult to relate varying diets to the disease because the latter has a long course of development before becoming clinically manifest (10 to 40 years).

The major strength of epidemiological studies, however, is their focus on human populations, thus avoiding the need to extrapolate from other species. They tend to afford an opportunity to examine different effects at different exposure levels, and they are always realistic, in contrast to the high exposure levels usually employed with animals (National Research Council 1982; International Agency for Research on Cancer 1990; Weisburger and Kroes 1994). In this connection, however, it should be noted that in specific investigations into the role of nutrients such as fat, the experimental design in laboratory animals usually faithfully mimics the situation of human populations at high or low risk, thus providing relatively reliable comparative data. But at the same time, as noted, it should also be recognized that the normal food patterns of laboratory animals differ from those of humans.

Mechanisms of Carcinogenesis

The concept that chemicals can induce cancer through a variety of modes of action is derived from a greater understanding of the complex processes of carcinogenesis (Williams and Weisburger 1991). Cancer causation and development involves a series of essential steps (Figure IV.F.7.1). In the first step, a reactive form of carcinogen (often produced metabolically from a procarcinogen) binds to DNA, or DNA is altered by the effective generation of hydroxy radicals. This reaction, in turn, leads to translocation and amplification of specific genes, proto-oncogenes, or a mutation in tumor suppressor genes, that translate to a distinct expression of the properties of the cells bearing such altered genes (Williams and Weisburger 1991; Ronai 1992; Miller 1994).

The property to bind to DNA is the basis for the development of specific rapid, efficient, and economical in vitro bioassays, such as a mutation assay in prokaryotic or eukaryotic cell systems. Advantage can also be taken of the presence of enzyme systems performing DNA repair; these can provide effective complementary test systems to outline the possible DNA-reactivity of chemicals (Weisburger and Williams 1991; Weisburger 1994). Moreover, the ^{32}P-postlabeling procedure of K. Randerath and colleagues (1989) yields information about the presence of reactive carcinogen–DNA adducts.

When a chemical displays properties of reacting with DNA and inducing mutations and DNA repair in a number of cell systems, it can be considered DNA-reactive or genotoxic. Most human carcinogens are genotoxic. Other agents, such as the hormonoïd diethylstilbestrol (DES) or the hormone estradiol, may give rise to genotoxic products (Liehr 1990). The fact that a given product is genotoxic may signal that, with sufficient dosage and chronicity of exposure, it poses a cancer risk to humans.

Reactive oxygen, hydroxy radicals, or hydrogen peroxide can be generated in metabolic processes. On the other hand, there are endogenous defense mechanisms, such as catalase-destroying hydrogen peroxide or superoxide dismutase or glutathione peroxidase (in turn, involving glutathione [GSH] or sulfhydryl amino acids), that neutralize reactive oxygen. Exogenous antioxidants (such as those in vegetables, tomatoes, and tea), carotene, vitamins C and E, selenium, and sources of GSH aid in the disposition of reactive species (Harris 1991; Olson and Kobayashi 1992; Packer 1992; Sai et al. 1992).

The consequences of DNA-carcinogen interactions are beginning to be explored in terms of proto-oncogene – oncogene codon translation and amplification that can be measured by highly specific and sensitive polymerase chain reaction techniques

(Brugge et al. 1991). Errors may be introduced into DNA during biosynthesis (Echols and Goodman 1991). Mutational events in tumor-suppressor genes also yield abnormal DNA, which is of growing interest (Brugge et al. 1991). The rate of cell duplication is important in generating abnormal DNA. A rapid rate decreases the chances of successful repair and is a reason that growing organisms or proliferating tissues are often more sensitive to carcinogens (Cohen and Ellwein 1992). For example, radiation exposure during the Hiroshima atom-bomb explosion caused a fourfold higher breast-cancer incidence in the 10- to 15-year-old age group (with mammary gland cells in rapid DNA synthesis and mitosis) than in younger or older groups (Land et al. 1980).

Reactive carcinogens modify not only DNA but also proteins. Both types of interactions can serve as sensitive markers for qualitative and quantitative analysis, especially the readily measured hemoglobin adducts (Brugge et al. 1991).

Nongenotoxic carcinogens and promoters cannot cause cancer without an antecedent mutational event and cell change. For example, mice with mammary tumor virus (MTV) develop mammary tumors proportional to the level of estrogen administered, but those without MTV do not, no matter what dose of estrogen is used (Highman, Norvell, and Shellenberg 1977). The action of promoters requires their presence at relatively high levels for a long time, and that action is often tissue specific. For example, bile acids are promoters of colon cancer, and very high dosages of sodium saccharin act as a promoter for cancer of the urinary bladder. The interruption of gap junctions and intercellular communication plays a key role in promotion, and promoters can be detected through this characteristic (Yamasaki 1990; Trosko and Goodman 1994).

As promoters are nongenotoxic substances, linear extrapolation for health-risk assessment seems unrealistic and, actually, scientifically improper (Kroes 1987; Williams and Weisburger 1991; Weisburger 1994). In order to better assess risk using appropriate epidemiological and biostatistical approaches, new procedures to define the mode of action of epigenetic (nongenotoxic) agents are being developed. Most likely, dose-response studies will yield a typical pharmacological S-shape response, with a definite no-effect level. This is especially important when fundamental insights into the properties of carcinogens and promoters are applied to the area of nutritional mechanisms in cancer causation.

Thus, chemical carcinogens can be classified into two main groups: (1) DNA-reactive substances that are genotoxic in appropriate test systems and (2) epigenetic (nongenotoxic) agents operating by producing some other specific biological effect as the basis for their carcinogenicity. Genotoxic carcinogens alter DNA, are mutagenic, and lead to transformed cells with neoplastic attributes. Nongenotoxic carcinogens involve other mechanisms, such as cytotoxicity, chronic tissue injury, hormonal imbalances, immunologic effects, or promotional activity.

Diet-Related Cancers

Several extensive reviews addressing diet-related neoplasms have been published in the past decades. In the Western world, cancers associated with nutrition account for a substantial percentage – about 35 to 45 percent – of premature deaths. In this section, characteristics of the different types of cancer, their established or suggested relationships with dietary factors, and their presumed mechanisms of action are described. In addition, possible measures to prevent or decrease the risk of developing the disease are discussed.[1]

Oral Cavity, Pharynx, and Esophagus

Cancers of the oral cavity and pharynx account for approximately 400,000 new cancer cases each year in the world. High incidences are noted in France, Switzerland, northern Italy, Central and South America, parts of Pakistan, and India. These cancers occur much more frequently in males than females, and differences between high- and low-incidence areas may be as much as 20-fold.

High-incidence rates of cancer of the esophagus are found in the so-called Asian esophageal cancer belt, which extends from eastern Iran, along the Caspian Sea, through Turkmenistan, Tajikistan, Uzbekistan, and Kyrgyzstan, and into parts of China. Except for the high-incidence areas, where the sex ratio almost equals 1:1, males show predominantly higher incidences. World incidence rates differ more than 100-fold, and globally more than 300,000 new cases occur each year.

Cancer of the esophagus is especially common among individuals who chew or smoke tobacco and drink alcoholic beverages. Consumption of alcohol alone – especially hard liquor – seems to be a risk factor as well (Seitz and Simanowski 1991; Castelleto et al. 1994). Smoking and alcohol consumption have a synergistic effect on carcinogenesis in the upper alimentary tract. In Asian and African populations, dietary deficiencies of zinc, riboflavin, vitamins A and C, manganese, and molybdenum may play a role, as well as mycotoxins, bracken fern, opium pyrolysates, and betel quids. The consumption of salted fish is an established risk factor in southern Chinese populations, probably because of the formation of specific nitrosamines (Craddock 1992; Zeng et al. 1993). Consumption of very hot beverages, along with the use of substances that irritate the oral cavity, pharynx, and esophagus, all of which lead to increased cell proliferation, may enhance the incidence of neoplasia.

However, substantial differences in incidence between high- and low-risk areas indicate that there exists considerable potential for prevention. Frequent consumption of fresh fruits and vegetables, as well as tea, appears to be associated with a lower risk for these types of cancer. The potential reduction has been estimated to be around 75 percent (Negri et al. 1993). Preventive measures involve the avoidance of tobacco and very hot beverages, along with moderate alcohol use and a well-balanced diet that includes a sizable increase in the regular consumption of vegetables and fruits (Block, Patterson, and Subar 1992).

Stomach
In the 1980s, gastric cancer was still considered to be the most common cancer in the world. Indeed, with almost 700,000 new cases per year, it represented approximately 10 percent of all cancers. Differences between high- and low-incidence areas vary by 40-fold. However, a large decrease in rates has occurred in most populations during the last four to five decades, indicating a reduction in exposure to tissue-specific carcinogens and/or the introduction of a protective agent.

Males suffer approximately twice the incidence and mortality of females, although the sex ratio is not constant by age group. The sex ratio equals 1:1 in people under the age of 30, but the disease is rare in this group. High-risk populations usually consume considerable quantities of pickled vegetables, dried salted fish, smoked fish, and other smoked, salted, and dried foods. Consumption of certain salted and pickled fish has yielded high levels of mutagenicity and evidence of carcinogenicity. One of the mutagens present has been identified as 2-chloro-4-methylthiobutanoic acid. This finding was totally unexpected, because in the past, nitroso compounds were associated with stomach cancer (Chen et al. 1995).

By contrast, a negative association has been established between mutagenicity and the regular intake of green leafy vegetables and citrus fruits. Laboratory experiments show that vitamins C and E block the formation of mutagens when fish is treated with nitrite, mimicking pickling (Weisburger 1991).

Infection with *Helicobacter pylori* and associated conditions, such as atrophic gastritis, ulceration, partial gastrectomy, bile acid reflux, and pernicious anemia, are additional risk factors. Several of these increase cell-duplication rates, rendering the gastric cells more sensitive to genotoxic carcinogens.

A high level of consumption of salted, pickled, or smoked food was once customary in the Western world. However, better access to home refrigeration, improved and cheaper transport – and, therefore, increased availability – of fresh fruit and vegetables seems to correlate well with the decline of this type of cancer (Howson, Hiyama, and Wynder 1986; Weisburger 1991). The relevant mechanism begins with the development of atrophic gastritis due to the cytotoxic activity of salt and vitamin deficiencies. The consequent decrease in gastric acidity permits uninhibited bacterial growth. Bacterial growth then converts dietary nitrates to nitrites, which are further metabolized into carcino-

genic nitroso derivatives or reactive carcinogens (Correa 1992; Chen et al. 1995). Because vitamins C and E are known to be effective inhibitors of nitrosation, it is plausible that an increased intake of these vitamins, or foods containing them, should reduce the risk of gastric cancer by inhibiting nitrosation.

Preventive measures are the introduction of food refrigeration, the reduction of salt and pickled food intake, and an increased consumption of fruits and vegetables. Especially in areas with high prevailing environmental nitrate levels, vitamin C and vitamin E supplementation may be useful for preventing formation of nitrite-derived reactive carcinogens and reducing nitrite produced by conversion of nitrate in the mouth. The preventive potential has been estimated to be about 50 percent but may well be much higher.

Colon and Rectum
Approximately 600,000 new cases of colorectal cancer are diagnosed worldwide each year. It is particularly a disease of the developed countries, which to some extent reflects increasing life expectancy. Differences in incidence may be 60-fold. The lowest incidence rates are found in Africa and Asia, although incidences are rising, especially in areas where the risk was formerly low, as in Japan. Colon cancer affects the sexes equally. The distribution for rectal cancer is similar to that for colon cancer. Incidences are usually lower, and there is a male–female ratio of 1.5:2.0, especially in high-incidence areas.

Epidemiological evidence suggests that (Western) lifestyle is an important determinant of risk for colorectal cancer: Migrants to Western countries acquire a higher risk for the disease in the first generation, and Mormons and Seventh Day Adventists enjoy a low risk. Familial polyposis, ulcerative colitis, and Crohn's disease are identified risk factors for colon cancer, but these are uncommon conditions.

Diets high in fats and low in fiber and vegetables are associated with increased risk for colon cancer. A fat–fiber interaction has been suggested, and the type of fiber is important as well (Kroes, Beems, and Bosland 1986; Weisburger 1992). It is interesting to note that some polyunsaturated fats found in fish and some vegetable seeds inhibit colon cancer formation. Moreover, olive oil intake, as in the Mediterranean countries, does not increase the risk of the nutritionally linked cancers or heart disease, a fact also documented in animal models (Reddy 1992). An inverse relationship has also been found for the consumption of fruits and vegetables, as well as for calcium intake and regular exercise; the same is true of coffee and tea for colon and rectal cancer, respectively (Baron, Gerhardson de Verdier, and Ekbom 1994).

Experimental and epidemiological research has revealed that bile acids promote cancer formation (Reddy 1992). The case is similar with alcohol, especially for rectal cancer, perhaps accounting for the higher male-to-female ratio (Seitz and Simanowski

1991). Recent surveys also indicate that intake of heavily fried or grilled meat and gravies is positively related to colorectal cancer, suggesting that chemicals produced during the frying or grilling of meats (heterocyclic aromatic amines) may be the initiating carcinogens, particularly for breast, colon, and, perhaps, prostate and pancreatic cancer (Adamson et al. 1995).

Suggested mechanisms in colon cancer development are the increased bile acid concentrations in individuals consuming high levels of many types of dietary fat. The higher concentrations of bile acids may lead to increased turnover of the epithelial cells of the intestines, reflecting increased risk of carcinogen–DNA adducts to cause translocation and amplification of abnormal genes or mutated tumor-suppressor genes. This phenomenon is inhibited by increased dietary calcium. The toxicity of bile acids is also reduced at a lower luminal pH. Alcohol may act as a promoter at the level of the rectum, and its metabolite acetaldehyde, which occurs at higher concentration in the rectum, may induce cytotoxicity, thus leading to increased cell proliferation and turnover.

Dietary fibers at adequate concentrations are thought to dilute and particularly bind the genotoxic agents present in the gut, decreasing fecal mutagenic activity. Fibers also modify the metabolic activity of the gut flora and lower luminal pH. Wheat bran increases the bulk of the gut contents, thus diluting bile acids and decreasing their adverse effect on the mucosal lining of the bowel (Reddy 1992). Regular physical exercise also lowers transit time of the luminal contents and appears to decrease risk of colorectal cancer. Fruits and vegetables generally reduce cancer risk through several mechanisms (Block et al. 1992). They provide fibers and antioxidants that can detoxify active genotoxins and also contain a number of chemopreventive agents, such as indole derivatives, that are anticarcinogenic. Tea antagonizes the effect of heterocyclic amines present in fried or broiled meats, which are thought to be carcinogens for the colon.

Potential reduction of colorectal cancers through prevention has been estimated at 35 percent, mainly of distal colon cancer and rectal cancer. The risk factors for proximal colon cancer are not well known, although general recommendations for lower risk may apply to colorectal cancer overall. This would involve a low fat intake (20 to 25 percent of calories), use of monounsaturated fats such as olive oil, an adequate fiber intake (25 to 30 g/day), moderate alcohol consumption (an average of 2 drinks/day), fish 2 to 3 times a week, an increased calcium (lowfat milk or yoghurt) intake (1,200 to 1,500 mg), increased consumption of vegetables and fruits (ideally 5 to 9 servings/day), tea (4 to 5 cups per day), and regular exercise.

Breast

Breast cancer is the third most common cancer in the world; every year about 600,000 new cases are detected, which is about 9 percent of the global cancer burden. It is important to distinguish between premenopausal breast cancer, in which diet plays a minor role (except for some protection afforded by consumption of vegetables and fruits, including soy products), and peri- and postmenopausal disease, in which diet may exert important controlling effects. Breast cancer occurs almost exclusively in women, and in high-risk areas (North America and western Europe), the incidence is about 4 to 30 times higher than in low-risk areas like China, Japan, and Sri Lanka, although there has been an appreciable increase in Japan during the last decade – the result of a westernization of dietary customs.

Important risk factors for breast cancer are a family history of the disease, a low number of offspring, avoidance of breast feeding of infants, a late age at first pregnancy, an early menarche, a late age at menopause, and high consumption of fats (about 30 to 40 percent of calories) and, possibly, alcohol. During the last decade, increasing evidence has been adduced indicating that there is an inverse relationship between breast cancer and increased intake of vegetables and fruits. Food antioxidants (such as selenium, retinoids, and polyphenols), as well as bran cereal fibers, have been suggested as inhibiting factors. Obviously, endocrine factors are important in breast cancer development. Fat may increase breast cancer risk by its control of hormonal regulation. In addition, high fat and high energy intakes, coupled with lack of exercise, lead to obesity, a possible contributory factor in breast cancer in postmenopausal women.

Obesity, however, seems inversely related to the risk of breast cancer in premenopausal women. F. De Waard has developed a unifying concept on the etiology of breast cancer, which focuses on the events that occur during adolescence and early reproductive ages (see Weisburger and Kroes 1994). He has suggested that preneoplastic lesions develop at early ages, from 15 years onward. Several factors, such as nutritional status, high fat intake, low consumption of protective vegetables, fruit, and fibers, along with reproductive life, interact in inducing a long period of cell proliferation without sufficient differentiation in the breast.

On the other hand, early pregnancy and long-term lactation will raise the differentiation of cells, thus limiting the proliferation of less differentiated cells, the latter being more vulnerable to genotoxic attack. Fat may also influence the immune system, increase prostaglandin synthesis, and increase membrane fluidity, all phenomena bearing on the promotion and growth of neoplastic cells. Therefore, the appropriate dietary preventive measures are avoidance of heavily fried or broiled meats, a limited fat intake (possibly as low as 20 to 25 percent of total calories), preference for monounsaturated fats such as olive oil, an increased intake of vegetables, fruits, tea, and insoluble bran cereal fiber, and an energy intake that balances energy need with the avoidance of obesity. In this latter connection, an increase of exercise has been shown to lower risk and assist in weight control.

Endometrium and Ovary

Endometrial cancer strikes approximately 150,000 women in the world each year, with tenfold differences in incidence, depending on location. High incidences are found in Argentina, the United States, Canada, and western Europe, whereas a low incidence has been noted in Asian populations. Identified risk factors are, in particular, endogenous estrogen and higher amounts of exogenous hormones employed for the management of menopausal and postmenopausal symptoms. Obesity and fat consumption are also associated with increased risk. Estrogen therapy, as practiced for postmenopausal symptoms between 1960 and 1975, has been documented as a causal element for endometrial cancer, most probably because it was given in relatively large dosages and was not balanced by progesterone. If the action of limited amounts of estrogens is balanced by progesterone, cancer risk is decreased.

The role of obesity or high fat consumption in endometrial cancer may be explained by the fact that fat cells produce estrogen, which itself is a key effector in neoplastic development through its specific effect on endometrial tissue and on overall endocrine balances. As dietary factors may be responsible for an appreciable percentage of cases, limited fat intake and avoidance of excessive energy intake are suggested preventive measures. Regular exercise, likewise, constitutes a protective element.

Ovarian cancer is common in western Europe and North America, whereas it has a low frequency in Indian, Japanese, and other Asian populations. Unlike that of many other types of cancer, the incidence of ovarian cancer in the Western world has remained rather constant over time. The risk factors for ovarian cancer are the same as those for breast and uterine cancer, meaning a positive association with endocrine factors and dietary fat intake and a negative association with parity and elements that suppress ovulation. Thus, oral contraceptives may substantially reduce the risk of ovarian cancer. Limited fat intake (perhaps 20 to 25 percent of calories or less) and consumption of vegetables and fruits are suggested as preventive measures.

Pancreas

Pancreatic cancer occurs more frequently in developed countries, comprising approximately 3 percent of the worldwide cancer burden. The disease, however, is increasing in incidence over time and has a very high mortality rate because of late diagnosis and, thus, has low success in therapy. Every year, approximately 140,000 new cases are diagnosed. In the last 40 years, pancreatic cancer incidence has doubled in western Europe and quadrupled in Japan (Hirayama 1989).

Tobacco smoking has been implicated as a major risk factor, which can explain the increasing incidence, especially in those countries where the pancreatic cancer incidence is still relatively low. Convincing evidence also exists from experimental animal research that carcinogens from tobacco and a high fat intake are positively related, whereas caloric restriction, selenium, and retinoids are inversely related. Of interest is the role shown by trypsin inhibitors in pancreatic carcinogenesis in experimental animals. These trypsin inhibitors do reduce trypsin levels in the gut, stimulating the secretion of cholecystokinin (CCK) as a feedback phenomenon. CCK stimulates pancreatic growth, thus promoting pancreatic carcinogenesis. Trypsin inhibitors, present in soy proteins, are heat labile. Soy proteins are high-quality foods, but they should be incorporated in foods and cooked (Watanapa and Williamson 1993).

Epidemiological research reveals a positive relationship for dietary fat, fried or grilled meats, and, possibly, alcohol or cholesterol, whereas an inverse relationship has been observed for caloric restriction, omega-3 fatty acids (fish and some seeds like flax seed), and fresh fruits and vegetables (Bueno de Mesquita 1992). Preventive potential has been estimated to be 70 percent. Cessation of tobacco smoking, moderate alcohol use, low fat consumption, and increased intake of vegetables and fruits are the main measures for prevention. This is particularly important because of its grim prognosis. Thus, control is optimal through prevention by lifestyle adjustment.

Prostate

Prostate cancer is the fifth most common cancer among males, and especially predominant in older males. Approximately 240,000 new cases of clinical invasive prostate cancer occur each year, and high-incidence areas are northwestern Europe and North America; in the latter, African-Americans have a particularly high incidence. Low rates are found in India, China, and Japan. There exists a 50-fold difference between populations with the highest rates of prostate cancer (blacks in Detroit, Michigan) and populations with the lowest incidence (Asians in Shanghai, China) (Nomura and Kolonel 1991). Endocrine factors may play a role in prostate carcinogenesis, but geographic pathology indicates that dietary factors are probably also important. Populations with a tradition of high fat and high protein intake have a high risk. The diet controls the endocrine balance.

Negative associations have been suggested for vitamin A, beta-carotene, vegetables, fruits, selenium, fish, and fiber. Sugar and egg consumption are weakly positive (Bosland 1986). Genetic, sexual, and dietary factors seem to play a role in prostate carcinogenesis, indicating a multifactorial process. As is true for other endocrine-controlled neoplasms, a dietary regime low in fat and rich in vegetables and fruits, coupled with regular exercise, may contribute to lower risk irrespective of sexual and genetic elements (Wynder, Rose, and Cohen 1994).

Lung

It is surprising to note that more and more data have become available to indicate that lung cancer is influenced by dietary factors. Clearly, the disease is associated with cigarette smoking, but since E. Bjelke (1975) and G. Kvale, Bjelke, and J. J. Gart (1983) found in metabolic epidemiological studies that smokers with a higher level of vitamin A in plasma had a lower risk of lung cancer, more attention has been given to dietary factors (Ziegler et al. 1992; Le Marchand et al. 1993). Also, for humans, an inverse relationship between lung cancer development and fruit and vegetable intake has been observed, whereas other data suggest a positive relationship between dietary fat intake and lung cancer (Wynder, Taioli, and Fujita 1992). In addition, the antioxidants in tea may provide a protective effect. Currently, there are more smokers in Japan than in the United States or the United Kingdom, but the incidence of lung cancer is lower in Japan. It has been suggested that the Japanese have a lower risk because of a lower total fat intake and more frequent intake of fish, soy foods, and tea.

Therefore, although the first recommendation should be to quit smoking – or, in fact, never to start – an increased intake of fruits and vegetables (especially those containing retinoids) and also of fish, soy-derived foods, and tea, coupled with a lowered fat consumption, may serve as preventive measures and could be particularly appropriate for ex-smokers.

Food Additives, Contaminants, and Natural Toxins

For decades, the possibility of cancer risks from food additives and contaminants has been widely publicized, especially in the developed countries, where there has been an increase in the addition of various substances to food for preservative and commercial purposes. Thus, food additives and contaminants are viewed by many as a major threat to human health – and one that may cause cancer. Scientific information, however, shows exactly the opposite: Food additives are safer than everyday traditional nutrients, and the same is true for most contaminants (Miller 1992; Weisburger 1994; Weisburger and Kroes 1994).

Such opposite perceptions may be explained by the misinterpretation of epidemiological reports in the late sixties, when the term "environmental" (as in "environmental factors") was used to account for major causes of cancer. In fact, what was meant was as lifestyle factors, but the general public (and especially the news media) misinterpreted this to mean synthetic chemicals, including food additives and contaminants.

In addition, several episodes have enhanced this misconception, as, for example, when certain food additives (that is, some food dyes in Western countries and the preservative AF-2 in Japan) were first permitted and later correctly withdrawn because of their demonstrated carcinogenicity in animals (Sugimura 1992). Regulatory action, especially in the United States, aimed at such chemicals as sodium saccharin and cyclamate, further deepened public suspicion. Yet the latter substances are now considered safe, at least at the normal intake levels that humans experience. In fact, certain substances with antioxidant properties, which are used as food additives, are even believed to reduce cancer risk. Thus, Wynder and Gori (1977), as well as Doll and Peto (1981), have estimated that cancer mortality from food additives ranges from –5 to +2 percent, the negative score specifically addressing the beneficial aspects of antioxidants used in foods.

Additives are used to improve the stability and storability of foods, as well as their flavor, consistency, appearance, texture, and nutritional quality. In certain cases, they are a necessity, such as in the case of preservatives that prevent food-borne microbial infections. And in any event, the risk of disease from food additives today is minimal, because efficient and effective control practices are available and applied to ensure safety.

Contaminants of human-made origin are, like food additives, extensively tested in animals before use, and the levels permissible in crops are well controlled internationally. Thus, the margin of safety for pesticide residues in food runs usually between 1,000 and several millions, whereas for several macro- and micronutrients, the margin of safety is as small as 2 to 10 (Kroes in press). In fact, B. N. Ames and colleagues (1990, 1992) have listed a number of naturally occurring substances in food that, because of uncontrolled exposure, provide much more concern for cancer risk than synthetic chemicals. About half of such natural chemicals that have undergone standard high-dose animal cancer tests proved to be animal carcinogens, such as the mold-generated hepatic carcinogen, aflatoxin (International Agency for Research on Cancer 1993b). In addition, as noted, powerful carcinogens are formed during the cooking of meats and during the salting and pickling of some fish and meats.

The natural defenses of humans, however, may make them capable of detoxifying low doses of most toxins, whether synthetic or natural. For example, despite a continuing low-level presence of aflatoxin B_1 in some foods, the incidence of primary liver cancer in the United States and Europe is not significant. Yet it is quite high in parts of Africa and China, where the dietary contamination is appreciable and where more people carry the hepatitis B antigen, potentiating the action.

Certainly, in light of the foregoing, it seems relevant to invest more research capacity in the identification of possible risks and benefits of naturally occurring substances. This is especially true because many are also known to possess anticarcinogenic properties – properties that are believed to be the reason for the inverse relationship between several cancers (and heart diseases) and the regular intake of vegetables, fruits, and tea.

Food preparation has entailed cancer risk in the past and will continue to do so in the future. Preservation methods, for example, such as the use of salt or pickling solutions, are associated with a high risk of stomach cancer and in some areas, such as China, with cancer of the esophagus. Salted fish causes nasopharyngeal cancer, and salt and high nitrate (saltpeter) concentrations in several meat products can lead to the formation of carcinogenic nitroso compounds, or of the chloro analog of methionine, either in the food itself or in the stomach. Salt is cytotoxic to the gastric mucosa, translated by increased cell duplication rates and, in turn, to more efficient carcinogenesis. Some salted, pickled foods contain direct-acting mutagens thought to be gastric carcinogens (Weisburger 1992; Chen et al. 1995). Salt, not balanced by potassium from vegetables, and calcium from dairy products is also a cause of hypertension and stroke. In Japan (Sugimura 1992) and in Belgium (Joossens, Hill, and Geboers 1985), formal plans were introduced to lower salt intake by people.

Charcoal-broiled meats or fish have at their surface polycyclic aromatic hydrocarbons that are established animal carcinogens. But it is important to note that the ordinary cooking (broiling, frying) of meats or fish can produce powerful mutagens, consisting of about 19 heterocyclic amines (also established animal carcinogens) for specific target organs. They are believed to be the key carcinogens causing increased incidence of several human cancers, such as those in the breast, prostate, colon, and pancreas. Certainly it has been shown that those who generally eat well-done meat increase their risk of colon cancer. The formation of heterocyclic amines during the heating of meats can be reduced by preliminary brief microwave cooking (removing essential creatinine) or by the addition of antioxidants, soy protein, or the indole amino acids tryptophan and proline, which all compete with creatinine in the so-called Maillard reaction, forming heterocyclic amines (Weisburger and Kroes 1994).

Prevention: An Integrated Approach

A substantial amount of solid epidemiological and experimental evidence indicates that the majority of human cancers, and indeed many other chronic diseases, such as heart disease, hypertension, and adult-onset diabetes, are largely preventable. Complex causes have been, or are being, identified, and the underlying mechanisms elucidated. Control of many major diseases of humankind in the past, such as scurvy, pellagra, rickets, polio, smallpox, rabies, and

tuberculosis, has been achieved by prevention strategies. Therefore, a clear and balanced prevention approach to the effective control of human cancers (and other chronic illnesses, such as cardiovascular diseases) is likely to be successful as well.

Experience in the past two decades with other chronic ailments, such as cardiovascular diseases, indicates that the application of sometimes even simple measures can have a considerable impact on their outcome (Meyskens 1992). In fact, cancer prevention runs a decade behind the scientific understanding of the disease, as a number of lifestyle-associated factors contributing significantly to cancer risk are well known. Tobacco and nutritional traditions, in particular, and – to a lesser extent – radiation, some chemicals, and certain viruses, are documented, avoidable risk factors.

Wynder and Gori (1977), Doll and Peto (1981), and J. H. Weisburger (1992) have contributed substantially to the evidence of preventive potential for many types of cancer through their listing and documentation of avoidable risks of cancer. Unfortunately, not only are such concrete factors as tobacco, diet, lifestyle, and radiation contributing to the cancer burden, but poverty does as well, because the need for essential lifestyle changes has been difficult to communicate effectively to the lower socioeconomic groups (Tomatis 1992).

Cancer prevention programs should be based on reliable epidemiological and laboratory evidence, and on ethical and moral responsibility, and ought to specify clearly achievable outcomes in mortality and morbidity reduction. Moreover, they should be integrated with other chronic-disease-prevention programs. The multifactorial elements, such as nutritional traditions, sedentary habits, and tobacco use, which represent a risk for diseases like coronary heart disease, hypertension, stroke, obesity, and many neoplastic diseases, have to do with lifestyle. In fact, these factors are the *major causes and modulators of these diseases.*

Table IV.F.2.1 depicts several realistic actions to take in order to lower the risk for certain common diseases. In the Western world, nutritional traditions with a relatively high fat intake (38 to 46 percent of energy intake), low cereal fiber, and low vegetable and fruit consumption, along with a lack of regular physical exercise, are associated with high incidence and high cost of the management of chronic diseases, such as cardiovascular diseases, diabetes, obesity, and specific types of cancer. In the Far East and in Central and South America, prevailing illnesses seem to stem from other nutritional traditions, such as the use of highly salted and pickled foods and a limited variety in diet. Currently, the changing nutritional habits in Japan to a Western style parallel an increase in heart disease and the kind of cancers common in the Western world. This provides strong additional support for the thesis that dietary customs and specific chronic diseases are related.

Today's knowledge enables us to recommend a healthy dietary regime in which fats should be

Table IV.F.2.1. *Chronic disease prevention and health promotion*

Action	Lower risk
1. Quit smoking or use a low-tar and nicotine cigarette.	Coronary heart disease; cancers of the lung, oropharynx, kidney, bladder, pancreas, cervix
2. Quit chewing tobacco or snuff dipping.	Cancer of oral cavity, esophagus
3. Lower the fat intake to at least 20–30% of energy (calorie) intake, preferably lower (15–20%).	Coronary heart disease; cancers of the distal colon, postmenopausal breast, prostate, pancreas, ovary, endometrium
4. Limit protein intake to 10–15% of calories; include vegetable proteins.	Colon cancer, kidney diseases, aging
5. Increase vegetables and fruits considerably (ideally 5–9 servings); provide sufficient essential micronutrients.	Most chronic diseases, aging
6. Increase fiber, soluble as well as insoluble (1:1), to 25–35 grams.	Cancer of colon, breast; constipation, diverticulosis, appendicitis
7. Increase Ca^{2+} intake (skim milk, yoghurt, some vegetables, sardines).	Cancer of colon, osteoporosis
8. Reduce intake of heavily fried or grilled foods, especially meats and gravies.	Cancers of colon, breast, pancreas; heart disease
9. Avoid pickled, smoked, and salted foods.	Cancer of stomach, esophagus, nasopharynx, liver; hypertension, stroke
10. Lower salt Na^+ intake; balance $K^+ + Ca^{++}/Na^+$ ratio.	Hypertension, stroke, cardiovascular disease
11. Have regular moderate exercise.	Coronary heart disease; cancer of the colon, breast; aging
12. Maintain proper weight; avoid obesity.	Coronary heart disease; cancer of the endometrium and kidneys; postmenopausal breast cancer; diabetes
13. Moderate use of alcoholic beverages.	Liver cirrhosis, liver cancer, cardiomyopathy, male impotence, oropharyngeal and esophageal cancer
14. Practice sexual hygiene.	Cancer of the cervix, penis; AIDS
15. Moderate sun exposure.	Skin cancer, melanoma, skin aging

replaced by complex carbohydrates (starches) that should provide around 70 to 75 percent of the calories needed for energy. Furthermore, a protein intake of between 10 to 15 percent from animal and vegetable sources (more in growing young children, less in older individuals) is recommended. Fats should consist of a fair proportion of monounsaturated oils, such as olive oil or canola oil, and omega-3 fatty acids as found in fish and some seeds, like flaxseed.

Excessive salting, pickling, and smoking of food as a mode of preservation should, ideally, be abandoned, and foods should be preserved by refrigeration or freezing, or eaten fresh. Caloric intake should be equal to energy need as an effective means to avoid obesity. The intake of fruits and vegetables should be increased considerably – ideally to more than 5 servings per day. Bran cereal fibers, or breads baked with high-fiber flour, increase stool bulk, avoid constipation, and lower the risk of colon and breast cancer and perhaps other diseases. A low intake of total salt, 3g/day or less, and adequate calcium (1,000 to 1,500 mg) and magnesium (300 mg) are beneficial; less is needed on a low-protein diet. Moderate, but regular, physical exercise is also part of a healthy lifestyle. Alcohol consumption ought to be moderate, but adequate fluid intake (2 to 2.5 liters daily for adults) is essential for maintenance of physiologic functions. Tea, an extract of the plant *Camellia sinensis*, is, after water, the second-most-used beverage in the world. Because it is made with boiling water, it is sterile even if the water source is not pure. Tea is rich in fluoride, potassium, and espe-

cially in antioxidants that lower the risk of coronary heart disease and many types of cancer (Weisburger 1996; Weisburger and Comer this volume).

These recommendations will contribute to better health by lowering the risk for major chronic diseases. In education and in medical practice, emphasis must be placed on the importance and the efficacy of available methods for chronic disease prevention. One task of practicing nutritionists and home economists ought to be that of devising practical recipes for cooks to incorporate the essence of a new, health-promoting lifestyle that the public will find attractive. Indeed, it is essential to devise appealing dishes and drinks for the public that are also designed for chronic disease prevention, and when such preventive approaches are successful, health-care costs should decrease. Good health into old age is not only a desirable goal for the individual but may have major economic savings for the population at large. To repeat our earlier quotation, the ultimate goal, as expressed by Ernst Wynder, should be "to die young, as late in life as possible" (Wynder et al. 1994).

Robert Kroes
J. H. Weisburger

Research in Weisburger's laboratory is supported by USPHS-NIH grants and contracts from the National Cancer Institute, grants from the Tea Trade Health Research Association and the American Cancer Society, and gifts from Texaco, Inc., and the Friends Against Cancer Team.

Note

1. For ease of reading, only specific references have been inserted. Our discussion has been based mainly on these publications: National Research Council 1982; Dutch Nutrition Council 1986; Kroes 1986; Reddy and Cohen 1986; U.S. Public Health Service 1988; Committee on Diet and Health, Food and Nutrition Board 1989; International Agency for Research on Cancer 1990, 1993a; Weisburger 1991, 1992; Weisburger and Kroes 1994; Levi, Lucchini, and La Vecchia 1994.

Bibliography

Adamson, R. H., J. A. Gustafsson, N. Ito, et al. 1995. Heterocyclic amines in cooked foods. *Proceedings of the 23rd International Symposium of the Princess Takamatsu Cancer Research Fund.* Princeton, N.J.

Ames, B. N., and L. S. Gold. 1992. Animal cancer tests and cancer prevention. *Journal of the National Cancer Institute Monographs,* no. 12: 125-32.

Ames, B. N., M. Profet, and L. S. Gold. 1990. Nature's chemicals and synthetic chemicals: Comparative toxicology. *Proceedings of the National Academy of Sciences* 87: 7782-6.

Baron, J. A., M. Gerhardson de Verdier, and A. Ekbom. 1994. Coffee, tea, tobacco, and cancer of the large bowel. *Cancer Epidemiology, Biomarkers, Prevention* 3: 565-70.

Bjelke, E. 1975. Dietary vitamin A and human lung cancer. *International Journal of Cancer* 15: 561-5.

Block, G., B. Patterson, and A. Subar. 1992. Fruit, vegetables and cancer prevention: A review of the epidemiological evidence. *Nutrition and Cancer* 18: 1-29.

Bosland, M. C. 1986. Diet and cancer of the prostate: Epidemiologic and experimental evidence. In *Diet, nutrition, and cancer: A critical evaluation,* Vol. 1, ed. B. S. Reddy and L. A. Cohen, 125-49. Boca Raton, Fla.

Brugge, J., T. Cuppan, E. Harlow, and F. McCormick. 1991. *Origins of human cancer; a comprehensive review.* Plainview, N.Y.

Bueno de Mesquita, H. B. 1992. On the causation of cancer of the exocrine pancreas; a population based case-control study in the Netherlands. Thesis, University of Utrecht.

Castelleto, R., X. Castellsague, M. Muñoz, et al. 1994. Alcohol, tobacco, mate drinking and esophageal cancer in Argentina. *Cancer Epidemiology, Biomarkers, Prevention* 3: 357-64.

Chen, W., J. H. Weisburger, E. S. Fiala, et al. 1995. 2-Chloro-4-Methylthiobutanoic acid, a newly identified mutagen in salt, nitrite-treated fish. *Nature* 374: 599.

Cohen, S. M., and L. B. Ellwein. 1992. Risk assessment based on high dose animal exposure experiments. *Chemical Research in Toxicology* 5: 742-8.

Committee on Diet and Health, Food and Nutrition Board. 1989. *Diet and health: Implication for reducing chronic disease risk.* Washington, D.C.

Correa, P. 1992. Human gastric carcinogenesis: A multistep and multifactorial process. First American Cancer Society Award Lecture on Cancer Epidemiology and Prevention. *Cancer Research* 52: 6735-40.

Craddock, V. M. 1992. Aetiology of oesophageal cancer: Some operative factors. *European Journal of Cancer Prevention* 1: 89-103.

Davidson, M. K., I. K. Davis, and J. R. Lindsey. 1987. Requirement and selection of an animal model. *International Journal of Medical Sciences* 23: 551-5.

Doll R., and R. Peto. 1981. The causes of cancer: Quantitative estimate of avoidable risks of cancer in the United States today. *Journal of The National Cancer Institute* 66: 1191-308.

Dutch Nutrition Council. 1986. Factoren in de voeding en het ontstaan van kanker (Dietary factors in relation to the causation of cancer). *Dutch Nutrition Council Report.* The Hague.

Echols, M., and M. F. Goodman. 1991. Fidelity mechanisms in DNA replication. *Annual Review of Biochemistry* 60: 477-511.

Galloway, D. J. 1989. Animal models in the study of colorectal cancer. *Cancer Surveys* 8: 170-88.

Harris, E. D. 1991. Regulation of anti-oxidant enzymes. *Federation of American Societies for Experimental Biology Journal* 6: 2675-83.

Highman, B., M. J. Norvell, and T. E. Shellenberg. 1977. Pathological changes in female C_3H mice continuously fed diets containing diethylstilbestrol or 17-beta-estradiol. *Journal of Environmental Pathology and Toxicology* 1: 1-30.

Hirayama, T. 1989. Epidemiology of pancreatic cancer in Japan. *Japanese Journal of Clinical Oncology* 19: 208-15.

Howson, C. P., T. Hiyama, and E. L. Wynder. 1986. Decline of gastric cancer: Epidemiology of an unplanned triumph. *Epidemiology Reviews* 8: 1-27.

International Agency for Research on Cancer. 1990. Cancer: Causes, occurrence and control. *International Agency for Research on Cancer Scientific Publication no. 100.* Lyon.

    1993. Some naturally occurring substances, food items and constituents, heterocyclic aromatic amines and mycotoxins. *Monographs on the evaluation of carcinogenic risk to humans, no. 56.* Lyon.

Joossens, J. V., M. J. Hill, and J. Geboers, eds. 1985. *Diet and human carcinogenesis.* Amsterdam.

Kroes, R. 1979. Animal data, interpretation and consequences. In *Environmental carcinogenesis,* ed. P. Emmelot and E. Kriek, 287-302. Amsterdam.

    1986. Diet in relation to cancer. In *New concepts and developments in toxicology,* ed. P. L. Chambers, P. Gehring, and F. Sakai, 91-105. New York.

    1987. Contribution of toxicology towards risk assessment of carcinogens. *Archives of Toxicology* 60: 224-8.

    In press. *Risk assessment: Past, present and future.* Proceedings of the 2d Princess Chulabhorn Science Congress. Thailand.

Kroes, R., R. B. Beems, M. C. Bosland, et al. 1986. Nutritional factors in lung, colon and prostate carcinogenesis in animal models. *Federation Proceedings* 45: 136-41.

Kvale, G., E. Bjelke, and J. J. Gart. 1983. Dietary habits and lung cancer risk. *International Journal of Cancer* 31: 397-405.

Land, C. E., J. D. Boice, C. E. Shore, et al. 1980. Breast cancer risk from low dose exposure to ionizing radiation: Results of parallel analysis of three exposed populations of women. *Journal of the National Cancer Institute* 65: 353-76.

Le Marchand, L., J. H. Hankin, L. N. Kolonel, et al. 1993. Intake of specific carotenoids and lung cancer risk. *Cancer Epidemiology, Biomarkers, Prevention* 2: 183-7.

Levi, F., F. Lucchini, and C. La Vecchia. 1994. Worldwide patterns of cancer mortality, 1985-1989. *European Journal of Cancer Prevention* 3: 109-43.

Liehr, J. G. 1990. Genotoxic effects of estrogens. *Mutation Research* 238: 269-76.

Meyskens, F. L. 1992. Strategies for prevention of cancer in humans. *Oncology* 6 (supplement): 15-24.

Miller, S. A. 1992. Food additives and contaminants. In *Toxicology: The basic science of poisons.* Fourth edition, ed. L. J. Casarett and J. Doull, 819-53. New York.

1994. A brief history of chemical carcinogenesis. *Cancer Letters* 83: 9-14.

National Research Council. 1982. *Diet, nutrition, and cancer.* Washington, D.C.

Negri, E., C. La Vecchia, S. Franceschi, and A. Tavani. 1993. Attributable risk for oral cancer in northern Italy. *Cancer Epidemiology, Biomarkers, Prevention* 2: 189-93.

Nomura, A. M. Y., and L. N. Kolonel. 1991. Prostate cancer: A current perspective. *American Journal of Epidemiology* 13: 200-27.

Olson, J. A., and S. Kobayashi. 1992. Antioxidants in health and disease: An overview. *Proceedings of the Society for Experimental Biology and Medicine* 200: 245-7.

Packer, L. 1992. Interactions among antioxidants in health and disease: Vitamin E and its redox cycle (43433). *Proceedings of the Society for Experimental Biology and Medicine* 200: 271-6.

Parkin, D. M. 1993. Studies of cancer in migrant populations. In *Cancer in Italian migrant populations,* eds. M. Geddels, D. M. Parkin, and M. Khlat et al. Lyon: International Agency for Research on Cancer, Scientific Publication no. 123, 1-10.

Randerath, K., E. Randerath, T. F. Danna, et al. 1989. A new sensitive ^{32}P-postlabeling assay based on the specific enzymatic conversion of bulky DNA lesions to radiolabeled dinucleotides and nucleoside 5'-monophosphates. *Carcinogenesis* 10: 1231-9.

Reddy, B. S. 1992. Animal experimental evidence on macronutrients and cancer. In *Macronutrients: Investigating their role in cancer,* ed. M. S. Micozzi and T. M. Moon, 33-54. New York.

Reddy, B. S., and L. A. Cohen. 1986. Diet, nutrition, and cancer: A critical evaluation. In *Macronutrients and cancer,* Vol. 1. Boca Raton, Fla.

Ronai, Z. 1992. Ras oncogene detection in preneoplastic lesions: Possible applications for diagnosis and prevention (Review). *Oncology Research* 4: 45-8.

Sai, K., T. Umemura, A. Tagaji, et al. 1992. The protective role of glutathione, cysteine and vitamin C against oxidative DNA damage induced in rat kidney by potassium bromate. *Japanese Journal of Cancer Research* 83: 45-51.

Seitz, H., and U. A. Simanowski. 1991. Alcohol and cancer: A critical review. In *Alcoholism: A molecular perspective,* ed. T. N. Palmer, 275-96. New York.

Sugimura, T. 1992. Multistep carcinogenesis: A 1992 perspective. *Science* 258: 603-7.

Tannenbaum, A. 1942a. The genesis and growth of tumors: II. Effects of caloric restriction per se. *Cancer Research* 2: 460-7.

1942b. The genesis and growth of tumors: III. Effect of a high fat diet. *Cancer Research* 2: 468-74.

Tannenbaum, A., and H. Silverstone. 1953. Nutrition in relation to cancer. *Advances in Cancer Research* 1: 453.

Tomatis, L. 1992. Poverty and cancer. *Cancer Epidemiology, Biomarkers, Prevention* 1: 167-75.

Trosko, J. E., and J. I. Goodman. 1994. Intercellular communication may facilitate apoptosis: Implications for tumor promotion (Review). *Molecular Carcinogenesis* 11: 8-12.

U.S. Public Health Service. 1988. *The Surgeon General's Report on Nutrition and Health, Department of Health and Human Services (Public Health Service) Publication no. 88-50210.* Washington, D.C.

Watanapa, P., and R. C. N. Williamson. 1993. Experimental pancreatic hyperplasia and neoplasia: Effects of dietary and surgical manipulation. *British Journal of Cancer* 67: 877-84.

Weisburger, J. H. 1991. Nutritional approach to cancer prevention with emphasis on vitamins, antioxidants and carcinogens. *American Journal of Clinical Nutrition* 53: 226-37.

1992. Mechanisms of macronutrient carcinogenesis. In *Macronutrients: Investigating their role in cancer,* ed. M. Dekker, M. S. Micozzi, and T. E. Moon, 3-31. New York.

1994. Commentary. Does the Delaney Clause of the U.S. Food and Drug Laws prevent human cancers? *Fundamental and Applied Toxicology* 22: 483-93.

1996. Tea antioxidants and health. In *Handbook of Antioxidants,* eds. Enrique Cajenas and Lester Packer. New York. 469-86.

Weisburger, J. H., and R. Kroes. 1994. Mechanisms in nutrition and cancer. Meeting report. *European Journal of Cancer Prevention* 3: 293-8.

Weisburger, J. H., and G. Williams. 1991. Critical effective methods to detect genotoxic carcinogens and neoplasm promoting agents. *Environmental Health Perspectives* 90: 121-6.

Williams, G. M., and J. H. Weisburger. 1991. Chemical carcinogens. In *Casarett and Doull's toxicology.* Fourth edition, ed. M. V. Amdur, J. Doull, and C. D. Klaassen, 127-200. New York.

World Cancer Research Fund. 1997. *Food, nutrition, and the prevention of cancer: A global perspective.* Washington, D.C.

Wynder, E. L., and G. B. Gori. 1977. Contribution of the environment to cancer incidence: An epidemiologic exercise. *Journal of the National Cancer Institute* 58: 825-32.

Wynder, E. L., J. A. Peters, and S. Vivona, eds. 1975. Nutrition in the causation of cancer, a symposium. *Cancer Research* 35: 3231-35.

Wynder, E. L., O. P. Rose, and L. A. Cohen. 1994. Nutrition and prostate cancer: A proposal for dietary intervention. *Nutrition and Cancer* 22: 1-10.

Wynder, E. L., E. Taioli, and Y. Fujita. 1992. Ecologic study of lung cancer risk factors in the U.S. and Japan with special reference to smoking and diet. *Japanese Cancer Research* 83: 418-23.

Yamasaki, H. 1990. Gap junctional intercellular communication and carcinogenesis. *Carcinogenesis* 11: 1051-8.

Zeng, Y., H. Oshima, G. Bouvier, et al. 1993. Urinary excretion of nitrosamino acids and nitrite by inhabitants of high and low risk areas for nasopharyngeal carcinoma in southern China. *Cancer Epidemiology, Biomarkers, Prevention* 2: 195-200.

Ziegler, R. G., A. F. Subar, N. E. Craft, et al. 1992. Does beta-carotene explain why reduced cancer risk is associated with vegetable and fruit intake? *Cancer Research* 52: 2060-6.

IV.F.3 ℞ Nutrition and Heart-Related Diseases

...When we have stuffed
These pipes and those conveyances of our blood
With wine and feeding ...

(Allbutt 1915: 239, citing Traube)

Over the course of the twentieth century, cardiovascular disease (CVD) has become the leading cause of death in the United States. CVD is also a significant cause of morbidity and mortality in many other industrialized countries and regions, such as Scandinavia, the United Kingdom, Australia, and Canada. Most CVD is manifested as coronary artery disease (CAD), usually based on atherosclerosis. This "epidemic" of CVD has been attributed to the poor lifestyle habits of members of late-twentieth-century industrialized, urban society, who smoke tobacco, exercise rarely, and indulge in fat-laden diets (Kannel 1987).

A striking similarity of these factors leading to disease is that each – in most cases – can be modified by an individual at risk for coronary disease, even without professional guidance and in the absence of public health initiatives. But risk factors are not always easily eliminated. Addiction to tobacco is difficult to overcome. Exercise may be problematic for some people, given constraints on time posed by other obligations. Everyone, however, must eat, and perhaps for this reason, of all the possible causes of heart-related diseases, diet has received the most attention.

This chapter explores the relationship between nutrition and heart-related diseases by describing selected nutrients that have been implicated in the pathogenesis, prevention, or treatment of CAD. Most of the available data come from population studies. It appears unlikely that any single nutrient will soon be identified as the specific dietary agent that causes atherosclerotic diseases. Moreover, any individual nutrient is but a small part of a larger group of chemicals that make up any particular "food." As of this writing, the overall relationship between diet and heart disease remains obscure. It will require many years of medical, nutritional, and food science research before we can hope to weave into a meaningful tapestry all of the puzzling threads of nutritional biochemistry and CAD pathophysiology.

Pathogenesis of Atherosclerosis

In the middle of the nineteenth century, it was discovered that lipids constituted a major component of atherosclerotic plaque (Vogel 1847). This observation led investigators to wonder how this lipid collection was formed and how it might be related to disease. They noted that when people with CAD died, examination of the vessels that supply blood to the heart (the coronary arterial endothelium) revealed greasy, yellow "plaques" adhering to the endothelial cells. These plaques varied in thickness and composition, reflecting both the age of the subjects and the severity of their disease. A few decades into the twentieth century it was widely recognized that CAD lesions were due to atherosclerosis, with cell death within the lesion (Leary 1935). Additional clues to disease severity – and the longevity of the disease process – were later found in the presence of blood substances, such as lipids and macrophages, and in structural damage to the surrounding endothelium.

Noting precisely which endothelium is diseased

may provide clues to the disease process. Although CAD is often conceptualized as a systemic disease, the location of atherosclerotic lesions is not random, nor are they necessarily "systemic." Some areas of the blood vessels are more "lesion-prone" than others, and these sections differ structurally and functionally from "non-lesion-prone" sites (Schwartz, Valente, and Sprague 1993). Lesion-prone sites are more permeable to substances that lead to the development of CAD. Any adequate explanation of the disease process must explain these morphological and topographical features.

Although autopsy findings may serve to document an underlying disease process, they represent only one moment in the lifetime of the affected individual and cannot alone explain the natural history of the disease. One approach to understanding the disease process is to conduct experiments using an animal that exhibits a similar set of lesions. In 1943, D. V. Dawber and L. N. Katz studied chickens that developed atheromata and suggested that their findings might be relevant to spontaneous disease (Dawber and Katz 1943).

Pigs also provide a useful model for studying human atherosclerotic CAD – a model used to good effect by investigators in the 1960s and early 1970s. When pigs were fed a low-fat, cholesterol-free diet, researchers initially noted a degeneration of smooth muscle cells. As the pigs aged, the degenerated smooth muscle cells accumulated and caused intimal thickening. If there was no injury to the blood vessel during this thickening stage, the pigs experienced no disruption of the endothelium of the artery. However, if the investigators mechanically injured the endothelium, intimal thickening progressed to form a more substantial plaque – one that could impede blood flow within the artery.

This early plaque contained not only degenerated smooth muscle cells but also collagen, a fibrous tissue that made the plaque less compliant. Plaque thickening could be further accelerated (in concert with mechanical injury) with dietary factors, including oxidized sterols, such as vitamin D_3 and 25-hydroxy cholesterol (a derivative of pure cholesterol). In advanced stages of atherosclerosis, lipid infiltrated the plaque. Other factors were found to influence development of the lesion. As the vessel lumen narrowed during plaque development, reduced blood flow through the area reduced oxygen delivery to the structures supplied by that blood vessel, and the hypoxemia thus produced sped up lipid accumulation in the plaque. As the plaque continued to thicken, the endothelium was stretched thin, sometimes thin enough to rupture.

The gap left by this process was then vulnerable to infiltration by lipoproteins. In animals that did not have the intimal injury, there was no progression past the intimal thickening. When investigators used electron microscopy to compare the experimentally induced atherosclerotic vessels of the mature pig with those obtained from a human who had undergone open heart surgery for CAD, they could detect no histological differences.

These animal studies were vital to our present understanding of the atherosclerotic process in humans. Recent research supports the concept that the arterial endothelium must sustain a mechanical injury to begin the process of pathologically significant plaque formation. Other blood components now known to be involved in this process are monocytes, platelets, and lipid–protein complexes, such as low-density lipoprotein (LDL) and lipoprotein(a). Also part of the process of plaque formation are chemical mediators, such as adhesive cytokines, chemoattractants, free radicals, and proteolytic enzymes.

Currently, most investigators believe that in early atherogenesis, monocytes (a type of white blood cell) are recruited to a "lesion-prone" area of the artery's innermost wall, or intima. Before the plaque can be formed, the monocyte has to attach to the endothelium, a process orchestrated by various chemoattractant substances (for example, oxidatively modified LDL cholesterol) and adhesive cytokines (for example, interleukin 1-beta). Once attached, the monocytes migrate through the endothelium and attach to its underside, away from the portion of the endothelium that is in contact with the bloodstream.

In this new space, the monocytes are transformed into a different type of cell, known as macrophages. As long ago as the early 1900s, pathologists observed macrophages associated with mature atherosclerotic plaques, but their presence was believed to be incidental. In the late twentieth century, however, macrophages have been assigned a pivotal role in atherogenesis. The macrophage synthesizes a variety of substances that activate the inflammatory response in the affected area, such as oxygen free radicals, proteases, and lipases. These cause the macrophage to take up oxidatively modified LDL and change its appearance so that the cell has a foamy appearance when viewed with a microscope. The cells are thus called "foam cells."

The next step in the process of atherosclerosis is necrosis of the foam cell, likely due to cytotoxicity from the oxidatively modified LDL. Smooth muscle migration and proliferation are mediated by a platelet-derived growth factor, a potent chemoattractant. Fibroblastic growth factors probably regulate smooth muscle cell proliferation. In the area of the plaque where there is the greatest density of macrophages, rupture may occur due to the high local concentration of macrophage-derived metalloproteases. This process ultimately results in blood clots that can obstruct blood flow – mural or occlusive thrombosis. Occlusion, whether temporary or not, creates a locally hypoxemic environment, which further enhances plaque growth. Oxidized LDL may initiate an autoimmune process that also adds to the inflammatory reaction occurring in the lesion-prone area.

The intricate atherosclerotic process provides investigators with many avenues of exploration for prevention and intervention. From a nutritional standpoint, the most obvious factors are cholesterol, dietary fat, and the biochemical precursors for the substances that may enhance or intervene in plaque formation: omega-3 fatty acids, protein, "antioxidant" nutrients (for example, vitamin E, beta-carotene, vitamin C), and other dietary substances. As an alternative approach to dietary prevention, one might consider dietary changes that would decrease the activities of the substances that enhance arteriosclerosis.

Cholesterol

Early Epidemiological Studies

In the mid-1940s, Ancel Keys (1963) and William Kannel (1971) and their colleagues designed two large-scale studies to examine longitudinally what caused people to develop coronary artery disease. These investigators believed that by recording the essential characteristics of a large group of at-risk people and by comparing those who went on to develop CAD with those who did not, they could identify particular risk factors for the disease. These two sets of studies have had a profound influence on the development of the field.

Keys and his associates studied 281 Minnesota business and professional men who were 45 to 55 years of age and clinically healthy at the start of a 15-year study period. Each year, the men were given a detailed physical examination, with particular attention to the cardiovascular system. Examiners noted each man's weight, relative body fatness, blood pressure, and serum cholesterol concentration. They measured two different pools of cholesterol in addition to total cholesterol: high-density lipoprotein (HDL) and low-density lipoprotein (LDL) cholesterol. During the 15 study years, 32 deaths occurred, 17 of which were directly attributable to CAD. Body weight and fatness were not predictive of disease, but the men in the upper part of the blood pressure distribution had a greater risk of CAD. Most compelling were the findings with regard to cholesterol. They indicated a direct relationship between blood cholesterol and risk of CAD, extending over all levels. The men who remained healthy had significantly higher HDL cholesterol than did subjects who developed CAD (mean 45.29 milligrams [mg] per deciliter as compared with 39.45). Detailed statistical analysis, however, failed to support the hypothesis that HDL cholesterol level was an independent predictor of CAD risk. Rather, high LDL and total cholesterol were more important predictors of CVD.

The Framingham Study (Kannel et al. 1971) followed 2,282 men and 2,845 women in Framingham, Massachusetts, for 14 years, starting in 1948. As in the Keys study, investigators were attempting to identify factors related to the onset of clinical coronary disease. Subjects were free of known coronary disease at the time of enrollment and were subdivided into groups based on their serum lipid content. After 14 years, 14 percent of the men and 6 percent of the women had developed some clinical manifestation of CAD. The incidence of CAD increased with age, and the baseline serum lipids and lipoproteins were higher in the CAD group than in the other subjects. Furthermore, the lipid profiles in the CAD subjects were high when compared to profiles in other parts of the world, such as France and Japan, where low CAD rates have been reported.

Investigators were unable to demonstrate that a particular lipid played a greater role than others. However, they did observe differences between men and women. In men and younger women (<55 years), the differences between those with CAD and those without the disease were more related to the total cholesterol. In older women (>55 years), prebeta lipoprotein (very low density lipoprotein or VLDL) discriminated better than total cholesterol between women with and without CAD. These two studies, coupled with what was known about atherosclerotic plaque composition, further supported the idea that one key to solving the mystery of atherosclerosis was to determine the relationship between blood lipids and plaque formation. Moreover, of all blood lipids, cholesterol appeared to be the most important.

Sources of Cholesterol

Cholesterol occurs naturally in eukaryotic cells (cells with a membrane-bound nucleus). In humans, cholesterol serves many vital functions. It acts as an integral part of the cellular membrane, serves as a chemical backbone for essential substances (for example, steroid hormones, vitamin D), and assists in digestion through its role in the formation of bile salts. Given the central role of cholesterol in biochemical and physiological functions, it is not surprising that the substance became a central focus for biochemical researchers. Although all human cholesterol was once thought to be ingested (Leary 1935), we now know that humans are able to manufacture cholesterol de novo, primarily in the liver and, to a lesser extent, in intestinal and other cells. Thus, even if one consumed a very low-cholesterol diet, the adult liver and intestine would still manufacture approximately 800 milligrams of cholesterol per day, which is enough for normal human functions. But cholesterol also reaches the body through dietary means for most humans, except those who are strict vegetarians and consume neither flesh nor dairy or egg products. Thus, cholesterol in atherosclerotic plaque formation could come from either de novo synthesis or dietary sources. The interaction between de novo cholesterol synthesis and dietary cholesterol, and the subsequent metabolism of cholesterol, is an intricate and fascinating phenomenon.

Serum cholesterol is transported bound to protein,

such as apoprotein, along with phospholipids and other circulating fat-soluble compounds. These lipoproteins (or lipid:apoprotein molecules) are classified according to increasing density: From lower to higher density they are called chylomicrons, very low density lipoproteins (VLDL), low-density lipoproteins (LDL), and high-density lipoproteins (HDL). LDL typically contains 60 to 70 percent of the total serum cholesterol and HDL about 15 to 20 percent. The remaining cholesterol is carried in VLDL and chylomicrons.

The apoprotein portions contain biochemical signals that regulate the entry and exit of particular lipids at specific targets. For instance, chylomicrons transport dietary cholesterol, triglycerides, and other lipids from the intestine to the liver and adipose tissue. VLDL transports de novo synthesized cholesterol and triglycerides from the liver to adipose tissue. The residue is transformed into LDL, which is very rich in cholesterol. LDL moves cholesterol to peripheral tissues and regulates de novo cholesterol synthesis. Nonhepatic target cells possess specific LDL receptors that allow the cell to take up LDL cholesterol. The receptor number can be increased and decreased depending on the needs of the target cell. HDL presumably carries cholesterol from peripheral tissues back to the liver.

LDL regulates cholesterol metabolism through feedback inhibition. First, the cholesterol that is released from the LDL after it is inside the cell suppresses the key synthetic enzyme, HMG-CoA reductase, slowing de novo cholesterol formation. Second, when cholesterol concentration within a cell is adequate for its needs, the cell shuts down the manufacture of additional LDL receptors, thus preventing it from taking up more cholesterol.

Relationship of Cholesterol to CAD

Perhaps the clearest link between cholesterol, LDL, and arteriosclerosis comes from people with homozygous or heterozygous familial hypercholesterolemia. People who inherit both genes of this autosomal recessive disorder (homozygotes) have extraordinarily high levels of total and LDL cholesterol in circulation. Depending on the type of inheritance, they suffer from premature CAD either as a child or as a young adult. The defect in most cases is an absence or deficiency of functional LDL receptors, impeding the movement of LDL-cholesterol into target cells. Because LDL cannot satisfactorily get cholesterol inside a cell, there is no mechanism to turn off HMG-CoA reductase, and cholesterol biosynthesis continues unchecked. The excess cholesterol, primarily found with LDL, is deposited in various tissues, including arterial endothelium. These cause myocardial infarctions at a very young age. Because dietary cholesterol restriction does not affect de novo synthesis, it is of very limited value alone in the management of these individuals.

Heterozygous familial hypercholesterolemia is relatively common (1:500 births), but is certainly far less common than CAD. Nonetheless, the association between cholesterol and CAD at extreme levels supports the idea that cholesterol is a factor in the development of CAD, particularly as it is consistent with numerous epidemiological studies that demonstrate a relationship between total and LDL cholesterol and CVD. Some of these are within-population studies, such as the Framingham and Minnesota studies discussed in the section "Early Epidemiological Studies." Others compare different populations or people who move from one population to another. These studies often consider the importance of culture – particularly as manifested in what people eat – and, thus, bring us closer to the overall topic of this chapter and this work, which is diet.

The observation that different communities have different rates of CAD provides an important counterbalance to overly deterministic theories of disease causation, as well as engendering a series of ideas leading toward an understanding of the possible impact of diet on cholesterol and on CAD. C. D. De Langen, a Dutch public health physician, noted in the 1910s and 1920s that the incidence of CAD was extraordinarily low among residents of the island of Java (Snapper 1963). He explained part of this difference as being the result of differences in diet; Javanese stewards who worked on Dutch steamships soon developed a pattern of coronary health similar to that of the native-born Dutchmen who worked on the ships.

In 1941, I. Snapper made a similar series of observations about people native to northern China. He said that the difference could, perhaps, be attributed to the "equanimity of the Chinese," but suggested that diet was probably a more important explanation. These observations led the American scientist Ancel Keys to wonder about the geographical variation in the incidence of CAD (Keys 1983). He initiated a massive study, published as *Seven Countries: A Multivariate Analysis of Death and Coronary Heart Disease*. This detailed work was begun in 1947 and eventually resulted in the study of a total of 12,763 men over 10 years in Yugoslavia, Finland, Italy, the Netherlands, Greece, the United States, and Japan. Conclusions are complex (on a scale with the study itself), but they show a clear relationship between the dietary intake of saturated fat and cholesterol and the incidence of coronary heart disease. Other between-population studies have shown that in countries where CVD rates are low, the serum LDL levels also tend to be low (for example, rural Japan and China compared to the United States and Finland).

Other investigations (following the lead of De Langen) have examined changes in CAD incidence with migration. Most have shown that when people move from a region with a low incidence of CAD to a region with a high incidence of CAD, and adopt the lifestyle of their new country, their likelihood of having CAD approaches that of the region to which they have moved. For instance, Japanese people living in their native Japan, in Hawaii, and in San Francisco, have an increasingly higher incidence of CVD: Age-adjusted rates among Japanese people were 1.6 per 1,000 person-years in Japan, 3.0 in Hawaii, and 3.7 in San Francisco (Kato et al. 1973). Saturated fat intake as a percentage of calories in the three populations was 7, 23, and 26 percent, respectively. The dietary trends among these populations emphasize the importance of the type of fat intake: Foods high in saturated fat also tend to be high in cholesterol. What happened to Japanese people moving from Japan to Hawaii to San Francisco seems clear enough. As they adopted a progressively more Western diet with a higher intake of saturated fats, their incidence of heart disease increased.

Cholesterol-Lowering Intervention

If the changing of diet results in a changing rate of heart disease, then public education efforts to heighten personal awareness of cholesterol levels may be serving as a broad and effective means of intervention. There are some encouraging signs. From 1980 to 1987, in the Minneapolis–St. Paul area, there was a significant decrease in total serum cholesterol and in the numbers of individuals with significant hypercholesterolemia (greater than 5.04 micromoles [mmol] per liter or 195 mg per deciliter) (Burke et al. 1991). However, despite the downward trend of cholesterol in the study population as a whole, many individuals (67 percent) with cholesterol levels high enough to require dietary and/or medical therapy remained unaware of their condition.

On a national level, the National Health and Nutrition Examination Survey (NHANES), undertaken between 1976 and 1980 (NHANES II) and from 1988 to 1991 (NHANES III), found an increase in the number of people with total cholesterol values less than 5.17 mmol per liter (200 mg per deciliter) and a decrease in those with total cholesterol values greater than 6.21 mmol per liter (240 mg per deciliter).

Although these population-based observations may reflect national public-health efforts to reduce total and saturated fat and cholesterol, such hopeful trends probably do not completely explain the decline in mortality from CVD. During the 1980s in the United States, there was also a decline in the use of tobacco, a major risk factor for CAD. In addition, there were changes in the diagnosis and management of CAD, including more widely available cardiac catheterization, angioplasty, functional cardiac studies (for example, dipyridamole and thallium stress echocardiograms), and development and utilization of new medications (for instance, thrombolytics, cardiospecific beta-blockers, and angiotensin converting enzyme inhibitors). Thus, at present, the relative importance of population-based cholesterol lowering in bringing about a declining CVD death rate remains unknown.

Nonetheless, although many factors could alter mortality from CAD, the lowering of cholesterol would intuitively seem both important and appropriate. Prevention of CAD among a community of individuals can be viewed from two perspectives: primary prevention and secondary prevention.

Primary prevention. Efforts to prevent persons from developing a particular disease fall under the rubric of primary prevention. In the case of CAD, primary prevention implies reducing the disease incidence for people with risk factors but who have not yet developed it. The Lipid Research Clinics Program (1984) and the Helsinki Heart Study (Frick et al. 1987) were large, randomized, controlled clinical trials that indicated that reducing serum cholesterol in persons without known CAD reduces the incidence of CAD onset. However, these trials were short (less than 10 years) and did not (or could not) demonstrate that primary prevention lengthens the life span by delaying or preventing the onset of CAD. Individuals who have hypercholesterolemia as their only risk factor for CAD likely do not add many years to their life by reducing their cholesterol level (Browner, Westenhouse, and Tice 1991). Indeed, some studies have even suggested a rise in the incidence of violent deaths among individuals with the lowest cholesterol levels, although the relevance of such observations remains controversial.

Secondary prevention. On average, however, 3 to 4 years of life can be gained by individuals who have CAD and reduce their serum cholesterol by dietary and/or by medical means. This approach – intervention in the presence of known disease – defines secondary prevention.

The idea that diet has some relationship with heart disease, and that changing the diet can help people with heart disease, has been around for some time. What entered and left the body were long held as being critically important to its general functioning. Thus, it should come as no surprise to see comments about treating heart disease with diet from, essentially, the very first speculations about heart diseases in general (Fothergill 1776, cited in Leibowitz 1970). We should not attempt, however, to read these comments as having the same sort of specificity we now associate with statements about disease causation and diet.

For the early twentieth century, some insight into generally accepted notions of diet and heart disease may be derived by consulting a series of articles published in 1913 by the American Medical Association (AMA), the "cordial reception" of which led to their presentation in book form. The opinions expressed in these articles may be regarded as reflecting a general consensus, at least among allopathic physicians. Some of what was advised for the patient with heart disease seems logical (if not necessarily appropriate) to the late-twentieth-century reader, such as the suggestion that coffee should be avoided or that obese patients should lose weight in order to help the functions of their hearts.

Other approaches, such as administering hydrochloric acid to aid in digestion, now seem clearly out of place. But what is most striking is the emphasis on the idea that diet should be individualized, at least in part because it is limited by "what the patient will do." Rather than being dogmatic about what constitutes a "correct" diet, advisers would do better to tailor their recommendations to the specific social and cultural setting of the person under treatment.

Across the Atlantic, the noted British physician Sir Clifford Allbutt, Regius Professor at Cambridge University in England, was also concerned about individual variation in dietary suggestions (Allbutt 1915, particularly 238–54 of Vol. 1). He considered the question of overfeeding to be a relative one: What was a good diet for one person might be gluttony for another. He noted that cholesterol was associated with atherosclerosis, but he saw also the wide variation in the diets of people who developed atherosclerosis.

More recently, many trials have examined the value of cholesterol reduction in the management of CAD. These studies usually randomized patients with known CAD to receive some type of treatment (diet, drug, lifestyle change) versus "usual care" or placebo. The outcomes of interest in these studies tended to be occurrence of angina, myocardial infarction, death, and regression of atherosclerosis. Most subjects had total serum cholesterol concentrations greater than 5.00 mmol per liter. To determine regression or progression of atherosclerosis, baseline coronary angiograms were compared with those at the end of the study period. The angiograms were assessed with quantitative angiography and/or global score assessment. Both methods asked the same question: Are the areas of stenosis the same, less, or greater than at baseline, and is there a relationship between the extent of plaque regression and the amount of cholesterol lowering?

The Cholesterol-Lowering Atherosclerosis Study (CLAS) (Blankenhorn et al. 1987) investigated the effects of drug therapy in a randomized, placebo-controlled trial using men ages 40 to 59 years who had undergone coronary artery bypass graft surgery. After two years of treatment, patients who had been given the cholesterol-lowering drugs colestipol and niacin instead of placebos exhibited a reduction in total cholesterol, a reduction in LDL-cholesterol, and a significant amount of atherosclerotic plaque regression and preservation of native coronary arteries. However, the incidence of coronary events was no different between the two groups.

A fairly recent study by D. Ornish and colleagues (1990) explored the influence of lifestyle changes on reversal of CAD in a randomized controlled trial that followed men and women for one year. The treatment group experienced aggressive lifestyle interventions, including the imposition of a very low cholesterol, strict vegetarian diet. Their overall dietary fat was reduced to 10 percent of calories, far lower than in the usual American diet, which contains 35 to 40 percent of calories from fat. The treatment group demonstrated regression of atherosclerotic lesions and reduction of serum cholesterol and LDL-cholesterol.

The investigation has been criticized for flaws in randomization. Morever, the practicality of implementing such a drastic dietary intervention for the general population with CAD has also been questioned. However, the findings are provocative and suggest that a radical reduction in dietary fat can greatly influence serum cholesterol and plaque regression. The study subjects also received psychological and behavioral interventions and increased their exercise. Whether such changes can alter morbidity and mortality from CAD over one's lifetime to a greater extent than more conservative, yet aggressive, approaches to cholesterol lowering remains to be elucidated.

The St. Thomas Atherosclerosis Regression Study (STARS) (Watts et al. 1992) focused on 90 men with CAD and mild hypercholesterolemia for approximately three years. It investigated the effects of usual care versus two interventions: a low-cholesterol diet and a low-cholesterol diet with the cholesterol-lowering drug, cholestyramine. Both interventions reduced the frequency of cardiovascular events and the progression of coronary artery narrowing.

The Monitored Atherosclerosis Regression Study (MARS) (Blankenhorn et al. 1993) was a randomized, double-blind, placebo-controlled study of 270 men and women with CAD that evaluated the effect of a low-cholesterol, reduced-fat diet with and without the HMG-CoA reductase inhibitor lovastatin. This trial demonstrated regression of atherosclerotic plaques; however, there was no difference in cardiac events between the treatment and placebo groups. At first glance, these results may seem to contradict the STARS trial, but the diet in the control group of the STARS study was not one designed to lower plasma lipids. In the STARS trial, both the lipid-lowering diet and the diet plus cholestyramine resin reduced coronary events to the same degree. They were significantly different from the usual care group, but not from each other.

The data on the role of cholesterol, particularly LDL-cholesterol, in the pathogenesis of CAD is compelling. Epidemiological population studies strongly suggest a positive relationship between elevated serum cholesterol and mortality rates from CAD. Primary and secondary prevention trials support the contention that reducing LDL-cholesterol, through a lipid-lowering diet with or without adjuvant medication, alters disease progression in middle-aged men. It is less clear if therapy will significantly reduce the incidence of subsequent cardiac events. The trials have not demonstrated an impact on longevity. However, it is certainly possible that future studies will do so. Studies in the Scandinavian Simvastatin Survival Study (known as 4S) seem to show an overall decrease in the death rate for people who already had heart disease when treated with potent cholesterol-lowering drugs (Scandinavian Simvastatin Survival Study Group 1994).

Dietary Fat

The influence of diet on CAD may reflect the amount of fat a person ingests. But the type of fat consumed may be just as important as the amount. Cholesterol is a type of fat found only in animal cells, not in plant cells. Low-cholesterol diets stress not only a reduction in dietary cholesterol but also a reduction in overall dietary fat, especially saturated fat. This approach is necessary because animal fat is laden with cholesterol. Animal fat is also primarily a saturated fat. Thus, the current recommendations by several national advisory panels are to decrease the consumption of saturated, cholesterol-rich animal fat, and to increase the amount of monounsaturated and polyunsaturated, or plant-derived, fat. Because poultry and fish contain more polyunsaturated fat than beef or pork, the recommendations also suggest consuming more poultry and fish as protein sources.

In dietary recommendations made in 1970 in the "Report of the Inter-Society Commission for Heart Disease Resources" (which were incorporated into "Dietary Goals for the United States by the United States Senate Select Committee on Nutrition and Human Needs"), the consumption of fat was expected to decrease from 42 to 30 percent of calories. Since 1909, Americans had consumed an average of 600 mg of cholesterol per day, but with these recommendations, cholesterol consumption was projected to decrease to 300 mg per capita per day. Such recommendations were considered radical at the time, and those who proposed diets based on them were concerned about the ability of patients to consume such a diet while maintaining normal protein nutrition.

More recently, however, the National Research Council's 1992 recommendations have emphasized that in order to better meet the national goal of reducing total cholesterol concentrations to less than 5.04 mmol per liter, daily calories from fat should not exceed 30 percent of total calories, and two-thirds of that fat should be monounsaturated and polyunsaturated.

Saturated versus Unsaturated Fats

Can the rise in CVD mortality seen in countries like the United States and Scandinavia be attributed to the type of dietary fat, as well as to dietary cholesterol? The answer to the question seems to be yes. In the first half of this century, although U.S. CVD mortality rates rose dramatically, the increase in consumption of total and saturated fat was much more modest. However, during the same period, consumption of polyunsaturated fat rose two to three times (Friend 1967; Page and Marston 1979). In Europe during World War II, as wartime deprivation curtailed animal fat and, in fact, total fat consumption, the number of deaths due to CAD fell dramatically. In the 1970s, rural Romanians consumed 900 mg of cholesterol per day – 50 percent more than Americans at the time – but Romanian CVD mortality rates were approximately 20 percent lower, perhaps because their dietary fat intake was 30 percent less than the average in the United States (WHO 1976).

Such observations implicate dietary fat, not just dietary cholesterol, in atherogenesis. Further, the nature of the fat (that is, saturated or unsaturated) may be important. Whether a fat is saturated or not has to do with how many hydrogen atoms are bound to carbon. Carbon atoms form the "backbone" of a fat molecule and can maximally bind to 4 other atoms. If 4 binding sites are used, the carbon atom is said to be "saturated." If only 2 binding sites are used, the carbon atom forms a double bond with another carbon atom and is said to be "unsaturated." Saturated fatty acids have no carbon double bonds, monounsaturated fatty acids have one carbon double bond, and polyunsaturated fatty acids have two or more carbon double bonds.

Epidemiological studies have observed that mortality from CVD is lower in southern European countries. There, total fat consumption is not remarkably low compared to other industrialized nations, but there is a greater consumption of monounsaturated fats, such as olive oil.

In 1928, two Chinese biochemists suggested that the low rate of CAD in China might be explained by the polyunsaturated fat linoleic acid (Snapper 1963). Others have later shown that this substance can lower serum cholesterol (Ahrens et al. 1959). In the United States, increased consumption of linoleic acid, primarily through greater consumption of corn oil products, parallels the decline in population serum cholesterol concentrations.

Marine Oils

Fish oils appear to lower serum lipids in animals and humans (Bronte-Stewart et al. 1956; Nelson 1972). In the 1970s, epidemiologists attempted to explain a striking difference in the incidence of CAD between Eskimos, who rarely suffer from CVD, and Danes. They found a major dietary difference, not in total fat consumption but in the amount of fish oil consumption. Eskimos who have diets high in omega-3 fatty acids (found in fish oil) have prolonged bleeding times, as well as a decreased number and aggregation of platelets – all features associated with a reduced incidence of coronary thrombosis. Several hypotheses have been presented to explain the antiatherogenic effects of marine oils. They include altered plasma

cholesterol and triglyceride concentrations, altered metabolism of prostaglandins and leukotrienes, and a variety of other physiological responses (Zhu and Parmley 1990).

Laboratory experiments have suggested possible mechanisms for the effects of marine oils. Animals fed a diet high in omega-3 long-chain polyunsaturated fatty acids and dietary cholesterol had a reduction in the number and size of atherosclerotic lesions. This may have resulted from chemical changes that affect how blood cells adhere to lesion-prone areas. Associated with these physiological changes were alterations in the prostaglandin synthetic pathway reflected by decreased thromboxane A2, increased prostacyclin, decreased leukotriene B4, and increased leukotriene B5. Most of these studies have also demonstrated significant lowering of plasma total cholesterol, LDL-cholesterol, and triglyceride levels. HDL-cholesterol has generally been unchanged.

Clinical investigations have shown that the consumption of fish oil in normal volunteers and in patients with hyperlipidemia can remarkably decrease plasma triglyceride levels, with inconsistent effects on plasma cholesterol and HDL-cholesterol. Perhaps as a result, fish oil supplements were widely marketed in the 1980s. But although epidemiological studies of Eskimos suggest a chemoprotective effect of fish oil, it is unclear that increasing fish oil in an American or northern European diet will impact CVD mortality rates. In addition, problems with fish oil supplements, including a bad flavor and unpalatable belching, pose compliance problems for patients with CVD risk.

Other Dietary Components

Dietary Protein

Sources of dietary protein include meat (for example, beef, pork, lamb, and wild game), poultry (such as chicken, turkey, and quail), fish, seafood, dairy products, eggs, grains, legumes (for example, peanuts, soy, and dried beans), nuts, and seeds. Depending on one's culture, religion, ethnicity, and other socioeconomic variables, the primary daily protein source will vary. Different protein sources contain varying amounts and types of fat. The discussion in the section "Dietary Fat" has pointed out that saturated animal fat is most relevant to hyperlipidemia, unlike plant lipids, which are unsaturated.

Milk protein has been implicated as an important nutrient in atherogenesis for more than 20 years, most notably in S. Seely's epidemiological analyses (1981, 1988). By reviewing the CVD mortality rates in men from 24 countries along with food consumption data, he found a significant correlation between CVD and the consumption of unfermented milk proteins, the only exception being cheese (1981). In 1988, Seely studied food consumption patterns of men and women in 21 countries that might be associated with

CVD mortality. He observed significant positive correlations between CVD mortality and milk, milk products, sugar, and oats. There were negative correlations with fish proteins, vegetable proteins, and fish fat.

Proteins are made of amino acids, and one of those amino acids - argininc - has become the subject of intense scrutiny. The discovery in the 1980s and 1990s that mammals endogenously synthesize nitric oxide, a toxic substance, has led to an enormous body of literature describing the physiology, immunology, and biochemistry of this substance. It is produced by the enzymatic conversion of L-arginine to nitric oxide by nitric oxide synthetase. This reaction occurs in several tissue types, including endothelium, macrophages, and the brain. Nitric oxide produced in endothelium causes relaxation of the vessel and, hence, vasodilation.

L. Castillo and colleagues (1995) demonstrated that up to 16 percent of dietary arginine may be converted to nitric oxide in healthy volunteers. Several investigators have reported abnormal coronary arterial vasodilation, probably related to nitric oxide production in patients with increased cholesterol (Creager et al. 1990), hypertension (Linder et al. 1990), and CAD (Zeiher et al. 1991; Egashira et al. 1993). M. Jeserich and colleagues (1992) found significantly lower plasma L-arginine concentrations in patients with hypercholesterolemia (greater than 270 mg per deciliter), as compared to patients with normal cholesterol levels (less than 220 mg per deciliter). The relationship of these findings to CVD pathogenesis remains to be elucidated. It is unclear whether this difference in arginine levels is because of diet or because of the process of atherogenesis.

Dietary Carbohydrates and Fiber

Carbohydrate foods provide the bulk of daily energy needs. Animal studies have found that if the ratio of energy to protein is low, serum cholesterol tends to be lower. In humans, decreased energy intake may be associated with less obesity, a lower incidence of diabetes, and reduced cholesterol (total and LDL) (Kannel 1987).

Thus, modification of these atherogenic risk factors by modifying energy intake may be beneficial. The other main dietary energy source is fat, which provides about twice the number of calories per gram as carbohydrate does. Thus, to reduce overall energy intake and reduce atherosclerotic risk, it is desirable to obtain energy calories primarily from carbohydrate sources.

The association of fiber with hyperlipidemia has also received attention. Soluble fiber consumption is associated with reduced serum cholesterol. D. J. A. Jenkins and colleagues (1993) studied soluble fiber supplementation in conjunction with a lipid-lowering diet in 43 healthy men and women of normal weight. They observed a significant reduction in total cholesterol in both groups compared to base-line, but the soluble fiber group attained an even greater reduction.

Vitamins

"Antioxidant" nutrients have recently gotten a great deal of media and scientific coverage. These compounds include beta-carotene, vitamin E, and vitamin C. There are several reasons for this interest. LDL-cholesterol is oxidatively modified through chemical mediators released from the macrophage during atherosclerotic pathogenesis. Nonnutrient antioxidant substances (for example, probucol, butylated hydroxytoluene) inhibit the progression of atherogenesis in rabbits, presumably due to an alteration in oxidatively modified LDL-cholesterol (Bjorkhem et al. 1991; Mao et al. 1991). Antioxidants such as vitamin E work by "grabbing" a hydrogen atom. Having done so, they are now the oxidized molecule, and they have thus prevented another moiety, such as LDL, from becoming oxidized. Epidemiological studies suggest that people with high plasma levels of vitamin E have a lower risk of CVD. Similar results have been obtained when examining beta-carotene intake and CVD incidence. In the Nurses' Health Study, CVD risk was reduced 30 to 40 percent in those individuals with high calculated intakes of vitamin E or beta-carotene. The data on vitamin C were unconvincing (Stampfer et al. 1987; Stampfer et al. 1993).

M. Abbey, P. J. Nestel, and P. A. Baghurst (1993) investigated LDL oxidation in nonsmoking men and women who were randomized to receive either a placebo or an "antioxidant" vitamin supplement (18 mg beta-carotene, 250 mg d-alpha-tocopheryl succinate, and 12 mg zinc) for 6 months. During the 6-month study period, the supplemented group's LDL was less able to oxidize than the control group. I. Jialal and S. M. Grundy (1993) also demonstrated a decrease in LDL oxidation rate in men supplemented with vitamin E.

There are, however, several problems with recommending supplements of vitamin E or any other of the "antioxidants." First, many of these vitamins have biochemically important interactions. For instance, vitamin C may reduce vitamin E needs by reducing oxidized vitamin E. The chemically reduced vitamin E can then be "recycled" and used again as an antioxidant. Second, no well-controlled randomized clinical trials have determined what dose of antioxidant may be needed to accomplish atherosclerosis prevention without adverse side effects. We do not even know which nutrient (or mixture of nutrients) should be tested. Further, it is not known if in vitro LDL oxidation is the best marker for what these nutrients may do in atherogenesis.

Thus, while it is probable that some of these nutrients play important roles in lipid metabolism (which may affect CVD), we simply do not know enough about them to make sweeping recommendations. If individuals would reduce their dietary fat to 30 percent of calories and increase their consumption of complex carbohydrates to 55 percent of calories (including fruits and vegetables), they would likely increase their ingestion of these "antioxidants," with numerous overall health benefits and without risk.

Alcohol

Several studies suggest a possible benefit of alcohol ingestion. LDL-cholesterol levels appear to be lower in individuals who consume moderate amounts of alcohol: 1 to 3 bottles of beer, glasses of wine, or shots of liquor per day. At higher levels of alcohol ingestion, LDL is further reduced, probably due to the replacement of alcohol for energy calories at the expense of ingesting foods containing cholesterol and fat. Alcohol is the only substance humans ingest (nonpharmacologically) that can raise HDL-cholesterol, a finding that probably explains the beneficial effect of alcohol ingestion in reducing CVD mortality. However, in addition to its beneficial effects on blood lipids, alcohol is a drug with significant potential for abuse. Thus, most public health officials, physicians, and scientists are concerned about advising alcohol as a therapeutic modality for hyperlipidemia and CVD prevention.

Miscellaneous Dietary Components

S. Warshafsky, R. S. Kamer, and S. L. Sivak (1993) examined five placebo-controlled randomized trials on the effects of garlic supplementation on serum cholesterol. About one-half to one clove of garlic per day decreases serum cholesterol by about 9 percent. Proposed mechanisms of garlic's effects on blood lipids include increased bile acid excretion and reduced HMG-CoA reductase activity in the liver. However, carefully controlled studies of garlic remain to be done.

In concert with the antioxidant hypothesis, certain minerals have been implicated in atherogenesis. Selenium is able to act as a free-radical scavenger through its role as a cofactor in the enzyme glutathione peroxidase. However, the epidemiological studies on selenium consumption and CVD mortality do not bear out a probable relationship.

Conclusion

We have reviewed several dietary components that have been implicated in the pathogenesis of cardiovascular disease. The contribution of most nutrients appears to revolve around their ability to influence the serum lipid profile – total cholesterol, LDL-cholesterol, HDL-cholesterol, triglycerides, and the various apoproteins.

There is a need to look beyond serum lipids, however. Besides influencing a specific set of measurable laboratory parameters, nutrients must impact the pathogenesis of disease through biochemical and molecular alterations at the cellular level. This milieu of biochemical reactions and interactions is ultimately the most consequential to the dietary pathogenesis, prevention, and therapy of cardiovascular disease. We will doubtless continue to receive information about the important benefits of "nutrient A" on "function B," and physicians, scientists, patients, and the public will try to make sense of these assertions.

Yet one must remember that nutrients are but small components of the whole chemical "package" that makes up a particular food or group of foods. Other properties of additional components in food may work synergistically or antagonistically, or act as innocent bystanders in cardiovascular disease chemoprotection and pathogenesis. It is unlikely that in years to come a single nutrient – will be uncovered as "the cause" of CAD. More likely, further investigation will describe the subtle interactions of various dietary components with an individual's genome, in concert with other cardiovascular risk factors, such as tobacco use, diabetes mellitus, hypertension, hypoestrogenemia, stress, and obesity. Researchers probably will demonstrate that it is not just one or two nutrients or dietary factors that are critical, but the diet as a whole.

Consider an 88-year-old, generally healthy man who had a verified consumption of 20 to 30 whole eggs per day (Kern 1991). Despite this incredibly high daily cholesterol intake (12,953 micromoles), his total cholesterol was only 5.18 mmol per liter (200 mg per deciliter), and his LDL-cholesterol was 3.68 mmol per liter (142 mg per deciliter). It appears that he had compensated for his dietary excess by excreting excess cholesterol bound in bile acids in his stool. Thus, how an individual utilizes the diet biochemically may be as important as the diet itself.

We are not yet in a position to predict which people will do well with high cholesterol intake and which will not. In the meantime, it is prudent to follow the recent dietary guidelines of the National Research Council, which stress a diet containing 15 to 20 percent of calories from protein, 25 to 30 percent of calories from dietary fat, and the remaining calories from complex carbohydrates, such as whole grains, vegetables, and fruits.

These guidelines were put forward as death rates from CAD were falling, and there is no shortage of advocacy groups ready and willing to take credit for this reduction. But it is most probably the result of many lifestyle changes, among them declining use of tobacco (at least in the United States, when considered for all members of the population combined); better emergency medical services; improved in-hospital treatments; and, of course, dietary modifications. As noted, change in diet has a particular appeal as an explanation because it is the only one of these factors that daily affects each and every member of society. And, as the new millennium dawns, it would seem that dietary intervention to prevent CAD has proved to be a successful means of secondary prevention for those people who have already incurred a cardiac event, even if the utility of such intervention as a means of primary prevention, applied to entire populations, remains controversial.

We should also bear in mind that the debate over diet and heart disease is being conducted in a very public arena, and an arena in which diet and heart disease are only one aspect of a more general tension over questions focusing on personal risk and responsibility. In the case of heart disease, these questions have stirred a broad-based popular reaction. No longer are discussions of diet and the heart confined to the pages of medical journals, but they can now be found in practically every issue of widely circulating newspapers and magazines. One good example is an extensive and detailed analysis questioning the overall importance of cholesterol in heart disease – indeed, dismissing "The Cholesterol Myth" – in the *Atlantic Magazine* (Moore 1989a). In the same year that this essay appeared, it was also published in expanded form as a book (Moore 1989b).

Public skepticism about the importance of diet in heart disease is also apparent in cartoons. One, in the *New Yorker* magazine (January 16, 1989: 39), shows a man starting to eat a huge oatmeal muffin. The caption reads: "Wellness update: Thirty-year-old man starting on the twenty-five-thousand-pound oat-bran muffin he must consume over forty years in order to reduce significantly his risk of death from high cholesterol."

This and countless other less-than-reverent cartoons constitute widespread cultural markers that express a number of popular reactions to the diet–heart hypothesis. First, they ventilate frustration at the gospel of eating for one's heart (or for health in general). And given a culture in which the average person is daily bombarded with images of food, with much of the easiest food to acquire and consume that which is likely to be least beneficial for preventing heart disease, this frustration is understandable. Such cartoons also reflect a general lack of conviction that altered diets will "work" against heart disease – a skepticism that primary prevention trials have thus far failed to address convincingly. At a lay level, most people know (or have heard of) someone who has lived to a ripe old age while engaging in near-constant dietary indiscretions, whereas someone who ate "right" and stayed fit may have suffered an early death. Epidemiologists might discount the relevance of such anecdotes, but they can have a major impact on popular perceptions of risk and disease, especially when the behavior that is being advocated may be neither easy nor (seemingly) pleasurable.

The popular reaction against dietary constraints also raises fundamental questions of personal versus public responsibility. If someone has CAD, whose fault is it? The choices people make about what to eat are limited by the cultural world in which they live, so to what extent is the larger society to be held responsible? And, if one is personally accountable for what foods are consumed, then should a "healthy lifestyle"

make a difference in terms of how much one pays for health or life insurance?

Finally, what is the disease here? Is it CAD, or is it high cholesterol? We should not lose sight of the fact that blood lipids are merely surrogates for what is most important – the disability and death that come from CAD and CVD. Keeping track of these differences is important. First, it can help to maintain focus on the ultimate goals of therapy and not allow us to become sidetracked by that which is easier to effect. Second, it will prevent the labeling of a large percentage of the population as "diseased" simply because of a high lipid profile. The answers to the questions raised in this chapter are unlikely to come purely from the accumulation of more and more data, because the prevention controversies are also fueled by "hidden ideological, structural, and professional factors" (Aronowitz 1994).

Melissa H. Olken
Joel D. Howell

Bibliography

Abbey, M., P. J. Nestel, and P. A. Baghurst. 1993. Antioxidant vitamins and low-density lipoprotein oxidation. *American Journal of Clinical Nutrition* 58: 525–32.

Ahrens, E. H., W. Insull, J. Hirsch, et al. 1959. The effect on human serum-lipids of a dietary fat, highly unsaturated but poor in essential fatty acids. *Lancet* 1: 117–19.

Allbutt, Clifford. 1915. *Diseases of the arteries, including angina pectoris.* 2 vols. London.

Armstrong, B. K., J. I. Mann, A. M. Adelstein, and F. Eskin. 1975. Commodity consumption and ischemic heart disease mortality, with special reference to dietary practices. *Journal of Chronic Disease* 28: 455–67.

Aronowitz, Robert. 1994. Trouble in prevention. *Journal of General Internal Medicine* 9: 475–8.

Bjorkhem, I., A. Henriksson-Freyschuss, O. Breuer, et al. 1991. The antioxidant butylated hydroxytoluene protects against atherosclerosis. *Atherosclerosis and Thrombosis* 11: 15–22.

Blankenhorn, D. H., S. P. Azen, D. M. Kramsch, et al. 1993. Coronary angiographic changes with lovastatin therapy. *Annals of Internal Medicine* 119: 969–76.

Blankenhorn, D. H., S. A. Nessim, R. L. Johnson, et al. 1987. Beneficial effects of combined colestipol-niacin therapy on coronary atherosclerosis and coronary venous bypass grafts. *Journal of the American Medical Association* 257: 3233–40.

Bronte-Stewart, B., A. Antonis, L. Eales, and J. F. Brock. 1956. Effects of feeding different fats on serum-cholesterol level. *Lancet* 2: 521–6.

Browner, Warren S., Janice Westenhouse, and Jeffrey A. Tice. 1991. What if Americans ate less fat? A quantitative estimate of the effect on mortality. *Journal of the American Medical Association* 265: 3285–91.

Burke, G. L., J. M. Sprafka, A. R. Folsom, et al. 1991. Trends in serum cholesterol levels from 1980–1987. *New England Journal of Medicine* 324: 941–6.

Castillo, L., M. Sanchez, J. Vogt, et al. 1995. Plasma arginine, citrulline, and ornithine kinetics in adults, with observations on nitric oxide synthesis. *American Journal of Physiology* 268: E360-7.

Creager, M. A., J. P. Cooke, M. E. Mendelsohn, et al. 1990. Impaired vasodilation of forearm resistance vessels in hypercholesterolemic humans. *Journal of Clinical Investigation* 86: 228-34.

Dalderup, L. M. 1973. Ozone, vitamin E, fatty acids, prostaglandins, atherosclerosis and its complications (letter to the editor). *Archives of Environmental Health* 27: 58.

Dawber, D. V., and L. N. Katz. 1943. Experimental atherosclerosis in the chick. *Archives of Pathology* 36: 473-92.

Egashira, K., T. Inou, Y. Hirooka, et al. 1993. Evidence of impaired endothelium-dependent coronary vasodilatation in patients with angina pectoris and normal coronary angiograms. *New England Journal of Medicine* 328: 1659-64.

Expert Panel on Detection, Evaluation, and Treatment of High Blood Cholesterol in Adults. 1993. Summary of the second report of the National Cholesterol Education Program (NCEP). *Journal of the American Medical Association* 269: 3015-23.

Frick, M. H., O. Elo, K. Happa, et al. 1987. Helsinki heart study: Primary-prevention trial with gemfibrozil in middle-aged men with dyslipidemia: Safety of treatment, changes in risk factors, and incidence of coronary heart disease. *New England Journal of Medicine* 817: 1237-45.

Friend, B. 1967. Nutrients in the United States food supply: A review of trends, 1909-1913 to 1965. *American Journal of Clinical Nutrition* 20: 907-14.

Godfried, S. L., G. F. Combs, J. M. Saroka, and L. A. Dillingham. 1989. Potentiation of atherosclerotic lesions in rabbits by a high dietary level of vitamin E. *British Journal of Nutrition* 61: 607-17.

Jenkins, D. J. A., T. M. S. Wolever, A. V. Rao, et al. 1993. Effect on blood lipids of very high intakes of fiber in diets low in saturated fat and cholesterol. *New England Journal of Medicine* 329: 21-6.

Jeserich, M., T. Munzel, H. Just, and H. Drexler. 1992. Reduced plasma L-arginine in hypercholesterolaemia (letter). *Lancet* 339: 561.

Jialal, I., and S. M. Grundy. 1993. Effect of combined supplementation with alpha-tocopherol, ascorbate, and beta carotene on low-density lipoprotein oxidation. *Circulation* 88: 2780-6.

Kannel, W. B. 1987. New perspectives on cardiovascular risk factors. *American Heart Journal* 114: 213-19.

Kannel, W. B., W. P. Castelli, T. Gordon, and P. M. McNamara. 1971. Serum cholesterol, lipoproteins, and the risk of coronary heart disease: The Framingham Study. *Annals of Internal Medicine* 74: 1-12.

Kato, H., J. Tillotson, M. Z. Nichamen, et al. 1973. Epidemiologic studies of coronary heart disease and stroke in Japanese men living in Japan, Hawaii and California: Serum lipids and diet. *American Journal of Epidemiology* 97: 372-85.

Kern, F. 1991. Normal plasma cholesterol in an 88-year-old man who eats 25 eggs a day. *New England Journal of Medicine* 324: 896-9.

Keys, Ancel. 1980. *Seven countries: A multivariate analysis of death and coronary heart disease.* Cambridge, Mass.

1983. From Naples to seven countries – A sentimental journey. *Progress in Biochemical Pharmacology* 19: 1-30.

Keys, Ancel, H. L. Taylor, H. Blackburn, et al. 1963. Coronary heart disease among Minnesota business and professional men followed for fifteen years. *Circulation* 28: 381-95.

Kummerow, F. A. 1979. Nutrition imbalance and angiotoxins as dietary risk factors in coronary heart disease. *American Journal of Clinical Nutrition* 32: 58-83.

Leary, Timothy. 1935. Pathology of coronary sclerosis. *American Heart Journal* 10: 328-37.

Leibowitz, J. O. 1970. *The history of coronary heart disease.* Berkeley, Calif.

Linder, L., W. Kiowski, F. R. Buhler, and T. P. Luscher. 1990. Indirect evidence for release of endothelium-derived relaxing factor in human forearm circulation in vivo: Blunted response in essential hypertension. *Circulation* 81: 1762-7.

Lipid Research Clinics Program. 1984. The lipid research clinics coronary primary prevention trial results: I. Reduction in incidence of coronary heart disease. *Journal of the American Medical Association* 251: 351-64.

Mao, S. J., M. T. Yates, A. E. Rechtin, et al. 1991. Antioxidant activity of probucol and its analogues in hypercholesterolemic Watanabe rabbits. *Journal of Medicinal Chemistry* 34: 298-302.

Moore, Thomas J. 1989a. The cholesterol myth. *Atlantic Magazine* 264 (September): 37-40.

1989b. *Heart failure: A critical inquiry into American medicine and the revolution in heart care.* New York.

Nelson, A. M. 1972. Diet therapy in coronary disease: Effect on mortality of high-protein, high-seafood, fat-controlled diet. *Geriatrics* 24: 103-16.

NIH Consensus Development Panel. 1993. Triglyceride, high-density lipoprotein, and coronary heart disease. *Journal of the American Medical Association* 269: 505-10.

Ornish, D., S. E. Brown, L. W. Scherwitz, et al. 1990. Can lifestyle changes reverse coronary heart disease? *Lancet* 336: 129-33.

Osborne, Oliver T. 1913. *Disturbances of the heart: Discussion of the treatment of the heart in various disorders.* Chicago.

Page, L., and R. M. Marston. 1979. Food consumption pattern – U.S. diet. In *Proceedings of the conference on the decline in coronary heart disease mortality,* ed. R. J Havilik and M. Feinleib, 236-43. U.S. Dept. of Health, Education and Welfare, Public Health Service, National Institute of Health, Washington, D.C. (NIH Pub. No. 79-1610).

Report of Inter-Society Commission for Heart Disease Resources. 1970. *Circulation* 42: A-55.

Sabate, J., G. E. Fraser, K. Burke, et al. 1993. Effects of walnuts on serum lipid levels and blood pressure in normal men. *New England Journal of Medicine* 328: 603-7.

Scandinavian Simvastatin Survival Study Group (4S). 1994. Randomized trial of cholesterol lowering in 4444 patients with coronary heart disease: The Scandinavian Simvastatin Survival Study. *Lancet* 344: 1383-9.

Schwartz, C. J., A. J. Valente, and E. A. Sprague. 1993. A modern view of atherogenesis. *American Journal of Cardiology* 71: 9B-14B.

Seely, S. 1981. Diet and coronary disease: A survey of mortality rates and food consumption statistics of 24 countries. *Medical Hypotheses* 7: 907-18.

1988. Diet and coronary arterial disease: A statistical study. *International Journal of Cardiology* 20: 183-92.

Sempos, C. T., J. I. Cleeman, M. D. Carroll, et al. 1993. Prevalence of high blood cholesterol among US adults. *Journal of the American Medical Association* 269: 3009-14.

Snapper, I. 1963. Diet and atherosclerosis: Truth and fiction. *American Journal of Cardiology* 11: 283-9.

Stampfer, M. J., G. A. Colditz, W. C. Willett, et al. 1987. Coronary heart disease risk factors in women: The Nurses' Health Study experience. In *Coronary heart disease in women,* ed. E. Eaker, B. Packard, N. K. Wenger, et al., 112–16. New York.

Stampfer, M. J., C. H. Hennekens, J. E. Manson, et al. 1993. Vitamin E consumption and risk of coronary heart disease in women. *New England Journal of Medicine* 328: 1444–9.

Steinberg, D. 1991. Alcohol and atherosclerosis. *Annals of Internal Medicine* 114: 967–76.

1992. Antioxidants in the prevention of human atherosclerosis: Summary of the proceedings of a National Heart, Lung, and Blood Institute workshop: September 5–6, 1991, Bethesda, Maryland. *Circulation* 85: 2338–43.

U.S. Senate Select Committee on Nutrition and Human Needs. 1977. *Dietary Goals for the United States.* Washington, D.C.

Vogel, Julius. [1847] 1847. *The Pathological anatomy of the human body,* trans. G. E. Day. Philadelphia, Pa.

Von Schacky, C. 1987. Prophylaxis of atherosclerosis with marine omega-3 fatty acids. *Annals of Internal Medicine* 107: 890–9.

Walldius, G., J. Regnstrom, J. Nilsson, et al. 1993. The role of lipids and antioxidative factors for development of atherosclerosis. *American Journal of Cardiology* 71: 15B–9B.

Warshafsky, S., R. S. Kamer, and S. L. Sivak. 1993. Effect of garlic on total serum cholesterol: A meta-analysis. *Annals of Internal Medicine* 119: 599–605.

Watts, G. F., B. Lewis, J. N. H. Brunt, et al. 1992. Effects on coronary artery disease of lipid-lowering diet, or diet plus cholestyramine, in the St. Thomas's Atherosclerosis Regression Study (STARS). *Lancet* 339: 563–9.

WHO (World Health Organization). 1976. *Myocardial infarction community registers.* Copenhagen.

Zeiher, A. M., H. Drexler, H. Wollschlager, and H. Just. 1991. Modulation of coronary vasomotor in humans: Progressive endothelial dysfunction with different early stages of coronary atherosclerosis. *Circulation* 83: 391–401.

Zhu, B-Q., and W. W. Parmley. 1990. Modification of experimental and clinical atherosclerosis by dietary fish oil. *American Heart Journal* 119: 168–78.

IV.F.4 ❧ The Cardiovascular System, Coronary Artery Disease, and Calcium: A Hypothesis

The Circulation

The central organ of the human circulatory system, the heart, must be among the most remarkable creations of nature. In the longest-living individuals, it works continuously for a hundred or more years, executing something like 4,000 million working strokes and moving 350,000 cubic meters of blood, enough to make a small lake. In individuals who die of heart disease, it is not, as a rule, the heart itself that fails but some auxiliary mechanism, like one of its arteries, or the pacemaker. If an artery, supplying a small part of the heart, is blocked, the tissues receiving oxygen and nutrients from that vessel die. If the area involved is not so large as to endanger the entire heart, the damage is gradually repaired by the immune system. The dead cells are removed but cannot be replaced; the gap they leave is filled with scar tissue. While the repair is carried out, the heart continues to work.

Among other remarkable properties of the heart is a virtual immunity from cancer and a good resistance to inflammatory diseases. When the body is at rest, the heart contracts approximately once every second. Its contraction – the systole – lasts about one-third of a second; its relaxation period – the diastole – two-thirds of a second. During hard physical exercise, the heart rate increases about three times.

The arterial system is like a many-branched tree. Its trunk, the aorta, is about three centimeters in diameter at its origin. The branches become progressively smaller and end in a network of capillaries of microscopic size. On the return side, blood is collected by small venules, which join to form veins and end in two large venous trunks. The entire length of the system is more than enough to encircle the earth.

The function of the circulatory system is to deliver nutrients to the cell population of the body and to collect their waste products. The system is waterborne, but a very small quantity of water carries a comparatively enormous cargo. The volume of water in the blood, and that of the substances dissolved or floating in it, are approximately equal.

A water-based transport system can readily transport water-soluble substances, but those are only a small part of the nutrients carried in blood. The most difficult technical problem is the transport of gases, notably oxygen and carbon dioxide. These are soluble, but only sparsely so in water. If they were carried only in aqueous solution, a very large quantity would be required for their transport. The problem is solved by the use of iron porphyrin, a substance that can readily take up oxygen and equally readily release it. The porphyrins are incorporated in large hemoglobin molecules, with molecular weight of 64,000, and these, in turn, are incorporated into red blood cells. It is interesting to note that the mammalian type of hemoglobin is the end product of a long process of development in evolutionary history. Invertebrate blood contains a large variety of hemoglobin-like substances (erythrocruorins), with molecular weights ranging from 17,000 to 1,250,000, in some cases copper-based compounds being used instead of iron. Red blood cells constitute about 40 percent of the blood by volume. Allowing an equal quantity of water for their flotation, 80 percent of the total capacity of the circulatory system is engaged in the task of oxygen transport.

Similar difficulties are presented by the transport of lipids and other hydrophobic substances. If they were simply released in water, they would stick to each other and to vessel walls. There are two solutions to the problem. One is the conjugation of a water-insoluble molecule with one or more other molecules to form a water-soluble complex. The other expedient is the use of carrier proteins. These are large molecules in comparison with the lipids they carry, serving, in effect, as packing cases for them. The protein molecule turns a hydrophilic outer surface to the watery medium in which it floats, and can pack a large quantity of hydrophobic molecules inside, shielded from contact with water.

The protein carrier with its lipid cargo constitutes a lipoprotein. As the carrier protein is heavier than water, the lipid it carries is lighter; the specific weight (or density) of their combination depends on the proportion of the two constituents. When the cargo of transport proteins is mainly cholesterol, they constitute low-density lipoproteins (LDL). Some lipoproteins carry cholesterol and other lipids from dead cells to the liver for reuse or excretion. They transport a small quantity of lipids; hence, they constitute high-density (HDL) lipoproteins.

The aqueous portion of the blood, the plasma, carries a variety of organic and inorganic substances, such as blood sugar (glucose) and salts. Among them are three kinds of proteins, albumin, globulin, and fibrinogen, serving various functions. The chemical messengers, hormones, which have to be transported from organs that produce them to receptors in other parts of the body, are always in transit in the blood, and so are enzymes, vitamins, and the like.

Moreover, the circulatory system is the highway that invading microorganisms try to use for spreading in the body, and cancers also spread by blood-borne fragments. To cope with these hazards, the system is defended by the immune mechanism, notably by several types of white blood cells (polymorphonuclear leukocytes, lymphocytes, and monocytes). The function of these cells is to seek out, ingest, and kill invading microorganisms, penetrate areas of infection, and phagocytose foreign matter and dead cells. The circulatory system is also the target organ of several plant toxins, some of which can act as vasodilators or constrictors, blood coagulants, or anticoagulants. The rye fungus ergot, for example, is such a powerful constrictor of peripheral blood vessels that, in the past, it created numerous epidemics in countries where rye was an important food item. The toxin ergotamine, mixed with rye flour, was capable of cutting off the circulation of the limbs, causing death by gangrene.

Apart from the effect of poisons upon them, arteries are subject to several other disorders (see the section "Specific Hazards of the Circulatory System). Larger arteries are more vulnerable than small arteries. Veins are not entirely trouble free but, in comparison with arteries, are notable for their smooth functioning and resistance to disease. They do, of course, work under less onerous conditions than arteries.

Not surprisingly, arterial disorders are among the leading causes of mortality in advanced countries with older populations. In a few countries, they are responsible for more mortality than all other causes combined. The current worldwide yearly toll of coronary artery disease is about two million deaths, to which cerebrovascular disease (strokes) add half a million. Disorders of the peripheral circulation can cause deaths, but since the elimination of ergotism, the numbers are small.

Specific Hazards of the Circulatory System

The foregoing review attempts to show the complexity and potential vulnerability of the circulation system. However, the exact causes of the most important arterial disorders are still not known, and the intent in this essay is to highlight a few specific hazards that could be relevant to their pathogenesis.

When the heart contracts, it compresses its own blood vessels, the coronary arteries, so that although it supplies all other organs in the body with blood, it cannot supply itself. The perfusion of the heart is effected by an auxiliary mechanism, working on the same principle as a flywheel in a mechanical system by drawing energy from a prime mover in one part of a power cycle and returning it in another part. The corresponding mechanism in the circulation is an elastic reservoir, consisting of the aorta and parts of its large-branch arteries. During systole the walls of the reservoir are distended, storing energy in their stretched elastic tissues; during diastole they contract, generating sufficient pressure to maintain blood flow in the circulation, including the by-then-relaxed coronary arteries. This arrangement, however, makes the nutrition of the heart dependent on the elasticity of the aorta and the other arteries that constitute the elastic reservoir. Several aspects of the aging process can bring about the deterioration of the elastic properties of tissues, representing a special hazard for the heart.

A similar problem arises in connection with the blood supply of the artery wall. The walls of arteries have a cell population that must be supplied with oxygen and nutrients like any other tissue. The difficulty in supplying them arises from the fact that the artery wall is compressed by the blood flowing through it, with a radial pressure gradient across it, the inside being more compressed than the outside. Large arteries have their own blood vessels, the *vasa vasorum*, which enter them on the outside and perfuse the outer half of the artery wall. They cannot perfuse the inner half, because the pressure available to force blood through these small arteries is insufficient to overcome the compression of that part of the artery. Consequently, the inner half of the artery wall must obtain oxygen and nutrients from blood flowing through the artery. The technical problems associated with this process are probably the basic causes of arterial disorders.

Oxygen and water-soluble nutrients can apparently diffuse through the layer of cells – the endothelium – that constitute the inner lining of the artery wall, and there are no known disorders caused by deficiencies of such nutrients. The main difficulty is the transfer of lipids from arterial blood to tissues in the inner half of the artery wall. As mentioned, lipids in the blood are carried by large protein molecules, which do not diffuse into tissues. Cells in need of them have to capture them by means of surface receptors that bind lipoproteins on contact (Goldstein and Brown 1977). The receptors are located in a special area of each cell's surface, the coated pit. When receptors have captured a sufficient quantity of lipoproteins, the coated pit sinks into the cell and unites with a lysosome, the digestive organ of the cell (Simonescu, Simonescu, and Palade 1976; Anderson, Brown, and Goldstein 1977).

A brief description of the construction of the artery wall is needed at this point. The artery wall is a three-layered structure. Its inside, the intima, consists of a single layer of flat endothelial cells and a thin, liquid-filled subendothelial space. The second layer, the media, forms the bulk of the artery wall. It consists of elastic laminae and smooth muscle in varying proportions. The largest arteries, such as the aorta, are mainly elastic; those next in size, mainly muscular. The muscles of the media form peripheral bands, the contraction of which can reduce the lumen of the artery, regulating blood flow through it. Thus they reduce blood flow to organs at rest and increase it to organs in a state of high activity. However, individual smooth muscle cells also exist in the artery wall and perform the same duties as fibroblasts in other tissues. They can secrete various types of elastic and nonelastic fibers that are used mainly in the repair of injuries. Lastly, the outer layer of the wall is a tough connective-tissue covering.

The exact causes of the most important artery disease, atherosclerosis, are not known with certainty. A plausible explanation of the pathogenesis of the disorder is the following: The endothelial cells of the intima, in direct contact with blood inside the artery, capture lipoproteins in the plasma, as do other cells, by means of surface receptors. They do this not only for their own use but also for the supply of other cells in the inner half of the artery wall. Receptors in coated pits sink, as usual, into the interior of the endothelial cell, but in this case, they travel through the cell to emerge on its other side, where they discharge their load of lipoproteins into the subendothelium (Schwartz et al. 1977).

The hazard of the process, at least in prosperous countries, is not that they cannot transfer enough lipids into the subendothelium, but that they transfer too much. Presumably, if a cell captures lipoproteins from blood for its own use, it ceases to produce surface receptors when its needs are satisfied, but if it does so for other cells, it does not receive clear signals when to stop. The quantity actually transferred may depend on the availability of lipoproteins in the plasma.

In developing countries where the population lives on a barely adequate, or less than adequate, diet, the lipoprotein concentration in the plasma is correspondingly low, and the risk of endothelial cells oversupplying the cell population of the median layer of the artery wall is small. In prosperous countries, hyperlipidemia is common, presumably resulting in the almost universal occurrence of fatty suffusions in the intima of some arteries.

Such accumulations of lipoproteins, beginning in infancy or early childhood, could be the initiating event in atherosclerosis, even if the given description is only a simplified – possibly oversimplified – account of the earliest stage of atherosclerosis. Fatty streaks make a patchy appearance in the aorta and some other large arteries. The coronary circulation is usually more heavily involved than others, so that the concentration of lipoproteins in the plasma cannot be the only factor involved in pathogenesis.

Another hazard arises from the fact that arteries must be self-sealing in case of injuries; otherwise, small injuries may cause fatal hemorrhages. Injuries are sealed in the first instance by platelets – small discs 2 to 4 micrometers (μm) in diameter – circulating in immense numbers in the bloodstream. When the wall of a blood vessel is injured, collagen – a tough connective tissue inside it – is exposed. Collagen apparently attracts platelets, which immediately adhere to it. The platelets then release a substance that attracts more platelets and that makes them sticky, causing them to aggregate and form a temporary plug. This is subsequently converted into a more stable clot, after a complicated set of reactions, by fibrin. The latter is produced by the conversion of the soluble plasma protein, fibrinogen, into an insoluble substance. The fibrin originally forms a loose mesh, but ultimately it becomes a dense, tight aggregate.

This essential defense mechanism can become a life-threatening hazard, because advanced atherosclerosis can result in the ulceration of the artery wall, which, in turn, may invoke the clotting reaction. The ultimate result can be a thrombus, occluding the artery.

Atherosclerosis

Atherosclerosis begins with the already mentioned lipid suffusions – the fatty streaks – in the subendothelium of some arteries. The space immediately beneath the single layer of endothelial cells inside the artery is originally small, but it is gradually extended by lipid deposits. The accumulating lipids are mainly cholesterol esters (cholesterol with an attached fatty acid molecule). Cholesterol can act as a weak base and, combined with a weak fatty acid, constitutes the equivalent of an inorganic salt. As there are many types of fatty acids that can combine with cholesterol, there are many types of cholesterol esters. The most important esters are oleates and linoleates, which are cholesterol combined with oleic and linoleic acid, respectively.

Cholesterol is a highly stable waxy substance, an essential constituent of every single cell in the body. The flexibility of the animal body, in comparison with the more rigid structure of plants, is due to the fact that the outer shell of plant cells is cellulose, a comparatively rigid substance, whereas that of animal cells is a complex, three-layered construction, containing proteins and lipids, including cholesterol. These cell membranes combine toughness with flexibility. In addition to the cell itself, its organelles have similar membranes.

The usefulness of cholesterol does not alter the fact that its accumulations in the artery wall can become harmful. Not known with certainty is why deposits of cholesterol esters accumulate inside artery walls. The possibility that if the density of lipoproteins in the plasma is high, endothelial cells transfer more than the required quantity from the blood to the subendothelium has been mentioned. The arising fatty streaks are visible without magnification as yellowish lines or small patches on the luminal surface of the artery. These streaks are flat, or only slightly raised, so that they do not obstruct blood flow and are not known to cause any clinical symptoms; hence, they appear to be harmless.

Fatty streaks appear in large arteries, particularly the aorta, at a very early age, probably in infancy. They are universal in children of all races in all parts of the world, but in developing countries they disappear in early childhood, whereas in prosperous countries they persist and spread. They occupy about 10 percent of the aorta in children; in adult life the affected area may increase to 30 to 50 percent.

In spite of their apparent innocuousness, fatty streaks may not be entirely harmless. They may, for instance, impede the diffusion of oxygen and water-soluble nutrients from blood flowing through the artery to tissues of the artery wall covered by them. But whatever the reason, the immune mechanism of the body treats them as foreign matter. The lipid accumulations are immediately invaded by phagocytes (monocytes), making their way into the lesions from arterial blood. They are apparently capable of separating adjacent endothelial cells slightly and slipping through the gap. Inside the fatty streak they engulf cholesterol esters until they are swollen with them. The lipid-laden phagocytes presumably attempt to leave the site of the lesion, but unlike other tissues, arteries are not drained by lymphatics, making it difficult for phagocytes to find their way out. Occasionally they can be found in the blood, and so some can escape, but many of them die in the attempt, so that ultimately dead foam cells, as lipid-laden monocytes are called, become the main constituents of fatty streaks.

Subsequently, fatty streaks are invaded by another type of cell: individual, motile smooth muscle cells,

migrating into the lesion from the media. These perform the same function as fibroblasts in other tissues. They are cells capable of secreting various elastic and nonelastic fibers, used mainly in the repair of injuries. The fibers bridge over gaps in tissues separated by the injury. As far as possible, they attempt to restore the status quo ante, but when this is not possible, they do a serviceable repair. The ends of a broken bone, for instance, would initially be held together by inelastic fibers until new bone is formed to fill the gap. Under natural conditions, the bone would heal crookedly because the repair mechanism does not have the power to reset it in its original form.

Another function of fibroblasts is to encapsulate foreign matter in the body. If the immune mechanism is powerless to deal with some invading microorganism, an attempt might be made to encapsulate its colonies, as, for instance, in tuberculosis. This is essentially the function that fibroblasts of smooth muscle origin appear to fulfill in fatty streaks. Probably they attempt to break up a continuous layer of lipids, dead phagocytes, and other cell debris into a number of separated accumulations, which are then encapsulated by layers of fibrous tissue. This is how the archetypal lesion of atherosclerosis, the fibrolipid plaque, is thought to arise. The two basic components of the fibrolipid plaque are a white cap of connective tissue and an underlying pool of necrotic debris. The proportion of the two components can vary considerably, and so can the extent of the lesion and the number of fibrous caps in it. In the advanced stage of the lesion, the fibrous caps can be so numerous that they give the luminal surface of the artery wall the porridge-like appearance from which the disorder takes its name.

The fibrolipid plaques are elevated above the surface of the intima and thus represent an obstruction to smooth blood flow. It must be remembered, however, that the lesions are virtually universal in the population of advanced countries. They begin in early childhood and last throughout life, causing no discomfort or inconvenience of any kind for decades. Indeed, in the majority of the population they remain silent until death from some other cause. They can be best conceptualized as a potentially lethal disorder, but one that is generally under the firm control of the defense mechanism of the body.

In the last, uncontrolled stage of atherosclerosis, arteries densely covered by fibrolipid plaques may ulcerate, possibly leading to the adhesion of platelets to the lesions and ultimate thrombus formation. Ulcerated arteries may calcify. The much-thickened intima of the artery wall can fissure, become partly detached, and cause the condition known as an aneurysm. If the lumen of the artery, already narrowed by fibrolipid plaques, is further obstructed by a thrombus or aneurysm, it may become completely occluded, cutting off the blood supply of tissues served by the given artery.

To repeat, the basic cause of atherosclerosis in prosperous countries is thought to be excess lipid intake, and preventive efforts throughout the century have been directed at the reduction of fats in the diet. The main difficulty has been that an effective reduction of lipids seems to require such a Spartan diet that the population of advanced countries has not been persuaded to adopt it. Much evidence, however, is available to suggest that even if this assumption is correct, it can be only a part of the story. There must be other contributory factors that determine why arterial disorders become a lethal disease in some individuals and remain in their harmless, controlled stage in others.

For example, there are considerable differences between the geographical distribution of coronary artery disease and cerebrovascular disease (strokes). The latter appears at a lower level of prosperity, the highest mortality rates occurring in moderately prosperous countries, such as Bulgaria and Portugal, where the consumption of animal fats is comparatively low. With increasing prosperity and increasing fat consumption, mortality from strokes tends to drop. Thus 40 years ago, the world leader in stroke mortality was Japan. The dramatic rise of prosperity in that country was accompanied by considerable changes in diet, the consumption of animal fats increasing by about 50 percent. At the same time, there was a sharp decrease in the incidence of strokes, and stroke mortality is now approximately half that of 40 years ago. The lipid theory of atherogenesis does not differentiate between atherosclerosis in coronary arteries and atherosclerosis in cerebrovascular arteries, and so the fall of cerebrovascular mortality in Japan (as well as a similar sharp fall in the United States in the first half of the twentieth century) provides directly contradictory evidence.

If possible, preventive measures should eliminate atherosclerosis completely, but if that is not a practical possibility, preventing the transition from the controlled to the uncontrollable stage would be nearly as useful. Therefore, an understanding of the basic process of atherogenesis is not enough. It is also necessary to investigate contributory causes and other factors that promote or retard its development. Well-known factors of this nature are cigarette smoking, diabetes, and hypothyroidism, all of which may promote atherogenesis and hasten the onset of its terminal stage, but which fall far short of providing a complete explanation. The low prevalence of coronary artery disease in Japan, for instance, has not been changed by heavy smoking habits. The effect of smoking, diabetes, and hypothyroidism is probably not specific to arterial disease, but is rather a general weakening of the immune mechanism.

Progress toward a better understanding of the causes of artery diseases can proceed along two lines. One is the study of the pathogenetic process itself. If that were completely understood, the causes might be self-evident. Until then, important pointers may be provided by epidemiological studies. Knowledge of the parts of the earth in which artery diseases are highly prevalent and of those in which they are not should throw light on the conditions that promote or retard the disorders and to help in an understanding of their causative agents.

Epidemiological Studies

Arterial disorders have a distinct geographical distribution. They are generally very low or nonexistent in poor countries but are the leading cause of mortality in some of the most prosperous countries. Such a pattern creates the impression that the circulatory system, in spite of its complexity and potential vulnerability, is well able to cope with its natural hazards. Prosperity may have introduced some new condition – perhaps a surfeit of food in place of scarcity – that has changed a trouble-free mechanism into one susceptible to trouble.

An alternative possibility is that the difference is the result of the prolongation of life in prosperous countries. Arterial disorders appear in old age; therefore, the longer duration of life increases their share among causes of mortality. Yet another possibility is that the difference is the result of racial characteristics, Europeans being more vulnerable than Asians or Africans. Climatic conditions could be another factor, with arterial disease being more prevalent in temperate than in warm climates.

Epidemiological studies have eliminated a number of these possibilities. For instance, immigrant studies have disposed of the racial hypothesis. Black people may be free of arterial disease in Africa, but in the United States they are as vulnerable as American whites. Nor is the prolongation of life a satisfactory explanation. When mortality rates are compared in the same age groups in developing and advanced countries, it is still only the population of prosperous countries that is highly vulnerable to arterial disease. The critical factor appears to be diet. Thus, when population groups migrate from poor to prosperous countries, they, or their descendants, gradually become subject to the mortality patterns of their hosts. Migrants going from prosperous to poor countries take their diseases with them. This is, presumably, because migrants from poor to prosperous countries are willing enough to adopt the food of their hosts, but those moving in the other direction are not willing to embrace the poorer diet of their hosts.

Yet although such epidemiological studies have produced useful results on general points, they have brought little progress in matters of detail, such as the identification of food items connected with specific disorders, or finding the reason for the epidemiological peculiarities of some disorders. Why, for example, is worldwide mortality from coronary disease highest in Finland and that from strokes in Bulgaria?

One reason for the apparently limited usefulness of epidemiology is the intrinsic difficulty of the task. The diet of prosperous countries consists of something like a thousand food items, containing a million chemical substances, all potential suspects. None, however, is strongly poisonous, suggesting that perhaps the pathogenic agent may not be present in just one food item but in several, in different proportions, so that the correlation between the disease they collectively cause and one of the food items may only be weakly positive.

Possibly an equally important factor retarding progress might be regarded as a self-inflicted injury. Although the identification of the true causes of artery diseases is difficult, nothing is easier than the presentation of suspects on the basis of superficial arguments. Some of the favorite concepts of popular medicine, such as the particularly harmful effect of saturated fats or the assumed protective effect of dietary fiber, garlic, onions, and the like, are not the results of epidemiological studies but of superficial observations, or they are simply guesses.

An early comparison was that between the "low-protein, lowfat, high-fiber" diet of this or that African tribe and the "high-protein, high-fat, low-fiber" diet of prosperous countries, giving rise to the fiber industry. In fact, the differences between the diets of African tribesmen and the population of rich countries are innumerable. The tribesmen eat fewer apples, chocolates, and cabbages than do people in the West and do not take a sleeping pill at night and a tranquilizer in the morning. The main virtue of fiber is probably the fact that it is a nonfood that may help to prevent overnutrition.

When it was pointed out that Eskimos – whose diet was not a lowfat, low protein, high fiber one – did not suffer from arterial diseases, the objection was sidestepped with the suggestion that they consumed the unsaturated fat of marine animals, not the hard fat of land animals. When it was pointed out that the French consumed as much animal fat and proteins as the British, yet the mortality from coronary disease in France was about a third of that in Britain, the "protective" effect of garlic, onions, and red wine was suggested as a possible explanation. Not even a guess is available as to how garlic, onions, and the like might protect the circulatory system. Yet such ideas, for some reason, are immediately taken up by the media and popular medicine, often impeding serious research. It may also be well to remember that the first task of research is to discover the causes of arterial disease. When those are known, attention can be turned to protective effects, but before they are known with certainty, protective effects are usually invoked to cover discrepancies between facts and theory.

A new line of approach emerged in the 1940s with the Framingham study. The basic idea was to recruit a large number of participants and keep a record of their food consumption until they all died. Then the diet of those who died of coronary disease could be compared with that of the participants who died of other diseases, providing valuable information about the dietary causes of coronary disease. In some of the later trials, the protocol was slightly changed. Some participants were persuaded to change their habits (for example, to reduce fat intake, or to give up smoking), whereas others were allowed to continue with their customary diets and other practices. Thus, prospective studies became intervention trials. A large number of these were conducted in many countries, among others by M. R. Garcia-Palmieri and colleagues (1980), the Multiple Risk Factor Intervention Research Group (1982), and G. Rose, H. D. Turnstall-Pedoe, and R. F. Heller (1983).

Neither the Framingham trial nor its many successors, however, have produced clear evidence identifying the causes of coronary disease, and some of the results have been contradictory. At least one of the reasons for the poor performance of prospective studies is likely to be the gross inaccuracy of the food consumption data they collect. The data are obtained by means of periodic samplings by the method of "24-hour recall," and are subject to several errors. A one-day sampling in, let us say, a month is unlikely to be truly representative of food consumption for the whole period. The data, as collected, are nonquantitative, and the quantities must be estimated by the conductors of the trial. There have to be errors of recall. These are in addition to several confounding factors, such as individual sensitivities to food toxin. If an individual dies of a food-related disorder, it is not necessarily because his consumption of the food was too high. Another possibility is that his resistance to its toxic effect was too low. Also to be remembered is that atherosclerosis is a virtually universal disorder in prosperous countries. Thus, those participants in a trial who die of other diseases may also be in an advanced stage of atherosclerosis. Finally in the case of intervention trials, the persuasion aimed at one group of participants to change habits (such as quitting smoking) is often little different from that directed at the other group by doctors and the media.

This writer suggests that food consumption statistics of advanced countries provide more reliable information regarding the type and quantity of food consumed in a community than do data collected individually in periodic samplings. Statistics are not free of errors, but they are unlikely to be of such magnitude that two studies can produce directly contradictory results. Comparing population groups rather than individuals has, at least, the advantage of eliminating individual susceptibilities. The results of a statistical study conducted by this writer (Seely 1988) is recapitulated in the following section.

A Statistical Study

When searching for the correlation between one or more food items and mortality from a given disease, statistics are likely to present a blurred image. This is partly on account of chance correlations and indirect correlations, and partly on account of statistical errors. Food consumption statistics of prosperous countries, for example, include a large amount of waste, whereas death certificates may give erroneous causes of death. Prosperity-related diseases can be positively correlated with virtually any aspect of that prosperity, such as the number of two-car families in a community, as well as with the consumption of the food item that is the presumed actual cause of disease. The consumption of a number of luxury foods increases together with prosperity. All such errors tend to mask the connection between real causes and effects. In an attempt to sharpen the image, the following expedient was tried.

Let us consider a statistical study in a group of prosperous countries, such as the 21 countries of the Organization of Economic Cooperation and Development (OECD), for which both mortality and food consumption statistics are available (Seely 1988). The object is to see if a consistent association can be found between mortality from coronary artery disease and the consumption of one or more food items. It may be advantageous to restrict the initial search to the four countries with the highest, and the four countries with the lowest, mortality from coronary disease because the contrast between the two groups may bring the critical differences between them into sharper focus. The range of mortality between the two groups is wide. Male coronary mortality in the leading country, Finland, is about eight times as high as in the country with the lowest mortality, Japan. The average male coronary mortality in the four leading countries – Finland, Ireland, United Kingdom, and Sweden – is four times as high as in the low-mortality group – Spain, France, Portugal, and Japan. Thus it seems unlikely that a food item, the consumption of which in the low-mortality group *exceeds* that in the high-mortality group, can play a significant part in the causation of coronary disease, and thus it can be excluded from the list of suspects with a reasonable degree of confidence.

In our statistical study, the source of mortality data are mortality statistics of the World Health Organization (1983–6) and that of food consumption are statistics of the Organisation for Economic Co-operation and Development (1981). Mortality statistics are for 1983, or the nearest available year; food consumption statistics are for 1973. The reason for the time interval between them is that foods containing some mildly noxious substance result in a disorder only after a long delay. The exact interval cannot be estimated, but empirical observations suggest that 10 years is reasonable.

In order to ensure that no food item for which consumption statistics are available is overlooked, it is necessary to consider *all* food appearing in them. As noted, the diet of prosperous countries includes about a thousand food items, yet the statistics give consumption figures for about 50 items. There is obviously no guarantee that foods not appearing in statistics cannot be causative agents for a disorder, but at least it can be said that all *major* food items are included in the statistics. The possible connection between a food item and a disease can be verified by the calculation of correlation coefficients. The simplest case of perfect correlation is exact proportionality between the consumption of a food item and mortality from a given disease. In other words, if in a country the consumption of x coexists with a number of deaths from a disease, y, then in other countries, where the consumption of that food is 2, 3, or 4 times higher than in the first country, mortality is also 2, 3, or 4 times higher. In a more realistic case the relationship is $y = ax + b$, where a and b are constants, and correlation is perfect if mortality in every country corresponds exactly to the value obtained from the equation. Perfect positive correlation is expressed by the correlation coefficient 1, entire lack of correlation by the coefficient 0, and perfect negative correlation by –1.

The results of the study are reproduced in Table IV.F.4.1. This shows the correlation coefficients calculated for each item appearing in the cited food consumption statistics for eight countries. Table IV.F.4.2 shows male age-compensated mortality rates in these countries and gives some of the more important food consumption figures from which the correlation coefficients in Table IV.F.4.1 were calculated. The highest positive correlations in Table IV.F.4.1 are as follows: oats 0.95, whole milk 0.91, milk proteins (excluding cheese) 0.91, milk fats (excluding butter and cheese) 0.91, sugar 0.90, total milk protein 0.86, beer 0.86, total milk fats 0.84, total animal fats 0.77, total animal proteins 0.74.

When correlations were checked for all 21 OECD countries, the high correlation with beer was found to be spurious. The countries with the highest beer consumption, notable Germany, Austria, the Netherlands, and Denmark, have only moderately high mortality from coronary disease. The other correlations, including that of oats, were confirmed.

The most surprising finding of the study is the near-perfect correlation between coronary mortality and the consumption of oats. At the time of the investigation, we could offer no explanation or even a suggestion as to what constituent of oats could have a connection with arterial disorders, but an attempt at an explanation follows shortly.

The connection between milk consumption and coronary disease has been suspected for a long time, based mainly on the geographical correspondence

Table IV.F.4.1. *Correlation coefficients between age-compensated male mortality rates from ischaemic heart disease and the consumption of various foods in 8 member countries of the Organization of Economic Cooperation and Development. The 8 countries comprise the 4 with the highest coronary mortality (Finland, Ireland, U.K., Sweden) and the 4 with the lowest mortality (Spain, Portugal, France, Japan). Source of mortality data: World Health Organization statistics for the year 1983 (or nearest); source of food consumption data: statistics of the Organisation of Economic Cooperation and Development for the year 1973*

Wheat	0.03	Eggs	0.11
Rye	0.33	Fish, fresh	−0.70
Barley	0.20	canned or smoked	−0.55
Oats	0.95	Molluscs, crustaceans	−0.56
Maize	0.27	Total fish	−0.77
Rice	−0.55	Fish, protein content	−0.79
Sugar	0.90	fat content	−0.77
Honey	0.44	Whole milk	0.91
Potatoes	0.30	Skimmed milk	0.61
Pulses	−0.62	Cheese	0.05
Nuts	−0.52	Dried & condensed milk	0.05
Pulses and nuts, total	−0.74	Butter	0.77
Other vegetables, protein content	−0.89	Total milk, proteins	0.86
Citrus fruit	0.26	Milk proteins without cheese	0.91
Other fresh fruit	−0.79	Total milk fats	0.84
Fruit, conserved or dried	0.62	Milk fats without butter	0.90
Total fruit	−0.55	Milk fats, without butter & cheese	0.91
Cocoa	0.22	Vegetable oils	−0.61
Beef and veal	0.45	Wine	−0.65
Pork	0.62	Beer	0.86
Mutton	0.30	Total animal proteins	0.74
Poultry	−0.36	Total animal fats	0.77
Horse meat	−0.35	Total plant proteins	−0.74
Other meats	−0.47	Total plant lipids	−0.62
Offal	0.38	Total protein	0.40
Total meat, proteins	0.33	Total fats	0.53
fats	0.55		

Source: S. Seely (1988). Reproduced from *International Journal of Cardiology,* 20 (1988) p. 185, with the permission of the publishers, Elsevier Science Publishers, Amsterdam.

between them. Figure IV.F.4.1 shows this graphically for member countries of the Organisation for Economic Co-operation and Development. Many papers have been published on the subject, notably by J. C. Annand (1961), K. A. Oster (1971), J. J. Segall (1980), and S. Seely (1981), although the authors could not agree on the mechanism of interaction between milk and the arteries. It is interesting to note from Table IV.F.4.1 that whatever the noxious constituent of milk may be, some process in cheese manufacture appears to destroy it.

Sugar is also a long-standing suspect. However, the main objection to the suspicion is that no reasonable proposal has ever been put forward to explain why and how sugar might have an adverse effect on arteries (Yudkin and Roddy 1964).

Table IV.F.4.2. *Sample data on which Table IV.F.4.1 is based. Mortality rates below denote age-compensated male mortality rates (European standard) from ischaemic heart disease. Food consumption in grams/day*

	High-mortality group				Low-mortality group			
	Finland	Ireland	U.K.	Sweden	Spain	Portugal	France	Japan
Mortality	406.4	400.1	390.6	349.2	114.6	110.3	110.1	61.4
Foods								
Wheat	125.9	221.1	177.1	151.7	207.7	197.8	192.4	84.8
Oats	7.4	6.1	3.8	5.1	–	–	0.3	–
Beef & veal	61.6	50.0	57.8	43.5	32.7	34.0	77.6	32.7
Eggs	29.4	32.1	42.1	35.0	34.6	11.9	34.5	44.1
Butter	25.5	29.6	17.1	16.0	0.9	1.4	20.1	1.2
Milk protein (without cheese)	39.4	31.8	19.3	24.9	10.2	5.5	10.9	4.0

Source: S. Seely (1988). Reproduced from *International Journal of Cardiology* with the permission of Elsevier Science Publishers.

Figure IV.F.4.1. Male coronary mortality in the 65–74 age group in OECD countries and the consumption of milk proteins (excluding cheese). Reproduced from *International Journal of Cardiology*, with the permission of the publishers, Elsevier Science Publishers, Amsterdam. *Note.* Mortality statistics are for 1987 (or the nearest year for which statistics were available); food consumption data precede mortality statistics by ten years.

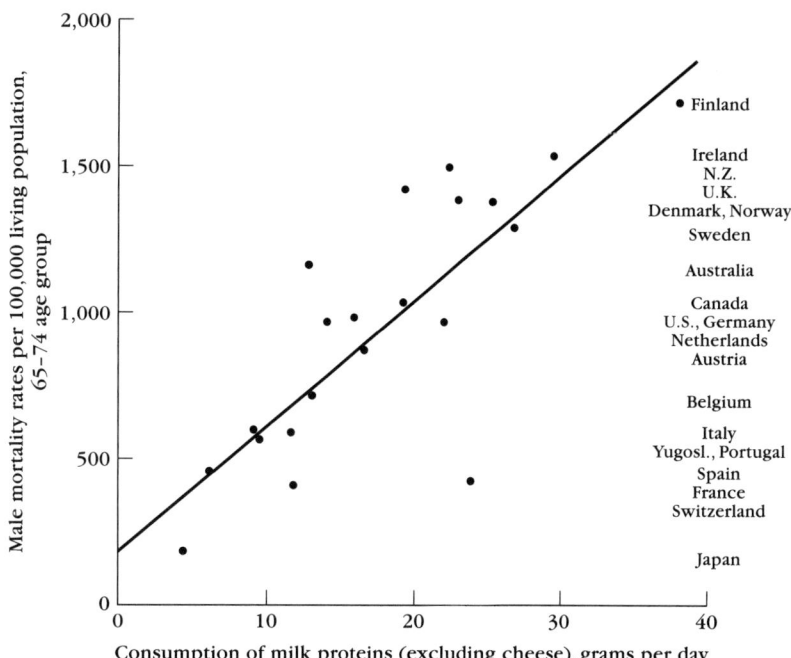

Consumption of milk proteins (excluding cheese), grams per day

The food items, for the possible atherogenic effect of which reasonable explanations *are* available, are animal fats and proteins. Yet, as shown by Table IV.F.4.1, the correlation coefficients between them and coronary mortality are considerably weaker than those found for oats, milk, and sugar. Clearly, this helps to demonstrate the complexity of the problem.

Perhaps a clue to the resolution of some of these difficulties can be found by considering one distinguishing feature that cow's milk and oats have in common: They both have a high calcium content. That of cow's milk is 120 milligrams (mg) per 100 grams (g) (as compared with 31 mg per 100 g of human milk); the calcium content of oats is 80 mg per 100 g (McCance and Widdowson 1980). Hence, we arrive at the possibility that the missing link in the pathogenesis of coronary disease is the excessively high calcium content of the Western diet.

Calcium in the Western Diet

What might be called the "natural human diet" is low in calcium, as are present-day diets in most developing countries, where the daily intake amounts to about 200 to 500 mg. The calcium content of the European diet was probably the same in past centuries, giving rise to the frequent occurrence of calcium deficiency disease – rickets – in children.

The large increase in the calcium content of the Western diet came with the increasing use of cow's milk as a staple food for all age groups. The calcium content of milk is high, and it serves the needs of infants whose rapidly growing skeletons need a com-

paratively large amount. Calves grow at 4 times the rate of human infants; hence, cow's milk contains 4 times as much calcium as human milk. The average intake of milk and dairy products in prosperous countries is usually between ¼ and ½ liter a day, containing 300 to 600 mg calcium. Three hundred mg is sufficient to convert the intake from other foods into an abundant 600 to 700 mg, and half a liter of milk into an excessive 900 to 1,000 mg. In many Western countries, the calcium intake from cow's milk is more than that from all other foods combined.

Calcium is an essential nutrient, but in the ideal case, the dietary intake should not exceed requirements because the excretion of the surplus is a difficult task. The requirement of the human body can be estimated from the following data: The adult body contains about 1,100 grams of calcium, 99 percent of which is in the skeleton. The remaining 1 percent is needed for various essential functions, such as the generation of nerve impulses, muscular contraction, blood coagulation, and so forth. The skeleton reaches its maximum size and weight at the age of 35 years. While the skeleton is growing, it takes up a daily average of 80 mg calcium. After the age of 50 years, the skeleton begins to shrink, releasing calcium.

All body fluids contain calcium. About 100 mg is lost daily in urine and about 15 mg in sweat, though with hard physical exercise, sweating can excrete 80 mg calcium in a day. In addition, digestive fluids, such as saliva and pancreatic juice, discharge calcium into the digestive tract, and this amount is not completely reabsorbed. Allowing 150 mg calcium daily for this loss, the calcium requirement of a young adult, depending on physical exercise, amounts to 330 to 390 mg/day, and that of an old person about 240 mg/day. The dietary intake should exceed the needs of the body by about 20 percent to allow for calcium passing unabsorbed through the intestines, making the daily requirement for a hard-working young adult 470 mg, that of old people 290 mg. When the risk of coronary heart disease is considered, we are mainly interested in the older age groups. In their case, a possible dietary calcium intake of the order of 1,000 mg is *several times* the quantity they need, and that from milk alone can be twice that amount.

The uptake of calcium from the small intestine is a controlled process, so that an excessive dietary intake does not necessarily mean that calcium finding its way into body fluids must also be excessive. Control is exercised by a vitamin D metabolite, cholecalciferol, synthesized in two steps in the liver and kidney. This metabolite is the signal for the synthesis of a carrier protein in the intestine, which is the actual transfer agent for calcium through the intestinal wall. If the calcium content of the plasma is already adequate, the synthesis of cholecalciferol is discontinued, and the excess calcium passes unabsorbed through the alimentary canal. However, newly born infants do not yet possess this control mechanism. In their case, milk sugar, lactose, facilitates the absorption of calcium from the small intestine by a simple diffusion process. Under natural conditions, this facility does not involve a health hazard because when infants are weaned, lactose disappears from their diet. In a prosperous society, however, infants are never weaned, in the sense that lactose remains in their diet from birth to death. Not only is milk, therefore, high in calcium but its lactose content also enables it to bypass the control mechanism of the body (Bronner 1987).

It might be mentioned that when milk is fermented, lactose is converted into lactic acid, a biologically inactive substance. Fermented milk and its products, such as cheese, are very high in calcium but do not provide the facility for evading the intestinal control for its absorption. This is the probable reason that the correlation between mortality from coronary disease and cheese consumption is much weaker than it is with the consumption of whole milk.

If the quantity of calcium absorbed from the intestine exceeds requirements, a good excretory mechanism exists for disposing of the excess. The kidneys normally excrete about 100 mg/day. Concentration of calcium in the urine (hypercalciuria) involves the risk of stone formation in the kidneys, but a second excretory mechanism is available to support them. The surplus calcium becomes protein bound and is excreted by the liver, not the kidneys. In individuals in prosperous countries, the concentration of protein-bound calcium in the plasma, 1.16 millimoles (mmol) per liter (l), is nearly as high as that of diffusible calcium, 1.34 mmol/l (Ganong 1987), demonstrating

that calcium intake in Western countries, indeed, tends to be excessive.

The effective excretory mechanism ensures that most of the surplus calcium is eliminated, but a small fraction escapes and is ultimately precipitated in soft tissues. Under normal conditions, this process is so slow that a large dietary calcium excess can be tolerated for decades, the calcification of soft tissues becoming a health hazard only in old age. Misuse, however, can overwhelm the excretory mechanism. In the 1950s, for example, it was customary to treat gastric ulcer patients with large quantities of milk, amounting to about 2 liters per day, until a disproportionately high mortality from coronary disease was observed among them (Briggs et al. 1960). Two liters of cow's milk contains 2.4 grams of calcium, together with lactose facilitating its absorption from the intestine. The calcium absorbed from this source by the body may amount to a daily intake of 1.8 grams, perhaps 6 times the amount needed by elderly individuals. The excretory mechanism may well be incapable of dealing with such a gross excess.

As noted, excess calcium that cannot be excreted ultimately finds its way into soft tissues. Large arteries, notably the aorta, are particularly vulnerable to calcification. The heavy calcification of the aorta in individuals who died of heart disease was already observed by the pioneers of medicine in the nineteenth century, who correspondingly called the disorder "the hardening of the arteries."

Calcium deposits in arteries have two important pathological effects. One is the calcification of atherosclerotic plaques. A recent autopsy study by A. Fleckenstein and his group (1990) has found that atherosclerotic lesions appear to attract calcium from their earliest stage onward. Fatty streaks already contain, at an average, 10 times as much calcium as the surrounding normal arterial tissue. Normal atherosclerotic plaques contain 25 times as much, advanced plaques in individuals who died of coronary disease, 80 times as much. Such advanced plaques are, in effect, calcium plaques. Calcium compounds, mainly apatite, constitute about half of their dry weight, cholesterol and its compounds about 3 percent. It is calcium that gives advanced plaques bulk and rigidity and makes them potential obstacles to blood flow.

Secondly, mural deposits of calcium in the aorta and other large elastic arteries encroach on their elasticity. As pointed out, these arteries constitute an elastic reservoir that is distended when the heart injects a volume of blood into it during systole, storing energy in its stretched elastic tissues. The contraction of the reservoir generates diastolic pressure and maintains blood flow in the circulatory system when the heart is at rest. As the heart compresses its own arteries when it contracts, its perfusion is entirely dependent on an adequate diastolic pressure.

If the elasticity of the reservoir deteriorates, an increasing systolic pressure is needed to maintain diastolic pressure at a given value. Perfusion failure in a part of the heart occurs when the aging, partly calcified elastic reservoir cannot generate sufficient pressure to force an adequate quantity of blood through narrowed and obstructed coronary arteries. Calcification is involved both in the reduction of diastolic pressure generated by the reservoir and in the obstructions presented by advanced atherosclerotic plaques. Thus, calcium excess in Western diets may well be the most important factor in the pathogenesis of coronary artery disease (Seely 1989, 1991). If the populations of Western countries were alerted to this possibility and advised to reduce their consumption, a large reduction in mortality could well be the result.

In a recent trial (Woods et al. 1992), coronary patients were treated with magnesium sulphate with beneficial results. A possible explanation is that the excretion of the four main electrolytes – sodium, potassium, calcium, and magnesium – is an interlinked process. The most difficult task of excretion for the kidneys arises when the intake of these minerals is unbalanced, high in some, low in others. Thus in the 1960s, rats on a high-cholesterol diet also had their food unbalanced in electrolytes, with an excessive sodium–potassium and calcium–magnesium ratio (Sos 1965). The rats died of repeated, humanlike heart attacks, but their lives could be prolonged if the imbalances were moderated. Thus, if human diet has an excessive calcium content, the best remedy would be its reduction, but failing that, an increase in magnesium intake can be beneficial.

As mentioned in the section "A Statistical Study," epidemiological studies show a positive correlation between mortality from coronary artery disease and the consumption of oats, as well as of milk. The calcium content of oats, 80 mg/100 g, is high, but the strong correlation with coronary disease would probably arise only if they also contained some substance promoting the absorption of their calcium from the intestines. An oat grass, *Trisetum flavescens*, is known to contain vitamin D_3, capable of causing calcinosis in grazing animals, but no data are available to show that this also applies to cultivated oats.

The apparent connection between mortality from coronary disease and climate has been noted. The countries with very high mortality, such as Finland, Latvia, Lithuania, and Russia, have cold climates. In warmer climates, mortality is generally lower and, in tropical countries, very low or nonexistent. This may be explained by corresponding differences in calcium excretion. In a cold climate, the amount of calcium excreted by sweating is usually small, whereas a person doing hard physical work in the tropics can lose more fluid, and possibly more calcium, in sweat than in urine.

If arterial calcification is one of the main causes of death from coronary disease – the "skeleton in the atherosclerosis closet," as a recent article called it (Demer 1995) – this could be a blessing in disguise.

The most important source of dietary calcium is one easily identifiable food item, cow's milk – hence, arterial calcification is *preventable*. The best way of achieving such prevention would be the reduction of milk consumption, particularly by elderly people. An alternative course might be the elimination of lactose from fresh milk. As mentioned, the worldwide toll of coronary disease is about two million deaths per year. The possibility deserves careful consideration.

Stephen Seely

Bibliography

Anderson, R. G. W., M. S. Brown, and J. L. Goldstein. 1977. Role of the coated endocytotic vesicle in the uptake of receptor-bound low-density lipo-proteins in human fibroblasts. *Cell* 10: 351–64.

Annand, J. C. 1961. Atherosclerosis: The case against protein. *Journal of the College of General Practitioners* 4: 567–96.

Briggs, E. D., M. L. Rubenberg, R. M. O'Neal, et al. 1960. Myocardial infraction in patients treated with Sippy and other high-milk diets: An autopsy study of fifteen hospitals in the USA and Great Britain. *Circulation* 21: 532–42.

Bronner, F. 1987. Intestinal calcium absorption: Mechanism and applications. *Journal of Nutrition* 117: 1347–52.

Demer, L. L. 1995. A skeleton in the atherosclerosis closet. *Circulation* 92: 2029–32.

Fleckenstein, A., M. Frey, F. Thimm, and G. Fleckenstein-Grun. 1990. Excessive mural calcium overload: A predominant causal factor in the development of stenosing coronary plaques in humans. *Cardiovascular Drugs and Therapy* 4: 1005–14

Ganong, W. F. 1987. *Review of medical physiology.* Thirteenth edition. Los Altos, Calif.

Garcia-Palmieri, M. R., P. Sorlie, J. Pillotson, et al. 1980. Relationship of dietary intake to subsequent coronary heart disease incidence: The Puerto-Rico Heart Health Program. *American Journal of Clinical Nutrition* 3: 1818–27.

Goldstein, J. L., and M. S. Brown. 1977. The low-density lipoprotein pathway and its relation to atherosclerosis. *Annual Review of Biochemistry* 46: 897–930.

Kornitzer, M., M. Dramaix, C. Thilly, et al. 1983. Belgian heart disease prevention project: Incidence and mortality results. *Lancet* 1: 1066–70.

Little, R. C. 1981. *Physiology of the heart and circulation.* Second edition. Chicago and London.

McCance, R. A., and E. M. Widdowson. 1980. *The composition of foods.* London.

Multiple Risk Factor Intervention Research Group. 1982. Multiple risk factor intervention trial: Risk factor changes and mortality results. *Journal of the American Medical Association* 248: 1465–77.

OECD (Organisation for Economic Co-operation and Development). 1981. *Food consumption statistics, 1964–1978.* Paris.

Oster, K. A. 1971. Plasmalogen diseases: A new concept of the etiology of the atherosclerotic process. *American Journal of Clinical Research* 2: 30–5.

Rose, G., H. D. Turnstall-Pedoe, and R. F. Heller. 1983. U.K. heart disease prevention project: Incidence and mortality results. *Lancet* 1: 1062–6.

Schwartz, C. J., R. J. Garrity, L. J. Lewis, et al. 1977. Arterial endothelial permeability to macromolecules. In *Proceedings of the fourth international symposium,* ed. G. Schettler and A. Weizel, 1–11.

Segall, J. J. 1980. Hypothesis: Is lactose a dietary risk factor for ischaemic heart disease? *International Journal of Epidemiology* 9: 271–6.

Seely, S. 1981. Diet and coronary disease: A survey of mortality rates and food consumption statistics of 24 countries. *Medical Hypotheses* 7: 907–18.

　　1988. Diet and coronary arterial disease: A statistical study. *International Journal of Cardiology* 20: 183–92.

　　1989. Atherosclerosis or hardening of the arteries? *International Journal of Cardiology* 22: 5–12.

　　1991. Is calcium excess in Western diet a major cause of arterial disease? *International Journal of Cardiology* 33: 191–8.

Simonescu, N., M. Simonescu, and C. E. Palade. 1976. Recent studies on vascular subendothelium. *Annals of the New York Academy of Sciences* 275: 64–75.

Sos, J. 1965. An investigation into the nutritional factors of experimental cardiopathy. In *Electrolytes and cardiovascular disease,* ed. E. Bajusz. Basel and New York.

WHO (World Health Organization). 1983–6. *World Health Statistics Annuals.* Geneva.

Woods, K., S. Fletcher, C. Roffe, and Y. Haider. 1992. Intravenous magnesium sulphate in suspected myocardial infarction: Results of the second Leicester Intravenous Magnesium Intervention Trial (LIMIT-2). *Lancet* 339: 344–7.

Yudkin, J., and J. Roddy. 1964. Levels of dietary sucrose in patients with occlusive atherosclerotic disease. *Lancet* 2: 6–8.